REFERENCE

REFERENCE

Income
Tax Regulations

Including Proposed Regulations

As of May 8, 2020

Volume 4

**Proposed Regulations
and Preambles**

Wolters Kluwer Editorial Staff Publication

This publication is designed to provide accurate and authoritative information in regard to the subject matter covered. It is sold with the understanding that the publisher is not engaged in rendering legal, accounting, or other professional service. If legal advice or other expert assistance is required, the services of a competent professional person should be sought.

ISBN 978-0-8080-5425-2 (Set)
ISBN 978-0-8080-5431-3 (Volume 1)
ISBN 978-0-8080-5432-0 (Volume 2)
ISBN 978-0-8080-5433-7 (Volume 3)
ISBN 978-0-8080-5434-4 (Volume 4)

2700 Lake Cook Road
Riverwoods, IL 60015
800 344 3734
CCHCPELink.com

Do not send returns to the above address. If for any reason you are not satisfied with your book purchase, it can easily be returned within 30 days of shipment. Please go to *support.cch.com/returns* to initiate your return. If you require further assistance with your return, please call: (800) 344-3734 M-F, 8 a.m. – 6 p.m CT.

Printed in the United States of America

SUSTAINABLE FORESTRY INITIATIVE
Certified Sourcing
www.sfiprogram.org
SFI-01681

CONTENTS

TABLE OF CONTENTS

INDEX
PROPOSED REGULATIONS UNDER THE 1986 CODE

[References are to Reg. § numbers.]

[Index to Final and Temporary Regulations Begins on Page 19,003.]

73,002

Index—Proposed Regulations Under 1986 Code
[References are to Reg. § numbers.]

Index—Proposed Regulations Under 1986 Code
[References are to Reg. § numbers.]

73,003

73,006

Index—Proposed Regulations Under 1986 Code
[References are to Reg. § numbers.]

Index—Proposed Regulations Under 1986 Code
[References are to Reg. § numbers.]

73,007

73,008

Index—Proposed Regulations Under 1986 Code
[References are to Reg. § numbers.]

[The next page is 73,031.]

List of Proposed Regulations—2020

Under the Administrative Procedure Act, most changes in regulations must be issued in proposed form, and interested parties are given, generally, 30 days after the date of publication of the Notice of Proposed Rulemaking in the Federal Register within which to file objections or suggestions. Sometime thereafter, the regulations are issued in permanent form. Proposed income, estate and excise tax regulations under the 1986 Code are included in this list.

1986 Code Sec.	Regs. Section	Date Proposed[1]	Date Adopted[2]	Paragraph (¶)
2	1.2-1, 1.2-2	1/19/17	. . . .	49,737
3	1.3-1	1/19/17	. . . .	49,737
21	1.21-1	1/19/17	. . . .	49,737
25	1.25-1—1.25-8	5/8/85	. . . .	49,054
	1.25-4	9/3/85	. . . .	49,059
25A	1.25A-0—1.25A-2, 1.25A-5	8/2/16	. . . .	49,709
32	1.32-2	1/19/17	. . . .	49,737
36B	1.36B-2	7/8/16	. . . .	49,704
	1.36B-6	5/3/13	. . . .	49,574
	1.36B-6	9/1/15	. . . .	49,664
	1.36B-2—1.36B-4	7/28/14	. . . .	49,624
40	1.40-1, 1.40-2	7/29/08	. . . .	49,389
40A	1.40A-1	7/29/08	. . . .	49,389
41	1.41-0, 1.41-6	12/13/13	. . . .	49,599
42	1.42-1	6/22/87	. . . .	49,080
	1.42-5	2/25/16	. . . .	49,687
	1.42-10	3/3/16	. . . .	49,689
45D	1.45D-1	8/11/08	. . . .	49,393
48	1.48-9	1/26/82	. . . .	49,020
56	1.56(g)-1	12/30/92	. . . .	49,130
59A	1.59A-1—1.59A-10	12/21/18	. . . .	49,783
	1.59A-2, 1.59A-3, 1.59A-7, 1.59A-9, 1.59A-10	12/6/19	. . . .	49,821
61	1.61-6, 1.61-7	4/8/86	. . . .	49,070
	1.61-16	2/3/78	. . . .	49,007
	1.61-21	10/9/92	. . . .	49,132
	1.61-21	8/23/19	TD 9893, 2/4/20	49,808
62	1.62-1	3/28/88	. . . .	49,092
63	1.63-1—1.63-3	1/19/17	. . . .	49,737
	1.63-3	9/19/17	. . . .	49,744
66	1.66-4, 1.66-5	8/13/13	. . . .	49,580
	1.66-0—1.66-5	11/20/15	. . . .	49,674
67	1.67-1, 1.67-2	3/28/88	. . . .	49,092
	1.67-3T	9/30/91	. . . .	49,124
	1.67-3T	9/3/92	. . . .	49,131
71	1.71-1	8/31/84	. . . .	49,041
72	1.72-4, 1.72-13	4/30/75	. . . .	49,003
	1.72-6	10/18/06	. . . .	49,280
	1.72(e)-1	2/4/86	. . . .	49,066
74	1.74-1, 1.74-2	1/9/89	. . . .	49,110
79	1.79-4	2/4/86	. . . .	49,066
83	1.83-3, 1.83-6	5/24/05	. . . .	49,242
101	1.101-2	4/30/75	. . . .	49,003
	1.101-8	12/15/92	. . . .	49,134
102	1.102-1	1/9/89	. . . .	49,110
103	5f.103-1	11/15/82	. . . .	49,021
	5f.103-1	12/19/86	. . . .	49,073
	5f.103-1	9/19/17	. . . .	49,744
	1.103-8	8/22/84	. . . .	49,038
	1.103-8	11/7/85	. . . .	49,062
	1.103-10	2/21/86	. . . .	49,067
	1.103-10	2/21/86	. . . .	49,068
103A	6a.103A-1—6a.103A-3	7/1/81	. . . .	49,017
	6a.103A-1, 6a.103A-2	11/10/81	. . . .	49,019

[1] Date published in the *Federal Register*.
[2] Date filed with the *Federal Register*.

1986 Code Sec.	Regs. Section	Date Proposed[1]	Date Adopted[2]	Paragraph (¶)
	6a.103A-2	5/8/85		49,054
	6a.103A-2	4/8/86		49,070
105	1.105-11	2/25/83		49,025
	1.105-11	9/30/19		49,814
106	1.106-1	6/15/87		49,078
117	1.117-0—1.117-6	6/9/88		49,100
120	1.120-1, 1.120-2	4/29/80		49,011
122	1.122-1	4/30/75		49,003
125	1.125-0—1.125-3	8/6/07		49,315
	1.125-5—1.125-7	8/6/07		49,315
126	16A.126-0—16A.126-2	5/21/81		49,016
133	1.133-1	2/4/86		49,066
150	1.150-1	4/10/02		49,187
	1.150-3	12/28/18		49,786
151	1.151-1—1.151-4	1/19/17		49,737
152	1.152-0—1.152-5	1/19/17		49,737
162	1.162-10	2/4/86		49,066
	1.162-15	12/17/19		49,823
	1.162-20	11/25/80		49,014
	1.162-25T	1/7/85		49,051
	1.162-25T	11/1/85		49,061
	1.162-27, 1.162-33	12/20/19		49,824
	1.162-30	2/26/04		49,216
	1.162-31	6/10/16		49,701
	1.162(l)-1	7/28/14		49,624
163	5f.163-1	11/15/82		49,021
	5f.163-1	4/8/86		49,070
	5f.163-1	9/19/17		49,744
	1.163-4	4/8/86		49,070
	1.163-5, 1.163-5T	9/19/17		49,744
	1.163-5T	5/19/88		49,097
	1.163-5T	5/19/88		49,098
	1.163-6	5/8/85		49,054
	1.163-8	7/2/87		49,081
	1.163-9, 1.163-10	12/22/87		49,087
	1.163(j)-0—1.163(j)-11	12/28/18		49,780
164	1.164-3	12/17/19		49,823
165	1.165-11	10/14/16		49,716
	1.165-12	9/19/17		49,744
166	1.166-4	12/19/83		49,030
167	1.167(a)-5	7/18/88		49,105
	1.167(a)-11	2/16/84		49,032
	1.167(a)-13	3/15/94		49,144
	1.167(n)-0—1.167(n)-7	5/31/02		49,190
168	1.168-1—1.168-6	2/16/84		49,032
	1.168(j)-1	7/2/85		49,055
	1.168(k)-0, 1.168(k)-2	9/24/19		49,813
170A	1.170A-1, 1.170A-13	12/17/19		49,823
	1.170A-9	4/24/20		49,833
172	1.172(h)-0—1.172(h)-5	9/17/12		49,548
178	1.178-1	2/16/84		49,032
179B	1.179B-1	6/27/08		49,376
183	1.183-1	8/7/80		49,013
197	1.197-1	3/15/94		49,144
	1.197-2	12/19/17	TD 9891, 1/17/20	49,738
199	1.199-0—1.199-9	6/19/19		49,803
199A	1.199A-0, 1.199A-3, 1.199A-6	2/8/19		49,787
	1.199A-7—1.199A-12	6/19/19		49,803
212	1.212-1	8/7/80		49,013
	1.212-1	2/26/04		49,216
215	1.215-1	8/31/84		49,041
219	1.219-1—1.219-3	7/14/81		49,018
	1.219(a)-1—1.219(a)-6	1/23/84		49,031
220	1.220-1	7/14/81		49,018
245A	1.245A-1—1.245A-5	6/18/19		49,802
	1.245A(e)-1	12/28/18	TD 9896, 4/7/20	49,785

[1] Date published in the *Federal Register*.

[2] Date filed with the *Federal Register*.

1986 Code Sec.	Regs. Section	Date Proposed[1]	Date Adopted[2]	Paragraph (¶)
	1.245A(e)-1	4/8/20	....	49,831
249	1.249-1	4/8/86	....	49,070
250	1.250-0, 1.250-1, 1.250(a)-1, 1.250(b)-1—1.250(b)-6	3/6/19	....	49,788
262	1.262-1	8/7/80	....	49,013
263	1.263(g)-1—1.263(g)-5	1/18/01	....	49,181
263A	1.263A-9	12/28/18	....	49,780
265	1.265-2	5/7/04	....	49,219
267	1.267(a)-2	11/30/84	....	49,048
	1.267(a)-3	10/2/19	....	49,815
269A	1.269A-1	3/31/83	....	49,026
	1.267A-1—1.267A-7	12/28/18	TD 9896, 4/7/20	49,785
274	1.274-1, 1.274-3, 1.274-8	1/9/89	....	49,110
	1.274-5T, 1.274-6T	11/1/85	....	49,061
	1.274-11, 1.274-12	2/26/20	....	49,829
275	51.2, 51.11	7/28/14	....	49,625
280A	1.280A-1—1.280A-3	8/7/80	....	49,013
	1.280A-1—1.280A-3	7/21/83	....	49,028
280F	1.280F-1—1.280F-5	10/24/84	....	49,045
	1.280F-1, 1.280F-3, 1.280F-5	11/1/85	....	49,061
280H	1.280H-0T, 1.280H-1T	5/27/88	....	49,099
301	1.301-1	3/26/19	....	49,792
305	1.305-1, 1.305-3, 1.305-7	4/13/16	....	49,695
312	1.312-10	11/15/00	....	49,175
316	1.316-2	11/7/19	....	49,818
332	1.332-8	10/2/19	....	49,815
337	1.337(d)-3	3/25/19	....	49,790
338	1.338-1	12/20/19	....	49,824
	1.338-11	4/2/20	....	49,830
351	1.351-1	12/23/14	....	49,635
355	1.355-0, 1.355-1, 1.355-3	5/8/07	....	49,297
	1.355-0, 1.355-2, 1.355-8, 1.355-9	7/15/16	....	49,706
	1.355-0, 1.355-8	12/19/16	TD 9888, 12/16/19	49,728
356	1.356-1	3/26/19	....	49,792
361	1.361-1	12/23/14	....	49,635
367	1.367(a)-1, 1.367(a)-6, 1.367(d)-1	5/16/86	....	49,071
	1.367(a)-1T	1/16/90	....	49,115
	1.367(a)-8	10/2/19	....	49,815
	1.367(a) 9	2/11/09	....	49,415
	1.367(b)-5, 1.367(b)-8, 1.367(e)-1	11/15/00	....	49,175
368	1.368-2	3/26/19	....	49,792
381	1.381(c)(20)-1	12/28/18	....	49,780
	1.381(c)(22)-1	4/2/20	....	49,830
382	1.382-1, 1.382-2, 1.382-5, 1.382-6	12/28/18	....	49,780
	1.382-1, 1.382-2, 1.382-7	9/10/19	....	49,812
	1.382-1, 1.382-2, 1.382-7	1/14/20	....	49,827
	1.382-2T	8/11/87	....	49,083
	1.382-2T	9/20/89	....	49,112
383	1.383-1	12/21/18	....	49,783
385	1.383-0, 1.383-1	12/28/18	....	49,780
385	1.385-3, 1.385-4	10/21/16	....	49,717
401	1.401(a)-1, 1.401(a)-3	11/10/04	....	49,228
	1.401(a)-1	1/27/16	....	49,678
	1.401(a)-13, 1.401(a)-20	10/9/08	....	49,401
	1.401(a)(9)-5, 1.401(a)(9)-6, 1.401(a)(9)-8, 1.401(a)(9)-9	11/8/19	....	49,819
402	1.402(a)-1, 1.402(e)-2, 1.402(e)-3	4/30/75	....	49,003
	1.402(a)-1, 1.402(e)-2, 1.402(e)-14	5/31/79	....	49,008
	1.402(a)(5)-1	2/4/86	....	49,066
	1.402(f)-1	10/9/08	....	49,401
403	1.403(a)-1, 1.403(a)-2	4/30/75	....	49,003
	1.403(a)-2	5/31/79	....	49,008
404	1.404(a)-1, 1.404(b)-1, 1.404(d)-1,1.404(k)-1	2/4/86	....	49,066
	1.404(h)-1	7/14/81	....	49,018
	1.404(k)-2	8/24/05	....	49,247
404A	1.404A-0—1.404A-7	5/7/93	....	49,142

[1] Date published in the *Federal Register*.

[2] Date filed with the *Federal Register*.

1986 Code Sec.	Regs. Section	Date Proposed[1]	Date Adopted[2]	Paragraph (¶)
408	1.408-2—1.408-4, 1.408-6—1.408-9	7/14/81	. . . .	49,018
	1.408-2, 1.408-3, 1.408-10	1/23/84	. . . .	49,031
	1.408-5	11/16/84	. . . .	49,047
409A	1.409A-0, 1.409A-4	12/8/08	. . . .	49,406
	1.409A-0—1.409A-4, 1.409A-6	6/22/16	. . . .	49,702
410	1.410(a)-3, 1.410(a)-8, 1.410(a)-9	1/6/88	. . . .	49,088
	1.410(a)-4A	4/8/88	. . . .	49,093
411	1.411(a)-1, 1.411(a)-7, 1.411(b)-2, 1.411(c)-1	4/11/88	. . . .	49,093
	1.411(a)-3, 1.411(a)-4, 1.411(a)-8	1/6/88	. . . .	49,088
	1.411(a)-11	10/9/08	. . . .	49,401
	1.411(b)-1	6/18/08	. . . .	49,374
	1.411(c)-1	12/22/95	. . . .	49,151
	1.411(d)-1	4/9/80	. . . .	49,010
	1.411(d)-1	6/12/80	. . . .	49,012
412	1.412(a)-1, 1.412(b)-1, 1.412(b)-4, 1.412(c)(2)-2,1.412(c)(4)-1— 1.412(c)(10)-1, 1.412(g)-1	12/1/82		49,022
413	1.413-1, 1.413-2	12/1/82	. . . .	49,022
	1.413-2	7/3/19	. . . .	49,805
414	1.414(m)-1—1.414(m)-4	2/25/83	. . . .	49,025
	1.414(o)-1	8/27/87	. . . .	49,084
	1.414(q)-1	2/19/88	. . . .	49,089
415	1.415(c)-2	11/15/13	. . . .	49,593
417	1.417(e)-1	10/9/08	. . . .	49,401
	1.417(e)-1	11/25/16	. . . .	49,722
419	1.419-1	2/4/86	. . . .	49,066
419A	1.419A-1	2/4/86	. . . .	49,066
	1.419A-2	7/3/85	. . . .	49,056
432	1.432(a)-1, 1.432(b)-1	3/18/08	. . . .	49,357
442	1.442-1	1/5/93	. . . .	49,139
444	1.444-0T—1.444-3T	5/27/88	. . . .	49,099
446	1.446-1	1/28/99	. . . .	49,169
	1.446-1, 1.446-2	9/9/19	. . . .	49,810
	1.446-2	12/22/92	. . . .	49,136
	1.446-3	7/10/91	. . . .	49,123
	1.446-3	2/26/04	. . . .	49,216
	1.446-3	9/16/11	. . . .	49,493
	1.446-3	5/8/15	. . . .	49,647
	1.446-3	12/28/18	. . . .	49,780
	1.446-4	12/19/2017	. . . .	49,753
448	1.448-1T	6/16/87	. . . .	49,079
451	1.451-1, 1.451-2	4/8/86	. . . .	49,070
	1.451-1, 1.451-3	9/9/19	. . . .	49,810
	1.451-8	9/9/19	. . . .	49,809
453	1.453-1	5/3/84	. . . .	49,034
	15A.453-0, 15A.453-1	2/4/81	. . . .	49,015
453B	1.453B-1	12/23/14	. . . .	49,635
454	1.454-1	4/8/86	. . . .	49,070
457	1.457-1, 1.457-2, 1.457-4, 1.457-6, 1.457-7, 1.457-9—1.457-13	6/22/16	. . . .	49,703
460	1.460-3, 1.460-4, 1.460-5, 1.460-6	8/4/08	. . . .	49,390
465	1.465-1—1.465-7, 1.465-9—1.465-13, 1.465-22—1.465-26, 1.465-38, 1.465-39, 1.465-41—1.465-45, 1.465-66—1.465-69, 1.465-75—1.465-79, 1.465-95	6/5/79	. . . .	49,009
468A	1.468A-1, 1.468A-5	12/29/16	. . . .	49,730
469	1.469-1T, 1.469-2T, 1.469-3T, 1.469-5T	2/24/88	. . . .	49,090
	1.469-0, 1.469-5, 1.469-5T, 1.469-9	11/28/11	. . . .	49,509
	1.469-9, 1.469-11	12/28/18	. . . .	49,780
471	1.471-12	1/28/99	. . . .	49,169
472	1.472-2	2/10/83	. . . .	49,024
475	1.475(a)-1, 1.475(a)-2, 1.475(b)-3	1/4/95	. . . .	49,145
	1.475(c)-1, 1.475(c)-2, 1.475(e)-1, 1.475(f)-1,1.475(f)-2, 1.475(g)-1	1/28/99	. . . .	49,169
	1.475(g)-2	3/6/98	. . . .	49,165
481	1.481-5, 1.481-6	11/7/19	. . . .	49,818

---

[1] Date published in the *Federal Register*.
[2] Date filed with the *Federal Register*.

1986 Code Sec.	Regs. Section	Date Proposed[1]	Date Adopted[2]	Paragraph (¶)
482	1.482-0—1.482-2, 1.482-8	3/6/98	. . . .	49,165
	1.482-1	9/16/15	. . . .	49,667
501	1.501(a)-1, 1.501(c)(3)-1	7/2/14	. . . .	49,619
	1.501(c)(4)-1	11/29/13	. . . .	49,595
	1.501(c)(9)-2	8/7/92	. . . .	49,129
	1.501(c)(20)-1	4/29/80	. . . .	49,011
505	1.505(c)-1	2/4/86	. . . .	49,066
508	1.508-1	7/2/14	. . . .	49,619
509	1.509(a)-3	4/24/20	. . . .	49,833
	1.509(a)-4	2/9/16	. . . .	49,682
511	1.511-2	6/22/15	. . . .	49,654
512	1.512(a)-1, 1.512(a)-6	4/24/20	. . . .	49,833
	1.512(a)-5	2/6/14	. . . .	49,609
	1.512(b)-1	9/16/11	. . . .	49,493
	1.512(b)-1	4/24/20	. . . .	49,833
513	1.513-1	6/22/15	. . . .	49,654
	1.513-1	4/24/20	. . . .	49,833
514	1.514(c)-2	11/23/16	. . . .	49,721
527	1.527-3	8/28/79	. . . .	49,009A
529	1.529-0—1.529-6	8/24/98	. . . .	49,167
529A	1.529A-0—1.529A-7	6/22/15	. . . .	49,654
	1.529A-0, 1.529A-1, 1.529A-8	10/10/19	. . . .	49,817
563	1.563-1	1/5/93	. . . .	49,139
581	1.581-2	12/19/83	. . . .	49,030
582	1.582-1	4/8/86	. . . .	49,070
591	1.591-1	12/19/83	. . . .	49,030
593	1.593-1—1.593-11	12/19/83	. . . .	49,030
612	1.612-3	2/8/00	. . . .	49,172
617	1.617-4	11/3/14	. . . .	49,633
636	1.636-1	4/8/86	. . . .	49,070
642	1.642(c)-1, 1.642(c)-2	5/5/88	. . . .	49,096
652	1.652(b)-1	4/30/75	. . . .	49,003
664	1.664-1	12/19/75	. . . .	49,004
671	1.671-1, 1.671-2	9/27/96	. . . .	49,154
672	1.672(f)-2	10/2/19	. . . .	49,815
702	1.702-3	12/23/87	. . . .	49,086
704	1.704-1	5/24/05	. . . .	49,242
	1.704-1	12/7/16	TD 9895, 3/20/20	49,725
	1.704-1	8/9/18	. . . .	49,767
	1.704-1, 1.704-3	11/3/14	. . . .	49,633
	1.704-1, 1.704-3	1/19/17	TD 9891, 1/17/20	49,738
	1.704-3, 1.704-4	8/22/07	. . . .	49,318
	1.704-3, 1.704-4	1/16/14	. . . .	49,604
705	1.705-1	8/9/18	. . . .	49,767
706	1.706-0, 1.706-2, 1.706-2T, 1.706-3, 1.706-4	8/3/15	. . . .	49,658
	1.706-1	10/2/19	. . . .	49,815
	1.706-2	11/30/84	. . . .	49,048
	1.706-3	5/24/05	. . . .	49,242
	1.706-4	8/9/18	. . . .	49,767
707	1.707-1	5/24/05	. . . .	49,242
	1.707-0, 1.707-1, 1.707-2, 1.707-9	7/23/15	. . . .	49,657
721	1.721-1	5/24/05	. . . .	49,242
	1.721-1	12/23/14	. . . .	49,635
	1.721(c)-1—1.721(c)-7	1/19/17	TD 9891, 1/17/20	49,738
732	1.732-1	11/3/14	. . . .	49,633
	1.732-2	1/16/14	. . . .	49,604
734	1.734-1, 1.734-2	1/16/14	. . . .	49,604
736	1.736-1	11/3/14	. . . .	49,633
	1.736-1	7/23/15	. . . .	49,657
737	1.737-1, 1.737-2, 1.737-5	8/22/07	. . . .	49,318
	1.737-1	1/16/14	. . . .	49,604
743	1.743-1	1/16/14	. . . .	49,604
751	1.751-1	11/3/14	. . . .	49,633
752	1.752-0, 1.752-2, 1.752-4, 1.752-5	12/16/13	. . . .	49,600
	1.752-2	10/21/16	. . . .	49,717
754	1.754-1	10/12/17	. . . .	49,749

[1] Date published in the *Federal Register*.

[2] Date filed with the *Federal Register*.

1986 Code Sec.	Regs. Section	Date Proposed[1]	Date Adopted[2]	Paragraph (¶)
755	1.755-1	1/16/14		49,604
	1.755-1	11/3/14		49,633
761	1.761-1	5/24/05		49,242
	1.761-3	2/5/13		49,564
801	1.801-2, 1.801-5, 1.801-7, 1.801-8	4/2/20		49,830
	1.801-4	1/2/97		49,156
806	1.806-4	4/2/20		49,830
807	1.807-1, 1.807-3, 1.807-4	4/2/20		49,830
809	1.809-2, 1.809-5	4/2/20		49,830
810	1.810-3	4/2/20		49,830
816	1.816-1	4/2/20		49,830
817A	1.817A-0, 1.817A-1	4/2/20		49,830
818	1.818-2, 1.818-4	4/2/20		49,830
	1.818-3	4/8/86		49,070
848	1.848-1	4/2/20		49,830
851	1.851-2	9/28/16		49,713
860A	1.860A-0	10/9/19		49,816
860C	1.860C-2	12/28/18		49,780
860D	1.860D-1	9/19/17		49,744
860F	1.860F-4	9/30/91		49,124
860G	1.860G-1	10/9/19		49,816
	1.860G-3	4/13/16		49,695
861	1.861-2	4/8/86		49,070
	1.861-3	4/13/16		49,695
	1.861-4	10/17/07		49,327
	1.861-7, 1.861-18, 1.861-19	8/14/19		49,807
	1.861-8—1.861-12, 1.861-14	9/14/88		49,109
	1.861-8—1.861-14, 1.861-17	12/7/18	TD 9882, 12/16/19	49,781
	1.861-8, 1.861-8T, 1.861-9, 1.861-9T, 1.861-12, 1.861-12T, 1.861-14, 1.861-14T, 1.861-17	12/17/19		49,822
	1.861-9T, 1.861-13T	8/2/89		49,111
863	1.863-1—3, 1.863-8	12/30/19		49,826
	1.863-3, 1.863-7	3/6/98		49,165
	1.863-3A	9/14/88		49,109
	1.863-7	9/16/11		49,493
	1.863-8, 1.863-9	10/2/19		49,815
864	1.864-4, 1.864-6	3/6/98		49,165
	1.864-6	12/30/19		49,826
	1.864-8	6/14/88		49,101
	1.864(b)-1	6/12/98		49,166
	1.864(c)(8)-1	12/27/18		49,784
	1.864(c)(8)-2	5/13/19		49,797
865	1.865-3	12/30/19		49,826
871	1.871-14	9/19/17		49,744
	1.871-15	1/24/17		49,740
881	1.881-3	9/19/17		49,744
	1.881-3	4/8/20		49,831
882	1.882-5	3/8/96		49,152
	1.882-5	12/28/18		49,780
	1.882-5	10/9/19		49,816
884	1.884-1	3/8/96		49,152
	1.884-2T, 1.884-3T	9/2/88		49,106
892	1.892-1—1.892-7	6/27/88		49,103
	1.892-4, 1.892-5	11/3/11		49,503
894	1.894-1	3/6/98		49,165
897	1.897-4A, 1.897-5—1.897-9	5/5/88		49,095
	1.897-7, 1.897-7T	12/27/18		49,784
	1.897(l)-1	6/7/19		49,800
898	1.898-0—1.898-4	1/5/93		49,139
	1.898-4	6/13/01		49,139
901	1.901-2	3/30/07		49,293
	1.901(j)-1	12/7/18	TD 9882, 12/16/19	49,781
	1.901(m)-1—1.901(m)-8	12/7/16	TD 9895, 3/20/20	49,725
902	1.902-1, 1.902-3	3/26/19		49,792
904	1.904-1—1.904-6, 1.904(b)-3, 1.904(f)-12	12/7/18	TD 9882, 12/16/19	49,781

[1] Date published in the *Federal Register*.

[2] Date filed with the *Federal Register*.

1986 Code Sec.	Regs. Section	Date Proposed[1]	Date Adopted[2]	Paragraph (¶)
	1.904-4, 1.904(g)-3	6/25/12	TD 9882, 12/16/19	49,542
	1.904-4, 1.904-6, 1.904(b)-3, 1.904(g)-3	12/17/19	. . . .	49,822
	1.904-5	7/13/99	. . . .	49,170
	1.904-5	10/2/19	. . . .	49,815
905	1.905-4, 1.905-5	6/23/88	. . . .	49,102
	1.905-4, 1.905-5	11/7/07	. . . .	49,329
	1.905-3, 1.905-4, 1.905-5	12/17/19	. . . .	49,822
921	1.921-1T	2/3/87	. . . .	49,074
927	1.927(a)-1, 1.927(d)-2	3/3/87	. . . .	49,075
936	1.936-2, 1.936-3, 1.936-3A, 7.936-1	1/21/86	. . . .	49,065
	1.936-10	5/13/91	. . . .	49,120
937	1.937-1	8/27/15	. . . .	49,662
	1.937-2, 1.937-3	12/30/19	. . . .	49,826
	1.937-3	8/14/19	. . . .	49,807
951	1.951-1	6/21/19	. . . .	49,801
951A	1.951A-0, 1.951A-2, 1.951A-7	6/21/19	. . . .	49,801
	1.951A-0, 1.951A-2, 1.951A-7	4/8/20	. . . .	49,831
952	1.952-1	12/7/18	TD 9882, 12/16/19	49,781
953	1.953-0—1.953-7	4/17/91	. . . .	49,119
954	1.954-0—1.954-2, 1.954-9	7/13/99	. . . .	49,170
	1.954-0—1.954-2	5/20/19	TD 9883, 11/18/19	49,798
	1.954-1	12/7/18	TD 9882, 12/16/19	49,781
	1.954-1	6/21/19	. . . .	49,801
	1.954-1, 1.954-2	12/17/19	. . . .	49,822
	1.954-1T	4/17/91	. . . .	49,119
	1.954-2	9/16/11	. . . .	49,493
	1.954-0, 1.954-2	12/19/2017	. . . .	49,753
	1.954(c)(6)-1	6/18/19	. . . .	49,802
956	1.956-1, 1.956-2	6/14/88	. . . .	49,101
	1.956-1	6/21/19	. . . .	49,801
	1.956-2	5/8/15	. . . .	49,647
	1.956-4	11/3/16	. . . .	49,720
958	1.958-1	6/21/19	. . . .	49,801
	1.958-2	5/20/19	TD 9883, 11/18/19	49,798
	1.958-2	10/2/19	. . . .	49,815
959	1.959-1—1.959-4	8/29/06	. . . .	49,277
960	1.960-1—1.960-7	12/7/18	TD 9882, 12/16/19	49,781
	1.960-7	12/17/19	. . . .	49,822
961	1.961-1—1.961-4	8/29/06	. . . .	49,277
962	1.962-1	3/6/19	. . . .	49,788
964	1.964-1	4/17/91	. . . .	49,119
	1.964-1	11/4/11	. . . .	49,504
965	1.965-5	12/7/18	TD 9882, 12/16/19	49,781
	1.965-5, 1.965-9	12/17/19	. . . .	49,822
987	1.987-1, 1.987-3, 1.987-6, 1.987-8	12/8/16	. . . .	49,726
988	1.988-1	3/17/92	. . . .	49,125
	1.988-1	9/16/11	. . . .	49,493
	1.988-2	3/17/92	. . . .	49,125
	1.988-4	3/6/98	. . . .	49,165
	1.988-5	3/17/92	. . . .	49,125
	1.988-7	12/19/2017	. . . .	49,753
991	1.991-1	2/3/87	. . . .	49,074
992	1.992-1, 1.992-2	2/3/87	. . . .	49,074
993	1.993-1	4/8/86	. . . .	49,070
995	1.995-2, 1.995-2A, 1.995-8, 1.995(f)-1	2/3/87	. . . .	49,074
	1.995-4	11/3/14	. . . .	49,633
996	1.996-1, 1.996-9	2/3/87	. . . .	49,074
999	1.999-1	2/24/77	. . . .	49,006
1001	1.1001-1	10/18/06	. . . .	49,280
	1.1001-3	12/28/18	. . . .	49,786
	1.1001-6	10/9/19	. . . .	49,816
1012	1.1012-2	4/8/86	. . . .	49,070
1014	1.1014-10	3/4/16	. . . .	49,690
1016	1.1016-3, 1.1016-4	2/16/84	. . . .	49,032
	1.1016-5	4/8/86	. . . .	49,070
1031	1.1031(d)-1	7/18/88	. . . .	49,105

[1] Date published in the *Federal Register*.

[2] Date filed with the *Federal Register*.

1986 Code Sec.	Regs. Section	Date Proposed[1]	Date Adopted[2]	Paragraph (¶)
1037	1.1037-1	4/8/86	....	49,070
1041	1.1041-1	8/31/84	....	49,041
1042	1.1042-1	2/4/86	....	49,066
	1.1042-1T	7/10/03	....	49,208
1058	1.1058-1, 1.1058-2	7/26/83	....	49,029
1092	1.1092(b)-1, 1.1092(b)-2, 1.1092(b)-5	1/24/85	....	49,052
	1.1092(b)-3, 1.1092(b)-4	1/24/85	....	49,053
	1.1092(d)-2	5/2/95	....	49,148
1223	1.1223-2	7/26/83	....	49,029
1231	1.1231-1	11/3/14	....	49,633
1232	1.1232-1—1.1232-3A	4/8/86	....	49,070
1234	1.1234-3	2/5/13	....	49,564
1234A	1.1234A-1	2/26/04	....	49,216
1245	1.1245-1, 1.1245-2, 1.1245-4	11/3/14	....	49,633
1248	1.1248-1	4/17/91	....	49,119
	1.1248-1	11/3/14	....	49,633
1250	1.1250-1	11/3/14	....	49,633
1252	1.1252-2	11/3/14	....	49,633
1254	1.1254-5	11/3/14	....	49,633
1255	16A.1255-1, 16A.1255-2	5/21/81	....	49,016
1256	1.1256(b)-1, 1.1256(g)-1	9/16/11	....	49,493
1271	1.1271-0	8/25/04	....	49,226
	1.1271-0	10/9/19	....	49,816
1275	1.1275-2	8/25/04	....	49,226
	1.1275-2	9/9/19	....	49,810
	1.1275-2	10/9/19	....	49,816
1287	1.1287-1	9/19/17	....	49,744
1291	1.1291-0	4/28/95	....	49,147
	1.1291-0, 1.1291-1	7/11/19	....	49,806
	1.1291-1—1.1291-7	4/1/92	....	49,126
1293	1.1293-1	4/1/92	....	49,126
	1.1293-2	12/24/96	....	49,155
1294	1.1294-1	3/2/88	....	49,091
1295	1.1295-1	4/1/92	....	49,126
	1.1295-2	12/24/96	....	49,155
1296	1.1296-4	1/2/98	....	49,164
	1.1296-4, 1.1296-6	4/28/95	....	49,147
1297	1.1297-0—1.1297-2, 1.1297-4, 1.1297-5	7/11/19	....	49,806
	1.1297-1	10/2/19	....	49,815
	1.1297-4	9/27/96	....	49,154
1298	1.1298-0, 1.1298-2, 1.1298-4	7/11/19	....	49,806
1361	18.0	1/26/83	....	49,023
	1.1361-5	3/6/15	....	49,640
1362	1.1362-3	3/6/15	....	49,640
1371	1.1371-1, 1.1371-2	11/7/19	....	49,818
1377	1.1377-2, 1.1377-3	11/7/19	....	49,818
1379	18.1379-1, 18.1379-2	1/26/83	....	49,023
1388	1.1388-1	6/19/19	....	49,803
1400Z	1.1400Z-2(a)-1, 1.1400Z-2(c)-1, 1.1400Z-2(d)-1, 1.1400Z-2(e)-1	10/29/18	TD 9889, 12/31/19	49,773
	1.1400Z2(a)-1—1.1400Z2(d)-1, 1.1400Z2(f)-1, 1.1400Z2(g)-1	5/1/19	TD 9889, 12/31/19	49,795
1402	1.1402(a)-2	1/13/97	....	49,157
1411	1.1411-0, 1.1411-3, 1.1411-4, 1.1411-7	12/2/13	....	49,594
1441	1.1441-1	10/14/97	....	49,160
	1.1441-1, 1.1441-6	12/18/18	TD 9890, 12/27/19	49,782
	1.1441-1, 1.1441-2, 1.1441-6, 1.1441-7	1/6/17	TD 9890, 12/27/19	49,733
	1.1441-3	10/14/97	....	49,161
	1.1441-3	10/17/07	....	49,326
	1.1441-3	6/7/19	....	49,800
1445	1.1445-10, 1.1445-11	5/5/88	....	49,095
	1.1445-2, 1.1445-5, 1.1445-8	5/13/19	....	49,797
	1.1445-2, 1.1445-4, 1.1445-5, 1.1445-8	6/7/19	....	49,800
1446	1.1446-3	7/20/17	TD 9892, 1/29/20	49,743
	1.1446-3, 1.1446-4, 1.1446-7	5/13/19	....	49,797
	1.1446-1, 1.1446-2, 1.1446-7	6/7/19	....	49,800

[1] Date published in the *Federal Register*.

[2] Date filed with the *Federal Register*.

1986 Code Sec.	Regs. Section	Date Proposed[1]	Date Adopted[2]	Paragraph (¶)
1461	1.1461-2	4/13/16,	. . . .	49,695
	1.1461-1, 1.1461-2	12/18/18	. . . .	49,782
	1.1461-1—1.1461-3	5/13/19	. . . .	49,797
1463	1.1463-1	5/13/19	. . . .	49,797
1464	1.1464-1	5/13/19	. . . .	49,797
1471	1.1471-2	4/13/16	. . . .	49,695
	1.1471-1, 1.1471-3, 1.1471-4	1/6/17	TD 9890, 12/27/19	49,732
	1.1471-1	12/18/18	TD 9890, 12/27/19	49,782
	1.1471-2—1.1471-5	12/18/18	. . . .	49,782
1473	1.1473-1	4/13/16	. . . .	49,695
	1.1473-1	12/18/18	. . . .	49,782
1474	1.1474-1	1/6/17	TD 9890, 12/27/19	49,732
	1.1474-1, 1.1474-2	12/18/18	. . . .	49,782
1502	1.1502-1, 1.1502-5, 1.1502-33,1.1502-55	12/30/92	. . . .	49,138
	1.1502-2, 1.1502-4, 1.1502-43, 1.1502-47, 1.1502-59A, 1.1502-100	12/21/18	. . . .	49,783
	1.1502-4, 1.1502-21	12/17/19	. . . .	49,822
	1.1502-11, 1.1502-12	6/11/15	. . . .	49,650
	1.1502-12	8/29/06	. . . .	49,277
	1.1502-12, 1.1502-13, 1.1502-50	3/6/19	. . . .	49,788
	1.1502-13	5/7/04	. . . .	49,219
	1.1502-13	1/16/14	. . . .	49,604
	1.1502-13	3/6/15	. . . .	49,640
	1.1502-13, 1.1502-21, 1.1502-36, 1.1502-79, 1.1502-90, 1.1502-91, 1.1502-95, 1.1502-98, 1.1502-99	12/28/18	. . . .	49,780
	1.1502-13	12/30/19	. . . .	49,826
	1.1502-21	5/31/02	. . . .	49,189
	1.1502-21	6/23/10	. . . .	49,450
	1.1502-21, 1.1502-72	9/17/12	. . . .	49,548
	1.1502-21, 1.1502-22, 1.1502-28	3/6/15	. . . .	49,640
	1.1502-21, 1.1502-21A, 1.1502-22, 1.1502-22A, 1.1502-23A,1.1502-24	6/11/15	. . . .	49,650
	1.1502-32	8/29/06	. . . .	49,277
	1.1502-51	6/21/19	. . . .	49,801
	1.1502-76	3/6/15	. . . .	49,640
	1.1502-80	11/14/01	. . . .	49,183
	1.1502-80	3/18/04	. . . .	49,217
	1.1502-81	3/18/87	. . . .	49,076
	1.1502-91	10/24/11	. . . .	49,499
1503	1.1503(d)-1, 1.1503(d)-3, 1.1503(d)-6, 1.1503(d)-7, 1.1503(d)-8	12/28/18	TD 9896, 4/7/20	49,785
1504	1.1504-4	12/28/18	. . . .	49,780
1552	1.1552-1	12/30/92	. . . .	49,138
2010	20.2010-1, 20.2010-3	11/23/18	. . . .	61,166
2031	20.2031-4	8/20/85	. . . .	61,104
2032	20.2032-1	5/7/09	. . . .	61,140
	20.2032-1	11/18/11	. . . .	61,150
2036	20.2036-2	8/3/83	. . . .	61,103
2039	20.2039-1T	1/29/86	. . . .	61,106
	20.2039-2, 20.2039-4	1/23/84	. . . .	61,105
2055	20.2055-2	12/19/75	. . . .	61,101
2501	25.2501-1	6/22/15	. . . .	61,157
2503	25.2503-3	6/22/15	. . . .	61,157
	25.2503-5	7/14/81	. . . .	61,102
	25.2503-6	6/22/15	. . . .	61,157
2511	25.2511-2	6/22/15	. . . .	61,157
2512	25.2512-4, 25.2512-8	4/8/86	. . . .	61,107
2642	26.2642-1	6/22/15	. . . .	61,157
	26.2642-7	4/17/08	. . . .	61,132
2652	26.2652-1	6/22/15	. . . .	61,157
2801	28.2801-0—28.2801-7	9/10/15	. . . .	61,158
3401	31.3401(a)-1T	1/7/85	. . . .	49,051
	31.3401(e)-1	2/13/20	. . . .	49,828

[1] Date published in the *Federal Register*.
[2] Date filed with the *Federal Register*.

1986 Code Sec.	Regs. Section	Date Proposed[1]	Date Adopted[2]	Paragraph (¶)
3402	31.3402(a)-1, 31.3402(b)-1, 31.3402(c)-1, 31.3402(f)(1)-1, 31.3402(f)(2)-1, 31.3402(f)(3)-1, 31.3402(f)(4)-1, 31.3402(f)(4)-2, 31.3402(f)(5)-1, 31.3402(f)(6)-1, 31.3402(g)-1, 31.3402(h)(4)-1, 31.3402(i)-1, 31.3402(i)-2, 31.3402(l)-1, 31.3402(m)-1, 31.3402(n)-1,	2/13/20	. . . .	49,828
3405	31.3405(e)-2	5/31/19	. . . .	49,799
3406	31.3406(b)(3)-2	12/17/09	. . . .	49,439
3501	31.3501(a)-1	1/7/85	. . . .	49,051
3508	31.3508-1	1/7/86	. . . .	49,064
3509	31.3509-1	1/7/86	. . . .	49,064
4001	48.0-1, 48.0-4	7/29/08	. . . .	62,153
	48.0-1, 48.0-2, 48.0-4	3/31/16	. . . .	62,166
4041	48.4041-0, 48.4041-18—48.4041-20	7/29/08	. . . .	62,153
	48.4041-8	3/31/16	. . . .	62,166
4051	48.4051-0, 48.4051-1, 145.4051-1, 48.4051-2	3/31/16	. . . .	62,166
4052	48.4052-1, 145.4052-1	3/31/16	. . . .	62,166
4061	48.4061(a)-1	3/31/16	. . . .	62,166
4071	48.4071-1—48.4071-4	3/31/16	. . . .	62,166
4072	48.4072-1	3/31/16	. . . .	62,166
4073	48.4073-1—48.4073-4	3/31/16	. . . .	62,166
4081	48.4081-1—48.4081-3, 48.4081-6	7/29/08	. . . .	62,153
	48.4081-1	3/31/16	. . . .	62,166
4082	48.4082-1	4/26/05	. . . .	62,149
	48.4082-4	7/29/08	. . . .	62,153
4101	48.4101-1	4/26/05	. . . .	62,149
	48.4101-1	7/29/08	. . . .	62,153
4221	48.4221-7, 48.4221-8	3/31/16	. . . .	62,166
4252	49.4252-0	4/1/03	. . . .	62,145
4377	46.4377-1	6/10/16	. . . .	62,167
4482	41.4482(a)-1	3/31/16	. . . .	62,166
4701	46.4701-1	9/19/17	. . . .	49,744
4941	53.4941(d)-2	8/20/85	. . . .	49,057
4968	53.4968-1	7/3/19	. . . .	49,804
4971	54.4971-1—54.4971-3	12/1/82	. . . .	49,022
4973	54.4973-1	7/14/81	. . . .	49,018
4974	54.4974-1	7/14/81	. . . .	49,018
4976	54.4976-1T	2/4/86	. . . .	49,066
4977	54.4977-1T	1/7/85	. . . .	49,051
4978	54.4978-1T	2/4/86	. . . .	49,066
4980	54.4980H-4, 54.4980H-5	9/30/19	. . . .	49,814
5000A	1.5000A-2	6/10/16	. . . .	49,701
	1.5000A-3	7/8/16	. . . .	49,704
6011	54.6011-1T	4/3/87	. . . .	49,077
	1.6011-2	2/3/87	. . . .	49,074
	1.6011-4	9/26/07	. . . .	49,322
	301.6011-2	6/22/15	. . . .	49,654
	301.6011-2	5/31/18	. . . .	49,760
	301.6011-6	9/14/10	. . . .	49,462
	301.6011-8	9/9/13	. . . .	49,587
	301.6011-9	9/9/13	. . . .	49,588
6012	1.6012-2	4/2/20	. . . .	49,830
	1.6012-6	7/20/17	TD 9892, 1/29/20	49,743
6013	1.6013-1	1/19/17	. . . .	49,737
6015	1.6015-0, 1.6015-5, 1.6015-9	8/13/13	. . . .	49,580
	1.6015-0—1.6015-9	11/20/15	. . . .	49,674
6031	1.6031(b)-1, 1.6031(c)-1	9/6/88	. . . .	49,107
	1.6031(a)-1	7/20/17	TD 9892, 1/29/20	49,743
	1.6031(a)-1	12/6/19	. . . .	49,821
6033	1.6033-2	11/25/80	. . . .	49,014
	1.6033-2	7/20/17	TD 9892, 1/29/20	49,743
	1.6033-2	9/10/19	. . . .	49,811
6035	1.6035-1	3/4/16	. . . .	49,690
6038	1.6038-2	6/18/19	. . . .	49,802
	1.6038-2, 1.6038-3	12/28/18	TD 9896, 4/7/20	49,785

[1] Date published in the *Federal Register*.

[2] Date filed with the *Federal Register*.

1986 Code Sec.	Regs. Section	Date Proposed[1]	Date Adopted[2]	Paragraph (¶)
	1.6038-2, 1.6038-3	3/6/19	. . . .	49,788
6038A	1.6038A-1, 1.6038A-2, 1.6038A-4	12/21/18	. . . .	49,783
	1.6038A-2	12/28/18	TD 9896, 4/7/20	49,785
	1.6038A-2	3/6/19	. . . .	49,788
6038B	1.6038B-1T	5/16/86	. . . .	49,071
	1.6038B-2	1/19/17	TD 9891, 1/17/20	49,738
6038C	1.6038C-1	12/10/90		49,118
6041	1.6041-2, 1.6041-6	7/20/17	TD 9892, 1/29/20	49,743
6041A	1.6041A-1	1/7/86		49,064
6042	301.6402-2	12/23/19	. . . .	49,825
6043	1.6043-4T	5/24/05	. . . .	49,239
6045	1.6045-1	4/8/86	. . . .	49,070
	1.6045-1	9/19/17	. . . .	49,744
	1.6045-1	10/17/18	. . . .	49,772
6045B	1.6045B-1	4/13/16	. . . .	49,695
6046	1.6046-1	4/17/91	. . . .	49,119
6049	1.6049-4—1.6049-6	4/8/86	. . . .	49,070
	1.6049-5	12/17/86	. . . .	49,072
	1.6049-5	9/19/17	. . . .	49,744
	1.6049-5	10/2/19	. . . .	49,815
	1.6049-7	9/30/91	. . . .	49,124
6050J	1.6050J-1T	8/31/84	. . . .	49,040
6050K	1.6050K-1	11/3/14	. . . .	49,633
	1.6050K-1	5/13/19	. . . .	49,797
6050S	1.6050S-1, 1.6050S-2	8/2/16	. . . .	49,709
6055	1.6055-1	8/2/16	. . . .	49,708
	1.6055-2	6/10/16	. . . .	49,701
6056	301.6056-2	6/10/16	. . . .	49,701
6057	301.6057-1, 301.6057-2	6/21/12	. . . .	49,539
6071	301.6071-2	9/14/10	. . . .	49,462
	31.6071(a)-1	7/20/17	TD 9892, 1/29/20	49,743
6072	1.6072-2	7/20/17	TD 9892, 1/29/20	49,743
6081	1.6081-11	6/21/12	. . . .	49,539
	1.6081-1—1.6081-3, 1.6081-5, 1.6081-6, 1.6081-9	7/20/17	TD 9892, 1/29/20	49,743
6103	301.6103(j)(1)-1	12/9/16	. . . .	49,727
	301.6103(n)-1	3/13/18	. . . .	49,758
6104	301.6104(c)-1	3/15/11	. . . .	49,475
6109	1.6109-2	2/15/12	. . . .	49,524
	301.6109-3	1/19/17	. . . .	49,737
6111	301.6111-1	8/15/84	. . . .	49,036
	301.6111-1	10/31/84	. . . .	49,046
	301.6111-1	3/4/86	. . . .	49,069
	301.6111-3	9/26/07	. . . .	49,322
6164	1.6164-4, 1.6164-8	3/26/84	. . . .	49,033
6225	301.6225-4	8/9/18	. . . .	49,767
6226	301.6226-4	8/9/18	. . . .	49,767
6227	301.6227-1	12/17/19	. . . .	49,822
6302	40.6302(c)-1	7/29/08	. . . .	62,153
6402	301.6402-7	6/11/15	. . . .	49,650
6416	48.6416(c)-1	3/31/16	. . . .	62,166
6421	48.6421-4	3/31/16	. . . .	62,166
6426	48.6426-1—48.6426-7	7/29/08	. . . .	62,153
6427	48.6427-8	7/29/08	. . . .	62,153
	48.6427-10	10/19/94	. . . .	62,124
	48.6427-12	7/29/08	. . . .	62,153
6601	301.6601-1	10/9/84	. . . .	49,044
6611	301.6611-1	10/9/84	. . . .	49,044
6621	301.6621-2	12/28/84	. . . .	49,049
6652	301.6652-4	1/23/84	. . . .	49,031
6655	1.6655-5	12/21/18	. . . .	49,783
6662	1.6662-8	3/4/16	. . . .	49,690
6689	301.6689-1	6/23/88	. . . .	49,102
	301.6689-1	11/7/07	. . . .	49,329
	301.6689-1	12/17/19	. . . .	49,822
6693	301.6693-1	7/14/81	. . . .	49,018

[1] Date published in the *Federal Register*.

[2] Date filed with the *Federal Register*.

1986 Code Sec.	Regs. Section	Date Proposed[1]	Date Adopted[2]	Paragraph (¶)
6708	301.6708-1	8/29/84	. . . .	49,039
6709	1.6709-1T	5/8/85	. . . .	49,054
6721	301.6721-1	3/4/16	. . . .	49,690
	301.6721-0, 301.6721-1	10/17/18	. . . .	49,772
	301.6721-1	5/31/18	. . . .	49,760
6722	301.6722-1	3/4/16	. . . .	49,690
	301.6722-1	10/17/18	. . . .	49,772
6724	301.6724-1	7/9/03	. . . .	49,206
	301.6724-1	8/2/16	. . . .	49,708
	301.6724-1	8/2/16	. . . .	49,709
	301.6724-1	10/17/18	. . . .	49,772
7519	1.7519-0T—1.7519-3T	5/27/88	. . . .	49,099
7602	301.7602-1	3/28/18	. . . .	49,759
7611	301.7611-1	8/5/09	. . . .	49,426
7701	301.7701-1	9/14/10	. . . .	49,462
	305.7701-1	5/7/84	. . . .	49,035
	301.7701-2	5/4/16	. . . .	49,696
	301.7701-3	12/28/18	TD 9896, 4/7/20	49,785
	301.7701-17	2/4/86	. . . .	49,066
	301.7701(b)-7	4/27/92	. . . .	49,127
7702	1.7702-1	7/5/91	. . . .	49,122
	1.7702-2, 1.7702A-1	12/15/92	. . . .	49,134
7871	305.7871-1	5/7/84	. . . .	49,035
7872	1.7872-1—1.7872-14	8/20/85	. . . .	49,057
	1.7872-4	4/8/86	. . . .	49,070
. . . .	57.2, 57.4, 57.10	6/10/16	. . . .	62,167
	57.2, 57.10	12/9/16	. . . .	62,169
	57.3, 57.10	12/9/16	. . . .	62,168
	300.3	10/13/16	TD 9894, 3/12/20	49,715
	300.12	4/16/20	. . . .	49,832
	301.9100-3	4/17/08	. . . .	49,363
	301.9100-6T	4/2/20	. . . .	49,830
9801	54.9801-1, 54.9801-2, 54.9801-4—54.9801-7	12/30/04	. . . .	49,234
	54.9801-2	6/10/16	. . . .	49,701
	54.9802-3	10/7/09	. . . .	49,435
9815	54.9815-2715A	11/27/19	. . . .	49,820
9831	54.9831-1	12/30/04	. . . .	49,234
	54.9831-1	6/10/16	. . . .	49,701
Procedural Rules	601.106	9/20/93	. . . .	49,143

[The next page is 73,601.]

---

[1] Date published in the *Federal Register*.

[2] Date filed with the *Federal Register*.

DETERMINATION OF TAX LIABILITY

Dependency Exemption: Authorized Placement Agency: Definition

Dependency Exemption: Authorized Placement Agency: Definition.—Amendments to Reg. §§1.2-1 and 1.2-2, relating to the definition of an authorized placement agency for purposes of a dependency exemption for a child placed for adoption that were issued prior to the changes made to the law by the Working Families Tax Relief Act of 2004, are proposed (published in the Federal Register on January 19, 2017) (REG-137604-07).

Par. 2. Section 1.2-1 is revised to read as follows:

§1.2-1. Returns of surviving spouse and head of household.— (a) *In general.*—Tax is determined under section 1(a) for a return of a surviving spouse, as defined in section 2(a) and §1.2-2(a). Tax is determined under section 1(b) for a return of a head of household, as defined in section 2(b) and §1.2-2(b).

(b) *Death of a spouse.*—If married taxpayers have different taxable years solely because of the death of either spouse, the taxable year of the deceased spouse is deemed to end on the last day of the surviving spouse's taxable year for purposes of determining their eligibility to file a joint return for that year. For rules relating to filing a joint return in the year a spouse dies, see section 6013 and the related regulations.

(c) *Tax tables.*—For rules on the use of the tax tables that apply to individuals, see section 3 and the related regulations.

(d) *Change in rates.*—For the treatment of taxable years during which a change in the tax rates occurs, see section 15.

(e) *Applicability date.*—This section applies to taxable years beginning after the date these regulations are published as final regulations in the **Federal Register**.

Par. 3. Section 1.2-2 is revised to read as follows:

§1.2-2. Definitions and special rules.—(a) *Surviving spouse.*— (1) *In general.*—If a taxpayer is eligible to file a joint return under section 6013 (without applying section 6013(a)(3)) for the taxable year in which the taxpayer's spouse dies, the taxpayer qualifies as a surviving spouse for each of the two taxable years immediately following the year of the spouse's death if the taxpayer—

(i) Has not remarried before the close of the taxable year; and

(ii) Maintains as the taxpayer's home a household that is for the taxable year the principal place of abode of a son or daughter (including by adoption), stepson, or stepdaughter who is a member of the taxpayer's household and who is a dependent of the taxpayer within the meaning of paragraph (a)(2) of this section.

(2) *Dependent.*—An individual is a dependent of a taxpayer for purposes of this paragraph (a) if the taxpayer may claim a deduction under section 151 for the individual, without applying sections 152(b)(1), (b)(2), and (d)(1)(B).

(b) *Head of household.*—(1) *In general.*—A taxpayer qualifies as a head of household if the taxpayer is not married at the end of the taxable year, is not a surviving spouse, as defined in paragraph (a) of this section, and either—

(i) Maintains as the taxpayer's home a household that is for more than one-half of the taxable year the principal place of abode of a qualifying child or dependent of the taxpayer, within the meaning of paragraph (b)(2) of this section, who is a member of the taxpayer's household during that period; or

(ii) Maintains a household, whether or not the taxpayer's home, that is for the taxable year the principal place of abode of a parent of the taxpayer, within the meaning of paragraph (b)(3) of this section.

(2) *Qualifying child or dependent.*—(i) *Qualifying child.*—An individual is a qualifying child for purposes of this paragraph (b) if the individual is a qualifying child of the taxpayer as defined in section 152(c) and the related regulations, determined without applying section 152(e). However, if the individual is married at the end of the taxpayer's taxable year, the individual is not a qualifying child for purposes of this section if the individual is not the taxpayer's dependent because of the limitations of section 152(b)(2) (relating to an individual filing a joint return with his or her spouse) or 152(b)(3) (relating to individuals who are citizens or nationals of other countries).

(ii) *Dependent.*—An individual is a dependent for purposes of this paragraph (b) if the individual is the taxpayer's dependent, within the meaning of section 152 without applying sections 152(d)(2)(H) (relating to an individual qualifying as a member of the household) and 152(d)(3) (relating to the special rule for multiple support agreements) for whom the taxpayer may claim a deduction under section 151.

(3) *Parent.*—An individual is a parent of the taxpayer for purposes of this paragraph (b) if the individual is the taxpayer's father or mother, including a father or mother who legally adopted the taxpayer, and is the taxpayer's dependent within the meaning of section 152 without applying section 152(d)(3), relating to the special rule for multiple support agreements, for whom the taxpayer may claim a deduction under section 151.

(4) *Limitation.*—An individual may qualify only one taxpayer as a head of household for taxable years beginning in the same calendar year.

(5) *Marital status.*—For purposes of this paragraph (b), the marital status of a taxpayer is determined at the end of the taxpayer's taxable year. A taxpayer is considered not married if the taxpayer is legally separated from the taxpayer's spouse under a decree of divorce or separate maintenance, if at any time during the taxable year the taxpayer's spouse is a nonresident alien, or if the provisions of section 7703(b) are satisfied. A taxpayer is considered married if the taxpayer's spouse, other than a spouse who is a nonresident alien, dies during the taxable year.

(6) *Nonresident alien.*—A taxpayer does not qualify as a head of household if the taxpayer is a nonresident alien, as defined in section 7701(b)(1)(B), at any time during the taxable year.

(c) *Member of the household.*—An individual is a member of a taxpayer's household if the individual and the taxpayer reside in the same living quarters and the taxpayer maintains the household, in part, for the benefit of the individual. An individual is a member of a taxpayer's household despite a temporary absence due to special circumstances. An individual is not treated as a member of the taxpayer's household if, at any time during the taxable year of the taxpayer, the relationship between the individual and the taxpayer violates local law. See §1.152-4(c)(2) for rules relating to temporary absences.

(d) *Maintaining a household.*—(1) *In general.*—A taxpayer maintains a household only if during the taxable year the taxpayer pays more than one-half of the cost of operating the household for the mutual benefit of the residents. These expenses include property taxes, mortgage interest, rent, utility charges, upkeep and repairs, property insurance, and food consumed on the premises. A taxpayer may treat a home's fair market rental value as a cost of maintaining a household, instead of the sum of payments for property taxes, mortgage interest, and property insurance. Expenses of maintaining a household do not include—

(i) The cost of clothing, education, medical treatment, vacations, life insurance, and transportation;

(ii) The value of services performed in the household by the taxpayer or any other person qualifying the taxpayer as a head of household or as a surviving spouse; or

(iii) An expense paid or reimbursed by any other person.

(2) *Proration of costs.*—In determining whether a taxpayer pays more than one-half of the cost of maintaining a household that is the principal place of abode of a qualifying child or dependent for less than a taxable year, the cost for the entire taxable year is prorated on the basis of the number of calendar months the qualifying child or dependent resides in the household. A period of less than a calendar month is treated as a full calendar month. Thus, for example, if the cost of maintaining a household for a taxable year is $30,000, and a taxpayer shares a principal place of abode with a qualifying child or dependent from May 20 to December 31, the taxpayer must furnish more than $10,000 (8/12 of $30,000 × 50 percent) in maintaining the household from May 1 to December 31 to satisfy the requirements of this paragraph (d).

(3) *New household.*—If a new household is established during the taxpayer's taxable year (for example, if spouses separate and one moves out of the family home with the child), the cost of maintaining

the new household for the year is the cost of maintaining that household beginning with the date the new household is established. If one spouse and the child remain in the family home and the other parent moves out of the home, the cost of maintaining the household for the year is the cost of maintaining the household beginning with the date the other spouse moves out.

(4) *Birth, death, adoption, or placement.*—If an individual is a member of a household for less than a taxable year as a result of the individual's birth, death, adoption, or placement with a taxpayer for adoption or in foster care during that year, the requirement that the individual be a member of the household for more than one-half of the taxable year is satisfied if the individual is a member of the household for more than one-half of the period after the individual's birth, adoption, or placement for adoption or in foster care or before the individual's death.

(5) *Shared residence.*—(i) *In general.*—If two or more taxpayers not filing a joint return reside in the same living quarters, each taxpayer may be treated as maintaining a separate household if each provides more than one-half of the cost of maintaining the separate household. For this purpose, two households in the same living quarters are not considered separate households if any individual in one household is the spouse of any individual in the other household, or if any individual in one household may claim, or would have priority under the tiebreaker rules in section 152(c)(4) to claim, any individual in the other household as a dependent.

(ii) *Examples.*—The following examples illustrate the rules in this paragraph (d)(5). In each example, assume that if a taxpayer may be treated as residing in a separate household, that taxpayer provides more than one-half of the cost of maintaining that household.

Example 1. Two sisters and their respective children reside in the same living quarters. Neither sister may claim the other sister as a dependent. Each sister pays more than one-half of the expenses for herself and her children, and each sister claims each of her own children as a dependent. Because neither sister may claim the other sister as a dependent, and because neither sister would have priority to claim any of the other sister's children as a qualifying child under the tiebreaker rules of section 152(c)(4), each sister is treated as maintaining a separate household.

Example 2. A and B, an unmarried couple, have two children together (C1 and C2) and all four individuals live in the same living quarters for the entire tax year. Both A and B contribute to paying the expenses of the couple and the two children. A has higher adjusted gross income than B. Each parent files a tax return. Under the tiebreaker rules in section 152(c)(4), the parent with the higher adjusted gross income (in this case, A) would have priority to claim

each child as a qualifying child if both claimed the child. As a result, B may not be treated as maintaining a separate household with either child or both children. Therefore, if B may be claimed as A's dependent, then all four individuals are members of the same household. However, if B may not be claimed as A's dependent, B may be treated as maintaining a separate household consisting solely of B, even if B claims one of the children as a dependent on B's return.

Example 3. The facts are the same as in *Example 2* of this paragraph (d)(5)(ii) except that A and B do not have any children together; C1 is the child of A and C2 is the child of B. Neither A nor B may claim the other as a dependent, and each parent pays more than one-half of the expenses for himself or herself and his or her child. Because neither A nor B may claim the other adult or the other adult's child as a dependent, each adult is treated as maintaining a separate household.

Example 4. Grandparent, Parent, and Child live together and Child meets the definition of a qualifying child for both Parent and Grandparent. Both Parent and Grandparent pay their respective expenses, and both contribute to paying Child's expenses. Neither Parent nor Grandparent may claim the other as a dependent. Under the tiebreaker rules of section 152(c)(4), Parent would have priority over Grandparent to claim Child as a qualifying child. Therefore, Grandparent may not be treated as maintaining a household for Grandparent and Child separate from the household of Parent. However, Parent may be treated as maintaining a household for Parent and Child separate from the household of Grandparent.

(e) *Special rules for maintaining a household.*—(1) *Principal place of abode.*—For purposes of this section, the term *principal place of abode* has the same meaning as in section 152 and § 1.152-4(c).

(2) *Part-year residence.*—If, during the taxable year, an individual who may qualify a taxpayer as head of household is born or dies, is adopted or lawfully placed for adoption with the taxpayer, is an eligible foster child, or is a missing child, whether the taxpayer maintained a household that is the principal place of abode of the individual for the required period is determined under § 1.152-4(d) and (e).

(3) *Change of location.*—A taxpayer may maintain a household even though the physical location of the household changes.

(f) *Certain married individuals living apart.*—An individual who is considered not married under section 7703(b) also is considered not married for all purposes of part I of subchapter A of chapter 1 of the Code.

(g) *Applicability date.*—This section applies to taxable years beginning after the date these regulations are published as final regulations in the **Federal Register**.

Dependency Exemption: Authorized Placement Agency: Definition

Dependency Exemption: Authorized Placement Agency: Definition.—Amendments to Reg. §§1.3-1, relating to the definition of an authorized placement agency for purposes of a dependency exemption for a child placed for adoption that were issued prior to the changes made to the law by the Working Families Tax Relief Act of 2004, are proposed (published in the Federal Register on January 19, 2017) (REG-137604-07).

Par. 4. Section 1.3-1 is revised to read as follows:

§1.3-1. Tax tables for individuals.—(a) *In general.*—Except as otherwise provided in paragraph (b) of this section, in lieu of the tax imposed by section 1, an individual who does not itemize deductions for the taxable year and whose taxable income for the taxable year does not exceed the ceiling amount as defined in paragraph (c) of this section, must determine his or her tax liability under the prescribed tax tables in tax forms and publications of the Internal Revenue Service. The individual must use the appropriate tax rate category under the tax tables. The tax imposed under section 3 and this section shall be treated as tax imposed by section 1.

(b) *Exceptions.*—Section 3 and this section do not apply to (1) an individual making a return for a period of fewer than 12 months as a

result of a change in annual accounting period, or (2) an estate or trust.

(c) *Ceiling amount defined.*—The ceiling amount means the highest amount of taxable income for which a tax amount is determined in the tax tables for the tax rate category in which the taxpayer falls.

(d) *Special rule for surviving spouse.*—A taxpayer filing as a surviving spouse uses the same tax rate category as a taxpayer filing a joint return.

(e) *Applicability date.*—This section applies to taxable years beginning after the date these regulations are published as final regulations in the **Federal Register**.

Dependency Exemption: Authorized Placement Agency: Definition

Dependency Exemption: Authorized Placement Agency: Definition.—Amendments to Reg. §1.21-1, relating to the definition of an authorized placement agency for purposes of a dependency exemption for a child placed for adoption that were issued prior to the changes made to the law by the Working Families Tax Relief Act of 2004, are proposed (published in the Federal Register on January 19, 2017) (REG-137604-07).

Par. 5. Section 1.21-1 is amended by revising paragraph (a)(1), removing paragraph (h), redesignating paragraphs (j), (k), and (l) as paragraphs (h), (j), and (k), and revising newly redesignated paragraph (k) to read as follows:

§1.21-1. Expenses for household and dependent care services necessary for gainful employment.—(a) *In general.*—(1) Section 21 allows a credit to a taxpayer against the tax imposed by chapter 1 for employment-related expenses for household services and care (as defined in paragraph (d) of this section) of a qualifying individual (as

defined in paragraph (b) of this section). The purpose of the expenses must be to enable the taxpayer to be gainfully employed (as defined in paragraph (c) of this section). For taxable years beginning after December 31, 2004, a qualifying individual must have the same principal place of abode (as defined by paragraph (g) of this section) as the taxpayer for more than one-half of the taxable year.

* * *

(k) *Applicability date.*—(1) *In general.*—Except as provide in paragraph (k)(2) of this section, this section and §§1.21-2 through 1.21-4 apply to taxable years ending after August 14, 2007.

(2) *Exception.*—Paragraph (a)(1) of this section applies to taxable years beginning after the date these regulations are published as final regulations in the **Federal Register**.

Mortgage Credit Certificates: Issuance: Penalties

Mortgage Credit Certificates: Issuance: Penalties.—Temporary Reg. §§1.25-1T—1.25-4T, relating to the issuance of mortgage credit certificates, are also proposed as final and, when adopted, would become Reg. §§1.25-1—1.25-4 (published in the Federal Register on May 8, 1985).

§1.25-1. Credit for interest paid on certain home mortgages.

§1.25-2. Amount of credit.

§1.25-3. Qualified mortgage credit certificate.

§1.25-4. Qualified mortgage credit certificate program.

Mortgage Credit Certificates: Information

Mortgage Credit Certificates: Information Reporting.—An amendment to Temporary Reg. §1.25-4T, dealing with information reporting and policy statement requirements, is also proposed to be finalized (published in the Federal Register on September 3, 1985).

§1.25-4. Qualified mortgage credit certificate program.

Mortgage Credit Certificates: Issuance

Mortgage Credit Certificates: Issuance: Penalties.—Temporary Reg. §§1.25-5T—1.25-8T, relating to the issuance of mortgage credit certificates, are also proposed as final and, when adopted, would become Reg. §§1.25-5—1.25-8 (published in the Federal Register on May 8, 1985).

§1.25-5. Limitation on aggregate amount of mortgage credit certificates.

§1.25-6. Form of qualified mortgage credit certificate.

§1.25-7. Public notice.

§1.25-8. Reporting requirements.

Qualified Tuition: Related Expenses: Reporting

Qualified Tuition: Related Expenses: Reporting.—Amendments to Reg. §§1.25A-0—1.25A-2 and 1.25A-5, revising the rules for reporting qualified tuition and related expenses under section 6050S on a Form 1098-T, "Tuition Statement," and conforming the regulations to changes made to section 6050S by the Protecting Americans from Tax Hikes Act of 2015, are proposed (published in the Federal Register on August 2, 2016) (corrected September 26, 2016) (REG-131418-14).

Par. 2. Section 1.25A-0 is amended by:

1. Revising the entry for §1.25A-1(e)(1) introductory text.
2. Adding entries for §1.25A-1(e)(1), (2), and (3).
3. Revising the entries for §1.25A-1(f) introductory text and (f)(2).
4. Adding entries for §1.25A-1(f)(3) and (4).
5. Revising the entries for §1.25A-1(g) and (h).
6. Adding an entry for §1.25A-1(i).
7. Revising the entries for §§1.25A-2(d)(3), (4), (5), and (6).
8. Adding entries for §§1.25A-2(d)(7) and (e).
9. Revising the entry for §1.25A-5(f)(6).
10. Adding entries for §§1.25A-5(f)(7) and (g).

The revisions and additions read as follows:

§1.25A-0. Table of Contents.

* * *

§1.25A-1. Calculation of Education Tax Credit and General Eligibility Requirements.

* * *

(e) Identification requirements.

(1) In general.

(2) Additional identification requirements for the American Opportunity Tax Credit.

(i) TIN must be issued on or before the due date of the original return.

(ii) Return must include the eligible educational institution's employer identification number (EIN).

(3) Applicability dates.

(f) Statement requirement.

* * *

(2) Exceptions.

(3) Transition rule.

(4) Applicability date.

(g) Claiming the credit in the case of a dependent.

(h) Married taxpayers.

(i) Nonresident alien taxpayers and dependents.

§1.25A-2. Definitions.

* * *

(d) * * *

(3) Course materials for the American Opportunity Tax Credit for taxable years beginning after December 31, 2008.

(4) Personal expenses.

(5) Treatment of a comprehensive or bundled fee.

(6) Hobby courses.

(7) Examples.

(e) Applicability date.

* * *

§1.25A-5. Special Rules Relating to Characterization and Timing of Payments.

* * *

(f) * * *

(6) Treatment of refunds where qualified tuition and related expenses paid in two taxable years for the same academic period.

(7) Examples.

(g) Applicability date.

Par. 3. Section 1.25A-1 is amended by:

1. Revising paragraph (e).

2. Redesignating paragraphs (f), (g), and (h) as paragraphs (g), (h), and (i), respectively.

3. Adding a new paragraph (f).

4. In newly redesignated paragraph (g)(2), removing the language "(f)" and adding "(g)" in its place.

The revisions and additions read as follows:

§1.25A-1. Calculation of education tax credit and general eligibility requirements.

* * *

(e) *Identification requirements.*—(1) *In general.*—No education tax credit is allowed unless a taxpayer includes on the federal income tax return claiming the credit the name and the taxpayer identification number (TIN) of the student for whom the credit is claimed. For rules relating to assessment for an omission of a correct taxpayer identification number, see section 6213(b) and (g)(2)(J).

(2) *Additional identification requirements for the American Opportunity Tax Credit (AOTC).*—(i) *TIN must be issued on or before the due date of the original return.*—For any federal income tax return (including an amended return) filed after December 18, 2015, no AOTC is allowed unless the TIN of the student and the TIN for the taxpayer claiming the credit are issued on or before the due date, or the extended due date if the extension request is timely filed, for filing the return for the taxable year for which the credit is claimed.

(ii) *Return must include the eligible educational institution's employer identification number (EIN).*—For taxable years beginning after December 31, 2015, no AOTC is allowed unless the taxpayer includes the EIN of each eligible educational institution to which qualified tuition and related expenses were paid.

(3) *Applicability dates.*—(i) Except as provided in paragraphs (e)(3)(ii) and (iii) of this section, this paragraph (e) applies on or after December 26, 2002.

(ii) Paragraph (e)(2)(i) of this section applies to federal income tax returns (including amended returns) filed after December 18, 2015.

(iii) Paragraph (e)(2)(ii) of this section applies to taxable years beginning after December 31, 2015.

(f) *Statement requirement.*—(1) *In general.*—Except as provided in paragraph (f)(2) of this section, for taxable years beginning after June 29, 2015, no education tax credit is allowed unless the taxpayer (or the taxpayer's dependent) receives a statement furnished by an eligi-ble educational institution, as defined in §1.25A-2(b), containing all of the information required under §1.6050S-1(b)(2). The amount of qualified tuition and related expenses reported on the statement furnished by an eligible educational institution may not reflect the total amount of the qualified tuition and related expenses paid during the taxable year for which a taxpayer may claim an education tax credit. A taxpayer that substantiates payment of qualified tuition and related expenses that are not reported on Form 1098-T, "Tuition Statement", may include those expenses in computing the amount of the education tax credit allowable for the taxable year.

(2) *Exceptions.*—Paragraph (f)(1) of this section does not apply—

(i) If the taxpayer or the taxpayer's dependent:

(A) Has not received such a statement from an eligible educational institution required to furnish such statement under section 6050S and the regulations thereunder as of January 31 of the year following the taxable year to which the education tax credit relates or the date the return is filed claiming the education tax credit, whichever is later;

(B) Has requested, in the manner prescribed in forms, instructions, or in other published guidance, the eligible educational institution to furnish the Form 1098-T after January 31 of the year following the taxable year to which the education tax credit relates but on or before the date the return is filed claiming the education tax credit; and

(C) Has cooperated fully with the eligible educational institution's efforts to obtain information necessary to furnish the statement;

(ii) If the eligible educational institution is not required to furnish a statement to the student under section 6050S and the regulations thereunder; or

(iii) As otherwise provided in published guidance of general applicability, see §601.601(d)(2) of this chapter.

(3) *Applicability date.*—Paragraph (f) of this section applies to credits claimed for taxable years beginning after June 29, 2015.

* * *

Par. 4. Section 1.25A-2 is amended by:

1. Revising paragraphs (d)(2)(i) and (ii).

2. In paragraph (d)(2)(iii), removing the language "(d)(3)" and adding "(d)(4)" in its place.

3. Redesignating paragraphs (d)(3), (4), (5), and (6) as paragraphs (d)(4), (5), (6), and (7), respectively.

4. Adding a new paragraph (d)(3).

5. In newly redesignated paragraph (d)(5), by removing the language "(d)(3)" and adding "(d)(4)" in its place.

6. In newly redesignated paragraph (d)(7), revising *Example 2*, redesignating *Examples 3, 4, 5,* and *6,* as *Examples 4, 5, 6,* and *7,* and adding a new *Example 3*.

7. Adding paragraph (e).

The revisions and additions read as follows:

§1.25A-2. Definitions.

* * *

(d) * * *

(2) *Required fees.*—(i) *In general.*—Except as provided in paragraphs (d)(3) and (4) of this section, the test for determining whether any fee is a qualified tuition and related expense is whether the fee is required to be paid to the eligible educational institution as a condition of the student's enrollment or attendance at the institution.

(ii) *Books, supplies, and equipment.*—For taxable years beginning before January 1, 2009, for purposes of the Hope Scholarship Credit, and for taxable years beginning after December 31, 1997, for purposes of the Lifetime Learning Credit, qualified tuition and related expenses include fees for books, supplies, and equipment used in a course of study only if the fees must be paid to the eligible educational institution for the enrollment or attendance of the student at the institution. For taxable years beginning after December 31, 2008, see paragraph (d)(3) of this section for rules relating to books, supplies and equipment for purposes of the American Opportunity Tax Credit.

* * *

(3) *Course materials for the American Opportunity Tax Credit for taxable years beginning after December 31, 2008.*—For taxable years beginning after December 31, 2008, the term "qualified tuition and related expenses" for purposes of the American Opportunity Tax Credit under section 25A(i) includes the amount paid for course materials (such as books, supplies, and equipment) required for enrollment or attendance at an eligible educational institution. For this purpose, "required for enrollment or attendance" means that the course materials are needed for meaningful attendance or enrollment in a course of study, regardless of whether the course materials are purchased from the institution.

* * *

(7) * * *

Example 2. First-year students attending College W during 2008 are required to obtain books and other materials used in its mandatory first-year curriculum. The books and other reading materials are not required to be purchased from College W and may be borrowed from other students or purchased from off-campus bookstores, as well as from College W's bookstore. College W bills students for any books and materials purchased from College W's bookstore. The expenses paid for the first-year books and materials purchased at College W's bookstore are not qualified tuition and related expenses because under §1.25A-2(d)(2)(ii) the books and materials are not required to be purchased from College W for enrollment or attendance at the institution. In addition, expenses paid for the first-year books and materials borrowed from other students or purchased from vendors other than College W's bookstore are also not qualified tuition and related expenses because under §1.25A-2(d)(2)(ii) the books and materials are not required to be purchased from College W for enrollment or attendance at the institution

Example 3. Assume the same facts as *Example 2,* except that the books and materials are required for first-year students attending College W during 2009. Because the expenses are paid with respect to enrollment or attendance after 2008, §1.25A-1(d)(3) applies rather than §1.25A-1(d)(2)(ii), if the taxpayer claims the American Opportunity Tax Credit under section 25A(i). Under §1.25A-1(d)(3), expenses for books and other course materials are qualified tuition and related expenses for purposes of the American Opportunity Tax Credit if they are needed for meaningful attendance in the student's course of study at College W. Accordingly, if the taxpayer claims the American Opportunity Tax Credit for 2009, the expenses paid for the first-year books and materials are qualified tuition and related expenses. However, if the taxpayer claims the Lifetime Learning Credit for 2009 under section 25A(c), §1.25A-2(d)(2)(ii) applies rather than §1.25A-1(d)(3). Accordingly, if the taxpayer claims the Lifetime Learning Credit, the expenses paid for the first-year books and materials purchased at College W's bookstore are not qualified tui-

Par. 5. Section 1.25A-5 is amended by:

1. In paragraph (e)(2)(ii), revising the *Example.*

2. Redesignating paragraph (f)(6) as paragraph (f)(7).

3. Adding a new paragraph (f)(6).

4. In newly redesignated paragraph (f)(7), adding *Example 4.*

5. Adding paragraph (g).

The revisions and additions read as follows:

§1.25A-5. Special rules relating to characterization and timing of payments.

* * *

(e) * * *

  (2) * * *

   (ii) * * *

Example. In December 2016, Taxpayer A, a calendar year taxpayer who is not a dependent of another taxpayer under section 151, receives a bill from College Z for $5,000 for qualified tuition and related expenses to attend College Z for the 2017 spring semester, which begins in January 2017. This is the first semester that Taxpayer A will attend College Z. On December 15, 2016, Taxpayer A pays College Z $1,000 in qualified tuition and related expenses for the 2017 spring semester. On February 15, 2017, Taxpayer A pays College Z the remaining $4,000 due for qualified tuition and related expenses for the 2017 spring semester. In August 2017, Taxpayer A receives a bill from College Z for $7,000 for qualified tuition and related expenses to attend College Z for the 2017 fall semester, which begins in September 2017. Taxpayer A pays the entire $7,000 on September 1, 2017. In December 2017, Taxpayer A receives a bill from College Z for $7,000 for qualified tuition and related expenses to attend for the 2018 spring semester. Taxpayer A pays $1,000 of the 2018 spring semester bill on December 15, 2017 and $6,000 of that bill in February 15, 2018. Taxpayer A does not enroll in an eligible educational institution for the 2018 fall semester or the 2019 spring semester. Taxpayer A may claim an education tax credit on Taxpayer A's 2016 Form 1040 with respect to the $1,000 taxpayer paid to College Z on December 15, 2016 for the 2017 spring semester. On Taxpayer A's 2017 Form 1040, Taxpayer A may claim an education credit with respect to the $12,000 Taxpayer A paid to College Z during 2017 ($4,000 paid on February 15, 2017 for the 2017 spring semester, $7,000 paid on September 1, 2017, for the 2017 fall semester, and $1,000 paid on December 15, 2017, for the 2018 spring semester). On Taxpayer A's 2018 Form 1040, Taxpayer A may claim an education credit with respect to the $6,000 taxpayer paid to College Z on February 15, 2018.

* * *

(f) * * *

(6) *Treatment of refunds where qualified tuition and related expenses paid in two taxable years for the same academic period.*—If a taxpayer or someone other than the taxpayer—

 (i) Pays qualified tuition and related expenses in one taxable year (prior taxable year) for a student's enrollment or attendance at an eligible educational institution during an academic period beginning in the first three months of the taxpayer's next taxable year (subsequent taxable year);

tion and related expenses because under §1.25A-2(d)(2)(ii) the books and materials are not required to be purchased from College W for enrollment or attendance at the institution.

* * *

(e) *Applicability date.*—(1) Except as provided in paragraph (e)(2) of this section, this section applies on or after December 26, 2002.

(2) Paragraphs (d)(2)(i), (d)(2)(ii), (d)(3), and *Examples 2* and *3* of paragraph (d)(7) of this section apply to qualified tuition and related expenses paid, and education furnished in academic periods beginning, on or after the date of publication of the Treasury decision adopting these rules as final regulations in the **Federal Register**. However, taxpayers may apply paragraphs (d)(2)(i), (d)(2)(ii), (d)(3), and *Examples 2* and *3* of paragraph (d)(7) of this section for taxable years beginning after December 31, 2008, for which the period of limitations on filing a claim for credit or refund under section 6511 has not expired.

 (ii) Pays qualified tuition and related expenses in the subsequent taxable year for the academic period beginning in the first three months of the subsequent taxable year; and

 (iii) Receives a refund of qualified tuition and related expenses during the subsequent taxable year for the academic period beginning in the first three months of the subsequent taxable year (including an amount treated as a refund under paragraph (f)(4) or (5) of this section), the taxpayer may allocate the refund in any proportion to qualified tuition and related expenses paid in the prior taxable year under paragraph (f)(2) or (3) of this section or the subsequent taxable year under paragraph (f)(1) of this section, except that the amount of the refund allocated to a taxable year may not exceed the qualified tuition and related expenses paid during the taxable year with respect to the academic period beginning in the subsequent taxable year. The sum of the amounts allocated to each taxable year cannot exceed the amount of the refund.

(7) * * *

Example 4. In December 2016, Taxpayer D, a calendar year taxpayer who is not a dependent of another taxpayer under section 151, receives a bill from University X for $2,000 for qualified tuition and related expenses to attend University X as a full-time student for the 2017 spring semester, which begins in January 2017. In December 2016, D pays $500 of qualified tuition and related expenses for the 2017 spring semester. In January 2017, D pays an additional $1,500 of qualified tuition and related expenses for the 2017 spring semester. Early in the 2017 spring semester, D withdraws from several courses and no longer qualifies as a full-time student. As a result of D's change in status from a full-time student to a part-time student, D receives a $750 refund from University X on February 16, 2017. D has no other qualified tuition and related expenses for 2017. Under paragraph (f)(6) of this section, D may allocate all, or a portion, of the $750 refund to reduce the $1,500 of qualified tuition and related expenses paid in 2017 or D may also allocate a portion of the $750 refund, up to $500, to reduce the qualified tuition and related expenses paid in 2016 and allocate the remainder of the refund to reduce the qualified tuition and related expenses paid in 2017.

(g) *Applicability date.*—(1) Except as provided in paragraph (g)(2) of this section, this section applies on or after December 26, 2002.

(2) Paragraphs (e)(2)(ii), (f)(6), and *Example 4* in paragraph (f)(7) of this section apply to qualified tuition and related expenses paid and education furnished in academic periods beginning on or after the date of publication of the Treasury decision adopting these rules as final regulations in the **Federal Register**. However, taxpayers may apply paragraphs (e)(2)(ii), (f)(6), and *Example 4* in paragraph (f)(7) of this section in taxable years for which the limitation on filing a claim for credit or refund under section 6511 has not expired.

Dependency Exemption: Authorized Placement Agency: Definition

Dependency Exemption: Authorized Placement Agency: Definition.—Amendments to Reg. §1.32-2, relating to the definition of an authorized placement agency for purposes of a dependency exemption for a child placed for adoption that were issued prior to the changes made to the law by the Working Families Tax Relief Act of 2004, are proposed (published in the Federal Register on January 19, 2017) (REG-137604-07).

Par. 6. Section 1.32-2 is amended by revising the section heading, adding paragraph (c)(3), and revising paragraph (e) to read as follows:

§1.32-2. Earned income credit.

* * *

(c) * * *

(3) *Qualifying child.*—(i) *In general.*—For purposes of this section, a qualifying child of the taxpayer is a qualifying child as defined in section 152(c), determined without applying sections 152(c)(1)(D) and 152(e).

(ii) *Application of tie-breaker rules.*—For purposes of determining whether a taxpayer is an eligible individual under section 32(c)(1)(A), if an individual meets the definition of a qualifying child under paragraph (c)(3)(i) of this section for more than one taxpayer and the individual is treated as the qualifying child of a taxpayer under the tiebreaker rules of section 152(c)(4) and the related regulations, then that taxpayer may be an eligible individual under section 32(c)(1)(A)(i) and may claim the earned income credit for a taxpayer with a qualifying child if all other requirements of section 32 are satisfied. If an individual meets the definition of a qualifying child under paragraph (c)(3)(i) of this section for more than one taxpayer and the individual is not treated as the qualifying child of a taxpayer under the tiebreaker rules of section 152(c)(4) and the related regulations, then the individual also is not treated as a qualifying child of that taxpayer in the taxable year for purposes of section 32(c)(1)(A). Thus, that taxpayer may be an eligible individual under section 32(c)(1)(A)(ii) and may claim the earned income credit for a taxpayer without a qualifying child if all other requirements are satisfied.

(iii) *Examples.*—The following examples illustrate the rules of this paragraph (c). In each example, the taxpayer uses the calendar year as the taxpayer's taxable year and, except to the extent indicated, each taxpayer meets the requirements to claim the benefits(s) described in the example.

Example 1. Child, Parent, and Grandparent share the same principal place of abode for the taxable year. Child meets the defini-

tion of a qualifying child under paragraph (c)(3)(i) of this section for both Parent and Grandparent (and for no other person) for the taxable year. Parent claims the earned income credit with Child as Parent's qualifying child. Under the tiebreaker rules of section 152(c)(4)(A) and the related regulations, Child is treated as the qualifying child of Parent and is not treated as the qualifying child of Grandparent. Under section 32(c)(1) and paragraph (c)(3)(ii) of this section, Parent is an eligible individual under section 32(c)(1)(A)(i) who may claim the earned income credit for a taxpayer with a qualifying child, and Grandparent is an eligible individual under section 32(c)(1)(A)(ii) who may claim the earned income credit for a taxpayer without a qualifying child.

Example 2. The facts are the same as in *Example 1* of this paragraph (c)(3)(iii), except that Grandparent, rather than Parent, claims Child as a qualifying child, and Grandparent's adjusted gross income is higher than Parent's adjusted gross income. Under the tiebreaker rules of section 152(c)(4)(C) and the related regulations, Child is treated as the qualifying child of Grandparent and is not treated as the qualifying child of Parent. Under section 32(c)(1) and paragraph (c)(3)(ii) of this section, Grandparent is an eligible individual under section 32(c)(1)(A)(i) who may claim the earned income credit for a taxpayer with a qualifying child, and Parent is an eligible individual under section 32(c)(1)(A)(ii) who may claim the earned income credit for a taxpayer without a qualifying child.

* * *

(e) *Applicability date.*—(1) *In general.*—Except as provided in paragraph (e)(2) of this section, this section applies to taxable years beginning after March 5, 2003.

(2) *Exception.*—Paragraph (c)(3) of this section applies to taxable years beginning after the date these regulations are published as final regulations in the **Federal Register**.

Premium Tax Credit: Individual Shared Responsibility

Premium Tax Credit: Individual Shared Responsibility.—Amendments to Reg. §1.36B-2, relating to the health insurance premium tax credit (premium tax credit) and the individual shared responsibility provision, are proposed (published in the Federal Register on July 8, 2016) (corrected September 14, 2016) (REG-109086-15).

Par. 4. Section 1.36B-2 is amended by:

6. Adding new paragraphs (c)(3)(v)(A)(7)

§1.36B-2. Eligibility for premium tax credit.

* * *

(c) * * *

(3) * * *

(v) * * *

(A) * * *

(7) *Opt-out arrangements.*—(i) *In general.*—Except as otherwise provided in this paragraph (c)(3)(v)(A)(7), the amount of an opt-out payment made available to an employee under an opt-out arrangement increases the employee's required contribution for purposes of determining the affordability of the eligible employer-sponsored plan to which the opt-out arrangement relates, regardless of whether the employee enrolls in the eligible employer-sponsored plan or declines to enroll in that coverage and is paid the opt-out payment.

(ii) *Eligible opt-out arrangements.*—The amount of an opt-out payment made available to an employee under an eligible opt-out arrangement does not increase the employee's required contribution for purposes of determining the affordability of the eligible employer-sponsored plan to which the eligible opt-out arrangement relates, regardless of whether the employee enrolls in the eligible employer-sponsored plan or is paid the opt-out payment.

(iii) *Definitions.*—The following definitions apply for purposes of this paragraph (c)(3)(v)(A)(7):

(A) *Opt-out payment.*—The term *opt-out payment* means a payment that is available only if an employee declines coverage, including waiving coverage in which the employee would otherwise be enrolled, under an eligible employer-sponsored plan and that is not permitted to be used to pay for coverage under the eligible employer-sponsored plan. An amount provided as an employer contribution to a cafeteria plan that is permitted to be used by the employee to purchase minimum essential coverage is not an opt-out payment, whether or not the employee may receive the amount as a taxable benefit. See paragraph (c)(3)(v)(A)(6) of this section for the treatment of employer contributions to a cafeteria plan.

(B) *Opt-out arrangement.*—The term *opt-out arrangement* means the arrangement under which an opt-out payment is made available.

(C) *Eligible opt-out arrangement.*—The term *eligible opt-out arrangement* means an arrangement under which an employee's right to receive an opt-out payment is conditioned on the employee providing reasonable evidence that the employee and all other individuals for whom the employee reasonably expects to claim a personal exemption deduction for the taxable year or years that begin or end in or with the employer's plan year to which the opt-out arrangement applies (employee's expected tax family) have or will have minimum essential coverage (other than coverage in the individual market, whether or not obtained through the Marketplace) during the period of coverage to which the opt-out arrangement applies. For this purpose, reasonable evidence of alternative coverage may include the employee's attestation that the employee and all other members of the employee's expected tax family have or will have minimum essential coverage (other than coverage in the individual market, whether or not obtained through the Marketplace) for the relevant period. Regardless of the evidence of alternative coverage required under the arrangement, to be an eligible opt-out arrangement, the arrangement must provide that the opt-out payment will not be made, and the employer in fact must not make the payment, if the employer knows or has reason to know that the employee or any other member of the employee's expected tax family does not have or will not have the alternative coverage. The arrangement must also require that the evidence of the alternative coverage be provided no less frequently than every plan year to which the eligible opt-out arrangement applies, and that it must be provided no earlier than a reasonable period of time before the commencement of the period of coverage to which the eligible opt-out arrangement applies. If the reasonable evidence (such as an attestation) is obtained as part of the regular annual open enrollment period that occurs within a few months before the commencement of the next plan year of employer-sponsored coverage, it will qualify as being provided no earlier than a reasonable period of time before commencement of the applicable period of coverage. An eligible opt-out arrangement is also permitted to require evidence of alternative coverage to be provided at a later date, such as after the plan year starts, which would enable the employer to require evidence that the employee and all other members of the employee's expected tax family have already obtained the alternative coverage. Nothing in this rule prohibits an employer from requiring reasonable evidence of alternative coverage other than an attestation in order for an employee to qualify for an opt-out payment under an eligible opt-out arrangement. Further, provided that the reasonable evidence requirement is met, the amount of an opt-out payment made available under an eligible opt-out arrangement continues to be excluded from the employee's required contribution for the remainder of the period of coverage to which the opt-out payment originally applied even if the alternative coverage subsequently terminates for the employee or for any other member of the employee's expected tax family, regardless of whether the opt-out payment is required to be adjusted or terminated due to the loss of alternative coverage, and regardless of whether the employee is required to provide notice of the loss of alternative coverage to the employer.

(iv) Examples.—The following examples illustrate the provisions of this paragraph (c)(3)(v)(A)(7). In each example, the eligible employer-sponsored plan's plan year is the calendar year.

Example 1. Taxpayer B is an employee of Employer X, which offers its employees coverage under an eligible employer-sponsored plan that requires B to contribute $3,000 for self-only coverage. X also makes available to B a payment of $500 if B declines to enroll in the eligible employer-sponsored plan. Therefore, the $500 opt-out payment made available to B under the opt-out arrangement increases B's required contribution under X's eligible employer-sponsored plan from $3,000 to $3,500, regardless of whether B enrolls in the eligible employer-sponsored plan or declines to enroll and is paid the opt-out payment.

Example 2. The facts are the same as in *Example 1*, except that availability of the $500 opt-out payment is conditioned not only on B declining to enroll in X's eligible employer-sponsored plan but also on B providing reasonable evidence no earlier than the regular annual open enrollment period for the next plan year that B and all other members of B's expected tax family are or will be enrolled in minimum essential coverage through another source (other than coverage in the individual market, whether or not obtained through the Marketplace). B's expected tax family consists of B and B's spouse, C, who is an employee of Employer Y. During the regular annual open enrollment period for the upcoming plan year, B declines coverage under X's eligible employer-sponsored plan and provides X with reasonable evidence that B and C will be enrolled in Y's employer-sponsored plan, which is minimum essential coverage. The opt-out arrangement provided by X is an eligible opt-out arrangement, and, therefore, the $500 opt-out payment made available to B does not increase B's required contribution under X's eligible

employer-sponsored plan. B's required contribution for self-only coverage under X's eligible employer-sponsored plan is $3,000.

Example 3. The facts are the same as in *Example 2*, except that B and C have two children that B expects to claim as dependents for the taxable year that coincides with the upcoming plan year. During the regular annual open enrollment period for the upcoming plan year, B declines coverage under X's eligible employer-sponsored plan and provides X with reasonable evidence that B and C will be enrolled in Y's employer-sponsored plan, which is minimum essential coverage. However, B does not provide reasonable evidence that B's children will be enrolled in minimum essential coverage (other than coverage in the individual market, whether or not obtained through the Marketplace); therefore, X determines B is not eligible for the opt-out payment, and B does not receive it. The $500 opt-out payment made available under the opt-out arrangement does not increase B's required contribution under X's eligible employer-sponsored plan because the opt-out arrangement provided by X is an eligible opt-out arrangement. B's required contribution for self-only coverage under X's eligible employer-sponsored plan is $3,000.

Example 4. Taxpayer D is married and is employed by Employer Z, which offers its employees coverage under an eligible employer-sponsored plan that requires D to contribute $2,000 for self-only coverage. Z also makes available to D a payment of $300 if D declines to enroll in the eligible employer-sponsored plan and provides reasonable evidence no earlier than the regular annual open enrollment period for the next plan year that D is or will be enrolled in minimum essential coverage through another source (other than coverage in the individual market, whether or not obtained through the Marketplace); the opt-out arrangement is not conditioned on whether the other members of D's expected tax family have other coverage. This opt-out arrangement is not an eligible opt-out arrangement because it does not condition the right to receive the opt-out payment on D providing reasonable evidence that D and the other members of D's expected tax family have (or will have) minimum essential coverage (other than coverage in the individual market, whether or not obtained through the Marketplace). Therefore, the $300 opt-out payment made available to D under the opt-out arrangement increases D's required contribution under Z's eligible employer-sponsored plan. D's required contribution for self-only coverage under Z's eligible employer-sponsored plan is $2,300.

* * *

Health Insurance Premium Tax Credit: Employer-Sponsored Plans: Minimum Value

Health Insurance Premium Tax Credit: Employer-Sponsored Plans: Minimum Value.—Reg. §1.36B-6, affecting individuals who enroll in qualified health plans through Affordable Insurance Exchanges and claim the health insurance premium tax credit and providing guidance on determining whether health coverage under an eligible employer-sponsored plan provides minimum value, is proposed (published in the Federal Register on May 3, 2013) (REG-125398-12). Reg. §1.36B-6(a) and (g), as proposed on May 3, 2013, were withdrawn and replaced on September 1, 2015 (REG-143800-14). Portions of proposed Reg. §1.36B-6 were adopted by T.D. 9745 on December 16, 2015; the remaining proposed amendments are below.

☐ Par. 6. Section 1.36B-6 is added [amended] to read as follows:

§1.36B-6. Minimum value.—(a) * * *

(2) The plan provides substantial coverage of inpatient hospital services and physician services.

(b) *MV standard population.*—The MV standard population is a standard population developed and described through summary statistics by the Department of Health and Human Services (HHS). The MV standard population is based on the population covered by typical self-insured group health plans.

(c) *MV percentage.*—(1) *In general.*—An eligible employer-sponsored plan's MV percentage is—

(i) The plan's anticipated covered medical spending for benefits provided under a particular essential health benefits (EHB) benchmark plan described in 45 CFR 156.110 (EHB coverage) for the MV standard population based on the plan's cost-sharing provisions;

(ii) Divided by the total anticipated allowed charges for EHB coverage provided to the MV standard population; and

(iii) Expressed as a percentage.

(2) * * *

(3) * * *

(4) * * *

(5) *Expected spending adjustments for health savings accounts and health reimbursement arrangements.*—The amount taken into account under paragraph (c)(3) or (c)(4) of this section is the amount of expected spending for health care costs in a benefit year.

(d) *Methods for determining MV.*—An eligible employer-sponsored plan may use one of the following methods to determine whether the plan provides MV—

(1) The MV Calculator made available by HHS and IRS, with adjustments permitted by paragraph (e) of this section;

(2) One of the safe harbors established by HHS and IRS and described in published guidance, see §601.601(d) of this chapter;

(3) Actuarial certification, as described in paragraph (f) of this section, if an eligible employer-sponsored plan has nonstandard features that are not compatible with the MV Calculator and may materially affect the MV percentage; or

(4) For plans in the small group market, conformance with the requirements for a level of metal coverage defined at 45 CFR 156.140(b) (bronze, silver, gold, or platinum).

(e) *Scope of essential health benefits and adjustment for benefits not included in MV Calculator.*—An eligible employer-sponsored plan may include in calculating its MV percentage all benefits included in any EHB benchmark (as defined in 45 CFR part 156). An MV percentage that is calculated using the MV Calculator may be adjusted based on an actuarial analysis that complies with the requirements of paragraph (f) of this section to the extent of the value of these benefits that are outside the parameters of the MV Calculator.

(f) *Actuarial certification.*—(1) *In general.*—An actuarial certification under paragraph (d)(3) of this section must satisfy the requirements of this paragraph (f).

(2) *Membership in American Academy of Actuaries.*—The actuary must be a member of the American Academy of Actuaries.

(3) *Actuarial analysis.*—The actuary's analysis must be performed in accordance with generally accepted actuarial principles and methodologies and specific standards that may be provided in published guidance, see §601.601(d) of this chapter.

(4) *Use of MV Calculator.*—The actuary must use the MV Calculator to determine the plan's MV percentage for coverage the plan provides that is measurable by the MV Calculator. The actuary may

perform an actuarial analysis of the plan's EHB coverage for the MV standard population for benefits not measured by the MV Calculator to determine the effect of nonstandard features that are not compatible with the MV Calculator. The actuary may certify the plan's MV percentage based on the MV percentage that results from use of the MV Calculator and the actuarial analysis of the plan's coverage that is not measured by the MV calculator.

(g) * * *

(2) *Exception.*—Paragraph (a)(2) of this section applies for plan years beginning after November 3, 2014.

Excise Taxes: Taxable Fuel: Returns: Definitions

Excise Taxes: Taxable Fuel: Returns: Definitions.—Reg. §§1.40-2 and 1.40A-1 and amendments to Reg. §1.40-1, relating to credits and payments for alcohol mixtures, biodiesel mixtures, renewable diesel mixtures, alternative fuel mixtures, and alternative fuel sold for use or used as a fuel and relating to the definition of gasoline and diesel fuel, are proposed (published in the Federal Register on July 29, 2008) (REG-155087-05).

Par. 2. Section 1.40-1 is revised to read as follows:

§1.40-1. Alcohol used as a fuel.—For the definition of "alcohol" for purposes of the credits allowed by section 40, see §48.6426-1(c) of this chapter.

Par. 3. Sections 1.40-2 is added to read as follows:

§1.40-2. Small ethanol producer credit.—(a) *In general.*—Section 40 provides a small ethanol producer credit for each gallon of qualified ethanol production of an eligible small ethanol producer. Section 40(b)(4)(B) defines "qualified ethanol production". Section 40(g)(1) defines "eligible small ethanol producer". Section 40(g)(5) provides authority to prescribe such regulations as may be necessary to prevent the credit from directly or indirectly benefiting any person with a direct or indirect productive capacity of more than 60 million gallons of alcohol during the taxable year. A person has produced ethanol if the person has title to the ethanol immediately after it is created.

(b) *Qualified ethanol production.*—Section 40(b)(4)(B) limits qualified ethanol production to ethanol that is produced by an eligible small ethanol producer. Ethanol is "produced" for this purpose only when a feedstock other than ethanol is transformed into ethanol.

(c) *Denial of credit for ethanol produced at certain facilities.*—The person at whose facilities ethanol is produced is treated for purposes of section 40(g)(5) as an indirect beneficiary of any credit allowed with respect to the ethanol. Accordingly, the small ethanol producer credit is not allowed with respect to ethanol that is produced at the facilities of a contract manufacturer or other person if such contract manufacturer or other person has a direct or indirect productive capacity of more than 60 million gallons of alcohol during the taxable

year. Similarly, if the manufacturer does not have a productive capacity of more than 60 million gallons but more than 15 million gallons of ethanol is produced at the manufacturer's facilities during the taxable year, the small ethanol producer credit is allowed with respect to only the first 15 million gallons of ethanol produced at the facilities during the taxable year.

(d) *Examples.*—The following examples illustrate the application of this section:

Example 1. X purchases hydrous ethanol and processes it into anhydrous ethanol. X is not the producer of the ethanol because X does not transform a feedstock other than ethanol into ethanol.

Example 2. Y arranges with contract manufacturer Z to produce 10 million gallons of ethanol. Y is not related to Z. Y provides the raw materials and retains title to them and to the finished ethanol. Z has the capacity to produce 100 million gallons of alcohol per year. The small producer credit is not allowed with respect to the 10 million gallons of ethanol because it is produced at the facilities of a contract manufacturer that has a productive capacity of more than 60 million gallons of alcohol during the taxable year.

(e) *Effective/applicability date.*—This section is applicable on and after the date of publication of these regulations in the **Federal Register** as final regulations. [Reg. §1.40-2.]

Par. 3. Sections 1.40A-1 is added to read as follows:

§1.40A-1. Biodiesel.—(a) *In general.*—Rules similar to the rules of §1.40-2 apply for purposes of the small agri-biodiesel producer credit allowed by section 40A.

(b) *Definitions.*—For the definitions of "biodiesel" and "renewable diese" for purposes of the credits allowed by section 40A, see §48.6426-1(b) of this chapter.

(c) *Effective/applicability date.*—This section is applicable on and after the date of publication of these regulations in the **Federal Register** as final regulations. [Reg. §1.40A-1.]

Qualified Research Expenditures (QREs): Credit for Increasing Research Activities: Intra-Group Gross Receipts

Qualified Research Expenditures (QREs): Credit for Increasing Research Activities: Intra-Group Gross Receipts.—Amendments to Reg. §1.41-0, relating to the treatment of qualified research expenditures (QREs) and gross receipts resulting from transactions between members of a controlled group of corporations or a group of trades or businesses under common control (intra-group transactions) for purposes of determining the credit under section 41 for increasing research activities (research credit), are proposed (published in the Federal Register on December 13, 2013) (REG-159420-04).

☐ Par. 2. In §1.41-0, the table of contents is amended by:
1. Revising the section heading for §1.41-6 and the entries for §1.41-6 (i), (i)(1), (i)(2), (i)(3), (i)(4), and (i)(5).
2. Adding a new entry for §1.41-6(i)(6).
3. Adding a new entry for §1.41-6(j)(4).
The addition reads as follows:

§1.41-0. Table of contents.

* * *

§1.41-6 Controlled groups.

* * *

(i) Transactions between controlled group members.
  (1) In general.
  (2) Exception for certain amounts received from foreign corporate controlled group members.

  (3) In-house research expenses.
  (4) Contract research expenses.
  (5) Payment for supplies.
  (6) Consistency requirement.
(j) * * *

* * *

  (4) Intra-group transactions.

* * *

Credit: Research Activities: Internal-Use Software Exclusion

Credit: Research Activities: Internal-Use Software Exclusion.—Amendments to Reg. §1.41-4, relating to the computation of the research credit under Code Sec. 41(c), the definition of qualified research under Code Sec. 41(d), and when computer software is excepted from the internal-use software exclusion contained in Code Sec. 41(d)(4)(E), are proposed (published in the Federal Register on December 26, 2001) (REG-112991-01) (corrected March 19, 2002). These proposed regulations have been designed to lay to rest many of the disputes that arose after T.D. 8930 was published. *Note:* Proposed amendments to Reg. §1.41-0 and portions of the proposed amendments to Reg. §1.41-4 were adopted by T.D. 9104 on December 30, 2003; however, proposed Reg. §1.41-4(c)(6), pertaining to internal use computer software, was specifically not adopted.

☐ Par. 4. Section 1.41-4 is revised to read as follows [see *Note*, above]:

§1.41-4. Qualified research for expenditures paid or incurred in taxable years ending on or after December 26, 2001.

* * *

(c) * * *

(6) *Internal use software for taxable years beginning on or after December 31, 1985.*—(i) *General rule.*—Research with respect to computer software that is developed by (or for the benefit of) the taxpayer primarily for the taxpayer's internal use is eligible for the research credit only if the software satisfies the requirements of paragraph (c)(6)(ii) of this section.

(ii) *Requirements.*—The requirements of this paragraph (c)(6)(ii) are—

(A) The software satisfies the requirements of section 41(d)(1);

(B) The software is not otherwise excluded under section 41(d)(4) (other than section 41(d)(4)(E)); and

(C) One of the following conditions is met—

(1) The taxpayer develops the software for use in an activity that constitutes qualified research (other than the development of the internal-use software itself);

(2) The taxpayer develops the software for use in a production process that satisfies the requirements of section 41(d)(1);

(3) The taxpayer develops the software for use in providing computer services to customers; or

(4) The software satisfies the high threshold of innovation test of paragraph (c)(6)(vi) of this section.

(iii) *Computer software and hardware developed as a single product.*—This paragraph (c)(6) does not apply to the development costs of a new or improved package of computer software and hardware developed together by the taxpayer as a single product (or to the costs to modify an acquired computer software and hardware package), of which the software is an integral part, that is used directly by the taxpayer in providing services in its trade or business to customers. In these cases, eligibility for the research credit is to be determined by examining the combined software-hardware product as a single product.

(iv) *Primarily for internal use.*—Unless computer software is developed to be commercially sold, leased, licensed, or otherwise marketed, for separately stated consideration to unrelated third parties, computer software is presumed developed by (or for the benefit of) the taxpayer primarily for the taxpayer's internal use. For example, the computer software may serve general and administrative functions of the taxpayer, or may be used in providing a noncomputer service. General and administrative functions include, but are not limited to, functions such as payroll, bookkeeping, financial management, financial reporting, personnel management, sales and marketing, fixed asset accounting, inventory management and cost accounting. Computer software that is developed to be commercially sold, leased, licensed, or otherwise marketed, for separately stated consideration to unrelated third parties is not developed primarily for the taxpayer's internal use. The requirements of this paragraph (c)(6) apply to computer software that is developed primarily for the taxpayer's internal use even though the taxpayer subsequently sells, leases, licenses, or otherwise markets the computer software for separately stated consideration to unrelated third parties.

(v) *Software used in the provisions of services.*—(A) *Computer services.*—For purposes of this section, a computer service is a service offered by a taxpayer to customers who conduct business with the taxpayer primarily for the use of the taxpayer's computer or software technology. A taxpayer does not provide a computer service merely because customers interact with the taxpayer's software.

(B) *Noncomputer services.*—For purposes of this section, a noncomputer service is a service offered by a taxpayer to customers who conduct business with the taxpayer primarily to obtain a service other than a computer service, even if such other service is enabled, supported, or facilitated by computer or software technology.

(vi) *High threshold of innovation test.*—Computer software satisfies this paragraph (c)(6)(vi) only if the taxpayer can establish that—

(A) The software is innovative in that the software is intended to be unique or novel and is intended to differ in a significant and inventive way from prior software implementations or methods;

(B) The software development involves significant economic risk in that the taxpayer commits substantial resources to the

development and there is substantial uncertainty, because of technical risk, that such resources would be recovered within a reasonable period; and

(C) The software is not commercially available for use by the taxpayer in that the software cannot be purchased, leased, or licensed and used for the intended purpose without modifications that would satisfy the requirements of paragraphs (c)(6)(vi)(A) and (B) of this section.

(vii) *Application of high threshold of innovation test.*—The costs of developing internal use software are eligible for the research credit only if the software satisfies the high threshold of innovation test of paragraph (c)(6)(vi) of this section. This test takes into account only the results attributable to the development of the new or improved software independent of the effect of any modifications to related hardware or other software.

(viii) *Illustrations.*—The following examples illustrate provisions contained in this paragraph (c)(6) of this section. No inference should be drawn from these examples concerning the application of section 41(d)(1) and paragraph (a) of this section to these facts. The examples are as follows:

Example 1. (i) *Facts.* X, an insurance company, has increased its number of insurance policies in force. In recent years, regulatory and financial accounting rules for computing actuarial reserves on these insurance policies have changed several times. In order to compute actuarial reserves in a more timely and cost-effective manner, X undertakes to create an improved reserve valuation software that will generate data for regulatory and financial accounting purposes.

(ii) *Conclusion.* The improved reserve valuation software created by X is internal use software because the software is not developed to be commercially sold, leased, licensed, or otherwise marketed, for separately stated consideration to unrelated third parties. The improved reserve valuation software was developed by X to serve X's general and administrative functions. X's costs of developing the reserve valuation software are eligible for the research credit only if the software satisfies the high threshold of innovation test of paragraph (c)(6)(vi) of this section.

Example 2. (i) *Facts.* Assume the same facts as in *Example 1.* Also assume that in order to create the improved reserve valuation software, X purchases updated hardware with a new operating system to build the new software system. Several other insurance companies using the same updated hardware and new operating system have in place software systems that can handle the volume of transactions that X seeks to handle, provide reserve computations within a similar time frame, and accommodate the most current regulatory and financial accounting requirements.

(ii) *Conclusion.* X's reserve valuation software system is internal use software that does not satisfy the high threshold of innovation test of paragraph (c)(6)(vi) of this section. The software is not intended to be unique or novel in that it is intended to be merely comparable to software developed by other insurance companies. The software does not differ in a significant or inventive way from prior software implementations because X's reserve valuation software system was developed using the same technologies and methods that were employed by other insurance companies. Further, X's reserve valuation software is not excluded from the application of paragraph (c)(6) of this section by the rule of paragraph (c)(6)(iii) of this section.

Example 3. (i) *Facts.* In 1986, X, a large regional bank with hundreds of branch offices, maintained separate software systems for each of its customer's accounts, including checking, deposit, loan, lease, and trust. X determined that improved customer service could be achieved by redesigning its disparate systems into one customer-centric system. X also determined that commercially available database management systems did not meet all of the critical requirements of the proposed system. Specifically, available relational database management systems were well suited for the proposed system's data modeling requirements but not the data integrity and transaction throughput (transactions-per-second) requirements. Rather than waiting several years for vendor offerings to mature and become viable for its purpose, X decided to embark upon the project utilizing older technology that satisfied the data integrity and transaction throughput requirements but that was severely challenged with respect to the data modeling capabilities. X commits substantial resources to this project and, because of technical risk, X cannot determine if it will recover its resources in a reasonable period. Early in the course of the project, industry analysts observed that the project appeared highly ambitious and risky. The limitations of the technology X was attempting to utilize required that X develop a new database architecture that could accommodate transaction volumes unheard-of in the industry. X was unable to successfully develop the system and X abandoned the project.

(ii) *Conclusion.* X intended to develop a computer software system primarily for X's internal use because X did not intend to commercially sell, lease, license, or otherwise market the software, for separately stated consideration to unrelated third parties, and X intended to use the software in providing noncomputer services to its customers. X's software development activities satisfy the high threshold of innovation test of paragraph (c)(6)(vi) of this section because the system was intended to be innovative in that it was intended to be novel and it was intended to differ in a significant and inventive way from prior software implementations. In addition, X's development activities involved significant economic risk in that X committed substantial resources to the development and there was substantial uncertainty, because of technical risk, that such resources would be recovered within a reasonable period. Finally, at the time X undertook the development of the system, software meeting X's requirements was not commercially available for use by X.

Example 4. (i) *Facts.* X wishes to improve upon its capabilities in the area of insurance fraud prevention, detection and control. X believes that it can exceed the capabilities of current commercial offerings in this area by developing and applying pattern matching algorithms that are not implemented in current vendor offerings. X has determined that many insurance fraud perpetrators can evade detection because its current system relies too heavily on exact matches and scrubbed data. Because a computer software system that will accomplish these objectives is not commercially available, X undertakes to develop and implement advanced pattern matching algorithms that would significantly improve upon the capabilities currently available from vendors. X commits substantial resources to the development of the software system and cannot determine, because of technical risk, if it will recover its investment within a reasonable period.

(ii) *Conclusion.* X's computer software system is developed primarily for X's internal use because X did not intend to sell, lease, license or otherwise market the software, for separately stated consideration to unrelated third parties. X's software development activities satisfy the high threshold of innovation test of paragraph (c)(6)(vi) of this section because the software system is innovative in that it was intended to be novel and it was intended to differ in a significant and inventive way from prior software implementations. In addition, X's development activities involved significant economic risk in that X committed substantial resources to the development and there was substantial uncertainty, because of technical risk, that such resources would be recovered within a reasonable period. Finally, at the time X undertook the development of the software, software satisfying X's requirements was not commercially available for use by X.

Example 5. (i) *Facts.* X is engaged in the business of designing, manufacturing, and selling widgets. X delivers its widgets in the same manner and time as its competitors. To improve customer service, X undertakes to develop computer software that will monitor the progress of the manufacture and delivery of X's widgets to enable X's customers to track their widget orders from origination to delivery, whether by air, land or ship. In addition, at the request of a customer, X will be able to intercept and return or reroute packages prior to delivery. At the time X undertakes its software development activities, X is uncertain whether it can develop the real-time communication software necessary to achieve its objective. None of X's competitors have a comparable tracking system. X commits substantial resources to the development of the system and, because of technical risk, X cannot determine if it will recover its investment within a reasonable period.

(ii) *Conclusion.* X's computer software is developed primarily for X's internal use because the software is not developed to be commercially sold, leased, licensed, or otherwise marketed, for separately stated consideration to unrelated third parties. X's computer software was developed to be used by X in providing noncomputer services to its customers. X's software satisfies the high threshold of innovation test of paragraph (c)(6)(vi) of this section because, at the time the research is undertaken, X's software is designed to provide a new tracking capability that is novel in that none of X's competitors have such a capability. Further, the new capability differs in a significant and inventive way from prior software implementations. In addition, X's development activities involved significant economic risk in that X committed substantial resources to the development and there was substantial uncertainty, because of technical risk, that such resources would be recovered within a reasonable period. Finally, at the time X undertook the development of the software, software satisfying X's requirements was not commercially available for use by X.

Example 6. (i) *Facts.* X, a multinational chemical manufacturer with different business and financial systems in each of its divisions, undertakes a software development project aimed at integrating the majority of the functional areas of its major software systems into a single enterprise resource management system supporting centralized financial systems, inventory, and management reporting. This project involves the detailed analysis of X's (as well as each of X's divisions') legacy systems to understand the actual current business processes and data requirements. X also has to develop programs to fill in the gaps between the software features and X's system requirements. X hires Y, a systems consulting firm to assist with this development effort. Y has experience in developing similar systems. X, working jointly with Y, evaluates its needs, establishes goals for the new system, re-engineers the business processes that will be made concurrently with the implementation of the new system, and chooses and purchases a software system upon which to base its enterprise-wide system.

(ii) *Conclusion.* X's enterprise-wide computer software is developed primarily for internal use because the software is not developed to be commercially sold, leased, licensed, or otherwise marketed, for separately stated consideration to unrelated third parties. X's computer software was developed to be used by X to serve X's general and administrative functions. However, the development of X's enterprise management system does not satisfy the high threshold of innovation test of paragraph (c)(6)(vi) of this section because the system that X is seeking to develop is not intended to be unique or novel. Further, the software does not differ in a significant or inventive way from software implemented by other manufacturers.

Example 7. (i) *Facts.* X, a financial services company specializing in commercial mortgages, decides to support its ongoing expansion by upgrading its information technology infrastructure. In order to accommodate its expanding efforts to acquire and maintain corporate borrowers and draw securitized loan investors, X builds a scalable and modular enterprise network to run its latest business applications, including web-based portfolio access for investors and staff, document imaging for customer service personnel, desktop access to information services for in-house securities traders and multimedia on-line training and corporate information delivery for all company personnel. As a result, X is able to access market information faster and function more efficiently and effectively than before. The new network is based on a faster local area network technology which is better able to meet the higher bandwidth requirements of X's current multimedia applications.

(ii) *Conclusion.* X's software is developed primarily for X's internal use because the software is not developed to be commercially sold, leased, licensed, or otherwise marketed, for separately stated consideration to unrelated third parties. X's software development activities do not meet the high threshold of innovation test of paragraph (c)(6)(vi) of this section because the system is not intended to be unique or novel. Further, the software does not differ in a significant or inventive way from other existing software implementations.

Example 8. (i) *Facts.* X, a corporation, undertook a software project to rewrite a legacy mainframe application using an object-oriented programming language, and to move the new application off the mainframe to a client/server environment. Both the object-oriented language and client/server technologies were new to X. This project was undertaken to develop a more maintainable application, and to be able to implement new features more quickly. X had to perform a detailed analysis of the old legacy application in order to determine the requirements of the rewritten application. To accomplish this task, X had to train the legacy mainframe programmers in the new object-oriented and client/server technologies that they would have to utilize. Several of X's competitors had successfully implemented similar systems using object-oriented programming language and client/server technologies.

(ii) *Conclusion.* X's software is developed primarily for internal use because the software is not developed to be commercially sold, leased, licensed, or otherwise marketed, for separately stated consideration to unrelated third parties. X's activities to rewrite a legacy mainframe application using an object-oriented programming language, and to move the application from X's mainframe to a client/server environment do not satisfy the high threshold of innovation test of paragraph (c)(6)(vi) of this section. The software developed is not intended to be either unique or novel and is not intended to differ in a significant and inventive way from prior software implementations or methods.

Example 9. (i) *Facts.* X, a retail and distribution company, wants to upgrade its warehouse management software. Therefore, X performs an analysis of the warehouse management products and vendors in the marketplace. X selects vendor V's software and, in turn, develops the software interfaces between X's legacy systems and V's warehouse management software in order to integrate the new warehouse management system with X's financial and inventory systems. The development of these interfaces requires a detailed understanding of all the input and output fields and their data formats, and how they map from the old system to the new system and vice-versa. Once X develops the interfaces, X has to perform extensive testing and validation work to ensure that the interfaces work correctly and accurately.

(ii) *Conclusion*. X's software is developed primarily for internal use because the software is not developed to be commercially sold, leased, licensed, or otherwise marketed, for separately stated consideration to unrelated third parties. X's software development activities do not satisfy the high threshold of innovation test of paragraph (c)(6)(vi) of this section because the software development does not involve significant economic risk in that there is no substantial uncertainty, because of technical risk, that such resources will be recovered within a reasonable period.

Example 10. (i) *Facts*. X, a credit card company, knows that its customers are not comfortable with purchasing products over the Internet because they feel the Web is not secure. X decides to build a payment system that provides customers with a single use, automatically generated, short-term time-based, transaction number. This single-use transaction number has a short expiration period that is just long enough to allow a merchant to process and fill the customer's order. Thus, when a customer wishes to make a purchase over the Internet, the customer requests X to generate automatically a single-use transaction number that merchant systems will accept as a legitimate card number. All purchases using single-use transaction numbers are automatically linked back to the customer's credit card account. X commits substantial resources to the development of the system and X cannot determine, because of technical risk, if it will recover its investment within a reasonable period. At the time of this project, nothing exists in the market that has these capabilities.

(ii) *Conclusion*. X's software is developed primarily for internal use because the software is not developed to be commercially sold, leased, licensed, or otherwise marketed, for separately stated consideration to unrelated third parties. X's computer software is developed primarily for X's internal use because it was intended to be used by X in providing noncomputer services to its customers. X's software satisfies the high threshold of innovation test of paragraph (c)(6)(vi) of this section because the system is a novel way to solve the security issue of making purchases over the Internet. Further, because of the secure payment capability, the software differs in a significant and inventive way from prior software implementations. In addition, X's development activities involved significant economic risk in that X committed substantial resources to the development and there was substantial uncertainty, because of technical risk, that such resources would be recovered within a reasonable period. Finally, at the time X undertook the development of the software, software satisfying X's requirements was not commercially available for use by X.

Example 11. (i) *Facts*. X, a corporation, wants to expand its internal computing power, and is aware that its PCs and workstations are idle at night, on the weekends, and for a significant part of any business day. Because the corporate computations that X needs to make could be done on workstations as well as PCs, X develops a screen-saver like application that runs on employee computers. When employees' computers have been idle for an amount of time set by each employee, the "screen-saver" starts to execute. However, instead of displaying moving lines, like the typical screen-saver, X's application goes back to a central server to get a new job to execute. This job will execute on the idle employee's computer until it has either finished, or the employee resumes working on his computer. X wants to ensure that it can manage all of the computation jobs distributed across its thousands of PCs and workstations. In addition, X wants to ensure that the additional load on its network caused by downloading the jobs and uploading the results, as well as in monitoring and managing the jobs, does not adversely impact the corporate computing infrastructure. At the time X undertook this software development project, X was uncertain, because of technical risk, it could develop a server application that could schedule and distribute the jobs across thousands of PCs and workstations, as well as handle all the error conditions that occur on a user's machine. Also, at the time X undertook this project, there was no commercial application available with such a capability.

(ii) *Conclusion*. X's computer software is developed primarily for internal use because the software is not developed to be commercially sold, leased, licensed, or otherwise marketed, for separately stated consideration to unrelated third parties. X's computer software was developed to be used by X to serve X's general and administrative functions. X's software satisfies the high threshold of innovation test of paragraph (c)(6)(vi) of this section because making use of idle corporate computing resources through what is ostensibly a screen-saver, was a novel approach to solving X's need for more computer intensive processing time. In addition, X's software development involves significant economic risk in that there was substan-

tial uncertainty, because of technical risk, that the server application that schedules and distributes the jobs across thousands of PCs and workstations, as well as handles all the error conditions that can occur on a user's machine, amounts to developing a new operating system with new capabilities. Finally, at the time X undertook the development of the software, software satisfying X's requirements was not commercially available for use by X.

Example 12. (i) *Facts*. (A) X, a corporation, wants to protect its internal documents without building a large public key infrastructure. In addition, X needs to implement a new highly secure encryption algorithm that has a "back-door" such that X can decrypt and read any document, even when the employee is on vacation or leaves the company. X wants to develop a new encryption algorithm that is both secure, easy to use, and difficult to break. Current commercial encryption/decryption products are too slow for high-level secure encryption processing. Furthermore, no commercial product exists that provides the capability of having a secure back-door key to decrypt files when the owner is unavailable.

(B) The development of the encryption/decryption software requires specialized knowledge of cryptography and computational methods. Due to the secret nature of X's work, the encryption algorithm has to be unbreakable, yet recoverable should the employee forget his key. X commits substantial resources to the development of the system and, because of technical risk, cannot estimate whether it will recover its investment within a reasonable period.

(ii) *Conclusion*. X's back-door file encryption software is developed primarily for internal use because the software is not developed to be commercially sold, leased, licensed, or otherwise marketed, for separately stated consideration to unrelated third parties. X's back-door file encryption software was developed to be used by X to serve X's general and administrative functions. X's encryption software satisfies the high threshold of innovation test of paragraph (c)(6)(vi) of this section because, at the time the research is undertaken, X's software is designed to provide encryption and back-door decryption capabilities that are unique in that no other product has these capabilities, which indicates the software encryption system differs in a significant way from prior software implementations. Further, the encryption and back-door decryption capabilities indicate that the software differs in a significant and inventive way from prior software implementations. In addition, X's development activities involved significant economic risk in that X committed substantial resources to the development and there was substantial uncertainty, because of technical risk, that such resources would be recovered within a reasonable period. Finally, at the time X undertook the development of the software, software satisfying X's requirements was not commercially available for use by X.

Example 13. (i) *Facts*. X, a large regional telephone company, is experiencing rapidly increasing customer demand. X would like to determine whether evolutionary algorithms such as genetic algorithms may improve its ability to design cost-effective networks and extend existing networks. X would also like to determine whether such adaptive algorithms may be used to optimize the routing of call traffic across existing networks in order to use efficiently the resources available without causing congestion. X first explores the use of evolutionary algorithms for the call routing task, because X determines that this type of complex, unpredictable problem is most appropriate for an adaptive algorithm solution. X develops and tests genetic algorithms until it determines that it has developed a software system it can test on a pilot basis on its existing networks. X commits substantial resources to the project, and cannot predict, because of technical risk, whether it will recover its resources within a reasonable period. Finally, at the time X undertook the development of the software, software satisfying X's requirements was not commercially available for use by X.

(ii) *Conclusion*. X's software is developed primarily for internal use because the software is not developed to be commercially sold, leased, licensed, or otherwise marketed, for separately stated consideration to unrelated third parties. X's computer software is intended to be used by X in providing noncomputer services to its customers. X's software satisfies the high threshold of innovation test of paragraph (c)(6)(vi) of this section because the software is intended to be novel and is intended to differ in a significant and inventive way from other existing software implementations. In addition, X's development activities involved significant economic risk in that X committed substantial resources to the development and there was substantial uncertainty, because of technical risk, that such resources would be recovered within a reasonable period. Finally, at the time X undertook the development of the software, software satisfying X's requirements was not commercially available.

(ix) *Effective date*.—This paragraph (c)(6) is applicable for taxable years beginning after December 31, 1985.

* * *

Qualified Research Expenditures (QREs): Credit for Increasing Research Activities: Intra-Group Gross Receipts

Qualified Research Expenditures (QREs): Credit for Increasing Research Activities: Intra-Group Gross Receipts.—Amendments to Reg. §1.41-6, relating to the treatment of qualified research expenditures (QREs) and gross receipts resulting from transactions between members of a controlled group of corporations or a group of trades or businesses under common control (intra-group transactions) for purposes of determining the credit under section 41 for increasing research activities (research credit), are proposed (published in the Federal Register on December 13, 2013) (REG-159420-04).

☐ Par. 3. Section 1.41-6 is amended by:

1. Revising the section heading.
2. Revising paragraph (i)(1).
3. Removing paragraph (i)(4).
4. Redesignating paragraphs (i)(2) and (3) as paragraphs (i)(3) and (4), respectively.
5. Adding new paragraph (i)(2).
6. Adding new paragraph (i)(6).
7. Revising the first sentence of paragraph (j)(1).
8. Adding new paragraph (j)(4).

The revisions and additions read as follows:

§1.41-6. Controlled groups.

* * *

(i) *Transactions between controlled group members.*—(1) *In general—Treatment of transactions.*—Except as otherwise provided in this paragraph, all activities giving rise to amounts included in gross receipts under §1.41-3(c) (transactions) between members of a controlled group as defined in paragraph (a)(3) of this section (intra-group transactions) are generally disregarded in determining the QREs and gross receipts of a member for purposes of the research credit.

(2) *Exception for certain amounts received from foreign corporate controlled group member.*—(i) *In general.*—Notwithstanding paragraph (i)(1) of this section, gross receipts (within the meaning of §1.41-3(c)) from an intra-group transaction are taken into account if—

(A) A foreign corporate controlled group member engages in a transaction with a party outside of the group (an external transaction) involving the same or a modified version of tangible or intangible property or a service that was previously the subject of one or more intra-group transactions (an internal transaction); and

(B) The external transaction does not give rise to gross receipts that are effectively connected with a trade or business within the United States, the Commonwealth of Puerto Rico, or any possession of the United States.

(ii) *Timing of inclusion.*—The amount described as taken into account in computing gross receipts in paragraph (i)(2)(i) of this section is taken into account in the year a foreign corporate controlled group member engages in the external transaction described in paragraph (i)(2)(i)(B) of this section.

(iii) *Multiple intra-group transactions.*—If there is more than one internal transaction, then only the last internal transaction giving rise to gross receipts (within the meaning of section 1.41-3(c)) is taken into account in the research credit computation pursuant to paragraph (i)(2)(i) of this section.

(iv) *Examples.*—The following examples illustrate the principles of paragraph (i)(2) of this section.

Example 1. Domestic Controlled Group Member Includes in Gross Receipts Proceeds From Intra-group Sale. D and F are members of the same controlled group. D is a domestic corporation. F is a foreign corporation that is organized under the laws of Country. F does not conduct a trade or business within the United States, Puerto Rico, or any U.S. possession. In Year 1, D sells Product to F for $8x. In Year 2, F sells Product to F's unrelated customer for $10x. Because the Product that F sells outside the group is the same Product that was the subject of an internal transaction (i.e., the sale from D to F), and the $10x that F receives upon sale of Product outside the group is not effectively connected with a trade or business within the United States, the Commonwealth of Puerto Rico, or any possession of the United States, the $8x that D receives from F is included in D's gross receipts for purposes of computing the amount of the group credit. The $8x of gross receipts is taken into account in Year 2, the year of the external transaction. See paragraph (i)(2) of this section. The $10x that F receives from F's customer is excluded from gross receipts under section 41(c)(7) because it is not effectively connected with the conduct of a trade or business within the United States, the Commonwealth of Puerto Rico, or any possession of the United States.

Example 2. Domestic Controlled Group Member Includes in Gross Receipts Amounts Received For Intra-group Transfer of License. Assume the same facts as in *Example 1*, except in Year 1, D licenses intellectual property (license) to F for $8x. F owns similar intellectual property that it plans to license to a customer together with the license it received from D. In Year 2, F licenses its intellectual property and sublicenses D's intellectual property to F's unrelated cus-

tomer for $20x. Because the intellectual property that F sublicenses outside the group is the same intellectual property that was the subject of an internal transaction (i.e., the license from D to F), and the $20x that F receives for the license and sublicense of intellectual property outside the group is not effectively connected with a trade or business within the United States, the Commonwealth of Puerto Rico, or any possession of the United States, the $8x that D receives from F is included in D's gross receipts for purposes of computing the amount of the group credit. The $8x of gross receipts is taken into account in Year 2, the year of the external transaction. See paragraph (i)(2) of this section. The $20x that F receives from F's customer is excluded from gross receipts under section 41(c)(7) because it is not effectively connected with the conduct of a trade or business within the United States, the Commonwealth of Puerto Rico, or any possession of the United States.

Example 3. Domestic Controlled Group Member Includes in Gross Receipts Proceeds From Intra-group Sale Following Multiple Internal Transactions. D, F1, and F2 are members of the same controlled group. D is a domestic corporation. F1 and F2 are foreign corporations that are organized under the laws of Country. F1 and F2 do not conduct a trade or business within the United States, Puerto Rico, or any U.S. possession. In Year 1, D sells Product to F1 for $8x. In Year 2, F1 sells Product to F2 for $9x, and F2 sells Product to F2's unrelated customer for $10x. Both D's sale to F1 and F1's sale to F2 are internal transactions involving Product that precede F2's external transaction involving Product. The $10x that F2 receives upon sale of Product outside the group is not effectively connected with a trade or business within the United States, the Commonwealth of Puerto Rico, or any possession of the United States. Accordingly, the group will include gross receipts from an internal transaction in its research credit computation pursuant to paragraph (i)(2)(i) of this section. Because F1's sale of Product to F2 does not produce gross receipts that are effectively connected with the conduct of a trade or business within the United States, the Commonwealth of Puerto Rico, or any possession of the United States, those gross receipts are not taken into account even though that sale is the most recent internal transaction preceding the external transaction. See section 41(c)(7) and paragraph (i)(2)(i) of this section. Therefore, D will include $8x of gross receipts in its research credit computation in Year 2, the year of the external transaction, because the transfer from D to F1 is the last internal transaction giving rise to includible gross receipts. See paragraph (i)(2)(iii) of this section.

Example 4. Foreign Partnership Controlled Group Member Includes in Gross Receipts Proceeds From Intra-group Sale. Assume the same facts as in *Example 3*, except that F1 is a foreign partnership for federal income tax purposes and is part of the controlled group (within the meaning of §1.41-6(a)(3)(ii)) that includes D and F2. Both D's sale to F1 and F1's sale to F2 are internal transactions involving Product that precede F2's external transaction involving Product. The $10x that F2 receives upon sale of Product outside the group is not effectively connected with a trade or business within the United States, the Commonwealth of Puerto Rico, or any possession of the United States. Accordingly, the group will include gross receipts from an internal transaction in its research credit computation pursuant to paragraph (i)(2)(i) of this section. F1's sale to F2 is the most recent internal transaction preceding the external transaction giving rise to gross receipts (see paragraph (i)(2)(iii)). The gross receipts from F1's sale to F2 are not excluded under section 41(c)(7) and paragraph (i)(2)(i) of this section because F1 is a partnership. Therefore, F1 will include $9x of gross receipts in its research credit computation in Year 2 because the transfer from F1 to F2 is the last internal transaction giving rise to gross receipts. See paragraph (i)(2)(iii) of this section.

Example 5. Domestic Controlled Group Member Includes in Gross Receipts Proceeds From Intra-group Sale Following Multiple Internal Transactions that Include a Section 721 Exchange. Assume the same facts as *Example 3*, except that in an exchange meeting the requirements of section 721(a), F2 transfers Product to PRS, a partnership that is not part of the controlled group within the meaning of §1.41-6(a)(3)(ii). Both D's sale to F1 and F1's sale to F2 are internal transactions involving Product that precede F2's transfer of Product to PRS. The exchange engaged in by F2 does not give rise to gross receipts that are effectively connected with a trade or business within the United States, the Commonwealth of Puerto Rico, or any possession of the United States. Because F1's sale of Product to F2 does not produce gross receipts that are effectively connected with the conduct of a trade or business within the United States, the Commonwealth of Puerto Rico, or any possession of the United States, those gross receipts are not taken into account even though that sale is the most recent internal transaction preceding the external transaction. See section 41(c)(7) and paragraph (i)(2)(i) of this section. Therefore, D will include $8x of gross receipts in its research credit computation in Year 2, the year of the external transaction, because the transfer from D to F1 is the last internal transaction giving rise to includible gross receipts. See paragraphs (i)(2)(i) and (i)(2)(iii) of this section.

* * *

(6) *Consistency requirement.*—In computing the research credit for taxable years beginning on or after the date of publication of these regulations as final regulations in the **Federal Register**, QREs and gross receipts taken into account in computing a taxpayer's fixed-base percentage and a taxpayer's base amount must be determined on a basis consistent with the definition of QREs and gross receipts for the credit year, without regard to the law in effect for the taxable years taken into account in computing the fixed-base percentage or the base amount. This consistency requirement applies even if the period for filing a claim for credit or refund has expired for any taxable year taken into account in computing the fixed-base percentage or the base amount.

(j) *Effective/applicability dates.*—(1) *In general.*—Except as otherwise provided in this paragraph (j), these regulations apply to taxable years ending on or after May 24, 2005.

* * *

(4) *Intra-group transactions.*—Paragraphs (i)(1) and (2) of this section apply to taxable years beginning on or after the date of publication of these regulations as final regulations in the **Federal Register**.

Low-Income Housing Credit

Low-Income Housing Credit.—Temporary Reg. §1.42-1T, relating to the low-income housing credit, is also proposed as a final regulation and, when adopted, would become Reg. §1.42-1 (published in the Federal Register on June 22, 1987).

§1.42-1. Limitation on low-income housing credit allowed with respect to qualified low-income buildings receiving housing credit allocations from a State or local housing credit agency.

Business Related Credits: New Markets Tax Credit

Business Related Credits: New Markets Tax Credit.—Amendments to Reg. §1.45D-1, revising and clarifying certain rules relating to recapture of the new markets tax credit and affecting certain taxpayers claiming the new markets tax credit, are proposed (published in the Federal Register on August 11, 2008) (REG-149404-07).

Par. 2. Section 1.45D-1 is amended by:

1. Redesignating the paragraph (a) entries for paragraphs (e)(4), (e)(5), (e)(6), and (e)(7) as paragraphs (e)(5), (e)(6), (e)(7), and (e)(8), respectively, adding a new entry for paragraph (e)(4), and revising the entry for paragraph (h)(2).

3. Revising paragraph (d)(6)(i).

4. Revising paragraph (e)(3)(iii) introductory text.

5. Redesignating paragraphs (e)(3)(iii)(B), (e)(3)(iii)(C), (e)(3)(iii)(D), and (e)(3)(iii)(E) as paragraphs (e)(3)(iii)(C), (e)(3)(iii)(D), (e)(3)(iii)(E), and (e)(3)(iii)(F), respectively, and adding new paragraph (e)(3)(iii)(B).

6. Revising newly-designated paragraph (e)(3)(iii)(D).

7. Redesignating paragraphs (e)(4), (e)(5), (e)(6), and (e)(7) as paragraphs (e)(5), (e)(6), (e)(7), and (e)(8), respectively, and adding new paragraph (e)(4).

8. Revising the heading for paragraph (h)(2) and adding a sentence at the end of the paragraph.

The additions and revisions read as follows:

§1.45D-1. New markets tax credit.

(a) * * *

(e) * * *

(4) Section 708(b)(1)(B) termination.

* * *

(h) * * *

(2) Exception for certain provisions.

* * *

(d) * * *

(6) * * *

(i) * * * Except as provided in paragraph (d)(6)(ii) of this section, an entity is treated as a qualified active low-income community business for the duration of the qualified community development entity's (CDE's) investment in the entity if the CDE reasonably expects, at the time the CDE makes the capital or equity investment in, or loan to, the entity, that the entity will satisfy the requirements to be a qualified active low-income community business under paragraphs (d)(4)(i) and (d)(5) of this section (including, if applicable, portions of business under paragraph (d)(4)(iii) of this section) throughout the entire period of the investment or loan. A CDE may rely on this paragraph (d)(6)(i) to treat an entity as a qualified active low-income community business even if the CDE's investment in or loan to the entity is made through other CDEs under paragraph (d)(1)(iv)(A) of this section.

(e) * * *

(3) * * *

(iii) *Capital interest in a partnership.*—In the case of an equity investment that is a capital interest in a CDE that is a partnership for Federal tax purposes, a pro rata cash distribution by the CDE to its partners based on each partner's capital interest in the CDE during the taxable year will not be treated as a redemption for purposes of paragraph (e)(2)(iii) of this section if the distribution does not exceed the sum of the CDE's "operating income" for the taxable year and the CDE's undistributed "operating income" (if any) for the prior taxable year. For purposes of this paragraph (e)(3)(iii), §1.704-1(b)(1)(vii) applies to treat an allocation to a partner of its share of partnership net or "bottom line" taxable income or loss as an allocation to such partner of the same share of each item of income, gain, loss, and deduction that is taken into account in computing the partner's net or "bottom line" taxable income or loss. In addition, a nonpro rata "de minimis" cash distribution by a CDE to a partner or partners during the taxable year will not be treated as a redemption. A non-pro rata "de minimis" cash distribution may not exceed the lesser of 5 percent of the CDE's "operating income" for that taxable year or 10 percent of the partner's capital interest in the CDE. For purposes of this paragraph (e)(3)(iii), with respect to any taxable year, "operating income" is the sum of:

* * *

(B) Tax-exempt income under section 103;

* * *

(D) Deductions under sections 167 and 168, including the additional first-year depreciation under section 168(k), and any other depreciation and amortization deductions under the Code;

* * *

(e) * * *

(4) *Section 708(b)(1)(B) termination.* A termination under section 708(b)(1)(B) of a CDE that is a partnership is not a recapture event.

* * *

(h) * * *

(2) *Exception for certain provisions.*—* * * Paragraph (d)(6)(i) of this section as it relates to a CDE's investment under paragraph (d)(1)(iv)(A), paragraph (e)(3)(iii) of this section as it relates to the distribution of undistributed "operating income" for the prior taxable year and to the application of §1.704-1(b)(1)(vii), paragraph

(e)(3)(iii)(B) of this section, paragraph (e)(3)(iii)(D) of this section as it relates to any other depreciation and amortization deductions under the Code, and paragraph (e)(4) of this section apply to taxable years ending on or after the date of publication of the Treasury decision adopting these rules as final regulation in the **Federal Register**.

Energy Credits: Subsidized Borrowings

Energy Credits: Subsidized Borrowings.—Reproduced below is the text of proposed amendments of Reg. §1.48-9, relating to the rule which reduces the energy credit where energy property is financed by subsidized energy financing or tax-exempt industrial development bonds (published in the Federal Register on January 26, 1982).

☐ The proposed amendments to the Income Tax Regulations (26 CFR Part 1) are as follows:

Section 1.48-9 is amended by adding a new paragraph (o) to read as follows:

§1.48-9. Definition of energy property.—

* * *

(o) *Energy property financed by subsidized energy financing or industrial development bonds.*—(1) *In general.*—(i) This paragraph (o) prescribes rules—

(A) For reducing the qualified investment for purposes of the energy credit. See section 48(1)(11) as amended by section 223(c)(1) of the Crude Oil Windfall Profit Tax Act of 1980 (P.L. 96-223) and paragraph (o)(2) of this section.

(B) For reducing the energy credit percentage. See section 48(1)(11) as amended by section 221(b)(2) of that Act and paragraph (o)(6) of this section.

(ii) For effective dates, see paragraph (o)(8) of this section.

(2) *General rule.*—For purposes of the energy credit, qualified investment in any energy property (determined without this paragraph (o)) is reduced by the amount of subsidized borrowed funds used to finance in whole or in part the energy property. Funds borrowed are subsidized if they are directly or indirectly attributable to the proceeds of exempt IDB's or subsidized energy financing.

(3) *Exempt IDB defined.*—For purposes of this paragraph (c), an exempt IDB is an industrial development bond (within the meaning of section 103(b)(2)) with respect to which the interest paid is excluded from gross income under section 103.

(4) *Subsidized energy financing.*—(i) Funds are attributable to subsidized energy financing if the source of the funds for financing (other than exempt IDB's) is provided directly or indirectly (such as in association with, or through the facilities of, a bank or other lender) by, or through, a government agency under a program a principal purpose of which is to provide (or assist in providing) financing for projects designed to conserve or produce energy. For purposes of this paragraph (o), a government agency is a State or local governmental unit referred to in §1.103-1(a) or the Federal government.

(ii) Subsidized energy financing does not include a grant includible in gross income under section 61, a nontaxable government grant, or a credit against State or local taxes. Loan guarantees, price guarantees, purchase commitments, price support loans, and similar arrangements are not considered subsidized energy financing unless the arrangement is essentially subsidized borrowing under subdivision (i) of this subparagraph (4).

(iii) The following examples illustrate this subparagraph (4).

Example (1). A law in State A requires, as part of its Statewide energy program, that public utilities in the State provide low-interest loans to business enterprises for the purchase of energy property. The utilities are able to make these low-interest loans available to the enterprises by charging a 2 percent surcharge on each utility service bill. The funds from the surcharge are kept separate in an escrow account. This type of low interest loan is not subsidized energy financing and will not reduce the qualified investment of any energy property purchased with these funds.

Example (2). Assume the same facts as in example (1) except that, in lieu of the surcharge, the utilities receive money from the State for the express purpose of providing energy loans. Any low-interest loans made from these funds will be considered subsidized energy financing.

Example (3). State B allows a tax credit to a financial institution which makes low interest loans to corporations for the purpose of acquiring energy devices. The financial institution receives a credit each year in the amount of the excess of the interest that would have been paid at market rates and the actual interest paid on such loans. The State B tax credit arrangement is an interest subsidy. Thus, any low-interest loans pursuant to this credit arrangement is considered subsidized energy financing.

Example (4). State C wishes to encourage the production of synthetic fuels. As an inducement to Corporation X to build a synthetic fuel production plant, C enters into a contract with X guaranteeing X a certain price for the first 1,000 barrels of daily production. Before the plant is operational and pursuant to the price guarantee commitment, X receives an interest free advance of $10,000. Since the advance of funds is essentially a subsidized energy loan, it is considered to be subsidized energy financing.

(5) *Allocation of proceeds.*—(i) For purposes of the general rule, this subparagraph (5) sets forth the manner of determining the amount of subsidized borrowed funds that are considered used to finance energy property.

(ii) If borrowings attributable to subsidized energy financing are used to finance a facility, the entire amount of the borrowings are considered used to finance the energy property included in that facility and thus is applied directly to reduce the qualified investment in the energy property.

(iii)(A) If borrowings attributable to the proceeds of exempt IDB's are used to finance a facility, the borrowings reduce the qualified investment in that energy property. The amount of those borrowings considered used to finance energy property included in that facility equals the amount of the borrowings multiplied by a fraction. The numerator of the fraction is the qualified investment in the energy property before the reduction and the denominator is the total cost of that facility.

(B) If borrowings are attributable to the proceeds of exempt IDB's the exempt status of which is derived solely under section 103(b)(4), and the proceeds of such borrowings are used solely to finance the type of property or facility described in section 103(b)(4) from which the issue derives its tax-exempt status, then the facility referred to in paragraph (o)(5)(iii)(A) of this section is the property or facility from which the issue derives its tax-exempt status.

(iv) If both borrowings attributable to subsidized energy financing and borrowings attributable to exempt IDB financing are used to finance a facility, the total amount of subsidized energy financing is first applied directly to reduce the qualified investment (determined without this subdivision (iv)) in the energy property included in the facility. Then, paragraph (o)(5)(iii) of this section is applied to the exempt IDB financing by reducing both the numerator and the denominator of the fraction by the same total amount.

(v) The following examples illustrate this subparagraph (5).

Example (1). In 1983, Corporation X builds a facility costing $10,000. The facility includes energy property having a useful life of 7 years and the qualified investment (before reduction) is $8,000. X receives in 1983 a $6,000 energy loan from the Department of Energy for this facility at a subsidized rate of interest. The qualified investment for the energy property is reduced by $6,000 to $2,000. See paragraph (o)(5)(ii) of this section.

Example (2). Assume the same facts as in example (1) except that the $6,000 is borrowed from a fund established by a local government unit from the proceeds of exempt IDB's. The qualified investment in the energy property is reduced by $4,800 (i.e., $6,000 × $8,000/$10,000). Thus, the qualified investment is reduced from $8,000 to $3,200. See paragraph (o)(5)(iii)(A) of this section.

Example (3). Assume the same facts as in example (1) except that the total $6,000 borrowed to finance the property is from two sources. $2,000 is a subsidized energy loan and $4,000 is attributable to the proceeds of exempt IDB's. First, the qualified investment in the energy property of $8,000 is reduced by the subsidized energy loan of $2,000 to $6,000. For purposes of allocating the proceeds from exempt IDB's, the numerator and denominator of the fraction in example (2) are both reduced by this $2,000 from $8,000/$10,000 to $6,000/$8,000. Thus, the amount attributed to the proceeds of exempt IDB's is $3,000 (i.e., $4,000 × $6,000/$8,000), and the qualified investment for the energy property is $3,000, i.e., $6,000 − $3,000. See paragraph (o)(5)(iv) of this section.

Example (4). (a) In 1983, Corporation Y constructs a coal gasification project having an estimated useful life of 20 years and consisting of a gasifier and air pollution control equipment. The total cost of the project is $60 million, allocable to various types of property as follows:

($000,000 omitted)

	Gasifier	Pollution control equipment
Energy property	$30	$10
Other	10	10
	$40	$20

(b) Y finances construction of the project with subsidized financing ($10 million) and conventional financing ($36 million). Y also receives proceeds of $14 million from an issue of exempt IDB's, the exempt status of which is derived solely under section 103(b)(4)(F). Y uses the proceeds of the exempt IDB's solely to provide the pollution control equipment.

(c) Qualified investment for the energy credit is determined as follows:

		Energy property	
	Gasifier		Pollution control equipment
1. Cost	$30		$ 10
2. Allocation of subsidized energy financing ($10) to energy property			
(a) $10 × 30/40	7.5		
(b) $10 × 10/40			2.5
3. Remainder after applying paragraph (o)(5)(ii) of this section	$22.5		$ 7.5
4. Allocation of proceeds ($14) of IDB exempt solely under section 103(b)(4):			
(a) Fraction of cost of pollution control equipment that is energy property			10/20
(b) Reduce numerator and denominator of fraction by line 2(b)			7.5/17.5
(c) Multiply by proceeds			$ 14
(d) Allocated proceeds (line (b) × (c))			$ 6
5. Qualified investment for energy credit after applying paragraph (o)(5)(i)—			
(iv) of this section (line 3—line 4(d))	$22.5		$ 1.5

(6) *One-half exempt IDB rule for certain periods.*—For periods beginning on or after October 1, 1978, to which the general rule of paragraph (o)(2) of this section does not apply, the energy percentage for property is one-half of the energy percentage determined under section 46(a)(2)(C) if any funds borrowed to finance the facility of which the energy property is a part are directly or indirectly attributable to the proceeds of exempt IDB's. For explanation of the effective date of this subparagraph (6), see paragraph (o)(8) of this section.

(7) *Add-on equipment rule.*—(i) Energy property is not considered to be financed with subsidized borrowings solely because it is installed in an existing facility which has been previously so financed.

(ii) The facts and circumstances determine if energy property installed in connection with existing property is a separate unit or installed pursuant to a design, plan, or as a component of a larger property (such as a project or facility).

(iii) The following example illustrates this subparagraph (7).

Example. In 1981, corporation X finances its energy facility with the proceeds of exempt IDB's. The facility meets all air pollution laws and regulations in existence, or anticipated, when it is placed in service. In 1982, a new State regulation requires the installation of additional air pollution control equipment which is alternative energy property under section 48(1)(3)(A)(vi). X receives subsidized energy financing and installs the added equipment pursuant to the new regulation. The added air pollution control equipment is a separate unit. Therefore, the subsidized energy loan for the facility is not imputed to the qualified investment in this new separate unit.

(8) *Effective dates.*—(i) The general rule in paragraph (o)(2) of this section applies to early application property for periods after December 31, 1979. Early application property is defined in paragraph (o)(9) of this section. For other property, it applies to periods after December 31, 1982.

(ii) Notwithstanding paragraph (o)(8)(i) of this section, funds attributable under paragraph (o)(4) of this section to subsidized energy financing made before January 1, 1980, shall not be taken into account for purposes of reducing qualified investment under the general rule of paragraph (o)(2) of this section. See section 223(c)(2)(D) of P.L. 96-223. Subsidized energy financing is considered made before January 1, 1980, if it meets the requirements of § 1.167(j)-4(c) (applied without reference to any dates therein).

(iii) The one-half-exempt IDB rule in paragraph (o)(6) of this section applies for periods beginning after October 1, 1978, to which the general rule of paragraph (o)(2) of this section does not apply.

(iv) For purposes of this subparagraph (8), whether qualified investment (without any reduction under this paragraph (o)) falls within a period is determined under section 48(m). If under section 48(m) this qualified investment for energy property is allocable to more than one period, the portion of subsidized borrowings used to finance the property (as determined under paragraph (o)(5) of this section) is ratably apportioned to this qualified investment for each period in proportion to this qualified investment for each period.

(v) The following examples illustrate this subparagraph (8).

Example (1). (a) Corporation Z begins building on February 1, 1980, a facility costing $100,000, $75,000 of which is solar energy property which generates electricity. The energy property has a useful life of seven years. The facility is completed in 1983. Z spent $45,000 for the energy property for the period ending on December 31, 1982, and $30,000 for periods after that date. In connection with this facility, Z receives a loan of $10,000 attributable to subsidized energy financing made in January 1980.

(b) The subsidized energy financing is allocated between the two periods in proportion to the amount of basis of energy property attributable to each period. Thus, $6,000 of the subsidized financing is allocated to the period before 1983 (*i.e.*, $10,000 × $45,000/$75,000) and $4,000 is allocated to the period after 1982 (*i.e.*, $10,000 × $30,000/$75,000). See paragraph (o)(8)(iv) of this section.

(c) The $6,000 of subsidized energy financing attributable to the period before 1983 does not reduce qualified investment in energy property (other than early application property) because the general rule in paragraph (o)(2) of this section does not apply. However, the qualified investment of $30,000 for the period after 1982 is reduced by $4,000 to $26,000.

Example (2). Assume the same facts as in example (1) except that the energy property is early application property. The general rule in paragraph (o)(2) of this section applies and the total amount of subsidized energy financing ($10,000) is subtracted from the total qualified investment. Thus, the qualified investment for the energy credit is reduced from $75,000 to $65,000.

Example (3). (a) Assume the same facts as in example (1) except that the $10,000 loan was attributable to the proceeds of exempt IDB financing. Exempt IDB financing allocated to pre-1983 periods does not reduce the qualified investment. Instead, the energy percentage is reduced by one-half from 15 percent to 7$^1/_2$ percent and applied against the qualified investment allocable to such periods, *i.e.*, $45,000. See section 46(a)(2)(C).

(b) The amount of exempt IDB financing attributable to qualified investment in energy property is $7,500 (*i.e.*, $10,000 × $75,000/$100,000). The portion of that amount attributable to periods after 1982 is $3,000 (*i.e.*, $7,500 × $30,000/$75,000). Accordingly, the qualified investment for the energy property attributable to periods after 1982 is reduced from $30,000 by $3,000 to $27,000. See paragraph (o)(8)(iv) of this section.

Example (4). Assume the same facts in example (3) except that the energy property is early application property. The general rule in paragraph (o)(2) of this section applies to the entire energy property, and the total amount of the proceeds of exempt IDB's is multiplied by the fraction in paragraph (o)(5)(iii) of this section. Thus, the qualified investment of $75,000 is reduced by $7,500 (*i.e.*, $10,000 × $75,000/$100,000) to $67,500.

(9) *Early application property.*—(i) Early application property is—

(A) Qualified hydroelectric generating property (described in section 48(1)(2)(A)(vii)),

(B) Cogeneration equipment (described in section 48(1)(2)(A)(viii)),

(C) Qualified intercity buses (described in section 48(1)(2)(A)(ix)),

(D) Ocean thermal property (described in section 48(1)(3)(A)(ix)), or

Reg. §1.48-9(o)(9)(i)(D)

(E) Expanded energy property.

(ii) Expanded energy property is—

(A) Property that is included for the first time as alternative energy property under clause (iii) or (v) of section 48(1)(3)(A) by reason of the amendments thereto by section 222(b)(1) and (2) of the Crude Oil Windfall Profit Tax Act of 1980 (Pub. L. 96-223, 94 Stat. 229),

(B) Solar or wind energy property that provides solar process heat referred to in section 49(1)(4)(C),

(C) Modifications to alumina electrolytic cells referred to in section 48(1)(5)(L), and

(D) Property described in the last sentence of section 48(1)(3)(A) (relating to storage equipment for refuse-derived fuel).

Consolidated Returns: AMT

Consolidated Returns: Alternative Minimum Tax.—Reproduced below is the text of a proposed amendment to Reg. §1.56(g)-1, relating to the computation of the alternative minimum tax by consolidated groups (published in the Federal Register on December 30, 1992).

☐ Par. 2. Section 1.56(g)-1 is amended by revising paragraph (n) to read as follows:

§1.56(g)-1. Adjusted current earnings.

* * *

(n) *Adjustment for adjusted current earnings of consolidated groups.*—For consolidated return years for which the due date of the income tax return (without regard to extensions) is on or after [the date that is sixty days after final regulations are filed with the Federal Register], the rules of §1.1502-55(b)(3) apply in computing the adjustment for adjusted current earnings of a consolidated group.

* * *

Base Erosion and Anti-Abuse Tax: Additional Rules

Base Erosion and Anti-Abuse Tax: Additional Rules.—Amendments to Reg. §§1.59A-2 and 1.59A-3, regarding the base erosion and anti-abuse tax imposed on certain large corporate taxpayers with respect to certain payments made to foreign related parties, are proposed (published in the Federal Register on December 6, 2019) (REG-112607-19).

Par. 2 Section1.59A-2, as added in a final rule [T.D. 9885], effective December 6, 2019, is amended by adding paragraphs (c)(2)(ii), (c)(4) through (6), and paragraph (f)(2) to read as follows:

§1.59A-2. Applicable taxpayer.

* * *

(c) * * *

(2) * * *

(ii) *Change in the composition of an aggregate group.*—A change in ownership of the taxpayer (for example, a sale of the taxpayer to a third party) does not cause the taxpayer to leave its own aggregate group. Instead, any members of the taxpayer's aggregate group before the change in ownership that are no longer members following the change in ownership are treated as having left the taxpayer's aggregate group, and any new members that become members of the taxpayer's aggregate group following the change in ownership are treated as having joined the taxpayer's aggregate group. A change in ownership of another member of the aggregate group of the taxpayer (for example, a sale of the member to a third party) may result in the member joining or leaving the aggregate group of the taxpayer. See paragraph (c)(4) of this section for the treatment of members joining or leaving the aggregate group of a taxpayer.

* * *

(4) *Periods before and after a corporation is a member of an aggregate group.*—Solely for purposes of this section, to determine the gross receipts and the base erosion percentage of the aggregate group of a taxpayer, the taxpayer takes into account only the portion of another corporation's taxable year during which the corporation is a member of the aggregate group of the taxpayer. The gross receipts of an aggregate group of a taxpayer attributable to a member of the aggregate group are not reduced as a result of the member leaving the aggregate group of the taxpayer. Solely for purposes of this paragraph (c), when a member joins or leaves the aggregate group of a taxpayer in a transaction that does not result in the member having a taxable year-end, the member is treated as having a taxable year end (deemed taxable year-end) immediately before joining or leaving the group. For purposes of this paragraph (c)(4), a corporation that has a deemed taxable year-end may determine gross receipts, base erosion tax benefits, and deductions attributable to that year by either treating the corporation's books as closing at the deemed taxable year-end or, in the case of items other than extraordinary items (as defined in §1.1502-76(b)(2)(ii)(C)), allocating those items on a pro-rata basis without a closing of the books.

(5) *Treatment of short taxable year.*—Solely for purposes of this section, if a taxpayer has a taxable year of fewer than 12 months (a short period), gross receipts are annualized by multiplying the gross receipts for the short period by 365 and dividing the result by the number of days in the short period. When a taxpayer has a taxable year that is a short period, the taxpayer must use a reasonable approach to determine the gross receipts and base erosion percentage of its aggregate group for the short period. A reasonable approach should neither over-count nor under-count the gross receipts, base erosion tax benefits, and deductions of the aggregate group of the taxpayer, even if the taxable year of a member or members of the aggregate group does not end with or within the short period.

(6) *Treatment of predecessors.*—(i) *In general.*—Solely for purposes of this section, in determining gross receipts under paragraph (d) of this section, any reference to a taxpayer includes a reference to any predecessor of the taxpayer. For this purpose, a predecessor includes the distributor or transferor corporation in a transaction described in section 381(a) in which the taxpayer is the acquiring corporation.

(ii) *No duplication.*—If the taxpayer or any member of its aggregate group is also a predecessor of the taxpayer or any member of its aggregate group, the gross receipts, base erosion tax benefits, and deductions of each member are taken into account only once.

* * *

(f) * * *

(2) *Example 2: Member leaving an aggregate group*—(i) *Facts.* Parent Corporation wholly owns Corporation 1 and Corporation 2. Each corporation is a domestic corporation and a calendar year taxpayer that does not file a consolidated return. The aggregate group of Corporation 1 includes Parent Corporation and Corporation 2. At noon on June 30, Year 1, Parent Corporation sells the stock of Corporation 2 to Corporation 3, an unrelated domestic corporation, in exchange for cash consideration. Before the acquisition, Corporation 3 was not a member of an aggregate group. Corporation 2 and Corporation 3 do not file a consolidated return.

(ii) *Analysis.* (A) For purposes of section 59A, to determine the gross receipts and base erosion percentage of the aggregate group of Corporation 1 for calendar Year 1, Corporation 2 is treated as having a taxable year end immediately before noon on June 30, Year 1, as a result of the sale. The aggregate group of Corporation 1 takes into account only the gross receipts, base erosion tax benefits, and deductions of Corporation 2 attributable to the period from January 1 to immediately before noon on June 30 of Year 1. The same results apply to the aggregate group of Parent Corporation for calendar Year 1.

(B) For purposes of section 59A, to determine the gross receipts and base erosion percentage of the aggregate group of Corporation 2 for calendar Year 1, each of Parent Corporation, Corporation 1, and Corporation 3 are treated as having a taxable year end at immediately before noon on June 30, Year 1. Because Corporation 2 does not have a short taxable year, paragraph (c)(5) of this section does not apply. The aggregate group of Corporation 2 takes into account the gross receipts, base erosion tax benefits, and deductions of Parent Corporation and Corporation 1 attributable to the period from January 1 to immediately before noon on June 30 of Year 1, and the gross receipts, base erosion tax benefits, and deductions of Corporation 3 attributable to the period from noon on June 30 to December 31 of Year 1.

Par. 3. Section 1.59A-3, as added in a final rule [T.D. 9885], effective December 6, 2019, is amended by adding paragraphs (c)(5) and (6) and (d)(8) and (9) to read as follows:

§1.59A-3. Base erosion payments and base erosion tax benefits.

* * *

(c) * * *

(5) *Allowed deduction.*—Solely for purposes of paragraph (c)(1) of this section, all deductions that could be properly claimed by a taxpayer for the taxable year (determined after giving effect to the taxpayer's permissible method of accounting or to any election, such as the election under section 173 to capitalize circulation expenditures or the election under section 168(g)(7) to use the alternative depreciation system of depreciation) are treated as allowed deductions under chapter 1 of subtitle A of the Internal Revenue Code.

(6) *Election to waive allowed deductions.*—(i) *In general.*—Solely for purposes of paragraph (c)(1) of this section, if a taxpayer elects to waive certain deductions, the amount of allowed deductions as defined in paragraph (c)(5) of this section is reduced by the amount of deductions that are properly waived under this paragraph (c)(6)(i). To make this election, a taxpayer must provide information related to each deduction waived as required by applicable forms and instructions issued by the Commissioner, including—

(A) A detailed description of the item or property to which the deduction relates, including sufficient information to identify that item or property on the taxpayer's books and records;

(B) The date on which, or period in which, the waived deduction was paid or accrued;

(C) The provision of the Internal Revenue Code (and regulations, as applicable) that allows the deduction for the item or property to which the election relates;

(D) The amount of the deduction that is claimed for the taxable year with respect to the item or property;

(E) The amount of the deduction being waived for the taxable year with respect to the item or property;

(F) A description of where the deduction is reflected (or would have been reflected) on the Federal income tax return (schedule and line number); and

(G) The name, EIN (if applicable), and country of organization of the foreign related party that is or will be the recipient of the payment that generates the deduction.

(ii) *Effect of election to waive deduction.*—(A) *In general.*—(1) *Consistent treatment.*—Except as otherwise provided in this paragraph (c)(6)(ii), any deduction waived under paragraph (c)(6) of this section is treated as having been waived for all purposes of the Code and regulations.

(2) *No allocation and apportionment of waived deductions.*—The waiver of deductions described in this paragraph (c)(6) is treated as occurring before the allocation and apportionment of deductions under §§ 1.861-8 through -14T and 1.861-17 (such as for purposes of section 904).

(3) *Effect of waiver of deductions described in §§ 1.861-10 and § 1.861-10T.* To the extent that any waived deduction is interest expense that would have been directly allocated under the rules of §§ 1.861-10 or § 1.861-10T and would have resulted in the reduction of value of any assets for purposes of allocating other interest expense under §§ 1.861-9 and 1.861-9T, the value of the assets is reduced to the same extent as if the taxpayer had not elected to waive the deduction.

(B) *Effect of the election to waive deductions disregarded for certain purposes.*—If a taxpayer makes the election to waive a deduction, in whole or in part, under paragraph (c)(6)(i) of this section, the election is disregarded for determining—

(1) The taxpayer's overall method of accounting, or the taxpayer's method of accounting for any item, under section 446 and the regulations in this part under section 446;

(2) Whether a change in the taxpayer's overall plan of accounting or the taxpayer's treatment of a material item is a change in method of accounting under section 446(e) and § 1.446-1(e);

(3) The amount allowable under subtitle A of the Code for depreciation or amortization for purposes of section 167(c) and section 1016(a)(2) or section 1016(a)(3) and any other adjustment to basis under section 1016(a);

(4) For purposes of applying the exclusive apportionment rule in § 1.861-17(b), the geographic source where the research and experimental activities which account for more than fifty percent of the amount of the deduction for research and experimentation was performed;

(5) The application of section 482 and the regulations under section 482;

(6) The amount of the taxpayer's earnings and profits; and

(7) Any other item as necessary to prevent a taxpayer from receiving the benefit of a waived deduction.

(C) *Not a method of accounting.*—The election described in paragraph (c)(6)(i) of this section is not a method of accounting under section 446 and the regulations in this part under section 446.

(D) *Effect of the election in determining section 481(a) adjustments.*—A taxpayer making the election described in paragraph (c)(6)(i) of this section agrees that if the method of accounting for a waived deduction is changed, the amount of adjustment taken into account under section 481(a)(2) is determined without regard to the election described in paragraph (c)(6)(i) of this section. As a result, a waived deduction has no effect on the amount of a section 481(a) adjustment compared to what the adjustment would have been if the deduction had not been waived.

(iii) *Time and manner for election to waive deduction.*—A taxpayer may make the election described in paragraph (c)(6)(i) of this section on its original filed Federal income tax return. In addition, a taxpayer may elect to waive deductions or increase the amount of deductions waived pursuant to the election described in paragraph (c)(6)(i) of this section on an amended Federal income tax return filed within the later of 3 years from the date the original return was filed, taking into account section 6501(b)(1), for the taxable year for which the election is made or the period described in section 6501(c)(4), or during the course of an examination of the taxpayer's income tax return for the relevant tax year pursuant to procedures prescribed by the Commissioner. However, a taxpayer may not decrease the amount of deductions waived by the election, or otherwise revoke the election that is described in paragraph (c)(6)(i) of this section on any amended Federal income tax return or during the course of an examination. To make the election, a taxpayer must complete the appropriate part of Form 8991, *Tax on Base Erosion Payments of Taxpayers With Substantial Gross Receipts*, (or successor), including the information described in paragraph (c)(6)(i) of this section and any other information required by the form or instructions. A taxpayer makes the election described in paragraph (c)(6)(i) of this section on an annual basis, and the taxpayer does not need the consent of the Commissioner if the taxpayer chooses not to make the election for a subsequent taxable year. The election described in paragraph (c)(6)(i) of this section may not be made in any other manner (for example, by filing an application for a change in accounting method).

(d) * * *

(8) *Example 8: Effect of election to waive deduction on method of accounting*— (i) *Facts.* DC, a domestic corporation, purchased and placed in service a depreciable asset (Asset A) from a foreign related party on the first day of its taxable year 1 for $100x. DC elects to use the alternative depreciation system under section 168(g) to depreciate all properties placed in service during taxable year 1. Asset A is not eligible for the additional first year depreciation deduction. Beginning in taxable year 1, DC depreciates Asset A under the alternative depreciation system using the straight-line depreciation method, a 5-year recovery period, and the half-year convention. This depreciation method, recovery period, and convention are permissible for Asset A under section 168(g). On its timely filed original Federal income tax return for taxable year 1, DC does not elect to waive any deductions and DC claims a depreciation deduction of $10x for Asset A. On its timely filed original Federal income tax return for taxable year 2, DC does not elect to waive any deductions and DC claims a depreciation deduction of $20x for Asset A. During taxable year 3, DC files an amended return for taxable year 1 to elect to waive the depreciation deduction for Asset A and reports in accordance with paragraph (c)(6)(i) of this section with its amended return for taxable year 1 that the amount of the waived depreciation deduction for Asset A is $10x and the amount of the claimed depreciation deduction is $0x.

(ii) *Analysis*— Pursuant to paragraph (c)(6)(ii)(B)(1) of this section, DC's election to waive the depreciation deduction for Asset A for taxable year 1 is disregarded for determining DC's method of accounting for Asset A. Accordingly, after DC's election to waive the depreciation deduction for Asset A for taxable year 1, DC's method of accounting for depreciation for Asset A continues to be the straight-line depreciation method, a 5-year recovery period, and the half-year convention. Pursuant to paragraph (c)(6)(ii)(C) of this section, the election made by DC in taxable year 3 on its amended return for taxable year 1 is not a method of accounting.

(9) *Example 9: Change of accounting method when taxpayer has waived a deduction*—(i) *Facts.* DC, a domestic corporation, purchased and placed in service a depreciable asset (Asset B) from a foreign related party on the first day of its taxable year 1 for $100x. DC elects to use the alternative depreciation system under section 168(g) to depreciate all properties placed in service during taxable year 1. Asset B is not eligible for the additional first year depreciation deduction. Beginning in taxable year 1, DC depreciates Asset B under the alternative depreciation system using the straight-line depreciation method, a 10-year recovery period, and the half-year convention. Under this method of accounting, the depreciation deductions for Asset B are $5x for taxable year 1 and $10x for taxable year 2. However, for taxable years 1 and 2, DC elects to waive $3x and $6x, respectively, of the depreciation deductions for Asset B and reports the information required under paragraph (c)(6)(i) of this section with its returns. In taxable year 3, DC realizes that the correct

recovery period for Asset B is 5 years. If DC had used the correct recovery period for Asset B, the depreciation deductions for Asset B would have been $10x for taxable year 1 and $20x for taxable year 2. DC timely files a Form 3115 to change its method of accounting for Asset B from a 10-year recovery period to a 5-year recovery period, beginning with taxable year 3. DC was not under examination as of the date on which it timely filed this Form 3115.

(ii) *Analysis*—(A) *Computation of the section 481(a) adjustment.* In determining the net negative section 481(a) adjustment for this method change, DC compares the depreciation deductions under its present method of accounting to the depreciation deductions under its proposed method of accounting. Pursuant to paragraph (c)(6)(ii)(D) of this section, DC agreed that, by making the election to waive depreciation deductions for Asset B, DC will not take into account the fact that depreciation deductions for Asset B were waived under paragraph (c)(6)(i) of this section. Accordingly, DC's

net negative section 481(a) adjustment for this method change is $15x, which is calculated by determining the difference between the depreciation deductions for Asset B for taxable years 1 and 2 under DC's present method of accounting ($15x) and the depreciation deductions that would have been allowable for Asset B for taxable years 1 and 2 under DC's proposed method of accounting ($30x).

(B) *Computation of basis adjustments.* Pursuant to paragraph (c)(6)(ii)(B)(3) of this section, DC's elections to waive the depreciation deductions for Asset B for taxable years 1 and 2 are disregarded for determining the amount allowable for depreciation for purposes of section 1016(a)(2). The amount allowable for depreciation of Asset B is determined based on the proper method of computing depreciation for Asset B. Accordingly, Asset B's adjusted basis at the end of taxable year 1 is $90x ($100x - $10x) and at the end of taxable year 2 is $70x ($90x - $20x).

Base Erosion and Anti-Abuse Tax: Additional Rules

Base Erosion and Anti-Abuse Tax: Additional Rules.—Amendments to Reg. §1.59A-7, regarding the base erosion and anti-abuse tax imposed on certain large corporate taxpayers with respect to certain payments made to foreign related parties, are proposed (published in the Federal Register on December 6, 2019) (REG-112607-19).

Par. 4. Section 1.59A-7, as added in a final rule [T.D. 9885], effective December 6, 2019, is amended by adding paragraphs (c)(5)(v) and (g)(2)(x) to read as follows:

§1.59A-7. Application of base erosion and anti-abuse tax to partnerships.

* * *

(c) * * *

(5) * * *

(v) *Allocations of income in lieu of deductions.*—If a partnership adopts the curative method of making section 704(c) allocations under §1.704-3(c), the allocation of income to the contributing partner in lieu of a deduction allocation to the noncontributing partner is treated as a deduction for purposes of section 59A in an amount equal to the income allocation. See paragraph (g)(2)(x) of this section (*Example 10*) for an example illustrating the application of this paragraph (c)(5)(v).

* * *

(g) * * *

(2) * * *

(x) *Example 10: Section 704(c) and curative allocations*—(A) *Facts.* The facts are the same as in paragraph (d)(2)(ii)(A) of this section (the facts in *Example 2*), except that DC's property is not depreciable, PRS uses the traditional method with curative allocations under §1.704-3(c), and the curative allocations are to be made from operating income. Also assume that the partnership has $20x of gross operating income in each year and a curative allocation of the operating income satisfies the "substantially the same effect" requirement of §1.704-3(c)(3)(iii)(A).

(B) *Analysis.* The analysis and results are the same as in paragraph (d)(2)(i)(B) of this section (the analysis in *Example 1*), except that actual depreciation is $8x ($40x/5) per year and the ceiling rule shortfall under §1.704-3(b)(1) of $2x per year is corrected with a curative allocation of income from DC to FC is $2x per year. Solely for U.S. federal income tax purposes, each year FC is allocated $12x of total operating income and DC is allocated $8x of operating income. Both the actual depreciation deduction to DC and the curative allocation of income from DC are base erosion tax benefits to DC under paragraph (d)(1) of this section.

Base Erosion and Anti-Abuse Tax: Additional Rules

Base Erosion and Anti-Abuse Tax: Additional Rules.—Amendments to Reg. §§1.59A-9 and 1.59A-10, regarding the base erosion and anti-abuse tax imposed on certain large corporate taxpayers with respect to certain payments made to foreign related parties, are proposed (published in the Federal Register on December 6, 2019) (REG-112607-19).

Par. 5. Section 1.59A-9, as added in a final rule [T.D. 9885], effective December 6, 2019, is amended by adding paragraphs (b)(5) and (6) to read as follows:

§1.59A-9. Anti-abuse and recharacterization rules.

* * *

(b) * * *

(5) *Transactions involving derivatives on a partnership interest.*—If a taxpayer acquires a derivative on a partnership interest (or partnership assets) as part of a transaction (or series of transactions), plan or arrangement that has as a principal purpose avoiding a base erosion payment (or reducing the amount of a base erosion payment) and the partnership interest (or partnership assets) would have resulted in a base erosion payment had the taxpayer acquired that interest (or partnership asset) directly, then the taxpayer is treated as having a direct interest instead of a derivative interest for purposes of applying section 59A. A derivative interest in a partnership includes any contract (including any financial instrument) the value of which, or any payment or other transfer with respect to which, is (directly or

indirectly) determined in whole or in part by reference to the partnership, including the amount of partnership distributions, the value of partnership assets, or the results of partnership operations.

(6) *Allocations to eliminate or reduce a base erosion payment.*—If a partnership receives (or accrues) income from a person not acting in a partner capacity (including a person who is not a partner) and allocates that income to its partners with a principal purpose of avoiding a base erosion payment (or reducing the amount of a base erosion payment), then the taxpayer transacting with the partnership will determine its base erosion payment as if the allocations had not been made and the items of income had been allocated proportionately. The preceding sentence applies only when the allocations, in combination with any related allocations, do not change the economic arrangement of the partners to the partnership.

* * *

Par. 6. Section 1.59A-10, as added in a final rule [T.D. 9885], effective December 6, 2019, is revised to read as follows:

§1.59A-10. Applicability date.—(a) *General applicability date.*—
Sections 1.59A-1 through 1.59A-9, other than the provisions described in the first sentence of paragraph (b) of this section, apply to taxable years ending on or after December 17, 2018. However, taxpayers may apply these regulations in their entirety for taxable years beginning after December 31, 2017, and ending before December 17, 2018. In lieu of applying these regulations, taxpayers may apply the provisions matching §§1.59A-1 through 1.59A-9 from the Internal Revenue Bulletin (IRB) 2019-02 (https://www.irs.gov/pub/irs-irbs/irb19-02.pdf) in their entirety for all taxable years ending on or before December 6, 2019.

(b) *Exception.*—Sections 1.59A-2(c)(2)(ii) and (c)(4) through (6) and 1.59A-3(c)(5) and (6) apply to taxable years beginning on or after [EFFECTIVE DATE OF FINAL RULE], and §§1.59A-7(c)(5)(v) and 1.59A-9(b)(5) and (6) apply to taxable years ending on or after December 2, 2019. However, taxpayers may apply these provisions in their entirety for taxable years beginning after December 31, 2017, and before the final regulations are applicable. If a taxpayer is applying the provisions described in the last sentence of paragraph (a) of this section, the taxpayer's failure to apply §1.59A-2(c)(2)(ii) and (c)(4) through (6) to taxable years ending on or before December 6, 2019 is not taken into account for purposes of applying the preceding sentence.

* * *

COMPUTATION OF TAXABLE INCOME

Imputed Interest: OID: Safe Haven Rates

Imputed Interest: Original Issue Discount: Safe Haven Interest Rates.—Reproduced below are the texts of proposed amendments of Reg §§1.61-6 and 1.61-7, relating to (1) the tax treatment of debt instruments issued after July 1, 1982, that contain original issue discount, (2) the imputation of and the accounting for interest with respect to sales and exchanges of property occurring after December 31, 1984, and (3) safe haven interest rates for loans or advances between commonly controlled taxpayers and safe haven leases between such taxpayers (published in the Federal Register on April 8, 1986).

☐ Par. 2. Paragraph (c)(3) of §1.61-6 is revised to read as follows:

§1.61-6. Gains derived from dealings in property.

* * *

(c) *Character of recognized gain.*—* * *

(3) Amounts received on retirement or sale or exchange of debt instruments, section 1271;

* * *

☐ Par. 3. In paragraph (d) of §1.61-7, the third sentence is amended by removing the phrase "section 1232" and adding in its place the phrase "section 1271".

§1.61-7. Interest.

Compensation Reduction Plans

Gross Income: Deferred: Compensation Reduction Plans or Arrangements.—Reproduced below is the text of proposed Reg. §1.61-16, relating to amounts payment of which are deferred under compensation reduction plans or arrangements (published in the Federal Register on February 3, 1978).

☐ 26 CFR Part 1 is amended by adding a new §1.61-16 immediately after §1.61-15. The new section reads as follows:

§1.61-16. Amounts payments of which are deferred under certain compensation reduction plans or arrangements.—(a) *In general.*—Except as otherwise provided in paragraph (b) of this section, if under a plan or arrangement (other than a plan or arrangement described in sections 401(a), 403(a) or (b), or 405(a)) payment of an amount of a taxpayer's basic or regular compensation fixed by contract, statute, or otherwise (or supplements to such compensation, such as bonuses, or increases in such compensation) is, at the taxpayer's individual option, deferred to a taxable year later than that in which such amount would have been payable but for his exercise of such option, the amount shall be treated as received by the taxpayer in such earlier taxable year. For purposes of this paragraph, it is immaterial that the taxpayer's rights in the amount payment of which is so deferred become forfeitable by reason of his exercise of the option to defer payment.

(b) *Exception.*—Paragraph (a) of this section shall not apply to an amount payment of which is deferred as described in paragraph (a) under a plan or arrangement in existence on February 3, 1978, if such amount would have been payable, but for the taxpayer's exercise of the option, at any time prior to [date 30 days following publication of this section as a Treasury Decision]. For purposes of this paragraph, a plan or arrangement in existence on February 3, 1978, which is significantly amended after such date will be treated as a new plan as of the date of such amendment. Examples of significant amendments would be extension of coverage to an additional class of taxpayers or an increase in the maximum percentage of compensation subject to the taxpayer's option.

Fringe Benefits: Employer-Provided Vehicle and Fuel: Lease Valuation Rule

Fringe Benefits: Employer-Provided Vehicle and Fuel: Lease Valuation Rule.—Reproduced below is the text of a proposed amendment to Reg. §1.61-21, relating to the valuation of an employee's personal use of employer-provided fuel when an employer-provided automobile is valued pursuant to the automobile lease valuation rule (published in the Federal Register on October 9, 1992).

☐ Par. 2. Section 1.61-21 is amended by revising paragraphs (d)(3)(ii)(A), (B), and (D) as follows:

§1.61-21. Taxation of fringe benefits.

* * *

(d) * * *

(3) * * *

(ii) *Fuel excluded.*—(A) *In general.*—The Annual Lease Values do not include the fair market value of fuel provided by the employer, whether fuel is provided in kind or its cost is reimbursed by or charged to the employer. Thus, if an employer provides fuel for the employee's personal use, the fuel must be valued separately for inclusion in income.

(B) *Valuation of fuel provided in kind.*—Fuel provided in kind may be valued at fair market value based on all the facts and circumstances or, in the alternative, may be valued at 5.5 cents per mile for all miles driven by the employee in calendar years 1989 through 1992. For subsequent calendar years, the applicable cents-per-mile rate is the amount specified in the annual Revenue Procedure concerning the optional standard mileage rates used in computing deductible costs of operating a passenger automobile for business. However, fuel provided in kind may not be valued at the alternative cents-per-mile rate for miles driven outside the United States, Canada, or Mexico.

* * *

(D) *Additional methods available to employers with fleets of at least 20 automobiles.*—(1) *Fleet-average cents-per-mile fuel cost.*—If an employer with a fleet of at least 20 automobiles (regardless of whether the requirements of paragraph (d)(5)(v)(D) of this section are met) reimburses employees for the cost of fuel or allows employees to charge the employer for the cost of fuel, the fair market value of fuel provided to those automobiles may be determined by reference to the employer's fleet-average cents-per-mile fuel cost. The fleet-average cents-per-mile fuel cost is equal to the fleet-average per-gallon fuel cost divided by the fleet-average miles-per-gallon rate. The averages described in the preceding sentence must be determined by averaging the per-gallon fuel costs and miles-per-gallon rates of a representative sample of the automobiles in the fleet equal to the greater of ten percent of the automobiles in the fleet or 20 automobiles for a representative period, such as a two-month period.

(2) *Alternative cents-per-mile method.*—In lieu of determining the fleet-average cents-per-mile fuel cost under paragraph (d)(3)(ii)(D)(1) of this section, an employer with a fleet of at least 20 automobiles may value the fuel provided for these automobiles by reference to the cents-per-mile rate set forth in paragraph (d)(3)(ii)(B) of this section (regardless of whether the requirements of paragraph (d)(5)(v)(D) of this section are met).

* * *

Individual Retirement Plans: Simplified Employee Pensions

Individual Retirement Plans: Simplified Employee Pensions.—Reproduced below is the text of proposed amendment of Reg. §1.62-1, relating to individual retirement plans and simplified employee pensions (published in the Federal Register on July 14, 1981).

☐ Par. 1. Section 1.62-1 is amended by revising paragraph (c)(13) to read as follows:

§1.62-1. Adjusted gross income.

* * *

(c) * * *

(13) Deductions allowed by sections 219 and 220 for contributions to an individual retirement account described in section 408(a), for an individual retirement annuity described in section 408(b), or for a retirement bond described in section 409;

* * *

Dependency Exemption: Authorized Placement Agency: Definition

Dependency Exemption: Authorized Placement Agency: Definition.—Reg. §1.63-3 and amendments to Reg. §§1.63-1 and 1.63-2, relating to the definition of an authorized placement agency for purposes of a dependency exemption for a child placed for adoption that were issued prior to the changes made to the law by the Working Families Tax Relief Act of 2004, are proposed (published in the Federal Register on January 19, 2017) (REG-137604-07).

Par. 7. Section 1.63-1 is amended by:

1. Removing the language "the zero bracket amount and" from the section heading.

2. Removing the language "section 63(g)" and replacing it with the language "section 63(e)" in paragraph (a).

§1.63-1. Change of treatment with respect to the zero bracket amount and itemized deductions.

Par. 8. Section 1.63-2 is revised to read as follows:

§1.63-2. Standard deduction.—The standard deduction means the sum of the basic standard deduction and the additional standard deduction.

Par. 9. Section 1.63-3 is added to read as follows:

§1.63-3. Additional standard deduction for the aged and blind.—(a) *In general.*—A taxpayer who, at the end of the taxable year, has attained age 65 or is blind is entitled to an additional standard deduction amount. The additional standard deduction amount is the sum of the amounts to which the taxpayer is entitled under paragraphs (b) and (c) of this section. If an individual meets the requirements for both the additional amount for the aged and the additional amount for the blind, the taxpayer is entitled to both additional amounts.

(b) *Additional amount for the aged.*—(1) *Aged taxpayer or spouse.*—A taxpayer is entitled to an additional amount under section 63(f)(1) if the taxpayer has attained age 65 before the end of the taxable year. If spouses file a joint return, each spouse who has attained age 65 before the end of the taxable year for which the spouses file the joint return is entitled to an additional amount. A married taxpayer who files a separate return is entitled to an additional amount for the taxpayer's spouse if the spouse has attained age 65 before the end of the taxable year and, for the calendar year in which the taxable year of the taxpayer begins, the spouse has no gross income and is not the dependent of another taxpayer. The taxpayer is not entitled to an additional amount if the spouse dies before attaining age 65, even though the spouse would have attained age 65 before the end of the taxpayer's taxable year.

(2) *Age determined.*—For purposes of section 63(f) and this paragraph (b), a taxpayer's age is determined as of the last day of the taxpayer's taxable year. A person attains the age of 65 on the first moment of the day preceding his or her sixty-fifth birthday.

(c) *Additional amount for the blind.*—(1) *Blind taxpayer or spouse.*—A taxpayer is entitled to an additional amount under section 63(f)(2) if the taxpayer is blind at the end of the taxable year. If spouses file a joint return, each spouse who is blind at the end of the taxable year for which the spouses file the joint return is entitled to an additional amount. A married taxpayer who files a separate return is entitled to an additional amount for the taxpayer's spouse if the spouse is blind and, for the calendar year in which the taxable year of the taxpayer begins, the spouse has no gross income and is not the dependent of another taxpayer. If the spouse dies during the taxable year, the date of death is the time for determining the spouse's blindness.

(2) *Blindness determined.*—A taxpayer who claims an additional amount allowed by section 63(f)(2) for the blind must maintain in the taxpayer's records a statement from a physician skilled in the diseases of the eye or a registered optometrist stating that the physician or optometrist has examined the person for whom the additional amount is claimed and, in the opinion of the physician or optometrist, the person's central visual acuity did not exceed 20/200 in the better eye with correcting lenses, or the person's visual acuity was accompanied by a limitation in the field of vision such that the widest diameter of the visual field subtends an angle no greater than 20 degrees. The statement must provide that the physician or optometrist examined the person in the taxpayer's taxable year for which the amount is claimed, or that the physician or optometrist examined the person in an earlier year and that the visual impairment is irreversible.

(d) *Applicability date.*—This section and §§1.63-1(a) and 1.63-2 apply to taxable years beginning after the date these regulations are published as final regulations in the **Federal Register**. [Reg. §1.63-3.]

Taxable Income: Relief from Joint and Several Liability

Taxable Income: Relief from Joint and Several Liability.—Amendments to Reg. §§1.66-1—1.66-5, relating to relief from joint and several liability under section 6015 of the Internal Revenue Code and reflecting changes in the law made by the Tax Relief and Health Care Act of 2006 as well as changes in the law arising from litigation, are proposed (published in the Federal Register on November 20, 2015) (REG-134219-08).

Par. 2. Section 1.66-1 is amended by adding paragraph (d) to read as follows:

§1.66-1. Treatment of community income.

* * *

(d) *Effective/applicability date.*—This section is applicable beginning July 10, 2003.

Par. 3. Section 1.66-2 is amended by adding paragraph (e) to read as follows:

§1.66-2. Treatment of community income where spouses live apart.

* * *

(e) *Effective/applicability date.*—This section is applicable beginning July 10, 2003.

Par. 4. Section 1.66-3 is amended by adding paragraph (d) to read as follows:

§1.66-3. Denial of the Federal income tax benefits resulting from the operation of community property law where spouses not notified.

* * *

(d) *Effective/applicability date.*—This section is applicable beginning July 10, 2003.

Par. 5. Section 1.66-4 is amended by:

1. The last sentence of paragraphs (a)(3) and (b) are revised.

2. Paragraph (l) is added and reserved.

3. Paragraph (m) is added.

The revisions and additions read as follows:

§ 1.66-4. Request for relief from the Federal income tax liability resulting from the operation of community property law.—(a) * * *

(3) * * * Factors relevant to whether it would be inequitable to hold a requesting spouse liable, more specifically described under the applicable administrative procedure issued under section 66(c) (Rev. Proc. 2013-34 (2013-2 CB 397) (See § 601.601(d)(2) of this chapter), or other applicable guidance published by the Secretary), are to be considered in making a determination under this paragraph (a).

(b) * * * Factors relevant to whether it would be inequitable to hold a requesting spouse liable, more specifically described under the applicable administrative procedure issues under section 66(c)

Par. 6. Section 1.66-5 is removed.

§ 1.66-5. Effective date.

(Rev. Proc. 2013-34 (2013-2 CB 397) (See § 601.601(d)(2) of this chapter), or other applicable guidance published by the Secretary), are to be considered in making a determination under this paragraph (b).

* * *

(l) [Reserved]

(m) *Effective/applicability date.*—This section is applicable beginning July 10, 2003, except that paragraphs (a)(3) and (b) of this section will be applicable on the date of publication of a Treasury Decision adopting these rules as final regulations in the **Federal Register**.

Tax Liability: Relief from Joint and Several Liability

Tax Liability: Relief from Joint and Several Liability.—Amendments to Reg. §§ 1.66-4 and 1.66-5, providing guidance to taxpayers on when and how to request relief under sections 66 and 6015, are proposed (published in the Federal Register on August 13, 2013) (REG-132251-11).

☐ Par. 2 In § 1.66-4, paragraph (j)(2)(ii) is revised to read as follows:

§ 1.66-4. Request for relief from the Federal income tax liability resulting from the operation of community property law.

* * *

(j) * * *

(2) * * *

(ii) *Equitable relief.*—The earliest time for submitting a request for equitable relief from the Federal income tax liability resulting from the operation of community property law under paragraph (b) of this section is the date the requesting spouse receives notification of an audit or a letter or notice from the IRS stating that there may be an outstanding liability with regard to that year (as described in paragraph (j)(2)(iii) of this section). A request for equitable relief from the Federal income tax liability resulting from the operation of community property law under paragraph (b) of this section for a liability that is properly reported but unpaid is properly submitted with the requesting spouse's individual Federal income tax return, or after the requesting spouse's individual Federal income tax return is filed. To request equitable relief under § 1.66-4, a requesting spouse must file Form 8857, "Request for Innocent Spouse Relief," or other

similar statement with the IRS within the period of limitation on collection of tax in section 6502 or within the period of limitation on credit or refund of tax in section 6511, as applicable to the tax liability. If a requesting spouse files a request for equitable relief under § 1.66-4 within the period of limitation on collection of tax, the IRS will consider the request for equitable relief, but the requesting spouse will be eligible for a credit or refund of tax only if the limitation period for credit or refund of tax is open when the request is filed (assuming all other requirements are met, including the limit on amount of credit or refund prescribed in section 6511(b)(2)). Alternatively, if a requesting spouse files a request for equitable relief after the period of limitation on collection of tax has expired but while the limitation period on credit or refund of tax remains open, the IRS will consider the request for equitable relief insofar as tax was paid by or collected from the requesting spouse, and the requesting spouse will be eligible for a potential credit or refund of tax. If neither the section 6502 nor section 6511 limitation period is open when a requesting spouse files a request for equitable relief, the IRS will not consider the request for equitable relief.

* * *

☐ Par. 3. Section 1.66-5 is revised to read as follows:

§ 1.66-5. Effective/applicability date.—Except for § 1.66-4(j)(2)(ii), sections 1.66-1 through 1.66-4 are applicable on July 10, 2003. Section 1.66-4(j)(2)(ii) applies to any request for relief filed on or after July 25,

2011 (the date that Notice 2011-70, 2011-32 IRB, was issued to the public).

Itemized Deductions

Itemized Deductions: Two-Percent Floor.—Temporary Reg. §§ 1.67-1T and 1.67-2T, relating to the two-percent floor on miscellaneous itemized deductions, are also proposed as final regulations and, when adopted, would become Reg. §§ 1.67-1 and 1.67-2 (published in the Federal Register on March 28, 1988).

§ 1.67-1. 2-percent floor on miscellaneous itemized deductions.

§ 1.67-2. Treatment of pass-through entities.

REMICs: Reporting Information: Extension of Time

REMICs: Reporting Information: Extension of Time.—Reproduced below is the text of a proposed amendment to Temporary Reg. § 1.67-3T, relating to real estate mortgage investment conduits (published in the Federal Register on September 30, 1991).

☐ Par. 2. Section 1.67-3T is amended by revising the last sentence of paragraph (f)(2)(ii)(A) to read as follows:

§ 1.67-3T. Allocation of expenses by real estate mortgage investment conduits (Temporary).

* * *

(f) * * *

(2) * * *

(ii) * * *

(A) * * * The separate statement provided in a separate mailing must be furnished to each pass-through interest holder no later than the 41st day following the close of the calendar year.

* * *

REMICs: Reporting Requirements: Allocable Investment Expenses

REMICs: Reporting Requirements: Allocable Investment Expenses.—Temporary Reg. § 1.67-3T(a) through (e), relating to reporting requirements with respect to real estate mortgage investment conduits (REMICs), is also proposed as final (published in the Federal Register on September 3, 1992).

§ 1.67-3. Allocation of expenses by real estate mortgage investment conduits.

Transfers Between Spouses

Transfers: Alimony, Separate Maintenance, and Dependency Exemption.—Temporary Reg. §1.71-1T, relating to the treatment of transfers of property between spouses and former spouses, the tax treatments of alimony and separate maintenance payments, and the dependency exemption in the case of a child of divorced parents, is also proposed as a final regulation and, when adopted, would become Reg. §1.71-1 (published in the Federal Register on August 31, 1984).

§1.71-1. Alimony and separate maintenance payments.

Exclusion Ratio

Exclusion Ratio.—Reproduced below is the text of a proposed amendment of Reg. §1.72-4, relating to the exclusion ratio (published in the Federal Register on April 30, 1975).

§1.72-4. Exclusion ratio.—(a) *General rule.*—(1)(i) To determine the proportionate part of the total amount received each year as an annuity which is excludable from the gross income of a recipient in the taxable year of receipt (other than amounts received under (A) certain employee annuities described in section 72(d) and §1.72-13, or (B) certain annuities described in section 72(n) and §1.122-1), an exclusion ratio is to be determined for each contract. In general, this ratio is determined by dividing the investment in the contract as found under §1.72-6 by the expected return under such contract as found under §1.72-5. Where a single consideration is given for a particular contract which provides for two or more annuity elements, an exclusion ratio shall be determined for the contract as a whole by dividing the investment in such contract by the aggregate of the expected returns under all the annuity elements provided thereunder. However, where the provisions of paragraph (b)(3) of §1.72-2 apply to payments received under such a contract, see paragraph (b)(3) of §1.72-6.

* * *

Annuity Contracts: Exchanges of Property

Annuity Contracts: Exchanges of Property.—Amendments to Reg. §1.72-6, providing guidance on the taxation of the exchange of property for an annuity contract, are proposed (published in the Federal Register on October 18, 2006) (REG-141901-05).

☐ Par. 2. In §1.72-6, paragraph (e) is added to read as follows:

§1.72-6. Investment in the contract.

* * *

(e) *Certain annuity contracts received in exchange for property.*—(1) *In general.*—If an annuity contract is received in an exchange subject to §1.1001-1(j), the aggregate amount of premiums or other consideration paid for the contract equals the amount realized attributable to the annuity contract, determined according to §1.1001-1(j).

(2) *Effective date.*—(i) *In general.*—Except as provided in paragraph (e)(2)(ii), this paragraph (e) is applicable for annuity contracts received after October 18, 2006, in an exchange subject to §1.1001-1(j).

(ii) This paragraph (e) is applicable for annuity contracts received after April 18, 2007, in an exchange subject to §1.1001-1(j) if the following conditions are met —

(A) The issuer of the annuity contract is an individual;

(B) The obligations under the annuity contract are not secured, either directly or indirectly; and

(C) The property transferred in exchange for the annuity contract is not subsequently sold or otherwise disposed of by the transferee during the two-year period beginning on the date of the exchange. For purposes of this provision, a disposition includes without limitation a transfer to a trust (whether a grantor trust, a revocable trust, or any other trust) or to any other entity even if solely owned by the transferor.

Exclusion Ratio: Special Rule

Exclusion Ratio.—Reproduced below is the text of a proposed amendment of Reg. §1.72-13, relating to the exclusion ratio (published in the Federal Register on April 30, 1975).

☐ Section 1.72-13(e)(3) is amended by deleting "72(o)" and inserting in lieu thereof "72(n)". As amended §1.72-13(e)(3) reads as follows:

§1.72-13. Special rule for employee contributions recoverable in three years.—

* * *

(e) *Inapplicability of section 72(d) and this section.*—Section 72(d) and this section do not apply to: * * *

(3) Amounts paid to an annuitant under chapter 73 of title 10 of the United States Code with respect to which section 72(n) and §1.122-1 apply.

Employee Trusts: Effective Dates

Employee Trusts: Tax Reform Act of 1984: Effective Dates.—Temporary Reg. §1.72(e)-1T is also proposed as a final regulation and, when adopted, would become Reg. §1.72(e)-1 (published in the Federal Register on February 4, 1986).

§1.72(e)-1. Treatment of distributions where substantially all contributions are employee contributions.

Prizes and Awards

Exclusions: Prizes and Awards: Employee Achievement Awards.—Reproduced below are the texts of proposed Reg. §1.74-2 and a proposed amendment of Reg. §1.74-1, relating to prizes and awards and employee achievement awards (published in the Federal Register on January 9, 1989).

☐ Paragraph 1. The authority for Part 1 continues to read in part:
Authority: 26 U.S.C. 7805. * * *

☐ Par. 2. Section 1.74-1 is amended as follows:

(a) Paragraph (a)(1) is amended by

(1) Removing the phrase "subsection (b)" and adding the phrase "subsections (b) and (c)" in its place, and

(2) Removing the word "any" in the last sentence and adding the word "most" in its place.

(b) Paragraph (b) is amended by

(1) Removing the word "and" from the first sentence, and

(2) Removing "award" at the end of the first sentence and adding the language set forth below in its place.

(c) Paragraph (c) is removed and new paragraphs (c), (d), (e), (f), and (g) are added directly following paragraph (b) to read as set forth below.

§1.74-1. Prizes and awards.—* * *

(b) *Exclusion from gross income* . . . award; and (4) the payor transfers the prize or award (and the prize or award is, in fact, transferred) to one or more governmental units or organizations described in paragraph (1) or (2) of section 170(c) pursuant to a designation by the recipient. Accordingly, awards such as the Nobel prize and the Pulitzer prize will qualify for the exclusion if the award is transferred by the payor to one or more qualifying organizations pursuant to a qualified designation by the recipient.

(c) *Designation by recipient.*—(1) *In general.*—To qualify for the exclusion under this section, the recipient must make a qualifying designation, in writing, within 45 days of the date the prize or award is granted (see paragraph (e)(3) of this section for a definition of "granted"). A qualifying designation is required to indicate only that a designation is being made. The document does not need to state on its face that the organization(s) are entities described in paragraph (1) and/or (2) of section 170(c) to result in a qualified designation. Furthermore, it is not necessary that the document do more than identify a class of entities from which the payor may select a recipient. However, designation of a specific nonqualified donee organization or designation of a class of recipients that may include nonqualified donee organizations is not a qualified designation. The following example illustrates the application of this section:

A distinguished ophthalmologist, S, is awarded the Nobel prize for medicine. S may designate that the prize money be given to a particular university that is described in section 170(c)(1), or to any university that is described in that section. However, S cannot designate that the award be given to a donee that is not described in section 170(c)(1), such as a foreign medical school. Selection of such a donee or inclusion of such a donee on a list of possible donees on S's designation would disqualify the designation.

(2) *Prizes and awards granted before 60 days after date of publication of final regulations.*—In the case of prizes and awards granted before 60 days after date of publication of final regulations, a qualifying designation may be made at any time prior to 105 days after date of publication of final regulations.

(d) *Transferred by payor.*—An exclusion will not be available under this section unless the designated items or amounts are transferred by the payor to one or more qualified donee organizations. The provisions of this paragraph shall not be satisfied unless the items or amounts are transferred by the payor to one or more qualifying donee organizations no later than the due date of the return (without regard to extensions) for the taxable year in which the items or amounts would otherwise be includible in the recipient's gross income. A transfer may be accomplished by any method that results in the receipt of the items or amounts by one or more qualified donee organizations from the payor and does not involve a

disqualifying use of the items or amounts. Delivery of items or amounts by a person associated with a payor (*e.g.,* a contractual agent, licensee, or other representative of the payor) will satisfy the requirements of this section so long as the items or amounts are received by, or on behalf of, one or more qualified donee organizations. Possession of a prize or an award by any person before a designation is made will not result in the disallowance of an exclusion unless a disqualifying use of the items or amounts is made before the items or amounts are returned to the payor for transfer to one or more qualified donee organizations (see paragraph (e)(2) of this section for a definition of "disqualifying use"). Accordingly, transfer of an item or amount to a nonqualified donee organization will not result in an ineffective transfer under this section if the item or amount is timely returned to the payor by the nonqualified donee organization before a disqualifying use of the item or amount is made and the item or amount is then transferred to a qualifying organization.

(e) *Definitions.*—(1) For purposes of this section, "qualified donee organizations" means entities defined in section 170(c)(1) or (2) of the Code.

(2) For purposes of this section, the term "disqualifying use" means, in the case of cash or other intangibles, spending, depositing, investing or otherwise using the prize or award so as to enure to the benefit of the recipient or any person other than the grantor or an entity described in section 170 (c)(1) or (2). In the case of tangible items, the term "disqualifying use" means physical possession of the item for more than a brief period of time by any person other than the grantor or an entity described in section 170(c)(1) or (2). Thus, physical possession by the recipient or a person associated with the recipient may constitute a disqualifying use if the item is kept for more than a brief period of time. For example, receipt of an unexpected tangible award at a ceremony that otherwise comports with the requirements of this section will not constitute a disqualifying use unless the recipient fails to return the item to the payor as soon as practicable after receipt.

(3) For purposes of this section, an item will be considered "granted" when it is subject to the recipient's dominion and control to such an extent that it otherwise would be includible in the recipient's gross income.

(f) *Charitable deduction not allowable.*—Neither the payor nor the recipient will be allowed a charitable deduction for the value of any prize or award that is excluded under this section.

(g) *Qualified scholarships.*—See section 117 and the regulations thereunder for provisions relating to qualified scholarships.

□ Par. 3. New section 1.74-2 is added to immediately follow section 1.74-1 as set forth below.

§1.74-2. Special exclusion for certain employee achievement awards.—(a) *General rule.*—(1) Section 74(c) provides an exclusion from gross income for the value of an employee achievement award (as defined in section 274(j)) received by an employee if the cost to the employer of the award does not exceed the amount allowable as a deduction to the employer for the cost of the award. Thus, where the cost to the employer of an employee achievement award is fully deductible after considering the limitation under section 274(j), the value representing the employer's cost of the award is excludable from the employee's gross income.

(2) Where the cost of an award to the employer is so disproportionate to the fair market value of the award that there is a significant likelihood that the award was given as disguised compensation, no portion of the award will qualify as an employee achievement award excludable under the provisions of this section (see also §1.274-8(c)(1) and (4)).

(b) *Excess deduction award.*—Where the cost to the employer of an employee achievement award exceeds the amount allowable as a deduction to the employer, the recipient must include in gross income an amount which is the greater of (1) the excess of such cost over the amount that is allowable as a deduction (but not to exceed the fair market value of the award) or (2) the excess of the fair market value of the award over the amount allowable as a deduction to the employer.

(c) *Examples.*—The operation of this section may be illustrated by the following examples:

Example (1). An employer makes a qualifying length of service award to an employee in the form of a television set. Assume that the deduction limitation under §274(j)(2) applicable to the award is $400. Assume also that the cost of the television set to the employer was $350, and that the fair market value of the television set is $475. The amount excludable is $475 (the full fair market value of the television set). This is true even though the fair market value exceeds both the cost of the television set to the employer and the $400 deduction

allowable to the employer for nonqualified plan awards under section 274(j)(2)(A).

Example (2). Assume the same facts as in example (1) except that the fair market value of the television set is $900. Under these circumstances, the fair market value of the television set is so disproportionate to the cost of the item to the employer that the item will be considered payment of disguised compensation. As a result, no portion of the award will qualify as an employee achievement award. Since no portion of the award is excludable by the employee, the employer must report the full fair market value of the award as compensation on the employee's Form W-2.

Example (3). An employer makes a qualifying safety achievement award to an employee in the form of a pearl necklace. Assume that the deduction limitation under section 274(j) is $400. Assume also that the cost of the necklace to the employer is $425 and that the fair market value of the necklace is $475. The amount includible by the employee in gross income is the greater of (a) $25 (the difference between the cost of the item ($425) and the employer's deductible amount of $400) or (b) $75 (the amount by which the fair market value of the award ($475) exceeds the employer's deductible amount of $400). Accordingly, $75 is the amount includible in the employee's gross income. The remaining portion of the fair market value of the award (*i.e.,* the $400 amount allowable as a deduction to the employer) is not included in the gross income of the employee. If the cost of the pearl necklace to the employer was $500 instead of $425, then $100 would be includible in the employee's gross income because the excess of the cost of the award over $400 (*i.e.,* $100) is greater than the excess of the fair market value of the award over $400 (*i.e.,* $75). The employer must report the $75, which is includible in the employee's gross income, as compensation on the employee's Form W-2.

Example (4). An employer invites its employees to attend a party it is sponsoring to benefit a charity. In order to encourage the employees to attend the party and to make contributions to the charity, the employer promises to match the employees' contributions and also provide expensive prizes to be awarded to contributing employees selected at random. Each employee receiving a prize must include the full fair market value of the prize in gross income because the prizes are not qualifying achievement awards under section 274(j) or de minimis fringe benefits under section 132(e). Since the prizes are not excludable, the employer must report the full fair market value of the prize as compensation on the employee's Form W-2.

(d) *Special rules.*—(1) The exclusion provided by this section shall not be available for any award made by a sole proprietorship to the sole proprietor.

(2) In the case of an employer exempt from taxation under Subtitle A of the Code, any reference in this section to the amount allowable as a deduction to the employer shall be treated as a reference to the amount which would be allowable as a deduction to the employer if the employer were not exempt from taxation under Subtitle A of the Code.

(e) *Exclusion for certain de minimis fringe benefits.*—Nothing contained in this section shall preclude the exclusion of the value of an employee award that is otherwise qualified for exclusion under section 132(e). [Reg. §1.74-2.]

Employee Trusts: Effective Dates

Employee Trusts: Tax Reform Act of 1984: Effective Date.—Temporary Reg. §1.79-4T is also proposed as a final regulation and, when adopted, would become Reg. §1.79-4 (published in the Federal Register on February 4, 1986).

§1.79-4. Questions and answers relating to the nondiscrimination requirements for group-term life insurance.

Partnerships: Equity for Services

Partnerships: Equity for Services.—Amendments to Reg. §1.83-3, providing that the transfer of a partnership interest in connection with the performance of services is subject to Code Sec. 83 and providing rules for coordinating Code Sec. 83 with partnership taxation principles, are proposed (published in the Federal Register on May 24, 2005) (REG-105346-03).

☐ Par. 2. Section 1.83-3 is amended as follows:

1. Paragraph (e) is amended by adding two new sentences after the first sentence.

2. Paragraph (l) is added.

The revision and addition read as follows:

§1.83-3. Meaning and use of certain terms.
* * *

(e) *Property.*—* * * Accordingly, property includes a partnership interest. The previous sentence is effective for transfers on or after the date final regulations are published in the Federal Register. * * *
* * *

(l) *Special rules for the transfer of a partnership interest.*—(1) Subject to such additional conditions, rules, and procedures that the Commissioner may prescribe in regulations, revenue rulings, notices, or other guidance published in the Internal Revenue Bulletin (see §601.601(d)(2)(ii)(*b*) of this chapter), a partnership and all of its partners may elect a safe harbor under which the fair market value of a partnership interest that is transferred in connection with the performance of services is treated as being equal to the liquidation value of that interest for transfers on or after the date final regulations are published in the **Federal Register** if the following conditions are satisfied:

(i) The partnership must prepare a document, executed by a partner who has responsibility for Federal income tax reporting by the partnership, stating that the partnership is electing, on behalf of the partnership and each of its partners, to have the safe harbor apply irrevocably as of the stated effective date with respect to all partnership interests transferred in connection with the performance of services while the safe harbor election remains in effect and attach the document to the tax return for the partnership for the taxable year that includes the effective date of the election.

(ii) Except as provided in paragraph (l)(1)(iii) of this section, the partnership agreement must contain provisions that are legally binding on all of the partners stating that—

(A) The partnership is authorized and directed to elect the safe harbor; and

(B) The partnership and each of its partners (including any person to whom a partnership interest is transferred in connec-

tion with the performance of services) agrees to comply with all requirements of the safe harbor with respect to all partnership interests transferred in connection with the performance of services while the election remains effective.

(iii) If the partnership agreement does not contain the provisions described in paragraph (l)(1)(ii) of this section, or the provisions are not legally binding on all of the partners of the partnership, then each partner in a partnership that transfers a partnership interest in connection with the performance of services must execute a document containing provisions that are legally binding on that partner stating that—

(A) The partnership is authorized and directed to elect the safe harbor; and

(B) The partner agrees to comply with all requirements of the safe harbor with respect to all partnership interests transferred in connection with the performance of services while the election remains effective.

(2) The specified effective date of the safe harbor election may not be prior to the date that the safe harbor election is executed. The partnership must retain such records as may be necessary to indicate that an effective election has been made and remains in effect, including a copy of the partnership's election statement under this paragraph (l), and, if applicable, the original of each document submitted to the partnership by a partner under this paragraph (l). If the partnership is unable to produce a record of a particular document, the election will be treated as not made, generally resulting in termination of the election. The safe harbor election also may be terminated by the partnership preparing a document, executed by a partner who has responsibility for Federal income tax reporting by the partnership, which states that the partnership, on behalf of the partnership and each of its partners, is revoking the safe harbor election on the stated effective date, and attaching the document to the tax return for the partnership for the taxable year that includes the effective date of the revocation.

Partnerships: Equity for Services

Partnerships: Equity for Services.—Amendments to Reg. §1.83-6, providing that the transfer of a partnership interest in connection with the performance of services is subject to Code Sec. 83 and providing rules for coordinating Code Sec. 83 with partnership taxation principles, are proposed (published in the Federal Register on May 24, 2005) (REG-105346-03).

☐ Par. 3. Section 1.83-6 is amended by revising the first sentence of paragraph (b) to read as follows:

§1.83-6. Deduction by employer.
* * *

(b) *Recognition of gain or loss.*—Except as provided in section 721 and section 1032, at the time of a transfer of property in connection

with the performance of services the transferor recognizes gain to the extent that the transferor receives an amount that exceeds the transferor's basis in the property. * * *

* * *

Employee Death Benefits

Employee Death Benefits.—Reproduced below is the text of a proposed amendment of Reg. §1.101-2, relating to employees' death benefits (published in the Federal Register on April 30, 1975).

☐ Paragraph (d) of §1.101-2 is amended by revising subparagraph (3)(i) and example (2) of subparagraph (3)(ii) to read as follows:

§1.101-2. Employees' death benefits.

* * *

(d) *Nonforfeitable rights.*—* * *

(3)(i) Notwithstanding the rule stated in paragraph (d)(1) of this section and illustrated in paragraph (d)(2) of this section, the exclusion from gross income provided by section 101(b) applies to a lump sum distribution (as defined in section 402(e)(4)(A) and the regulations thereunder) with respect to which the deceased employee possessed, immediately before his death, a nonforfeitable right to receive the amounts while living (see section 101(b)(2)(B) (i) and (ii)). See paragraph (d)(4) of this section relating to the exclusion of amounts which are received under annuity contracts purchased by certain exempt organizations and with respect to which the deceased employee possessed, immediately before his death, a nonforfeitable right to receive the amounts while living.

(ii) The application of the provisions of paragraph (d)(3)(i) of this section may be illustrated by the following examples:

* * *

Example (2). The trustee of the X Corporation noncontributory, "qualified," profit-sharing plan is required under the provisions of the plan to pay to the beneficiary of B, an employee of the X Corporation who died on July 1, 1974, the benefit due on account of the death of B. The provisions of the profit-sharing plan give each participating employee, in case of termination of employment, a 10 percent vested interest in the amount accumulated in his account for each of the first 10 years of participation in the plan, but, in case of death, the entire balance to the credit of the participant's account is to be paid to his beneficiary. At the time of B's death, he had been a participant for five years. The accumulation in his account was $8,000, and the amount which would have been distributable to him in the event of termination of employment was $4,000 (50 percent of $8,000). After his death, $8,000 is paid to his beneficiary in a lump sum. (It may be noted that these are the same facts as in example (5)

of subparagraph (2) of this paragraph except that the employee has been a participant for five years instead of three and the plan is a "qualified" plan.) It is immaterial that the employee had a nonforfeitable right to $4,000, because the payment of the $8,000 to the beneficiary is the payment of a lump sum distribution to which subdivision (i) of this subparagraph applies. Assuming no other death benefits are involved, the beneficiary may exclude $5,000 of the $8,000 payment from gross income.

Example (3). The facts are the same as in example (2) except that the beneficiary is entitled to receive only the $4,000 to which the employee had a nonforfeitable right and elects, 30 days after B's death, to receive it over a period of ten years. Because the distribution is not a lump sum distribution and because B's interest is nonforfeitable, no exclusion from gross income is allowable with respect to the $4,000.

Example (4). The X Corporation instituted a trust, forming part of a "qualified" profit-sharing plan for its employees, the cost thereof being borne entirely by the corporation. The plan provides, in part, that if an employee leaves the employ of the corporation, either voluntarily or involuntarily, before retirement, 10 percent of the account balance provided for the employee in the trust fund will be paid to the employee for each of the first 10 years of service. The plan further provides that if an employee dies before reaching retirement age, his beneficiary will receive a percentage of the account balance provided for the employee in the trust fund, on the same basis as shown in the preceding sentence. A, an employee of the X Corporation for 5 years, died before attaining retirement age while in the employ of the corporation. At the time of his death, $15,000 was the account balance provided for him in the trust fund. His beneficiary receives $7,500 in a lump sum, an amount equal to 50 percent of the account balance provided for A's retirement. The beneficiary may exclude from gross income (assuming no other death benefits are involved) $5,000 of the $7,500, since the latter amount constitutes a lump sum distribution to which subdivision (i) of this subparagraph applies.

Life Insurance Contracts: Qualified Accelerated Death Benefits

Life Insurance Contracts: Qualified Accelerated Death Benefits.—Reproduced below is the text of proposed Reg. §1.101-8, relating to the definition of a life insurance contract for federal tax purposes and the tax treatment of amounts received as qualified accelerated death benefits (published in the Federal Register on December 15, 1992).

☐ Par. 2. Section 1.101-8 is added to read as follows:

§1.101-8. Amounts paid with respect to terminally ill individuals.—For purposes of section 101(a), a qualified accelerated death benefit (as defined in §1.7702-2(d)), received on or after [date on

which final regulations are published in the Federal Register], is treated as an amount paid by reason of the death of the insured. [Reg. §1.101-8.]

Prizes and Awards

Exclusions: Prizes and Awards: Employee Achievement Awards.—Reproduced below is the text of a proposed amendment of Reg. §1.102-1, relating to prizes and awards and employee achievement awards (published in the Federal Register on January 9, 1989).

☐ Par. 4. Section 1.102-1 is amended as follows:

(a) The last sentence of paragraph (a) is removed.

(b) A new paragraph (f) is added immediately following paragraph (e) to read as follows.

§1.102-1. Gifts and inheritances.

* * *

(f) *Exclusions.*—(1) *In general.*—Section 102 does not apply to prizes and awards (including employee achievement awards) (see section 74); certain de minimis fringe benefits (see section 132); any amount transferred by or for an employer to, or for the benefit of, an employee (see section 102(c)); or to qualified scholarships (see section 117).

(2) *Employer/Employee transfers.*—For purposes of section 102(c), extraordinary transfers to the natural objects of an employer's bounty will not be considered transfers to, or for the benefit of, an employee if the employee can show that the transfer was not made in recognition of the employee's employment. Accordingly, section 102(c) shall not apply to amounts transferred between related parties (*e.g.*, father and son) if the purpose of the transfer can be substantially attributed to the familial relationship of the parties and not to the circumstances of their employment.

Registration Requirements: Debt Obligations: Interest Deduction

Obligations of the United States: Registration Requirement: Deduction of Interest.—The text of Temporary Reg. §5f.103-1, relating to registration requirements with respect to debt obligations, has also been proposed as a final regulation and, when adopted, would become Reg. §1.103-8(a)(7) (published in the Federal Register on November 15, 1982). *NOTE: Code Sec. 103 has been amended to remove special exempt bond issue rules and provide similar rules in Code Secs. 141-150. This proposed regulation was issued under Code Sec. 103 as it read before amendment.*

§5f.103-1. Obligations issued after December 31, 1982, required to be in registered form (temporary).

Debt Obligations: Registration Requirements: Withholding

Registration-Required Obligations: Withholding.—An amendment to Temporary Reg. §5f.103-1, relating to the definition of the term "registration-required" with respect to certain types of obligations and to the repeal of the 30 percent withholding tax on certain types of interest, is also proposed as final (published in the Federal Register on December 19, 1986). *NOTE: Code Sec. 103 has been amended to remove special exempt bond issue rules and provide similar rules in Code Secs. 141-150. This proposed amendment was issued under Code Sec. 103 as it read before amendment.*

§ 5f.103-1. **Obligations issued after December 31, 1982, required to be in registered form (temporary).**

Definition of Registered Form: Guidance

Definition of Registered Form: Guidance.—Amendments to Reg. § 5f.103-1, providing guidance on the definitions of registration-required obligation and registered form, including guidance on the issuance of pass-through certificates and participation interests in registered form, are proposed (published in the Federal Register on September 19, 2017) (REG-125374-16).

Par. 13. Section 5f.103-1(d) is amended by revising the paragraph heading and adding two sentences at the end of the paragraph to read as follows:

§ 5f.103-1. **Obligations issued after December 31, 1982, required to be in registered form.**

* * *

(d) *Applicability date.*—* * * For the purpose of determining whether bonds satisfy the requirements of section 149(a), this section applies to bonds issued prior to the date 90 days after the publication of the Treasury decision adopting these rules as final regulations in the **Federal Register**, and § 1.149(a)-1 of this chapter applies to bonds issued on or after the date 90 days after the publication of the Treasury decision adopting these rules as final regulations in the **Federal Register**. For all other purposes, see § 1.163-5(a)(2) and (b) of this chapter for obligations issued after March 18, 2012.

* * *

Industrial Development Bonds for Water Facilities

Industrial Development Bonds: Issuance to Finance Certain Water Facilities.—Reproduced below is the text of a proposed amendment of Reg. § 1.103-8, relating to the income tax exemption for interest on industrial development bonds issued to finance certain water facilities (published in the Federal Register on August 22, 1984). *NOTE: Code Sec. 103 has been amended to remove special exempt bond issue rules and provide similar rules in Code Secs. 141-150. This proposed amendment was issued under Code Sec. 103 as it read before amendment.*

☐ Section 1.103-8 (relating to exemption for interest on bonds to finance certain exempt facilities) is amended by revising paragraph (h) thereof. The revised provisions read as follows:

§ 1.103-8. **Interest on bonds to finance certain exempt facilities.**

* * *

(h) *Water facilities.*—(1) *General rule for obligations issued after November 6, 1978.*—Section 103(b)(4)(G) provides that section 103(b)(1) shall not apply to any obligation issued after November 6, 1978, by (or on behalf of) a State or local governmental unit which is issued as part of an issue substantially all of the proceeds of which are to be used to provide facilities for the furnishing of water for any purpose if certain requirements are met. In order to qualify under section 103(b)(4)(G) and this paragraph as an exempt facility, the facility must satisfy the requirements established by subparagraph (3) of this paragraph.

(2) *Facilities for the furnishing of water defined.*—For purposes of section 103(b)(4)(G) and this paragraph, the term "facilities for the furnishing of water" means those components of a system for the distribution of water to customers that are necessary for the collection, treatment, and distribution of water to a service area, and other functionally related and subordinate components as defined in § 1.103-8(a)(3). For a component to come within this definition, it must be part of a system which, when viewed as a whole, is for the distribution of water to customers. A system or component does not come within this definition if it is a production facility that merely uses water in the production process (*e.g.*, a cooling pond, or equipment using water internally within a manufacturing plant). For example, an extension of a pipeline to carry water to a single industrial user from a qualified system is a qualified component because the system as a whole qualifies, but the internal water facilities of a private plant would not be a qualified component. In general, a series of dams will not constitute a single system, but each will constitute a separate system. Components of a dam or reservoir used to generate electric energy, such as generators and turbines, will not qualify as facilities for the furnishing of water (of course they may qualify as components for the local furnishing of electric energy under section 103(b)(4)(E) or as components used in hydroelectric generating facilities qualifying under section 103(b)(4)(H)). However, a reservoir or dam does not necessarily fail to qualify as facilities for the furnishing of water solely because one use of the water is to produce electricity if at least 90 percent of the water is available for other purposes, such as irrigation and domestic consumption, in addition to producing electricity.

(3) *Additional requirements.*—(i) The facility must make its water available to members of the general public. For this purpose, the general public includes electric utility, industrial, agricultural, and commercial users. In order to make its water available to the general public, a facility must make available to residential users within its service area, municipal water districts within its service area, or any combination thereof, at least 25 percent of its capacity (which must be a considerable quantity in absolute terms). Except with respect to residential users and municipal water districts, a water facility is not required to make available water to all segments of the general public in order to qualify under this subdivision (i). For example, if an industrial user agrees to "take or pay for" the entire capacity of a reservoir (but is guaranteed only 25 to 75 percent of the capacity), the facility will comply with this subdivision (i), provided the remainder of the water will be made available to residential users or municipal water districts within the service area. However, a facility is not considered to make water available to the general public merely because it is available for swimming, water skiing, and other recreational activities. A water facility is not required to make its water available to the general public immediately after its construction in order to qualify under this subdivision (i); it is sufficient that the facility is available to serve the general public. For example, if a pipeline is built to serve a sparsely inhabited region which lacks water, the pipeline meets the requirement of this subdivision (i) if it will serve the general public that the new source of water reasonably may be expected to cause to move into the region.

(ii) The facility must be operated either by—

(A) A governmental unit, within the meaning of § 1.103-7(b)(2), or the United States government or an agency or instrumentality thereof, or

(B) A regulated public water utility whose rates for the furnishing or sale of the water are required to be established or approved by a State or political subdivision thereof, by an agency or instrumentality of the United States, or by a public service or public utility commission or other similar body of any State or political subdivision thereof.

A governmental unit or a regulated public water utility is considered to operate a facility only if it has responsibility and control over the repairs and maintenance of the facility. For example, if an industrial user leases the facility on a long-term basis, and it either controls the maintenance and repair of the facility, or bears these costs, then the facility fails to meet the requirement that it be operated by a governmental unit or a regulated public water utility.

* * *

Tax Exempt Status of Industrial Development Bonds

Nontaxables: Government Obligations: Tax-Exempt Industrial Development Bonds.—Reproduced below is the text of a proposed amendment of Reg. § 1.103-8, relating to the definition of low or moderate income made by the Tax Reform Act of 1984 (published in the Federal Register on November 7, 1985). *NOTE: Code Sec. 103 has been amended to remove special exempt bond issue rules and provide similar rules in Code Secs. 141-150. This proposed amendment was issued under Code Sec. 103 as it read before amendment.*

☐ Par. 2. Section 1.103-8 is amended by revising paragraph (b)(1), (b)(3) and paragraph (b)(4)(i) and (ii), by adding a new paragraph (b)(4)(v), by revising paragraph (b)(5), paragraph (b)(7)(ii), and paragraph (b)(8)(v), by revising *Example (3)* of paragraph (b)(9), and by adding new *Example (12)* and *Example (13)* to follow *Example (11)* of paragraph (b)(9). These revised and added provisions read as follows:

§ 1.103-8. **Interest on bonds to finance certain exempt facilities.**

* * *

(b) *Residential rental property.*—(1) *General rule for obligations issued after April 24, 1979.*—Section 103(b)(1) shall not apply to any obligation which is issued after April 24, 1979, and is part of an issue substantially all of the proceeds of which are to be used to provide a residential rental project in which 20 percent or more of the units in the project that are to be provided with the proceeds of the issue (other than those units to be provided with an insubstantial amount of the proceeds of the issue as permitted under paragraph (a)(3) of this section) are to be occupied by individuals or families of low or moderate income (as defined in paragraph (b)(8)(v) of this section). See paragraph (b)(4)(v) with respect to mixed-use projects. In the case of a targeted area project, the minimum percentage is 15 percent. See generally § 1.103-7 for rules relating to refunding issues.

* * *

(3) *Transitional rule.*—For purposes of this section, obligations issued after April 24, 1979, may be treated as issued before April 25, 1979, if the transitional requirements of section 1104 of the Mortgage Subsidy Bond Tax Act of 1980 (94 Stat. 2670), as amended by section 614 of the Tax Reform Act of 1984 (98 Stat. 914), are satisfied.

(4) *Residential rental project.*—(i) *In general.*—A residential rental project is a building or structure, together with any facilities functionally related and subordinate thereto, containing one or more similarly constructed units that—

(a) Are not used on a transient basis, and

(b) Satisfy the requirements of paragraph (b)(5)(i) of this section and are available to members of the general public in accordance with the requirements of paragraph (a)(2) of this section.

Although a residential rental project may include other property, such as commercial office space, special rules apply to such mixed-use projects (see paragraph (b)(4)(v)). Hotels, motels, dormitories, fraternity and sorority houses, rooming houses, hospitals, nursing homes, sanitariums, and rest homes are not residential rental projects (but, with respect to obligations issued prior to January 1, 1986, only if such facilities are for use on a transient basis). In addition, trailer parks and courts for use on a transient basis are not residential rental projects.

(ii) *Multiple buildings and partial use of buildings.*—(a) Proximate buildings or structures that have similarly constructed units are treated as part of the same project if they are owned for Federal tax purposes by the same person and they are financed pursuant to a common plan.

(b) Buildings or structures are proximate if they are located on a single tract of land. The term "tract" means any parcel or parcels of land that either are contiguous or are contiguous except for the interposition of a road, street, stream or similar property. Parcels are contiguous if their boundaries meet at one or more points.

(c) Similarly constructed units located in a single building and financed pursuant to a common plan of financing are treated as part of the same project.

(d) A common plan of financing exists if, for example, all such buildings or similarly constructed units are provided by the same issue or several issues subject to a common indenture.

* * *

(v) *Mixed-use projects.*—(a) For purposes of this paragraph (b), a mixed-use project is a building or structure, together with any facilities functionally related and subordinate thereto, containing—

(1) One or more similarly constructed units rented or available for rental that, in the aggregate, meet the low or moderate income occupancy requirement of paragraph (b)(5)(ii), and

(2) Other property the use of which is unrelated to such units, *e.g.*, commercial office space, owner-occupied residences, and units that, in the aggregate, do not meet the low or moderate income occupancy requirement of paragraph (b)(5)(ii) ("nonqualifying property").

(b) For purposes of determining whether, in the case of a mixed-use project, substantially all of the proceeds of the issue are to be used to provide a residential rental project, only the proceeds to be used to provide the units described in paragraph (b)(4)(v)(a)(1) and the other portions of the project allocable to such units are treated as being used to provide a residential rental project. Other portions of the project allocable to such units include—

(1) The allocable portion of property benefitting both such units and the nonqualifying property (*e.g.*, common elements), and

(2) All property benefitting only such units (*e.g.*, recreational facilities used only by occupants of the units described in paragraph (b)(4)(v)(a)(1)).

(c) In determining whether, in the case of a mixed-use project, substantially all of the proceeds of an issue are to be used to provide a residential rental project, the cost of property that will benefit, directly or indirectly, both the units described in paragraph (b)(4)(v)(a)(1) and the nonqualifying property must be allocated between such units and the nonqualifying property. For example, in the case of a mixed-use project part of which is to be used for commercial

purposes, the cost of the building's foundation must be allocated between the commercial portion of the building and the units described in paragraph (b)(4)(v)(a)(1). The allocation of the cost of such common elements may be made according to any reasonable method that properly reflects the proportionate benefit to be derived, directly or indirectly, by the units described in paragraph (b)(4)(v)(a)(1) and the nonqualifying property. Allocating the cost of such common elements based on the ratio of the total floor space in the building or structure that is to be used for nonqualifying property to all other floor space in the building or structure is, generally, a reasonable method; however, in the case of any common elements with respect to which an allocation according to this method does not reasonably reflect the relative benefits to be derived, directly or indirectly, by the units described in paragraph (b)(4)(v)(a)(1) and the nonqualifying property, the allocation may not be made according to this method. For example, this method would not be a reasonable method for making the allocation in the case of a residential rental project one-half of the floor space of which is used for shopping space where three-fourths of the parking lot for the building will be used to serve the shopping space and the balance of the parking lot will be used to serve tenants of the units described in paragraph (b)(4)(v)(a)(1); the cost of constructing the parking lot must be allocated based on the proportion of the parking lot to be used, directly or indirectly, by the tenants of the units described in paragraph (b)(4)(v)(a)(1) and by the owners and tenants of the nonqualifying portion of the project.

(5) *Requirements must be continuously satisfied.*—(i) *Rental requirement.*—Once available for occupancy, each unit (as defined in paragraph (b)(8)(i) of this section) in a residential rental project that was provided with the proceeds of an issue described in section 103(b)(4)(A) (other than those units provided with an insubstantial amount of the proceeds of the issue as permitted under paragraph (a)(3) of this section) must be rented or available for rental on a continuous basis for the longer of—

(a) The remaining term of the obligation, or

(b) The qualified project period (as defined in paragraph (b)(7) of this section).

(ii) *Low or moderate income occupancy requirement.*—Individuals or families of low or moderate income must occupy that percentage of completed units in the project that were provided with the proceeds of an issue described in section 103(b)(4)(A) (other than those units provided with an insubstantial amount of the proceeds of the issue as permitted under paragraph (a)(3) of this section) applicable to the project under paragraph (b)(1) of this section continuously during the qualified project period. For this purpose, a unit occupied by an individual or family who at the commencement of the occupancy is of low or moderate income is treated as occupied by an individual or family of low or moderate income even though the individual or family ceases to be of low or moderate income during the period of their occupancy. Moreover, such unit is treated as occupied by an individual or family of low or moderate income until reoccupied, other than for a temporary period not in excess of 31 days, at which time a redetermination of whether the unit is occupied by an individual or family of low or moderate income shall be made.

* * *

(7) *Qualified project period.*—* * *

(ii) For obligations issued after September 3, 1982, a period beginning on the later of the first day on which at least 10 percent of the units in the project that are provided with the proceeds of the issue are first occupied or the date of issue of an obligation described in section 103(b)(4)(A) and this paragraph and ending on the later of the date—

(a) Which is 10 years after the date on which at least 50 percent of the units in the project that are provided with the proceeds of the issue are first occupied,

(b) Which is a qualified number of days after the date on which any of the units in the project that are provided with the proceeds of the issue are first occupied, or

(c) On which any assistance provided with respect to the project under section 8 of the United States Housing Act of 1937 terminates. For purposes of this paragraph (b)(7)(ii), the term "qualified number of days" means 50 percent of the total number of days comprising the term of the obligation with the longest maturity in the issue used to provide the project. In the case of a refunding of such an issue, the longest maturity is equal to the sum of the period the prior issue was outstanding and the longest term of any refunding obligations.

(8) *Other definitions.*—* * *

(v) *Low or moderate income.*—Individuals and families of low or moderate income shall be determined in a manner consistent with determinations of lower income families under section 8 of the United States Housing Act of 1937, as amended, except that the percentage of median gross income that qualifies as low or moderate income shall be 80 percent of the median gross income for the area with adjustments for smaller and larger families. Therefore, occupants of a unit are considered individuals or families of low or moderate income only if their adjusted income (computed in the manner prescribed in § 1.167(k)-3(b)(3)) does not exceed 80 percent of the median gross income for the area with adjustments for smaller and larger families. With respect to obligations issued prior to January 1, 1986, determinations of low or moderate income shall be made in accordance with the requirements of this paragraph (b)(8)(v) except that median gross income for the area need not be adjusted for family size. Notwithstanding the foregoing, the occupants of a unit shall not be considered to be of low or moderate income if all the occupants are students (as defined in section 151(e)(4)), no one of whom is entitled to file a joint return under section 6013. The method of determining low or moderate income in effect on the date of issue will be determinative for such issue even if such method is subsequently changed. In the event programs under section 8(f) of the Housing Act of 1937, as amended, are terminated prior to the date of issue, the applicable method shall be that in effect immediately prior to the date of such termination.

(9) *Examples.*—* * *

Example (3). The facts are the same as in example (1), except that the proceeds of the obligation are provided to N, a cooperative housing corporation. N uses the proceeds to finance the construction of a portion of a cooperative housing project. The balance of the project is financed with the proceeds of a note that is not described in section 103(a). Shares in the cooperative carrying the rights to occupy the units in the portion of the project financed with the proceeds of the obligation issued by City X will be sold to shareholders who will rent the units to other persons. The balance of the shares in the cooperative, carrying the rights to occupy more than half of the space in the project, will be sold to individuals who will occupy the units themselves. The project is a residential rental project within the meaning of section 103(b)(4)(A) and this paragraph (b).

* * *

Example (12). In July 1985, County X issues a $10 million issue of industrial development bonds to be used to finance the construction of a building to be owned by Corporation W. Corporation W will construct a 10 story building. The first 2 floors of the building will be made available for commercial use. The remaining 8 floors will consist of similarly constructed units that will be made available as residences on a rental basis to members of the general public. Corporation W uses substantially all of the proceeds of the issue to finance the 8 floors of the building to be made available as rental units, the portions of the building benefitting, directly or indirectly, only the rental units, and the portions of the building benefitting, directly or indirectly, both the rental units and the commercial space that are properly allocable to the rental units. The remainder of the building is financed other than with the proceeds of an obligation described in section 103(a). Corporation W will make 20 percent of the rental units available to low or moderate income individuals, and all of the other requirements of this section are met. The obligations are used to provide a residential rental project within the meaning of section 103(b)(4)(A) and this section, and the obligations are described in section 103(a).

Example (13). The facts are the same as in example (12), except that Corporation W uses the proceeds of the issue to finance the entire building including the 2 floors to be available for commercial use. The cost of the 2 floors available for commercial use, including those portions of the building that benefit both the commercial space and the rental units that are properly allocable to the commercial space, is $2 million. Under paragraph (b)(4)(v) of this section, the building is a residential rental project. However, substantially all of the proceeds of the issue are not used to provide a residential rental project since, in making this determination, proceeds used to provide nonqualifying property are treated as not used to provide a residential rental project. Therefore, the obligations are not described in section 103(b)(4)(A) and this paragraph (b).

* * *

Industrial Development Bonds: Small Issues

Interest Received: Governmental Obligations: Industrial Development Bonds: Principal User.—Reproduced below is the text of a proposed amendment of Reg. § 1.103-10, which would define the term "principal user" for purposes of Code Sec. 103(b)(6), (15) (published in the Federal Register on February 21, 1986). NOTE: Code Sec. 103 has been amended to remove special exempt bond issue rules and provide similar rules in Code Secs. 141-150. This proposed amendment was issued under Code Sec. 103 as it read before amendment.

☐ Par. 2. Section 1.103-10 is amended by adding a new sentence after the second sentence of paragraph (b)(2)(i); by deleting "(e)" and adding "(f)" in lieu thereof in the first sentence of paragraph (b)(2)(iv) and by adding a new subdivision (f) at the end of subdivision (iv) thereof; by adding two new sentences after the first sentence of paragraph (d)(1); by revising paragraph (d)(2)(ii); by adding two new sentences at the end of paragraph (d)(2); by revising the first sentence of paragraph (g); and by adding a new paragraph (h). The revised and added provisions read as follows:

§ 1.103-10. Exemption for certain small issues of industrial development bonds.

* * *

(b) *Small issue exemption.*—* * *

(2) *$10 million or less.*—(i) * * * All capital expenditures described in paragraph (b)(2)(ii) with respect to each principal user and each related person must be aggregated with the issue of obligations in question for purposes of determining whether the $10 million limitation of section 103(b)(6)(D) is exceeded. * * *

(iv) * * *

(f) A capital expenditure with respect to a facility other than the bond-financed facility ("other facility") is an excluded expenditure if the principal user of the other facility does not become a principal user of the facility financed by the proceeds of the issue in question ("bond-financed facility") until after the last day of the test period described in paragraph (i)(3)(ii) of this section. In addition, a capital expenditure with respect to an "other facility" becomes an excluded expenditure on and after the date the principal user of the other facility ceases to use the bond-financed facility; if, however, the issue financing the bond-financed facility lost its tax-exempt status on or before that date, this sentence will not apply to restore its tax-exempt status. * * *

* * *

(d) *Certain prior issues taken into account.*—(1) *In general.*—* * * Thus, the outstanding face amount of all prior issues specified in paragraph (d)(2) with respect to each principal user and each related person and taken into account under this paragraph (d)(1) must be aggregated with the issue of obligations in question for purposes of determining whether the $1 million limitation of section 103(b)(6)(A) or the $10 million limitation of section 103(b)(6)(D) has been exceeded with respect to the issue in question. The outstanding face amount of the prior exempt small issue is the principal amount outstanding at the time of issuance of the subsequent exempt small issue. * * *

(2) *Prior issues specified.*—* * *

(ii) The principal user of the facilities described in paragraph (d)(2)(i) of this section is the same person or two or more related persons (as defined in section 103(b)(6)(C) and in paragraph (e) of this section) at any time on or after the date of issue of the subsequent issue but before the expiration of the test period described in paragraph (i)(3)(ii) of this section with respect to the subsequent issue.

The loss of tax exemption with respect to the interest on the subsequent issue shall be effective on the date of issue of the subsequent issue. For purposes of this paragraph (d), when a person ceases to use a facility financed by either the prior issue or the subsequent issue, the prior issue will no longer be taken into account under paragraph (d)(1) with respect to the subsequent issue; if, however, the subsequent issue loses its tax-exempt status on or before the date the person ceases to use either of the facilities described in this subparagraph, this paragraph will not apply to restore the tax-exempt status of the subsequent issue. * * *

* * *

(g) *Examples.*—The application of the rules contained in section 103(b)(6) and in paragraphs (a) through (f) of this section are illustrated by the following examples: * * *

* * *

(h) *Rules relating to principal users.*—(1) *Definition of principal user.*—For purposes of section 103(b)(6) and § 1.103-10, the term "principal user" means a person who is a principal owner, a principal lessee, a principal output purchaser, or an "other" principal user. The term "principal user" also includes a person who is related to another person who is a principal user under section 103(b)(6)(C) and paragraph (e) of this section, unless the other person ceased to use the facility before the two persons became related. For purposes of this paragraph (h)—

(i) *Principal owner.*—A principal owner is a person who at any time holds more than a 10-percent ownership interest (by value) in the facility or, if no person holds more than a 10-percent ownership interest, then the person (or persons in the case of multiple equal owners) who holds the largest ownership interest in the facility. A person is treated as holding an ownership interest if such person is an owner for Federal income tax purposes generally. Thus, for example, where a facility constructed on land subject to a ground lease has an economic useful life less than the noncancellable portion of the term of the ground lease, the ground lessor shall not, merely by reason of that reversionary interest, be treated as the principal user of the facility before the ground lease expires.

(ii) *Principal lessee.*—A principal lessee is a person who at any time leases more than 10 percent of the facility (disregarding portions used by the lessee under a short-term lease). The portion of a facility leased to a lessee is generally determined by reference to its fair rental value. A short-term lease is one which has a term of one year or less, taking into account all options to renew and reasonably anticipated renewals.

(iii) *Principal output purchaser.*—A principal output purchaser is any person who purchases output of an electric or thermal energy, gas, water, or other similar facility, unless the total output purchased by such person during each one-year period beginning with the date the facility is placed in service is 10 percent or less of the facility's output during each such period.

(iv) *Other principal user.*—An "other" principal user is a person who enjoys a use of the facility (other than a short-term use) in a degree comparable to the enjoyment of a principal owner or a principal lessee, taking into account all the relevant facts and circumstances, such as the person's participation in control over use of the facility or its remote or proximate geographic location. For example, a party to a contract who would be treated as a lessee using more than 10 percent of a facility on a long-term basis but for the special rules of section 7701(e)(3) and (5) (relating to service contracts for certain energy and water facilities and low-income housing) is an "other" principal user. A short-term use means use that is comparable to use under a short-term lease.

(2) *Operating rules.*—(i) In determining whether a person is a principal user of a facility, it is irrelevant where in a chain of use such person's use occurs. For example, where a sublessee subleases more than 10 percent of a facility from a lessee, both the lessee and the sublessee are principal lessees.

(ii) In determining whether a person owns or uses more than 10 percent of a facility or whether he uses it for more than one year, the person is treated as owning or using the facility to the extent that any person related to such person under section 103(b)(6)(C) and paragraph (e) of this section owns or uses the facility. For purposes of the preceding sentence, the term "use" includes use pursuant to an output purchase arrangement.

(iii) Co-owners or co-lessees who are collectively treated as a partnership subject to subchapter K under section 761(a) are not treated as principal users merely by reason of their ownership of partnership interests; such ownership is, however, taken into account in determining whether persons are related under section 103(b)(6)(C) and paragraph (e) of this section.

(iv) For purposes of this section, a principal user of a facility is treated as ceasing to use the facility when he ceases to own, lease, purchase the output of, or otherwise use the facility, as the case may be. A person who is a principal user of a facility because he is related to another person who is a principal user is treated as ceasing to use the facility when the other person ceases to use the facility or when the two persons cease to be related. A principal user who ceases to use a facility continues to be a principal user. See, however, paragraph (b)(2)(iv)(f) of this section (relating to excluded expenditures), paragraph (d)(2) (relating to prior issues), and paragraph (h)(1) (defining principal user), which may apply when a principal user ceases to use a facility.

(3) *Special rule for exempt persons.*—If an exempt person, as defined in section 103(b)(3) and § 1.103-7(b)(2), is a principal user of a facility financed with an issue of obligations described in section 103(b)(6), the following amounts must be aggregated with the issue in determining whether the $1 million limit of section 103(b)(6)(A) or the $10 million limit of section 103(b)(6)(D) has been exceeded:

(i) The outstanding face amount of any prior exempt small issue of industrial development bonds described in paragraph (d) of this section that financed a facility of which the exempt person is a principal user,

(ii) For purposes of the $10 million limitation, capital expenditures described in paragraph (b)(2)(ii) of this section paid or incurred with respect to other facilities used by the exempt person in an unrelated trade or business (within the meaning of section 513 and § 1.513-1) and of which the exempt person is a principal user, and

(iii) Any section 103(b)(6)(D) capital expenditures paid or incurred with respect to the facility financed by the issue in question.

(4) *Examples.*—The application of the rules of section 103(b)(6) and this paragraph (h) is illustrated by the following examples:

Example (1). On September 1, 1986, City L, after making the section 103(b)(6)(D) election, issues $8 million of obligations to finance the costs of acquiring a newly constructed warehouse within City L, owned by Corporation Z, a non-exempt person, which thus is a principal user of the warehouse. Beginning on September 1, 1986, the entire warehouse is leased to Corporation Y, an unrelated non-exempt person, for a 2-year term; thus, Y is also a principal user of the warehouse. On June 30, 1988, Y ceases to lease the warehouse. On October 1, 1988, Y incurs $20 million of capital expenditures in connection with its purchase of an office building in City L. Although Y continues to be a principal user of the warehouse under paragraph (h)(2)(iv) of this section, Y's capital expenditures after the date it ceases to use the warehouse are excluded expenditures under paragraph (b)(2)(iv)(f) of this section. Accordingly, the $20 million Y incurred with respect to the office building is not taken into account for purposes of determining whether the $10 million limitation of section 103(b)(6)(D) has been exceeded.

Example (2). The facts are the same as in Example (1), except that on October 1, 1985, City L issued an exempt small issue to finance acquisition of a newly constructed office building in the amount of $5 million, of which $4 million is outstanding on September 1, 1986. On December 1, 1988, Corporation Z leases 15 percent (by fair rental value) of the office building financed by the 1985 issue for a 2-year term. Thus, beginning on December 1, 1988, Z is a principal user of the office building. On December 1, 1988, Z still owns the warehouse financed by the 1986 issue. Because Z became a principal user of the office building before the end of the 3-year test period described in paragraph (i)(3)(ii) of this section with respect to the 1986 issue, the $4 million outstanding amount of the 1985 issue must be aggregated with the $8 million 1986 issue for purposes of determining whether the 1986 issue has exceeded the $10 million limitation of section 103(b)(6)(D). Because the sum of the two issues ($4 million of the prior 1985 issue outstanding on September 1, 1986, and the $8 million subsequent issue issued on September 1, 1986) exceeds $10 million, the interest on the 1986 issue ceases to be tax-exempt on September 1, 1986. Had Z's lease begun after September 1, 1989, the two issues would not have to be aggregated.

Example (3). On June 1, 1985, City O issues $15 million of its obligations to finance an expansion of a hospital owned by H, an organization described in section 501(c)(3) exempt from taxation under section 501(a). None of the proceeds of the issue will be used by H in an unrelated trade or business or in the trade or business of non-exempt persons. On November 1, 1986, City O, after making the section 103(b)(6)(D) election, issues $5 million of its obligations to construct a medical office building which will be owned by H for Federal income tax purposes and which will be entirely leased (for terms in excess of one year) to physicians, none of whom will lease over 10 percent of the building by value. On July 1, 1987, H incurs a $500,000 capital expenditure for permanent improvements to the medical office building. In addition, on August 1, 1987, W, a non-exempt person related to H, incurs a $1 million capital expenditure with respect to a facility that W owns within City O and uses in its trade or business. For purposes of determining whether the $10 million limitation of section 103(b)(6)(D) has been exceeded with respect to the November 1, 1986, issue for the medical office building, H must take into account the $5 million issue, the $500,000 of capital expenditures made with respect to the medical office building, and W's $1 million capital expenditure. Because the sum of these amounts is less than $10 million, interest on the issue does not cease to be tax-exempt. H is not required to take into account the June 1, 1985, issue financing the hospital expansion because that issue is not an exempt small issue as defined in section 103(b)(6) (see paragraph (h)(3)(i) of this section) and because the cost of the facility financed by the June 1, 1985, issue is neither a section 103(b)(6)(D) capital expenditure with respect to the medical office building owned by H (see paragraph (h)(3)(iii) of this section) nor a section 103(b)(6)(D) capital expenditure for a separate facility used by H in an unrelated trade or business (see paragraph (h)(3)(ii) of this section).

* * *

Industrial Development Bonds: Limitations

Interest Received: Governmental Obligations: Limitation on Beneficiaries.—Reproduced below is the text of a proposed amendment of Reg. § 1.103-10, relating to industrial development bonds and the beneficiaries of such bond issues (published in the Federal Register on February 21, 1986). NOTE: *Code Sec. 103 has been amended to remove special exempt bond issue rules and provide similar rules in Code Secs. 141-150. This proposed amendment was issued under Code Sec. 103 as it read before amendment.*

☐ Par. 2. Section 1.103-10 is revised by adding a new paragraph (i) immediately following paragraph (h) therein. The new paragraph reads as follows:

§1.103-10. Exemption for certain small issues of industrial development bonds.

* * *

(i) *$40 million limitation for beneficiaries of small issues of industrial development bonds.*—(1) *General rule.*—Section 103(b)(6) and §1.103-10(a) do not apply to an issue of obligations ("issue in question") if—

(i) The portion of the aggregate authorized face amount of the issue in question allocated to any test-period beneficiary as defined in paragraph (i)(3) of this section, of the issue, plus

(ii) The portion of the outstanding principal amount of prior bonds, as defined in paragraph (i)(2) of this section, allocated—

(*a*) To the test-period beneficiary described in paragraph (i)(1)(i) of this section, or

(*b*) To a person who at any time during the test period of the issue in question is related to such beneficiary,

exceeds $40 million. If interest on the issue in question would, but for this paragraph and section 103(b)(15), be exempt from Federal income taxation solely because of section 103(b)(6), the issue is treated as an issue of obligations not described in section 103(a) on and after the date of issuance. For purposes of this paragraph (i), the aggregate authorized face amount of the issue in question and the outstanding principal amount of a prior bond shall be determined without regard to section 103(b)(6)(B) or (D) (requiring certain amounts of prior issues or capital expenditures to be taken into account in determining the aggregate face amount of the issue in question or of the prior bond).

(2) *Prior bonds.*—For purposes of this paragraph (i), "prior bonds" means prior or simultaneous issues of industrial development bonds described in paragraph (4), (5), or (6) of section 103(b) the interest on which is exempt from tax pursuant to section 103(a), including such bonds issued before January 1, 1984. For purposes of paragraph (i)(1)(ii) of this section, "outstanding principal amount of prior bonds" means the principal amount that is outstanding at the time of issuance of the issue in question, not including the amount to be redeemed from the proceeds of the issue in question. Thus, the outstanding principal amount of prior bonds does not include the portion of the original face amount that has been discharged, nor does it include any amount to be issued in the future.

(3) *Test-period beneficiary.*—(i) *In general.*—For purposes of this paragraph (i), a "test-period beneficiary" of the issue in question or of an issue of prior bonds means any person who at any time during the test period for the issue is a principal user, as defined in paragraph (h)(1) of this section, of a facility financed by the proceeds of the issue, including a person who is related to a principal user. For purposes of the preceding sentence, a person shall be treated as related to a principal user only if that person is related to such user within the meaning of section 103(b)(6)(C) and paragraph (e) of this section at any time during the test period, and such user has not ceased to use the facility before the persons became related. See paragraph (h)(2)(iv) of this section for circumstances in which a person will be treated as ceasing to use a facility. A test-period beneficiary does not cease to be a test-period beneficiary if he ceases to use the facility; the portion of the issue allocated to the test-period beneficiary continues to be so allocated until the issue is no longer outstanding.

(ii) *Test period.*—The "test period" for an issue means the 3-year period beginning on the later of the date the facility financed by the proceeds of the issue is placed in service or the date of issue of such issue. A facility shall be considered as being placed in service at the time the facility is placed in a condition or state of readiness and availability for a specifically assigned function. If separate facilities are financed by an issue and the facilities are placed in service at different times, there shall be separate test periods for the portions of the issue financing each separate facility. If a single facility (consisting of separately depreciable items of property) is placed in service in stages, then the entire facility will be deemed placed in service when its last portion is placed in service.

(4) *Allocation of issue.*—(i) *In general.*—The portion of the amount of an issue allocated to a test-period beneficiary is the highest percent of the facility financed by proceeds of the issue that the beneficiary owned or used on a regular basis during the test period. For example, a person that owns the entire facility shall be allocated 100 percent of the issue; a person that leases 90 percent of a facility for two years of the test period and leases 35 percent for the third year shall be allocated 90 percent of the issue.

(ii) *Portion allocable to lessee and output purchaser.*—The portion of a facility used by a lessee is generally determined by reference to its fair rental value. The portion of a facility used by a principal output purchaser, as defined in paragraph (h)(1)(iii) of this section, is the highest portion of the facility's total output purchased by such purchaser during any of the three years of the test period.

(iii) *Portion allocable to related person.*—The portion of an issue allocable to a person who is a test-period beneficiary because he is related to a principal user is the same portion allocated to such principal user.

(iv) *Double allocation.*—The total amount of an issue allocated to test-period beneficiaries may exceed 100 percent of its outstanding face amount, such as when one test-period beneficiary is an owner and another person leases the facility for over a year. However, if a beneficiary is the owner of all or a portion of a facility that is leased to or otherwise used by such beneficiary or by a related person, then the portion of the issue the proceeds of which were used to finance the facility is allocated only once to the beneficiary. For example, if Corporation X owns an undivided 50 percent of a facility while related Corporation Y is the lessee of 60 percent of the facility, the portion of the issue financing the facility allocable to X is 80 percent (50 percent plus 30 percent), because one-half of the 60-percent portion used by Y (30 percent) is considered attributable to the portion owned by X.

(v) *Allocation of remainder of issue to owners.*—If the portion of an issue allocated to all test-period beneficiaries of the bond-financed facility (other than related persons) is less than 100 percent, the remainder shall be allocated to test-period beneficiaries who are owners of the facility in proportion to the amount of the issue otherwise allocable to such persons by reason of their ownership interests during the test period.

(vi) *Bond redeemed before person becomes principal user.*—If all or some of the outstanding principal amount of the issue in question or of prior bonds is redeemed other than from the proceeds of a refunding issue described in section 103(a) either before or as soon as reasonably practicable after a person becomes a test-period beneficiary with respect to the issue in question, but in no event later than 180 days after the date such person becomes a test-period beneficiary, then the amount of the issue so redeemed will not be allocated to such person (or to a related person) in determining whether the issue in question exceeds the $40 million limitation. With respect to obligations that are issued after August 20, 1986, paragraph (i)(4)(vi) shall not apply if the terms of the issue provide for a delay in redemption a principal purpose of which is to benefit from the 180-day period referred to therein. In the case of a person who becomes a test-period beneficiary before February 21, 1986, bonds redeemed before August 20, 1986, shall be considered redeemed as soon as reasonably practicable for purposes of the first sentence of this paragraph (i)(4)(vi) and the 180-day limitation referred to therein shall not apply.

(5) *Treatment of certain successors as test-period beneficiaries.*—If a corporation, partnership, or other entity which is a test-period beneficiary with respect to one or more issues transfers substantially all of its properties to another person (or to two or more related persons within the meaning of section 103(b)(6)(C)), or if a corporation acquires the assets of a test-period beneficiary in a transaction described in section 381(a), the transferee shall be treated as a test-period beneficiary with respect to such issues and shall be allocated the portion of such issues that were allocated to the transferor prior to the transfer. The preceding sentence shall not apply to the extent that it would result in double allocation of an issue, such as in the case of a transfer to a related person. This paragraph (i)(5) shall apply regardless of whether gain is required to be recognized by the transferor for Federal income tax purposes and regardless of whether the transferor remains in existence after the transfer. If the transferor remains in existence after the transfer, this paragraph (i)(5) shall not relieve the transferor of its allocation of any issue. This paragraph (i)(5) shall apply only for purposes of determining the tax exemption of issues of which the transferee becomes the test-period beneficiary after the transfer described herein.

(6) *Examples.*—The application of section 103(b)(15) and this paragraph (i) may be illustrated by the following examples:

Example (1). On September 1, 1986, City M issues a $9 million obligation to finance acquisition of a newly constructed shopping center that is placed in service on September 1, 1986, and is owned and managed by Corporation X. Half of the shopping center (determined by fair rental value) is leased for a term exceeding 1 year to Corporation Y. X owns 60 percent of the shares of Y. The other half of the shopping center (also determined by fair rental value) is leased in equal shares for a term exceeding 1 year to A and B, two unrelated corporations. As of September 1, 1986, $30 million of prior issues of obligations are outstanding and are allocable to X as a test-period beneficiary under the rules of § 1.103-10(i)(4). As of that date there is no prior issue of obligations outstanding and allocable to Y, A, or B as test-period beneficiaries. Because X owns 100 percent of the shopping center, 100 percent of the 1986 issue ($9 million) is allocated to X. Therefore, for purposes of determining whether the 1986 issue exceeds the $40 million limitation of section 103(b)(15), the $30 million of outstanding prior issues must be added to the $9 million 1986 issue. Because Y leases 50 percent of the shopping center, 50 percent of the 1986 issue ($4.5 million) is allocated to Y. Although Y is related to X under section 103(b)(15)(E), the $4.5 million of the 1986 issue that is allocated to Y is not added to the $39 million allocated to X under paragraph (i)(4)(iv) of this section since such amount has already been allocated to X as owner of the shopping center. Because A and B each leases 25 percent of the shopping center, each is allocated 25 percent ($2.25 million) of the 1986 issue.

Example (2). The facts are the same as in *Example (1)* except that A owns a 60-percent interest in an airport hotel described in § 1.103-8(e)(2)(ii)(*d*) and, because of such ownership interest, is allocated $15 million of prior outstanding obligations described in section 103(b)(4)(D). In addition, County N issues $25 million of obligations described in section 103(b)(4)(E) on October 1, 1986, to finance construction of a solid-waste disposal facility that will be owned by C, A's wholly-owned subsidiary corporation. In this case, with respect to the September 1, 1986, issue, A is allocated the $15 million prior issue that is outstanding with respect to A's share of the airport hotel bond and the $2.25 million that is A's allocable share of the September 1, 1986, issue for a total of $17.25 million. Because the solid-waste disposal facility bonds had not yet been issued when the September 1, 1986, obligation was issued, no portion of the $25 million of obligations to finance C's solid-waste disposal facility will be treated as part of A's allocable obligations with respect to the September 1, 1986, issue even though A and C are related persons. In addition, even though A and C are related persons and even though on the date of issue of the solid-waste disposal bonds C will be allocated more than $40 million of outstanding obligations for purposes of section 103(b)(15) (including A's $17.25 million of outstanding prior obligations), the $40 million limitation of section 103(b)(15) does not render the interest on the October 1, 1986, bonds taxable since the October 1, 1986, issue qualifies for tax exemption under section 103(b)(4), and the $40 million limitation of section 103(b)(15) does not apply to render taxable bonds issued under section 103(b)(4).

Example (3). On October 1, 1986, City K issues an $8 million issue of obligations exempt under section 103(b)(6) to finance acquisition of a newly-constructed manufacturing plant owned by Corporation L. On October 1, 1986, Corporation M has $35 million of prior outstanding obligations allocable to it under section 103(b)(15). On October 1, 1986, L has no prior outstanding obligations allocable to itself. On April 1, 1988, M acquires 100 percent of the stock of L, which still owns the plant financed by the 1986 issue. Since M and L became related to each other during the 3-year test period of the 1986 issue and L had not ceased to use the facility, the $8 million issue is allocated to M under section 103 (b)(15). This allocation causes the 1986 issue to exceed the $40 million limitation of section 103(b)(15) and the interest upon the issue to become taxable on and after October 1, 1986. However, if at least $3 million of the 1986 issue or of other issues allocated to M are redeemed as soon as reasonably practicable, and no later than 180 days after M's acquisition of L's stock, then the 1986 issue would not exceed the $40 million limitation.

Example (4). The facts are the same as in *Example (3)*, except the October 1, 1986, bonds were issued on January 1, 1985, the plant acquired with the proceeds of the issue was placed in service on January 1, 1985, and M had $39 million of prior outstanding obligations allocable to it on January 1, 1985. Because M and L became related to each other after the test period for the January 1, 1985, issue ended, M is not a test-period beneficiary, and the January 1, 1985, issue does not exceed the $40 million limitation of section 103(b)(15). However, if either M or L subsequently becomes a test-period beneficiary of an issue of obligations, then the outstanding principal amount of the January 1, 1985, issue and of the other issues allocable to M would be taken into account in applying the $40 million limitation to that issue.

Mortgage Subsidy Bonds

Interest on Mortgage Subsidy Bonds: Exemption.—Temporary Reg. §§ 6a.103A-1—6a.103A-3, relating to the exemption of interest on mortgage subsidy bonds, are also proposed as final regulations (published in the Federal Register on July 1, 1981). *NOTE: Code Sec. 103A has been repealed. Similar exempt bond issue rules have been provided in Code Secs. 141-150. These proposed regulations were issued under Code Sec. 103A as it read before amendment.*

§ 6a.103A-1. Interest on mortgage subsidy bonds.

§ 6a.103A-2. Qualified mortgage bond.

§ 6a.103A-3. Qualified veteran's mortgage bonds.

Mortgage Subsidy Bonds: Interest Exemption

Interest on Mortgage Subsidy Bonds: Exemption.—Amendments to Temporary Reg. §§ 6a.103A-1 and 6a.103A-2, relating to mortgage subsidy bonds, are also proposed as final regulations (published in the Federal Register on November 10, 1981). *NOTE: Code Sec. 103A has been repealed. Similar exempt bond issue rules have been provided in Code Secs. 141-150. These proposed regulations were issued under Code Sec. 103A as it read before amendment.*

§ 6a.103A-1. Interest on mortgage subsidy bonds.

§ 6a.103A-2. Qualified mortgage bond.

Mortgage Credit Certificates: Qualified Mortgage Bond

Mortgage Credit Certificates Issuance: Penalties.—An amendment to Temporary Reg. § 6a.103A-2, relating to the issuance of mortgage credit certificates, is also proposed as final (published in the Federal Register on May 8, 1985). *NOTE: Code Sec. 103A has been repealed. Similar exempt bond issue rules have been provided in Code Secs. 141-150. This proposed amendment was issued under Code Sec. 103A as it read before amendment.*

§ 6a.103A-2. Qualified mortgage bond.

Imputed Interest: OID: Safe Haven Interest Rates

Imputed Interest: Original Issue Discount: Safe Haven Interest Rates.—Reproduced below is the text of a proposed amendment of Temporary Reg. § 6a.103A-2, relating to (1) the tax treatment of debt instruments issued after July 1, 1982, that contain original issue discount, (2) the imputation of and the accounting for interest with respect to sales and exchanges of property occurring after December 31, 1984, and (3) safe haven interest rates for loans or advances between commonly controlled taxpayers and safe haven leases between such taxpayers (published in the Federal Register on April 8, 1986). *NOTE: Code Sec. 103A has been repealed. Similar exempt bond issue rules have been provided in Code Secs. 141-150. This proposed amendment was issued under Code Sec. 103A as it read before amendment.*

☐ Par. 41. Paragraph (i)(2)(vi)(B) of § 6a.103A-2 is amended by removing the phrase "section 1232(b)(2)" and adding in its place the phrase "section 1273(b)".

§ 6a.103A-2. Qualified mortgage bond.

Affiliated Service Groups

Employees' Trusts: Affiliated Service Groups.—Reproduced below is the text of a proposed amendment of Reg. §1.105-11, which prescribes rules for determining whether two or more separate service organizations constitute an affiliated group and which detail how certain requirements are satisfied by a qualified retirement plan maintained by a member of an affiliated service group (published in the Federal Register on February 28, 1983).

☐ Paragraph 1. Paragraph (f) of section 1.105-11 is amended by striking out "section 414(b) and (c)" and inserting in lieu thereof "section 414(b), (c) or (m),"

§1.105-11. Self-insured medical reimbursement plan.

HRAs: Group Health Plans: Employer Shared Responsibility: Nondiscrimination Rules

HRAs: Group Health Plans: Employer Shared Responsibility: Nondiscrimination Rules.—Amendments to Reg. §1.105-11, clarifying the application of the employer shared responsibility provisions and certain nondiscrimination rules under the Internal Revenue Code to health reimbursement arrangements and other account-based group health plans integrated with individual health insurance coverage or Medicare (individual coverage HRAs), and to provide certain safe harbors with respect to the application of those provisions to individual coverage HRAs, are proposed (published in the Federal Register on September 30, 2019) (REG-136401-18).

Par. 2. Section 1.105-11 is amended by revising paragraphs (c)(3)(i) and (j) to read as follows:

§1.105-11. Self-insured medical reimbursement plan.

* * *

(c) * * *

(3) * * *

(i) *In general.*—(A) *Benefits.*—In general, benefits subject to reimbursement under a plan must not discriminate in favor of highly compensated individuals. Plan benefits will not satisfy the requirements of this paragraph (c)(3)(i)(A) unless all the benefits provided for participants who are highly compensated individuals are provided for all other participants. In addition, all the benefits available for the dependents of employees who are highly compensated individuals must also be available on the same basis for the dependents of all other employees who are participants. A plan that provides optional benefits to participants will be treated as providing a single benefit with respect to the benefits covered by the option provided that all eligible participants may elect any of the benefits covered by the option and there are either no required employee contributions or the required employee contributions are the same amount. This test is applied to the benefits subject to reimbursement under the plan rather than the actual benefit payments or claims under the plan. The presence or absence of such discrimination will be determined by considering the type of benefit subject to reimbursement provided highly compensated individuals, as well as the amount of the benefit subject to reimbursement.

(B) *Maximum limits.*—(1) *Uniformity rule.*—A plan may establish a maximum limit for the amount of reimbursement which may be paid a participant for any single benefit, or combination of benefits. However, except as otherwise provided in paragraph (c)(3)(i)(B)(2) of this section, any maximum limit attributable to employer contributions must be uniform for all participants and for all dependents of employees who are participants and may not be modified by reason of a participant's age or years of service.

(2) *Exception to uniformity rule.*—With respect to an individual coverage HRA, as defined in §54.9802-4(b) of this chapter, if the maximum dollar amount made available varies for participants within a class of employees set forth in §54.9802-4(d) of this chapter, or varies between classes of employees offered the individual coverage HRA, the plan does not violate the requirements of this paragraph (c)(3) by virtue of that variance; provided that, within a class of employees, the maximum dollar amount made available varies only in accordance with the same terms requirement set forth in §54.9802-4(c)(3) of this chapter, and, with respect to differences in the maximum dollar amount made available for different classes of employees, each of the classes of employees is one of the classes of employees set forth in §54.9802-4(d) of this chapter. Specifically, with respect to age-based variances, in the case of an individual coverage HRA, if the maximum dollar amount made available to participants who are members of a particular class of employees increases based on the age of each participant and the increases in the maximum dollar amount comply with the age-variation rule under the same terms requirement set forth under §54.9802-4(c)(3)(iii)(B) of this chapter, the plan does not violate the requirements of this paragraph (c)(3) with respect to those increases.

(C) *Reference to employee compensation.*—If a plan covers employees who are highly compensated individuals, and the type or the amount of benefits subject to reimbursement under the plan are in proportion to employee compensation, the plan discriminates as to benefits.

* * *

(j) *Applicability date.*—Section 105(h) and this section, except for paragraph (c)(3)(i)(B)(2) of this section, are applicable for taxable years beginning after December 31, 1979 and for amounts reimbursed after December 31, 1979. In determining plan discrimination and the taxability of excess reimbursements made for a plan year beginning in 1979 and ending in 1980, a plan's eligibility and benefit requirements as well as actual reimbursements made in the plan year during 1979, will not be taken into account. In addition, this section does not apply to expenses which are incurred in 1979 and paid in 1980. Paragraph (c)(3)(i)(B)(2) of this section is applicable for plan years beginning after December 31, 2019.

* * *

Sickness and Disability Payments: Group Health Plan

Business Expenses: Sickness and Disability Payments: Group Health Plan.—Reproduced below is the text of a proposed amendment of Reg. §1.106-1, relating to the requirement that a group health plan offer continuation coverage to people who would otherwise lose coverage as a result of certain events (published in the Federal Register on June 15, 1987).

☐ Par. 2. Section 1.106-1 is amended by redesignating the existing text as paragraph (a), revising the first sentence of paragraph (a), and adding a new paragraph (b). The revised and added provisions read as follows:

§1.106-1. Contributions by employer to accident and health plans.—(a) Except as set forth in paragraph (b) of this section, the gross income of an employee does not include contributions which his employer makes to an accident or health plan for compensation (through insurance or otherwise) to the employee for personal injuries or sickness incurred by him, his spouse, or his dependents, as defined in section 152. * * *

(b) In situations involving group health plans that do not comply with section 162(k), the exclusion described in paragraph (a) of this section is not available to highly compensated employees (as defined in section 414(q)). See §1.162-26 (regarding continuation coverage requirements of group health plans).

* * *

Scholarships

Exclusions: Scholarships: Payment for Services.—Reproduced below are the texts of proposed Reg. §§1.117-0 and 1.117-6 and proposed amendments of Reg. §§1.117-1—1.117-5, relating to the exclusion from gross income of qualified scholarships (published in the Federal Register on June 9, 1988).

☐ Par. 2. A new §1.117-0 is added to read as follows:

§1.117-0. Outline of regulations pertaining to scholarships and fellowship grants.—(a) §1.117-1.—Exclusion of amounts received as a scholarship or fellowship grant in taxable years beginning before 1987, but only in the case of scholarships and fellowships granted before August 17, 1986.

(b) *§1.117-2.*—Limitations applicable to taxable years beginning before 1987, but only in the case of scholarships and fellowships granted before August 17, 1986.

(c) *§1.117-3.*—Definitions applicable to taxable years beginning before 1987, but only in the case of scholarships and fellowships granted before August 17, 1986.

(d) *§1.117-4.*—Items not considered as scholarships or fellowship grants in taxable years beginning before 1987, but only in the case of scholarships and fellowships granted before August 17, 1986.

(e) *§1.117-5.*—Federal grants requiring future service as a federal employee pertaining to taxable years beginning before 1987, but only in the case of scholarships and fellowships granted before August 17, 1986.

(f) *§1.117-6.*—Qualified scholarships. [Reg. §1.117-0.]

□ Par. 3. Section 1.117-1 is amended by revising the heading to read as set forth below, inserting "and before August 17, 1986," after "July 28, 1956," in the first sentence of paragraph (b)(2)(i), and adding a new paragraph (c) to read as follows:

§1.117-1. Exclusion of amounts received as a scholarship or fellowship grant in taxable years beginning before 1987, but only in the case of scholarships and fellowships granted before August 17, 1986.

* * *

(c) *Special rule; termination date; cross reference.*—For purposes of this section, all references to section 117 within this section are to

section 117 as in effect prior to its amendment by the Tax Reform Act of 1986, unless otherwise indicated. This section does not apply to amounts granted after August 16, 1986, except to the extent that amounts granted after August 16, 1986, and before January 1, 1987, and received prior to January 1, 1987, are attributable to expenditures incurred before January 1, 1987. See §1.117-6(f) for rules relating to when a scholarship or fellowship is granted for purposes of section 117 as amended by the 1986 Act.

□ Par. 4. Section 1.117-2 is amended by revising the heading to read as set forth below, inserting "and before August 17, 1986," after "December 31, 1961," in the first sentence of paragraph (b)(1)(iii), and adding a new paragraph (c) to read as follows:

§1.117-2. Limitations applicable to taxable years beginning before 1987, but only in the case of scholarships and fellowships granted before August 17, 1986.—

* * *

(c) *Special rule; termination date; cross reference.*—For purposes of this section, all references to section 117 within this section are to section 117 as in effect prior to its amendment by the Tax Reform Act

of 1986, unless otherwise indicated. This section does not apply to amounts granted after August 16, 1986, except to the extent that amounts granted after August 16, 1986, and before January 1, 1987, and received prior to January 1, 1987, are attributable to expenditures incurred before January 1, 1987. See §1.117-6(f) for rules relating to when a scholarship or fellowship is granted for purposes of section 117 as amended by the 1986 Act.

□ Par. 5. Section 1.117-3 is amended by revising the heading to read as set forth below, inserting "of the Internal Revenue Code of 1954" after "151(e)(4)" in the first sentence of paragraph (b), inserting "of the Internal Revenue Code of 1954" after "151(e)(4)" in the last sentence of paragraph (b), and adding a new paragraph (f) to read as follows:

§1.117-3. Definitions applicable to taxable years beginning before 1987, but only in the case of scholarships and fellowships granted before August 17, 1986.—

* * *

(f) *Special rule; termination date; cross reference.*—For purposes of this section, all references to section 117 within this section are to section 117 as in effect prior to its amendment by the Tax Reform Act

of 1986, unless otherwise indicated. This section does not apply to amounts granted after August 16, 1986, except to the extent that amounts granted after August 16, 1986, and before January 1, 1987, and received prior to January 1, 1987, are attributable to expenditures incurred before January 1, 1987. See §1.117-6(f) for rules relating to when a scholarship or fellowship is granted for purposes of section 117 as amended by the 1986 Act.

□ Par. 6. Section 1.117-4 is amended as follows: 1. the heading is revised as set forth below; 2. the first sentence is revised by inserting "(a) *Applicability.*" before "The", 3. paragraphs (a), (b), and (c) are redesignated as paragraphs (1), (2), and (3); 4. paragraphs (1) and (2) of paragraph (3) as redesignated are redesignated as paragraphs (i) and (ii); 5. the second sentence of paragraph (3)(ii) as redesignated is amended by removing "subparagraph (1)" and adding in its place "subparagraph (i)"; and 6. a new paragraph (b) is added to read as set forth below.

§1.117-4. Items not considered as scholarships or fellowship grants in taxable years beginning before 1987, but only in the case of scholarships and fellowships granted before August 17, 1986.—

* * *

(b) *Special rule; termination date; cross reference.*—For purposes of this section, all references to section 117 within this section are to section 117 as in effect prior to its amendment by the Tax Reform Act

of 1986, unless otherwise indicated. This section does not apply to amounts granted after August 16, 1986, except to the extent that amounts granted after August 16, 1986, and before January 1, 1987, and received prior to January 1, 1987, are attributable to expenditures incurred before January 1, 1987. See §1.117-6(f) for rules relating to when a scholarship or fellowship is granted for purposes of section 117 as amended by the 1986 Act.

□ Par. 7. Section 1.117-5 is amended by revising the heading to read as set forth below, adding a second sentence to paragraph (f), and adding a new paragraph (g) to read as follows:

§1.117-5. Federal grants requiring future service as a federal employee pertaining to taxable years beginning before 1987, but only in the case of scholarships and fellowships granted before August 17, 1986.—

* * *

(f) *Effective date.*—* * * This section does not apply to amounts granted after August 16, 1986, except to the extent that amounts granted after August 16, 1986, and before January 1, 1987, and

received prior to January 1, 1987, are attributable to expenditures incurred before January 1, 1987.

(g) *Special rule; cross reference.*—For purposes of this section, all references to section 117 within this section are to section 117 as in effect prior to its amendment by the Tax Reform Act of 1986, unless otherwise indicated. See §1.117-6(f) for rules relating to when a scholarship or fellowship is granted for purposes of section 117 as amended by the 1986 Act.

□ Par. 8. A new §1.117-6 is added to read as follows:

§1.117-6. Qualified scholarships.—(a) *Outline of provisions.*
  (b) Exclusion of qualified scholarships.
  (c) Definitions.
    (1) Qualified scholarship.
    (2) Qualified tuition and related expenses.
    (3) Scholarship or fellowship grant.
      (i) In general

      (ii) Items not considered as scholarships or fellowship grants.
    (4) Candidate for a degree.
    (5) Educational organization.
    (6) Examples.
  (d) Inclusion of qualified scholarships and qualified tuition reductions representing payment for services.

(1) In general.

(2) Payment for services.

(3) Determination of amount of scholarship or fellowship grant representing payment for services.

(4) Characterization of scholarship or fellowship grants representing payment for services for purposes of the reporting and withholding requirements.

(5) Examples.

(e) Recordkeeping requirements.

(f) Effective date.

(1) In general.

(2) When a scholarship or fellowship is granted.

(3) Scholarships or fellowships granted before August 17, 1986.

(i) In general.

(ii) Amounts received in subsequent academic periods that were not initially described as fixed cash amounts or readily determinable amounts.

(iii) Examples.

(4) Expenditures incurred before January 1, 1987.

(g) Reporting and withholding requirements.

(h) Characterization of scholarship or fellowship grants exceeding amounts permitted to be excluded from gross income for purposes of the standard deduction and filing requirements for dependents.

(b) *Exclusion of qualified scholarships.*—(1) Gross income does not include any amount received as a qualified scholarship by an individual who is a candidate for a degree at an educational organization described in section 170(b)(1)(A)(ii), subject to the rules set forth in paragraph (d) of this section. Generally, any amount of a scholarship or fellowship grant that is not excludable under section 117 is includable in the gross income of the recipient for the taxable year in which such amount is received, notwithstanding the provisions of section 102 (relating to exclusion from gross income of gifts). However, see section 127 and the regulations thereunder for rules permitting an exclusion from gross income for certain educational assistance payments. See also section 162 and the regulations thereunder for the deductibility as a trade or business expense of the educational expenses of an individual who is not a candidate for a degree.

(2) If the amount of a scholarship or fellowship grant eligible to be excluded as a qualified scholarship under this paragraph cannot be determined when the grant is received because expenditures for qualified tuition and related expenses have not yet been incurred, then that portion of any amount received as a scholarship or fellowship grant that is not used for qualified tuition and related expenses within the academic period to which the scholarship or fellowship grant applies must be included in the gross income of the recipient for the taxable year in which such academic period ends.

(c) *Definitions.*—(1) *Qualified scholarship.*—For purposes of this section, a qualified scholarship is any amount received by an individual as a scholarship or fellowship grant (as defined in paragraph (c)(3) of this section), to the extent the individual establishes that, in accordance with the conditions of the grant, such amount was used for qualified tuition and related expenses (as defined in paragraph (c)(2) of this section). To be considered a qualified scholarship, the terms of the scholarship or fellowship grant need not expressly require that the amounts received be used for tuition and related expenses. However, to the extent that the terms of the grant specify that any portion of the grant cannot be used for tuition and related expenses or designate any portion of the grant for purposes other than tuition and related expenses (such as for room and board, or for a meal allowance), such amounts are not amounts received as a qualified scholarship. See paragraph (e) of this section for rules relating to recordkeeping requirements for establishing amounts used for qualified tuition and related expenses.

(2) *Qualified tuition and related expenses.*—For purposes of this section, qualified tuition and related expenses are—

(i) Tuition and fees required for the enrollment or attendance of a student at an educational organization described in section 170(b)(1)(A)(ii); and

(ii) Fees, books, supplies, and equipment required for courses of instruction at such an educational organization.

In order to be treated as related expenses under this section, the fees, books, supplies, and equipment must be required of all students in the particular course of instruction. Incidental expenses are not considered related expenses. Incidental expenses include expenses incurred for room and board, travel, research, clerical help, and equipment and other expenses that are not required for either enrollment or attendance at an educational organization, or in a course of instruction at such educational organization. See paragraph (c)(6), Example (1) of this section.

(3) *Scholarship or fellowship grant.*—(i) *In general.*—Generally, a scholarship or fellowship grant is a cash amount paid or allowed to, or for the benefit of, an individual to aid such individual in the pursuit of study or research. A scholarship or fellowship grant also may be in the form of a reduction in the amount owed by the recipient to an educational organization for tuition, room and board, or any other fee. A scholarship or fellowship grant may be funded by a governmental agency, college or university, charitable organization, business, or any other source. To be considered a scholarship or fellowship grant for purposes of this section, any amount received need not be formally designated as a scholarship. For example, an "allowance" is treated as a scholarship if it meets the definition set forth in this paragraph. However, a scholarship or fellowship grant does not include any amount provided by an individual to aid a relative, friend, or other individual in the pursuit of study or research if the grantor is motivated by family or philanthropic considerations.

(ii) *Items not considered as scholarships or fellowship grants.*—The following payments or allowances are not considered to be amounts received as a scholarship or fellowship grant for purposes of section 117:

(A) Educational and training allowances to a veteran pursuant to section 400 of the Servicemen's Readjustment Act of 1944 (58 Stat. 287) or pursuant to 38 U.S.C. 1631 (formerly section 231 of the Veterans' Readjustment Assistance Act of 1952).

(B) Tuition and subsistence allowances to members of the Armed Forces of the United States who are students at an educational institution operated by the United States or approved by the United States for their education and training, such as the United States Naval Academy and the United States Military Academy.

(4) *Candidate for a degree.*—For purposes of this section, a candidate for a degree is—

(i) A primary or secondary school student;

(ii) An undergraduate or graduate student at a college or university who is pursuing studies or conducting research to meet the requirement for an academic or professional degree; or

(iii) A full-time or part-time student at an educational organization described in section 170(b)(1)(A)(ii) that—

(A) Provides an educational program that is acceptable for full credit towards a bachelor's or higher degree, or offers a program of training to prepare students for gainful employment in a recognized occupation, and

(B) Is authorized under Federal or State law to provide such a program and is accredited by a nationally recognized accreditation agency.

The student may pursue studies or conduct research at an educational organization other than the one conferring the degree provided that such study or research meets the requirements of the educational organization granting the degree. See paragraph (c)(6), Examples (2) and (3) of this section.

(5) *Educational organization.*—For purposes of this section, an educational organization is an organization described under section 170(b)(1)(A)(ii) and the regulations thereunder. An educational organization is described in section 170(b)(1)(A)(ii) if it has as its primary function the presentation of formal instruction, and it normally maintains a regular faculty and curriculum and normally has a regularly enrolled body of pupils or students in attendance at the place where its educational activities are regularly carried on. See paragraph (c)(6), Example (4) of this section.

(6) *Examples.*—The provisions of this paragraph may be illustrated by the following examples:

Example (1). On September 1, 1987, A receives a scholarship from University U for academic year 1987-1988. A is enrolled in a writing course at U. Suggested supplies for the writing course in which A is enrolled include a word processor, but students in the course are not required to obtain a word processor. Any amount used for suggested supplies is not an amount used for qualified tuition and related expenses for purposes of this section. Thus, A may not include the cost of a word processor in determining the amount received by A as a qualified scholarship.

Example (2). B is a scholarship student during academic year 1987-1988 at Technical School V located in State W. B is enrolled in a program to train individuals to become data processors. V is authorized by State W to provide this program and is accredited by an appropriate accreditation agency. B is a candidate for a degree for purposes of this section. Thus, B may exclude from gross income any amount received as a qualified scholarship, subject to the rules set forth in paragraph (d) of this section.

Example (3). C holds a Ph.D. in chemistry. On January 31, 1988, Foundation X awards C a fellowship. During 1988 C pursues chemistry research at Research Foundation Y, supported by the fellowship grant from X. C is not an employee of either foundation. C is not a candidate for a degree for purposes of this section. Thus, the fellowship grant from X must be included in C's gross income.

Example (4). On July 1, 1987, D receives a $500 scholarship to take a correspondence course from School Z. D receives and returns all lessons to Z through the mail. No students are in attendance at Z's place of business. D is not attending an educational organization described in section 170(b)(1)(A)(ii) for purposes of this section. Thus, the $500 scholarship must be included in D's gross income.

(d) *Inclusion of qualified scholarships and qualified tuition reductions representing payment for services.*—(1) *In general.*—The exclusion from gross income under this section does not apply to that portion of any amount received as a qualified scholarship or qualified tuition reduction (as defined under section 117(d)) that represents payment for teaching, research, or other services by the student required as a condition to receiving the qualified scholarship or qualified tuition reduction, regardless of whether all candidates for the degree are required to perform such services. The provisions of this paragraph (d) apply not only to cash amounts received in return for such services, but also to amounts by which the tuition or related expenses of the person who performs services are reduced, whether or not pursuant to a tuition reduction plan described in section 117(d).

(2) *Payment for services.*—For purposes of this section, a scholarship or fellowship grant represents payment for services when the grantor requires the recipient to perform services in return for the granting of the scholarship or fellowship. A requirement that the recipient pursue studies, research, or other activities primarily for the benefit of the grantor is treated as a requirement to perform services. A requirement that a recipient furnish periodic reports to the grantor for the purpose of keeping the grantor informed as to the general progress of the individual, however, does not constitute the performance of services. A scholarship or fellowship grant conditioned upon either past, present, or future teaching, research, or other services by the recipient represents payment for services under this section. See paragraph (d)(5), Examples (1), (2), (3) and (4) of this section.

(3) *Determination of amount of scholarship or fellowship grant representing payment for services.*—If only a portion of a scholarship or fellowship grant represents payment for services, the grantor must determine the amount of the scholarship or fellowship grant (including any reduction in tuition or related expenses) to be allocated to payment for services. Factors to be taken into account in making this allocation include, but are not limited to, compensation paid by—

(i) The grantor for similar services performed by students with qualifications comparable to those of the scholarship recipient, but who do not receive scholarship or fellowship grants;

(ii) The grantor for similar services performed by full-time or part-time employees of the grantor who are not students; and

(iii) Educational organizations, other than the grantor of the scholarship or fellowship, for similar services performed either by students or other employees.

If the recipient includes in gross income the amount allocated by the grantor to payment for services and such amount represents reasonable compensation for those services, then any additional amount of a scholarship or fellowship grant received from the same grantor that meets the requirements of paragraph (b) of this section is excludable from gross income. See paragraph (d)(5), Examples (5) and (6) of this section.

(4) *Characterization of scholarship or fellowship grants representing payment for services for purposes of the reporting and withholding requirements.*—Any amount of a scholarship or fellowship grant that represents payment for services (as defined in paragraph (d)(2) of this section) is considered wages for purposes of sections 3401 and 3402 (relating to withholding for income taxes), section 6041 (relating to returns of information), and section 6051 (relating to reporting wages of employees). The application of sections 3101 and 3111 (relating to the Federal Insurance Contributions Act (FICA)), or section 3301 (relating to the Federal Unemployment Tax Act (FUTA)) depends upon the nature of the employment and the status of the organization. See sections 3121(b), 3306(c), and the regulations thereunder.

(5) *Examples.*—The provisions of this paragraph may be illustrated by the following examples:

Example (1). On November 15, 1987, A receives a $5,000 qualified scholarship (as defined in paragraph (c)(1) of this section) for academic year 1988-1989 under a federal program requiring A's future service as a federal employee. The $5,000 scholarship represents payment for services for purposes of this section. Thus, the $5,000 must be included in A's gross income as wages.

Example (2). B receives a $10,000 scholarship from V Corporation on June 4, 1987, for academic year 1987-1988. As a condition to receiving the scholarship, B agrees to work for V after graduation. B has no previous relationship with V. The $10,000 scholarship represents payment for future services for purposes of this section. Thus, the $10,000 scholarship must be included in B's gross income as wages.

Example (3). On March 15, 1987, C is awarded a fellowship for academic year 1987-1988 to pursue a research project the nature of which is determined by the grantor, University W. C must submit a paper to W that describes the research results. The paper does not fulfill any course requirements. Under the terms of the grant, W may publish C's results, or otherwise use the results of C's research. C is treated as performing services for W. Thus, C's fellowship from W represents payment for services and must be included in C's gross income as wages.

Example (4). On September 27, 1987, D receives a qualified scholarship (as defined in paragraph (c)(1) of this section) from University X for academic year 1987-1988. As a condition to receiving the scholarship, D performs services as a teaching assistant for X. Such services are required of all candidates for a degree at X. The amount of D's scholarship from X is equal to the compensation paid by X to teaching assistants who are part-time employees and not students at X. D's scholarship from X represents payment for services. Thus, the entire amount of D's scholarship from X must be included in D's gross income as wages.

Example (5). On June 11, 1987, E receives a $6,000 scholarship for academic year 1987-1988 from University Y. As a condition to receiving the scholarship, E performs services as a researcher for Y. Other researchers who are not scholarship recipients receive $2,000 for similar services for the year. Therefore, Y allocates $2,000 of the scholarship amount to compensation for services performed by E. Thus, the portion of the scholarship that represents payment for services, $2,000, must be included in E's gross income as wages. However, if E establishes expenditures of $4,000 for qualified tuition and related expenses (as defined in paragraph (c)(2) of this section), then $4,000 of E's scholarship is excludable from E's gross income as a qualified scholarship.

Example (6). During 1987 F is employed as a research assistant to a faculty member at University Z. F receives a salary from Z that represents reasonable compensation for the position of research assistant. In addition to salary, F receives from Z a qualified tuition reduction (as defined in section 117(d)) to be used to enroll in an undergraduate course at Z. F includes the salary in gross income. Thus, the qualified tuition reduction does not represent payment for services and therefore, is not includable in F's gross income.

(e) *Recordkeeping requirements.*—In order to be eligible to exclude from gross income any amount received as a qualified scholarship (as defined in paragraph (c)(1) of this section), the recipient must maintain records that establish amounts used for qualified tuition and related expenses (as defined in paragraph (c)(2) of this section) as well as the total amount of qualified tuition and related expenses. Such amounts may be established by providing to the Service, upon request, copies of relevant bills, receipts, cancelled checks, or other documentation or records that clearly reflect the use of the money. The recipient must also submit, upon request, documentation that establishes receipt of the grant, notification date of the grant, and the conditions and requirements of the particular grant. Subject to the rules set forth in paragraph (d) of this section, qualified scholarship amounts are excludable without the need to trace particular grant dollars to particular expenditures for qualified tuition and related expenses.

(f) *Effective date.*—(1) *In general.*—The rules of this section generally apply to taxable years beginning on or after January 1, 1987. However, section 117, as in effect prior to its amendment by the Tax Reform Act of 1986 (1986 Act), continues to apply to scholarships and fellowships granted before August 17, 1986, whenever received. In addition, section 117, as in effect prior to its amendment by the 1986 Act, applies in the case of scholarships and fellowships granted after August 16, 1986, and before January 1, 1987, to the extent of any amount received prior to January 1, 1987, that is attributable to expenditures incurred before January 1, 1987.

(2) *When a scholarship or fellowship is granted.*—For purposes of this section, a scholarship or fellowship is granted when the grantor either notifies the recipient of the award or notifies an organization or institution acting on behalf of a specified recipient of the award to be provided to such recipient. If the notification is sent by mail, notification occurs as of the date the notice is postmarked. If evidence of a postmark does not exist, the date on the award letter is treated as the notification date.

(3) *Scholarships or fellowships granted before August 17, 1986.*— (i) *In general.*—For purposes of this section, a scholarship or fellowship is considered granted before August 17, 1986, to the extent that, in a notice of award made before that date, the grantor made a firm commitment to provide the recipient with a fixed cash amount or a readily determinable amount. A notice of award is treated as containing a firm commitment even if the scholarship or fellowship grant is subject to a condition that the recipient remain in good standing or maintain a specific grade point average. In addition, a requirement that the recipient file a financial statement on an annual basis to show

Reg. §1.117-6(f)(3)(i)

continuing financial need is not treated as a requirement to reapply to the grantor. If a scholarship or fellowship, initially awarded before August 17, 1986, is granted for a period exceeding one academic period (for example, a semester), amounts received in subsequent academic periods are treated as granted before August 17, 1986, only if—

(A) The amount awarded for the first academic period is described in the original notice of award as a fixed cash amount or readily determinable amount;

(B) The original notice of award contains a firm commitment by the grantor to provide the scholarship or fellowship grant for more than one academic period; and

(C) The recipient is not required to reapply to the grantor in order to receive the scholarship or fellowship grant in future academic periods.

Scholarship or fellowship amounts treated as granted before August 17, 1986, must be applied against qualified tuition and related expenses before any amount of a scholarship or fellowship treated as granted after August 16, 1986, may be eligible for exclusion as a qualified scholarship.

(ii) *Amounts received in subsequent academic periods that were not initially described as fixed cash amounts or readily determinable amounts.*—If the notice of award of a scholarship or fellowship grant satisfies the requirements of paragraph (f)(3)(i) of this section but does not describe the amount to be received in subsequent academic periods as either a fixed cash amount or readily determinable amount, then the amount received in each subsequent academic period that is treated as granted before August 17, 1986, may not exceed the amount granted for the initial academic period. To the extent that any amount received in a subsequent academic period, under the same notice of award, exceeds the amount received in the initial academic period, the excess amount is treated as a scholarship or fellowship granted after August 16, 1986.

(iii) *Examples.*—The provisions of this paragraph may be illustrated by the following examples:

Example (1). On January 7, 1985, A receives a notice of award under a federal program of a $500 scholarship for the academic period Spring 1985. A receives the $500 in February 1988. For purposes of this section the $500 scholarship is granted before August 17, 1986, and thus is subject to section 117 prior to its amendment by the 1986 Act.

Example (2). On May 7, 1986, B receives a notice of award of a scholarship in the amount of $4,000 annually for four years. The total amount of this scholarship is a fixed cash amount. Thus, $16,000, the total amount of the scholarship for all four years, is subject to section 117 prior to its amendment by the 1986 Act.

Example (3). On May 7, 1986, C is notified of the award of the Y scholarship that will pay for C's tuition, room, and board for four years. The total amount of the Y scholarship is readily determinable. Thus, the total amount of the Y scholarship for all four years is subject to section 117 prior to its amendment by the 1986 Act.

Example (4). On May 7, 1986, D is notified that she is the recipient of a scholarship to attend University Z. The scholarship is not conditioned upon the performance of services by D. The notice provides that Z will award scholarship funds for four years and specifies that D will receive $5,000 during the first year. D is not required to reapply in order to receive scholarship funds during years 2 through 4. However, the notice does not specify the scholarship funds to be received in years 2 through 4. The $5,000 received in year 1 is treated as granted before August 17, 1986, because this amount is a fixed cash amount described in the notice of award. In addition, because Z has made a specific commitment to provide scholarship funds during years 2 through 4 without requiring D to reapply for the scholarship, an amount from Z not exceeding $5,000 per year is treated as granted before August 17, 1986, during years 2 through 4. Thus, if D receives $4,000 from Z in year 2, the entire $4,000 is treated as granted before August 17, 1986. If, in year 3, D receives $6,000 from Z, only $5,000 of the amount received is treated as granted before August 17, 1986. The additional $1,000 received in year 3 is treated as granted after August 16, 1986. Whether this additional $1,000 is excludable from D's gross income depends upon

the amount of qualified tuition and related expenses (as defined in paragraph (c)(2) of this section) incurred by D in year 3. Thus, if D's qualified tuition and related expenses for year 3 are $6,000, the entire $6,000 is excludable from D's gross income.

Example (5). Assume the same facts as in Example (4) except that D's qualified tuition and related expenses in year 3 are $5,500. D excludes the $5,000 that is treated as granted before August 17, 1986. However, this $5,000 must be applied against the total qualified tuition and related expenses of $5,500 owed by D for year 3 before any amount received from a scholarship or fellowship granted after August 16, 1986, may be excluded. The additional $1,000 received by D that is treated as granted after August 16, 1986, is excludable to the extent of $500, the amount by which qualified tuition and related expenses exceed the amount that is treated as granted before August 17, 1986. The remaining $500 scholarship amount must be included in D's gross income.

Example (6). Assume the same facts as in Example (4) except that D's qualified tuition and related expenses for year 3 are $5,000. The amount of D's qualified tuition and related expenses for year 3 is equal to the scholarship amount from Z treated as granted before August 17, 1986. Thus, no part of the $1,000 treated as granted after August 16, 1986, is excludable from D's gross income.

(4) *Expenditures incurred before January 1, 1987.*—In the case of scholarships and fellowships granted after August 16, 1986, and before January 1, 1987, amounts received prior to January 1, 1987, that are attributable to expenditures incurred prior to January 1, 1987, are subject to section 117 as in effect prior to its amendment by the 1986 Act. For purposes of this section, an expenditure is incurred when it becomes properly due and payable by the recipient. However, expenditures relating to an academic period beginning after December 31, 1986, paid by the recipient before January 1, 1987, prior to the time when the recipient is billed for such expenditures, are not treated as expenditures incurred before January 1, 1987. Thus, if in December 1986 an educational organization billed a scholarship recipient for expenses relating to the academic period beginning in January 1987, and the recipient used scholarship amounts received prior to January 1, 1987, to pay the expenses on January 5, 1987, the scholarship amounts used to pay such expenses are considered attributable to expenditures incurred prior to January 1, 1987. If, however, on December 31, 1986, a scholarship recipient used scholarship amounts to pay expenses relating to the academic period beginning in January 1987, before the recipient was billed for such expenses, the amounts used are not treated as attributable to expenditures incurred before January 1, 1987.

(g) *Reporting and withholding requirements.*—For return of information requirements, see sections 6041, 6051, and the regulations thereunder. For withholding from scholarships or fellowship grants representing payment for services, see sections 3401, 3402, and the regulations thereunder. For withholding from scholarships or fellowship grants of nonresident aliens, see section 1441 and the regulations thereunder. For the application of FICA, see sections 3101 and 3111. For the application of FUTA, see section 3301.

(h) *Characterization of scholarship or fellowship grants exceeding amounts permitted to be excluded from gross income for purposes of the standard deduction and filing requirements for dependents.*—For purposes of section 63(c)(5) (relating to the standard deduction for dependents) and section 6012(a)(1)(C)(i) (relating to dependents required to make returns of income), any amount of a scholarship or fellowship grant in excess of the amount permitted to be excluded from gross income under paragraph (b) of this section is considered earned income. For example, on June 11, 1987, A, a student who has no other earned or unearned income for the year and can be claimed as a dependent on another taxpayer's return of tax, receives a $1,000 scholarship for room and board. The $1,000 must be included in A's gross income because it is not a qualified scholarship under paragraph (b) of this section. However, for purposes of sections 63(c)(5) and 6012(a)(1)(C)(i), the $1,000 is earned income. Accordingly, A is not required to file a return of tax for 1987 because A's gross income ($1,000) does not exceed A's standard deduction ($1,000) and A has no unearned income. [Reg. § 1.117-6.]

Qualified Group Legal Services Plans

Qualified Group Legal Services Plans.—Reproduced below are the texts of proposed Reg. §§ 1.120-1 and 1.120-2, relating to qualified group legal services plans (published in the Federal Register on April 29, 1980).

☐ Par. 2. New §§ 1.120-1 and 1.120-2 are added to the appropriate place:

§ 1.120-1. Amounts received under a qualified group legal services plan.—(a) *Exclusion from gross income.*—The gross income of an employee, or the employee's spouse or dependent, does not include—

(1) Amounts contributed by an employer on behalf of the employee, spouse or dependent under a qualified group legal services plan described in § 1.120-2;

(2) The value of legal services provided the employee, spouse or dependent under the plan, or

(3) Amounts paid to the employee, spouse or dependent under the plan as reimbursement for the cost of personal legal services provided to the employee, spouse or dependent.

(b) *Definitions.*—For rules relating to the meaning of the terms "employee," "employer," "spouse," and "dependent" see paragraph (d)(3) and (4) and paragraph (i) of §1.120-2.

(c) *Effective date.*—This section is effective with respect to employer contributions made on behalf of, and legal services provided to, an employee, spouse or dependent on or after the first day of the period of plan qualification (as determined under §1.120-3(d)) and in taxable years of the employee, spouse or dependent beginning after December 31, 1976, and ending before January 1, 1982. [Reg. §1.120-1.]

§1.120-2. Qualified group legal services plan.—(a) *In general.*—In general, a qualified group legal services plan is a plan established and maintained by an employer under which the employer provides employees, or their spouses or dependents, personal legal services by prepaying, or providing in advance for, all or part of the legal fees for the services. To be a qualified plan, the plan must satisfy the requirements described in paragraphs (b) through (h) of this section and be recognized as a qualified plan by the Internal Revenue Service. Section 1.120-3 provides rules under which a plan must apply to the Internal Revenue Service for recognition as a qualified plan.

(b) *Separate written plan.*—The plan must be a separate written plan of the employer. For purposes of this section—

(1) *Plan.*—The term "plan" implies a permanent as distinguished from a temporary program. Thus, although the employer may reserve the right to change or terminate the plan, and to discontinue contributions thereunder, the abandonment of the plan for any reason other than a business necessity soon after it has taken effect will be evidence that the plan from its inception was not a *bona fide* plan for the benefit of employees generally (see paragraph (d) of this section). Such evidence will be given special weight if, for example, a plan is abandoned soon after extensive benefits are provided to persons with respect to whom discrimination in plan benefits is prohibited (see paragraph (e) of this section).

(2) *Separate plan.*—The requirement that the plan be a separate plan means that the plan may not provide benefits which are not personal legal services within the meaning of paragraph (c) of this section. For example, the requirement for a separate plan is not satisfied if personal legal services are provided under an employee benefit plan that also provides pension, disability, life insurance, medical or other such non-legal benefits. The requirement for a separate plan does not, however, preclude a single plan from being adopted by more than one employer.

(c) *Personal legal services.*—(1) *In general.*—In general, benefits under the plan must consist of, or be provided with respect to, only personal legal services that are specified in the plan. The plan must specifically prohibit a diversion or use of any funds of the plan for purposes other than the providing of personal legal services for the participants. In general, a personal legal service is a legal service (within the meaning of subparagraph (3) of this paragraph) provided to a participant employee, spouse or dependent which is not directly connected with or pertaining to—

(i) A trade or business of the employee, spouse or dependent,

(ii) The management, conservation or preservation of property held by the employee, spouse or dependent for the production of income, or

(iii) The production or collection of income by the employee, spouse or dependent.

(2) *Certain personal legal services.*—Notwithstanding subparagraph (1)(ii) and (iii) of this paragraph, the following (if legal services within the meaning of subparagraph (3)) are considered personal legal services—

(i) A legal service provided to a participant with respect to securing, increasing or collecting alimony under a decree of divorce (or payments in lieu of alimony) or the division or redivision of community property under the community property laws of a State,

(ii) A legal service provided to a participant as heir or legatee of a decedent, or as beneficiary under a testamentary trust, in protecting or asserting rights to property of a decedent, or

(iii) A legal service provided to a participant with respect to the participant's claim for damages, other than compensatory damages, for personal injury.

(3) *Legal services.*—(i) *Services of a lawyer.*—In general, a legal service is a service performed by a lawyer if the performing of the service constitutes the practice of law.

(ii) *Services of a person not a lawyer.*—A legal service may include a service performed by a person who is not a lawyer, if the service is performed under the direction or control of a lawyer, in connection with a legal service (within the meaning of subdivision (i)) performed by the lawyer, and the fee for the service is included in the legal fee of the lawyer. Examples of services to which this subdivision (ii) may apply are the services of an accountant, a researcher, a paralegal, a law clerk, an investigator or a searcher of title to real property.

(iii) *Court fees.*—Amounts payable to a court in connection with the presentation, litigation or appeal from a matter before a court is considered the cost of a legal service. For example, benefits under the plan may be provided with respect to a court filing fee, a fee for service of summons or other process, the cost of a transcript of trial or the posting of bail bond.

(iv) *Other fees or charges.*—An amount payable to a competent governmental authority (for example, the United States, a State or any subdivision thereof) is considered the cost of a legal service, if the amount is payable with respect to the filing or registration of a legal document (for example, a deed or will). However, any amount payable directly or indirectly to a governmental authority is not the cost of a legal service, if the amount is in the nature of a tax. For example, although a plan may provide for payment of an amount payable to a county for the filing or registration of a deed to real property, a plan may not provide for payment of an amount in the nature of a tax on the transfer of title to real property.

(4) *Limited initial consultation.*—A plan is not other than a qualified plan merely because, in connection with providing personal legal services, the plan provides a specified "limited initial consultation" benefit without restricting the benefit to personal legal services. An "initial consultation" is a consultation, the purpose of which is to determine whether a plan participant is in need of a personal legal service and, if so, whether the required personal legal service may be provided under the plan. An initial consultation must not include document preparation or review, or representation of the participant. An initial consultation benefit is "limited", if under the plan it is limited either in time (*e. g.,* no more than 4 hours of initial consultation during any year) or number (*e. g.,* no more than 4 initial consultations during any year).

(d) *Exclusive benefit.*—(1) *In general.*—The plan must benefit only employees of the employer, including individuals who are employees within the meaning of paragraph (i)(1) of this section, or the spouses or dependents of employees.

(2) *Plans to which more than one employer contributes.*—In the case of a plan to which more than one employer contributes, in determining whether the plan is for the exclusive benefit of an employer's employees, or their spouses or dependents, the employees of any employer who maintains the plan are considered the employees of each employer who maintains the plan.

(3) *Spouses of employees.*—In general, for purposes of determining whether a plan is for the exclusive benefit of an employer's employees, or their spouses or dependents, the determination of whether an individual is a spouse of an employee is made at the time the legal services are provided to the individual. The term "spouse" includes a surviving spouse of a deceased employee. Although, in general, the term "spouse" does not include a person legally separated from an employee under a decree of divorce or separate maintenance, a legal service provided to an employee's former spouse after the issuing of a decree of divorce, annulment or separate maintenance from the employee is considered a service provided to the spouse of an employee, if the service relates to the divorce, annulment or separation. For purposes of this section and §1.120-1, the term "spouse" includes an individual to whom benefits may be provided under this subparagraph.

(4) *Dependents of employees.*—For purposes of determining whether a plan is for the exclusive benefit of an employer's employees, or their spouses or dependents, benefits provided to the following individuals are considered benefits provided to a dependent of an employee:

(i) An individual who is a dependent of an employee within the meaning of section 152 for the taxable year of the employee within which the legal services are provided to the individual;

(ii) An individual who is described in paragraph (h)(2) of this section (relating to certain surviving dependents) at the time the legal services are provided to the individual; or

(iii) An individual who is a dependent of an employee within the meaning of section 152 for the taxable year of the employee ending on the date of the employee's death, under age 21 on the date of the employee's death, and under age 21 at the time the legal services are provided to the individual.

For purposes of this section and §1.120-1, the term "dependent" means an individual to whom benefits may be provided under this subparagraph.

(5) *Estates of employees.*—A plan is for the exclusive benefit of the employer's employees, or their spouses or dependents, notwithstanding that the plan provides benefits to the personal representative of a deceased employee, or spouse or dependent, with respect to the estate of the deceased.

(e) *Prohibited discrimination.*—(1) *In general.*—The plan must benefit the employer's employees generally. Among those benefited may be employees who are officers, shareholders, self-employed or highly compensated. A plan is not for the benefit of employees generally, however, if the plan discriminates in favor of employees described in the preceding sentence, or their spouses or dependents, in eligibility requirements (see subparagraph (2) of this paragraph) or in contributions or benefits (see subparagraph (3) of this paragraph).

(2) *Eligibility to participate.*—A plan need not provide benefits for all employees (or their spouses or dependents). A plan must, however, benefit those employees (or their spouses or dependents) who qualify under a classification of employees set up by the employer which is found by the Internal Revenue Service not to discriminate in favor of employees who are officers, shareholders, self-employed or highly compensated, or their spouses or dependents. In general, this determination shall be made by applying the same standards as are applied under section 410(b)(1)(B) (relating to qualified pension, profit-sharing and stock bonus plans), without regard to section 401(a)(5). For purposes of making this determination, there shall be excluded from consideration employees not covered by the plan who are included in a unit of employees covered by an agreement which the Secretary of Labor finds to be a collective bargaining agreement between employee representatives and one or more employers, if the Internal Revenue Service finds that group legal services plan benefits were the subject of good faith bargaining between the employee representatives and the employer or employers. For purposes of determining whether such bargaining occurred, it is not material that the employees are not covered by another plan or that the employer's present plan was not considered in the bargaining.

(3) *Contributions and benefits.*—(i) *In general.*—Employer contributions under the plan or benefits provided under the plan must not discriminate in favor of employees who are officers, shareholders, self-employed or highly compensated, or their spouses or dependents, as against other employees, or their spouses or dependents, covered by the plan. This does not mean that contributions or benefits may not vary. Variations in contributions or benefits may be provided so long as the plan, viewed as a whole for the benefit of employees in general, with all its attendant circumstances, does not discriminate in favor of those with respect to whom discrimination is prohibited. Thus, contributions or benefits which vary by reason of a formula which takes into account years of service with the employer, or other factors, are not prohibited unless those factors discriminate in favor of employees who are officers, shareholders, self-employed or highly compensated, or their spouses or dependents. Under this subparagraph (3), if a plan covers employees who are highly compensated, and benefits under the plan uniformly increase as compensation increases, the plan is not a qualified plan.

(ii) *Relative utilization of plan benefits.*—Not only must a plan not discriminate on its face in employer contributions or plan benefits in favor of employees who are officers, shareholders, self-employed or highly compensated, or their spouses or dependents, the plan also must not discriminate in favor of such employees, or their spouses or dependents, in actual operation. Accordingly, the extent to which such employees, or their spouses or dependents, as a group, utilize plan benefits must be compared to the extent to which all other employees, or their spouses or dependents, as a group, utilize plan benefits. A plan is not other than a qualified plan for a plan year merely because, relative to their number, those employees, or their spouses or dependents, with respect to whom discrimination is prohibited utilize plan benefits to a greater extent than do other employees, or their spouses or dependents. However, a persistent pattern of greater relative utilization of plan benefits by the group of employees who are officers, shareholders, self-employed or highly compensated, or their spouses or dependents, may be evidence that the plan discriminates in favor of such employees and is not for the benefit of employees generally. Such evidence will be considered, together with all other pertinent facts and circumstances, to determine whether the plan improperly discriminates in actual operation.

(f) *Contribution limitation.*—(1) *In general.*—Under section 120(c)(3), a plan is a qualified plan for a plan year only if no more than 25% of the amount contributed by the employer under the plan for the plan year is contributed on behalf of the limitation class described in subparagraph (2). A plan satisfies the requirements of

section 120(c)(3) for a plan year (as determined under the plan) if either—

(i) The plan satisfies the requirements of subparagraph (3), or

(ii) The percentage determined under subparagraph (4) is 25% or less, and the plan is not other than a qualified plan by reason of subparagraph (5).

(2) *Limitation class.*—The limitation class consists of—

(i) *Shareholders.*—Individuals who, on any day of the plan year, own more than 5% of the total number of shares of outstanding stock of the employer, or

(ii) *Owners.*—In the case of an employer's trade or business which is not incorporated, individuals who on any day of the plan year, own more than 5% of the capital or profits interest in the employer, and

(iii) *Spouses and dependents.*—Individuals who are spouses or dependents of shareholders or owners described in subdivisions (i) and (ii).

For purposes of determining stock ownership, the attribution rules described in paragraph (i)(4) of this section apply. The regulations prescribed under section 414(c) are applicable in determining an individual's interest in the capital or profits of an unincorporated trade or business.

(3) *Disregarding allocation rules.*—(i) *Plans providing legal services directly.*—If a plan is one under which legal services are provided directly to a participant, the plan will satisfy the requirements of section 120(c)(3), without regard to the allocation rules described in subparagraphs (4) and (5) of this paragraph, if the plan satisfies the following requirement. The plan must provide and be operated so that no legal service may be provided to a member of the limitation class if to provide the service would cause the fair market value of legal services provided to date during the plan year to members of the limitation class to exceed 25% of the fair market value of the legal services provided under the plan to date during the plan year.

(ii) *Plans providing reimbursement for the cost of legal services.*—If a plan is one under which a participant is reimbursed for the cost of legal services, the plan will satisfy the requirements of section 120(c)(3), without regard to the allocation rules described in subparagraphs (4) and (5) of this paragraph, if the plan satisfies the following requirement. The plan must provide and be operated so that no amount may be paid to a member of the limitation class if the payment would cause amounts paid to date during the plan year to members of the limitation class to exceed 25% of the amounts paid under the plan to date during the plan year.

(iii) *Limitation class; special rule.*—For purposes of this subparagraph (3), an individual is a member of the limitation class only if the individual is a member (within the meaning of subparagraph (2)) on or before the date on which the determination described in subdivision (ii) or (iii) is required to be made.

(iv) *Example.*—The provisions of subdivision (iii) of this subparagraph may be illustrated by the following example:

Example. (A) Plan X is a qualified group legal services plan under which plan participants are reimbursed for the cost of personal legal services specified in the plan. The plan includes a provision satisfying the requirements of subdivision (ii) of this subparagraph. The plan year is the calendar year.

(B) A, an individual, is a participant in Plan X. On March 18, 1981, A is paid an amount under the plan. On June 21, 1981, A purchases shares of stock of the employer maintaining the plan. As a result of the purchase A owns more than 5% of the total number of shares of outstanding stock of the employer. Accordingly, under subparagraph (2) of this paragraph, A is a member of the limitation class for the plan year 1981. On August 14, 1981, A sells the shares of stock purchased on June 21, 1981, and no longer owns more than 5% of the total number of shares of outstanding stock of the employer. On October 9, 1981, A is paid an additional amount under the plan.

(C) For purposes of the determination required by subdivision (ii) of this subparagraph, if the determination is made for a date after March 17, 1981, and before June 21, 1981, the amount paid to A on March 18, 1981, is not considered an amount paid to a member of the limitation class. If the determination is made for a date after June 20, 1981, the amount paid to A on March 18, 1981, is considered an amount paid to a member of the limitation class. With respect to a determination made for a date after October 8, 1981, the amount paid to A on October 9, 1981, is considered an amount paid to a member of the limitation class.

(4) *Contribution allocation.*—(i) *Equal benefits.*—In general, if under a plan the same benefits are made available to each participant, the percentage of the amount contributed by the employer for a plan year that is considered contributed on behalf of the limitation

class is equal to the number of participants who are members of the limitation class at any time during the plan year, divided by the number of individuals who are participants in the plan at any time during the plan year.

(ii) *Unequal benefits.*—In general, if under the plan different benefits are made available to different participants or different classes of participants, the percentage of the amount contributed by the employer for a plan year that is considered contributed on behalf of the limitation class is equal to the fair market value (as of the first day of the plan year) of those benefits available under the plan to participants who are members of the limitation class at any time during the plan year, divided by the fair market value (as of the first day of the plan year) of those benefits available under the plan to all individuals who are participants in the plan at any time during the plan year.

(iii) *Individual premiums.*—Notwithstanding subdivision (i) or (ii) of this subparagraph, if benefits are provided under the plan in exchange for the employer's prepayment or payment of a premium, and the amount of the prepayment or premium is determined by taking into account the circumstances of individual participants or classes of participants, the percentage of the amount contributed by the employer for a plan year that is considered contributed on behalf of the limitation class is equal to the sum of the prepayments or premiums paid for the plan year on behalf of participants who are members of the limitation class at any time during the plan year, divided by the sum of the prepayments or premiums paid for the plan year. A prepayment or premium is paid for the plan year if it is paid with respect to legal services provided or made available during the plan year. This subdivision (iii) will apply if, for example, equal benefits are provided each participant under the plan in exchange for the employer's payment of a premium with respect to each participant employee, and the amount of the premium varies, taking into account the employee's income level, the number and ages of the employee's dependents or other such factors.

(5) *Relative utilization of plan benefits.*—(i) *Application.*—The extent to which members of the limitation class, as a class, utilize plan benefits shall be taken into account in determining the percentage of amounts contributed by the employer that is considered contributed on behalf of the limitation class. The rules described in this subparagraph (5) are in addition to those described in subparagraph (4) of this paragraph, and a plan may be other than a qualified plan by reason of the application of this subparagraph (5), notwithstanding that the percentage determined under subparagraph (4) is 25% or less.

(ii) *Computation.*—Under this subparagraph (5), if during any three successive plan years, benefits paid to or with respect to the limitation class (as determined for each plan year) exceed 25% of all benefits paid under the plan during the three years, the plan is not a qualified plan for the next succeeding plan year.

(iii) *Reapplication for recognition as a qualified plan.*—A plan that is not a qualified plan for a plan year by reason of this subparagraph (5), may reapply under §1.120-3 for recognition as a qualified plan for any plan year following the first plan year for which it is not a qualified plan. A plan so reapplying will be recognized as a qualified plan for any plan year for which recognition is sought only if the plan is a qualified plan under this subparagraph (5) for the first plan year for which such recognition is sought and otherwise satisfies the requirements of section 120 and this section.

(g) *Employer contributions.*—(1) *In general.*—Employer contributions under the plan may be made only—

(i) To insurance companies, or to organizations or persons that provide personal legal services, or indemnification against the cost of personal legal services, in exchange for a prepayment or payment of a premium,

(ii) To organizations or trusts described in section 501(c)(20),

(iii) To organizations described in section 501(c) that are permitted by that section to receive payments from an employer for support of a qualified group legal services plan, except that the organization shall pay or credit the contribution to an organization or trust described in section 501(c)(20),

(iv) As prepayment to providers of legal services under the plan, or

(v) A combination of the above.

(2) *Prepayment required.*—For purposes of subparagraph (1)(i) and (iv), employer contributions are considered prepayments or premiums only if a contribution made with respect to benefits reasonably anticipated to be provided under the plan during any month is made on or before the tenth day of the month.

(h) *Employee contributions.*—(1) *In general.*—A plan is not a qualified plan if it permits participants to contribute under the plan other than as described in subparagraphs (2) and (3) of this paragraph.

(2) *Certain separated employees and surviving spouses and dependents.*—A plan will not be other than a qualified plan merely because the plan allows—

(i) A separated former employee,

(ii) A surviving spouse of a deceased employee, or

(iii) An individual who is a dependent of an employee within the meaning of section 152 for the taxable year of the employee ending on the date of the death of the employee,

to elect to continue as a participant under the plan on a self-contributory basis for a period not to exceed one year after the separation or death.

(3) *Certain employee contributions in lieu of employer contributions.*—This subparagraph (3) applies with respect to a plan that—

(i) Is maintained pursuant to an agreement that the Secretary of Labor finds to be a collective bargaining agreement between employee representatives and one or more employers, and

(ii) Provides that an employer is required to contribute (or contribute in full) on behalf of a participant employee only if the employee completes a minimum number of hours of service with the employer within a stated period ending on or before the date the contribution is otherwise required to be made by the employer.

Such a plan is not other than a qualified plan merely because it permits a participant employee to contribute under the plan an amount not required to be contributed by the employer because the employee fails to complete the minimum number of hours. However, no amount may be contributed by an employee under this subparagraph (3) unless employer contributions on behalf of participant employees are required to be made monthly or more often, and at least one employer contribution is made on behalf of the employee under the plan before the contribution by the employee is made under the plan. In addition, a plan shall not be a qualified plan for a plan year by reason of this subparagraph (3), if amounts contributed by employees under this subparagraph (3) during the plan year exceed 5% of the total amount contributed under the plan during the plan year.

(i) *Definitions.*—For purposes of this section, §1.120-1 and §1.120-3—

(1) *Employee.*—The term "employee" includes—

(i) A retired, disabled or laid-off employee,

(ii) A present employee who is on leave, as, for example, in the Armed Forces of the United States,

(iii) An individual who is self-employed within the meaning of section 401(c)(1), or

(iv) A separated former employee who is covered by the plan by reason of paragraph (h)(2)(i) of this section (relating to employee contributions).

(2) *Employer.*—An individual who owns the entire interest in an unincorporated trade or business is treated as his or her own employer. A partnership is treated as the employer of each partner who is an employee within the meaning of section 401(c)(1).

(3) *Officer.*—An officer is an individual who is an officer within the meaning of regulations prescribed under section 414(c).

(4) *Shareholder.*—The term "shareholder" includes an individual who is a shareholder as determined by the attribution rules under section 1563(d) and (e), without regard to §1563(e)(3)(C).

(5) *Highly compensated.*—The term "highly compensated" has the same meaning as it does for purposes of section 410(b)(1)(B). [Reg. §1.120-2.]

Reduced Retirement Pay

Reduced Retirement Pay: Uniformed Services: Applicable Rules.—Reproduced below is the text of a proposed amendment of Reg. §1.122-1, relating to the applicable rules regarding reduced uniformed services retirement pay (published in the Federal Register on April 30, 1975).

☐ Section 1.122-1 is amended by deleting "72(o)" each place it appears and inserting in lieu thereof "72(n)". As amended, §1.122-1(b)(2)(ii) and examples (2) and (3) of §1.122-(d) read as follows:

§1.122-1. Applicable rules relating to certain reduced uniformed services retirement pay.

* * *

(b) *Rule applicable after December 31, 1965.*—* * *

(2) * * *

(ii) Upon the death of a member or former member of the uniformed services, where the "consideration for the contract" (as described in paragraph (b)(2)(iii) of this section) has not been excluded in whole or in part from gross income under section 122(b) and (b)(2)(i) of this section, the survivor of such member who is receiving an annuity under chapter 73 of title 10 of the United States Code shall, after December 31, 1965, exclude from gross income under section 72(n) and this subdivision such annuity payments received after December 31, 1965, until there has been so excluded annuity payments equalling the portion of the "consideration for the contract" not previously excluded under paragraph (b)(2)(i) of this section.

* * *

(d) *Examples.*—The rules discussed in paragraph (a) of this section may be illustrated by the following examples:

* * *

Example (2). Assume the facts in Example (1) except that A retires on disability resulting from active service and his disability is rated at 40 percent. The entire amount of disability retirement pay, prior to and including 1966, is excludable from gross income under sections 104(a)(4) and 105(d), and in 1966, section 122(a). Assume further that A attains retirement age on December 31, 1966, dies on January 1, 1967, and his widow then begins receiving a survivor annuity under the Retired Serviceman's Family Protection Plan (10 U.S.C. 1431). A's widow may exclude from gross income in 1967 and 1968 under section 72(n) and paragraph (b)(2)(ii) of this section, the $1,800 of "consideration for the contract" i.e., the reductions in 1963, 1964, and 1965 to provide the survivor annuity. Thus, A's widow will exclude all of the survivor annuity she receives in 1967 ($1,350) and $450 of the $1,350 annuity received in 1968. In addition, if A had not attained retirement age at the time of his death, his widow would, under section 101 and paragraph (a)(2) of §1.101-2, exclude up to $5,000 subject to the limitations of paragraph (b)(2)(ii) of this section.

Example (3). Assume, in the previous example, that A dies on January 1, 1965, and his widow then begins receiving a survivor annuity. Assume further that A's widow is entitled to exclude under section 72(b) $1,000 of the $1,350 she received in 1965. Under section 72(n) and paragraph (b)(2)(ii) of this section, A's widow for 1966 will exclude the $200 remaining consideration for the contract ($1,200 – $1,000) and will include $1,150 of the survivor annuity in gross income.

* * *

Employee Benefits: Cafeteria Plans

Employee Benefits: Cafeteria Plans.—Reg. §§1.125-0, 1.125-1, 1.125-2, 1.125-5, 1.125-6 and 1.125-7, providing guidance on cafeteria plans, are proposed (published in the Federal Register on August 6, 2007) (REG-142695-05).

☐ Par. 2. Sections 1.125-0, 1.125-1 and 1.125-2 are added to read as follows:

§1.125-1. Cafeteria plans; general rules.—(a) *Definitions.*—The definitions set forth in this paragraph (a) apply for purposes of section 125 and the regulations.

(1) The term *cafeteria plan* means a separate written plan that complies with the requirements of section 125 and the regulations, that is maintained by an employer for the benefit of its employees and that is operated in compliance with the requirements of section 125 and the regulations. All participants in a cafeteria plan must be employees. A cafeteria plan must offer at least one permitted taxable benefit (as defined in paragraph (a)(2) of this section) and at least one qualified benefit (as defined in paragraph (a)(3) of this section). A cafeteria plan must not provide for deferral of compensation (except as specifically permitted in paragraph (o) of this section).

(2) The term *permitted taxable benefit* means cash and certain other taxable benefits treated as cash for purposes of section 125. For purposes of section 125, *cash* means cash compensation (including salary reduction), payments for annual leave, sick leave, or other

paid time off and severance pay. A distribution from a trust described in section 401(a) is not cash for purposes of section 125. *Other taxable benefits treated as cash* for purposes of section 125 are:

(i) Property;

(ii) Benefits attributable to employer contributions that are currently taxable to the employee upon receipt by the employee; and

(iii) Benefits purchased with after-tax employee contributions, as described in paragraph (h) of this section.

(3) *Qualified benefit.*—Except as otherwise provided in section 125(f) and paragraph (q) of this section, the term *qualified benefit* means any benefit attributable to employer contributions to the extent that such benefit is not currently taxable to the employee by reason of an express provision of the Internal Revenue Code (Code) and which does not defer compensation (except as provided in paragraph (o) of this section). The following benefits are qualified benefits that may be offered under a cafeteria plan and are excludible from employees' gross income when provided in accordance with the applicable provisions of the Code—

(A) Group-term life insurance on the life of an employee in an amount that is less than or equal to the $50,000 excludible from gross income under section 79(a), but not combined with any permanent benefit within the meaning of § 1.79-0;

(B) An accident and health plan excludible from gross income under section 105 or 106, including self-insured medical reimbursement plans (such as health FSAs described in § 1.125-5);

(C) Premiums for COBRA continuation coverage (if excludible under section 106) under the accident and health plan of the employer sponsoring the cafeteria plan or premiums for COBRA continuation coverage of an employee of the employer sponsoring the cafeteria plan under an accident and health plan sponsored by a different employer;

(D) An accidental death and dismemberment insurance policy (section 106);

(E) Long-term or short-term disability coverage (section 106);

(F) Dependent care assistance program (section 129);

(G) Adoption assistance (section 137);

(H) A qualified cash or deferred arrangement that is part of a profit-sharing plan or stock bonus plan, as described in paragraph (o)(3) of this section (section 401(k));

(I) Certain plans maintained by educational organizations (section 125(d)(2)(C) and paragraph (o)(3)(iii) of this section); and

(J) Contributions to Health Savings Accounts (HSAs) (sections 223 and 125(d)(2)(D)).

(4) *Dependent.*—The term *dependent* generally means a dependent as defined in section 152. However, the definition of dependent is modified to conform with the underlying Code section for the qualified benefit. For example, for purposes of a benefit under section 105, the term dependent means a dependent as defined in section 152, determined without regard to section 152(b)(1), (b)(2) or (d)(1)(B).

(5) *Premium-only-plan.*—A *premium-only-plan* is a cafeteria plan that offers as its sole benefit an election between cash (for example, salary) and payment of the employee share of the employer-provided accident and health insurance premium (excludible from the employee's gross income under section 106).

(b) *General rules.*—(1) *Cafeteria plans.*—Section 125 is the exclusive means by which an employer can offer employees an election between taxable and nontaxable benefits without the election itself resulting in inclusion in gross income by the employees. Section 125 provides that cash (including certain taxable benefits) offered to an employee through a nondiscriminatory cafeteria plan is not includible in the employee's gross income merely because the employee has the opportunity to choose among cash and qualified benefits (within the meaning of section 125(e)) through the cafeteria plan. Section 125(a), (d)(1). However, if a plan offering an employee an election between taxable benefits (including cash) and nontaxable qualified benefits does not meet the section 125 requirements, the election between taxable and nontaxable benefits results in gross income to the employee, regardless of what benefit is elected and when the election is made. An employee who has an election among nontaxable benefits and taxable benefits (including cash) that is not through a cafeteria plan that satisfies section 125 must include in gross income the value of the taxable benefit with the greatest value that the employee could have elected to receive, even if the employee elects to receive only the nontaxable benefits offered. The amount of the taxable benefit is includible in the employee's income in the year in which the employee would have actually received the taxable benefit if the employee had elected such benefit. This is the result even if the employee's election between the nontaxable benefits and taxable benefits is made prior to the year in which the employee would

actually have received the taxable benefits. See paragraph (q) in § 1.125-1 for nonqualified benefits.

(2) *Nondiscrimination rules for qualified benefits.*—Accident and health plan coverage, group-term life insurance coverage, and benefits under a dependent care assistance program or adoption assistance program do not fail to be qualified benefits under a cafeteria plan merely because they are includible in gross income because of applicable nondiscrimination requirements (for example, sections 79(d), 105(h), 129(d), 137(c)(2)). See also § § 1.105-11(k) and 1.125-7.

(3) *Examples.*—The following examples illustrate the rules of paragraph (b)(1) of this section.

Example 1. Distributions from qualified pension plan used for health insurance premiums. (i) Employer A maintains a qualified section 401(a) retirement plan for employees. Employer A also provides accident and health insurance (as described in section 106) for employees and former employees, their spouses and dependents. The health insurance premiums are partially paid through a cafeteria plan. None of Employer A's employees are public safety officers. Employer A's health plan allows former employees to elect to have distributions from the qualified retirement plan applied to pay for the health insurance premiums through the cafeteria plan.

(ii) Amounts distributed from the qualified retirement plan which the former employees elect to have applied to pay health insurance premiums through the cafeteria plan are includible in their gross income. The same result occurs if distributions from the qualified retirement plan are applied directly to reimburse section 213(d) medical care expenses incurred by a former employee or his or her spouse or dependents. These distributions are includible in their income, and are not cash for purposes of section 125. The plan is not a cafeteria plan with respect to former employees.

Example 2. Severance pay used to pay COBRA premiums. Employer B maintains a cafeteria plan, which offers employees an election between cash and employer-provided accident and health insurance (excludible from employees' gross income under section 106). Employer B pays terminating employees severance pay. The cafeteria plan also allows a terminating employee to elect between receiving severance pay and using the severance pay to pay the COBRA premiums for the accident and health insurance. These provisions in the cafeteria plan are consistent with the requirements in section 125.

(4) *Election by participants.*—(i) *In general.*—A cafeteria plan must offer participants the opportunity to elect between at least one permitted taxable benefit and at least one qualified benefit. For example, if employees are given the opportunity to elect only among two or more nontaxable benefits, the plan is not a cafeteria plan. Similarly, a plan that only offers the election among salary, permitted taxable benefits, paid time off or other taxable benefits is not a cafeteria plan. See section 125(a), (d). See § 1.125-2 for rules on elections.

(ii) *Premium-only-plan.*—A cafeteria plan may be a premium-only-plan.

(iii) *Examples.*—The following examples illustrate the rules of paragraph (b)(4)(i) of this section.

Example 1. No election. Employer C covers all its employees under its accident and health plan (excludible from employees' gross income under section 106). Coverage is mandatory (that is, employees have no election between cash and the Employer C's accident and health plan). This plan is not a cafeteria plan, because the plan offers employees no election between taxable and nontaxable benefits. The accident and health coverage is excludible from employees' gross income

Example 2. Election between cash and at least one qualified benefit. Employer D offers its employees a plan with an election between cash and an employer-provided accident and health plan (excludible from employees' gross income under section 106). If the plan also satisfies all the other requirements of section 125, the plan is a cafeteria plan because it offers an election between at least one taxable benefit and at least one nontaxable qualified benefit.

Example 3. Election between employer flex-credits and qualified benefits. Employer E offers its employees an election between an employer flex-credit (as defined in paragraph (b) in § 1.125-5) and qualified benefits. If an employee does not elect to apply the entire employer flex-credit to qualified benefits, the employee will receive no cash or other taxable benefit for the unused employer flex-credit. The plan is not a cafeteria plan because it does not offer an election between at least one taxable benefit and at least one nontaxable qualified benefit.

Example 4. No election between cash and qualified benefits for certain employees. (i) Employer F maintains a calendar year plan offering employer-provided accident and health insurance coverage which includes employee-only and family coverage options.

Reg. § 1.125-1(b)(4)(iii)

(ii) The plan provides for an automatic enrollment process when a new employee is hired, or during the annual election period under the plan: only employees who certify that they have other health coverage are permitted to elect to receive cash. Employees who cannot certify are covered by the accident and health insurance on a mandatory basis. Employer F does not otherwise request or collect information from employees regarding other health coverage as part of the enrollment process. If the employee has a spouse or child, the employee can elect between cash and family coverage.

(iii) When an employee is hired, the employee receives a notice explaining the plan's automatic enrollment process. The notice includes the salary reduction amounts for employee-only coverage and family coverage, procedures for certifying whether the employee has other health coverage, elections for family coverage, information on the time by which a certification or election must be made, and the period for which a certification or election will be effective. The notice is also given to each current employee before the beginning of each plan year, (except that the notice for a current employee includes a description of the employee's existing coverage, if any).

(iv) For a new employee, an election to receive cash or to have family coverage is effective if made when the employee is hired. For a current employee, an election is effective if made prior to the start of each calendar year or under any other circumstances permitted under §1.125-4. An election for any prior year carries over to the next succeeding plan year unless changed. Certification that the employee has other health coverage must be made annually.

(v) Contributions used to purchase employer-provided accident and health coverage under section 125 are not includible in an employee's gross income if the employee can elect cash. Section 125 does not apply to the employee-only coverage of an employee who cannot certify that he or she has other health coverage and, therefore, does not have the ability to elect cash in lieu of health coverage.

(5) *No deferred compensation.*—Except as provided in paragraph (o) of this section, in order for a plan to be a cafeteria plan, the qualified benefits and the permitted taxable benefits offered through the cafeteria plan must not defer compensation. For example, a cafeteria plan may not provide for retirement health benefits for current employees beyond the current plan year or group-term life insurance with a permanent benefit, as defined under §1.79-0.

(c) *Written plan requirements.*—(1) *General rule.*—A cafeteria plan must contain in writing the information described in this paragraph (c), and depending on the qualified benefits offered in the plan, may also be required to contain additional information described in paragraphs (c)(2) and (c)(3) of this section. The cafeteria plan must be adopted and effective on or before the first day of the cafeteria plan year to which it relates. The terms of the plan must apply uniformly to all participants. The cafeteria plan document may be comprised of multiple documents. The written cafeteria plan must contain all of the following information—

(i) A specific description of each of the benefits available through the plan, including the periods during which the benefits are provided (the periods of coverage);

(ii) The plan's rules governing participation, and specifically requiring that all participants in the plan be employees;

(iii) The procedures governing employees' elections under the plan, including the period when elections may be made, the periods with respect to which elections are effective, and providing that elections are irrevocable, except to the extent that the optional change in status rules in §1.125-4 are included in the cafeteria plan;

(iv) The manner in which employer contributions may be made under the plan, (for example, through an employee's salary reduction election or by nonelective employer contributions (that is, flex-credits, as defined in paragraph (b) in §1.125-5) or both);

(v) The maximum amount of employer contributions available to any employee through the plan, by stating:

(A) The maximum amount of elective contributions (i.e., salary reduction) available to any employee through the plan, expressed as a maximum dollar amount or a maximum percentage of compensation or the method for determining the maximum dollar amount; and

(B) For contributions to section 401(k) plans, the maximum amount of elective contributions available to any employee through the plan, expressed as a maximum dollar amount or maximum percentage of compensation that may be contributed as elective contributions through the plan by employees.

(vi) The plan year of the cafeteria plan;

(vii) If the plan offers paid time off, the required ordering rule for use of nonelective and elective paid time off in paragraph (o)(4) of this section;

(viii) If the plan includes flexible spending arrangements (as defined in §1.125-5(a)), the plan's provisions complying with any additional requirements for those FSAs (for example, the uniform coverage rule and the use-or-lose rules in paragraphs (d) and (c) in §1.125-5);

(ix) If the plan includes a grace period, the plan's provisions complying with paragraph (e) of this section; and

(x) If the plan includes distributions from a health FSA to employees' HSAs, the plan's provisions complying with paragraph (n) in §1.125-5.

(2) *Additional requirements under sections 105(h), 129, and 137.*— A written plan is required for self-insured medical reimbursement plans (§1.105-11(b)(1)(i)), dependent care assistance programs (section 129(d)(1)), and adoption assistance (section 137(c)). Any of these plans or programs offered through a cafeteria plan that satisfies the written plan requirement in this paragraph (c) for the benefits under these plans and programs also satisfies the written plan requirements in §1.105-11(b)(1)(i), section 129(d)(1), and section 137(c) (whichever is applicable). Alternatively, a self-insured medical reimbursement plan, a dependent care assistance program, or an adoption assistance program is permitted to satisfy the requirements in §1.105-11(b)(1)(i), section 129(d)(1), or section 137(c) (whichever is applicable) through a separate written plan, and not as part of the written cafeteria plan.

(3) *Additional requirements under section 401(k).*—See §1.401(k)-1(e)(7) for additional requirements that must be satisfied in the written plan if the plan offers deferrals into a section 401(k) plan.

(4) *Cross-reference allowed.*—In describing the benefits available through the cafeteria plan, the written cafeteria plan need not be self-contained. For example, the written cafeteria plan may incorporate by reference benefits offered through other *separate written plans*, such as a section 401(k) plan, or coverage under a dependent care assistance program (section 129), without describing in full the benefits established through these other plans. But, for example, if the cafeteria plan offers different maximum levels of coverage for dependent care assistance programs, the descriptions in the separate written plan must specify the available maximums.

(5) *Amendments to cafeteria plan.*—Any amendment to the cafeteria plan must be in writing. A cafeteria plan is permitted to be amended at any time during a plan year. However, the amendment is only permitted to be effective for periods after the later of the adoption date or effective date of the amendment. For an amendment adding a new benefit, the cafeteria plan must pay or reimburse only those expenses for new benefits incurred after the later of the amendment's adoption date or effective date.

(6) *Failure to satisfy written plan requirements.*—If there is no written cafeteria plan, or if the written plan fails to satisfy any of the requirements in this paragraph (c) (including cross-referenced requirements), the plan is not a cafeteria plan and an employee's election between taxable and nontaxable benefits results in gross income to the employee.

(7) *Operational failure.*—(i) *In general.*—If the cafeteria plan fails to operate according to its written plan or otherwise fails to operate in compliance with section 125 and the regulations, the plan is not a cafeteria plan and employees' elections between taxable and nontaxable benefits result in gross income to the employees.

(ii) *Failure to operate according to written cafeteria plan or section 125.*—Examples of failures resulting in section 125 not applying to a plan include the following—

(A) Paying or reimbursing expenses for qualified benefits incurred before the later of the adoption date or effective date of the cafeteria plan, before the beginning of a period of coverage or before the later of the date of adoption or effective date of a plan amendment adding a new benefit;

(B) Offering benefits other than permitted taxable benefits and qualified benefits;

(C) Operating to defer compensation (except as permitted in paragraph (o) of this section);

(D) Failing to comply with the uniform coverage rule in paragraph (d) in §1.125-5;

(E) Failing to comply with the use-or-lose rule in paragraph (c) in §1.125-5;

(F) Allowing employees to revoke elections or make new elections, except as provided in §1.125-4 and paragraph (a) in §1.125-2;

(G) Failing to comply with the substantiation requirements of §1.125-6;

(H) Paying or reimbursing expenses in an FSA other than expenses expressly permitted in paragraph (h) in §1.125-5;

(I) Allocating experience gains other than as expressly permitted in paragraph (o) in §1.125-5;

(J) Failing to comply with the grace period rules in paragraph (e) of this section; or

(K) Failing to comply with the qualified HSA distribution rules in paragraph (n) in §1.125-5.

(d) *Plan year requirements.*—(1) *Twelve consecutive months.*—The plan year must be specified in the cafeteria plan. The plan year of a cafeteria plan must be twelve consecutive months, unless a short plan year is allowed under this paragraph (d). A plan year is permitted to begin on any day of any calendar month and must end on the preceding day in the immediately following year (for example, a plan year that begins on October 15, 2007, must end on October 14, 2008). A calendar year plan year is a period of twelve consecutive months beginning on January 1 and ending on December 31 of the same calendar year. A plan year specified in the cafeteria plan is effective for the first plan year of a cafeteria plan and for all subsequent plan years, unless changed as provided in paragraph (d)(2) of this section.

(2) *Changing plan year.*—The plan year is permitted to be changed only for a valid business purpose. A change in the plan year is not permitted if a principal purpose of the change in plan year is to circumvent the rules of section 125 or these regulations. If a change in plan year does not satisfy this subparagraph, the attempt to change the plan year is ineffective and the plan year of the cafeteria plan remains the same.

(3) *Short plan year.*—A short plan year of less than twelve consecutive months is permitted for a valid business purpose.

(4) *Examples.*—The following examples illustrate the rules in paragraph (d) of this section:

Example 1. Employer with calendar year. Employer G, with a calendar taxable year, first establishes a cafeteria plan effective July 1, 2009. The cafeteria plan specifies a calendar plan year. The first cafeteria plan year is the period beginning on July 1, 2009, and ending on December 31, 2009. Employer G has a business purpose for a short first cafeteria plan year.

Example 2. Employer changes insurance carrier. Employer H establishes a cafeteria plan effective January 1, 2009, with a calendar year plan year. The cafeteria plan offers an accident and health plan through Insurer X. In March 2010, Employer H contracts to provide accident and health insurance through another insurance company, Y. Y's accident and health insurance is offered on a July 1-June 30 benefit year. Effective July 1, 2010, Employer H amends the plan to change to a July 1-June 30 plan year. Employer H has a business purpose for changing the cafeteria plan year and for the short plan year ending June 30, 2010.

(5) *Significance of plan year.*—The plan year generally is the coverage period for benefits provided through the cafeteria plan to which annual elections for these benefits apply. Benefits elected pursuant to the employee's election for a plan year generally may not be carried forward to subsequent plan years. However, see the grace period rule in paragraph (e) of this section.

(e) *Grace period.*—(1) *In general.*—A cafeteria plan may, at the employer's option, include a grace period of up to the fifteenth day of the third month immediately following the end of each plan year. If a cafeteria plan provides for a grace period, an employee who has unused benefits or contributions relating to a qualified benefit (for example, health flexible spending arrangement (health FSA) or dependent care assistance) from the immediately preceding plan year, and who incurs expenses for that same qualified benefit during the grace period, may be paid or reimbursed for those expenses from the unused benefits or contributions as if the expenses had been incurred in the immediately preceding plan year. A grace period is available for all qualified benefits described in paragraph (a)(3) of this section, except that the grace period does not apply to paid time off and elective contributions under a section 401(k) plan. The effect of the grace period is that the employee may have as long as 14 months and 15 days (that is, the 12 months in the current cafeteria plan year plus the grace period) to use the benefits or contributions for a plan year before those amounts are *forfeited* under the *use-or-lose* rule in paragraph (c) in § 1.125-5. If the grace period is added to a cafeteria plan through an amendment, all requirements in paragraph (c) of this section must be satisfied.

(2) *Grace period optional features.*—A grace period provision may contain any or all of the following—

(i) The grace period may apply to some qualified benefits described in paragraph (a)(3) of this section, but not to others;

(ii) The grace period provision may limit the amount of unused benefits or contributions available during the grace period. The limit must be uniform and apply to all participants. However, the limit must not be based on a percentage of the amount of the unused benefits or contributions remaining at the end of the immediately prior plan year;

(iii) The last day of the grace period may be sooner than the fifteenth day of the third month immediately following the end of the plan year (that is, the grace period may be shorter than two and one half months);

(iv) The grace period provision is permitted to treat expenses for qualified benefits incurred during the grace period either as expenses incurred during the immediately preceding plan year or as expenses incurred during the current plan year (for example, the plan may first apply the unused contributions or benefits from the immediately preceding year to pay or reimburse grace period expenses and then, when the unused contributions and benefits from the prior year are exhausted, the grace period expenses may be paid from current year contributions and benefits.); and

(v) The grace period provision may permit the employer to defer the allocation of expenses described in paragraph (e)(2)(iv) of this section until after the end of the grace period.

(3) *Grace period requirements.*—A grace period must satisfy the requirements in paragraph (c) of this section and all of the following requirements:

(i) The grace period provisions in the cafeteria plan (including optional provisions in paragraph (e)(2) of this section) must apply uniformly to all participants in the cafeteria plan, determined as of the last day of the plan year. Participants in the cafeteria plan through COBRA and participants who were participants as of the last day of the plan year but terminate during the grace period are participants for purposes of the grace period. See § 54.4980B-2, Q & A-8 of this chapter;

(ii) The grace period provision in the cafeteria plan must state that unused benefits or contributions relating to a particular qualified benefit may only be used to pay or reimburse expenses incurred with respect to the same qualified benefit. For example, unused amounts elected to pay or reimburse medical expenses in a health FSA may not be used to pay or reimburse dependent care expenses incurred during the grace period; and

(iii) The grace period provision in the cafeteria plan must state that to the extent any unused benefits or contributions from the immediately preceding plan year exceed the expenses for the qualified benefit incurred during the grace period, those remaining unused benefits or contributions may not be carried forward to any subsequent period (including any subsequent plan year), cannot be cashed-out and must be forfeited under the use-or-lose rule. See paragraph (c) in § 1.125-5

(4) *Examples.*—The following examples illustrate the rules in this paragraph (e).

Example 1. Expenses incurred during grace period and immediately following plan year. (i) Employer I's calendar year cafeteria plan includes a grace period allowing all participants to apply unused benefits or contributions remaining at the end of the plan year to qualified benefits incurred during the grace period immediately following that plan year. The grace period for the plan year ending December 31, 2009, ends on March 15, 2010.

(ii) Employee X timely elected salary reduction of $1,000 for a health FSA for the plan year ending December 31, 2009. As of December 31, 2009, X has $200 remaining unused in his health FSA. X timely elected salary reduction for a health FSA of $1,500 for the plan year ending December 31, 2010.

(iii) During the grace period from January 1 through March 15, 2010, X incurs $300 of unreimbursed medical expenses (as defined in section 213(d)). The unused $200 from the plan year ending December 31, 2009, is applied to pay or reimburse $200 of X's $300 of medical expenses incurred during the grace period. Therefore, as of March 16, 2010, X has no unused benefits or contributions remaining for the plan year ending December 31, 2009.

(iv) The remaining $100 of medical expenses incurred between January 1 and March 15, 2010, is paid or reimbursed from X's health FSA for the plan year ending December 31, 2010. As of March 16, 2010, X has $1,400 remaining in the health FSA for the plan year ending December 31, 2010.

Example 2. Unused benefits exceed expenses incurred during grace period. Same facts as *Example 1*, except that X incurs $150 of section 213(d) medical expenses during the grace period (January 1 through March 15, 2010). As of March 16, 2010, X has $50 of unused benefits or contributions remaining for the plan year ending December 31, 2009. The unused $50 cannot be cashed-out, converted to any other taxable or nontaxable benefit, or used in any other plan year (including the plan year ending December 31, 2009). The unused $50 is subject to the use-or-lose rule in paragraph (c) in § 1.125-5 and is forfeited. As of March 16, 2010, X has the entire $1,500 elected in the health FSA for the plan year ending December 31, 2010.

Example 3. Terminated participants. (i) Employer J's cafeteria plan includes a grace period allowing all participants to apply unused benefits or contributions remaining at the end of the plan year to qualified benefits incurred during the grace period immediately following that plan year. For the plan year ending on December 31, 2009, the grace period ends March 15, 2010.

(ii) Employees A, B, C, and D each timely elected $1,200 salary reduction for a health FSA for the plan year ending December 31, 2009. Employees A and B terminated employment on September 15, 2009. Each has $500 of unused benefits or contributions in the health FSA.

(iii) Employee A elected COBRA for the health FSA. Employee A is a participant in the cafeteria plan as of December 31, 2009, the last day of the 2009 plan year. Employee A has $500 of unused benefits or contributions available during the grace period for the 2009 plan year (ending March 15, 2010).

(iv) Employee B did not elect COBRA for the health FSA. Employee B is not a participant in a cafeteria plan as of December 31, 2009. The grace period does not apply to Employee B.

(v) Employee C has $500 of unused benefits in his health FSA as of December 31, 2009, and terminated employment on January 15, 2010. Employee C is a participant in the cafeteria plan as of December 31, 2009 and has $500 of unused benefits or contributions available during the grace period ending March 15, 2010, even though he terminated employment on January 15, 2010.

(vi) Employee D continues to work for Employer H throughout 2009 and 2010, also has $500 of unused benefits or contributions in his health FSA as of December 31, 2009, but made no health FSA election for 2010. Employee D is a participant in the cafeteria plan as of December 31, 2009 and has $500 of unused benefits or contributions available during the grace period ending March 15, 2010, even though he is not a participant in a health FSA for the 2010 plan year.

(f) *Run-out period.*—A cafeteria plan is permitted to contain a run-out period as designated by the employer. A run-out period is a period after the end of the plan year (or grace period) during which a participant can submit a claim for reimbursement for a qualified benefit incurred during the plan year (or grace period). Thus, a plan is also permitted to provide a deadline on or after the end of the plan year (or grace period) for submitting a claim for reimbursement for the plan year. Any run-out period must be provided on a uniform and consistent basis with respect to all participants.

(g) *Employee for purposes of section 125.*—(1) *Current employees, former employees.*—The term employee includes any current or former employee (including any laid-off employee or retired employee) of the employer. See paragraph (g)(3) of this section concerning limits on participation by former employees. Specifically, the term *employee* includes the following—

(i) Common law employee;

(ii) Leased employee described in section 414(n);

(iii) Full-time life insurance salesman (as defined in section 7701(a)(20)); and

(iv) A current employee or former employee described in paragraphs (g)(1)(i) through (iii) of this section.

(2) *Self-employed individual not an employee.*—(i) *In general.*—The term *employee* does not include a self-employed individual or a 2-percent shareholder of an S corporation, as defined in paragraph (g)(2)(ii) of this subsection. For example, a sole proprietor, a partner in a partnership, or a director solely serving on a corporation's board of directors (and not otherwise providing services to the corporation as an employee) is not an employee for purposes of section 125, and thus is not permitted to participate in a cafeteria plan. However, a sole proprietor may sponsor a cafeteria plan covering the sole proprietor's employees (but not the sole proprietor). Similarly, a partnership or S corporation may sponsor a cafeteria plan covering employees (but not a partner or 2-percent shareholder of an S corporation).

(ii) *Two percent shareholder of an S corporation.*—A 2-percent shareholder of an S corporation has the meaning set forth in section 1372(b).

(iii) *Certain dual status individuals.*—If an individual is an employee of an employer and also provides services to that employer as an independent contractor or director (for example, an individual is both a director and an employee of a C corp), the individual is eligible to participate in that employer's cafeteria plan solely in his or her capacity as an employee. This rule does not apply to partners or to 2-percent shareholders of an S corporation.

(iv) *Examples.*—The following examples illustrate the rules in paragraphs (g)(2)(ii) and (g)(2)(iii) of this section:

Example 1. Two-percent shareholders of an S corporation. (i) Employer K, an S corporation, maintains a cafeteria plan for its employees (other than 2-percent shareholders of an S corporation). Employer K's taxable year and the plan year are the calendar year. On January 1, 2009, individual Z owns 5 percent of the outstanding stock in Employer K. Y, who owns no stock in Employer K, is married to Z. Y and Z are employees of Employer K. Z is a 2-percent shareholder in Employer K (as defined in section 1372(b)). Y is also a 2-percent shareholder in Employer K by operation of the attribution rules in section 318(a)(1)(A)(i).

(ii) On July 15, 2009, Z sells all his stock in Employer K to an unrelated third party, and ceases to be a 2-percent shareholder. Y and Z continue to work as employees of Employer K during the entire

2009 calendar year. Y and Z are ineligible to participate in Employer K's cafeteria plan for the 2009 plan year.

Example 2. Director and employee. T is an employee and also a director of Employer L, a C corp that sponsors a cafeteria plan. The cafeteria plan allows only employees of Employer L to participate in the cafeteria plan. T's annual compensation as an employee is $50,000; T is also paid $3,000 annually in director's fees. T makes a timely election to salary reduce $5,000 from his employee compensation for dependent care benefits. T makes no election with respect to his compensation as a director. T may participate in the cafeteria plan in his capacity as an employee of Employer L.

(3) *Limits on participation by former employees.*—Although former employees are treated as employees, a cafeteria plan may not be established or maintained predominantly for the benefit of former employees of the employer. Such a plan is not a cafeteria plan.

(4) *No participation by the spouse or dependent of an employee.*—(i) *Benefits allowed to participant's spouse or dependents but not participation.*—The spouse or dependents of employees may not be participants in a cafeteria plan unless they are also employees. However, a cafeteria plan may provide benefits to spouses and dependents of participants. For example, although an employee's spouse may benefit from the employee's election of accident and health insurance coverage or of coverage through a dependent care assistance program, the spouse may not participate in a cafeteria plan (that is, the spouse may not be given the opportunity to elect or purchase benefits offered by the plan).

(ii) *Certain elections after employee's death.*—An employee's spouse is not a participant in a cafeteria plan merely because the spouse has the right, upon the death of the employee, to elect among various settlement options or to elect among permissible distribution options with respect to the deceased employee's benefits through a section 401(k) plan, Health Savings Account, or certain group-term life insurance offered through the cafeteria plan. See § 54.4980B-2, Q & A 8 and § 54.4980B-4, Q & A-1 of this chapter on COBRA rights of a participant's spouse or dependents.

(5) *Employees of certain controlled groups.*—All employees who are treated as employed by a single employer under section 414(b), (c), (m), or (o) are treated as employed by a single employer for purposes of section 125. Section 125(g)(4); section 414(t).

(h) *After-tax employee contributions.*—(1) *Certain after-tax employee contributions treated as cash.*—In addition to the cash benefits described in paragraph (a)(2) of this section, in general, a benefit is treated as cash for purposes of section 125 if the benefit does not defer compensation (except as provided in paragraph (o) of this section) and an employee who receives the benefit purchases such benefit with after-tax employee contributions or is treated, for all purposes under the Code (including, for example, reporting and withholding purposes), as receiving, at the time that the benefit is received, cash compensation equal to the full value of the benefit at that time and then purchasing the benefit with after-tax employee contributions. Thus, for example, long-term disability coverage is treated as cash for purposes of section 125 if the cafeteria plan provides that an employee may purchase the coverage through the cafeteria plan with after-tax employee contributions or provides that the employee receiving such coverage is treated as having received cash compensation equal to the value of the coverage and then as having purchased the coverage with after-tax employee contributions. Also, for example, a cafeteria plan may offer employees the opportunity to purchase, with after-tax employee contributions, group-term life insurance on the life of an employee (providing no permanent benefits), an accident and health plan, or a dependent care assistance program.

(2) *Accident and health coverage purchased for someone other than the employee's spouse or dependents with after-tax employee contributions.*—If the requirements of section 106 are satisfied, employer-provided accident and health coverage for an employee and his or her spouse or dependents is excludible from the employee's gross income. The fair market value of coverage for any other individual, provided with respect to the employee, is includible in the employee's gross income. § 1.106-1; § 1.61-21(a)(4), and § 1.61-21(b)(1). A cafeteria plan is permitted to allow employees to elect accident and health coverage for an individual who is not the spouse or dependent of the employee as a taxable benefit.

(3) *Example.*—The following example illustrates the rules of this paragraph (h):

Example. Accident and health plan coverage for individuals who are not a spouse or dependent of an employee. (i) Employee C participates in Employer M's cafeteria plan. Employee C timely elects salary reduction for employer-provided accident and health coverage for himself and for accident and health coverage for his former spouse. C's former spouse is not C's dependent. A former spouse is not a spouse as defined in section 152.

(ii) The fair market value of the coverage for the former spouse is $1,000. Employee C has $1,000 includible in gross income for the accident and health coverage of his former spouse, because the section 106 exclusion applies only to employer-provided accident and health coverage for the employee or the employee's spouse or dependents.

(iii) No payments or reimbursements received under the accident and health coverage result in gross income to Employee C or to the former spouse. The result is the same if the $1,000 for coverage of C's former spouse is paid from C's after-tax income outside the cafeteria plan.

(i) *Prohibited taxable benefits.*—Any taxable benefit not described in paragraph (a)(2) of this section and not treated as cash for purposes of section 125 in paragraph (h) of this section is not permitted to be included in a cafeteria plan. A plan that offers taxable benefits other than the taxable benefits described in paragraph (a)(2) and (h) of this section is not a cafeteria plan.

(j) *Coordination with other rules.*—(1) *In general.*—If a benefit is excludible from an employee's gross income when provided separately, the benefit is excludible from gross income when provided through a cafeteria plan. Thus, a qualified benefit is excludible from gross income if both the rules under section 125 and the specific rules providing for the exclusion of the benefit from gross income are satisfied. For example, if the nondiscrimination rules for specific qualified benefits (for example, sections 79(d), 105(h), 129(d)(2), 137(c)(2)) are not satisfied, those qualified benefits are includible in gross income. Thus, if $50,000 in group-term life insurance is offered through a cafeteria plan, the nondiscrimination rules in section 79(d) must be satisfied in order to exclude the coverage from gross income.

(2) *Section 125 nondiscrimination rules.*—Qualified benefits are includible in the gross income of highly compensated participants or key employees if the nondiscrimination rules of section 125 are not satisfied. See § 1.125-7.

(3) *Taxable benefits.*—If a benefit that is includible in gross income when offered separately is offered through a cafeteria plan, the benefit continues to be includible in gross income.

(k) *Group-term life insurance.*—(1) *In general.*—In addition to offering up to $50,000 in group-term life insurance coverage excludible under section 79(a), a cafeteria plan may offer coverage in excess of that amount. The cost of coverage in excess of $50,000 in group-term life insurance coverage provided under a policy or policies carried directly or indirectly by one or more employers (taking into account all coverage provided both through a cafeteria plan and outside a cafeteria plan) is includible in an employee's gross income. Group-term life insurance combined with permanent benefits, within the meaning of § 1.79-0, is a prohibited benefit in a cafeteria plan.

(2) *Determining cost of insurance includible in employee's gross income.*—(i) *In general.*—If the aggregate group-term life insurance coverage on the life of the employee (under policies carried directly or indirectly by the employer) exceeds $50,000, all or a portion of the insurance is provided through a cafeteria plan, and the group-term life insurance is provided through a plan that meets the nondiscrimination rules of section 79(d), the amount includible in an employee's gross income is determined under paragraphs (k)(2)(i)(A) through (C) of this section. For each employee—

(A) The entire amount of salary reduction and employer flex-credits through a cafeteria plan for group-term life insurance coverage on the life of the employee is excludible from the employee's gross income, regardless of the amount of employer-provided group-term life insurance on the employee's life (that is, whether or not the coverage provided to the employee both through the cafeteria plan and outside the cafeteria plan exceeds $50,000);

(B) The cost of the group-term life insurance in excess of $50,000 of coverage is includible in the employee's gross income. The amount includible in the employee's income is determined using the rules of § 1.79-3 and Table I (*Uniform Premiums for $1,000 of Group-Term Life Insurance Protection*). See subparagraph (C) of this paragraph (k)(2)(i) for determining the amount paid by the employee for purposes of reducing the Table I amount includible in income under § 1.79-3.

(C) In determining the amount paid by the employee toward the purchase of the group-term life insurance for purposes of § 1.79-3, only an employee's after-tax contributions are treated as an amount paid by the employee.

(ii) *Examples.*—The rules in this paragraph (k) are illustrated by the following examples, in which the group-term life insurance coverage satisfies the nondiscrimination rules in section 79(d), provides no permanent benefits, is for a 12-month period, is the only group-term life insurance coverage provided under a policy carried directly or indirectly by the employer, and applies Table I (*Uniform Premiums for $1,000 of Group-Term Life Insurance Protection*) effective July 1, 1999:

Example 1. Excess group-term life insurance coverage provided through salary reduction in a cafeteria plan. (i) Employer N provides group-term life insurance coverage to its employees only through its cafeteria plan. Employer N's cafeteria plan allows employees to elect salary reduction for group-term life insurance. Employee B, age 42, elected salary reduction of $200 for $150,000 of group-term life insurance. None of the group-term life insurance is paid through after-tax employee contributions.

(ii) B's $200 of salary reduction for group-term life insurance is excludible from B's gross income under paragraph (k)(2)(i)(A).

(iii) B has a total of $150,000 of group-term life insurance. The group-term life insurance in excess of the dollar limitation of section 79 is $100,000 (150,000 – 50,000).

(iv) The Table I cost is $120 for $100,000 of group-term life insurance for an individual between ages 40 to 44. The Table I cost of $120 is reduced by zero (because B paid no portion of the group-term life insurance with after-tax employee contributions), under paragraphs (k)(2)(i)(A)-(B) of this section.

(v) The amount includible in B's gross income for the $100,000 of excess group-term life insurance is $120.

Example 2. Excess group-term life insurance coverage provided through salary reduction in a cafeteria plan where employee purchases a portion of group-term life insurance coverage with after-tax contributions. (i) Same facts as *Example 1*, except that B elected salary reduction of $100 and makes an after-tax contribution of $100 toward the purchase of group-term life insurance coverage.

(ii) B's $100 of salary reduction for group-term life insurance is excludible from B's gross income, under paragraph (k)(2)(i)(A) of this section.

(iii) B has a total of $150,000 of group-term life insurance. The group-term life insurance in excess of the dollar limitation of section 79 is $100,000 (150,000 – 50,000).

(iv) The Table I cost is $120 for $100,000 of group-term life insurance for an individual between ages 40 to 44, under (k)(2)(i)(B). The Table I cost of $120 is reduced by $100 (because B paid $100 for the group-term life insurance with after-tax employee contributions), under paragraphs (k)(2)(i)(B) and (k)(2)(i)(C) of this section.

(v) The amount includible in B's gross income for the $100,000 of excess group-term life insurance coverage is $20.

Example 3. Excess group-term life insurance coverage provided through salary reduction in a cafeteria plan and outside a cafeteria plan. (i) Same facts as *Example 1* except that Employer N also provides (at no cost to employees) group-term life insurance coverage equal to each employee's annual salary. Employee B's annual salary is $150,000. B has $150,000 of group-term life insurance directly from Employer N, and also $150,000 coverage through Employer N's cafeteria plan.

(ii) B's $200 of salary reduction for group-term life insurance is excludible from B's gross income, under paragraph (k)(2)(i)(A) of this section.

(iii) B has a total of $300,000 of group-term life insurance. The group-term life insurance in excess of the dollar limitation of section 79 is $250,000 (300,000 – 50,000).

(iv) The Table I cost is $300 for $250,000 of group-term life insurance for an individual between ages 40 to 44. The Table I cost of $300 is reduced by zero (because B paid no portion of the group-term life insurance with after-tax employee contributions), under paragraphs (k)(2)(i)(B) and (k)(2)(i)(C) of this section.

(v) The amount includible in B's gross income for the $250,000 of excess group-term life insurance is $300.

Example 4. Excess group-term life insurance coverage provided through salary reduction in a cafeteria plan and outside a cafeteria plan. (i) Same facts as *Example 3* except that Employee C's annual salary is $30,000. C has $30,000 of group-term life insurance coverage provided directly from Employer N, and elects an additional $30,000 of coverage for $40 through Employer N's cafeteria plan. C is 42 years old.

(ii) C's $40 of salary reduction for group-term life insurance is excludible from C's gross income, under paragraph (k)(2)(i)(A) of this section.

(iii) C has a total of $60,000 of group-term life insurance. The group-term life insurance in excess of the dollar limitation of section 79 is $10,000 (60,000 – 50,000).

(iv) The Table I cost is $12 for $10,000 of group-term life insurance for an individual between ages 40 to 44. The Table I cost of $12 is reduced by zero (because C paid no portion of the group-term life insurance with after-tax employee contributions), under paragraphs (k)(2)(i)(B) and (k)(2)(i)(C) of this section.

(v) The amount includible in C's gross income for the $10,000 of excess group-term life insurance coverage is $12.

(l) *COBRA premiums.*—(1) *Paying COBRA premiums through a cafeteria plan.*—Under §1.125-4(c)(3)(iv), COBRA premiums for an employer-provided group health plan are qualified benefits if:

(i) The premiums are excludible from an employee's income under section 106; or

(ii) The premiums are for the accident and health plan of the employer sponsoring the cafeteria plan, even if the fair market value of the premiums is includible in an employee's gross income. See also paragraph (e)(2) in §1.125-5 and §54.4980B-2, Q & A-8 of this chapter for COBRA rules for health FSAs.

(2) *Example.*—The following example illustrates the rules of this paragraph (l):

Example. COBRA premiums. (i) Employer O maintains a cafeteria plan for full-time employees, offering an election between cash and employer-provided accident and health insurance and other qualified benefits. Employees A, B, and C participate in the cafeteria plan. On July 1, 2009, Employee A has a qualifying event (as defined in §54.4980B-4 of this chapter).

(ii) Employee A was a full-time employee and became a part-time employee and for that reason, is no longer covered by Employer O's accident and health plan. Under §1.125-4(f)(3)(ii), Employee A changes her election to salary reduce to pay her COBRA premiums.

(iii) Employee B previously worked for another employer, quit and elected COBRA. Employee B begins work for Employer O on July 1, 2009, and becomes eligible to participate in Employer O's cafeteria plan on July 1, 2009, but will not be eligible to participate in Employer O's accident and health plan until October 1, 2009. Employee B elects to salary reduce to pay COBRA premiums for coverage under the accident and health plan sponsored by B's former employer.

(iv) Employee C and C's spouse are covered by Employer O's accident and health plan until July 1, 2009, when C's divorce from her spouse became final. C continues to be covered by the accident and health plan. On July 1, 2009, C requests to pay COBRA premiums for her former spouse (who is not C's dependent (as defined in section 152)) with after-tax employee contributions.

(v) Salary reduction elections for COBRA premiums for Employees A and B are qualified benefits for purposes of section 125 and are excludible from the gross income of Employees A and B. Employer O allows A and B to salary reduce for these COBRA premiums.

(vi) Employer O allows C to pay for COBRA premiums for C's former spouse, with after-tax employee contributions because although accident and health coverage for C's former spouse is permitted in a cafeteria plan, the premiums are includible in C's gross income.

(vii) The operation of Employer O's cafeteria plan satisfies the requirements of this paragraph (l).

(m) *Payment or reimbursement of employees' individual accident and health insurance premiums.*—(1) *In general.*—The payment or reimbursement of employees' substantiated individual health insurance premiums is excludible from employees' gross income under section 106 and is a qualified benefit for purposes of section 125.

(2) *Example.*—The following example illustrates the rule of this paragraph (m):

Example. Payment or reimbursement of premiums. (i) Employer P's cafeteria plan offers the following benefits for employees who are covered by an individual health insurance policy. The employee substantiates the expenses for the premiums for the policy (as required in paragraph (b)(2) in §1.125-6) before any payments or reimbursements to the employee for premiums are made. The payments or reimbursements are made in the following ways:

(ii) The cafeteria plan reimburses each employee directly for the amount of the employee's substantiated health insurance premium;

(iii) The cafeteria plan issues the employee a check payable to the health insurance company for the amount of the employee's health insurance premium, which the employee is obligated to tender to the insurance company;

(iv) The cafeteria plan issues a check in the same manner as (iii), except that the check is payable jointly to the employee and the insurance company; or

(v) Under these circumstances, the individual health insurance policies are accident and health plans as defined in §1.106-1. This benefit is a qualified benefit under section 125.

(n) *Section 105 rules for accident and health plan offered through a cafeteria plan.*—(1) *General rule.*—In order for an accident and health plan to be a qualified benefit that is excludible from gross income if elected through a cafeteria plan, the cafeteria plan must satisfy section 125 and the accident and health plan must satisfy section 105(b) and (h).

(2) *Section 105(b) requirements in general.*—Section 105(b) provides an exclusion from gross income for amounts paid to an employee from an employer-funded accident and health plan specifically to reimburse the employee for certain expenses for medical care (as defined in section 213(d)) incurred by the employee or the employee's spouse or dependents during the period for which the benefit is provided to the employee (that is, when the employee is covered by the accident and health plan).

(o) *Prohibition against deferred compensation.*—(1) *In general.*—Any plan that offers a benefit that defers compensation (except as provided in this paragraph (o)) is not a cafeteria plan. See section 125(d)(2)(A). A plan that permits employees to carry over unused elective contributions, after-tax contributions, or plan benefits from one plan year to another (except as provided in paragraphs (e), (o)(3) and (4) and (p) of this section) defers compensation. This is the case regardless of how the contributions or benefits are used by the employee in the subsequent plan year (for example, whether they are automatically or electively converted into another taxable or nontaxable benefit in the subsequent plan year or used to provide additional benefits of the same type). Similarly, a cafeteria plan also defers compensation if the plan permits employees to use contributions for one plan year to purchase a benefit that will be provided in a subsequent plan year (for example, life, health or disability if these benefits have a savings or investment feature, such as whole life insurance). See also Q & A-5 in §1.125-3, prohibiting deferring compensation from one cafeteria plan year to a subsequent cafeteria plan year. See paragraph (e) of this section for grace period rules. A plan does not defer compensation merely because it allocates experience gains (or forfeitures) among participants in compliance with paragraph (o) in §1.125-5.

(2) *Effect if a plan includes a benefit that defers the receipt of compensation or a plan operates to defer compensation.*—If a plan violates paragraph (o)(1) of this section, the availability of an election between taxable and nontaxable benefits under such a plan results in gross income to the employees.

(3) *Cash or deferred arrangements that may be offered in a cafeteria plan.*—(i) *In general.*—A cafeteria plan may offer the benefits set forth in this paragraph (o)(3), even though these benefits defer compensation.

(ii) *Elective contributions to a section 401(k) plan.*—A cafeteria plan may permit a covered employee to elect to have the employer, on behalf of the employee, pay amounts as contributions to a trust that is part of a profit-sharing or stock bonus plan or rural cooperative plan (within the meaning of section 401(k)(7)), which includes a qualified cash or deferred arrangement (as defined in section 401(k)(2)). In addition, after-tax employee contributions under a qualified plan subject to section 401(m) are permitted through a cafeteria plan. The right to make such contributions does not cause a plan to fail to be a cafeteria plan merely because, under the qualified plan, employer matching contributions (as defined in section 401(m)(4)(A)) are made with respect to elective or after-tax employee contributions.

(iii) *Additional permitted deferred compensation arrangements.*—A plan maintained by an educational organization described in section 170(b)(1)(A)(ii) to the extent of amounts which a covered employee may elect to have the employer pay as contributions for post-retirement group life insurance is permitted through a cafeteria plan, if—

(A) All contributions for such insurance must be made before retirement; and

(B) Such life insurance does not have a cash surrender value at any time.

(iv) *Contributions to HSAs.*—Contributions to covered employees' HSAs as defined in section 223 (but not contributions to Archer MSAs).

(4) *Paid time off.*—(i) *In general.*—A cafeteria plan is permitted to include elective paid time off (that is, vacation days, sick days or personal days) as a permitted taxable benefit through the plan by permitting employees to receive more paid time off than the employer otherwise provides to the employees on a nonelective basis, but only if the inclusion of elective paid time off through the plan does not operate to permit the deferral of compensation. In addition, a plan that only offers the choice of cash or paid time off is not a cafeteria plan and is not subject to the rules of section 125. In order to avoid deferral of compensation, the cafeteria plan must preclude any employee from using the paid time off or receiving cash, in a subsequent plan year, for any portion of such paid time off remaining unused as of the end of the plan year. (See paragraph (o)(4)(iii) of this section for the deadline to cash out unused elective paid time off.) For example, a plan that offers employees the opportunity to purchase paid time off (or to receive cash or other benefits through

the plan in lieu of paid time off) is not a cafeteria plan if employees who purchase the paid time off for a plan year are allowed to use any unused paid time off in a subsequent plan year. This is the case even though the plan does not permit the employee to convert, in any subsequent plan year, the unused paid time off into any other benefit.

(ii) *Ordering of elective and nonelective paid time off.*—In determining whether a plan providing paid time off operates to permit the deferral of compensation, a cafeteria plan must provide that employees are deemed to use paid time off in the following order:

(A) *Nonelective paid time off.*—Nonelective paid time off (that is, paid time off with respect to which the employee has no election) is used first;

(B) *Elective paid time off.*—Elective paid time off is used after all nonelective paid time off is used.

(iii) *Cashing out or forfeiture of unused elective paid time off, in general.*—The cafeteria plan must provide that all unused elective paid time off (determined as of the last day of the plan year) must either be paid in cash (within the time specified in this paragraph (o)(4)) or be forfeited. This provision must apply uniformly to all participants in the cafeteria plan.

(A) *Cash out of unused elective paid time off.*—A plan does not operate to permit the deferral of compensation merely because the plan provides that an employee who has not used all elective paid time off for a plan year receives in cash the value of such unused paid time off. The employee must receive the cash on or before the last day of the cafeteria plan's plan year to which the elective contributions used to purchase the unused elective paid time off relate.

(B) *Forfeiture of unused elective paid time off.*—If the cafeteria plan provides for forfeiture of unused elective paid time off, the forfeiture must be effective on the last day of the plan year to which the elective contributions relate.

(iv) *No grace period for paid time off.*—The grace period described in paragraph (e) of this section does not apply to paid time off.

(v) *Examples.*—The following examples illustrate the rules of this paragraph (o)(4):

Example 1. Plan cashes out unused elective paid time off on or before the last day of the plan year. (i) Employer Q provides employees with two weeks of paid time off for each calendar year. Employer Q's human resources policy (that is, outside the cafeteria plan), permits employees to carry over one nonelective week of paid time off to the next year. Employer Q maintains a calendar year cafeteria plan that permits the employee to purchase, with elective contributions, an additional week of paid time off.

(ii) For the 2009 plan year, Employee A (with a calendar tax year), timely elects to purchase one additional week of paid time off. During 2009, Employee A uses only two weeks of paid time off. Employee A is deemed to have used two weeks of nonelective paid time off and zero weeks of elective paid time off.

(iii) Pursuant to the cafeteria plan, the plan pays Employee A the value of the unused elective paid time off week in cash on December 31, 2009. Employer Q includes this amount on the 2009 Form W-2 for Employee A. This amount is included in Employee A's gross income in 2009. The cafeteria plan's terms and operations do not violate the prohibition against deferring compensation.

Example 2. Unused nonelective paid time off carried over to next plan year. (i) Same facts as *Example 1*, except that Employee A uses only one week of paid time off during the year. Pursuant to the cafeteria plan, Employee A is deemed to have used one nonelective week, and having retained one nonelective week and one elective week of paid time off. Employee A receives in cash the value of the unused elective paid time off on December 31, 2009. Employer Q includes this amount on the 2009 Form W-2 for Employee A. Employee A must report this amount as gross income in 2009.

(ii) Pursuant to Employer Q's human resources policy, Employee A is permitted to carry over the one nonelective week of paid time off to the next year. Nonelective paid time off is not part of the cafeteria plan (that is, neither Employer Q nor the cafeteria plan permit employees to exchange nonelective paid time off for other benefits).

(iii) The cafeteria plan's terms and operations do not violate the prohibition against deferring compensation.

Example 3. Forfeiture of unused elective paid time off. Same facts as *Example 2*, except that pursuant to the cafeteria plan, Employee A forfeits the remaining one week of elective paid time off. The cafeteria plan's terms and operations do not violate the prohibition against deferring compensation.

Example 4. Unused elective paid time off carried over to next plan year. Same facts as *Example 1*, except that Employee A uses only two weeks of paid time off during the 2009 plan year, and, under the terms of the cafeteria plan, Employee A is treated as having used the two nonelective weeks and as having retained the one elective week. The one remaining week (that is, the elective week) is carried over to the next plan year (or the value thereof used for any other purpose in the next plan year). The plan operates to permit deferring compensation and is not a cafeteria plan.

Example 5. Paid time off exchanged for accident and health insurance premiums. Employer R provides employees with four weeks of paid time off for a year. Employer R's calendar year cafeteria plan permits employees to exchange up to one week of paid time off to pay the employee's share of accident and health insurance premiums. For the 2009 plan year, Employee B (with a calendar tax year), timely elects to exchange one week of paid time off (valued at $769) to pay accident and health insurance premiums for 2009. The $769 is excludible from Employee B's gross income under section 106. The cafeteria plan's terms and operations do not violate the prohibition against deferring compensation.

(p) *Benefits relating to more than one year.*—(1) *Benefits in an accident and health insurance policy relating to more than one year.*—Consistent with section 125(d), an accident and health insurance policy may include certain benefits, as set forth in this paragraph (p)(1), without violating the prohibition against deferred compensation.

(i) *Permitted benefits.*—The following features or benefits of insurance policies do not defer compensation—

(A) Credit toward the deductible for unreimbursed covered expenses incurred in prior periods;

(B) Reasonable lifetime maximum limit on benefits;

(C) Level premiums;

(D) Premium waiver during disability;

(E) Guaranteed policy renewability of coverage, without further evidence of insurability (but not guaranty of the amount of premium upon renewal);

(F) Coverage for a specified accidental injury;

(G) Coverage for a specified disease or illness, including payments at initial diagnosis of the specified disease or illness, and progressive payments of a set amount per month following the initial diagnosis (sometimes referred to as progressive diagnosis payments); and

(H) Payment of a fixed amount per day (or other period) of hospitalization.

(ii) *Requirements of permitted benefits.*—All benefits described in paragraph (p)(1)(i) of this section must in addition satisfy all of the following requirements—

(A) No part of any benefit is used in one plan year to purchase a benefit in a subsequent plan year;

(B) The policies remain in force only so long as premiums are timely paid on a current basis, and, irrespective of the amount of premiums paid in prior plan years, if the current premiums are not paid, all coverage for new diseases or illnesses lapses. See paragraph (p)(1)(i)(D), allowing premium waiver during disability;

(C) There is no investment fund or cash value to rely upon for payment of premiums; and

(D) No part of any premium is held in a separate account for any participant or beneficiary, or otherwise segregated from the assets of the insurance company.

(2) *Benefits under a long-term disability policy relating to more than one year.*—A long-term disability policy paying disability benefits over more than one year does not violate the prohibition against deferring compensation.

(3) *Reasonable premium rebates or policy dividends.*—Reasonable premium rebates or policy dividends paid with respect to benefits provided through a cafeteria plan do not constitute impermissible deferred compensation if such rebates or dividends are paid before the close of the 12-month period immediately following the cafeteria plan year to which such rebates and dividends relate.

(4) *Mandatory two-year election for vision or dental insurance.*—When a cafeteria plan offers vision or dental insurance that requires a mandatory two-year coverage period, but not longer (sometimes referred to as a "two-year lock-in"), the mandatory two-year coverage period does not result in deferred compensation in violation of section 125(d)(2), provided both of the following requirements are satisfied—

(i) The premiums for each plan year are paid no less frequently than annually; and

(ii) In no event does a cafeteria plan use salary reduction or flex-credits relating to the first year of a two-year election to apply to vision or dental insurance for the second year of the two-year election.

Reg. §1.125-1(p)(4)(ii)

(5) *Using salary reduction amounts from one plan year to pay accident and health insurance premiums for the first month of the immediately following plan year.*—(i) *In general.*—Salary reduction amounts from the last month of one plan year of a cafeteria plan may be applied to pay accident and health insurance premiums for insurance during the first month of the immediately following plan year, if done on a uniform and consistent basis with respect to all participants (based on the usual payroll interval for each group of participants).

(ii) *Example.*—The following example illustrates the rules in this paragraph (p)(5):

Example. Salary reduction payments in December of calendar plan year to pay accident and health insurance premiums for January. Employer S maintains a calendar year cafeteria plan. The cafeteria plan offers employees a salary reduction election for accident and health insurance. The plan provides that employees' salary reduction amounts for the last pay period in December are applied to pay accident and health insurance premiums for the immediately following January. All employees are paid bi-weekly. For the plan year ending December 31, 2009, Employee C elects salary reduction of $3,250 for accident and health coverage. For the last pay period in December 2009, $125 (3,250/26) is applied to the accident and health insurance premium for January 2010. This plan provision does not violate the prohibition against deferring compensation.

(q) *Nonqualified benefits.*—(1) *In general.*—The following benefits are nonqualified benefits that are not permitted to be offered in a cafeteria plan—

(i) Scholarships described in section 117;

(ii) Employer-provided meals and lodging described in section 119;

(iii) Educational assistance described in section 127;

(iv) Fringe benefits described in section 132;

(v) Long-term care insurance, or any product which is advertised, marketed or offered as long-term care insurance;

(vi) Long-term care services (but see paragraph (q)(3) of this section);

(vii) Group-term life insurance on the life of any individual other than an employee (whether includible or excludible from the employee's gross income);

(viii) Health reimbursement arrangements (HRAs) that provide reimbursements up to a maximum dollar amount for a coverage period and that all or any unused amount at the end of a coverage period is carried forward to increase the maximum reimbursement amount in subsequent coverage periods;

(ix) Contributions to Archer MSAs (section 220); and

(x) Elective deferrals to a section 403(b) plan.

(2) *Nonqualified benefits not permitted in a cafeteria plan.*—The benefits described in this paragraph (q) are not qualified benefits or taxable benefits or cash for purposes of section 125 and thus may not be offered in a cafeteria plan regardless of whether any such benefit is purchased with after-tax employee contributions or on any other basis. A plan that offers a nonqualified benefit is not a cafeteria plan. Employees' elections between taxable and nontaxable benefits through such plan result in gross income to the participants for any benefit elected. See section 125(f). See paragraph (q)(3) of this section for special rule on long-term care insurance purchased through an HSA.

(3) *Long-term care insurance or services purchased through an HSA.*—Although long-term care insurance is not a qualified benefit and may not be offered in a cafeteria plan, a cafeteria plan is permitted to offer an HSA as a qualified benefit, and funds from the HSA may be used to pay eligible long-term care premiums on a qualified long-term care insurance contract or for qualified long-term care services.

(r) *Employer contributions to a cafeteria plan.*—(1) *Salary reduction—in general.*—The term *employer contributions* means amounts that are not currently available (after taking section 125 into account) to the employee but are specified in the cafeteria plan as amounts that an employee may use for the purpose of electing benefits through the plan. A plan may provide that employer contributions may be made, in whole or in part, pursuant to employees' elections to reduce their compensation or to forgo increases in compensation and to have such amounts contributed, as employer contributions, by the employer on their behalf. See also § 1.125-5 (flexible spending arrangements). Also, a cafeteria plan is permitted to require employees to elect to pay the employees' share of any qualified benefit through salary reduction and not with after tax employee contributions. A cafeteria plan is also permitted to pay reasonable cafeteria plan administrative fees through salary reduction amounts, and these salary reduction amounts are excludible from an employee's gross income.

(2) *Salary reduction as employer contribution.*—Salary reduction contributions are employer contributions. An employee's salary reduction election is an election to receive a contribution by the employer in lieu of salary or other compensation that is not currently available to the employee as of the effective date of the election and that does not subsequently become currently available to the employee.

(3) *Employer flex-credits.*—A cafeteria plan may also provide that the employer contributions will or may be made on behalf of employees equal to (or up to) specified amounts (or specified percentages of compensation) and that such nonelective contributions are available to employees for the election of benefits through the plan.

(4) *Elective contributions to a section 401(k) plan.*—See § 1.401(k)-1 for general rules relating to contributions to section 401(k) plans.

(s) *Effective/applicability date.*—It is proposed that these regulations apply on and after plan years beginning on or after January 1, 2009, except that the rule in paragraph (k)(2)(i)(B) of this section is effective as of the date the proposed regulations are published in the **Federal Register**. [Reg. § 1.125-1.]

§ 1.125-2. Cafeteria plans; elections.—(a) *Rules relating to making and revoking elections.*—(1) *Elections in general.*—A plan is not a cafeteria plan unless the plan provides in writing that employees are permitted to make elections among the permitted taxable benefits and qualified benefits offered through the plan for the plan year (and grace period, if applicable). All elections must be irrevocable by the date described in paragraph (a)(2) of this section except as provided in paragraph (a)(4) of this section. An election is not irrevocable if, after the earlier of the dates specified in paragraph (a)(2) of this section, employees have the right to revoke their elections of qualified benefits and instead receive the taxable benefits for such period, without regard to whether the employees actually revoke their elections.

(2) *Timing of elections.*—In order for employees to exclude qualified benefits from employees' gross income, benefit elections in a cafeteria plan must be made before the earlier of—

(i) The date when taxable benefits are currently available; or

(ii) The first day of the plan year (or other coverage period).

(3) *Benefit currently available to an employee—in general.*—Cash or another taxable benefit is currently available to the employee if it has been paid to the employee or if the employee is able currently to receive the cash or other taxable benefit at the employee's discretion. However, cash or another taxable benefit is not currently available to an employee if there is a significant limitation or restriction on the employee's right to receive the benefit currently. Similarly, a benefit is not currently available as of a date if the employee may under no circumstances receive the benefit before a particular time in the future. The determination of whether a benefit is currently available to an employee does not depend on whether it has been constructively received by the employee for purposes of section 451.

(4) *Exceptions to rule on making and revoking elections.*—If a cafeteria plan incorporates the change in status rules in § 1.125-4, to the extent provided in those rules, an employee who experiences a change in status (as defined in § 1.125-4) is permitted to revoke an existing election and to make a new election with respect to the remaining portion of the period of coverage, but only with respect to cash or other taxable benefits that are not yet currently available. See paragraph (c)(1) of this section for a special rule for changing elections prospectively for HSA contributions and paragraph (r)(4) in § 1.125-1 for section 401(k) elections. Also, only an employee of the employer sponsoring a cafeteria plan is allowed to make, revoke or change elections in the employer's cafeteria plan. The employee's spouse, dependent or any other individual other than the employee may not make, revoke or change elections under the plan.

(5) *Elections not required on written paper documents.*—A cafeteria plan does not fail to meet the requirements of section 125 merely because it permits employees to use electronic media for such transactions. The safe harbor in § 1.401(a)-21 applies to electronic elections, revocations and changes in elections under section 125.

(6) *Examples.*—The following examples illustrate the rules in this paragraph (a):

Example 1. Election not revocable during plan year. Employer A's cafeteria plan offers each employee the opportunity to elect, for a plan year, between $5,000 cash for the plan year and a dependent care assistance program of up to $5,000 of dependent care expenses incurred by the employee during the plan year. The cafeteria plan requires employees to elect between these benefits before the beginning of the plan year. After the year has commenced, employees are prohibited from revoking their elections. The cafeteria plan allows revocation of elections based on changes in status (as described in §1.125-4). Employees who elected the dependent care assistance program do not include the $5,000 cash in gross income. The cafeteria plan satisfies the requirements in this paragraph (a).

Example 2. Election revocable during plan year. Same facts as Example 1 except that Employer A's cafeteria plan allows employees to revoke their elections for dependent care assistance at any time during the plan year and receive the unused amount of dependent care assistance as cash. The cafeteria plan fails to satisfy the requirements in this paragraph (a), and is not a cafeteria plan. All employees are treated as having received the $5,000 in cash even if they do not revoke their elections. The same result occurs even though the cash is not payable until the end of the plan year.

(b) *Automatic elections.*—(1) *In general.*—For new employees or current employees who fail to timely elect between permitted taxable benefits and qualified benefits, a cafeteria plan is permitted, but is not required, to provide default elections for one or more qualified benefits (for example, an election made for any prior year is deemed to be continued for every succeeding plan year, unless changed).

(2) *Example.*—The following example illustrates the rules in this paragraph (b):

Example. Automatic elections for accident and health insurance.

(i) Employer B maintains a calendar year cafeteria plan. The cafeteria plan offers accident and health insurance with an option for employee-only or family coverage. All employees are eligible to participate in the cafeteria plan immediately upon hire.

(ii) The cafeteria plan provides for an automatic enrollment process: each new employee and each current employee is automatically enrolled in employee-only coverage under the accident and health insurance plan, and the employee's salary is reduced to pay the employee's share of the accident and health insurance premium, unless the employee affirmatively elects cash. Alternatively, if the employee has a spouse or child, the employee can elect family coverage.

(iii) When an employee is hired, the employee receives a notice explaining the automatic enrollment process and the employee's right to decline coverage and have no salary reduction. The notice includes the salary reduction amounts for employee-only coverage and family coverage, procedures for exercising the right to decline coverage, information on the time by which an election must be made, and the period for which an election is effective. The notice is also given to each current employee before the beginning of each subsequent plan year, except that the notice for a current employee includes a description of the employee's existing coverage, if any.

(iv) For a new employee, an election to receive cash or to have family coverage rather than employee-only coverage is effective if made when the employee is hired. For a current employee, an election is effective if made prior to the start of each calendar year or under any other circumstances permitted under §1.125-4. An election made for any prior year is deemed to be continued for every succeeding plan year, unless changed.

(v) Contributions used to purchase accident and health insurance through a cafeteria plan are not includible in the gross income of the employee solely because the plan provides for automatic enroll-ment as a default election whereby the employee's salary is reduced each year to pay for a portion of the accident and health insurance through the plan (unless the employee affirmatively elects cash).

(c) *Election rules for salary reduction contributions to HSAs.*—(1) *Prospective elections and changes in salary reduction elections allowed.*—Contributions may be made to an HSA through a cafeteria plan. A cafeteria plan offering HSA contributions through salary reduction may permit employees to make prospective salary reduction elections or change or revoke salary reduction elections for HSA contributions (for example, to increase or decrease salary reduction elections for HSA contributions) at any time during the plan year, effective before salary becomes currently available. If a cafeteria plan offers HSA contributions as a qualified benefit, the plan must—

(i) Specifically describe the HSA contribution benefit;

(ii) Allow a participant to prospectively change his or her salary reduction election for HSA contributions on a monthly basis (or more frequently); and

(iii) Allow a participant who becomes ineligible to make HSA contributions to prospectively revoke his or her salary reduction election for HSA contributions.

(2) *Example.*—The following example illustrates the rules in this paragraph (c):

Example. Prospective HSA salary reduction elections. (i) A cafeteria plan with a calendar plan year allows employees to make salary reduction elections for HSA contributions through the plan. The cafeteria plan permits employees to prospectively make, change or revoke salary contribution elections for HSA contributions, limited to one election, change or revocation per month.

(ii) Employee M participates in the cafeteria plan. Before salary becomes currently available to M, M makes the following elections. On January 2, 2009, M elects to contribute $100 for each pay period to an HSA, effective January 3, 2009. On March 15, 2009, M elects to reduce the HSA contribution to $35 per pay period, effective April 1, 2009. On May 1, 2009, M elects to discontinue all HSA contributions, effective May 15, 2009. The cafeteria plan implements all of Employee M's elections,

(iii) The cafeteria plan's operation is consistent with the section 125 election, change and revocation rules for HSA contributions.

(d) *Optional election for new employees.*—A cafeteria plan may provide new employees 30 days after their hire date to make elections between cash and qualified benefits. The election is effective as of the employee's hire date. However, salary reduction amounts used to pay for such an election must be from compensation not yet currently available on the date of the election. The written cafeteria plan must provide that any employee who terminates employment and is rehired within 30 days after terminating employment (or who returns to employment following an unpaid leave of absence of less than 30 days) is not a new employee eligible for the election in this paragraph (d).

(e) *Effective/applicability date.*—It is proposed that these regulations apply on and after plan years beginning on or after January 1, 2009. [Reg. §1.125-2.]

□ Par. 3. Sections 1.125-5, 1.125-6 and 1.125-7 are added to read as follows:

§1.125-5. Flexible spending arrangements.—(a) *Definition of flexible spending arrangement.*—(1) *In general.*—An FSA generally is a benefit program that provides employees with coverage which reimburses specified, incurred expenses (subject to reimbursement maximums and any other reasonable conditions). An expense for qualified benefits must not be reimbursed from the FSA unless it is incurred during a period of coverage. See paragraph (e) of this section. After an expense for a qualified benefit has been incurred, the expense must first be substantiated before the expense is reimbursed. See paragraphs (a) through (f) in §1.125-6.

(2) *Maximum amount of reimbursement.*—The maximum amount of reimbursement that is reasonably available to an employee for a period of coverage must not be substantially in excess of the total salary reduction and employer flex-credit for such participant's coverage. A maximum amount of reimbursement is not substantially in excess of the total salary reduction and employer flex-credit if such maximum amount is less than 500 percent of the combined salary reduction and employer flex-credit. A single FSA may provide participants with different levels of coverage and maximum amounts of reimbursement. See paragraph (r) in §1.125-1 and paragraphs (b) and (d) in this section for the definition of salary reduction, employer flex-credit, and uniform coverage rule.

(b) *Flex-credits allowed.*—(1) *In general.*—An FSA in a cafeteria plan must include an election between cash or taxable benefits (including salary reduction) and one or more qualified benefits, and may include, in addition, "employer flex-credits." For this purpose, flex-credits are non-elective employer contributions that the employer makes for every employee eligible to participate in the employer's cafeteria plan, to be used at the employee's election only for one or more qualified benefits (but not as cash or a taxable benefit). See §1.125-1 for definitions of qualified benefits, cash and taxable benefits.

(2) *Example.*—The following example illustrates the rules in this paragraph (b):

Example. Flex-credit. Contribution to health FSA for employees electing employer-provided accident and health plan. Employer A maintains a cafeteria plan offering employees an election between cash or taxable benefits and premiums for employer-provided accident and health insurance or coverage through an HMO. The plan also provides an employer contribution of $200 to the health FSA of every employee who elects accident and health insurance or HMO coverage. In addition, these employees may elect to reduce their salary to make additional contributions to their health FSAs. The benefits offered in this cafeteria plan are consistent with the requirements of section 125 and this paragraph (b).

(c) *Use-or-lose rule.*—(1) *In general.*—An FSA may not defer compensation. No contribution or benefit from an FSA may be carried over to any subsequent plan year or period of coverage. See paragraph (k)(3) in this section for specific exceptions. Unused benefits or contributions remaining at the end of the plan year (or at the end of a grace period, if applicable) are forfeited.

(2) *Example.*—The following example illustrates the rules in this paragraph (c):

Example. Use-or-lose rule. (i) Employer B maintains a calendar year cafeteria plan, offering an election between cash and a health FSA. The cafeteria plan has no grace period.

(ii) Employee A plans to have eye surgery in 2009. For the 2009 plan year, Employee A timely elects salary reduction of $3,000 for a health FSA. During the 2009 plan year, Employee A learns that she cannot have eye surgery performed, but incurs other section 213(d) medical expenses totaling $1,200. As of December 31, 2009, she has $1,800 of unused benefits and contributions in the health FSA. Consistent with the rules in this paragraph (c), she forfeits $1,800.

(d) *Uniform coverage rules applicable to health FSAs.*—(1) *Uniform coverage throughout coverage period- in general.*—The maximum amount of reimbursement from a health FSA must be available at all times during the period of coverage (properly reduced as of any particular time for prior reimbursements for the same period of coverage). Thus, the maximum amount of reimbursement at any particular time during the period of coverage cannot relate to the amount that has been contributed to the FSA at any particular time prior to the end of the plan year. Similarly, the payment schedule for the required amount for coverage under a health FSA may not be based on the rate or amount of covered claims incurred during the coverage period. Employees' salary reduction payments must not be accelerated based on employees' incurred claims and reimbursements.

(2) *Reimbursement available at all times.*—Reimbursement is deemed to be available at all times if it is paid at least monthly or when the total amount of the claims to be submitted is at least a specified, reasonable minimum amount (for example, $50).

(3) *Terminated participants.*—When an employee ceases to be a participant, the cafeteria plan must pay the former participant any amount the former participant previously paid for coverage or benefits to the extent the previously paid amount relates to the period from the date the employee ceases to be a participant through the end of that plan year. See paragraph (e)(2) in this section for COBRA elections for health FSAs.

(4) *Example.*—The following example illustrates the rules in this paragraph (d):

Example. Uniform coverage. (i) Employer C maintains a calendar year cafeteria plan, offering an election between cash and a health FSA. The cafeteria plan prohibits accelerating employees' salary reduction payments based on employees' incurred claims and reimbursements.

(ii) For the 2009 plan year, Employee N timely elects salary reduction of $3,000 for a health FSA. Employee N pays the $3,000 salary reduction amount through salary reduction of $250 per month throughout the coverage period. Employee N is eligible to receive the maximum amount of reimbursement of $3,000 at all times throughout the coverage period (reduced by prior reimbursements).

(iii) N incurs $2,500 of section 213(d) medical expenses in January, 2009. The full $2,500 is reimbursed although Employee N has made only one salary reduction payment of $250. N incurs $500 in medical expenses in February, 2009. The remaining $500 of the $3,000 is reimbursed. After Employee N submits a claim for reimbursement and substantiates the medical expenses, the cafeteria plan reimburses N for the $2,500 and $500 medical expenses. Employer C's cafeteria plan satisfies the uniform coverage rule.

(5) *No uniform coverage rule for FSAs for dependent care assistance or adoption assistance.*—The uniform coverage rule applies only to health FSAs and does not apply to FSAs for dependent care assistance or adoption assistance. See paragraphs (i) and (j) of this section for the rules for FSAs for dependent care assistance and adoption assistance.

(e) *Required period of coverage for a health FSA, dependent care FSA and adoption assistance FSA.*—(1) *Twelve-month period of coverage—in general.*—An FSA's period of coverage must be 12 months. However, in the case of a short plan year, the period of coverage is the entire short plan year. See paragraph (d) in § 1.125-1 for rules on plan years and changing plan years.

(2) *COBRA elections for health FSAs.*—For the application of the health care continuation rules of section 4980B of the Code to health FSAs, see Q & A-2 in § 54.4980B-2 of this chapter.

(3) *Separate period of coverage permitted for each qualified benefit offered through FSA.*—Dependent care assistance, adoption assistance, and a health FSA are each permitted to have a separate period of coverage, which may be different from the plan year of the cafeteria plan.

(f) *Coverage on a month-by-month or expense-by-expense basis prohibited.*—In order for reimbursements from an accident and health plan to qualify for the section 105(b) exclusion, an employer-funded accident and health plan offered through a cafeteria plan may not operate in a manner that enables employees to purchase the accident and health plan coverage only for periods when employees expect to incur medical care expenses. Thus, for example, if a cafeteria plan permits employees to receive accident and health plan coverage on a month-by-month or an expense-by-expense basis, reimbursements from the accident and health plan fail to qualify for the section 105(b) exclusion. If, however, the period of coverage under an accident and health plan offered through a cafeteria plan is twelve months and the cafeteria plan does not permit an employee to elect specific amounts of coverage, reimbursement, or salary reduction for less than twelve months, the cafeteria plan does not operate to enable participants to purchase coverage only for periods during which medical care will be incurred. See § 1.125-4 and paragraph (a) in § 1.125-2 regarding the revocation of elections during a period of coverage on account of changes in family status.

(g) *FSA administrative practices.*—(1) *Limiting health FSA enrollment to employees who participate in the employer's accident and health plan.*—At the employer's option, a cafeteria plan is permitted to provide that only those employees who participate in one or more specified employer-provided accident and health plans may participate in a health FSA. See § 1.125-7 for nondiscrimination rules.

(2) *Interval for employees' salary reduction contributions.*—The cafeteria plan is permitted to specify any interval for employees' salary reduction contributions. The interval specified in the plan must be uniform for all participants.

(h) *Qualified benefits permitted to be offered through an FSA.*—Dependent care assistance (section 129), adoption assistance (section 137) and a medical reimbursement arrangement (section 105(b)) are permitted to be offered through an FSA in a cafeteria plan.

(i) *Section 129 rules for dependent care assistance program offered through a cafeteria plan.*—(1) *General rule.*—In order for dependent care assistance to be a qualified benefit that is excludible from gross income if elected through a cafeteria plan, the cafeteria plan must satisfy section 125 and the dependent care assistance must satisfy section 129.

(2) *Dependent care assistance in general.*—Section 129(a) provides an employee with an exclusion from gross income both for an employer-funded dependent care assistance program and for amounts paid or incurred by the employer for dependent care assistance provided to the employee, if the amounts are paid or incurred through a dependent care assistance program. See paragraph (a)(4) in § 1.125-6 on when dependent care expenses are incurred.

(3) *Reimbursement exclusively for dependent care assistance.*—A dependent care assistance program may not provide reimbursements other than for dependent care expenses; in particular, if an employee has dependent care expenses less than the amount specified by salary reduction, the plan may not provide other taxable or nontaxable benefits for any portion of the specified amount not used for the reimbursement of dependent care expenses. Thus, if an employee has elected coverage under the dependent care assistance program and the period of coverage has commenced, the employee must not have the right to receive amounts from the program other than as reimbursements for dependent care expenses. This is the case regardless of whether coverage under the program is purchased with contributions made at the employer's discretion, at the employee's discretion, or pursuant to a collective bargaining agreement. Arrangements formally outside of the cafeteria plan providing for the adjustment of an employee's compensation or an employee's receipt of any other benefits on the basis of the assistance or reimbursements received by the employee are considered in determining whether a dependent care benefit is a dependent care assistance program under section 129.

(j) *Section 137 rules for adoption assistance program offered through a cafeteria plan.*—(1) *General rule.*—In order for adoption assistance to be a qualified benefit that is excludible from gross income if elected through a cafeteria plan, the cafeteria plan must satisfy section 125 and the adoption assistance must satisfy section 137.

(2) *Adoption assistance in general.*—Section 137(a) provides an employee with an exclusion from gross income for amounts paid or expenses incurred by the employer for qualified adoption expenses in connection with an employee's adoption of a child, if the amounts are paid or incurred through an adoption assistance program. Certain limits on amount of expenses and employee's income apply.

(3) *Reimbursement exclusively for adoption assistance.*—Rules and requirements similar to the rules and requirements in paragraph

(i)(3) of this section for dependent care assistance apply to adoption assistance.

(k) *FSAs and the rules governing the tax-favored treatment of employer-provided health benefits.*—(1) *Medical expenses.*—Health plans that are flexible spending arrangements, as defined in paragraph (a)(1) of this section, must conform to the generally applicable rules under sections 105 and 106 in order for the coverage and reimbursements under such plans to qualify for tax-favored treatment under such sections. Thus, health FSAs must qualify as accident and health plans. See paragraph (n) in § 1.125-1. A health FSA is only permitted to reimburse medical expenses as defined in section 213(d). Thus, for example, a health FSA is not permitted to reimburse dependent care expenses.

(2) *Limiting payment or reimbursement to certain section 213(d) medical expenses.*—A health FSA is permitted to limit payment or reimbursement to only certain section 213(d) medical expenses (except health insurance, long-term care services or insurance). See paragraph (q) in § 1.125-1. For example, a health FSA in a cafeteria plan is permitted to provide in the written plan that the plan reimburses all section 213(d) medical expenses allowed to be paid or reimbursed under a cafeteria plan except over-the-counter drugs.

(3) *Application of prohibition against deferred compensation to medical expenses.*—(i) *Certain advance payments for orthodontia permitted.*—A cafeteria plan is permitted, but is not required to, reimburse employees for orthodontia services before the services are provided but only to the extent that the employee has actually made the payments in advance of the orthodontia services in order to receive the services. These orthodontia services are deemed to be incurred when the employee makes the advance payment. Reimbursing advance payments does not violate the prohibition against deferring compensation.

(ii) *Example.*—The following example illustrates the rules in paragraph (k)(3):

Example. Advance payment to orthodontist. Employer D sponsors a calendar year cafeteria plan which offers a health FSA. Employee K elects to salary reduce $3,000 for a health FSA for the 2009 plan year. Employee K's dependent requires orthodontic treatment. K's accident and health insurance does not cover orthodontia. The orthodontist, following the normal practice, charges $3,000, all due in 2009, for treatment, to begin in 2009 and end in 2010. K pays the $3,000 in 2009. In 2009, Employer D's cafeteria plan may reimburse $3,000 to K, without violating the prohibition against deferring compensation in section 125(d)(2).

(iii) *Reimbursements for durable medical equipment*—A health FSA in a cafeteria plan that reimburses employees for equipment (described in section 213(d)) with a useful life extending beyond the period of coverage during which the expense is incurred does not provide deferred compensation. For example, a health FSA is permitted to reimburse the cost of a wheelchair for an employee.

(4) *No reimbursement of premiums for accident and health insurance or long-term care insurance or services.*—A health FSA is not permitted to treat employees' premium payments for other health coverage as reimbursable expenses. Thus, for example, a health FSA is not permitted to reimburse employees for payments for other health plan coverage, including premiums for COBRA coverage, accidental death and dismemberment insurance, long-term disability or short-term disability insurance or for health coverage under a plan maintained by the employer of the employee or the employer of the employee's spouse or dependent. Also, a health FSA is not permitted to reimburse expenses for long-term care insurance premiums or for long-term care services for the employee or employee's spouse or dependent. See paragraph (q) in § 1.125-1 for nonqualified benefits

(l) *Section 105(h) requirements.*—Section 105(h) applies to health FSAs. Section 105(h) provides that the exclusion provided by section 105(b) is not available with respect to certain amounts received by a highly compensated individual (as defined in section 105(h)(5)) from a discriminatory self-insured medical reimbursement plan, which includes health FSAs. See § 1.105-11. For purposes of section 105(h), coverage by a self-insured accident and health plan offered through a cafeteria plan is an optional benefit (even if only one level and type of coverage is offered) and, for purposes of the optional benefit rule in § 1.105-11(c)(3)(i), employer contributions are treated as employee contributions to the extent that taxable benefits are offered by the plan.

(m) *HSA-compatible FSAs-limited-purpose health FSAs and post-deductible health FSAs.*—(1) *In general.*—Limited-purpose health FSAs and *post-deductible health FSAs* which satisfy all the requirements of section 125 are permitted to be offered through a cafeteria plan.

(2) *HSA-compatible FSAs.*—Section 223(a) allows a deduction for certain contributions to a "Health Savings Account" (HSA) (as defined in section 223(d)). An *eligible individual* (as defined in section 223(c)(1)) may contribute to an HSA. An eligible individual must be covered under a "high deductible health plan" (HDHP) and not, while covered under an HDHP, under any health plan which is not an HDHP. A general purpose health FSA is not an HDHP and an individual covered by a general purpose health FSA is not eligible to contribute to an HSA. However, an individual covered by an HDHP (and who otherwise satisfies section 223(c)(1)) does not fail to be an eligible individual merely because the individual is also covered by a limited-purpose health FSA or post-deductible health FSA (as defined in this paragraph (m)) or a combination of a limited-purpose health FSA and a post-deductible health FSA.

(3) *Limited-purpose health FSA.*—A limited-purpose health FSA is a health FSA described in the cafeteria plan that only pays or reimburses permitted coverage benefits (as defined in section 223(c)(2)(C)), such as vision care, dental care or preventive care (as defined for purposes of section 223(c)(2)(C)). See paragraph (k) in this section.

(4) *Post-deductible health FSA.*—(i) *In general.*—A post-deductible health FSA is a health FSA described in the cafeteria plan that only pays or reimburses medical expenses (as defined in section 213(d)) for preventive care or medical expenses incurred after the minimum annual HDHP deductible under section 223(c)(2)(A)(i) is satisfied. See paragraph (k) in this section. No medical expenses incurred before the annual HDHP deductible is satisfied may be reimbursed by a post-deductible FSA, regardless of whether the HDHP covers the expense or whether the deductible is later satisfied. For example, even if chiropractic care is not covered under the HDHP, expenses for chiropractic care incurred before the HDHP deductible is satisfied are not reimbursable at any time by a post-deductible health FSA.

(ii) *HDHP and health FSA deductibles.*—The deductible for a post-deductible health FSA need not be the same amount as the deductible for the HDHP, but in no event may the post-deductible health FSA or other coverage provide benefits before the minimum annual HDHP deductible under section 223(c)(2)(A)(i) is satisfied (other than benefits permitted under a limited-purpose health FSA). In addition, although the deductibles of the HDHP and the other coverage may be satisfied independently by separate expenses, no benefits may be paid before the minimum annual deductible under section 223(c)(2)(A)(i) has been satisfied. An individual covered by a post-deductible health FSA (if otherwise an eligible individual) is an eligible individual for the purpose of contributing to the HSA.

(5) *Combination of limited-purpose health FSA and post-deductible health FSA.*—An FSA is a combination of a limited-purpose health FSA and post-deductible health FSA if each of the benefits and reimbursements provided under the FSA are permitted under either a limited-purpose health FSA or post-deductible health FSA. For example, before the HDHP deductible is satisfied, a combination limited-purpose and post-deductible health FSA may reimburse only preventive, vision or dental expenses. A combination limited-purpose and post-deductible health FSA may also reimburse any medical expense that may otherwise be paid by an FSA (that is, no insurance premiums or long-term care benefits) that is incurred after the HDHP deductible is satisfied.

(6) *Substantiation.*—The substantiation rules in this section apply to limited-purpose health FSAs and to post-deductible health FSAs. In addition to providing third-party substantiation of medical expenses, a participant in a post-deductible health FSA must provide information from an independent third party that the HDHP deductible has been satisfied. A participant in a limited-purpose health FSA must provide information from an independent third-party that the medical expenses are for vision care, dental care or preventive care.

(7) *Plan amendments.*—See paragraph (c) in § 1.125-1 on the required effective date for amendments adopting or changing limited-purpose, post-deductible or combination limited-purpose and post-deductible health FSAs.

(n) *Qualified HSA distributions.*—(1) *In general.*—A health FSA in a cafeteria plan is permitted to offer employees the right to elect qualified HSA distributions described in section 106(e). No qualified HSA distribution may be made in a plan year unless the employer amends the health FSA written plan with respect to all employees, effective by the last day of the plan year, to allow a qualified HSA distribution satisfying all the requirements in this paragraph (n). See also section 106(e)(5)(B). In addition, a distribution with respect to an employee is not a qualified HSA distribution unless all of the following the requirements are satisfied—

(i) No qualified HSA distribution has been previously made on behalf of the employee from this health FSA;

(ii) The employee elects to have the employer make a qualified HSA distribution from the health FSA to the HSA of the employee;

(iii) The distribution does not exceed the lesser of the balance of the health FSA on—

(A) September 21, 2006; or

(B) The date of the distribution;

(iv) For purposes of this paragraph (n)(1), balances as of any date are determined on a cash basis, without taking into account expenses incurred but not reimbursed as of a date, and applying the uniform coverage rule in paragraph (d) in this section;

(v) The distribution is made no later than December 31, 2011; and

(vi) The employer makes the distribution directly to the trustee of the employee's HSA.

(2) *Taxation of qualified HSA distributions.*—A qualified HSA distribution from the health FSA covering the participant to his or her HSA is a rollover to the HSA (as defined in section 223(f)(5)) and thus is generally not includible in gross income. However, if the participant is not an eligible individual (as defined in section 223(c)(1)) at any time during a testing period following the qualified HSA distribution, the amount of the distribution is includible in the participant's gross income and he or she is also subject to an additional 10 percent tax (with certain exceptions). Section 106(e)(3).

(3) *No effect on health FSA elections, coverage, use-or-lose rule.*—A qualified HSA distribution does not alter an employee's irrevocable election under paragraph (a) of §1.125-2, or constitute a change in status under §1.125-4(a). If a qualified HSA distribution is made to an employee's HSA, even if the balance in a health FSA is reduced to zero, the employee's health FSA coverage continues to the end of the plan year. Unused benefits and contributions remaining at the end of a plan year (or at the end of a grace period, if applicable) must be forfeited.

(o) *FSA experience gains or forfeitures.*—(1) *Experience gains in general.*—An FSA experience gain (sometimes referred to as forfeitures in the use-or-lose rule in paragraph (c) in this section) with respect to a plan year (plus any grace period following the end of a plan year described in paragraph (e) in §1.125-1), equals the amount of the employer contributions, including salary reduction contributions, and after-tax employee contributions to the FSA minus the FSA's total claims reimbursements for the year. Experience gains (or forfeitures) may be—

(i) Retained by the employer maintaining the cafeteria plan; or

(ii) If not retained by the employer, may be used only in one or more of the following ways—

(A) To reduce required salary reduction amounts for the immediately following plan year, on a reasonable and uniform basis, as described in paragraph (o)(2) of this section;

(B) Returned to the employees on a reasonable and uniform basis, as described in paragraph (o)(2) of this section; or

(C) To defray expenses to administer the cafeteria plan.

(2) *Allocating experience gains among employees on reasonable and uniform basis.*—If not retained by the employer or used to defray expenses of administering the plan, the experience gains must be allocated among employees on a reasonable and uniform basis. It is permissible to allocate these amounts based on the different coverage levels of employees under the FSA. Experience gains allocated in compliance with this paragraph (o) are not a deferral of the receipt of compensation. However, in no case may the experience gains be allocated among employees based (directly or indirectly) on their individual claims experience. Experience gains may not be used as contributions directly or indirectly to any deferred compensation benefit plan.

(3) *Example.*—The following example illustrates the rules in this paragraph (o):

Example. Allocating experience gains. (i) Employer L maintains a cafeteria plan for its 1,200 employees, who may elect one of several different annual coverage levels under a health FSA in $100 increments from $500 to $2,000.

(ii) For the 2009 plan year, 1,000 employees elect levels of coverage under the health FSA. For the 2009 plan year, the health FSA has an experience gain of $5,000.

(iii) The $5,000 may be allocated to all participants for the plan year on a per capita basis weighted to reflect the participants' elected levels of coverage.

(iv) Alternatively, the $5,000 may be used to reduce the required salary reduction amount under the health FSA for all 2009 participants (for example, a $500 health FSA for the next year is priced at $480) or to reimburse claims incurred above the elective limit in 2010 as long as such reimbursements are made on a reasonable and uniform level.

(p) *Effective/applicability date.*—It is proposed that these regulations apply on and after plan years beginning on or after January 1, 2009. [Reg. §1.125-5.]

§1.125-6. Substantiation of expenses for all cafeteria plans.—(a) *Cafeteria plan payments and reimbursements.*—(1) *In general.*—A cafeteria plan may pay or reimburse only those substantiated expenses for qualified benefits incurred on or after the later of the effective date of the cafeteria plan and the date the employee is enrolled in the plan. This requirement applies to all qualified benefits offered through the cafeteria plan. See paragraph (b) of this section for substantiation rules.

(2) *Expenses incurred.*—(i) *Employees' medical expenses must be incurred during the period of coverage.*—In order for reimbursements to be excludible from gross income under section 105(b), the medical expenses reimbursed by an accident and health plan elected through a cafeteria plan must be incurred during the period when the participant is covered by the accident and health plan. A participant's period of coverage includes COBRA coverage. See §54.4980B-2 of this chapter. Medical expenses incurred before the later of the effective date of the plan and the date the employee is enrolled in the plan are not incurred during the period for which the employee is covered by the plan. However, the actual reimbursement of covered medical care expenses may be made after the applicable period of coverage.

(ii) *When medical expenses are incurred.*—For purposes of this rule, medical expenses are incurred when the employee (or the employee's spouse or dependents) is provided with the medical care that gives rise to the medical expenses, and not when the employee is formally billed, charged for, or pays for the medical care.

(iii) *Example.*—The following example illustrates the rules in this paragraph (a)(2):

Example. Medical expenses incurred after termination. (i) Employer E maintains a cafeteria plan with a calendar year plan year. The cafeteria plan provides that participation terminates when an individual ceases to be an employee of Employer E, unless the former employee elects to continue to participate in the health FSA under the COBRA rules in §54.4980B-2 of this chapter. Employee G timely elects to salary reduce $1,200 to participate in a health FSA for the 2009 plan year. As of June 30, 2009, Employee G has contributed $600 toward the health FSA, but incurred no medical expenses. On June 30, 2009, Employee G terminates employment and does not continue participation under COBRA. On July 15, 2009, G incurs a section 213(d) medical expense of $500.

(ii) Under the rules in paragraph (a)(2) of this section, the cafeteria plan is prohibited from reimbursing any portion of the $500 medical expense because, at the time the medical expense is incurred, G is not a participant in the cafeteria plan.

(3) *Section 105(b) requirements for reimbursement of medical expenses through a cafeteria plan.*—(i) *In general.*—In order for medical care reimbursements paid to an employee through a cafeteria plan to be excludible under section 105(b), the reimbursements must be paid pursuant to an employer-funded *accident and health plan,* as defined in section 105(e) and §§1.105-2 and 1.105-5.

(ii) *Reimbursement exclusively for section 213(d) medical expenses.*—A cafeteria plan benefit through which an employee receives reimbursements of medical expenses is excludable under section 105(b) only if reimbursements from the plan are made specifically to reimburse the employee for medical expenses (as defined in section 213(d)) incurred by the employee or the employee's spouse or dependents during the period of coverage. Amounts paid to an employee as reimbursement are not paid specifically to reimburse the employee for medical expenses if the plan provides that the employee is entitled, or operates in a manner that entitles the employee, to receive the amounts, in the form of cash (for example, routine payment of salary) or any other taxable or nontaxable benefit irrespective of whether the employee (or the employee's spouse or dependents) incurs medical expenses during the period of coverage. This rule applies even if the employee will not receive such amounts until the end or after the end of the period. A plan under which employees (or their spouses and dependents) will receive reimbursement for medical expenses up to a specified amount and, if they incur no medical expenses, will receive cash or any other benefit in lieu of the reimbursements is not a benefit qualifying for the exclusion under sections 106 and 105(b). See §1.105-2. This is the case without regard to whether the benefit was purchased with contributions made at the employer's discretion, at the employee's discretion (for example, by salary reduction election), or pursuant to a collective bargaining agreement.

(iii) *Other arrangements.*—Arrangements formally outside of the cafeteria plan that adjust an employee's compensation or an employee's receipt of any other benefits on the basis of the expenses incurred or reimbursements the employee receives are considered in determining whether the reimbursements are through a plan eligible for the exclusions under sections 106 and 105(b).

(4) *Reimbursements of dependent care expenses.*—(i) *Dependent care expenses must be incurred.*—In order to satisfy section 129, dependent care expenses may not be reimbursed before the expenses are incurred. For purposes of this rule, dependent care expenses are incurred when the care is provided and not when the employee is formally billed, charged for, or pays for the dependent care.

(ii) *Dependent care provided during the period of coverage.*—In order for dependent care assistance to be provided through a dependent care assistance program eligible for the section 129 exclusion, the care must be provided to or on behalf of the employee during the period for which the employee is covered by the program. For example, if for a plan year, an employee elects a dependent care assistance program providing for reimbursement of dependent care expenses, only reimbursements for dependent care expenses incurred during that plan year are provided from a dependent care assistance program within the scope of section 129. Also, for purposes of this rule, expenses incurred before the later of the program's effective date and the date the employee is enrolled in the program are not incurred during the period when the employee is covered by the program. Similarly, if the dependent care assistance program furnishes the dependent care in-kind (for example, through an employer-maintained child care facility), only dependent care provided during the plan year of coverage is provided through a dependent care assistance program within the meaning of section 129. See also § 1.125-5 for FSA rules.

(iii) *Period of coverage.*—In order for dependent care assistance through a cafeteria plan to be provided through a dependent care assistance program eligible for the section 129 exclusion, the plan may not operate in a manner that enables employees to purchase dependent care assistance only for periods during which the employees expect to receive dependent care assistance. If the period of coverage for a dependent care assistance program offered through a cafeteria plan is twelve months (or, in the case of a short plan year, at least equal to the short plan year) and the plan does not permit an employee to elect specific amounts of coverage, reimbursement, or salary reduction for less than twelve months, the plan is deemed not to operate to enable employees to purchase coverage only for periods when dependent care assistance will be received. See paragraph (a) in § 1.125-2 and § 1.125-4 regarding the revocation of elections during the period of coverage on account of changes in family status. See paragraph (e) in this section for required period of coverage for dependent care assistance.

(iv) *Examples.*—The following examples illustrate the rules in paragraphs (a)(4)(i)-(iii) of this section:

Example 1. Initial non-refundable fee for child care. (i) Employer F maintains a calendar year cafeteria plan, offering employees an election between cash and qualified benefits, including dependent care assistance. Employee M has a one-year old dependent child. Employee M timely elected $5,000 of dependent care assistance for 2009. During the entire 2009 plan year, Employee M satisfies all the requirements in section 129 for dependent care assistance.

(ii) On February 1, 2009, Employee M pays an initial non-refundable fee of $500 to a licensed child care center (unrelated to Employer F or to Employee M), to reserve a space at the child care center for M's child. The child care center's monthly charges for child care are $1,200. When the child care center first begins to care for M's child, the $500 non-refundable fee is applied toward the first month's charges for child care.

(iii) On March 1, 2009, the child care center begins caring for Employee M's child, and continues to care for the child through December 31, 2009. On March 1, 2009, M pays the child care center $700 (the balance of the $1,200 in charges for child care to be provided in March 2009). On April 1, 2009, M pays the child care center $1,200 for the child care to be provided in April 2009.

(iv) Dependent care expenses are incurred when the services are provided. For dependent care services provided in March 2009, the $500 nonrefundable fee paid on February 1, 2009, and the $700 paid on March 1, 2009 may be reimbursed on or after the later of the date when substantiated or April 1, 2009. For dependent care services provided in April 2009, the $1,200 paid on April 1, 2009 may be reimbursed on or after the later of the date when substantiated or May 1, 2009.

Example 2. Non-refundable fee forfeited. Same facts as *Example 1,* except that the child care center never cared for M's child (who was instead cared for at Employer F's onsite child care facility). Because the child care center never provided child care services to Employee M's child, the $500 non-refundable fee is not reimbursable.

(v) *Optional spend-down provision.*—At the employer's option, the written cafeteria plan may provide that dependent care expenses incurred after the date an employee ceases participation in

the cafeteria plan (for example, after termination) and through the last day of that plan year (or grace period immediately after that plan year) may be reimbursed from unused benefits, if all of the requirements of section 129 are satisfied.

(vi) *Example.*—The following example illustrates the rules in paragraph (a)(4)(v) of this section:

Example. Terminated employee's post-termination dependent care expenses. (i) For calendar year 2009, Employee X elects $5,000 salary reduction for dependent care assistance through Employer G's cafeteria plan. X works for Employer G from January 1 through June 30, 2009, when X terminates employment. As of June 30, 2009, X had paid $2,500 in salary reduction and had incurred and was reimbursed for $2,000 of dependent care expenses.

(ii) X does not work again until October 1, 2009, when X begins work for Employer H. X was employed by Employer H from October 1, 2009 through December 31, 2009. During this period, X also incurred $500 of dependent care expenses. During all the periods of employment in 2009, X satisfied all requirements in section 129 for excluding payments for dependent care assistance from gross income.

(iii) Employer G's cafeteria plan allows terminated employees to "spend down" unused salary reduction amounts for dependent care assistance, if all requirements of section 129 are satisfied. After X's claim for $500 of dependent care expenses is substantiated, Employer G's cafeteria plan reimburses X for $500 (the remaining balance) of dependent care expenses incurred during X's employment for Employer H between October 1, 2009 and December 31, 2009. Employer G's cafeteria plan and operation are consistent with section 125.

(b) *Rules for claims substantiation for cafeteria plans.*—(1) *Substantiation required before reimbursing expenses for qualified benefits.*—This paragraph (b) sets forth the substantiation requirements that a cafeteria plan must satisfy before paying or reimbursing any expense for a qualified benefit.

(2) *All claims must be substantiated.*—As a precondition of payment or reimbursement of expenses for qualified benefits, a cafeteria plan must require substantiation in accordance with this section. Substantiating only a percentage of claims, or substantiating only claims above a certain dollar amount, fails to comply with the substantiation requirements in § 1.125-1 and this section.

(3) *Substantiation by independent third-party.*—(i) *In general.*—All expenses must be substantiated by information from a third-party that is independent of the employee and the employee's spouse and dependents. The independent third-party must provide information describing the service or product, the date of the service or sale, and the amount. Self-substantiation or self certification of an expense by an employee does not satisfy the substantiation requirements of this paragraph (b). The specific requirements in sections 105(b), 129, and 137 must also be satisfied as a condition of reimbursing expenses for qualified benefits. For example, a health FSA does not satisfy the requirements of section 105(b) if it reimburses employees for expenses where the employees only submit information describing medical expenses, the amount of the expenses and the date of the expenses but fail to provide a statement from an independent third-party (either automatically or subsequent to the transaction) verifying the expenses. Under § 1.105-2, all amounts paid under a plan that permits self-substantiation or self-certification are includible in gross income, including amounts reimbursed for medical expenses, whether or not substantiated. See paragraph (m) in § 1.125-5 for additional substantiation rules for limited-purpose and post-deductible health FSAs.

(ii) *Rules for substantiation of health FSA claims using an explanation of benefits provided by an insurance company.*—(A) *Written statement from an independent third-party.*—If the employer is provided with information from an independent third-party (such as an "*explanation of benefits*" (*EOB*) from an insurance company) indicating the date of the section 213(d) medical care and the employee's responsibility for payment for that medical care (that is, coinsurance payments and amounts below the plan's deductible), and the employee certifies that any expense paid through the health FSA has not been reimbursed and that the employee will not seek reimbursement from any other plan covering health benefits, the claim is fully substantiated without the need for submission of a receipt by the employee or further review.

(B) *Example.*—The following example illustrates the rules in this paragraph (b)(3):

Example. Explanation of benefits. (i) During the plan year ending December 31, 2009, Employee Q is a participant in the health FSA sponsored by Employer J and is enrolled in Employer J's accident and health plan.

(ii) On March 1, 2009, Q visits a physician's office for medical care as defined in section 213(d). The charge for the physician's services is $150. Under the plan, Q is responsible for 20 percent of the charge for the physician's services (that is, $30). Q has sufficient FSA coverage for the $30 claim.

(iii) Employer J has coordinated with the accident and health plan so that Employer J or its agent automatically receives an EOB from the plan indicating that Q is responsible for payment of 20 percent of the $150 charged by the physician. Because Employer J has received a statement from an independent third-party that Q has incurred a medical expense, the date the expense was incurred, and the amount of the expense, the claim is substantiated without the need for J to submit additional information regarding the expense. Employer J's FSA reimburses Q the $30 medical expense without requiring Q to submit a receipt or a statement from the physician. The substantiation rules in paragraph (b) in this section are satisfied.

(4) *Advance reimbursement of expenses for qualified benefits prohibited.*—Reimbursing expenses before the expense has been incurred or before the expense is substantiated fails to satisfy the substantiation requirements in § 1.105-2, § 1.125-1 and this section.

(5) *Purported loan from employer to employee.*—In determining whether, under all the facts and circumstances, employees are being reimbursed for unsubstantiated claims, special scrutiny will be given to other arrangements such as employer-to-employee loans based on actual or projected employee claims.

(6) *Debit cards.*—For purposes of this section, a *debit card* is a debit card, credit card, or stored value card. See also paragraphs (c) through (g) of this section for additional rules on payments or reimbursements made through debit cards.

(c) *Debit cards-overview.*—(1) *Mandatory rules for all debit cards usable to pay or reimburse medical expenses.*—Paragraph (d) of this section sets forth the mandatory procedures for debit cards to substantiate section 213(d) medical expenses. These rules apply to all debit cards used to pay or reimburse medical expenses. Paragraph (e) of this section sets forth additional substantiation rules that may be used for medical expenses incurred at medical care providers and certain stores with the Drug Stores and Pharmacies merchant category code. Paragraph (f) in this section sets forth the requirements for an inventory information approval system which must be used to substantiate medical expenses incurred at merchants or service providers that are not medical care providers or certain stores with the Drug Stores and Pharmacies merchant category code and that may be used for medical expenses incurred at all merchants.

(2) *Debit cards used for dependent care assistance.*—Paragraph (g) of this section sets forth additional rules for debit cards usable for reimbursing dependent care expenses.

(3) *Additional guidance.*—The Commissioner may prescribe additional guidance of general applicability, published in the Internal Revenue Bulletin (see § 601.601(d)(2)(ii)(*b*) of this chapter), to provide additional rules for debit cards.

(d) *Mandatory rules for all debit cards usable to pay or reimburse medical expenses.*—A health FSA paying or reimbursing section 213(d) medical expenses through a debit card must satisfy all of the following requirements—

(1) Before any employee participating in a health FSA receives the debit card, the employee agrees in writing that he or she will only use the card to pay for medical expenses (as defined in section 213(d)) of the employee or his or her spouse or dependents, that he or she will not use the debit card for any medical expense that has already been reimbursed, that he or she will not seek reimbursement under any other health plan for any expense paid for with a debit card, and that he or she will acquire and retain sufficient documentation (including invoices and receipts) for any expense paid with the debit card.

(2) The debit card includes a statement providing that the agreements described in paragraph (d)(1) of this section are reaffirmed each time the employee uses the card.

(3) The amount available through the debit card equals the amount elected by the employee for the health FSA for the cafeteria plan year, and is reduced by amounts paid or reimbursed for section 213(d) medical expenses incurred during the plan year.

(4) The debit card is automatically cancelled when the employee ceases to participate in the health FSA.

(5) The employer limits use of the debit card to—

(i) Physicians, dentists, vision care offices, hospitals, other medical care providers (as identified by the merchant category code);

(ii) Stores with the merchant category code for Drugstores and Pharmacies if, on a location by location basis, 90 percent of the store's gross receipts during the prior taxable year consisted of items which qualify as expenses for medical care described in section 213(d); and

(iii) Stores that have implemented the inventory information approval system under paragraph (f).

(6) The employer substantiates claims based on payments to medical care providers and stores described in paragraphs (d)(5)(i) and (ii) of this section in accordance with either paragraph (e) or paragraph (f) of this section.

(7) The employer follows all of the following correction procedures for any improper payments using the debit card—

(i) Until the amount of the improper payment is recovered, the debit card must be de-activated and the employee must request payments or reimbursements of medical expenses from the health FSA through other methods (for example, by submitting receipts or invoices from a merchant or service provider showing the employee incurred a section 213(d) medical expense);

(ii) The employer demands that the employee repay the cafeteria plan an amount equal to the improper payment;

(iii) If, after the demand for repayment of improper payment (as described in paragraph (d)(7)(ii) of this section), the employee fails to repay the amount of the improper charge, the employer withholds the amount of the improper charge from the employee's pay or other compensation, to the full extent allowed by applicable law;

(iv) If any portion of the improper payment remains outstanding after attempts to recover the amount (as described in paragraph (d)(7)(ii) and (iii) of this section), the employer applies a claims substitution or offset to resolve improper payments, such as a reimbursement for a later substantiated expense claim is reduced by the amount of the improper payment. So, for example, if an employee has received an improper payment of $200 and subsequently submits a substantiated claim for $250 incurred during the same coverage period, a reimbursement for $50 is made; and

(v) If, after applying all the procedures described in paragraph (d)(7)(ii) through (iv) of this section, the employee remains indebted to the employer for improper payments, the employer, consistent with its business practice, treats the improper payment as it would any other business indebtedness.

(e) *Substantiation of expenses incurred at medical care providers and certain other stores with Drug Stores and Pharmacies merchant category code.*—(1) *In general.*—A health FSA paying or reimbursing section 213(d) medical expenses through a debit card is permitted to comply with the substantiation provisions of this paragraph (e), instead of complying with the provisions of paragraph (f), for medical expenses incurred at providers described in paragraph (e)(2) of this section.

(2) *Medical care providers and certain other stores with Drug Stores and Pharmacies merchant category code.*—Medical expenses may be substantiated using the methods described in paragraph (e)(3) of this section if incurred at physicians, pharmacies, dentists, vision care offices, hospitals, other medical care providers (as identified by the merchant category code) and at stores with the Drug Stores and Pharmacies merchant category code, if, on a store location-by-location basis, 90 percent of the store's gross receipts during the prior taxable year consisted of items which qualify as expenses for medical care described in section 213(d).

(3) *Claims substantiation for copayment matches, certain recurring medical expenses and real-time substantiation.*—If all of the requirements in this paragraph (e)(3) are satisfied, copayment matches, certain recurring medical expenses and medical expenses substantiated in real-time are substantiated without the need for submission of receipts or further review.

(i) *Matching copayments-multiples of five or fewer.*—If an employer's accident or health plan covering the employee (or the employee's spouse or dependents) has copayments in specific dollar amounts, and the dollar amount of the transaction at a medical care provider equals an exact multiple of not more than five times the dollar amount of the copayment for the specific service (for example, pharmacy benefit copayment, copayment for a physician's office visit) under the accident or health plan covering the specific employee-cardholder, then the charge is fully substantiated without the need for submission of a receipt or further review.

(A) *Tiered copayments.*—If a health plan has multiple copayments for the same benefit, (for example, tiered copayments for a pharmacy benefit), exact matches of multiples or combinations of up to five copayments are similarly fully substantiated without the need for submission of a receipt or further review.

(B) *Copayment match must be exact multiple.*—If the dollar amount of the transaction is not an exact multiple of the copayment (or an exact match of a multiple or combination of different copayments for a benefit in the case of multiple copayments), the transaction must be treated as conditional pending confirmation of the charge, even if the amount is less than five times the copayment.

(C) *No match for multiple of six or more times copayment.*—If the dollar amount of the transaction at a medical care provider equals a multiple of six or more times the dollar amount of the copayment for the specific service, the transaction must be treated as conditional pending confirmation of the charge by the submission of additional third-party information. See paragraph (d) of this section. In the case of a plan with multiple copayments for the same benefit, if the dollar amount of the transaction exceeds five times the maximum copayment for the benefit, the transaction must also be treated as conditional pending confirmation of the charge by the submission of additional third-party information. In these cases, the employer must require that additional third-party information, such as merchant or service provider receipts, be submitted for review and substantiation, and the third-party information must satisfy the requirements in paragraph (b)(3) of this section.

(D) *Independent verification of copayment required.*—The copayment schedule required under the accident or health plan must be independently verified by the employer. Statements or other representations by the employee are not sufficient. Self-substantiation or self-certification of an employee's copayment in connection with copayment matching procedures through debit cards or otherwise does not constitute substantiation. If a plan's copayment matching system relies on an employee to provide a copayment amount without verification of the amount, claims have not been substantiated, and all amounts paid from the plan are included in gross income, including amounts paid for medical care whether or not substantiated. See paragraph (b) in this section.

(4) *Certain recurring medical expenses.*—Automatic payment or reimbursement satisfies the substantiation rules in this paragraph (e) for payment of recurring expenses that match expenses previously approved as to amount, medical care provider and time period (for example, for an employee who refills a prescription drug on a regular basis at the same provider and in the same amount). The payment is substantiated without the need for submission of a receipt or further review.

(5) *Real-time substantiation.*—If a third party that is independent of the employee and the employee's spouse and dependents (for example, medical care provider, merchant, or pharmacy benefit manager) provides, at the time and point of sale, information to verify to the employer (including electronically by email, the internet, intranet or telephone) that the charge is for a section 213(d) medical expense, the expense is substantiated without the need for further review.

(6) *Substantiation requirements for all other medical expenses paid or reimbursed through a health FSA debit card.*—All other charges to the debit card (other than substantiated copayments, recurring medical expenses or real-time substantiation, or charges substantiated through the inventory information approval system described in paragraph (f) of this section) must be treated as conditional, pending substantiation of the charge through additional independent third-party information describing the goods or services, the date of the service or sale and the amount of the transaction. All such debit card payments must be substantiated, regardless of the amount of the payment.

(f) *Inventory information approval system.*—(1) *In general.*—An inventory information approval system that complies with this paragraph (f) may be used to substantiate payments made using a debit card, including payments at merchants and service providers that are not described in paragraph (e)(2) of this section. Debit card transactions using this system are fully substantiated without the need for submission of a receipt by the employee or further review.

(2) *Operation of inventory information approval system.*—An inventory information approval system must operate in the manner described in this paragraph (f)(2).

(i) When an employee uses the card, the payment card processor's or participating merchant's system collects information about the items purchased using the inventory control information (for example, *stock keeping units* (SKUs)). The system compares the inventory control information for the items purchased against a list of items, the purchase of which qualifies as expenses for medical care under section 213(d) (including nonprescription medications).

(ii) The section 213(d) medical expenses are totaled and the merchant's or payment card processor's system approves the use of the card only for the amount of the section 213(d) medical expenses eligible for coverage under the health FSA (taking into consideration the uniform coverage rule in paragraph (d) of § 1.125-5);

(iii) If the transaction is only partially approved, the employee is required to tender additional amounts, resulting in a split-tender transaction. For example, if, after matching inventory information, it is determined that all items purchased are section 213(d) medical expenses, the entire transaction is approved, subject to the coverage limitations of the health FSA;

(iv) If, after matching inventory information, it is determined that only some of the items purchased are section 213(d) medical expenses, the transaction is approved only as to the section 213(d) medical expenses. In this case, the merchant or service-pro-

vider must request additional payment from the employee for the items that do not satisfy the definition of medical care under section 213(d);

(v) The merchant or service-provider must also request additional payment from the employee if the employee does not have sufficient health FSA coverage to purchase the section 213(d) medical items;

(vi) Any attempt to use the card at non-participating merchants or service-providers must fail.

(3) *Employer's responsibility for ensuring inventory information approval system's compliance with §1.105-2, §1.125-1, §1.125-6 and recordkeeping requirements.*—An employer that uses the inventory information approval system must ensure that the inventory information approval system complies with the requirements in § § 1.105-2, 1.125-1, and § 1.125-6 for substantiating, paying or reimbursing section 213(d) medical expenses and with the recordkeeping requirements in section 6001.

(g) *Debit cards used to pay or reimburse dependent care assistance.*—(1) *In general.*—An employer may use a debit card to provide benefits under its dependent care assistance program (including a dependent care assistance FSA). However, dependent care expenses may not be reimbursed before the expenses are incurred. See paragraph (a)(4) in this section. Thus, if a dependent care provider requires payment before the dependent care services are provided, the expenses cannot be reimbursed at the time of payment through use of a debit card or otherwise.

(2) *Reimbursing dependent care assistance through a debit card.*—An employer offering a dependent care assistance FSA may adopt the following method to provide reimbursements for dependent care expenses through a debit card—

(i) At the beginning of the plan year or upon enrollment in the dependent care assistance program, the employee pays initial expenses to the dependent care provider and substantiates the initial expenses by submitting to the employer or plan administrator a statement from the dependent care provider substantiating the dates and amounts for the services provided.

(ii) After the employer or plan administrator receives the substantiation (but not before the date the services are provided as indicated by the statement provided by the dependent care provider), the plan makes available through the debit card an amount equal to the lesser of—

(A) The previously incurred and substantiated expense; or

(B) The employee's total salary reduction amount to date.

(iii) The card may be used to pay for subsequently incurred dependent care expenses.

(iv) The amount available through the card may be increased in the amount of any additional dependent care expenses only after the additional expenses have been incurred.

(3) *Substantiating recurring dependent care expenses.*—Card transactions that collect information matching expenses previously substantiated and approved as to dependent care provider and time period may be treated as substantiated without further review if the transaction is for an amount equal to or less than the previously substantiated expenses. Similarly, dependent care expenses previously substantiated and approved through nonelectronic methods may also be treated as substantiated without further review. In both cases, if there is an increase in previously substantiated amounts or a change in the dependent care provider, the employee must submit a statement or receipt from the dependent care provider substantiating the claimed expenses before amounts relating to the increased amounts or new providers may be added to the card.

(4) *Example.*—The following example illustrates the rules in this paragraph (g):

Example. Recurring dependent care expenses. (i) Employer K sponsors a dependent care assistance FSA through its cafeteria plan. Salary reduction amounts for participating employees are made on a weekly payroll basis, which are available for dependent care coverage on a weekly basis. As a result, the amount of available dependent care coverage equals the employee's salary reduction amount minus claims previously paid from the plan. Employer K has adopted a payment card program for its dependent care FSA.

(ii) For the plan year ending December 31, 2009, Employee F is a participant in the dependent care FSA and elected $5,000 of dependent care coverage. Employer K reduces F's salary by $96.15 on a weekly basis to pay for coverage under the dependent care FSA.

(iii) At the beginning of the 2009 plan year, F is issued a debit card with a balance of zero. F's childcare provider, ABC Daycare Center, requires a $250 advance payment at the beginning of the week for dependent care services that will be provided during the week. The dependent care services provided for F by ABC qualify for reimbursement under section 129. However, because as of the begin ning of the plan year, no services have yet been provided, F cannot be reimbursed for any of the amounts until the end of the first week of the plan year (that is, the week ending January 5, 2009), after the services have been provided.

(iv) F submits a claim for reimbursement that includes a statement from ABC with a description of the services, the amount of the services, and the dates of the services. Employer K increases the balance of F's payment card to $96.15 after the services have been provided (i.e., the lesser of F's salary reduction to date or the incurred dependent care expenses). F uses the card to pay ABC $96.15 on the first day of the next week (January 8, 2009) and pays ABC the remaining balance due for that week ($153.85) by check.

(v) To the extent that this card transaction and each subsequent transaction is with ABC and is for an amount equal to or less than the previously substantiated amount, the charges are fully substantiated without the need for the submission by F of a statement from the provider or further review by the employer. However, the subsequent amount is not made available on the card until the end of the week when the services have been provided. Employer K's dependent care debit card satisfies the substantiation requirements of this paragraph (g).

(h) *Effective/applicability date.*—It is proposed that these regulations apply on and after plan years beginning on or after January 1, 2009. However, the effective dates for the previously issued guidance on debit cards, which is incorporated in this section, remain applicable. [Reg. § 1.125-6.]

§ 1.125-7. Cafeteria plan nondiscrimination rules.—
(a) *Definitions.*—(1) *In general.*—The definitions set forth in this paragraph (a) apply for purposes of section 125(b), (c), (e) and (g) and this section.

(2) *Compensation.*—The term *compensation* means compensation as defined in section 415(c)(3).

(3) *Highly compensated individual.*—(i) *In general.*—The term *highly compensated individual* means an individual who is—

(A) An officer;

(B) A five percent shareholder (as defined in paragraph (a)(8) of this section); or

(C) Highly compensated.

(ii) *Spouse or dependent.*—A spouse or a dependent of any highly compensated individual described in (a)(3)(i) of this section is a highly compensated individual. Section 125(e).

(4) *Highly compensated participant.*—The term *highly compensated participant* means a highly compensated individual who is eligible to participate in the cafeteria plan.

(5) *Nonhighly compensated individual.*—The term *nonhighly compensated individual* means an individual who is not a highly compensated individual.

(6) *Nonhighly compensated participant.*—The term *nonhighly compensated participant* means a participant who is not a highly compensated participant.

(7) *Officer.*—The term *officer* means any individual or participant who for the preceding plan year (or the current plan year in the case of the first year of employment) was an officer. Whether an individual is an *officer* is determined based on all the facts and circumstances, including the source of the individual's authority, the term for which he or she is elected or appointed, and the nature and extent of his or her duties. Generally, the term officer means an administrative executive who is in regular and continued service. The term officer implies continuity of service and excludes individuals performing services in connection with a special and single transaction. An individual who merely has the title of an officer but not the authority of an officer, is not an officer. Similarly, an individual without the title of an officer but who has the authority of an officer is an officer. Sole proprietorships, partnerships, associations, trusts and labor organizations also may have officers. See §§ 301.7701-1 through -3

(8) *Five percent shareholder.*—A *five percent shareholder* is an individual who in either the preceding plan year or current plan year owns more than five percent of the voting power or value of all classes of stock of the employer, determined without attribution.

(9) *Highly compensated.*—The term *highly compensated* means any individual or participant who for the preceding plan year (or the current plan year in the case of the first year of employment) had compensation from the employer in excess of the compensation amount specified in section 414(q)(1)(B), and, if elected by the employer, was also in the top-paid group of employees (determined by reference to section 414(q)(3)) for such preceding plan year (or for the current plan year in the case of the first year of employment).

(10) *Key employee.*—A *key employee* is a participant who is a key employee within the meaning of section 416(i)(1) at any time during the preceding plan year. A key employee covered by a collective bargaining agreement is a key employee.

(11) *Collectively bargained plan.*—A *collectively bargained plan* is a plan or the portion of a plan maintained under an agreement which is a collective bargaining agreement between employee representatives and one or more employers, if there is evidence that cafeteria plan benefits were the subject of good faith bargaining between such employee representatives and such employer or employers.

(12) *Year of employment.*—For purposes of section 125(g)(3)(B)(i), a *year of employment* is determined by reference to the elapsed time method of crediting service. See § 1.410(a)-7.

(13) *Premium-only-plan.*—A *premium-only-plan* is described in paragraph (a)(5) in § 1.125-1.

(14) *Statutory nontaxable benefits.*—*Statutory nontaxable benefits* are qualified benefits that are excluded from gross income (for example, an employer-provided accident and health plan excludible under section 106 or a dependent care assistance program excludible under section 129). Statutory nontaxable benefits also include group-term life insurance on the life of an employee includible in the employee's gross income solely because the coverage exceeds the limit in section 79(a).

(15) *Total benefits.*—*Total benefits* are qualified benefits and permitted taxable benefits.

(b) *Nondiscrimination as to eligibility.*—(1) *In general.*—A cafeteria plan must not discriminate in favor of highly compensated individuals as to eligibility to participate for that plan year. A cafeteria plan does not discriminate in favor of highly compensated individuals if the plan benefits a group of employees who qualify under a reasonable classification established by the employer, as defined in § 1.410(b)-4(b), and the group of employees included in the classification satisfies the safe harbor percentage test or the unsafe harbor percentage component of the facts and circumstances test in § 1.410(b)-4(c). (In applying the § 1.410(b)-4 test, substitute highly compensated individual for highly compensated employee and substitute nonhighly compensated individual for nonhighly compensated employee).

(2) *Deadline for participation in cafeteria plan.*—Any employee who has completed three years of employment (and who satisfies any conditions for participation in the cafeteria plan that are not related to completion of a requisite length of employment) must be permitted to elect to participate in the cafeteria plan no later than the first day of the first plan year beginning after the date the employee completed three years of employment (unless the employee separates from service before the first day of that plan year).

(3) *The safe harbor percentage test.*—(i) *In general.*—For purposes of the safe harbor percentage test and the unsafe harbor percentage component of the facts and circumstances test, if the cafeteria plan provides that only employees who have completed three years of employment are permitted to participate in the plan, employees who have not completed three years of employment may be excluded from consideration. However, if the cafeteria plan provides that employees are allowed to participate before completing three years of employment, all employees with less than three years of employment must be included in applying the safe harbor percentage test and the unsafe harbor percentage component of the facts and circumstances test. See paragraph (g) of this section for a permissive disaggregation rule.

(ii) *Employees excluded from consideration.*—In addition, for purposes of the safe harbor percentage test and the unsafe harbor percentage component of the facts and circumstances test, the following employees are excluded from consideration —

(A) Employees (except key employees) covered by a collectively bargained plan as defined in paragraph (a)(11) of this section;

(B) Employees who are nonresident aliens and receive no earned income (within the meaning of section 911(d)(2)) from the employer which constitutes income from sources within the United States (within the meaning of section 861(a)(3)); and

(C) Employees participating in the cafeteria plan under a COBRA continuation provision.

(iv) *Examples.*—The following examples illustrate the rules in paragraph (b) of this section:

Example 1. Same qualified benefit for same salary reduction amount. Employer A has one employer-provided accident and health insurance plan. The cost to participants electing the accident and health plan is $10,000 per year for single coverage. All employees have the same opportunity to salary reduce $10,000 for accident and health plan. The cafeteria plan satisfies the eligibility test.

Example 2. Same qualified benefit for unequal salary reduction amounts. Same facts as *Example 1* except the cafeteria plan offers nonhighly compensated employees the election to salary reduce $10,000 to pay premiums for single coverage. The cafeteria plan provides an $8,000 employer flex-credit to highly compensated employees to pay a portion of the premium, and provides an election to them to salary reduce $2,000 to pay the balance of the premium. The cafeteria plan fails the eligibility test.

Example 3. Accident and health plans of unequal value. Employer B's cafeteria plan offers two employer-provided accident and health insurance plans: Plan X, available only to highly compensated participants, is a low-deductible plan. Plan Y, available only to nonhighly compensated participants, is a high deductible plan (as defined in section 223(c)(2)). The annual premium for single coverage under Plan X is $15,000 per year, and $8,000 per year for Plan Y. Employer B's cafeteria plan provides that highly compensated participants may elect salary reduction of $15,000 for coverage under Plan X, and that nonhighly compensated participants may elect salary reduction of $8,000 for coverage under Plan Y. The cafeteria plan fails the eligibility test.

Example 4. Accident and health plans of unequal value for unequal salary reduction amounts. Same facts as *Example 3*, except that the amount of salary reduction for highly compensated participants to elect Plan X is $8,000. The cafeteria plan fails the eligibility test.

(c) *Nondiscrimination as to contributions and benefits.*—(1) *In general.*—A cafeteria plan must not discriminate in favor of highly compensated participants as to contributions and benefits for a plan year.

(2) *Benefit availability and benefit election.*—A cafeteria plan does not discriminate with respect to contributions and benefits if either qualified benefits and total benefits, or employer contributions allocable to statutory nontaxable benefits and employer contributions allocable to total benefits, do not discriminate in favor of highly compensated participants. A cafeteria plan must satisfy this paragraph (c) with respect to both benefit availability and benefit utilization. Thus, a plan must give each similarly situated participant a uniform opportunity to elect qualified benefits, and the actual election of qualified benefits through the plan must not be disproportionate by highly compensated participants (while other participants elect permitted taxable benefits). Qualified benefits are disproportionately elected by highly compensated participants if the aggregate qualified benefits elected by highly compensated participants, measured as a percentage of the aggregate compensation of highly compensated participants, exceed the aggregate qualified benefits elected by nonhighly compensated participants measured as a percentage of the aggregate compensation of nonhighly compensated participants. A plan must also give each similarly situated participant a uniform election with respect to employer contributions, and the actual election with respect to employer contributions for qualified benefits through the plan must not be disproportionate by highly compensated participants (while other participants elect to receive employer contributions as permitted taxable benefits). Employer contributions are disproportionately utilized by highly compensated participants if the aggregate contributions utilized by highly compensated participants, measured as a percentage of the aggregate compensation of highly compensated participants, exceed the aggregate contributions utilized by nonhighly compensated participants measured as a percentage of the aggregate compensation of nonhighly compensated participants.

(3) *Example.*—The following example illustrates the rules in paragraph (c) of this section:

Example. Contributions and benefits test. Employer C's cafeteria plan satisfies the eligibility test in paragraph (b) of this section. Highly compensated participants in the cafeteria plan elect aggregate qualified benefits equaling 5 percent of aggregate compensation; nonhighly compensated participants elect aggregate qualified benefits equaling 10 percent of aggregate compensation. Employer C's cafeteria plan passes the contribution and benefits test.

(d) *Key employees.*—(1) *In general.*—If for any plan year, the statutory nontaxable benefits provided to key employees exceed 25 percent of the aggregate of statutory nontaxable benefits provided for all employees through the cafeteria plan, each key employee includes in gross income an amount equaling the maximum taxable benefits that he or she could have elected for the plan year. However, see safe harbor for premium-only-plans in paragraph (f) of this section.

(2) *Example.*—The following example illustrates the rules in paragraph (d) of this section:

Example. (i) *Key employee concentration test.* Employer D's cafeteria plan offers all employees an election between taxable benefits and qualified benefits. The cafeteria plan satisfies the eligibility test

in paragraph (b) of this section. Employer D has two key employees and four nonhighly compensated employees. The key employees each elect $2,000 of qualified benefits. Each nonhighly compensated employee also elects $2,000 of qualified benefits. The qualified benefits are statutory nontaxable benefits.

(ii) Key employees receive $4,000 of statutory nontaxable benefits and nonhighly compensated employees receive $8,000 of statutory nontaxable benefits, for a total of $12,000. Key employees receive 33 percent of statutory nontaxable benefits (4,000/12,000). Because the cafeteria plan provides more than 25 percent of the aggregate of statutory nontaxable benefits to key employees, the plan fails the key employee concentration test.

(e) *Safe harbor for cafeteria plans providing health benefits.*—(1) *In general.*—A cafeteria plan that provides health benefits is not treated as discriminatory as to benefits and contributions if:

(i) Contributions under the plan on behalf of each participant include an amount which equals 100 percent of the cost of the health benefit coverage under the plan of the majority of the highly compensated participants similarly situated, or equals or exceeds 75 percent of the cost of the health benefit coverage of the participant (similarly situated) having the highest cost health benefit coverage under the plan, and

(ii) Contributions or benefits under the plan in excess of those described in paragraph (e)(1)(i) of this section bear a uniform relationship to compensation.

(2) *Similarly situated.*—In determining which participants are similarly situated, reasonable differences in plan benefits may be taken into account (for example, variations in plan benefits offered to employees working in different geographical locations or to employees with family coverage versus employee-only coverage).

(3) *Health benefits.*— Health benefits for purposes of this rule are limited to major medical coverage and exclude dental coverage and health FSAs.

(4) *Example.*—The following example illustrates the rules in paragraph (e) of this section:

Example. (i) All 10 of Employer E's employees are eligible to elect between permitted taxable benefits and salary reduction of $8,000 per plan year for self-only coverage in the major medical health plan provided by Employer E. All 10 employees elect $8,000 salary reduction for the major medical plan.

(ii) The cafeteria plan satisfies the section 125(g)(2) safe harbor for cafeteria plans providing health benefits.

(f) *Safe harbor test for premium-only-plans.*—(1) *In general.*—A premium-only-plan (as defined in paragraph (a)(13) of this section) is deemed to satisfy the nondiscrimination rules in section 125(c) and this section for a plan year if, for that plan year, the plan satisfies the safe harbor percentage test for eligibility in paragraph (b)(3) of this section.

(2) *Example.*—The following example illustrates the rules in paragraph (f) of this section:

Example. Premium-only-plan. (i) Employer F's cafeteria plan is a premium-only-plan (as defined in paragraph (a)(13) of this section). The written cafeteria plan offers one employer-provided accident and health plan and offers all employees the election to salary reduce same amount or same percentage of the premium for self-only or family coverage. All key employees and all highly compensated employees elect salary reduction for the accident and health plan, but only 20 percent of nonhighly compensated employees elect the accident and health plan.

(ii) The premium-only-plan satisfies the nondiscrimination rules in section 125(b) and (c) and this section.

(g) *Permissive disaggregation for nondiscrimination testing.*—(1) *General rule.*—If a cafeteria plan benefits employees who have not completed three years of employment, the cafeteria plan is permitted to test for nondiscrimination under this section as if the plan were two separate plans—

(i) One plan benefiting the employees who completed one day of employment but less than three years of employment; and

(ii) Another plan benefiting the employees who have completed three years of employment.

(2) *Disaggregated plans tested separately for eligibility test and contributions and benefits test.*—If a cafeteria plan is disaggregated into two separate plans for purposes of nondiscrimination testing, the two separate plans must be tested separately for both the nondiscrimination as to eligibility test in paragraph (b) of this section and the nondiscrimination as to contributions and benefits test in paragraph (c) of this section.

(h) *Optional aggregation of plans for nondiscrimination testing.*—An employer who sponsors more than one cafeteria plan is permitted to aggregate two or more of the cafeteria plans for purposes of nondiscrimination testing. If two or more cafeteria plans are aggregated into a combined plan for this purpose, the combined plan must satisfy the nondiscrimination as to eligibility test in paragraph (b) of this section and the nondiscrimination as to contributions and benefits test in paragraph (c) of this section, as though the combined plan were a single plan. Thus, for example, in order to satisfy the benefit availability and benefit election requirements in paragraph (c)(2) of this section, the combined plan must give each similarly situated participant a uniform opportunity to elect qualified benefits and the actual election of qualified benefits by highly compensated participants must not be disproportionate. However, if a principal purpose of the aggregation is to manipulate the nondiscrimination testing requirements or to otherwise discriminate in favor of highly compensated individuals or participants, the plans will not be permitted to be aggregated for nondiscrimination testing.

(i) *Employees of certain controlled groups.*—All employees who are treated as employed by a single employer under section 414(b), (c), (m), or (o) are treated as employed by a single employer for purposes of section 125. Section 125(g)(4); section 414(t).

(j) *Time to perform nondiscrimination testing.*—(1) *In general.*—Nondiscrimination testing must be performed as of the last day of the plan year, taking into account all non-excludable employees (or former employees) who were employees on any day during the plan year.

(2) The following example illustrates the rules in paragraph (j) of this section:

Example. When to perform discrimination testing. (i) Employer H employs three employees and maintains a calendar year cafeteria plan. During the 2009 plan year, Employee J was an employee the entire calendar year, Employee K was an employee from May 1, through August 31, 2009, and Employee L worked from January 1, 2009 to April 15, 2009, when he retired.

(ii) Nondiscrimination testing for the 2009 plan year must be performed on December 31, 2009, taking into account employees J, K, and L's compensation in the preceding year.

(k) *Discrimination in actual operation prohibited.*—In addition to not discriminating as to either benefit availability or benefit utilization, a cafeteria plan must not discriminate in favor of highly compensated participants in actual operation. For example, a plan may be discriminatory in actual operation if the duration of the plan (or of a particular nontaxable benefit offered through the plan) is for a period during which only highly compensated participants utilize the plan (or the benefit). See also the key employee concentration test in section 125(b)(2).

(l) *Anti-abuse rule.*—(1) *Interpretation.*—The provisions of this section must be interpreted in a reasonable manner consistent with the purpose of preventing discrimination in favor of highly compensated individuals, highly compensated participants and key employees.

(2) *Change in plan testing procedures.*—A plan will not be treated as satisfying the requirements of this section if there are repeated changes to plan testing procedures or plan provisions that have the effect of manipulating the nondiscrimination testing requirements of this section, if a principal purpose of the changes was to achieve this result.

(m) *Tax treatment of benefits in a cafeteria plan.*—(1) *Nondiscriminatory cafeteria plan.*—A participant in a nondiscriminatory cafeteria plan (including a highly compensated participant or key employee) who elects qualified benefits is not treated as having received taxable benefits offered through the plan, and thus the qualified benefits elected by the employee are not includible in the employee's gross income merely because of the availability of taxable benefits. But see paragraph (j) in §1.125-1 on nondiscrimination rules for sections 79(d), 105(h), 129(d), and 137(c)(2), and limitations on exclusion.

(2) *Discriminatory cafeteria plan.*—A highly compensated participant or key employee participating in a discriminatory cafeteria plan must include in gross income (in the participant's taxable year within which ends the plan year with respect to which an election was or could have been made) the value of the taxable benefit with the greatest value that the employee could have elected to receive, even if the employee elects to receive only the nontaxable benefits offered.

(n) *Employer contributions to employees' Health Savings Accounts.*—If an employer contributes to employees' Health Savings Accounts (HSAs) through a cafeteria plan (as defined in §54.4980G-5 of this chapter) those contributions are subject to the nondiscrimination rules in section 125 and this section and are not subject to the comparability rules in section 4980G. See §§ 54.4980G-0 through 54.4980G-5 of this chapter.

(o) *Effective/applicability date.*—It is proposed that these regulations apply on and after plan years beginning on or after January 1, 2009. [Reg. §1.125-7.]

Cost-Sharing Payments: Conservation Payments

Cost-Sharing Payments: Conservation Payments: Exclusions: Recapture.—Temporary Reg. §§16A.126-0—16A.126-2, relating to cost-sharing payments, are also proposed as final regulations (published in the Federal Register on May 21, 1981).

§16A.126-0.   Effective dates.

§16A.126-1.   Certain cost sharing payments—In general.

§16A.126-2.   Section 126 elections.

Employee Trusts: Effective Dates

Employee Trusts: Tax Reform Act of 1984: Effective Dates.—Temporary Reg. §1.133-1T is also proposed as a final regulation and, when adopted, would become Reg. §1.133-1 (published in the Federal Register on February 4, 1986).

§1.133-1.   Questions and answers relating to interest on certain loans used to acquire employer securities.

Definition of Registered Form: Guidance

Definition of Registered Form: Guidance.—Reg. §1.149(a)-1, providing guidance on the definitions of registration-required obligation and registered form, including guidance on the issuance of pass-through certificates and participation interests in registered form, is proposed (published in the Federal Register on September 19, 2017) (REG-125374-16).

Par. 2. Section 1.149(a)-1 is added to read as follows:

§1.149(a)-1. Obligations required to be in registered form.—(a) *General rule.*—Interest on a registration-required bond shall not be exempt from tax notwithstanding section 103(a) or any other provision of law, exclusive of any treaty obligation of the United States, unless the bond is issued in registered form (as defined in §1.163-5(b)). For this purpose, registration-required bond has the same meaning as registration-required obligation in §1.163-5(a)(2).

(b) *Applicability date.*—This section applies to bonds issued on or after the date 90 days after the publication of the Treasury decision adopting these rules as final regulations in the **Federal Register**. For bonds issued before the date 90 days after the publication of the Treasury decision adopting these rules as final regulations in the **Federal Register**, see §5f.103-1 of this chapter. [Reg. §1.149(a)-1.]

Tax-Exempt Bonds: State and Local Governments: Refunding Issue: Definition

Tax-Exempt Bonds: State and Local Governments: Refunding Issue: Definition. Amendments to Reg. §1.150-1, relating to the definition of refunding issue applicable to tax-exempt bonds issued by States and local governments, are proposed (published in the Federal Register on April 10, 2007) (REG-165706-01).

☐ Par. 2. Section 1.150-1 is amended as follows:

1. Paragraph (a)(2)(iii) is added.

2. Paragraphs (d)(2)(ii) and (d)(2)(v) are revised.

The added and revised provisions read as follows:

§1.150-1. Definitions.—(a) * * *

(2) * * *

(iii) *Special effective date for paragraphs (d)(2)(ii) and (d)(2)(v).*—Paragraphs (d)(2)(ii) and (d)(2)(v) of this section apply to bonds sold on or after the date of publication of final regulations in the Federal Register, and may be applied by issuers in whole, but not in part, to any issue that is sold on or after April 10, 2002.

* * *

(d) * * *

(2) * * *

(ii) *Certain issues with different obligors.*—(A) *In general.*—An issue is not a refunding issue to the extent that the obligor (as defined in paragraph (d)(2)(ii)(B) of this section) of one issue is neither the obligor of the other issue nor a related party with respect to the obligor of the other issue. The determination of whether persons are related for this purpose is generally made immediately before the issuance of the refinancing issue. This paragraph (d)(2)(ii)(A) does not apply to any issue that is issued in connection with a transaction to which section 381(a) applies.

(B) *Definition of obligor.*—The obligor of an issue means the actual issuer of the issue, except that the obligor of the portion of an issue properly allocable to an investment in a purpose investment means the conduit borrower under that purpose investment. The obligor of an issue used to finance qualified mortgage loans, qualified student loans, or similar program investments (as defined in §1.148-1) does not include the ultimate recipient of the loan (e.g., the homeowner, the student).

(C) *Certain integrated transactions.*—If, within six months before or after a person assumes (including taking subject to) obligations of an unrelated party in connection with an acquisition transaction (other than a transaction to which section 381(a) applies), the assumed issue is refinanced, the refinancing issue is not a refunding issue. An acquisition transaction is a transaction in which a person acquires from an unrelated party—

(1) Assets (other than an equity interest in an entity);

(2) Stock of a corporation with respect to which a valid election under section 338 is made; or

(3) Control of a governmental unit or a 501(c)(3) organization through the acquisition of stock, membership interests or otherwise.

(D) *Special rule for affiliated persons.*—Paragraphs (d)(2)(ii)(A) and (C) of this section do not apply to any issue that is issued in connection with a transaction between affiliated persons (as defined in paragraph (d)(2)(ii)(E) of this section), unless—

(1) The refinanced issue is redeemed on the earliest date on which it may be redeemed (or otherwise within 90 days after the date of issuance of the refinancing issue); and

(2) The refinancing issue is treated for all purposes of sections 103 and 141 through 150 as financing the assets that were financed with the refinanced issue.

(E) *Affiliated persons.*—For purposes of paragraph (d)(2)(ii)(D) of this section, persons are affiliated persons if—

(1) At any time during the six months prior to the transaction, more than 5 percent of the voting power of the governing body of either person is in the aggregate vested in the other person and its directors, officers, owners, and employees; or

(2) During the one-year period beginning six months prior to the transaction, the composition of the governing body of the acquiring person (or any person that controls the acquiring person) is modified or established to reflect (directly or indirectly) representation of the interests of the acquired person or the person from whom assets are acquired (or there is an agreement, understanding, or arrangement relating to such a modification or establishment during that one-year period).

(F) *Reverse acquisitions.*—Notwithstanding any other provision of this paragraph (d)(2)(ii), a refinancing issue is a refunding issue if the obligor of the refinanced issue (or any person that is related to the obligor of the refinanced issue immediately before the transaction) has or obtains in the transaction the right to appoint the majority of the members of the governing body of the obligor of the refinancing issue (or any person that controls the obligor of the refinancing issue). See paragraph (d)(2)(v) *Example* 2 of this section.

* * *

(v) *Examples.*—The provisions of this paragraph (d)(2) are illustrated by the following examples:

Example 1. Consolidation of 501(c)(3) hospital organizations. (i) A and B are unrelated hospital organizations described in section 501(c)(3). A has assets with a fair market value of $175 million, and is the obligor of outstanding tax-exempt bonds in the amount of $75 million. B has assets with a fair market value of $145 million, and is the obligor of outstanding tax-exempt bonds in the amount of $50 million. In response to significant competitive pressures in the healthcare industry, and for other substantial business reasons, A and B agree to consolidate their operations. To accomplish the consolidation, A and B form a new 501(c)(3) hospital organization, C. A and B each appoint one-half of the members of the initial governing body of C. Subsequent to the initial appointments, C's governing body is self-perpetuating. On December 29, 2003, State Y issues bonds with sale proceeds of $129 million and lends the entire sale proceeds to C. The 2003 bonds are collectively secured by revenues of A, B and C. Simultaneously with the issuance of the 2003 bonds, C acquires the sole membership interest in each of A and B. C's ownership of these membership interests entitles C to exercise exclusive control over the assets and operations of A and B. C uses the $129 million of sale proceeds of the 2003 bonds to defease the $75 million of bonds on which A was the obligor, and the $50 million of bonds on which B was the obligor. All of the defeased bonds will be redeemed on the first date on which they may be redeemed. In addition, C treats the 2003 bonds as financing the same assets as the defeased bonds. The 2003 bonds do not constitute a refunding issue because the obligor of the 2003 bonds (C) is neither the obligor of the defeased bonds nor a related party with respect to the obligors of those bonds immediately before the issuance of the 2003 bonds. In addition, the requirements of paragraph (d)(2)(ii)(D) of this section have been satisfied.

(ii) The facts are the same as in paragraph (i) of this *Example 1*, except that C acquires the membership interests in A and B subject to the obligations of A and B on their respective bonds, and the 2003 bonds are sold within six months after the acquisition by C of the membership interests. The 2003 bonds do not constitute a refunding issue.

Example 2. Reverse acquisition. D and E are unrelated hospital organizations described in section 501(c)(3). D has assets with a fair market value of $225 million, and is the obligor of outstanding tax-exempt bonds in the amount of $100 million. E has assets with a fair market value of $100 million. D and E agree to consolidate their operations. On May 18, 2004, Authority Z issues bonds with sale proceeds of $103 million and lends the entire sale proceeds to E. Simultaneously with the issuance of the 2004 bonds, E acquires the sole membership interest in D. In addition, D obtains the right to appoint the majority of the members of the governing body of E. E uses the $103 million of sale proceeds of the 2004 bonds to defease the bonds of which D was the obligor. All of the defeased bonds will be redeemed on the first date on which they may be redeemed. In addition, E treats the 2004 bonds as financing the same assets as the defeased bonds. The 2004 bonds constitute a refunding issue because the obligor of the defeased bonds (D) obtains in the transaction the right to appoint the majority of the members of the governing body of the obligor of the 2004 bonds (E). See paragraph (d)(2)(ii)(F) of this section.

Example 3. Relinquishment of control. The facts are the same as in *Example 2*, except that D does not obtain the right, directly or indirectly, to appoint any member of the governing body of E. Rather, E obtains the right both to approve and to remove without cause each member of the governing body of D. In addition, prior to being acquired by E, D experiences financial difficulties as a result of mismanagement. Thus, as part of E's acquisition of D, all of the former members of D's governing body resign their positions and are replaced with persons appointed by E. The 2004 bonds do not constitute a refunding issue.

* * *

State and Local Governments: Tax-Exempt Bonds

State and Local Governments: Tax-Exempt Bonds.—Reg. §1.150-3, addressing when tax-exempt bonds are treated as retired for purposes of section 103 and sections 141 through 150 of the Internal Revenue Code, is proposed (published in the Federal Register on December 31, 2018) (REG-141739-08).

Par. 2. Section 1.150-3 is added to read as follows:

§1.150-3. Retirement standards for state and local bonds.—(a) *General purpose and scope.*—This section provides rules to determine when a tax-exempt bond is retired for purposes of sections 103 and 141 through 150.

(b) *General rules for retirement of a tax-exempt bond.*—Except as otherwise provided in paragraph (c) of this section, a tax-exempt bond is retired when:

(1) A significant modification of the bond occurs under §1.1001-3;

(2) The issuer or its agent acquires the bond in a manner that liquidates or extinguishes the bondholder's investment in the bond; or

(3) The bond is otherwise redeemed (for example, redeemed at maturity).

(c) *Exceptions to retirement of a tax-exempt bond.*—(1) *Qualified tender right does not result in a modification.*—In applying §1.1001-3 to a qualified tender bond for purposes of paragraph (b)(1) of this section, both the existence and exercise of a qualified tender right are disregarded. Thus, a change in the interest rate mode made in connection with the exercise of a qualified tender right generally is not a modification because the change occurs by operation of the terms of the bond and the holder's resulting right to put the bond to the issuer or its agent does not prevent the issuer's option from being a unilateral option.

(2) *Acquisition pursuant to a qualified tender right.*—Acquisition of a qualified tender bond by the issuer or its agent does not result in retirement of the bond under paragraph (b)(2) of this section if the acquisition is pursuant to the operation of a qualified tender right and neither the issuer nor its agent continues to hold the bond after the close of the 90-day period beginning on the date of the tender.

(3) *Acquisition of a tax-exempt bond by a guarantor or liquidity facility provider.*—Acquisition of a tax-exempt bond by a guarantor or liquidity facility provider acting on the issuer's behalf does not result in retirement of the bond under paragraph (b)(2) of this section if the acquisition is pursuant to the terms of the guarantee or liquidity facility and the guarantor or liquidity facility provider is not a related party (as defined in §1.150-11(b)) to the issuer.

(d) *Effect of retirement.*—If a bond is retired pursuant to paragraph (b)(1) of this section (that is, in a transaction treated as an exchange of the bond for a bond with modified terms), the bond is treated as a new bond issued at the time of the modification as determined under §1.1001-3. If the issuer or its agent resells a bond retired pursuant to paragraph (b)(2) of this section, the bond is treated as a new bond issued on the date of resale. In both cases, the rules of §1.150-1(d) apply to determine if the new bond is part of a refunding issue.

(e) *Definitions.*—For purposes of this section, the following definitions apply:

(1) *Issuer* means the State or local governmental unit (as defined in §1.103-1) that actually issues the tax-exempt bond and any related party (as defined in §1.150-1(b)) to the actual issuer (as distinguished, for example, from a conduit borrower that is not a related party to the actual issuer).

(2) *Qualified tender bond* means a tax-exempt bond that, pursuant to the terms of its governing contract, has all of the features described in this paragraph (e)(2). During each authorized interest rate mode, the bond bears interest at a fixed interest rate, a qualified floating rate under §1.1275-5(b), or an objective rate for a tax-exempt bond under §1.1275-5(c)(5). Interest on the bond is unconditionally payable at periodic intervals of no more than one year. The bond has a stated maturity date that is not later than 40 years after the issue date of the bond. The bond includes a qualified tender right.

(3) *Qualified tender right* means a right or obligation of a holder of the bond to tender the bond for purchase as described in this paragraph (e)(3). The purchaser under the tender may be the issuer, its agent, or another party. The tender right is available on at least one date before the stated maturity date. For each such tender, the purchase price of the bond is equal to par (plus any accrued interest). Following each such tender, the issuer or its remarketing agent either redeems the bond or uses reasonable best efforts to resell the bond within the 90-day period beginning on the date of the tender. Upon any such resale, the purchase price of the bond is equal to par (plus any accrued interest).

(f) *Applicability date.*—This section applies to events and actions taken with respect to bonds that occur on or after the date that is 90 days after the date of publication of the Treasury decision adopting these rules as final regulations in the **Federal Register**. [Reg. §1.150-3.]

Dependency Exemption: Authorized Placement Agency: Definition

Dependency Exemption: Authorized Placement Agency: Definition.—Amendments to Reg. §§1.151-1—1.151-4, relating to the definition of an authorized placement agency for purposes of a dependency exemption for a child placed for adoption that were issued prior to the changes made to the law by the Working Families Tax Relief Act of 2004, are proposed (published in the Federal Register on January 19, 2017) (REG-137604-07).

Par. 10. Section 1.151-1 is amended by revising paragraphs (a)(1), (c), and (d) to read as follows:

§1.151-1. Deductions for personal exemptions.—(a) * * *

(1) In computing taxable income, an individual is allowed a deduction for the exemptions for an individual taxpayer and spouse (the personal exemptions) and the exemption for a dependent of the taxpayer.

* * *

Par. 11. Sections 1.151-2, 1.151-3, and 1.151-4 are removed.

§1.151-2. Additional exemptions for dependents.

§1.151-3. Definitions.

§1.151-4. Amount of deduction for each exemption under section 151.

(c) *Additional exemption for dependent.*—Section 151(c) allows a taxpayer an exemption for each individual who is a dependent (as defined in section 152) of the taxpayer for the taxable year. See §§1.152-1 through 1.152-5 for rules relating to dependents.

(d) *Applicability date.*—Paragraphs (a)(1) and (c) of this section apply to taxable years beginning after the date these regulations are published as final regulations in the **Federal Register**.

Dependency Exemption: Authorized Placement Agency: Definition

Dependency Exemption: Authorized Placement Agency: Definition.—Reg. §§1.152-0 and 1.152-4 and amendments to Reg. §§1.152-1—1.152-5, relating to the definition of an authorized placement agency for purposes of a dependency exemption for a child placed for adoption that were issued prior to the changes made to the law by the Working Families Tax Relief Act of 2004, are proposed (published in the Federal Register on January 19, 2017) (REG-137604-07).

Par. 12. Section 1.152-0 is added under the undesignated center heading Deductions for Personal Exemptions to read as follows:

§1.152-0. Table of contents.—This section lists the captions contained in §1.152-1 through §1.152-5.

§1.152-1 General rules for dependents.

(a) In general.

(1) Dependent defined.

(2) Exceptions.

(i) Dependents ineligible.

(ii) Married dependents.

(iii) Citizens or nationals of other countries.

(b) Definitions.

(1) Child.

(i) In general.

(ii) Adopted child.

(iii) Eligible foster child.

Par. 13. Section 1.152-1 is revised to read as follows:

§1.152-1. General rules for dependents.—(a) *In general.*—(1) *Dependent defined.*—Except as provided in section 152(b) and paragraph (a)(2) of this section, the term *dependent* means a qualifying child as described in §1.152-2 or a qualifying relative as described in §1.152-3. In general, an individual may be treated as the dependent of only one taxpayer for taxable years beginning in the same calendar year.

(2) *Exceptions.*—(i) *Dependents ineligible.*—If an individual is a dependent of a taxpayer for a taxable year of the taxpayer, the individual is treated as having no dependents for purposes of section 152 and the related regulations in the individual's taxable year beginning in the calendar year in which that taxable year of the taxpayer begins. For purposes of this paragraph (a)(2)(i), an individual is not a dependent of a person if that person is not required to file an income tax return under section 6012 and either does not file an income tax return or files an income tax return solely to claim a refund of estimated or withheld taxes.

(ii) *Married dependents.*—An individual is not treated as a dependent of a taxpayer for a taxable year of the taxpayer if the individual files a joint return, other than solely to claim a refund of estimated or withheld taxes, with the individual's spouse under section 6013 for the taxable year beginning in the calendar year in which that taxable year of the taxpayer begins.

(iii) *Citizens or nationals of other countries.*—An individual who is not a citizen or national of the United States is not treated as a dependent of a taxpayer unless the individual is a resident, as defined in section 7701(b), of the United States or of a country contiguous to the United States (Canada or Mexico). This limitation, however, does not apply to an adopted child, as defined in section 152(f)(1)(B) and paragraph (b)(1)(ii) of this section, if the taxpayer is a citizen or national of the United States and the child has the same principal place of abode as the taxpayer and is a member of the taxpayer's household, within the meaning of §§1.152-4(c) and 1.2-2(c), respectively, for the taxpayer's taxable year. See §1.152-4(d)(2) for rules relating to residence for a portion of a taxable year. A taxpayer and the child have the same principal place of abode for the taxpayer's taxable year if the taxpayer and child have the same principal place of abode for the entire portion of the taxable year following the placement of the child with the taxpayer.

(b) *Definitions.*—The following definitions apply for purposes of section 152 and the related regulations.

(1) *Child.*—(i) *In general.*—The term *child* means a son, daughter, stepson, or stepdaughter, or an eligible foster child, within the meaning of paragraph (b)(1)(iii) of this section, of the taxpayer.

(ii) *Adopted child.*—In determining whether an individual bears any of the relationships described in paragraph (b)(1)(i) of this section, §1.152-2(b), or §1.152-3(b), a legally adopted child of a person, or a child who is lawfully placed with a person for legal adoption by that person, is treated as a child by blood of that person. A child lawfully placed with a person for legal adoption by that person includes a child placed for legal adoption by a parent, an authorized placement agency, or any other person(s) authorized by law to place a child for legal adoption.

(iii) *Eligible foster child.*—The term *eligible foster child* means a child who is placed with a person by an authorized placement agency or by judgment, decree, or other order of any court of competent jurisdiction.

(iv) *Authorized placement agency.*—The term *authorized placement agency* means a State, the District of Columbia, a possession of the United States, a foreign country, an Indian Tribal Government (ITG) (as defined in section 7701(a)(40)), or an agency or organization that is authorized by a State, the District of Columbia, a possession of the United States, a foreign country, an ITG, or a political subdivision of any of the foregoing, to place children for legal adoption or in foster care.

(2) *Student.*—The term *student* means an individual who, for some part of each of five calendar months, whether or not consecutive, during the calendar year in which the taxable year of the taxpayer begins, either is a full-time student at an educational organization, as defined in section 170(b)(1)(A)(ii), or is pursuing a full-time course of institutional on-farm training under the supervision of an accredited agent of an educational organization or of a State or political subdivision of a State. A full-time student is one who is enrolled for the number of hours or courses that the educational organization considers full-time attendance.

(3) *Brother and sister.*—The terms *brother* and *sister* include a brother or sister by half blood.

(4) *Parent.*—The term *parent* refers to a biological or adoptive parent of an individual. It does not include a stepparent who has not adopted the individual.

(c) *Applicability date.*—This section, and §§1.152-2, 1.152-3, and 1.152-4 apply to taxable years beginning after the date these regulations are published as final regulations in the **Federal Register**.

Par. 14. Section 1.152-2 is revised to read as follows:

§1.152-2. Qualifying child.—(a) *In general.*—The term *qualifying child* of a taxpayer for a taxable year means an individual who satisfies the tests described in paragraphs (b), (c), (d), (e), and (f) of this section. If an individual satisfies the definition of a qualifying child for more than one taxpayer, then the tiebreaker rules in paragraph (g) of this section apply. See, however, section 152(e) and §1.152-5 for a special rule for a child of divorced or separated parents or parents who live apart.

(b) *Qualifying child relationship test.*—The individual must bear one of the following relationships to the taxpayer—

(1) A child of the taxpayer or descendant of such a child; or

(2) A brother, sister, stepbrother, or stepsister of the taxpayer, or a descendant of any of these relatives.

(c) *Residency test.*—The individual must have the same principal place of abode as the taxpayer for more than one-half of the taxable year. Generally, an individual has the same principal place of abode as the taxpayer for more than one-half of the taxable year if the individual resides with the taxpayer for more than one-half of the taxable year. See §1.152-4(c) for rules relating to principal place of abode and temporary absence and for determining whether an individual resides with the taxpayer for more than one-half of the taxable year.

(d) *Age test.*—(1) *In general.*—The individual must be younger than the taxpayer claiming the individual as a qualifying child and must not have attained the age of 19, or age 24 if the individual is a student within the meaning of §1.152-1(b)(2), as of the end of the calendar year in which the taxpayer's taxable year begins. For purposes of this section, an individual attains an age on the anniversary of the individual's birth.

(2) *Disabled individual.*—This age requirement is treated as satisfied if the individual is permanently and totally disabled, as defined in section 22(e)(3), at any time during the calendar year.

(e) *Qualifying child support test.*—The individual must not provide more than one-half of the individual's own support for the calendar year in which the taxpayer's taxable year begins. See §1.152-4(a) for rules relating to the definition and sources of an individual's support.

(f) *Joint return test.*—The individual must not file a joint return, other than solely to claim a refund of estimated or withheld taxes, under section 6013 with the individual's spouse for the taxable year beginning in the calendar year in which the taxpayer's taxable year begins.

(g) *Child who is eligible to be claimed as a qualifying child by more than one taxpayer.*—(1) *In general.*—Under section 152(c)(4), if an individual satisfies the definition of a qualifying child for two or more taxpayers (eligible taxpayers) for a taxable year beginning in the same calendar year, the following rules apply.

(i) *More than one eligible parent.*—If more than one eligible taxpayer is a parent of the individual (eligible parent), any one of the eligible parents may claim the individual as a qualifying child. However, if more than one eligible parent claims the individual as a qualifying child, and those eligible parents do not file a joint return with each other, the individual is treated as the qualifying child of the eligible parent claiming the individual with whom the individual resides for the longest period of time during the taxable year as determined under §1.152-4(c)(3). If the individual resides for the same amount of time during the taxable year with each eligible parent claiming the child, the individual is treated as the qualifying child of the eligible parent with the highest adjusted gross income who claims the individual.

(ii) *Eligible parent not claiming.*—If at least one eligible taxpayer is a parent of the individual, but no eligible parent claims the individual as a qualifying child, the individual may be treated as the qualifying child of another eligible taxpayer only if that taxpayer's adjusted gross income exceeds both the adjusted gross income of each eligible parent of the individual and the adjusted gross income of each other eligible taxpayer, if any.

(iii) *One eligible parent and other eligible taxpayer(s).*—Except as provided in paragraph (g)(1)(i) or (ii) of this section, if there are two or more eligible taxpayers, only one of whom is the parent of the individual, the individual is treated as the qualifying child of the eligible parent.

(iv) *No eligible parent.*—If no eligible taxpayer is a parent of the individual, the individual is treated as the qualifying child of the eligible taxpayer with the highest adjusted gross income for the taxable year.

(2) *Determination of adjusted gross income of a person who files a joint return.*—For purposes of section 152 and the related regulations, the adjusted gross income of each person who files a joint return is the total adjusted gross income shown on the joint return.

(3) *Coordination with other provisions.*—Except to the extent that section 152(e) and §1.152-5 apply, if more than one taxpayer may claim a child as a qualifying child, the child is treated as the qualifying child of only one taxpayer for purposes of head of household filing status under section 2(b), the child and dependent care credit under section 21, the child tax credit under section 24, the earned income credit under section 32, the exclusion from income for dependent care assistance under section 129, and the dependency exemption under section 151. Thus, the taxpayer claiming the individual as a qualifying child under any one of these sections is the only taxpayer who may claim any credit or exemption under these other sections for that same individual for a taxable year beginning in the same calendar year as the taxpayer's taxable year. If section 152(e) applies, however, the noncustodial parent may claim the child as a qualifying child for purposes of the dependency exemption and the child tax credit, and another person may claim the child for purposes of one or more of these other provisions. See §1.152-5 for rules under section 152(e).

(4) *Examples.*—The following examples illustrate the rules in this paragraph (g). In the examples, each taxpayer uses the calendar year as the taxpayer's taxable year, the child is a qualifying child (as described in section 152(c) and this section) of each taxpayer, and, except to the extent indicated, each taxpayer meets the requirements to claim the benefit(s) described in the example.

Example 1. (i) A and B, parents of Child, are married to each other. A, B, and Child share the same principal place of abode for the first 8 months of the year. Thus, both parents satisfy the qualifying child residency test of paragraph (c) of this section. For the last 4 months of the year, the parents live apart from each other, and B and Child share the same principal place of abode. Section 152(e), relating to divorced or separated parents, does not apply. The parents file as married filing separately for the taxable year, and both parents claim Child as a qualifying child.

(ii) Under paragraph (g)(1)(i) of this section, Child is treated as a qualifying child of B for all purposes, because Child resided with B for the longer period of time during the taxable year. Because section 152(e) does not apply, Child may not be treated as a qualifying child of A for any purpose.

Example 2. (i) The facts are the same as in *Example 1* of this paragraph (g)(4), except that B does not claim Child as a qualifying child.

(ii) Because A and B are not both claiming the same child as a qualifying child, under paragraph (g)(1)(i) of this section, Child is treated as a qualifying child of A.

Example 3. (i) Child, Child's parent (D), and Grandparent share the same principal place of abode. D is not married and is not a qualifying child or dependent of Grandparent, and Grandparent is not D's dependent. Section 152(e), relating to divorced or separated parents, does not apply. Under paragraph (a) of this section, Child meets the definition of a qualifying child of both D and Grandparent. D claims Child as a qualifying child for purposes of the child and dependent care credit under section 21, the earned income credit under section 32, and the dependency exemption under section 151. Grandparent claims Child as a qualifying child for purposes of head of household filing status under section 2(b).

(ii) Under paragraph (g)(1)(iii) of this section, Child is treated as the qualifying child of D for all purposes, because D is eligible to claim and claims Child as D's qualifying child. Because D is eligible to claim and claims Child as D's qualifying child, under paragraph (g)(3) of this section, Child may not be treated as a qualifying child of Grandparent for any purpose. Grandparent erroneously claimed Child as Grandparent's qualifying child for purposes of head of household filing status under section 2(b). If D had not claimed Child as D's qualifying child for any purpose, under paragraph (g)(1)(ii) of this section, Grandparent could have claimed Child as Grandparent's qualifying child if Grandparent's adjusted gross income (AGI) exceeded D's AGI. In that situation, under paragraph (g)(3) of this section, Grandparent could have claimed Child as Grandparent's

Par. 15. Section 1.152-3 is revised to read as follows:

§1.152-3. Qualifying relative.—(a) *In general.*—The term *qualifying relative* of a taxpayer for a taxable year means an individual who satisfies the tests described in paragraphs (b), (c), (d), and (e) of this section. See, however, section 152(e) and §1.152-5 for a special rule for a child of divorced or separated parents or parents who live apart.

(b) *Qualifying relative relationship test.*—The individual must bear one of the following relationships to the taxpayer:

(1) A child or descendant of a child;

(2) A brother, sister, stepbrother, or stepsister;

(3) A father or mother, or an ancestor of either;

(4) A stepfather or stepmother;

(5) A niece or nephew;

(6) An aunt or uncle;

(7) A son-in-law, daughter-in-law, father-in-law, mother-in-law, brother-in-law, or sister-in-law; or

(8) An individual (other than one who at any time during the taxable year was the taxpayer's spouse, determined without regard to section 7703) who for the taxable year of the taxpayer has the same principal place of abode as the taxpayer and is a member of the taxpayer's household. See §1.2-2(c) for the definition of a member of the household, and §1.152-4(c) for rules relating to the meaning of principal place of abode and the meaning of temporary absence.

(c) *Gross income test.*—(1) *In general.*—The individual's gross income for the calendar year in which the taxable year begins must be less than the exemption amount as defined in section 151(d).

(2) *Income of disabled or handicapped individuals.*—For purposes of paragraph (c)(1) of this section, the gross income of an individual who is permanently and totally disabled, as defined in section 22(e)(3), at any time during the taxable year does not include income for services performed by the individual at a sheltered workshop, as defined in section 152(d)(4)(B), if—

(i) The principal reason for the individual's presence at the workshop is the availability of medical care there; and

(ii) The individual's income arises solely from activities at the workshop that are incident to the medical care.

(d) *Qualifying relative support test.*—(1) *In general.*—The individual must receive over one-half of the individual's support from the

qualifying child for purposes of any of the child-related tax benefits, provided that Grandparent had met the requirements of those sections.

Example 4. (i) The facts are the same as in *Example 3* of this paragraph (g)(4), except that Child's parents, D and E, are married to each other and share the same principal place of abode with Child and Grandparent for the entire taxable year. Under paragraph (a) of this section, Child meets the definition of a qualifying child of both parents and Grandparent. D and E file a joint return for the taxable year and do not claim Child as a qualifying child for any purpose.

(ii) Because D or E may claim Child as a qualifying child but neither claims Child as a qualifying child for any purpose, under paragraph (g)(1)(ii) of this section, Grandparent may claim Child as a qualifying child if Grandparent's AGI exceeds the total AGI reported on the joint return of D and E.

Example 5. (i) The facts are the same as in *Example 4* of this paragraph (g)(4), except that D and E are divorced from each other, E moved into a separate residence during that year and is the noncustodial parent, and section 152(e), relating to divorced or separated parents, applies. E attaches to E's return a Form 8332 on which D agrees to release D's claim to a dependency exemption for Child and E claims Child as a qualifying child for purposes of the dependency exemption and the child tax credit.

(ii) Under paragraph (g)(3) of this section, Child is treated as a qualifying child of E for purposes of the dependency exemption and the child tax credit. Child may be treated as a qualifying child of D for purposes of the earned income credit. If D claims Child as a qualifying child for purposes of the earned income credit, under paragraph (g)(1)(iii) of this section, Child may not be treated as a qualifying child of Grandparent for any purpose.

Example 6. (i) F and G, parents of two children, are married to each other. F, G, and both children share the same principal place of abode for the entire taxable year. F and G file as married filing separately for the taxable year. F claims the older child as a qualifying child for purposes of the child tax credit, dependency exemption, and the child and dependent care credit. G claims the younger child as a qualifying child for purposes of the same three tax benefits.

(ii) The older child is treated as a qualifying child of F and the younger child is treated as a qualifying child of G. The tiebreaker rule of paragraph (g)(1)(i) of this section does not apply because F and G are not claiming the same child as a qualifying child.

taxpayer for the calendar year in which the taxpayer's taxable year begins. See §1.152-4(a) for rules relating to support.

(2) *Certain income of taxpayer's spouse.*—A payment to a spouse that is includible in the payee spouse's gross income under section 71 (relating to alimony and separate maintenance payments) or section 682 (relating to income of an estate or trust in the case of divorce) is not treated as a payment by the payor spouse for the support of any dependent.

(3) *Support from stepparent.*—Any support provided to or for the benefit of an individual by a stepparent of the individual is treated as support provided by the individual's parent who is married to the stepparent.

(4) *Multiple support agreements.*—If more than one-half of an individual's support is provided by two or more persons together, a taxpayer is treated as having contributed over one-half of the support of that individual for the calendar year if—

(i) No one person contributes more than one-half of the individual's support;

(ii) Each member of the group that collectively contributes more than one-half of the support of the individual would have been entitled to claim the individual as a dependent for a taxable year beginning in that calendar year but for the fact that the group member alone did not contribute more than one-half of the individual's support;

(iii) The taxpayer claiming the individual as a qualifying relative contributes more than 10 percent of the individual's support; and

(iv) Each other group member who contributes more than 10 percent of the support of the individual furnishes to the taxpayer claiming the individual as a dependent a written declaration that the other person will not claim the individual as a dependent for any taxable year beginning in that calendar year.

(e) *Not a qualifying child test.*—(1) *In general.*—The individual must not be a qualifying child of the taxpayer or of any other taxpayer for any taxable year beginning in the calendar year in which the taxpayer's taxable year begins. An individual is not a qualifying child of a person, however, if that person is not required to file an income tax return under section 6012, and either does not file an income tax return or files an income tax return solely to claim a refund of estimated or withheld taxes.

(2) *Examples.*—The following examples illustrate the rules in this paragraph (e). In each example, each taxpayer uses the calendar year as the taxpayer's taxable year, and except to the extent otherwise indicated, each taxpayer meets the requirements to claim the benefits described in the example.

Example 1. For the taxable year, B provides more than one-half of the support of an unrelated friend, C, and C's 3-year-old child, D, who are members of B's household. No taxpayer other than C is eligible to claim D as a qualifying child. C has no gross income, is not required by section 6012 to file a Federal income tax return, and does not file a Federal income tax return for the taxable year. Under paragraph (e)(1) of this section, because C does not have a filing requirement and does not file an income tax return, D is not treated as a qualifying child of C, and B may claim both C and D as B's qualifying relatives.

Par. 16. Redesignate § 1.152-4 as § 1.152-5, and add a new § 1.152-4 to read as follows:

§1.152-4. Rules for a qualifying child and a qualifying relative.—(a) *Support.*—(1) *In general.*—The term *support* includes food, shelter, clothing, medical and dental care, education, and similar items. Support does not include an individual's Federal, State, and local income taxes paid from the individual's own income or assets, Social Security and Medicare taxes under section 3101 paid from the individual's own income, life insurance premiums, or funeral expenses. In determining whether an individual provided more than one-half of the individual's own support for purposes of § 1.152-2(e), or whether a taxpayer provided more than one-half of an individual's support for purposes of § 1.152-3(d), the amount of support provided by the individual, or the taxpayer, is compared to the total amount of the individual's support from all sources. For these purposes, except as otherwise provided in this paragraph (a), the amount of an individual's total support is the amount of support from all sources, and includes support the individual provides and amounts that are excludable from gross income. Generally, the amount of an item of support is the amount of expense paid or incurred to furnish the item of support. If the item of support furnished is property or a benefit, such as lodging, however, the amount of the item of support is the fair market value of the item.

(2) *Payments made during the year for unpaid or future support.*— For purposes of determining the amount of support provided in a calendar year, an amount paid in a calendar year after the calendar year in which the liability is incurred is treated as paid in the year of payment. An amount paid in a calendar year before due, whether or not made in the form of a lump sum payment in settlement of a person's liability for support, is treated as support paid during the calendar year of payment rather than the calendar year when payment is due. A payment of a liability from amounts set aside in trust in a prior year is treated as made in the year in which the liability is paid.

(3) *Governmental payments.*—(i) *Governmental payments as support.*—(A) *In general.*—Except as provided in paragraph (a)(3)(iii) of this section, governmental payments and subsidies for an item of support are support provided by a third party, the government.

(B) *Examples.*—Payments of Temporary Assistance for Needy Families (42 U.S.C. 601-619), low-income housing assistance (42 U.S.C. 1437f), Supplemental Nutrition Assistance Program benefits (7 U.S.C. chapter 51), Supplemental Security Income payments (42 U.S.C. 1381-1383f), foster care maintenance payments, and adoption assistance payments are governmental payments and subsidies for an item of support as described in paragraph (a)(3)(i)(A) of this section.

(ii) *Governmental payments based on a taxpayer's contributions.*—(A) *In general.*—Except as provided in paragraph (a)(3)(iii) of this section, governmental payments based on a taxpayer's earnings and contributions into the Social Security system are support provided by the individual for whose benefit the payments are made to the extent those payments are used for that individual's support.

(B) *Examples.*—Social Security old age benefits under section 202(b) of Title II of the Social Security Act (SSA) (42 U.S.C. 402) are governmental payments based on a taxpayer's earnings and contributions into the Social Security system as described in paragraph (a)(3)(ii)(A) of this section. Similarly, Social Security survivor and disability insurance benefits paid under section 202(d) of the SSA to, or for the benefit of, the child of a deceased or disabled parent are treated as support provided by the child to the extent those payments are used for the child's support.

Example 2. The facts are the same as in *Example 1* of this paragraph (e)(2) except that C has earned income of $1,500 during the taxable year, had income tax withheld from C's wages, and is not required by section 6012 to file an income tax return. C files an income tax return solely to obtain a refund of withheld taxes and does not claim the earned income credit under section 32. Under paragraph (e)(1) of this section, because C does not have a filing requirement and files only to obtain a refund of withheld taxes, D is not treated as a qualifying child of C, and B may claim both C and D as B's qualifying relatives.

Example 3. The facts are the same as in *Example 2* of this paragraph (e)(2) except that C's earned income is more than the amount of the dependency exemption for that year. C files an income tax return for the taxable year to obtain a refund of withheld taxes and claims the earned income credit. Because C filed an income tax return to obtain the earned income credit and not solely to obtain a refund of withheld taxes, D is a qualifying child of a taxpayer (C), and B may not claim D as a qualifying relative. B also may not claim C as a qualifying relative because C fails the gross income test under paragraph (c) of this section.

(iii) *Payments used for support of another individual.*—Governmental payments and subsidies described in paragraph (a)(3)(i) of this section and governmental payments described in paragraph (a)(3)(ii) of this section that are used by the recipient or other intended beneficiary to support another person are support of that person provided by the recipient or other intended beneficiary, rather than support provided by a third party, the government.

(4) *Medical insurance.*—Medical insurance premiums, including Part A Basic Medicare premiums, if any, under Title XVIII of the Social Security Act (42 U.S.C. 1395c to 1395i-5), Part B Supplemental Medicare premiums under Title XVIII of the Social Security Act (42 U.S.C. 1395j to 1395w-6), Part C Medicare + Choice Program premiums under Title XVIII of the Social Security Act (42 U.S.C. 1395w-21 to 1395w-29), and Part D Voluntary Prescription Drug Benefit Medicare premiums under Title XVIII of the Social Security Act (42 U.S.C. 1395w-101 to 1395w-154), are treated as support. Medical insurance proceeds, including benefits received under Medicare Part A, Part B, Part C, and Part D, are not treated as items of support and are disregarded in determining the amount of the individual's support. Services provided to an individual under the medical and dental care provisions of the Armed Forces Act (10 U.S.C. chapter 55) are not treated as support and are disregarded in determining the amount of the individual's support.

(5) *Medical care payments from personal injury claim.*—Payments for the medical care of an injured individual from a third party, including a third party's insurance company, in satisfaction of a legal claim for the personal injury of the individual are not treated as items of support and are disregarded in determining the amount of the individual's support.

(6) *Scholarships.*—Amounts a student who is the child of the taxpayer receives as a scholarship for study at an educational organization described in section 170(b)(1)(A)(ii) are not treated as an item of support and are disregarded in determining the amount of the student's support.

(b) *Relationship test.*—(1) *Joint return.*—A taxpayer may satisfy the relationship test described in § 1.152-2(b) (relating to a qualifying child) or in § 1.152-3(b) (relating to a qualifying relative) if a described relationship exists between an individual and the taxpayer claiming that individual as a qualifying child or qualifying relative, even though the taxpayer files a joint return with his or her spouse who does not have a described relationship with the individual.

(2) *Divorce or death of spouse.*—If the relationship between the taxpayer and an individual claimed by that taxpayer as a dependent results from a marriage, the taxpayer's qualifying relationship with the individual continues after the termination of the marriage by divorce or death.

(c) *Principal place of abode.*—(1) *In general.*—The term *principal place of abode* of a person means the primary or main home or dwelling where the person resides. A person's principal place of abode need not be the same physical location throughout the taxable year and may be temporary lodging such as a homeless shelter or relief housing resulting from displacement caused by a natural disaster.

(2) *Temporary absence.*—The taxpayer and an individual have the same principal place of abode despite a temporary absence by either person because of special circumstances. An absence is temporary if the person would have resided at the place of abode but for the absence and, under the facts and circumstances, it is reasonable to

assume that the person will return to reside at the place of abode. An individual who does not reside with the taxpayer because of a temporary absence is treated as residing with the taxpayer. For example, a nonpermanent failure to occupy the abode by reason of illness, education, business, vacation, military service, institutionalized care for a child who is totally and permanently disabled (as defined in section 22(e)(3)), or incarceration may be treated as a temporary absence because of special circumstances. If an infant must remain in a hospital for a period of time after birth and would have resided with the taxpayer during that period but for the hospitalization, the infant is treated as having the same principal place of abode as the taxpayer during the period of hospitalization.

(3) *Residing with taxpayer for more than one-half of the taxable year.*—(i) *In general.*—An individual has the same principal place of abode as the taxpayer for more than one-half of the taxable year if the individual resides with the taxpayer for at least 183 nights during the taxpayer's taxable year, or 184 nights if the taxable year includes a leap day.

(ii) *Nights of residence.*—(A) *Nights counted.*—For purposes of determining whether an individual resides with the taxpayer for more than one-half of the taxable year, an individual resides with a taxpayer for a night if the individual sleeps

(1) At the taxpayer's principal place of abode, whether or not the taxpayer is present; or

(2) In the company of the taxpayer when the individual does not sleep at the taxpayer's principal place of abode (for example, when the taxpayer and the individual are on vacation).

(B) *Night straddling two taxable years.*—If an individual resides with a taxpayer for a night that extends over two taxable years, that night is allocated to the taxable year in which the night begins.

(C) *Exception for a parent who works at night.*—If, in a calendar year, because of a taxpayer's nighttime work schedule, an individual resides for at least 183 days, or 184 days if the taxable year includes a leap day, but not nights with the taxpayer, the individual is treated as residing with the taxpayer for more than one-half of the taxable year.

(D) *Absences.*—An individual who does not reside with a taxpayer for a night because of a temporary absence as described in paragraph (c)(2) of this section is treated as residing with the taxpayer for that night if the individual would have resided with the taxpayer for that night but for the absence.

(4) *Examples.*—The following examples illustrate the rules of this paragraph (c). In each example, each taxpayer uses the calendar taxable year, and section 152(e) does not apply.

Example 1. B and C are the divorced parents of Child. In 2015, Child sleeps at B's principal place of abode for 210 nights and at C's principal place of abode for 155 nights. Under paragraph (c)(3) of this section, Child resides with B for at least 183 nights during 2015 and has the same principal place of abode as B for more than one-half of 2015.

Example 2. D and E are the divorced parents of Child, and Grandparent is E's parent. In 2015, Child resides with D for 140 nights, with E for 135 nights, and with Grandparent for the last 90 nights of the year. None of these periods is a temporary absence. Under paragraph (c)(3) of this section, Child does not have the same principal place of abode as D, E, or Grandparent for more than one-half of 2015.

Example 3. The facts are the same as in *Example 2* of this paragraph (c)(4), except that, for the 90-day period that Child lives with Grandparent, E is temporarily absent on military service. Child would have lived with E if E had not been absent during that period. Under paragraphs (c)(2) and (c)(3)(ii)(D) of this section, Child is treated as residing with E for 225 nights in 2015 and, therefore, Child has the same principal place of abode as E for more than one-half of 2015.

Example 4. The facts are the same as in *Example 2* of this paragraph (c)(4), except that, for the last 90 days of the year Child, who is 18, moves into Child's own apartment and begins full-time employment. Because Child's absence is not temporary, under paragraph (c)(2) of this section, Child is not treated as residing with D or E for the 90 nights. Under paragraph (c) of this section, Child does not have the same principal place of abode as D or E for more than one-half of 2015.

Example 5. F and G are the divorced parents of Child. In 2015, Child sleeps at F's principal place of abode for 170 nights and at G's principal place of abode for 170 nights. Child spends 25 nights of the year away from F and G at a summer camp. Child would have spent those nights with F if Child had not gone to summer camp. Under paragraphs (c)(2) and (c)(3)(ii)(D) of this section, Child is treated as residing with F for 195 nights and, therefore, Child has the same principal place of abode as F for more than one-half of 2015.

Example 6. H and J are the divorced parents of Child. In 2015, Child sleeps at H's principal place of abode for 180 nights and at J's principal place of abode for 180 nights. For 5 nights during that year, Child sleeps at Grandparent's abode or at the house of a friend. Child would have spent all 5 nights at H's house if Child had not slept at Grandparent's or a friend's house. Under paragraphs (c)(2) and (c)(3)(ii)(D) of this section, Child is treated as residing with H for 185 nights and, therefore, Child has the same principal place of abode as H for more than one-half of 2015.

(d) *Residence for a portion of a taxable year because of special circumstances.*—(1) *Individual who is born or dies during the year.*—If an individual is born or dies during a taxpayer's taxable year, the residency test for a qualifying child is treated as met if the taxpayer and the individual have the same principal place of abode for more than one-half of the portion of the taxable year during which the individual is alive. If an individual is born or dies during a taxpayer's taxable year, the relationship test for a qualifying relative who is a member of the taxpayer's household is treated as met if the taxpayer and the individual have the same principal place of abode for the entire portion of the taxable year during which the individual is alive.

(2) *Adopted child or foster child.*—If, during a taxpayer's taxable year, the taxpayer adopts a child, a child is lawfully placed with a taxpayer for legal adoption by that taxpayer, or an eligible foster child is placed with a taxpayer, the residency test for a qualifying child and the residency requirement under §1.152-1(a)(2)(iii) for a child who is not a citizen or national of the United States are treated as met if the taxpayer and the child have the same principal place of abode for more than one-half of the portion of the taxable year as required for a qualifying child, or for the entire taxable year as required for a noncitizen, following the placement of the child with the taxpayer.

(e) *Missing child.*—(1) *Qualifying child.*—A child of the taxpayer who is presumed by law enforcement authorities to have been kidnapped by someone who is not a member of the family of either the child or the taxpayer, and who had for the taxable year in which the kidnapping occurred the same principal place of abode as the taxpayer for more than one-half of the portion of the taxable year before the date of the kidnapping, is treated as meeting the residency test for a qualifying child, as described in §1.152-2(c), of the taxpayer for all taxable years ending during the period that the child is missing. Also, the child is treated as meeting the residency test in the year of the child's return if the child has the same principal place of abode as the taxpayer for more than one-half of the portion of the taxable year following the date of the child's return.

(2) *Qualifying relative.*—A child of the taxpayer who is presumed by law enforcement authorities to have been kidnapped by someone who is not a member of the family of either the child or the taxpayer, and who was a qualifying relative of the taxpayer for the portion of the taxable year before the date of the kidnapping, is treated as a qualifying relative, as described in section 152(d) and §1.152-3, of the taxpayer for all taxable years ending during the period that the child is missing. Also, the child is treated as a qualifying relative of the taxpayer in the year of the child's return if the child is a qualifying relative of the taxpayer for the portion of the taxable year following the date of the child's return.

(3) *Age limitation.*—The special rules provided in this paragraph (e) cease to apply as of the first taxable year of the taxpayer beginning after the calendar year in which there is a determination that the child is dead or, if earlier, in which the child would have attained age 18.

(4) *Application.*—This paragraph (e) applies solely for purposes of determining surviving spouse or head of household filing status under section 2, the child tax credit under section 24, the earned income credit under section 32, and the dependency exemption under section 151.

Par. 17. In newly redesignated §1.152-5, paragraphs (e)(2), (e)(3)(iii), and (h) are revised to read as follows:

§1.152-5. Special rule for a child of divorced or separated parents or parents who live apart.

* * *

(e) * * *

(2) *Attachment to return.*—(i) *In general.*—A noncustodial parent must attach a copy of the written declaration to the parent's original or amended return for each taxable year for which the noncustodial parent claims an exemption for the child. A noncus-

todial parent may submit a copy of the written declaration to the IRS during an examination to substantiate a claim to a dependency exemption for a child. A copy of a written declaration attached to an amended return, or provided during an examination, will not meet the requirement of this paragraph (e) if the custodial parent signed the written declaration after the custodial parent filed a return claiming a dependency exemption for the child for the year at issue, and the custodial parent has not filed an amended return to remove that claim to a dependency exemption for the child.

      (ii) *Examples.*—The following examples illustrate the rules of this paragraph (e).

      Example 1. Custodial parent (CP) files her 2015 return on March 1, 2016, and claims a dependency exemption for Child. At noncustodial parent's (NCP) request, CP signs a Form 8332 for the 2015 tax year on April 15, 2016. On April 15, NCP files his return claiming a dependency exemption for Child and attaches the signed Form 8332 to his return. Under section 152(e) and paragraph (b) of this section, NCP is allowed a dependency exemption for Child for 2015, and CP is not allowed a dependency exemption for Child for that year.

      Example 2. The facts are the same as in *Example 1* of this paragraph (e)(2)(ii), except NCP files on April 15, 2016, a request for an extension to file his tax return because he does not have a signed Form 8332. CP signs the Form 8332 for the 2015 tax year in August of 2016, and NCP files his return a week later. NCP claims a dependency exemption for Child and attaches the signed Form 8332 to his return. Under section 152(e) and paragraph (b) of this section, NCP is allowed a dependency exemption for Child for 2015, and CP is not allowed a dependency exemption for Child for that year.

      Example 3. CP files his 2015 return on March 1, 2016, and claims a dependency exemption for Child. NCP files her return on April 15, 2016, and does not claim a dependency exemption for Child, even though her divorce decree allocates the dependency exemption for Child to her. CP signs a Form 8332 for the 2015 tax year in August of 2016, and NCP files an amended return a week later and attaches the signed Form 8332 to her amended return claiming a dependency exemption for Child. Under paragraph (e)(2) of this section, NCP is not allowed a dependency exemption for Child for 2015 if CP has not amended his return to remove a claim to the dependency exemption for Child for that year.

      (3) * * *

      (iii) *Attachment to return.*—The parent revoking the written declaration must attach a copy of the revocation to the parent's original or amended return for each taxable year for which the parent claims a child as a dependent as a result of the revocation. The parent revoking the written declaration must keep a copy of the revocation and evidence of delivery of the notice to the other parent, or of the reasonable efforts to provide actual notice. A parent may submit a copy of a revocation to the IRS during an examination to substantiate a claim to a dependency exemption for the child.

* * *

      (h) *Applicability date.*—(1) *In general.*—Except as provided in paragraph (h)(2) of this section, this section applies to taxable years beginning after July 2, 2008.

      (2) *Exception.*—Paragraphs (e)(2) and (e)(3)(iii) of this section apply to taxable years beginning after the date these regulations are published as final regulations in the **Federal Register**.

Employee Trusts: Effective Dates

Employee Trusts: Tax Reform Act of 1984: Effective Dates.—Temporary Reg. § 1.162-10T is also proposed as a final regulation and, when adopted, would become Reg. § 1.162-10 (published in the Federal Register on February 4, 1986).

§ 1.162-10. Certain employee benefits.

Treatment of Payments to Charitable Entities: Return for Consideration

Treatment of Payments to Charitable Entities: Return for Consideration.—Amendments to Reg. § 1.162-15, updating the regulations under section 162 to reflect current law regarding the application of section 162 to a taxpayer that makes a payment or transfer to an entity described in section 170(c) for a business purpose, are proposed (published in the Federal Register on December 17, 2019) (REG-107431-19).

Par. 2. Section 1.162-15 is amended by revising paragraph (a) to read as follows:

§ 1.162-15. Contributions, dues, etc.—(a) *Payments and transfers to entities described in section 170(c).*—(1) *In general.*—A payment or transfer to or for the use of an entity described in section 170(c) that bears a direct relationship to the taxpayer's trade or business and that is made with a reasonable expectation of financial return commensurate with the amount of the payment or transfer may constitute an allowable deduction as a trade or business expense rather than a charitable contribution deduction under section 170. For payments or transfers in excess of the amount deductible under section 162(a), see § 1.170A-1(h).

      (2) *Examples.*—The following examples illustrate the rules of paragraph (a)(1) of this section:

      (i) *Example 1. A*, an individual, is a sole proprietor who manufactures musical instruments and sells them through a website. *A* makes a $1,000 payment to a local church (which is a charitable organization described in section 170(c)) for a half-page advertisement in the church's program for a concert. In the program, the church thanks its concert sponsors, including *A. A*'s advertisement includes the URL for the website through which *A* sells its instruments. *A* reasonably expects that the advertisement will attract new customers to *A*'s website and will help *A* to sell more musical instruments. *A* may treat the $1,000 payment as an expense of carrying on a trade or business under section 162.

      (ii) *Example 2. P*, a partnership, operates a chain of supermarkets, some of which are located in State N. *P* operates a promotional program in which it sets aside the proceeds from one percent of its sales each year, which it pays to one or more charities described in section 170(c). The funds are earmarked for use in projects that improve conditions in State N. *P* makes the final determination on which charities receive payments. *P* advertises the program. *P* reasonably believes the program will generate a significant degree of name recognition and goodwill in the communities where it operates and thereby increase its revenue. As part of the program, *P* makes a $1,000 payment to a charity described in section 170(c). *P* may treat the $1,000 payment as an expense of carrying on a trade or business under section 162. This result is unchanged if, under State N's tax credit program, *P* expects to receive a $1,000 income tax credit on account of *P*'s payment, and under State N law, the credit can be passed through to *P*'s partners.

      (3) *Safe harbors for C corporations and specified passthrough entities making payments in exchange for state or local tax credits.*—(i) *Safe harbor for C corporations.*—If a C corporation makes a payment to or for the use of an entity described in section 170(c) and receives or expects to receive in return a state or local tax credit that reduces a state or local tax imposed on the C corporation, the C corporation may treat such payment as meeting the requirements of an ordinary and necessary business expense for purposes of section 162(a) to the extent of the amount of the credit received or expected to be received.

      (ii) *Safe harbor for specified passthrough entities.*— (A) *Definition of specified passthrough entity.*—For purposes of this paragraph (a)(3)(ii), an entity is a specified passthrough entity if each of the following requirements is satisfied—

      (*1*) The entity is a business entity other than a C corporation and is regarded for all Federal income tax purposes as separate from its owners under § 301.7701-3 of this chapter;

      (*2*) The entity operates a trade or business within the meaning of section 162;

      (*3*) The entity is subject to a state or local tax incurred in carrying on its trade or business that is imposed directly on the entity; and

      (*4*) In return for a payment to an entity described in section 170(c), the entity described in paragraph (a)(3)(ii)(A)(*1*) of this section receives or expects to receive a state or local tax credit that this entity applies or expects to apply to offset a state or local tax described in paragraph (a)(3)(ii)(A)(*3*) of this section.

      (B) *Safe harbor.*—Except as provided in paragraph (a)(3)(ii)(C) of this section, if a specified passthrough entity makes a payment to or for the use of an entity described in section 170(c), and receives or expects to receive in return a state or local tax credit that reduces a state or local tax described in paragraph (a)(3)(ii)(A)(*3*) of this section, the specified passthrough entity may treat such payment as meeting the requirements of an ordinary and necessary business expense for purposes of section 162(a) to the extent of the amount of credit received or expected to be received.

      (C) *Exception.*—The safe harbor described in this paragraph (a)(3)(ii) does not apply if the credit received or expected to be received reduces a state or local income tax.

(iii) *Definition of payment.*—For purposes of this paragraph (a)(3), payment is defined as a payment of cash or cash equivalent.

(iv) *Examples.*—The following examples illustrate the rules of paragraph (a)(3) of this section.

(A) *Example 1: C corporation that receives or expects to receive dollar-for-dollar state or local tax credit. A*, a C corporation engaged in a trade or business, makes a payment of $1,000 to an entity described in section 170(c). In return for the payment, *A* expects to receive a dollar-for-dollar state tax credit to be applied to *A*'s state corporate income tax liability. Under paragraph (a)(3)(i) of this section, *A* may treat the $1,000 payment as an expense of carrying on a trade or business under section 162.

(B) *Example 2: C corporation that receives or expects to receive percentage-based state or local tax credit. B*, a C corporation engaged in a trade or business, makes a payment of $1,000 to an entity described in section 170(c). In return for the payment, *B* expects to receive a local tax credit equal to 80 percent of the amount of this payment ($800) to be applied to *B*'s local real property tax liability. Under paragraph (a)(3)(i) of this section, *B* may treat $800 as an expense of carrying on a trade or business under section 162. The treatment of the remaining $200 will depend upon the facts and circumstances and is not affected by paragraph (a)(3)(i) of this section.

(C) *Example 3: Partnership that receives or expects to receive dollar-for-dollar state or local tax credit. P* is a limited liability company classified as a partnership for Federal income tax purposes under §301.7701-3 of this chapter. *P* is engaged in a trade or business and makes a payment of $1,000 to an entity described in section 170(c). In return for the payment, *P* expects to receive a dollar-for-dollar state tax credit to be applied to *P*'s state excise tax liability incurred by *P* in carrying on its trade or business. Under applicable state law, the state's excise tax is imposed at the entity level (not the owner level). Under paragraph (a)(3)(ii) of this section, *P* may treat the $1,000 as an expense of carrying on a trade or business under section 162.

(D) *Example 4: S corporation that receives or expects to receive percentage-based state or local tax credit. S* is an S corporation engaged in a trade or business and is owned by individuals *C* and *D. S* makes a payment of $1,000 to an entity described in section 170(c). In return for the payment, *S* expects to receive a local tax credit equal to 80 percent of the amount of this payment ($800) to be applied to *S*'s local real property tax liability incurred by *S* in carrying on its trade or business. Under applicable state and local law, the real property tax is imposed at the entity level (not the owner level). Under paragraph (a)(3)(ii) of this section, *S* may treat $800 of the payment as an expense of carrying on a trade or business under section 162. The treatment of the remaining $200 will depend upon the facts and circumstances and is not affected by paragraph (a)(3)(ii) of this section.

(v) *Applicability of section 170 to payments in exchange for state or local tax benefits.*—For rules regarding the availability of a charitable contribution deduction under section 170 where a taxpayer makes a payment or transfers property to or for the use of an entity described in section 170(c) and receives or expects to receive a state or local tax benefit in return for such payment, see §1.170A-1(h)(3).

(4) *Applicability dates.*—Paragraphs (a)(1) and (2) of this section, regarding the application of section 162 to taxpayers making payments or transfers to entities described in section 170(c), apply to payments or transfers on or after December 17, 2019. However, taxpayers may choose to apply paragraphs (a)(1) and (2) to payments and transfers on or after January 1, 2018. Paragraph (a)(3) of this section, regarding the safe harbors for C corporations and specified passthrough entities making payments to section 170(c) entities in exchange for state or local tax credits applies to payments made by these entities on or after December 17, 2019. However, taxpayers may choose to apply the safe harbors of paragraph (a)(3) to payments on or after January 1, 2018.

* * *

Expenditures Incurred in Attempts to Influence Legislation

Business Expenses: Private Foundations, Excise Taxes: Expenditures Incurred in Attempts to Influence Legislation.—Reproduced below is the text of a proposed amendment of Reg. §1.162-20, relating to the treatment, for federal income tax purposes, of expenditures incurred in attempts to influence legislation (published in the Federal Register on November 25, 1980).

§1.162-20. Expenditures attributable to lobbying, political campaigns, attempts to influence legislation, etc., and certain advertising.—(a) *In general.*—(1) *Scope of section.*—This section contains rules governing the deductibility or nondeductibility of expenditures for lobbying purposes, for the promotion or defeat of legislation, for political campaign purposes (including the support of or opposition to any candidate for public office) or for carrying on propaganda (including advertising) related to any of the foregoing purposes. This section also deals with expenditures for institutional or "good will" advertising.

(2) *Institutional or "good will" advertising.*—Expenditures for institutional or "good will" advertising which keeps the taxpayer's name before the public are generally deductible as ordinary and necessary business expenses provided the expenditures are related to the patronage the taxpayer reasonably expects in the future. For example, a deduction will ordinarily be allowed for the cost of advertising which keeps the taxpayer's name before the public in connection with encouraging contributions to such organizations as the Red Cross, the purchase of United States Savings Bonds, or participation in similar causes. In like fashion, expenditures for advertising which presents views on economic, financial, social, or other such issues, but which does not attempt to influence the public with respect to legislative matters (see paragraph (c)(4) of this section) or involve any of the other activities specified in paragraph (c) of this section for which a deduction is not allowable, are deductible if they otherwise meet the requirements of the regulations under section 162.

(b) *Taxable years beginning before January 1, 1963.*—For rules with respect to taxable years beginning before January 1, 1963, see 26 CFR 1.162-20(b) (Rev. as of April 1, 1980).

(c) *Taxable years beginning after December 31, 1962.*—(1) *In general.*—For taxable years beginning after December 31, 1962, certain types of expenses incurred with respect to legislative matters are deductible under section 162(a) if they otherwise meet the requirements of the regulations under section 162. These deductible expenses are described in subparagraph (2) of this paragraph. All other expenditures for lobbying purposes, for the promotion or defeat of legislation, for political campaign purposes (including the support of or opposition to any candidate for public office), or for carrying on propaganda (including advertising) relating to any of the foregoing purposes (see subparagraph (4) of this paragraph) are not deductible from gross income for such taxable years. For the disallowance of

deductions for bad debts and worthless securities of a political party, see §1.271-1. For the disallowance of deductions for certain indirect political contributions, such as the cost of certain advertising and the cost of admission to certain dinners, programs, and inaugural events, see §1.276-1.

* * *

(3) *Deductibility of dues and other payments to an organization.*—If part of the activities of an organization, such as a labor union or a trade association, consists of one or more of the activities to which this paragraph relates (legislative matters, political campaigns, etc.) exclusive of any activity constituting an appearance or communication with respect to legislation or proposed legislation of direct interest to the organization (see subparagraph (2)(ii)(*b*)(1)), a deduction will be allowed only for such portion of the dues or other payments to the organization as the taxpayer can clearly establish is attributable to activities to which this paragraph does not relate and to any activity constituting an appearance or communication with respect to legislation or proposed legislation of direct interest to the organization. In no event shall a deduction be allowed for that portion of a special assessment or similar payment (including an increase in dues) made to any organization for any activity to which this paragraph relates if the activity does not constitute an appearance or communication with respect to legislation or proposed legislation of direct interest to the organization. If an organization pays or incurs expenses allocable to legislative activities which meet the tests of subdivisions (i) and (ii) of subparagraph (2) of this paragraph (appearances or communications with respect to legislation or proposed legislation of direct interest to the organization) on behalf of its members, the dues paid by a taxpayer are deductible to the extent used for such activities. Dues paid by a taxpayer will be considered to be used for such an activity, and thus deductible, although the legislation or proposed legislation involved is not of direct interest to the taxpayer, if, pursuant to the provisions of subparagraph (2)(ii)(*b*)(1) of this paragraph, the legislation or proposed legislation is of direct interest to the organization, as such, or is of direct interest to one or more members of the organization. For other provisions relating to the deductibility of dues and other payments to an organization, such as a labor union or trade association, see paragraph (c) of §1.162-15. For requirement that an organization furnish to members and contributors a statement about expenditures, see §1.6033-2(k). This subparagraph applies to expenditures made after 1980. For corresponding rules for expenditures made before 1981, see 26 CFR §1.162-20(c)(3) (Rev. as of April 1, 1980).

(4) *Limitations with respect to legislative matters.*—(i) *In general.*—No deduction shall be allowed under section 162(a) for any amount paid or incurred (whether by way of contribution, gift, or otherwise) in connection with any attempt (including what is commonly referred to as a grassroots campaign) to influence the general public, or any segment thereof, with respect to legislative matters. A communication shall be considered an attempt to influence the general public, or a segment thereof, with respect to legislative matters if, and only if, the communication satisfies all of the following three tests:

(A) It pertains to legislation being considered by, or likely in the immediate future to be proposed to, a legislative body, or seeks or opposes legislation;

(B) It reflects a view with respect to the desirability of legislation (for this purpose, a communication that pertains to legislation but expresses no explicit view on the legislation shall be deemed to reflect a view on legislation if the communication is selectively disseminated to persons likely to share a common view of the legislation); and

(C) It is communicated in a form and distributed in a manner so as to reach individuals as members of the general public, that is, as voters or constituents, as opposed to a communication designed for academic, scientific, or similar purposes. A communication may meet this test even if it reaches the public only indirectly as in a news release submitted to the media. No portion of an expenditure in connection with an advertisement is deductible if any part of the advertisement constitutes an attempt to influence the general public with respect to legislative matters.

(ii) *Definitions.*—For purposes of this subparagraph—

(A) The term "legislation" includes action by the Congress, any state legislature, any local council, or similar legislative body, or by the public in a referendum, initiative, constitutional amendment, or similar procedure. The term "legislation" includes a proposed treaty required to be submitted by the President to the Senate for its advice and consent from the time the President's representative begins to negotiate its position with the prospective parties to the proposed treaty.

(B) The term "action" includes the introduction, amendment, enactment, defeat, or repeal of Acts, bills, resolutions, or similar items.

(C) The term "legislative body" does not include executive, judicial, or administrative bodies.

(D) The term "administrative bodies" includes school boards, housing authorities, sewer and water districts, zoning boards, and other similar Federal, State, or local special purpose bodies, whether elective or appointive.

(iii) *Examples.*—The provisions of this subparagraph relating to attempts to influence the public with respect to legislative matters may be illustrated by the following examples:

Example (1). Several major businesses in State W place in local newspapers an advertisement asserting that lack of new capital is hurting the state's economy. The advertisement recommends that residents either invest more in local businesses or increase their savings so that funds will be available to others interested in making investments. Although the advertisement expresses a view with respect to a general problem that might receive legislative attention and is distributed in a manner so as to reach many individuals, it does not constitute an attempt to influence the public with respect to legislative matters because it pertains to private conduct rather than legislation.

Example (2). Assume the same facts as in example (1), except that the advertisement, although not expressly calling for legislative action, also asserts that particular kinds of state tax incentives (which could not be implemented without legislation) would substantially increase capital formation. Thus, the advertisement is seeking action by the legislature and, at least in part, is addressed to individuals as voters or constituents rather than as potential investors. The advertisement reflects a view with respect to the desirability of the legisla-

tion. The advertisement constitutes an attempt to influence the public with respect to a legislative matter, and no portion of any expenditures in connection with the advertisement may be deducted.

Example (3). There is pending in the legislature of State X a proposal to amend certain laws concerning voting in state elections. As a public service, M, a manufacturer in State X, places in local newspapers an advertisement that explains both the current voting laws and the proposed amendments. The advertisement takes no position on the merits of the proposal. Under these circumstances, the advertisement does not reflect a view with respect to the desirability of the proposal and does not constitute an attempt to influence the general public with respect to the proposal.

Example (4). The legislature of State Y is considering a proposal to prohibit hunting on land owned by the state. Hunters in State Y are generally opposed to the measure. N, a manufacturer of hunting equipment, prepares a pamphlet that outlines the proposal and its effects but expresses no view on its merits. N arranges for distribution of the pamphlet to customers of stores in State Y that specialize in hunting equipment. The pamphlet pertains to legislation and is deemed to reflect a view with respect to the desirability of the legislation by reason of its selective distribution to an audience likely to oppose the prohibition on hunting. The information is communicated in a form and distributed in a manner so as to reach individuals as voters or constituents. Expenditures in connection with the preparation and distribution of the pamphlet are nondeductible.

Example (5). The legislature in State Z is considering a proposal to require pharmaceutical firms to test the safety of their products through certain laboratory procedures. P, a pharmaceutical firm in State Z, prepares a detailed report on the usefulness of the tests that would be required under the proposal. The report concludes that the tests specified in the proposal are poorly designed. P distributes copies of the report to university professors in the field of health science without suggesting that the recipients make any attempt to influence the public with respect to the proposal. Although the report pertains to legislation and implies that the legislative proposal under consideration should not be enacted, the form of the report and its limited distribution indicate that copies were furnished to the recipients as scholars in the field rather than as members of the general public, that is, as voters or constituents. The expenditures for the report, therefore, are not expenditures in connection with an attempt to influence the public with respect to the proposal.

Example (6). Assume the same facts as in example (5) except that, instead of distributing copies of the report to university professors, P distributes to various civic groups leaflets summarizing the conclusions and recommendations of the report. The information is communicated in a form and distributed in a manner so as to reach individuals as voters or constituents. Expenditures in connection with the report and the leaflet are nondeductible.

Example (7). Corporation Q pays for the radio broadcast of an advertisement that refers to a current controversy and urges citizens to "become involved". The advertisement does not discuss the merits of any legislative proposal, but it does offer a free booklet which analyzes and takes positions on various legislative proposals relating to the controversy. Expenditures in connection with the advertisement and the booklet are nondeductible because together they constitute an attempt by Q to influence the public with respect to this legislative matter.

Example (8). Corporation R makes the services of B, one of its executives, available to S, a trade association of which R is a member. B works for several weeks to assist S to develop materials designed to influence public opinion on legislation. In performing this work, B uses office space and clerical assistance provided by R. R pays full salary and benefits to B during this period and receives no reimbursement from S for these payments or for the other facilities and assistance provided. All expenditures of R, including the allocable office expenses, that are attributable to this assignment are nondeductible because B was engaged in an attempt to influence the public on legislative matters.

* * *

Fringe Benefits: Taxability

Fringe Benefits: Taxability.—Reg. §1.162-25T, relating to the treatment of taxable and nontaxable fringe benefits, is proposed (published in the Federal Register on January 7, 1985) (LR-216-84).

§1.162-25T. Deductions with respect to noncash fringe benefits.

Substantiation: Travel, Entertainment, Gifts, Listed Property, Etc.

Business Expenses: Substantiation: Recordkeeping Requirements: Listed Property.—An amendment to Temporary Reg. §1.162-25T, relating to the requirement that any deduction or credit with respect to certain business-related expenses be substantiated with adequate or sufficient evidence to corroborate a taxpayer's own statement and to the limitations on cost recovery deductions and the investment tax credit for listed property, is also proposed as final (published in the Federal Register on November 6, 1985).

§1.162-25T. Deductions with respect to noncash fringe benefits.

Employee Remuneration in Excess of $1,000,000: Deductibility

Employee Remuneration in Excess of $1,000,000: Deductibility.—Amendments to Reg. §1.162-27, limiting the deduction for certain employee remuneration in excess of $1,000,000 for federal income tax purposes, are proposed (published in the Federal Register on December 20, 2019) (REG-122180-18).

Par. 2. Section 1.162-27 is amended by revising paragraphs (a) and (j)(1) to read as follows:

§1.162-27. Certain employee remuneration in excess of $1,000,000 not deductible for taxable years beginning on or after January 1, 1994, and for taxable years beginning prior to January 1, 2018.—(a) *Scope.*—This section provides rules for the application of the $1 million deduction limitation under section 162(m)(1) for taxable years beginning on or after January 1, 1994, and beginning prior to January 1, 2018, and, as provided in paragraph (j) of this section, for taxable years beginning after December 31, 2017. For rules concerning the applicability of section 162(m)(1) to taxable years beginning after December 31, 2017, see §1.162-33. Paragraph (b) of this section provides the general rule limiting deductions under section 162(m)(1). Paragraph (c) of this section provides definitions of generally applicable terms. Paragraph (d) of this section provides an exception from the deduction limitation for compensation payable on a commission basis. Paragraph (e) of this section provides an exception for qualified performance-based compensation. Paragraphs (f) and (g) of this section provide special rules for corporations that become publicly held corporations and payments that are subject to section 280G, respectively. Paragraph (h) of this section provides transition rules, including the rules for contracts that are grandfathered and not subject to section 162(m)(1). Paragraph (j) of this section contains the effective date provisions, which also specify when these rules apply to the deduction for compensation otherwise deductible in a taxable year beginning after December 31, 2017. For rules concerning the deductibility of compensation for services that are not covered by section 162(m)(1) and this section, see section 162(a)(1) and §1.162-7. This section is not determinative as to whether compensation meets the requirements of section 162(a)(1). For rules concerning the deduction limitation under section 162(m)(6) applicable to certain health insurance providers, see §1.162-31.

* * *

(j) *Effective date.*—(1) *In general.*—Section 162(m) and this section apply to the deduction for compensation that is otherwise deductible by the corporation in taxable years beginning on or after January 1, 1994, and beginning prior to January 1, 2018. Section 162(m) and this section also apply to compensation that is a grandfathered amount (as defined in §1.162-33(g)) at the time it is paid to the covered employee. For examples of the application of the rules of this section to grandfathered amounts paid during taxable years beginning after December 31, 2017, see §1.162-33(g).

* * *

Notional Principal Contracts: Contingent Nonperiodic Payments

Notional Principal Contracts: Contingent Nonperiodic Payments.—Reg. §1.162-30, relating to the inclusion into income or deduction of a contingent nonperiodic payment provided for under a notional principal contract, is proposed (published in the Federal Register on February 26, 2004) (REG-166012-02).

☐ Par. 2. Section 1.162-30 is added to read as follows:

§1.162-30. Notional principal contract payments.—(a) *In general.*—Amounts taken into account by a taxpayer pursuant to §1.446-3(d)(1) (including mark-to-market deductions) with respect to a notional principal contract as defined in §1.446-3(c)(1)(i), are deductible as ordinary and necessary business expenses. However, this section will not apply to any amount representing interest expense on the deemed loan component of a significant nonperiodic payment as described in §1.446-3(g)(4). For any loss arising from a termination payment as defined in §1.446-3(h)(1), see section 1234A and the regulations thereunder. For the timing of deductions with respect to notional principal contracts, see §1.446-3.

(b) *Effective date.*—Paragraph (a) of this section is applicable to notional principal contracts entered into on or after 30 days after the date a Treasury decision based on these proposed regulations is published in the Federal Register. [Reg. §1.162-30.]

Expatriate Health Plans: Issuers: Excepted Benefits

Expatriate Health Plans: Issuers: Excepted Benefits.—Amendments to Reg. §1.162-31, relating to the rules for expatriate health plans, expatriate health plan issuers, and qualified expatriates under the Expatriate Health Coverage Clarification Act of 2014 (EHCCA), are proposed (published in the Federal Register on June 10, 2016) (REG-135702-15).

2. Section 1.162-31 is amended by adding paragraph (b)(5)(v) to read as follows:

§1.162-31. The $500,000 deduction limitation for remuneration provided by certain health insurance providers.

* * *

(b) * * *

(5) * * *

(v) *Expatriate health plan coverage.* For purposes of this section, amounts received in payment for expatriate health plan coverage, as defined in §54.9831-1(f)(3), are not premiums.

* * *

Employee Remuneration in Excess of $1,000,000: Deductibility

Employee Remuneration in Excess of $1,000,000: Deductibility.—Reg. §1.162-33, limiting the deduction for certain employee remuneration in excess of $1,000,000 for federal income tax purposes, is proposed (published in the Federal Register on December 20, 2019) (REG-122180-18).

Par. 3. Section 1.162-33 is added to read as follows:

§1.162-33. Certain employee remuneration in excess of $1,000,000 not deductible for taxable years beginning after December 31, 2017.—(a) *Scope.*—This section provides rules for the application of the $1 million deduction limitation under section 162(m)(1) for taxable years beginning after December 31, 2017. For rules concerning the applicability of section 162(m)(1) to taxable years beginning on or after January 1, 1994, and prior to January 1, 2018, see §1.162-27. Paragraph (b) of this section provides the general rule limiting deductions under section 162(m)(1). Paragraph (c) of this section provides definitions of generally applicable terms. Paragraph (d) of this section provides rules for determining when a corporation becomes a publicly held corporation. Paragraph (e) of this section provides rules for payments that are subject to section 280G. Paragraph (f) of this section provides a special rule for coordination with section 4985. Paragraph (g) of this section provides transition rules, including the rules for contracts that are grandfathered. Paragraph (h) of this section sets forth the effective date provisions. For rules concerning the deductibility of compensation for services that are not covered by section 162(m)(1) and this section, see section 162(a)(1) and §1.162-7. This section is not determinative as to whether compensation meets the requirements of section 162(a)(1). For rules concerning the deduction limitation under section 162(m)(6) applicable to certain health insurance providers, see §1.162-31.

(b) *Limitation on deduction.*—Section 162(m)(1) precludes a deduction under chapter 1 of the Internal Revenue Code by any publicly held corporation for compensation paid to any covered employee to the extent that the compensation for the taxable year exceeds $1,000,000.

(c) *Definitions.*—(1) *Publicly held corporation.*—(i) *General rule.*—A publicly held corporation means any corporation that issues securities required to be registered under section 12 of the Exchange Act or that is required to file reports under section 15(d) of the Exchange Act. In addition, a publicly held corporation means any S corporation (as defined in section 1361(a)(1)) that issues securities that are required to be registered under section 12(b) of the Exchange Act, or that is required to file reports under section 15(d) of the Exchange Act. For purposes of this section, whether a corporation is publicly held is determined based solely on whether, as of the last day of its taxable year, the securities issued by the corporation are required to be registered under section 12 of the Exchange Act or the corporation is required to file reports under section 15(d) of the Exchange Act. Whether registration under the Exchange Act is required by rules other than those of the Exchange Act is irrelevant to this determination. A publicly traded partnership that is treated as a corporation under section 7704 (or otherwise) is a publicly held corporation if, as of the last day of its taxable year, its securities are required to be registered under section 12 of the Exchange Act or it is required to file reports under section 15(d) of the Exchange Act.

    (ii) *Affiliated groups.*—(A) *In general.*—A publicly held corporation includes an affiliated group of corporations, as defined in section 1504 (determined without regard to section 1504(b)) that includes one or more publicly held corporations (as defined in paragraph (c)(1)(i) of this section). In the case of an affiliated group that includes two or more publicly held corporations as defined in paragraph (c)(1)(i) of this section, each member of the affiliated group that is a publicly held corporation as defined in paragraph (c)(1)(i) of this section is separately subject to this section, and the affiliated group as a whole is subject to this section. Thus, for example, assume that a publicly held corporation (as defined in paragraph (c)(1)(i) of this section) is a wholly-owned subsidiary of another publicly held corporation (as defined in paragraph (c)(1)(i) of this section), which is a wholly-owned subsidiary of a privately held corporation. In this case, the two subsidiaries are separately subject to this section, and all three corporations are members of an affiliated group that is subject to this section. Furthermore, each subsidiary has its own set of covered employees as defined in paragraphs (c)(2)(i) through (iv) of this section (although it is possible that the same individual may be a covered employee of both subsidiaries).

    (B) *Proration of amount disallowed as a deduction.*—If, in a taxable year, a covered employee (as defined in paragraphs (c)(2)(i) through (iv) of this section) of one member of an affiliated group is paid compensation by more than one member of the affiliated group, compensation paid by each member of the affiliated group is aggregated with compensation paid to the covered employee by all other members of the affiliated group (excluding compensation paid by any other publicly held corporation in the affiliated group, as defined in paragraph (c)(1)(i) of this section, of which the individual is also a covered employee as defined in paragraphs (c)(2)(i) through (iv) of this section). In the event that, in a taxable year, a covered employee (as defined in paragraphs (c)(2)(i) through (iv) of this section) is paid compensation by more than one publicly held corporation in an affiliated group and is also a covered employee of more than one publicly held payor corporation (as defined in paragraph (c)(1)(i) of this section) in the affiliated group, the amount disallowed as a deduction is determined separately with respect to each publicly held corporation of which the individual is a covered employee. Any amount disallowed as a deduction by this section must be prorated among the payor corporations (excluding any other publicly held payor corporation of which the individual is also a covered employee) in proportion to the amount of compensation paid to the covered employee (as defined in paragraphs (c)(2)(i) through (iv) of this section) by each such corporation in the taxable year. This process is repeated for each publicly held payor corporation of which the individual is a covered employee.

    (iii) *Disregarded entities.*—For purposes of paragraph (c)(1) of this section, a publicly held corporation includes a corporation that owns an entity that is disregarded as an entity separate from its owner within the meaning of § 301.7701-2(c)(2)(i) of this chapter if the disregarded entity issues securities required to be registered under section 12(b) of the Exchange Act, or is required to file reports under section 15(d) of the Exchange Act.

    (iv) *Qualified subchapter S subsidiaries.*—For purposes of paragraph (c)(1) of this section, a publicly held corporation includes an S corporation that owns a qualified subchapter S subsidiary as defined in section 1361(b)(3)(B) (QSub) if the QSub issues securities required to be registered under section 12(b) of the Exchange Act, or is required to file reports under section 15(d) of the Exchange Act.

    (v) *Examples.*—The following examples illustrate the provisions of this paragraph (c)(1). For each example, assume that no corporation is a predecessor of a publicly held corporation within the meaning of this paragraph (c)(2)(ii). Furthermore, for each example, unless provided otherwise, a reference to a publicly held corporation means a publicly held corporation as defined in paragraph (c)(1)(i) of this section. Additionally, for each example, assume that the corporation is a calendar year taxpayer and has a fiscal year ending December 31 for reporting purposes under the Exchange Act. These examples are not intended to provide guidance on the legal requirements of the Securities Act and Exchange Act and the rules thereunder (17 CFR part 240).

    (A) *Example 1 (Corporation required to file reports under section 15(d) of the Exchange Act)*—(1) *Facts.* Corporation Z plans to issue debt securities in a public offering registered under the Securities Act.

Corporation Z is not required to file reports under section 15(d) of the Exchange Act with respect to any other class of securities and does not have another class of securities required to be registered under section 12 of the Exchange Act. On April 1, 2021, the Securities Act registration statement for Corporation Z's debt securities is declared effective by the SEC. As a result, Corporation Z is required to file reports under section 15(d) of the Exchange Act. Accordingly, as of December 31, 2021, the last day of its taxable year, Corporation Z is required to file reports under section 15(d) of the Exchange Act.

    (2) *Conclusion.* Corporation Z is a publicly held corporation for its 2021 taxable year because it is required to file reports under section 15(d) of the Exchange Act as of the last day of its taxable year.

    (B) *Example 2 (Corporation not required to file reports under section 15(d) of the Exchange Act)*—(1) *Facts.* The facts are the same as in paragraph (c)(1)(v)(A) of this section (*Example 1*), except that, on January 1, 2022, pursuant to section 15(d) of the Exchange Act, Corporation Z's obligation to file reports under section 15(d) is automatically suspended for the fiscal year ending December 31, 2022, because Corporation Z meets the statutory requirements for an automatic suspension to file reports under section 15(d). Accordingly, as of December 31, 2022, Corporation Z is not required to file reports under section 15(d) of the Exchange Act.

    (2) *Conclusion.* Corporation Z is not a publicly held corporation for its 2022 taxable year because it is not required to file reports under section 15(d) of the Exchange Act as of as of the last day of its taxable year.

    (C) *Example 3 (Corporation not required to file reports under section 15(d) of the Exchange Act)*—(1) *Facts.* The facts are the same as in paragraph (c)(1)(v)(B) of this section (*Example 2*), except that, on January 1, 2022, pursuant to section 15(d) of the Exchange Act, Corporation Z's obligation to file reports under section 15(d) is not automatically suspended for the fiscal year ending December 31, 2022 because Corporation Z does not meet the statutory requirements for automatic suspension. Instead, on May 2, 2022, Corporation Z is eligible to suspend its section 15(d) reporting obligation under Rule 12h-3 of the Exchange Act (17 CFR 240.12h-3) and files Form 15, Certification and Notice of Termination of Registration under Section 12(g) of the Securities Exchange Act of 1934 or Suspension of Duty to File Reports under Sections 13 and 15(d) of the Securities Exchange Act of 1934 (or its successor), to suspend its section 15(d) reporting obligation for its fiscal year ending December 31, 2022. Accordingly, as of December 31, 2022, Corporation Z is not required to file reports under section 15(d) of the Exchange Act.

    (2) *Conclusion.* Corporation Z is not a publicly held corporation for its 2022 taxable year because it is not required to file reports under section 15(d) of the Exchange Act as of the last day of its taxable year.

    (D) *Example 4 (Corporation required to file reports under section 15(d) of the Exchange Act)*—(1) *Facts.* The facts are the same as in paragraph (c)(1)(v)(C) of this section (*Example 3*), except that, Corporation Z does not utilize Rule 12h-3 under the Exchange Act (17 CFR 240.12h-3) to file a Form 15, Certification and Notice of Termination of Registration under Section 12(g) of the Securities Exchange Act of 1934 or Suspension of Duty to File Reports under Sections 13 and 15(d) of the Securities Exchange Act of 1934 (or its successor), to suspend its section 15(d) reporting obligation during its fiscal year ending December 31, 2022. Accordingly, Corporation Z's reporting obligation under section 15(d) of the Exchange Act is not suspended for its fiscal year ending December 31, 2022.

    (2) *Conclusion.* Corporation Z is a publicly held corporation for its 2022 taxable year because it is required to file reports under section 15(d) of the Exchange Act as of the last day of its taxable year.

    (E) *Example 5 (Corporation required to file reports under section 15(d) of the Exchange Act)*—(1) *Facts.* Corporation Y is a wholly-owned subsidiary of Corporation X, which is required to file reports under the Exchange Act. Corporation Y issued a class of debt securities in a public offering registered under the Securities Act, and therefore is required to file reports under Exchange Act Section 15(d), including for its fiscal year ending December 31, 2020. Corporation Y has no other class of securities registered under the Exchange Act. In its Form 10-K, Annual Report Pursuant to Section 13 or 15(d) of the Securities Exchange Act of 1934 (or its successor), for the 2020 fiscal year, Corporation Y may omit Item 11 Executive Compensation (required by Part III of Form 10-K), which requires disclosure of compensation of certain executive officers because it is wholly-owned by Corporation X and the other conditions of General Instruction I to Form 10-K are satisfied.

    (2) *Conclusion.* Corporation Y is a publicly held corporation for its 2020 taxable year because it is required to file reports under section 15(d) of the Exchange Act as of the last day of its taxable year.

    (F) *Example 6 (Corporation not required to file reports under section 15(d) of the Exchange Act and not required to register securities under section 12 of the Exchange Act)*—(1) *Facts.* Corporation A has a class of securities registered under section 12(g) of the Exchange Act. For its 2020 taxable year, Corporation A is a publicly held corporation. On September 30, 2021, Corporation A is eligible to terminate the registration of its securities under section 12(g) of the Exchange Act pursuant to Rule 12g-4(a)(2) of the Exchange Act (17 CFR 240.12g-4(a)(2)), but does not terminate the registration of its securities prior to December 31, 2021. Because Corporation A did not issue securities in a public offering registered under the Securities Act, Corporation A is not required to file reports under section 15(d) of the Exchange Act.

(2) *Conclusion.* Corporation A is not a publicly held corporation for its 2021 taxable year because, as of the last day of its taxable year, the securities issued by Corporation A are not required to be registered under section 12 of the Exchange Act and Corporation A is not required to file reports under section 15(d) of the Exchange Act.

(G) *Example 7 (Corporation required to file reports under section 15(d) of the Exchange Act)*—(1) *Facts.* The facts are the same as in paragraph (c)(1)(v)(F) of this section (*Example 6*), except that Corporation A previously issued a class of securities in a public offering registered under the Securities Act. Furthermore, on October 1, 2021, Corporation A terminates the registration of its securities under section 12(g) of the Exchange Act. Because Corporation A issued a class of securities in a public offering registered under the Securities Act and is not eligible to suspend its reporting obligation under section 15(d) of the Exchange Act, as of December 31, 2021, Corporation A is required to file reports under section 15(d) of the Exchange Act.

(2) *Conclusion.* Corporation A is a publicly held corporation for its 2021 taxable year because it is required to file reports under section 15(d) of the Exchange Act as of the last day of its taxable year.

(H) *Example 8 (Corporation not required to file reports under section 15(d) of the Exchange Act and not required to register securities under section 12 of the Exchange Act)*—(1) *Facts.* On November 1, 2021, Corporation B is an issuer with only one class of equity securities. On November 5, 2021, Corporation B files a registration statement for its equity securities under section 12(g) of the Exchange Act. Corporation B's filing of its registration statement is voluntary because the Exchange Act does not require Corporation B to register its class of securities under section 12(g) of the Exchange Act based on the number and composition of its record holders. On December 1, 2021, the Exchange Act registration statement for Corporation B's securities is declared effective by the SEC. As of December 31, 2021, the last day of its taxable year, Corporation B continues to have its class of equity securities registered voluntarily under section 12 of the Exchange Act. Furthermore, Corporation B is not required to file reports under section 15(d) of the Exchange Act because it did not register any class of securities in a public offering under the Securities Act.

(2) *Conclusion.* Corporation B is not a publicly held corporation for its 2021 taxable year because, as of the last day of that taxable year, the securities issued by Corporation B are not required to be registered under section 12 of the Exchange Act and Corporation B is not required to file reports under section 15(d) of the Exchange Act.

(I) *Example 9 (Corporation not required to file reports under section 15(d) of the Exchange Act and not required to register securities under section 12 of the Exchange Act)*—(1) *Facts.* The facts are the same as in paragraph (c)(1)(v)(H) of this section (*Example 8*), except that, on December 31, 2022, because of a change in circumstances, under the Exchange Act, Corporation B must register its class of equity securities under section 12(g) of the Exchange Act within 120 days of December 31, 2022. On February 1, 2023, the Exchange Act registration statement for Corporation B's securities is declared effective by the SEC.

(2) *Conclusion.* Corporation B is not a publicly held corporation for its 2022 taxable year because, as of the last day of that taxable year, Corporation B is not required to file reports under section 15(d) of the Exchange Act, and the class of equity securities issued by Corporation B is not yet required to be registered under section 12 of the Exchange Act. Corporation B has 120 days following December 31, 2022, to file a registration statement to register its class of equity securities under section 12(g) of the Exchange Act.

(J) *Example 10 (Securities of foreign private issuer in the form of ADRs traded in the over-the-counter market)*—(1) *Facts.* For its fiscal and taxable years ending December 31, 2021, Corporation W is a foreign private issuer. Because Corporation W has not registered an offer or sale of securities under the Securities Act, it is not required to file reports under section 15(d) of the Exchange Act. Corporation W qualifies for an exemption from registration of its securities under section 12(g) of the Exchange Act pursuant to Rule 12g3-2(b) under the Exchange Act (17 CFR 240.12g3-2(b)). Corporation W wishes to have its securities traded in the U.S. in the over-the-counter market in the form of ADRs. Because Corporation W qualifies for an exemption pursuant to Rule 12g3-2(b) under the Exchange Act (17 CFR 240.12g3-2(b)), Corporation W is not required to register its securities underlying the ADRs under section 12 of the Exchange Act. However, the depositary bank is required to register the ADRs under the Securities Act. Even though the depositary bank is required to register the ADRs under the Securities Act, such registration of the ADRs does not create a requirement for either the depositary bank or

Corporation W to file reports under section 15(d) of the Exchange Act. On February 3, 2021, the Securities Act registration statement for the ADRs is declared effective by the SEC. On February 4, 2021, Corporation W's ADRs begin trading in the over-the-counter market. On December 31, 2021, the securities of Corporation W are not required to be registered under Section 12 of the Exchange Act because Corporation W qualifies for an exemption pursuant to Rule 240.12g3-2(b) of the Exchange Act. Furthermore, on December 31, 2021, Corporation W is not required to file reports under section 15(d) of the Exchange Act.

(2) *Conclusion.* Corporation W is not a publicly held corporation for its 2021 taxable year because, as of the last day of that taxable year, the securities underlying the ADRs are not required to be registered under section 12 of the Exchange Act and Corporation W is not required to file reports under section 15(d) of the Exchange Act. The conclusion would be the same if Corporation W had its securities traded in the over-the-counter market other than in the form of ADRs.

(K) *Example 11 (Securities of foreign private issuer in the form of ADRs quoted on Over the Counter Bulletin Board)*—(1) *Facts.* The facts are the same as in paragraph (c)(1)(v)(J) of this section (*Example 10*), except that Corporation W has its securities quoted on the Over the Counter Bulletin Board (OTCBB) in the form of ADRs. Because Corporation W qualifies for an exemption pursuant to Rule 12g3-2(b) of the Exchange Act (17 CFR 240.12g3-2(b)), Corporation W is not required to register its securities underlying the ADRs under section 12 of the Exchange Act. However, the depositary bank is required to register the ADRs under the Securities Act. Section 6530(b)(1) of the OTCBB Rules requires that a foreign equity security may be quoted on the OTCBB only if the security is registered with the SEC pursuant to section 12 of the Exchange Act and the issuer of the security is current in its reporting obligations. To comply with section 6530(b)(1) of the OTCBB Rules, on February 5, 2021, Corporation W files a registration statement for its class of securities underlying the ADRs under section 12(g) of the Exchange Act. On February 26, 2021, the Exchange Act registration statement for Corporation W's securities is declared effective by the SEC. As of December 31, 2021, Corporation W is subject to the reporting obligations under the section 12 of the Exchange Act as a result of section 12 registration.

(2) *Conclusion.* Corporation W is not a publicly held corporation for its 2021 taxable year because, as of the last day of that taxable year, its ADRs and the securities underlying the ADRs are not required by the Exchange Act to be registered under section 12, and Corporation W is not required to file reports under section 15(d) of the Exchange Act. The conclusion would be the same if Corporation W had its securities traded on the OTCBB other than in the form of ADRs.

(L) *Example 12 (Securities of foreign private issuer in the form of ADRs listed on a national securities exchange without a capital raising transaction)*—(1) *Facts.* For its fiscal and taxable years ending December 31, 2021, Corporation V is a foreign private issuer. Corporation V wishes to list its securities on the New York Stock Exchange (NYSE) in the form of ADRs without a capital raising transaction. Under the Exchange Act, Corporation V is required to register its securities underlying the ADRs under section 12(b) of the Exchange Act. Because the ADRs and the deposited securities are separate securities, the depositary bank is required to register the ADRs under the Securities Act. On February 2, 2021, Corporation V's registration statement under section 12(b) of the Exchange Act in connection with the underlying securities, and the depositary bank's registration statement under the Securities Act in connection with the ADRs, are declared effective by the SEC. On March 1, 2021, Corporation V's securities begin trading on the NYSE in the form of ADRs. As of December 31, 2021, Corporation V is not required to file reports under section 15(d) of the Exchange Act; however, the securities underlying the ADRs are required to be registered under section 12(b) of the Exchange Act.

(2) *Conclusion.* Corporation V is a publicly held corporation for its 2021 taxable year because, as of the last day of that taxable year, the securities underlying the ADRs are required to be registered under section 12 of the Exchange Act. The conclusion would be the same if Corporation V had its securities listed on the NYSE other than in the form of ADRs.

(M) *Example 13 (Securities of foreign private issuer in the form of ADRs listed on a national securities exchange with a capital raising transaction)*—(1) *Facts.* The facts are the same as in paragraph (c)(1)(v)(L) of this section (*Example 12*), except that Corporation V wishes to raise capital and have its securities listed on the NYSE in the form of ADRs. Corporation V is required to register the offer of securities underlying the ADRs under the Securities Act and to register the class of those securities under section 12(b) of the Exchange Act. The depositary bank is required to register the ADRs under the Securities Act. On February 2, 2021, Corporation V's registration statements under the Securities Act and section 12(b) of the Exchange Act, and the registration statement for the ADRs under the Securities Act, are declared effective by the SEC. As of December

31, 2021, Corporation V is not required to file reports under section 15(d) of the Exchange Act; however, the securities underlying the ADRs are required to be registered under section 12(b) of the Exchange Act.

(2) *Conclusion.* Corporation V is a publicly held corporation for its 2021 taxable year because, as of the last day of that taxable year, its securities underlying the ADRs are required to be registered under section 12 of the Exchange Act. The conclusion would be the same if Corporation V had its securities listed on the NYSE other than in the form of ADRs.

(N) *Example 14 (Foreign private issuer incorporates subsidiary in the United States to issue debt securities and subsequently issues a guarantee)*—(1) *Facts.* Corporation T is a corporation incorporated in Country S (which is not the United States). For its fiscal and taxable years ending December 31, 2021, Corporation T is a foreign private issuer. Corporation T wishes to access the U.S. capital markets. Corporation T incorporates Corporation U in the United States to issue debt securities. On January 15, 2021, the SEC declares Corporation U's Securities Act registration statement effective. Corporation U is a wholly-owned subsidiary of Corporation T. To enhance the credit of Corporation U and the marketability of Corporation U's debt securities, Corporation T issues a guarantee of Corporation U's securities and, as required, registers the guarantee under the Securities Act on the registration statement that the SEC declares effective on January 15, 2021. On December 31, 2021, Corporations T and U are required to file reports under section 15(d) of the Exchange Act.

(2) *Conclusion.* Corporations T and U are publicly held corporations for their 2021 taxable years because they are required to file reports under section 15(d) of the Exchange Act as of the last day of their taxable years.

(O) *Example 15 (Affiliated group composed of two corporations, one of which is a publicly held corporation)*—(1) *Facts.* Employee D, a covered employee of Corporation N, performs services and receives compensation from Corporations N and O, members of an affiliated group of corporations. Corporation N, the parent corporation, is a publicly held corporation. Corporation O is a direct subsidiary of Corporation N and is a privately held corporation. The total compensation paid to Employee D from all affiliated group members is $3,000,000 for the taxable year, of which Corporation N pays $2,100,000 and Corporation O pays $900,000.

(2) *Conclusion.* Because the compensation paid by all affiliated group members is aggregated for purposes of section 162(m)(1), $2,000,000 of the aggregate compensation paid is nondeductible. Corporations N and O each are treated as paying a ratable portion of the nondeductible compensation. Thus, two thirds of each corporation's payment will be nondeductible. Corporation N has a nondeductible compensation expense of $1,400,000 ($2,100,000 x $2,000,000/$3,000,000). Corporation O has a nondeductible compensation expense of $600,000 ($900,000 x $2,000,000/$3,000,000).

(P) *Example 16 (Affiliated group composed of two corporations, one of which is a publicly held corporation)*—(1) *Facts.* The facts are the same as in paragraph (c)(1)(v)(O) of this section (*Example 15*), except that, Corporation O is a publicly held corporation and Corporation N is a privately held corporation, and Employee D is a covered employee of Corporation O (instead of Corporation N).

(2) *Conclusion.* The result is the same as in paragraph (c)(1)(v)(T) of this section (*Example 15*). Even though Corporation O is a subsidiary that is a publicly held corporation, it is still a member of the affiliated group comprised of Corporations N and O. Accordingly, $2,000,000 of the aggregate compensation paid is nondeductible. Thus, Corporations N and O each are treated as paying a ratable portion of the nondeductible compensation.

(Q) *Example 17 (Affiliated group composed of two publicly held corporations)*—(1) *Facts.* The facts are the same as in paragraph (c)(1)(v)(O) of this section (*Example 15*), except that Corporation O is also a publicly held corporation. As in paragraph (c)(1)(v)(O) of this section (*Example 15*), Employee D is not a covered employee of Corporation O.

(2) *Conclusion.* The result is the same as in paragraph (c)(1)(v)(O) of this section (*Example 15*). Even though Corporation O is a subsidiary that is a publicly held corporation, it is still a member of the affiliated group comprised of Corporations N and O. Corporations N and O are payor corporations that are members of an affiliated group for purposes of prorating the amount disallowed as a deduction. Accordingly, $2,000,000 of the aggregate compensation paid is nondeductible. Thus, Corporations N and O each are treated as paying a ratable portion of the nondeductible compensation.

(R) *Example 18 (Affiliated group composed of two publicly held corporations)*—(1) *Facts.* The facts are the same as in paragraph (c)(1)(v)(Q) of this section (*Example 17*), except that Employee D is also a covered employee of Corporation O.

(2) *Conclusion.* Even though Corporations N and O are each publicly held corporations and separately subject to this section, they are still members of the affiliated group comprised of Corporations N and O. Because Employee D is a covered employee of both Corpora-

tions N and O, which are each a separate publicly held corporation, the determination of the amount disallowed as a deduction is made separately for each publicly held corporation. Accordingly, Corporation N has a nondeductible compensation expense of $1,100,000 (the excess of $2,100,000 over $1,000,000), and Corporation O has no nondeductible compensation expense because the amount it paid to Employee D was below $1,000,000.

(S) *Example 19 (Affiliated group composed of three corporations, one of which is a publicly held corporation)*—(1) *Facts.* Employee C, a covered employee of Corporation P, performs services for, and receives compensation from, Corporations P, Q, and R, members of an affiliated group of corporations. Corporation P, the parent corporation, is a publicly held corporation. Corporation Q is a direct subsidiary of Corporation P, and Corporation R is a direct subsidiary of Corporation Q. Corporations Q and R are both privately held corporations. The total compensation paid to Employee C from all affiliated group members is $3,000,000 for the taxable year, of which Corporation P pays $1,500,000, Corporation Q pays $900,000, and Corporation R pays $600,000.

(2) *Conclusion.* Because the compensation paid by all affiliated group members is aggregated for purposes of section 162(m)(1), $2,000,000 of the aggregate compensation paid is nondeductible. Corporations P, Q, and R are each treated as paying a ratable portion of the nondeductible compensation. Thus, two thirds of each corporation's payment will be nondeductible. Corporation P has a nondeductible compensation expense of $1,000,000 ($1,500,000 x $2,000,000/$3,000,000). Corporation Q has a nondeductible compensation expense of $600,000 ($900,000 x $2,000,000/$3,000,000). Corporation R has a nondeductible compensation expense of $400,000 ($600,000 x $2,000,000/$3,000,000).

(T) *Example 20 (Affiliated group composed of three corporations, one of which is a publicly held corporation)*—(1) *Facts.* The facts are the same as in paragraph (c)(1)(v)(S) of this section (*Example 19*), except that Corporation Q is a publicly held corporation and Corporation P is a privately held corporation, and Employee C is a covered employee of Corporation Q (instead of Corporation P).

(2) *Conclusion.* The result is the same as in paragraph (c)(1)(v)(S) of this section (*Example 19*). Even though Corporation Q is a subsidiary that is a publicly held corporation, it is still a member of the affiliated group comprised of Corporations P, Q, and R. Accordingly, $2,000,000 of the aggregate compensation paid is nondeductible. Thus, Corporations P, Q, and R are each treated as paying a ratable portion of the nondeductible compensation.

(U) *Example 21 (Affiliated group composed of three corporations, two of which are publicly held corporations)*—(1) *Facts.* The facts are the same as in paragraph (c)(1)(v)(T) of this section (*Example 20*), except that Corporation R is also a publicly held corporation. As in paragraph (c)(1)(v)(T) of this section (*Example 20*), Corporation Q is a publicly held corporation, Corporation P is a privately held corporation, and Employee C is a covered employee of Corporation Q but not a covered employee of Corporation R.

(2) *Conclusion.* The result is the same as in paragraph (c)(1)(v)(T) of this section (*Example 20*). Even though Corporation R is a subsidiary that is a publicly held corporation, it is still a member of the affiliated group comprised of Corporations P, Q, and R. Accordingly, $2,000,000 of the aggregate compensation paid is nondeductible. Thus, Corporations P, Q, and R are each treated as paying a ratable portion of the nondeductible compensation.

(V) *Example 22 (Affiliated group composed of three publicly held corporations)*—(1) *Facts.* The facts are the same as in paragraph (c)(1)(v)(S) of this section (*Example 19*), except that, Corporations Q and R are also publicly held corporations, and Employee C is a covered employee of both Corporations P and Q, but is not a covered employee of Corporation R.

(2) *Conclusion.* Even though Corporations Q and R are subsidiaries that are publicly held corporations and separately subject to this section, they are still members of the affiliated group comprised of Corporations P, Q, and R. Because Employee C is a covered employee of both Corporations P and Q, the determination of the amount disallowed as a deduction is prorated among Corporation P and R, and separately prorated among Corporations Q and R. With respect to Corporations P and R, $1,100,000 of the aggregate compensation is nondeductible (the difference between the total compensation of $2,100,000 paid by Corporations P and R and the $1,000,000 deduction limitation). Corporations P and R are each treated as paying a ratable portion of the nondeductible compensation. Accordingly, Corporation P has a nondeductible compensation expense of $785,714 ($1,500,000 x $1,100,000/$2,100,000), and Corporation R has a nondeductible compensation expense of $314,285 ($600,000 x $1,100,000/$2,100,000). With respect to Corporations Q and R, $500,000 of the aggregate compensation is nondeductible (the difference between the total compensation of $1,500,000 paid by Corporations Q and R and the $1,000,000 deduction limitation). Accordingly, Corporation Q has a nondeductible compensation expense of $300,000 ($900,000 x $500,000/$1,500,000), and Corporation R has a nondeductible compensation expense of $200,000 ($600,000 x

$500,000/$1,500,000). The total amount of nondeductible compensation expense with respect to Corporation R is $514,285.

(W) *Example 23 (Affiliated group composed of three publicly held corporations)*—(1) *Facts.* The facts are the same as in paragraph (c)(1)(v)(V) of this section (*Example 22*), except that Employee C does not perform any services for Corporation R and does not receive any compensation from Corporation R.

(2) *Conclusion.* Even though Corporations Q and R are subsidiaries that are publicly held corporations and separately subject to this section, they are still members of the affiliated group comprised of Corporations P, Q, and R. Because Employee C performs services only for Corporations P and Q and because Employee C is a covered employee of both Corporations P and Q, which are each a separate publicly held corporation, the determination of the amount disallowed as a deduction is made separately for each publicly held corporation. Accordingly, Corporation P has a nondeductible compensation expense of $500,000 (the excess of $1,500,000 over $1,000,000), and Corporation Q has no nondeductible compensation expense because the amount it paid to Employee C was below $1,000,000.

(X) *Example 24 (Affiliated group composed of three corporations, one of which is a publicly held corporation*—(1) *Facts.* The facts are the same as in paragraph (c)(1)(v)(S) of this section (*Example 19*), except that Corporation R is a direct subsidiary of Corporation P instead of being a direct subsidiary of Corporation Q.

(2) *Conclusion.* The result is the same as in paragraph (c)(1)(v)(S) of this section (*Example 19*). Corporations P, Q, and R are members of an affiliated group. Accordingly, $2,000,000 of the aggregate compensation paid is nondeductible. Thus, Corporations P, Q, and R are each treated as paying a ratable portion of the nondeductible compensation.

(Y) *Example 25 (Affiliated group composed of three publicly held corporations)*—(1) *Facts.* The facts are the same as in paragraph (c)(1)(v)(X) of this section (*Example 24*), except that Corporations Q and R are also publicly held corporations, and Employee C is a covered employee of both Corporations P and Q.

(2) *Conclusion.* The result is the same as in paragraph (c)(1)(v)(V) of this section (*Example 22*). Even though Corporations Q and R are subsidiaries that are publicly held corporations and separately subject to this section, they are still members of the affiliated group comprised of Corporations P, Q, and R. Because Employee C is a covered employee of both Corporations P and Q, the determination of the amount disallowed as a deduction is prorated among Corporation P and R, and separately among Corporations Q and R.

(Z) *Example 26 (Disregarded entity)*—(1) *Facts.* Corporation G is a privately held corporation for its 2020 taxable year. Entity H, a limited liability company, is wholly-owned by Corporation G and is disregarded as an entity separate from its owner under § 301.7701-2(c)(2)(i). As of December 31, 2020, Entity H is required to file reports under section 15(d) of the Exchange Act.

(2) *Conclusion.* Because Entity H is required to file reports under section 15(d) of the Exchange Act and is disregarded as an entity separate from its owner Corporation G, Corporation G is a publicly held corporation under paragraph (c)(1)(iii) of this section for its 2020 taxable year.

(2) *Covered employee.*—(i) *General rule.*—Except as provided in paragraph (c)(2)(v) of this section, with respect to a publicly held corporation as defined in paragraph (c)(1) of this section (without regard to paragraph (c)(1)(ii) of this section), for the publicly held corporation's taxable year, a covered employee means any of the following—

(A) The principal executive officer (PEO) or principal financial officer (PFO) of the publicly held corporation serving at any time during the taxable year, including individuals acting in either such capacity.

(B) The three highest compensated executive officers of the publicly held corporation for the taxable year (other than the principal executive officer or principal financial officer, or an individual acting in such capacity), regardless of whether the executive officer is serving at the end of the publicly held corporation's taxable year, and regardless of whether the executive officer's compensation is subject to disclosure for the last completed fiscal year under the executive compensation disclosure rules under the Exchange Act. The amount of compensation used to identify the three most highly compensated executive officers for the taxable year is determined pursuant to the executive compensation disclosure rules under the Exchange Act (using the taxable year as the fiscal year for purposes of making the determination), regardless of whether the corporation's fiscal year and taxable year end on the same date.

(C) Any individual who was a covered employee of the publicly held corporation (or any predecessor of a publicly held corporation, as defined in paragraph (c)(2)(ii) of this section) for any preceding taxable year beginning after December 31, 2016. For taxable years beginning prior to January 1, 2018, covered employees are identified in accordance with the rules in § 1.162-27(c)(2).

(ii) *Predecessor of a publicly held corporation.*—(A) *Publicly held corporations that become privately held.*—For purposes of this paragraph (c)(2)(ii), a predecessor of a publicly held corporation includes a publicly held corporation that, after becoming a privately held corporation, again becomes a publicly held corporation for a taxable year ending before the 36-month anniversary of the due date for the corporation's U.S. Federal income tax return (disregarding any extensions) for the last taxable year for which the corporation was previously publicly held.

(B) *Corporate reorganizations.*—A predecessor of a publicly held corporation includes a publicly held corporation the stock or assets of which are acquired in a corporate reorganization (as defined in section 368(a)(1)).

(C) *Corporate divisions.*—A predecessor of a publicly held corporation includes a publicly held corporation that is a distributing corporation (within the meaning of section 355(a)(1)(A)) that distributes the stock of a controlled corporation (within the meaning of section 355(a)(1)(A)) to its shareholders in a distribution or exchange qualifying under section 355(a)(1) (corporate division). The rule of this paragraph (c)(2)(ii)(C) applies only with respect to covered employees of the distributing corporation who commence the performance of services for the controlled corporation (or for a corporation affiliated with the controlled corporation that receives stock of the controlled corporation in the corporate division) within the period beginning 12 months before and ending 12 months after the distribution.

(D) *Affiliated groups.*—A predecessor of a publicly held corporation includes a publicly held corporation that becomes a member of an affiliated group (as defined in paragraph (c)(1)(ii) of this section).

(E) *Asset acquisitions.*—If a publicly held corporation, including one or more members of an affiliated group as defined in paragraph (c)(1)(ii) of this section (acquiror), acquires at least 80% of the operating assets (determined by fair market value on the date of acquisition) of another publicly held corporation (target), then the target is a predecessor of the acquiror. For an acquisition of assets that occurs over time, only assets acquired within a 12-month period are taken into account to determine whether at least 80% of the target's operating assets were acquired. However, this 12-month period is extended to include any continuous period that ends on, or begins on, any day during which the acquiror has an arrangement to purchase, directly or indirectly, assets of the target. Additions to the assets of target by a shareholder made as part of a plan or arrangement to avoid the application of this subsection to acquiror's purchase of target's assets are disregarded in applying this paragraph. This paragraph (c)(2)(ii)(E) applies only with respect to covered employees of the target who commence the performance of services for the acquiror (or a corporation affiliated with the acquiror) within the period beginning 12 months before and ending 12 months after the date of the transaction as defined in paragraph (c)(2)(ii)(I) of this section (incorporating any extensions to the 12-month period made pursuant to this paragraph).

(F) *Predecessor of a predecessor.*—For purposes of this paragraph (c)(2)(ii), a reference to a predecessor of a corporation includes each predecessor of the corporation and the predecessor or predecessors of any prior predecessor or predecessors.

(G) *Corporations that are not publicly held at the time of the transaction and sequential transactions.*—(1) *Predecessor corporation is not publicly held at the time of the transaction.*—If a corporation that was previously publicly held (the first corporation) would be a predecessor to another corporation (the second corporation) under the rules of this paragraph (c)(2)(ii) but for the fact that it is not a publicly held corporation at the time of the relevant transaction (or transactions), the first corporation is a predecessor of a publicly held corporation if the second corporation is a publicly held corporation at the time of the relevant transaction (or transactions) and the relevant transaction (or transactions) take place during a taxable year ending before the 36-month anniversary of the due date for the first corporation's U.S. Federal income tax return (excluding any extensions) for the last taxable year for which the first corporation was previously publicly held.

(2) *Second corporation is not publicly held at the time of the transaction.*—If a corporation that is publicly held (the first corporation) at the time of the relevant transaction (or transactions) would be a predecessor to another corporation (the second corporation) under the rules of this paragraph (c)(2)(ii) but for the fact that the second corporation is not a publicly held corporation at the time of the relevant transaction (or transactions), the first corporation is a predecessor of a publicly held corporation if the second corporation becomes a publicly held corporation for a taxable year ending before the 36-month anniversary of the due date for the first corporation's

U.S. Federal income tax return (excluding any extensions) for the first corporation's last taxable year in which the transaction is taken into account.

(3) *Neither corporation is publicly held at the time of the transaction.*—If a corporation that was previously publicly held (the first corporation) would be a predecessor to another corporation (the second corporation) under the rules of this paragraph (c)(2)(ii) but for the fact that neither it nor the second corporation is a publicly held corporation at the time of the relevant transaction (or transactions), the first corporation is a predecessor of a publicly held corporation if the second corporation becomes a publicly held corporation for a taxable year ending before the 36-month anniversary of the due date for the first corporation's U.S. Federal income tax return (excluding any extensions) for the last taxable year for which the first corporation was previously publicly held.

(4) *Sequential transactions.*—If a corporation that was previously publicly held (the first corporation) would be a predecessor to another corporation (the second corporation) under the rules of this paragraph (c)(2)(ii) but for the fact that the first corporation is (or its assets are) transferred to one or more intervening corporations prior to being transferred to the second corporation, and if each intervening corporation would be a predecessor of a publicly held corporation with respect to the second corporation if the intervening corporation or corporations were publicly held corporations, then paragraphs (c)(2)(ii)(G)(1) through (3) of this section also apply without regard to the intervening corporations.

(H) *Elections under sections 336(e) and 338.*—For purposes of this paragraph (c)(2), when a corporation makes an election to treat as an asset purchase either the sale, exchange, or distribution of stock pursuant to regulations under section 336(e) or the purchase of stock pursuant to regulations under section 338, the corporation that issued the stock is treated as the same corporation both before and after such transaction.

(I) *Date of transaction.*—For purposes of this paragraph (c)(2)(ii), the date that a transaction is treated as having occurred is the date on which all events necessary for the transaction to be described in the relevant provision have occurred.

(J) *Publicly traded partnership.*—For purposes of applying this paragraph (c)(2)(ii), a publicly traded partnership is a predecessor of a publicly held corporation if under the same facts and circumstances a corporation substituted for the publicly traded partnership would be a predecessor of the publicly held corporation, and at the time of the transaction the publicly traded partnership is treated as a publicly held corporation as defined in paragraph (c)(1)(i) of this section. In making this determination, the rules in paragraphs (c)(2)(ii)(A) through (I) of this section apply to publicly traded partnerships by analogy.

(iii) *Disregarded entities.*—If a publicly held corporation under paragraph (c)(1) of this section owns an entity that is disregarded as an entity separate from its owner under § 301.7701-2(c)(2)(i) of this chapter, then the covered employees of the publicly held corporation are determined pursuant to paragraphs (c)(2)(i) and (ii) of this section. The executive officers of the entity that is disregarded as an entity separate from its corporate owner under § 301.7701-2(c)(2)(i) of this chapter are neither covered employees of the entity nor of the publicly held corporation unless they meet the definition of covered employee in paragraphs (c)(2)(i) and (ii) of this section with respect to the publicly held corporation, in which case they are covered employees for its taxable year.

(iv) *Qualified subchapter S subsidiaries.*—If a publicly held corporation under paragraph (c)(1) of this section owns an entity that is a QSub under section 1361(b)(3)(B), then the covered employees of the publicly held corporation are determined pursuant to paragraphs (c)(2)(i) and (ii) of this section. The executive officers of the QSub are neither covered employees of the QSub nor of the publicly held corporation unless they meet the definition of covered employee in paragraphs (c)(2)(i) and (ii) of this section with respect to the publicly held corporation, in which case they are covered employees for its taxable year.

(v) *Covered employee of an affiliated group.*—A person who is identified as a covered employee in paragraphs (c)(2)(i) through (iv) of this section for a publicly held corporation's taxable year is also a covered employee for the taxable year of a publicly held corporation as defined in paragraph (c)(1)(ii) of this section.

(vi) *Examples.*—The following examples illustrate the provisions of this paragraph (c)(2). For each example, assume that the corporation has a taxable year that is a calendar year and has a fiscal year ending December 31 for reporting purposes under the Exchange Act. Additionally, for each example, unless explicitly provided, assume that none of the employees were covered employees for any

taxable year preceding the first taxable year set forth in that example (since being a covered employee for a preceding taxable year would provide a separate and independent basis for classifying that employee as a covered employee for a subsequent taxable year).

(A) *Example 1 (Covered employees of members of an affiliated group)*—(1) *Facts.* Corporations A, B, and C are direct wholly-owned subsidiaries of Corporation D. Corporation D is a publicly held corporation as defined in paragraph (c)(1)(i) of this section because its class of securities is required to be registered under section 12 of the Exchange Act as of December 31, 2020. Corporation A is a publicly held corporation as defined in paragraph (c)(1)(i) of this section because it is required to file reports under section 15(d) of the Exchange Act as of December 31, 2020. Corporations B and C are not publicly held corporations for their 2020 taxable years. Employee E served as the PEO of Corporation D from January 1, 2020, to March 31, 2020. Employee F served as the PEO of Corporation D from April 1, 2020, to December 31, 2020. Employee G served as the PEO of Corporation A for its entire 2020 taxable year. Employee H served as the PEO of Corporation B for its entire 2020 taxable year. Employee I served as the PEO of Corporation C for its entire 2020 taxable year. From April 1, 2020, through September 30, 2020, Employee E served as an advisor (not as a PEO) to Employee I and received compensation from Corporation C for these services. In 2020, all four corporations paid compensation to their respective PEOs.

(2) *Conclusion (Employees F and E).* Because both Employees E and F served as the PEO during Corporation D's 2020 taxable year, both Employees E and F are covered employees for Corporation D's 2020 and subsequent taxable years. Corporations D and C are members of an affiliated group as defined in paragraph (c)(1)(ii) of this section. Because Employee E received compensation from Corporations D and C, the compensation paid by both corporations is aggregated. Any amount disallowed as a deduction by this section is prorated between Corporations D and C in proportion to the amount of compensation paid to Employee E by each corporation in 2020.

(3) *Conclusion (Employee G).* Because Employee G served as a PEO of Corporation A, a publicly held corporation, Employee G is a covered employee of Corporation A for its 2020 and subsequent taxable years.

(4) *Conclusion (Employee H).* Even though Employee H served as the PEO of Corporation B, Employee H is not a covered employee of Corporation B for its 2020 taxable year, because Corporation B is considered a publicly held corporation solely by reason of being a member of an affiliated group as defined in paragraph (c)(1)(ii) of this section.

(5) *Conclusion (Employee I).* Even though Employee I served as the PEO of Corporation C, Employee I is not a covered employee of Corporation C for its 2020 taxable year, because Corporation C is considered a publicly held corporation solely by reason of being a member of an affiliated group as defined in paragraph (c)(1)(ii) of this section. The aggregation of the compensation paid to Employee E by Corporations D and C (for purposes of determining the amount of deduction disallowed by this section) is immaterial to determining whether Employee I is a covered employee of Corporation C.

(B) *Example 2 (Covered employees of a publicly held corporation)*—(1) *Facts.* Corporation J is a publicly held corporation. Corporation J is not a smaller reporting company or emerging growth company for purposes of reporting under the Exchange Act. For 2020, Employee K served as the sole PEO of Corporation J and Employees L and M both served as the PFO of Corporation J at different times during the year. Employees N, O, and P were, respectively, the first, second, and third highest compensated executive officers of Corporation J for 2020 other than the PEO and PFO, and all three retired before the end of 2020. Employees Q, R, and S were, respectively, Corporation J's fourth, fifth, and sixth highest compensated executive officers other than the PEO and PFO for 2020, and all three were serving at the end of 2020. On March 1, 2021, Corporation J filed its Form 10-K, Annual Report Pursuant to Section 13 or 15(d) of the Securities Exchange Act of 1934 with the SEC. With respect to Item 11, Executive Compensation (as required by Part III of Form 10-K, or its successor), Corporation J disclosed the compensation of Employee K for serving as the PEO, Employees L and M for serving as the PFO, and Employees Q, R, and S pursuant to Item 402 of Regulation S-K, 17 CFR 229.402(a)(3)(iii). Corporation J also disclosed the compensation of Employees N and O pursuant to Item 402 of Regulation S-K, 17 CFR 229.402(a)(3)(iv).

(2) *Conclusion (PEO).* Because Employee K served as the PEO during 2020, Employee K is a covered employee for Corporation J's 2020 taxable year.

(3) *Conclusion (PFO).* Because Employees L and M served as the PFO during 2020, Employees L and M are covered employees for Corporation J's 2020 taxable year.

(4) *Conclusion (Three Highest Compensated Executive Officers).* Even though the executive compensation disclosure rules under the Exchange Act require Corporation J to disclose the compensation of Employees N, O, Q, R, and S for 2020, Corporation J's three highest

compensated executive officers who are covered employees for its 2020 taxable year are Employees N, O, and P, because these are the three highest compensated executive officers other than the PEO and PFO for 2020.

(C) *Example 3 (Covered employees of a smaller reporting company)*—(1) *Facts.* The facts are the same as in paragraph (c)(2)(vi)(B) of this section (*Example 2*), except that Corporation J is a smaller reporting company or emerging growth company for purposes of reporting under the Exchange Act. Accordingly, with respect to Item 11, Executive Compensation (as required by Part III of Form 10-K, or its successor), Corporation J disclosed the compensation of Employee K for serving as the PEO, Employees Q and R pursuant to Item 402(m) of Regulation S-K, 17 CFR 229.402(m)(2)(ii), and Employees N and O pursuant to Item 402(m) of Regulation S-K, 17 CFR 229.402(m)(2)(iii).

(2) *Conclusion.* The result is the same as in paragraph (c)(2)(vi)(L) of this section (*Example 2*). For purposes of identifying a corporation's covered employees, it is not relevant whether the reporting obligation under the Exchange Act for smaller reporting companies and emerging growth companies apply to the corporation, nor is it relevant whether the specific executive officers' compensation must be disclosed pursuant to the disclosure rules under the Exchange Act applicable to the corporation.

(D) *Example 4 (Covered employees of a publicly held corporation that is not required to file a Form 10-K)*—(1) *Facts.* The facts are the same as in paragraph (c)(2)(vi)(B) of this section (*Example 2*), except that on February 4, 2021, Corporation J files Form 15, Certification and Notice of Termination of Registration under Section 12(g) of the Securities Exchange Act of 1934 or Suspension of Duty to File Reports under Sections 13 and 15(d) of the Securities Exchange Act of 1934 (or its successor), to terminate the registration of its securities. Corporation J's duty to file reports under Section 13(a) of the Exchange Act is suspended upon the filing of the Form 15 and, as a result, Corporation J is not required to file a Form 10-K and disclose the compensation of its executive officers for 2020.

(2) *Conclusion.* The result is the same as in paragraph (c)(2)(vi)(B) of this section (*Example 2*). Covered employees include executive officers of a publicly held corporation even if the corporation is not required to disclose the compensation of its executive officers under the Exchange Act. Therefore, Employees K, L, M, N, O, and P are covered employees for 2020. The conclusion would be different if Corporation J filed Form 15, Certification and Notice of Termination of Registration under Section 12(g) of the Securities Exchange Act of 1934 or Suspension of Duty to File Reports under Sections 13 and 15(d) of the Securities Exchange Act of 1934 (or its successor), to terminate the registration of its securities prior to December 31, 2020. In that case, Corporation J would not be a publicly held corporation for its 2020 taxable year, and, therefore, Employees K, L, M, N, O, and P would not be covered employees for Corporation J's 2020 taxable year.

(E) *Example 5 (Covered employees of two publicly held corporations after a corporate transaction)*—(1) *Facts.* Corporation T is a domestic publicly held corporation for its 2019 taxable year. Corporation U is a domestic privately held corporation for its 2019 and 2020 taxable years. On July 31, 2020, Corporation U acquires for cash 80% of the only class of outstanding stock of Corporation T. The group (comprised of Corporations U and T) elects to file a consolidated Federal income tax return. As a result of this election, Corporation T has a short taxable year ending on July 31, 2020. Corporation T does not change its fiscal year for reporting purposes under the Exchange Act to correspond to the short taxable year. Corporation T remains a domestic publicly held corporation for its short taxable year ending on July 31, 2020, and its subsequent taxable year ending on December 31, 2020, for which it files a consolidated Federal income tax return with Corporation U. For Corporation T's taxable year ending July 31, 2020, Employee V serves as the only PEO, and Employee W serves as the only PFO. Employees X, Y, and Z are the three most highly compensated executive officers of Corporation T for the taxable year ending July 31, 2020, other than the PEO and PFO. As a result of the acquisition, effective July 31, 2020, Employee V ceases to serve as the PEO of Corporation T. Instead, Employee AA begins serving as the PEO of Corporation T on August 1, 2020. Employee V continues to provide services for Corporation T and never serves as PEO again (or as an individual acting in such capacity). For Corporation T's taxable year ending December 31, 2020, Employee AA serves as the only PEO, and Employee W serves as the only PFO. Employees X, Y, and Z continue to serve as executive officers of Corporation T during the taxable year ending December 31, 2020. Employees BB, CC, and DD are the three most highly compensated executive officers of Corporation T, other than the PEO and PFO, for the taxable year ending December 31, 2020.

(2) *Conclusion (Employee V).* Because Employee V served as the PEO during Corporation T's short taxable year ending July 31, 2020, Employee V is a covered employee for Corporation T's short taxable year ending July 31, 2020. Furthermore, Employee V is a covered employee for Corporation T's short taxable year ending July 31, 2020, even though Employee V's compensation is required to be disclosed pursuant to the executive compensation disclosure rules under the Exchange Act only for the fiscal year ending December 31, 2020. Because Employee V was a covered employee for Corporation T's short taxable year ending July 31, 2020, Employee V is also a covered employee for Corporation T's short taxable year ending December 31, 2020.

(3) *Conclusion (Employee W).* Because Employee W served as the PFO during Corporation T's short taxable years ending July 31, 2020, and December 31, 2020, Employee W is a covered employee for both taxable years. Furthermore, Employee W is a covered employee for Corporation T's short taxable year ending July 31, 2020, even though Employee W's compensation is required to be disclosed pursuant to the executive compensation disclosure rules under the Exchange Act only for the fiscal year ending December 31, 2020. Employee W would be a covered employee for Corporation T's short taxable year ending December 31, 2020, even if Employee W did not serve as the PFO during this taxable year because Employee W was a covered employee for Corporation T's short taxable year ending July 31, 2020.

(4) *Conclusion (Employee AA).* Because Employee AA served as the PEO during Corporation T's short taxable year ending December 31, 2020, Employee AA is a covered employee for this taxable year.

(5) *Conclusion (Employees X, Y, and Z).* Employees X, Y, and Z are covered employees for Corporation T's short taxable years ending July 31, 2020, and December 31, 2020. Employees X, Y, and Z are covered employees for Corporation T's short taxable year ending July 31, 2020, because these employees are the three highest compensated executive officers for this taxable year. Employees X, Y, and Z are covered employees for Corporation T's short taxable year ending December 31, 2020, because they were covered employees for Corporation T's short taxable year ending July 31, 2020. Accordingly, Employees X, Y, and Z would be covered employees for Corporation T's short taxable years ending July 31, 2020, and December 31, 2020, even if their compensation would not be required to be disclosed pursuant to the executive compensation disclosure rules under the Exchange Act.

(6) *Conclusion (Employees BB, CC, and DD).* Employees BB, CC, and DD are covered employees for Corporation T's short taxable year ending December 31, 2020 because these employees are the three highest compensated executive officers for this taxable year.

(F) *Example 6 (Predecessor of a publicly held corporation)*—(1) *Facts.* Corporation EE is a publicly held corporation for its 2021 taxable year. Corporation EE is a privately held corporation for its 2022 and 2023 taxable years. For its 2024 taxable year, Corporation EE is a publicly held corporation.

(2) *Conclusion.* Corporation EE is a predecessor of a publicly held corporation within the meaning of paragraph (c)(2)(ii)(A) of this section because it became a publicly held corporation for a taxable year ending prior to April 15, 2025. Therefore, for Corporation EE's 2024 taxable year, the covered employees of Corporation EE include the covered employees of Corporation EE for its 2021 taxable year and any additional covered employees determined pursuant to paragraph (c)(2) of this section.

(G) *Example 7 (Predecessor of a publicly held corporation)*—(1) *Facts.* The facts are the same as in paragraph (c)(2)(vi)(F) of this section (*Example 6*), except that Corporation EE remains a privately held corporation until it becomes a publicly held corporation for its 2027 taxable year.

(2) *Conclusion.* Corporation EE is not a predecessor of a publicly held corporation within the meaning of paragraph (c)(2)(ii)(A) of this section because it became a publicly held corporation for a taxable year ending after April 15, 2025. Therefore, any covered employee of Corporation EE for its 2021 taxable year is not a covered employee of Corporation EE for its 2027 taxable year due to that individual's status as a covered employee of Corporation EE for a preceding taxable year beginning after December 31, 2016 (but may be a covered employee due to status during the 2027 taxable year).

(H) *Example 8 (Predecessor of a publicly held corporation that is party to a merger)*—(1) *Facts.* On June 30, 2021, Corporation FF (a publicly held corporation) merged into Corporation GG (a publicly held corporation) in a transaction that qualifies as a reorganization under section 368(a)(1)(A), with Corporation GG as the surviving corporation. As a result of the merger, Corporation FF has a short taxable year ending June 30, 2021. Corporation FF is a publicly held corporation for this short taxable year. Corporation GG does not have a short taxable year and is a publicly held corporation for its 2021 taxable year.

(2) *Conclusion.* Corporation FF is a predecessor of a publicly held corporation within the meaning of paragraph (c)(2)(ii)(B) of this section. Therefore, any covered employee of Corporation FF for its short taxable year ending June 30, 2021, is a covered employee of Corporation GG for its 2021 taxable year. Accordingly, for Corporation GG's 2021 and subsequent taxable years, the covered employees of Corporation GG include the covered employees of Corporation FF

(for a preceding taxable year beginning after December 31, 2016) and any additional covered employees determined pursuant to paragraph (c)(2) of this section.

(I) *Example 9 (Predecessor of a publicly held corporation that is party to a merger)*—(1) *Facts*. The facts are the same as in paragraph (c)(2)(vi)(H) of this section (*Example 8*), except that, after the merger, Corporation GG is a privately held corporation for its 2021 taxable year.

(2) *Conclusion*. Because Corporation GG is a privately held corporation for its 2021 taxable year, it is not subject to section 162(m)(1) for this taxable year.

(J) *Example 10 (Predecessor of a publicly held corporation that is party to a merger)*—(1) *Facts*. The facts are the same as in paragraph (c)(2)(vi)(I) of this section (*Example 9*), except Corporation GG becomes a publicly held corporation on June 30, 2023, and is a publicly held corporation for its 2023 taxable year.

(2) *Conclusion*. Because Corporation GG became a publicly held corporation for a taxable year ending prior to April 15, 2025, Corporation FF is a predecessor of a publicly held corporation within the meaning of paragraph (c)(2)(ii)(G) of this section. Therefore, any covered employee of Corporation FF for its short taxable year ending June 30, 2021, is a covered employee of Corporation GG for its 2023 and subsequent taxable years. Accordingly, for Corporation GG's 2023 and subsequent taxable years, the covered employees of Corporation GG include the covered employees of Corporation FF (for a preceding taxable year beginning after December 31, 2016) and any additional covered employees determined pursuant to paragraph (c)(2) of this section.

(K) *Example 11 (Predecessor of a publicly held corporation that is party to a merger)*—(1) *Facts*. The facts are the same as in paragraph (c)(2)(vi)(J) of this section (*Example 10*), except that Corporation FF is a privately held corporation for its taxable year ending June 30, 2021, but was a publicly held corporation for its 2020 taxable year.

(2) *Conclusion*. Even though Corporation FF was a privately held corporation when it merged with Corporation GG on June 30, 2021, Corporation FF may still be a considered a predecessor corporation if Corporation GG becomes a publicly held corporation within a taxable year ending prior to April 15, 2024. Because Corporation GG became a publicly held corporation for a taxable year ending December 31, 2023, Corporation FF is a predecessor of a publicly held corporation within the meaning of paragraph (c)(2)(ii)(G) of this section. Therefore, any covered employee of Corporation FF for its 2020 taxable year is a covered employee of Corporation GG for its 2024 and subsequent taxable years. Accordingly, for Corporation GG's 2023 and subsequent taxable years, the covered employees of Corporation GG include the covered employees of Corporation FF (for a preceding taxable year beginning after December 31, 2016) and any additional covered employees determined pursuant to paragraph (c)(2) of this section.

(L) *Example 12 (Predecessor of a publicly held corporation that is party to a merger and subsequently becomes member of an affiliated group)*—(1) *Facts*. The facts are the same as in paragraph (c)(2)(vi)(I) of this section (*Example 9*). Additionally, on June 30, 2022, Corporation GG becomes a member of an affiliated group (as defined in paragraph (c)(1)(ii) of this section) that files a consolidated Federal income tax return. Corporation II is the parent corporation of the group and is a publicly held corporation. Employee HH was a covered employee of Corporation FF for its taxable year ending June 30, 2021. On July 1, 2022, Employee HH becomes an employee of Corporation II.

(2) *Conclusion*. By becoming a member of an affiliated group (as defined in paragraph (c)(1)(ii) of this section) on June 30, 2022, Corporation GG became a publicly held corporation for a taxable year ending prior to April 15, 2025. Therefore, Corporation FF is a predecessor of a publicly held corporation (Corporation GG) within the meaning of paragraph (c)(2)(ii)(G) of this section. Furthermore, Corporation FF is a predecessor of a publicly held corporation (Corporation II) within the meaning of paragraph (c)(2)(ii)(G) of this section. Accordingly, for Corporation II's 2022 and subsequent taxable years, Employee HH is a covered employee of Corporation II because Employee HH was a covered employee of Corporation FF for its taxable year ending June 30, 2021.

(M) *Example 13 Predecessor of a publicly held corporation that is party to a merger and subsequently becomes member of an affiliated group)*—(1) *Facts*. The facts are the same as in paragraph (c)(2)(vi)(L) of this section (*Example 12*), except that, Corporation FF was a privately held corporation for its taxable year ending June 30, 2021, and Employee HH was a covered employee of Corporation FF for its taxable year ending December 31, 2020.

(2) *Conclusion*. Even though Corporation FF was a privately held corporation when it merged with Corporation GG on June 30, 2021, Corporation FF may still be a considered a predecessor corporation if Corporation GG becomes a publicly held corporation for a taxable year ending prior to April 15, 2024. Because Corporation GG became a publicly held corporation for its 2022 taxable year by

becoming a member of an affiliated group (as defined in paragraph (c)(1)(ii) of this section), Corporation FF is a predecessor of a publicly held corporation (Corporation GG) within the meaning of paragraph (c)(2)(ii)(G) of this section. Furthermore, Corporation FF is a predecessor of a publicly held corporation (Corporation II) within the meaning of paragraph (c)(2)(ii)(G) of this section. Therefore, any covered employee of Corporation FF for its 2020 taxable year is a covered employee of Corporation II for its 2022 and subsequent taxable years. Accordingly, for Corporation II's 2022 taxable year, Employee HH is a covered employee of Corporation II because Employee HH was a covered employee of Corporation FF for its 2020 taxable year.

(N) *Example 14 (Predecessor of a publicly held corporation that is a party to a merger)*—(1) *Facts*. Corporation JJ is a publicly held corporation for its 2019 taxable year. Corporation JJ is incorporated in State KK. On June 1, 2019, Corporation JJ formed a wholly-owned subsidiary, Corporation LL. Corporation LL is a publicly held corporation incorporated in State MM. On June 30, 2021, Corporation JJ merged into Corporation LL under State MM law in a transaction that qualifies as a reorganization under section 368(a)(1)(A), with Corporation LL as the surviving corporation. As a result of the merger, Corporation JJ has a short taxable year ending June 30, 2021. Corporation JJ is a publicly held corporation for this short taxable year.

(2) *Conclusion*. Corporation JJ is a predecessor of a publicly held corporation within the meaning of paragraph (c)(2)(ii)(B) of this section. Therefore, any covered employee of Corporation JJ for its short taxable year ending June 30, 2021, is a covered employee of Corporation LL for its taxable years ending after June 30, 2021. Accordingly, for taxable years ending after June 30, 2021, the covered employees of Corporation LL include the covered employees of Corporation JJ (for a preceding taxable year beginning after December 31, 2016) and any additional covered employees determined pursuant to paragraph (c)(2) of this section.

(O) *Example 15 (Predecessor of a publicly held corporation becomes member of an affiliated group)*—(1) *Facts*. Corporations NN and OO are publicly held corporations for their 2021 and 2022 taxable years. On June 30, 2021, Corporation OO acquires for cash 100% of the only class of outstanding stock of Corporation NN. The group (comprised of Corporations NN and OO) elects to file a consolidated income tax return. As a result of this election, Corporation NN has a short taxable year ending on June 30, 2021. Corporation NN is a publicly held corporation for its taxable year ending June 30, 2021, and a privately held corporation for subsequent taxable years. On June 30, 2022, Corporation OO completely liquidates Corporation NN.

(2) *Conclusion*. After Corporation OO acquired Corporation NN, Corporations NN and OO comprised an affiliated group as defined in paragraph (c)(1)(ii) of this section. Thus, Corporation NN is a predecessor of a publicly held corporation within the meaning of paragraph (c)(2)(ii)(D) of this section. Therefore, any covered employee of Corporation NN for its short taxable year ending June 30, 2021, is a covered employee of Corporation OO for its taxable years ending after June 30, 2021. Accordingly, for taxable years ending after June 30, 2021, the covered employees of Corporation OO include the covered employees of Corporation NN (for a preceding taxable year beginning after December 31, 2016) and any additional covered employees determined pursuant to paragraph (c)(2) of this section.

(P) *Example 16 (Predecessor of a publicly held corporation becomes member of an affiliated group)*—(1) *Facts*. The facts are the same as in paragraph (c)(2)(vi)(O) of this section (*Example 15*), except that Corporation OO is a privately held corporation on June 30, 2021, and for its 2021 and 2022 taxable years.

(2) *Conclusion*. Because Corporation OO is a privately held corporation for its 2021 and 2022 taxable years, it is not subject to section 162(m)(1) for these taxable years.

(Q) *Example 17 (Predecessor of a publicly held corporation becomes member of an affiliated group)*—(1) *Facts*. The facts are the same as in paragraph (c)(2)(vi)(P) of this section (*Example 16*), except that on October 1, 2022, Corporation OO's Securities Act registration statement in connection with its initial public offering is declared effective by the SEC, and Corporation OO is a publicly held corporation for its 2022 taxable year.

(2) *Conclusion (Taxable Year Ending December 31, 2021)*. Because Corporation OO is a privately held corporation for its 2021 taxable year, it is not subject to section 162(m)(1) for this taxable year.

(3) *Conclusion (Taxable Year Ending December 31, 2022)*. For the 2022 taxable year, Corporations NN and OO comprised an affiliated group as defined in paragraph (c)(1)(ii) of this section. Corporation NN is a predecessor of a publicly held corporation within the meaning of paragraph (c)(2)(ii)(D) and (F) of this section because Corporation OO became a publicly held corporation for a taxable year ending prior to April 15, 2025. Therefore, any covered employee of Corporation NN for its short taxable year ending June 30, 2021, is a

covered employee of Corporation OO for its 2022 and subsequent taxable years. Accordingly, for Corporation OO's 2022 and subsequent taxable years, the covered employees of Corporation OO include the covered employees of Corporation NN (for a preceding taxable year beginning after December 31, 2016) and any additional covered employees determined pursuant to paragraph (c)(2) of this section.

(R) *Example 18 (Predecessor of a publicly held corporation and asset acquisition)*—(1) *Facts.* Corporations PP and QQ are publicly held corporations for their 2020 and 2021 taxable years. On June 30, 2021, Corporation PP acquires for cash 80% of the operating assets (determined by fair market value) of Corporation QQ. Employees RR, SS, TT, and UU were covered employees for Corporation QQ's taxable year ending December 31, 2020. On April 1, 2020, Employee RR becomes an employee of Corporation PP. On June 30, 2021, Employee SS becomes an employee of Corporation PP. On October 1, 2021, Employee TT becomes an employee of Corporation PP. On August 1, 2022, Employee UU becomes an employee of Corporation PP.

(2) *Conclusion.* Because Corporation PP acquired 80% of Corporation QQ's operating assets (determined by fair market value), Corporation QQ is a predecessor of a publicly held corporation within the meaning of paragraph (c)(2)(ii)(E) of this section. Therefore, any covered employee of Corporation QQ for its 2020 taxable year (who commenced services for Corporation PP within the 12 months before or the 12 months after the acquisition) is a covered employee of Corporation PP for its 2021 and subsequent taxable years. Accordingly, for Corporation PP's 2021 and subsequent taxable years, the covered employees of Corporation PP include Employees RR, SS, and TT, and any additional covered employees determined pursuant to paragraph (c)(2) of this section. Because Employee UU became an employee of Corporation PP after June 30, 2022, Employee UU is not a covered employee of Corporation PP for its 2022 taxable year, but may be a covered employee of Corporation PP by application of paragraph (c)(2) of this section to Employee UU's employment at Corporation PP.

(S) *Example 19 (Predecessor of a publicly held corporation and asset acquisition)*—(1) *Facts.* The facts are the same as in paragraph (c)(2)(vi)(R) of this section (*Example 18*), except that Corporation PP is a privately held corporation on June 30, 2021 and for its 2021 taxable year.

(2) *Conclusion.* Because Corporation PP is a privately held corporation for its 2021 taxable year, it is not subject to section 162(m)(1) for this taxable year.

(T) *Example 20 (Predecessor of a publicly held corporation and asset acquisition)*—(1) *Facts.* The facts are the same as in paragraph (c)(2)(vi)(S) of this section (*Example 19*), except that, on October 1, 2022, Corporation PP's Securities Act registration statement in connection with its initial public offering is declared effective by the SEC, and Corporation PP is a publicly held corporation for 2022 taxable year.

(2) *Conclusion (2021 taxable year).* Because Corporation PP is a privately held corporation for its 2021 taxable year, it is not subject to section 162(m)(1) for this taxable year.

(3) *Conclusion (2022 taxable year).* Corporation QQ is a predecessor of a publicly held corporation within the meaning of paragraph (c)(2)(ii)(G) of this section because Corporation PP became a publicly held corporation for a taxable year ending prior to April 15, 2025. Therefore, any covered employee of Corporation QQ for its 2020 taxable year is a covered employee of Corporation PP for its 2022 and subsequent taxable years. Accordingly, for Corporation PP's 2022 and subsequent taxable years, the covered employees of Corporation PP include the covered employees of Corporation QQ and any additional covered employees determined pursuant to paragraph (c)(2) of this section.

(U) *Example 21 (Predecessor of a publicly held corporation and asset acquisition)*—(1) *Facts.* Corporations VV, WW, and XX are publicly held corporations for their 2020 and 2021 taxable years. Corporations VV and WW are members of an affiliated group. Corporation WW is a direct subsidiary of Corporation VV. On June 30, 2021, Corporation VV acquires for cash 40% of the operating assets (determined by fair market value) of Corporation XX. On January 31, 2022, Corporation WW acquires an additional 40% of the operating assets (determined by fair market value) of Corporation XX. Employees YY, ZZ, and AAA are covered employees for Corporation XX's 2020 taxable year. Employees BBB and CCC are covered employees for Corporation XX's 2021 taxable year. On January 15, 2021, Employee AAA becomes an employee of Corporation WW. On July 1, 2021, Employee YY becomes an employee of Corporation WW. On February 1, 2022, Employees ZZ and BBB become employees of Corporation WW. On June 30, 2023, Employee CCC becomes an employee of Corporation WW.

(2) *Conclusion.* Because an affiliated group, comprised of Corporations VV and WW, acquired 80% of Corporation XX's operating assets (determined by fair market value), Corporation XX is a

predecessor of a publicly held corporation within the meaning of paragraph (c)(2)(ii)(E) of this section. Therefore, any covered employee of Corporation XX for its 2020 and 2021 taxable years (who commenced services for Corporation WW within the period beginning 12 months before and ending 12 months after the acquisition), is a covered employee of Corporation WW for its 2021, 2022 and subsequent taxable years. Accordingly, for Corporation WW's 2021 and subsequent taxable years, the covered employees of Corporation WW include Employees AAA and YY, and any additional covered employees determined pursuant to paragraph (c)(2) of this section. For Corporation WW's 2022 and subsequent taxable years, the covered employees of Corporation WW include Employees AAA, YY, ZZ and BBB, and any additional covered employees determined pursuant to paragraph (c)(2) of this section. Because Employee CCC became an employee of Corporation WW after January 31, 2023, Employee CCC is not a covered employee of Corporation WW for its 2023 taxable year, but may be a covered employee of Corporation WW by application of this paragraph (c)(2) to Employee CCC's employment at Corporation WW.

(V) *Example 22 (Predecessor of a publicly held corporation and asset acquisition)*—(1) *Facts.* The facts are the same as in paragraph (c)(2)(vi)(U) of this section (*Example 21*), except that Corporations VV and WW are not publicly held corporations on June 30, 2021, and for their 2021 taxable years.

(2) *Conclusion.* Because Corporations VV and WW are not publicly held corporations for their 2021 taxable years, they are not subject to section 162(m)(1) for this taxable year.

(W) *Example 23 (Predecessor of a publicly held corporation and asset acquisition)*—(1) *Facts.* The facts are the same as in paragraph (c)(2)(vi)(V) of this section (*Example 22*), except that, on October 1, 2022, Corporation VV's Securities Act registration statement in connection with its initial public offering is declared effective by the SEC, and Corporation VV is a publicly held corporation for its 2022 taxable year.

(2) *Conclusion (2021 taxable year).* Because Corporations VV and WW are not publicly held corporations for their 2021 taxable years, they are not subject to section 162(m)(1) for this taxable year.

(3) *Conclusion (2022 taxable year).* Corporation XX is a predecessor of a publicly held corporation within the meaning of paragraph (c)(2)(ii)(G) of this section because the affiliated group, comprised of Corporations VV and WW, became a publicly held corporation for a taxable year ending prior to April 15, 2024. Therefore, any covered employee of Corporation XX for its 2020 taxable year is a covered employee of Corporation WW for its 2022 taxable year. Accordingly, for Corporation WW's 2022 and subsequent taxable years, the covered employees of Corporation WW include the covered employees of Corporation XX (for a preceding taxable year beginning after December 31, 2016) and any additional covered employees determined pursuant to this paragraph (c)(2).

(X) *Example 24 (Predecessor of a publicly held corporation and a division)*—(1) *Facts.* Corporation DDD is a publicly held corporation for its 2021 and 2022 taxable years. On March 2, 2021, Corporation DDD forms a wholly-owned subsidiary, Corporation EEE, and transfers assets to it. On April 1, 2022, Corporation DDD distributes all shares of Corporation EEE to its shareholders in a transaction described in section 355(a)(1). On April 1, 2022, Corporation EEE's Securities Act registration statement in connection with its initial public offering is declared effective by the SEC. Corporation EEE is a publicly held corporation for its 2022 taxable year. Employee FFF serves as the PFO of Corporation DDD from January 1, 2022, to March 31, 2022. On April 2, 2022, Employee FFF joins Corporation EEE to serve as an advisor (as a common law employee) to the PFO of Corporation EEE. After March 31, 2022, Employee FFF ceases to provide services for Corporation EEE.

(2) *Conclusion.* Because the distribution of the stock of Corporation EEE is a transaction described under section 355(a)(1), Corporation DDD is a predecessor of Corporation EEE within the meaning of paragraph (c)(2)(ii)(C) of this section. Accordingly, Corporation DDD is a predecessor of Corporation EEE within the meaning of paragraph (c)(2)(ii)(A) of this section even if Corporation EEE was a privately held corporation prior to its 2022 taxable year. Because Employee FFF was a covered employee of Corporation DDD for its 2022 taxable year, Employee FFF is a covered employee of Corporation EEE for its 2022 taxable year. The result is the same whether Employee FFF performs services for Corporation EEE as a common law employee or an independent contractor.

(Y) *Example 25 (Predecessor of a publicly held corporation and a division)*—(1) *Facts.* The facts are the same as in paragraph (c)(2)(vi)(X) of this section (*Example 24*), except that, Corporation DDD exchanges 100% of the shares of Corporation EEE with Corporation GGG in a transaction described in section 355(a)(1) and Corporation EEE does not register any class of securities with the SEC. Furthermore, Employee FFF performs services for Corporation GGG instead of for Corporation EEE. Corporation GGG is a privately held corporation for its 2022 taxable year. On October 1, 2023, Corporation GGG's Securities Act registration statement in connection with its initial public offering is declared effective by the SEC. Corporation GGG is a publicly held corporation for its 2023 taxable year. On January 1, 2028, Employee FFF begins serving as a director of Corporation DDD. Corporation DDD is a publicly held corporation for its 2028 taxable year.

(2) *Conclusion (2022 taxable year)*. Because Corporation GGG is a privately held corporation for its 2022 taxable year, section 162(m)(1) does not limit the deduction for compensation deductible for this taxable year.

(3) *Conclusion (2023 taxable year)*. Because the exchange of the stock of Corporation EEE is a transaction described under section 355(a)(1), because Corporations EEE and GGG are an affiliated group, and because Corporation GGG became a publicly held corporation for a taxable year ending prior to April 15, 2025, Corporation DDD is a predecessor of Corporation GGG within the meaning of paragraphs (c)(2)(ii)(D) and (G) of this section. Employee FFF was a covered employee of Corporation DDD for its 2022 taxable year, and began performing services for Corporation GGG following April 1, 2021, and before April 1, 2023. Therefore, Employee FFF is a covered employee of Corporation GGG for its 2023 taxable year.

(4) *Conclusion (2028 taxable year)*. Because Employee FFF served as the PFO of Corporation DDD from January 1, 2022, to March 31, 2022, Employee FFF was a covered employee of Corporation DDD for its 2022 taxable year. Because an individual who is a covered employee for a taxable year remains a covered employee for all subsequent taxable years (even after the individual has separated from service), Employee FFF is a covered employee of Corporation DDD for its 2028 taxable year.

(Z) *Example 26 (Predecessor of a publicly held corporation and a division)*—(1) *Facts*. The facts are the same as in paragraph (c)(2)(vi)(Y) of this section (*Example 25*), except that, Employee FFF begins performing services for Corporation GGG on June 30, 2023, instead of on April 2, 2022, and never performs services for Corporation DDD after June 30, 2023. Furthermore, on June 30, 2023, Employee HHH, a covered employee of Corporation EEE for all of its taxable years, begins performing services for Corporation GGG as an independent contractor advising its PEO but not serving as a PEO.

(2) *Conclusion (2023 taxable year)*. Because the exchange of the stock of Corporation EEE is a transaction described under section 355(a)(1) and because Corporation GGG became a publicly held corporation for a taxable year ending before April 15, 2025, Corporation DDD is a predecessor of Corporation GGG within the meaning of paragraphs (c)(2)(ii)(D) and (G) of this section. Even though Employee FFF was a covered employee of Corporation DDD for its 2022 taxable year, because Employee FFF began performing services for Corporation GGG after April 1, 2023, Employee FFF is not a covered employee of Corporation GGG for its 2023 taxable year. However, if Employee FFF is a PEO, PFO, or one of the three highest compensated executives (other than the PEO or PFO) of Corporation GGG for its 2023 or subsequent taxable years, then Employee FFF is a covered employee of Corporation GGG for such taxable year (and subsequent taxable years). Because Employee HHH was a covered employee of Corporation EEE for its 2022 taxable year, Employee is a covered employee of Corporation GGG for its 2023 taxable year.

(AA) *Example 27 (Predecessor of a publicly held corporation and election under section 338(h)(10))*—(1) *Facts*. Corporation III is the common parent of a group of corporations filing consolidated returns that includes Corporation JJJ as a member. Corporation III wholly-owns Corporation JJJ, a publicly held corporation within the meaning of paragraph (c)(1)(i) of this section. On June 30, 2021, Corporation LLL purchases Corporation JJJ from Corporation III. Corporation III and Corporation LLL make a timely election under section 338(h)(10) with respect to the purchase of Corporation JJJ stock. For its taxable year after the purchase ending December 31, 2021, Corporation JJJ continues to be a publicly held corporation within the meaning of paragraph (c)(1)(i) of this section.

(2) *Conclusion*. As provided in paragraph (c)(2)(ii)(H), Corporation JJJ is treated as the same corporation for purposes for purposes of paragraph (c)(2). Accordingly, any covered employee of Corporation JJJ for its short taxable year ending June 30, 2021, is a covered employee of Corporation JJJ for its short taxable year ending on December 31, 2021, and subsequent taxable years.

(BB) *Example 28 (Disregarded entity)*–(1) *Facts*. Corporation MMM is a privately held corporation for its 2020 taxable year. Entity NNN is a wholly-owned limited liability company and is disregarded as an entity separate from its owner, Corporation MMM, under § 301.7701-2(c)(2)(i) of this chapter. As of December 31, 2020, Entity NNN is required to file reports under section 15(d) of the Exchange Act. For the 2020 taxable year, Employee OOO is the PEO and Employee PPP is the PFO of Corporation MMM. Employees QQQ, RRR, and SSS are the three most highly compensated executive officers of Corporation MMM (other than Employees OOO and PPP). Employee TTT is the PFO of Entity NNN and does not perform any policy making functions for Corporation MMM. Entity NNN has no other executive officers,

(2) *Conclusion*. Because Entity NNN is disregarded as an entity separate from its owner, Corporation MMM, and is required to file reports under section 15(d) of the Exchange Act, Corporation MMM is a publicly held corporation under paragraph (c)(1)(iii) of this section for its 2020 taxable year. Even though Employee TTT is a PFO of Entity NNN, Employee TTT is not considered a PFO of Corporation MMM under paragraph (c)(2)(iii) of this section. As PEO and PFO, Employees OOO and PPP are covered employees of Corporation MMM under paragraph (c)(2)(i) of this section. Additionally, as the three most highly compensated executive officers of Corporation MMM (other than Employees OOO and PPP), Employees QQQ, RRR, and SSS are also covered employees of Corporation MMM under paragraph (c)(2)(i) of this section for Corporation MMM's 2020 taxable year because their compensation would be disclosed if Corporation MMM were subject to the SEC executive compensation disclosure rules. The conclusion would be the same if Entity NNN was not required to file reports under section 15(d) of the Exchange Act and Corporation MMM was a publicly held corporation pursuant to paragraph (c)(1)(i) instead of paragraph (c)(1)(iii) of this section.

(CC) *Example 29 (Disregarded entity)*—(1) *Facts*. The facts are the same as in paragraph (c)(2)(vi)(BB) of this section (*Example 28*), except that Employee TTT performs a policy making function for Corporation MMM. If Corporation MMM were subject to the SEC executive compensation disclosure rules, then Employee TTT would be treated as an executive officer of Corporation MMM pursuant to 17 CFR 240.3b-7 for purposes of determining the three highest compensated executive officers for Corporation MMM's 2020 taxable year. Employees QQQ, RRR and SSS are the three most highly compensated executive officers of Corporation MMM (other than Employees OOO and PPP). Employee TTT is compensated more than Employee QQQ, but less than Employees RRR and SSS.

(2) *Conclusion*. Because Entity NNN is disregarded as an entity separate from its owner, Corporation MMM, and is required to file reports under section 15(d) of the Exchange Act, Corporation MMM is a publicly held corporation under paragraph (c)(1)(iii) of this section for its 2020 taxable year. As PEO and PFO, Employees OOO and PPP are covered employees of Corporation MMM under paragraph (c)(2)(i) of this section. Employee TTT is one of the three highest compensated executive officers for Corporation MMM's taxable year. Because Employees TTT, RRR, and SSS are the three most highly compensated executive officers of Corporation MMM (other than Employees OOO and PPP), they are covered employees of Corporation MMM under paragraph (c)(2)(i) of this section for Corporation MMM's 2020 taxable year because their compensation would be disclosed if Corporation MMM were subject to the SEC executive compensation disclosure rules. The conclusion would be the same if Entity NNN was not required to file reports under section 15(d) of the Exchange Act and Corporation MMM was a publicly held corporation pursuant to paragraph (c)(1)(i) instead of paragraph (c)(1)(iii) of this section.

(DD) *Example 30 (Individual as covered employee of a publicly held corporation that includes the affiliated group)*—(1) *Facts*. Corporations UUU and VVV are publicly held corporations for their 2020, 2021, and 2022 taxable years. Corporation VVV is a direct subsidiary of Corporation UUU. Employee WWW is an employee, but not a covered employee, of Corporation UUU for its 2020, 2021, and 2022 taxable years. From April 1, 2020, to September 30, 2020, Employee WWW performs services for Corporation VVV. Employee WWW does not perform any services for Corporation VVV for its 2021 and 2022 taxable years. Employee WWW is a covered employee of Corporation VVV for its 2020, 2021, and 2022 taxable years. For the 2020 taxable year, Employee WWW receives compensation for services provided to Corporations UUU and VVV only from Corporation UUU in the amount of $1,500,000. Employee WWW receives $2,000,000 from Corporation UUU for performing services for Corporation UUU during each of its 2021 and 2022 taxable years. On June 30, 2022, Corporation VVV pays $500,000 to Employee WWW from a nonqualified deferred compensation plan that complies with section 409A.

(2) *Conclusion (2020 taxable year)*. Because Employee WWW is a covered employee of Corporation VVV and because the affiliated group of corporations (composed of Corporations UUU and VVV) is a publicly held corporation, Employee WWW is a covered employee of the publicly held corporation that is the affiliated group pursuant to paragraph (c)(2)(v) of this section. Accordingly, compensation paid by Corporations UUU and VVV is aggregated for purposes of section 162(m)(1) and, as a result, $500,000 of the aggregate compensation paid is nondeductible. The conclusion would be the same if Corporation UUU was a privately held corporation for its 2020 taxable year.

(3) *Conclusion (2021 taxable year)*. Because Employee WWW is a covered employee of Corporation VVV pursuant to paragraph (c)(2)(i)(C) of this section and because the affiliated group of corporations (composed of Corporations UUU and VVV) is a publicly held corporation, Employee WWW is a covered employee of the publicly

held corporation that is the affiliated group pursuant to paragraph (c)(2)(v) of this section. Accordingly, compensation paid by Corporations UUU and VVV is aggregated for purposes of section 162(m)(1) and, as a result, $1,000,000 of the aggregate compensation paid is nondeductible. The conclusion would be the same if Corporation UUU was a privately held corporation for its 2021 taxable year.

(4) *Conclusion (2022 taxable year).* Because Employee WWW is a covered employee of Corporation VVV pursuant to paragraph (c)(2)(i)(C) of this section and because the affiliated group of corporations (composed of Corporations UUU and VVV) is a publicly held corporation, Employee WWW is a covered employee of the publicly held corporation that is the affiliated group pursuant to paragraph (c)(2)(v) of this section. Accordingly, compensation paid by Corporations UUU and VVV is aggregated for purposes of section 162(m)(1) and, as a result, $1,500,000 of the aggregate compensation paid is nondeductible. The conclusion would be the same if Corporation UUU was a privately held corporation for its 2022 taxable year.

(EE) *Example 31 (Individual as covered employee of a publicly held corporation that includes the affiliated group)*—(1) *Facts.* Corporation BBBB is a publicly held corporation for its 2020 through 2022 taxable years. Corporations YYY and ZZZ are direct subsidiaries of Corporation BBBB and are privately held corporations for their 2020 through 2022 taxable years. Employee AAAA serves as the PFO of Corporation BBBB from January 1, 2020 to December 31, 2020, when Employee AAAA separates from service. On January 1, 2021, Employee AAAA commences employment with Corporation YYY. In 2021, Employee AAAA receives compensation from Corporation YYY in excess of $1,000,000. On April 1, 2022, Employee AAAA commences employment with Corporation ZZZ. On September 30, 2022, Employee AAAA separates from service from Corporations YYY and ZZZ. In 2022, Employee AAAA receives compensation from Corporations YYY and ZZZ in excess of $1,000,000. For the 2021 and 2022 taxable years, Employee AAA does not serve as either the PEO or PFO of Corporations YYY and ZZZ, and is not one of the three highest compensated executive officers (other than the PEO or PFO) of Corporations YYY and ZZZ.

(2) *Conclusion (2021 taxable year).* Employee AAAA is a covered employee of Corporation BBBB for the 2020 taxable year and subsequent taxable years. Because Employee AAAA is a covered employee of Corporation BBBB and because the affiliated group of corporations (composed of Corporations BBBB, YYY, and ZZZ) is a publicly held corporation, Employee AAAA is a covered employee of the publicly held corporation that is the affiliated group pursuant to paragraph (c)(2)(v) of this section for the 2020 taxable year and subsequent taxable years. Therefore, Corporation YYY's deduction for compensation paid to Employee AAAA for the 2021 taxable year is subject to limitation under section 162(m)(1). The result would be the same if Corporation YYY was a publicly held corporation as defined in paragraph (c)(1)(i) of this section.

(3) *Conclusion (2022 taxable year).* Because Employee AAAA is a covered employee of Corporation BBBB and because the affiliated group of corporations (composed of Corporations BBBB, YYY, and ZZZ) is a publicly held corporation, Employee AAAA is a covered employee of the publicly held corporation that is the affiliated group pursuant to paragraph (c)(2)(v) of this section. Therefore, Corporation YYY's and ZZZ's deduction for compensation paid to Employee AAAA for the 2022 taxable year is subject to limitation under section 162(m)(1). Because the compensation paid by all affiliated group members is aggregated for purposes of section 162(m)(1), $1,000,000 of the aggregate compensation paid is nondeductible. Corporations YYY and ZZZ each are treated as paying a ratable portion of the nondeductible compensation. The result would be the same if either Corporation YYY or ZZZ (or both) was a publicly held corporation as defined in paragraph (c)(1)(i).

(3) *Compensation.*—(i) *In general.*—For purposes of the deduction limitation described in paragraph (b) of this section, compensation means the aggregate amount allowable as a deduction under chapter 1 of the Internal Revenue Code for the taxable year (determined without regard to section 162(m)(1)) for remuneration for services performed by a covered employee in any capacity, whether or not the services were performed during the taxable year. Compensation includes an amount that is includible in the income of, or paid to, a person other than the covered employee (including a beneficiary after the death of the covered employee) for services performed by the covered employee.

(ii) *Compensation paid by a partnership.*—For purposes of paragraph (c)(3)(i) of this section, compensation includes an amount equal to a publicly held corporation's distributive share of a partnership's deduction for compensation expense attributable to the remuneration paid by the partnership for services performed by a covered employee of the publicly held corporation.

(iii) *Exceptions.*—Compensation does not include—

(A) Remuneration covered in section 3121(a)(5)(A) through (D) (concerning remuneration that is not treated as wages for purposes of the Federal Insurance Contributions Act);

(B) Remuneration consisting of any benefit provided to or on behalf of an employee if, at the time the benefit is provided, it is reasonable to believe that the employee will be able to exclude it from gross income; or

(C) Salary reduction contributions described in section 3121(v)(1).

(iv) *Examples.*—The following examples illustrate the provisions of this paragraph (c)(3). For each example, assume that the corporation is a calendar year taxpayer.

(A) *Example 1*—(1) *Facts.* Corporation Z is a publicly held corporation for its 2020 taxable year, during which Employee A serves as the PEO of Corporation Z and also serves on the board of directors of Corporation Z. In 2020, Corporation Z paid $1,200,000 to Employee A plus an additional $50,000 fee for serving as chair of the board of directors of Corporation Z. These amounts are otherwise deductible for Corporation Z's 2020 taxable year.

(2) *Conclusion.* The $1,200,000 paid to Employee A in 2020 plus the additional $50,000 director's fee paid to Employee A in 2020 are compensation within the meaning of paragraph (c)(3) of this section. Therefore, Corporation Z's $1,250,000 deduction for the 2020 taxable year is subject to limitation under section 162(m)(1).

(B) *Example 2*—(1) *Facts.* Corporation X is a publicly held corporation for its 2020 through 2024 taxable years. Employee B serves as the PEO of Corporation X for its 2020 taxable year. In 2020, Corporation X established a new nonqualified retirement plan for its executive officers. The retirement plan provides for the distribution of benefits over a three-year period beginning after a participant separates from service. Employee B separates from service in 2021 and becomes a member of the board of directors of Corporation X in 2022. In 2022, Employee B receives a $75,000 fee for services as a director and $1,500,000 as the first payment under the retirement plan. Employee B continues to serve on the board of directors until 2023 when Employee B dies before receiving the retirement benefit for 2023 and before becoming entitled to any director's fees for 2023. In 2023 and 2024, Corporation X pays the $1,500,000 annual retirement benefits to Person C, a beneficiary of Employee B.

(2) *Conclusion (2022 Taxable Year).* In 2022, Corporation X paid Employee B $1,575,000, including $1,500,000 under the retirement plan and $75,000 in director's fees. The retirement benefit and the director's fees are compensation within the meaning of this paragraph (c)(3). Therefore, Corporation X's $1,575,000 deduction for the 2022 taxable year is subject to limitation under section 162(m)(1).

(3) *Conclusion (2023 and 2024 Taxable Years).* In 2023 and 2024, Corporation X made payments to Person C of $1,500,000 under the retirement plan. The retirement benefits are compensation within the meaning of this paragraph (c)(3). Therefore, Corporation X's deduction for each annual payment of $1,500,000 for the 2023 and 2024 taxable years is subject to limitation under section 162(m)(1).

(D) *Example 3*—(1) *Facts.* Corporation T is a publicly held corporation for its 2021 taxable year. Corporation S is a privately held corporation for its 2021 taxable year. On January 2, 2021, Corporations S and T form a general partnership. Under the partnership agreement, Corporations S and T each have a 50% share of the partnership's income, loss, and deductions. For the taxable year ending December 31, 2021, Employee D, a covered employee of Corporation T, performs services for the partnership, and the partnership pays $800,000 to Employee D for these services, $400,000 of which is allocated to Corporation T.

(2) *Conclusion.* Because Corporation T's distributive share of the partnership's $400,000 deduction is attributable to the compensation paid by the partnership for services performed by Employee D, a covered employee of Corporation T, the $400,000 is compensation within the meaning of this paragraph (c)(3) and section 162(m)(1) limits Corporation T's deduction for this expense for the 2021 taxable year. Corporation T's $400,000 share of the partnership's deduction is aggregated with Corporation T's deduction for compensation paid to Employee D, if any, in determining the amount allowable as a deduction to Corporation T for remuneration paid to Employee D for Corporation T's 2021 taxable year. See § 1.702-1(a)(8)(iii). The result is the same whether the covered employee performs services for the partnership as a common law employee, an independent contractor, or a partner, and whether the payment for services is a payment under section 707(a) or a guaranteed payment under section 707(c).

(4) *Securities Act.*—The Securities Act means the Securities Act of 1933.

(5) *Exchange Act.*—The Exchange Act means the Securities Exchange Act of 1934.

(6) *SEC.*—The SEC means the United States Securities and Exchange Commission.

(7) *Foreign Private Issuer.*—A foreign private issuer means an issuer as defined in 17 CFR 240.3b-4(c).

(8) *American Depositary Receipt (ADR).*—An American Depositary Receipt means a negotiable certificate that evidences ownership of a specified number (or fraction) of a foreign private issuer's securities held by a depositary (typically, a U.S. bank).

(9) *Privately held corporation.*—A privately held corporation is a corporation that is not a publicly held corporation as defined in paragraph (c)(1) of this section (without regard to paragraph (c)(1)(ii) of this section).

(d) *Corporations that become publicly held.*—(1) *In general.*—In the case of a corporation that was a privately held corporation and then becomes a publicly held corporation, the deduction limitation of paragraph (b) of this section applies to any compensation that is otherwise deductible for the taxable year ending on or after the date that the corporation becomes a publicly held corporation. A corporation is considered to become publicly held on the date that its registration statement becomes effective either under the Securities Act or the Exchange Act. The rules in this section apply to a partnership that becomes a publicly traded partnership that is a publicly held corporation within the meaning of paragraph (c)(1)(i) of this section.

(2) *Example.*—The following example illustrates the provision of this paragraph (d).

(i) *Facts.* In 2021, Corporation E plans to issue debt securities in a public offering registered under the Securities Act. Corporation E is not required to file reports under section 15(d) of the Exchange Act with respect to any other class of securities and does not have another class of securities required to be registered under section 12 of the Exchange Act. On December 18, 2021, the Securities Act registration statement for Corporation Z's debt securities is declared effective by the SEC.

(ii) *Conclusion.* Corporation E is considered to become a publicly held corporation on December 18, 2021 because it is now required to file reports under section 15(d) of the Exchange Act. The deduction limitation of paragraph (b) of this section applies to any remuneration that is otherwise deductible for Corporation E's taxable year ending on or after December 18, 2021.

(e) *Coordination with disallowed excess parachute payments under section 280G.*—The $1,000,000 limitation in paragraph (b) of this section is reduced (but not below zero) by the amount (if any) that would have been included in the compensation of the covered employee for the taxable year but for being disallowed by reason of section 280G. For example, assume that during a taxable year a corporation pays $1,500,000 to a covered employee. Of the $1,500,000, $600,000 is an excess parachute payment, as defined in section 280G(b)(1), and a deduction for that excess parachute payment is disallowed by reason of section 280G(a). Because the $1,000,000 limitation in paragraph (b) of this section is reduced by the amount of the excess parachute payment, the corporation may deduct $400,000 ($1,000,000 - $600,000), and $500,000 of the otherwise deductible amount is nondeductible by reason of section 162(m)(1). Thus $1,100,000 (of the total $1,500,000 payment) is nondeductible, reflecting the disallowance related to the excess parachute payment under section 280G and the application of section 162(m)(1).

(f) *Coordination with excise tax on specified stock compensation.*—The $1,000,000 limitation in paragraph (b) of this section is reduced (but not below zero) by the amount (if any) of any payment (with respect to such employee) of the tax imposed by section 4985 directly or indirectly by the expatriated corporation (as defined in section 4985(e)(2)) or by any member of the expanded affiliated group (as defined in section 4985(e)(4)) that includes such corporation.

(g) *Transition rules.*—(1) *Amount of compensation payable under a written binding contract which was in effect on November 2, 2017.*—(i) *General rule.*—This section does not apply to the deduction for remuneration payable under a written binding contract that was in effect on November 2, 2017, and that is not modified in any material respect on or after such date (a grandfathered amount). Instead, section 162(m), as in effect prior to its amendment by Public Law 115-97, applies to limit the deduction for such remuneration. Accordingly, because § 1.162-27 implemented section 162(m), as in effect prior to its amendment by Public Law 115-97, the rules of § 1.162-27 determine the applicability of the deduction limitation under section 162(m) with respect to the payment of a grandfathered amount. Remuneration is a grandfathered amount only to the extent that as of November 2, 2017, the corporation was and remains obligated under applicable law (for example, state contract law) to pay the remuneration under the contract if the employee performs services or satisfies the applicable vesting conditions. Accordingly, this section applies to the deduction for any amount of remuneration that exceeds the grandfathered amount if the employee performs services or satisfies the applicable vesting conditions. If a grandfathered amount and non-grandfathered amount are otherwise deductible for the same taxable year and, under the rules of § 1.162-27, the deduction of some or all of the grandfathered amount may be limited (for example, the grandfathered amount does not satisfy the requirements of § 1.162-27(e)(2) through (5) as qualified performance-based compensation), then the grandfathered amount is aggregated with the non-grandfathered amount to determine the deduction disallowance for the taxable year under section 162(m)(1) (so that the deduction limit applies to the excess of the aggregated amount over $1 million). If a portion of the remuneration payable under a contract is a grandfathered amount and a portion is subject to this section and payment under the contract is made in a series of payments, the grandfathered amount is allocated to the first payment of an amount under the contract that is otherwise deductible. If the grandfathered amount exceeds the initial payment, the excess is allocated to the next payment of an amount under the contract that is otherwise deductible, and this process is repeated until the entire grandfathered amount has been paid.

(ii) *Contracts that are terminable or cancelable.*—If a written binding contract is renewed after November 2, 2017, this section (and not § 1.162-27) applies to any payments made after the renewal. A written binding contract that is terminable or cancelable by the corporation without the employee's consent after November 2, 2017, is treated as renewed as of the earliest date that any such termination or cancellation, if made, would be effective. Thus, for example, if the terms of a contract provide that it will be automatically renewed or extended as of a certain date unless either the corporation or the employee provides notice of termination of the contract at least 30 days before that date, the contract is treated as renewed as of the date that termination would be effective if that notice were given. Similarly, for example, if the terms of a contract provide that the contract will be terminated or canceled as of a certain date unless either the corporation or the employee elects to renew within 30 days of that date, the contract is treated as renewed by the corporation as of that date (unless the contract is renewed before that date, in which case, it is treated as renewed on that earlier date). Alternatively, if the corporation will remain legally obligated by the terms of a contract beyond a certain date at the sole discretion of the employee, the contract will not be treated as renewed as of that date if the employee exercises the discretion to keep the corporation bound to the contract. A contract is not treated as terminable or cancelable if it can be terminated or canceled only by terminating the employment relationship of the employee. A contract is not treated as renewed if upon termination or cancellation of the contract the employment relationship continues but would no longer be covered by the contract. However, if the employment continues after such termination or cancellation, payments with respect to such post-termination or post-cancellation employment are not made pursuant to the contract (and, therefore, are not grandfathered amounts).

(iii) *Compensation payable under a plan or arrangement.*—If a compensation plan or arrangement is binding, the deduction for the amount that the corporation is obligated to pay pursuant to written binding contract in effect on November 2, 2017, to an employee pursuant to the plan or arrangement is not subject to this section even if the employee was not eligible to participate in the plan or arrangement as of November 2, 2017, if the employee was employed on November 2, 2017, by the corporation that maintained the plan or arrangement, or the employee had the right to participate in the plan or arrangement under a written binding contract as of that date.

(iv) *Compensation subject to recovery by corporation.*—If the corporation is obligated or has discretion to recover compensation paid in a taxable year only upon the future occurrence of a condition that is objectively outside of the corporation's control, then the corporation's right to recovery is disregarded for purposes of determining the grandfathered amount for the taxable year. If the condition occurs, only the amount the corporation is obligated to pay under applicable law remains grandfathered taking into account the occurrence of the condition. Whether or not the corporation exercises its discretion to recover any compensation does not affect the amount of compensation that the corporation remains obligated to pay under applicable law.

(2) *Material modifications.*—(i) If a written binding contract is modified after November 2, 2017, this section (and not § 1.162-27) applies to any payments made after the modification. A material modification occurs when the contract is amended to increase the amount of compensation payable to the employee. If a written binding contract is materially modified, it is treated as a new contract entered into as of the date of the material modification. Thus, amounts received by an employee under the contract before a material modification are not affected, but amounts received subsequent to the material modification are treated as paid pursuant to a new

contract, rather than as paid pursuant to a written binding contract in effect on November 2, 2017.

(ii) A modification of the contract that accelerates the payment of compensation is a material modification unless the amount of compensation paid is discounted to reasonably reflect the time value of money. If the contract is modified to defer the payment of compensation, any compensation paid or to be paid that is in excess of the amount that was originally payable to the employee under the contract will not be treated as resulting in a material modification if the additional amount is based on applying to the amount originally payable either a reasonable rate of interest or the rate of return on a predetermined actual investment as defined in §31.3121(v)(2)-1(d)(2)(i)(B) of this chapter, (whether or not assets associated with the amount originally owed are actually invested therein) such that the amount payable by the employer at the later date will be based on the reasonable rate of interest or the actual rate of return on the predetermined actual investment (including any decrease, as well as any increase, in the value of the investment).

(iii) The adoption of a supplemental contract or agreement that provides for increased compensation, or the payment of additional compensation, is a material modification of a written binding contract if the facts and circumstances demonstrate that the additional compensation to be paid is based on substantially the same elements or conditions as the compensation that is otherwise paid pursuant to the written binding contract. However, a material modification of a written binding contract does not include a supplemental payment that is equal to or less than a reasonable cost-of-living increase over the payment made in the preceding year under that written binding contract. In addition, the failure, in whole or in part, to exercise negative discretion under a contract does not result in the material modification of that contract.

(iv) If a grandfathered amount is subject to a substantial risk of forfeiture (as defined in §1.409A-1(d)), then a modification of the contract that results in a lapse of the substantial risk of forfeiture is not considered a material modification. For compensation received pursuant to the substantial vesting of restricted property, or the exercise of a stock option or stock appreciation right that do not provide for a deferral of compensation (as defined in §1.409A-1(b)(5)(i) and (ii)), a modification of a written binding contract in effect on November 2, 2017, that results in a lapse of the substantial risk of forfeiture (as defined §1.83-3(c)) is not considered a material modification.

(3) *Examples.*—The following examples illustrate the provisions of this paragraph (g). For each example, assume for all relevant years that the corporation is a publicly held corporation within the meaning of paragraph (c)(1) of this section and is a calendar year taxpayer. Furthermore, assume that, for each example, if any arrangement is subject to section 409A, then the arrangement complies with section 409A, and that no arrangement is subject to section 457A.

(i) *Example 1 (Multi-year agreement for annual salary)*—(A) *Facts.* On October 2, 2017, Corporation X executed a 3-year employment agreement with Employee A for an annual salary of $2,000,000 beginning on January 1, 2018. Employee A serves as the PFO of Corporation X for the 2017 through 2020 taxable years. The agreement provides for automatic extensions after the 3-year term for additional 1-year periods, unless the corporation exercises its option to terminate the agreement within 30 days before the end of the 3-year term or, thereafter, within 30 days before each anniversary date. Termination of the employment agreement does not require the termination of Employee A's employment with Corporation X. Under applicable law, the agreement for annual salary constitutes a written binding contract in effect on November 2, 2017, to pay $2,000,000 of annual salary to Employee A for three years through December 31, 2020.

(B) *Conclusion.* If this §1.162-33 applies, Employee A is a covered employee for Corporation X's 2018 through 2020 taxable years. Because the October 2, 2017, employment agreement is a written binding contract to pay Employee A an annual salary of $2,000,000, this section does not apply (and §1.162-27 does apply) to the deduction for Employee A's annual salary. Pursuant to §1.162-27(c)(2), Employee A is not a covered employee for Corporation X's 2018 through 2020 taxable years. Accordingly, the deduction for Employee A's annual salary for the 2018 through 2020 taxable years is not subject to section 162(m)(1). However, the employment agreement is treated as renewed on January 1, 2021, unless it is previously terminated, and the deduction limit of this section (and not §1.162-27) will apply to the deduction for any payments made under the employment agreement on or after that date.

(ii) *Example 2 (Agreement for severance based on annual salary and discretionary bonus)*—(A) *Facts.* The facts are the same as in paragraph (g)(3)(i) of this section (*Example 1*), except that the employment agreement also requires Corporation X to pay Employee A severance if Corporation X terminates the employment relationship without cause within the term of the agreement. The amount of severance is

equal to the sum of two times Employee A's annual salary plus two times Employee A's discretionary bonus (if any) paid within 12 months preceding termination. Under applicable law, the agreement for severance constitutes a written binding contract in effect on November 2, 2017, to pay $4,000,000 (two times Employee A's $2,000,000 annual salary) if Corporation X terminates Employee A's employment without cause within the term of the agreement.

(B) *Conclusion.* If this §1.162-33 applies, Employee A is a covered employee for Corporation X's 2018 through 2020 taxable years. Because the October 2, 2017, employment agreement is a written binding contract to pay Employee A $4,000,000 if Employee A is terminated without cause prior to December 31, 2020, this section does not apply (and §1.162-27 does apply) to the deduction for $4,000,000 of Employee A's severance. Pursuant to §1.162-27(c)(2), Employee A is not a covered employee for Corporation X's 2018 through 2020 taxable years. Accordingly, the deduction for $4,000,000 of Employee A's severance is not subject to section 162(m)(1). However, the employment agreement is treated as renewed on January 1, 2021, unless it is previously terminated, and this section (and not §1.162-27) will apply to the deduction for any payments made under the employment agreement, including for severance, on or after that date.

(iii) *Example 3 (Agreement for severance based on annual salary and discretionary bonus)*—(A) *Facts.* The facts are the same as in paragraph (g)(3)(ii) of this section (*Example 2*), except that, on October 31, 2017, Corporation X paid Employee A a discretionary bonus of $10,000. Under applicable law, the agreement for severance constitutes a written binding contract in effect on November 2, 2017, to pay $4,000,000 (two times Employee A's $2,000,000 annual salary) if Corporation X terminates Employee A's employment without cause prior to December 31, 2020, and $20,000 if Corporation X terminates Employee A's employment without cause prior to October 31, 2018. On June 30, 2018, Corporation X terminates Employee A without cause and makes a $4,020,000 severance payment to Employee A.

(B) *Conclusion.* If this §1.162-33 applies, Employee A is a covered employee for Corporation X's 2018 taxable year. Because the October 2, 2017, agreement is a written binding contract to pay Employee A $4,000,000 if Employee A is terminated without cause prior to December 31, 2020, and $20,000 if Corporation X terminates Employee A's employment without cause prior to October 31, 2018, this section does not apply (and §1.162-27 does apply) to the deduction for Employee A's severance payment of $4,020,000. Pursuant to §1.162-27(c)(2), Employee A is not a covered employee for Corporation X's 2018 taxable year. Accordingly, the deduction for the entire $4,020,000 of Employee A's severance payment is not subject to section 162(m)(1).

(iv) *Example 4 (Effect of discretionary bonus payment on agreement for severance based on annual salary and discretionary bonus)*—(A) *Facts.* The facts are the same as in paragraph (g)(3)(ii) of this section (*Example 2*), except that, on May 14, 2018, Corporation X paid a $600,000 discretionary bonus to Employee A and, on April 30, 2019, terminated Employee A's employment without cause. Pursuant to the terms of the employment agreement for severance, on May 1, 2019, Corporation X made a $5,200,000 severance payment (the sum of two times the $2,000,000 annual salary and two times the $600,000 discretionary bonus) to Employee A.

(B) *Conclusion.* If this §1.162-33 applies, Employee A is a covered employee for Corporation X's 2019 taxable year. Because the October 2, 2017, agreement is a written binding contract to pay Employee A $4,000,000 if Employee A is terminated without cause prior to December 31, 2020, this section does not apply (and §1.162-27 does apply) to the deduction for $4,000,000 of Employee A's severance payment. Accordingly, the deduction for $4,000,000 of Employee A's severance payment is not subject to section 162(m)(1). Because the October 2, 2017, agreement is not a written binding contract to pay Employee A a discretionary bonus, the deduction for $1,200,000 (based on the discretionary bonus) of the $5,200,000 payment is subject to this section (and not §1.162-27).

(v) *Example 5 (Effect of adjustment to annual salary on severance)*—(A) *Facts.* The facts are the same as in paragraph (g)(3)(ii) of this section (*Example 2*), except that the employment agreement provides for discretionary increases in salary and, on January 1, 2019, Corporation X increased Employee A's annual salary from $2,000,000 to $2,050,000, an increase that was less than a reasonable, cost-of-living adjustment.

(B) *Conclusion (Annual salary):* If this §1.162-33 applies, Employee A is a covered employee for Corporation X's 2018 through 2020 taxable years. Because the October 2, 2017, agreement is a written binding contract to pay Employee A an annual salary of $2,000,000, this section does not apply (and §1.162-27 does apply) to the deduction for Employee A's annual salary unless the change in the salary is a material modification. Even though the $50,000 increase is paid on the basis of substantially the same elements or conditions as the salary that is otherwise paid under the contract, the $50,000 increase does not constitute a material modification because it is less than or equal to a reasonable cost-of-living increase to the

$2,000,000 annual salary Corporation X is required to pay under applicable law as of November 2, 2017. However, the deduction for the $50,000 increase is subject to this section (and not § 1.162-27).

(C) *Conclusion (Severance payment):* Because the October 2, 2017, agreement is a written binding contract to pay Employee A severance of $4,000,000, this section would not apply (and § 1.162-27 would apply) to the deduction for this amount of severance unless the change in the employment agreement is a material modification. Even though the $100,000 increase in severance (two times the $50,000 increase in salary) would be paid on the basis of substantially the same elements or conditions as the severance that would otherwise be paid pursuant to the written binding contract, the $50,000 increase in salary on which it is based does not constitute a material modification of the written binding contract since it is less than or equal to a reasonable cost-of-living increase. However, the deduction for the $100,000 increase in severance is subject to this section (and not § 1.162-27).

(vi) *Example 6 (Effect of adjustment to annual salary on severance)*—(A) Facts. The facts are the same as in paragraph (g)(3)(v) of this section (*Example 5*), except that, on January 1, 2019, Corporation X increased Employee A's annual salary from $2,000,000 to $3,000,000, an increase that exceeds a reasonable, cost-of-living adjustment.

(B) *Conclusion (Annual salary):* If this § 1.162-33 applies, Employee A is a covered employee for Corporation X's 2018 through 2020 taxable years. Because the October 2, 2017, agreement is a written binding contract to pay Employee A an annual salary of $2,000,000, this section does not apply (and § 1.162-27 does apply) to the deduction for Employee A's annual salary unless the change in the employment agreement is a material modification. The $1,000,000 increase is a material modification of the written binding contract because the additional compensation is paid on the basis of substantially the same elements or conditions as the compensation that is otherwise paid pursuant to the written binding contract, and it exceeds a reasonable, annual cost-of-living increase from the $2,000,000 annual salary for 2018 that Corporation X is required to pay under applicable law as of November 2, 2017. Because the written binding contract is materially modified as of January 1, 2019, the deduction for all annual salary paid to Employee A in 2019 and thereafter is subject to this section (and not § 1.162-27).

(C) *Conclusion (Severance payment):* Because the October 2, 2017, agreement is a written binding contract to pay Employee A severance of $4,000,000, this section would not apply (and § 1.162-27 would apply) to the deduction for this amount of severance unless the change in the employment agreement is a material modification. The additional $2,000,000 (two times the $1,000,000 increase in annual salary) constitutes a material modification of the written binding contract because the $1,000,000 increase in salary on which it is based constitutes a material modification of the written binding contract since it exceeds a reasonable cost-of-living increase from the $2,000,000 annual salary for 2018 that Corporation X is required to pay under applicable law as of November 2, 2017. Because the agreement is materially modified as of January 1, 2019, the deduction for any amount of severance payable to Employee A under the severance agreement is subject to this section (and not § 1.162-27).

(vii) *Example 7 (Elective deferral of an amount that corporation was obligated to pay under applicable law)*—(A) Facts. The facts are the same as in paragraph (g)(3)(i) of this section (*Example 1*), except that, on December 15, 2018, Employee A makes a deferral election under a NQDC plan to defer $200,000 of annual salary earned and payable in 2019. Pursuant to the deferred compensation agreement, the $200,000, including earnings, is to be paid in a lump sum at Employee A's separation from service. The earnings are based on the Standard & Poor's 500 Index. Under applicable law, pursuant to the written binding contract in effect on November 2, 2017, (and absent the deferral agreement) Corporation X would have been obligated to pay $200,000 to Employee A in 2019, but is not obligated to pay any earnings on the $200,000 deferred pursuant to the deferral election Employee A makes on December 15, 2018. Employee A separates from service on December 15, 2020. On December 15, 2020, Corporation X pays $250,000 (the deferred $200,000 of salary plus $50,000 in earnings).

(B) *Conclusion.* If this § 1.162-33 applies, Employee A is a covered employee for Corporation X's 2020 taxable year. Employee A's deferred compensation agreement is not a material modification of the written binding contract in effect on November 2, 2017, because the earnings to be paid under the deferred compensation agreement are based on a predetermined actual investment (as defined in § 31.3121(v)(2)-1(d)(2)(i)(B)). The deduction for the $50,000 of earnings to be paid that exceed the amount originally payable to Employee A under the written binding contract ($200,000 of salary) are subject to this section (and not § 1.162-27). This section does not apply (and § 1.162-27 does apply) to the deduction for the $200,000 portion of the $250,000 payment because Corporation X was obligated under applicable law to pay as of November 2, 2017. Pursuant to § 1.162-27(c)(2), Employee A is not a covered employee for Corpo-

ration X's 2020 taxable year; thus, the deduction for the $200,000 payment is not subject to section 162(m)(1).

(viii) *Example 8 (Compensation subject to mandatory recovery by corporation)*-(A) Facts. Employee B serves as the PFO of Corporation Z for its 2017 through 2019 taxable years. On October 2, 2017, Corporation Z executed a bonus agreement with Employee B that provides for a performance bonus of $3,000,000 to be paid on May 1, 2019, if Corporation Z's net earnings increase by at least 10% for its 2018 taxable year based on the financial statements filed with the SEC. The agreement prohibits Corporation Z from reducing the amount of the bonus for any reason but provides that, if the bonus is paid and subsequently the financial statements are restated to show that the net earnings did not increase by at least 10%, then Corporation Z shall recover the $3,000,000 from Employee B within six months of the restatement. Under applicable law, the agreement for the performance bonus constitutes a written binding contract in effect on November 2, 2017, to pay $3,000,000 to Employee B if Corporation Z's net earnings increase by at least 10% for its 2018 taxable year based on the financial statements filed with the SEC. On May 1, 2019, Corporation Z pays $3,000,000 to Employee B because its net earnings increased by at least 10% of its 2018 taxable year.

(B) *Conclusion.* If this § 1.162-33 applies, Employee B is a covered employee for Corporation Z's 2019 taxable year. The terms of the contract providing for recovery of the $3,000,000 do not preclude Corporation Z from being contractually obligated under applicable law to pay $3,000,000 to Employee B if the net earnings increase by at least 10% for its 2018 taxable year. Because the October 2, 2017, agreement is a written binding contract to pay Employee B $3,000,000 if Corporation Z's net earnings increase by at least 10% for its 2018 taxable year based on the financial statements filed with the SEC, this section does not apply (and § 1.162-27 does apply) to the deduction for the $3,000,000 payment. Pursuant to § 1.162-27(c)(2), Employee B is not a covered employee for Corporation Z's 2019 taxable year, so the deduction for the $3,000,000 payment is not subject to section 162(m)(1).

(ix) *Example 9 (Compensation subject to discretionary recovery by corporation)*— (A) Facts. The facts are the same as in paragraph (g)(3)(viii) of this section (*Example 8*), except that the agreement provides that, if the financial statements are restated to show that the net earnings did not increase by at least 10%, then Corporation Z may, in its discretion, recover all or a portion of the $3,000,000 bonus from Employee B within six months of the restatement. Under applicable law, the agreement constitutes a written binding contract in effect on November 2, 2017, to pay $3,000,000 to Employee B if the conditions are met. However, under applicable law, taking into account the employer's ability to exercise discretion and the employer's past exercise of such discretion with respect to a recovery in the event of an earnings restatement, on November 2, 2017, the bonus plan is a written binding contract only with respect to $500,000 if Corporation Z's financial statements are restated to show that the net earnings did not increase by at least 10%. On May 1, 2019, Corporation Z pays $3,000,000 to Employee B. On July 1, 2019, Corporation Z's financial statements are restated to show that its net earnings did not increase by at least 10% for its 2018 taxable year. On July 30, 2019, Corporation Z recovers $1,000,000 from Employee B.

(B) *Conclusion.* If this § 1.162-33 applies, Employee B is a covered employee for Corporation Z's 2019 taxable year. Because the October 2, 2107, agreement is a written binding contract to pay Employee B $3,000,000 if the applicable conditions are met, this section does not apply (and § 1.162-27 does apply) to the deduction for the $3,000,000 provided Corporation Z's financial statements are not restated to show that its net earnings did not increase by at least 10%. However, because Corporation Z's financial statements were so restated, then, on November 2, 2017, under applicable law, taking into account the employer's ability to exercise discretion and the employer's past exercise of such discretion, the bonus plan constitutes a written binding contract to pay only $500,000. Because Corporation Z recovered $1,000,000 of the $3,000,000 payment, this section does not apply (and § 1.162-27 does apply) to the deduction for $500,000 of the $2,000,000 that Corporation Z did not recover. Pursuant to § 1.162-27(c)(2), Employee B is not a covered employee for Corporation Z's 2019 taxable year, so the deduction for the $500,000 is not subject to section 162(m)(1). The deduction for the remaining $1,500,000 is subject to this section (and not § 1.162-27).

(x) *Example 10 (Compensation subject to discretionary recovery by corporation based on a condition)*—(A) Facts. The facts are the same as in paragraph (g)(3)(viii) of this section (*Example 8*), except that the agreement does not include a provision regarding an earnings restatement. Instead, the agreement provides that Corporation Z may, in its discretion, require Employee B to repay the $3,000,000 bonus if, within three years from the date of payment, Employee B engages in willful or reckless behavior that has a material adverse impact on Corporation Z, or is convicted of, or pleads *nolo contendere* or guilty to a felony. Under applicable law, the agreement constitutes a written binding contract in effect on November 2, 2017, to pay $3,000,000 to Employee B if the conditions are met. However, under applicable law, taking into account the employer's ability to exercise discretion and the employer's past exercise of such discretion, if conditions arise to permit Corporation Z to recover the $3,000,000 bonus from Employee B, then the bonus plan established on October 2, 2017, constitutes a written binding contract to pay only $2,000,000 to Employee B if Corporation Z's net earnings increase by at least 10% for its 2018 taxable year based on the financial statements filed with the SEC. On May 1, 2019, Corporation Z pays $3,000,000 to Employee B. Prior to May 1, 2022, Employee B does not engage in willful or reckless behavior that has a material adverse impact on Corporation Z, and is not convicted of, or plead *nolo contendere* or guilty to a felony.

(B) *Conclusion.* If this §1.162-33 applies, Employee B is a covered employee for Corporation Z's 2019 taxable year. Because the October 2, 2017, agreement is a written binding contract under applicable law to pay Employee B $3,000,000 if the applicable conditions are met, this section does not apply (and §1.162-27 does apply) to the deduction for the $3,000,000. Pursuant to §1.162-27(c)(2), Employee B is not a covered employee for Corporation Z's 2019 taxable year, so the deduction for the $3,000,000 is not subject to section 162(m)(1).

(xi) *Example 11 (Compensation subject to discretionary recovery by corporation based on a condition)*—(A) *Facts.* The facts are the same as in paragraph (g)(3)(x) of this section (*Example 10*), except that, on April 1, 2021, Employee B pleads guilty to a felony. Because Employee B pled guilty to a felony prior to May 1, 2022, Corporation Z has discretion to recover the $3,000,000 bonus from Employee B. Corporation Z chooses not to recover any amount of the $3,000,000 from Employee B.

(B) *Conclusion.* If this §1.162-33 applies, Employee B is a covered employee for Corporation Z's 2019 taxable year. Because Employee B pled guilty to a felony prior to May 1, 2022, the bonus plan constitutes a written binding contract in effect on November 2, 2017, to pay only $2,000,000 to Employee B if the applicable conditions were met. Accordingly, this section does not apply (and §1.162-27 does apply) to the deduction for the $2,000,000 portion of the $3,000,000. Pursuant to §1.162-27(c)(2), Employee B is not a covered employee for Corporation Z's 2019 taxable year; thus, the deduction for the $2,000,000 portion of the $3,000,000 is not subject to section 162(m)(1). The deduction for the remaining $1,000,000 of the $3,000,000 is subject to this section (and not §1.162-27).

(xii) *Example 12 (Election to defer bonus)*—(A) *Facts.* On December 31, 2015, Employee C, an employee of Corporation Y, makes an election under a NQDC plan to defer the entire amount that would otherwise be paid to Employee C on December 31, 2016, under Corporation Y's 2016 annual bonus plan. Pursuant to the NQDC plan, the earnings on the deferred amount may be based on either of the following two investment choices (but not the greater of the two): annual total shareholder return for Corporation Y or Moody's Average Corporate Bond Yield. On a prospective basis, Employee C may change the investment measure. The deferred amount and the earnings thereon are to be paid in a lump sum at Employee C's separation from service. Employee C initially elects to have earnings based on annual total shareholder return for Corporation Y. On December 31, 2018, Employee C elects to have earnings based on Moody's Average Corporate Bond Yield. The bonus plan provides that Corporation Y may not reduce the bonus or any applicable earnings. Employee C earns a $200,000 bonus for the 2016 taxable year. Under applicable law, the deferred compensation agreement constitutes a written binding contract in effect on November 2, 2017, to pay the $200,000 bonus plus earnings. Specifically, Corporation Y is obligated to pay earnings on the $200,000 deferred pursuant to the deferral election Employee C makes on December 31, 2015. On January 1, 2018, Employee C is promoted to serve as PEO of Corporation Y and becomes a covered employee for the first time. On December 15, 2020, Employee C separates from service and Corporation Y pays $225,000 (the deferred $200,000 bonus plus $25,000 in earnings) to Employee C.

(B) *Conclusion.* If this §1.162-33 applies, Employee C is a covered employee for Corporation Y's 2020 taxable year because Employee C served as the PEO of Corporation Y during the taxable year. The December 31, 2015, agreement is a written binding contract to pay the $200,000 bonus plus earnings. Furthermore, Employee C's December 31, 2018, election to change the earnings measure does not constitute a material modification. Accordingly, this section does not apply (and §1.162-27 does apply) to the deduction for the $225,000 payment from Corporation Y to Employee C. Pursuant to §1.162-27(c)(2), Employee C is not a covered employee because Employee C did not serve as the PEO at the close of the Corporation Y's taxable year, so the deduction for the $225,000 payment is not subject to section 162(m)(1).

(xii) *Example 13 (Nonaccount balance plan)*—(A) *Facts.* On November 2, 2012, Employee D commences employment with Corporation W as its PFO. Employee D separates from service as PFO on January 7, 2020. For each taxable year, Employee D receives a base salary of $2,000,000. On January 1, 2016, Corporation W and Employee D enter into a NQDC arrangement that is a nonaccount

balance plan (as defined in §1.409A-1(c)(2)(i)(C). Under the terms of the plan, Corporation W will pay Employee D a lump sum payment equal to 25% of Employee D's base salary in the year of separation from service multiplied by 1/12 for each month of service. The plan provides that this payment will be made six months after separation from service and that Corporation W may, at any time, amend the plan to reduce the amount of future benefits; however, Corporation W may not reduce the benefit accrued prior to the date of the amendment. Furthermore, under the terms of the plan and in accordance with §1.409A-3(j)(4)(ix)(C)(3), if Corporation W terminates the plan, the payments due under the plan may be accelerated to any date no earlier than 12 months after the date of termination and no later than 24 months after the date of termination. Under applicable law, if an employer terminates a NQDC plan and does not make a payment until 12 months after the date of termination, then, to reflect the time value of money, the employer is obligated to pay a reasonable rate of interest (compounded annually) on any benefit accrued under the plan at the date of termination until the date of payment. Assume for this purpose that for all applicable periods 3% is a reasonable rate of interest. As of November 2, 2017, Employee D has 60 months of service for Corporation W as calculated under the NQDC plan terms. Under applicable law, the plan constitutes a written binding contract in effect on November 2, 2017, to pay $2,575,000. The $2,575,000 is equal to the amount Corporation W is obligated to pay if it terminated the plan on November 2, 2017 (25% x $2,000,000 x 1/12 x 60 months of service ($2,500,000)), plus a 3% reasonable rate of interest that the $2,500,000 earns after plan termination ($75,000)). On January 7, 2020, when Employee D separates from service, Corporation D pays $3,583,333.33 (25% x $2,000,000 x 1/12 x 86 months of service).

(B) *Conclusion.* If this §1.162-33 applies, Employee D is a covered employee for Corporation W's 2020 taxable year. Because, as of November 2, 2017, the plan is a written binding contract with respect to $2,575,000, this section does not apply (and §1.162-27 does apply) to the deduction for the $2,575,000 portion of the $3,583,333.33 payment. Pursuant to §1.162-27(c)(2), Employee D is not a covered employee, so the deduction for the $2,575,000 portion of the $3,583,333.33 payment is not subject to section 162(m)(1). The deduction for the remaining $1,008,333.33 portion of the $3,583,333.33 payment is subject to this section (and not §1.162-27).

(xiv) *Example 14 (Nonaccount balance plan with offset)*—(A) *Facts.* The facts are the same as in paragraph (g)(3)(xiii) of this section (*Example 13*), except that the plan provides that the amount to be paid to an employee is decreased by the employee's account balance in Corporation W's 401(k) plan on the date of separation from service. The terms of the offset comply with section 409A. On November 2, 2017, and July 7, 2020, Employee D's account balance in the 401(k) plan is $500,000 and $600,000, respectively. Under applicable law, the NQDC plan constitutes a written binding contract in effect on November 2, 2017, to pay $2,075,000, which is equal to the amount of remuneration Corporation W is obligated to pay if it terminated the NQDC plan on November 2, 2017. The $2,075,000 is the difference between the $500,000 401(k) plan account balance on November 2, 2017, and the $2,500,000 accumulated benefit (25% x $2,000,000 x 1/12 x 60 months of service), plus the 3% interest that the $2,500,000 earns after plan termination ($75,000). On July 7, 2020, under the terms of the NQDC plan, Corporation D pays $2,983,333.33 (the difference between the $600,000 401(k) account balance on July 7, 2020, and $3,583,333.33 (25% x $2,000,000 x 1/12 x 86 months of service)).

(B) *Conclusion.* If this §1.162-33 applies, Employee D is a covered employee for Corporation W's 2020 taxable year. Because, as of November 2, 2017, the plan is a written binding contract with respect to $2,075,000, this section does not apply (and §1.162-27 does apply) to the deduction for $2,075,000 of the $2,983,333.33 payment. Pursuant to §1.162-27(c)(2), Employee D is not a covered employee, so the deduction for the $2,075,000 portion of the $2,983,333.33 payment is not subject to section 162(m)(1). The deduction for the remaining $908,333.33 portion of the $2,983,333.33 payment is subject to this section (and not §1.162-27).

(xv) *Example 15 (Nonaccount balance plan)*—(A) *Facts.* The facts are the same as in paragraph (g)(3)(xiii) of this section (*Example 13*), except that the nonaccount balance plan provides that Corporation W will pay Employee D a lump sum payment of $5,000,000 on November 7, 2020, if Employee D provides services from January 1, 2016, through June 30, 2017. Under applicable law, the plan constitutes a written binding contract in effect on November 2, 2017, to pay $4,712,979.55, which is the sum of $4,575,708.30 (the amount of remuneration Corporation W is obligated to pay if it reduced the amount of future benefits to $0 on November 2, 2017) and the increase in present value of $137,271.55 (the difference between $4,575,708.30 and $4,712,979.55 (the present value of $5,000,000 on November 2, 2018)). On November 7, 2020, Corporation W makes a lump sum payment of $5,000,000 to Employee D.

(B) *Conclusion.* If this §1.162-33 applies, Employee D is a covered employee for Corporation W's 2020 taxable year. Because, as of November 2, 2017, the plan is a written binding contract with respect to $4,712,979.55, this section does not apply (and §1.162-27 does apply) to the deduction for the $4,712,979.55 portion of the $5,000,000 payment. Pursuant to §1.162-27(c)(2), Employee D is not a covered employee, so the deduction for the $4,712,979.55 portion of the $5,000,000 payment is not subject to section 162(m)(1). The deduction for the remaining $287,020.45 portion of the $5,000,000 payment is subject to this section (and not §1.162-27).

(xvi) *Example 16 (Performance bonus plan with negative discretion)*—(A) *Facts.* Employee E serves as the PEO of Corporation V for the 2017 and 2018 taxable years. On February 1, 2017, Corporation V establishes a bonus plan, under which Employee E will receive a cash bonus of $1,500,000 if a specified performance goal is satisfied. The compensation committee retains the right, if the performance goal is met, to reduce the bonus payment to no less than $400,000 if, in its judgment, other subjective factors warrant a reduction. On November 2, 2017, under applicable law which takes into account the employer's ability to exercise negative discretion, the bonus plan established on February 1, 2017, constitutes a written binding contract to pay $400,000. On March 1, 2018, the compensation committee certifies that the performance goal was satisfied, but exercises its discretion to reduce the award to $500,000. On April 1, 2018, Corporation V pays $500,000 to Employee E. The payment satisfies the requirements of §1.162-27(e)(2) through (5) as qualified performance-based compensation.

(B) *Conclusion.* If this §1.162-33 applies, Employee E is a covered employee for Corporation V's 2018 taxable year. Because the February 1, 2017, plan is a written binding contract to pay Employee E $400,000 if the performance goal is satisfied, this section does not apply (and §1.162-27 does apply) to the deduction for the $400,000 portion of the $500,000 payment. Furthermore, the failure of the compensation committee to exercise its discretion to reduce the award further to $400,000, instead of $500,000, does not result in a material modification of the contract. Pursuant to §1.162-27(e)(1), the deduction for the $400,000 payment is not subject to section 162(m)(1) because the payment satisfies the requirements of §1.162-27(e)(2) through (5) as qualified performance-based compensation. The deduction for the remaining $100,000 of the $500,000 payment is subject to this section (and not §1.162-27) and therefore the status as qualified performance-based compensation is irrelevant to the application of section 162(m)(1) to this remaining portion.

(xvii) *Example 17 (Account balance plan)*—(A) *Facts.* Employee F serves as the PFO of Corporation U for the 2016 through 2018 taxable years. On January 4, 2016, Corporation U and Employee F enter into a NQDC arrangement that is an account balance plan. Under the terms of the plan, Corporation A will pay Employee X's account balance on June 30, 2019, but only if Employee F continues to serve as the PFO through December 31, 2018. Pursuant to the terms of the plan, Corporation U credits $100,000 to Employee F's account annually on December 31 of each year for three years beginning on December 31, 2016, and credits earnings and losses on the account balance daily. The plan also provides that Corporation U may, in its discretion and at any time, amend the plan either to stop or to reduce the amount of future credits; however, Corporation U may not reduce Employee F's account balance credited before the date of any such amendment. Under the terms of the plan and in accordance with §1.409A-3(j)(4)(ix)(C)(3), if Corporation U terminates the plan, the payment under the plan may be accelerated, but may not be made within 12 months of the date of termination. Under the plan terms and applicable law, if Corporation U terminates the plan, then it is obligated to pay any earnings that accumulated through the date of payment. Under applicable law, the plan constitutes a written binding contract in effect on November 2, 2017, to pay $100,000 of remuneration that Corporation U credited to the account balance on December 31, 2016, plus any earnings credited on that amount through November 2, 2018, which is equal to the amount Corporation U is obligated to pay if it terminates the plan on November 2, 2017 (i.e., after that date, Corporation U is obligated to credit earnings but not any further contributions). On November 2, 2017, Employee E's account balance under the plan is $110,000. On November 2, 2018, Employee E's account balance under the plan would be $115,000 (the $110,000 account balance on November 2, 2017, plus $5,000 earnings on that amount). On June 30, 2019, Corporation U pays Employee F $350,000, the account balance on June 30, 2019.

(B) *Conclusion.* If this §1.162-33 applies, Employee F is a covered employee for Corporation U's 2019 taxable year because Employee F served as the PFO of Corporation U during the taxable year. Because the January 4, 2016, agreement constitutes a written binding contract to pay $115,000, this section does not apply (and §1.162-27 does apply) to the deduction for the $115,000 portion of the $350,000. Pursuant to §1.162-27(c)(2), Employee F is not a covered employee of Corporation U for the 2019 taxable year, so the deduction for the $115,000 portion of the $350,000 is not subject to section 162(m)(1). The deduction for the remaining $235,000 portion of the payment is subject to this section (and not §1.162-27).

(xviii) *Example 18 (Effect of increasing credits to an account balance plan)*—(A) *Facts.* The facts are the same as in paragraph (g)(3)(xvii) of this section (*Example 17*), except that on January 1, 2018, Corporation U increased the amount it would credit to Employee F's account on December 31, 2018 to $200,000. The amount of the increase exceeds a reasonable, annual cost-of-living increase. On June 30, 2019, Corporation U pays Employee F the account balance of $455,000 (including earnings).

(B) *Conclusion.* If this §1.162-33 applies, Employee F is a covered employee for Corporation U's 2019 taxable year. The January 1, 2018 increase in the amount credited to the account balance plan is a material modification of the plan because the additional compensation (the excess of $200,000 over $100,000) credited under the plan is credited on the basis of substantially the same elements or conditions as the compensation that would otherwise be credited pursuant to the plan ($100,000), and it exceeds a reasonable, annual cost-of-living increase. Because the plan is materially modified as of January 1, 2018, and all payments under the plan are made on or after January 1, 2018, the deduction for all payments under the plan is subject to this section (and not §1.162-27).

(xix) *Example 19 (Equity-based compensation with underlying grants made prior to November 2, 2017)*—(A) *Facts.* On January 2, 2017, Corporation T executed a 4-year employment agreement with Employee G to serve as its PEO, and Employee G serves as the PEO for the four-year term. Pursuant to the employment agreement, on January 2, 2017, Corporation T executed a grant agreement and granted to Employee G nonqualified stock options to purchase 1,000 shares of Corporation T stock, stock appreciation rights (SARs) on 1,000 shares, and 1,000 shares of Corporation T restricted stock. On the date of grant, the stock options had no readily ascertainable fair market value as defined in §1.83-7(b), and neither the stock options nor the SARs provided for a deferral of compensation under §§1.409A-1(b)(5)(i)(A) and (B). The stock options, SARs, and shares of restricted stock are subject to a substantial risk of forfeiture and all substantially vest on January 2, 2020. Employee G may exercise the stock options and the SARs at any time from January 2, 2020, through January 2, 2027. On January 2, 2020, Employee G exercises the stock options and the SARs, and the 1,000 shares of restricted stock become substantially vested (as defined in §1.83-3(b)). The grant agreement pursuant to which grants of the stock options, SARs, and shares of restricted stock are made constitutes a written binding contract under applicable law. The compensation attributable to the stock options and the SARs satisfy the requirements of §1.162-27(e)(2) through (5) as qualified performance-based compensation.

(B) *Conclusion.* If this §1.162-33 applies, Employee G is a covered employee for Corporation T's 2020 taxable year. Because the January 2, 2017, grant agreement constitutes a written binding contract, this section does not apply (and §1.162-27 does apply) to the deduction for compensation received pursuant to the exercise of the stock options and the SARs, or the restricted stock becoming substantially vested (as defined in §1.83-3(b)). Pursuant to §1.162-27(e)(1), the deduction attributable to the stock options and the SARs is not subject to section 162(m)(1) because the compensation satisfies the requirements of §1.162-27(e)(2) through (5) as qualified performance-based compensation. However, the deduction attributable to the restricted stock is subject to section 162(m)(1) because the compensation does not satisfy the requirements of §1.162-27(e)(2) through (5) as qualified performance-based compensation.

(xx) *Example 20 (Equity-based compensation with underlying grants made prior to November 2, 2017 for which vesting is accelerated)*—(A) *Facts.* The facts are the same as in paragraph (g)(3)(xix) of this section (*Example 19*), except that, on December 31, 2018, Corporation T modifies the grant agreement pursuant to which grants are made to provide that the stock options, SARs, and shares of Corporation T restricted stock are vested as of January 2, 2019. On January 3, 2019, Employee G exercises the stock options and the SARs.

(B) *Conclusion.* If this §1.162-33 applies, Employee G is a covered employee for Corporation T's 2019 taxable year. The modification of the January 2, 2017, grant agreement is not a material modification. Because the January 2, 2017, agreement under which grants were made constitutes a written binding contract, this section does not apply (and §1.162-27 does apply) to the deduction for compensation received pursuant to the exercise of the stock options and the SARs, or the restricted stock becoming vested. Pursuant to §1.162-27(e)(2)(iii)(B), the acceleration of substantial vesting of the stock options and SARs is not an impermissible increase in compensation to disqualify the compensation attributable to the stock options and SARs from satisfying the requirements of §1.162-27(e)(2) through (5) as qualified performance-based compensation, so the deduction attributable to the stock options and the SARs is not subject to section 162(m)(1). However, the deduction attributable to the restricted stock is subject to section 162(m)(1) because the compensation does not satisfy the requirements of §1.162-27(e)(2) through (5) as qualified performance-based compensation.

(xxi) *Example 21 (Plan in which an employee is not a participant on November 2, 2017)*—(A) *Facts.* On October 2, 2017, Employee H executes an employment agreement with Corporation Y to serve as its PFO, and commences employment with Corporation Y. The employment agreement, which is a written binding contract under applicable law, provides that if Employee H continues in his position through April 1, 2018, Employee H will become eligible to participate in the NQDC plan of Corporation Y and that Employee H's benefit accumulated on that date will be $3,000,000. On April 1, 2021, Employee H receives a payment of $4,500,000 (the increase from $3,000,000 to $4,500,000 is not a result of a material modification as defined in paragraph (g)(2) of this section), which is the entire benefit accumulated under the plan through the date of payment.

(B) *Conclusion.* If this § 1.162-33 applies, Employee H is a covered employee for Corporation Y's 2021 taxable year. Even though Employee H was not eligible to participate in the NQDC plan on November 2, 2017, Employee H had the right to participate in the plan under a written binding contract as of that date. Because the amount required to be paid pursuant to the written binding contract is $3,000,000, this section does not apply (and § 1.162-27 does apply) to the deduction for the $3,000,000 portion of the $4,500,000. Pursuant to § 1.162-27(c)(2), Employee H is not a covered employee of Corporation Y for the 2021 taxable year. Accordingly, the deduction for the $3,000,000 portion of the $4,500,000 is not subject to section 162(m)(1). The deduction for the remaining $1,500,000 portion of the payment is subject to this section (and not § 1.162-27).

(xxii) *Example 22 (Material modification of annual salary)*—(A) *Facts.* On January 2, 2017, Corporation R executed a 5-year employment agreement with Employee I to serve as Corporation R's PFO, providing for an annual salary of $1,800,000. The agreement constitutes a written binding contract under applicable law. In 2017 and 2018, Employee I receives the salary of $1,800,000 per year. In 2019, Corporation R increases Employee I's salary by $40,000, which is less than a reasonable cost-of-living increase from $1,800,000. On January 1, 2020, Corporation R increases Employee I's salary to $2,400,000. The $560,000 increase exceeds a reasonable, annual cost-of-living increase from $1,840,000.

(B) *Conclusion ($1,840,000 Payment in 2019).* If this § 1.162-33 applies, Employee I is a covered employee for Corporation R's 2018 through 2020 taxable years. Because the January 1, 2017, agreement is a written binding contract to pay Employee I an annual salary of $1,800,000, this section does not apply (and § 1.162-27 does apply) to the deduction for Employee I's annual salary unless the change in employment agreement is a material modification. Pursuant to § 1.162-27(c)(2), Employee I is not a covered employee of Corporation R for the 2019 taxable year, so the deduction for the $1,800,000 salary is not subject to section 162(m)(1). Even though the $40,000 increase is made on the basis of substantially the same elements or conditions as the salary, the $40,000 increase does not constitute a material modification of the written binding contract because the $40,000 is less than or equal to a reasonable cost-of-living increase applied to the $1,800,000 annual salary Corporation R owes under the agreement. However, the deduction for the $40,000 increase is subject to this section (and not § 1.162-27).

(C) *Conclusion (Salary increase to $2,400,000 in 2020).* The $560,000 increase in salary in 2020 is a material modification of the written binding contract because the additional compensation is paid on the basis of substantially the same elements or conditions as the salary, and it exceeds a reasonable, annual cost-of-living increase from $1,840,000. Because the written binding contract is materially modified as of January 1, 2020, the deduction for all salary paid to Employee I on and after January 1, 2020 is subject is subject to this section (and not § 1.162-27).

(xxiii) *Example 23 (Additional payment not considered a material modification)*—(A) *Facts.* The facts are the same as in paragraph (g)(3)(xxii) of this section (*Example 22*), except that instead of an increase in salary, in 2020 Employee I receives a restricted stock grant subject to Employee I's continued employment for the balance of the contract.

(B) *Conclusion.* The restricted stock grant is not a material modification of the written binding contract because any additional compensation paid to Employee I under the grant is not paid on the basis of substantially the same elements and conditions as Employee I's salary. However, the deduction attributable to the restricted stock grant is subject to this section (and not § 1.162-27).

(xxiv) *Example 24 (Modification of written binding contract to provide for accelerated vesting)*—(A) *Facts.* Employee J serves as the PFO of Corporation Q for the 2017 through 2020 taxable years. On July 14, 2017, Corporation Q and Employee J enter into an agreement providing that Corporation Q will pay $2,000,000 to Employee J if Employee J continues to serve as the PFO until the third anniversary of the agreement (July 14, 2020). The agreement provides that Corporation Q will make the payment on the date Employee J meets the service requirement. The right to the $2,000,000 payment is subject to a substantial risk of forfeiture as defined in § 1.409A-1(d). Under applicable law, the plan constitutes a written binding contract in effect on November 2, 2017, to pay $2,000,000 to Employee J if

Employee J serves as the PFO through July 14, 2020. On November 29, 2019, Corporation Q modifies the written binding contract to provide for substantial vesting of the $2,000,000 on that date and pays the $2,000,000 to Employee J.

(B) *Conclusion.* If this § 1.162-33 applies, Employee J is a covered employee for Corporation Q's 2019 taxable year because Employee J served as the PFO of Corporation Q during the taxable year. Because the July 14, 2017, agreement constitutes a written binding contract to pay $2,000,000, this section does not apply (and § 1.162-27 does apply) to the deduction for the $2,000,000 unless the contract is materially modified. Pursuant to § 1.162-27(c)(2), Employee J is not a covered employee of Corporation Q for the 2019 taxable year. The change in terms of the contract on November 29, 2019, to accelerate vesting but to otherwise pay the amounts under the original terms is not a material modification. Accordingly, the deduction for the $2,000,000 is not subject to section 162(m)(1).

(h) *Effective/Applicability dates.*—(1) *Effective date.*—These regulations are effective on [DATE OF PUBLICATION OF THE FINAL RULE IN THE FEDERAL REGISTER].

(2) *Applicability dates.*—(i) *General applicability date.*—Except as otherwise provided in paragraph (h)(2)(ii) of this section, these regulations apply to taxable years beginning on or after [DATE OF PUBLICATION OF THE FINAL RULE IN THE FEDERAL REGISTER].

(ii) *Special applicability dates.*—(A) *Definition of covered employee.*—The definition of covered employee in paragraph (c)(2)(i) of this section applies to taxable years ending on or after September 10, 2018. However, for a corporation whose fiscal year and taxable year do not end on the same date, the rule in paragraph (c)(2)(i)(B) requiring the determination of the three most highly compensated executive officers to be made pursuant to the rules under the Exchange Act applies to taxable years ending on or after December 20, 2019.

(B) *Definition of predecessor of a publicly held corporation.*— (1) *Publicly held corporations that become privately held.*—The definition of predecessor of a publicly held corporation in paragraph (c)(2)(ii)(A) of this section applies to any publicly held corporation that becomes a privately held corporation for a taxable year beginning after December 31, 2017, and, subsequently, again becomes a publicly held corporation on or after [DATE OF PUBLICATION OF THE FINAL RULE IN THE FEDERAL REGISTER]. Accordingly, the definition of predecessor of a publicly held corporation in paragraph (c)(2)(ii)(A) of this section does not apply to any publicly held corporation that became a privately held corporation for a taxable year beginning before January 1, 2018, with respect to the earlier period as a publicly held corporation; or a publicly held corporation that becomes a privately held corporation for a taxable year beginning after December 31, 2017, and, subsequently, again becomes a publicly held corporation before [DATE OF PUBLICATION OF THE FINAL RULE IN THE FEDERAL REGISTER].

(2) *Corporate transactions.*—The definition of predecessor of a publicly held corporation in paragraphs (c)(2)(ii)(B) through (H) of this section applies to corporate transactions that occur (as provided in the transaction timing rule of paragraph (c)(2)(ii)(I) of this section) on or after [DATE OF PUBLICATION OF THE FINAL RULE IN THE FEDERAL REGISTER].

(C) *Definition of compensation.*—The definition of compensation provided in paragraph (c)(3)(ii) of this section (relating to allocable shares of partnership deductions for compensation paid) applies to any deduction for compensation that is otherwise allowable for a taxable year ending on or after December 20, 2019. However, this definition of compensation does not apply to compensation paid pursuant to a written binding contract that is in effect on December 20, 2019 and that is not materially modified after that date. For purposes of this paragraph (h)(3), written binding contract and material modification have the same meanings as provided in paragraphs (g)(1) and (g)(2) of this section.

(D) *Corporations that become publicly held.*—The rule in paragraph (d) of this section (providing that the deduction limitation of paragraph (b) of this section applies to a deduction for any compensation that is otherwise deductible for the taxable year ending on or after the date that a privately held corporation becomes a publicly held corporation) applies to corporations that become publicly held on or after December 20, 2019. A privately held corporation that becomes a publicly held corporation before December 20, 2019 may rely on the transition rules provided in § 1.162-27(f)(1) until the earliest of the events provided in § 1.162-27(f)(2).

(E) *Transition rules.*—The transition rules in paragraphs (g)(1) and (2) of this section (providing that this section does not apply to remuneration payable under a written binding contract which was in effect on November 2, 2017, and which is not modified in any material respect on or after such date) apply to taxable years ending on or after September 10, 2018. [Reg. § 1.162-33.]

Registration Requirements with Respect to Debt Obligations

Obligations of the United States: Registration Requirements: Deduction of Interest.—The text of Temporary Reg. § 5f.163-1, relating to registration requirements with respect to debt obligations, has also been proposed as a final regulation and, when adopted, would become Reg. § 1.163-5 (published in the Federal Register on November 15, 1982).

§ 5f.163-1. Denial of interest deduction on certain obligations issued after December 31, 1982, unless issued in registered form.

Imputed Interest: OID: Safe Haven Interest Rates

Reproduced below is the text of a proposed amendment to Temporary Reg. § 5f.163-1, relating to (1) the tax treatment of debt instruments issued after July 1, 1982, that contain original issue discount, (2) the imputation of and the accounting for interest with respect to sales and exchanges of property occurring after December 31, 1984, and (3) safe haven interest rates for loans or advances between commonly controlled taxpayers and safe haven leases between such taxpayers (published in the Federal Register on April 8, 1986).

§ 5f.163-1. Denial of interest deduction on certain obligations issued after December 31, 1982, unless issued in registered form.

☐ Par. 39. Paragraph (f) of § 5f.163-1 is amended by removing the word "1232(d)" from each place that it appears and adding in its

place the word "1287", and by removing the phrase "section 1232B" from each place that it appears and adding in its place the phrase "section 1286".

* * *

Definition of Registered Form: Guidance

Definition of Registered Form: Guidance.—Amendments to Reg. § 5f.163-1, providing guidance on the definitions of registration-required obligation and registered form, including guidance on the issuance of pass-through certificates and participation interests in registered form, are proposed (published in the Federal Register on September 19, 2017) (REG-125374-16).

Par. 14. Section 5f.163-1(d) is amended by revising the paragraph heading and adding a sentence at the end of the paragraph to read as follows:

§ 5f.163-1. Denial of interest deduction on certain obligations issued after December 31, 1982, unless issued in registered form.

* * *

(d) *Applicability date.*—* * * For obligations issued after March 18, 2012, see § 1.163-5 of this chapter.

* * *

Imputed Interest: OID: Safe Haven Leases

Imputed Interest: Original Issue Discount: Safe Haven Interest Rates.—Reproduced below is the text of a proposed amendment to Reg. § 1.163-4, relating to (1) the tax treatment of debt instruments issued after July 1, 1982, that contain original issue discount, (2) the imputation of and the accounting for interest with respect to sales and exchanges of property occurring after December 31, 1984, and (3) safe haven interest rates for loans or advances between commonly controlled taxpayers and safe haven leases between such taxpayers (published in the Federal Register on April 8, 1986).

§ 1.163-4. Deduction for original issue discount on certain obligations issued after May 27, 1969.

☐ Par. 4. Section 1.163-4 is amended as follows:

1. The heading is revised by adding a comma and the phrase "and before July 2, 1982" after the word "1969".

2. In paragraph (a)(1), the second sentence is amended by removing the phrase "section 1232(b)(1)" and adding in its place the phrase "section 1273(a)(1)", and the second sentence is further amended by removing the phrase "the second sentence thereof" in parenthetical and adding in its place the phrase "section 1273(a)(3)".

3. Paragraph (b) is amended by removing the phrase "section 1232(b)(1)" from each place that it appears in the paragraph and adding its place the phrase "section 1273(a)(1)", by removing the phrase "the second sentence thereof" from each place it appears in the paragraph and adding in its place the phrase "section 1273(a)(3)", and by removing the phrase "section 1232(a)(3)(A)" from *Example (4)* and adding in its place the phrase "section 1271(a)(3)(A)".

4. Paragraph (d) is amended by adding the phrase "and before July 2, 1982," after the word "1969," each place that it appears.

Pass-Through Certificates: Registration: Sanctions

Interest Paid: Pass-Through Certificates: Registration Requirements.—Temporary Reg. § 1.163-5T, relating to registration requirements with respect to certain debt obligations and sanctions on issuers of registration-required obligations not in registered form, is also proposed as a final regulation and, when adopted, would become Reg. § 1.163-5 (published in the Federal Register on May 19, 1988).

§ 1.163-5. Denial of interest deduction on certain obligations issued after December 31, 1982, unless issued in registered form.

Pass-Through Certificates: Registration: Transfers

Interest Paid: Pass-Through Certificates: Registration Requirements.—Reproduced below is the text of a proposed amendment of Temporary Reg. § 1.163-5T, relating to registration requirements with respect to certain debt obligations and sanctions on issuers of registration-required obligations not in registered form (published in the Federal Register on May 19, 1988).

☐ Par. 2. Paragraph (d)(7) is added immediately after paragraph (d)(6) of § 1.163-5T. The added paragraph reads as follows:

§ 1.163-5T. Denial of interest deduction on certain obligations issued after December 31, 1982, unless issued in registered form (temporary).

(d) *Pass-through certificates.*

* * *

(7)(i) For purposes of section 4701, any person who holds a registration-required obligation that is in registered form within the meaning of § 5f.103-1(c)(1) and transfers the obligation through a method not described in § 5f.103-1(c)(1) is considered to have issued the obligation so transferred on the date of the transfer in the principal amount of the obligation received by the transferee. Such person is therefore liable for any excise tax under section 4701 that may be

imposed. This paragraph (d)(7) applies to transfers of obligations occurring after August 17, 1988.

(ii) The provisions of this paragraph (d)(7) may be illustrated by the following examples:

Example (1). X, a corporation, holds a registration required obligation in registered form in the principal amount of 10x with a maturity date of December 31, 1999. X transfers the obligation through a method not described in § 5f.103-1(c)(1) on June 30, 1990. For purposes of section 4701, X is considered to have issued an obligation on June 30, 1990 in the principal amount of 10x with a maturity date of December 31, 1999. Because X has issued a registration required obligation not in registered form, X is liable for the tax imposed by section 4701 in an amount computed with reference to the principal amount of 10x and the period beginning on June 30, 1990 and ending on December 31, 1999.

Example (2). X, a corporation, holds a registration required obligation in registered form as nominee of Y, a corporation. The principal amount of the obligation is 10x and the maturity date of the obligation is December 31, 1999. On June 30, 1990, X issued a bearer receipt to Y for the obligation. For purposes of section 4701, X is considered to have issued an obligation on June 1990 in the principal amount of 10x with a maturity date of December 31, 1999. Because X has issued a registration-required obligation not in registered form, X is liable for the tax imposed by section 4701 in an amount computed with reference to the principal amount of 10x and the period beginning June 30, 1990 and ending December 31, 1999.

Example (3). The facts are the same as in *Example* (1) except that X transfers 5x of the 10x obligation held by X. X is considered to have issued an obligation on June 30, 1990 in the principal amount of 5x with a maturity date of December 31, 1999. Because X has issued a registration required obligation not in registered form, X is liable for the tax imposed by section 4701 in an amount computed with reference to the principal amount of 5x and the period beginning on June 30, 1990 and ending on December 31, 1999.

Example (4). The facts are the same as in *Example* (1) except that X is a natural person. X is considered to have issued an obligation on June 30, 1990 in the principal amount of 10x with a maturity date of December 31, 1999. Because X is a natural person, the obligation is not a registration required obligation and, therefore, X is not subject to the tax imposed under section 4701.

Definition of Registered Form: Guidance

Definition of Registered Form: Guidance.—Amendments to Reg. §§1.163-5 and 1.163-5T, providing guidance on the definitions of registration-required obligation and registered form, including guidance on the issuance of pass-through certificates and participation interests in registered form, are proposed (published in the Federal Register on September 19, 2017) (REG-125374-16).

Par. 3. Section 1.163-5 is amended by revising the section heading and adding paragraphs (a), (b), and (c)(3)(iii) to read as follows:

§1.163-5. Denial of interest deduction on certain obligations unless issued in registered form.—(a) *Denial of deduction.*—(1) *In general.*—No deduction shall be allowed a taxpayer under section 163 for interest paid or accrued on a registration-required obligation (as defined in section 163(f) and paragraph (a)(2) of this section) unless such obligation is issued in registered form (as defined in paragraph (b) of this section). An obligation that is not in registered form under paragraph (b) of this section is an obligation in bearer form.

(2) *Registration-required obligation.*—(i) *In general.*—The term *registration-required obligation* means any obligation (including a pass-through certificate or participation interest described in paragraph (a)(3) of this section and a regular interest in a REMIC described in paragraph (a)(4) of this section) other than—

(A) An obligation issued by a natural person;

(B) An obligation not of a type offered to the public (as described in paragraph (a)(2)(ii) of this section); or

(C) An obligation that has a maturity at the date of issue of not more than 1 year.

(ii) *Obligation not of a type offered to the public.*—For purposes of section 163(f)(2)(A)(ii) and paragraph (a)(2)(i)(B) of this section, an obligation is not of a type offered to the public unless the obligation is traded on an established market as determined under §1.1273-2(f) without regard to §1.1273-2(f)(6).

(3) *Pass-through certificates and participation interests.*—(i) *Pass-through certificate.*—(A) *In general.*—A pass-through certificate is considered to be a registration-required obligation if the pass-through certificate is described in paragraph (a)(2)(i) of this section without regard to whether any obligation held by the entity to which the pass-through certificate relates is described in paragraph (a)(2)(i) of this section.

(B) *Definition of pass-through certificate.*—For purposes of paragraph (a) of this section, a *pass-through certificate* is an instrument evidencing an interest in a grantor trust under Subpart E of Part I of Subchapter J of the Code, or a similar fund, that principally holds debt instruments. For purposes of this paragraph (a)(3)(i)(B), a similar fund includes an entity that, under §§301.7701-1 through 301.7701-3 of this chapter, is disregarded as an entity separate from its owner or classified as a partnership for federal tax purposes, without regard to whether the fund has the power to vary the assets in the fund or the sequence of payments made to holders. In addition, for purposes of this paragraph (a)(3)(i)(B), a similar fund does not include a business entity that is classified as a corporation under §301.7701-2 of this chapter.

(ii) *Participation interest.*—A participation interest that evidences ownership of some or all of one or more obligations and that is treated as conveying ownership of a specified portion of the obligation or obligations (and not ownership of an entity treated as created under §301.7701-1(a)(2) of this chapter) is considered to be a registration-required obligation if the participation interest is described in paragraph (a)(2)(i) of this section without regard to whether any obligation to which the participation interest relates is described in paragraph (a)(2)(i) of this section.

(iii) *Treatment of obligation held by a trust or fund.*—An obligation held by a trust or a fund in which ownership interests are represented by pass-through certificates is considered to be in registered form or to be a registration-required obligation if the obligation held by the trust or fund is in registered form (as defined in paragraph (b) of this section) or is a registration-required obligation described in paragraph (a)(2)(i) of this section, without regard to whether the pass-through certificates are so considered.

(iv) *Examples.*—The application of paragraph (a)(3) of this section may be illustrated by the following examples:

Example 1. Fund, a partnership under the laws of the state in which it is organized, acquires a pool of student loans. The student loans are issued by natural persons and, therefore, are not registration-required obligations as described in paragraph (a)(2)(i) of this section. Fund contributes the student loans to Trust, a business trust under the laws of the state in which Trust is organized. Trust has the power to vary the investments in Trust, and is not treated as a trust of which the grantor is the owner under Subpart E of Part I of Subchapter J of the Code. Trust issues certificates evidencing an interest in Trust. The certificates issued by Trust are offered to the public. The certificates issued by Trust are pass-through certificates (as described in paragraph (a)(3)(i)(B) of this section) and are described in paragraph (a)(2)(i) of this section, and thus, are registration-required obligations described in paragraph (a)(2)(i) of this section, even though the student loans held by Trust are not registration-required obligations.

Example 2. Partnership U purchases a building from Partnership V. Partnership U makes a cash down payment and issues a note secured by a mortgage in the building to Partnership V for the remaining purchase price of the building. The note is not a registration-required obligation described in paragraph (a)(2)(i) of this section because it is not an obligation of a type offered to the public. Partnership V offers participations in the underlying note to the public. Under the terms of the participation, each participant will own an interest in the note that will entitle the participant to a specified portion of the interest and principal generated by the note. The participation is a participation interest described in paragraph (a)(3)(ii) of this section and is described in paragraph (a)(2)(i) of this section, and, thus, is a registration-required obligation described in paragraph (a)(2)(i) of this section, even though the underlying note is not a registration-required obligation.

(4) *REMICs.*—(i) *Regular interest in a REMIC.*—A regular interest in a REMIC, as defined in sections 860D and 860G and the regulations thereunder, is considered to be a registration-required obligation if the regular interest is described in paragraph (a)(2)(i) of this section, without regard to whether one or more of the obligations held by the REMIC to which the regular interest relates is described in paragraph (a)(2)(i) of this section.

(ii) *Treatment of obligation held by a REMIC.*—An obligation described in paragraph (a)(2)(i) of this section and held by a REMIC is treated as a registration-required obligation regardless of whether the regular interests in the REMIC are so treated.

(5) *Applicability date.*—(i) *In general.*—Except as otherwise provided in paragraphs (a)(5)(ii) and (iii) of this section, paragraph (a) of this section applies to obligations issued after March 18, 2012. For obligations issued on or before March 18, 2012, see §5f.163-1 of this chapter.

(ii) *Obligations not of a type offered to the public.*—Paragraph (a)(2)(ii) of this section applies to obligations issued after the date of publication of a Treasury decision adopting these rules as final regulations in the **Federal Register**.

(iii) *Pass-through certificates, participation interests, and regular interests in REMICs.*—Paragraph (a) of this section applies to pass-through certificates, participation interests, and regular interests in REMICs issued after the date of publication of a Treasury decision adopting these rules as final regulations in the **Federal Register**. For pass-through certificates or regular interests in REMICs issued on or before the date of publication of a Treasury decision adopting these rules as final regulations in the **Federal Register**, see §1.163-5T.

(b) *Registered form.*—(1) *General rule.*—Except as provided in paragraph (b)(4) of this section, an obligation is in registered form if a transfer of the right to receive both principal and any stated interest on the obligation may be effected only—

(i) By surrender of the old obligation and either the reissuance of the old obligation to the new holder or the issuance of a new obligation to the new holder;

(ii) Through a book entry system (as described in paragraph (b)(2) of this section) maintained by the issuer of the obligation (or its agent) or by a clearing organization (as defined in paragraph (b)(3) of this section); or

(iii) Through both of the methods described in paragraphs (b)(1)(i) and (ii) of this section.

(2) *Book entry system.*—(i) *In general.*—An obligation will be considered transferable through a book entry system, including a dematerialized book entry system, if ownership of the obligation or an interest in the obligation is required to be recorded in an electronic or physical register maintained by the issuer of the obligation (or its agent) or by a clearing organization (as defined in paragraph (b)(3) of this section).

(ii) *Book entry system maintained by clearing organization that effectively immobilizes a bearer form obligation.*—An obligation represented by one or more physical certificates in bearer form will be considered to be in registered form if the physical certificates are effectively immobilized. A physical certificate is effectively immobilized only if—

(A) The physical certificate is issued to and held by a clearing organization (as defined in paragraph (b)(3) of this section) for the benefit of purchasers of interests in the obligation under arrangements that prohibit the transfer of the physical certificate except to a successor clearing organization subject to terms that effectively immobilize the physical certificate, as provided in paragraph (b)(2)(ii) of this section, in the hands of the successor clearing organization; and

(B) Ownership of the obligation or an interest in the obligation is transferable only through a book entry system (as described in paragraph (b)(2)(i) of this section) maintained by the clearing organization (as defined in paragraph (b)(3) of this section).

(3) *Definition of clearing organization.*—For purposes of paragraph (b) of this section, *clearing organization* means an entity that is in the business of holding obligations for or reflecting the ownership interests of member organizations and transferring obligations among such member organizations by credit or debit to the account of a member organization without the necessity of physical delivery of the obligation.

(4) *Temporal limitations on registered form.*—(i) *In general.*—Except as provided in paragraphs (b)(4)(ii) and (iii) of this section, an obligation is not considered to be in registered form as of a particular time if the obligation may be transferred at that time or at a time or times on or before the maturity of the obligation by any means not described in paragraph (b)(1) of this section.

(ii) *Events that permit issuance of physical certificates in bearer form.*—(A) *In general.*—An obligation transferrable through a dematerialized book entry system is not in bearer form pursuant to paragraph (b)(4)(i) of this section solely because a holder of the obligation (or an interest therein) has a right to obtain a physical certificate in bearer form upon the occurrence of one or both of the following events—

(1) A termination of business without a successor by the clearing organization that maintains the book entry system; or

(2) The issuance of physical securities at the issuer's request upon a change in tax law that would be adverse to the issuer but for the issuance of physical securities in bearer form.

(B) *Treatment upon issuance of physical certificate in bearer form.*—Upon the occurrence of one or both of the events described in paragraph (b)(4)(ii)(A) of this section, any obligation with respect to which a holder, or a group of holders acting collectively, may obtain a physical certificate in bearer form will no longer be in registered form, regardless of whether a physical certificate in bearer form has actually been issued.

(iii) *Obligations in registered form until maturity.*—An obligation that as of a particular time is not considered to be in registered form because the obligation may be transferred at a time or times before the maturity of the obligation by a means not described in paragraph (b)(1) of this section and that during the period beginning at a later time and ending at maturity may be transferred only by a means described in paragraph (b)(1) of this section is considered to be in registered form during the period beginning at that later time.

(5) *Examples.*—The application of paragraph (b) of this section may be illustrated by the following examples:

Example 1. X issues an obligation that is a registration-required obligation as described in paragraph (a)(2)(i) of this section. At issuance, X issues the obligation in the purchaser's name evidencing the purchaser's ownership of the principal and interest under the obligation. The purchaser may transfer the obligation only by surrendering the obligation to X and by X issuing a new instrument to the new holder. X's obligation is issued in registered form under paragraph (b)(1) of this section.

Example 2. Corporation A issues US$500 million of debt (the Note) evidenced by a physical certificate that is registered in the name of ABC, a clearing organization (as defined in paragraph (b)(3) of this section). Under the terms of the Note, Corporation A must maintain an electronic register identifying the owners of interests in the Note, and a transfer of the right to receive either principal or any stated interest on such ownership interests may be effected only through a change to the electronic register. Pursuant to an agreement with Corporation A, ABC takes custody of the physical certificate evidencing the Note and receives all principal and interest on the Note from Corporation A. Independently of its agreement with Corporation A, ABC maintains electronic records of its members' ownership interests in the Note and distributes principal and interest to members' accounts in accordance with those interests. ABC's members, in turn, maintain electronic records of their customers' ownership interests in the Note and similarly distribute principal and interest to their customers' accounts. Corporation A's electronic register identifies ABC as the sole owner of the Note. Corporation A does not record transfers of ownership interests in the Note to or among ABC's members, and ABC does not record transfers of ownership interests in the Note to or among its members' customers. Corporation A's electronic register is a book entry system as described in paragraph (b)(2)(i) of this section, and the Note is in registered form under paragraph (b)(1) of this section.

Example 3. The facts are the same as in *Example 2* of paragraph (b)(5) of this section, except that, instead of maintaining an electronic register, Corporation A issues a global bearer certificate (Certificate) to ABC pursuant to an agreement that prohibits the transfer of Certificate except to a successor clearing organization subject to terms that effectively immobilize Certificate, as provided in paragraph (b)(2)(ii) of this section, in the hands of the successor clearing organization. Further, holders of interests in Certificate may only obtain physical bearer certificates upon cessation of ABC's operations without a successor or, at Corporation A's request, upon a change in tax law that would be adverse to Corporation A but for the issuance of physical bearer certificates. Because ownership of interests in Certificate may be transferred only through a dematerialized book entry system maintained by ABC, and because the circumstances under which definitive bearer certificates may be issued to holders of interests in Certificate are limited to the circumstances described in paragraph (b)(4)(ii)(A) of this section, Certificate is an immobilized bearer form obligation described in paragraph (b)(2)(ii) of this section and is accordingly in registered form under paragraph (b)(2)(ii) of this section.

Example 4. The facts are the same as in *Example 3* of paragraph (b)(5) of this section, except that purchasers of interests in Certificate have the right to obtain definitive bearer certificates upon request at any time until maturity of Certificate. Because the circumstances under which definitive bearer obligations may be issued to holders of interests in Certificate are not limited to the circumstances described in paragraph (b)(4)(ii)(A) of this section, Certificate is not considered to be issued in registered form under paragraph (b)(4)(i) of this section.

Example 5. Bank makes a loan to borrower secured by real property (Loan). Participations in Loan are traded on an established market. The participations are participation interests described in paragraph (a)(3)(ii) of this section and are accordingly registration-required obligations described in paragraph (a)(2)(i) of this section. Bank remains the registered owner of Loan and maintains an electronic book entry system that identifies participants. Participation interests may be transferred only by surrender of the old participation interest and reissuance of the participation interest in the name of the new participant, or by transfer of the participation interest from the name of the old participant to the name of the new participant in the book entry system of Bank. Bank's book entry system is described in paragraph (b)(2)(i) of this section, and, accordingly, under paragraph (b)(1)(iii) of this section, the participation interests are in registered form.

(6) *Applicability date.*—Paragraph (b) of this section applies to obligations issued after March 18, 2012. Taxpayers may apply the rules in section 3 of Notice 2012-20, 2012-13 IRB 574, for obligations issued prior to the date of publication of the Treasury decision adopting these rules as final regulations in the **Federal Register**. For obligations issued on or before March 18, 2012, see §5f.103-1 of this chapter.

(c) * * *

(3) * * *

    (iii) *Applicability to obligations issued after March 18, 2012.*— For purposes of section 163(f), paragraph (c) of this section does not apply to obligations issued after March 18, 2012. However, for pur-

poses of determining whether an obligation is described in section 4701(b)(1)(B) or whether the exception in section 6049 from information reporting of interest or original discount with respect to obligations that have an original term of 183 days or less applies, paragraph (c) of this section continues to apply to obligations issued after March 18, 2012. See §§1.4701-1(b)(3) and 1.6049-5(b)(10).

Par. 4. Section 1.163-5T is amended by adding paragraph (f) to read as follows:

§1.163-5T. Denial of interest deduction on certain obligations issued after December 31, 1982, unless issued in registered form (temporary).

* * *

    (f) *Applicability date.*—This section applies to obligations to which §5f.163-1 of this chapter applies. See §5f.163-1(d) of this chapter.

Mortgage Credit Certificates

Mortgage Credit Certificates: Issuance: Penalties.—Temporary Reg. §1.163-6T, relating to the issuance of mortgage credit certificates, is also proposed as final and when adopted, would become Reg. §1.163-6 (published in the Federal Register on May 8, 1985).

§1.163-6. Reduction of deduction where section 25 credit taken.

Interest Paid: Allocation

Interest Paid or Payable: Allocation.—Temporary Reg. §1.163-8T, relating to the allocation of interest expense among a taxpayer's expenditures, is also proposed as a final regulation and, when adopted, would become Reg. §1.163-8 (Published in the Federal Register on July 12, 1987).

§1.163-8. Allocation of interest expense among expenditures.

Personal Interest: Qualified Residence Interest

Personal Interest: Paid or Accrued: Qualified Residence Interest.—Temporary Reg. §§1.163-9T, and 1.163-10T, relating to the treatment of personal interest and the treatment and determination of qualified residence interest, are also proposed as final regulations and, when adopted, would become Reg. §§1.163-9 and 1.163-10 (published in the Federal Register on December 22, 1987).

§1.163-9. Personal interest.

§1.163-10. Qualified residence interest.

Deduction for Business Interest Expense: Limitation

Deduction for Business Interest Expense: Limitation.—Reg. §§1.163(j)-0—1.163(j)-11, regarding the limitation on the deduction for business interest expense after the enactment of recent tax legislation, are proposed (published in the Federal Register on December 28, 2018) (REG-106089-18).

    Par. 2. Section 1.163(j)-0 is added to read as follows:

§1.163(j)-0. Table of contents.—This section lists the table of contents for §§1.163(j)-1 through 1.163(j)-11.
§1.163(j)-1 Definitions.
  (a) In general.
  (b) Definitions.
    (1) Adjusted taxable income.
      (i) Additions.
      (ii) Subtractions.
      (iii) Depreciation, amortization, or depletion expenses capitalized to inventory under section 263A.
      (iv) Other adjustments.
      (v) Additional rules relating to adjusted taxable income in other sections.
    (2) Business interest expense.
      (i) In general.
      (ii) Special rules.
    (3) Business interest income.
      (i) In general.
      (ii) Special rules.
    (4) C corporation.
    (5) Cleared swap.
    (6) Consolidated group.
    (7) Consolidated return year.
    (8) Disallowed business interest expense.
    (9) Disallowed business interest expense carryforward.
    (10) Disallowed disqualified interest.
    (11) Electing farming business.
    (12) Electing real property trade or business.
    (13) Excepted regulated utility trade or business.
      (i) In general.
      (ii) Excepted and non-excepted utility trades or businesses.
    (14) Excess business interest expense.
    (15) Excess taxable income.
    (16) Floor plan financing indebtedness.
    (17) Floor plan financing interest expense.
    (18) Group.
    (19) Intercompany transaction.
    (20) Interest.
      (i) In general.
      (ii) Swaps with significant nonperiodic payments.
        (A) Non-cleared swaps.
        (B) [Reserved]
      (iii) Other amounts treated as interest.
        (A) Treatment of premium.
          (1) Issuer.
          (2) Holder.
        (B) Treatment of ordinary income or loss on certain debt instruments.
        (C) Substitute interest payments.
        (D) Section 1258 gain.
        (E) Amounts affecting a taxpayer's effective cost of borrowing.
        (F) Yield adjustments.
        (G) Certain amounts labeled as fees.
          (1) Commitment fees.
          (2) [Reserved]
        (H) Debt issuance costs.
        (I) Guaranteed payments.
        (J) Factoring income.
      (iv) Anti-avoidance rule for amounts predominantly associated with the time value of money.
      (v) Examples.
    (21) Interest expense.
    (22) Interest income.
    (23) Inventory.
    (24) Member.
    (25) Motor vehicle.
    (26) Old section 163(j).
    (27) Real estate investment trust.
    (28) Real property.
    (29) Regulated investment company.
    (30) S corporation.

(e) Adjusted taxable income and business interest income of partners.

(1) Modification of adjusted taxable income for partners.

(2) Partner basis items and remedial items.

(3) Disposition of partnership interests.

(4) Double counting of business interest income and floor plan financing interest expense prohibited.

(f) Allocation and determination of section 163(j) excess items made in the same manner as nonseparately stated taxable income or loss of the partnership.

(1) Overview.

(i) In general.

(ii) Relevance solely for purposes of section 163(j).

(2) Steps for allocating deductible business interest expense and section 163(j) excess items.

(i) Partnership-level calculation required by section 163(j)(4)(A).

(ii) Determination of each partner's relevant section 163(j) items.

(iii) Partner-level comparison of business interest income and business interest expense.

(iv) Matching partnership and aggregate partner excess business interest income.

(v) Remaining business interest expense determination.

(vi) Determination of final allocable ATI.

(A) Positive allocable ATI.

(B) Negative allocable ATI.

(C) Final allocable ATI.

(vii) Partner-level comparison of thirty percent of adjusted taxable income and remaining business interest expense.

(viii) Partner priority right to ATI capacity excess determination.

(ix) Matching partnership and aggregate partner excess taxable income.

(x) Matching partnership and aggregate partner excess business interest expense.

(xi) Final section 163(j) excess item and deductible business interest expense allocation.

(g) Carryforwards.

(1) In general.

(2) Treatment of excess of business interest expense allocated to partners.

(3) Excess taxable income and excess business interest income ordering rule.

(h) Basis adjustments.

(1) Section 704(d) ordering.

(2) Excess business interest expense basis adjustments.

(3) Basis adjustments upon disposition of partnership interest.

(i) Complete disposition of partnership interest.

(ii) Partial disposition of partnership interest.

(i) [Reserved]

(j) Investment items.

(k) [Reserved]

(l) S corporations.

(1) In general.

(2) Character of deductible business interest expense.

(3) Adjusted taxable income of an S corporation.

(4) Adjusted taxable income and business interest income of S corporation shareholders.

(i) Adjusted taxable income of S corporation shareholders.

(ii) Disposition of S corporation stock.

(iii) Double counting of business interest income and floor plan financing interest expense prohibited.

(5) Carryforwards.

(6) Basis adjustments and disallowed business interest expense carryforwards.

(7) Accumulated adjustment accounts.

(8) Termination of qualified subchapter S subsidiary election.

(9) Investment items.

(m) Partnerships and S corporations not subject to section 163(j).

(1) Partnerships and S corporations not subject to section 163(j) by reason of the small business exemption.

(2) Partnerships and S corporations not subject to section 163(j) by reason of an excepted trade or business.

(3) Partnerships that allocated excess business interest expense prior to becoming not subject to section 163(j).

(4) S corporations with disallowed business interest expense carryforwards prior to becoming not subject to section 163(j).

(n) [Reserved]

(o) Examples.

(p) Applicability date.

§1.163(j)-7 Application of the business interest deduction limitation to foreign corporations and United States shareholders.

(a) Overview.

(b) Application of section 163(j) to an applicable CFC and certain partnerships.

(1) Scope.

(2) General application of section 163(j) to an applicable CFC and a partnership with at least one partner that is an applicable CFC.

(3) Alternative approach for computing the deduction for business interest expense.

(4) Treatment of certain partnerships as a CFC group member.

(i) General rule.

(ii) Exception for certain partnerships engaged in a United States trade or business.

(5) CFC group election.

(i) Manner of making a CFC group election.

(ii) Consistency requirement.

(iii) Duration of a CFC group election.

(c) Rules concerning the computation of adjusted taxable income of an applicable CFC and certain CFC group members.

(1) Computation of taxable income.

(2) Treatment of certain dividends.

(3) Treatment of CFC excess taxable income.

(i) In general.

(ii) Ordering rules.

(d) Rules concerning the computation of adjusted taxable income of a United States shareholder.

(1) In general.

(i) Treatment of gross income inclusions that are properly allocable to a non-excepted trade or business.

(ii) Treatment of deemed inclusions of a domestic partnership that are not allocable to any trade or business.

(2) Additional rule after application of paragraph (d)(1) of this section for a United States shareholder of a CFC group member with a CFC group election in effect.

(i) In general.

(ii) Eligible CFC group ETI.

(iii) CFC group inclusions.

(3) Special rules if a domestic partnership is a United States shareholder of a CFC group member with a CFC group election in effect.

(4) Inclusions under section 951A(a).

(e) Effect on earnings and profits.

(f) Definitions.

(1) Allocable share.

(i) General rule.

(ii) Special rule if there is a financial services subgroup.

(2) Applicable CFC.

(3) Applicable net business interest expense.

(4) Applicable subgroup net business interest expense.

(5) CFC excess taxable income.

(i) In general.

(ii) CFC group member is a partnership.

(6) CFC group.

(i) In general.

(ii) Aggregation rules.

(7) CFC group election.

(8) CFC group member.

(9) Financial services subgroup.

(10) Financial services subgroup member.

(11) Majority U.S. shareholder taxable year.

(12) Net business interest expense.

(13) Passthrough entity.

(14) Specified ETI ratio.

(i) In general.

(ii) Includable CFC group members.

(iii) Numerator.

(iv) Denominator.

(15) Specified highest-tier member.

(16) Specified lower-tier member.

(17) Specified taxable year.

(18) United States shareholder.

(g) Examples.

(h) Applicability date.

§1.163(j)-8 Application of the business interest deduction limitation to foreign persons with effectively connected income.

(a) Overview.

(b) Application of section 163(j) and the section 163(j) regulations to specified foreign persons with effectively connected taxable income.

(1) In general.

(ii) Partnership interests; stock in non-consolidated domestic corporations.

   (A) Partnership interests.

     (1) Calculation of asset basis.

     (2) Allocation of asset basis.

      (i) In general.

      (ii) De minimis rule.

      (iii) Partnership assets not properly allocable to a trade or business.

      (iv) Inapplicability of partnership look-through rule.

   (B) Stock in non-consolidated domestic corporations.

     (1) In general.

     (2) Domestic non-consolidated C corporations.

      (i) Allocation of asset basis.

      (ii) De minimis rule.

      (iii) Inapplicability of corporate look-through rule.

     (3) S corporations.

      (i) Calculation of asset basis.

      (ii) Allocation of asset basis.

      (iii) De minimis rule.

      (iv) Inapplicability of S corporation look-through rule.

   (C) Stock in CFCs.

   (D) Inapplicability of look-through rule to partnerships or non-consolidated corporations to which the small business exemption applies.

   (E) Tiered entities.

  (iii) Cash and cash equivalents and customer receivables.

  (iv) Deemed asset sale.

  (v) Other adjustments.

(6) Determination dates; determination periods; reporting requirements.

  (i) Definitions.

  (ii) Application of look-through rules.

  (iii) Reporting requirements.

   (A) Books and records.

   (B) Information statement.

  (iv) Failure to file statement.

(7) Ownership threshold for look-through rules.

  (i) Corporations.

   (A) Asset basis.

   (B) Dividends.

  (ii) Partnerships.

  (iii) Inapplicability of look-through rule.

(8) Anti-abuse rule.

(d) Direct allocations.

  (1) In general.

  (2) Financial services entities.

  (3) Assets used in more than one trade or business.

  (4) Adjustments to basis of assets to account for direct allocations.

  (5) Example.

(e) Examples.

(f) Applicability date.

§ 1.163(j)-11 Transition rules.

(a) Application of section 163(j) limitation if a corporation joins a consolidated group with a taxable year beginning before January 1, 2018.

  (1) In general.

  (2) Example.

(b) Treatment of disallowed disqualified interest.

  (1) In general.

  (2) Earnings and profits.

  (3) Disallowed disqualified interest of members of an affiliated group.

   (i) Scope.

   (ii) Allocation of disallowed disqualified interest to members of the affiliated group.

    (A) In general.

    (B) Definitions.

     (1) Allocable share of the affiliated group's disallowed disqualified interest.

     (2) Disallowed disqualified interest ratio.

     (3) Exempt related person interest expense.

   (iii) Treatment of carryforwards.

  (4) Application of section 382.

   (i) Ownership change occurring before the date the Treasury decision adopting these regulations as final regulations is published in the **Federal Register**.

    (A) Pre-change loss.

    (B) Loss corporation.

   (ii) Ownership change occurring on or after the date the Treasury decision adopting these regulations as final regulations is published in the **Federal Register**.

    (A) Pre-change loss.

    (B) Loss corporation.

   (iii) Definitions.

  (5) [Reserved]

  (6) Treatment of excess limitation from taxable years beginning before January 1, 2018.

  (7) Example.

(c) Applicability date.

[Reg. § 1.163(j)-0.]

Par. 3. Sections 1.163(j)-1 through 1.163(j)-11 are added to read as follows:

§ 1.163(j)-1. Definitions.—(a) *In general.*—This section defines terms used in the section 163(j) regulations. For purposes of the rules sets forth in §§ 1.163(j)-2 through 1.163(j)-11, additional definitions for certain terms are provided in those sections.

(b) *Definitions.*—(1) *Adjusted taxable income.*—The term *adjusted taxable income* (ATI) means the taxable income of the taxpayer for the taxable year, with the adjustments in this paragraph (b).

  (i) *Additions.*—The amounts of the following items (if any) are added to taxable income to determine ATI —

   (A) Any business interest expense;

   (B) Any net operating loss deduction under section 172;

   (C) Any deduction under section 199A;

   (D) For taxable years beginning before January 1, 2022, any deduction for depreciation under section 167, section 168, or section 168 of the Internal Revenue Code of 1954 (former section 168);

   (E) For taxable years beginning before January 1, 2022, any deduction for the amortization of intangibles (for example, under section 167 or 197) and other amortized expenditures (for example, under section 195(b)(1)(B), 248, or 1245(a)(2)(C));

   (F) For taxable years beginning before January 1, 2022, any deduction for depletion under section 611;

   (G) Any deduction for a capital loss carryback or carryover; and

   (H) Any deduction or loss that is not properly allocable to a non-excepted trade or business (for rules governing the allocation of items to an excepted trade or business, see §§ 1.163(j)-1(b)(38) and 1.163(j)-10).

  (ii) *Subtractions.*—The amounts of the following items (if any) are subtracted from taxable income to determine ATI—

   (A) Any business interest income;

   (B) Any floor plan financing interest expense for the taxable year;

   (C) With respect to the sale or other disposition of property, the lesser of:

    (1) Any gain recognized on the sale or other disposition of such property; and

    (2) Any depreciation, amortization, or depletion deductions for the taxable years beginning after December 31, 2017, and before January 1, 2022, with respect to such property;

   (D) With respect to the sale or other disposition of stock of a member of a consolidated group that includes the selling member, the investment adjustments, as defined under § 1.1502-32, with respect to such stock that are attributable to deductions described in paragraph (b)(1)(ii)(C) of this section;

   (E) With respect to the sale or other disposition of an interest in a partnership, the taxpayer's distributive share of deductions described in paragraph (b)(1)(ii)(C) of this section with respect to property held by the partnership at the time of such sale or other disposition to the extent such deductions were allowable under section 704(d); and

   (F) Any income or gain that is not properly allocable to a non-excepted trade or business (for rules governing the allocation of items to an excepted trade or business, see §§ 1.163(j)-1(b)(38) and 1.163(j)-10)).

  (iii) *Depreciation, amortization, or depletion expenses capitalized to inventory under section 263A.*—Depreciation, amortization, or depletion expense that is capitalized to inventory under section 263A is not a depreciation, amortization, or depletion deduction for purposes of this paragraph (b)(1).

  (iv) *Other adjustments.*—ATI is computed with the other adjustments provided in §§ 1.163(j)-2 through 1.163(j)-11.

  (v) *Additional rules relating to adjusted taxable income in other sections.*—(A) For rules governing the ATI of C corporations, see §§ 1.163(j)-4(b)(2) and (3) and 1.163(j)-10(a)(2)(ii).

   (B) For rules governing the ATI of RICs and REITs, see § 1.163(j)-4(b)(4).

(C) For rules governing the ATI of tax-exempt corporations, see § 1.163(j)-4(b)(5).

(D) For rules governing the ATI of consolidated groups, see § 1.163(j)-4(d)(2)(iv) and (v).

(E) For rules governing the ATI of partnerships, see § 1.163(j)-6(d).

(F) For rules governing the ATI of partners, see § 1.163(j)-6(e).

(G) For rules governing partnership basis adjustments impacting ATI, see § 1.163(j)-6(h)(2).

(H) For rules governing the ATI of S corporations, see § 1.163(j)-6(l)(3).

(I) For rules governing the ATI of S corporation shareholders, see § 1.163(j)-6(l)(4).

(J) For rules governing the ATI of applicable CFCs and certain CFC group members, as defined in § 1.163(j)-7(f), see § 1.163(j)-7(c).

(K) For rules governing the ATI of United States shareholders of applicable CFCs, including the treatment of inclusions under sections 78, 951(a), and 951A(a), see § 1.163(j)-7(d).

(L) For rules governing the ATI of specified foreign persons, as defined in § 1.163(j)-8(g)(7), with effectively connected income, see § 1.163(j)-8(b)(2).

(M) For rules governing the ATI of specified foreign partners, as defined in § 1.163(j)-8(g)(6), other than applicable CFCs, as defined in § 1.163(j)-8(g)(1), see § 1.163(j)-8(c)(1).

(N) For rules governing the ATI of certain beneficiaries of trusts and estates, see § 1.163(j)-2(f).

(2) *Business interest expense.*—(i) *In general.*—The term *business interest expense* means interest expense that is properly allocable to a non-excepted trade or business or that is floor plan financing interest expense. Business interest expense also includes disallowed business interest expense carryforwards (as defined in paragraph (b)(9) of this section). For the treatment of investment interest, see section 163(d); and for the treatment of personal interest, see section 163(h).

(ii) *Special rules.*—For special rules for defining business interest expense in certain circumstances, see §§ 1.163(j)-3(b)(2) (regarding disallowed interest expense), 1.163(j)-4(b) (regarding C corporations) and (d)(2)(iii) (regarding consolidated groups), and 1.163(j)-8(b)(3) (regarding foreign persons engaged in a U.S. trade or business).

(3) *Business interest income.*—(i) *In general.*—The term *business interest income* means interest income which is properly allocable to a non-excepted trade or business. For the treatment of investment income, see section 163(d).

(ii) *Special rules.*—For special rules defining business interest income in certain circumstances, see §§ 1.163(j)-4(b) (regarding C corporations) and (d)(2)(iii) (regarding consolidated groups) and 1.163(j)-8(b)(4) (regarding foreign persons engaged in a U.S. trade or business).

(4) *C corporation.*—The term *C corporation* has the meaning provided in section 1361(a)(2).

(5) *Cleared swap.*—The term *cleared swap* means a swap that is cleared by a derivatives clearing organization, as such term is defined in section 1a of the Commodity Exchange Act (7 U.S.C. 1a), or by a clearing agency, as such term is defined in section 3 of the Securities Exchange Act of 1934 (15 U.S.C. 78c), that is registered as a derivatives clearing organization under the Commodity Exchange Act or as a clearing agency under the Securities Exchange Act of 1934, respectively, if the derivatives clearing organization or clearing agency requires the parties to the swap to post and collect margin or collateral.

(6) *Consolidated group.*—The term *consolidated group* has the meaning provided in § 1.1502-1(h).

(7) *Consolidated return year.*—The term *consolidated return year* has the meaning provided in § 1.1502-1(d).

(8) *Disallowed business interest expense.*—The term *disallowed business interest expense* means the amount of business interest expense for a taxable year in excess of the amount allowed as a deduction for the taxable year under section 163(j)(1) and § 1.163(j)-2(b).

(9) *Disallowed business interest expense carryforward.*—The term *disallowed business interest expense carryforward* means any business interest expense described in § 1.163(j)-2(c).

(10) *Disallowed disqualified interest.*—The term *disallowed disqualified interest* means interest expense, including carryforwards, for which a deduction was disallowed under old section 163(j) (as defined in paragraph (b)(26) of this section) in the taxpayer's last

taxable year beginning before January 1, 2018, and that was carried forward pursuant to old section 163(j).

(11) *Electing farming business.*—The term *electing farming business* means a trade or business that makes an election as provided in § 1.163(j)-9 or other published guidance and that is—

(i) A farming business, as defined in section 263A(e)(4) or § 1.263A-4(a)(4); or

(ii) Any trade or business of a specified agricultural or horticultural cooperative, as defined in section 199A(g)(4).

(12) *Electing real property trade or business.*—The term *electing real property trade or business* means a trade or business that makes an election as provided in § 1.163(j)-9 or other published guidance and that is described in—

(i) Section 469(c)(7)(C) and § 1.469-9(b)(2); or

(ii) Section 1.163(j)-9(g).

(13) *Excepted regulated utility trade or business.*—(i) *In general.*—The term *excepted regulated utility trade or business* means a trade or business—

(A) That furnishes or sells:

(1) Electrical energy, water, or sewage disposal services;

(2) Gas or steam through a local distribution system; or

(3) Transportation of gas or steam by pipeline; and

(B) To the extent that the rates for the furnishing or sale of the items in paragraph (b)(13)(i)(A) of this section—

(1) Have been established or approved by a State or political subdivision thereof, by any agency or instrumentality of the United States, or by a public service or public utility commission or other similar body of any State or political subdivision thereof and are determined on a cost of service and rate of return basis; or

(2) Have been established or approved by the governing or ratemaking body of an electric cooperative.

(ii) *Excepted and non-excepted utility trades or businesses.*—If a taxpayer is engaged in both an excepted trade or business and a non-excepted trade or business described in this paragraph (b)(13), the taxpayer must allocate items between the trades or businesses. See §§ 1.163(j)-1(b)(38) and 1.163(j)-10(c)(3)(iii)(C). Some trades or businesses with de minimis furnishing or sales of items described in paragraph (b)(13)(i)(A) of this section that are not sold pursuant to rates determined on a cost of service and rate of return basis as required in paragraph (b)(13)(i)(B)(1) of this section, or by the governing or ratemaking body of an electric cooperative as required in paragraph (b)(13)(i)(B)(2) of this section are treated as excepted trades or businesses. See § 1.163(j)-10(c)(3)(iii)(C)(3).

(14) *Excess business interest expense.*—The term *excess business interest expense* means, with respect to a partnership, the amount of disallowed business interest expense of the partnership for a taxable year under section § 1.163(j)-2(b), except as provided in § 1.163(j)-6(h)(2).

(15) *Excess taxable income.*—With respect to any partnership or S corporation, the term *excess taxable income* means the amount which bears the same ratio to the partnership's ATI as—

(i) The excess (if any) of—

(A) The amount determined for the partnership or S corporation under section 163(j)(1)(B); over

(B) The amount (if any) by which the business interest expense of the partnership, reduced by the floor plan financing interest expense, exceeds the business interest income of the partnership or S corporation; bears to

(ii) The amount determined for the partnership or S corporation under section 163(j)(1)(B).

(16) *Floor plan financing indebtedness.*—The term *floor plan financing indebtedness* means indebtedness—

(i) Used to finance the acquisition of motor vehicles held for sale or lease; and

(ii) Secured by the inventory so acquired.

(17) *Floor plan financing interest expense.*—The term *floor plan financing interest expense* means interest paid or accrued on floor plan financing indebtedness. For purposes of the section 163(j) regulations, all floor plan financing interest expense is treated as business interest expense. See paragraph (b)(2) of this section.

(18) *Group.*—The term *group* has the meaning provided in § 1.1502-1(a).

(19) *Intercompany transaction.*—The term *intercompany transaction* has the meaning provided in § 1.1502-13(b)(1)(i).

(20) *Interest.*—The term *interest* means any amount described in paragraph (b)(20)(i), (ii), (iii), or (iv) of this section.

(i) *In general.*—Interest is an amount paid, received, or accrued as compensation for the use or forbearance of money under the terms of an instrument or contractual arrangement, including a series of transactions, that is treated as a debt instrument for purposes of section 1275(a) and §1.1275-1(d), and not treated as stock under §1.385-3, or an amount that is treated as interest under other provisions of the Internal Revenue Code (Code) or the regulations thereunder. Thus, for example, interest includes—

(A) Original issue discount (OID), as adjusted by the holder for any acquisition premium or amortizable bond premium;

(B) Qualified stated interest, as adjusted by the holder for any amortizable bond premium or by the issuer for any bond issuance premium;

(C) Acquisition discount;

(D) Amounts treated as taxable OID under section 1286 (relating to stripped bonds and stripped coupons);

(E) Accrued market discount on a market discount bond to the extent includible in income by the holder under either section 1276(a) or 1278(b);

(F) OID includible in income by a holder that has made an election under §1.1272-3 to treat all interest on a debt instrument as OID;

(G) OID on a synthetic debt instrument arising from an integrated transaction under §1.1275-6;

(H) Repurchase premium to the extent deductible by the issuer under §1.163-7(c);

(I) Deferred payments treated as interest under section 483;

(J) Amounts treated as interest under a section 467 rental agreement;

(K) Amounts treated as interest under section 988;

(L) Forgone interest under section 7872;

(M) De minimis OID taken into account by the issuer;

(N) Amounts paid or received in connection with a sale-repurchase agreement treated as indebtedness under Federal tax principles; in the case of a sale-repurchase agreement relating to tax-exempt bonds, however, the amount is not tax-exempt interest;

(O) Redeemable ground rent treated as interest under section 163(c); and

(P) Amounts treated as interest under section 636.

(ii) *Swaps with significant nonperiodic payments.*—(A) *Non-cleared swaps.*—A swap other than a cleared swap with significant nonperiodic payments is treated as two separate transactions consisting of an on-market, level payment swap and a loan. The loan must be accounted for by the parties to the contract independently of the swap. The time value component associated with the loan, determined in accordance with §1.446-3(f)(2)(iii)(A), is recognized as interest expense to the payor and interest income to the recipient.

(B) [Reserved]

(iii) *Other amounts treated as interest.*—(A) *Treatment of premium.*—(1) *Issuer.*—If a debt instrument is issued at a premium within the meaning of §1.163-13, any ordinary income under §1.163-13(d)(4) is treated as interest income of the issuer.

(2) *Holder.*—If a taxable debt instrument is acquired at a premium within the meaning of §1.171-1 and the holder elects to amortize the premium, any amount otherwise deductible under section 171(a)(1) as a bond premium deduction under §1.171-2(a)(4)(i)(A) or (C) is treated as interest expense of the holder.

(B) *Treatment of ordinary income or loss on certain debt instruments.*—If an issuer of a contingent payment debt instrument subject to §1.1275-4(b), a nonfunctional currency contingent payment debt instrument subject to §1.988-6, or an inflation-indexed debt instrument subject to §1.1275-7 recognizes ordinary income on the debt instrument in accordance with the rules in §1.1275-4(b), §1.988-6(b)(2), or §1.1275-7(f), whichever is applicable, the ordinary income is treated as interest income of the issuer. If a holder of a contingent payment debt instrument subject to §1.1275-4(b), a nonfunctional currency contingent payment debt instrument subject to §1.988-6, or an inflation-indexed debt instrument subject to §1.1275-7 recognizes an ordinary loss on the debt instrument in accordance with the rules in §1.1275-4(b), §1.988-6(b)(2), or §1.1275-7(f), whichever is applicable, the ordinary loss is treated as interest expense of the holder.

(C) *Substitute interest payments.*—A substitute interest payment described in §1.861-2(a)(7) is treated as interest expense to the payor or interest income to the recipient; in the case of a sale-repurchase agreement or a securities lending transaction relating to tax-exempt bonds, however, the recipient of a substitute payment does not receive tax-exempt interest income.

(D) *Section 1258 gain.*—Any gain treated as ordinary gain under section 1258 is treated as interest income.

(E) *Amounts affecting a taxpayer's effective cost of borrowing.*—Income, deduction, gain, or loss from a derivative, as defined in section 59A(h)(4)(A), that alters a taxpayer's effective cost of borrowing with respect to a liability of the taxpayer is treated as an adjustment to interest expense of the taxpayer. For example, a taxpayer that is obligated to pay interest at a floating rate on a note and enters into an interest rate swap that entitles the taxpayer to receive an amount that is equal to or that closely approximates the interest rate on the note in exchange for a fixed amount is, in effect, paying interest expense at a fixed rate by entering into the interest rate swap. Income, deduction, gain, or loss from the swap is treated as an adjustment to interest expense. Similarly, any gain or loss resulting from a termination or other disposition of the swap is an adjustment to interest expense, with the timing of gain or loss subject to the rules of §1.446-4.

(F) *Yield adjustments.*—Income, deduction, gain, or loss from a derivative, as defined in section 59A(h)(4)(A), that alters a taxpayer's effective yield with respect to a debt instrument held by the taxpayer is treated as an adjustment to interest income by the taxpayer.

(G) *Certain amounts labeled as fees.*—(1) *Commitment fees.*—Any fees in respect of a lender commitment to provide financing are treated as interest if any portion of such financing is actually provided.

(2) [Reserved]

(H) *Debt issuance costs.*—Any debt issuance costs subject to §1.446-5 are treated as interest expense of the issuer.

(I) *Guaranteed payments.*—Any guaranteed payments for the use of capital under section 707(c) are treated as interest.

(J) *Factoring income.*—The excess of the amount that a taxpayer collects on a factored receivable (or realizes upon the sale or other disposition of the factored receivable) over the amount paid for the factored receivable by the taxpayer is treated as interest income. For purposes of this paragraph (b)(20)(iii)(J), the term *factored receivable* includes any account receivable or other evidence of indebtedness, whether or not issued at a discount and whether or not bearing stated interest, arising out of the disposition of property or the performance of services by any person, if such account receivable or evidence of indebtedness is acquired by a person other than the person who disposed of the property or provided the services that gave rise to the account receivable or evidence of indebtedness.

(iv) *Anti-avoidance rule for amounts predominantly associated with the time value of money.*—Any expense or loss, to the extent deductible, incurred by a taxpayer in a transaction or series of integrated or related transactions in which the taxpayer secures the use of funds for a period of time is treated as interest expense of the taxpayer if such expense or loss is predominantly incurred in consideration of the time value of money.

(v) *Examples.*—The examples in this paragraph (b)(20)(v) illustrate the application of paragraphs (b)(20)(i) through (iv) of this section. Unless otherwise indicated, assume the following: A, B, C, D, and Bank are domestic C corporations that are publicly traded; the exemption for certain small businesses in §1.163(j)-2(d) does not apply; A is not engaged in an excepted trade or business; and all amounts of interest expense are deductible except for the potential application of section 163(j).

(A) *Example 1*—(1) *Facts.* (i) A is a calendar year taxpayer that is engaged in a manufacturing business. In January 2019, A, which has an investment-grade credit rating, enters into the following transactions (the transactions): Bank transfers a portfolio of U.S. Treasury bonds (the Treasury portfolio) to A; A agrees to pay Bank an amount equivalent to any interest paid on the Treasury portfolio during the transactions and a fee for lending the Treasury portfolio to A; A agrees to return to Bank securities that are substantially identical to the Treasury portfolio upon request, regardless of any value increases or decreases in the market value of the Treasury portfolio; A rehypothecates the Treasury portfolio in exchange for cash, which A uses to purchase a portfolio of corporate bonds (the debt portfolio); and the transactions remain in place for the duration of the 2019 calendar year until Bank delivers a notice to A recalling the Treasury portfolio 5 business days before December 31, 2019.

(ii) The obligations undertaken with respect to the transactions are not collateralized. Assume that the transactions do not result in a sale-repurchase agreement treated as indebtedness under Federal tax principles. During the course of the transactions, the debt portfolio generates $70x of interest income. The Treasury portfolio generates $60x of interest income during the course of the transactions and A pays $60x to Bank under its obligation to pay amounts equivalent to the interest paid on the Treasury portfolio.

(2) *Analysis.* The transactions involving Bank and A are transactions described in paragraph (b)(20)(iii)(C) of this section.

Consequently, the $60x of substitute interest payments that A paid to Bank in 2019 is treated as interest expense for purposes of section 163(j). In addition, the $70x of interest income generated by the debt portfolio is interest income to A.

(B) *Example 2*—(1) *Facts.* A is a calendar year taxpayer that is engaged in a manufacturing business. In early 2019, A enters into the following transactions:

(i) A enters into a loan obligation in which A borrows Japanese yen from Bank in an amount equivalent to $2000x with an interest rate of 1 percent (at the time of the loan, the U.S. dollar equivalent interest rate on a loan of $2,000x is 5 percent); and

(ii) A enters into a foreign currency swap transaction (FX Swap) with Bank with a notional principal amount of $2000x under which A receives Japanese yen at 1 percent multiplied by the amount of Japanese yen borrowed from Bank (which for 2019 equals $20x) and pays U.S. dollars at 5 percent multiplied by a notional amount of $2000x ($100x per year). The FX Swap is not integrated with the loan obligation under §1.988-5.

(2) *Analysis.* The FX Swap alters A's cost of borrowing within the meaning of paragraph (b)(20)(iii)(E) of this section. As a result, for purposes of section 163(j), the $100x paid by A to Bank on the FX Swap is treated by A as interest expense and the $20x paid by Bank to A on the FX Swap is treated by A as a reduction of interest expense.

(C) *Example 3*—(1) *Facts.* A borrows from B two ounces of gold at a time when the spot price for gold is $500x per ounce. A agrees to return the two ounces of gold in six months. A sells the two ounces of gold to C for $1,000x. A then enters into a contract with D to purchase two ounces of gold six months in the future for $1,013x. In exchange for the use of $1,000x in cash, A has sustained a loss of $13x on related transactions.

(2) *Analysis.* A has obtained the use of $1,000x and, in a series of related transactions, created a loss of $13x predominantly associated with the time value of money. As a result, for purposes of section 163(j), the loss of $13x is treated as interest expense under paragraph (b)(20)(iv) of this section.

(21) *Interest expense.*—The term *interest expense* means interest that is paid or accrued, or treated as paid or accrued, for the taxable year.

(22) *Interest income.*—The term *interest income* means interest that is included in gross income for the taxable year.

(23) *Inventory.*—The term *inventory* means property held for sale or for lease, or both, by a taxpayer in the ordinary course of its trade or business.

(24) *Member.*—The term *member* has the meaning provided in §1.1502-1(b).

(25) *Motor vehicle.*—The term *motor vehicle* means a motor vehicle as defined in section 163(j)(9)(C).

(26) *Old section 163(j).*—The term *old section 163(j)* means section 163(j) immediately prior to its amendment by Public Law 115-97, 131 Stat. 2054 (2017).

(27) *Real estate investment trust.*—The term *real estate investment trust* (REIT) has the meaning provided in section 856.

(28) *Real property.*—The term *real property* includes—

(i) Real property as defined in §1.469-9(b)(2); and

(ii) Any direct or indirect right, including a license or other contractual right, to share in the appreciation in value of, or the gross or net proceeds or profits generated by, an interest in real property, including net proceeds or profits associated with tolls, rents or other similar fees.

(29) *Regulated investment company.*—The term *regulated investment company* (RIC) has the meaning provided in section 851.

(30) *S corporation.*—The term *S corporation* has the meaning provided in section 1361(a)(1).

(31) *Section 163(j) limitation.*—The term *section 163(j) limitation* means the limit on the amount of business interest expense that a taxpayer may deduct in a taxable year under section 163(j) and §1.163(j)-2(b).

(32) *Section 163(j) regulations.*—The term *section 163(j) regulations* means this section and §§1.163(j)-2 through 1.163(j)-11.

(33) *Separate return limitation year.*—The term *separate return limitation year* (SRLY) has the meaning provided in §1.1502-1(f).

(34) *Separate return year.* The term *separate return year* has the meaning provided in §1.1502-1(e).

(35) *Separate taxable income.*—The term *separate taxable income* has the meaning provided in §1.1502-12.

(36) *Tax-exempt corporation.*—The term *tax-exempt corporation* means any corporation subject to tax under section 511.

(37) *Taxable income.*—(i) *In general.*—The term *taxable income*, with respect to a taxpayer and a taxable year, has the meaning provided in section 63, but for this purpose computed without regard to the application of section 163(j) and the section 163(j) regulations.

(ii) *General rules to coordinate the application of sections 163(j) and 250.*—If for a taxable year a taxpayer is allowed a deduction under section 250(a)(1) that is properly allocable to a non-excepted trade or business, then taxable income for the taxable year is determined without regard to the limitation in section 250(a)(2). For this purpose, the amount of the deduction allowed under section 250(a)(1), without regard to the limitation in section 250(a)(2), is determined without regard to the application of section 163(j) and the section 163(j) regulations.

(iii) [Reserved]

(iv) *Special rules for defining taxable income.*—(A) For special rules defining the taxable income of a RIC or REIT, see §1.163(j)-4(b)(4)(ii).

(B) For special rules defining the taxable income of consolidated groups, see §1.163(j)-4(d)(2)(iv).

(C) For special rules defining the taxable income of a partnership, see §1.163(j)-6(d)(1).

(D) For special rules defining the taxable income of an S corporation, see §1.163(j)-6(l)(3).

(E) For special rules defining the taxable income of certain controlled foreign corporations, see §1.163(j)-7(c)(1).

(38) *Trade or business.*—(i) *In general.*—The term *trade or business* means a trade or business within the meaning of section 162.

(ii) *Excepted trade or business.*—The term *excepted trade or business* means a trade or business that is described in paragraphs (b)(38)(ii)(A) through (D) of this section. For additional rules related to excepted trades or businesses, including elections made under section 163(j)(7)(B) and (C), see §1.163(j)-9.

(A) The trade or business of performing services as an employee.

(B) Any electing real property trade or business.

(C) Any electing farming business.

(D) Any excepted regulated utility trade or business.

(iii) *Non-excepted trade or business.*—The term *non-excepted trade or business* means any trade or business that is not an excepted trade or business.

(39) *Unadjusted basis.*—The term *unadjusted basis* means the basis as determined under section 1012 or other applicable sections of chapter 1 of subtitle A of the Code, including subchapters O (relating to gain or loss on dispositions of property), C (relating to corporate distributions and adjustments), K (relating to partners and partnerships), and P (relating to capital gains and losses) of the Code. Unadjusted basis is determined without regard to any adjustments described in section 1016(a)(2) or (3), to any adjustments for tax credits claimed by the taxpayer (for example, under section 50(c)), or to any adjustments for any portion of the basis for which the taxpayer has elected to treat as an expense (for example, under section 179, 179B, or 179C).

(c) *Applicability date.*—This section applies to taxable years ending after the date the Treasury decision adopting these regulations as final regulations is published in the **Federal Register**. However, taxpayers and their related parties, within the meaning of sections 267(b) and 707(b)(1), may apply the rules of this section to a taxable year beginning after December 31, 2017, so long as the taxpayers and their related parties consistently apply the rules of the section 163(j) regulations, and if applicable, §§1.263A-9, 1.381(c)(20)-1, 1.382-6, 1.383-1, 1.469-9, 1.882-5, 1.1502-13, 1.1502-21, 1.1502-36, 1.1502-79, 1.1502-91 through 1.1502-99, (to the extent they effectuate the rules of §§1.382-6 and 1.383-1), and 1.1504-4 to those taxable years. [Reg. §1.163(j)-1.]

§1.163(j)-2. Deduction for business interest expense limited.— (a) *Overview.*—This section provides general rules regarding the section 163(j) limitation. Paragraph (b) of this section provides rules regarding the basic computation of the section 163(j) limitation. Paragraph (c) of this section provides rules for disallowed business interest expense carryforwards. Paragraph (d) of this section provides rules regarding the small business exemption from the section 163(j) limitation. Paragraph (e) of this section provides rules regarding real estate mortgage investment conduits (REMICs). Paragraph (f) of this section provides examples illustrating the application of this section. Paragraph (g) of this section provides an anti-avoidance rule.

(b) *General rule.*—Except as otherwise provided in this section or in §§1.163(j)-3 through 1.163(j)-11, the amount allowed as a deduction for business interest expense for the taxable year cannot exceed the sum of—

(1) The taxpayer's business interest income for the taxable year;

(2) 30 percent of the taxpayer's ATI for the taxable year, or zero if the taxpayer's ATI for the taxable year is less than zero; and

(3) The taxpayer's floor plan financing interest expense for the taxable year.

(c) *Disallowed business interest expense carryforward.*—(1) *In general.*—Under section 163(j)(2), any business interest expense disallowed under paragraph (b) of this section, or any disallowed disqualified interest that is properly allocable to a non-excepted trade or business under §1.163(j)-10, is carried forward to the succeeding taxable year as business interest expense that is subject to paragraph (b) of this section in such succeeding taxable year (a disallowed business interest expense carryforward).

(2) *Coordination with small business exemption.*—If disallowed business interest expense is carried forward under the rules of paragraph (c)(1) of this section to a taxable year in which the small business exemption in paragraph (d) of this section applies to the taxpayer, then the general rule in paragraph (b) of this section does not apply to limit the deduction of the disallowed business interest expense carryforward in that taxable year.

(3) *Cross-references.*—(i) For special rules regarding disallowed business interest expense carryforwards for taxpayers that are C corporations, including members of a consolidated group, see §1.163(j)-5.

(ii) For special rules regarding disallowed business interest expense carryforwards of S corporations, see §§1.163(j)-5(b)(2) and 1.163(j)-6(l)(5).

(iii) For special rules regarding disallowed business interest expense carryforwards from partnerships, see §1.163(j)-6.

(iv) For special rules regarding disallowed business interest expense carryforwards from partnerships engaged in a U.S. trade or business, see §1.163(j)-8(c)(2).

(d) *Small business exemption.*—(1) *Exemption.*—The general rule in paragraph (b) of this section does not apply to any taxpayer, other than a tax shelter as defined in section 448(d)(3), in any taxable year if the taxpayer meets the gross receipts test of section 448(c) and the regulations thereunder for the taxable year.

(2) *Application of the gross receipts test.*—(i) *In general.*—In the case of any taxpayer that is not a corporation or a partnership, and except as provided in paragraphs (d)(2)(ii), (iii), and (iv) of this section, the gross receipts test and aggregation rules of section 448(c) and the regulations thereunder are applied in the same manner as if such taxpayer were a corporation or partnership.

(ii) *Gross receipts of individuals.*—Except as provided in paragraph (d)(2)(iii) of this section regarding partnership and S corporation interests and when the aggregation rules of section 448(c) apply, an individual taxpayer's gross receipts include all items specified as gross receipts in regulations under section 448(c), whether or not derived in the ordinary course of the taxpayer's trade or business. For purposes of section 163(j), an individual taxpayer's gross receipts do not include inherently personal amounts, including, but not limited to, personal injury awards or settlements with respect to an injury of the individual taxpayer, disability benefits, Social Security benefits received by the taxpayer during the taxable year, and wages received as an employee that are reported on Form W-2.

(iii) *Partners and S corporation shareholders.*—Except when the aggregation rules of section 448(c) apply, each partner in a partnership includes a share of partnership gross receipts in proportion to such partner's distributive share (as determined under section 704) of items of gross income that were taken into account by the partnership under section 703. Additionally, each shareholder in an S corporation includes a pro rata share of S corporation gross receipts.

(iv) *Tax-exempt organizations.*—For purposes of section 163(j), the gross receipts of an organization subject to tax under section 511 includes only gross receipts taken into account in determining its unrelated business taxable income.

(e) *REMICs.*—For the treatment of interest expense by a REMIC as defined in section 860D, see §1.860C-2(b)(2)(ii).

(f) *Calculation of ATI with respect to certain beneficiaries.*—The ATI of a trust or estate beneficiary is reduced by any income (including any distributable net income) received from the trust or estate by the beneficiary to the extent such income supported a deduction for business interest expense under section 163(j)(1)(B) or §1.163(j)-2(b)(2) in computing the trust or estate's taxable income.

(g) *Examples.*—The examples of this paragraph (g) illustrate the application of section 163(j) and the provisions of this section. Unless otherwise indicated, assume the following: X and Y are domestic C corporations; C and D are U.S. resident individuals not subject to any foreign income tax; PRS is a domestic partnership with partners who are all individuals; all taxpayers use a calendar taxable year; the exemption for certain small businesses in section 163(j)(3) and paragraph (d) of this section does not apply; and the interest expense would be deductible but for section 163(j).

(1) *Example 1: Limitation on business interest expense deduction*—(i) *Facts.* During its taxable year ending December 31, 2019, X has ATI of $100x. X has business interest expense of $50x, which includes $10x of floor plan financing interest expense, and business interest income of $20x.

(ii) *Analysis.* X's section 163(j) limitation is $60x, which is the sum of its business interest income ($20x), plus 30 percent of its ATI ($100x x 30 percent = $30x), plus its floor plan financing interest expense ($10x). See §1.163(j)-2(b). Because X's business interest expense ($50x) does not exceed X's section 163(j) limitation ($60x), X can deduct all $50x of its business interest expense for the 2019 taxable year.

(2) *Example 2: Carryforward of business interest expense*—(i) *Facts.* The facts are the same as in *Example 1* in paragraph (g)(1)(i) of this section, except that X has $80x of business interest expense, which includes $10x of floor plan financing interest expense.

(ii) *Analysis.* As in *Example 1* in paragraph (g)(1)(ii) of this section, X's section 163(j) limitation is $60x. Because X's business interest expense ($80x) exceeds X's section 163(j) limitation ($60x), X may only deduct $60x of its business interest expense for the 2019 taxable year, and the remaining $20x of its business interest expense will be carried forward to the succeeding taxable year as a disallowed business interest expense carryforward. See §1.163(j)-2(c).

(3) *Example 3: ATI computation*—(i) *Facts.* During the 2019 taxable year, Y has taxable income of $30x (without regard to the application of section 163(j)), which includes the following: $20x of business interest income; $50x of business interest expense, which includes $10x of floor plan financing interest expense; $25x of net operating loss deduction under section 172; and $15x of depreciation deduction under section 167.

(ii) *Analysis.* (A) For purposes of determining the section 163(j) limitation, Y's ATI is $90x, calculated as follows:

Table 1 to paragraph (g)(3)(ii)(A)

Taxable income:	$30x
Less:	
Floor plan financing interest	10x
Business interest income	*20x*
	0x

(B) Plus:

Table 1 to paragraph (g)(3)(ii)(B)

Business interest expense	$50x
Net operating loss deduction	25x
Depreciation deduction	*15x*
ATI	$90x

(4) *Example 4: Floor plan financing interest expense*—(i) *Facts.* C is the sole proprietor of an automobile dealership that uses a cash method of accounting. In the 2019 taxable year, C paid $30x of interest on a loan that was obtained to purchase sedans for sale by the dealership. The indebtedness is secured by the sedans purchased with the loan proceeds. In addition, C paid $20x of interest on a loan, secured by the dealership's office equipment, which C obtained to purchase convertibles for sale by the dealership.

(ii) *Analysis.* For the purpose of calculating C's section 163(j) limitation, only the $30x of interest paid on the loan to purchase the sedans is floor plan financing interest expense. The $20x paid on the loan to purchase the convertibles is not floor plan financing interest expense for purposes of section 163(j) because the indebtedness was not secured by the inventory of convertibles. However, because under §1.163(j)-10 the interest paid on the loan to purchase the convertibles is properly allocable to C's dealership trade or business, and because floor plan financing interest expense is also business interest expense, C has $50x of business interest expense for the 2019 taxable year.

(5) *Example 5: Interest not properly allocable to non-excepted trade or business*—(i) *Facts.* The facts are the same as in *Example 4* in paragraph (g)(4)(i) of this section, except that the $20x of interest C pays is on acquisition indebtedness obtained to purchase C's personal residence and not to purchase convertibles for C's dealership trade or business.

(ii) *Analysis.* Because the $20x of interest expense is not properly allocable to a non-excepted trade or business, and therefore is not business interest expense as defined in §1.163(j)-1(b)(2), C's only business interest expense is the $30x that C pays on the loan used to purchase sedans for sale in C's dealership trade or business. C deducts the $20x of interest related to his residence under the rules of section 163(h), without regard to section 163(j).

(6) *Example 6: Small business exemption*—(i) *Facts.* During the 2019 taxable year, D, the sole proprietor of a trade or business reported on Schedule C, has interest expense properly allocable to that trade or business. D also earns gross income from providing services as an employee that is reported on a Form W-2. Under section 448(c) and the regulations thereunder, D has average annual gross receipts of $21 million, including $1 million of wages in each of the three prior taxable years and $2 million of income from investments not related to a trade or business in each of the three prior taxable years. Also, in each of the three prior taxable years, D received $5 million in periodic payments of compensatory damages awarded in a personal injury lawsuit.

(ii) *Analysis.* Section 163(j) does not apply to D for the taxable year, because D qualifies for the small business exemption under §1.163(j)-2(d). The wages that D receives as an employee and the compensatory damages that D received from D's personal injury lawsuit are not gross receipts, as provided in §1.163(j)-2(d)(2)(ii). D may deduct all of its business interest expense for the 2019 taxable year without regard to section 163(j).

(7) *Example 7: Aggregation of gross receipts*—(i) *Facts.* X and Y are domestic C corporations under common control, within the meaning of section 52(a) and §1.52-1(b). X's only trade or business is a farming business described in §1.263A-4(a)(4). During the taxable year ending December 31, 2019, X has average annual gross receipts under section 448(c) of $6 million. During the same taxable year, Y has average annual gross receipts under section 448(c) of $21 million.

(ii) *Analysis.* Because X and Y are under common control, they must aggregate gross receipts for purposes of section 448(c) and the small business exemption in §1.163(j)-2(d). See section 448(c)(2). Therefore, X and Y are both considered to have $27 million in average annual gross receipts for 2019. X and Y must separately apply section 163(j) to determine any limitation on the deduction for business interest expense. Assuming X otherwise meets the requirements in §1.163(j)-9 in 2019, X may elect for its farming business to be an excepted trade or business.

(h) *Anti-avoidance rule.*—Arrangements entered into with a principal purpose of avoiding the rules of section 163(j) or the section 163(j) regulations, including the use of multiple entities to avoid the gross receipts test of section 448(c), may be disregarded or recharacterized by the Commissioner of the IRS to the extent necessary to carry out the purposes of section 163(j).

(i) *Applicability date.*—This section applies to taxable years ending after the date the Treasury decision adopting these regulations as final regulations is published in the **Federal Register**. However, taxpayers and their related parties, within the meaning of sections 267(b) and 707(b)(1), may apply the rules of this section to a taxable year beginning after December 31, 2017, so long as the taxpayers and their related parties consistently apply the rules of the section 163(j) regulations, and if applicable, §§1.263A-9, 1.381(c)(20)-1, 1.382-6, 1.383-1, 1.469-9, 1.882-5, 1.1502-13, 1.1502-21, 1.1502-36, 1.1502-79, 1.1502-91 through 1.1502-99, (to the extent they effectuate the rules of §§1.382-6 and 1.383-1), and 1.1504-4 to those taxable years. [Reg. §1.163(j)-2.]

§1.163(j)-3. Relationship of business interest deduction limitation to other provisions affecting interest.—(a) *Overview.*—This section contains rules regarding the relationship between section 163(j) and certain other provisions of the Code. Paragraph (b) of this section provides the general rules concerning the relationship between section 163(j) and certain other provisions of the Code. Paragraph (c) of this section provides examples illustrating the application of this section. For rules regarding the relationship between sections 163(j) and 704(d), see §1.163(j)-6(h)(1) and (2).

(b) *Coordination of section 163(j) with certain other provisions.*—(1) *In general.*—Section 163(j) and the section 163(j) regulations generally apply only to business interest expense that would be deductible in the current taxable year without regard to section 163(j). Except as otherwise provided in this section, section 163(j) applies after the application of provisions that subject interest expense to disallowance, deferral, capitalization, or other limitation. For the rules that must be applied in determining whether excess business interest is paid or accrued by a partner, see section 163(j)(4)(B)(ii) and §1.163(j)-6.

(2) *Disallowed interest provisions.*—For purposes of section 163(j), business interest expense does not include interest expense that is permanently disallowed as a deduction under another provi-

sion of the Code, such as in section 163(e)(5)(A)(i), (f), (l), or (m), or section 264(a), 265, 267A, or 279.

(3) *Deferred interest provisions.*—Other than sections 461(l), 465, and 469, Code provisions that defer the deductibility of interest expense, such as section 163(e)(3) and (e)(5)(A)(ii), 267(a)(2) and (3), 1277, or 1282, apply before the application of section 163(j). For purposes other than sections 465 and 469, interest expense is taken into account for section 163(j) purposes in the taxable year when it is no longer deferred under another section of the Code.

(4) *At risk rules, passive activity loss provisions, and limitation on excess business losses of noncorporate taxpayers.*—Section 163(j) applies before the application of sections 461(l), 465, and 469.

(5) *Capitalized interest expenses under sections 263A and 263(g).*—Sections 263A and 263(g) apply before the application of section 163(j). Capitalized interest expense under those sections is not treated as business interest expense for purposes of section 163(j). For ordering rules that determine whether interest expense is capitalized under section 263A(f), see the regulations under section 263A(f), including §1.263A-9(g).

(6) *Reductions under section 246A.*—Section 246A applies before section 163(j). Any reduction in the dividends received deduction under section 246A reduces the amount of business interest expense taken into account under section 163(j).

(7) *Section 381.*—Disallowed business interest expense carryforwards are items to which an acquiring corporation succeeds under section 381(a). See section 381(c)(20), and §§1.163(j)-5(c) and 1.381(c)(20)-1.

(8) *Section 382.*—For rules governing the interaction of sections 163(j) and 382, see section 382(d)(3) and (k)(1), §§1.163(j)-5(e) and 1.163(j)-11(b), the regulations under sections 382 and 383, and §§1.1502-91 through 1.1502-99.

(9) *Other types of interest provisions.*—Except as otherwise provided in the section 163(j) regulations, provisions that characterize interest expense as something other than business interest expense under section 163(j), such as section 163(d), govern the treatment of that interest expense, and such interest expense will not be treated as business interest expense for any purpose under section 163(j).

(10) [Reserved]

(c) *Examples.*—The examples of this paragraph (c) illustrate the application of section 163(j) and the provisions of this section. Unless otherwise indicated, assume the following: X and Y are domestic C corporations with a calendar taxable year; D is a U.S. resident individual not subject to any foreign income tax; none of the taxpayers have floor plan financing interest expense; and the exemption for small businesses in §1.163(j)-2(d) does not apply.

(1) *Example 1: Disallowed interest expense*—(i) *Facts.* In 2019, X has $30x of interest expense. Of X's interest expense, $10x is permanently disallowed under section 265. X's business interest income is $3x and X's ATI is $90x.

(ii) *Analysis.* Under paragraph (b)(2) of this section, the $10x interest expense that is permanently disallowed under section 265 cannot be taken into consideration for purposes of section 163(j) in the 2019 taxable year. X's section 163(j) limitation, or the amount of business interest expense that X may deduct is limited to $30x under §1.163(j)-2(b), determined by adding X's business interest income ($3x) and 30 percent of X's 2018 ATI ($27x). Therefore, in the 2019 taxable year, none of the $20x of X's deduction for its business interest expense is disallowed under section 163(j).

(2) *Example 2: Deferred interest expense*—(i) *Facts.* In 2019, Y has no business interest income, $120x of ATI, and $70x of interest expense. Of Y's interest expense, $30x is not currently deductible under section 267(a)(2). Assume that the $30x expense will be allowed as a deduction under section 267(a)(2) in 2020.

(ii) *Analysis.* Under paragraph (b)(3) of this section, section 267(a)(2) is applied before section 163(j). Accordingly, $30x of Y's interest expense cannot be taken into consideration for purposes of section 163(j) in 2019 because it is not currently deductible under section 267(a)(2). Accordingly, in 2019, if the interest expense is properly allocable to a non-excepted trade or business, Y will have $4x of disallowed business interest expense because the $40x of business interest expense in 2019 ($70x - $30x) exceeds 30 percent of its ATI for the taxable year ($36x). The $30x of interest expense not allowed as a deduction in the 2019 taxable year under section 267(a)(2) will be taken into account in determining the business interest expense deduction under section 163(j) in 2020, the taxable year in which it is allowed as a deduction under section 267(a)(2), if it is allocable to a trade or business. Additionally, the $4x of disallowed business interest expense in 2019 will be carried forward to 2020 as a disallowed business interest expense carryforward. See §1.163(j)-2(c)

(3) *Example 3: Passive activity loss*—(i) *Facts.* D is engaged in a rental activity treated as a passive activity within the meaning of section 469. For tax year 2019, D receives $200x of rental income and incurs $300x of expenses all properly allocable to the rental activity, consisting of $150x of interest expense, $60x of maintenance expenses, and $90x of depreciation expense. D's ATI is $400x.

(ii) *Analysis.* Under paragraph (b)(4) of this section, section 163(j) is applied before the section 469 passive loss rules apply. D's section 163(j) limitation is $120x, determined by adding to D's business interest income ($0), floor plan financing ($0), and 30 percent of D's ATI ($120x). See § 1.163(j)-2(b). Because D's business interest expense of $150x exceeds D's section 163(j) limitation for 2019, $30x of D's business interest expense is disallowed under section 163(j) and will be carried forward as a disallowed business interest expense carryforward. See § 1.163(j)-2(c). Because the section 163(j) limitation is applied before the limitation under section 469, only $120x of the business interest expense allowable under section 163(j) is included in determining D's passive activity loss limitation for the 2019 tax year under section 469. The $30x of disallowed business interest expense is not an allowable deduction under section 163(j) and, therefore, is not a deduction under section 469 in the current taxable year. See § 1.469-2(d)(8).

(4) *Example 4: Passive activity loss by taxpayer that also participates in a non-passive activity*—(i) *Facts.* For 2019, D has no business interest income and ATI of $1,000x, entirely attributable to a passive activity within the meaning of section 469. D has business interest expense of $1,000x, $900x of which is properly allocable to a passive activity and $100x of which is properly allocable to a non-passive activity in which D materially participates. D has other business deductions that are not subject to section 469 of $600x, and a section 469 passive loss from the previous year of $250x.

(ii) *Analysis.* Under paragraph (b)(4) of this section, section 163(j) is applied before the section 469 passive loss rules apply. D's section 163(j) limitation is $300x, determined by adding D's business interest income ($0), floor plan financing ($0), and 30 percent of D's ATI ($300x)). Next, applying the limitation under section 469 to the $300x business interest expense deduction allowable under sections 163(a) and (j), $270x (a proportionate amount of the $300x (0.90 x $300x)) is business interest expense included in determining D's passive activity loss limitation under section 469, and $30x (a proportionate amount of the $300x (0.10 x $300)) is business interest expense not included in determining D's passive activity loss limitation under section 469. Because D's interest expense of $1,000x exceeds 30 percent of its ATI for 2019, $700x of D's interest expense is disallowed under section 163(j) and will be carried forward as a disallowed business interest expense carryforward. Section 469 does not apply to any portion of the $700x disallowed business interest expense because that business interest expense is not an allowable deduction under section 163(j) and, therefore, is not an allowable deduction under section 469 in the current taxable year. See § 1.469-2(d)(8).

(d) *Applicability date.*—The provisions of this section apply to taxable years ending after the date the Treasury decision adopting these regulations as final regulations is published in the **Federal Register**. However, taxpayers and their related parties, within the meaning of sections 267(b) and 707(b)(1), may apply the rules of this section to a taxable year beginning after December 31, 2017, so long as the taxpayers and their related parties consistently apply the rules of the section 163(j) regulations, and if applicable, §§ 1.263A-9, 1.381(c)(20)-1, 1.382-6, 1.383-1, 1.469-9, 1.882-5, 1.1502-13, 1.1502-21, 1.1502-36, 1.1502-79, 1.1502-91 through 1.1502-99 (to the extent they effectuate the rules of §§ 1.382-6 and 1.383-1), and 1.1504-4 to those taxable years. [Reg. § 1.163(j)-3.]

§ 1.163(j)-4. General rules applicable to C corporations (including REITs, RICs, and members of consolidated groups) and tax-exempt corporations.—(a) *Scope.*—This section provides certain rules regarding the computation of items of income and expense under section 163(j) for taxpayers that are C corporations (including members of a consolidated group, REITs, and RICs) and tax-exempt corporations. Paragraph (b) of this section provides rules regarding the characterization of items of income, gain, deduction, or loss. Paragraph (c) of this section provides rules regarding adjustments to earnings and profits. Paragraph (d) of this section provides special rules applicable to members of a consolidated group. Paragraph (e) of this section provides cross-references to other rules within the 163(j) regulations that may be applicable to C corporations.

(b) *Characterization of items of income, gain, deduction, or loss.*—(1) *Interest expense and interest income.*—Solely for purposes of section 163(j), all interest expense of a taxpayer that is a C corporation is treated as properly allocable to a trade or business. Similarly, solely for purposes of section 163(j), all interest income of a taxpayer that is a C corporation is treated as properly allocable to a trade or business. For rules governing the allocation of interest expense and interest income between excepted and non-excepted trades or businesses, see § 1.163(j)-10.

(2) *Adjusted taxable income.*—Solely for purposes of section 163(j), all items of income, gain, deduction, or loss of a taxpayer that is a C corporation are treated as properly allocable to a trade or business. For rules governing the allocation of tax items between excepted and non-excepted trades or businesses, see § 1.163(j)-10.

(3) *Investment interest, investment income, and investment expenses of a partnership with a C corporation partner.*—(i) *Characterization as expense or income properly allocable to a trade or business.*—For purposes of section 163(j), any investment interest, within the meaning of section 163(d), that a partnership pays or accrues and that is allocated to a C corporation partner is treated by the C corporation as interest expense that is properly allocable to a trade or business of that partner. Similarly, for purposes of section 163(j), except as provided in § 1.163(j)-7(d)(1)(ii), any investment income or investment expenses, within the meaning of section 163(d), that a partnership receives, pays, or accrues and that is allocated to a C corporation partner is treated by the C corporation as properly allocable to a trade or business of that partner.

(ii) *Impact of characterization on partnership.*—The characterization of a partner's investment interest, investment income, or investment expenses pursuant to paragraph (b)(3)(i) of this section will not affect the characterization of these items as investment interest, investment income, or investment expenses at the partnership level.

(iii) *Investment interest expense and investment interest income of a partnership not treated as excess business interest expense or excess taxable income of a C corporation partner.*—Investment interest expense of a partnership that is treated as business interest expense by a C corporation partner is not treated as excess business interest expense. Investment interest income of a partnership that is treated as business interest income by a C corporation partner is not treated as excess taxable income. For rules governing excess business interest expense and excess taxable income, see § 1.163(j)-6.

(4) *Application to RICs and REITs.*—(i) *In general.*—Except as otherwise provided in paragraphs (b)(4)(ii) and (iii) of this section, the rules in this paragraph (b) apply to RICs and REITs.

(ii) *Taxable income for purposes of calculating the adjusted taxable income of RICs and REITs.*—The taxable income of a RIC or REIT for purposes of calculating adjusted taxable income (ATI) is the taxable income of the corporation, without any adjustment that would be made under section 852(b)(2) or 857(b)(2) to compute investment company taxable income or real estate investment trust taxable income, respectively. For example, the taxable income of a RIC or REIT is not reduced by the deduction for dividends paid, but is reduced by the dividends received deduction (DRD) and the other deductions described in sections 852(b)(2)(C) and 857(b)(2)(A), taking into account § 1.163(j)-1(b)(37)(ii). See paragraph (b)(4)(iii) of this section for an adjustment to adjusted taxable income in respect of these items.

(iii) *Other adjustments to adjusted taxable income for RICs and REITs.*—In the case of a taxpayer that, for a taxable year, is a RIC to which section 852(b) applies or a REIT to which section 857(b) applies, the taxpayer's ATI for the taxable year is increased by the amounts of any deductions described in section 852(b)(2)(C) or 857(b)(2)(A), taking into account § 1.163(j)-1(b)(37)(ii).

(5) *Application to tax-exempt corporations.*—The rules in this paragraph (b) apply to a corporation that is subject to the unrelated business income tax under section 511 only with respect to that corporation's items of income, gain, deduction, or loss that are taken into account in computing the corporation's unrelated business taxable income, as defined in section 512.

(6) *Examples.*—The principles of this paragraph (b) are illustrated by the following examples. For purposes of the examples in this paragraph (b)(6), T is a taxable domestic C corporation whose taxable year ends on December 31; T is neither a consolidated group member nor a RIC or a REIT; neither T nor PS1, a domestic partnership, owns at least 80 percent of the stock of any corporation; neither T nor PS1 qualifies for the small business exemption in § 1.163(j)-2(d) or is engaged in an excepted trade or business; T has no floor plan financing expense; all interest expense is deductible except for the potential application of section 163(j); and the facts set forth the only corporate or partnership activity.

(i) *Example 1: C corporation items properly allocable to a trade or business*—(A) *Facts.* In taxable year 2019, T's taxable income (without regard to the application of section 163(j)) is $320x. This amount is comprised of the following tax items: $1,000x of revenue from inventory sales; $500x of ordinary and necessary business expenses (excluding interest and depreciation); $200x of interest expense; $50x of interest income; $50x of depreciation deductions under section 168; and a $20x gain on the sale of stock.

(B) *Analysis.* For purposes of section 163(j), each of T's tax items is treated as properly allocable to a trade or business. Thus, T's

ATI for the 2019 taxable year is $520x ($320x of taxable income + $200x business interest expense - $50x business interest income + $50x depreciation deductions = $520x), and its section 163(j) limitation for the 2019 taxable year is $206x ($50x of business interest income + 30 percent of its ATI (30 percent x $520x) = $206x). As a result, all $200x of T's interest expense is deductible in the 2019 taxable year under section 163(j).

(C) *Taxable year beginning in 2022.* The facts are the same as in *Example 1* in paragraph (b)(6)(i)(A) of this section, except that the taxable year is 2022 and therefore depreciation deductions are not added back to ATI under § 1.163(j)-1(b)(1)(i)(E). As a result, T's ATI for 2022 is $470x ($320x of taxable income + $200x business interest expense - $50x business interest income = $470x), and its section 163(j) limitation for the 2022 taxable year is $191x ($50x of business interest income + 30 percent of its ATI (30 percent x $470x) = $191x). As a result, T may only deduct $191x of its business interest expense for the taxable year, and the remaining $9x will be carried forward to the 2023 taxable year as a disallowed business interest expense carryforward. See § 1.163(j)-2(c).

(ii) *Example 2: C corporation partner*—(A) *Facts.* T and individual A each own a 50 percent interest in PS1, a general partnership. PS1 borrows funds from a third party (Loan 1) and uses those funds to buy stock in publicly-traded corporation X. PS1's only activities are holding X stock (and receiving dividends) and making payments on Loan 1. In the 2019 taxable year, PS1 receives $150x in dividends and pays $100x in interest on Loan 1.

(B) *Analysis.* For purposes of section 163(d) and (j), PS1 has investment interest expense of $100x and investment income of $150x, and PS1 has no interest expense or interest income that is properly allocable to a trade or business. PS1 allocates its investment interest expense and investment income to its two partners pursuant to § 1.163(j)-6(j). Pursuant to paragraph (b)(3) of this section, T's allocable share of PS1's investment interest expense is treated as a business interest expense of T, and T's allocable share of PS1's investment income is treated as properly allocable to a trade or business of T. This business interest expense is not treated as excess business interest expense, and this income is not treated as excess taxable income. See paragraph (b)(3)(iii) of this section. T's treatment of its allocable share of PS1's investment interest expense and investment income as business interest expense and income properly allocable to a trade or business, respectively, does not affect the character of these items at the PS1 level and does not affect the character of A's allocable share of PS1's investment interest and investment income.

(C) *Partnership engaged in a trade or business.* The facts are the same as in *Example 2* in paragraph (b)(6)(ii)(A) of this section, except that PS1 also is engaged in Business 1, and PS1 borrows funds from a third party to finance Business 1 (Loan 2). In 2019, Business 1 earns $150x of net income (excluding interest expense and depreciation), and PS1 pays $100x of interest on Loan 2. For purposes of § 1.163-8T, the interest paid on Loan 2 is allocated to a trade or business (and is therefore not treated as investment interest expense under section 163(d)). As a result, PS1 has investment interest expense of $100x (attributable to Loan 1), business interest expense of $100x (attributable to Loan 2), $150x of investment income, and $150x of income from Business 1. PS1's ATI is $150x (its net income from Business 1 excluding interest and depreciation), and its section 163(j) limitation is $45x (30 percent x $150x). Pursuant to § 1.163(j)-6, PS1 has $55x of excess business interest expense ($100x - $45x), half of which ($27.5x) is allocable to T. Additionally, pursuant to paragraph (b)(3)(i) of this section, T's allocable share of PS1's investment interest expense ($50x) is treated as a business interest expense of T for purposes of section 163(j), and T's allocable share of PS1's investment income ($75x) is treated as properly allocable to a trade or business of T. Therefore, with respect to T's interest in PS1, T is treated as having $50x of business interest expense that is not treated as excess business interest expense, $75x of income that is properly allocable to a trade or business, and $27.5x of excess business interest expense.

(c) *Effect on earnings and profits.*—(1) *In general.*—In the case of a taxpayer that is a C corporation, except as otherwise provided in paragraph (c)(2) of this section, the disallowance and carryforward of a deduction for the taxpayer's business interest expense under § 1.163(j)-2 will not affect whether or when the business interest expense reduces the taxpayer's earnings and profits.

(2) *Special rule for RICs and REITs.*—In the case of a taxpayer that is a RIC or a REIT for the taxable year in which a deduction for the taxpayer's business interest expense is disallowed under § 1.163(j)-2(b), or in which the RIC or REIT is allocated any excess business interest expense from a partnership under section 163(j)(4)(B)(i) and § 1.163(j)-6, the taxpayer's earnings and profits are adjusted in the taxable year or years in which the business interest expense is deductible or, if earlier, in the first taxable year for which the taxpayer no longer is a RIC or a REIT.

(3) *Special rule for partners that are C corporations.*—If a taxpayer that is a C corporation is allocated any excess business interest

expense from a partnership under section 163(j)(4)(B)(i) and § 1.163(j)-6, and if any amount of the excess business interest expense has not yet been treated as business interest expense by the taxpayer at the time of the taxpayer's disposition of all or substantially all of its interest in the partnership, then the taxpayer must increase its earnings and profits by that amount immediately prior to its disposition of the partnership interest.

(4) *Examples.*—The principles of this paragraph (c) are illustrated by the following examples. For purposes of the examples in this paragraph (c)(4), except as otherwise provided in the examples, X is a taxable domestic C corporation whose taxable year ends on December 31; X is not a member of a consolidated group; X does not qualify for the small business exemption under § 1.163(j)-2(d); X is not engaged in an excepted trade or business; X has no floor plan financing indebtedness; all interest expense is deductible except for the potential application of section 163(j); X has no accumulated earnings and profits at the beginning of the 2019 taxable year; and the facts set forth the only corporate activity.

(i) *Example 1: Earnings and profits of a taxable domestic C corporation other than a RIC or a REIT*—(A) *Facts.* X is a corporation that does not intend to qualify as a RIC or a REIT for its 2019 taxable year. In that year, X has taxable income (without regard to the application of section 163(j)) of $0, which includes $100x of gross income and $100x of interest expense on a loan from an unrelated third party. X also makes a $100x distribution to its shareholders that year.

(B) *Analysis.* The $100x of interest expense is business interest expense for purposes of section 163(j) (see paragraph (b)(1) of this section). X's ATI in the 2019 taxable year is $100x ($0 of taxable income computed without regard to $100x of business interest expense). Thus, X may deduct $30x of its $100x of business interest expense in the 2019 taxable year under § 1.163(j)-2(b) (30 percent x $100x), and X may carry forward the remainder ($70x) to X's 2020 taxable year as a disallowed business interest expense carryforward under § 1.163(j)-2(c). Although X may not currently deduct all $100x of its business interest expense in the 2019 taxable year, X must reduce its earnings and profits in that taxable year by the full amount of its business interest expense ($100x) in that taxable year. As a result, no portion of X's distribution of $100x to its shareholders in the 2019 taxable year is a dividend within the meaning of section 316(a).

(ii) *Example 2: RIC adjusted taxable income and earnings and profits*—(A) *Facts.* X is a corporation that intends to qualify as a RIC for its 2019 taxable year. In that taxable year, X's only items are $100x of interest income, $50x of dividend income from C corporations that only issue common stock and in which X has less than a twenty percent interest (by vote and value), $10x of net capital gain, and $125x of interest expense. None of the dividends are received on debt financed portfolio stock under section 246A. The DRD determined under section 243(a) with respect to X's $50x of dividend income is $25x. X pays $42x in dividends to its shareholders, meeting the requirements of section 562 during X's 2019 taxable year, including $10x that X reports as capital gain dividends in written statements furnished to X's shareholders.

(B) *Analysis.* (1) Under paragraph (b) of this section, all of X's interest expense is considered business interest expense, all of X's interest income is considered business interest income, and all of X's other income is considered to be properly allocable to a trade or business. Under paragraph (b)(4)(ii) of this section, prior to the application of section 163(j), X's taxable income is $10x ($100x business interest income + $50x dividend income + $10x net capital gain - $125x business interest expense - $25x DRD = $10x). Under paragraph (b)(4)(iii) of this section, X's ATI is increased by the DRD. As such, X's ATI for the 2019 taxable year is $60x ($10x taxable income + $125x business interest expense - $100x business interest income + $25x DRD = $60x).

(2) X may deduct $118x of its $125x of business interest expense in the 2019 taxable year under section 163(j)(1) ($100x business interest income + (30 percent x $60x of ATI) = $118x), and X may carry forward the remainder ($7x) to X's taxable year ending December 31, 2020. See § 1.163(j)-2(b) and (c).

(3) After the application of section 163(j), X has taxable income of $17x ($100x interest income + $50x dividend income + $10x capital gain - $25x DRD - $118x allowable interest expense = $17x) for the 2019 taxable year. X will have investment company taxable income (ICTI) in the amount of $0 ($17x taxable income - $10x capital gain + $25x DRD - $32x dividends paid deduction for ordinary dividends = 0). The excess of X's net capital gain ($10x) over X's dividends paid deduction determined with reference to capital gain dividends ($10x) is also $0.

(4) Under paragraph (c)(2) of this section, X will not reduce its earnings and profits by the amount of interest expense disallowed as a deduction in the 2019 taxable year under section 163(j). Thus, X has current earnings and profits in the amount of $42x ($100x interest income + $50x dividend income + $10x capital gain - $118x allowable

business interest expense = $42x) before giving effect to dividends paid during the 2019 taxable year.

(iii) *Example 3: Carryforward of disallowed interest expense*—(A) *Facts.* The facts are the same as the facts in *Example 2* in paragraph (c)(4)(ii)(A) of this section for the 2019 taxable year. In addition, X has $50x of interest income and $20x of interest expense for the 2020 taxable year.

(B) *Analysis.* Under paragraph (b) of this section, all of X's interest expense is considered business interest expense, all of X's interest income is considered business interest income, and all of X's other income is considered to be properly allocable to a trade or business. Because X's $50x of business interest income exceeds the $20x of business interest expense from the 2020 taxable year and the $7x of disallowed business interest expense carryforward from the 2019 taxable year, X may deduct $27x of business interest expense in the 2020 taxable year. Under paragraph (c)(2) of this section, X must reduce its current earnings and profits for the 2020 taxable year by the full amount of the deductible business interest expense ($27x).

(iv) *Example 4: REIT adjusted taxable income and earnings and profits*—(A) *Facts.* X is a corporation that intends to qualify as a REIT for its 2019 taxable year. X is not engaged in an excepted trade or business and is not engaged in a trade or business that is eligible to make any election under section 163(j)(7). In that year, X's only items are $100x of mortgage interest income, $30x of dividend income from C corporations that only issue common stock and in which X has less than a ten percent interest (by vote and value) in each C corporation, $10x of net capital gain from the sale of mortgages on real property that is not property described in section 1221(a)(1), and $125x of interest expense. None of the dividends are received on debt financed portfolio stock under section 246A. The DRD determined under section 243(a) with respect to X's $30x of dividend income is $15x. X pays $28x in dividends meeting the requirements of section 562 during X's 2019 taxable year, including $10x that X properly designates as capital gain dividends under section 857(b)(3)(B).

(B) *Analysis.* (1) Under paragraph (b) of this section, all of X's interest expense is considered business interest expense, all of X's interest income is considered business interest income, and all of X's other income is considered to be properly allocable to a trade or business. Under paragraph (b)(4)(ii) of this section, prior to the application of section 163(j), X's taxable income is $0 ($100x business interest income + $30x dividend income + $10x net capital gain - $125x business interest expense - $15x DRD = $0). Under paragraph (b)(4)(iii) of this section, X's ATI is increased by the DRD. As such, X's ATI for the 2019 taxable year is $40x ($0 taxable income + $125x business interest expense - $100x business interest income + $15x DRD = $40x).

(2) X may deduct $112x of its $125x of business interest expense in the 2019 taxable year under section 163(j)(1) ($100x business interest income + (30 percent x $40x of ATI) = $112x), and X may carry forward the remainder of its business interest expense ($13x) to X's 2020 taxable year.

(3) After the application of section 163(j), X has taxable income of $13x ($100x business interest income + $30x dividend income + $10x capital gain - $15x DRD - $112x allowable business interest expense = $13x) for the 2019 taxable year. X will have real estate investment trust taxable income (REITTI) in the amount of $0 ($13x taxable income + $15x of DRD - $28x dividends paid deduction = $0).

(4) Under paragraph (c)(2) of this section, X will not reduce earnings and profits by the amount of business interest expense disallowed as a deduction in the 2019 taxable year. Thus, X has current earnings and profits in the amount of $28x ($100x business interest income + $30x dividend income + $10x capital gain - $112x allowable business interest expense = $28x) before giving effect to dividends paid during X's 2019 taxable year.

(v) *Example 5: Carryforward of disallowed interest expense*—(A) *Facts.* The facts are the same as in *Example 4* in paragraph (c)(4)(iv)(A) of this section for the 2019 taxable year. In addition, X has $50x of mortgage interest income and $20x of interest expense for the 2020 taxable year. X has no other tax items for the 2020 taxable year.

(B) *Analysis.* Because X's $50x of business interest income exceeds the $20x of business interest expense from the 2020 taxable year and the $13x of disallowed business interest expense carryforwards from the 2019 taxable year, X may deduct $33x of business interest expense in 2020. Under paragraph (c)(2) of this section, X must reduce its current earnings and profits for 2020 by the full amount of the deductible interest expense ($33x).

(d) *Special rules for consolidated groups.*—(1) *Scope.*—This paragraph (d) provides certain rules applicable to members of a consolidated group. For all members of a consolidated group for a consolidated return year, the computations required by section 163(j) and the section 163(j) regulations are made in accordance with the rules of this paragraph (d) unless otherwise provided elsewhere in the section 163(j) regulations. For rules governing the carryforward of disallowed business interest expense, including rules governing the treatment of disallowed business interest expense carryforwards when members enter or leave a group, see §1.163(j)-5.

(2) *Calculation of the section 163(j) limitation for members of a consolidated group.*—(i) *In general.*—A consolidated group has a single section 163(j) limitation, the absorption of which is governed by §1.163(j)-5(b)(3)(ii).

(ii) *Interest.*—For purposes of determining whether amounts, other than amounts in respect of intercompany obligations, as defined in §1.1502-13(g)(2)(ii), intercompany items, as defined in §1.1502-13(b)(2), or corresponding items, as defined in §1.1502-13(b)(3), are treated as interest within the meaning of §1.163(j)-1(b)(20), all members of a consolidated group are treated as a single taxpayer.

(iii) *Calculation of business interest expense and business interest income for a consolidated group.*—For purposes of calculating the section 163(j) limitation for a consolidated group, the consolidated group's current-year business interest expense (as defined in §1.163(j)-5(a)(2)(i)) and business interest income, respectively, are the sum of each member's current-year business interest expense and business interest income, including amounts treated as business interest expense and business interest income under paragraph (b)(3) of this section.

(iv) *Calculation of adjusted taxable income.*—For purposes of calculating the ATI for a consolidated group, the relevant taxable income is the consolidated group's consolidated taxable income, determined under §1.1502-11 without regard to any carryforwards or disallowances under section 163(j). Additionally, if for a taxable year a member of a consolidated group is allowed a deduction under section 250(a)(1) that is properly allocable to a non-excepted trade or business, then, for purposes of calculating ATI, consolidated taxable income for the taxable year is determined as if the deduction were not subject to the limitation in section 250(a)(2). For this purpose, the amount of the deduction allowed under section 250(a)(1) is determined without regard to the application of section 163(j) and the section 163(j) regulations. Further, for purposes of calculating the ATI of the group, intercompany items and corresponding items are disregarded to the extent that they offset in amount. Thus, for example, certain portions of the intercompany items and corresponding items of a group member engaged in a non-excepted trade or business will not be included in ATI to the extent that the counterparties to the relevant intercompany transactions are engaged in one or more excepted trades or businesses.

(v) *Treatment of intercompany obligations.*—For purposes of determining a member's business interest expense and business interest income, and for purposes of calculating the consolidated group's ATI, all intercompany obligations, as defined in §1.1502 13(g)(2)(ii), are disregarded. Therefore, interest expense and interest income from intercompany obligations are not treated as business interest expense and business interest income.

(3) *Investment adjustments.*—For rules governing investment adjustments within a consolidated group, see §1.1502-32(b).

(4) *Ownership of partnership interests by members of a consolidated group.*—(i) *Dispositions of partnership interests.*—The transfer of a partnership interest in an intercompany transaction that does not result in the termination of the partnership is treated as a disposition for purposes of the basis adjustment rule in section 163(j)(4)(B)(iii)(II), regardless of whether the transfer is one in which gain or loss is recognized. See §1.1502-13 for rules applicable to the redetermination of attributes of group members. A change in status of a member (becoming or ceasing to be a member) is not treated as a disposition for purposes of section 163(j)(4)(B)(iii)(II).

(ii) *Basis adjustments under §1.1502-32.*—A member's allocation of excess business interest expense from a partnership and the resulting decrease in basis in the partnership interest under section 163(j)(4)(B) is not a noncapital, nondeductible expense for purposes of §1.1502-32(b)(3)(iii). Additionally, an increase in a member's basis in a partnership interest under section 163(j)(4)(B)(iii)(II) to reflect excess business interest expense not deducted by the consolidated group is not tax-exempt income for purposes of §1.1502-32(b)(3)(ii). Investment adjustments are made under §1.1502-32(b)(3)(i) when the excess business interest expense from the partnership is absorbed by the consolidated group. See §1.1502-32(b).

(iii) [Reserved]

(5) *Examples.*—The principles of this paragraph (d) are illustrated by the following examples (see also §1.1502-13(c)(7)(ii)(R) and (S)). For purposes of the examples in this paragraph (d)(5), S is a member of the calendar-year consolidated group of which P is the common parent; the P group does not qualify for the small business exemption in §1.163(j)-2(d); no member of the P group is engaged in an excepted trade or business; all interest expense is deductible

except for the potential application of section 163(j); and the facts set forth the only corporate activity.

(i) *Example 1: Calculation of the section 163(j) limitation*—(A) *Facts.* In the 2019 taxable year, P has $50x of separate taxable income after taking into account $65x of interest paid on a loan from a third party (without regard to any disallowance under section 163(j)) and $35x of depreciation deductions under section 168. In turn, S has $40x of separate taxable income in the 2019 taxable year after taking into account $10x of depreciation deductions under section 168. S has no interest expense in the 2019 taxable year. The P group's consolidated taxable income for the 2019 taxable year is $90x, determined under §1.1502-11 without regard to any disallowance under section 163(j).

(B) *Analysis.* As provided in paragraph (b)(1) of this section, P's interest expense is treated as business interest expense for purposes of section 163(j). If P and S were to apply the section 163(j) limitation on a separate-entity basis, then P's ATI would be $150x ($50x + $65x + $35x = $150x), its section 163(j) limitation would be $45x (30 percent x $150x = $45x), and a deduction for $20x of its $65x of business interest expense would be disallowed in the 2019 taxable year under section 163(j). However, as provided in paragraph (d)(2) of this section, the P group computes a single section 163(j) limitation, and that computation begins with the P group's consolidated taxable income (as determined prior to the application of section 163(j)), or $90x. The P group's ATI is $200x ($50x + $40x + $65x + $35x + $10x = $200x). Thus, the P group's section 163(j) limitation for the 2019 taxable year is $60x (30 percent x $200x = $60x). As a result, all but $5x of the P group's business interest expense is deductible in the 2019 taxable year. P carries over the $5x of disallowed business interest expense to the succeeding taxable year.

(ii) *Example 2: Intercompany obligations*—(A) *Facts.* On January 1, 2019, G, a corporation unrelated to P and S, lends P $100x in exchange for a note that accrues interest at a 10 percent annual rate. A month later, P lends $100x to S in exchange for a note that accrues interest at a 12 percent annual rate. In 2019, P accrues and pays $10x of interest to G on P's note, and S accrues and pays $12x of interest to P on S's note. For that year, the P group's only other items of income, gain, deduction, and loss are $40x of income earned by S from the sale of inventory, and a $30x deductible expense arising from P's payment of tort liability claims.

(B) *Analysis.* As provided in paragraph (d)(2)(v) of this section, the intercompany obligation between P and S is disregarded in determining P and S's business interest expense and business interest income and in determining the P group's ATI. For purposes of section 163(j), P has $10x of business interest expense and a $30x deduction for the payment of tort liability claims, and S has $40x of income. The P group's ATI is $10x ($40x - $30x = $10x), and its section 163(j) limitation is $3x (30 percent x $10x = $3x). The P group may deduct $3x of its business interest expense in the 2019 taxable year. A deduction for P's remaining $7x of business interest expense is disallowed in the 2019 taxable year, and this amount is carried forward to the 2020 taxable year.

(e) *Cross-references.*—For rules governing the treatment of disallowed business interest expense carryforwards for C corporations, see §1.163(j)-5. For rules governing the application of section 163(j) to a C corporation or a consolidated group engaged in both excepted and non-excepted trades or businesses, see §1.163(j)-10.

(f) *Applicability date.*—The provisions of this section apply to taxable years ending after the date the Treasury decision adopting these regulations as final regulations is published in the **Federal Register**. However, taxpayers and their related parties, within the meaning of sections 267(b) and 707(b)(1), may apply the rules of this section to a taxable year beginning after December 31, 2017, so long as the taxpayers and their related parties consistently apply the rules of the section 163(j) regulations, and if applicable, §§1.263A-9, 1.381(c)(20)-1, 1.382-6, 1.383-1, 1.469-9, 1.882-5, 1.1502-13, 1.1502-21, 1.1502-36, 1.1502-79, 1.1502-91 through 1.1502-99 (to the extent they effectuate the rules of §§1.382-6 and 1.383-1), and 1.1504-4 to those taxable years. [Reg. §1.163(j)-4.]

§1.163(j)-5. General rules governing disallowed business interest expense carryforwards for C corporations.—(a) *Scope and definitions.*—(1) *Scope.*—This section provides certain rules regarding disallowed business interest expense carryforwards for taxpayers that are C corporations, including members of a consolidated group. Paragraph (b) of this section provides rules regarding the treatment of disallowed business interest expense carryforwards. Paragraph (c) of this section provides cross-references to other rules regarding disallowed business interest expense carryforwards in transactions to which section 381(a) applies. Paragraph (d) of this section provides rules regarding limitations on disallowed business interest expense carryforwards from separate return limitation years (SRLYs). Paragraph (e) of this section provides cross-references to other rules regarding the application of section 382 to disallowed business interest expense carryforwards. Paragraph (f) of this section provides rules regarding the overlap of the SRLY limitation with section 382.

(2) *Definitions.*—(i) *Current-year business interest expense.*—The term *current-year business interest expense* means business interest expense (as defined in §1.163(j)-1(b)(2)) that would be deductible in the current taxable year without regard to section 163(j) and that is not a disallowed business interest expense carryforward (as defined in §1.163(j)-1(b)(9)) from a prior taxable year.

(ii) *Allocable share of the consolidated group's remaining section 163(j) limitation.*—The term *allocable share of the consolidated group's remaining section 163(j) limitation* means, with respect to any member of a consolidated group, the product of the consolidated group's remaining section 163(j) limitation and the member's remaining current-year interest ratio.

(iii) *Consolidated group's remaining section 163(j) limitation.*—The term *consolidated group's remaining section 163(j) limitation* means the amount of the consolidated group's section 163(j) limitation calculated pursuant to §1.163(j)-4(d)(2), reduced by the amount of interest deducted by members of the consolidated group pursuant to paragraph (b)(3)(ii)(C)(2) of this section.

(iv) *Remaining current-year interest ratio.*—The term *remaining current-year interest ratio* means, with respect to any member of a consolidated group for a particular taxable year, the ratio of the remaining current-year business interest expense of the member after applying the rule in paragraph (b)(3)(ii)(C)(2) of this section, to the sum of the amounts of remaining current-year business interest expense for all members of the consolidated group after applying the rule in paragraph (b)(3)(ii)(C)(2) of this section.

(b) *Treatment of disallowed business interest expense carryforwards.*—(1) *In general.*—The amount of any business interest expense of a C corporation not allowed as a deduction for any taxable year as a result of the limitation under section 163(j)(1) and §1.163(j)-2(b) is carried forward to the succeeding taxable year as a disallowed business interest expense carryforward under section 163(j)(2) and §1.163(j)-2(c).

(2) *Deduction of business interest expense.*—For a taxpayer that is a C corporation, current-year business interest expense is deducted in the current taxable year before any disallowed business interest expense carryforwards from a prior taxable year are deducted in that year. Disallowed business interest expense carryforwards are deducted in the order of the taxable years in which they arose, beginning with the earliest taxable year, subject to certain limitations (for example, the limitation under section 382). For purposes of section 163(j), disallowed disqualified interest is treated as carried forward from the taxable year in which a deduction was disallowed under old section 163(j).

(3) *Consolidated groups.*—(i) *In general.*—A consolidated group's disallowed business interest expense carryforwards for the current consolidated return year (the current year) are the carryforwards from the group's prior consolidated return years plus any carryforwards from separate return years.

(ii) *Deduction of business interest expense.*—(A) *General rule.*—All current-year business interest expense of members of a consolidated group is deducted in the current year before any disallowed business interest expense carryforwards from prior taxable years are deducted in the current year. Disallowed business interest expense carryforwards from prior taxable years are deducted in the order of the taxable years in which they arose, beginning with the earliest taxable year, subject to the limitations described in this section.

(B) *Section 163(j) limitation is equal to or exceeds the current-year business interest expense and disallowed business interest expense carryforwards from prior taxable years.*—If a consolidated group's section 163(j) limitation for the current year is equal to or exceeds the aggregate amount of its members' current-year business interest expense and disallowed business interest expense carryforwards from prior taxable years that are available for deduction, then none of the current-year business interest expense or disallowed business interest expense carryforwards will be subject to disallowance in the current year under section 163(j). However, a deduction for the members' business interest expense may be subject to limitation under other provisions of the Code or the regulations promulgated thereunder (see, for example, paragraphs (c), (d), (e), and (f) of this section).

(C) *Current-year business interest expense and disallowed business interest expense carryforwards exceed section 163(j) limitation.*—If the aggregate amount of members' current-year business interest expense and disallowed business interest expense carryforwards from prior taxable years exceeds the consolidated group's section 163(j) limitation for the current year, then the following rules apply in the order provided.

(1) The group first determines whether its section 163(j) limitation for the current year equals or exceeds the aggregate amount of the members' current-year business interest expense.

(i) If the group's section 163(j) limitation for the current year equals or exceeds the aggregate amount of the members' current-year business interest expense, then no amount of the group's current-year business interest expense will be subject to disallowance in the current year under section 163(j). Once the group has taken into account its members' current-year business interest expense, the group applies the rules of paragraph (b)(3)(ii)(C)(4) of this section.

(ii) If the aggregate amount of members' current-year business interest expense exceeds the group's section 163(j) limitation for the current year, then the group applies the rule in paragraph (b)(3)(ii)(C)(2) of this section.

(2) If this paragraph (b)(3)(ii)(C)(2) applies (see paragraph (b)(3)(ii)(C)(1)(*ii*) of this section), then each member with current-year business interest expense and with current-year business interest income or floor plan financing interest deducts current-year business interest expense in an amount that does not exceed the sum of the member's business interest income and floor plan financing interest expense for the current year.

(3) After applying the rule in paragraph (b)(3)(ii)(C)(2) of this section, if the group has any section 163(j) limitation remaining for the current year, then each member with remaining current-year business interest expense deducts a portion of its expense based on its allocable share of the consolidated group's remaining section 163(j) limitation.

(4) If this paragraph (b)(3)(ii)(C)(4) applies (see paragraph (b)(3)(ii)(C)(1)(*i*) of this section), and if the group has any section 163(j) limitation remaining for the current year after applying the rules in paragraph (b)(3)(ii)(C)(1) of this section, then disallowed business interest expense carryforwards permitted to be deducted in the current year will be deducted in the order of the taxable years in which they arose, beginning with the earliest taxable year. Disallowed business interest expense carryforwards from taxable years ending on the same date that are available to offset consolidated taxable income for the current year generally will be deducted on a pro rata basis, under the principles of paragraph (b)(3)(ii)(C)(3) of this section. For example, assume that P and S are the only members of a consolidated group with a section 163(j) limitation for the current year (Year 2) of $200x; the amount of current-year business interest expense deducted in Year 2 is $100x; and P and S, respectively, have $140x and $60x of disallowed business interest expense carryforwards from Year 1 that are not subject to limitation under paragraph (c), (d), or (e) of this section. Under these facts, P would be allowed to deduct $70x of its carryforwards from Year 1 ($100x × ($140x / ($60x + $140x)) = $70x), and S would be allowed to deduct $30x of its carryforwards from Year 1 ($100x × ($60x / ($60x + $140x)) = $30x). But see § 1.383-1(d)(1)(ii), providing that, if losses subject to and not subject to the section 382 limitation are carried from the same taxable year, losses subject to the limitation are deducted before losses not subject to the limitation.

(5) Each member with remaining business interest expense after applying the rules of this paragraph (b)(3)(ii), taking into account the limitations in paragraphs (c), (d), (e), and (f) of this section, will carry the expense forward to the succeeding taxable year as a disallowed business interest expense carryforward under section 163(j)(2) and § 1.163(j)-2(c).

(iii) *Departure from group.*—If a corporation ceases to be a member during a consolidated return year, the corporation's current-year business interest expense from the taxable period ending on the day of the corporation's change in status as a member, as well as the corporation's disallowed business interest expense carryforwards from prior taxable years that are available to offset consolidated taxable income in the consolidated return year, are first made available for deduction during that consolidated return year. See § 1.1502-76(b)(1)(i); see also § 1.1502-36(d) (regarding reductions of deferred deductions on the transfer of loss shares of subsidiary stock). Only the amount that is neither deducted by the group in that consolidated return year nor otherwise reduced under the Code or regulations may be carried to the corporation's first separate return year after its change in status.

(iv) *Example: Deduction of interest expense*—(A) *Facts.* (1) P wholly owns A, which is a member of the consolidated group of which P is the common parent. P and A each borrow money from Z, an unrelated third party. The business interest expense of P and A in Years 1, 2, and 3, and the P group's section 163(j) limitation for those years, are as follows:

Table 1 to paragraph (b)(3)(iv)(A)(*1*)

Year	P's business interest expense	A's business interest expense	P group's section 163(j) limitation
1	$150x	$50x	$100x
2	60x	90x	120x
3	25x	50x	185x

(2) P and A have neither business interest income nor floor plan financing interest expense in Years 1, 2, and 3. Additionally, the P group is neither eligible for the small business exemption in § 1.163(j)-2(d) nor engaged in an excepted trade or business within the meaning of § 1.163(j)-1(b)(38)(ii).

(B) *Analysis*—(1) *Year 1.* In Year 1, the aggregate amount of the P group members' current-year business interest expense ($150x + $50x) exceeds the P group's section 163(j) limitation ($100x). As a result, the rules of paragraph (b)(3)(ii)(C) of this section apply. Because the P group members' current-year business interest expense exceeds the group's section 163(j) limitation for Year 1, P and A must apply the rule in paragraph (b)(3)(ii)(C)(2) of this section. Pursuant to paragraph (b)(3)(ii)(C)(2) of this section, each of P and A must deduct its current-year business interest expense to the extent of its business interest income and floor plan financing interest expense. Neither P nor A has business interest income or floor plan financing interest expense in Year 1. Next, pursuant to paragraph (b)(3)(ii)(C)(3) of this section, each of P and A must deduct a portion of its current-year business interest expense based on its allocable share of the consolidated group's remaining section 163(j) limitation ($100x). P's allocable share is $75x ($100x × ($150x / $200x) = $75x), and A's allocable share is $25x ($100x × ($50x / $200x) = $25x). Accordingly, in Year 1, P deducts $75x of its current-year business interest expense, and A deducts $25x of its current-year business interest expense. P has a disallowed business interest expense carryforward from Year 1 of $75x ($150x - $75x = $75x), and A has a disallowed business interest expense carryforward from Year 1 of $25x ($50x - $25x = $25x).

(2) *Year 2.* In Year 2, the aggregate amount of the P group members' current-year business interest expense ($60x + $90x) and disallowed business interest expense carryforwards ($75x + $25x) exceeds the P group's section 163(j) limitation ($120x). As a result, the rules of paragraph (b)(3)(ii)(C) of this section apply. Because the P group members' current-year business interest expense exceeds the group's section 163(j) limitation for Year 2, P and A must apply the rule in paragraph (b)(3)(ii)(C)(2) of this section. Pursuant to paragraph (b)(3)(ii)(C)(2) of this section, each of P and A must deduct its current-year business interest expense to the extent of its business interest income and floor plan financing interest expense. Neither P nor A has business interest income or floor plan financing interest expense in Year 2. Next, pursuant to paragraph (b)(3)(ii)(C)(3) of this section, each of P and A must deduct a portion of its current-year business interest expense based on its allocable share of the consolidated group's remaining section 163(j) limitation ($120x). P's allocable share is $48x (($120x × ($60x / $150x)) = $48x), and A's allocable share is $72x (($120x × ($90x / $150x)) = $72x). Accordingly, in Year 2, P deducts $48x of current-year business interest expense, and A deducts $72x of current-year business interest expense. P has a disallowed business interest expense carryforward from Year 2 of $12x ($60x - $48x = $12x), and A has a disallowed business interest expense carryforward from Year 2 of $18x ($90x - $72x = $18x). Additionally, because the P group has no section 163(j) limitation remaining after deducting current-year business interest expense in Year 2, the full amount of P and A's disallowed business interest expense carryforwards from Year 1 ($75x and $25x, respectively) also are carried forward to Year 3. As a result, at the beginning of Year 3, P and A's respective disallowed business interest expense carryforwards are as follows:

Table 1 to paragraph (b)(3)(iv)(B)(2)

	Year 1 disallowed business interest expense carryforwards	Year 2 disallowed business interest expense carryforwards	Total disallowed business interest expense carryforwards
P	$75x	$12x	$87x
A	25x	18x	43x

	Year 1 disallowed business interest expense carryforwards	Year 2 disallowed business interest expense carryforwards	Total disallowed business interest expense carryforwards
Total	100x	30x	130x

(3) *Year 3*. In Year 3, the aggregate amount of the P group members' current-year business interest expense ($25x + $50x = $75x) and disallowed business interest expense carryforwards ($130x) exceeds the P group's section 163(j) limitation ($185x). As a result, the rules of paragraph (b)(3)(ii)(C) of this section apply. Because the P group's section 163(j) limitation for Year 3 equals or exceeds the P group members' current-year business interest expense, no amount of the members' current-year business interest expense will be subject to disallowance under section 163(j) (see paragraph (b)(3)(ii)(C)(*1*) of this section). After each of P and A deducts its current-year business interest expense, the P group has $110x of section 163(j) limitation remaining for Year 3 ($185x - $25x - $50x = $110x). Next, pursuant to paragraph (b)(3)(ii)(C)(*4*) of this section, $110x of disallowed business interest expense carryforwards are deducted on a pro rata basis, beginning with carryforwards from Year 1. Because the total amount of carryforwards from Year 1 ($100x) is less than the section 163(j) limitation remaining after the deduction of Year 3 business interest expense ($110x), all of the Year 1 carryforwards are deducted in Year 3. After current-year business interest expense and Year 1 carryforwards are deducted, the P group's remaining section 163(j) limitation in Year 3 is $10x. Because the Year 2 carryforwards ($30x) exceed the remaining section 163(j) limitation ($10x), under paragraph (b)(3)(ii)(C)(*4*) of this section, each of P and A will deduct a portion of its Year 2 carryforwards based on its allocable share of the consolidated group's remaining section 163(j) limitation. P's allocable share is $4x (($10x x ($12x / $30x)) = $4x), and A's allocable share is $6x (($10x x ($18x / $30x)) = $6x). Accordingly, P and A may deduct $4x and $6x, respectively, of their Year 2 carryforwards. For Year 4, P and A have $8x and $12x of disallowed business interest expense carryforwards from Year 2, respectively.

(c) *Disallowed business interest expense carryforwards in transactions to which section 381(a) applies.*—For rules governing the application of section 381(c)(20) to disallowed business interest expense carryforwards, including limitations on an acquiring corporation's use of the disallowed business interest expense carryforwards of the transferor or distributor corporation in the acquiring corporation's first taxable year ending after the date of distribution or transfer, see § 1.381(c)(20)-1.

(d) *Limitations on disallowed business interest expense carryforwards from separate return limitation years.*—(1) *General rule.*—Except as provided in paragraph (f) of this section (relating to an overlap with section 382), the disallowed business interest expense carryforwards of a member arising in a separate return limitation year (or SRLY (see § 1.1502-1(f))) that are included in the consolidated group's business interest expense deduction for any taxable year under paragraph (b) of this section may not exceed the group's section 163(j) limitation for that year, determined by reference only to the member's items of income, gain, deduction, and loss for that year (section 163(j) SRLY limitation). For purposes of this paragraph (d), the SRLY subgroup principles of § 1.1502-21(c)(2) apply with appropriate adjustments.

(2) *Deduction of disallowed business interest expense carryforwards arising in a SRLY.*—Notwithstanding paragraph (d)(1) of this section, disallowed business interest expense carryforwards of a member arising in a SRLY are available for deduction by the consolidated group in the current year only to the extent the group has any remaining section 163(j) limitation for the current year after the deduction of current-year business interest expense and disallowed business interest expense carryforwards from earlier taxable years that are permitted to be deducted in the current year (see paragraph (b)(3)(ii)(A) of this section), and only to the extent the section 163(j) SRLY limitation for the current year exceeds the amount of the member's business interest expense already deducted by the group in that year under paragraph (b)(3)(ii) of this section. SRLY-limited disallowed business interest expense carryforwards are deducted on a pro rata basis (under the principles of paragraph (b)(3)(ii)(C)(3) of this section) with non-SRLY limited disallowed business interest expense carryforwards from taxable years ending on the same date.

(3) *Examples.*—The principles of this paragraph (d) are illustrated by the following examples. For purposes of the examples in this paragraph (d)(3), unless otherwise stated, P, R, S, and T are taxable domestic C corporations that are not regulated investment companies (RICs) or real estate investment trusts (REITs) and that file their tax returns on a calendar-year basis; none of P, R, S, or T qualifies for the small business exemption under section 163(j)(3) or is engaged in an excepted trade or business; all interest expense is deductible except for the potential application of section 163(j); and the facts set forth the only corporate activity.

(i) *Example 1: Determination of SRLY limitation*—(A) *Facts*. Individual A owns P. In 2019, A forms T, which pays or accrues a $100x business interest expense for which a deduction is disallowed under section 163(j) and that is carried forward to 2020. P does not pay or accrue business interest expense in 2019, and P has no disallowed business interest expense carryforwards from prior taxable years. At the close of 2019, P acquires all of the stock of T, which joins with P in filing a consolidated return beginning in 2020. Neither P nor T pays or accrues business interest expense in 2020, and the P group has a section 163(j) limitation of $300x in that year. This limitation would be $70x if determined solely by reference to T's items for 2020.

(B) *Analysis*. T's $100x of disallowed business interest expense carryforwards from 2019 arose in a SRLY. P's acquisition of T was not an ownership change as defined by section 382(g); thus, T's disallowed business interest expense carryforwards are subject to the SRLY limitation in paragraph (d)(1) of this section. The section 163(j) SRLY limitation for 2020 is the P group's section 163(j) limitation, determined by reference solely to T's items for 2020 ($70x). See paragraph (d)(1) of this section. Thus, $70x of T's disallowed business interest expense carryforwards are available to be deducted by the P group in 2020, and the remaining $30x of T's disallowed business interest expense carryforwards are carried forward to 2021.

(C) *Section 163(j) limitation of $0*. The facts are the same as in paragraph (A) of this *Example 1*, except that the section 163(j) SRLY limitation for 2020 (computed by reference solely to T's items for that year) is $0. Because the amount of T's disallowed business interest expense carryforwards that may be deducted by the P group in 2020 may not exceed the section 163(j) SRLY limitation for that year, none of T's carryforwards from 2019 may be deducted by the P group in 2020.

(ii) *Example 2: Deduction of disallowed business interest expense carryforwards arising in a SRLY*—(A) *Facts*. P and S are the only members of a consolidated group. P has neither current-year business interest expense nor disallowed business interest expense carryforwards. S has $100x of disallowed business interest expense carryforwards that arose in a SRLY and $150x of current-year business interest. The section 163(j) SRLY limitation for the current year (computed by reference solely to S's items for that year) is $200x. Assume that the P group's section 163(j) limitation for the current year would permit all of S's current-year business interest expense and disallowed business interest expense carryforwards to be deducted in the current year but for the rules of this paragraph (d).

(B) *Analysis*. Under paragraph (d)(1) of this section, the section 163(j) SRLY limitation for the current year of $200x (computed by reference solely to S's items for that year) exceeds the amount of S's business interest expense taken into account by the P group in the current year under paragraph (b)(3)(ii) of this section ($150x) by $50x. Thus, $50x of S's disallowed business interest expense carryforwards that arose in a SRLY may be taken into account by the P group in the current year.

(e) *Application of section 382.*—(1) *Pre-change loss.*—For rules governing the treatment of a disallowed business interest expense as a pre-change loss for purposes of section 382, see §§ 1.382-2(a) and 1.382-6. For rules governing the application of section 382 to disallowed disqualified interest carryforwards, see § 1.163(j)-11(b)(4).

(2) *Loss corporation.*—For rules governing when a disallowed business interest expense causes a corporation to be a loss corporation within the meaning of section 382(k)(1), see § 1.382-2(a). For the application of section 382 to disallowed disqualified interest carryforwards, see § 1.163(j)-11(b)(4).

(3) *Ordering rules for utilization of pre-change losses and for absorption of the section 382 limitation.*—For ordering rules for the utilization of disallowed business interest expense, net operating losses, and other pre-change losses, and for the absorption of the section 382 limitation, see § 1.383-1(d).

(4) *Disallowed business interest expense from the pre-change period in the year of a testing date.*—For rules governing the treatment of disallowed business interest expense from the pre-change period (within the meaning of § 1.382-6(g)(2)) in the year of a testing date, see § 1.382-2.

(f) *Overlap of SRLY limitation with section 382.*—The limitation provided in paragraph (d) of this section does not apply to disallowed business interest expense carryforwards when the application of paragraph (d) of this section results in an overlap with the application of section 382. For purposes of applying this paragraph (f), the principles of § 1.1502-21(g) apply with appropriate adjustments.

(g) *Additional limitations.*—Additional rules provided under the Code or regulations also apply to limit the use of disallowed business interest expense carryforwards. For rules governing the relationship between section 163(j) and other provisions affecting the deductibility of interest, see § 1.163(j)-3.

(h) *Applicability date.*—This section applies to taxable years ending after the date the Treasury decision adopting these regulations as final regulations is published in the **Federal Register**. However, taxpayers and their related parties, within the meaning of sections 267(b) and 707(b)(1), may apply the rules of this section to a taxable year beginning after December 31, 2017, so long as the taxpayers and their related parties consistently apply the rules of the section 163(j) regulations, and if applicable, §§ 1.263A-9, 1.381(c)(20)-1, 1.382-6, 1.383-1, 1.469-9, 1.882-5, 1.1502-13, 1.1502-21, 1.1502-36, 1.1502-79, 1.1502-91 through 1.1502-99 (to the extent they effectuate the rules of §§ 1.382-6 and 1.383-1), and 1.1504-4 to those taxable years. [Reg. § 1.163(j)-5.]

§ 1.163(j)-6. Application of the business interest deduction limitation to partnerships and subchapter S corporations.—(a) *Overview.*—If a deduction for business interest expense of a partnership or S corporation is subject to limitation under section 163(j), section 163(j)(4) provides that the section 163(j) limitation applies at the partnership or S corporation level and any deduction for business interest expense within the meaning of section 163(j) is taken into account in determining the nonseparately stated taxable income or loss of the partnership or S corporation. Once a partnership or S corporation determines its business interest expense, business interest income, ATI, and floor plan financing interest expense, the partnership or S corporation calculates its section 163(j) limitation by applying the rules of § 1.163(j)-2(b) and this section. Paragraph (b) of this section provides definitions used in this section. Paragraph (c) of this section provides rules regarding the character of a partnership's deductible business interest expense and excess business interest expense. Paragraph (d) of this section provides rules regarding the calculation of a partnership's ATI and floor plan financing interest expense. Paragraph (e) of this section provides rules regarding a partner's ATI and business interest income. Paragraph (f) of this section provides an eleven-step computation necessary for properly allocating a partnership's deductible business interest expense and section 163(j) excess items to its partners. Paragraph (g) of this section applies carryforward rules at the partner level if a partnership has excess business interest expense, as defined in § 1.163(j)-1(b)(14). Paragraph (h) of this section provides basis adjustment rules and paragraph (j) of this section provides rules regarding investment items of a partnership. Paragraph (l) of this section provides rules regarding S corporations. Paragraph (m) of this section provides rules for partnerships and S corporations not subject to section 163(j). Paragraph (o) of this section provides examples illustrating the rules of this section. Paragraph (p) provides the applicability date of the rules in this section.

(b) *Definitions.*—In addition to the definitions contained in § 1.163(j)-1, the following definitions apply for purposes of this section.

(1) *Section 163(j) items.*—The term *section 163(j) items* means the partnership or S corporation's business interest expense, business interest income, and items comprising ATI, as defined in § 1.163(j)-1(b)(1).

(2) *Partner basis items.*—The term *partner basis items* means any items of income, gain, loss, or deduction resulting from either an adjustment to the basis of partnership property used in a non-excepted trade or business made pursuant to section 743(b) or the operation of section 704(c)(1)(C)(i) with respect to such property. Partner basis items also include section 743(b) basis adjustments used to increase or decrease a partner's share of partnership gain or loss on the sale of partnership property used in a non-excepted trade or business (as described in § 1.743-1(j)(3)(i)) and amounts resulting from the operation of section 704(c)(1)(C)(i) used to decrease a partner's share of partnership gain or increase a partner's share of partnership loss on the sale of such property.

(3) *Remedial items.*—The term *remedial items* means any allocation to a partner of remedial items of income, gain, loss, or deduction pursuant to section 704(c) and § 1.704-3(d).

(4) *Excess business interest income.*—The term *excess business interest income* means the amount by which a partnership's or S corporation's business interest income exceeds its business interest expense in a taxable year.

(5) *Deductible business interest expense.*—The term *deductible business interest expense* means the amount of a partnership's or S corporation's business interest expense that is deductible under section 163(j) in the current taxable year following the application of the limitation contained in § 1.163(j)-2(b).

(6) *Section 163(j) excess items.*—The term *section 163(j) excess items* means the partnership's excess business interest expense, excess taxable income, and excess business interest income.

(7) *Non-excepted assets.*—The term *non-excepted assets* means assets from a trade or business other than assets from an excepted regulated utility trade or business, electing farming business, or electing real property trade or business, as such terms are defined in § 1.163(j)-1.

(8) *Excepted assets.*—The term *excepted assets* means assets from an excepted regulated utility trade or business, electing farming business, or electing real property trade or business, as such terms are defined in § 1.163(j)-1.

(c) *Character of business interest expense.*—If a partnership has deductible business interest expense, such deductible business interest expense is not subject to any additional application of section 163(j) at the partner-level because it is taken into account in determining the nonseparately stated taxable income or loss of the partnership. For all other purposes of the Code, however, deductible business interest expense and excess business interest expense retain their character as business interest expense at the partner-level. For example, for purposes of section 469, such business interest expense retains its character as either passive or non-passive in the hands of the partner. Additionally, for purposes of section 469, deductible business interest expense and excess business interest expense from a partnership remain interest derived from a trade or business in the hands of a partner even if the partner does not materially participate in the partnership's trade or business activity. For additional rules regarding the interaction between sections 465, 469, and 163(j), see § 1.163(j)-3.

(d) *Adjusted taxable income of the partnership.*—(1) *Modification of adjusted taxable income for partnerships.*—The ATI of the partnership generally is determined in accordance with § 1.163(j)-1(b)(1). For purposes of computing the partnership's ATI, the taxable income of the partnership is determined under section 703(a) and includes any items described in section 703(a)(1) to the extent such items are otherwise included under § 1.163(j)-1(b)(1).

(2) *Section 734(b), partner basis items, and remedial items.*—A partnership takes into account items resulting from adjustments made to the basis of its property pursuant to section 734(b) for purposes of calculating its ATI pursuant to § 1.163(j)-1(b)(1). However, partner basis items and remedial items are not taken into account in determining a partnership's ATI under § 1.163(j)-1(b)(1). Instead, partner basis items and remedial items are taken into account by the partner in determining the partner's ATI pursuant to § 1.163(j)-1(b)(1). See *Example 8* in paragraph (o)(8) of this section.

(e) *Adjusted taxable income and business interest income of partners.*—(1) *Modification of adjusted taxable income for partners.*—The ATI of a partner in a partnership generally is determined in accordance with § 1.163(j)-1(b)(1) without regard to such partner's distributive share of any items of income, gain, deduction, or loss of such partnership, and is increased by such partner's distributive share of such partnership's excess taxable income determined under paragraph (f) of this section. For rules regarding corporate partners, see § 1.163(j)-4(b)(3).

(2) *Partner basis items and remedial items.*—Partner basis items and remedial items are taken into account as items derived directly by the partner in determining the partner's ATI for purposes of the partner's section 163(j) limitation. If a partner is allocated remedial items, such partner's ATI is increased or decreased by the amount of such items. Additionally, to the extent a partner is allocated partner basis items, such partner's ATI is increased or decreased by the amount of such item. See *Example 8* in paragraph (o)(8) of this section.

(3) *Disposition of partnership interests.*—If a partner recognizes gain or loss upon the disposition of interests in a partnership, and the partnership in which the interest is being disposed owns only non-excepted trade or business assets, the gain or loss on the disposition of the partnership interest is included in the partner's ATI. For dispositions of interests in partnerships that own:

(i) Non-excepted assets and excepted assets; or

(ii) Investment assets; or

(iii) Both. See § 1.163(j)-10(b)(4)(ii).

(4) *Double counting of business interest income and floor plan financing interest expense prohibited.*—For purposes of calculating a partner's section 163(j) limitation, the partner does not include—

(i) Business interest income from a partnership that is subject to section 163(j) except to the extent it is allocated excess business interest income from that partnership pursuant to paragraph (f)(2) of this section; and

(ii) The partner's allocable share of the partnership's floor plan financing interest expense because such floor plan financing interest expense has already been taken into account by the partnership in determining its nonseparately stated taxable income or loss for purposes of section 163(j).

(f) *Allocation and determination of section 163(j) excess items made in the same manner as nonseparately stated taxable income or loss of the partnership.*—(1) *Overview.*—(i) *In general.*—The purpose of this section is to provide guidance regarding how a partnership must allocate its deductible business interest expense and section 163(j) excess items, if any, among its partners. For purposes of section 163(j)(4) and this section, allocations and determinations of deductible business interest expense and section 163(j) excess items are considered made in the same manner as the nonseparately stated taxable income or loss of the partnership if, and only if, such allocations and determinations are made in accordance with the eleven-step computation set forth in paragraphs (f)(2)(i) through (xi) of this section. A partnership first determines its section 163(j) limitation, total amount of deductible business interest expense, and section 163(j) excess items under paragraph (f)(2)(i) of this section. The partnership then applies paragraphs (f)(2)(ii) through (xi) of this section, in that order, to determine how those items of the partnership are allocated among its partners. At the conclusion of the eleven-step computation set forth in paragraphs (f)(2)(i) through (xi) of this section, the total amount of deductible business interest expense and section 163(j) excess items allocated to each partner will equal the partnership's total amount of deductible business interest expense and section 163(j) excess items.

(ii) *Relevance solely for purposes of section 163(j).*—No rule set forth in paragraph (f)(2) of this section prohibits a partnership from making an allocation to a partner of any item of partnership income, gain, loss, or deduction that is otherwise permitted under section 704 and the regulations thereunder. Accordingly, any calculations in paragraphs (f)(2)(i) through (xi) of this section are solely for the purpose of determining each partner's deductible business interest expense and section 163(j) excess items, and do not otherwise affect any other provision under the Code, such as section 704(b). Additionally, floor plan financing interest expense is not allocated in accordance with paragraph (f)(2) of this section. Instead, floor plan financing interest expense of a partnership is allocated to its partners under section 704(b) and is taken into account as a nonseparately stated item of loss for purposes of section 163(j).

(2) *Steps for allocating deductible business interest expense and section 163(j) excess items.*—(i) *Partnership-level calculation required by section 163(j)(4)(A).*—First, a partnership must determine its section 163(j) limitation pursuant to §1.163(j)-2(b). This calculation determines a partnership's total amounts of excess business interest income, excess taxable income, excess business interest expense (that is, the partnership's section 163(j) excess items), and deductible business interest expense under section 163(j) for a taxable year.

(ii) *Determination of each partner's relevant section 163(j) items.*—Second, a partnership must determine each partner's allocable share of each section 163(j) item under section 704(b) and the regulations thereunder including any allocations under section 704(c), other than remedial items as defined in paragraph (b)(3) of this section. Only section 163(j) items that were actually taken into account in the partnership's section 163(j) calculation under paragraph (f)(2)(i) of this section are taken into account for purposes of this paragraph (f)(2)(ii). Partner basis items, allocations of investment income and expense, remedial items, and amounts determined for the partner under §1.163(j)-8T are not taken into account for purposes of this paragraph (f)(2)(ii). For purposes of this paragraph (f)(2)(ii) through (xi) of this section, the term *allocable ATI* means a partner's distributive share of the partnership's ATI (i.e., a partner's distributive share of gross income and gain items comprising ATI less such partner's distributive share of gross loss and deduction items comprising ATI), the term *allocable business interest income* means a partner's distributive share of the partnership's business interest income, and the term *allocable business interest expense* means a partner's distributive share of the partnership's business interest expense that is not floor plan financing interest expense.

(iii) *Partner-level comparison of business interest income and business interest expense.*—Third, a partnership must compare each partner's allocable business interest income to such partner's allocable business interest expense. Paragraphs (f)(2)(iii) through (v) of this section determine how a partnership must allocate its excess business interest income among its partners, as well as the amount of each partner's allocable business interest expense that is not deductible business interest expense after taking the partnership's business interest income into account. To the extent a partner's allocable business interest income exceeds its allocable business interest expense, the partner has an *allocable business interest income excess.* The aggregate of all the partners' allocable business interest income excess amounts is the *total allocable business interest income excess.* To the

extent a partner's allocable business interest expense exceeds its allocable business interest income, the partner has an *allocable business interest income deficit.* The aggregate of all the partners' allocable business interest income deficit amounts is the *total allocable business interest income deficit.* These amounts are required to perform calculations in paragraphs (f)(2)(iv) and (v) of this section, which appropriately reallocate allocable business interest income excess to partners with allocable business interest income deficits in order to reconcile the partner-level calculation under paragraph (f)(2)(iii) of this section with the partnership-level result under paragraph (f)(2)(i) of this section.

(iv) *Matching partnership and aggregate partner excess business interest income.*—Fourth, a partnership must determine each partner's final allocable business interest income excess. A partner's *final allocable business interest income excess* is determined by reducing, but not below zero, such partner's allocable business interest income excess (if any) by the partner's step four adjustment amount. A partner's *step four adjustment amount* is the product of the total allocable business interest income deficit and the ratio of such partner's allocable business interest income excess to the total allocable business interest income excess. The rules of this paragraph (f)(2)(iv) ensure that, following the application of paragraph (f)(2)(xi) of this section, the aggregate of all the partners' allocations of excess business interest income equals the total amount of the partnership's excess business interest income as determined in paragraph (f)(2)(i) of this section.

(v) *Remaining business interest expense determination.*—Fifth, a partnership must determine each partner's remaining business interest expense. A partner's *remaining business interest expense* is calculated by reducing, but not below zero, such partner's allocable business interest income deficit (if any) by such partner's step five adjustment amount. A partner's *step five adjustment amount* is the product of the total allocable business interest income excess and the ratio of such partner's allocable business interest income deficit to the total allocable business interest income deficit. Generally, a partner's remaining business interest expense is a partner's allocable business interest income deficit adjusted to reflect a reallocation of allocable business interest income excess from other partners. Determining a partner's remaining business interest expense is necessary to perform an ATI calculation that begins in paragraph (f)(2)(vii) of this section.

(vi) *Determination of final allocable ATI.*—Sixth, a partnership must determine each partner's final allocable ATI. Paragraphs (f)(2)(vi) through (x) of this section determine how a partnership must allocate its excess taxable income and excess business interest expense among its partners.

(A) *Positive allocable ATI.*—To the extent a partner's income and gain items comprising its allocable ATI exceed its deduction and loss items comprising its allocable ATI, the partner has *positive allocable ATI.* The aggregate of all the partners' positive allocable ATI amounts is the *total positive allocable ATI.*

(B) *Negative allocable ATI.*—To the extent a partner's deduction and loss items comprising its allocable ATI exceed its income and gain items comprising its allocable ATI, the partner has negative allocable ATI. The aggregate of all the partners' negative allocable ATI amounts is the *total negative allocable ATI.*

(C) *Final allocable ATI.*—Any partner with a negative allocable ATI, or an allocable ATI of $0, has a positive allocable ATI of $0. Any partner with a positive allocable ATI of $0 has a final allocable ATI of $0. The final allocable ATI of any partner with a positive allocable ATI greater than $0 is such partner's positive allocable ATI reduced, but not below zero, by the partner's step six adjustment amount. A partner's *step six adjustment amount* is the product of the total negative allocable ATI and the ratio of such partner's positive allocable ATI to the total positive allocable ATI. The total of the partners' final allocable ATI amounts must equal the partnership's ATI amount used to compute its section 163(j) limitation pursuant to §1.163(j)-2(b).

(vii) *Partner-level comparison of thirty percent of adjusted taxable income and remaining business interest expense.*—Seventh, a partnership must compare each partner's ATI capacity to such partner's remaining business interest expense as determined under paragraph (f)(2)(v) of this section. A partner's *ATI capacity* is the amount that is thirty percent of such partner's final allocable ATI as determined under paragraph (f)(2)(vi) of this section. A partner's final allocable ATI is grossed down to thirty percent prior to being compared to its remaining business interest expense in this calculation to parallel the partnership's adjustment to its ATI under section 163(j)(1)(B). To the extent a partner's ATI capacity exceeds its remaining business interest expense, the partner has an *ATI capacity excess.* The aggregate of all the partners' ATI capacity excess amounts is the *total ATI capacity excess.* To the extent a partner's remaining business interest expense exceeds its ATI capacity, the partner has an *ATI capacity deficit.* The aggregate of all the partners' ATI capacity deficit amounts is the *total ATI capacity deficit*. These amounts (which may be subject to adjustment under paragraph (f)(2)(viii) of this section) are required to perform calculations in paragraphs (f)(2)(ix) and (x) of this section, which appropriately reallocate ATI capacity excess to partners with ATI capacity deficits in order to reconcile the partner-level calculation under paragraph (f)(2)(vii) of this section with the partnership-level result under paragraph (f)(2)(i) of this section.

(viii) *Partner priority right to ATI capacity excess determination.*—(A) Eighth, the partnership must determine whether it is required to make any adjustments described in this paragraph (f)(2)(viii) and, if it is, make such adjustments. The rules of this paragraph (f)(2)(viii) are necessary to account for adjustments made to a partner's allocable ATI in paragraph (f)(2)(vi) of this section to ensure that the partners who had a negative allocable ATI do not inappropriately benefit under the rules of paragraphs (f)(2)(ix) through (xi) of this section to the detriment of the partners who had positive allocable ATI. The partnership must perform the calculations and make the necessary adjustments described under paragraphs (f)(2)(viii)(B) and (C) or paragraph (f)(2)(viii)(D) of this section if, and only if, there is—

(1) An excess business interest expense amount greater than $0 under paragraph (f)(2)(i) of this section;

(2) A total negative allocable ATI amount greater than $0 under paragraph (f)(2)(vi) of this section; and

(3) A total ATI capacity excess amount greater than $0 under paragraph (f)(2)(vii) of this section.

(B) A partnership must determine each partner's priority amount and usable priority amount. A partner's *priority amount* is thirty percent of the amount by which a partner's positive allocable ATI under paragraph (f)(2)(vi)(A) of this section exceeds such partner's final allocable ATI under paragraph (f)(2)(vi)(C) of this section. However, only partners with an ATI capacity deficit as determined under paragraph (f)(2)(vii) of this section can have a priority amount greater than $0. The aggregate of all the partners' priority amounts is the *total priority amount*. A partner's *usable priority amount* is the lesser of such partner's priority amount and such partner's ATI capacity deficit as determined under paragraph (f)(2)(vii) of this section. The aggregate of all the partners' usable priority amounts is the *total usable priority amount*. If the total ATI capacity excess amount, as determined under paragraph (f)(2)(vii) of this section, is greater than or equal to the total usable priority amount, then the partnership must perform the adjustments described in paragraph (f)(2)(viii)(C) of this section. If the total usable priority amount is greater than the total ATI capacity excess amount, as determined under paragraph (f)(2)(vii) of this section, then the partnership must perform the adjustments described in paragraph (f)(2)(viii)(D) of this section.

(C) For purposes of paragraph (f)(2)(ix) of this section, each partner's final ATI capacity excess amount is $0. For purposes of paragraph (f)(2)(x) of this section, the following terms have the following meanings for each partner:

(1) Each partner's *ATI capacity deficit* is such partner's ATI capacity deficit as determined under paragraph (f)(2)(vii) of this section reduced by such partner's usable priority amount.

(2) The *total ATI capacity deficit* is the total ATI capacity deficit as determined under paragraph (f)(2)(vii) of this section reduced by the total usable priority amount.

(3) The *total ATI capacity excess* is the total ATI capacity excess as determined under paragraph (f)(2)(vii) of this section reduced by the total usable priority amount.

(D) Any partner with a priority amount greater than $0 is a *priority partner*. Any partner that is not a priority partner is a *non-priority partner*. For purposes of paragraph (f)(2)(ix) of this section, each partner's final ATI capacity excess amount is $0. For purposes of paragraph (f)(2)(x) of this section, each non-priority partner's final ATI capacity deficit amount is such partner's ATI capacity deficit as determined under paragraph (f)(2)(vii) of this section. For purposes of paragraph (f)(2)(x) of this section, the following terms have the following meanings for priority partners.

(1) Each priority partner must determine its step eight excess share. A partner's *step eight excess share* is the product of the total ATI capacity excess as determined under paragraph (f)(2)(vii) of this section and the ratio of the partner's priority amount to the total priority amount.

(2) To the extent a priority partner's step eight excess share exceeds its ATI capacity deficit as determined under paragraph (f)(2)(vii) of this section, such excess amount is the priority partner's *ATI capacity excess* for purposes of paragraph (f)(2)(x) of this section. The *total ATI capacity excess* is the aggregate of the priority partners' ATI capacity excess amounts as determined under this paragraph (f)(2)(viii)(D)(2).

(3) To the extent a priority partner's ATI capacity deficit as determined under paragraph (f)(2)(vii) of this section exceeds its step eight excess share, such excess amount is the priority part-

ner's *ATI capacity deficit* for purposes of paragraph (f)(2)(x) of this section. The *total ATI capacity deficit* is the aggregate of the priority partners' ATI capacity deficit amounts as determined under this paragraph (f)(2)(viii)(D)(3).

(ix) *Matching partnership and aggregate partner excess taxable income.*—Ninth, a partnership must determine each partner's final ATI capacity excess. A partner's *final ATI capacity excess* amount is determined by reducing, but not below zero, such partner's ATI capacity excess (if any) by the partner's step nine adjustment amount. A partner's *step nine adjustment amount* is the product of the total ATI capacity deficit and the ratio of such partner's ATI capacity excess to the total ATI capacity excess. The rules of this paragraph (f)(2)(ix) ensure that, following the application of paragraph (f)(2)(xi) of this section, the aggregate of all the partners' allocations of excess taxable income equals the total amount of the partnership's excess taxable income as determined in paragraph (f)(2)(i) of this section.

(x) *Matching partnership and aggregate partner excess business interest expense.*—Tenth, a partnership must determine each partner's final ATI capacity deficit. A partner's *final ATI capacity deficit* amount is determined by reducing, but not below zero, such partner's ATI capacity deficit (if any) by the partner's step ten adjustment amount. A partner's *step ten adjustment amount* is the product of the total ATI capacity excess and the ratio of such partner's ATI capacity deficit to the total ATI capacity deficit. Generally, a partner's final ATI capacity deficit is a partner's ATI capacity deficit adjusted to reflect a reallocation of ATI capacity excess from other partners. The rules of this paragraph (f)(2)(x) ensure that, following the application of paragraph (f)(2)(xi) of this section, the aggregate of all the partners' allocations of excess business interest expense equals the total amount of the partnership's excess business interest expense as determined in paragraph (f)(2)(i) of this section.

(xi) *Final section 163(j) excess item and deductible business interest expense allocation.*—Eleventh, a partnership must allocate section 163(j) excess items and deductible business interest expense to its partners. Excess business interest income calculated under paragraph (f)(2)(i) of this section, if any, is allocated dollar for dollar by the partnership to its partners with final allocable business interest income excess amounts. Excess business interest expense calculated under paragraph (f)(2)(i) of this section, if any, is allocated dollar for dollar to partners with final ATI capacity deficit amounts. After grossing up each partner's final ATI capacity excess amount by ten-thirds, excess taxable income calculated under paragraph (f)(2)(i) of this section, if any, is allocated dollar for dollar to partners with final ATI capacity excess amounts. A partner's allocable business interest expense is deductible business interest expense to the extent it exceeds such partner's share of excess business interest expense. See paragraphs (o)(11) through (15) of this section.

(g) *Carryforwards.*—(1) *In general.*—The amount of any business interest expense not allowed as a deduction to a partnership by reason of §1.163(j)-2(b) and paragraph (f)(2) of this section for any taxable year is—

(i) Not treated as business interest expense of the partnership in the succeeding taxable year; and

(ii) Subject to paragraph (g)(2) of this section, treated as excess business interest expense which is allocated to each partner pursuant to paragraph (f)(2) of this section.

(2) *Treatment of excess business interest expense allocated to partners.*—If a partner is allocated excess business interest expense from a partnership under paragraph (f)(2) of this section for any taxable year—

(i) Solely for purposes of section 163(j), such excess business interest expense is treated as business interest expense paid or accrued by the partner in the next succeeding taxable year in which the partner is allocated excess taxable income or excess business interest income from such partnership, but only to the extent of such excess taxable income or excess business interest income; and

(ii) Any portion of such excess business interest expense remaining after the application of paragraph (g)(2)(i) of this section is excess business interest expense that is subject to the limitations of paragraph (g)(2)(i) of this section in succeeding years, unless paragraph (m)(3) of this section applies. See paragraphs (o)(1) through (10) of this section.

(3) *Excess taxable income and excess business interest income ordering rule.*—In the event a partner has excess business interest expense from a prior taxable year and is allocated excess taxable income or excess business interest income from the same partnership in a succeeding taxable year, the partner must treat, for purposes of section 163(j), the excess business interest expense as business interest expense paid or accrued by the partner in an amount equal to the partner's share of the partnership's excess taxable income or excess business interest income in such succeeding taxable year. See paragraphs (o)(2) through (10) of this section.

(h) *Basis adjustments.*—(1) *Section 704(d) ordering.*—Deductible business interest expense and excess business interest expense are subject to section 704(d). If a partner is subject to a limitation on loss under section 704(d) and a partner is allocated losses from a partnership in a taxable year, §1.704-1(d)(2) requires that the limitation on losses under section 704(d) be apportioned amongst these losses based on the character of each loss (each grouping of loses based on character being a "section 704(d) loss class"). If there are multiple section 704(d) loss classes in a given year, §1.704-1(d)(2) requires the partner to apportion the limitation on losses under section 704(d) to each section 704(d) loss class proportionately. For purposes of applying this proportionate rule, any deductible business interest expense (whether allocated to the partner in the current taxable year or suspended under section 704(d) in a prior taxable year), any excess business interest expense allocated to the partner in the current taxable year, and any excess business interest expense from a prior taxable year that was suspended under section 704(d) ("negative section 163(j) expense") shall comprise the same section 704(d) loss class. Once the partner determines the amount of limitation on losses apportioned to this section 704(d) loss class, any deductible business interest expense is taken into account before any excess business interest expense or negative section 163(j) expense. See paragraph (o)(9) of this section.

(2) *Excess business interest expense basis adjustments.*—The adjusted basis of a partner in a partnership interest is reduced, but not below zero, by the amount of excess business interest expense allocated to the partner pursuant to paragraph (f)(2) of this section. Negative section 163(j) expense is not treated as excess business interest expense in any subsequent year until such negative section 163(j) expense is no longer suspended under section 704(d). Therefore, negative section 163(j) expense does not affect, and is not affected by, any allocation of excess taxable income to the partner. Accordingly, any excess taxable income allocated to a partner from a partnership while the partner still has negative section 163(j) expense will be included in the partner's ATI. However, once the negative section 163(j) expense is no longer suspended under section 704(d), it becomes excess business interest expense, which is subject to the general rules in paragraph (g) of this section. See paragraph (o)(10) of this section.

(3) *Basis adjustments upon disposition of partnership interest.*—(i) *Complete disposition of partnership interest.*—If a partner disposes of all or substantially all of a partnership interest (whether by sale, exchange, or redemption), the adjusted basis of the partnership interest is increased immediately before the disposition by the amount of the excess (if any) of the amount of the basis reduction under paragraph (h)(2) of this section over the portion of any excess business interest expense allocated to the partner under paragraph (f)(2) of this section which has previously been treated under paragraph (g) of this section as business interest expense pair or accrued by the partner, regardless of whether the disposition was a result of a taxable or non-taxable transaction. Therefore, the adjusted basis of a partner in a partnership interest is not increased by any negative section 163(j) expense upon the disposition of a partnership interest. No deduction under section 163(j) is allowed to the transferor or transferee under chapter 1 of subtitle A of the Code for any excess business interest expense resulting in a basis increase under this section or any negative section 163(j) expense.

(ii) *Partial disposition of partnership interest.*—If a partner disposes of less than substantially all of its interest in a partnership (whether by sale, exchange, or redemption), a partner shall not increase its basis in its partnership interest by the amount of any excess business interest expense that has not yet been treated as business interest expense paid or accrued by the partner in accordance with paragraph (g) of this section. Any such excess business interest expense shall remain excess business interest expense of the transferor partner until such time as the transferor partner is allocated an appropriate amount of excess taxable income or excess business interest income from the partnership or the partner disposes of its partnership interest in accordance with paragraph (h)(2)(i) of this section. Additionally, any negative section 163(j) expense shall remain negative section 163(j) expense of the transferor partner until such negative section 163(j) expense is no longer suspended under section 704(d).

(i) [Reserved]

(j) *Investment items.*—Any item of a partnership's income, gain, deduction, or loss that is investment interest income or expense pursuant to §1.163-8T is allocated to each partner in accordance with section 704(b) and the regulations thereunder and the effect of such allocation for purposes of section 163 is determined at the partner-level. See §1.163(j)-4(b)(3), section 163(d), and §1.163-8T.

(k) [Reserved]

(l) *S corporations.*—(1) *In general.*—In the case of any S corporation, the section 163(j) limitation is applied at the S corporation level,

and any deduction allowed for business interest expense is taken into account in determining the nonseparately stated taxable income or loss of the S corporation. An S corporation determines its section 163(j) limitation in the same manner as set forth in §1.163(j)-2(b). Allocations of excess taxable income and excess business interest income are made in accordance with the shareholders' respective pro rata interests in the S corporation pursuant to section 1366(a)(1) after determining the S corporation's section 163(j) limitation pursuant to §1.163(j)-2(b).

(2) *Character of deductible business interest expense.*—If an S corporation has deductible business interest expense, such deductible business interest expense is not subject to any additional application of section 163(j) at the shareholder-level because such deductible business interest expense is taken into account in determining the nonseparately stated taxable income or loss of the S corporation. For all other purposes of the Code, however, deductible business interest expense retains its character as business interest expense at the shareholder-level. For example, for purposes of section 469, such deductible business interest expense retains its character as either passive or non-passive in the hands of the shareholder. Additionally, for purposes of section 469, deductible business interest expense from an S corporation remains interest derived from a trade or business in the hands of a shareholder even if the shareholder does not materially participate in the S corporation's trade or business activity. For additional rules regarding the interaction between sections 465, 469, and 163(j), see §1.163(j)-3.

(3) *Adjusted taxable income of an S corporation.*—The ATI of an S corporation generally is determined in accordance with §1.163(j)-1(b)(1). For purposes of computing the S corporation's ATI, the taxable income of the S corporation is determined under section 1363(b) and includes—

(i) Any item described in section 1363(b)(1); and

(ii) Any item described in §1.163(j)-1(b)(1), to the extent such item is consistent with subchapter S of the Code.

(4) *Adjusted taxable income and business interest income of S corporation shareholders.*—(i) *Adjusted taxable income of S corporation shareholders.*—The ATI of an S corporation shareholder is determined in accordance with §1.163(j)-1(b)(1) without regard to such shareholder's distributive share of any items of income, gain, deduction, or loss of such S corporation, and is increased by such shareholder's distributive share of such S corporation's excess taxable income, as defined in §1.163(j)-1(b)(15).

(ii) *Disposition of S corporation stock.*—If a shareholder of an S corporation recognizes gain or loss upon the disposition of stock of the S corporation, and the corporation in which the stock is being disposed only owns non-excepted trade or business assets, the gain or loss on the disposition of the stock is included in the shareholder's ATI. For dispositions of stock of S corporations that own:

(A) Non-excepted assets and excepted assets; or

(B) Investment assets; or

(C) Both. See §1.163(j)-10(b)(4)(ii).

(iii) *Double counting of business interest income and floor plan financing interest expense prohibited.*—For purposes of calculating an S corporation shareholder's section 163(j) limitation, the shareholder does not include—

(A) Business interest income from an S corporation that is subject to section 163(j) except to the extent it is allocated excess business interest income from that S corporation pursuant to paragraph (l)(1) of this section; and

(B) The shareholder's share of the S corporation's floor plan financing interest expense because such floor plan financing interest expense has already been taken into account by the S corporation in determining its nonseparately stated taxable income or loss for purposes of section 163(j).

(5) *Carryforwards.*—The amount of any business interest expense not allowed as a deduction for any taxable year by reason of the limitation contained in §1.163(j)-2(b) is carried forward in the succeeding taxable year as a disallowed business interest expense carryforward under the rules set forth in §1.163(j)-2(c) (whether to an S corporation or C corporation taxable year). S corporations are subject to:

(i) The same ordering rules as a C corporation that is not a member of a consolidated group; and

(ii) The limitation under section 382. See §1.163(j)-5(b)(2) and (e).

(6) *Basis adjustments and disallowed business interest expense carryforwards.*—An S corporation shareholder's adjusted basis in its S corporation stock is reduced, but not below zero, when a disallowed business interest expense carryforward becomes deductible under section 163(j).

(7) *Accumulated adjustment accounts.*—The accumulated adjustment account of an S corporation is adjusted to take into account business interest expense in the year in which the S corporation treats such business interest expense as deductible under the section 163(j) limitation. See section 1368(e)(1).

(8) *Termination of qualified subchapter S subsidiary election.*—If a corporation's qualified subchapter S subsidiary election terminates and any disallowed business interest expense carryforward is attributable to the activities of the qualified subchapter S subsidiary at the time of termination, such disallowed business interest expense carryforward remains with the parent S corporation and no portion of these items is allocable to the former qualified subchapter S subsidiary.

(9) *Investment items.*—Any item of an S corporation's income, gain, deduction, or loss that is investment interest income or expense pursuant to § 1.163-8T is allocated to each shareholder in accordance with the shareholders' pro rata interests in the S corporation pursuant to section 1366(a)(1). See section 163(d), § 1.163-8T.

(m) *Partnerships and S corporations not subject to section 163(j).*— (1) *Partnerships and S corporations not subject to section 163(j) by reason of the small business exemption.*—If a partnership or S corporation is not subject to section 163(j) by reason of § 1.163(j)-2(d) (exempt entity), the exempt entity does not calculate the section 163(j) limitation under § 1.163(j)-2 and these regulations. Because an exempt entity is not subject to section 163(j)(4), it does not take its deduction for business interest expense into account in determining its non-separately stated taxable income or loss within the meaning of section 163(j)(4)(A)(i) and retains its character as business interest expense. See § 1.163(j)-6(c). Thus, if a partner or S corporation shareholder is allocated business interest expense from an exempt entity, that allocated business interest expense will be subject to the partner's or S corporation shareholder's section 163(j) limitations. Additionally, contrary to the general rule in § 1.163(j)-6(e)(1), a partner or S corporation shareholder includes items of income, gain, loss, or deduction of such exempt entity when calculating its ATI. Finally, business interest income of such exempt entity is included in the partner's or S corporation shareholder's section 163(j) limitation regardless of the exempt entity's business interest expense amount.

(2) *Partnerships and S corporations not subject to section 163(j) by reason of an excepted trade or business.*—To the extent a partnership or S corporation is not subject to section 163(j) because it has an excepted trade or business as defined in § 1.163(j)-1(b)(38)(ii) (excepted entity), the entity does not apply its section 163(j) limitation under § 1.163(j)-2 and this section with respect to the business interest expense that is allocable to such excepted trade or business. If a partner or S corporation shareholder is allocated any section 163(j) item that is allocable to the partnership's or S corporation's excepted trade or business (excepted 163(j) items), such excepted 163(j) items are excluded from the partner or shareholder's section 163(j) deduction calculation. See § 1.163(j)-10(c) (regarding the allocation of items between excepted and non-excepted trades or businesses).

(3) *Partnerships that allocated excess business interest expense prior to becoming not subject to section 163(j).*—If a partnership allocates excess business interest expense to one or more of its partners, and in a succeeding taxable year becomes not subject to the requirements of section 163(j), the excess business interest expense from the prior taxable years is treated as paid or accrued by the partner in such succeeding taxable year. See paragraphs (o)(6) and (7) of this section.

(4) *S corporations with disallowed business interest expense carryforwards prior to becoming not subject to section 163(j).*—If an S corporation has a disallowed business interest expense carryforward for a taxable year, and in the succeeding taxable year becomes not subject to the requirements of section 163(j), then such disallowed business interest expense carryforward—

(i) Continues to be carried forward at the S corporation level;

(ii) Is no longer subject to the section 163(j) limitation; and

(iii) Is taken into account in determining the nonseparately stated taxable income or loss of the S corporation.

(n) [Reserved]

(o) *Examples.*—The examples in this paragraph illustrate the provisions of section 163(j) as applied to partnerships and subchapter S corporations. For purposes of these examples, each partnership is subject to the provisions of section 163(j), was created or organized in the United States, and is a calendar year taxpayer. Unless stated otherwise, all partners are subject to the provisions of section 163(j), are not subject to a limitation under section 704(d) or 1366(d), have no tax items other than those listed in the example, are U.S. citizens, and are calendar year taxpayers. The phrase "section 163(j) limit" shall equal the maximum potential deduction allowed under section 163(j)(1). Unless stated otherwise, business interest expense means

business interest expense that is not floor plan financing interest expense. With respect to partnerships, all allocations are in accordance with section 704(b) and the regulations thereunder.

(1) *Example 1*—(i) *Facts.* X and Y are equal partners in partnership PRS. In Year 1, PRS has $100 of ATI and $40 of business interest expense. PRS allocates the items comprising its $100 of ATI $50 to X and $50 to Y. PRS allocates its $40 of business interest expense $20 to X and $20 to Y. X has $100 of ATI and $20 of business interest expense from its sole proprietorship. Y has $0 of ATI and $20 of business interest expense from its sole proprietorship.

(ii) *Partnership-level.* In Year 1, PRS's section 163(j) limit is 30 percent of its ATI, or $30 ($100 x 30 percent). Thus, PRS has $30 of deductible business interest expense and $10 of excess business interest expense. Such $30 of deductible business interest expense is includable in PRS's non-separately stated income or loss, and is not subject to further limitation under section 163(j) at the partners' level.

(iii) *Partner-level allocations.* Pursuant to § 1.163(j)-6(f)(2), X and Y are each allocated $15 of deductible business interest expense and $5 of excess business interest expense. At the end of Year 1, X and Y each have $5 of excess business interest expense from PRS, which is not treated as paid or accrued by the partner until such partner is allocated excess taxable income or excess business interest income from PRS in a succeeding taxable year. Pursuant to § 1.163(j)-6(e)(1), X and Y, in computing their limit under section 163(j), do not increase any of their section 163(j) items by any of PRS's section 163(j) items. X and Y each increase their outside basis in PRS by $30 ($50 - $20).

(iv) *Partner-level computations.* X, in computing its limit under section 163(j), has $100 of ATI and $20 of business interest expense from its sole proprietorship. X's section 163(j) limit is $30 ($100 x 30 percent). Thus, X's $20 of business interest expense is deductible business interest expense. Y, in computing its limit under section 163(j), has $20 of business interest expense from its sole proprietorship. Y's section 163(j) limit is $0 ($0 x 30 percent). Thus, Y's $20 of business interest expense is not allowed as a deduction and is treated as business interest expense paid or accrued by Y in Year 2.

(2) *Example 2*—(i) *Facts.* The facts are the same as in *Example 1* in paragraph (o)(1)(i) of this section. In Year 2, PRS has $200 of ATI, $0 of business interest income, and $30 of business interest expense. PRS allocates the items comprising its $200 of ATI $100 to X and $100 to Y. PRS allocates its $30 of business interest expense $15 to X and $15 to Y. X has $100 of ATI and $20 of business interest expense from its sole proprietorship. Y has $0 of ATI and $20 of business interest expense from its sole proprietorship.

(ii) *Partnership-level.* In Year 2, PRS's section 163(j) limit is 30 percent of its ATI plus its business interest income, or $60 ($200 x 30 percent). Thus, PRS has $100 of excess taxable income, $30 of deductible business interest expense, and $0 of excess business interest expense. Such $30 of deductible business interest expense is includable in PRS's non-separately stated income or loss, and is not subject to further limitation under section 163(j) at the partners' level.

(iii) *Partner-level allocations.* Pursuant to § 1.163(j)-6(f)(2), X and Y are each allocated $50 of excess taxable income, $15 of deductible business interest expense, and $0 of excess business interest expense. As a result, X and Y each increase their ATI by $50. Because X and Y are each allocated $50 of excess taxable income from PRS, and excess business interest expense from a partnership is treated as paid or accrued by a partner to the extent excess taxable income and excess business interest income are allocated from such partnership to a partner, X and Y each treat $5 of excess business interest expense (the carryforward from Year 1) as paid or accrued in Year 2. X and Y each increase their outside basis in PRS by $85 ($100 - $15).

(iv) *Partner-level computations.* X, in computing its limit under section 163(j), has $150 of ATI ($100 from its sole proprietorship, plus $50 excess taxable income) and $25 of business interest expense ($20 from its sole proprietorship, plus $5 excess business interest expense treated as paid or accrued in Year 2). X's section 163(j) limit is $45 ($150 x 30 percent). Thus, X's $25 of business interest expense is deductible business interest expense. At the end of Year 2, X has $0 of excess business interest expense from PRS ($5 from Year 1, less $5 treated as paid or accrued in Year 2). Y, in computing its limit under section 163(j), has $50 of ATI ($0 from its sole proprietorship, plus $50 excess taxable income) and $45 of business interest expense ($20 from its sole proprietorship, plus $20 disallowed business interest expense from Year 1, plus $5 excess business interest expense treated as paid or accrued in Year 2). Y's section 163(j) limit is $15 ($50 x 30 percent). Thus, $15 of Y's business interest expense is deductible business interest expense. The $30 of Y's business interest expense not allowed as a deduction ($45 business interest expense, less $15 section 163(j) limit) is treated as business interest expense paid or accrued by Y in Year 3. At the end of Year 2, Y has $0 of excess business interest expense from PRS ($5 from Year 1, less $5 treated as paid or accrued in Year 2).

(3) *Example 3*—(i) *Facts.* The facts are the same as in *Example 1* in paragraph (o)(1)(i) of this section. In Year 2, PRS has $0 of ATI, $60 of business interest income, and $40 of business interest expense. PRS

allocates its $60 of business interest income $30 to X and $30 to Y. PRS allocates its $40 of business interest expense $20 to X and $20 to Y. X has $100 of ATI and $20 of business interest expense from its sole proprietorship. Y has $0 of ATI and $20 of business interest expense from its sole proprietorship.

(ii) *Partnership-level.* In Year 2, PRS's section 163(j) limit is 30 percent of its ATI plus its business interest income, or $60 (($0 × 30 percent) + $60). Thus, PRS has $20 of excess business interest income, $0 of excess taxable income, $40 of deductible business interest expense, and $0 of excess business interest expense. Such $40 of deductible business interest expense is includable in PRS's non-separately stated income or loss, and is not subject to further limitation under section 163(j) at the partners' level.

(iii) *Partner-level allocations.* Pursuant to §1.163(j)-6(f)(2), X and Y are each allocated $10 of excess business interest income, and $20 of deductible business interest expense. As a result, X and Y each increase their business interest income by $10. Because X and Y are each allocated $10 of excess business interest income from PRS, and excess business interest expense from a partnership is treated as paid or accrued by a partner to the extent excess taxable income and excess business interest income are allocated from such partnership to a partner, X and Y each treat $5 of excess business interest expense (the carryforward from Year 1) as paid or accrued in Year 2. X and Y each increase their outside basis in PRS by $10 ($30 - $20).

(iv) *Partner-level computations.* X, in computing its limit under section 163(j), has $100 of ATI (from its sole proprietorship), $10 of business interest income (from the allocation of $10 of excess business interest income from PRS), and $25 of business interest expense ($20 from its sole proprietorship, plus $5 excess business interest expense treated as paid or accrued in Year 2). X's section 163(j) limit is $40 (($100 × 30 percent) + $10). Thus, X's $25 of business interest expense is deductible business interest expense. At the end of Year 2, X has $0 of excess business interest expense from PRS ($5 from Year 1, less $5 treated as paid or accrued in Year 2). Y, in computing its limit under section 163(j), has $0 of ATI (from its sole proprietorship), $10 of business interest income, and $45 of business interest expense ($20 from its sole proprietorship, plus $20 disallowed business interest expense from Year 1, plus $5 excess business interest expense treated as paid or accrued in Year 2). Y's section 163(j) limit is $10 (($0 × 30 percent) + $10). Thus, $10 of Y's business interest expense is deductible business interest expense. The $35 of Y's business interest expense not allowed as a deduction ($45 business interest expense, less $10 section 163(j) limit) is treated as business interest expense paid or accrued by Y in Year 3. At the end of Year 2, Y has $0 of excess business interest expense from PRS ($5 from Year 1, less $5 treated as paid or accrued in Year 2).

(4) *Example 4—*(i) *Facts.* The facts are the same as in *Example 1* in paragraph (o)(1)(i) of this section. In Year 2, PRS has $100 of ATI, $60 of business interest income, and $40 of business interest expense. PRS allocates the items comprising its $100 of ATI $50 to X and $50 to Y. PRS allocates its $60 of business interest income $30 to X and $30 to Y. PRS allocates its $40 of business interest expense $20 to X and $20 to Y. X has $100 of ATI and $20 of business interest expense from its sole proprietorship. Y has $0 of ATI and $20 of business interest expense from its sole proprietorship.

(ii) *Partnership-level.* In Year 2, PRS's section 163(j) limit is 30 percent of its ATI plus its business interest income, or $90 (($100 × 30 percent)) + $60). Thus, PRS has $20 of excess business interest income, $100 of excess taxable income, $40 of deductible business interest expense, and $0 of excess business interest expense. Such $40 of deductible business interest expense is includable in PRS's non-separately stated income or loss, and is not subject to further limitation under section 163(j) at the partners' level.

(iii) *Partner-level allocations.* Pursuant to §1.163(j)-6(f)(2), X and Y are each allocated $10 of excess business interest income, $50 of excess taxable income, and $20 of deductible business interest expense. As a result, X and Y each increase their business interest income by $10 and ATI by $50. Because X and Y are each allocated $10 of excess business interest income and $50 of excess taxable income from PRS, and excess business interest expense from a partnership is treated as paid or accrued by a partner to the extent excess taxable income and excess business interest income are allocated from such partnership to a partner, X and Y each treat $5 of excess business interest expense (the carryforward from Year 1) as paid or accrued in Year 2. X and Y each increase their outside basis in PRS by $60 ($80 - $20).

(iv) *Partner-level computations.* X, in computing its limit under section 163(j), has $150 of ATI ($100 from its sole proprietorship, plus $50 excess taxable income), $10 of business interest income, and $25 of business interest expense ($20 from its sole proprietorship, plus $5 excess business interest expense treated as paid or accrued in Year 2). X's section 163(j) limit is $55 (($150 × 30 percent) + $10). Thus, $25 of X's business interest expense is deductible business interest expense. At the end of Year 2, X has $0 of excess business interest expense from PRS ($5 from Year 1, less $5 treated as paid or accrued in Year 2). Y, in computing its limit under section 163(j), has $50 of ATI ($0

from its sole proprietorship, plus $50 excess taxable income), $10 of business interest income, and $45 of business interest expense ($20 from its sole proprietorship, plus $20 disallowed business interest expense from Year 1, plus $5 excess business interest expense treated as paid or accrued in Year 2). Y's section 163(j) limit is $25 (($50 × 30 percent) + $10). Thus, $25 of Y's business interest expense is deductible business interest expense. Y's $20 of business interest expense not allowed as a deduction ($45 business interest expense, less $25 section 163(j) limit) is treated as business interest expense paid or accrued by Y in Year 3. At the end of Year 2, Y has $0 of excess business interest expense from PRS ($5 from Year 1, less $5 treated as paid or accrued in Year 2).

(5) *Example 5—*(i) *Facts.* The facts are the same as in *Example 1* in paragraph (o)(1)(i) of this section. In Year 2, PRS has $100 of ATI, $11.20 of business interest income, and $40 of business interest expense. PRS allocates the items comprising its $100 of ATI $50 to X and $50 to Y. PRS allocates its $11.20 of business interest income $5.60 to X and $5.60 to Y. PRS allocates its $40 of business interest expense $20 to X and $20 to Y. X has $100 of ATI and $20 of business interest expense from its sole proprietorship. Y has $0 of ATI and $20 of business interest expense from its sole proprietorship.

(ii) *Partnership-level.* In Year 2, PRS's section 163(j) limit is 30 percent of its ATI plus its business interest income, or $41.20 (($100 × 30 percent) + $11.20). Thus, PRS has $0 of excess business interest income, $4 of excess taxable income, and $40 of deductible business interest expense. Such $40 of deductible business interest expense is includable in PRS's non-separately stated income or loss, and is not subject to further limitation under section 163(j) at the partners' level.

(iii) *Partner-level allocations.* Pursuant to §1.163(j)-6(f)(2), X and Y are each allocated $2 of excess taxable income, $20 of deductible business interest expense, and $0 of excess business interest expense. As a result, X and Y each increase their ATI by $2. Because X and Y are each allocated $2 of excess taxable income from PRS, and excess business interest expense from a partnership is treated as paid or accrued by a partner to the extent excess taxable income and excess business interest income are allocated from such partnership to a partner, X and Y each treat $2 of excess business interest expense (a portion of the carryforward from Year 1) as paid or accrued in Year 2. X and Y each increase their outside basis in PRS by $35.60 ($55.60 - $20).

(iv) *Partner-level computations.* X, in computing its limit under section 163(j), has $102 of ATI ($100 from its sole proprietorship, plus $2 excess taxable income), $0 of business interest income, and $22 of business interest expense ($20 from its sole proprietorship, plus $2 excess business interest expense treated as paid or accrued). X's section 163(j) limit is $30.60 ($102 × 30 percent). Thus, X's $22 of business interest expense is deductible business interest expense. At the end of Year 2, X has $3 of excess business interest expense from PRS ($5 from Year 1, less $2 treated as paid or accrued in Year 2). Y, in computing its limit under section 163(j), has $2 of ATI ($0 from its sole proprietorship, plus $2 excess taxable income), $0 of business interest income, and $42 of business interest expense ($20 from its sole proprietorship, plus $20 disallowed business interest expense from Year 1, plus $2 excess business interest expense treated as paid or accrued in Year 2). Y's section 163(j) limit is $0.60 ($2 × 30 percent). Thus, $0.60 of Y's business interest expense is deductible business interest expense. Y's $41.40 of business interest expense not allowed as a deduction ($42 business interest expense, less $0.60 section 163(j) limit) is treated as business interest expense paid or accrued by Y in Year 3. At the end of Year 2, Y has $3 of excess business interest expense from PRS ($5 from Year 1, less $2 treated as paid or accrued in Year 2).

(6) *Example 6—*(i) *Facts.* The facts are the same as in *Example 5* in paragraph (o)(5)(i) of this section, except in Year 2 Y becomes not subject to section 163(j) under section 163(j)(3).

(ii) *Partnership-level.* Same analysis as *Example 5* in paragraph (o)(5)(ii) of this section.

(iii) *Partner-level allocations.* Same analysis as *Example 5* in paragraph (o)(5)(iii) of this section.

(iv) *Partner-level computations.* For X, same analysis as *Example 5* in paragraph (o)(5)(iv) of this section. Y is not subject to section 163(j) under section 163(j)(3). Thus, all $42 of business interest expense ($20 from its sole proprietorship, plus $20 disallowed business interest expense from Year 1, plus $2 excess business interest expense treated as paid or accrued in Year 2) is not subject to limitation under §1.163(j)-2(d). At the end of Year 2, Y has $3 of excess business interest expense from PRS ($5 from Year 1, less $2 treated as paid or accrued in Year 2).

(7) *Example 7—*(i) *Facts.* The facts are the same as in *Example 5* in paragraph (o)(5)(i) of this section, except in Year 2 PRS and Y become not subject to section 163(j) under section 163(j)(3).

(ii) *Partnership-level.* In Year 2, PRS becomes not subject to section 163(j)(4) by reason of section 163(j)(3). As a result, none of PRS's $30 of business interest expense is subject to limitation at the partnership level.

(iii) *Partner-level allocations.* Because section 163(j) does not apply, PRS's $30 of business interest expense is not taken into account in determining its non-separately stated taxable income or loss. Thus, PRS's $30 of business interest expense retains its character as business interest expense for purposes of section 163(j), and is potentially subject to limitation at the partners' level. As a result, X and Y each increase their business interest expense by $15. Further, because PRS is not subject to section 163(j)(4) by reason of section 163(j)(3), the provision requiring each partner of the partnership to determine their ATI without regard to such partner's distributive share of any items of income, gain, deduction, or loss of such partnership (section 163(j)(4)(ii)(I)) is no longer applicable under §1.163(j)-6(m)(1). As a result, X and Y each increase their ATI by $100. Further, because PRS is not subject to section 163(j)(4) by reason of section 163(j)(3), the excess business interest expense from Year 1 is treated as paid or accrued by the partners pursuant to §1.163(j)-6(m)(3). As a result, X and Y each treat their $5 of excess business interest expense from Year 1 as paid or accrued in Year 2, and increase their business interest expense by $5.

(iv) *Partner-level computations.* X, in computing its limit under section 163(j), has $200 of ATI ($100 from its sole proprietorship, plus $100 ATI from PRS) and $40 of business interest expense ($20 from its sole proprietorship, plus $15 from PRS, plus $5 of excess business interest expense treated as paid or accrued in Year 2). X's section 163(j) limit is $60 ($200 x 30 percent). Thus, $40 of X's business interest expense is deductible business interest expense. Y is not subject to section 163(j) under section 163(j)(3). As a result, Y's business interest expense is not subject to limitation under section 163(j). Thus, all $60 of Y's business interest expense ($20 from its sole proprietorship, plus $20 disallowed from year 1, plus $15 from PRS from year 2, plus $5 of excess business interest expense treated as paid or accrued in Year 2) is not subject to limitation under section 163(j).

(8) *Example 8*—(i) *Facts.* In Year 1, X, Y, and Z formed partnership PRS. Upon formation, X and Y each contributed $100, and Z contributed non-excepted and non-depreciable trade or business property with a basis of $0 and fair market value of $100 (Blackacre). PRS allocates all items pro rata between its partners. Immediately after the formation of PRS, Z sold all of its interest in PRS to A for $100 (assume the interest sale is respected for U.S. federal income tax purposes). In connection with the interest transfer, PRS made a valid election under section 754. Therefore, after the interest sale, A had a $100 positive section 743(b) adjustment in Blackacre. In Year 1, PRS had $0 of ATI, $15 of business interest expense, and $0 of business interest income. Pursuant to §1.163(j)-6(f)(2), PRS allocated each of the partners $5 of excess business interest expense. In Year 2, PRS sells Blackacre for $100 which generated $100 of ATI. The sale of Blackacre was PRS's only item of income in Year 2. In accordance with section 704(c), PRS allocates all $100 of gain resulting from the sale of Blackacre to A. Additionally, PRS has $15 of business interest expense, all of which it allocates to X. A has $50 of ATI and $20 of business interest expense from its sole proprietorship.

(ii) *Partnership-level.* In Year 2, PRS's section 163(j) limit is 30 percent of its ATI, or $30 ($100 x 30 percent). Thus, PRS has $15 of deductible business interest expense and $50 of excess taxable income. Such $15 of deductible business interest expense is includable in PRS's non-separately stated income or loss, and is not subject to further limitation under section 163(j) at X's level.

(iii) *Partner-level allocations.* Pursuant to §1.163(j)-6(f)(2), X is allocated $15 of deductible business interest expense and X's outside basis in PRS is reduced by $15. A is allocated $50 of excess taxable income and, as a result, A increases its ATI by $50. Because A is allocated $50 of excess taxable income, and excess business interest expense from a partnership is treated as paid or accrued by a partner to the extent excess taxable income and excess business interest income are allocated from such partnership to a partner, A treats $5 of excess business interest expense (the carryforward from Year 1) as paid or accrued in Year 2. PRS's $100 of gain allocated to A in Year 2 is fully reduced by A's $100 section 743(b) adjustment. Therefore, at the end of Year 2, there is no change to A's outside basis in PRS.

(iv) *Partner-level.* A, in computing its limit under section 163(j), has $0 of ATI ($50 from its sole proprietorship, plus $50 excess taxable income, less $100 ATI reduction as a result of A's section 743(b) adjustment under §1.163(j)-6(e)(2)) and $25 of business interest expense ($20 from its sole proprietorship, plus $5 excess business interest expense treated as paid or accrued in Year 2). A's section 163(j) limit is $0 ($0 x 30 percent). Thus, all $25 of A's business interest expense is not allowed as a deduction and is treated as business interest expense paid or accrued by A in Year 3.

(9) *Example 9*—(i) *Facts.* X and Y are equal partners in partnership PRS. At the beginning of Year 1, X and Y each have an outside basis in PRS of $5. In Year 1, PRS has $0 of ATI, $20 of business interest income, and $40 of business interest expense. PRS allocates its $20 of business interest income $10 to X and $10 to Y. PRS allocates $40 of business interest expense $20 to X and $20 to Y. X has $100 of ATI and $20 of business interest expense from its sole propri-

etorship. Y has $0 of ATI and $20 of business interest expense from its sole proprietorship.

(ii) *Partnership-level.* In Year 1, PRS's section 163(j) limit is 30 percent of its ATI plus its business interest income, or $20 (($0 x 30 percent) + $20). Thus, PRS has $0 of excess business interest income, $0 of excess taxable income, $20 of deductible business interest expense, and $20 of excess business interest expense. Such $20 of deductible business interest expense is includable in non-separately stated income or loss of PRS, and not subject to further limitation under section 163(j) by the partners.

(iii) *Partner-level allocations.* Pursuant to §1.163(j)-6(f)(2), X and Y are each allocated $10 of deductible business interest expense and $10 of excess business interest expense. After adjusting each partners respective basis for business interest income under section 705(a)(1)(A), pursuant to §1.163(j)-6(h)(1), X and Y each take their $10 of deductible business interest expense into account when reducing their outside basis in PRS before taking the $10 of excess business interest expense into account. Following each partner's reduction in outside basis due to the $10 of deductible business interest expense, each partner has $5 of outside basis remaining in PRS. Pursuant to §1.163(j)-6(h)(2), each partner has $5 of excess business interest expense and $5 of negative section 163(j) expense. In sum, at the end of Year 1, X and Y each have $5 of excess business interest expense from PRS which reduces each partner's outside basis to $0 (and is not treated as paid or accrued by the partners until such partner is allocated excess taxable income or excess business interest income from PRS in a succeeding taxable year), and $5 of negative section 163(j) expense (which is suspended under section 704(d) and not treated as excess business interest expense of the partners until such time as the negative section 163(j) expense is no longer subject to a limitation under section 704(d)).

(iv) *Partner-level computations.* X, in computing its limit under section 163(j), has $100 of ATI (from its sole proprietorship) and $20 of business interest expense (from its sole proprietorship). X's section 163(j) limit is $30 ($100 x 30 percent). Thus, $20 of X's business interest expense is deductible business interest expense. Y, in computing its limit under section 163(j), has $20 of business interest expense (from its sole proprietorship). Y's section 163(j) limit is $0 ($0 x 30 percent). Thus, $20 of Y's business interest expense is not allowed as a deduction in Year 1, and is treated as business interest expense paid or accrued by Y in Year 2.

(10) *Example 10*—(i) *Facts.* The facts are the same as in *Example 9* in paragraph (o)(9)(i) of this section. In Year 2, PRS has $20 of gross income that is taken into account in determining PRS's ATI (i.e., properly allocable to a trade or business), $30 of gross deductions from an investment activity, and $0 of business interest expense. PRS allocates the items comprising its $20 of ATI $10 to X and $10 to Y. PRS allocates the items comprising its $30 of gross deductions $15 to X and $15 to Y. X has $100 of ATI and $20 of business interest expense from its sole proprietorship. Y has $0 of ATI and $20 of business interest expense from its sole proprietorship.

(ii) *Partnership-level.* In Year 2, PRS's section 163(j) limit is 30 percent of its ATI plus its business interest income, or $6 ($20 x 30 percent). Because PRS has no business interest expense, all $20 of its ATI is excess taxable income.

(iii) *Partner-level allocations.* Pursuant to §1.163(j)-6(f)(2), X and Y are each allocated $10 of excess taxable income. Because X and Y are each allocated $10 of excess taxable income from PRS, X and Y each increase their ATI by $10. Pursuant to §1.704-1(d)(2), each partner's limitation on losses under section 704(d) must be allocated to its distributive share of each such loss. Thus, each partner reduces its adjusted basis of $10 (attributable to the allocation of items comprising PRS's ATI in Year 2) by $7.50 of gross deductions from Year 2 ($10 x ($15 of total gross deductions from Year 2 / $20 of total losses disallowed)), and $2.50 of excess business interest expense that was carried over as negative section 163(j) expense from Year 1 ($10 x ($5 of negative section 163(j) expense treated as excess business interest expense solely for the purposes of section 704(d) / $20 of total losses disallowed)). Following the application of section 704(d), each partner has $7.50 of excess business interest expense from PRS ($5 excess business interest expense from Year 1, plus $2.50 of excess business interest expense that was formerly negative section 163(j) expense carried over from Year 1). Excess business interest expense from a partnership is treated as paid or accrued by a partner to the extent excess taxable income and excess business interest income are allocated from such partnership to the partner. As a result, X and Y each treat $7.50 of excess business interest expense as paid or accrued in Year 2.

(iv) *Partner-level computations.* X, in computing its limit under section 163(j), has $110 of ATI ($100 from its sole proprietorship, plus $10 excess taxable income) and $27.50 of business interest expense ($20 from its sole proprietorship, plus $7.50 excess business interest expense treated as paid or accrued in Year 2). X's section 163(j) limit is $33 ($110 x 30 percent). Thus, $27.50 of X's business interest expense is deductible business interest expense. At the end of Year 2, X has $0 of excess business interest expense from PRS ($5 from Year

1, plus $2.50 treated as excess business interest expense in Year 2, less $7.50 treated as paid or accrued in Year 2), and $2.50 of negative section 163(j) expense from PRS. Y, in computing its limit under section 163(j), has $10 of ATI ($0 from its sole proprietorship, plus $10 excess taxable income) and $47.50 of business interest expense ($20 from its sole proprietorship, plus $20 disallowed business interest expense from Year 1, plus $7.50 excess business interest expense treated as paid or accrued in Year 2). Y's section 163(j) limit is $3 ($10 x 30 percent). Thus, $3 of Y's business interest expense is deductible business interest expense. The $44.50 of Y's business interest expense not allowed as a deduction ($47.50 business interest expense, less $3 section 163(j) limit) is treated as business interest expense paid or accrued by Y in Year 3. At the end of Year 2, Y has $0 of excess business interest expense from PRS ($5 from Year 1, plus $2.50 treated as excess business interest expense in Year 2, less $7.50 treated as paid or accrued in Year 2), and $2.50 of negative section 163(j) expense from PRS.

(11) *Example 11: Facts.* A (an individual) and B (a corporation) own all of the interests in partnership PRS. In Year 1, PRS has $100 of ATI, $10 of investment interest income, $20 of business interest income (BII), $60 of business interest expense (BIE), and $10 of floor plan financing interest expense. PRS's ATI consists of $100 of gross income and $0 of gross deductions. PRS allocates its items comprising ATI $100 to A and $0 to B. PRS allocates its business interest income $10 to A and $10 to B. PRS allocates its business interest expense $30 to A and $30 to B. PRS allocates all $10 of its investment interest income and all $10 of its floor plan financing interest expense to B. A has ATI from a sole proprietorship, unrelated to PRS, in the amount of $300.

(i) First, PRS determines its limitation pursuant to § 1.163(j)-2. PRS's section 163(j) limit is 30 percent of its ATI plus its business interest income, or $50 (($100 x 30 percent) + $20). Thus, PRS has $0 of excess business interest income (EBII), $0 of excess taxable income, $50 of deductible business interest expense, and $10 of excess business interest expense. PRS takes its $10 of floor plan financing into account in determining its nonseparately stated taxable income or loss.

(ii) Second, PRS determines each partner's allocable share of section 163(j) items used in its own section 163(j) calculation. B's $10 of investment interest income is not included in B's allocable business interest income amount because the $10 of investment interest income was not taken into account in PRS's section 163(j) calculation. B's $10 of floor plan financing interest expense is not included in B's allocable business interest expense. The $300 of ATI from A's sole proprietorship is not included in A's allocable ATI amount because the $300 was not taken into account in PRS's section 163(j) calculation.

Table 1 to paragraph (o)(11)(ii)

	A	B	Total
Allocable ATI	$100	$0	$100
Allocable BII	$10	$10	$20
Allocable BIE	$30	$30	$60

(iii) Third, PRS compares each partner's allocable business interest income to such partner's allocable business interest expense. Because each partner's allocable business interest expense exceeds its allocable business interest income by $20 ($30 - $10), each partner has an allocable business interest income deficit of $20. Thus, the total allocable business interest income deficit is $40 ($20 + $20). No partner has allocable business interest income excess because no partner has allocable business interest income in excess of its allocable business interest expense. Thus, the total allocable business interest income excess is $0.

Table 1 to paragraph (o)(11)(iii)

	A	B	Total
Allocable BII	$10	$10	N/A
Allocable BIE	$30	$30	N/A
If allocable BII exceeds allocable BIE, then such amount = Allocable BII excess	$0	$0	$0
If allocable BIE exceeds allocable BII, then such amount = Allocable BII deficit	$20	$20	$40

(iv) Fourth, PRS determines each partner's final allocable business interest income excess. Because no partner had any allocable business interest income excess, each partner has final allocable business interest income excess of $0.

(v) Fifth, PRS determines each partner's remaining business interest expense. PRS determines A's remaining business interest expense by reducing, but not below $0, A's allocable business interest income deficit ($20) by the product of the total allocable business interest income excess ($0) and the ratio of A's allocable business interest income deficit to the total business interest income deficit ($20/$40). Therefore, A's allocable business interest income deficit of $20 is reduced by $0 ($0 x 50 percent). As a result, A's remaining business interest expense is $20. PRS determines B's remaining business interest expense by reducing, but not below $0, B's allocable business interest income deficit ($20) by the product of the total allocable business interest income excess ($0) and the ratio of B's allocable business interest income deficit to the total business interest income deficit ($20/$40). Therefore, B's allocable business interest income deficit of $20 is reduced by $0 ($0 x 50 percent). As a result, B's remaining business interest expense is $20.

Table 1 to paragraph (o)(11)(v)

	A	B	Total
Allocable BII deficit	$20	$20	$40
Less: (Total allocable BII excess) x (Allocable BII deficit / Total allocable BII deficit)	$0	$0	N/A
= Remaining BIE	$20	$20	$40

(vi) Sixth, PRS determines each partner's final allocable ATI. Any partner with a negative allocable ATI, or an allocable ATI of $0, has a positive allocable ATI of $0. Therefore, B has a positive allocable ATI of $0. Because A's allocable ATI is comprised of $100 of income and gain and $0 of deduction and loss, A has positive allocable ATI of $100. Thus, the total positive allocable ATI is $100 ($100 + $0). PRS determines A's final allocable ATI by reducing, but not below $0, A's positive allocable ATI ($100) by the product of total negative allocable ATI ($0) and the ratio of A's positive allocable ATI to the total positive allocable ATI ($100/$100). Therefore, A's positive allocable ATI is reduced by $0 ($0 x 100 percent). As a result, A's final allocable ATI is $100. Because B has a positive allocable ATI of $0, B's final allocable ATI is $0.

Table 1 to paragraph (o)(11)(vi)

	A	B	Total
Allocable ATI	$100	$0	$100
If deduction and loss items comprising allocable ATI exceed income and gain items comprising allocable ATI, then such excess amount = Negative allocable ATI	$0	$0	$0

Table 1 to paragraph (o)(11)(vi)	A	B	Total
If income and gain items comprising allocable ATI equal or exceed deduction and loss items comprising allocable ATI, then such amount = Positive allocable ATI	$100	$0	$100

Table 2 to paragraph (o)(11)(vi)	A	B	Total
Positive allocable ATI	$100	$0	$100
Less: (Total negative allocable ATI) x (Positive allocable ATI / Total positive allocable ATI)	$0	$0	N/A
= Final allocable ATI	$100	$0	$100

(vii) Seventh, PRS compares each partner's ATI capacity (ATIC) amount to such partner's remaining business interest expense. A's ATIC amount is $30 ($100 x 30 percent) and B's ATIC amount is $0 ($0 x 30 percent). Because A's ATIC amount exceeds its remaining business interest expense by $10 ($30 - $20), A has an ATIC excess of $10. B does not have any ATIC excess. Thus, the total ATIC excess is $10 ($10 + $0). A does not have any ATIC deficit. Because B's remaining business interest expense exceeds its ATIC amount by $20 ($20 - $0), B has an ATIC deficit of $20. Thus, the total ATIC deficit is $20 ($0 + $20).

Table 1 to paragraph (o)(11)(vii)	A	B	Total
ATIC (Final allocable ATI x 30 percent)	$30	$0	N/A
Remaining BIE	$20	$20	N/A
If ATIC exceeds remaining BIE, then such excess = ATIC excess	$10	$0	$10
If remaining BIE exceeds ATIC, then such excess = ATIC deficit	$0	$20	$20

(viii)(A) Eighth, PRS must perform the calculations and make the necessary adjustments described under paragraph (f)(2)(viii) of this section if, and only if, PRS has:

(1) An excess business interest expense greater than $0 under paragraph (f)(2)(i) of this section;

(2) A total negative allocable ATI greater than $0 under paragraph (f)(2)(vi) of this section; and

(3) A total ATIC excess amount greater than $0 under paragraph (f)(2)(vii) of this section.

(B) Because PRS does not meet all three requirements in paragraph (o)(11)(viii)(A) of this section, PRS does not perform the calculations or adjustments described in paragraph (f)(2)(viii) of this section. In sum, the correct amounts to be used in paragraphs (o)(11)(ix) and (x) of this section are as follows.

Table 1 to paragraph (o)(11)(viii)(B)	A	B	Total
ATIC excess	$10	$0	$10
ATIC deficit	$0	$20	$20

(ix) Ninth, PRS determines each partner's final ATIC excess amount. Because A has an ATIC excess, PRS must determine A's final ATIC excess amount. A's final ATIC excess amount is A's ATIC excess ($10), reduced, but not below $0, by the product of the total ATIC deficit ($20) and the ratio of A's ATIC excess to the total ATIC excess ($10/$10). Therefore, A has $0 of final ATIC excess ($10 — ($20 x 100 percent)).

Table 1 to paragraph (o)(11)(ix)	A	B	Total
ATIC excess	$10	$0	N/A
Less: (Total ATIC deficit) x (ATIC excess / Total ATIC excess)	$20	$0	N/A
= Final ATIC excess	$0	$0	$0

(x) Tenth, PRS determines each partner's final ATIC deficit amount. Because B has an ATIC deficit, PRS must determine B's final ATIC deficit amount. B's final ATIC deficit amount is B's ATIC deficit ($20), reduced, but not below $0, by the product of the total ATIC excess ($10) and the ratio of B's ATIC deficit to the total ATIC deficit ($20/$20). Therefore, B has $10 of final ATIC deficit ($20 — ($10 x 100 percent)).

Table 1 to paragraph (o)(11)(x)	A	B	Total
ATIC deficit	$0	$20	N/A
Less: (Total ATIC excess) x (ATIC deficit / Total ATIC deficit)	$0	$10	N/A
= Final ATIC deficit	$0	$10	$10

(xi) Eleventh, PRS allocates deductible business interest expense and section 163(j) excess items to the partners. Pursuant to paragraph (f)(2)(i) of this section, PRS has $10 of excess business interest expense. PRS allocates the excess business interest expense dollar for dollar to the partners with final ATIC deficits amounts. Thus, PRS allocates all $10 of its excess business interest expense to B. A partner's allocable business interest expense is deductible business interest expense to the extent it exceeds such partner's share of excess business interest expense. Therefore, A has deductible business interest expense of $30 ($30 - $0) and B has deductible business interest expense of $20 ($30 - $10).

Table 1 to paragraph (o)(11)(xi)	A	B	Total
Deductible BIE	$30	$20	$50
EBIE allocated	$0	$10	$10

Table 1 to paragraph (o)(11)(xi)			
	A	B	Total
ETI allocated	$0	$0	$0
EBII allocated	$0	$0	$0

(12) *Example 12: Facts.* A, B, and C own all of the interests in partnership PRS. In Year 1, PRS has $150 of ATI, $10 of business interest income, and $40 of business interest expense. PRS's ATI consists of $200 of gross income and $50 of gross deductions. PRS allocates its items comprising ATI ($50) to A, $200 to B, and $0 to C. PRS allocates its business interest income $0 to A, $0 to B, and $10 to C. PRS allocates its business interest expense $30 to A, $10 to B, and $0 to C.

(i) First, PRS determines its limitation pursuant to §1.163(j)-2. PRS's section 163(j) limit is 30 percent of its ATI plus its business interest income, or $55 (($150 x 30 percent) + $10). Thus, PRS has $0 of excess business interest income, $50 of excess taxable income, $40 of deductible business interest expense, and $0 of excess business interest expense.

(ii) Second, PRS determines each partner's allocable share of section 163(j) items used in its own section 163(j) calculation.

Table 1 to paragraph (o)(12)(ii)				
	A	B	C	Total
Allocable ATI	($50)	$200	$0	$150
Allocable BII	$0	$0	$10	$10
Allocable BIE	$30	$10	$0	$40

(iii) Third, PRS compares each partner's allocable business interest income to such partner's allocable business interest expense. Because A's allocable business interest expense exceeds its allocable business interest income by $30 ($30 - $0), A has an allocable business interest income deficit of $30. Because B's allocable business interest expense exceeds its allocable business interest income by $10 ($10 - $0), B has an allocable business interest income deficit of $10. C does not have any allocable business interest income deficit. Thus, the total allocable business interest income deficit is $40 ($30 + $10 + $0). A and B do not have any allocable business interest income excess. Because C's allocable business interest income exceeds its allocable business interest expense by $10 ($10 - $0), C has an allocable business interest income excess of $10. Thus, the total allocable business interest income excess is $10 ($0 + $0 + $10).

Table 1 to paragraph (o)(12)(iii)				
	A	B	C	Total
Allocable BII	$0	$0	$10	N/A
Allocable BIE	$30	$10	$0	N/A
If allocable BII exceeds allocable BIE, then such amount = Allocable BII excess	$0	$0	$10	$10
If allocable BIE exceeds allocable BII, then such amount = Allocable BII deficit	$30	$10	$0	$40

(iv) Fourth, PRS determines each partner's final allocable business interest income excess. Because A and B do not have any allocable business interest income excess, each partner has final allocable business interest income excess of $0. PRS determines C's final allocable business interest income excess by reducing, but not below $0, C's allocable business interest income excess ($10) by the product of the total allocable business interest income deficit ($40) and the ratio of C's allocable business interest income excess to the total allocable business interest income excess ($10/$10). Therefore, C's allocable business interest income excess of $10 is reduced by $10 ($40 x 100 percent). As a result, C's allocable business interest income excess is $0.

Table 1 to paragraph (o)(12)(iv)				
	A	B	C	Total
Allocable BII excess	$0	$0	$10	N/A
Less: (Total allocable BII deficit) x (Allocable BII excess / Total allocable BII excess)	$0	$0	$40	N/A
= Final Allocable BII Excess	$0	$0	$0	$10

(v) Fifth, PRS determines each partner's remaining business interest expense. PRS determines A's remaining business interest expense by reducing, but not below $0, A's allocable business interest income deficit ($30) by the product of the total allocable business interest income excess ($10) and the ratio of A's allocable business interest income deficit to the total business interest income deficit ($30/$40). Therefore, A's allocable business interest income deficit of $30 is reduced by $7.50 ($10 x 75 percent). As a result, A's remaining business interest expense is $22.50. PRS determines B's remaining business interest expense by reducing, but not below $0, B's allocable business interest income deficit ($10) by the product of the total allocable business interest income excess ($10) and the ratio of B's allocable business interest income deficit to the total business interest income deficit ($10/$40). Therefore, B's allocable business interest income deficit of $10 is reduced by $2.50 ($10 x 25 percent). As a result, B's remaining business interest expense is $7.50. Because C does not have any allocable business interest income deficit, C's remaining business interest expense is $0.

Table 1 to paragraph (o)(12)(v)				
	A	B	C	Total
Allocable BII deficit	$30	$10	$0	$40
Less: (Total allocable BII excess) x (Allocable BII deficit / Total allocable BII deficit)	$7.50	$2.50	$0	N/A
= Remaining BIE	$22.50	$7.50	$0	N/A

(vi) Sixth, PRS determines each partner's final allocable ATI. Because A's allocable ATI is comprised of $50 of items of deduction and loss and $0 of income and gain, A has negative allocable ATI of $50. A is the only partner with negative allocable ATI. Thus, the total negative allocable ATI amount is $50. Any partner with a negative allocable ATI, or an allocable ATI of $0, has a positive allocable ATI of $0. Therefore, A and C have a positive allocable ATI of $0. Because B's allocable ATI is comprised of $200 of items of income and gain and $0 of deduction and loss, B has positive allocable ATI of $200. Thus, the total positive allocable ATI is $200 ($0 + $200 + $0). PRS determines B's final allocable ATI by reducing, but not below $0, B's positive allocable ATI ($200) by the product of total negative allocable ATI ($50) and the ratio of B's positive allocable ATI to the total positive allocable ATI ($200/$200). Therefore, B's positive allocable ATI is reduced by $50 ($50 x 100 percent). As a result, B's final allocable ATI is $150.

Table 1 to paragraph (o)(12)(vi)

	A	B	C	Total
Allocable ATI	($50)	$200	$0	$150
If deduction and loss items comprising allocable ATI exceed income and gain items comprising allocable ATI, then such excess amount = Negative allocable ATI	$50	$0	$0	$50
If income and gain items comprising allocable ATI equal or exceed deduction and loss items comprising allocable ATI, then such amount = Positive allocable ATI	$0	$200	$0	$200

Table 2 to paragraph (o)(12)(vi)

	A	B	C	Total
Positive allocable ATI	$0	$200	$0	$200
Less: (Total negative allocable ATI) x (Positive allocable ATI / Total positive allocable ATI)	$0	$50	$0	N/A
= Final allocable ATI	$0	$150	$0	$150

(vii) Seventh, PRS compares each partner's ATI capacity (ATIC) amount to such partner's remaining business interest expense. A's ATIC amount is $0 ($0 x 30 percent), B's ATIC amount is $45 ($150 x 30 percent), and C's ATIC amount is $0 ($0 x 30 percent). A does not have any ATIC excess. Because B's ATIC amount exceeds its remaining business interest expense by $37.50 ($45 - $7.50), B has an ATIC excess amount of $37.50. C does not have any ATIC excess. Thus, the total ATIC excess amount is $37.50 ($0 + $37.50 + $0). Because A's remaining business interest expense exceeds its ATIC amount by $22.50 ($22.50 - $0), A has an ATIC deficit of $22.50. B and C do not have any ATIC deficit. Thus, the total ATIC deficit is $22.50 ($22.50 + $0 + $0).

Table 1 to paragraph (o)(12)(vii)

	A	B	C	Total
ATIC (Final allocable ATI x 30 percent)	$0	$45	$0	N/A
Remaining BIE	$22.50	$7.50	$0	N/A
If ATIC exceeds remaining BIE, then such excess = ATIC excess	$0	$37.50	$0	$37.50
If remaining BIE exceeds ATIC, then such excess = ATIC deficit	$22.50	$0	$0	$22.50

(viii)(A) Eighth, PRS must perform the calculations and make the necessary adjustments described under paragraph (f)(2)(viii) of this section if, and only if, PRS has:

(1) An excess business interest expense greater than $0 under paragraph (f)(2)(i) of this section;

(2) A total negative allocable ATI greater than $0 under paragraph (f)(2)(vi) of this section; and

(3) A total ATIC excess amount greater than $0 under paragraph (f)(2)(vii) of this section.

(B) Because PRS does not meet all three requirements in paragraph (o)(12)(viii)(A) of this section, PRS does not perform the calculations or adjustments described in paragraph (f)(2)(viii) of this section. In sum, the correct amounts to be used in paragraphs (o)(12)(ix) and (x) of this section are as follows.

Table 1 to paragraph (o)(12)(viii)(B)

	A	B	C	Total
ATIC excess	$0	$37.50	$0	$37.50
ATIC deficit	$22.50	$0	$0	$22.50

(ix) Ninth, PRS determines each partner's final ATIC excess amount. Because B has ATIC excess, PRS must determine B's final ATIC excess amount. B's final ATIC excess amount is B's ATIC excess ($37.50), reduced, but not below $0, by the product of the total ATIC deficit ($22.50) and the ratio of B's ATIC excess to the total ATIC excess ($37.50/$37.50). Therefore, B has $15 of final ATIC excess ($37.50 — ($22.50 x 100 percent)).

Table 1 to paragraph (o)(12)(ix)

	A	B	C	Total
ATIC excess	$0	$37.50	$0	N/A
Less: (Total ATIC deficit) x (ATIC excess / Total ATIC excess)	$0	$22.50	$0	N/A
= Final ATIC excess	$0	$15	$0	$15

(x) Tenth, PRS determines each partner's final ATIC deficit amount. Because A has an ATIC deficit, PRS must determine A's final ATIC deficit amount. A's final ATIC deficit amount is A's ATIC deficit ($22.50), reduced, but not below $0, by the product of the total ATIC excess ($37.50) and the ratio of A's ATIC deficit to the total ATIC deficit ($22.50/$22.50). Therefore, A has $0 of final ATIC deficit ($22.50 — ($37.50 x 100 percent)).

Table 1 to paragraph (o)(12)(x)

	A	B	C	Total
ATIC deficit	$22.50	$0	$0	N/A
Less: (Total ATIC excess) x (ATIC deficit / Total ATIC deficit)	$37.50	$0	$0	N/A
= Final ATIC deficit	$0	$0	$0	$0

(xi) Eleventh, PRS allocates deductible business interest expense and section 163(j) excess items to the partners. Pursuant to paragraph (f)(2)(i) of this section, PRS has $50 of excess taxable income and $40 of deductible business interest expense. After grossing up each partner's final ATIC excess amounts by ten-thirds, excess taxable income is allocated dollar for dollar to partners with final ATIC excess amounts. Thus, PRS allocates its excess taxable income (ETI) $50 to B.

A partner's allocable business interest expense is deductible business interest expense to the extent it exceeds such partner's share of excess business interest expense (EBIE). Therefore, A has deductible business interest expense of $30 ($30 - $0), B has deductible business interest expense of $10 ($10 - $0), and C has deductible business interest expense of $0 ($0 - $0).

Table 1 to paragraph (o)(12)(xi)				
	A	B	C	Total
Deductible BIE	$30	$10	$0	$40
EBIE allocated	$0	$0	$0	$0
ETI allocated	$0	$50	$0	$50
EBII allocated	$0	$0	$0	$0

(13) *Example 13: Facts.* A, B, and C own all of the interests in partnership PRS. In Year 1, PRS has $100 of ATI, $0 of business interest income, and $50 of business interest expense. PRS's ATI consists of $200 of gross income and $100 of gross deductions. PRS allocates its items comprising ATI $100 to A, $100 to B, and ($100) to C. PRS allocates its business interest expense $0 to A, $25 to B, and $25 to C.

(i) First, PRS determines its limitation pursuant to § 1.163(j)-2. PRS's section 163(j) limit is 30 percent of its ATI plus its business interest income, or $30 ($100 x 30 percent). Thus, PRS has $30 of deductible business interest expense and $20 of excess business interest expense.

(ii) Second, PRS determines each partner's allocable share of section 163(j) items used in its own section 163(j) calculation.

Table 1 to paragraph (o)(13)(ii)				
	A	B	C	Total
Allocable ATI	$100	$100	($100)	$100
Allocable BII	$0	$0	$0	$0
Allocable BIE	$0	$25	$25	$50

(iii) Third, PRS compares each partner's allocable business interest income to such partner's allocable business interest expense. No partner has allocable business interest income. Consequently, each partner's allocable business interest income deficit is equal to such partner's allocable business interest expense. Thus, A's allocable business interest income deficit is $0, B's allocable business interest income deficit is $25, and C's allocable business interest income deficit is $25. The total allocable business interest income deficit is $50 ($0 + $25 + $25). No partner has allocable business interest income excess because no partner has allocable business interest income in excess of its allocable business interest expense. Thus, the total allocable business interest income excess is $0.

Table 1 to paragraph (o)(13)(iii)				
	A	B	C	Total
Allocable BII	$0	$0	$0	N/A
Allocable BIE	$0	$25	$25	N/A
If allocable BII exceeds allocable BIE, then such amount = Allocable BII excess	$0	$0	$0	$0
If allocable BIE exceeds allocable BII, then such amount = Allocable BII deficit	$0	$25	$25	$50

(iv) Fourth, PRS determines each partner's final allocable business interest income excess. Because no partner had any allocable business interest income excess, each partner has final allocable business interest income excess of $0.

(v) Fifth, PRS determines each partner's remaining business interest expense. Because no partner has any allocable business interest income excess, each partner's remaining business interest expense equals its allocable business interest income deficit. Thus, A's remaining business interest expense is $0, B's remaining business interest expense is $25, and C's remaining business interest expense is $25.

Table 1 to paragraph (o)(13)(v)				
	A	B	C	Total
Allocable BII deficit	$0	$25	$25	$50
Less: (Total allocable BII excess) x (Allocable BII deficit / Total allocable BII deficit)	$0	$0	$0	N/A
= Remaining BIE	$0	$25	$25	N/A

(vi) Sixth, PRS determines each partner's final allocable ATI. Because C's allocable ATI is comprised of $100 of items of deduction and loss and $0 of income and gain, C has negative allocable ATI of $100. C is the only partner with negative allocable ATI. Thus, the total negative allocable ATI amount is $100. Any partner with a negative allocable ATI, or an allocable ATI of $0, has a positive allocable ATI of $0. Therefore, C has a positive allocable ATI of $0. Because A's allocable ATI is comprised of $100 of items of income and gain and $0 of deduction and loss, A has positive allocable ATI of $100. Because B's allocable ATI is comprised of $100 of income and gain and $0 of deduction and loss, B has positive allocable ATI of $100. Thus, the total positive allocable ATI is $200 ($100 + $100 + $0). PRS determines A's final allocable ATI by reduc-

ing, but not below $0, A's positive allocable ATI ($100) by the product of total negative allocable ATI ($100) and the ratio of A's positive allocable ATI to the total positive allocable ATI ($100/$200). Therefore, A's positive allocable ATI is reduced by $50 ($100 x 50 percent). As a result, A's final allocable ATI is $50. PRS determines B's final allocable ATI by reducing, but not below $0, B's positive allocable ATI ($100) by the product of total negative allocable ATI ($100) and the ratio of B's positive allocable ATI to the total positive allocable ATI ($100/$200). Therefore, B's positive allocable ATI is reduced by $50 ($100 x 50 percent). As a result, B's final allocable ATI is $50. Because C has a positive allocable ATI of $0, C's final allocable ATI is $0.

Table 1 to paragraph (o)(13)(vi)				
	A	B	C	Total
Allocable ATI	$100	$100	($100)	$100
If deduction and loss items comprising allocable ATI exceed income and gain items comprising allocable ATI, then such excess amount = Negative allocable ATI	$0	$0	$100	$100
If income and gain items comprising allocable ATI equal or exceed deduction and loss items comprising allocable ATI, then such amount = Positive allocable ATI	$100	$100	$0	$200

Table 2 to paragraph (o)(13)(vi)	A	B	C	Total
Positive allocable ATI	$100	$100	$0	$200
Less: (Total negative allocable ATI) x (Positive allocable ATI / Total positive allocable ATI)	$50	$50	$0	N/A
= Final allocable ATI	$50	$50	$0	$100

(vii) Seventh, PRS compares each partner's ATI capacity (ATIC) amount to such partner's remaining business interest expense. A's ATIC amount is $15 ($50 x 30 percent), B's ATIC amount is $15 ($50 x 30 percent), and C's ATIC amount is $0 ($0 x 30 percent). Because A's ATIC amount exceeds its remaining business interest expense by $15 ($15 - $0), A has an ATIC excess of $15. B and C do not have any ATIC excess. Thus, the total ATIC excess is $15 ($15 + $0 + $0). A does not have any ATIC deficit. Because B's remaining business interest expense exceeds its ATIC amount by $10 ($25 - $15), B has an ATIC deficit of $10. Because C's remaining business interest expense exceeds its ATIC amount by $25 ($25 - $0), C has an ATIC deficit of $25. Thus, the total ATIC deficit is $35 ($0 + $10 + $25).

Table 1 to paragraph (o)(13)(vii)	A	B	C	Total
ATIC (Final allocable ATI x 30 percent)	$15	$15	$0	N/A
Remaining BIE	$0	$25	$25	N/A
If ATIC exceeds remaining BIE, then such excess = ATIC excess	$15	$0	$0	$15
If remaining BIE exceeds ATIC, then such excess = ATIC deficit	$0	$10	$25	$35

(viii)(A) Eighth, PRS must perform the calculations and make the necessary adjustments described under paragraph (f)(2)(viii) of this section if, and only if, PRS has:

(1) An excess business interest expense greater than $0 under paragraph (f)(2)(i) of this section;

(2) A total negative allocable ATI greater than $0 under paragraph (f)(2)(vi) of this section; and

(3) A total ATIC excess greater than $0 under paragraph (f)(2)(vii) of this section. Because PRS satisfies each of these three requirements, PRS must perform the calculations and make the necessary adjustments described under paragraph (f)(2)(viii)(B) and (C) or (D) of this section.

(B) PRS must determine each partner's priority amount and usable priority amount. Only partners with an ATIC deficit under paragraph (f)(2)(vii) of this section can have a priority amount greater than $0. Thus, only partners B and C can have a priority amount greater than $0. PRS determines a partner's priority amount as thirty percent of the amount by which such partner's allocable positive ATI exceeds its final allocable ATI. Therefore, A's priority amount is $0, B's priority amount is $15 (($100 - $50) x 30 percent), and C's priority amount is $0 (($0 - $0) x 30 percent). Thus, the total priority amount is $15 ($0 + $15 + $0). Next, PRS must determine each partner's usable priority amount. Each partner's usable priority amount is the lesser of such partner's priority amount or ATIC deficit. Thus, A has a usable priority amount of $0, B has a usable priority amount of $10, and C has a usable priority amount of $0. As a result, the total usable priority amount is $10 ($0 + $10 + $0). Because the total ATIC excess under paragraph (f)(2)(vii) of this section ($15) is greater than the total usable priority amount ($10), PRS must perform the adjustments described in paragraph (f)(2)(viii)(C) of this section.

Table 1 to paragraph (o)(13)(viii)(B)	A	B	C	Total
(Positive allocable ATI - Final allocable ATI)	$0	$50	$0	N/A
Multiplied by 30 percent	30 percent	30 percent	30 percent	N/A
= Priority amount	$0	$15	$0	$15

Table 2 to paragraph (o)(13)(viii)(B)	A	B	C	Total
Priority amount	$0	$15	$0	N/A
ATIC deficit	$0	$10	$25	N/A
Lesser of priority amount or ATIC deficit = Usable priority amount	$0	$10	$0	$10

(C) For purposes of paragraph (f)(2)(ix) of this section, each partner's final ATIC excess is $0. For purposes of paragraph (f)(2)(x) of this section, the following terms shall have the following meanings. Each partner's ATIC deficit is such partner's ATIC deficit as determined pursuant to paragraph (f)(2)(vii) of this section reduced by such partner's usable priority amount. Thus, A's ATIC deficit is $0 ($0 - $0), B's ATIC deficit is $0 ($10 - $10), and C's ATIC deficit is $25 ($25 - $0). The total ATIC deficit is the total ATIC deficit determined pursuant to paragraph (f)(2)(vii) ($35) reduced by the total usable priority amount ($10). Thus, the total ATIC deficit is $25 ($35 - $10). The total ATIC excess is the total ATIC excess determined pursuant to paragraph (f)(2)(vii) of this section ($15) reduced by the total usable priority amount ($10). Thus, the total ATIC excess is $5 ($15 - $5).

Table 1 to paragraph (o)(13)(viii)(C)	A	B	C	Total
ATIC deficit	$0	$10	$25	N/A
Less: Usable priority amount	$0	$10	$0	N/A
= ATIC deficit for purposes of paragraph (f)(2)(x) of this section	$0	$0	$25	$25

(D) In light of the fact that the total ATIC excess was greater than the total usable priority amount under paragraph (f)(2)(viii)(B) of this section, paragraph (f)(2)(viii)(D) of this section does not apply. In sum, the correct amounts to be used in paragraph (f)(2)(x) of this section are as follows.

Table 1 to paragraph (o)(13)(viii)(C)	A	B	C	Total
ATIC excess	$5	$0	$0	$5

Table 1 to paragraph (o)(13)(viii)(C)				
	A	B	C	Total
ATIC deficit	$0	$0	$25	$25

(ix) Ninth, PRS determines each partner's final ATIC excess amount. Pursuant to paragraph (f)(2)(viii)(C) of this section, each partner's final ATIC excess amount is $0.

(x) Tenth, PRS determines each partner's final ATIC deficit amount. Because C has an ATIC deficit, PRS must determine C's final

ATIC deficit amount. C's final ATIC deficit amount is C's ATIC deficit ($25), reduced, but not below $0, by the product of the total ATIC excess ($5) and the ratio of C's ATIC deficit to the total ATIC deficit ($25/$25). Therefore, C has $20 of final ATIC deficit ($25 — ($5 x 100 percent)).

Table 1 to paragraph (o)(13)(x)				
	A	B	C	Total
ATIC deficit	$0	$0	$25	N/A
Less: (Total ATIC excess) x (ATIC deficit / Total ATIC deficit)	$0	$0	$5	N/A
= Final ATIC deficit	$0	$0	$20	$20

(xi) Eleventh, PRS allocates deductible business interest expense and section 163(j) excess items to the partners. Pursuant to paragraph (f)(2)(i) of this section, PRS has $20 of excess business interest expense. PRS allocates the excess business interest expense dollar for dollar to the partners with final ATIC deficits. Thus, PRS allocates its excess business interest expense $20 to C. A partner's allocable

business interest expense is deductible business interest expense to the extent it exceeds such partner's share of excess business interest expense. Therefore, A has deductible business interest expense of $0 ($0 - $0), B has deductible business interest expense of $25 ($25 - $0), and C has deductible business interest expense of $5 ($25 - $20).

Table 1 to paragraph (o)(13)(xi)				
	A	B	C	Total
Deductible BIE	$0	$25	$5	$30
EBIE allocated	$0	$0	$20	$20
ETI allocated	$0	$0	$0	$0
EBII allocated	$0	$0	$0	$0

(14) *Example 14: Facts.* A, B, C, and D own all of the interests in partnership PRS. In Year 1, PRS has $200 of ATI, $0 of business interest income, and $140 of business interest expense. PRS's ATI consists of $600 of gross income and $400 of gross deductions. PRS allocates its items comprising ATI $100 to A, $100 to B, $400 to C, and ($400) to D. PRS allocates its business interest expense $0 to A, $40 to B, $60 to C, and $40 to D.

(i) First, PRS determines its limitation pursuant to §1.163(j)-2. PRS's section 163(j) limit is 30 percent of its ATI plus its business interest income, or $60 ($200 x 30 percent). Thus, PRS has $60 of deductible business interest expense and $80 of excess business interest expense.

(ii) Second, PRS determines each partner's allocable share of section 163(j) items used in its own section 163(j) calculation.

Table 1 to paragraph (o)(14)(ii)					
	A	B	C	D	Total
Allocable ATI	$100	$100	$400	($400)	$200
Allocable BII	$0	$0	$0	$0	$0
Allocable BIE	$0	$40	$60	$40	$140

(iii) Third, PRS compares each partner's allocable business interest income to such partner's allocable business interest expense. No partner has allocable business interest income. Consequently, each partner's allocable business interest income deficit is equal to such partner's allocable business interest expense. Thus, A's allocable business interest income deficit is $0, B's allocable business interest income deficit is $40, C's allocable business interest income deficit is

$60, and D's allocable business interest income deficit is $40. The total allocable business interest income deficit is $140 ($0 + $40 + $60 + $40). No partner has allocable business interest income excess because no partner has allocable business interest income in excess of its allocable business interest expense. Thus, the total allocable business interest income excess is $0.

Table 1 to paragraph (o)(14)(iii)					
	A	B	C	D	Total
Allocable BII	$0	$0	$0	$0	N/A
Allocable BIE	$0	$40	$60	$40	N/A
If allocable BII exceeds allocable BIE, then such amount = Allocable BII excess	$0	$0	$0	$0	$0
If allocable BIE exceeds allocable BII, then such amount = Allocable BII deficit	$0	$40	$60	$40	$140

(iv) Fourth, PRS determines each partner's final allocable business interest income excess. Because no partner has any allocable business interest income excess, each partner has final allocable business interest income excess of $0.

(v) Fifth, PRS determines each partner's remaining business interest expense. Because no partner has any allocable business inter-

est income excess, each partner's remaining business interest expense equals its allocable business interest income deficit. Thus, A's remaining business interest expense is $0, B's remaining business interest expense is $40, C's remaining business interest expense is $60, and D's remaining business interest expense is $40.

Table 1 to paragraph (o)(14)(v)					
	A	B	C	D	Total
Allocable BII deficit	$0	$40	$60	$40	$140
Less: (Total allocable BII excess) x (Allocable BII deficit / Total allocable BII deficit)	$0	$0	$0	$0	N/A
= Remaining BIE	$0	$40	$60	$40	N/A

(vi) Sixth, PRS determines each partner's final allocable ATI. Because D's allocable ATI is comprised of $400 of items of deduction and loss and $0 of income and gain, D has negative allocable ATI of $400. D is the only partner with negative allocable ATI. Thus, the total negative allocable ATI amount is $400. Any partner with a negative allocable ATI, or an allocable ATI of $0, has a positive allocable ATI of $0. Therefore, D has a positive allocable ATI of $0. PRS determines A's final allocable ATI by reducing, but not below $0, A's positive allocable ATI ($100) by the product of total negative allocable ATI ($400) and the ratio of A's positive allocable ATI to the total positive allocable ATI ($100/$600). Therefore, A's positive allocable ATI is reduced by $66.67 ($400 x 16.67 percent). As a result, A's final allocable ATI is $33.33. PRS determines B's final allocable ATI by reducing, but not below $0, B's positive allocable ATI ($100) by the product of total negative allocable ATI ($400) and the ratio of B's positive allocable ATI to the total positive allocable ATI ($100/$600). Therefore, B's positive allocable ATI is reduced by $66.67 ($400 x 16.67 percent). As a result, B's final allocable ATI is $33.33. PRS determines C's final allocable ATI by reducing, but not below $0, C's positive allocable ATI ($400) by the product of total negative allocable ATI ($400) and the ratio of C's positive allocable ATI to the total positive allocable ATI ($400/$600). Therefore, C's positive allocable ATI is reduced by $266.67 ($400 x 66.67 percent). As a result, C's final allocable ATI is $133.33. Because D has a positive allocable ATI of $0, D's final allocable ATI is $0.

Table 1 to paragraph (o)(14)(vi)

	A	B	C	D	Total
Allocable ATI	$100	$100	$400	($400)	$200
If deduction and loss items comprising allocable ATI exceed income and gain items comprising allocable ATI, then such excess amount = Negative allocable ATI	$0	$0	$0	$400	$400
If income and gain items comprising allocable ATI equal or exceed deduction and loss items comprising allocable ATI, then such amount = Positive allocable ATI	$100	$100	$400	$0	$600

Table 2 to paragraph (o)(14)(vi)

	A	B	C	D	Total
Positive allocable ATI	$100	$100	$400	$0	$600
Less: (Total negative allocable ATI) x (Positive allocable ATI / Total positive allocable ATI)	$66.67	$66.67	$266.67	$0	N/A
= Final allocable ATI	$33.33	$33.33	$133.33	$0	$200

(vii) Seventh, PRS compares each partner's ATI capacity (ATIC) amount to such partner's remaining business interest expense. A's ATIC amount is $10 ($33.33 x 30 percent), B's ATIC amount is $10 ($33.33 x 30 percent), C's ATIC amount is $40 ($133.33 x 30 percent), and D's ATIC amount is $0 ($0 x 30 percent). Because A's ATIC amount exceeds its remaining business interest expense by $10 ($10 - $0), A has an ATIC excess of $10. B, C, and D do not have any ATIC excess. Thus, the total ATIC excess is $10 ($10 + $0 + $0 + $0). A does not have any ATIC deficit. Because B's remaining business interest expense exceeds its ATIC amount by $30 ($40 - $10), B has an ATIC deficit of $30. Because C's remaining business interest expense exceeds its ATIC amount by $20 ($60 - $40), C has an ATIC deficit of $20. Because D's remaining business interest expense exceeds its ATIC amount by $40 ($40 - $0), D has an ATIC deficit of $40. Thus, the total ATIC deficit is $90 ($0 + $30 + $20 + $40).

Table 1 to paragraph (o)(14)(vii)

	A	B	C	D	Total
ATIC (Final allocable ATI x 30 percent)	$10	$10	$40	$0	N/A
Remaining BIE	$0	$40	$60	$40	N/A
If ATIC exceeds remaining BIE, then such excess = ATIC excess	$10	$0	$0	$0	$10
If remaining BIE exceeds ATIC, then such excess = ATIC deficit	$0	$30	$20	$40	$90

(viii)(A) Eighth, PRS must perform the calculations and make the necessary adjustments described under paragraph (f)(2)(viii) of this section if, and only if, PRS has (1) an excess business interest expense greater than $0 under paragraph (f)(2)(i) of this section, (2) a total negative allocable ATI greater than $0 under paragraph (f)(2)(vi) of this section, and (3) a total ATIC excess amount greater than $0 under paragraph (f)(2)(vii) of this section. Because PRS satisfies each of these three requirements, PRS must perform the calculations and make the necessary adjustments described under paragraphs (f)(2)(viii)(B) and (C) or paragraph (f)(2)(viii)(D) of this section.

(B) PRS must determine each partner's priority amount and usable priority amount. Only partners with an ATIC deficit under paragraph (f)(2)(vii) of this section can have a priority amount greater than $0. Thus, only partners B, C, and D can have a priority amount greater than $0. PRS determines a partner's priority amount as thirty percent of the amount by which such partner's allocable positive ATI exceeds its final allocable ATI. Therefore, B's priority amount is $20 (($100 - $33.33) x 30 percent), C's priority amount is $80 (($400 - $133.33) x 30 percent), and D's priority amount is $0 (($0 - $0) x 30 percent). Thus, the total priority amount is $100 ($0 + $20 + $80 + $0). Next, PRS must determine each partner's usable priority amount. Each partner's usable priority amount is the lesser of such partner's priority amount or ATIC deficit. Thus, A has a usable priority amount of $0, B has a usable priority amount of $20, C has a usable priority amount of $20, and D has a usable priority amount of $0. As a result, the total usable priority amount is $40 ($0 + $20 + $20 + $0). Because the total usable priority amount ($40) is greater than the total ATIC excess under paragraph (f)(2)(vii) ($10), PRS must perform the adjustments described in paragraph (f)(2)(viii)(D) of this section.

Table 1 to paragraph (o)(14)(viii)(B)

	A	B	C	D	Total
(Positive allocable ATI - Final allocable ATI)	$0	$66.67	$266.67	$0	N/A
Multiplied by 30 percent	30 percent	30 percent	30 percent	30 percent	N/A
= Priority amount	$0	$20	$80	$0	$100

Table 2 to paragraph (o)(14)(viii)(B)

	A	B	C	D	Total
Priority amount	$0	$20	$80	$0	N/A
ATIC deficit	$0	$30	$20	$40	N/A

Table 2 to paragraph (o)(14)(viii)(B)					
	A	B	C	D	Total
Lesser of priority amount or ATIC deficit = Usable priority amount	$0	$20	$20	$0	$40

(C) In light of the fact that the total usable priority amount is greater than the total ATIC excess under paragraph (f)(2)(viii)(B) of this section, paragraph (f)(2)(viii)(C) of this section does not apply.

(D)(1) Because B and C are the only partners with priority amounts greater than $0, B and C are priority partners, while A and D are non-priority partners. For purposes of paragraph (f)(2)(ix) of this section, each partner's final ATIC excess amount is $0. For purposes of paragraph (f)(2)(x) of this section, each non-priority partner's final ATIC deficit amount is such partner's ATIC deficit determined pursuant to paragraph (f)(2)(vii) of this section. Therefore, A has a final ATIC deficit of $0 and D has a final ATIC deficit of $40. Additionally, for purposes of paragraph (f)(2)(x) of this section, PRS must determine each priority partner's step eight excess share. A priority partner's step eight excess share is the product of the total

ATIC excess and the ratio of the partner's priority amount to the total priority amount. Thus, B's step eight excess share is $2 ($10 x ($20/$100)) and C's step eight excess share is $8 ($10 x ($80/$100)). To the extent a priority partner's step eight excess share exceeds its ATIC deficit, the excess shall be the partner's ATIC excess for purposes of paragraph (f)(2)(x) of this section. Thus, B and C each have an ATIC excess of $0, resulting in a total ATIC excess is $0. To the extent a priority partner's ATIC deficit exceeds its step eight excess share, the excess shall be the partner's ATIC deficit for purposes of paragraph (f)(2)(x) of this section. Because B's ATIC deficit ($30) exceeds its step eight excess share ($2), B's ATIC deficit for purposes of paragraph (f)(2)(x) of this section is $28 ($30 -$2). Because C's ATIC deficit ($20) exceeds its step eight excess share ($8), C's ATIC deficit for purposes of paragraph (f)(2)(x) of this section is $12 ($20 - $8). Thus, the total ATIC deficit is $40 ($28 + $12).

Table 1 to paragraph (o)(14)(viii)(D)(1)					
	A	B	C	D	Total
Non-priority partners ATIC deficit in paragraph (f)(2)(vii) = Final ATIC deficit for purposes of paragraph (f)(2)(x) of this section	$0	N/A	N/A	$40	N/A

Table 2 to paragraph (o)(14)(viii)(D)(1)					
	A	B	C	D	Total
Priority partners step eight excess share = (Total ATIC excess) x (Priority / Total priority)	N/A	$2	$8	N/A	N/A
ATIC deficit	N/A	$30	$20	N/A	N/A
If step eight excess share exceeds ATIC deficit, then such excess = ATIC excess for purposes of paragraph (f)(2)(x) of this section	N/A	$0	$0	N/A	$0
If ATIC deficit exceeds step eight excess share, then such excess = ATIC deficit for purposes of paragraph (f)(2)(x) of this section	N/A	$28	$12	N/A	$40

(2) In sum, the correct amounts to be used in paragraph (f)(2)(x) of this section are as follows:

Table 1 to paragraph (o)(14)(viii)(D)(2)					
	A	B	C	D	Total
ATIC excess	$0	$0	$0	$0	$0
ATIC deficit	$0	$28	$12	$0	$40
Non-priority partner final ATIC deficit	$0	$0	$0	$40	N/A

(ix) Ninth, PRS determines each partner's final ATIC excess amount. Pursuant to paragraph (f)(2)(viii)(D) of this section, each priority and non-priority partner's final ATIC excess amount is $0.

(x) Tenth, PRS determines each partner's final ATIC deficit amount. Because B has an ATIC deficit, PRS must determine B's final ATIC deficit amount. B's final ATIC deficit amount is B's ATIC deficit ($28), reduced, but not below $0, by the product of the total ATIC excess ($0) and the ratio of B's ATIC deficit to the total ATIC deficit

($28/$40). Therefore, B has $28 of final ATIC deficit ($28 — ($0 x 70 percent)). Because C has an ATIC deficit, PRS must determine C's final ATIC deficit amount. C's final ATIC deficit amount is C's ATIC deficit ($12), reduced, but not below $0, by the product of the total ATIC excess ($0) and the ratio of C's ATIC deficit to the total ATIC deficit ($12/$40). Therefore, C has $12 of final ATIC deficit ($12 — ($0 x 30 percent)). Pursuant to paragraph (f)(2)(viii)(D) of this section, D's final ATIC deficit amount is $40.

Table 2 to paragraph (o)(14)(x)					
	A	B	C	D	Total
ATIC deficit	N/A	$28	$12	N/A	N/A
Less: (Total ATIC excess) x (ATIC deficit / Total ATIC deficit)	N/A	$0	$0	N/A	N/A
= Final ATIC deficit	$0	$28	$12	$40	$80

(xi) Eleventh, PRS allocates deductible business interest expense and section 163(j) excess items to the partners. Pursuant to paragraph (f)(2)(i) of this section, PRS has $80 of excess business interest expense. PRS allocates the excess business interest expense dollar for dollar to the partners with final ATIC deficits. Thus, PRS allocates its excess business interest expense $28 to B, $12 to C, and $40 to D. A partner's allocable business interest expense is deductible business

interest expense to the extent it exceeds such partner's share of excess business interest expense. Therefore, A has deductible business interest expense of $0 ($0 - $0), B has deductible business interest expense of $12 ($40 - $28), C has deductible business interest expense of $48 ($60 - $12), and D has deductible business interest expense of $0 ($40 - $40).

Table 1 to paragraph (o)(14)(xi)					
	A	B	C	D	Total
Deductible BIE	$0	$12	$48	$0	$60
EBIE allocated	$0	$28	$12	$40	$80

Table 1 to paragraph (o)(14)(xi)

	A	B	C	D	Total
ETI allocated	$0	$0	$0	$0	$0
EBII allocated	$0	$0	$0	$0	$0

(15) *Example 15: Facts.* A, B, C, and D own all of the interests in partnership PRS. In Year 1, PRS has $200 of ATI, $0 of business interest income, and $150 of business interest expense. PRS's ATI consists of $500 of gross income and $300 of gross deductions. PRS allocates its items comprising ATI $50 to A, $50 to B, $400 to C, and ($300) to D. PRS allocates its business interest expense $0 to A, $50 to B, $50 to C, and $50 to D.

(i) First, PRS determines its limitation pursuant to §1.163(j)-2. PRS's section 163(j) limit is 30 percent of its ATI plus its business interest income, or $60 ($200 x 30 percent). Thus, PRS has $60 of deductible business interest expense, and $90 of excess business interest expense.

(ii) Second, PRS determines each partner's allocable share of section 163(j) items used in its own section 163(j) calculation.

Table 1 to paragraph (o)(15)(ii)

	A	B	C	D	Total
Allocable ATI	$50	$50	$400	($300)	$200
Allocable BII	$0	$0	$0	$0	$0
Allocable BIE	$0	$50	$50	$50	$150

(iii) Third, PRS compares each partner's allocable business interest income to such partner's allocable business interest expense. No partner has allocable business interest income. Consequently, each partner's allocable business interest income deficit is equal to such partner's allocable business interest expense. Thus, A's allocable business interest income deficit is $0, B's allocable business interest income deficit is $50, C's allocable business interest income deficit is $50, and D's allocable business interest income deficit is $50. The total allocable business interest income deficit is $150 ($0 + $50 + $50 + $50). No partner has allocable business interest income excess because no partner has allocable business interest income in excess of its allocable business interest expense. Thus, the total allocable business interest income excess is $0.

Table 1 to paragraph (o)(15)(iii)

	A	B	C	D	Total
Allocable BII	$0	$0	$0	$0	N/A
Allocable BIE	$0	$50	$50	$50	N/A
If allocable BII exceeds allocable BIE, then such amount = Allocable BII excess	$0	$0	$0	$0	$0
If allocable BIE exceeds allocable BII, then such amount = Allocable BII deficit	$0	$50	$50	$50	$150

(iv) Fourth, PRS determines each partner's final allocable business interest income excess. Because no partner has any allocable business interest income excess, each partner has final allocable business interest income excess of $0.

(v) Fifth, PRS determines each partner's remaining business interest expense. Because no partner has any allocable business interest income excess, each partner's remaining business interest expense equals its allocable business interest income deficit. Thus, A's remaining business interest expense is $0, B's remaining business interest expense is $50, C's remaining business interest expense is $50, and D's remaining business interest expense is $50.

Table 1 to paragraph (o)(15)(v)

	A	B	C	D	Total
Allocable BII deficit	$0	$50	$50	$50	$150
Less: (Total allocable BII excess) x (Allocable BII deficit / Total allocable BII deficit)	$0	$0	$0	$0	N/A
= Remaining BIE	$0	$50	$50	$50	N/A

(vi) Sixth, PRS determines each partner's final allocable ATI. Because D's allocable ATI is comprised of $300 of items of deduction and loss and $0 of income and gain, D has negative allocable ATI of $300. D is the only partner with negative allocable ATI. Thus, the total negative allocable ATI amount is $300. Any partner with a negative allocable ATI, or an allocable ATI of $0, has a positive allocable ATI of $0. Therefore, D has a positive allocable ATI of $0. PRS determines A's final allocable ATI by reducing, but not below $0, A's positive allocable ATI ($50) by the product of total negative allocable ATI ($300) and the ratio of A's positive allocable ATI to the total positive allocable ATI ($50/$500). Therefore, A's positive allocable ATI is reduced by $30 ($300 x 10 percent). As a result, A's final allocable ATI is $20. PRS determines B's final allocable ATI by reduc-ing, but not below $0, B's positive allocable ATI ($50) by the product of total negative allocable ATI ($300) and the ratio of B's positive allocable ATI to the total positive allocable ATI ($50/$500). Therefore, B's positive allocable ATI is reduced by $30 ($300 x 10 percent). As a result, B's final allocable ATI is $20. PRS determines C's final allocable ATI by reducing, but not below $0, C's positive allocable ATI ($400) by the product of total negative allocable ATI ($300) and the ratio of C's positive allocable ATI to the total positive allocable ATI ($400/$500). Therefore, C's positive allocable ATI is reduced by $240 ($300 x 80 percent). As a result, C's final allocable ATI is $160. Because D has a positive allocable ATI of $0, D's final allocable ATI is $0.

Table 1 to paragraph (o)(15)(vi)

	A	B	C	D	Total
Allocable ATI	$50	$50	$400	($300)	$200
If deduction and loss items comprising allocable ATI exceed income and gain items comprising allocable ATI, then such excess amount = Negative allocable ATI	$0	$0	$0	$300	$300
If income and gain items comprising allocable ATI equal or exceed deduction and loss items comprising allocable ATI, then such amount = Positive allocable ATI	$50	$50	$400	$0	$500

Table 2 to paragraph (o)(15)(vi)	A	B	C	D	Total
Positive allocable ATI	$50	$50	$400	$0	$500
Less: (Total negative allocable ATI) x (Positive allocable ATI / Total positive allocable ATI)	$30	$30	$240	$0	N/A
= Final allocable ATI	$20	$20	$160	$0	$200

(vii) Seventh, PRS compares each partner's ATI capacity (ATIC) amount to such partner's remaining business interest expense. A's ATIC amount is $6 ($20 x 30 percent), B's ATIC amount is $6 ($20 x 30 percent), C's ATIC amount is $48 ($160 x 30 percent), and D's ATIC amount is $0 ($0 x 30 percent). Because A's ATIC amount exceeds its remaining business interest expense by $6 ($6 - $0), A has an ATIC excess of $6. B, C, and D do not have any ATIC excess. Thus, the total ATIC excess amount is $6 ($6 + $0 + $0 + $0). A does not have any

ATIC deficit. Because B's remaining business interest expense exceeds its ATIC amount by $44 ($50 - $6), B has an ATIC deficit of $44. Because C's remaining business interest expense exceeds its ATIC amount by $2 ($50 - $48), C has an ATIC deficit of $2. Because D's remaining business interest expense exceeds its ATIC amount by $50 ($50 - $0), D has an ATIC deficit of $50. Thus, the total ATIC deficit is $96 ($0 + $44 + $2 + $50).

Table 1 to paragraph (o)(15)(vii)	A	B	C	D	Total
ATIC (Final allocable ATI x 30 percent)	$6	$6	$48	$0	N/A
Remaining BIE	$0	$50	$50	$50	N/A
If ATIC exceeds remaining BIE, then such excess = ATIC excess	$6	$0	$0	$0	$6
If remaining BIE exceeds ATIC, then such excess = ATIC deficit	$0	$44	$2	$50	$96

(viii)(A) Eighth, PRS must perform the calculations and make the necessary adjustments described under paragraph (f)(2)(viii) of this section if, and only if, PRS has:

(1) An excess business interest expense greater than $0 under paragraph (f)(2)(i) of this section;

(2) A total negative allocable ATI greater than $0 under paragraph (f)(2)(vi) of this section; and

(3) A total ATIC excess amount greater than $0 under paragraph (f)(2)(vii) of this section. Because PRS satisfies each of these three requirements, PRS must perform the calculations and make the necessary adjustments described under paragraph (f)(2)(viii) of this section.

(B) PRS must determine each partner's priority amount and usable priority amount. Only partners with an ATIC deficit under paragraph (f)(2)(vii) of this section of this section can have a priority

amount greater than $0. Thus, only partners B, C, and D can have a priority amount greater than $0. PRS determines a partner's priority amount as thirty percent of the amount by which such partner's allocable positive ATI exceeds its final allocable ATI. Therefore, B's priority amount is $9 (($50 - $20) x 30 percent), C's priority amount is $72 (($400 - $160) x 30 percent), and D's priority amount is $0 (($0 - $0) x 30 percent). Thus, the total priority amount is $81 ($0 + $9 + $72 + $0). Next, PRS must determine each partner's usable priority amount. Each partner's usable priority amount is the lesser of such partner's priority amount or ATIC deficit. Thus, B has a usable priority amount of $9, C has a usable priority amount of $2, and D has a usable priority amount of $0. As a result, the total usable priority amount is $11 ($0 + $9 + $2 + $0). Because the total usable priority amount ($11) is greater than the total ATIC excess ($6) under paragraph (f)(2)(vii) of this section, PRS must perform the adjustments described in paragraph (f)(2)(viii)(D) of this section.

Table 1 to paragraph (o)(15)(viii)(B)	A	B	C	D	Total
(Positive allocable ATI - Final allocable ATI)	$0	$30	$240	$0	N/A
Multiplied by 30 percent	30 percent	30 percent	30 percent	30 percent	N/A
= Priority amount	$0	$9	$72	$0	$81

Table 2 to paragraph (o)(15)(viii)(B)	A	B	C	D	Total
Priority amount	$0	$9	$72	$0	N/A
ATIC deficit	$0	$44	$2	$50	N/A
Lesser of priority amount or ATIC deficit = Usable priority amount	$0	$9	$2	$0	$11

(C) In light of the fact that the total usable priority amount is greater than the total ATIC excess under paragraph (f)(2)(viii)(B) of this section, paragraph (f)(2)(viii)(C) of this section does not apply.

(D)(1) Because B and C are the only partners with priority amounts greater than $0, B and C are priority partners, while A and D are non-priority partners. For purposes of paragraph (f)(2)(ix) of this section, each partner's final ATIC excess amount is $0. For purposes of paragraph (f)(2)(x) of this section, each non-priority partner's final ATIC deficit amount is such partner's ATIC deficit determined pursuant to paragraph (f)(2)(vii) of this section. Therefore, A has a final ATIC deficit of $0 and D has a final ATIC deficit of $50. Additionally, for purposes of paragraph (f)(2)(x) of this section, PRS must determine each priority partner's step eight excess share. A priority partner's step eight excess share is the product of the total ATIC excess and the ratio of the partner's priority amount to the total priority amount. Thus, B's step eight excess share is $0.67 ($6 x

($9/$81)) and C's step eight excess share is $5.33 ($6 x ($72/$81)). To the extent a priority partner's step eight excess share exceeds its ATIC deficit, the excess shall be the partner's ATIC excess for purposes of paragraph (f)(2)(x) of this section. B's step eight excess share does not exceed its ATIC deficit. Because C's step eight excess share ($5.33) exceeds its ATIC deficit ($2), C's ATIC excess for purposes of paragraph (f)(2)(x) of this section is $3.33 ($5.33 - $2). Thus, the total ATIC excess for purposes of paragraph (f)(2)(x) of this section is $3.33 ($0 + $3.33). To the extent a priority partner's ATIC deficit exceeds its step eight excess share, the excess shall be the partner's ATIC deficit for purposes of paragraph (f)(2)(x) of this section. Because B's ATIC deficit ($44) exceeds its step eight excess share ($0.67), B's ATIC deficit for purposes of paragraph (f)(2)(x) of this section is $43.33 ($44 - $0.67). C's ATIC deficit does not exceed its step eight excess share. Thus, the total ATIC deficit for purposes of paragraph (f)(2)(x) of this section is $43.33 ($43.33 + $0).

Table 1 to paragraph (o)(15)(viii)(D)(1)	A	B	C	D	Total
Non-priority partners ATIC deficit in paragraph (f)(2)(vii) = Final ATIC deficit for purposes of paragraph (f)(2)(x) of this section	$0	N/A	N/A	$50	N/A

Table 2 to paragraph (o)(15)(viii)(D)(1)

	A	B	C	D	Total
Priority partners step eight excess share = (Total ATIC excess) x (Priority / Total priority)	N/A	$0.67	$5.33	N/A	N/A
ATIC deficit	N/A	$44	$2	N/A	N/A
If step eight excess share exceeds ATIC deficit, then such excess = ATIC excess for purposes of paragraph (f)(2)(x) of this section	N/A	$0	$3.33	N/A	$3.33
If ATIC deficit exceeds step eight excess share, then such excess = ATIC deficit for purposes of paragraph (f)(2)(x) of this section	N/A	$43.33	$0	N/A	$43.33

(2) In sum, the correct amounts to be used in paragraph (f)(2)(x) of this section are as follows.

Table 1 to paragraph (o)(15)(viii)(D)(2)

	A	B	C	D	Total
ATIC excess	$0	$0	$3.33	$0	$3.33
ATIC deficit	$0	$43.33	$0	$0	$43.33
Non-priority partner final ATIC deficit	$0	$0	$0	$50	N/A

(ix) Ninth, PRS determines each partner's final ATIC excess amount. Pursuant to paragraph (f)(2)(viii)(D) of this section, each priority and non-priority partner's final ATIC excess amount is $0.

(x) Tenth, PRS determines each partner's final ATIC deficit amount. Because B has an ATIC deficit, PRS must determine B's final ATIC deficit amount. B's final ATIC deficit amount is B's ATIC deficit ($43.33), reduced, but not below $0, by the product of the total ATIC excess ($3.33) and the ratio of B's ATIC deficit to the total ATIC deficit ($43.33/$43.33). Therefore, B has $40 of final ATIC deficit ($43.33 — ($3.33 x 100 percent)). Pursuant to paragraph (f)(2)(viii)(D) of this section, D's final ATIC deficit amount is $40.

Table 1 to paragraph (o)(15)(x)

	A	B	C	D	Total
ATIC deficit	$0	$43.33	$0	N/A	N/A
Less: (Total ATIC excess) x (ATIC deficit / Total ATIC deficit)	$0	$3.33	$0	N/A	N/A
= Final ATIC deficit	$0	$40	$0	$50	$90

(xi) Eleventh, PRS allocates deductible business interest expense and section 163(j) excess items to the partners. Pursuant to paragraph (f)(2)(i) of this section, PRS has $90 of excess business interest expense. PRS allocates the excess business interest expense dollar for dollar to the partners with final ATIC deficits. Thus, PRS allocates its excess business interest expense $40 to B and $50 to D. A partner's allocable business interest expense is deductible business interest expense to the extent it exceeds such partner's share of excess business interest expense. Therefore, A has deductible business interest expense of $0 ($0 - $0), B has deductible business interest expense of $10 ($50 - $40), C has deductible business interest expense of $50 ($50 - $0), and D has deductible business interest expense of $0 ($50 - $50).

Table 1 to paragraph (o)(15)(xi)

	A	B	C	D	Total
Deductible BIE	$0	$10	$50	$0	$60
EBIE allocated	$0	$40	$0	$50	$90
ETI allocated	$0	$0	$0	$0	$0
EBII allocated	$0	$0	$0	$0	$0

(16) *Example 16*—(i) *Facts.* A and B are equal shareholders in X, a subchapter S corporation. In Year 1, X has $100 of ATI and $40 of business interest expense. A has $100 of ATI and $20 of business interest expense from its sole proprietorship. B has $0 of ATI and $20 of business interest expense from its sole proprietorship.

(ii) *S corporation-level.* In Year 1, X's section 163(j) limit is 30 percent of its ATI, or $30 ($100 x 30 percent). Thus, X has $30 of deductible business interest expense and $10 of disallowed business interest expense. Such $30 of deductible business interest expense is includable in X's non-separately stated income or loss, and is not subject to further limitation under section 163(j). X carries forward the $10 of disallowed business interest expense to Year 2 as a disallowed business interest expense carryforward under §1.163(j)-2(c). X may not currently deduct all $40 of its business interest expense in Year 1. X only reduces its accumulated adjustments account in Year 1 by the $30 of deductible business interest expense in Year 1 under §1.163(j)-6(l)(7).

(iii) *Shareholder allocations.* A and B are each allocated $35 of nonseparately stated taxable income ($50 items of income or gain, less $15 of deductible business interest expense) from X. A and B do not reduce their basis in X by the $10 of disallowed business interest expense.

(iv) *Shareholder-level computations.* A, in computing its limit under section 163(j), has $100 of ATI and $20 of business interest expense from its sole proprietorship. A's section 163(j) limit is $30 ($100 x 30 percent). Thus, A's $20 of business interest expense is deductible business interest expense. B, in computing its limit under section 163(j), has $20 of business interest expense from its sole proprietorship. B's section 163(j) limit is $0 ($0 x 30 percent). Thus, B's $20 of business interest expense is not allowed as a deduction and is treated as business interest expense paid or accrued by B in Year 2.

(17) *Example 17*—(i) *Facts.* The facts are the same as in *Example 16* in paragraph (o)(16) of this section. In Year 2, X has $233.33 of ATI, $0 of business interest income, and $30 of business interest expense. A has $100 of ATI and $20 of business interest expense from its sole proprietorship. B has $0 of ATI and $20 of business interest expense from its sole proprietorship.

(ii) *S corporation-level.* In Year 2, X's section 163(j) limit is 30 percent of its ATI plus its business interest income, or $70 ($233.33 x 30 percent). Because X's section 163(j) limit exceeds X's $40 of business interest expense ($30 from Year 2, plus the $10 disallowed business interest expense carryforwards from Year 1), X may deduct all $40 of business interest expense in Year 2. Such $40 of deductible business interest expense is includable in X's non-separately stated income or loss, and is not subject to further limitation under section 163(j). Pursuant to §1.163(j)-6(l)(7), X must reduce its accumulated adjustments account by $40. Additionally, X has $100 of excess taxable income under §1.163(j)-1(b)(15).

(iii) *Shareholder allocations.* A and B are each allocated $96.67 of nonseparately stated taxable income ($116.67 items of income or gain, less $20 of deductible business interest expense) from X. Additionally, A and B are each allocated $50 of excess taxable income under §1.163(j)-6(l)(4). As a result, A and B each increase their ATI by $50.

(iv) *Shareholder-level computations.* A, in computing its limit under section 163(j), has $150 of ATI ($100 from its sole proprietorship, plus $50 excess taxable income) and $20 of business interest expense (from its sole proprietorship). A's section 163(j) limit is $45 ($150 x 30 percent). Thus, A's $20 of business interest expense is deductible business interest expense. B, in computing its limit under section 163(j), has $50 of ATI ($0 from its sole proprietorship, plus $50 excess taxable income) and $40 of business interest expense ($20 from its sole proprietorship, plus $20 disallowed business interest expense from its sole proprietorship in Year 1). B's section 163(j) limit is $15 ($50 × 30 percent). Thus, $15 of B's business interest expense is deductible business interest expense. The $25 of B's business interest expense not allowed as a deduction ($40 business interest expense, less $15 section 163(j) limit) is treated as business interest expense paid or accrued by B in Year 3.

(p) *Applicability date.*—This section applies to taxable years ending after the date the Treasury decision adopting these regulations as final regulations is published in the **Federal Register**. However, taxpayers and their related parties, within the meaning of sections 267(b) and 707(b)(1), may apply the rules of this section to a taxable year beginning after December 31, 2017, so long as the taxpayers and their related parties consistently apply the rules of the section 163(j) regulations, and if applicable, §§ 1.263A-9, 1.381(c)(20)-1, 1.382-6, 1.383-1, 1.469-9, 1.882-5, 1.1502-13, 1.1502-21, 1.1502-36, 1.1502-79, 1.1502-91 through 1.1502-99 (to the extent they effectuate the rules of §§ 1.382-6 and 1.383-1), and 1.1504-4 to those taxable years. [Reg. § 1.163(j)-6.]

§ 1.163(j)-7. Application of the business interest deduction limitation to foreign corporations and United States shareholders.—
(a) *Overview.*—This section provides rules for the application of section 163(j) to foreign corporations with shareholders that are United States persons. Paragraph (b) of this section provides rules regarding the application of section 163(j) to certain controlled foreign corporations. Paragraph (c) of this section provides rules concerning the computation of adjusted taxable income (ATI) of certain controlled foreign corporations. Paragraph (d) of this section provides rules concerning the computation of ATI of a United States shareholder of certain controlled foreign corporations (CFC). Paragraph (e) of this section provides a rule regarding the effect of section 163(j) on the earnings and profits of foreign corporations. Paragraph (f) of this section provides definitions that apply for purposes of this section. Paragraph (g) of this section provides examples illustrating the application of this section. Paragraph (h) of this section provides dates of applicability.

(b) *Application of section 163(j) to an applicable CFC and certain partnerships.*—(1) *Scope.*—This paragraph (b) provides rules regarding the application of section 163(j) to an applicable CFC and certain partnerships. Paragraph (b)(2) of this section describes the general application of section 163(j) to an applicable CFC and certain partnerships in which an applicable CFC is a partner. Paragraph (b)(3) of this section provides an election to use an alternative method for computing the deduction for business interest expense of a member of a CFC group. Paragraph (b)(4) of this section treats certain partnerships as members of a CFC group for purposes of this paragraph (b). Paragraph (b)(5) of this section provides the rules regarding an election to apply paragraph (b)(3) of this section.

(2) *General application of section 163(j) to an applicable CFC and a partnership with at least one partner that is an applicable CFC.*—Except as otherwise provided in this paragraph (b) or in the section 163(j) regulations, section 163(j) and the section 163(j) regulations apply to determine the deductibility of an applicable CFC's business interest expense for purposes of computing its taxable income in the same manner as those provisions apply to determine the deductibility of a domestic C corporation's business interest expense for purposes of computing its taxable income. Furthermore, if an applicable CFC is a partner in a partnership, except as otherwise provided in this paragraph (b) or in the section 163(j) regulations, section 163(j) and the section 163(j) regulations apply to the partnership in the same manner as those provisions would apply if the applicable CFC were a domestic C corporation. If an applicable CFC has income that is, or is treated as, effectively connected with the conduct of a trade or business in the United States or if a partnership is engaged in a trade or business conducted in the United States, see also §§ 1.163(j)-8(d) and 1.882-5 for additional rules concerning the deduction for interest.

(3) *Alternative approach for computing the deduction for business interest expense.*—If a CFC group election is properly made and in effect with respect to a specified taxable year of a CFC group member of a CFC group, then—

(i) The portion of the CFC group member's business interest expense that is subject to the general rule under § 1.163(j)-2(b) is the amount equal to the CFC group member's allocable share of the CFC group's applicable net business interest expense, or, in the case in which the CFC group member is also a member of a financial services subgroup, the allocable share of the applicable subgroup net business interest expense; and

(ii) The limitation provided in § 1.163(j)-2(b) is applied without regard to § 1.163(j)-2(b)(1) and (3).

(4) *Treatment of certain partnerships as a CFC group member.*—(i) *General rule.*—If one or more CFC group members of the same CFC group, in the aggregate, own more than 80 percent of the interests in the capital or profits in a partnership, then, except as provided in paragraph (b)(4)(ii) of this section, the partnership is treated as a CFC group member. If there is a financial services subgroup with respect to the CFC group, this paragraph (b)(4) will apply only if all of the CFC group members described in the preceding sentence are financial services subgroup members or none of them are financial services subgroup members. If a partnership is treated as a CFC group member, then an interest in the partnership is treated as stock for purposes of applying this section.

(ii) *Exception for certain partnerships engaged in a United States trade or business.*—Notwithstanding paragraph (b)(4)(i) of this section, a partnership is not treated as a CFC group member if the partnership is engaged in a trade or business in the United States, directly or indirectly through another passthrough entity, and one or more partners has income that is effectively connected with the conduct of a trade or business in the United States, including any income that is treated as effectively connected income under an applicable provision of the Code or regulations, and at least one of the partners is not exempt from U.S. tax by reason of a U.S. income tax treaty. Notwithstanding the preceding sentence, a partnership that, without regard to this paragraph (b)(4)(ii), would be treated as a CFC group member under paragraph (b)(4)(i) of this section, is treated as a CFC group member solely for purposes of determining if another entity is a CFC group member with respect to the CFC group.

(5) *CFC group election.*—(i) *Manner of making a CFC group election.*—Subject to paragraph (b)(5)(ii) of this section, a CFC group election is made by applying paragraph (b)(3) of this section for purposes of computing the amount of a CFC group member's deduction for business interest expense. Except as otherwise provided in publications, forms, instructions, or other guidance, a separate statement or form evidencing the election need not be filed.

(ii) *Consistency requirement.*—An election under paragraph (b)(5)(i) of this section is not effective unless all CFC group members of the CFC group make the election. If an entity becomes a CFC group member of a CFC group for which a CFC group election is in effect, the entity must make the CFC group election.

(iii) *Duration of a CFC group election.*—A CFC group election is irrevocable. If an entity ceases to be a CFC group member of a CFC group for which a CFC group election is in effect, the election terminates solely with respect to such entity. If a CFC group ceases to exist, a CFC group election terminates with respect to all CFC group members of the CFC group.

(c) *Rules concerning the computation of adjusted taxable income of an applicable CFC and certain CFC group members.*—(1) *Computation of taxable income.*—For purposes of computing taxable income of an applicable CFC for a taxable year, the applicable CFC's gross income and allowable deductions are determined under the principles of § 1.952-2 or the rules of section 882 for determining taxable income that is effectively connected with the conduct of a trade or business in the United States, as applicable.

(2) *Treatment of certain dividends.*—For purposes of computing the ATI of an applicable CFC for a taxable year, any dividend included in gross income that is received from a related person, within the meaning of section 954(d)(3), with respect to the distributee is subtracted from taxable income.

(3) *Treatment of CFC excess taxable income.*—(i) *In general.*—If a CFC group election is in effect for a specified taxable year of a CFC group member and if the CFC group member (*upper-tier member*) directly owns stock in one or more other CFC group members (*lower-*

tier member), then, for purposes of computing ATI of the upper-tier member for the specified taxable year, there is added to taxable income the sum of the products of the following amounts with respect to each lower-tier member—

(A) The CFC excess taxable income (if any) of the lower-tier member for the lower-tier member's specified taxable year; and

(B) The percentage (by value) of the stock of the lower-tier member that is directly owned by the upper-tier member on the last day of the lower-tier member's specified taxable year.

(ii) *Ordering rules.*—For purposes of applying paragraph (c)(3)(i) of this section, if a CFC group member is an upper-tier member with respect to a CFC group member and a lower-tier member with respect to another CFC group member, paragraph (c)(3)(i) of this section is applied starting with the lowest-tier CFC group member in the chain of ownership. If an upper-tier member is a partner in a lower-tier member that is a partnership, which is an entity that does not have CFC excess taxable income but that may have excess taxable income (as defined in §1.163(j)-1(b)(15)), see §1.163(j)-6(f) for determining the upper-tier member's share of the lower-tier member's excess taxable income (if any).

(d) *Rules concerning the computation of adjusted taxable income of a United States shareholder.*—(1) *In general.*—(i) *Treatment of gross income inclusions that are properly allocable to a non-excepted trade or business.*—If for a taxable year a United States shareholder with respect to one or more applicable CFCs includes amounts in gross income under section 78, 951(a), or 951A(a) that are properly allocable to a non-excepted trade or business (each amount, a *specified deemed inclusion* and such amounts, collectively *specified deemed inclusions*), then, for purposes of computing ATI of the United States shareholder, there is subtracted from taxable income an amount equal to the specified deemed inclusions, reduced by the portion of the deduction allowed under section 250(a)(1), without regard to the taxable income limitation of section 250(a)(2), by reason of the specified deemed inclusions (such a deduction, a *specified section 250 deduction*). For rules concerning inclusions under sections 78, 951(a), and 951A(a) and deductions allowable under section 250 that are not properly allocable to a non-excepted trade or business, see §1.163(j)-1(b)(1)(ii)(F) and (b)(1)(i)(H), respectively.

(ii) *Treatment of deemed inclusions of a domestic partnership that are not allocable to any trade or business.*—If a United States shareholder that is a domestic partnership includes amounts in gross income under section 951(a) or 951A(a) that are not properly allocable to trade or business of the domestic partnership, then, notwithstanding §1.163(j)-4(b)(3), to the extent a C corporation partner, including an indirect partner in the case of tiered partnerships, takes such amounts into account as a distributive share in accordance with section 702 and §1.702-1(a)(8)(ii), the C corporation partner may not treat such amounts as properly allocable to a trade or business of the C corporation partner.

(2) *Additional rule after application of paragraph (d)(1) of this section for a United States shareholder of a CFC group member with a CFC group election in effect.*—(i) *In general.*—Subject to paragraph (d)(3) of this section, if for a taxable year, a United States shareholder owns directly, or indirectly through one or more foreign pass-through entities, stock of one or more CFC group members of a CFC group for which a CFC group election is in effect for the specified taxable year of each CFC group member that ends with or within the taxable year of the United States shareholder, then, for purposes of computing ATI of the United States shareholder, in addition to the subtraction described in paragraph (d)(1) of this section, there is added to taxable income the amount equal to the sum of the amounts of eligible CFC group ETI, as defined in paragraph (d)(2)(ii) of this section, with respect to each specified highest-tier member of the United States shareholder, but not in excess of the amount of the CFC group inclusions, as defined in paragraph (d)(2)(iii) of this section, of the United States shareholder for the taxable year. For purposes of this paragraph (d)(2)(i), members of a consolidated group are treated as a single United States shareholder.

(ii) *Eligible CFC group ETI.*—The term *eligible CFC group ETI* means, with respect to a specified highest-tier member and a specified taxable year, the amount equal to the product of the following three amounts—

(A) The specified highest-tier member's CFC excess taxable income for the specified taxable year, taking into account the application of paragraph (c)(3) of this section;

(B) The specified highest-tier member's specified ETI ratio for the specified taxable year; and

(C) The percentage, by value, of the stock of the specified highest-tier member that is owned directly, or indirectly through one or more foreign passthrough entities, by the United States shareholder on the last day of the specified taxable year.

(iii) *CFC group inclusions.*—The term *CFC group inclusions* means, with respect to a United States shareholder and a taxable year, the amounts of the specified deemed inclusions subtracted from taxable income under paragraph (d)(1)(i) of this section that are with respect to CFC group members, other than amounts included in gross income by reason of section 78, reduced by the portion of any specified section 250 deduction described in paragraph (d)(1)(i) of this section that is allowable by reason of such specified deemed inclusions.

(3) *Special rules if a domestic partnership is a United States shareholder of a CFC group member with a CFC group election in effect.*—Paragraph (d)(2) of this section does not apply with respect to a United States shareholder described in paragraph (d)(2) of this section that is a domestic partnership (such a partnership, a *U.S. shareholder partnership*). If a U.S. shareholder partnership has a domestic C corporation partner, including an indirect partner in the case of tiered partnerships, (such a partner, a *U.S. corporate partner*), then, for purposes of computing ATI of the U.S. corporate partner, paragraph (d)(2) of this section is applied by treating the U.S. shareholder partnership, and in case of tiered partnerships, any tiered partnership that is a domestic partnership, as if it were a foreign partnership and by making the following modifications—

(i) The term "U.S. corporate partner" is substituted for the term "United States shareholder" each place it appears in paragraph (d)(2) of this section; and

(ii) If a U.S. shareholder partnership includes an amount in gross income under section 951(a) or 951(A) with respect to a CFC group member, then to the extent the amount is taken into account by a U.S. corporate partner as a distributive share in accordance with section 702 and §1.702-1(a)(8)(ii), such amount is treated as a specified deemed inclusion of the U.S. corporate partner with respect to the CFC group member for purposes of applying paragraph (d)(2)(iii) of this section.

(4) *Inclusions under section 951A(a).*—For purposes of applying paragraph (d) of this section, the portion of a United States shareholder's inclusion under section 951A(a) treated as being with respect to a CFC group member is determined under section 951A(f)(2) and §1.951A-6(b)(2).

(e) *Effect on earnings and profits.*—In the case of a foreign corporation, the disallowance and carryforward of a deduction for the corporation's business interest expense under §1.163(j)-2 will not affect whether and when such business interest expense reduces the corporation's earnings and profits. Thus, for example, if a United States person has elected under section 1295 to treat a passive foreign investment company (as defined in section 1297) (PFIC) as a qualified electing fund, then the disallowance and carryforward of a deduction for the PFIC's business interest expense under §1.163(j)-2 will not affect whether or when such business interest expense reduces the PFIC's earnings and profits. Similarly, the disallowance and carryforward of a deduction for an applicable CFC's business interest expense will not affect the earnings and profits limitation for subpart F income under section 952(c). See also §1.163(j)-4(c).

(f) *Definitions.*—The following definitions apply for purposes of this section.

(1) *Allocable share.*—(i) *General rule.*—The term *allocable share* means, with respect to a CFC group member of a CFC group and a specified taxable year, the amount equal to the product of the CFC group's applicable net business interest expense (multiplicand), if any, and a fraction, the numerator of which is equal to the amount of the CFC group member's net business interest expense, and the denominator of which is equal to the sum of the amounts of the net business interest expense of each CFC group member.

(ii) *Special rule if there is a financial services subgroup.*—If there is a financial services subgroup with respect to a CFC group, then paragraph (f)(1)(i) of this section is applied with the following modifications—

(A) With respect to a CFC group member that is also a financial services subgroup member—

(1) The multiplicand is equal to the amount of the applicable subgroup net business interest expense; and

(2) The denominator of the fraction is determined by replacing the term "CFC group member" with the term "financial services subgroup member."

(B) With respect to a CFC group member this is not a financial services subgroup member—

(1) The multiplicand is reduced by the amount of the applicable subgroup net business interest expense; and

(2) The denominator of the fraction is reduced by the sum of the amounts of the net business interest expense of each financial services subgroup member.

(2) *Applicable CFC.*—The term *applicable CFC* means a controlled foreign corporation described in section 957, but only if the foreign corporation has at least one United States shareholder that owns, within the meaning of section 958(a), stock of the foreign corporation.

(3) *Applicable net business interest expense.*—The term *applicable net business interest expense* means, with respect to a CFC group and a majority U.S. shareholder taxable year, the excess, if any, of the sum of the amounts of the business interest expense of each CFC group member for the specified taxable year, over the sum of the amounts of the business interest income of each CFC group member for the specified taxable year.

(4) *Applicable subgroup net business interest expense.*—The term *applicable subgroup net business interest expense* means, with respect to a financial services subgroup of a CFC group and a majority U.S. shareholder taxable year, the excess, if any, of the sum of the amounts of the business interest expense of each financial services subgroup member for the specified taxable year, over the sum of the amounts of the business interest income of each financial services subgroup member for the specified taxable year.

(5) *CFC excess taxable income.*—(i) *In general.*—The term *CFC excess taxable income* means, with respect to a CFC group member, other than a partnership described in paragraph (b)(4)(i) of this section, and a specified taxable year, the amount which bears the same ratio to the CFC group member's ATI, as—

(A) The excess (if any) of—

(1) The amount determined for the CFC group member under § 1.163(j)-2(b)(2); over

(2) The CFC group member's allocable share of either the applicable net business interest expense or the applicable subgroup net business interest expense, as applicable; bears to

(B) The amount determined for the CFC group member under § 1.163(j)-2(b)(2).

(ii) *CFC group member is a partnership.*—If a CFC group member is a partnership, see § 1.163(j)-1(b)(15) for determining the extent to which the partnership has excess taxable income. For rules concerning a partner's share of a partnership's excess taxable income, see § 1.163(j)-6(f).

(6) *CFC group.*—(i) *In general.*—The term *CFC group* means two or more applicable CFCs if 80 percent or more of the total value of shares of all classes of stock of each applicable CFC is owned, within the meaning of section 958(a), either by a single United States shareholder or by multiple U.S. shareholders that are related persons, within the meaning of section 267(b) or 707(b)(1), (each a *related United States shareholder* and collectively *related United States shareholders*), provided the stock of each applicable CFC is owned in the same proportion by each related United States shareholder.

(ii) *Aggregation rules.*—The following rules apply for the purpose of applying paragraph (f)(6)(i) of this section—

(A) Members of a consolidated group and individuals described in section 318(a)(1)(A)(i) who file a joint tax return are treated as a single person; and

(B) If a single United States person, as defined in section 957(c), taking into account the application of paragraph (f)(6)(ii)(A) of this section, owns, directly or indirectly through one or more passthrough entities, more than 80 percent of the interests in a pass-through entity that is a United States shareholder that owns, within the meaning of section 958(a), stock in an applicable CFC, then that United States person is treated as owning the stock of the applicable CFC that is owned by the passthrough entity. For purposes of applying the 80-percent threshold described in the preceding sentence, if the pass-through entity is a partnership, then the 80-percent threshold is satisfied if the United States person owns at least 80 percent of the interests in the capital or the profits of the partnership, and if the passthrough entity is not a partnership, then the 80-percent threshold is satisfied if the United States person owns at least 80 percent of the value of all interests of the passthrough entity.

(7) *CFC group election.*—The term *CFC group election* means an election to apply paragraph (b)(3) of this section.

(8) *CFC group member.*—The term *CFC group member* means, with respect to a CFC group, an entity included in the CFC group. An entity that has, including through ownership of an interest in a passthrough entity, income which is effectively connected with a trade or business conducted in the United States, including any income that is treated as effectively connected income under an applicable provision of the Code or regulations, and not exempt from U.S. tax by reason of a U.S. income tax treaty is not treated as a member of a CFC group, other than solely for purposes of determining if another entity is a CFC group member with respect to the CFC group.

(9) *Financial services subgroup.*—The term *financial services subgroup* means, with respect to a CFC group, a group comprised of each CFC group member of the CFC group that is an eligible controlled foreign corporation (as defined in section 954(h)(2)(A)), a qualified insurance company (as defined in section 953(e)(3)), or eligible for the dealer exception in computing foreign personal holding company income (as described in section 954(c)(2)(C)).

(10) *Financial services subgroup member.*—The term *financial services subgroup member* means, with respect to a financial services subgroup of a CFC group, a CFC group member that is also a member of the financial services subgroup.

(11) *Majority U.S. shareholder taxable year.*—The term *majority U.S. shareholder taxable year* means, with respect to a CFC group, one of the following taxable years, applied sequentially—

(i) If there is a single United States shareholder of the CFC group for purposes of paragraph (f)(6)(i) of this section, then the taxable year of the United States shareholder;

(ii) If paragraph (f)(11)(i) of this section does not apply and a related United States shareholder owns, within the meaning of section 958(a), more stock of the members of the CFC group, by value, than is owned, within the meaning of section 958(a), by any other related United States shareholder, then the taxable year of the first-mentioned related United States shareholder;

(iii) If paragraphs (f)(11)(i) and (ii) of this section do not apply and if one or more related United States shareholders with the same taxable year, in aggregate, own, within the meaning of section 958(a), more stock of the members of the CFC group (by value) than is, in aggregate, owned, within the meaning of section 958(a), by other related United States shareholders with the same taxable year, then the taxable year of the first-mentioned related United States shareholders; and

(iv) If paragraphs (f)(11)(i), (ii), and (iii) of this section do not apply, then the calendar year.

(12) *Net business interest expense.*—The term *net business interest expense* means, with respect to a CFC group member of a CFC group and a specified taxable year, the excess, if any, of the amount of the CFC group member's business interest expense over the amount of the CFC group member's business interest income, in each case determined without regard to section 163(j) and the section 163(j) regulations.

(13) *Passthrough entity.*—The term *passthrough entity* means a partnership, S corporation, or any other entity (domestic or foreign) that is not a corporation if all items of income and deduction of the entity are included in the income of its owners or beneficiaries. An *interest in a passthrough entity* means an interest in the capital or profits of the entity or stock of an S corporation, as applicable.

(14) *Specified ETI ratio.*—(i) *In general.*—The term *specified ETI ratio* means, with respect to a specified highest-tier member of a CFC group and a specified taxable year, the ratio computed as a fraction (expressed as a percentage), the numerator of which is the sum of the amounts described in paragraph (f)(14)(iii) of this section with respect to each CFC group member described in paragraph (f)(14)(ii) of this section, and the denominator of which is the sum of the amounts described in paragraph (f)(14)(iv) of this section with respect to each CFC group member described in paragraph (f)(14)(ii) of this section that has amounts included in the numerator. The specified ETI ratio may not exceed 100 percent. If the numerator and the denominator of the fraction are not both greater than zero, the specified ETI ratio is treated as being equal to zero.

(ii) *Includable CFC group members.*—For purposes of applying paragraph (f)(14)(i) of this section, a CFC group member is described in this paragraph (f)(14)(ii) if—

(A) The CFC group member is the specified highest-tier member or a specified lower-tier member with respect to the specified highest-tier member; and

(B) The CFC group member has CFC excess taxable income without regard to paragraph (c)(3) of this section.

(iii) *Numerator.*—For purposes of applying (f)(14)(i) of this section, the amount described in this paragraph (f)(14)(iii) is, with respect to a CFC group member and a specified taxable year, the sum of the amounts included in gross income under sections 951(a) and 951A(a) of each United States shareholder with respect to the CFC group member for the taxable years of the United States shareholders in which or with which the specified taxable year of the CFC group member ends. For purposes of this paragraph (f)(14)(iii), the portion of a United States shareholder's inclusion under section 951A(a) treated as being with respect to a CFC group member is determined under section 951A(f)(2) and § 1.951A-6(b)(2).

(iv) *Denominator.*—For purposes of applying (f)(14)(i) of this section, the amount described in this paragraph (f)(14)(iv) is, with respect to a CFC group member and a specified taxable year, the taxable income of the CFC group member for the specified taxable year.

(15) *Specified highest-tier member.*—The term *specified highest-tier member* means, with respect to a CFC group, a CFC group member in which a United States shareholder owns directly, or indirectly through one or more foreign passthrough entities, stock of the CFC group member.

(16) *Specified lower-tier member.*—The term *specified lower-tier member* means, with respect to a specified highest-tier member of a CFC group, a CFC group member in which the specified highest-tier member owns stock directly or indirectly through a chain of ownership.

(17) *Specified taxable year.*—The term *specified taxable year* means, with respect to a CFC group member of a CFC group, the taxable year that ends with or within a majority U.S. shareholder year.

(18) *United States shareholder.*—The term *United States shareholder* has the meaning provided in section 951(b).

(g) *Examples.*—The following examples illustrate the application of this section. For each example, unless otherwise stated, the referenced business interest expense is deductible but for the application of section 163(j), no exemptions from the application of section 163(j) are available, none of the business interest expense is floor plan financing interest expense, and no foreign corporation has income that is effectively connected with a trade or business conducted in the United States or is an entity described in paragraph (f)(9) of this section (regarding entities that provide certain types of financial services).

(1) *Example 1: Computation of section 163(j) limitation of CFC group members*—(i) *Facts.* USP, a domestic C corporation, wholly owns US1 and US2, each of which is a domestic C corporation. USP, US1, and US2 are members of a consolidated group of which USP is the common parent (USP group). US1 wholly owns CFC1, a foreign corporation, and US2 wholly owns CFC2 and CFC3, each of which is a foreign corporation. The USP group has a calendar year taxable year. For U.S. tax purposes, CFC1, CFC2, and CFC3 each have a fiscal taxable year ending on November 30. CFC1 has an outstanding loan of $1,000x from a third-party (CFC1 note). CFC1 has a receivable of $500x from each of CFC2 and CFC3 (CFC2 note and CFC3 note, respectively). Interest on all debt is paid and accrued annually on November 30. During the taxable year ending November 30, 2019, CFC1 has business interest expense of $90x attributable to CFC1 note and business interest income of $100x attributable to CFC2 note and CFC3 note, and CFC2 and CFC3 each have $50x of business interest expense attributable to CFC2 note and CFC3 note, respectively. Assume that each of CFC1, CFC2, and CFC3 has ATI of $100x computed on a separate company basis for the taxable year ending November 30, 2019. The USP group has no business interest expense.

(ii) *Analysis*—(A) *Determination of CFC group.* US1 owns (within the meaning of section 958(a)) all of the stock of CFC1, and US2 owns (within the meaning of section 958(a)) all of the stock of each of CFC2 and CFC3. Under paragraph (f)(2) of this section, each of CFC1, CFC2, and CFC3 is an applicable CFC. Under paragraph (f)(6)(ii)(A) of this section, because US1 and US2 are members of a consolidated group, US1 and US2 are treated as a single person for purposes determining a CFC group under paragraph (f)(6)(i) of this section. Therefore, because 80 percent or more of the stock of each of CFC1, CFC2, and CFC3 is owned (within the meaning of section 958(a)) by a single United States shareholder, under paragraph (f)(6)(i) of this section, CFC1, CFC2, and CFC3 are members of a CFC group (USP CFC group).

(B) *CFC group election is made.* Assume a CFC group election is properly made. Under paragraph (f)(11)(i) of this section, because there is a single United States shareholder of the USP CFC group with a calendar taxable year, the majority U.S. shareholder taxable year with respect to the USP CFC group ends on December 31, 2019. Under paragraph (f)(17) of this section, the specified taxable year of each of CFC1, CFC2, and CFC3 is November 30, 2019, which is the taxable year that ends with or within the majority U.S. shareholder taxable year ending on December 31, 2019. Under paragraph (f)(3) of this section, the applicable net business interest expense of the USP CFC group is $90x. The $90x is the excess of $190x, which is the sum of the amounts of the business interest expense of each of CFC1, CFC2, and CFC3 ($90x, $50x, and $50x, respectively), over $100x, which is the sum of the amounts of the business interest income of each of CFC1, CFC2, and CFC3 ($100x, $0, and $0, respectively). Under paragraph (f)(12) of this section, CFC1 has $0 of net business interest expense ($90x business interest expense does not exceed $100x of business interest income), and CFC2 and CFC3 each have $50x of net business interest expense (each has $50x business interest expense and $0 business interest income). Because CFC2 and CFC3 each has net business interest expense, under paragraph (f)(1) of this

section, each has an allocable share of the applicable net business interest expense of the USP CFC group. The allocable share of each of CFC2 and CFC3 is $45x, computed as $90x (the applicable net business interest expense) multiplied by the fraction equal to $50x / $100x (the net business interest expense of the member and the sum of the amounts of net business interest expense of all members, respectively). Under paragraph (b)(3)(i) of this section, none of CFC1's $90x of business interest expense and $45x of each of CFC2's and CFC3's $50x of business interest expense is subject to the general rule under §1.163(j)-2(b) (and $5x of each of CFC2's and CFC3's business interest expense is not subject to limitation under §1.163(j)-2(b)), and, under paragraph (b)(3)(ii) of this section, the general rule under §1.163(j)-2(b), as applied to CFC2 and CFC3, is computed without regard to §1.163(j)-2(b)(1) and (3). Thus, under §1.163(j)-2(b), CFC2's limitation is $30x ($100x ATI computed on a separate company basis x 30 percent). The amount of CFC2's business interest expense subject to limitation under paragraph (b)(3) of this section, $45x, exceeds CFC2's limitation under §1.163(j)-2(b), $30x. Accordingly, $35x ($5x not subject to limitation + $30x) of CFC2's business interest expense is deductible, and under §1.163(j)-2(c), the remaining $15x of business interest expense is not deductible and will be carried forward as a disallowed business interest expense carryforward. The analysis for CFC3 is the same as for CFC2. Because the USP group has no business interest expense, the application of paragraph (d) of this section is not relevant.

(C) *CFC group election is not made.* Instead, assume a CFC group election is not made. In this case, each of CFC1, CFC2, and CFC3 must compute its interest deduction limitation under §1.163(j)-2(b), without regard to paragraph (b)(3) of this section. CFC1's business interest expense of $90x is deductible because it has business interest income of $100x. CFC2's business interest expense limitation is $30x ($100x ATI computed on a separate company basis x 30 percent). Accordingly, $30x of CFC2's business interest expense is deductible, and under §1.163(j)-2(c), the remaining $20x of business interest expense is disallowed business interest expense and will be carried forward as a disallowed business interest expense carryforward. The analysis for CFC3 is the same as for CFC2.

(2) *Example 2: Computation and allocation of CFC excess taxable income*—(i) *Facts.* USP, a domestic C corporation, wholly owns CFC1, a foreign corporation. CFC1 wholly owns CFC2, a foreign corporation, and CFC2 wholly owns each of CFC3 and CFC4, both of which are foreign corporations (CFC1, CFC2, CFC3, and CFC4, collectively, the USP CFC group). All entities have a calendar year for U.S. tax purposes. For Year 1, assume the following additional facts: Prior to the application of section 163(j), CFC1 has no items of income, gain, deduction, or loss; CFC2 has a taxable loss of $5x (including $5x of business interest expense); CFC3 has taxable income of $85x (including $15x of business interest expense); CFC4 has $60x of taxable income (including $40x of business interest expense); a CFC group election is in effect for the CFC group; there is no intercompany debt between any CFC group member; 50 percent of CFC3's items of income and gain are subpart F income (as defined in section 952), and 50 percent of CFC3's items of deduction and loss are properly allocable to subpart F income, and with respect to the remaining portion of CFC3's items of income, gain, deduction, and loss, no portion is taken into account in computing tested income (as defined in section 951A(c)(2)(A)) or tested loss (as defined in section 951A(c)(2)(B)) of CFC3; CFC4's items of income and gain are all tested income, and CFC4's items of deduction are all properly allocable to such income; no portion of CFC2's items of income, gain, deduction, or loss is taken into account in computing tested income or tested loss; no CFC group member has qualified business asset investment (as defined in section 951A(d)); for purposes of computing ATI, there are no subtractions or additions to taxable income described in §1.163(j)-1(b)(1) with respect to any CFC group member of the USP CFC group other than for business interest expense; for simplicity, no foreign income taxes are paid by any CFC group member of the USP CFC group; in addition to the inclusions in gross income under sections 951(a)(1) and 951A(a) with respect to the CFC group members of the USP CFC group, USP has business interest expense of $20x.

(ii) *Analysis*—(A) *Application of section 163(j) to CFC group members of the USP CFC group; computation of USP CFC group's applicable net business interest expense.* Under paragraph (f)(3) of this section, the USP CFC group's applicable net business interest expense is $60x ($0 + $5x + $15x + $40x with respect to CFC1, CFC2, CFC3, and CFC4, respectively). Because there is no debt between the CFC group members of the USP CFC group, under paragraph (b)(3) of this section, each of the CFC group members allocable share of the $60x is equal to its separate company business interest expense. In particular, CFC1's allocable share of the USP CFC group's applicable net interest expense is zero, CFC2's allocable share is $5x, CFC3's allocable share is $15x, and CFC4's allocable share is $40x.

(B) *Application of section 163(j) to CFC4.* Under §1.163(j)-1(b)(1), CFC4's ATI is $100x ($60x taxable income + $40x business interest expense). Under §1.163(j)-2(b), CFC4's limitation is $30x ($100x ATI computed on a separate company basis x 30 percent). The amount of CFC4's business interest expense subject to limitation, $40x, exceeds CFC4's limitation, $30x. Accordingly, under §1.163(j)-2(c), $10x of business interest expense is not deductible and will be carried forward as a disallowed business interest expense carryforward. Because $10x of business interest expense is not currently deductible, CFC4's tested income is $70x ($60x taxable income prior to application of section 163(j), increased by $10x of disallowed business interest expense).

(C) *Application of section 163(j) to CFC3.* Under §1.163(j)-1(b)(1), CFC3's ATI is $100x ($85x taxable income + 15x business interest expense). Under §1.163(j)-2(b), CFC3's limitation is $30x ($100x ATI computed on a separate company basis x 30 percent). Because the amount of CFC3's business interest expense subject to limitation, $15x, does not exceed CFC3's limitation, $30x, all of CFC3's business interest expense is currently deductible. Accordingly, CFC3's subpart F income is $42.50x ($85x taxable income x 50 percent). Furthermore, CFC3 has CFC excess taxable income of $50x ($100x x ($15x / $30x)).

(D) *Application of section 163(j) to CFC2.* Under §1.163(j)-1(b)(1), taking into account the application of paragraph (c)(3) of this section, CFC2's ATI is $50x ((-$5x) taxable loss + $5x business interest expense + $50x (100 percent x $50x of CFC3's excess taxable income)). Under §1.163(j)-2(b), CFC2's limitation is $15x ($50x ATI x 30 percent). Because the amount of CFC2's business interest expense subject to limitation, $5x, does not exceed CFC2's limitation, $15x, all of CFC2's business interest expense is currently deductible. Furthermore, CFC2 has CFC excess taxable income of $33.33x ($50x x ($10x / $15x)).

(E) *Application of section 163(j) to CFC1.* Under §1.163(j)-1(b)(1), taking into account the application of paragraph (c)(3) of this section, CFC1's ATI is $33.33x ($0 taxable income + $33.33x (100 percent x $33.33x of CFC2's excess taxable income)). CFC1 has no business interest expense subject to limitation and therefore CFC1 has CFC excess taxable income of $33.33x.

(F) *Application of section 163(j) to USP.* Under section 951(a)(1), USP includes $42.50x in gross income with respect to CFC3. Under section 951A(a), USP includes $70x in gross income, all of which is allocable to CFC4 under section 951A(f)(2), and under section 250(a)(1)(B), USP is allowed a deduction of $35x. Thus, the amount of USP's CFC group inclusions is $77.50x ($42.50 + $70x - $35x), and USP's taxable income prior to the application of section 163(j) is $57.50x ($77.50x - $20x business interest expense). Under §1.163(j)-1(b)(1), taking into account the application of paragraph (d)(2) of this section, USP's ATI is $16.67x. USP's ATI, $16.67x, is equal to $57.50x of taxable income + $20x of business interest expense - $77.50x of CFC group inclusions + $16.67x of eligible CFC group ETI. The eligible CFC group ETI, $16.67x, is determined as $33.33x (CFC1's excess taxable income) x 50 percent (CFC1's specified ETI ratio) x 100 percent (percentage of stock of CFC1 owned directly by USP)). Under paragraph (f)(14) of this section, the specified ETI ratio of CFC1 is 50 percent ($42.50x / $85x). The numerator of the fraction, $42.50x, is equal to the amount of USP's gross income inclusion under section 951(a) with respect to CFC3. The denominator of the fraction, $85x, is equal to the amount of the taxable income of CFC3. The numerator and the denominator of the fraction do not include amounts with respect to CFC1, CFC2, and CFC4, because none of them has CFC excess taxable income without regard to the application of paragraph (c)(3) of this section. Furthermore, USP includes no amounts in gross income under section 951(a) or 951A(a) with respect to CFC1 or CFC2. Under §1.163(j)-2(b), USP's section 163(j) limitation is $5x ($16.67x ATI x 30 percent). The amount of USP's business interest expense, $20x, exceeds USP's section 163(j) limitation, $5x. Accordingly, under §1.163(j)-2(c), $15x of business interest expense is not deductible and is carried forward as a disallowed business interest expense carryforward.

(h) *Applicability date.*—This section applies to a taxable year of a foreign corporation ending after the date the Treasury decision adopting these regulations as final regulations is published in the **Federal Register** and to a taxable year of a shareholder of the foreign corporation ending with or within the taxable year of the foreign corporation. However, a foreign corporation and its shareholders and their related parties, within the meaning of sections 267(b) and 707(b)(1), may apply this section to a taxable year of the foreign corporation beginning after December 31, 2017, and to a taxable year of a shareholder of the foreign corporation ending with or within the taxable year of the foreign corporation, if the foreign corporation and its shareholders and their related parties consistently apply all of the section 163(j) regulations, and if applicable, §§1.263A-9, 1.381(c)(20)-1, 1.382-6, 1.383-1, 1.469-9, 1.882-5, 1.1502-13, 1.1502-21, 1.1502-36, 1.1502-79, 1.1502-91 through 1.1502-99 (to the extent they effectuate the rules of §§1.382-6 and 1.383-1), and 1.1504-4 to those taxable years. [Reg. §1.163(j)-7.]

§1.163(j)-8. Application of the business interest deduction limitation to foreign persons with effectively connected income.— (a) *Overview.* This section provides rules concerning the application

of section 163(j) to foreign persons engaged in a trade or business in the United States. Paragraph (b) of this section modifies the application of section 163(j) for specified foreign persons with effectively connected taxable income. Paragraph (c) of this section modifies the application of section 163(j) for specified foreign partners in a partnership engaged in a trade or business in the United States. Paragraph (d) of this section provides rules for certain controlled foreign corporations with effectively connected taxable income. Paragraph (e) of this section coordinates the application of section 163(j) and §1.882-5. Paragraph (f) of this section provides a coordination rule for determining effectively connected earnings and profits for purposes of the branch profits tax under section 884. Paragraph (g) of this section provides definitions that apply for purposes of this section. Paragraph (h) of this section provides examples that illustrate the application of this section. Paragraph (i) of this section provides dates of applicability.

(b) *Application of section 163(j) and the section 163(j) regulations to specified foreign persons with effectively connected taxable income.*—(1) *In general.*—If a taxpayer is a specified foreign person, then the modifications described in this paragraph (b) are made to the application of section 163(j) and the section 163(j) regulations. If a specified foreign person is also a specified foreign partner, then the modifications described in this paragraph (b) are subject to the partner-level modifications described in paragraph (c) of this section.

(2) *Modification of adjusted taxable income.*—ATI for a specified foreign person for a taxable year means the specified foreign person's effectively connected taxable income for the taxable year, adjusted for the items described in §1.163(j)-1(b)(1)(i) through (iv) that are taken into account in determining effectively connected taxable income.

(3) *Modification of business interest expense.*—(i) *General rule.*— Business interest expense for a specified foreign person means interest described in §1.163(j)-1(b)(2) that is determined under §1.882-5, in the case of a foreign corporation, or under §1.861-9T(d)(2), in the case of a non-resident alien individual, and allocable to income which is effectively connected taxable income.

(ii) *Exclusion of certain business interest expense of a specified foreign partner.*—If a foreign corporation is a specified foreign partner in a partnership engaged in a trade or business in the United States, then, for purposes of paragraph (b)(3)(i) of this section, business interest expense excludes the portion of interest expense determined under §1.882-5 that is attributable to interest on U.S. booked liabilities of the partnership determined under §1.882-5(d)(2)(vii).

(4) *Modification of business interest income.*—The business interest income of a specified foreign person means interest described in §1.163(j)-1(b)(3) that is effectively connected taxable income.

(5) *Modification of floor plan financing interest expense.*—The floor plan financing interest expense of a specified foreign person means interest described §1.163(j)-1(b)(17) that is allocable to income which is effectively connected taxable income.

(6) *Modification of allocation of interest expense and interest income that is properly allocable to a trade or business.*—For purposes of §1.163(j)-10(c), a specified foreign person's interest expense and interest income that is properly allocable to a trade or business is only allocated to the specified foreign person's excepted or non-excepted trades or business that have effectively connected taxable income. If the specified foreign person is also a specified foreign partner, this rule only applies to the trades or business not in the partnership.

(c) *Partner-level modifications to §1.163(j)-6 for partnerships engaged in a U.S. trade or business.*—(1) *Modification related to a partnership's excess taxable income.*—If for a taxable year a specified foreign partner, other than an applicable CFC, has allocable excess taxable income with respect to a partnership, then, for purposes of computing the specified foreign partner's ATI for the taxable year, the excess, if any, of the amount of the allocable excess taxable income over the amount of the specified excess taxable income is subtracted from ATI.

(2) *Modification related to a partnership's excess business interest expense.*—If for a taxable year a specified foreign partner, other than an applicable CFC, has allocable excess business interest expense with respect to a partnership, then, for purposes of determining the specified foreign partner's business interest expense for a succeeding taxable year, the amount of the allocable excess business interest expense treated as disallowed business interest expense carryforward under §1.163(j)-6(f) is determined by taking into account only the portion of allocable excess business interest expense that is specified excess business interest expense and such excess business interest expense is limited to the portion of allocable excess taxable income for the succeeding taxable year that is specified excess taxable income.

(3) *Modification related to a partnership's excess business interest income.*—If for a taxable year a specified foreign partner, other than an applicable CFC, has allocable excess business interest income (as defined in §1.163(j)-6(b)(4)) with respect to a partnership, then, for purposes of determining the specified foreign partner's section 163(j) limitation, the amount of allocable excess business interest income that can be used by the specified foreign partner cannot exceed the amount of ECI excess business interest income.

(d) *An applicable CFC with effectively connected taxable income.*—If an applicable CFC has effectively connected taxable income for a taxable year in which the applicable CFC has disallowed business interest expense, then a portion of the disallowed business interest expense is treated as being with respect to the applicable CFC's interest expense determined under §1.882-5. That portion is equal to the amount of the applicable CFC's disallowed business interest expense multiplied by a fraction, the numerator of which is the applicable CFC's effectively connected taxable income for the taxable year, adjusted for the items described in §1.163(j)-1(b)(1)(i) through (iv) that are taken into account in determining effectively connected taxable income, and the denominator of which is the applicable CFC's ATI for the taxable year. However, in no case will such portion exceed the amount of interest expense determined under §1.882-5. See also §1.163(j)-7(b)(2) (concerning the general application of section 163(j) to an applicable CFC).

(e) *Coordination of section 163(j) and §1.882-5.*—(1) *General rules.*—(i) *Ordering rule.*—A foreign corporation first determines its interest expense under §1.882-5 and then determines the amount of disallowed business interest expense.

(ii) *Treatment of disallowed business interest expense carryforward.*—If a foreign corporation has a disallowed business interest expense carryforward from a taxable year, then such carryforward is not taken into account for purposes of determining interest expense under §1.882-5 in the succeeding taxable year.

(iii) *Treatment of allocable excess business interest expense.*—If a foreign corporation has allocable excess business interest expense from a taxable year that is treated under §1.163(j)-6(g)(2) as disallowed business interest expense carryforward, such interest is not taken into account for purposes of determining interest expense under §1.882-5 in the succeeding taxable year.

(iv) *Scaling ratio.*—If a foreign corporation determines its interest expense under the method described in §1.882-5(b) through (d) and has U.S. booked liabilities in excess of U.S. connected liabilities, the foreign corporation must apply the scaling ratio (as defined in §1.882-5(d)(4)(ii)) pro rata to all interest expense paid or accrued by the foreign corporation consistent with §1.882-5(d)(4)(i), including for purposes of paragraph (b)(3)(ii) of this section.

(2) *Amount of interest determined under §1.882-5 that is disallowed business interest expense.*—(i) *Foreign corporation is not a specified foreign partner.*—If a foreign corporation is not a specified foreign partner for a taxable year, then the amount of the foreign corporation's interest expense determined under §1.882-5 for which a deduction is disallowed for the taxable year is either—

(A) The amount of disallowed business interest expense computed under §1.163(j)-2(b) with respect to business interest expense described in paragraph (b)(3)(i) of this section, in the case of a foreign corporation that is not an applicable CFC; or

(B) The amount of disallowed business interest expense determined under paragraph (d) of this section, in the case of an applicable CFC.

(ii) *Foreign corporation is a specified foreign partner.*—If a foreign corporation is a specified foreign partner with respect to one or more partnerships engaged in a trade or business in the United States for a taxable year, then the portion of the foreign corporation's business interest expense determined under §1.882-5 for which a deduction is disallowed for the taxable year is equal to the sum of the following amounts—

(A) Either—

(1) The amount described in paragraph (e)(2)(i)(A) of this section, in the case of a foreign corporation that is not an applicable CFC; or

(2) The amount described in paragraph (e)(2)(i)(B) of this section, in the case of an applicable CFC; and

(B) With respect to each partnership that has excess business interest expense for the taxable year that ends with or within the foreign corporation's taxable year, the amount of the foreign corporation's specified excess business interest expense.

(f) *Coordination with branch profits tax.*—(1) *Effect on effectively connected earnings and profits.*—The disallowance and carryforward of business interest expense under §1.163(j)-2(b) and (c) will not affect when such business interest expense reduces the effectively con-

nected earnings and profits of a foreign corporation, as defined in §1.884-1(f).

(2) *Effect on U.S. net equity.*—The disallowance and carryforward of business interest expense under §1.163(j)-2(b) and (c) will not affect the computation of the U.S. net equity of a foreign corporation, as defined in §1.884-1(c).

(g) *Definitions.*—The following definitions apply for purposes of this section.

(1) *Applicable CFC.*—The term *applicable CFC* means a foreign corporation described in section 957, but only if the foreign corporation has at least one United States shareholder that owns, within the meaning of section 958(a), stock of the foreign corporation.

(2) *ECI excess business interest income.*—The term *ECI excess business interest income* means, with respect to a specified foreign partner and a partnership, the excess, if any, of the specified foreign partner's allocable business interest income (as defined in §1.163(j)-6(f)(2)(ii)) over its allocable business interest expense (as defined in §1.163(j)-6(f)(2)(ii)), but, for purposes of determining a specified foreign partner's allocable business interest income and allocable business interest expense, taking into account only the portion of the partnership's business interest income determined under paragraph (b)(4) of this section as if the partnership were a specified foreign person, over the business interest expense on the U.S. booked liabilities of the partnership as determined under §1.882-5(d)(2)(vii).

(3) *Effectively connected taxable income.*—The term *effectively connected taxable income* means taxable income of a person that is, or is treated as. effectively connected with the conduct of a trade business in the United States under an applicable provision of the Code or regulations or, if an income tax treaty applies, business profits attributable to a U.S. permanent establishment of a tax treaty resident eligible for benefits under an income tax treaty between the United States and the treaty country.

(4) *Specified excess business interest expense.*—The term *specified excess business interest expense* means, with respect to a specified foreign partner and a partnership, the amount determined by multiplying the specified foreign partner's allocable excess business interest expense (as determined under §1.163(j)-6(f)) by the partnership's specified ratio for the taxable year.

(5) *Specified excess taxable income.*—The term *specified excess taxable income* means, with respect to a specified foreign partner and a partnership, the amount determined by multiplying the amount of the specified foreign partner's allocable excess taxable income (as determined under §1.163(j)-6(f)) by the amount of the partnership's specified ratio for the taxable year.

(6) *Specified foreign partner.*—The term *specified foreign partner* means, with respect to a partnership that is engaged in a U.S. trade or business, a partner that is a specified foreign person or an applicable CFC.

(7) *Specified foreign person.*—The term *specified foreign person* means a nonresident alien individual, as defined in section 7701(b) and the regulations thereunder, or a foreign corporation other than an applicable CFC.

(8) *Specified ratio.*—The term *specified ratio* means, with respect to a partnership, a fraction (expressed as a percentage), the numerator of which is the ATI for the partnership determined under paragraph (b)(2) of this section as if the partnership were a specified foreign person, and the denominator of which is the ATI for the partnership determined under §1.163(j)-6(d).

(h) *Examples.*—The following examples illustrate the application of this section. For all examples, assume that all referenced interest expense is deductible but for the application of section 163(j), the small business exemption under §1.163(j)-2(d) is not available, no party is engaged in an excepted trade or business, and no business interest expense is floor plan financing interest expense.

(1) *Example 1: Limitation on business interest deduction of a foreign corporation*—(i) *Facts.* FC, a foreign corporation that is not an applicable CFC, has $100x of gross income that is effectively connected income. FC has $60x of other income which is not effectively connected income. FC has total expenses of $100x. Assume that under §1.882-5, FC has $30x of interest expense allocable to income which is effectively connected income. Under section 882(c) and the regulations thereunder, FC has $40x of other expenses properly allocated and apportioned to income which is effectively connected taxable income. FC does not have any business interest income.

(ii) *Analysis.* FC is a specified foreign person under paragraph (g)(7) of this section. Under paragraph (e)(2) of this section, the amount of FC's interest expense determined under §1.882-5 that is disallowed is the disallowed business interest expense computed under §1.163(j)-2(b) with respect to interest expense described in paragraph (b)(3) of this section. Under §1.163(j)-4(b)(1), all interest paid or accrued by FC is properly allocable to a trade or business and therefore under paragraph (b)(3) of this section, FC has business interest expense of $30x. FC has $30x of effectively connected taxable income described in paragraph (g)(3) of this section ($100x - $30x - $40x). Under paragraph (b)(2) of this section, FC has ATI of $60x, determined as $30x of effectively connected taxable income, increased by $30x of business interest expense. Accordingly, FC's section 163(j) limitation is $18x ($60x x 30 percent). Because FC's business interest expense ($30x) exceeds the section 163(j) limitation ($18x), FC may only deduct $18x of business interest expense. Under §1.163(j)-2(c), the remaining $12x is disallowed business interest expense carryforward and under paragraph (e)(1)(ii) of this section, the $12x is not taken into account for purposes of applying §1.882-5 in the succeeding taxable year.

(2) *Example 2: Use of a disallowed business interest expense carryforward*—(i) *Facts.* The facts are the same as in *Example 1* in paragraph (h)(1)(i) of this section except that FC has $300x of gross income which is all effectively connected income. Furthermore assume that FC has a disallowed business interest expense carryforward of $25x from the prior taxable year.

(ii) *Analysis.* Under paragraph (e)(1)(ii) of this section, FC's $25x of disallowed business interest expense carryforward is not taken into account for purposes of determining FC's interest under §1.882-5. Therefore, FC has $30x of business interest expense determined under §1.882-5. Under paragraph (g)(3) of this section, FC has effectively connected taxable income of $205x ($300x gross income - $55x interest expense ($30x + $25x) - $40x other expenses). Under paragraph (b)(2) of this section, FC has ATI of $260x, determined as $205x of effectively connected taxable income, increased by $55x of business interest expense. Accordingly, FC's section 163(j) limitation is $78x ($260x x 30 percent). Under paragraph (b)(3) of this section, FC has business interest expense of $55x ($30x + $25x disallowed interest carryforward) for the taxable year. Because FC's business interest expense ($55x) does not exceed the section 163(j) limitation ($78x), FC may deduct all $55x of business interest expense.

(3) *Example 3: Foreign corporation is engaged in a U.S. trade or business and a specified foreign partner in a partnership engaged in a U.S. trade or business*—(i) *Facts.* FC, a foreign corporation that is not an applicable CFC, owns a 50-percent interest in ABC, a foreign partnership that is engaged in a trade or business in the United States. ABC has two lines of businesses, Business A and Business B. Business A produces $120x of taxable income (including interest expense) and Business B produces $80x of taxable income. FC is allocated 50 percent of all items of income and expense of Business A and Business B. Business A has business interest expense of $20x on $400x of liabilities but has no business interest income. Business B does not have any business interest expense or business interest income. With respect to FC, only Business A produces effectively connected income. FC has an outside basis of $500x in the ABC partnership for purposes of §1.882-5(b), step 1. All of the liabilities of Business A are U.S. booked liabilities for purposes of §1.882-5(d). In addition to owning a 50-percent interest in ABC, FC conducts a separate business that is engaged in a trade or business in the United States (Business X). Business X has effectively connected taxable income of $50x, U.S. assets with an adjusted basis of $300x, U.S. booked liabilities of $160x, and interest on U.S. booked liabilities of $15x. FC computes its interest expense under the three-step method described in §1.882-5(b) through (d) and uses the fixed ratio of 50 percent for purposes of §1.882-5(c), step 2. Assume the interest rate on excess U.S. connected liabilities is 5 percent. For the taxable year, FC has total interest expense of 500x for purposes of §1.882-5(a)(3).

(ii) *Analysis*—(A) *Application of section 163(j) to ABC.* Under §1.163(j)-6(a), ABC computes a section 163(j) limitation at the partnership level. Under §1.163(j)-6(d), ABC has ATI of $220x, determined as $200x of taxable income ($120x from Business A + $80x from Business B), increased by $20x of business interest expense of Business A. Under §1.163(j)-2(b), ABC's section 163(j) limitation is $66x ($220x x 30 percent). Because ABC's business interest expense ($20x) does not exceed the section 163(j) limitation ($66x), ABC can deduct all of its business interest expense for the taxable year. Under §1.163(j)-1(b)(15), ABC has excess taxable income of $153.33x ($220x x ($46x/$66x)). Under §1.163(j)-6(f), FC is allocated 50 percent of the $153.33x of ABC's excess taxable income, or $76.67x of allocable excess taxable income, but, under paragraph (c)(1) of this section, the amount by which the allocable excess taxable income exceeds FC's specified excess taxable income (as defined in paragraph (g)(5) of this section) is a subtraction from FC's ATI. Under paragraph (g)(5) of this section, FC's specified excess taxable income is $48.79x, which is equal to the product of $76.67x and ABC's specified ratio of 63.64 percent. Under paragraph (g)(8) of this section, ABC's specified ratio of 63.64 percent is determined as $140x / $220x (where the numerator of $140x is the ATI of ABC determined under paragraph (b)(2) of this section as if ABC were a specified foreign person ($120x taxable income of Business A, increased by $20x of business interest ex-

pense), and the denominator of $220x is the ATI of ABC under §1.163(j)-6(d)). FC's allocable excess taxable income ($76.67x) exceeds its specified excess taxable income ($48.79x) by $27.88x.

(B) *Application of §1.882-5 to FC.* FC is a specified foreign partner under paragraph (g)(6) of this section. Under paragraph (e)(1) of this section, FC first determines its interest expense under §1.882-5 and then determines its disallowed business interest expense. Under §1.882-5(b), step 1, FC has U.S. assets of $800x ($500x (FC's basis in its interest in ABC) + $300x (FC's basis in Business X assets). Under §1.882-5(c), step 2, applying the 50-percent safe harbor in §1.882-5 for a non-banking business, FC has U.S. connected liabilities of $400x ($800x x 50 percent). Under §1.882-5(d), step 3, FC has U.S. booked liabilities of $360x ($200x (50-percent share of Business A liabilities of ABC of $400x) + $160x (Business X liabilities) and interest on U.S. booked liabilities of $25x ($10x (50-percent share of $20x interest expense of Business A) + $15x (interest expense of Business X)). FC has excess U.S. connected liabilities of $40x ($400x – $360x) and interest on such excess liabilities of $2x ($40x x 5 percent). FC's interest expense determined under §1.882-5 is $27x ($25x + $2x).

(C) *Application of section 163(j) to FC.* Under paragraph (e)(2)(ii) of this section, the amount of business interest expense that is disallowed for FC is equal to only the amount of interest described in paragraph (b)(3) of this section that is disallowed because there is no specified excess business interest expense with respect to ABC. Under paragraph (b)(3) of this section, FC's business interest expense (at the corporate level) is $17x, the amount determined under §1.882-5 ($27x) less the amount of interest on U.S. booked liabilities from ABC determined under §1.882-5(d)(2)(vii) ($10x), which was subject to the section 163(j) limitation at the ABC partnership level. Under §1.163(j)-6(e)(1), FC's ATI is determined under §1.163(j)-1(b)(1) without regard to FC's distributive share of any items of income, gain, deduction, or loss of ABC. Under paragraph (b)(2) of this section, taking into account the application of paragraph (c)(1) of this section, FC's ATI is $115.77x ($50x effectively connected taxable income with respect to Business X, + $17x (business interest expense under §1.882-5 of 27x less the amount of interest on U.S. booked liabilities from ABC determined under §1.882-5(d)(2)(vii) of $10x) + $76.65x (excess taxable income from ABC) - $27.88x (amount excess taxable income exceeds specified excess taxable income)). FC's section 163(j) limitation is $34.73x ($115.77x x 30 percent). Because FC's business interest expense ($17x) is less than FC's section 163(j) limitation ($34.73x) and all of its share of ABC's interest is deductible, FC may deduct all $27x of interest determined under §1.882-5.

(4) *Example 4: Scaleback of interest expense under §1.882-5*—(i) *Facts.* Assume the same facts in *Example 3* in paragraph (h)(3)(i) of this section except that Business X has U.S. booked liabilities of $300x and interest on U.S. booked liabilities of $20x.

(ii) *Analysis*—(A) *Application of section 163(j) to ABC.* The analysis is the same as *Example 3* in paragraph (h)(3)(ii)(A) of this section.

(B) *Application of §1.882-5 to FC.* Under §1.882-5(b), step 1, FC has U.S. assets of $800x ($500x (FC's basis in its interest in ABC) + $300x (FC's basis in Business X assets)). Under §1.882-5(c), step 2, applying the 50-percent safe harbor in §1.882-5 for a non-banking business, FC has U.S. connected liabilities of $400x ($800x x 50 percent). Under §1.882-5(d), step 3, FC has U.S. booked liabilities of $500x ($200x (50-percent share of Business A liabilities of ABC of $400x) + $300x (Business X liabilities) and interest on U.S. booked liabilities of $30x ($10x (50-percent share of $20x interest expense of Business A) + $20x (interest expense of Business X)). FC has excess U.S. booked liabilities of $100x ($500x – $400x) and the interest expense on U.S. booked liabilities must be reduced by the scaling ratio as provided in §1.882-5(d)(4). FC's interest expense determined under §1.882-5 is $24x ($30x x (400/500 scaling ratio)).

(C) *Application of section 163(j) to FC.* Under paragraph (b)(3) of this section, FC's business interest expense is $16x, the amount determined under §1.882-5 ($24x) less the amount of interest on U.S. booked liabilities from ABC determined under §1.882-5(d)(2)(vii) after applying the scaling ratio ($8x, determined as interest expense of Business A of $10x x scaling ratio of 400/500), which was subject to the section 163(j) limitation at the ABC partnership level. Under §1.163(j)-6(e)(1), FC's ATI is determined under §1.163(j)-1(b)(1) without regard to FC's distributive share of any items of income, gain, deduction, or loss of ABC. Under paragraph (b)(2) of this section, taking into account the application of paragraph (c)(1) of this section, FC's ATI is $114.79x ($50x effectively connected taxable income with respect to Business X + $16x (business interest expense under §1.882-5 of 24x less the amount of interest on U.S. booked liabilities from ABC determined under §1.882-5(d)(2)(vii), after applying the scaleback, of $8x) + $76.67x (excess taxable income from ABC) - $27.88x (amount excess taxable income exceeds specified excess taxable income). FC's section 163(j) limitation is $34.44x ($114.79x x 30 percent). Because FC's business interest expense ($16x) is less than FC's section 163(j) limitation ($34.44x) and all of ABC's interest is deductible, FC may deduct all $24x of interest determined under §1.882-5

(5) *Example 5: Separate currency pools method*—(i) *Facts.* Assume the same facts in *Example 3* in paragraph (h)(3)(i) of this section except that FC does not conduct Business X; the value of FC's interest in ABC for purposes of § 1.882-5(e)(i), step 1, is $1,000x; and FC computes its interest expense under the separate currency pools method in § 1.882-5(e) and for purposes of applying such method, the prescribed interest rate is 5 percent.

(ii) *Analysis*—(A) *Application of section 163(j) to ABC.* The analysis is the same as in *Example 3* in paragraph (h)(1)(ii)(A) of this section.

(B) *Application of § 1.882-5 to FC.* Under § 1.882-5(e)(i), step 1, FC has U.S. assets of $1,000x (FC's basis in its partnership interest in ABC). Under § 1.882-5(e)(1)(ii), step 2, FC has U.S. connected liabilities of $500x ($1,000x x 50 percent) applying the 50 percent safe harbor for non-banking business. Under § 1.882-5(e)(1)(iii), step 3, the interest expense under § 1.882-5 is $25x ($500x x 5 percent).

(C) *Application of section 163(j) to FC.* Under paragraph (b)(3) of this section, FC's business interest expense is $15x, the amount determined under § 1.882-5 ($25x) less the amount of interest on U.S. booked liabilities from ABC determined under § 1.882-5(d)(2)(vii) of $10x, which was subject to the section 163(j) limitation at the ABC partnership level. Under § 1.163(j)-6(e)(1), FC's ATI is determined under § 1.163(j)-1(b)(1) without regard to FC's distributive share of any items of income, gain, deduction, or loss of ABC. Under paragraph (b)(2) of this section, taking into account the application of paragraph (c)(1) of this section, FC's ATI is $48.79x ($76.67x (excess taxable income from ABC) — $27.88x (amount excess taxable income exceeds specified excess taxable income)). FC's section 163(j) limitation is $14.64x ($48.79x x 30 percent). Because FC's business interest expense ($15x) exceeds the 163(j) limitation ($14.64x), FC may only deduct $14.64x of its business interest expense. Under § 1.163(j)-2(c), the remaining $0.36x is disallowed business interest expense carryforward and under paragraph (e)(1)(ii) of this section, the $0.36x is not taken into account for purposes of applying § 1.882-5 in the succeeding taxable year. Accordingly, FC may deduct 24.64x of the $25x interest determined under § 1.882-5.

(6) *Example 6: Specified foreign partner with excess business interest expense*—(i) *Facts - Year 1.* FC, a foreign corporation that is not an applicable CFC, owns a 50-percent interest in XYZ, a foreign partnership that is engaged in a trade or business in the United States. XYZ has two lines of businesses, Business S and Business T. Business S produces $50x of taxable income (including interest expense), and Business T produces $40x of taxable income (including interest expense). FC is allocated 50 percent of all items of income and expenses of Business S and Business T. Business S has business interest expense of $30x on $500x of liabilities but has no business interest income. Business T has business interest expense of $50x on $500x of liabilities but has no business interest income. With respect to FC, only Business S produces effectively connected income. FC has an adjusted basis of $500x in XYZ for purposes of § 1.882-5(b), step 1. All of the liabilities of Business S are U.S. booked liabilities for purposes of § 1.882-5(d). FC computes its interest expense under the three-step method described in § 1.882-5(b) through (d) and uses the fixed ratio of 50 percent for purposes of § 1.882-5(c), step 2.

(ii) *Analysis with respect to Year 1*—(A) *Application of section 163(j) to XYZ.* Under § 1.163(j)-6(a), XYZ computes a section 163(j) limitation at the partnership-level. Under § 1.163(j)-6(d), XYZ has ATI of $170x, determined as $90x of taxable income ($50x from Business S + $40x from Business T), increased by $80x of business interest expense ($30x from Business S + $50x from Business T). Under § 1.163(j)-2(b), XYZ's section 163(j) limitation is $51x ($170x x 30 percent). Because XYZ's business interest expense ($80x) exceeds the section 163(j) limitation ($51x), XYZ may only deduct $51x of business interest expense and $29x is disallowed under section 163(j). Under § 1.163(j)-6(f), FC is allocated $14.5x of excess business interest expense (50 percent x $29x). Under paragraph (c)(2) of this section, the amount of allocable business interest expense that can be used by FC is equal to the amount of specified excess business interest, and the amount of such interest that is treated as paid or accrued by FC in the succeeding taxable year is limited to the amount of FC's specified excess taxable income allocated to FC in the succeeding taxable year.

(B) *Application of § 1.882-5 to FC.* FC is a specified foreign partner under paragraph (g)(6) of this section. Under paragraph (e)(1) of this section, FC first determines its interest expense under § 1.882-5 and then determines its disallowed business interest expense. Under § 1.882-5(b), step 1, FC has U.S. assets of $500x (FC's adjusted basis in its interest in XYZ). Under § 1.882-5(c), step 2, applying the 50-percent fixed ratio in § 1.882-5 for a non-banking business, FC has U.S. connected liabilities of $250x ($500x x 50 percent). Under § 1.882-5(d), step 3, FC has U.S. booked liabilities of $250x ($500x x 50-percent share of Business S liabilities of XYZ) and interest on U.S. booked liabilities of $15x (50 percent share of $30x interest expense of Business S). Because FC has U.S. connected liabilities equal to its U.S. booked liabilities, its interest expense under § 1.882-5 is $15x (the amount of interest expense on its U.S. booked liabilities).

(C) *Application of section 163(j) to FC.* Under paragraph (e)(2)(ii) of this section, the amount of business interest expense that is disal-

lowed for FC is equal to the sum of the amount of interest described in paragraph (b)(3) of this section that is disallowed plus the amount of FC's specified excess business interest expense. FC's business interest expense (at the corporate level) under paragraph (b)(3) of this section is $0, the amount determined under § 1.882-5 ($15x) less the amount of interest on U.S. booked liabilities from XYZ determined under § 1.882-5(d)(2)(vii) ($15x), which was subject to the section 163(j) limitation at the XYZ partnership level. Because FC (at the corporate level) has no business interest expense, there is no business interest expense subject to the section 163(j) limitation. However, because FC has excess business interest expense with respect to XYZ, a deduction for a portion of the $15x of interest on U.S. booked liabilities from XYZ determined under § 1.882-5(d)(2)(vii) will be disallowed for the taxable year. The amount of such interest that is limited is equal to the amount of the FC's specified excess business interest expense determined under paragraph (g)(4) of this section. The specified excess business interest expense is $6.82x, determined by multiplying FC's distributive share of excess business interest expense ($14.5x) by XYZ's specified ratio of 47.06 percent, determined under paragraph (g)(8) of this section. The specified ratio of 47.06 percent is determined by dividing $80x ATI determined under paragraph (b)(2) of the section as if XYZ were a specified foreign person (determined as $50x taxable income from Business S + $30x business interest expense from Business S) by $170x of XYZ ATI. FC may only deduct $8.18x ($15x - $6.82x) of business interest expense. Under § 1.163(j)-2(c), the remaining $6.82x is disallowed business interest expense carryforward and under paragraph (e)(1)(ii) of this section, the $6.82x is not taken into account for purposes of applying § 1.882-5 in the succeeding taxable year.

(iii) *Facts - Year 2.* During Year 2, Business S produces $170x of taxable income (including interest expense) and Business T produces $150x (including interest expense) of taxable income. Business S has business interest expense of $30x on $500x of liabilities but has no business interest income. Business T has business interest expense of $50x on $500x of liabilities but no business interest income. With respect to FC, only Business S produces effectively connected taxable income. FC has an adjusted basis of $600x in XYZ for purposes of § 1.882-5(b), step 1. All of the liabilities of Business S are U.S. booked liabilities for purposes of § 1.882-5(d). FC computes its interest expense under the three-step method described in § 1.882-5(b) through (d) and uses the fixed ratio of 50 percent for purposes of § 1.882-5(c), step 2. The interest rate on excess U.S. connected liabilities is 5 percent. For the taxable year, FC has total interest expense of $1,000x for purposes of § 1.882-5(a)(3).

(iv) *Analysis with respect to Year 2*—(A) *Application of section 163(j) to XYZ.* Under § 1.163(j)-6(a), XYZ computes a section 163(j) limitation at the partnership-level. Under § 1.163(j)-6(d), XYZ has ATI of $400x, determined as $320x of taxable income ($170x from Business S + $150x from Business T), increased by $80x of business interest expense ($30x from Business S + $50x from Business T). Under § 1.163(j)-2(b), XYZ's section 163(j) limitation is $120x ($400x x 30 percent). Because XYZ's business interest expense ($80x) does not exceed the section 163(j) limitation ($120x), XYZ can deduct all of its business interest expense for the taxable year. Under § 1.163(j)-1(b)(15), XYZ has excess taxable income of $133.30x ($400x x ($40x/$120x)). Under § 1.163(j)-6(f), FC is allocated 50 percent of the $133.33x of XYZ's excess taxable income, or $66.66x of allocable excess taxable income but, under paragraph (c)(1) of this section, the amount by which the allocable excess taxable income exceeds FC's specified excess taxable income (as defined in paragraph (g)(5) of this section) is a subtraction from FC's ATI. Under paragraph (g)(5) of this section, FC's specified excess taxable income is $33.33x, which is equal to the product of FC's allocable excess taxable income of $66.66x and XYZ's specified ratio of 50 percent. Under paragraph (g)(8) of this section, XYZ's specified ratio of 50 percent is determined as $200x / $400x (where the numerator of $200x is the ATI of XYZ determined under paragraph (b)(2) of this section as if XYZ were a specified foreign person ($170x taxable income of Business S, increased by $30x of business interest expense), and the denominator of $400x is the ATI of XYZ under § 1.163(j)-6(d)). FC's allocable excess taxable income ($66.66x) exceeds its specified excess taxable income ($33.33x) by $33.33x.

(B) *Treatment of excess business interest expense from Year 1.* In Year 1, XYZ had disallowed business interest expense of $29x and under § 1.163(j)-6(f), FC's allocable excess business interest expense was $14.50x. Under paragraph (c)(2) of this section, FC may use its allocable excess business interest expense in a succeeding taxable year only to the extent of its specified excess business interest expense, which, in this case, was determined to be $6.82x, and, with respect to Year 2, the amount of specified excess business interest expense treated as paid or accrued by FC is limited to FC's specified excess taxable income ($33.33x). Thus, FC can treat the entire $6.82x as business interest expense paid or accrued in Year 2.

(C) *Application of § 1.882-5 to FC.* Under § 1.882-5(b), step 1, FC has U.S. assets of $600x (FC's adjusted basis in its interest in XYZ). Under § 1.882-5(c), step 2, applying the 50 percent fixed ratio in

§1.882-5 for a non-banking business, FC has U.S. connected liabilities of $300x ($600x x 50 percent). Under §1.882-5(d), step 3, FC has U.S. booked liabilities of $250x ($500x x 50-percent share of Business S liabilities of XYZ) and interest on U.S. booked liabilities of $15x (50 percent share of $30x interest expense of Business S). FC has excess U.S. connected liabilities of $50x ($300x – $250x) and interest on such excess liabilities of $2.5x ($50x x 5 percent). FC's interest expense determined under §1.882-5 is $17.5x ($15x + $2.5x).

(D) *Application of section 163(j) to FC.* Under paragraph (e)(2)(ii) of this section, the amount of business interest expense that is disallowed for FC is equal to only the amount of interest described in paragraph (b)(3) of this section that is disallowed because there is no excess business interest expense with respect to XYZ. FC's business interest expense (at the corporate level) under paragraphs (b)(3) and (e)(1) of this section is $9.32x, determined as the sum of $2.50x (the amount determined under §1.882-5 ($17.50x) less the amount of interest on U.S. booked liabilities from XYZ determined under §1.882-5(d)(2)(vii) ($15x) that is excluded under paragraph (b)(3)(ii) of this section) + $6.82x (allocable business interest expense from Year 1 treated as paid or accrued in Year 2). Under §1.163(j)-6(e)(1), FC's ATI is determined under §1.163(j)-1(b)(1) without regard to FC's distributive share of any items of income, gain, deduction, or loss of XYZ. Under paragraph (b)(2) of this section, taking into account the application of paragraph (c)(1) of this section, FC's ATI is $33.33x, determined as $66.66x (excess taxable income from XYZ) — $33.33x (amount excess taxable income exceeds specified excess taxable income). FC's section 163(j) limitation is $10x ($33.33x x 30 percent). Because FC's business interest expense (at the corporate level) of $9.32x is less than FC's section 163(j) limitation of $10x, FC may deduct all $9.32x of business interest expense ($2.50x from Year 2 and $6.82x from Year 1). Because all of XYZ's business interest expense is deductible, FC may also deduct the $15x of business interest expense on U.S. booked liabilities of XYZ for Year 2.

(7) *Example 7: Coordination of section 163(j) and branch profits tax*— (i) *Facts.* FC, a foreign corporation that is not an applicable CFC, uses cash that is treated as a U.S. asset under §1.884-1(d) in order to pay interest described in paragraph (b)(3) of this section for which a deduction for such interest is disallowed under §1.163(j)-2(b).

(ii) *Analysis.* Assuming that FC's U.S. assets otherwise remain constant during the year, the U.S. assets of FC will have decreased by the amount of cash used to pay the interest expense, and the U.S. net equity of FC will be computed accordingly.

(i) *Applicability date.*—This section applies to taxable years ending after the date the Treasury decision adopting these regulations as final regulations is published in the **Federal Register**. However, taxpayers and their related parties, within the meaning of sections 267(b) and 707(b)(1), may apply this section to a taxable year beginning after December 31, 2017, if the taxpayers and their related parties consistently apply all of the section 163(j) regulations, and if applicable, §§1.263A-9, 1.381(c)(20)-1, 1.382-6, 1.383-1, 1.469-9, 1.882-5, 1.1502-13, 1.1502-21, 1.1502-36, 1.1502-79, 1.1502-91 through 1.1502-99 (to the extent they effectuate the rules of §§1.382-6 and 1.383-1), and 1.1504-4 to those taxable years. [Reg. §1.163(j)-8.]

§1.163(j)-9. Elections for excepted trades or businesses; safe harbor for certain REITs.—(a) *Overview.*—This section provides rules and procedures for making an election under section 163(j)(7)(B) to be an electing real property trade or business, as defined in §1.163(j)-1(b)(12), and an election under section 163(j)(7)(C) to be an electing farming business, as defined in §1.163(j)-1(b)(11).

(b) *Scope and effect of election.*—(1) *In general.*—An election under this section is made with respect to each eligible trade or business of the taxpayer and applies only to such trade or business for which the election is made. An election under this section applies to the taxable year in which the election is made and to all subsequent taxable years, except as otherwise provided in this section.

(2) *Irrevocability.*—An election under this section is irrevocable.

(c) *Time and manner of making election.*—(1) *In general.*—Subject to paragraph (e) of this section, a taxpayer makes an election under this section by attaching an election statement to the taxpayer's timely filed original Federal income tax return, including extensions. A taxpayer may make elections for multiple trades or businesses on a single election statement.

(2) *Election statement contents.*—The election statement should be titled "Section 1.163(j)-9 Election" and must contain the following information for each trade or business:

(i) The taxpayer's name;

(ii) The taxpayer's address;

(iii) The taxpayer's social security number (SSN) or employer identification number (EIN);

(iv) A description of the taxpayer's electing trade or business, including the principal business activity code; and

(v) A statement that the taxpayer is making an election under section 163(j)(7)(B) or (C), as applicable.

(3) *Consolidated group's trade or business.*—For a consolidated group's trade or business, the election under this section is made by the agent for the group, as defined in §1.1502-77, on behalf of itself and members of the consolidated group. Only the name and taxpayer identification number (TIN) of the agent for the group, as defined in §1.1502-77, must be provided on the election statement.

(4) *Partnership's trade or business.*—An election for a partnership must be made on the partnership's return with respect to any trade or business that the partnership conducts. An election by a partnership does not apply to a trade or business conducted by a partner outside the partnership.

(d) *Termination of election.*—(1) *In general.*—An election under this section automatically terminates if a taxpayer ceases to engage in the electing trade or business. A taxpayer is considered to cease to engage in an electing trade or business if the taxpayer sells or transfers substantially all of the assets of the electing trade or business to an acquirer that is not a related party in a taxable asset transfer. A taxpayer is also considered to cease to engage in an electing trade or business if the taxpayer terminates its existence for Federal income tax purposes or ceases operation of the electing trade or business, except to the extent that such termination or cessation results in the sale or transfer of substantially all of the assets of the electing trade or business to an acquirer that is a related party, or in a transaction that is not a taxable asset transfer.

(2) *Taxable asset transfer defined.*—For purposes of this paragraph (d), the term taxable asset transfer means a transfer in which the acquirer's basis or adjusted basis in the assets is not determined, directly or indirectly, in whole or in part, by reference to the transferor's basis in the assets.

(3) *Related party defined.*—For purposes of this paragraph (d), the term *related party* means any person who bears a relationship to the taxpayer which is described section 267(b) or 707(b)(1).

(4) *Anti-abuse rule.*—If, within 60 months of a sale or transfer of assets described in paragraph (d)(1) of this section, the taxpayer or a related party reacquires substantially all of the assets that were used in the taxpayer's prior electing trade or business, or substantially similar assets, and resumes conducting such prior electing trade or business, the taxpayer's previously terminated election under this section is reinstated and is effective on the date the prior electing trade or business is reacquired.

(e) *Additional guidance.*—The rules and procedures regarding the time and manner of making an election under this section and the election statement contents in paragraph (c) of this section may be modified through other guidance (see §§601.601(d) and 601.602 of this chapter). Additional situations in which an election may terminate under paragraph (d) of this section may be provided through guidance published in the **Federal Register** or in the Internal Revenue Bulletin (see §601.601(d) of this chapter).

(f) *Examples.*—The examples of this paragraph (f) illustrate the application of this section. Unless otherwise indicated, assume the following: X and Y are domestic C corporations; D and E are U.S. resident individuals not subject to any foreign income tax; and the exemption for certain small businesses in §1.163(j)-2(d) does not apply.

(1) *Example 1: Scope of election*—(i) *Facts.* During her taxable year ending December 31, 2019, D, a sole proprietor, owned and operated a dairy farm and a tree farm as separate farming businesses described in section 263A(e)(4). D filed its original Federal income tax return for the 2019 taxable year on August 1, 2020, and included with the return an election statement meeting the requirements of paragraph (c)(2) of this section. The election statement identified D's dairy farm business as an electing trade or business under this section. On March 1, 2021, D sold some but not all or substantially all of the assets from her dairy farm business to her neighbor, E, who is unrelated to D. After the sale, D continued to operate the dairy farm trade or business.

(ii) *Analysis.* D's election under this section was properly made and is effective for the 2019 taxable year and subsequent years. D's dairy farm business is an excepted trade or business because D made the election with her timely filed Federal income tax return. D's tree farm business is a non-excepted trade or business. The sale of some but not all or substantially all of the assets from D's dairy farm business has no impact on D's election under this section.

(2) *Example 2: Cessation of entire trade or business*—(i) *Facts.* X has a real property trade or business for which X made an election under this section by attaching an election statement to A's 2019 Federal income tax return. On March 1, 2020, X sold all of the assets used in its real property trade or business to Y, an unrelated party, and ceased to engage in the electing trade or business. On June 1, 2027, X

started a new real property trade or business that was substantially similar to X's prior electing trade or business.

(ii) *Analysis.* X's election under this section terminated on March 1, 2020, under paragraph (d)(1) of this section. X may choose whether to make an election under this section for X's new real property trade or business that A started in 2027.

(3) *Example 3: Anti-abuse rule*—(i) *Facts.* The same facts are the same as in *Example 2* in paragraph (f)(2)(i) of this section, except that X re-started her previous real property trade or business on February 1, 2021, when X reacquired substantially all of the assets that X had sold on March 1, 2020.

(ii) *Analysis.* X's election under this section terminated on March, 1, 2020, under paragraph (d)(1) of this section. On February 1, 2021, X's election was reinstated under paragraph (d)(4) of this section. X's new real property trade or business is treated as a resumption of X's prior electing trade or business and is therefore treated as an electing real property trade or business.

(4) *Example 4: Trade or business continuing after acquisition*—(i) *Facts.* X has a farming business for which X made an election under this section by attaching an election statement to X's timely filed 2019 Federal income tax return. Y, unrelated to X, also has a farming business, but Y has not made an election under this section. On July 1, 2020, X transferred all of its assets to Y in a transaction described in section 368(a)(1)(D) (a "D reorganization"). After the transfer, Y continues to operate the farming trade or business acquired from X.

(ii) *Analysis.* Under paragraph (d)(1) of this section, Y is subject to X's election under this section for the trade or business that uses X's assets because the sale or transfer was not in a taxable transaction. Y cannot revoke X's election, but X's election has no effect on Y's existing farming business for which Y has not made an election under this section.

(5) *Example 5: Trade or business merged after acquisition*—(i) *Facts.* The facts are the same as in *Example 4* in paragraph (f)(4)(i) of this section, except that Y uses the assets acquired from X in a trade or business that is neither a farming business (as defined in section 263A(e)(4) or §1.263A-4(a)(4)) nor a trade or business of a specified agricultural or horticultural cooperative (as defined in section 199A(g)(4)).

(ii) *Analysis.* Y is not subject to X's election for Y's farming business because the farming trade or business ceased to exist after the acquisition.

(g) *Safe harbor for REITs.*—(1) *In general.*—If a REIT holds real property, as defined in §1.856-10, interests in partnerships holding real property, as defined in §1.856-10, or shares in other REITs holding real property, as defined in §1.856-10, the REIT is eligible to make the election described in paragraph (b)(1) of this section to be an electing real property trade or business for purposes of sections 163(j)(7)(B) and 168(g)(1)(F) for all or part of its assets. The portion of the REIT's assets eligible for this election is determined under paragraph (g)(2) or (3) of this section.

(2) *REITs that do not significantly invest in real property financing assets.*—If a REIT makes an election described in paragraph (g)(1) of this section and the value of the REIT's real property financing assets, as defined in paragraphs (g)(5) and (6) of this section, at the close of the taxable year is 10 percent or less of the value of the REIT's total assets at the close of the taxable year, as determined under section 856(c)(4)(A), then all of the REIT's assets are treated as assets of an excepted trade or business.

(3) *REITs that significantly invest in real property financing assets.*—If a REIT makes an election described in paragraph (g)(1) of this section and the value of the REIT's real property financing assets, as defined in paragraphs (g)(5) and (6) of this section, at the close of the taxable year is more than 10 percent of the value of the REIT's total assets at the close of the taxable year, as determined under section 856(c)(4)(A), then for allocation of interest expense, interest income, and other items of expense and gross income to excepted and non-excepted trades or businesses, the REIT must apply the rules set forth in §1.163(j)-10 as modified by paragraph (g)(4) of this section.

(4) *REIT real property assets, interests in partnerships, and shares in other REITs.*—(i) *Real property assets.*—Assets held by a REIT described in paragraph (g)(3) of this section that meet the definition of real property under §1.856-10 are treated as assets of an excepted trade or business.

(ii) *Partnership interests.*—If a REIT described in paragraph (g)(3) of this section holds an interest in a partnership, in applying the partnership look-through rule described in §1.163(j)-10(c)(5)(ii)(A)(2), the REIT treats assets of the partnership that meet the definition of real property under §1.856-10 as assets of an excepted trade or business. This application of the definition of real property under §1.856-10 does not affect the characterization of

the partnership's assets at the partnership level or for any non-REIT partner.

(iii) *Shares in other REITs.*—If a REIT (shareholder REIT) described in paragraph (g)(3) of this section holds an interest in another REIT, then for purposes of applying the allocation rules in §1.163(j)-10, the partnership look-through rule described in §1.163(j)-10(c)(5)(ii)(A)(2) applies to the assets of the other REIT (as if the other REIT were a partnership) in determining the extent to which shareholder REIT's adjusted basis in the shares of the other REIT is allocable to an excepted or non-excepted trade or business of shareholder REIT. However, no portion of the adjusted basis of shareholder REIT's shares in the other REIT is allocated to a non-excepted trade or business if all of the other REIT's assets are treated as assets of an excepted trade or business under paragraph (g)(2) of this section. If shareholder REIT does not receive from the other REIT the information necessary to determine whether and the extent that the assets of the other REIT are investments in real property financing assets, then shareholder REIT's shares in the other REIT are treated as assets of a non-excepted trade or business under §1.163(j)-10(c).

(5) *Value of shares in other REITs.*—If a REIT (shareholder REIT) holds shares in another REIT, then for purposes of applying the value tests under paragraphs (g)(2) and (3) of this section, the value of shareholder REIT's real property financing assets includes the portion of the value of shareholder REIT's shares in the other REIT that is attributable to the other REIT's investments in real property financing assets. However, no portion of the value of shareholder REIT's shares in the other REIT is included in the value of shareholder REIT's real property financing assets if all of the other REIT's assets are treated as assets of an excepted trade or business under paragraph (g)(2) of this section. If shareholder REIT does not receive from the other REIT the information necessary to determine whether and the extent that the assets of the other REIT are investments in real property financing assets, then shareholder REIT's shares in the other REIT are treated as real property financing assets for purposes of paragraphs (g)(2) and (3) of this section.

(6) *Real property financing assets.*—For purposes of this paragraph (g), *real property financing assets* include interests, including participation interests, in the following: mortgages, deeds of trust, and installment land contracts; mortgage pass-thru certificates guaranteed by Government National Mortgage Association (GNMA), Federal National Mortgage Association (FNMA), Federal Home Loan Mortgage Corporation (FHLMC), or Canada Mortgage and Housing Corporation (CMHC); REMIC regular interests; other interests in investment trusts classified as trusts under §301.7701-4(c) of this chapter that represent undivided beneficial ownership in a pool of obligations principally secured by interests in real property and related assets that would be permitted investments if the investment trust were a REMIC; obligations secured by manufactured housing treated as single family residences under section 25(e)(10), without regard to the treatment of the obligations or the properties under state law; and debt instruments issued by publicly offered REITs.

(h) *Special anti-abuse rule for certain real property trades or businesses.*—(1) *In general.* Except as provided in paragraph (h)(2) of this section, a real property trade or business does not constitute a trade or business eligible for an election described in paragraph (b)(1) of this section to be an electing real property trade or business if at least 80 percent, determined by fair market value, of the business's real property is leased, whether or not the arrangement is pursuant to a written lease or pursuant to a service contract or another agreement that is not denominated as a lease, to a trade or business under common control with the real property trade or business. For purposes of this paragraph (h), two trades or businesses are under common control if 50 percent of the direct and indirect ownership of both businesses are held by related parties within the meaning of sections 267(b) and 707(b).

(2) *Exception for certain REITs.*—The special anti-abuse rule in paragraph (h)(1) does not apply to REITs that lease qualified lodging facilities, as defined in section 856(d)(9)(D), and qualified health care properties, as defined in section 856(e)(6)(D).

(i) *Applicability date.*—This section applies to taxable years ending after the date the Treasury decision adopting these regulations as final regulations is published in the **Federal Register**. However, taxpayers and their related parties, within the meaning of sections 267(b) and 707(b)(1), may apply the rules of this section to a taxable year beginning after December 31, 2017, so long as the taxpayers and their related parties consistently apply the rules of the section 163(j) regulations, and if applicable, §§1.263A-9, 1.381(c)(20)-1, 1.382-6, 1.383-1, 1.469-9, 1.882-5, 1.1502-13, 1.1502-21, 1.1502-36, 1.1502-79, 1.1502-91 through 1.1502-99 (to the extent they effectuate the rules of §§1.382-6 and 1.383-1), and 1.1504-4 to those taxable years. [Reg. §1.163(j)-9]

§1.163(j)-10. Allocation of interest expense, interest income, and other items of expense and gross income to an excepted trade or business.—(a) *Overview.*—(1) *In general.*—(i) *Purposes.*—This section provides the exclusive rules for allocating tax items that are properly allocable to a trade or business between excepted trades or businesses and non-excepted trades or businesses for purposes of section 163(j). The amount of a taxpayer's interest expense that is properly allocable to excepted trades or businesses is not subject to limitation under section 163(j). The amount of a taxpayer's other items of income, gain, deduction, or loss, including interest income, that is properly allocable to excepted trades or businesses is excluded from the calculation of the taxpayer's section 163(j) limitation. See section 163(j)(6) and (j)(8)(A)(i); see also §1.163(j)-1(b)(1)(i)(H), (b)(1)(ii)(F), and (b)(3). The general method of allocation set forth in paragraph (c) of this section is based on the approach that money is fungible and that interest expense is attributable to all activities and property, regardless of any specific purpose for incurring an obligation on which interest is paid. In no event may the amount of interest expense allocated under this section exceed the amount of interest paid or accrued, or treated as paid or accrued, by the taxpayer within the taxable year.

(ii) *Application of section.*—The amount of a taxpayer's tax items properly allocable to a trade or business, other than interest expense and interest income, that is properly allocable to excepted trades or businesses for purposes of section 163(j) is determined as set forth in paragraph (b) of this section. The amount of a taxpayer's interest expense and interest income that is properly allocable to excepted trades or businesses for purposes of section 163(j) generally is determined as set forth in paragraph (c) of this section, except as otherwise provided in paragraph (d) of this section. For purposes of this section, a taxpayer's activities are not treated as a trade or business if those activities do not involve the provision of services or products to a person other than the taxpayer. For example, if a taxpayer engaged in a manufacturing trade or business has in-house legal personnel that provide legal services solely to the taxpayer, the taxpayer is not treated as also engaged in the trade or business of providing legal services.

(2) *Coordination with other rules.*—(i) *In general.*—The rules of this section apply after a taxpayer has determined whether any interest expense or interest income paid, received, or accrued is properly allocable to a trade or business. Similarly, the rules of this section apply to other tax items after a taxpayer has determined whether those items are properly allocable to a trade or business. For instance, a taxpayer must apply §1.163-8T to determine which items of interest expense are investment interest under section 163(d) before applying the rules in paragraph (c) of this section to allocate interest expense between excepted and non-excepted trades or businesses. After determining whether its tax items are properly allocable to a trade or business, a taxpayer that is engaged in both excepted and non-excepted trades or businesses must apply the rules of this section to determine the amount of interest expense that is business interest expense subject to limitation under section 163(j) and to determine which items are included or excluded in computing its section 163(j) limitation.

(ii) *Treatment of investment interest, investment income, and investment expenses of a partnership with a C corporation or tax-exempt corporation as a partner.*—For rules governing the treatment of investment interest, investment income, and investment expenses of a partnership with a C corporation or tax-exempt corporation as a partner, see §§1.163(j)-4(b)(3) and 1.163(j)-6(j).

(3) *Application of allocation rules to foreign corporations and foreign partnerships.*—The rules of this section apply to foreign corporations and foreign partnerships. See §§1.163(j)-7 and 1.163(j)-8.

(4) *Application of allocation rules to members of a consolidated group.*—(i) *In general.*—As provided in §1.163(j)-4(d), the computations required by section 163(j) and the section 163(j) regulations generally are made for a consolidated group on a consolidated basis. In this regard, for purposes of applying the allocation rules of this section, all members of a consolidated group are treated as one corporation. Therefore, the rules of this section apply to the activities conducted by the group as if those activities were conducted by a single corporation. For example, the group (rather than a particular member) is treated as engaged in excepted or non-excepted trades or businesses. In the case of intercompany obligations, within the meaning of §1.1502-13(g)(2)(ii), for purposes of allocating asset basis between excepted and non-excepted trades or businesses, the obligation of the member borrower is not considered an asset of the creditor member. Similarly, intercompany transactions, within the meaning of §1.1502-13(b)(1)(i), are disregarded for purposes of this section, as are the resulting offsetting items, and property is not treated as used in a trade or business to the extent the use of such property in that trade or business derives from an intercompany

transaction. Further, stock of a group member that is owned by another member of the same group is not treated as an asset for purposes of this section, and the transfer of any amount of member stock to a non-member is treated by the group as a transfer of the member's assets proportionate to the amount of member stock transferred. Additionally, stock of a corporation that is not a group member is treated as owned by the group.

(ii) *Application of excepted business percentage to members of a consolidated group.*—After a consolidated group has determined the percentage of the group's interest expense allocable to excepted trades or businesses for the taxable year (and thus not subject to limitation under section 163(j)), this exempt percentage is applied to the interest paid or accrued by each member during the taxable year to any lender that is not a group member. Therefore, except to the extent paragraph (d) of this section (providing rules for certain qualified nonrecourse indebtedness) applies, an identical percentage of the interest paid or accrued by each member of the group to any lender that is not a group member will be treated as allocable to excepted trades or businesses, regardless of whether any particular member actually engaged in an excepted trade or business.

(iii) *Basis in assets transferred in an intercompany transaction.*—For purposes of allocating interest expense and interest income under paragraph (c) of this section, the basis of property does not include any gain or loss realized with respect to the property by another member in an intercompany transaction, as defined in §1.1502-13(b), whether or not the gain or loss is deferred.

(5) *Tax-exempt organizations.*—For organizations subject to tax under section 511, section 512 and the regulations thereunder determine the rules for allocating all income and expenses among multiple trades or businesses.

(6) [Reserved]

(7) *Examples.*—The following examples illustrate the principles of this paragraph (a).

(i) *Example 1: Items properly allocable to a trade or business*—(A) *Facts.* Individual T operates Business X, a non-excepted trade or business, as a sole proprietor. In Year 1, T pays or accrues $40x of interest expense and receives $100x of gross income with respect to Business X that is not eligible for a section 199A deduction. T borrows money to buy a car for personal use, and T pays or accrues $20x of interest expense with respect to the car loan. T also invests in corporate bonds, and, in Year 1, T receives $50x of interest income on those bonds.

(B) *Analysis.* Under paragraphs (a)(1) and (2) of this section, T must determine which items of income and expense, including items of interest income and interest expense, are properly allocable to a trade or business. T's $100x of gross income and T's $40x of interest expense with respect to Business X are properly allocable to a trade or business. However, the interest expense on T's car loan is personal interest within the meaning of section 163(h)(2) rather than interest properly allocable to a trade or business. Similarly, T's interest income from corporate bonds is not properly allocable to a trade or business because it is interest from investment activity. See section 163(d)(4)(B).

(ii) *Example 2: Intercompany transaction*—(A) *Facts.* S is a member of a consolidated group of which P is the common parent. P conducts an electing real property trade or business (Business X), and S conducts a non-excepted trade or business (Business Y). P leases Building V (which P owns) to S for use in Business Y.

(B) *Analysis.* Under paragraph (a)(4)(i) of this section, a consolidated group is treated as a single corporation for purposes of applying the allocation rules of this section, and the consolidated group (rather than a particular member of the group) is treated as engaged in excepted and non-excepted trades or businesses. Thus, intercompany transactions are disregarded for purposes of this section. As a result, the lease of Building V by P to S is disregarded. Moreover, because Building V is used in Business Y, basis in this asset is allocated to Business Y rather than Business X for purposes of these allocation rules, regardless of which member (P or S) owns the building.

(b) *Allocation of tax items other than interest expense and interest income.*—(1) *In general.*—For purposes of calculating ATI, tax items other than interest expense and interest income are allocated to a particular trade or business in the manner described in this paragraph (b). It is not necessary to allocate items under this paragraph (b) for purposes of calculating ATI if all of the taxpayer's items subject to allocation under this paragraph (b) are allocable to excepted trades or businesses, or if all of those items are allocable to non-excepted trades or businesses.

(2) *Gross income other than dividends and interest income.*—A taxpayer's gross income other than dividends and interest income is allocated to the trade or business that generated the gross income.

(3) *Dividends.*—(i) *Look-through rule.*—If a taxpayer receives a dividend, within the meaning of section 316, that is not investment income, within the meaning of section 163(d), and if the taxpayer looks through to the assets of the payor corporation under paragraph (c)(5)(ii) of this section for the taxable year, then, solely for purposes of allocating amounts received as a dividend during the taxable year to excepted or non-excepted trades or businesses under this paragraph (b), the dividend income is treated as allocable to excepted or non-excepted trades or businesses based upon the relative amounts of the payor corporation's adjusted basis in the assets used in its trades or businesses, determined pursuant to paragraph (c) of this section. If at least 90 percent of the payor corporation's adjusted basis in its assets during the taxable year, determined pursuant to paragraph (c) of this section, is allocable to either excepted trades or businesses or to non-excepted trades or businesses, all of the taxpayer's dividend income from the payor corporation for the taxable year is treated as allocable to either excepted or non-excepted trades or businesses, respectively.

(ii) *Inapplicability of the look-through rule.*—If a taxpayer receives a dividend that is not investment income, within the meaning of section 163(d), and if the taxpayer does not look through to the assets of the payor corporation under paragraph (c)(5)(ii) of this section for the taxable year, then the taxpayer must treat the dividend as allocable to a non-excepted trade or business.

(4) *Gain or loss from the disposition of non-consolidated C corporation stock, partnership interests, or S corporation stock.*—(i) *Non-consolidated C corporations.*—If a taxpayer recognizes gain or loss upon the disposition of stock in a non-consolidated C corporation that is not property held for investment, within the meaning of section 163(d)(5), and if the taxpayer looks through to the assets of the C corporation under paragraph (c)(5)(ii) of this section for the taxable year, then the taxpayer must allocate gain or loss from the disposition of stock to excepted or non-excepted trades or businesses based upon the relative amounts of the corporation's adjusted basis in the assets used in its trades or businesses, determined pursuant to paragraph (c) of this section. However, if a taxpayer recognizes gain or loss upon the disposition of stock in a non-consolidated C corporation that is not property held for investment, within the meaning of section 163(d)(5), and if the taxpayer does not look through to the assets of the C corporation under paragraph (c)(5)(ii) of this section for the taxable year, then the taxpayer must treat the gain or loss from the disposition of stock as allocable to a non-excepted trade or business. For rules governing the transfer of stock of a member of a consolidated group, see paragraph (a)(4)(i) of this section.

(ii) *Partnerships and S corporations.*—(A) If a taxpayer recognizes gain or loss upon the disposition of interests in a partnership or stock in an S corporation that owns:

(1) Non-excepted assets and excepted assets;

(2) Investment assets; or

(3) Both;

(B) The taxpayer determines a proportionate share of the amount properly allocable to a non-excepted trade or business in accordance with the allocation rules set forth in paragraph (c)(5)(ii)(A) or (c)(5)(ii)(B)(3) of this section, as appropriate, and includes such proportionate share of gain or loss in the taxpayer's ATI. This rule also applies to tiered passthrough entities, as defined in § 1.163(j)-7(f)(13), by looking through each passthrough entity tier (for example, an S corporation that is the partner of the highest-tier partnership would look through each lower-tier partnership), subject to paragraph (c)(5)(ii)(D) of this section. With respect to a partner that is a C corporation or tax-exempt corporation, a partnership's investment assets are taken into account and treated as non-excepted trade or business assets.

(5) *Expenses, losses, and other deductions.*—(i) *Expenses, losses, and other deductions that are definitely related to a trade or business.*—Expenses (other than interest expense), losses, and other deductions (collectively, *deductions* for purposes of this paragraph (b)(5)) that are definitely related to a trade or business are allocable to the trade or business to which they relate. A deduction is considered definitely related to a trade or business if the item giving rise to the deduction is incurred as a result of, or incident to, an activity of the trade or business or in connection with property used in the trade or business (see § 1.861-8(b)(2)). If a deduction is definitely related to one or more excepted trades or businesses and one or more non-excepted trades or businesses, the deduction is apportioned between the excepted and non-excepted trades or businesses based upon the relative amounts of the taxpayer's adjusted basis in the assets used in those trades or businesses, as determined under paragraph (c) of this section.

(ii) *Other deductions.*—Deductions that are not described in paragraph (b)(5)(i) of this section are ratably apportioned to all gross income.

(6) *Treatment of certain investment items of a partnership with a C corporation partner.*—Any investment income or investment expenses that a partnership receives, pays, or accrues and that is treated as properly allocable to a trade or business of a C corporation partner under § 1.163(j)-4(b)(3)(i) is treated as properly allocable to a non-excepted trade or business of the C corporation partner.

(7) *Example: Allocation of income and expense.*—The following example illustrates the principles of this paragraph (b):

(i) *Facts.* T conducts an electing real property trade or business (Business Y), which is an excepted trade or business. T also operates a lumber yard (Business Z), which is a non-excepted trade or business. In Year 1, T receives $100x of gross rental income from real property leasing activities. T also pays or accrues $60x of expenses in connection with its real property leasing activities and $20x of legal services performed on behalf of both Business Y and Business Z. T receives $60x of gross income from lumber yard customers and pays or accrues $50x of expenses related to the lumber yard business. For purposes of expense allocations under paragraphs (b) and (c) of this section, T has $240x of adjusted basis in its Business Y assets and $80x of adjusted basis in its Business Z assets.

(ii) *Analysis.* Under paragraph (b)(2) of this section, for Year 1, $100x of rental income is allocated to Business Y, and $60x of income from lumber yard customers is allocated to Business Z. Under paragraph (b)(5)(i) of this section, $60x of expenses paid or accrued in connection with real property leasing activities are allocated to Business Y, and $50x of expenses related to the lumber yard are allocated to Business Z. The $20x of remaining expenses for legal services performed on behalf of both Business Y and Business Z are allocated according to the relative amounts of T's basis in the assets used in each business. The total amount of T's basis in the assets used in Businesses Y and Z is $320x, of which 75 percent ($240x / $320x) is used in Business Y and 25 percent ($80x / $320x) is used in Business Z. Accordingly, $15x of the expenses for legal services are allocated to Business Y and $5x are allocated to Business Z.

(c) *Allocating interest expense and interest income that is properly allocable to a trade or business.*—(1) *General rule.*—(i) *In general.*—Except as otherwise provided in this section, the amount of a taxpayer's interest expense and interest income that is properly allocable to a trade or business is allocated to the taxpayer's excepted or non-excepted trades or businesses for purposes of section 163(j) based upon the relative amounts of the taxpayer's adjusted basis in the assets, as determined under paragraph (c)(5) of this section, used in its excepted or non-excepted trades or businesses. The taxpayer must determine the adjusted basis in its assets as of the close of each determination date, as defined in paragraph (c)(6) of this section, in the taxable year and average those amounts to determine the relative amounts of asset basis for its excepted and non-excepted trades or businesses for that year. It is not necessary to allocate interest expense or interest income under this paragraph (c) for purposes of determining a taxpayer's business interest expense and business interest income if all of the taxpayer's interest income and expense is allocable to excepted trades or businesses (in which case the taxpayer is not subject to the section 163(j) limitation) or if all of the taxpayer's interest income and expense is allocable to non-excepted trades or businesses.

(ii) *De minimis exception.*—If 90 percent or more of the taxpayer's basis in its assets for the taxable year is allocable to either excepted or non-excepted trades or businesses pursuant to this paragraph (c), then all of the taxpayer's interest expense and interest income for that year that is properly allocable to a trade or business is treated as allocable to either excepted or non-excepted trades or businesses, respectively.

(2) *Example.*—The following example illustrates the principles of paragraph (c)(1) of this section: T is a calendar-year C corporation engaged in an electing real property trade or business, the business of selling wine, and the business of selling hand-carved wooden furniture. In Year 1, T has $100x of interest expense that is deductible except for the potential application of section 163(j). Based upon determinations made on the determination dates of March 31, June 30, September 30, and December 31, T's average adjusted basis in the assets used in the electing real property trade or business (an excepted trade or business) in Year 1 is $800x, and T's total average adjusted basis in the assets used in the other two businesses in Year 1 is $200x. Thus, $80x (($800x / ($800x + $200x)) x $100x) of T's interest expense for Year 1 is allocable to T's electing real property trade or business and is not business interest expense subject to limitation under section 163(j). The remaining $20x of T's interest expense is business interest expense for Year 1 that is subject to limitation under section 163(j).

(3) *Asset used in more than one trade or business.*—(i) *General rule.*—If an asset is used in more than one trade or business during a determination period, as defined in paragraph (c)(6) of this section, the taxpayer's adjusted basis in the asset is allocated to each trade or

business using the permissible methodology under this paragraph (c)(3) that most reasonably reflects the use of the asset in each trade or business during that determination period. An allocation methodology most reasonably reflects the use of the asset in each trade or business if it most properly reflects the proportionate benefit derived from the use of the asset in each trade or business. If none of the permissible methodologies set forth in paragraph (c)(3)(ii) of this section reasonably reflects the use of the asset in each trade or business, the taxpayer's basis in the asset is not taken into account for purposes of this paragraph (c).

(ii) *Permissible methodologies for allocating asset basis between or among two or more trades or businesses.*— Subject to the special rules in paragraphs (c)(3)(iii) and (c)(5) of this section, a taxpayer's basis in an asset used in two or more trades or businesses during a determination period may be allocated to those trades or businesses based upon—

(A) The relative amounts of gross income that an asset generates, has generated, or may reasonably be expected to generate, within the meaning of § 1.861-9T(g)(3), with respect to the trades or businesses;

(B) If the asset is land or an inherently permanent structure, the relative amounts of physical space used by the trades or businesses; or

(C) If the trades or businesses generate the same unit of output, the relative amounts of output of those trades or businesses (for example, if an asset is used in two trades or businesses, one of which is an excepted regulated utility trade or business, and the other of which is a non-excepted regulated utility trade or business, the taxpayer may allocate basis in the asset based upon the relative amounts of kilowatt-hours generated by each trade or business).

(iii) *Special rules.*—(A) *Consistent allocation methodologies.*— (1) *In general.*—Except as otherwise provided in paragraph (c)(3)(iii)(A)(2) of this section, a taxpayer may not vary its allocation methodology from one determination period to the next within a taxable year or from one taxable year to the next.

(2) *Consent to change allocation methodology.*—If a taxpayer determines that a different allocation methodology properly reflects the proportionate benefit derived from the use of assets in its trades or businesses, the taxpayer may change its method of allocation under paragraphs (c)(3)(i) and (ii) of this section with the consent of the Commissioner. To obtain consent, a taxpayer must submit a request for a letter ruling under the applicable administrative procedures, and consent only will be granted in extraordinary circumstances.

(B) *De minimis exceptions.*—(1) *De minimis amount of gross income from trades or businesses.*—If at least 90 percent of gross income that an asset generates, has generated, or may reasonably be expected to generate, within the meaning of § 1.861-9T(g)(3), during a determination period is with respect to either excepted trades or businesses or non-excepted trades or businesses, the taxpayer's entire basis in the asset for the determination period must be allocated to either excepted or non-excepted trades or businesses, respectively.

(2) *De minimis amount of asset basis allocable to a trade or business.*—If 90 percent or more of the taxpayer's basis in an asset would be allocated to either excepted trades or businesses or non-excepted trades or businesses during a determination period pursuant to this paragraph (c)(3), the taxpayer's entire basis in the asset for the determination period must be allocated to either excepted or non-excepted trades or businesses, respectively.

(C) *Allocations of excepted regulated utility trades or businesses.*—(1) *In general.*—Except as provided in the de minimis rule in paragraph (c)(3)(iii)(C)(3) of this section, if a taxpayer is engaged in the trade or business of the furnishing or sale of items described in § 1.163(j)-1(b)(13)(i)(A), the taxpayer is engaged in an excepted regulated utility trade or business only to the extent the rates for the items furnished and sold are described in § 1.163(j)-1(b)(13)(i)(B). Thus, for example, electricity sold at market rates rather than on a cost of service and rate of return basis must be treated as electricity sold by a non-excepted regulated utility trade or business. The taxpayer must allocate under this paragraph (c) the basis of assets used in the utility trade or business between its excepted and non-excepted trades or businesses.

(2) *Permissible method for allocating asset basis for utility trades or businesses.*—In the case of a utility trade or business described in paragraph (c)(3)(iii)(C)(1) of this section, and except as provided in the de minimis rule in paragraph (c)(3)(iii)(C)(3) of this section, the method described in paragraph (c)(3)(ii)(C) of this section is the only permissible method for allocating the taxpayer's basis in assets used in the trade or business between the taxpayer's excepted and non-excepted trades or businesses of selling or furnishing the items described in § 1.163(j)-1(b)(13)(i)(A).

(3) *De minimis rule for excepted utility trades or businesses.*—If a taxpayer is engaged in a utility trade or business described in paragraph (c)(3)(iii)(C)(1) of this section, and if more than 90 percent of the items described in § 1.163(j)-1(b)(13)(i)(A) are furnished or sold at rates determined in the manner described in § 1.163(j)-1(b)(13)(i)(B), the taxpayer's entire trade or business is an excepted regulated utility trade or business, and paragraph (c)(3)(iii)(C)(2) of this section does not apply.

(4) *Example.*—The following example illustrates the principles of this paragraph (c)(3)(iii)(C):

(i) *Facts.* X, a C corporation, is engaged in the trade or business of generating electrical energy. During each determination period in the taxable year, 80 percent of the kilowatts generated in the electricity generation trade or business is sold at rates established by a public utility commission on a rate of return basis. The remaining 20 percent of the kilowatts is sold on the wholesale markets at rates not established on a rate of return basis or by the governing or ratemaking body of an electric cooperative. None of the assets used in X's utility generation trade or business are used in any other trade or business.

(ii) *Analysis.* For purposes of section 163(j), under paragraph (c)(3)(iii)(C)(1) of this section, 80 percent of X's electricity generation business is an excepted regulated utility trade or business, and the remaining 20 percent of X's business is a non-excepted utility trade or business. Under paragraph (c)(3)(iii)(C)(2) of this section, X must allocate 80 percent of the basis of the assets used in its utility business to excepted trades or business and the remaining 20 percent of the basis in its assets to non-excepted trades or businesses.

(4) *Disallowed business interest expense carryforwards; floor plan financing interest expense.*—Disallowed business interest expense carryforwards (which were treated as allocable to a non-excepted trade or business in a prior taxable year) are not re-allocated between non-excepted and excepted trades or businesses in a succeeding taxable year. Instead, the carryforwards continue to be treated as allocable to a non-excepted trade or business. Floor plan financing interest expense also is not subject to allocation between excepted and non-excepted trades or businesses (see § 1.163(j)-1(b)(17)) and is always treated as allocable to non-excepted trades or businesses.

(5) *Additional rules relating to basis.*—(i) *Calculation of adjusted basis.*—(A) *Non-depreciable property other than land.*—Except as otherwise provided in paragraph (c)(5)(i)(E) of this section, for purposes of this section, the adjusted basis of an asset other than land with respect to which no deduction is allowable under section 167, section 168 of the Internal Revenue Code of 1954 (former section 168), or section 197, as applicable, is the adjusted basis of the asset for determining gain or loss from the sale or other disposition of that asset as provided in § 1.1011-1. Self-created intangible assets are not taken into account for purposes of this paragraph (c).

(B) *Depreciable property other than inherently permanent structures.*—For purposes of this section, the adjusted basis of any tangible asset with respect to which a deduction is allowable under section 167, other than inherently permanent structures, is determined by using the alternative depreciation system under section 168(g) before any application of the additional first-year depreciation deduction (for example, under section 168(k) or (m)), and the adjusted basis of any tangible asset with respect to which a deduction is allowable under former section 168, other than inherently permanent structures, is determined by using the taxpayer's method of computing depreciation for the asset under former section 168. The depreciation deduction with respect to the property described in this paragraph (c)(5)(i)(B) is allocated ratably to each day during the period in the taxable year to which the depreciation relates.

(C) *Special rule for land and inherently permanent structures.*—Except as otherwise provided in paragraph (c)(5)(i)(E) of this section, for purposes of this section, the adjusted basis of any asset that is land, including nondepreciable improvements to land, or an inherently permanent structure is its unadjusted basis.

(D) *Depreciable or amortizable intangible property and depreciable income forecast method property.*—For purposes of this section, the adjusted basis of any intangible asset with respect to which a deduction is allowable under section 167 or 197, as applicable, is determined in accordance with section 167 or 197, as applicable, and the adjusted basis of any asset described in section 167(g)(6) for which the deduction allowable under section 167 is determined by the taxpayer under section 167(g), is determined in accordance with section 167(g). The depreciation or amortization deduction with respect to the property described in this paragraph (c)(5)(i)(D) is allocated ratably to each day during the period in the taxable year to which the depreciation or amortization relates.

(E) *Assets not yet used in a trade or business.*—Assets that have been acquired or that are under development but that are not yet used in a trade or business are not taken into account for purposes of this paragraph (c). For example, construction works in progress (such as buildings, airplanes, or ships) are not taken into account for purposes of this paragraph (c). Similarly, land acquired by a taxpayer for construction of a building by the taxpayer to be used in a trade or business is not taken into account for purposes of this paragraph (c) until the building is placed in service. This rule does not apply to interests in a partnership or stock in a corporation.

(F) *Trusts established to fund specific liabilities.*—Trusts required by law to fund specific liabilities (for example, pension trusts and plant decommissioning trusts) are not taken into account for purposes of this paragraph (c).

(G) *Inherently permanent structure.*—For purposes of this section, the term *inherently permanent structure* has the meaning provided in §1.856-10(d)(2).

(ii) *Partnership interests; stock in non-consolidated domestic corporations.*—(A) *Partnership interests.*—(1) *Calculation of asset basis.*—For purposes of this section, a partner's interest in a partnership is treated as an asset of the partner. For these purposes, the partner's adjusted basis in a partnership interest is reduced, but not below zero, by the partner's share of partnership liabilities, as determined under section 752, and is further reduced as provided in paragraph (c)(5)(ii)(A)(2)(*iii*) of this section.

(2) *Allocation of asset basis.*—(i) *In general.*—For purposes of determining the extent to which a partner's adjusted basis in its partnership interest is allocable to an excepted or non-excepted trade or business, the partner may look through to such partner's share of the partnership's basis in the partnership's assets, taking into account any adjustments under sections 734(b) and 743(b), and adjusted to the extent required under paragraph (d)(4) of this section, except as otherwise provided in paragraph (c)(5)(ii)(D) of this section. For purposes of the preceding sentence, such partner's share of partnership assets is determined using a reasonable method taking into account special allocations under section 704(b). Notwithstanding paragraph (c)(7) of this section, if a partner's direct and indirect interest in a partnership is greater than or equal to 80 percent of the partnership's capital or profits, the partner must apply the rules in this paragraph (c)(5)(ii)(A) to look through to the partnership's basis in the partnership's assets.

(ii) *De minimis rule.*—If, after applying paragraph (c)(5)(ii)(A)(2)(*iii*) of this section, at least 90 percent of a partner's share of a partnership's basis in its assets (including adjustments under sections 734(b) and 743(b)) is allocable to either excepted trades or businesses or non-excepted trades or businesses, without regard to assets not properly allocable to a trade or business, the partner's entire basis in its partnership interest is treated as allocable to either excepted or non-excepted trades or businesses, respectively. For purposes of the preceding sentence, such partner's share of partnership assets is determined using a reasonable method taking into account special allocations under section 704(b).

(iii) *Partnership assets not properly allocable to a trade or business.*—For purposes of applying paragraphs (c)(5)(ii)(A)(2)(*i*) and (*ii*) of this section with respect to a partner that is a C corporation or tax-exempt corporation, such partner's share of a partnership's assets that are not properly allocable to a trade or business is treated as properly allocable to an excepted or non-excepted trade or business with respect to such partner in the same manner that such assets would be treated if held directly by such partner. With respect to a partner other than a C corporation or tax-exempt corporation, a partnership's assets that are not properly allocable to a trade or business are treated as neither excepted nor non-excepted trade or business assets, and such partner's adjusted basis in its partnership interest is reduced by that partner's share of the partnership's asset basis with respect to those assets. For purposes of this paragraph (c)(5)(ii)(A)(2)(*iii*), such partner's share of a partnership's assets is determined under a reasonable method taking into account special allocations under section 704(b).

(iv) *Inapplicability of partnership look-through rule.*—If a partner, other than a C corporation or a tax-exempt corporation, chooses not to look through to the partnership's basis in the partnership's assets under paragraph (c)(5)(ii)(A)(2)(*i*) of this section or is precluded by paragraph (c)(5)(ii)(D) of this section from applying such partnership look-through rule, the partner generally will treat its basis in the partnership interest as either an asset held for investment or a non-excepted trade or business asset as determined under section 163(d). If a partner that is a C corporation or a tax-exempt corporation chooses not to look through to the partnership's basis in the partnership's assets under paragraph (c)(5)(ii)(A)(2)(*i*) of this section or is precluded by paragraph (c)(5)(ii)(D) of this section from applying such partnership look-through rule, the taxpayer must treat

its entire basis in the partnership interest as allocable to a non-excepted trade or business.

(B) *Stock in non-consolidated domestic corporations.*—(1) *In general.*—For purposes of this section, if a taxpayer owns stock in a domestic C corporation that is not a member of the taxpayer's consolidated group, or if the taxpayer owns stock in an S corporation, the stock is treated as an asset of the taxpayer.

(2) *Domestic non-consolidated C corporations.*—(i) *Allocation of asset basis.*—If a shareholder satisfies the minimum ownership threshold in paragraph (c)(7) of this section, then, for purposes of determining the extent to which the shareholder's basis in its stock in the domestic non-consolidated C corporation is allocable to an excepted or non-excepted trade or business, the shareholder must look through to the corporation's basis in the corporation's assets, adjusted to the extent required under paragraph (d)(4) of this section, except as otherwise provided in paragraph (c)(5)(ii)(D) of this section.

(ii) *De minimis rule.*—If at least 90 percent of the domestic non-consolidated C corporation's basis in the corporation's assets is allocable to either excepted trades or businesses or non-excepted trades or businesses, the shareholder's entire interest in the corporation's stock is treated as allocable to either excepted or non-excepted trades or businesses, respectively.

(iii) *Inapplicability of corporate look-through rule.*—If a shareholder other than a C corporation or a tax-exempt corporation does not satisfy the minimum ownership threshold in paragraph (c)(7) of this section or is precluded by paragraph (c)(5)(ii)(D) of this section from applying the corporation look-through rule of paragraph (c)(5)(ii)(B)(2)(*i*) of this section, the shareholder generally will treat its entire basis in the corporation's stock as an asset held for investment. If a shareholder that is a C corporation or a tax-exempt corporation does not satisfy the minimum ownership threshold in paragraph (c)(7) of this section or is precluded by paragraph (c)(5)(ii)(D) of this section from applying the corporation look-through rule of paragraph (c)(5)(ii)(B)(2)(*i*) of this section, the shareholder must treat its entire basis in the corporation's stock as allocable to a non-excepted trade or business.

(3) *S corporations.*—(i) *Calculation of asset basis.*—For purposes of this section, a shareholder's share of stock in an S corporation is treated as an asset of the shareholder. Additionally, for these purposes, the shareholder's adjusted basis in a share of S corporation stock is adjusted to take into account the modifications in paragraph (c)(5)(i)(A) of this section with respect to the assets of the S corporation (for example, a shareholder's adjusted basis in its S corporation stock is increased by the shareholder's share of depreciation with respect to an inherently permanent structure owned by the S corporation).

(ii) *Allocation of asset basis.*—For purposes of determining the extent to which a shareholder's basis in its stock of an S corporation is allocable to an excepted or non-excepted trade or business, the shareholder may look through to such shareholder's share of the S corporation's basis in the S corporation's assets, allocated on a pro rata basis, adjusted to the extent required under paragraph (d)(4) of this section, except as otherwise provided in paragraph (c)(5)(ii)(D) of this section. Notwithstanding paragraph (c)(7) of this section, if a shareholder's direct and indirect interest in an S corporation is greater than or equal to 80 percent of the S corporation's stock by vote and value, the shareholder must apply the rules in this paragraph (c)(5)(ii)(B)(3) to look through to the S corporation's basis in the S corporation's assets.

(iii) *De minimis rule.*—If at least 90 percent of a shareholder's share of an S corporation's basis in its assets is allocable to either excepted trades or businesses or non-excepted trades or businesses, the shareholder's entire basis in its S corporation stock is treated as allocable to either excepted or non-excepted trades or businesses, respectively.

(iv) *Inapplicability of S corporation look-through rule.*—If a shareholder chooses not to look through to the S corporation's basis in the S corporation's assets under paragraph (c)(5)(ii)(B)(3)(*ii*) of this section or is precluded by paragraph (c)(5)(ii)(D) of this section from applying such S corporation look-through rule, the shareholder generally will treat its basis in the S corporation stock as either an asset held for investment or a non-excepted trade or business asset as determined under section 163(d).

(C) *Stock in CFCs.*—The rules applicable to domestic non-consolidated C corporations in paragraph (c)(5)(ii)(B) of this section also apply to CFCs.

(D) *Inapplicability of look-through rule to partnerships or non-consolidated corporations to which the small business exemption applies.*—

A taxpayer may not apply the look-through rules in paragraphs (b)(3) and (c)(5)(ii)(A), (B), and (C) of this section to a partnership, S corporation, or non-consolidated corporation that is eligible for the small business exemption under section 163(j)(3) and §1.163(j)-2(d)(1).

(E) *Tiered entities.*—If a taxpayer applies the look-through rules of this paragraph (c)(5)(ii), the taxpayer must do so for all lower-tier entities with respect to which the taxpayer satisfies, directly or indirectly, the minimum ownership threshold in paragraph (c)(7) of this section, subject to the limitation in paragraph (c)(5)(ii)(D) of this section, beginning with the lowest-tier entity.

(iii) *Cash and cash equivalents and customer receivables.*—Except as otherwise provided in paragraph (d)(2) of this section, a taxpayer's basis in its cash and cash equivalents and customer receivables is not taken into account for purposes of this paragraph (c). This rule also applies to a lower-tier entity if a taxpayer looks through to the assets of that entity under paragraph (c)(5)(ii) of this section. For purposes of this paragraph (c)(5)(iii), the term *cash and cash equivalents* includes cash, foreign currency, commercial paper, any interest in an investment company registered under the Investment Company Act of 1940 (1940 Act) and regulated as a money market fund under 17 CFR 270.2a-7 (Rule 2a-7 under the 1940 Act), any obligation of a government, and any derivative that is substantially secured by an obligation of a government, or any similar asset. For purposes of this paragraph (c)(5)(iii), a *derivative* is a derivative described in section 59A(h)(4)(A), without regard to section 59A(h)(4)(C). For purposes of this paragraph (c)(5)(iii), the term *government* means the United States or any agency or instrumentality of the United States; a State or any political subdivision thereof, including the District of Columbia and any possession or territory of the United States, within the meaning of section 103 and §1.103-1; or any foreign government, any political subdivision of a foreign government, or any wholly owned agency or instrumentality of any one of the foregoing within the meaning of §1.1471-6(b).

(iv) *Deemed asset sale.*—Solely for purposes of determining the amount of basis allocable to excepted and non-excepted trades or businesses under this section, an election under section 336, 338, or 754, as applicable, is deemed to have been made for any acquisition of corporate stock or partnership interests with respect to which the taxpayer demonstrates to the satisfaction of the Commissioner, in the information statement required by paragraph (c)(6)(iii)(B) of this section, that the taxpayer was eligible to make an election but was actually or effectively precluded from doing so by a regulatory agency with respect to an excepted regulated utility trade or business. Any additional basis taken into account under this rule is reduced ratably over a 15-year period beginning with the month of the acquisition and is not subject to the anti-abuse rule in paragraph (c)(8) of this section.

(v) *Other adjustments.*—The Commissioner may make appropriate adjustments to prevent a taxpayer from intentionally and artificially increasing its basis in assets attributable to an excepted trade or business.

(6) *Determination dates; determination periods; reporting requirements.*—(i) *Definitions.*—For purposes of this section, the term *determination date* means the last day of each quarter of the taxpayer's taxable year (and the last day of the taxpayer's taxable year, if the taxpayer has a short taxable year), and the term *determination period* means the period beginning the day after one determination date and ending on the next determination date.

(ii) *Application of look-through rules.*—If a taxpayer that applies the look-through rules of paragraph (c)(5)(ii) of this section has a different taxable year than the partnership or non-consolidated corporation to which the taxpayer is applying those rules, then, for purposes of this paragraph (c)(6), the taxpayer must use the most recent quarterly figures from the partnership or non-consolidated corporation. For example, assume that PS1 is a partnership with a May 31 taxable year, and that C (a calendar-year C corporation) is a partner whose ownership interest satisfies the ownership threshold in paragraph (c)(7) of this section. PS1's determination dates are February 28, May 31, August 31, and November 30. In turn, C's determination dates are March 31, June 30, September 30, and December 31. If C looks through to PS1's basis in its assets under paragraph (c)(5)(ii) of this section, then, for purposes of determining the amount of C's asset basis that is attributable to its excepted and non-excepted businesses on March 31, C must use PS1's asset basis calculations for February 28.

(iii) *Reporting requirements.*—(A) *Books and records.*—A taxpayer must maintain books of account and other records cond data as necessary to substantiate the taxpayer's use of an asset in an excepted trade or business and to substantiate the adjustments to asset basis for purposes of applying paragraph (c) of this section. One indication

demonstrating that a particular asset is used in a particular trade or business is if the taxpayer maintains separate books and records for all of its excepted and non-excepted trades or businesses, and can show the asset in the books and records of a particular excepted or non-excepted trade or business. For rules governing record retention, see §1.6001-1.

(B) *Information statement.*—Except as otherwise provided in publications, forms, instructions, or other guidance, each taxpayer that is making an allocation under this paragraph (c) must prepare a statement containing the information described in this paragraph (c)(6)(iii) and must attach the statement to its timely filed Federal income tax return for the taxable year. The statement, which must be titled "Section 163(j) Asset Basis Calculations," must include the following information:

(1) The taxpayer's adjusted basis in the assets used in its excepted and non-excepted businesses, determined on a quarterly basis as set forth in this section, including detailed information for the different groups of assets identified in paragraphs (c)(5)(i), (c)(5)(ii), and (d) of this section;

(2) The determination dates on which asset basis was measured during the taxable year;

(3) The names and taxpayer identification numbers (TINs) of all entities for which basis information is being provided, including partnerships and corporations if the taxpayer that owns an interest in a partnership or corporation looks through to the partnership's or corporation's basis in the partnership's or corporation's assets under paragraph (c)(5)(ii) of this section. If the taxpayer is a member of a consolidated group, the name and TIN of the agent for the group, as defined in §1.1502-77, must be provided, but the taxpayer need not provide the names and TINs of all other consolidated group members;

(4) Asset basis information for corporations or partnerships if the taxpayer looks through to the corporation's or partnership's basis in the corporation's or partnership's assets under paragraph (c)(5)(ii) of this section; and

(5) A summary of the method or methods used to determine asset basis in property used in both excepted and non-excepted businesses, as well as information regarding any deemed sale under paragraph (c)(5)(iv) of this section.

(iv) *Failure to file statement.*—If a taxpayer fails to file the statement described in paragraph (c)(6)(iii) of this section or files a statement that does not comply with the requirements of paragraph (c)(6)(iii) of this section, the Commissioner may treat the taxpayer as if all of its interest expense is properly allocable to a non-excepted trade or business, unless the taxpayer shows that there was reasonable cause for failing to comply with, and the taxpayer acted in good faith with respect to, the requirements of paragraph (c)(6)(iii) of this section, taking into account all pertinent facts and circumstances.

(7) *Ownership threshold for look-through rules.*—(i) *Corporations.*—(A) *Asset basis.*—A shareholder must look through to the assets of a non-consolidated domestic C corporation or a CFC under paragraph (c)(5)(ii) of this section for purposes of allocating the shareholder's basis in its stock in the corporation between excepted and non-excepted trades or businesses if the shareholder's direct and indirect interest in the corporation satisfies the ownership requirements of section 1504(a)(2). A shareholder may look through to the assets of an S corporation under paragraph (c)(5)(ii) of this section for purposes of allocating the shareholder's basis in its stock in the S corporation between excepted and non-excepted trades or businesses regardless of the shareholder's direct and indirect interest in the S corporation.

(B) *Dividends.*—A shareholder must look through to the activities of a non-consolidated domestic C corporation or a CFC under paragraph (b)(3) of this section if the shareholder's direct and indirect interest in the corporation satisfies the ownership requirements of section 1504(a)(2). A shareholder may look through to the activities of an S corporation under paragraph (b)(3) of this section regardless of the shareholder's direct and indirect interest in the S corporation.

(ii) *Partnerships.*—A partner may look through to the assets of a partnership under paragraph (c)(5)(ii) of this section for purposes of allocating the partner's basis in its partnership interest between excepted and non-excepted trades or businesses regardless of the partner's direct and indirect interest in the partnership.

(iii) *Inapplicability of look-through rule.*—For circumstances in which a taxpayer that satisfies the ownership threshold in this paragraph (c)(7) may not apply the look-through rules in paragraphs (b)(3) and (c)(5)(ii) of this section, see paragraph (c)(5)(ii)(D) of this section.

(8) *Anti-abuse rule.*—If a principal purpose for the acquisition, disposition, or change in use of an asset was to artificially shift the

amount of basis allocable to excepted or non-excepted trades or businesses on a determination date, the additional basis or change in use will not be taken into account for purposes of this section. For example, if an asset is used in a non-excepted trade or business for most of the taxable year, and if the taxpayer begins using the asset in an excepted trade or business towards the end of the year with a principal purpose of shifting the amount of basis in the asset that is allocable to the excepted trade or business, the change in use is disregarded for purposes of this section. A purpose may be a principal purpose even though it is outweighed by other purposes (taken together or separately). In determining whether a taxpayer has a principal purpose described in this paragraph (c)(8), factors to be considered include, for example, the following: the business purpose for the acquisition, disposition, or change in use; the length of time the asset was used in a trade or business; whether the asset was acquired from a related person; and whether the taxpayer's aggregate basis in its assets increased or decreased temporarily on or around a determination date. A principal purpose is presumed to be present in any case in which the acquisition, disposition, or change in use lacks a substantial business purpose and increases the taxpayer's basis in assets used in its excepted trades or businesses by more than 10 percent during the taxable year.

(d) *Direct allocations.*—(1) *In general.*—For purposes of this section, a taxpayer with qualified nonrecourse indebtedness, within the meaning of §1.861-10T(b), must directly allocate interest expense from the indebtedness to the taxpayer's assets in the manner and to the extent provided in §1.861-10T(b).

(2) *Financial services entities.*—For purposes of this section, a taxpayer that is engaged in the trade or business of banking, within the meaning of section 581, insurance, financing, or a similar business that derives active financing income as described in §1.904-4(e)(2) (an active financing business) must directly allocate interest expense and interest income from that business to the taxpayer's assets used in that business. The special rule for cash and cash equivalents in paragraph (c)(5)(iii) of this section does not apply to an entity that qualifies as a financial services entity as described in §1.904-4(e)(3).

(3) *Assets used in more than one trade or business.*—If an asset is used in more than one trade or business, the taxpayer must apply the rules in paragraph (c)(3) of this section to determine the extent to which interest that is directly allocated under this paragraph (d) is allocable to excepted or non-excepted trades or businesses.

(4) *Adjustments to basis of assets to account for direct allocations.*—In determining the amount of a taxpayer's basis in the assets used in its excepted and non-excepted trades or businesses for purposes of paragraph (c) of this section, adjustments must be made to reflect direct allocations under this paragraph (d). These adjustments consist of reductions in the amount of the taxpayer's basis in its assets for purposes of paragraph (c) of this section to reflect assets to which interest expense is directly allocated under this paragraph (d). These adjustments must be made before the taxpayer averages the adjusted basis in its assets as determined on each determination date during the taxable year.

(5) *Example: Direct allocation of interest expense.*—(i) *Facts.* T conducts an electing real property trade or business (Business X) and operates a retail store that is a non-excepted trade or business (Business Y). In Year 1, T issues Note A to a third party in exchange for $1,000x for the purpose of acquiring Building B. Note A is qualified nonrecourse indebtedness (within the meaning of §1.861-10T(b)) secured by Building B. T then uses those funds to acquire Building B for $1,200x, and T uses Building B in Business X. During Year 1, T pays $500x of interest, of which $100x is interest payments on Note A. For Year 1, T's basis in its assets used in Business X (as determined under paragraph (c) of this section) is $3,600x (excluding cash and cash equivalents), and T's basis in its assets used in Business Y (as determined under paragraph (c) of this section) is $800x (excluding cash and cash equivalents). Each of Business X and Business Y also has $100x of cash and cash equivalents.

(ii) *Analysis.* Because Note A is qualified nonrecourse indebtedness that is secured by Building B, in allocating interest expense between Businesses X and Y, T first must directly allocate the $100x of interest expense it paid with respect to Note A to Business X in accordance with paragraph (d)(1) of this section. Thereafter, T must allocate the remaining $400x of interest expense between Businesses X and Y under paragraph (c) of this section. After excluding T's $1,200x cost basis in Building B (see paragraph (d)(4) of this section), and without regard to T's $200x of cash and cash equivalents (see paragraph (c)(5)(iv) of this section), T's basis in assets used in Businesses X and Y is $2,400x and $800x (75 percent and 25 percent), respectively. Thus, $300x of the remaining $400x of interest expense would be allocated to Business X, and $100x would be allocated to Business Y.

(e) *Examples.*—The examples in this paragraph (e) illustrate the principles of this section. For purposes of these examples, assume that no taxpayer is eligible for the small business exemption under section 163(j)(3) and §1.163(j)-2(d), no taxpayer has floor plan financing interest expense, and no taxpayer has qualified nonrecourse indebtedness within the meaning of §1.163-10T(b).

(1) *Example 1: Interest allocation within a consolidated group*—(i) *Facts.* S is a member of a consolidated group of which P is the common parent. P conducts an electing real property trade or business (Business X), and S conducts a non-excepted trade or business (Business Y). In Year 1, P pays or accrues (without regard to section 163(j)) $35x of interest expense and receives $10x of interest income, and S pays or accrues (without regard to section 163(j)) $115x of interest expense and receives $5x of interest income (for a total of $150x of interest expense and $15x of interest income). For purposes of this example, assume that, pursuant to paragraph (c) of this section, $30x of the P group's interest expense and $3x of the P group's interest income is allocable to Business X, and the remaining $120x of interest expense and $12x of interest income is allocable to Business Y.

(ii) *Analysis.* Under paragraph (a)(4) of this section, 20 percent of the P group's Year 1 interest expense ($30x / $150x) and interest income ($3x / $15x) is allocable to an excepted trade or business. Thus, $7x ($35x x 20 percent) of P's interest expense and $2x ($10x x 20 percent) of P's interest income is allocable to an excepted trade or business. The remaining $28x of P's interest expense is business interest expense subject to limitation under section 163(j), and the remaining $8x of P's interest income is business interest income that increases the group's section 163(j) limitation. In turn, $23x ($115x x 20 percent) of S's interest expense and $1x ($5x x 20 percent) of S's interest income is allocable to an excepted trade or business. The remaining $92x of S's interest expense is business interest expense subject to limitation under section 163(j), and the remaining $4x of S's interest income is business interest income that increases the group's section 163(j) limitation.

(2) *Example 2: Interest allocation within a consolidated group with assets used in more than one trade or business*—(i) *Facts.* S is a member of a consolidated group of which P is the common parent. P conducts an electing real property trade or business (Business X), and S conducts a non-excepted trade or business (Business Y). In Year 1, P pays or accrues (without regard to section 163(j)) $50x of interest expense, and S pays or accrues $100x of interest expense (without regard to section 163(j)). P leases 40 percent of space in Building V (which P owns) to S for use in Business Y, and P leases the remaining 60 percent of space in Building V to third parties. For purposes of allocating interest expense under paragraph (c) of this section, the P group's basis in its assets (excluding Building V) used in Businesses X and Y is $180x and $620x, respectively. The P group's basis in Building V for purposes of allocating interest expense under paragraph (c) of this section is $200x.

(ii) *Analysis.* Under paragraph (c)(3)(ii) of this section, the P group's basis in Building V ($200x) is allocated to excepted and non-excepted trades or businesses in accordance with the use of space by Business Y (40 percent) and Business X (the remainder, or 60 percent). Accordingly, $120x of the basis in Building V is allocated to excepted trades or businesses (60 percent x $200x), and $80x is allocated to non-excepted trades or businesses (40 percent x $200x). After allocating the basis in Building V, the P group's total basis in the assets used in excepted and non-excepted trades or businesses is $300x and $700x, respectively. Under paragraphs (a)(4) and (c) of this section, 30 percent ($300x / $1000x) of the P group's Year 1 interest expense is properly allocable to an excepted trade or business. Thus, $15x ($50x x 30 percent) of P's interest expense is properly allocable to an excepted trade or business, and the remaining $35x of P's interest expense is business interest expense subject to limitation under section 163(j). In turn, $30x ($100x x 30 percent) of S's interest expense is properly allocable to an excepted trade or business, and the remaining $70x of S's interest expense is business interest expense subject to limitation under section 163(j).

(3) *Example 3: Application of look-through rules*—(i) *Facts.* (A) A and B are unrelated individual taxpayers. A owns 100 percent of the stock of Corp 1, a calendar-year domestic C corporation. The basis of A's stock in Corp 1 is $500x. Corp 1 owns 10 percent of the interests in PS1 (a domestic partnership), and B owns the remaining 90 percent. Corp 1's basis in its PS1 interests is $25x, and B's basis in its PS1 interests is $225x. PS1 owns 100 percent of the stock of Corp 2, a calendar-year domestic C corporation. PS1 has a basis of $1000x in its Corp 2 stock.

(B) In 2020, Corp 1 was engaged solely in a non-excepted trade or business. That same year, PS1's only activity was holding Corp 2 stock. In turn, Corp 2 was engaged in both an electing farming business and a non-excepted trade or business. Under the allocation rules in paragraph (c) of this section, 50 percent of Corp 2's asset basis in 2020 was allocable to the electing farming business. The remaining 50 percent was allocable to the non-excepted trade or business.

(C) Individuals A and B each paid or accrued (without regard to section 163(j)) $150x of interest expense allocable to a trade or business under §1.163-8T (along with personal interest and investment interest). A's trade or business was an excepted trade or business, and B's trade or business was a non-excepted trade or business. A's basis in the assets used in its trade or business was $100x, and B's basis in the assets used in its trade or business was $112.5x.

(ii) *Analysis.* (A) As provided in paragraph (c)(5)(ii)(E) of this section, if a taxpayer applies the look-through rules of paragraph (c)(5)(ii) of this section, the taxpayer must begin with the lowest-tier entity to which it is eligible to apply the look-through rules. A directly owns 100 percent of the stock of Corp 1; thus, A satisfies the 80 percent minimum ownership threshold with respect to Corp 1. A also owns 10 percent of the interests in PS1. There is no minimum ownership threshold for partnerships; thus, A may apply the look-through rules to PS1. However, A does not directly or indirectly own at least 80 percent of the stock of Corp 2; thus, A may not look through its indirect interest in Corp 2. In turn, B directly owns 90 percent of the interests in PS1, and B indirectly owns at least 80 percent of the stock of Corp 2. Thus, B may apply the look-through rules to both PS1 and Corp 2.

(B) From A's perspective, PS1 is not engaged in a trade or business for purposes of section 163(j); instead, PS1 is merely holding its Corp 2 stock as an investment. Under paragraph (c)(5)(ii)(A)(2) of this section, if a partnership is not engaged in a trade or business, then its C corporation partner must treat its entire basis in the partnership interest as allocable to a non-excepted trade or business. Thus, for purposes of A's application of the look-through rules, Corp 1's entire basis in its PS1 interest ($25x) is allocable to a non-excepted trade or business. Corp 1's basis in its other assets also is allocable to a non-excepted trade or business (the only trade or business in which Corp 1 is engaged). Thus, under paragraph (c) of this section, A's $500x basis in its Corp 1 stock is allocable entirely to a non-excepted trade or business. A's $100x basis in its other business assets is allocable to an excepted trade or business. Thus, 5/6 (or $125x) of A's $150x of interest expense is properly allocable to a non-excepted trade or business and is business interest expense subject to limitation under section 163(j), and the remaining $25x of A's $150x of interest expense is allocable to an excepted trade or business and is not subject to limitation under section 163(j).

(C) From B's perspective, PS1 must look through its stock in Corp 2 to determine the extent to which PS1's basis in the stock is allocable to an excepted or non-excepted trade or business. Half of Corp 2's basis in its assets is allocable to an excepted trade or business, and the other half is allocable to a non-excepted trade or business. Thus, from B's perspective, $500x of PS1's basis in its Corp 2 stock (PS1's only asset) is allocable to an excepted trade or business, and the other half is allocable to a non-excepted trade or business. B's basis in its PS1 interests is $225x. Applying the look-through rules to B's PS1 interests, $112.5x of B's basis in its PS1 interests is allocable to an excepted trade or business, and $112.5x of B's basis in its PS1 interests is allocable to a non-excepted trade or business. Since B's basis in the assets used in its non-excepted trade or business also was $112.5x, two-thirds of B's interest expense ($100x) is properly allocable to a non-excepted trade or business and is business interest expense subject to limitation under section 163(j), and one-third of B's interest expense ($50x) is allocable to an excepted trade or business and is not subject to limitation under section 163(j).

(4) *Example 4: Excepted and non-excepted trades or businesses in a consolidated group*—(i) *Facts.* P is the common parent of a consolidated group of which A and B are the only other members. A conducts an electing real property trade or business (Business X), and B conducts a non-excepted trade or business (Business Y). In Year 1, A pays or accrues (without regard to section 163(j)) $50x of interest expense and earns $70x of gross income in the conduct of Business X, and B pays or accrues (without regard to section 163(j)) $100x of interest expense and earns $150x of gross income in the conduct of Business Y. B owns Building V, which it uses in Business Y. For purposes of allocating the P group's Year 1 business interest expense between excepted and non-excepted trades or businesses under paragraph (c) of this section, the P group's basis in its assets (other than Building V) used in Businesses X and Y is $180x and $620x, respectively, and the P group's basis in Building V is $200x. At the end of Year 1, B sells Building V to a third party and realizes a gain of $60x in addition to the $150x of gross income B earned that year from the conduct of Business Y.

(ii) *Analysis.* (A) Under paragraphs (a)(4) and (c) of this section, the P group's basis in its assets used in its trades or businesses is allocated between the P group's excepted trade or business (Business X) and its non-excepted trade or business (Business Y) as though these trades or businesses were conducted by a single corporation. Under paragraph (c) of this section, the P group's basis in its assets used in Businesses X and Y is $180x and $820x, respectively. Accordingly, 18 percent ($180x / $1,000x) of the P group's total interest expense ($150x) is properly allocable to an excepted trade or business ($27x), and the remaining 82 percent of the P group's total interest

expense is business interest expense properly allocable to a non-excepted trade or business ($123x).

(B) To determine the P group's section 163(j) limitation, paragraph (a) of this section requires that certain items of income and deduction be allocated to the excepted and non-excepted trades or businesses of the P group as though these trades or businesses were conducted by a single corporation. In Year 1, the P group's excepted trade or business (Business X) has gross income of $70x, and the P group's non-excepted trade or business (Business Y) has gross income of $150x. Because Building V was used exclusively in Business Y, the $60x of gain from the sale of Building V in Year 1 is attributed to Business Y under paragraph (b)(2) of this section. The P group's section 163(j) limitation is $63x (30 percent x $210x), which allows the P group to deduct $63x of its $123x of business interest expense allocated to the P group's non-excepted trades or businesses. The group's $27x of interest expense that is allocable to excepted trades or businesses may be deducted without limitation under section 163(j).

(iii) *Intercompany transaction.* The facts are the same as in *Example* 4 in paragraph (e)(4)(i) of this section, except that A owns Building V and leases it to B in Year 1 for $20x for use in Business Y, and A sells Building V to a third party for a $60 gain at the end of Year 1. Under paragraphs (a)(4) and (c) of this section, all members of the P group are treated as a single corporation. As a result, the P group's basis in its assets used in its trades or businesses is allocated between the P group's excepted trade or business (Business X) and its non-excepted trade or business (Business Y) as though these trades or businesses were conducted by a single corporation. A lease between two divisions of a single corporation would produce no rental income or expense. Thus, the $20x of rent paid by B to A does not affect the P group's ATI. Moreover, under paragraph (c) of this section, Building V is an asset used in the P group's non-excepted trade or business (Business Y). Accordingly, although A owns Building V, the basis in Building V is added to the P group's basis in assets used in Business Y for purposes of allocating interest expense under paragraph (c) of this section. In the same vein, when A sells Building V to a third party at a gain of $60x, the gain is included in the P group's ATI because Building V was used in a non-excepted trade or business of the P group (Business Y) prior to its sale.

(5) *Example 5: Captive activities*—(i) *Facts.* S and T are members of a consolidated group of which P is the common parent. P conducts an electing real property trade or business (Business X), S conducts a non-excepted trade or business (Business Y), and T provides transportation services to Businesses X and Y but does not have any customers outside of the P group. For Year 1, T provides transportation services using a single bus with a basis of $120x.

(ii) *Analysis.* Under paragraph (a)(4) of this section, activities conducted by a consolidated group are treated as though those activities were conducted by a single corporation. Because the activities of T are limited to providing intercompany transportation services, T does not conduct a trade or business for purposes of section 163(j). Under paragraph (c)(3) of this section, business interest expense is allocated to excepted and non-excepted trades or businesses based on the relative basis of the assets used in those businesses. The basis in T's only asset, a bus, is therefore allocated between Business X and Business Y according to the use of T's bus by these businesses. Business X uses one-third of T's services, and Business Y uses two-thirds of T's services. Thus, $40x of the basis of T's bus is allocated to Business X, and $80x of the basis of T's bus is allocated to Business Y.

(f) *Applicability date.*—This section applies to taxable years ending after the date the Treasury decision adopting these regulations as final regulations is published in the **Federal Register**. However, taxpayers and their related parties, within the meaning of sections 267(b) and 707(b)(1), may apply the rules of this section to a taxable year beginning after December 31, 2017, so long as the taxpayers and their related parties consistently apply the rules of the section 163(j) regulations, and if applicable, §§1.263A-9, 1.381(c)(20)-1, 1.382-6, 1.383-1, 1.469-9, 1.882-5, 1.1502-13, 1.1502-21, 1.1502-36, 1.1502-79, 1.1502-91 through 1.1502-99 (to the extent they effectuate the rules of §§1.382-6 and 1.383-1), and 1.1504-4 to those taxable years. [Reg. §1.163(j)-10.]

§1.163(j)-11. Transition rules.—(a) *Application of section 163(j) limitation if a corporation joins a consolidated group with a taxable year beginning before January 1, 2018.*—(1) *In general.*—If a corporation (S) joins a consolidated group whose taxable year began before January 1, 2018, and if S is subject to the section 163(j) limitation at the time of its change in status, then section 163(j) will apply to S's short taxable year that ends on the day of S's change in status, but section 163(j) will not apply to S's short taxable year that begins the next day (when S is a member of the acquiring consolidated group). Any business interest expense paid or accrued (without regard to section 163(j)) by S in its short taxable year ending on the day of S's change in status for which a deduction is disallowed under section 163(j) will be carried forward to the acquiring group's first taxable year beginning after December 31, 2017. Those disallowed business interest expense carryforwards may be subject to limitation under other provisions of these regulations (see, for example, § 1.163(j)-5(c), (d), (e), and (f)).

(2) *Example.*—Acquiring Group is a consolidated group with a fiscal year end of November 30; Target is a stand-alone calendar-year C corporation. On May 31, 2018, Acquiring Group acquires Target in a transaction that is not an ownership change for purposes of section 382. Acquiring Group is not subject to the section 163(j) limitation during its taxable year beginning December 1, 2017. As a result of the acquisition, Target has a short taxable year beginning January 1, 2018 and ending May 31, 2018. Target is subject to the section 163(j) limitation during this short taxable year. However, Target (as a member of Acquiring Group) is not subject to the section 163(j) limitation during Acquiring Group's taxable year ending November 30, 2018. Any disallowed business interest expense carryforwards from Target's taxable year ending May 31, 2018, will not be available for use in Acquiring Group's taxable year ending November 30, 2018. However, that disallowed business interest expense is carried forward to Acquiring Group's taxable year beginning December 1, 2018, and can be deducted by the group, subject to the separate return limitation year (SRLY) limitation. See § 1.163(j)-5(d).

(b) *Treatment of disallowed disqualified interest.*—(1) *In general.*—Disallowed disqualified interest is carried forward to the taxpayer's first taxable year beginning after December 31, 2017, and is subject to disallowance as a disallowed business interest expense carryforward under section 163(j) and § 1.163(j)-2, except to the extent the interest is properly allocable to an excepted trade or business under § 1.163(j)-10. See § 1.163(j)-10(a)(6).

(2) *Earnings and profits.*—A taxpayer may not reduce its earnings and profits in a taxable year beginning after December 31, 2017, to reflect any disallowed disqualified interest carryforwards to the extent the payment or accrual of the disallowed disqualified interest reduced the earnings and profits of the taxpayer in a prior taxable year.

(3) *Disallowed disqualified interest of members of an affiliated group.*—(i) *Scope.*—This paragraph (b)(3)(i) applies to corporations that were treated as a single taxpayer under old section 163(j)(6)(C) and that had disallowed disqualified interest.

(ii) *Allocation of disallowed disqualified interest to members of the affiliated group.*—(A) *In general.*—Each member of the affiliated group is allocated its allocable share of the affiliated group's disallowed disqualified interest as provided in paragraph (b)(3)(ii)(B) of this section.

(B) *Definitions.*—The following definitions apply for purposes of paragraph (b)(3)(ii) of this section.

(1) *Allocable share of the affiliated group's disallowed disqualified interest.*—The term *allocable share of the affiliated group's disallowed disqualified interest* means, with respect to any member of an affiliated group for the member's last taxable year beginning before January 1, 2018, the product of the total amount of the disallowed disqualified interest of all members of the affiliated group under old section 163(j)(6)(C) and the member's disallowed disqualified interest ratio.

(2) *Disallowed disqualified interest ratio.*—The term *disallowed disqualified interest ratio* means, with respect to any member of an affiliated group for the member's last taxable year beginning before January 1, 2018, the ratio of the exempt related person interest expense of the member for the last taxable year beginning before January 1, 2018, to the sum of the amounts of exempt related person interest expense for all members of the affiliated group.

(3) *Exempt related person interest expense.*—The term *exempt related person interest expense* means interest expense that is, or is treated as, paid or accrued by a domestic C corporation, or by a foreign corporation with income, gain, or loss that is effectively connected, or treated as effectively connected, with the conduct of a trade or business in the United States, to—

(i) Any person related to the taxpayer, within the meaning of sections 267(b) or 707(b)(1), applying the constructive ownership and attribution rules of section 267(c), if no U.S. tax is imposed with respect to the interest under subtitle A of the Internal Revenue Code, determined without regard to net operating losses or net operating loss carryovers, and taking into account any applicable treaty obligation of the United States. For this purpose, interest that is subject to a reduced rate of tax under any treaty obligation of the United States applicable to the recipient is treated as in part subject to the statutory tax rate under sections 871 or 881 and in part not subject to tax, based on the proportion that the rate of tax under the treaty bears to the statutory tax rate. Thus, for purposes of section 163(j), if the statutory tax rate is 30 percent, and pursuant to a treaty U.S. tax is instead limited to a rate of 10 percent, two-thirds of the interest is

considered interest not subject to U.S. tax under subtitle A of the Internal Revenue Code;

(ii) A person that is not related to the taxpayer, within the meaning of sections 267(b) or 707(b)(1), applying the constructive ownership and attribution rules of section 267(c), with respect to indebtedness on which there is a disqualified guarantee, within the meaning of paragraph (6)(D) of old section 163(j), of such indebtedness, and no gross basis U.S. tax is imposed with respect to the interest. For purposes of this paragraph (b)(3)(ii)(B)(3)(ii), a *gross basis U.S. tax* means any tax imposed by this subtitle A of the Internal Revenue Code that is determined by reference to the gross amount of any item of income without any reduction for any deduction allowed by subtitle A of the Internal Revenue Code. Interest that is subject to a gross basis U.S. tax that is eligible for a reduced rate of tax under any treaty obligation of the United States applicable to the recipient is treated as, in part, subject to the statutory tax rate under sections 871 or 881 and, in part, not subject to a gross basis U.S. tax, based on the proportion that the rate of tax under the treaty bears to the statutory tax rate. Thus, for purposes of section 163(j), if the statutory tax rate is 30 percent, and pursuant to a treaty U.S. tax is instead limited to a rate of 10 percent, two-thirds of the interest is considered interest not subject to a gross basis U.S. tax under subtitle A of the Internal Revenue Code; or

(iii) A REIT, directly or indirectly, to the extent that the domestic C corporation, or a foreign corporation with income, gain, or loss that is effectively connected, or treated as effectively connected, with the conduct of a trade or business in the United States, is a taxable REIT subsidiary, as defined in section 856(l), with respect to the REIT.

(iii) *Treatment of carryforwards.*—The amount of disallowed disqualified interest allocated to a taxpayer pursuant to paragraph (b)(3)(ii) of this section is treated in the same manner as described in paragraph (b)(1) of this section.

(4) *Application of section 382.*—(i) *Ownership change occurring before the date the Treasury decision adopting these regulations as final regulations is published in the* **Federal Register**.—(A) *Pre-change loss.*—For purposes of section 382(d)(3), unless the rules of § 1.382-2(a)(7) apply, disallowed disqualified interest is not a pre-change loss under § 1.382-2(a) subject to a section 382 limitation with regard to an ownership change on a change date occurring before the date the Treasury decision adopting these regulations as final regulations is published in the **Federal Register**. But see section 382(h)(6)(B) (regarding built-in deduction items).

(B) *Loss corporation.*—For purposes of section 382(k)(1), unless the rules of § 1.382-2(a)(7) apply, disallowed disqualified interest is not a carryforward of disallowed interest described in section 381(c)(20) with regard to an ownership change on a change date occurring before the date the Treasury decision adopting these regulations as final regulations is published in the **Federal Register**. But see section 382(h)(6) (regarding built-in deductions).

(ii) *Ownership change occurring on or after the date the Treasury decision adopting these regulations as final regulations is published in the* **Federal Register**.—(A) *Pre-change loss.*—For rules governing the treatment of disallowed disqualified interest as a pre-change loss for purposes of section 382 with regard to an ownership change on a change date occurring on or after the date the Treasury decision adopting these regulations as final regulations is published in the **Federal Register**, see §§ 1.382-2(a)(2) and 1.382-6(c)(3).

(B) *Loss corporation.*—For rules governing when disallowed disqualified interest causes a corporation to be a loss corporation with regard to an ownership change occurring on or after the date the Treasury decision adopting these regulations as final regulations is published in the **Federal Register**, see § 1.382-2(a)(1)(i)(A).

(iii) *Definitions.*—For purposes of this paragraph (b)(4), the terms *ownership change* and *change date* have the meanings provided in section 382 and the regulations thereunder.

(5) [Reserved]

(6) *Treatment of excess limitation from taxable years beginning before January 1, 2018.*—No amount of excess limitation under old section 163(j)(2)(B) may be carried forward to taxable years beginning after December 31, 2017.

(7) *Example: Members of an affiliated group.*—(i) *Facts.* A, B, and C are calendar-year domestic C corporations that are members of an affiliated group (within the meaning of section 1504(a)) that was treated as a single taxpayer under old section 163(j)(6)(C) and the proposed regulations thereunder (see formerly proposed § 1.163(j)-5). For the taxable year ending December 31, 2017, the separately determined amounts of exempt related person interest expense of A, B, and C were $0, $600x, and $150x, respectively (for a total of $750x). The affiliated group has $200x of disallowed disqualified interest in that year

(ii) *Analysis.* The affiliated group's disallowed disqualified interest expense for the 2017 taxable year ($200x) is allocated among A, B, and C based on the ratio of each member's exempt related person interest expense to the group's exempt related person interest expense. Because A has no exempt related person interest expense, no disallowed disqualified interest is allocated to A. Disallowed disqualified interest of $160x is allocated to B (($600x / $750x) x $200x), and disallowed disqualified interest of $40x is allocated to C (($150x / $750x) x $200x). Thus, B and C have $160x and $40x, respectively, of disallowed disqualified interest that is carried forward to the first taxable year beginning after December 31, 2017. No excess limitation that was allocated to A, B, or C under old section 163(j) will carry forward to the first taxable year beginning after December 31, 2017.

(iii) *Carryforward of disallowed disqualified interest to 2018 taxable year.* The facts are the same as in the *Example* in paragraph (b)(7)(i) of this section, except that, for the taxable year ending December 31, 2018, A, B, and C are members of a consolidated group that has a section 163(j) limitation of $140x, current-year business interest expense (as defined in §1.163(j)-5(a)(2)(i)) of $80x, and no excepted trade or business. Under paragraph (b)(1) of this section, disallowed disqualified interest is carried to the taxpayer's first taxable year beginning after December 31, 2017, and is subject to disallowance under section 163(j) and §1.163(j)-2. Under §1.163(j)-5(b)(3)(ii)(D)(*1*), a consolidated group that has section 163(j) limitation remaining for the current year after deducting all current-year business interest expense deducts each member's disallowed disqualified interest car-

ryforwards from prior taxable years, starting with the earliest taxable year, on a pro rata basis (subject to certain limitations). In accordance with paragraph (b)(1) of this section, the rule in §1.163(j)-5(b)(3)(ii)(D)(*1*) applies to disallowed disqualified interest carried forward to the taxpayer's first taxable year beginning after December 31, 2017. Accordingly, after deducting $80x of current-year business interest expense in 2018, the group may deduct $60x of its $200x disallowed disqualified interest carryforwards. Under paragraph (b)(3) of this section, B has $160x of disallowed disqualified interest carryforwards, and C has $40x of disallowed disqualified interest carryforwards. Thus, $48x (($160x / $200x) x $60x) of B's disallowed disqualified interest carryforwards, and $12x (($40x / $200x) x $60x) of C's disallowed disqualified interest carryforwards, are deducted by the consolidated group in the 2018 taxable year.

(c) *Applicability date.*—This section applies to taxable years ending after the date the Treasury decision adopting these regulations as final regulations is published in the **Federal Register**. However, taxpayers and their related parties, within the meaning of sections 267(b) and 707(b)(1), may apply the rules of this section to a taxable year beginning after December 31, 2017, so long as the taxpayers and their related parties consistently apply the rules of the section 163(j) regulations, and if applicable, §§1.263A-9, 1.381(c)(20)-1, 1.382-6, 1.383-1, 1.469-9, 1.882-5, 1.1502-13, 1.1502-21, 1.1502-36, 1.1502-79, 1.1502-91 through 1.1502-99 (to the extent they effectuate the rules of §§1.382-6 and 1.383-1), and 1.1504-4 to those taxable years. [Reg. §1.163(j)-11.]

Treatment of Payments to Charitable Entities: Return for Consideration

Treatment of Payments to Charitable Entities: Return for Consideration.—Amendments to Reg. §1.164-3, updating the regulations under section 162 to reflect current law regarding the application of section 162 to a taxpayer that makes a payment or transfer to an entity described in section 170(c) for a business purpose, are proposed (published in the Federal Register on December 17, 2019) (REG-107431-19).

Par. 3. Section 1.164-3 is amended by adding paragraph (j) to read as follows:

§1.164-3. Definitions and special rules.

*   *   *

(j) *Safe harbor for payments by individuals in exchange for state or local tax credits.*—(1) *In general.*—An individual who itemizes deductions and who makes a payment to or for the use of an entity described in section 170(c) in consideration for a state or local tax credit may treat as a payment of state or local tax for purposes of section 164 the portion of such payment for which a charitable contribution deduction under section 170 is disallowed under §1.170A-1(h)(3). This treatment as payment of state or local tax under section 164(a) is allowed in the taxable year in which the payment is made to the extent that the resulting credit is applied, consistent with applicable state or local law, to offset the individual's state or local tax liability for such taxable year or the preceding taxable year.

(2) *Credits carried forward.*—To the extent that a state or local tax credit described in paragraph (j)(1) of this section is not applied to offset the individual's applicable state or local tax liability for the taxable year of the payment or the preceding taxable year, any excess state or local tax credit permitted to be carried forward may be treated as a payment of state or local tax under section 164(a) in the taxable year or years for which the carryover credit is applied in accordance with state or local law.

(3) *Limitation on individual deductions.*—Nothing in this paragraph (j) may be construed as permitting a taxpayer who applies this safe harbor to avoid the limitations of section 164(b)(6) for any amount paid as a tax or treated under this paragraph (j) as a payment of tax.

(4) *No safe harbor for transfers of property.*—The safe harbor provided in this paragraph (j) applies only to a payment of cash or cash equivalent.

(5) *Coordination with other deductions.*—An individual who deducts a payment under section 164 may not also deduct the same payment under any other Code section.

(6) *Examples.*—In the following examples, assume that the taxpayer is an individual who itemizes deductions for Federal income tax purposes.

(i) *Example 1.* In year 1, Taxpayer A makes a payment of $500 to an entity described in section 170(c). In return for the payment, A

receives a dollar-for-dollar state income tax credit. Prior to application of the credit, A's state income tax liability for year 1 was more than $500. A applies the $500 credit to A's year 1 state income tax liability. Under paragraph (j)(1) of this section, A treats the $500 payment as a payment of state income tax in year 1. To determine A's deduction amount, A must apply the provisions of section 164 applicable to payments of state and local taxes, including the limitation in section 164(b)(6). See paragraph (j)(3) of this section.

(ii) *Example 2.* In year 1, Taxpayer B makes a payment of $7,000 to an entity described in section 170(c). In return for the payment, B receives a dollar-for-dollar state income tax credit, which under state law may be carried forward for three taxable years. Prior to application of the credit, B's state income tax liability for year 1 was $5,000; B applies $5,000 of the $7,000 credit to B's year 1 state income tax liability. Under paragraph (j)(1) of this section, B treats $5,000 of the $7,000 payment as a payment of state income tax in year 1. Prior to application of the remaining credit, B's state income tax liability for year 2 exceeds $2,000. B applies the excess credit of $2,000 to B's year 2 state income tax liability. For year 2, under paragraph (j)(2) of this section, B treats the $2,000 as a payment of state income tax under section 164. To determine B's deduction amounts in years 1 and 2, B must apply the provisions of section 164 applicable to payments of state and local taxes, including the limitation under section 164(b)(6). See paragraph (j)(3) of this section.

(iii) *Example 3.* In year 1, Taxpayer C makes a payment of $7,000 to an entity described in section 170(c). In return for the payment, C receives a local real property tax credit equal to 25 percent of the amount of this payment ($1,750). Prior to application of the credit, C's local real property tax liability in year 1 was more than $1,750. C applies the $1,750 credit to C's year 1 local real property tax liability. Under paragraph (j)(1) of this section, for year 1, C treats $1,750 of her $7,000 payment as a payment of local real property tax for purposes of section 164. To determine C's deduction amount, C must apply the provisions of section 164 applicable to payments of state and local taxes, including the limitation under section 164(b)(6). See paragraph (j)(3) of this section.

(7) *Applicability date.*—This paragraph (j) applies to payments made to section 170(c) entities on or after June 11, 2019. However, a taxpayer may choose to apply this paragraph (j) to payments made to section 170(c) entities after August 27, 2018.

Definition of Registered Form: Guidance

Definition of Registered Form: Guidance.—Amendments to Reg. §1.165-12, providing guidance on the definitions of registration-required obligation and registered form, including guidance on the issuance of pass-through certificates and participation interests in registered form, are proposed (published in the Federal Register on September 19, 2017) (REG 125371-16).

Par. 5. Section 1.165-12 is amended by:

1. Revising paragraph (a).

2. Redesignating paragraphs (b)(1) and (2) as (b)(2) and (3), respectively.

3. Adding a new paragraph (b)(1).

4. Revising the paragraph heading and first sentence of newly redesignated paragraph (b)(2).

5. Redesignating paragraph (d) as paragraph (d)(1).

6. Revising the paragraph heading and the first sentence of newly redesignated paragraph (d)(1).

7. Adding a new paragraph heading for paragraph (d).

8. Adding paragraph (d)(2).

The revisions and additions read as follows:

§1.165-12. Denial of deduction for losses on registration-required obligations not in registered form.—(a) *In general.*—Except as provided in paragraph (c) of this section, nothing in section 165(a) and the regulations thereunder, or in any other provision of law, shall be construed to provide a deduction for any loss sustained on any registration-required obligation held after December 31, 1982, unless the obligation is in registered form or the issuance of the obligation was subject to tax under section 4701. The term *registration-required obligation* has the meaning given to that term in section 163(f)(2) and §1.163-5(a)(2)(i). For purposes of this section, the term *holder* means the person that would be denied a loss deduction under section 165(j)(1) or denied capital gain treatment under section 1287(a). For purposes of this section, the term *United States* means the United States and its possessions within the meaning of §1.163-5(c)(2)(iv).

(b) *Registered form.*—(1) *Obligations issued after March 18, 2012.*—With respect to obligations issued after March 18, 2012, the term *registered form* has the meaning given that term in §1.163-5(b).

(2) *Obligations issued after September 21, 1984 and on or before March 18, 2012.*—With respect to any obligation originally issued after September 21, 1984, and on or before March 18, 2012, the term *registered form* has the meaning given that term in §5f.103-1 of this chapter. * * *

* * *

(d) *Applicability date.*—(1) *In general.*—Except as provided in paragraph (d)(2) of this section, these regulations apply generally to obligations issued after January 20, 1987. * * *

(2) *Obligations issued after March 18, 2012.*—Paragraph (a) of this section applies to obligations issued after March 18, 2012. For the rules that apply to obligations issued on or before March 18, 2012, see §1.165-12 as contained in 26 CFR part 1, revised as of the date of the most recent annual revision.

Minimum Addition to Reserves for Losses: Mutual Savings Banks

Minimum Addition to Reserves for Losses: Mutual Savings Banks.—Reproduced below is the text of a proposed amendment of Reg. §1.166-4, relating to the minimum addition to reserves for losses on loans of mutual savings banks and other organizations (published in the Federal Register on December 19, 1983).

☐ Paragraph 1. Paragraph (d)(3) of §1.166-4 is amended by removing "§§1.593-1 through 1.593-11" and inserting "§§1.593-1 through 1.593-8" in lieu thereof.

§1.166-4. Reserve for bad debts.

Allocation Rules

Gains and Losses: Asset Acquisitions: Allocation Rules.—Temporary Reg. §1.167(a)-5T, relating to allocation rules for certain asset acquisitions under Code Sec. 1060, is also proposed as a final regulation and, when adopted, would become Reg. §1.167(a)-5 (published in the Federal Register on July 18, 1988).

§1.167(a)-5. Apportionment of basis.

Accelerated Cost Recovery System

Accelerated Cost Recovery System.—Reproduced below is the text of a proposed amendment of Reg. §1.167(a)-11, relating to the Accelerated Cost Recovery System for recovering capital costs of eligible property (published in the Federal Register on February 16, 1984).

§1.167(a)-11. Depreciation based on class lives and asset depreciation ranges for property placed in service after December 31, 1970.—(a) *In general.*—(1) *Summary.*—This section does not apply with respect to recovery property (within the meaning of section 168 and the regulations thereunder) placed in service after December 31, 1980. * * *

* * *

(d) *Special rules for salvage, repairs and retirements.*—* * *

(2) *Treatment of repairs.*—(i) *In general.*—(a) *Treatment of repair expenditures.*—* * *

(b) *Property placed in service after December 31, 1980.*—This paragraph (d)(2) does not apply to any expenditures with respect to property first placed in service after December 31, 1980, but may apply to expenditures paid or incurred after such date with respect to property first placed in service before January 1, 1981. Expenditures with respect to property first placed in service after December 31, 1980, shall be treated as capital expenditures or as deductible expenses for the taxable year in which paid or incurred in accordance with the general rules provided in sections 162, 212, and 263. Property is considered first placed in service for purposes of this paragraph (d)(2)(i)(b) under the rules of paragraph (e)(1)(i) and (ii) of this section.

(ii) *Election of repair allowance.*—* * * For taxable years ending after December 31, 1980, and before February 16, 1984, notwith-standing paragraph (f)(1) of this section, the taxpayer may elect (in the original return or in an amended return) to apply this section and the asset guideline class repair allowance described in paragraph (d)(2)(iii) of this section on or before the later of the due date (including extensions) of the taxpayer's tax return for the taxable year or November 16, 1984.

* * *

(viii) *Treatment of property improvements and excluded additions.*—* * *

(d) Paragraph (d)(2)(viii)(a), (b), and (c) of this section does not apply to a property improvement, excluded addition, or part thereof considered first placed in service by the taxpayer after December 31, 1980. Such property improvement, excluded addition, or part thereof shall generally be treated as a separate item of recovery property (as defined in section 168(c)(1)), and shall be assigned to the appropriate class of recovery property in accordance with section 168(c)(2). See §1.168-2(e)(2). For taxable years ending after December 31, 1980, notwithstanding the succeeding sentence, for purposes of this paragraph (d)(2)(viii)(d), a property improvement, excluded addition, or part thereof is considered first placed in service under the rules provided in paragraph (e)(1)(i) and (ii) of this section and not under the rules provided in paragraph (e)(1)(iii) and (iv) of this section. * * *

* * *

Deductions: Elections: Depreciation: Intangible Property

Deductions: Elections: Depreciation: Intangible Property.—Temporary Reg. §1.167(a)-13T, relating to the procedures for making elections under the intangibles provisions of the Omnibus Budget Reconciliation Act of 1993 (P.L. 103-66), is also proposed as a final regulation and, when adopted, would become Reg. §1.167(a)-13 (published in the Federal Register on March 15, 1994).

☐ Par. 2. Section 1.167(a)-13 is added to read as follows:

§1.167(a)-13. Certain elections for intangible property.—For rules applying the elections under sections 13261(g)(2) and (3) of the Omnibus Budget Reconciliation Act of 1993 to intangible property described in section 167(f), see §1.197-1. [Reg. §1.167(a)-13.]

Depreciation: Income Forecast Method: Guidance on Cost Recovery

Depreciation: Income Forecast Method: Guidance on Cost Recovery.—Reg. §§1.167(n)-0—1.167(n)-7, relating to deductions available to taxpayers using the income forecast method of depreciation under Code Sec. 167(g), are proposed (published in the Federal Register on May 31, 2002) (REG-103823-99) (corrected August 6, 2002).

☐ Par. 2. Sections 1.167(n)-0 through 1.167(n)-7 are added to read as follows:

§1.167(n)-0. Outline of regulation sections for section 167(g).—This section lists the major captions contained in §1.167(n)-1 through §1.167(n)-7.

    §1.167(n)-1. Income forecast method.
    (a) Overview.
    (b) Method of accounting.
       (1) In general.
       (2) Election of the income forecast method.

    §1.167(n)-2. Basis.
    (a) Depreciable basis.
       (1) In general.
       (2) Timing of basis determinations and redeterminations.
       (3) Separate Property.
    (b) Basis redeterminations.
    (c) Unrecovered depreciable basis.
    (d) Example.

    §1.167(n)-3. Income from the property.
    (a) Current year income.
       (1) In general.
       (2) Special rule for advance payments.
    (b) Forecasted total income.
    (c) Revised forecasted total income.
    (d) Special rules.
       (1) Disposition of the property.
       (2) Syndication income from television series.
       (3) Apportionment of income in certain circumstances.
       (4) Examples.

    §1.167(n)-4. Computation of depreciation using the income forecast method.
    (a) Computation of depreciation allowance.
    (b) Revised computation.
       (1) Change in estimated income.
       (2) Requirement to use the revised computation.
    (c) Basis redeterminations.
       (1) Calculation of depreciation allowance.
       (2) Example.
    (d) Special rules.
       (1) Final year depreciation.
       (2) Certain basis redeterminations.
       (3) Disposition of property.
       (4) Separate property.
    (e) Examples.

    §1.167(n)-5. Property for which the income forecast method may be used.
    (a) In general.
    (b) Specific exclusions.
    (c) Costs treated as separate property.
       (1) Costs giving rise to a significant increase in income.
       (2) Significant increase in income.
       (3) Special rule for costs paid or incurred after the end of the final year.
       (4) Time separate property is placed in service.
       (5) Examples.
    (d) Aggregations treated as a single income forecast property.
       (1) Multiple episodes of a television series produced in the same taxable year.
       (2) Multiple episodes of a television series produced in more than one taxable year.
       (3) Multiple interests acquired pursuant to a single contract.
       (4) Videocassettes and DVDs.

    §1.167(n)-6. Look-back method.
    (a) Application of the look-back method.
    (b) Operation of the look-back method.
       (1) In general.
       (2) Property-by-property application.
    (c) Recalculation of depreciation allowances.

       (1) Computation.
       (2) Revised forecasted total income from the property.
       (3) Special rule for basis redeterminations.
    (d) Hypothetical overpayment or underpayment of tax.
       (1) In general.
       (2) Hypothetical overpayment or underpayment, actual recomputation.
       (3) Hypothetical overpayment or underpayment, simplified method.
       (4) Definitions.
    (e) Recomputation year.
       (1) In general.
       (2) Look-back method inapplicable in certain de minimis cases.
    (f) De minimis basis exception.
    (g) Treatment of look-back interest.
       (1) In general.
       (2) Additional interest due on interest only after tax liability due.
       (3) Timing of look-back interest.
       (4) Statute of limitations; compounding of interest on look-back interest.
    (h) Example.

    §1.167(n)-7. Effective date.
[Reg. §1.167(n)-0.]

§1.167(n)-1. Income forecast method.—(a) *Overview.*—This section and §§1.167(n)-2 through 1.167(n)-7 provide rules for computing depreciation allowances under section 167 for property depreciated using the income forecast method. Because the income forecast method is only appropriate for property with unique income earning characteristics, only property specified in §1.167(n)-5 may be depreciated under the income forecast method. A taxpayer using the income forecast method generally computes depreciation allowances each year based upon the ratio of current year income to forecasted total income from the property as described in §1.167(n)-4. Current year income and forecasted total income are determined in accordance with the provisions of §1.167(n)-3. In addition, a taxpayer must determine depreciable basis for income forecast property in accordance with the basis rules of §1.167(n)-2. Property depreciated under the income forecast method generally is subject to the look-back rules of §1.167(n)-6 whereby taxpayers must determine the amount of interest owed on any hypothetical underpayment of tax, or due on any hypothetical overpayment of tax, attributable to the use of estimated income in the computation of income forecast depreciation. Under these rules, look-back computations must be performed in specified recomputation years, which are generally the 3rd and 10th taxable years after the taxable year that the property is placed in service.

(b) *Method of accounting.*—(1) *In general.*—The computation of depreciation under the income forecast method is elected on a property-by-property basis, and is a method of accounting under section 446 that may not be changed without the consent of the Commissioner. However, a change in forecasted total income in accordance with the rules of §1.167(n)-4 is not a change in method of accounting requiring the Commissioner's consent.

(2) *Election of the income forecast method.*—A taxpayer elects the income forecast method by computing allowances for depreciation for the eligible property in accordance with the provisions of this section and §§1.167(n)-2 through §1.167(n)-6. See §1.167(n)-5 for rules regarding eligible property. [Reg. §1.167(n)-1.]

§1.167(n)-2. Basis.—(a) *Depreciable basis.*—(1) *In general.*—The basis upon which the allowance for depreciation is computed with respect to income forecast property is the basis of the income forecast property for purposes of section 1011 without regard to the adjustments described in section 1016(a)(2) and (3).

(2) *Timing of basis determinations and redeterminations.*—Costs paid or incurred in or after the taxable year in which the income forecast property is placed in service are taken into account in

accordance with a taxpayer's method of accounting in redetermining the basis of income forecast property in the taxable year paid or incurred (i.e., when all events have occurred that establish the fact of the liability, the amount of the liability can be determined with reasonable accuracy, and economic performance has occurred with respect to the liability). See §§ 1.446-1(c)(1)(i) and (ii), 1.461-1(a)(1) and (2), and 1.263A-1(c). Accordingly, contingent payments may not be included in the basis of income forecast property when the property is placed in service, but are included in the basis of income forecast property in the taxable year in which they are paid or incurred, even if the forecasted total income used in the computation of income forecast depreciation allowances is sufficient to indicate that the contingency will be satisfied.

(3) *Separate property.*—Certain amounts paid or incurred in taxable years after income forecast property is placed in service are treated as separate property for purposes of computing depreciation allowances under the income forecast method. See § 1.167(n)-5(c).

(b) *Basis redeterminations.*—If an amount required to be capitalized into the basis of income forecast property is paid or incurred after the income forecast property is placed in service, and if the amount required to be capitalized is not treated as separate property in accordance with § 1.167(n)-5(c), the basis of the income forecast property is redetermined and the amount required to be capitalized is the basis redetermination amount. The redetermined basis of the income forecast property is the depreciable basis of the income forecast property increased by the basis redetermination amount. In the year basis is redetermined (and in subsequent taxable years), the redetermined basis must be used to determine depreciation under the income forecast method. An additional allowance for depreciation under the income forecast method is allowed in the taxable year the basis of certain income forecast property is redetermined. See § 1.167(n)-4(c).

(c) *Unrecovered depreciable basis.*—For any taxable year, the unrecovered depreciable basis of an income forecast property is the depreciable basis of the property less the adjustments described in section 1016(a)(2) and (3).

(d) *Example.*—The provisions of § 1.167(n)-2 are illustrated by the following example:

(i) *Studio* contracts with *Actor* to star in a motion picture film to be produced by *Studio*. Both *Studio* and *Actor* are calendar year taxpayers; *Studio* is an accrual basis taxpayer and *Actor* is a cash basis taxpayer. As compensation for *Actor*'s services, the contract guarantees *Actor* a payment of five percent of the gross income from the film, beginning after the film has earned a total gross income (net of distribution costs) of $ 100x. *Studio* estimates that the film will earn a total gross income of $160x by the end of the 10th taxable year following the taxable year that the film is placed in service. The film is placed in service and earns $ 65x of gross income in year one, $ 30x in year two, and $ 25x in year three. Because the income from the film does not exceed $100x in either year one or year two, *Studio* pays nothing under the contract to *Actor* in years one and two. In year three, the cumulative income from the film reaches $120x, which exceeds the $100x threshold by $20x. Based on this excess, *Studio* calculates that it owes *Actor* $ 1x, calculated by multiplying $20x by *Actor*'s contractual percentage of five percent. *Studio* pays $1x to *Actor* 20 days after the end of year three.

(ii) *Studio* may not include the $1x paid to *Actor* in the basis of the film in years one or two because *Studio* does not have a fixed liability to pay *Actor* any amount under the contract in years one and two. Furthermore, while *Studio* does have a fixed liability to pay *Actor* $1x in year three, the requirements of section 404 are not met in year three and *Studio* thus may not include the $1x in the basis of the film in year three. In year four, when section 404 is satisfied, *Studio* incurs the $1x in accordance with § 1.263A-1(c) and increases its basis in the film. The $1x is treated as a basis redetermination amount under § 1.167(n)-2(b) in year four.

[Reg. § 1.167(n)-2.]

§1.167(n)-3. Income from the property.—(a) *Current year income.*—(1) *In general.*—Current year income is the income from an income forecast property for the current year (less the distribution costs of the income forecast property for such year), determined in accordance with the taxpayer's method of accounting. All income earned in connection with the income forecast property is included in current year income, except as provided in paragraph (d) of this section. In the case of a film, television show, or similar property, such income includes, but is not limited to—

(i) Income from foreign and domestic theatrical, television, and other releases and syndications;

(ii) Income from releases, sales, rentals, and syndications of video tape, DVD, and other media; and

(iii) Incidental income associated with the property, such as income from the financial exploitation of characters, designs, titles,

scripts, and scores, but only to the extent that such incidental income is earned in connection with the ultimate use of such items by, or the ultimate sale of merchandise to, persons who are not related to the taxpayer (within the meaning of section 267(b)).

(2) *Special rule for advance payments.*—In the year that income forecast property is placed in service, current year income for an income forecast property includes income included in gross income for any prior taxable year in connection with the property. This paragraph applies separately to any cost treated as separate property under § 1.167(n)-5(c).

(b) *Forecasted total income.*—Forecasted total income is the sum of current year income for the year that income forecast property is placed in service, plus all income from the income forecast property that the taxpayer reasonably believes will be includible in current year income in subsequent taxable years (as adjusted for distribution costs) up to and including the 10th taxable year after the year in which the income forecast property is placed in service. Forecasted total income is based on the conditions known to exist at the end of the taxable year for which the income forecast property is placed in service.

(c) *Revised forecasted total income.*—If information is discovered in a taxable year following the year in which income forecast property is placed in service that indicates that forecasted total income is inaccurate, a taxpayer must compute revised forecasted total income for the taxable year. Revised forecasted total income is based on the conditions known to exist at the end of the taxable year for which the revised forecast is being made. Revised forecasted total income for the taxable year is the sum of current year income for the taxable year and all prior taxable years, plus all income from the income forecast property that the taxpayer reasonably believes will be includible in current year income in taxable years after the current taxable year up to and including the 10th taxable year after the year in which the income forecast property is placed in service. Where a taxpayer computes revised forecasted total income in accordance with this § 1.167(n)-3(c), see § 1.167(n)-4(b) for the computation of the allowance for income forecast depreciation.

(d) *Special rules.*—(1) *Disposition of the property.*—In computing the depreciation allowance for an income forecast property, income from the sale or other disposition of income forecast property is not included in current year income. However, if the income forecast property is disposed of prior to the end of the 10th taxable year following the taxable year in which the property is placed in service, income from the sale or other disposition of income forecast property is taken into account in calculating revised forecasted total income both for purposes of calculating the allowance for depreciation in the year of disposition and for purposes of applying look-back. See § 1.167(n)-4(d)(3) and § 1.167(n)-6(c)(2).

(2) *Syndication income from television series.*—(i) In the case of a television series produced for distribution on television networks, current year income and forecasted total income (or, if applicable, revised forecasted total income) used in the computation of the depreciation allowance for such property under § 1.167(n)-4 need not include income from syndication of the television series before the earlier of—

(A) The fourth taxable year beginning after the date the first episode in the series is placed in service; or

(B) The earliest taxable year in which the taxpayer has an arrangement relating to the syndication of the series.

(ii) For purposes of this paragraph (d)(2), an arrangement relating to syndication of a series of television shows means any arrangement other than the first run exhibition agreement. For example, an arrangement for exhibition of a television series by individual television stations is an arrangement for syndication if it results in an exhibition of one or more episodes of the series beginning after one or more episodes of the series have been exhibited on a television network. A first run exhibition agreement is an agreement under which any episode (including a pilot episode) of a television series is first placed in service within a particular market.

(3) *Apportionment of income in certain circumstances.*—When income from a particular source relates to more than one income forecast property the taxpayer must make a reasonable allocation of the income among those properties based on all relevant factors. Situations where allocation is necessary include income generated by a syndication arrangement involving more than one income forecast property, incidental income described in paragraph (a)(1)(iii) of this section that relates to more than one motion picture, and income associated with income forecast property when expenditures relating to the property have given rise to separate property as defined in § 1.167(n)-5(c). For example, when a taxpayer sells or licenses merchandise that features the likeness of a character that has appeared in more than one film, relevant factors might include merchandise sales figures prior to the release of the subsequent film, specific identifica-

tion of certain merchandise with one particular film, and the taxpayer's prior experience with similar situations.

(4) *Examples.*—The provisions of this section are illustrated by the following examples:

Example 1. C produces a motion picture film featuring the adventures of a fictional character. C sells merchandise using the character's image, enters into licensing agreements with unrelated parties for the use of the image, and uses the image to promote a ride at an amusement park that is wholly owned by C. Pursuant to paragraph (a)(1) of this section, income from the sales of merchandise by C to consumers and income from the licensing agreements are included in current year income. No portion of the admission fees for the amusement park is included in current year income because the amusement part is wholly owned by C.

Example 2. Assume the same facts as in *Example 1.* C forecasts that the cumulative amount of current year income it will earn (net of distribution costs) from the year it places the motion picture film in service through the end of the 7th taxable year thereafter to be $345x. C also forecasts that the motion picture film will earn current year income of $155x from the beginning of the 8th taxable year through the end of the 10th taxable year after the year the income forecast property is placed in service. C anticipates the sale of the motion picture film at the end of the 7th taxable year after the year the property is placed in service and in fact sells the motion picture film for $200x on the last day of the 7th taxable year after the year the property is placed in service. C's computations of forecasted total income must reflect the fact that C forecasts that $500x will be earned by the motion picture film through the end of the 10th taxable year after the year the property is placed in service ($345x from the year the film is placed in service through the end of the 7th taxable year after the taxable year that the property was placed in service, plus $155x C forecasts from the beginning of the 8th taxable year through the end of the 10th taxable year after the year the property is placed in service). Even though C only expects to earn $345x prior to the sale of the film, C may not use $345x as forecasted total income in computing its depreciation allowance under the income forecast method. Similarly, C may not use the combination of the amounts it expects to earn prior to the sale ($345x) plus the anticipated sales proceeds ($200x) or $545x as forecasted total income, except when computing its depreciation allowance for the 7th taxable year after the year in which the income forecast property was placed in service and for purposes of computing look-back interest.

[Reg. § 1.167(n)-3.]

§1.167(n)-4. Computation of depreciation using the income forecast method.—(a) *Computation of depreciation allowance.*—Generally, the depreciation allowance for an income forecast property for a given taxable year is computed by multiplying the depreciable or redetermined basis of the property (as defined in §1.167(n)-2) by a fraction, the numerator of which is current year income (as defined in §1.167(n)-3(a)) and the denominator of which is forecasted total income (as defined in §1.167(n)-3(b)).

(b) *Revised computation.*—(1) *Change in estimated income.*—The depreciation allowance for an income forecast property for any taxable year following the year in which income forecast property is placed in service may be computed using the computation provided in this paragraph (b)(1) if revised forecasted total income differs from forecasted total income. Thus, for example, a taxpayer using the income forecast method for a motion picture may revise upward the forecast of total income from the motion picture (to arrive at revised forecasted total income) in a taxable year wherein the taxpayer discovers that the motion picture is more popular than originally expected, and may thereafter use the revised computation to compute the allowance for income forecast depreciation for the motion picture. Under the revised computation, the unrecovered depreciable basis of the income forecast property (as defined in §1.167(n)-2(c)) is multiplied by a fraction, the numerator of which is current year income and the denominator of which is obtained by subtracting from revised forecasted total income the amounts of current year income from prior taxable years.

(2) *Requirement to use the revised computation.*—The revised computation described in paragraph (b)(1) of this section must be used in any taxable year following the year in which income forecast property is placed in service if forecasted total income (as defined in §1.167(n)-3(b)) (or, if applicable, revised forecasted total income (as defined in §1.167(n)-3(c)) in the immediately preceding taxable year is either—

(i) Less than 90 percent of revised forecasted total income for the taxable year; or

(ii) Greater than 110 percent of revised forecasted total income for the taxable year.

(c) *Basis redeterminations.*—(1) *Calculation of depreciation allowance.*—An additional depreciation allowance is available under this

paragraph in the taxable year that basis is redetermined under §1.167(n)-2(b) when that taxable year is subsequent to the taxable year in which income forecast property is placed in service, but prior to the 10th taxable year following the taxable year in which the property is placed in service. The additional depreciation allowance is that portion of the basis redetermination amount that would have been recovered through depreciation allowances in prior taxable years if the basis redetermination amount had been included in depreciable basis in the taxable year that the property was placed in service. This §1.167(n)-4(c) does not apply to property treated as a single income forecast property pursuant to §1.167(n)-5(d)(1) through (4).

(2) *Example.*—The provisions of paragraph (c)(1) of this section are illustrated by the following example:

Example. D, an accrual basis movie producer, enters into a contract with E, an author, under which D will make a film based on E's book. E performs no services for D, but merely permits D to use the book as a basis for D's film. D pays E a fixed dollar amount upon entry into the agreement and promises to pay E a contingent payment of five percent of D's income from the film, beginning after the film has earned $100,000 (net of distribution costs). D estimates that forecasted total income from the film will be $200,000. The film earns $65,000 of current year income in year one, $30,000 in year two, and $25,000 in year three. D takes allowances for depreciation in year one ($65,000 divided by $200,000, multiplied by the basis of the film) and year two ($30,000 divided by $200,000, multiplied by the basis of the film). In year three, D's liability to E becomes fixed and D pays E $1,000. The $1,000 incurred by D is a basis redetermination amount that increases the basis of the film for purposes of computing D's depreciation allowance for the film for year three. In addition to the year three allowance based on current year income ($25,000 divided by $200,000 multiplied by the basis of the film, which includes for year three the $1,000 basis redetermination amount), D is entitled to an additional allowance for depreciation for year three under paragraph (c)(1). This additional allowance is $475, the sum of the allowance of $325 that would have been allowed in year one ($65,000 divided by $200,000, multiplied by the $1,000 payment to E) and the allowance of $150 that would have been allowed in year two ($30,000 divided by $200,000, multiplied by $1,000) if the $1,000 had been included in basis in the year that the film was placed in service.

(d) *Special rules.*—(1) *Final year depreciation.*—Except as provided in paragraphs (d)(2) and (3) of this section, a taxpayer may deduct as a depreciation allowance the remaining depreciable basis of income forecast property depreciated under the income forecast method in the earlier of—

(i) The year in which the taxpayer reasonably believes, based on the conditions known to exist at the end of the taxable year, that no income from the income forecast property will be included in current year income in any subsequent taxable year up to and including the 10th taxable year following the taxable year the income forecast property is placed in service; or

(ii) The 10th taxable year following the taxable year the income forecast property is placed in service.

(2) *Certain basis redeterminations.*—A taxpayer may deduct as a depreciation allowance the amount of any basis redetermination that occurs in a taxable year in which the taxpayer reasonably believes, based on the conditions known to exist at the end of the taxable year, that no income from the income forecast property will be included in current year income in any subsequent taxable year. In addition, a taxpayer may deduct as a depreciation allowance the amount of any basis redetermination that occurs in a taxable year following a taxable year in which a deduction is allowable under paragraph (d)(1) of this section.

(3) *Disposition of property.*—Paragraph (d)(1) of this section does not apply to income forecast property that is sold or otherwise disposed of before the end of the 10th taxable year following the taxable year that the property is placed in service. In the case of such a disposition, the allowance for depreciation in the year of disposition is calculated by multiplying the depreciable basis (or, if applicable, the redetermined basis) of the property by a fraction, the numerator of which is current year income and the denominator of which is the sum of the amount realized on the disposition of the property plus all amounts included in current year income in the year of disposition and in taxable years prior to the year of disposition.

(4) *Separate property.*—The deductions provided in paragraphs (d)(1) and (2) of this section apply separately to property that is treated as separate property under §1.167(n)-5(c).

(e) *Examples.*—The provisions of this section are illustrated by the following examples:

Example 1. F places in service income forecast property with a depreciable basis of $100x, and estimates that forecasted total income from the property will be $200x. In taxable year one, current year income is $80x. The depreciation allowance for year one is $40x, computed by multiplying the depreciable basis of the property of $100x by the fraction obtained by dividing current year income of $80x by forecasted total income of $200x.

Example 2. Assume the same facts as in *Example 1.* In year two, *F*'s current year income is $40x. In addition, *F* computes revised forecasted total income to be $176x. *F* is required to compute its depreciation allowance for this property using the revised computation of paragraph (b)(1) of this section because forecasted total income in year one of $200x is greater than 110 percent of revised forecasted total income in year two (110 percent of $176x = $193.6x). The depreciation allowance for taxable year two computed under the revised computation is $25x, computed by multiplying the unrecovered depreciable basis of $60x by the fraction obtained by dividing current year income of $40x by $96x (revised forecasted total income of $176x less current year income from prior taxable years of $80x).

Example 3. Assume the same facts as in *Example 2.* Because *F* used the revised computation in year two, the revised computation applies in year three. In year three, *F*'s current year income is $32x. The depreciation allowance for year three computed under the revised computation is $20x, computed by multiplying the unrecovered depreciable basis of $60x by the fraction obtained by dividing current year income of $32x by $96x (revised forecasted total income of $176x less current year income from taxable years prior to the change in estimate taxable year of $80x).

[Reg. § 1.167(n)-4.]

§ 1.167(n)-5. Property for which the income forecast method may be used.—(a) *In general.*—The depreciation allowance under § 1.167(n)-4 may be computed under the income forecast method only with respect to eligible property. Eligible property is limited to an interest (including interests involving limited rights in property) in the following property—

(1) Property described in section 168(f)(3) and (4);

(2) Copyrights;

(3) Books;

(4) Patents;

(5) Theatrical productions; and

(6) Other property as designated in published guidance by the Commissioner.

(b) *Specific exclusions.*—The income forecast method does not apply to any amortizable section 197 intangible (as defined in section 197(c) and § 1.197-2(d)).

(c) *Costs treated as separate property.*—(1) *Costs giving rise to a significant increase in income.*—(i) *In general.*—For purposes of § 1.167(n)-1 through § 1.167(n)-6, any amount paid or incurred after the income forecast property is placed in service must be treated as a separate property if the cost is significant and gives rise to an increase in income that is significant and that was not included in either forecasted total income or revised forecasted total income in a prior taxable year.

(ii) *Exception for de minimis amounts.*—For purposes of this paragraph, a cost that is less than the lesser of 5 percent of the depreciable basis (as of the date the amount is paid or incurred) of the income forecast property to which the amount relates or $100,000 is not significant. Such a cost is therefore not treated as separate property but is instead treated as a basis redetermination amount in accordance with § 1.167(n)-2(b).

(2) *Significant increase in income.*—For purposes of this paragraph, whether an increase in income is significant is determined by comparing the amount that would be considered revised forecasted total income from the amounts treated as separate property to the most recent estimate of forecasted total income or revised forecasted total income used in calculating an allowance for depreciation with respect to the income forecast property.

(3) *Special rule for costs paid or incurred after the end of the final year.*—For purposes of § 1.167(n)-1 through § 1.167(n)-6, any amount paid or incurred with respect to an income forecast property in a taxable year following the year in which the taxpayer claims a depreciation allowance in accordance with the final year depreciation rules of § 1.167(n)-4(d)(1) is treated as a basis redetermination amount under § 1.167(n)-2(b) provided the amount is not expected to give rise to a significant increase in current year income in any taxable year.

(4) *Time separate property is placed in service.*—Separate property is treated as placed in service in the year the amount giving rise to the property is paid or incurred.

(5) *Examples.*—The provisions of this paragraph (c) are illustrated in the following examples:

Example 1. G releases a film in 2001 and begins to recover the depreciable basis in the film using the income forecast method in the year 2001. In 2003, the film is re-edited and restored, and director's commentary is added in order to prepare the film for release on DVD. The total cost of preparing the film for the DVD release exceeds both 5 percent of the depreciable basis of the film and $100,000. G did not anticipate the income from the DVD market, and did not include any DVD release income in the income projections for the film in prior years. If G anticipates that the additional DVD release income will be significant in relation to the forecasted total income used in calculating an allowance for depreciation for 2002 (the previous taxable year), the additional amount gives rise to separate property and must be recovered over the forecasted total income from the DVD. If not, G must treat the additional amounts as additions to basis under § 1.167(n)-2(b).

Example 2. G releases a film in 2001 and recovers the depreciable basis in the film using the income forecast method in the years 2001 through 2011. In 2018, the film is re-edited and restored, and director's commentary is added in order to prepare the film for release on a newly discovered technology. If G anticipates that the additional new technology release income will be significant in relation to the revised forecasted total income used in calculating an allowance for depreciation for 2011 (the last taxable year for which an allowance was claimed), the cost of preparing the release gives rise to separate property and must be recovered over the forecasted total income from the new technology release. If not, G may deduct the cost in 2018, the year paid or incurred.

(d) *Aggregations treated as a single income forecast property.*—Taxpayers must apply the income forecast method on a property-by-property basis, unless one of the aggregation rules provided in paragraphs (d)(1) through (4) of this section applies. If a taxpayer applies one of the aggregation rules provided in paragraphs (d)(1) through (4) of this section, costs incurred in taxable years after the initial income forecast property is placed in service are treated as basis redeterminations under § 1.167(n)-2; however, the additional allowance for depreciation provided in § 1.167(n)-4(c)(1) does not apply. The application of the provisions of paragraphs (d)(1) through (d)(4) is a method of accounting that may not be changed without the consent of the Commissioner. Permissible aggregations are limited to the following:

(1) *Multiple episodes of a television series produced in the same taxable year.*—The producer of a television series may treat multiple episodes of a single television series produced in the same taxable year as a single unit of property for purposes of the income forecast method.

(2) *Multiple episodes of a television series produced in more than one taxable year.*—The producer of a television series may treat multiple episodes of a single television series that are produced as a single season of episodes and placed in service over a period not in excess of twelve consecutive calendar months as a single unit of property for purposes of the income forecast method notwithstanding that the twelve-month period may span more than one taxable year.

(3) *Multiple interests acquired pursuant to a single contract.*—Multiple interests in specifically identified income forecast properties acquired for broadcast pursuant to a single contract may be treated as a single unit of property for purposes of the income forecast method.

(4) *Videocassettes and DVDs.*—The purchaser or licensee of videocassettes and DVDs for rental to the public may treat multiple copies of the same title purchased or licensed in the same taxable year as a single unit of property for purposes of the income forecast method. [Reg. § 1.167(n)-5.]

§ 1.167(n)-6. Look-back method.—(a) *Application of the look-back method.*—If a taxpayer claims a depreciation deduction under the income forecast method for any eligible income forecast property, such taxpayer is required to pay (or is entitled to receive) interest computed as described in this paragraph for any year to which the look-back method applies (a recomputation year). The look-back method generally must be applied when income forecast property is disposed of or ceases to generate income. Further, the look-back method generally applies in the 3rd and 10th taxable years following the year in which income forecast property is placed in service. Under the look-back method, taxpayers must pay interest on deductions accelerated by the underestimation of either forecasted total income or revised forecasted total income from income forecast property. Conversely, taxpayers are entitled to receive interest on deductions delayed by the overestimation of either forecasted total income or revised forecasted total income from income forecast property. If either forecasted total income or revised forecasted total income are overestimated or underestimated, interest may arise from basis redeterminations. The computation of adjusted tax liability as part of the look-back method is hypothetical; application of the look-back method does not require a taxpayer to adjust tax liability as reported on the taxpayer's tax returns, on an amended return, or as adjusted on examination for prior years.

(b) *Operation of the look-back method.*—(1) *In general.*—Under the look-back method, a taxpayer must perform a series of computations to determine look-back interest that the taxpayer is either required to pay or entitled to receive. As specified in paragraph (c) of this section, a taxpayer must first recompute depreciation allowances using revised forecasted total income rather than forecasted total income from income forecast property for the recomputation year (as defined in paragraph (e) of this section) and each prior year. These recomputed depreciation amounts are then used to determine a hypothetical tax liability that would have arisen had the taxpayer used revised forecasted total income rather than forecasted total income in determining depreciation allowances. The hypothetical tax liability is compared to the taxpayer's prior tax liability and interest is calculated in accordance with paragraph (d) of this section on the resulting hypothetical overpayments or underpayments of tax for each year. Reporting requirements and special rules for the resulting amounts of interest are specified in paragraph (g) of this section.

(2) *Property-by-property application.*—Except as provided in this section, the look-back method applies to each property for which the income forecast method is used. Aggregations properly treated as a single income forecast property pursuant to §1.167(n)-5(d) are treated as a single property for purposes of applying the look-back method.

(c) *Recalculation of depreciation allowances.*—(1) *Computation.*—Under the look-back method, a taxpayer must compute the depreciation allowances for each income forecast property subject to the look-back method that would have been allowable under §1.167(n)-1 through §1.167(n)-5 for prior taxable years if the computation of the amounts so allowable had been made using revised forecasted total income as calculated at the end of the recomputation year.

(2) *Revised forecasted total income from the property.*—(i) *In general.*—Except as provided in this paragraph (c)(2), revised forecasted total income is determined in accordance with §1.167(n)-3(c).

(ii) *Syndication income from television-series.*—Income excluded from forecasted total income (or, if appropriate revised forecasted total income) in any prior taxable year pursuant to §1.167(n)-3(d)(2) is excluded from revised forecasted total income for purposes of this section for that year.

(iii) *Disposition of income forecast property.*—For purposes of this section, income from the disposition of property must be taken into account in determining the amount of revised forecasted total income. Thus, when income forecast property is disposed of prior to the end of the 10th taxable year following the taxable year the property is placed in service, revised forecasted total income from the property for the year of disposition is deemed to be the sum of the amount realized on the disposition of the property plus all amounts included in current year income in the year of disposition and in taxable years prior to the year of disposition.

(3) *Special rule for basis redeterminations.*—For purposes of the look-back calculation, any amount that is not treated as a separate property under §1.167(n)-5(c) that is paid or incurred with respect to income forecast property after the property is placed in service is taken into account by discounting (using the Federal mid-term rate determined under section 1274(d) as of the time the cost is paid or incurred) the amount to its value as of the date the property is placed in service. The taxpayer may elect for the recomputation year with respect to any income forecast property to have the preceding sentence not apply to the property by taking the amount into account in the year that the amount was paid or incurred in the same manner as it was taken into account under §1.167(n)-2.

(d) *Hypothetical overpayment or underpayment of tax.*—(1) *In general.*—(i) *Years for which a hypothetical overpayment or underpayment must be computed.*—After recalculating depreciation allowances in accordance with paragraph (c) of this section, a taxpayer must calculate a hypothetical overpayment or underpayment of tax for each prior taxable year for which income tax liability is affected by the change in depreciation allowances. A redetermination of income tax liability is required for every tax year for which the income tax liability would have been affected by a change in the allowance for income forecast depreciation in any year. For example, if the change in depreciation allowance results in a net operating loss carryforward that affects income tax liability in a subsequent taxable year, income tax liability must be recomputed for such subsequent year.

(ii) *Methods of determining a hypothetical overpayment or underpayment.*—Generally, the calculation of the hypothetical overpayment or underpayment of tax must be made under the method described in paragraph (d)(2) of this section. Certain taxpayers are required to use the simplified method contained in paragraph (d)(3) of this section.

(iii) *Cumulative determination of hypothetical income tax liability.*—The redetermination of income tax liability in any prior taxable year for which income tax liability is affected by the change in depreciation allowances must take into account all previous applications of the look-back calculation. Thus, for example, in computing the amount of a hypothetical overpayment or underpayment of tax for a prior taxable year for which income tax liability is affected by the change in depreciation allowances, the hypothetical income tax liability is compared to the hypothetical income tax liability for that year determined as of the previous application of the look-back method.

(2) *Hypothetical overpayment or underpayment, actual recomputation.*—(i) *Computation of change in income tax liability.*—The hypothetical overpayment or underpayment is calculated first by redetermining the tax liability for each prior taxable year (either as originally reported, or as subsequently adjusted on examination or by amended return) using depreciation allowances calculated in paragraph (c) of this section for each prior taxable year in which depreciation allowances were determined under the income forecast method for the income forecast property (affected year). These recomputed depreciation allowances are then substituted for the depreciation allowances allowed (or allowable) for each affected year (whether originally reported, or as subsequently adjusted on examination or by amended return) and a revised taxable income is computed. A hypothetical income tax liability is then computed for each affected year using revised taxable income for that year. The hypothetical income tax liability for any affected year must be computed by taking into account all applicable additions to tax, credits, and net operating loss carrybacks and carryforwards. The tax, if any, imposed under section 55 (relating to alternative minimum tax) must be taken into account. Hypothetical income tax liability for each affected year is then compared to the tax liability determined as of the latest of the following dates—

(A) The original due date of the return (including extensions);

(B) The date of a subsequently amended or adjusted return; or

(C) The date of the previous application of the look-back method, in which case the hypothetical income tax liability for the affected year used in the most recent previous application of the look-back method (previous hypothetical tax liability) is used.

(ii) *Determination of interest.*—Once the hypothetical overpayment or underpayment for each year is computed, the adjusted overpayment rate under section 460(b)(7), compounded daily, is applied to the overpayment or underpayment determined under paragraph (d)(2)(i) of this section for the period beginning with the due date of the return (determined without regard to extensions) for the year in which either an overpayment or underpayment arises, and ending on the earlier of the due date of the return (determined without regard to extensions) for the redetermination year, or the first date by which both the income tax return for the filing year is filed and the tax for that year has been paid in full. The amounts of interest on overpayments are then netted against interest on underpayments to arrive at look-back interest that must be paid by the taxpayer or that the taxpayer is entitled to receive.

(iii) *Changes in the amount of a loss or credit carryback or carryforward.*—If a recomputation of income forecast depreciation results in an increase or decrease to a net operating loss carryback (but not a carryforward), the interest a taxpayer is entitled to receive or required to pay must be computed on the decrease or increase in tax attributable to the change to the carryback only from the due date (not including extensions) of the return for the prior taxable year that generated the carryback and not from the due date of the return for the prior taxable year in which the carryback was absorbed. In the case of a change in the amount of a carryforward as a result of applying the look-back method, interest is computed from the due date of the return for the years in which the carryforward was absorbed.

(iv) *Changes in the amount of income tax liability that generated a subsequent refund.*—If the hypothetical income tax liability for any affected year is less than the amount of the affected year tax liability (as reported on the taxpayer's original return, as subsequently adjusted on examination, as adjusted by amended return, or as redetermined by the last previous application of the look-back method), and any portion of the affected year tax liability was refunded as a result of a loss or credit carryback arising in a year subsequent to the affected year, the look-back method applies as follows to properly reflect the time period of the use of the tax overpayment. To the extent the amount of refund because of the carryback exceeds the hypothetical income tax liability for the affected year, the taxpayer is entitled to receive interest only until the due date (not including extensions) of the return for the year in which the carryback arose.

(v) *Example.*—The provisions of this paragraph (d)(2) are illustrated by the following example:

Example. Upon the cessation of income from an income forecast property in 2003, the taxpayer computes a hypothetical income tax liability for 2001 under the look-back method. This computation results in a hypothetical income tax liability ($1,200x) that is less than the actual income tax liability the taxpayer originally reported ($1,500x). In addition, the taxpayer had already received a refund of some or all of the actual 2001 income tax liability by carrying back a net operating loss (NOL) that arose in 2002. The time period over which interest would be computed on the hypothetical overpayment of $300x for 2001 would depend on the amount of the refund generated by the carryback, as illustrated by the following three alternative situations:

(i) If the amount refunded because of the NOL is $1,500x, interest is credited to the taxpayer on the entire hypothetical overpayment of $300x from the due date of the 2001 return, when the hypothetical overpayment occurred, until the due date of the 2002 return, when the taxpayer received a refund for the entire amount of the 2001 tax, including the hypothetical overpayment.

(ii) If the amount refunded because of the NOL is $1,000x, interest is credited to the taxpayer on the entire amount of the hypothetical overpayment of $300x from the due date of the 2001 return, when the hypothetical overpayment occurred, until the due date of the 2003 return. In this situation interest is credited until the due date of the return for the recomputation year, rather than the due date of the return for the year in which the carryback arose, because the amount refunded was less than the hypothetical income tax liability of $1,200x. Therefore, no portion of the hypothetical overpayment is treated as having been refunded to the taxpayer before the recomputation year.

(iii) If the amount refunded because of the NOL is $1,300x, interest is credited to the taxpayer on $100x ($1,300x-$1,200x) from the due date of the 2001 return until the due date of the 2002 return because only this portion of the total hypothetical overpayment is treated as having been refunded to the taxpayer before the recomputation year. However, the taxpayer did not receive a refund for the remaining $200x of the overpayment at that time and, therefore, is credited with interest on $200x through the due date of the tax return for 2003, the recomputation year.

(3) *Hypothetical overpayment or underpayment, simplified method.*—(i) *Introduction.*—This paragraph provides a simplified method for calculating look-back interest. A pass-through entity that is not a closely held pass-through entity is required to apply the simplified method at the entity level with respect to income forecast property and the owners of the entity do not calculate look-back interest for the property. Under the simplified method, a taxpayer calculates the hypothetical underpayments or overpayments of tax for a prior year based on an assumed marginal tax rate.

(ii) *Operation of the simplified method.*—Under the simplified method, depreciation allowances for income forecast property are first recomputed in accordance with the procedures contained in paragraph (c) of this section. These recomputed depreciation allowances are then compared with depreciation allowances allowed (or allowable) for each prior taxable year (whether originally reported, as subsequently adjusted on examination or by amended return, or as recomputed in the most recent previous application of the look-back method) to arrive at changes in depreciation allowances for the income forecast property. When multiple properties are subject to the look-back method in any given affected year, the changes in depreciation allowances attributable to each income forecast property determined in accordance with paragraph (c) of this section for each such year are cumulated or netted against one another to arrive at a net change in income forecast depreciation for purposes of computing the hypothetical overpayment or underpayment attributable to the year. The hypothetical underpayment or overpayment of tax for each affected year is then determined by multiplying the applicable regular tax rate (as defined in paragraph (d)(3)(iv) of this section) by the increase or decrease in depreciation allowances.

(iii) *Determination of interest.*—Interest is credited to the taxpayer on the net overpayment and is charged to the taxpayer on the net underpayment for each affected year by applying the adjusted overpayment rate under section 460(b)(7), compounded daily, to the overpayment or underpayment determined under paragraph (d)(3)(ii) of this section for the period beginning with the due date of the return (determined without regard to extensions) for the affected year, and ending on the earlier of the due date of the return (determined without regard to extensions) for the recomputation year, or the first date by which both the income tax return for the recomputation year is filed and the tax for that year has been paid in full. The

resulting amounts of interest are then netted to arrive at look-back interest that must be paid by the taxpayer or that the taxpayer is entitled to receive.

(iv) *Applicable tax rate.*—For purposes of determining hypothetical underpayments or overpayments of tax under the simplified method, the applicable regular rate is generally the highest rate of tax in effect for corporations under section 11. However, the applicable regular tax rate is the highest rate of tax imposed on individuals under section 1 if, at all times during all affected years, more than 50 percent of the interests in the entity were held by individuals directly or through 1 or more pass-through entities. The highest rate of tax imposed on individuals is determined without regard to any additional tax imposed for the purpose of phasing out multiple tax brackets or exemptions.

(4) *Definitions.*—(i) *Pass-through entity.*—For purposes of this section, a pass-through entity is either a partnership, an S corporation, an estate or a trust.

(ii) *Closely-held pass-through entity.*—A closely-held pass-through entity is a pass-through entity that, at any time during any year for which allowances for depreciation are recomputed, 50 percent or more (by value) of the beneficial interests in that entity are held (directly or indirectly) by or for 5 or fewer persons. For this purpose, the term *person* has the same meaning as in section 7701(a)(1), except that a pass-through entity is not treated as a person. In addition, the constructive ownership rules of section 1563(e) apply by substituting the term *beneficial interest* for the term *stock* and by substituting the term *pass-through entity* for the term *corporation* used in that section, as appropriate, for purposes of determining whether a beneficial interest in a pass-through entity is indirectly owned by any person.

(e) *Recomputation year.*—(1) *In general.*—Except as provided in this paragraph (e), the term *recomputation year* means, with respect to any income forecast property—

(i) The earlier of—

(A) The year the income from the income forecast property ceases with respect to the taxpayer (and with respect to any person who would be treated as a single taxpayer with the taxpayer under rules similar to those in section 41(f)(1)); or

(B) The 3rd taxable year beginning after the taxable year in which the income forecast property was placed in service; and

(ii) The earlier of—

(A) The year the income from the income forecast property ceases with respect to the taxpayer (and with respect to any person who would be treated as a single taxpayer with the taxpayer under rules similar to those in section 41(f)(1)); or

(B) The 10th taxable year following the taxable year the income forecast property is placed in service.

(2) *Look-back method inapplicable in certain de minimis cases.*—(i) *De minimis difference between actual and forecasted income.*—A taxable year described in paragraph (e)(1) of this section is not a recomputation year if forecasted total income (as defined in § 1.167(n)-3(b)) or, where applicable, revised forecasted total income (as defined in § 1.167(n)-3(c)), for each preceding taxable years is—

(A) Greater than 90 percent of revised forecasted total income for the taxable year that would otherwise be a recomputation year; and

(B) Less than 110 percent of revised forecasted total income for the taxable year that would otherwise be a recomputation year.

(ii) *Application of the de minimis rule where the look-back method was previously applied.*—For purposes of applying paragraph (e)(2)(i) of this section in any taxable year after a taxable year in which the look-back method has previously been applied, revised forecasted total income for the year the look-back method was applied, forecasted total income for the year the income forecast property was placed in service, and revised forecasted total income for all taxable years preceding the taxable year in which the look-back method was previously applied are deemed to be equal to the amount of revised forecasted total income that was used for purposes of applying the look-back method in the most recent taxable year for which the look-back method was applied.

(f) *De minimis basis exception.*—The look-back method does not apply to any income forecast property with an adjusted basis, determined in accordance with section 1011 but without regard to the adjustments described in section 1016(a)(2) and (3), as of the close of any year that would otherwise be a recomputation year of $100,000 or less.

(g) *Treatment of look-back interest.*—(1) *In general.*—The amount of interest a taxpayer is required to pay is treated as an income tax under Subtitle A of the Internal Revenue Code, but only for purposes of Subtitle F of the Internal Revenue Code (other than sections 6654 and 6655), which addresses tax procedure and administration. Thus, a taxpayer that fails to report look-back interest when due is subject to any penalties under Subtitle F of the Internal Revenue Code applicable to a failure to report and pay a tax liability. However, look-back interest to be paid is treated as interest arising from an underpayment of tax under Subtitle A of the Internal Revenue Code, even though it is treated as an income tax liability for penalty purposes. Thus, look-back interest required to be paid by an individual, or by a pass-through entity on behalf of an individual owner (or beneficiary) under the simplified method, is personal interest and, therefore, is not deductible in accordance with § 1.163-9T(b)(2). Interest received under the look-back method is treated as taxable interest income for all purposes, and is not treated as a reduction in tax liability. The determination of whether interest computed under the look-back method is treated as income tax under Subtitle A of the Internal Revenue Code is determined on a net basis for each recomputation year. Thus, if a taxpayer computes both hypothetical overpayments of tax and hypothetical underpayments of tax for years prior to any given recomputation year, the taxpayer has an increase in tax only if the total interest computed on underpayments for all prior taxable years for which income tax liability is affected by the application of the look-back method exceeds the total interest computed on overpayments for such years, taking into account all income forecast property for which the look-back method is required. Interest determined at the entity level under the simplified method is allocated among the owners (or beneficiaries) for reporting purposes in the same manner that interest income and interest expense are allocated to owners (or beneficiaries) and subject to the allocation rules applicable to such entities.

(2) *Additional interest due on interest only after tax liability due.*—For each recomputation year, taxpayers are required to file a Form 8866, "Interest Computation Under the Look-back Method for Property Depreciated Under the Income Forecast Method," at the time the return for that recomputation year is filed to report the interest a taxpayer is required to pay or entitled to receive under the look-back method. Even if the taxpayer has received an extension to file its income tax return for the recomputation year, look-back interest is computed with respect to the hypothetical increase (or decrease) in the tax liability determined under the look-back method only until the initial due date of that return (without regard to the extension). Interest is charged, unless the taxpayer otherwise has a refund that fully offsets the amount of interest due, (or credited) with respect to the amount of look-back interest due (or to be refunded) under the look-back method from the initial due date of the return through the date the return is filed. No interest is charged (or credited) after the due date of the return with respect to the amount of the hypothetical increases (or decreases) in tax liability determined under the look-back method.

(3) *Timing of look-back interest.*—For purposes of determining taxable income under Subtitle A of the Internal Revenue Code, any amount refunded to the taxpayer as a result of the application of the look-back method is includible in gross income in accordance with the taxpayer's method of accounting for interest income. Any amount required to be paid is taken into account as interest expense arising from an underpayment of income tax in the tax year it is properly taken into account under the taxpayer's method of accounting for interest expense.

(4) *Statute of limitations; compounding of interest on look-back interest.*—For guidance on the statute of limitations applicable to the assessment and collection of look-back interest owed by a taxpayer,

see sections 6501 and 6502. A taxpayer's claim for credit or refund of look-back interest *previously paid by or collected from a taxpayer* is a claim for credit or refund of an overpayment of tax and is subject to the statute of limitations provided in section 6511. A taxpayer's claim for look-back interest (or interest payable on look-back interest) that is not attributable to an amount previously paid or collected from a taxpayer is a general claim against the federal government. For guidance on the statute of limitations that applies to general claims against the federal government, see 28 U.S.C. 2401 and 2501. For guidance applicable to the compounding of interest when the look-back interest is not paid, see sections 6601 to 6622.

(h) *Example.*—The provisions of this section are illustrated by the following example:

Example. (i) H, a calendar year corporation, creates a motion picture at a cost of $60x. H completes the motion picture in 2001 and begins exhibition of the film that same year. Assume that $60x is greater than $100,000. In 2001, H anticipates that it will earn $200x from the motion picture (net of distribution costs). H therefore uses this amount as Forecasted Total Income when computing depreciation allowances for the motion picture.

(ii) H earns current year income of $80x in 2001, $60x in 2002, and $40x in 2003. During the period from 2001 to 2004, one of the actors who appeared in H's film became more popular, and this increase in the actor's popularity increased the demand for H's film. In 2004, therefore, H revised its forecast of income from the film upward to $240x. H earns $20x in 2004 from the motion picture and $10x in 2005.

(iii) Based on these facts, H's allowances for depreciation for the motion picture for 2001 would be $24x, computed by multiplying the depreciable basis of the motion picture of $60x by current year income of $80x divided by forecasted total income of $200x under § 1.167(n)-4(a). Similarly, H's allowances for depreciation for the motion picture for 2002 would be $18x, computed by multiplying the depreciable basis of the motion picture of $60x by current year income of $60x divided by forecasted total income of $200x, and H's allowances for depreciation for the motion picture for 2003 would be $12x, computed by multiplying the depreciable basis of the motion picture of $60x by current year income of $40x divided by forecasted total income of $200x.

(iv) In 2004, H determines revised forecasted total income of $240x in accordance with § 1.167(n)-3(c). Because revised forecasted total income in 2004 of $240x is greater than 110 percent of forecasted total income used in computing the allowance for depreciation in the immediately preceding year (110 percent of $200x equals $220x), H is required under § 1.167(n)-4(b)(2) to compute the allowance for depreciation in 2004 and thereafter using the revised computation. H first computes its unrecovered depreciable basis in the motion picture under § 1.167(n)-2(c) of $6x by subtracting from the depreciable basis of $60x the depreciation allowances for 2001, 2002, and 2003 of $24x, $18x, and $12x. H then multiplies the unrecovered depreciable basis of $6x by the current year income for 2004 of $20x divided by $60x (revised forecasted total income $240x less current year income for all years prior to 2004 ($80x + $60x + $40x or $180x), resulting in a depreciation allowance for 2004 of $2x.

(v) In 2005, H is required to use the revised computation because H used it in 2004. Thus, H multiplies the unrecovered depreciable basis of $6x times current year income for 2005 of $10x divided by $60x (revised forecasted total income as computed in 2004), resulting in a depreciation allowance for 2005 of $1x.

(vi) Thus, H's allowances for depreciation may be summarized as follows:

Year	Current Year Income	Forecasted Total Income	Revised Forecasted Total Income	Depreciable Basis	Unrecovered Depreciable Basis	Depreciation Allowance
2001	80x	200x		60x		24x
2002	60x	200x		60x		18x
2003	40x	200x		60x		12x
2004	20x		240x		6x	2x
2005	10x		240x		6x	1x

(vii) Under paragraph (e)(l)(i)(B) of this section, 2004 is a recomputation year (because 2004 is the third taxable year after the year in which the motion picture was placed in service) unless a de minimis rule applies. The de minimis rule in paragraph (e)(2) of this section does not apply in 2004 because forecasted total income of $200x used in the computation of income forecast depreciation in 2001, 2002 and 2003 is not greater than 90 percent of the 2004 revised forecasted total income of $240x (90 percent of $240x = $216x). Thus, H must apply the look-back method for 2004.

(viii) If H sells the motion picture in 2006 for $25x prior to earning any current year income from the motion picture, H would not be entitled to any allowance for depreciation in 2006. (The special rule of § 1.167(n)-3(d)(l) precludes H from including income from the

sale of the motion picture in current year income, H has no other current year income, and § 1.167(n)-4(d)(3) precludes the use of the final year depreciation rule of § 1.167(n)-4(d)(1)). Under paragraph (e)(1)(ii)(A) of this section, 2006 is a recomputation year (because in 2006 the income from the property to H ceases) unless a de minimis rule applies.

(ix) To determine whether the de minimis rule applies, H is required to determine revised forecasted total income for 2006. Under paragraph (c)(2) of this section, revised forecasted total income for 2006 is deemed to be the sum of current year income for the years 2001—2006 of $210x ($80x + $60x + $40x + $20x + $10x + $0x) plus the amount realized from the sale of the motion picture of $25x or $235x. Revised forecasted total income for 2005 is $240x, and pursuant to paragraph (e)(2)(ii) of this section, revised forecasted total income for the years 2001—2004 is deemed (for purposes of determining whether 2006 is a recomputation year) to be the amount of revised forecasted total income used in the 2004 application of the look-back method of $240x. Because $240x is greater than $212x (90 percent of $235x) and less than $259x (110 percent of $235x), the de minimis rule applies and H is not required to apply the look-back method in 2006.

[Reg. § 1.167(n)-6.]

§1.167(n)-7. Effective date.—The regulations under §1.167(n)-1 through §1.167(n)-6 are applicable for property placed in service on or after the date that final regulations are published in the Federal Register. [Reg. § 1.167(n)-7.]

Accelerated Cost Recovery System

Accelerated Cost Recovery System.—Reproduced below are the texts of proposed Reg. §§ 1.168-1—1.168-4, 1.168-5(b)—(f) and 1.168-6, relating to the Accelerated Cost Recovery System for recovering capital costs of eligible property (published in the Federal Register on February 16, 1984). Proposed Reg. §1.168-5(a) was adopted by T.D. 8116 on 12/23/86. Proposed Reg. §1.168-2(n) was withdrawn by REG-209682-94 on 1/29/98.

☐ Par. 2. New §§1.168-1 through 1.168-6 are added. The new sections read as follows:

§1.168-1. Accelerated Cost Recovery System; in general.—
(a) *Cost recovery deduction allowed.*—Section 168 of the Internal Revenue Code of 1954 provides a system for determining cost recovery deductions for recovery property, the Accelerated Cost Recovery System ("ACRS"). The deduction allowable under section 168 is deemed to constitute the reasonable allowance for depreciation allowed as a deduction under section 167(a). Operating rules regarding determination of the allowable cost recovery deduction are provided in § 1.168-2. The definition of recovery property and the classification of recovery property into recovery categories of 3, 5, 10, and 15 years are provided in §1.168-3. ACRS must be applied with respect to recovery property placed in service after December 31, 1980, except for certain property which does not qualify under section 168 or which may be excluded from ACRS; § 1.168-4 provides rules regarding such exclusions and non-qualifications. Special rules regarding ACRS are provided in § 1.168-5. Rules relating to the recognition of gain or loss on dispositions are provided in § 1.168-6.

(b) *Cross references.*—See § 1.167(a)-11(d)(2) regarding the election after 1980 of the repair allowance for certain property. See § 1.178-1 regarding the availability of ACRS deductions for, or the amortization of, improvements on leased property. See § 1.1016-3(a)(3) regarding the basis adjustment for the amount allowable where no ACRS deduction is claimed. [Reg. § 1.168-1.]

§1.168-2. Amount of deduction for recovery property.—
(a) *Computation of recovery allowance.*—(1) *General rule.*—Except as otherwise provided in section 168 and the regulations thereunder, the recovery allowance for any taxable year equals the aggregate amount determined by multiplying the unadjusted basis (as defined in § 1.168-2(d)) of recovery property (as defined in §1.168-3) by the appropriate applicable percentage provided in paragraph (b) of this section. For purposes of determining the recovery allowance, salvage value shall be disregarded.

(2) *No allowance in year of disposition.*—Except for 15-year real property and except as otherwise provided in §1.168-5, no recovery allowance shall be allowed in the year of disposition of recovery property.

(3) *Proration of allowance in year of disposition of 15-year real property.*—In the taxable year in which 15-year real property is disposed of, the recovery allowance shall be determined by multiplying the allowance (determined without regard to this subparagraph) by a fraction, the numerator of which equals the number of months in the taxable year that the property is in service in the taxpayer's trade or business or for the production of income and the denominator of which is 12. In the case of 15-year real property that is disposed of in the first recovery year, the denominator shall equal the number of months in the taxpayer's taxable year after the recovery property was placed in service by the taxpayer (including the month the property was placed in service). If the recovery allowance for the taxable year is limited by reason of the short taxable year rules of section 168(f)(5) and paragraph (f) of this section (e.g., if the taxpayer dies, or if the taxpayer is a corporation which becomes a member, or ceases being a member, of an affiliated group of corporations filing a consolidated return), then the denominator shall equal the number of months in the taxpayer's taxable year. For purposes of this subparagraph, 15-year real property shall be treated as disposed of as of the last day of the month preceding the month in which it is withdrawn from service.

(b) *Applicable percentage.*—(1) *Property other than 15-year real property.*—The applicable percentage for recovery property, other than 15-year real property, is as follows:

If the recovery year is:	3-year	5-year	10-year	15-year Public Utility
			The applicable percentage is:	
1	25	15	8	5
2	38	22	14	10
3	37	21	12	9
4		21	10	8
5		21	10	7
6			10	7
7			9	6
8			9	6
9			9	6
10			9	6
11				6
12				6
13				6
14				6
15				6

(2) *15-year real property.*—(i) The applicable percentage for 15-year real property, other than low-income housing is as follows:

If the recovery year is:	1	2	3	4	5	6	7	8	9	10	11	12
				And the month in the 1st recovery year the property is placed in service is:								
					The applicable percentage is:							
1	12	11	10	9	8	7	6	5	4	3	2	1
2	10	10	11	11	11	11	11	11	11	11	11	12
3	9	9	9	9	10	10	10	10	10	10	10	10
4	8	8	8	8	8	8	9	9	9	9	9	9
5	7	7	7	7	7	7	8	8	8	8	8	8
6	6	6	6	6	7	7	7	7	7	7	7	7
7	6	6	6	6	6	6	6	6	6	6	6	6
8	6	6	6	6	6	6	5	6	6	6	6	6
9	6	6	6	6	5	6	5	5	5	6	6	6

If the recovery year is:	1	2	3	4	5	6	7	8	9	10	11	12
					And the month in the 1st recovery year the property is placed in service is:							
					The applicable percentage is:							
10	5	6	5	6	5	5	5	5	5	5	6	5
11	5	5	5	5	5	5	5	5	5	5	5	5
12	5	5	5	5	5	5	5	5	5	5	5	5
13	5	5	5	5	5	5	5	5	5	5	5	5
14	5	5	5	5	5	5	5	5	5	5	5	5
15	5	5	5	5	5	5	5	5	5	5	5	5
16	—	—	1	1	2	2	3	3	4	4	4	5

(ii) The applicable percentage for 15-year real property that is low-income housing is as follows:

If the recovery year is:	1	2	3	4	5	6	7	8	9	10	11	12
					And the month in the 1st recovery year the property is placed in service is:							
					The applicable percentage is:							
1	13	12	11	10	9	8	7	6	4	3	2	1
2	12	12	12	12	12	12	12	13	13	13	13	13
3	10	10	10	10	11	11	11	11	11	11	11	11
4	9	9	9	9	9	9	9	9	10	10	10	10
5	8	8	8	8	8	8	8	8	8	8	8	9
6	7	7	7	7	7	7	7	7	7	7	7	7
7	6	6	6	6	6	6	6	6	6	6	6	6
8	5	5	5	5	5	5	5	5	5	6	6	6
9	5	5	5	5	5	5	5	5	5	5	5	5
10	5	5	5	5	5	5	5	5	5	5	5	5
11	4	5	5	5	5	5	5	5	5	5	5	5
12	4	4	4	4	5	5	5	5	5	5	5	5
13	4	4	4	4	4	4	5	4	5	5	5	5
14	4	4	4	4	4	4	4	4	4	5	4	4
15	4	4	4	4	4	4	4	4	4	4	4	4
16	—	—	1	1	2	2	2	3	3	3	4	4

(iii) For purposes of this section, the term "low-income housing" means property described in clause (i), (ii), (iii), or (iv) of section 1250(a)(1)(B).

(iv) For purposes of this subparagraph (2), 15-year real property placed in service on or after the first day of a month shall be treated as placed in service in that month.

(c) *Election of optional recovery percentage.*—(1) *Straight line method.*—Except as provided by section 168(f)(2) and §1.168-2(g)

Class of property
3-year property
5-year property
10-year property
15-year real property
15-year public utility property

Such election is irrevocable without the consent of the Commissioner. See subparagraph (4) of this paragraph for tables containing the applicable percentages to be used in computing the recovery allowance.

(2) *Election for property other than 15-year real property.*—Except in the case of 15-year real property, a single recovery period must be elected under this paragraph for all recovery property which is in the same recovery class and which is placed in service in the same taxable year. A different recovery period may be elected (or the tables provided in section 168(b)(1) and §1.168-2(b)(1) may be used) for

(relating to property used predominantly outside the United States), in lieu of using the applicable percentages prescribed in section 168(b)(1) and (2) and §1.168-2(b), the taxpayer may elect (in accordance with §1.168-5(e)), for recovery property placed in service during the taxable year, to determine the recovery allowance by using the straight line method over one of the recovery periods elected by the taxpayer and set forth in the following table:

Recovery periods
3, 5, or 12 years
5, 12, or 25 years
10, 25, or 35 years
15, 35, or 45 years
15, 35, or 45 years

recovery property in different recovery classes placed in service during the same taxable year, or for recovery property placed in service in different taxable years, whether or not in the same recovery class.

(3) *Election for 15-year real property.*—In the case of 15-year real property, the election provided in paragraph (c)(1) may be made separately with respect to each property.

(4) *Applicable percentage.*—(i) For property other than 15-year real property—

If the recovery year is:	3	5	10	12	15	25	35	45
			And the period elected is:					
				The applicable percentage is:				
1	17	10	5	4	3	2	1	1.1
2	33	20	10	9	7	4	3	2.3
3	33	20	10	9	7	4	3	2.3
4	17	20	10	9	7	4	3	2.3
5		20	10	9	7	4	3	2.3
6		10	10	8	7	4	3	2.3
7			10	8	7	4	3	2.3
8			10	8	7	4	3	2.3
9			10	8	7	4	3	2.3
10			10	8	7	4	3	2.3
11			5	8	7	4	3	2.3
12				8	6	4	3	2.2
13				4	6	4	3	2.2
14					6	4	3	2.2
15					6	4	3	2.2
16					3	4	3	2.2
17						4	3	2.2
18						4	3	2.2
19						4	3	2.2

If the recovery year is:	And the period elected is:							
	3	5	10	12	15	25	35	45
				The applicable percentage is:				
20						4	3	2.2
21						4	3	2.2
22						4	3	2.2
23						4	3	2.2
24						4	3	2.2
25						4	3	2.2
26						2	3	2.2
27							3	2.2
28							3	2.2
29							3	2.2
30							3	2.2
31							3	2.2
32							2	2.2
33							2	2.2
34							2	2.2
35							2	2.2
36							1	2.2
37								2.2
38								2.2
39								2.2
40								2.2
41								2.2
42								2.2
43								2.2
44								2.2
45								2.2
46								1.1

(ii) For 15-year real property—

(A) For which a 15-year period is elected—

If the recovery year is:	And the month in the 1st recovery year that the property is placed in service is:						
	1	2-3	4	5-6	7-8	9-10	11-12
				The applicable percentage is:			
1	7	6	5	4	3	2	1
2	7	7	7	7	7	7	7
3	7	7	7	7	7	7	7
4	7	7	7	7	7	7	7
5	7	7	7	7	7	7	7
6	7	7	7	7	7	7	7
7	7	7	7	7	7	7	7
8	7	7	7	7	7	7	7
9	7	7	7	7	7	7	7
10	7	7	7	7	7	7	7
11	6	6	6	6	6	6	6
12	6	6	6	6	6	6	6
13	6	6	6	6	6	6	6
14	6	6	6	6	6	6	6
15	6	6	6	6	6	6	6
16		1	2	3	4	6	6

(B) For which a 35-year period is elected—

If the recovery year is:	And the month in the 1st recovery year that the property is placed in service is:		
	1-2	3-6	7-12
		The applicable percentage is:	
1	3	2	1
2	3	3	3
3	3	3	3
4	3	3	3
5	3	3	3
6	3	3	3
7	3	3	3
8	3	3	3
9	3	3	3
10	3	3	3
11	3	3	3
12	3	3	3
13	3	3	3
14	3	3	3
15	3	3	3
16	3	3	3
17	3	3	3
18	3	3	3
19	3	3	3
20	3	3	3
21	3	3	3
22	3	3	3
23	3	3	3
24	3	3	3
25	3	3	3
26	3	3	3

If the recovery year is:

And the month in the 1st recovery year that the property is placed in service is:

If the recovery year is:	1-2	3-6	7-12
		The applicable percentage is:	
27	3	3	3
28	3	3	3
29	3	3	3
30	3	3	3
31	2	2	2
32	2	2	2
33	2	2	2
34	2	2	2
35	2	2	2
36		1	2

(C) For which a 45-year period is elected—

If the recovery year is:

And the month in the 1st recovery year that the property is placed in service is:

If the recovery year is:	1	2	3	4	5	6	7	8	9	10	11	12
					The applicable percentage is:							
1	2.3	2.0	1.9	1.7	1.5	1.3	1.2	.9	.7	.6	.4	.2
2	2.3	2.3	2.3	2.3	2.3	2.3	2.3	2.3	2.3	2.3	2.3	2.3
3	2.3	2.3	2.3	2.3	2.3	2.3	2.3	2.3	2.3	2.3	2.3	2.3
4	2.3	2.3	2.3	2.3	2.3	2.3	2.3	2.3	2.3	2.3	2.3	2.3
5	2.3	2.3	2.3	2.3	2.3	2.3	2.3	2.3	2.3	2.3	2.3	2.3
6	2.3	2.3	2.3	2.3	2.3	2.3	2.3	2.3	2.3	2.3	2.3	2.3
7	2.3	2.3	2.3	2.3	2.3	2.3	2.3	2.3	2.3	2.3	2.3	2.3
8	2.3	2.3	2.3	2.3	2.3	2.3	2.3	2.3	2.3	2.3	2.3	2.3
9	2.3	2.3	2.3	2.3	2.3	2.3	2.3	2.3	2.3	2.3	2.3	2.3
10	2.3	2.3	2.3	2.3	2.3	2.3	2.3	2.3	2.3	2.3	2.3	2.3
11	2.2	2.2	2.2	2.2	2.2	2.2	2.2	2.2	2.2	2.2	2.2	2.2
12	2.2	2.2	2.2	2.2	2.2	2.2	2.2	2.2	2.2	2.2	2.2	2.2
13	2.2	2.2	2.2	2.2	2.2	2.2	2.2	2.2	2.2	2.2	2.2	2.2
14	2.2	2.2	2.2	2.2	2.2	2.2	2.2	2.2	2.2	2.2	2.2	2.2
15	2.2	2.2	2.2	2.2	2.2	2.2	2.2	2.2	2.2	2.2	2.2	2.2
16	2.2	2.2	2.2	2.2	2.2	2.2	2.2	2.2	2.2	2.2	2.2	2.2
17	2.2	2.2	2.2	2.2	2.2	2.2	2.2	2.2	2.2	2.2	2.2	2.2
18	2.2	2.2	2.2	2.2	2.2	2.2	2.2	2.2	2.2	2.2	2.2	2.2
19	2.2	2.2	2.2	2.2	2.2	2.2	2.2	2.2	2.2	2.2	2.2	2.2
20	2.2	2.2	2.2	2.2	2.2	2.2	2.2	2.2	2.2	2.2	2.2	2.2
21	2.2	2.2	2.2	2.2	2.2	2.2	2.2	2.2	2.2	2.2	2.2	2.2
22	2.2	2.2	2.2	2.2	2.2	2.2	2.2	2.2	2.2	2.2	2.2	2.2
23	2.2	2.2	2.2	2.2	2.2	2.2	2.2	2.2	2.2	2.2	2.2	2.2
24	2.2	2.2	2.2	2.2	2.2	2.2	2.2	2.2	2.2	2.2	2.2	2.2
25	2.2	2.2	2.2	2.2	2.2	2.2	2.2	2.2	2.2	2.2	2.2	2.2
26	2.2	2.2	2.2	2.2	2.2	2.2	2.2	2.2	2.2	2.2	2.2	2.2
27	2.2	2.2	2.2	2.2	2.2	2.2	2.2	2.2	2.2	2.2	2.2	2.2
28	2.2	2.2	2.2	2.2	2.2	2.2	2.2	2.2	2.2	2.2	2.2	2.2
29	2.2	2.2	2.2	2.2	2.2	2.2	2.2	2.2	2.2	2.2	2.2	2.2
30	2.2	2.2	2.2	2.2	2.2	2.2	2.2	2.2	2.2	2.2	2.2	2.2
31	2.2	2.2	2.2	2.2	2.2	2.2	2.2	2.2	2.2	2.2	2.2	2.2
32	2.2	2.2	2.2	2.2	2.2	2.2	2.2	2.2	2.2	2.2	2.2	2.2
33	2.2	2.2	2.2	2.2	2.2	2.2	2.2	2.2	2.2	2.2	2.2	2.2
34	2.2	2.2	2.2	2.2	2.2	2.2	2.2	2.2	2.2	2.2	2.2	2.2
35	2.2	2.2	2.2	2.2	2.2	2.2	2.2	2.2	2.2	2.2	2.2	2.2
36	2.2	2.2	2.2	2.2	2.2	2.2	2.2	2.2	2.2	2.2	2.2	2.2
37	2.2	2.2	2.2	2.2	2.2	2.2	2.2	2.2	2.2	2.2	2.2	2.2
38	2.2	2.2	2.2	2.2	2.2	2.2	2.2	2.2	2.2	2.2	2.2	2.2
39	2.2	2.2	2.2	2.2	2.2	2.2	2.2	2.2	2.2	2.2	2.2	2.2
40	2.2	2.2	2.2	2.2	2.2	2.2	2.2	2.2	2.2	2.2	2.2	2.2
41	2.2	2.2	2.2	2.2	2.2	2.2	2.2	2.2	2.2	2.2	2.2	2.2
42	2.2	2.2	2.2	2.2	2.2	2.2	2.2	2.2	2.2	2.2	2.2	2.2
43	2.2	2.2	2.2	2.2	2.2	2.2	2.2	2.2	2.2	2.2	2.2	2.2
44	2.2	2.2	2.2	2.2	2.2	2.2	2.2	2.2	2.2	2.2	2.2	2.2
45	2.2	2.2	2.2	2.2	2.2	2.2	2.2	2.2	2.2	2.2	2.2	2.2
46		.3	.4	.6	.8	1.0	1.1	1.4	1.6	1.7	1.9	2.1

(iii) For purposes of this paragraph, 15-year real property that is placed in service on or after the first day of a month shall be treated as placed in service in that month.

(5) *Property financed with the proceeds of industrial development bonds.*—If, in accordance with section 168(f)(12) and §1.168-2(m), the recovery allowance for property financed with the proceeds of an industrial development bond (as described in section 103(b)) is determined using the straight line method, then an election as provided in section 168(b)(3) and this paragraph shall be deemed to have been made with respect to such property.

(d) *Unadjusted basis.*—(1) *Computation.*—Except as provided in paragraph (j)(6)(ii) of this section (relating to change of status), the unadjusted basis of recovery property is equal to the difference between—

(i) The basis of the property for purposes of determining gain under sections 1011 through 1024 but without regard to any adjustments to basis described in section 1016(a)(2) and (3), and

(ii) Any portion of the basis for which the taxpayer properly elects amortization in lieu of cost recovery (*e.g.*, under section 167(k)) or treatment as an expense under section 179.

The unadjusted basis of recovery property shall be first taken into account under this section for the taxable year in which the property is placed in service (as defined in paragraph (1)(2) of this §1.168-2) as recovery property.

(2) *Reductions in basis.*—(i) If an investment tax credit is determined under section 46(a)(2) with respect to recovery property, then, unless the taxpayer makes an election provided under section 48(q)(4), for purposes of this section the unadjusted basis shall be reduced by 50 percent of the amount of the credit so determined. In the case of a credit determined under section 46(a)(2) for any qualified rehabilitation expenditure made in connection with a qualified rehabilitated building (other than a certified historic structure), the unadjusted basis shall be reduced by 100 percent of the amount of the credit so determined. See section 48(q) and the regulations thereunder. For rules relating to the treatment of such basis adjustment

upon the disposition of an asset from a mass asset account, see §1.168-2(h)(4).

(ii) Subject to the rules of other applicable provisions of the Code (*e.g.*, section 280A), for recovery property which is used in the taxpayer's trade or business (or for the production of income) as well as in a personal or tax-exempt activity throughout a taxable year, the unadjusted basis shall be determined by multiplying the unadjusted basis (determined without regard to this subdivision) by a fraction, the numerator of which equals the taxpayer's use of the property during the taxable year in his trade or business (or for the production of income) and the denominator of which equals the taxpayer's total use of the property during the taxable year. For property converted from personal or tax-exempt use to use in the taxpayer's trade or business (or for the production of income), or for property devoted to increased use in the taxpayer's trade or business (or for the production of income), see §1.168-2(j).

Example. In 1981, A, a calendar year taxpayer, purchases a car for $10,000 to be used in his business as well as for his personal enjoyment. During 1981, A drives the car a total of 20,000 miles of which 8,000 miles (*i.e.*, 40 percent) is in the course of A's business. During 1982, A drives the car a total of 30,000 miles of which 21,000 miles (*i.e.*, 70 percent) is in the course of A's business. During 1983, A drives the car a total of 10,000 miles of which 3,000 miles (*i.e.*, 30 percent) is in the course of A's business. The optional straight line method provided under §1.168-2(c) is not elected. Thus, A's recovery allowance in 1981 equals $1,000 (*i.e.*, ($10,000 × .40) × .25), in 1982 equals $2,660 (*i.e.*, ($10,000 × .70) × .38) and in 1983 equals $1,110 (*i.e.*, ($10,000 × .30) × .37). If A continues to use the car in his business after 1983, additional recovery may be allowed. See §1.168-2(j).

(3) *Redeterminations.*—(i) For the taxable year (and subsequent taxable years) in which the unadjusted basis of recovery property is redetermined (*e.g.*, due to contingent purchase price or discharge of indebtedness), the recovery allowance shall be the amount determined by multiplying the redetermined adjusted basis by the redetermined applicable percentage. For purposes of this subparagraph, the redetermination adjusted basis is the unadjusted basis reduced by the recovery allowance previously allowed or allowable to the taxpayer with respect to the property and adjusted to reflect the redetermination. The redetermined applicable percentage is the percentage determined by dividing the applicable percentage otherwise provided in paragraph (b), (c), (g), or (m) of §1.168-2 for the recovery year by an amount equal to the unrecovered percentage (*i.e.*, 100 percent minus the applicable percentage for recovery years prior to the year in which the basis is redetermined). Thus, the increase or decrease in basis shall be accounted for over the remaining recovery years beginning with the recovery year in which the basis is redetermined.

(ii) The following examples illustrate the provisions of this subparagraph (3):

Example (1). On July 15, 1984, A places in service 5-year recovery property with an unadjusted basis of $100,000. In order to purchase the property, A borrowed $80,000 from B. On December 1, 1984, B forgives $10,000 of the indebtedness. A makes the election provided in section 108(d)(4). The recovery allowance for the property in 1984 is $15,000. Under section 1017(a), as of January 1, 1985, the adjusted basis of the property is $75,000. In 1985 the recovery allowance is $19,411.77 (*i.e.*, .22/(1.00 − .15) × ($100,000 − ($10,000 + $15,000))). In 1986, 1987, and 1988 the recovery allowance is $18,529.41 in each year (*i.e.*, .21/(1.00 − .15) × ($100,000 − ($10,000 + $15,000))).

Example (2). On July 15, 1984, C purchases and places in service 5-year recovery property with an unadjusted basis of $100,000. In addition to the $100,000, C agrees to pay the seller 25 percent of the gross profits from the operation of the property in the first year. On July 15, 1985, C pays to the seller an additional $10,000. The recovery allowance for the property in 1984 is $15,000. In 1985 the recovery allowance is $24,588.23 (*i.e.*, .22/(1.00 − .15) × ($100,000 + ($10,000 − $15,000))). In 1986, 1987, and 1988 the recovery allowance is $23,470.59 in each year (*i.e.*, .21/(1.00 − .15) × ($100,000 + ($10,000 − $15,000))).

(e) *Components and improvements.*—(1) *Component cost recovery not permitted.*—In general, the unadjusted basis of structural components (as defined in §1.48-1(e)(2)) of a building must be recovered as a whole. Thus, the same recovery period and method must be used for all structural components, and such components must be recovered as constituent parts of the building of which they are a part. The recovery period for a component begins on the later of the first day of the month in which the component is placed in service as recovery property or the first day of the month in which the building of which the component is a part is placed in service as recovery property. See subparagraph (3) of this paragraph for the treatment of components of a building which is made available in stages.

(2) *Treatment of amounts added to capital account.*—(i) Sections 162, 212, and 263 provide rules for the treatment of certain expenditures for the repair, maintenance, rehabilitation, or improvement of property. An expenditure which is treated as a capital expenditure under such sections (after application of the repair allowance rules of §1.167(a)-11(d)(2)) is treated as the purchase of recovery property if the improvement for which the expenditure is made is placed in service after December 31, 1980. The recovery of such expenditure shall begin when the improvement is placed in service. See subparagraph (3) of this paragraph for the treatment of a building which is made available in stages.

(ii) For capital expenditures (which are section 1250 class property) made with respect to an improvement of a building which is recovery property, the taxpayer must use the same recovery period and method as are used with respect to the building, unless the improvement qualifies as a substantial improvement. See subparagraph (4) of this paragraph. If capital expenditures (which are section 1250 class property) are made with respect to improvements of a building which is not recovery property under section 168(e) and §1.168-4, then the taxpayer may select any applicable recovery period and method for the recovery of the first of such expenditures. The recovery period and method so selected shall apply to each subsequent expenditure (unless the improvement qualifies as a substantial improvement).

(iii) A capital expenditure made with respect to the improvement of property, other than a building, is assigned to the same recovery class (as defined in §1.168-3(b)) as the property of which the improvement is a part. For such an expenditure, the taxpayer need not use the same recovery period and method as are used with respect to the property of which the improvement is a part.

(3) *Recovery for a building which is made available in stages.*—This subparagraph (3) (and not subparagraphs (1) and (2) of this paragraph) applies to a building which is made available in stages. For purposes of this section, a building shall be considered placed in service (and, therefore, recovery will begin) only when a significant portion is made available for use in a finished condition (*e.g.*, when a certificate of occupancy is issued with respect to such portion). If less than the entire building is made available, then the unadjusted basis which is taken into account under this section shall be that amount of the unadjusted basis of the building (including capital expenditures for any components) as is properly allocable to the portion made available. If another portion of the building is subsequently made available, then that amount of the unadjusted basis (including capital expenditures for any components) as is properly allocable to the ensuing portion shall be taken into account under this section when such portion becomes available. The taxpayer must use the same recovery period and method for all portions of the building.

(4) *Substantial improvements.*—(i) A substantial improvement to a building shall be treated as a separate building. Thus, the taxpayer may use a different period and method for computing the recovery allowance for the substantial improvement than are used for computing the allowance for the building.

(ii) An improvement is a substantial improvement if—

(A) Over 24 consecutive months the aggregate expenditures properly chargeable to the capital account for a building equal at least 25 percent of the adjusted basis of the building (disregarding adjustments provided in section 1016(a)(2) and (3)) as of the day on which the first expenditure is made, and

(B) All expenditures for the improvement are made 3 or more years after the building is placed in service by the taxpayer.

For purposes of the preceding sentence, a building acquired in a transaction to which section 1031 or 1033 applies is considered placed in service when the building that was replaced was placed in service. Similarly, a building acquired in a transaction to which section 168(f)(10)(A) applies is deemed placed in service by the transferee when such building was placed in service by the transferor. An expenditure which is allocated to a 24-month period shall not be allocated to another 24-month period. For example, an expenditure may not be part of one substantial improvement when considered together with an expenditure incurred 15 months earlier and also be part of another substantial improvement when combined with an expenditure incurred 10 months later.

(iii) It is possible that an improvement will not be part of a substantial improvement in the taxable year in which the improvement is placed in service but will become part of a substantial improvement in a subsequent taxable year. In such case, if the taxpayer uses a different method and recovery period with respect to the substantial improvement, then the tax return filed for the taxable year in which the first improvement is placed in service shall be amended accordingly.

(5) *Examples.*—The provisions of this paragraph may be illustrated by the following examples:

Example (1). In 1985, A spends $10,000 to improve machinery used in his trade or business. The $10,000 is added to capital account under the principles of sections 162, 212, and 263. The machinery would be 5-year property if placed in service after 1980. The $10,000 expenditure is treated as the purchase of 5-year recovery property, placed in service in 1985. Any election made by A with respect to the underlying machinery will not affect the recovery allowance for the improvement.

Example (2). B, a calendar year taxpayer, begins constructing a 10-story office building in 1982. All floors will have approximately the same amount of usable floor space. By 1983, B has paid or incurred $10 million for the building's shell (and other items not directly related to any specific portion of the building), $4 million for work with respect to the first three floors, and $5 million for work directly related to other floors (including installation of components). In March 1983, B receives a certificate of occupancy for the first three floors and begins offering the floors for rental to tenants. The building is considered placed in service in March 1983. No deduction is allowable under this section with respect to the building for 1982. No election is made under §1.168-2(c) to use the optional recovery percentages. B's recovery for 1983 is the properly allocable unadjusted basis times the applicable percentage (10 percent). The properly allocable unadjusted basis is $7 million, consisting of the amount of unadjusted basis directly related to the portion of the building which is made available for use ($4 million), plus that amount of the unadjusted basis which is not directly related to any specific portion of the building ($10 million) properly allocable to the portion which is made available for use (*i.e.*, 3 floors/10 floors equals 30 percent or $3 million). No deduction is allowable in 1983 for the $5 million paid or incurred for work directly related to portions of the building not made available for use. B will recover the $7 million unadjusted basis over the 15-year recovery period, beginning in March 1983.

Example (3). The facts are the same as in example (2) except that, in January 1984, B receives a certificate of occupancy for the remaining seven floors and begins offering them for rental to tenants. B has spent an additional $7 million to complete the building as of the date on which the remaining seven floors are offered for rental. In January 1984, B takes into account as unadjusted basis the $12 million not previously taken into account, plus the $7 million of later expenditures. B will recover the $19 million unadjusted basis over a 15-year recovery period beginning in January 1984. B may not use a different recovery period and method for such amount than were used for the amount taken into account in March 1983.

Example (4). The facts are the same as in examples (2) and (3) except that in 1990 B spends $1 million, which is added to capital account to rehabilitate certain portions of the building. The $1 million is treated as the purchase by B of 15-year real property in 1990. B must use the same recovery period and method with respect to that improvement as were used for the underlying building. The improvement has a 15-year recovery period, and the recovery begins when the improvement is placed in service.

Example (5). In 1983 C spends $1 million, which is added to capital account, to rehabilitate certain portions of a building placed in service by C in 1975. The $1 million is treated as the purchase by C of 15-year real property in 1983. C may use any applicable recovery period and method with respect to such expenditure, and the recovery begins when the improvement is placed in service. The recovery period and method selected with respect to such expenditure, however, will apply to all ensuing capital expenditures made by C with respect to the building, unless an expenditure qualifies as part of a substantial improvement. The result in this example would be the same if the building were placed in service by C after 1980, but did not qualify as recovery property by reason of the provisions of section 168(e)(4) and §1.168-4(d).

(f) *Short taxable years.*—(1) *General rule.*—For any recovery year in which there are less than 12 months (hereinafter in this section referred to as a "short taxable year"), the recovery allowance shall be determined by multiplying the deduction which would have been allowable if the recovery year were not a short taxable year by a fraction the numerator of which equals the number of months and part-months in the short taxable year and the denominator of which is 12. This paragraph shall not apply to 15-year real property for the year the property is placed in service or disposed of.

(2) *Subsequent years' allowance.*—Recovery allowances for years in a recovery period following a short taxable year shall be determined in accordance with paragraph (a), (c), (g), or (m) of this section without reference to the short taxable year.

(3) *Unrecovered allowance.*—In the taxable year following the last year in the recovery period, a recovery allowance is permitted to the extent of any unrecovered allowance. If the optional recovery percentages are elected under §1.168-2(c) or (g)(3) and the short taxable year is the last recovery year, then the unrecovered allowance shall be allowed in the year following the short taxable year. The term "unrecovered allowance" means the difference between—

(i) The recovery allowance properly allowed for the short taxable year, and

(ii) The recovery allowance which would have been allowable if such year were not a short taxable year.

In no event shall the recovery allowance for any taxable year following the last year in the recovery period be greater than what the recovery allowance would be for the last year in the recovery period assuming that such year consists of 12 months. Any amount in excess of such recovery allowance for the last year in the recovery period shall be taken into account in the following taxable year or years in the same manner as provided in this subparagraph (3).

(4) *When a taxable year begins.*—For purposes of this section, a taxable year of a person placing property in service does not include any month prior to the month in which the person begins engaging in a trade or business or holding recovery or depreciable property for the production of income. For purposes of applying the preceding sentence to an employee, an employee is not considered engaged in a trade or business by virtue of his employment except that, for purposes of applying this section to recovery property used for purposes of employment, the taxable year includes any month during which a person is engaged in trade or business as an employee. In addition, if a person engages in a small amount of trade or business activity for the purpose of obtaining a disproportionately large recovery allowance for assets for the taxable year in which they are placed in service, and if placing those assets in service represents a substantial increase in the person's level of business activity, then for purposes of the recovery allowance for such assets the person will not be treated as beginning a trade or business until the increased amount of business activity begins. For property held for the production of income, the principle of the preceding sentence also applies.

(5) *Successive short taxable years.*—In applying the rule of subparagraph (1) of this paragraph, no month shall be taken into account more than once. Thus, if a taxpayer has successive short taxable years, with one taxable year ending and the following taxable year beginning in the same calendar month, then the recovery year which is ending shall not include the month in which the taxable year terminates.

(6) *Examples.*—The following examples illustrate the application of this paragraph:

Example (1). On October 10, 1983, A and B enter into an agreement to form a partnership (P), for the purpose of leasing sailboats. The partnership adopts a calendar year as its taxable year pursuant to §1.706-1(b)(1). On November 5, 1983, P purchases four sailboats for a total of $20,000 and places the sailboats in service immediately. For purposes of section 168, P's taxable year begins on November 5, 1983. Sailboats are 5-year recovery property as defined in section 168(c)(2). No straight line election is made under §1.168-2(c). The recovery allowance for the sailboats in 1983, a short taxable year, is $500 (*i.e.*, .15 × $20,000 × 2/12). In 1984, the recovery allowance is $4,400 (.22 × $20,000). In 1985, 1986, and 1987, the recovery allowance is $4,200 annually (.21 × $20,000). In 1988, the taxable year following the last year in the recovery period, the unrecovered allowance equal to $2,500 may be deducted by A and B.

Example (2). In November 1984, Corporation L is incorporated and places in service two race horses which it acquired for a total of $18,500. The corporation adopts a calendar year as its taxable year. For purposes of section 168, the race horses are 3-year recovery property. No straight line election is made under §1.168-2(c). In 1984, the recovery allowance permitted to L for the race horses is $770.83 (*i.e.*, (.25 × $18,500) × 2/12). At the close of business on June 30, 1985, all of the stock of L is acquired by Corporation M. M elects in accordance with section 1501 to file a consolidated return with respect to M and L. M's taxable year begins on July 1. By reason of becoming included in the consolidated return, under §1.1502-76 L's second taxable year ending June 30, 1985, is also a short taxable year containing 6 months. In the second taxable year, L is permitted a recovery allowance equal to $3,515 (*i.e.*, .38 × $18,500 × 6/12). In the third taxable year ending June 30, 1986, L is entitled to a recovery allowance of $6,845 (*i.e.*, .37 × $18,500). Thus, the unrecovered allowance as of July 1, 1986, equals $7,369.17. Since the unrecovered allowance exceeds the recovery allowance for the third recovery year (the last year in the recovery period), the recovery allowance for the taxable year ending June 30, 1987, equals the allowance for such year, $6,845. The recovery allowance in the taxable year ending June 30, 1988, equals $524.17, the remaining unrecovered allowance.

Example (3). On August 1, 1984, Partnership M is formed and places in service a warehouse which will be leased to an unrelated person. M acquires the warehouse for $250,000. M adopts a calendar year as its taxable year pursuant to §1.706-1(b)(1). In 1984, M has a short taxable year within the meaning of §1.168-2(f)(1). Since the property is 15-year real property, however, the recovery allowance is computed as though 1984 were a full taxable year. Because the recovery property would have been placed in service in the eighth month of M's normal taxable year, the recovery property is deemed placed in service in the eighth month of the first recovery year. The recovery allowance in 1984 is $12,500 (*i.e.*, .05 × $250,000).

Example (4). In July 1983, D, who has been an employee of Corporation N since 1982, purchases an automobile for use in the performance of his employment for N. On June 5, 1984, D purchases a truck for use in another business. D begins the new business on June 5, 1984. In 1984, D holds no other depreciable or recovery property for the production of income. D does not have a short taxable year for the automobile purchased in 1983 since the automobile is used by D in his trade or business as an employee. Since an employee is not considered engaged in a trade or business by virtue of employment, however, for purposes of determining when a taxable year begins with respect to property not used in the trade or business of employment, D has a short taxable year in 1984 for the truck purchased in that year. The recovery allowance permitted D in 1984 with respect to the truck must be adjusted in accordance with the provisions of § 1.168-2(f).

Example (5). A has been actively engaged in the trade or business of selling used cars since 1981. On July 1, 1983, A accepts employment with Corporation M and on that same date purchases a truck for $10,000 for use in the performance of his employment for M. A does not have a short taxable year for the truck because the taxable year of a person placing property in service includes all months during which that person is engaged in a trade or business.

Example (6). In 1983, C graduates from college and on July 1, 1983, is employed by N. On that same day, C purchases an automobile for $10,000 for use in the performance of his employment for N. C has a short taxable year for the automobile purchased in 1983. Although, for recovery property used for purposes of employment, the taxable year includes any month during which a person is an employee, C does not begin that trade or business until July. In addition, C is engaged in no other trade or business (and does not hold any depreciable or recovery property for the production of income) during the taxable year. The recovery allowance permitted C in 1983 with respect to the automobile must be adjusted in accordance with the provisions of § 1.168-2(f).

Example (7). Corporation X, a calendar year taxpayer, has been in the trade or business of selling household appliances since 1979.

On July 1, 1983, X purchases a restaurant. On that same day, X purchases restaurant equipment for use in its new business. X does not have a short taxable year for the restaurant equipment because the taxable year of a person placing property in service includes all months during which that person is engaged in a trade or business.

(g) *Special rules for property used predominantly outside the United States.*—(1) *General rule.*—(i) In lieu of the deduction allowed under paragraphs (a) and (c) of this § 1.168-2, except as provided in subparagraphs (3) and (4) of this paragraph, and except as otherwise provided in section 168 and the regulations thereunder, the recovery allowance for recovery property used predominantly outside the United States (as described in § 1.168-2(g)(5)) during the taxable year equals the aggregate amount determined by multiplying the unadjusted basis (as defined in § 1.168-2(d)) of such recovery property by the applicable percentage provided in paragraph (g)(2) of this section. For purposes of determining the recovery allowance, salvage value shall be disregarded.

(ii) The recovery period for recovery property used predominantly outside the United States, other than 15-year real property, shall be the present class life. For recovery property (other than 15-year real property) which is not assigned a present class life, the recovery period shall be 12 years. For 15-year real property used predominantly outside the United States, the recovery period shall be 35 years.

(iii) Except for 15-year real property and except as otherwise provided in § 1.168-5, no recovery allowance shall be allowed in the year of disposition of recovery property described in this paragraph.

(iv) For purposes of this paragraph, rules similar to the rules of paragraph (e) of this section shall apply.

(2) *Applicable percentages.*—(i) For property other than 15-year real property—

If the recovery year is: / *And the recovery period is:* / *The applicable percentage is:*

If the recovery year is:	2.5	3	3.5	4	5	6	6.5	7	7.5	8
1	40	33	29	25	20	17	15	14	13	13
2	48	45	41	38	32	28	26	25	23	22
3	12	15	17	19	19	18	18	17	17	16
4		7	13	12	12	12	13	13	13	12
5				6	12	10	10	9	9	9
6					5	10	9	9	9	8
7						5	9	9	8	8
8								4	8	8
9										4

If the recovery year is:	8.5	9	9.5	10	10.5	11	11.5	12	12.5	13
1	12	11	11	10	10	9	9	8	8	8
2	21	20	19	18	17	17	16	15	15	14
3	16	15	15	14	14	13	13	13	12	12
4	12	12	12	12	11	11	11	11	10	10
5	9	9	9	9	9	9	9	9	9	9
6	8	8	7	7	7	7	7	7	7	7
7	8	7	7	7	7	7	6	6	6	6
8	7	7	7	7	7	6	6	6	6	6
9	7	7	7	7	6	6	6	6	6	5
10		4	6	6	6	6	6	6	6	5
11				3	6	6	6	5	5	5
12						3	5	5	5	5
13								3	5	5
14										3

If the recovery year is:	13.5	14	15	16	16.5	17	18	19	20	22
1	7	7	7	6	6	6	6	5	5	5
2	14	13	12	12	11	11	10	10	10	9
3	12	11	11	10	10	10	9	9	9	8
4	10	10	9	9	9	9	8	8	8	7
5	8	8	8	8	8	8	7	7	7	6
6	7	7	7	7	7	7	7	6	6	6
7	6	6	6	6	6	6	6	6	6	6
8	6	6	5	5	5	5	5	5	5	5
9	5	5	5	5	5	5	5	5	4	4
10	5	5	5	5	5	4	4	4	4	4
11	5	5	5	5	4	4	4	4	4	4
12	5	5	4	4	4	4	4	4	4	4
13	5	5	4	4	4	4	4	4	4	4
14	5	4	4	4	4	4	4	4	4	3
15		3	4	4	4	4	4	4	3	3
16			2	4	4	4	4	4	3	3
17				2	4	3	4	3	3	3
18						2	3	3	3	3
19							2	3	3	3
20								2	3	3
21									2	3
22										3
23										2

If the recovery year is:

And the recovery period is:

If the recovery year is:	25	26.5	28	30	35	45	50
			The applicable percentage is:				
1	4	4	4	3	3	2	2
2	8	7	7	6	6	4	4
3	7	7	6	6	5	4	4
4	6	6	6	6	5	4	4
5	6	6	6	5	5	4	3
6	6	5	5	5	4	4	3
7	5	5	5	5	4	3	3
8	5	5	4	4	4	3	3
9	4	4	4	4	4	3	3
10	4	4	4	4	3	3	3
11	4	4	4	3	3	3	3
12	3	3	3	3	3	3	2
13	3	3	3	3	3	3	2
14	3	3	3	3	3	3	2
15	3	3	3	3	3	2	2
16	3	3	3	3	3	2	2
17	3	3	3	3	2	2	2
18	3	3	3	3	2	2	2
19	3	3	3	3	2	2	2
20	3	3	3	3	2	2	2
21	3	3	3	2	2	2	2
22	3	3	2	2	2	2	2
23	3	3	2	2	2	2	2
24	2	2	2	2	2	2	2
25	2	2	2	2	2	2	2
26	1	2	2	2	2	2	2
27		1	2	2	2	2	2
28			2	2	2	2	2
29			1	2	2	2	2
30				2	2	2	2
31				1	2	2	2
32					2	2	2
33					2	2	2
34					2	2	2
35					2	2	2
36					1	2	1
37						1	1
38						1	1
39						1	1
40						1	1
41						1	1
42						1	1
43						1	1
44						1	1
45						1	1
46						1	1
47							1
48							1
49							1
50							1
51							1

(ii) For 15-year real property—

If the recovery year is

And the month in the 1st recovery year in which the property is placed in service is:

If the recovery year is	1	2,3	4,5,6	7,8	9,10,11,12
			The applicable percentage is:		
1	4	4	3	2	1
2	4	4	4	4	4
3	4	4	4	4	4
4	4	4	4	4	4
5	4	4	4	4	4
6	3	3	3	3	3
7	3	3	3	3	3
8	3	3	3	3	3
9	3	3	3	3	3
10	3	3	3	3	3
11	3	3	3	3	3
12	3	3	3	3	3
13	3	3	3	3	3
14	3	3	3	3	3
15	3	3	3	3	3
16	3	3	3	3	3
17	3	3	3	3	3
18	3	3	3	3	3
19	3	3	3	3	3
20	3	3	3	3	3
21	3	3	3	3	3
22	3	3	3	3	3
23	3	3	3	3	3
24	3	3	3	3	3
25	3	2	3	2	3
26	2	2	2	2	2
27	2	2	2	2	2
28	2	2	2	2	2
29	2	2	2	2	2
30	2	2	2	2	2
31	2	2	2	2	2
32	2	2	2	2	2
33	2	2	2	2	2
34	2	2	2	2	2
35	2	2	2	2	2
36		1	1	2	2

(3) *Election of optional recovery percentage method.*—(i) In lieu of the applicable percentage provided by subparagraphs (1) and (2), the taxpayer may elect (in accordance with §1.168-5(e)), for recovery property used predominantly outside the United States that is placed in service during the taxable year, to determine the recovery allow-

ance by using the straight line method over one of the recovery periods elected by the taxpayer and set forth in the following table:

CLASS OF PROPERTY	RECOVERY PERIOD
3-year property	5 or 12 years or present class life
5-year property	12 or 25 years or present class life
10-year property	25 or 35 years or present class life
15-year real property	35 or 45 years
15-year public utility property	35 or 45 years or present class life

Such election is irrevocable without the consent of the Commissioner. See subdivision (iv) of this subparagraph for tables containing the applicable percentages to be used in computing the recovery allowance.

(ii) Except in the case of 15-year real property, a single recovery period must be elected under this subparagraph for all recovery property placed in service in the same taxable year which is in the same recovery class and which has the same present class life. For property other than 15-year real property the recovery period elected may not be shorter than the present class life (or, if none, 12

years). A different recovery period may be elected (or the tables provided in subparagraph (2) may be used) for recovery property in different recovery classes, or with different present class lives, placed in service during the taxable year, or for recovery property placed in service in a different taxable year, whether or not in the same recovery class or with the same present class life.

(iii) In the case of 15-year real property, the election provided by this subparagraph may be made separately with respect to each property.

(iv)(A) For property other than 15-year real property—

If the recovery year is:	And the period elected is:								
	2.5	3	3.5	4	5	6	6.5	7	7.5
	The applicable percentage is:								
1	20	17	14	13	10	8	8	8	7
2	40	33	29	25	20	17	16	14	14
3	40	33	29	25	20	17	16	14	14
4		17	28	25	20	17	15	14	13
5				12	20	17	15	14	13
6					10	17	15	14	13
7						7	15	14	13
8								8	13

If the recovery year is:	And the period elected is:								
	8	8.5	9	9.5	10	10.5	11	11.5	12
	The applicable percentage is:								
1	6	6	6	5	5	5	5	4	4
2	13	12	11	11	10	10	9	9	9
3	13	12	11	11	10	10	9	9	9
4	13	12	11	11	10	10	9	9	9
5	13	12	11	11	10	10	9	9	9
6	12	12	11	11	10	10	9	9	8
7	12	12	11	10	10	9	9	9	8
8	12	11	11	10	10	9	9	9	8
9	6	11	11	10	10	9	9	9	8
10			6	10	10	9	9	8	8
11					5	9	9	8	8
12								5	8	8
13									4

If the recovery year is:	And the period elected is:								
	12.5	13	13.5	14	15	16	16.5	17	18
	The applicable percentage is:								
1	4	4	4	4	3	3	3	3	3
2	8	8	8	8	7	7	7	6	6
3	8	8	8	7	7	7	6	6	6
4	8	8	8	7	7	7	6	6	6
5	8	8	8	7	7	7	6	6	6
6	8	8	8	7	7	7	6	6	6
7	8	8	7	7	7	7	6	6	6
8	8	8	7	7	7	7	6	6	6
9	8	8	7	7	7	7	6	6	6
10	8	8	7	7	7	6	6	6	6
11	8	7	7	7	7	6	6	6	6
12	8	7	7	7	6	6	6	6	5
13	8	7	7	7	6	6	6	6	5
14		3	7	7	6	6	6	6	5
15				4	6	6	6	6	5
16					3	6	6	6	5
17						3	6	5	5
18								2	5	5
19									2

If the recovery year is:	And the period elected is:								
	19	20	22	25	26.5	28	30	35
	The applicable percentage is:							
1	3	3	2	2	2	2	2	1
2	6	5	5	4	4	4	4	3
3	6	5	5	4	4	4	4	3
4	6	5	5	4	4	4	4	3
5	6	5	5	4	4	4	4	3
6	6	5	5	4	4	4	4	3
7	5	5	5	4	4	4	4	3
8	5	5	5	4	4	4	4	3
9	5	5	5	4	4	4	4	3
10	5	5	5	4	4	4	3	3
11	5	5	5	4	4	4	3	3
12	5	5	5	4	4	4	3	3
13	5	5	5	4	4	4	3	3
14	5	5	4	4	4	4	3	3
15	5	5	4	4	4	4	3	3
16	5	5	4	4	4	4	3	3
17	5	5	4	4	4	3	3	3
18	5	5	4	4	4	3	3	3
19	5	5	4	4	4	3	3	3
20	2	5	4	4	4	3	3	3
21		2	4	4	4	3	3	3
22			4	4	3	3	3	3

Reg. § 1.168-2(g)(3)(iv)(A)

If the recovery year is:	19	20	22	25	26.5	28	30	35
					The applicable percentage is:			
23		2	4	3	3	3	3	3
24			4	3	3	3	3	3
25			4	3	3	3	3	3
26			2	3	3	3	3	3
27				3	3	3	3	3
28					3	3	3	3
29					2	3	3	3
30						3	3	3
31						3	3	3
32						2	2	2
33							2	2
34							2	2
35							2	2
36								1

If the recovery year is:	45	50
	The applicable percentage is:	
1	1.1	1
2	2.3	2
3	2.3	2
4	2.3	2
5	2.3	2
6	2.3	2
7	2.3	2
8	2.3	2
9	2.3	2
10	2.3	2
11	2.3	2
12	2.2	2
13	2.2	2
14	2.2	2
15	2.2	2
16	2.2	2
17	2.2	2
18	2.2	2
19	2.2	2
20	2.2	2
21	2.2	2
22	2.2	2
23	2.2	2
24	2.2	2
25	2.2	2
26	2.2	2
27	2.2	2
28	2.2	2
29	2.2	2
30	2.2	2
31	2.2	2
32	2.2	2
33	2.2	2
34	2.2	2
35	2.2	2
36	2.2	2
37	2.2	2
38	2.2	2
39	2.2	2
40	2.2	2
41	2.2	2
42	2.2	2
43	2.2	2
44	2.2	2
45	2.2	2
46	1.1	2
47		2
48		2
49		2
50		2
51		1

(B) *For 15-year real property.*—*(1)* If a 35-year period is elected—

If the recovery year is:	And the month in the 1st recovery year the property is placed in service is:		
	1-2	3-6	7-12
		The applicable percentage is:	
1	3	2	1
2	3	3	3
3	3	3	3
4	3	3	3
5	3	3	3
6	3	3	3
7	3	3	3
8	3	3	3
9	3	3	3
10	3	3	3
11	3	3	3
12	3	3	3
13	3	3	3
14	3	3	3
15	3	3	3
16	3	3	3
17	3	3	3
18	3	3	3
19	3	3	3
20	3	3	3
21	3	3	3
22	3	3	3

If the recovery year is:	And the month in the 1st recovery year the property is placed in service is:		
	1-2	3-6	7-12
	The applicable percentage is:		
23	3	3	3
24	3	3	3
25	3	3	3
26	3	3	3
27	3	3	3
28	3	3	3
29	3	3	3
30	2	3	3
31	2	2	2
32	2	2	2
33	2	2	2
34	2	2	2
35	2	2	2
36		1	2

(2) If a 45-year period is elected—

If the recovery year is:	And the month in the 1st recovery year the property is placed in service is:											
	1	2	3	4	5	6	7	8	9	10	11	12
	The applicable percentage is:											
1	2.3	2.0	1.9	1.7	1.5	1.3	1.2	.9	.7	.6	.4	.2
2	2.3	2.3	2.3	2.3	2.3	2.3	2.3	2.3	2.3	2.3	2.3	2.3
3	2.3	2.3	2.3	2.3	2.3	2.3	2.3	2.3	2.3	2.3	2.3	2.3
4	2.3	2.3	2.3	2.3	2.3	2.3	2.3	2.3	2.3	2.3	2.3	2.3
5	2.3	2.3	2.3	2.3	2.3	2.3	2.3	2.3	2.3	2.3	2.3	2.3
6	2.3	2.3	2.3	2.3	2.3	2.3	2.3	2.3	2.3	2.3	2.3	2.3
7	2.3	2.3	2.3	2.3	2.3	2.3	2.3	2.3	2.3	2.3	2.3	2.3
8	2.3	2.3	2.3	2.3	2.3	2.3	2.3	2.3	2.3	2.3	2.3	2.3
9	2.3	2.3	2.3	2.3	2.3	2.3	2.3	2.3	2.3	2.3	2.3	2.3
10	2.3	2.3	2.3	2.3	2.3	2.3	2.3	2.3	2.3	2.3	2.3	2.3
11	2.2	2.2	2.2	2.2	2.2	2.2	2.2	2.2	2.2	2.2	2.2	2.2
12	2.2	2.2	2.2	2.2	2.2	2.2	2.2	2.2	2.2	2.2	2.2	2.2
13	2.2	2.2	2.2	2.2	2.2	2.2	2.2	2.2	2.2	2.2	2.2	2.2
14	2.2	2.2	2.2	2.2	2.2	2.2	2.2	2.2	2.2	2.2	2.2	2.2
15	2.2	2.2	2.2	2.2	2.2	2.2	2.2	2.2	2.2	2.2	2.2	2.2
16	2.2	2.2	2.2	2.2	2.2	2.2	2.2	2.2	2.2	2.2	2.2	2.2
17	2.2	2.2	2.2	2.2	2.2	2.2	2.2	2.2	2.2	2.2	2.2	2.2
18	2.2	2.2	2.2	2.2	2.2	2.2	2.2	2.2	2.2	2.2	2.2	2.2
19	2.2	2.2	2.2	2.2	2.2	2.2	2.2	2.2	2.2	2.2	2.2	2.2
20	2.2	2.2	2.2	2.2	2.2	2.2	2.2	2.2	2.2	2.2	2.2	2.2
21	2.2	2.2	2.2	2.2	2.2	2.2	2.2	2.2	2.2	2.2	2.2	2.2
22	2.2	2.2	2.2	2.2	2.2	2.2	2.2	2.2	2.2	2.2	2.2	2.2
23	2.2	2.2	2.2	2.2	2.2	2.2	2.2	2.2	2.2	2.2	2.2	2.2
24	2.2	2.2	2.2	2.2	2.2	2.2	2.2	2.2	2.2	2.2	2.2	2.2
25	2.2	2.2	2.2	2.2	2.2	2.2	2.2	2.2	2.2	2.2	2.2	2.2
26	2.2	2.2	2.2	2.2	2.2	2.2	2.2	2.2	2.2	2.2	2.2	2.2
27	2.2	2.2	2.2	2.2	2.2	2.2	2.2	2.2	2.2	2.2	2.2	2.2
28	2.2	2.2	2.2	2.2	2.2	2.2	2.2	2.2	2.2	2.2	2.2	2.2
29	2.2	2.2	2.2	2.2	2.2	2.2	2.2	2.2	2.2	2.2	2.2	2.2
30	2.2	2.2	2.2	2.2	2.2	2.2	2.2	2.2	2.2	2.2	2.2	2.2
31	2.2	2.2	2.2	2.2	2.2	2.2	2.2	2.2	2.2	2.2	2.2	2.2
32	2.2	2.2	2.2	2.2	2.2	2.2	2.2	2.2	2.2	2.2	2.2	2.2
33	2.2	2.2	2.2	2.2	2.2	2.2	2.2	2.2	2.2	2.2	2.2	2.2
34	2.2	2.2	2.2	2.2	2.2	2.2	2.2	2.2	2.2	2.2	2.2	2.2
35	2.2	2.2	2.2	2.2	2.2	2.2	2.2	2.2	2.2	2.2	2.2	2.2
36	2.2	2.2	2.2	2.2	2.2	2.2	2.2	2.2	2.2	2.2	2.2	2.2
37	2.2	2.2	2.2	2.2	2.2	2.2	2.2	2.2	2.2	2.2	2.2	2.2
38	2.2	2.2	2.2	2.2	2.2	2.2	2.2	2.2	2.2	2.2	2.2	2.2
39	2.2	2.2	2.2	2.2	2.2	2.2	2.2	2.2	2.2	2.2	2.2	2.2
40	2.2	2.2	2.2	2.2	2.2	2.2	2.2	2.2	2.2	2.2	2.2	2.2
41	2.2	2.2	2.2	2.2	2.2	2.2	2.2	2.2	2.2	2.2	2.2	2.2
42	2.2	2.2	2.2	2.2	2.2	2.2	2.2	2.2	2.2	2.2	2.2	2.2
43	2.2	2.2	2.2	2.2	2.2	2.2	2.2	2.2	2.2	2.2	2.2	2.2
44	2.2	2.2	2.2	2.2	2.2	2.2	2.2	2.2	2.2	2.2	2.2	2.2
45	2.2	2.2	2.2	2.2	2.2	2.2	2.2	2.2	2.2	2.2	2.2	2.2
46		.3	.4	.6	.8	1.0	1.1	1.4	1.6	1.7	1.9	2.1

(4) *Rules for year of disposition and placement in service of 15-year real property.*—(i) In the taxable year in which 15-year real property is disposed of, the recovery allowance shall be determined by multiplying the allowance (determined without regard to this subdivision) by a fraction, the numerator of which equals the number of months in the taxable year that the property is in service in the taxpayer's trade or business or for the production of income and the denominator of which is 12. In the case of 15-year real property that is disposed of during the first recovery year, the denominator shall equal the number of months in the taxpayer's taxable year after the property was placed in service by the taxpayer (including the month the property was placed in service). If the recovery allowance for the taxable year is limited by reason of the short taxable year rules of section 168(f)(5) and paragraph (f) of this section (*e.g.*, if the taxpayer dies, or if the taxpayer is a corporation which becomes a member, or ceases being a member, of an affiliated group of corporations filing a consolidated return), then the denominator shall equal the number of months in the taxpayer's taxable year.

(ii) For purposes of this paragraph—

(A) 15-year real property that is placed in service on or after the first day of a month shall be treated as placed in service in that month; and

(B) 15-year real property that is disposed of during the recovery year shall be treated as disposed of as of the last day of the month preceding the month in which it is withdrawn from service.

(5) *Determination of whether property is used predominantly outside the United States.*—(i) The determination of whether property is used predominantly outside the United States (as defined in section 7701(a)(9)) during the taxable year shall be made by comparing the period in such year during which the property is physically located outside of the United States with the period during which the property is physically located within the United States. If the property is physically located outside the United States during more than 50 percent of the taxable year, such property shall be considered used predominantly outside the United States during the year. If property is placed in service after the first day of the taxable year, the determination of whether such property is physically located outside the United States during more than 50 percent of the taxable year shall be made with respect to the period beginning on the date on which the property is placed in service and ending on the last day of such taxable year.

(ii) This paragraph applies whether recovery property is used predominantly outside the United States by the owner or by the lessee of the property. For recovery property which is leased, the determination of whether such property is physically located outside the United States during the taxable year shall be made with respect to the taxable year of the lessor.

(iii) For purposes of this §1.168-2(g), the following property is not "property used predominantly outside the United States":

(A) Any aircraft which is registered by the Administrator of the Federal Aviation Agency, and which (*1*) is operated, whether on a scheduled or nonscheduled basis, to and from the United States, or (2) is operated under contract with the United States, provided that the use of the aircraft under the contract constitutes its principal use outside the United States during the taxable year. The term "to and from the United States" shall not exclude an aircraft which makes flights from one point in a foreign country to another such point, as long as such aircraft returns to the United States with some degree of frequency;

(B) Rolling stock which is used within and without the United States and which is (1) of a domestic railroad corporation subject to part I of the Interstate Commerce Act or (2) of a United States person (other than a corporation subject to part I of the Interstate Commerce Act) but only if the rolling stock is not leased to one or more foreign persons for periods totaling more than 12 months in any 24-month period. For purposes of this subdivision (iii)(B), the term "rolling stock" means locomotives, freight and passenger train cars, floating equipment, and miscellaneous transportation equipment on wheels, the expenditures for which are of the type chargeable to the equipment investment accounts in the uniform system of accounts for railroad companies prescribed by the Interstate Commerce Commission.

(C) Any vessel documented under the laws of the United States which is operated in the foreign or domestic commerce of the United States. A vessel is documented under the laws of the United States if it is registered, enrolled, or licensed under the laws of the United States by the Commandant, United States Coast Guard. Vessels operated in the foreign or domestic commerce of the United States include those documented for use in foreign trade, coast-wise trade, or fisheries;

(D) Any motor vehicle of a United States person (as defined in section 7701(a)(30)) which is operated to and from the United States with some degree of frequency;

(E) Any container of a United States person which is used in the transportation of property to and from the United States;

(F) Any property (other than a vessel or an aircraft) of a United States person which is used for the purpose of exploring for, developing, removing, or transporting resources from the Outer Continental Shelf (within the meaning of section 2 of the Outer Continental Shelf Lands Act, as amended and supplemented, 43 U.S.C. section 1331), e.g., offshore drilling equipment;

(G) Any property which (1) is owned by a domestic corporation (other than a corporation which has an election in effect under section 936 or which is entitled to the benefits of section 934(b)), by a United States citizen (other than a citizen entitled to the benefits of section 931, 932, 933, or 934(c)), or by a domestic partnership, all of whose partners are domestic corporations (none of which has an election in effect under section 936 or is entitled to the benefits of section 934(b)) or United States citizens (none of whom is entitled to the benefits of section 931, 932, 933, or 934(c)), and (2) which is used predominantly in a possession of the United States during the taxable year by such a corporation, citizen, or partnership, or by a corporation created or organized in, or under the law of, a possession of the United States. The determination of whether property is used predominantly in a possession of the United States during the taxable year shall be made under principles similar to those described in subdivision (i) of this subparagraph. For example, if a machine is placed in service in a possession of the United States on July 1, 1981, by a calendar year taxpayer and if it is physically located in such a possession during more than 50 percent of the period beginning on July 1, 1981, and ending on December 31, 1981, then such machine shall be considered used predominantly in a possession of the United States during the taxable year 1981;

(H) Any communications satellite (as defined in section 103(3) of the Communications Satellite Act of 1962, 47 U.S.C. section 702(3)), or any interest therein, of a United States person;

(I) Any cable, or any interest therein, of a domestic corporation engaged in furnishing telephone service to which section 46(c)(3)(B)(iii) applies (or of a wholly owned domestic subsidiary of such corporation), if such cable is part of a submarine cable system which constitutes part of a communications link exclusively between the United States and one or more foreign countries;

(J) Any property (other than a vessel or an aircraft) of a United States person which is used in international or territorial waters within the northern portion of the Western Hemisphere for the purpose of exploring for, developing, removing, or transporting resources from ocean waters or deposits under such waters. The term "northern portion of the Western Hemisphere" means the area lying west of the 30th meridian west of Greenwich, east of the international dateline, and north of the Equator, but not including any foreign country which is a country of South America; and

(K) Any property described in section 48(l)(3)(A)(ix) which is owned by a United States person and which is used in international or territorial waters to generate energy for use in the United States.

(h) *Mass asset accounts.*—(1) *In general.*—In accordance with the provisions of §1.168-5(e), a taxpayer may elect to account for mass assets (as defined in §1.168-2(h)(2)) in the same mass asset account, as though such assets were a single asset. If such treatment is elected, the taxpayer, upon disposition of an asset in the account, shall include as ordinary income (as defined in section 64) all proceeds realized to the extent of the unadjusted basis in the account (as defined in paragraph (d) of this section), less any amounts previously so included, and shall include as capital gain any excess, unless gain on such disposition is not recognized under another provision of the Code. With respect to the recovery allowance, the account shall be treated as though the asset were not disposed of.

(2) *Definition.*—For purposes of this section, the term "mass assets" means a mass or group of individual items of recovery property (i) not necessarily homogenous, (ii) each of which is minor in value relative to the total value of such mass or group, (iii) numerous in quantity, (iv) usually accounted for only on a total dollar or quantity basis, (v) with respect to which separate identification is impracticable, (vi) with the same present class life, and (vii) placed in service in the same taxable year.

(3) *Election.*—The election under this paragraph shall be made for the taxable year in which the assets in the account are placed in service. The election shall apply, with respect to the account, throughout the applicable recovery period and for all subsequent taxable years. The taxpayer is not bound by such election with respect to assets placed in service in other taxable years, or with respect to other assets placed in service in the same taxable year, which may properly be included in another mass asset account (e.g., assets with a different present class life).

(4) *Recovery of an increase in basis.*—To the extent that §1.168-2(d)(2)(i) (relating to reductions in basis) applies, if as a result of early disposition of an asset in a mass asset account (determined in accordance with the provision of subparagraph (5) of this paragraph), the investment tax credit is recaptured (in accordance with section 47 and the regulations thereunder), then the basis of the account shall be increased by an amount equal to one-half of the amount of the recapture. Such increase shall be treated in a manner similar to §1.168-2(d)(3), relating to redeterminations. For purposes of subparagraph (1) of this paragraph, such increase will be taken into account as unadjusted basis in determining the inclusion of proceeds as ordinary income.

(5) *Identification of dispositions for purposes of basis increase.*—For purposes of subparagraph (4) of this paragraph, disposition of assets from a mass asset account shall be determined by the use of an appropriate mortality dispersion table. If the taxpayer adopts record-keeping practices consistent with his prior practices and consonant with good accounting and engineering practices, and supplies such reasonable information as may be required by the Commissioner, the mortality dispersion table may be based upon an acceptable sampling of the taxpayer's actual experience or other acceptable statistical or engineering techniques. Alternatively, the taxpayer may use the following standard mortality dispersion table:

STANDARD MORTALITY DISPERSION TABLE
PERCENTAGE OF BASIS OF MASS ASSET ACCOUNT CONSIDERED
DISPOSED OF EACH 12-MONTH PERIOD AFTER THE
ACCOUNT IS PLACED IN SERVICE

Present Class Life	1st (1)	2nd (2)	3rd (3)	4th (4)	5th (5)	6th (6)	7th (7)	8th (8)	9th (9)	10th (10)
2.5	3.59	23.84	45.14	23.84	3.59	...	...	...	...	...
3.0	2.28	13.59	34.13	34.13	13.59	2.28	...	...	...	...
3.5	1.62	8.23	23.51	33.28	23.51	8.23	1.62	...	...	...
4.0	1.22	5.46	15.98	27.34	27.34	15.98	5.46	1.22	...	...
5.0	.82	2.77	7.92	15.91	22.58	22.58	15.91	7.92	2.77	.82
6.0	.62	1.66	4.40	9.19	14.98	19.15	19.15	14.98	9.19	4.40
6.5	.55	1.33	3.38	7.25	12.00	16.39	18.20	16.39	12.00	7.25
7.0	.51	1.11	2.74	5.49	9.64	13.87	16.64	16.64	13.87	9.64
7.5	.47	.92	2.20	4.49	7.79	11.55	14.65	15.86	14.65	11.55
8.0	.44	.78	1.85	3.61	6.46	9.52	12.91	14.43	14.43	12.91
8.5	.40	.70	1.52	2.97	5.16	8.19	10.87	13.05	14.28	13.05

STANDARD MORTALITY DISPERSION TABLE
PERCENTAGE OF BASIS OF MASS ASSET ACCOUNT CONSIDERED
DISPOSED OF EACH 12-MONTH PERIOD AFTER THE
ACCOUNT IS PLACED IN SERVICE

Present Class Life	1st (1)	2nd (2)	3rd (3)	4th (4)	5th (5)	6th (6)	7th (7)	8th (8)	9th (9)	10th (10)
9.0	.38	.61	1.29	2.47	4.43	6.69	9.27	11.93	12.93	12.93
9.5	.37	.52	1.13	2.07	3.69	5.57	8.13	10.44	11.72	12.72
10 and 10.5	.35	.47	.97	1.80	3.09	4.83	6.90	9.01	10.79	11.79
11 and 11.5	.32	.39	.75	1.35	2.24	3.64	5.10	6.82	8.51	10.24
12 and 12.5	.30	.32	.60	1.06	1.73	2.67	3.88	5.31	6.79	8.19
13 and 13.5	.28	.27	.49	.84	1.34	2.04	3.12	4.13	5.37	6.63
14	.27	.24	.40	.71	1.06	1.68	2.32	3.17	4.38	5.26
15	.26	.21	.35	.57	.89	1.31	1.89	2.60	3.43	4.36
16 and 16.5	.25	.18	.29	.49	.75	1.10	1.48	2.13	2.83	3.83
17	.24	.16	.28	.42	.60	.92	1.30	1.67	2.34	2.82
18	.23	.15	.24	.37	.51	.78	1.08	1.39	1.93	2.50
19	.23	.14	.20	.32	.47	.66	.92	1.15	1.61	2.08
20-24	.22	.13	.19	.28	.40	.57	.77	1.03	1.36	1.73
25-29	.20	.09	.12	.18	.23	.31	.41	.53	.67	.85
30-50	.19	.07	.09	.12	.15	.20	.25	.32	.40	.49

Present Class Life	11th (11)	12th (12)	13th (13)	14th (14)	15th (15)	16th (16)	17th (17)	18th (18)	19th (19)	20th (20)
2.5	...	...	...	...	...	...	...	...	...	...
3.0	...	...	...	...	...	...	...	...	...	...
3.5	...	...	...	...	...	...	...	...	...	...
4.0	...	...	...	...	...	...	...	...	...	...
5.0	...	...	...	...	...	...	...	...	...	...
6.0	1.66	.62								
6.5	3.38	1.33	.55							
7.0	5.49	2.74	1.11	.51						
7.5	7.70	4.49	2.20	.92	.47					
8.0	9.52	6.46	3.61	1.85	.78	.44				
8.5	10.87	8.19	5.16	2.97	1.52	.70	.40			
9.0	11.93	9.27	6.69	4.43	2.47	1.29	.61	.38		
9.5	11.72	10.44	8.13	5.57	3.69	2.07	1.13	.52	.37	
10 and 10.5	11.79	10.79	9.01	6.90	4.83	3.09	1.80	.97	.47	.35
11 and 11.5	10.64	10.64	10.24	8.51	6.82	5.10	3.64	2.24	1.35	.75
12 and 12.5	9.28	9.87	9.87	9.28	8.19	6.79	5.31	3.88	2.67	1.73
13 and 13.5	7.77	8.62	9.10	9.10	8.62	7.77	6.63	5.37	4.13	3.12
14	6.62	7.25	8.32	8.32	8.32	8.32	7.25	6.62	5.26	4.38
15	5.32	6.23	7.04	7.61	7.93	7.93	7.61	7.04	6.23	5.32
16 and 16.5	4.22	5.30	6.11	6.80	6.89	7.54	7.54	6.89	6.80	6.11
17	3.71	4.48	4.94	5.93	6.51	6.54	7.14	7.14	6.54	6.51
18	3.12	3.57	4.46	4.81	5.71	6.19	6.21	6.75	6.75	6.21
19	2.60	2.97	3.76	4.37	4.96	5.48	5.53	6.19	6.36	6.36
20-24	2.17	2.66	3.18	3.72	4.25	4.76	5.22	5.57	5.83	5.96
25-29	1.06	1.29	1.55	1.85	2.18	2.50	2.84	3.19	3.54	3.84
30-50	.59	.72	.87	1.02	1.20	1.40	1.60	1.83	2.86	2.30

Present Class Life	21st (21)	22nd (22)	23rd (23)	24th (24)	25th (25)	26th (26)	27th (27)	28th (28)	29th (29)	30th (30)
2.5	...	...	...	...	...	...	...	...	...	...
3.0	...	...	...	...	...	...	...	...	...	...
3.5	...	...	...	...	...	...	...	...	...	...
4.0	...	...	...	...	...	...	...	...	...	...
5.0	...	...	...	...	...	...	...	...	...	...
6.0	...	...	...	...	...	...	...	...	...	...
6.5	...	...	...	...	...	...	...	...	...	...
7.0	...	...	...	...	...	...	...	...	...	...
7.5	...	...	...	...	...	...	...	...	...	...
8.0	...	...	...	...	...	...	...	...	...	...
8.5	...	...	...	...	...	...	...	...	...	...
9.0	...	...	...	...	...	...	...	...	...	...
9.5	...	...	...	...	...	...	...	...	...	...
10 and 10.5	...	...	...	...	...	...	...	...	...	...
11 and 11.5	.39	.32								
12 and 12.5	1.06	.60	.32	.30						
13 and 13.5	2.04	1.34	.84	.49	.27	.28				
14	3.17	2.32	1.68	1.06	.71	.40	.24	.27		
15	4.36	3.43	2.60	1.89	1.31	.89	.57	.35	.21	.26
16 and 16.5	5.30	4.22	3.83	2.83	2.13	1.48	1.10	.75	.49	.29
17	5.93	4.94	4.48	3.71	2.82	2.34	1.67	1.30	.92	.60
18	6.19	5.71	4.81	4.46	3.57	3.12	2.50	1.93	1.39	1.08
19	6.19	5.53	5.48	4.96	4.37	3.76	2.97	2.60	2.08	1.61
20-24	5.96	5.83	5.57	5.22	4.76	4.25	3.72	3.18	2.66	2.17
25-29	4.13	4.38	4.58	4.70	4.78	4.78	4.70	4.58	4.38	4.13
30-50	2.54	2.78	3.01	3.23	3.42	3.61	3.75	3.86	3.95	3.98

For purposes of applying the standard mortality dispersion table, all assets in a mass asset account placed in service during a taxable year are considered to be placed in service on the same day. If the taxpayer uses the standard mortality dispersion table for a taxable year, such table must be used for all subsequent taxable years unless the taxpayer obtains the consent of the Commissioner.

(6) *Transitional rule.*—Unless the taxpayer establishes to the contrary (by statistical methods or otherwise), all proceeds realized upon the disposition of assets from one or more mass asset accounts shall be considered realized with respect to accounts placed in service by the taxpayer after December 31, 1980.

(i) [Reserved]

(j) *Changes in use.*—(1) *Conversion from personal use or use in tax-exempt activity.*—If property which was previously used by the taxpayer for personal purposes or in a tax-exempt activity is converted to use in a trade or business or for the production of income during the taxable year, then the recovery allowance for the taxable year (and subsequent taxable years) shall be determined as though the property were placed in service by the taxpayer as recovery property on the date on which the conversion occurs. Thus, the recovery allowance shall be determined by multiplying the unadjusted basis (as provided in subparagraph (6)(ii) of this paragraph) by the applicable percentage.

(2) *Increased business use of property.*—If a taxpayer uses property in a trade or business (or for the production of income) and for personal (or tax-exempt) purposes during a recovery period, and increases the business (or income-producing) use of such property after the recovery for that period is completed, then a recovery allowance shall continue to be allowed with respect to such property. The amount of the allowance shall be determined as though, to the extent of the increase in business (or income-producing) use, the property were placed in service by the taxpayer as recovery property at the beginning of the taxable year in which such increased use occurs. Thus, the recovery allowance for the taxable year shall be determined first by multiplying the unadjusted basis (as provided in subparagraph (6)(ii) of this paragraph) by the applicable percentage, and then by the excess of the percentage of the business (or income-producing) use during the taxable year over the average of such use during the prior recovery period (or periods). The combined recovery under this subparagraph and subparagraph (1) shall not exceed the original cost of the property. See Example (2) of subparagraph (7) of this paragraph.

(3) *Domestic property changing recovery classes.*—(i) When the class of recovery property not used predominantly outside the United States changes during the taxable year, and the property continues to be used as recovery property by the taxpayer (*e.g.,* when property ceases to be used predominantly in connection with research and experimentation) the following rules apply:

(A) If the change results in the property's being assigned to a class with a shorter recovery period, then the recovery allowance for the taxable year in which the change occurs (and subsequent taxable years) shall be determined as though the property were placed in service as recovery property in the year of the change. Thus, the recovery allowance shall be determined by multiplying the unadjusted basis (as provided in subparagraph (6)(ii) of this paragraph) by the applicable percentage. Alternatively, the taxpayer may continue to treat the property as though the change had not occurred.

(B) If the change results in the property's being assigned to a class with a longer recovery period, then the recovery allowance for the taxable year of the change (and subsequent taxable years) shall be determined as though the property had originally been assigned to that longer recovery class. Proper adjustment shall be made under the principles of §1.168-2(d)(3) (relating to redeterminations) to account for the deductions allowable to the taxpayer with respect to the property prior to the year of the change in excess of those which would have been allowable had the taxpayer used the applicable percentages for the longer recovery class for those years.

(4) *Foreign property.*—(i) If recovery property ceases being used predominantly outside the United States during a taxable year, and the property continues to be used as recovery property by the taxpayer, then the recovery allowance for the taxable year (and subsequent taxable years) shall be determined as though the property were placed in service as recovery property in the year of the cessation. Thus, the recovery allowance shall be determined by multiplying the unadjusted basis (as provided in subparagraph (6)(ii) of this paragraph) by the applicable percentage. Alternatively, the taxpayer may continue to treat the property as though the cessation had not occurred. See §§1.168-5(e)(5) and 1.1016-3a(3)(iii) and (iv).

(ii) If the recovery property begins to be used by the taxpayer predominantly outside the United States during a taxable year after having been used otherwise by the taxpayer as recovery property in the previous taxable year, then the recovery allowance for the taxable year in which the change occurs (and subsequent years) shall be determined as though the property had originally been placed in service by the taxpayer as recovery property used predominantly outside the United States. Proper adjustment shall be made under the principles of §1.168-2(d)(3) to account for the difference between the deductions allowable with respect to the property prior to the year of the change and those which would have been allowable had the taxpayer used the applicable percentages for property used predominantly outside the United States for those years.

(5) *Low income housing.*—If 15-year real property begins or ceases to be low income housing (as defined in §1.168-2(b)(2) (iii)) during a taxable year, then the recovery allowance for the taxable year in which the change occurs (and subsequent taxable years) shall be determined under the principles of paragraph (j)(3)(i)(B) and (4) (ii) of this section.

(6) *Special rules.*—(i) For purposes of this paragraph, if, prior to a change in status, the taxpayer used the optional applicable percentages (under paragraph (c) or (g)(3) of this section) with respect to recovery property, then similar optional percentages shall be used with respect to the property after the change.

(ii) For purposes of subparagraphs (1) and (2) of this paragraph, the unadjusted basis shall be the lesser of the fair market value or the adjusted basis of the property (taking into account the adjustments described in section 1016(a)(3)) at the time of the conversion to use in the taxpayer's trade or business (or for the production of income), or at the beginning of the taxable year in which the increase in business (or income-producing) use occurs, as the case may be. For purposes of subparagraphs (3)(i)(A) and (4)(i) of this paragraph, the unadjusted basis shall be the adjusted basis of the property (taking into account the adjustments described in section 1016(a)(2) and (3)) at the beginning of the year in which the change or cessation occurs.

(7) *Examples.*—The following examples illustrate the application of this paragraph:

Example (1). A, a calendar year taxpayer, purchases a house in 1981 which he occupies as his principal residence. In June 1985, A ceases to occupy the house and converts it to rental property. Under paragraph (j)(1) of this section, for purposes of determining the recovery allowance, A is deemed to have placed the house in service as recovery property in June 1985. A does not elect to compute the recovery allowance by use of the optional recovery method provided in §1.168-2(c). Thus, A's recovery allowance under section 168 for 1985 is determined by multiplying the unadjusted basis of the property by .07. Under paragraph (j)(6)(ii) of this section, the unadjusted basis is the lesser of the property's basis or its fair market value in June 1985. See also section 280A and the regulations thereunder.

Example (2). In 1981, B (a calendar year taxpayer) purchases an automobile for $10,000. In taxable years 1981 through 1983, B's business use of the automobile is 60 percent of his total use. B does not elect use of the optional percentages provided in §1.168-2(c). The fair market value of the automobile at the beginning of 1984 is $7,500. In 1984, B's business use of the automobile is 70 percent of the total. B's allowable deduction for 1984 is $187.50, computed as follows: $7,500 (lesser of basis or fair market value) × .25 (applicable percentage) × .10 (increase in the percentage business use in 1984 (70 percent) over the average business use during 1981-1983 (60 percent)). In 1985, B's business use of the automobile is 50 percent of the total. B is entitled to no recovery allowance with respect to the automobile for 1985 since B's business use of the automobile in that year does not exceed the average business use during 1981-1983 (60 percent). In 1986, B's business use of the automobile is 75 percent of the total. B's allowable deduction for 1986 is $416.25 computed as follows: $7,500 (lesser of basis or fair market value in 1984) × .37 (applicable percentage) × .15 (increase in the percentage business use in 1986 (75 percent) over the average business use during 1981-1983 (60 percent)).

Example (3). In 1981 C, a calendar year taxpayer, purchases for $20,000 and places in service section 1245 class property used predominantly in connection with research and experimentation. C does not elect to compute the recovery allowance by use of the optional method as provided in §1.168-2(c). In 1981 C's allowable deduction is $5,000 (*i.e.,* .25 × $20,000). In 1982 C continues to use the property as recovery property, but not predominantly in connection with research and experimentation. As a result, in 1982 the property is treated as 5-year property. C's recovery allowance for 1982 (and subsequent taxable years) is determined as though C had placed the property in service in 1981 as 5-year property. The excess recovery allowance allowed in 1981 is accounted for in accordance with §1.168-2(d)(3). Thus, the difference between the recovery allowance which would have been allowed had the applicable percentage for 5-year property been used (*i.e.,* .15 × $20,000 = $3,000) and the recovery allowance allowed in 1981 (*i.e.,* .25 × $20,000 = $5,000) equals $2,000 and is accounted for as follows:

Unadjusted basis × applicable percentage for second recovery year ($20,000.00 × .22)	$4,400.00
Excess allowance × applicable percentage for second recovery year ÷ the sum of the remaining unused applicable percentages (($2,000.00 × .22)/.85)	− 517.65
Difference—allowable deduction for 1982	$3,882.35

Example (4). In 1981 D, a calendar year taxpayer, places in service 5-year recovery property with an unadjusted basis of $100,000 and a present class life of 8 years. D uses the property predominantly outside the United States in 1981, 1982, and 1983. D does not elect to compute the recovery allowance by use of the optional method as

provided in §1.168-2(g)(3). In 1984 D uses the property as recovery property but not predominantly outside the United States. D's allowable deduction for 1984 (and subsequent taxable years) is determined as though D placed the property in service in 1984 as recovery property not used predominantly outside the United States. The basis of the property is deemed to be the adjusted basis in 1984. Thus, D's allowable deduction for 1984 is $7,350 (*i.e.*, .15 × $49,000 (basis)) and for 1985 is $10,780 (*i.e.*, .22 × $49,000 (basis)). If D elected to use the optional method based on the present class life, D would use the optional percentages based on a 5-year recovery period. Alternatively, D may continue to treat the property as though it continued to be used predominantly outside the United States. If so treated D's allowable deductions for 1984 and 1985 would be $12,000 (*i.e.*, .12 × $100,000) and $9,000 (.09 × $100,000), respectively.

Example (5). The facts are the same as in example (4) except that the recovery property is not used predominantly outside the

United States for 1981 through 1983. In 1984, however, D begins using the property predominantly outside the United States. D's allowable deduction for 1984 is determined as though D placed the property in service in 1981 as property used predominantly outside the United States. Additionally, D accounts for the difference between the recovery allowance for 1981 through 1983 ($58,000) and the allowance which would have been allowable for those years had the applicable percentages for property used predominantly outside the United States been used ($51,000) in accordance with §1.168-2(d)(3). Thus, the recovery allowance in 1984 is $10,285.71, determined as follows:

Unadjusted basis × applicable percentage for 4th recovery year for property with an 8-year present class life ($100,000.00 × .12)	$12,000.00
Excess recovery from 1981 through 1983 × applicable percentage for 4th recovery year ÷ the sum of the remaining unused applicable percentages (($7,000.00 × .12)/.49)	– 1,714.29
Difference	$10,285.71

If, for 1981 through 1983, D elected to use the optional method based on a 5-year recovery period, then the allowable deduction for 1984 and subsequent taxable years would be determined using the optional percentages over the 8-year present class life.

(k) *Ratable inclusion rule.*—(1) *General rule.*—In general, the recovery allowance provided by section 168 and this section shall be considered as accruing ratably over the taxable year. Thus, for example, the distributive share of the recovery allowance for each partner in a partnership in which a partner's partnership interest varies so as to be subject to section 706(c)(2)(B) shall be determined by allocating to each partner a pro rata share of such allowance for the entire taxable year of the partnership. This paragraph does not apply, however, in determining the recovery allowance for the taxable year in which 15-year real property is placed in service or disposed of.

(2) *Example.*—The provisions of this subparagraph are illustrated by the following example:

Example. In 1978 A and B each acquire 50 percent interests in partnership P which is in the business of renting and managing beach resort property. On December 1, 1983, C and D each acquire from the partnership 25 percent interests in the partnership. On December 15, 1983, the partnership acquires for rental and places in service two sailboats (5-year recovery property) for $10,000 each. No election is made to use the optional recovery percentages provided by §1.168-2(c). The recovery allowance for P for the sailboats in 1983 equals $3,000 (*i.e.*, .15 × $20,000). The recovery allowance, however, must be allocated pro rata over the taxable year. As such, the distributive share of the recovery allowance for A and B is $1,437.50 each. The distributive share of the recovery allowance for C and D is $62.50 each.

(l) *Definitions.*—For purposes of section 168 and §§1.168-1 through 1.168-6—

(1) *Disposition.*—The term "disposition" means the permanent withdrawal of property from use in the taxpayer's trade or business or use for the production of income. Withdrawal may be made in several ways, including sale, exchange, retirement, abandonment, or destruction. A disposition does not include a transfer of property by gift or by reason of the death of the taxpayer. See §1.168-5(f)(3) and (4). A disposition also does not include the retirement of a structural component of 15-year real property. The manner of disposition (*e.g.*, ordinary retirement, abnormal retirement) is not a consideration. For rules relating to nonrecognition transactions see section 168(f)(7) and (10)) and the regulations thereunder. For rules relating to the recognition of gain or loss on dispositions, see §1.168-6.

(2) *Placed in service.*—The term "placed in service" means the time that property is first placed by the taxpayer in a condition or state of readiness and availability for a specifically assigned function, whether for use in a trade or business, for the production of income, in a tax-exempt activity, or in a personal activity. In the case of a building which is intended to house machinery and equipment, such readiness and availability shall be determined without regard to whether the machinery or equipment which the building houses, or is intended to house, has been placed in service. However, in an appropriate case, as, for example, where the building is essentially an item of machinery or equipment, or the use of the building is so closely related to the use of the machinery or equipment that it clearly can be expected to be replaced or retired when the property it initially houses is replaced or retired, the determination of readiness or availability of the building shall be made by taking into account the readiness and availability of such machinery or equipment. For a building which becomes available for use in separate stages, see paragraph (e)(3) of this section.

(3) *Recovery year.*—The term "recovery year" means the taxable year during which recovery property is placed in service by the taxpayer and each subsequent taxable year for which a deduction is

allowable to the taxpayer under this section with respect to such property.

(4) *Recovery period.*—The term "recovery period" means the actual period of years assigned, or elected by the taxpayer, for the computation under this section of the recovery allowance with respect to the unadjusted basis of the recovery property (*e.g.*, 3 years, 5 years, 12 years, present class life). The recovery period does not include any year after the end of the period assigned or elected, even though under paragraph (c), (g)(3), or (m) of this section a year following the recovery period may be a recovery year (as defined in subparagraph (3)).

(m) *Limitation on property financed with proceeds of industrial development bonds.*—[Reserved]

(n) [Withdrawn.]

[Reg. §1.168-2.]

§1.168-3. Recovery property.—(a) *Recovery property.*—(1) *In general.*—Except as provided in §1.168-4, "recovery property" to which ACRS applies means tangible property of a character subject to the allowance for depreciation which is—

(i) Used in a trade or business, or

(ii) Held for the production of income. Property is considered recovery property only if such property would have been depreciable under section 167. Thus, ACRS applies only to that part of the property which is subject to wear and tear, to decay or decline from natural causes, to exhaustion, and to obsolescence. ACRS does not apply to inventories or stock in trade, works of art, or to land apart from the improvements or physical development added to it. ACRS does not apply to natural resources which are subject to the allowance for depletion provided in section 611. No deduction shall be allowed under ACRS for automobiles or other vehicles used solely for pleasure, for a building used by the taxpayer solely as his residence, or for furniture or furnishings therein, personal effects, or clothing; but properties and costumes used exclusively in a business, such as a theatrical business, may be recovery property. For rules regarding the recovery allowance for property which is used partly for business and partly for personal purposes, or which is converted from personal to business use, see §§1.168-2(d)(2)(ii) and 1.168-2(j)(1) and (2).

(2) *Intangible property.*—[Reserved]

(3) *Boilers fueled by oil or gas.*—The term "recovery property" includes property described in section 167(p), relating to boilers fueled by oil or gas, if such property otherwise qualifies as "recovery property" under section 168 and subparagraph (1) of this paragraph.

(b) *Classes of recovery property.*—Each item of recovery property shall be assigned to one of the following classes of property:

(1) 3-year property,

(2) 5-year property,

(3) 10-year property,

(4) 15-year real property, or

(5) 15-year public utility property.

Any property which is treated as included in a class of property by reason of paragraph (c)(1), (2), (3), (4), or (5) of this §1.168-3 shall not be treated as property included in any other class.

(c) *3-, 5-, 10-, and 15-year recovery property; definitions.*—(1) *3-year property.*—The following recovery property is included in the 3-year class:

(i) Section 1245 class property (as defined in paragraph (c)(6) of this §1.168-3) with a present class life (as defined in paragraph (c)(8)) of 4 years or less,

(ii) Section 1245 class property predominantly used in connection with research and experimentation (as described in section 174 and §1.174-2(a)). Property is used in connection with research and experimentation if the property is used (A) by its owner to conduct research and experimentation in its owner's trade or business, (B) by its owner to conduct research and experimentation for another person, (C) by a lessee to conduct research and experimentation in its trade or business, or (D) by the lessee to conduct research and experimentation for another person, and

(iii) Any race horse which is more than 2 years old at the time the horse is placed in service and any other horse which is more than 12 years old at the time the horse is placed in service. A horse is more than 2 (or 12) years old after 24 (or 144) months after its actual birthdate.

Examples of 3-year recovery property are automobiles and light-duty trucks.

(2) *5-year property.*—The following recovery property is included in the 5-year class: Section 1245 class property which is not 3-year property (as defined in paragraph (c)(1)), or 10-year property (as defined in paragraph (c)(3)), or 15-year public utility property (as defined in paragraph (c)(5) and (10)). Included in the 5-year recovery property class are horses which are not included in the 3-year recovery property class, property which, prior to January 1, 1981, may have been depreciated under the retirement-replacement-betterment method (subject to the provisions of §1.168-5(a)), single-purpose agricultural and horticultural structures, and storage facilities (other than buildings and their structural components) used in connection with the distribution of petroleum or any of its primary products. Primary products of petroleum are products described in §1.993-3(g)(3)(i).

(3) *10-year property.*—The following recovery property is included in the 10-year class:

(i) Public utility property with a present class life of more than 18 years but not more than 25 years, other than section 1250 class property (as defined in paragraph (c)(7)) or 3-year property,

(ii) Section 1250 class property with a present class life of 12.5 years or less,

(iii) Railroad tank cars,

(iv) Manufactured homes (as defined in 42 U.S.C. section 5402(6)) which are section 1250 class property used as dwelling units, and

(v) Qualified coal utilization property (as defined in paragraph (c)(9)) which would otherwise be 15-year public utility property.

A building (and its structural components, if any) is not treated as having a present class life of 12.5 years or less if, in its original use (as defined in paragraph (c)(11) of this §1.168-3), the building (and its structural components, if any) does not have a present class life of 12.5 years or less. Thus, for example, a theme park structure is considered 10-year property only if the original use of such structure is as a theme park structure.

(4) *15-year real property.*—Fifteen-year real property is section 1250 class property which does not have a present class life of 12.5 years or less (including section 1250 class property which does not have a present class life). Examples of 15-year real property are office buildings and elevators and escalators.

(5) *15-year public utility property.*—Fifteen-year public utility property is public utlity property, other than section 1250 class property or 3-year property, with a present class life of more than 25 years. Examples of 15-year public utility property are: most property in electric utility steam production plants, gas utility manufactured gas production plants, water utility property, and telephone distribution plants.

(6) *Section 1245 class property defined.*—For purposes of section 168 and §§1.168-1 through 1.168-6, section 1245 class property is tangible property described in section 1245(a)(3) (other than subparagraphs (C) and (D)). See §1.168-4 for exclusion of certain "section 1245 class property" from recovery property.

(7) *Section 1250 class property defined.*—For purposes of section 168 and §§1.168-1 through 1.168-6, section 1250 class property is property described in section 1250(c) and property described in section 1245(a)(3)(C). See §1.168-4 for exclusion of certain "section 1250 class property" from recovery property.

(8) *Present class life defined.*—(i) For purposes of section 168 and §§1.168-1 through 1.168-6, present class life is the asset depreciation range (ADR) class life ("midpoint" or "asset guideline period") (if any) applicable with respect to the property as of January 1, 1981, published in Rev. Proc. 83-35. No changes will be made to the classes or class lives which are set forth in Rev. Proc. 83-35.

(ii) The application of subdivision (i) may be illustrated by the following example:

Example. X purchases a light-duty truck to be used in his trade or business. The ADR midpoint life of this asset as of January 1, 1981, determined under Rev. Proc. 83-35 is 4 years. Since this truck is

section 1245 class property with a present class life of 4 years or less, it is 3-year recovery property under section 168.

(9) *Qualified coal utilization property.*—See section 168(g)(8) for the definition of "qualified coal utilization property".

(10) *Public utility property.*—(i) For purposes of section 168 and §§1.168-1 through 1.168-6, the term "public utility property" means property used predominantly in the trade or business of the furnishing or sale of—

(A) Electrical energy, water, or sewage disposal services,

(B) Gas or steam through a local distribution system,

(C) Telephone services, or other communication services if furnished or sold by the Communications Satellite Corporation for purposes authorized by the Communications Satellite Act of 1962 (47 U.S.C. section 701), or

(D) Transportation of gas or steam by pipeline, if the rates for such furnishing or sale, as the case may be, are regulated, *i.e.*, are established or approved by a State (including the District of Columbia) or political subdivision thereof, by any agency or instrumentality of the United States, or by a public service or public utility commission or other similar body of any State or political subdivision thereof. A taxpayer's rates are "regulated" if they are established or approved on a rate-of-return basis. Rates regulated on a rate-of-return basis are an authorization to collect revenues that cover the taxpayer's cost of providing goods or services, including a fair return on the taxpayer's investment in providing such goods or services, where the taxpayer's costs and investment are determined by use of a uniform system of accounts prescribed by the regulatory body. A taxpayer's rates are not "regulated" if they are established or approved on the basis of maintaining competition within an industry, insuring adequate service to customers of an industry, insuring adequate security for loans, or charging "reasonable" rates within an industry since the taxpayer is not authorized to collect revenues based on the taxpayer's cost of providing goods or services. Rates are considered to be "established or approved" if a schedule of rates is filed with a regulatory body that has the power to approve such rates, even though the regulatory body takes no action on the filed schedule or generally leaves undisturbed rates filed by the taxpayer.

(ii) Public utility property includes property which is leased to others by a taxpayer, where the leasing of such property is part of the lessor's public utility activity, as described in subdivision (i). Public utility property also includes property leased to a person who uses such property predominantly in a public utility activity, as described in subdivision (i).

(11) *"Original use".*—The term "original use" means the first use to which the property is put, whether or not such use corresponds to the use of such property by the taxpayer. [Reg. §1.168-3.]

§1.168-4. Exclusions from ACRS.—(a) *Property placed in service by the taxpayer before January 1, 1981.*—ACRS does not apply with respect to property placed in service by the taxpayer before January 1, 1981. See §1.168-2(l)(2) for when property is placed in service. As provided in paragraph (d) of this section, ACRS does not apply with respect to property placed in service before January 1, 1981, which is transferred in certain "churning" transactions. If property is excluded from ACRS, the provisions of section 167 (and related provisions) apply in determining the allowable depreciation deduction with respect to such property.

(b) *Property amortized or depreciated other than in terms of years.*—(1) *Depreciation.*—If—

(i) Property can properly be depreciated under a method not expressed in a term of years (such as unit-of-production) which, before January 1, 1981, was a recognized method within the particular industry for the type of property in question, and

(ii) The taxpayer properly elects such treatment for such property in accordance with section 168(f)(4) and §1.168-5(e) for the first taxable year for which an ACRS deduction would (but for this election) be allowable with respect to such property in the hands of the taxpayer,

then such property shall be entirely excluded from ACRS so long as it remains in the hands of such taxpayer. A taxpayer may elect to apply a depreciation method not expressed in a term of years (and thereby exclude the property from ACRS) with respect to some or all property within the same recovery class and placed in service in the same taxable year.

(2) *Amortization.*—If—

(i) The basis of a recovery property may be amortized, in lieu of being depreciated, under any section of the Code (such as section 167(k), relating to expenditures to rehabilitate low-income rental housing, or section 169, relating to pollution control facilities), and

(ii) The taxpayer properly elects to amortize such property in accordance with the relevant amortization provision, then the amount subject to such amortization shall be excluded from the property's unadjusted basis as defined in section 168(d)(1)(A) and §1.168-2(d). A taxpayer may elect amortization with respect to one property (or a portion thereof) and apply ACRS with respect to other property (or the remaining portion) within the same recovery class and placed in service in the same taxable year.

(c) *Special rule for public utility property.*—[Reserved]

(d) *Anti-churning rules for certain transactions in property placed in service before 1981.*—(1) *In general.*—To be eligible for ACRS, property must be placed in service by the taxpayer after 1980. The anti-churning rules of section 168(e)(4) and this paragraph (d) are designed generally to deny ACRS to property in service before 1981 in the absence of a significant change in ownership or use.

(2) *Section 1245 class property.*—(i) *In general.*—Section 1245 class property, as defined in section 168(g)(3) and §1.168-3(c)(6), acquired by the taxpayer after December 31, 1980, will not qualify for ACRS if—

(A) The property was owned or used at any time during 1980 by the taxpayer or a related person,

(B) The property is acquired from a person who owned such property at any time during 1980, and, as part of the transaction, the user of the property does not change,

(C) The property is leased by the taxpayer for more than 3 months to a person (or a person related to such person) who owned or used such property at any time during 1980, or

(D) The property is acquired in a transaction in which the user of such property does not change, and the property does not qualify for ACRS in the hands of the person from whom the property is so acquired due to subdivisions (B) and (C) of this paragraph (d)(2)(i).

See section 168(e)(4)(D) and subparagraph (6) of this paragraph (d) for definition of the term "related person". See subparagraph (3) of this paragraph (d) for the treatment of the acquisition of section 1245 class property acquired incidental to the acquisition of section 1250 class property. See subparagraph (4) of this paragraph (d) for other special rules.

(ii) *Change in user.*—For purposes of subdivision (i) of this paragraph (d)(2), the user of a section 1245 class property shall not be considered to have changed as part of a transaction if the property is physically used, for more than 3 months after its transfer, by the same person (or a related person) who used such property before the transfer, or if such person, pursuant to a plan, resumes use of the property after the transfer. If the former owner (or a related person) continues to operate section 1245 class property through an arrangement such as a management contract for more than 3 months after the transfer, then all facts and circumstances will be taken into account in determining whether the user of the property has changed as part of such transaction for purposes of section 168(e)(4)(A) and subdivision (i) of this paragraph (d)(2). Among the factors which would indicate that the user of section 1245 property has changed in such case are—

(A) The arrangement in question is a customary commercial practice,

(B) The transaction in question has been arranged at arm's length, and

(C) The new owner has assumed all benefits and burdens of ownership. For purposes of this subdivision (ii)(C), the former owner will not be considered to have retained any benefits and burdens of ownership solely by reason of receiving contingent payments if such payments—

(1) Represent the real value of services rendered,

(2) Are reasonable in amount, and

(3) Are ordinary and customary in both nature and amount within the industry and region for the transaction in question.

(3) *Section 1250 class property.*—A section 1250 class property, as defined in section 168(g)(4) and §1.168-3(c)(7), acquired by the taxpayer after December 31, 1980, will not qualify for ACRS if—

(i) The property was owned at any time during 1980 by the taxpayer or a related person,

(ii) The property is leased by the taxpayer for more than 3 months to a person (or a person related to such person) who owned such property at any time during 1980, or

(iii) The property is acquired in an exchange described in section 1031 (relating to exchange of property held for productive use or investment), section 1033 (relating to involuntary conversions), section 1038 (relating to certain reacquisitions of real property), or section 1039 (relating to certain sales of low-income housing projects), to the extent that the basis of such property includes an amount representing the adjusted basis of other property owned by the taxpayer or a related person at any time during 1980. The excess

of the basis of the property acquired over the adjusted basis of such other property shall be considered a separate item of property, eligible for ACRS, provided that the exchange is not otherwise treated as a "churning" transaction under section 168(e)(4) and this paragraph. Property which does not qualify for ACRS under this subdivision shall be considered, for purposes of this section, as owned by the taxpayer during 1980.

See section 168(e)(4)(D) and subparagraph (6) of this paragraph (d) for definition of the term "related person". If, in a transaction, section 1245 class property is acquired incidental to the acquisition of section 1250 class property, then the rules of section 168(e)(4)(B) and this subparagraph shall apply with respect to the section 1245 property acquired in such transaction instead of the rules of section 168(e)(4)(A) and paragraph (d)(2) of this section. The preceding sentence will not apply in transactions where section 1245 property constitutes a significant portion of the property acquired.

(4) *Special rules.*—(i) *Property under construction during 1980.*—For purposes of paragraph (d)(2) and (3) of this section, a taxpayer shall not be deemed to own property under construction during 1980 until it is placed in service, as described in §1.168-2(1)(2).

(ii) *Entire property excluded.*—Except as provided in paragraph (d)(3)(iii) of this section (relating to excess basis in substituted basis transactions), subdivision (iii) of this paragraph (d)(4) (relating to the lease of a portion of section 1250 class property), and paragraph (d)(6)(ii)(C) of this section (relating to transactions between persons related by reason of the application of §1.267(b)-1(b)), if property is acquired in a transaction described in paragraph (d)(2) or (3) of this section, the entire property shall be excluded from ACRS.

(iii) *Lease of portion of section 1250 class property.*—Paragraph (d)(3)(ii) of this section (relating to the lease of section 1250 class property) shall apply only with respect to that portion of the property (determined on a fair market value basis) that is leased to the person (or to a person related to such person) who owned the property during 1980. The portion of the property excluded from ACRS shall not exceed the portion of the property which was owned by the lessee (or a person related to the lessee) during 1980.

(iv) *Undivided interests.*—Subject to the provisions of paragraph (d)(7) of this section (relating to avoidance), if an undivided interest in property is acquired, and the resulting arrangement is not a partnership for tax purposes, then such interest shall be treated as a separate item of property for purposes of paragraph (d)(2) and (3) of this section.

(v) *Acquisition by or lease to 1980 owner or user.*—If recovery property is acquired by, or leased to, its 1980 owner (or, in the case of section 1245 class property, its 1980 owner or user), or a related person, then the property shall cease to qualify for ACRS.

(vi) *Sale-leaseback of disqualified property.*—If property which does not qualify for ACRS under this section becomes the subject of a sale-leaseback transaction, then the property shall not become ACRS property by virtue of that transaction.

(5) *Certain nonrecognition transactions.*—(i) *In general.*—With respect to property placed in service by the transferor or distributor before January 1, 1981, and which is acquired by the taxpayer after December 31, 1980, in a nonrecognition transaction described in section 168(e)(4)(C) and in subdivision (ii) of this paragraph (d)(5), ACRS shall not apply to the extent that the property's basis in the hands of the taxpayer is determined by reference to its basis in the hands of the transferor or distributor. In such a transaction, the taxpayer shall be treated as the transferor or distributor for purposes of computing the depreciation allowance under section 167 with respect to so much of the basis of the acquired property in the hands of the taxpayer as does not exceed its adjusted basis in the hands of the transferor or distributor. However, the taxpayer shall treat the portion of the basis of the acquired property which exceeds the adjusted basis in the hands of the transferor or distributor as a separate item of property, eligible for ACRS, provided that sale or exchange of such property by the transferor or distributor to the taxpayer would not be treated as a "churning" transaction under section 168(e)(4) and this paragraph.

(ii) *Nonrecognition transactions affected.*—Subdivision (i) of this paragraph (d)(5) applies to transactions described in any of the following provisions:

(A) Section 332 (relating to distributions in complete liquidation of an 80 percent or more controlled subsidiary corporation) except where the basis of the assets distributed is determined under section 334(b)(2) (as in effect on August 31, 1982);

(B) Section 351 (relating to transfer to a corporation controlled by transferor);

(C) Section 361 (relating to exchanges pursuant to certain corporate reorganizations);

(D) Section 371(a) (relating to exchanges pursuant to certain receivership and bankruptcy proceedings);

(E) Section 374(a) (relating to exchanges pursuant to certain railroad reorganizations);

(F) Section 721 (relating to transfers to a partnership in exchange for a partnership interest); and

(G) Section 731 (relating to distributions by a partnership to a partner).

A distribution of property by a partnership to a partner in liquidation of the partner's interest in the partnership (where the basis of the distributed property to the partner is determined under section 732(b)) is not a transaction described in section 168(e)(4)(C) and this subdivision (ii) since, in such case, the basis of the property is determined by reference to the partner's adjusted basis in his interest in the partnership and not by reference to the basis of the property in the hands of the partnership. However, such distribution may be described in paragraph (d)(2) or (3) of this section.

(iii) *Successive application.*—Property which does not qualify for ACRS by reason of its acquisition in a nonrecognition transaction will not qualify for ACRS if it is subsequently transferred in another nonrecognition transaction. The preceding sentence shall apply to the extent that the basis of the property in the hands of the transferee does not exceed the basis that does not qualify for ACRS in the hands of the transferor.

(6) *Related person defined.*—(i) *In general.*—For purposes of this paragraph (d) except as provided in section 168(e)(4)(E) and in subparagraph (11) of this paragraph (d), persons are related if—

(A) They bear a relationship specified in section 267(b) or section 707(b)(1) and the regulations thereunder, or

(B) They are engaged in trades or businesses under common control (as defined by subsections (a) and (b) of section 52 and the regulations thereunder).

For purposes of applying section 267(b) and 707(b)(1) with respect to this paragraph (d)(6), "10 percent" shall be substituted for "50 percent".

(ii) *Special rules.*—(A) In general, persons are related if they are related either immediately before or immediately after the taxpayer's acquisition of the property in question. When a partnership's acquisition of property results from the termination of another partnership under section 708(b)(1)(B), whether the acquiring partnership is related to such other partnership shall be determined by comparing the ownership of the acquiring partnership immediately after the acquisition with that of the terminated partnership as it existed immediately before the event resulting in such termination occurs. Similarly, when the acquisition of property by a partner results from the termination of a partnership under section 708(b)(1)(A), whether the acquiring person is related to the partnership shall be determined immediately before the event resulting in such termination occurs.

(B) If a person would be related to a corporation, partnership, or trust which owned (or, in the case of section 1245 class property, owned or used) property during 1980 but for the fact that such corporation, partnership, or trust is no longer in existence when the taxpayer acquires such property, then, for purposes of this subparagraph (6), such corporation, partnership, or trust is deemed to be in existence when the taxpayer acquires such property. Similarly, when a taxpayer leases property to a newly-created corporation, partnership, or trust, and a person who owned (or, in the case of section 1245 class property, owned or used) such property during 1980 would be related to the lessee but for the fact that such corporation, partnership, or trust is not in existence when the taxpayer acquires such property, then, for purposes of this subparagraph (6), such corporation, partnership, or trust is deemed to be in existence when the taxpayer acquires such property.

(C) If persons are related by reason of the application of § 1.267(b)-1(b), then only a portion of the property shall be excluded from ACRS, consistent with the principles of § 1.267(b)-1(b). See, however, paragraph (d)(7) of this section (relating to avoidance).

(D) If persons are not considered to be engaged in trades or businesses under common control (as defined by subsections (a) and (b) of section 52 and the regulations thereunder), but are considered to be related persons by substituting "10 percent" for "50 percent" within the provisions of section 267(b) or 707(b)(1), then such persons are considered to be related persons for purposes of this subparagraph (6).

(7) *Avoidance purpose indicated.*—Property acquired by the taxpayer after December 31, 1980, does not qualify for ACRS if it is acquired in a transaction one of whose principal purposes is to avoid the operation of the effective date rule of section 168(e)(1) and the "anti-churning" rules of section 168(e)(4), and the rules of this section. A transaction will be presumed to have a principal purpose of avoidance if it does not effect a significant change in ownership or use of property in service before 1981 commensurate with that otherwise required for ACRS to apply. Among the circumstances in which

a principal avoidance purpose may be indicated, and in which the property involved in the transfer may therefore be ineligible for ACRS, are—

(i) The same person owns (other than as a nominee), directly or indirectly, more than a 10 percent interest in the taxpayer (or the taxpayer's lessee) and in a person who owned (or, in the case of section 1245 class property, owned or used) the property during 1980;

(ii) There is a mere change in form of the ownership of property owned by a person during 1980 (such as from a partnership to undivided interests);

(iii) The taxpayer (or the taxpayer's lessee) and a person who owned (or, in the case of section 1245 class property, owned or used) the property during 1980 are engaged in trades or businesses under common control within the meaning of section 52(a) and (b) and the regulations thereunder, substituting a 25 percent test for the 50 percent tests of § 1.52-1, or there is a similar 25 percent common ownership in the property (or in a leasehold of the property) and in a person who owned (or, in the case of section 1245 class property, owned or used) the property during 1980;

(iv) The taxpayer (or the taxpayer's lessee) is related during 1980 to the person who owned (or, in the case of section 1245 class property, owned or used) the property during 1980;

(v) Section 1250 class property is operated by a person who owned such property during 1980 (or by a related person) under a management contract and, had such property been section 1245 class property instead of section 1250 class property, the user would be considered not to have changed as part of the transaction (see § 1.168-4(d)(2)(ii));

(vi) The taxpayer leases section 1250 class property to a person and, through one or more subleases, the property is leased to a person who owned such property during 1980 (or to a related person); or

(vii) Section 1245 class property is acquired in an exchange described in section 1031, relating to exchange of property held for productive use or investment, to the extent that the basis of such property includes an amount representing the adjusted basis of other property owed by the taxpayer or a related person at any time during 1980. In the case of property which does not qualify for ACRS under this subdivision, rules similar to those of paragraph (d)(3)(iii) of this section shall apply.

In general, the avoidance intent indicated in subdivisions (i) through (vii) may be rebutted by evidence of an overriding business purpose (or purposes) for the transaction. However, even if the taxpayer demonstrates an overriding business purpose (or purposes) for the transaction, the property will not qualify for ACRS if the Internal Revenue Service establishes that one of the principal purposes of the transaction is to avoid the operation of the effective date rule of section 168(e)(1) and the "anti-churning" rules of section 168(e)(4), and the rules of this section.

(8) *Adjustment to basis of partnership property.*—ACRS shall not apply with respect to any adjustment to the basis of partnership property made under section 734(b) (relating to the optional adjustment to the basis of undistributed partnership property) or section 743(b) (relating to the optional adjustment to the basis of partnership property) if the partnership property itself does not qualify for ACRS because of section 168(e) and this section. If a partnership has property which qualifies for ACRS, see § 1.168-2(n) for the application of ACRS to the adjustments, pursuant to section 734(b) or 743(b), to the basis of such property.

(9) *Acquisitions by reason of death.*—Property acquired by the taxpayer after December 31, 1980, by reason of death, for which the basis is determined under section 1014(a), is eligible for ACRS.

(10) *Reduction in unadjusted basis.*—The unadjusted basis of property for purposes of section 168(d)(1) and § 1.168-2(d) shall be reduced to the extent that such property does not qualify for ACRS due to the application of this paragraph (d). The basis not taken into account for ACRS purposes pursuant to the preceding sentence shall be taken into account by the taxpayer for purposes of other provisions of the Code.

(11) *Certain corporate transactions.*—For purposes of section 168(e)(4) and § 1.168-4(d)(6), a corporation is not related to a distributee (or, in the case of a transaction described in section 338, the new target corporation) if—

(i) Such corporation is a distributing corporation in a transaction to which section 334(b)(2)(B) (as in effect on August 31, 1982) applies, or is a target corporation for which an election under section 338 is made, and at least 80 percent of the stock of such corporation (as described in section 334(b)(2)(B) or 338(d)(3)) is acquired by purchase after December 31, 1980, or

(ii) Such corporation is a distributing corporation in a complete liquidation to which section 331(a) applies, or a partial liquidation to which section 331(a) (as in effect on August 31, 1982) applies, or to which section 302(b)(4) applies, and the distributee (or a related person) by himself or together with one or more persons acquires the amount of stock specified in subdivision (i) of this paragraph (d)(11) by purchase after December 31, 1980.

(e) *Examples.*—The application of this section may be illustrated by the following examples:

Example (1). In 1978 A buys a house which he uses as his family residence. In 1983, A's family moves out, and A converts the house into rental property. A may not use ACRS with respect to the property because he placed it in service before 1981. A must depreciate the property in accordance with section 167 and the regulations thereunder, subject to the other applicable provisions of the Code.

Example (2). In 1982 X Corp. purchases and places in service two major pieces of manufacturing equipment. One is newly constructed, while the other is a used machine expected to produce only 5,000 additional units. X elects to depreciate the used machine under the unit-of-production method. Such method was properly used within X's industry before 1981. Assuming that X has met the requirements of section 168(f)(4) and §1.168-5(e), the used machine will not be recovery property as defined in section 168(c)(1) and §1.168-3(a). X will apply ACRS with respect to the new machine even though it properly elected to apply the unit-of-production method with respect to the used machine.

Example (3). On November 15, 1984, B, a calendar year taxpayer, places in service a 10-unit apartment building for individuals and families of low income under section 8 of the United States Housing Act of 1937. B acquired the building for $100,000 and has incurred an additional $100,000 of expenditures for its rehabilitation, which B elects to amortize under section 167(k). In 1984, B is entitled to an allowance under ACRS of $2,000 (*i.e.*, .02 × $100,000). The $100,000 which B amortizes under section 167(k) is not included in the unadjusted basis and therefore is not recovered under the provisions of ACRS.

Example (4). C is an individual engaged in the trucking business. On February 1, 1983, C purchases a new truck from a dealer. As is his normal business practice, C financed the transaction partly by trading in a truck C had used in his business for the previous 3 years. Although this transaction is described in section 1031, it does not have as one of its principal purposes avoidance of the rules of section 168(e)(1) and (4). C therefore will use ACRS with respect to the entire unadjusted basis of the truck purchased in 1983, including cash paid, indebtedness incurred, and the amount attributable to the adjusted basis of the used truck traded in.

Example (5). On June 1, 1983, in a transaction described in section 1031, Corporation M exchanges a corporate jet, acquired before 1981, for a very similar corporate jet owned and also acquired before 1981 by unrelated Corporation N. There is no significant difference to M or N in the use of the jet acquired from that of the jet exchanged, and the operations of each corporation do not change significantly as a result of the transaction. These facts and circumstances indicate that one of the principal purposes of this transaction is to avoid the principles of paragraphs (1) and (4) of section 168(e). Thus, absent evidence of an overriding business purpose (or purposes) for the transaction, neither of the jets will be treated as recovery property. Further, even if an overriding business purpose (or purposes) for the transaction is (or are) demonstrated, the property will not be eligible for ACRS if the Internal Revenue Service establishes that one of the principal purposes of the transaction is to avoid the principles of paragraphs (1) and (4) of section 168(e). The result in this example would be the same if, after the exchange, M or N sold the acquired property and leased it back, or sold the property to a related person.

Example (6). Z Corp., owner and largest occupant of the Z Building since 1965, sells this building to an institutional investor, M Corp., on May 1, 1983. After this sale, 25 percent of the Z Building is leased to Z until May 1, 1985. Because 25 percent of the Z Building is leased for more than 3 months by Z, which owned the building during 1980, M may not take ACRS deductions with respect to this 25 percent portion. Such portion must be depreciated in accordance with section 167. However, ACRS will apply with respect to the portion of the Z Building which is not leased by Z for more than 3 months after the above-described sale. If Z had leased the building only until July 31, 1983, then M Corp. would apply ACRS with respect to the entire building.

Example (7). During 1980 O Corp. undertakes construction of a department store which becomes available for its assigned business function on April 1, 1981. For purposes of section 168(e)(4)(B), O is not treated as owning the department store building under construction until it placed it in service on April 1, 1981. Accordingly, ACRS will apply with respect to the building, beginning on the day it is placed in service.

Example (8). On June 1, 1983, P Corp. sells an undivided 70 percent interest in a building it has owned since March 1, 1980, to Q Corp. which is not related to P. R Corp., which is not related to P, has occupied the building as a tenant since June 1980 and will continue to occupy it after this sale. P and Q will own the building as tenants-in-common. Q, but not P, will take ACRS deductions with respect to its portion of the building. The fact that the user of the building did not change will not affect this result. However, if P and Q had formed a partnership which owned the building after the sale, no portion of the building would qualify for ACRS because the taxpayer acquiring the property after 1980 (the partnership) would be related under section 168(e)(4)(D) to a person (P) which owned the building in 1980.

Example (9). On January 1, 1984, D, a 20 percent partner in Partnership W, sells his entire partnership interest to E for $400,000. Partnership W has one asset, a building it placed in service before 1981. D's adjusted basis in his partnership interest, allocable entirely to the building, is $200,000 when it is sold. A valid election under section 754 is in effect with respect to the sale of the partnership interest. Accordingly, Partnership W makes an adjustment pursuant to section 743(b) to increase the basis of the building with respect to E from $200,000 to $400,000. Under the provisions of §1.168-4(d)(8) no portion of the increase in the basis of the partnership property with respect to E is eligible for ACRS because the partnership property itself does not qualify for ACRS due to the provisions of section 168(e)(1) and §1.168-4(a).

Example (10). In 1983, F, an individual, sells a piece of business equipment he placed in service in 1980 to X, a partnership in which F owns a 20 percent interest. No portion of such equipment will qualify for ACRS since it was acquired after 1980 by the taxpayer (Partnership X) and was owned during 1980 by a related person (partner P). The result in this example would not be changed if F owned no interest in X in 1980.

Example (11). G, an individual, has owned an apartment building containing furnished apartments since 1979. On June 1, 1983, G sells the building and its furnishings to unrelated Partnership Y. The furniture was purchased by G before 1981. Most of these apartments will continue to be occupied by the same tenants who occupied them before the sale. For purposes of section 168(e)(4)(I) and §1.168-4(d)(3), the furniture is acquired incidental to the acquisition of the building. Therefore, ACRS will apply with respect to the furniture, notwithstanding that many of the tenants who use the furniture do not change as part of the transaction.

Example (12). On June 1, 1983, Partnership Z purchases a factory which has been leased by Corporation S, an unrelated person, since 1979. Corporation S continues to use this factory for more than 3 months after the sale. The pre-1981 section 1245 class property transferred in this transaction, such as machinery and equipment, represents a significant portion of the unadjusted basis of the property purchased by Z. Since the unadjusted basis of such section 1245 class property is significant in relation to the factory's unadjusted basis, for purposes of section 168(e)(4)(I) and §1.168-4(d)(3), the machinery and equipment are not acquired incidental to the acquisition of the factory. Since the user of such machinery and equipment does not change as part of the transaction, Partnership Z may not use ACRS with respect to such section 1245 class property. However, Z will use ACRS with respect to the factory and the other section 1250 class property acquired.

Example (13). Partnership W, in which Partner E holds a 25 percent interest, has as its sole asset an office building it placed in service in 1980. On May 1, 1983, E dies, and his partnership interest, whose basis is determined under section 1014, passes to his daughter, D. ACRS is not available with respect to any increase in the basis of the partnership property with respect to D, because the partnership property itself does not qualify for ACRS due to the provisions of section 168(e)(1) and §1.168-4(a).

Example (14). On July 1, 1983, Corporation X sells a building it had owned in 1980 to Corporation Y, an unrelated person. X retains an option to repurchase this building within 5 years. This building qualifies as recovery property in Y's hands, and Y will take ACRS deductions under section 168 with respect to it. On July 1, 1985, X exercises its option and repurchases the building. When X repurchases the building, it ceases to be recovery property because the taxpayer (X) owned the building during 1980. X may not take ACRS deductions with respect to the repurchased building. Instead, X must depreciate it under section 167 and the regulations thereunder.

Example (15). F, an individual, sells his business (including section 1245 class property owned in 1980) to G, on August 1, 1983. Under their arrangement, F continues to manage the business for G, using the same equipment he had previously used. F receives as compensation for managing the business a fixed salary plus 5 percent of the gross profits. The arrangement follows customary commercial practice and was negotiated by F and G at arm's length. In addition, the amounts received (including the 5 percent of gross profits) represent the real value of the services rendered by F and are reasonable in amount. Further, receipt of 5 percent of gross profits under these circumstances is an ordinary and customary feature in the sale of a business in the industry and region in question. This arrangement results in a sufficient change in the ownership and use of the equipment that G will recover the cost of such equipment under ACRS.

Example (16). Individuals J and K each own a 50 percent interest in Partnership X, whose only asset is a building placed in service before 1981. On August 1, 1983, H, an individual, purchases a 25 percent interest each from J and K. Partnership X is deemed under section 708(b)(1)(B) to have terminated when H purchases the 50 percent interest. The building is not eligible for ACRS because the taxpayer acquiring the property after 1980 (the new partnership formed by H, J, and K) is related to the person who owned the property during 1980 (the old partnership), since J and K own more than a 10 percent interest in each of the two partnerships.

Example (17). In 1980, individual A owns all of the stock of Corporation T, which in turn owns depreciable property. In 1982, A sells the stock of T to unrelated Corporation V. Shortly thereafter, T sells some of the depreciable property it owned in 1980 to A. Under section 168(e)(4)(D), the property is not owned during 1980 by a person related to the taxpayer (A) since A is not related to the 1980 owner (T) when A acquires the property. However, an avoidance purpose is indicated under §1.168-4(d)(7)(iv) since A was related in 1980 to the 1980 owner (T). Also, A broke the relationship with T shortly before acquiring the property. Accordingly, A may not use ACRS with respect to the property acquired, unless he can demonstrate an overriding business purpose (or purposes) for the transaction. Further, even if an overriding business purpose (or purposes) for the transaction is (or are) demonstrated, the property will not be eligible for ACRS if the Internal Revenue Service establishes that one of the principal purposes of the transaction is to avoid the principles of paragraphs (1) and (4) of section 168(e).

Example (18). In 1980, individual B owns all of the stock of Corporations X and Y. In 1980, X owns depreciable property. In 1981, X liquidates. In 1982, B sells to Y property owned by X in 1980. Y may not use ACRS with respect to the acquired property. Since the taxpayer (Y) would be related to the 1980 owner (X) but for the fact that X is no longer in existence when Y acquires the property, then, under §1.168-4(d)(6)(ii)(B), X is considered to be in existence for purposes of determining whether the property was owned (or used) by a related person during 1980.

Example (19). In 1980, individual C owns all of the stock of Corporation M, which in turn owns all of the stock of Corporation N. In 1980, N owns depreciable property. In 1981, N distributes such 1980 property to M. In 1982, M sells the N stock to an unrelated person. In 1983, M distributes to C the property it received from N. Under section 168(e)(4)(D), the property is not owned during 1980 by a person related to the taxpayer (C), since C is not related to the 1980 owner (N) when C acquires the property. However, under §1.168-4(d)(7)(iv) an avoidance purpose is indicated since the taxpayer (C) is related in 1980 to the 1980 owner (N). Also, upon acquisition, C is related to the person from whom the property is acquired (M). Therfore, C may not use ACRS with respect to the property unless he demonstrates an overriding business purpose (or purposes) for the transaction. Further, even if an overriding business purpose (or purposes) for the transaction is (or are) demonstrated, the property will not be eligible for ACRS if the Internal Revenue Service establishes that one of the principal purposes of the transaction is to avoid the principles of paragraphs (1) and (4) of section 168(e).

Example (20). D owns 20 percent of Corporation X and a 20 percent interest in Partnership P. X owns depreciable property in 1980. In 1981, X sells the property to P. Under §1.267(b)-1(b), the sale is considered as occurring between X and the members of the partnership (including D) separately. Accordingly, under the principles of §1.267(b)-1(b), 20 percent of the unadjusted basis of the property is excluded from ACRS. In addition, under §1.168-4(d)(7)(i) an avoidance purpose is indicated since D owns more than a 10 percent interest in the taxpayer (P) and the person who owned the property during 1980 (X). Therefore, ACRS is not available with respect to the remainder of the unadjusted basis of the property unless an overriding business purpose (or purposes) for the transaction is (or are) demonstrated. Further, even if an overriding business purpose (or purposes) for the transaction is (or are) demonstrated, the property will not be eligible for ACRS if the Internal Revenue Service establishes that one of the principal purposes of the transaction is to avoid the principles of paragraphs (1) and (4) of section 168(e).

Example (21). In 1980, E leases section 1245 class property to F. In 1982, at the termination of the lease, F purchases the property from E and continues to use it for more than 3 months after the sale. F is not entitled to use ACRS with respect to the property since, as part of the transaction, the user of the property did not change. The result in this example would be the same if, instead of selling the property to F, E sold the property to G, subject to F's lease, with F's use continuing for more than 3 months after the sale.

Example (22). In 1980, H and I each own section 1245 class property which they use in their respective businesses. In 1981, H and I swap titles to the property, with the parties continuing to use the same property as before the exchange. Neither H nor I is entitled to use ACRS with respect to the acquired property, since the user of the property does not change as part of the transaction.

Example (23). A owns section 1250 class property in 1980. In 1981, A sells the property to B who leases it back to A. B later sells the property to C, subject to A's lease. ACRS is not available with respect to the property in the hands of C since the taxpayer (C) leases the property to a person who owned it during 1980 (A).

Example (24). D owns section 1250 class property in 1980. In 1981, D transfers the property to E (an unrelated person) in exchange for property of a like kind in a transaction described in section 1031. Subsequently, D sells to and leases back from F the property acquired from E. Under §1.168-4(d)(3)(iii), the property acquired from E is considered to have been owned by D in 1980. Therefore, ACRS is not available with respect to such property in the hands of F since the taxpayer (F) leases the property to a person who owned it during 1980 (D). The result in this example would be the same if, instead of selling the property to F, D sold it to G (regardless of whether G leased it back to D), a person related to D under section 168(e)(4)(D) and §1.168-4(d)(6).

Example (25). In 1980, Corporation X places in service section 1245 class property. In 1981, X merges into Corporation Y in a transaction described in section 368(a)(1)(A). Subsequently, Y sells to and leases back from Z the 1980 section 1245 class property acquired from X in the merger. Under §1.168-4(d)(4)(vi), ACRS is not available with respect to the property in the hands of Z. [Reg. §1.168-4.]

§1.168-5. Special rules.

* * *

(b) *Transferee bound by transferor's period and method in certain transactions.*—(1) *In general.*—In the case of recovery property which is transferred in a transaction described in section 168(f)(10)(B) and subparagraph (2) of this §1.168-5(b), the transferee shall be treated as the transferor for purposes of computing the recovery allowance under section 168(a) and §1.168-2 with respect to so much of the basis of such property in the hands of the transferee as does not exceed its adjusted basis (determined before the application of the section 48(q)(2) adjustment, if any) in the hands of the transferor immediately before the transfer.

(2) *Transactions covered.*—The provisions of subparagraph (1) of this paragraph (b) apply to the following transactions:

(i) A transaction described in—

(A) Section 332 (relating to distributions in complete liquidation of an 80 percent or more controlled subsidiary corporation) except where the basis of the assets distributed is determined under section 334(b)(2) (as in effect on August 31, 1982);

(B) Section 351 (relating to transfer to a corporation controlled by transferor);

(C) Section 361 (relating to exchanges pursuant to certain corporate reorganizations);

(D) Section 371(a) (relating to exchanges pursuant to certain receivership and bankruptcy proceedings);

(E) Section 374(a) (relating to exchanges pursuant to certain railroad reorganizations);

(F) Section 721 (relating to transfers to a partnership in exchange for a partnership interest); and

(G) Section 731 (relating to distributions by a partnership to a partner);

(ii) An acquisition (other than one described in subdivision (i) of this paragraph (2)) from a related person (as defined in section 168(e)(4)(D) and §1.168-4(d)(6)). Property acquired from a decedent is not property acquired in a transaction included in this subdivision (ii); and

(iii) An acquisition followed by a leaseback to the person from whom the property is acquired. A leaseback does not exist for purposes of this subdivision (iii) if the former owner in turn subleases the property to another person.

(3) *Transactions excluded.*—The provisions of section 168(f)(10)(A) and paragraph (b)(1) of this section do not apply—

(i) To recovery property which is transferred within 12 months after the property is placed in service by the transferor. The exception of this subdivision (i) shall not apply in the case of a transaction also described in section 168(f)(7) (*i.e.,* a transaction in which gain or loss is not recognized in whole or in part); or

(ii) To any transaction described in section 168(e)(4) and §1.168-4(d).

(4) *Allowable deduction when transferor and transferee are calendar year taxpayers or have the same fiscal year.*—When the transferor and transferee are calendar year taxpayers or when both the transferee and transferor have the same fiscal year—

(i) *Allowable deduction in year of transfer.*—The allowable deduction for the recovery year in which the property is transferred shall be prorated between the transferor and the transferee on a monthly basis. For property other than 15-year real property, the transferor's deduction for such year is the deduction allowable to the transferor (determined without regard to this subdivision) multiplied by a fraction, the numerator of which is the number of months in the transferor's taxable year before the month in which the transfer occurs, and the denominator of which is the total number of months in the transferor's taxable year. The remaining portion of the transferor's allowable deduction for the taxable year of the transfer (determined without regard to this subdivision) shall be allocated to the transferee. For property transferred in a transaction described in section 332, 361, 371(a), 374(a), or 731, the two preceding sentences shall be applied by disregarding that the taxable year of the transferor may end on the date of the transfer. In the case of 15-year real property, the transferor's deduction for the year of the transfer is the deduction allowable to the transferor under the disposition rules of § 1.168-2(a)(3) or (g)(4) (as the case may be). The remaining portion of the transferor's allowable deduction for the taxable year of the transfer (determined as if the transfer had not occurred) shall be allocated to the transferee. See subdivision (ii) of this paragraph (4) for a special rule applicable to certain nonrecognition transactions.

(ii) *Special rule for certain nonrecognition transactions occurring as of the close of business on the last day of any calendar month.*—For purposes of this paragraph (b), in the case of a transaction described in section 168(f)(10)(B)(i) and paragraph (b)(2)(i) of this section, if the transfer occurs as of the close of business on the last day of any calendar month, such transfer is deemed to occur on the first day of the next calendar month.

(iii) *Transferee's allowable deduction for a taxable year subsequent to the year of transfer.*—The allowable deduction to the transferee for taxable years subsequent to the year of transfer shall be determined as if the cost of the property were being recovered in the transferor's hands (i.e., by multiplying the transferor's applicable recovery percentage for the current recovery year by the transferor's unadjusted basis in the transferred property).

Thus, for example, A, a calendar year taxpayer, purchases for $30,000 and places in service 15-year real property (other than low income housing) on February 15, 1981, and transfers the property to partnership B, a calendar year partnership, on March 15, 1981, in a transaction described in section 721. A does not elect to use the optional recovery percentages provided in § 1.168-2(c). For 1981, A's allowable deduction is $300 (i.e., $30,000 × .11 × 1/11). B's allowable deductions for 1981 and 1982 are $3,000 (i.e., $3,300 − $300) and $3,000 (i.e., .10 × $30,000), respectively.

(5) *Allowable deduction when transferor and transferee have different taxable years.*—When the transferor and the transferee have different taxable years—

(i) *Transferor's allowable deduction.*—The allowable deduction to the transferor for any taxable year in which the property is transferred shall be determined as under paragraph (b)(4)(i) and (ii) of this section.

(ii) *Transferee's allowable deduction.*—In computing the transferee's allowable deduction for the year of transfer and for subsequent taxable years, the property shall similarly be treated as if its cost were being recovered by the transferor. However, the allowable deduction for any taxable year shall be allocated to the transferee based on the transferee's taxable year.

Thus, for example, B, a calendar year taxpayer, purchases for $30,000 and places in service 15-year real property (other than low income housing) on February 15, 1981. B's allowable deduction for 1981 is $3,300 (i.e., .11 × $30,000). B transfers the property to C on March 15, 1982. C's taxable year is a fiscal year ending June 30. For 1982, B's allowable deduction is $500 (i.e., $30,000 × .10 × 2/12). For fiscal year 1982, C's allowable deduction is $1,000 (i.e., the remainder of B's 1982 deduction ($2,500), allocated to the period March 1 through June 30, 1982 (4 months/10 months)). For fiscal year 1983, C's allowable deduction is $2,850 (i.e., the remainder of B's allowable 1982 deduction ($1,500), plus $1,350 which is B's allowable 1983 deduction of $2,700 ($30,000 × .09) allocated to the period January 1 through June 30, 1983 (i.e., $2,700 × 6 months/12 months).

(6) *Transferee's basis lower than transferor's.*—If the adjusted basis of the property in the hands of the transferee is lower than the adjusted basis of the property in the hands of the transferor immediately before the transfer, see § 1.168-2 (d) (3) for rules relating to redeterminations of basis.

(7) *Portion of basis in hands of transferee which exceeds transferor's adjusted basis.*—The transferee shall treat as newly purchased ACRS property that portion of the basis of the property in the hands of the transferee that exceeds the adjusted basis (determined before the application of the section 48 (q) (2) adjustment, if any) of the property in the hands of the transferor immediately before the transfer. Thus, such excess shall be treated as recovery property placed in service by the transferee in the year of the transfer. The transferee may choose any applicable recovery period and recovery method with respect to

such excess and need not use the transferor's recovery period and recovery method.

(8) *Examples.*—The application of this paragraph (b) may be illustrated by the following examples:

Example (1). In 1981, A, a calendar year taxpayer, purchases for $12,000 and places in service 3-year recovery property. Under section 168 (b) (1) and § 1.168-2 (b) (1), the recovery allowances for the first and second recovery years are $3,000 (i.e., .25 × $12,000) and $4,560 (i.e., .38 × $12,000), respectively. On February 15, 1983, A transfers the property to M Corporation, a calendar year taxpayer, in exchange for M's stock and $2,000 cash in a transaction described in section 351. A's recovery allowance for 1983 is $370 (i.e., (1/12 × .37) × $12,000). A's adjusted basis immediately before the exchange is $4,070 (i.e., $12,000 − $7,930). Assume A recognizes gain of $2,000 on the transaction. The basis attributable to the property under section 362 is determined to be $6,070 in the hands of M Corporation. Under the provisions of section 168 (f) (10) (A) and this paragraph (b), M, the transferee, is treated the same as A, the transferor, with respect to $4,070, which is so much of M's basis as does not exceed A's adjusted basis. However, in computing the deduction allowable with respect to such basis, A's unadjusted basis ($12,000) is used. Thus, in the third recovery year, M may deduct $4,070 (i.e., (11/12 × .37) × $12,000) under section 168 (f) (10) (A) and § 1.168-5 (b) (1) and (4). The remaining $2,000 of basis in the property is treated as newly purchased ACRS property placed in service in 1983. M may choose any applicable recovery period and recovery method with respect to such $2,000 and need not use A's recovery period and recovery method.

Example (2). In 1983, B, a calendar year taxpayer, purchases for $12,000 and places in service 5-year recovery property. Under section 46, B's investment tax credit for such property is $1,200. Under section 48 (q) (1) and § 1.168-2 (d) (2), B reduces his basis of $600 (i.e., .50 × $1,200). Therefore, B's unadjusted basis for purposes of section 168 is $11,400 (i.e., $12,000 − $600). Under section 168 (b) (1) and § 1.168-2 (b) (1), the recovery allowances for the first and second recovery years are $1,710 (i.e., .15 × $11,400) and $2,508 (i.e., .22 × $11,400), respectively. On February 15, 1985, B sells the property for $13,000 to C, a related party (as defined in section 168 (e) (4) (D) and § 1.168-4 (d)(6)) who is a calendar year taxpayer. B's recovery allowance for 1985 is $199.50 (i.e., (1/12 × .21) × $11,400). B's adjusted basis (determined without regard to the section 48 (q) (2) adjustment), immediately before the sale is $6,982.50 (i.e., $11,400 − $4,417.50). The basis of the property under section 1012 is $13,000 in C's hands. Under the provisions of section 168 (f) (10) (A) and this paragraph (b), C, the transferee, is treated the same as B, the transferor, with respect to $6,982.50, which is so much of C's basis as does not exceed B's adjusted basis. However, in computing the deduction allowable with respect to such basis, B's unadjusted basis ($11,400) is used. Thus, in the third recovery year, C may deduct $2,194.50 (i.e., (11/12 × .21) × $11,400) under section 168 (f) (10) (A) and § 1.168-5 (b) (1) and (4). In the fourth and fifth recovery years, C may deduct $2,394 (i.e., .21 × $11,400) each year. The remaining basis of $6,017.50 (i.e., $13,000 − $6,982.50) in property is treated as newly purchased ACRS property placed in service in 1985. C may choose any applicable period and recovery method with respect to such amount and need not use B's recovery period and recovery method.

Example (3). In 1981, D, a calendar year taxpayer, purchases for $12,000 and places in service 5-year recovery property. Under section 168 (b) (1) and § 1.168-2 (b) (1), the recovery allowances for the first and second recovery years are $1,800 (i.e., .15 × $12,000) and $2,640 (i.e., .22 × $12,000), respectively. On March 15, 1983, D transfers the property to N Corporation, a taxpayer having a fiscal year ending June 30, in exchange for N's stock and $2,000 cash in a transaction described in section 351. D's recovery allowance for 1983 is $420 (i.e., (2/12 × .21) × $12,000). D's adjusted basis in the property immediately before the exchange is $7,140 (i.e., $12,000 − $4,860). Assume D recognizes gain of $2,000 on the transaction. The basis attributable to the property under section 362 is determined to be $9,140 in the hands of N Corporation. Under the provisions of section 168(f) (10) (A) and this paragraph (b), N, the transferee, is treated the same as D, the transferor, with respect to $7,140, which is so much of N's basis as does not exceed D's adjusted basis. However, in computing the deduction allowable with respect to such basis, D's unadjusted basis ($12,000) is used. Thus, for fiscal year 1983, N Corporation's allowable deduction with respect to the carryover basis is $840 (i.e., (4/12 × .21) × $12,000). For fiscal years 1984 and 1985, N Corporation's allowable deduction is $2,520 (i.e., [(6/12 × .21) + (6/12 × .21)] × $12,000). For fiscal year 1986, N Corporation's allowable deduction is $1,260 (i.e., (6/12 × .21) × $12,000). The remaining $2,000 of basis in the property is treated as newly purchased ACRS property. N may choose any applicable recovery period and recovery method with respect to such basis and need not use D's recovery period and recovery method. N elects to use the optional recovery percentage based on a 5-year recovery period with respect to the $2,000 of basis which is treated as newly purchased ACRS property. For fiscal years

1983, 1984, 1985, 1986, 1987, and 1988, N's recovery allowance with respect to such $2,000 basis are $200, $400, $400, $400, $400, and $200, respectively. If N's fiscal year ending June 30, 1983, were a short taxable year, the provisions of §1.168-2(f) would apply with respect to the $2,000 considered newly purchased ACRS property, but not with respect to N's basis carried over from D.

Example (4). On May 1, 1981, E, a calendar year taxpayer, purchases for $100,000 and places in service 5-year recovery property. On April 1, 1982, E sells the property for $100,000 to F who leases it back to E. Under the provisions of paragraph (b) (3), section 168 (f) (10) (A) and §1.168-5 (b) (1) do not apply. Thus, F may choose any applicable recovery period and recovery method with respect to its unadjusted basis of $100,000, with recovery beginning in 1982.

Example (5). Assume the same facts as in example (4) except that the property is sold to F and leased back to E on June 15, 1982. Assume further that F's fiscal year ends on July 31, 1982. For 1981, E's allowable deduction is $15,000 (i.e., .15 × $100,000), and for 1982 is $9,166.67 (i.e., $100,000 × .22 × 5/12). E's adjusted basis in the property immediately before the transfer is $75,833.33 (i.e., $100,000 − $24,166.67). Under the provisions of section 168(f)(10)(A) and this paragraph (b), F, the transferee, is treated the same as E, the transferor, with respect to $75,833.33 which is so much of F's basis as does not exceed E's adjusted basis. However, in computing the deduction allowable with respect to such basis, E's unadjusted basis ($100,000) is used. Thus, for the fiscal year ending July 31, 1982, F's allowable deduction with respect to the carryover basis is $3,666.66 (i.e., 2/12 × .22 × $100,000). For fiscal year 1983, F's allowable deduction is $21,416.67 (i.e., (5/12 × .22 × $100,000) + (7/12 × .21 × $100,000)). For fiscal years 1984 and 1985, F's allowable deductions are $21,000 (i.e., (.21 × 5/12 × $100,000) + (.21 × 7/12 × $100,000)). For the fiscal year ending July 31, 1986, F's allowable deduction is $8,750 (i.e., 5/12 × .21 × $100,000). The remaining $24,166.67 of basis is treated as newly-purchased property, placed in service by F in 1981. F may choose any applicable recovery period and method for such amount and need not use E's recovery period and method.

Example (6). On January 1, 1981, G, a calendar year taxpayer, purchases for $1 million and places in service 15-year real property (other than low income housing). On July 15, 1988, G sells the property to H for $1.5 million, who leases it back to G. H's taxable year is a fiscal year ending September 30. G does not elect use of the optional percentages provided by §1.168-2(c). For 1988, G's allowable deduction is $30,000 (i.e., .06 × $1,000,000 × 6/12). H is treated the same as G with respect to $390,000, which is so much of the basis of the property in the hands of H as does not exceed its adjusted basis to G immediately before the transfer (i.e., $1,000,000 − $610,000). H's allowable deduction for its fiscal year ending September 30, 1988, with respect to such basis is $15,000 (i.e., the remainder of G's allowable deduction for 1988 ($30,000) allocated to the period July 1 through September 30, 1988 (3 months/6 months)). For H's fiscal year ending September 30, 1989, H's allowable deduction is $60,000 (i.e., the remainder of G's allowable 1988 deduction ($15,000) plus G's allowable 1989 deduction ($60,000) allocated to the period January 1 through September 30, 1989 (9 months/12 months) or $45,000). For H's fiscal year ending September 30, 1990, H's allowable deduction is $52,500 (i.e., the remainder of G's allowable deduction for 1989 ($15,000), plus G's allowable deduction for 1990 ($50,000), allocated to the period January 1 through September 30, 1990 (9 months/12 months), or $37,500). For H's fiscal year ending September 30, 1996, H is entitled to G's allowable deduction for 1995 ($50,000), allocated to the period October 1 through December 31, 1995 (3 months/12 months), or $12,500. The amount of H's basis in excess of G's adjusted basis (i.e., $1,500,000 less $390,000, or $1,110,000) is treated as newly purchased ACRS property placed in service by H on July 15, 1988. H may use any applicable recovery period and method with respect to such basis. Thus, assuming H does not elect the optional percentages provided by §1.168-2(c), H has an additional allowable deduction for its year ending September 30, 1988, of $33,300 (i.e., .03 × $1,110,000). For its fiscal year ending September 30, 1989, H's allowable deduction with respect to such basis is $122,100 (i.e., .11 × $1,110,000).

Example (7). On January 1, 1981, partnership P, a calendar year taxpayer, purchases for $1,000,000 and places in service 15-year real property (other than low income housing) which is the only asset of the partnership. At no time does the partnership have an election under section 754 in effect. P is owned equally by partners A, B, and C. On April 18, 1985, individual D purchases the interests of B and C for $1,500,000, thereby terminating the partnership under section 708(b)(1)(B). The deduction allowable with respect to the property for 1985 prior to the termination is $17,500 (i.e., $1,000,000 × .07 × 3/12). The partnership's adjusted basis in the property immediately before the termination is $592,500 (i.e., $1,000,000 − $407,500). Under the provisions of section 168(f)(10)(A) and §1.168-5(b)(1), the new partnership which is created by A and D is treated the same as the old partnership with respect to $592,500, which is so much of the adjusted basis of the property to the new partnership as does not exceed its adjusted basis to the old partnership. However, in comput-

ing the allowable deduction with respect to such basis the old partnership's unadjusted basis ($1,000,000) is used. Thus, for 1985, the deduction allowable to the new partnership with respect to such basis is $52,500 (i.e., $1,000,000 × .07 × 9/12) and for 1986 is $60,000 (i.e., $1,000,000 × .06). This result would be the same if D purchased a 95 percent interest in the partnership. Recovery of such basis will be completed in 1995. The new partnership's basis in the property in excess of that of the old partnership is taken into account under ACRS as if it were newly-purchased recovery property placed in service in 1985. Any applicable period and method may be used with respect to such basis.

Example (8). In 1981, Corporation X, a calendar year taxpayer, purchases for $100,000 and places in service 5-year recovery property. Under section 168(b)(1) and §1.168-2(b)(1), X's recovery allowance for 1981 is $15,000. On March 15, 1982, X merges into Corporation Y in a transaction described in section 368(a)(1)(A) solely in exchange for Y stock. Y's taxable year is a fiscal year ending August 31. X's recovery allowance for 1982 is $3,666.66 (i.e., 2/12 × .22 × $100,000). Under section 362, Y's basis in the property is the same as the property's adjusted basis in the hands of X immediately before the transfer. Therefore, for fiscal year 1982, Y's allowable deduction is $11,000 which is the remainder of X's allowable deduction for 1982, $18,333.34 (i.e., $22,000 − $3,666.66) allocated to the period March 1, 1982, through August 31, 1982 (i.e., 6 months/10 months). For fiscal year 1983, Y's allowable deduction is $21,333.34 which is the remainder of X's allowable deduction for 1982 ($7,333.34) plus the deduction which would be allowable to X in 1983 (i.e., $100,000 × .21, or $21,000) allocated to the period January 1 through August 31, 1983 (i.e., $21,000 × 8 months/12 months or $14,000). In computing the deductions allowable to X and Y, the fact that X's taxable year ends on the date of the merger is disregarded.

(c) *Recovery property reacquired by the taxpayer.*—(1) *In general.*—Recovery property which is disposed of and then reacquired by the taxpayer shall be treated (for purposes of computing the allowable deduction under section 168(a) and §1.168-2) as if such property had not been disposed of by the taxpayer. This paragraph (c)(1) generally applies only to so much of the taxpayer's adjusted basis in the reacquired property as does not exceed his adjusted basis at the time he disposed of the property.

(2) *Taxpayers to whom provisions apply.*—The provisions of section 168(f)(10)(C) and paragraph (c)(1) of this section apply only to a taxpayer who, at the time of the disposition of the property, anticipates a reacquisition of the same property.

(3) *Exceptions.*—Section 168(f)(10)(C) and paragraph (c)(1) of this section shall not apply—

(i) To recovery property which is disposed of during the same taxable year that the property is placed in service by the taxpayer, or

(ii) To any transaction described in section 168(e)(4) and §1.168-4(d).

(4) *Taxpayer resumes prior recovery.*—For purposes of paragraph (c)(1) of this §1.168-5, the reacquiring taxpayer shall resume the recovery under §1.168-2 applicable at the time of the disposition. For example, if the taxpayer originally uses a 3-year recovery period and the applicable percentages prescribed in section 168(b)(1) and §1.168-2(b)(1), in the year of reacquisition the recovery allowance is computed by applying the applicable percentage for the year of disposition to the original unadjusted basis (i.e., the unadjusted basis at the time the taxpayer originally placed the recovery property in service).

(5) *Portion of unadjusted basis in reacquired property which exceeds taxpayer's adjusted basis at the time of disposition.*—That part of the unadjusted basis in the reacquired property which exceeds the taxpayer's adjusted basis in the property at the time of disposition shall be treated generally as newly purchased ACRS property. For property other than a building, any appropriate recovery period and method may be used with respect to such excess. For a building, the taxpayer must use the same recovery period and method with respect to such excess as are used for the building, unless such excess would qualify as a substantial improvement under §1.168-2(e)(4) if paid or incurred by the taxpayer for an improvement if he had continued to own the building.

(6) *Unadjusted basis in reacquired property lower than taxpayer's adjusted basis at time of disposition.*—If the unadjusted basis in the reacquired property is lower than the taxpayer's adjusted basis in the property at the time of disposition, see §1.168-2(d)(3) for rules relating to redetermination of basis.

(7) *Examples.*—The provisions of this paragraph may be illustrated by the following examples:

Example (1). In 1981 A, a calendar year taxpayer, purchases for $6,000 and places in service 3-year recovery property. A does not elect an optional recovery percentage under §1.168-2(c). Under section 168(b)(1) and §1.168-2(b)(1), A's recovery allowance for 1981 is $1,500 (i.e., .25 × $6,000). A wants to change his method of cost recovery from the use of the accelerated percentages to the use of the optional straight line percentages. To effectuate this change, A sells the property to B in 1982 for $7,000 anticipating that B will sell the property back to A. B does not elect to use an optional recovery percentage. B's recovery deduction for 1982 is $1,750 (i.e., .25 × $7,000). In 1983 A reacquires the property from B for $9,000. With respect to that portion of A's unadjusted basis in the reacquired property which does not exceed the adjusted basis at the time of disposition (i.e., $4,500), A's recovery allowance for 1983 is determined as if A had not disposed of the property, that is, by applying the percentage (38 percent) applicable for the second recovery year (i.e., 1982, the year of disposition) to the original unadjusted basis ($6,000). Thus, A's allowable deduction is $2,280 (i.e., .38 × $6,000). That portion of the unadjusted basis in the reacquired property which exceeds A's adjusted basis at the time of disposition (i.e., $4,500) is treated as newly purchased ACRS property placed in service in 1983. A may use any appropriate recovery period and method for such excess. Thus, if A uses the tables under §1.168-2(b)(1), A's recovery allowance for 1983 also includes $1,125 (i.e., .25 × $4,500). A's recovery allowances for 1984 are $2,220 (i.e., .37 × $6,000) plus $1,710 (i.e., .38 × $4,500). A's recovery allowance for 1985 is $1,665 (i.e., .37 × $4,500).

Example (2). In 1981 C, a calendar year taxpayer, purchases for $15,000 and places in service 3-year recovery property and elects under §1.168-2(c) the optional 5-year recovery period using the straight line method. Under §1.168-2(c)(4), C's recovery allowance for 1981 is $1,500 (i.e., .10 × $15,000). C wants to change his method of cost recovery from the use of the optional straight line percentages to the use of the accelerated percentages. Consent to change is not granted to C under section 168(f)(4). Therefore, C tries to effectuate this change by selling the property to D in 1982 for $16,000 anticipating that D will sell the property back to C. D does not elect to use the optional recovery percentages. D's recovery allowance for 1982 is $4,000 (i.e., .25 × $16,000). In 1983, C reacquires the property from D for $17,000. With respect to that portion of C's unadjusted basis in the reacquired property that does not exceed the adjusted basis at the time of disposition (i.e., $13,500), C must use the option recovery percentages originally elected. C's recovery allowances for 1983, 1984, 1985, 1986, and 1987 are determined as if C had not disposed of the property, that is, by applying the applicable percentages beginning in the second recovery year to the original unadjusted basis ($15,000). Thus, C's allowable deductions are $3,000, $3,000, $3,000, $3,000, and $1,500, respectively. With respect to that portion of the unadjusted basis in the reacquired property which exceeds C's adjusted basis at the time of disposition (i.e., $3,500), C may use any appropriate recovery period and method. Cost recovery for this portion of the reacquired property begins in 1983 as if C placed the property in service in that year.

Example (3). On February 15, 1981, E, a calendar year taxpayer, purchases for $30,000 and places in service 15-year real property (other than low income housing) and does not elect the optional straight line percentages under §1.168-2(c). Under §1.168-2(b)(2), E's recovery allowance for 1981 is $3,000 (i.e., .11 × $30,000). E wants to change his method of cost recovery from the use of the accelerated percentages to the use of the optional straight line percentages. To effectuate this change, E sells the property to F on February 15, 1983, anticipating that F will sell the property back to E. E's recovery allowance for 1982 is $3,000 (i.e., .10 × $30,000) and for 1983 is $225 (i.e., .09 × 1/12 × $30,000). In 1985 E reacquires the property from F for $28,000. With respect to that portion of E's unadjusted basis in the reacquired property which does not exceed the adjusted basis at the time of disposition (i.e., $23,475) E's recovery allowance for 1985 is determined as if E had not disposed of the property, that is, by applying the percentage (9 percent) applicable for the third recovery year to the original unadjusted basis ($30,000). The recovery for the year of reacquisition must be adjusted to reflect the number of months the property is used by the taxpayer in that year as recovery property. Thus, if E reacquired the property in July, E's recovery allowance for 1985 would be $1,350 (i.e., .09 × 6/12 × $30,000). The unrecovered allowance for the third recovery year, $1,125 ($30,000 × .09 × 5/12), must be recovered in the year following the last recovery year. With respect to that portion of the unadjusted basis in the reacquired property which exceeds E's adjusted basis at the time of disposition (i.e., $4,525), E may not elect an optional recovery period. Cost recovery for this portion of the reacquired property will begin in 1985. Thus, if the reacquisition occurred in July, E's allowable deduction for 1985 with respect to this portion would be $271.50 (i.e., .06 × $4,525).

(d) *Treatment of leasehold improvements.*—(1) *In general.*—Capital expenditures made by a lessee for the erection of buildings or the construction of other permanent improvements on leased property are recoverable through ACRS deductions or amortization deduc-tions. If the recovery period of such improvements in the hands of the taxpayer is equal to or shorter than the remaining period of the lease, the allowances shall take the form of ACRS deductions under section 168. If, on the other hand, the recovery period of such property in the hands of the taxpayer would be longer than the remaining period of such lease, the allowances shall take the form of annual deductions from gross income in an amount equal to the unrecovered cost of such capital expenditures divided by the number of years remaining on the term of the lease. Such deductions shall be in lieu of ACRS deductions. See section 162 and the regulations thereunder.

(2) *Determination of recovery period.*—For purposes of determining whether the recovery period is longer than the lease term, an election of an optional recovery period under section 168(b)(3) or (f)(2)(C) shall be taken into account.

(3) *Determination of the effect given to lease renewal options; related lessee and lessor.*—Section 178 governs the effect to be given renewal options in determining whether the recovery period of the improvements exceeds the remaining period of the lease. Section 178 also provides rules for determining the period of a lease when the lessee and lessor are related. In making any determination under section 178, the "recovery period" of the improvement shall be taken into account in lieu of its useful life. See §1.178-1.

(4) *Improvements made by lessor.*—If a lessor makes an improvement to the leased property, the cost of the improvement must be recovered under the general provisions of section 168. The provisions of 168(f)(6) and this paragraph (d) do not apply to improvements made by the lessor.

(5) *Example.*—The application of this paragraph may be illustrated by the following example:

Example. In 1981, A leases B's land for a term of 99 years. The lease provisions do not include any options to renew the lease. In 2034, A places in service 15-year real property which he built on the leased premises. Since the remaining term of the lease (46 years) is longer than any recovery period which A could select under section 168 (i.e., 15, 35, or 45 years), A must recover the costs of the improvement under section 168.

(e) *Manner and time for making election.*—(1) *Elections to which this paragraph applies.*—The rules in this paragraph apply to the following elections provided under section 168:

(i) Section 168(b)(3)(A) and (B)(i) and §1.168-2(c)(1) and (2), relating to election of optional recovery percentage with respect to property in the same recovery class (i.e., all 3-year recovery property);

(ii) Section 168(b)(3)(A) and (B)(ii) and §1.168-2(c)(1) and (3), relating to election of optional recovery percentage on a property-by-property basis for 15 year real property;

(iii) Section 168(d)(2)(A) and §1.168-2(h), relating to election to account for mass assets in the same mass asset account and to include in income all proceeds realized on disposition;

(iv) Section 168(e)(2) and §1.168-4(b), relating to election to exclude property from ACRS by use of a method of depreciation not expressed in a term of years;

(v) Section 168(f)(2)(C)(i) and (ii)(I) and §1.168-2(g)(3)(i) and (ii), relating to election of optional recovery percentage for property used predominantly outside the United States in the same recovery class and with the same present class life (e.g., 3-year recovery property with a present class life of 4 years); and

(vi) Section 168(f)(2)(C)(i) and (ii)(II) and §1.168-2(g)(3)(i) and (iii), relating to election of optional recovery percentage on a property-by-property basis for 15-year real property used predominantly outside the United States.

Use by a taxpayer of a method of cost recovery described in section 168(b)(1) and (2) and §1.168-2(b)(1) and (2) or section 168(f)(2)(A) and (B) and §1.168-2(g)(1) and (2) (relating to the use of the accelerated percentages) is not an election for purposes of section 168 and this paragraph (e). Thus, no consent will be granted to change from such a method to another method described in section 168. The provisions of section 168(f)(4) and this paragraph (e) do not apply to elections which must be made under another section of the Code. Thus, for example, if a taxpayer wants to amortize property under section 167(k), the rules under section 167(k) apply with respect to such election and the revocation of such election.

(2) *Time for making elections.*—Except as provided in subparagraph (4) or (5), the elections specified in subparagraph (1) of this paragraph (e) shall be made on the taxpayer's income tax return filed for the taxable year in which the property is placed in service as recovery property (as defined in §1.168-3(a)) by the taxpayer. If the taxpayer does not file a timely return (taking into account extensions of the time for filing) for such taxable year, the election shall be made at the time the taxpayer files his first return for such year. The election may be made on a return, as amended, filed within the time prescribed by law (including extensions) for filing the return for such

taxable year. A separate election may be made for each corporation which is a member of an affiliated group (as defined in section 1504) and which joins in the making of a consolidated return in accordance with section 1502 and the regulations thereunder. See § 1.1502-77.

(3) *Manner of making elections.*—Except as provided in subparagraph (5), Form 4562 is provided for making an election under this paragraph and for submitting the information required. The taxpayer must specify in the election—

    (i) The name of the taxpayer;

    (ii) The taxpayer's identification number;

    (iii) The year the recovery property was placed in service (or, in the case of 15-year real property, the month the property was placed in service);

    (iv) The unadjusted basis of the recovery property; and

    (v) Such other information as may be required.

An election will not be rendered invalid so long as there is substantial compliance, in good faith, with the requirements of this subparagraph (3).

(4) *Special rule for qualified rehabilitated buildings.*—In the case of any qualified rehabilitated building (as defined in section 48(g)(1)), an election under section 168(b)(3) and § 1.168-2(c) (relating to election of optional recovery percentage) may be made at any time before the date 3 years after the building was placed in service by the taxpayer.

(5) *Special rule for foreign taxpayers.*—(i) *Foreign corporations subject to section 964.*—In the case of a foreign corporation whose earnings and profits are determined under section 964, the elections specified in subparagraph (1) of this paragraph (e) shall be made at the time and in the manner provided in § 1.964-1(c). Except as provided in the regulations under section 952 and section 1248, any election made under this subdivision (i) shall apply with respect to the recovery property affected by the election from the taxable year in which such property is placed in service. Such election may be revoked only as provided in § 1.964-1(c)(7) and subparagraph (9) of this paragraph.

(ii) *Foreign taxpayers other than corporations subject to section 964.*—In the case of a foreign taxpayer other than a corporation described in subdivision (i) of this subparagraph (5), the elections specified in subparagraph (1) of this paragraph (e) shall be made at the time and in the manner provided in subparagraphs (2) and (3) of this paragraph, except that the election shall be made on the taxpayer's income tax return for the later of the taxable year in which the property is placed in service as recovery property by the taxpayer or the first taxable year in which the taxpayer is subject to United States tax. Any election made under this subdivision (ii) shall apply with respect to the recovery property affected by the election from the taxable year in which such property is placed in service. Such election may be revoked only as provided in subparagraph (9) of this paragraph. No election may be made under this subdivision (ii) by a taxpayer who was required to, but did not make the election at the time and in the manner prescribed under subdivision (i). For purposes of this subdivision (ii)—

(A) "Foreign taxpayer" means a taxpayer that is not a United States person as defined in section 7701(a)(30), and

(B) "United States tax" means tax under subtitle A of the Code (relating to income taxes) other than sections 871(a)(1) and 881 thereof.

(6) *Failure to elect optional recovery percentages.*—If a taxpayer does not elect to use the optional recovery percentages within the time and in the manner prescribed in subparagraphs (2), (3), (4), and (5) (or is not considered to have elected under § 1.168-2(c)(5)), the amount allowable under section 168 must be determined under section 168(b)(1) or (2) (or under section 168(f)(2)(A) or (B), where applicable) for the year in which the recovery property is placed in service and for all subsequent recovery years. Thus, no election to use such optional percentages may be made by the taxpayer in any other manner (*e.g.,* through a request under section 446(e) to change the taxpayer's method of accounting).

(7) *Individuals, partnerships, trusts, estates, and corporations.*—Except as provided in subparagraph (8) of this paragraph with respect to transactions to which section 168(f)(10)(A) and (B) applies, and subject to other applicable provisions of the Code and regulations, if recovery property is placed in service by an individual, trust, estate, partnership, or corporation, an election under this paragraph shall be made by the individual, trust, estate, partnership, or corporation placing such property in service.

(8) *Transactions to which section 168(f)(10)(A) and (B) applies.*—In a transaction to which section 168(f)(10)(A) and (B) and paragraph (b) of this § 1.168-5 apply, the transferee is bound by the transferor's election (or nonelection) under this paragraph with respect to the property so acquired. The rule of the preceding sentence shall apply

with respect to so much of the basis of the property in the hands of the transferee as does not exceed the adjusted basis of the property in the hands of the transferor immediately before the transfer.

(9) *Revocation of election.*—An election under this paragraph, once made, may be revoked only with the consent of the Commissioner. Such consent will be granted only in extraordinary circumstances. Requests for consent must be filed with the Commissioner of Internal Revenue, Washington, D.C. 20224.

(f) *Treatment of certain nonrecognition transactions.*—(1) *Section 1033 transactions.*—(i) *Allowable deduction for section 1033 converted property.*—For any taxable year in which a transaction described in section 1033 occurs, the full year's allowable deduction shall be prorated on a monthly basis under the principles of paragraph (b)(4)(i) of this section. Thus, for example, on March 3, 1981, A, a calendar year taxpayer, purchases for $25,000 and places in service 3-year recovery property. On August 14, 1981, the property is converted. A's 1981 allowable deduction for the converted property is $3,645.83 (*i.e.,* $25,000 × .25 × 7/12). If the property were 15-year real property (other than low income housing) A's 1981 allowable deduction for the converted property would be $1,250 (*i.e.,* $25,000 × .10 × 5/10).

(ii) *Allowable deduction for section 1033 replacement property in year of replacement and subsequent taxable years.*—(A) Replacement property acquired in a transaction to which section 1033 applies, which qualifies as recovery property, shall be treated the same as the converted property. Thus, the replacement property shall be recovered over the remaining recovery period using the same recovery method as the converted property. The preceding sentence applies only with respect to so much of the basis (as determined under section 1033(b)) in the replacement property as does not exceed the adjusted basis in the converted property. Any excess of the unadjusted basis of the replacement property over the adjusted basis of the converted property shall be treated as newly purchased ACRS property. Any excess of the adjusted basis of the converted property over the unadjusted basis of the replacement property shall be recovered under the principles of § 1.168-2(d)(3) (relating to redeterminations).

(B) The allowable deduction for the replacement property in the year of replacement (whether such replacement year is the same as the year of conversion or a later year) shall be based on the number of months the replacement property is in service as recovery property during the replacement year.

(1) If the number of months in the conversion year after the property is converted (including the month of conversion) is greater than or equal to the number of months the replacement property is in service during the replacement year, the allowable deduction for the replacement year shall equal—

$$(a/b \times c) \times d$$

where

    a = number of months replacement property is in service as recovery property during replacement year,

    b = 12 or, in the case of 15-year real property converted in the first recovery year, the number of months in the taxpayer's taxable year after the converted property was placed in service by the taxpayer (including the month the property was placed in service),

    c = applicable recovery percentage for converted property in year of conversion, and

    d = unadjusted basis of converted property.

An allowance is permitted to the extent of any unrecovered allowance in the taxable year following the final recovery year. The term "unrecovered allowance" means the difference between—

    (i) The sum of recovery allowances for the year of the conversion and the year of the replacement, and

    (ii) The recovery allowance which would have been allowable in the year of conversion had such conversion not occurred.

In a year following the year of replacement, the allowable deduction shall be computed by multiplying the applicable recovery percentage for the next recovery year to the unadjusted basis of the converted property.

(2) If the number of months in the conversion year after the property is converted (including the month of conversion) is less than the number of months the replacement property is in service during the replacement year, the allowable deduction for the replacement year shall equal—

$$[(a/b \times c) + (d/12 \times e)] \times f$$

where

    a = number of months in conversion year after the property is converted (including the month of conversion),

    b = 12 or, in the case of 15-year real property converted in the first recovery year, the number of months in the taxpayer's taxable year after the converted property was placed in service by the taxpayer (including the month the property was placed in service), c = applicable recovery percentage for converted property in the year of conversion,

d = number of months replacement property is in service as recovery property during replacement year minus a,

e = applicable recovery percentage for the next recovery year, and

f = unadjusted basis of converted property.

An allowance is permitted to the extent of any unrecovered allowance in the taxable year following the final recovery year. The term "unrecovered allowance" means the difference between—

(i) The sum of the recovery allowances for the year of conversion and the year of replacement, and

(ii) The sum of the recovery allowances which would have been allowable in the year of conversion and the next recovery year had such conversion not occurred.

In a year following the year of replacement, the allowable deduction shall be computed by multiplying the unadjusted basis of the converted property by the applicable recovery percentage for the second recovery year after the year of conversion.

(iii) *Examples.*—The provisions of paragraph (f)(1)(i) and (ii) may be illustrated by the following examples:

Example (1). On January 1, 1981, A, a calendar year taxpayer, purchases for $40,000 and places in service recovery property which is 15-year real property (other than low income housing). Under section 168(b)(2) and §1.168-2(b)(2), the allowable deductions for the first and second recovery years are $4,800 (*i.e.,* .12 × $40,000) and $4,000 (*i.e.,* .10 × $40,000). On March 3, 1983, A's property is involuntarily converted. Under the provisions of subdivision (i), A's 1983 allowable deduction for the converted property is $600 (*i.e.,* 2/12 × .09 × $40,000). On May 15, 1984, A acquires replacement property. A's unadjusted basis in the replacement property is the same as his adjusted basis in the converted property (*i.e.,* $30,600). Under the provisions of subdivision (ii), the replacement property is treated the same as the converted property with respect to such $30,600 of basis. However, in computing the allowable deduction with respect to such basis, A's unadjusted basis in the converted property ($40,000) is used. Thus, A's allowable deduction for 1984 is $2,400 (*i.e.,* 8/12 × .09 × $40,000). Under the provisions of subdivision (ii)(B)(1), the unrecovered allowance is $600 (*i.e.,* $3,600 – $3,000), and it must be recovered in the taxable year following the final recovery year, that is, in the taxable year following the fifteenth recovery year. A's allowable deduction for 1985 is $3,200 (*i.e.,* .08 × $40,000).

Example (2). Assume the same facts as in example (1) except that A acquires the replacement property on January 1, 1984. A's allowable deduction for 1984 is $3,533.33 (*i.e.,* [(10/12 × .09) = (2/12 × .08)] × $40,000). Under the provisions of subdivision (ii)(B)(2), the unrecovered allowance is $2,666.67 (*i.e.,* $6,800 – $4,133.33), and it must be recovered in the taxable year following the final recovery year, that is, in the taxable year following the fifteenth recovery year. A's allowance deduction for 1985 is $2,800 (*i.e.,* .07 × $40,000).

Example (3). Assume the same facts as in example (1) except that A acquires the replacement property on the same day as the conversion (March 3, 1983). A's allowable deduction for 1983 for the converted property is $600 (*i.e.,* (2/12 × .09) × $40,000). A's allowable deduction for 1983 for the replacement property is $3,000 (*i.e.,* (10/12 × .09) × $40,000). A's allowable deduction for 1984 is $3,200 (*i.e.,* $40,000 × .08).

Example (4). On February 3, 1981, B, a calendar year taxpayer, purchases for $100,000 and places in service recovery property which is 15-year real property (other than low income housing). On June 25, 1981, B's property is involuntarily converted. On that same day B acquires replacement property with the same basis as the converted property. B's allowable deduction for 1981 for the converted property is $4,000 (*i.e.,* 4/11 × .11 × $100,000). B's allowable deduction for 1981 for the replacement property is $7,000 (*i.e.,* 7/11 × .11 × $100,000). B's allowable deduction for 1982 is $10,000 (*i.e.,* $100,000 × .10).

(2) *Section 1031 transactions.*—(i) *Allowable deductions.*—In a transaction to which section 1031 applies, the allowable deduction for the exchanged and acquired properties shall be determined under the principles of subparagraph (1) of this paragraph. Similarly, any excess of the unadjusted basis of the acquired property over the adjusted basis of the exchanged property shall be treated as newly purchased ACRS property, and any excess of the adjusted basis of the exchanged property over the unadjusted basis of the acquired property shall be recovered under the principles of §1.168-2(d)(3) (relating to redeterminations).

(ii) *Examples.*—The provisions of paragraph (f)(2)(i) may be illustrated by the following examples:

Example (1). In 1981 A, a calendar year taxpayer, purchases for $12,000 and places in service recovery property which is 3-year recovery property. Under section 168(b)(1) and §1.168-2(b)(1), the allowable deductions for the first and second recovery years are $3,000 (*i.e.,* .25 × $12,000) and $4,560 (*i.e.,* .38 × $12,000), respectively. On March 3, 1983, A exchanges this property and $1,000 cash for property of a "like kind." A's 1983 allowable deduction for the exchanged property is $740 (*i.e.,* 2/12 × .37 × $12,000). A's basis in the acquired property is $4,700. The acquired property is treated the same as the exchanged property with respect to $3,700, which is so much of the basis in the acquired property as does not exceed the adjusted basis in the exchanged property. However, in computing the allowable deduction with respect to such basis, A's unadjusted basis in the exchanged property ($12,000) is used. Therefore, A's 1983 allowable deduction for the acquired property with respect to the substituted basis is $3,700 (*i.e.,* 10/12 × .37 × $12,000). The remaining $1,000 of basis in the acquired property is treated as newly purchased ACRS property placed in service in 1983. A may choose any applicable recovery period and recovery method for such basis and need not use the same recovery period and recovery method used for the exchanged property. If A uses the tables provided in section 168(b)(1) and §1.168-2(b)(1), for 1983, 1984, and 1985, A is entitled to additional allowable deductions of $250, $380, and $370, respectively.

Example (2). On February 8, 1981, B, a calendar year taxpayer, purchases for $80,000 and places in service 15-year real property (other than low income housing). Under the provisions of section 168(b)(2) and §1.168-2(b)(2), the allowable deduction for 1981 is $8,800 (*i.e.,* .11 × $80,000). On March 3, 1982, B exchanges this property and $20,000 cash for property of a "like kind." B's 1982 allowable deduction for the exchanged property is $1,333.33 (*i.e.,* 2/12 × .10 × $80,000). B's basis in the acquired property is $89,866.67. The acquired property is treated the same as the exchanged property with respect to $69,866.67, which is so much of the basis in the acquired property as does not exceed the adjusted basis in the exchanged property. However, in computing the allowable deduction with respect to such basis, B's unadjusted basis in the exchanged property ($80,000) is used. Therefore, B's 1982 and 1983 allowable deductions for the acquired property with respect to the substituted basis are $6,666.66 (*i.e.,* 10/12 × .10 × $80,000) and $7,200 (*i.e.,* .09 × $80,000), respectively. The remaining $20,000 of basis in the acquired property is treated as newly purchased ACRS property placed in service in March 1982. B may choose any applicable recovery period and recovery method for this basis and need not use the same period and method used for the exchanged property. If B uses the tables prescribed in §1.168-2(b)(2), B's 1982 allowable deduction for this basis is $2,000 (*i.e.,* $20,000 × .10).

(3) *Transfers of property by gift.*—(i) *Allowable deductions.*—With respect to recovery property which is transferred by gift (where the donee's basis is determined under section 1015), the allowable deduction for the taxable year of the gift shall be apportioned between the donor and donee under the principles of paragraphs (b) (including paragraph (b)(4)(ii) and (f)(1) of this section, and the donee shall be treated as the donor for subsequent taxable years to the extent that the donee's basis is carried over from the donor. That portion of the donee's basis (as determined under section 1015) in the property that exceeds the donor's adjusted basis immediately preceding the gift shall be treated as newly purchased ACRS property. The donee may choose any applicable recovery period and recovery method with respect to such excess and need not use the donor's recovery period and recovery method.

(ii) *Example.*—The provisions of paragraph (f)(3)(i) may be illustrated by the following example:

Example. In 1981 A, a calendar year taxpayer, purchases for $12,000 and places in service 5-year recovery property. Under section 168(b)(1) and §1.168-2(b)(1), the allowable deduction for 1981 is $1,800 (*i.e.,* .15 × $12,000). On March 15, 1982, A transfers the property by gift to B (another calendar year taxpayer) who continues to use it as recovery property. A's 1982 allowable deduction is $440 (*i.e.,* 2/12 × .22 × $12,000). Under section 1015, B's basis in the property is determined to be $11,000. In the hands of B, the donee, the property is treated the same as in the hands of the donor with respect to $9,760, which is so much of the carryover basis as does not exceed the donor's adjusted basis in the property immediately preceding the gift. However, in computing the allowable deduction with respect to such basis, the donor's unadjusted basis ($12,000) is used. Therefore, B's 1982 allowable deduction with respect to such basis is $2,200 (*i.e.,* 10/12 × .22 × $12,000). The remaining $1,240 (*i.e.,* $11,000 – $9,760) of basis is treated as newly purchased ACRS property. B may choose any applicable recovery period and recovery method for such basis and need not use the donor's recovery period and recovery method.

(4) *Transfers of property by reason of death.*—Where recovery property is transferred by reason of the death of the taxpayer, the allowable deduction for the taxpayer's taxable year which ends upon his death shall be governed by the rules applicable to short taxable years. See §1.168-2(f). [Reg. §1.168-5.]

§1.168-6. Gain or loss on dispositions.—(a) *General rule*—Except as provided in §1.168-2(h) (relating to mass assets), where recovery property is disposed of during a taxable year, the following rules shall apply:

(1) If the asset is disposed of by sale or exchange, gain or loss shall be recognized as provided under the applicable provisions of the Code.

(2) If the asset is disposed of by physical abandonment, loss shall be recognized in the amount of the adjusted basis of the asset at the time of the abandonment. For a loss to qualify for recognition under this subparagraph (2), the taxpayer must intend to discard the asset irrevocably so that he will neither use the asset again, nor retrieve it for sale, exchange, or other disposition.

(3) If the asset is disposed of other than by sale or exchange or physical abandonment (as, for example, where the asset is transferred to a supplies or scrap account), gain shall not be recognized. Loss shall be recognized in the amount of the excess of the adjusted basis of the asset over its fair market value at the time of the disposition. No loss shall be recognized upon the conversion of property to personal use.

(b) *Definitions.*—(1) See § 1.168-2(l)(1) for the definition of "disposition," which excludes the retirement of a structural component of 15-year real property. Thus, no loss shall be recognized on such retirement, and the unadjusted basis of the property under § 1.168-2(d) shall not be reduced. For example, if a taxpayer replaces the roof on 15-year real property, no loss is recognized upon the retirement of the replaced roof, and the unadjusted basis of the property continues to be recovered over the remaining period. For determination of the deductions allowable under section 168 with respect to the expenditures paid or incurred to replace the roof, see § 1.168-2(e).

(2) The adjusted basis of an asset at the time of its disposition is its unadjusted basis, as provided in § 1.168-2, adjusted as prescribed in § 1.1011-1. [Reg. § 1.168-6.]

Tax-Exempt Entity Leasing

Accelerated Cost Recovery System: Tax-Exempt Entity Leasing.—Temporary Reg. § 1.168(j)-1T, regarding tax-exempt entity leasing is also proposed as a final regulations and, when adopted, would become Reg. § 1.168(j)-1 (published in the Federal Register on July 2, 1985).

§ 1.168(j)-1. Questions and answers concerning tax-exempt entity leasing rules.

Qualified Property: Additional First Year Depreciation Deduction

Qualified Property: Additional First Year Depreciation Deduction.—Amendments to Reg. § 1.168(k)-0, regarding the additional first year depreciation deduction under section 168(k) of the Internal Revenue Code, are proposed (published in the Federal Register on September 24, 2019) (REG-106808-19).

Par. 2. Section 1.168(k)-0 is amended by adding entries for § 1.168(k)-2(b)(3)(iii)(C), (b)(3)(v), (b)(5)(iii)(G), (b)(5)(v), (c), and (g)(11); and adding an entry for § 1.168(k)-2(h)(4) to read as follows:

§ 1.168(k)-0. Table of contents.

* * *

§ 1.168(k)-2 Additional first year depreciation deduction for property acquired and placed in service after September 27, 2017.

* * *

(b) * * *

  (3) * * *

    (iii) * * *

      (C) Special rules for a series of related transactions.

* * *

    (v) Application to members of a consolidated group.

* * *

  (5) * * *

    (iii) * * *

      (G) Acquisition of a trade or business or an entity.

* * *

    (v) Determination of acquisition date for property not acquired pursuant to a written binding contract.

* * *

(c) Election for components of larger self-constructed property for which the manufacture, construction, or production begins before September 28, 2017.

  (1) In general.

  (2) Eligible larger self-constructed property.

    (i) In general.

    (ii) Exceptions.

  (3) Eligible components.

    (i) In general.

    (ii) Acquired components.

    (iii) Self-constructed components.

  (4) Special rules.

    (i) Installation costs.

    (ii) Property described in section 168(k)(2)(B).

  (5) Computation of additional first year depreciation deduction.

    (i) Election is made.

    (ii) Election is not made.

  (6) Time and manner for making election.

    (i) Time for making election.

    (ii) Manner of making election.

  (7) Examples.

(g) * * *

  (11) Mid-quarter convention.

(h) * * *

  (4) Regulation project REG-106808-19.

Qualified Property: Additional First Year Depreciation Deduction

Qualified Property: Additional First Year Depreciation Deduction.—Reg. § 1.168(k)-2, providing guidance regarding the additional first year depreciation deduction under section 168(k) of the Internal Revenue Code, is proposed (published in the Federal Register on August 8, 2018) (REG-104397-18). Proposed amendments to Reg. § 1.168(k)-2(b)(3)(iii)(B)(3)(*i*) through (*iii*), § 1.168(k)-2(b)(3)(iii)(C), and § 1.168(k)-2(b)(3)(vi) *Examples 18* through 22 withdrawn by REG-106808-19 on September 24, 2019.

   ⟫⟫→ *Caution: Prop. Reg. § 1.168(k)-2, below, was adopted by T.D. 9874 on September 17, 2019, but it may be relied on for qualified property acquired and placed in service or planted or grafted, as applicable, after September 27, 2017, and in a tax year that ends before September 24, 2019.*

Par. 9. Section 1.168(k)-2 is added to read as follows:

§ 1.168(k)-2. Additional first year depreciation deduction for property acquired and placed in service after September 27, 2017.—(a) *Scope and definitions.*—(1) *Scope.*—This section provides rules for determining the additional first year depreciation deduction allowable under section 168(k) for qualified property acquired and placed in service after September 27, 2017.

(2) *Definitions.*—For purposes of this section—

(i) *Act* is the Tax Cuts and Jobs Act, Public Law 115-97 (131 Stat. 2054 (December 22, 2017)); and

(ii) *Applicable percentage* is the percentage provided in section 168(k)(6).

(b) *Qualified property.*—(1) *In general.*—Qualified property is depreciable property, as defined in § 1.168(b)-1a)(1), that meets all the following requirements in the first taxable year in which the property

is subject to depreciation by the taxpayer whether or not depreciation deductions for the property are allowable:

(i) The requirements in § 1.168(k)-2(b)(2) (description of qualified property);

(ii) The requirements in § 1.168(k)-2(b)(3) (original use or used property acquisition requirements);

(iii) The requirements in § 1.168(k)-2(b)(4) (placed-in-service date); and

(iv) The requirements in § 1.168(k)-2(b)(5) (acquisition of property).

(2) *Description of qualified property.*—(i) *In general.*—Depreciable property will meet the requirements of this paragraph (b)(2) if the property is—

(A) MACRS property, as defined in § 1.168(b)-1(a)(2), that has a recovery period of 20 years or less. For purposes of this paragraph (b)(2)(i)(A) and section 168(k)(2)(A)(i)(I), the recovery period is determined in accordance with section 168(c) regardless of any election made by the taxpayer under section 168(g)(7). This paragraph (b)(2)(i)(A) includes the following MACRS property that is acquired by the taxpayer after September 27, 2017, and placed in service by the taxpayer after September 27, 2017, and before January 1, 2018:

(1) Qualified leasehold improvement property as defined in section 168(e)(6) as in effect on the day before amendment by section 13204(a)(1) of the Act;

(2) Qualified restaurant property, as defined in section 168(e)(7) as in effect on the day before amendment by section 13204(a)(1) of the Act, that is qualified improvement property as defined in §1.168(b)-1(a)(5)(i)(C) and (a)(5)(ii); and

(3) Qualified retail improvement property as defined in section 168(e)(8) as in effect on the day before amendment by section 13204(a)(1) of the Act;

(B) Computer software as defined in, and depreciated under, section 167(f)(1) and the regulations under section 167(f)(1);

(C) Water utility property as defined in section 168(e)(5) and depreciated under section 168;

(D) Qualified improvement property as defined in §1.168(b)-1a(5)(i)(C) and (a)(5)(ii) and depreciated under section 168;

(E) Qualified film or television production, as defined in section 181(d) and §1.181-3, for which a deduction would have been allowable under section 181 without regard to section 181(a)(2) and (g), or section 168(k);

(F) Qualified live theatrical production, as defined in section 181(e), for which a deduction would have been allowable under section 181 without regard to section 181(a)(2) and (g), or section 168(k); or

(G) A specified plant, as defined in section 168(k)(5)(B), for which the taxpayer has properly made an election to apply section 168(k)(5) for the taxable year in which the specified plant is planted, or grafted to a plant that has already been planted, by the taxpayer in the ordinary course of the taxpayer's farming business, as defined in section 263A(e)(4) (for further guidance, see paragraph (e) of this section).

(ii) *Property not eligible for additional first year depreciation deduction.*—Depreciable property will not meet the requirements of this paragraph (b)(2) if the property is—

(A) Described in section 168(f) (for example, automobiles for which the taxpayer uses the optional business standard mileage rate);

(B) Required to be depreciated under the alternative depreciation system of section 168(g) pursuant to section 168(g)(1)(A), (B), (C), (D), (F), or (G), or other provisions of the Internal Revenue Code (for example, property described in section 263A(e)(2)(A) if the taxpayer or any related person, as defined in section 263A(e)(2)(B), has made an election under section 263A(d)(3), or property described in section 280F(b)(1));

(C) Included in any class of property for which the taxpayer elects not to deduct the additional first year depreciation (for further guidance, see paragraph (e) of this section);

(D) A specified plant that is placed in service by the taxpayer during the taxable year and for which the taxpayer made an election to apply section 168(k)(5) for a prior taxable year;

(E) Included in any class of property for which the taxpayer elects to apply section 168(k)(4). This paragraph (b)(2)(ii)(E) applies to property placed in service in any taxable year beginning before January 1, 2018;

(F) Described in section 168(k)(9)(A) and placed in service in any taxable year beginning after December 31, 2017; or

(G) Described in section 168(k)(9)(B) and placed in service in any taxable year beginning after December 31, 2017.

(3) *Original use or used property acquisition requirements.*—(i) *In general.*—Depreciable property will meet the requirements of this paragraph (b)(3) if the property meets the original use requirements in paragraph (b)(3)(ii) of this section or if the property meets the used property acquisition requirements in paragraph (b)(3)(iii) of this section.

(ii) *Original use.*—(A) *In general.*—Depreciable property will meet the requirements of this paragraph (b)(3)(ii) if the original use of the property commences with the taxpayer. Except as provided in paragraphs (b)(3)(ii)(B) and (C) of this section, original use means the first use to which the property is put, whether or not that use corresponds to the use of the property by the taxpayer. Additional capital expenditures incurred by a taxpayer to recondition or rebuild property acquired or owned by the taxpayer satisfy the original use requirement. However, the cost of reconditioned or rebuilt property does not satisfy the original use requirement (but may satisfy the used property acquisition requirements in paragraph (b)(3)(iii) of this

section). The question of whether property is reconditioned or rebuilt property is a question of fact. For purposes of this paragraph (b)(3)(ii)(A), property that contains used parts will not be treated as reconditioned or rebuilt if the cost of the used parts is not more than 20 percent of the total cost of the property, whether acquired or self-constructed.

(B) *Conversion to business or income-producing use.*—(1) *Personal use to business or income-producing use.*—If a taxpayer initially acquires new property for personal use and subsequently uses the property in the taxpayer's trade or business or for the taxpayer's production of income, the taxpayer is considered the original user of the property. If a person initially acquires new property for personal use and a taxpayer subsequently acquires the property from the person for use in the taxpayer's trade or business or for the taxpayer's production of income, the taxpayer is not considered the original user of the property.

(2) *Inventory to business or income-producing use.*—If a taxpayer initially acquires new property and holds the property primarily for sale to customers in the ordinary course of the taxpayer's business and subsequently withdraws the property from inventory and uses the property primarily in the taxpayer's trade or business or primarily for the taxpayer's production of income, the taxpayer is considered the original user of the property. If a person initially acquires new property and holds the property primarily for sale to customers in the ordinary course of the person's business and a taxpayer subsequently acquires the property from the person for use primarily in the taxpayer's trade or business or primarily for the taxpayer's production of income, the taxpayer is considered the original user of the property. For purposes of this paragraph (b)(3)(ii)(B)(2), the original use of the property by the taxpayer commences on the date on which the taxpayer uses the property primarily in the taxpayer's trade or business or primarily for the taxpayer's production of income.

(C) *Fractional interests in property.*—If, in the ordinary course of its business, a taxpayer sells fractional interests in new property to third parties unrelated to the taxpayer, each first fractional owner of the property is considered as the original user of its proportionate share of the property. Furthermore, if the taxpayer uses the property before all of the fractional interests of the property are sold but the property continues to be held primarily for sale by the taxpayer, the original use of any fractional interest sold to a third party unrelated to the taxpayer subsequent to the taxpayer's use of the property begins with the first purchaser of that fractional interest. For purposes of this paragraph (b)(3)(ii)(C), persons are not related if they do not have a relationship described in section 267(b) or 707(b) and the regulations under section 267(b) or 707(b).

(iii) *Used property acquisition requirements.*—(A) *In general.*—Depreciable property will meet the requirements of this paragraph (b)(3)(iii) if the acquisition of the used property meets the following requirements:

(1) Such property was not used by the taxpayer or a predecessor at any time prior to such acquisition;

(2) The acquisition of such property meets the requirements of section 179(d)(2)(A), (B), and (C), and §1.179-4(c)(1)(ii), (iii), and (iv), or 1.179-4(c)(2) (property is acquired by purchase); and

(3) The acquisition of such property meets the requirements of section 179(d)(3) and §1.179-4(d) (cost of property) (for further guidance regarding like-kind exchanges and involuntary conversions, see paragraph (f)(5) of this section).

(B) *Property was not used by the taxpayer at any time prior to acquisition.*—(1) *In general.*—Solely for purposes of paragraph (b)(3)(iii)(A)(1) of this section, the property is treated as used by the taxpayer or a predecessor at any time prior to acquisition by the taxpayer or predecessor if the taxpayer or the predecessor had a depreciable interest in the property at any time prior to such acquisition, whether or not the taxpayer or the predecessor claimed depreciation deductions for the property. If a lessee has a depreciable interest in the improvements made to leased property and subsequently the lessee acquires the leased property of which the improvements are a part, the unadjusted depreciable basis, as defined in §1.168(b)-1(a)(3), of the acquired property that is eligible for the additional first year depreciation deduction, assuming all other requirements are met, must not include the unadjusted depreciable basis attributable to the improvements.

(2) *Taxpayer has a depreciable interest in a portion of the property.*—If a taxpayer initially acquires a depreciable interest in a portion of the property and subsequently acquires a depreciable interest in an additional portion of the same property, such additional depreciable interest is not treated as used by the taxpayer at any time prior to its acquisition by the taxpayer. This paragraph (b)(3)(iii)(B)(2) does not apply if the taxpayer or a predecessor previously had a depreciable interest in the subsequently acquired addi-

tional portion. For purposes of this paragraph (b)(3)(iii)(B)(2), a portion of the property is considered to be the percentage interest in the property. If a taxpayer holds a depreciable interest in a portion of the property, sells that portion or a part of that portion, and subsequently acquires a depreciable interest in another portion of the same property, the taxpayer will be treated as previously having a depreciable interest in the property up to the amount of the portion for which the taxpayer held a depreciable interest in the property before the sale.

     (3) [(*i*) through (*iii*) withdrawn by REG-106808-19 on September 24, 2019.]

     (C) [Withdrawn by REG-106808-19 on September 24, 2019.]

     (iv) *Application to partnerships.*—(A) *Section 704(c) remedial allocations.*—Remedial allocations under section 704(c) do not satisfy the requirements of paragraph (b)(3) of this section. See §1.704-3(d)(2).

     (B) *Basis determined under section 732.*—Any basis of distributed property determined under section 732 does not satisfy the requirements of paragraph (b)(3) of this section.

     (C) *Section 734(b) adjustments.*—Any increase in basis of depreciable property under section 734(b) does not satisfy the requirements of paragraph (b)(3) of this section.

     (D) *Section 743(b) adjustments.*—(1) *In general.*—For purposes of determining whether the transfer of a partnership interest meets the requirements of paragraph (b)(3)(iii)(A) of this section, each partner is treated as having a depreciable interest in the partner's proportionate share of partnership property. Any increase in basis of depreciable property under section 743(b) satisfies the requirements of paragraph (b)(3)(iii)(A) of this section if—

     (i) At any time prior to the transfer of the partnership interest that gave rise to such basis increase, neither the transferee partner nor a predecessor of the transferee partner had any depreciable interest in the portion of the property deemed acquired to which the section 743(b) adjustment is allocated under section 755 and the regulations under section 755; and

     (ii) The transfer of the partnership interest that gave rise to such basis increase satisfies the requirements of paragraphs (b)(3)(iii)(A)(2) and (3) of this section.

     (2) *Relatedness tested at partner level.*—Solely for purposes of paragraph (b)(3)(iv)(D)(1)(ii) of this section, whether the parties are related or unrelated is determined by comparing the transferor and the transferee of the transferred partnership interest.

     (v) *Syndication transaction.*—If a lessor has a depreciable interest in the property and the lessor and any predecessor did not previously have a depreciable interest in the property, and the property is sold by the lessor or any subsequent purchaser within three months after the date the property was originally placed in service by the lessor (or, in the case of multiple units of property subject to the same lease, within three months after the date the final unit is placed in service, so long as the period between the time the first unit is placed in service and the time the last unit is placed in service does not exceed 12 months), and the user of the property after the last sale during the three-month period remains the same as when the property was originally placed in service by the lessor, the purchaser of the property in the last sale during the three-month period is considered the taxpayer that acquired the property for purposes of applying paragraphs (b)(3)(ii) and (iii) of this section.

     (vi) *Examples.*—The application of this paragraph (b)(3) is illustrated by the following examples. Unless the facts specifically indicate otherwise, assume that the parties are not related within the meaning of section 179(d)(2)(A) or (B) and §1.179-4(c), no corporation is a member of a consolidated or controlled group, and the parties do not have predecessors:

     Example 1. (i) On August 1, 2018, *A* buys a new machine for $35,000 from an unrelated party for use in *A*'s trade or business. On July 1, 2020, *B* buys that machine from *A* for $20,000 for use in *B*'s trade or business. On October 1, 2020, *B* makes a $5,000 capital expenditure to recondition the machine. *B* did not have any depreciable interest in the machine before *B* acquired it on July 1, 2020.

     (ii) *A*'s purchase price of $35,000 satisfies the original use requirement of paragraph (b)(3)(ii) of this section and, assuming all other requirements are met, qualifies for the additional first year depreciation deduction.

     (iii) *B*'s purchase price of $20,000 does not satisfy the original use requirement of paragraph (b)(3)(ii) of this section, but it does satisfy the used property acquisition requirements of paragraph (b)(3)(iii) of this section. Assuming all other requirements are met, the $20,000 purchase price qualifies for the additional first year depreciation deduction. Further, *B*'s $5,000 expenditure satisfies the original use requirement of paragraph (b)(3)(ii) of this section and

assuming all other requirements are met, qualifies for the additional first year depreciation deduction, regardless of whether the $5,000 is added to the basis of the machine or is capitalized as a separate asset.

     Example 2. C, an automobile dealer, uses some of its automobiles as demonstrators in order to show them to prospective customers. The automobiles that are used as demonstrators by *C* are held by *C* primarily for sale to customers in the ordinary course of its business. On November 1, 2017, *D* buys from *C* an automobile that was previously used as a demonstrator by *C*. *D* will use the automobile solely for business purposes. The use of the automobile by *C* as a demonstrator does not constitute a "use" for purposes of the original use requirement and, therefore, *D* will be considered the original user of the automobile for purposes of paragraph (b)(3)(ii) of this section. Assuming all other requirements are met, *D*'s purchase price of the automobile qualifies for the additional first year depreciation deduction for *D*, subject to any limitation under section 280F.

     Example 3. On April 1, 2015, *E* acquires a horse to be used in *E*'s thoroughbred racing business. On October 1, 2018, *F* buys the horse from *E* and will use the horse in *F*'s horse breeding business. *F* did not have any depreciable interest in the horse before *F* acquired it on October 1, 2018. The use of the horse by *E* in its racing business prevents *F* from satisfying the original use requirement of paragraph (b)(3)(ii) of this section. However, *F*'s acquisition of the horse satisfies the used property acquisition requirements of paragraph (b)(3)(iii) of this section. Assuming all other requirements are met, *F*'s purchase price of the horse qualifies for the additional first year depreciation deduction for *F*.

     Example 4. In the ordinary course of its business, *G* sells fractional interests in its aircraft to unrelated parties. *G* holds out for sale eight equal fractional interests in an aircraft. On October 1, 2017, *G* sells five of the eight fractional interests in the aircraft to *H* and *H* begins to use its proportionate share of the aircraft immediately upon purchase. On February 1, 2018, *G* sells to *I* the remaining unsold $3/8$ fractional interests in the aircraft. *H* is considered the original user as to its $5/8$ fractional interest in the aircraft and *I* is considered the original user as to its $3/8$ fractional interest in the aircraft. Thus, assuming all other requirements are met, *H*'s purchase price for its $5/8$ fractional interest in the aircraft qualifies for the additional first year depreciation deduction and *I*'s purchase price for its $3/8$ fractional interest in the aircraft qualifies for the additional first year depreciation deduction.

     Example 5. On September 1, 2017, *J*, an equipment dealer, buys new tractors that are held by *J* primarily for sale to customers in the ordinary course of its business. On October 15, 2017, *J* withdraws the tractors from inventory and begins to use the tractors primarily for producing rental income. The holding of the tractors by *J* as inventory does not constitute a "use" for purposes of the original use requirement and, therefore, the original use of the tractors commences with *J* on October 15, 2017, for purposes of paragraph (b)(3)(ii) of this section. However, the tractors are not eligible for the 100-percent additional first year depreciation deduction because *J* acquired the tractors before September 28, 2017.

     Example 6. K is in the trade or business of leasing equipment to others. During 2016, *K* buys a new machine (Machine #1) and then leases it to *L* for use in *L*'s trade or business. The lease between *K* and *L* for Machine #1 is a true lease for federal income tax purposes. During 2018, *L* enters into a written binding contract with *K* to buy Machine #1 at its fair market value on May 15, 2018. *L* did not have any depreciable interest in Machine #1 before *L* acquired it on May 15, 2018. As a result, *L*'s acquisition of Machine #1 satisfies the used property acquisition requirements of paragraph (b)(3)(iii) of this section. Assuming all other requirements are met, *L*'s purchase price of Machine #1 qualifies for the additional first year depreciation deduction for *L*.

     Example 7. The facts are the same as in *Example 6* of this paragraph (b)(3)(vi), except that *K* and *L* are related parties within the meaning of section 179(d)(2)(A) or (B) and §1.179-4(c). As a result, *L*'s acquisition of Machine #1 does not satisfy the used property acquisition requirements of paragraph (b)(3)(iii) of this section. Thus, Machine #1 is not eligible for the additional first year depreciation deduction for *L*.

     Example 8. The facts are the same as in *Example 6* of this paragraph (b)(3)(vi), except *L* incurred capital expenditures of $5,000 to improve Machine #1 on September 5, 2017, and has a depreciable interest in such improvements. *L*'s purchase price of $5,000 for the improvements to Machine #1 satisfies the original use requirement of §1.168(k)-1(b)(3)(i) and, assuming all other requirements are met, qualifies for the 50-percent additional first year depreciation deduction. Because *L* had a depreciable interest only in the improvements to Machine #1, *L*'s acquisition of Machine #1, excluding *L*'s improvements to such machine, satisfies the used property acquisition requirements of paragraph (b)(3)(iii) of this section. Assuming all other requirements are met, *L*'s unadjusted depreciable basis of Machine #1, excluding the amount of such unadjusted depreciable basis attributable to *L*'s improvements to Machine #1, qualifies for the 100-percent additional first year depreciation deduction.

Example 9. During 2016, *M* and *N* purchased used equipment for use in their trades or businesses and each own a 50 percent interest in such equipment. Prior to this acquisition, *M* and *N* did not have any depreciable interest in the equipment. Assume this ownership arrangement is not a partnership. During 2018, *N* enters into a written binding contract with *M* to buy *M*'s interest in the equipment. Pursuant to paragraph (b)(3)(iii)(B)(2) of this section, *N* is not treated as using *M*'s interest in the equipment prior to *N*'s acquisition of *M*'s interest. As a result, *N*'s acquisition of *M*'s interest in the equipment satisfies the used property acquisition requirements of paragraph (b)(3)(iii) of this section. Assuming all other requirements are met, *N*'s purchase price of *M*'s interest in the equipment qualifies for the additional first year depreciation deduction for *N*.

Example 10. The facts are the same as in *Example 9* of this paragraph (b)(3)(vi), except *N* had a 100 percent depreciable interest in the equipment prior to 2016 and *M* purchased from *N* a 50 percent interest in the equipment during 2016. As a result, *N*'s acquisition of *M*'s interest in the equipment during 2018 does not satisfy the used property acquisition requirements of paragraphs (b)(3)(iii)(A)(1) and (b)(3)(iii)(B)(1) of this section. Paragraph (b)(3)(iii)(B)(2) of this section does not apply because *N* initially acquired a 100 percent depreciable interest in the equipment. Accordingly, *N*'s purchase price of *M*'s interest in the equipment during 2018 does not qualify for the additional first year depreciation deduction for *N*.

Example 11. The facts are the same as in *Example 9* of this paragraph (b)(3)(vi), except during 2018, *M* also enters into a written binding contract with *N* to buy *N*'s interest in the equipment. Pursuant to paragraph (b)(3)(iii)(B)(2) of this section, both *M* and *N* are treated as previously having a depreciable interest in a 50-percent portion of the equipment. Accordingly, the acquisition by *M* of *N*'s 50-percent interest and the acquisition by *N* of *M*'s 50-percent interest in the equipment during 2018 do not qualify for the additional first year depreciation deduction.

Example 12. *O* and *P* form an equal partnership, *OP*, in 2018. *O* contributes cash to *OP*, and *P* contributes equipment to *OP*. *OP*'s basis in the equipment contributed by *P* is determined under section 723. Because *OP*'s basis in such equipment is determined in whole or in part by reference to *P*'s adjusted basis in such equipment, *OP*'s acquisition of such equipment does not satisfy section 179(d)(2)(C) and §1.179-4(c)(1)(iv) and, thus, does not satisfy the used property acquisition requirements of paragraph (b)(3)(iii) of this section. Accordingly, *OP*'s acquisition of such equipment is not eligible for the additional first year depreciation deduction.

Example 13. *Q*, *R*, and *S* form an equal partnership, *QRS*, in 2019. Each partner contributes $100, which *QRS* uses to purchase a retail motor fuels outlet for $300. Assume this retail motor fuels outlet is *QRS*' only property and is qualified property under section 168(k)(2)(A)(i). *QRS* makes an election not to deduct the additional first year depreciation for all qualified property placed in service during 2019. *QRS* has a section 754 election in effect. *QRS* claimed depreciation of $15 for the retail motor fuels outlet for 2019. During 2020, when the retail motor fuels outlet's fair market value is $600, *Q* sells all of his partnership interest to *T* in a fully taxable transaction for $200. *T* never previously had a depreciable interest in the retail motor fuels outlet. *T* takes an outside basis of $200 in the partnership interest previously owned by *Q*. *T*'s share of the partnership's previously taxed capital is $95. Accordingly, *T*'s section 743(b) adjustment is $105 and is allocated entirely to the retail motor fuels outlet under section 755. Assuming all other requirements are met, *T*'s section 743(b) adjustment qualifies for the additional first year depreciation deduction.

Example 14. The facts are the same as in *Example 13* of this paragraph (b)(3)(vi), except that *Q* sells his partnership interest to *U*, a related person within the meaning of section 179(d)(2)(A) or (B) and §1.179-4(c). *U*'s section 743(b) adjustment does not qualify for the additional first year depreciation deduction.

Example 15. The facts are the same as in *Example 13* of this paragraph (b)(3)(vi), except that *Q* dies and his partnership interest is transferred to *V*. *V* takes a basis in *Q*'s partnership interest under section 1014. As a result, section 179(d)(2)(C)(ii) and §1.179-4(c)(1)(iv) are not satisfied, and *V*'s section 743(b) adjustment does not qualify for the additional first year depreciation deduction.

Example 16. The facts are the same as in *Example 13* of this paragraph (b)(3)(vi), except that *QRS* purchased the retail motor fuels outlet from *T* prior to *T* purchasing *Q*'s partnership interest in *QRS*. *T* had a depreciable interest in such retail motor fuels outlet. Because *T* had a depreciable interest in the retail motor fuels outlet before *T* acquired its interest in *QRS*, *T*'s section 743(b) adjustment does not qualify for the additional first year depreciation deduction.

Example 17. In November 2017, AA Corporation purchases a used drill press costing $10,000 and is granted a trade-in allowance of $2,000 on its old drill press. The used drill press is qualified property under section 168(k)(2)(A)(i). The old drill press had a basis of $1,200. Under sections 1012 and 1031(d), the basis of the used drill press is $9,200 ($1,200 basis of old drill press plus cash expended of $8,000). Only $8,000 of the basis of the used drill press satisfies the require-

ments of section 179(d)(3) and §1.179-4(d) and, thus, satisfies the used property acquisition requirement of paragraph (b)(3)(iii) of this section. The remaining $1,200 of the basis of the used drill press does not satisfy the requirements of section 179(d)(3) and §1.179-4(d) because it is determined by reference to the old drill press. Accordingly, assuming all other requirements are met, only $8,000 of the basis of the used drill press is eligible for the additional first year depreciation deduction.

[*Examples 18* through *22* withdrawn by REG-106808-19 on September 24, 2019.]

Example 23. (i) J Corporation, K Corporation, and L Corporation are unrelated parties within the meaning of section 179(d)(2)(A) or (B) and §1.179-4(c). None of J Corporation, K Corporation, and L Corporation is a member of a consolidated group. J Corporation has a depreciable interest in Equipment #5. During 2018, J Corporation sells Equipment #5 to K Corporation. During 2020, J Corporation merges into L Corporation in a transaction described in section 368(a)(1)(A). In 2021, L Corporation acquires Equipment #5 from K Corporation.

(ii) Because J Corporation is the predecessor of L Corporation and J Corporation previously had a depreciable interest in Equipment #5, L Corporation's acquisition of Equipment #5 does not satisfy paragraphs (b)(3)(iii)(A)(1) and (b)(3)(iii)(B)(1) of this section and, thus, does not satisfy the used property acquisition requirements of paragraph (b)(3)(iii) of this section. Accordingly, L Corporation's acquisition of Equipment #5 is not eligible for the additional first year depreciation deduction.

Example 24. (i) M Corporation acquires and places in service a used airplane on March 26, 2018. Prior to this acquisition, M Corporation never had a depreciable interest in this airplane. On March 26, 2018, M Corporation also leases the used airplane to N Corporation, an airline company. On May 27, 2018, M Corporation sells to O Corporation the used airplane subject to the lease with N Corporation. M Corporation and O Corporation are related parties within the meaning of section 179(d)(2)(A) or (B) and §1.179-4(c). As of May 27, 2018, N Corporation is still the lessee of the used airplane. Prior to this acquisition, O Corporation never had a depreciable interest in the used airplane. O Corporation is a calendar-year taxpayer.

(ii) The sale transaction of May 27, 2018, satisfies the requirements of paragraph (b)(3)(v) of this section. As a result, O Corporation is considered the taxpayer that acquired the used airplane for purposes of applying the used property acquisition requirements in paragraph (b)(3)(iii) of this section. In applying these rules, the fact that M Corporation and O Corporation are related parties is not taken into account because O Corporation, not M Corporation, is treated as acquiring the used airplane. Further, pursuant to paragraph (b)(4)(iv) of this section, the used airplane is treated as originally placed in service by O Corporation on May 27, 2018. Because O Corporation never had a depreciable interest in the used airplane and assuming all other requirements are met, O Corporation's purchase price of the used airplane qualifies for the 100-percent additional first year depreciation deduction for O Corporation.

Example 25. (i) The facts are the same as in *Example 24* of this paragraph (b)(3)(vi). Additionally, on September 5, 2018, O Corporation sells to P Corporation the used airplane subject to the lease with N Corporation. Prior to this acquisition, P Corporation never had a depreciable interest in the used airplane.

(ii) Because O Corporation, a calendar-year taxpayer, placed in service and disposed of the used airplane during 2018, the used airplane is not eligible for the additional first year depreciation deduction for O Corporation pursuant to paragraph (f)(1)(i) of this section.

(iii) Because P Corporation never had a depreciable interest in the used airplane and assuming all other requirements are met, P Corporation's purchase price of the used airplane qualifies for the 100-percent additional first year depreciation deduction for P Corporation.

(4) *Placed-in-service date.*—(i) *In general.*—Depreciable property will meet the requirements of this paragraph (b)(4) if the property is placed in service by the taxpayer for use in its trade or business or for production of income after September 27, 2017; and, except as provided in paragraphs (b)(2)(i)(A) and (D) of this section, before January 1, 2027, or, in the case of property described in section 168(k)(2)(B) or (C), before January 1, 2028.

(ii) *Specified plant.*—If the taxpayer has properly made an election to apply section 168(k)(5) for a specified plant, the requirements of this paragraph (b)(4) are satisfied only if the specified plant is planted before January 1, 2027, or is grafted before January 1, 2027, to a plant that has already been planted, by the taxpayer in the ordinary course of the taxpayer's farming business, as defined in section 263A(e)(4).

(iii) *Qualified film, television, or live theatrical production.*—(A) For purposes of this paragraph (b)(4), a qualified film or television production is treated as placed in service at the time of initial release or broadcast as defined under § 1.181-1(a)(7).

(B) For purposes of this paragraph (b)(4), a qualified live theatrical production is treated as placed in service at the time of the initial live staged performance. Solely for purposes of this paragraph, the term *initial live staged performance* means the first commercial exhibition of a production to an audience. However, the term *initial live staged performance* does not include limited exhibition, prior to commercial exhibition to general audiences, if the limited exhibition is primarily for purposes of publicity, determining the need for further production activity, or raising funds for the completion of production. For example, an initial live staged performance does not include a preview of the production if the preview is primarily to determine the need for further production activity.

(iv) *Syndication transaction.*—If a lessor has a depreciable interest in the property and the lessor and any predecessor did not previously have a depreciable interest in the property, and the property is sold by the lessor or any subsequent purchaser within three months after the date the property was originally placed in service by the lessor (or, in the case of multiple units of property subject to the same lease, within three months after the date the final unit is placed in service, so long as the period between the time the first unit is placed in service and the time the last unit is placed in service does not exceed 12 months), and the user of the property after the last sale during this three-month period remains the same as when the property was originally placed in service by the lessor, the property is treated as originally placed in service by the purchaser of the property in the last sale during the three-month period but not earlier than the date of the last sale.

(v) *Technical termination of a partnership.*—For purposes of this paragraph (b)(4), in the case of a technical termination of a partnership under section 708(b)(1)(B) occurring in a taxable year beginning before January 1, 2018, qualified property placed in service by the terminated partnership during the taxable year of termination is treated as originally placed in service by the new partnership on the date the qualified property is contributed by the terminated partnership to the new partnership.

(vi) *Section 168(i)(7) transactions.*—For purposes of this paragraph (b)(4), if qualified property is transferred in a transaction described in section 168(i)(7) in the same taxable year that the qualified property is placed in service by the transferor, the transferred property is treated as originally placed in service on the date the transferor placed in service the qualified property. In the case of multiple transfers of qualified property in multiple transactions described in section 168(i)(7) in the same taxable year, the placed-in-service date of the transferred property is deemed to be the date on which the first transferor placed in service the qualified property.

(5) *Acquisition of property.*—(i) *In general.*—This paragraph (b)(5) provides rules for the acquisition requirements in section 13201(h) of the Act. These rules apply to all property, including self-constructed property or property described in section 168(k)(2)(B) or (C).

(ii) *Acquisition date.*—Except as provided in paragraph (b)(5)(vi) of this section, depreciable property will meet the requirements of this paragraph (b)(5) if the property is acquired by the taxpayer after September 27, 2017, or is acquired by the taxpayer pursuant to a written binding contract entered into by the taxpayer after September 27, 2017. Property that is manufactured, constructed, or produced for the taxpayer by another person under a written binding contract that is entered into prior to the manufacture, construction, or production of the property for use by the taxpayer in its trade or business or for its production of income is acquired pursuant to a written binding contract. If a taxpayer acquired the property pursuant to a written binding contract and such contract states the date on which the contract was entered into and a closing date, delivery date, or other similar date, the date on which the contract was entered into is the date the taxpayer acquired the property. See paragraph (b)(5)(v) of this section for when a qualified film, television, or live theatrical production is treated as acquired for purposes of this paragraph (b)(5).

(iii) *Definition of binding contract.*—(A) *In general.*—A contract is binding only if it is enforceable under State law against the taxpayer or a predecessor, and does not limit damages to a specified amount (for example, by use of a liquidated damages provision). For this purpose, a contractual provision that limits damages to an amount equal to at least 5 percent of the total contract price will not be treated as limiting damages to a specified amount. In determining whether a contract limits damages, the fact that there may be little or no damages because the contract price does not significantly differ from fair market value will not be taken into account. For example, if a taxpayer entered into an irrevocable written contract to purchase an asset for $100 and the contract did not contain a provision for

liquidated damages, the contract is considered binding notwithstanding the fact that the asset had a fair market value of $99 and under local law the seller would only recover the difference in the event the purchaser failed to perform. If the contract provided for a full refund of the purchase price in lieu of any damages allowable by law in the event of breach or cancellation, the contract is not considered binding.

(B) *Conditions.*—A contract is binding even if subject to a condition, as long as the condition is not within the control of either party or a predecessor. A contract will continue to be binding if the parties make insubstantial changes in its terms and conditions or if any term is to be determined by a standard beyond the control of either party. A contract that imposes significant obligations on the taxpayer or a predecessor will be treated as binding notwithstanding the fact that certain terms remain to be negotiated by the parties to the contract.

(C) *Options.*—An option to either acquire or sell property is not a binding contract.

(D) *Letter of intent.*—A letter of intent for an acquisition is not a binding contract.

(E) *Supply agreements.*—A binding contract does not include a supply or similar agreement if the amount and design specifications of the property to be purchased have not been specified. The contract will not be a binding contract for the property to be purchased until both the amount and the design specifications are specified. For example, if the provisions of a supply or similar agreement state the design specifications of the property to be purchased, a purchase order under the agreement for a specific number of assets is treated as a binding contract.

(F) *Components.*—A binding contract to acquire one or more components of a larger property will not be treated as a binding contract to acquire the larger property. If a binding contract to acquire the component does not satisfy the requirements of this paragraph (b)(5), the component does not qualify for the additional first year depreciation deduction.

(iv) *Self-constructed property.*—(A) *In general.*—If a taxpayer manufactures, constructs, or produces property for use by the taxpayer in its trade or business or for its production of income, the acquisition rules in paragraph (b)(5)(ii) of this section are treated as met for the property if the taxpayer begins manufacturing, constructing, or producing the property after September 27, 2017. This paragraph (b)(5)(iv) does not apply to property that is manufactured, constructed, or produced for the taxpayer by another person under a written binding contract that is entered into prior to the manufacture, construction, or production of the property for use by the taxpayer in its trade or business or for its production of income (for further guidance, see paragraphs (b)(5)(ii) and (iii) of this section).

(B) *When does manufacture, construction, or production begin.*—(1) *In general.*—For purposes of paragraph (b)(5)(iv)(A) of this section, manufacture, construction, or production of property begins when physical work of a significant nature begins. Physical work does not include preliminary activities such as planning or designing, securing financing, exploring, or researching. The determination of when physical work of a significant nature begins depends on the facts and circumstances. For example, if the taxpayer constructs a retail motor fuels outlet on-site for use by the taxpayer in its trade or business, construction begins when physical work of a significant nature commences at the site by the taxpayer; that is, when work begins on the excavation for footings, pouring the pads for the outlet, or the driving of foundation pilings into the ground. Preliminary work, such as clearing a site, test drilling to determine soil condition, or excavation to change the contour of the land (as distinguished from excavation for footings) does not constitute the beginning of construction. However, if the taxpayer assembles a retail motor fuels outlet on-site from modular units manufactured off-site by the taxpayer and delivered to the site where the outlet will be used, manufacturing begins when physical work of a significant nature commences at the off-site location by the taxpayer.

(2) *Safe harbor.*—For purposes of paragraph (b)(5)(iv)(B)(1) of this section, a taxpayer may choose to determine when physical work of a significant nature begins in accordance with this paragraph (b)(5)(iv)(B)(2). Physical work of a significant nature will be considered to begin at the time the taxpayer incurs (in the case of an accrual basis taxpayer) or pays (in the case of a cash basis taxpayer) more than 10 percent of the total cost of the property (excluding the cost of any land and preliminary activities such as planning or designing, securing financing, exploring, or researching). A taxpayer chooses to apply this paragraph (b)(5)(iv)(B)(2) by filing a federal income tax return for the placed-in-service year of the property that determines when physical work of a significant nature begins consistent with this paragraph (b)(5)(iv)(B)(2).

(C) *Components of self-constructed property.—(1) Acquired components.*—If a binding contract, as defined in paragraph (b)(5)(iii) of this section, to acquire a component does not satisfy the requirements of paragraph (b)(5)(ii) of this section, the component does not qualify for the additional first year depreciation deduction. A binding contract described in the preceding sentence to acquire one or more components of a larger self-constructed property will not preclude the larger self-constructed property from satisfying the acquisition rules in paragraph (b)(5)(iv)(A) of this section. Accordingly, the unadjusted depreciable basis of the larger self-constructed property that is eligible for the additional first year depreciation deduction, assuming all other requirements are met, must not include the unadjusted depreciable basis of any component that does not satisfy the requirements of paragraph (b)(5)(ii) of this section. If the manufacture, construction, or production of the larger self-constructed property begins before September 28, 2017, the larger self-constructed property and any acquired components related to the larger self-constructed property do not qualify for the additional first year depreciation deduction under this section.

(2) Self-constructed components.—If the manufacture, construction, or production of a component by the taxpayer does not satisfy the requirements of this paragraph (b)(5)(iv), the component does not qualify for the additional first year depreciation deduction. However, if the manufacture, construction, or production of a component does not satisfy the requirements of this paragraph (b)(5)(iv), but the manufacture, construction, or production of the larger self-constructed property satisfies the requirements of this paragraph (b)(5)(iv), the larger self-constructed property qualifies for the additional first year depreciation deduction, assuming all other requirements are met, even though the component does not qualify for the additional first year depreciation deduction. Accordingly, the unadjusted depreciable basis of the larger self-constructed property that is eligible for the additional first year depreciation deduction, assuming all other requirements are met, must not include the unadjusted depreciable basis of any component that does not qualify for the additional first year depreciation deduction. If the manufacture, construction, or production of the larger self-constructed property began before September 28, 2017, the larger self-constructed property and any self-constructed components related to the larger self-constructed property do not qualify for the additional first year depreciation deduction under this section.

(v) *Qualified film, television, or live theatrical production.*—(A) For purposes of section 13201(h)(1)(A) of the Act, a qualified film or television production is treated as acquired on the date principal photography commences.

(B) For purposes of section 13201(h)(1)(A) of the Act, a qualified live theatrical production is treated as acquired on the date when all of the necessary elements for producing the live theatrical production are secured. These elements may include a script, financing, actors, set, scenic and costume designs, advertising agents, music, and lighting.

(vi) *Specified plant.*—If the taxpayer has properly made an election to apply section 168(k)(5) for a specified plant, the requirements of this paragraph (b)(5) are satisfied if the specified plant is planted after September 27, 2017, or is grafted after September 27, 2017, to a plant that has already been planted, by the taxpayer in the ordinary course of the taxpayer's farming business, as defined in section 263A(e)(4).

(vii) *Examples.*—The application of this paragraph (b)(5) is illustrated by the following examples. Unless the facts specifically indicate otherwise, assume that the parties are not related within the meaning of section 179(d)(2)(A) or (B) and § 1.179-4(c), and the parties do not have predecessors:

Example 1. On September 1, 2017, *BB*, a corporation, entered into a written agreement with *CC*, a manufacturer, to purchase 20 new lamps for $100 each within the next two years. Although the agreement specifies the number of lamps to be purchased, the agreement does not specify the design of the lamps to be purchased. Accordingly, the agreement is not a binding contract pursuant to paragraph (b)(5)(iii)(E) of this section.

Example 2. The facts are the same as in *Example 1* of this paragraph (b)(5)(vii). On December 1, 2017, *BB* placed a purchase order with *CC* to purchase 20 new model XPC5 lamps for $100 each for a total amount of $2,000. Because the agreement specifies the number of lamps to be purchased and the purchase order specifies the design of the lamps to be purchased, the purchase order placed by *BB* with *CC* on December 1, 2017, is a binding contract pursuant to paragraph (b)(5)(iii)(E) of this section. Accordingly, assuming all other requirements are met, the cost of the 20 lamps qualifies for the 100-percent additional first year depreciation deduction.

Example 3. The facts are the same as in *Example 1* of this paragraph (b)(5)(vii), except that the written agreement between *BB* and *CC* is to purchase 100 model XPC5 lamps for $100 each within the next two years. Because this agreement specifies the amount and design of the lamps to be purchased, the agreement is a binding contract pursuant to paragraph (b)(5)(iii)(E) of this section. However, because the agreement was entered into before September 28, 2017, no lamp acquired by *BB* under this contract qualifies for the 100-percent additional first year depreciation deduction.

Example 4. On September 1, 2017, *DD* began constructing a retail motor fuels outlet for its own use. On November 1, 2018, *DD* ceases construction of the retail motor fuels outlet prior to its completion. Between September 1, 2017, and November 1, 2018, *DD* incurred $3,000,000 of expenditures for the construction of the retail motor fuels outlet. On May 1, 2019, *DD* resumed construction of the retail motor fuels outlet and completed its construction on August 31, 2019. Between May 1, 2019, and August 31, 2019, *DD* incurred another $1,600,000 of expenditures to complete the construction of the retail motor fuels outlet and, on September 1, 2019, *DD* placed the retail motor fuels outlet in service. None of *DD*'s total expenditures of $4,600,000 qualify for the 100-percent additional first year depreciation deduction because, pursuant to paragraph (b)(5)(iv)(A) of this section, *DD* began constructing the retail motor fuels outlet before September 28, 2017.

Example 5. The facts are the same as in *Example 4* of this paragraph (b)(5)(vii) except that *DD* began constructing the retail motor fuels outlet for its own use on October 1, 2017, and *DD* incurred the $3,000,000 between October 1, 2017, and November 1, 2018. *DD*'s total expenditures of $4,600,000 qualify for the 100-percent additional first year depreciation deduction because, pursuant to paragraph (b)(5)(iv)(A) of this section, *DD* began constructing the retail motor fuels outlet after September 27, 2017, and *DD* placed the retail motor fuels outlet in service on September 1, 2019. Accordingly, assuming all other requirements are met, the additional first year depreciation deduction for the retail motor fuels outlet will be $4,600,000, computed as $4,600,000 multiplied by 100 percent.

Example 6. On August 15, 2017, *EE* entered into a written binding contract with *FF* to manufacture an aircraft described in section 168(k)(2)(C) for use in *EE*'s trade or business. *FF* begins to manufacture the aircraft on October 1, 2017. *EE* places the aircraft in service on March 1, 2018. Pursuant to paragraph (b)(5)(ii) of this section, the aircraft is acquired by *EE* pursuant to a written binding contract. Because *EE* entered into such contract before September 28, 2017, the aircraft does not qualify for the 100-percent additional first year depreciation deduction.

Example 7. On June 1, 2017, *HH* entered into a written binding contract to acquire a new component part of property that is being constructed by *HH* for its own use in its trade or business. *HH* commenced construction of the property in November 2017, and placed the property in service in November 2018. Because *HH* entered into a written binding contract to acquire a component part prior to September 28, 2017, pursuant to paragraphs (b)(5)(ii) and (b)(5)(iv)(C)(1) of this section, the component part does not qualify for the 100-percent additional first year depreciation deduction. However, pursuant to paragraphs (b)(5)(iv)(A) and (b)(5)(iv)(C)(1) of this section, the property constructed by *HH* will qualify for the 100-percent additional first year depreciation deduction, because construction of the property began after September 27, 2017, assuming all other requirements are met. Accordingly, the unadjusted depreciable basis of the property that is eligible for the 100-percent additional first year depreciation deduction must not include the unadjusted depreciable basis of the component part.

Example 8. The facts are the same as in *Example 7* of this paragraph (b)(5)(vii) except that *HH* entered into the written binding contract to acquire the new component part on September 30, 2017, and *HH* commenced construction of the property on August 1, 2017. Pursuant to paragraphs (b)(5)(iv)(A) and (C) of this section, neither the property constructed by *HH* nor the component part will qualify for the 100-percent additional first year depreciation deduction, because *HH* began construction of the property prior to September 28, 2017.

Example 9. On September 1, 2017, *II* acquired and placed in service equipment. On October 15, 2017, *II* sells the equipment to *JJ* and leases the property back from *JJ* in a sale-leaseback transaction. Pursuant to paragraph (b)(5)(ii) of this section, *II*'s cost of the equipment does not qualify for the 100-percent additional first year depreciation deduction because *II* acquired the equipment prior to September 28, 2017. However, *JJ* acquired used equipment from an unrelated party after September 27, 2017, and, assuming all other requirements are met, *JJ*'s cost of the used equipment does qualify for the 100-percent additional first year depreciation deduction for *JJ*.

Example 10. On July 1, 2017, *KK* began constructing property for its own use in its trade or business. *KK* placed this property in service on September 15, 2017. On October 15, 2017, *KK* sells the property to *LL* and leases the property back from *LL* in a sale-leaseback transaction. Pursuant to paragraph (b)(5)(iv) of this section, *KK*'s cost of the property does not qualify for the 100-percent additional first year depreciation deduction because construction began prior to September 28, 2017. However, *LL* acquired used property from an unrelated party after September 27, 2017, and, assuming all other requirements are met, *LL*'s cost of the used property does qualify for the 100-percent additional first year depreciation deduction for *LL*.

(c) *Property described in section 168(k)(2)(B) or (C).*—(1) *In general.*—Property described in section 168(k)(2)(B) or (C) will meet the acquisition requirements of section 168(k)(2)(B)(i)(III) or (k)(2)(C)(i) if the property is acquired by the taxpayer before January 1, 2027, or acquired by the taxpayer pursuant to a written binding contract that is entered into before January 1, 2027. Property described in section 168(k)(2)(B) or (C) also must meet the acquisition requirement in section 13201(h)(1)(A) of the Act (for further guidance, see paragraph (b)(5) of this section).

(2) *Definition of binding contract.*—For purposes of this paragraph (c), the rules in paragraph (b)(5)(iii) of this section for a binding contract apply.

(3) *Self-constructed property.*—(i) *In general.*—If a taxpayer manufactures, constructs, or produces property for use by the taxpayer in its trade or business or for its production of income, the acquisition rules in paragraph (c)(1) of this section are treated as met for the property if the taxpayer begins manufacturing, constructing, or producing the property before January 1, 2027. Property that is manufactured, constructed, or produced for the taxpayer by another person under a written binding contract, as defined in paragraph (b)(5)(iii) of this section, that is entered into prior to the manufacture, construction, or production of the property for use by the taxpayer in its trade or business or for its production of income is considered to be manufactured, constructed, or produced by the taxpayer. If a taxpayer enters into a written binding contract, as defined in paragraph (b)(5)(iii) of this section, before January 1, 2027, with another person to manufacture, construct, or produce property described in section 168(k)(2)(B) or (C) and the manufacture, construction, or production of this property begins after December 31, 2026, the acquisition rule in paragraph (c)(1) of this section is met.

(ii) *When does manufacture, construction, or production begin.*—(A) *In general.*—For purposes of this paragraph (c)(3), manufacture, construction, or production of property begins when physical work of a significant nature begins. Physical work does not include preliminary activities such as planning or designing, securing financing, exploring, or researching. The determination of when physical work of a significant nature begins depends on the facts and circumstances. For example, if a retail motor fuels outlet is to be constructed on-site, construction begins when physical work of a significant nature commences at the site; that is, when work begins on the excavation for footings, pouring the pads for the outlet, or the driving of foundation pilings into the ground. Preliminary work, such as clearing a site, test drilling to determine soil condition, or excavation to change the contour of the land (as distinguished from excavation for footings) does not constitute the beginning of construction. However, if a retail motor fuels outlet is to be assembled on-site from modular units manufactured off-site and delivered to the site where the outlet will be used, manufacturing begins when physical work of a significant nature commences at the off-site location.

(B) *Safe harbor.*—For purposes of paragraph (c)(3)(ii)(A) of this section, a taxpayer may choose to determine when physical work of a significant nature begins in accordance with this paragraph (c)(3)(ii)(B). Physical work of a significant nature will be considered to begin at the time the taxpayer incurs (in the case of an accrual basis taxpayer) or pays (in the case of a cash basis taxpayer) more than 10 percent of the total cost of the property (excluding the cost of any land and preliminary activities such as planning or designing, securing financing, exploring, or researching). When property is manufactured, constructed, or produced for the taxpayer by another person, this safe harbor test must be satisfied by the taxpayer. For example, if a retail motor fuels outlet is to be constructed for an accrual basis taxpayer by another person for the total cost of $200,000 (excluding the cost of any land and preliminary activities such as planning or designing, securing financing, exploring, or researching), construction is deemed to begin for purposes of this paragraph (c)(3)(ii)(B) when the taxpayer has incurred more than 10 percent (more than $20,000) of the total cost of the property. A taxpayer chooses to apply this paragraph (c)(3)(ii)(B) by filing a federal income tax return for the placed-in-service year of the property that determines when physical work of a significant nature begins consistent with this paragraph (c)(3)(ii)(B).

(iii) *Components of self-constructed property.*—(A) *Acquired components.*—If a binding contract, as defined in paragraph (b)(5)(iii) of this section, to acquire a component does not satisfy the requirements of paragraph (c)(1) of this section, the component does not qualify for the additional first year depreciation deduction. A binding contract described in the preceding sentence to acquire one or more components of a larger self-constructed property will not pre-clude the larger self-constructed property from satisfying the acquisition rules in paragraph (c)(3)(i) of this section. Accordingly, the unadjusted depreciable basis of the larger self-constructed property that is eligible for the additional first year depreciation deduction, assuming all other requirements are met, must not include the unadjusted depreciable basis of any component that does not satisfy the requirements of paragraph (c)(1) of this section. If a binding contract to acquire the component is entered into before January 1, 2027, but the manufacture, construction, or production of the larger self-constructed property does not begin before January 1, 2027, the component qualifies for the additional first year depreciation deduction, assuming all other requirements are met, but the larger self-constructed property does not.

(B) *Self-constructed components.*—If the manufacture, construction, or production of a component by the taxpayer does not satisfy the requirements of paragraph (c)(3)(i) of this section, the component does not qualify for the additional first year depreciation deduction. However, if the manufacture, construction, or production of a component does not satisfy the requirements of paragraph (c)(3)(i) of this section, but the manufacture, construction, or production of the larger self-constructed property satisfies the requirements of paragraph (c)(3)(i) of this section, the larger self-constructed property qualifies for the additional first year depreciation deduction, assuming all other requirements are met, even though the component does not qualify for the additional first year depreciation deduction. Accordingly, the unadjusted depreciable basis of the larger self-constructed property that is eligible for the additional first year depreciation deduction, assuming all other requirements are met, must not include the unadjusted depreciable basis of any component that does not qualify for the additional first year depreciation deduction. If the manufacture, construction, or production of a component begins before January 1, 2027, but the manufacture, construction, or production of the larger self-constructed property does not begin before January 1, 2027, the component qualifies for the additional first year depreciation deduction, assuming all other requirements are met, but the larger self-constructed property does not.

(iv) *Examples.*—The application of this paragraph (c) is illustrated by the following examples:

Example 1. On June 1, 2017, *MM* decided to construct property described in section 168(k)(2)(B) for its own use. However, one of the component parts of the property had to be manufactured by another person for *MM*. On August 15, 2017, *MM* entered into a written binding contract with *NN* to acquire this component part of the property for $100,000. The manufacture of the component part commenced on September 1, 2018, and *MM* received the completed component part on February 1, 2020. The cost of this component part is 9 percent of the total cost of the property to be constructed by *MM*. *MM* began constructing the property described in section 168(k)(2)(B) on January 15, 2020, and placed this property, including all component parts, in service on November 1, 2021. Pursuant to paragraphs (b)(5)(iv)(C)(*1*) and (c)(1) of this section, the component part of $100,000 manufactured by *NN* for *MM* is not eligible for the 100-percent additional first year depreciation deduction because the written binding contract to acquire such component part was entered into before September 28, 2017. However, pursuant to paragraph (c)(3)(i) of this section, the cost of the property described in section 168(k)(2)(B), excluding the cost of the component part of $100,000 manufactured by *NN* for *MM*, is eligible for the 100-percent additional first year depreciation deduction, assuming all other requirements are met, because construction of the property began after September 27, 2017, and before January 1, 2027, and the property described in section 168(k)(2)(B) was placed in service by *MM* before January 1, 2028.

Example 2. On June 1, 2026, *OO* decided to construct property described in section 168(k)(2)(B) for its own use. However, one of the component parts of the property had to be manufactured by another person for *OO*. On August 15, 2026, *OO* entered into a written binding contract with *PP* to acquire this component part of the property for $100,000. The manufacture of the component part commenced on September 1, 2026, and *OO* received the completed component part on February 1, 2027. The cost of this component part is 9 percent of the total cost of the property to be constructed by *OO*. *OO* began constructing the property described in section 168(k)(2)(B) on January 15, 2027, and placed this property, including all component parts, in service on November 1, 2027. Pursuant to paragraph (c)(3)(iii)(B) of this section, the self-constructed component part of $100,000 manufactured by *PP* for *OO* is eligible for the additional first year depreciation deduction, assuming all other requirements are met, because the manufacturing of the component part began before January 1, 2027, and the property described in section 168(k)(2)(B), the larger self-constructed property, was placed in service by *OO* before January 1, 2028. However, pursuant to paragraph (c)(3)(i) of this section, the cost of the property described in section 168(k)(2)(B), excluding the cost of the self-constructed component part of $100,000 manufactured by *PP* for *OO*, is not eligible for the additional first year depreciation deduction because construction of the property began after December 31, 2026.

Example 3. On December 1, 2026, *QQ* entered into a written binding contract, as defined in paragraph (b)(5)(iii) of this section, with *RR* to manufacture an aircraft described in section 168(k)(2)(C) for use in *QQ's* trade or business. *RR* begins to manufacture the aircraft on February 1, 2027. *QQ* places the aircraft in service on August 1, 2027. Pursuant to paragraph (c)(3)(i) of this section, the aircraft meets the requirements of paragraph (c)(1) of this section because the aircraft was acquired by *QQ* pursuant to a written binding contract entered into before January 1, 2027. Further, the aircraft was placed in service by *QQ* before January 1, 2028. Thus, assuming all other requirements are met, *QQ's* cost of the aircraft is eligible for the additional first year depreciation deduction.

(d) *Computation of depreciation deduction for qualified property.*—(1) *Additional first year depreciation deduction.*—(i) *Allowable taxable year.*—The additional first year depreciation deduction is allowable—

(A) Except as provided in paragraph (d)(1)(i)(B) or (f) of this section, in the taxable year in which the qualified property is placed in service by the taxpayer for use in its trade or business or for the production of income; or

(B) In the taxable year in which the specified plant is planted, or grafted to a plant that has already been planted, by the taxpayer in the ordinary course of the taxpayer's farming business, as defined in section 263A(e)(4), if the taxpayer properly made the election to apply section 168(k)(5) (for further guidance, see paragraph (e) of this section).

(ii) *Computation.*—Except as provided in paragraph (f)(5) of this section, the allowable additional first year depreciation deduction for qualified property is determined by multiplying the unadjusted depreciable basis, as defined in § 1.168(b)-1a(3), of the qualified property by the applicable percentage. Except as provided in paragraph (f)(1) of this section, the additional first year depreciation deduction is not affected by a taxable year of less than 12 months. See paragraph (f)(1) of this section for qualified property placed in service or planted or grafted, as applicable, and disposed of during the same taxable year. See paragraph (f)(5) of this section for qualified property acquired in a like-kind exchange or as a result of an involuntary conversion.

(iii) *Property described in section 168(k)(2)(B).*—For purposes of paragraph (d)(1)(ii) of this section, the unadjusted depreciable basis, as defined in § 1.168(b)-1(a)(3), of qualified property described in section 168(k)(2)(B) is limited to the property's unadjusted depreciable basis attributable to the property's manufacture, construction, or production before January 1, 2027.

(iv) *Alternative minimum tax.*—(A) *In general.*—The additional first year depreciation deduction is allowable for alternative minimum tax purposes—

(1) Except as provided in paragraph (d)(1)(iv)(A)(2) of this section, in the taxable year in which the qualified property is placed in service by the taxpayer; or

(2) In the taxable year in which a specified plant is planted by the taxpayer, or grafted by the taxpayer to a plant that was previously planted, if the taxpayer properly made the election to apply section 168(k)(5) (for further guidance, see paragraph (e) of this section).

(B) *Special rules.*—In general, the additional first year depreciation deduction for alternative minimum tax purposes is based on the unadjusted depreciable basis of the property for alternative minimum tax purposes. However, see paragraph (f)(5)(iii)(E) of this section for qualified property acquired in a like-kind exchange or as a result of an involuntary conversion.

(2) *Otherwise allowable depreciation deduction.*—(i) *In general.*—Before determining the amount otherwise allowable as a depreciation deduction for the qualified property for the placed-in-service year and any subsequent taxable year, the taxpayer must determine the remaining adjusted depreciable basis of the qualified property. This remaining adjusted depreciable basis is equal to the unadjusted depreciable basis, as defined in § 1.168(b)-1(a)(3), of the qualified property reduced by the amount of the additional first year depreciation allowed or allowable, whichever is greater. The remaining adjusted depreciable basis of the qualified property is then depreciated using the applicable depreciation provisions under the Internal Revenue Code for the qualified property. The remaining adjusted depreciable basis of the qualified property that is MACRS property is also the basis to which the annual depreciation rates in the optional depreciation tables apply (for further guidance, see section 8 of Rev. Proc. 87-57 (1987-2 C.B. 687) and § 601.601(d)(2)(ii)(b) of this chapter). The depreciation deduction allowable for the remaining adjusted depreciable basis of the qualified property is affected by a taxable year of less than 12 months.

(ii) *Alternative minimum tax.*—For alternative minimum tax purposes, the depreciation deduction allowable for the remaining adjusted depreciable basis of the qualified property is based on the remaining adjusted depreciable basis for alternative minimum tax purposes. The remaining adjusted depreciable basis of the qualified property for alternative minimum tax purposes is depreciated using the same depreciation method, recovery period (or useful life in the case of computer software), and convention that apply to the qualified property for regular tax purposes.

(3) *Examples.*—This paragraph (d) is illustrated by the following examples:

Example 1. On March 1, 2023, *SS*, a calendar-year taxpayer, purchased and placed in service qualified property that costs $1 million and is 5-year property under section 168(e). *SS* depreciates its 5-year property placed in service in 2023 using the optional depreciation table that corresponds with the general depreciation system, the 200-percent declining balance method, a 5-year recovery period, and the half-year convention. For 2023, *SS* is allowed an 80-percent additional first year depreciation deduction of $800,000 (the unadjusted depreciable basis of $1 million multiplied by 0.80). Next, *SS* must reduce the unadjusted depreciable basis of $1 million by the additional first year depreciation deduction of $800,000 to determine the remaining adjusted depreciable basis of $200,000. Then, *SS'* depreciation deduction allowable in 2023 for the remaining adjusted depreciable basis of $200,000 is $40,000 (the remaining adjusted depreciable basis of $200,000 multiplied by the annual depreciation rate of 0.20 for recovery year 1).

Example 2. On June 1, 2023, *TT*, a calendar-year taxpayer, purchased and placed in service qualified property that costs $1,500,000. The property qualifies for the expensing election under section 179 and is 5-year property under section 168(e). *TT* did not purchase any other section 179 property in 2023. *TT* makes the election under section 179 for the property and depreciates its 5-year property placed in service in 2023 using the optional depreciation table that corresponds with the general depreciation system, the 200-percent declining balance method, a 5-year recovery period, and the half-year convention. Assume the maximum section 179 deduction for 2023 is $1,000,000. For 2023, *TT* is first allowed a $1,000,000 deduction under section 179. Next, *TT* must reduce the cost of $1,500,000 by the section 179 deduction of $1,000,000 to determine the unadjusted depreciable basis of $500,000. Then, for 2023, *TT* is allowed an 80-percent additional first year depreciation deduction of $400,000 (the unadjusted depreciable basis of $500,000 multiplied by 0.80). Next, *TT* must reduce the unadjusted depreciable basis of $500,000 by the additional first year depreciation deduction of $400,000 to determine the remaining adjusted depreciable basis of $100,000. Then, *TT's* depreciation deduction allowable in 2023 for the remaining adjusted depreciable basis of $100,000 is $20,000 (the remaining adjusted depreciable basis of $100,000 multiplied by the annual depreciation rate of 0.20 for recovery year 1).

(e) *Elections under section 168(k).*—(1) *Election not to deduct additional first year depreciation.*—(i) *In general.*—A taxpayer may make an election not to deduct the additional first year depreciation for any class of property that is qualified property placed in service during the taxable year. If this election is made, the election applies to all qualified property that is in the same class of property and placed in service in the same taxable year, and no additional first year depreciation deduction is allowable for the property placed in service during the taxable year in the class of property, except as provided in § 1.743-1(j)(4)(i)(B)(1).

(ii) *Definition of class of property.*—For purposes of this paragraph (e)(1), the term *class of property* means:

(A) Except for the property described in paragraphs (e)(1)(ii)(B), and (D), and (e)(2) of this section, each class of property described in section 168(e) (for example, 5-year property);

(B) Water utility property as defined in section 168(e)(5) and depreciated under section 168;

(C) Computer software as defined in, and depreciated under, section 167(f)(1) and the regulations under section 167(f)(1);

(D) Qualified improvement property as defined in § 1.168(b)-1(a)(5)(i)(C) and (a)(5)(ii), and depreciated under section 168;

(E) Each separate production, as defined in § 1.181-3(b), of a qualified film or television production;

(F) Each separate production, as defined in section 181(e)(2), of a qualified live theatrical production; or

(G) A partner's basis adjustment in partnership assets under section 743(b) for each class of property described in paragraphs (e)(1)(ii)(A) through (F), and (e)(2) of this section (for further guidance, see § 1.743-1(j)(4)(i)(B)(1)).

(iii) *Time and manner for making election.*—(A) *Time for making election.*—Any election specified in paragraph (e)(1)(i) of this section must be made by the due date, including extensions, of the

Federal tax return for the taxable year in which the qualified property is placed in service by the taxpayer.

(B) *Manner of making election.*—Any election specified in paragraph (e)(1)(i) of this section must be made in the manner prescribed on Form 4562, "Depreciation and Amortization," and its instructions. The election is made separately by each person owning qualified property (for example, for each member of a consolidated group by the common parent of the group, by the partnership (including basis adjustments in the partnership assets under section 743(b)), or by the S corporation). If Form 4562 is revised or renumbered, any reference in this section to that form shall be treated as a reference to the revised or renumbered form.

(iv) *Failure to make election.*—If a taxpayer does not make the election specified in paragraph (e)(1)(i) of this section within the time and in the manner prescribed in paragraph (e)(1)(iii) of this section, the amount of depreciation allowable for that property under section 167(f)(1) or 168, as applicable, must be determined for the placed-in-service year and for all subsequent taxable years by taking into account the additional first year depreciation deduction. Thus, any election specified in paragraph (e)(1)(i) of this section shall not be made by the taxpayer in any other manner (for example, the election cannot be made through a request under section 446(e) to change the taxpayer's method of accounting).

(2) *Election to apply section 168(k)(5) for specified plants.*—(i) *In general.*—A taxpayer may make an election to apply section 168(k)(5) to one or more specified plants that are planted, or grafted to a plant that has already been planted, by the taxpayer in the ordinary course of the taxpayer's farming business, as defined in section 263A(e)(4). If this election is made for a specified plant, such plant is not treated as qualified property under section 168(k) and this section in its placed-in-service year.

(ii) *Time and manner for making election.*—(A) *Time for making election.*—Any election specified in paragraph (e)(2)(i) of this section must be made by the due date, including extensions, of the Federal tax return for the taxable year in which the taxpayer planted or grafted the specified plant to which the election applies.

(B) *Manner of making election.*—Any election specified in paragraph (e)(2)(i) of this section must be made in the manner prescribed on Form 4562, "Depreciation and Amortization," and its instructions. The election is made separately by each person owning specified plants (for example, for each member of a consolidated group by the common parent of the group, by the partnership, or by the S corporation). If Form 4562 is revised or renumbered, any reference in this section to that form shall be treated as a reference to the revised or renumbered form.

(iii) *Failure to make election.*—If a taxpayer does not make the election specified in paragraph (e)(2)(i) of this section for a specified plant within the time and in the manner prescribed in paragraph (e)(2)(ii) of this section, the specified plant is treated as qualified property under section 168(k), assuming all requirements are met, in the taxable year in which such plant is placed in service by the taxpayer. Thus, any election specified in paragraph (e)(2)(i) of this section shall not be made by the taxpayer in any other manner (for example, the election cannot be made through a request under section 446(e) to change the taxpayer's method of accounting).

(3) *Election for qualified property placed in service during the 2017 taxable year.*—(i) *In general.*—A taxpayer may make an election to deduct 50 percent, instead of 100 percent, additional first year depreciation for all qualified property acquired after September 27, 2017, by the taxpayer and placed in service by the taxpayer during its taxable year that includes September 28, 2017. If a taxpayer makes an election to apply section 168(k)(5) for its taxable year that includes September 28, 2017, the taxpayer also may make an election to deduct 50 percent, instead of 100 percent, additional first year depreciation for all specified plants that are planted, or grafted to a plant that has already been planted, after September 27, 2017, by the taxpayer in the ordinary course of the taxpayer's farming business during such taxable year.

(ii) *Time and manner for making election.*—(A) *Time for making election.*—Any election specified in paragraph (e)(3)(i) of this section must be made by the due date, including extensions, of the Federal tax return for the taxpayer's taxable year that includes September 28, 2017.

(B) *Manner of making election.*—Any election specified in paragraph (e)(3)(i) of this section must be made in the manner prescribed on the 2017 Form 4562, "Depreciation and Amortization," and its instructions. The election is made separately by each person owning qualified property (for example, for each member of a consolidated group by the common parent of the group, by the partnership, or by the S corporation).

(iii) *Failure to make election.*—If a taxpayer does not make the election specified in paragraph (e)(3)(i) of this section within the time and in the manner prescribed in paragraph (e)(3)(ii) of this section, the amount of depreciation allowable for qualified property under section 167(f)(1) or 168, as applicable, acquired and placed in service, or planted or grafted, as applicable, by the taxpayer after September 27, 2017, must be determined for the taxable year that includes September 28, 2017, and for all subsequent taxable years by taking into account the 100-percent additional first year depreciation deduction, unless the taxpayer makes the election specified in paragraph (e)(1)(i) of this section within the time and in the manner prescribed in paragraph (e)(1)(iii) of this section for the class of property in which the qualified property is included. Thus, any election specified in paragraph (e)(3)(i) of this section shall not be made by the taxpayer in any other manner (for example, the election cannot be made through a request under section 446(e) to change the taxpayer's method of accounting).

(4) *Alternative minimum tax.*—If a taxpayer makes an election specified in paragraph (e)(1) of this section for a class of property or in paragraph (e)(2) of this section for a specified plant, the depreciation adjustments under section 56 and the regulations under section 56 do not apply to the property or specified plant, as applicable, to which that election applies for purposes of computing the taxpayer's alternative minimum taxable income. If a taxpayer makes an election specified in paragraph (e)(3) of this section for all qualified property, see paragraphs (d)(1)(iv) and (d)(2)(ii) of this section.

(5) *Revocation of election.*—(i) *In general.*—Except as provided in paragraph (e)(5)(ii) of this section, an election specified in this paragraph (e), once made, may be revoked only by filing a request for a private letter ruling and obtaining the Commissioner of Internal Revenue's written consent to revoke the election. The Commissioner may grant a request to revoke the election if the taxpayer acted reasonably and in good faith, and the revocation will not prejudice the interests of the Government. See generally § 301.9100-3 of this chapter. An election specified in this paragraph (e) may not be revoked through a request under section 446(e) to change the taxpayer's method of accounting.

(ii) *Automatic 6-month extension.*—If a taxpayer made an election specified in this paragraph (e), an automatic extension of 6 months from the due date of the taxpayer's Federal tax return, excluding extensions, for the placed-in-service year or the taxable year in which the specified plant is planted or grafted, as applicable, is granted to revoke that election, provided the taxpayer timely filed the taxpayer's Federal tax return for the placed-in-service year or the taxable year in which the specified plant is planted or grafted, as applicable, and, within this 6-month extension period, the taxpayer, and all taxpayers whose tax liability would be affected by the election, file an amended Federal tax return for the placed-in-service year or the taxable year in which the specified plant is planted or grafted, as applicable, in a manner that is consistent with the revocation of the election.

(f) *Special rules.*—(1) *Property placed in service and disposed of in the same taxable year.*—(i) *In general.*—Except as provided in paragraphs (f)(1)(ii) and (iii) of this section, the additional first year depreciation deduction is not allowed for qualified property placed in service or planted or grafted, as applicable, and disposed of during the same taxable year. Also if qualified property is placed in service and disposed of during the same taxable year and then reacquired and again placed in service in a subsequent taxable year, the additional first year depreciation deduction is not allowable for the property in the subsequent taxable year.

(ii) *Technical termination of a partnership.*—In the case of a technical termination of a partnership under section 708(b)(1)(B) in a taxable year beginning before January 1, 2018, the additional first year depreciation deduction is allowable for any qualified property placed in service or planted or grafted, as applicable, by the terminated partnership during the taxable year of termination and contributed by the terminated partnership to the new partnership. The allowable additional first year depreciation deduction for the qualified property shall not be claimed by the terminated partnership but instead shall be claimed by the new partnership for the new partnership's taxable year in which the qualified property was contributed by the terminated partnership to the new partnership. However, if qualified property is both placed in service or planted or grafted, as applicable, and contributed to a new partnership in a transaction described in section 708(b)(1)(B) by the terminated partnership during the taxable year of termination, and if such property is disposed of by the new partnership in the same taxable year the new partnership received such property from the terminated partnership, then no additional first year depreciation deduction is allowable to either partnership.

(iii) Section 168(i)(7) transactions.—If any qualified property is transferred in a transaction described in section 168(i)(7) in the same taxable year that the qualified property is placed in service or planted or grafted, as applicable, by the transferor, the additional first year depreciation deduction is allowable for the qualified property. The allowable additional first year depreciation deduction for the qualified property for the transferor's taxable year in which the property is placed in service or planted or grafted, as applicable, is allocated between the transferor and the transferee on a monthly basis. This allocation shall be made in accordance with the rules in § 1.168(d)-1(b)(7)(ii) for allocating the depreciation deduction between the transferor and the transferee. However, solely for purposes of this section, if the qualified property is transferred in a section 721(a) transaction to a partnership that has as a partner a person, other than the transferor, who previously had a depreciable interest in the qualified property, in the same taxable year that the qualified property is placed in service or planted or grafted, as applicable, by the transferor, the allowable additional first year depreciation deduction is allocated entirely to the transferor, and not to the partnership. Additionally, if qualified property is both placed in service or planted or grafted, as applicable, and transferred in a transaction described in section 168(i)(7) by the transferor during the same taxable year, and if such property is disposed of by the transferee, other than by a transaction described in section 168(i)(7), during the same taxable year the transferee received such property from the transferor, then no additional first year depreciation deduction is allowable to either party.

(iv) Examples.—The application of this paragraph (f)(1) is illustrated by the following examples:

Example 1. UU and *VV* are equal partners in *Partnership JL,* a general partnership. *Partnership JL* is a calendar-year taxpayer. On October 1, 2017, *Partnership JL* purchased and placed in service qualified property at a cost of $30,000. On November 1, 2017, *UU* sells its entire 50 percent interest to *WW* in a transfer that terminates the partnership under section 708(b)(1)(B). As a result, terminated *Partnership JL* is deemed to have contributed the qualified property to new *Partnership JL.* Pursuant to paragraph (f)(1)(ii) of this section, new *Partnership JL,* not terminated *Partnership JL,* is eligible to claim the 100-percent additional first year depreciation deduction allowable for the qualified property for the taxable year 2017, assuming all other requirements are met.

Example 2. On January 5, 2018, *XX* purchased and placed in service qualified property for a total amount of $9,000. On August 20, 2018, *XX* transferred this qualified property to *Partnership BC* in a transaction described in section 721(a). No other partner of *Partnership BC* has ever had a depreciable interest in the qualified property. *XX* and *Partnership BC* are calendar-year taxpayers. Because the transaction between *XX* and *Partnership BC* is a transaction described in section 168(i)(7), pursuant to paragraph (f)(1)(iii) of this section, the 100-percent additional first year depreciation deduction allowable for the qualified property is allocated between *XX* and *Partnership BC* in accordance with the rules in § 1.168(d)-1(b)(7)(ii) for allocating the depreciation deduction between the transferor and the transferee. Accordingly, the 100-percent additional first year depreciation deduction allowable of $9,000 for the qualified property for 2018 is allocated between *XX* and *Partnership BC* based on the number of months that *XX* and *Partnership BC* held the qualified property in service during 2018. Thus, because the qualified property was held in service by *XX* for 7 of 12 months, which includes the month in which *XX* placed the qualified property in service but does not include the month in which the qualified property was transferred, *XX* is allocated $5,250 ($7/12 × $9,000 additional first year depreciation deduction). *Partnership BC* is allocated $3,750, the remaining 5/12 of the $9,000 additional first year depreciation deduction allowable for the qualified property.

(2) Redetermination of basis.—If the unadjusted depreciable basis, as defined in § 1.168(b)-1(a)(3), of qualified property is redetermined (for example, due to contingent purchase price or discharge of indebtedness) before January 1, 2027, or in the case of property described in section 168(k)(2)(B) or (C), is redetermined before January 1, 2028, the additional first year depreciation deduction allowable for the qualified property is redetermined as follows:

(i) Increase in basis.—For the taxable year in which an increase in basis of qualified property occurs, the taxpayer shall claim an additional first year depreciation deduction for qualified property by multiplying the amount of the increase in basis for this property by the applicable percentage for the taxable year in which the underlying property was placed in service by the taxpayer. For purposes of this paragraph (f)(2)(i), the additional first year depreciation deduction applies to the increase in basis only if the underlying property is qualified property. To determine the amount otherwise allowable as a depreciation deduction for the increase in basis of qualified property, the amount of the increase in basis of the qualified property

must be reduced by the additional first year depreciation deduction allowed or allowable, whichever is greater, for the increase in basis and the remaining increase in basis of—

(A) Qualified property, except for computer software described in paragraph (b)(2)(i)(B) of this section, is depreciated over the recovery period of the qualified property remaining as of the beginning of the taxable year in which the increase in basis occurs, and using the same depreciation method and convention applicable to the qualified property that applies for the taxable year in which the increase in basis occurs; and

(B) Computer software, as defined in paragraph (b)(2)(i)(B) of this section, that is qualified property is depreciated ratably over the remainder of the 36-month period, the useful life under section 167(f)(1), as of the beginning of the first day of the month in which the increase in basis occurs.

(ii) Decrease in basis.—For the taxable year in which a decrease in basis of qualified property occurs, the taxpayer shall reduce the total amount otherwise allowable as a depreciation deduction for all of the taxpayer's depreciable property by the excess additional first year depreciation deduction previously claimed for the qualified property. If, for such taxable year, the excess additional first year depreciation deduction exceeds the total amount otherwise allowable as a depreciation deduction for all of the taxpayer's depreciable property, the taxpayer shall take into account a negative depreciation deduction in computing taxable income. The excess additional first year depreciation deduction for qualified property is determined by multiplying the amount of the decrease in basis for this property by the applicable percentage for the taxable year in which the underlying property was placed in service by the taxpayer. For purposes of this paragraph (f)(2)(ii), the additional first year depreciation deduction applies to the decrease in basis only if the underlying property is qualified property. Also, if the taxpayer establishes by adequate records or other sufficient evidence that the taxpayer claimed less than the additional first year depreciation deduction allowable for the qualified property before the decrease in basis, or if the taxpayer claimed more than the additional first year depreciation deduction allowable for the qualified property before the decrease in basis, the excess additional first year depreciation deduction is determined by multiplying the amount of the decrease in basis by the additional first year depreciation deduction percentage actually claimed by the taxpayer for the qualified property before the decrease in basis. To determine the amount to reduce the total amount otherwise allowable as a depreciation deduction for all of the taxpayer's depreciable property for the excess depreciation previously claimed, other than the additional first year depreciation deduction, resulting from the decrease in basis of the qualified property, the amount of the decrease in basis of the qualified property must be adjusted by the excess additional first year depreciation deduction that reduced the total amount otherwise allowable as a depreciation deduction, as determined under this paragraph (f)(2)(ii), and the remaining decrease in basis of—

(A) Qualified property, except for computer software described in paragraph (b)(2)(i)(B) of this section, reduces the amount otherwise allowable as a depreciation deduction over the recovery period of the qualified property remaining as of the beginning of the taxable year in which the decrease in basis occurs, and using the same depreciation method and convention of the qualified property that applies in the taxable year in which the decrease in basis occurs. If, for any taxable year, the reduction to the amount otherwise allowable as a depreciation deduction, as determined under this paragraph (f)(2)(ii)(A), exceeds the total amount otherwise allowable as a depreciation deduction for all of the taxpayer's depreciable property, the taxpayer shall take into account a negative depreciation deduction in computing taxable income; and

(B) Computer software, as defined in paragraph (b)(2)(i)(B) of this section, that is qualified property reduces the amount otherwise allowable as a depreciation deduction over the remainder of the 36-month period, the useful life under section 167(f)(1), as of the beginning of the first day of the month in which the decrease in basis occurs. If, for any taxable year, the reduction to the amount otherwise allowable as a depreciation deduction, as determined under this paragraph (f)(2)(ii)(B), exceeds the total amount otherwise allowable as a depreciation deduction for all of the taxpayer's depreciable property, the taxpayer shall take into account a negative depreciation deduction in computing taxable income.

(iii) Definitions.—Except as otherwise expressly provided by the Internal Revenue Code (for example, section 1017(a)), the regulations under the Internal Revenue Code, or other guidance published in the Internal Revenue Bulletin for purposes of this paragraph (f)(2)—

(A) An increase in basis occurs in the taxable year an amount is taken into account under section 461; and

(B) A decrease in basis occurs in the taxable year an amount would be taken into account under section 451.

(iv) *Examples.*—The application of this paragraph (f)(2) is illustrated by the following examples:

Example 1. (i) On May 15, 2023, *YY*, a cash-basis taxpayer, purchased and placed in service qualified property that is 5-year property at a cost of $200,000. In addition to the $200,000, *YY* agrees to pay the seller 25 percent of the gross profits from the operation of the property in 2023. On May 15, 2024, *YY* paid to the seller an additional $10,000. *YY* depreciates the 5-year property placed in service in 2023 using the optional depreciation table that corresponds with the general depreciation system, the 200-percent declining balance method, a 5-year recovery period, and the half-year convention.

(ii) For 2023, *YY* is allowed an 80-percent additional first year depreciation deduction of $160,000 (the unadjusted depreciable basis of $200,000 multiplied by 0.80). In addition, *YY*'s depreciation deduction for 2023 for the remaining adjusted depreciable basis of $40,000 (the unadjusted depreciable basis of $200,000 reduced by the additional first year depreciation deduction of $160,000) is $8,000 (the remaining adjusted depreciable basis of $40,000 multiplied by the annual depreciation rate of 0.20 for recovery year 1).

(iii) For 2024, *YY*'s depreciation deduction for the remaining adjusted depreciable basis of $40,000 is $12,800 (the remaining adjusted depreciable basis of $40,000 multiplied by the annual depreciation rate of 0.32 for recovery year 2). In addition, pursuant to paragraph (f)(2)(i) of this section, *YY* is allowed an additional first year depreciation deduction for 2024 for the $10,000 increase in basis of the qualified property. Consequently, *YY* is allowed an additional first year depreciation deduction of $8,000 (the increase in basis of $10,000 multiplied by 0.80, the applicable percentage for 2023). Also, *YY* is allowed a depreciation deduction for 2024 attributable to the remaining increase in basis of $2,000 (the increase in basis of $10,000 reduced by the additional first year depreciation deduction of $8,000). The depreciation deduction allowable for 2024 attributable to the remaining increase in basis of $2,000 is $889 (the remaining increase in basis of $2,000 multiplied by 0.4444, which is equal to 1/remaining recovery period of 4.5 years at January 1, 2024, multiplied by 2). Accordingly, for 2024, *YY*'s total depreciation deduction allowable for the qualified property is $21,689 ($12,800 plus $8,000 plus $889).

Example 2. (i) On May 15, 2023, *ZZ*, a calendar-year taxpayer, purchased and placed in service qualified property that is 5-year property at a cost of $400,000. To purchase the property, *ZZ* borrowed $250,000 from Bank1. On May 15, 2024, Bank1 forgives $50,000 of the indebtedness. *ZZ* makes the election provided in section 108(b)(5) to apply any portion of the reduction under section 1017 to the basis of the depreciable property of the taxpayer. *ZZ* depreciates the 5-year property placed in service in 2023 using the optional depreciation table that corresponds with the general depreciation system, the 200-percent declining balance method, a 5-year recovery period, and the half-year convention.

(ii) For 2023, *ZZ* is allowed an 80-percent additional first year depreciation deduction of $320,000 (the unadjusted depreciable basis of $400,000 multiplied by 0.80). In addition, *ZZ*'s depreciation deduction allowable for 2023 for the remaining adjusted depreciable basis of $80,000 (the unadjusted depreciable basis of $400,000 reduced by the additional first year depreciation deduction of $320,000) is $16,000 (the remaining adjusted depreciable basis of $80,000 multiplied by the annual depreciation rate of 0.20 for recovery year 1).

(iii) For 2024, *ZZ*'s deduction for the remaining adjusted depreciable basis of $80,000 is $25,600 (the remaining adjusted depreciable basis of $80,000 multiplied by the annual depreciation rate 0.32 for recovery year 2). Although Bank1 forgave the indebtedness in 2024, the basis of the property is reduced on January 1, 2025, pursuant to sections 108(b)(5) and 1017(a) under which basis is reduced at the beginning of the taxable year following the taxable year in which the discharge of indebtedness occurs.

(iv) For 2025, *ZZ*'s deduction for the remaining adjusted depreciable basis of $80,000 is $15,360 (the remaining adjusted depreciable basis of $80,000 multiplied by the annual depreciation rate 0.192 for recovery year 3). However, pursuant to paragraph (f)(2)(ii) of this section, *ZZ* must reduce the amount otherwise allowable as a depreciation deduction for 2025 by the excess depreciation previously claimed for the $50,000 decrease in basis of the qualified property. Consequently, *ZZ* must reduce the amount of depreciation otherwise allowable for 2025 by the excess additional first year depreciation of $40,000 (the decrease in basis of $50,000 multiplied by 0.80, the applicable percentage for 2023). Also, *ZZ* must reduce the amount of depreciation otherwise allowable for 2025 by the excess depreciation attributable to the remaining decrease in basis of $10,000 (the decrease in basis of $50,000 reduced by the excess additional first year depreciation of $40,000). The reduction in the amount of depreciation otherwise allowable for 2025 for the remaining decrease in basis of $10,000 is $5,714 (the remaining decrease in basis of $10,000 multiplied by 0.5714, which is equal to (1/remaining recovery period of 3.5 years at January 1, 2025) multiplied by 2). Accordingly, assuming the qualified property is the only depreciable property owned by

ZZ, for 2025, ZZ has a negative depreciation deduction for the qualified property of $30,354 ($15,360 minus $40,000 minus $5,714).

(3) *Sections 1245 and 1250 depreciation recapture.*—For purposes of section 1245 and the regulations under section 1245, the additional first year depreciation deduction is an amount allowed or allowable for depreciation. Further, for purposes of section 1250(b) and the regulations under section 1250(b), the additional first year depreciation deduction is not a straight line method.

(4) *Coordination with section 169.*—The additional first year depreciation deduction is allowable in the placed-in-service year of a certified pollution control facility, as defined in § 1.169-2(a), that is qualified property even if the taxpayer makes the election to amortize the certified pollution control facility under section 169 and the regulations under section 169 in the certified pollution control facility's placed-in-service year.

(5) *Like-kind exchanges and involuntary conversions.*—(i) *Scope.*—The rules of this paragraph (f)(5) apply to replacement MACRS property or replacement computer software that is qualified property at the time of replacement provided the time of replacement is after September 27, 2017, and before January 1, 2027; or, in the case of replacement MACRS property or replacement computer software that is qualified property described in section 168(k)(2)(B) or (C), the time of replacement is after September 27, 2017, and before January 1, 2028.

(ii) *Definitions.*—For purposes of this paragraph (f)(5), the following definitions apply:

(A) *Replacement MACRS property* has the same meaning as that term is defined in § 1.168(i)-6(b)(1).

(B) *Relinquished MACRS property* has the same meaning as that term is defined in § 1.168(i)-6(b)(2).

(C) *Replacement computer software* is computer software, as defined in paragraph (b)(2)(i)(B) of this section, in the hands of the acquiring taxpayer that is acquired for other computer software in a like-kind exchange or in an involuntary conversion.

(D) *Relinquished computer software* is computer software that is transferred by the taxpayer in a like-kind exchange or in an involuntary conversion.

(E) *Time of disposition* has the same meaning as that term is defined in § 1.168(i)-6(b)(3) for relinquished MACRS property. For relinquished computer software, *time of disposition* is when the disposition of the relinquished computer software takes place under the convention determined under § 1.167(a)-14(b).

(F) Except as provided in paragraph (f)(5)(iv) of this section, the *time of replacement* has the same meaning as that term is defined in § 1.168(i)-6(b)(4) for replacement MACRS property. For replacement computer software, the *time of replacement* is, except as provided in paragraph (f)(5)(iv) of this section, the later of—

(1) When the replacement computer software is placed in service under the convention determined under § 1.167(a)-14(b); or

(2) The time of disposition of the relinquished property.

(G) *Exchanged basis* has the same meaning as that term is defined in § 1.168(i)-6(b)(7) for MACRS property, as defined in § 1.168(b)-1(a)(2). For computer software, the *exchanged basis* is determined after the amortization deductions for the year of disposition are determined under § 1.167(a)-14(b) and is the lesser of—

(1) The basis in the replacement computer software, as determined under section 1031(d) and the regulations under section 1031(d), or section 1033(b) and the regulations under section 1033(b); or

(2) The adjusted depreciable basis of the relinquished computer software.

(H) *Excess basis* has the same meaning as that term is defined in § 1.168(i)-6(b)(8) for replacement MACRS property. For replacement computer software, the *excess basis* is any excess of the basis in the replacement computer software, as determined under section 1031(d) and the regulations under section 1031(d), or section 1033(b) and the regulations under section 1033(b), over the exchanged basis as determined under paragraph (f)(5)(ii)(G) of this section.

(I) *Remaining exchanged basis* is the exchanged basis as determined under paragraph (f)(5)(ii)(G) of this section reduced by—

(1) The percentage of such basis attributable to the taxpayer's use of property for the taxable year other than in the taxpayer's trade or business or for the production of income; and

(2) Any adjustments to basis provided by other provisions of the Code and the regulations under the Code (including section 1016(a)(2) and (3)) for periods prior to the disposition of the relinquished property.

(J) *Remaining excess basis* is the excess basis as determined under paragraph (f)(5)(ii)(H) of this section reduced by—

(1) The percentage of such basis attributable to the taxpayer's use of property for the taxable year other than in the taxpayer's trade or business or for the production of income;

(2) Any portion of the basis the taxpayer properly elects to treat as an expense under section 179 or 179C; and

(3) Any adjustments to basis provided by other provisions of the Code and the regulations under the Code.

(K) *Year of disposition* has the same meaning as that term is defined in § 1.168(i)-6(b)(5).

(L) *Year of replacement* has the same meaning as that term is defined in § 1.168(i)-6(b)(6).

(M) *Like-kind exchange* has the same meaning as that term is defined in § 1.168(i)-6(b)(11).

(N) *Involuntary conversion* has the same meaning as that term is defined in § 1.168(i)-6(b)(12).

(iii) *Computation.*—(A) *In general.*—If the replacement MACRS property or the replacement computer software, as applicable, meets the original use requirement in paragraph (b)(3)(ii) of this section and all other requirements of section 168(k) and this section, the remaining exchanged basis for the year of replacement and the remaining excess basis, if any, for the year of replacement for the replacement MACRS property or the replacement computer software, as applicable, are eligible for the additional first year depreciation deduction. If the replacement MACRS property or the replacement computer software, as applicable, meets the used property acquisition requirements in paragraph (b)(3)(iii) of this section and all other requirements of section 168(k) and this section, only the remaining excess basis for the year of replacement for the replacement MACRS property or the replacement computer software, as applicable, is eligible for the additional first year depreciation deduction. See paragraph (b)(3)(iii)(A)(3) of this section. The additional first year depreciation deduction applies to the remaining exchanged basis and any remaining excess basis, as applicable, of the replacement MACRS property or the replacement computer software, as applicable, if the time of replacement is after September 27, 2017, and before January 1, 2027; or, in the case of replacement MACRS property or replacement computer software, as applicable, described in section 168(k)(2)(B) or (C), the time of replacement is after September 27, 2017, and before January 1, 2028. The additional first year depreciation deduction is computed separately for the remaining exchanged basis and any remaining excess basis, as applicable.

(B) *Year of disposition and year of replacement.*—The additional first year depreciation deduction is allowable for the replacement MACRS property or replacement computer software in the year of replacement. However, the additional first year depreciation deduction is not allowable for the relinquished MACRS property or the relinquished computer software, as applicable, if the relinquished MACRS property or the relinquished computer software, as applicable, is placed in service and disposed of in a like-kind exchange or in an involuntary conversion in the same taxable year.

(C) *Property described in section 168(k)(2)(B).*—For purposes of paragraph (f)(5)(iii)(A) of this section, the total of the remaining exchanged basis and the remaining excess basis, if any, of the replacement MACRS property that is qualified property described in section 168(k)(2)(B) and meets the original use requirement in paragraph (b)(3)(ii) of this section is limited to the total of the property's remaining exchanged basis and remaining excess basis, if any, attributable to the property's manufacture, construction, or production after September 27, 2017, and before January 1, 2027. For purposes of paragraph (f)(5)(iii)(A) of this section, the remaining excess basis, if any, of the replacement MACRS property that is qualified property described in section 168(k)(2)(B) and meets the used property acquisition requirements in paragraph (b)(3)(iii) of this section is limited to the property's remaining excess basis, if any, attributable to the property's manufacture, construction, or production after September 27, 2017, and before January 1, 2027.

(D) *Effect of § 1.168(i)-6(i)(1) election.*—If a taxpayer properly makes the election under § 1.168(i)-6(i)(1) not to apply § 1.168(i)-6 for any MACRS property, as defined in § 1.168(b)-1(a)(2), involved in a like-kind exchange or involuntary conversion and either of the following:

(1) The replacement MACRS property meets the original use requirement in paragraph (b)(3)(ii) of this section and all other requirements of section 168(k) and this section, the total of the exchanged basis, as defined in § 1.168(i)-6(b)(7), and the excess basis, as defined in § 1.168(i)-6(b)(8), if any, in the replacement MACRS property is eligible for the additional first year depreciation deduction; or

(2) The replacement MACRS property meets the used property acquisition requirements in paragraph (b)(3)(iii) of this section and all other requirements of section 168(k) and this section, only the excess basis, as defined in § 1.168(i)-6(b)(8), if any, in the

replacement MACRS property is eligible for the additional first year depreciation deduction.

(E) *Alternative minimum tax.*—The additional first year depreciation deduction is allowed for alternative minimum tax purposes for the year of replacement of replacement MACRS property or replacement computer software, as applicable, that is qualified property. If the replacement MACRS property or the replacement computer software, as applicable, meets the original use requirement in paragraph (b)(3)(ii) of this section and all other requirements of section 168(k) and this section, the additional first year depreciation deduction for alternative minimum tax purposes is based on the remaining exchanged basis and the remaining excess basis, if any, of the replacement MACRS property or the replacement computer software, as applicable, for alternative minimum tax purposes. If the replacement MACRS property or the replacement computer software, as applicable, meets the used property acquisition requirements in paragraph (b)(3)(iii) of this section and all other requirements of section 168(k) and this section, the additional first year depreciation deduction for alternative minimum tax purposes is based on the remaining excess basis, if any, of the replacement MACRS property or the replacement computer software, as applicable, for alternative minimum tax purposes.

(iv) *Replacement MACRS property or replacement computer software that is acquired and placed in service before disposition of relinquished MACRS property or relinquished computer software.*—If, in an involuntary conversion, a taxpayer acquires and places in service the replacement MACRS property or the replacement computer software, as applicable, before the time of disposition of the involuntarily converted MACRS property or the involuntarily converted computer software, as applicable; and the time of disposition of the involuntarily converted MACRS property or the involuntarily converted computer software, as applicable, is after December 31, 2026, or, in the case of property described in service 168(k)(2)(B) or (C), after December 31, 2027, then—

(A) The time of replacement for purposes of this paragraph (f)(5) is when the replacement MACRS property or replacement computer software, as applicable, is placed in service by the taxpayer, provided the threat or imminence of requisition or condemnation of the involuntarily converted MACRS property or involuntarily converted computer software, as applicable, existed before January 1, 2027, or, in the case of property described in section 168(k)(2)(B) or (C), existed before January 1, 2028; and

(B) The taxpayer depreciates the replacement MACRS property or replacement computer software, as applicable, in accordance with paragraph (d) of this section. However, at the time of disposition of the involuntarily converted MACRS property, the taxpayer determines the exchanged basis, as defined in § 1.168(i)-6(b)(7), and the excess basis, as defined in § 1.168(i)-6(b)(8), of the replacement MACRS property and begins to depreciate the depreciable exchanged basis, as defined in § 1.168(i)-6(b)(9), of the replacement MACRS property in accordance with § 1.168(i)-6(c). The depreciable excess basis, as defined in § 1.168(i)-6(b)(10), of the replacement MACRS property continues to be depreciated by the taxpayer in accordance with the first sentence of this paragraph (f)(5)(iv)(B). Further, in the year of disposition of the involuntarily converted MACRS property, the taxpayer must include in taxable income the excess of the depreciation deductions allowable, including the additional first year depreciation deduction allowable, on the unadjusted depreciable basis of the replacement MACRS property over the additional first year depreciation deduction that would have been allowable to the taxpayer on the remaining exchanged basis of the replacement MACRS property at the time of replacement, as defined in paragraph (f)(5)(v)(A) of this section, plus the depreciation deductions that would have been allowable, including the additional first year depreciation deduction allowable, to the taxpayer on the depreciable excess basis of the replacement MACRS property from the date the replacement MACRS property was placed in service by the taxpayer, taking into account the applicable convention, to the time of disposition of the involuntarily converted MACRS property. Similar rules apply to replacement computer software.

(v) *Examples.*—The application of this paragraph (f)(5) is illustrated by the following examples:

Example 1. (i) In April 2016, *CSK*, a calendar-year corporation, acquired for $200,000 and placed in service Canopy V1, a gas station canopy. Canopy V1 is qualified property under section 168(k)(2), as in effect on the day before amendment by the Act, and is 5-year property under section 168(e). *CSK* depreciated Canopy V1 under the general depreciation system of section 168(a) by using the 200-percent declining balance method of depreciation, a 5-year recovery period, and the half-year convention. *CSK* elected to use the optional depreciation tables to compute the depreciation allowance for Canopy V1. In November 2017, Canopy V1 was destroyed in a fire and was no longer usable in CSK's business. In December 2017, in an involuntary conversion, *CSK* acquired and placed in service

Canopy W1 with all of the $160,000 of insurance proceeds *CSK* received due to the loss of Canopy V1. Canopy W1 is qualified property under section 168(k)(2) and this section, and is 5-year property under section 168(e). Canopy W1 also meets the original use requirement in paragraph (b)(3)(ii) of this section. *CSK* did not make the election under § 1.168(i)-6(i)(1).

(ii) For 2016, *CSK* is allowed a 50-percent additional first year depreciation deduction of $100,000 for Canopy V1 (the unadjusted depreciable basis of $200,000 multiplied by 0.50), and a regular MACRS depreciation deduction of $20,000 for Canopy V1 (the remaining adjusted depreciable basis of $100,000 multiplied by the annual depreciation rate of 0.20 for recovery year 1).

(iii) For 2017, *CSK* is allowed a regular MACRS depreciation deduction of $16,000 for Canopy V1 (the remaining adjusted depreciable basis of $100,000 multiplied by the annual depreciation rate of 0.32 for recovery year 2 × ½ year).

(iv) Pursuant to paragraph (f)(5)(iii)(A) of this section, the additional first year depreciation deduction allowable for Canopy W1 for 2017 equals $64,000 (100 percent of Canopy W1's remaining exchanged basis at the time of replacement of $64,000 (Canopy V1's remaining adjusted depreciable basis of $100,000 minus 2016 regular MACRS depreciation deduction of $20,000 minus 2017 regular MACRS depreciation deduction of $16,000)).

Example 2. (i) The facts are the same as in *Example 1* of this paragraph (f)(5)(v), except *CSK* elected not to deduct the additional first year depreciation for 5-year property placed in service in 2016. *CSK* deducted the additional first year depreciation for 5-year property placed in service in 2017.

(ii) For 2016, *CSK* is allowed a regular MACRS depreciation deduction of $40,000 for Canopy V1 (the unadjusted depreciable basis of $200,000 multiplied by the annual depreciation rate of 0.20 for recovery year 1).

(iii) For 2017, *CSK* is allowed a regular MACRS depreciation deduction of $32,000 for Canopy V1 (the unadjusted depreciable basis of $200,000 multiplied by the annual depreciation rate of 0.32 for recovery year 2 × ½ year).

(iv) Pursuant to paragraph (f)(5)(iii)(A) of this section, the additional first year depreciation deduction allowable for Canopy W1 for 2017 equals $128,000 (100 percent of Canopy W1's remaining exchanged basis at the time of replacement of $128,000 (Canopy V1's unadjusted depreciable basis of $200,000 minus 2016 regular MACRS depreciation deduction of $40,000 minus 2017 regular MACRS depreciation deduction of $32,000)).

Example 3. The facts are the same as in *Example 1* of this paragraph (f)(5)(v), except Canopy W1 meets the used property acquisition requirements in paragraph (b)(3)(iii) of this section. Because the remaining excess basis of Canopy W1 is zero, *CSK* is not allowed any additional first year depreciation for Canopy W1 pursuant to paragraph (f)(5)(iii)(A) of this section.

Example 4. (i) In December 2016, *AB*, a calendar-year corporation, acquired for $10,000 and placed in service Computer X2. Computer X2 is qualified property under section 168(k)(2), as in effect on the day before amendment by the Act, and is 5-year property under section 168(e). *AB* depreciated Computer X2 under the general depreciation system of section 168(a) by using the 200-percent declining balance method of depreciation, a 5-year recovery period, and the half-year convention. *AB* elected to use the optional depreciation tables to compute the depreciation allowance for Computer X2. In November 2017, *AB* acquired Computer Y2 by exchanging Computer X2 and $1,000 cash in a like-kind exchange. Computer Y2 is qualified property under section 168(k)(2) and this section, and is 5-year property under section 168(e). Computer Y2 also meets the original use requirement in paragraph (b)(3)(ii) of this section. *AB* did not make the election under § 1.168(i)-6(i)(1).

(ii) For 2016, *AB* is allowed a 50-percent additional first year depreciation deduction of $5,000 for Computer X2 (unadjusted basis of $10,000 multiplied by 0.50), and a regular MACRS depreciation deduction of $1,000 for Computer X2 (the remaining adjusted depreciable basis of $5,000 multiplied by the annual depreciation rate of 0.20 for recovery year 1).

(iii) For 2017, *AB* is allowed a regular MACRS depreciation deduction of $800 for Computer X2 (the remaining adjusted depreciable basis of $5,000 multiplied by the annual depreciation rate of 0.32 for recovery year 2 × ½ year).

(iv) Pursuant to paragraph (f)(5)(iii)(A) of this section, the 100-percent additional first year depreciation deduction for Computer Y2 for 2017 is allowable for the remaining exchanged basis at the time of replacement of $3,200 (Computer X2's unadjusted depreciable basis of $10,000 minus additional first year depreciation deduction allowable of $5,000 minus the 2016 regular MACRS depreciation deduction of $1,000 minus the 2017 regular MACRS depreciation deduction of $800) and for the remaining excess basis at the time of replacement of $1,000 (cash paid for Computer Y2). Thus, the 100-percent additional first year depreciation deduction allowable for Computer Y2 totals $4,200 for 2017.

Example 5. (i) In July 2017, *BC*, a calendar-year corporation, acquired for $20,000 and placed in service Equipment X3. Equipment X3 is qualified property under section 168(k)(2), as in effect on the day before amendment by the Act, and is 5-year property under section 168(e). *BC* depreciated Equipment X3 under the general depreciation system of section 168(a) by using the 200-percent declining balance method of depreciation, a 5-year recovery period, and the half-year convention. *BC* elected to use the optional depreciation tables to compute the depreciation allowance for Equipment X3. In December 2017, *BC* acquired Equipment Y3 by exchanging Equipment X3 and $5,000 cash in a like-kind exchange. Equipment Y3 is qualified property under section 168(k)(2) and this section, and is 5-year property under section 168(e). Equipment Y3 also meets the used property acquisition requirements in paragraph (b)(3)(iii) of this section. *BC* did not make the election under § 1.168(i)-6(i)(1).

(ii) Pursuant to § 1.168(k)-1(f)(5)(iii)(B), no additional first year depreciation deduction is allowable for Equipment X3 and, pursuant to § 1.168(d)-1(b)(3)(ii), no regular depreciation deduction is allowable for Equipment X3, for 2017.

(iii) Pursuant to paragraph (f)(5)(iii)(A) of this section, no additional first year depreciation deduction is allowable for Equipment Y3's remaining exchanged basis at the time of replacement of $20,000 (Equipment X3's unadjusted depreciable basis of $20,000). However, pursuant to paragraph (f)(5)(iii)(A) of this section, the 100-percent additional first year depreciation deduction is allowable for Equipment Y3's remaining excess basis at the time of replacement of $5,000 (cash paid for Equipment Y3). Thus, the 100-percent additional first year depreciation deduction allowable for Equipment Y3 is $5,000 for 2017.

Example 6. (i) The facts are the same as in *Example 5* of this paragraph (f)(5)(v), except *BC* properly makes the election under § 1.168(i)-6(i)(1) not to apply § 1.168(i)-6 to Equipment X3 and Equipment Y3.

(ii) Pursuant to § 1.168(k)-1(f)(5)(iii)(B), no additional first year depreciation deduction is allowable for Equipment X3 and, pursuant to § 1.168(d)-1(b)(3)(ii), no regular depreciation deduction is allowable for Equipment X3, for 2017.

(iii) Pursuant to § 1.168(i)-6(i)(1), *BC* is treated as placing Equipment Y3 in service in December 2017 with a basis of $25,000 (the total of the exchanged basis of $20,000 and the excess basis of $5,000). However, pursuant to paragraph (f)(5)(iii)(D)(2) of this section, the 100-percent additional first year depreciation deduction is allowable only for Equipment Y3's excess basis at the time of replacement of $5,000 (cash paid for Equipment Y3). Thus, the 100-percent additional first year depreciation deduction allowable for Equipment Y3 is $5,000 for 2017.

(6) *Change in use.*—(i) *Change in use of depreciable property.*—The determination of whether the use of depreciable property changes is made in accordance with section 168(i)(5) and § 1.168(i)-4.

(ii) *Conversion to personal use.*—If qualified property is converted from business or income-producing use to personal use in the same taxable year in which the property is placed in service by a taxpayer, the additional first year depreciation deduction is not allowable for the property.

(iii) *Conversion to business or income-producing use.*—(A) *During the same taxable year.*—If, during the same taxable year, property is acquired by a taxpayer for personal use and is converted by the taxpayer from personal use to business or income-producing use, the additional first year depreciation deduction is allowable for the property in the taxable year the property is converted to business or income-producing use, assuming all of the requirements in paragraph (b) of this section are met. See paragraph (b)(3)(ii) of this section relating to the original use rules for a conversion of property to business or income-producing use.

(B) *Subsequent to the acquisition year.*—If property is acquired by a taxpayer for personal use and, during a subsequent taxable year, is converted by the taxpayer from personal use to business or income-producing use, the additional first year depreciation deduction is allowable for the property in the taxable year the property is converted to business or income-producing use, assuming all of the requirements in paragraph (b) of this section are met. For purposes of paragraphs (b)(4) and (5) of this section, the property must be acquired by the taxpayer for personal use after September 27, 2017, and converted by the taxpayer from personal use to business or income-producing use by January 1, 2027. See paragraph (b)(3)(ii) of this section relating to the original use rules for a conversion of property to business or income-producing use.

(iv) *Depreciable property changes use subsequent to the placed-in-service year.*—(A) If the use of qualified property changes in the hands of the same taxpayer subsequent to the taxable year the qualified property is placed in service and, as a result of the change in use, the property is no longer qualified property, the additional first year depreciation deduction allowable for the qualified property is not redetermined.

(B) If depreciable property is not qualified property in the taxable year the property is placed in service by the taxpayer, the additional first year depreciation deduction is not allowable for the property even if a change in the use of the property subsequent to the taxable year the property is placed in service results in the property being qualified property in the taxable year of the change in use.

(v) *Examples.*—The application of this paragraph (f)(6) is illustrated by the following examples:

Example 1. (i) On January 1, 2019, *FFF*, a calendar year corporation, purchased and placed in service several new computers at a total cost of $100,000. *FFF* used these computers within the United States for 3 months in 2019 and then moved and used the computers outside the United States for the remainder of 2019. On January 1, 2020, *FFF* permanently returns the computers to the United States for use in its business.

(ii) For 2019, the computers are considered as used predominantly outside the United States in 2019 pursuant to § 1.48-1(g)(1)(i). As a result, the computers are required to be depreciated under the alternative depreciation system of section 168(g). Pursuant to paragraph (b)(2)(ii)(B) of this section, the computers are not qualified property in 2019, the placed-in-service year. Thus, pursuant to paragraph (f)(6)(iv)(B) of this section, no additional first year depreciation deduction is allowed for these computers, regardless of the fact that the computers are permanently returned to the United States in 2020.

Example 2. (i) On February 8, 2023, GGG, a calendar year corporation, purchased and placed in service new equipment at a cost of $1,000,000 for use in its California plant. The equipment is 5-year property under section 168(e) and is qualified property under section 168(k). GGG depreciates its 5-year property placed in service in 2023 using the optional depreciation table that corresponds with the general depreciation system, the 200-percent declining balance method, a 5-year recovery period, and the half-year convention. On June 4, 2024, due to changes in GGG's business circumstances, GGG permanently moves the equipment to its plant in Mexico.

(ii) For 2023, GGG is allowed an 80-percent additional first year depreciation deduction of $800,000 (the adjusted depreciable basis of $1,000,000 multiplied by 0.80). In addition, GGG's depreciation deduction allowable in 2023 for the remaining adjusted depreciable basis of $200,000 (the unadjusted depreciable basis of $1,000,000 reduced by the additional first year depreciation deduction of $800,000) is $40,000 (the remaining adjusted depreciable basis of $200,000 multiplied by the annual depreciation rate of 0.20 for recovery year 1).

(iii) For 2024, the equipment is considered as used predominantly outside the United States pursuant to § 1.48-1(g)(1)(i). As a result of this change in use, the adjusted depreciable basis of $160,000 for the equipment is required to be depreciated under the alternative depreciation system of section 168(g) beginning in 2024. However, the additional first year depreciation deduction of $800,000 allowed for the equipment in 2023 is not redetermined.

(7) *Earnings and profits.*—The additional first year depreciation deduction is not allowable for purposes of computing earnings and profits.

(8) *Limitation of amount of depreciation for certain passenger automobiles.*—For a passenger automobile as defined in section 280F(d)(5), the limitation under section 280F(a)(1)(A)(i) is increased by $8,000 for qualified property acquired and placed in service by a taxpayer after September 27, 2017.

(9) *Coordination with section 47.*—(i) *In general.*—If qualified rehabilitation expenditures, as defined in section 47(c)(2) and § 1.48-12(c), incurred by a taxpayer with respect to a qualified rehabilitated building, as defined in section 47(c)(1) and § 1.48-12(b), are qualified property, the taxpayer may claim the rehabilitation credit provided by section 47(a), provided the requirements of section 47 are met—

(A) With respect to the portion of the basis of the qualified rehabilitated building that is attributable to the qualified rehabilitation expenditures if the taxpayer makes the applicable election under paragraph (e)(1)(i) of this section not to deduct any additional first year depreciation for the class of property that includes the qualified rehabilitation expenditures; or

(B) With respect to the portion of the remaining rehabilitated basis of the qualified rehabilitated building that is attributable to the qualified rehabilitation expenditures if the taxpayer claims the additional first year depreciation deduction on the unadjusted depreciable basis, as defined in § 1.168(b)-1(a)(3) but before the reduction

in basis for the amount of the rehabilitation credit, of the qualified rehabilitation expenditures; and the taxpayer depreciates the remaining adjusted depreciable basis, as defined in paragraph (d)(2)(i) of this section, of such expenditures using straight line cost recovery in accordance with section 47(c)(2)(B)(i) and § 1.48-12(c)(7)(i). For purposes of this paragraph (f)(9)(i)(B), the remaining rehabilitated basis is equal to the unadjusted depreciable basis, as defined in § 1.168(b)-1(a)(3) but before the reduction in basis for the amount of the rehabilitation credit, of the qualified rehabilitation expenditures that are qualified property reduced by the additional first year depreciation allowed or allowable, whichever is greater.

(ii) *Example.*—The application of this paragraph (f)(9) is illustrated by the following example:

Example. (i) Between February 8, 2023, and June 4, 2023, *JM*, a calendar-year taxpayer, incurred qualified rehabilitation expenditures of $200,000 with respect to a qualified rehabilitated building that is nonresidential real property under section 168(e). These qualified rehabilitation expenditures are qualified property and qualify for the 20-percent rehabilitation credit under section 47(a)(1). *JM*'s basis in the qualified rehabilitated building is zero before incurring the qualified rehabilitation expenditures and *JM* placed the qualified rehabilitated building in service in July 2023. *JM* depreciates its nonresidential real property placed in service in 2023 under the general depreciation system of section 168(a) by using the straight line method of depreciation, a 39-year recovery period, and the mid-month convention. *JM* elected to use the optional depreciation tables to compute the depreciation allowance for its depreciable property placed in service in 2023. Further, for 2023, *JM* did not make any election under paragraph (e) of this section.

(ii) Because *JM* did not make any election under paragraph (e) of this section, *JM* is allowed an 80-percent additional first year depreciation deduction of $160,000 for the qualified rehabilitation expenditures for 2023 (the unadjusted depreciable basis of $200,000 (before reduction in basis for the rehabilitation credit) multiplied by 0.80). *JM* also is allowed to claim a rehabilitation credit of $8,000 for the remaining rehabilitated basis of $40,000 (the unadjusted depreciable basis (before reduction in basis for the rehabilitation credit) of $200,000 less the additional first year depreciation deduction of $160,000, multiplied by 0.20 to calculate the rehabilitation credit). For 2023, the ratable share of the rehabilitation credit of $8,000 is $1,600. Further, *JM*'s depreciation deduction for 2023 for the remaining adjusted depreciable basis of $32,000 (the unadjusted depreciable basis (before reduction in basis for the rehabilitation credit) of $200,000 less the additional first year depreciation deduction of $160,000 less the rehabilitation credit of $8,000) is $376.64 (the remaining adjusted depreciable basis of $32,000 multiplied by the depreciation rate of 0.01177 for recovery year 1, placed in service in month 7).

(10) *Coordination with section 514(a)(3).*—The additional first year depreciation deduction is not allowable for purposes of section 514(a)(3).

(g) *Applicability dates.*—(1) *In general.*—Except as provided in paragraph (g)(2) of this section, the rules of this section apply to—

(i) Qualified property under section 168(k)(2) that is placed in service by the taxpayer during or after the taxpayer's taxable year that includes the date of publication of a Treasury decision adopting these rules as final regulations in the **Federal Register**; and

(ii) A specified plant for which the taxpayer properly made an election to apply section 168(k)(5) and that is planted, or grafted to a plant that was previously planted, by the taxpayer during or after the taxpayer's taxable year that includes the date of publication of a Treasury decision adopting these rules as final regulations in the **Federal Register**.

(2) *Early application.*—A taxpayer may rely on the provisions of this section in these proposed regulations for—

(i) Qualified property under section 168(k)(2) acquired and placed in service after September 27, 2017, by the taxpayer during taxable years ending on or after September 28, 2017, and ending before the taxpayer's taxable year that includes the date of publication of a Treasury decision adopting these rules as final regulations in the **Federal Register**; and

(ii) A specified plant for which the taxpayer properly made an election to apply section 168(k)(5) and that is planted, or grafted to a plant that was previously planted, after September 27, 2017, by the taxpayer during taxable years ending on or after September 28, 2017, and ending before the taxpayer's taxable year that includes the date of publication of a Treasury decision adopting these rules as final regulations in the **Federal Register**. [Reg. § 1.168(k)-2.]

Reg. § 1.168(k)-2(g)(2)(ii)

Qualified Property: Additional First Year Depreciation Deduction

Qualified Property: Additional First Year Depreciation Deduction.—Amendments to Reg. §1.168(k)-2, regarding the additional first year depreciation deduction under section 168(k) of the Internal Revenue Code, are proposed (published in the Federal Register on September 24, 2019) (REG-106808-19).

Par. 3. Section 1.168(k)-2 is amended by:

1. At the end of paragraph (a)(1), adding ", except as provided in paragraph (c) of this section";

2. Revising paragraph (b)(2)(ii)(F);

3. Adding three sentences at the end of paragraph (b)(2)(ii)(G);

4. Adding paragraphs (b)(2)(iii)(F), (G), and (H);

5. Adding paragraphs (b)(3)(iii)(B)(*4*) and (5), (b)(3)(iii)(C), (b)(3)(v), and (b)(3)(vii)(Y) through (HH);

6. Revising the last sentence in paragraph (b)(5)(ii)(A);

7. In the first sentence in paragraph (b)(5)(iii)(A), removing the word "A" at the beginning of the sentence and adding "Except as provided in paragraph (b)(5)(iii)(G) of this section, a" in its place;

8. In the first sentence in paragraph (b)(5)(iii)(B), removing the word "A" at the beginning of the sentence and adding "Except as provided in paragraph (b)(5)(iii)(G) of this section, a" in its place;

9. Adding paragraph (b)(5)(iii)(G);

10. In the penultimate sentence in paragraph (b)(5)(iv)(C)(*1*), removing the period at the end of the sentence and adding ", except as provided in paragraph (c) of this section." in its place;

11. In the penultimate sentence in paragraph (b)(5)(iv)(C)(*2*), removing the period at the end of the sentence and adding ", except as provided in paragraph (c) of this section." in its place;

12. Adding paragraph (b)(5)(v);

13. Revising the second sentence in paragraph (b)(5)(viii) introductory text;

14. Adding paragraph (c);

15. Adding two sentences at the end of paragraph (e)(1)(iii);

16. Adding paragraph (g)(11);

17. In introductory paragraph (h)(1), removing "paragraphs (h)(2) and (3)" and adding "paragraphs (h)(2), (3), and (4)" in its place; and

18. Adding paragraph (h)(4).

The additions and revisions read as follows:

§1.168(k)-2. Additional first year depreciation deduction for property acquired and placed in service after September 27, 2017.

* * *

(b) * * *

(2) * * *

(ii) * * *

(F) Primarily used in a trade or business described in section 163(j)(7)(A)(iv), and placed in service by the taxpayer in any taxable year beginning after December 31, 2017. For purposes of section 168(k)(9)(A) and this paragraph (b)(2)(ii)(F), the term *primarily used* has the same meaning as that term is used in §1.167(a)-11(b)(4)(iii)(*b*) and (e)(3)(iii) for classifying property. This paragraph (b)(2)(ii)(F) does not apply to property that is leased to a trade or business described in section 163(j)(7)(A)(iv) by a lessor's trade or business that is not described in section 163(j)(7)(A)(iv) for the taxable year; or

(G) * * * Solely for purposes of section 168(k)(9)(B) and this paragraph (b)(2)(ii)(G), floor plan financing interest is not taken into account for the taxable year by a trade or business that has had floor plan financing indebtedness if the sum of the amounts calculated under section 163(j)(1)(A) and (B) for the trade or business for the taxable year equals or exceeds the business interest, as defined in section 163(j)(5), of the trade or business for the taxable year (which includes floor plan financing interest). If the trade or business has taken floor plan financing interest into account pursuant to this paragraph (b)(2)(ii)(G) for a taxable year, this paragraph (b)(2)(ii)(G) applies to any property placed in service by that trade or business in that taxable year. This paragraph (b)(2)(ii)(G) does not apply to property that is leased to a trade or business that has had floor plan financing indebtedness by a lessor's trade or business that has not had floor plan financing indebtedness during the taxable year or that has had floor plan financing indebtedness but did not take into account floor plan financing interest for the taxable year pursuant to this paragraph (b)(2)(ii)(G).

(iii) * * *

(F) *Example 6.*—In 2019, a financial institution buys new equipment for $1 million and then leases this equipment to a lessee that primarily uses the equipment in a trade or business described in section 163(j)(7)(A)(iv). The financial institution is not described in section 163(j)(7)(A)(iv). As a result, paragraph (b)(2)(ii)(F) of this section does not apply to this new equipment. Assuming all other requirements are met, the financial institution's purchase price of $1 million for the new equipment qualifies for the additional first year depreciation deduction under this section.

(G) *Example 7.*—In 2019, F, an automobile dealer, buys new computers for $50,000 for use in its trade or business of selling automobiles. For purposes of section 163(j), F has the following for 2019: $1,000 of adjusted taxable income, $40 of business interest income, $400 of business interest (which includes $100 of floor plan financing interest). The sum of the amounts calculated under section 163(j)(1)(A) and (B) for F for 2019 is $340 ($40 + ($1,000 x 30 percent)). F's business interest, which includes floor plan financing interest, for 2019 is $400. As a result, F's floor plan financing interest is taken into

account by F for 2019 pursuant to paragraph (b)(2)(ii)(G) of this section. Accordingly, F's purchase price of $50,000 for the computers does not qualify for the additional first year depreciation deduction under this section.

(H) *Example 8.*—The facts are the same as in *Example 7* in paragraph (b)(2)(iii)(G) of this section. In 2020, F buys new copiers for $30,000 for use in its trade or business of selling automobiles. For purposes of section 163(j), F has the following for 2020: $1,300 of adjusted taxable income, $40 of business interest income, $400 of business interest (which includes $100 of floor plan financing interest). The sum of the amounts calculated under section 163(j)(1)(A) and (B) for F for 2020 is $430 ($40 + ($1,300 x 30 percent)). F's business interest, which includes floor plan financing interest, for 2020 is $400. As a result, F's floor plan financing interest is not taken into account by F for 2020 pursuant to paragraph (b)(2)(ii)(G) of this section. Assuming all other requirements are met, F's purchase price of $30,000 for the copiers qualifies for the additional first year depreciation deduction under this section.

(3) * * *

(iii) * * *

(B) * * *

(4) *De minimis use of property.*—If a taxpayer acquires and places in service property, the taxpayer or a predecessor did not previously have a depreciable interest in the property, the taxpayer disposes of the property to an unrelated party within 90 calendar days after the date the property was originally placed in service by the taxpayer, without taking into account the applicable convention, and the taxpayer reacquires and again places in service the property, the taxpayer's depreciable interest in the property during that 90-day period is not taken into account for determining whether the property was used by the taxpayer or a predecessor at any time prior to its reacquisition by the taxpayer under paragraphs (b)(3)(iii)(A)(*1*) and (b)(3)(iii)(B)(*1*) of this section. This paragraph (b)(3)(iii)(B)(4) does not apply if the taxpayer reacquires and again places in service the property during the same taxable year the taxpayer disposed of the property. For purposes of this paragraph (b)(3)(iii)(B)(4), an *unrelated party* is a person not described in section 179(d)(2)(A) or (B), and §1.179-4(c)(1)(ii) or (iii), or (c)(2).

(5) *Partner's prior depreciable interest in property held by partnership.*—Solely for purposes of applying paragraphs (b)(3)(iii)(A)(*1*) and (b)(3)(iii)(B)(*1*) and (2) of this section, a person is treated as having a depreciable interest in a portion of property prior to the person's acquisition of the property if the person was a partner in a partnership at any time the partnership owned the property. For purposes of the preceding sentence, the portion of property that a partner is treated as having a depreciable interest in is equal to the total share of depreciation deductions with respect to the property allocated to the partner as a percentage of the total depreciation deductions with respect to that property allocated to all partners during the current calendar year and five calendar years immediately prior to the partnership's current placed-in-service year of the property. If the person was not a partner in the partnership for this entire period, or if the partnership did not own the property for the entire

period, only the period during which the person was a partner and the partnership owned the property is taken into account for purposes of determining a partner's share of depreciation deductions.

(C) *Special rules for a series of related transactions.—(1) In general.*—Solely for purposes of paragraph (b)(3)(iii) of this section, the relationship between parties under section 179(d)(2)(A) or (B) in a series of related transactions is tested immediately after each step in the series, and between the original transferor and the ultimate transferee immediately after the last transaction in the series. A series of related transactions may include, for example, a transfer of partnership assets followed by a transfer of an interest in the partnership that owned the assets; or a disposition of property and disposition, directly or indirectly, of the transferor or transferee of the property.

(2) *Special rules.—(i) Property placed in service and disposed of in same taxable year or property not placed in service.*—Any party in a series of related transactions that is neither the original transferor nor the ultimate transferee is disregarded (disregarded party) for purposes of testing the relationships under paragraph (b)(3)(iii)(C)(1) of this section if the party places in service and disposes of the depreciable property subject to the series, other than in a transaction described in paragraph (g)(1)(iii) of this section, during the party's same taxable year or if the party does not place in service the depreciable property subject to the series for use in the party's trade or business or production of income. In this case, the relationship is tested between the party from which the disregarded party acquired the depreciable property and the party to which the disregarded party disposed of the depreciable property. If the series has consecutive disregarded parties, the relationship is tested between the party from which the first disregarded party acquired the depreciable property and the party to which the last disregarded party disposed of the depreciable property. The rules for testing the relationships in paragraph (b)(3)(iii)(C)(1) of this section continue to apply for the other transactions in the series and for the last transaction in the series.

(ii) *All section 168(i)(7) transactions.*—This paragraph (b)(3)(iii)(C) does not apply if all transactions in a series of related transactions are described in paragraph (g)(1)(iii) of this section (section 168(i)(7) transactions in which property is transferred in the same taxable year that the property is placed in service by the transferor).

(iii) *One or more section 168(i)(7) transactions.*—Any step in a series of related transactions that is neither the original step nor the ultimate step is disregarded (disregarded step) for purposes of testing the relationships under paragraph (b)(3)(iii)(C)(1) of this section if the step is a transaction described in paragraph (g)(1)(iii) of this section. In this case, the relationship is not tested between the transferor and transferee of that transaction. Instead, the relationship is tested between the transferor in the disregarded step and the party to which the transferee in the disregarded step disposed of the depreciable property, and the transferee in the disregarded step and the party to which the transferee in the disregarded step disposed of the depreciable property. If the series has consecutive disregarded steps, the relationship is tested between the transferor in the first disregarded step and the party to which the transferee in the last disregarded step disposed of the depreciable property, and the transferee in the last disregarded step and the party to which the transferee in the last disregarded step disposed of the depreciable property. The rules for testing the relationships in paragraph (b)(3)(iii)(C)(1) of this section continue to apply for the other transactions in the series and for the last transaction in the series.

(iv) *Syndication transaction.*—This paragraph (b)(3)(iii)(C) does not apply to a syndication transaction described in paragraph (b)(3)(vi) of this section.

(v) *Application of paragraph (g)(1) of this section.*—Paragraph (g)(1) of this section applies to each step in a series of related transactions.

* * *

(v) *Application to members of a consolidated group.—(A) In general.*—Solely for purposes of applying paragraph (b)(3)(iii)(A)(1) of this section, if a member of a consolidated group, as defined in §1.1502-1(h), acquires depreciable property in which the group had a depreciable interest at any time prior to the member's acquisition of the property, the member is treated as having a depreciable interest in the property prior to the acquisition. For purposes of this paragraph (b)(3)(v)(A), a consolidated group is treated as having a depreciable interest in property during the time any current or previous member of the group had a depreciable interest in the property while a member of the group.

(B) *Certain acquisitions pursuant to a series of related transactions.*—Solely for purposes of applying paragraph (b)(3)(v)(A) of this section, if a series of related transactions includes one or more

transactions in which property is acquired by a member of a consolidated group, and one or more transactions in which a corporation that had a depreciable interest in the property, determined without regard to the application of paragraph (b)(3)(v)(A) of this section, becomes a member of the group, the member that acquires the property is treated as having a depreciable interest in the property prior to the time of its acquisition.

(C) *Sale of depreciable property to a member that leaves the group.*—Except as otherwise provided in paragraph (b)(3)(v)(E) of this section, if a member of a consolidated group (transferee member) acquires from another member of the same group (transferor member) depreciable property in an acquisition meeting the requirements of paragraph (b)(3)(iii)(A) of this section without regard to section 179(d)(2)(A) or (B) or paragraph (b)(3)(v)(A) of this section, and if, as part of the same series of related transactions that includes the acquisition, the transferee member ceases to be a member of the consolidated group within 90 calendar days of the date of the acquisition, then—

(1) The transferor member is treated as disposing of, and the transferee member is treated as acquiring, the depreciable property one day after the date on which the transferee member ceases to be a member of the consolidated group (Deconsolidation Date) for all Federal income tax purposes; and

(2) The transferee member is treated as placing the depreciable property in service not earlier than one day after the Deconsolidation Date for purposes of sections 167 and 168 and §§1.46-3(d) and 1.167(a)-11(e)(1).

(D) *Deemed sales of depreciable property under section 338 or 336(e) to a member that leaves the group.*—This paragraph (b)(3)(v)(D) applies only if a member of a consolidated group (transferee member) acquires the stock of another member of the same group that holds depreciable property (target) in either a qualified stock purchase for which a section 338 election is made or a qualified stock disposition described in §1.336-2(b)(1) for which a section 336(e) election is made. Except as otherwise provided in paragraph (b)(3)(v)(E) of this section, if the target would be eligible for the additional first year depreciation deduction under this section with respect to the depreciable property without regard to paragraph (b)(2)(v)(A) of this section, and if the transferee member and the target cease to be members of the group within 90 calendar days of the acquisition date, within the meaning of §1.338-2(c)(1), or disposition date, within the meaning of §1.336-1(b)(8), as part of the same series of related transactions that includes the acquisition, then—

(1) The acquisition date or disposition date, as applicable, is treated as the date that is one day after the Deconsolidation Date for all Federal income tax purposes; and

(2) New target is treated as placing the depreciable property in service not earlier than one day after the Deconsolidation Date for purposes of sections 167 and 168 and §§1.46-3(d) and 1.167(a)-11(e)(1).

(E) *Disposition of depreciable property pursuant to the same series of related transactions.*—Paragraph (b)(3)(v)(C) of this section does not apply if, following the acquisition of depreciable property, the transferee member disposes of such property pursuant to the same series of related transactions that includes the property acquisition. Paragraph (b)(3)(v)(D) of this section does not apply if, following the deemed acquisition of depreciable property, the target disposes of such property pursuant to the same series of related transactions that includes the deemed acquisition. See paragraph (b)(3)(iii)(C) of this section for rules regarding the transfer of property in a series of related transactions. See also paragraph (g)(1) of this section for rules regarding property placed in service and disposed of in the same taxable year.

* * *

(vii) * * *

(Y) *Example 25.—(1)* On September 5, 2017, *Y*, a calendar-year taxpayer, acquires and places in service a new machine (Machine #1), and begins using Machine #1 in its manufacturing trade or business. On November 1, 2017, *Y* sells Machine #1 to *Z*, then *Z* leases Machine #1 back to *Y* for 4 years, and *Y* continues to use Machine #1 in its manufacturing trade or business. The lease agreement contains a purchase option provision allowing *Y* to buy Machine #1 at the end of the lease term. On November 1, 2021, *Y* exercises the purchase option in the lease agreement and buys Machine #1 from *Z*. The lease between *Y* and *Z* for Machine #1 is a true lease for Federal tax purposes.

(2) Because *Y*, a calendar-year taxpayer, placed in service and disposed of Machine #1 during 2017, Machine #1 is not eligible for the additional first year depreciation deduction for *Y* pursuant to §1.168(k)-1(g)(1)(i).

(3) The use of Machine #1 by *Y* prevents *Z* from satisfying the original use requirement of paragraph (b)(3)(ii) of this section. However, *Z*'s acquisition of Machine #1 satisfies the used property

acquisition requirements of paragraph (b)(3)(iii) of this section. Assuming all other requirements are met, Z's purchase price of Machine #1 qualifies for the additional first year depreciation deduction for Z under this section.

(4) During 2017, *Y* sold Machine #1 within 90 calendar days of placing in service Machine #1. Pursuant to paragraph (b)(3)(iii)(B)(4) of this section, *Y*'s depreciable interest in Machine #1 during that 90-day period is not taken into account for determining whether Machine #1 was used by *Y* or a predecessor at any time prior to its reacquisition by *Y* on November 1, 2021. Accordingly, assuming all other requirements are met, *Y*'s purchase price of Machine #1 on November 1, 2021, qualifies for the additional first year depreciation deduction for *Y* under this section.

(Z) Example 26.—Parent owns all of the stock of B and C, which are members of the Parent consolidated group. C has a depreciable interest in Equipment #1. During 2018, C sells Equipment #1 to B. Prior to this acquisition, B never had a depreciable interest in Equipment #1. B's acquisition of Equipment #1 does not satisfy the used property acquisition requirements of paragraph (b)(3)(iii) of this section for two reasons. First, B and C are related parties within the meaning of section 179(d)(2)(B) and § 1.179-4(c)(2)(iii). Second, pursuant to paragraph (b)(3)(v)(A) of this section, B is treated as previously having a depreciable interest in Equipment #1 because B is a member of the Parent consolidated group and C, while a member of the Parent consolidated group, had a depreciable interest in Equipment #1. Accordingly, B's acquisition of Equipment #1 is not eligible for the additional first year depreciation deduction.

(AA) Example 27.—(1) Facts.—Parent owns all of the stock of D and E, which are members of the Parent consolidated group. D has a depreciable interest in Equipment #2. No other current or previous member of the Parent consolidated group has ever had a depreciable interest in Equipment #2 while a member of the Parent consolidated group. During 2018, D sells Equipment #2 to BA, a person not related, within the meaning of section 179(d)(2)(A) or (B) and § 1.179-4(c), to any member of the Parent consolidated group. In an unrelated transaction during 2019, E acquires Equipment #2 from BA or another person not related to any member of the Parent consolidated group within the meaning of section 179(d)(2)(A) or (B) and § 1.179-4(c).

(2) Analysis.—Pursuant to paragraph (b)(3)(v)(A) of this section, E is treated as previously having a depreciable interest in Equipment #2 because E is a member of the Parent consolidated group and D, while a member of the Parent consolidated group, had a depreciable interest in Equipment #2. As a result, E's acquisition of Equipment #2 does not satisfy the used property acquisition requirements of paragraph (b)(3)(iii) of this section. Thus, E's acquisition of Equipment #2 is not eligible for the additional first year depreciation deduction. The results would be the same if, after selling Equipment #2 to BA, D had ceased to be a member of the Parent consolidated group prior to E's acquisition of Equipment #2.

(BB) Example 28.—(1) Facts.—Parent owns all of the stock of B and S, which are members of the Parent consolidated group. S has a depreciable interest in Equipment #3. No other current or previous member of the Parent consolidated group has ever had a depreciable interest in Equipment #3 while a member of the Parent consolidated group. X is the common parent of a consolidated group and is not related, within the meaning of section 179(d)(2)(A) or (B) and § 1.179-4(c), to any member of the Parent consolidated group. No member of the X consolidated group has ever had a depreciable interest in Equipment #3 while a member of the X consolidated group. On January 1, 2019, B purchases Equipment #3 from S. On February 15, 2019, as part of the same series of related transactions that includes B's purchase of Equipment #3, Parent sells all of the stock of B to X. Thus, B leaves the Parent consolidated group at the end of the day on February 15, 2019, and joins the X consolidated group on February 16, 2019. See § 1.1502-76(b).

(2) Application of paragraph (b)(3)(v)(C) of this section.—B was a member of the Parent consolidated group when B acquired Equipment #3 from S, another member of the same group. Paragraph (b)(3)(v)(A) of this section generally treats each member of a consolidated group as having a depreciable interest in property during the time any member of the group had a depreciable interest in such property while a member of the group. However, B acquired Equipment #3 in a transaction meeting the requirements of paragraph (b)(3)(iii)(A) of this section, without regard to section 179(d)(2)(A) or (B) or paragraph (b)(3)(v)(A) of this section, and Parent sold all of the stock of B to X within 90 calendar days of B's acquisition of Equipment #3 as part of the same series of related transactions that included B's acquisition of Equipment #3. Thus, under paragraph (b)(3)(v)(C) of this section, B's acquisition of Equipment #3 is treated as occurring on February 16, 2019, for all Federal income tax purposes.

(3) Eligibility for the additional first year depreciation deduction.—B's acquisition of Equipment #3 on February 16, 2019, under paragraph (b)(3)(v)(C) of this section satisfies the requirement in paragraph (b)(3)(iii)(A)(1) of this section because B does not have a prior depreciable interest in Equipment #3. In addition, because no member of the X consolidated group previously had a depreciable interest in Equipment #3 while a member of the X consolidated group, B is not treated as previously having a depreciable interest in Equipment #3 under paragraph (b)(3)(v)(A) of this section. Further, because the relation between S and B is tested as if B acquired Equipment #3 while a member of the X consolidated group, S and B are neither members nor component members of the same controlled group on February 16, 2019. Therefore, section 179(d)(2)(A) and (B) and § 1.179-4(c)(1)(ii) and (iii) are satisfied. If the other requirements of paragraph (b)(3)(iii)(A) of this section are satisfied, B is treated as placing Equipment #3 in service on a date not earlier than February 16, 2019, while a member of the X consolidated group. Accordingly, assuming all other requirements of this section are satisfied, B is eligible to claim the additional first year depreciation deduction for Equipment #3 on that date. In addition, because the sale of Equipment #3 is deemed to occur between S, a member of the Parent consolidated group, and B, a member of the X consolidated group, the transaction is not between members of the same consolidated group and thus is not covered by section 168(i)(7)(B)(ii). Therefore, B's deduction is not limited by section 168(i)(7)(A) when B is treated, under paragraph (b)(3)(v)(C) of this section, as placing Equipment #3 in service on a date not earlier than February 16, 2019.

(CC) Example 29.—(1) Facts.—The facts are the same as Example 28 in paragraph (b)(3)(viii)(BB)(1) of this section, except that S owns all of the stock of T (rather than a depreciable interest in Equipment #3), which is a member of the Parent consolidated group; T has a depreciable interest in Equipment #3; B acquires all of the stock of T (instead of a depreciable interest in Equipment #3) on January 1, 2019; and S and B make a section 338(h)(10) election for B's qualified stock purchase.

(2) Application of paragraph (b)(3)(v)(D) of this section.—As a result of the section 338(h)(10) election, Old T is treated as transferring all of its assets, including Equipment #3, to an unrelated person in a single transaction in exchange for consideration at the close of the acquisition date and then transferring the consideration received to S in liquidation. In turn, New T is treated as acquiring all of its assets, including Equipment #3, from an unrelated person in exchange for consideration on the following day. See § 1.338-1(a)(1). New T was a member of the Parent consolidated group on January 1, 2019, the date that New T acquired Equipment #3. Paragraph (b)(3)(v)(A) of this section generally treats each member of a consolidated group as having a depreciable interest in property during the time any member of the group had a depreciable interest in such property while a member of the group. However, New T would be eligible for the additional first year depreciation deduction under this section without regard to paragraph (b)(3)(v)(A) of this section, and Parent sold all of its B stock to X within 90 calendar days of New T's acquisition of Equipment #3 as part of the same series of related transactions that included the acquisition, thereby causing B and New T to cease to be members of the Parent consolidated group at the end of the day on February 15, 2019. Thus, paragraph (b)(3)(v)(D) applies to treat the acquisition date as February 16, 2019, for all Federal income tax purposes.

(3) Eligibility for the additional first year depreciation deduction.—Pursuant to paragraph (b)(3)(v)(D), Old T is treated as selling its assets to an unrelated person on February 16, 2019, and New T is treated as acquiring those assets on the following day, February 17, 2019. If the other requirements of paragraph (b)(3)(iii)(A) of this section are satisfied, New T is treated as placing Equipment #3 in service on a date not earlier than February 17, 2019, while a member of the X consolidated group. Accordingly, assuming all other requirements of this section are satisfied, New T is eligible to claim the additional first year depreciation deduction for Equipment #3 when New T places Equipment #3 in service. In addition, the amount of the deduction is not limited by section 168(i)(7)(A).

(DD) Example 30.—(1) Facts.—G, which is not a member of a consolidated group, has a depreciable interest in Equipment #4. Parent owns all the stock of H, which is a member of the Parent consolidated group. No member of the Parent consolidated group has ever had a depreciable interest in Equipment #4 while a member of the Parent consolidated group, and neither Parent nor H is related to G within the meaning of section 179(d)(2)(A) or (B) and § 1.179-4(c). During 2018, G sells Equipment #4 to a person not related to G, Parent, or H within the meaning of section 179(d)(2)(A) or (B) and § 1.179-4(c). In a series of related transactions, during 2019, Parent acquires all of the stock of G, and H purchases Equipment #4 from an unrelated person.

(2) Analysis.—In a series of related transactions, G became a member of the Parent consolidated group, and H, also a member of the Parent consolidated group, acquired Equipment #4. Because G previously had a depreciable interest in Equipment #4, pursuant to paragraph (b)(3)(v)(B) of this section, H is treated as having a depreciable interest in Equipment #4. As a result, H's acquisition of Equipment #4 does not satisfy the used property acquisition requirements of paragraph (b)(3)(iii) of this section. Accordingly, H's acquisition of Equipment #4 is not eligible for the additional first year depreciation deduction.

(EE) *Example 31.*—(1) In a series of related transactions, a father sells a machine to an unrelated individual in December 2019 who sells the machine to the father's daughter in January 2020 for use in the daughter's trade or business. Pursuant to paragraph (b)(3)(iii)(C)(1) of this section, the time to test whether the parties are related is immediately after each step in the series, and between the original transferor and the ultimate transferee immediately after the last transaction in the series. As a result, the following relationships are tested under section 179(d)(2)(A): the father and the unrelated individual, the unrelated individual and the father's daughter, and the father and his daughter.

(2) Because the individual is not related to the father within the meaning of section 179(d)(2)(A) and §1.179-4(c)(ii), the individual's acquisition of the machine satisfies the used property acquisition requirement of paragraph (b)(3)(iii)(A)(2) of this section. Accordingly, assuming all other requirements of this section are satisfied, the individual's purchase price of the machine qualifies for the additional first year depreciation deduction under this section.

(3) The individual and the daughter are not related parties within the meaning of section 179(d)(2)(A) and §1.179-4(c)(ii). However, the father and his daughter are related parties within the meaning of section 179(d)(2)(A) and §1.179-4(c)(ii). Accordingly, daughter's acquisition of the machine does not satisfy the used property acquisition requirements of paragraph (b)(3)(iii) of this section and is not eligible for the additional first year depreciation deduction.

(FF) *Example 32.*—(1) The facts are the same as in *Example 31* of paragraph (b)(3)(viii)(EE)(1) of this section, except that instead of selling to an unrelated individual, the father sells the machine to his son in December 2019 who sells the machine to his sister (the father's daughter) in January 2020. Pursuant to paragraph (b)(3)(iii)(C)(1) of this section, the time to test whether the parties are related is immediately after each step in the series, and between the original transferor and the ultimate transferee immediately after the last transaction in the series. As a result, the following relationships are tested under section 179(d)(2)(A): the father and his son, the father's son and his sister, and the father and the father's daughter.

(2) Because the father and his son are related parties within the meaning of section 179(d)(2)(A) and §1.179-4(c)(ii), the son's acquisition of the machine does not satisfy the used property acquisition requirements of paragraph (b)(3)(iii) of this section. Accordingly, the son's acquisition of the machine is not eligible for the additional first year depreciation deduction.

(3) The son and his sister are not related parties within the meaning of section 179(d)(2)(A) and §1.179-4(c)(ii). However, the father and his daughter are related parties within the meaning of section 179(d)(2)(A) and §1.179-4(c)(ii). Accordingly, the daughter's acquisition of the machine does not satisfy the used property acquisition requirements of paragraph (b)(3)(iii) of this section and is not eligible for the additional first year depreciation deduction.

(GG) *Example 33.*—(1) In June 2018, *DA*, an individual, bought and placed in service a new machine from an unrelated party for use in its trade or business. In a series of related transactions, *DA* sells the machine to *DB* and *DB* places it in service in October 2019, *DB* sells the machine to *DC* and *DC* places it in service in December 2019, and *DC* sells the machine to *DD* and *DD* places it in service in January 2020. *DA* and *DB* are related parties within the meaning of section 179(d)(2)(A) and §1.179-4(c)(ii). *DB* and *DC* are related parties within the meaning of section 179(d)(2)(B) and §1.179-4(c)(iii). *DC* and *DD* are not related parties within the meaning of section 179(d)(2)(A) and §1.179-4(c)(ii), or section 179(d)(2)(B) and §1.179-4(c)(iii). *DA* is not related to *DC* or to *DD* within the meaning of section 179(d)(2)(A) and §1.179-4(c)(ii). All parties are calendar year taxpayers.

(2) *DA*'s purchase of the machine in June 2018 satisfies the original use requirement of paragraph (b)(3)(ii) of this section and, assuming all other requirements of this section are met, qualifies for the additional first year depreciation deduction under this section.

(3) Pursuant to paragraph (b)(3)(iii)(C)(1) of this section, the time to test whether the parties in the series of related transactions are related is immediately after each step in the series, and between the original transferor and the ultimate transferee im-

mediately after the last transaction in the series. However, because *DB* placed in service and disposed of the machine in the same taxable year, *DB* is disregarded pursuant to paragraph (b)(3)(iii)(C)(2)(*i*) of this section. As a result, the following relationships are tested under section 179(d)(2)(A) and (B): *DA* and *DC*, *DC* and *DD*, and *DA* and *DD*.

(4) Because *DA* is not related to *DC* within the meaning of section 179(d)(2)(A) and §1.179-4(c)(ii), *DC*'s acquisition of the machine satisfies the used property acquisition requirement of paragraph (b)(3)(iii)(A)(2) of this section. Accordingly, assuming all other requirements of this section are satisfied, *DC*'s purchase price of the machine qualifies for the additional first year depreciation deduction under this section.

(5) Because *DC* is not related to *DD* and *DA* is not related to *DD* within the meaning of section 179(d)(2)(A) and §1.179-4(c)(ii), or section 179(d)(2)(B) and §1.179-4(c)(iii), *DD*'s acquisition of the machine satisfies the used property acquisition requirement of paragraph (b)(3)(iii)(A)(2) of this section. Accordingly, assuming all other requirements of this section are satisfied, *DD*'s purchase price of the machine qualifies for the additional first year depreciation deduction under this section.

(HH) *Example 34.*—(1) In June 2018, *EA*, an individual, bought and placed in service a new machine from an unrelated party for use in his trade or business. In a series of related transactions, *EA* sells the machine to *EB* and *EB* places it in service in September 2019, *EB* transfers the machine to *EC* in a transaction described in paragraph (g)(1)(iii) of this section and *EC* places it in service in November 2019, and *EC* sells the machine to *ED* and *ED* places it in service in January 2020. *EA* and *EB* are not related parties within the meaning of section 179(d)(2)(A) and §1.179-4(c)(ii). *EB* and *EC* are related parties within the meaning of section 179(d)(2)(B) and §1.179-4(c)(iii). *EB* and *ED* are related parties within the meaning of section 179(d)(2)(A) and §1.179-4(c)(ii), or section 179(d)(2)(B) and §1.179-4(c)(iii). *EC* and *ED* are not related parties within the meaning of section 179(d)(2)(A) and §1.179-4(c)(ii), or section 179(d)(2)(B) and §1.179-4(c)(iii). *EA* is not related to *EC* or to *ED* within the meaning of section 179(d)(2)(A) and §1.179-4(c)(ii). All parties are calendar year taxpayers.

(2) *EA*'s purchase of the machine in June 2018 satisfies the original use requirement of paragraph (b)(3)(ii) of this section and, assuming all other requirements of this section are met, qualifies for the additional first year depreciation deduction under this section.

(3) Pursuant to paragraph (b)(3)(iii)(C)(1) of this section, the time to test whether the parties in the series of related transactions are related is immediately after each step in the series, and between the original transferor and the ultimate transferee immediately after the last transaction in the series. However, because *EB* placed in service and transferred the machine in the same taxable year in a transaction described in paragraph (g)(1)(iii) of this section, the section 168(i)(7) transaction between *EB* and *EC* is disregarded pursuant to paragraph (b)(3)(iii)(C)(2)(*iii*) of this section. As a result, the following relationships are tested under section 179(d)(2)(A) and (B): *EA* and *EB*, *EB* and *ED*, *EC* and *ED*, and *EA* and *ED*.

(4) Because *EA* is not related to *EB* within the meaning of section 179(d)(2)(A) and §1.179-4(c)(ii), *EB*'s acquisition of the machine satisfies the used property acquisition requirement of paragraph (b)(3)(iii)(A)(2) of this section. Accordingly, assuming all other requirements of this section are satisfied, *EB*'s purchase price of the machine qualifies for the additional first year depreciation deduction under this section. Pursuant to paragraph (g)(1)(iii) of this section, *EB* is allocated 2/12 of its 100-percent additional first year depreciation deduction for the machine, and *EC* is allocated the remaining portion of *EB*'s 100-percent additional first year depreciation deduction for the machine.

(5) *EC* is not related to *ED* and *EA* is not related to *ED* within the meaning of section 179(d)(2)(A) and §1.179-4(c)(ii), or section 179(d)(2)(B) and §1.179-4(c)(iii). However, *EB* and *ED* are related parties within the meaning of section 179(d)(2)(A) and §1.179-4(c)(ii), or section 179(d)(2)(B) and §1.179-4(c)(iii). Accordingly, *ED*'s acquisition of the machine does not satisfy the used property acquisition requirements of paragraph (b)(3)(iii) of this section and is not eligible for the additional first year depreciation deduction.

* * *

(5) * * *

(ii) * * *

(A) * * * For determination of acquisition date, see paragraph (b)(5)(ii)(B) of this section for property acquired pursuant to a written binding contract, paragraph (b)(5)(iv) of this section for self-constructed property, and paragraph (b)(5)(v) of this section for property not acquired pursuant to a written binding contract.

* * *

(iii) * * *

Reg. §1.168(k)-2(b)(5)(iii)

(G) *Acquisition of a trade or business or an entity.*—A contract to acquire all or substantially all of the assets of a trade or business or to acquire an entity (for example, a corporation, a partnership, or a limited liability company) is binding if it is enforceable under State law against the parties to the contract. The presence of a condition outside the control of the parties, including, for example, regulatory agency approval, will not prevent the contract from being a binding contract. Further, the fact that insubstantial terms remain to be negotiated by the parties to the contract, or that customary conditions remain to be satisfied, does not prevent the contract from being a binding contract. This paragraph (b)(5)(iii)(G) also applies to a contract for the sale of the stock of a corporation that is treated as an asset sale as a result of an election under section 338.

* * *

(v) *Determination of acquisition date for property not acquired pursuant to a written binding contract.*—Except as provided in paragraphs (b)(5)(iv), (vi), and (vii) of this section, the acquisition date of property that the taxpayer acquires pursuant to a contract that does not meet the definition of a written binding contract in paragraph (b)(5)(iii) of this section, is the date on which the taxpayer paid (in the case of a cash basis taxpayer) or incurred (in the case of an accrual basis taxpayer) more than 10 percent of the total cost of the property, excluding the cost of any land and preliminary activities such as planning and designing, securing financing, exploring, or researching. This paragraph (b)(5)(v) does not apply to an acquisition described in paragraph (b)(5)(iii)(G) of this section.

* * *

(viii) * * * Unless the facts specifically indicate otherwise, assume that the parties are not related within the meaning of section 179(d)(2)(A) or (B) and §1.179-4(c), paragraph (c) of this section does not apply, and the parties do not have predecessors:

* * *

(c) *Election for components of larger self-constructed property for which the manufacture, construction, or production begins before September 28, 2017.*—(1) *In general.*—A taxpayer may elect to treat any acquired or self-constructed component, as described in paragraph (c)(3) of this section, of the larger self-constructed property, as described in paragraph (c)(2) of this section, as being eligible for the additional first year depreciation deduction under this section, assuming all requirements of section 168(k) and this section are met. The taxpayer may make this election for one or more such components.

(2) *Eligible larger self-constructed property.*—(i) *In general.*— Solely for purposes of this paragraph (c) and except as provided in paragraph (c)(2)(ii) of this section, the larger self-constructed property must be qualified property under section 168(k)(2), as in effect on the day before the date of the enactment of the Act, for which the taxpayer begins the manufacture, construction, or production before September 28, 2017. The determination of when manufacture, construction, or production of the larger self-constructed property begins is made in accordance with the rules in §1.168(k)-1(b)(4)(iii)(B). A larger self-constructed property is property that is manufactured, constructed, or produced by the taxpayer for its own use in its trade or business or for its production of income, or property that is manufactured, constructed, or produced for the taxpayer by another person under a written binding contract, as defined in §1.168(k)-1(b)(4)(ii), that is entered into prior to the manufacture, construction, or production of the property for use by the taxpayer in its trade or business or for its production of income. If the taxpayer enters into a written binding contract, as defined in paragraph (b)(5)(iii) of this section, before September 28, 2017, with another person to manufacture, construct, or produce the larger self-constructed property and the manufacture, construction, or production of this property begins after September 27, 2017, paragraph (b)(5)(iv) of this section applies and paragraph (c) of this section does not apply.

(ii) *Exceptions.*—This paragraph (c) does not apply to any larger self-constructed property that meets at least one of the following criteria:

(A) Is placed in service by the taxpayer before September 28, 2017;

(B) Is placed in service by the taxpayer after December 31, 2019, or for property described in section 168(k)(2)(B) or (C) as in effect on the day before the date of the enactment of the Act, after December 31, 2020;

(C) Does not meet the original use requirement in section 168(k)(2)(A)(ii) as in effect on the day before the date of the enactment of the Act;

(D) Is described in section 168(k)(9) and §1.168(k)-2(b)(2)(ii)(F) or (G);

(E) Is described in section 168(g)(1)(F) and (g)(8) (electing real property trade or business) or section 168(g)(1)(G) (electing farming business) and placed in service by the taxpayer in any taxable year beginning after December 31, 2017;

(F) Is qualified leasehold improvement property, as defined in section 168(e)(6) as in effect on the day before amendment by section 13204(a)(1) of the Act, and placed in service by the taxpayer after December 31, 2017;

(G) Is qualified restaurant property, as defined in section 168(e)(7) as in effect on the day before amendment by section 13204(a)(1) of the Act, and placed in service by the taxpayer after December 31, 2017;

(H) Is qualified retail improvement property, as defined in section 168(e)(8) as in effect on the day before amendment by section 13204(a)(1) of the Act, and placed in service by the taxpayer after December 31, 2017;

(I) Is qualified improvement property as defined in §1.168(b)-1(a)(5)(i)(A) (placed in service by the taxpayer after December 31, 2017); or

(J) Is included in a class of property for which the taxpayer made an election under section 168(k)(7) (formerly section 168(k)(2)(D)(iii)) not to deduct the additional first year depreciation deduction.

(3) *Eligible components.*—(i) *In general.*—Solely for purposes of this paragraph (c), a component of the larger self-constructed property, as described in paragraph (c)(2) of this section, must be qualified property under section 168(k)(2) and paragraph (b) of this section.

(ii) *Acquired components.*—Solely for purposes of this paragraph (c), a binding contract, as defined in paragraph (b)(5)(iii) of this section, to acquire a component of the larger self-constructed property must be entered into by the taxpayer after September 27, 2017.

(iii) *Self-constructed components.*—Solely for purposes of this paragraph (c), the manufacture, construction, or production of a component of the larger self-constructed property must begin after September 27, 2017. The determination of when manufacture, construction, or production of the component begins is made in accordance with the rules in paragraph (b)(5)(iv)(B) of this section.

(4) *Special rules.*—(i) *Installation costs.*—If the taxpayer pays or incurs costs, including labor costs, to install a component of the larger self-constructed property, as described in paragraph (c)(2) of this section, such costs are eligible for additional first year depreciation under this section, assuming all requirements are met, only if the component being installed meets the requirements in paragraph (c)(3) of this section.

(ii) *Property described in section 168(k)(2)(B).*—For purposes of this paragraph (c), the unadjusted depreciable basis, as defined in §1.168(b)-1(a)(3), of qualified property in section 168(k)(2)(B), as in effect on the day before the date of the enactment of the Act, is limited to the property's unadjusted depreciable basis attributable to the property's manufacture, construction, or production before January 1, 2020. The amounts of unadjusted depreciable basis attributable to the property's manufacture, construction, or production before January 1, 2020, are referred to as "progress expenditures." Rules similar to the rules in section 4.02(1)(b) of Notice 2007-36 (2007-17 I.R.B. 1000) (see §601.601(d)(2)(ii)(*b*) of this chapter) apply for determining progress expenditures.

(5) *Computation of additional first year depreciation deduction.*— (i) *Election is made.*—Before determining the allowable additional first year depreciation deduction for property for which the taxpayer makes the election specified in this paragraph (c), the taxpayer must determine the portion of the unadjusted depreciable basis, as defined in §1.168(b)-1(a)(3), of the larger self-constructed property, including all components, attributable to the component that meets the requirements of paragraph (c)(3) of this section (component basis). The additional first year depreciation deduction for the component basis is determined by multiplying such component basis by the applicable percentage for the placed-in-service year of the larger self-constructed property. The additional first year depreciation deduction for the remaining unadjusted depreciable basis of the larger self-constructed property, as described in paragraph (c)(2) of this section, is determined by multiplying such remaining unadjusted depreciable basis by the phase-down percentage in section 168(k)(8) applicable to the placed-in-service year of the larger self-constructed property. For purposes of this paragraph (c), the remaining unadjusted depreciable basis of the larger self-constructed property is equal to the unadjusted depreciable basis, as defined in §1.168(b)-1(a)(3), of the larger self-constructed property, including all components, reduced by the sum of the component basis of the components for which the taxpayer makes the election specified in this paragraph (c). If the phase-down percentage in section 168(k)(8) is zero for the placed-in-service year of the larger self-constructed property, none of the components of the larger self-constructed property qualify for the additional first year depreciation deduction under this section.

(ii) *Election is not made.*—If the taxpayer does not make the election specified in this paragraph (c), the additional first year depreciation deduction for the larger self-constructed property, including all components, that is qualified property under section 168(k)(2), as in effect on the day before the date of the enactment of the Act, is determined by multiplying the unadjusted depreciable basis, as defined in § 1.168(b)-1(a)(3), of the larger self-constructed property, including all components, by the phase-down percentage in section 168(k)(8) applicable to the placed-in-service year of the larger self-constructed property.

(6) *Time and manner for making election.*—(i) *Time for making election.*—The election specified in this paragraph (c) must be made by the due date, including extensions, of the Federal tax return for the taxable year in which the taxpayer placed in service the larger self-constructed property.

(ii) *Manner of making election.*—The election specified in this paragraph (c) must be made by attaching a statement to such return indicating that the taxpayer is making the election provided in this paragraph (c) and whether the taxpayer is making the election for all or some of the components described in paragraph (c)(3) of this section. The election is made separately by each person owning qualified property (for example, for each member of a consolidated group by the common parent of the group, by the partnership (including a lower-tier partnership), or by the S corporation).

(7) *Examples.*—The application of this paragraph (c) is illustrated by the following examples. Unless the facts specifically indicate otherwise, assume that the larger self-constructed property is qualified property under section 168(k)(2) as in effect on the day before the date of the enactment of the Act, and the components acquired or self-constructed after September 27, 2017, are qualified property under section 168(k)(2) and paragraph (b) of this section.

(i) *Example 1.* (A) *BC*, a calendar year taxpayer, is engaged in a trade or business described in section 163(j)(7)(A)(iv). In December 2015, *BC* decided to construct an electric generation power plant for its own use. This plant is property described in section 168(k)(2)(B) as in effect on the day before the date of the enactment of the Act. However, the turbine for the plant had to be manufactured by another person for *BC*. In January 2016, *BC* entered into a written binding contract with *CD* to acquire the turbine. *BC* received the completed turbine in August 2017 at which time *BC* incurred the cost of the turbine. The cost of the turbine is 11 percent of the total cost of the electric generation power plant to be constructed by *BC*. *BC* began constructing the electric generation power plant in October 2017 and placed in service this new power plant, including all component parts, in 2020.

(B) *BC* uses the safe harbor test in § 1.168(k)-1(b)(4)(iii)(B)(2) to determine when physical work of a significant nature begins for the electric generation power plant. Because the turbine that was manufactured by *CD* for *BC* is more than 10 percent of the total cost of the electric generation power plant, physical work of a significant nature for this plant began before September 28, 2017. None of *BC*'s expenditures for components of the power plant that are acquired or self-constructed after September 27, 2017, are eligible for the election specified in this paragraph (c) because the power plant is described in section 168(k)(9)(A) and paragraph (b)(2)(ii)(F) of this section and, therefore, are not eligible for the election pursuant to paragraph (c)(2)(ii)(D) of this section. Assuming all requirements are met under section 168(k)(2) as in effect on the day before the date of the enactment of the Act, the unadjusted depreciable basis of the power plant, including all components, attributable to its construction before January 1, 2020, is eligible for the 30-percent additional first year depreciation deduction pursuant to section 168(k)(8).

(ii) *Example 2.* (A) In August 2017, *BD*, a calendar-year taxpayer, entered into a written binding contract with *CE* for *CE* to manufacture a locomotive for *BD* for use in its trade or business. Before September 28, 2017, *BD* incurred $500,000 of expenses for the locomotive, which is more than 10 percent of the total cost of the locomotive. After September 27, 2017, *BD* incurred $4,000,000 of expenses for components of the locomotive. These components were acquired or self-constructed after September 27, 2017. In February 2019, *CE* delivered the locomotive to *BD* and *BD* placed in service the locomotive. The total cost of the locomotive is $4,500,000. The locomotive is property described in section 168(k)(2)(B) as in effect on the day before the date of the enactment of the Act. On its timely filed Federal income tax return for 2019, *BD* made the election specified in this paragraph (c).

(B) *BD* uses the safe harbor test in § 1.168(k)-1(b)(4)(iii)(B)(2) to determine when physical work of a significant nature begins for the locomotive. Because *BD* had incurred more than 10 percent of the total cost of the locomotive before September 28, 2017, physical work of a significant nature for this locomotive began before September 28, 2017. Because *BD* made the election specified in this paragraph (c), the cost of $1,000,000 for the locomotive's components acquired or

self-constructed after September 27, 2017, qualifies for the 100-percent additional first year depreciation deduction, assuming all other requirements are met. The remaining cost of the locomotive is $500,000 and such amount qualifies for the 40-percent additional first year depreciation deduction pursuant to section 168(k)(8).

(iii) *Example 3.* (A) In March 2017, *BE*, a calendar-year taxpayer, decided to construct qualified leasehold improvement property, as defined in section 168(e)(6) as in effect on the day before enactment of the Act, for its own use in its trade or business. This qualified leasehold improvement property also met the definition of qualified improvement property as defined in section 168(k)(3) as in effect on the day before enactment of the Act. Physical work of a significant nature for this qualified leasehold improvement property began before September 28, 2017. After September 27, 2017, *BE* acquired components of the qualified leasehold improvement property at a cost of $100,000. *BE* placed in service the qualified leasehold improvement property in February 2018.

(B) Because *BE* placed in service the qualified leasehold improvement property after December 31, 2017, none of *BE*'s expenditures of $100,000 for components of the qualified leasehold improvement property that are acquired after September 27, 2017, are eligible for the election specified in this paragraph (c) pursuant to paragraph (c)(2)(ii)(F) of this section. Additionally, *BE*'s unadjusted depreciable basis of the qualified leasehold improvement property, including all components, is not eligible for any additional first year depreciation deduction under section 168(k) and this section nor under section 168(k) as in effect on the day before enactment of the Act.

* * *

(e) * * *

(1) * * *

(iii) * * * The amounts of unadjusted depreciable basis attributable to the property's manufacture, construction, or production before January 1, 2020, are referred to as "progress expenditures." Rules similar to the rules in section 4.02(1)(b) of Notice 2007-36 (2007-17 I.R.B. 1000) (see § 601.601(d)(2)(ii)(b) of this chapter) apply for determining progress expenditures.

* * *

(g) * * *

(11) *Mid-quarter convention.*—In determining whether the mid-quarter convention applies for a taxable year under section 168(d)(3) and § 1.168(d)-1, the depreciable basis, as defined in § 1.168(d)-1(b)(4), for the taxable year the qualified property is placed in service by the taxpayer is not reduced by the allowed or allowable additional first year depreciation deduction for that taxable year. See § 1.168(d)-1(b)(4).

(h) * * *

(4) *Regulation project REG-106808-19.*—(i) *In general.*—Except as provided in paragraph (h)(4)(ii) of this section, the rules of this section in this regulation project REG-106808-19 apply to—

(A) Qualified property under section 168(k)(2) that is placed in service by the taxpayer during or after the taxpayer's taxable year that includes the date of publication of a Treasury decision adopting these rules as final regulations in the **Federal Register**;

(B) A specified plant for which the taxpayer properly made an election to apply section 168(k)(5) and that is planted, or grafted to a plant that was previously planted, by the taxpayer during or after the taxpayer's taxable year that includes the date of publication of a Treasury decision adopting these rules as final regulations in the **Federal Register**; and

(C) Components acquired or self-constructed after September 27, 2017, of larger self-constructed property for which manufacture, construction, or production begins before September 28, 2017, and that is qualified property under section 168(k)(2) as in effect before the enactment of the Act and placed in service by the taxpayer during or after the taxpayer's taxable year that includes the date of publication of a Treasury decision adopting these rules as final regulations in the **Federal Register**.

(ii) *Early application of regulation project REG-106808-19.*—A taxpayer may rely on the provisions of this section in this regulation project REG-106808-19, in its entirety, for—

(A) Qualified property under section 168(k)(2) acquired and placed in service after September 27, 2017, by the taxpayer during the taxpayer's taxable year ending on or after September 28, 2017, and ending before the taxpayer's taxable year that includes the date of publication of a Treasury decision adopting these rules as final regulations in the **Federal Register**;

(B) A specified plant for which the taxpayer properly made an election to apply section 168(k)(5) and that is planted, or grafted to a plant that was previously planted, after September 27, 2017, by the taxpayer during the taxpayer's taxable year ending on or after September 28, 2017, and ending before the taxpayer's taxable year that includes the date of publication of a Treasury decision adopting these rules as final regulations in the **Federal Register**; and

(C) Components acquired or self-constructed after September 27, 2017, of larger self-constructed property for which manufacture, construction, or production begins before September 28, 2017, and that is qualified property under section 168(k)(2) as in effect before the enactment of the Act and placed in service by the taxpayer during the taxpayer's taxable year ending on or after September 28, 2017, and ending before the taxpayer's taxable year that includes the date of publication of a Treasury decision adopting these rules as final regulations in the **Federal Register**.

Treatment of Payments to Charitable Entities: Return for Consideration

Treatment of Payments to Charitable Entities: Return for Consideration.—Amendments to Reg. §1.170A-1, updating the regulations under section 162 to reflect current law regarding the application of section 162 to a taxpayer that makes a payment or transfer to an entity described in section 170(c) for a business purpose, are proposed (published in the Federal Register on December 17, 2019) (REG-107431-19).

Par. 4. Section 1.170A-1 is amended as follows:

1. Paragraph (c)(5) is revised.

2. In paragraph (h)(1), remove the cross-references to §1.170A-13(f)(6)" and §1.170A-13(f)(5)" and add in their places "paragraph (h)(4)(i) of this section" and "paragraph (h)(4)(ii) of this section", respectively.

3. Paragraphs (h)(2)(i)(B) and (h)(3)(iii) are revised.

4. Paragraph (h)(3)(viii) is redesignated as paragraph (h)(3)(x).

5. New paragraph (h)(3)(viii) and paragraph (h)(3)(ix) are added.

6. Paragraphs (h)(4) through (6) are redesignated as paragraphs (h)(5) through (7).

7. New paragraph (h)(4) is added.

The revisions and additions read as follows:

§1.170A-1. Charitable, etc., contributions and gifts; allowance of deduction.

* * *

(c) * * *

(5) For payments or transfers to an entity described in section 170(c) by a taxpayer carrying on a trade or business, see §1.162-15(a).

* * *

(h) * * *

(2) * * *

(i) * * *

(B) The fair market value of the goods or services received or expected to be received in return.

* * *

(3) * * *

(iii) *In consideration for*.—For purposes of paragraph (h) of this section, the term *in consideration for* has the meaning set forth in paragraph (h)(4)(i) of this section.

* * *

(viii) *Safe harbor for payments by C corporations and specified passthrough entities*.—For payments by a C corporation or by a specified passthrough entity to an entity described in section 170(c), where the C corporation or specified passthrough entity receives or expects to receive a state or local tax credit that reduces the charitable contribution deduction for such payments under paragraph (h)(3) of this section, see §1.162-15(a)(3) (providing safe harbors under section 162(a) to the extent of that reduction).

(ix) *Safe harbor for individuals*.—Under certain circumstances, an individual who itemizes deductions and makes a payment to an entity described in section 170(c) in consideration for a state or local tax credit may treat the portion of such payment for which a charitable contribution deduction is disallowed under paragraph (h)(3) of this section as a payment of state or local taxes under section 164. See §1.164-3(j), providing a safe harbor for certain payments by individuals in exchange for state or local tax.

* * *

(4) *Definitions*.—For purposes of this paragraph (h), the following definitions apply:

(i) *In consideration for*.—A taxpayer receives goods or services in consideration for a taxpayer's payment or transfer to an entity described in section 170(c) if, at the time the taxpayer makes the payment to such entity, the taxpayer receives or expects to receive goods or services from that entity or any other party in return.

(ii) *Goods or services*.—Goods or services means cash, property, services, benefits, and privileges.

(iii) *Applicability date*.—The definitions provided in this paragraph (h)(4) are applicable for amounts paid or property transferred on or after December 17, 2019.

* * *

Exempt Organization: Unrelated Business Taxable Income

Exempt Organization: Unrelated Business Taxable Income.—Amendments to Reg. §1.170A-9, providing guidance on how an exempt organization subject to the unrelated business income tax described in section 511 of the Internal Revenue Code (Code) determines if it has more than one unrelated trade or business, and, if so, how the exempt organization calculates unrelated business taxable income, are proposed (published in the Federal Register on April 24, 2020) (REG-106864-18).

Par. 2. Section 1.170A-9 is proposed to be amended by:

1. Adding new paragraph (f)(7)(v).

2. Adding new paragraph (k)(3).

The additions read as follows:

§1.170A-9. Definition of section 170(b)(1)(A) organization.

* * *

(f) * * *

(7) * * *

(v) *Unrelated business activities*.—The term *net income from unrelated business activities* in section 509(d)(3) includes (but is not limited to) an organization's unrelated business taxable income (UBTI) within the meaning of section 512. However, when calculating UBTI for purposes of determining support (within the meaning of paragraph (f)(7)(i) of this section), section 512(a)(6) does not apply.

Accordingly, in the case of an organization that derives gross income from the regular conduct of two or more unrelated business activities, support includes the aggregate of gross income from all such unrelated business activities less the aggregate of the deductions allowed with respect to all such unrelated business activities.

* * *

(k) * * *

(3) *Applicability date*.—Paragraph (f)(7)(v) of this section applies to taxable years beginning on or after [DATE OF PUBLICATION OF THE FINAL RULES IN THE **Federal Register**].

Treatment of Payments to Charitable Entities: Return for Consideration

Treatment of Payments to Charitable Entities: Return for Consideration.—Amendments to Reg. §1.170A-13, updating the regulations under section 162 to reflect current law regarding the application of section 162 to a taxpayer that makes a payment or transfer to an entity described in section 170(c) for a business purpose, are proposed (published in the Federal Register on December 17, 2019) (REG-107431-19).

Par. 5. Section 1.170A-13(f)(7) is amended by removing the cross-reference to §1.170A-1(h)(5)" and adding in its place §1.170A-1(h)(6)."

§1.170A-13. Recordkeeping and return requirements for deductions for charitable contributions.

Application of Section 172(h): Regulations: Consolidated Groups

Application of Section 172(h): Regulations: Consolidated Groups.—Reg. §§1.172(h)-0—1.172(h)-5, providing guidance regarding the treatment of corporate equity reduction transactions (CERTs), including the treatment of multiple step plans for the acquisition of stock and CERTs involving members of a consolidated group, are proposed (published in the Federal Register on September 17, 2012) (REG-140668-07) (corrected October 23, 2012).

□ Par. 2. Sections 1.172(h)-0 through 1.172(h)-5 are added to read as follows:

§1.172(h)-0. Table of Contents.—This section lists the paragraphs contained in §§1.172(h)-1 through 1.172(h)-5.

§1.172(h)-1. Existence of CERT and loss limitation years.—(a) *In general.*—If there is a corporate equity reduction transaction (CERT) and an applicable corporation has a corporate equity reduction interest loss (CERIL) for any loss limitation year, section 172(b)(1)(E) and (h), this section, §§1.172(h)-2 through 1.172(h)-5, and §1.1502-72 (collectively, the *CERT rules*) limit the amount of net operating loss that can be carried back to any taxable year preceding the taxable year in which the CERT occurs. This section provides rules regarding the determination of whether a CERT has occurred and whether a taxable year constitutes a loss limitation year. See §1.172(h)-2 for rules regarding the computation of a CERIL.

(b) *Applicable corporation.*—(1) *In general.*—The CERT rules apply only to applicable corporations. The term *applicable corporation* means a C corporation that acquires stock, or the stock of which is acquired, in a major stock acquisition (MSA), a C corporation making distributions with respect to, or redeeming, its stock in connection with an excess distribution (ED), or a C corporation that is a successor of any corporation described in this paragraph (b)(1). For special rules regarding the definition of an applicable corporation with regard to members that join and leave a consolidated group, see §1.1502-72(a) and (b).

(2) *Predecessor and successor.*—For purposes of the CERT rules, the term *predecessor* means a transferor or distributor of assets to a transferee or distributee (the successor) in a transaction to which section 381(a) applies. A corporation is a successor to its predecessor, and to all predecessors of that predecessor. If an applicable corporation transfers or distributes its assets to a successor, the successor is treated as an applicable corporation in the successor's taxable year during which the transfer or distribution occurs and any subsequent years.

(c) *CERT defined.*—(1) *In general.*—A CERT can be an MSA or an ED.

(2) *MSA defined.*—An *MSA* is the acquisition by a corporation pursuant to a plan of such corporation (or any group of persons acting in concert with such corporation) of stock in another corporation representing 50 percent or more (by vote or value) of the stock in such other corporation.

(3) *ED defined.*—An *ED* is any excess of the aggregate distributions made during a taxable year by a corporation with respect to its stock, over the greater of—

(i) 150 percent of the average of such distributions (the three-year distribution average) during the three taxable years immediately preceding such taxable year (the distribution lookback period); or

(ii) 10 percent of the fair market value of the stock of such corporation as of the beginning of such taxable year. For purposes of testing a potential ED, distributions include redemptions.

(d) *Transactions tested as CERTs.*—(1) *Tax-free transactions.*—A transaction may constitute a CERT and must be tested under the CERT rules regardless of whether gain or loss is recognized by any party. For example, a distribution that qualifies for tax-free treatment under section 355 is tested as a potential ED (or part of a potential ED). Likewise, the acquisition by a corporation of 50 percent or more of the stock of another corporation in a transaction meeting the requirements of section 351, section 368(a)(1)(A) and (a)(2)(E), or section 368(a)(1)(B) constitutes an MSA.

(2) *Multiple step plan of acquisition.*—Solely for purposes of determining whether an MSA has occurred and determining the consequences of an MSA, all steps of an integrated plan (including redemptions and other distributions) are tested as a single potential MSA. If an integrated plan qualifies as an MSA and includes one or more distributions, then, for purposes of applying the CERT rules, the distributions are treated solely as a part of the MSA, regardless of whether such distributions would otherwise constitute an ED (or would so qualify in conjunction with other distributions). Any distributions during the year that are not part of the integrated plan qualifying as an MSA are tested as a potential ED.

(3) *Examples.*—The following examples illustrate the rules of this paragraph (d). For purposes of these examples, unless otherwise stated, assume that all entities are domestic C corporations that do not join in the filing of a consolidated return and that the entities have no history of paying dividends or otherwise making distributions:

Example 1. Spin-off. Distributing corporation (D) distributes stock of controlled corporation (C) to its shareholders in a transaction that satisfies the requirements of section 355. There is no taxable "boot" associated with the distribution. Pursuant to paragraph (d)(1) of this section, D's distribution of C stock is tested as a potential ED (in conjunction with any other distributions by D during the same taxable year). The same result would obtain if D distributes boot to its shareholders in addition to C stock.

Example 2. Bootstrap acquisition. (i) *Facts.* T is a publicly-traded, widely-held corporation with a single class of stock outstanding with a fair market value of $100. The following steps occur as part of an integrated plan. Corporation A acquires 10 percent of the outstanding stock of T for $10. A forms a new corporation, S, with a contribution of $25. S obtains a loan of $65 from an unrelated lender, and then merges with and into T, with T surviving. In the merger, all shareholders of T except A receive cash in exchange for their shares, and as a consequence, A owns all of the outstanding stock of T. As a result of the merger, T becomes liable for S's $65 loan. Assume that the $90 cash payment from T to the T shareholders should be treated as a redemption to the extent of the $65 loan assumed by T, and as a stock acquisition by A to the extent of the remaining $25.

(ii) *Analysis.* A's direct acquisition of 10 percent of T's outstanding stock and the steps culminating with the merger are part of an integrated plan. Therefore, the multiple steps are tested together as a potential MSA. Because the steps of the integrated plan resulted in A's acquisition of 100 percent of T, the transaction is treated as a single MSA. Furthermore, because the $65 redemption is part of an MSA, it is treated solely as part of the MSA and is not tested as a potential ED. See paragraph (d)(2) of this section.

(e) *Loss limitation years.*—The taxable year in which a CERT occurs and each of the two succeeding taxable years constitute loss limitation years with regard to the CERT. See §1.172(h)-4(b) (addressing loss limitation years of successors) and §1.1502-72(a)(3) (addressing loss limitation years of consolidated groups and former members of consolidated groups).

(f) *Computation of three-year distribution average relevant to a potential ED.*—(1) *Integrated plan.*—Section 172(h)(3)(C)(ii)(I) and paragraph (c)(3) of this section treat as an ED the excess of distributions in a taxable year over the taxpayer's average distributions (three-year distribution average) made in the three taxable years preceding the taxable year in which a potential ED occurs (distribution lookback period). The computation of a taxpayer's three-year distribution average under this paragraph (f) excludes any distribution during the distribution lookback period that is treated as part of an integrated plan qualifying as an MSA pursuant to paragraph (d)(2) of this section. See §1.1502-72(f)(2) and (3) for rules relating to distributions (including intercompany distributions) made during a consolidated return year.

(2) *Short taxable year.*—For purposes of computing the three-year distribution average under this paragraph (f), if the year of the potential ED is less than a full 12-month year, the distribution history with regard to any year of the taxpayer during a distribution lookback period (distribution lookback period year) equals the amount of distributions made during the distribution lookback period year multiplied by a fraction, the numerator of which equals the number of days in the short taxable year of the potential ED, and the denominator of which equals the number of days in the distribution lookback period year. The value of the fraction may not exceed 100 percent. No distributions are deemed made (in excess of amounts actually distributed) in a distribution lookback period year that is shorter than the year of the potential ED.

(g) *Effective/applicability date.*—This section is applicable to CERTs occurring on or after the date of publication of the Treasury decision adopting these rules as final regulations in the **Federal Register**. This section is also applicable to the deconsolidation of a member from, or the acquisition of a corporation by, a consolidated group that occurs on or after the date of publication of the Treasury decision adopting these rules as final regulations in the **Federal Register**. However, in each case, this section does not apply to any CERT, deconsolidation, or acquisition occurring pursuant to a written agreement that is binding before the date of publication of the Treasury decision adopting these rules as final regulations in the **Federal Register**. [Reg. §1.172(h)-1.]

§1.172(h)-2. Computation of a CERIL.—(a) *In general.*—(1) *Scope.*—The portion of a net operating loss (NOL) that is treated as a corporate equity reduction interest loss (CERIL) (as defined in paragraph (a)(2) of this section) cannot be carried back to a taxable year preceding the taxable year in which the corporate equity reduction transaction (CERT) occurs. This section provides rules for computing allocable interest deductions necessary to compute a CERIL for purposes of applying section 172(b)(1)(E) and (h), §§1.172(h)-1 through 1.172(h)-5, and §1.1502-72 (the CERT rules).

(2) *CERIL defined.*—A CERIL means, with respect to any loss limitation year, the excess (if any) of the NOL for such taxable year over the NOL for such taxable year determined without regard to any allocable interest deductions otherwise taken into account in computing such loss.

(b) *Computation of allocable interest deductions.*—(1) *In general.*—Allocable interest deductions are deductions allowed for interest on the portion of indebtedness allocable to a CERT. Except as provided in section 172(h)(2)(E) (relating to adjustments for certain unforeseeable events), indebtedness is allocated to a CERT in the manner prescribed in section 263A(f)(2)(A), without regard to clause (i) thereof (relating to traced debt). Generally, interest deductions are allocable to a CERT if the interest expense could have been avoided if the CERT had not been undertaken (for example, if the amount of CERT costs (as defined in paragraph (b)(3)) had instead been used to pay down debt). See section 263A(f)(2)(A)(ii) and §1.263A-9(a)(1). For purposes of applying the avoided cost rules of section 263A(f)(2)(A)(ii), all CERT costs are treated as if they were cash expenditures.

(2) *Operating rules.*—This section provides a method for identifying the pool of costs to be treated as arising from a CERT (CERT costs). The interest allocable to those CERT costs is then computed under the principles of the avoided cost rules under section 263A(f)(2)(A) (without regard to paragraph (i) thereof) and the regulations thereunder, but substituting "CERT costs" or "accumulated CERT costs" (as defined in paragraph (b)(4)) for "production expenditures" or "accumulated production expenditures," where those terms appear. In addition, for purposes of applying the avoided cost rules to compute interest allocable to a CERT, the "production period" is treated as beginning on the first date of the taxable year in which the CERT occurs (year of the CERT) on which there are accumulated CERT costs. Because the principles of section 263A(f)(2)(A)(i) are inapplicable to CERT computations, the principles of §1.263A-9(b) (relating to traced debt) are also inapplicable. Instead, accumulated CERT costs are treated in their entirety as expenditures allocable to non-traced debt as that term is defined under §1.263A-9(c)(5), and interest allocable to a CERT is calculated without tracing debt under the provisions of §1.263A-9(d)(1). Limitations apply to the amount of interest allocable to a CERT. See, for example, section 172(h)(2)(C)(ii) and §1.172(h)-3 (generally relating to three-year average interest history).

(3) *CERT costs defined.*—(i) *Major stock acquisition.*—CERT costs with regard to a major stock acquisition (MSA) include the fair market value of the stock acquired, whether that stock is acquired in exchange for cash, for stock of the acquirer, or for other property. In addition, CERT costs include the fair market value of any distributions to shareholders that are treated as part of the MSA under §1.172(h)-1(d)(2). CERT costs also include the sum of amounts paid or incurred to facilitate any step of the MSA to the extent that those amounts are required to be capitalized under section 263(a), and any amounts disallowed under section 162(k). See also §1.1502-72(a)(4) for additional rules regarding CERT costs in the case of a reverse acquisition.

(ii) *Excess distribution.*—CERT costs with regard to an excess distribution (ED) include the fair market value of any distributions to shareholders during the year of the CERT. CERT costs also include the sum of amounts paid or incurred to facilitate the distributions to the extent that those amounts are required to be capitalized under section 263(a), and any amounts disallowed under section 162(k). To the extent that neither section 263(a) nor section 162(k) applies or if only section 162(k) applies to a distribution included in an ED, additional CERT costs associated with the distribution are determined under the principles of §1.263(a)-4(e) (relating to the capitalization of certain costs incurred to acquire or create intangibles), applied as if the distribution were a transaction within the scope of §1.263(a)-4.

(iii) *Borrowing costs included in CERT costs.*—For purposes of identifying CERT costs with regard to an MSA or ED under this paragraph (b)(3), the determination of whether costs facilitate an MSA or ED is made without regard to §§1.263(a)-5(c)(1) and 1.263(a)-4(e)(1)(iv) (excluding borrowing costs). Therefore, certain costs of debt financing are included in CERT costs.

(4) *Accumulated CERT costs.*—(i) *Major stock acquisition.*—Except as otherwise provided in this paragraph (b)(4), accumulated CERT costs with regard to an MSA as of a particular date are the total CERT costs described in paragraph (b)(3) of this section that have been taken into account as of that date under the applicable corporation's method of accounting. For example, CERT costs incurred in the taxable year after the year of the CERT are not included in accumulated CERT costs in the year of the CERT, but are included in accumulated CERT costs during the taxable year in which they are incurred and in any succeeding loss limitation year. Similarly, CERT costs include costs incurred after the date on which a CERT occurs if the CERT consists of multiple steps. See §1.172(h)-5(a).

(ii) *Excess distribution.*—Except as provided otherwise in this paragraph (b)(4), accumulated CERT costs as of a particular date with regard to an ED are the total CERT costs described in paragraph (b)(3) of this section that have been taken into account as of that date under the applicable corporation's method of accounting, multiplied by a fraction, the numerator of which equals the amount of distributions constituting an ED during the year of the CERT pursuant to §1.172(h)-1(c)(3), and the denominator of which equals the total amount of distributions made during the year of the CERT. CERT costs include costs incurred after date on which a CERT occurs if the CERT consists of multiple steps. See §1.172(h)-5(a).

(iii) *CERT costs incurred in a year prior to a CERT year.*—CERT costs incurred in a year prior to the year of the CERT are treated as incurred on the first day of the year of the CERT.

(iv) *Year constitutes loss limitation year with regard to multiple CERTs.*—If a single taxable year constitutes a loss limitation year with regard to more than one CERT, the accumulated CERT costs on any particular date during that year include accumulated CERT costs under this paragraph (b)(4) with regard to all such CERTs. See §1.172(h)-3(d) for rules regarding computation of a CERIL if a year constitutes a loss limitation year with regard to multiple CERTs.

(5) *No netting of interest income and deductions.*—Allocable interest deductions under paragraph (b)(1) of this section are the deductions allowed for interest on any indebtedness allocable to a CERT. Allocable interest deductions are not netted against a taxpayer's interest income.

(6) *Certain unforeseeable events.*—[Reserved].

(7) *Examples.*—The following examples illustrate the rules of this paragraph (b). Unless otherwise provided, assume that all entities are domestic C corporations that do not join in the filing of consolidated returns and are accrual method taxpayers. Assume that all applicable corporations have substantial NOLs in their loss limitation years:

Example 1. CERT costs in MSA. (i) *Facts.* On February 1, Year 5, Corporation A begins investigating the possible acquisition of Corporation T. On March 1, Year 5, A enters into an exclusivity agreement with T. On July 1, Year 5, A engages in an MSA when it acquires all of the stock of T in exchange for cash. A incurs costs for services rendered by its outside counsel and an investment banker. A's outside counsel and the investment banker conduct due diligence on T, determine the value of T, negotiate and structure the transaction with T, draft the purchase agreement, secure shareholder approval, and prepare SEC filings. In addition, the investment banker arranges borrowings to fund both the stock acquisition and A's operations. A also pays a bonus to one of its corporate officers, who negotiated the acquisition of T. Before and after the acquisition is consummated, A incurs costs to relocate personnel and equipment, and to integrate records and information systems.

(ii) *Analysis.* The CERT costs taken into account by A in computing interest allocable to the CERT include the fair market value of the T stock. See paragraph (b)(3)(i) of this section. The costs incurred on or after the date of the exclusivity agreement, March 1, Year 5, (but not before) to conduct due diligence are also included in A's CERT costs. See paragraph (b)(3)(i) of this section and §1.263(a)-5(e)(1). A's CERT costs also include all amounts incurred to determine the value of T, negotiate and structure the transaction with T, draft the purchase agreement, secure shareholder approval, and prepare SEC filings. See §1.263(a)-5(e)(2). In addition, A's CERT costs

include borrowing costs that facilitate the CERT. See paragraph (b)(3)(iii) of this section. A's CERT costs do not include any portion of the bonus paid to the corporate officer or the costs incurred to relocate personnel and equipment, and to integrate records and information systems. See §1.263(a)-5(c)(6) and (d).

Example 2. CERT costs in ED. (i) *Facts.* X corporation is a calendar-year taxpayer. On July 1, Year 5, X makes a distribution of $80,000 to its shareholders, $60,000 of which constitutes an ED. X makes no other distributions during Year 5. At previous regular quarterly board of directors meetings, the directors discussed the July 1, Year 5 distribution. On March 30, Year 5, X incurs $2,500 in borrowing costs that constitute CERT costs under paragraph (b)(3)(iii) of this section. In addition, on March 30 and April 15, Year 5, X incurs $500 and $3,000, respectively, for work performed by its outside counsel which facilitates the ED under the principles of §1.263(a)-4(e). During Year 5, X pays its directors for attendance at the regular quarterly board of directors meetings. No additional CERT costs are incurred in Years 6 and 7.

(ii) *CERT costs.* X's CERT costs include the fair market value of all distributions made during the year of the CERT ($80,000), as well as the $2,500 of borrowing costs. See paragraph (b)(3)(ii) and (iii) of this section. In addition, under the principles of §1.263(a)-4(e), X's CERT costs include the costs incurred for work performed by A's outside counsel related to the ED. See paragraph (b)(3)(ii) of this section and §1.263(a)-4(e)(1)(i). X's CERT costs do not include amounts paid to X's board of directors to attend the regular board of directors meetings. See §1.263(a)-4(e)(4)(ii)(B).

(iii) *Accumulated CERT costs.* Under paragraph (b)(4)(ii) of this section, X's accumulated CERT costs as of a particular date with regard to its ED are the total CERT costs that have been taken into account as of that date multiplied by a fraction the numerator of which equals the amount of distributions constituting ED during the year of the CERT, and the denominator of which equals the total amount of distributions made during the year of the CERT. Here $60,000 is divided by $80,000, which equals 3/4. The CERT occurs during X's Year 5, and that year is a loss limitation year with regard to the CERT. X's accumulated CERT costs on March 30, Year 5 are $2,250 (3,000 x 3/4). X's accumulated CERT costs are $4,500 (6,000 x 3/4) on April 15, Year 5 and $64,500 (86,000 x 3/4) on July 1, Year 5. X's Years 6 and 7 are also loss limitation years. Because no additional CERT costs are incurred in Years 6 and 7, throughout those years, X's accumulated CERT costs are $64,500.

Example 3. Accumulated CERT costs in an MSA. (i) *All CERT costs incurred in year of CERT.* X corporation is a calendar-year taxpayer. On March 1, Year 5, X acquires all of the stock of unrelated corporation T in an MSA. X's loss limitation years are calendar Years 5, 6, and 7. During Year 5, X incurs the following CERT costs: $4,000 on January 30; $50,000 on March 1; and $9,000 on March 15. During Year 5, X's accumulated CERT costs are: $4,000 as of January 30; $54,000 as of March 1; and $63,000 as of March 15. See paragraph (b)(4)(i) of this section. No additional CERT costs are incurred in Years 6 and 7. As a result, throughout Years 6 and 7, X's accumulated CERT costs are $63,000.

(ii) *Portion of CERT costs incurred prior to year of CERT.* The facts are the same as in paragraph (i) of this *Example 3*, except during Year 4, X incurs $2,000 of CERT costs. During Year 5, X's accumulated CERT costs are: $2,000 as of January 1 (reflecting costs incurred during Year 4); $6,000 as of January 30; $56,000 as of March 1; and $65,000 as of March 15. See paragraph (b)(4)(i) and (iii) of this section. X is treated as having no accumulated CERT costs during Year 4.

(c) *Effective/applicability date.*—This section is applicable to CERTs occurring on or after the date of publication of the Treasury decision adopting these rules as final regulations in the **Federal Register**. This section is also applicable to the deconsolidation of a member from, or the acquisition of a corporation by, a consolidated group that occurs on or after the date of publication of the Treasury decision adopting these rules as final regulations in the **Federal Register**. However, in each case, this section does not apply to any CERT, deconsolidation, or acquisition occurring pursuant to a written agreement that is binding before the date of publication of the Treasury decision adopting these rules as final regulations in the **Federal Register**. [Reg. §1.172(h)-2.]

§1.172(h)-3. Limitation on allocable interest deductions.—(a) *General rule.*—The amount of allocable interest deductions (determined under §1.172(h)-2(b)) for any loss limitation year is limited to the excess (if any) of the amount allowable as a deduction for interest paid or accrued by the taxpayer during the loss limitation year, over the average of interest paid or accrued by the taxpayer (the three-year average) for the three taxable years preceding the taxable year in which the corporate equity reduction transaction (CERT) occurred (the lookback period). This section provides additional rules for computing the three-year average relevant to any loss limitation year for purposes of applying section 172(b)(1)(F) and (h), §§1.172(h) 1 through 1.172(h)-5, and §1.1502-72 (the CERT rules).

(b) *Three-year average for a short loss limitation year.*—(1) *General rule.*—For purposes of computing the three-year average if the relevant loss limitation year is less than a full 12-month year, the interest paid or accrued with regard to any year of the taxpayer during a lookback period (lookback period year) equals the amount of interest treated as paid or accrued multiplied by a fraction, the numerator of which equals the number of days in the short loss limitation year, and the denominator of which equals the number of days in the lookback period year. The value of the fraction may not exceed 100 percent. Zero interest is deemed paid or accrued (in excess of amounts actually paid or accrued) in a lookback period year that is shorter than the loss limitation year.

(2) *Example.*—The following example illustrates the short loss limitation year rule of this paragraph (b):

Example. (i) *Facts.* T, a domestic C corporation, was organized on July 1, Year 1. T's first taxable year is a short taxable year, which includes July 1 through December 31, Year 1 (184 days). T's next two taxable years are full calendar years: Calendar Year 2 and Calendar Year 3. T's Year 4 ends on September 30 as a result of a change in accounting period. T engages in a CERT during its taxable Year 4, which includes January 1, Year 4, through September 30, Year 4 (273 days). T's next two taxable periods are full 12-month fiscal years ending on September 30, Year 5, and September 30, Year 6.

(ii) *Year 4 analysis.* T's taxable Year 4 is a short loss limitation year. Therefore, in computing its three-year average applicable to loss limitation Year 4, T multiplies its interest treated as paid or accrued during each of the three years of the lookback period by the fraction specified in paragraph (b)(1) of this section. The pertinent fraction with regard to Year 1 of the lookback period is 273/184 (number of days in short loss limitation year divided by the number of days in the lookback period year). However, under paragraph (b)(1) of this section, the value of the fraction cannot exceed 100 percent. As a result, T includes in the computation of its three-year average its actual interest paid or accrued in Year 1. As to Years 2 and 3, T includes in the computation of its three-year average its actual interest paid or accrued in each of those years, multiplied by a fraction equal to 273/365.

(iii) *Year 5 and 6 analysis.* Because T's taxable Years 5 and 6 are full 12- month loss limitation years, T includes in the computation of its three-year average applicable to those loss limitation years its actual interest paid or accrued in each year of the lookback period, without adjustment.

(c) *Computation of interest paid or accrued by corporation with incomplete lookback period.*—(1) *Lookback period for corporation not in existence.*—If an applicable corporation was not in existence for three taxable years preceding the taxable year in which the CERT occurred (the lookback period), for purposes of determining the limitation on allocable interest deductions under section 172(h)(2)(C) and paragraph (a) of this section, the applicable corporation's lookback period is deemed to have additional 12-month periods that end on the calendar date that is one day prior to the date of the corporation's organization. See § 1.172(h)-4(c)(2)(i)(B) (regarding determination of lookback period for successor applicable corporations not in existence on date of CERT) and § 1.1502-72(d)(4)(ii) (regarding consolidated groups not in existence during the entire lookback period).

(2) *Interest history of corporation not in existence.*—If an applicable corporation was not in existence for the entire lookback period, it is treated as having paid or accrued zero interest during periods deemed to exist under paragraph (c)(1) of this section in computing any three-year average. However, if the applicable corporation is a successor corporation pursuant to § 1.172(h)-1(b)(2), the computation of any three-year average for the successor includes interest paid or accrued by any predecessor during the lookback period. See § 1.172(h)-4(c)(2)(ii)(A).

(3) *Example.*—The following example illustrates the rules of this paragraph (c):

Example. Corporation not in existence for entire lookback period. C is a domestic C corporation that does not join in the filing of a consolidated return and maintains a calendar taxable year. C is formed on October 1, Year 3, and engages in a CERT during Year 5. For purposes of computing any CERIL related to the CERT, paragraph (a) of this section requires that C must measure its interest deductions for the lookback period. However, C was not in existence for three taxable years preceding the year in which the CERT occurred. Rather, C was in existence for one full calendar taxable year (Year 4) and one short taxable year (October 1 through December 31, Year 3). Pursuant to paragraph (c)(1) of this section, C's lookback period is deemed to include an additional taxable period (October 1, Year 2, through September 30, Year 3). Further, in computing any three-year average, C is treated as having paid or accrued zero interest during the deemed additional period. See paragraph (c)(2) of this section.

(d) *Computation of a CERIL if single year constitutes loss limitation year with regard to multiple CERTs.*—(1) *Single CERIL computation.*—This paragraph (d) applies if a taxable year constitutes a loss limitation year of the taxpayer with regard to more than one CERT. In that case, a single corporate equity reduction interest loss (CERIL) is computed under section 172(h)(1) and § 1.172(h)-2(a)(2) for that year. This computation takes into account accumulated CERT costs for every CERT, determined under § 1.172(h)-2(b)(4)(iv) for the loss limitation year.

(2) *Limitation on allocable interest deductions.*—In computing the single CERIL under this paragraph (d), section 172(h)(2)(C) and paragraph (a) of this section are applied a single time to limit the cumulative amount of interest allocable to all of the CERTs to the excess (if any) of the amount allowable as a deduction for interest paid or accrued by the taxpayer during the loss limitation year over the three-year average for the lookback period. The limitation is not applied separately with respect to interest allocable to a particular CERT.

(3) *Computation of three-year average if CERTs have different lookback periods.*—(i) *In general.*—If the lookback periods (as defined in paragraph (a) of this section or in § 1.1502-72(d)(4)) relevant to all of the CERTs pertinent to a loss limitation year are not identical, a cumulative three-year average is computed by applying the rules of paragraph (d)(3)(ii) of this section. The cumulative three-year average is treated as the three-year average relevant to the loss limitation year, and is applied to determine the limitation on the amount of interest allocable to all of the CERTs under section 172(h)(2)(C) and paragraph (a) of this section.

(ii) *Cumulative three-year average.*—The cumulative three-year average applicable to any loss limitation year is computed under this paragraph (d)(3)(ii). With regard to each lookback period relevant to a loss limitation year, a modified three-year average is computed. The modified three-year average is the three-year average relevant to a particular lookback period (determined under section 172(h)(2)(C) and this section) multiplied by a fraction, the numerator of which equals the accumulated CERT costs as of the close of the loss limitation year that are attributable to the particular CERT or CERTs to which the three-year average corresponds, and the denominator of which equals the total accumulated CERT costs as of the close of the loss limitation year that are attributable to all CERTs relevant to the loss limitation year. See § 1.172(h)-2(b)(4) defining accumulated CERT costs. The sum of all modified three-year averages is the cumulative three-year average for that year.

(4) *Allocation of a CERIL among CERTS.*—After the computation of the single CERIL for a loss limitation year that is attributable to all CERTs, the total CERIL is allocated to particular CERTs, if CERILs attributable to different CERTs are subject to different limitations on carryback. See section 172(b)(1)(E)(i) and § 1.172(h)-5(b) (regarding prohibition on carrybacks). For purposes of this allocation, the CERT costs attributable to each particular CERT are identified. The total CERIL is then attributed to each CERT by multiplying the total CERIL by a fraction, the numerator of which equals the accumulated CERT costs as of the close of the loss limitation year that are attributable to a particular CERT, and the denominator of which equals the total accumulated CERT costs as of the close of the loss limitation year that are attributable to all CERTs relevant to the loss limitation year. See § 1.172(h)-2(b)(4) defining accumulated CERT costs.

(5) *Examples.*—The following examples illustrate the rules of this paragraph (d). Unless otherwise provided, assume that all entities are domestic C corporations that do not join in the filing of consolidated returns and that maintain calendar taxable years. Assume that all applicable corporations have substantial net operating losses in their loss limitation years:

Example 1. Multiple CERTs with identical lookback period. (i) *Facts.* Corporation A maintains a calendar taxable year. A engages in two separate CERTs during its taxable Year 4. The lookback period for both CERTs is January 1, Year 1, through December 31, Year 3. The total amount of interest deductions allocable to CERT 1 and CERT 2 (before application of section 172(h)(2)(C) and paragraph (a) of this section) is $50. A's total interest expense during Year 4 was $150, and its three-year average interest for the lookback period was $120.

(ii) *Analysis.* Year 4 constitutes a loss limitation year with regard to both CERT 1 and CERT 2. A single CERIL is computed with regard to Year 4, and the limitation on allocable interest under section 172(h)(2)(C) and paragraph (a) of this section is applied a single time. See paragraphs (d)(1) and (2) of this section. The limitation under section 172(h)(2)(C) and paragraph (a) of this section is applied to the cumulative amount of interest allocable to the two CERTs ($50). See paragraph (d)(2) of this section. The limitation under section 172(h)(2)(C) and paragraph (a) of this section equals the excess of the amount of interest allowable in Year 4 ($150) over the three-year average ($120), or $30. Therefore, the CERIL is limited to $30.

Example 2. Multiple CERTs with different lookback periods. (i) *Facts.* Corporation A maintains a calendar taxable year. A engages in CERT 1 during its taxable Year 4. The lookback period relevant to CERT 1 is January 1, Year 1, through December 31, Year 3. A also engages in CERT 2 during its taxable Year 5. The lookback period relevant to CERT 2 is January 1, Year 2, through December 31, Year 4. The total amount of interest deductions allocable to CERT 1 and CERT 2 (before application of section 172(h)(2)(C) and paragraph (a) of this section) during taxable Year 5 is $50. A's total interest expense during Year 5 is $126. A's three-year average interest that is relevant to loss limitation Year 5 for the CERT 1 lookback period is $100, and its three-year average interest that is relevant to loss limitation Year 5 for the CERT 2 lookback period is $110. A's accumulated CERT costs attributable to CERT 1 are $400. A's accumulated CERT costs attributable to CERT 2 are $600.

(ii) *Cumulative three-year average.* Year 5 is a loss limitation year with regard to both CERT 1 and CERT 2. A single CERIL is computed with regard to Year 5, and the limitation on allocable interest under section 172(h)(2)(C) and paragraph (a) of this section is applied a single time. See paragraph (d)(1) and (2) of this section. The limitation under section 172(h)(2)(C) and paragraph (a) of this section is applied to the cumulative amount of interest allocable to the two CERTs ($50). See paragraph (d)(2) of this section. Because Year 5 constitutes a loss limitation year with regard to CERTs with different lookback periods, the relevant three-year average applied under section 172(h)(2)(C) and paragraph (a) of this section is the cumulative three-year average, which is the sum of all modified three-year averages. See paragraph (d)(3)(ii) of this section. The modified three-year average with regard to CERT 1 is the three-year average for CERT 1 multiplied by $400/$1,000 (accumulated CERT costs attributable to CERT 1 divided by the total accumulated CERT costs attributable to CERTs 1 and 2), or 2/5. Therefore, the modified three-year average with regard to CERT 1 is $40 (100 × 2/5). The modified three-year average with regard to CERT 2 is the three-year average for CERT 2 multiplied by $600/$1,000 (accumulated CERT costs attributable to CERT 2 divided by the total accumulated CERT costs attributable to CERTs 1 and 2), or 3/5. Therefore, the modified three-year average with regard to CERT 2 is $66 (110 × 3/5). Thus, the cumulative threeyear average interest for Year 5 is $106 ($40 + $66). See paragraph (d)(3) of this section. The limitation under section 172(h)(2)(C) and paragraph (a) of this section equals the excess of the amount of interest allowable in Year 5 ($126) over the cumulative three-year average interest ($106), or $20. Therefore, the CERIL for Year 5 is limited to $20.

(iii) *Allocation of a CERIL to different CERTs.* Because Year 5 constitutes a loss limitation year with regard to more than one CERT, and a CERIL associated with each CERT is subject to different limitations on carryback, the total CERIL must be allocated between CERT 1 and CERT 2. See paragraph (d)(4) of this section. The portion of the total CERIL allocated to CERT 1 is the total CERIL multiplied by $400/$1,000 (accumulated CERT costs attributable to CERT 1 divided by the total accumulated CERT costs attributable to CERTs 1 and 2), or 2/5. Therefore, the portion of the total CERIL allocated to CERT 1 is $8 ($20 × 2/5). The portion of the total CERIL allocated to CERT 2 is the total CERIL multiplied by $600/$1,000 (accumulated CERT costs attributable to CERT 2 divided by the total accumulated CERT costs attributable to CERTs 1 and 2), or 3/5. Therefore, the portion of the total CERIL allocated to CERT 2 is $12 ($20 × 3/5). See paragraph (d)(4) of this section. See also section 172(b)(1)(E)(i) and § 1.172(h)-5(b)(1) for rules regarding the prohibition on carryback of a CERIL.

Example 3. CERTs of multiple corporations with identical lookback period. (i) *Facts.* Corporation T maintains a taxable year ending on June 30. On August 31, Year 5, T engages in CERT 1. Unrelated P is the parent of a group that maintains a calendar taxable year. On October 31, Year 5, P acquires all the stock of T in an MSA (CERT 2). T is first included in the P group on November 1, Year 5. For its calendar Year 5, the P group is treated as an applicable corporation with respect to CERT 1 and CERT 2. See § 1.1502-72(a)(2)(iv)(A). The P group's lookback period for both CERTs is January 1, Year 2, through December 31, Year 4. The total CERIL of the group in Year 5 is $80. The P group's accumulated CERT costs attributable to CERT 1 are $500. The P group's accumulated CERT costs attributable to CERT 2 are $1,500. The P group has a consolidated net operating loss (CNOL) in Year 5, a portion of which is allocable to T under § 1.1502-21(b)(2)(iv)(B).

(ii) *Allocation of a CERIL to different CERTs.* Year 5 constitutes a loss limitation year with regard to two CERTs that share a common lookback period. However, the CERIL associated with the different CERTs is subject to different limitations on carryback under § 1.172(h)-5(b)(1) (some CNOL will be carried back to the group's consolidated return years and some will be carried back to T's separate return years). Therefore, the total CERIL must be allocated between CERT 1 and CERT 2. The portion of the total CERIL allocated to CERT 1 is the total CERIL multiplied by $500/$2,000 (accumulated CERT costs attributable to CERT 1 divided by the total

accumulated CERT costs attributable to CERTs 1 and 2), or 1/4. See paragraph (d)(4) of this section. Therefore, the portion of the total CERIL allocated to CERT 1 is $20 ($80 × 1/4). The portion of the total CERIL allocated to CERT 2 is the total CERIL multiplied by $1,500/$2,000 (accumulated CERT costs attributable to CERT 2 divided by the total accumulated CERT costs attributable to CERTs 1 and 2), or 3/4. Therefore, the portion of the total CERIL allocated to CERT 2 is $60 ($80 × 3/4).

(e) *Effective/applicability date.*—This section is applicable to CERTs occurring on or after the date of publication of the Treasury decision adopting these rules as final regulations in the **Federal Register**. This section is also applicable to the deconsolidation of a member from, or the acquisition of a corporation by, a consolidated group that occurs on or after the date of publication of the Treasury decision adopting these rules as final regulations in the **Federal Register**. However, in each case, this section does not apply to any CERT, deconsolidation, or acquisition occurring pursuant to a written agreement that is binding before the date of publication of the Treasury decision adopting these rules as final regulations in the **Federal Register**. [Reg. § 1.172(h)-3.]

§ 1.172(h)-4. Special rules for predecessors and successors.— (a) *Scope.*—This section provides guidance with regard to the application of section 172(b)(1)(E) and (h), §§ 1.172(h)-1 through 1.172(h)-5, and § 1.1502-72 (the CERT rules) to predecessors and successors (as defined in § 1.172(h)-1(b)(2)).

(b) *Loss limitation years.*—(1) *In general.*—This paragraph (b)(1) applies to identify loss limitation years of a successor. The taxable year in which a corporate equity reduction transaction (CERT) actually occurs is a loss limitation year. See § 1.172(h)-1(e). Any taxable year of a successor (potential loss limitation year) of any applicable corporation is a loss limitation year with regard to the CERT if, under the carryover rules of sections 172(b)(1)(A)(ii) and 381(c)(1), the potential loss limitation year constitutes the first or second taxable year following the taxable year of the corporation that actually engaged in the CERT which includes the date on which the CERT occurred. See § 1.172(h)-5(a) (defining date on which CERT occurs in multiple-step transaction); but see § 1.1502-72(a)(3) (defining loss limitation years of consolidated groups and corporations that were previously members of a consolidated group).

(2) *Example.*—The following example illustrates the rules of this paragraph (b):

Example. Loss limitation years of successor. T is a domestic C corporation that maintains a calendar taxable year and does not join in the filing of a consolidated return. On March 31, Year 6, T engages in a CERT. On June 30, Year 6, T merges into Corporation A, a calendar-year taxpayer, in a transaction to which section 381(a) applies. T's taxable Year 6 ends on the date of the merger, and A succeeds to T's tax attributes. See section 381(a) and (b)(1). T's only loss limitation year with respect to the Year 6 CERT is its short taxable year ending June 30, Year 6. See section 172(b)(1)(E)(ii) and § 1.172(h)-1(e). Following the merger, A is the successor to T, and A is treated as an applicable corporation with regard to the Year 6 CERT. See § 1.172(h)-1(b)(2). A's calendar Years 6 and 7 are the second and third loss limitation years with regard to the Year 6 CERT. See section 172(b)(1)(E)(ii) and paragraph (b)(1) of this section.

(c) *Computation of a CERIL.*—(1) *CERT costs.*—For purposes of computing any corporate equity reduction interest loss (CERIL) under section 172(h)(1) and § 1.172(h)-2(a)(2), any CERT costs incurred (or treated as incurred under this paragraph (c)) by a predecessor are attributed to the successor. However, such costs are treated as having been incurred by the successor only for purposes of applying the avoided cost rules of section 263A(f)(2)(A) to any measurement date (as defined in § 1.263A-9(f)(2)) after the date of the section 381(a) transaction.

(2) *Limitation on allocable interest deductions.*—(i) *Lookback period.*—(A) *In general.*—The *lookback period* with regard to a CERT is the three taxable years preceding the taxable year in which the CERT occurs. See § 1.172(h)-3(a). The lookback period that is relevant to the calculation of any CERIL of a successor (successor's lookback period) is the three years preceding the taxable year of the successor that includes the date on which the CERT occurred. See § 1.172(h)-5(a) (defining the date on which a CERT occurs if the CERT consists of multiple steps) and § 1.172(h)-3(c) (regarding corporations with insufficient lookback periods).

(B) *Successor not in existence on date of CERT.*—If a successor was not in existence on the date on which the CERT occurred, for purposes of determining the lookback period, the successor is deemed to have additional 12-month periods that end on the calendar date that is one day prior to the date of the corporation's organization. The successor is deemed to have a sufficient number of such additional periods such that the successor is treated as having a year that includes the date on which the CERT occurred and as having three years (the lookback period) immediately preceding the deemed year that includes the date of the CERT. See §1.172(h)-3(c)(1) regarding lookback period for corporation lacking three-year history.

(ii) *Computation of three-year average.*—(A) *In general.*—Except as otherwise provided in this paragraph (c)(2)(ii), for purposes of determining any three-year average of a successor under section 172(h)(2)(C)(ii) and §1.172(h)-3, the interest paid or accrued by a successor includes interest paid or accrued by all corporations that are its predecessors as of the end of the successor's taxable year. If the dates of any taxable year of a predecessor do not precisely correspond to the dates of a taxable year of the successor, the interest paid or accrued by the predecessor is apportioned equally to each date of the predecessor's taxable year. The successor is treated as having paid or accrued in any year during the lookback period all predecessor interest that is apportioned to a date within that lookback period year.

(B) *Year of successor transaction.*—In computing the three-year average that is relevant to the taxable year of a successor that includes the date of the section 381(a) transaction that resulted in successor status, the successor includes only a pro rata portion of the predecessor's amount of interest paid or accrued during the successor's lookback period. The pro rata amount equals the predecessor's interest treated as paid or accrued for the dates of the successor's lookback period, multiplied by a fraction, the numerator of which equals the number of days in the loss limitation year of the successor that follow the date of the transaction that resulted in successor status, and the denominator of which equals the number of days in the successor's loss limitation year. The predecessor's amount of interest treated as paid or accrued that is subject to proration under this paragraph (c)(2)(ii)(B) is the interest history of the predecessor that would otherwise be fully combined with the interest history of the successor under paragraph (c)(2)(ii)(A) of this section.

(3) *Examples.*—The following examples illustrate the rules of this paragraph (c). Unless otherwise provided, assume that all entities are domestic C corporations that do not join in the filing of consolidated returns and that maintain calendar taxable years. Assume that all applicable corporations have substantial net operating losses in their loss limitation years:

Example 1. Predecessor corporation engages in CERT. (i) *Facts.* Corporation X is a calendar-year taxpayer. On February 1, Year 5, X engages in a CERT. On August 1, Year 5, X merges into unrelated corporation Y in a transaction to which section 381(a) applies. Y is a calendar-year taxpayer and all of its taxable years are full calendar years. All of X's taxable years prior to the year of the merger are full calendar years.

(ii) *Analysis.* X's only loss limitation year is its short year ending August 1, Year 5. X's lookback period relevant to the Year 5 CERT includes X's calendar Years 2, 3, and 4. See paragraph (c)(2)(i)(A) of this section; see also §1.172(h)-3(b)(1) (computation of three-year average for a short loss limitation year). Following the merger, Y is the successor to X, and Y is treated as an applicable corporation with regard to the Year 5 CERT. See §1.172(h)-1(b)(2). Because Y's calendar Year 5 follows a single loss limitation year of X with regard to the same CERT, Y's calendar Years 5 and 6 are loss limitation years with regard to the Year 5 CERT. See paragraph (b)(1) of this section and §1.381(c)(1)-1(e)(3). Y's lookback period for the Year 5 CERT is its calendar Years 2, 3, and 4. See paragraph (c)(2)(i)(A) of this section. The computations of Y's three-year averages relevant to its loss limitation Years 5 and 6 include interest paid or accrued by Y and by all of Y's predecessors, including X, during the lookback period. See paragraph (c)(2)(ii)(A) of this section. However, because Year 5 is Y's taxable year that includes the date of the section 381(a) transaction that resulted in Y's successor status, for purposes of computing Y's three-year average for Y's loss limitation Year 5, Y includes only a pro rata portion of X's amount of interest paid or accrued. In the proration, X's amount of interest paid or accrued during the three-year lookback period is multiplied by 151/365 (the number of days in Y's loss limitation Year 5 that follow the date of the section 381(a) transaction that resulted in Y's successor status, divided by the number of days in Y's loss limitation Year 5). See paragraph (c)(2)(ii)(B) of this section.

(iii) *Predecessor and successor have different taxable years.* The facts are the same as in paragraph (i) of this *Example 1*, except that X maintained a taxable year ending June 30 before its merger in Y. X's full taxable year ending June 30, Year 5, and its short year ending August 1, Year 5, are its loss limitation years with regard to its February 1, Year 5 CERT. See section 172(b)(1)(E)(ii) and §1.172(h)-1(e). Following the merger of X into Y, Y is a successor to X and is treated as an applicable corporation with regard to the Year 5 CERT. Y's calendar Year 5 is the third loss limitation year with regard to the CERT. See paragraph (b)(1) of this section. Y's lookback period is Y's three taxable years preceding Y's taxable year that includes the date of the CERT, which are Years 2, 3, and 4. Further, because the

dates of X's taxable years do not precisely correspond to the dates of Y's taxable years, X's interest paid or accrued is apportioned equally to each date within each of X's taxable years. Y is treated as having paid or accrued in any year during the lookback period all of X's interest that is so apportioned. See paragraph (c)(2)(ii)(A) of this section. However, because Y's taxable Year 5 includes the date of the section 381(a) transaction that resulted in Y's successor status, for purposes of computing Y's three-year average for loss limitation Year 5, Y includes only a pro rata portion of X's interest history. See paragraphs (c)(2)(ii)(B) of this section.

Example 2. Successor corporation not in existence for entire lookback period. (i) *Facts.* Corporation A is formed on October 1, Year 3, and thereafter maintains a calendar taxable year. Immediately after A is formed in Year 3, a second corporation, T, merges into A in a transaction that meets the requirements of section 368(a)(1)(A). During Year 5, A engages in a CERT.

(ii) *Analysis.* A's loss limitation years are its calendar Years 5, 6, and 7. See section 172(b)(1)(E)(ii). For purposes of computing any CERIL related to the Year 5 CERT, section 172(h)(2)(C)(ii) and §1.172(h)-3 require that A measure its interest deductions for the three years preceding the taxable year of the CERT (three-year average). However, A is in existence for only two taxable years before the year in which the CERT occurs. Therefore, pursuant to §1.172(h)-3(c)(1), A is deemed to have an additional taxable period (October 1, Year 2, through September 30, Year 3). Further, in computing the three-year average, A is treated as having paid or accrued zero interest during the deemed year. See §1.172(h)-3(c)(2). However, because T is the predecessor of A, the computation of A's three-year average relevant to its loss limitation Year 5 includes interest paid or accrued by T during the lookback period (October 1, Year 2, through December 31, Year 4). See paragraph (c)(2)(ii)(A) of this section and §1.172(h)-3(c)(2). Because T merges into A in a year prior to any loss limitation year, there is no proration of T's interest history under paragraph (c)(2)(ii)(B) of this section.

(d) *Three-year distribution average.*—For purposes of determining any three-year distribution average of a successor under section 172(h)(3)(C)(ii)(I) and §1.172(h)-1(c)(3), the distributions made by a successor include distributions made by all corporations that are its predecessors as of the end of the successor's taxable year. If the dates of any taxable year of a predecessor do not correspond to the dates of a taxable year of the successor, the distributions made by the predecessor are apportioned equally to each date of the predecessor's taxable year. The successor is treated as having made in its taxable years all predecessor distributions that are apportioned to a date within those taxable years.

(e) *Effective/applicability date.*—This section is applicable to CERTs occurring on or after the date of publication of the Treasury decision adopting these rules as final regulations in the **Federal Register**. This section is also applicable to the deconsolidation of a member from, or the acquisition of a corporation by, a consolidated group that occurs on or after the date of publication of the Treasury decision adopting these rules as final regulations in the **Federal Register**. However, in each case, this section does not apply to any CERT, deconsolidation, or acquisition occurring pursuant to a written agreement that is binding before the date of publication of the Treasury decision adopting these rules as final regulations in the **Federal Register**. [Reg. §1.172(h)-4.]

§1.172(h)-5. Operating rules.—(a) *Date on which CERT occurs in a multi-step transaction.*—For purposes of applying section 172(b)(1)(E) and (h), §§1.172(h)-1 through 1.172(h)-4, and this section, and §1.1502-72 (the CERT rules), if a corporate equity reduction transaction (CERT) consists of multiple steps, the date on which the CERT occurs is the earliest date on which the requirements for CERT status are satisfied. For example, if multiple distributions are made in a single year, an excess distribution (ED) is treated as occurring on the earliest date on which the amount of distributions satisfies the greater of the two thresholds contained in section 172(h)(3)(C)(ii) and §1.172(h)-1(c)(3). A major stock acquisition (MSA) is treated as occurring on the earliest date on which at least 50 percent of the stock of a corporation is acquired, subject to the provisions of section 172(h)(3)(B) and §1.172(h)-1(c)(2).

(b) *Prohibition on carryback.*—(1) *In general.*—No corporate equity reduction interest loss (CERIL) attributable to a CERT may be carried back under section 172 or §1.1502-21(b) to any taxable year (including a consolidated return year) that includes solely dates that precede the date on which the CERT occurred. In addition, if a corporation becomes a member of a consolidated group as a result of a CERT, no CERIL allocable to that CERT may be carried back under section 172 or §1.1502-21(b) to the taxable year of the acquired corporation that includes the date on which the CERT occurred, or to any preceding taxable year. See §1.172(h)-3(d)(4) regarding allocation of a CERIL among CERTs, and §1.1502-21(b)(2)(iv)(C)(1) for the apportionment of a CERIL among consolidated group members.

(2) *Example.*—The following example illustrates the rules of this paragraph (b):

Example. Prohibition on carryback. (i) *Facts.* T corporation maintains a taxable year ending June 30. X corporation is the parent of a group that maintains a calendar taxable year. On March 31, Year 5, the X group acquires all of the T stock in a CERT, and T is first included in the X group on April 1, Year 5. During its consolidated return Year 5, the X group has a consolidated net operating loss (CNOL), a portion of which constitutes a CERIL, pursuant to section 172(h)(1) and §1.172(h)-2(a)(2). Part of the CERIL is apportioned to T, pursuant to §1.1502-21(b)(2)(iv)(C)(1).

(ii) *Analysis.* On the date of the acquisition, both the X group and T constitute applicable corporations with regard to the Year 5 CERT. See section 172(b)(1)(E)(iii)(I) and §1.172(h)-1(b). T's short taxable year ending on March 31, Year 5, was T's taxable year in which the CERT occurred. The X group's year in which the CERT occurred was its consolidated return Year 5. Section 172(b)(1)(E)(i) and paragraph (b) of this section prohibit the carryback of a CERIL to years preceding the taxable year in which the CERT occurs. Pursuant to paragraph (b)(1) of this section, no portion of a CERIL relating to the X group CNOL can be carried back to any taxable year that includes solely dates that precede the date on which the CERT occurred. As a result, no portion of the CERIL can be carried back to the X group's Year 4, or any preceding year. Moreover, because T becomes a member of the X group as a result of the CERT, no portion of the CERIL can be carried back to T's short taxable year ending March 31, Year 5, or any preceding taxable year. See paragraph (b)(1) of this section.

(c) *Stock issuances and computation of three-year distribution average.*—(1) *In general.*—In determining whether an ED has occurred, aggregate distributions made during a taxable year are reduced by the aggregate amount of stock issued by the applicable corporation during the year in which the potential ED occurred in exchange for money or property other than stock of the applicable corporation. Similarly, the computation of any three-year distribution average under section 172(h)(3)(C)(ii)(I) and §1.172(h)-1(f) is reduced by the average of the stock issuances described in section 172(h)(3)(E)(ii)

and this paragraph (c)(1) during the three years of the distribution lookback period (threeyear stock issuance average).

(2) *Example.*—The following example illustrates the rules of this paragraph (c):

Example. (i) *Facts.* C is a corporation that maintains a calendar taxable year. During Year 5, C makes a large distribution to its shareholders. During taxable Years 2, 3, and 4, C distributes an average of $100,000 per year. In addition, during taxable Year 2, C issued stock in exchange for $90,000 cash. During taxable Year 3, C issued stock in exchange for $15,000 cash. C issued no stock during taxable Year 4.

(ii) *Analysis.* C must test its Year 5 distribution as a potential ED. C's three-year distribution average without respect to any stock issued during the distribution lookback period is $100,000. C's three-year distribution average is reduced by the average of the stock issued by the corporation in exchange for money or property other than stock in C during the years of the distribution lookback period (three-year stock issuance average). See paragraph (c)(1) of this section. C's three-year stock issuance average is $35,000 [($90,000 + $15,000 + 0)/3]. Therefore, T's three-year distribution average is $65,000 ($100,000 - $35,000).

(d) *Computation of the alternative minimum tax net operating loss deduction.*—The CERT rules governing the carryback of net operating losses following a CERT also apply to the carryback of an alternative minimum tax net operating loss.

(e) *Effective/applicability date.*—This section is applicable to CERTs occurring on or after the date of publication of the Treasury decision adopting these rules as final regulations in the **Federal Register**. This section is also applicable to the deconsolidation of a member from, or the acquisition of a corporation by, a consolidated group that occurs on or after the date of publication of the Treasury decision adopting these rules as final regulations in the **Federal Register**. However, in each case, this section does not apply to any CERT, deconsolidation, or acquisition occurring pursuant to a written agreement that is binding before the date of publication of the Treasury decision adopting these rules as final regulations in the **Federal Register**. [Reg. §1.172(h)-5.]

Accelerated Cost Recovery System

Accelerated Cost Recovery System.—Reproduced below is the text of a proposed amendment of Reg. §1.178-1, relating to the Accelerated Cost Recovery System for recovering capital costs of eligible property (published in the Federal Register on February 16, 1984).

☐ Par. 3. Section 1.178-1 is amended as follows:

1. Paragraph (a) is amended by removing the term "section 167 or 611" and inserting "section 167, 168, or 611" in its place.

2. Paragraph (b)(1)(i) and (3) is amended by removing the term "estimated useful life" in each of the three places it appears and removing the term "section 167" in the one place it appears and by inserting "estimated useful life or, in the case of recovery property (as defined in section 168), the recovery period (including, where applicable, any optional recovery period under section 168(b)(3) or (f)(2)(C))" and by inserting "section 167 or 168", respectively, in its place.

3. Paragraph (b)(2) is amended by removing the term "(or depreciation)" and by inserting "(or depreciation under section 167 or accelerated cost recovery under section 168)" in lieu thereof.

4. Paragraph (d)(1)(i) is amended by removing the term "remaining estimated useful life" and by inserting "remaining estimated useful life or, in the case of recovery property (as defined in section 168), the recovery period (including, where applicable, any optional recovery period under section 168(b)(3) or (f)(2)(C))" in its place.

5. Paragraph (b)(6) is amended by adding two examples immediately after example (5), which read as follows:

§1.178-1. Depreciation or amortization of improvements on leased property and cost of acquiring a lease.

* * *

(b) *Determination of amount of deduction.*—* * *

(6) * * *

Example (6). Lessee C, a calendar year taxpayer, constructs a building on land leased from lessor D. The construction is completed and the building is placed in service on January 1, 1984, at which time C has 8 years remaining on the lease with no options to renew. On January 1, 1988, D grants C an option to renew the lease for a 10-year period. As of January 1, 1988, the date the renewal option is granted, section 178(a) and paragraph (b)(1) of this section become applicable, since the portion of the term of the lease remaining upon completion of the building (8 years) is less than 60 percent of any recovery period applicable to the building (60 percent of the shortest recovery period (15 years) is 9 years). As of the January 1, 1988, the term of the lease shall be treated as including the remaining portion of the original lease (4 years) and the 10-year renewal, or 14 years,

unless C can establish that, as of the close of 1988, it is more probable that the lease will not be renewed than that it will be. In such case, since the term of the lease as of January 1, 1988 (14 years), is less than the ACRS recovery period, a deduction is not allowed under section 168 with respect to such building.

Example (7). The facts are the same as in example (6), except that the option to renew is for 15 years. If, as of the close of 1988, C cannot establish that it is more probable that the lease will not be renewed than that it will be, the term of the lease as of January 1, 1988, will be 19 years. Since the term of the lease would be longer than the ACRS recovery period (unless a 35- or 45-year optional recovery period were desired), the provisions of section 168 will be applicable with respect to this building. For purposes of section 168, C is considered as having placed the building in service on January 1, 1988, with a 15-year recovery period extending from that time. C's unadjusted basis for purposes of section 168 is the adjusted basis in the building as of January 1, 1988.

* * *

Capital Costs: Deduction: EPA Sulfur Regulations

Capital Costs: Deduction: EPA Sulfur Regulations.—Reg. §1.179B-1, relating to the deduction for qualified capital costs paid or incurred by a small business refiner to comply with the highway diesel fuel sulfur control requirements of the Environmental Protection Agency (EPA), is proposed (published in the Federal Register on June 27, 2008) (REG-143453-05).

☐ Par. 2. Section 1.179B-1 is added to read as follows:

§1.179B-1. Deduction for capital costs incurred in complying with Environmental Protection Agency sulfur regulations.

[The text of this proposed §1.179B-1 is the same as the text of §1.179B-1T as added by T.D. 9404].

Business Use or Rental of Dwelling Unit

Business Use or Rental of Dwelling Unit.—Reproduced below is the text of a proposed amendment of Reg. §1.183-1, relating to the deductibility of expenses in connection with the business use, or the rental of others, of a dwelling unit that the taxpayer is deemed to have used for personal purposes during the taxable year (published in the Federal Register on August 7, 1980).

☐ Paragraph 1. Section 1.183-1 is amended by adding at the end thereof the following new paragraph:

§1.183-1. Activities not engaged in for profit.
* * *

(g) *Coordination with section 280A.*—If section 280A(a) (relating to disallowance of deductions for certain expenses with respect to the use of a dwelling unit used as a residence) applies with respect to any dwelling unit (or portion thereof) for the taxable year—

(1) Section 183 and this section shall not apply to that unit (or portion thereof) for that year, but

(2) That year shall be taken into account as a taxable year for purposes of applying section 183(d).

See section 280A and the regulations thereunder for definitions and rules relating to use of dwelling units. Note that the limitations of section 280A(e) and §1.280A-3(c) applies in any case where an individual or an electing small business corporation uses a dwelling unit for personal purposes on any day during the taxable year.

* * *

Deductions: Elections: Depreciation: Intangible Property

Deductions: Elections: Depreciation: Intangible Property.—Temporary Reg. §1.197-1T, relating to the procedures for making elections under the intangibles provisions of the Omnibus Budget Reconciliation Act of 1993 (P.L. 103-66), is also proposed as a final regulation and, when adopted, would become Reg. §1.197-1 (published in the Federal Register on March 15, 1994).

☐ Par 3. Section 1.197-1 is added to read as follows:

§1.197-1. Certain elections for intangible property.—[The text of this proposed section is the same as the text of Temporary Reg. §1.197-1T as added by T.D. 8528.]

Section 199A Rules: Cooperatives and Patrons

Section 199A Rules: Cooperatives and Patrons.—Amendments to Reg. §§1.199-0—1.199-9, providing guidance to cooperatives to which sections 1381 through 1388 of the Code apply (Cooperatives) and their patrons regarding the deduction for qualified business income under section 199A(a) of the Code as well as guidance to specified agricultural or horticultural cooperatives (Specified Cooperatives) and their patrons regarding the deduction for domestic production activities under section 199A(g) of the Code, are proposed (published in the Federal Register on June 19, 2019) (REG-118425-18).

Par. 2. Sections 1.199-0 through 1.199-9 are removed.

§1.199-0. Table of contents.

§1.199-1. Income attributable to domestic production activities.

§1.199-2. Wage limitation.

§1.199-3. Domestic production gross receipts.

§1.199-4. Costs allocable to domestic production gross receipts.

§1.199-5. Application of section 199 to pass-thru entities for taxable years beginning after May 17, 2006, the enactment date of the Tax Increase Prevention and Reconciliation Act of 2005.

§1.199-6. Agricultural and horticultural cooperatives.

§1.199-7. Other rules.

§1.199-8. Expanded affiliated groups.

§1.199-9. Application of section 199 to pass-thru entities for taxable years beginning on or before May 17, 2006, the enactment date of the Tax Increase Prevention and Reconciliation Act of 2005.

Qualified Business Income: Deduction

Qualified Business Income: Deduction.—Amendments to Reg. §1.199A-0, concerning the deduction for qualified business income under section 199A of the Internal Revenue Code, are proposed (published in the Federal Register on February 8, 2019) (REG-134652-18).

Par. 2. Section 1.199A-0 is amended by:

1. Adding entries for §1.199A-3(b)(1)(iv)(A) and (B).

2. Adding entries for §1.199A-3(d), (d)(1) and (2), (d)(2)(i) through (iii), (d)(2)(iii)(A) and (B), (d)(3), (d)(3)(i) through (v), (d)(4), (d)(4)(i) and (ii), and (d)(5) and (6).

3. Adding entries for §1.199A-6(d)(3)(iii) and (v).

The additions read as follows:

§1.199A-0. Table of contents.

* * *

§1.199A-3 Qualified business income, qualified REIT dividends, and qualified PTP income.

* * *

(b) ***

(1) ***

(iv) ***

(A) In general.

(B) Attributes of disallowed loss determined in year loss is incurred.

* * *

(d) Section 199A dividends paid by a regulated investment company.

(1) In general.

(2) Definition of section 199A dividend.

(i) In general.

(ii) Reduction in the case of excess reported amounts.

(iii) Allocation of excess reported amount

(A) In general.
(B) Special rule for noncalendar-year RICs.
(3) Definitions.
  (i) Reported section 199A dividend amount.
  (ii) Excess reported amount.
  (iii) Aggregate reported amount.
  (iv) Post-December reported amount.
  (v) Qualified REIT dividend income.
(4) Treatment of section 199A dividends by shareholders.
  (i) In general.
  (ii) Holding period.
(5) Example.

(6) Applicability date.

* * *

§1.199A-6 *Relevant passthrough entities (RPEs), publicly traded partnerships (PTPs), trusts, and estates.*

* * *

(d) ***
  (3) ***
    (iii) Separate shares.

* * *

  (v) Charitable remainder trusts.

* * *

Qualified Business Income: Deduction

Qualified Business Income: Deduction.—Amendments to Reg. §1.199A-3, concerning the deduction for qualified business income under section 199A of the Internal Revenue Code, are proposed (published in the Federal Register on February 8, 2019) (REG-134652-18).

Par. 3. Section 1.199A-3 is amended by revising paragraph (b)(1)(iv) and adding paragraph (d) to read as follows:

§1.199A-3. Qualified business income, qualified REIT dividends, and qualified PTP income.

* * *

(b) ***
  (1) * * *

    (iv) *Previously disallowed losses.*—(A) *In general.*—Previously disallowed losses or deductions (including losses disallowed under sections 465, 469, 704(d), and 1366(d)) allowed in the taxable year generally are taken into account for purposes of computing QBI to the extent the disallowed loss or deduction is otherwise allowed by section 199A and this section. These losses shall be used, for purposes of section 199A and these regulations, in order from the oldest to the most recent on a first-in, first-out (FIFO) basis and shall be treated as losses from a separate trade or business. To the extent such losses relate to a PTP, they must be treated as a loss from a separate PTP in the taxable year the losses are taken into account. However, losses or deductions that were disallowed, suspended, limited, or carried over from taxable years ending before January 1, 2018 (including under sections 465, 469, 704(d), and 1366(d)), are not taken into account in a later taxable year for purposes of computing QBI.

    (B) *Attributes of disallowed loss determined in year loss is incurred.*—Whether a disallowed loss or deduction is attributable to a trade or business, and otherwise meets the requirements of this section is determined in the year the loss is incurred. Whether a disallowed loss or deduction is attributable to a specified service trade or business (including whether an individual has taxable income under the threshold amount, within the phase-in range, or in excess of the phase-in range) also is determined in the year the loss is incurred. To the extent a loss is partially disallowed, QBI in the year of disallowance must be reduced proportionately.

* * *

(d) *Section 199A dividends paid by a regulated investment company.*—(1) *In general.*—If section 852(b) applies to a regulated investment company (RIC) for a taxable year, the RIC may pay section 199A dividends, as defined in this paragraph (d).

  (2) *Definition of section 199A dividend.*—(i) *In general.*—Except as provided in paragraph (d)(2)(ii) of this section, a section 199A dividend is any dividend or part of such a dividend that a RIC pays to its shareholders and reports as a section 199A dividend in written statements furnished to its shareholders.

    (ii) *Reduction in the case of excess reported amounts.*—If the aggregate reported amount with respect to the RIC for any taxable year exceeds the RIC's qualified REIT dividend income for the taxable year, then a section 199A dividend is equal to—
    (A) The reported section 199A dividend amount, reduced by;
    (B) The excess reported amount that is allocable to that reported section 199A dividend amount.

    (iii) *Allocation of excess reported amount.*—(A) *In general.*—Except as provided in paragraph (d)(2)(iii)(B) of this section, the excess reported amount (if any) that is allocable to the reported section 199A dividend amount is that portion of the excess reported amount that bears the same ratio to the excess reported amount as the reported section 199A dividend amount bears to the aggregate reported amount.

    (B) *Special rule for noncalendar-year RICs.*—In the case of any taxable year that does not begin and end in the same calendar year, if the post-December reported amount equals or exceeds the excess reported amount for that taxable year, paragraph (d)(2)(iii)(A) of this section is applied by substituting "post-December reported amount" for "aggregate reported amount," and no excess reported

amount is allocated to any dividend paid on or before December 31 of that taxable year.

  (3) *Definitions.*—For purposes of paragraph (d) of this section—

    (i) *Reported section 199A dividend amount.*—The term *reported section 199A dividend amount* means the amount of a dividend distribution reported to the RIC's shareholders under paragraph (d)(2)(i) of this section as a section 199A dividend.

    (ii) *Excess reported amount.*—The term *excess reported amount* means the excess of the aggregate reported amount over the RIC's qualified REIT dividend income for the taxable year.

    (iii) *Aggregate reported amount.*—The term *aggregate reported amount* means the aggregate amount of dividends reported by the RIC under paragraph (d)(2)(i) of this section as section 199A dividends for the taxable year (including section 199A dividends paid after the close of the taxable year and described in section 855).

    (iv) *Post-December reported amount.*—The term *post-December reported amount* means the aggregate reported amount determined by taking into account only dividends paid after December 31 of the taxable year.

    (v) *Qualified REIT dividend income.*—The term *qualified REIT dividend income* means, with respect to a taxable year of a RIC, the excess of the amount of qualified REIT dividends, as defined in §1.199A-3(c)(2), includible in the RIC's taxable income for the taxable year over the amount of the RIC's deductions that are properly allocable to such income.

  (4) *Treatment of section 199A dividends by shareholders.*—(i) *In general.*—For purposes of section 199A and the regulations under section 199A, a section 199A dividend is treated by a taxpayer that receives the section 199A dividend as a qualified REIT dividend.

    (ii) *Holding period.*—Paragraph (d)(4)(i) does not apply to any dividend received with respect to a share of RIC stock—
    (A) That is held by the shareholder for 45 days or less (taking into account the principles of section 246(c)(3) and (4)) during the 91-day period beginning on the date which is 45 days before the date on which the share becomes ex-dividend with respect to such dividend; or
    (B) To the extent that the shareholder is under an obligation (whether pursuant to a short sale or otherwise) to make related payments with respect to positions in substantially similar or related property.

  (5) *Example.*—The following example illustrates the provisions of this paragraph (d).
    (i) *Example.* (A) X is a corporation that has elected to be a RIC. For its taxable year ending March 31, 2019, X has $25,000x of net long-term capital gain, $60,000x of qualified dividend income, $25,000x of taxable interest income, $15,000x of net short-term capital gain, and $25,000x of qualified REIT dividends. X has $15,000x of deductible expenses, of which $3,000x is allocable to the qualified REIT dividends. On December 31, 2018, X pays a single dividend of $100,000x on December 31, and reports $20,000x of the dividend as a section 199A dividend in written statements to its shareholders. On March 31, 2019, X pays a dividend of $35,000x, and reports $5,000x of the dividend as a section 199A dividend in written statements to its shareholders.
    (B) X's qualified REIT dividend income under paragraph (d)(3)(v) of this section is $22,000x, which is the excess of X's $25,000x of qualified REIT dividends over $3,000x in allocable expenses. The reported section 199A dividend amounts for the December 31, 2018, and March 31, 2019, distributions are $20,000x and $5,000x, respec-

tively. For the taxable year ending March 31, 2019, the aggregate reported amount of section 199A dividends is $25,000x, and the excess reported amount under paragraph (d)(3)(ii) of this section is $3,000x. Because X is a noncalendar-year RIC and the post-December reported amount of $5,000x exceeds the excess reported amount of $3,000x, the entire excess reported amount is allocated under paragraphs (d)(2)(iii)(A) and (B) of this section to the reported section 199A dividend amount for the March 31, 2019, distribution. No portion of the excess reported amount is allocated to the reported section 199A dividend amount for the December 31, 2018, distribution. Thus, the section 199A dividend on March 31, 2019, is $2,000x, which is the reported section 199A dividend amount of $5,000x reduced by the $3,000x of allocable excess reported amount. The section 199A dividend on December 31, 2018, is the $20,000x that X reports as a section 199A dividend.

(C) Shareholder A, a United States person, receives a dividend from X of $100x on December 31, 2018, of which $20x is reported as a

section 199A dividend. If A meets the holding period requirements in paragraph (d)(4)(ii) of this section with respect to the stock of X, A treats $20x of the dividend from X as a qualified REIT dividend for purposes of section 199A for A's 2018 taxable year.

(D) A receives a dividend from X of $35x on March 31, 2019, of which $5x is reported as a section 199A dividend. If A meets the holding period requirements in paragraph (d)(4)(ii) of this section with respect to the stock of X, A may only treat $2x of the dividend from X as a section 199A dividend for A's 2019 taxable year.

(6) *Applicability date.*—The provisions of paragraph (d) of this section apply to taxable years ending after the date the Treasury decision adopting these regulations as final regulations is published in the Federal Register. However, taxpayers may rely on the rules of this section until the date the Treasury decision adopting these regulations as final regulations is published in the Federal Register.

* * *

Qualified Business Income: Deduction

Qualified Business Income: Deduction.—Amendments to Reg. §1.199A-6, concerning the deduction for qualified business income under section 199A of the Internal Revenue Code, are proposed (published in the Federal Register on February 8, 2019) (REG-134652-18).

Par. 4. Section 1.199A-6 is amended by adding paragraphs (d)(3)(iii) and (v) to read as follows:

§1.199A-6. Relevant passthrough entities (RPEs), publicly traded partnerships (PTPs), trusts, and estates.

* * *

(d) ***

(3) ***

(iii) *Separate shares.*—In the case of a trust described in section 663(c) with substantially separate and independent shares for multiple beneficiaries, such trust will be treated as a single trust for purposes of determining whether the taxable income of the trust exceeds the threshold amount.

* * *

(v) *Charitable remainder trusts.*—A charitable remainder trust described in section 664 is not entitled to and does not calculate a section 199A deduction and the threshold amount described in section 199A(e)(2) does not apply to the trust. However, any taxable recipient of a unitrust or annuity amount from the trust must determine and apply the recipient's own threshold amount for purposes of section 199A taking into account any annuity or unitrust amounts received from the trust. A recipient of a unitrust or annuity amount from a trust may take into account QBI, qualified REIT dividends, or qualified PTP income for purposes of determining the recipient's section 199A deduction for the taxable year to the extent that the unitrust or annuity amount distributed to such recipient consists of such section 199A items under §1.664-1(d). For example, if a charitable remainder trust has investment income of $500, qualified dividend income of $200, and qualified REIT dividends of $1,000, and distributes $1,000 to the recipient, the trust would be treated as having income in two classes within the category of income described in §1.664-1(d)(1)(i)(a)(1), for purposes of §1.664-1(d)(1)(ii)(b). Because the annuity amount first carries out income in the class subject to the highest income tax rate, the entire annuity payment

comes from the class with the investment income and qualified REIT dividends. Thus, the charitable remainder trust would be treated as distributing a proportionate amount of the investment income ($500/(1,000+500)*1,000 = $333) and qualified REIT dividends ($1000/(1,000+500)*1000 = $667) because the investment income and qualified REIT dividends are taxed at the same rate and within the same class, which is higher than the rate of tax for the qualified dividend income which is in a separate class. The charitable remainder trust in this example would not be treated as distributing any of the qualified dividend income until it distributed all of the investment income and qualified REIT dividends (more than $1,500 in total) to the recipient. To the extent that a trust is treated as distributing QBI, qualified REIT dividends, or qualified PTP income to more than one unitrust or annuity recipient in the taxable year, the distribution of such income will be treated as made to the recipients proportionately, based on their respective shares of the total of QBI, qualified REIT dividends, or qualified PTP income distributed for that year. The trust allocates and reports any W-2 wages or UBIA of qualified property to the taxable recipient of the annuity or unitrust interest based on each recipient's share of the trust's total QBI (whether or not distributed) for that taxable year. Accordingly, if 10 percent of the QBI of a charitable remainder trust is distributed to the recipient and 90 percent of the QBI is retained by the trust, 10 percent of the W-2 wages and UBIA of qualified property is allocated and reported to the recipient and 90 percent of the W-2 wages and UBIA of qualified property is treated as retained by the trust. However, any W-2 wages retained by the trust do not carry over to subsequent taxable years for section 199A purposes. Any QBI, qualified REIT dividends, or qualified PTP income of the trust that is unrelated business taxable income is subject to excise tax and that tax must be allocated to the corpus of the trust under §1.664-1(c).

* * *

Section 199A Rules: Cooperatives and Patrons

Section 199A Rules: Cooperatives and Patrons.—Reg. §§1.199A-7—1.199A-12, providing guidance to cooperatives to which sections 1381 through 1388 of the Code apply (Cooperatives) and their patrons regarding the deduction for qualified business income under section 199A(a) of the Code as well as guidance to specified agricultural or horticultural cooperatives (Specified Cooperatives) and their patrons regarding the deduction for domestic production activities under section 199A(g) of the Code, are proposed (published in the Federal Register on June 19, 2019) (corrected August 6, 2019) (REG-118425-18).

Par. 3. Sections 1.199A-7 through 1.199A-12 are added to read as follows:

§1.199A-7. Section 199A(a) Rules for Cooperatives and their Patrons.—(a) *Overview.*—(1) *In general.*—This section provides guidance and special rules on the application of the rules of §§1.199A-1 through 1.199A-6 regarding the deduction for qualified business income (QBI) under section 199A(a) (section 199A(a) deduction) of the Internal Revenue Code (Code) by patrons (patrons) of cooperatives to which Part I of subchapter T of chapter 1 of subtitle A of the Code applies (Cooperatives). Unless otherwise provided in this section, all of the rules in §§1.199A-1 through 1.199A-6 relating to calculating the section 199A(a) deduction apply to patrons and Cooperatives. Paragraph (b) of this section provides special rules for patrons relating to trades or businesses. Paragraph (c) of this section provides special rules for patrons and Cooperatives relating to the definition of QBI. Paragraph (d) of this section provides special rules for patrons and Cooperatives relating to specified service trades or businesses (SSTBs). Paragraph (e) of this section provides special rules for patrons relating to the statutory limitations based on W-2 wages and unadjusted basis immediately after acquisition (UBIA) of

qualified property. Paragraph (f) of this section provides special rules for specified agricultural or horticultural cooperatives (Specified Cooperatives) and paragraph (g) of this section provides examples for Specified Cooperatives and their patrons. Paragraph (h) of this section sets forth the applicability date of this section and a special transition rule relating to Specified Cooperatives and their patrons.

(2) *At patron level.*—The section 199A(a) deduction is applied at the patron level, and patrons who are individuals (as defined in §1.199A-1(a)(2)) may take the section 199A(a) deduction.

(3) *Definitions.*—For purposes of section 199A and §1.199A-7, the following definitions apply—

(i) *Individual* is defined in §1.199A-1(a)(2).

(ii) *Patron* is defined in §1.1388-1(e).

(iii) *Patronage and nonpatronage* is defined in §1.1388-1(f).

(iv) *Relevant Passthrough Entity (RPE)* is defined in §1.199A-1(a)(9).

(v) *Qualified payment* is defined in §1.199A-8(d)(2)(ii).

(vi) *Specified Cooperative* is defined in §1.199A-8(a)(2) and is a subset of Cooperatives defined in §1.199A-7(a)(1).

(b) *Trade or business.*—A patron (whether the patron is an RPE or an individual) must determine whether it has one or more trades or businesses that it directly conducts as defined in §1.199A-1(b)(14). To the extent a patron operating a trade or business has income directly from that business, the patron must follow the rules of §§1.199A-1 through 1.199A-6 to calculate the section 199A deduction. Patronage dividends or similar payments are considered to be generated from the trade or business the Cooperative conducts on behalf of or with the patron, and are tested by the Cooperative at its trade or business level. A patron that receives patronage dividends or similar payments, as described in paragraph (c)(1) of this section, from a Cooperative must follow the rules of paragraphs (c) through (e) of this section to calculate the section 199A deduction.

(c) *Qualified Business Income:*—(1) *In general.*—QBI means the net amount of qualified items of income, gain, deduction, and loss with respect to any trade or business as determined under the rules of §1.199A-3(b). A qualified item of income includes distributions for which the Cooperative is allowed a deduction under section 1382(b) and (c)(2) (including patronage dividends or similar payments, such as money, property, qualified written notices of allocations, and qualified per-unit retain certificates, as well as money or property paid in redemption of a nonqualified written notice of allocation (collectively patronage dividends or similar payments)), provided such distribution is otherwise a qualified item of income, gain, deduction, or loss. *See* special rule in paragraph (d)(3) of this section relating to SSTBs that may affect QBI.

(2) *QBI determinations made by patron.*—A patron must determine QBI for each trade or business it directly conducts. In situations where the patron receives distributions described in paragraph (c)(1) of this section, the Cooperative must determine whether those distributions include qualified items of income, gain, deduction, and loss. These distributions may be included in the QBI of the patron's trade or business:

(i) To the extent that those payments are related to the patron's trade or business;

(ii) Are qualified items of income, gain, deduction, and loss at the Cooperative's trade or business level;

(iii) Are not income from an SSTB at the Cooperative's trade or business level (except as permitted by the threshold rules (*see* §1.199A-5(a)(2)); and

(iv) Provided the patron receives certain information from the Cooperative about these payments as provided in paragraphs (c)(3) and (d)(3) of this section.

(3) *Qualified items of income, gain, deduction, and loss determinations made and reported by Cooperatives.*—In the case of a Cooperative that makes distributions described in paragraph (c)(1) of this section to a patron, the Cooperative must determine the amount of qualified items of income, gain, deduction, and loss in those distributions. Pursuant to this paragraph (c)(3), the Cooperative must report the amounts of qualified items with respect to any non-SSTB of the Cooperative in the distributions made to the patron on an attachment to or on the Form 1099-PATR, Taxable Distributions Received From Cooperatives (Form 1099-PATR), (or any successor form) issued by the Cooperative to the patron, unless otherwise provided by the instructions to the Form. If the Cooperative does not report on or before the due date of the Form 1099-PATR the amount of such qualified items of income, gain, deduction, and loss in the distributions to the patron, the amount of distributions from the Cooperative that may be included in the patron's QBI is presumed to be zero. *See* special rule in paragraph (d)(3) of this section relating to reporting of qualified items of income, gain, deduction, and loss with respect to SSTBs of the Cooperative.

(d) *Specified Service Trades or Businesses.*—(1) *In general.*—This section provides guidance on the determination of SSTBs. Unless otherwise provided in this section, all of the rules in §1.199A-5 relating to SSTBs apply to patrons of Cooperatives.

(2) *SSTB determinations made by patron.*—A patron (whether an RPE or an individual) must determine whether each trade or business it directly conducts is an SSTB.

(3) *SSTB determinations made and reported by Cooperatives.*—In the case of a Cooperative that makes distributions described in paragraph (c)(1) of this section to a patron, the Cooperative must determine whether the distributions from the Cooperative include items of income, gain, deduction, and loss from an SSTB directly conducted by the Cooperative, and whether such items are qualified items of income, gain, deduction, and loss with respect to such SSTB. The Cooperative must report to the patron the amount of income, gain, deduction, and loss in the distributions that is a qualified item of income, gain, deduction, and loss with respect to such SSTB. The

Cooperative must report the amount on an attachment to or on the Form 1099-PATR (or any successor form) issued by the Cooperative to the patron, unless otherwise provided by the instructions to the Form. If the Cooperative does not report the amount on or before the due date of the Form 1099-PATR, then only the amount that a Cooperative reports as qualified items of income, gain, deduction, and loss under §1.199A-7(c)(3) may be included in the patron's QBI, and the remaining amount of distributions from the Cooperative that may be included in the patron's QBI is presumed to be zero.

(e) *W-2 wages and unadjusted basis immediately after acquisition of qualified property.*—(1) *In general.*—This section provides guidance on calculating a trade or business's W-2 wages and the UBIA of qualified property properly allocable to QBI.

(2) *Determinations made by patron.*—The determination of W-2 wages and UBIA of qualified property must be made for each trade or business by the patron (whether an RPE or individual) that directly conducts the trade or business before applying the aggregation rules of §1.199A-4. Unlike RPEs, Cooperatives do not allocate their W-2 wages and UBIA of qualified property to patrons.

(f) *Special rules for patrons of Specified Cooperatives.*—(1) *Section 199A(b)(7) reduction.*—A patron of a Specified Cooperative that receives a qualified payment must reduce its section 199A(a) deduction as provided in §1.199A-1(e)(7). This reduction applies whether the Specified Cooperative passes through all, some, or none of the Specified Cooperative's section 199A(g) deduction to the patron in that taxable year. The proposed rules relating to the section 199A(g) deduction can be found in §§1.199A-8 through 1.199A-12.

(2) *Deduction Calculation.*—(i) *Allocation method.*—If in any taxable year, a patron receives both qualified payments and income that is not a qualified payment in a trade or business, the patron must allocate those items and related deductions using a reasonable method based on all the facts and circumstances. Different reasonable methods may be used for different items and related deductions of income, gain, deduction, and loss. The chosen reasonable method for each item must be consistently applied from one taxable year of the patron to another, and must clearly reflect the income and expenses of each trade or business. The overall combination of methods must also be reasonable based on all the facts and circumstances. The books and records maintained for a trade or business must be consistent with any allocations under this paragraph (f)(2)(i).

(ii) *Safe harbor.*—A patron with taxable income under the threshold amount set forth in section 199A(e)(2) is eligible to use the safe harbor set forth in this paragraph (f)(2)(ii) instead of the allocation method set forth in paragraph (f)(2)(i) of this section for any taxable year in which the patron receives qualified payments and income from other than qualified payments in its trade or business. Under the safe harbor the patron may apportion its deductions and W-2 wages ratably between income from qualified payments and income from other than qualified payments for purposes of calculating the reduction in paragraph (f)(1) of this section. Accordingly, the amount of deductions apportioned to determine QBI allocable to qualified payments is equal to the proportion of the total deductions that the amount of qualified payments bears to total gross receipts used to determine QBI. The same proportion applies to determine the amount of W-2 wages allocable to the portion of the trade or business that received qualified payments.

(3) *Qualified payments notice requirement.*—A Specified Cooperative must report the amount of the qualified payments made to the eligible taxpayer, as defined in section 199A(g)(2)(D), on an attachment to or on the Form 1099-PATR (or any successor form) issued by the Cooperative to the patron, unless otherwise provided by the instructions to the Form.

(g) *Examples.*—The following examples illustrate the provisions of paragraph (f) of this section. For purposes of these examples, assume that the Specified Cooperative has satisfied the applicable written notice requirements in paragraphs (c)(3), (d)(3) and (f)(3) of this section.

(1) *Example 1. Patron of Specified Cooperative with W-2 wages.* (i) P, a grain farmer and patron of nonexempt Specified Cooperative (C), delivered to C during 2018 2% of all grain marketed through C during such year. During 2019, P receives $20,000 in patronage dividends and $1,000 of allocated section 199A(g) deduction from C related to the grain delivered to C during 2018.

(ii) P has taxable income of $75,000 for 2019 (determined without regard to section 199A) and has a filing status of married filing jointly. P's QBI related to its grain trade or business for 2019 is $50,000, which consists of gross receipts of $150,000 from sales to an independent grain elevator, per-unit retain allocations received from C during 2019 of $80,000, patronage dividends received from C during 2019 related to C's 2018 net earnings of $20,000, and expenses of $200,000 (including $50,000 of W-2 wages).

(iii) The portion of QBI from P's grain trade or business related to qualified payments received from C during 2019 is $10,000, which consists of per-unit retain allocations received from C during 2019 of $80,000, patronage dividends received from C during 2019 related to C's 2018 net earnings of $20,000, and properly allocable expenses of $90,000 (including $25,000 of W-2 wages).

(iv) P's deductible amount related to the grain trade or business is 20% of QBI ($10,000) reduced by the lesser of 9% of QBI related to qualified payments received from C ($900) or 50% of W-2 wages related to qualified payments received from C ($12,500), or $9,100. As P does not have any other trades or businesses, the combined QBI amount is also $9,100.

(v) P's deduction under section 199A for 2019 is $10,100, which consists of the combined QBI amount of $9,100, plus P's deduction passed through from C of $1,000.

(2) *Example 2. Patron of Specified Cooperative without W-2 wages.* (i) C and P have the same facts for 2018 and 2019 as *Example 1*, except that P has expenses of $200,000 that include zero W-2 wages during 2019.

(ii) P's deductible amount related to the grain trade or business is 20% of QBI ($10,000) reduced by the lesser of 9% of QBI related to qualified payments received from C ($900) or 50% of W-2 wages related to qualified payments received from C ($0), or $10,000.

(iii) P's deduction under section 199A for 2019 is $11,000, which consists of the combined QBI amount of $10,000, plus P's deduction passed through from C of $1,000.

(3) *Example 3. Patron of Specified Cooperative – Qualified Payments do not equal QBI and no section 199A(g) passthrough.* (i) P, a grain farmer and a patron of a nonexempt Specified Cooperative (C), during 2019, receives $60,000 in patronage dividends, $100,000 in per-unit retain allocations, and $0 of allocated section 199A(g) deduction from C related to the grain delivered to C. C notifies P that only $150,000 of the patronage dividends and per-unit retain allocations are qualified payments because $10,000 of the payments are not attributable to C's qualified production activities income (QPAI).

(ii) P has taxable income of $90,000 (determined without regard to section 199A) and has a filing status of married filing jointly. P's QBI related to its grain trade or business is $45,000, which consists of gross receipts of $95,000 from sales to an independent grain elevator, plus $160,000 from C (all payments from C qualify as qualified items of income, gain, deduction, and loss), less expenses of $210,000 (including $30,000 of W-2 wages).

(iii) The portion of QBI from P's grain trade or business related to qualified payments received from C is $25,000, which consists of the qualified payments received from C of $150,000, less the properly allocable expenses of $125,000 (including $18,000 of W-2 wages), which were determined using a reasonable method under paragraph (f)(2)(ii) of this section.

(iv) P's patron reduction is $2,250, which is the lesser of 9% of QBI related to qualified payments received from C, $2,250 (9% x $25,000), or 50% of W-2 wages related to qualified payments received from C, $9,000 (50% x $18,000). As P does not have any other trades or businesses, the combined QBI amount is $6,750 (20% of P's total QBI, $9,000 (20% x $45,000), reduced by the patron reduction of $2,250).

(v) P's deduction under section 199A is $6,750, which consists of the combined QBI amount of $6,750.

(4) *Example 4. Patron of Specified Cooperative – Reasonable Method under paragraph (f)(2)(ii) of this section.* P is a grain farmer that has $45,000 of QBI related to P's grain trade or business in 2019. P's QBI consists of $105,000 of sales to an independent grain elevator, $100,000 of per-unit retain allocations, and $50,000 of patronage dividends from a nonexempt Specified Cooperative (C), for which C reports $150,000 of qualified payments to P as required by paragraph (f)(3) of this section. P's grain trade or business has $210,000 of expenses (including $30,000 of W-2 wages). P delivered 65x bushels of grain to C and sold 35x bushels of comparable grain to the independent grain elevator. To allocate the expenses between qualified payments ($150,000) and other income ($105,000), P compares the bushels of grain delivered to C (65x) to the total bushels of grain delivered to C and sold to the independent grain elevator (100x). P determines $136,500 (65% x $210,000) of expenses (including $19,500 of W-2 wages) are properly allocable to the qualified payments. The portion of QBI from P's grain trade or business related to qualified payments received from C is $13,500, which consists of qualified payments of $150,000 less the properly allocable expenses of $136,500 (including $19,500 of W-2 wages). P's method of allocating expenses is a reasonable method under paragraph (f)(2)(ii) of this section.

(5) *Example 5. Patron of Specified Cooperative using safe harbor to allocate.* (i) P is a grain farmer with taxable income of $100,000 for 2019 (determined without regard to section 199A) and has a filing status of married filing jointly. P's QBI related to P's grain trade or business for 2019 is $50,000, which consists of gross receipts of $180,000 from sales to an independent grain elevator, per-unit retain allocations received from a Specified Cooperative (C) during 2019 of

$15,000, patronage dividends received from C during 2019 related to C's 2018 net earnings of $5,000, and expenses of $150,000 (including $50,000 of W-2 wages). C also passed through $1,800 of the section 199A(g) deduction to P, which related to the grain delivered by P to the Specified Cooperative during 2018. P uses the safe harbor in paragraph (f)(2)(iii) of this section to determine the expenses (including W-2 wages) allocable to the qualified payments.

(ii) Using the safe harbor to allocate P's $150,000 of expenses, P allocates $15,000 of the expenses to the qualified payments ($150,000 of expenses multiplied by the ratio (0.10) of qualified payments ($20,000) to total gross receipts ($200,000)). Using the same ratio, P also determines there are $5,000 of W-2 wages allocable ($50,000 multiplied by 0.10) to the qualified payments.

(iii) The portion of QBI from P's grain trade or business related to qualified payments received from C during 2019 is $5,000, which consists of per-unit retain allocations received from C during 2019 of $15,000, patronage dividends of $5,000, and properly allocable expenses of $15,000 (including $5,000 of W-2 wages).

(iv) P's QBI related to the grain trade or business is 20% of QBI ($10,000) reduced by the lesser of 9% of QBI related to qualified payments received from C ($450) or 50% of W-2 wages related to qualified payments received from C ($2,500), or $9,550. As P does not have any other trades or businesses, the combined QBI amount is also $9,550.

(v) P's deduction under section 199A for 2019 is $11,350, which consists of the combined QBI amount of $9,550, plus P's deduction passed through from C of $1,800.

(h) *Effective/applicability date.*—(1) *General rule.*—Except as provided in paragraph (h)(2) of this section, the provisions of this section apply to taxable years ending after the date the Treasury decision adopting these regulations as final regulations is published in the *Federal Register*. Taxpayers, however, may rely on these regulations until that date, but only if the taxpayers apply the rules in their entirety and in a consistent manner.

(2) *Transition rule for qualified payments of patrons of Cooperatives.*—No deductions under section 199A are allowed to patrons for any qualified payments that are attributable to QPAI with respect to which a deduction is allowable to the Specified Cooperative under section 199 as in effect on and before December 31, 2017, for a taxable year of the Specified Cooperative beginning before January 1, 2018.

(3) *Notice from the Cooperative.*—If a patron of a Cooperative cannot claim a deduction under section 199A for any qualified payments described in the transition rule set forth in paragraph (h)(2) of this section, the Cooperative must report this information on an attachment to or on the Form 1099-PATR (or any successor form) issued by the Cooperative to the patron, unless otherwise provided by the instructions to the Form. [Reg. § 1.199A-7.]

§1.199A-8. Deduction for income attributable to domestic production activities of specified agricultural or horticultural cooperatives.—(a) *Overview.*—(1) *In general.*—This section provides rules relating to the deduction for income attributable to domestic production activities of a specified agricultural or horticultural cooperative (Specified Cooperative). This paragraph (a) provides an overview and definitions of certain terms. Paragraph (b) of this section provides rules explaining the steps a nonexempt Specified Cooperative performs to calculate its section 199A(g) deduction and includes definitions of relevant terms. Paragraph (c) of this section provides rules explaining the steps an exempt Specified Cooperative performs to calculate its section 199A(g) deduction. Paragraph (d) of this section provides rules for Specified Cooperatives passing through the section 199A(g) deduction to patrons. Paragraph (e) of this section provides examples that illustrate the provisions of paragraphs (b), (c), and (d) of this section. Paragraph (f) of this section provides guidance for Specified Cooperatives that are partners in a partnership. Paragraph (g) of this section provides guidance on the recapture of a claimed section 199A(g) deduction. Paragraph (h) of this section provides effective dates. For additional rules addressing an expanded affiliated group (EAG) *see* § 1.199A-12. The principles of this section apply to the EAG rules in § 1.199A-12.

(2) *Specified Cooperative.*—(i) *In general.*—Specified Cooperative means a cooperative to which Part I of subchapter T of chapter 1 of subtitle A of the Internal Revenue Code (Code) applies and which—

(A) Manufactures, produces, grows, or extracts (MPGE) in whole or significant part within the United States any agricultural or horticultural product, or

(B) Is engaged in the marketing of agricultural or horticultural products that have been MPGE in whole or significant part within the United States by the patrons of the cooperative.

(ii) *Additional rules.*—See § 1.199A-9 for rules to determine if a Specified Cooperative has MPGE an agricultural or horticultural product in whole or significant part within the United States.

(iii) *Types of Specified Cooperatives.*—A Specified Cooperative that is qualified as a farmer's cooperative organization under section 521 is an *exempt Specified Cooperative*, while a Specified Cooperative not so qualified is a *nonexempt Specified Cooperative.*

(3) *Patron* is defined in § 1.1388-1(e).

(4) *Agricultural or horticultural products* are agricultural, horticultural, viticultural, and dairy products, livestock and the products thereof, the products of poultry and bee raising, the edible products of forestry, and any and all products raised or produced on farms and processed or manufactured products thereof within the meaning of the Cooperative Marketing Act of 1926, 44 Stat. 802 (1926). Agricultural or horticultural products also include aquatic products that are farmed whether by an exempt or a nonexempt Specified Cooperative. In addition, agricultural or horticultural products include fertilizer, diesel fuel, and other supplies used in agricultural or horticultural production that are MPGE by a Specified Cooperative. Agricultural or horticultural products, however, do not include intangible property (other than as provided in the exception in § 1.199A-9(b)(2)); for example, an agricultural or horticultural product includes a seed that is grown, but does not include the intangible property right to reproduce a seed for sale. This exclusion of intangible property does not apply to intangible characteristics of any particular agricultural or horticultural product. For example, gross receipts from the sale of different varieties of oranges would all qualify as DPGR from the disposition of agricultural or horticultural products (assuming all other requirements of section 199A(g) are met). However, gross receipts from the license of the right to produce and sell a certain variety of an orange would be considered separate from the orange and not from an agricultural or horticultural product.

(b) *Steps for a nonexempt Specified Cooperative in calculating deduction.*—(1) *In general.*—Except as provided in paragraph (c)(3) of this section, this paragraph (b) applies only to nonexempt Specified Cooperatives.

(2) *Step 1 - Gross receipts and related deductions.*—(i) *Identify.*—To determine the section 199A(g) deduction, a Specified Cooperative first identifies its patronage and nonpatronage gross receipts and related cost of goods sold (COGS), deductible expenses, W-2 wages, etc. (deductions) and allocates them between patronage and nonpatronage. A single definition for the term *patronage and nonpatronage* is found in § 1.1388-1(f).

(ii) *Applicable gross receipts and deductions.*—For all purposes of the section 199A(g) deduction, a Specified Cooperative can use only patronage gross receipts and related deductions to calculate qualified production activities income (QPAI) as defined in paragraph (b)(4)(ii) of this section, oil-related QPAI as defined in paragraph (b)(7)(ii) of this section, or the W-2 wage limitation in paragraph (b)(5)(ii)(B) of this section. A Specified Cooperative cannot use its nonpatronage gross receipts and related deductions to calculate its section 199A(g) deduction.

(iii) *Gross receipts* are the Specified Cooperative's receipts for the taxable year that are recognized under the Specified Cooperative's methods of accounting used for Federal income tax purposes for the taxable year. See § 1.199A-12 if the gross receipts are recognized in an intercompany transaction within the meaning of § 1.1502-13. Gross receipts include total sales (net of returns and allowances) and all amounts received for services. In addition, gross receipts include any income from investments and from incidental or outside sources. For example, gross receipts include interest (except interest under section 103 but including original issue discount), dividends, rents, royalties, and annuities, regardless of whether the amounts are derived in the ordinary course of the Specified Cooperative's trade or business. Gross receipts are not reduced by COGS or by the cost of property sold if such property is described in section 1221(a)(1), (2), (3), (4), or (5). Finally, gross receipts do not include amounts received by the Specified Cooperative with respect to sales tax or other similar state or local taxes if, under the applicable state or local law, the tax is legally imposed on the purchaser of the good or service and the Specified Cooperative merely collects and remits the tax to the taxing authority. If, in contrast, the tax is imposed on the Specified Cooperative under the applicable law, then gross receipts include the amounts received that are allocable to the payment of such tax.

(3) *Step 2 – Determine gross receipts that are DPGR.*—(i) *In general.*—A Specified Cooperative examines its patronage gross receipts to determine which of these are DPGR. A Specified Cooperative does not use nonpatronage gross receipts to determine DPGR.

(ii) *DPGR* are the gross receipts of the Specified Cooperative that are derived from any lease, rental, license, sale, exchange, or other disposition of an agricultural or horticultural product that is MPGE by the Specified Cooperative or its patrons in whole or significant part within the United States. DPGR does not include gross receipts derived from services or the lease, rental, license, sale,

exchange, or other disposition of land unless a de minimis or other exception applies. See § 1.199A-9 for additional rules on determining if gross receipts are DPGR.

(4) *Step 3 – Determine QPAI.*—(i) *In general.*—A Specified Cooperative determines QPAI from patronage DPGR and patronage deductions identified in paragraphs (b)(3)(ii) and (b)(2)(i) of this section, respectively. A Specified Cooperative does not use nonpatronage gross receipts or deductions to determine QPAI.

(ii) *QPAI* for the taxable year means an amount equal to the excess (if any) of—

(A) DPGR for the taxable year, over

(B) The sum of—

(1) COGS that are allocable to DPGR, and

(2) Other expenses, losses, or deductions (other than the section 199A(g) deduction) that are properly allocable to DPGR.

(C) *QPAI computational rules.*—QPAI is computed without taking into account the section 199A(g) deduction or any deduction allowed under section 1382(b). See § 1.199A-10 for additional rules on calculating QPAI.

(5) *Step 4 – Calculate deduction.*—(i) *In general.*—From QPAI and taxable income, a Specified Cooperative calculates its section 199A(g) deduction as provided in paragraph (b)(5)(ii) of this section.

(ii) *Deduction.*—(A) *In general.*—A Specified Cooperative is allowed a deduction equal to 9 percent of the lesser of—

(1) QPAI of the Specified Cooperative for the taxable year, or

(2) Taxable income of the Specified Cooperative for the taxable year.

(B) *W-2 wage limitation.*—The deduction allowed under paragraph (b)(5)(ii)(A) of this section for any taxable year cannot exceed 50 percent of the patronage W-2 wages attributable to DPGR for the taxable year. See § 1.199A-11 for additional rules on calculating the patronage W-2 wage limitation.

(C) *Taxable income.*—Taxable income is defined in section 1382 and § 1.1382-1 and § 1.1382-2. For purposes of determining the amount of the deduction allowed under paragraph (b)(5)(ii) of this section, taxable income is limited to taxable income and related deductions from patronage sources. Patronage net operating losses (NOLs) reduce taxable income. Taxable income is computed without taking into account the section 199A(g) deduction or any deduction allowable under section 1382(b). Taxable income is determined using the same method of accounting used to determine distributions under section 1382(b) and qualified payments to eligible taxpayers.

(6) *Use of patronage section 199A(g) deduction.*—Except as provided in § 1.199A-12(c)(2) related to the rules for EAGs, the patronage section 199A(g) deduction cannot create or increase a patronage or nonpatronage NOL or the amount of a patronage or nonpatronage NOL carryover or carryback, if applicable, in accordance with section 172. A patronage section 199A(g) deduction can be applied only against patronage income and deductions. A patronage section 199A(g) deduction that is not used in the appropriate taxable year is lost.

(7) *Special rules for nonexempt Specified Cooperatives that have oil-related QPAI.*—(i) *Reduction of section 199A(g) deduction.*—If a Specified Cooperative has oil-related QPAI for any taxable year, the amount otherwise allowable as a deduction under paragraph (b)(5)(ii) of this section must be reduced by 3 percent of the least of—

(A) Oil-related QPAI of the Specified Cooperative for the taxable year,

(B) QPAI of the Specified Cooperative for the taxable year, or

(C) Taxable income of the Specified Cooperative for the taxable year.

(ii) *Oil-related QPAI* means, for any taxable year, the patronage QPAI that is attributable to the production, refining, processing, transportation, or distribution of oil, gas, or any primary product thereof (within the meaning of section 927(a)(2)(C), as in effect before its repeal) during such taxable year. Oil-related QPAI for any taxable year is an amount equal to the excess (if any) of patronage DPGR derived from the production, refining or processing of oil, gas, or any primary product thereof (oil-related DPGR) over the sum of—

(A) COGS of the Specified Cooperative that is allocable to such receipts; and

(B) Other expenses, losses, or deductions (other than the section 199A(g) deduction) that are properly allocable to such receipts.

(iii) *Special rule for patronage oil-related DPGR.*—Oil-related DPGR does not include gross receipts derived from the transportation or distribution of oil, gas, or any primary product thereof.

However, to the extent that the nonexempt Specified Cooperative treats gross receipts derived from transportation or distribution of oil, gas, or any primary product thereof as part of DPGR under §1.199A-9(j)(3)(i), or under §1.199A-9(j)(3)(i)(B), then the Specified Cooperative must treat those patronage gross receipts as oil-related DGPR.

(iv) *Oil* includes oil recovered from both conventional and non-conventional recovery methods, including crude oil, shale oil, and oil recovered from tar/oil sands. The *primary product from oil* includes all products derived from the destructive distillation of oil, including volatile products, light oils such as motor fuel and kerosene, distillates such as naphtha, lubricating oils, greases and waxes, and residues such as fuel oil. The *primary product from gas* means all gas and associated hydrocarbon components from gas wells or oil wells, whether recovered at the lease or upon further processing, including natural gas, condensates, liquefied petroleum gases such as ethane, propane, and butane, and liquid products such as natural gasoline. The primary products from oil and gas provided in this paragraph (b)(7)(iv) are not intended to represent either the only primary products from oil or gas, or the only processes from which primary products may be derived under existing and future technologies. Examples of non-primary products include, but are not limited to, petrochemicals, medicinal products, insecticides, and alcohols.

(c) *Exempt Specified Cooperatives.*—(1) *In general.*—This paragraph (c) applies only to exempt Specified Cooperatives.

(2) *Two section 199A(g) deductions.*—The Specified Cooperative must calculate two separate section 199A(g) deductions, one patronage sourced and the other nonpatronage sourced. Patronage and nonpatronage gross receipts, related COGS that are allocable to DPGR, and other expenses, losses, or deductions (other than the section 199A(g) deduction) that are properly allocable to DPGR (deductions), DPGR, QPAI, NOLs, W-2 wages, etc. are not netted to calculate these two separate section 199A(g) deductions.

(3) *Exempt Specified Cooperative patronage section 199A(g) deduction.*—The Specified Cooperative calculates its patronage section 199A(g) deduction following steps 1 through 4 in paragraphs (b)(2) through (5) of this section as if it were a nonexempt Specified Cooperative.

(4) *Exempt Specified Cooperative nonpatronage section 199A(g) deduction.*—(i) *In general.*—The Specified Cooperative calculates its nonpatronage section 199A(g) deduction following steps 2 through 4 in paragraphs (b)(2) through (5) of this section using only nonpatronage gross receipts and related nonpatronage deductions. For purposes of determining the amount of the nonpatronage section 199A(g) deduction allowed under paragraph (b)(5)(ii) of this section, taxable income is limited to taxable income and related deductions from nonpatronage sources. Nonpatronage NOLs reduce taxable income. Taxable income is computed without taking into account the section 199A(g) deduction or any deduction allowable under section 1382(c). Taxable income is determined using the same method of accounting used to determine distributions under section 1382(c)(2).

(ii) *Use of nonpatronage section 199A(g) deduction.*—Except as provided in §1.199A-12(c)(2) related to the rules for EAGs, the nonpatronage section 199A(g) deduction cannot create or increase a nonpatronage NOL or the amount of nonpatronage NOL carryover or carryback, if applicable, in accordance with section 172. A Specified Cooperative cannot allocate its nonpatronage section 199A(g) deduction under paragraph (d) of this section and can apply the nonpatronage section 199A(g) deduction only against its nonpatronage income and deductions. As is the case for the patronage section 199A(g) deduction, the nonpatronage section 199A(g) deduction that a Specified Cooperative does not use in the appropriate taxable year is lost.

(d) *Discretion to pass through deduction.*—(1) *In general.*—A Specified Cooperative may, at its discretion, pass through all, some, or none of its patronage section 199A(g) deduction to an eligible taxpayer. An eligible taxpayer is a patron other than a C corporation or a Specified Cooperative. A Specified Cooperative member of a federated cooperative may pass through the patronage section 199A(g) deduction it receives from the federated cooperative to its member patrons that are eligible taxpayers.

(2) *Amount of deduction being passed through.*—(i) *In general.*—A Specified Cooperative is permitted to pass through to an eligible taxpayer an amount equal to the portion of the Specified Cooperative's section 199A(g) deduction that is allowed with respect to the portion of the cooperative's QPAI that is attributable to the qualified payments the Specified Cooperative distributed to the eligible taxpayer during the taxable year and identified on the notice required in §1.199A-7(f)(3) on an attachment to or on the Form 1099-PATR, Taxable Distributions Received From Cooperatives (Form 1099-PATR), (or any successor form) issued by the Specified Coopera-

tive to the eligible taxpayer, unless otherwise provided by the instructions to the Form. The notice requirement to pass through the section 199A(g) deduction is in paragraph (d)(3) of this section.

(ii) *Qualified payment* means any amount of a patronage dividend or per-unit retain allocation, as described in section 1385(a)(1) or (3) received by a patron from a Specified Cooperative that is attributable to the portion of the Specified Cooperative's QPAI, for which the cooperative is allowed a section 199A(g) deduction. For this purpose, patronage dividends include any advances on patronage and per-unit retain allocations include per-unit retains paid in money during the taxable year. A Specified Cooperative calculates its qualified payment using the same method of accounting it uses to calculate its taxable income.

(3) *Notice requirement to pass through deduction.*—A Specified Cooperative must identify in a written notice the amount of the section 199A(g) deduction being passed through to the eligible taxpayer. This written notice must be mailed by the Specified Cooperative to the eligible taxpayer no later than the 15th day of the ninth month following the close of the taxable year of the Specified Cooperative. The Specified Cooperative may use the same written notice, if any, that it uses to notify the eligible taxpayer of the eligible taxpayer's respective allocations of patronage distributions, or may use a separate timely written notice(s) to comply with this section. The Specified Cooperative must report the amount of section 199A(g) deduction passed through to the eligible taxpayer on an attachment to or on the Form 1099-PATR (or any successor form) issued by the Specified Cooperative to the eligible taxpayer, unless otherwise provided by the instructions to the Form.

(4) *Section 199A(g) deduction allocated to eligible taxpayer.*—An eligible taxpayer may deduct the lesser of the section 199A(g) deduction identified on the notice described in paragraph (d)(3) of this section or the eligible taxpayer's taxable income in the taxable year in which the eligible taxpayer receives the timely written notice described in paragraph (d)(3) of this section. For this purpose, the eligible taxpayer's taxable income is determined without taking into account the section 199A(g) deduction being passed through to the eligible taxpayer and after taking into account any section 199A(a) deduction allowed to the eligible taxpayer. Any section 199A(g) deduction the eligible taxpayer does not use in the taxable year in which the eligible taxpayer receives the notice (received on or before the due date of the Form 1099-PATR) is lost and cannot be carried forward or back to other taxable years. The taxable income limitation for the section 199A(a) deduction set forth in section 199A(b)(3) and §1.199A-1(a) and (b) does not apply to limit the deductibility of the section 199A(g) deduction passed through to the eligible taxpayer.

(5) *Special rules for eligible taxpayers that are Specified Cooperatives.*—A Specified Cooperative that receives a section 199A(g) deduction as an eligible taxpayer can take the deduction only against patronage gross income and related deductions.

(6) *W-2 wage limitation.*—The W-2 wage limitation described in paragraph (b)(5)(ii)(B) of this section is applied at the cooperative level whether or not the Specified Cooperative chooses to pass through some or all of the section 199A(g) deduction. Any section 199A(g) deduction that has been passed through by a Specified Cooperative to an eligible taxpayer is not subject to the W-2 wage limitation a second time at the eligible taxpayer's level.

(7) *Specified Cooperative denied section 1382 deduction for portion of qualified payments.*—A Specified Cooperative must reduce its section 1382 deduction under section 1382(b) and/or (c), as applicable, by an amount equal to the portion of any qualified payment that is attributable to the Specified Cooperative's section 199A(g) deduction passed through to the eligible taxpayer. This means the Specified Cooperative must reduce its section 1382 deduction in an amount equal to the section 199A(g) deduction passed through to its eligible taxpayers.

(8) *No double counting.*—A qualified payment received by a Specified Cooperative that is a patron of a Specified Cooperative is not taken into account by the patron for purposes of section 199A(g).

(e) *Examples.*—The following examples illustrate the application of paragraphs (b), (c), and (d) of this section. Assume for each example that the Specified Cooperative sent all required notices to patrons on or before the due date of the Form 1099-PATR.

(1) *Example 1. Nonexempt Specified Cooperative calculating section 199A(g) deduction.* (i) C is a grain marketing nonexempt Specified Cooperative, with $5,250,000 in gross receipts during 2018 from the sale of grain grown by its patrons. C paid $4,000,000 to its patrons at the time the grain was delivered in the form of per-unit retain allocations pursuant to an agreement and another $1,000,000 in patronage dividends after the close of the 2018 taxable year. C has other expenses of $250,000 during 2018, including $100,000 of W-2 wages.

(ii) C has DPGR of $5,250,000 and QPAI as defined in §1.199A-8(b)(4)(ii) of $5,000,000 for 2018. C's section 199A(g) deduction is equal to the least of 9% of QPAI ($450,000), 9% of taxable income ($450,000), or 50% of W-2 wages ($50,000). C passes through the entire section 199A(g) deduction to its patrons. Accordingly, C reduces its $5,000,000 deduction allowable under section 1382(b) (relating to the $1,000,000 patronage dividends and $4,000,000 per-unit retain allocations) by $50,000.

(2) *Example 2. Nonexempt Specified Cooperative calculating section 199A(g) deduction with purchases.* Same facts as *Example 1*, except C purchased grain from its patrons for $4,000,000 and these purchases are not per-unit retain allocations described in section 1388(f). C allocated and reported the $1,000,000 patronage dividends to its patrons and provided notification (in accordance with the requirements of §1.199A-7(f)(3)) that only the patronage dividends are treated as qualified payments for purposes of its section 199A(g) deduction. C has QPAI and taxable income of $1,000,000 ($5,250,000 – $4,000,000 – $250,000). C's section 199A(g) deduction is the lesser of 9% of QPAI ($90,000), 9% of taxable income without taking into account any deduction under section 1382(b) ($90,000), or 50% of W-2 wages ($50,000). C passes through the entire section 199A(g) deduction to its patrons. Accordingly, C reduces its $1,000,000 deduction allowable under section 1382(b) by $50,000. Patrons do not include any of the $4,000,000 of payments when determining the reduction amount under section 199A(b)(7).

(3) *Example 3. Nonexempt Specified Cooperative determines amounts included in QPAI and taxable income.* (i) C, a nonexempt Specified Cooperative, offers harvesting services and markets the grain of patrons and nonpatrons. C had gross receipts from harvesting services and grain sales, and expenses related to both. All of C's harvesting services were performed for their patrons, and 75% of the grain sales were for patrons.

(ii) C identifies 75% of the gross receipts and related expenses from grain sales and 100% of the gross receipts and related expenses from the harvesting services as patronage sourced. C identifies 25% of the gross receipts and related expenses from grain sales as nonpatronage sourced.

(iii) C does not include any nonpatronage gross receipts or related expenses from grain sales in either QPAI or taxable income when calculating the section 199A(g) deduction. C's QPAI includes the patronage DPGR, less related expenses (allocable COGS, wages and other expenses). C's taxable income includes the patronage gross receipts, whether such gross receipts are DPGR or non-DPGR.

(iv) C allocates and reports patronage dividends to its harvesting patrons and grain marketing patrons. C also notifies its grain marketing patrons (in accordance with the requirements of §1.199A-7(f)(3)) that their patronage dividends are qualified payments used in C's section 199A(g) computation. The patrons must use this information for purposes of computing their section 199A(b)(7) reduction to their section 199A(a) deduction (*see* §1.199A-7(f)).

(4) *Example 4. Nonexempt Specified Cooperative with patronage and nonpatronage gross receipts and related deductions.* (i) C, a nonexempt Specified Cooperative, markets corn grown by its patrons in the United States. For the calendar year ending December 31, 2020, C derives gross receipts from the marketing activity of $1,800. Such gross receipts qualify as DPGR. Assume C has $800 of expenses (including COGS, other expenses, and $400 of W-2 wages) properly allocable to DPGR, and a $1,000 deduction allowed under section 1382(b). C also derives gross receipts from nonpatronage sources in the amount of $500, and has nonpatronage deductions in the amount of $400 (including COGS, other expenses, and $100 of W-2 wages).

(ii) C does not include any gross receipts or deductions from nonpatronage sources when calculating the deduction under paragraph (b)(5)(ii) of this section. C's QPAI and taxable income both equal $1,000 ($1,800 – 800). C's deduction under paragraph (b)(5)(ii) of this section for the taxable year is equal to $90 (9% of $1,000), which does not exceed $200 (50% of C's W-2 wages properly allocable to DPGR). C passes through $90 of the deduction to patrons and C reduces its section 1382(b) deduction by $90.

(5) *Example 5. Exempt Specified Cooperative with patronage and nonpatronage income and deductions.* (i) C, an exempt Specified Cooperative, markets corn MPGE by its patrons in the United States. For the calendar year ending December 31, 2020, C derives gross receipts from the marketing activity of $1,800. For this activity assume C has $800 of expenses (including COGS, other expenses, and $400 of W-2 wages) properly allocable to DPGR, and a $1,000 deduction under section 1382(b). C also derives gross receipts from nonpatronage sources in the amount of $500. Assume the gross receipts qualify as DPGR. For this activity assume C has $400 of expenses (including COGS, other expenses, and $20 of W-2 wages) properly allocable to DPGR and no deduction under section 1382(c).

(ii) C calculates two separate section 199A(g) deduction amounts. C's section 199A(g) deduction attributable to patronage sources is the same as the deduction calculated by the nonexempt Specified Cooperative in *Example 1* in paragraph (e)(1) of this section.

(iii) C's nonpatronage QPAI and taxable income is equal to $100 ($500 – $400). C's deduction under paragraph (c)(3) of this section that directs C to use paragraph (b)(5)(ii) of this section attributable to nonpatronage sources is equal to $9 (9% of $100), which does not exceed $10 (50% of C's W-2 wages properly allocable to DPGR). C cannot pass through any of the nonpatronage section 199A(g) deduction amount to its patrons.

(6) *Example 6. NOL.* C, a nonexempt Specified Cooperative, MPGE agricultural or horticultural products. C is not part of an EAG as defined in §1.199A-12. In 2018, C generates QPAI and taxable income is $600, without taking into account any of its deductions under section 1382(b), the deduction under section 199A(g), or an NOL deduction. During 2018, C incurs W-2 wages as defined in §1.199A-11 of $300. C has an NOL carryover to 2018 of $500. C's deduction under this section for 2018 is $9 (9% × (lesser of QPAI of $600 and taxable income of $100 ($600 taxable income – $500 NOL)). Under these facts the wage limitation does not act to limit the deduction because the wage limitation is $150 (50% × $300).

(7) *Example 7. NOL.* (i) C, a nonexempt Specified Cooperative, MPGE agricultural or horticultural products. C is not part of an EAG. In 2018, C generates QPAI and taxable income of $100, without taking into account any of its deductions under section 1382(b), the deduction under section 199A(g), or an NOL deduction. C has an NOL carryover to 2018 of $500 that reduces its taxable income for 2018 to $0. C's section 199A(g) deduction for 2018 is $0 (9% × (lesser of QPAI of $100 and taxable income of $0)).

(ii) *Carryover to 2019.* C's taxable income for purposes of determining its NOL carryover to 2019 is $100. Accordingly, for purposes of section 199A(g), C's NOL carryover to 2019 is $400 ($500 NOL carryover to 2018 – $100 NOL used in 2018).

(f) *Special rule for Specified Cooperative partners.*—In the case described in section 199A(g)(5)(B), where a Specified Cooperative is a partner in a partnership, the partnership must separately identify and report on the Schedule K-1 of the Form 1065, U.S. Return of Partnership Income (or any successor form) issued to the Specified Cooperative the cooperative's share of gross receipts and related deductions, unless otherwise provided by the instructions to the Form. The Specified Cooperative determines what gross receipts reported by the partnership qualify as DPGR and includes these gross receipts and related deductions to calculate one section 199A(g) deduction (in the case of a nonexempt Specified Cooperative) or two section 199A(g) deductions (in the case of an exempt Specified Cooperative) using the steps set forth in paragraphs (b) and (c) of this section.

(g) *Recapture of section 199A(g) deduction.*—If the amount of the section 199A(g) deduction that was passed through to eligible taxpayers exceeds the amount allowable as a section 199A(g) deduction as determined on examination or reported on an amended return, then recapture of the excess will occur at the Specified Cooperative level in the taxable year the Specified Cooperative took the excess section 199A(g) deduction.

(h) *Applicability date.*—Except as provided in paragraph (h)(2) of §1.199A-7, the provisions of this section apply to taxable years ending after the date the Treasury decision adopting these regulations as final regulations is published in the *Federal Register*. Taxpayers, however, may rely on these regulations until that date, but only if the taxpayers apply the rules in their entirety and in a consistent manner. [Reg. 1.199A-8.]

§1.199A-9. Domestic production gross receipts.—(a) *Domestic production gross receipts.*—(1) *In general.*—The provisions of this section apply solely for purposes of section 199A(g) of the Internal Revenue Code (Code). The provisions of this section provide guidance to determine what gross receipts (defined in §1.199A-8(b)(2)(iii)) are domestic production gross receipts (DPGR) (defined in §1.199A-8(b)(3)(ii)). DPGR does not include gross receipts derived from services or the lease, rental, license, sale, exchange, or other disposition of land unless a de minimis or other exception applies. Partners, including partners in an EAG partnership described in §1.199A-12(i)(1), may not treat guaranteed payments under section 707(c) as DPGR.

(2) *Application to marketing cooperatives.*—For purposes of determining DPGR, a Specified Cooperative (defined in §1.199A-8(a)(2)) will be treated as having manufactured, produced, grown, or extracted (MPGE) (defined in paragraph (f) of this section) in whole or significant part (defined in paragraph (h) of this section) any agricultural or horticultural product (defined in §1.199A-8(a)(4)) within the United States (defined in paragraph (i) of this section) marketed by the Specified Cooperative which its patrons (defined in §1.1388-1(e)) have so MPGE.

(b) *Related persons.*—(1) *In general.*—Pursuant to 199A(g)(3)(D)(ii), DPGR does not include any gross receipts derived from agricultural or horticultural products leased, licensed, or rented by the Specified Cooperative for use by any related person. A person is treated as related to another person if both persons are treated as a single employer under either section 52(a) or (b) (without regard to section 1563(b)), or section 414(m) or (o). Any other person is an unrelated person for purposes of the section 199A(g) deduction.

(2) *Exceptions.*—Notwithstanding paragraph (b)(1) of this section, gross receipts derived from any agricultural or horticultural product leased or rented by the Specified Cooperative to a related person may qualify as DPGR if the agricultural or horticultural product is held for sublease or rent, or is subleased or rented, by the related person to an unrelated person for the ultimate use of the unrelated person. Similarly, notwithstanding paragraph (b)(1) of this section, gross receipts derived from a license of the right to reproduce an agricultural or horticultural product to a related person for reproduction and sale, exchange, lease, or rental to an unrelated person for the ultimate use of the unrelated person are treated as gross receipts from a disposition of an agricultural or horticultural product and may qualify as DPGR.

(c) *Allocating gross receipts.*—(1) *In general.*—A Specified Cooperative must determine the portion of its gross receipts for the taxable year that is DPGR and the portion of its gross receipts that is non-DPGR using a reasonable method based on all the facts and circumstances. Applicable Federal income tax principles apply to determine whether a transaction is, in substance, a lease, rental, license, sale, exchange, or other disposition the gross receipts of which may constitute DPGR, whether it is a service the gross receipts of which may constitute non-DPGR, or some combination thereof. For example, if a Specified Cooperative sells an agricultural or horticultural product and, in connection with that sale, also provides services, the Specified Cooperative must allocate its gross receipts from the transaction using a reasonable method based on all the facts and circumstances that accurately identifies the gross receipts that constitute DPGR and non-DPGR in accordance with the requirements of §§ 1.199A-8(b) and/or (c). The chosen reasonable method must be consistently applied from one taxable year to another and must clearly reflect the portion of gross receipts for the taxable year that is DPGR and the portion of gross receipts that is non-DPGR. The books and records maintained for gross receipts must be consistent with any allocations under this paragraph (c)(1).

(2) *Reasonable method of allocation.*—If a Specified Cooperative has the information readily available and can, without undue burden or expense, specifically identify whether the gross receipts are derived from an item (and thus, are DPGR), then the Specified Cooperative must use that specific identification to determine DPGR. If the Specified Cooperative does not have information readily available to specifically identify whether gross receipts are derived from an item or cannot, without undue burden or expense, specifically identify whether gross receipts are derived from an item, then the Specified Cooperative is not required to use a method that specifically identifies whether the gross receipts are derived from an item but can use a reasonable allocation method. Factors taken into consideration in determining whether the Specified Cooperative's method of allocating gross receipts between DPGR and non-DPGR is reasonable include whether the Specified Cooperative uses the most accurate information available; the relationship between the gross receipts and the method used; the accuracy of the method chosen as compared with other possible methods; whether the method is used by the Specified Cooperative for internal management or other business purposes; whether the method is used for other Federal or state income tax purposes; the time, burden, and cost of using alternative methods; and whether the Specified Cooperative applies the method consistently from year to year.

(3) *De minimis rules.*—(i) *DPGR.*—A Specified Cooperative's applicable gross receipts as provided in §§ 1.199A-8(b) and/or (c) may be treated as DPGR if less than 5 percent of the Specified Cooperative's total gross receipts are non-DPGR (after application of the exceptions provided in § 1.199A-9(j)(3)). If the amount of the Specified Cooperative's gross receipts that are non-DPGR equals or exceeds 5 percent of the Specified Cooperative's total gross receipts, then, except as provided in paragraph (c)(3)(ii) of this section, the Specified Cooperative is required to allocate all gross receipts between DPGR and non-DPGR in accordance with paragraph (c)(1) of this section. If a Specified Cooperative is a member of an expanded affiliated group (EAG) (defined in § 1.199A-12), but is not a member of a consolidated group, then the determination of whether less than 5 percent of the Specified Cooperative's total gross receipts are non-DPGR is made at the Specified Cooperative level. If a Specified Cooperative is a member of a consolidated group, then the determination of whether less than 5 percent of the Specified Cooperative's total gross receipts are non-DPGR is made at the consolidated group level. *See* § 1.199A-12(d).

(ii) *Non-DPGR.*—A Specified Cooperative's applicable gross receipts as provided in §§ 1.199A-8(b) and/or (c) may be treated as

non-DPGR if less than 5 percent of the Specified Cooperative's total gross receipts are DPGR. If a Specified Cooperative is a member of an EAG, but is not a member of a consolidated group, then the determination of whether less than 5 percent of the Specified Cooperative's total gross receipts are DPGR is made at the Specified Cooperative level. If a Specified Cooperative is a member of a consolidated group, then the determination of whether less than 5 percent of the Specified Cooperative's total gross receipts are DPGR is made at the consolidated group level.

(d) *Use of historical data for multiple-year transactions.*—If a Specified Cooperative recognizes and reports gross receipts from upfront payments or other similar payments on a Federal income tax return for a taxable year, then the Specified Cooperative's use of historical data in making an allocation of gross receipts from the transaction between DPGR and non-DPGR may constitute a reasonable method. If a Specified Cooperative makes allocations using historical data, and subsequently updates the data, then the Specified Cooperative must use the more recent or updated data, starting in the taxable year in which the update is made.

(e) *Determining DPGR item-by-item.*—(1) *In general.*—For purposes of the section 199A(g) deduction, a Specified Cooperative determines, using a reasonable method based on all the facts and circumstances, whether gross receipts qualify as DPGR on an item-by-item basis (and not, for example, on a division-by-division, product line-by-product line, or transaction-by-transaction basis). The chosen reasonable method must be consistently applied from one taxable year to another and must clearly reflect the portion of gross receipts that is DPGR. The books and records maintained for gross receipts must be consistent with any allocations under this paragraph (e)(1).

(i) The term *item* means the agricultural or horticultural product offered by the Specified Cooperative in the normal course of its trade or business for lease, rental, license, sale, exchange, or other disposition (for purposes of this paragraph (e), collectively referred to as disposition) to customers, if the gross receipts from the disposition of such product qualify as DPGR; or

(ii) If paragraph (e)(1)(i) of this section does not apply to the product, then any component of the product described in paragraph (e)(1)(i) of this section is treated as the item, provided that the gross receipts from the disposition of the product described in paragraph (e)(1)(i) of this section that are attributable to such component qualify as DPGR. Each component that meets the requirements under this paragraph (e)(1)(ii) must be treated as a separate item and a component that meets the requirements under this paragraph (e)(1)(ii) may not be combined with a component that does not meet these requirements.

(2) *Special rules.*—(i) For purposes of paragraph (e)(1)(i) of this section, in no event may a single item consist of two or more products unless those products are offered for disposition, in the normal course of the Specified Cooperative's trade or business, as a single item (regardless of how the products are packaged).

(ii) In the case of agricultural or horticultural products customarily sold by weight or by volume, the item is determined using the most common custom of the industry (for example, barrels of oil).

(3) *Exception.*—If the Specified Cooperative MPGE agricultural or horticultural products within the United States that it disposes of, and the Specified Cooperative leases, rents, licenses, purchases, or otherwise acquires property that contains or may contain the agricultural or horticultural products (or a portion thereof), and the Specified Cooperative cannot reasonably determine, without undue burden and expense, whether the acquired property contains any of the original agricultural or horticultural products MPGE by the Specified Cooperative, then the Specified Cooperative is not required to determine whether any portion of the acquired property qualifies as an item for purposes of paragraph (e)(1) of this section. Therefore, the gross receipts derived from the disposition of the acquired property may be treated as non-DPGR. Similarly, the preceding sentences apply if the Specified Cooperative can reasonably determine that the acquired property contains agricultural or horticultural products (or a portion thereof) MPGE by the Specified Cooperative, but cannot reasonably determine, without undue burden or expense, how much, or what type, grade, etc., of the agricultural or horticultural MPGE by the Specified Cooperative the acquired property contains.

(f) *Definition of manufactured, produced, grown, or extracted (MPGE).*—(1) *In general.*—Except as provided in paragraphs (f)(2) and (3) of this section, the term *MPGE* includes manufacturing, producing, growing, extracting, installing, developing, improving, and creating agricultural or horticultural products; making agricultural or horticultural products out of material by processing, manipulating, refining, or changing the form of an article, or by combining or assembling two or more articles; cultivating soil, raising livestock, and farming aquatic products. The term MPGE also includes storage, handling, or other processing activities (other than transportation activities)within the United States related to the sale, exchange, or other disposition of agricultural or horticultural products only if the products are consumed in connection with or incorporated into the MPGE of agricultural or horticultural products, whether or not by the Specified Cooperative. The Specified Cooperative (or the patron if section 1.199A-9(a)(2) applies) must have the benefits and burdens of ownership of the agricultural or horticultural products under Federal income tax principles during the period the MPGE activity occurs in order for the gross receipts derived from the MPGE of the agricultural or horticultural products to qualify as DPGR.

(2) *Packaging, repackaging, or labeling.*—If the Specified Cooperative packages, repackages, or labels agricultural or horticultural products and engages in no other MPGE activity with respect to those agricultural or horticultural products, the packaging, repackaging, or labeling does not qualify as MPGE with respect to those agricultural or horticultural products.

(3) *Installing.*—If a Specified Cooperative installs agricultural or horticultural products and engages in no other MPGE activity with respect to the agricultural or horticultural products, the Specified Cooperative's installing activity does not qualify as an MPGE activity. Notwithstanding paragraph (j)(3)(i)(A) of this section, if the Specified Cooperative installs agricultural or horticultural products MPGE by the Specified Cooperative and the Specified Cooperative has the benefits and burdens of ownership of the agricultural or horticultural products under Federal income tax principles during the period the installing activity occurs, then the portion of the installing activity that relates to the agricultural or horticultural products is an MPGE activity.

(4) *Consistency with section 263A.*—A Specified Cooperative that has MPGE agricultural or horticultural products for the taxable year must treat itself as a producer under section 263A with respect to the agricultural or horticultural products unless the Specified Cooperative is not subject to section 263A. A Specified Cooperative that currently is not properly accounting for its production activities under section 263A, and wishes to change its method of accounting to comply with the producer requirements of section 263A, must follow the applicable administrative procedures issued under §1.446-1(e)(3)(ii) for obtaining the Commissioner's consent to a change in accounting method (for further guidance, for example, *see* Rev. Proc. 2015-13, 2015-5 IRB 419, or any applicable subsequent guidance (*see* §601.601(d)(2) of this chapter)).

(g) *By the taxpayer.*—With respect to the exception of the rules applicable to an EAG and EAG partnerships under §1.199A-12, only one Specified Cooperative may claim the section 199A(g) deduction with respect to any qualifying activity under paragraph (f) of this section performed in connection with the same agricultural or horticultural product. If an unrelated party performs a qualifying activity under paragraph (f) of this section pursuant to a contract with a Specified Cooperative (or its patron as relevant under paragraph (a)(2) of this section), then only if the Specified Cooperative (or its patron) has the benefits and burdens of ownership of the agricultural or horticultural product under Federal income tax principles during the period in which the qualifying activity occurs is the Specified Cooperative (or its patron) treated as engaging in the qualifying activity.

(h) *In whole or significant part defined.*—(1) *In general.*—Agricultural or horticultural products must be MPGE in whole or significant part by the Specified Cooperative (or its patrons in the case described in paragraph (a)(2) of this section) and in whole or significant part within the United States to qualify under section 199A(g)(3)(D)(i). If a Specified Cooperative enters into a contract with an unrelated person for the unrelated person to MPGE agricultural or horticultural products for the Specified Cooperative and the Specified Cooperative has the benefits and burdens of ownership of the agricultural or horticultural products under applicable Federal income tax principles during the period the MPGE activity occurs, then, pursuant to paragraph (g) of this section, the Specified Cooperative is considered to MPGE the agricultural or horticultural products under this section. The unrelated person must perform the MPGE activity on behalf of the Specified Cooperative in whole or significant part within the United States in order for the Specified Cooperative to satisfy the requirements of this paragraph (h)(1).

(2) *Substantial in nature.*—Agricultural or horticultural products will be treated as MPGE in whole or in significant part by the Specified Cooperative (or its patrons in the case described in paragraph (a)(2) of this section) within the United States for purposes of paragraph (h)(1) of this section if the MPGE of the agricultural or horticultural products by the Specified Cooperative within the United States is substantial in nature taking into account all the facts and circumstances, including the relative value added by, and relative cost of, the Specified Cooperative's MPGE within the United

States, the nature of the agricultural or horticultural products, and the nature of the MPGE activity that the Specified Cooperative performs within the United States. The MPGE of a key component of an agricultural or horticultural product does not, in itself, meet the substantial-in-nature requirement with respect to an agricultural or horticultural product under this paragraph (h)(2). In the case of an agricultural or horticultural product, research and experimental activities under section 174 and the creation of intangible assets are not taken into account in determining whether the MPGE of the agricultural or horticultural product is substantial in nature.

(3) *Safe harbor.*—(i) *In general.*—A Specified Cooperative (or its patrons in the case described in paragraph (a)(2) of this section) will be treated as having MPGE an agricultural or horticultural product in whole or in significant part within the United States for purposes of paragraph (h)(1) of this section if the direct labor and overhead of such Specified Cooperative to MPGE the agricultural or horticultural product within the United States account for 20 percent or more of the Specified Cooperative's COGS of the agricultural or horticultural product, or in a transaction without COGS (for example, a lease, rental, or license), account for 20 percent or more of the Specified Cooperative's unadjusted depreciable basis (as defined in paragraph (h)(3)(ii) of this section) in property included in the definition of agricultural or horticultural products. For Specified Cooperatives subject to section 263A, overhead is all costs required to be capitalized under section 263A except direct materials and direct labor. For Specified Cooperatives not subject to section 263A, overhead may be computed using a reasonable method based on all the facts and circumstances, but may not include any cost, or amount of any cost, that would not be required to be capitalized under section 263A if the Specified Cooperative were subject to section 263A. Research and experimental expenditures under section 174 and the costs of creating intangible assets are not taken into account in determining direct labor or overhead for any agricultural or horticultural product. In the case of agricultural or horticultural products, research and experimental expenditures under section 174 and any other costs incurred in the creation of intangible assets may be excluded from COGS or unadjusted depreciable basis for purposes of determining whether the Specified Cooperative meets the safe harbor under this paragraph (h)(3). For Specified Cooperatives not subject to section 263A, the chosen reasonable method to compute overhead must be consistently applied from one taxable year to another and must clearly reflect the Specified Cooperative's portion of overhead not subject to section 263A. The method must also be reasonable based on all the facts and circumstances. The books and records maintained for overhead must be consistent with any allocations under this paragraph (h)(3)(i).

(ii) *Unadjusted depreciable basis.*—The term unadjusted depreciable basis means the basis of property for purposes of section 1011 without regard to any adjustments described in section 1016(a)(2) and (3). This basis does not reflect the reduction in basis for—

(A) Any portion of the basis the Specified Cooperative properly elects to treat as an expense under sections 179 or 179C; or

(B) Any adjustments to basis provided by other provisions of the Code and the regulations under the Code (for example, a reduction in basis by the amount of the disabled access credit pursuant to section 44(d)(7)).

(4) *Special rules.*—(i) *Contract with an unrelated person.*—If a Specified Cooperative enters into a contract with an unrelated person for the unrelated person to MPGE an agricultural or horticultural product within the United States for the Specified Cooperative, and the Specified Cooperative is considered to MPGE the agricultural or horticultural product pursuant to paragraph (f)(1) of this section, then, for purposes of the substantial-in-nature requirement under paragraph (h)(2) of this section and the safe harbor under paragraph (h)(3)(i) of this section, the Specified Cooperative's MPGE activities or direct labor and overhead must include both the Specified Cooperative's MPGE activities or direct labor and overhead to MPGE the agricultural or horticultural product within the United States as well as the MPGE activities or direct labor and overhead of the unrelated person to MPGE the agricultural or horticultural product within the United States under the contract.

(ii) *Aggregation.*—In determining whether the substantial-in-nature requirement under paragraph (h)(2) of this section or the safe harbor under paragraph (h)(3)(i) of this section is met at the time the Specified Cooperative disposes of an agricultural or horticultural product—

(A) An EAG member must take into account all of the previous MPGE activities or direct labor and overhead of the other members of the EAG;

(B) An EAG partnership as defined in §1.199A-12(i)(1) must take into account all of the previous MPGE activities or direct labor and overhead of all members of the EAG in which the partners of the EAG partnership are members (as well as the previous MPGE activities of any other EAG partnerships owned by members of the same EAG); and

(C) A member of an EAG in which the partners of an EAG partnership are members must take into account all of the previous MPGE activities or direct labor and overhead of the EAG partnership (as well as those of any other members of the EAG and any previous MPGE activities of any other EAG partnerships owned by members of the same EAG).

(i) *United States defined.*—For purposes of section 199A(g), the term *United States* includes the 50 states, the District of Columbia, the territorial waters of the United States, and the seabed and subsoil of those submarine areas that are adjacent to the territorial waters of the United States and over which the United States has exclusive rights, in accordance with international law, with respect to the exploration and exploitation of natural resources. Consistent with its definition in section 7701(a)(9), the term *United States* does not include possessions and territories of the United States or the airspace or space over the United States and these areas.

(j) *Derived from the lease, rental, license, sale, exchange, or other disposition.*—(1) *In general.*—(i) *Definition.*—The term *derived from the lease, rental, license, sale, exchange, or other disposition* is defined as, and limited to, the gross receipts directly derived from the lease, rental, license, sale, exchange, or other disposition of agricultural or horticultural products even if the Specified Cooperative has already recognized receipts from a previous lease, rental, license, sale, exchange, or other disposition of the same agricultural or horticultural products. Applicable Federal income tax principles apply to determine whether a transaction is, in substance, a lease, rental, license, sale, exchange, or other disposition, whether it is a service, or whether it is some combination thereof.

(ii) *Lease income.*—The financing and interest components of a lease of agricultural or horticultural products are considered to be derived from the lease of such agricultural or horticultural products. However, any portion of the lease income that is attributable to services or non-qualified property as defined in paragraph (j)(3) of this section is not derived from the lease of agricultural or horticultural products.

(iii) *Income substitutes.*—The proceeds from business interruption insurance, governmental subsidies, and governmental payments not to produce are treated as gross receipts derived from the lease, rental, license, sale, exchange, or other disposition to the extent they are substitutes for gross receipts that would qualify as DPGR.

(iv) *Exchange of property.*—(A) *Taxable exchanges.*—The value of property received by the Specified Cooperative in a taxable exchange of agricultural or horticultural products MPGE in whole or in significant part by the Specified Cooperative within the United States is DPGR for the Specified Cooperative (assuming all the other requirements of this section are met). However, unless the Specified Cooperative meets all of the requirements under this section with respect to any additional MPGE by the Specified Cooperative of the agricultural or horticultural products received in the taxable exchange, any gross receipts derived from the sale by the Specified Cooperative of the property received in the taxable exchange are non-DPGR, because the Specified Cooperative did not MPGE such property, even if the property was an agricultural or horticultural product in the hands of the other party to the transaction.

(B) *Safe harbor.*—For purposes of paragraph (j)(1)(iv)(A) of this section, the gross receipts derived by the Specified Cooperative from the sale of eligible property (as defined in paragraph (j)(1)(iv)(C) of this section) received in a taxable exchange, net of any adjustments between the parties involved in the taxable exchange to account for differences in the eligible property exchanged (for example, location differentials and product differentials), may be treated as the value of the eligible property received by the Specified Cooperative in the taxable exchange. For purposes of the preceding sentence, the taxable exchange is deemed to occur on the date of the sale of the eligible property received in the taxable exchange by the Specified Cooperative, to the extent the sale occurs no later than the last day of the month following the month in which the exchanged eligible property is received by the Specified Cooperative. In addition, if the Specified Cooperative engages in any further MPGE activity with respect to the eligible property received in the taxable exchange, then, unless the Specified Cooperative meets the in-whole-or-in-significant-part requirement under paragraph (h)(1) of this section with respect to the property sold, for purposes of this paragraph (j)(1)(iv)(B), the Specified Cooperative must also value the property sold without taking into account the gross receipts attributable to the further MPGE activity.

(C) *Eligible property.*—For purposes of paragraph (j)(1)(iv)(B) of this section, eligible property is—

(1) Oil, natural gas, or petrochemicals, or products derived from oil, natural gas, or petrochemicals; or

(2) Any other property or product designated by publication in the Internal Revenue Bulletin (*see* § 601.601(d)(2)(ii)(b) of this chapter).

(3) For this purpose, the term *natural gas* includes only natural gas extracted from a natural deposit and does not include, for example, methane gas extracted from a landfill. In the case of natural gas, production activities include all activities involved in extracting natural gas from the ground and processing the gas into pipeline quality gas.

(2) *Hedging transactions.*—(i) *In general.*—For purposes of this section, if a transaction is a hedging transaction within the meaning of section 1221(b)(2)(A) and § 1.1221-2(b), is properly identified as a hedging transaction in accordance with § 1.1221-2(f), and the risk being hedged relates to property described in section 1221(a)(1) that gives rise to DPGR or to property described in section 1221(a)(8) that is consumed in an activity that gives rise to DPGR, then—

(A) In the case of a hedge of purchases of property described in section 1221(a)(1), income, deduction, gain, or loss on the hedging transaction must be taken into account in determining COGS;

(B) In the case of a hedge of sales of property described in section 1221(a)(1), income, deduction, gain, or loss on the hedging transaction must be taken into account in determining DPGR; and

(C) In the case of a hedge of purchases of property described in section 1221(a)(8), income, deduction, gain, or loss on the hedging transaction must be taken into account in determining DPGR.

(ii) *Allocation.*—The income, deduction, gain and loss from hedging transactions described in paragraph (j)(2) of this section must be allocated between the patronage and nonpatronage (defined in § 1.1388-1(f)) sourced income and related deductions of the Specified Cooperatives consistent with the cooperative's method for determining patronage and nonpatronage income and deductions.

(iii) *Effect of identification and nonidentification.*—The principles of § 1.1221-2(g) apply to a Specified Cooperative that identifies or fails to identify a transaction as a hedging transaction, except that the consequence of identifying as a hedging transaction a transaction that is not in fact a hedging transaction described in paragraph (j)(2) of this section, or of failing to identify a transaction that the Specified Cooperative has no reasonable grounds for treating as other than a hedging transaction described in paragraph (j)(2) of this section, is that deduction or loss (but not income or gain) from the transaction is taken into account under paragraph (j)(2) of this section.

(iv) *Other rules.*—See § 1.1221-2(e) for rules applicable to hedging by members of a consolidated group and § 1.446-4 for rules regarding the timing of income, deductions, gains or losses with respect to hedging transactions.

(3) *Allocation of gross receipts to embedded services and non-qualified property.*—(i) *Embedded services and non-qualified property.*—(A) *In general.*—Except as otherwise provided in paragraph (j)(3)(i)(B) of this section, gross receipts derived from the performance of services do not qualify as DPGR. In the case of an embedded service, that is, a service the price of which, in the normal course of the business, is not separately stated from the amount charged for the lease, rental, license, sale, exchange, or other disposition of agricultural or horticultural products, DPGR includes only the gross receipts derived from the lease, rental, license, sale, exchange, or other disposition of agricultural or horticultural products (assuming all the other requirements of this section are met) and not any receipts attributable to the embedded service. In addition, DPGR does not include gross receipts derived from the lease, rental, license, sale, exchange, or other disposition of property that does not meet all of the requirements under this section (non-qualified property). The allocation of the gross receipts attributable to the embedded services or non-qualified property will be deemed to be reasonable if the allocation reflects the fair market value of the embedded services or non-qualified property.

(B) *Exceptions.*—There are five exceptions to the rules under paragraph (j)(3)(i)(A) of this section regarding embedded services and non-qualified property. A Specified Cooperative may include in DPGR, if all the other requirements of this section are met with respect to the underlying item of agricultural or horticultural products to which the embedded services or non-qualified property relate, the gross receipts derived from—

(1) A qualified warranty, that is, a warranty that is provided in connection with the lease, rental, license, sale, exchange, or other disposition of agricultural or horticultural products if, in the normal course of the Specified Cooperative's business—

(i) The price for the warranty is not separately stated from the amount charged for the lease, rental, license, sale, exchange, or other disposition of the agricultural or horticultural products; and

(ii) The warranty is neither separately offered by the Specified Cooperative nor separately bargained for with customers (that is, a customer cannot purchase the agricultural or horticultural products without the warranty);

(2) A qualified delivery, that is, a delivery or distribution service that is provided in connection with the lease, rental, license, sale, exchange, or other disposition of agricultural or horticultural products if, in the normal course of the Specified Cooperative's business—

(i) The price for the delivery or distribution service is not separately stated from the amount charged for the lease, rental, license, sale, exchange, or other disposition of the agricultural or horticultural products; and

(ii) The delivery or distribution service is neither separately offered by the Specified Cooperative nor separately bargained for with customers (that is, a customer cannot purchase the agricultural or horticultural products without the delivery or distribution service).

(3) A qualified operating manual, that is, a manual of instructions that is provided in connection with the lease, rental, license, sale, exchange, or other disposition of the agricultural or horticultural products if, in the normal course of the Specified Cooperative's business—

(i) The price for the manual is not separately stated from the amount charged for the lease, rental, license, sale, exchange, or other disposition of the agricultural or horticultural products;

(ii) The manual is neither separately offered by the Specified Cooperative nor separately bargained for with customers (that is, a customer cannot purchase the agricultural or horticultural products without the manual); and

(iii) The manual is not provided in connection with a training course for customers.

(4) A qualified installation, that is, an installation service for agricultural or horticultural products that is provided in connection with the lease, rental, license, sale, exchange, or other disposition of the agricultural or horticultural products if, in the normal course of the Specified Cooperative's business—

(i) The price for the installation service is not separately stated from the amount charged for the lease, rental, license, sale, exchange, or other disposition of the agricultural or horticultural products; and

(ii) The installation is neither separately offered by the Specified Cooperative nor separately bargained for with customers (that is, a customer cannot purchase the agricultural or horticultural products without the installation service).

(5) A de minimis amount of gross receipts from embedded services and non-qualified property for each item of agricultural or horticultural products may qualify. For purposes of this exception, a de minimis amount of gross receipts from embedded services and non-qualified property is less than 5 percent of the total gross receipts derived from the lease, rental, license, sale, exchange, or other disposition of each item of agricultural or horticultural products. In the case of gross receipts derived from the lease, rental, license, sale, exchange, or other disposition of agricultural or horticultural products that are received over a period of time (for example, a multi-year lease or installment sale), this de minimis exception is applied by taking into account the total gross receipts for the entire period derived (and to be derived) from the lease, rental, license, sale, exchange, or other disposition of the item of agricultural or horticultural products. For purposes of the preceding sentence, if a Specified Cooperative treats gross receipts as DPGR under this de minimis exception, then the Specified Cooperative must treat the gross receipts recognized in each taxable year consistently as DPGR. The gross receipts that the Specified Cooperative treats as DPGR under paragraphs (j)(3)(i)(B)(1) through (4) of this section are treated as DPGR for purposes of applying this de minimis exception. This de minimis exception does not apply if the price of a service or non-qualified property is separately stated by the Specified Cooperative, or if the service or non-qualified property is separately offered or separately bargained for with the customer (that is, the customer can purchase the agricultural or horticultural products without the service or non-qualified property).

(ii) *Non-DPGR.*—Applicable gross receipts as provided in §§1.199A-8(b) and/or (c) derived from the lease, rental, license, sale, exchange or other disposition of an item of agricultural or horticultural products may be treated as non-DPGR if less than 5 percent of the Specified Cooperative's total gross receipts derived from the lease, rental, license, sale, exchange or other disposition of that item are DPGR (taking into account embedded services and non-qualified property included in such disposition, but not part of the item). In the case of gross receipts derived from the lease, rental, license, sale, exchange, or other disposition of agricultural or horticultural products that are received over a period of time (for example, a multi-year lease or installment sale), this paragraph (j)(5)(ii) is applied by taking into account the total gross receipts for the entire period derived (and

to be derived) from the lease, rental, license, sale, exchange, or other disposition of the item of agricultural or horticultural products. For purposes of the preceding sentence, if the Specified Cooperative treats gross receipts as non-DPGR under this de minimis exception, then the Specified Cooperative must treat the gross receipts recognized in each taxable year consistently as non-DPGR.

(k) *Applicability date.*—The provisions of this section apply to taxable years ending after the date the Treasury decision adopting these regulations as final regulations is published in the *Federal Register.* Taxpayers, however, may rely on these regulations until that date, but only if the taxpayers apply the rules in their entirety and in a consistent manner. [Reg. §1.199A-9.]

§1.199A-10. Allocation of costs of goods sold (COGS) and other deductions to domestic production gross receipts (DPGR), and other rules.—(a) *In general.*—The provisions of this section apply solely for purposes of section 199A(g) of the Internal Revenue Code (Code). The provisions of this section provide additional guidance on determining qualified production activities income (QPAI) as described and defined in §1.199A-8(b)(4)(ii).

(b) *COGS allocable to DPGR.*—(1) *In general.*—When determining its QPAI, the Specified Cooperative (defined in §1.199A-8(a)(2)) must subtract from its DPGR (defined in §1.199A-8(b)(3)(ii)) the COGS allocable to its DPGR. The Specified Cooperative determines its COGS allocable to DPGR in accordance with this paragraph (b)(1) or, if applicable, paragraph (f) of this section. In the case of a sale, exchange, or other disposition of inventory, COGS is equal to beginning inventory of the Specified Cooperative plus purchases and production costs incurred during the taxable year and included in inventory costs by the Specified Cooperative, less ending inventory of the Specified Cooperative. In determining its QPAI, the Specified Cooperative does not include in COGS any payment made, whether during the taxable year, or included in beginning inventory, for which a deduction is allowed under section 1382(b) and/or (c), as applicable. *See* §1.199A-8(b)(4)(C). COGS is determined under the methods of accounting that the Specified Cooperative uses to compute taxable income. *See* sections 263A, 471, and 472. If section 263A requires the Specified Cooperative to include additional section 263A costs (as defined in §1.263A-1(d)(3)) in inventory, additional section 263A costs must be included in determining COGS. COGS also includes the Specified Cooperative's inventory valuation adjustments such as write-downs under the lower of cost or market method. In the case of a sale, exchange, or other disposition (including, for example, theft, casualty, or abandonment) by the Specified Cooperative of non-inventory property, COGS for purposes of this section includes the adjusted basis of the property.

(2) *Allocating COGS.*—(i) *In general.*—A Specified Cooperative must use a reasonable method based on all the facts and circumstances to allocate COGS between DPGR and non-DPGR. Whether an allocation method is reasonable is based on all the facts and circumstances, including whether the Specified Cooperative uses the most accurate information available; the relationship between COGS and the method used; the accuracy of the method chosen as compared with other possible methods; whether the method is used by the Specified Cooperative for internal management or other business purposes; whether the method is used for other Federal or state income tax purposes; the availability of costing information; the time, burden, and cost of using alternative methods; and whether the Specified Cooperative applies the method consistently from year to year. Depending on the facts and circumstances, reasonable methods may include methods based on gross receipts (defined in §1.199A-8(b)(2)(iii)), number of units sold, number of units produced, or total production costs. Ordinarily, if a Specified Cooperative uses a method to allocate gross receipts between DPGR and non-DPGR, then the use of a different method to allocate COGS that is not demonstrably more accurate than the method used to allocate gross receipts will not be considered reasonable. However, if a Specified Cooperative has information readily available to specifically identify COGS allocable to DPGR and can specifically identify that amount without undue burden or expense, COGS allocable to DPGR is that amount irrespective of whether the Specified Cooperative uses another allocation method to allocate gross receipts between DPGR and non-DPGR. A Specified Cooperative that does not have information readily available to specifically identify COGS allocable to DPGR and that cannot, without undue burden or expense, specifically identify that amount is not required to use a method that specifically identifies COGS allocable to DPGR. The chosen reasonable method must be consistently applied from one taxable year to another and must clearly reflect the portion of COGS between DPGR and non-DPGR. The method must also be reasonable based on all the facts and circumstances. The books and records maintained for COGS must be consistent with any allocations under this paragraph (b)(2).

(ii) *Gross receipts recognized in an earlier taxable year.*—If the Specified Cooperative (other than a Specified Cooperative that uses the small business simplified overall method of paragraph (f) of this section) recognizes and reports gross receipts on a Federal income tax return for a taxable year, and incurs COGS related to such gross receipts in a subsequent taxable year, then regardless of whether the gross receipts ultimately qualify as DPGR, the Specified Cooperative must allocate the COGS to—

(A) DPGR if the Specified Cooperative identified the related gross receipts as DPGR in the prior taxable year; or

(B) Non-DPGR if the Specified Cooperative identified the related gross receipts as non-DPGR in the prior taxable year or if the Specified Cooperative recognized under the Specified Cooperative's methods of accounting those gross receipts in a taxable year to which section 199A(g) does not apply.

(iii) *COGS associated with activities undertaken in an earlier taxable year.*—(A) *In general.*—A Specified Cooperative must allocate its COGS between DPGR and non-DPGR under the rules provided in paragraphs (b)(2)(i) and (iii) of this section, regardless of whether certain costs included in its COGS can be associated with activities undertaken in an earlier taxable year (including a year prior to the effective date of section 199A(g)). A Specified Cooperative may not segregate its COGS into component costs and allocate those component costs between DPGR and non-DPGR.

(B) *Example.*—The following example illustrates an application of paragraph (b)(2)(iii)(A) of this section.

(1) *Example.* During the 2018 taxable year, nonexempt Specified Cooperative X grew and sold Horticultural Product A. All of the patronage gross receipts from sales recognized by X in 2018 were from the sale of Horticultural Product A and qualified as DPGR. Employee 1 of X was involved in X's production process until he retired in 2013. In 2018, X paid $30 directly from its general assets for Employee 1's medical expenses pursuant to an unfunded, self-insured plan for retired X employees. For purposes of computing X's 2018 taxable income, X capitalized those medical costs to inventory under section 263A. In 2018, the COGS for a unit of Horticultural Product A was $100 (including the applicable portion of the $30 paid for Employee 1's medical costs that was allocated to COGS under X's allocation method for additional section 263A costs). X has information readily available to specifically identify COGS allocable to DPGR and can identify that amount without undue burden and expense because all of X's gross receipts from sales in 2018 are attributable to the sale of Horticultural Product A and qualify as DPGR. The inventory cost of each unit of Horticultural Product A sold in 2018, including the applicable portion of retiree medical costs, is related to X's gross receipts from the sale of Horticultural Product A in 2018. X may not segregate the 2018 COGS by separately allocating the retiree medical costs, which are components of COGS, to DPGR and non-DPGR. Thus, even though the retiree medical costs can be associated with activities undertaken in prior years, $100 of inventory cost of each unit of Horticultural Product A sold in 2018, including the applicable portion of the retiree medical expense cost component, is allocable to DPGR in 2018.

(3) *Special allocation rules.*—Section 199A(g)(3)(C) provides the following two special rules—

(i) For purposes of determining the COGS that are allocable to DPGR, any item or service brought into the United States (defined in §1.199A-9(i)) is treated as acquired by purchase, and its cost is treated as not less than its value immediately after it entered the United States. A similar rule applies in determining the adjusted basis of leased or rented property where the lease or rental gives rise to DPGR.

(ii) In the case of any property described in paragraph (b)(3)(i) of this section that has been exported by the Specified Cooperative for further manufacture, the increase in cost or adjusted basis under paragraph (b)(3)(i) of this section cannot exceed the difference between the value of the property when exported and the value of the property when brought back into the United States after the further manufacture. For the purposes of this paragraph (b)(3), the value of property is its customs value as defined in section 1059A(b)(1).

(4) *Rules for inventories valued at market or bona fide selling prices.*—If part of COGS is attributable to the Specified Cooperative's inventory valuation adjustments, then COGS allocable to DPGR includes inventory adjustments to agricultural or horticultural products that are MPGE in whole or significant part within the United States. Accordingly, a Specified Cooperative that values its inventory under §1.471-4 (inventories at cost or market, whichever is lower) or §1.471-2(c) (subnormal goods at bona fide selling prices) must allocate a proper share of such adjustments (for example, write-downs) to DPGR based on a reasonable method based on all the facts and circumstances. Factors taken into account in determining whether the method is reasonable include whether the Specified Cooperative uses the most accurate information available; the relationship between the adjustment and the allocation base chosen; the accuracy of the

method chosen as compared with other possible methods; whether the method is used by the Specified Cooperative for internal management or other business purposes; whether the method is used for other Federal or state income tax purposes; the time, burden, and cost of using alternative methods; and whether the Specified Cooperative applies the method consistently from year to year. If the Specified Cooperative has information readily available to specifically identify the proper amount of inventory valuation adjustments allocable to DPGR, then the Specified Cooperative must allocate that amount to DPGR. The Specified Cooperative that does not have information readily available to specifically identify the proper amount of its inventory valuation adjustments allocable to DPGR and that cannot, without undue burden or expense, specifically identify the proper amount of its inventory valuation adjustments allocable to DPGR, is not required to use a method that specifically identifies inventory valuation adjustments to DPGR. The chosen reasonable method must be consistently applied from one taxable year to another and must clearly reflect inventory adjustments. The method must also be reasonable based on all the facts and circumstances. The books and records maintained for inventory adjustments must be consistent with any allocations under this paragraph (b)(4).

(5) *Rules applicable to inventories accounted for under the last-in, first-out inventory method.*—(i) *In general.*—This paragraph (b)(5) applies to inventories accounted for using the specific goods last-in, first-out (LIFO) method or the dollar-value LIFO method. Whenever a specific goods grouping or a dollar-value pool contains agricultural or horticultural products that produce DPGR and goods that do not, the Specified Cooperative must allocate COGS attributable to that grouping or pool between DPGR and non-DPGR using a reasonable method based on all the facts and circumstances. Whether a method of allocating COGS between DPGR and non-DPGR is reasonable must be determined in accordance with paragraph (b)(2) of this section. In addition, this paragraph (b)(5) provides methods that a Specified Cooperative may use to allocate COGS for a Specified Cooperative's inventories accounted for using the LIFO method. If the Specified Cooperative uses the LIFO/FIFO ratio method provided in paragraph (b)(5)(ii) of this section or the change in relative base-year cost method provided in paragraph (b)(5)(iii) of this section, then the Specified Cooperative must use that method for all of the Specified Cooperative's inventory accounted for under the LIFO method. The chosen reasonable method must be consistently applied from one taxable year to another and must clearly reflect the inventory method. The method must also be reasonable based on all the facts and circumstances. The books and records maintained for the inventory method must be consistent with any allocations under this paragraph (b)(5).

(ii) *LIFO/FIFO ratio method.*—The LIFO/FIFO ratio method is applied with respect to the LIFO inventory on a grouping-by-grouping or pool-by-pool basis. Under the LIFO/FIFO ratio method, a Specified Cooperative computes the COGS of a grouping or pool allocable to DPGR by multiplying the COGS of agricultural or horticultural products (defined in §1.199A-8(a)(4)) in the grouping or pool that produced DPGR computed using the FIFO method by the LIFO/FIFO ratio of the grouping or pool. The LIFO/FIFO ratio of a grouping or pool is equal to the total COGS of the grouping or pool computed using the LIFO method over the total COGS of the grouping or pool computed using the FIFO method.

(iii) *Change in relative base-year cost method.*—A Specified Cooperative using the dollar-value LIFO method may use the change in relative base-year cost method. The change in relative base-year cost method for a Specified Cooperative using the dollar-value LIFO method is applied to all LIFO inventory on a pool-by-pool basis. The change in relative base-year cost method determines the COGS allocable to DPGR by increasing or decreasing the total production costs (section 471 costs and additional section 263A costs) of agricultural or horticultural products that generate DPGR by a portion of any increment or liquidation of the dollar-value pool. The portion of an increment or liquidation allocable to DPGR is determined by multiplying the LIFO value of the increment or liquidation (expressed as a positive number) by the ratio of the change in total base-year cost (expressed as a positive number) of agricultural or horticultural products that will generate DPGR in ending inventory to the change in total base-year cost (expressed as a positive number) of all goods in ending inventory. The portion of an increment or liquidation allocable to DPGR may be zero but cannot exceed the amount of the increment or liquidation. Thus, a ratio in excess of 1.0 must be treated as 1.0.

(6) *Specified Cooperative using a simplified method for additional section 263A costs to ending inventory.*—A Specified Cooperative that uses a simplified method specifically described in the section 263A regulations to allocate additional section 263A costs to ending inventory must follow the rules in paragraph (b)(2) of this section to determine the amount of additional section 263A costs allocable to

DPGR. Allocable additional section 263A costs include additional section 263A costs included in the Specified Cooperative's beginning inventory as well as additional section 263A costs incurred during the taxable year by the Specified Cooperative. Ordinarily, if the Specified Cooperative uses a simplified method specifically described in the section 263A regulations to allocate its additional section 263A costs to its ending inventory, the additional section 263A costs must be allocated in the same proportion as section 471 costs are allocated.

(c) *Other deductions properly allocable to DPGR or gross income attributable to DPGR.*—(1) *In general.*—In determining its QPAI, the Specified Cooperative must subtract from its DPGR (in addition to the COGS), the deductions that are properly allocable and apportioned to DPGR. A Specified Cooperative generally must allocate and apportion these deductions using the rules of the section 861 method provided in paragraph (d) of this section. In lieu of the section 861 method, an eligible Specified Cooperative may apportion these deductions using the simplified deduction method provided in paragraph (e) of this section. Paragraph (f) of this section provides a small business simplified overall method that may be used by a qualifying small Specified Cooperative. A Specified Cooperative using the simplified deduction method or the small business simplified overall method must use that method for all deductions. A Specified Cooperative eligible to use the small business simplified overall method may choose at any time for any taxable year to use the small business simplified overall method or the simplified deduction method for a taxable year.

(2) *Treatment of net operating losses.*—A deduction under section 172 for a net operating loss (NOL) is not allocated or apportioned to DPGR or gross income attributable to DPGR.

(3) *W-2 wages.*—Although only W-2 wages as described in §1.199A-11 are taken into account in computing the W-2 wage limitation, all wages paid (or incurred in the case of an accrual method taxpayer) in the taxable year are taken into account in computing QPAI for that taxable year.

(d) *Section 861 method.*—Under the section 861 method, the Specified Cooperative must allocate and apportion its deductions using the allocation and apportionment rules provided under the section 861 regulations under which section 199A(g) is treated as an operative section described in §1.861-8(f). Accordingly, the Specified Cooperative applies the rules of the section 861 regulations to allocate and apportion deductions (including, if applicable, its distributive share of deductions from passthrough entities) to gross income attributable to DPGR. If the Specified Cooperative applies the allocation and apportionment rules of the section 861 regulations for section 199A(g) and another operative section, then the Specified Cooperative must use the same method of allocation and the same principles of apportionment for purposes of all operative sections. Research and experimental expenditures must be allocated and apportioned in accordance with §1.861-17 without taking into account the exclusive apportionment rule of §1.861-17(b). Deductions for charitable contributions (as allowed under section 170 and section 873(b)(2) or 882(c)(1)(B)) must be ratably apportioned between gross income attributable to DPGR and gross income attributable to non-DPGR based on the relative amounts of gross income.

(e) *Simplified deduction method.*—(1) *In general.*—An eligible Specified Cooperative (defined in paragraph (e)(2) of this section) may use the simplified deduction method to apportion business deductions between DPGR and non-DPGR. The simplified deduction method does not apply to COGS. Under the simplified deduction method, the business deductions (except the NOL deduction) are ratably apportioned between DPGR and non-DPGR based on relative gross receipts. Accordingly, the amount of deductions for the current taxable year apportioned to DPGR is equal to the proportion of the total business deductions for the current taxable year that the amount of DPGR bears to total gross receipts.

(2) *Eligible Specified Cooperative.*—For purposes of this paragraph (e), an eligible Specified Cooperative is—

(i) A Specified Cooperative that has average annual total gross receipts (as defined in paragraph (g) of this section) of $100,000,000 or less; or

(ii) A Specified Cooperative that has total assets (as defined in paragraph (e)(3) of this section) of $10,000,000 or less.

(3) *Total assets.*—(i) *In general.*—For purposes of the simplified deduction method, total assets mean the total assets the Specified Cooperative has at the end of the taxable year.

(ii) *Members of an expanded affiliated group.*—To compute the total assets of an *expanded affiliated group* (EAG) at the end of the taxable year, the total assets at the end of the taxable year of each member of the EAG at the end of the taxable year that ends with or within the taxable year of the computing member (as described in §1.199A-12(g)) are aggregated.

(4) *Members of an expanded affiliated group.*—(i) *In general.*—Whether the members of an EAG may use the simplified deduction method is determined by reference to all the members of the EAG. If the average annual gross receipts of the EAG are less than or equal to $100,000,000 or the total assets of the EAG are less than or equal to $10,000,000, then each member of the EAG may individually determine whether to use the simplified deduction method, regardless of the cost allocation method used by the other members.

(ii) *Exception.*—Notwithstanding paragraph (e)(4)(i) of this section, all members of the same consolidated group must use the same cost allocation method.

(f) *Small business simplified overall method.*—(1) *In general.*—A qualifying small Specified Cooperative may use the small business simplified overall method to apportion COGS and deductions between DPGR and non-DPGR. Under the small business simplified overall method, a Specified Cooperative's total costs for the current taxable year (as defined in paragraph (f)(3) of this section) are apportioned between DPGR and non-DPGR based on relative gross receipts. Accordingly, the amount of total costs for the current taxable year apportioned to DPGR is equal to the proportion of total costs for the current taxable year that the amount of DPGR bears to total gross receipts.

(2) *Qualifying small Specified Cooperative.*—For purposes of this paragraph (f), a qualifying small Specified Cooperative is a Specified Cooperative that has average annual total gross receipts (as defined in paragraph (g) of this section) of $25,000,000 or less.

(3) *Total costs for the current taxable year.*—For purposes of the small business simplified overall method, total costs for the current taxable year means the total COGS and deductions for the current taxable year. Total costs for the current taxable year are determined under the methods of accounting that the Specified Cooperative uses to compute taxable income.

(4) *Members of an expanded affiliated group.*—(i) *In general.*—Whether the members of an EAG may use the small business simplified overall method is determined by reference to all the members of the EAG. If the average annual gross receipts of the EAG are less than or equal to $25,000,000 then each member of the EAG may individually determine whether to use the small business simplified overall method, regardless of the cost allocation method used by the other members.

(ii) *Exception.*—Notwithstanding paragraph (f)(4)(i) of this section, all members of the same consolidated group must use the same cost allocation method.

(g) *Average annual gross receipts.*—(1) *In general.*—For purposes of the simplified deduction method and the small business simplified overall method, average annual gross receipts means the average annual gross receipts of the Specified Cooperative for the 3 taxable years (or, if fewer, the taxable years during which the taxpayer was in existence) preceding the current taxable year, even if one or more of such taxable years began before the effective date of section 199A(g). In the case of any taxable year of less than 12 months (a short taxable year), the gross receipts of the Specified Cooperative are annualized by multiplying the gross receipts for the short period by 12 and dividing the result by the number of months in the short period.

(2) *Members of an expanded affiliated group.*—(i) *In general.*—To compute the average annual gross receipts of an EAG, the gross receipts for the entire taxable year of each member that is a member of the EAG at the end of its taxable year that ends with or within the taxable year are aggregated. For purposes of this paragraph (g)(2), a consolidated group is treated as one member of an EAG.

(ii) *Exception.*—Notwithstanding paragraph (g)(1)(i) of this section, all members of the same consolidated group must use the same cost allocation method.

(h) *Cost allocation methods for determining oil-related QPAI.*—(1) *Section 861 method.*—A Specified Cooperative that uses the section 861 method to determine deductions that are allocated and apportioned to gross income attributable to DPGR must use the section 861 method to determine deductions that are allocated and apportioned to gross income attributable to oil-related DPGR.

(2) *Simplified deduction method.*—A Specified Cooperative that uses the simplified deduction method to apportion deductions between DPGR and non-DPGR must determine the portion of deductions allocable to oil-related DPGR by multiplying the deductions allocable to DPGR by the ratio of oil-related DPGR to DPGR from all activities.

(3) *Small business simplified overall method.*—A Specified Cooperative that uses the small business simplified overall method to apportion total costs (COGS and deductions) between DPGR and non-DPGR must determine the portion of total costs allocable to oil-related DPGR by multiplying the total costs allocable to DPGR by the ratio of oil-related DPGR to DPGR from all activities.

(i) *Applicability date.*—The provisions of this section apply to taxable years ending after the date the Treasury decision adopting these regulations as final regulations is published in the *Federal Register*. Taxpayers, however, may rely on these regulations until that date, but only if the taxpayers apply the rules in their entirety and in a consistent manner. [Reg. § 1.199A-10.]

§ 1.199A-11. Wage limitation for the section 199A(g) deduction.—(a) *Rules of application.*—(1) *In general.*—The provisions of this section apply solely for purposes of section 199A(g) of the Internal Revenue Code (Code). The provisions of this section provide guidance on determining the W-2 wage limitation as defined in § 1.199A-8(b)(5)(ii)(B). Except as provided in paragraph (d)(2) of this section, the Form W-2, Wage and Tax Statement, or any subsequent form or document used in determining the amount of W-2 wages, are those issued for the calendar year ending during the taxable year of the Specified Cooperative (defined in § 1.199A-8(a)(2)) for wages paid to employees (or former employees) of the Specified Cooperative for employment by the Specified Cooperative. Employees are limited to employees defined in section 3121(d)(1) and (2) (that is, officers of a corporate taxpayer and employees of the taxpayer under the common law rules). See paragraph (a)(5) of this section for the requirement that W-2 wages must have been included in a return filed with the Social Security Administration (SSA) within 60 days after the due date (including extensions) of the return. *See also* section 199A(a)(4)(C).

(2) *Wage limitation for section 199A(g) deduction.*—The amount of the deduction allowable under section 199A(g) to the Specified Cooperative for any taxable year cannot exceed 50 percent of the W-2 wages (as defined in section 199A(g)(1)(B)(ii) and paragraph (b) of this section) for the taxable year that are attributable to domestic production gross receipts (DPGR), defined in § 1.199A-8(b)(3)(ii), of agricultural or horticultural products defined in § 1.199A-8(a)(4).

(3) *Wages paid by entity other than common law employer.*—In determining W-2 wages, the Specified Cooperative may take into account any W-2 wages paid by another entity and reported by the other entity on Forms W-2 with the other entity as the employer listed in Box c of the Forms W-2, provided that the W-2 wages were paid to common law employees or officers of the Specified Cooperative for employment by the Specified Cooperative. In such cases, the entity paying the W-2 wages and reporting the W-2 wages on Forms W-2 is precluded from taking into account such wages for purposes of determining W-2 wages with respect to that entity. For purposes of this paragraph (a)(4), entities that pay and report W-2 wages on behalf of or with respect to other taxpayers can include, but are not limited to, certified professional employer organizations under section 7705, statutory employers under section 3401(d)(1), and agents under section 3504.

(4) *Requirement that wages must be reported on return filed with the Social Security Administration.*—(i) *In general.*—Pursuant to section 199A(g)(1)(B)(ii) and section 199A(b)(4)(C), the term W-2 wages does not include any amount that is not properly included in a return filed with SSA on or before the 60th day after the due date (including extensions) for such return. Under § 31.6051-2 of this chapter, each Form W-2 and the transmittal Form W-3, Transmittal of Wage and Tax Statements, together constitute an information return to be filed with SSA. Similarly, each Form W-2c, Corrected Wage and Tax Statement, and the transmittal Form W-3 or W-3c, Transmittal of Corrected Wage and Tax Statements, together constitute an information return to be filed with SSA. In determining whether any amount has been properly included in a return filed with SSA on or before the 60th day after the due date (including extensions) for such return, each Form W-2 together with its accompanying Form W-3 is considered a separate information return and each Form W-2c together with its accompanying Form W-3 or Form W-3c is considered a separate information return. Section 6071(c) provides that Forms W-2 and W-3 must be filed on or before January 31 of the year following the calendar year to which such returns relate (but see the special rule in § 31.6071(a)-1T(a)(3)(1) of this chapter for monthly returns filed under § 31.6011(a)-5(a) of this chapter). Corrected Forms W-2 are required to be filed with SSA on or before January 31 of the year following the year in which the correction is made.

(ii) *Corrected return filed to correct a return that was filed within 60 days of the due date.*—If a corrected information return (Return B) is filed with SSA on or before the 60th day after the due date (including extensions) of Return B to correct an information return (Return A) that was filed with SSA on or before the 60th day after the due date

(including extensions) of the information return (Return A) and paragraph (a)(5)(iii) of this section does not apply, then the wage information on Return B must be included in determining W-2 wages. If a corrected information return (Return D) is filed with SSA later than the 60th day after the due date (including extensions) of Return D to correct an information return (Return C) that was filed with SSA on or before the 60th day after the due date (including extensions) of the information return (Return C), then if Return D reports an increase (or increases) in wages included in determining W-2 wages from the wage amounts reported on Return C, such increase (or increases) on Return D is disregarded in determining W-2 wages (and only the wage amounts on Return C may be included in determining W-2 wages). If Return D reports a decrease (or decreases) in wages included in determining W-2 wages from the amounts reported on Return C, then, in determining W-2 wages, the wages reported on Return C must be reduced by the decrease (or decreases) reflected on Return D.

(iii) *Corrected return filed to correct a return that was filed later than 60 days after the due date.*—If an information return (Return F) is filed to correct an information return (Return E) that was not filed with SSA on or before the 60th day after the due date (including extensions) of Return E, then Return F (and any subsequent information returns filed with respect to Return E) will not be considered filed on or before the 60th day after the due date (including extensions) of Return F (or the subsequent corrected information return). Thus, if a Form W-2c is filed to correct a Form W-2 that was not filed with SSA on or before the 60th day after the due date (including extensions) of the Form W-2 (or to correct a Form W-2c relating to a Form W-2 that had not been filed with SSA on or before the 60th day after the due date (including extensions) of the Form W-2), then this Form W-2c is not to be considered to have been filed with SSA on or before the 60th day after the due date (including extensions) for this Form W-2c, regardless of when the Form W-2c is filed.

(b) *Definition of W-2 wages.*—(1) *In general.*—Section 199A(g)(1)(B)(ii) provides that the W-2 wages of the Specified Cooperative must be determined in the same manner as under section 199A(b)(4) (without regard to section 199A(b)(4)(B) and after application of section 199A(b)(5)). Section 199A(b)(4)(A) provides that the term W-2 wages means with respect to any person for any taxable year of such person, the amounts described in paragraphs (3) and (8) of section 6051(a) paid by such person with respect to employment of employees by such person during the calendar year ending during such taxable year. Thus, the term W-2 wages includes the total amount of wages as defined in section 3401(a); the total amount of elective deferrals (within the meaning of section 402(g)(3)); the compensation deferred under section 457; and the amount of designated Roth contributions (as defined in section 402A).

(2) *Section 199A(g) deduction.*—Pursuant to section 199A(g)(3)(A), W-2 wages do not include any amount which is not properly allocable to DPGR for purposes of calculating qualified production activities income (QPAI) as defined in § 1.199A-8(b)(4)(ii). The Specified Cooperative may determine the amount of wages that is properly allocable to DPGR using a reasonable method based on all the facts and circumstances. The chosen reasonable method must be consistently applied from one taxable year to another and must clearly reflect the wages allocable to DPGR for purposes of QPAI. The books and records maintained for wages allocable to DPGR for purposes of QPAI must be consistent with any allocations under this paragraph (b)(2).

(c) *Methods for calculating W-2 wages.*—The Secretary may provide for methods to be used in calculating W-2 wages, including W-2 wages for short taxable years by publication in the Internal Revenue Bulletin (*see* § 601.601(d)(2)(ii)(b) of this chapter).

(d) *Wage limitation — acquisitions, dispositions, and short taxable years.*—(1) *In general.*—For purposes of computing the deduction under section 199A(g) of the Specified Cooperative, in the case of an acquisition or disposition (as defined in section 199A(b)(5) and paragraph (d)(3) of this section) that causes more than one Specified Cooperative to be an employer of the employees of the acquired or disposed of Specified Cooperative during the calendar year, the W-2 wages of the Specified Cooperative for the calendar year of the acquisition or disposition are allocated between or among each Specified Cooperative based on the period during which the employees of the acquired or disposed of Specified Cooperatives were employed by the Specified Cooperative, regardless of which permissible method is used for reporting predecessor and successor wages on Form W-2, Wage and Tax Statement.

(2) *Short taxable year that does not include December 31.*—If the Specified Cooperative has a short taxable year that does not contain a calendar year ending during such short taxable year, wages paid to employees for employment by the Specified Cooperative during the short taxable year are treated as W-2 wages for such short taxable

year for purposes of paragraph (a) of this section (if the wages would otherwise meet the requirements to be W-2 wages under this section but for the requirement that a calendar year must end during the short taxable year).

(3) *Acquisition or disposition.*—For purposes of paragraph (d)(1) and (2) of this section, the terms *acquisition* and *disposition* include an incorporation, a liquidation, a reorganization, or a purchase or sale of assets.

(e) *Application in the case of a Specified Cooperative with a short taxable year.*—In the case of a Specified Cooperative with a short taxable year, subject to the rules of paragraph (a) of this section, the W-2 wages of the Specified Cooperative for the short taxable year can include only those wages paid during the short taxable year to employees of the Specified Cooperative, only those elective deferrals (within the meaning of section 402(g)(3)) made during the short taxable year by employees of the Specified Cooperative, and only compensation actually deferred under section 457 during the short taxable year with respect to employees of the Specified Cooperative.

(f) *Non-duplication rule.*—Amounts that are treated as W-2 wages for a taxable year under any method cannot be treated as W-2 wages of any other taxable year. Also, an amount cannot be treated as W-2 wages by more than one taxpayer. Finally, an amount cannot be treated as W-2 wages by the Specified Cooperative both in determining patronage and nonpatronage W-2 wages.

(g) *Wage expense safe harbor.*—(1) *In general.*—A Specified Cooperative using either the section 861 method of cost allocation under §1.199A-10(d) or the simplified deduction method under §1.199A-10(e) may determine the amount of W-2 wages that are properly allocable to DPGR for a taxable year by multiplying the amount of W-2 wages determined under paragraph (b)(1) of this section for the taxable year by the ratio of the Specified Cooperative's wage expense included in calculating QPAI for the taxable year to the Specified Cooperative's total wage expense used in calculating the Specified Cooperative's taxable income for the taxable year, without regard to any wage expense disallowed by section 465, 469, 704(d), or 1366(d). A Specified Cooperative that uses either the section 861 method of cost allocation or the simplified deduction method to determine QPAI must use the same expense allocation and apportionment methods that it uses to determine QPAI to allocate and apportion wage expense for purposes of this safe harbor. For purposes of this paragraph (g)(1), the term wage expense means wages (that is, compensation paid by the employer in the active conduct of a trade or business to its employees) that are properly taken into account under the Specified Cooperative's method of accounting.

(2) *Wage expense included in cost of goods sold.*—For purposes of paragraph (g)(1) of this section, a Specified Cooperative may determine its wage expense included in cost of goods sold (COGS) using a reasonable method based on all the facts and circumstances, such as using the amount of direct labor included in COGS or using section 263A labor costs (as defined in §1.263A-1(h)(4)(ii)) included in COGS. The chosen reasonable method must be consistently applied from one taxable year to another and must clearly reflect the portion of wage expense included in COGS. The method must also be reasonable based on all the facts and circumstances. The books and records maintained for wage expense included in COGS must be consistent with any allocations under this paragraph (g)(2).

(3) *Small business simplified overall method safe harbor.*—The Specified Cooperative that uses the small business simplified overall method under §1.199A-10(f) may use the small business simplified overall method safe harbor for determining the amount of W-2 wages determined under paragraph (b)(1) of this section that is properly allocable to DPGR. Under this safe harbor, the amount of W-2 wages determined under paragraph (b)(1) of this section that is properly allocable to DPGR is equal to the same proportion of W-2 wages determined under paragraph (b)(1) of this section that the amount of DPGR bears to the Specified Cooperative's total gross receipts.

(h) *Applicability date.*—The provisions of this section apply to taxable years ending after the date the Treasury decision adopting these regulations as final regulations is published in the *Federal Register*. Taxpayers, however, may rely on these regulations until that date, but only if the taxpayers apply the rules in their entirety and in a consistent manner. [Reg. §1.199A-11.]

§1.199A-12. Expanded affiliated groups.—(a) *In general.*—The provisions of this section apply solely for purposes of section 199A(g) of the Internal Revenue Code (Code). Except as otherwise provided in the Code or regulations issued under the relevant section of the Code (for example, sections 199A(g)(3)(D)(ii) and 267, §1.199A-8(c), paragraph (a)(3) of this section, and the consolidated return regulations under section 1502), each Specified Cooperative whether exempt or nonexempt (as defined in §1.199A-8(a)(2)(iii)) that is a member of

an expanded affiliated group (EAG) (defined in paragraph (a)(1) of this section) computes its own taxable income or loss, qualified production activities income (QPAI) (defined in §1.199A-8(b)(4)(ii)), and W-2 wages (defined in §1.199A-11(b)). If a Specified Cooperative is also a member of a consolidated group, see paragraph (d) of this section.

(1) *Definition of an expanded affiliated group.*—An EAG is an affiliated group as defined in section 1504(a), determined by substituting "more than 50 percent" for "at least 80 percent" in each place it appears and without regard to section 1504(b)(2) and (4).

(2) *Identification of members of an expanded affiliated group.*—(i) *In general.*—Each Specified Cooperative must determine if it is a member of an EAG on a daily basis.

(ii) *Becoming or ceasing to be a member of an expanded affiliated group.*—If a Specified Cooperative becomes or ceases to be a member of an EAG, the Specified Cooperative is treated as becoming or ceasing to be a member of the EAG at the end of the day on which its status as a member changes.

(3) *Attribution of activities.*—(i) *In general.*—Except as provided in paragraph (a)(3)(iv) of this section, if a Specified Cooperative that is a member of an EAG (disposing member) derives gross receipts (defined in §1.199A-8(b)(2)(iii)) from the lease, rental, license, sale, exchange, or other disposition (defined in §1.199A-9(j))of agricultural or horticultural products (defined in §1.199A-8(a)(4)) that were manufactured, produced, grown or extracted (MPGE) (as defined in §1.199A-9(f)), in whole or significant part (as defined in §1.199A-9(h)) in the United States (as defined in §1.199A-9(i)) by another Specified Cooperative, then the disposing member is treated as conducting the previous activities conducted by such other Specified Cooperative with respect to the agricultural or horticultural products in determining whether its gross receipts are domestic production gross receipts (DPGR) (defined in §1.199A-8(b)(3)(ii)) if—

(A) Such property was MPGE by such other Specified Cooperative, and

(B) The disposing member is a member of the same EAG as such other Specified Cooperative at the time that the disposing member disposes of the agricultural or horticultural products.

(ii) *Date of disposition for leases, rentals, or licenses.*—Except as provided in paragraph (a)(3)(iv) of this section, with respect to a lease, rental, or license, the disposing member described in paragraph (a)(3)(i) of this section is treated as having disposed of the agricultural or horticultural products on the date or dates on which it takes into account the gross receipts derived from the lease, rental, or license under its methods of accounting.

(iii) *Date of disposition for sales, exchanges, or other dispositions.*—Except as provided in paragraph (a)(3)(iv) of this section, with respect to a sale, exchange, or other disposition, the disposing member is treated as having disposed of the agricultural or horticultural products on the date on which it ceases to own the agricultural or horticultural products for Federal income tax purposes, even if no gain or loss is taken into account.

(iv) *Exception.*—Nonexempt Specified Cooperatives. A nonexempt Specified Cooperative is not attributed nonpatronage activities conducted by another Specified Cooperative. See §1.199A-8(b)(2)(ii).

(4) *Marketing Specified Cooperatives.*—A Specified Cooperative will be treated as having MPGE in whole or significant part any agricultural or horticultural product within the United States marketed by the Specified Cooperative which its patrons have so MPGE. Patrons are defined in §1.1388-1(e).

(5) *Anti-avoidance rule.*—If a transaction between members of an EAG is engaged in or structured with a principal purpose of qualifying for, or increasing the amount of, the section 199A(g) deduction of the EAG or the portion of the section 199A(g) deduction allocated to one or more members of the EAG, the Secretary may make adjustments to eliminate the effect of the transaction on the computation of the section 199A(g) deduction.

(b) *Computation of EAG's section 199A(g) deduction.*—(1) *In general.*—The section 199A(g) deduction for an EAG is determined by separately computing the section 199A(g) deduction from the patronage sources of Specified Cooperatives that are members of the EAG and the section 199A(g) deduction from the nonpatronage sources of exempt Specified Cooperatives that are members of the EAG. The section 199A(g) deduction from patronage sources of Specified Cooperatives is determined by aggregating the income or loss, QPAI, and W-2 wages, if any, of each patronage source of a Specified Cooperative that is a member of the EAG (whether an exempt or nonexempt Specified Cooperative). The section 199A(g) deduction from nonpatronage sources of exempt Specified Cooperatives is determined by aggregating the income or loss, QPAI, and W-2 wages, if any, of each nonpatronage source of exempt Specified Cooperatives that are members of the EAG. For purposes of this determination, a member's QPAI may be positive or negative. A Specified Cooperative's taxable income or loss and QPAI will be determined by reference to the Specified Cooperative's method of accounting. For purposes of determining the section 199A(g) deduction for an EAG, taxable income or loss, QPAI, and W-2 wages of a nonexempt Specified Cooperative from nonpatronage sources are considered to be zero. See § 1.199A-8(b)(2)(ii).

(2) *Example.*—The following examples illustrates the application of paragraph (b)(1) of this section.

(i) *Example.* Nonexempt Specified Cooperatives X, Y, and Z, calendar year taxpayers, are the only members of an EAG and are not members of a consolidated group. X's patronage source has taxable income of $50,000, QPAI of $15,000, and W-2 wages of $0. Y has patronage source taxable income of ($20,000), QPAI of ($1,000), and W-2 wages of $750. Z's patronage source has taxable income of $0, QPAI of $0, and W-2 wages of $3,000. In determining the EAG's section 199A(g) deduction, the EAG aggregates each member's patronage source's taxable income or loss, QPAI, and W-2 wages. Thus, the EAG's patronage source has taxable income of $30,000, the sum of X's patronage source taxable income of $50,000, Y's patronage source taxable income of ($20,000), and Z's patronage source taxable income of $0. The EAG has QPAI of $14,000, the sum of X's QPAI of $15,000, Y's QPAI of ($1,000), and Z's QPAI of $0. The EAG has W-2 wages of $3,750, the sum of X's W-2 wages of $0, Y's W-2 wages of $750, and Z's W-2 wages of $3,000. Accordingly, the EAG's section 199A(g) deduction equals $1,260, 9% of $14,000, the lesser of the QPAI and patronage source taxable income, but not greater than $1,875, 50% of its W-2 wages of $3,750. This result would be the same if X had a nonpatronage source income or loss, because nonpatronage source income of a nonexempt Specified Cooperative is not taken into account in determining the section 199A(g) deduction.

(3) *Net operating loss carryovers/carrybacks.*—In determining the taxable income of an EAG, if a Specified Cooperative has a net operating loss (NOL) from its patronage sources that may be carried over or carried back, if applicable, (in accordance with section 172), to the taxable year, then for purposes of determining the taxable income of the Specified Cooperative, the amount of the NOL used to offset taxable income cannot exceed the taxable income of the patronage source of that Specified Cooperative. Similarly, if a Specified Cooperative has an NOL from its nonpatronage sources that may be carried over to the taxable year, then for purposes of determining the taxable income of the Specified Cooperative, the amount of the NOL used to offset taxable income cannot exceed the taxable income of the nonpatronage sources of that Specified Cooperative.

(4) *Losses used to reduce taxable income of an expanded affiliated group.*—The amount of an NOL sustained by a Specified Cooperative member of an EAG that is used in the year sustained in determining an EAG's taxable income limitation under § 1.199A-8(b)(5)(ii)(C) (for nonexempt Specified Cooperatives) or § 1.199A-8(c)(4)(i) (for exempt Specified Cooperatives), as applicable, is not treated as an NOL carryover to any taxable year in determining the taxable income limitation under § 1.199A-8(b)(5)(ii)(C) or § 1.199A-8(c)(4)(i), as applicable. For purposes of this paragraph (b)(4), an NOL is considered to be used if it reduces an EAG's aggregate taxable income from patronage source or nonpatronage source, as the case may be, regardless of whether the use of the NOL actually reduces the amount of the section 199A(g) deduction that the EAG would otherwise derive. An NOL is not considered to be used to the extent that it reduces an EAG's aggregate taxable income from patronage source or nonpatronage source, as the case may be, to an amount less than zero. If more than one Specified Cooperative has an NOL used in the same taxable year to reduce the EAG's taxable income from patronage or nonpatronage sources, as the case may be, the respective NOLs are deemed used in proportion to the amount of each Specified Cooperative's NOL.

(5) *Example.*—The following example illustrates the application of paragraph (b)(4) of this section.

(i) *Example*—(A) *Facts.* Nonexempt Specified Cooperatives A and B are the only two members of an EAG. A and B are both calendar year taxpayers and they do not join in the filing of a consolidated Federal income tax return. Neither A nor B had taxable income or loss prior to 2018. In 2018, A has patronage QPAI and taxable income of $1,000 and B has patronage QPAI of $1,000 and a patronage NOL of $1,500. A also has nonpatronage income of $3,000. B has no activities other than from its patronage activities. In 2019, A has patronage QPAI of $2,000 and patronage taxable income of $1,000 and B has patronage QPAI of $2,000 and patronage taxable income prior to the NOL deduction allowed under section 172 of $2,000. Neither A nor B has nonpatronage activities in 2019. A's and B's patronage activities have aggregate W-2 wages in excess of the section 199A(g)(1)(B) wage limitation in both 2018 and 2019.

(B) *Section 199A(g) deduction for 2018.* In determining the EAG's section 199A(g) deduction for 2018, A's $1,000 of QPAI and B's $1,000 of QPAI are aggregated, as are A's $1,000 of taxable income from its patronage activities and B's $1,500 NOL from its patronage activities. A's nonpatronage income is not included. Thus, for 2018, the EAG has patronage QPAI of $2,000 and patronage taxable income of ($500). The EAG's section 199A(g) deduction for 2018 is 9% of the lesser of its patronage QPAI or its patronage taxable income. Because the EAG has a taxable loss from patronage sources in 2018, the EAG's section 199A(g) deduction is $0.

(C) *Section 199A(a) deduction for 2019.* In determining the EAG's section 199A deduction for 2019, A's patronage QPAI of $2,000 and B's patronage QPAI of $2,000 are aggregated, resulting in the EAG having patronage QPAI of $4,000. Also, $1,000 of B's patronage NOL from 2018 was used in 2018 to reduce the EAG's taxable income from patronage sources to $0. The remaining $500 of B's patronage NOL from 2018 is not considered to have been used in 2018 because it reduced the EAG's patronage taxable income to less than $0. Accordingly, for purposes of determining the EAG's taxable income limitation under § 1.199A-8(b)(5) in 2019, B is deemed to have only a $500 NOL carryover from its patronage sources from 2018 to offset a portion of its 2019 taxable income from its patronage sources. Thus, B's taxable income from its patronage sources in 2019 is $1,500, which is aggregated with A's $1,000 of taxable income from its patronage sources. The EAG's taxable income limitation in 2019 is $2,500. The EAG's section 199A(g) deduction is 9% of the lesser of its patronage sourced QPAI of $4,000 and its taxable income from patronage sources of $2,500. Thus, the EAG's section 199A(g) deduction in 2019 is 9% of $2,500, or $225. The results for 2019 would be the same if neither A nor B had patronage sourced QPAI in 2018.

(c) *Allocation of an expanded affiliated group's section 199A(g) deduction among members of the expanded affiliated group.*—(1) *In general.*— An EAG's section 199A(g) deduction from its patronage sources, as determined in paragraph (b) of this section, is allocated among the Specified Cooperatives that are members of the EAG in proportion to each Specified Cooperative's patronage QPAI, regardless of whether the Specified Cooperative has patronage taxable income or W-2 wages for the taxable year. An EAG's section 199A(g) deduction from its nonpatronage sources, as determined in paragraph (b) of this section, is allocated among the Specified Cooperatives that are members of the EAG in proportion to each Specified Cooperative's nonpatronage QPAI, regardless of whether the Specified Cooperative has nonpatronage taxable income or W-2 wages for the taxable year. For these purposes, if a Specified Cooperative has negative patronage or nonpatronage QPAI, such QPAI is treated as zero. Pursuant to § 1.199A-8(b)(6), a patronage section 199A(g) deduction can be applied only against patronage income and deductions. Pursuant to § 1.199A-8(c)(ii), a nonpatronage section 199A(g) deduction and can be applied only against nonpatronage income and deductions.

(2) *Use of section 199A(g) deduction to create or increase a net operating loss.*—If a Specified Cooperative that is a member of an EAG has some or all of the EAG's section 199A(g) deduction allocated to it under paragraph (c)(1) of this section and the amount allocated exceeds patronage or nonpatronage taxable income, determined as described in this section and prior to allocation of the section 199A(g) deduction, the section 199A(g) deduction will create an NOL for the patronage source or nonpatronage source. Similarly, if a Specified Cooperative that is a member of an EAG, prior to the allocation of some or all of the EAG's section 199A(g) deduction to the member, has a patronage or nonpatronage NOL for the taxable year, the portion of the EAG's section 199A(g) deduction allocated to the member will increase such NOL.

(d) *Special rules for members of the same consolidated group.*—(1) *Intercompany transactions.*—In the case of an intercompany transaction between consolidated group members S and B (as the terms intercompany transaction, S and B are defined in § 1.1502-13(b)(1)), S takes the intercompany transaction into account in computing the section 199A(g) deduction at the same time and in the same proportion as S takes into account the income, gain, deduction, or loss from the intercompany transaction under § 1.1502-13.

(2) *Application of the simplified deduction method and the small business simplified overall method.*—For purposes of applying the simplified deduction method under § 1.199A-10(e) and the small business simplified overall method under § 1.199A-10(f), a Specified Cooperative that is part of a consolidated group determines its QPAI using its members' DPGR, non-DPGR, cost of goods sold (COGS), and all other deductions, expenses, or losses (hereinafter deductions), determined after application of § 1.1502-13.

(3) *Determining the section 199A(g) deduction.*—(i) *Expanded affiliated group consists of consolidated group and non-consolidated group members.*—In determining the section 199A(g) deduction, if an EAG includes Specified Cooperatives that are members of the same consolidated group and Specified Cooperatives that are not members of

the same consolidated group, the consolidated taxable income or loss, QPAI, and W-2 wages, from patronage sources, if any, of the consolidated group (and not the separate taxable income or loss, QPAI, and W-2 wages from patronage sources of the members of the consolidated group), are aggregated with the taxable income or loss, QPAI, and W-2 wages, from patronage sources, if any, of the non-consolidated group members. A similar rule applies with respect to nonpatronage taxable income or loss, QPAI, and W-2 wages. For example, if A, B, C, S1, and S2 are Specified Cooperatives that are members of the same EAG, and A, S1, and S2 are members of the same consolidated group (the A consolidated group), then the A consolidated group is treated as one member of the EAG. Accordingly, the EAG is considered to have three members, the A consolidated group, B, and C. The consolidated taxable income or loss, QPAI, and W-2 wages from patronage sources, if any, of the A consolidated group are aggregated with the taxable income or loss from patronage sources, QPAI, and W-2 wages, if any, of B and C in determining the EAG's section 199A(g) deduction from patronage sources. Similarly, the consolidated taxable income or loss, QPAI, and W-2 wages from nonpatronage sources, if any, of the A consolidated group are aggregated with the taxable income or loss from nonpatronage sources, QPAI, and W-2 wages, if any, of B and C in determining the EAG's section 199A(g) deduction from nonpatronage sources. Pursuant to §1.199A-8(b)(6), a patronage section 199A(g) deduction can be applied only against patronage income and deductions. Pursuant to §1.199A-8(c)(ii), a nonpatronage section 199A(g) deduction and can be applied only against nonpatronage income and deductions.

(ii) *Expanded affiliated group consists only of members of a single consolidated group.*—If all of the Specified Cooperatives that are members of an EAG are also members of the same consolidated group, the consolidated group's section 199A(g) deduction is determined using the consolidated group's consolidated taxable income or loss, QPAI, and W-2 wages, from patronage sources or nonpatronage sources, as the case may be, rather than the separate taxable income or loss, QPAI, and W-2 wages from patronage sources or nonpatronage sources of its members.

(4) *Allocation of the section 199A(g) deduction of a consolidated group among its members.*—The section 199A(g) deduction from patronage sources of a consolidated group (or the section 199A(g) deduction allocated to a consolidated group that is a member of an EAG) is allocated among the patronage sources of Specified Cooperatives in proportion to each Specified Cooperative's patronage QPAI, regardless of whether the Specified Cooperative has patronage separate taxable income or W-2 wages for the taxable year. In allocating the section 199A(g) deduction of a patronage source of a Specified Cooperative that is part of a consolidated group among patronage sources of other members of the same group, any redetermination of a member's patronage receipts, COGS, or other deductions from an intercompany transaction under §1.1502-13(c)(1)(i) or (c)(4) is not taken into account for purposes of section 199A(g). Also, for purposes of this allocation, if a patronage source of a Specified Cooperative that is a member of a consolidated group has negative QPAI, the QPAI of the patronage source is treated as zero.

(e) *Examples.*—The following examples illustrate the application of paragraphs (a) through (d) of this section.

(i) *Example 1.* Specified Cooperatives X, Y, and Z are members of the same EAG but are not members of a consolidated group. X, Y, and Z each files Federal income tax returns on a calendar year basis. None of X, Y, or Z have activities other than from its patronage sources. Prior to 2018, X had no taxable income or loss. In 2018, X has taxable income of $0, QPAI of $2,000, and W-2 wages of $0, Y has taxable income of $4,000, QPAI of $3,000, and W-2 wages of $500, and Z has taxable income of $4,000, QPAI of $5,000, and W-2 wages of $2,500. Accordingly, the EAG's patronage source taxable income is $8,000, the sum of X's taxable income of $0, Y's taxable income of $4,000, and Z's taxable income of $4,000. The EAG has QPAI of $10,000, the sum of X's QPAI of $2,000, Y's QPAI of $3,000, and Z's QPAI of $5,000. The EAG's W-2 wages are $3,000, the sum of X's W-2 wages of $0, Y's W-2 wages of $500, and Z's W-2 wages of $2,500. Thus, the EAG's section 199A(g) deduction for 2018 is $720 (9% of the lesser of the EAG's patronage source taxable income of $8,000 and the EAG's QPAI of $10,000, but no greater than 50% of its W-2 wages of $3,000, i.e., $1,500). Pursuant to paragraph (c)(1) of this section, the $720 section 199A(g) deduction is allocated to X, Y, and Z in proportion to their respective amounts of QPAI, that is $144 to X ($720 × $2,000/$10,000), $216 to Y ($720 × $3,000/$10,000), and $360 to Z ($720 × $5,000/$10,000). Although X's patronage source taxable income for 2018 determined prior to allocation of a portion of the EAG's section 199A(g) deduction to it was $0, pursuant to paragraph (c)(2) of this section, X will have an NOL from its patronage source for 2018 equal to $144, which will be a carryover to 2019.

(ii) *Example 2.* (A) *Facts.* Corporation X is the common parent of a consolidated group, consisting of X and Y, which has filed a consoli-

dated Federal income tax return for many years. Corporation P is the common parent of a consolidated group, consisting of P and S, which has filed a consolidated Federal income tax return for many years. The X and P consolidated groups each file their consolidated Federal income tax returns on a calendar year basis. X, Y, P, and S are each Specified Cooperatives, and none of X, Y, P, or S has ever had activities other than from its patronage sources. The X consolidated group and the P consolidated group are members of the same EAG in 2019. In 2018, the X consolidated group incurred a consolidated net operating loss (CNOL) of $25,000. Neither P nor S (nor the P consolidated group) has ever incurred an NOL. In 2019, the X consolidated group has (prior to the deduction under section 172) taxable income of $8,000 and the P consolidated group has taxable income of $20,000. X's QPAI is $8,000, Y's QPAI is ($13,000), P's QPAI is $16,000 and S's QPAI is $4,000. There are sufficient W-2 wages to exceed the section 199A(g)(1)(B) limitation.

(B) *Analysis.* The X consolidated group uses $8,000 of its CNOL from 2018 to offset the X consolidated group's taxable income in 2019. None of the X consolidated group's remaining CNOL may be used to offset taxable income of the P consolidated group under paragraph (b)(3) of this section. Accordingly, for purposes of determining the EAG's section 199A(g) deduction for 2019, the EAG has taxable income of $20,000 (the X consolidated group's taxable income, after the deduction under section 172, of $0 plus the P consolidated group's taxable income of $20,000). The EAG has QPAI of $15,000 (the X consolidated group's QPAI of ($5,000) (X's $8,000 + Y's ($13,000)), and the P consolidated group's QPAI of $20,000 (P's $16,000 + S's $4,000)). The EAG's section 199A(g) deduction equals $1,350, 9% of the lesser of its taxable income of $20,000 and its QPAI of $15,000. The section 199A(g) deduction is allocated between the X and P consolidated groups in proportion to their respective QPAI. Because the X consolidated group has negative QPAI, all of the section 199A(g) deduction of $1,350 is allocated to the P consolidated group. This $1,350 is allocated between P and S, the members of the P consolidated group, in proportion to their QPAI. Accordingly, P is allocated $1,080 ($1,350 x ($16,000/$20,000) and S is allocated $270 ($1,350 x $4,000/$20,000)).

(f) *Allocation of patronage income and loss by a Specified Cooperative that is a member of the expanded affiliated group for only a portion of the year.*—(1) *In general.*—A Specified Cooperative that becomes or ceases to be a member of an EAG during its taxable year must allocate its taxable income or loss, QPAI, and W-2 wages between the portion of the taxable year that the Specified Cooperative is a member of the EAG and the portion of the taxable year that the Specified Cooperative is not a member of the EAG. This allocation of items is made by using the pro rata allocation method described in this paragraph (f)(1). Under the pro rata allocation method, an equal portion of patronage taxable income or loss, QPAI, and W-2 wages, and nonpatronage taxable income or loss, QPAI, and W-2 wages for the taxable year is assigned to each day of the Specified Cooperative's taxable year. Those items assigned to those days that the Specified Cooperative was a member of the EAG are then aggregated.

(2) *Coordination with rules relating to the allocation of income under §1.1502-76(b).*—If §1.1502-76(b) (relating to items included in a consolidated return) applies to a Specified Cooperative that is a member of an EAG, then any allocation of items required under this paragraph (f) is made only after the allocation of the items pursuant to §1.1502-76(b).

(g) *Total section 199A(g) deduction for a Specified Cooperative that is a member of an expanded affiliated group for some or all of its taxable year.*—(1) *Member of the same EAG for the entire taxable year.*—If a Specified Cooperative is a member of the same EAG for its entire taxable year, the Specified Cooperative's section 199A(g) deduction for the taxable year (whether patronage sourced or nonpatronage sourced) is the amount of the section 199A(g) deduction allocated to it by the EAG under paragraph (c)(1) of this section.

(2) *Member of the expanded affiliated group for a portion of the taxable year.*—If a Specified Cooperative is a member of an EAG for only a portion of its taxable year and is either not a member of any EAG or is a member of another EAG, or both, for another portion of the taxable year, the Specified Cooperative's section 199A(g) deduction for the taxable year (whether patronage sourced or nonpatronage sourced) is the sum of its section 199A(g) deductions for each portion of the taxable year.

(3) *Example.*—The following example illustrates the application of paragraphs (f) and (g) of this section.

(i) *Example*—(A) *Facts.* Specified Cooperatives X and Y, calendar year taxpayers, are members of the same EAG for the entire 2018 taxable year. Specified Cooperative Z, also a calendar year taxpayer, is a member of the EAG of which X and Y are members for the first half of 2018 and not a member of any EAG for the second half of 2018. Assume that X, Y, and Z each has W-2 wages in excess of the section 199A(g)(1)(B) wage limitation for all relevant periods. In 2018, X's patronage source has taxable income of $2,000 and QPAI of $600, Y's patronage source has a taxable loss of $400 and QPAI of ($200), and Z's patronage source has taxable income of $1,400 and QPAI of $2,400.

(B) *Analysis.* Pursuant to the pro rata allocation method, $700 of Z's 2018 patronage taxable income and $1,200 of its 2018 QPAI are allocated to the first half of the 2018 taxable year (the period in which Z is a member of the EAG) and $700 of Z's 2018 patronage taxable income and $1,200 of its 2018 QPAI are allocated to the second half of the 2018 taxable year (the period in which Z is not a member of any EAG). Accordingly, in 2018, the EAG has taxable income from patronage source of $2,300 (X's $2,000 + Y's ($400) + Z's $700) and QPAI of $1,600 (X's $600 + Y's ($200) + Z's $1,200). The EAG's section 199A(g) deduction for 2018 is $144 (9% of the lesser of the EAG's taxable income from patronage source of $2,300 or QPAI of $1,600). Pursuant to §1.199A-14(c)(1), this $144 deduction is allocated to X's, Y's, and Z's patronage source in proportion to their respective QPAI. Accordingly, X's patronage source is allocated $48 of the EAG's section 199A(g) deduction ($144 x ($600/($600 + $0 + $1,200))), Y's patronage source is allocated $0 of the EAG's section 199A(g) deduction ($144 x ($0 / ($600 + $0 + $1,200))), and Z's patronage source is allocated $96 of the EAG's section 199A(g) deduction ($144 x ($1,200 / ($600 + $0 + $1,200))). For the second half of 2018, Z's patronage source has taxable income of $700 and QPAI of $1,200. Therefore, for the second half of 2018, Z's patronage source has a section 199A(g) deduction of $63 (9% of the lesser of its taxable income of $700 or its QPAI of $1,200 for the second half of 2018). Accordingly, X's 2018 section 199A(g) deduction is $48 and Y's 2018 section 199A(g) deduction is $0. Z's 2018 section 199A(g) deduction is $159, the sum of the $96 section 199A(g) deduction of the EAG allocated to Z for the first half of 2018 and Z's $63 section 199A(g) deduction for the second half of 2018.

(h) *Computation of section 199A(g) deduction for members of an expanded affiliated group with different taxable years.*—(1) *In general.*—If Specified Cooperatives that are members of an EAG have different taxable years, in determining the section 199A(g) deduction of a member (the computing member), the computing member is required to take into account the taxable income or loss, determined without regard to the section 199A(g) deduction, QPAI, and W-2 wages of each other group member that are both—

(i) Attributable to the period that each other member of the EAG and the computing member are members of the EAG; and

(ii) Taken into account in a taxable year that begins after the effective date of section 199A(g) and ends with or within the taxable year of the computing member with respect to which the section 199A(g) deduction is computed.

(2) *Example.*—The following example illustrates the application of this paragraph (h).

(i) *Example.* (A) Specified Cooperatives X, Y, and Z are members of the same EAG. Neither X, Y, nor Z is a member of a consolidated group. X and Y are calendar year taxpayers and Z is a June 30 fiscal year taxpayer. Z came into existence on July 1, 2017. All of X's, Y's, and Z's activities are patronage sourced. Each Specified Cooperative has taxable income that exceeds its QPAI and W-2 wages in excess of the section 199A(g)(1)(B) wage limitation. For the taxable year ending December 31, 2018, X's QPAI is $8,000 and Y's QPAI is ($6,000). For its taxable year ending June 30, 2019, Z's QPAI is $2,000.

(B) In computing X's and Y's respective section 199A(g) deductions for their taxable years ending December 31, 2018, X's taxable income or loss, QPAI and W-2 wages and Y's taxable income or loss, QPAI, and W-2 wages from their respective taxable years ending December 31, 2018, are aggregated. The EAG's QPAI for this purpose is $2,000 (X's QPAI of $8,000 + Y's QPAI of ($6,000)). The $180 deduction is allocated to each of X and Y in proportion to their respective QPAI as a percentage of the QPAI of each member of the EAG that was taken into account in computing the EAG's section 199A(g) deduction. Pursuant to paragraph (c)(1) of this section, in allocating the section 199A(g) deduction between X and Y, because Y's QPAI is negative, Y's QPAI is treated as being $0. Accordingly, X's section 199A(g) deduction for its taxable year ending December 31, 2018, is $180 ($180 × $8,000/($8,000 + $0)). Y's section 199A(g) deduction for its taxable year ending December 31, 2018, is $0 ($180 × $0/($8,000 + $0)).

(C) In computing Z's section 199A(g) deduction for its taxable year ending June 30, 2019, X's and Y's items from their respective taxable years ending December 31, 2018, are taken into account. Therefore, X's taxable income or loss and Y's taxable income or loss, determined without regard to the section 199A(g) deduction, QPAI, and W-2 wages from their taxable years ending December 31, 2018, are aggregated with Z's taxable income or loss, QPAI, and W-2 wages from its taxable year ending June 30, 2019. The EAG's QPAI is $4,000 (X's QPAI of $8,000 + Y's QPAI of ($6,000) + Z's QPAI of $2,000). The

EAG's section 199A(g) deduction is $360 (9% × $4,000). A portion of the $360 deduction is allocated to Z in proportion to its QPAI as a percentage of the QPAI of each member of the EAG that was taken into account in computing the EAG's section 199A(g) deduction. Pursuant to paragraph (c)(1) of this section, in allocating a portion of the $360 deduction to Z, Y's QPAI is treated as being $0 because Y's QPAI is negative. Z's section 199A(g) deduction for its taxable year ending June 30, 2019, is $72 ($360 × ($2,000/($8,000 + $0 + $2,000))).

(i) *Partnership owned by expanded affiliated group.*—(1) *In general.*—For purposes of section 199A(g)(3)(D) relating to DPGR, if all of the interests in the capital and profits of a partnership are owned by members of a single EAG at all times during the taxable year of such partnership (EAG partnership), then the EAG partnership and all members of that EAG are treated as a single taxpayer during such period.

(2) *Attribution of activities.*—(i) *In general.*—If a Specified Cooperative which is a member of an EAG (disposing member) derives gross receipts from the lease, rental, license, sale, exchange, or other disposition of property that was MPGE by an EAG partnership, all the partners of which are members of the same EAG to which the disposing member belongs at the time that the disposing member disposes of such property, then the disposing member is treated as conducting the MPGE activities previously conducted by the EAG partnership with respect to that property. The previous sentence applies only for those taxable years in which the disposing member is a member of the EAG of which all the partners of the EAG partnership are members for the entire taxable year of the EAG partnership. With respect to a lease, rental, or license, the disposing member is treated as having disposed of the property on the date or dates on which it takes into account its gross receipts from the lease, rental, or license under its method of accounting. With respect to a sale, exchange, or other disposition, the disposing member is treated as having disposed of the property on the date it ceases to own the property for Federal income tax purposes, even if no gain or loss is taken into account. Likewise, if an EAG partnership derives gross receipts from the lease, rental, license, sale, exchange, or other disposition of property that was MPGE by a member (or members) of the same EAG (the producing member) to which all the partners of the EAG partnership belong at the time that the EAG partnership disposes of such property, then the EAG partnership is treated as conducting the MPGE activities previously conducted by the producing member with respect to that property. The previous sentence applies only for those taxable years in which the producing member is a member of the EAG of which all the partners of the EAG partnership are members for the entire taxable year of the EAG partnership. With respect to a lease, rental, or license, the EAG partnership is treated as having disposed of the property on the date or dates on which it takes into account its gross receipts derived from the lease, rental, or license under its method of accounting. With respect to a sale, exchange, or other disposition, the EAG partnership is treated as having disposed of the property on the date it ceases to own the property for Federal income tax purposes, even if no gain or loss is taken into account.

(ii) *Attribution between expanded affiliated group partnerships.*—If an EAG partnership (disposing partnership) derives gross receipts from the lease, rental, license, sale, exchange, or other disposition of property that was MPGE by another EAG partnership (producing partnership), then the disposing partnership is treated as conducting the MPGE activities previously conducted by the producing partnership with respect to that property, provided that each of these partnerships (the producing partnership and the disposing partnership) is owned for its entire taxable year in which the disposing partnership disposes of such property by members of the same EAG. With respect to a lease, rental, or license, the disposing partnership is treated as having disposed of the property on the date or dates on which it takes into account its gross receipts from the lease, rental, or license under its method of accounting. With respect to a sale, exchange, or other disposition, the disposing partnership is treated as having disposed of the property on the date it ceases to own the property for Federal income tax purposes, even if no gain or loss is taken into account.

(iii) *Exception.*—No member of an EAG other than an exempt Specified Cooperative is attributed nonpatronage activities conducted by an EAG partnership. An EAG partnership is not attributed nonpatronage activities conducted by any member of the EAG or by another EAG partnership.

(j) *Applicability date.*—The provisions of this section apply to taxable years ending after the date the Treasury decision adopting these regulations as final regulations is published in the *Federal Register*. Taxpayers, however, may rely on these regulations until that date, but only if the taxpayers apply the rules in their entirety and in a consistent manner. [Reg. §1.199A-12.]

Itemized Deductions for Individuals

Business Use or Rental of Dwelling Unit.—Reproduced below is the text of a proposed amendment of Reg. §1.212-1, relating to the deductibility of expenses in connection with the business use, or the rental to others, of a dwelling unit that the taxpayer is deemed to have used for personal purposes during the taxable year (published in the Federal Register on August 7, 1980).

☐ Par. 2. Paragraph (h) of §1.212-1 is amended by adding at the end thereof a new sentence to read as follows:

§1.212-1. Nontrade or nonbusiness expenses.—

* * *

(h) * * * But see section 280A and the regulations thereunder.

* * *

Notional Principal Contracts: Contingent Nonperiodic Payments

Notional Principal Contracts: Contingent Nonperiodic Payments.—Amendments to Reg. §1.212-1, relating to the inclusion into income or deduction of a contingent nonperiodic payment provided for under a notional principal contract, are proposed (published in the Federal Register on February 26, 2004) (REG-166012-02).

☐ Par. 3. In §1.212-1, paragraph (q) is added to read as follows:

§1.212-1. Nontrade or nonbusiness expenses.

* * *

(q) *Notional principal contract payments.*—(1) Amounts taken into account by an individual pursuant to §1.446-3(d)(1) (including mark-to-market deductions) with respect to a notional principal contract as defined in §1.446-3(c)(1)(i), are ordinary and necessary, and are deductible to the extent these amounts are paid or incurred in connection with the production or collection of income. However, this section will not apply to any amount representing interest ex-

pense on the deemed loan component of a significant nonperiodic payment as described in §1.446-3(g)(4). For any loss arising from a termination payment as defined in §1.446-3(h)(1), see section 1234A and the regulations thereunder. For the timing of deductions with respect to notional principal contracts, see §1.446-3.

(2) *Effective date.*—Paragraph (q) of this section is applicable to notional principal contracts entered into on or after 30 days after the date a Treasury decision based on these proposed regulations is published in the Federal Register.

Transfers Between Spouses

Transfers: Alimony, Separate Maintenance, and Dependency Exemption.—Temporary Reg. §1.215-1T, relating to the treatment of transfers of property between spouses and former spouses, the tax treatments of alimony and separate maintenance payments, and the dependency exemption in the case of a child of divorced parents, is also proposed as a final regulation and, when adopted, would become Reg. §1.215-1 (published in the Federal Register on August 31, 1984).

§1.215-1. Alimony, etc., payments.

IRAs: SEPs: Deduction

Individual Retirement Plans: Simplified Employee Pensions.—Reproduced below are the texts of proposed Reg. §1.219-3 and proposed amendments of Reg. §§1.219-1 and 1.219-2, relating to individual retirement plans and simplified employee pensions (published in the Federal Register on July 14, 1981).

☐ Par. 2. Section 1.219-1 is revised by adding: (1) a new subdivision (iv) to paragraph (b)(2), and (2) new paragraphs (d) and (e) to read as follows:

§1.219-1. Deduction for retirement savings.—

* * *

(b) *Limitations and restrictions.*—* * *

(2) *Restrictions.*—* * *

(iv) *Alternative deduction.*—No deduction is allowed under subsection (a) for the taxable year if the individual claims the deduction allowed by section 220 (relating to retirement savings for certain married individuals) for the taxable year.

* * *

(d) *Time when contributions deemed made.*—(1) *Taxable years beginning before January 1, 1978.*—For taxable years beginning before January 1, 1977, a taxpayer must make a contribution to an individual retirement plan during a taxable year in order to receive a deduction for such taxable year. For taxable years beginning after December 31, 1976, and before January 1, 1978, a taxpayer shall be deemed to have made a contribution on the last day of the preceding taxable year if the contribution is made on account of such taxable year and is made not later than 45 days after the end of such taxable year. A contribution made not later than 45 days after the end of a taxable year shall be treated as made on account of such taxable year if the individual specifies in writing to the trustee, insurance company, or custodian that the amounts contributed are for such taxable year.

(2) *Taxable years beginning after December 31, 1977.*—For taxable years beginning after December 31, 1977, a taxpayer shall be deemed to have made a contribution on the last day of the preceding taxable year if the contribution is made on account of such taxable year and is made not later than the time prescribed by law for filing the return for such taxable year (including extensions thereof). A contribution made not later than the time prescribed by law for filing the return for a taxable year (including extensions thereof) shall be treated as made on account of such taxable year if it is irrevocably specified in writing to the trustee, insurance company, or custodian that the amounts contributed are for such taxable year.

(3) *Time when individual retirement plan must be established.*—For purposes of this paragraph, an individual retirement plan need not be established until the contribution is made.

(4) *Year of inclusion in income.*—Any amount paid by an employer to an individual retirement account, for an individual retirement annuity or for an individual retirement bond (including an individual retirement account or individual retirement annuity maintained as part of a simplified employee pension plan) shall be included in the gross income of the employee for the taxable year for which the contribution is made.

(e) *Excess contributions treated as contribution made during subsequent year for which there is an unused limitation.*—(1) *In general.*—If for the taxable year the maximum amount allowable as a deduction under this section exceeds the amount contributed, then the taxpayer, whether or not a deduction is actually claimed, shall be treated as having made an additional contribution for the taxable year in an amount equal to the lesser of—

(i) The amount of such excess, or

(ii) The amount of the excess contributions for such taxable year (determined under section 4973(b)(2) without regard to subparagraph (C) thereof).

(2) *Amount contributed.*—For purposes of this paragraph, the amount contributed—

(i) Shall be determined without regard to this paragraph, and

(ii) Shall not include any rollover contribution.

(3) *Special rule where excess deduction was allowed for closed year.*—Proper reduction shall be made in the amount allowable as a deduction by reason of this paragraph for any amount allowed as a deduction under this section or section 220 for a prior taxable year for which the period for assessing a deficiency has expired if the amount so allowed exceeds the amount which should have been allowed for such prior taxable year.

(4) *Effective date.*—(i) This paragraph shall apply to the determination of deductions for taxable years beginning after December 31, 1975.

(ii) If, but for this subdivision, an amount would be allowable as a deduction by reason of section 219(c)(5) for a taxable year beginning before January 1, 1978, such amount shall be allowable only for the taxpayer's first taxable year beginning in 1978.

Reg. §1.219-1(e)(4)(ii)

(5) *Examples.*—The provisions of this paragraph may be illustrated by the following examples. (Assume in each example, unless otherwise stated, that B is less than age $70^{1}/_{2}$ and is not covered by a simplified employee pension or a plan described in section 219(b)(2).)

Example (1). (i) B, a calendar-year taxpayer, earns $8,000 in compensation includible in gross income for 1979. On December 1, 1979, B establishes an individual retirement account (IRA) and contributes $1,500 to the account. B does not withdraw any money from the IRA after the initial contribution. Under section 219(b)(l), the maximum amount that B can deduct for 1979 is 15% of $8,000 or $1,200. B has an excess contribution for 1979 of $300.

(ii) For 1980, B has compensation includible in gross income of $12,000. B makes a $1,000 contribution to his IRA for 1980.

(iii) Although B made only a $1,000 contribution to his IRA for 1980, under the rules contained in this paragraph, B is treated as having made an additional contribution of $300 for 1980 and will be allowed to deduct $1,300 as his 1980 IRA contribution.

Example (2). (i) For 1979, the facts are the same as in *Example (1).*

(ii) For 1980, B has compensation includible in gross income of $12,000. B makes a $1,500 contribution to his IRA for 1980.

(iii) B will be allowed a $1,500 deduction for 1980 (the amount of his contribution). B will not be allowed a deduction for the $300 excess contribution made in 1979 because the maximum amount allowable for 1980 does not exceed the amount contributed.

Example (3). (i) For 1979, the facts are the same as in *Example (1).*

(ii) For 1980, B has compensation includible in gross income of $12,000. B makes a $1,400 contribution to his IRA for 1980.

(iii) For 1980, B will be allowed to deduct his contribution of $1,400 and $100 of the excess contribution made for 1979. He will not be allowed to deduct the remaining $200 of the excess contribution made for 1979 because that would make his deduction for 1980 more than $1,500, his allowable deduction for 1980.

(iv) For 1981, B has compensation includible in gross income of $15,000. B makes a $1,300 contribution to his IRA for 1981.

(v) B will be allowed to deduct the remaining $200 and his $1,300 contribution for 1981.

Example (4). (i) For 1979, the facts are the same as in *Example (1).*

(ii) For 1980, B has compensation includible in gross income of $12,000. B makes a $1,000 contribution to his IRA for 1980. B is allowed to deduct the $300 excess contribution for 1980 but fails to do so on his return. Consequently, B deducts only $1,000 for 1980.

(iii) Under no circumstances will B be allowed to deduct the $300 excess contribution made for 1979 for any taxable year after 1980 because B is treated as having made the contribution for 1980.

Example (5). (i) For 1979, the facts are the same as in *Example (1).*

(ii) For 1980, B has compensation includible in gross income of $15,000 and is an active participant in a plan described in section 219(b)(2)(A).

(iii) B will not be allowed to deduct for 1980 the $300 excess contribution for 1979 because the maximum amount allowable as a deduction under sections 219(b)(1) and 219(b)(2) is $0.

☐ Par. 3. Section 1.219-2 is amended by: (1) revising the first sentence of paragraph (b)(1); (2) renumbering paragraph (b)(2), (3), and (4) as paragraph (b)(3), (4) and (5), respectively, and adding a new paragraph (b)(2) before the renumbered paragraph (b)(3), (4) and (5); (3) revising paragraph (f) and (4) adding new examples (3), (4) and (5) after *Example (2)* in paragraph (h). These revised and added provisions read as follows:

§1.219-2. Definition of active participant.—

* * *

(b) *Defined benefit plans.*—(1) *In general.*—Except as provided in subparagraphs (2), (3), (4) and (5) of this paragraph, an individual is an active participant in a defined benefit plan if for any portion of the plan year ending with or within such individual's taxable year he is not excluded under the eligibility provisions of the plan. * * *

(2) *Special rule for offset plans.*—For taxable years beginning after December 31, 1980, an individual who satisfies the eligibility requirements of a plan under which benefits are offset by Social Security or Railroad Retirement benefits is not considered an active participant by virtue of participation in such plan for a particular plan year if such individual's compensation for the calendar year during which such plan year ends does not exceed the offset plan's breakpoint compensation amount for such plan year. Breakpoint compensation is the maximum compensation determined for the plan for a plan year that any participant could earn and have a projected benefit from the offset plan of $0. For purposes of determining the projected plan benefit, the following assumptions are made: plan participation begins at age 25 and maximum credited service is earned for participation from age 25 to age 65 regardless of the participant's actual participation; plan benefits, including the offset, are based on W-2 earnings from the employer for such calendar year regardless of the definition of compensation on which plan benefits are based; and the projected Social Security Primary Insurance Amount (PIA) is computed under a formula that the Commissioner may, from time to time, prescribe for this purpose.

* * *

(f) *Certain individuals not active participants.*—(1) *Election out of plan.*—For purposes of this section, an individual who elects pursuant to the plan not to participate in the plan will be considered to be ineligible for participation for the period to which the election applies. In the case of a defined benefit plan, such an election shall be effective no earlier than the first plan year commencing after the date of the election.

(2) *Members of reserve components.*—A member of a reserve component of the armed forces (as defined in section 261(a) of Title 10 of the United States Code) is not considered to be an active participant in a plan described in section 219(b)(2)(A)(iv) for a taxable year solely because he is a member of a reserve component unless he has served in excess of 90 days on active duty (other than military duty for training) during the year.

(3) *Volunteer firefighters.*—An individual whose participation in a plan described in section 219(b)(2)(A)(iv) is based solely upon his activity as a volunteer firefighter and whose accrued benefit as of the beginning of the taxable year is not more than an annual benefit of $1,800 (when expressed as a single life annuity commencing at age

65) is not considered to be an active participant in such a plan for the taxable year.

* * *

(h) *Examples.*—* * *

Example (3). (i) For plan year X the annual projected Social Security PIA is determined as follows:

Compensation Range*	PIA Formula*
$0 to $1,626	PIA = $1,464
$1,627 to $2,160	PIA = .90 (compensation)
$2,161 to $13,020	PIA = .32 (compensation) + $1,253
$13,021 to $22,900	PIA = .15 (compensation) + $3,466
$22,901 and over	PIA = $6,901

* These numbers are for illustrative purposes only.

(ii) V is a defined benefit plan which provides a normal retirement benefit of 1.5% of high five-year average earnings excluding overtime pay, minus 2% of Social Security PIA, the difference multiplied by years of plan participation up to a maximum of 30 years. V provides that individuals commence plan participation on their date of employment. Normal retirement age is 62. V's breakpoint compensation for the plan year ending in year X can be determined as follows:

I. Determine V's projected benefit:

An individual credited with 40 years of service (from age 25 to 65) would have a projected benefit of:

(30) (1.5% (compensation) – 2% (PIA))

or

45% (compensation) – 60% (PIA).

Note that in the determination of the projected benefit, the normal retirement age is assumed to be age 65 rather than the actual normal retirement age of 62, the participant is assumed to have 40 years of credited service, and the plan definition of compensation is assumed to be the same as is used to compute the Social Security benefit.

II. Determine V's formula compensation changepoints. The formula compensation changepoints are amounts where the projected benefit formula, expressed in terms of compensation, changes:

Since V's benefit formula applies uniformly to all compensation, the compensation changepoints are determined by the PIA portion only, and are

a.	$ 1,626
b.	2,160
c.	13,020
d.	22,900

III. Determine which of the formula compensation changepoints first produces a projected benefit greater than 0. This can be done by testing the projected benefit for compensation amounts equal to V's compensation changepoints:

a. Formula compensation changepoint equal to $1,626.

i. Projected benefit = 45% × 1,626 – 60% × 1,464 = 0

V's compensation breakpoint, therefore, exceeds $1,626.

b. Formula compensation changepoint equal to $2,160.

i. Projected benefit = $45\% \times 2,160 - 60\% \times (.90 \times 2,160) = 0$

V's compensation breakpoint, therefore, exceeds $2,160.

c. Formula compensation changepoint equal to $13,020.

i. Projected benefit = $45\% \times 13,020 - 60\% \times (.32 \times 13,020 + 1,253) = 2,607$.

V's compensation breakpoint is, therefore, in the compensation range $2,161 to $13,020.

IV. Determine V's compensation breakpoint within the $2,161 to $13,020 compensation range.

V's compensation breakpoint can be determined by finding the greatest compensation that will result in a projected benefit of 0 for this compensation range:

a. $45\% \times$ compensation $- 60\% \times (.32 \times$ compensation $+ 1,253) = 0$.

b. Eliminate the parentheses in equation a by multiplying each of the terms within the parentheses by $- 60\%$. $45\% \times$ compensation $- 19.2\% \times$ compensation $- 751.80 = 0$.

c. Add 751.80 to both sides of equation in b and combine the first two terms. $25.8\% \times$ compensation $= 751.80$.

d. Dividing both sides of the equation in c by 25.8%, V's breakpoint compensation for 1979 = $2,914.

V. Therefore, individuals whose W-2 earnings from the employer do not exceed $2,914 in year X are not considered active participants by virtue of participating in Plan V.

Example (4). For year X the annual projected Social Security PIA is determined as in *Example (3).*

T is a defined benefit plan which provides a normal retirement benefit equal to 20% of final average earnings plus 10% of such earnings in excess of $2,000 minus 45% of PIA, the net result reduced pro rata for participation less than 15 years. Participation commences upon attainment of age 20. Normal retirement age is 65.

I. Determine T's projected benefit for year X.

An individual credited with 40 years of service (from age 25 to 65) would have a projected benefit of:

20% of compensation plus 10% of compensation in excess of $2,000, if any

minus

45% of PIA

II. Determine T's formula compensation changepoints.

$2,000 is a formula compensation changepoint, in addition to the four PIA changepoints, since T's benefit formula changes at this compensation amount. The five formula compensation changepoints are:

a. $ 1,626
b. 2,000
c. 2,160
d. 13,020
e. 22,900

III. Determine which of T's formula compensation changepoints first produces a projected benefit greater than 0.

a. Compensation changepoint equal to $1,626

i. Projected benefit = $20\% \times 1,626 + 10\% \times 0 - 45\% \times 1,424 = 0$

[T]'s compensation breakpoint, therefore, exceeds $1,626.

b. Compensation changepoint equal to $2,000

i. Projected benefit = $20\% \times 2,000 + 10\% \times 0 - 45\% \times (.90 \times 2,000) = 0$.

T's compensation breakpoint, therefore, exceeds $2,000.

c. Compensation changepoint equal to $2,160

i. Projected benefit = $20\% \times 2,160 + 10\% \times (2,160 - 2,000) - 45\% \times (.90 \times 2,160) = 0$.

T's compensation breakpoint, therefore, exceeds $2,160.

d. Compensation changepoint equal to $13,020

i. Projected benefit = $20\% \times 13,020 + 10\% (13,020 - 2,000) - 45\% \times (.32 \times 13,020 + 1,253) = 1,267$.

T's compensation breakpoint is, therefore, in the compensation range $2,160 to $13,020.

IV. Determine T's breakpoint compensation within the $2,160 to $13,020 range.

T's compensation breakpoint can be determined by finding the greatest compensation that will result in a projected benefit of 0 for this range:

a. $20\% \times$ comp. $+ 10\% \times$ (comp. $- 2,000) - 45\% \times (.32 \times$ comp. $+ 1,253) = 0$.

b. Eliminating both parentheses in equation a. by multiplying each of the terms within by the appropriate percentage.

$20\% \times$ comp. $+ 10\% \times$ comp. $- 200 - 14.4\% \times$ comp. $- 563.85 = 0$.

c. Add 763.85 to both sides of equation and combine remaining terms in equation b.

$15.6\% \times$ comp. $= 763.85$.

d. Dividing each side of equation c. by 15.6%, T's breakpoint compensation for year X = $4,896.

V. Therefore, individuals whose W-2 earnings do not exceed $4,896 in year X are not considered active participants by virtue of participating in Plan T.

Example (5). Assume the same facts as *Example (4),* except that T also provides a minimum monthly benefit of $100 for participants with 15 or more years of plan participation. There is no compensation amount which will produce a projected benefit of $0. Therefore, all individuals who satisfy T's eligibility requirements are considered active participants.

☐ Par. 4. There are added after §1.219-2 the following new sections:

§1.219-3. Limitation on simplified employee pension deductions.—(a) *General rule.*—(1) *In general.*—Under section 219(b)(7), if an employer contribution is made on behalf of an employee to a simplified employee pension described in section 408(k), the limitations of this section, and not section 219(b)(1) and §1.219-1(b)(1), shall apply for purposes of computing the maximum allowable deduction for that individual employee. The other rules of section 219 and §§1.219-1 and 1.219-2 apply for purposes of computing an individual's deduction except as modified by this section.

(2) *Employer limitation.*—The maximum deduction limitation under section 219(a) for an employee with respect to an employer contribution to the employee's simplified employee pension under that employer's arrangement cannot exceed an amount equal to the lesser of—

(i) 15 percent of the employee's compensation from that employer (determined without regard to the employer contribution to the simplified employee pension) includible in the employee's gross income for the taxable year, or

(ii) The amount contributed by that employer to the employee's simplified employee pension and included in gross income (but not in excess of $7,500).

(3) *Special rules.*—(i) *Compensation.*—Compensation referred to in paragraph (a)(2)(i) has the same meaning as under §1.219-1(c)(1) except that it includes only the compensation from the employer making the contribution to the simplified employee pension. Thus, if an individual earns $50,000 from employer A and $20,000 from employer B and employer B contributes $4,000 to a simplified employee pension on behalf of the individual, the maximum amount the individual will be able to deduct under section 219(b)(7) is 15 percent of $20,000, or $3,000.

(ii) *Special rule for officers, shareholders, and owner-employees.*—In the case of an employee who is an officer, shareholder, or owner-employee described in section 408(k)(3) with respect to a particular employer, the $7,500 amount referred to in paragraph (a)(2)(ii) shall be reduced by the amount of tax taken into account with respect to such individual under section 408(k)(3)(D).

(iii) *More than one employer arrangement.*—Except as provided in paragraph (c), below, the maximum deduction under paragraph (a)(2) for an individual who receives simplified employee pension contributions under two or more employers' simplified employee pension arrangements cannot exceed the sum of the maximum deduction limitations computed separately for that individual under each such employer's arrangement.

(iv) *Section 408 rules.*—Under section 408(j), for purposes of applying the $7,500 limitations under section 408(a)(1), (b), (b)(2)(B) and (d)(5) (§1.408-2(b)(1), §1.408-3(b)(2) and §1.408-4(h)(3)(i), respectively), the $7,500 limitations shall be applied separately with respect to each employer's contributions to an individual's simplified employee pension.

(b) *Limitations not applicable to SEP contributions*—

(1) *Active participant.*—The limitations on coverage by certain other plans in section 219(b)(2) and §1.219-1(b)(2)(i) shall not apply with respect to the employer contribution to a simplified employee pension. Thus, an employee is allowed a deduction for an employer's contribution to a simplified employee pension even though he is an active participant in an employer's qualified plan.

(2) *Contributions to simplified employee pensions after age 70 1/2.*—The denial of deductions for contributions after age 70½ contained in section 219(b)(3) and §1.219-1(b)(2)(ii) shall not apply with respect to the employer contribution to a simplified employee pension.

(c) *Multiple employer, etc. limitations.*—(1) *Section 414(b) and (c) employers.*—In the case of a controlled group of employers within the meaning of section 414(b) or (c), the maximum deduction limitation for an employee under paragraph (a)(2) shall be computed by treating such employers as one employer maintaining a single simplified pension arrangement and by treating the compensation of that employee from such employers as if from one employer. Thus, for example, for a particular employee the 15 percent limitation on compensation would be determined with regard to the compensation from all employers within such group. Further, the maximum deduction with respect to such group could not exceed $7,500.

(2) *Self-employed individuals.*—In the case of an employee who is a self-employed individual within the meaning of section 401(c)(1) with respect to more than one trade or business, the maximum deduction limitation for such an employee under paragraph (a)(2) shall not exceed the lesser of the sum of such limitation applied separately with respect to the simplified employee pension arrangement of each trade or business or such limitation determined by treating such trades or businesses as if they constituted a single employer.

(d) *Additional deduction for employee contributions.*—If the maximum allowable deduction for an individual employee determined under paragraph (a) for employer contributions to that individual's simplified employee pensions is less than $1,500, the individual shall be entitled to an additional deduction for contributions to individual retirement programs maintained on his behalf. The additional deduction shall equal the excess, if any, of the section 219(b)(1) and §1.219-1(b)(1) maximum deduction limitation over the maximum deduction limitation determined under paragraph (a). For purpose of determining the compensation limit of section 219(b)(1), employer simplified employee pension contributions shall not be taken into account. Thus, for example, if $1,000 is deductible by individual A for employer contributions under a simplified employee pension arrangement and A's compensation, not including the $1,000 SEP

Employee	Compensation	Lesser of $7500 or 15% of Comp.
A	$10,000	$1,500
B	20,000	3,000
C	30,000	4,500
D	60,000	7,500

Example (3). Corporations A and B are calendar year taxpayers. Corporations A and B are not members of a controlled group of employers within the meaning of section 414(b) or (c). Individual M is employed full-time by Corporation A and part-time by Corporation B. Corporation A adopts a simplified employee pension agreement for calendar year 1980 and agrees to contribute 15% of compensation for each participant. M is a participant under Corporation A's simplified employee pension agreement and earns $15,000 for 1980 from Corporation A before A's contribution to his simplified employee pension. M also earns $5,000 as a part-time employee of Corporation B for 1980. Corporation A contributes $2,500 to M's simplified employee pension. The maximum amount that M will be allowed to deduct under section 219(b)(7) for 1980 is 15% of $15,000 or $2,250. The remaining $250 is an excess contribution because M cannot consider the compensation earned from Corporation B under §1.219-3(a)(3)(i).

contribution, is $10,000, than A would be entitled to an additional deduction of $500.

(e) *Examples.*—The provisions of this section may be illustrated by the following examples:

Example (1). Corporation X is a calendar-year, cash basis taxpayer. It adopts a simplified employee pension agreement in 1980 and wishes to contribute the maximum amount on behalf of each employee for 1980. Individual E is a calendar-year taxpayer who is employed solely by Corporation X in 1980. Beginning in June, 1980, Corporation X pays $100 each month into a simplified employee pension maintained on behalf of E. X makes a total payment to E's simplified employee pension during the year of $700. E's other compensation from X for the year totals $15,000. The maximum amount which E will be allowed to deduct as a simplified employee pension contribution is 15% of $15,000, or $2,250. Therefore, X may make an additional contribution for 1980 to E's simplified employee pension of $1,550. X makes this additional contribution to E's simplified employee pension in February of 1981. E's total compensation for 1980 includible in gross income is $15,000 + $2,250 or $17,250.

Example (2). (i) Corporation G is a calendar-year taxpayer which does not maintain an integrated plan as defined in section 408(k)(3)(E). It adopts a simplified employee pension agreement for 1980. It wishes to contribute 15% of compensation on behalf of each employee reduced by its tax under section 3111(a). The corporation has 4 employees, A, B, C, and D. D is a shareholder. The compensation for these employees for 1980 is as follows:

A = $10,000
B = 20,000
C = 30,000
D = 60,000

(ii) The amount of money which the corporation will be allowed to contribute on behalf of each employee under this allocation formula and the amount of the employer contribution each employee will be allowed to deduct is set forth in the following table:

3111(a)[1] Tax	SEP[2] Contribution	Sec. 219(b)(7) deduction
$508.00	$992.00	$992.00
1,016.00	1,984.00	1,984.00
1,315.72	3,184.28	3,184.28
1,315.72	6,184.28	6,184.28

[1] The section 3111(a) tax is computed by multiplying compensation up to the taxable wage base ($25,900 for 1980) by the tax rate (5.08% for 1980).
[2] Simplified Employee Pension

Example (4). Individual P is employed by Corporation H and Corporation O. Corporation H and O are not members of a controlled group of employers within the meaning of section 414(b) or (c). Both Corporation H and Corporation O maintain a simplified employee pension arrangement and contribute 15 percent of compensation on behalf of each employee. P earns $50,000 from Corporation H and $60,000 from Corporation O. Corporation H and O each contributes $7,500 under its simplified employee pension arrangement to an individual retirement account maintained on behalf of P. P will be allowed to deduct $15,000 for employer contributions to simplified employee pensions because each employer has a simplified employee pension arrangement and the SEP contributions by Corporation H and O do not exceed the applicable $7,500-15 percent limitation. [Reg. §1.219-3.]

IRAs: SEPs: Qualified Voluntary Employee Contributions

Individual Retirement Plans: Simplified Employee Pensions: Qualified Voluntary Employee Contributions.—Reproduced below are the texts of proposed Reg. §§1.219(a)-1—1.219(a)-6, relating to individual retirement plans, simplified employee pensions and qualified voluntary employee contributions (published in the Federal Register on January 23, 1984).

☐ Paragraph 1. There are added after proposed §1.219-3, 46 Fed. Reg. 36202 (1981), the following new sections 1.219(a)-1 through 1.219(a)-6:

§1.219(a)-1. Deduction for contributions to individual retirement plans and employer plans under the Economic Recovery Tax Act of 1981.—(a) *In general.*—Under section 219, as amended by the Economic Recovery Tax Act of 1981, an individual is allowed a deduction from gross income for amounts paid on his behalf to an individual retirement plan or to certain employer retirement plans. The following is a table of contents for the rules for deductions on behalf of individuals to individual retirement plans or employer plans.

(b) *Definitions.*—The following is a list of terms and their definitions to be used for purposes of this section and §§1.219(a)-2 through 1.219(a)-6:

(1) *Individual retirement plan.*—The term "individual retirement plan" means an individual retirement account described in section 408(a), an individual retirement annuity described in section 408(b), and a retirement bond described in section 409.

(2) *Simplified employee pension.*—The term "simplified employee pension" has the meaning set forth in §1.408-7(a).

(3) *Compensation.*—The term "compensation" means wages, salaries, professional fees, or other amounts derived from or received for personal service actually rendered (including, but not limited to, commissions paid salesmen, compensation for services on the basis

of a percentage of profits, commissions on insurance premiums, tips, and bonuses), but does not include amounts derived from or received as earnings or profits from property (including, but not limited to, interest and dividends) or amounts not includible in gross income such as amounts excluded under section 911. Compensation includes earned income, as defined in section 401(c)(2), reduced by amounts deductible under sections 404 and 405. Compensation does not include amounts received as deferred compensation, including any pension or annuity payment. Compensation does not include unemployment compensation within the meaning of section 85(c).

(4) *Qualified voluntary employee contribution.*—The term "qualified voluntary employee contribution" means any employee contribution which is not a mandatory contribution within the meaning of section 411(c)(2)(C) made by an individual as an employee under a qualified employer plan or government plan, which plan allows an employee to make such contributions, and which the individual has not designated as a contribution other than a qualified voluntary employee contribution. Thus, if employee contributions are required as a condition of plan participation, they are mandatory contributions within the meaning of section 411(c)(2)(C) and cannot be treated as qualified voluntary employee contributions.

(5) *Qualified retirement contribution.*—The term "qualified retirement contribution" means any amount paid in cash for the taxable year by or on behalf of an individual for his benefit to an individual retirement plan and any qualified voluntary employee contribution paid in cash by the individual for the taxable year.

(6) *Deductible employee contribution.*—The term "deductible employee contribution" means any qualified voluntary employee contribution made after December 31, 1981, in a taxable year beginning after such date and allowable as a deduction under section 219(a) for such taxable year.

(7) *Qualified employer plan.*—The term "qualified employer plan" means—

(i) A plan described in section 401(a) which includes a trust exempt from tax under section 501(a),

(ii) An annuity plan described in section 403(a),

(iii) A qualified bond purchase plan described in section 405(a), and

(iv) A plan under which amounts are contributed by an individual's employer for an annuity contract described in section 403(b).

(8) *Government plan.*—The term "government plan" means any retirement plan, whether or not qualified, established and maintained for its employees by the United States, by a State or political subdivision thereof, or by an agency or instrumentality of any of the foregoing.

(c) *Effective date.*—This section and §§ 1.219(a)-2 through 1.219(a)-6 are effective for taxable years of individuals beginning after December 31, 1981. [Reg. § 1.219(a)-1.]

§ 1.219(a)-2. Deduction for contributions to individual retirement plans under the Economic Recovery Tax Act of 1981.—(a) *In general.*—Subject to the limitations and restrictions of paragraph (b) and the special rules of paragraph (c)(3) of this section, there shall be allowed a deduction under section 62 from gross income of amounts paid for the taxable year of an individual by or on behalf of such individual to an individual retirement plan. The deduction described in the preceding sentence shall be allowed only to the individual on whose behalf such individual retirement plan is maintained and only in the case of a contribution of cash. No deduction is allowable under this section for a contribution of property other than cash. In the case of a retirement bond, no deduction is allowed if the bond is redeemed within 12 months of its issue date.

(b) *Limitations and restrictions.*—(1) *Maximum deduction.*—The amount allowable as a deduction for contributions to an individual retirement plan to an individual for any taxable year cannot exceed the lesser of—

(i) $2,000, or

(ii) An amount equal to the compensation includible in the individual's gross income for the taxable year, reduced by the amount of the individual's qualified voluntary employee contributions for the taxable year.

(2) *Contributions after age 70 ½.*—No deduction is allowable for contributions to an individual retirement plan to an individual for the taxable year of the individual if he has attained the age of 70½ before the close of such taxable year.

(3) *Rollover contributions.*—No deduction is allowable under § 1.219(a)-2(a) for any taxable year of an individual with respect to a rollover contribution described in section 402(a)(5), 402(a)(7), 403(a)(4), 403(b)(8), 405(d)(3), 408(d)(3), or 409(b)(3)(C).

(4) *Amounts contributed under endowment contracts.*—(i) For any taxable year, no deduction is allowable under § 1.219(a)-2(a) for amounts paid under an endowment contract described in § 1.408-3(e) which is allowable under subdivision (ii) of this subparagraph to the cost of life insurance.

(ii) For any taxable year, the cost of current life insurance protection under an endowment contract described in paragraph (b)(4)(i) of this section is the product of the net premium cost, as determined by the Commissioner, and the excess, if any, of the death benefit payable under the contract during the policy year beginning in the taxable year over the cash value of the contract at the end of such policy year.

(c) *Special rules.*—(1) *Separate deduction for each individual.*—The maximum deduction allowable for contributions to an individual retirement plan is computed separately for each individual. Thus, if a husband and wife each has compensation of $15,000 for the taxable year, the maximum amount allowable as a deduction on their joint return is $4,000. See § 1.219(a)-3 for the maximum deduction for a spousal individual retirement plan when one spouse has no compensation.

(2) *Community property.*—Section 219 is to be applied without regard to any community property laws. Thus, if, for example, a husband and wife, live in a community property jurisdiction, the husband has compensation of $30,000 for the taxable year, and the wife has no compensation for the taxable year, then the maximum amount allowable as a deduction for contributions to an individual retirement plan, other than a spousal individual retirement plan, is $2,000.

(3) *Employer contributions.*—For purposes of this chapter, any amount paid by an employer to an individual retirement plan of an employee (other than a self-employed individual who is an employee within the meaning of section 401(c)(1)) constitutes the payment of compensation to the employee. The payment is includible in the employee's gross income, whether or not a deduction for such payment is allowable under section 219 to this employee. An employer will be entitled to a deduction for compensation paid to an employee for amounts the employer contributes on the employee's behalf to an individual retirement plan if such deduction is otherwise allowable under section 162. See § 1.404(h)-1 for certain limitations on this deduction in the case of employer contributions to a simplified employee pension.

(4) *Year of inclusion in income.*—Any amount paid by an employer to an individual retirement plan (including an individual retirement account or individual retirement annuity maintained as part of a simplified employee pension arrangement) shall be included in the gross income of the employee for the taxable year for which the contribution was made.

(5) *Time when contributions deemed made.*—A taxpayer shall be deemed to have made a contribution on the last day of the preceding taxable year if the contribution is made on account of the taxable year which includes such last day and is made not later than the time prescribed by law for filing the return for such taxable year (including extensions thereof). A contribution made not later than the time prescribed by law for filing the return for a taxable year (including extensions thereof) shall be treated as made on account of such taxable year if it is irrevocably specified in writing to the trustee, insurance company, or custodian that the amounts contributed are for such taxable year.

(d) *Excess contributions treated as contribution made during subsequent year for which there is an unused limitation.*—(1) *In general.*—This paragraph sets forth rules for the possible deduction of excess contributions made to an individual retirement plan for the taxable years following the taxable year of the excess contribution. If for a taxable year subsequent to the taxable year for which the excess contribution was made, the maximum amount allowable as a deduction for contributions to an individual retirement plan exceeds the amount contributed, then the taxpayer, whether or not a deduction is actually claimed, shall be treated as having made an additional contribution for the taxable year in an amount equal to the lesser of—

(i) The amount of such excess, or

(ii) The amount of the excess contributions for such taxable year (determined under section 4973(b)(2) without regard to subparagraph (C) thereof).

(2) *Amount contributed.*—For purposes of this paragraph, the amount contributed—

(i) Shall be determined without regard to this paragraph, and

(ii) Shall not include any rollover contribution.

(3) *Special rule where excess deduction was allowed for closed year.*—Proper reduction shall be made in the amount allowable as a

deduction by reason of this paragraph for any amount allowed as a deduction for contributions to an individual retirement plan for a prior taxable year for which the period for assessing a deficiency has expired if the amount so allowed exceeds the amount which should have been allowed for such prior taxable year.

(4) *Excise tax consequences.*—See section 4973 and the regulations thereunder for the excise tax applicable to excess contributions made to individual retirement plans.

(5) *Examples.*—The provisions of this paragraph may be illustrated by the following examples. (Assume in each example, unless otherwise stated, that T is less than age 70$\frac{1}{2}$ and is not married.)

Example (1). (i) T, a calendar-year taxpayer, earns $1,500 in compensation includible in gross income for 1982. On December 1, 1982, T establishes an individual retirement account (IRA) and contributes $2,000 to the account. T does not withdraw any money from the IRA after the initial contribution. Under section 219(b)(1), the maximum amount that T can deduct for 1982 is $1,500. T has an excess contribution for 1982 of $500.

(ii) For 1983, T has compensation includible in gross income of $12,000. T makes a $1,000 contribution to his IRA for 1983.

(iii) Although T made only a $1,000 contribution to his IRA for 1983, under the rules contained in this paragraph, T is treated as having made an additional contribution of $500 for 1983 and will be allowed to deduct $1,500 as his 1983 IRA contribution.

Example (2). (i) For 1982, the facts are the same as in *Example (1).*

(ii) For 1983, T has compensation includible in gross income of $12,000. T makes a $2,000 contribution to his IRA for 1983.

(iii) T will be allowed a $2,000 deduction for 1983 (the amount of his contribution). T will not be allowed a deduction for the $500 excess contribution made in 1982 because the maximum amount allowable for 1983 does not exceed the amount contributed.

Example (3). (i) For 1982, the facts are the same as in *Example (1).*

(ii) For 1983, T has compensation includible in gross income of $12,000. T makes a $1,800 contribution to his IRA for 1983.

(iii) For 1983, T will be allowed to deduct his contribution of $1,800 and $200 of the excess contribution made for 1982. He will not be allowed to deduct the remaining $300 of the excess contribution made for 1982 because his deduction for 1983 would then exceed $2,000, his allowable deduction for 1983.

(iv) For 1984, T has compensation includible in gross income of $15,000. T makes a $1,300 contribution to his IRA for 1984.

(v) T will be allowed to deduct both his $1,300 contribution for 1984 and the remaining $300 contribution made for 1982.

Example (4). (i) For 1982, the facts are the same as in *Example (1).*

(ii) For 1983, T has compensation includible in gross income of $12,000. T makes a $1,000 contribution to his IRA for 1983. T is allowed to deduct the $500 excess contribution for 1983 but fails to do so on his return. Consequently, T deducts only $1,000 for 1983.

(iii) Under no circumstances will T be allowed to deduct the $500 excess contribution made for 1982 for any taxable year after 1983 because T is treated as having made the contribution for 1983.

Example (5). (i) For 1982, the facts are the same as in *Example (1).*

(ii) For 1983, T has no compensation includible in gross income.

(iii) T will not be allowed to deduct for 1983 the $500 excess contribution for 1982 because the maximum amount allowable as a deduction under section 219(b)(1) is $0. [Reg. § 1.219(a)-2.]

§1.219(a)-3. Deduction for retirement savings for certain married individuals.—(a) *In general.*—Subject to the limitations and restrictions of paragraphs (c) and (d) and the special rules of paragraph (e) of this section, there shall be allowed a deduction under section 62 from gross income of amounts paid for the taxable year of an individual by or on behalf of such individual for the benefit of his spouse to an individual retirement plan. The amounts contributed to an individual retirement plan by or on behalf of an individual for the benefit of his spouse shall be deductible only by such individual and only in the case of a contribution of cash. No deduction is allowable under this section for a contribution of property other than cash. In the case of an individual retirement bond, no deduction is allowed if the bond is redeemed within 12 months of its issue date.

(b) *Definition of compensation.*—For purposes of this section, the term "compensation" has the meaning set forth in §1.219(a)-1(b)(3).

(c) *Maximum deduction.*—The amount allowable as a deduction under this section to an individual for any taxable year may not exceed the smallest of—

(1) $2,000,

(2) An amount equal to the compensation includible in the individual's gross income for the taxable year less the amount allowed as a deduction under section 219(a) (determined without regard to contributions to a simplified employee pension allowed under section 219(b)(2)), §1.219(a)-2 and §1.219(a)-5 for the taxable year, or

(3) $2,250 less the amount allowed as a deduction under section 219(a) (determined without regard to contributions to a simplified employee pension allowed under section 219(b)(2)), §1.219(a)-2 and §1.219(a)-5 for the taxable year.

(d) *Limitations and restrictions.*—(1) *Requirement to file joint return.*—No deduction is allowable under this section for a taxable year unless the individual and his spouse file a joint return under section 6013 for the taxable year.

(2) *Employed spouses.*—No deduction is allowable under this section if the spouse of the individual has any compensation for the taxable year of such spouse ending with or within the taxable year of the individual. For purposes of this subparagraph, compensation has the meaning set forth in §1.219(a)-1(b)(3), except that compensation shall include amounts excluded under section 911.

(3) *Contributions after age 70 1/2.*—No deduction is allowable under this section with respect to any payment which is made for a taxable year of an individual if the individual for whose benefit the individual retirement plan is maintained has attained age 70$\frac{1}{2}$ before the close of such taxable year.

(4) *Recontributed amounts.*—No deduction is allowable under this section for any taxable year of an individual with respect to a rollover contribution described in section 402(a)(5), 402(a)(7), 403(a)(4), 403(b)(8), 405(d)(3), 408(d)(3), or 409(b)(3)(C).

(5) *Amounts contributed under endowment contracts.*—The rules for endowment contracts under this section are the same as the provisions for such contracts under §1.219(a)-2(b)(4).

(e) *Special rules.*—(1) *Community property.*—This section is to be applied without regard to any community property laws.

(2) *Time when contributions deemed made.*—The time when contributions are deemed made is determined under section 219(f)(3). See §1.219(a)-2(c)(5). [Reg. §1.219(a)-3.]

§1.219(a)-4. Deduction for contributions to simplified employee pensions.—(a) *General rule.*—(1) *In general.*—Under section 219(b)(2), if an employer contribution is made on behalf of an employee to a simplified employee pension described in section 408(k), the limitations of this section, and not section 219(b)(1) and §1.219(a)-2, shall apply for purposes of computing the maximum allowable deduction with respect to that contribution for that individual employee.

(2) *Employer limitation.*—The maximum deduction under section 219(b)(2) for an employee with respect to an employer contribution to the employee's simplified employee pension under that employer's arrangement cannot exceed an amount equal to the lesser of—

(i) 15 percent of the employee's compensation from that employer (determined without regard to the employer contribution to the simplified employee pension) includible in the employee's gross income for the taxable year, or

(ii) The amount contributed by that employer to the employee's simplified employee pension and included in gross income (but not in excess of $15,000).

(3) *Special rules.*—(i) *Compensation.*—Compensation referred to in paragraph (a)(2)(i) has the same meaning as under §1.219(a)-1(b)(3) except that it includes only the compensation from the employer making the contribution to the simplified employee pension. Thus, if an individual earns $50,000 from employer A and $20,000 from employer B and employer B contributes $4,000 to a simplified employee pension on behalf of the individual, the maximum amount the individual will be able to deduct under section 219(b)(2) is 15 percent of $20,000, or $3,000.

(ii) *Special rule for officers, shareholders, and owner-employees.*—In the case of an employee who is an officer, shareholder, or owner-employee described in section 408(k)(3) with respect to a particular employer, the $15,000 amount referred to in paragraph (a)(2)(ii) shall be reduced by the amount of tax taken into account with respect to such individual under section 408(k)(3)(D).

(iii) *More than one employer arrangement.*—Except as provided in paragraph (c), below, the maximum deduction under paragraph (a)(2) for an individual who receives simplified employee pension contributions under two or more employers' simplified employee pension arrangements cannot exceed the sum of the maximum deduction limitations computed separately for that individual under each such employer's arrangement.

(iv) *Section 408 rules.*—Under section 408(j), the limitations under section 408(a)(1) and (b)(2)(B) (§1.408-2(b)(1) and §1.408-3(b)(2)), shall be applied separately with respect to each employer's contributions to an individual's simplified employee pension.

(4) *Additional deduction for individual retirement plan and qualified voluntary employee contribution.*—The deduction under this paragraph is in addition to any deduction allowed under section 219(a) to the individual for qualified retirement contributions.

(b) *Contributions to simplified employee pensions after age 70 1/2.*—The denial of deductions for contributions after age 70½ contained in section 219(d)(1) and §1.219(a)-2(b)(2) shall not apply with respect to employer contributions to a simplified employee pension.

(c) *Multiple employer, etc. limitations.*—(1) *Section 414(b), (c) and (m) employers.*—In the case of a controlled group of employers within the meaning of section 414(b) or (c) or employers aggregated under section 414(m), the maximum deduction limitation for an employee under paragraph (a)(2) shall be computed by treating such employers as one employer maintaining a single simplified employee pension arrangement and by treating the compensation of that employee from such employers as if from one employer. Thus, for example, for a particular employee the 15 percent limitation on compensation would be determined with regard to the compensation from all employers within such group. Further, the maximum deduction with respect to contributions made by employers included within such group could not exceed $15,000.

(2) *Self-employed individuals.*—In the case of an employee who is a self-employed individual within the meaning of section 401(c)(1) with respect to more than one trade or business, the maximum deduction limitation for such an employee under paragraph (a)(2) shall not exceed the lesser of the sum of such limitation applied

separately with respect to the simplified employee pension arrangement of each trade or business or such limitation determined by treating such trades or businesses as if they constituted a single employer.

(d) *Examples.*—The provisions of this section may be illustrated by the following examples:

Example (1). Corporation X is a calendar-year, cash basis taxpayer. It adopts a simplified employee pension agreement in 1982 and wishes to contribute the maximum amount on behalf of each employee for 1982. Individual E is a calendar-year taxpayer who is employed solely by Corporation X in 1982. Beginning in June, 1982, Corporation X pays $100 each month into a simplified employee pension maintained on behalf of E. X makes a total payment to E's simplified employee pension during the year of $700. E's other compensation from X for the year totals $15,000. The maximum amount which E will be allowed to deduct as a simplified employee pension contribution is 15% of $15,000, or $2,250. Therefore, X may make an additional contribution for 1982 to E's simplified employee pension in February of 1983. E's total compensation includible in gross income for 1982 is $15,000 + $2,250 or $17,250.

Example (2). (i) Corporation G is a calendar-year taxpayer which adopts a simplified employee pension agreement for 1982. It does not maintain an integrated plan as defined in section 408(k)(3)(E). It wishes to contribute 15% of compensation on behalf of each employee reduced by its tax under section 3111(a). The corporation has 4 employees, A, B, C, and D. D is a shareholder. The compensation for these employees for 1982 is as follows:

A = $10,000
B = 20,000
C = 30,000
D = 120,000

(ii) The amount of money which the corporation will be allowed to contribute on behalf of each employee under this allocation formula and the amount of the employer contribution each employee will be allowed to deduct is set forth in the following table:

Employee	Compensation	Lesser of $15,000 or 15% of Comp.	3111(a)[1] Tax	SEP Contribution[2]	Sec. 219(b)(2) deduction
A	$10,000	$1,500	$540.00	$960.00	$960.00
B	20,000	3,000	1,080.00	1,920.00	1,920.00
C	30,000	4,500	1,620.00	2,880.00	2,880.00
D	120,000	15,000	1,749.60	13,250.40	13,250.40

[1] The section 3111(a) tax is computed by multiplying compensation up to the taxable wage base ($32,400 for 1982) by the tax rate (5.40% for 1982).
[2] Simplified Employee Pension.

Example (3). Corporations A and B are calendar year taxpayers. Corporations A and B are not aggregated employers under section 414(b), (c) or (m). Individual M is employed full-time by Corporation A and part-time by Corporation B. Corporation A adopts a simplified employee pension agreement for calendar year 1982 and agrees to contribute 15% of compensation for each participant. M is a participant under Corporation A's simplified employee pension agreement and earns $15,000 for 1982 from Corporation A before A's contribution to his simplified employee pension. M also earns $5,000 as a part-time employee of Corporation B for 1982. Corporation A contributes $2,500 to M's simplified employee pension. The maximum amount that M will be allowed to deduct under section 219(b)(2) for 1982 is 15% of $15,000 or $2,250. In addition, M would be allowed to deduct the remaining $250 under section 219(a) for qualified retirement contributions.

Example (4). Individual P is employed by Corporation H and Corporation O. Corporations H and O are not aggregated employers under section 414(b), (c) or (m). Both Corporation H and Corporation O maintain a simplified employee pension arrangement and contribute 15 percent of compensation on behalf of each employee, up to a maximum of 5,000. P earns $100,000 from Corporation H and $120,000 from Corporation O. Corporation H and O each contribute $15,000 under its simplified employee pension arrangement to an individual retirement account maintained on behalf of P. P will be allowed to deduct $30,000 for employer contributions to simplified employee pensions because each employer has a simplified employee pension arrangement and the SEP contributions by Corporation H and O do not exceed the applicable $15,000-15 percent limitation with respect to compensation received from each employer. In addition, P would be allowed to deduct $2,000 under section 219(a) for qualified retirement contributions. [Reg. §1.219(a)-4.]

§1.219(a)-5. Deduction for employee contributions to employer plans.—(a) *Deduction allowed.*—In the case of an individual, there is allowed as a deduction amounts contributed in cash to a qualified employer plan or government plan (as defined, respectively, in paragraphs (b)(7) and (b)(8) of §1.219(a)-1) and designated as qualified voluntary employee contributions. If an employee transfers an

amount of cash from one account in a plan to the qualified voluntary employee contribution account, such transfer is a distribution for purposes of sections 72, 402 and 403, and the amounts are considered recontributed as qualified voluntary employee contributions. No deduction will be allowed for a contribution of property other than cash.

(b) *Limitations.*—(1) *Maximum amount of deduction.*—The amount allowable as a deduction under paragraph (a) to any individual for any taxable year shall not exceed the lesser of $2,000 or an amount equal to the compensation (from the employer who maintains the plan) includible in the individual's gross income for such taxable year.

(2) *Contributions after age 70 1/2.*—No deduction is allowable for contributions under paragraph (a) to an individual for the taxable year of the individual if he has attained the age of 70½ before the close of such taxable year.

(3) *Rollover contributions.*—No deduction is allowable under paragraph (a) for any taxable year of an individual with respect to a rollover contribution described in section 402(a)(5), 402(a)(7), 403(a)(4), 403(b)(8), 405(d)(3), 408(d)(3), or 409(b)(3)(C).

(c) *Rules for plans accepting qualified voluntary employee contributions.*—(1) *Plan provision, etc.*—(i) No plan may receive qualified voluntary employee contributions unless the plan document provides for acceptance of voluntary contributions. No plan may receive qualified voluntary employee contributions unless either the plan document provides for acceptance of qualified voluntary employee contributions or the employer or the plan administrator manifests an intent to accept such contributions. Such intention must be communicated to the employees. Any manner of communication that satisfies §1.7476-2(c)(1) shall satisfy the requirements of this subparagraph.

(ii) If the plan document provides for the acceptance of voluntary contributions, but does not specifically provide for acceptance of qualified voluntary employee contributions, the plan qualification limitation on voluntary contributions (the limit of 10 percent of the employee's cumulative compensation less prior voluntary contributions) would apply to both qualified voluntary employee contributions and other voluntary contributions. On the other hand, if the plan document provides for acceptance of both qualified voluntary employee contributions and other voluntary contributions, the plan qualification limitation on voluntary contributions would apply only to the contributions other than the qualified voluntary employee contributions.

(2) *Plans accepting only qualified voluntary employee contributions.*—A qualified pension plan or stock bonus plan may be established that provides only for qualified voluntary employee contributions. Similarly, a government plan may be established that provides only for qualified voluntary employee contributions. A plan that provides only for qualified voluntary employee contributions would not satisfy the qualification requirements for a profit-sharing plan.

(3) *Recordkeeping provisions.*—Separate accounting for qualified voluntary employee contributions that are deductible under this section is not required as a condition for receiving qualified voluntary employee contributions. However, failure to properly account for such contributions may result in adverse tax consequences to employees upon subsequent plan distributions and reporting and recordkeeping penalties for employers. See section 72(o) for rules for accounting for such contributions.

(4) *Status as employee.*—An amount will not be considered as a qualified voluntary employee contribution on behalf of an individual unless the individual is an employee of the employer at some time during the calendar year for which the voluntary contribution is made. See section 415(c) concerning the effect of a nondeductible voluntary employee contribution on plan qualification.

(5) *Contribution before receipt of compensation.*—A plan may allow an individual to make a qualified voluntary employee contribution greater than the amount he has received in compensation from the employer at the time the contribution is made. However, see paragraph (f) of this section.

(d) *Designations, procedures, etc.*—(1) *Plan procedures.*—(i) A plan which accepts qualified voluntary employee contributions may adopt procedures by which an employee can designate the character of the employee's voluntary contributions as either qualified voluntary employee contributions or other employee contributions. Such procedures may, but need not, be in the plan document.

(ii) In the absence of such plan procedures, all voluntary employee contributions shall be deemed to be qualified voluntary employee contributions unless the employee notifies the employer that the contributions are not qualified voluntary employee contributions. Such notification must be received by April 15 following the calendar year for which such contributions were made. If such notification is not received, contributions are deemed to be qualified voluntary employee contributions for the prior year.

(2) *Characterization procedures, etc.*—(i) The plan procedures may allow an employee to elect whether or not an employee contribution is to be treated as a qualified voluntary employee contribution or as other voluntary contributions. This election can be required either prior to or after the contribution is made. If a contribution may be treated under such procedures as a qualified voluntary employee contribution or other voluntary contribution for a calendar year and the employee has not by April 15 of the subsequent calendar year designated the character of the contribution, the contribution must be treated as a qualified voluntary employee contribution for the calendar year. An employer may allow the election to be irrevocable or revocable. A procedure allowing revocable elections may limit the time within which an election may be revoked. The revocation of an election after April 15 following the calendar year for which the contribution was made is deemed to be ineffective in changing the character of employee contributions.

(ii) For purposes of this section, if the plan procedures allow employees to make contributions on account of the immediately preceding calendar year, a taxpayer shall be deemed to have made a qualified voluntary employee contribution to such plan on the last day of the preceding calendar year if the contribution is on account of such year and is made by April 15 of the calendar year or such earlier time as provided by the plan procedure.

(e) *Nondiscrimination requirements.*—(1) *General rule.*—Plans subject to the nondiscrimination requirements of section 401(a)(4) which accept qualified voluntary employee contributions must permit such contributions in a nondiscriminatory manner in order to satisfy section 401(a)(4). If a plan permits participants to make qualified voluntary employee contributions, the opportunity to make such contributions must be reasonably available to a nondiscriminatory group of employees. The availability standard will be satisfied if a nondiscriminatory group of employees is eligible to make qualified voluntary employee contributions under the terms of the plan and if a nondiscriminatory group of employees actually has the opportu-

nity to make qualified voluntary employee contributions when plan restrictions are taken into account.

(2) *Eligible employees.*—A nondiscriminatory group of employees is eligible to make qualified voluntary employee contribution under the terms of the plan if the group either meets the percentage requirements of section 410(b)(1)(A) or comprises a classification of employees that does not discriminate in favor of employees who are officers, shareholders, or highly compensated, as provided in section 410(b)(1)(B).

(3) *Plan restrictions.*—In some cases, an employee may not be permitted to make qualified voluntary employee contributions until a plan restriction (such as making a certain level of mandatory employee contributions) is satisfied. In this case, it is necessary to determine whether a nondiscriminatory group of employees actually has the opportunity to make qualified voluntary employee contributions. For this purpose, only employees who have satisfied the plan restriction will be considered to have the opportunity to make deductible contributions. Thus, for example, if a plan requires an employee to make mandatory contributions of 6 percent of compensation in order to make qualified voluntary employee contributions and if only a small percentage of employees make the 6 percent mandatory contributions, then the group of employees who have the opportunity to make qualified voluntary employee contributions may not satisfy either test under section 410(b). A similar rule is applicable to integrated plans: employees who are not permitted to make qualified voluntary employee contributions to such a plan because they earn less than the integration level amount will be considered as employees who do not have the opportunity to make qualified voluntary employee contributions.

(4) *Permissible contributions.*—If the availability standards are met, and if the qualified voluntary employee contributions permitted are not higher, as a percentage of compensation, for officers, shareholders or highly compensated employees than for other participants, the qualified voluntary employee contribution feature will meet the requirement that contributions or benefits not discriminate in favor of employees who are officers, shareholders, or highly compensated. This is so because the contributions are made by the employee, not the employer.

(5) *Acceptable contributions.*—A plan may accept qualified voluntary employee contributions in an amount less than the maximum deduction allowable to an individual.

(f) *Excess qualified voluntary employee contributions.*—Voluntary employee contributions which exceed the amount allowable as a deduction under paragraph (b) of this section will be treated as nondeductible voluntary employee contributions to the plan. See § 1.415-6(b)(8).

(g) *Reports.*—(1) *Requirements.*—Each employer who maintains a plan which accepts qualified voluntary employee contributions must furnish to each employee—

(i) A report showing the amount of qualified voluntary employee contributions the employee made for the calendar year, and

(ii) A report showing the amount of withdrawals made by the employee of qualified voluntary employee contributions during the calendar year.

(2) *Times.*—(i) The report required by paragraph (g)(1)(i) of this section must be furnished by the later of January 31 following the year for which the contribution was made or the time the contribution is made.

(ii) The report required by paragraph (g)(1)(ii) of this section must be furnished by January 31 following the year of withdrawal.

(3) *Authority for additional reports.*—The Commissioner may require additional reports to be given to individuals or to be filed with the Service. Such reports shall be furnished at the time and in the manner that the Commissioner specifies.

(4) *Authority to modify reporting requirements.*—The Commissioner may, in his discretion, modify the reporting requirements of this paragraph. Such modification may include: the matters to be reported, the forms to be used for the reports, the time when the reports must be filed or furnished, who must receive the reports, the substitution of the plan administrator for the employer as the person required to file or furnish the reports, and the deletion of some or all of the reporting requirements. The Commissioner may, in his discretion, relieve employers from making the reports required by section 219(f)(4) and this paragraph (g). This discretion includes the ability to relieve categories of employers (but not individual employers) from furnishing or filing any report required by section 219(f)(4) and this paragraph (g).

(5) *Effective date.*—This paragraph shall apply to reports for calendar years after 1982. [Reg. § 1.219(a)-5.]

§1.219(a)-6. Alternative deduction for divorced individuals.—(a) *In general.*—a divorced individual may use the provisions of this section rather than §1.219(a)-2 in computing the maximum amount he may deduct as a contribution to an individual retirement plan. A divorced individual is not required to use the provisions of this section; he may use the provisions of §1.219(a)-2 in computing the maximum amount he may deduct as a contribution to an individual retirement plan.

(b) *Individuals who may use this section.*—An individual may compute the deduction for a contribution to an individual retirement plan under this section if—

(1) An individual retirement plan was established for the benefit of the individual at least five years before the beginning of the calendar year in which the decree of divorce or spearate maintenance was issued, and

(2) For at least three of the former spouse's most recent five taxable years ending before the taxable year in which the decree was issued, such former spouse was allowed a deduction under section 219(c) (or the corresponding provisions of prior law) for contributions to such individual retirement plan.

(c) *Limitations.*—(1) *Amount of deduction.*—An individual who computes his deduction for contributions to an individual retirement plan under this section may deduct the smallest of—

(i) The amount contributed to the individual retirement plan for the taxable year,

(ii) $1,125, or

(iii) The sum of the amount of compensation includible in the individual's gross income for the taxable year and any qualifying alimony received by the individual during the taxable year.

(2) *Contributions after age 70 1/2.*—No deduction is allowable for contributions to an individual retirement plan to an individual for the taxable year of the individual if he has attained the age of 70 1/2 before the close of such taxable year.

(3) *Rollover contributions.*—No deduction is allowable under this section for any taxable year of an individual with respect to a rollover contribution described in section 402(a)(5), 402(a)(7), 403(a)(4), 403(b)(8), 405(d)(3), 408(d)(3), or 409(b)(3)(C).

(d) *Qualifying alimony.*—For purposes of this section, the term "qualifying alimony" means amounts includible in the individual's gross income under section 71(a)(1) (relating to a decree of divorce or separate maintenance). [Reg. § 1.219(a)-6.]

* * *

IRAs: SEPs: Married Individuals

Individual Retirement Plans: Simplified Employee Pensions.—Reproduced below is the text of proposed Reg. §1.220-1, relating to individual retirement plans and simplified employee pensions (published in the Federal Register on July 14, 1981).

§1.220-1. Deduction for retirement savings for certain married individuals.—(a) *In general.*—Subject to the limitations and restrictions of paragraphs (c), (d) and (e) and the special rules of paragraph (f) of this section, there shall be allowed a deduction under section 62 from gross income of amounts paid for the taxable year of an individual by or on behalf of such individual for the benefit of himself and his spouse to an individual retirement account described in section 408(a), for an individual retirement annuity described in section 408(b), or for an individual retirement bond described in section 409. The amounts contributed to an individual retirement account, for an individual retirement annuity, or for an individual retirement bond by or on behalf of an individual for the benefit of himself and his spouse shall be deductible only by such individual. The first sentence of this paragraph shall apply only in the case of a contribution of cash; a contribution of property other than cash is not allowable as a deduction. In the case of an individual retirement bond, a deduction will not be allowed if the bond is redeemed within 12 months of its issue date.

(b) *Definitions.*—(1) *Compensation.*—For purposes of this section, the term "compensation" has the meaning set forth in §1.219-1(c)(1).

(2) *Active participant.*—For purposes of this section, the term "active participant" has the meaning set forth in §1.219-2.

(3) *Individual retirement subaccount.*—For purposes of this section, the term individual retirement subaccount is that part of an individual retirement account maintained for the exclusive benefit of the individual or the individual's spouse and which meets the following requirements:

(i) The individual or spouse for whom the subaccount is maintained has exclusive control over the subaccount after deposits have been made,

(ii) The subaccount, by itself, meets the requirements of section 408(a), except that it is not a separate trust,

(iii) The trustee or custodian maintains records indicating the ownership of the funds, and

(iv) The individual and spouse do not jointly own the individual retirement account of which the subaccount is a part.

(c) *Types of funding arrangements permitted.*—The deduction under paragraph (a) of this section shall be allowed only if one of the following types of funding arrangements is used:

(1) A separate individual retirement account, individual retirement annuity, or individual retirement bond is established or purchased for the benefit of the individual and a separate individual retirement account, individual retirement annuity or individual retirement bond is established or purchased for the individual's spouse.

(2) A single individual retirement account described in section 408 (a) is established or purchased and such account has an individual retirement subaccount for the benefit of the individual and an individual retirement subaccount for the benefit of the spouse. The single individual retirement account cannot be owned jointly by the husband and wife.

(3) An individual retirement account described in section 408(c) is maintained by an employer or employee association and such account has arrangements described in subparagraphs (1) or (2).

(d) *Maximum deduction.*—The amount allowable as a deduction under section 220(a) to an individual for any taxable year may not exceed—

(1) Twice the amount paid (including prior excess contributions) to the account, subaccount, annuity, or for the bond, established for the individual or for the spouse to or for which the lesser amount was paid for the taxable year,

(2) An amount equal to 15 percent of the compensation includible in the individual's gross income for the taxable year, or

(3) $1,750 whichever is the smallest amount.

(e) *Limitations and restrictions.*—(1) *Alternative deduction.*—No deduction is allowable under section 220(a) for the taxable year if the individual claims the deduction allowed by section 219(a) for the taxable year.

(2) *Individual or spouse covered by certain other plans.*—No deduction is allowable under section 220(a) to an individual for the taxable year if for any part of such year—

(i) He or his spouse was an active participant (as defined in §1.219-2), or

(ii) Amounts were contributed by his employer, or his spouse's employer, on the individual's or spouse's behalf for an annuity contract described in section 403(b) (whether or not his, or his spouse's, rights in such contract are nonforfeitable).

(3) *Contributions after age 70 1/2.*—No deduction is allowable under section 220(a) with respect to any payment which is made for a taxable year of an individual if either the individual or his spouse has attained age 70 1/2 before the close of such taxable year.

(4) *Recontributed amounts.*—No deduction is allowable under section 220(a) for any taxable year of an individual with respect to a rollover contribution described in section 402(a)(5), 402(a)(7), 403(a)(4), 403(b)(8), 408(d)(3), or 409(b)(3)(C).

(5) *Amounts contributed under endowment contracts.*—The rules for endowment contracts under section 220 are the same as the provisions for such contracts under §1.219-1(b)(3).

(6) *Employed spouses.*—No deduction is allowable under section 220(a) if the spouse of the individual has any compensation (as defined in §1.219-1(c)(1) determined without regard to section 911) for the taxable year of such spouse ending with or within the taxable year of the individual.

(f) *Special rules.*—(1) *Community property.*—Section 220 is to be applied without regard to any community property laws.

(2) *Time when contributions deemed made.*—The time when contributions are deemed made is determined in the same manner as under section 219(c)(3). See §1.219-1(d).

(g) *Excess contributions treated as contribution made during subsequent year for which there is an unused limitation.*—(1) *In general.*—If for the taxable year the maximum amount allowable as a deduction under this section exceeds the amount contributed, then the taxpayer, whether or not a deduction is actually claimed, shall be treated as having made an additional contribution for the taxable year in an amount equal to the lesser of—

(i) The amount of such excess, or

(ii) The amount of the excess contributions for such taxable year (determined under section 4973(b)(2) without regard to subparagraph (C) thereof).

For purposes of computing the maximum deduction under section 220(b)(1), the excess contribution for a previous year shall be treated as made for the current year.

(2) *Amount contributed.*—For purposes of this paragraph, the amount contributed—

(i) Shall be determined without regard to this paragraph, and

(ii) Shall not include any rollover contribution.

(3) *Special rule where excess contribution was allowed for closed year.*—Proper reduction shall be made in the amount allowable as a deduction by reason of this paragraph for any amount allowed as a deduction under this section or section 219 for a prior taxable year for which the period for assessing a deficiency has expired if the amount so allowed exceeds the amount which should have been allowed for such prior taxable year.

(4) *Examples.*—The provisions of this paragraph may be illustrated by the following examples:

Example (1). (i) H, a calendar-year taxpayer, earns $10,000 in compensation includible in gross income for 1979. H is married to W, also a calendar-year taxpayer, who has no compensation for 1979. For 1979, neither H nor W is covered by certain other plans within the meaning of section 220(b)(3). On November 24, 1979, H establishes an individual retirement account (IRA) for himself and an individual retirement account for W. H contributes $850 to each account. Neither H nor W withdraws any money from either account after the initial contribution. Under section 220(b)(1) the maximum amount that H can deduct for 1979 is 15 percent of the compensation includible in his gross income or $1,500. H has made an excess contribution of $200 for 1979.

(ii) For 1980, H has compensation includible in gross income of $12,000. W has no compensation for 1980. For 1980, neither H nor

W is covered by certain other plans within the meaning of section 220(b)(3). No contributions are made to the IRA of H or W for 1980.

(iii) Although H made no contributions to either his or W's IRA for 1980, under the rules contained in this paragraph, H is treated as having made an additional contribution of $100 to his IRA and $100 to W's IRA for 1980 and will be allowed to deduct $200 as his 1980 IRA contribution.

Example (2). (i) For 1979, the facts are the same as in *Example (1).*

(ii) For 1980, H has compensation of $15,000 includible in gross income and is not covered by any other plans within the meaning of section 219(b)(2). W also goes to work in 1980 and has compensation of $6,000, but is not covered by certain other plans within the meaning of section 219(b)(2). H will not be treated as having made a deductible contribution of a previous year's excess contribution within the meaning of section 220(c)(6) because W has compensation for 1980. However, both H and W now meet the deduction standards of section 219 and each will be treated as having made a deductible contribution of $100 to their separate IRA's for 1980 under section 219(c)(5).

Example (3). (i) For 1979, the facts are the same as in *Example (1).*

(ii) For 1980, H has compensation of $15,000 includible in gross income and is covered by certain other plans within the meaning of section 220(b)(3). W has no compensation for 1980 and is not covered by certain other plans within the meaning of section 220(b)(3). H will not be treated as having made a deductible contribution of a previous year's excess contribution within the meaning of section 219(c)(5) or 220(c)(6) because H is covered by other plans for 1980 and has no allowable deduction under section 219 or 220.

(iii) W will not be treated as having made a deductible contribution of a previous year's excess contribution within the meaning of section 219(c)(5) because W has no compensation for 1980 and thus no allowable deduction under section 219.

(h) *Effective date.*—(1) This section is effective for taxable years beginning after December 31, 1976.

(2) If, but for this subparagraph, an amount would be allowable as a deduction by reason of section 220(c)(6) and paragraph (g) for a taxable year beginning before January 1, 1978, such amount shall be allowable only for the taxpayer's first taxable year beginning in 1978. [Reg. § 1.220-1]

Foreign Corporations: Limitation on Deduction for Dividends

Foreign Corporations: Limitation on Deduction for Dividends.—Reg. §§ 1.245A-1—1.245A-5, limiting the dividends received deduction available for certain dividends received from current or former controlled foreign corporations, are proposed (published in the Federal Register on June 18, 2019) (corrected August 8, 2019) (REG-106282-18).

Par. 2. Add and reserve §§ 1.245A-1 through 1.245A-4 and add § 1.245A-5 to read as follows:

§ 1.245A-1. [Reserved].

§ 1.245A-2. [Reserved].

§ 1.245A-3. [Reserved].

§ 1.245A-4. [Reserved].

§ 1.245A-5. Limitation of section 245A deduction and section 954(c)(6) exception.—[The text of proposed § 1.245A-5 is the same as the text of § 1.245A-5T as added by T.D. 9865].

GILTI: Hybrid Arrangements: Allocation of Deductions

GILTI: Hybrid Arrangements: Allocation of Deductions.—Amendments to Reg. § 1.245A(e)-1, adjusting hybrid deduction accounts to take into account earnings and profits of a controlled foreign corporation that are included in income by a United States shareholder, are proposed (published in the Federal Register on April 8, 2020) (REG-106013-19).

Par. 2. Section 1.245A(e)-1 is amended by:

1. Adding paragraphs (d)(4)(i)(B) and (d)(4)(ii).
2. Adding a sentence at the end of the introductory text of paragraph (g).
3. Adding paragraphs (g)(1)(v) and (h)(2).

The additions read as follows:

§ 1.245A(e)-1. Special rules for hybrid dividends.

* * *

(d) * * *

(4) * * *

(i) * * *

(B) Second, the account is decreased (but not below zero) pursuant to the rules of paragraphs (d)(4)(i)(B)(*1*) through (3) of this section, in the order set forth in this paragraph (d)(4)(i)(B).

(*1*) *Adjusted subpart F inclusions.*—(i) *In general.*—Subject to the limitation in paragraph (d)(4)(i)(B)(*1*)(*ii*) of this section, the account is reduced by an adjusted subpart F inclusion with respect to

the share for the taxable year, as determined pursuant to the rules of paragraph (d)(4)(ii) of this section.

(*ii*) *Limitation.*—The reduction pursuant to paragraph (d)(4)(i)(B)(*1*)(*i*) of this section cannot exceed the hybrid deductions of the CFC allocated to the share for the taxable year multiplied by a fraction, the numerator of which is the subpart F income of the CFC for the taxable year and the denominator of which is the taxable income (as determined under § 1.952-2(b)) of the CFC for the taxable year. However, if the denominator of the fraction would be zero or less, then the fraction is considered to be zero.

(*iii*) *Special rule allocating reductions across accounts in certain cases.*—This paragraph (d)(4)(i)(B)(*1*)(*iii*) applies after each of the specified owner's hybrid deduction accounts with respect to its shares of stock of the CFC are adjusted pursuant to paragraph (d)(4)(i)(B)(1)(i) of this section but before the accounts are adjusted pursuant to paragraph (d)(4)(i)(B)(2) of this section, to the extent that one or more of the hybrid deduction accounts would have been reduced by an amount pursuant to paragraph (d)(4)(i)(B)(1)(i) of this section but for the limitation in paragraph (d)(4)(i)(B)(1)(ii) of this section (the aggregate of the amounts that would have been reduced but for the limitation, the *excess amount*, and the accounts that would have been reduced by the excess amount, the *excess amount accounts*). When this paragraph (d)(4)(i)(B)(1)(iii) applies, the specified owner's hybrid deduction accounts other than the excess amount accounts (if any) are ratably reduced by the lesser of the excess amount and the difference of the following two amounts: the hybrid deductions of the CFC allocated to the specified owner's shares of stock of the CFC for the taxable year multiplied by the fraction described in paragraph (d)(4)(i)(B)(1)(ii) of this section; and the reductions pursuant to paragraph (d)(4)(i)(B)(1)(i) of this section with respect to the specified owner's shares of stock of the CFC.

(2) *Adjusted GILTI inclusions.*—(i) *In general.*—Subject to the limitation in paragraph (d)(4)(i)(B)(2)(ii) of this section, the account is reduced by an adjusted GILTI inclusion with respect to the share for the taxable year, as determined pursuant to the rules of paragraph (d)(4)(ii) of this section.

(ii) *Limitation.*—The reduction pursuant to paragraph (d)(4)(i)(B)(2)(i) of this section cannot exceed the hybrid deductions of the CFC allocated to the share for the taxable year multiplied by a fraction, the numerator of which is the tested income of the CFC for the taxable year and the denominator of which is the taxable income (as determined under §1.952-2(b)) of the CFC for the taxable year. However, if the denominator of the fraction would be zero or less, then the fraction is considered to be zero.

(iii) *Special rule allocating reductions across accounts in certain cases.*—This paragraph (d)(4)(i)(B)(2)(iii) applies after each of the specified owner's hybrid deduction accounts with respect to its shares of stock of the CFC are adjusted pursuant to paragraph (d)(4)(i)(B)(2)(i) of this section but before the accounts are adjusted pursuant to paragraph (d)(4)(i)(B)(3) of this section, to the extent that one or more of the hybrid deduction accounts would have been reduced by an amount pursuant to paragraph (d)(4)(i)(B)(2)(i) of this section but for the limitation in paragraph (d)(4)(i)(B)(2)(ii) of this section (the aggregate of the amounts that would have been reduced but for the limitation, the *excess amount*, and the accounts that would have been reduced by the excess amount, the *excess amount accounts*). When this paragraph (d)(4)(i)(B)(2)(iii) applies, the specified owner's hybrid deduction accounts other than the excess amount accounts (if any) are ratably reduced by the lesser of the excess amount and the difference of the following two amounts: the hybrid deductions of the CFC allocated to the specified owner's shares of stock of the CFC for the taxable year multiplied by the fraction described in paragraph (d)(4)(i)(B)(2)(ii) of this section; and the reductions pursuant to paragraph (d)(4)(i)(B)(2)(i) of this section with respect to the specified owner's shares of stock of the CFC.

(3) *Certain section 956 inclusions.*—The account is reduced by an amount included in the gross income of a domestic corporation under sections 951(a)(1)(B) and 956 with respect to the share for the taxable year of the domestic corporation in which or with which the CFC's taxable year ends, to the extent so included by reason of the application of section 245A(e) and this section to the hypothetical distribution described in §1.956-1(a)(2).

* * *

(ii) *Rules regarding adjusted subpart F and GILTI inclusions.*—(A) The term *adjusted subpart F inclusion* means, with respect to a share of stock of a CFC for a taxable year of the CFC, a domestic corporation's pro rata share of the CFC's subpart F income included in gross income under section 951(a)(1)(A) for the taxable year of the domestic corporation in which or with which the CFC's taxable year ends, to the extent attributable to the share (as determined under the principles of section 951(a)(2) and §1.951-1(b) and (e)), adjusted by—

(1) Adding to the amount the associated foreign income taxes with respect to the amount; and

(2) Subtracting from such sum the quotient of the associated foreign income taxes divided by the percentage described in section 11(b).

(B) The term *adjusted GILTI inclusion* means, with respect to a share of stock of a CFC for a taxable year of the CFC, a domestic corporation's GILTI inclusion amount (within the meaning of §1.951A-1(c)(1)) for the U.S. shareholder inclusion year (within the meaning of §1.951A-1(f)(7)), to the extent attributable to the share (as determined under paragraph (d)(4)(ii)(C) of this section), adjusted by—

(1) Adding to the amount the associated foreign income taxes with respect to the amount;

(2) Multiplying such sum by the difference of 100 percent and the percentage described in section 250(a)(1)(B); and

(3) Subtracting from such product the quotient of 80 percent of the associated foreign income taxes divided by the percentage described in section 11(b).

(C) A domestic corporation's GILTI inclusion amount for a U.S. shareholder inclusion year is attributable to a share of stock of the CFC based on a fraction—

(1) The numerator of which is the domestic corporation's pro rata share of the tested income of the CFC for the U.S. shareholder inclusion year, to the extent attributable to the share (as determined under the principles of §1.951A-1(d)(2)); and

(2) The denominator of which is the aggregate of the domestic corporation's pro rata share of the tested income of each tested income CFC (as defined in §1.951A-2(b)(1)) for the U.S. shareholder inclusion year.

(D) The term *associated foreign income taxes* means—

(1) With respect to a domestic corporation's pro rata share of the subpart F income of the CFC included in gross income under section 951(a)(1)(A) and attributable to a share of stock of a CFC for a taxable year of the CFC, current year tax (as described in §1.960-1(b)(4)) allocated and apportioned under §1.960-1(d)(3)(ii) to the subpart F income groups (as described in §1.960-1(b)(30)) of the CFC for the taxable year, to the extent allocated to the share under paragraph (d)(4)(ii)(E) of this section; and

(2) With respect to a domestic corporation's GILTI inclusion amount under section 951A attributable to a share of stock of a CFC for a taxable year of the CFC, current year tax (as described in §1.960-1(b)(4)) allocated and apportioned under §1.960-1(d)(3)(ii) to the tested income groups (as described in §1.960-1(b)(33)) of the CFC for the taxable year, to the extent allocated to the share under paragraph (d)(4)(ii)(F) of this section, multiplied by the domestic corporation's inclusion percentage (as described in §1.960-2(c)(2)).

(E) Current year tax allocated and apportioned to a subpart F income group of a CFC for a taxable year is allocated to a share of stock of the CFC by multiplying the foreign income tax by a fraction—

(1) The numerator of which is the domestic corporation's pro rata share of the subpart F income of the CFC for the taxable year, to the extent attributable to the share (as determined under the principles of section 951(a)(2) and §1.951-1(b) and (e)); and

(2) The denominator of which is the subpart F income of the CFC for the taxable year.

(F) Current year tax allocated and apportioned to a tested income group of a CFC for a taxable year is allocated to a share of stock of the CFC by multiplying the foreign income tax by a fraction—

(1) The numerator of which is the domestic corporation's pro rata share of tested income of the CFC for the taxable year, to the extent attributable to the share (as determined under the principles §1.951A-1(d)(2)); and

(2) The denominator of which is the tested income of the CFC for the taxable year.

* * *

(g) * * * No amounts are included in the gross income of US1 under sections 951(a)(1)(A), 951A(a), or 951(a)(1)(B) and 956.

(1) * * *

(v) *Alternative facts – account reduced by adjusted GILTI inclusion.* The facts are the same as in paragraph (g)(1)(i) of this section, except that for taxable year 1 FX has $130x of gross tested income and $10.5x of current year tax (as described in §1.960-1(b)(4)) that is allocated and apportioned under §1.960-1(d)(3)(ii) to the tested income groups of FX. In addition, FX has $119.5x of tested income ($130x of gross tested income, less the $10.5x of current year tax deductions properly allocable to the gross tested income). Further, of US1's pro rata share of the tested income ($119.5x), $80x is attributable to Share A and $39.5x is attributable to Share B (as determined under the principles of §1.951A-1(d)(2)). Moreover, US1's net deemed tangible income return (as defined in §1.951A-1(c)(3)) for taxable year 1 is $71.7x, and US1 does not own any stock of a CFC other than its stock of FX. Thus, US1's GILTI inclusion amount (within the meaning of §1.951A-1(c)(1)) for taxable year 1, the U.S. shareholder inclusion year, is $47.8x (net CFC tested income of $119.5x, less net deemed tangible income return of $71.7x) and US1's inclusion percentage (as described in §1.960-2(c)(2)) is 40 ($47.8x/$119.5x). At the end of year 1, US1's hybrid deduction account with respect to Share A is: first, increased by $80x (the amount of hybrid deductions allocated to Share A); and second, decreased by $10x (the sum of the adjusted GILTI inclusion with respect to Share A, and the adjusted GILTI inclusion with respect to Share B that is allocated to the hybrid deduction account with respect to Share A) to $70x. *See* paragraphs (d)(4)(i)(A) and (B) of this section. In year 2, the entire $30x of each dividend received by US1 from FX during year 2 is a hybrid dividend, because the sum of US1's hybrid deduction accounts with respect to each of its shares of FX stock at the end of year 2 ($70x) is at least equal to the amount of the dividends ($60x). *See* paragraph (b)(2) of this section. At the end of year 1, US1's hybrid deduction account with respect to Share A is decreased by $60x (the amount of the hybrid deductions in the account that give rise to a hybrid dividend or tiered hybrid dividend during year 1) to $10x. *See* paragraph (d)(4)(i)(C) of this section. Paragraphs (g)(1)(v)(A) through (C) of this section describe the computations pursuant to paragraph (d)(4)(i)(B)(2) of this section.

(A) To determine the adjusted GILTI inclusion with respect to Share A for taxable year 1, it must be determined to what extent US1's $47.8x GILTI inclusion amount is attributable to Share A. *See* paragraph (d)(4)(ii)(B) of this section. Here, $32x of the inclusion is attributable to Share A, calculated as $47.8x multiplied by a fraction, the numerator of which is $80x (US1's pro rata share of the tested income of FX attributable to Share A) and denominator of which is $119.5x (US1's pro rata share of the tested income of FX, its only CFC). *See* paragraph (d)(4)(ii)(C) of this section. Next, the associated foreign income taxes with respect to the $32x GILTI inclusion amount attributable to Share A must be determined. *See* paragraphs (d)(4)(ii)(B) and (D) of this section. Such associated foreign income taxes are $2.8x, calculated as $10.5x (the current year tax allocated and apportioned to the tested income groups of FX) multiplied by a fraction, the numerator of which is $80x (US1's pro rata share of the tested income of FX attributable to Share A) and the denominator of which is $119.5x (the tested income of FX), multiplied by 40% (US1's inclusion percentage). *See* paragraphs (d)(4)(ii)(D) and (F) of this section. Thus, pursuant to paragraph (d)(4)(ii)(B) of this section, the adjusted GILTI inclusion with respect to Share A is $6.7x, computed by—

(1) Adding $2.8x (the associated foreign income taxes with respect to the $32x GILTI inclusion attributable to Share A) to $32x, which is $34.8x;

(2) Multiplying $34.8x (the sum of the amounts in paragraph (g)(1)(v)(A)(1) of this section) by 50% (the difference of 100 percent and the percentage described in section 250(a)(1)(B)), which is $17.4x; and

(3) Subtracting $10.7x (calculated as $2.24x (80% of the $2.8x of associated foreign income taxes) divided by .21 (the percentage described in section 11(b)) from $17.4x (the product of the amounts in paragraph (g)(1)(v)(A)(2) of this section), which is $6.7x.

(B) Pursuant to computations similar to those discussed in paragraph (g)(1)(v)(A) of this section, the adjusted GILTI inclusion with respect to Share B is $3.3x. However, the hybrid deduction account with respect to Share B is not reduced by such $3.3x, because of the limitation in paragraph (d)(4)(i)(B)(2)(ii) of this section, which, with respect to Share B, limits the reduction pursuant to paragraph (d)(4)(i)(B)(2)(i) of this section to $0 (calculated as $0, the hybrid deductions allocated to the share for the taxable year, multiplied by 1, the fraction described in paragraph (d)(4)(i)(B)(2)(ii) of this section (computed as the $119.5x of tested income divided by the $119.5x of taxable income)). *See* paragraphs (d)(4)(i)(B)(2)(i) and (ii) of this section.

(C) US1's hybrid deduction account with respect to Share A is reduced by the entire $6.7x adjusted GILTI inclusion with respect to the share, as such $6.7x does not exceed the limit in paragraph (d)(4)(i)(B)(2)(ii) of this section ($80x, calculated as $80x, the hybrid deductions allocated to the share for the taxable year, multiplied by 1, the fraction described in paragraph (d)(4)(i)(B)(2)(ii) of this section). *See* paragraphs (d)(4)(i)(B)(2)(i) and (ii) of this section. In addition, the hybrid deduction account is reduced by another $3.3x, the amount of the adjusted GILTI inclusion with respect to Share B that is allocated to the hybrid deduction account with respect to Share A. *See* paragraph (d)(4)(i)(B)(2)(iii) of this section. As a result, pursuant to paragraph (d)(4)(i)(B)(2) of this section, US1's hybrid deduction account with respect to Share A is reduced by $10x ($6.7x plus $3.3x).

* * *

(h) * * *

(2) *Special rules.*—Paragraphs (d)(4)(i)(B) and (d)(4)(ii) of this section (decrease of hybrid deduction accounts; rules regarding adjusted subpart F and GILTI inclusions) apply to taxable years ending on or after [date of publication of the final regulations in the **Federal Register**]. However, a taxpayer may apply those paragraphs to taxable years ending before that date, so long as the taxpayer consistently applies paragraphs (d)(4)(i)(B) and (d)(4)(ii) to those taxable years.

Imputed Interest: Original Issue Discount

Imputed Interest: Original Issue Discount: Safe Haven Interest Rates.—Reproduced below is the text of a proposed amendment of Reg. §1.249-1, relating to (1) the tax treatment of debt instruments issued after July 1, 1982, that contain original issue discount, (2) the imputation of and the accounting for interest with respect to sales and exchanges of property occurring after December 31, 1984, and (3) safe haven interest rates for loans or advances between commonly controlled taxpayers and safe haven leases between such taxpayers (published in the Federal Register on April 8, 1986).

☐ Par. 6. Section 1.249-1 is amended as follows:

1. In paragraph (c)(2) by removing the phrase "section 1232(b)" and adding in its place the phrase "sections 1273(b) and 1274", and by removing the phrase "§§1.163-3 and 1.163-4," and adding in its place the phrase "§§1.163-3, 1.163-4, and 1.163-7."

2. In paragraph (d)(2), the first sentence, by removing the phrase "§§1.163-3 and 1.163-4," and adding in its place the phrase "§§1.163-3, 1.163-4, and 1.163-7."

3. In paragraph (f)(2), the second sentence, by removing the phrase "§§1.163-3(c) and 1.163-4(c)," and adding in its place the phrase "§§1.163-3(c), 1.163-4(c), and 1.163-7(f)."

§1.249-1. Limitation on deduction of bond premium on repurchase.

Foreign-Derived Intangible Income: Global Intangible Low-Taxed Income: Deduction

Foreign-Derived Intangible Income: Global Intangible Low-Taxed Income: Deduction.—Reg. §§1.250-0, 1.250-1 and 1.250(a)-1 through 1.250(b)-6, providing guidance to determine the amount of the deduction for foreign-derived intangible income and global intangible low-taxed income, are proposed (published in the Federal Register on March 6, 2019) (corrected April 11, 2019) (corrected April 12, 2019) (REG-104464-18).

Par. 2. Sections 1.250-0, 1.250-1, and 1.250(a)-1 through 1.250(b)-6 are added to read as follows:

§1.250-0. Table of contents.—This section lists the table of contents for §§1.250-1 through 1.250(b)-6.

§1.250-1. Introduction.—(a) *Overview.*—Sections 1.250(a)-1 through 1.250(b)-6 provide rules to determine a domestic corporation's section 250 deduction. Section 1.250(a)-1 provides rules to determine the amount of a domestic corporation's deduction for foreign-derived intangible income and global intangible low-taxed income. Section 1.250(b)-1 provides general rules and definitions regarding the computation of foreign-derived intangible income. Section 1.250(b)-2 provides rules for determining a domestic corporation's qualified business asset investment. Section 1.250(b)-3 provides general rules and definitions regarding the determination of gross foreign-derived deduction eligible income. Section 1.250(b)-4 provides rules regarding the determination of gross foreign-derived deduction eligible income from the sale of property. Section 1.250(b)-5 provides rules regarding the determination of gross foreign-derived deduction eligible income from the provision of a service. Section 1.250(b)-6 provides rules regarding the sale of property or provision of a service to a related party.

(b) *Applicability dates.*—Sections 1.250(a)-1 through 1.250(b)-6 apply to taxable years ending on or after March 4, 2019. However, for taxable years beginning on or before March 4, 2019, taxpayers may use any reasonable documentation maintained in the ordinary course of the taxpayer's business that establishes that a recipient is a foreign person, property is for a foreign use (within the meaning of § 1.250(b)-4(d) and (e)), or a recipient of a general service is located outside the United States (within the meaning of § 1.250(b)-5(d)(2) and (e)(2)), as applicable, in lieu of the documentation required in § § 1.250(b)-4(c)(2), (d)(3), and (e)(3) and 1.250(b)-5(d)(3) and (e)(3), provided that such documentation meets the reliability requirements described in § 1.250(b)-3(d). [Reg. § 1.250-1.]

§1.250(a)-1. Deduction for foreign-derived intangible income and global intangible low-taxed income.—(a) *Scope.*—This section provides rules for determining the amount of a domestic corporation's deduction for foreign-derived intangible income and global intangible low-taxed income. Paragraph (b) of this section provides general rules for determining the amount of the deduction. Paragraph (c) of this section provides definitions relevant for determining the amount of the deduction. Paragraph (d) of this section provides reporting requirements for a domestic corporation claiming the deduction. Paragraph (e) of this section provides a rule for determining the amount of the deduction of a member of a consolidated group. Paragraph (f) of this section provides examples illustrating the application of this section.

(b) *Allowance of deduction.*—(1) *In general.*—A domestic corporation is allowed a deduction for any taxable year equal to the sum of—

   (i) 37.5 percent of its foreign-derived intangible income for the year; and

   (ii) 50 percent of—

     (A) Its global intangible low-taxed income for the year; and

     (B) The amount treated as a dividend received by the corporation under section 78 which is attributable to its global intangible low-taxed income for the year.

(2) *Taxable income limitation.*—In the case of a domestic corporation with a section 250(a)(2) amount for a taxable year, for purposes of applying paragraph (b)(1) of this section for the year—

   (i) The corporation's foreign-derived intangible income for the year (if any) is reduced (but not below zero) by an amount that bears the same ratio to the corporation's section 250(a)(2) amount that the corporation's foreign-derived intangible income for the year bears to the sum of the corporation's foreign-derived intangible income and global intangible low-taxed income for the year; and

   (ii) The corporation's global intangible low-taxed income for the year (if any) is reduced (but not below zero) by the excess of the corporation's section 250(a)(2) amount over the amount of the reduction described in paragraph (b)(2)(i) of this section.

(3) *Reduction in deduction for taxable years after 2025.*—For any taxable year of a domestic corporation beginning after December 31, 2025, paragraph (b)(1) of this section applies by substituting—

   (i) 21.875 percent for 37.5 percent in paragraph (b)(1)(i) of this section; and

   (ii) 37.5 percent for 50 percent in paragraph (b)(1)(ii) of this section.

(4) *Treatment under section 4940.*—For purposes of section 4940(c)(3)(A), a deduction under section 250(a) is not treated as an ordinary and necessary expense paid or incurred for the production or collection of gross investment income.

(c) *Definitions.*—The following definitions apply for purposes of this section.

(1) *Domestic corporation.*—The term *domestic corporation* has the meaning set forth in section 7701(a), but does not include a regulated investment company (as defined in section 851), a real estate investment trust (as defined in section 856), or an S corporation (as defined in section 1361).

(2) *Foreign-derived intangible income.*—The term *foreign-derived intangible income* has the meaning set forth in § 1.250(b)-1(b).

(3) *Global intangible low-taxed income.*—The term *global intangible low-taxed income* means, with respect to a domestic corporation for a taxable year, the sum of the corporation's GILTI inclusion amount under § 1.951A-1(c) for the taxable year and the corporation's distributive share of any U.S. shareholder partnership's GILTI inclusion amount under § 1.951A-5(b)(2).

(4) *Section 250(a)(2) amount.*—The term *section 250(a)(2) amount* means, with respect to a domestic corporation for a taxable year, the excess (if any) of the sum of the corporation's foreign-derived intangible income and global intangible low-taxed income (determined without regard to section 250(a)(2) and paragraph (b)(2) of this section), over the corporation's taxable income determined with regard to all items of income, deduction, or loss, except for the deduction allowed under section 250 and this section. Therefore, for example, a domestic corporation's taxable income under the previous sentence is determined taking into account the application of sections 163(j) and 172(a). For a corporation that is subject to the unrelated business income tax under section 511, taxable income is determined only by reference to that corporation's unrelated business taxable income defined under section 512.

(d) *Reporting requirement.*—Each domestic corporation (or individual making an election under section 962) that claims a deduction under section 250 for a taxable year must make an annual return on Form 8993, "Section 250 Deduction for Foreign-Derived Intangible Income (FDII) and Global Intangible Low-Taxed Income (GILTI)" (or any successor form) for such year, setting forth the information, in such form and manner, as Form 8993 (or any successor form) or its instructions prescribe. Returns on Form 8993 (or any successor form) for a taxable year must be filed with the domestic corporation's (or in the case of a section 962 election, the individual's) income tax return on or before the due date (taking into account extensions) for filing the corporation's (or in the case of a section 962 election, the individual's) income tax return.

(e) *Determination of deduction for consolidated groups.*—A member of a consolidated group (as defined in § 1.1502-1(h)) determines its deduction under section 250(a) and this section under the rules provided in § 1.1502-50(b).

(f) *Examples.*—The following examples illustrate the application of this section. For purposes of the examples, it is assumed that DC is a domestic corporation that is not a member of a consolidated group and the taxable year of DC begins after 2017 and before 2026.

(1) *Example 1: Application of the taxable income limitation*—(i) *Facts.* For the taxable year, without regard to section 250(a)(2) and paragraph (b)(2) of this section, DC has foreign-derived intangible income of $100x and global intangible low-taxed income of $300x. DC's taxable income (without regard to section 250(a) and this section) is $300x.

(ii) *Analysis.* DC has a section 250(a)(2) amount of $100x, which is equal to the excess of the sum of DC's foreign-derived intangible income and global intangible low-taxed income of $400x ($100x + $300x) over its taxable income of $300x. As a result, DC's foreign-derived intangible income and global intangible low-taxed income are reduced, in the aggregate, by $100x under section 250(a)(2) and paragraph (b)(2) of this section for purposes of calculating DC's deduction allowed under section 250(a)(1) and paragraph (b)(1) of this section. DC's foreign-derived intangible income is reduced by $25x, the amount that bears the same ratio to the section 250(a)(2) amount ($100x) as DC's foreign-derived intangible income ($100x) bears to the sum of DC's foreign-derived intangible income and global intangible low-taxed income ($400x). DC's global intangible low-taxed income is reduced by $75x, which is the remainder of the section 250(a)(2) amount ($100x - $25x). Therefore, for purposes of calculating its deduction under section 250(a)(1) and paragraph (b)(1) of this section, DC's foreign-derived intangible income is $75x ($100x - $25x) and its global intangible low-taxed income is $225x ($300x - $75x). Accordingly, DC is allowed a deduction for the taxable year under section 250(a)(1) and paragraph (b)(1) of this section of $140.63x ($75x x 0.375 + $225x x 0.50).

(2) *Example 2: Interaction of sections 163(j), 172, and 250*—(i) *Facts.* For the taxable year, DC has gross DEI (as defined in § 1.250(b)-1(c)(14)) and gross FDDEI (as defined in § 1.250(b)-1(c)(15)) of $300x. DC has no income for the taxable year other than income included in gross DEI. DC also has a net operating loss carryover to the taxable year under section 172(b) of $130x and business interest (as defined in section 163(j)(5), without regard to any carryforwards described in section 163(j)(2)) of $100x. Under § 1.250(b)-1(d)(2), all of DC's interest expense is allocable to gross FDDEI and the net operating loss carryover, to the extent absorbed in the taxable year, is allocable to gross FDDEI. DC has no other allowable deductions, qualified business asset investment (as defined in § 1.250(b)-2(b)), or global intangible low-taxed income for the taxable year. DC has no floor plan financing interest (as defined in section 163(j)(9)) for the taxable year and no business interest income (as defined in section 163(j)(6)) for the taxable year.

(ii) *Analysis*—(A) *Calculation of tentative section 250 deduction for purposes of section 163(j).* First, for purposes of applying section 163(j), the amount of the deduction allowed to DC under section 250(a)(1) is determined without regard to the application of section 163(j) and the section 163(j) regulations, without regard to section 172, and without regard to section 250(a)(2) and paragraph (b)(2) of this section (*tentative section 250 deduction*). See § 1.163(j)-1(b)(37)(ii); see also § 1.250(b)-1(d)(2)(ii). Therefore, solely for purposes of calculating DC's tentative section 250 deduction, DC's allowable deductions under § 1.250(b)-1(d)(2)(ii) for computing its foreign-derived intangible income are $100x, the amount of its business interest before the application of section 163(j). DC's deduction eligible income (as defined in § 1.250(b)-1(c)(2)) is $200x, the excess of its gross DEI (as defined in § 1.250(b)-1(c)(14)) of $300x, over its deductions properly allocable to gross DEI of $100x. DC's foreign-derived deduction eligible income (as defined in § 1.250(b)-1(c)(12)) is also $200x, the excess of its gross FDDEI of $300x over its deductions properly allocable to gross FDDEI of $100x. DC's foreign-derived ratio (as defined in § 1.250(b)-1(c)(13)) is 100%, which is the ratio of DC's foreign-derived deduction eligible income of $200x to DC's deduction eligible income of $200x. DC's deemed intangible income (as defined § 1.250(b)-1(c)(3)) is $200x, the excess of its deduction eligible income of $200x over its qualified business asset investment of $0. Therefore, DC's foreign-derived intangible income for purposes of the tentative section 250 deduction is $200x, which is equal to DC's deemed intangible income of $200x multiplied by its foreign-derived ratio of 100%. Accordingly, DC's tentative section 250 deduction is $75x ($200x x 0.375).

(B) *Calculation of disallowance under section 163(j)(1).* Second, the amount of DC's business interest deduction allowed under section 163(j) is determined taking into account the tentative section 250 deduction, but without regard to section 172(a). See section 163(j)(8)(A)(iii). Under section 163(j)(1) and § 1.163(j)-2(b), DC's deduction for business interest is limited to 30% of adjusted taxable income plus the amount of any business interest income for the taxable year and the amount of any floor plan financing interest for the taxable year. In this case, DC has no business interest income or floor plan financing interest for the taxable year and therefore DC's deduction for business interest is limited to 30% of DC's adjusted taxable income for the taxable year. DC's adjusted taxable income is equal to DC's taxable income with the relevant adjustments set forth under section 163(j)(8) and the regulations under section 163(j). For

this purpose, DC's taxable income is computed without regard to DC's business interest and the amount of any net operating loss deduction under section 172, but taking into account the tentative section 250 deduction. Taking into account the tentative section 250 deduction, DC's adjusted taxable income is $225x ($300x - $75x). Therefore, the amount of DC's allowable deduction for business interest is $67.5x ($225x x 0.30) and the remaining $32.5x of DC's business interest expense will be carried forward to the succeeding taxable year.

(C) *Calculation of net operating loss deduction under section 172(a).* Third, the amount of DC's net operating loss deduction under section 172(a) is determined taking into account section 163(j), but without regard to section 250(a) and paragraph (b)(1) of this section. See § 1.250(b)-1(d)(2)(ii). Under section 172(a)(2), the amount of DC's net operating loss deduction is limited to 80% of taxable income. Taking into account the allowable deduction for business interest (but not its deduction allowed under section 250(a)), DC's taxable income is $232.5x ($300x - $67.5x), and its taxable income limitation under section 172(a)(2) is $186x ($232.5x x 0.80). DC is entitled to a net operating loss deduction equal to its entire net operating loss carryover of $130x, because such amount is less than $186x.

(D) *Calculation of FDII.* Fourth, the amount of DC's foreign-derived intangible income is determined, taking into account the deductions allowed after the application of sections 163(j) and 172(a). DC's allowable deductions under § 1.250(b)-1(d)(2)(ii) for computing its foreign-derived intangible income are $197.5x, which is equal to its allowed deduction for business interest of $67.5x plus its net operating loss deduction of $130x. Accordingly, DC's deduction eligible income (as defined in § 1.250(b)-1(c)(2)) is $102.5x, the excess of its gross DEI (as defined in § 1.250(b)-1(c)(14)) of $300x, over its deductions properly allocable to gross DEI of $197.5x. DC's foreign-derived deduction eligible income (as defined in § 1.250(b)-1(c)(12)) is also $102.5x, the excess of its gross FDDEI of $300x, over its deductions properly allocable to gross FDDEI of $197.5x. DC's foreign-derived ratio (as defined in § 1.250(b)-1(c)(13)) is 100%, which is the ratio of DC's foreign-derived deduction eligible income of $102.5x to DC's deduction eligible income of $102.5x. DC's deemed intangible income (as defined in § 1.250(b)-1(c)(3)) is $102.5x, the excess of its deduction eligible income of $102.5x over its qualified business asset investment of $0. Accordingly, DC's foreign-derived intangible income before application of section 250(a)(2) and paragraph (b)(2) of this section is $102.5x, which is equal to DC's deemed intangible income of $102.5x multiplied by its foreign-derived ratio of 100%.

(E) *Calculation of section 250 deduction.* Finally, the amount of DC's deduction under section 250 is determined after the application of section 250(a)(2), which is applied taking into account DC's business interest allowed under section 163(j) and its net operating loss deduction under section 172(a). DC's taxable income for purposes of section 250(a)(2) and paragraph (b)(2) of this section is $102.5x, which is $300x of gross income minus $197.5x, which is equal to its deduction for business interest of $67.5x plus its net operating loss deduction of $130x. DC does not have a section 250(a)(2) amount (as defined in paragraph (c)(4) of this section) for the year because DC's foreign-derived intangible income of $102.5x, determined without regard to section 250(a)(2) and paragraph (b)(2) of this section, does not exceed DC's taxable income of $102.5x. Therefore, the amount of DC's foreign-derived intangible income is not reduced under section 250(a)(2) and paragraph (b)(2) of this section. Accordingly, for the taxable year, DC is allowed a deduction under section 250(a)(1) and paragraph (b)(1) of this section of $38.44x ($102.5x x 0.375). [Reg. § 1.250(a)-1.]

§ 1.250(b)-1. Computation of foreign-derived intangible income (FDII).—(a) *Scope.*—This section provides rules for computing foreign-derived intangible income. Paragraph (b) of this section defines foreign-derived intangible income. Paragraph (c) of this section provides definitions that are relevant for computing foreign-derived intangible income. Paragraph (d) of this section provides rules for computing gross income and allocating and apportioning deductions for purposes of computing deduction eligible income and foreign-derived deduction eligible income. Paragraph (e) of this section provides rules for computing the deduction eligible income and foreign-derived deduction eligible income of a domestic corporate partner. Paragraph (f) of this section provides a rule for computing the foreign-derived intangible income of a member of a consolidated group. Paragraph (g) of this section provides a rule for computing the foreign-derived intangible income of a tax-exempt corporation.

(b) *Definition of foreign-derived intangible income.*—Subject to the provisions of this section, the term *foreign-derived intangible income* means, with respect to a domestic corporation for a taxable year, the corporation's deemed intangible income for the year multiplied by the corporation's foreign-derived ratio for the year.

(c) *Definitions.*—This paragraph (c) provides definitions that apply for purposes of this section and §§ 1.250(b)-2 through 1.250(b)-6.

(1) *Controlled foreign corporation.*—The term *controlled foreign corporation* has the meaning set forth in section 957(a).

(2) *Deduction eligible income.*—The term *deduction eligible income* means, with respect to a domestic corporation for a taxable year, the excess (if any) of the corporation's gross DEI for the year, over the deductions properly allocable to gross DEI for the year, as determined under paragraph (d)(2) of this section.

(3) *Deemed intangible income.*—The term *deemed intangible income* means, with respect to a domestic corporation for a taxable year, the excess (if any) of the corporation's deduction eligible income for the year, over the corporation's deemed tangible income return for the year.

(4) *Deemed tangible income return.*—The term *deemed tangible income return* means, with respect to a domestic corporation and a taxable year, 10 percent of the corporation's qualified business asset investment for the year.

(5) *Dividend.*—The term *dividend* has the meaning set forth in section 316, and includes any amount treated as a dividend under any other provision of subtitle A of the Internal Revenue Code or the regulations thereunder (for example, under section 78, 356(a)(2), 367(b), or 1248).

(6) *Domestic corporation.*—The term *domestic corporation* has the meaning set forth in § 1.250(a)-1(c)(1).

(7) *Domestic oil and gas extraction income.*—The term *domestic oil and gas extraction income* means income described in section 907(c)(1), substituting "within the United States" for "without the United States."

(8) *FDDEI sale.*—The term *FDDEI sale* has the meaning set forth in § 1.250(b)-4(b).

(9) *FDDEI service.*—The term *FDDEI service* has the meaning set forth in § 1.250(b)-5(b).

(10) *FDDEI transaction.*—The term *FDDEI transaction* means a FDDEI sale or a FDDEI service.

(11) *Foreign branch income.*—The term *foreign branch income* means gross income attributable to a foreign branch of a domestic corporation or a partnership under § 1.904-4(f)(2), except that the term also includes any income or gain that would not be treated as gross income attributable to a foreign branch under § 1.904-4(f) but that arises from the direct or indirect sale (as defined in § 1.250(b)-3(b)(7)) of any asset (other than stock) that produces gross income attributable to a foreign branch, including by reason of the sale of a disregarded entity or interest in a partnership. See also § 1.904-4(f)(2)(v) (providing that if a principal purpose of recording or failing to record an item of gross income on the books and records of a foreign branch is the avoidance of the purposes of section 250 (in connection with section 250(b)(3)(A)(i)(VI)), the item must be attributed to one or more foreign branches of the foreign branch owner in a manner that reflects the substance of the transaction).

(12) *Foreign-derived deduction eligible income.*—The term *foreign-derived deduction eligible income* means, with respect to a domestic corporation for a taxable year, the excess (if any) of the corporation's gross FDDEI for the year, over the deductions properly allocable to gross FDDEI for the year, as determined under paragraph (d)(2) of this section.

(13) *Foreign-derived ratio.*—The term *foreign-derived ratio* means, with respect to a domestic corporation for a taxable year, the ratio (not to exceed one) of the corporation's foreign-derived deduction eligible income for the year to the corporation's deduction eligible income for the year. If a domestic corporation has no foreign-derived deduction eligible income for a taxable year, the corporation's foreign-derived ratio is zero for the year.

(14) *Gross DEI.*—The term *gross DEI* means, with respect to a domestic corporation or a partnership for a taxable year, the gross income of the corporation or partnership for the year determined without regard to the following items of gross income—

    (i) Amounts included in gross income under section 951(a)(1);

    (ii) Global intangible low-taxed income (as defined in § 1.250(a)-1(c)(3));

    (iii) Financial services income (as defined in section 904(d)(2)(D) and § 1.904-4(e)(1)(ii));

    (iv) Dividends received from a controlled foreign corporation with respect to which the corporation or partnership is a United States shareholder;

    (v) Domestic oil and gas extraction income; and

    (vi) Foreign branch income.

(15) *Gross FDDEI.*—The term *gross FDDEI* means, with respect to a domestic corporation or a partnership for a taxable year, the portion of the gross DEI of the corporation or partnership for the year which is derived from all of its FDDEI transactions.

(16) *Gross non-FDDEI.*—The term *gross non-FDDEI* means, with respect to a domestic corporation for a taxable year, the portion of the corporation's gross DEI that is not included in gross FDDEI.

(17) *Modified affiliated group.*—(i) *In general.*—The term *modified affiliated group* means an affiliated group as defined in section 1504(a) determined by substituting "more than 50 percent" for "at least 80 percent" each place it appears, and without regard to section 1504(b)(2) and (3).

    (ii) *Special rule for noncorporate entities.*—Any person (other than a corporation) that is controlled by one or more members of a modified affiliated group (including one or more persons treated as a member or members of a modified affiliated group by reason of this paragraph (c)(17)(ii)) or that controls any such member is treated as a member of the modified affiliated group.

    (iii) *Definition of control.*—For purposes of paragraph (c)(17)(ii) of this section, the term *control* has the meaning set forth in section 954(d)(3).

(18) *Qualified business asset investment.*—The term *qualified business asset investment* has the meaning set forth in § 1.250(b)-2(b).

(19) *Related party.*—The term *related party* means, with respect to any person, any member of a modified affiliated group that includes such person.

(20) *United States shareholder.*—The term *United States shareholder* has the meaning set forth in section 951(b) and § 1.951-1(g).

(d) *Treatment of cost of goods sold and allocation and apportionment of deductions.*—(1) *Cost of goods sold for determining gross DEI and gross FDDEI.*—For purposes of determining the gross income included in gross DEI and gross FDDEI of a domestic corporation or a partnership, the cost of goods sold of the corporation or partnership is attributed to gross receipts with respect to gross DEI or gross FDDEI under any reasonable method. Cost of goods sold must be attributed to gross receipts with respect to gross DEI or gross FDDEI regardless of whether certain costs included in cost of goods sold can be associated with activities undertaken in an earlier taxable year (including a year before the effective date of section 250). A domestic corporation or partnership may not segregate cost of goods sold with respect to a particular product into component costs and attribute those component costs disproportionately to gross receipts with respect to amounts excluded from gross DEI or gross FDDEI, as applicable.

(2) *Deductions properly allocable to gross DEI and gross FDDEI.*—(i) *In general.*—For purposes of determining a domestic corporation's deductions that are properly allocable to gross DEI and gross FDDEI, the corporation's deductions are allocated and apportioned to gross DEI and gross FDDEI under the rules of § § 1.861-8 through 1.861-14T and 1.861-17 by treating section 250(b) as an operative section described in § 1.861-8(f). In allocating and apportioning deductions under § § 1.861-8 through 1.861-14T and 1.861-17, gross FDDEI and gross non-FDDEI are treated as separate statutory groupings. The deductions allocated and apportioned to gross DEI equal the sum of the deductions allocated and apportioned to gross FDDEI and gross non-FDDEI. All items of gross income described in paragraphs (c)(14)(i) through (vi) of this section are in the residual grouping. For purposes of this paragraph (d)(2)(i), research and experimental expenditures are allocated and apportioned in accordance with § 1.861-17 without taking into account the exclusive apportionment rule of § 1.861-17(b).

    (ii) *Determination of deductions to allocate.*—All deductions allowed to a domestic corporation are allocated and apportioned to gross DEI and gross FDDEI for a taxable year under paragraph (d)(2)(i) of this section, other than the deduction allowed under section 250(a) and § 1.250(a)-1(b). For this purpose, the amount of the net operating loss deduction under section 172(a) is determined without regard to section 250. See also § 1.163(j)-1(b)(37)(ii) (for purposes of determining the limitation under section 163(j)(1), the deduction under section 250(a)(1) is determined without regard to the application of section 163(j) and the section 163(j) regulations and without regard to the taxable income limitation of section 250(a)(2) and § 1.250(a)-1(b)(2)).

(3) *Examples.*—The following example illustrates the application of this paragraph (d).

    (i) *Presumed facts.*—The following facts are assumed for purposes of the examples—

(A) DC is a domestic corporation that is not a member of a consolidated group.

(B) All sales and services are provided to persons that are not related parties.

(C) All sales and services to foreign persons qualify as FDDEI transactions.

(ii) *Examples.*—(A) *Example 1: Allocation of deductions*—(1) *Facts.* For a taxable year, DC manufactures products A and B in the United States. DC sells products A and B and provides services associated with products A and B to United States and foreign persons. DC's qualified business asset investment for the taxable year is $1,000x. DC has $300x of deductible interest expense allowed under section 163. DC has assets with a tax book value of $2,500x. The tax book value of DC's assets used to produce products A and B and services is split evenly between assets that produce gross FDDEI

and assets that produce gross non-FDDEI. DC has $840x of supportive deductions, as defined in §1.861-8(b)(3), attributable to general and administrative expenses incurred for the purpose of generating the class of gross income that consists of gross DEI. DC apportions the $840x of deductions on the basis of gross income in accordance with §1.861-8T(c)(1). For purposes of determining gross FDDEI and gross DEI under paragraph (d)(1) of this section, DC attributes $200x of cost of goods sold to Product A and $400x of cost of goods sold to Product B, and then attributes the cost of goods sold for each product ratably between the gross receipts of such product sold to foreign persons and the gross receipts of such product sold to United States persons. The manner in which DC attributes the cost of goods sold is a reasonable method. DC has no other items of income, loss, or deduction. For the taxable year, DC has the following income tax items relevant to the determination of its foreign-derived intangible income:

Table 1 To Paragraph (d)(3)(ii)(A)(1)	Product A	Product B	Services	Total
Gross receipts from U.S. persons	$200x	$800x	$100x	$1,100x
Gross receipts from foreign persons	$200x	$800x	$100x	$1,100x
Total gross receipts	$400x	$1,600x	$200x	$2,200x
Cost of goods sold for gross receipts from U.S. persons	$100x	$200x	$0	$300x
Cost of goods sold for gross receipts from foreign persons	$100x	$200x	$0	$300x
Total cost of goods sold	$200x	$400x	$0	$600x
Gross income	$200x	$1,200x	$200x	$1,600x
Tax book value of assets used to produce products/services	$500x	$500x	$1,500x	$2,500x

(2) *Analysis*—(i) *Determination of gross FDDEI and gross non-FDDEI.* Because DC does not have any income described in section 250(b)(3)(A)(i)(I) through (VI) and paragraphs (c)(14)(i) through (vi) of this section, none of its gross income is excluded from gross DEI. DC's gross DEI is $1,600x ($2,200x total gross receipts less $600x total cost of goods sold). DC's gross FDDEI is $800x ($1,100x of gross receipts from foreign persons minus attributable cost of goods sold of $300x).

(ii) *Determination of foreign-derived deduction eligible income.* To calculate its foreign-derived deduction eligible income, DC must determine the amount of its deductions that are allocated and apportioned to gross FDDEI and then subtract those amounts from gross FDDEI. DC's interest deduction of $300x is allocated and apportioned to gross FDDEI on the basis of the average total value of DC's assets in each grouping. DC has assets with a tax book value of $2,500x split evenly between assets that produce gross FDDEI and assets that produce gross non-FDDEI. Accordingly, an interest expense deduction of $150x is apportioned to DC's gross FDDEI. With respect to DC's supportive deductions of $840x that are related to DC's gross DEI, DC apportions such deductions between gross FDDEI and gross non-FDDEI on the basis of gross income. Accordingly, supportive deductions of $420x are apportioned to DC's gross FDDEI. Thus, DC's foreign-derived deduction eligible income is $230x, which is equal to its gross FDDEI of $800x less $150x of interest expense deduction and $420x of supportive deductions.

(iii) *Determination of deemed intangible income.* DC's deemed tangible income return is $100x, which is equal to 10% of its qualified business asset investment of $1,000x. DC's deduction eligible income is $460x, which is equal to its gross DEI of $1,600x less $300x of interest expense deductions and $840x of supportive deductions.

Therefore, DC's deemed intangible income is $360x, which is equal to the excess of its deduction eligible income of $460x over its deemed tangible income return of $100x.

(iv) *Determination of foreign-derived intangible income.* DC's foreign-derived ratio is 50%, which is the ratio of DC's foreign-derived deduction eligible income of $230x to DC's deduction eligible income of $460x. Therefore, DC's foreign-derived intangible income is $180x, which is equal to DC's deemed intangible income of $360x multiplied by its foreign-derived ratio of 50%.

(B) *Example 2: Allocation of deductions with respect to a partnership*—(1) *Facts*—(i) *DC's operations.* DC is engaged in the production and sale of products consisting of two separate product groups in three-digit Standard Industrial Classification (SIC) Industry Groups, hereafter referred to as Group AAA and Group BBB. All of the gross income of DC is included in gross DEI. DC incurs $250x of research and experimental (R&E) expenditures in the United States that are deductible under section 174. None of the R&E is legally mandated as described in §1.861-17(a)(4) and none is included in cost of goods sold. For purposes of determining gross FDDEI and gross DEI under paragraph (d)(1) of this section, DC attributes $210x of cost of goods sold to Group AAA products and $900x of cost of goods sold to Group BBB products, and then attributes the cost of goods sold with respect to each such product group ratably between the gross receipts with respect to such product group sold to foreign persons and the gross receipts with respect to such product group not sold to foreign persons. The manner in which DC attributes the cost of goods sold is a reasonable method. For the taxable year, DC has the following income tax items relevant to the determination of its foreign-derived intangible income:

Table 2 To Paragraph (d)(3)(ii)(B)(1)(i)	Group AAA Products	Group BBB Products	Total
Gross receipts from U.S. persons	$200x	$800x	$1,000x
Gross receipts from foreign persons	$100x	$400x	$500x
Total gross receipts	$300x	$1,200x	$1,500x
Cost of goods sold for gross receipts from U.S. persons	$140x	$600x	$750x
Cost of goods sold for gross receipts from foreign persons	$70x	$300x	$370x
Total cost of goods sold	$210x	$900x	$1,110x
Gross income	$90x	$300x	$390x
R&E deductions	$40x	$210x	$250x

(ii) *PRS's operations.* In addition to its own operations, DC is a partner in PRS, a partnership that also produces products described in SIC Group AAA. DC is allocated 50% of all income, gain, loss, and deductions of PRS. During the taxable year, PRS sells Group AAA products solely to foreign persons, and all of its gross income is included in gross DEI. PRS has $400 of gross receipts from sales of Group AAA products for the taxable year and incurs $100x of re-

search and experimental (R&E) expenditures in the United States that are deductible under section 174. None of the R&E is legally mandated as described in §1.861-17(a)(4) and none is included in cost of goods sold. For purposes of determining gross FDDEI and gross DEI under paragraph (d)(1) of this section, PRS attributes $200x of cost of goods sold to Group AAA products, and then attributes the cost of goods sold with respect to such product group ratably between the gross receipts with respect to such product group sold to foreign persons and the gross receipts with respect to such product group not sold to foreign persons. The manner in which PRS attributes the cost of goods sold is a reasonable method. DC's distributive share of PRS taxable items is $100x of gross income and $50x of R&E deductions, and DC's share of PRS's gross receipts from sales of Group AAA products for the taxable year is $200x under §1.861-17(f)(3).

(*iii*) *Election to use sales method to allocate and apportion R&E.* DC has elected to use the sales method to apportion its R&E deductions under §1.861-17. Neither DC nor PRS licenses or sells its intangible property to controlled or uncontrolled corporations in a manner that necessitates including the sales by such corporations for purposes of apportioning DC's R&E deductions.

(2) *Analysis*—(*i*) *Determination of gross DEI and gross FDDEI.* Under paragraph (e)(1) of this section, DC's gross DEI, gross FDDEI, and deductions allocable to those amounts include its distributive share of gross DEI, gross FDDEI, and deductions of PRS. Thus, DC's gross DEI for the year is $490x ($390x attributable to DC and $100x attributable to DC's interest in PRS). DC's gross income from sales of Group AAA products to foreign persons is $30x ($100x of gross receipts minus attributable cost of goods sold of $70x). DC's gross income from sales of Group BBB products to foreign persons is $100x ($400x of gross receipts minus attributable cost of goods sold of $300x). DC's gross FDDEI for the year is $230x ($30x from DC's sale of Group AAA products plus $100x from DC's sale of Group BBB products plus DC's distributive share of PRS's gross FDDEI of $100x).

(*ii*) *Allocation and apportionment of R&E deductions.* To determine foreign-derived deduction eligible income, DC must allocate and apportion its R&E expense of $300x ($250x incurred directly by DC and $50x incurred indirectly through DC's interest in PRS). In accordance with §1.861-17, R&E expenses are first allocated to a class of gross income related to a three-digit SIC group code. DC's R&E expenses related to products in Group AAA are $90x ($40x incurred directly by DC and $50x incurred indirectly through DC's interest in PRS) and its expenses related to Group BBB are $210x. None of those expenses were legally mandated by a particular country and therefore do not require the allocation of R&E expense solely to income arising from that jurisdiction. The exclusive apportionment rule in §1.861-17(b) does not apply for purposes of apportioning R&E to gross DEI and gross FDDEI. See paragraph (d)(2)(i) of this section. Accordingly, all R&E expense attributable to a particular SIC group code is apportioned on the basis of the amounts of sales within that SIC group code. Total sales within Group AAA were $500x ($300x directly by DC and $200x attributable to DC's interest in PRS), $300x of which were made to foreign persons ($100x directly by DC and $200x attributable to DC's interest in PRS). Therefore, the $90x of R&E expense related to Group AAA is apportioned $54x to gross FDDEI ($90x x $300x/$500x) and $36x to gross non-FDDEI ($90x x $200x/$500x). Total sales within Group BBB were $1,200x, $400x of which were made to foreign persons. Therefore, the $210x of R&E expense related to products in Group BBB is apportioned $70x to gross FDDEI ($210x x $400x/$1,200x) and $140x to gross non-FDDEI ($210x x $800x/$1,200x). Accordingly, DC's foreign-derived deduction eligible income for the tax year is $106x ($230x gross FDDEI minus $124x of R&E ($54x + $70x) allocated and apportioned to gross FDDEI).

(e) *Domestic corporate partners.*—(1) *In general.*—A domestic corporation's deduction eligible income and foreign-derived deduction eligible income for a taxable year are determined taking into account the corporation's share of gross DEI, gross FDDEI, and deductions of any partnership (whether domestic or foreign) in which the corporation is a direct or indirect partner. For purposes of the preceding sentence, a domestic corporation's share of each such item of a partnership is determined in accordance with the corporation's distributive share of the underlying items of income, gain, deduction, and loss of the partnership that comprise such amounts. See §1.250(b)-2(g) for rules calculating the increase to a domestic corporation's qualified business asset investment by the corporation's share of partnership QBAI.

(2) *Reporting requirement for partnership with domestic corporate partners.*—A partnership that has one or more direct or indirect partners that are domestic corporations and that is required to file a return under section 6031 must furnish to each such partner on or with such partner's Schedule K-1 (Form 1065 or any successor form) by the due date (including extensions) for furnishing Schedule K-1 the partner's share of the partnership's gross DEI, gross FDDEI, deductions that are definitely related to the partnership's gross DEI and gross FDDEI, and partnership QBAI (as determined under §1.250(b)-2(g)) for each taxable year in which the partnership has gross DEI, gross FDDEI, deductions that are definitely related to the partnership's gross DEI or gross FDDEI, or partnership specified tangible property (as defined in §1.250(b)-2(g)(2)(iii)).

(3) *Examples.*—The following examples illustrate the application of this paragraph (e).

(i) *Presumed facts.*—The following facts are assumed for purposes of the examples—

(A) DC, a domestic corporation, is a partner in PRS, a partnership.

(B) FP and FP2 are foreign persons.

(C) FC is a foreign corporation.

(D) The allocations under PRS's partnership agreement satisfy the requirements of section 704.

(E) No partner of PRS is a related party of DC.

(F) DC, PRS, and FC all use the calendar year as their taxable year.

(G) PRS has no items of income, loss, or deduction for its taxable year, except the items of income described.

(ii) *Examples.*—(A) *Example 1: Sale by partnership to foreign person*—(1) *Facts.* Under the terms of the partnership agreement, DC is allocated 50% of all income, gain, loss, and deductions of PRS. For the taxable year, PRS recognizes $20x of gross income on the sale of general property (as defined in §1.250(b)-3(b)(3)) to FP, a foreign person (as determined under §1.250(b)-4(c)), for a foreign use (as determined under §1.250(b)-4(d)). The gross income recognized on the sale of property is not described in section 250(b)(3)(A)(I) through (VI) or paragraphs (c)(14)(i) through (vi) of this section.

(2) *Analysis.* PRS's sale of property to FP is a FDDEI sale as described in §1.250(b)-4(b). Therefore, the gross income derived from the sale ($20x) is included in PRS's gross DEI and gross FDDEI, and DC's share of PRS's gross DEI and gross FDDEI ($10x) is included in DC's gross DEI and gross FDDEI for the taxable year.

(B) *Example 2: Sale by partnership to foreign person attributable to foreign branch*—(1) *Facts.* The facts are the same as in paragraph (e)(3)(ii)(A)(1) of this section (the facts in *Example 1*), except the income from the sale of property to FP is attributable to a foreign branch of PRS.

(2) *Analysis.* PRS's sale of property to FP is excluded from PRS's gross DEI under section 250(b)(3)(A)(VI) and paragraph (c)(14)(vi) of this section. Accordingly, DC's share of PRS's gross income of $10x from the sale is not included in DC's gross DEI or gross FDDEI for the taxable year.

(C) *Example 3: Partnership with a loss in gross FDDEI*—(1) *Facts.* The facts are the same as in paragraph (e)(3)(ii)(A)(1) of this section (the facts in *Example 1*), except that in the same taxable year, PRS also sells property to FP2, a foreign person (as determined under §1.250(b)-4(c)), for a foreign use (as determined under §1.250(b)-4(d)). After taking into account both sales, PRS has a gross loss of $30x.

(2) *Analysis.* Both the sale of property to FP and the sale of property to FP2 are FDDEI sales because each sale is described in §1.250(b)-4(b). DC's share of PRS's gross loss ($15x) from the sales is included in DC's gross DEI and gross FDDEI.

(D) *Example 4: Sale by partnership to foreign related party of the partnership*—(1) *Facts.* Under the terms of the partnership agreement, DC has 25% of the capital and profits interest in the partnership and is allocated 25% of all income, gain, loss, and deductions of PRS. PRS owns 100% of the single class of stock of FC. In the taxable year, PRS has $20x of gain on the sale of general property (as defined in §1.250(b)-3(b)(3)) to FC, and FC makes a material physical change to the property within the meaning of §1.250(b)-4(d)(2)(iii) outside the United States before selling the property to customers in the United States. PRS satisfies the documentation requirement of §1.250(b)-4(d)(3) with respect to the sale.

(2) *Analysis.* The sale of property by PRS to FC is described in §1.250(b)-4(b) without regard to the application of §1.250(b)-6, since the sale is to a foreign person (as determined under §1.250(b)-4(c)) for a foreign use (as determined under §1.250(b)-4(d)). However, FC is a foreign related party of PRS within the meaning of section 250(b)(5)(D) and §1.250(b)-6(b)(1), because FC and PRS are members of a modified affiliated group within the meaning of paragraph (c)(17) of this section. Therefore, the sale by PRS to FC is a related party sale within the meaning of §1.250(b)-6(b)(3). Under section 250(b)(5)(C)(i) and §1.250(b)-6(c), because FC did not sell the property, or use the property in connection with other property sold or the provision of a service, to a foreign unrelated party before the property was subject to a domestic use, the sale by PRS to FC is not a FDDEI sale. See §1.250(b)-6(c)(1). Accordingly, the gain from the sale ($20x) is included in PRS's gross DEI but not its gross FDDEI, and DC's share of PRS's gain ($5x) is included in DC's gross DEI but not gross FDDEI. This is the result notwithstanding that FC is not a related party of DC because FC and DC are not members of a modified affiliated group within the meaning of paragraph (c)(17) of this section.

(f) *Determination of foreign-derived intangible income for consolidated groups.*—A member of a consolidated group (as defined in

§ 1.1502-1(h)) determines its foreign-derived intangible income under the rules provided in § 1.1502-50.

(g) *Determination of foreign-derived intangible income for tax-exempt corporations.*—The foreign-derived intangible income of a corporation that is subject to the unrelated business income tax under section 511 is determined only by reference to that corporation's items of income, gain, deduction, or loss, and adjusted bases in property, that are taken into account in computing the corporation's unrelated business taxable income (as defined in section 512). For example, if a corporation that is subject to the unrelated business income tax under section 511 has tangible property used in the production of both unrelated business income and gross income that is not unrelated business income, only the portion of the basis of such property taken into account in computing the corporation's unrelated business taxable income is taken into account in determining the corporation's qualified business asset investment. Similarly, if a corporation that is subject to the unrelated business income tax under section 511 has tangible property that is used in both the production of gross DEI and the production of gross income that is not gross DEI, only the corporation's unrelated business income is taken into account in determining the corporation's dual use ratio with respect to such property under § 1.250(b)-2(d)(2). [Reg. § 1.250(b)-1.]

§ 1.250(b)-2. Qualified business asset investment.—(a) *Scope.*—This section provides general rules for determining the qualified business asset investment of a domestic corporation for purposes of determining its deemed tangible income return under § 1.250(b)-1(c)(4). Paragraph (b) of this section defines qualified business asset investment. Paragraph (c) of this section defines tangible property and specified tangible property. Paragraph (d) of this section provides rules for determining the portion of property that is specified tangible property when the property is used in the production of both gross DEI and gross income that is not gross DEI. Paragraph (e) of this section provides rules for determining the adjusted basis of specified tangible property. Paragraph (f) of this section provides rules for determining qualified business asset investment of a domestic corporation with a short taxable year. Paragraph (g) of this section provides rules for increasing the qualified business asset investment of a domestic corporation by reason of property owned through a partnership. Paragraph (h) of this section provides an anti-avoidance rule that disregards certain transfers when determining the qualified business asset investment of a domestic corporation.

(b) *Definition of qualified business asset investment.*—The term *qualified business asset investment* means the average of a domestic corporation's aggregate adjusted bases as of the close of each quarter of a domestic corporation's taxable year in specified tangible property that is used in a trade or business of the domestic corporation and is of a type with respect to which a deduction is allowable under section 167. See paragraph (f) of this section for rules relating to the qualified business asset investment of a domestic corporation with a short taxable year.

(c) *Specified tangible property.*—(1) *In general.*—The term *specified tangible property* means, subject to paragraph (d) of this section, tangible property used in the production of gross DEI.

(2) *Tangible property.*—For purposes of paragraph (c)(1) of this section, the term *tangible property* means property for which the depreciation deduction provided by section 167(a) is eligible to be determined under section 168 without regard to section 168(f)(1), (2), or (5) and the date placed in service.

(d) *Dual use property.*—(1) *In general.*—In the case of tangible property (as defined in paragraph (c)(2) of this section) of a domestic corporation that is used in both the production of gross DEI and the production of gross income that is not gross DEI in a domestic corporation's taxable year, the portion of the adjusted basis in the property treated as adjusted basis in specified tangible property for the domestic corporation's taxable year is determined by multiplying the average of the domestic corporation's adjusted basis in the property by the dual use ratio with respect to the property for the domestic corporation's taxable year.

(2) *Dual use ratio.*—The term *dual use ratio* means, with respect to specified tangible property—

(i) In the case of specified tangible property that produces directly identifiable income for a domestic corporation's taxable year, the ratio of the gross DEI produced by the property for the taxable year to the total amount of gross income produced by the property for the taxable year.

(ii) In the case of specified tangible property that does not produce directly identifiable income for a domestic corporation's taxable year, the ratio of the gross DEI of the domestic corporation for the taxable year to the total amount of gross income of the domestic corporation for the taxable year.

(3) *Example.*—The following example illustrates the application of this paragraph (d).

(i) *Facts.* DC, a domestic corporation, owns a machine that produces both gross DEI and domestic oil and gas extraction income. For the taxable year, the machine produces gross DEI of $750x and domestic oil and gas extraction income of $250x. The average adjusted basis of the machine for the taxable year in the hands of DC is $4,000x. DC also owns an office building for its administrative functions with an average adjusted basis for the taxable year of $10,000x. The office building does not produce directly identifiable income. DC has no other specified tangible property. For the taxable year, DC's gross DEI is $2,000x and its gross income is $5,000x.

(ii) *Analysis.* The machine and office building are both property for which the depreciation deduction provided by section 167(a) are eligible to be determined under section 168. Therefore, under paragraph (c)(2) of this section, the machine and office building are tangible property. The machine and office building are used in both the production of gross income that is included in gross DEI and gross income that is not included in gross DEI, because domestic oil and gas extraction income is an item of gross income excluded from gross DEI under section 250(b)(3)(A)(i)(V) and § 1.250(b)-1(c)(14)(v). Therefore, under paragraph (d)(1) of this section, the portion of the basis in the machine treated as basis in specified tangible property is equal to DC's average basis in the machine for the year ($4,000x), multiplied by the dual use ratio under paragraph (d)(2)(i) of this section (0.75), which is the proportion that the gross DEI produced by the property ($750x) bears to the total gross income produced with respect to the property ($1,000x). Accordingly, $3,000x ($4,000x x 0.75) of DC's adjusted basis in the machine is taken into account in determining DC's qualified business asset investment. Under paragraph (d)(1) of this section, the portion of the basis in the office building treated as basis in specified tangible property is equal to DC's average basis in the office building for the year ($10,000x), multiplied by the dual use ratio under paragraph (d)(2)(ii) of this section (0.40), which is the ratio of DC's gross DEI for the taxable year ($2,000x) to DC's total gross income for the taxable year ($5,000x). Accordingly, $4,000x ($10,000x x 0.40) of DC's adjusted basis in the office building is taken into account in determining DC's qualified business asset investment under paragraph (b) of this section. Accordingly, DC's total qualified business asset investment is $7,000x ($3,000x + $4,000x).

(e) *Determination of adjusted basis of specified tangible property.*—(1) *In general.*—The adjusted basis in specified tangible property is determined by using the alternative depreciation system under section 168(g), and by allocating the depreciation deduction with respect to such property for the domestic corporation's taxable year ratably to each day during the period in the taxable year to which such depreciation relates.

(2) *Effect of change in law.*—The determination of adjusted basis for purposes of paragraph (b) of this section is made without regard to any provision of law enacted after December 22, 2017, unless such later enacted law specifically and directly amends the definition of qualified business asset investment under section 250 or section 951A.

(3) *Specified tangible property placed in service before enactment of section 250.*—The adjusted basis in property placed in service before December 22, 2017, is determined using the alternative depreciation system under section 168(g), as if this system had applied from the date that the property was placed in service.

(f) *Special rules for short taxable years.*—(1) *In general.*—In the case of a domestic corporation that has a taxable year that is less than twelve months (a *short taxable year*), the rules for determining the qualified business asset investment of the domestic corporation under this section are modified as provided in paragraphs (f)(2) and (3) of this section with respect to the taxable year.

(2) *Determination of quarter closes.*—For purposes of determining quarter closes, in computing the qualified business asset investment of a domestic corporation for a short taxable year, the quarters of the domestic corporation for purposes of this section are the full quarters beginning and ending within the short taxable year (if any), determining quarter length as if the domestic corporation did not have a short taxable year, plus one or more short quarters (if any).

(3) *Reduction of qualified business asset investment.*—The qualified business asset investment of a domestic corporation for a short taxable year is the sum of—

(i) The sum of the domestic corporation's aggregate adjusted bases in specified tangible property as of the close of each full quarter (if any) in the domestic corporation's taxable year divided by four; plus

(ii) The domestic corporation's aggregate adjusted bases in specified tangible property as of the close of each short quarter (if any) in the domestic corporation's taxable year multiplied by the sum of the number of days in each short quarter divided by 365.

(4) *Example.*—The following example illustrates the application of this paragraph (f).

(i) *Facts.* A, an individual, owns all of the stock of DC, a domestic corporation. A owns DC from the beginning of the taxable year. On July 15 of the taxable year, A sells DC to USP, a domestic corporation that is unrelated to A. DC becomes a member of the consolidated group of which USP is the common parent and as a result, under § 1.1502-76(b)(2)(ii), DC's taxable year is treated as ending on July 15. USP and DC both use the calendar year as their taxable year. DC's aggregate adjusted bases in specified tangible property for the taxable year are $250x as of March 31, $300x as of June 30, $275x as of July 15, $500x as of September 30, and $450x as of December 31.

(ii) *Analysis*—(A) *Determination of short taxable years and quarters.* DC has two short taxable years during the taxable year. The first short taxable year is from January 1 to July 15, with two full quarters (January 1-March 31 and April 1-June 30) and one short quarter (July 1-July 15). The second taxable year is from July 16 to December 31, with one short quarter (July 16-September 30) and one full quarter (October 1-December 31).

(B) *Calculation of qualified business asset investment for the first short taxable year.* Under paragraph (f)(2) of this section, for the first short taxable year, DC has three quarter closes (March 31, June 30, and July 15). Under paragraph (f)(3) of this section, the qualified business asset investment of DC for the first short taxable year is $148.80x, the sum of $137.50x (($250x + $300x)/4) attributable to the two full quarters and $11.30x ($275x x 15/365) attributable to the short quarter.

(C) *Calculation of qualified business asset investment for the second short taxable year.* Under paragraph (f)(2) of this section, for the second short taxable year, DC has two quarter closes (September 30 and December 31). Under paragraph (f)(3) of this section, the qualified business asset investment of DC for the second short taxable year is $217.98x, the sum of $112.50x ($450x/4) attributable to the one full quarter and $105.48x ($500x x 77/365) attributable to the short quarter.

(g) *Partnership property.*—(1) *In general.*—For purposes of paragraph (b) of this section, if a domestic corporation holds an interest in one or more partnerships as of the close of the domestic corporation's taxable year, the qualified business asset investment of the domestic corporation for its taxable year is increased by the sum of the domestic corporation's partnership QBAI with respect to each partnership for the domestic corporation's taxable year.

(2) *Definitions related to partnership QBAI.*—(i) *In general.*—The term *partnership QBAI* means the sum of the domestic corporation's share of the partnership's adjusted basis in partnership specified tangible property as of the close of a partnership taxable year that ends with or within a domestic corporation's taxable year. A domestic corporation's share of the partnership's adjusted basis in partnership specified tangible property is determined separately with respect to each partnership specified tangible property of the partnership by multiplying the partnership's adjusted basis in the property by the partnership QBAI ratio with respect to the property. If the partnership's taxable year is less than twelve months, the principles of paragraph (f) of this section apply in determining a domestic corporation's partnership QBAI with respect to the partnership.

(ii) *Partnership QBAI ratio.*—The term *partnership QBAI ratio* means, with respect to partnership specified tangible property—

(A) In the case of partnership specified tangible property that produces directly identifiable income for a partnership taxable year, the ratio of the domestic corporation's distributive share of the gross income produced by the property for the partnership taxable year that is included in the gross DEI of the domestic corporation for its taxable year to the total gross income produced by the property for the partnership taxable year.

(B) In the case of partnership specified tangible property that does not produce directly identifiable income for a partnership taxable year, the ratio of the domestic corporation's distributive share of the gross income of the partnership for the partnership taxable year that is included in the gross DEI of the domestic corporation for its taxable year to the total amount of gross income of the partnership for the partnership taxable year.

(iii) *Partnership specified tangible property.*—The term *partnership specified tangible property* means tangible property (as defined in paragraph (c)(2) of this section) of a partnership that is—

(A) Used in the trade or business of the partnership;

(B) Of a type with respect to which a deduction is allowable under section 167; and

(C) Used in the production of gross DEI.

(3) *Determination of adjusted basis.*—For purposes of this paragraph (g), a partnership's adjusted basis in partnership specified tangible property is determined based on the average of the partnership's adjusted basis in the property as of the close of each quarter in the partnership taxable year. The principles of paragraphs (e) and (h) of this section apply for purposes of determining a partnership's adjusted basis in partnership specified tangible property and the portion of such adjusted basis taken into account in determining a domestic corporation's partnership QBAI.

(4) *Example.*—The following example illustrates the rules of this paragraph (g).

(i) *Facts.* DC, a domestic corporation, is a partner in PRS. Both DC and PRS use the calendar year as their taxable year. PRS owns two assets, Asset A and Asset B, both of which are tangible property used in PRS's trade or business that it depreciates under section 168. Asset A and Asset B are used solely in the production of gross DEI. The average of PRS's adjusted basis as of the close of each quarter of PRS's taxable year in Asset A is $100x, and the average of PRS's adjusted basis as of the close of each quarter of PRS's taxable year in Asset B is $50x. Asset A produces $10x of directly identifiable gross income for the taxable year, and Asset B produces $50x of directly identifiable gross income for the taxable year. DC's distributive share of the gross income from Asset A is $8x and its distributive share of the gross income from Asset B is $10x. DC's entire distributive share of income from Asset A and Asset B is included in DC's gross DEI for the taxable year. See § 1.250(b)-1(e)(1). DC's distributive share satisfies the requirements of section 704(b).

(ii) *Analysis.* Each of Asset A and Asset B is partnership specified tangible property because each is tangible property, of a type with respect to which a deduction is allowable under section 167, used in PRS's trade or business, and used in the production of gross DEI. DC's partnership QBAI ratio for Asset A is 80%, the ratio of DC's distributive share of the gross income from Asset A for the taxable year that is included in DC's gross DEI ($8x) to the total gross income produced by Asset A for the taxable year ($10x). DC's partnership QBAI ratio for Asset B is 20%, the ratio of DC's distributive share of the gross income from Asset B for the taxable year that is included in DC's gross DEI ($10x) to the total gross income produced by Asset B for the taxable year ($50x). DC's share of the average of PRS's adjusted basis of Asset A is $80x, PRS's adjusted basis in Asset A of $100x multiplied by DC's partnership QBAI ratio for Asset A of 80%. DC's share of the average of PRS's adjusted basis of Asset B is $10x, PRS's adjusted basis in Asset B of $50x multiplied by DC's partnership QBAI ratio for Asset B of 20%. Therefore, DC's partnership QBAI with respect to PRS is $90x ($80x + $10x). Accordingly, under paragraph (g)(1) of this section, DC increases its qualified business asset investment for the taxable year by $90x.

(h) *Anti-avoidance rule for certain transfers of property.*—(1) *In general.*—If, with a principal purpose of decreasing the amount of its deemed tangible income return, a domestic corporation transfers specified tangible property (*transferred property*) to a specified related party of the domestic corporation and, within the disqualified period, the domestic corporation or an FDII-eligible related party of the domestic corporation leases the same or substantially similar property from any specified related party, then, solely for purposes of determining the qualified business asset investment of the domestic corporation under paragraph (b) of this section, the domestic corporation is treated as owning the transferred property from the later of the beginning of the term of the lease or date of the transfer of the property until the earlier of the end of the term of the lease or the end of the recovery period of the property.

(2) *Rule for structured arrangements.*—For purposes of paragraph (h)(1) of this section, a transfer of specified tangible property to a person that is not a related party or lease of property from a person that is not a related party is treated as a transfer to or lease from a specified related party if the transfer or lease is pursuant to a structured arrangement. A structured arrangement exists only if either paragraph (h)(2)(i) or (ii) of this section is satisfied.

(i) The reduction in the domestic corporation's deemed tangible income return is a material factor in the pricing of the arrangement with the transferee.

(ii) Based on all the facts and circumstances, the reduction in the domestic corporation's deemed tangible income return is a principal purpose of the arrangement. Facts and circumstances that indicate the reduction in the domestic corporation's deemed tangible income return is a principal purpose of the arrangement include—

(A) Marketing the arrangement as tax-advantaged where some or all of the tax advantage derives from the reduction in the domestic corporation's deemed tangible income return;

(B) Primarily marketing the arrangement to domestic corporations which earn foreign-derived deduction eligible income;

(C) Features that alter the terms of the arrangement, including the return, in the event the reduction in the domestic corporation's deemed tangible income return is no longer relevant; or

(D) A below-market return absent the tax effects or benefits resulting from the reduction in the domestic corporation's deemed tangible income return.

(3) *Per se rules for certain transactions.*—For purposes of paragraph (h)(1) of this section, a transfer of property by a domestic corporation to a specified related party (including a party deemed to be a specified related party under paragraph (h)(2) of this section) followed by a lease of the same or substantially similar property by the domestic corporation or an FDII-eligible related party from a specified related party (including a party deemed to be a specified related party under paragraph (h)(2) of this section) is treated per se as occurring pursuant to a principal purpose of decreasing the amount of the domestic corporation's deemed tangible income return if both the transfer and the lease occur within a six-month period.

(4) *Definitions related to anti-avoidance rule.*—The following definitions apply for purpose of this paragraph (h).

(i) *Disqualified period.*—The term *disqualified period* means, with respect to a transfer, the period beginning one year before the date of the transfer and ending the earlier of the end of the remaining recovery period (under the system described in section 951A(d)(3)(A)) of the property or one year after the date of the transfer.

(ii) *FDII-eligible related party.*—The term *FDII-eligible related party* means, with respect to a domestic corporation, a member of the same consolidated group as the domestic corporation or a partnership with respect to which at least 80 percent of the interests in partnership capital and profits are owned, directly or indirectly, by the domestic corporation or one or more members of the consolidated group that includes the domestic corporation.

(iii) *Specified related party.*—The term *specified related party* means, with respect to a domestic corporation, a related party (as defined in §1.250(b)-1(c)(19)) other than an FDII-eligible related party.

(iv) *Transfer.*—The term *transfer* means any disposition, exchange, contribution, or distribution of property, and includes an indirect transfer. For example, a transfer of an interest in a partnership is treated as a transfer of the assets of the partnership. In addition, if paragraph (h)(1) of this section applies to treat a domestic corporation as owning specified tangible property by reason of a lease of the property, the termination or lapse of the lease of the property is treated as a transfer of the property by the domestic corporation to the lessor.

(5) *Examples.*—The following examples illustrate the application of this paragraph (h).

(i) *Example 1: Sale-leaseback with a related party*—(A) *Facts.* DC, a domestic corporation, owns Asset A, which is specified tangible property. DC also owns all the single class of stock of DS, a domestic corporation, and FS1 and FS2, each a controlled foreign corporation. DC and DS are members of the same consolidated group. On January 1, Year 1, DC sells Asset A to FS1. At the time of the sale, Asset A had a remaining recovery period of 10 years under the alternative depreciation system. On February 1, Year 1, FS2 leases Asset B, which is substantially similar to Asset A, to DS for a five-year term ending on January 31, Year 6.

(B) *Analysis.* Because DC transfers specified tangible property (Asset A), to a specified related party of DC (FS1), and, within a six month period (January 1, Year 1 to February 1, Year 1), an FDII-eligible related party of DC (DS) leases a substantially similar property (Asset B), DC's transfer of Asset A and lease of Asset B are treated as per se occurring pursuant to a principal purpose of decreasing the amount of its deemed tangible income return. Accordingly, for purposes of determining DC's qualified business asset investment, DC is treated as owning Asset A from February 1, Year 1, the later of the date of the transfer of Asset A (January 1, Year 1) and the beginning of the term of the lease of Asset B (February 1, Year 1), until January 31, Year 6, the earlier of the end of the term of the lease of Asset B (January 31, Year 6) or the remaining recovery period of Asset A (December 31, Year 10).

(ii) *Example 2: Sale-leaseback with a related party; lapse of initial lease*—(A) *Facts.* The facts are the same as in paragraph (h)(5)(i)(A) of this section (the facts in *Example 1*). In addition, DS allows the lease of Asset B to expire on February 1, Year 6. On June 1, Year 6, DS and FS2 renew the lease for a five-year term ending on May 31, Year 11.

(B) *Analysis.* Because DC is treated as owning Asset A under paragraph (h)(1) of this section, the lapse of the lease of Asset B is treated as a transfer of Asset A to FS2 on February 1, Year 6, under paragraph (h)(4)(iv) of this section. Further, because DC is deemed to transfer specified tangible property (Asset A) to a specified related party (FS2) upon the lapse of the lease, and within a six month period (February 1, Year 6 to June 1, Year 6), an FDII-eligible related party of DC (DS) leases a substantially similar property (Asset B), DC's

deemed transfer of Asset A under paragraph (h)(4)(iv) of this section and lease of Asset B are treated as per se occurring pursuant to a principal purpose of decreasing the amount of its deemed tangible income return. Accordingly, for purposes of determining DC's qualified business asset investment, DC is treated as owning Asset A from June 1, Year 6, the later of the date of the deemed transfer of Asset A (February 1, Year 6) and the beginning of the term of the lease of Asset B (June 1, Year 6), until December 31, Year 10, the earlier of the end of the term of the lease of Asset B (May 31, Year 11) or the remaining recovery period of Asset A (December 31, Year 10). [Reg. §1.250(b)-2.]

§1.250(b)-3. FDDEI transactions.—(a) *Scope.*—This section provides rules related to the determination of whether a sale of property or provision of a service is a FDDEI transaction. Paragraph (b) of this section provides definitions related to the determination of whether a sale of property or provision of a service is a FDDEI transaction. Paragraph (c) of this section provides rules regarding a sale of property or provision of a service to a foreign government or an international organization. Paragraph (d) of this section provides rules for determining the reliability of documentation. Paragraph (e) of this section provides a rule for characterizing a transaction with both sales and services elements. Paragraph (f) of this section provides a rule for treating certain loss transactions as FDDEI transactions. Paragraph (g) of this section provides a rule for determining whether a sale of property or provision of a service to a partnership is a FDDEI transaction.

(b) *Definitions.*—This paragraph (b) provides definitions that apply for purposes of this section and §§1.250(b)-4 through 1.250(b)-6.

(1) *FDII filing date.*—The term *FDII filing date* means, with respect to a sale of property by a seller or provision of a service by a renderer, the date, including extensions, by which the seller or renderer is required to file an income tax return (or in the case of a seller or renderer that is a partnership, a return of partnership income) for the taxable year in which the gross income from the sale of property or provision of a service is included in the gross income of the seller or renderer.

(2) *Foreign person.*—The term *foreign person* means a person that is not a United States person, and includes a foreign government or an international organization.

(3) *General property.*—The term *general property* means any property other than—
(i) Intangible property;
(ii) A security (as defined in section 475(c)(2)); or
(iii) A commodity (as defined in section 475(e)(2)(B) through (D)).

(4) *Intangible property.*—The term *intangible property* has the meaning set forth in section 367(d)(4).

(5) *Recipient.*—The term *recipient* means a person that purchases property or services from a seller or renderer.

(6) *Renderer.*—The term *renderer* means a person that provides a service to a recipient.

(7) *Sale.*—The term *sale* means any sale, lease, license, exchange, or disposition of property, and includes any transfer of property in which gain or income is recognized under section 367.

(8) *Seller.*—The term *seller* means a person that sells property to a recipient.

(9) *United States.*—The term *United States* has the meaning set forth in section 7701(a)(9), as expanded by section 638(1) with respect to mines, oil and gas wells, and other natural deposits.

(10) *United States person.*—The term *United States person* has the meaning set forth in section 7701(a)(30), except that the term does not include an individual that is a bona fide resident of a United States territory within the meaning of section 937(a).

(11) *United States territory.*—The term *United States territory* means American Samoa, Guam, the Northern Mariana Islands, Puerto Rico, or the U.S. Virgin Islands.

(c) *Foreign military sales.*—For purposes of determining whether a sale of property or a provision of a service is a FDDEI transaction, if a sale of property or a provision of a service is made to the United States or an instrumentality thereof pursuant to 22 U.S.C. 2751 et seq. under which the United States or an instrumentality thereof purchases the property or service for resale or on-service, on commercial terms, to a foreign government or agency or instrumentality thereof, and the contract between the seller or renderer and the United States or an instrumentality thereof provides that the sale or service is purchased for resale or on-service to such foreign government or agency or instrumentality thereof, then the sale of property or provision of a service is treated as a sale of property or a provision of a service to the foreign government.

(d) *Reliability of documentation.*—For purposes of the documentation requirements described in §§ 1.250(b)-4 through 1.250(b)-6, documentation is reliable only if each of the requirements described in paragraphs (d)(1) through (3) of this section is satisfied.

(1) As of the FDII filing date, the seller or renderer does not know and does not have reason to know that the documentation is unreliable or incorrect. For this purpose, a seller or renderer has reason to know that documentation is unreliable or incorrect if its knowledge of all the relevant facts or statements contained in the documentation is such that a reasonably prudent person in the position of the seller or renderer would question the accuracy or reliability of the documentation.

(2) The documentation is obtained by the seller or renderer by the FDII filing date with respect to the sale or service.

(3) The documentation is obtained no earlier than one year before the date of the sale or service.

(e) *Transactions with multiple elements.*—If a transaction includes both a sale component and a service component, the transaction is classified according to the overall predominant character of the transaction for purposes of determining whether the transaction is subject to § 1.250(b)-4 or § 1.250(b)-5.

(f) *Treatment of certain loss transactions.*—(1) *In general.*—If a seller knows or has reason to know that property is sold to a foreign person for a foreign use (within the meaning of § 1.250(b)-4(d)(2) or (e)(2)) or a renderer knows or has reason to know that a general service (as defined in § 1.250(b)-5(c)(4)) is provided to a person located outside the United States (within the meaning of § 1.250(b)-5(d)(2) or (e)(2)), but the seller or renderer does not satisfy

the documentation requirements described in § 1.250(b)-4(c)(2), (d)(3), or (e)(3) or § 1.250(b)-5(d)(3) or (e)(3), as applicable, the transaction is deemed to be a FDDEI transaction with respect to a domestic corporation if not treating the transaction as a FDDEI transaction would increase the amount of the corporation's foreign-derived deduction eligible income for the taxable year relative to its foreign-derived deduction eligible income that would be determined if the transaction were treated as a FDDEI transaction. If a seller or renderer engages in more than one transaction described in the preceding sentence in a taxable year, the previous sentence applies by comparing the corporation's foreign-derived deduction eligible income if each such transaction were not treated as a FDDEI transaction to its foreign-derived deduction eligible income if each such transaction were treated as a FDDEI transaction.

(2) *Example.*—The following example illustrates the application of this paragraph (f).

(i) *Facts.* During a taxable year, DC, a domestic corporation, manufactures products A and B in the United States. DC sells product A for $200x and product B for $800x. DC knows or has reason to know that all of its sales of product A and product B are to foreign persons for a foreign use. DC establishes that its sales of product B are to foreign persons for a foreign use but does not obtain documentation establishing that any sales of product A are to foreign person for a foreign use. DC's cost of goods sold is $450x. For purposes of determining gross FDDEI, under § 1.250(b)-1(d)(1) DC attributes $250x of cost of goods sold to product A and $200x of cost of goods sold to product B, and then attributes the cost of goods sold for each product ratably between the gross receipts of such product sold to foreign persons and the gross receipts of such product not sold to foreign persons. The manner in which DC attributes the cost of goods sold is a reasonable method. DC has no other items of income, loss, or deduction.

Table 1 to paragraph (f)(2)(i)	Product A	Product B	Total
Gross receipts	$200x	$800x	$1,000x
Cost of Goods Sold	$250x	$200x	$450x
Gross Income (Loss)	($50x)	$600x	$550x

(ii) *Analysis.* By not treating the sales of product A as FDDEI sales, the amount of DC's foreign-derived deduction eligible income would increase by $50x relative to its foreign-derived deduction eligible income if the sales of product A were treated as FDDEI sales. Accordingly, because DC knows or has reason to know that its sales of product A are to foreign persons for a foreign use, the sales of product A constitute FDDEI sales under paragraph (f)(1) of this section, and thus the $50x loss from the sale of product A is included in DC's gross FDDEI.

(g) *Treatment of partnerships.*—(1) *In general.*—For purposes of determining whether a sale of property to or by a partnership or a provision of a service to or by a partnership is a FDDEI transaction, a partnership is treated as a person. Accordingly, for example, a partnership may be a seller, renderer, recipient, or related party, including a foreign related party (as defined in § 1.250(b)-6(b)(1)).

(2) *Examples.*—The following examples illustrate the application of this paragraph (g).

(i) *Example 1: Domestic partner sale to foreign partnership with a foreign branch*-(A) *Facts.* DC, a domestic corporation, is a partner in PRS, a foreign partnership. DC and PRS are not related parties. PRS has a foreign branch within the meaning of § 1.904-4(f)(3)(iii). DC and PRS both use the calendar year as their taxable year. For the taxable year, DC recognizes $20x of gain on the sale of general property to PRS for a foreign use (as determined under § 1.250(b)-4(d)). During the same taxable year, PRS recognizes an additional $20x of gain on the sale of the property to a foreign person for a foreign use (as determined under § 1.250(b)-4(d)). PRS's income on the sale of the property is attributable to its foreign branch.

(B) *Analysis.* DC's sale of property to PRS, a foreign partnership, is a FDDEI sale because it is a sale to a foreign person for a foreign use. Therefore, DC's gain of $20x on the sale to PRS is included in DC's gross DEI and gross FDDEI. However, PRS's gain of $20x is not included in the gross DEI or gross FDDEI of PRS because the gain is foreign branch income within the meaning of § 1.250(b)-1(c)(11). Accordingly, none of PRS's gain on the sale of property is included in DC's gross DEI or gross FDDEI under § 1.250(b)-1(e)(1).

(ii) *Example 2: Domestic partner sale to domestic partnership without a foreign branch*—(A) *Facts.* The facts are the same as in paragraph (g)(2)(i)(A) of this section (the facts in *Example 1*), except PRS is a domestic partnership that does not have a foreign branch within the meaning of § 1.904-4(f)(3)(iii).

(B) *Analysis.* DC's sale of property to PRS, a domestic partnership, is not a FDDEI sale because the sale is to a United States person.

Therefore, the gross income from DC's sale to PRS is included in DC's gross DEI, but is not included in its gross FDDEI. However, PRS's subsequent sale is a FDDEI sale, and therefore the gain of $20x is included in the gross DEI and gross FDDEI of PRS. Accordingly, DC includes its distributive share of PRS's gain from the sale in determining DC's gross DEI and gross FDDEI for the taxable year under § 1.250(b)-1(e)(1). [Reg. § 1.250(b)-3.]

§ 1.250(b)-4. FDDEI sales.—(a) *Scope.*—This section provides rules for determining whether a sale of property is a FDDEI sale. Paragraph (b) of this section defines a FDDEI sale. Paragraph (c) of this section provides rules for determining whether a recipient is a foreign person. Paragraph (d) of this section provides rules for determining whether general property is sold for a foreign use. Paragraph (e) of this section provides rules for determining whether intangible property is sold for a foreign use. Paragraph (f) of this section provides a special rule for the sale of certain financial instruments.

(b) *Definition of FDDEI sale.*—Except as provided in § 1.250(b)-6(c), the term *FDDEI sale* means a sale of general property or intangible property to a foreign person (as determined under paragraph (c) of this section) for a foreign use (as determined under paragraphs (d) and (e) of this section).

(c) *Foreign person.*—(1) *In general.*—A recipient is a foreign person for purposes of paragraph (b) of this section only if the seller establishes that the recipient is a foreign person by obtaining the documentation described in paragraph (c)(2) of this section (which meets the reliability requirements described in § 1.250(b)-3(d)) and, as of the FDII filing date, the seller does not know or have reason to know that the recipient is not a foreign person.

(2) *Documentation of status as a foreign person.*—(i) *In general.*—Except as provided in paragraph (c)(2)(ii) of this section, a seller establishes the status of a recipient as a foreign person by obtaining one or more of the following types of documentation with respect to the person—

(A) A written statement by the recipient that the recipient is a foreign person;

(B) With respect to a recipient that is an entity, documentation that establishes that the entity is organized or created under the laws of a foreign jurisdiction;

(C) With respect to an individual, any valid identification issued by a foreign government or an agency thereof that is typically used for identification purposes;

(D) Documents filed with a government or an agency or instrumentality thereof that provide the foreign jurisdiction of organization or residence of an entity (for example, a publicly traded corporation's annual report filed with the U.S. Securities and Exchange Commission that includes the jurisdiction of organization or residence of foreign subsidiaries of the corporation); or

(E) Any other forms of documentation as prescribed by the Secretary in forms, instructions, or other guidance.

(ii) *Special rules.*—(A) *Special rule for small businesses.*—A seller that receives less than $10,000,000 in gross receipts during a prior taxable year establishes the status of any recipient as a foreign person for a taxable year if the seller's shipping address for the recipient is outside the United States. If the seller's prior taxable year was less than 12 months (a short period), gross receipts are annualized by multiplying the gross receipts for the short period by 365 and dividing the result by the number of days in the short period.

(B) *Special rule for small transactions.*—A seller that receives less than $5,000 in gross receipts during a taxable year from a recipient establishes the status of such recipient as a foreign person for such taxable year if the seller's shipping address for the recipient is outside the United States.

(d) *Foreign use for general property.*—(1) *In general.*—The sale of general property is for a foreign use only if the seller establishes that the property is for a foreign use within the meaning of paragraph (d)(2) of this section by obtaining the documentation described in paragraph (d)(3) of this section (which meets the reliability requirements described in § 1.250(b)-3(d)) and, as of the FDII filing date, the seller does not know or have reason to know that the property is not for a foreign use within the meaning of paragraph (d)(2) of this section.

(2) *Determination of foreign use.*—(i) *In general.*—Except as provided in paragraph (d)(2)(iv) of this section, the sale of general property is for a foreign use if—

(A) The property is not subject to a domestic use within three years of the date of delivery; or

(B) The property is subject to manufacture, assembly, or other processing outside the United States before the property is subject to a domestic use.

(ii) *Determination of domestic use.*—General property is subject to domestic use if—

(A) The property is subject to any use, consumption, or disposition within the United States; or

(B) The property is subject to manufacture, assembly, or other processing within the United States.

(iii) *Determination of manufacture, assembly, or other processing.*—(A) *In general.*—General property is subject to manufacture, assembly, or other processing only if the property is physically and materially changed (as described in paragraph (d)(2)(iii)(B) of this section) or the property is incorporated as a component into a second product (as described in paragraph (d)(2)(iii)(C) of this section).

(B) *Property subject to a physical and material change.*—For purposes of paragraph (d)(2)(iii)(A) of this section, the determination of whether general property is subject to a physical and material change is made based on all the relevant facts and circumstances. However, general property is not considered subject to physical and material change if it is subject only to minor assembly, packaging, or labeling.

(C) *Property incorporated into second product as a component.*—For purposes of paragraph (d)(2)(iii)(A) of this section, general property is treated as a component incorporated into a second product only if the fair market value of such property when it is delivered to the recipient constitutes no more than 20 percent of the fair market value of the second product, determined when the second product is completed. For purposes of the preceding sentence, all general property that is sold by the seller and incorporated into the second product is treated as a single item of property.

(iv) *Determination of foreign use for transportation property.*—In the case of aircraft, railroad rolling stock, vessel, motor vehicle, or similar property that provides a mode of transportation and is capable of traveling internationally (*international transportation property*), such property is for a foreign use only if, during the three year period from the date of delivery, the property is located outside the United States more than 50 percent of the time and more than 50 percent of the miles traversed in the use of the property are traversed outside the United States. For purposes of the preceding sentence, international transportation property is deemed to be within the United States at all times during which it is engaged in transport between any two points within the United States, except where the transport constitutes uninterrupted international air transportation within the meaning of section 4262(c)(3) and the regulations under that section (relating to tax on air transportation of persons).

(3) *Documentation of foreign use of general property.*—(i) *In general.*—Except as provided in paragraphs (d)(3)(ii) and (iii) of this section, a seller establishes that general property, or a portion of a particular class of fungible general property, is for a foreign use only if the seller obtains one or more of the following types of documentation with respect to the sale—

(A) A written statement from the recipient or a related party of the recipient that the recipient's use or intended use of the property is for a foreign use (within the meaning of paragraph (d)(2) of this section);

(B) A binding contract between the seller and the recipient which provides that the recipient's use or intended use of the property is for a foreign use (within the meaning of paragraph (d)(2) of this section);

(C) Except in the case of international transportation property, documentation of shipment of the general property (including both property located within the United States or outside the United States, such as in a warehouse, storage facility, or assembly site located outside the United States) to a location outside the United States (for example, a copy of the export bill of lading issued by the carrier which delivered the property, or a copy of the certificate of lading for the property executed by a customs officer of the country to which the property is delivered); or

(D) Any other forms of documentation as prescribed by the Secretary in forms, instructions, or other guidance.

(ii) *Special rules.*—(A) *Special rule for small businesses.*—A seller that receives less than $10,000,000 in gross receipts during the prior taxable year establishes that the sale of general property in a taxable year to any recipient is for a foreign use for the taxable year if the seller's shipping address for the recipient is outside the United States. If the seller's prior taxable year was a short period, gross receipts are annualized by multiplying the gross receipts for the short period by 365 and dividing the result by the number of days in the short period.

(B) *Special rule for small transactions.*—A seller that receives less than $5,000 in gross receipts during a taxable year from a recipient establishes that the sale of general property to the recipient is for a foreign use for the taxable year if the seller's shipping address for the recipient is outside the United States.

(iii) *Sales of fungible mass of general property.*—In the case of sales of multiple items of general property, which because of their fungible nature cannot reasonably be specifically traced to the location of use (*fungible mass*), as an alternative to obtaining the documentation described in paragraphs (d)(3)(i)(A) through (D) of this section, a seller may establish that a portion of the fungible mass is for a foreign use through market research, including statistical sampling, economic modeling and other similar methods indicating that the property will be subject to a foreign use. If, under the preceding sentence, the seller establishes that 90 percent or more of a fungible mass is for a foreign use, then the entire fungible mass is for a foreign use. If, under the first sentence of this paragraph (d)(3)(iii), the seller does not establish that 10 percent or more of the sale of a fungible mass is for a foreign use, then no portion of the fungible mass is for a foreign use.

(4) *Examples.*—The following examples illustrate the application of this paragraph (d).

(i) *Presumed facts.*—The following facts are assumed for purposes of the examples—

(A) DC is a domestic corporation.

(B) FP is a foreign person that is a foreign unrelated party (as defined in § 1.250(b)-6(b)(2)) with respect to DC, and DC obtains documentation establishing that FP is a foreign person.

(C) Any documentation obtained meets the reliability requirements described in § 1.250(b)-3(d).

(D) The treatment of any sale as a FDDEI sale would not reduce DC's foreign-derived deduction eligible income for the year.

(ii) *Examples.*—(A) *Example 1: Manufacturing outside the United States*—(1) *Facts.* DC sells general property for $18x to FP for manufacture outside the United States and obtains documentation of shipment of the property to a location outside the United States. DC does not know or have reason to know that the property will be subject to a domestic use before manufacture, but DC knows or has reason to know that the property will be subject to a domestic use after manufacture and within three years of delivery to FP. FP will incorporate the property into a second product outside the United States that FP will sell to a United States person for $100x. The property is not physically or materially changed in the process of its incorporation into the second product.

(2) *Analysis.* Because the fair market value of the general property FP purchases from DC and incorporates into the second product does not exceed 20% of the fair market value of the second product, the general property FP purchases from DC is a component, and therefore the property is treated as subject to manufacture, assembly, or other processing outside the United States. See paragraphs (d)(2)(iii)(A) and (B) of this section. As a result, notwithstanding that DC knows or has reason to know that the property will be subject to a domestic use within three years of delivery, DC does not know or have reason to know that its sale of general property to FP is not for a foreign use. See paragraph (d)(2)(i)(B) of this section. Accordingly, DC's sale of property to FP is for a foreign use under paragraph (d)(2) of this section, and the sale is a FDDEI sale.

(B) *Example 2: Manufacturing outside the United States*—(1) *Facts.* The facts are the same as in paragraph (d)(2)(iv)(A)(1) of this section (the facts in *Example 1*), except FP purchases the general property from DC for $25x.

(2) *Analysis.* Because the fair market value of the general property FP purchases from DC and incorporates into the second product exceeds 20% of the fair market value of the second product, the general property is not treated as a component of the second product. Because the property is also not subject to a physical and material change in the process of incorporation into the second product, the property is not subject to manufacture, assembly, or other processing outside the United States. As a result, because DC knows or has reason to know that FP will sell the second product, which includes the property, for domestic use, DC knows or has reason to know that its sale of general property to FP is not for a foreign use. Accordingly, DC's sale of the property to FP is not for a foreign use under paragraph (d)(2) of this section, and the sale is not a FDDEI sale.

(C) *Example 3: Sale of a fungible mass of products*—(1) *Facts.* DC and persons other than DC sell multiple units of fungible general property to FP during the taxable year. DC obtains documentation of shipment of the property to a location outside the United States, but it knows or has reason to know that some portion of the property will be resold back to customers in the United States. DC also engages in reliable market research that determines that approximately 25% of the fungible general property FP sold during the taxable year is for domestic use.

(2) *Analysis.* Notwithstanding that the documentation of shipment meets the reliability requirements of §1.250(b)-3(d), DC knows or has reason to know that certain units of the property are not for a foreign use. See paragraphs (d)(1) and (2) of this section. However, DC can establish foreign use of a portion of the fungible property through its market research. See paragraphs (d)(1) and (d)(3)(iii) of this section. Based on its market research, DC knows that approximately 25% of the total units of fungible general property that FP purchased from all persons in the taxable year is sold by FP for domestic use. Accordingly, DC satisfies the test for a foreign use under paragraph (d)(2) of this section with respect to 75% of its sales of the property to FP.

(e) *Foreign use for intangible property.*—(1) *In general.*—A sale of intangible property is for a foreign use only to the extent the seller establishes that the sale is for a foreign use within the meaning of paragraph (e)(2) of this section by obtaining documentation described in paragraph (e)(3) of this section (which meets the reliability requirements described in §1.250(b)-3(d)) and, as of the FDII filing date, the seller does not know or have reason to know that the portion of the sale of the intangible property for which the seller establishes foreign use is not for a foreign use within the meaning of paragraph (e)(2) of this section.

(2) *Determination of foreign use.*—(i) *In general.*—A sale of intangible property is for a foreign use only to the extent that the intangible property generates revenue from exploitation outside the United States. A sale of intangible property rights providing for exploitation both within the United States and outside the United States is for a foreign use in proportion to the revenue generated from exploitation of the intangible property outside the United States over the total revenue generated from the exploitation of the intangible property. For intangible property used in the development, manufacture, sale, or distribution of a product, the intangible property is treated as exploited at the location of the end user when the product is sold to the end user. Paragraphs (e)(2)(ii) and (iii) of this section provide rules for how and when to determine revenue from exploitation with respect to different types of sales of intangible property.

(ii) *Sales in exchange for periodic payments.*—In the case of a sale of intangible property to a foreign person in exchange for periodic payments, the extent to which the sale is for a foreign use is determined on an annual basis based on the actual revenue earned by the recipient for the taxable year in which a periodic payment is received.

(iii) *Sales in exchange for a lump sum.*—In the case of a sale of intangible property to a foreign person for a lump sum, the extent to which the sale is for a foreign use is determined based on the ratio of the total net present value of revenue the seller would have reasonably expected to earn from the exploitation of the intangible property outside the United States to the total net present value of revenue the seller would have reasonably expected to earn from the exploitation of the intangible property.

(3) *Documentation of foreign use of intangible property.*—(i) *Documentation for sales for periodic payments.*—Except as provided in paragraph (e)(3)(ii) of this section, a seller establishes the extent to which a sale of intangible property described in paragraph (e)(2)(ii) of this section is for a foreign use by obtaining one or more of the following types of documentation with respect to the sale—

(A) A written statement from the recipient providing the amount of the annual revenue from sales or sublicenses of the intangible property or sales of products with respect to which the intangible property is used that is generated as a result of exploitation of the intangible property outside the United States and the total amount of revenue from such sales or sublicenses worldwide;

(B) A binding contract for the sale of the intangible property that provides that the intangible property can be exploited solely outside the United States;

(C) Audited financial statements or annual reports of the recipient stating the amount of annual revenue earned within the United States and outside the United States from sales of products with respect to which the intangible property is used;

(D) Any statements or documents used by the seller and the recipient to determine the amount of payment due for exploitation of the intangible property if those statements or documents provide reliable data on revenue earned within the United States and outside the United States; or

(E) Any other forms of documentation as prescribed by the Secretary in forms, instructions, or other guidance.

(ii) *Certain sales to foreign unrelated parties.*—In the case of a sale of intangible property described in paragraph (e)(2)(ii) of this section that are not contingent on revenue or profit to a foreign unrelated party (as defined in §1.250(b)-6(b)(2)), where the seller is unable to obtain the documentation described in paragraph (e)(3)(i) of this section without undue burden, a seller establishes the extent to which the sale of intangible property is for a foreign use using the principles of paragraph (e)(3)(iii) of this section, except that the seller must make reasonable projections on an annual basis.

(iii) *Documentation for sales in exchange for a lump sum.*—A seller establishes the extent to which a sale of intangible property described in paragraph (e)(2)(iii) of this section is for a foreign use through documentation containing reasonable projections of the amount and location of revenue that the seller would have reasonably expected to earn from exploiting the intangible property. To be considered reasonable, the projections must be consistent with the financial data and projections used by the seller to determine the price it sold the intangible property to the foreign person.

(4) *Examples.*—The following examples illustrate the application of this paragraph (e).

(i) *Presumed facts.*—The following facts are assumed for purposes of the examples—

(A) DC is a domestic corporation.

(B) Except as otherwise provided, FP and FP2 are foreign persons that are foreign unrelated parties (as defined in §1.250(b)-6(b)(2)) with respect to DC.

(C) Any documentation obtained meets the reliability requirements described in §1.250(b)-3(d).

(D) All of DC's income is deduction eligible income.

(E) The treatment of any sale as a FDDEI sale would not reduce DC's foreign-derived deduction eligible income for the year.

(ii) *Examples.*—(A) *Example 1: License of worldwide rights with documentation*—(1) *Facts.* DC licenses to FP worldwide rights to the copyright to composition A in exchange for annual royalties of $60x. FP sells composition A to customers through digital downloads from servers. In the taxable year, FP earns $100x in revenue from sales of copies of composition A to customers, of which $60x is from customers located in the United States and the remaining $40x is from customers located outside the United States. FP provides DC with records showing the amount of revenue earned in the taxable year from sales of composition A to establish the royalties owed to DC. These records also provide DC with the amount of revenue earned from sales of composition A in different countries, including the United States.

(2) *Analysis.* Based on the information provided, DC has obtained documentation establishing that 40% ($40x/$100x) of the revenue generated by the copyright during the taxable year is earned

outside the United States. Accordingly, a portion of DC's license to FP is for a foreign use under paragraph (e)(2) of this section and therefore such portion is a FDDEI sale. The $24x of royalty (0.40 x $60x) derived with respect to such portion is included in DC's gross FDDEI for the taxable year.

(B) *Example 2: License of worldwide rights without documentation*—(1) *Facts.* The facts are the same as in paragraph (e)(4)(ii)(A)(1) of this section (the facts in *Example 1*), except FP does not provide DC with data showing how much revenue was earned from sales in different countries.

(2) *Analysis.* DC has not obtained documentation establishing the amount of revenue FP earned from sales of composition A outside the United States. Accordingly, DC's license of the copyright is not for a foreign use under paragraph (e)(2) of this section and is not a FDDEI sale.

(C) *Example 3: Sale of patent rights protected in the United States and other countries; documentation through financial projections*—(1) *Facts.* DC owns a patent for an active pharmaceutical ingredient ("API") approved for treatment of disease A ("indication A") in the United States and in Countries A, B, and C. The patent is registered in the United States and in Countries A, B, and C. DC sells to FP all of its patent rights to the API for indication A for a lump sum payment of $1,000x. DC has no basis in the patent rights. To determine the sales price for the patent rights, DC projected that the net present value of the revenue it would earn from selling a pharmaceutical product incorporating the API for indication A was $5,000x, with 15% of the revenue earned from sales within the United States and 85% of the revenue earned from sales outside the United States.

(2) *Analysis.* Based on the financial projections DC used to determine the sales price, DC has obtained documentation establishing that 85% of the revenue that will be generated by the patent rights will be outside the United States. Accordingly, a portion of DC's sale to FP is for a foreign use under paragraph (e)(2) of this section and such portion is a FDDEI sale. The $850x (85% x $1,000x) of gain derived with respect to such portion is included in DC's gross FDDEI for the taxable year.

(D) *Example 4: Limited use license of copyrighted computer software; documentation through public filing*—(1) *Facts.* DC provides FP with a limited use license to copyrighted computer software in exchange for an annual fee of $100x. The limited use license restricts FP's use of the computer software to 100 of FP's employees. The limited use license prohibits FP from using the computer software in any way other than as an end-user, which includes prohibiting sublicensing, selling, reverse engineering, or modifying the computer software. FP's annual report for the taxable year indicates that all of FP's employees are physically located outside the United States.

(2) *Analysis.* The software licensed to FP is exploited where its employees that use the software are located. The revenue DC earns from the limited use license to FP is based on the number of FP's employees allowed to use the computer software as end-users. Based on FP's annual report for the taxable year, DC has obtained documentation establishing that all the revenue generated for the use of the copyrighted computer software is earned outside the United States for the taxable year. Accordingly, DC's license to FP is for a foreign use and therefore a FDDEI sale. The entire $100x of the license fee is included in DC's gross FDDEI for the taxable year.

(E) *Example 5: Limited use license of copyrighted computer software; documentation through public filing*—(1) *Facts.* The facts are the same as in paragraph (e)(4)(ii)(D)(1) of this section (the facts in *Example 4*), except that FP's annual report for the taxable year indicates that FP has offices both within and outside the United States, and that 50% of FP's revenue is earned within the United States.

(2) *Analysis.* Based on FP's annual report for the taxable year, DC has obtained documentation establishing that 50% of the revenue generated from the use of the copyrighted computer software is outside the United States for the taxable year. Accordingly, a portion of DC's license to FP is for a foreign use and therefore such portion is a FDDEI sale. The $50x of license fee derived with respect to such portion is included in DC's gross FDDEI for the taxable year.

(F) *Example 6: Deemed sale in exchange for contingent payments under section 367(d)*—(1) *Facts.* DC owns 100% of the stock of FP, a foreign related party (as defined in §1.250(b)-6(b)(1)) with respect to DC. FP manufactures and sells product A. For the taxable year, DC contributes to FP exclusive worldwide rights to patents, trademarks, knowhow, customer lists, and goodwill and going concern value (collectively, intangible property) related to product A in an exchange described in section 351. As a result, DC is required to report an annual income inclusion on its Federal income tax return based on the productivity, use, or disposition of the contributed intangible property under section 367(d). DC includes a percentage of FP's revenue in its gross income under section 367(d) each year. In the current taxable year, FP earns $1,000x of revenue from sales of product A. Based on FP's sales records for the taxable year, $300x of its revenue is earned from sales of product A to customers within the

United States, and $700x of its revenue is earned from sales of product A to customers outside the United States.

(2) *Analysis.* DC's deemed sale of the intangible property to FP in exchange for payments contingent upon the productivity, use, or disposition of the intangible property related to product A under section 367(d) is a sale for purposes of section 250 and this section. See §1.250(b)-3(b)(7). Based on FP's sales records, DC has obtained documentation that 70% ($700/$1,000x) of the revenue generated by the intangible property is generated outside the United States in the taxable year. Accordingly, for the taxable year, 70% of DC's deemed sale to FP is for a foreign use, and 70% of DC's income inclusion under section 367(d) derived with respect to such portion is included in DC's gross FDDEI for the taxable year.

(f) *Special rule for certain financial instruments.*—The sale of a security (as defined in section 475(c)(2)) or a commodity (as defined in section 475(e)(2)(B) through (D)) is not a FDDEI sale. [Reg. §1.250(b)-4.]

§1.250(b)-5. FDDEI services.—(a) *Scope.*—This section provides rules for determining whether a provision of a service is a FDDEI service. Paragraph (b) of this section defines a FDDEI service. Paragraph (c) of this section provides definitions relevant for determining whether a provision of a service is a FDDEI service. Paragraph (d) of this section provides rules for determining whether a general service is provided to a consumer located outside the United States. Paragraph (e) of this section provides rules for determining whether a general service is provided to a business recipient located outside the United States. Paragraph (f) of this section provides rules for determining whether a proximate service is provided to a recipient located outside the United States. Paragraph (g) of this section provides rules for determining whether a service is provided with respect to property located outside the United States. Paragraph (h) of this section provides rules for determining whether a transportation service is provided to a recipient, or with respect to property, located outside the United States.

(b) *Definition of FDDEI service.*—Except as provided in §1.250(b)-6(d), the term *FDDEI service* means a provision of a service described in one of paragraphs (b)(1) through (5) of this section. If only a portion of a service is treated as provided to a person, or with respect to property, outside the United States, the provision of the service is a FDDEI service only to the extent of the gross income derived with respect to such portion.

(1) The provision of a general service to a consumer located outside the United States (as determined under paragraph (d) of this section).

(2) The provision of a general service to a business recipient located outside the United States (as determined under paragraph (e) of this section).

(3) The provision of a proximate service to a recipient located outside the United States (as determined under paragraph (f) of this section).

(4) The provision of a property service with respect to tangible property located outside the United States (as determined under paragraph (g) of this section).

(5) The provision of a transportation service to a recipient, or with respect to property, located outside the United States (as determined under paragraph (h) of this section).

(c) *Definitions.*—This paragraph (c) provides definitions that apply for purposes of this section and §1.250(b)-6.

(1) *Benefit.*—The term *benefit* has the meaning set forth in §1.482-9(l)(3).

(2) *Business recipient.*—The term *business recipient* means a recipient other than a consumer.

(3) *Consumer.*—The term *consumer* means a recipient that is an individual that purchases a general service for personal use.

(4) *General service.*—The term *general service* means any service other than a property service, proximate service, or transportation service.

(5) *Property service.*—The term *property service* means a service, other than a transportation service, provided with respect to tangible property, but only if substantially all of the service is performed at the location of the property and results in physical manipulation of the property such as through assembly, maintenance, or repair. Substantially all of a service is performed at the location of property if the renderer spends more than 80 percent of the time providing the service at or near the location of the property.

(6) *Proximate service.*—The term *proximate service* means a service, other than a property service or a transportation service, provided to a recipient, but only if substantially all of the service is performed in the physical presence of the recipient or, in the case of a

business recipient, its employees. Substantially all of a service is performed in the physical presence of the recipient or its employees if the renderer spends more than 80 percent of the time providing the service in the physical presence of the recipient or its employees.

(7) *Transportation service.*—The term *transportation service* means a service to transport a person or property using aircraft, railroad rolling stock, vessel, motor vehicle, or any similar mode of transportation.

(d) *General services provided to consumers.*—(1) *In general.*—A general service is provided to a consumer located outside the United States only if the renderer establishes that the consumer is located outside the United States by obtaining the documentation described in paragraph (d)(3) of this section (which meets the reliability requirements described in § 1.250(b)-3(d)) and, as of the FDII filing date, the renderer does not know or have reason to know that the consumer is located within the United States (as determined under paragraph (d)(2) of this section) when the service is provided.

(2) *Location of consumer.*—For purposes of paragraph (d)(1) of this section, the consumer of a general service is located where the consumer resides when the service is provided.

(3) *Documentation of location of consumer.*—(i) *In general.*—Except as provided in paragraph (d)(3)(ii) of this section, a renderer establishes that a consumer is located outside the United States only if the renderer obtains one or more of the following types of documentation with respect to the consumer—

(A) A written statement by the consumer indicating that the consumer resides outside the United States when the service is provided;

(B) Any valid identification issued by a foreign government or an agency thereof that is typically used for identification purposes; or

(C) Any other forms of documentation as prescribed by the Secretary in forms, instructions, or other guidance.

(ii) *Special rules.*—(A) *Special rule for small businesses.*—A renderer that receives less than $10,000,000 in gross receipts during the prior taxable year establishes that any consumer of a service provided in the taxable year is located outside the United States if the renderer's billing address for the consumer is outside of the United States. If a renderer has a prior taxable year of fewer than 12 months (a short period), gross receipts are annualized by multiplying the gross receipts for the short period by 365 and dividing the result by the number of days in the short period.

(B) *Special rule for small transactions.*—A renderer that receives less than $5,000 in gross receipts during a taxable year from a consumer establishes that such consumer is located outside the United States for such taxable year if the renderer's billing address for the consumer is outside the United States.

(e) *General services provided to business recipients.*—(1) *In general.*—A general service is provided to a business recipient located outside the United States only to the extent that the renderer establishes that the service is provided to a business recipient located outside the United States (as determined under paragraph (e)(2) of this section) by obtaining the documentation described in paragraph (e)(3) of this section (which meets the reliability requirements described in § 1.250(b)-3(d)) and, as of the FDII filing date, the renderer does not know or have reason to know that the portion of the service which the seller establishes is provided to a business recipient located outside the United States is provided to a business recipient that is located within the United States when the service is provided.

(2) *Location of business recipient.*—(i) *In general.*—A service is provided to a business recipient located outside of the United States to the extent that the gross income derived by the renderer from such service is allocated to the business recipient's operations outside the United States under the rules in paragraphs (e)(2)(i)(A) and (B) of this section. A service is provided to a business recipient located within the United States to the extent that a service is not provided to a business recipient located outside the United States.

(A) *Determination of business operations that benefit from the service.*—If the renderer provides a service that provides a benefit to the operations of the business recipient in specific locations, gross income of the renderer is allocated to a business recipient's operations outside the United States to the extent that the benefit of the service is conferred on operations of the business recipient that are located outside the United States. However, if the renderer is unable to obtain reliable information regarding the specific locations of the operations of the business recipient to which a benefit is conferred, or if the renderer provides a service that does not provide a benefit to specific locations of the business recipient's operations but rather will generally confer a benefit on all locations of the business recipient's

operations, gross income of the renderer is allocated ratably to all of the business recipient's operations at the time the service is provided.

(B) *Determination of amount of benefit conferred on operations outside the United States.*—The amount of the benefit conferred on a business recipient's operations located outside the United States is determined under any method that is reasonable under the circumstances. In determining whether a method is reasonable, the principles of § 1.482-9(k) apply, treating the business recipient's operations in different locations as if they were "recipients" and treating the renderer's gross income as if they were "costs" as those terms are used in § 1.482-9(k). Reasonable methods may include, for example, allocations based on time spent or costs incurred by the renderer or gross receipts, revenue, profits, or assets of the business recipient.

(ii) *Location of business recipient's operations.*—For purposes of this paragraph (e), a business recipient is treated as having operations in any location where it maintains an office or other fixed place of business.

(3) *Documentation of location of business recipient.*—(i) *In general.*—A renderer establishes that a business recipient is located outside the United States only if the renderer obtains one or more of the types of documentation described in paragraphs (e)(3)(i)(A) through (E) of this section. The documentation must also support the renderer's allocation of income described in paragraph (e)(2)(i) of this section.

(A) A written statement from the business recipient that specifies the locations of the operations of the business recipient that benefit from the service.

(B) A binding contract that specifies the locations of the operations of the business recipient that benefit from the service.

(C) Documentation obtained in the ordinary course of the provision of the service that specifies the locations of the operations of the business recipient that benefit from the service.

(D) Publicly available information that establishes the locations of the operations of the business recipient.

(E) Any other forms of documentation as prescribed by the Secretary in forms, instructions, or other guidance.

(ii) *Special rules.*—(A) *Special rule for small businesses.*—A renderer that receives less than $10,000,000 in gross receipts during a prior taxable year establishes that a business recipient of a service provided in a taxable year is located outside the United States if the renderer's billing address for the business recipient is outside of the United States. If the renderer's prior taxable year is less than 12 months (a short period), gross receipts are annualized by multiplying the gross receipts for the short period by 365 and dividing the result by the number of days in the short period.

(B) *Special rule for small transactions.*—A renderer that receives less than $5,000 in gross receipts during a taxable year from services provided to a business recipient in such taxable year establishes that such business recipient is located outside the United States if the renderer's billing address for the business recipient is outside the United States.

(4) *Related parties.*—For purposes of this paragraph (e), a reference to a business recipient includes a reference to any related party of the business recipient.

(5) *Examples.*—The following examples illustrate the application of this paragraph (e).

(i) *Presumed facts.*—The following facts are assumed for purposes of the examples—

(A) DC is a domestic corporation.

(B) A and R are not related parties of DC.

(C) Any documentation obtained meets the reliability requirements described in § 1.250(b)-3(d).

(D) The treatment of any service as a FDDEI service would not reduce DC's foreign-derived deduction eligible income for the year.

(ii) *Examples.*—(A) *Example 1: Service that benefits specific aspects of the business recipient's business*—(1) *Facts.* For the taxable year, DC provides a marketing service to R, a company that operates restaurants within and outside of the United States, in exchange for $150x. Publicly available information indicates that 50% of the revenue earned by R and its related parties is from customers located outside of the United States. However, the marketing service that DC provides relates specifically to a single chain of restaurants that R operates. Sales information that R provides to DC indicates that 70% of the revenue of the restaurant chain is from locations within the United States and 30% of the revenue is from locations outside the United States.

(2) *Analysis.* R is located outside the United States in part under paragraph (e)(2)(i) of this section because DC's services benefit

both R's operations within the United States and its operations outside the United States. Under paragraph (e)(2)(i) of this section, the portion of the service provided by DC that is treated as provided to a person located outside the United States is determined by the amount of DC's gross income from the service that is allocated to R's operations outside the United States. Because DC provides a service that provides a benefit to R's operations in specific locations, and reliable information about the specific locations of the operations that receive a benefit is available, DC must determine R's location based on information relating specifically to R's business operations that benefits from DC's service. See paragraph (e)(2)(i)(A) of this section. In this case, allocation of DC's gross income based on the revenue of the business recipient is a reasonable method. See paragraph (e)(2)(i)(B) of this section. Therefore, 30% of the provision of the marketing service is treated as the provision of a service to a person located outside the United States and a FDDEI service under paragraph (b)(2) of this section. Accordingly, $45x ($150x × 0.30) of DC's gross income from the provision of the marketing service is included in DC's gross FDDEI for the taxable year.

(B) *Example 2: Service that benefits the business recipient's operations generally*—(1) *Facts.* The facts are the same as in paragraph (e)(5)(ii)(A)(1) of this section (the facts in *Example 1*), except that DC provides an information technology service to R that benefits R's entire business.

(2) *Analysis.* Because the service that DC provides relate to R's entire business, DC may rely on publicly available information indicating that 50% of R's operations are outside of the United States. See paragraph (e)(2)(i)(A) of this section. Therefore, 50% of the provision of the information technology service is treated as a service to a person located outside the United States and a FDDEI service under paragraph (b)(2) of this section. Accordingly, $75x ($150x x 0.50) of DC's gross income from the provision of the information technology service is included in DC's gross FDDEI for the taxable year.

(C) *Example 3: No reliable information about which operations benefit from the service*—(1) *Facts.* The facts are the same as in paragraph (e)(5)(ii)(A) (1) of this section (the facts in *Example 1*), except that no information is available to DC about the specific chain of restaurants for which the service is provided.

(2) *Analysis.* Because the only information available to DC relates to R's entire business, DC may rely on publicly available information indicating that 50% of R's operations are outside of the United States to determine the portion of the service treated as provided to a person located outside the United States. See paragraph (e)(2)(i)(A) of this section. Therefore, 50% of the provision of the marketing service is treated as a service to a person located outside the United States and a FDDEI service under paragraph (b)(2) of this section. Accordingly, $75x ($150x x 0.50) of DC's gross income from the provision of the marketing service is included in DC's gross FDDEI for the taxable year.

(D) *Example 4: Service provided to a domestic intermediary*—(1) *Facts.* A, a domestic corporation that operates solely in the United States, enters into a services agreement with R, a company that operates solely outside the United States. Under the agreement, A agrees to perform a consulting service for R. A hires DC to provide a service to A that A will use in the provision of a consulting service to R.

(2) *Analysis.* A is located within the United States because the service that DC provides A confers a benefit solely to A's operations within the United States. R is located outside the United States because the service that A provides to R confers a benefit solely to R's operations outside the United States. See paragraph (e)(2)(i) of this section. Because DC provides a service to A, a person located within the United States, DC's provision of the service to A is not a FDDEI service under paragraph (b)(2) of this section, even though the service is used by A in providing a service to R, a person located outside the United States. See also section 250(b)(5)(B)(ii). However, A's provision of the consulting service to R may be a FDDEI service, in which case A's gross income from the provision of such service would be included in A's gross FDDEI.

(f) *Proximate services.*—A proximate service is provided with respect to a recipient located outside the United States if the proximate service is performed outside the United States. In the case of a proximate service performed partly within the United States and partly outside of the United States, a proportionate amount of the service is treated as provided to a recipient located outside the United States corresponding to the portion of time the renderer spends providing the service outside of the United States.

(g) *Property services.*—A property service is provided with respect to tangible property located outside the United States only if the property is located outside the United States for the duration of the period the service is performed.

(h) *Transportation services.*—Except as provided in this paragraph (h), a transportation service is provided to a recipient, or with respect to property, located outside the United States only if both the origin

and the destination of the service are outside of the United States. However, in the case of a transportation service provided to a recipient, or with respect to property, where either the origin or the destination of the service is outside of the United States, but not both, then 50 percent of the transportation service is considered provided to a recipient, or with respect to property, located outside the United States. [Reg. § 1.250(b)-5.]

§ 1.250(b)-6. Related party transactions.—(a) *Scope.*—This section provides additional rules for determining whether a sale of property or a provision of a service to a related party is a FDDEI transaction. Paragraph (b) of this section provides additional definitions relevant for determining whether a sale of property or a provision of a service to a related party is a FDDEI transaction. Paragraph (c) of this section provides additional rules for determining whether a sale of general property to a foreign related party is a FDDEI sale. Paragraph (d) of this section provides additional rules for determining whether the provision of a general service to a business recipient that is a related party is a FDDEI service.

(b) *Definitions.*—This paragraph (b) provides definitions that apply for purposes of this section.

(1) *Foreign related party.*—The term *foreign related party* means, with respect to a seller or renderer, any foreign person that is a related party of the seller or renderer.

(2) *Foreign unrelated party.*—The term *foreign unrelated party* means, with respect to a seller, a foreign person that is not a related party of the seller.

(3) *Related party sale.*—The term *related party sale* means a sale of general property to a foreign related party that satisfies the requirements described in § 1.250(b)-4(b) without regard to paragraph (c) of this section. See § 1.250(b)-1(e)(3)(ii)(D) (*Example 4*) for an illustration of a related party sale in the case of a seller that is a partnership.

(4) *Related party service.*—The term *related party service* means a provision of a general service to a business recipient that is a related party of the renderer and that is described in § 1.250(b)-5(b)(2) without regard to paragraph (d) of this section.

(5) *Unrelated party transaction.*—The term *unrelated party transaction* means, with respect to property purchased in a related party sale from a seller—

(i) A sale of the property by a foreign related party to a foreign unrelated party with respect to the seller;

(ii) A sale of property by a foreign related party to a foreign unrelated party with respect to the seller if the property sold in the related party sale is a component of the property sold to the foreign unrelated party;

(iii) A sale of property by a foreign related party to a foreign unrelated party with respect to the seller, other than a sale described in paragraph (b)(5)(ii) of this section, if the property sold in the related party sale is used in connection with the property sold to the foreign unrelated party; or

(iv) A provision of a service by a foreign related party to a foreign unrelated party with respect to the seller, if the property sold in the related party sale was used in connection with the provision of the service.

(c) *Related party sales.*—(1) *In general.*—A related party sale is a FDDEI sale only if the requirements described in either paragraph (c)(1)(i) or (ii) of this section are satisfied with respect to the related party sale. Section 250(b)(5)(C)(i) and this paragraph (c) does not apply to determine whether a sale of intangible property to a foreign related party is a FDDEI sale.

(i) *Sale of property in an unrelated party transaction.*—A related party sale is a FDDEI sale if an unrelated party transaction described in paragraph (b)(5)(i) or (ii) of this section occurs with respect to the property purchased in the related party sale, such unrelated party transaction is described in § 1.250(b)-4(b), and, except as provided in this paragraph (c)(1)(i), the unrelated party transaction occurs on or before the FDII filing date. In the case of an unrelated party transaction that occurs after the FDII filing date with respect to a related party sale, a taxpayer may file an amended return for the taxable year in which the related party sale occurred, within the period of limitations provided by section 6511, claiming the related party sale as a FDDEI sale for purposes of determining the taxpayer's foreign-derived intangible income for that taxable year.

(ii) *Use of property in an unrelated party transaction.*—A related party sale is a FDDEI sale if, as of the FDII filing date, the seller in the related party sale reasonably expects that one or more unrelated party transactions described in paragraph (b)(5)(iii) or (iv) of this section will occur with respect to the property purchased in the related party sale, such unrelated party transaction or transactions would be described in §1.250(b)-4(b) or §1.250(b)-5(b) without regard to the documentation rules in §1.250(b)-4 or §1.250(b)-5, and more than 80 percent of the revenue earned by the foreign related party with respect to the property will be earned from such unrelated party transaction or transactions.

(2) *Treatment of foreign related party as seller or renderer.*—For purposes of determining whether a sale of property or provision of a service by a foreign related party is, or would be, described in §1.250(b)-4 or §1.250(b)-5 (except for purposes of obtaining documentation), the foreign related party that sells the property or provides the service is treated as a seller or renderer, as applicable, and the foreign unrelated party is treated as the recipient. In the case of an unrelated party transaction described in paragraph (b)(5)(i) or (ii) of this section, the seller in the related party sale must obtain the documentation required in §1.250(b)-4.

(3) *Transactions between a foreign related party and other foreign related parties.*—All foreign related parties of the seller are treated as if they were a single foreign related party for purposes of applying paragraphs (c)(1) and (2) of this section. Accordingly, if a foreign related party sells or uses property purchased in a related party sale in a transaction with a second foreign related party of the seller, transactions between the second foreign related party and unrelated parties may be treated as an unrelated party transaction for purposes of applying paragraph (c)(1) of this section to a related party sale.

(4) *Example.*—The following example illustrates the application of paragraph (c) of this section.

(i) *Facts.* DC, a domestic corporation, sells a machine to FC, a foreign related party of DC in a transaction described in §1.250(b)-4(b) (without regard to §1.250(b)-6(c)). FC uses the machine solely to manufacture product A. As of the FDII filing date for the taxable year, FC reasonably expects that more than 80% of future revenue from sales of product A will be from sales that would be described in §1.250(b)-4(b) without regard to the documentation requirements of §1.250(b)-4(c) and (d).

(ii) *Analysis.* The sale by DC to FC is a related party sale. Because FC uses the machine to make product A, but the machine is not a component of product A, FC's sale of product A is an unrelated party transaction described in paragraph (b)(5)(iii) of this section. Therefore, DC's sale of the machine is only a FDDEI sale if the requirements of paragraph (c)(1)(ii) of this section are satisfied. Because DC reasonably expects that more than 80% of the revenue from future sales of product A will be from unrelated party transactions that would be described in §1.250(b)-4(b), DC's sale of the machine to FC is a FDDEI sale.

(d) *Related party services.*—(1) *In general.*—Except as provided in this paragraph (d)(1), a related party service is a FDDEI service only if the related party service is not substantially similar to a service provided by the related party to a person located within the United States. However, if a related party service is substantially similar to a service provided (in whole or in part) by the related party to a person located in the United States solely by reason of paragraph (d)(2)(ii) of this section, the amount of gross income from the related party service attributable to a FDDEI service is equal to the gross income from the related party service multiplied by a fraction, the numerator of which is the sum of the benefits conferred by the related party service to persons not located within the United States and the denominator of which is the sum of all benefits conferred by the related party service. Section 250(b)(5)(C)(ii) and this paragraph (d)(1) apply only to a general service provided to a business recipient and are not applicable with respect to any other service provided to a foreign related party.

(2) *Substantially similar services.*—A related party service is substantially similar to a service provided by the related party to a person located within the United States only if the related party service is used by the related party to provide a service to a person located within the United States and either—

(i) 60 percent or more of the benefits conferred by the related party service are to persons located within the United States; or

(ii) 60 percent or more of the price paid by persons located within the United States for the service provided by the related party is attributable to the related party service.

(3) *Location of recipient of services provided by related party.*—For purposes of paragraph (d) of this section, the location of a consumer or business recipient with respect to a related party service is determined under the principles of §1.250(b)-5(d)(2) and (e)(2), respectively.

(4) *Examples.*—The following examples illustrate the application of this paragraph (d).

(i) *Presumed facts.*—The following facts are assumed for purposes of the examples—

(A) DC is a domestic corporation.

(B) FC is a foreign corporation and a foreign related party of DC that operates solely outside the United States.

(C) The service DC provides to FC is a general service provided to a business recipient located outside the United States as described in §1.250(b)-5(b)(2) without regard to the application of paragraph (d) of this section.

(D) The benefits conferred by DC's service to FC's customers are not indirect or remote within the meaning of §1.482-9(l)(3)(ii).

(ii) *Examples.*—(A) *Example 1: Services that are substantially similar services under paragraph (d)(2)(i) of this section*—(1) *Facts.* FC enters into a services agreement with R, a company that operates restaurant chains within and outside the United States. Under the agreement, FC agrees to furnish a design for the renovation of a chain of restaurants that R owns, which design will include architectural plans. FC hires DC to provide an architectural service to FC that FC will use in the provision of its design service to R. The architectural service that DC provides to FC will serve no other purpose than to enable FC to provide its service to R. The architectural service will benefit solely R's operations within the United States. FC pays an arm's length price of $50x to DC for the architectural service and DC recognizes $50x of gross income from the service. FC incurs additional costs to add additional design elements to the plans and charges R a total of $100x for its service.

(2) *Analysis.* The service that DC provides to FC is used in the provision of a service to R. R is treated as entirely located within the United States under paragraph (d)(3) of this section and the principles of §1.250(b)-5(e)(2) because only its U.S. operations benefit from the service provided by DC. Because FC uses DC's architectural service to provide its design service to R, and the architectural service that DC provides to FC will serve no purpose other than to enable FC to provide its service to R, 100% of the benefits conferred by DC's architectural service are to R, a person located within the United States. Therefore, the service provided by DC to FC is substantially similar to the service provided by FC to R under paragraph (d)(2)(i) of this section. Accordingly, DC's provision of the architectural service to FC is not a FDDEI service under paragraph (d)(1) of this section and DC's gross income from the architectural service ($50x) is not included in its gross FDDEI.

(B) *Example 2: Services that are substantially similar services under paragraph (d)(2)(ii) of this section*—(1) *Facts.* The facts are the same as paragraph (d)(4)(ii)(A)(1) (the facts in *Example 1*), except that FC pays an arm's length price of $75x to DC for the architectural service, DC recognizes $75x of gross income from the service, and 90% of the benefits of DC's architectural service are conferred on R's operations outside the United States.

(2) *Analysis*—(i) *Analysis under paragraph (d)(2)(i) of this section.* R is treated as located within the United States with respect to DC's architectural service under paragraph (d)(3) of this section to the extent of the benefits conferred on its operations within the United States by the architectural service. See §1.250(b)-5(e)(2). Because 90% of the benefits of DC's architectural service are conferred on R's operations outside the United States, only 10% of the benefits of DC's architectural service are treated as conferred on persons located within the United States under paragraph (d)(3) of this section. Therefore, the architectural service provided by DC to FC is not substantially similar to the design service provided by FC to persons located within the United States under paragraph (d)(2)(i) of this section.

(ii) *Analysis under paragraph (d)(2)(ii) of this section.* Because 10% of the benefits of FC's architectural design services are conferred on R's operations within the United States, $10x of the amount paid by R for FC's services (10% x $100) is treated as paid by persons located within the United States. Similarly, because 10% of the benefits of DC's architectural services are conferred on R's operations within the United States, of the $10x paid with respect to R's operations within the United States, $7.5x (10% × $75x) is attributable to DC's architectural service. Accordingly, because 75% ($7.5x/$10x) of the price paid by R to FC for the design service is attributable to the architectural service provided by DC to FC, and R is a person located within the United States under paragraph (d)(3) of this section and the principles of §1.250(b)-5(e)(2), the architectural service provided by DC to FC is substantially similar to the design service provided by FC to persons located within the United States under paragraph (d)(2)(ii) of this section.

(iii) *Application of paragraph (d)(1) of this section.* Because DC's architectural service is substantially similar to FC's design service provided to R, a person located in the United States, solely by reason of paragraph (d)(2)(ii) of this section, the amount of gross income from DC's architectural service included in its gross FDDEI is $67.5x, which is equal to DC's gross income from the architectural service ($75x) multiplied by 90%, which is the percentage of the benefits of

DC's architectural service that are conferred on R's operations outside the United States. [Reg. § 1.250(b)-6.]

Business Use or Rental of Dwelling Unit

Business Use or Rental of Dwelling Unit.—Reproduced below is the text of a proposed amendment of § 1.262-1, relating to the deductibility of expenses in connection with the business use, or the rental to others, of a dwelling unit that the taxpayer is deemed to have used for personal purposes during the taxable year (published in the Federal Register on August 7, 1980).

* * *

☐ Par. 3. Paragraph (b)(3) of § 1.262-1 is amended to read as follows:

§ 1.262-1. Personal, living and family expenses.—

* * *

(b) *Examples of personal, living, and family expenses.*—* * *

(3) Expenses and maintaining a household, including amounts paid for rent, water, utilities, domestic service, and the like

are not deductible. For rules relating to expenses incurred in connection with dwelling units used for both business purposes and personal purposes, see section 280A and the regulations thereunder.

* * *

Straddles: Capitalization of Interest: Carrying Charges: Personal Property

Straddles: Capitalization of Interest: Carrying Charges: Personal Property.—Reg. §§ 1.263(g)-1—1.263(g)-5, clarifying what constitutes interest and carrying charges and when interest and carrying charges are properly allocable to personal property that is part of a straddle and clarifying that a taxpayer's obligation under a debt instrument can be a position in personal property that is part of a straddle, are proposed (published in the Federal Register on January 18, 2001) (REG-105801-00) (corrected April 2, 2001).

☐ Par. 2. Sections 1.263(g)-1, 1.263(g)-2, 1.263(g)-3, 1.263(g)-4, and 1.263(g)-5 are added to read as follows:

§ 1.263(g)-1. Treatment of interest and carrying charges in the case of straddles; in general.—(a) Under section 263(g), no deduction is allowed for interest and carrying charges allocable to personal property that is part of a straddle (as defined in section 1092(c)). The purpose of section 263(g) is to coordinate the character and the timing of items of income and loss attributable to a taxpayer's positions that are part of a straddle. In order to prevent payments or accruals related to a straddle transaction from giving rise to recognition of deductions or losses before related income is recognized and to prevent the items of loss and income from having different character, no deduction is allowed for interest and carrying charges properly allocable to personal property that is part of a straddle. Rather, such amounts are chargeable to the capital account of the personal property to which the interest and carrying charges are properly allocable.

(b) Section 263(g) does not apply if none of the taxpayer's positions that are part of the straddle are personal property. Section 263(g) also does not apply to hedging transactions as defined in section 1256(e) (see section 263(g)(3)) or to securities to which the mark-to-market accounting method provided by section 475 applies (see section 475(d)(1)).

(c) Section 1.263(g)-2 provides a definition of personal property for purposes of section 263(g) and §§ 1.263(g)-1 through 1.263(g)-5. Section 1.263(g)-3 provides a definition of interest and carrying charges for purposes of section 263(g), section 1092, §§ 1.263(g)-1 through 1.263(g)-5, and § 1.1092(b)-4T. Section 1.263(g)-4 provides a set of allocation rules governing the capitalization of amounts to which section 263(g) applies. [Reg. § 1.263(g)-1.]

§ 1.263(g)-2. Personal property to which interest and carrying charges may properly be allocable.—(a) *Definition of personal property.*—For purposes of section 263(g) and of §§ 1.263(g)-1 through 1.263(g)-5, *personal property* means property, whether or not actively traded, that is not real property. For purposes of the preceding sentence, a position in personal property may itself be property. In general, however, a position in personal property is not property of a taxpayer unless the position confers or may confer substantial rights on the taxpayer.

(1) *Application to certain financial instruments.*—Personal property includes a stockholder's ownership of common stock, a holder's ownership of a debt instrument, and either party's position in a forward contract or in a conventional swap agreement. Personal property does not include a position that imposes obligations but does not confer substantial rights on the taxpayer. Therefore, the obligor's position in a debt instrument generally is not personal property, even though the obligor may have typical rights of a debtor, such as the right to prepay the debt. However, the obligor on a debt instrument has a position in any personal property underlying the debt instrument. See § 1.1092(d)-1(d).

(2) *Options.*—For the purposes of applying this section, a put option or call option imposes obligations but does not confer substantial rights on the grantor, whether or not the option is cash-settled.

(b) *Example.*—The following example illustrates the rules stated in paragraph (a) of this section:

Example. (i) *Facts.* A purchases 100 ounces of gold at a cost of x. A transfers the 100 ounces of gold to a trust that issues multiple

classes of trust certificates and is treated as a partnership for tax purposes. In return, A receives two trust certificates that are not personal property of a type that is actively traded within the meaning of section 1092(d)(1). One certificate entitles A to a payment on termination of the trust at the end of four years equal to the value of the 100 ounces of gold up to a maximum value of $(x + y)$. The other certificate entitles A to a payment equal to the amount by which the value of 100 ounces of gold exceeds $(x + y)$ on termination of the trust. A sells the second certificate and keeps the first certificate.

(ii) *Analysis.* The trust certificate retained by A is property that is not real property. In addition, ownership of the trust certificate confers certain substantial rights on A. Therefore, although the trust certificate is not personal property of a type that is actively traded, A's interest in the trust certificate is personal property for purposes of section 263(g).
[Reg. § 1.263(g)-2.]

§ 1.263(g)-3. Interest and carrying charges properly allocable to personal property that is part of a straddle.—(a) *In general.*—For purposes of section 263(g), section 1092, §§ 1.263(g)-1 through 1.263(g)-5, and § 1.1092(b)-4T, *interest and carrying charges properly allocable to personal property that is part of a straddle* means the excess of interest and carrying charges (as defined in paragraph (b) of this section) over the allowable income offsets (as defined in paragraph (e) of this section).

(b) *Interest and carrying charges.*—Interest and carrying charges are otherwise deductible amounts paid or accrued with respect to indebtedness or other financing incurred or continued to purchase or carry personal property that is part of a straddle and otherwise deductible amounts paid or incurred to carry personal property that is part of a straddle. As provided in section 263(g)(2), interest includes any amount paid or incurred in connection with personal property used in a short sale. Interest and carrying charges include—

(1) Otherwise deductible payments or accruals (including interest and original issue discount) on indebtedness or other financing issued or continued to purchase or carry personal property that is part of a straddle;

(2) Otherwise deductible fees or expenses paid or incurred in connection with acquiring or holding personal property that is part of a straddle including, but not limited to, fees or expenses incurred to purchase, insure, store, maintain or transport the personal property; and

(3) Other otherwise deductible payments or accruals on financial instruments that are part of a straddle or that carry part of a straddle.

(c) *Indebtedness or other financing incurred or continued to purchase or carry personal property that is part of a straddle.*—For purposes of paragraph (b)(1) of this section, indebtedness or other financing that is incurred or continued to purchase or carry personal property that is part of a straddle includes—

(1) Indebtedness or other financing the proceeds of which are used directly or indirectly to purchase or carry personal property that is part of the straddle;

(2) Indebtedness or other financing that is secured directly or indirectly by personal property that is part of the straddle; and

(3) Indebtedness or other financing the payments on which are determined by reference to payments with respect to the personal property or the value of, or change in value of, the personal property.

(d) *Financial instruments that are part of a straddle or that carry part of a straddle.*—For purposes of paragraph (b)(3), financial instruments that are part of a straddle or that carry part of a straddle include—

(1) A financial instrument that is part of the straddle;

(2) A financial instrument that is issued in connection with the creation or acquisition of a position in personal property if that position is part of the straddle;

(3) A financial instrument that is sold or marketed as part of an arrangement that involves a taxpayer's position in personal property that is part of the straddle and that is purported to result in either economic realization of all or part of the appreciation in an asset without simultaneous recognition of taxable income or a current tax deduction (for interest, carrying charges, payments on a notional principal contract, or otherwise) reflecting a payment or expense that is economically offset by an increase in value that is not concurrently recognized for tax purposes or has a different tax character (for example, an interest payment that is economically offset by an increase in value that may result in a capital gain in a later tax period); and

(4) Any other financial instrument if the totality of the facts and circumstances support a reasonable inference that the issuance, purchase, or continuation of the financial instrument by the taxpayer was intended to purchase or carry personal property that is part of the straddle.

(e) *Allowable income offsets.*—The allowable income offsets are:

(1) The amount of interest (including original issue discount) includible in gross income for the taxable year with respect to such personal property;

(2) Any amount treated as ordinary income under section 1271(a)(3)(A), 1278, or 1281(a) with respect to such personal property for the taxable year;

(3) The excess of any dividends includible in gross income with respect to such property for the taxable year over the amount of any deductions allowable with respect to such dividends under section 243, 244, or 245;

(4) Any amount that is a payment with respect to a security loan (within the meaning of section 512(a)(5)) includible in income with respect to the personal property for the taxable year; and

(5) Any amount that is a receipt or accrual includible in income for the taxable year with respect to a financial instrument described in §1.263(g)-3(d) to the extent the financial instrument is entered into to purchase or carry the personal property. [Reg. §1.263(g)-3.]

§1.263(g)-4. Rules for allocating amounts to personal property that is part of a straddle.—(a) *Allocation rules.*—(1) Interest and carrying charges paid or accrued on indebtedness or other financing issued or continued to purchase or carry personal property that is part of a straddle are allocated, in the order listed—

(i) To personal property that is part of the straddle purchased, directly or indirectly, with the proceeds of the indebtedness or other financing;

(ii) To personal property that is part of the straddle and directly or indirectly secures the indebtedness or other financing; or

(iii) If all or a portion of such interest and carrying charges are determined by reference to the value or change in value of personal property, to such personal property.

(2) Fees and expenses described in §1.263(g)-3(b)(2) are allocated to the personal property, the acquisition or holding of which resulted in the fees and expenses being paid or incurred.

(3) In all other cases, interest and carrying charges are allocated to personal property that is part of a straddle in the manner that under all the facts and circumstances is most appropriate.

(b) *Coordination with other provisions.*—In the case of a short sale, section 263(g) applies after section 263(h). See sections 263(g)(4)(A) and (h)(6). In case of an obligation to which section 1277 (dealing with deferral of interest deduction allocable to accrued market discount) or 1282 (dealing with deferral of interest deduction allocable to certain accruals on short-term indebtedness) applies, section 263(g) applies after section 1277 and section 1282. See section 263(g)(4)(B). Capitalization under section 263(g) applies before loss deferral under section 1092.

(c) *Examples.*—The following examples illustrate the rules stated in §§1.263(g)-2, 1.263(g)-3, and 1.263(g)-4.

Example 1. Cash and Carry Silver.

(i) *Facts.* On January 1, 2002, A borrows $x at 6% interest and uses the proceeds to purchase y ounces of silver from B. At approximately the same time, A enters into a forward contract with C to deliver y ounces of silver to C in one year.

(ii) *Analysis.* The y ounces of silver and the forward contract to deliver y ounces of silver in one year are offsetting positions with respect to the same personal property and therefore constitute a straddle. See sections 1092(c)(1), (c)(3)(A)(i). The proceeds of the debt

instrument were used to purchase personal property that is part of the straddle. Consequently, A's interest payments are interest and carrying charges properly allocable to personal property that is part of a straddle. See §1.263(g)-3(b)(1) & (c)(1). Under §1.263(g)-4(a)(1)(i), the interest payments must be charged to the capital account for the y ounces of silver purchased by A with the proceeds of the borrowing.

Example 2. Additional indebtedness issued to carry personal property.

(i) *Facts.* The facts are the same as for Example 1 except that during the year 2002, the market price of silver increases and A is required to post variation margin as security for its obligation to deliver y ounces of silver to C. A incurs additional indebtedness to obtain funds necessary to meet A's variation margin requirement.

(ii) *Analysis.* The additional indebtedness is incurred to continue to carry A's holding of y ounces of silver. Consequently, A's interest payments on the additional indebtedness are interest and carrying charges properly allocable to personal property that is part of a straddle and must be charged to the capital account for the y ounces of silver.

Example 3. Contingent payment debt instrument.

(i) *Facts.* On January 1, 2002, D enters into a contract to deliver x barrels of fuel oil to E on July 1, 2004, at an aggregate price equal to $y. Soon afterward, D issues a contingent payment debt instrument to F with a principal amount of $z and a 2-year term that pays interest quarterly at a rate determined at the beginning of each quarter equal to the greater of zero and the London Interbank Offered Rate (LIBOR) adjusted by an index that varies inversely with changes in the price of fuel oil (so that the interest rate increases as the price of fuel oil decreases and vice versa). The change in the aggregate amount of interest paid on the $z of debt due to the functioning of the index approximates the concurrent aggregate change in value of x barrels of fuel oil and, thus, the value of D's interest in the forward contract.

(ii) *Analysis.* The debt instrument and the forward contract are offsetting positions with respect to the same personal property and constitute a straddle. See section 1092(c)(1), (c)(3)(A)(i). When issued, the debt instrument is a position in personal property that is part of a straddle. See §1.1092(d)-1(d). Consequently, D's interest payments are interest and carrying charges properly allocable to personal property that is part of a straddle and must be allocated to the capital account for the forward contract for the delivery of x barrels of fuel oil to E. See §§1.263(g)-3(b)(1), (b)(3), (c)(3), and (d)(1) and -4(a)(1)(iii).

Example 4. Financial instrument issued to carry personal property that is part of a straddle.

(i) *Facts.* The facts are the same as for Example 3 except that D also enters into a two-year interest rate swap under which D receives LIBOR times a notional principal amount equal to $z and pays 7% times $z.

(ii) *Analysis.* Because of the relationship between the two-year debt instrument issued by D and the interest rate swap, the interest rate swap is a financial instrument that carries personal property that is part of a straddle. See §1.263(g)-3(d)(4). Net payments made by D under the interest rate swap are chargeable to the capital account for the forward contract for the delivery of x barrels of fuel oil to E. Similarly, net payments received by D under the interest rate swap are allowable offsets. See §1.263(g)-3(e)(5).

Example 5. Contingent payment debt instrument with embedded short position.

(i) *Facts.* On January 1, 1998, G purchases 100,000 shares of the common stock of XYZ corporation (which is publicly traded). On January 1, 2002, the 100,000 shares of XYZ corporation common stock were worth $x per share. On that date, G issued a contingent payment debt instrument for $100,000x. The terms of the debt instrument provided that the holders would receive an annual payment of $2,000x on December 31 of each year up to and including the maturity date of December 31, 2007. On the maturity date, the holders would also receive a payment of $100,000x plus an additional amount, if the price of an XYZ share exceeded $1.2x on such date, equal to 100,000 times three-quarters of the amount of such excess per share. Thus, G's aggregate payments on the debt instrument varied directly with the increase in value in the XYZ shares.

(ii) *Analysis.* The debt instrument is a position in XYZ stock. See §1.1092(d)-1(d). The XYZ stock is personal property within the meaning of section 1092(d)(3)(B) because the debt instrument is a position with respect to substantially similar or related property (other than stock) within the meaning of section 1092(d)(3)(B)(i)(II). See §1.1092(d)-2(c). The debt instrument and the XYZ shares are offsetting positions with respect to the same personal property and constitute a straddle. See sections 1092(c)(1), (c)(3)(A)(i). Consequently, G's interest payments are interest and carrying charges properly allocable to personal property that is part of a straddle, see §§1.263(g)-3(b)(1), (b)(3), (c)(3), and (d)(1), and must be allocated to the capital account for the XYZ common stock, see §1.263(g)-4(a)(1)(iii) and (a)(3).

Example 6. Straddle including partnership interest.

(i) *Facts.* H borrows money from *I* to purchase 100 ounces of gold at a cost of $*u*. H transfers the 100 ounces of gold and $*v* to a newly created trust that issues multiple classes of trust certificates and is treated as a partnership for tax purposes. In return, H receives two trust certificates. One certificate entitles the holder to a payment on termination of the trust at the end of four years equal to the value of the 100 ounces of gold up to a maximum value of $(*u* + *w*). The other certificate entitles the holder to a payment equal to the amount by which the value of 100 ounces of gold exceeds $(*u* + *w*) on termination of the trust. H sells the second certificate and keeps the first certificate. H also enters into a forward contract to sell 100 ounces of gold for $1.12*u* per ounce on a date two years after creation of the trust. The trust uses part of the $*v* and similar cash contributions from other investors to pay costs of storing the gold held by the trust and allocates H's share of the expenses to H.

(ii) *Analysis.* The trust certificate retained by H and the forward contract entered into by H are personal property for the purposes of section 263(g). See §1.263(g)-2(a). They are also offsetting positions and constitute a straddle. Section 1092(c)(1). The borrowing from *I* is an indebtedness incurred to purchase personal property that is part of a straddle. See §§1.263(g)-3(b)(1) and (c)(1). Similarly, the gold storage expenses are expenses incurred due to the taxpayer's holding personal property that is part of a straddle. See §1.263(g)-3(b)(2). Therefore both the interest on the borrowing and the gold storage expenses must be allocated to the capital account for the partnership interest represented by the retained trust certificate. See §1.263(g)-4(a)(1)(i) and (a)(2).

Example 7. Equity Swap.

(i) *Facts.* On January 1, 1998, *J* purchases 100,000 shares of the common stock of *XYZ* corporation (which is publicly traded). On December 31, 2001, the 100,000 shares of *XYZ* corporation common stock were worth $*x* per share. On that date, *J* entered into a NPC with *K*. The terms of the NPC provided that *K* would receive an annual payment on December 31 of each year equal to 100,000 times any appreciation in the value of a share of *XYZ* corporation stock

above its price at the end of trading on December 31 of the preceding year and 100,000 times the dividends paid during the year on each share of *XYZ* corporation stock. In return, on December 31 of each year, *J* would receive an amount equal to LIBOR times the value of 100,000 *XYZ* shares at the end of trading on December 31 of the preceding year plus 100,000 times the amount of any decrease in the value of a share of *XYZ* corporation stock below its price at the end of trading on December 31 of the preceding year. Payments between *J* and *K* would be netted and continue up to and including the maturity date of the NPC on December 31, 2008. Thus, *J*'s aggregate payments on the NPC varied directly with the increase in value in the *XYZ* shares.

(ii) *Analysis.* The NPC is a position in *XYZ* stock. See §1.1092(d)-2(c). The *XYZ* stock is personal property within the meaning of section 1092(d)(3)(B) because the NPC is a position with respect to substantially similar or related property (other than stock) within the meaning of section 1092(b)(3)(B)(i)(II). See §1.1092(d)-2(a)(1)(ii). The NPC and the *XYZ* shares are offsetting positions with respect to the same personal property and constitute a straddle. See sections 1092(c)(1), (c)(3)(A)(i). Consequently, *J*'s payments are interest and carrying charges properly allocable to personal property that is part of a straddle. See §§1.263(g)-3(b)(3) and (d)(1). Therefore, they should be allocated to the personal property that is part of the straddle in the manner that is most appropriate under all the facts and circumstances. In this case, because these payments are incurred to carry the *XYZ* shares, they should be allocated to the capital account for the *XYZ* common stock. See §1.263(g)-4(a)(3).

[Reg. §1.263(g)-4.]

§1.263(g)-5. Effective dates.—Sections 1.263(g)-1, 1.263(g)-2, 1.263(g)-3, and 1.263(g)-4 apply to interest and carrying charges properly allocable to personal property that are paid, incurred, or accrued after the date these regulations are adopted as final regulations by publication in the Federal Register for a straddle established on or after January 17, 2001. [Reg. §1.263(g)-5.]

Deduction for Business Interest Expense: Limitation

Deduction for Business Interest Expense: Limitation.—Amendments to Reg. §1.263A-9, regarding the limitation on the deduction for business interest expense after the enactment of recent tax legislation, are proposed (published in the Federal Register on December 28, 2018) (REG-106089-18).

Par. 4. Section 1.263A-9 is amended by revising the first and third sentences of paragraph (g)(1)(i) to read as follows:

§1.263A-9. The avoided cost method.

* * *

(g) * * *

(1) * * *

(i) Interest must be capitalized under section 263A(f) before the application of section 163(d) (regarding the investment interest limitation), section 163(j) (regarding the limitation on business interest expense), section 266 (regarding the election to capitalize carrying

charges), section 469 (regarding the limitation on passive losses), and section 861 (regarding the allocation of interest to United States sources). * * * However, in applying section 263A(f) with respect to the excess expenditure amount, the taxpayer must capitalize all interest that is neither investment interest under section 163(d), business interest expense under section 163(j), nor passive interest under section 469 before capitalizing any interest that is either investment interest, business interest expense, or passive interest. * * *

* * *

Consolidated Returns: Intercompany Obligations: Disallowance of Interest Expense Deductions

Consolidated Returns: Intercompany Obligations: Disallowance of Interest Expense Deductions.—Amendments to Reg. §1.265-2, affecting corporations filing consolidated returns by providing special rules for the treatment of certain intercompany transactions involving interest on intercompany obligations, are proposed (published in the Federal Register on May 7, 2004) (REG-128590-03).

☐ Par. 2. In §1.265-2, paragraph (c) is added to read as follows:

§1.265-2. Interest relating to tax-exempt income.

* * *

(c) *Special rule for consolidated groups.*—(1) *Treatment of intercompany obligations.*—(i) *Direct tracing to nonmember indebtedness.*—If a member of a consolidated group incurs or continues indebtedness to a nonmember, that indebtedness is directly traceable to all or a portion of an intercompany obligation (as defined in §1.1502-13(g)(2)(ii)) extended to a member of the group (B) by another member of the group (S), and section 265(a)(2) applies to disallow a deduction for all or a portion of B's interest expense incurred with respect to the intercompany obligation, then §1.1502-13(c)(6)(i) will not apply to exclude an amount of S's interest income with respect to the intercompany obligation that equals the amount of B's disallowed interest deduction.

(ii) *Limitation.*—The amount of interest income to which §1.1502-13(c)(6)(i) will not apply as a result of the application of paragraph (c)(1)(i) of this section cannot exceed the interest expense on the portion of the indebtedness to the nonmember that is directly traceable to the intercompany obligation.

(2) *Examples.*—The rules of this paragraph (c) are illustrated by the following examples. For purposes of these examples, unless otherwise stated, P and S are members of a consolidated group of

which P is the common parent. P owns all of the outstanding stock of S. The taxable year of the P group is the calendar year and all members of the P group use the accrual method of accounting. L is a bank unrelated to any member of the consolidated group. All obligations are on the same terms and conditions, remain outstanding at the end of the applicable year, and provide for payments of interest on December 31 of each year that are greater than the appropriate applicable Federal rate (AFR). The examples are as follows:

Example 1. (i) *Facts.* On January 1, 2005, P borrows $100x from L and lends the entire $100x of borrowed proceeds to S. S uses the $100x of borrowed proceeds to purchase tax-exempt securities. P's indebtedness to L is directly traceable to the intercompany obligation between P and S. In addition, there is direct evidence that the proceeds of S's intercompany obligation to P were used to fund S's purchase or carrying of tax-exempt obligations. During the 2005 taxable year, P incurs $10x of interest expense on its loan from L, and S incurs $10x of interest expense on its loan from P. Under section 265(a)(2), the entire $10x of S's interest expense on the intercompany obligation to P is disallowed as a deduction.

(ii) *Analysis.* Because section 265(a)(2) permanently and explicitly disallows $10x of S's interest expense, ordinarily $10x of P's interest income on the intercompany obligation would be redetermined to be excluded from P's gross income under §1.1502-13(c)(6)(i). However, under this paragraph (c),

§1.1502-13(c)(6)(i) will not apply to exclude P's interest income with respect to the intercompany obligation in an amount that equals S's disallowed interest deduction with respect to the intercompany obligation. Accordingly, §1.1502-13(c)(6)(i) will not apply to exclude P's $10x of interest income on the intercompany obligation and P must include in income $10x of interest income from the intercompany obligation.

Example 2. (i) *Facts.* The facts are the same as in Example 1, except that P incurs only $8x of interest expense on its loan from L.

(ii) *Analysis.* Section 1.1502-13(c)(6)(i) will apply to exclude only a portion of P's $10x of interest income on the intercompany

obligation. Under paragraph (c)(1)(ii) of this section, the amount of P's interest income that §1.1502-13(c)(6)(i) will not apply to exclude is $8x, the total interest expense incurred by P on its indebtedness to L. Consequently, P must include in income $8x of interest income from the intercompany obligation and §1.1502-13(c)(6)(i) will apply to exclude $2x of interest income from the intercompany obligation.

(3) *Effective date.*—The provisions of this section shall apply to taxable years beginning on or after the date these regulations are published as final regulations in the Federal Register.

Deductions and Losses Between Related Taxpayers

Deductions: Losses: Interest: Transactions Between Related Taxpayers.—Temporary Reg. §1.267(a)-2T, relating to deductions, timing of deductions and losses in transactions between certain related taxpayers, is also proposed as a final regulation and, when adopted, would become Reg. §1.267(a)-2 (published in the Federal Register on November 30, 1984).

§1.267(a)-2. Temporary regulations; questions and answers arising under the Tax Reform Act of 1984.

CFCs: U.S. Shareholders: Ownership Attribution

CFCs: U.S. Shareholders: Ownership Attribution.—Amendments to Reg. §1.267(a)-3, relating to the modification of section 958(b) of the Internal Revenue Code by the Tax Cuts and Jobs Act, which was enacted on December 22, 2017, are proposed (published in the Federal Register on October 2, 2019) (REG-104223-18).

Par. 2. Section 1.267(a)-3 is amended by:

1. Removing the language "or (a)(3)" from paragraph (c)(2).

2. Revising paragraph (c)(4).

3. In paragraph (d), revising the second sentence and adding five sentences at the end of the paragraph.

The revisions and addition read as follows:

§1.267(a)-3. Deduction of amounts owed to related foreign persons.

* * *

(c) * * *

(4) *Certain amounts owed to certain controlled foreign corporations.*—An amount (other than interest) that is income of a related foreign person with respect to which the related foreign person is exempt from United States taxation on the amount owed pursuant to a treaty obligation of the United States (such as under an article relating to the taxation of business profits) is exempt from the application of section 267(a)(3)(B)(i) if the related foreign person is a controlled foreign corporation that does not have any United States shareholders (as defined in section 951(b)) that own (within the meaning of section 958(a)) stock of the controlled foreign corporation.

* * *

(d) * * * Except as otherwise provided in this paragraph (d), the regulations in this section issued under section 267 apply to all other

deductible amounts that are incurred after July 31, 1989, but do not apply to amounts that are incurred pursuant to a contract that was binding on September 29, 1983, and at all times thereafter (unless the contract was renegotiated, extended, renewed, or revised after that date). Paragraph (c)(2) of this section applies to payments accrued on or after October 22, 2004. For payments accrued before October 22, 2004, see §1.267(a)-3(c)(2), as contained in 26 CFR part 1, revised as of April 1, 2004. Paragraph (c)(4) of this section applies to payments accrued on or after October 1, 2019. For payments accrued before October 1, 2019, a taxpayer may apply paragraph (c)(4) of this section for payments accrued during the last taxable year of a foreign corporation beginning before January 1, 2018, and each subsequent taxable year of the foreign corporation, provided that the taxpayer and United States persons that are related (within the meaning of section 267 or 707) to the taxpayer consistently apply such paragraph with respect to all foreign corporations. For payments accrued before October 22, 2004, see §1.267(a)-3(c)(4), as contained in 26 CFR part 1, revised as of April 1, 2004.

Personal Service Corporations

Personal Service Corporations: Allocation of Income and Deductions.—Reproduced below is the text of proposed Reg. §1.269A-1, relating to the reallocation of income, deductions, credits, and exclusions between a personal service corporation and its employee-owners if the corporation was formed or availed of primarily to evade or avoid Federal income taxes (published in the Federal Register on March 31, 1983).

☐ The Income Tax Regulations (26 CFR Part 1) are proposed to be amended by adding the new §1.269A-1, in the appropriate place:

§1.269A-1. Personal service corporations.—(a) *In general.*—Section 269A permits the Internal Revenue Service to reallocate income and tax benefits between personal service corporations and their employee-owners to prevent evasion or avoidance of Federal income taxes or to reflect clearly the income of the personal service corporation or any of its employee-owners, if:

(1) Substantially all of the services of the personal service corporation are performed for or on behalf of one other entity, and

(2) The principal purpose for which the corporation was formed or availed of is the evasion or avoidance of Federal income tax. Such purpose is evidenced when use of the corporation either reduces the income of any employee-owner, or secures for any employee-owner one or more tax benefits which would not otherwise be available.

(b) *Definitions.*—For purposes of section 269A and the regulations thereunder, the following definitions will apply:

(1) *Personal service corporation.*—The term "personal service corporation" means a corporation the principal activity of which is the performance of personal services that are substantially performed by employee-owners.

(2) *Employee-owner.*—The term "employee-owner" means an employee who owns, directly or indirectly, on any day of the corporation's taxable year, more than 10 percent of the outstanding stock of the personal service corporation. Section 318 will apply to deter-

mine indirect stock ownership, except that "5 percent" is to be substituted for "50 percent" in section 318(a)(2)(C).

(3) *Entity.*—The term "entity" means a corporation, partnership, or other entity. All persons related to such entity will be treated as one entity. A related person is a related person within the meaning of section 103(b)(6)(C).

(4) *Not otherwise be available.*—The term "not otherwise be available" refers to any tax benefit that would not be available to an employee-owner had such employee-owner performed the personal services in an individual capacity.

(5) *Qualified employer plan.*—The term "qualified employer plan" means a qualified employer plan as defined in section 219(e)(3).

(6) *Tax benefits.*—The term "tax benefits" means any expense, deduction, credit, exclusion or other allowance which would not otherwise be available. The term includes, but is not limited to: multiple surtax exemptions being claimed by the owners of a single integrated business operation conducted through multiple corporate entities, accumulation of income by the corporation, the corporate dividends received deduction under section 243, deferral of income of an employee-owner through the use of a corporation with a fiscal year or accounting method differing from that of such employee-owner, the use of multiple classes of stock to deflect income to taxpayers in lower tax brackets, group-term life insurance (section

79), certain accident and health plans (section 105 and 106), certain employee death benefits (section 101), meals and lodging furnished for the convenience of the employer (section 119), and qualified transportation expenses (section 124). Except as otherwise provided in paragraph (d)(2)(ii) of this section, the term "tax benefits" does not include contributions to a qualified employer plan.

(c) *Safe harbor.*—In general, a personal service corporation will be deemed not to have been formed or availed of for the principal purpose of avoiding or evading Federal income taxes if the Federal income tax liability of no employee-owner is reduced in a 12 month period by more than the lesser of (1) $2,500 or (2) 10 percent of the Federal income tax liability of the employee-owner that would have resulted in that 12 month period had the employee-owner performed the personal services in an individual capacity. For purposes of the computation required by this paragraph, any current corporate tax liability incurred for that 12 month period by the personal service corporation will be considered to be the tax liability of the employee-owners in proportion to the employee-owners' stock holdings in the personal service corporation.

(d) *Special rules relating to qualified employer plans.*—(1) *In general.*—Contributions to, and benefits under, qualified employer plans will not be taken into account in determining the presence or absence of a principal purpose of the personal service corporation for purposes of paragraph (c) of this section, except as provided in this paragraph.

(2) *Taxable years beginning before January 1, 1984.*—For taxable years beginning before January 1, 1984.

(i) *Corporations in existence on or before September 3, 1982.*—For corporations in existence on or before September 3, 1982, the general rule provided in paragraph (d)(1) of this section will apply unless:

(A) The corporation adopts a new qualified employer plan after September 3, 1982 that has a plan year differing from either the taxable year of the corporation or the calendar year; or

(B) The corporation changes the plan year of an existing qualified employer plan, or its taxable year, after September 3, 1982, in a manner that would extend the period during which section 416 (relating to restrictions on "top heavy" plans), or section 269A (if this (B) did not apply) would be inapplicable to such corporation. If (A) or (B) applies, the corporation will be treated as a corporation formed after September 3, 1982 for purposes of this paragraph.

(ii) *Corporations formed after September 3, 1982.*—For corporations formed after September 3, 1982, contributions to, and benefits under, a qualified employer plan that are in excess of those that would have been available to an employee-owner performing the personal services in an individual capacity are to be taken into account in determining the principal purpose of the personal service corporation and will be considered to be tax benefits.

(e) *Effective dates.*—(1) *In general.*—In general, section 269A and this section are effective for taxable years of personal service corporations beginning after December 31, 1982. Taxable years of employee-owners generally are not considered for purposes of this paragraph.

(2) *Exceptions.*—If a personal service corporation changes its taxable year or qualified employer plan year after September 3, 1982, in a manner that would delay the effective date of section 416 (relating to restrictions on top-heavy plans), or section 269A (but for this (2)), section 269A will be applied to the corporation and its employee-owners on the earlier of the first day of the first taxable year of the corporation or any of its employee-owners beginning after December 31, 1982.

(f) *Effect on section 269A on other sections.*—Nothing in section 269A or the regulations thereunder, including the safe harbor provided in paragraph (c) of this section, precludes application with respect to personal service corporations or their employee-owners of any other Code section (*e.g.,* sections 61 or 482) or tax law principle (*e.g.,* assignment of income doctrine) to reallocate or reapportion income, deductions, credits, etc., so as to reflect the true earner of income. [Reg. § 1.269A-1.]

Prizes and Awards

Exclusions: Prizes and Awards: Employee Achievement Awards.—Reproduced below are the texts of proposed amendments to Reg. §§ 1.274-1 and 1.274-3, relating to prizes and awards and employee achievement awards (published in the Federal Register on January 9, 1989).

☐ Par. 5. Section 1.274-1 is amended by removing everything after the word "business" in the last sentence of paragraph (d) and adding in its place "activity, see § 1.274-6"; revising paragraph (e) and adding paragraph (f) to read as follows:

§ 1.274-1. Disallowance of certain entertainment, gift and travel expenses.—* * * (e) treatment of personal portion of entertainment facility, see § 1.274-7, and (f) employee achievement awards, see § 1.274-8.

☐ Par. 6. Section 1.274-3 is amended as follows:

§ 1.274-3. Disallowance of deduction for gifts.
(a) The last sentence of paragraph (b)(1) is amended by substituting "subsections (b) and (c) of section 74" for "section 74(b)".
(b) The language "recipient, or" at the end of paragraph (b)(2)(ii) is replaced by the language "recipient".
(c) Subdivisions (iii) and (iv) of paragraph (b)(2) are removed.
(d) The first, second, and fourth sentences of the flush material immediately following subdivision (iv) are removed and the last sentence is amended by substituting "sections 61, 74, 102, and 132" for "sections 61, 74, and 102".
(e) Paragraph (d) is removed and paragraphs (e), (f), and (g) are redesignated as paragraphs (d), (e), and (f).

Meals and Entertainment Expenses: Disallowance of Deductions

Meals and Entertainment Expenses: Disallowance of Deductions.—Reg. §§ 1.274-11 and 1.274-12, addressing the elimination of the deduction under Code Sec. 274 for expenditures related to entertainment, amusement, or recreation activities, and providing guidance to determine whether an activity is of a type generally considered to be entertainment, are proposed (published in the Federal Register on February 26, 2020) (REG-100814-19).

Par. 2. Section 1.274-11 is added to read as follows:

§ 1.274-11. Disallowance of deductions for certain entertainment, amusement, or recreation expenditures paid or incurred after December 31, 2017.—(a) *In general.*—Except as provided in this section, no deduction otherwise allowable under chapter 1 of the Internal Revenue Code (Code) is allowed for any expenditure with respect to an activity that is of a type generally considered to be entertainment, or with respect to a facility used in connection with an entertainment activity. For purposes of this paragraph (a), dues or fees to any social, athletic, or sporting club or organization are treated as items with respect to facilities and, thus, are not deductible. In addition, no deduction otherwise allowable under chapter 1 of the Code is allowed for amounts paid or incurred for membership in any club organized for business, pleasure, recreation, or other social purpose.

(b) *Definitions.*—(1) *Entertainment.*—(i) *In general.*—For section 274 purposes, the term *entertainment* means any activity which is of a type generally considered to constitute entertainment, amusement, or recreation, such as entertaining at bars, theaters, country clubs, golf and athletic clubs, sporting events, and on hunting, fishing, vacation and similar trips, including such activity relating solely to the taxpayer or the taxpayer's family. These activities are treated as entertainment under this section, subject to the objective test, regardless of whether the expenditure for the activity is related to or associated with the active conduct of the taxpayer's trade or business. The term *entertainment* may include an activity, the cost of which otherwise is a business expense of the taxpayer, which satisfies the personal, living, or family needs of any individual, such as a hotel suite or an automobile to a business customer or the customer's family. The term *entertainment* does not include activities which, although satisfying personal, living, or family needs of an individual, are clearly not regarded as constituting entertainment, such as a hotel room maintained by an employer for lodging of employees while in business travel status or an automobile used in the active conduct of trade or business even though used for routine personal purposes such as commuting to and from work. On the other hand, the providing of a hotel room or an automobile by an employer to an employee who is on vacation would constitute entertainment of the employee.

(ii) Food or beverages.—Under this section, the term *entertainment* does not include food or beverages unless the food or beverages are provided during or at an entertainment activity. Food or beverages provided during or at an entertainment activity generally are treated as part of the entertainment activity. However, in the case of food or beverages provided during or at an entertainment activity, the food or beverages are not considered entertainment if the food or beverages are purchased separately from the entertainment, or the cost of the food or beverages is stated separately from the cost of the entertainment on one or more bills, invoices, or receipts. The amount charged for food or beverages on a bill, invoice, or receipt must reflect the venue's usual selling cost for those items if they were to be purchased separately from the entertainment, or must approximate the reasonable value of those items. Unless the food or beverages are purchased separately from the entertainment, or the cost of the food or beverages is stated separately from the cost of the entertainment on one or more bills, invoices, or receipts, no allocation can be made and the entire amount is a nondeductible entertainment expenditure.

(iii) Objective test.—An objective test is used to determine whether an activity is of a type generally considered to be entertainment. Thus, if an activity is generally considered to be entertainment, it will be treated as entertainment for purposes of this section and section 274(a) regardless of whether the expenditure can also be described otherwise, and even though the expenditure relates to the taxpayer alone. This objective test precludes arguments that *entertainment* means only entertainment of others or that an expenditure for entertainment should be characterized as an expenditure for advertising or public relations. However, in applying this test the taxpayer's trade or business is considered. Thus, although attending a theatrical performance generally would be considered entertainment, it would not be so considered in the case of a professional theater critic, attending in a professional capacity. Similarly, if a manufacturer of dresses conducts a fashion show to introduce its products to a group of store buyers, the show generally would not be considered entertainment. However, if an appliance distributor sponsors a fashion show, the fashion show generally would be considered to be entertainment.

(2) Expenditure.—The term *expenditure* as used in this section includes amounts paid or incurred for goods, services, facilities, and other items, including items such as losses and depreciation.

(3) Expenditures for production of income.—For purposes of this section, any reference to *trade or business* includes an activity described in section 212.

(c) *Exceptions.*—Paragraph (a) of this section does not apply to any expenditure described in section 274(e)(1), (2), (3), (4), (5), (6), (7), (8), or (9).

(d) *Examples.*—The following examples illustrate the application of paragraphs (a) and (b) of this section. In each example, neither the taxpayer nor the business associate is engaged in a trade or business that relates to the entertainment activity.

(1) Example 1.—Taxpayer A invites, B, a business associate, to a baseball game to discuss a proposed business deal. A purchases tickets for A and B to attend the game. The baseball game is entertainment as defined in paragraph (b)(1) of this section and thus, the cost of the game tickets is an entertainment expenditure and is not deductible by A.

(2) Example 2.—Assume the same facts as in paragraph (d)(1) of this section (*Example 1*), except that A also buys hot dogs and drinks for A and B from a concession stand. The cost of the hot dogs and drinks, which are purchased separately from the game tickets, is not an entertainment expenditure and is not subject to the section 274(a)(1) disallowance. Therefore, A may deduct 50 percent of the expenses associated with the hot dogs and drinks purchased at the game if they meet the requirements of section 162 and § 1.274-12.

(3) Example 3.—Taxpayer C invites D, a business associate, to a basketball game. C purchases tickets for C and D to attend the game in a suite, where they have access to food and beverages. The cost of the basketball game tickets, as stated on the invoice, includes the cost of the food or beverages. The basketball game is entertainment as defined in paragraph (b)(1) of this section and, thus, the cost of the game tickets is an entertainment expenditure and is not deductible by C. The cost of the food and beverages, which are not purchased separately from the game tickets, is not stated separately on the invoice. Thus, the cost of the food and beverages is an entertainment expenditure that is subject to the section 274(a)(1) disallowance. Therefore, C may not deduct the cost of the tickets or the food and beverages associated with the basketball game.

(4) Example 4.—Assume the same facts as in paragraph (d)(3) of this section (*Example 3*), except that the invoice for the basketball game tickets separately states the cost of the food and beverages and reflects the venue's usual selling price if purchased separately. As in paragraph (d)(3) (*Example 3*), the basketball game is entertainment as defined in paragraph (b)(1) of this section and, thus, the cost of the game tickets, other than the cost of the food and beverages, is an entertainment expenditure and is not deductible by C. However, the cost of the food and beverages, which is stated separately on the invoice for the game tickets, is not an entertainment expenditure and is not subject to the section 274(a)(1) disallowance. Therefore, C may deduct 50 percent of the expenses associated with the food and beverages provided at the game if they meet the requirements of section 162 and § 1.274-12.

(e) *Applicability date.*—This section applies for taxable years that begin on or after **[DATE OF PUBLICATION OF FINAL REGULATIONS IN THE FEDERAL REGISTER]**. [Reg. § 1.274-11.]

Par. 3. Section 1.274-12 is added to read as follows:

§1.274-12. Limitation on deductions for certain food or beverage expenses paid or incurred after December 31, 2017.—(a) *Food or beverage expenses.*—(1) *In general.*—Except as provided in this section, no deduction is allowed for the expense of any food or beverages provided by the taxpayer (or an employee of the taxpayer) to another person or persons unless—

(i) The expense is not lavish or extravagant under the circumstances;

(ii) The taxpayer, or an employee of the taxpayer, is present at the furnishing of such food or beverages; and

(iii) The food or beverages are provided to a business associate.

(2) Only 50 percent of food or beverage expenses allowed as deduction.—Except as provided in this section, the amount allowable as a deduction for any expense for food or beverages provided by the taxpayer, or an employee of the taxpayer, to a business associate may not exceed 50 percent of the amount of the expense that otherwise would be allowable.

(3) Examples.—The following examples illustrate the application of paragraph (a)(1) and (2) of this section. In each example, the food or beverage expenses are ordinary and necessary expenses under section 162(a) that are paid or incurred during the taxable year in carrying on a trade or business and are not lavish or extravagant under the circumstances.

(i) Example 1.—Taxpayer A takes client B out to lunch. While eating lunch, A and B discuss A's trade or business activities. Under section 274(k) and (n) and paragraph (a) of this section, A may deduct 50 percent of the food or beverage expenses.

(ii) Example 2.—Taxpayer C takes employee D out to lunch. While eating lunch, C and D discuss D's annual performance review. Under section 274(k) and (n) and paragraph (a) of this section, C may deduct 50 percent of the food and beverage expenses.

(4) Special rules for travel meals.—(i) *In general.*—Food or beverage expenses paid or incurred while traveling away from home in pursuit of a trade or business generally are subject to the deduction limitations in section 274(k) and (n) and paragraph (a)(1) and (2) of this section, as well as the substantiation requirements in section 274(d). In addition, travel expenses generally are subject to the limitations in section 274(m)(1), (2) and (3).

(ii) Substantiation.—Except as provided in this section, no deduction is allowed for the expense of any food or beverages paid or incurred while traveling away from home in pursuit of a trade or business unless the taxpayer meets the substantiation requirements in section 274(d).

(iii) Travel meal expenses of spouse, dependent, or others.—No deduction is allowed under chapter 1 of the Internal Revenue Code (Code), except under section 217 for certain members of the Armed Forces of the United States, for the expense of any food or beverages paid or incurred with respect to a spouse, dependent, or other individual accompanying the taxpayer, or an officer or employee of the taxpayer, on business travel, unless—

(A) The spouse, dependent, or other individual is an employee of the taxpayer;

(B) The travel of the spouse, dependent, or other individual is for a bona fide business purpose of the taxpayer; and

(C) The expenses would otherwise be deductible by the spouse, dependent or other individual.

(D) The following example illustrates the application of paragraph (a)(4)(iii) of this section. Taxpayer E and Taxpayer E's spouse travel from New York to Boston to attend a series of business meetings. E's spouse is not an employee of E, does not travel to Boston for a bona fide business purpose of E, and the expenses would not otherwise be deductible. While in Boston, E and E's spouse go out to dinner. Under section 274(m)(3) and paragraph (a)(4)(iii) of this section, the expenses associated with the food and beverages consumed by E's spouse are not deductible. Therefore, the cost of E's spouse's dinner is not deductible. E may deduct 50 percent of the expense associated with the food and beverages E consumed while on business travel if E meets the requirements in sections 162 and 274, including section 274(k) and (d).

(b) *Definitions.*—Except as otherwise provided in this section, the following definitions apply for purposes of section 274(k) and (n), § 1.274-11(b)(1)(ii) and (d), and this section:

(1) *Food or beverages.*—*Food or beverages* means all food and beverage items, regardless of whether characterized as meals, snacks, or other types of food and beverages, and regardless of whether the food and beverages are treated as *de minimis* fringes under section 132(e).

(2) *Food or beverage expenses.*—*Food or beverage expenses* mean the full cost of food or beverages, including any delivery fees, tips, and sales tax. In the case of employer-provided meals furnished at an eating facility on the employer's business premises, *food or beverage expenses* do not include expenses for the operation of the eating facility such as salaries of employees preparing and serving meals, and other overhead costs.

(3) *Business associate.*—*Business associate* means a person with whom the taxpayer could reasonably expect to engage or deal in the active conduct of the taxpayer's trade or business such as the taxpayer's customer, client, supplier, employee, agent, partner, or professional adviser, whether established or prospective.

(4) *Independent contractor.*—For purposes of the reimbursement or other expense allowance arrangements described in paragraph (c)(2)(ii) of this section, *independent contractor* means a person who is not an employee of the payor.

(5) *Client or customer.*—For purposes of the reimbursement or other expense allowance arrangements described in paragraph (c)(2)(ii) of this section, *client or customer* means a person who receives services from an independent contractor and enters into a reimbursement or other expense allowance arrangement with the independent contractor.

(6) *Payor.*—For purposes of the reimbursement or other expense allowance arrangements described in paragraph (c)(2)(ii) of this section, *payor* means a person that enters into a reimbursement or other expense allowance arrangement with an employee and may include an employer, its agent, or a third party.

(7) *Reimbursement or other expense allowance arrangement.*—For purposes of the reimbursement or other expense allowance arrangements described in paragraph (c)(2)(ii) of this section, *reimbursement or other expense allowance arrangement* means—

(i) For purposes of paragraph (c)(2)(ii)(B) of this section, an arrangement under which an employee receives an advance, allowance, or reimbursement from a payor (the employer, its agent, or a third party) for expenses the employee pays or incurs; and

(ii) For purposes of paragraph (c)(2)(ii)(C) of this section, an arrangement under which an independent contractor receives an advance, allowance, or reimbursement from a client or customer for expenses the independent contractor pays or incurs if either—

(A) A written agreement between the parties expressly states that the client or customer will reimburse the independent contractor for expenses that are subject to the limitations on deductions in paragraph (a) of this section; or

(B) A written agreement between the parties expressly identifies the party subject to the limitations.

(8) *Primarily consumed.*—For purposes of paragraph (c)(2)(iv) of this section, *primarily consumed* means greater than 50 percent of actual or reasonably estimated consumption.

(9) *General public.*—For purposes of paragraph (c)(2)(iv) of this section, the *general public* includes, but is not limited to, customers, clients, and visitors. The *general public* does not include employees, partners or independent contractors of the taxpayer. Also, an exclusive list of guests is not the *general public.*

(c) *Exceptions.*—(1) *In general.*—The limitations on the deduction of food or beverage expenses in paragraph (a) of this section do not apply to any expense described in paragraph (c)(2) of this section.

These expenses are deductible to the extent allowable under chapter 1 of the Code.

(2) *Exceptions.*—(i) *Expenses treated as compensation.*—(A) *In general.*—Any expense paid or incurred by a taxpayer for food or beverages, including food or beverages provided during travel described in section 274(m)(3), if an employee is the recipient of the food or beverages, is not subject to the deduction limitations in paragraph (a) of this section to the extent that the expense is treated by the taxpayer—

(1) On the taxpayer's income tax return as originally filed, as compensation paid to the employee; and

(2) As wages to the employee for purposes of withholding under chapter 24 of the Code, relating to collection of income tax at source on wages.

(B) *Expenses includible in income of persons who are not employees.*—An expense paid or incurred by a taxpayer for food or beverages, including food or beverages provided during travel described in section 274(m)(3), is not subject to the deduction limitations in paragraph (a) of this section to the extent the expenditure is includible in gross income as compensation for services rendered, or as a prize or award under section 74 by a recipient of the expense who is not an employee of the taxpayer. The preceding sentence does not apply to any amount paid or incurred by the taxpayer if the amount is required to be included, or would be so required except that the amount is less than $600, in any information return filed by such taxpayer under part III of subchapter A of chapter 61 of the Code and is not so included.

(C) *Expenses for which value is improperly included or for which amount required to be included is zero.*—The exception in section 274(e)(2) and (e)(9) and paragraph (c)(2)(i) of this section does not apply to expenses paid or incurred for food or beverages for which the value that is included in gross income is less than the amount required to be included in gross income under § 1.61-21. Furthermore, if the amount required to be included in gross income under § 1.61-21 is zero, the exception in section 274(e)(2) and (e)(9) and paragraph (c)(2)(i) of this section does not apply.

(D) *Examples.*—The following examples illustrate the application of paragraph (c)(2)(i) of this section. In each example, the food or beverage expenses are ordinary and necessary expenses under section 162(a) that are paid or incurred during the taxable year in carrying on a trade or business and that are not lavish or extravagant under the circumstances.

(1) *Example 1.*—Employer F provides food and beverages to its employees without charge at a company cafeteria on its premises. The food and beverages do not meet the definition of a *de minimis* fringe under section 132(e). F treats the food and beverage expenses as compensation and wages, and determines the amount of the inclusion under § 1.61-21. Under section 274(e)(2) and paragraph (c)(2)(i) of this section, the expenses associated with the food and beverages provided to the employees are not subject to the 50 percent deduction limitations in paragraph (a) of this section. Thus, F may deduct 100 percent of the food and beverage expenses.

(2) *Example 2.*—Employer G provides meals to its employees without charge. The meals are properly excluded from the employees' income under section 119 as meals provided for the convenience of the employer. Under § 1.61-21(b)(1), an employee must include in gross income the amount by which the fair market value of a fringe benefit exceeds the sum of the amount, if any, paid for the benefit by or on behalf of the recipient, and the amount, if any, specifically excluded from gross income by some other section of subtitle A of the Code. Because the entire value of the employees' meals is excluded from the employees' income under section 119, the fair market value of the fringe benefit does not exceed the amount excluded from gross income under subtitle A of the Code, so there is nothing to be included in the employees' income under § 1.61-21. Thus, the exception in section 274(e)(2) and paragraph (c)(2)(i) of this section does not apply and G may only deduct 50 percent of the expenses for the food and beverages provided to employees.

(ii) *Reimbursed food or beverage expenses.*—(A) *In general.*—In the case of expenses for food or beverages paid or incurred by one person in connection with the performance of services for another person, whether or not the other person is an employer, under a reimbursement or other expense allowance arrangement, the deduction limitations in paragraph (a) of this section apply either to the person who makes the expenditure or to the person who actually bears the expense, but not to both. If an expense of a type described in paragraph (c)(2)(ii) of this section properly constitutes a dividend paid to a shareholder, unreasonable compensation paid to an employee, a personal expense, or other nondeductible expense, nothing in this paragraph (c)(2)(ii)(A) prevents disallowance of the deduction to the taxpayer under other provisions of the Code.

(B) *Reimbursement arrangements involving employees.*—In the case of expenses paid or incurred by an employee for food or beverages in performing services as an employee under a reimbursement or other expense allowance arrangement with a payor (the employer, its agent, or a third party) the limitations on deductions in paragraph (a) of this section apply—

    (1) To the employee to the extent the employer treats the reimbursement or other payment of the expense on the employer's income tax return as originally filed as compensation paid to the employee and as wages to the employee for purposes of withholding under chapter 24 relating to collection of income tax at source on wages; or

    (2) To the payor to the extent the reimbursement or other payment of the expense is not treated as compensation and wages paid to the employee in the manner provided in paragraph (c)(2)(ii)(B)(*1*) of this section. However, see paragraph (c)(2)(ii)(C) of this section if the payor receives a payment from a third party that may be treated as a reimbursement arrangement under paragraph (c)(2)(ii)(C).

    (C) *Reimbursement arrangements involving persons that are not employees.*—In the case of expenses for food or beverages paid or incurred by an independent contractor in connection with the performance of services for a client or customer under a reimbursement or other expense allowance arrangement with the independent contractor, the limitations on deductions in paragraph (a) of this section apply to the party expressly identified in an agreement between the parties as subject to the limitations. If an agreement between the parties does not expressly identify the party subject to the limitations, then the deduction limitations in paragraph (a) of this section apply—

    (1) To the independent contractor (which may be a payor) to the extent the independent contractor does not account to the client or customer within the meaning of section 274(d); or

    (2) To the client or customer if the independent contractor accounts to the client or customer within the meaning of section 274(d).

    (D) *Section 274(d) substantiation.*—If the reimbursement or other expense allowance arrangement involves persons who are not employees and the agreement between the parties does not expressly identify the party subject to the limitations on deductions in paragraph (a) of this section, the limitations on deductions in paragraph (a) of this section apply to the independent contractor unless the independent contractor accounts to the client or customer with substantiation that satisfies the requirements of section 274(d).

    (E) *Examples.*—The following examples illustrate the application of paragraph (c)(2)(ii) of this section.

    (1) *Example 1.*—(*i*) Employee I performs services under an arrangement in which J, an employee leasing company, pays I a per diem allowance of $10x for each day that I performs services for J's client, K, while traveling away from home. The per diem allowance is a reimbursement of travel expenses for food or beverages that I pays in performing services as an employee. J enters into a written agreement with K under which K agrees to reimburse J for any substantiated reimbursements for travel expenses, including meal expenses, that J pays to I. The agreement does not expressly identify the party that is subject to the limitations on deductions in paragraph (a) of this section. I performs services for K while traveling away from home for 10 days and provides J with substantiation that satisfies the requirements of section 274(d) of $100x of meal expenses incurred by I while traveling away from home. J pays I $100x to reimburse those expenses pursuant to their arrangement. J delivers a copy of I's substantiation to K. K pays J $300x, which includes $200x compensation for services and $100x as reimbursement of J's payment of I's travel expenses for meals. Neither J nor K treats the $100x paid to I as compensation or wages.

    (*ii*) Under paragraph (b)(7)(i) of this section, I and J have established a reimbursement or other expense allowance arrangement for purposes of paragraph (c)(2)(ii)(B) of this section. Because the reimbursement payment is not treated as compensation and wages paid to I, under section 274(e)(3)(A) and paragraph (c)(2)(ii)(B)(*1*) of this section, I is not subject to the limitations on deductions in paragraph (a) of this section. Instead, under paragraph (c)(2)(ii)(B)(*2*) of this section, J, the payor, is subject to limitations on deductions in paragraph (a) of this section unless J can meet the requirements of section 274(e)(3)(B) and paragraph (c)(2)(ii)(C) of this section.

    (*iii*) Because the agreement between J and K expressly states that K will reimburse J for substantiated reimbursements for travel expenses that J pays to I, under paragraph (b)(7)(ii)(A) of this section, J and K have established a reimbursement or other expense allowance arrangement for purposes of paragraph (c)(2)(ii)(C) of this section. J accounts to K for K's reimbursement in the manner required by section 274(d) by delivering to K a copy of the substantia-

tion J received from I. Therefore, under section 274(e)(3)(B) and paragraph (c)(2)(ii)(C)(*2*) of this section, K and not J is subject to the deduction limitations in paragraph (a) of this section.

    (2) *Example 2.*—(*i*) The facts are the same as in paragraph (c)(2)(ii)(E)(*1*) of this section (*Example 1*) except that, under the arrangements between I and J and between J and K, I provides the substantiation of the expenses directly to K, and K pays the per diem directly to I.

    (*ii*) Under paragraph (b)(7)(i) of this section, I and K have established a reimbursement or other expense allowance arrangement for purposes of paragraph (c)(2)(ii)(C) of this section. Because I substantiates directly to K and the reimbursement payment was not treated as compensation and wages paid to I, under section 274(e)(3)(A) and paragraph (c)(2)(ii)(C)(*1*) of this section I is not subject to the limitations on deductions in paragraph (a) of this section. Under paragraph (c)(2)(ii)(C)(*2*) of this section, K, the payor, is subject to the limitations on deductions in paragraph (a) of this section.

    (3) *Example 3.*—(*i*) The facts are the same as in paragraph (c)(2)(ii)(E)(*1*) of this section (*Example 1*), except that the written agreement between J and K expressly provides that the limitations of this section will apply to K.

    (*ii*) Under paragraph (b)(7)(ii)(B) of this section, J and K have established a reimbursement or other expense allowance arrangement for purposes of paragraph (c)(2)(ii)(C) of this section. Because the agreement provides that the 274 deduction limitations apply to K, under section 274(e)(3)(B) and paragraph (c)(2)(ii)(C) of this section, K and not J is subject to the limitations on deductions in paragraph (a) of this section.

    (4) *Example 4.*—(*i*) The facts are the same as in paragraph (c)(2)(ii)(E)(*1*) of this section (*Example 1*), except that the agreement between J and K does not provide that K will reimburse J for travel expenses.

    (*ii*) The arrangement between J and K is not a reimbursement or other expense allowance arrangement within the meaning of section 274(e)(3)(B) and paragraph (b)(7)(ii) of this section. Therefore, even though J accounts to K for the expenses, J is subject to the limitations on deductions in paragraph (a) of this section.

    (iii) *Recreational expenses for employees.*—(A) *In general.*— Any food or beverage expense paid or incurred by a taxpayer for a recreational, social, or similar activity, primarily for the benefit of taxpayer's employees (other than employees who are highly compensated employees (within the meaning of paragraph (c)(2)(iii)(B) of this section)) is not subject to the deduction limitations in paragraph (a) of this section. This paragraph (c)(2)(iii)(A) applies to expenses paid or incurred for events such as holiday parties, annual picnics, or summer outings. This paragraph (c)(2)(iii)(A) does not apply to expenses for meals the value of which is excluded from employees' income under section 119 because the meals are provided for the convenience of the employer.

    (B) *Highly compensated employees.*—The exception in this paragraph (c)(2)(iii) applies only to expenses for food or beverages made primarily for the benefit of employees of the taxpayer other than employees who are officers, shareholders or other owners who own a 10-percent or greater interest in the business, or other highly compensated employees. For purposes of the preceding sentence, an employee is treated as owning any interest owned by a member of the employee's family, within the meaning of section 267(c)(4). Any expense for food or beverages that is made under circumstances which discriminate in favor of employees who are officers, shareholders or other owners, or highly compensated employees is not considered to be made primarily for the benefit of employees generally. An expense for food or beverages is not to be considered outside of the exception of this paragraph (c)(2)(iii) merely because, due to the large number of employees involved, the provision of food or beverages is intended to benefit only a limited number of employees at one time, provided the provision of food or beverages does not discriminate in favor of officers, shareholders, other owners, or highly compensated employees.

    (C) *Examples.*—The following examples illustrate the application of this paragraph (c)(2)(iii). In each example, the food or beverage expenses are ordinary and necessary expenses under section 162(a) that are paid or incurred during the taxable year in carrying on a trade or business and that are not lavish or extravagant under the circumstances.

    (1) *Example 1.*—Employer L invites all employees to a holiday party in a hotel ballroom that includes a buffet dinner and an open bar. Under section 274(e)(4), this paragraph (c)(2)(iii), and §1.274-11(c), the cost of the party, including food and beverage expenses, is not subject to the deduction limitations in paragraph (a)

of this section because the holiday party is a recreational, social, or similar activity primarily for the benefit of non-highly compensated employees. Thus, L may deduct 100 percent of the cost of the party.

(2) *Example 2.*—The facts are the same as in paragraph (c)(2)(iii)(C)(1) of this section (*Example 1*), except that Employer L invites only highly-compensated employees to the holiday party, and the invoice provided by the hotel lists the costs for food and beverages separately from the cost of the rental of the ballroom. The costs reflect the venue's usual selling price for food or beverages. The exception in this paragraph (c)(2)(iii) does not apply because L invited only highly-compensated employees to the holiday party. However, under §1.274-11(b)(1)(ii), the food and beverage expenses are not treated as entertainment. L may deduct 50 percent of the food and beverage costs that are separately stated on the invoice under paragraph (a)(2) of this section.

(3) *Example 3.*—Employer M provides free coffee, soda, bottled water, chips, donuts, and other snacks in a break room available to all employees. The expenses associated with the food and beverages are subject to the deduction limitations in paragraph (a) of this section because the break room is not a recreational, social, or similar activity primarily for the benefit of the employees. Thus, the exception in section 274(e)(4) and this paragraph (c)(2)(iii) does not apply and M may only deduct 50 percent of the expenses for food and beverages provided in the break room.

(4) *Example 4.*—Employer N has a written policy that employees in a certain medical services-related position must be available for emergency calls due to the nature of the position that requires frequent emergency response. Because these emergencies can and do occur during meal periods, N furnishes food and beverages to employees in this position without charge in a cafeteria on N's premises. N excludes food and beverage expenses from the employees' income as meals provided for the convenience of the employer excludable under section 119. Because these food and beverages are furnished for the employer's convenience, and therefore are not primarily for the benefit of the employees, the exception in section 274(e)(4) and this paragraph (c)(2)(iii) does not apply, even if some socializing related to the food and beverages provided occurs. Thus, N may only deduct 50 percent of the expenses for food and beverages provided to employees in the cafeteria.

(5) *Example 5.*—Employer O invites an employee and a client to dinner at a restaurant. Because it is the birthday of the employee, O orders a special dessert in celebration. Because the meal is a business meal, and therefore not primarily for the benefit of the employee, the exception in section 274(e)(4) and this paragraph (c)(2)(iii) does not apply, even though an employee social activity in the form of a birthday celebration occurred during the meal. Thus, O may only deduct 50 percent of the meal expenses.

(iv) *Items available to the public.*—(A) *In general.*—Any expense paid or incurred by a taxpayer for food or beverages to the extent the food or beverages are made available to the general public is not subject to the deduction limitations in paragraph (a) of this section. If a taxpayer provides food or beverages to employees, this paragraph (c)(2)(iv)(A) applies to the entire amount of expenses for those food or beverages if the same types of food or beverages are provided to, and are primarily consumed by, the general public.

(B) *Examples.*—The following examples illustrate the application of this paragraph (c)(2)(iv). In each example, the food and beverage expenses are ordinary and necessary expenses under section 162(a) that are paid or incurred during the taxable year in carrying on a trade or business and that are not lavish or extravagant under the circumstances.

(1) *Example 1.*—Employer P is a real estate agent and provides refreshments at an open house for a home available for sale to the public. The refreshments are consumed by P's employees, potential buyers of the property, and other real estate agents. Under section 274(e)(7) and this paragraph (c)(2)(iv), the expenses associated with the refreshments are not subject to the deduction limitations in paragraph (a) of this section if over 50 percent of the food

and beverages are primarily consumed by potential buyers and other real estate agents. If the food and beverages are not primarily consumed by the general public, only the costs attributable to the food and beverages provided to the general public are excepted under section 274(e)(7) and this paragraph (c)(2)(iv).

(2) *Example 2.*—Employer Q is an automobile service center and provides refreshments in its waiting area. The refreshments are consumed by Q's employees and customers. Under section 274(e)(7) and this paragraph (c)(2)(iv), the expenses associated with the refreshments are not subject to the deduction limitations provided for in paragraph (a) of this section if over 50 percent of the food and beverages are primarily consumed by customers. If the food and beverages are not primarily consumed by the general public, only the costs attributable to the food and beverages provided to the general public are excepted under section 274(e)(7) and this paragraph (c)(2)(iv).

(3) *Example 3.*—Employer R operates a summer camp open to the general public for children and provides breakfast and lunch, as part of the fee to attend camp, both to camp counselors, who are employees, and to camp attendees, who are customers. There are 20 camp counselors and 100 camp attendees. The same type of meal is available to each counselor and attendee, and attendees consume more than 50 percent of the food and beverages. Under section 274(e)(7) and this paragraph (c)(2)(iv), the expenses associated with the food and beverages are not subject to the deduction limitations in paragraph (a) of this section, because over 50 percent of the food and beverages are primarily consumed by camp attendees. Thus, R may deduct 100 percent of the food and beverage expenses.

(4) *Example 4.*—Employer S provides food and beverages to its employees without charge at a company cafeteria on its premises. Occasionally, customers or other visitors also eat without charge in the cafeteria. The occasional consumption of food and beverages at the company cafeteria by customers and visitors is less than 50 percent of the total amount of food and beverages consumed at the cafeteria. Therefore, only the costs attributable to the food and beverages provided to the general public are excepted under section 274(e)(7) and this paragraph (c)(2)(iv).

(v) *Goods or services sold to customers.*—(A) *In general.*—An expense paid or incurred for food or beverages, to the extent the food or beverages are sold to customers in a bona fide transaction for an adequate and full consideration in money or money's worth, is not subject to the deduction limitations in paragraph (a) of this section. However, *money or money's worth* does not include payment through services provided. Under this paragraph (c)(2)(v), a restaurant or catering business may deduct 100 percent of its costs for food or beverage items, purchased in connection with preparing and providing meals to its paying customers, which are also consumed at the worksite by employees who work in the employer's restaurant or catering business. In addition, for purposes of this paragraph (c)(2)(v), the term *customer* includes anyone, including an employee of the taxpayer, who is sold food or beverages in a bona fide transaction for an adequate and full consideration in money or money's worth.

(B) *Example.*—The following example illustrates the application of this paragraph (c)(2)(v). Employer T operates a restaurant. T provides food and beverages to its food service employees before, during, and after their shifts for no consideration. Under section 274(e)(8) and this paragraph (c)(2)(v), the expenses associated with the food and beverages provided to the employees are not subject to the 50 percent deduction limitation in paragraph (a) of this section because the restaurant sells food and beverages to customers in a bona fide transaction for an adequate and full consideration in money or money's worth. Thus, T may deduct 100 percent of the food and beverage expenses.

(d) *Applicability date.*—This section applies for taxable years that begin on or after **[DATE OF PUBLICATION OF FINAL REGULATIONS IN THE FEDERAL REGISTER]**. [Reg. §1.274-12.]

Substantiation: Travel, Entertainment, Gifts, Listed Property, Etc.

Business Expenses: Substantiation: Recordkeeping Requirements: Listed Property.—Temporary Reg. §§1.274-5T and 1.274-6T, relating to the requirement that any deduction or credit with respect to certain business-related expenses be substantiated with adequate or sufficient evidence to corroborate a taxpayer's own statement and to the limitations on cost recovery deductions and the investment tax credit for listed property, are proposed (published in the Federal Register on November 6, 1985) (LR-145-84). Portions of Reg. §1.274-5T were adopted by T.D. 8864 on January 21, 2000.

§1.274-5. Substantiation requirements.

§1.274-6. Substantiation with respect to certain types of listed property for taxable years beginning after 1985.

Prizes and Awards

Exclusions: Prizes and Awards: Employee Achievement Awards.—Reproduced below is the text of proposed Reg. §1.274-8 relating to prizes and awards and employee achievement awards (published in the Federal Register on January 9, 1989).

☐ Par. 7. Section 1.274-8 is redesignated as §1.274-9 and a new §1.274-8 is added immediately following §1.274-7 to read as set forth below.

§1.274-8. Disallowance of certain employee achievement award expenses.—(a) *In general.*—No deduction is allowable under section 162 or 212 for any portion of the cost of an employee achievement award (as defined in section 274(j)(3)(A)) in excess of the deduction limitations of section 274(j)(2).

(b) *Deduction limitations.*—The deduction for the cost of an employee achievement award made by an employer to an employee: (1) which is not a qualified plan award, when added to the cost to the employer for all other employee achievement awards made to such employee during the taxable year which are not qualified plan awards, shall not exceed $400, and (2) which is a qualified plan award, when added to the cost to the employer for all other employee achievement awards made to such employee during the taxable year (including employee achievement awards which are not qualified plan awards), shall not exceed $1,600. Thus, the $1,600 limitation is the maximum amount that may be deducted by an employer for all employee achievement awards granted to any one employee during the taxable year.

(c) *Definitions.*—(1) *Employee achievement award.*—The term "employee achievement award", for purposes of this section, means an item of tangible personal property that is transferred to an employee by reason of the employee's length of service or safety achievement. The item must be awarded as part of a meaningful presentation, and under conditions and circumstances that do not create a significant likelihood of the payment of disguised compensation. For purposes of section 274(j), an award made by a sole proprietorship to the sole proprietor is not an award made to an employee.

(2) *Tangible personal property.*—For purposes of this section, the term "tangible personal property" does not include cash or a certificate (other than a nonnegotiable certificate conferring only the right to receive tangible personal property). If a certificate entitles an employee to receive a reduction of the balance due on his account with the issuer of the certificate, the certificate is a negotiable certificate and is not tangible personal property for purposes of this section. Other items that will not be considered to be items of tangible personal property include vacations, meals, lodging, tickets to theater and sporting events, and stocks, bonds, and other securities.

(3) *Meaningful presentation.*—Whether an award is presented as part of a meaningful presentation is determined by a facts and circumstances test. While the presentation need not be elaborate, it must be a ceremonious observance emphasizing the recipient's achievement in the area of safety or length of service.

(4) *Disguised compensation.*—An award will be considered disguised compensation if the conditions and circumstances surrounding the award create a significant likelihood that it is payment of compensation. Examples include the making of employee achievement awards at the time of annual salary adjustments or as a substitute for a prior program of awarding cash bonuses, the providing of employee achievement awards in a manner that discriminates in favor of highly paid employees, or, with respect to awards the cost of which would otherwise be fully deductible by the employer under the deduction limitations of section 274(j)(2), the making of an employee achievement award the cost of which to the employer is grossly disproportionate to the fair market value of the item.

(5) *Qualified plan awards.*—(i) *In general.*—Except as provided in paragraph (c)(5)(ii) of this section, the term "qualified plan award" means an employee achievement award that is presented pursuant to an established written plan or program that does not discriminate in terms of eligibility or benefits in favor of highly compensated employees. See section 414(q) of the Code for the definition of highly compensated employees. Whether an award plan is established shall be determined from all the facts and circumstances of the particular case, including the frequency and timing of any changes to the plan. Whether or not an award plan is discriminatory shall be determined from all the facts and circumstances of the particular case. An award plan may fail to qualify because it is discriminatory in its actual operation even though the written provisions of the award plan are nondiscriminatory.

(ii) *Items not treated as qualified plan awards.*—No award presented by an employer during the taxable year will be considered a qualified plan award if the average cost of all employee achievement awards presented during the taxable year by the taxpayer under any plan described in paragraph (c)(5)(i) of this section exceeds $400. The average cost of employee achievement awards shall be computed by dividing (A) the sum of the costs to the employer for all employee achievement awards (without regard to the deductibility of those costs) by (B) the total number of employee achievement awards presented. For purposes of the preceding sentence, employee achievement awards of nominal value shall not be taken into account in the computation of average cost. An employee achievement award that costs the employer $50 or less shall be considered to be an employee achievement award of nominal value.

(d) *Special rules.*—(1) *Partnership.*—Where employee achievement awards are made by a partnership, the deduction limitations of section 274(j)(2) shall apply to the partnership as well as to each member thereof.

(2) *Length of service awards.*—An item shall not be treated as having been provided for length of service achievement if the item is presented for less than 5 years employment with the taxpayer or if the award recipient received a length of service achievement award (other than an award excludable under section 132(e)(1)) during that year or any of the prior 4 calendar years. An award presented upon the occasion of a recipient's retirement is a length of service award subject to the rules of this section. However, under appropriate circumstances, a traditional retirement award will be treated as a de minimis fringe. For example, assume that an employer provides a gold watch to each employee who completes 25 years of service with the employer. The value of the gold watch is excluded from gross income as a de minimis fringe. However, if the employer provides a gold watch to an employee who has not completed lengthy service with the employer or on an occasion other than retirement, the value of the watch is not excludable from gross income under section 132(e).

(3) *Safety achievement awards.*—(i) *In general.*—An item shall not be treated as having been provided for safety achievement if—

(A) During the taxable year, employee achievement awards (other than awards excludable under section 132(e)(1)) for safety achievement have previously been awarded by the taxpayer to more than 10 percent of the eligible employees of the taxpayer, or

(B) Such item is awarded to a manager, administrator, clerical employee, or other professional employee.

(ii) *"Eligible employee" defined.*—An eligible employee is one not described in paragraph (d)(3)(i)(B) of this section and who has worked in a full-time capacity for the taxpayer for a minimum of one year immediately preceding the date on which the safety achievement award is presented.

(iii) *Special rules.*—Where safety achievement awards are presented to more than 10 percent of the taxpayer's eligible employees, only those awards presented to eligible employees before 10 percent of the taxpayer's eligible employees are exceeded shall be treated as having been provided for safety achievement. Where the only safety achievement awards presented by an employer consist of items that are presented at one time during the calendar year, then, if safety achievement awards are presented to more than 10 percent of the taxpayer's eligible employees, the taxpayer may deduct an amount equal to the product of the cost of the item (subject to the applicable deduction limitation) and 10 percent of the taxpayer's eligible employees. Except as provided in the preceding sentence, no award shall be treated as having been provided for safety achievement except to the extent that it can be reasonably demonstrated that that award was made before the 10 percent limitation was exceeded. [Reg. §1.274-8.]

Business Use or Rental of Dwelling Unit

Business Use or Rental of Dwelling Unit.—Reproduced below are the texts of proposed Reg. §§1.280A-1—1.280A-3, relating to the deductibility of expenses in connection with the business use, or the rental to others, of a dwelling unit that the taxpayer is deemed to have used for personal purposes during the taxable year (published in the Federal Register on August 7, 1980, with amendments published in the Federal Register on July 21, 1983; Reg. §1.280A-2(b)(2) and (3) were withdrawn on May 20, 1994).

§1.280A-1. Limitations on deductions with respect to a dwelling unit which is used by the taxpayer during the taxable year as a residence.—(a) *General rule.*—In the case of an individual, a partnership, a trust, an estate, or an electing small business corporation (as defined in section 1371 (b)), no deductions which would otherwise be allowable under chapter 1 of the Code shall be allowed with respect to the use of a dwelling unit used by such person during the taxable year as a residence except as provided in section 280A and in §§1.280A-1 through 1.280A-3. The requirements imposed by section 280A are in addition to the requirements imposed by other provisions of the Code. If a deduction is claimed for an item attributable to a dwelling unit used by the taxpayer during the taxable year as a residence, the taxpayer must first establish that it is otherwise allowable as a deduction under chapter 1 of the Code before the provisions of section 280A become applicable. Section 1.280A-2 sets forth the rules relating to the deductibility of expenses attributable to the business use of a dwelling unit used as a residence. Section 1.280A-3 sets forth the rules relating to the deductibility of expenses attributable to the rental of a dwelling unit used as a residence. Note that the allocation rule of section 280A(e) and §1.280A-3(c) applies to expenses attributable to any dwelling unit used by the taxpayer for personal purposes on any day during the taxable year, whether or not the taxpayer is treated as using the unit as a residence.

(b) *Deductions allowable without regard to any connection with a trade or business or an income-producing activity.*—Deductions which are allowable without regard to any connection with a trade or business or an income-producing activity are allowed with respect to the use of dwelling units. Such deductions include the deduction for interest under section 163, the deduction for taxes under section 164, and the deduction for casualty losses under section 165.

(c) *Dwelling unit.*—(1) *In general.*—For purposes of this section and §§1.280A-2 and 1.280A-3, the term "dwelling unit" includes a house, apartment, condominium, mobile home, boat, or similar property, which provides basic living accommodations such as sleeping space, toilet, and cooking facilities. A single structure may contain more than one dwelling unit. For example, each apartment in an apartment building is a separate dwelling unit. Similarly, if the basement of a house contains basic living accommodations, the basement constitutes a separate dwelling unit. All structures and other property appurtenant to a dwelling unit which do not themselves constitute dwelling units are considered part of the unit. For example, an individual who rents to another person space in a garage which is appurtenant to a house which the individual owns and occupies may claim deductions with respect to that rental activity only to the extent allowed under section 280A, paragraph (b) of this section, and §1.280A-3.

(2) *Exception.*—Notwithstanding the provisions of paragraph (c)(1) of this section, the term "dwelling unit" does not include any unit or portion of a unit which is used exclusively as a hotel, motel, inn, or similar establishment. Property is so used only if it is regularly available for occupancy by paying customers and only if no person having an interest in the property is deemed under the rules of this section to have used the unit (or the portion of the unit) as a residence during the taxable year. Thus, this exception may apply to a portion of a home used to furnish lodging to tourists or to long-term boarders such as students. This exception may also apply to a unit entered in a rental pool (see 1.280A-3 (e)) if the owner of the unit does not use it as a residence during the taxable year.

(d) *Use as a residence.*—(1) *In general.*—For purposes of this section and §§1.280A-2 and 1.280A-3, a taxpayer uses a dwelling unit during the taxable year as a residence if the taxpayer uses the unit for personal purposes for a number of days which exceeds the greater of—

(i) 14 days, or

(ii) 10 percent of the number of days during the year for which the unit is rented at a fair rental.

For purposes of this determination, a unit shall not be treated as rented at fair rental for any day on which it is used for personal purposes.

(2) *Examples.*—The provisions of this paragraph (e) may be illustrated by the following examples:

Example (1). B owns a boat suitable for overnight use. B is deemed, under paragraph (d) of this section, to have used the boat for personal purposes for 16 days during B's taxable year. B rents the boat at fair rental for 163 days during B's taxable year. B is not deemed to have used the boat for personal purposes on any of the 163 days for which it is rented at fair rental. Since the number of days on which B used the boat for personal purposes does not exceed 16.3 (10 percent of 163, the number of days on which the boat is treated as rented at a fair rental for purposes of this determination), B has not used the boat as a residence for the taxable year.

Example (2). Assume the same facts as in example (1) of this subparagraph, except that 5 of the 16 days on which B is deemed to have used the boat for personal purposes were included in the 163 days on which the boat was rented at fair rental. On those 5 days the boat is not treated as rented at a fair rental for purposes of this

paragraph. Since the number of days on which B used the boat for personal purposes exceeds 15.8 (10 percent of 158, the number of days on which the boat is treated as rented at a fair rental for purposes of this determination), B has used the boat as a residence for the taxable year.

(e) *Personal use of dwelling unit.*—(1) *General rule.*—For purposes of this section and §§1.280A-2 and 1.280A-3, a taxpayer shall be deemed to have used a dwelling unit for personal purposes on any day on which, for any part of the day, any portion of the unit is used—

(i) For personal purposes by the taxpayer or any other person who has an interest in the unit;

(ii) By brother or sister (whether by the whole or half blood), spouse, ancestor, or lineal descendant of the taxpayer or of any other person who has an interest in the unit;

(iii) By any individual who uses the unit under an arrangement which enables the taxpayer to use some other dwelling unit for any period of time, whether or not a rental is charged for the use of the other unit and regardless of the length of time that the taxpayer uses the other unit; or

(iv) By any individual, other than an employee with respect to whose use section 119 (relating to meals or lodging furnished for the convenience of the employer) applies, unless for such day the dwelling unit is rented for a rental which, under the facts and circumstances, is fair rental.

For purposes of this paragraph, a person is considered to have an interest in a dwelling unit if that person holds any interest in the unit (other than a security interest or an interest under a lease for a fair rental) even if there are no immediate rights to possession and enjoyment under the interest.

(2) *Rental at fair rental to other persons for use as principal residence.*—Notwithstanding paragraph (e) (1) of this section, a taxpayer shall not be treated as using a dwelling unit for personal purposes by reason of a rental arrangement for any day on which the taxpayer rents the dwelling unit at a fair rental to any person for use as that person's principal residence. If a taxpayer actually makes personal use of a unit on any such day, however, that personal use is taken into account because it arises other than "by reason of a rental arrangement." For purposes of the preceding sentence, a brief visit during which the taxpayer is a guest of the occupant of the unit shall not be considered personal use by the taxpayer. For the meaning of the term "principal residence," see section 1034 and §1.1034-1 (c) (3).

(3) *Rental to persons having interest in the unit.*—(i) *In general.*—Paragraph (e) (2) of this section shall apply in the case of a rental of a unit to a person who has an interest in the unit only if the rental is pursuant to a shared equity financing agreement.

(ii) *Shared equity financing agreement.*—A shared equity financing agreement is any written agreement under which—

(A) Two or more persons acquire qualified ownership interests in the dwelling unit, and

(B) A person (or persons) holding one or more of the interests is—

(1) Entitled to occupy the dwelling unit for use as a principal residence, and

(2) Required to pay rent to one or more persons holding a qualified ownership interest in the unit.

(iii) *Fair rental.*—For purposes of this paragraph (e)(3), the determination whether a unit is rented at a fair rental (within the meaning of paragraph (g) of this section) shall be made in light of all the facts and circumstances that existed at the time the agreement was entered into. The totality of rights and obligations of all parties under the agreement is taken into account in determining fair rental.

(iv) *Qualified ownership interest.*—For purposes of this paragraph (e)(3), the term "qualified ownership interest" means an undivided interest for more than 50 years in the entire dwelling unit and appurtenant land being acquired in the transaction to which the shared equity financing agreement relates.

(v) *Not necessary that all owners charge fair rental.*—A shared equity financing arrangement may exist even if one or more of the owners does not charge the occupant fair rental for use of the unit. Paragraph (e)(2) of this section, however, applies only to those owners who do charge fair rental.

(4) *Special rule for "qualified rental period".*—For purposes of determining whether section 280A(c)(5) and §1.280A-3(d) limit deductions for expenses allocable to a "qualified rental period," a taxpayer shall not be considered to have used the rented unit for personal purposes on any day during the taxable year before or after a "qualified rental period" described in paragraph (e)(4)(i) of this section, or before a "qualified rental period" described in paragraph (e)(4)(ii) of this section, if the rented unit was the principal residence

of the taxpayer with respect to that day. The use of the unit for personal purposes shall, however, be taken into account for all other purposes of section 280A. A "qualified rental period" is a consecutive period of—

(i) 12 or more months which begins or ends during the taxable year, or

(ii) less than 12 months which begins in the taxable year and at the end of which the rented unit is sold or exchanged, and for which the unit is rented, or is held for rental, at a fair rental. For the meaning of the term "principal residence," see section 1034 and §1.1034-1(c)(3).

(5) *Dwelling units in which a partnership, a trust, an estate, or an electing small business corporation has an interest.*—(i) *In general.*—This paragraph (e)(5) sets out special rules for purposes of applying paragraph (e)(1) and (2) of this section to a dwelling unit in which a partnership, a trust, an estate, an electing small business corporation (as defined in section 1371(b), as it read before the enactment of the Subchapter S Revision Act of 1982), or an S corporation (as defined in section 1361(a)) has an interest. For purposes of this paragraph (e)(5), these entities shall be referred to as pass-through entities, and any partner, beneficiary, or shareholder that owns an interest in such an entity shall be referred to as beneficial owner of the entity.

(ii) *Personal use under paragraph (e)(1).*—For purposes of paragraph (e)(1) of this section, a pass-through entity shall be considered to have made personal use of a dwelling unit on any day on which any beneficial owner of the entity would be considered to have made personal use of the unit. Personal use under the preceding sentence shall be determined as if each beneficial owner had an interest in the unit. Thus, for example, personal use by a sister of a partner is considered personal use by the partnership.

(iii) *Personal use under paragraph (e)(2).*—(A) *In general.*—For purposes of applying the second sentence of paragraph (e)(2) of this section to a dwelling unit in which a pass-through entity has an interest, actual personal use by any beneficial owner of that pass-through entity shall be treated as personal use by the entity. Deemed personal use by a beneficial owner under paragraph (e)(1), for example, by reason of the personal use of the unit by a sister of the beneficial owner, shall not be treated as personal use by the entity.

(B) *Exception for certain partnerships.*—If—

(1) A partnership owns an interest in a dwelling unit,

(2) A partner rents the unit from the partnership at a fair rental for use as the partner's principal residence, and

(3) The items of income, gain, loss, deduction or credit of the partnership related to the unit are allocated among the partners in accordance with their percentage ownership interest in the partnership, use of the unit by that partner as that partner's principal residence shall not be treated as personal use of the unit by the partnership for purposes of paragraph (e)(2). The partner actually making use of the unit, however, is subject to the limitations of section 280A(c)(5) with respect to items related to the unit that are allocated to that partner.

(C) *Example.*—The provisions of paragraph (e)(5)(iii)(B) of this section may be illustrated by the following example.

Example. A, B, and C form partnership P, in which each holds a one-third interest. P acquires a dwelling unit that C rents from P at fair rental for use as C's principal residence. All items of income, gain, loss, deduction, or credit of P that are related to the unit are allocated one-third to each partner. Under these circumstances, the personal use of the unit by C is not treated as personal use by P. Consequently, the use of the unit by C does not subject A and B to the limitations of section 280A(c)(5) with respect to their shares of items related to the unit. C, however, is subject to the limitations of section 280A(c)(5) with respect to C's share of those items.

(6) *Use of the unit for repairs and maintenance.*—Notwithstanding the provisions of paragraph (e)(1) of this section, a dwelling unit shall not be deemed to have been used by the taxpayer for personal purposes on any day on which the principal purpose of the use of the unit is to perform repair or maintenance work on the unit. Whether the principal purpose of the use of the unit is to perform repair or maintenance work shall be determined in light of all the facts and circumstances including, but not limited to, the following: the amount of time devoted to repair and maintenance work, the frequency of the use for repair and maintenance purposes during a taxable year, and the presence and activities of companions. In no case, however, shall a day on which the taxpayer engages in repair and maintenance of the unit on a substantially full-time basis be considered a day of personal use by the taxpayer.

(7) *Examples.*—The provisions of this paragraph (e) may be illustrated by the following examples:

Example (1). B owns a vacation home which B rents to S, B's sister, at fair rental for 10 days. B also rents the home to C at fair rental for 11 days as a part of an arrangement whereby B is entitled to use D's home for 6 days. As a favor, B rents the home to F at a discount rate for 15 days. On the basis of the rental activity described, B is deemed to have used the home for personal purposes for 36 days.

Example (2). X Inc., an electing small business corporation in which A and B are shareholders, is the owner of a fully equipped recreational vehicle. During the month of July, the vehicle is used by three individuals. A uses the vehicle on a 7-day camping trip. D, who is B's daughter, rents the vehicle from X Inc. at fair rental for 10 days. E rents the vehicle at fair rental for 12 days under an arrangement whereby B is entitled to use an apartment owned by F, a friend of E, for 9 days. X Inc. is deemed to have used the dwelling unit for personal purposes on any day on which any of its shareholders would be deemed to have so used the unit. Therefore, X Inc. is deemed to have used the recreational vehicle for personal purposes on 29 days.

Example (3). A owns a lakeside cottage which A rents during the summer. A and B, A's spouse, arrive late Thursday evening after a long drive to prepare the cottage for the rental season. A and B prepare dinner but do no work on the unit that evening. A spends a normal work day working on the unit on Friday and Saturday; B helps for a few hours each day but spends most of the time relaxing. By Saturday evening, the necessary maintenance work is complete. Neither A nor B works on the unit on Sunday; they depart shortly before noon. The principal purpose of the use of the unit from Thursday evening through Sunday morning is to perform maintenance work on the unit. Consequently, the use during this period will not be considered personal use by A.

Example (4). C owns a mountain cabin which C rents for most of the year. C spends a week at the cabin with family members. C works on maintenance of the cabin 3 or 4 hours each day during the week. C spends the rest of the time fishing, hiking, and relaxing. C's family members, however, work substantially fulltime on the cabin on each day during the week. The principal purpose of the use of the cabin is to perform maintenance work. Therefore, the use during this period will not be considered personal use by C.

Example (5). B, an individual whose taxable year is the calendar year, uses a dwelling unit as a principal residence from January 1, 1978, to June 30, 1978. On July 1, 1978, B rents the unit at a fair rental to D, an unrelated individual, for a two-year period beginning immediately. In determining whether section 280A(c)(5) and §1.280A-3(d) limit deductions for expenses allocable to this "qualified rental period", B is not considered to have used the unit for personal purposes from January 1, 1978, to June 30, 1978. Note, however, that section 280A(e) and §1.280A-3(c) limit the portion of the total 1978 expenses with respect to the unit which may be attributed to the "qualified rental period." B's personal use of the unit is similarly taken into account in applying section 280A(c)(5) to any other use of the unit during the taxable year, *e.g.*, the use of a portion of the unit as a place of business.

(f) *"Day" defined.*—For purposes of section 280A, this section, and §1.280A-3, the term "day" means generally the 24-hour period for which a day's rental would be paid. Thus, a person using a dwelling unit from Saturday afternoon through the following Saturday morning would generally be treated as having used the unit for 7 days even though the person was on the premises on 8 calendar days.

(g) *Fair rental in the case of co-owners.*—(1) *In general.*—For purposes of sections 280A, this section, and §1.280A-3, a co-owner of a dwelling unit shall be treated as renting the unit at a fair rental if the co-owner charges an amount that is equal to the fair rental of the entire unit multiplied by that co-owner's fractional interest in the unit.

(2) *Example.*—The provisions of this paragraph may be illustrated by the following example:

Example: B and C own undivided one-half interests in a dwelling unit, fair rental for which would be $100x per month. D rents the unit from B and C for a month. B charges D $50x for the month's rental, but C charges D only $20x. B is treated as renting the unit at a fair rental for that month because B charges D $50x, which is equal to the fair rental of the entire unit ($100x), multiplied by B's one-half interest in the unit.

(h) *Coordination with section 162(a)(2).*—Nothing in section 280A or this section shall be construed to disallow any deduction allowable under section 162(a)(2) (or any deduction which meets the tests of section 162(a)(2) but is allowable under another provision of the Internal Revenue Code) by reason of the taxpayer's being away from home in pursuit of a trade or business (other than the trade or business of renting dwelling units).

(i) *Coordination with section 183.*—If a dwelling unit is used by the taxpayer during the taxable year as a residence, section 183 (relating to activities not engaged in for profit) shall not apply with respect to the unit for the taxable year. The taxable year shall, however, be taken into account as a taxable year for purposes of determining whether the presumption described in section 183(d) applies.

Example. B owns a cottage which B rents for part of the summer in 1976, 1977, and 1978. B also uses the cottage as a residence in 1976 and 1977, but not in 1978. B's rental income for 1976 exceeds the expenses allocable to the rental activity, but in 1977 the expenses exceed the rental income. In determining whether B may claim for 1978 the benefit of the presumption described in section 183(d), the rental activity in 1976 and 1977 is taken into account even though section 183 did not apply with respect to the cottage for those years.

(j) *Effective date.*—This section and §§1.280A-2 and 1.280A-3 apply to taxable years beginning after December 31, 1975. [Reg. §1.280A-1.]

§1.280A-2. Deductibility of expenses attributable to business use of a dwelling unit used as a residence.—(a) *Scope.*—This section describes the business uses of a dwelling unit used as a residence for which items may be deductible under an exception to the general rule of section 280A and explains the general conditions for the deductibility of items attributable to those uses. Deductions are allowable only to the extent provided in section 280A(c)(5) and in paragraph (i) of this section. See §1.280A-1 for the general rules under section 280A.

(b) *Use as the taxpayer's principal place of business.*—(1) *In general.*—Section 280A(c)(1)(A) provides an exception to the general rule of section 280A(a) for any item to the extent that the item is allocable to a portion of the dwelling unit which is used exclusively and on a regular basis as the principal place of business for any trade or business of the taxpayer.

(2) [*Withdrawn by the IRS on 5-20-94.*]

(3) [*Withdrawn by the IRS on 5-20-94.*]

(c) *Use by patients, clients, or customers in meeting or dealing with the taxpayer in the normal course of business.*—Section 280A(c)(1)(B) provides an exception to the general rule of section 280A for any item to the extent the item is allocable to a portion of the dwelling unit which is used exclusively and on a regular basis as a place of business in which patients, clients, or customers meet or deal with the taxpayer in the normal course of the taxpayer's business. Property is so used only if the patients, clients, or customers are physically present on the premises; conversations with the taxpayer by telephone do not constitute use of the premises by patients, clients or customers. This exception applies only if the use of the dwelling unit by patients, clients, or customers is substantial and integral to the conduct of the taxpayer's business. Occasional meetings are insufficient to make this exception applicable.

(d) *Use of a separate structure not attached to the dwelling unit in connection with the taxpayer's trade or business.*—Section 280A(c)(1)(C) provides an exception to the general rule of section 280A(a) for any item to the extent that the item is allocable to a separate structure which is appurtenant to, but not attached to, the dwelling unit and is used exclusively and on a regular basis in connection with the taxpayer's trade or business. An artist's studio, a florist's greenhouse, and a carpenter's workshop are examples of structures that may be within the description of this paragraph.

(e) *Use as a storage unit for taxpayer's inventory.*—Section 280A(c)(2) provides an exception to the general rule of section 280A(a) for any item to the extent such item is allocable to space within the dwelling unit which is used on a regular basis as a storage unit for the inventory of the taxpayer held for use in the taxpayer's trade or business of selling products at retail or wholesale. The storage unit includes only the space actually used for storage; thus, if a taxpayer stores inventory in one portion of a basement, the storage unit includes only that portion even if the taxpayer makes no use of the rest of the basement. The exception provided under section 280A(c)(2) applies only if—

(1) The dwelling unit is the sole fixed location of that trade or business, and

(2) The space used is a separately identifiable space suitable for storage.

(f) *Use in providing day care services.*—(1) *In general.*—Section 280A(c)(4) provides an exception to the general rule of section 280A(a) for any item to the extent that the item is allocable to the use of any portion of the dwelling unit on a regular basis in the taxpayer's trade or business of providing day care services for children, for individuals who have attained age 65, or for individuals who are physically or mentally incapable of caring for themselves.

(2) *Day care services.*—Day care services are services which are primarily custodial in nature and which, unlike foster care, are

provided for only certain hours during the day. Day care services may include educational, developmental, or enrichment activities which are incidental to the primary custodial services. If the services performed in the home are primarily educational or instructional in nature, however, they do not qualify as day care services. The determination whether particular activities are incidental to the primary custodial services generally depends upon all the facts and circumstances of the case. Educational instruction to children of nursery school age shall be considered incidental to the custodial services. Further, educational instruction to children of kindergarten age would ordinarily be considered incidental to the custodial services if the instruction is not in lieu of public instruction under a State compulsory education requirement. In addition, enrichment instruction in arts and crafts to children, handicapped individuals, or the elderly would ordinarily be considered incidental to the custodial services rendered.

(3) *State law requirements.*—This paragraph, applies to items accruing after August 31, 1977, only if the owner or operator of the day care business is, at the time the item accrues, acting in accordance with the applicable State law relating to the licensing, certification, registration, or approval of day care centers or family or group day care homes. A person satisfies the condition stated in the preceding sentence for any period for which—

(i) There is no applicable State law of the type described;

(ii) The person is exempt from the requirements of the applicable State law;

(iii) The person has whatever license, etc., is required under the applicable State law; or

(iv) The person has applied for whatever license, etc., is required under the applicable State law, provided, that the application has not been rejected, and provided that the person has corrected or removed any deficiencies that resulted in the revocation of any previous license, etc., or in the rejection of any previous application.

(g) *Exclusive use requirement.*—(1) *In general.*—Paragraph (b), (c), or (d) of this section may apply to the use of a portion of a dwelling unit for a taxable year only if there is no use of that portion of the unit at any time during the taxable year other than for business purposes. For purposes of section 280A(c)(1) and this section, the phrase "a portion of the dwelling unit" refers to a room or other separately identifiable space; it is not necessary that the portion be marked off by a permanent partition. Paragraph (b), (c), or (d) of this section may apply to a portion of a unit which is used for more than one business purpose. Necessary repair or maintenance does not constitute use for purposes of this paragraph.

(2) *Convenience of the employer.*—In the case of an employee, paragraph (b), (c), or (d) shall apply to a use of a portion of a dwelling unit only if that use is for the convenience of the employer.

(h) *Use on a regular basis.*—The determination whether a taxpayer has used a portion of a dwelling unit for a particular purpose on a regular basis must be made in light of all the facts and circumstances.

(i) *Limitation on deductions.*—(1) *In general.*—The deductions allowable under chapter 1 of the Code for a taxable year with respect to the use of a dwelling unit for one of the purposes described in paragraphs (b) through (f) of this section shall not exceed the gross income derived from such use of the unit during the taxable year, as determined under subparagraph (2) of this paragraph. Subparagraphs (3) and (4) of this paragraph provide rules for determining the expenses allocable to the business use of a unit. Subparagraph (5) of this paragraph prescribes the order in which deductions are allowable.

(2) *Gross income derived from use of unit.*—(i) *Only income from qualifying business use to be taken into account.*—For purposes of section 280A and this section, the taxpayer shall take into account, in applying the limitation on deductions, only gross income from a business use described in section 280A(c). For example, a taxpayer who teaches at school may also be engaged in a retail sales business. If the taxpayer uses a home office on a regular basis as the principal place of business for the retail sales business (a use described in section 280A(c)(1)(A)) and makes no non-business use of the office, the taxpayer shall take the gross income from the use of the office for the retail sales business into account in applying the limitation on deductions. Even if the taxpayer also corrects student papers and prepares class presentations in the home office (not a use described in section 280A(c)), no portion of the taxpayer's gross income from teaching may be taken into account in applying the limitation on deductions.

(ii) *More than one location.*—If the taxpayer engages in a business in the dwelling unit and in one or more other locations, the taxpayer shall allocate the gross income from the business to the different locations on a reasonable basis. In making this determination, the taxpayer shall take into account the amount of time that the taxpayer engages in activity related to the business at each location, the capital investment related to the business at each location, and any other facts and circumstances that may be relevant.

(iii) *Exclusion of certain amounts.*—For purposes of section 280A(c)(5)(A) and this section, gross income derived from use of a unit means gross income from the business activity in the unit reduced by expenditures required for the activity but not allocable to use of the unit itself, such as expenditures for supplies and compensation paid to other persons. For example, a physician who uses a portion of a dwelling unit for treating patients shall compute gross income derived from use of the unit by subtracting from the gross income attributable to the business activity in the unit any expenditures for nursing and secretarial services, supplies, etc.

(3) *Expenses allocable to portion of unit.*—The taxpayer may determine the expenses allocable to the portion of the unit used for business purposes by any method that is reasonable under the circumstances. If the rooms in the dwelling unit are of approximately equal size, the taxpayer may ordinarily allocate the general expenses for the unit according to the number of rooms used for the business purpose. The taxpayer may also allocate general expenses according to the percentage of the total floor space in the unit that is used for the business purpose. Expenses which are attributable only to certain portions of the unit, *e.g.*, repairs to kitchen fixtures, shall be allocated in full to those portions of the unit. Expenses which are not related to the use of the unit for business purposes, *e.g.*, expenditures for lawn care, are not taken into account for purposes of section 280A.

(4) *Time allocation for use in providing day care services.*—If the taxpayer uses a portion of a dwelling unit in providing day care services, as described in paragraph (f) of this section, and the taxpayer makes any use of that portion of the unit for nonbusiness purposes during the taxable year, the taxpayer shall make further allocation of the amounts determined under subparagraph (3) of this paragraph to be allocable to the portion of the unit used in providing day care services. The amounts allocated to the business use of the unit under this subparagraph shall bear the same proportion to the amounts determined under subparagraph (3) of this paragraph as the length of time that the portion of the unit is used for day care services bears to the length of time that the portion of the unit is available for all purposes. For example, if a portion of the unit is used for day care services for an average of 36 hours each week during the taxable

year, the fraction to be used for making the allocation required under this subparagraph is 36/168 the ratio of the number of hours of day care use in a week to the total number of hours in a week.

(5) *Order of deductions.*—Business deductions with respect to the business use of a dwelling unit are allowable in the following order and only to the following extent:

(i) The allocable portions of amounts allowable as deductions for the taxable year under chapter 1 of the Code with respect to the dwelling unit without regard to any use of the unit in trade or business, *e.g.*, mortgage interest and real estate taxes, are allowable as business deductions to the extent of the gross income derived from use of the unit.

(ii) Amounts otherwise allowable as deductions for the taxable year under chapter 1 of the Code by reason of the business use of the dwelling unit (other than those which would result in an adjustment to the basis of property) are allowable to the extent the gross income derived from use of the unit exceeds the deductions allowed or allowable under subdivision (i) of this subparagraph.

(iii) Amounts otherwise allowable as deductions for the taxable year under chapter 1 of the Code by reason of the business use of the dwelling unit which would result in an adjustment to the basis of property are allowable to the extent the gross income derived from use of the unit exceeds the deductions allowed or allowable under subdivisions (i) and (ii) of this subparagraph.

(6) *Cross reference.*—For rules with respect to the deductions to be taken into account in computing adjusted gross income in the case of employees, see section 62 and the regulations prescribed thereunder.

(7) *Example.*—The provisions of this subparagraph may be illustrated by the following example:

Example. A, a self-employed individual, uses an office in the home on a regular basis as a place of business for meeting with clients of A's consulting service. A makes no other use of the office during the taxable year and uses no other premises for the consulting activity. A has a special telephone line for the office and occasionally employs secretarial assistance. A also has a gardener care for the lawn around the home during the year. A determines that 10% of the general expenses for the dwelling unit are allocable to the office. On the basis of the following figures, A determines that the sum of the allowable business deductions for the use of the office is $1,050.

Gross income from consulting services		$1,900
Expense for secretary	$500	
Business telephone	150	
Supplies	200	
Total expenditures not allocable to use of unit		850
Gross income derived from use of unit		$1,050

Deductions allowable under subparagraph (5)(i) of this paragraph

	Total	Allocable to Office	
Mortgage interest	$5,000	$500	
Real estate taxes	2,000	200	
Amount allowable			700
Limit on further deductions			$350

Deductions allowable under subparagraph (5)(ii) of this paragraph

	Total	Allocable to Office	
Insurance	$600	$60	
Utilities (other than residential telephone)	900	90	
Lawn care	500	0	
Amount allowable			150
Limit on further deductions			$200

Deductions allowable under subparagraph (5)(iii) of this paragraph

	Total	Allocable to Office	
Depreciation	$3,200	$320	
Amount allowable			200

No portion of the lawn care expense is allocable to the business use of the dwelling unit. A may claim the remaining $6,300 paid for mortgage interest and real estate taxes as itemized deductions. [Reg. §1.280A-2.]

§1.280A-3. Deductibility of expenses attributable to the rental of a dwelling unit used as a residence.—(a) *Scope.*—This section provides rules for determining the deductibility of expenses attributable to the rental of a dwelling unit used as a residence. Note that paragraph (c) of this section applies to any dwelling unit used by the taxpayer for personal purposes on any day during the taxable year, whether or not the taxpayer is treated as using the unit as a residence. See §1.280A-1 for the general rules under section 280A.

(b) *Short rental period.*—If a dwelling unit used by the taxpayer as a residence during the taxable year is actually rented for less than 15 days during the taxable year,

(1) No deduction otherwise allowable because of the rental use shall be allowed, and

(2) The rental income shall not be included in gross income.

(c) *Allocation.*—(1) *In general.*—If a taxpayer uses a dwelling unit for personal purposes on any day during the taxable year, the amount deductible by reason of the rental use of the unit during the taxable year shall not exceed an amount which bears the same relationship to the total expenses paid or incurred with respect to the unit during the taxable year as the number of days on which the unit is rented at fair rental during the year bears to the total number of days that the unit is used for any purpose during the taxable year.

For purposes of section 280A(e) and this section, the fact that a unit is deemed to be used for personal purposes on a particular day does not prevent that day from being counted as a day on which the unit is rented at fair rental. Use of a unit for repair and maintenance which is disregarded under §1.280A-1(e)(6) shall be disregarded for purposes of this paragraph.

(2) *Portion of unit rented.*—If the taxpayer rents only a portion of the dwelling unit, the rule prescribed in subparagraph (1) of this paragraph shall be applied to the expenses attributable to that portion of the unit, and the days to be taken into account shall be the days on which that portion of the unit is rented at fair rental during the taxable year and the days on which that portion of the unit is used for any purpose during the taxable year. The expenses attributable to any portion of a unit shall be determined in accordance with the rules prescribed in §1.280A-2(i)(3).

(3) *Deductions allowable without regard to rental use.*—This paragraph shall not disallow any part of those deductions with respect to a dwelling unit which are allowable without regard to the rental use of the unit.

(4) *Example.*—The provisions of this paragraph may be illustrated by the following example:

Example. A, an individual, owns a cottage which A rents to vacationers at fair rental for 120 days during the taxable year. A is deemed to have made personal use of the cottage on 15 of those 120 days. The unit is used for one or more purposes (other than repair or maintenance) on 160 days during the taxable year. The amount that A may claim as rental expenses may not exceed 120/160 of the total expenses paid or incurred with respect to the unit during the taxable year. If A itemizes deductions, A may claim the remaining 40/160 of items, such as mortgage interest and taxes, which are deductible without regard to the rental use of the unit.

(d) *Limitation on deductions if taxpayer has used dwelling unit as a residence.*—(1) *In general.*—The deductions allowable under chapter 1 of the Code for a taxable year with respect to the rental use of a dwelling unit which the taxpayer is treated as having used as a residence during such year shall not exceed the gross rental income from the unit for such year. See section 280A(d)(4) and §1.280A-1(e)(4) for special rules affecting the determination whether the taxpayer has used a unit as a residence if any day during the taxable year is part of a "qualified rental period."

(2) *Gross rental income.*—For purposes of section 280A and this section gross rental income from a unit equals the gross receipts from rental of the unit reduced by expenditures to obtain tenants for the unit, such as realtors' fees and advertising expense. The gross rental income from a unit for a taxable year includes rental income for periods during which the unit is rented at less than a fair rental as well as rental income for periods during which the unit is rented at fair rental.

(3) *Order of deductions.*—Deductions with respect to the rental use of a dwelling unit are allowable in the following order and only to the following extent:

(i) The allocable portions of amounts otherwise allowable as deductions for the taxable year under chapter 1 of the Code with respect to the dwelling unit without regard to the rental use of the unit, *e.g.*, mortgage interest and real estate taxes, are deductible as rental expenses to the extent of the gross rental income from the unit.

(ii) The allocable portions of amounts otherwise allowable as deductions for the taxable year under chapter 1 of the Code by reason of the rental use of the dwelling unit (other than those which would result in an adjustment to the basis of property) are allowable to the extent the gross rental income exceeds the deductions allowed or allowable under subdivision (i) of this subparagraph.

(iii) The allocable portions of amounts otherwise allowable as deductions for the taxable year under chapter 1 of the Code by reason of the rental use of the dwelling unit which would result in an adjustment to the basis of property are allowable to the extent the gross rental income exceeds the deductions allowed or allowable under subdivisions (i) and (ii) of this subparagraph.

For purposes of this subparagraph, the portion of any item which is allocable to the rental use of a unit during a taxable year shall be that amount which bears the same relationship to the total amount of the item as the number of days on which the unit is rented at a fair rental during the taxable year bears to the number of days on which the unit is used for any purpose (other than repair or maintenance) during the taxable year.

(4) *Example.*—The provisions of this paragraph may be illustrated by the following example:

Example. B owns a lakeside home which B rents at a fair rental for 90 days during the taxable year. B uses the home for personal purposes on 20 other days during the taxable year and also rents it to a friend at a discount for 10 days. Thus, the home is used for some purpose (other than repair or maintenance) on 120 days during the taxable year, and the rental allocation fraction may not exceed 90/120. On the basis of the following figures, B determines that the sum of the rental expenses for the home for the taxable year that are deductible under subparagraph (3) of this paragraph is $2,200. The advertising expense and the realtor's fee are also deductible.

Gross receipts from rental:			
90 days at $25 per day		$2,250	
10 days at $15 per day		150	
Total			$2,400
Computation of gross rental income:			
Gross receipts from rental		$2,400	
Less: Advertising and realtor's fee		200	
Gross rental income			$2,200

Deductions allowable under subparagraph (3)(i) of this paragraph:

	Total	Allocable to rental	
Mortgage interest	$1,000	$750	
Real estate taxes	800	600	
Amount allowable			1,350
Limit on further deductions			$850

Deductions allowable under subparagraph (3)(ii) of this paragraph:

Insurance	$400	$300	
Utilities	600	450	
Amount allowable			750
Limit on further deductions			$100

Deductions allowable under subparagraph (3)(iii) of this paragraph:

Depreciation	$1,500	$1,125	
Amount allowable			100

NOTE.—If B itemizes deductions, B may claim the other $250 in mortgage interest and the other $200 in real estate taxes as itemized deductions.

(e) *Application of the provisions of §1.280A-1 and this section to rental pools.*—(1) *In general.*—In the case of a dwelling unit which is entered in a rental pool, as defined in subparagraph (2) of this paragraph, during the taxable year, the provisions of §1.280A-1 and this section shall be applied in accordance with this paragraph.

(2) *Rental pool.*—For purposes of this section, the term "rental pool" means any arrangement whereby two or more dwelling units are made available for rental and those persons with interests in the units agree to share at least a substantial part of the rental income from the units without regard to the actual use of the various units. The fact that those persons with interests in a particular unit are entitled to an occupancy fee or other payment for the actual use of the unit does not prevent the arrangement from constituting a rental pool if the percentage of the rental income in which the participants in the arrangement share is substantial.

(3) *Gross rental income of participants.*—Participants in a rental pool shall include in gross rental income all amounts received or accrued by reason of participation in the rental pool (including

payments such as occupancy fees) except amounts which are clearly not rental income, *e.g.*, interest earned on deposits held in escrow on behalf of the rental pool participants. Thus, a taxpayer who participates in a rental pool may have gross rental income although the unit in which the taxpayer has an interest is not actually rented during the taxable year.

(4) *Determination of use when averaging is not elected.*—(i) *Applicability.*—This paragraph (e)(4) applies with respect to a rental pool unit only for periods for which the unit is not subject to paragraph (e)(5) of this section.

(ii) *Actual use rule.*—For purposes of §1.280A-1(d)(1) and paragraph (c) of this section, the number of days on which the unit is rented at fair rental and the number of days on which the unit is used for any purpose shall be determined by reference to the actual use of the unit. Availability for rental through the rental pool does not constitute rental at a fair rental or use of the unit for any purpose. If the taxpayer's unit is actually rented at a fair rental on any day during the taxpayer's participation in the rental pool, the taxpayer may count that day as a day on which the unit is rented at a fair rental although the taxpayer receives only a portion of the rent paid.

(iii) *Furnishing information.*—The rental agency managing the rental pool shall furnish the taxpayer within 60 days after the end of the pool season a written statement indicating the number of days the taxpayer's unit was actually rented at fair rental and the number of days the unit was used for any other purpose (other than repair and maintenance) during the pool season.

(5) *Election to average rental use.*—(i) *Applicability.*—This paragraph (e)(5) applies to a taxpayer with respect to participation in a rental pool for a pool season only if—

(A) The taxpayer signs and furnishes to the pool management a document stating that the taxpayer irrevocably consents to the application of this paragraph (e)(5) for that pool season, and

(B) The pool management sends to the taxpayer a written notice stating that there has been unanimous consent by all pool participants to the application of this paragraph (e)(5) for the pool season and providing the taxpayer with the information necessary to enable the taxpayer to comply with the rules of this paragraph (e)(5). It is not necessary that the taxpayer furnish a separate consent for each pool season; a consent may provide that it applies to more than one pool season. If the Commissioner determines that there has not been unanimous consent to the application of this paragraph (e)(5) or that the pool management has failed to provide the required notice to pool participants, the Commissioner may require all pool participants to determine the use of their units under paragraph (e)(4) of this section.

(ii) *General rules.*—All taxpayers with interests in units participating in a rental pool during a pool season with respect to which this paragraph (e)(5) applies shall determine the number of days that the unit is rented at fair rental during its participation in the rental pool in that pool season under paragraph (e)(5)(iii) of this section. All use of the unit on days other than participation days and all use of the unit on participation days other than use at fair rental shall be determined by reference to actual use of the unit. These determinations are for purposes of applying §1.280-1(d)(1) and paragraph (c) of this section.

(iii) *Averaging formula.*—The aggregate number of days that units in the rental pool were rented at fair rental during the pool season shall be apportioned among the units in the pool according to the following ratio:

$$\frac{\text{number of participation days}}{\text{of a particular unit}}$$
$$\overline{\begin{array}{c}\text{aggregate number of participation}\\\text{days of all units.}\end{array}}$$

Thus, if the aggregate number of days of rental at fair rental for all units in a pool were 300, the number of participation days of a particular unit were 80, and the aggregate number of participation days of all units in the pool were 480, the number of days of rental at fair rental to be allocated to the particular unit would be 50, computed as follows:

$$\frac{80}{480} \times 300 = 50.$$

(iv) *When pool season overlaps 2 taxable years.*—If a pool season with respect to which this paragraph (e)(5) applies overlaps 2 taxable years of a person with an interest in a unit participating in the rental pool during that pool season, that person shall apportion the number of days of fair rental allocated to that unit for that season under paragraph (e)(5)(iii) of this section between the taxable years according to the following ratio:

$$\frac{\begin{array}{c}\text{number of participation days of}\\\text{the unit during the pool season}\\\text{that fall in the taxable year}\end{array}}{\begin{array}{c}\text{number of participation days of the unit}\\\text{during the pool season}\end{array}}$$

(v) *"Participation day" defined.*—A "participation day" of a unit is a day for which that unit is entered in the rental pool.

(6) *Reciprocal arrangements.*—If the rental pool agreement provides that a participant whose unit is rented on a given day may make use of another unit in the pool on that day, a taxpayer who has an interest in a unit so used by another participant shall be deemed to have used the unit for personal purposes on any day on which another participant uses the unit under that provision of the agreement.

(f) *Application of the rules of §1.280A-1 and this section to time sharing arrangement.*—(1) *In general.*—In the case of a dwelling unit which is used during the taxable year under a time sharing arrangement, as defined in subparagraph (2) of this paragraph, the provisions of §1.280A-1 and this section shall be applied in accordance with this paragraph.

(2) *Time sharing arrangement.*—For purposes of this section, the term "time sharing arrangement" means any arrangement whereby two or more persons with interests in a dwelling unit agree to exercise control over the unit for different periods during the taxable year. For example, an arrangement under which each of twelve persons with interests in a unit is entitled to exercise control over the unit for one month during the taxable year is a time sharing arrangement. Whether all twelve persons have undivided interests in the unit for the entire year or each has the sole interest in the unit for a single month during the year is immaterial.

(3) *Use for personal purposes.*—For purposes of §1.280A-1(d) and (e), each of the persons with an interest in the unit subject to the time sharing arrangements shall be considered to have a continuing interest in the unit regardless of the terms of the interest under local law.

(4) *Short rental period.*—The provisions of paragraph (b) of this section shall be applied on the basis of the number of days that the unit is actually rented during the entire taxable year.

(5) *Allocation rule.*—The provisions of paragraph (c) of this section shall apply if any person with an interest in the unit is deemed to use the unit for personal purposes on any day during the taxable year. The provisions of paragraph (c) of this section shall be applied on the basis of the taxpayer's expenses for the unit, the number of days during the taxable year that the unit is rented at a fair rental (determined without regard to the provisions of §1.280A-1(g)), and the number of days during the taxable year that the unit is used for any purpose.

(6) *Limitation on deductions.*—The provisions of paragraph (d) of this section shall be applied on the basis of the taxpayer's rental income and expenses with respect to the unit. [Reg. §1.280A-3.]

Investment Tax Credit: Luxury Automobiles

Investment Tax Credit: Luxury Automobiles: Limitation on Amount of Depreciation.—Reg. §§1.280F-1T—1.280F-5T, relating to the limitations placed on the amount of cost recovery deductions and investment tax credit allowed for taxpayers who purchase passenger automobiles for use in a trade or business or for use in the production of income, are proposed as final and, when adopted, would become Reg. §§1.280F-1—1.280F-5 (published in the Federal Register on October 24, 1984).

§1.280F-1. Limitations on investment tax credit and recovery deductions under section 168 for passenger automobiles and certain other listed property; overview of regulations.

§1.280F-2. Limitations on recovery dedcutions and the invvestment tax credit for certain passenger automobiles.

§1.280F-3. Limitations on recovery deductions and the investment tax credit when the business use percentage of listed property is not greater than 50 percent.

§1.280F-4. Special rules for listed property.

§1.280F-5. Leased property.

Substantiation Travel, Entertainment, Gifts, Listed Property, Etc.

Business Expenses: Substantiation: Recordkeeping Requirements: Listed Property.—Amendments to Temporary Reg. §§1.280F-1T, 1.280F-3T and 1.280F-5T, relating to the requirement that any deduction or credit with respect to certain business-related expenses be substantiated with adequate or sufficient evidence to corroborate a taxpayer's own statement and to the limitations on cost recovery deductions and the investment tax credit for listed property, are also proposed as final (published in the Federal Register on November 6, 1985).

§1.280F-1. Limitations on investment tax credit and recovery deductions under section 168 for passenger automobiles and certain other listed property; overview of regulations.

§1.280F-3. Limitations on recovery deductions and the investment tax credit when the business use percentage of listed property is not greater than 50 percent.

§1.280F-5. Leased property.

Tax Year: Partnerships, S Corporations, Personal Service Corporations

Tax Year: Election: Partnerships: S Corporations: Personal Service Corporation.—Temporary Reg. §§1.280H-0T and 1.280H-1T, relating to the election of a taxable year by a partnership, S corporation or personal service corporation, are also proposed as final regulations (published in the Federal Register on May 27, 1988).

§1.280H-0. Table of contents.

§1.280H-1. Limitation on certain amounts paid to employee-owners by personal service corporations electing alternative taxable years.

CORPORATE DISTRIBUTIONS AND ADJUSTMENTS

Section 301 Regulations: Statutory Changes Reflected

Section 301 Regulations: Statutory Changes Reflected.—Amendments to Reg. §1.301-1, updating existing regulations under section 301 to reflect statutory changes made by the Technical and Miscellaneous Revenue Act of 1988, which changes provide that the amount of a distribution of property made by a corporation to its shareholder is the fair market value of the distributed property, are proposed (published in the Federal Register on March 26, 2019) (corrected April 23, 2019) (REG-121694-16).

Par. 2. Section 1.301-1 is revised to read as follows:

§1.301-1. Rules applicable with respect to distributions of money and other property.—(a) *General.*—Section 301 provides the general rule for treatment of distributions made in taxable years beginning after December 31, 1986, of property by a corporation to a shareholder with respect to its stock. The term *property* is defined in section 317(a). Such distributions, except as otherwise provided in this chapter, shall be treated as provided in section 301(c). Under section 301(c), distributions may be included in gross income to the extent the amount distributed is considered a dividend under section 316, applied against and reduce the adjusted basis of the stock, treated as gain from the sale or exchange of property, or (in the case of certain distributions out of increase in value accrued before March 1, 1913) may be exempt from tax. The amount of the distributions to which section 301 applies is determined in accordance with the provisions of section 301(b). The basis of property received in a distribution to which section 301 applies is determined in accordance with the provisions of section 301(d).

(b) *Amount of distribution and determination of fair market value.*—The amount of a distribution to which section 301 applies shall be the amount of money received in the distribution, plus the fair market value of other property received in the distribution. The fair market value of any property distributed shall be determined as of the date of the distribution.

(c) *Time of inclusion in gross income and time of determination of fair market value.*—A distribution made by a corporation to its shareholders shall be included in the gross income of the distributees when the cash or other property is unqualifiedly made subject to their demands without regard to whether such date is the same as that on which the corporation made the distribution. For example, if a corporation distributes a taxable dividend in property on December 30, 2018, which is received by, or unqualifiedly made subject to the demand of, its shareholders on January 3, 2019, the amount to be included in the gross income of the shareholders will be the fair market value of such property on December 30, 2018, although such

amount will not be includible in the gross income of the shareholders until January 3, 2019.

(d) *Application of section to shareholders.*—Section 301 is not applicable to an amount paid by a corporation to a shareholder unless the amount is paid to the shareholder in the shareholder's capacity as such.

(e) *Example.*—Corporation M, formed in 1998, has never been an acquiring corporation in a transaction to which section 381(a) applies. On January 1, 2019, A, an individual owned all of the stock of Corporation M, consisting of a single share, with an adjusted basis of $2,000. During 2019, A received distributions from Corporation M totaling $30,000, consisting of $10,000 in cash and listed securities having a basis in the hands of Corporation M and a fair market value on the date distributed of $20,000. Corporation M's taxable year is the calendar year. As of December 31, 2018, Corporation M had accumulated earnings and profits in the amount of $26,000, and it had no earnings and profits and no deficit for 2019. Of the $30,000 received by A, $26,000 will be treated as an ordinary dividend; the remaining $4,000 will be applied against the adjusted basis of his stock; the $2,000 in excess of the adjusted basis of his stock will be treated as gain from the sale or exchange of property under section 301(c)(3)(A). If A subsequently sells his stock in Corporation M, the basis for determining gain or loss on the sale will be zero.

(f) *Reduction for liabilities.*—(1) *General rule.*—For purposes of section 301(b)(2), no reduction in the amount of a distribution shall be made for the amount of any liability, except to the extent the liability is assumed by the shareholder within the meaning of section 357(d).

(2) *No reduction below zero.*—Any reduction pursuant to paragraph (f)(1) of this section shall not cause the amount of the distribution to be reduced below zero.

(3) *Effective dates.*—(i) *In general.*—This paragraph (f) applies to distributions occurring after January 4, 2001.

(ii) *Retroactive application.*—This paragraph (f) also applies to distributions made on or before January 4, 2001, if the distribution is made as part of a transaction described in, or substantially similar to the transaction in, Notice 99-59 (1999-2 C.B. 761), including transactions designed to reduce gain (*see* §601.601(d)(2) of this chapter). For rules for distributions on or before January 4, 2001 (other than distributions on or before that date to which this paragraph (f) applies), see rules in effect on January 4, 2001 (see §1.301-1(g) as contained in 26 CFR part 1 revised April 1, 2001).

(g) *Basis.*—The basis of property received in a distribution to which section 301 applies shall be the fair market value of such property. See paragraph (b) of this section.

(h) *Transfers for less than fair market value.*—If property is transferred by a corporation to a shareholder for an amount less than its fair market value in a sale or exchange, such shareholder shall be treated as having received a distribution to which section 301 applies. In such case, the amount of the distribution shall be the excess of the fair market value of the property over the amount paid for such property at the time of the transfer. For example, on January 3, 2019, A, a shareholder of Corporation X, purchased property from X for $20. The fair market value of such property on January 3, 2019 was $100. The amount of the distribution to A determined under section 301(b) is $80.

(i) [Reserved]

(j) *Transactions treated as distributions.*—A distribution to shareholders with respect to their stock is within the terms of section 301 although it takes place at the same time as another transaction if the distribution is in substance a separate transaction whether or not connected in a formal sense. This is most likely to occur in the case of a recapitalization, a reincorporation, or a merger of a corporation with a newly organized corporation having substantially no property. For example, if a corporation having only common stock outstanding, exchanges one share of newly issued common stock and one bond in the principal amount of $10 for each share of outstanding common stock, the distribution of the bonds will be a distribution of property (to the extent of their fair market value) to which section 301 applies, even though the exchange of common stock for common stock may be pursuant to a plan of reorganization under the terms of section 368(a)(1)(E) (recapitalization) and even though the exchange of common stock for common stock may be tax free by virtue of section 354.

(k) *Cancellation of indebtedness.*—The cancellation of indebtedness of a shareholder by a corporation shall be treated as a distribution of property.

(l) *Cross references.*—For certain rules relating to adjustments to earnings and profits and for determining the extent to which a distribution is a dividend, see sections 312 and 316 and regulations thereunder.

(m) *Split-dollar and other life insurance arrangements.*—(1) *Split-dollar life insurance arrangements.*—(i) *Distribution of economic benefits.*—The provision by a corporation to its shareholder pursuant to a split-dollar life insurance arrangement, as defined in §1.61-22(b)(1) or (2), of economic benefits described in §1.61-22(d) or of amounts described in §1.61-22(e) is treated as a distribution of property, the amount of which is determined under §1.61-22(d) and (e), respectively.

(ii) *Distribution of entire contract or undivided interest therein.*—A transfer (within the meaning of §1.61-22(c)(3)) of the ownership of a life insurance contract (or an undivided interest therein) that is part of a split-dollar life insurance arrangement is a distribution of property, the amount of which is determined pursuant to §1.61-22(g)(1) and (2).

(2) *Other life insurance arrangements.*—A payment by a corporation on behalf of a shareholder of premiums on a life insurance contract or an undivided interest therein that is owned by the shareholder constitutes a distribution of property, even if such payment is not part of a split-dollar life insurance arrangement under §1.61-22(b).

(3) *When distribution is made.*—(i) *In general.*—Except as provided in paragraph (m)(3)(ii) of this section, paragraph (c) of this section shall apply to determine when a distribution described in paragraph (m)(1) or (2) of this section is taken into account by a shareholder.

(ii) *Exception.*—Notwithstanding paragraph (c) of this section, a distribution described in paragraph (m)(1)(ii) of this section shall be treated as made by a corporation to its shareholder at the time that the life insurance contract, or an undivided interest therein, is transferred (within the meaning of §1.61-22(c)(3)) to the shareholder.

(4) *Effective date.*—(i) *General rule.*—This paragraph (m) applies to split-dollar and other life insurance arrangements entered into after September 17, 2003. For purposes of this paragraph (m)(4), a split-dollar life insurance arrangement is entered into as determined under §1.61-22(j)(1)(ii).

(ii) *Modified arrangements treated as new arrangements.*—If a split-dollar life insurance arrangement entered into on or before September 17, 2003 is materially modified (within the meaning of §1.61-22(j)(2)) after September 17, 2003, the arrangement is treated as a new arrangement entered into on the date of the modification.

(n) *Applicability date.*—Paragraphs (a) through (c), (e), (g), and (h) of this section apply to distributions under section 301 made after the date of publication of the Treasury decision adopting these rules as final regulations in the **Federal Register**.

Stock and Rights to Acquire Stock: Deemed Distributions

Stock and Rights to Acquire Stock: Deemed Distributions.—Amendments to Reg. §§1.305-1, 1.305-3 and 1.305-7, regarding deemed distributions of stock and rights to acquire stock and resolving ambiguities concerning the amount and timing of deemed distributions that are or result from adjustments to rights to acquire stock, are proposed (published in the Federal Register on April 13, 2016) (corrected July 5, 2016) (REG-133673-15).

Par. 2. Section 1.305-1 is amended by:
1. Revising paragraphs (b)(3) and (d).
2. Adding paragraph (e).
The revisions and addition read as follows:

§1.305-1. Stock dividends.

* * *

(b) * * *

(3) For rules determining the amount of the distribution for certain transactions, such as periodic redemptions or applicable adjustments (as defined in §1.305-7(a)) of rights to acquire stock that are treated as distributions under section 305(b) and (c), *see* §1.305-7 and *Examples 6, 7, 8, 9*, and *15* of §1.305-3(e).

* * *

(d) *Definitions.*—For purposes of section 305, this section, and §§1.305-2 through 1.305-7:

(1) *Stock.*—The term *stock* means actual stock or a right to acquire stock.

(2) *Actual stock.*—The term *actual stock* means stock issued by a corporation, excluding rights to acquire stock as defined in paragraph (d)(3) of this section.

(3) *Right to acquire stock.*—The term *right to acquire stock* means—

(i) A right of a holder of a convertible instrument (including a debt instrument that is convertible into shares of stock and stock that is convertible into shares of another class of stock) to convert the instrument into one or more shares of stock of the corporation issuing the instrument;

(ii) A warrant, subscription right, stock right, or other option to acquire shares of stock of the corporation issuing the instrument;

(iii) A right to acquire stock of the corporation issuing such right similar to the rights described in paragraphs (d)(3)(i) and (ii) of this section; and

(iv) A right to receive an amount of cash or other property determined in whole or in part by reference to the value of a specified number of shares of stock (whether or not in lieu of such stock) of the corporation issuing the right.

(4) *Shareholder.*—The term *shareholder* means a holder of actual stock or a holder of a right to acquire stock.

(5) *Actual shareholder.*—The term *actual shareholder* means a holder of actual stock.

(6) *Deemed shareholder.*—The term *deemed shareholder* means a holder of a right to acquire stock.

(7) *Deemed distribution.*—The term *deemed distribution* means a transaction or event, other than an actual distribution of cash or property, that constitutes a distribution under section 305(b) and (c). An applicable adjustment to a right to acquire stock is not and does not result in a deemed distribution if either—

(i) The right to acquire stock is a nonqualified stock option without a readily ascertainable fair market value (*see* section 83(e) and § 1.83-7), or

(ii) Section 83(a) applies to the right to acquire stock or the stock to which the right relates or the stock is subject to a substantial

Par. 3. Section 1.305-3 is amended by:
1. Revising paragraph (e) introductory text,
Example (6)(ii),
Example (7)(ii) and (iii).
2. Adding paragraph (f).
The revisions and addition read as follows:

§ 1.305-3. Disproportionate distributions.
* * *

(e) *Examples.*—The following examples illustrate the application of section 305(b)(2) to distributions of stock and rights to acquire stock and the application of section 305(c) to deemed distributions of stock and rights to acquire stock.

* * *

Example 6. * * *
(ii) M pays an annual cash dividend on the class A stock. At the beginning of the second year, when the conversion ratio is increased to 1.05 shares of class A stock for each share of class B stock, an applicable adjustment occurs, as defined in § 1.305-7(a), and a distribution of rights to acquire 0.05 shares of class A stock is deemed made under section 305(c) and § 1.305-7(c)(1) with respect to each share of class B stock. The proportionate interests of the class B shareholders in the assets or earnings and profits of M are increased, and the transaction has the effect described in section 305(b)(2). Accordingly, sections 305(b)(2) and 301 apply to the transaction. The amount of the deemed distribution is determined in accordance with 1.305-7(c)(4)(i) and the date and time of the deemed distribution are determined in accordance with § 1.305-7(c)(5).

Example 7. * * *
(ii) In 2017, a $1 cash dividend per share is declared and paid on the class B stock. Pursuant to the terms of the class B stock, on the date of payment, the conversion ratio of the class B stock is reduced. The reduction in conversion ratio is an applicable adjustment, as defined in § 1.305-7(a). Under section 305(c) and § 1.305-7(c)(2), the reduction is a deemed distribution of stock to the class A shareholders, since their proportionate interest in the assets or earnings and profits of the corporation is increased, and the transaction has the

Par. 4. Section 1.305-7 is revised to read as follows:

§ 1.305-7. Certain transactions treated as distributions.—
(a) *Applicable adjustment.*—For purposes of section 305, §§ 1.305-1 through 1.305-6, and this section, the term *applicable adjustment* means an adjustment to a right to acquire stock (as defined in § 1.305-1(d)(3)), including—

(1) With respect to a convertible instrument and a holder thereof, an increase in the conversion ratio or a reduction in the conversion price of such instrument;

(2) With respect to a warrant, subscription right, stock right, option, or other similar right and a holder thereof, an increase in the number of shares to be received by the holder upon exercise or a reduction in exercise price;

(3) With respect to a convertible instrument and a holder of actual stock into which such instrument may be converted, an increase in the conversion price or a reduction in the conversion ratio of such instrument;

(4) With respect to a warrant, subscription right, stock right, option, or similar right and a holder of actual stock into which such instrument is exercisable, an increase in the exercise price or a reduction in the number of shares to be received by the holder upon exercise; and

(5) An adjustment in the terms of a right to acquire stock having an effect similar to the effects of the adjustments described in paragraphs (a)(1) through (a)(4) of this section, including, for example, an extension or reduction of the term during which a right to acquire stock may be exercised.

(b) *Transactions treated as distributions.*—(1) *In general.*—Under section 305(c), an applicable adjustment, a change in redemption

risk of forfeiture, and the holder of the right has not made an election under section 83(b).

(e) *Effective/applicability date.*—Paragraphs (b)(3) and (d) of this section apply to deemed distributions under section 305(b) and (c) occurring on or after the date of publication of the Treasury decision adopting these rules as final regulations in the **Federal Register**. A taxpayer, however, may rely on these proposed regulations for deemed distributions under section 305(c) that occur prior to such date. For purposes of determining the amount of a deemed distribution to a deemed shareholder occurring prior to such date, a taxpayer may determine the amount of the deemed distribution by treating such distribution either as a distribution of a right to acquire stock or as a distribution of the actual stock to which the right relates.

effect described in section 305(b)(2). Accordingly, sections 305(b)(2) and 301 apply to the transaction. The amount of the distribution is determined in accordance with § 1.305-7(c)(4)(ii), and the date and time of the deemed distribution are determined in accordance with § 1.305-7(c)(5).

(iii) In the following year a cash dividend is paid on the class A stock but not on the class B stock, and the conversion ratio of the class B stock increases. The increase in the conversion ratio of the class B shares is an applicable adjustment. Under section 305(c) and § 1.305-7(c)(1), the adjustment is a deemed distribution of rights to acquire stock to the class B shareholders since their proportionate interest in the assets or earnings and profits of the corporation is increased, and the transaction has the effect described in section 305(b)(2). Accordingly, sections 305(b)(2) and 301 apply to the transaction. The amount of the distribution is determined in accordance with § 1.305-7(c)(4)(i), and the date and time of the deemed distribution are determined in accordance with § 1.305-7(c)(5).

* * *

(f) *Effective/applicability date.*—The first sentence of paragraph (e) of this section and *Examples 6* and *7* of paragraph (e) of this section apply to deemed distributions under section 305(c) occurring on or after the date of publication of the Treasury decision adopting these rules as final regulations in the **Federal Register**. A taxpayer, however, may rely on these proposed regulations for deemed distributions under section 305(c) that occur prior to such date. For purposes of determining the amount of a deemed distribution to a deemed shareholder occurring prior to the date of publication, a taxpayer may determine the amount of the deemed distribution by treating such distribution either as a distribution of a right to acquire stock or as a distribution of the actual stock to which the right relates.

price, a difference between redemption price and issue price, a redemption that is treated as a distribution to which section 301 applies, or any transaction (including a recapitalization) having a similar effect on the interest of any shareholder is treated as a distribution of stock to which sections 305(b) and 301 apply if such transaction increases a shareholder's proportionate interest in the assets or earnings and profits of the corporation deemed to make such distribution, and the distribution has the result described in section 305(b)(2), (3), (4), or (5). Depending upon the facts presented, the distribution may be deemed to be made in shares of actual stock or in additional rights to acquire stock (which, in either case, may be common or preferred stock).

(c) *Applicable adjustment to right to acquire stock.*—(1) *Increase in deemed shareholder's proportionate interest.*—Under section 305(c), if an applicable adjustment has the effect of increasing a deemed shareholder's proportionate interest in the assets or earnings and profits of the corporation, and if such increase has the effect described in section 305(b)(2), (3), (4) or (5), the applicable adjustment is a deemed distribution to the deemed shareholder of a right to acquire stock, and section 301 applies to the deemed distribution. Applicable adjustments that can have this effect include, with respect to a convertible instrument, an increase in the conversion ratio or the number of shares of stock to be received upon conversion or a reduction in the conversion price.

(2) *Increase in actual shareholder's proportionate interest.*—If an applicable adjustment has the effect of reducing a deemed shareholder's proportionate interest in the assets or earnings and profits of

the corporation and thereby increasing an actual shareholder's proportionate interest, and if such increase has the effect described in section 305(b)(2), (3), (4) or (5), then the applicable adjustment is a deemed distribution of stock to the actual shareholder, and section 301 applies to the deemed distribution. Applicable adjustments that can have this effect include, with respect to a convertible instrument, a reduction in the conversion ratio or in the number of shares to be received upon conversion, or an increase in the conversion price.

(3) *Exception.*—For purposes of applying section 305(c) in conjunction with section 305(b), an applicable adjustment that is made pursuant to a bona fide, reasonable adjustment formula (including but not limited to an applicable adjustment made to compensate for a distribution of stock to another shareholder) and that has the effect of preventing dilution of the proportionate interest of the holders of actual stock or rights to acquire stock does not result in a deemed distribution of stock. An applicable adjustment that is made to compensate for a cash or property distribution to another shareholder and that is taxable under section 301, 356(a)(2), 871(a)(1)(A), 881(a)(1), 852(b), or 857(b) is not made pursuant to a bona fide adjustment formula described in the preceding sentence.

(4) *Amount of deemed distribution.*—(i) *Deemed distribution to deemed shareholder.*—For a deemed distribution under section 305(b) and (c) that is made to a deemed shareholder and is an applicable adjustment, the amount of the deemed distribution is the excess of—

(A) The fair market value of the right to acquire stock held by the deemed shareholder immediately after the applicable adjustment, over

(B) The fair market value, determined immediately after the applicable adjustment, of such right to acquire stock as if no applicable adjustment had occurred.

(ii) *Deemed distribution to actual shareholder.*—For a deemed distribution under section 305(b) and (c) that is made to an actual shareholder and results from an applicable adjustment, the amount of the deemed distribution is the fair market value of the stock deemed distributed, determined in accordance with the methodology set forth in §1.305-3(e), *Examples 8* and *9*.

(iii) *Fair market value standard.*—In determining the fair market value of a right to acquire stock for purposes of this paragraph (c)(4),

(A) Any particular facts pertaining to the deemed shareholder, including the number of rights or shares such deemed shareholder owns, will be disregarded, and

(B) Any value or reduction in value attributable to the possibility of future applicable adjustments that may result from actual or deemed distributions will not be taken into account.

(5) *Date and time of deemed distribution.*—When an applicable adjustment is a deemed distribution under paragraphs (c)(1) or (2) of this section, the deemed distribution occurs at the time such applicable adjustment occurs, in accordance with the instrument setting forth the terms of the right to acquire stock, but in no event later than the date of the distribution of cash or property that results in the deemed distribution (taking into account §1.305-3(b)). For such applicable adjustment relating to a right to acquire publicly-traded stock, if the instrument setting forth the terms of such right does not set forth the time the applicable adjustment occurs, the deemed distribution occurs immediately prior to the opening of business on the ex-dividend date for the distribution of the cash or property that results in the deemed distribution. For such an applicable adjustment relating to a right to acquire non-publicly traded stock, if the instrument setting forth the terms of such right does not set forth the time the applicable adjustment occurs, the deemed distribution occurs on the date that a holder is legally entitled to the distribution of cash or property that results in the deemed distribution.

(6) *Examples.*—The following examples and the examples in §§1.305-3(e) and 1.305-5(d) illustrate the application of section 305(c) and paragraphs (a), (b) and (c) of this section.

Example 1. (i) *Facts.* Corporation U has two classes of actual stock outstanding, class A and class B. Each class B share is convertible into class A stock. In accordance with a bona fide, reasonable antidilution provision, the conversion price is adjusted downward if the corporation transfers class A stock to anyone for consideration below the conversion price. The corporation sells class A stock to the public at the current market price, which is below the conversion price. Pursuant to the antidilution provision, the conversion price is adjusted downward.

(ii) *Analysis.* Although such a reduction in conversion price is an applicable adjustment, under paragraph (c)(3) of this section the reduction is not a distribution under section 305(c) for the purposes of section 305(b).

Example 2. (i) *Facts.* Corporation X has outstanding one class of actual common stock and convertible debt securities. The convertible

securities have a bona fide, reasonable antidilution provision that provides for an increase in conversion ratio in the event stock dividends or rights to acquire stock are distributed to the common shareholders. Corporation X distributes to the common shareholders an actual stock dividend that results in an increase in the conversion ratio of the convertible securities. Pursuant to the antidilution provision, the conversion ratio is increased.

(ii) *Analysis.* Under section 305(d) and §1.305-1(d)(4), the holders of convertible securities are shareholders for purposes of section 305(b) and (c). The convertible securities are rights to acquire stock and are stock for purposes of section 305. The increase in conversion ratio caused by the distribution of the stock dividend to the common shareholders is an applicable adjustment. Because the applicable adjustment is made pursuant to a bona fide, reasonable adjustment formula within the meaning of paragraph (c)(3) of this section, the applicable adjustment is not a deemed distribution under section 305(c) of rights to acquire stock.

Example 3. (i) *Facts.* Corporation X has outstanding one class of publicly-traded common stock and convertible debt securities. The terms of the convertible securities provide for an increase in conversion ratio in the event stock, cash, or property is distributed to the holders of the common stock. Corporation X distributes cash to the holders of the common stock, and the distribution results in an increase in the conversion ratio of the convertible securities.

(ii) *Analysis.* Under section 305(d) and §1.305-1(d)(4), the holders of the convertible securities are shareholders for purposes of section 305(b) and (c). The conversion rights in the convertible securities are rights to acquire stock (as defined in §1.305-1(d)(3)) and is stock for purposes of section 305. The increase in conversion ratio resulting from the cash distribution to the holders of common stock is an applicable adjustment. Because the applicable adjustment is not made pursuant to a bona fide, reasonable adjustment formula within the meaning of paragraph (c)(3) of this section, it is a deemed distribution to the holders of the convertible securities of rights to acquire stock under section 305(c) and paragraph (c)(1) of this section. Because the proportionate interests of these deemed shareholders in the assets or earnings and profits of Corporation X are increased by the change in conversion ratio, the distribution has the result described in section 305(b)(2) and is treated as a distribution to which section 301 applies. The amount of the deemed distribution is determined in accordance with paragraph (c)(4)(i) of this section, and the date and time of the deemed distribution are determined in accordance with paragraph (c)(5) of this section.

(d) *Recapitalizations.*—(1) *In general.*—A recapitalization (whether or not an isolated transaction) will be deemed to result in a distribution to which section 305(c) and this section apply if—

(i) It is pursuant to a plan to periodically increase a shareholder's proportionate interest in the assets or earnings and profits of the corporation, or

(ii) A shareholder owning preferred stock with dividends in arrears exchanges his stock for other stock and, as a result, increases his proportionate interest in the assets or earnings and profits of the corporation. An increase in a preferred shareholder's proportionate interest occurs in any case where the fair market value or the liquidation preference, whichever is greater, of the stock received in the exchange (determined immediately following the recapitalization), exceeds the issue price of the preferred stock surrendered.

(2) *Amount of distribution.*—In a case to which paragraph (d)(1)(ii) of this section applies, the amount of the distribution deemed under section 305(c) to result from the recapitalization is the lesser of—

(i) The amount by which the fair market value or the liquidation preference, whichever is greater, of the stock received in the exchange (determined immediately following the recapitalization) exceeds the issue price of the preferred stock surrendered, or

(ii) The amount of the dividends in arrears.

(3) *Definition.*—For purposes of applying paragraphs (d)(1) and (2) of this section with respect to stock issued before July 12, 1973, the term *issue price of the preferred stock surrendered* shall mean the greater of the issue price or the liquidation preference (not including dividends in arrears) of the stock surrendered.

(4) *Examples.*—For an illustration of the application of this paragraph (d), *see Example 12* of §1.305-3(e) and *Examples 1, 2, 3*, and *6* of §1.305-5(d).

(e) *Redemption premiums with respect to preferred stock.*—Under section 305(c), if a redemption premium exists with respect to a class of preferred stock under the circumstances described in §1.305-5(b) and the other requirements of this section are met, the distribution will be deemed made with respect to such preferred stock, in stock of the same class. Accordingly, the preferred shareholders are considered under section 305(b)(4) and (c) to have received a deemed distribution of preferred stock to which section 301 applies.

(f) *Coordination with section 871(m).*—For coordination of sections 305 and 871(m), *see* § 1.871-15(c)(2)(ii).

(g) *Effective date.*—This section applies to deemed distributions under section 305(c) occurring on or after the date of publication of the Treasury decision adopting these rules as final regulations in the **Federal Register**. A taxpayer, however, may rely on these proposed regulations for deemed distributions under section 305(c) that occur prior to such date. For purposes of determining the amount of a deemed distribution to a deemed shareholder occurring prior to the date of publication, a taxpayer may determine the amount of the deemed distribution by treating such distribution either as a distribution of a right to acquire stock or as a distribution of the actual stock to which the right relates.

Foreign Corporations: Stock Transfer Rules: Carryover of Earnings and Taxes

Foreign Corporations: Stock Transfer Rules: Carryover of Earnings and Taxes.—Amendments to Reg. §1.312-10, addressing **(1)** the carryover of certain tax attributes, such as earnings and profits and foreign income tax accounts, when two corporations combine in a section 367(b) transaction and **(2)** the allocation of certain tax attributes when a corporation distributes stock of another corporation in a section 367(b) transaction, are proposed (published in the Federal Register on November 15, 2000) (REG-116050-99).

☐ Par. 2. Section 1.312-10 is amended by adding paragraph (d) to read as follows:

§1.312-10. Allocation of earnings in certain corporate separations.

* * *

(d) For additional rules involving foreign corporations, see § 1.367(b)-8.

Eligible Terminated S Corporations: Definition: Distributions of Money

Eligible Terminated S Corporations: Definition: Distributions of Money.—Amendments to Reg. §1.316-2, regarding the definition of an eligible terminated S corporation (ETSC) and providing rules relating to distributions of money by an ETSC after the post-termination transition period, are proposed (published in the Federal Register on November 7, 2019) (REG-131071-18).

Par. 2. Section 1.316-2 is amended by removing "consist only of money and" from the second sentence of paragraph (b).

§1.316-2. Sources of distribution in general.

CFCs: U.S. Shareholders: Ownership Attribution

CFCs: U.S. Shareholders: Ownership Attribution.—Reg. §1.332-8, relating to the modification of section 958(b) of the Internal Revenue Code by the Tax Cuts and Jobs Act, which was enacted on December 22, 2017, is proposed (published in the Federal Register on October 2, 2019) (REG-104223-18).

Par. 3. Section 1.332-8 is added to read as follows:

§1.332-8. Recognition of gain on liquidation of certain holding companies.—(a) *Definition of controlled foreign corporation.*—For purposes of section 332(d)(3), a controlled foreign corporation has the meaning provided in section 957, determined without applying subparagraphs (A), (B), and (C) of section 318(a)(3) so as to consider a United States person as owning stock which is owned by a person who is not a United States person.

(b) *Applicability date.*—This section applies to distributions in complete liquidation occurring on or after October 1, 2019, and to distributions in complete liquidation occurring before October 1, 2019, that result from an entity classification election made under § 301.7701-3 of this chapter that is filed on or after October 1, 2019. For distributions in complete liquidation occurring before October 1, 2019, other than distributions in complete liquidation occurring before October 1, 2019, that result from an entity classification election made under § 301.7701-3 of this chapter that is filed on or after October 1, 2019, a taxpayer may apply this section to distributions in complete liquidation occurring during the last taxable year of a distributee foreign corporation beginning before January 1, 2018, and each subsequent taxable year of the foreign corporation, provided that the taxpayer and United States persons that are related (within the meaning of section 267 or 707) to the taxpayer consistently apply this section with respect to all foreign corporations. [Reg. § 1.332-8.]

Partnership Transactions: Equity Interests

Partnership Transactions: Equity Interests.—Amendments to Reg. §1.337(d)-3, preventing a corporate partner from avoiding corporate-level gain through transactions with a partnership involving equity interests of the partner or certain related entities, are proposed (published in the Federal Register on March 25, 2019) REG-135671-17).

Par. 2. Section 1.337(d)-3 is amended by revising paragraphs (c)(2), (f)(2)(ii) and (i) to read as follows:

§1.337(d)-3. Gain recognition upon certain partnership transactions involving a partner's stock.

* * *

(c) * * *

(2) *Stock of the Corporate Partner.*—(i) *In general.*—With respect to a Corporate Partner, Stock of the Corporate Partner includes stock, warrants and other options to acquire stock, and similar interests (each an equity interest) in the Corporate Partner. Stock of the Corporate Partner also includes equity interests in a corporation that controls the Corporate Partner within the meaning of section 304(c), and which also has a direct or indirect equity interest in the Corporate Partner. Solely for purposes of determining whether a corporation that controls the Corporate Partner also has a direct or indirect equity interest in the Corporate Partner under this paragraph (c)(2), a direct or indirect ownership of an equity interest in the Corporate Partner includes ownership of Stock of the Corporate Partner that would be attributed to a person under section 318(a)(2) (except that the 50-percent ownership limitation in section 318(a)(2)(C) does not apply) and under section 318(a)(4) (but otherwise without regard to section 318).

(ii) *Equity Interests with value attributable to Stock of the Corporate Partner.*—If an equity interest in an entity is not Stock of the Corporate Partner within the meaning of paragraph (c)(2)(i) of this section, then the equity interest will be treated as Stock of the Corporate Partner to the extent that the value of that equity interest is attributable to Stock of the Corporate Partner. The preceding sentence will apply only if either—

(A) The Corporate Partner is in control (within the meaning of section 304(c)) of that entity; or

(B) That entity owns directly or indirectly 5 percent or more, by vote or value, of the stock in the Corporate Partner.

(iii) *Determination of value attributable to Stock of the Corporate Partner.*—The value of an equity interest in an entity that is attributable to Stock of the Corporate Partner under paragraph (c)(2)(ii) of this section is equal to the product of—

(A) The fair market value of the equity interest; and

(B) The lesser of—

(1) The ratio of the fair market value of the Stock of the Corporate Partner owned (directly or indirectly (as defined in paragraph (c)(2)(i) of this section), by the entity to the fair market value of all the equity interests in the entity; or

(2) One.

* * *

(f) * * *

(2) * * *

(ii) Is not distributed to the Corporate Partner or a corporation that controls the Corporate Partner within the meaning of section 304(c) and owns directly or indirectly stock or other interests in the Corporate Partner. For purposes of this paragraph (f)(2), a direct or indirect ownership of an equity interest in the Corporate Partner means ownership of Stock of the Corporate Partner that would be attributed to a person under section 318(a)(2) (except that the 50-percent ownership limitation in section

318(a)(2)(C) does not apply) and under section 318(a)(4) (but otherwise without regard to section 318).

* * *

Employee Remuneration in Excess of $1,000,000: Deductibility

Employee Remuneration in Excess of $1,000,000: Deductibility.—Amendments to Reg. §1.338-1, limiting the deduction for certain employee remuneration in excess of $1,000,000 for federal income tax purposes, are proposed (published in the Federal Register on December 20, 2019) (REG-122180-18).

Par. 4. Section 1.338-1 is amended by revising paragraph (b)(2)(i) to read as follows:

§1.338-1. General principles, status of old target and new target.

* * *

(b) * * *

(2) * * *

(i) The rules applicable to employee benefit plans (including those plans described in sections 79, 104, 105, 106, 125, 127, 129, 132, 137, and 220), qualified pension, profit-sharing, stock bonus and annuity plans (sections 401(a) and 403(a)), simplified employee pensions (section 408(k)), tax qualified stock option plans (sections 422 and 423), welfare benefit funds (sections 419, 419A, 512(a)(3), and 4976), voluntary employee benefit associations (section 501(c)(9) and the regulations thereunder (26 CFR 1.501(c)(9)-1 through 1.501(c)(9)-8)) and certain excessive employee remuneration (section 162(m) and the regulations thereunder (26 CFR 1.162-27 and §1.162-31));

* * *

Life Insurance Companies: Computation and Reporting of Reserves

Life Insurance Companies: Computation and Reporting of Reserves.—Amendments to Reg. §1.338-11, providing guidance on the computation of life insurance reserves and the change in basis of computing certain reserves of insurance companies, are proposed (published in the Federal Register on April 2, 2020) (REG-132529-17).

Par. 2. Section 1.338-11 is amended by:

1. Revising paragraph (d)(2).
2. Removing the language "and (d)(3)(iii)" from the first sentence in paragraph (d)(3)(i) and adding "through (iv)" in its place.
3. Redesignating paragraph (d)(3)(iii) as paragraph (d)(3)(iv).
4. Adding a new paragraph (d)(3)(iii).
5. Revising newly redesignated paragraph (d)(3)(iv).
6. Adding paragraph (d)(7)(iii).

The revisions and additions read as follows:

§1.338-11. Effect of section 338 election on insurance company targets.

* * *

* * *

(d) * * *

(2) *Exception.*—New target is not treated as receiving additional premium under paragraph (d)(1) of this section if it is under state receivership as of the close of the taxable year for which the increase in reserves occurs.

(3)

* * *

(iii) *Increases in section 807(c) reserves.*—The positive amounts with respect to the items referred to in section 807(c) other than discounted unpaid loss reserves is the sum of the net increases in such items that are required to be taken into account under section 807(f).

(iv) *Increases in other reserves.*—The positive amount with respect to reserves other than discounted unpaid loss reserves and other items referred to in section 807(c) is the net increase of those reserves due to changes in estimate, methodology, or other assumptions used to compute the reserves (including the adoption by new target of a methodology or assumptions different from those used by old target).

* * *

(7) * * *

(iii) *Application of paragraphs (d)(2) and (3) of this section.*—Paragraphs (d)(2) and (3) of this section apply to taxable years beginning on or after **[DATE FINAL REGULATIONS ARE PUBLISHED IN THE FEDERAL REGISTER]**. For taxable years beginning before such date, see paragraph (d) of this section as contained in 26 CFR part 1 revised as of April 1, 2019.

* * *

Installment Obligations: Dispositions: Nonrecognition of Gain or Loss

Installment Obligations: Dispositions: Nonrecognition of Gain or Loss—Amendments to Reg. §1.351-1, relating to the nonrecognition of gain or loss on certain dispositions of an installment obligation, are proposed (published in the Federal Register on December 23, 2014) (REG-109187-11).

☐ Par. 2. Section 1.351-1(a)(1) is amended by adding a heading and new second and third sentences to read as follows:

§1.351-1. Transfer to corporation controlled by transferor.—

(a)(1) *In general.*—* * * See §1.453B-1(c) for rules requiring a transferor to recognize gain or loss upon the satisfaction of an installment obligation of a corporation when the obligation is exchanged for stock in that corporation. The preceding sentence applies to satisfactions of installment obligations after the date these regulations are published as final regulations in the **Federal Register.*** * *

* * *

Active Trade or Business Requirement: Guidance

Active Trade or Business Requirement: Guidance.—Amendments to Reg. §§1.355-0 and 1.355-1, providing guidance regarding active trade or business requirements, is proposed (published in the Federal Register on May 8, 2007) (REG-123365-03) (corrected June 5, 2007).

☐ Par. 2. Section 1.355-0 is amended by revising the entries under §1.355-3.

The revisions are as follows:

§1.355-0. Outline of sections.

* * *

§1.355-3 Active conduct of a trade or business.

(a) General requirements.
(b) Active conduct of a trade or business defined.
  (1) In general.
    (i) Directly engaged in a trade or business.
    (ii) Treatment of a separate affiliated group.
    (iii) Separate affiliated group defined.
  (2) Active conduct of a trade or business immediately after the distribution.

    (i) In general.
    (ii) Trade or business.
    (iii) Active conduct.
    (iv) Limitations.
    (v) Partner attributed the trade or business assets and activities of a partnership.
      (A) In general.
      (B) Significant interest.
      (C) Meaningful interest.
      (D) Other factors.
  (3) Active conduct for the pre-distribution period.

(i) *Effective/applicability date.*—The regulations in this section are effective as of the date of their publication as final regulations in the **Federal Register.**

(i) In general.

(ii) Change and expansion.

(iii) Certain transactions with partnerships that do not constitute acquisitions.

(4) Special rules for an acquisition of a trade or business.

(i) In general.

(A) Application of section 355(b)(2)(C).

(B) Application of section 355(b)(2)(D).

(C) Gain or loss recognized.

(ii) Certain transactions treated as transactions in which gain or loss is recognized.

(A) Certain tax-free acquisitions made in exchange for assets.

(B) Distributions from partnerships.

(iii) Certain transactions in which recognized gain or loss is disregarded.

(A) Transfers to controlled.

(B) Cash for fractional shares.

(C) Certain acquisitions of control of distributing.

(iv) Operating rules for acquisitions.

(A) Predecessors.

(B) Certain multi-step acquisitions of control of distributing or controlled.

(C) Certain multi-step acquisitions of a subsidiary SAG member.

(D) Certain multi-step asset acquisitions.

(E) Acquisitions involving the issuance of subsidiary stock.

(F) Acquisitions of controlled stock where controlled is or becomes a DSAG member.

(G) Treatment of stock received in certain tax-free exchanges.

(H) Situations where the separate existence of a subsidiary SAG member is respected.

(c) Definitions.

(1) Affiliate.

(2) Controlled.

(3) Distributing.

(4) Pre-distribution period.

(d) Conventions and examples.

(1) Conventions.

(2) Examples.

* * *

☐ Par. 3. Section 1.355-1 is amended by revising paragraph (a) to read as follows:

§1.355-1. Distribution of stock and securities of a controlled corporation.—(a) *Effective date of certain sections.*—Except as otherwise provided, §§1.355-1, 1.355-2, and 1.355-4 apply to transactions occurring after February 6, 1989. Section 1.355-3 applies to distributions after the date these regulations are published as final regulations in the **Federal Register.** For transactions occurring on or before that date but after February 6, 1989, see 26 CFR 1.355-3 (revised as of April 1, 2007). For all transactions occurring on or before February 6, 1989, see 26 CFR 1.355-1 through 1.355-4 (revised as of April 1, 1987). Sections 1.355-1, 1.355-2, and 1.355-4 do not reflect the amendments to section 355 made by the Revenue Act of 1987 and the Technical and Miscellaneous Revenue Act of 1988. For the effective date of §§1.355-6 and 1.355-7, see §§1.355-6(g) and 1.355-7(k), respectively.

* * *

Distribution of Stock: Device and Active Trade or Business: Guidance

Distribution of Stock: Device and Active Trade or Business: Guidance.—Amendments to Reg. §§1.355-0 and 1.355-2, clarifying the application of the device prohibition and the active business requirement of section 355 and affecting corporations that distribute the stock of controlled corporations, their shareholders, and their security holders, are proposed (published in the Federal Register on July 15, 2016) (REG-134016-15).

Par. 2. Section 1.355-0 is amended by:

1. Removing from the introductory text "1.355-7" and adding "1.355-9" in its place.

2. Revising the entry for §1.355-2(d)(2)(iv)(B).

3. Adding entries for §1.355-2(d)(2)(iv)(B)(*1*), (*2*), (*3*), (*4*), (*5*), (*6*), and (*7*).

4. Redesignating the entry for §1.355-2(d)(2)(iv)(C) as the entry for §1.355-2(d)(2)(iv)(F).

5. Adding a new entry for §1.355-2(d)(2)(iv)(C).

6. Adding entries for §1.355-2(d)(2)(iv)(C)(*1*), (*2*), and (*3*).

7. Adding an entry for §1.355-2(d)(2)(iv)(D).

8. Adding entries for §1.355-2(d)(2)(iv)(D)(*1*), (*2*), (*3*), and (*4*).

9. Adding entries for §1.355-2(d)(2)(iv)(D)(*4*)(*i*) and (*ii*).

10. Adding entries for §1.355-2(d)(2)(iv)(D)(*5*) and (*6*).

11. Adding entries for §1.355-2(d)(2)(iv)(D)(*6*)(*i*) and (*ii*).

12. Adding an entry for §1.355-2(d)(2)(iv)(D)(*7*).

13. Adding entries for §1.355-2(d)(2)(iv)(D)(*7*)(*i*) and (*ii*).

14. Adding an entry for §1.355-2(d)(2)(iv)(D)(*8*).

15. Adding an entry for §1.355-2(d)(2)(iv)(E).

16. Redesignating the entry for §1.355-2(d)(5) as the entry for §1.355-2(d)(6).

17. Adding a new entry for §1.355-2(d)(5).

18. Adding entries for §1.355-2(d)(5)(i), (ii), (iii), and (iv).

19. Adding entries for §1.355-2(i)(1), (i)(1)(i) and (ii), and (i)(2).

20. Adding an entry for §1.355-8.

21. Adding entries for §1.355-9.

The revisions and additions read as follows:

§1.355-0. Outline of sections.

* * *

§1.355-2. Limitations.

* * *

(d) * * *

(2) * * *

(iv) * * *

(B) Definitions.

(*1*) Business.

(*2*) Business Assets.

(*3*) Nonbusiness Assets.

(*4*) Total Assets.

(*5*) Nonbusiness Asset Percentage.

(*6*) Separate Affiliated Group, SAG, CSAG, and DSAG.

(*7*) 50-Percent-Owned Group, Member of a 50-Percent-Owned Group.

(C) Presence of Nonbusiness Assets as evidence of device.

(*1*) Ownership of Nonbusiness Assets.

(*2*) Difference between Nonbusiness Asset Percentages.

(*3*) Cross-reference.

(D) Operating rules.

(*1*) Multiple controlled corporations.

(*2*) Treatment of SAG as a single corporation.

(*3*) Time to identify assets and determine character of assets.

(*4*) Time to determine fair market value of assets.

(*i*) In general.

(*ii*) Consistency.

(*5*) Fair market value.

(*6*) Interest in partnership.

(*i*) In general.

(*ii*) Exception for certain interests in partnerships.

(*7*) Stock in corporation.

(*i*) In general.

(ii) Exception for stock in Member of a 50-Percent-Owned Group.

(8) Obligation between distributing corporation or controlled corporation and certain partnerships or Members of 50-Percent-Owned Groups.

(E) Anti-abuse rule.

* * *

(5) Distributions involving separation of Business Assets from Nonbusiness Assets.

(i) In general.

(ii) Definitions and operating rules.

(iii) Certain distributions involving separation of Nonbusiness Assets from Business Assets.

(iv) Anti-abuse rule.

* * *

(i) * * *

(1) Paragraph (d) of this section.

(i) In general.

(ii) Transition rule.

(2) Paragraph (g) of this section.

* * *

§ 1.355-8 Reserved.

Par. 3. Section 1.355-2 is amended by:

1. Adding the language "federal" before the language "tax avoidance" in the second sentence of paragraph (d)(1).

2. Removing the last sentence of paragraph (d)(1) and adding two sentences at the end of the paragraph.

3. Revising paragraphs (d)(2)(iv)(A) and (B).

4. Redesignating paragraph (d)(2)(iv)(C) as (d)(2)(iv)(F).

5. Adding new paragraphs (d)(2)(iv)(C), (D), and (E).

6. Revising paragraph (d)(3)(ii).

7. Removing from paragraph (d)(3)(ii)(A) the language "the business" and adding the language "one or more Businesses (as defined in paragraph (d)(2)(iv)(B)(1) of this section) of the distributing corporation, the controlled corporation, or both" in its place.

8. Revising paragraph (d)(4).

9. Redesignating paragraph (d)(5) as (d)(6).

10. Adding a new paragraph (d)(5).

11. Revising newly designated paragraph (d)(6)(i).

12. Removing from newly designated paragraph (d)(6)(v) the language "subparagraph (5)" and adding the language "paragraph (d)(6)" in its place.

13. Removing from the last sentence of newly designated paragraph (d)(6)(v) *Example 1* the language "(d)(5)(i)" and adding the language "(d)(6)(i)" in its place.

14. Removing from the sixth sentence of newly designated paragraph (d)(6)(v) *Example 2* the language "(d)(5)(i)" and adding the language "(d)(6)(i)" in its place.

15. Removing from the last sentence of newly designated paragraph (d)(6)(v) *Example 2* the language "made from all the facts" and adding the language "made from either the presence of a separation of Business Assets from Nonbusiness Assets as described in paragraph (d)(5) of this section or from all the facts" in its place.

16. Adding to paragraph (h) the language "and § 1.355-9 (relating to Minimum Percentage of Five-Year-Active-Business Assets)" immediately before the language "are satisfied".

17. Revising paragraph (i).

The revisions and additions read as follows:

§ 1.355-2. Limitations.

* * *

(d) * * *

(1) * * * However, if a transaction is specified in paragraph (d)(5)(iii) of this section, then it is considered to have been used principally as a device unless it is also specified in paragraph (d)(3)(iv) of this section or paragraph (d)(6) of this section. If a transaction is specified in paragraph (d)(6) of this section, then it is ordinarily considered not to have been used principally as a device.

(2) * * *

(iv) * * *

(A) *In general.*—The determination of whether a transaction was used principally as a device will take into account the nature, kind, amount, and use of the assets of the distributing corporation and the controlled corporation.

(B) *Definitions.*—The following definitions apply for purposes of this paragraph (d)(2)(iv):

(1) *Business.*—*Business* means the active conduct of a trade or business, within the meaning of section 355(b) and § 1.355-3, without regard to—

(i) The requirements of section 355(b)(2)(B), (C), and (D), and § 1.355-3(b)(3) and (4) (relating to active conduct throughout the five-year period preceding a distribution and acquisitions during such period);

(ii) The collection of income requirement in § 1.355-3(b)(2)(ii); and

(iii) The requirement of § 1.355-9 (relating to Minimum Percentage of Five-Year-Active-Business Assets (as defined in § 1.355-9(a)(3))).

§ 1.355-9 Minimum percentage of Five-Year-Active-Business Assets.

(a) Definitions.

(1) Distributing, Controlled.

(2) Five-Year-Active Business.

(3) Five-Year-Active-Business Assets.

(4) Non-Five-Year-Active-Business Assets.

(5) Total Assets.

(6) Five-Year-Active-Business Asset Percentage.

(7) Separate Affiliated Group, CSAG, and DSAG.

(b) Five percent minimum Five-Year-Active-Business Asset Percentage.

(c) Operating rules.

(1) Treatment of SAG and fair market value.

(2) Time to identify assets, determine character of assets, and determine fair market value of assets.

(3) Interest in partnership.

(i) In general.

(ii) Exception for certain interests in partnerships.

(d) Anti-abuse rule.

(e) Effective/applicability date.

(1) In general.

(2) Transition rule.

(2) *Business Assets.*—*Business Assets* of a corporation means its gross assets used in one or more Businesses. Such assets include cash and cash equivalents held as a reasonable amount of working capital for one or more Businesses. Such assets also include assets required (by binding commitment or legal requirement) to be held to provide for exigencies related to a Business or for regulatory purposes with respect to a Business. For this purpose, such assets include assets the holder is required (by binding commitment or legal requirement) to hold to secure or otherwise provide for a financial obligation reasonably expected to arise from a Business and assets held to implement a binding commitment to expend funds to expand or improve a Business.

(3) *Nonbusiness Assets.*—*Nonbusiness Assets* of a corporation means its gross assets other than its Business Assets.

(4) *Total Assets.*—*Total Assets* of a corporation means its Business Assets and its Nonbusiness Assets.

(5) *Nonbusiness Asset Percentage.*—The *Nonbusiness Asset Percentage* of a corporation is the percentage determined by dividing the fair market value of its Nonbusiness Assets by the fair market value of its Total Assets.

(6) *Separate Affiliated Group, SAG, CSAG, and DSAG.*—*Separate Affiliated Group* (or *SAG*) means a separate affiliated group as defined in section 355(b)(3)(B), *CSAG* means a SAG with respect to which a controlled corporation is the common parent, and *DSAG* means a SAG with respect to which a distributing corporation is the common parent, excluding the controlled corporation and any other members of the CSAG.

(7) 50-Percent-Owned Group, Member of a 50-Percent-Owned Group.—*50-Percent-Owned Group* has the same meaning as SAG, except that "50-percent" is substituted for "80-percent" each place it appears in section 1504(a)(2), for purposes of section 355(b)(3)(B). A *Member of a 50-Percent-Owned Group* is a corporation that would be a member of a DSAG or a CSAG, with the substitution provided in this paragraph (d)(2)(iv)(B)(7).

(C) Presence of Nonbusiness Assets as evidence of device.—**(1) Ownership of Nonbusiness Assets.**—Ownership of Nonbusiness Assets by the distributing corporation or the controlled corporation is evidence of device. The strength of the evidence will be based on all the facts and circumstances, including the Nonbusiness Asset Percentage for each corporation. The larger the Nonbusiness Asset Percentage of either corporation, the stronger is the evidence of device. Ownership of Nonbusiness Assets ordinarily is not evidence of device if the Nonbusiness Asset Percentage of each of the distributing corporation and the controlled corporation is less than 20 percent.

(2) Difference between Nonbusiness Asset Percentages.—A difference between the Nonbusiness Asset Percentage of the distributing corporation and the Nonbusiness Asset Percentage of the controlled corporation is evidence of device, and the larger the difference, the stronger is the evidence of device. Such a difference ordinarily is not itself evidence of device (but may be considered in determining the presence or the strength of other device factors) if—

(i) The difference is less than 10 percentage points; or

(ii) The distribution is not pro rata among the shareholders of the distributing corporation, and the difference is attributable to a need to equalize the value of the controlled stock and securities (if any) distributed and the value of the distributing stock and securities (if any) exchanged therefor by the distributees.

(3) Cross-reference.—*See* paragraph (d)(5) of this section for a rule under which a distribution is considered to have been used principally as a device when the distributing corporation or the controlled corporation has a large Nonbusiness Asset Percentage and there is a large difference between Nonbusiness Asset Percentages of the two corporations.

(D) Operating rules.—The following operating rules apply for purposes of this paragraph (d)(2)(iv):

(1) Multiple controlled corporations.—If a transaction involves distributions by a distributing corporation of the stock of more than one controlled corporation, this paragraph (d)(2)(iv) applies to all such controlled corporations. If any provision in this paragraph (d)(2)(iv) requires a comparison between characteristics of the distributing corporation and the controlled corporation, the provision also requires such a comparison between the distributing corporation and each of the controlled corporations and between each controlled corporation and each other controlled corporation. If any distribution involved in the transaction is determined to have been used principally as a device by reason of this paragraph (d)(2)(iv), all distributions involved in the transaction are considered to have been used principally as a device.

(2) Treatment of SAG as a single corporation.—The members of a DSAG are treated as a single corporation, the members of a CSAG are treated as a single corporation, references to the distributing corporation include all members of the DSAG, and references to the controlled corporation include all members of the CSAG.

(3) Time to identify assets and determine character of assets.—The assets of the distributing corporation and the controlled corporation that are relevant in connection with this paragraph (d)(2)(iv), and the character of these assets as Business Assets or Nonbusiness Assets, must be determined by the distributing corporation and the controlled corporation immediately after the distribution. Accordingly, for purposes of this paragraph (d)(2)(iv), the assets of the distributing corporation do not include any asset, including stock of the controlled corporation, that is distributed in the transaction.

(4) Time to determine fair market value of assets.—**(i) In general.**—The distributing corporation and the controlled corporation each must determine the fair market value of its assets at the time of the distribution as of one of the following dates: immediately before the distribution; on any date within the 60-day period before the distribution; on the date of an agreement with respect to the distribution that was binding on the distributing corporation on such date and at all times thereafter; or on the date of a public announcement or filing with the Securities and Exchange Commission with respect to the distribution.

(ii) Consistency.—The distributing corporation and the controlled corporation must make the determinations described in paragraph (d)(2)(iv)(D)(4)(i) of this section in a manner consistent with each other and as of the same date for purposes of this para-

graph (d)(2)(iv), paragraph (d)(5) of this section, and §1.355-9. If these consistency requirements are not met, the fair market value of assets will be determined immediately before the distribution for purposes of all such provisions, unless the Commissioner determines that the use of such date is inconsistent with the purposes of section 355 and the regulations thereunder.

(5) Fair market value.—The fair market value of an asset is determined under general federal tax principles but reduced (but not below the adjusted basis of the asset) by the amount of any liability that is described in section 357(c)(3) (relating to exclusion of certain liabilities, including liabilities the payment of which would give rise to a deduction, from the amount of liabilities assumed in certain exchanges) and relates to the asset (or to a Business with which the asset is associated). Any other liability is disregarded for purposes of determining the fair market value of an asset.

(6) Interest in partnership.—**(i) In general.**—Except as provided in paragraph (d)(2)(iv)(D)(6)(ii) of this section, an interest in a partnership is a Nonbusiness Asset.

(ii) Exception for certain interests in partnerships.—A distributing corporation or controlled corporation may be considered to be engaged in one or more Businesses conducted by a partnership. This determination will be made using the same criteria that would be used to determine for purposes of section 355(b) and §1.355-3 whether the corporation is considered to be engaged in the active conduct of a trade or business conducted by the partnership (relating to the corporation's ownership interest or to its ownership interest and participation in management of the partnership). If a distributing corporation or controlled corporation is considered to be engaged in one or more Businesses conducted by a partnership, the fair market value of the corporation's interest in the partnership will be allocated between Business Assets and Nonbusiness Assets in the same proportion as the proportion of the fair market values of the Business Assets and Nonbusiness Assets of the partnership.

(7) Stock in corporation.—**(i) In general.**—Except as provided in paragraph (d)(2)(iv)(D)(7)(ii) of this section, stock in a corporation other than a member of the DSAG or the CSAG is a Nonbusiness Asset.

(ii) Exception for stock in Member of a 50-Percent-Owned Group.—If a Member of a 50-Percent-Owned Group with respect to the distributing corporation or the controlled corporation owns stock in another Member of the 50-Percent-Owned Group (other than a member of the DSAG or the CSAG, respectively), the fair market value of such stock will be allocated between Business Assets and Nonbusiness Assets in the same proportion as the proportion of the fair market values of the Business Assets and Nonbusiness Assets of the issuing corporation. This computation will be made with respect to lower-tier Members of the 50-Percent-Owned Group before the computations with respect to higher-tier members.

(8) Obligation between distributing corporation or controlled corporation and certain partnerships or Members of 50-Percent-Owned Groups.—If an obligation of the distributing corporation or the controlled corporation is held by a partnership described in paragraph (d)(2)(iv)(D)(6)(ii) of this section or by a Member of its 50-Percent-Owned Group, or if an obligation of a partnership described in paragraph (d)(2)(iv)(D)(6)(ii) of this section or of a Member of its 50-Percent-Owned Group, with respect to the distributing corporation or the controlled corporation, is held by the distributing corporation or the controlled corporation, proper adjustments will be made to prevent double inclusion of assets or inappropriate allocation between Business Assets and Nonbusiness Assets of the distributing corporation or the controlled corporation on account of such obligation. *See Examples 6* and *7* of paragraph (d)(4) of this section.

(E) Anti-abuse rule.—A transaction or series of transactions undertaken with a principal purpose of affecting the Nonbusiness Asset Percentage of any corporation will not be given effect for purposes of applying this paragraph (d)(2)(iv). For this purpose, a transaction or series of transactions includes a change in the form of ownership of an asset; an issuance, assumption, or repayment of indebtedness or other obligations; or an issuance or redemption of stock. However, this paragraph (d)(2)(iv)(E) generally does not apply to a non-transitory acquisition or disposition of assets, other than an acquisition from or disposition to a person the ownership of whose stock would, under section 318(a) (other than paragraph (4) thereof), be attributed to the distributing corporation or the controlled corporation, or to a non-transitory transfer of assets between the distributing corporation and the controlled corporation.

* * *

(3) * * *

(ii) Corporate business purpose.—A corporate business purpose for the transaction is evidence of nondevice. The stronger the evidence of device (such as the presence of the device factors specified in paragraph (d)(2) of this section), the stronger the corporate business purpose must be to prevent the determination that the transaction is being used principally as a device. Evidence of device presented by ownership of Nonbusiness Assets (as defined in paragraph (d)(2)(iv)(B)(3) of this section) can be outweighed by the existence of a corporate business purpose for the ownership. Evidence of device presented by a difference between the Nonbusiness Asset Percentages (as defined in paragraph (d)(2)(iv)(B)(5) of this section) of the distributing corporation and the controlled corporation can be outweighed by the existence of a corporate business purpose for the difference. A corporate business purpose that relates to a separation of Nonbusiness Assets from one or more Businesses or Business Assets (as defined in paragraph (d)(2)(iv)(B) of this section) is not evidence of nondevice unless the business purpose involves an exigency that requires an investment or other use of the Nonbusiness Assets in one or more Businesses of the distributing corporation, the controlled corporation, or both. The assessment of the strength of a corporate business purpose will be based on all of the facts and circumstances, including, but not limited to, the following factors:

* * *

(4) *Examples.*—The provisions of paragraphs (d)(1) through (3) of this section may be illustrated by the following examples. For purposes of these examples, A and B are individuals; P is a partnership; D and C are the distributing corporation and the controlled corporation, respectively; D and C each has no assets other than those described; there is no other evidence of device or nondevice other than as described; D has accumulated earnings and profits; and D distributes the stock of C in a distribution which, but for the issue of whether the transaction has been used principally as a device, satisfies the requirements of section 355(a).

Example 1. Sale after distribution (device). A owns all of the stock of D, which is engaged in the warehousing business. D owns all of the stock of C, which is engaged in the transportation business. All of D's and C's assets are Business Assets. D employs B, who is extremely knowledgeable of the warehousing business in general and the operations of D in particular. B has informed A that he will seriously consider leaving D if he is not given the opportunity to purchase a significant amount of stock of D. Because of his knowledge and experience, the loss of B would seriously damage the business of D. B cannot afford to purchase any significant amount of stock of D as long as D owns C. Accordingly, D distributes the stock of C to A and A subsequently sells a portion of his D stock to B. However, instead of A selling a portion of the D stock, D could have issued additional shares to B after the distribution. In light of the fact that D could have issued additional shares to B, the sale of D stock by A is substantial evidence of device. The transaction is considered to have been used principally as a device. See paragraph (d)(1), (2)(i), (ii), and (iii)(A), (B), and (D), and (3)(i) and (ii) of this section.

Example 2. Disproportionate division of Nonbusiness Assets (device)—(i) Facts. D owns and operates a fast food restaurant in State M and owns all of the stock of C, which owns and operates a fast food restaurant in State N. The value of the Business Assets of D's and C's fast food restaurants are $100 and $105, respectively. D also has $195 cash which D holds as a Nonbusiness Asset. D and C operate their businesses under franchises granted by competing businesses F and G, respectively. G has recently changed its franchise policy and will no longer grant or renew franchises to subsidiaries or other members of the same affiliated group of corporations operating businesses under franchises granted by its competitors. Thus, C will lose its franchise if it remains a subsidiary of D. The franchise is about to expire. The lease for the State M location will expire in 24 months, and D will be forced to relocate at that time. While D has not made any plans, it is weighing its option to purchase a building for the relocation. D contributes $45 to C, which C will retain, and distributes the stock of C pro rata among D's shareholders.

(ii) *Analysis.* After the distribution, D's Nonbusiness Asset Percentage is 60 percent ($150/$250), and C's Nonbusiness Asset Percentage is 30 percent ($45/$150). D's and C's ownership of Nonbusiness Assets of at least 20 percent of their respective Total Assets is evidence of device with respect to each. The difference between D's Nonbusiness Asset Percentage and C's Nonbusiness Asset Percentage is 30 percentage points, which is also evidence of device. The corporate business purpose for the distribution does not relate to a separation of Nonbusiness Assets from one or more Businesses or Business Assets and is evidence of nondevice. However, D has no corporate business purpose for the difference of Nonbusiness Asset Percentages. While D is considering purchasing a building for use in the State M location, this purchase is not required by any exigency. The fact that the distribution is pro rata is also evidence of device. Based on all the facts and circumstances, the transaction is considered to have been used principally as a device. See paragraph (d)(1), (2)(i), (ii), (iv)(A) and (C), and (3)(i) and (ii)(A), (B), and (C) of this section.

Example 3. Proportionate division of Nonbusiness Assets (nondevice). The facts are the same as in *Example 2*, except that D

contributes $95 of the cash to C instead of $45. After the distribution, D's Nonbusiness Asset Percentage is 50 percent ($100/$200) and C's Nonbusiness Asset Percentage is 47.5 percent ($95/$200), each of which is evidence of device. The difference between D's Nonbusiness Asset Percentage and C's Nonbusiness Asset Percentage (2.5 percentage points) is less than 10 percentage points and thus is not evidence of device. The corporate business purpose for the distribution is evidence of nondevice. Based on all the facts and circumstances, the transaction is considered not to have been used principally as a device. See paragraph (d)(1), (2)(i), (ii), (iv)(A) and (C), and (3)(i) and (ii)(A), (B), and (C) of this section.

Example 4. Disproportionate division of Nonbusiness Assets (nondevice). The facts are the same as in *Example 2*, except that the lease for the State M location will expire in 6 months instead of 24 months, and D will use $80 of the $150 cash it retains to purchase a nearby building for the relocation. After the distribution, D's Nonbusiness Asset Percentage is 60 percent, and C's Nonbusiness Asset Percentage is 30 percent. D's and C's ownership of Nonbusiness Assets of at least 20 percent of their respective Total Assets is evidence of device with respect to each. The difference between D's Nonbusiness Asset Percentage and C's Nonbusiness Asset Percentage is 30 percentage points, which is also evidence of device. However, D has a corporate business purpose for a significant part of the difference of Nonbusiness Asset Percentages because D's use of $80 is required by business exigencies. The fact that the distribution is pro rata is also evidence of device. The corporate business purpose for the distribution is evidence of nondevice. Based on all the facts and circumstances, the transaction is not considered to have been used principally as a device. See paragraph (d)(1), (2)(i), (ii), (iv)(A) and (C), and (3)(i) and (ii)(A), (B), and (C) of this section.

Example 5. Nonbusiness Asset Percentage (50-Percent-Owned Group)—(i) Facts. C's assets consist of 50% of the stock of S1 and other assets consisting of $10,000 of Business Assets and $5,000 of Nonbusiness Assets. S1's assets consist of 40% of the stock of S2, 60% of the stock of S3 and other assets consisting of $1,000 of Business Assets and $500 of Nonbusiness Assets. S1 has $500 of liabilities, owed to unrelated persons. S2's assets consist of $500 Business Assets and $100 Nonbusiness Assets. S2 has $200 of liabilities. S3's assets consist of $3,000 Business Assets and $1,500 Nonbusiness Assets. S3 has $3,500 of liabilities, owed to unrelated persons.

(ii) *Determination of S1's Business Assets and Nonbusiness Assets.* Because C owns at least 50% of the stock of S1, S1 is a member of C's 50-Percent-Owned Group. See paragraph (d)(2)(iv)(B)(7) of this section. In determining the amount of C's Business Assets and Nonbusiness Assets, whether S1's stock in S2 and S3 are Nonbusiness Assets or partially Nonbusiness Assets and partially Business Assets must first be determined. See paragraph (d)(2)(iv)(D)(7)(ii) of this section (computations are made with respect to lower-tier Members of a 50-Percent-Owned Group before the computations with respect to higher-tier members). The fair market value of S1's stock in S2 is $160 (40% of $400 ($500 + $100 - $200)). Because S1 owns less than 50% of the stock of S2, S2 is not a member of C's 50-Percent-Owned Group, and thus the S2 stock is a $160 Nonbusiness Asset in the hands of S1. See paragraph (d)(2)(iv)(B)(7) and (D)(7)(i) of this section. The fair market value of S1's stock in S3 is $600 (60% of $1,000 ($3,000 + $1,500 - $3,500)). Because C owns at least 50% of the stock of S1 and S1 owns at least 50% of the stock of S3, S3 is a member of C's 50-Percent-Owned Group. See paragraph (d)(2)(iv)(B)(7) of this section. Thus, the fair market value of the S3 stock is allocated between Business Assets and Nonbusiness Assets in the same proportion as S3's proportion of Business Assets and Nonbusiness Assets. See paragraph (d)(2)(iv)(D)(7)(ii) of this section. Because S3 has Business Assets of $3,000 and Nonbusiness Assets of $1,500, this proportion is 66 2/3% Business Assets ($3,000/$4,500) and 33 1/3% Nonbusiness Assets ($1,500/$4,500). The $600 fair market value of S1's stock in S3 is allocated $400 to Business Assets ($600 × 66 2/3%) and $200 to Nonbusiness Assets ($600 × 33 1/3%). Thus, S1's assets consist of $1,400 of Business Assets ($1,000 held directly + $400 allocated from S3) and $860 of Nonbusiness Assets ($500 held directly + $160 fair market value of its S2 stock + $200 allocated from S3).

(iii) *Determination of C's Business Assets and Nonbusiness Assets.* The fair market value of C's stock in S1 is $880 (50% of $1,760 ($160 + $600 + $1,000 + $500 - $500)). Because C owns at least 50% of the stock of S1, S1 is a member of C's 50-Percent-Owned Group. See paragraph (d)(2)(iv)(B)(7) of this section. Thus, the fair market value of the S1 stock is allocated between Business Assets and Nonbusiness Assets in the same proportion as the proportion of S1's Business Assets and Nonbusiness Assets. See paragraph (d)(2)(iv)(D)(7)(ii) of this section. Because S1 has Business Assets of $1,400 and Nonbusiness Assets of $860, this proportion is 61.95% Business Assets ($1,400/$2,260) and 38.05% Nonbusiness Assets ($860/$2,260). The $880 fair market value of C's S1 stock is allocated $545 to Business Assets ($880 × 61.95%) and $335 to Nonbusiness Assets ($880 × 38.05%). Thus, C's assets consist of $10,545 of Business Assets ($10,000 + $545) and $5,335 of Nonbusiness Assets ($5,000 + $335), for

Total Assets of $15,880. C's Nonbusiness Asset Percentage is 33.6% ($5,335/$15,880).

Example 6. Partnership interest held by Distributing. (i) *Facts.* D has directly-held Business Assets of $1,000, directly held Nonbusiness Assets of $2,000, and a 40% partnership interest in P. P has $450 of Business Assets and $1,350 of cash, which P holds as a Nonbusiness Asset, and owes a liability of $800.

(ii) *Analysis.* Pursuant to paragraph (d)(2)(iv)(D)(6)(ii) of this section, D is allocated $100 of Business Assets from P ($400 (value of D's 40% interest in P) × 25% ($450/$1,800)) and $300 of Nonbusiness Assets from P ($400 (value of D's 40% interest in P) × 75% ($1,350/$1,800)), which are added to D's directly held Business Assets and Nonbusiness Assets, respectively. D's Nonbusiness Asset Percentage is 67.6% ($2,300 Nonbusiness Assets/$3,400 Total Assets).

Example 7. Borrowing by Distributing from partnership. (i) *Facts.* The facts are the same as in Example 6, except that D borrows $500 from P and invests the proceeds in a Nonbusiness Asset. P's directly-held Nonbusiness Assets increase by $500. The D obligation is a Nonbusiness Asset in P's hands.

(ii) *Analysis.* D's directly-held Nonbusiness Assets increase by $500, to $2,500. There is no corresponding decrease in the amount of Business Assets or Nonbusiness Assets allocated to D from P, because a Nonbusiness Asset of P ($500 cash) has been replaced by another $500 Nonbusiness Asset, the obligation from D. Effectively, because D has a 40% interest in P, D has borrowed $200 (40% of $500) from itself. Accordingly, D's Nonbusiness Assets must be decreased by $200. D's Business Assets will continue to be $1,100 ($1,000 directly held plus $100 allocated from P), and D's Nonbusiness Assets will be $2,600 ($2,500 directly held, plus $300 allocated from P less the $200 decrease to prevent double inclusion of the obligation and the obligation proceeds).

* * *

(5) *Distributions involving separation of Business Assets from Nonbusiness Assets.*—(i) *In general.*—A distribution specified in paragraph (d)(5)(iii) of this section is considered to have been used principally as a device, notwithstanding the presence of nondevice factors described in paragraph (d)(3) of this section or other facts and circumstances. However, this paragraph (d)(5)(i) does not apply to a distribution that is described in paragraph (d)(3)(iv) of this section (distributions to domestic corporations entitled to certain dividends received deductions absent application of section 355(a)) or paragraph (d)(6) of this section (transactions ordinarily not considered to be a device).

(ii) *Definitions and operating rules.*—The definitions in paragraph (d)(2)(iv)(B) of this section and the operating rules in paragraph (d)(2)(iv)(D) of this section apply for purposes of this paragraph (d)(5). For purposes of paragraph (d)(2)(iv)(D)(1), (2), and (3), references to paragraph (d)(2)(iv) of this section are treated as references to this paragraph (d)(5).

(iii) *Certain distributions involving separation of Nonbusiness Assets from Business Assets.*—A distribution is specified in this paragraph (d)(5)(iii) if both—

(A) The Nonbusiness Asset Percentage of the distributing corporation or the controlled corporation is 66 2/3 percent or more, and

(B) If the Nonbusiness Asset Percentage of the distributing corporation or the controlled corporation is—

(1) 66 2/3 percent or more but less than 80 percent, and the Nonbusiness Asset Percentage of the other corporation (the controlled corporation or the distributing corporation, as the case may be) is less than 30 percent;

(2) 80 percent or more but less than 90 percent, and the Nonbusiness Asset Percentage of the other corporation (the controlled corporation or the distributing corporation, as the case may be) is less than 40 percent; or

(3) 90 percent or more, and the Nonbusiness Asset Percentage of the other corporation (the controlled corporation or the distributing corporation, as the case may be) is less than 50 percent.

(iv) *Anti-abuse rule.*—The anti-abuse rule in paragraph (d)(2)(iv)(E) of this section applies for purposes of this paragraph (d)(5), with references to paragraph (d)(2)(iv) of this section treated as references to this paragraph (d)(5) and references to paragraph (d)(2)(iv)(E) of this section treated as references to this paragraph (d)(5)(iv).

(6) *Transactions ordinarily not considered as a device.*—(i) *In general.*—This paragraph (d)(6) specifies three distributions that ordinarily do not present the potential for federal tax avoidance described in paragraph (d)(1) of this section. Accordingly, such distributions are ordinarily considered not to have been used principally as a device, notwithstanding the presence of any of the device factors described in paragraph (d)(2) of this section or a separation of Business Assets from Nonbusiness Assets as described in paragraph (d)(5) of this section. A transaction described in paragraph (d)(6)(iii) or (iv) of this section is not protected by this paragraph (d)(6) from a determination that it was used principally as a device if it involves the distribution of the stock of more than one controlled corporation and facilitates the avoidance of the dividend provisions of the Code through the subsequent sale or exchange of stock of one corporation and the retention of the stock of another corporation.* * *

* * *

(i) *Effective/applicability date.*—(1) *Paragraph (d) of this section.*—(i) *In general.*—Except as provided in paragraph (i)(1)(ii) of this section, paragraph (d) of this section applies to transactions occurring on or after the date the Treasury decision adopting these regulations as final regulations is published in the **Federal Register**.

(ii) *Transition rule.*—Paragraph (d) of this section does not apply to a distribution that is—

(A) Made pursuant to an agreement, resolution, or other corporate action that is binding on or before the date the Treasury decision adopting these regulations as final regulations is published in the **Federal Register** and at all times thereafter;

(B) Described in a ruling request submitted to the Internal Revenue Service on or before July 15, 2016; or

(C) Described in a public announcement or filing with the Securities and Exchange Commission on or before the date the Treasury decision adopting these regulations as final regulations is published in the **Federal Register**.

(2) *Paragraph (g) of this section.*—Paragraph (g) of this section applies to distributions occurring after October 20, 2011. For rules regarding distributions occurring on or before October 20, 2011, *see* §1.355-2T(i), as contained in 26 CFR part 1, revised as of April 1, 2011.

Active Trade or Business Requirement: Guidance

Active Trade or Business Requirement: Guidance.—Amendments to Reg. §1.355-3, providing guidance regarding active trade or business requirements, is proposed (published in the Federal Register on May 8, 2007) (REG-123365-03) (corrected June 5, 2007).

☐ Par. 4. Section 1.355-3 is revised to read as follows:

§1.355-3. Active conduct of a trade or business.—(a) *General requirements.*—Under section 355(b)(1), a distribution of stock, or stock and securities, of controlled (as defined in paragraph (c)(2) of this section) qualifies under section 355 only if—

(1) Distributing (as defined in paragraph (c)(3) of this section) and controlled are each engaged in the active conduct of a trade or business immediately after the distribution (section 355(b)(1)(A)); or

(2) Immediately before the distribution, distributing had no assets other than stock or securities of the controlled corporations (without regard to paragraph (b)(1)(ii) of this section), and each of the controlled corporations is engaged in the active conduct of a trade or business immediately after the distribution (section 355(b)(1)(B)). A de minimis amount of assets held by distributing shall be disregarded for purposes of this paragraph (a)(2).

(b) *Active conduct of a trade or business defined.*—(1) *In general.*—(i) *Directly engaged in a trade or business.*—Section 355(b)(2) provides rules for determining whether a corporation is treated as engaged in the active conduct of a trade or business under section 355(b)(1).

Section 355(b)(2)(A) and (b)(3)(A) provides that a corporation is treated as engaged in the active conduct of a trade or business if and only if such corporation is engaged in the active conduct of a trade or business. Accordingly, except as provided in paragraph (b)(1)(ii) of this section, a corporation is not treated as engaged in the active conduct of a trade or business under such Internal Revenue Code section solely as a result of substantially all of its assets consisting of stock, or stock and securities, of one or more corporations controlled by it (immediately after the distribution) each of which is engaged in the active conduct of a trade or business.

(ii) *Treatment of a separate affiliated group.*—Under section 355(b)(3)(B), solely for purposes of determining whether a corporation is engaged in the active conduct of a trade or business, all members of a corporation's separate affiliated group (SAG) (as defined in paragraph (b)(1)(iii) of this section) shall be treated as one corporation. This treatment applies for all purposes of determining whether a corporation is engaged in the active conduct of a trade or business. Accordingly, for this purpose, transfers of assets (or activities) that are owned (or performed) by the SAG immediately before and immediately after the transfer are disregarded and are not acquisitions under paragraph (b)(4) of this section. Further, a transaction that results in a corporation becoming a subsidiary SAG member (a SAG member that is not the common parent of such SAG) is treated as an acquisition of any assets (or activities) that are owned (or performed) by the acquired corporation at such time. Therefore, the acquisition of additional stock of a current subsidiary SAG member has no effect for purposes of applying paragraph (b)(4)(i)(A) of this section.

(iii) *Separate affiliated group defined.*—A corporation's SAG is the affiliated group which would be determined under section 1504(a) if such corporation were the common parent and section 1504(b) did not apply. Thus, the separate affiliated group of distributing (DSAG) is the affiliated group that consists of distributing as the common parent and all corporations affiliated with distributing through stock ownership described in section 1504(a)(1)(B) (regardless of whether the corporations are includible corporations under section 1504(b)). The separate affiliated group of controlled (CSAG) is determined in a similar manner (with controlled as the common parent). Accordingly, prior to a distribution, the DSAG may include CSAG members if the applicable ownership requirements are met. Further, the determination of whether a corporation is a DSAG or CSAG member shall be made separately for each distribution, and without regard to whether such corporation is a SAG member with respect to any other distribution. Any reference to DSAG or CSAG is a reference to distributing or controlled, respectively, if such corporation is not the common parent of a SAG (that is, such corporation does not own stock in any corporation that is a subsidiary member of its SAG). Further, any reference to a SAG is a reference to distributing or controlled, as the context may require, if such corporation is not the common parent of a SAG.

(2) *Active conduct of a trade or business immediately after the distribution.*—(i) *In general.*—For purposes of section 355(b), a corporation shall be treated as engaged in the active conduct of a trade or business immediately after the distribution if the assets and activities of the corporation satisfy the requirements and limitations described in paragraphs (b)(2)(ii), (b)(2)(iii), and (b)(2)(iv) of this section. See paragraph (b)(2)(v) of this section for additional special rules that apply to determine whether a corporation is attributed the trade or business assets and activities of a partnership.

(ii) *Trade or business.*—A corporation shall be treated as engaged in a trade or business immediately after the distribution if a specific group of activities is being carried on by the corporation for the purpose of earning income or profit, and the activities included in such group include every operation that forms a part of, or a step in, the process of earning income or profit. Such group of activities ordinarily must include the collection of income and the payment of expenses.

(iii) *Active conduct.*—For purposes of section 355(b), the determination of whether a trade or business is actively conducted will be made from all of the facts and circumstances. Generally, the corporation is required itself to perform active and substantial management and operational functions. Activities performed by a corporation include activities performed by employees of an affiliate (as defined in paragraph (c)(1) of this section), and in certain cases by shareholders of a closely held corporation, if such activities are performed for the corporation. For example, activities performed by a corporation include activities performed for the corporation by its sole shareholder. However, the activities of employees of affiliates (or, in certain cases, shareholders) are only taken into account during the period such corporations are affiliates (or persons are shareholders) of the corporation. A corporation will not be treated as engaged in the active conduct of a trade or business unless it (or its SAG, or a partnership from which the trade or business assets and activities are attributed) is the principal owner of the goodwill and significant assets of the trade or business for Federal income tax purposes. Activities performed by a corporation generally do not include activities performed by persons outside the corporation, including independent contractors, unless those activities are performed by employees of an affiliate (or, in certain cases, by shareholders). However, a corporation may satisfy the requirements of this paragraph (b)(2)(iii) through the activities that it performs itself, even though some of its activities are performed by persons that are not its employees, or employees of an affiliate (or, in certain cases, shareholders). Separations of real property all or substantially all of which is occupied before the distribution by the DSAG or CSAG will be carefully scrutinized in applying the requirements of section 355(b) and this section.

(iv) *Limitations.*—The active conduct of a trade or business does not include—

(A) The holding for investment purposes of stock, securities, land, or other property; or

(B) The ownership and operation (including leasing) of real or personal property used in a trade or business, unless the owner performs significant services with respect to the operation and management of the property.

(v) *Partner attributed the trade or business assets and activities of a partnership.*—(A) *In general.*—For purposes of section 355(b), a partner in a partnership will be attributed the trade or business assets and activities of that partnership during the period that such partner satisfies the requirements of paragraph (b)(2)(v)(B) or (b)(2)(v)(C) of this section. However, for purposes of this paragraph (b)(2)(v), the stock of a corporation owned by the partnership is not attributed to a partner. For purposes of determining the activities that are conducted by the partnership that may be attributed to the partner under this paragraph (b)(2)(v), the activities of independent contractors, and partners that are not affiliates (or, in certain cases, shareholders) of the partner, are not taken into account. For this purpose, the activities of partners that are affiliates (or, in certain cases, shareholders) of the partner are only taken into account during the period that such partners are affiliates (or, in certain cases, shareholders) of the partner.

(B) *Significant interest.*—The trade or business assets and activities of a partnership will be attributed to a partner if the partner (or its SAG) directly (or indirectly through one or more other partnerships) owns a significant interest in the partnership.

(C) *Meaningful interest.*—The trade or business assets and activities of a partnership will be attributed to a partner if the partner or affiliates (or, in certain cases, shareholders) of the partner performs active and substantial management functions for the partnership with respect to the trade or business assets and activities (for example, makes decisions regarding significant business issues of the partnership and regularly participates in the overall supervision, direction, and control of the employees performing the operational functions for the partnership), and the partner (or its SAG) directly (or indirectly through one or more other partnerships) owns a meaningful interest in the partnership. Whether such active and substantial management functions are performed with respect to the trade or business assets and activities of the partnership will be determined from all of the facts and circumstances. The number of partners providing management functions will not be determinative.

(D) *Other factors.*—In deciding whether the requirements of paragraph (b)(2)(v)(B) or (b)(2)(v)(C) of this section are satisfied, the formal description of the partnership interest (for example, general or limited) will not be determinative and the extent to which the partner is responsible for liabilities of the partnership will not be relevant.

(3) *Active conduct for the pre-distribution period.*—(i) *In general.*—Under section 355(b)(2), a trade or business that is relied upon to meet the requirements of section 355(b) must have been actively conducted throughout the pre-distribution period (as defined in paragraph (c)(4) of this section) by the DSAG or CSAG, or actively conducted throughout the pre-distribution period and acquired during such period by the DSAG or CSAG in a transaction in which no gain or loss is recognized as provided in paragraph (b)(4) of this section. For purposes of section 355(b)(2)(B), activities that constitute a trade or business under paragraph (b)(2) of this section shall be treated as described in the preceding sentence if such activities were actively conducted throughout the pre-distribution period.

(ii) *Change and expansion.*—The fact that a trade or business underwent change during the pre-distribution period (for example, by the addition of new or the dropping of old products, changes in production capacity, and the like) shall be disregarded, provided that the changes are not of such a character as to constitute the acquisition of a new or different business. In particular, if a SAG engaged in the active conduct of one trade or business during the pre-distribution period (the original business) purchased, created, or otherwise acquired (either directly, through an interest in a partnership, or as a result of a corporation becoming a subsidiary SAG member) another trade or business (the acquired business) in the same line of business, the acquisition of the acquired business is ordinarily treated as an expansion of the original business, all of which is treated as having been actively conducted by the acquiring SAG during the pre-distribution period, unless the acquired business effects a change of such a character as to constitute the acquisition of a new or different business. For purposes of this paragraph (b)(3)(ii), in determining whether an acquired business is in the same line of business as the original business, all facts and circumstances shall be considered, including the following—

(A) Whether the product of the acquired business is similar to that of the original business;

(B) Whether the business activities associated with the operation of the acquired business are the same as the business activities associated with the operation of the original business; and

(C) Whether the operation of the acquired business involves the use of the experience and know-how that the owner of the original business developed in the operation of the original business or, alternatively, whether the operation of the acquired business draws to a significant extent on the existing experience and know-how of the owner of the original business and the success of the acquired business will depend in large measure on the goodwill associated with the original business and the name of the original business.

(iii) *Certain transactions with partnerships that do not constitute acquisitions.*—If a partner is attributed the trade or business assets and activities of a partnership under paragraph (b)(2)(v) of this section, the partner's acquisition of such trade or business assets and activities from the partnership is not, in and of itself, the acquisition of a new or different trade or business. In addition, if a partner transfers to a partnership trade or business assets and activities that the partner actively conducted immediately before the transfer and, immediately after the transfer, the partner is attributed the trade or business assets and activities of the partnership under paragraph (b)(2)(v) of this section, such transfer is not, in and of itself, the acquisition of a new or different trade or business by the transferor partner.

(4) *Special rules for an acquisition of a trade or business.*—(i) *In general.*—(A) *Application of section 355(b)(2)(C).*—Under section 355(b)(2)(C) and (b)(3), a trade or business or an interest in a partnership engaged in a trade or business relied on to meet the requirements of section 355(b) must not have been acquired by either the DSAG or CSAG during the pre-distribution period unless it was acquired in a transaction in which no gain or loss was recognized. Further, a trade or business must not have been acquired by either the DSAG or CSAG during the pre-distribution period as a result of a corporation becoming a subsidiary SAG member unless such corporation became a subsidiary SAG member as a result of one or more transactions in which no gain or loss was recognized or by reason of such transactions combined with acquisitions before the pre-distribution period. This paragraph (b)(4)(i)(A) also applies with respect to any acquisition during the pre-distribution period of a trade or business, an interest in a partnership engaged in a trade or business, or stock of a corporation engaged in a trade or business by a corporation that later becomes a subsidiary SAG member. See paragraphs (b)(4)(iv)(C) and (b)(4)(iv)(D) of this section regarding the application of this paragraph (b)(4)(i)(A) to certain multi-step acquisitions.

(B) *Application of section 355(b)(2)(D).*—Under section 355(b)(2)(D), control of distributing must not have been acquired (at the time it was conducting the trade or business to be relied on) directly or indirectly by any distributee corporation, and control of controlled must not have been acquired (at the time it was conducting the trade or business to be relied on) directly or indirectly by the DSAG, during the pre-distribution period in one or more transactions in which gain or loss was recognized. This paragraph (b)(4)(i)(B) also applies with respect to any acquisition of stock of controlled during the pre-distribution period by a corporation that later becomes a DSAG member. For purposes of this paragraph (b)(4)(i)(B), and paragraphs (b)(4)(iii)(C) and (b)(4)(iv)(B) of this section, all distributee corporations shall be treated as one distributee corporation. This paragraph (b)(4)(i)(B) does not apply with respect to an acquisition of stock of any corporation other than distributing or controlled. See paragraph (b)(4)(iv)(B) of this section regarding the application of this paragraph (b)(4)(i)(B) to certain multi-step acquisitions of control. Further, see paragraph (b)(4)(iv)(F) of this section regarding certain acquisitions of stock in controlled to which paragraph (b)(4)(i)(A) of this section (and not this paragraph (b)(4)(i)(B)) applies.

(C) *Gain or loss recognized.*—Any reference to gain or loss recognized includes gain or loss treated as recognized under paragraphs (b)(4)(ii) or (b)(4)(iv) of this section.

(ii) *Certain transactions treated as transactions in which gain or loss is recognized.*—The common purpose of section 355(b)(2)(C) and (D) is to prevent the direct or indirect acquisition of the trade or business to be relied on by a corporation in exchange for assets in anticipation of a distribution to which section 355 would otherwise apply. Generally, if a DSAG member or controlled acquires the trade or business solely in exchange for distributing stock, distributing acquires control of controlled solely in exchange for distributing stock, or controlled acquires the trade or business from distributing solely in exchange for stock of controlled, in a transaction in which no gain or loss was recognized, the requirements of section 355(b)(2)(C) and (D) are satisfied. On the other hand, if the trade or business is acquired in exchange for assets of distributing (other than stock of a corporation in control of distributing used in a reorganization) the requirements of section 355(b)(2)(C) and (D) are generally

not satisfied. For example, acquisitions by controlled (while controlled by distributing) from an unrelated party made in exchange for controlled stock have the effect of an indirect acquisition by distributing in exchange for distributing's assets. Such acquisitions violate the purpose of section 355(b)(2)(C) even if no gain or loss is recognized. Therefore, as provided in paragraphs (b)(4)(ii)(A) and (b)(4)(ii)(B) of this section, if the DSAG or CSAG acquires a trade or business, an interest in a partnership engaged in a trade or business, or stock of a corporation engaged in a trade or business in exchange for assets of the DSAG in a transaction in which no gain or loss is recognized, for purposes of paragraph (b)(4)(i) of this section such acquisition will be treated as one in which gain or loss is recognized.

(A) *Certain tax-free acquisitions made in exchange for assets.*—An acquisition paid for in whole or in part, directly or indirectly, with assets of the DSAG will be treated as an acquisition in which gain or loss is recognized even if no gain or loss is actually recognized. Acquisitions described in this paragraph (b)(4)(ii)(A) include for example, a transaction in which the DSAG or CSAG acquires stock of a corporation engaged in the trade or business to be relied on by transferring assets not constituting the trade or business to be relied on to such corporation in exchange for stock of such corporation, the DSAG or CSAG acquires an interest in a partnership engaged in the trade or business to be relied on by contributing assets not constituting the trade or business to be relied on to the partnership, the DSAG or CSAG acquires stock of a corporation engaged in the trade or business in an exchange to which section 304(a)(1) applies, or distributing acquires a trade or business in exchange for its stock and assets in a transaction in which no loss is recognized by virtue of section 351(b). See also paragraph (b)(4)(iv)(E) of this section regarding the extent to which an acquisition involving the issuance of subsidiary stock constitutes an acquisition paid for with assets. However, the assumption by the DSAG or CSAG of liabilities of a transferor shall not, in and of itself, be treated as the payment of assets if such assumption is not treated as the payment of money or other property under any other applicable provision. In addition, an acquisition in which no gain or loss is recognized consisting of a pro rata distribution to which section 355 applies (to the extent the stock with respect to which the distribution is made was not acquired during the pre-distribution period in a transaction in which gain or loss was recognized), a distribution from a partnership that is explicitly excluded from paragraph (b)(4)(ii)(B) of this section, a reorganization described in section 368(a)(1)(E) or (F), and an exchange to which section 1036 applies, are not acquisitions described in this paragraph (b)(4)(ii)(A).

(B) *Distributions from partnerships.*—An acquisition consisting of a distribution from a partnership is generally an acquisition paid for with assets of the DSAG, and will be treated as an acquisition in which gain or loss is recognized even if no gain or loss is actually recognized. However, an acquisition consisting of a pro rata distribution from a partnership of stock or an interest in lower-tier partnership is not an acquisition described in this paragraph (b)(4)(ii)(B) (and consequently not described in paragraph (b)(4)(ii)(A) of this section) to the extent the distributee partner did not acquire the interest in the distributing partnership during the pre-distribution period in a transaction in which gain or loss was recognized and to the extent the distributing partnership did not acquire the distributed stock or partnership interest within such period. This paragraph (b)(4)(ii)(B) (and consequently paragraph (b)(4)(ii)(A) of this section) does not apply to any partnership distribution to which paragraph (b)(3)(iii) of this section (regarding distributions from partnerships that are not, in and of themselves, the acquisition of a new or different trade or business) applies.

(iii) *Certain transactions in which recognized gain or loss is disregarded.*—The common purpose of section 355(b)(2)(C) and (D) is to prevent the direct or indirect acquisition of the trade or business to be relied on by a corporation in exchange for assets in anticipation of a distribution to which section 355 would otherwise apply. An additional purpose of section 355(b)(2)(D) is to prevent a distributee corporation from acquiring control of distributing in anticipation of a distribution to which section 355 would otherwise apply, enabling the disposition of controlled stock without recognizing the appropriate amount of gain. The acquisitions described in paragraphs (b)(4)(iii)(A) through (b)(4)(iii)(C) of this section are not the types of acquisitions to which section 355(b)(2)(C) or (D) is intended to apply. Therefore, for purposes of paragraph (b)(4)(i) of this section, the recognition of gain or loss is disregarded if a trade or business, an interest in a partnership engaged in a trade or business, or stock of a corporation engaged in a trade or business is acquired in a transaction described in any of paragraphs (b)(4)(iii)(A) through (b)(4)(iii)(C) of this section.

(A) *Transfers to controlled.*—An acquisition by the CSAG from the DSAG provided the DSAG controls controlled immediately after the acquisition.

(B) *Cash for fractional shares.*—An acquisition that would satisfy the requirements of paragraph (b)(4)(i) of this section but for the payment of cash to shareholders for fractional shares in the transaction, provided that the cash paid represents a mere rounding off of the fractional shares in the exchange and is not separately bargained for consideration.

(C) *Certain acquisitions of control of distributing.*—A direct or indirect acquisition by a distributee corporation of control of distributing, in one or more transactions, where the basis of the acquired distributing stock in the hands of the distributee corporation is determined in whole by reference to the transferor's basis. This paragraph (b)(4)(iii)(C) is only applicable with respect to a distribution by the acquired distributing, and does not apply for purposes of any subsequent distribution by any distributee corporation.

(iv) *Operating rules for acquisitions.*—(A) *Predecessors.*—References to a corporation shall include references to a predecessor of such corporation. For this purpose, a predecessor of a corporation is a corporation that transfers its assets to such corporation in a transaction to which section 381 applies.

(B) *Certain multi-step acquisitions of control of distributing or controlled.*—A distributee corporation's acquisition of stock in distributing or a DSAG's acquisition of stock in controlled in one or more transactions in which gain or loss was recognized during the pre-distribution period will not prevent a distributee corporation's acquisition of distributing stock or a DSAG's acquisition of controlled stock constituting control of distributing or controlled in one or more separate transactions in which no gain or loss is recognized from satisfying the requirements of paragraph (b)(4)(i)(B) of this section, provided that, at the time control of distributing or controlled is first acquired, the acquiring distributee corporation owns an amount of distributing stock or the acquiring DSAG owns an amount of controlled stock, as the case may be, constituting control that was acquired in one or more transactions in which no gain or loss was recognized or by reason of such transactions combined with acquisitions before the pre-distribution period. The principles of this paragraph (b)(4)(iv)(B) will be applied with respect to an indirect acquisition of distributing or controlled stock.

(C) *Certain multi-step acquisitions of a subsidiary SAG member.*—An acquisition of stock in a corporation (target) by a SAG in one or more transactions in which gain or loss was recognized during the pre-distribution period will not prevent a SAG's acquisition of target stock resulting in target becoming a subsidiary SAG member in one or more separate transactions in which no gain or loss is recognized from satisfying the requirements of paragraph (b)(4)(i)(A) of this section, provided that, at the time that target first becomes a subsidiary SAG member, the SAG owns an amount of target stock meeting the requirements of section 1504(a)(2) that was acquired in one or more transactions in which no gain or loss was recognized or by reason of such transactions combined with acquisitions before the pre-distribution period. The principles of this paragraph (b)(4)(iv)(C) will be applied with respect to an indirect acquisition of target stock by the SAG.

(D) *Certain multi-step asset acquisitions.*—Notwithstanding paragraph (b)(4)(i)(A) of this section, if immediately before a SAG's direct acquisition of a trade or business (or an interest in a partnership engaged in a trade or business) held by a corporation (owner) in a transaction to which section 381 applies and in which no gain or loss is recognized, the SAG owns an amount of stock of the owner that it acquired in one or more transactions during the pre-distribution period in which gain or loss was recognized such that all of the other stock of the owner does not meet the requirements of section 1504(a)(2), such direct acquisition shall be treated as a transaction in which gain or loss was recognized. The principles of this paragraph (b)(4)(iv)(D) will be applied with respect to an indirect acquisition of the owner stock by the SAG.

(E) *Acquisitions involving the issuance of subsidiary stock.*—If a SAG directly or indirectly owns stock of a subsidiary (including a subsidiary SAG member) and the subsidiary directly or indirectly acquires a trade or business, an interest in a partnership engaged in a trade or business, or stock of a corporation engaged in a trade or business from a person other than such SAG in exchange for stock of such subsidiary in a transaction in which no gain or loss is recognized (the acquisition), solely for purposes of applying this paragraph (b)(4) with respect to the trade or business, partnership interest, or stock acquired by the subsidiary in the acquisition, the subsidiary's stock directly or indirectly owned by the SAG immediately after the acquisition is treated as acquired at the time of the acquisition in a transaction in which gain or loss is recognized.

(F) *Acquisitions of controlled stock where controlled is or becomes a DSAG member.*—With respect to an acquisition of stock in

controlled, if controlled is or becomes a DSAG member, paragraph (b)(4)(i)(A) of this section applies and paragraph (b)(4)(i)(B) of this section does not apply for purposes of determining whether the requirements of section 355(b) are satisfied with respect to controlled.

(G) *Treatment of stock received in certain tax-free exchanges.*—Any stock received in a reorganization described in section 368(a)(1)(E) or (F), or in an exchange to which section 1036 applies, in which no gain or loss is recognized is treated as acquired in the same manner as the stock surrendered.

(H) *Situations where the separate existence of a subsidiary SAG member is respected.*—The separate existence of a subsidiary SAG member will be respected for purposes of determining whether a transaction qualifies for nonrecognition treatment under other provisions of the Internal Revenue Code. For example, for purposes of determining whether section 351 applies or whether the transaction qualifies as a reorganization described in section 368(a), the separate existence of the subsidiary SAG member is respected.

(c) *Definitions.*—For purposes of this section the following definitions apply:

(1) *Affiliate.*—An affiliate is any member of an affiliated group as defined in section 1504(a) (without regard to section 1504(b)).

(2) *Controlled.*—Controlled is the controlled corporation.

(3) *Distributing.*—Distributing is the distributing corporation.

(4) *Pre-distribution period.*—The *pre-distribution period* is the five-year period ending on the date of the distribution.

(d) *Conventions and examples.*—(1) *Conventions.*—The examples in paragraph (d)(2) of this section illustrate section 355(b) and this section. No inference should be drawn from any of these examples as to whether any requirements of section 355 other than those of section 355(b), as specified, are satisfied. Throughout these examples, C, D, D2, P, S, S1, S2, S3, T, X, Y, and Z are corporations, and Partnership is an entity that is treated as a partnership for Federal income tax purposes under §301.7701-3 of this chapter. Further, assume any transfer described in *Examples 1* through *25* that is not identified as a purchase (defined in paragraph (d)(1)(iii) of this section) satisfies all the requirements of paragraph (b)(4) of this section as a transaction in which no gain or loss is recognized. Except as otherwise provided, for more than five years D has owned section 368(c) stock (as defined in paragraph (d)(1)(iv) of this section) but not section 1504(a)(2) stock (as defined in paragraph (d)(1)(v) of this section) of C. Furthermore, the following definitions apply:

(i) *ATB.*—ATB is any active trade or business. ATB1 and ATB2 are not in the same line of business under paragraph (b)(3)(ii) of this section.

(ii) *New subsidiary.*—A *new subsidiary* is a newly formed wholly owned corporation.

(iii) *Purchase.*—A *purchase* is an acquisition for cash.

(iv) *Section 368(c) stock.*—Section 368(c) stock is stock constituting control within the meaning of section 368(c).

(v) *Section 1504(a)(2) stock.*—Section 1504(a)(2) stock is stock meeting the requirements of section 1504(a)(2).

(2) *Examples.*—Generally, *Examples 1* and *2* illustrate the general requirements in paragraph (a) of this section, *Examples 3* through *9* illustrate the SAG rules in paragraphs (b)(1)(ii) and (b)(1)(iii) of this section, *Examples 10* through *25* illustrate the rules regarding the active trade or business and active conduct for the pre-distribution period in paragraphs (b)(2) and (b)(3) of this section, *Examples 26* through *40* illustrate the acquisition rules in paragraphs (b)(4)(i) through (b)(4)(iii) of this section, and *Examples 41* through *51* illustrate the operating rules for acquisitions in paragraph (b)(4)(iv) of this section. The examples are as follows:

Example 1. Spin-off. For more than five years, D and C have engaged in the active conduct of ATB1 and ATB2, respectively. D distributes the C stock to the D shareholders, and each corporation continues the active conduct of its respective trade or business. Because both D and C are engaged in the active conduct of a trade or business immediately after the distribution and such trades or businesses have been actively conducted by such corporations throughout the pre-distribution period, the requirements of section 355(b) have been satisfied. See paragraphs (a)(1) and (b)(3) of this section.

Example 2. Split-up. The facts are the same as *Example 1* except that D transfers all of its assets (including ATB1) other than the C stock to new subsidiary S, and then distributes the C stock and S stock to the D shareholders. Because C and S are respectively engaged in the active conduct of ATB2 and ATB1 immediately after the distribution, ATB2 has been actively conducted by C throughout the pre-distribution period, and together D (prior to the transfer to S) and S (after the transfer to S) have actively conducted ATB1 throughout the pre-distribution period, the requirements of section 355(b) have been satisfied. See paragraphs (a)(2) and (b)(3) of this section.

Example 3. Subsidiary SAG member's business. For more than five years, D has owned section 1504(a)(2) stock but not section 368(c) stock of S. Throughout this period, C and S have engaged in the active conduct of ATB1 and ATB2, respectively. In year 8, D distributes the C stock to the D shareholders. Because D owns section 1504(a)(2) stock of S, S is a DSAG member. See paragraph (b)(1)(iii) of this section. D and S are treated as one corporation for purposes of determining whether D is engaged in an active trade or business. See paragraph (b)(1)(ii) of this section. Therefore, D is engaged in the active conduct of ATB2 both throughout the pre-distribution period and immediately after the distribution. Accordingly, D and C both satisfy the requirements of section 355(b).

Example 4. Additional subsidiary SAG member shares acquired. The facts are the same as *Example 3* except that in year 6, D acquires the remaining S stock. D's acquisition of the remaining S stock in year 6 has no effect for purposes of determining whether D satisfies the requirements of section 355(b)(2)(C) because the DSAG is already engaged in the active conduct of ATB2. See paragraph (b)(1)(ii) of this section. Section 355(b)(2)(D) does not apply to D's acquisition of S stock. See paragraph (b)(4)(i)(B) of this section. Accordingly, D and C both satisfy the requirements of section 355(b).

Example 5. Segmented CSAG business. For more than five years, C has owned all the stock of S1, S2, and S3. Throughout this period, D has engaged in the active conduct of ATB1. Throughout this same period, S1, S2, and S3 have each engaged in a different essential segment of ATB2. While the three segments of ATB2 would together constitute the active conduct of a trade or business, none of S1, S2, or S3 would be considered engaged in the active conduct of an ATB individually. In year 6, D distributes the C stock to the D shareholders. C owns section 1504(a)(2) stock of S1, S2, and S3, therefore, C, S1, S2, and S3 are CSAG members. See paragraph (b)(1)(iii) of this section. C, S1, S2, and S3 are treated as one corporation for purposes of determining whether C is engaged in the active conduct of a trade or business. See paragraph (b)(1)(ii) of this section. Therefore, C is engaged in the active conduct of ATB2 both throughout the pre-distribution period and immediately after the distribution. Accordingly, D and C both satisfy the requirements of section 355(b).

Example 6. Segmented DSAG business. The facts are the same as *Example 5* except that D owns all of the C stock and all of the S3 stock, and D transfers the S3 stock to C immediately prior to the distribution. Prior to D's transfer of the S3 stock to C, D owns section 1504(a)(2) stock of S3 and C, and C owns section 1504(a)(2) stock of S1 and S2, therefore, D, C, S1, S2, and S3 are DSAG members. See paragraph (b)(1)(iii) of this section. D, C, S1, S2, and S3 are treated as one corporation for purposes of determining whether D and C are engaged in the active conduct of a trade or business, and accordingly the transfer of the S3 stock to C is disregarded. See paragraph (b)(1)(ii) of this section. After the transfer, C owns section 1504(a)(2) stock of S3, and the CSAG includes C, S1, S2, and S3. See paragraph (b)(1)(iii) of this section. C, S1, S2, and S3 are treated as one corporation for purposes of determining whether C is engaged in the active conduct of a trade or business. See paragraph (b)(1)(ii) of this section. Throughout the pre-distribution period, D, C, S1, S2, and S3 are treated as one corporation and both D and C are engaged in the active conduct of ATB1 and ATB2. See paragraphs (b)(1) and (b)(2) of this section. Immediately after the distribution, D is engaged in the active conduct of ATB1 and C is engaged in the active conduct of ATB2. Because D and C were engaged in the active conduct of ATB1 and ATB2 throughout the pre-distribution period and, immediately after the distribution, D is engaged in the active conduct of ATB1 and C is engaged in the active conduct of ATB2, D and C both satisfy the requirements of section 355(b).

Example 7. Failed segmented business. The facts are the same as *Example 6* except that D owns section 368(c) stock but not section 1504(a)(2) stock of C. Prior to D's transfer of the S3 stock, the DSAG includes only D and S3, and the CSAG includes only C, S1, and S2. See paragraph (b)(1)(iii) of this section. Therefore, prior to the transfer of the S3 stock, ATB2 does not exist because no one SAG conducts all three of the essential segments of the trade or business. Accordingly, C does not satisfy the requirements of section 355(b) because ATB2 was not actively conducted throughout the pre-distribution period. See paragraph (b)(3)(i) of this section.

Example 8. Jointly owned partnership. For more than five years, D has owned all of the stock of C, and D and C each have owned a 17-percent interest in Partnership. Throughout this period, D and Partnership have engaged in the active conduct of ATB1 and ATB2, respectively. In year 6, D transfers its 17-percent interest in Partnership to C and distributes all of the C stock to the D shareholders. Because D owns section 1504(a)(2) stock of C, C is a DSAG member. See paragraph (b)(1)(iii) of this section. D and C are treated as one corporation for purposes of determining whether D and C are engaged in the active conduct of a trade or business. See paragraph (b)(1)(ii) of this section. Accordingly, throughout the pre-distribution

period, D and C are each treated as owning a 34-percent interest in Partnership. As such, both D and C are treated as engaged in the active conduct of both ATB1 and ATB2 throughout the pre-distribution period. See paragraphs (b)(2)(v)(A) and (b)(2)(v)(B) of this section. The transfer of the Partnership interest is disregarded because it is between SAG members. See paragraph (b)(1)(ii) of this section. After the distribution, C owns 34 percent of Partnership and is therefore engaged in the active conduct of ATB2. See paragraphs (b)(2)(v)(A) and (b)(2)(v)(B) of this section. Therefore, D and C both satisfy the requirements of section 355(b).

Example 9. Sequential application of the SAG rule—(i) Facts. For more than five years, D2 has owned all of the stock of D, and D has owned all of the stock of C. Throughout this period, D2 has engaged in the active conduct of ATB1 and ATB2, and D has engaged in the active conduct of ATB1. C, individually, has not engaged in the active conduct of any ATB. In year 6, D distributes all of the C stock to D2 (first distribution). Immediately thereafter, D2 transfers ATB2 to C and distributes all of the C stock to the D2 shareholders (second distribution).

(ii) *Analysis - first distribution.* Because D owns section 1504(a)(2) stock of C, C is a DSAG member prior to the first distribution. See paragraph (b)(1)(iii) of this section. D and C are treated as one corporation for purposes of determining whether D and C are engaged in the active conduct of a trade or business with respect to the first distribution. See paragraphs (b)(1)(ii) and (b)(1)(iii) of this section. Accordingly, throughout the pre-distribution period, D and C are each treated as engaged in ATB1 with respect to the first distribution. However, for purposes of determining whether D's distribution of the C stock to D2 satisfies the requirements of section 355(b) immediately after the first distribution, C is the only CSAG member (D2 is not a member of any SAG with respect to the first distribution). See paragraph (b)(1)(iii) of this section. Accordingly, C does not satisfy the requirements of section 355(b) with respect to the first distribution because C is not engaged in the active conduct of an ATB immediately after the first distribution.

(iii) *Analysis - second distribution.* Because D2 owns section 1504(a)(2) stock of D and C (and D owned section 1504(a)(2) stock of C before the first distribution), D2, D, and C are D2 SAG members throughout the pre-distribution period with respect to the second distribution. See paragraph (b)(1)(iii) of this section. Further, for purposes of the second distribution D's distribution of the C stock to D2 is disregarded because it is between D2 SAG members. See paragraphs (b)(1)(ii) and (b)(1)(iii) of this section. D2, D, and C are treated as one corporation for purposes of determining whether D2 and C are engaged in the active conduct of a trade or business with respect to the second distribution. See paragraphs (b)(1)(ii) and (b)(1)(iii) of this section. Accordingly, throughout the pre-distribution period, D2 and C are each treated as engaged in the active conduct of ATB1 and ATB2 with respect to the second distribution. The transfer of ATB2 to C is disregarded because it is between D2 SAG members. See paragraph (b)(1)(ii) of this section. Immediately after the second distribution, C is engaged in the active conduct of ATB2. Therefore, D2 and C both satisfy the requirements of section 355(b) with respect to the second distribution.

Example 10. Limitations - securities and vacant land. For more than five years, D has owned investment securities and vacant land. D has conducted no activities with respect to the vacant land, but D will subsequently subdivide the vacant land, install streets and utilities, and sell the developed lots to various homebuilders. D cannot currently satisfy the requirements of section 355(b) because the holding of investment securities does not constitute the active conduct of a trade or business. See paragraph (b)(2)(iv)(A) of this section. Furthermore, no significant development activities have been conducted with respect to the vacant land. See paragraph (b)(3) of this section.

Example 11. Limitations - occupied real estate - active. For more than five years, D, a bank, has owned an eleven-story office building, the ground floor of which D has occupied while engaged in the active conduct of its banking business. The remaining ten floors are rented to various tenants. Throughout this period, the building has been managed, operated, repaired, and maintained by employees of D. D transfers the building along with the significant assets used to operate the building and the goodwill associated with the building to new subsidiary C and distributes the C stock to the D shareholders. Henceforth, C's employees will manage, operate, repair, and maintain the building. D and C both satisfy the requirements of section 355(b). See paragraph (b)(3) of this section.

Example 12. Limitations - occupied real estate - not active. For more than five years, D, a bank, has owned a two-story building, the ground floor and one half of the second floor of which D has occupied while engaged in the active conduct of its banking business. The other half of the second floor has been rented as storage space to a neighboring retail merchant. D transfers the building and the goodwill associated with the building to new subsidiary C and distributes the C stock to the D shareholders. After the distribution, D leases from C the space in the building that it formerly occupied. Under the lease, D will repair and maintain its portion of the building and pay property taxes and insurance. C does not satisfy the requirements of section 355(b) because it is not engaged in the active conduct of a trade or business immediately after the distribution. See paragraph (b)(2)(iv)(A) of this section. This example does not address the question of whether the activities of D with respect to the building prior to the separation would constitute the active conduct of a trade or business.

Example 13. No significant activities. For more than five years, D owned land on which it has engaged in the active conduct of the ranching business. Oil has been discovered in the area, and it is apparent that oil may be found under the land on which the ranching business is conducted. D has engaged in no significant activities in connection with its mineral rights. D transfers its mineral rights to new subsidiary C and distributes the C stock to the D shareholders. C will actively pursue the development of the oil producing potential of the property. C does not satisfy the requirements of section 355(b) after the distribution because D was not engaged in significant exploitation activities with respect to the mineral rights throughout the pre-distribution period. See paragraph (b)(3) of this section.

Example 14. Vertical division - state contracts. For more than five years, D has engaged in the active conduct of a single business of constructing sewage disposal plants and other facilities. D transfers one half of its assets to new subsidiary C. These assets include a contract for the construction of a sewage disposal plant in State M, construction equipment, cash, goodwill, and other tangible and significant assets. D retains a contract for the construction of a sewage disposal plant in State N, construction equipment, cash, goodwill, and other tangible and significant assets. D distributes the C stock to one of D's shareholders in exchange for all of his D stock. D and C both satisfy the requirements of section 355(b). See paragraphs (b)(2) and (b)(3)(i) of this section.

Example 15. Vertical division - location. For more than five years, D has engaged in the active conduct of owning and operating two men's retail clothing stores, one in the downtown area of the City of G and one in a suburban area of G. D transfers the store building, fixtures, inventory, and other significant assets related to the operations of the suburban store and the goodwill attributable to that store to new subsidiary C. D also transfers to C the delivery trucks and delivery personnel that formerly served both stores. Henceforth, D will contract with a local public delivery service to make its deliveries. D retains the warehouses that formerly served both stores. Henceforth, C will lease warehouse space from an unrelated public warehouse company. D then distributes the C stock to the D shareholders. D and C both satisfy the requirements of section 355(b). See paragraphs (b)(2) and (b)(3)(i) of this section.

Example 16. Horizontal division - research. For more than five years, D has engaged in the active conduct of manufacturing and sale of household products. Throughout this period, D has maintained a research department for use in connection with its manufacturing activities. The research department has 30 employees actively engaged in the development of new products. D transfers the research department (which has significant assets and goodwill) to new subsidiary C and distributes the C stock to the D shareholders. After the distribution, C continues its research operations on a contractual basis with several corporations, including D. D and C both satisfy the requirements of section 355(b). See paragraphs (b)(2) and (b)(3)(i) of this section. The result is the same if, after the distribution, C continues its research operations but furnishes its services only to D. See paragraphs (b)(2) and (b)(3)(i) of this section. However, see § 1.355-2(d)(2)(iv)(C) (related function device factor) for possible evidence of device.

Example 17. Horizontal division - sales. For more than five years, D has engaged in the active conduct of processing and selling meat products. D derives income from no other source. D separates the sales function from the processing function by transferring the significant business assets related to the sales function, the goodwill associated with the sales function, and cash for working capital to new subsidiary C. D then distributes the C stock to the D shareholders. After the distribution, C purchases for resale the meat products processed by D. D and C both satisfy the requirements of section 355(b). See paragraphs (b)(2) and (b)(3)(i) of this section. However, see § 1.355-2(d)(2)(iv)(C) (related function device factor) for possible evidence of device.

Example 18. Expansion and vertical division - location. For more than five years, D has engaged in the active conduct of owning and operating hardware stores in several states. In year 6, D purchased all of the assets of a hardware store in State M, where D had not previously conducted business. In year 8, D transfers the State M hardware store and related significant assets and goodwill to new subsidiary C and distributes the C stock to the D shareholders. After the distribution, the State M hardware store has its own manager and is operated independently of the other stores. Because—

(i) The product of the State M hardware store is similar to the product of D's hardware stores in the other states;

(ii) The business activities associated with the operation of the State M hardware store are the same as the business activities associated with the operation of D's hardware stores in the other states; and

(iii) The operation of a hardware store in State M involves the use of the experience and know-how that D developed in the operation of the hardware stores in the other states, the hardware store in State M is in the same line of business as the hardware stores in the other states. Therefore, the acquisition of the State M hardware store constitutes an expansion of D's existing business and its acquisition does not constitute the acquisition of a new or different business under paragraph (b)(3)(ii) of this section. Accordingly, D and C both satisfy the requirements of section 355(b).

Example 19. Expansion and horizontal division - Internet. For more than five years, D has engaged in the active conduct of operating a retail shoe store business, under the name D. Throughout this period, D's sales are made exclusively to customers who frequent its retail stores in shopping malls and other locations. D's business enjoys favorable name recognition, customer loyalty, and other elements of goodwill in the retail shoe market. D creates an Internet web site and begins selling shoes at retail on the web site. To a significant extent, the operation of the web site draws upon D's existing experience and know-how. The web site is named "D.com" to take advantage of the name recognition, customer loyalty, and other elements of goodwill associated with D and the D name and to enhance the web site's chances for success in its initial stages. Eight months after beginning to sell shoes on the web site, D transfers all of the web site's assets and liabilities (all of which include the significant assets and goodwill associated with the web site's business) to new subsidiary C and distributes the C stock to the D shareholders. The product of the retail shoe store business and the product of the web site are the same (shoes), and the principal business activities of the retail shoe store business are the same as those of the web site (purchasing shoes at wholesale and reselling them at retail). Although selling shoes on a web site requires some know-how not associated with operating a retail store, such as familiarity with different marketing approaches, distribution chains, and technical operations issues, the web site's operation does draw to a significant extent on D's existing experience and know-how, and the web site's success will depend in large measure on the goodwill associated with D and the D name. Therefore, the creation by D of the Internet web site does not constitute the acquisition of a new or different business under paragraph (b)(3)(ii) of this section. Accordingly, it is an expansion of D's retail shoe store business, all of which is treated as having been actively conducted throughout the pre-distribution period. Therefore, D and C both satisfy the requirements of section 355(b).

Example 20. Expansion - acquiring a SAG member. For more than five years, D has owned all of the stock of C. Throughout this period, C and unrelated T have engaged in the active conduct of ATB1. In year 6, D purchases all of the T stock. In year 8, D distributes all of the C stock to the D shareholders. Throughout the period that C is a DSAG member, D is engaged in the active conduct of ATB1. See paragraph (b)(1)(ii) of this section. Moreover, because D acquired section 1504(a)(2) stock of T, D is treated as having acquired T's assets (and activities), and that acquisition constitutes an expansion of ATB1. See paragraphs (b)(1)(ii) and (b)(3)(ii) of this section. Therefore, D and C both satisfy the requirements of section 355(b). The result would be the same if D had owned all of the T stock for more than five years, and purchased all of the C stock in year 6. See paragraphs (b)(1)(ii), (b)(3)(ii), (b)(4)(i), and (b)(4)(iv)(F) of this section.

Example 21. No expansion - acquiring only control of controlled. For more than five years, D and unrelated C have engaged in the active conduct of ATB1. In year 6, D purchases section 368(c) stock but not section 1504(a)(2) stock of C. In year 8, D distributes the C stock to the D shareholders. While D and C are in the same line of business, the acquisition does not result in an expansion of D's business under paragraph (b)(3)(ii) of this section because D is not treated as having acquired C's assets (and activities). Accordingly, D has acquired control of C in violation of section 355(b)(2)(D). See paragraph (b)(4)(i)(B) of this section. However, if D acquires additional C stock thereby causing C to become a DSAG member, D would be treated as having acquired C's assets (and activities) and the acquisition would constitute an expansion of ATB1. See paragraphs (b)(1)(ii), (b)(3)(ii), (b)(4)(i), and (b)(4)(iv)(F) of this section. In such a case, D and C both would satisfy the requirements of section 355(b).

Example 22. Partnership - meaningful but not significant. For more than five years, unrelated X and Y have owned a 20-percent and 33 1/3-percent interest, respectively, in Partnership. The remaining interests in Partnership are owned by unrelated parties. For more than five years, Partnership has manufactured power equipment. But for the performance of all its management functions by employees of X, Partnership would satisfy all the requirements of paragraph (b)(2)(i) this section. X and/or Y will be attributed the trade or business assets and activities of Partnership only if the corporation satisfies the requirements of paragraph (b)(2)(v)(B) or (b)(2)(v)(C) of this section. See paragraph (b)(2)(iv)(A) of this section. While X does not satisfy the requirements of paragraph (b)(2)(v)(B) of this section because X's interest in Partnership is not significant, under paragraph (b)(2)(v)(C) of this section, X owns a meaningful interest in Partnership and performs active and substantial management functions for the trade or business assets and activities of Partnership. Therefore, X is attributed the trade or business assets and activities of Partnership. Accordingly, X is engaged in the active conduct of the business of manufacturing power equipment. See paragraph (b)(2) of this section. In determining whether Y is engaged in the business of manufacturing power equipment, the management functions performed by X for Partnership are not taken into account. See paragraph (b)(2)(v)(A) of this section. Therefore, although Y is attributed Partnership's trade or business assets and activities under paragraph (b)(2)(v)(B) of this section because Y owns a significant interest in Partnership, Y is not engaged in the business of manufacturing power equipment because neither Y nor Partnership perform any management functions for the business. See paragraph (b)(2)(iii) of this section.

Example 23. Partnership - significant but not meaningful. The facts are the same as *Example 22* except that all the management functions related to the business of Partnership are performed by employees of Partnership. Because employees of Partnership perform all of the management functions related to the trade or business assets and activities of manufacturing power equipment, Partnership itself satisfies all the requirements of paragraph (b)(2)(i) of this section. X neither owns a significant interest in Partnership nor performs active and substantial management functions with respect to the trade or business assets and activities of Partnership. Accordingly, X does not satisfy the requirements of paragraph (b)(2)(v)(B) or (b)(2)(v)(C) of this section, X is not attributed the trade or business assets and activities of Partnership's business of manufacturing power equipment, and X is not engaged in the active conduct of the business of manufacturing power equipment. On the other hand, because Y owns a significant interest in Partnership, Y satisfies the requirements of paragraph (b)(2)(v)(B) of this section. Therefore, Y is attributed the trade or business assets and activities of Partnership's business. Accordingly, Y satisfies the requirements of paragraph (b)(2)(i) of this section and is engaged in the active conduct of the business of manufacturing power equipment.

Example 24. Partnership - significant by many. The facts are the same as *Example 23* except that X, Y, and Z each own a 33 1/3-percent interest in Partnership. Because X, Y, and Z each own a significant interest in Partnership, each of X, Y, and Z satisfies the requirements of paragraph (b)(2)(v)(B) of this section. Accordingly, each of X, Y, and Z is attributed the trade or business assets and activities of Partnership, satisfies the requirements of paragraph (b)(2)(i) of this section, and is engaged in the active conduct of the business of manufacturing power equipment.

Example 25. Non-SAG affiliates—(i) *Facts.* For more than five years, X has owned 10 percent of the stock of D2, D2 has owned all the stock of D and S, and D has owned all the stock of C. Throughout this period, D has manufactured furniture that it sells to furniture stores and has been the principal owner of the goodwill and significant assets associated with that business and C has owned and operated a laundry business and has been the principal owner of the goodwill and significant assets associated with that business. Throughout this period, however, employees of S have performed all the active and substantial management and operational functions of the furniture business for D and the laundry business for C. D distributes the C stock to D2 (first distribution) and D2 distributes the C stock to X in exchange for all of X's D2 stock (second distribution). After the distributions, employees of X perform all the active and substantial management and operational functions of the laundry business for C that the employees of S performed before the distributions and the employees of S continue to perform the same activities for D as they did before the distributions.

(ii) *Analysis - first distribution.* In determining whether the furniture manufacturing business and laundry business have been actively conducted throughout the pre-distribution period and immediately after the first distribution, the activities performed for those businesses include activities performed by employees of affiliates of D and C (even if they are not DSAG or CSAG members). Accordingly, such activities include the activities performed by the employees of S for D and C. See paragraph (b)(2)(iii) of this section. D and C own the goodwill and significant assets associated with their respective businesses both throughout the pre-distribution period and immediately after the first distribution, and are treated as performing active and substantial management and operational functions for their respective businesses both throughout the pre-distribution period and immediately after the first distribution. Therefore, D and C both satisfy the requirements of section 355(b) with respect to the first distribution.

(iii) *Analysis - second distribution.* Because D2 owns section 1504(a)(2) stock of D, C, and S (and D owned section 1504(a)(2) stock of C before the first distribution), D2, D, C, and S are D2 SAG members throughout the pre-distribution period with respect to the

second distribution. See paragraph (b)(1)(iii) of this section. Accordingly, D2, D, C, and S are treated as one corporation for purposes of determining whether D2 is engaged in an active trade or business with respect to the second distribution. See paragraph (b)(1)(ii) of this section. Accordingly, for purposes of the second distribution, D2 has been engaged in the furniture manufacturing business and the laundry business throughout the pre-distribution period. Further, for purposes of the second distribution D's distribution of the C stock to D2 is disregarded because it is between D2 SAG members. See paragraph (b)(1)(ii) of this section. D and S continue to be D2 SAG members immediately after the second distribution. See paragraph (b)(1)(iii) of this section. Accordingly, D2 is engaged in the furniture manufacturing business immediately after the second distribution. In determining whether C is engaged in the active conduct of a trade or business immediately after the second distribution, the activities performed for the laundry business include activities performed by employees of affiliates of C (even if they are not CSAG members). Accordingly, immediately after the second distribution, such activities include the activities performed for C by the employees of X. See paragraph (b)(2)(iii) of this section. C owns the goodwill and significant assets associated with the laundry business both throughout the pre-distribution period and immediately after the second distribution, and is treated as performing active and substantial management and operational functions both throughout the pre-distribution period and immediately after the second distribution. Therefore, D2 and C both satisfy the requirements of section 355(b) with respect to the second distribution.

Example 26. Purchased ATB and SAG member. For more than five years, P has owned all of the stock of D and S1, and D and S1 have owned all of the stock of S2 and S3, respectively. Throughout this period, S1 and S3 have engaged in the active conduct of ATB1 and ATB2, respectively. In year 6, S2 purchases ATB1 and all of the S3 stock from S1 on the same day. In year 6, the DSAG acquired ATB1 and ATB2 (as a result of S3 becoming a DSAG member) in a transaction in which gain or loss was recognized. Accordingly, if D were to make a distribution, it could not rely on ATB1 or ATB2 to satisfy the requirements of section 355(b) unless the DSAG's year 6 acquisition of ATB1 and ATB2 is not in the pre-distribution period. See paragraph (b)(4)(i)(A) of this section. The fact that S2 acquired ATB1 and the S3 stock from an affiliate is not relevant.

Example 27. Purchased ATB prior to entering. For more than five years, T has engaged in the active conduct of ATB1. In year 6, S purchased ATB1 from T. In year 7, D acquired all of the S stock from the S shareholders solely in exchange for D stock in a transaction to which section 351 applied and in which no gain or loss was recognized. As a result, S became a DSAG member. Although S became a DSAG member in a transaction in which no gain or loss was recognized, S, a corporation that later became a DSAG member, acquired ATB1 in a transaction in which gain or loss was recognized. Accordingly, if D were to make a distribution, it could not rely on ATB1 to satisfy the requirements of section 355(b) unless S's year 6 acquisition of ATB1 is not in the pre-distribution period. See paragraph (b)(4)(i)(A) of this section.

Example 28. ATB (or new SAG member) for stock of distributing or a corporation in control of distributing in a reorganization - transfer of ATB to controlled. For more than five years, unrelated T and Z have owned all of the stock of X and Y, respectively, and X and Y have engaged in the active conduct of ATB1 and ATB2, respectively. Unrelated P owns all of the stock of D. In year 6, D acquires all of X's assets (including ATB1) from X solely in exchange for D stock in a reorganization described in section 368(a)(1)(A), and all of Y's assets (including ATB2) from Y solely in exchange for P stock in a reorganization described in section 368(a)(1)(A) by reason of section 368(a)(2)(D). No gain or loss is recognized on either acquisition. In a separate transaction, D transfers ATB2 to new subsidiary C in exchange for all of the C stock in a transaction that satisfies the requirements of section 351 and in which no gain or loss is recognized. If D were to distribute the C stock in a separate transaction, D and C can rely on ATB1 and ATB2, respectively, to satisfy the requirements of section 355(b). ATB1 and ATB2 were acquired in transactions in which no gain or loss was recognized, and were not acquired in exchange for assets of the DSAG. See paragraph (b)(4)(ii) of this section. The result would be the same if D acquired all of the assets of T (including the X stock) and Z (including the Y stock) in the reorganizations instead of acquiring the assets of X and Y, and then transferred the Y stock to C. See paragraphs (b)(1)(ii) and (b)(4)(ii) of this section.

Example 29. Taxable transfer of ATB by distributing to controlled. The facts are the same as the original facts in *Example 28* except that before and after the transfer to C, D owned section 368(c) stock but not section 1504(a)(2) stock of C, and recognized gain under section 357(c) on the transfer of ATB2 to C. D and C can rely on ATB1 and ATB2, respectively, to satisfy the requirements of section 355(b). See paragraph (b)(4)(iii)(A) of this section. The result would be the same if C purchased ATB2 from D. The result would also be the same if D acquired all of the assets of T (including the X stock) and Z (including the Y stock) in the reorganizations instead of acquiring the assets of X and Y, and then C purchased the Y stock from D. See paragraphs (b)(1)(ii) and (b)(4)(iii)(A) of this section.

Example 30. Assets for controlled stock in a section 351 transaction. For more than five years, unrelated D and C have engaged in the active conduct of ATB1 and ATB2, respectively. In year 6, D transfers trucks to C to be used in ATB2 in exchange for section 368(c) stock of C in a transaction to which section 351 applies and in which no gain or loss is recognized. If D were to distribute the C stock, C could not rely on ATB2 to satisfy the requirements of section 355(b) unless D's year 6 acquisition of the C stock is not in the pre-distribution period because D acquired section 368(c) stock of C, a corporation engaged in ATB2, in exchange for assets not constituting the trade or business. See paragraphs (b)(4)(i)(B) and (b)(4)(ii)(A) of this section. The result would be the same even if C became a DSAG member as a result of the year 6 transfer. See paragraphs (b)(4)(i)(A) and (b)(4)(ii)(A) of this section.

Example 31. ATB for controlled stock in a reorganization. For more than five years, unrelated D and T have engaged in the active conduct of ATB1 and ATB2, respectively. Throughout this period, D has owned all of the sole class of C stock. In year 6, T merges into C solely in exchange for C stock in a reorganization described in section 368(a)(1)(A) and in which no gain or loss is recognized. As a result, the T shareholders receive 20 percent of the sole class of C stock. Because C acquired ATB2 in exchange for C stock, solely for purposes of determining whether ATB2 can be relied on to satisfy the requirements of section 355(b), D is treated as having acquired its 80 percent of the C stock in year 6 in a transaction in which gain or loss was recognized. See paragraph (b)(4)(iv)(E) of this section. Accordingly, if D were to distribute the C stock, C could not rely on ATB2 to satisfy the requirements of section 355(b) unless C's year 6 acquisition of ATB2 is not in the pre-distribution period because ATB2 was in effect indirectly acquired in exchange for D's assets. See paragraphs (b)(4)(i)(A), (b)(4)(ii)(A), and (b)(4)(iv)(E) of this section.

Example 32. ATB and controlled stock for distributing stock in a section 351 transaction. For more than five years, T and unrelated C have engaged in the active conduct of ATB1 and ATB2, respectively. Unrelated P owns all of the stock of D. In year 6, P purchases ATB1 from T, and section 368(c) stock of C from the C shareholders. In year 6, P contributes the C stock and ATB1 to D solely in exchange for additional D stock in a transaction to which section 351 applies and in which no gain or loss is recognized. If D were to subsequently distribute the C stock in a separate transaction, D can rely on ATB1, and C can rely on ATB2 to satisfy the requirements of section 355(b) because neither ATB1 nor control of C was acquired in exchange for assets of the DSAG. See paragraphs (b)(4)(i)(A), (b)(4)(i)(B), and (b)(4)(ii) of this section. The fact that P, an affiliate of D, purchased ATB1 and section 368(c) stock of C in year 6 is not relevant.

Example 33. ATB for distributing stock in a section 351 transaction with section 357(c) gain. The facts are the same as *Example 32* except that D has owned section 368(c) stock of C for more than five years, P only purchases ATB1 from T, and P recognizes under section 357(c) gain on the transfer of ATB1 to D as a result of D assuming liabilities of P. D cannot rely on ATB1 to satisfy the requirements of section 355(b) until D's year 6 acquisition of ATB1 is no longer in the pre-distribution period because D acquired ATB1 in a transaction in which gain or loss was recognized. See paragraph (b)(4)(i)(A) of this section.

Example 34. Partnership distributions. For more than five years, X and Y have engaged in the active conduct of ATB1 and ATB2, respectively. Throughout this period, unrelated D has owned a 90-percent interest in Partnership. D is attributed any trade or business assets and activities of Partnership under paragraph (b)(2)(v) of this section. In year 6, Partnership purchases ATB1 from X and all of the Y stock from its owner. In year 9, Partnership distributes ATB1 and all of the Y stock to D in a non-liquidating distribution. Assume that no gain or loss is recognized by Partnership or any partner on the distribution. As a result of the distribution, Y becomes a DSAG member, and D is treated as having acquired Y's assets (and activities). See paragraphs (b)(1)(ii) and (b)(1)(iii) of this section. If D were to make a distribution, ATB1 could not be relied on to satisfy the requirements of section 355(b) unless Partnership's year 6 acquisition of ATB1 is not in the pre-distribution period. See paragraphs (b)(2)(v), (b)(3)(iii), and (b)(4)(ii)(B) of this section. If D were to make a distribution, ATB2 could not be relied on to satisfy the requirements of section 355(b) unless D's year 9 acquisition of the Y stock is not in the pre-distribution period. See paragraphs (b)(2)(v)(A) and (b)(4)(ii)(B) of this section. Alternatively, if in year 9 Partnership only makes a pro rata distribution of all the Y stock to its partners such that D receives 90 percent of the Y stock, ATB2 cannot be relied on until Partnership's year 6 acquisition of all of the Y stock is no longer in the pre-distribution period. See paragraph (b)(4)(ii)(B) of this section.

Example 35. Partnership distribution (new SAG member). For more than five years, D has owned a 50-percent interest in Partnership. The remaining interests in Partnership are owned by unrelated parties. Throughout this period, Partnership has engaged in the

active conduct of ATB1, and D has been attributed the trade or business assets and activities of Partnership's ATB1 under paragraph (b)(2)(v) of this section. In year 6, pursuant to an integrated plan, Partnership contributes ATB1 to new subsidiary S, and distributes all of the S stock to D in liquidation of D's 50-percent interest in Partnership. Assume that no gain or loss is recognized by Partnership or any partner on the distribution. As a result, S becomes a DSAG member, and D is treated as having acquired S's assets (and activities). See paragraphs (b)(1)(ii) and (b)(1)(iii) of this section. Because D was attributed ATB1 immediately before the incorporation and distribution by Partnership, and S became a DSAG member as a result of the distribution, Partnership's distribution of the S stock to D is not an acquisition of ATB1. See paragraphs (b)(3)(iii) and (b)(4)(ii)(B) of this section. Accordingly, if D were to make a distribution, it could rely on ATB1 to satisfy the requirements of section 355(b).

Example 36. Transfer of partnership in a reorganization and distribution. For more than five years, T has owned a 40-percent interest in Partnership which has engaged in the active conduct of ATB1. Throughout this period, T has been attributed the trade or business assets and activities of Partnership's ATB1 under paragraph (b)(2)(v) of this section. In year 6, T merges into S, a wholly owned subsidiary of unrelated D, solely in exchange for D stock in a reorganization described in section 368(a)(1)(A) by reason of section 368(a)(2)(D). No gain or loss is recognized. If D were to make a distribution, D can rely on ATB1 because ATB1 has been actively conducted throughout the pre-distribution period, and the interest in Partnership was acquired in a transaction in which no gain or loss was recognized and was not acquired in exchange for assets of the DSAG. See paragraphs (b)(2)(v), (b)(3)(i), and (b)(4)(ii) of this section. The results would be the same if T owned only a 20-percent interest in Partnership, employees of T performed active and substantial management functions for Partnership's trade or business assets and activities prior to the merger, and employees of S (or an affiliate of S) performed active and substantial management functions for Partnership's trade or business assets and activities after the merger. See paragraphs (b)(2)(iii), (b)(2)(v), (b)(3), and (b)(4)(ii) of this section.

Example 37. Transferred ATB sold (SAG member). For more than five years, D and unrelated T have engaged in the active conduct of ATB1 and ATB2, respectively. In year 6, D contributes ATB1 to T in exchange for T stock in a transaction to which section 351 applies. No gain or loss is recognized on the contribution. Immediately after the contribution T is a DSAG member. In year 8, in response to unanticipated market changes, T sells ATB1 to an unrelated third party. Although T became a DSAG member as a result of D acquiring T stock in exchange for ATB1 in a transaction in which no gain or loss was recognized, ATB1 is not the trade or business to be relied upon. Accordingly, D cannot rely on ATB2 until the year 6 transaction is no longer in the pre-distribution period because D acquired ATB2 in exchange for D's assets not constituting the active trade or business to be relied on. See paragraphs (b)(4)(i)(A) and (b)(4)(ii)(A) of this section.

Example 38. Transferred ATB sold (partnership). The facts are the same as *Example 37* except that, in year 6, D and T contribute ATB1 and ATB2, respectively, to Partnership in a transaction to which section 721 applies. In the exchange, D and T each receive a 50-percent interest in Partnership. In year 8, in response to unanticipated market changes, Partnership sells ATB1 to an unrelated third party. If D were to make a distribution, D could not rely on ATB2 under paragraph (b)(2)(v)(B) of this section unless the year 6 transaction is not in the pre-distribution period because D acquired ATB2 in exchange for D's assets not constituting the trade or business to be relied on. See paragraphs (b)(4)(i)(A) and (b)(4)(ii)(A) of this section.

Example 39. Indirect acquisition of control of distributing's ATB. For more than five years, D and T have engaged in the active conduct of ATB1 and ATB2, respectively. All of the T stock is owned by individuals. In year 6, T purchases all the stock of D in a transaction in which gain or loss is recognized. In a separate transaction, T merges downstream into D solely in exchange for D stock in a reorganization described in section 368(a)(1)(A) and (D). No gain or loss is recognized. In year 7, D transfers ATB2 formerly conducted by T to new subsidiary C, and then distributes the C stock to the D shareholders. Although D acquired ATB2 solely in exchange for D stock in a transaction in which no gain or loss was recognized, the requirements of section 355(b) are not satisfied because ATB1, the business of D, was indirectly acquired by T, a predecessor of D, during the pre-distribution period in a transaction in which gain or loss was recognized. See paragraphs (b)(4)(i)(A) and (b)(4)(iv)(A) of this section. The result would be the same if prior to the year 6 acquisition D and wholly owned subsidiary C were engaged in the active conduct of ATB1 and ATB2, respectively, and T had no ATB.

Example 40. Exception for corporate distributee. For more than five years, T has owned all of the stock of D which in turn owned all of the stock of C. Throughout this period, D and C have engaged in the active conduct of ATB1 and ATB2, respectively. In year 6, P purchases all the stock of T. In year 7, P liquidates T in a transaction in which no gain or loss is recognized under section 332. Under section 334(b), P's basis in the D stock is determined in whole by reference to T's basis in the D stock. In year 8, D distributes the C stock to P. While the D stock was indirectly acquired in a taxable transaction, the adjusted basis that P, the distributee corporation, has in the D stock was determined in whole by reference to T's adjusted basis. Accordingly, D and C satisfy the requirements of section 355(b). See paragraph (b)(4)(iii)(C) of this section. If P were to distribute either the D stock or C stock, neither ATB1 nor ATB2 could be relied on unless the year 6 acquisition of the T stock is not in the pre-distribution period. See paragraph (b)(4)(iii)(C) of this section. The results would be the same if P acquired all of T's assets in exchange for P stock and other property in a reorganization described in section 368(a)(1)(A).

Example 41. Acquisition of section 368(c) stock of controlled, DSAG member. For more than five years, D has owned section 1504(a)(2) stock but not section 368(c) stock of C. Throughout this period, C has engaged in the active conduct of ATB1. In year 6, D purchased additional shares of C stock. As a result, D acquired section 368(c) stock of C. If D were to make a distribution of the C stock, C could rely on ATB1 to satisfy the requirement of section 355(b). C was a DSAG member, so D was engaged in ATB1 prior to the year 6 purchase of additional C stock. Accordingly, D's acquisition of additional stock of a DSAG member is disregarded in applying paragraph (b)(4)(i)(A) of this section, and paragraph (b)(4)(i)(B) of this section does not apply to this acquisition of additional C stock. See paragraphs (b)(1)(ii) and (b)(4)(iv)(F) of this section.

Example 42. Controlled becoming a DSAG member. For more than five years, D has owned section 368(c) stock but not section 1504(a)(2) stock of C. Throughout this period, D and C have engaged in the active conduct of ATB1 and ATB2, respectively. In year 6, D purchases the remaining C stock. If D distributes all the C stock, C cannot rely on ATB2 to satisfy the requirements of section 355(b) because C became a DSAG member (and thus D acquired ATB2) in a transaction in which gain or loss was recognized. See paragraphs (b)(1)(ii), (b)(4)(i)(A), and (b)(4)(iv)(F) of this section.

Example 43. Nontaxable multi-step acquisition of control. For more than five years, unrelated D and C have engaged in the active conduct of ATB1 and ATB2, respectively. C has two classes of stock outstanding. X owns all 95 shares of the class A stock of C, representing 95 percent of the voting power and 70 percent of the value, and Y owns all of the class B stock of C, representing five percent of the voting power and 30 percent of the value. In year 6, D acquires 10 shares of class A C stock from X in a transaction in which gain or loss was recognized. In year 7, in a separate transaction, D acquires an additional 80 shares of class A C stock from X solely in exchange for D voting stock in a reorganization described in section 368(a)(1)(B). No gain or loss is recognized. In year 8, in a separate transaction, D acquires the remaining five shares of class A C stock from X in a transaction in which gain or loss was recognized. Because D only acquires 70 percent of the value of C stock, C does not become a DSAG member. In year 9, D distributes the 95 shares of class A C stock to the D shareholders. At the time D first acquired control of C, D owned an amount of C stock constituting control that was acquired in a transaction in which no gain or loss was recognized. Accordingly, D and C both satisfy the requirements of section 355(b). See paragraphs (b)(4)(i)(B) and (b)(4)(iv)(B) of this section.

Example 44. Taxable multi-step acquisition of control. The facts are the same as *Example 43* except that in year 7 D acquires 70 shares of class A C stock solely in exchange for D voting stock in a reorganization described in section 368(a)(1)(B). No gain or loss is recognized. At the time D first acquired control of C, D did not own an amount of C stock constituting control that was acquired in one or more transactions in which no gain or loss was recognized or by reason of such transactions combined with acquisitions before the pre-distribution period. Accordingly, C cannot rely on ATB2 to satisfy the requirements of section 355(b) until D's year 6 acquisition of the 10 shares of class A C stock is no longer in the pre-distribution period. See paragraphs (b)(4)(i)(B) and (b)(4)(iv)(B) of this section.

Example 45. Taxable acquisition of control. For more than five years, unrelated D and C have engaged in the active conduct of ATB1 and ATB2, respectively. In year 6, D acquires section 368(c) stock but not section 1504(a)(2) stock of C from unrelated T in a reorganization described in section 368(a)(1)(A) by reason of section 368(a)(2)(E) through the use of a newly created transitory subsidiary of D. In the reorganization, T receives consideration 95 percent of which is D voting common stock and five percent of which is cash. Because D acquired control of C in a single transaction in which gain or loss was recognized, paragraph (b)(4)(iv)(B) of this section does not apply. Accordingly, C cannot rely on ATB2 to satisfy the requirements of section 355(b) until D's year 6 acquisition of control of C is no longer in the pre-distribution period. See paragraph (b)(4)(i)(B) of this section.

Example 46. Taxable multi-step indirect acquisition of control. For more than five years, C has engaged in the active conduct of ATB1. T owns exactly 80 percent of the total combined voting power of all classes of C stock entitled to vote and 80 percent of the total number of shares of all other classes of C stock, but T owns less than 80 percent of the total value of the C stock. In year 6, unrelated D acquires 10 percent of the sole outstanding class of stock of T in a transaction in which gain or loss is recognized. In year 8, in a separate transaction, T merges into D solely in exchange for D stock in a reorganization described in section 368(a)(1)(A). No gain or loss is recognized. As a result, D owns section 368(c) stock of C. Because D indirectly acquired 10 percent of the C stock owned by T in year 6, at the time D first acquired control of C, D did not own stock constituting control of C that it acquired in one or more transactions in which no gain or loss was recognized or by reason of such transactions combined with acquisitions before the pre-distribution period. Accordingly, C cannot rely on ATB1 to satisfy the requirements of section 355(b) until D's year 6 acquisition of the T stock is no longer in the pre-distribution period. See paragraphs (b)(4)(i)(B) and (b)(4)(iv)(B) of this section.

Example 47. Nontaxable multi-step acquisition of SAG member (or ATB). For more than five years, S has engaged in the active conduct of ATB1. X owns all 100 shares of the sole outstanding class of S stock. In year 6, unrelated D acquires 10 shares of S stock from X in a transaction in which gain or loss was recognized. In year 7, in a separate transaction, D acquires an additional 80 shares of S stock from X solely in exchange for D voting stock in a reorganization described in section 368(a)(1)(B). No gain or loss is recognized. As a result, S becomes a DSAG member. In year 8, in a separate transaction, D acquires another 5 shares of S stock from X in a transaction in which gain or loss was recognized. Because at the time S first became a DSAG member, D owned an amount of S stock meeting the requirements of section 1504(a)(2) that was acquired in a transaction in which no gain or loss was recognized, D can rely on ATB1 to satisfy the requirements of section 355(b) as of the year 7 transaction. See paragraphs (b)(4)(i)(A) and (b)(4)(iv)(C) of this section. The acquisition by D of other S stock in a separate transaction in which gain or loss was recognized during the pre-distribution period is disregarded. See paragraph (b)(1)(ii) of this section. The result would be the same if, in year 7, instead of acquiring S stock in a reorganization described in section 368(a)(1)(B), S merged into D in exchange for D stock in a reorganization described in section 368(a)(1)(A) in which no gain or loss was recognized. See paragraphs (b)(4)(i)(A) and (b)(4)(iv)(D) of this section.

Example 48. Taxable multi-step acquisition of SAG member (or ATB). The facts are the same as *Example 47* except that in year 6 D acquires 21 shares of S stock in a transaction in which gain or loss was recognized, and in year 7, in a separate transaction, D acquires an additional 79 shares of S stock solely in exchange for D voting stock in a reorganization described in section 368(a)(1)(B). No gain or loss is recognized, and S becomes a DSAG member. D cannot rely on ATB1 to satisfy the requirements of section 355(b) until D's year 6 acquisition of the 21 shares of S stock is no longer in the pre-distribution period because at the time S first became a DSAG member D did not own an amount of S stock meeting the requirements of section 1504(a)(2) that was acquired in one or more transactions in which no gain or loss was recognized or by reason of such transactions combined with acquisitions before the pre-distribution period. See paragraphs (b)(4)(i)(A) and (b)(4)(iv)(C) of this section. The result would be the same if, in year 7, in a separate transaction, S merged into D in exchange for D stock in a reorganization described in section 368(a)(1)(A) in which no gain or loss was recognized. See paragraphs (b)(4)(i)(A) and (b)(4)(iv)(D) of this section. The result would also be the same if in year 6 D acquired 10 shares of S stock in a transaction in which gain or loss was recognized and, in year 7, in a separate transaction, D acquired an additional 70 shares of S stock solely in exchange for D voting stock in a reorganization described in section 368(a)(1)(B). See paragraphs (b)(4)(i)(A) and (b)(4)(iv)(C) of this section.

Example 49. Nontaxable multi-step indirect acquisition using subsidiary stock. For more than five years, X has owned all of the sole outstanding class of S stock. Throughout this period, S and unrelated T have engaged in the active conduct of ATB1 and ATB2, respectively. In year 6, T merges into S solely in exchange for S stock in a reorganization described in section 368(a)(1)(A). No gain or loss is recognized. Immediately after the merger, X and the former T shareholders own 80 percent and 20 percent of the S stock, respectively. In year 8, unrelated D acquires all of the S shares held by X solely in exchange for D voting stock in a reorganization described in section 368(a)(1)(B). No gain or loss is recognized. As a result, S becomes a DSAG member. Because D acquired ATB1 and ATB2 in a transaction in which no gain or loss was recognized, solely in exchange for D stock, D can rely on both ATB1 and ATB2 to satisfy the requirements of section 355(b). Because X is neither a predecessor of D nor a DSAG member, paragraph (b)(4)(iv)(E) of this section is not applicable.

Example 50. Taxable multi-step indirect acquisition using subsidiary stock. The facts are the same as *Example 49* except that, for more than five years, D has owned 50 percent of the sole outstanding class of X stock. In year 8, instead of D acquiring the S stock, S merges into D solely in exchange for D stock in a reorganization described in section 368(a)(1)(A). No gain or loss is recognized. Because D indirectly owned S stock and S acquired ATB2 in exchange for S stock, paragraph (b)(4)(iv)(E) of this section is applicable. Under paragraph (b)(4)(iv)(E) of this section, for purposes of applying paragraph (b)(4) of this section with respect to ATB2, D is treated as having indirectly acquired in year 6 the S stock it indirectly owns immediately after the merger of T into S in a transaction in which gain or loss was recognized. Thus, D is treated as having indirectly acquired 40 percent of the S stock in a transaction in which gain or loss is recognized at the time of the merger of T into S. Further, if the merger of T into S is in the pre-distribution period, under paragraph (b)(4)(iv)(D) of this section, D will be treated as having acquired ATB2 in a transaction in which gain or loss is recognized because, immediately before the merger of S into D, D indirectly owned 40 percent of the S stock that had been acquired in a transaction in which gain or loss was recognized. Accordingly, D cannot rely on ATB2 to satisfy the requirements of section 355(b) until the year 6 merger of T into S is no longer in the pre-distribution period. However, D can rely on ATB1 to satisfy the requirements of section 355(b). Alternatively, if X, instead of S, merged into D, S would become a DSAG member and X would be a predecessor of D. If so, for purposes of applying paragraph (b)(4) of this section with respect to ATB2, D is treated as having acquired 80 percent of the S stock in year 6 in a transaction in which gain or loss was recognized. Accordingly, D cannot rely on ATB2 to satisfy the requirements of section 355(b) until the year 6 merger of T

into S is no longer in the pre-distribution period. See paragraphs (b)(1)(iii), (b)(4)(i)(A), (b)(4)(iv)(A), and (b)(4)(iv)(E) of this section. However, D can rely on ATB1 to satisfy the requirements of section 355(b).

Example 51. Taxable multi-step indirect acquisition of SAG member (or ATB). For more than five years, T has engaged in the active conduct of ATB1. Throughout this period, X owned all of the sole outstanding class of T stock, and D owned 50 percent of the sole outstanding stock of S. In year 6, S acquires 50 percent of the sole outstanding class of the X stock in a transaction in which gain or loss is recognized. In year 8, X merges into D solely in exchange for D stock. No gain or loss is recognized. As a result, T becomes a DSAG member. Because D indirectly acquired more than 20 percent of the T stock (D indirectly acquired 25 percent of T) in year 6, at the time T first became a DSAG member D did not own an amount of T stock meeting the requirements of section 1504(a)(2) that it acquired in one or more transactions in which no gain or loss was recognized or by reason of such transactions combined with acquisitions before the predistribution period. Accordingly, D cannot rely on ATB1 to satisfy the requirements of section 355(b) until D's year 6 indirect acquisition of the T stock is no longer in the pre-distribution period. See paragraphs (b)(4)(i)(A) and (b)(4)(iv)(C) of this section. The result would be the same if, instead of X, in year 8, T merged into D solely in exchange for D stock. See paragraphs (b)(4)(i) and (b)(4)(iv) of this section.

Distribution of Stock: Device and Active Trade or Business: Guidance

Distribution of Stock: Device and Active Trade or Business: Guidance.—Reg. §§1.355-8 and 1.355-9, clarifying the application of the device prohibition and the active business requirement of section 355 and affecting corporations that distribute the stock of controlled corporations, their shareholders, and their security holders, are proposed (published in the Federal Register on July 15, 2016) (REG-134016-15).

Par. 5. Reserved §1.355-8 is added to read as follows:

§1.355-8. Definition of predecessors and successors and limitations on gain recognition.—[Reserved]

Par. 6. Section 1.355-9 is added to read as follows:

§1.355-9. Minimum percentage of Five-Year-Active-Business Assets.—(a) *Definitions.*—The following definitions apply for purposes of this section:

(1) *Distributing, Controlled.*—*Distributing* means the distributing corporation within the meaning of §1.355-1(b). *Controlled* means the controlled corporation within the meaning of §1.355-1(b).

(2) *Five-Year-Active Business.*—*Five-Year-Active Business* means the active conduct of a trade or business that satisfies the requirements and limitations of section 355(b)(2) and §1.355-3(b).

(3) *Five-Year-Active-Business Assets.*—*Five-Year-Active-Business Assets* of a corporation means its gross assets used in one or more Five-Year-Active Businesses. Such assets include cash and cash equivalents held as a reasonable amount of working capital for one or more Five-Year-Active Businesses. Such assets also include assets required (by binding commitment or legal requirement) to be held to provide for exigencies related to a Five-Year-Active Business or for regulatory purposes with respect to a Five-Year-Active Business. For this purpose, such assets include assets the holder is required (by binding commitment or legal requirement) to hold to secure or otherwise provide for a financial obligation reasonably expected to arise from a Five-Year-Active Business and assets held to implement a binding commitment to expend funds to expand or improve a Five-Year-Active Business.

(4) *Non-Five-Year-Active-Business Assets.*—*Non-Five-Year-Active-Business Assets* of a corporation means its gross assets other than its Five-Year-Active-Business Assets.

(5) *Total Assets.*—*Total Assets* of a corporation means its Five-Year-Active-Business Assets and its Non-Five-Year-Active-Business Assets.

(6) *Five-Year-Active-Business Asset Percentage.*—The *Five-Year-Active-Business Asset Percentage* of a corporation is the percentage determined by dividing the fair market value of its Five-Year-Active-Business Assets by the fair market value of its Total Assets.

(7) *Separate Affiliated Group, SAG, CSAG, and DSAG.*—*Separate Affiliated Group* (or *SAG*), *CSAG*, and *DSAG* have the same meanings as in §1.355-2(d)(2)(iv)(B)(6).

(b) *Five percent minimum Five-Year-Active-Business Asset Percentage.*—For the requirements of section 355(a)(1)(C) and section 355(b) to be satisfied with respect to a distribution, the Five-Year-Active-Business Asset Percentage of each of Distributing and Controlled must be at least five percent.

(c) *Operating rules.*—The following operating rules apply for purposes of this section:

(1) *Treatment of SAG and fair market value.*—The operating rules in §1.355-2(d)(2)(iv)(D)(2) (treatment of SAG as a single corporation) and (5) (fair market value) apply.

(2) *Time to identify assets, determine character of assets, and determine fair market value of assets.*—The provisions of §1.355-2(d)(2)(iv)(D)(3) (time to identify assets and determine character of assets) apply, except that references to paragraph (d)(2)(iv) are treated as references to this section and "Business Assets or Nonbusiness Assets" is replaced with "Five-Year-Active-Business Assets or Non-Five-Year-Active-Business Assets," and the provisions of §1.355-2(d)(2)(iv)(D)(4) (time to determine fair market value of assets) apply.

(3) *Interest in partnership.*—(i) *In general.*—Except as provided in paragraph (c)(3)(ii) of this section, an interest in a partnership is a Non-Five-Year-Active-Business Asset.

(ii) *Exception for certain interests in partnerships.*—If Distributing or Controlled is considered to be engaged in one or more Five-Year-Active-Businesses conducted by a partnership, the fair market value of the corporation's interest in the partnership will be allocated between Five-Year-Active-Business Assets and Non-Five-Year-Active-Business Assets in the same proportion as the proportion of the fair market values of the Five-Year-Active-Business Assets and Non-Five-Year-Active-Business Assets of the partnership.

(d) *Anti-abuse rule.*—A transaction or series of transactions undertaken with a principal purpose of affecting the Five-Year-Active-Business Asset Percentage of any corporation will not be given effect for purposes of applying this §1.355-9. For this purpose, a transaction or series of transactions includes a change in the form of ownership of an asset; an issuance, assumption, or repayment of indebtedness or other obligations; or an issuance or redemption of stock. However, this paragraph (d) generally does not apply to a non-transitory acquisition or disposition of assets, other than an acquisition from or disposition to a person the ownership of whose stock would, under section 318(a) (other than paragraph (4) thereof), be attributed to Distributing or Controlled, or to a non-transitory transfer of assets between Distributing and Controlled.

(e) *Effective/applicability date.*—(1) *In general.*—Except as provided in paragraph (e)(2) of this section, this section applies to transactions occurring on or after the date the Treasury decision adopting these regulations as final regulations is published in the **Federal Register**.

(2) *Transition rule.*—This section does not apply to a distribution that is—

(i) Made pursuant to an agreement, resolution, or other corporate action that is binding on or before the date the Treasury decision adopting these regulations as final regulations is published in the **Federal Register** and at all times thereafter;

(ii) Described in a ruling request submitted to the Internal Revenue Service on or before July 15, 2016; or

(iii) Described in a public announcement or filing with the Securities and Exchange Commission on or before the date the Treasury decision adopting these regulations as final regulations is published in the **Federal Register**. [Reg. § 1.355-9.]

Section 301 Regulations: Statutory Changes Reflected

Section 301 Regulations: Statutory Changes Reflected.—Amendments to Reg. § 1.356-1, updating existing regulations under section 301 to reflect statutory changes made by the Technical and Miscellaneous Revenue Act of 1988, which changes provide that the amount of a distribution of property made by a corporation to its shareholder is the fair market value of the distributed property, are proposed (published in the Federal Register on March 26, 2019) (REG-121694-16).

Par. 3. Section 1.356-1 is amended by revising paragraph (f) to read as follows:

§ 1.356-1. Receipt of additional consideration in connection with an exchange.

* * *

(f) See § 1.301–1(j) for certain transactions which are not within the scope of section 356.

* * *

Installment Obligations: Dispositions: Nonrecognition of Gain or Loss

Installment Obligations: Dispositions: Nonrecognition of Gain or Loss—Amendments to Reg. § 1.361-1, relating to the nonrecognition of gain or loss on certain dispositions of an installment obligation, are proposed (published in the Federal Register on December 23, 2014) (REG-109187-11).

☐ Par. 3. Section 1.361-1 is amended by adding new second and third sentences to read as follows:

§ 1.361-1. Nonrecognition of gain or loss to corporations.—* * * See § 1.453B-1(c) for rules requiring a corporation transferring an installment obligation to the acquiring corporation (as that term is used in § 1.368-1) to recognize gain or loss upon the receipt of stock of the acquiring corporation or another party to the reorganization (as defined in § 1.368-2(f)) in satisfaction of that installment obligation. The preceding sentence applies to satisfactions of installment obligations after the date these regulations are published as final regulations in the **Federal Register**.* * *

Reorganizations: Foreign Corporations: Transfer of Property

Reorganizations: Foreign Corporations: Transfer of Property.—Reg. § § 1.367(a)-1T and 1.367(a)-6T, relating to transfers of property to foreign corporations, are proposed (published in the Federal Register on May 16, 1986) (LR-3-86). Reg. § 1.367(a)-3T was adopted as Reg. § 1.367(a)-3 by T.D. 8702 on December 27, 1996. Reg. § § 1.367(a)-2T and 1.367(a)-4T were adopted and § 1.367(a)-5T was removed by T.D. 9803 on December 15, 2016.

§ 1.367(a)-1. Transfers to foreign corporations subject to section 367(a): In general.

§ 1.367(a)-6. Transfer of foreign branch with previously deducted losses.

Corporate Reorganizations: Foreign Corporations: Liquidating Distribution

Corporate Distributions: Foreign Corporation.—Amendments to Temporary Reg. § § 1.367(a)-1T, relating to the distribution of stock and securities by a domestic corporation to a person who is not a United States person, and also relating to a liquidating distribution of property by a domestic or foreign corporation to a foreign corporation, are proposed (published in the Federal Register on January 16, 1990). Reg. § 7.367(b)-1 was removed by T.D. 8862, effective February 23, 2000.

§ 1.367(a)-1T. Transfers to foreign corporations subject to section 367(a): In general (temporary).

CFCs: U.S. Shareholders: Ownership Attribution

CFCs: U.S. Shareholders: Ownership Attribution.—Amendments to Reg. § 1.367(a)-8, relating to the modification of section 958(b) of the Internal Revenue Code by the Tax Cuts and Jobs Act, which was enacted on December 22, 2017, are proposed (published in the Federal Register on October 2, 2019) (REG-104223-18).

Par. 4. Section 1.367(a)-8 is amended by:

1. Revising the second sentence of paragraph (k)(14)(ii).

2. In paragraph (p)(3), designating Examples 1 through 3 as paragraphs (p)(3)(i) through (iii), respectively.

3. In newly redesignated paragraphs (p)(3)(i) through (iii), redesignating the paragraphs in the first column as the paragraphs in the second column:

Old Paragraphs	New Paragraphs
(p)(3)(i)(i) and (ii)	(p)(3)(i)(A) and (B)
(p)(3)(ii)(i) and (ii)	(p)(3)(ii)(A) and (B)
(p)(3)(iii)(i) and (ii)	(p)(3)(iii)(A) and (B)

4. In each newly redesignated paragraph listed in the first column, removing the language in the second column and adding in its place the language in the third column:

Paragraph	Remove	Add
(p)(3)(i)(B)	this *Example 1*	In paragraph (p)(3)(i)(A) of this section (the facts of this *Example 1*)
(p)(3)(ii)(B)	this *Example 2*	In paragraph (p)(3)(ii)(A) of this section (the facts of this *Example 1*)

5. In paragraph (q)(2):

a. Removing the language "at least 5% (applying the attribution rules of section 318, as modified by section 958(b))" each place that it appears and adding "at least 5% (determined as provided in paragraph (k)(14)(ii) of this section)" in its place.

b. Designating *Examples 1* through 25 as paragraphs (q)(2)(i) through (xxv), respectively.

6. In newly redesignated paragraphs (q)(2)(i) through (xxv), redesignating the paragraphs in the first column as the paragraphs in the second column:

Old Paragraphs	New Paragraphs
(q)(2)(i)(i) and (ii)	(q)(2)(i)(A) and (B)
(q)(2)(ii)(i) and (ii)	(q)(2)(ii)(A) and (B)
(q)(2)(ii)(B)(A) and (B)	(q)(2)(ii)(B)(*1*) and (*2*)
(q)(2)(iii)(i) and (ii)	(q)(2)(iii)(A) and (B)
(q)(2)(iv)(i) and (ii)	(q)(2)(iv)(A) and (B)
(q)(2)(iv)(B)(A) and (B)	(q)(2)(iv)(B)(*1*) and (*2*)
(q)(2)(iv)(B)(2)(*1*) through (*3*)	(q)(2)(iv)(B)(2)(*i*) through (*iii*)
(q)(2)(v)(i) and (ii)	(q)(2)(v)(A) and (B)
(q)(2)(vi)(i) through (iii)	(q)(2)(vi)(A) through (C)
(q)(2)(vi)(B)(A) and (B)	(q)(2)(vi)(B)(*1*) and (*2*)
(q)(2)(vi)(B)(2)(*1*) through (*3*)	(q)(2)(vi)(B)(2)(*i*) through (*iii*)
(q)(2)(vii)(i) and (ii)	(q)(2)(vii)(A) and (B)
(q)(2)(viii)(i) and (ii)	(q)(2)(viii)(A) and (B)
(q)(2)(ix)(i) and (ii)	(q)(2)(ix)(A) and (B)
(q)(2)(x)(i) and (ii)	(q)(2)(x)(A) and (B)
(q)(2)(x)(B)(A) through (C)	(q)(2)(x)(B)(*1*) through (*3*)
(q)(2)(xi)(i) through (iii)	(q)(2)(xi)(A) through (C)
(q)(2)(xii)(i) and (ii)	(q)(2)(xii)(A) and (B)
(q)(2)(xii)(B)(A) through (C)	(q)(2)(xii)(B)(*1*) through (*3*)
(q)(2)(xiii)(i) and (ii)	(q)(2)(xiii)(A) and (B)
(q)(2)(xiv)(i) and (ii)	(q)(2)(xiv)(A) and (B)
(q)(2)(xiv)(B)(A) and (B)	(q)(2)(xiv)(B)(*1*) and (*2*)
(q)(2)(xv)(i) and (ii)	(q)(2)(xv)(A) and (B)
(q)(2)(xvi)(i) and (ii)	(q)(2)(xvi)(A) and (B)
(q)(2)(xvii)(i) and (ii)	(q)(2)(xvii)(A) and (B)
(q)(2)(xvii)(B)(A) through (C)	(q)(2)(xvii)(B)(1) through (3)
(q)(2)(xvii)(B)(3)(*1*) through (*3*)	(q)(2)(xvii)(B)(3)(*i*) through (*iii*)
(q)(2)(xviii)(i) and (ii)	(q)(2)(xviii)(A) and (B)
(q)(2)(xix)(i) and (ii)	(q)(2)(xix)(A) and (B)
(q)(2)(xx)(i) through (vi)	(q)(2)(xx)(A) through (F)
(q)(2)(xx)(B)(A) and (B)	(q)(2)(xx)(B)(1) and (2)
(q)(2)(xx)(B)(*1*)(1) and (2)	(q)(2)(xx)(B)(*1*)(*i*) and (*ii*)
(q)(2)(xxi)(i) and (ii)	(q)(2)(xxi)(A) and (B)
(q)(2)(xxi)(B)(A) through (C)	(q)(2)(xxi)(B)(*1*) through (*3*)
(q)(2)(xxii)(i) through (iii)	(q)(2)(xxii)(A) through (C)
(q)(2)(xxii)(B)(A) through (C)	(q)(2)(xxii)(B)(*1*) through (*3*)
(q)(2)(xxii)(C)(A) through (C)	(q)(2)(xxii)(C)(*1*) through (*3*)
(q)(2)(xxiii)(i) through (iv)	(q)(2)(xxiii)(A) through (D)
(q)(2)(xxiii)(B)(A) through (D)	(q)(2)(xxiii)(B)(*1*) through (*4*)
(q)(2)(xxiii)(C)(A) and (B)	(q)(2)(xxiii)(C)(*1*) and (*2*)
(q)(2)(xxiv)(i) and (ii)	(q)(2)(xxiv)(A) and (B)
(q)(2)(xxv)(i) and (ii)	(q)(2)(xxv)(A) and (B)

7. In each newly redesignated paragraph listed in the first column, removing the language in the second column and adding in its place the language in the third column:

Paragraph	Remove	Add
(q)(2)(ii)(B)(*2*)	paragraph (ii)(A) of this *Example 2*	paragraph (q)(2)(ii)(B)(*1*) of this section (paragraph (*1*) in the results in this *Example 2*)
(q)(2)(iv)(B)(2)(*i*)	paragraph (ii)(A) of this *Example 4*	paragraph (q)(2)(iv)(B)(*1*) of this section (paragraph (*1*) in the results in this *Example 4*)
(q)(2)(vi)(B)(*1*)	paragraph (ii)(B) of this *Example 6*	paragraph (q)(2)(vi)(B)(*2*) of this section (paragraph (*2*) in the results in this *Example 6*)
(q)(2)(vi)(C)	paragraph (i) of this *Example 6*	paragraph (q)(2)(vi)(A) of this section (the facts in this *Example 6*)
(q)(2)(xi)(C)	paragraph (i) of this *Example 11*	paragraph (q)(2)(xi)(A) of this section (the facts in this *Example 11*)
(q)(2)(xx)(C)	paragraph (i) of this *Example 20*	paragraph (q)(2)(xx)(A) of this section (the facts in this *Example 20*)
(q)(2)(xx)(C)	paragraph (ii) of this *Example 20*	paragraph (q)(2)(xx)(B) of this section (the results in this *Example 20*)
(q)(2)(xx)(D)	paragraph (i) of this *Example 20*	paragraph (q)(2)(xx)(A) of this section (the facts in this *Example 20*)

Paragraph	Remove	Add
(q)(2)(xx)(D)	paragraph (ii) of this *Example 20*	paragraph (q)(2)(xx)(B) of this section (the facts in this *Example 20*)
(q)(2)(xx)(E)	paragraph (i) of this *Example 20*	paragraph (q)(2)(xx)(A) of this section (the facts in this *Example 20*)
(q)(2)(xx)(F)	paragraph (i) of this *Example 20*	paragraph (q)(2)(xx)(A) of this section (the facts in this *Example 20*)
(q)(2)(xxii)(C) introductory text	in paragraph (i) of this *Example 22*	paragraph (q)(2)(xxii)(A) of this section (the facts in this *Example 22*)
(q)(2)(xxiii)(C) introductory text	paragraph (i) of this *Example 23*	paragraph (q)(2)(xxiii)(A) of this section (the facts in this *Example 23*)
(q)(2)(xxiii)(C) introductory text	paragraph (ii) of this *Example 23*	paragraph (q)(2)(xxiii)(B) of this section (the results in this *Example 23*)
(q)(2)(xxiii)(D)	paragraph (i) of this *Example 23*	paragraph (q)(2)(xxiii)(A) of this section (the facts in this *Example 23*)
(q)(2)(xxiv)(A)	in paragraph (i) of *Example 6*	paragraph (q)(2)(vi)(A) of this section (the facts in *Example 6*)

8. Amend each paragraph listed in the first column, by removing the language in the second column and adding in its place the language in the third column:

Paragraph	Remove	Add
(c)(1)(ii)	(q)(2) of this section, Example 6	(q)(2)(vi) of this section
(c)(4)(iv)	paragraph (q)(2) of this section, Examples 1, 2, 3, and 5	paragraphs (q)(2)(i), (ii), (iii), and (v) of this section
(j)(1)	(q)(2) of this section, Example 2	(q)(2)(ii) of this section
(k)(1) introductory language	(q)(2) of this section, Example 4	(q)(2)(iv) of this section
(k)(1)(ii)	(q)(2) of this section, Example 3	(q)(2)(iii) of this section
(k)(1)(iii)	(q)(2) of this section, Example 11	(q)(2)(xi) of this section
(k)(6)(i)	(q)(2) of this section, Example 5	(q)(2)(v) of this section
(k)(6)(i)	(q)(2) of this section, Example 6	(q)(2)(vi) of this section
(k)(6)(ii)	(q)(2) of this section, Example 7	(q)(2)(vii) of this section
(k)(6)(iii)	(q)(2) of this section, Example 8	(q)(2)(viii) of this section
(k)(8)	(q)(2) of this section, Example 9	(q)(2)(ix) of this section
(k)(12)(i)	(q)(2) of this section, Example 20	(q)(2)(xx) of this section
(k)(14) introductory language	paragraph (q)(2), Examples 4, 6, 10, 12, 17, 21, and 23 of this section	paragraphs (q)(2)(iv), (vi), (x), (xii), (xvii), (xxi), and (xxiii) of this section
(m)(1)	(q)(2) of this section, Example 13	(q)(2)(xiii) of this section
(n)(1)	(q)(2) of this section, Example 14	(q)(2)(xiv) of this section
(o)(1)(ii)	(q)(2) of this section, Example 15	(q)(2)(xv) of this section
(o)(1)(iii) introductory language	(q)(2) of this section, Example 16	(q)(2)(xvi) of this section
(o)(5)(i)(A)	(q)(2) of this section, Example 18	(q)(2)(xviii) of this section
(o)(5)(i)(B)	(q)(2) of this section, Example 19	(q)(2)(ixx) of this section
(o)(5)(i)(C)	(q)(2) of this section, Example 22	(q)(2)(xxii) of this section
(o)(5)(i)(D)	(q)(2) of this section, Example 22	(q)(2)(xxii) of this section
(o)(6)	(q)(2) of this section, Example 20	(q)(2)(xx) of this section
(r)(2)(i)	paragraph (q)(2) of this section, Examples 24 and 25	paragraphs (q)(2)(xxiv) and (xxv) of this section

9. Revising the heading of paragraph (r).

10. Adding two sentences at the end of paragraph (r)(1)(i).

The revision and addition read as follows:

§1.367(a)-8. Gain recognition agreement requirements.

* * *

(k) * * *

(14) * * *

(ii) * * * If, as a result of the disposition or other event, a foreign corporation acquires the transferred stock or securities or, as applicable, substantially all the assets of the transferred corporation, the condition of this paragraph (k)(14)(ii) is satisfied only if the U.S. transferor owns at least five percent (applying the attribution rules of section 318, as modified by section 958(b), without applying subparagraphs (A), (B), and (C) of section 318(a)(3) so as to consider the U.S. transferor as owning stock which is owned by a person who is not a United States person) of the total voting power and the total value of the outstanding stock of such foreign corporation.

* * *

(r) *Applicability dates.*—(1) * * *

(i) * * * Paragraph (k)(14)(ii) of this section applies to transfers occurring on or after October 1, 2019, and to transfers occurring before October 1, 2019, that result from an entity classification election made under §301.7701-3 of this chapter that is filed on or after October 1, 2019. For transfers occurring before October 1, 2019, other than transfers occurring before October 1, 2019, that result from an entity classification election made under §301.7701-3 of this chapter that is filed on or after October 1, 2019, a taxpayer may apply paragraph (k)(14)(ii) of this section to transfers occurring during the last taxable year of a transferee foreign corporation beginning before January 1, 2018, and each subsequent taxable year of the foreign corporation, provided that the taxpayer and United States persons that are related (within the meaning of section 267 or 707) to the taxpayer consistently apply such paragraph with respect to all foreign corporations.

* * *

Foreign Corporations: Transfers of Stock by U.S. Person

Foreign Corporations: Transfers of Stock by U.S. Person.—Reg. §1.367(a)-9, providing rules under Code Sec. 367(a) and (b) that apply to certain transfers of stock by a United States person to a foreign corporation described in Code Sec. 304(a)(1), is proposed (published in the Federal Register on February 11, 2009) (REG-147636-08).

Par. 2. Section 1.367(a)-9 is added to read as follows:

§1.367(a)-9. Treatment of deemed section 351 exchanges pursuant to section 304(a)(1).

[The text of proposed §1.367(a)-9 is the same as the text of §1.367(a)-9T as added by T.D. 9444].

Foreign Corporations: Stock Transfer Rules: Carryover of Earnings and Taxes

Foreign Corporations: Stock Transfer Rules: Carryover of Earnings and Taxes.—Reg. §1.367(b)-8 and amendments to Reg. §1.367(b)-5, addressing (1) the carryover of certain tax attributes, such as earnings and profits and foreign income tax accounts, when two corporations combine in a section 367(b) transaction and (2) the allocation of certain tax attributes when a corporation distributes stock of another corporation in a section 367(b) transaction, are proposed (published in the Federal Register on November 15, 2000) (REG-116050-99) (corrected March 12, 2001).

☐ Par. 7. Section 1.367(b)-5 is amended by: **1.** Revising paragraphs (b)(1)(ii) and (c)(2). **2.** Adding paragraph (e)(3). The revisions and addition read as follows:

§1.367(b)-5. Distributions of stock described in section 355.

* * *

(b) * * *

(1) * * *

(ii) If the distributee is an individual or a tax-exempt entity as described in §1.337(d)-4(c)(2) then, solely for purposes of determining the gain recognized by the distributing corporation, the controlled corporation shall not be considered to be a corporation, and the distributing corporation shall recognize any gain (but not loss) realized on the distribution.

* * *

(c) * * *

(2) *Adjustment to basis in stock and income inclusion.*—(i) *In general.*—If the distributee's postdistribution amount (as defined in paragraph (e)(2) of this section) with respect to the distributing or controlled corporation is less than the distributee's predistribution amount (as defined in paragraph (e)(1) of this section) with respect to such corporation, then the distributee's basis in such stock immediately after the distribution (determined under the normal principles of section 358) shall be reduced by the amount of the difference. However, the distributee's basis in such stock shall not be reduced below zero, and to the extent the foregoing reduction would have reduced basis below zero, the distributee shall instead include such amount in income as a deemed dividend from such corporation. See, e.g., paragraph (g) *Example 1* of this section.

(ii) *Exception.*—The basis reduction rule of paragraph (c)(2)(i) of this section shall apply only to the extent such reduction increases the distributee's section 1248 amount (as defined in §1.367(b)-2(c)(1)) with respect to the distributing or controlled corporation; otherwise such basis reduction shall be replaced by the income inclusion rule of paragraph (c)(2)(i) of this section. See, e.g., §1.367(b)-8(d)(6) *Example 2.*

* * *

(e) * * *

(3) *Divisive D reorganization with a preexisting controlled corporation.*—In the case of a transaction described in §1.367(b)-8(b)(4), the predistribution amount with respect to a distributing or controlled corporation shall be computed after the allocation of the distributing corporation's earnings and profits described in §1.367(b)-8(b)(4)(i)(A) and (b)(4)(ii)(A) (without regard to the parenthetical phrase in §1.367(b)-8(b)(4)(ii)(A)), but before the reduction in the distributing corporation's earnings and profits described in §1.367(b)-8(b)(4)(i)(B). See, e.g., §1.367(b)-8(d)(6) *Example 3* and §1.367(b)-8(e)(7) *Example 3.*

* * *

☐ Par. 10. Section 1.367(b)-8 is added to read as follows:

§1.367(b)-8. Allocation of earnings and profits and foreign income taxes in certain foreign corporate separations.—(a) *Scope.*—This section applies to distributions to which section 355 (or so much of section 356 as relates to section 355) applies, whether or not in connection with a section 368(a)(1)(D) reorganization (D reorganization), in which the distributing corporation or the controlled corporation (or both) is a foreign corporation (foreign divisive transaction). For purposes of this section, the terms distributing corporation and controlled corporation have the same meaning as used in section 355 and the regulations thereunder. Paragraph (b) of this section provides general rules governing the allocation and reduction of a distributing corporation's earnings and profits and foreign income taxes (pre-transaction earnings and pre-transaction taxes, respectively) in foreign divisive transactions. Paragraphs (c), (d), and (e) of this section describe special rules for the application of paragraph (b) of this section to specific situations, depending upon whether the distributing corporation or the controlled corporation (or both the distributing and the controlled corporation) is a foreign corporation.

(b) *General rules.*—(1) *Application of §1.312-10.*—(i) *In general.*—Pre-transaction earnings of a distributing corporation shall be allocated between the distributing corporation and the controlled corporation in accordance with the rules of §1.312-10(a) and shall be reduced in accordance with the rules of §1.312-10(b), except to the extent otherwise provided in this section.

(ii) *Special rules for application of §1.312-10(b).*—(A) *Distributing corporation.*—The pre-transaction earnings of a distributing corporation shall be reduced without taking into account §1.312-10(b)(2).

(B) *Controlled corporation.*—Section 1.312-10(b) shall not apply to increase or replace the earnings and profits of a controlled corporation by the amount of any decrease in the pre-transaction earnings of a distributing corporation.

(iii) *Net deficit in pre-transaction earnings.*—Nothing in this section shall permit any portion of the pre-transaction earnings of a distributing corporation that has a net deficit in pre-transaction earnings to be allocated or reduced under paragraph (b)(1)(i) of this section. See §1.312-10(c). Compare paragraph (b)(2) of this section (requiring an allocation or reduction of a pro rata portion of deficits in statutory groupings of earnings and profits when a distributing corporation has a net positive amount of pre-transaction earnings).

(iv) *Use of net bases.*—All allocations and reductions described in paragraph (b)(1)(i) of this section shall be determined in accordance with the net bases in assets. Net basis shall have the same meaning as under §1.312-10(a).

(v) *Gain recognized by distributing corporation.*—The pre-transaction earnings that are subject to allocation or reduction under paragraph (b)(1)(i) of this section shall include any increase in earnings and profits from gain recognized or income included by the distributing corporation as a result of the foreign divisive transaction. See, for example, section 367(a) and (e), section 1248(f), and §1.367(b)-5(b).

(vi) *Coordination with branch profits tax.*—An allocation or reduction in a distributing corporation's pre-transaction earnings under paragraph (b)(1)(i) of this section shall not be out of or reduce effectively connected earnings and profits or non-previously taxed accumulated effectively connected earnings and profits, as defined in section 884. See also §1.884-2T(d)(5)(iii) (providing that such earnings and profits are not subject to reduction under §1.312-10(b)).

(2) *Cross-section of earnings and profits.*—Except to the extent provided in paragraphs (b)(1)(iii), (b)(1)(vi), (d)(2)(ii), (d)(4), and (e)(4) of this section and other than any portion attributable to an inclusion under §1.367(b)-5 or paragraph (d)(2)(i) of this section, an allocation or reduction of pre-transaction earnings described in paragraph (b)(1)(i) of this section shall decrease, on a pro rata basis, the statutory groupings of earnings and profits (or deficits in statutory

groupings of earnings and profits) of the distributing corporation. Thus, for example, a pro rata portion of a foreign distributing corporation's separate categories, post-1986 undistributed earnings, and annual layers of pre-1987 accumulated profits and pre-1987 section 960 earnings and profits shall be allocated or reduced.

(3) *Foreign income taxes.*—Pre-transaction taxes of a distributing corporation shall be ratably allocated or reduced only to the extent described in paragraphs (d)(3) and (e)(3) of this section. Thus, a distributing corporation's excess foreign taxes described in section 904(c) shall not be allocated or reduced under this section.

(4) *Divisive D reorganization with a preexisting controlled corporation.*—In the case of a foreign divisive transaction that includes a D reorganization with a controlled corporation that is not newly created (a preexisting controlled corporation), paragraph (b)(1)(i) of this section shall apply in the following manner:

(i) *Calculation of earnings and profits of distributing corporation.*—The pre-transaction earnings of a distributing corporation shall be reduced by the sum of—

(A) The amount of the reduction in the pre-transaction earnings of the distributing corporation as described in § 1.312-10(a) (as determined under this section); and

(B) The amount of the reduction in the pre-transaction earnings of the distributing corporation as described in § 1.312-10(b) (as determined under this section).

(ii) *Calculation of earnings and profits of controlled corporation.*—The amount of earnings and profits of the controlled corporation immediately after the foreign divisive transaction shall equal the sum of—

(A) The amount described in paragraph (b)(4)(i)(A) of this section (except to the extent such amounts are included in income as a deemed dividend pursuant to the foreign divisive transaction or are subject to the rule of § 1.367(b)-3(f)); and

(B) The amount of earnings and profits of the controlled corporation immediately before the foreign divisive transaction.

(c) *Foreign divisive transactions involving a domestic distributing corporation and a foreign controlled corporation.*—(1) *Scope.*—The rules of this paragraph (c) apply to a foreign divisive transaction involving a domestic distributing corporation and a foreign controlled corporation.

(2) *Earnings and profits allocated to a foreign controlled corporation.*—Pre-transaction earnings of a domestic distributing corporation that are allocated to a foreign controlled corporation under the rules described in paragraph (b)(1)(i) of this section shall not be included in the foreign controlled corporation's post-1986 undistributed earnings, pre-1987 accumulated profits, or pre-1987 section 960 earnings and profits. In addition, if a distribution by the domestic distributing corporation out of pre-transaction earnings immediately before the foreign divisive transaction would have been treated as a U.S. source dividend under section 861(a)(2)(A) that would not be exempt from tax under section 871(i)(2)(B) or 881(d), a distribution out of such earnings and profits by the foreign controlled corporation shall be treated as a U.S. source dividend under section 904(g) and for purposes of Chapter 3 of subtitle A of the Internal Revenue Code. See *Georday Enterprises v. Commissioner*, 126 F.2d 384 (4th Cir. 1942). See also sections 243(e) and 861(a)(2)(C) and § 1.367(b)-2(j) for other rules that may apply.

(3) *Examples.*—The following examples illustrate the application of the rules of this section to transactions described in paragraph (c)(1) of this section. The examples presume the following facts: USD is a domestic corporation engaged in manufacturing and shipping activities through Business A and Business B, respectively. FC is a foreign corporation that is wholly owned by USD. USD and FC use calendar taxable years. FC (and all of its qualified business units as defined in section 989) maintains a "u" functional currency and, except as otherwise specified, 1u = US$1 at all times. The examples are as follows:

Example 1—(i) *Facts.* The stock of USD is owned in equal parts by three shareholders, USP (a domestic corporation), USI (a United States citizen), and FP (a foreign corporation). USD owns assets with total net bases of $260 (including $100 attributable to the Business B shipping assets, which have a $160 fair market value). USD has $500 of earnings and profits (that it accumulated). The entire $500 would have been treated as a U.S. source dividend under section 861(a)(2)(A) that would not be exempt from tax under sections 871(i)(2)(B) or 881(d) if distributed by USD immediately before the foreign divisive transaction. On January 1, 2002, USD incorporates FC and transfers to FC the Business B shipping assets. USD then distributes the FC stock pro rata to USP, USI, and FP. The transaction meets the requirements of sections 368(a)(1)(D) and 355.

(ii) *Result*—(A) *Gain Recognition.* Under section 367(a)(5), USD recognizes gain equal to the difference between the fair market value

and USD's adjusted basis in the Business B shipping assets ($160 – $100 = $60).

(B) *Calculation of USD's earnings and profits.* Under paragraph (b)(1)(v) of this section, USD's pre-transaction earnings include any gain recognized or income included as a result of the foreign divisive transaction. As described in this *Example 1* (ii)(A), USD recognizes $60 of gain as a result of the foreign divisive transaction. Accordingly, USD has $560 of pre-transaction earnings ($500 + $60). Under paragraph (b)(1)(i) of this section, USD's pre-transaction earnings are reduced by an amount equal to its pre-transaction earnings times the net bases of the assets transferred to FC divided by the net bases of the assets held by USD immediately before the foreign divisive transaction ($560 × ($160 ÷ $320) = $280). Following this reduction, USD has $280 of earnings and profits ($560 – $280).

(C) *Calculation of FC's earnings and profits.* Under paragraph (b)(1)(i) of this section, the $280 reduction in USD's pre-transaction earnings is allocated to FC. Under § 1.367(b)-2(j)(1), the $280 is translated into "u" at the spot rate on January 1, 2002, to 280u. Under paragraph (c)(2) of this section, the 280u is not included as part of FC's post-1986 undistributed earnings, pre-1987 accumulated profits, or section 960 earnings and profits.

(iii) *Post-transaction distribution.* During 2002, FC does not accumulate any earnings and profits or pay or accrue any foreign income taxes. On December 31, 2002, at a time when US$1 = 0.5u, FC distributes 180u (or $360) to its shareholders. Thus, FP, USP, and USI each receive a $120 dividend. See section 989(b)(1). Under paragraph (c)(2) of this section and § 1.367(b)-2(j)(4), $93.33 of the distribution to FP is subject to withholding under Chapter 3 of subtitle A of the Internal Revenue Code ($280 ÷ 3 = $93.33). Under section 243(e) and § 1.367(b)-2(j)(3), $93.33 of the distribution to USP is eligible for the dividends received deduction. See also section 861(a)(2)(C). Under paragraph (c)(2) of this section, the remaining $26.67 distribution to USP is treated as U.S. source under section 904(g) (and is not eligible for the dividends received deduction under section 243(e)). Under paragraph (c)(2) of this section, the $120 dividend distribution to USI is treated as U.S. source under section 904(g).

Example 2—(i) *Facts.* The stock of USD is owned by the following unrelated persons: 20 percent by USP (a domestic corporation), 20 percent by USI (a United States citizen), and 60 percent by FP (a foreign corporation). FC is a preexisting controlled corporation that was incorporated in 1995 and USD always has owned all of the FC stock. USD owns assets with total net bases of $320 (including $160 attributable to the FC stock), and USD has $500 of earnings and profits. FC has 150u of earnings and profits in the section 904(d)(1)(D) shipping separate category and has $60 of related foreign income taxes. FC's earnings and profits qualified for the high tax exception from subpart F income under section 954(b)(4), and USD elected to exclude the earnings and profits from subpart F income under section 954(b)(4) and § 1.954-1(d)(5). On January 1, 2002, USD distributes the stock of FC to its shareholders in a transaction that meets the requirements of section 355. FC is not a controlled foreign corporation after the foreign divisive transaction. On the date of the foreign divisive transaction, the FC stock has a $460 fair market value.

(ii) *Result*—(A) *Gain Recognition.* Under § 1.367(b)-5(b)(1)(ii), USD recognizes gain equal to the difference between the fair market value and USD's adjusted basis in the FC stock distributed to USI. Under § 1.367(e)-1(b)(1), USD recognizes gain equal to the difference between the fair market value and USD's adjusted basis in the FC stock distributed to FP. As a result of the transfers to USI and FP, USD recognizes gain of $240 (4/5 × ($460 – $160)), $120 of which is included in USD's income as a dividend under section 1248(a) and (f)(1) (4/5 × 150u, translated at the spot rate under section 989(b)(2)). Under section 1248(a) and (f)(1), USD includes as a dividend the difference between the fair market value and its adjusted basis in the FC stock distributed to USP to the extent of FC's earnings and profits attributable to the distributed stock. For further guidance, see also Notice 87-64 (1987-2 C.B. 375) (see also § 601.601(d)(2) of this chapter). As a result of this transfer, USD includes a $30 dividend under section 1248(a) and (f)(1) (1/5 × 150u). USD qualifies for a section 902 deemed paid foreign tax credit with respect to its $150 of section 1248 dividends.

(B) *Calculation of USD's earnings and profits.* Under paragraph (b)(1)(v) of this section, USD's pre-transaction earnings include any gain recognized or income included as a result of the foreign divisive transaction. As described in this *Example 2* (ii)(A), USD recognizes and includes a total of $270 of gain and dividend income as a result of the foreign divisive transaction. Accordingly, USD has $770 of pre-transaction earnings ($500 + $270). Under paragraphs (b)(1)(i) and (b)(1)(ii)(A) of this section, USD's pre-transaction earnings are reduced by the amount of the reduction that would have been required if USD had transferred the stock of FC to a new corporation in a D reorganization. Thus, USD's pre-transaction earnings are reduced by an amount equal to its pre-transaction earnings times its net basis in the FC stock divided by the net bases of the assets held by USD immediately before the foreign divisive transaction ($770 × ($430 ÷

$590) = \$561.19$). Following this reduction, USD has \$208.81 of earnings and profits (\$770 – \$561.19).

(C) *Calculation of FC's earnings and profits.* Under paragraph (b)(1)(ii)(B) of this section, FC's earnings and profits are not increased (or replaced) as a result of the foreign divisive transaction.

Example 3—(i) *Facts.* USP, a domestic corporation, owns all of the stock of USD. FC is a preexisting controlled corporation and USD has owned all of the FC stock since FC was incorporated in 1995. USD owns assets with total net bases of \$320 (including \$100 attributable to the FC stock and \$160 attributable to the Business B shipping assets). USD has \$500 of pre-transaction earnings. FC has 150u of earnings and profits in the section 904(d)(1)(D) shipping separate category and has \$60 of related foreign income taxes. FC's earnings and profits qualified for the high tax exception from subpart F income under section 954(b)(4), and USD elected to exclude the earnings and profits from subpart F income under section 954(b)(4) and §1.954-1(d)(5). On January 1, 2002, USD transfers to FC the Business B shipping assets. USD then distributes the FC stock to USP. The transaction meets the requirements of sections 368(a)(1)(D) and 355. USD's transfer of the Business B shipping assets to FC falls within the active trade or business exception to section 367(a)(1) described in §1.367(a)-2T. Immediately after the foreign divisive transaction, the FC stock has a \$460 fair market value. USP and USD meet and comply with the requirements of section 367(a)(5) and 1248(f)(2) (and any regulations thereunder). (Sections 1.367(b)-5(b)(1)(ii) and 1.367(e)-1(b)(1) do not apply with respect to the foreign divisive transaction because the distributee, USP, is a domestic corporation.)

(ii) *Result*—(A) *Calculation of USD's earnings and profits.* Under paragraph (b)(4)(i) of this section, USD's pre-transaction earnings are reduced by the sum of the amounts described in paragraphs (b)(4)(i)(A) and (b)(4)(i)(B) of this section. Under paragraph (b)(4)(i)(A) of this section, USD's pre-transaction earnings are reduced by an amount equal to USD's pre-transaction earnings times the net bases of the assets transferred to FC divided by the total net bases of the assets held by USD immediately before the foreign divisive transaction ($\$500 \times (\$160 \div \$320) = \$250$). Under paragraph (b)(4)(i)(B) of this section, USD's pre-transaction earnings are reduced by an amount equal to USD's pre-transaction earnings times USD's net basis in the stock of FC (immediately before USD's transfer of the shipping assets) divided by the total net bases of the assets held by USD immediately before the foreign divisive transaction ($\$500 \times (\$100 \div \$320) = \$156.25$). The sum of the amounts described in paragraphs (b)(4)(i)(A) and (B) of this section is \$406.25 (\$250 + \$156.25). Following the reduction described in paragraph (b)(4)(i) of this section, USD has \$93.75 of earnings and profits (\$500 – \$406.25).

(B) *Calculation of FC's earnings and profits.* Under paragraphs (b)(4)(ii) of this section, the earnings and profits of FC immediately after the foreign divisive transaction are increased by the amount of the reduction in USD's pre-transaction earnings described in paragraph (b)(4)(i)(A) of this section (\$250). Under §1.367(b)-2(j)(1), this \$250 is translated into "u" at the spot rate on January 1, 2002, to 250u. Under paragraph (c)(2) of this section, the 250u is not included as part of FC's post-1986 undistributed earnings. FC has 400u in earnings and profits (250u + 150u) immediately after the foreign divisive transaction.

(iii) *Post-transaction distribution.* FC does not accumulate any earnings and profits or pay or accrue any foreign income taxes during 2002. On December 31, 2002, FC distributes 100u as a dividend to USP, which has remained its sole shareholder. Under section 989(b)(1), the 100u distribution is translated into US$ at the spot rate on December 31, 2002, to \$100. Proportionate parts of the \$100 dividend are attributable to the pre-transaction earnings of FC (\$37.50 = \$100 × (150 ÷ 400)) and USD (\$62.50 = \$100 × (250 ÷ 400)). See sections 243(e) and 245. Thus, under sections 243(e) and §1.367(b)-2(j)(3), \$62.50 of the distribution is eligible for the dividends received deduction. See also section 861(a)(2)(C). The remaining \$37.50 of the distribution (and \$15 of related foreign income taxes) is subject to the generally applicable rules concerning dividends paid by foreign corporations.

(d) *Foreign divisive transactions involving a foreign distributing corporation and a domestic controlled corporation.*—(1) *Scope.* The rules of this paragraph (d) apply to a foreign divisive transaction involving a foreign distributing corporation and a domestic controlled corporation.

Separate Category	
General	. . . .
Shipping	. . . .

(B) On January 1, 2002, FD incorporates USC and transfers to USC the Business B shipping assets. FD then distributes the USC stock to USP. The transaction meets the requirements of sections 368(a)(1)(D) and 355. Immediately after the foreign divisive transac-

(2) *Coordination with §1.367(b)-3.*—(i) *In general.*—In the case of a foreign divisive transaction that includes a D reorganization, the rules of §1.367(b)-3 are applicable with respect to the pre-transaction earnings of a foreign distributing corporation that are allocable to a domestic controlled corporation under paragraph (b)(1)(i) of this section.

(ii) *Determination of all earnings and profits amount.*—An all earnings and profits amount inclusion under paragraph (d)(2)(i) of this section shall be computed with respect to the pre-transaction earnings that are allocable to the domestic controlled corporation, without regard to the parenthetical phrase in paragraph (b)(4)(ii)(A) of this section.

(iii) *Interaction with section 358 and §1.367(b)-2(e)(3)(ii).*—The basis increase provided in §1.367(b)-2(e)(3)(ii) shall apply to an all earnings and profits amount inclusion under paragraph (d)(2)(i) of this section, subject to the following rules—

(A) Section 358 shall apply to determine the distributee's basis in the foreign distributing and domestic controlled corporation without regard to the all earnings and profits amount inclusion;

(B) After application of the rule in paragraph (d)(2)(iii)(A) of this section, the basis increase provided in §1.367(b)-2(e)(3)(ii) shall be applied in a manner that attributes such basis increase solely to the exchanging shareholder's stock in the domestic controlled corporation; and

(C) the rule of paragraph (d)(2)(iii)(B) of this section shall apply prior to §1.367(b)-5(c)(4) and (d)(4).

(iv) *Coordination with §1.367(b)-3(c).*—In applying the rule of §1.367(b)-3(c)(2), an exchanging shareholder described in §1.367(b)-3(c)(1) shall recognize gain with respect to the stock of the domestic controlled corporation after the foreign divisive transaction.

(v) *Special rule for U.S. persons that own foreign distributing corporation stock after a non pro rata distribution.*—[Reserved]

(3) *Foreign income taxes.*—Pre-transaction taxes related to a foreign distributing corporation's pre-transaction earnings that are allocable or are reduced under the rules described in paragraph (b)(1)(i) of this section shall be ratably reduced. Pre-transaction taxes related to a foreign distributing corporation's pre-transaction earnings that are allocable to a domestic controlled corporation under the rules described in paragraph (b)(1)(i) of this section shall not carry over to the domestic controlled corporation. Nothing in this paragraph (d)(3) shall affect the deemed paid taxes that otherwise would accompany an inclusion under §1.367(b)-5 or paragraph (d)(2)(i) of this section.

(4) *Previously taxed earnings and profits.*—[Reserved]

(5) *Coordination with §1.367(b)-5.*—See also §1.367(b)-5(c) and (d) for other rules that may apply to a foreign divisive transaction described in paragraph (d)(1) of this section.

(6) *Examples.*—The following examples illustrate the application of the rules of this section to transactions described in paragraph (d)(1) of this section. The examples presume the following facts: FD is a foreign corporation engaged in manufacturing and shipping activities through Business A and Business B, respectively. Any earnings and profits of FD described in section 904(d)(1)(D) (shipping income) qualified for the high tax exception from subpart F income under section 954(b)(4), and FD's United States shareholders elected to exclude the earnings and profits from subpart F income under section 954(b)(4) and §1.954-1(d)(5). USC is a domestic corporation that is wholly owned by FD. FD and USC use calendar taxable years. FD (and all of its qualified business units as defined in section 989) maintains a "u" functional currency, and 1u = US$1 at all times. The examples are as follows:

Example 1—(i) *Facts.* (A) USP, a domestic corporation, has owned all of the stock of FD since FD's incorporation in 1995. USP's adjusted basis in the FD stock is \$100, and the FD stock has a fair market value of \$800. FD owns assets with total net bases of 320u (including 160u attributable to the Business B shipping assets), and has the following pre-transaction earnings and pre-transaction taxes accounts:

	E&P	Foreign Taxes
General	300u	\$60
Shipping	200u	\$80
	500u	\$140

tion, the FD stock and the USC stock each have a fair market value of \$400.

(ii) *Results*—(A) *Calculation of FD's earnings and profits.* Under paragraph (b)(1)(i) of this section, FD's pre-transaction earnings are reduced by an amount equal to its pre-transaction earnings times the net bases of the assets transferred to USC divided by the net bases of the assets held by FD immediately before the foreign divisive transaction (500u × (160u ÷ 320u) = 250u). Following this reduction, FD has 250u of earnings and profits (500u – 250u).

(B) *All earnings and profits amount inclusion.* Under §1.367(b)-3 and paragraph (d)(2)(i) of this section, USP includes in income as an all earnings and profits amount the pre-transaction earnings of FD that are allocable to USC under paragraph (b)(1)(i) of this section.

Separate Category		
General	150u	$30
Shipping	100u	$40
	250u	$70

(C) *Calculation of USP's basis in USC and USC's earnings and profits.* Under paragraph (d)(2)(iii) of this section, the §1.367(b)-2(e)(3)(ii) basis increase applies with respect to USP's all earnings and profits amount inclusion from FD and is attributed solely to USP's basis in USC (after application of section 358). Accordingly, USP has a $300 basis in the USC stock ($50 section 358 basis, determined by reference to the relative values of USP's FD and USC stock: $100 pre-transaction basis × ($400 ÷ $800) + $250 §1.367(b)-2(e)(3)(ii) basis increase = $300). Because USP included in income as a deemed dividend under §1.367(b)-3 and paragraph (d)(2) of this section the pre-transaction earnings of FD that are allocable to USC under paragraph (b)(1)(i) of this section, such earnings and profits are not available to increase USC's earnings and profits. As a result, USC has zero earnings and profits immediately after the foreign divisive transaction.

(D) *Application of §1.367(b)-5(c).* The basis adjustment and income inclusion rules of §1.367(b)-5(c)(2) apply if USP's postdistribution amount with respect to FD stock is less than its predistribution amount with respect to FD stock. Under §1.367(b)-5(e)(1), USP's predistribution amount with respect to FD stock is USP's section 1248

Separate Category		
General	150u	$30
Shipping	100u	$40
	250u	$70

Example 2—(i) Facts. (A) USP, a domestic corporation, has owned all of the stock of FD since FD's incorporation in 1995. USP's adjusted basis in the FD stock is $400 and the FD stock has a fair market value of $800. USC is a preexisting controlled corporation. FD

Separate Category		
General	300u	$60
Shipping	200u	$80
	500u	$140

(B) On January 1, 2002, FD distributes the USC stock to USP in a transaction that meets the requirements of section 355. Immediately after the foreign divisive transaction, the FD stock and the USC stock each have a $400 fair market value.

(ii) *Results*—(A) *Calculation of FD's earnings and profits.* Under paragraphs (b)(1)(i) and (b)(1)(ii)(A) of this section, FD's pre-transaction earnings are reduced by the amount of the reduction that would have been required if FD had transferred the stock of USC to a new corporation in a D reorganization. Thus, FD's pre-transaction earnings are reduced by an amount equal to its pre-transaction earnings times its net basis in the USC stock divided by the net bases of the assets held by FD immediately before the foreign divisive transaction (500u × (160u ÷ 320u) = 250u). Following this reduction, FD has 250u of earnings and profits (500u – 250u).

(B) *Calculation of USC's earnings and profits.* Under paragraph (b)(1)(ii)(B) of this section, USC's earnings and profits are not increased (or replaced) as a result of the foreign divisive transaction. As a result, USP is not required to include an amount in income under paragraph (d)(2)(i) of this section.

(C) *Application of §1.367(b)-5(c).* The basis adjustment and income inclusion rules of §1.367(b)-5(c)(2) apply if USP's postdistribution amount with respect to FD stock is less than its predistribution amount with respect to FD stock. Under §1.367(b)-5(e)(1), USP's predistribution amount with respect to FD stock is USP's section 1248

Separate Category		
General	90u	$18
Shipping	60u	$24
	150u	$42

(D) *Basis adjustment.* Under §1.367(b)-5(c)(3), USP does not increase its basis in FD stock as a result of USP's $150 deemed dividend from FD. Under §1.367(b)-5(c)(4), USP increases its basis in the USC stock by the amount by which it decreased its basis in the FD stock, as well as by the amount of its deemed dividend inclusion. The §1.367(b)-5(c)(4) basis increase applies in full because USP's basis in the USC stock is not increased above the fair market value of such stock. Thus, USP increases its basis in USC stock to $400 ($200 + $50 + $150).

Thus, USP's all earnings and profits amount inclusion is $250. See also section 989(b)(1) and paragraph (d)(2)(ii) of this section. Under §1.367(b)-3(b)(3)(i) and §1.367(b)-2(e), USP includes the all earnings and profits amount as a deemed dividend received from FD immediately before the foreign divisive transaction. Because the requirements of section 902 are met, USP qualifies for a deemed paid foreign tax credit with respect to the deemed dividend that it receives from FD. Under §1.902-1(d)(1), the $250 deemed dividend is out of FD's separate categories and reduces foreign income taxes as follows:

	E&P	Foreign Taxes
General	150u	$30
Shipping	100u	$40
	250u	$70

amount attributable to such stock computed immediately before the distribution but after taking into account the allocation of earnings and profits as a result of the D reorganization. Thus, USP's predistribution amount with respect to FD stock is $250 (500u – 250u). See also section 989(b)(2). Under section 358, USP allocates its $100 basis in FD stock between FD stock and USC stock according to the stock blocks' relative values, yielding a $50 ($100 × ($400 ÷ $800)) basis in FD stock. See also paragraph (d)(2)(iii) of this section. Under §1.367(b)-5(e)(2), USP's postdistribution amount with respect to FD stock is USP's section 1248 amount with respect to such stock, computed immediately after the distribution. Accordingly, USP's postdistribution amount with respect to FD stock is $250. Because USP's, postdistribution amount with respect to FD stock is not less than its predistribution amount, USP is not required to make any basis adjustment or include any income under §1.367(b)-5(c).

(E) *FD's earnings and profits after the foreign divisive transaction.* Following the reduction described in this *Example 1* (ii)(A) and (B), FD has the following earnings and profits and foreign income taxes accounts:

	E&P	Foreign Taxes
General	150u	$30
Shipping	100u	$40
	250u	$70

owns assets with net total bases of 320u (including 160u attributable to the USC stock), and has the following pre-transaction earnings and pre-transaction taxes accounts:

	E&P	Foreign Taxes
General	300u	$60
Shipping	200u	$80
	500u	$140

amount attributable to such stock computed immediately before the distribution. Thus, USP's predistribution amount with respect to FD stock is $400 (the predistribution amount is limited to USP's built-in gain in FD stock immediately before the distribution ($800 – $400)). See also section 989(b)(2). Under section 358, USP allocates its $400 basis in FD stock between FD stock and USC stock according to the stock blocks' relative values, yielding a $200 ($400 × ($400 ÷ $800)) basis in each block. Under §1.367(b)-5(e)(2), USP's postdistribution amount with respect to FD stock is USP's section 1248 amount with respect to such stock, computed immediately after the distribution. Accordingly, USP's postdistribution amount with respect to FD stock is $200 (the postdistribution amount is limited to USP's built-in gain in FD stock immediately after the distribution ($400 – $200)). Because USP's postdistribution amount with respect to FD stock is $200 less than its predistribution amount with respect to such stock ($400 – $200), §1.367(b)-5(c)(2)(i) and (ii) require USP to reduce its basis in FD stock by the $200 difference, but only to the extent such reduction increases USP's section 1248 amount with respect to the FD stock. As a result, USP reduces its basis in the FD stock from $200 to $150 and includes $150 in income as a deemed dividend from FD. Because the requirements of section 902 are met, USP qualifies for a deemed paid foreign tax credit with respect to the deemed dividend that it receives from FD. Under §1.902-1(d)(1), the $150 deemed dividend is out of FD's separate categories and reduces foreign income taxes as follows:

	E&P	Foreign Taxes
General	90u	$18
Shipping	60u	$24
	150u	$42

(E) *Reduction in FD's statutory groupings of earnings and profits.* Under paragraph (b)(2) of this section, the reduction in FD's pre-transaction earnings that is not attributable to USP's inclusion under §1.367(b)-5 decreases FD's statutory groupings of earnings and profits on a pro rata basis. Under paragraph (d)(3) of this section, FD's pre-transaction taxes also are ratably reduced. As described in this *Example 2* (ii)(A), the reduction in FD's pre-transaction earnings is 250u. As described in this *Example 2* (ii)(C), 150u of the 250u reduction is attributable to an inclusion under §1.367(b)-5. As a result, under paragraphs (b)(2) and (d)(3) of this section the remaining 100u

Separate Category		
General	60u	$12
Shipping	40u	$16
	100u	$28

(F) *FD's earnings and profits after the foreign divisive transaction.* After the reductions described in this *Example* 2 (ii)(C) and (E), FD

Separate Category		
General	150u	$30
Shipping	100u	$40
	250u	$70

Example 3—(i) *Facts.* (A) USP, a domestic corporation, has owned all of the stock of FD since FD's incorporation in 1995. USP's adjusted basis in the FD stock is $400 and the FD stock has a fair market value of $800. USC is a preexisting controlled corporation. FD

Separate Category		
General	300u	$60
Shipping	200u	$80
	500u	$140

(B) On January 1, 2002, FD transfers to USC the Business B shipping assets. FD then distributes the USC stock to USP. The transaction meets the requirements of sections 368(a)(1)(D) and 355. Immediately after the foreign divisive transaction, the FD stock has a $200 fair market value and the USC stock has a $600 fair market value.

(ii) *Results*—(A) *Calculation of FD's earnings and profits.* Under paragraph (b)(4)(i) of this section, FD's pre-transaction earnings are reduced by the sum of the amounts described in paragraphs (b)(4)(i)(A) and (B) of this section. Under paragraph (b)(4)(i)(A) of this section, FD's pre-transaction earnings are reduced by an amount equal to FD's pre-transaction earnings times the net bases of the Business B shipping assets transferred to USC divided by the total net bases of the assets held by FD immediately before the foreign divisive transaction (500u × (80u ÷ 320u) = 125u). Under paragraph (b)(4)(i)(B) of this section, FD's pre-transaction earnings are reduced by an amount equal to FD's pre-transaction earnings times FD's net basis in the stock of USC divided by the total net bases of the assets

Separate Category		
General	75u	$15
Shipping	50u	$20
	125u	$35

(C) *Calculation of USP's basis in USC and USC's earnings and profits.* Under paragraph (d)(2)(iii) of this section, the §1.367(b)-2(e)(3)(ii) basis increase applies with respect to USP's all earnings and profits amount inclusion and is attributed solely to USP's basis in USC (after application of section 358). Accordingly, USP has a $425 basis in the USC stock ($300 section 358 basis, determined by reference to the relative values of USP's FD and USC stock: $400 pre-transaction basis × ($600 ÷ $800) + $125 §1.367(b)-2(e)(3)(ii) basis increase = $425. Because USP included in income as a deemed dividend under §1.367(b)-3 and paragraph (d)(2) of this section the pre-transaction earnings of FD that are allocable to USC under paragraph (b)(1)(i) of this section, such earnings and profits are not available to increase USC's earnings and profits. As a result, USC's earnings and profits are not increased as a result of the foreign divisive transaction.

(D) *Application of §1.367(b)-5(c).* The basis adjustment and income inclusion rules of §1.367(b)-5(c)(2) apply if USP's postdistribution amount with respect to FD stock is less than its predistribution amount with respect to FD stock. Under §1.367(b)-5(e)(1) and (3), USP's predistribution amount with respect to FD stock is USP's section 1248 amount attributable to such stock computed immediately before the distribution, after the allocation of FD's pre-transaction earnings described in paragraphs (b)(4)(i)(A) and (ii)(A) of this section, but without regard to the reduction in FD's pre-transaction

Separate Category		
General	150u	$30
Shipping	100u	$40
	250u	$70

(E) *Basis adjustment.* Under §1.367(b)-5(c)(3), USP does not increase its basis in FD stock as a result of USP's $250 deemed dividend from FD. Under §1.367(b)-5(c)(4), USP increases its basis in the USC stock by the amount by which it decreased its basis in the FD stock, as well as by the amount of its deemed dividend inclusion, but only up to the fair market value of USP's USC stock. As described in this *Example 3* (ii)(C), USP has already increased its basis in the USC stock to $425. Because the fair market value of FD's USC stock is $600, USP's basis increase under §1.367(b)-5(c)(4) is limited to $175. See also paragraph (d)(2)(iii)(C) of this section. Thus, USP has a $600 basis in the USC stock immediately after the foreign divisive transaction.

reduction in FD's pre-transaction earnings is out of the following separate categories of earnings and profits and foreign income taxes:

	E&P	Foreign Taxes
	60u	$12
	40u	$16
	100u	$28

has the following earnings and profits and foreign income taxes accounts:

	E&P	Foreign Taxes
	150u	$30
	100u	$40
	250u	$70

owns assets with total net bases of 320u (including 160u attributable to the USC stock and 80u attributable to the Business B shipping assets), and has the following pre-transaction earnings and pre-transaction taxes accounts:

	E&P	Foreign Taxes
	300u	$60
	200u	$80
	500u	$140

held by FD immediately before the foreign divisive transaction (500u × (160u ÷ 320u) = 250u). The sum of the amounts described in paragraphs (b)(4)(i)(A) and (B) of this section is 375u (125u + 250u).

(B) *All earnings and profits amount inclusion.* Under §1.367(b)-3 and paragraph (d)(2)(i) of this section, USP is required to include in income as an all earnings and profits amount the pre-transaction earnings of FD that are allocable to USC under paragraph (b)(1)(i) of this section. Under paragraph (b)(4)(ii)(A) of this section, the 125u of pre-transaction earnings described in paragraph (b)(4)(i)(A) are allocable to USC. Thus, the all earnings and profits amount is $125. See also section 989(b)(1) and paragraph (d)(2)(ii) of this section. Under §§1.367(b)-3(b)(3)(i) and 1.367(b)-2(e), USP includes the all earnings and profits amount as a deemed dividend received from FD immediately before the foreign divisive transaction. Because the requirements of section 902 are met, USP qualifies for a deemed paid foreign tax credit with respect to the deemed dividend that it receives from FD. Under §1.902-1(d)(1), the $125 deemed dividend is out of FD's separate categories and reduces foreign income taxes as follows:

	E&P	Foreign Taxes
	75u	$15
	50u	$20
	125u	$35

earnings described in paragraph (b)(4)(i)(B) of this section. Thus, USP's predistribution amount with respect to FD stock is $375 ($500 – $125). See also section 989(b)(2). Under section 358, USP allocates its $400 basis in FD stock between FD stock and USC stock according to the stock blocks' relative values, yielding a $100 ($400 × ($200 ÷ $800)) basis in FD stock. See also paragraph (d)(2)(iii) of this section. Under §1.367(b)-5(e)(2), USP's postdistribution amount with respect to FD stock is USP's section 1248 amount with respect to such stock, computed immediately after the distribution. Accordingly, USP's postdistribution amount with respect to FD stock is $100. (While FD has earnings and profits of 125u immediately after the foreign divisive transaction, USP's postdistribution amount is limited to its built-in gain in FD stock immediately after the distribution ($200 – $100).) Because USP's postdistribution amount with respect to FD stock is $275 less than its predistribution amount with respect to such stock ($375 – $100), §1.367(b)-5(c)(2)(i) and (ii) require USP to reduce its basis in FD stock, but only to the extent such reduction increases USP's section 1248 amount with respect to the FD stock. As a result, USP reduces its basis in the FD stock from $100 to $75 and includes $250 in income as a deemed dividend from FD. Because the requirements of section 902 are met, USP qualifies for a deemed paid foreign tax credit with respect to the deemed dividend that it receives from FD. Under §1.902-1(d)(1), the $250 deemed dividend is out of FD's separate categories and reduces foreign income taxes as follows:

	E&P	Foreign Taxes
	150u	$30
	100u	$40
	250u	$70

(F) *Reduction in FD's statutory groupings of earnings and profits.* Under paragraph (b)(2) of this section, the reduction in FD's pre-transaction earnings that is not attributable to USP's inclusion under paragraph (d)(2)(i) of this section or §1.367(b)-5 decrease FD's statutory groupings of earnings and profits on a pro rata basis. Under paragraph (d)(3) of this section, FD's pre-transaction taxes are also ratably reduced. As described in this *Example 3* (ii)(A), the reduction in FD's pre-transaction earnings is 375u. As described in this *Example 3* (ii)(B) and (D), the entire 375u reduction was subject to inclusion as a deemed dividend by USP under paragraph (d)(2)(i) of this section or §1.367(b)-5. Thus, none of FD's pre-transaction earnings remain to be reduced under paragraph (b)(2) of this section.

(G) *FD's earnings and profits after the foreign divisive transaction.* After the reductions described in this *Example 3* (ii)(B) and (D), FD

Separate Category	E&P	Foreign Taxes
General	75u	$15
Shipping	50u	$20
	125u	$35

(e) *Foreign divisive transactions involving a foreign distributing corporation and a foreign controlled corporation.*—(1) *Scope.*—The rules of this paragraph (e) apply to a foreign divisive transaction involving a foreign distributing corporation and a foreign controlled corporation.

(2) *Earnings and profits of foreign controlled corporation.*—(i) *In general.*—Except to the extent specified in paragraph (e)(2)(ii) of this section, pre-transaction earnings of a foreign distributing corporation that are allocated to a foreign controlled corporation under the rules described in paragraphs (b)(1)(i) and (4) of this section shall carry over to the foreign controlled corporation in accordance with the rules described in §1.367(b)-7.

(ii) *Special rule for pre-transaction earnings allocated to a newly created controlled corporation.*—Section 1.367(b)-9 shall apply to pre-transaction earnings that are allocated from a foreign distributing corporation to a newly created foreign controlled corporation under the rules described in paragraph (b)(1)(i) of this section.

(3) *Foreign income taxes.*—Pre-transaction taxes related to a foreign distributing corporation's pre-transaction earnings that are allocated or reduced under the rules described in paragraph (b)(1)(i) of this section shall be ratably reduced. Pre-transaction taxes related to a foreign distributing corporation's pre-transaction earnings that are allocated to a foreign controlled corporation under the rules described in paragraph (b)(1)(i) of this section shall carry over to the foreign controlled corporation in accordance with the rules of §1.367(b)-7. Section 1.367(b)-9 shall apply to pre-transaction taxes that are allocated from a foreign distributing corporation to a newly

Separate Category	E&P	Foreign Taxes
General	300u	$60
Shipping	200u	$80
	500u	$140

(B) On January 1, 2002, FD incorporates FC and transfers to FC the Business B shipping assets. FD then distributes the FC stock to USP. The transaction meets the requirements of sections 368(a)(1)(D) and 355. Immediately after the foreign divisive transaction, the FD stock and the FC stock each have a $400 fair market value.

(ii) *Result*—(A) *Calculation of FD's earnings and profits.* Under paragraph (b)(1)(i) of this section, FD's pre-transaction earnings are reduced by an amount equal to its pre-transaction earnings times the net bases of the assets transferred to FC divided by the net bases of the assets held by FD immediately before the foreign divisive transaction (500u × (160u ÷ 320u) = 250u). Following this reduction, FD has 250u of earnings and profits (500u – 250u).

(B) *Application of §1.367(b)-5(c).* The basis adjustment and income inclusion rules of §1.367(b)-5(c)(2) apply if USP's postdistribution amount with respect to FD or FC stock is less than its predistribution amount with respect to such stock. Under §1.367(b)-5(e)(1), USP's predistribution amount with respect to FD or FC stock is USP's section 1248 amount attributable to such stock computed immediately before the distribution but after taking into account the allocation of earnings and profits as a result of the D

Separate Category	E&P	Foreign Taxes
General	150u	$30
Shipping	100u	$40
	250u	$70

(D) *Calculation of FC's earnings and profits.* Under paragraph (e)(2) of this section, the pre-transaction earnings of FD that are allocated to FC under paragraph (b)(1)(i) of this section carry over to FC in accordance with the rules of §1.367(b)-7, subject to the rule of §1.367(b)-9. Under paragraph (e)(3) of this section, FD's pre-transaction taxes related to the pre-transaction earnings that are allocated to

Separate Category	E&P	Foreign Taxes
General	150u	$30
Shipping	100u	$40
	250u	$70

Example 2—(i) *Facts.* (A) USP, a domestic corporation, has owned all of the stock of FD since FD's incorporation in 1995. USP's adjusted basis in the FD stock is $300 and the FD stock has a fair market value of $1,500. FC is a preexisting controlled corporation and FD:

Separate Category	E&P	Foreign Taxes
General	400u	$50
Passive	(100u)	$6
Shipping	200u	$80
	500u	$136

has the following earnings and profits and foreign income taxes accounts:

	E&P	Foreign Taxes
General	75u	$15
Shipping	50u	$20
	125u	$35

created foreign controlled corporation under the rules described in paragraph (b)(1)(i) of this section.

(4) *Previously taxed earnings and profits.*—[Reserved]

(5) *Coordination with §1.367(b)-5.*—See also §1.367(b)-5(c) and (d) for other rules that may apply to a foreign divisive transaction described in paragraph (e)(1) of this section.

(6) *Examples.*—The following examples illustrate the application of the rules of this section to transactions described in paragraph (e)(1) of this section. The examples presume the following facts: FD is a foreign corporation engaged in manufacturing and shipping activities through Business A and Business B, respectively. FC is a foreign corporation that is wholly owned by FD. Any earnings and profits of FD or FC described in section 904(d)(1)(D) (shipping income) qualified for the high tax exception from subpart F income under section 954(b)(4), and FD's and FC's United States shareholders elected to exclude the earnings and profits from subpart F income under section 954(b)(4) and §1.954-1(d)(1). FD and FC have calendar taxable years. FD and FC (and all of their respective qualified business units as defined in section 989) maintain a "u" functional currency, and 1u = US$1 at all times. The examples are as follows:

Example 1—(i) *Facts.* (A) USP, a domestic corporation, has owned all of the stock of FD since FD's incorporation in 1995. USP's adjusted basis in the FD stock is $400 and the FD stock has a fair market value of $800. FD owns assets with total net bases of 320u (including 160u attributable to the Business B shipping assets), and has the following pre-transaction earnings and pre-transaction taxes accounts:

	E&P	Foreign Taxes
General	300u	$60
Shipping	200u	$80
	500u	$140

reorganization. Thus, USP's predistribution amounts with respect to FD and FC stock are both $200. See also section 989(b)(2) and §1.1248-1(d)(3). Under section 358, USP allocates its $400 basis in FD stock between FD stock and FC stock according to the stock blocks' relative values, yielding a $200 ($400 × ($400 ÷ $800)) basis in each block. Under §1.367(b)-5(e)(2), USP's postdistribution amount with respect to FD or FC stock is USP's section 1248 amount with respect to such stock, computed immediately after the distribution. Accordingly, USP's postdistribution amounts with respect to FD and FC stock are both $200. Because USP's postdistribution amounts with respect to FD and FC stock are not less than USP's respective predistribution amounts, USP is not required to make any basis adjustment or include any income under §1.367(b)-5(c).

(C) *Reduction in FD's statutory groupings of earnings and profits.* Under paragraph (b)(2) of this section, the 250u reduction in FD's pre-transaction earnings decreases FD's statutory groupings of earnings and profits on a pro rata basis. Under paragraph (e)(3) of this section, FD's pre-transaction taxes also are ratably reduced. Accordingly, FD's pre-transaction earnings and pre-transaction taxes are reduced by the following amounts:

	E&P	Foreign Taxes
General	150u	$30
Shipping	100u	$40
	250u	$70

FC similarly carry over to FC in accordance with the rules of §1.367(b)-7, subject to the rule of §1.367(b)-9. As a result, under §1.367(b)-7(d), FC has the following earnings and profits and foreign income taxes accounts immediately after the foreign divisive transaction:

	E&P	Foreign Taxes
General	150u	$30
Shipping	100u	$40
	250u	$70

FD has always owned all of the FC stock. FD owns assets with total net bases of 320u (including 160u attributable to the FC stock). FD and FC have the following earnings and profits and foreign income taxes accounts:

FC:

Separate Category	E&P	Foreign Taxes
General	600u	$100
Passive	(50u)	$6
Shipping	100u	$40
	650u	$146

(B) On January 1, 2002, FD distributes the FC stock to USP in a transaction that meets the requirements of section 355. Immediately after the foreign divisive transaction, the FD stock and the FC stock each have a $750 fair market value.

(ii) *Result*—(A) *Calculation of FD's earnings and profits.* Under paragraph (b)(1)(i) and (ii)(A) of this section, FD's pre-transaction earnings are reduced by the amount of the reduction that would have been required if FD had transferred the stock of FC to a new corporation in a D reorganization. Thus, FD's pre-transaction earnings are reduced by an amount equal to its pre-transaction earnings times its net basis in the FC stock divided by the net bases of the assets held by FD immediately before the foreign divisive transaction (500u × (160u ÷ 320u) = 250u). Following this reduction, FD has 250u of earnings and profits (500u – 250u).

(B) *Application of §1.367(b)-5(c).* The basis adjustment and income inclusion rules of §1.367(b)-5(c) apply if USP's postdistribution amount with respect to FD or FC stock is less than its predistribution amount with respect to such stock. Under §1.367(b)-5(e)(1), USP's predistribution amount with respect to FD or FC stock is USP's section 1248 amount attributable to such stock computed immediately before the distribution. Thus, USP's predistribution amounts with respect to FD and FC stock are $500 and $650, respectively. See also section 989(b)(2). Under section 358, USP allocates its $300 basis in FD stock between FD stock and FC stock according to the stock blocks' relative values, yielding a $150 ($300 × ($750 ÷ $1,500)) basis in each block. Under §1.367(b)-5(e)(2), USP's postdistribution amount with respect to FD or FC stock is USP's section 1248 amount with respect to such stock, computed immediately after the distribution. Accordingly, USP's postdistribution amount with respect to FD

Separate Category	E&P	Foreign Taxes
General	166.67u	$25
Passive	0u	$0
Shipping	83.33u	$40
	250u	$65

(C) *Basis adjustments.* Under §1.367(b)-5(c)(3), USP does not increase its basis in FD stock as a result of USP's $250 deemed dividend from FD. Under §1.367(b)-5(c)(4), USP increases its basis in the FD and FC stock by the amount of its basis decrease or deemed dividend inclusion with respect to the other corporation, but only to the extent such basis increase does not diminish USP's postdistribution amount with respect to that other corporation and only to the extent of the other corporation's fair market value. Under these rules, USP increases its basis in the FD stock by the full amount by which it decreased its basis in FC ($150 + $50 = $200). USP does not increase

Separate Category	E&P	Foreign Taxes
General	233.33u	$25
Passive	(100u)	$6
Shipping	116.67u	$40
	250u	$71

(E) *Calculation of FC's earnings and profits.* Under paragraph (b)(1)(ii)(B) of this section, FC's earnings and profits are not increased (or replaced) as a result of the foreign divisive transaction. FC's earnings and profits also are not reduced because USP was not required to include a deemed dividend out of FC under §1.367(b)-5.

Example 3—(i) *Facts.* (A) USP, a domestic corporation, has owned all of the stock of FD since FD's incorporation in 1995. USP's

FD:

Separate Category	E&P	Foreign Taxes
General	300u	$50
10/50 dividends from FC1, a noncontrolled section 902 corporation	100u	$6
Shipping	200u	$80
	600u	$136

FC:

Separate Category	E&P	Foreign Taxes
General	100u	$10
Passive	(50u)	$6
Shipping	100u	$40
	150u	$56

(B) On January 1, 2002, FD transfers to FC the Business B shipping assets. FD then distributes the FC stock to USP. The transaction meets the requirements of sections 368(a)(1)(D) and 355. Immediately after the foreign divisive transaction, the FD stock and the FC stock each have a $1,000 fair market value.

stock is $250 (500u – 250u), and its postdistribution amount with respect to FC stock is $600 (while FC has 650u of earnings and profits immediately after the foreign divisive transaction, USP's postdistribution amount is limited to its built-in gain in FC stock immediately after the distribution ($750 – $150)). USP's postdistribution amount with respect to both the FD and FC stock is less than its predistribution amount with respect to such stock. This difference is $50 with respect to FC ($650 – $600), and $250 with respect to FD ($500 – $250). Under §1.367(b)-5(c)(2)(i) and (ii), USP is required to reduce its basis in the FD and FC stock, but only to the extent such reductions increase USP's section 1248 amount with respect to the stock. Accordingly, USP reduces its basis in the FC stock by $50, and thereafter USP has a $100 basis in such stock ($150 – $100). Because a reduction in USP's basis in FD stock would not increase any of USP's section 1248 amount with respect to such stock, USP includes the entire $250 difference between its predistribution and postdistribution amounts with respect to the FD stock as a deemed dividend from FD. Because the requirements of section 902 are met, USP qualifies for a deemed paid foreign tax credit with respect to the deemed dividend that it receives from FD. Under §1.960-1(i)(4), the 100u deficit in the section 904(d)(1)(A) passive separate category is allocated proportionately against the other separate categories for purposes of computing the deemed paid credit on the distribution. Thus, there are 333.33u (400u – (100u × (400u ÷ 600u))) of available earnings in the section 904(d)(1)(I) general separate category (along with $50 of foreign income taxes) and 166.67u (200u – (100u × (200u ÷ 600u))) of available earnings in the section 904(d)(1)(D) shipping separate category (along with $80 of foreign income taxes). Under §1.902-1(d)(1), the $250 deemed dividend is out of FD's separate categories and reduces foreign income taxes as follows:

its basis in the FC stock as a result of its deemed dividend from FD because any increase in the FC stock basis would diminish USP's postdistribution amount with respect to such stock.

(D) *FD's earnings and profits after the foreign divisive transaction.* Because the entire $250 reduction in FD's pre-transaction earnings was subject to inclusion under §1.367(b)-5 (as described in this *Example 2* (ii)(B)), paragraph (b)(2) of this section does not apply. FD has the following earnings and profits and foreign income taxes accounts immediately after the foreign divisive transaction (see §1.960-1(i)(4)):

adjusted basis in the FD stock is $100 and the FD stock has a fair market value of $2,000. FC is a preexisting controlled corporation and FD has always owned all of the FC stock. FD owns assets with total net bases of 320u (including 100u attributable to the FC stock and 160u attributable to the Business B shipping assets). FD and FC have the following earnings and profits and foreign income taxes accounts:

(ii) *Result*—(A) *Calculation of FD's earnings and profits.* Under paragraph (b)(4)(i) of this section, FD's pre-transaction earnings are reduced by the sum of the amounts described in paragraphs (b)(4)(i)(A) and (B) of this section. Under paragraph (b)(4)(i)(A) of this section, FD's pre-transaction earnings are reduced by an amount equal to FD's pre-transaction earnings times the net bases of the

Business B shipping assets transferred to FC divided by the total net bases in the assets held by FD immediately before the foreign divisive transaction (600u × (160u ÷ 320u) = 300u). Under paragraph (b)(4)(i)(B) of this section, FD's pre-transaction earnings are reduced by an amount equal to FD's pre-transaction earnings times FD's net bases in the stock of FC divided by the total net bases of the assets held by FD immediately before the foreign divisive transaction (600u × (100u ÷ 320u) = 187.50u). The sum of the amounts described in paragraphs (b)(4)(i)(A) and (B) of this section is 487.50u.

(B) *Application of § 1.367(b)-5(c).* The basis adjustment and income inclusion rules of § 1.367(b)-5(c)(2) apply if USP's postdistribution amount with respect to FD or FC stock is less than its predistribution amount with respect to such stock. Under § 1.367(b)-5(e)(1) and (3), USP's predistribution amount with respect to FD or FC stock is USP's section 1248 amount attributable to such stock computed immediately before the distribution, after the allocation of FD's pre-transaction earnings described in paragraphs (b)(4)(i)(A) and (ii)(A) of this section, but before the reduction in FD's pre-transaction earnings described in paragraph (b)(4)(i)(B) of this section. Thus, USP's predistribution amounts with respect to FD and FC stock are $300 (600u − 300u) and $450 (150u + 300u), respectively. See also section 989(b)(2). Under section 358, USP allocates its $100 basis in FD stock between FD stock and FC stock according to the stock blocks' relative values, yielding a $50 ($100 × ($1,000 ÷ $2,000))

Separate Category	E&P	Foreign Taxes
General	93.75u	$15.63
10/50 dividends from FC1	31.25u	$1.88
Shipping	62.50u	$25
	187.50u	$42.51

(C) *Basis adjustment.* Under § 1.367(b)-5(c)(3), the basis increase provided in § 1.367(b)-2(e)(3)(ii) does not apply with respect to USP's $187.50 deemed dividend from FD. Under § 1.367(b)-5(c)(4), USP increases its basis in the FC stock by the amount of its deemed dividend inclusion from FD, but only to the extent such basis increase does not diminish USP's postdistribution amount with respect to FC stock and only up to the fair market value of the FC stock. Under these rules, USP increases its basis in the FC stock by the full amount of its deemed dividend from FD ($50 + $187.50 = $237.50).

(D) *Reduction in FD's statutory groupings of earnings and profits.* Under paragraph (b)(2) of this section, the reduction in FD's pre-

Separate Category	E&P	Foreign Taxes
General	150u	$25
10/50 dividends from FC1	50u	$3
Shipping	100u	$40
	300u	$68

(E) *Calculation of FC's earnings and profits.* Under paragraph (b)(4)(ii) of this section, FC's earnings and profits immediately after the foreign divisive transaction equal the sum of FC's earnings and profits immediately before the foreign divisive transaction, plus the amount of the reduction in FD's earnings and profits described in paragraph (b)(4)(i)(A) of this section, except to the extent such amount was included in income as a deemed dividend pursuant to the foreign divisive transaction. The reduction in FD's earnings and profits described in paragraph (b)(4)(i)(A) of this section is 300u,

Separate Category	E&P
General	250u
10/50 dividends from FC1	50u
Passive	
Shipping	200u
	500u

(F) *FD's earnings and profits after the foreign divisive transaction.* Following the reductions described in this *Example 3* (ii)(B) and (D),

Separate Category	E&P	Foreign Taxes
General		
10/50 dividends from FC1		
Shipping		

(f) *Effective date.*—This section shall apply to section 367(b) exchanges that occur on or after the date 30 days after these regulations

basis in each block. Under § 1.367(b)-5(e)(2), USP's postdistribution amount with respect to FD or FC stock is USP's section 1248 amount with respect to such stock, computed immediately after the distribution. Accordingly, USP's postdistribution amount with respect to FD stock is $112.50 (600u − 300u − 187.50u), and its postdistribution amount with respect to FC stock is $450 (150u + 300u). Because USP's postdistribution amount with respect to FC stock is not less than its predistribution amount with respect to such stock, the § 1.367(b)-5(c)(2) basis adjustment and income inclusion rules do not apply with respect to the FC stock. Because USP's postdistribution amount with respect to FD stock is $187.50 less than its predistribution amount with respect to such stock ($300 − $112.50), § 1.367(b)-5(c)(2)(i) and (ii) require USP to reduce its basis in FD stock, but only to the extent such reduction increases USP's section 1248 amount with respect to the FD stock. Because a reduction in USP's basis in the FD stock would not increase any of USP's section 1248 amount with respect to such stock, USP includes the entire $187.50 difference between its predistribution and postdistribution amounts with respect to the FD stock as a deemed dividend from FD. Because the requirements of section 902 are met, USP qualifies for a deemed paid foreign tax credit with respect to the deemed dividend that it receives from FD. Under § 1.902-1(d)(1), the $187.50 deemed dividend is out of FD's separate categories and reduces foreign income taxes as follows:

transaction earnings that is not attributable to USP's inclusion under § 1.367(b)-5 decreases FD's statutory groupings of earnings and profits on a pro rata basis. Under paragraph (e)(3) of this section, FD's pre-transaction taxes are also ratably reduced. As described in this *Example 3* (ii)(A), the reduction in FD's pre-transaction earnings is 487.50u. As described in this *Example 3* (ii)(B), 187.50u of the 487.50u reduction is attributable to a deemed dividend inclusion by USP under § 1.367(b)-5. Thus, under paragraphs (b)(2) and (c)(3) of this section, the remaining 300u reduction in FD's pre-transaction earnings and related pre-transaction taxes is out of FD's separate categories and reduces foreign income taxes as follows:

none of which was included in income by USP as a deemed dividend pursuant to the foreign divisive transaction. Under paragraphs (e)(2) and (3) of this section, the 300u of pre-transaction earnings and related pre-transaction taxes carry over to FC and combine with FC's earnings and profits and foreign income taxes accounts in accordance with the rules described in § 1.367(b)-7. Under § 1.367(b)-7(d), FC has the following earnings and profits and foreign income taxes accounts immediately after the foreign divisive transaction:

Hovering Deficit	Taxes	Taxes Associated w/ Hovering Deficit
	$35	
	$3	
(50u)		$6
	$80	
(50u)	$118	$6

FD has the following earnings and profits and foreign income taxes accounts:

	E&P	Foreign Taxes
	56.25u	$9.37
	18.75u	$1.12
	37.50u	$15
	112.50u	$25.49

are published as final regulations in the Federal Register. [Reg. § 1.367(b)-8.]

Corporate Reorganizations: Foreign Corporations

Reorganizations: Foreign Corporations: Transfer of Property.—Temporary Reg. § 1.367(d)-1T, relating to transfers of property to foreign corporations, is proposed (published in the Federal Register on May 16, 1986) (LR-3-86).

§ 1.367(d)-1. Transfers of intangible property to foreign corporations.

Foreign Corporations: Stock Transfer Rules: Carryover of Earnings and Taxes

Foreign Corporations: Stock Transfer Rules: Carryover of Earnings and Taxes.—Amendments to Reg. §1.367(e)-1, addressing (1) the carryover of certain tax attributes, such as earnings and profits and foreign income tax accounts, when two corporations combine in a section 367(b) transaction and (2) the allocation of certain tax attributes when a corporation distributes stock of another corporation in a section 367(b) transaction, are proposed (published in the Federal Register on November 15, 2000) (REG-116050-99).

☐ Par. 12. In §1.367(e)-1, paragraph (a) is amended by adding a sentence at the end of the paragraph to read as follows:

§1.367(e)-1. **Distributions described in section 367(e)(1).**—(a) * *
* See §1.367(b)-8(c)(3) for an example illustrating the interaction of

§1.367(e)-1 with other sections of the Internal Revenue Code (such as sections 367(b) and 1248).

* * *

Section 301 Regulations: Statutory Changes Reflected

Section 301 Regulations: Statutory Changes Reflected.—Amendments to Reg. §1.368-2, updating existing regulations under section 301 to reflect statutory changes made by the Technical and Miscellaneous Revenue Act of 1988, which changes provide that the amount of a distribution of property made by a corporation to its shareholder is the fair market value of the distributed property, are proposed (published in the Federal Register on March 26, 2019) (REG-121694-16).

Par. 4. Section 1.368-2 is amended by revising the last sentence of paragraph (m)(3)(iii) to read as follows:

§1.368-2. **Definition of terms.**

* * *

(m) * * *

(3) * * *

(iii) * * * See §1.301-1(j).

* * *

Deduction for Business Interest Expense: Limitation

Deduction for Business Interest Expense: Limitation.—Reg. §1.381(c)(20)-1, regarding the limitation on the deduction for business interest expense after the enactment of recent tax legislation, is proposed (published in the Federal Register on December 28, 2018) (REG-106089-18).

Par. 5. Section 1.381(c)(20)-1 is added to read as follows:

§1.381(c)(20)-1. **Carryforward of disallowed business interest.**—(a) *Carryover requirement.*—Section 381(c)(20) provides that the acquiring corporation in a transaction described in section 381(a) will succeed to and take into account the carryover of disallowed business interest described in section 163(j)(2) to taxable years ending after the date of distribution or transfer.

(b) *Carryover of disallowed business interest described in section 163(j)(2).*—For purposes of section 381(c)(20) and this section, the term *carryover of disallowed business interest described in section 163(j)(2)* means the disallowed business interest expense carryforward (within the meaning of §1.163(j)-1(b)(9)), including any disallowed disqualified interest (within the meaning of §1.163(j)-1(b)(10)), and including the distributor or transferor corporation's disallowed business interest expense from the taxable year that ends on the date of distribution or transfer. For the application of section 382 to disallowed business interest expense described in section 163(j)(2), see the regulations under section 382, including but not limited to §1.382-2.

(c) *Limitation on use of disallowed business interest expense carryforwards in the acquiring corporation's first taxable year ending after the date of distribution or transfer.*—(1) *In general.*—In determining the extent to which the acquiring corporation may use disallowed business interest expense carryforwards in its first taxable year ending after the date of distribution or transfer, the principles of §§1.381(c)(1)-1 and 1.381(c)(1)-2 apply with appropriate adjustments, including but not limited to the adjustments described in paragraphs (c)(2) and (3) of this section.

(2) *One date of distribution or transfer within the acquiring corporation's taxable year.*—If the acquiring corporation succeeds to the disallowed business interest expense carryforwards of one or more distributor or transferor corporations on a single date of distribution or transfer within one taxable year of the acquiring corporation, then, for the acquiring corporation's first taxable year ending after the date of distribution or transfer, that part of the acquiring corporation's business interest expense deduction (if any) that is attributable to the disallowed business interest expense carryforwards of the distributor or transferor corporation is limited under this paragraph (c) to an amount equal to the post-acquisition portion of the acquiring corporation's section 163(j) limitation, as defined in paragraph (c)(4) of this section.

(3) *Two or more dates of distribution or transfer in the taxable year.*—If the acquiring corporation succeeds to the disallowed business interest expense carryforwards of two or more distributor or transferor corporations on two or more dates of distribution or transfer within one taxable year of the acquiring corporation, the limitation to be applied under this paragraph (c) is determined by applying the principles of §1.381(c)(1)-2(b) to the post-acquisition portion of the acquiring corporation's section 163(j) limitation, as defined in paragraph (c)(4) of this section.

(4) *Definition.*—For purposes of this paragraph (c), the term *post-acquisition portion of the acquiring corporation's section 163(j) limitation* means the amount that bears the same ratio to the acquiring corporation's section 163(j) limitation (within the meaning of

§1.163(j)-1(b)(31)) (or, if the acquiring corporation is a member of a consolidated group, the consolidated group's section 163(j) limitation) for the first taxable year ending after the date of distribution or transfer (taking into account items to which the acquiring corporation succeeds under section 381, other than disallowed business interest expense carryforwards) as the number of days in that year after the date of distribution or transfer bears to the total number of days in that year.

(5) *Examples.*—For purposes of this paragraph (c)(5), unless otherwise stated, X, Y, and Z are taxable domestic C corporations that were incorporated on January 1, 2018 and that file their tax returns on a calendar-year basis; none of X, Y, or Z is a member of a consolidated group; the small business exemption in §1.163(j)-2(d) does not apply; interest expense is deductible except to the extent of the potential application of section 163(j); and the facts set forth the only corporate activity. The principles of this paragraph (c) are illustrated by the following examples.

(i) *Example 1: Transfer before last day of acquiring corporation's taxable year*—(A) *Facts.* On October 31, 2019, X transferred all of its assets to Y in a statutory merger to which section 361 applies. For the 2018 taxable year, X had $400x of disallowed business interest expense, and Y had $0 of disallowed business interest expense. For the taxable year ending October 31, 2019, X had an additional $350x of disallowed business interest expense (X did not deduct any of its 2018 carryforwards in its 2019 taxable year). For the taxable year ending December 31, 2019, Y had business interest expense of $100x, business interest income of $200x, and adjusted taxable income (ATI) of $1,000x. Y's section 163(j) limitation for the 2019 taxable year was $500x ($200x + (30 percent x $1,000x) = $500x).

(B) *Analysis.* Pursuant to §1.163(j)-5(b)(2), Y deducts its $100x of current-year business interest expense (as defined in §1.163(j)-5(a)(2)(i)) before any disallowed business interest expense carryforwards (including X's carryforwards) from a prior taxable year are deducted. The aggregate disallowed business interest expense of X carried forward under section 381(c)(20) to Y's taxable year ending December 31, 2019, is $750x. However, pursuant to paragraph (c)(2) of this section, for Y's first taxable year ending after the date of distribution or transfer, the maximum amount of X's disallowed business interest expense carryforwards that Y can deduct is equal to the post-acquisition portion of Y's section 163(j) limitation. Pursuant to paragraph (c)(4) of this section, the post-acquisition portion of Y's section 163(j) limitation means Y's section 163(j) limitation times the ratio of the number of days in the taxable year after the date of distribution or transfer to the total number of days in that year. Therefore, only $84x of the aggregate amount ($500x x (61/365) = $84x) may be deducted by Y in that year, and the remaining $666x ($750x - $84x = $666x) is carried forward to the succeeding taxable year.

(C) *Transfer on last day of acquiring corporation's taxable year.* The facts are the same as in *Example 1* in paragraph (c)(5)(i)(A) of this section, except that X's transfer of its assets to Y occurred on December 31, 2019. For the taxable year ending December 31, 2019, X had an additional $350x of disallowed business interest expense (X did not deduct any of its 2018 carryforwards in its 2019 taxable year). For the taxable year ending December 31, 2020, Y had business interest expense of $100x, business interest income of $200x, and ATI of $1,000x. Y's section 163(j) limitation for the 2020 taxable year was $500x ($200x + (30 percent x $1,000x) = $500x). The aggregate disallowed business interest expense of X carried under section 381(c)(20) to Y's taxable year ending December 31, 2020, is $750x. Paragraph (c)(2) of this section does not limit the amount of X's disallowed business interest expense carryforwards that may be deducted by Y in the 2020 taxable year. Since the amount of Y's section 163(j) limit for the 2020 taxable year was $500x, Y may deduct the full amount ($100x) of its own business interest expense for the 2020 taxable year, along with $400x of X's disallowed business interest expense carryforwards.

(ii) *Example 2: Multiple transferors on same date*—(A) *Facts.* On October 31, 2019, X and Y transferred all of their assets to Z in statutory mergers to which section 361 applies. For the 2018 taxable year, X had $300x of disallowed business interest expense, Y had $200x, and Z had $0. For the taxable year ending October 31, 2019, each of X and Y had an additional $125x of disallowed business interest expense (neither X nor Y deducted any of its 2018 carryforwards in 2019). For the taxable year ending December 31, 2019, Z had business interest expense of $100x, business interest income of $200x,

and ATI of $1,000x. Z's section 163(j) limitation for the 2019 taxable year was $500x ($200x + (30 percent x $1,000x) = $500x).

(B) *Analysis.* The aggregate disallowed business interest expense of X and Y carried under section 381(c)(20) to Z's taxable year ending December 31, 2019, is $750x. However, pursuant to paragraph (c)(2) of this section, only $84x of the aggregate amount ($500x x (61/365) = $84x) may be deducted by Z in that year. Moreover, under paragraph (b)(2) of this section, this amount only may be deducted by Z in that year after Z has deducted its $100 of current-year business interest expense (as defined in § 1.163(j)-5(a)(2)(i)).

(d) *Applicability date.*—This section applies to taxable years ending after the date the Treasury decision adopting these regulations as final regulations is published in the **Federal Register**. However, taxpayers and their related parties, within the meaning of sections 267(b) and 707(b)(1), may apply the rules of this section to a taxable year beginning after December 31, 2017, so long as the taxpayers and their related parties consistently apply the rules of this section, the section 163(j) regulations (within the meaning of § 1.163(j)-1(b)(32)), and if applicable, §§ 1.263A-9, 1.381(c)(20)-1, 1.382-6, 1.383-1, 1.469-9, 1.882-5, 1.1502-13, 1.1502-21, 1.1502-36, 1.1502-79, 1.1502-91 through 1.1502-99 (to the extent they effectuate the rules of §§ 1.382-6 and 1.383-1), and 1.1504-4 to those taxable years. [Reg. § 1.381(c)(20)-1.]

Life Insurance Companies: Computation and Reporting of Reserves

Life Insurance Companies: Computation and Reporting of Reserves.—Amendments to Reg. § 1.381(c)(22)-1, providing guidance on the computation of life insurance reserves and the change in basis of computing certain reserves of insurance companies, are proposed (published in the Federal Register on April 2, 2020) (REG-132529-17).

Par. 3. In § 1.381(c)(22)-1, paragraph (b)(6) is removed and reserved.

§ 1.381(c)(22)-1. Successor life insurance company.

Deduction for Business Interest Expense: Limitation

Deduction for Business Interest Expense: Limitation.—Amendments to Reg. §§ 1.382-1 and 1.382-2, regarding the limitation on the deduction for business interest expense after the enactment of recent tax legislation, are proposed (published in the Federal Register on December 28, 2018) (REG-106089-18).

Par. 6. Section 1.382-1 is amended by:

1. Adding entries for § 1.382-2(a)(7) and (8);
2. Revising the entry for § 1.382-2(b)(3);
3. Adding entries for § 1.382-6(b)(4), (b)(4)(i), and (b)(4)(ii);
4. Revising the entry for § 1.382-6(h); and
5. Adding entries for § 1.382-6(h)(1) and (2).

The additions and revisions read as follows:

§ 1.382-1. Table of contents.

* * *

§ 1.382-2 General rules for ownership change.

(a) * * *

(7) Section 382 disallowed business interest carryforward.
(8) Testing period.

(b) * * *

(3) Rules provided in paragraphs (a)(1)(i)(A), (a)(1)(ii), (iv), and (v), (a)(2)(iv) through (vi), (a)(3)(i), and (a)(4) through (8) of this section.

* * *

Par. 7. Section 1.382-2 is amended by:

1. Revising paragraph (a)(1)(i)(A);
2. Removing ", or" and adding "; or" in its place at the end of paragraph (a)(1)(i)(B);
3. Revising paragraphs (a)(1)(ii) introductory text and (a)(1)(ii)(A);
4. Removing ", and" and adding "; and" in its place at the end of paragraph (a)(1)(ii)(B);
5. Removing the last sentence in paragraphs (a)(1)(iv) and (v);
6. Removing the commas and adding semicolons in their place at the end of paragraphs (a)(2)(i) and (iii);
7. Removing the period and adding a semicolon in its place at the end of paragraph (a)(2)(ii);
8. Removing ", and" and adding a semicolon in its place at the end of paragraph (a)(2)(iv);
9. Removing "1.383-1T(c)(3)." and adding § 1.383-1T(c)(3); and" in its place in paragraph (a)(2)(v);
10. Adding paragraph (a)(2)(vi);
11. Removing the last sentence in paragraphs (a)(3)(i), (a)(4)(i), and (a)(5) and (6);
12. Adding paragraphs (a)(7) and (8); and
13. Revising paragraph (b)(3).

The revisions and additions read as follows:

§ 1.382-2. General rules for ownership change.—(a) * * *

(1) * * *

(i) * * *

(A) Is entitled to use a net operating loss carryforward, a capital loss carryover, a carryover of excess foreign taxes under section 904(c), a carryforward of a general business credit under section 39, a carryover of a minimum tax credit under section 53, or a

§ 1.382-6 Allocation of income and loss to periods before and after the change date for purposes of section 382.

* * *

(b) * * *

(4) Allocation of business interest expense.
(i) In general.
(ii) Example.

* * *

(h) Applicability date.
(1) In general.
(2) Paragraphs (b)(1) and (4) of this section.

* * *

section 382 disallowed business interest carryforward described in paragraph (a)(7) of this section;

* * *

(ii) *Distributor or transferor loss corporation in a transaction under section 381.*—Notwithstanding that a loss corporation ceases to exist under state law, if its disallowed business interest expense carryforwards, net operating loss carryforwards, excess foreign taxes, or other items described in section 381(c) are succeeded to and taken into account by an acquiring corporation in a transaction described in section 381(a), such loss corporation shall be treated as continuing in existence until—

    (A) Any pre-change losses (excluding pre-change credits described in § 1.383-1(c)(3)), determined as if the date of such transaction were the change date, are fully utilized or expire under section 163(j), 172, or 1212;

* * *

    (2) * * *

    (vi) Any section 382 disallowed business interest carryforward.

* * *

    (7) *Section 382 disallowed business interest carryforward.*—The term *section 382 disallowed business interest carryforward* includes the following items:

    (i) The loss corporation's disallowed business interest expense carryforwards, as defined in § 1.163(j)-1(b)(9), including disallowed disqualified interest, within the meaning of § 1.163(j)-1(b)(10), as of the ownership change.

    (ii) The carryforward of the loss corporation's disallowed business interest expense (within the meaning of § 1.163(j)-1(b)(8)) paid or accrued (without regard to section 163(j)) in the pre-change period (within the meaning of § 1.382-6(g)(2)) in the year of the testing date, determined by allocating an equal portion of the disallowed business interest expense paid or accrued (without regard to section 163(j)) in the year of the testing date to each day in that year, regardless of whether the loss corporation has made a closing-of-the-books election under § 1.382-6(b)(2).

    (8) *Testing period.*—Notwithstanding the temporal limitations provided in § 1.382-2T(d)(3)(i), the testing period for a loss corporation can begin as early as the first day of the first taxable year from which there is a section 382 disallowed business interest carryforward to the first taxable year ending after the testing date.

    (b) * * *

    (3) *Rules provided in paragraphs (a)(1)(i)(A), (a)(1)(ii), (iv), and (v), (a)(2)(iv) through (vi), (a)(3)(i), and (a)(4) through (8) of this section.*—The rules provided in paragraphs (a)(1)(i)(A), (a)(1)(ii), (iv), and (v), (a)(2)(iv) through (vi), (a)(3)(i), and (a)(4) through (8) of this section apply to testing dates occurring on or after the date the Treasury decision adopting these regulations as final regulations is published in the **Federal Register.** For loss corporations that have testing dates occurring before the date the Treasury decision adopting these regulations as final regulations is published in the **Federal Register**, see § 1.382-2 as contained in 26 CFR part 1, revised April 1, 2018. However, taxpayers and their related parties, within the meaning of sections 267(b) and 707(b)(1), may apply the rules of this section to testing dates occurring during a taxable year beginning after December 31, 2017, so long as the taxpayers and their related parties consistently apply the rules of this section, the section 163(j) regulations (within the meaning of § 1.163(j)-1(b)(32)), § § 1.382-5, 1.382-6, and 1.383-1, and if applicable, § § 1.263A-9, 1.381(c)(20)-1, 1.469-9, 1.882-5, 1.1502-13, 1.1502-21, 1.1502-36, 1.1502-79, 1.1502-91 through 1.1502-99 (to the extent they effectuate the rules of § § 1.382-2, 1.382-5, 1.382-6, and 1.383-1), and 1.1504-4 to taxable years beginning after December 31, 2017.

Built-in Gain and Loss: Under Section 382(h)

    Built-in Gain and Loss: Under Section 382(h).—Amendments to Reg. § § 1.382-1 and 1.382-2, regarding the items of income and deduction which are included in the calculation of built-in gains and losses under section 382 of the Internal Revenue Code, and reflecting numerous changes made to the Code by the enactment of recent tax legislation, are proposed (published in the Federal Register on September 10, 2019) (REG-125710-18). Proposed amendments to Reg. § 1.382-2(b)(4) withdrawn by REG-125710-18 on January 14, 2020.

    Par. 2. Section 1.382-1 is amended by:

    a. Under § 1.382-2, adding reserved entries for (a)(7) and (8) and entries for (a)(9) through (13), and (b)(4); and

    b. Revising the entry for § 1.382-7.

    The additions and revision read as follows:

§ 1.382-1. Table of contents.

* * *

§ 1.382-2 General rules for ownership change.
  (a) * * *
    (7) [Reserved]
    (8) [Reserved]
    (9) Net unrealized built-in gain.
    (10) Net unrealized built-in loss.
    (11) Recognized built-in gain.
    (12) Recognized built-in loss.
    (13) Section 382 regulations.
  (b) * * *
    (4) Rules provided in paragraphs (a)(9) through (13) of this section.

* * *

§ 1.382-7 Built-in gains and losses.
  (a) Overview.
  (b) Definitions.
    (1) Change year.
    (2) Cost recovery deduction.
    (3) First-year nonrecourse COD income.
    (4) First-year recourse COD income.
    (5) Inadequately secured nonrecourse liabilities.
    (6) Negative section 163(j) expense.
    (7) Nonrecourse liabilities.
    (8) Pre-change excess recourse liabilities.
    (9) Recognition period.
    (10) Section 382 asset.
    (11) Section 382 excess business interest expense.
    (12) Taxable income or timing limitation.
  (c) Net unrealized built-in gains and losses.
    (1) In general.
    (2) Consistency rules.
      (i) In general.
      (ii) Members of consolidated groups.
    (3) Computation of net unrealized built-in gain and net unrealized built-in loss.
      (i) In general.
      (ii) Adjustments related to discharge of indebtedness.
        (A) In general.

      (B) Exception for first-year recourse COD income.
        (1) Discharge of indebtedness income included in gross income.
        (2) Excluded discharge of indebtedness income reducing post-ownership change attributes.
        (3) Excluded discharge of indebtedness income reducing basis.
      (iii) Additional operating rules.
        (A) Value of contingent liabilities.
        (B) Inventory.
        (C) Limitation on total amount of adjustment to NUBIL/NUBIG regarding recourse COD income.
        (D) Timing of adjustments described in paragraphs (c)(3)(ii)(B)(1) through (3) of this section.
        (E) Adjusted basis of the loss corporation's section 382 assets.
        (F) [Reserved]
  (d) Recognized built-in gain and loss.
    (1) In general.
    (2) Recognized built-in gain.
      (i) In general.
      (ii) Disposition of an asset.
      (iii) Income from discharge of indebtedness attributable to certain recourse liabilities.
      (iv) Income from discharge of indebtedness attributable to certain nonrecourse liabilities.
        (A) Treatment as RBIG.
        (B) Adjustment to basis.
        (C) Limitation on total amount of RBIG regarding nonrecourse COD income.
        (D) No adjustment to the NUBIG/NUBIL computation.
      (v) Installment method.
      (vi) Prepaid income.
    (3) Recognized built-in loss.
      (i) In general.
      (ii) Disposition of an asset.
      (iii) Cost recovery deductions.
      (iv) Bad debt expense.
      (v) Deductions for payments on certain liabilities.
      (vi) Deduction for section 382 excess business interest expense.

(A) In general.

(B) No adjustment to the NUBIG/NUBIL computation.

(4) Additional recognized built-in gain and loss items.

(5) Section 382 disallowed business interest carryforwards.

(e) General operating rules.

(1) Anti-duplication rule.

Par. 3. Section 1.382-2 is amended by adding reserved paragraphs (a)(7) and (8) and paragraphs (a)(9) through (13) and (b)(4) to read as follows:

§1.382-2. General rules for ownership change.—(a) * * *

(7) - (8) [Reserved]

(9) *Net unrealized built-in gain.*—The term *net unrealized built-in gain* means a positive amount determined under §1.382-7(c)(3).

(10) *Net unrealized built-in loss.*—The term *net unrealized built-in loss* means a negative amount determined under §1.382-7(c)(3).

(11) *Recognized built-in gain.*—The term *recognized built-in gain* has the meaning provided in §1.382-7(d)(2).

(2) References to the principles of regulations under section 1374.

(f) Examples.

(g) Applicability dates.

(1) In general.

(2) Paragraph (d)(2)(vi) of this section.

* * *

(12) *Recognized built-in loss.*—The term *recognized built-in loss* has the meaning provided in §1.382-7(d)(3).

(13) *Section 382 regulations.*—The term *section 382 regulations* means this section and §§1.382-3 through 1.382-12.

(b) * * *

(4) [Proposed amendments withdrawn by REG-125710-18 on January 14, 2020.]

Built-in Gain and Loss: Under Section 382(h): Revised Applicability Dates

Built-in Gain and Loss: Revised Applicability Dates.—Amendments to Reg. §§1.382-1 and 1.382-2, providing guidance regarding the items of income and deduction that are included in the calculation of built-in gains and losses under section 382 of the Internal Revenue Code, are proposed (published in the Federal Register on January 14, 2020) (REG-125710-18).

Par. 2. Section 1.382-1, as proposed to be revised by 84 FR 47455, September 10, 2019, is further amended by revising the entry for §1.382-7(g) to read as follows:

§1.382-1. Table of Contents.

* * *

§1.382-7 Built-in gains and losses.

* * *

(g) Applicability dates.

(1) In general.

(2) Transition relief.

(3) Paragraph (d)(2)(vi) of this section.

* * *

Par. 3. Section 1.382-2, as proposed to be amended by 84 FR 47455, September 10, 2019, is further amended by revising paragraph (b)(4) to read as follows:

§1.382-2. General rules for ownership change.

* * *

(b) * * *

(4) *Rules provided in paragraphs (a)(9) through (13) of this section.*—The rules of paragraphs (a)(9) through (13) of this section apply to any ownership change that occurs after the date that is 30 days after the date of publication in the **Federal Register** of a Treasury decision adopting these proposed regulations as final regulations, if §1.382-7(g)(2) does not apply to that ownership change. Notwithstanding the preceding sentence, a taxpayer may apply the rules of paragraphs (a)(9) through (13) of this section to an ownership change to which §1.382-7(g)(2) applies if the taxpayer applies the rules of §1.382-7 to such ownership change.

Carryforwards: Ownership Change: Limitations

Carryforwards: Ownership Change: Limitations.—Reg. §1.382-2T, relating to the limitation on net operating loss carryforwards and certain built-in losses following ownership changes, is proposed (published in the Federal Register on August 11, 1987) (LR-106-86). Reg. §1.382-1T was redesignated as Reg. §1.382-1 on 10/2/92 by T.D. 8440.

§1.382-2T. Definition of ownership change under section 382, as amended by the Tax Reform Act of 1986 (temporary).

Carryovers: Excess Credits: Use of Pre-change Attributes

Carryovers: Excess Credits: Use of Pre-change Attributes.—Amendments to Reg. §1.382-2T, relating to the manner and method of absorbing the Code Sec. 382 limitation with respect to certain capital losses and excess credits after there has been an ownership change of a corporation, are proposed (published in the Federal Register on September 20, 1989) (CO-69-87). Reg. §§1.383-1 and 1.383-2 were adopted by T.D. 8352 on 6/26/91.

§1.382-2T. Definition of ownership change under section 382, as amended by the Tax Reform Act of 1986 (temporary).

Deduction for Business Interest Expense: Limitation

Deduction for Business Interest Expense: Limitation.—Amendments to Reg. §§1.382-5 and 1.382-6, regarding the limitation on the deduction for business interest expense after the enactment of recent tax legislation, are proposed (published in the Federal Register on December 28, 2018) (REG-106089-18).

Par. 8. Section 1.382-5 is amended by revising the first and second sentences of paragraph (d)(1) and by adding three sentences to the end of paragraph (f) to read as follows:

§1.382-5. Section 382 limitation.

* * *

(d) * * *

(1) * * * If a loss corporation has two (or more) ownership changes, any losses or section 382 disallowed business interest carryforwards (within the meaning of §1.382-2(a)(7)) attributable to the period preceding the earlier ownership change are treated as pre-change losses with respect to both ownership changes. Thus, the later

ownership change may result in a lesser (but never in a greater) section 382 limitation with respect to such pre-change losses. * * *

* * *

(f) * * * Paragraph (d)(1) of this section applies with respect to an ownership change occurring on or after the date the Treasury decision adopting these regulations as final regulations is published in the **Federal Register**. For loss corporations that have undergone an ownership change before or after the date the Treasury decision adopting these regulations as final regulations is published in the

Federal Register, see §1.382-5 as contained in 26 CFR part 1, revised April 1, 2018. However, taxpayers and their related parties, within the meaning of sections 267(b) and 707(b)(1), may apply the rules of this section to testing dates occurring during a taxable year beginning after December 31, 2017, so long as the taxpayers and their related parties consistently apply the rules of this section, the section

Par. 9. Section 1.382-6 is amended by:

1. Removing "Subject to paragraphs (b)(3)(ii) and (d)" in the first sentence of paragraph (b)(1) and adding "Subject to paragraphs (b)(3)(ii), (b)(4), and (d)" in its place;

2. Adding paragraph (b)(4); and

3. Revising paragraph (h).

The addition and revision read as follows:

§1.382-6. Allocation of income and loss to periods before and after the change date for purposes of section 382.

* * *

(b) * * *

(4) *Allocation of business interest expense.*—(i) *In general.*—Regardless of whether a loss corporation has made a closing-of-the-books election pursuant to paragraph (b) of this section, for purposes of calculating the taxable income of a loss corporation attributable to the pre-change period, the amount of the loss corporation's deduction for current-year business interest expense, within the meaning of §1.163(j)-5(a)(2)(i), is calculated based on a single tax year and is allocated between the pre-change period and the post-change period by ratably allocating an equal portion to each day in the year.

(ii) *Example.*—(A) *Facts.* X is a calendar-year C corporation that is not a member of a consolidated group. On May 26, 2019, X is acquired by Z (an unrelated third-party) in a transaction that qualifies as an ownership change under section 382(g). For calendar year 2019, X has paid or accrued $100x of current-year business interest expense (within the meaning of §1.163(j)-5(a)(2)(i)) and has an $81x section 163(j) limitation (within the meaning of §1.163(j)-1(b)(31)).

(B) *Analysis.* Pursuant to paragraph (b)(4)(i) of this section, regardless of whether X has made a closing-of-the-books election pursuant to paragraph (b) of this section, X's business interest expense deduction is ratably allocated between the pre-change and post-change periods. For calendar year 2019, X may deduct $81x of business interest expense (see §1.163(j)-2(b)), of which $32.4x ($81x x (146 days/365 days) = $32.4x) is allocable to the pre-change period.

The remaining $19x of interest that was paid or accrued in calendar year 2019 is disallowed business interest expense, of which $7.6x ($19x x (146 days/365 days) = $7.6x) is allocable to the pre-change period. The $7.6x of disallowed business interest expense is treated as a section 382 disallowed business interest carryforward (see §1.382-2(a)(7)), and thus is a pre-change loss within the meaning of §1.382-2(a)(2).

* * *

(h) *Applicability date.*—(1) *In general.*—This section applies to ownership changes occurring on or after June 22, 1994.

(2) *Paragraphs (b)(1) and (4) of this section.*—Paragraphs (b)(1) and (4) of this section apply with respect to an ownership change occurring during a taxable year ending after the date the Treasury decision adopting these regulations as final regulations is published in the **Federal Register**. For ownership changes occurring during a taxable year ending before the date the Treasury decision adopting these regulations is published in the **Federal Register**, see §1.382-6 as contained in 26 CFR part 1, revised April 1, 2018. However, taxpayers and their related parties, within the meaning of sections 267(b) and 707(b)(1), may apply the rules of this section to testing dates occurring during a taxable year beginning after December 31, 2017, so long as the taxpayers and their related parties consistently apply the rules of this section, and the section 163(j) regulations (within the meaning of §1.163(j)-1(b)(32)) and §1.383-1, and if applicable, §§1.263A-9, 1.381(c)(20)-1, 1.469-9, 1.882-5, 1.1502-13, 1.1502-21, 1.1502-36, 1.1502-79, 1.1502-91 through 1.1502-99 (to the extent they effectuate the rules of §§1.382-6 and 1.383-1), and 1.1504-4 to taxable years beginning after December 31, 2017.

Built-in Gain and Loss: Under Section 382(h)

Built-in Gain and Loss: Under Section 382(h).—Amendments to Reg. §1.382-7, regarding the items of income and deduction which are included in the calculation of built-in gains and losses under section 382 of the Internal Revenue Code, and reflecting numerous changes made to the Code by the enactment of recent tax legislation, are proposed (published in the Federal Register on September 10, 2019) (REG-125710-18). Proposed amendments to Reg. §1.382-7(g) withdrawn by REG-125710-18 on January 14, 2020.

Par. 4. Section 1.382-7 is revised to read as follows:

§1.382-7. Built-in gains and losses.—(a) *Overview.*—This section provides rules governing the determination of a loss corporation's net unrealized built-in gain or net unrealized built-in loss, as well as its recognized built-in gains and recognized built-in losses for purposes of section 382 and the section 382 regulations. Paragraph (b) of this section provides definitions of terms used for purposes of this section. Paragraph (c) of this section provides the rules regarding the determination of a loss corporation's net unrealized built-in gain or net unrealized built-in loss. Paragraph (d) of this section provides the rules regarding the determination of a loss corporation's recognized built-in gain or recognized built-in loss. Paragraph (e) of this section provides an anti-duplication rule to prevent duplicate inclusion of items in the computation of net unrealized built-in gain or net unrealized built-in loss, or in the computation of recognized built-in gain or recognized built-in loss. Paragraph (f) of this section provides examples illustrating the rules of this section. Paragraph (g) of this section provides applicability dates for the rules of this section.

(b) *Definitions.*—The following definitions apply for purposes of this section.

(1) *Change year.*—The term *change year* has the meaning provided in §1.382-6(g)(1).

(2) *Cost recovery deduction.*—The term *cost recovery deduction* means any deduction for depreciation under section 167 or section 168, any deduction for the amortization of intangibles (for example, under section 167 or 197) and amortizable expenditures (for example, under section 195(b)(1)(B), section 248 or section 1245(a)(2)(C)), or any deduction for depletion under section 611.

(3) *First-year nonrecourse COD income.*—The term *first-year nonrecourse COD income* means any income from discharge of indebtedness that the loss corporation recognizes (including income that is

excluded from gross income under section 108(a)(1)) during the first twelve months of the recognition period on inadequately secured nonrecourse liabilities.

(4) *First-year recourse COD income.*—The term *first-year recourse COD income* means any income from discharge of indebtedness (including from liabilities described in paragraph (c)(3)(i)(C) of this section) that the loss corporation recognizes (including income that is excluded from gross income under section 108(a)(1)) during the first twelve months of the recognition period on all of the loss corporation's liabilities immediately before the ownership change (excluding nonrecourse liabilities) to the extent of its pre-change excess recourse liabilities.

(5) *Inadequately secured nonrecourse liabilities.*—The term *inadequately secured nonrecourse liabilities* means any nonrecourse liability of which, immediately before the ownership change:

(i) The adjusted issue price (within the meaning of §1.1275-1(b)) of the nonrecourse liability; exceeds

(ii) The fair market value of the property (determined without regard to section 7701(g) and §1.1001-2(a)(4)(i)) which secures such nonrecourse liability.

(6) *Negative section 163(j) expense.*—The term *negative section 163(j) expense* has the meaning provided in §1.163(j)-6(h)(1).

(7) *Nonrecourse liabilities.*—The term *nonrecourse liabilities* has the same meaning as the term nonrecourse liability has in §1.1001-2(a)(4)(i).

(8) *Pre-change excess recourse liabilities.*—The term *pre-change excess recourse liabilities* means:

(i) If the loss corporation is under the jurisdiction of a court under title 11 of the United States Code on the change date, in an action that results in a discharge of recourse liabilities of the loss corporation, then the amount of all of the loss corporation's liabilities immediately before the ownership change (excluding nonrecourse liabilities) that are discharged by order of the court in that action; or

(ii) In all other cases, an amount equal to the excess, if any, of:

(A) The aggregate adjusted issue price (within the meaning of §1.1275-1(b)) of the loss corporation's liabilities immediately before the ownership change, excluding—

(1) Recourse liabilities to the extent that they would not be included in the determination of whether the loss corporation is insolvent within the meaning of section 108(d)(3), and

(2) Nonrecourse liabilities; over

(B) The sum of the fair market value of the assets that the loss corporation owns immediately before the ownership change, reduced, but not below zero, by the amount of nonrecourse liabilities that is secured by such assets immediately before the ownership change.

(9) *Recognition period.*—The term *recognition period* has the meaning provided in section 382(h)(7)(A).

(10) *Section 382 asset.*—The term *section 382 asset* means any asset that the loss corporation owns immediately before the ownership change, including goodwill and other intangible assets, but excluding those assets described in section 382(h)(3)(B)(ii). For purposes of this definition, all accounts receivable, other than those that were acquired in the ordinary course of the loss corporation's business, are treated as items described in section 382(h)(3)(B)(ii).

(11) *Section 382 excess business interest expense.*—The term *section 382 excess business interest expense* means the amount of business interest expense of a partnership for a taxable year that was disallowed under §1.163(j)-2(b) but not suspended under section 704(d).

(12) *Taxable income or timing limitation.*—The term *taxable income or timing limitation* means:

(i) A limitation set forth in the Internal Revenue Code of 1986, as amended (Code), on the amount of a deduction that may otherwise be claimed by a loss corporation, based on, or derived from, any amount of a loss corporation's taxable income (see, for example, section 170(b)(2)(A)); or

(ii) A limitation set forth in the Code that defers the timing of a deduction that is otherwise allowable under the Code or regulations (see, for example, sections 267(a)(2) and 469).

(c) *Net unrealized built-in gains and losses.*—(1) *In general.* This paragraph (c) provides rules regarding the calculation of a loss corporation's net unrealized built-in gain or net unrealized built-in loss for purposes of section 382 and the section 382 regulations. See paragraph (e)(1) of this section (regarding anti-duplication).

(2) *Consistency rules.*—(i) *In general.*—No amount is included in the calculation of net unrealized built-in gain or net unrealized built-in loss if the amount is properly allocable to the pre-change period (within the meaning of §1.382-6(g)(2)) pursuant to §1.382-6 and is included in the determination of the loss corporation's taxable income or net operating loss for the change year.

(ii) *Members of consolidated groups.*—If a loss corporation enters or leaves a consolidated group on the date of an ownership change for purposes of section 382, the principles of §1.1502-76(b) apply in determining the treatment of any taxable item for purposes of this section. Accordingly, items that are includible (under the end of the day rule (within the meaning of §1.1502-76(b)(1)(ii)(A)) or otherwise) in the taxable year that ends as a result of the change in status of a loss corporation (S) are not treated as recognized or taken into account during the recognition period for purposes of section 382 and the section 382 regulations. See §1.1502-28(b)(11) (regarding allocation of excluded COD income under end of the day rule principles). Moreover, no such item is included in the determination of net unrealized built-in gain or net unrealized built-in loss. For example, if income from the discharge of indebtedness is includable in the taxable year that ends as a result of S's change in status, that income is neither treated as taken into account during the recognition period nor included in the determination of net unrealized built-in gain or net unrealized built-in loss. Further, the determination of net unrealized built-in gain or net unrealized built-in loss excludes the fair market value and basis of any asset that is disposed of on the change date if the gain or loss from that asset is includible in the taxable year that ends as a result of S's change in status. In contrast, items that are includible (under the next day rule (within the meaning of §1.1502-76(b)(1)(ii)(B)) or otherwise) in the taxable year that begins as a result of S's change in status are treated as occurring in the recognition period, and those items (and the basis and fair market value of any assets that generate those items) are among the amounts included in the determination of net unrealized built-in gain or loss.

(3) *Computation of net unrealized built-in gain and net unrealized built-in loss.*—(i) *In general.*—A loss corporation's *net unrealized built-in gain*, if positive, or *net unrealized built-in loss*, if negative, is the amount equal to—

(A) The sum of the amount that would be realized (taking into account section 382(h)(8)) if, immediately before the ownership change, the loss corporation—

(1) Had satisfied each inadequately secured nonrecourse liabilities by surrendering to the creditor all of the assets securing that debt; and

(2) Had sold all of its section 382 assets (other than those assets described in paragraph (c)(3)(i)(A)(1) of this section) at fair market value to an unrelated third party with the hypothetical buyer assuming no liabilities; decreased by

(B) The aggregate adjusted basis of the loss corporation's section 382 assets immediately before the ownership change; decreased by

(C) The amount of any non-contingent liability of the loss corporation immediately before the ownership change for which the loss corporation would be allowed a deduction (including a deduction for a capital loss) on payment of the liability (determined without regard to any taxable income or timing limitation); decreased by

(D) The estimated value of any liability of the loss corporation that is contingent immediately before the ownership change, for which, upon the removal of the contingency, the loss corporation would be allowed a deduction (including a deduction for a capital loss) on payment or accrual (determined without regard to any taxable income or timing limitation); increased or decreased by

(E) The loss corporation's section 481 adjustments that would be taken into account on the sale referred to in paragraph (c)(3)(i)(A) of this section; increased by

(F) The amount that would be treated as recognized built-in gain under paragraph (d)(2) of this section if all amounts (except for amounts described in paragraph (d)(2)(ii) of this section) were properly taken into account during the recognition period; decreased by

(G) The amount that would be treated as recognized built-in loss under paragraph (d)(3) of this section if all amounts (except for amounts described in paragraph (d)(3)(ii) of this section) were properly taken into account during the recognition period.

(ii) *Adjustments related to discharge of indebtedness.*—(A) *In general.*—Except as provided in paragraph (c)(3)(ii)(B) of this section, no amount of discharge of indebtedness income recognized during the recognition period that is included in gross income under section 61(a)(12) or excluded under section 108(a) is added to the computation of the loss corporation's net unrealized built-in gain or net unrealized built-in loss. See paragraphs (c)(2) and (c)(3)(iii)(C) of this section for limitations on amounts that can be included in the computation of net unrealized built-in gain and net unrealized built-in loss.

(B) *Exception for first-year recourse COD income.*—A loss corporation may apply the provisions of this paragraph (c)(3)(ii)(B) to all of its first-year recourse COD income, subject to the timing rules of paragraphs (c)(3)(iii)(D) of this section. An adjustment that is made pursuant to this paragraph (c)(3)(ii)(B) can cause a loss corporation that would otherwise have a net unrealized built-in loss to have a net unrealized built-in gain or to meet the requirements of section 382(h)(3)(B) such that the loss corporation's net unrealized built-in gain or net unrealized built-in loss is zero. See paragraphs (c)(2) and (c)(3)(iii)(C) of this section for limitations on amounts that can be included in the computation of net unrealized built-in gain and net unrealized built-in loss.

(1) *Discharge of indebtedness income included in gross income.*—The amount calculated under paragraph (c)(3)(i) of this section is increased by the amount of all first-year recourse COD income that is included in gross income under section 61(a)(12). This amount of first-year recourse COD income is treated as recognized built-in gain. See paragraph (d)(2)(iii) of this section.

(2) *Excluded discharge of indebtedness income reducing post-ownership change attributes.*—The amount calculated under paragraph (c)(3)(i) of this section is increased by the amount of all first-year recourse COD income that is excluded under section 108(a), to the extent section 108(b) reduces attributes that are not pre-change losses, as defined in §1.382-2(a)(2), including reduction under section 1017(a) of the basis of the loss corporation's assets that were not held at the time of the ownership change. This amount of first-year recourse COD income is treated as recognized built-in gain. See paragraph (d)(2)(iii) of this section. This paragraph (c)(3)(ii)(B)(2) does not apply to amounts of first-year recourse COD income corresponding to debt whose discharge results in reduction under section 1017(a) of the basis of the loss corporation's assets that were held at the time of the ownership change.

(3) Excluded discharge of indebtedness income reducing basis.—A loss corporation decreases the amount of basis that is described in paragraph (c)(3)(i)(B) of this section by the amount of first-year recourse COD income that is excluded under section 108(a), to the extent that section 1017(a) reduces the basis of the loss corporation's section 382 assets. No other adjustment to the computation in paragraph (c)(3)(i) of this section is made with respect to the first-year recourse COD income described in this paragraph (c)(3)(ii)(B)(3), and this amount of first-year recourse COD income is not treated as recognized built-in gain.

(iii) Additional operating rules.—*(A) Value of contingent liabilities.*—If any liability described in paragraph (c)(3)(i)(C) of this section is reflected on the face of the most recently issued applicable financial statement, within the meaning of section 451(b)(3) and the regulations in this part under section 451 of the Internal Revenue Code (determined without regard to whether the taxpayer has another statement described in section 451(b)(3) and the regulations in this part under section 451 of the Internal Revenue Code), then the estimated value of a liability is the amount of such liability reflected on the most current applicable financial statement as of the change date. The estimated value of any liability described in paragraph (c)(3)(i)(C) of this section is not adjusted to reflect the actual amount of liability that is established on removal of the contingency.

(B) Inventory.—The principles of §1.1374-7 apply to determine the amount realized under paragraph (c)(3)(i)(A) of this section with regard to inventory.

(C) Limitation on total amount of adjustment to NUBIL/ NUBIG regarding recourse COD income.—The total amount of increases in the calculation of net unrealized built-in gain or loss under paragraph (c)(3)(i) of this section related to first-year recourse COD income under paragraph (c)(3)(ii)(B) of this section is limited to the loss corporation's liabilities immediately before the ownership change (excluding nonrecourse liabilities) to the extent of its pre-change excess recourse liabilities defined in paragraph (b)(8)(i) or (ii) of this section, as applicable.

(D) Timing of adjustments described in paragraphs (c)(3)(ii)(B)(1) through (3) of this section.—If a loss corporation chooses to apply the provisions of this paragraph (c)(3)(iii)(D) to all of its first-year recourse COD income, then it must make the adjustments described in paragraphs (c)(3)(ii)(B)(1) through (3) of this section, in their entirety as of the change date. However, a loss corporation may make these adjustments only if—

(1) The statement described in §1.382-11 reflects such adjustments or;

(2) The loss corporation files an amended return for the taxable year that includes the change date and includes an amended §1.382-11 statement (entitled "AMENDED STATEMENT PURSUANT TO §1.382-11(a) BY [INSERT NAME AND EMPLOYER IDENTIFICATION NUMBER OF TAXPAYER], A LOSS CORPORATION,") to reflect such adjustments.

(E) Adjusted basis of the loss corporation's section 382 assets.—The adjustments of this paragraph (c)(3)(iii)(E) apply for purposes of determining the adjusted basis of loss corporation's assets under section 382(h)(2)(A)(ii)(II) and (B)(ii)(I) and the computation of net unrealized built-in gain and loss under section 382(h)(6)(C) and paragraph (c)(3)(i)(B) of this section. The loss corporation's basis in its section 382 assets is adjusted immediately before the ownership change by the amount of any adjustment that would apply if the section 382 asset were sold immediately before the ownership change. For example, the loss corporation's basis in a partnership interest is adjusted to the extent §1.163(j)-6(h)(3)(i) would have required an adjustment if the loss corporation had disposed of all or substantially all of its partnership interest immediately before the ownership change.

(F) [Reserved]

(d) Recognized built-in gain and loss.—*(1) In general.*—This paragraph (d) provides rules for determining whether an item is recognized built-in gain or recognized built-in loss for purposes of section 382(h) and the section 382 regulations. Except as expressly provided in this paragraph (d), no amount is treated as recognized built-in gain or recognized built-in loss if that amount was not properly included in the computation of the loss corporation's net unrealized built-in gain or net unrealized built-in loss pursuant to paragraph (c)(3) of this section.

(2) Recognized built-in gain.—*(i) In general.*—Except as otherwise provided in this paragraph (d)(2) and in paragraph (d)(4) of this section, subject to section 382(h)(1)(A)(ii), an item of income that is properly taken into account during the recognition period is a recognized built-in gain only if the item would have been properly included in gross income before the change date by an accrual method taxpayer (disregarding any method of accounting for which an elec-

tion by the taxpayer must be made unless the taxpayer actually elected that method). As a result, for example, cost recovery deductions on an appreciated asset claimed during the recognition period are not treated as generating recognized built-in gain.

(ii) Disposition of an asset.—The gain recognized on the disposition of an asset during the recognition period is recognized built-in gain to the extent provided in section 382(h)(2)(A). Income included as a dividend under section 61(a)(7) (including amounts treated as dividends under section 1248) and inclusions of income with respect to stock (excluding gain recognized on the disposition of stock), for example under section 951(a) and 951A(a), are not treated as recognized built-in gain.

(iii) Income from discharge of indebtedness attributable to certain recourse liabilities.—If a loss corporation chooses to apply the provisions of paragraph (c)(3)(ii)(B) of this section, then the amounts described in paragraphs (c)(3)(ii)(B)(1) and (2) of this section are treated as recognized built-in gain on the date recognized. Otherwise, no income from the discharge of indebtedness attributable to recourse liabilities is recognized built-in gain.

(iv) Income from discharge of indebtedness attributable to certain nonrecourse liabilities.—Except as provided in this paragraph (d)(2)(iv), no income from the discharge of indebtedness attributable to nonrecourse liabilities is recognized built-in gain.

(A) Treatment as RBIG.—Notwithstanding paragraph (d)(2)(i) of this section, the amount of all first-year nonrecourse COD income that is included in gross income under section 61(a)(12) or first-year nonrecourse COD income that is excluded under section 108(a), to the extent section 108(b) reduces attributes that are not pre-change losses, as defined in §1.382-2(a)(2), is recognized built-in gain on the date recognized. This paragraph (d)(2)(iv)(A) does not apply to amounts of first-year nonrecourse COD income corresponding to debt whose discharge results in reduction of basis described in section 1017(a).

(B) Adjustment to basis.—First-year nonrecourse COD income that is excluded under section 108(a) and reduces the basis of the loss corporation's assets that the loss corporation owned immediately before the ownership change is not recognized built-in gain. However, first-year nonrecourse COD income that is excluded under section 108(a) and reduces the basis of assets that the loss corporation did not own immediately before the ownership change is recognized built-in gain.

(C) Limitation on total amount of RBIG regarding nonrecourse COD income.—The amount of first-year non-recourse COD income treated as recognized built-in gain under this paragraph (d)(2)(iv) is limited to the excess of adjusted issue price of debt over fair market value of property measured under paragraph (e)(5) of this section.

(D) No adjustment to the NUBIG/NUBIL computation.—The computation under paragraph (c)(3)(i) of this section is not adjusted to reflect recognized built-in gain amounts related to this paragraph (d)(2)(iv). Nonetheless, for purposes of determining the limitations on amounts of recognized built-in gain or loss under section 382(h)(2)(A)(ii)(II) and (B)(ii)(I), the adjusted basis of the loss corporation's section 382 assets reflects the reduction, if any, described in paragraph (d)(2)(iv)(B) of this section.

(v) Installment method.—The amount of income reported under the installment method (see section 453) that is treated as recognized built-in gain is determined under the principles of §1.1374-4(h) (determined without regard to §1.1374-2(a)(2)). Further, if a loss corporation that is a member (selling or distributing member) of a consolidated group (as defined in §1.1502-1(h)) transfers a built-in gain asset to a member of the same consolidated group (transferee member) before or during the recognition period, the gain is deferred under §1.1502-13, and before the close of the recognition period, the transferee member sells the built-in gain asset in a sale reportable under the installment method, then any deferred gain is RBIG when taken into account by the selling or distributing member, even if the gain is taken into account after the close of the recognition period.

(vi) Prepaid income.—Any amount received prior to the change date that is attributable to performance occurring on or after the change date is not recognized built-in gain. Examples to which this paragraph (c)(2)(vi) applies include income received prior to the change date that is deferred under sections 451(c) or 455.

(3) Recognized built-in loss.—*(i) In general.*—Except as otherwise provided in paragraphs (d)(3) and (4) of this section, subject to section 382(h)(1)(B)(ii), any deduction properly allowed during the recognition period is treated as recognized built-in loss if an accrual-method taxpayer would have been allowed a deduction for the item against gross income before the change date (taking into account any

additional methods of accounting actually used by the loss corporation). For purposes of this paragraph (d)(3), in determining whether an accrual-method taxpayer would have been allowed a deduction before the change date, no taxable income or timing limitation applies. See paragraph (e) of this section for an anti-duplication rule.

(ii) *Disposition of an asset.*—The loss recognized on the disposition of an asset during the recognition period is treated as a recognized built-in loss to the extent provided in section 382(h)(2)(B).

(iii) *Cost recovery deductions.*—The amount of cost recovery deductions with respect to any section 382 asset for any taxable year during the recognition period is treated as recognized built-in loss to the extent of the excess, if any, of—

(A) The greater of the amount of cost recovery deductions allowed or allowable with respect to the period; over

(B) The amount of cost recovery deductions that would have been allowable if the adjusted basis on the change date equaled the fair market value of the section 382 asset, taking into account the depreciation or amortization method, as applicable; the useful life; the recovery period or amortization period, as applicable; and the convention (cost recovery schedule) actually used by the loss corporation.

(iv) *Bad debt expense.*—Any bad debt deduction under section 166 that arises during the recognition period from debt owed to the loss corporation immediately before the ownership change is a recognized built-in loss to the extent it does not exceed the amount described in section 382(h)(2)(B)(ii).

(v) *Deductions for payments on certain liabilities.*—A deduction for the payment of a liability that is described in paragraph (c)(3)(i)(C) or (D) of this section is a recognized built-in loss to the extent of the amount or the estimated amount of the liability, as applicable, immediately before the ownership change, that was included in the loss corporation's computation of net unrealized built-in loss or net unrealized built-in gain under paragraph (c)(3) of this section.

(vi) *Deduction for section 382 excess business interest expense.*—(A) *In general.*—A deduction attributable to section 382 excess business interest expense during the recognition period is recognized built-in loss to the extent the section 382 excess business interest expense is allocated to the loss corporation pursuant to §1.163(j)-6(f)(2) and is attributable to either a pre-change period (within the meaning of §1.382-6(g)(2)) or a taxable year prior to the ownership change. Solely for purposes of determining whether this paragraph (d)(3)(vi) applies;

(1) The principles of §1.382-6(a) apply (unless the taxpayer made an election pursuant to §1.382-6(b), in which case the principles of §1.382-6(b) apply) to determine the extent the section 382 excess business interest expense is attributable to a pre-change period and

(2) Section 1.163(j)-6(g)(2)(i) applies to section 382 excess business interest expense that was allocated to the loss corporation in the order of the taxable years in which the section 382 excess business interest expense was allocated to the loss corporation pursuant to §1.163(j)-6(f)(2), beginning with the earliest taxable year.

(B) *No adjustment to the NUBIG/NUBIL computation.*—The computation of a loss corporation's net unrealized built-in gain or net unrealized built-in loss is not adjusted to reflect recognized built-in loss amounts related to this paragraph (d)(3)(vi).

(4) *Additional recognized built-in gain and loss items.*—The following additional items of income, gain, deduction, or loss are treated as recognized built-in gain or recognized built-in loss, as applicable:

(i) Positive and negative section 481(a) adjustments, to the extent provided in §1.1374-4(d)(1);

(ii) Any item of income properly taken into account during the recognition period under the completed contract method (as described in §1.460-4(d)) and similar items of deduction, to the extent provided in §1.1374-4(g); and

(iii) The distributive share of a partnership item to the extent provided by the principles of §1.1374-4(i).

(5) *Section 382 disallowed business interest carryforwards.*—Section 382 disallowed business interest carryforwards are not treated as recognized built-in losses.

(e) *General operating rules.*—(1) *Anti-duplication rule.*—Appropriate adjustments must be made in applying the provisions of this section to ensure that no item of economic gain or loss is duplicated in the computation of net unrealized built-in gain or net unrealized built-in loss, or in the computation of recognized built-in gain or recognized built-in loss. Additionally, appropriate adjustments must be made in applying the provisions of this section to ensure that no amount of net unrealized built-in gain or net unrealized built-in loss

is utilized in a duplicative manner, and that the limitations on the total amount of adjustment to net unrealized built-in loss and net unrealized built-in gain take into account amounts of income from discharge of indebtedness that are excluded under section 108(a) and reduce the basis of the loss corporation's assets.

(2) *References to the principles of other regulatory provisions under section 1374.*—All references in this section to the principles cross-referenced in other regulatory provisions in this part under section 1374 of the Internal Revenue Code must be interpreted, as necessary, to be consistent with the requirements and principles of this section.

(f) *Examples.*—The examples in this paragraph (f) illustrate the application of the provisions of this section. For purposes of the examples in this paragraph (f), LossCo is a loss corporation that files its return on a calendar year basis, that uses the accrual method of accounting, and that has an ownership change on the last day of the taxable year (Year 0). Further, LossCo satisfies the threshold requirement of section 382(h)(3)(B)(i). Additionally, the stated facts of the example include all relevant corporate activity, property, and taxable items.

(1) *Example 1. Impact of certain liabilities on computation of net unrealized built-in loss and amount treated as recognized built-in loss*—(i) *Facts.* Immediately before the ownership change, LossCo has a section 382 asset with a fair market value of $100 and an adjusted basis of $90, a liability of $30 for which LossCo will be allowed a deduction upon payment (fixed liability), and an estimated contingent liability of $20, for which, upon removal of the contingency and payment, LossCo will be allowed a deduction (contingent liability). In Year 1, LossCo settles and pays off the contingent liability for $25. In Year 2, LossCo pays off the fixed liability for $30.

(ii) *Analysis*—(A) *Computation of net unrealized built-in loss.* Under paragraph (c)(3)(i) of this section, LossCo has a net unrealized built-in loss of $40 ($100, the amount LossCo would realize if it sold all its assets to an unrelated third party (paragraph (c)(i)(A)(2) of this section), decreased by $140 (the sum of the fixed liability ($30) (paragraph (c)(i)(B) of this section), the estimated value of the contingent liability ($20) (paragraph (c)(i)(C) of this section) and the aggregate adjusted basis in the asset ($90) (paragraph (c)(i)(D) of this section)).

(B) *Settlement of the contingent liability.* Upon settlement and payment of the contingent liability in Year 1, LossCo is entitled to a deduction of $25 (disregarding application of any limitation). Under paragraph (d)(3)(vi) of this section, $20 of the deduction (the estimated value of the liability at the time of the ownership change) is recognized built-in loss and $5 is not subject to section 382. After Year 1, pursuant to section 382(h)(1)(B)(ii), the maximum amount of recognized built-in loss that LossCo can have is $20 ($40 net unrealized built-in loss, less the $20 recognized built-in loss in Year 1).

(C) *Payment of the fixed liability.* Upon paying the fixed liability in Year 2, LossCo is entitled to a deduction of $30 (disregarding application of any limitation). Under paragraph (d)(3)(vi) of this section, $30 of the deduction would have been recognized built-in loss, but the amount of recognized built-in loss is limited by section 382(h)(1)(B)(ii). As a result, of the $30 deduction, $20 is a recognized built-in loss and $10 is not subject to section 382.

(2) *Example 2. Cost recovery deductions*—(i) *Facts.* Immediately before the ownership change, LossCo has a net unrealized built-in loss of $300 that is attributable to a non-depreciable asset with a fair market value of $500 and an adjusted basis of $650, and a patent with a fair market value of $125 and an adjusted basis of $275. The patent is an "amortizable section 197 intangible" as defined in section 197(c) and has a 15-year amortization period. As of the change date in Year 0, the patent has a remaining amortization period under section 197 of 5 years. For Year 1, LossCo calculates a $55 amortization deduction for the patent.

(ii) *Analysis.* Under paragraph (d)(3)(iii) of this section, the amount of cost recovery deduction on the patent that is a recognized built-in loss is the excess, if any, of the amount of cost recovery deductions allowed or allowable over the amount of cost recovery deductions that would have been allowable if the adjusted basis on the change date had equaled the fair market value of the patent, taking into account the amortization method, amortization period, and convention (cost recovery schedule) actually used by the loss corporation. LossCo would have been allowed a cost recovery deduction of $25 if the adjusted basis of the patent on the change date had equaled its fair market value taking into account the cost recovery schedule actually used by LossCo, ($125 fair market value divided by remaining amortization period of 5 years). Accordingly, $30 of the Year 1 cost recovery deduction is recognized built-in loss ($55 allowed and allowable cost recovery deduction, less the $25 cost recovery deduction that would have been allowable if the adjusted basis on the change date equaled the fair market value of the patent). The remaining $25 is not subject to section 382.

(3) *Example 3. Forgiveness of pre-change excess recourse liabilities*—(i) *Facts.* On Date 1, immediately before the ownership change, LossCo

has two assets: Asset 1, which has a fair market value of $100, an adjusted basis of $80, and is subject to a nonrecourse liability with an adjusted issue price of $120 (Liability 1); and Asset 2, which has a fair market value of $100, an adjusted basis of $90, and is subject to a nonrecourse liability with an adjusted issue price of $60 (Liability 2). Additionally, LossCo has a recourse liability with an adjusted issue price of $60. On Date 2, eleven months after the change date, the creditor forgives $20 of the recourse liability, which gives rise to discharge of indebtedness income that is excluded under 108(a), and for which LossCo elects to reduce the basis of Asset 1 and Asset 2 pursuant to section 108(b)(5).

(ii) *Analysis*—(A) *Calculation of net unrealized built-in gain.* The nonrecourse liability to which Asset 1 is subject is an inadequately secured nonrecourse liability, because the adjusted issue price of the liability ($120) exceeds the fair market value of the property securing the liability ($100). As a result, pursuant to paragraph (c)(3)(i)(A)(*1*) of this section, in determining its net unrealized built-in gain, LossCo is treated as satisfying Liability 1 by surrendering to the creditor Asset 1, resulting in an amount realized of $120. Additionally, pursuant to paragraph (c)(3)(i)(A)(2) of this section, LossCo is treated as selling Asset 2 and having an amount realized of $100. As a result, LossCo has a net unrealized built-in gain of $50 ($120 amount realized on Asset 1, plus the $100 amount realized on Asset 2, less the $170 aggregate adjusted basis of LossCo's section 382 assets). See paragraph (c)(3)(i) of this section.

(B) *Forgiveness of the recourse liability.* Pursuant to paragraph (c)(3)(ii)(A) of this section, the forgiveness of the recourse liability will not impact the calculation of LossCo's net unrealized built-in gain, unless it chooses to apply the provisions of paragraph (c)(3)(ii)(B) of this section to all of its first-year recourse COD income. The recourse liability is a pre-change excess recourse liability to the extent its adjusted issue price ($60) exceeds the fair market value of LossCo's section 382 assets, reduced, but not below zero, by the amount of nonrecourse liability that is secured by such assets immediately before the ownership change ($0 for Asset 1 and $40 for Asset 2), or $20. As a result, the first-year recourse COD income is $20 (the $20 income to the extent of the pre-change excess recourse liability). If LossCo chooses to apply the provisions of (c)(3)(ii)(B) of this section, then, pursuant to paragraph (c)(3)(ii)(B)(3) of this section, LossCo decreases by $20 the amount of basis it uses to compute its net unrealized built-in gain. As a result, LossCo has a net unrealized built-in gain of $70 ($120 amount realized on Asset 1, plus $100 amount realized on Asset 2, less $150 aggregate adjusted basis of LossCo's section 382 assets. See paragraph (c)(3)(i)(D) of this section. The first-year recourse COD income is not recognized built-in gain.

(4) *Example 4. Forgiveness of a recourse liability that is not a pre-change excess recourse liability*—(i) *Facts.* The facts are the same as in paragraph (f)(3)(i) (*Example 3*) of this section, except that, as of the date of the ownership change, LossCo also owns Asset 3, which has a fair market value of $80 and an adjusted basis of $50. Additionally, LossCo includes the $20 of cancellation of indebtedness income in gross income that was recognized on Date 2 under section 61(a)(12).

(ii) *Analysis*—(A) *Calculation of net unrealized built-in gain.* As in paragraph (f)(3)(ii)(A) (*Example 3*) of this section, the nonrecourse liability on Asset 1 is an inadequately secured nonrecourse liability, and as a result, pursuant to paragraph (c)(3)(i)(A)(*1*) of this section, the amount realized with respect to Asset 1 is $120. Additionally, pursuant to paragraph (c)(3)(i)(A)(2) of this section, LossCo is treated as selling Asset 2 and Asset 3 for an amount realized of $180 ($100, plus $80). As a result, LossCo has a net unrealized built-in gain of $80 ($120 amount realized on Asset 1, plus $100 amount realized on Asset 2, plus $80 amount realized on Asset 3, less $220 aggregate adjusted basis of LossCo's section 382 assets. See paragraph (c)(3)(i)(D) of this section.

(B) *Forgiveness of the recourse liability.* The forgiveness of the recourse liability will not impact the calculation of LossCo's net unrealized built-in gain under paragraph (c)(3)(ii)(A) of this section. The adjustment provided under paragraph (c)(3)(ii)(B) of this section for certain recourse liabilities is not available (and the cancellation of indebtedness is not recognized built-in loss) because the recourse liability does not constitute a pre-change excess recourse liability. See

paragraph (b)(4) and (8) of this section. The recourse liability is not a pre-change excess recourse liability because its adjusted issue price ($60) does not exceed the fair market value of the LossCo's section 382 assets, reduced, but not below zero, by the amount of nonrecourse liability that is secured by such assets immediately before the ownership change ($0 for Asset 1, $40 for Asset 2, and $80 for Asset 3).

(5) *Example 5. Computing net unrealized built-in gain or loss of a partner that is allocated section 382 excess business interest expense*—(i) *Facts.* LossCo and unrelated Corp A are equal partners in partnership PRS. LossCo has a basis of $100 in its PRS interest, which has a fair market value of $90. In Year 1, PRS pays or accrues $100 of section 382 excess business interest expense, which is allocated equally to LossCo and Corp A. At the end of Year 1, LossCo has an ownership change. In Year 2, PRS has $80 of excess taxable income (within the meaning of §1.163(j)-1(b)(15)), of which $40 is allocated to LossCo pursuant to §1.163(j)-6(f)(2). LossCo's section 163(j) limitation (within the meaning of §1.163(j)-1(b)(31)) for Year 2 is $25, and LossCo pays or accrues $60 of other business interest expense in Year 2. LossCo's section 382 limitation for Year 2 is $30.

(ii) *Analysis*—(A) *Year 1*—(1) *Basis reduction to reflect allocation of excess business interest expense.* Pursuant to section 163(j)(4) and §1.163(j)-6, a partner in a partnership reduces its adjusted basis in its partnership interest by the amount of excess business interest expense allocated to that partner. As a result, LossCo's basis in its PRS interest is reduced from $100 to $50 in Year 1.

(2) *Calculation of net unrealized built-in gain or loss.* LossCo experiences an ownership change at the end of Year 1. Paragraph (c)(3)(iii)(E) of this section provides that, in computing a loss corporation's net unrealized built-in gain or loss, the amount of the corporation's basis in its section 382 assets is adjusted immediately before the ownership change by the amount of any adjustment that would apply if the section 382 asset were sold immediately before the ownership change. If LossCo had sold its PRS interest immediately before the ownership change, §1.163(j)-6(h)(3)(i) would have required LossCo to increase its basis in the PRS interest by $50, the amount of its remaining excess business interest expense. As a result, for purposes of section 382(h)(6)(C) and paragraph (c)(3)(i)(B) of this section, LossCo's basis in its PRS interest is adjusted by the same amount. Thus, for purposes of computing LossCo's net unrealized gain or loss, LossCo's basis in its PRS interest is increased to $100 immediately before the ownership change.

(B) *Year 2*—(1) *Treatment of excess business interest expense as paid or accrued.* Pursuant to §1.163(j)-6(g)(2)(i), because LossCo is allocated $40 of excess taxable income from PRS in Year 2, LossCo treats $40 of its excess business interest expense (from Year 1) as paid or accrued in Year 2. LossCo's remaining $10 of excess business interest expense from Year 1 continues to be characterized as excess business interest expense in succeeding years. See §1.163(j)-6(g)(2)(ii).

(2) *Section 163(j) deduction.* In Year 2, LossCo is treated as having paid or accrued $100 of business interest expense ($40 of excess business interest expense that is treated as business interest expense under §1.163(j)-6(g)(2)(i), and $60 of business interest expense that LossCo actually paid or accrued in Year 2). Because LossCo has a section 163(j) limitation of $25, LossCo can deduct only $25 of its $100 Year 2 business interest expense (see §1.163(j)-2(b)). Pursuant to §1.383-1(d)(1)(ii), LossCo is treated as deducting $25 of its section 382 excess business interest expense that is treated as business interest expense in Year 2, because this amount is a recognized built-in loss. No adjustment is made to the computation of LossCo's net unrealized built-in gain or loss to reflect the $25 of LossCo's recognized built-in loss. See paragraph (c)(3)(vi) of this section. Both LossCo's $15 of Year 1 excess business interest expense that was treated as business interest expense in Year 2 and the $60 of other business interest expense that was paid or accrued in Year 2 is disallowed in Year 2 under §1.163(j)-2(b). These amounts are treated as disallowed business interest expense carryforwards into Year 3 under §1.163(j)-2(c), with the $15 carryforward being subject to section 382 limitation. See paragraph (d)(3)(vi) of this section.

(g) [Proposed amendments withdrawn by REG-125710-18 on January 14, 2020.]

Built-in Gain and Loss: Revised Applicability Dates

Built-in Gain and Loss: Revised Applicability Dates.—Amendments to Reg. §1.382-7, providing guidance regarding the items of income and deduction that are included in the calculation of built-in gains and losses under section 382 of the Internal Revenue Code, are proposed (published in the Federal Register on January 14, 2020) (REG-125710-18).

Par. 4. Section 1.382-7, as proposed to be revised by 84 FR 47455, September 10, 2019, is further amended by revising paragraph (g) to read as follows:

§1.382-7. Built-in gains and losses.

* * *

(g) *Applicability dates.*—(1) *In general.*—Except as otherwise provided in this paragraph (g), this section applies to any ownership change that occurs after the date that is 30 days after the date of

publication in the **Federal Register** of a Treasury decision adopting the rules of this section as final regulations (applicability date), if paragraph (g)(2) of this section does not apply to that ownership change. For ownership changes occurring on or before the applicability date and ownership changes to which paragraph (g)(2) of this section applies, see § 1.382-7 as contained in 26 CFR part 1, revised April 1, 2019, and other applicable guidance, including Notice 2003-65 (2003-2 CB 747) (see § 601.601(d)(2)(ii)(*b*) of this chapter). Notwithstanding the preceding sentences of this paragraph (g)(1), a taxpayer may apply this section to an ownership change to which paragraph (g)(2) of this section applies.

(2) *Certain ownership changes eligible for transition relief.*—This paragraph (g)(2) applies to an ownership change after the applicability date that occurs immediately after an owner shift or equity structure shift, if the owner shift or equity structure shift occurs—

(i) Pursuant to a binding agreement in effect on or before the applicability date and at all times thereafter;

(ii) Pursuant to a specific transaction described in a public announcement made on or before the applicability date;

(iii) Pursuant to a specific transaction described in a filing with the Securities and Exchange Commission submitted on or before the applicability date;

(iv) By order of a court (or pursuant to a plan confirmed, or a sale approved, by order of a court) in a title 11 or similar case (as defined in section 382(l)(5)(F)), provided that the taxpayer was a debtor in a case before such court on or before the applicability date; or

(v) Pursuant to a transaction described in a ruling request submitted to the IRS on or before the applicability date.

(3) *Paragraph (d)(2)(vi) of this section.*—Paragraph (d)(2)(vi) of this section applies to loss corporations that have undergone an ownership change on or after June 11, 2010. For loss corporations that have undergone an ownership change before June 11, 2010, see § 1.382-7T as contained in 26 CFR part 1, revised April 1, 2009.

Deduction for Business Interest Expense: Limitation

Deduction for Business Interest Expense: Limitation.—Amendments to Reg. §§1.383-0 and 1.383-1, regarding the limitation on the deduction for business interest expense after the enactment of recent tax legislation, are proposed (published in the Federal Register on December 28, 2018) (REG-106089-18).

Par. 10. Section 1.383-0 is amended by revising paragraph (a) to read as follows:

1.383-0. Effective date.—(a) The regulations under section 383 (other than the regulations described in paragraph (b) of this section) reflect the amendments made to sections 382 and 383 by the Tax

Reform Act of 1986 and the amendments made to section 382 by the Tax Cuts and Jobs Act of 2017. See § 1.383-1(j) for effective date rules.

* * *

Par. 11. Section 1.383-1 is amended by:
1. In paragraph (a):
a. Adding entries for paragraphs (d)(1)(i) and (ii);
b. Revising the entries for paragraphs (e)(3) and (j);
c. Adding entries for paragraphs (j)(1) and (2); and
d. Removing the entry for paragraph (k).
2. Removing "(iv)" and adding "(v)" in its place in paragraph (c)(6)(i)(B).
3. Revising paragraphs (c)(6)(ii) and (d)(1).
4. Removing the commas and adding semicolons in their place at ends of paragraphs (d)(2)(i) through (vi).
5. Revising paragraph (d)(2)(iii).
6. Redesignating paragraphs (d)(2)(iv) through (vii) as paragraphs (d)(2)(v) through (viii), respectively.
7. Adding a new paragraph (d)(2)(iv).
8. Revising newly redesignated paragraph (d)(2)(v) and paragraph (d)(3)(ii).
9. Removing "(iv)" and adding "(v)" in its place in paragraph (e)(1).
10. In paragraph (e)(2):
a. Removing "sections 11(b)(2) and (15)" and adding "section 15" in its place in the fourth sentence; and
b. Removing the last two sentences.
11. Removing and reserving paragraph (e)(3).
12. In paragraph (f):
a. Removing *Example 4;*
b. Designating *Examples 1* through 3 as paragraphs (f)(1) through (3), respectively; and
c. Revising newly designated paragraphs (f)(2) and (3).
13. In the last sentence of paragraph (g), removing "(e.g., 0.34 for taxable years beginning in 1989)".
14. In paragraph (j):
a. Revising the paragraph heading;
b. Designating the text of paragraph (j) as paragraph (j)(1) and adding a heading to newly designated paragraph (j)(1); and
c. Adding paragraph (j)(2).
15. Removing paragraph (k).
The revisions and additions read as follows:

1.383-1. Special limitations on certain capital losses and excess credits.—(a) * * *

* * *

(d) * * *
   (1) * * *
      (i) In general.
      (ii) Ordering rule for losses or credits from same taxable year.

* * *

(e) * * *
   (3) [Reserved]

* * *

(j) Applicability date.
   (1) In general.
   (2) Interaction with section 163(j).

* * *

(c) * * *
   (6) * * *

      (ii) *Example.*—L, a new loss corporation, is a calendar-year taxpayer. L has an ownership change on December 31, 2019. For 2020, L has taxable income (prior to the use of any pre-change losses) of $100,000. In addition, L has a section 382 limitation of $25,000, a pre-change net operating loss carryover of $12,000, a pre-change

general business credit carryforward under section 39 of $50,000, and no items described in § 1.383-1(d)(2)(i) through (iv). L's section 383 credit limitation for 2020 is the excess of its regular tax liability computed after allowing a $12,000 net operating loss deduction (taxable income of $88,000; regular tax liability of $18,480), over its regular tax liability computed after allowing an additional deduction in the amount of L's section 382 limitation remaining after the application of paragraphs (d)(2)(i) through (v) of this section, or $13,000 (taxable income of $75,000; regular tax liability of $15,750). L's section 383 credit limitation is therefore $2,730 ($18,480 minus $15,750).

(d) * * *

(1) *In general.*—(i) *In general.*—The amount of taxable income of a new loss corporation for any post-change year that may be offset by pre-change losses shall not exceed the amount of the section 382 limitation for the post-change year. The amount of the regular tax liability of a new loss corporation for any post-change year that may be offset by pre-change credits shall not exceed the amount of the section 383 credit limitation for the post-change year.

(ii) *Ordering rule for losses or credits from same taxable year.*—A loss corporation's taxable income is offset first by losses subject to a section 382 limitation, to the extent the section 382 limitation for that taxable year has not yet been absorbed, before being offset by losses of the same type from the same taxable year that are not subject to a section 382 limitation. For example, assume that Corporation X has an ownership change in Year 1 and carries over disallowed business interest expense within the meaning of §1.163(j)-1(b)(8), some of which constitutes a section 382 disallowed business interest carryforward, from Year 1 to Year 2. To the extent of its section 163(j) limitation, within the meaning of §1.163(j)-1(b)(31), and its remaining section 382 limitation, Corporation X offsets its Year 2 income with the section 382 disallowed business interest carryforward before using any of the disallowed business interest expense that is not a section 382 disallowed business interest carryforward. Similar principles apply to the use of tax credits.

(2) * * *

(iii) Pre-change losses that are described in §1.382-2(a)(2)(iii), other than losses that are pre-change capital losses, that are recognized and are subject to the section 382 limitation in such post-change year;

(iv)(A) With respect to an ownership change date occurring prior to the date the Treasury decision adopting these regulations as final regulations is published in the **Federal Register**, but during the taxable year which includes the date the Treasury decision adopting these regulations as final regulations is published in the **Federal Register**, the pre-change loss described in section 382(d)(3);

(B) With respect to an ownership change date occurring on or after the date the Treasury decision adopting these regulations as final regulations is published in the **Federal Register**, section 382 disallowed business interest carryforwards (within the meaning of §1.382-2(a)(7));

(v) Pre-change losses not described in paragraphs (d)(2)(i) through (iv) of this section;

* * *

(3) * * *

(ii) *Example.*—L, a calendar-year taxpayer, has an ownership change on December 31, 2019. For 2020, L has taxable income of $300,000 and a regular tax liability of $63,000. L has no pre-change losses, but it has a business credit carryforward from 2018 of $25,000. L has a section 382 limitation for 2020 of $50,000. L's section 383 credit limitation is $10,500, an amount equal to the excess of L's regular tax liability ($63,000) over its regular tax liability calculated by allowing an additional deduction of $50,000 ($52,500). Pursuant to the limitation contained in section 38(c), however, L is entitled to use only $9,500 (($63,000 - $25,000) x 25 percent) of its business credit carryforward in 2020. The unabsorbed portion of L's section 382 limitation (computed pursuant to paragraph (e) of this section) is carried forward under section 382(b)(2). The unused portion of L's business credit carryforward, $1,000, is carried forward to the extent provided in section 39.

* * *

(f) * * *

(2) *Example 2*—(i) *Facts.* L, a calendar-year taxpayer, has an ownership change on December 31, 2019. For 2020, L has $750,000 of ordinary taxable income (before the application of carryovers) and a section 382 limitation of $1,500,000. L's only carryovers are from pre-2019 taxable years and consist of a $500,000 net operating loss (NOL) carryover, and a $200,000 foreign tax credit carryover (all of which may be used under the section 904 limitation). The NOL carryover is a pre-change loss, and the foreign tax credit carryover is a pre-change credit. L has no other pre-change losses or credits that can be used in 2020.

(ii) *Analysis.* The following computation illustrates the application of this section for 2020:

1. Taxable income before carryovers	$750,000
2. Pre-change NOL carryover	$500,000
3. Section 382 limitation	$1,500,000
4. Amount of pre-change NOL carryover that can be used (least of line 1, 2, or 3)	$500,000
5. Taxable income (line 1 minus line 4)	$250,000
6. Section 382 limitation remaining (line 3 minus line 4)	$1,000,000
7. Pre-change credit carryover	$200,000
8. Regular tax liability (line 5 x section 11 rates)	$52,500
9. Modified tax liability (line 5 minus line 6 (but not less than zero) x section 11 rates)	$0
10. Section 383 credit limitation (line 8 minus line 9)	$52,500
11. Amount of pre-change credits that can be used in 2020 (lesser of line 7 or line 10)	$52,500
12. Amount of pre-change credits to be carried over to 2021 under section 904(c) (line 7 minus line 11)	$147,500
13. Section 383 credit reduction amount: $52,500/0.21	$250,000
14. Section 382 limitation to be carried to 2021 under section 382(b)(2) (line 6 minus line 13)	$750,000

(3) *Example 3*—(i) *Facts.* L, a calendar-year taxpayer, has an ownership change on December 31, 2019. L has $80,000 of ordinary taxable income (before the application of carryovers) and a section 382 limitation of $25,000 for 2020, a post-change year. L's only carryover is from a pre-2019 taxable year and is a general business credit carryforward under section 39 in the amount of $10,000 (no portion of which is attributable to the investment tax credit under section 46). The general business credit carryforward is a pre-change credit. L has no other credits which can be used in 2020.

(ii) *Analysis.* The following computation illustrates the application of this section:

1. Taxable income before carryovers	$80,000
2. Section 382 limitation	$25,000
3. Pre-change credit carryover	$10,000
4. Regular tax liability (line 1 x section 11 rates)	$16,800
5. Modified tax liability ((line 1 minus line 2) x section 11 rates)	$11,550
6. Section 383 credit limitation (line 4 minus line 5)	$5,250
7. Amount of pre-change credits that can be used (lesser of line 3 or line 6)	$5,250
8. Amount of pre-change credits to be carried over to 2021 under sections 39 and 382(l)(2) (line 3 minus line 7)	$4,750
9. Regular tax payable (line 4 minus line 7)	$11,550
10. Section 383 credit reduction amount: $5,250/0.21	$25,000
11. Section 382 limitation to be carried to 2021 under section 382(b)(2) (line 2 minus line 10)	$0

* * *

(j) Applicability date.—(1) *In general.*—* * *

(2) *Interaction with section 163(j).*—Paragraphs (c)(6)(i)(B) and (c)(6)(ii), (d)(1), (d)(2)(iii) through (viii), (d)(3)(ii), (e)(1) through (3), (f), and (g) of this section apply with respect to ownership changes occurring during a taxable year ending after the Treasury decision adopting these regulations as final regulations is published in the **Federal Register**. For loss corporations that have undergone an ownership change during a taxable year ending before the date the Treasury decision adopting these regulations as final regulations is published in the **Federal Register**, see §1.383-1 as contained in 26 CFR part 1, revised April 1, 2018. However, taxpayers and their related parties, within the meaning of sections 267(b) and 707(b)(1), may apply the rules of this section to an ownership change occurring during a taxable year beginning after December 31, 2017, so long as the taxpayers and their related parties consistently apply either the rules of this section, except paragraph (d)(2)(iv)(B) of this section, the section 163(j) regulations, within the meaning of §1.163(j)-1(b)(32), and §1.382-6, and if applicable, §§1.263A-9, 1.381(c)(20)-1, 1.469-9,

1.882-5, 1.1502-13, 1.1502-21, 1.1502-36, 1.1502-79, 1.1502-91 through 1.1502-99 (to the extent they effectuate the rules of §§1.382-6 and 1.383-1), and 1.1504-4; or the rules of this section (except paragraph (d)(2)(iv)(A) of this section), the section 163(j) regulations, within the meaning of §1.163(j)-1(b)(32), and §§1.382-2, 1.382-5, 1.382-6, and

1.383-1, and if applicable, §§1.263A-9, 1.381(c)(20)-1, 1.469-9, 1.882-5, 1.1502-13, 1.1502-21, 1.1502-36, 1.1502-79, 1.1502-91 through 1.1502-99 (to the extent they effectuate the rules of §§1.382-2, 1.382-5, 1.382-6, and 1.383-1), and 1.1504-4, to those ownership changes.

Certain Interests in Corporations: Treated as Stock or Indebtedness

Certain Interests in Corporations: Treated as Stock or Indebtedness.—Reg. §1.385-4 and amendments to Reg. §1.385-3, addressing the treatment of instruments issued by partnerships, consolidated groups, and certain transactions involving qualified cash-management arrangements, are proposed (published in the Federal Register on October 21, 2016) (REG-130314-16).

Par. 2. Section 1.385-3 is amended by:

1. Revising paragraph (b)(3)(vii).
2. Revising paragraph (d)(4).
3. Revising paragraph (f).
4. Revising paragraphs (g)(5)-(8), (15)-(17), and (22)-(23).
5. Revising *Example 12* through *Example 19* in paragraph (h)(3).
6. Adding paragraph (k).

The revisions and additions read as follows:

§1.385-3. Transactions in which debt proceeds are distributed or that have a similar effect.

* * *

(b) * * *

(3) * * *

(vii) [The text of the proposed amendment to §1.385-3(b)(3)(vii) is the same as the text of §1.385-3T(b)(3)(vii) as added by T.D. 9790.]

* * *

(d) * * *

(4) [The text of the proposed amendment to §1.385-3(d)(4) is the same as the text of §1.385-3T(d)(4) as added by T.D. 9790.]

* * *

(f) [The text of the proposed amendment to §1.385-3(f) is the same as the text of §1.385-3T(f) as added by T.D. 9790.]

(g) * * *

(5) [The text of the proposed amendment to §1.385-3(g)(5) is the same as the text of §1.385-3T(g)(5) as added by T.D. 9790.]

(6) [The text of the proposed amendment to §1.385-3(g)(6) is the same as the text of §1.385-3T(g)(6) as added by T.D. 9790.]

(7) [The text of the proposed amendment to §1.385-3(g)(7) is the same as the text of §1.385-3T(g)(7) as added by T.D. 9790.]

(8) [The text of the proposed amendment to §1.385-3(g)(8) is the same as the text of §1.385-3T(g)(8) as added by T.D. 9790.]

* * *

(15) [The text of the proposed amendment to §1.385-3(g)(15) is the same as the text of §1.385-3T(g)(15) as added by T.D. 9790.]

(16) [The text of the proposed amendment to §1.385-3(g)(16) is the same as the text of §1.385-3T(g)(16) as added by T.D. 9790.]

(17) [The text of the proposed amendment to §1.385-3(g)(16) is the same as the text of §1.385-3T(g)(17) as added by T.D. 9790.]

* * *

Par. 3. Section 1.385-4 is added to read as follows:

§1.385-4. Treatment of consolidated groups.—[The text of proposed §1.385-4 is the same as the text of §1.385-4T as added by T.D. 9790.]

(22) [The text of the proposed amendment to §1.385-3(g)(22) is the same as the text of §1.385-3T(g)(22) as added by T.D. 9790.]

(23) [The text of the proposed amendment to §1.385-3(g)(23) is the same as the text of §1.385-3T(g)(23) as added by T.D. 9790.]

* * *

(h) * * *

(3) * * *

Example 12. [The text of the proposed amendment to §1.385-3(h)(3), *Example 12* is the same as the text of §1.385-3T(h)(3), *Example 12* as added by T.D. 9790.]

Example 13. [The text of the proposed amendment to §1.385-3(h)(3), *Example 13* is the same as the text of §1.385-3T(h)(3), *Example 13* as added by T.D. 9790.]

Example 14. [The text of the proposed amendment to §1.385-3(h)(3), *Example 14* is the same as the text of §1.385-3T(h)(3), *Example 14* as added by T.D. 9790.]

Example 15. [The text of the proposed amendment to §1.385-3(h)(3), *Example 15* is the same as the text of §1.385-3T(h)(3), *Example 15* as added by T.D. 9790.]

Example 16. [The text of the proposed amendment to §1.385-3(h)(3), *Example 16* is the same as the text of §1.385-3T(h)(3), *Example 16* as added by T.D. 9790.]

Example 17. [The text of the proposed amendment to §1.385-3(h)(3), *Example 17* is the same as the text of §1.385-3T(h)(3), *Example 17* as added by T.D. 9790.]

Example 18. [The text of the proposed amendment to §1.385-3(h)(3), *Example 18* is the same as the text of §1.385 3T(h)(3), *Example 18* as added by T.D. 9790.]

Example 19. [The text of the proposed amendment to §1.385-3(h)(3), *Example 19* is the same as the text of §1.385-3T(h)(3), *Example 19* as added by T.D. 9790.]

* * *

(k) [The text of the proposed amendment to §1.385-3(k) is the same as the text of §1.385-3T(k) as added by T.D. 9790.]

DEFERRED COMPENSATION

Pension Plans: Distributions: Phased Retirement Programs

Pension Plans: Distributions: Phased Retirement Programs.—Reg. §1.401(a)-3 and amendments to Reg. §1.401(a)-1, providing rules that permit distributions to be made from a pension plan under a phased retirement program and setting forth requirements for a bona fide phased retirement program, are proposed (published in the Federal Register on November 10, 2004) (REG-114726-04).

☐ Par. 2. In §1.401(a)-1, paragraph (b)(1)(i) is amended by adding text before the period at the end of the current sentence and a new second sentence [*proposed amendment to (b)(1)(i) adopted by T.D. 9325, 5-21-2007*], and paragraph (b)(1)(iv) to read as follows:

§1.401(a)-1. Post-ERISA qualified plans and qualified trusts; in general.

* * *

(b) * * *

(1) * * *

(i) [*Proposed amendment to (b)(1)(i) adopted by T.D. 9325, 5-21-2007.*]

* * *

☐ Par. 3. Section 1.401(a)-3 is added to read as follows:

(iv) Benefits may not be distributed prior to normal retirement age solely due to a reduction in hours. However, notwithstanding anything provided elsewhere in paragraph (b) of this section (including the pre-ERISA rules under §1.401-1), an employee may be treated as partially retired for purposes of paragraph (b)(1)(i) of this section to the extent provided under §1.401(a)-3 relating to a bona fide phased retirement program.

* * *

§1.401(a)-3. Benefits during phased retirement.—
(a) *Introduction.*—(1) *General rule.*—Under section 401(a), a qualified pension plan may provide for the distribution of phased retirement benefits in accordance with the limitations of this paragraph (a) to the extent that an employee is partially retired under a bona fide phased retirement program, as defined in paragraph (c) of this section, provided the requirements set forth in paragraphs (d) and (e) of this section are satisfied.

(2) *Limitation on benefits paid during phased retirement period.*—(i) *Benefits limited to pro rata retirement benefit.*—The phased retirement benefits paid during the phased retirement period cannot exceed the phased retirement accrued benefit payable in the optional form of benefit applicable at the annuity starting date for the employee's phased retirement benefit.

(ii) *Availability of early retirement subsidies, etc.*—Except as provided in paragraph (a)(2)(iii) of this section, all early retirement benefits, retirement-type subsidies, and optional forms of benefit available upon full retirement must be available with respect to the portion of an employee's phased retirement accrued benefit that is payable as a phased retirement benefit.

(iii) *Limitation on optional forms of payment.*—Phased retirement benefits may not be paid in the form of a single sum or other form that constitutes an eligible rollover distribution under section 402(c)(4).

(3) *Limited to full-time employees who are otherwise eligible to commence benefits.*—Phased retirement benefits are only permitted to be made available to an employee who, prior to the phased retirement period, normally maintains a full-time work schedule and who would otherwise be eligible to commence retirement benefits immediately if he or she were to fully retire.

(4) *Authority of Commissioner to adopt other rules.*—The Commissioner, in revenue rulings, notices, or other guidance published in the Internal Revenue Bulletin (see §601.601(d)(2)(ii)(*b*) of this chapter), may adopt additional rules regarding the coordination of partial retirement under a phased retirement program and the qualification rules of section 401(a).

(b) *Definitions.*—(1) *In general.*—The definitions set forth in this paragraph (b) apply for purposes of this section.

(2) *Phased retirement program.*—The term *phased retirement program* means a written, employer-adopted program pursuant to which employees may reduce the number of hours they customarily work beginning on or after a date specified under the program and commence phased retirement benefits during the phased retirement period, as provided under the plan.

(3) *Phased retirement period.*—The term *phased retirement period* means the period of time that the employee and employer reasonably expect the employee to work reduced hours under the phased retirement program.

(4) *Phased retirement accrued benefit.*—The term *phased retirement accrued benefit* means the portion of the employee's accrued benefit equal to the product of the employee's total accrued benefit on the annuity starting date for the employee's phased retirement benefit, and one minus the employee's work schedule fraction.

(5) *Phased retirement benefit.*—The term *phased retirement benefit* means the benefit paid to an employee upon the employee's partial retirement under a phased retirement program, based on some or all of the employee's phased retirement accrued benefit, and payable in the optional form of benefit applicable at the annuity starting date.

(6) *Work schedule.*—With respect to an employee, the term *work schedule* means the number of hours the employee is reasonably expected to work annually during the phased retirement period (determined in accordance with paragraph (c)(4) of this section).

(7) *Full-time work schedule.*—With respect to an employee, the term *full-time work schedule* means the number of hours the employee would normally work during a year if the employee were to work on a full-time basis, determined in a reasonable and consistent manner.

(8) *Work schedule fraction.*—With respect to an employee, the term *work schedule fraction* means a fraction, the numerator of which is the employee's work schedule and the denominator of which is the employee's full-time work schedule.

(c) *Bona fide phased retirement program.*—(1) *Definition generally.*—The term *bona fide phased retirement program* means a phased retirement program that satisfies paragraphs (c)(2) through (5) of this section.

(2) *Limitation to individuals who have attained age 59 ½.*—A bona fide phased retirement program must be limited to employees who have attained age 59 ½. A plan is permitted to impose additional requirements for eligibility to participate in a bona fide phased retirement program, such as limiting eligibility to either employees who have satisfied additional age or service conditions (or combination thereof) specified in the program or employees whose benefit may not be distributed without consent under section 411(a)(11).

(3) *Participation must be voluntary.*—An employee's participation in a bona fide phased retirement program must be voluntary.

(4) *Reduction in hours requirement.*—An employee who participates in a bona fide phased retirement program must reasonably be expected (by both the employer and employee) to reduce, by 20 percent or more, the number of hours the employee customarily works. This requirement is satisfied if the employer and employee enter into an agreement, in good faith, under which they agree that the employee will reduce, by 20 percent or more, the number of hours the employee works during the phased retirement period.

(5) *Limited to employees who are not key-employee owners.*—Phased retirement benefits are not permitted to be made available to a key employee who is described in section 416(i)(1)(A)(ii) or (iii).

(d) *Conditions for commencement of phased retirement benefit.*—(1) *Imputed accruals based on full-time schedule.*—(i) *General rule.*—During the phased retirement period, in addition to being entitled to payment of the phased retirement benefit, the employee must be entitled to participate in the plan in the same manner as if the employee still maintained a full-time work schedule (including calculation of average earnings, imputation of compensation in accordance with §1.414(s)-1(f), and imputation of service in accordance with the service-crediting rules under §1.401(a)(4)-11(d)), and must be entitled to the same benefits (including early retirement benefits, retirement-type subsidies, and optional forms of benefits) upon full retirement as a similarly situated employee who has not elected phased retirement, except that the years of service credited under the plan for any plan year during the phased retirement period is determined under paragraph (d)(1)(ii) or (iii) of this section, whichever is applicable.

(ii) *Method for crediting years of service for full plan years.*—The years of service credited under the plan for any full plan year during the phased retirement period is multiplied by an adjustment ratio that is equal to the ratio of the employee's actual hours worked during that year to the number of hours that would be worked by the employee during that year under a full-time work schedule. Alternatively, on a reasonable and consistent basis, the adjustment ratio may be based on the ratio of an employee's actual compensation during the year to the compensation that would be paid to the employee during the year if he or she had maintained a full-time work schedule.

(iii) *Method for crediting years of service for partial plan years.*—In the case of a plan year only a portion of which is during a phased retirement period for an employee, the method described in paragraphs (d)(1)(i) and (ii) of this section is applied with respect to that portion of the plan year. Thus, for example, if an employee works full time until October 1 of a calendar plan year and works one-third time from October 1 through December 31 of the year, then the employee is credited with 10 months for that year (9 months plus 1/3 of 3 months).

(2) *Ancillary benefits during phased retirement period.*—(i) *Death benefits.*—If an employee dies while receiving phased retirement benefits, death benefits are allocated between the phased retirement benefit and the benefit that would be payable upon subsequent full retirement. See also §1.401(a)-20, A-9. Thus, if an employee dies after the annuity starting date for the phased retirement benefit, death benefits are paid with respect to the phased retirement benefit in accordance with the optional form elected for that benefit, and death benefits are paid with respect to the remainder of the employee's benefit in accordance with the plan's provisions regarding death during employment.

(ii) *Other ancillary benefits.*—To the extent provided under the terms of the plan, ancillary benefits, other than death benefits described in paragraph (d)(2)(i) of this section, are permitted to be provided during the phased retirement period.

(3) *Calculation of benefit at full retirement.*—(i) *In general.*—Upon full retirement following partial retirement under a phased retirement program, the employee's total accrued benefit under the plan (including the employee's accruals during the phased retirement period, determined in accordance with paragraph (d)(1) of this section) is offset by the portion of the employee's phased retirement accrued benefit that is being distributed as a phased retirement benefit at the time of full retirement.

(ii) *Adjustment for prior payments.*—If, before full retirement, the employee's phased retirement benefit has been reduced under paragraph (d)(4) of this section, then the employee's accrued benefit under the plan is also offset upon full retirement by an amount that is actuarially equivalent to the phased retirement benefit payments that have been made during the phased retirement period that were not made with respect to the portion of the phased retirement accrued benefit that is applied as an offset under paragraph (d)(3)(i) of this section at the time of full retirement.

(iii) *Election of optional form with respect to net benefit.*—Upon full retirement, an employee is entitled to elect, in accordance with section 417, an optional form of benefit with respect to the net accrued benefit determined under paragraph (d)(3)(i) and (ii) of this section.

(iv) *New election permitted for phased retirement benefit.*—A plan is permitted to provide that, upon full retirement, an employee may elect, in accordance with section 417 and without regard to paragraph (a)(2)(iii) of this section, a new optional form of benefit with respect to the portion of the phased retirement accrued benefit that is being distributed as a phased retirement benefit. Any such new optional form of benefit is calculated at the time of full retirement as the actuarial equivalent of the future phased retirement benefits (without offset for the phased retirement benefits previously paid).

(4) *Prospective reduction in phased retirement benefit if hours are materially greater than expected.*—(i) *General rule.*—Except as otherwise provided in this paragraph (d)(4), a plan must compare annually the number of hours actually worked by an employee during the phased retirement testing period and the number of hours the employee was reasonably expected to work during the testing period for purposes of calculating the work schedule fraction. For this purpose, the phased retirement testing period is the 12 months preceding the comparison date (or such longer period permitted under paragraph(d)(4)(iv) of this section, or any shorter period that applies if there is a comparison date as a result of an agreed increase under paragraph (d)(4)(vi) of this section). In the event that the actual hours worked (determined on an annual basis) during the phased retirement testing period exceeds the work schedule, then, except as provided in paragraph (d)(4)(ii) or (v) of this section, the employee's phased retirement benefit must be reduced in accordance with the method provided in paragraph (d)(4)(iii) of this section, effective as of an adjustment date specified in the plan that is not more than 3 months later than the comparison date.

(ii) *Permitted variance in hours.*—A plan is not required to reduce the phased retirement benefit unless the hours worked during the phased retirement testing period are materially greater than the hours that would be expected to be worked under the work schedule. For this purpose, the employee's hours worked (determined on annual basis) are materially greater than the employee's work schedule if either—

(A) The employee's hours worked (determined on an annual basis) are more than 133-1/3 percent of the employee's work schedule; or

(B) The employee's hours worked (determined on an annual basis) exceed 90 percent of the full-time work schedule.

(iii) *Adjustment method.*—If a phased retirement benefit must be reduced under paragraph (d)(4) of this section, a new (i.e., reduced) phased retirement benefit must be calculated as provided in this paragraph (d)(4)(iii). First, an adjusted work schedule is determined. The adjusted work schedule is an annual schedule based on the number of hours the employee actually worked during the phased retirement testing period. The adjusted work schedule is applied to the employee's accrued benefit that was used to calculate the prior phased retirement benefit. This results in a new phased retirement accrued benefit for purposes of paragraph (b)(4) of this section. Second, a new phased retirement benefit is determined, based on the new phased retirement accrued benefit and payable in the same optional form of benefit (i.e., using the same annuity starting date and the same early retirement factor and other actuarial adjustments) as the prior phased retirement benefit. If an employee is receiving more than one phased retirement benefit (as permitted under paragraph (e)(2) of this section) and a reduction is required under paragraph (d)(4) of this section, then the reduction is applied first to the most recently commencing phased retirement benefit (and then, if necessary, to the next most recent phased retirement benefit, etc.).

(iv) *Comparison date for phased retirement testing period.*—The comparison date is any date chosen by the employer on a reasonable and consistent basis and specified in the plan, such as the last day of the plan year, December 31, or the anniversary of the annuity starting date for the employee's phased retirement benefit. As an alternative to testing the hours worked during the 12 months preceding the comparison date, the plan may, on a reasonable and consistent basis, provide that the comparison of actual hours worked to the work schedule be based on a cumulative period that exceeds 12 months beginning with either the annuity starting date for the employee's phased retirement benefit or any later date specified in the plan.

(v) *Exceptions to comparison requirement.*—(A) *In general.*—The comparison of hours described in paragraph (d)(4) of this section is not required in the situations set forth in this paragraph (d)(4)(v).

(B) *Employees recently commencing phased retirement.*—No comparison is required for an employee who commenced phased retirement benefits within the 12-month period preceding the comparison date.

(C) *Employees with short phased retirement periods.*—No comparison is required during the first 2 years of an employee's phased retirement period if—

(1) The employee has entered into an agreement with the employer under which the employee's phased retirement period will not exceed 2 years and the employee will fully retire at the end of such period; and

(2) The employee fully retires after a phased retirement period not in excess of 2 years.

(D) *Employees with proportional pay reduction.*—No comparison is required for any phased retirement testing period if the amount of compensation paid to the employee during that period does not exceed the compensation that would be paid to the employee if he or she had maintained a full-time work schedule multiplied by the work schedule fraction.

(E) *Employees at or after normal retirement age.*—No comparison is required for any phased retirement testing period ending within 3 months before the employee's normal retirement age or any time thereafter.

(vi) *Agreement to increase hours.*—(A) *General rule.*—In the event that the employer and the employee agree to increase prospectively the hours under the employee's work schedule prior to normal retirement age, then, notwithstanding the exceptions provided in paragraphs (d)(4)(v)(B) through (D) of this section, the plan must treat the effective date of the agreement to increase the employee's hours as a comparison date for purposes of paragraph (d)(4)(iv) of this section. For purposes of this paragraph (d)(4)(vi), with respect to an employee, the term *new work schedule* means the greater of the actual number of hours the employee worked (determined on an annual basis) during the prior phased retirement testing period or the annual number of hours the employee reasonably expects to work under the new agreement.

(B) *Required adjustments.*—If the employee's hours under the new work schedule are materially greater (within the meaning of paragraph (d)(4)(ii) of this section) than the hours the employee would be expected to work (based on the employee's prior work schedule), the employer is required to reduce the employee's phased retirement benefit, effective as of the date of the increase, based on the new work schedule. In this case, the employee's new work schedule is used for future comparisons under paragraph (d)(4) of this section.

(C) *Permitted adjustments.*—If the employee's hours under the new work schedule are not materially greater (within the meaning of paragraph (d)(4)(ii) of this section) than the hours the employee would be expected to work (based on the employee's prior work schedule), the employer is permitted, but not required, to reduce the employee's phased retirement benefit, effective as of the date of the increase, based on the new work schedule. If the benefit is so reduced, the employee's new work schedule is used for future comparisons under paragraph (d)(4) of this section. If the employee's phased retirement benefit is not so reduced, future comparisons are determined using the employee's prior work schedule.

(e) *Other rules.*—(1) *Highly compensated employees.*—An employee who partially retires under a phased retirement program and who was a highly compensated employee, as defined in section 414(q), immediately before the partial retirement is considered to be a highly compensated employee during the phased retirement period, without regard to the compensation actually paid to the employee during the phased retirement period.

(2) *Multiple phased retirement benefits permitted.*—(i) *In general.*—A plan is permitted to provide one or more additional phased retirement benefits prospectively to an employee who is receiving a phased retirement benefit if the conditions set forth in paragraph (e)(2)(ii) of this section are satisfied. At the later annuity starting date for the additional phased retirement benefit, the additional phased retirement benefits may not exceed the amount permitted to be paid based on the excess of—

(A) The employee's phased retirement accrued benefit at the later annuity starting date, over

(B) The portion of the employee's phased retirement accrued benefit at the earlier annuity starting date that is being distributed as a phased retirement benefit.

(ii) *Conditions.*—The additional phased retirement benefit described in paragraph (e)(2)(i) of this section may be provided only if—

(A) The prior phased retirement benefit was not based on the employee's entire phased retirement accrued benefit at the annuity starting date for the prior phased retirement benefit, or

(B) The employee's work schedule at the later annuity starting date is less than the employee's work schedule that was used to calculate the prior phased retirement benefit.

(3) *Application of section 411(d)(6).*—In accordance with §1.411(d)-4, A-1(b)(1), the right to receive a partial distribution of an employee's accrued benefit as a phased retirement benefit is treated as an optional form of payment that is separate from the right to receive a full distribution of the accrued benefit upon full retirement.

(4). *Application of nondiscrimination rules.*—The right to receive a phased retirement benefit is a benefit, right, or feature that is subject to §1.401(a)(4)-4.

(f) *Examples.*—The following examples illustrate the application of this section:

Example 1. (i) *Employer's Plans.* Plan X (as in effect prior to amendment to reflect the phased retirement program described below) is a defined benefit plan maintained by Employer M. Plan X provides an accrued benefit of 1.5% of the average of an employee's highest three years of pay (based on the highest 36 consecutive months of pay), times years of service (with 1,000 hours of service required for a year of service), payable as a life annuity beginning at age 65. Plan X permits employees to elect to commence actuarially reduced distributions at any time after the later of termination of employment or attainment of age 50, except that if an employee retires after age 55 and completion of 20 years of service, the applicable reduction is only 3% per year for the years between ages 65 and 62 and 6% per year for the years between ages 62 to 55. Plan X permits employees to select, with spousal consent, a single life annuity, a joint and contingent annuity with the employee having the right to select any beneficiary and a continuation percentage of 50%, 75%, or 100%, or a 10-year certain and life annuity.

(ii) *Phased Retirement Program.* Employer M adopts a voluntary phased retirement program that will only be available for employees who retire during the two-year period from February 1, 2006 to January 31, 2008. The program will not be available to employees who are not entitled to an immediate pension or who are 1 percent owners. Employer M has determined that employees typically begin to retire after attainment of age 55 with at least 15 years of service. Accordingly, to increase retention of certain employees, the program will provide that employees in certain specified work positions who have reached age 59^1/$_2$ and completed 15 years of service may elect phased retirement. The program permits phased retirement to be implemented through a reduction of 25%, 50%, or 75% in the number of hours expected to be worked for up to 5 years following phased retirement (other reduced schedules may be elected with the approval of M), with the employee's compensation during the phased retirement period to be based on what a similar full-time employee would be paid, reduced by the applicable percentage reduction in hours expected to be worked. In order to participate in the program, the employee and the employer must enter into an agreement under which the employee will reduce his or her hours accordingly. The agreement also provides that the employee's compensation during phased retirement will be reduced by that same percentage. The program is announced to employees in the fall of 2005.

(iii) *Plan Provisions Regarding Phased Retirement Benefit.* (A) Plan X is amended, prior to February 1, 2006, to provide that an employee who elects phased retirement under M's phased retirement program is permitted to commence benefits with respect to a portion of his or her accrued retirement benefit (the employee's phased retirement accrued benefit), based on the applicable percentage reduction in hours expected to be worked. For example, for a 25% reduction in hours, the employee is entitled to commence benefits with respect to 25% of his or her accrued benefit. Plan X permits an employee who commences phased retirement to elect, with spousal consent, from any of the optional forms provided under the plan.

(B) During the phased retirement period, the employee will continue to accrue benefits (without regard to the plan's 1,000 hour requirement), with his or her pay for purposes of calculating benefits under Plan X increased by the ratio of 100 percent to the percentage of full-time pay that will be paid during phased retirement and with the employee's service credit to be equal to the product of the same percentage times the service credit that would apply if the employee were working full time. Upon the employee's subsequent full retire-

ment, his or her total accrued benefit will be based on the resulting highest three years of pay and total years of service, offset by the phased retirement accrued benefit. The retirement benefit payable upon subsequent full retirement is in addition to the phased retirement benefit. Plan X does not provide for a new election with respect to the phased retirement benefit.

(C) In the case of death during the phased retirement period, the employee will be treated as a former employee to the extent of his or her phased retirement benefit and as an active employee to the extent of the retirement benefit that would be due upon full retirement.

(D) Because the terms of the phased retirement program provide that the employee's compensation during phased retirement will be reduced by that same percentage as applies to calculate phased retirement benefits, Plan X does not have provisions requiring annual testing of hours actually worked.

(iv) *Application to a Specific Employee*—(A) *Phased retirement benefit.* Employee E is age 59^1/$_2$ with 20 years of credited service. Employee E's compensation is $90,000, and E's highest three years of pay is $85,000. Employee E elects phased retirement on April 1, 2006 and elects to reduce hours by 50% beginning on July 1, 2006. Thus, E's annuity starting date for the phased retirement benefit is July 1, 2006. Employee E's total accrued benefit as of July 1, 2006 as a single life annuity payable at normal retirement age is equal to $25,500 per year (1.5% times $85,000 times 20 years of service). Thus, Employee E's phased retirement accrued benefit as of July 1, 2006 as a single life annuity payable at normal retirement age is equal to $12,750 per year ($25,500 times 1 minus E's work schedule fraction of 50%). Accordingly, Employee E's phased retirement benefit payable as a straight life annuity commencing on July 1, 2006 is equal to $9,690 per year ($12,750 per year times 76% (100% minus the applicable reduction for early retirement equal to 3% for 3 years and 6% for an additional 2^1/$_2$ years)). Employee E elects a joint and 50% survivor annuity, with E's spouse as the contingent annuitant. Under Plan X, the actuarial factor for this form of benefit is 90%, so E's benefit is $8,721 per year.

(B) *Death during phased retirement.* If Employee E were to die on or after July 1, 2006 and before subsequent full retirement, E's spouse would be entitled to a 50% survivor annuity based on the joint and 50% survivor annuity being paid to E, plus a qualified preretirement survivor annuity that complies with section 417 with respect to the additional amount that would be paid to E if he or she had fully retired on the date of E's death.

(C) *Subsequent full retirement benefit.* Three years later, Employee E fully retires from Employer M. Throughout this period, E's compensation has been 50% of the compensation that would have been paid to E if he or she were working full time. Consequently, no adjustment in E's phased retirement benefit is required. E's highest consecutive 36 months of compensation would be $95,000 if E had not elected phased retirement and E has been credited with 1^1/$_2$ years of service credit for the 3 years of phased retirement (.50 times 3 years). Accordingly, prior to offset for E's phased retirement accrued benefit, E's total accrued benefit as of July 1, 2009 as a single life annuity commencing at normal retirement age is equal to $30,637.50 per year ($95,000 times 1.5% times 21.5 years of service) and, after the offset for E's phased retirement accrued benefit, E's retirement benefit as a single life annuity commencing at normal retirement age is equal to $17,887.50 ($30,637.50 minus $12,750). Thus, the amount of E's additional early retirement benefit payable as a straight life annuity at age 62^1/$_2$ is equal to $16,545.94 per year ($17,887.50 per year times 92.5% (100% minus 3% for 2^1/$_2$ years)). Employee E elects, with spousal consent, a 10-year certain and life annuity that applies to the remainder of E's accrued benefit. This annuity is in addition to the previously elected joint and 50% survivor annuity payable as E's phased retirement benefit.

Example 2. (i) *Same Plan and Phased Retirement Program, Except Annual Testing Required.* The facts with respect to the Plan X and M's phased retirement program are the same as in *Example 1*, except that the program does not provide that the employee's compensation during phased retirement will be reduced by that same percentage as is applied to calculate phased retirement benefits, but instead the compensation depends on the number of hours worked by the employee. Plan X provides for annual testing on a calendar year basis and for an employee's phased retirement benefit to be reduced proportionately if the hours worked exceed a threshold, under provisions which reflect the variance permitted paragraph (d)(4)(ii) of this section.

(ii) *Employee Has Small Increase in Hours.* The facts with respect to Employee E are the same as in *Example 1*, except that E's full time work schedule would result in 2,000 hours worked annually, E's work schedule fraction is 50%, and E works 500 hours from July 1, 2006 through December 31, 2006, 1,000 hours in 2007, 1,200 hours in 2008, and 600 hours from January 1, 2009 through E's full retirement on June 30, 2009.

(iii) *Application of Testing Rules.* No comparison of hours is required for the partial testing period that occurs in 2006. For 2007, no reduction is required in E's phased retirement benefit as a result of the hours worked by E during 2007 because the hours did not exceed

E's work schedule (50% of 2,000). For 2008, although the hours worked by E exceeded E's work schedule, no reduction is required because the hours worked in 2008 were not materially greater than E's work schedule (1,200 is not more than the variance permitted under paragraph (d)(4)(ii) of this section, which is 133-1/3% of 1,000). E's total accrued benefit upon E's retirement on July 1, 2009 would be based on 21.65 years of service to reflect the actual hours worked from July 1, 2006 through June 30, 2009.

Example 3. (i) *Same Plan and Phased Retirement Program, Except Material Increase in Hours.* The facts with respect to the Plan X and M's phased retirement program are the same as in *Example 2,* except E works 1,400 hours in 2008 and 700 hours in the first half of 2009.

(ii) *Application of Testing Rules.* No comparison of hours is required for the partial testing period that occurs in 2006. For 2007, no reduction is required in E's phased retirement benefit as a result of the hours worked by E during 2007 because the hours did not exceed 50% of 2,000. However, the hours worked by E during 2008 exceed 133-1/3% of E's work schedule (50% of 2,000), so that the phased retirement benefit paid to E during 2009 must be reduced. The reduction is effective March 1, 2009. The new phased retirement benefit of $5,232.60 is based on 30% of the participant's accrued benefit as of July 1, 2006, payable as a joint and 50% survivor annuity commencing on that date (30% times $25,500 times the early retirement factor of 76% times the joint and 50% factor of 90%). This is equivalent to reducing the previously elected joint and 50% survivor annuity payable with respect to E by 40% (400 "excess" hours divided by the 1,000 hour expected reduction). When E retires fully on July 1, 2009, E's total accrued benefit as of July 1, 2009 as a single life annuity commencing at normal retirement age is $31,065 per year ($95,000 times 1.5% times 21.8 years of service). This accrued benefit is offset by (A) E's phased retirement accrued benefit (which is $7,650 (600 divided by 2,000 times $25,500)) plus (B) the actuarial equivalent

of 40% of the payments that were made to E from January 1, 2008 through February 28, 2009.

Example 4. (i) *Same Plan and Phased Retirement Program, Except Employer and Employee Agree to Decrease Hours.* The facts with respect to the Plan X and M's phased retirement program are the same as in *Example 2,* except before 2008, E enters into an agreement with M to decrease E's number of hours worked from 50% of full time to 25% of full time. E works 500 hours in 2008 and 250 hours in 2009.

(ii) *Application of Multiple Benefit Rule.* Under paragraph (e)(2) of this section, Plan M may provide for an additional phased retirement benefit to be offered to E for 2008. The maximum increase would be for the phased retirement benefit paid to E during 2009 to be increased based on a phased retirement accrued benefit equal to 75% of E's accrued benefit (1,500 divided by 2,000). Thus, the amount being paid to E would be increased, effective January 1, 2008, based on the excess of 75% of E's total accrued benefit on December 31, 2007, over E's original phased retirement accrued benefit of $12,750. Employee E would have the right to elect, with spousal consent, any annuity form offered under Plan X (with the actuarial adjustment for time of commencement and form of payment to be based on the age of E and any contingent beneficiary (and E's service, if applicable) on June 1, 2008), which would be in addition to the previously elected joint and 50% survivor annuity payable as E's original phased retirement benefit. When E retires fully on July 1, 2009, Employee E's total accrued benefit as of July 1, 2009 would be offset by (A) E's original phased retirement accrued benefit plus (B) the phased retirement accrued benefit for which additional phased retirement benefits were payable beginning in 2008.

(g) *Effective date.*—The rules of this section apply to plan years beginning on or after the date of publication of the Treasury decision adopting these rules as final regulations in the Federal Register.

Governmental Pension Plans: Applicability of Normal Retirement Age Regulations

Governmental Pension Plans: Applicability of Normal Retirement Age Regulations.—Amendments to Reg. § 1.401(a)-1, providing rules relating to the determination of whether the normal retirement age under a governmental plan (within the meaning of section 414(d) of the Code) that is a pension plan satisfies the requirements of section 401(a) and whether the payment of definitely determinable benefits that commence at the plan's normal retirement age satisfies these requirements, are proposed (published in the Federal Register on January 27, 2016) (REG-147310-12).

Par. 2. Section 1.401(a)-1 is amended by:

1. Revising paragraph (b)(2)(v).

2. Adding paragraph (b)(2)(vi).

3. Revising the heading and the second sentence of paragraph (b)(4).

The revisions read as follows:

§ 1.401(a)-1. Post-ERISA qualified plans and qualified trusts; in general.

* * *

(b) * * *

(2) * * *

(v) *Rules of application for governmental plans.*—(A) *In general.*—In the case of a governmental plan (within the meaning of section 414(d)) that provides for distributions before retirement, the general rule described in paragraph (b)(2)(i) of this section may be satisfied in accordance with paragraph (b)(2)(ii) of this section or this paragraph (b)(2)(v). In the case of a governmental plan that does not provide for distributions before retirement, the plan's normal retirement age is not required to comply with the general rule described in paragraph (b)(2)(i) of this section or this paragraph (b)(2)(v).

(B) *Age 60 and 5 years of service safe harbor.*—A normal retirement age under a governmental plan that is the later of age 60 or the age at which the participant has been credited with at least 5 years of service under the plan is deemed to be not earlier than the earliest age that is reasonably representative of the typical retirement age for the industry in which the covered workforce is employed.

(C) *Age 55 and 10 years of service safe harbor.*—A normal retirement age under a governmental plan that is the later of age 55 or the age at which the participant has been credited with at least 10 years of service under the plan is deemed to be not earlier than the earliest age that is reasonably representative of the typical retirement age for the industry in which the covered workforce is employed.

(D) *Sum of 80 safe harbor.*—A normal retirement age under a governmental plan that is the participant's age at which the sum of the participant's age plus the number of years of service that have been credited to the participant under the plan equals 80 or more is deemed to be not earlier than the earliest age that is reasonably representative of the typical retirement age for the industry in which the covered workforce is employed. For example, a normal retirement age under a governmental plan that is age 55 for a participant who has been credited with 25 years of service would satisfy the rule described in this paragraph.

(E) *Service-based combination safe harbor.*—A normal retirement age under a governmental plan that is the earlier of the participant's age at which the participant has been credited with at least 25 years of service under the plan and an age that satisfies any other safe harbor provided under paragraphs (b)(2)(v)(B) through (D) of this section is deemed to be not earlier than the earliest age that is reasonably representative of the typical retirement age for the industry in which the covered workforce is employed. For example, a normal retirement age under a governmental plan that is the earlier of the participant's age at which the participant has been credited with 25 years of service under the plan and the later of age 60 or the age at which the participant has been credited with 5 years of service under the plan would satisfy this safe harbor.

(F) *Age 50 safe harbor for qualified public safety employees.*—A normal retirement age under a governmental plan that is age 50 or later is deemed to be not earlier than the earliest age that is reasonably representative of the typical retirement age for the industry in which the covered workforce is employed if the participants to which this normal retirement age applies are qualified public safety employees (within the meaning of section 72(t)(10)(B)).

(G) *Sum of 70 safe harbor for qualified public safety employees.*—A normal retirement age under a governmental plan that is the participant's age at which the sum of the participant's age plus the number of years of service that have been credited to the participant under the plan equals 70 or more, is deemed to be not earlier than the earliest age that is reasonably representative of the typical retirement age for the industry in which the covered workforce is employed if the participants to which this normal retirement age applies are qualified public safety employees (within the meaning of section 72(t)(10)(B)).

(H) *Service-based safe harbor for qualified public safety employees.*—A normal retirement age under a governmental plan that is the age at which the participant has been credited with at least 20 years of service under the plan is deemed to be not earlier than the earliest age that is reasonably representative of the typical retirement age for the industry in which the covered workforce is employed if the participants to which this normal retirement age applies are qualified public safety employees (within the meaning of section 72(t)(10)(B)). For example, a normal retirement age that covers only qualified public safety employees and that is an employee's age when the employee has been credited with 25 years of service under a governmental plan would satisfy this safe harbor.

(I) *Reserved.*

(J) *Other normal retirement ages.*—In the case of a normal retirement age under a governmental plan that fails to satisfy any safe harbor described in paragraph (b)(2)(ii) of this section or this paragraph (b)(2)(v), whether the age is not earlier than the earliest age that is reasonably representative of the typical retirement age for the industry in which the covered workforce is employed is based on all of the relevant facts and circumstances.

(vi) *Special normal retirement age rule for certain plans.*—See section 411(f), which provides a special rule for determining a permissible normal retirement age under certain defined benefit plans.

* * *

(4) *Effective/applicability date.*—* * * In the case of a governmental plan (as defined in section 414(d)), the rules in paragraph (b)(2)(v) of this section are effective for employees hired during plan years beginning on or after the later of: January 1, 2017; or the close of the first regular legislative session of the legislative body with the authority to amend the plan that begins on or after the date that is 3 months after the final regulations are published in the **Federal Register**. However, a governmental plan sponsor may elect to apply the rules of paragraph (b)(2)(v) of this section to earlier periods. * * *

Retirement Plans: Distributions: Deferral of Receipt: Notification of Consequences

Retirement Plans: Distributions: Deferral of Receipt: Notification of Consequences.—Amendments to Reg. §§1.401(a)-13 and 1.401(a)-20, specifying that the notice required under Code Sec. 411(a)(11) to be provided to a participant of his or her right, if any, to defer receipt of an immediately distributable benefit must also describe the consequences of failing to defer receipt of the distribution, are proposed (published in the Federal Register on October 9, 2008) (REG-107318-08).

Par. 2. For each entry listed in the "Location" column, remove the language in the "Remove" column and add the language in the "Add" column in its place.

§1.401(a)-13. Assignment or alienation of benefits.

Location	Remove	Add
1.401(a)-13(g)(4)(ii), first sentence	90 days	180 days

Par. 2. For each entry listed in the "Location" column, remove the language in the "Remove" column and add the language in the "Add" column in its place.

§1.401(a)-20. Requirements of qualified joint and survivor annuity and qualified preretirement survivor annuity.

Location	Remove	Add
1.401(a)-20, A-4, third sentence	90 days	180 days
1.401(a)-20, A-10(a), fifth and sixth sentences	90 days	180 days
1.401(a)-20, A-16, sixth sentence	90 days	180 days
1.401(a)-20, A-24(a)(1), fifth sentence	90 days	180 days

Closed Defined Benefit Pensions Plans: Nondiscrimination Relief

Closed Defined Benefit Pensions Plans: Nondiscrimination Relief.—Amendments to Reg. §§1.401(a)(4)-0, 1.401(a)(4)-2—1.401(a)(4)-4, 1.401(a)(4)-8, 1.401(a)(4)-9, 1.401(a)(4)-12 and 1.401(a)(4)-13, modifying the nondiscrimination requirements applicable to certain retirement plans that provide additional benefits to a grandfathered group of employees following certain changes in the coverage of a defined benefit plan or a defined benefit plan formula, are proposed (published in the Federal Register on January 29, 2016) (REG-125761-14).

Par. 2. Section 1.401(a)(4)-0 is amended by:
1. Adding paragraph (c)(5) to the entry for §1.401(a)(4)-2.
2. Adding paragraph (d)(8) to the entry for §1.401(a)(4)-4.
3. Adding paragraph (a)(4) to the entry for §1.401(a)(4)-13.
The additions read as follows:

§1.401(a)(4)-0. Table of contents.

* * *

§1.401(a)(4)-2. Nondiscrimination in amount of employer contributions under a defined contribution plan.

* * *

(c) * * *

(5) Effective/applicability date.

* * *

Par. 3. Section 1.401(a)(4)-2 is amended by:
1. Revising paragraph (c)(3)(ii).
2. Revising *Examples 4* and *5* in paragraph (c)(4).
3. Adding *Examples 6* and *7* to paragraph (c)(4).
4. Adding paragraph (c)(5).
The revisions and additions read as follows:

§1.401(a)(4)-2. Nondiscrimination in amount of employer contributions under a defined contribution plan.

* * *

(c) * * *

(3) * * *

§1.401(a)(4)-4. Nondiscriminatory availability of benefits, rights, and features.

* * *

(d) * * *

(8) Special testing rule for grandfathered group of employees.

* * *

§1.401(a)(4)-13. Effective dates and fresh-start rules.
(a) * * *

(4) Effective/applicability date.

* * *

(ii) *Application of nondiscriminatory classification test.*—A rate group satisfies the nondiscriminatory classification test of §1.410(b)-4 if and only if—

(A) The formula that is used to determine the allocation for the HCE with respect to whom the rate group is established applies to a group of employees that satisfies the reasonable classification requirement of §1.410(b)-4(b); and

(B) The ratio percentage of the rate group is greater than or equal to the midpoint between the safe and unsafe harbor percentages applicable to the plan (or the ratio percentage of the plan, if that percentage is less).

* * *

(4) * * *

Example 4. (a) The facts are the same as in *Example 3*, except that N4 has an allocation rate of 8.0 percent. In addition, the formula that is used to determine the allocation for H2 is the same formula that is used to determine the allocation for all other employees in Plan D.

(b) There are two rate groups in Plan D. Rate group 1 consists of H1 and all those employees who have an allocation rate greater than or equal to H1's allocation rate (5.0 percent). Thus, rate group 1 consists of H1, H2 and N1 through N4. Rate group 2 consists of H2, and all those employees who have an allocation rate greater than or equal to H2's allocation rate (7.5 percent). Thus, rate group 2 consists of H2 and N4.

(c) Rate group 1 satisfies the ratio percentage test under §1.410(b)-2(b)(2) because the ratio percentage of the rate group is 100 percent—that is, 100 percent (the percentage of all nonhighly compensated nonexcludable employees who are in the rate group) divided by 100 percent (the percentage of all highly compensated nonexcludable employees who are in the rate group).

(d) Rate group 2 does not satisfy the ratio percentage test of §1.410(b)-2(b)(2) because the ratio percentage of the rate group is 50 percent—that is, 25 percent (the percentage of all nonhighly compensated nonexcludable employees who are in the rate group) divided by 50 percent (the percentage of all highly compensated nonexcludable employees who are in the rate group).

(e) However, under paragraph (c)(3)(ii) of this section rate group 2 satisfies the nondiscriminatory classification test of §1.410(b)-4 because (i) the formula that is used to determine the allocation for H2 applies to a group of employees that satisfies the reasonable classification requirement of §1.410(b)-4(b) (in this case, because it applies to all the employees) and (ii) the ratio percentage of the rate group (50 percent) is greater than the midpoint between the safe harbor and unsafe harbor percentages applicable to the plan under §1.410(b)-4(c)(4) (40.5 percent).

(f) Under paragraph (c)(3)(iii) of this section, rate group 2 satisfies the average benefit percentage test if Plan D satisfies the average benefit percentage test. (The requirement that Plan D satisfy the average benefit percentage test applies even though Plan D satisfies the ratio percentage test and would ordinarily not need to run the average benefit percentage test.) If Plan D satisfies the average benefit percentage test, then rate group 2 satisfies section 410(b); thus, Plan D satisfies the general test in paragraph (c)(1) of this section because each rate group under the plan satisfies section 410(b).

Example 5. (a) Plan E satisfies section 410(b) by satisfying the nondiscriminatory classification test of §1.410(b)-4 and the average benefit percentage test of §1.410(b)-5 (without regard to §1.410(b)-5(f)). See §1.410(b)-2(b)(3). Plan E uses the facts-and-circumstances requirements of §1.410(b)-4(c)(3) to satisfy the nondis-

criminatory classification test of §1.410(b)-4. The safe and unsafe harbor percentages applicable to the plan under §1.410(b)-4(c)(4) are 29 and 20 percent, respectively. Plan E has a ratio percentage of 22 percent. Rate group 1 under Plan E has a ratio percentage of 23 percent. The formula that is used to determine the allocation for the HCE with respect to whom rate group 1 was formed applies to all other employees.

(b) Under paragraph (c)(3)(ii) of this section, rate group 1 satisfies the nondiscriminatory classification requirement of §1.410(b)-4, because (i) the formula that is used to determine the allocation for the HCE with respect to whom the rate group was formed applies to a group of employees that satisfies the reasonable classification requirement of §1.410(b)-4(b) (in this case, because it applies to all the employees) and (ii) the ratio percentage of the rate group (23 percent) is greater than the lesser of—

(1) The ratio percentage for the plan as a whole (22 percent); and

(2) The midpoint between the safe and unsafe harbor percentages (24.5 percent).

(c) Under paragraph (c)(3)(iii) of this section, the rate group satisfies section 410(b) because the plan satisfies the average benefit percentage test of §1.410(b)-5.

Example 6. (a) Employer Z maintains a defined contribution plan, Plan F. Employer Z has six nonexcludable employees, all of whom benefit under Plan F. There is one HCE (H1) and five NHCEs (N1 through N5). There is one rate group under Plan F. The formula that is used to determine the allocation for H1 is the greater of $20,000 or 10% of compensation for the year. The formula that applies to determine the allocation for N1 through N5 is 10% of compensation.

(b) Under paragraph (c)(3)(ii) of this section, the rate group with respect to H1 does not satisfy the nondiscriminatory classification test under §1.410(b)-4 because the formula that is used to determine the allocation for H1 (with respect to whom the rate group is established) only applies to H1. Therefore, the rate group will satisfy paragraph (c)(3) of this section only if the ratio percentage of the rate group is greater than or equal to 70 percent. This ratio percentage test applies even if H1's compensation is greater than $200,000. In such a case, the rate group will pass the ratio percentage test (and accordingly the plan will satisfy the general test of this paragraph (c)) because each employee receives an allocation of 10% of compensation and therefore the ratio percentage for the rate group is equal to 100%.

Example 7. The facts are the same as in *Example 6*, except that the classification of employees who are entitled to benefit under the formula that applies to H1 includes N1 and N2, who are identified by name. Under paragraph (c)(3)(ii) of this section, the rate group with respect to H1 does not satisfy the nondiscriminatory classification test under §1.410(b)-4 because the classification of H1, N1 and N2 by name does not satisfy the reasonable classification requirement of §1.410(b)-4(b). Therefore, the rate group with respect to H1 will satisfy paragraph (c)(3) of this section only if the ratio percentage of the rate group is greater than or equal to 70 percent.

(5) *Effective/applicability date.*—See §1.401(a)(4)-13(a)(4) for rules on the effective/applicability date of this paragraph (c).

Par. 4. In §1.401(a)(4)-3, paragraph (c)(2) is revised to read as follows:

§1.401(a)(4)-3. Nondiscrimination in amount of employer-provided benefits under a defined benefit plan.

* * *

(c) * * *

(2) *Satisfaction of section 410(b) by a rate group.*—For purposes of determining whether a rate group satisfies section 410(b), the rules

of §1.401(a)(4)-2(c)(3) apply except that §1.401(a)(4)-2(c)(3)(ii)(A) is applied by substituting "benefit formula" for "formula that is used to determine the allocation." See paragraph (c)(4) of this section and §1.401(a)(4)-2(c)(4), *Example 3* through *Example 6*, for examples of this rule. See §1.401(a)(4)-13(a)(4) for rules on the effective/applicability date of this paragraph (c)(2).

* * *

Par. 5. In §1.401(a)(4)-4, paragraph (d)(8) is added to read as follows:

§1.401(a)(4)-4. Nondiscriminatory availability of benefits, rights, and features.

* * *

(d) * * *

(8) *Special testing rule for grandfathered group of employees.*—(i) *General rule.*—For a plan year that begins on or after the fifth anniversary of the closure date with respect to a closed defined benefit plan, a benefit, right, or feature under a defined benefit or defined contribution plan that is available only to a grandfathered group of employees with respect to the closed defined benefit plan is treated as satisfying paragraphs (b) and (c) of this section for the plan year, provided that—

(A) No plan amendment that affects the availability of the benefit, right, or feature (other than the closure amendment) has

an applicable amendment date (within the meaning of §1.411(d)-3(g)(4)) that is within the period that begins on the closure date and ends on the last day of the plan year; and

(B) The additional requirements of paragraph (d)(8)(ii) or (iii) of this section, whichever is applicable, are satisfied.

(ii) *Additional requirements in the case of a benefit, right, or feature provided under a defined benefit plan.*—If the benefit, right, or feature is provided under a defined benefit plan, then the following additional requirements apply—

(A) The defined benefit plan under which the benefit, right, or feature is provided is the closed defined benefit plan;

(B) No plan amendment that affects the availability of the benefit, right, or feature (other than the closure amendment) has an applicable amendment date that is within the 5-year period ending on the closure date; and

(C) The closure amendment that restricted the availability of the benefit, right, or feature, making it available only to the grandfathered group of employees, must also have provided for a significant change in the type of benefit formula under the plan (such as a change from a benefit formula that is not a statutory hybrid benefit formula to a lump sum-based benefit formula).

(iii) *Additional requirements in the case of a benefit, right, or feature provided under a defined contribution plan.*—If the benefit, right, or feature is provided under a defined contribution plan, then the following additional requirements apply—

(A) The benefit, right, or feature must be a right to a rate of matching contributions provided under the defined contribution plan;

(B) The rate of matching contributions must be reasonably designed so that the matching contributions will replace some or all of the value of the benefit accruals that each employee in the grandfathered group of employees would have been provided under the closed defined benefit plan in the absence of a closure amendment (based on the terms of that plan and the section 415(b)(1)(A) dollar limit in effect immediately prior to the closure date);

(C) The closed defined benefit plan must satisfy the conditions set forth in § 1.401(a)(4)-8(b)(1)(iii)(D)(3); and

(D) The rate of matching contributions must be provided in a consistent manner to all similarly situated employees.

(iv) *Certain amendments not taken into account.*—For purposes of applying the rules under this paragraph (d)(8), the following plan amendments are not taken into account (and, in the case of an amendment described in paragraph (d)(8)(iv)(C) or (D) of this section, the rules of this paragraph (d)(8) are applied as if the benefit, right, or feature provided after the amendment were the benefit, right, or feature provided before the amendment):

(A) An amendment adopted during the 5-year period ending on the closure date that extends eligibility for the benefit, right, or feature to an acquired group of employees provided that all similarly situated employees within that group are treated in a consistent manner.

(B) An amendment adopted after the closure date that expands or restricts the eligibility for the benefit, right, or feature, provided that, as of the applicable amendment date, the ratio percentage of the group of employees eligible for the benefit, right, or feature (taking into account the plan amendment) is not less than the ratio percentage of the group of employees eligible for the benefit, right, or feature provided before the amendment.

(C) An amendment adopted after the closure date that results in a replacement of the benefit, right, or feature with another benefit, right, or feature that is available to the same group of employees as the original benefit, right, or feature, provided that the original benefit, right, or feature is of inherently equal or greater value (within the meaning of paragraph (d)(4)(i)(A) of this section) than the benefit, right, or feature that replaces it.

(D) An amendment adopted after the closure date that results in a replacement of the benefit, right, or feature with another benefit, right, or feature that is available to the same group of employees as the original benefit, right, or feature, provided that there is only a *de minimis* difference between the amount payable under the original benefit, right, or feature and the amount payable under the benefit, right, or feature that replaces it.

(E) An amendment that is permitted by guidance published by the Commissioner in the Internal Revenue Bulletin.

(v) *Examples.*—The following examples illustrate the rules in this paragraph (d)(8):

Example 1—(i) *Pre-amendment defined benefit plan.* Employer A maintains Plan P, a defined benefit plan that provides for an annual benefit equal to 2% of an employee's average annual compensation multiplied by the employee's years of service. Plan P also provides for a subsidized early retirement benefit available to employees who retire between the ages of 55 and 65 with 20 years of service. Plan P was established in 2003. The plan year is a calendar year. For the 2015 plan year, Plan P satisfied the nondiscrimination requirements under sections 410(b) and 401(a)(4) without regard to the special rules under section 410(b)(6)(C) and without aggregation with any other plan.

(ii) *Plan conversion amendment.* On November 1, 2015, Employer A amends Plan P to cease future accruals under its benefit formula effective as of the close of the plan year ending December 31, 2015 and to provide future benefit accruals under a cash balance formula. The cash balance formula provides for pay credits equal to 5% of compensation and annual interest credits at an interest crediting rate of 6%. Early retirement benefits payable with respect to benefits accrued under the cash balance formula are determined as the actuarial equivalent of the hypothetical account balance, deter-

mined using reasonable actuarial assumptions that are specified in Plan P. Under the terms of the conversion amendment, an employee's benefit is equal to the employee's benefit under the prior benefit formula as of the close of the plan year ending December 31, 2015, plus the amount determined under the cash balance formula. However, any employee who had attained the age of 50 and had completed 15 years of service on or before December 31, 2015 is entitled to a plan benefit that is the greater of the benefit determined under the pre-amendment formula, or the benefit described in the prior sentence. Except for the closure amendment, there is no other plan amendment that affects the availability of Plan P's early retirement subsidy. No other significant change to Plan P's coverage or benefit formula is made with an applicable amendment date that is during the period beginning on January 1, 2011 and ending on December 31, 2015 (the 5-year period ending on the closure date).

(iii) *Applicability of special testing rule.* The plan conversion amendment is a closure amendment with a closure date of December 31, 2015. Plan P's subsidized early retirement benefit available solely to the grandfathered group of employees is a separate benefit, right, or feature that must be tested for current and effective availability under paragraphs (b) and (c) of this section. For a plan year that begins on or after January 1, 2021, Plan P's subsidized early retirement benefit is eligible for the relief provided by the special testing rule of this paragraph (d)(8) because all of the applicable requirements are satisfied. The requirement under paragraph (d)(8)(i)(A) of this section is satisfied because no other plan amendment that affects the availability of the subsidized early retirement benefit has an applicable amendment date that is on or after December 31, 2015. The additional requirements pertaining to a benefit, right, or feature provided under a defined benefit plan are also satisfied: the subsidized early retirement benefit is provided under a closed defined benefit plan as required by paragraph (d)(8)(ii)(A) of this section; no amendment that affected the availability of the subsidized early retirement benefit was made with an applicable amendment date during the 5-year period ending on the closure date as required by paragraph (d)(8)(ii)(B) of this section; and Plan P has undergone a significant change in benefit formula in connection with the closure amendment that resulted in a restriction on the availability of the subsidized early retirement benefit as required by paragraph (d)(8)(ii)(C) of this section.

Example 2—(i) *Closure of defined benefit plan.* The facts are the same as in *Example 1* of this paragraph (d)(8)(v), except that, instead of adopting a plan conversion amendment, Employer A amends Plan P to cease future accruals under the original benefit formula for all employees.

(ii) *Plan amendment to profit-sharing plan that provides enhanced rate of matching contributions.* Employer A has a profit-sharing plan that includes a qualified cash or deferred arrangement and matching contributions with respect to elective deferrals of up to 3% of compensation. On November 1, 2015, Employer A amends the plan to provide, effective January 1, 2016, for additional matching contributions of up to an additional 4% of compensation solely for employees who (1) were previously covered under the defined benefit plan, and (2) had attained the age of 50 and had 15 years of service on or before December 31, 2015. This enhanced rate of matching contributions is reasonably designed so that the matching contributions will replace some or all of the value of the benefit accruals that would have otherwise been provided to this grandfathered group of employees under Plan P. Employer A makes no other change to this enhanced rate of matching contribution after the enhanced rate is established.

(iii) *Applicability of special testing rule.* The plan amendment is a closure amendment with a closure date of December 31, 2015. The enhanced rate of matching contribution that is available solely to the grandfathered group of employees is a separate benefit, right, or feature that must be tested for current and effective availability under paragraphs (b) and (c) of this section. For a plan year that begins on or after January 1, 2021, Plan P's enhanced rate of matching contribution is eligible for the relief provided by the special testing rule of this paragraph (d)(8) because all applicable requirements are satisfied. The requirement under paragraph (d)(8)(i)(A) of this section is satisfied because no change was made to the enhanced rate of match with an applicable amendment date that is on or after December 31, 2015. The following applicable additional requirements are also satisfied: the benefit, right, or feature provided under the defined contribution plan is a rate of matching contribution as required by paragraph (d)(8)(iii)(A) of this section; the enhanced rate of matching contribution is reasonably designed so that the matching contributions will replace some of the value of the benefit accruals that each employee in the grandfathered group of employees would have otherwise been provided under Plan P immediately prior to the closure date as required by paragraph (d)(8)(iii)(B) of this section; and the rate of matching contributions is provided in a consistent manner to all similarly situated employees as required by paragraph (d)(8)(iii)(D) of this section.

(iv) *Applicability of § 1.401(a)(4)-8(b)(1)(iii)(D)(3).* In addition to the requirements described in paragraph (iii) of this *Example 2*,

Plan P meets the conditions for a closed defined benefit plan specified in §1.401(a)(4)-8(b)(1)(iii)(D)(3) as required by paragraph (d)(8)(iii)(C) of this section because Plan P's prior benefit formula generated equivalent normal allocation rates that increased as employees attained higher ages; Plan P satisfied the minimum coverage and nondiscrimination requirements under sections 410(b) and 401(a)(4) without regard to the special rules under section 410(b)(6)(C) and without aggregating with any other plan for the plan year preceding the closure date; and Plan P was in effect for the

Par. 6. Section 1.401(a)(4)-8 is amended by:
1. Revising paragraphs (b)(1)(iii)(B) through (E).
2. Removing paragraph (b)(1)(iii)(F).
3. Adding paragraph (b)(1)(iv)(E).
The revisions and additions read as follows:

§1.401(a)(4)-8. Cross-testing.

* * *

(b) * * *

   (1) * * *

      (iii) * * *

(B) *Defined benefit replacement allocations disregarded.*—In determining whether a plan has broadly available allocation rates for the plan year within the meaning of paragraph (b)(1)(iii)(A) of this section, the following rules in paragraphs (b)(1)(iii)(B)(1) and (2) of this section apply:

(1) If an employee receives a defined benefit replacement allocation (within the meaning of paragraph (b)(1)(iii)(D) of this section) for the plan year in addition to the employee's otherwise applicable allocation under the plan for the plan year, then the employee's allocation rate is determined without regard to the defined benefit replacement allocation.

(2) If an employee receives an allocation for the plan year that is the greater of the allocation for which the employee would otherwise be eligible and the defined benefit replacement allocation (within the meaning of paragraph (b)(1)(iii)(D) of this section), then the allocation for which the employee would otherwise be eligible is considered currently available to the employee, even if the employee's defined benefit replacement allocation is greater. See paragraph (b)(1)(iii)(C)(2) of this section for additional rules relating to "greater-of" plan provisions.

(C) *Plan provisions.*—(1) *In general.*—Plan provisions providing for defined benefit replacement allocations (within the meaning of paragraph (b)(1)(iii)(D) of this section) for the plan year must specify both the group of employees who are eligible for the defined benefit replacement allocations and the amount of the defined benefit replacement allocations.

(2) *"Greater-of" plan provisions.*—An allocation does not fail to be a defined benefit replacement allocation within the meaning of paragraph (b)(1)(iii)(D) of this section merely because the plan provides that each employee who is eligible for a defined benefit replacement allocation receives the greater of that allocation and the allocation for which the employee would otherwise be eligible under the plan.

(3) *Limited plan amendments.*—Except as provided in paragraph (b)(1)(iii)(D)(5) of this section, an allocation is not a defined benefit replacement allocation within the meaning of paragraph (b)(1)(iii)(D) of this section for the plan year if the plan provisions relating to the allocation are amended after the date those plan provisions are both adopted and effective.

(D) *Defined benefit replacement allocation.*—(1) *In general.*—A defined benefit replacement allocation is an allocation under a defined contribution plan provided only to a grandfathered group of employees with respect to a closed defined benefit plan. An allocation is treated as a defined benefit replacement allocation if—

(i) The allocation satisfies the conditions to be a replacement allocation with respect to a closed defined benefit plan in paragraph (b)(1)(iii)(D)(2) of this section;

(ii) The closed defined benefit plan satisfies the conditions in paragraph (b)(1)(iii)(D)(3) of this section; and

(iii) For each plan year that begins before the fifth anniversary of the closure date of the closed defined benefit plan, the grandfathered group of employees is a nondiscriminatory group of employees within the meaning of paragraph (b)(1)(iii)(D)(4) of this section.

(2) *Replacement allocation.*—An allocation is a replacement allocation with respect to a closed defined benefit plan under this paragraph (b)(1)(iii)(D)(2) if—

five-year period ending on the closure date and neither the benefit formula nor the coverage of the plan was significantly changed during this period.

(vi) *Effective/applicability dates.*—The rules of this paragraph (d)(8) apply to plan years beginning on or after the date of publication of the Treasury decision adopting these rules as final in the **Federal Register**. Taxpayers may apply the rules of this paragraph (d)(8) for plan years beginning on or after January 1, 2014.

* * *

(i) The allocation is designed so that it is reasonably expected to replace some or all of the value of the benefit accruals that each employee in the grandfathered group of employees would have been provided under the closed defined benefit plan in the absence of a closure amendment (based on the terms of that plan and the section 415(b)(1)(A) dollar limit in effect immediately prior to the closure date); and

(ii) The allocation is provided in a consistent manner to all similarly situated employees.

(3) *Closed defined benefit plan.*—A closed defined benefit plan satisfies the conditions in this paragraph (b)(1)(iii)(D)(3) if—

(i) The closed defined benefit plan's benefit formula applicable to the grandfathered group of employees generated equivalent normal allocation rates that increased from year to year as employees attained higher ages or were credited with additional years of service;

(ii) The closed defined benefit plan satisfied the minimum coverage and nondiscrimination requirements under sections 410(b) and 401(a)(4) without regard to the special rules under section 410(b)(6)(C) and without aggregating with any other plan, for the plan year preceding the closure date; and

(iii) The closed defined benefit plan was in effect for the 5-year period ending on the closure date and neither the benefit formula nor the coverage of the plan was significantly changed by plan amendment with an effective date during this period.

(4) *Nondiscriminatory group of employees.*—A group of employees is a nondiscriminatory group of employees for purposes of this paragraph (b)(1)(iii)(D)(4) if the group of employees satisfies section 410(b) for the plan year (without regard to §1.410(b)-5).

(5) *Certain amendments not taken into account.*—For purposes of determining whether the requirements of paragraphs (b)(1)(iii)(C)(3) and (b)(1)(iii)(D)(3) of this section are satisfied, the following plan amendments are not taken into account:

(i) An amendment to the closed defined benefit plan adopted during the 5-year period ending on the closure date, provided that the accrued benefit or future accruals for any employee are not increased, coverage is not expanded, and the amendment is not discriminatory within the meaning of paragraph (b)(1)(iii)(D)(6) of this section.

(ii) An amendment to the defined contribution plan under which the defined benefit replacement allocation is provided that makes *de minimis* changes in the calculation of that allocation (such as a change in the definition of compensation to include section 132(f) elective reductions).

(iii) An amendment to the defined contribution plan under which the defined benefit replacement allocation is provided that adds or removes a "greater-of" provision described under paragraph (b)(1)(iii)(C)(2) of this section.

(iv) An amendment to the defined contribution plan under which the defined benefit replacement allocation is provided that makes changes in the calculation of that allocation in a manner that is not discriminatory within the meaning of paragraph (b)(1)(iii)(D)(6) of this section.

(v) An amendment that guidance published by the Commissioner in the Internal Revenue Bulletin provides will not be taken into account.

(6) *Nondiscriminatory amendment.*—(i) *General rule.*—An amendment to a plan is not discriminatory if the ratio percentage of the plan is not decreased as a result of the amendment and, in the case of a plan that demonstrates compliance with the nondiscrimination in amount requirement of §1.401(a)(4)-1(b)(2) using a method other than a safe harbor test under §1.401(a)(4)-2(b), §1.401(a)(4)-3(b), or paragraph (b)(3) or (c)(3) of this section, the ratio percentage for the rate group with respect to any HCE is not decreased as a result of the amendment.

(ii) Timing of nondiscrimination testing.—In determining whether the ratio percentage of the plan or the rate group is decreased as a result of an amendment, an amendment that is not in effect for an entire plan year is treated as if it were in effect for the entire plan year. In the case of an amendment that has separate portions with separate effective dates, each portion of the amendment is treated as a separate amendment that must satisfy the requirements of paragraph (b)(1)(iii)(D)(6)(i) of this section for the plan year in which it takes effect.

(7) Special rules for former employers and acquired employees.—The following special rules apply in the case of former employers and acquired employees:

(i) If the closed defined benefit plan was sponsored by a former employer and not by the employer, then the rules in paragraph (b)(1)(iii)(D)(3)(ii) of this section do not apply and one year is substituted for 5 years with respect to paragraph (b)(1)(iii)(D)(3)(iii) of this section;

(ii) An amendment adopted during the 5-year period ending on the closure date that extends the coverage or benefit formula of the closed defined benefit plan to an acquired group of employees may be applied (in addition to the amendments described in paragraph (b)(1)(iii)(D)(5) of this section) provided that all similarly situated employees within that group are treated in a consistent manner; and

(iii) If the employees of a former employer become the employees of the new employer as a result of a transaction that is a merger, acquisition, or similar event, then the transaction is treated as a closure amendment with respect to the former employer's plan as of the effective date of the acquisition.

(E) Effective/applicability date.—See § 1.401(a)(4)-13(a)(4) for rules on the effective/applicability date of this section.

(iv) * * *

(E) Defined benefit replacement allocation may be disregarded.—In determining whether a plan has a gradual age or service schedule for the plan year within the meaning of paragraph (b)(1)(iv)(A) of this section, if an employee receives a defined benefit replacement allocation (within the meaning of paragraph (b)(1)(iii)(D) of this section) for the plan year, then the plan's schedule is determined without regard to the defined benefit replacement allocation. For this purpose, the rules under paragraph (b)(1)(iii)(B) of this section apply. See § 1.401(a)(4)-13(a)(4) for rules on the effective/applicability date of this paragraph (b)(1)(iv)(E).

* * *

Par. 7. Section 1.401(a)(4)-9 is amended by:

1. Revising paragraphs (b)(2)(v)(A) and (b)(2)(v)(D)(3).
2. Adding paragraphs (b)(2)(v)(D)(4) and (5).
3. Redesignating paragraph (b)(2)(v)(F) as paragraph (b)(2)(v)(H).
4. Adding paragraphs (b)(2)(v)(F) and (b)(2)(v)(G). The revisions and additions read as follows:

§ 1.401(a)(4)-9. Plan aggregation and restructuring.

* * *

(b) * * *

(2) * * *

(v) *Eligibility for testing on a benefits basis.*—(A) *General rule.*—(1) *In general.*—Unless, for the plan year, a DB/DC plan is primarily defined benefit in character (within the meaning of paragraph (b)(2)(v)(B) of this section) or consists of broadly available separate plans (within the meaning of paragraph (b)(2)(v)(C) of this section), in order to be permitted to demonstrate satisfaction of the nondiscrimination in amount requirement of § 1.401(a)(4)-1(b)(2) on the basis of benefits, the DB/DC plan must satisfy the minimum aggregate allocation gateway (as described in paragraph (b)(2)(v)(D) of this section) except as provided in paragraph (b)(2)(v)(A)(2) of this section.

(2) Additional testing options.—A DB/DC plan that is not eligible to demonstrate satisfaction of the nondiscrimination in amount requirement of § 1.401(a)(4)-1(b)(2) on the basis of benefits under paragraph (b)(2)(v)(A)(1) of this section is permitted to demonstrate satisfaction of that requirement on the basis of benefits if the DB/DC plan satisfies either the closed plan rule of paragraph (b)(2)(v)(F) of this section or the lower interest rate rule of paragraph (b)(2)(v)(G) of this section.

(3) Effective/applicability date.—See § 1.401(a)(4)-13(a)(4) for rules on the effective/applicability date of this paragraph (b)(2)(v)(A).

* * *

(D) * * *

(3) Averaging of rates for NHCEs.—*(i) Defined benefit plan.*—For purposes of this paragraph (b)(2)(v)(D), a plan is permitted to treat each NHCE who benefits under a defined benefit plan that is part of the DB/DC plan as having an equivalent normal allocation rate equal to the average of the equivalent normal allocation rates under the defined benefit plan for all NHCEs benefitting under that plan.

(ii) Defined contribution plan.—For purposes of this paragraph (b)(2)(v)(D), a plan is permitted to treat each NHCE who benefits under a defined contribution plan that is part of the DB/DC plan as having an allocation rate equal to the average of the allocation rates under the defined contribution plan for all NHCEs benefitting under that plan.

(iii) Limitations on the averaging of rates.—For purposes of applying paragraphs (b)(2)(v)(D)(3)(i) and (ii) of this section, any equivalent normal allocation rate or allocation rate in excess of 15% of plan year compensation is treated as being 15%. The preceding sentence is applied by substituting 25% for 15% each time it appears, but only if any allocation rate or equivalent normal allocation rate higher than 15% results solely from a plan design providing allocation rates or generating equivalent normal allocation rates that are a function of age or service under which higher rates are provided to older or longer-service employees.

(4) Use of matching contributions.—For purposes of this paragraph (b)(2)(v)(D), if an NHCE is eligible for a matching contribution under a defined contribution plan that is part of the DB/DC plan, then the lesser of 3% and the average matching contribution percentage for the group of eligible NHCEs in that plan is permitted to be added to the allocation rate for that NHCE. For this purpose, the average matching contribution percentage for the group of eligible NHCEs in a plan is the actual contribution percentage (within the meaning of § 1.401(m)-5) for that group, determined without taking into account any employee contributions.

(5) Effective/applicability date.—See § 1.401(a)(4)-13(a)(4) for rules on the effective/applicability date of this paragraph (b)(2)(v)(D).

* * *

(F) Closed plan rule.—*(1) In general.*—For a plan year that begins on or after the fifth anniversary of the closure date with respect to a closed defined benefit plan, a DB/DC plan that includes a closed defined benefit plan satisfies the closed plan rule of this paragraph (b)(2)(v)(F) for the plan year if—

(i) The closed defined benefit plan was in effect for the 5-year period ending on the closure date and neither the benefit formula nor the coverage of the plan was significantly changed by plan amendment (other than the closure amendment) with an effective date during the period that begins five years before the closure date and ends on the last day of the plan year; and

(ii) For each plan year that begins on or after the closure date and before the fifth anniversary of the closure date, one of the requirements in paragraph (b)(2)(v)(F)(2) of this section is satisfied.

(2) Testing for 5 years post-closure.—A DB/DC plan meets the requirements of this paragraph (b)(2)(v)(F)(2) if—

(i) Each defined benefit plan that is part of the DB/DC plan satisfies the nondiscrimination in amount requirement of § 1.401(a)(4)-1(b)(2) on the basis of benefits without aggregation with any defined contribution plan;

(ii) The DB/DC plan satisfies the nondiscrimination in amount requirement of § 1.401(a)(4)-1(b)(2) on the basis of contributions; or

(iii) The DB/DC plan satisfies the primarily defined benefit in character requirement of paragraph (b)(2)(v)(B) of this section, or the broadly available separate plans requirement of paragraph (b)(2)(v)(C) of this section.

(3) Certain amendments not taken into account.—For purposes of this paragraph (b)(2)(v)(F), the following plan amendments are not taken into account:

(i) An amendment to the closed defined benefit plan adopted during the 5-year period ending on the closure date, provided that the accrued benefit or future accruals for any employee are not increased, coverage is not expanded, and the amendment is not discriminatory within the meaning of § 1.401(a)(4)-8(b)(1)(iii)(D)(6).

(ii) An amendment adopted during the 5-year period ending on the closure date that extends the benefit formula with respect to the closed benefit plan to an acquired group of employees provided that all similarly situated employees within that group are treated in a consistent manner.

(iii) An amendment to the closed defined benefit plan that is adopted after the closure date that is not discriminatory within the meaning of §1.401(a)(4)-8(b)(1)(iii)(D)(6).

(iv) An amendment to the closed defined benefit plan that makes *de minimis* changes in the benefit formula.

Par. 8. In §1.401(a)(4)-12, add definitions for *Closed defined benefit plan, Closure amendment, Closure date,* and *Grandfathered group of employees* in alphabetical order to read as follows:

§1.401(a)(4)-12. Definitions.

* * *

Closed defined benefit plan. Closed defined benefit plan means a defined benefit plan that has been amended to—

(1) Cease accruals under a benefit formula provided by the defined benefit plan for some or all employees whose benefits were previously determined under that benefit formula; or

(2) Limit participation in the defined benefit plan to a group of employees that consists of some or all of the plan participants who participated in the plan as of the closure date.

Closure amendment. A closure amendment is a plan amendment that results in a closed defined benefit plan.

Par. 9. In §1.401(a)(4)-13, paragraph (a)(4) is added to read as follows:

§1.401(a)(4)-13. Effective dates and fresh-start rules.—(a) * * *

(4) *Effective/applicability date.*—(i) *In general.*—Except as otherwise provided in this paragraph (a)(4), the rules of §1.401(a)(4)-2(c), §1.401(a)(4)-3(c)(2), §1.401(a)(4)-8(b), and §1.401(a)(4)-9(b)(2)(v)(A) and (D) apply to plan years beginning on or after the date of publication of the Treasury decision adopting these rules as final in the **Federal Register**.

(ii) *Application for earlier plan years.*—Except as provided in paragraph (a)(4)(iii) of this section, taxpayers may apply §1.401(a)(4)-2(c), §1.401(a)(4)-3(c)(2), §1.401(a)(4)-8(b), or

(v) An amendment that guidance published by the Commissioner in the Internal Revenue Bulletin provides will not be taken into account.

(G) *Lower interest rate rule.*—A DB/DC plan satisfies the lower interest rate rule of this paragraph (b)(2)(v)(G) if the plan can demonstrate satisfaction of the nondiscrimination in amount requirement of §1.401(a)(4)-1(b)(2) on the basis of benefits, provided that benefits are normalized using an interest rate of 6% rather than a standard interest rate.

* * *

Closure date. A closure date is the last day before accruals cease or participation is limited pursuant to the closure amendment.

* * *

Grandfathered group of employees. A grandfathered group of employees with respect to a closure amendment means the group of employees who, after the closure date, either continue accruals under the closed defined benefit plan's benefit formula or are entitled to an allocation formula under a defined contribution plan because those employees previously participated in the closed defined benefit plan.

* * *

§1.401(a)(4)-9(b)(2)(v)(A) and (D) for plan years beginning on or after January 1, 2014 and before the effective/applicability date specified under paragraph (a)(4)(i) of this section. Alternatively, for these plan years, taxpayers may apply §1.401(a)(4)-2(c), §1.401(a)(4)-3(c)(2), §1.401(a)(4)-8(b), or §1.401(a)(4)-9(b)(2)(v)(A) and (D) as contained in 26 CFR part 1 revised April 1, 2015.

(iii) *Certain rules not applicable until finalized.*—The rules of §1.401(a)(4)-9(b)(2)(v)(D)(3)(ii), (b)(2)(v)(D)(4), and (b)(2)(v)(G) are not permitted to be applied for plan years before the effective/applicability date specified in paragraph (a)(4)(i) of this section.

* * *

Minimum Required Distribution Calculation: Life Expectancy and Distribution Period Tables

Minimum Required Distribution Calculation: Life Expectancy and Distribution Period Tables.—Amendments to Reg. §§1.401(a)(9)-5 and 1.401(a)(9)-6, relating to the life expectancy and distribution period tables that are used to calculate required minimum distributions from qualified retirement plans, individual retirement accounts and annuities, and certain other tax-favored employer-provided retirement arrangements, are proposed (published in the Federal Register on November 8, 2019) (REG-132210-18).

Par. 2. Section 1.401(a)(9)-5 is amended by:

1. Removing the language "A-1 of §1.401(a)(9)-9" wherever it appears and adding "§1.401(a)(9)-9(b)" in its place.
2. Removing the language "A-2 of §1.401(a)(9)-9" wherever it appears and adding "§1.401(a)(9)-9(c)" in its place.
3. Removing the language "A-3 of §1.401(a)(9)-9" wherever it appears and adding "§1.401(a)(9)-9(d)" in its place.

§1.401(a)(9)-5. Required minimum distributions from defined contribution plans.

Par. 3. Section 1.401(a)(9)-6 is amended by:

1. Removing the language "A-1 of §1.401(a)(9)-9" wherever it appears and adding "§1.401(a)(9)-9(b)" in its place.
2. Removing the language "A-2 of §1.401(a)(9)-9" wherever it appears and adding "§1.401(a)(9)-9(d)" in its place.
3. Removing the language "A-3 of §1.401(a)(9)-9" wherever it appears and adding "§1.401(a)(9)-9(e)" in its place.

§1.401(a)(9)-6. Required minimum distributions for defined benefit plans and annuity contracts.

Minimum Required Distribution Calculation: Life Expectancy and Distribution Period Tables

Minimum Required Distribution Calculation: Life Expectancy and Distribution Period Tables.—Amendments to Reg. §§1.401(a)(9)-8 and 1.401(a)(9)-9, relating to the life expectancy and distribution period tables that are used to calculate required minimum distributions from qualified retirement plans, individual retirement accounts and annuities, and certain other tax-favored employer-provided retirement arrangements, are proposed (published in the Federal Register on November 8, 2019) (REG-132210-18).

Par. 4. Section 1.401(a)(9)-8 is amended by removing the language "A-2 of §1.401(a)(9)-9" wherever it appears and adding "§1.401(a)(9)-9(d)" in its place.

§1.401(a)(9)-8. Special rules.

Par. 5. Section 1.401(a)(9)-9 is amended to read as follows:

§1.401(a)(9)-9. Life Expectancy and Distribution Period Tables.—

(a) *In general.*—This section specifies the life expectancy and applicable distribution period tables that apply for purposes of determining required minimum distributions under section 401(a)(9). Paragraphs

(b), (c), and (d) of this section set forth these tables. Paragraph (e) of this section provides the mortality rates that are used to develop these tables. Paragraph (f) of this section provides applicability date rules.

(b) *Single Life Table.*—Table 1 to paragraph (b), referred to as the Single Life Table, sets forth the life expectancy of an individual at each age.

Table 1 to paragraph (b) — Single Life Table

Age	Life expectancy	Age	Life expectancy	Age	Life expectancy
0	84.5	41	44.7	81	10.5
1	83.7	42	43.8	82	9.9
2	82.7	43	42.8	83	9.2
3	81.7	44	41.8	84	8.6
4	80.8	45	40.9	85	8.1
5	79.8	46	39.9	86	7.5
6	78.8	47	39.0	87	7.0
7	77.8	48	38.0	88	6.6
8	76.8	49	37.1	89	6.1
9	75.8	50	36.1	90	5.7
10	74.8	51	35.2	91	5.3
11	73.8	52	34.3	92	4.9
12	72.8	53	33.3	93	4.6
13	71.9	54	32.4	94	4.2
14	70.9	55	31.5	95	3.9
15	69.9	56	30.6	96	3.7
16	68.9	57	29.7	97	3.4
17	67.9	58	28.8	98	3.2
18	66.9	59	27.9	99	3.0
19	66.0	60	27.1	100	2.8
20	65.0	61	26.2	101	2.6
21	64.0	62	25.3	102	2.5
22	63.0	63	24.5	103	2.3
23	62.0	64	23.6	104	2.2
24	61.1	65	22.8	105	2.1
25	60.1	66	22.0	106	2.1
26	59.1	67	21.2	107	2.1
27	58.2	68	20.4	108	2.0
28	57.2	69	19.5	109	2.0
29	56.2	70	18.7	110	2.0
30	55.3	71	17.9	111	2.0
31	54.3	72	17.1	112	2.0
32	53.4	73	16.3	113	1.9
33	52.4	74	15.6	114	1.9
34	51.4	75	14.8	115	1.8
35	50.5	76	14.0	116	1.8
36	49.5	77	13.3	117	1.6
37	48.6	78	12.6	118	1.4
38	47.6	79	11.9	119	1.1
39	46.6	80	11.2	120 +	1.0
40	45.7				

(c) *Uniform Lifetime Table.*—Table 2 to paragraph (c), referred to as the Uniform Lifetime Table, sets forth the distribution period that applies for lifetime distributions to an employee in situations in which the employee's surviving spouse is not the sole designated beneficiary. This table is also used if the employee's surviving spouse is the sole designated beneficiary but is not more than 10 years younger than the employee.

Table 2 to paragraph (c) — Uniform Lifetime Table

Age of employee	Distribution period
70	29.1
71	28.2
72	27.3
73	26.4
74	25.5
75	24.6
76	23.7
77	22.8
78	21.9
79	21.0
80	20.2
81	19.3
82	18.4
83	17.6
84	16.8
85	16.0
86	15.2
87	14.4
88	13.6
89	12.9
90	12.1
91	11.4
92	10.8
93	10.1

Age of employee	Distribution period
94	9.5
95	8.9
96	8.3
97	7.8
98	7.3
99	6.8
100	6.4
101	5.9
102	5.6
103	5.2
104	4.9
105	4.6
106	4.3
107	4.1
108	3.9

Age of employee	Distribution period
109	3.7
110	3.5
111	3.4
112	3.2
113	3.1
114	3.0
115	2.9
116	2.8
117	2.7
118	2.5
119	2.3
120 +	2.0

(d) *Joint and Last Survivor Table.*—Table 3 to paragraph (d), referred to as the Joint and Last Survivor Table, is used for determining the joint and last survivor life expectancy of two individuals.

Table 3 to paragraph (d) — Joint and Last Survivor Table

Ages	0	1	2	3	4	5	6	7	8
0	91.8	91.4	90.9	90.5	90.1	89.7	89.3	89.0	88.7
1	91.4	90.9	90.4	89.9	89.5	89.1	88.7	88.3	88.0
2	90.9	90.4	89.9	89.4	88.9	88.5	88.1	87.7	87.3
3	90.5	89.9	89.4	88.9	88.4	87.9	87.5	87.1	86.7
4	90.1	89.5	88.9	88.4	87.9	87.4	86.9	86.5	86.1
5	89.7	89.1	88.5	87.9	87.4	86.9	86.4	85.9	85.5
6	89.3	88.7	88.1	87.5	86.9	86.4	85.9	85.4	84.9
7	89.0	88.3	87.7	87.1	86.5	85.9	85.4	84.9	84.4
8	88.7	88.0	87.3	86.7	86.1	85.5	84.9	84.4	83.9
9	88.4	87.7	87.0	86.3	85.7	85.1	84.5	83.9	83.4
10	88.1	87.4	86.7	86.0	85.3	84.7	84.1	83.5	82.9
11	87.9	87.1	86.4	85.7	85.0	84.4	83.7	83.1	82.5
12	87.6	86.9	86.1	85.4	84.7	84.0	83.4	82.7	82.1
13	87.4	86.7	85.9	85.1	84.4	83.7	83.0	82.4	81.7
14	87.2	86.4	85.7	84.9	84.2	83.4	82.7	82.0	81.4
15	87.0	86.2	85.5	84.7	83.9	83.2	82.4	81.7	81.0
16	86.9	86.1	85.3	84.5	83.7	82.9	82.2	81.4	80.7
17	86.7	85.9	85.1	84.3	83.5	82.7	81.9	81.2	80.4
18	86.6	85.7	84.9	84.1	83.3	82.5	81.7	80.9	80.2
19	86.4	85.6	84.7	83.9	83.1	82.3	81.5	80.7	79.9
20	86.3	85.5	84.6	83.8	82.9	82.1	81.3	80.5	79.7
21	86.2	85.3	84.5	83.6	82.8	81.9	81.1	80.3	79.5
22	86.1	85.2	84.3	83.5	82.6	81.8	80.9	80.1	79.3
23	86.0	85.1	84.2	83.4	82.5	81.6	80.8	79.9	79.1
24	85.9	85.0	84.1	83.2	82.4	81.5	80.6	79.8	78.9
25	85.8	84.9	84.0	83.1	82.2	81.4	80.5	79.6	78.8
26	85.7	84.8	83.9	83.0	82.1	81.2	80.4	79.5	78.6
27	85.6	84.8	83.9	82.9	82.0	81.1	80.3	79.4	78.5
28	85.6	84.7	83.8	82.9	82.0	81.0	80.1	79.3	78.4
29	85.5	84.6	83.7	82.8	81.9	81.0	80.1	79.2	78.3
30	85.4	84.6	83.6	82.7	81.8	80.9	80.0	79.1	78.2
31	85.4	84.5	83.6	82.6	81.7	80.8	79.9	79.0	78.1
32	85.3	84.4	83.5	82.6	81.6	80.7	79.8	78.9	78.0
33	85.3	84.4	83.5	82.5	81.6	80.7	79.7	78.8	77.9
34	85.2	84.3	83.4	82.5	81.5	80.6	79.7	78.7	77.8
35	85.2	84.3	83.4	82.4	81.5	80.5	79.6	78.7	77.7
36	85.2	84.3	83.3	82.4	81.4	80.5	79.5	78.6	77.7
37	85.1	84.2	83.3	82.3	81.4	80.4	79.5	78.5	77.6
38	85.1	84.2	83.2	82.3	81.3	80.4	79.4	78.5	77.6
39	85.1	84.2	83.2	82.3	81.3	80.3	79.4	78.4	77.5
40	85.0	84.1	83.2	82.2	81.3	80.3	79.3	78.4	77.4
41	85.0	84.1	83.1	82.2	81.2	80.3	79.3	78.4	77.4
42	85.0	84.1	83.1	82.2	81.2	80.2	79.3	78.3	77.4
43	84.9	84.0	83.1	82.1	81.2	80.2	79.2	78.3	77.3

Ages	0	1	2	3	4	5	6	7	8
44	84.9	84.0	83.1	82.1	81.1	80.2	79.2	78.2	77.3
45	84.9	84.0	83.0	82.1	81.1	80.1	79.2	78.2	77.3
46	84.9	84.0	83.0	82.1	81.1	80.1	79.2	78.2	77.2
47	84.9	84.0	83.0	82.0	81.1	80.1	79.1	78.2	77.2
48	84.8	83.9	83.0	82.0	81.0	80.1	79.1	78.1	77.2
49	84.8	83.9	83.0	82.0	81.0	80.1	79.1	78.1	77.1
50	84.8	83.9	82.9	82.0	81.0	80.0	79.1	78.1	77.1
51	84.8	83.9	82.9	82.0	81.0	80.0	79.0	78.1	77.1
52	84.8	83.9	82.9	81.9	81.0	80.0	79.0	78.0	77.1
53	84.8	83.9	82.9	81.9	81.0	80.0	79.0	78.0	77.1
54	84.7	83.9	82.9	81.9	80.9	80.0	79.0	78.0	77.0
55	84.7	83.8	82.9	81.9	80.9	79.9	79.0	78.0	77.0
56	84.7	83.8	82.9	81.9	80.9	79.9	79.0	78.0	77.0
57	84.7	83.8	82.9	81.9	80.9	79.9	78.9	78.0	77.0
58	84.7	83.8	82.8	81.9	80.9	79.9	78.9	78.0	77.0
59	84.7	83.8	82.8	81.9	80.9	79.9	78.9	77.9	77.0
60	84.7	83.8	82.8	81.8	80.9	79.9	78.9	77.9	76.9
61	84.7	83.8	82.8	81.8	80.9	79.9	78.9	77.9	76.9
62	84.7	83.8	82.8	81.8	80.9	79.9	78.9	77.9	76.9
63	84.6	83.8	82.8	81.8	80.8	79.9	78.9	77.9	76.9
64	84.6	83.8	82.8	81.8	80.8	79.9	78.9	77.9	76.9
65	84.6	83.8	82.8	81.8	80.8	79.8	78.9	77.9	76.9
66	84.6	83.7	82.8	81.8	80.8	79.8	78.9	77.9	76.9
67	84.6	83.7	82.8	81.8	80.8	79.8	78.8	77.9	76.9
68	84.6	83.7	82.8	81.8	80.8	79.8	78.8	77.9	76.9
69	84.6	83.7	82.8	81.8	80.8	79.8	78.8	77.9	76.9
70	84.6	83.7	82.8	81.8	80.8	79.8	78.8	77.8	76.9
71	84.6	83.7	82.8	81.8	80.8	79.8	78.8	77.8	76.9
72	84.6	83.7	82.8	81.8	80.8	79.8	78.8	77.8	76.9
73	84.6	83.7	82.7	81.8	80.8	79.8	78.8	77.8	76.8
74	84.6	83.7	82.7	81.8	80.8	79.8	78.8	77.8	76.8
75	84.6	83.7	82.7	81.8	80.8	79.8	78.8	77.8	76.8
76	84.6	83.7	82.7	81.8	80.8	79.8	78.8	77.8	76.8
77	84.6	83.7	82.7	81.8	80.8	79.8	78.8	77.8	76.8
78	84.6	83.7	82.7	81.8	80.8	79.8	78.8	77.8	76.8
79	84.6	83.7	82.7	81.8	80.8	79.8	78.8	77.8	76.8
80	84.6	83.7	82.7	81.8	80.8	79.8	78.8	77.8	76.8
81	84.6	83.7	82.7	81.8	80.8	79.8	78.8	77.8	76.8
82	84.6	83.7	82.7	81.7	80.8	79.8	78.8	77.8	76.8
83	84.6	83.7	82.7	81.7	80.8	79.8	78.8	77.8	76.8
84	84.6	83.7	82.7	81.7	80.8	79.8	78.8	77.8	76.8
85	84.6	83.7	82.7	81.7	80.8	79.8	78.8	77.8	76.8
86	84.5	83.7	82.7	81.7	80.8	79.8	78.8	77.8	76.8
87	84.5	83.7	82.7	81.7	80.8	79.8	78.8	77.8	76.8
88	84.5	83.7	82.7	81.7	80.8	79.8	78.8	77.8	76.8
89	84.5	83.7	82.7	81.7	80.8	79.8	78.8	77.8	76.8
90	84.5	83.7	82.7	81.7	80.8	79.8	78.8	77.8	76.8
91	84.5	83.7	82.7	81.7	80.8	79.8	78.8	77.8	76.8
92	84.5	83.7	82.7	81.7	80.8	79.8	78.8	77.8	76.8
93	84.5	83.7	82.7	81.7	80.8	79.8	78.8	77.8	76.8
94	84.5	83.7	82.7	81.7	80.8	79.8	78.8	77.8	76.8
95	84.5	83.7	82.7	81.7	80.8	79.8	78.8	77.8	76.8
96	84.5	83.7	82.7	81.7	80.8	79.8	78.8	77.8	76.8
97	84.5	83.7	82.7	81.7	80.8	79.8	78.8	77.8	76.8
98	84.5	83.7	82.7	81.7	80.8	79.8	78.8	77.8	76.8
99	84.5	83.7	82.7	81.7	80.8	79.8	78.8	77.8	76.8
100	84.5	83.7	82.7	81.7	80.8	79.8	78.8	77.8	76.8
101	84.5	83.7	82.7	81.7	80.8	79.8	78.8	77.8	76.8
102	84.5	83.7	82.7	81.7	80.8	79.8	78.8	77.8	76.8
103	84.5	83.7	82.7	81.7	80.8	79.8	78.8	77.8	76.8
104	84.5	83.7	82.7	81.7	80.8	79.8	78.8	77.8	76.8

Ages	0	1	2	3	4	5	6	7	8
105	84.5	83.7	82.7	81.7	80.8	79.8	78.8	77.8	76.8
106	84.5	83.7	82.7	81.7	80.8	79.8	78.8	77.8	76.8
107	84.5	83.7	82.7	81.7	80.8	79.8	78.8	77.8	76.8
108	84.5	83.7	82.7	81.7	80.8	79.8	78.8	77.8	76.8
109	84.5	83.7	82.7	81.7	80.8	79.8	78.8	77.8	76.8
110	84.5	83.7	82.7	81.7	80.8	79.8	78.8	77.8	76.8
111	84.5	83.7	82.7	81.7	80.8	79.8	78.8	77.8	76.8
112	84.5	83.7	82.7	81.7	80.8	79.8	78.8	77.8	76.8
113	84.5	83.7	82.7	81.7	80.8	79.8	78.8	77.8	76.8
114	84.5	83.7	82.7	81.7	80.8	79.8	78.8	77.8	76.8
115	84.5	83.7	82.7	81.7	80.8	79.8	78.8	77.8	76.8
116	84.5	83.7	82.7	81.7	80.8	79.8	78.8	77.8	76.8
117	84.5	83.7	82.7	81.7	80.8	79.8	78.8	77.8	76.8
118	84.5	83.7	82.7	81.7	80.8	79.8	78.8	77.8	76.8
119	84.5	83.7	82.7	81.7	80.8	79.8	78.8	77.8	76.8
120+	84.5	83.7	82.7	81.7	80.8	79.8	78.8	77.8	76.8

Ages	9	10	11	12	13	14	15	16	17
0	88.4	88.1	87.9	87.6	87.4	87.2	87.0	86.9	86.7
1	87.7	87.4	87.1	86.9	86.7	86.4	86.2	86.1	85.9
2	87.0	86.7	86.4	86.1	85.9	85.7	85.5	85.3	85.1
3	86.3	86.0	85.7	85.4	85.1	84.9	84.7	84.5	84.3
4	85.7	85.3	85.0	84.7	84.4	84.2	83.9	83.7	83.5
5	85.1	84.7	84.4	84.0	83.7	83.4	83.2	82.9	82.7
6	84.5	84.1	83.7	83.4	83.0	82.7	82.4	82.2	81.9
7	83.9	83.5	83.1	82.7	82.4	82.0	81.7	81.4	81.2
8	83.4	82.9	82.5	82.1	81.7	81.4	81.0	80.7	80.4
9	82.9	82.4	81.9	81.5	81.1	80.7	80.4	80.0	79.7
10	82.4	81.9	81.4	80.9	80.5	80.1	79.7	79.4	79.0
11	81.9	81.4	80.9	80.4	79.9	79.5	79.1	78.7	78.4
12	81.5	80.9	80.4	79.9	79.4	78.9	78.5	78.1	77.7
13	81.1	80.5	79.9	79.4	78.9	78.4	77.9	77.5	77.1
14	80.7	80.1	79.5	78.9	78.4	77.9	77.4	76.9	76.5
15	80.4	79.7	79.1	78.5	77.9	77.4	76.9	76.4	75.9
16	80.0	79.4	78.7	78.1	77.5	76.9	76.4	75.9	75.4
17	79.7	79.0	78.4	77.7	77.1	76.5	75.9	75.4	74.9
18	79.4	78.7	78.0	77.4	76.7	76.1	75.5	75.0	74.4
19	79.2	78.4	77.7	77.0	76.4	75.7	75.1	74.5	74.0
20	78.9	78.2	77.4	76.7	76.0	75.4	74.7	74.1	73.5
21	78.7	77.9	77.2	76.4	75.7	75.0	74.4	73.7	73.1
22	78.5	77.7	76.9	76.2	75.4	74.7	74.0	73.4	72.7
23	78.3	77.5	76.7	75.9	75.2	74.4	73.7	73.1	72.4
24	78.1	77.3	76.5	75.7	74.9	74.2	73.5	72.7	72.1
25	77.9	77.1	76.3	75.5	74.7	73.9	73.2	72.5	71.7
26	77.8	76.9	76.1	75.3	74.5	73.7	72.9	72.2	71.5
27	77.6	76.8	75.9	75.1	74.3	73.5	72.7	71.9	71.2
28	77.5	76.6	75.8	74.9	74.1	73.3	72.5	71.7	71.0
29	77.4	76.5	75.6	74.8	73.9	73.1	72.3	71.5	70.7
30	77.3	76.4	75.5	74.6	73.8	73.0	72.1	71.3	70.5
31	77.2	76.3	75.4	74.5	73.7	72.8	72.0	71.1	70.3
32	77.1	76.2	75.3	74.4	73.5	72.7	71.8	71.0	70.1
33	77.0	76.1	75.2	74.3	73.4	72.5	71.7	70.8	70.0
34	76.9	76.0	75.1	74.2	73.3	72.4	71.5	70.7	69.8
35	76.8	75.9	75.0	74.1	73.2	72.3	71.4	70.5	69.7
36	76.7	75.8	74.9	74.0	73.1	72.2	71.3	70.4	69.5
37	76.7	75.7	74.8	73.9	73.0	72.1	71.2	70.3	69.4
38	76.6	75.7	74.7	73.8	72.9	72.0	71.1	70.2	69.3
39	76.6	75.6	74.7	73.8	72.8	71.9	71.0	70.1	69.2
40	76.5	75.6	74.6	73.7	72.8	71.8	70.9	70.0	69.1
41	76.5	75.5	74.6	73.6	72.7	71.8	70.8	69.9	69.0
42	76.4	75.5	74.5	73.6	72.6	71.7	70.8	69.8	68.9

Ages	9	10	11	12	13	14	15	16	17
43	76.4	75.4	74.5	73.5	72.6	71.6	70.7	69.8	68.9
44	76.3	75.4	74.4	73.5	72.5	71.6	70.6	69.7	68.8
45	76.3	75.3	74.4	73.4	72.5	71.5	70.6	69.6	68.7
46	76.3	75.3	74.3	73.4	72.4	71.5	70.5	69.6	68.7
47	76.2	75.3	74.3	73.3	72.4	71.4	70.5	69.5	68.6
48	76.2	75.2	74.3	73.3	72.3	71.4	70.4	69.5	68.5
49	76.2	75.2	74.2	73.3	72.3	71.4	70.4	69.4	68.5
50	76.1	75.2	74.2	73.2	72.3	71.3	70.4	69.4	68.5
51	76.1	75.2	74.2	73.2	72.2	71.3	70.3	69.4	68.4
52	76.1	75.1	74.2	73.2	72.2	71.3	70.3	69.3	68.4
53	76.1	75.1	74.1	73.2	72.2	71.2	70.3	69.3	68.3
54	76.1	75.1	74.1	73.1	72.2	71.2	70.2	69.3	68.3
55	76.0	75.1	74.1	73.1	72.1	71.2	70.2	69.2	68.3
56	76.0	75.0	74.1	73.1	72.1	71.2	70.2	69.2	68.3
57	76.0	75.0	74.1	73.1	72.1	71.1	70.2	69.2	68.2
58	76.0	75.0	74.0	73.1	72.1	71.1	70.1	69.2	68.2
59	76.0	75.0	74.0	73.0	72.1	71.1	70.1	69.2	68.2
60	76.0	75.0	74.0	73.0	72.1	71.1	70.1	69.1	68.2
61	76.0	75.0	74.0	73.0	72.0	71.1	70.1	69.1	68.1
62	75.9	75.0	74.0	73.0	72.0	71.0	70.1	69.1	68.1
63	75.9	75.0	74.0	73.0	72.0	71.0	70.1	69.1	68.1
64	75.9	74.9	74.0	73.0	72.0	71.0	70.0	69.1	68.1
65	75.9	74.9	73.9	73.0	72.0	71.0	70.0	69.1	68.1
66	75.9	74.9	73.9	73.0	72.0	71.0	70.0	69.0	68.1
67	75.9	74.9	73.9	72.9	72.0	71.0	70.0	69.0	68.1
68	75.9	74.9	73.9	72.9	72.0	71.0	70.0	69.0	68.0
69	75.9	74.9	73.9	72.9	71.9	71.0	70.0	69.0	68.0
70	75.9	74.9	73.9	72.9	71.9	71.0	70.0	69.0	68.0
71	75.9	74.9	73.9	72.9	71.9	70.9	70.0	69.0	68.0
72	75.9	74.9	73.9	72.9	71.9	70.9	70.0	69.0	68.0
73	75.9	74.9	73.9	72.9	71.9	70.9	70.0	69.0	68.0
74	75.9	74.9	73.9	72.9	71.9	70.9	69.9	69.0	68.0
75	75.9	74.9	73.9	72.9	71.9	70.9	69.9	69.0	68.0
76	75.8	74.9	73.9	72.9	71.9	70.9	69.9	68.9	68.0
77	75.8	74.9	73.9	72.9	71.9	70.9	69.9	68.9	68.0
78	75.8	74.9	73.9	72.9	71.9	70.9	69.9	68.9	68.0
79	75.8	74.8	73.9	72.9	71.9	70.9	69.9	68.9	68.0
80	75.8	74.8	73.9	72.9	71.9	70.9	69.9	68.9	67.9
81	75.8	74.8	73.9	72.9	71.9	70.9	69.9	68.9	67.9
82	75.8	74.8	73.9	72.9	71.9	70.9	69.9	68.9	67.9
83	75.8	74.8	73.9	72.9	71.9	70.9	69.9	68.9	67.9
84	75.8	74.8	73.8	72.9	71.9	70.9	69.9	68.9	67.9
85	75.8	74.8	73.8	72.9	71.9	70.9	69.9	68.9	67.9
86	75.8	74.8	73.8	72.9	71.9	70.9	69.9	68.9	67.9
87	75.8	74.8	73.8	72.9	71.9	70.9	69.9	68.9	67.9
88	75.8	74.8	73.8	72.9	71.9	70.9	69.9	68.9	67.9
89	75.8	74.8	73.8	72.9	71.9	70.9	69.9	68.9	67.9
90	75.8	74.8	73.8	72.9	71.9	70.9	69.9	68.9	67.9
91	75.8	74.8	73.8	72.9	71.9	70.9	69.9	68.9	67.9
92	75.8	74.8	73.8	72.9	71.9	70.9	69.9	68.9	67.9
93	75.8	74.8	73.8	72.8	71.9	70.9	69.9	68.9	67.9
94	75.8	74.8	73.8	72.8	71.9	70.9	69.9	68.9	67.9
95	75.8	74.8	73.8	72.8	71.9	70.9	69.9	68.9	67.9
96	75.8	74.8	73.8	72.8	71.9	70.9	69.9	68.9	67.9
97	75.8	74.8	73.8	72.8	71.9	70.9	69.9	68.9	67.9
98	75.8	74.8	73.8	72.8	71.9	70.9	69.9	68.9	67.9
99	75.8	74.8	73.8	72.8	71.9	70.9	69.9	68.9	67.9
100	75.8	74.8	73.8	72.8	71.9	70.9	69.9	68.9	67.9
101	75.8	74.8	73.8	72.8	71.9	70.9	69.9	68.9	67.9
102	75.8	74.8	73.8	72.8	71.9	70.9	69.9	68.9	67.9
103	75.8	74.8	73.8	72.8	71.9	70.9	69.9	68.9	67.9
104	75.8	74.8	73.8	72.8	71.9	70.9	69.9	68.9	67.9

Reg. §1.401(a)(9)-9(d)

Ages	9	10	11	12	13	14	15	16	17
105	75.8	74.8	73.8	72.8	71.9	70.9	69.9	68.9	67.9
106	75.8	74.8	73.8	72.8	71.9	70.9	69.9	68.9	67.9
107	75.8	74.8	73.8	72.8	71.9	70.9	69.9	68.9	67.9
108	75.8	74.8	73.8	72.8	71.9	70.9	69.9	68.9	67.9
109	75.8	74.8	73.8	72.8	71.9	70.9	69.9	68.9	67.9
110	75.8	74.8	73.8	72.8	71.9	70.9	69.9	68.9	67.9
111	75.8	74.8	73.8	72.8	71.9	70.9	69.9	68.9	67.9
112	75.8	74.8	73.8	72.8	71.9	70.9	69.9	68.9	67.9
113	75.8	74.8	73.8	72.8	71.9	70.9	69.9	68.9	67.9
114	75.8	74.8	73.8	72.8	71.9	70.9	69.9	68.9	67.9
115	75.8	74.8	73.8	72.8	71.9	70.9	69.9	68.9	67.9
116	75.8	74.8	73.8	72.8	71.9	70.9	69.9	68.9	67.9
117	75.8	74.8	73.8	72.8	71.9	70.9	69.9	68.9	67.9
118	75.8	74.8	73.8	72.8	71.9	70.9	69.9	68.9	67.9
119	75.8	74.8	73.8	72.8	71.9	70.9	69.9	68.9	67.9
120+	75.8	74.8	73.8	72.8	71.9	70.9	69.9	68.9	67.9

Ages	18	19	20	21	22	23	24	25	26
0	86.6	86.4	86.3	86.2	86.1	86.0	85.9	85.8	85.7
1	85.7	85.6	85.5	85.3	85.2	85.1	85.0	84.9	84.8
2	84.9	84.7	84.6	84.5	84.3	84.2	84.1	84.0	83.9
3	84.1	83.9	83.8	83.6	83.5	83.4	83.2	83.1	83.0
4	83.3	83.1	82.9	82.8	82.6	82.5	82.4	82.2	82.1
5	82.5	82.3	82.1	81.9	81.8	81.6	81.5	81.4	81.2
6	81.7	81.5	81.3	81.1	80.9	80.8	80.6	80.5	80.4
7	80.9	80.7	80.5	80.3	80.1	79.9	79.8	79.6	79.5
8	80.2	79.9	79.7	79.5	79.3	79.1	78.9	78.8	78.6
9	79.4	79.2	78.9	78.7	78.5	78.3	78.1	77.9	77.8
10	78.7	78.4	78.2	77.9	77.7	77.5	77.3	77.1	76.9
11	78.0	77.7	77.4	77.2	76.9	76.7	76.5	76.3	76.1
12	77.4	77.0	76.7	76.4	76.2	75.9	75.7	75.5	75.3
13	76.7	76.4	76.0	75.7	75.4	75.2	74.9	74.7	74.5
14	76.1	75.7	75.4	75.0	74.7	74.4	74.2	73.9	73.7
15	75.5	75.1	74.7	74.4	74.0	73.7	73.5	73.2	72.9
16	75.0	74.5	74.1	73.7	73.4	73.1	72.7	72.5	72.2
17	74.4	74.0	73.5	73.1	72.7	72.4	72.1	71.7	71.5
18	73.9	73.4	73.0	72.5	72.1	71.7	71.4	71.1	70.8
19	73.4	72.9	72.4	72.0	71.5	71.1	70.8	70.4	70.1
20	73.0	72.4	71.9	71.4	71.0	70.5	70.1	69.8	69.4
21	72.5	72.0	71.4	70.9	70.4	70.0	69.5	69.1	68.8
22	72.1	71.5	71.0	70.4	69.9	69.4	69.0	68.5	68.1
23	71.7	71.1	70.5	70.0	69.4	68.9	68.4	68.0	67.6
24	71.4	70.8	70.1	69.5	69.0	68.4	67.9	67.4	67.0
25	71.1	70.4	69.8	69.1	68.5	68.0	67.4	66.9	66.5
26	70.8	70.1	69.4	68.8	68.1	67.6	67.0	66.5	65.9
27	70.5	69.8	69.1	68.4	67.8	67.2	66.6	66.0	65.5
28	70.2	69.5	68.8	68.1	67.4	66.8	66.2	65.6	65.0
29	70.0	69.2	68.5	67.8	67.1	66.4	65.8	65.2	64.6
30	69.7	69.0	68.2	67.5	66.8	66.1	65.4	64.8	64.2
31	69.5	68.7	68.0	67.2	66.5	65.8	65.1	64.4	63.8
32	69.3	68.5	67.7	67.0	66.2	65.5	64.8	64.1	63.4
33	69.1	68.3	67.5	66.7	66.0	65.2	64.5	63.8	63.1
34	69.0	68.1	67.3	66.5	65.8	65.0	64.2	63.5	62.8
35	68.8	68.0	67.2	66.3	65.5	64.8	64.0	63.3	62.5
36	68.7	67.8	67.0	66.2	65.4	64.6	63.8	63.0	62.3
37	68.5	67.7	66.8	66.0	65.2	64.4	63.6	62.8	62.0
38	68.4	67.6	66.7	65.8	65.0	64.2	63.4	62.6	61.8
39	68.3	67.4	66.6	65.7	64.9	64.0	63.2	62.4	61.6
40	68.2	67.3	66.4	65.6	64.7	63.9	63.0	62.2	61.4
41	68.1	67.2	66.3	65.4	64.6	63.7	62.9	62.0	61.2
42	68.0	67.1	66.2	65.3	64.5	63.6	62.7	61.9	61.0

Ages	18	19	20	21	22	23	24	25	26
43	67.9	67.0	66.1	65.2	64.3	63.5	62.6	61.7	60.9
44	67.9	66.9	66.0	65.1	64.2	63.4	62.5	61.6	60.7
45	67.8	66.9	66.0	65.0	64.1	63.3	62.4	61.5	60.6
46	67.7	66.8	65.9	65.0	64.1	63.2	62.3	61.4	60.5
47	67.7	66.7	65.8	64.9	64.0	63.1	62.2	61.3	60.4
48	67.6	66.7	65.7	64.8	63.9	63.0	62.1	61.2	60.3
49	67.6	66.6	65.7	64.8	63.8	62.9	62.0	61.1	60.2
50	67.5	66.6	65.6	64.7	63.8	62.8	61.9	61.0	60.1
51	67.5	66.5	65.6	64.6	63.7	62.8	61.9	60.9	60.0
52	67.4	66.5	65.5	64.6	63.7	62.7	61.8	60.9	60.0
53	67.4	66.4	65.5	64.5	63.6	62.7	61.7	60.8	59.9
54	67.4	66.4	65.4	64.5	63.6	62.6	61.7	60.7	59.8
55	67.3	66.4	65.4	64.5	63.5	62.6	61.6	60.7	59.8
56	67.3	66.3	65.4	64.4	63.5	62.5	61.6	60.6	59.7
57	67.3	66.3	65.3	64.4	63.4	62.5	61.5	60.6	59.7
58	67.2	66.3	65.3	64.4	63.4	62.5	61.5	60.6	59.6
59	67.2	66.3	65.3	64.3	63.4	62.4	61.5	60.5	59.6
60	67.2	66.2	65.3	64.3	63.3	62.4	61.4	60.5	59.5
61	67.2	66.2	65.2	64.3	63.3	62.4	61.4	60.5	59.5
62	67.2	66.2	65.2	64.3	63.3	62.3	61.4	60.4	59.5
63	67.1	66.2	65.2	64.2	63.3	62.3	61.4	60.4	59.4
64	67.1	66.2	65.2	64.2	63.3	62.3	61.3	60.4	59.4
65	67.1	66.1	65.2	64.2	63.2	62.3	61.3	60.3	59.4
66	67.1	66.1	65.2	64.2	63.2	62.2	61.3	60.3	59.4
67	67.1	66.1	65.1	64.2	63.2	62.2	61.3	60.3	59.3
68	67.1	66.1	65.1	64.2	63.2	62.2	61.3	60.3	59.3
69	67.1	66.1	65.1	64.1	63.2	62.2	61.2	60.3	59.3
70	67.0	66.1	65.1	64.1	63.2	62.2	61.2	60.3	59.3
71	67.0	66.1	65.1	64.1	63.1	62.2	61.2	60.2	59.3
72	67.0	66.1	65.1	64.1	63.1	62.2	61.2	60.2	59.3
73	67.0	66.0	65.1	64.1	63.1	62.1	61.2	60.2	59.3
74	67.0	66.0	65.1	64.1	63.1	62.1	61.2	60.2	59.2
75	67.0	66.0	65.0	64.1	63.1	62.1	61.2	60.2	59.2
76	67.0	66.0	65.0	64.1	63.1	62.1	61.2	60.2	59.2
77	67.0	66.0	65.0	64.1	63.1	62.1	61.1	60.2	59.2
78	67.0	66.0	65.0	64.1	63.1	62.1	61.1	60.2	59.2
79	67.0	66.0	65.0	64.0	63.1	62.1	61.1	60.2	59.2
80	67.0	66.0	65.0	64.0	63.1	62.1	61.1	60.2	59.2
81	67.0	66.0	65.0	64.0	63.1	62.1	61.1	60.1	59.2
82	67.0	66.0	65.0	64.0	63.1	62.1	61.1	60.1	59.2
83	67.0	66.0	65.0	64.0	63.0	62.1	61.1	60.1	59.2
84	67.0	66.0	65.0	64.0	63.0	62.1	61.1	60.1	59.2
85	67.0	66.0	65.0	64.0	63.0	62.1	61.1	60.1	59.2
86	67.0	66.0	65.0	64.0	63.0	62.1	61.1	60.1	59.1
87	66.9	66.0	65.0	64.0	63.0	62.1	61.1	60.1	59.1
88	66.9	66.0	65.0	64.0	63.0	62.1	61.1	60.1	59.1
89	66.9	66.0	65.0	64.0	63.0	62.1	61.1	60.1	59.1
90	66.9	66.0	65.0	64.0	63.0	62.1	61.1	60.1	59.1
91	66.9	66.0	65.0	64.0	63.0	62.1	61.1	60.1	59.1
92	66.9	66.0	65.0	64.0	63.0	62.0	61.1	60.1	59.1
93	66.9	66.0	65.0	64.0	63.0	62.0	61.1	60.1	59.1
94	66.9	66.0	65.0	64.0	63.0	62.0	61.1	60.1	59.1
95	66.9	66.0	65.0	64.0	63.0	62.0	61.1	60.1	59.1
96	66.9	66.0	65.0	64.0	63.0	62.0	61.1	60.1	59.1
97	66.9	66.0	65.0	64.0	63.0	62.0	61.1	60.1	59.1
98	66.9	66.0	65.0	64.0	63.0	62.0	61.1	60.1	59.1
99	66.9	66.0	65.0	64.0	63.0	62.0	61.1	60.1	59.1
100	66.9	66.0	65.0	64.0	63.0	62.0	61.1	60.1	59.1
101	66.9	66.0	65.0	64.0	63.0	62.0	61.1	60.1	59.1
102	66.9	66.0	65.0	64.0	63.0	62.0	61.1	60.1	59.1
103	66.9	66.0	65.0	64.0	63.0	62.0	61.1	60.1	59.1
104	66.9	66.0	65.0	64.0	63.0	62.0	61.1	60.1	59.1

Ages	18	19	20	21	22	23	24	25	26
105	66.9	66.0	65.0	64.0	63.0	62.0	61.1	60.1	59.1
106	66.9	66.0	65.0	64.0	63.0	62.0	61.1	60.1	59.1
107	66.9	66.0	65.0	64.0	63.0	62.0	61.1	60.1	59.1
108	66.9	66.0	65.0	64.0	63.0	62.0	61.1	60.1	59.1
109	66.9	66.0	65.0	64.0	63.0	62.0	61.1	60.1	59.1
110	66.9	66.0	65.0	64.0	63.0	62.0	61.1	60.1	59.1
111	66.9	66.0	65.0	64.0	63.0	62.0	61.1	60.1	59.1
112	66.9	66.0	65.0	64.0	63.0	62.0	61.1	60.1	59.1
113	66.9	66.0	65.0	64.0	63.0	62.0	61.1	60.1	59.1
114	66.9	66.0	65.0	64.0	63.0	62.0	61.1	60.1	59.1
115	66.9	66.0	65.0	64.0	63.0	62.0	61.1	60.1	59.1
116	66.9	66.0	65.0	64.0	63.0	62.0	61.1	60.1	59.1
117	66.9	66.0	65.0	64.0	63.0	62.0	61.1	60.1	59.1
118	66.9	66.0	65.0	64.0	63.0	62.0	61.1	60.1	59.1
119	66.9	66.0	65.0	64.0	63.0	62.0	61.1	60.1	59.1
120+	66.9	66.0	65.0	64.0	63.0	62.0	61.1	60.1	59.1

Ages	27	28	29	30	31	32	33	34	35
0	85.6	85.6	85.5	85.4	85.4	85.3	85.3	85.2	85.2
1	84.8	84.7	84.6	84.6	84.5	84.4	84.4	84.3	84.3
2	83.9	83.8	83.7	83.6	83.6	83.5	83.5	83.4	83.4
3	82.9	82.9	82.8	82.7	82.6	82.6	82.5	82.5	82.4
4	82.0	82.0	81.9	81.8	81.7	81.6	81.6	81.5	81.5
5	81.1	81.0	81.0	80.9	80.8	80.7	80.7	80.6	80.5
6	80.3	80.1	80.1	80.0	79.9	79.8	79.7	79.7	79.6
7	79.4	79.3	79.2	79.1	79.0	78.9	78.8	78.7	78.7
8	78.5	78.4	78.3	78.2	78.1	78.0	77.9	77.8	77.7
9	77.6	77.5	77.4	77.3	77.2	77.1	77.0	76.9	76.8
10	76.8	76.6	76.5	76.4	76.3	76.2	76.1	76.0	75.9
11	75.9	75.8	75.6	75.5	75.4	75.3	75.2	75.1	75.0
12	75.1	74.9	74.8	74.6	74.5	74.4	74.3	74.2	74.1
13	74.3	74.1	73.9	73.8	73.7	73.5	73.4	73.3	73.2
14	73.5	73.3	73.1	73.0	72.8	72.7	72.5	72.4	72.3
15	72.7	72.5	72.3	72.1	72.0	71.8	71.7	71.5	71.4
16	71.9	71.7	71.5	71.3	71.1	71.0	70.8	70.7	70.5
17	71.2	71.0	70.7	70.5	70.3	70.1	70.0	69.8	69.7
18	70.5	70.2	70.0	69.7	69.5	69.3	69.1	69.0	68.8
19	69.8	69.5	69.2	69.0	68.7	68.5	68.3	68.1	68.0
20	69.1	68.8	68.5	68.2	68.0	67.7	67.5	67.3	67.2
21	68.4	68.1	67.8	67.5	67.2	67.0	66.7	66.5	66.3
22	67.8	67.4	67.1	66.8	66.5	66.2	66.0	65.8	65.5
23	67.2	66.8	66.4	66.1	65.8	65.5	65.2	65.0	64.8
24	66.6	66.2	65.8	65.4	65.1	64.8	64.5	64.2	64.0
25	66.0	65.6	65.2	64.8	64.4	64.1	63.8	63.5	63.3
26	65.5	65.0	64.6	64.2	63.8	63.4	63.1	62.8	62.5
27	65.0	64.5	64.0	63.6	63.2	62.8	62.5	62.1	61.8
28	64.5	64.0	63.5	63.0	62.6	62.2	61.8	61.5	61.1
29	64.0	63.5	63.0	62.5	62.0	61.6	61.2	60.8	60.5
30	63.6	63.0	62.5	62.0	61.5	61.0	60.6	60.2	59.8
31	63.2	62.6	62.0	61.5	61.0	60.5	60.1	59.6	59.2
32	62.8	62.2	61.6	61.0	60.5	60.0	59.5	59.1	58.6
33	62.5	61.8	61.2	60.6	60.1	59.5	59.0	58.5	58.1
34	62.1	61.5	60.8	60.2	59.6	59.1	58.5	58.0	57.5
35	61.8	61.1	60.5	59.8	59.2	58.6	58.1	57.5	57.0
36	61.5	60.8	60.1	59.5	58.8	58.2	57.6	57.1	56.6
37	61.3	60.5	59.8	59.2	58.5	57.9	57.2	56.7	56.1
38	61.0	60.3	59.6	58.9	58.2	57.5	56.9	56.3	55.7
39	60.8	60.0	59.3	58.6	57.9	57.2	56.5	55.9	55.3
40	60.6	59.8	59.0	58.3	57.6	56.9	56.2	55.5	54.9
41	60.4	59.6	58.8	58.1	57.3	56.6	55.9	55.2	54.5
42	60.2	59.4	58.6	57.8	57.1	56.3	55.6	54.9	54.2

Reg. § 1.401(a)(9)-9(d)

Ages	27	28	29	30	31	32	33	34	35
43	60.1	59.2	58.4	57.6	56.8	56.1	55.3	54.6	53.9
44	59.9	59.1	58.2	57.4	56.6	55.9	55.1	54.4	53.6
45	59.8	58.9	58.1	57.3	56.4	55.7	54.9	54.1	53.4
46	59.6	58.8	57.9	57.1	56.3	55.5	54.7	53.9	53.1
47	59.5	58.6	57.8	56.9	56.1	55.3	54.5	53.7	52.9
48	59.4	58.5	57.7	56.8	56.0	55.1	54.3	53.5	52.7
49	59.3	58.4	57.5	56.7	55.8	55.0	54.1	53.3	52.5
50	59.2	58.3	57.4	56.6	55.7	54.8	54.0	53.2	52.3
51	59.1	58.2	57.3	56.5	55.6	54.7	53.9	53.0	52.2
52	59.0	58.1	57.2	56.4	55.5	54.6	53.7	52.9	52.0
53	59.0	58.1	57.2	56.3	55.4	54.5	53.6	52.7	51.9
54	58.9	58.0	57.1	56.2	55.3	54.4	53.5	52.6	51.8
55	58.8	57.9	57.0	56.1	55.2	54.3	53.4	52.5	51.7
56	58.8	57.9	56.9	56.0	55.1	54.2	53.3	52.4	51.6
57	58.7	57.8	56.9	56.0	55.0	54.1	53.2	52.3	51.5
58	58.7	57.7	56.8	55.9	55.0	54.1	53.2	52.3	51.4
59	58.6	57.7	56.8	55.8	54.9	54.0	53.1	52.2	51.3
60	58.6	57.7	56.7	55.8	54.9	53.9	53.0	52.1	51.2
61	58.6	57.6	56.7	55.7	54.8	53.9	53.0	52.1	51.1
62	58.5	57.6	56.6	55.7	54.8	53.8	52.9	52.0	51.1
63	58.5	57.5	56.6	55.7	54.7	53.8	52.9	51.9	51.0
64	58.5	57.5	56.6	55.6	54.7	53.8	52.8	51.9	51.0
65	58.4	57.5	56.5	55.6	54.7	53.7	52.8	51.9	50.9
66	58.4	57.5	56.5	55.6	54.6	53.7	52.7	51.8	50.9
67	58.4	57.4	56.5	55.5	54.6	53.7	52.7	51.8	50.8
68	58.4	57.4	56.5	55.5	54.6	53.6	52.7	51.7	50.8
69	58.4	57.4	56.4	55.5	54.5	53.6	52.7	51.7	50.8
70	58.3	57.4	56.4	55.5	54.5	53.6	52.6	51.7	50.7
71	58.3	57.4	56.4	55.5	54.5	53.6	52.6	51.7	50.7
72	58.3	57.3	56.4	55.4	54.5	53.5	52.6	51.6	50.7
73	58.3	57.3	56.4	55.4	54.5	53.5	52.6	51.6	50.7
74	58.3	57.3	56.4	55.4	54.5	53.5	52.5	51.6	50.6
75	58.3	57.3	56.3	55.4	54.4	53.5	52.5	51.6	50.6
76	58.3	57.3	56.3	55.4	54.4	53.5	52.5	51.6	50.6
77	58.2	57.3	56.3	55.4	54.4	53.5	52.5	51.6	50.6
78	58.2	57.3	56.3	55.4	54.4	53.4	52.5	51.5	50.6
79	58.2	57.3	56.3	55.4	54.4	53.4	52.5	51.5	50.6
80	58.2	57.3	56.3	55.3	54.4	53.4	52.5	51.5	50.6
81	58.2	57.3	56.3	55.3	54.4	53.4	52.5	51.5	50.6
82	58.2	57.2	56.3	55.3	54.4	53.4	52.5	51.5	50.5
83	58.2	57.2	56.3	55.3	54.4	53.4	52.5	51.5	50.5
84	58.2	57.2	56.3	55.3	54.4	53.4	52.4	51.5	50.5
85	58.2	57.2	56.3	55.3	54.4	53.4	52.4	51.5	50.5
86	58.2	57.2	56.3	55.3	54.3	53.4	52.4	51.5	50.5
87	58.2	57.2	56.3	55.3	54.3	53.4	52.4	51.5	50.5
88	58.2	57.2	56.3	55.3	54.3	53.4	52.4	51.5	50.5
89	58.2	57.2	56.3	55.3	54.3	53.4	52.4	51.5	50.5
90	58.2	57.2	56.3	55.3	54.3	53.4	52.4	51.5	50.5
91	58.2	57.2	56.3	55.3	54.3	53.4	52.4	51.5	50.5
92	58.2	57.2	56.2	55.3	54.3	53.4	52.4	51.5	50.5
93	58.2	57.2	56.2	55.3	54.3	53.4	52.4	51.5	50.5
94	58.2	57.2	56.2	55.3	54.3	53.4	52.4	51.5	50.5
95	58.2	57.2	56.2	55.3	54.3	53.4	52.4	51.5	50.5
96	58.2	57.2	56.2	55.3	54.3	53.4	52.4	51.5	50.5
97	58.2	57.2	56.2	55.3	54.3	53.4	52.4	51.5	50.5
98	58.2	57.2	56.2	55.3	54.3	53.4	52.4	51.5	50.5
99	58.2	57.2	56.2	55.3	54.3	53.4	52.4	51.5	50.5
100	58.2	57.2	56.2	55.3	54.3	53.4	52.4	51.5	50.5
101	58.2	57.2	56.2	55.3	54.3	53.4	52.4	51.4	50.5
102	58.2	57.2	56.2	55.3	54.3	53.4	52.4	51.4	50.5
103	58.2	57.2	56.2	55.3	54.3	53.4	52.4	51.4	50.5
104	58.2	57.2	56.2	55.3	54.3	53.4	52.4	51.4	50.5

Reg. §1.401(a)(9)-9(d)

Ages	27	28	29	30	31	32	33	34	35
105	58.2	57.2	56.2	55.3	54.3	53.4	52.4	51.4	50.5
106	58.2	57.2	56.2	55.3	54.3	53.4	52.4	51.4	50.5
107	58.2	57.2	56.2	55.3	54.3	53.4	52.4	51.4	50.5
108	58.2	57.2	56.2	55.3	54.3	53.4	52.4	51.4	50.5
109	58.2	57.2	56.2	55.3	54.3	53.4	52.4	51.4	50.5
110	58.2	57.2	56.2	55.3	54.3	53.4	52.4	51.4	50.5
111	58.2	57.2	56.2	55.3	54.3	53.4	52.4	51.4	50.5
112	58.2	57.2	56.2	55.3	54.3	53.4	52.4	51.4	50.5
113	58.2	57.2	56.2	55.3	54.3	53.4	52.4	51.4	50.5
114	58.2	57.2	56.2	55.3	54.3	53.4	52.4	51.4	50.5
115	58.2	57.2	56.2	55.3	54.3	53.4	52.4	51.4	50.5
116	58.2	57.2	56.2	55.3	54.3	53.4	52.4	51.4	50.5
117	58.2	57.2	56.2	55.3	54.3	53.4	52.4	51.4	50.5
118	58.2	57.2	56.2	55.3	54.3	53.4	52.4	51.4	50.5
119	58.2	57.2	56.2	55.3	54.3	53.4	52.4	51.4	50.5
120+	58.2	57.2	56.2	55.3	54.3	53.4	52.4	51.4	50.5

Ages	36	37	38	39	40	41	42	43	44
0	85.2	85.1	85.1	85.1	85.0	85.0	85.0	84.9	84.9
1	84.3	84.2	84.2	84.2	84.1	84.1	84.1	84.0	84.0
2	83.3	83.3	83.2	83.2	83.2	83.1	83.1	83.1	83.1
3	82.4	82.3	82.3	82.3	82.2	82.2	82.2	82.1	82.1
4	81.4	81.4	81.3	81.3	81.3	81.2	81.2	81.2	81.1
5	80.5	80.4	80.4	80.3	80.3	80.3	80.2	80.2	80.2
6	79.5	79.5	79.4	79.4	79.3	79.3	79.3	79.2	79.2
7	78.6	78.5	78.5	78.4	78.4	78.4	78.3	78.3	78.2
8	77.7	77.6	77.6	77.5	77.4	77.4	77.4	77.3	77.3
9	76.7	76.7	76.6	76.6	76.5	76.5	76.4	76.4	76.3
10	75.8	75.7	75.7	75.6	75.6	75.5	75.5	75.4	75.4
11	74.9	74.8	74.7	74.7	74.6	74.6	74.5	74.5	74.4
12	74.0	73.9	73.8	73.8	73.7	73.6	73.6	73.5	73.5
13	73.1	73.0	72.9	72.8	72.8	72.7	72.6	72.6	72.5
14	72.2	72.1	72.0	71.9	71.8	71.8	71.7	71.6	71.6
15	71.3	71.2	71.1	71.0	70.9	70.8	70.8	70.7	70.6
16	70.4	70.3	70.2	70.1	70.0	69.9	69.8	69.8	69.7
17	69.5	69.4	69.3	69.2	69.1	69.0	68.9	68.9	68.8
18	68.7	68.5	68.4	68.3	68.2	68.1	68.0	67.9	67.9
19	67.8	67.7	67.6	67.4	67.3	67.2	67.1	67.0	66.9
20	67.0	66.8	66.7	66.6	66.4	66.3	66.2	66.1	66.0
21	66.2	66.0	65.8	65.7	65.6	65.4	65.3	65.2	65.1
22	65.4	65.2	65.0	64.9	64.7	64.6	64.5	64.3	64.2
23	64.6	64.4	64.2	64.0	63.9	63.7	63.6	63.5	63.4
24	63.8	63.6	63.4	63.2	63.0	62.9	62.7	62.6	62.5
25	63.0	62.8	62.6	62.4	62.2	62.0	61.9	61.7	61.6
26	62.3	62.0	61.8	61.6	61.4	61.2	61.0	60.9	60.7
27	61.5	61.3	61.0	60.8	60.6	60.4	60.2	60.1	59.9
28	60.8	60.5	60.3	60.0	59.8	59.6	59.4	59.2	59.1
29	60.1	59.8	59.6	59.3	59.0	58.8	58.6	58.4	58.2
30	59.5	59.2	58.9	58.6	58.3	58.1	57.8	57.6	57.4
31	58.8	58.5	58.2	57.9	57.6	57.3	57.1	56.8	56.6
32	58.2	57.9	57.5	57.2	56.9	56.6	56.3	56.1	55.9
33	57.6	57.2	56.9	56.5	56.2	55.9	55.6	55.3	55.1
34	57.1	56.7	56.3	55.9	55.5	55.2	54.9	54.6	54.4
35	56.6	56.1	55.7	55.3	54.9	54.5	54.2	53.9	53.6
36	56.0	55.6	55.1	54.7	54.3	53.9	53.6	53.2	52.9
37	55.6	55.1	54.6	54.1	53.7	53.3	52.9	52.6	52.2
38	55.1	54.6	54.1	53.6	53.1	52.7	52.3	51.9	51.6
39	54.7	54.1	53.6	53.1	52.6	52.1	51.7	51.3	50.9
40	54.3	53.7	53.1	52.6	52.1	51.6	51.2	50.7	50.3
41	53.9	53.3	52.7	52.1	51.6	51.1	50.6	50.2	49.7
42	53.6	52.9	52.3	51.7	51.2	50.6	50.1	49.6	49.2

Ages	36	37	38	39	40	41	42	43	44
43	53.2	52.6	51.9	51.3	50.7	50.2	49.6	49.1	48.6
44	52.9	52.2	51.6	50.9	50.3	49.7	49.2	48.6	48.1
45	52.6	51.9	51.3	50.6	50.0	49.3	48.7	48.2	47.7
46	52.4	51.7	50.9	50.3	49.6	49.0	48.3	47.8	47.2
47	52.1	51.4	50.7	50.0	49.3	48.6	48.0	47.4	46.8
48	51.9	51.2	50.4	49.7	49.0	48.3	47.6	47.0	46.4
49	51.7	50.9	50.2	49.4	48.7	48.0	47.3	46.6	46.0
50	51.5	50.7	49.9	49.2	48.4	47.7	47.0	46.3	45.7
51	51.4	50.5	49.7	49.0	48.2	47.5	46.7	46.0	45.3
52	51.2	50.4	49.6	48.8	48.0	47.2	46.5	45.7	45.0
53	51.0	50.2	49.4	48.6	47.8	47.0	46.2	45.5	44.8
54	50.9	50.1	49.2	48.4	47.6	46.8	46.0	45.3	44.5
55	50.8	49.9	49.1	48.2	47.4	46.6	45.8	45.0	44.3
56	50.7	49.8	48.9	48.1	47.3	46.4	45.6	44.8	44.1
57	50.6	49.7	48.8	48.0	47.1	46.3	45.5	44.7	43.9
58	50.5	49.6	48.7	47.8	47.0	46.1	45.3	44.5	43.7
59	50.4	49.5	48.6	47.7	46.9	46.0	45.2	44.3	43.5
60	50.3	49.4	48.5	47.6	46.8	45.9	45.0	44.2	43.4
61	50.2	49.3	48.4	47.5	46.7	45.8	44.9	44.1	43.2
62	50.2	49.3	48.4	47.5	46.6	45.7	44.8	43.9	43.1
63	50.1	49.2	48.3	47.4	46.5	45.6	44.7	43.8	43.0
64	50.0	49.1	48.2	47.3	46.4	45.5	44.6	43.7	42.9
65	50.0	49.1	48.2	47.2	46.3	45.4	44.5	43.6	42.8
66	50.0	49.0	48.1	47.2	46.3	45.4	44.5	43.6	42.7
67	49.9	49.0	48.0	47.1	46.2	45.3	44.4	43.5	42.6
68	49.9	48.9	48.0	47.1	46.2	45.2	44.3	43.4	42.5
69	49.8	48.9	48.0	47.0	46.1	45.2	44.3	43.3	42.4
70	49.8	48.9	47.9	47.0	46.1	45.1	44.2	43.3	42.4
71	49.8	48.8	47.9	47.0	46.0	45.1	44.2	43.2	42.3
72	49.7	48.8	47.9	46.9	46.0	45.0	44.1	43.2	42.3
73	49.7	48.8	47.8	46.9	45.9	45.0	44.1	43.1	42.2
74	49.7	48.8	47.8	46.9	45.9	45.0	44.0	43.1	42.2
75	49.7	48.7	47.8	46.8	45.9	44.9	44.0	43.1	42.1
76	49.7	48.7	47.8	46.8	45.9	44.9	44.0	43.0	42.1
77	49.6	48.7	47.7	46.8	45.8	44.9	43.9	43.0	42.1
78	49.6	48.7	47.7	46.8	45.8	44.9	43.9	43.0	42.0
79	49.6	48.7	47.7	46.8	45.8	44.9	43.9	43.0	42.0
80	49.6	48.7	47.7	46.7	45.8	44.8	43.9	42.9	42.0
81	49.6	48.6	47.7	46.7	45.8	44.8	43.9	42.9	42.0
82	49.6	48.6	47.7	46.7	45.8	44.8	43.9	42.9	42.0
83	49.6	48.6	47.7	46.7	45.8	44.8	43.8	42.9	41.9
84	49.6	48.6	47.7	46.7	45.7	44.8	43.8	42.9	41.9
85	49.6	48.6	47.7	46.7	45.7	44.8	43.8	42.9	41.9
86	49.6	48.6	47.6	46.7	45.7	44.8	43.8	42.9	41.9
87	49.6	48.6	47.6	46.7	45.7	44.8	43.8	42.9	41.9
88	49.6	48.6	47.6	46.7	45.7	44.8	43.8	42.8	41.9
89	49.6	48.6	47.6	46.7	45.7	44.8	43.8	42.8	41.9
90	49.5	48.6	47.6	46.7	45.7	44.8	43.8	42.8	41.9
91	49.5	48.6	47.6	46.7	45.7	44.7	43.8	42.8	41.9
92	49.5	48.6	47.6	46.7	45.7	44.7	43.8	42.8	41.9
93	49.5	48.6	47.6	46.7	45.7	44.7	43.8	42.8	41.9
94	49.5	48.6	47.6	46.7	45.7	44.7	43.8	42.8	41.9
95	49.5	48.6	47.6	46.7	45.7	44.7	43.8	42.8	41.9
96	49.5	48.6	47.6	46.7	45.7	44.7	43.8	42.8	41.9
97	49.5	48.6	47.6	46.7	45.7	44.7	43.8	42.8	41.9
98	49.5	48.6	47.6	46.7	45.7	44.7	43.8	42.8	41.9
99	49.5	48.6	47.6	46.7	45.7	44.7	43.8	42.8	41.9
100	49.5	48.6	47.6	46.7	45.7	44.7	43.8	42.8	41.9
101	49.5	48.6	47.6	46.7	45.7	44.7	43.8	42.8	41.9
102	49.5	48.6	47.6	46.7	45.7	44.7	43.8	42.8	41.9
103	49.5	48.6	47.6	46.7	45.7	44.7	43.8	42.8	41.9
104	49.5	48.6	47.6	46.7	45.7	44.7	43.8	42.8	41.9

Ages	36	37	38	39	40	41	42	43	44
105	49.5	48.6	47.6	46.7	45.7	44.7	43.8	42.8	41.9
106	49.5	48.6	47.6	46.7	45.7	44.7	43.8	42.8	41.9
107	49.5	48.6	47.6	46.7	45.7	44.7	43.8	42.8	41.9
108	49.5	48.6	47.6	46.7	45.7	44.7	43.8	42.8	41.9
109	49.5	48.6	47.6	46.6	45.7	44.7	43.8	42.8	41.9
110	49.5	48.6	47.6	46.6	45.7	44.7	43.8	42.8	41.9
111	49.5	48.6	47.6	46.6	45.7	44.7	43.8	42.8	41.9
112	49.5	48.6	47.6	46.6	45.7	44.7	43.8	42.8	41.9
113	49.5	48.6	47.6	46.6	45.7	44.7	43.8	42.8	41.9
114	49.5	48.6	47.6	46.6	45.7	44.7	43.8	42.8	41.9
115	49.5	48.6	47.6	46.6	45.7	44.7	43.8	42.8	41.9
116	49.5	48.6	47.6	46.6	45.7	44.7	43.8	42.8	41.8
117	49.5	48.6	47.6	46.6	45.7	44.7	43.8	42.8	41.8
118	49.5	48.6	47.6	46.6	45.7	44.7	43.8	42.8	41.8
119	49.5	48.6	47.6	46.6	45.7	44.7	43.8	42.8	41.8
120+	49.5	48.6	47.6	46.6	45.7	44.7	43.8	42.8	41.8

Ages	45	46	47	48	49	50	51	52	53
0	84.9	84.9	84.9	84.8	84.8	84.8	84.8	84.8	84.8
1	84.0	84.0	84.0	83.9	83.9	83.9	83.9	83.9	83.9
2	83.0	83.0	83.0	83.0	83.0	82.9	82.9	82.9	82.9
3	82.1	82.1	82.0	82.0	82.0	82.0	82.0	81.9	81.9
4	81.1	81.1	81.1	81.0	81.0	81.0	81.0	81.0	81.0
5	80.1	80.1	80.1	80.1	80.1	80.0	80.0	80.0	80.0
6	79.2	79.2	79.1	79.1	79.1	79.1	79.0	79.0	79.0
7	78.2	78.2	78.2	78.1	78.1	78.1	78.1	78.0	78.0
8	77.3	77.2	77.2	77.2	77.1	77.1	77.1	77.1	77.1
9	76.3	76.3	76.2	76.2	76.2	76.1	76.1	76.1	76.1
10	75.3	75.3	75.3	75.2	75.2	75.2	75.2	75.1	75.1
11	74.4	74.3	74.3	74.3	74.2	74.2	74.2	74.2	74.1
12	73.4	73.4	73.3	73.3	73.3	73.2	73.2	73.2	73.2
13	72.5	72.4	72.4	72.3	72.3	72.3	72.2	72.2	72.2
14	71.5	71.5	71.4	71.4	71.4	71.3	71.3	71.3	71.2
15	70.6	70.5	70.5	70.4	70.4	70.4	70.3	70.3	70.3
16	69.6	69.6	69.5	69.5	69.4	69.4	69.4	69.3	69.3
17	68.7	68.7	68.6	68.5	68.5	68.5	68.4	68.4	68.3
18	67.8	67.7	67.7	67.6	67.6	67.5	67.5	67.4	67.4
19	66.9	66.8	66.7	66.7	66.6	66.6	66.5	66.5	66.4
20	66.0	65.9	65.8	65.7	65.7	65.6	65.6	65.5	65.5
21	65.0	65.0	64.9	64.8	64.8	64.7	64.6	64.6	64.5
22	64.1	64.1	64.0	63.9	63.8	63.8	63.7	63.7	63.6
23	63.3	63.2	63.1	63.0	62.9	62.8	62.8	62.7	62.7
24	62.4	62.3	62.2	62.1	62.0	61.9	61.9	61.8	61.7
25	61.5	61.4	61.3	61.2	61.1	61.0	60.9	60.9	60.8
26	60.6	60.5	60.4	60.3	60.2	60.1	60.0	60.0	59.9
27	59.8	59.6	59.5	59.4	59.3	59.2	59.1	59.0	59.0
28	58.9	58.8	58.6	58.5	58.4	58.3	58.2	58.1	58.1
29	58.1	57.9	57.8	57.7	57.5	57.4	57.3	57.2	57.2
30	57.3	57.1	56.9	56.8	56.7	56.6	56.5	56.4	56.3
31	56.4	56.3	56.1	56.0	55.8	55.7	55.6	55.5	55.4
32	55.7	55.5	55.3	55.1	55.0	54.8	54.7	54.6	54.5
33	54.9	54.7	54.5	54.3	54.1	54.0	53.9	53.7	53.6
34	54.1	53.9	53.7	53.5	53.3	53.2	53.0	52.9	52.7
35	53.4	53.1	52.9	52.7	52.5	52.3	52.2	52.0	51.9
36	52.6	52.4	52.1	51.9	51.7	51.5	51.4	51.2	51.0
37	51.9	51.7	51.4	51.2	50.9	50.7	50.5	50.4	50.2
38	51.3	50.9	50.7	50.4	50.2	49.9	49.7	49.6	49.4
39	50.6	50.3	50.0	49.7	49.4	49.2	49.0	48.8	48.6
40	50.0	49.6	49.3	49.0	48.7	48.4	48.2	48.0	47.8
41	49.3	49.0	48.6	48.3	48.0	47.7	47.5	47.2	47.0
42	48.7	48.3	48.0	47.6	47.3	47.0	46.7	46.5	46.2

Ages	45	46	47	48	49	50	51	52	53
43	48.2	47.8	47.4	47.0	46.6	46.3	46.0	45.7	45.5
44	47.7	47.2	46.8	46.4	46.0	45.7	45.3	45.0	44.8
45	47.1	46.7	46.2	45.8	45.4	45.0	44.7	44.4	44.1
46	46.7	46.2	45.7	45.2	44.8	44.4	44.0	43.7	43.4
47	46.2	45.7	45.2	44.7	44.2	43.8	43.4	43.1	42.7
48	45.8	45.2	44.7	44.2	43.7	43.3	42.8	42.4	42.1
49	45.4	44.8	44.2	43.7	43.2	42.7	42.3	41.9	41.5
50	45.0	44.4	43.8	43.3	42.7	42.2	41.7	41.3	40.9
51	44.7	44.0	43.4	42.8	42.3	41.7	41.2	40.8	40.3
52	44.4	43.7	43.1	42.4	41.9	41.3	40.8	40.3	39.8
53	44.1	43.4	42.7	42.1	41.5	40.9	40.3	39.8	39.3
54	43.8	43.1	42.4	41.7	41.1	40.5	39.9	39.3	38.8
55	43.5	42.8	42.1	41.4	40.8	40.1	39.5	38.9	38.4
56	43.3	42.5	41.8	41.1	40.4	39.8	39.1	38.5	38.0
57	43.1	42.3	41.6	40.8	40.1	39.5	38.8	38.2	37.6
58	42.9	42.1	41.3	40.6	39.9	39.2	38.5	37.8	37.2
59	42.7	41.9	41.1	40.4	39.6	38.9	38.2	37.5	36.9
60	42.5	41.7	40.9	40.1	39.4	38.6	37.9	37.2	36.6
61	42.4	41.6	40.7	40.0	39.2	38.4	37.7	37.0	36.3
62	42.2	41.4	40.6	39.8	39.0	38.2	37.5	36.7	36.0
63	42.1	41.3	40.4	39.6	38.8	38.0	37.2	36.5	35.8
64	42.0	41.1	40.3	39.5	38.6	37.8	37.0	36.3	35.5
65	41.9	41.0	40.2	39.3	38.5	37.7	36.9	36.1	35.3
66	41.8	40.9	40.0	39.2	38.4	37.5	36.7	35.9	35.1
67	41.7	40.8	39.9	39.1	38.2	37.4	36.6	35.7	35.0
68	41.6	40.7	39.8	39.0	38.1	37.3	36.4	35.6	34.8
69	41.5	40.6	39.8	38.9	38.0	37.1	36.3	35.5	34.6
70	41.5	40.6	39.7	38.8	37.9	37.0	36.2	35.3	34.5
71	41.4	40.5	39.6	38.7	37.8	36.9	36.1	35.2	34.4
72	41.3	40.4	39.5	38.6	37.7	36.9	36.0	35.1	34.3
73	41.3	40.4	39.5	38.6	37.7	36.8	35.9	35.0	34.2
74	41.2	40.3	39.4	38.5	37.6	36.7	35.8	34.9	34.1
75	41.2	40.3	39.4	38.4	37.5	36.6	35.7	34.9	34.0
76	41.2	40.2	39.3	38.4	37.5	36.6	35.7	34.8	33.9
77	41.1	40.2	39.3	38.4	37.4	36.5	35.6	34.7	33.9
78	41.1	40.2	39.2	38.3	37.4	36.5	35.6	34.7	33.8
79	41.1	40.1	39.2	38.3	37.4	36.4	35.5	34.6	33.7
80	41.1	40.1	39.2	38.2	37.3	36.4	35.5	34.6	33.7
81	41.0	40.1	39.1	38.2	37.3	36.4	35.4	34.5	33.6
82	41.0	40.1	39.1	38.2	37.3	36.3	35.4	34.5	33.6
83	41.0	40.0	39.1	38.2	37.2	36.3	35.4	34.5	33.6
84	41.0	40.0	39.1	38.1	37.2	36.3	35.4	34.4	33.5
85	41.0	40.0	39.1	38.1	37.2	36.3	35.3	34.4	33.5
86	41.0	40.0	39.1	38.1	37.2	36.2	35.3	34.4	33.5
87	40.9	40.0	39.0	38.1	37.2	36.2	35.3	34.4	33.5
88	40.9	40.0	39.0	38.1	37.1	36.2	35.3	34.4	33.4
89	40.9	40.0	39.0	38.1	37.1	36.2	35.3	34.3	33.4
90	40.9	40.0	39.0	38.1	37.1	36.2	35.3	34.3	33.4
91	40.9	40.0	39.0	38.1	37.1	36.2	35.2	34.3	33.4
92	40.9	40.0	39.0	38.1	37.1	36.2	35.2	34.3	33.4
93	40.9	40.0	39.0	38.1	37.1	36.2	35.2	34.3	33.4
94	40.9	40.0	39.0	38.1	37.1	36.2	35.2	34.3	33.4
95	40.9	40.0	39.0	38.0	37.1	36.2	35.2	34.3	33.4
96	40.9	39.9	39.0	38.0	37.1	36.2	35.2	34.3	33.4
97	40.9	39.9	39.0	38.0	37.1	36.2	35.2	34.3	33.4
98	40.9	39.9	39.0	38.0	37.1	36.1	35.2	34.3	33.4
99	40.9	39.9	39.0	38.0	37.1	36.1	35.2	34.3	33.3
100	40.9	39.9	39.0	38.0	37.1	36.1	35.2	34.3	33.3
101	40.9	39.9	39.0	38.0	37.1	36.1	35.2	34.3	33.3
102	40.9	39.9	39.0	38.0	37.1	36.1	35.2	34.3	33.3
103	40.9	39.9	39.0	38.0	37.1	36.1	35.2	34.3	33.3
104	40.9	39.9	39.0	38.0	37.1	36.1	35.2	34.3	33.3

Reg. §1.401(a)(9)-9(d)

Ages	45	46	47	48	49	50	51	52	53
105	40.9	39.9	39.0	38.0	37.1	36.1	35.2	34.3	33.3
106	40.9	39.9	39.0	38.0	37.1	36.1	35.2	34.3	33.3
107	40.9	39.9	39.0	38.0	37.1	36.1	35.2	34.3	33.3
108	40.9	39.9	39.0	38.0	37.1	36.1	35.2	34.3	33.3
109	40.9	39.9	39.0	38.0	37.1	36.1	35.2	34.3	33.3
110	40.9	39.9	39.0	38.0	37.1	36.1	35.2	34.3	33.3
111	40.9	39.9	39.0	38.0	37.1	36.1	35.2	34.3	33.3
112	40.9	39.9	39.0	38.0	37.1	36.1	35.2	34.3	33.3
113	40.9	39.9	39.0	38.0	37.1	36.1	35.2	34.3	33.3
114	40.9	39.9	39.0	38.0	37.1	36.1	35.2	34.3	33.3
115	40.9	39.9	39.0	38.0	37.1	36.1	35.2	34.3	33.3
116	40.9	39.9	39.0	38.0	37.1	36.1	35.2	34.3	33.3
117	40.9	39.9	39.0	38.0	37.1	36.1	35.2	34.3	33.3
118	40.9	39.9	39.0	38.0	37.1	36.1	35.2	34.3	33.3
119	40.9	39.9	39.0	38.0	37.1	36.1	35.2	34.3	33.3
120+	40.9	39.9	39.0	38.0	37.1	36.1	35.2	34.3	33.3

Ages	54	55	56	57	58	59	60	61	62
0	84.7	84.7	84.7	84.7	84.7	84.7	84.7	84.7	84.7
1	83.9	83.8	83.8	83.8	83.8	83.8	83.8	83.8	83.8
2	82.9	82.9	82.9	82.9	82.8	82.8	82.8	82.8	82.8
3	81.9	81.9	81.9	81.9	81.9	81.9	81.8	81.8	81.8
4	80.9	80.9	80.9	80.9	80.9	80.9	80.9	80.9	80.9
5	80.0	79.9	79.9	79.9	79.9	79.9	79.9	79.9	79.9
6	79.0	79.0	79.0	78.9	78.9	78.9	78.9	78.9	78.9
7	78.0	78.0	78.0	78.0	78.0	77.9	77.9	77.9	77.9
8	77.0	77.0	77.0	77.0	77.0	77.0	76.9	76.9	76.9
9	76.1	76.0	76.0	76.0	76.0	76.0	76.0	76.0	75.9
10	75.1	75.1	75.0	75.0	75.0	75.0	75.0	75.0	75.0
11	74.1	74.1	74.1	74.1	74.0	74.0	74.0	74.0	74.0
12	73.1	73.1	73.1	73.1	73.1	73.0	73.0	73.0	73.0
13	72.2	72.1	72.1	72.1	72.1	72.1	72.1	72.0	72.0
14	71.2	71.2	71.2	71.1	71.1	71.1	71.1	71.1	71.0
15	70.2	70.2	70.2	70.2	70.1	70.1	70.1	70.1	70.1
16	69.3	69.2	69.2	69.2	69.2	69.2	69.1	69.1	69.1
17	68.3	68.3	68.3	68.2	68.2	68.2	68.2	68.1	68.1
18	67.4	67.3	67.3	67.3	67.2	67.2	67.2	67.2	67.2
19	66.4	66.4	66.3	66.3	66.3	66.3	66.2	66.2	66.2
20	65.4	65.4	65.4	65.3	65.3	65.3	65.3	65.2	65.2
21	64.5	64.5	64.4	64.4	64.4	64.3	64.3	64.3	64.3
22	63.6	63.5	63.5	63.4	63.4	63.4	63.3	63.3	63.3
23	62.6	62.6	62.5	62.5	62.5	62.4	62.4	62.4	62.3
24	61.7	61.6	61.6	61.5	61.5	61.5	61.4	61.4	61.4
25	60.7	60.7	60.6	60.6	60.6	60.5	60.5	60.5	60.4
26	59.8	59.8	59.7	59.7	59.6	59.6	59.5	59.5	59.5
27	58.9	58.8	58.8	58.7	58.7	58.6	58.6	58.6	58.5
28	58.0	57.9	57.9	57.8	57.7	57.7	57.7	57.6	57.6
29	57.1	57.0	56.9	56.9	56.8	56.8	56.7	56.7	56.6
30	56.2	56.1	56.0	56.0	55.9	55.8	55.8	55.7	55.7
31	55.3	55.2	55.1	55.0	55.0	54.9	54.9	54.8	54.8
32	54.4	54.3	54.2	54.1	54.1	54.0	53.9	53.9	53.8
33	53.5	53.4	53.3	53.2	53.2	53.1	53.0	53.0	52.9
34	52.6	52.5	52.4	52.3	52.3	52.2	52.1	52.1	52.0
35	51.8	51.7	51.6	51.5	51.4	51.3	51.2	51.1	51.1
36	50.9	50.8	50.7	50.6	50.5	50.4	50.3	50.2	50.2
37	50.1	49.9	49.8	49.7	49.6	49.5	49.4	49.3	49.3
38	49.2	49.1	48.9	48.8	48.7	48.6	48.5	48.4	48.4
39	48.4	48.2	48.1	48.0	47.8	47.7	47.6	47.5	47.5
40	47.6	47.4	47.3	47.1	47.0	46.9	46.8	46.7	46.6
41	46.8	46.6	46.4	46.3	46.1	46.0	45.9	45.8	45.7
42	46.0	45.8	45.6	45.5	45.3	45.2	45.0	44.9	44.8

Ages	54	55	56	57	58	59	60	61	62
43	45.3	45.0	44.8	44.7	44.5	44.3	44.2	44.1	43.9
44	44.5	44.3	44.1	43.9	43.7	43.5	43.4	43.2	43.1
45	43.8	43.5	43.3	43.1	42.9	42.7	42.5	42.4	42.2
46	43.1	42.8	42.5	42.3	42.1	41.9	41.7	41.6	41.4
47	42.4	42.1	41.8	41.6	41.3	41.1	40.9	40.7	40.6
48	41.7	41.4	41.1	40.8	40.6	40.4	40.1	40.0	39.8
49	41.1	40.8	40.4	40.1	39.9	39.6	39.4	39.2	39.0
50	40.5	40.1	39.8	39.5	39.2	38.9	38.6	38.4	38.2
51	39.9	39.5	39.1	38.8	38.5	38.2	37.9	37.7	37.5
52	39.3	38.9	38.5	38.2	37.8	37.5	37.2	37.0	36.7
53	38.8	38.4	38.0	37.6	37.2	36.9	36.6	36.3	36.0
54	38.3	37.9	37.4	37.0	36.6	36.2	35.9	35.6	35.3
55	37.9	37.4	36.9	36.4	36.0	35.6	35.3	34.9	34.6
56	37.4	36.9	36.4	35.9	35.5	35.1	34.7	34.3	34.0
57	37.0	36.4	35.9	35.4	35.0	34.5	34.1	33.7	33.4
58	36.6	36.0	35.5	35.0	34.5	34.0	33.6	33.2	32.8
59	36.2	35.6	35.1	34.5	34.0	33.5	33.1	32.6	32.2
60	35.9	35.3	34.7	34.1	33.6	33.1	32.6	32.1	31.7
61	35.6	34.9	34.3	33.7	33.2	32.6	32.1	31.6	31.2
62	35.3	34.6	34.0	33.4	32.8	32.2	31.7	31.2	30.7
63	35.0	34.4	33.7	33.0	32.4	31.8	31.3	30.7	30.2
64	34.8	34.1	33.4	32.7	32.1	31.5	30.9	30.3	29.8
65	34.6	33.8	33.1	32.5	31.8	31.2	30.5	30.0	29.4
66	34.4	33.6	32.9	32.2	31.5	30.9	30.2	29.6	29.0
67	34.2	33.4	32.7	32.0	31.3	30.6	29.9	29.3	28.7
68	34.0	33.2	32.5	31.7	31.0	30.3	29.6	29.0	28.4
69	33.8	33.1	32.3	31.5	30.8	30.1	29.4	28.7	28.1
70	33.7	32.9	32.1	31.3	30.6	29.9	29.1	28.5	27.8
71	33.6	32.7	32.0	31.2	30.4	29.7	28.9	28.2	27.5
72	33.4	32.6	31.8	31.0	30.2	29.5	28.7	28.0	27.3
73	33.3	32.5	31.7	30.9	30.1	29.3	28.6	27.8	27.1
74	33.2	32.4	31.6	30.7	29.9	29.2	28.4	27.6	26.9
75	33.1	32.3	31.5	30.6	29.8	29.0	28.2	27.5	26.7
76	33.1	32.2	31.4	30.5	29.7	28.9	28.1	27.3	26.6
77	33.0	32.1	31.3	30.4	29.6	28.8	28.0	27.2	26.4
78	32.9	32.0	31.2	30.3	29.5	28.7	27.9	27.1	26.3
79	32.9	32.0	31.1	30.3	29.4	28.6	27.8	27.0	26.2
80	32.8	31.9	31.1	30.2	29.3	28.5	27.7	26.9	26.1
81	32.7	31.9	31.0	30.1	29.3	28.4	27.6	26.8	26.0
82	32.7	31.8	30.9	30.1	29.2	28.4	27.5	26.7	25.9
83	32.7	31.8	30.9	30.0	29.2	28.3	27.5	26.7	25.8
84	32.6	31.7	30.9	30.0	29.1	28.3	27.4	26.6	25.8
85	32.6	31.7	30.8	29.9	29.1	28.2	27.4	26.5	25.7
86	32.6	31.7	30.8	29.9	29.0	28.2	27.3	26.5	25.7
87	32.6	31.7	30.8	29.9	29.0	28.2	27.3	26.5	25.6
88	32.5	31.6	30.7	29.9	29.0	28.1	27.3	26.4	25.6
89	32.5	31.6	30.7	29.8	29.0	28.1	27.2	26.4	25.5
90	32.5	31.6	30.7	29.8	28.9	28.1	27.2	26.4	25.5
91	32.5	31.6	30.7	29.8	28.9	28.1	27.2	26.3	25.5
92	32.5	31.6	30.7	29.8	28.9	28.0	27.2	26.3	25.5
93	32.5	31.6	30.7	29.8	28.9	28.0	27.2	26.3	25.5
94	32.5	31.6	30.7	29.8	28.9	28.0	27.1	26.3	25.4
95	32.5	31.5	30.6	29.8	28.9	28.0	27.1	26.3	25.4
96	32.4	31.5	30.6	29.7	28.9	28.0	27.1	26.3	25.4
97	32.4	31.5	30.6	29.7	28.9	28.0	27.1	26.3	25.4
98	32.4	31.5	30.6	29.7	28.8	28.0	27.1	26.2	25.4
99	32.4	31.5	30.6	29.7	28.8	28.0	27.1	26.2	25.4
100	32.4	31.5	30.6	29.7	28.8	28.0	27.1	26.2	25.4
101	32.4	31.5	30.6	29.7	28.8	28.0	27.1	26.2	25.4
102	32.4	31.5	30.6	29.7	28.8	28.0	27.1	26.2	25.4
103	32.4	31.5	30.6	29.7	28.8	27.9	27.1	26.2	25.4
104	32.4	31.5	30.6	29.7	28.8	27.9	27.1	26.2	25.4

Reg. §1.401(a)(9)-9(d)

Ages	54	55	56	57	58	59	60	61	62
105	32.4	31.5	30.6	29.7	28.8	27.9	27.1	26.2	25.4
106	32.4	31.5	30.6	29.7	28.8	27.9	27.1	26.2	25.4
107	32.4	31.5	30.6	29.7	28.8	27.9	27.1	26.2	25.4
108	32.4	31.5	30.6	29.7	28.8	27.9	27.1	26.2	25.4
109	32.4	31.5	30.6	29.7	28.8	27.9	27.1	26.2	25.4
110	32.4	31.5	30.6	29.7	28.8	27.9	27.1	26.2	25.4
111	32.4	31.5	30.6	29.7	28.8	27.9	27.1	26.2	25.4
112	32.4	31.5	30.6	29.7	28.8	27.9	27.1	26.2	25.4
113	32.4	31.5	30.6	29.7	28.8	27.9	27.1	26.2	25.4
114	32.4	31.5	30.6	29.7	28.8	27.9	27.1	26.2	25.4
115	32.4	31.5	30.6	29.7	28.8	27.9	27.1	26.2	25.4
116	32.4	31.5	30.6	29.7	28.8	27.9	27.1	26.2	25.3
117	32.4	31.5	30.6	29.7	28.8	27.9	27.1	26.2	25.3
118	32.4	31.5	30.6	29.7	28.8	27.9	27.1	26.2	25.3
119	32.4	31.5	30.6	29.7	28.8	27.9	27.1	26.2	25.3
120+	32.4	31.5	30.6	29.7	28.8	27.9	27.1	26.2	25.3

Ages	63	64	65	66	67	68	69	70	71
0	84.6	84.6	84.6	84.6	84.6	84.6	84.6	84.6	84.6
1	83.8	83.8	83.8	83.7	83.7	83.7	83.7	83.7	83.7
2	82.8	82.8	82.8	82.8	82.8	82.8	82.8	82.8	82.8
3	81.8	81.8	81.8	81.8	81.8	81.8	81.8	81.8	81.8
4	80.8	80.8	80.8	80.8	80.8	80.8	80.8	80.8	80.8
5	79.9	79.9	79.8	79.8	79.8	79.8	79.8	79.8	79.8
6	78.9	78.9	78.9	78.9	78.8	78.8	78.8	78.8	78.8
7	77.9	77.9	77.9	77.9	77.9	77.9	77.9	77.8	77.8
8	76.9	76.9	76.9	76.9	76.9	76.9	76.9	76.9	76.9
9	75.9	75.9	75.9	75.9	75.9	75.9	75.9	75.9	75.9
10	75.0	74.9	74.9	74.9	74.9	74.9	74.9	74.9	74.9
11	74.0	74.0	73.9	73.9	73.9	73.9	73.9	73.9	73.9
12	73.0	73.0	73.0	73.0	72.9	72.9	72.9	72.9	72.9
13	72.0	72.0	72.0	72.0	72.0	72.0	71.9	71.9	71.9
14	71.0	71.0	71.0	71.0	71.0	71.0	71.0	71.0	70.9
15	70.1	70.0	70.0	70.0	70.0	70.0	70.0	70.0	70.0
16	69.1	69.1	69.1	69.0	69.0	69.0	69.0	69.0	69.0
17	68.1	68.1	68.1	68.1	68.1	68.0	68.0	68.0	68.0
18	67.1	67.1	67.1	67.1	67.1	67.1	67.1	67.0	67.0
19	66.2	66.2	66.1	66.1	66.1	66.1	66.1	66.1	66.1
20	65.2	65.2	65.2	65.2	65.1	65.1	65.1	65.1	65.1
21	64.2	64.2	64.2	64.2	64.2	64.2	64.1	64.1	64.1
22	63.3	63.3	63.2	63.2	63.2	63.2	63.2	63.2	63.1
23	62.3	62.3	62.3	62.2	62.2	62.2	62.2	62.2	62.2
24	61.4	61.3	61.3	61.3	61.3	61.3	61.2	61.2	61.2
25	60.4	60.4	60.3	60.3	60.3	60.3	60.3	60.3	60.2
26	59.4	59.4	59.4	59.4	59.3	59.3	59.3	59.3	59.3
27	58.5	58.5	58.4	58.4	58.4	58.4	58.4	58.3	58.3
28	57.5	57.5	57.5	57.5	57.4	57.4	57.4	57.4	57.4
29	56.6	56.6	56.5	56.5	56.5	56.5	56.4	56.4	56.4
30	55.7	55.6	55.6	55.6	55.5	55.5	55.5	55.5	55.5
31	54.7	54.7	54.7	54.6	54.6	54.6	54.5	54.5	54.5
32	53.8	53.8	53.7	53.7	53.7	53.6	53.6	53.6	53.6
33	52.9	52.8	52.8	52.7	52.7	52.7	52.7	52.6	52.6
34	51.9	51.9	51.9	51.8	51.8	51.7	51.7	51.7	51.7
35	51.0	51.0	50.9	50.9	50.8	50.8	50.8	50.7	50.7
36	50.1	50.0	50.0	50.0	49.9	49.9	49.8	49.8	49.8
37	49.2	49.1	49.1	49.0	49.0	48.9	48.9	48.9	48.8
38	48.3	48.2	48.2	48.1	48.0	48.0	48.0	47.9	47.9
39	47.4	47.3	47.2	47.2	47.1	47.1	47.0	47.0	47.0
40	46.5	46.4	46.3	46.3	46.2	46.2	46.1	46.1	46.0
41	45.6	45.5	45.4	45.4	45.3	45.2	45.2	45.1	45.1
42	44.7	44.6	44.5	44.5	44.4	44.3	44.3	44.2	44.2

Ages	63	64	65	66	67	68	69	70	71
43	43.8	43.7	43.6	43.6	43.5	43.4	43.3	43.3	43.2
44	43.0	42.9	42.8	42.7	42.6	42.5	42.4	42.4	42.3
45	42.1	42.0	41.9	41.8	41.7	41.6	41.5	41.5	41.4
46	41.3	41.1	41.0	40.9	40.8	40.7	40.6	40.6	40.5
47	40.4	40.3	40.2	40.0	39.9	39.8	39.8	39.7	39.6
48	39.6	39.5	39.3	39.2	39.1	39.0	38.9	38.8	38.7
49	38.8	38.6	38.5	38.4	38.2	38.1	38.0	37.9	37.8
50	38.0	37.8	37.7	37.5	37.4	37.3	37.1	37.0	36.9
51	37.2	37.0	36.9	36.7	36.6	36.4	36.3	36.2	36.1
52	36.5	36.3	36.1	35.9	35.7	35.6	35.5	35.3	35.2
53	35.8	35.5	35.3	35.1	35.0	34.8	34.6	34.5	34.4
54	35.0	34.8	34.6	34.4	34.2	34.0	33.8	33.7	33.6
55	34.4	34.1	33.8	33.6	33.4	33.2	33.1	32.9	32.7
56	33.7	33.4	33.1	32.9	32.7	32.5	32.3	32.1	32.0
57	33.0	32.7	32.5	32.2	32.0	31.7	31.5	31.3	31.2
58	32.4	32.1	31.8	31.5	31.3	31.0	30.8	30.6	30.4
59	31.8	31.5	31.2	30.9	30.6	30.3	30.1	29.9	29.7
60	31.3	30.9	30.5	30.2	29.9	29.6	29.4	29.1	28.9
61	30.7	30.3	30.0	29.6	29.3	29.0	28.7	28.5	28.2
62	30.2	29.8	29.4	29.0	28.7	28.4	28.1	27.8	27.5
63	29.8	29.3	28.9	28.5	28.1	27.8	27.4	27.1	26.9
64	29.3	28.8	28.4	28.0	27.6	27.2	26.8	26.5	26.2
65	28.9	28.4	27.9	27.4	27.0	26.6	26.3	25.9	25.6
66	28.5	28.0	27.4	27.0	26.5	26.1	25.7	25.4	25.0
67	28.1	27.6	27.0	26.5	26.1	25.6	25.2	24.8	24.4
68	27.8	27.2	26.6	26.1	25.6	25.1	24.7	24.3	23.9
69	27.4	26.8	26.3	25.7	25.2	24.7	24.2	23.8	23.4
70	27.1	26.5	25.9	25.4	24.8	24.3	23.8	23.3	22.9
71	26.9	26.2	25.6	25.0	24.4	23.9	23.4	22.9	22.4
72	26.6	26.0	25.3	24.7	24.1	23.5	23.0	22.5	22.0
73	26.4	25.7	25.0	24.4	23.8	23.2	22.6	22.1	21.6
74	26.2	25.5	24.8	24.1	23.5	22.9	22.3	21.7	21.2
75	26.0	25.3	24.6	23.9	23.2	22.6	22.0	21.4	20.8
76	25.8	25.1	24.4	23.7	23.0	22.4	21.7	21.1	20.5
77	25.7	24.9	24.2	23.5	22.8	22.1	21.5	20.8	20.2
78	25.5	24.8	24.0	23.3	22.6	21.9	21.2	20.6	20.0
79	25.4	24.6	23.9	23.2	22.4	21.7	21.0	20.4	19.7
80	25.3	24.5	23.8	23.0	22.3	21.6	20.9	20.2	19.5
81	25.2	24.4	23.6	22.9	22.1	21.4	20.7	20.0	19.3
82	25.1	24.3	23.5	22.8	22.0	21.3	20.5	19.8	19.1
83	25.0	24.2	23.4	22.7	21.9	21.2	20.4	19.7	19.0
84	25.0	24.2	23.4	22.6	21.8	21.0	20.3	19.6	18.8
85	24.9	24.1	23.3	22.5	21.7	21.0	20.2	19.4	18.7
86	24.8	24.0	23.2	22.4	21.7	20.9	20.1	19.3	18.6
87	24.8	24.0	23.2	22.4	21.6	20.8	20.0	19.3	18.5
88	24.8	23.9	23.1	22.3	21.5	20.7	20.0	19.2	18.4
89	24.7	23.9	23.1	22.3	21.5	20.7	19.9	19.1	18.4
90	24.7	23.9	23.0	22.2	21.4	20.6	19.9	19.1	18.3
91	24.7	23.8	23.0	22.2	21.4	20.6	19.8	19.0	18.3
92	24.6	23.8	23.0	22.2	21.4	20.6	19.8	19.0	18.2
93	24.6	23.8	23.0	22.2	21.3	20.5	19.7	18.9	18.2
94	24.6	23.8	22.9	22.1	21.3	20.5	19.7	18.9	18.1
95	24.6	23.8	22.9	22.1	21.3	20.5	19.7	18.9	18.1
96	24.6	23.7	22.9	22.1	21.3	20.5	19.7	18.9	18.1
97	24.6	23.7	22.9	22.1	21.3	20.5	19.7	18.9	18.1
98	24.6	23.7	22.9	22.1	21.3	20.4	19.6	18.8	18.0
99	24.5	23.7	22.9	22.1	21.2	20.4	19.6	18.8	18.0
100	24.5	23.7	22.9	22.1	21.2	20.4	19.6	18.8	18.0
101	24.5	23.7	22.9	22.0	21.2	20.4	19.6	18.8	18.0
102	24.5	23.7	22.9	22.0	21.2	20.4	19.6	18.8	18.0
103	24.5	23.7	22.9	22.0	21.2	20.4	19.6	18.8	18.0
104	24.5	23.7	22.9	22.0	21.2	20.4	19.6	18.8	18.0

Reg. §1.401(a)(9)-9(d)

Ages	63	64	65	66	67	68	69	70	71
105	24.5	23.7	22.9	22.0	21.2	20.4	19.6	18.8	18.0
106	24.5	23.7	22.9	22.0	21.2	20.4	19.6	18.8	18.0
107	24.5	23.7	22.8	22.0	21.2	20.4	19.6	18.8	18.0
108	24.5	23.7	22.8	22.0	21.2	20.4	19.6	18.8	18.0
109	24.5	23.7	22.8	22.0	21.2	20.4	19.6	18.8	18.0
110	24.5	23.7	22.8	22.0	21.2	20.4	19.6	18.8	18.0
111	24.5	23.7	22.8	22.0	21.2	20.4	19.6	18.8	18.0
112	24.5	23.7	22.8	22.0	21.2	20.4	19.6	18.8	18.0
113	24.5	23.7	22.8	22.0	21.2	20.4	19.6	18.8	18.0
114	24.5	23.7	22.8	22.0	21.2	20.4	19.6	18.8	18.0
115	24.5	23.7	22.8	22.0	21.2	20.4	19.6	18.8	18.0
116	24.5	23.7	22.8	22.0	21.2	20.4	19.6	18.8	18.0
117	24.5	23.7	22.8	22.0	21.2	20.4	19.6	18.7	17.9
118	24.5	23.7	22.8	22.0	21.2	20.4	19.6	18.7	17.9
119	24.5	23.6	22.8	22.0	21.2	20.4	19.5	18.7	17.9
120+	24.5	23.6	22.8	22.0	21.2	20.4	19.5	18.7	17.9

Ages	72	73	74	75	76	77	78	79	80
0	84.6	84.6	84.6	84.6	84.6	84.6	84.6	84.6	84.6
1	83.7	83.7	83.7	83.7	83.7	83.7	83.7	83.7	83.7
2	82.8	82.7	82.7	82.7	82.7	82.7	82.7	82.7	82.7
3	81.8	81.8	81.8	81.8	81.8	81.8	81.8	81.8	81.8
4	80.8	80.8	80.8	80.8	80.8	80.8	80.8	80.8	80.8
5	79.8	79.8	79.8	79.8	79.8	79.8	79.8	79.8	79.8
6	78.8	78.8	78.8	78.8	78.8	78.8	78.8	78.8	78.8
7	77.8	77.8	77.8	77.8	77.8	77.8	77.8	77.8	77.8
8	76.9	76.8	76.8	76.8	76.8	76.8	76.8	76.8	76.8
9	75.9	75.9	75.9	75.9	75.8	75.8	75.8	75.8	75.8
10	74.9	74.9	74.9	74.9	74.9	74.9	74.9	74.8	74.8
11	73.9	73.9	73.9	73.9	73.9	73.9	73.9	73.9	73.9
12	72.9	72.9	72.9	72.9	72.9	72.9	72.9	72.9	72.9
13	71.9	71.9	71.9	71.9	71.9	71.9	71.9	71.9	71.9
14	70.9	70.9	70.9	70.9	70.9	70.9	70.9	70.9	70.9
15	70.0	70.0	69.9	69.9	69.9	69.9	69.9	69.9	69.9
16	69.0	69.0	69.0	69.0	68.9	68.9	68.9	68.9	68.9
17	68.0	68.0	68.0	68.0	68.0	68.0	68.0	68.0	67.9
18	67.0	67.0	67.0	67.0	67.0	67.0	67.0	67.0	67.0
19	66.1	66.0	66.0	66.0	66.0	66.0	66.0	66.0	66.0
20	65.1	65.1	65.1	65.0	65.0	65.0	65.0	65.0	65.0
21	64.1	64.1	64.1	64.1	64.1	64.1	64.1	64.0	64.0
22	63.1	63.1	63.1	63.1	63.1	63.1	63.1	63.1	63.1
23	62.2	62.1	62.1	62.1	62.1	62.1	62.1	62.1	62.1
24	61.2	61.2	61.2	61.2	61.2	61.1	61.1	61.1	61.1
25	60.2	60.2	60.2	60.2	60.2	60.2	60.2	60.2	60.2
26	59.3	59.3	59.2	59.2	59.2	59.2	59.2	59.2	59.2
27	58.3	58.3	58.3	58.3	58.3	58.2	58.2	58.2	58.2
28	57.3	57.3	57.3	57.3	57.3	57.3	57.3	57.3	57.3
29	56.4	56.4	56.4	56.3	56.3	56.3	56.3	56.3	56.3
30	55.4	55.4	55.4	55.4	55.4	55.4	55.4	55.4	55.3
31	54.5	54.5	54.5	54.4	54.4	54.4	54.4	54.4	54.4
32	53.5	53.5	53.5	53.5	53.5	53.5	53.4	53.4	53.4
33	52.6	52.6	52.5	52.5	52.5	52.5	52.5	52.5	52.5
34	51.6	51.6	51.6	51.6	51.6	51.6	51.5	51.5	51.5
35	50.7	50.7	50.6	50.6	50.6	50.6	50.6	50.6	50.6
36	49.7	49.7	49.7	49.7	49.7	49.6	49.6	49.6	49.6
37	48.8	48.8	48.8	48.7	48.7	48.7	48.7	48.7	48.7
38	47.9	47.8	47.8	47.8	47.8	47.7	47.7	47.7	47.7
39	46.9	46.9	46.9	46.8	46.8	46.8	46.8	46.8	46.7
40	46.0	45.9	45.9	45.9	45.9	45.8	45.8	45.8	45.8
41	45.0	45.0	45.0	44.9	44.9	44.9	44.9	44.9	44.8
42	44.1	44.1	44.0	44.0	44.0	43.9	43.9	43.9	43.9

Ages	72	73	74	75	76	77	78	79	80
43	43.2	43.1	43.1	43.1	43.0	43.0	43.0	43.0	42.9
44	42.3	42.2	42.2	42.1	42.1	42.1	42.0	42.0	42.0
45	41.3	41.3	41.2	41.2	41.2	41.1	41.1	41.1	41.1
46	40.4	40.4	40.3	40.3	40.2	40.2	40.2	40.1	40.1
47	39.5	39.5	39.4	39.4	39.3	39.3	39.2	39.2	39.2
48	38.6	38.6	38.5	38.4	38.4	38.4	38.3	38.3	38.2
49	37.7	37.7	37.6	37.5	37.5	37.4	37.4	37.4	37.3
50	36.9	36.8	36.7	36.6	36.6	36.5	36.5	36.4	36.4
51	36.0	35.9	35.8	35.7	35.7	35.6	35.6	35.5	35.5
52	35.1	35.0	34.9	34.9	34.8	34.7	34.7	34.6	34.6
53	34.3	34.2	34.1	34.0	33.9	33.9	33.8	33.7	33.7
54	33.4	33.3	33.2	33.1	33.1	33.0	32.9	32.9	32.8
55	32.6	32.5	32.4	32.3	32.2	32.1	32.0	32.0	31.9
56	31.8	31.7	31.6	31.5	31.4	31.3	31.2	31.1	31.1
57	31.0	30.9	30.7	30.6	30.5	30.4	30.3	30.3	30.2
58	30.2	30.1	29.9	29.8	29.7	29.6	29.5	29.4	29.3
59	29.5	29.3	29.2	29.0	28.9	28.8	28.7	28.6	28.5
60	28.7	28.6	28.4	28.2	28.1	28.0	27.9	27.8	27.7
61	28.0	27.8	27.6	27.5	27.3	27.2	27.1	27.0	26.9
62	27.3	27.1	26.9	26.7	26.6	26.4	26.3	26.2	26.1
63	26.6	26.4	26.2	26.0	25.8	25.7	25.5	25.4	25.3
64	26.0	25.7	25.5	25.3	25.1	24.9	24.8	24.6	24.5
65	25.3	25.0	24.8	24.6	24.4	24.2	24.0	23.9	23.8
66	24.7	24.4	24.1	23.9	23.7	23.5	23.3	23.2	23.0
67	24.1	23.8	23.5	23.2	23.0	22.8	22.6	22.4	22.3
68	23.5	23.2	22.9	22.6	22.4	22.1	21.9	21.7	21.6
69	23.0	22.6	22.3	22.0	21.7	21.5	21.2	21.0	20.9
70	22.5	22.1	21.7	21.4	21.1	20.8	20.6	20.4	20.2
71	22.0	21.6	21.2	20.8	20.5	20.2	20.0	19.7	19.5
72	21.5	21.1	20.7	20.3	20.0	19.6	19.4	19.1	18.9
73	21.1	20.6	20.2	19.8	19.4	19.1	18.8	18.5	18.2
74	20.7	20.2	19.7	19.3	18.9	18.6	18.2	17.9	17.6
75	20.3	19.8	19.3	18.9	18.5	18.1	17.7	17.4	17.1
76	20.0	19.4	18.9	18.5	18.0	17.6	17.2	16.9	16.5
77	19.6	19.1	18.6	18.1	17.6	17.2	16.8	16.4	16.0
78	19.4	18.8	18.2	17.7	17.2	16.8	16.3	15.9	15.6
79	19.1	18.5	17.9	17.4	16.9	16.4	15.9	15.5	15.1
80	18.9	18.2	17.6	17.1	16.5	16.0	15.6	15.1	14.7
81	18.6	18.0	17.4	16.8	16.2	15.7	15.2	14.7	14.3
82	18.4	17.8	17.2	16.6	16.0	15.4	14.9	14.4	14.0
83	18.3	17.6	17.0	16.3	15.7	15.2	14.6	14.1	13.6
84	18.1	17.4	16.8	16.1	15.5	14.9	14.4	13.8	13.3
85	18.0	17.3	16.6	16.0	15.3	14.7	14.1	13.6	13.1
86	17.9	17.2	16.5	15.8	15.2	14.5	13.9	13.4	12.8
87	17.8	17.1	16.4	15.7	15.0	14.4	13.8	13.2	12.6
88	17.7	17.0	16.2	15.6	14.9	14.2	13.6	13.0	12.4
89	17.6	16.9	16.2	15.4	14.8	14.1	13.5	12.9	12.3
90	17.5	16.8	16.1	15.4	14.7	14.0	13.4	12.7	12.1
91	17.5	16.7	16.0	15.3	14.6	13.9	13.2	12.6	12.0
92	17.4	16.7	15.9	15.2	14.5	13.8	13.2	12.5	11.9
93	17.4	16.6	15.9	15.2	14.4	13.7	13.1	12.4	11.8
94	17.4	16.6	15.8	15.1	14.4	13.7	13.0	12.4	11.7
95	17.3	16.6	15.8	15.1	14.3	13.6	12.9	12.3	11.6
96	17.3	16.5	15.8	15.0	14.3	13.6	12.9	12.2	11.6
97	17.3	16.5	15.7	15.0	14.3	13.5	12.9	12.2	11.5
98	17.3	16.5	15.7	15.0	14.2	13.5	12.8	12.1	11.5
99	17.2	16.5	15.7	14.9	14.2	13.5	12.8	12.1	11.4
100	17.2	16.4	15.7	14.9	14.2	13.5	12.8	12.1	11.4
101	17.2	16.4	15.7	14.9	14.2	13.4	12.7	12.0	11.4
102	17.2	16.4	15.7	14.9	14.2	13.4	12.7	12.0	11.4
103	17.2	16.4	15.6	14.9	14.1	13.4	12.7	12.0	11.3
104	17.2	16.4	15.6	14.9	14.1	13.4	12.7	12.0	11.3

Reg. §1.401(a)(9)-9(d)

Ages	72	73	74	75	76	77	78	79	80
105	17.2	16.4	15.6	14.9	14.1	13.4	12.7	12.0	11.3
106	17.2	16.4	15.6	14.9	14.1	13.4	12.7	12.0	11.3
107	17.2	16.4	15.6	14.9	14.1	13.4	12.7	12.0	11.3
108	17.2	16.4	15.6	14.9	14.1	13.4	12.7	12.0	11.3
109	17.2	16.4	15.6	14.9	14.1	13.4	12.7	12.0	11.3
110	17.2	16.4	15.6	14.9	14.1	13.4	12.7	12.0	11.3
111	17.2	16.4	15.6	14.9	14.1	13.4	12.7	12.0	11.3
112	17.2	16.4	15.6	14.9	14.1	13.4	12.7	12.0	11.3
113	17.2	16.4	15.6	14.9	14.1	13.4	12.7	12.0	11.3
114	17.2	16.4	15.6	14.8	14.1	13.4	12.6	12.0	11.3
115	17.2	16.4	15.6	14.8	14.1	13.4	12.6	11.9	11.3
116	17.2	16.4	15.6	14.8	14.1	13.3	12.6	11.9	11.3
117	17.1	16.4	15.6	14.8	14.1	13.3	12.6	11.9	11.2
118	17.1	16.4	15.6	14.8	14.1	13.3	12.6	11.9	11.2
119	17.1	16.3	15.6	14.8	14.0	13.3	12.6	11.9	11.2
120+	17.1	16.3	15.6	14.8	14.0	13.3	12.6	11.9	11.2

Ages	81	82	83	84	85	86	87	88	89
0	84.6	84.6	84.6	84.6	84.6	84.5	84.5	84.5	84.5
1	83.7	83.7	83.7	83.7	83.7	83.7	83.7	83.7	83.7
2	82.7	82.7	82.7	82.7	82.7	82.7	82.7	82.7	82.7
3	81.8	81.7	81.7	81.7	81.7	81.7	81.7	81.7	81.7
4	80.8	80.8	80.8	80.8	80.8	80.8	80.8	80.8	80.8
5	79.8	79.8	79.8	79.8	79.8	79.8	79.8	79.8	79.8
6	78.8	78.8	78.8	78.8	78.8	78.8	78.8	78.8	78.8
7	77.8	77.8	77.8	77.8	77.8	77.8	77.8	77.8	77.8
8	76.8	76.8	76.8	76.8	76.8	76.8	76.8	76.8	76.8
9	75.8	75.8	75.8	75.8	75.8	75.8	75.8	75.8	75.8
10	74.8	74.8	74.8	74.8	74.8	74.8	74.8	74.8	74.8
11	73.9	73.9	73.9	73.8	73.8	73.8	73.8	73.8	73.8
12	72.9	72.9	72.9	72.9	72.9	72.9	72.9	72.9	72.9
13	71.9	71.9	71.9	71.9	71.9	71.9	71.9	71.9	71.9
14	70.9	70.9	70.9	70.9	70.9	70.9	70.9	70.9	70.9
15	69.9	69.9	69.9	69.9	69.9	69.9	69.9	69.9	69.9
16	68.9	68.9	68.9	68.9	68.9	68.9	68.9	68.9	68.9
17	67.9	67.9	67.9	67.9	67.9	67.9	67.9	67.9	67.9
18	67.0	67.0	67.0	67.0	67.0	67.0	66.9	66.9	66.9
19	66.0	66.0	66.0	66.0	66.0	66.0	66.0	66.0	66.0
20	65.0	65.0	65.0	65.0	65.0	65.0	65.0	65.0	65.0
21	64.0	64.0	64.0	64.0	64.0	64.0	64.0	64.0	64.0
22	63.1	63.1	63.0	63.0	63.0	63.0	63.0	63.0	63.0
23	62.1	62.1	62.1	62.1	62.1	62.1	62.1	62.1	62.1
24	61.1	61.1	61.1	61.1	61.1	61.1	61.1	61.1	61.1
25	60.1	60.1	60.1	60.1	60.1	60.1	60.1	60.1	60.1
26	59.2	59.2	59.2	59.2	59.2	59.2	59.1	59.1	59.1
27	58.2	58.2	58.2	58.2	58.2	58.2	58.2	58.2	58.2
28	57.3	57.2	57.2	57.2	57.2	57.2	57.2	57.2	57.2
29	56.3	56.3	56.3	56.3	56.3	56.3	56.3	56.3	56.3
30	55.3	55.3	55.3	55.3	55.3	55.3	55.3	55.3	55.3
31	54.4	54.4	54.4	54.4	54.4	54.3	54.3	54.3	54.3
32	53.4	53.4	53.4	53.4	53.4	53.4	53.4	53.4	53.4
33	52.5	52.5	52.5	52.4	52.4	52.4	52.4	52.4	52.4
34	51.5	51.5	51.5	51.5	51.5	51.5	51.5	51.5	51.5
35	50.6	50.5	50.5	50.5	50.5	50.5	50.5	50.5	50.5
36	49.6	49.6	49.6	49.6	49.6	49.6	49.6	49.6	49.6
37	48.6	48.6	48.6	48.6	48.6	48.6	48.6	48.6	48.6
38	47.7	47.7	47.7	47.7	47.7	47.6	47.6	47.6	47.6
39	46.7	46.7	46.7	46.7	46.7	46.7	46.7	46.7	46.7
40	45.8	45.8	45.8	45.7	45.7	45.7	45.7	45.7	45.7
41	44.8	44.8	44.8	44.8	44.8	44.8	44.8	44.8	44.8
42	43.9	43.9	43.8	43.8	43.8	43.8	43.8	43.8	43.8

Ages	81	82	83	84	85	86	87	88	89
43	42.9	42.9	42.9	42.9	42.9	42.9	42.9	42.8	42.8
44	42.0	42.0	41.9	41.9	41.9	41.9	41.9	41.9	41.9
45	41.0	41.0	41.0	41.0	41.0	41.0	40.9	40.9	40.9
46	40.1	40.1	40.0	40.0	40.0	40.0	40.0	40.0	40.0
47	39.1	39.1	39.1	39.1	39.1	39.1	39.0	39.0	39.0
48	38.2	38.2	38.2	38.1	38.1	38.1	38.1	38.1	38.1
49	37.3	37.3	37.2	37.2	37.2	37.2	37.2	37.1	37.1
50	36.4	36.3	36.3	36.3	36.3	36.2	36.2	36.2	36.2
51	35.4	35.4	35.4	35.4	35.3	35.3	35.3	35.3	35.3
52	34.5	34.5	34.5	34.4	34.4	34.4	34.4	34.4	34.3
53	33.6	33.6	33.6	33.5	33.5	33.5	33.5	33.4	33.4
54	32.7	32.7	32.7	32.6	32.6	32.6	32.6	32.5	32.5
55	31.9	31.8	31.8	31.7	31.7	31.7	31.7	31.6	31.6
56	31.0	30.9	30.9	30.9	30.8	30.8	30.8	30.7	30.7
57	30.1	30.1	30.0	30.0	29.9	29.9	29.9	29.9	29.8
58	29.3	29.2	29.2	29.1	29.1	29.0	29.0	29.0	29.0
59	28.4	28.4	28.3	28.3	28.2	28.2	28.2	28.1	28.1
60	27.6	27.5	27.5	27.4	27.4	27.3	27.3	27.3	27.2
61	26.8	26.7	26.7	26.6	26.5	26.5	26.5	26.4	26.4
62	26.0	25.9	25.8	25.8	25.7	25.7	25.6	25.6	25.5
63	25.2	25.1	25.0	25.0	24.9	24.8	24.8	24.8	24.7
64	24.4	24.3	24.2	24.2	24.1	24.0	24.0	23.9	23.9
65	23.6	23.5	23.4	23.4	23.3	23.2	23.2	23.1	23.1
66	22.9	22.8	22.7	22.6	22.5	22.4	22.4	22.3	22.3
67	22.1	22.0	21.9	21.8	21.7	21.7	21.6	21.5	21.5
68	21.4	21.3	21.2	21.0	21.0	20.9	20.8	20.7	20.7
69	20.7	20.5	20.4	20.3	20.2	20.1	20.0	20.0	19.9
70	20.0	19.8	19.7	19.6	19.4	19.3	19.3	19.2	19.1
71	19.3	19.1	19.0	18.8	18.7	18.6	18.5	18.4	18.4
72	18.6	18.4	18.3	18.1	18.0	17.9	17.8	17.7	17.6
73	18.0	17.8	17.6	17.4	17.3	17.2	17.1	17.0	16.9
74	17.4	17.2	17.0	16.8	16.6	16.5	16.4	16.2	16.2
75	16.8	16.6	16.3	16.1	16.0	15.8	15.7	15.6	15.4
76	16.2	16.0	15.7	15.5	15.3	15.2	15.0	14.9	14.8
77	15.7	15.4	15.2	14.9	14.7	14.5	14.4	14.2	14.1
78	15.2	14.9	14.6	14.4	14.1	13.9	13.8	13.6	13.5
79	14.7	14.4	14.1	13.8	13.6	13.4	13.2	13.0	12.9
80	14.3	14.0	13.6	13.3	13.1	12.8	12.6	12.4	12.3
81	13.9	13.5	13.2	12.9	12.6	12.3	12.1	11.9	11.7
82	13.5	13.1	12.8	12.4	12.1	11.9	11.6	11.4	11.2
83	13.2	12.8	12.4	12.0	11.7	11.4	11.2	10.9	10.7
84	12.9	12.4	12.0	11.7	11.3	11.0	10.7	10.5	10.3
85	12.6	12.1	11.7	11.3	11.0	10.7	10.4	10.1	9.9
86	12.3	11.9	11.4	11.0	10.7	10.3	10.0	9.7	9.5
87	12.1	11.6	11.2	10.7	10.4	10.0	9.7	9.4	9.1
88	11.9	11.4	10.9	10.5	10.1	9.7	9.4	9.1	8.8
89	11.7	11.2	10.7	10.3	9.9	9.5	9.1	8.8	8.5
90	11.6	11.0	10.5	10.1	9.6	9.2	8.9	8.5	8.2
91	11.4	10.9	10.4	9.9	9.5	9.0	8.7	8.3	8.0
92	11.3	10.8	10.2	9.7	9.3	8.9	8.5	8.1	7.8
93	11.2	10.6	10.1	9.6	9.1	8.7	8.3	7.9	7.6
94	11.1	10.5	10.0	9.5	9.0	8.6	8.1	7.7	7.4
95	11.0	10.5	9.9	9.4	8.9	8.4	8.0	7.6	7.2
96	11.0	10.4	9.8	9.3	8.8	8.3	7.9	7.5	7.1
97	10.9	10.3	9.7	9.2	8.7	8.2	7.8	7.4	7.0
98	10.9	10.3	9.7	9.1	8.6	8.1	7.7	7.3	6.9
99	10.8	10.2	9.6	9.1	8.6	8.1	7.6	7.2	6.8
100	10.8	10.2	9.6	9.0	8.5	8.0	7.6	7.1	6.7
101	10.7	10.1	9.5	9.0	8.5	8.0	7.5	7.1	6.7
102	10.7	10.1	9.5	8.9	8.4	7.9	7.4	7.0	6.6
103	10.7	10.1	9.5	8.9	8.4	7.9	7.4	7.0	6.6
104	10.7	10.1	9.5	8.9	8.4	7.9	7.4	6.9	6.5

Reg. §1.401(a)(9)-9(d)

Ages	81	82	83	84	85	86	87	88	89
105	10.7	10.0	9.5	8.9	8.3	7.8	7.4	6.9	6.5
106	10.7	10.0	9.4	8.9	8.3	7.8	7.4	6.9	6.5
107	10.7	10.0	9.4	8.9	8.3	7.8	7.3	6.9	6.5
108	10.7	10.0	9.4	8.9	8.3	7.8	7.3	6.9	6.5
109	10.7	10.0	9.4	8.9	8.3	7.8	7.3	6.9	6.5
110	10.7	10.0	9.4	8.9	8.3	7.8	7.3	6.9	6.5
111	10.6	10.0	9.4	8.8	8.3	7.8	7.3	6.9	6.4
112	10.6	10.0	9.4	8.8	8.3	7.8	7.3	6.9	6.4
113	10.6	10.0	9.4	8.8	8.3	7.8	7.3	6.8	6.4
114	10.6	10.0	9.4	8.8	8.3	7.8	7.3	6.8	6.4
115	10.6	10.0	9.4	8.8	8.3	7.7	7.3	6.8	6.4
116	10.6	10.0	9.4	8.8	8.2	7.7	7.2	6.8	6.3
117	10.6	9.9	9.3	8.7	8.2	7.7	7.2	6.7	6.3
118	10.5	9.9	9.3	8.7	8.2	7.6	7.1	6.7	6.2
119	10.5	9.9	9.3	8.7	8.1	7.6	7.1	6.6	6.2
120+	10.5	9.9	9.2	8.6	8.1	7.5	7.0	6.6	6.1

Ages	90	91	92	93	94	95	96	97	98
0	84.5	84.5	84.5	84.5	84.5	84.5	84.5	84.5	84.5
1	83.7	83.7	83.7	83.7	83.7	83.7	83.7	83.7	83.7
2	82.7	82.7	82.7	82.7	82.7	82.7	82.7	82.7	82.7
3	81.7	81.7	81.7	81.7	81.7	81.7	81.7	81.7	81.7
4	80.8	80.8	80.8	80.8	80.8	80.8	80.8	80.8	80.8
5	79.8	79.8	79.8	79.8	79.8	79.8	79.8	79.8	79.8
6	78.8	78.8	78.8	78.8	78.8	78.8	78.8	78.8	78.8
7	77.8	77.8	77.8	77.8	77.8	77.8	77.8	77.8	77.8
8	76.8	76.8	76.8	76.8	76.8	76.8	76.8	76.8	76.8
9	75.8	75.8	75.8	75.8	75.8	75.8	75.8	75.8	75.8
10	74.8	74.8	74.8	74.8	74.8	74.8	74.8	74.8	74.8
11	73.8	73.8	73.8	73.8	73.8	73.8	73.8	73.8	73.8
12	72.9	72.9	72.9	72.8	72.8	72.8	72.8	72.8	72.8
13	71.9	71.9	71.9	71.9	71.9	71.9	71.9	71.9	71.9
14	70.9	70.9	70.9	70.9	70.9	70.9	70.9	70.9	70.9
15	69.9	69.9	69.9	69.9	69.9	69.9	69.9	69.9	69.9
16	68.9	68.9	68.9	68.9	68.9	68.9	68.9	68.9	68.9
17	67.9	67.9	67.9	67.9	67.9	67.9	67.9	67.9	67.9
18	66.9	66.9	66.9	66.9	66.9	66.9	66.9	66.9	66.9
19	66.0	66.0	66.0	66.0	66.0	66.0	66.0	66.0	66.0
20	65.0	65.0	65.0	65.0	65.0	65.0	65.0	65.0	65.0
21	64.0	64.0	64.0	64.0	64.0	64.0	64.0	64.0	64.0
22	63.0	63.0	63.0	63.0	63.0	63.0	63.0	63.0	63.0
23	62.1	62.1	62.0	62.0	62.0	62.0	62.0	62.0	62.0
24	61.1	61.1	61.1	61.1	61.1	61.1	61.1	61.1	61.1
25	60.1	60.1	60.1	60.1	60.1	60.1	60.1	60.1	60.1
26	59.1	59.1	59.1	59.1	59.1	59.1	59.1	59.1	59.1
27	58.2	58.2	58.2	58.2	58.2	58.2	58.2	58.2	58.2
28	57.2	57.2	57.2	57.2	57.2	57.2	57.2	57.2	57.2
29	56.3	56.3	56.2	56.2	56.2	56.2	56.2	56.2	56.2
30	55.3	55.3	55.3	55.3	55.3	55.3	55.3	55.3	55.3
31	54.3	54.3	54.3	54.3	54.3	54.3	54.3	54.3	54.3
32	53.4	53.4	53.4	53.4	53.4	53.4	53.4	53.4	53.4
33	52.4	52.4	52.4	52.4	52.4	52.4	52.4	52.4	52.4
34	51.5	51.5	51.5	51.5	51.5	51.5	51.5	51.5	51.5
35	50.5	50.5	50.5	50.5	50.5	50.5	50.5	50.5	50.5
36	49.5	49.5	49.5	49.5	49.5	49.5	49.5	49.5	49.5
37	48.6	48.6	48.6	48.6	48.6	48.6	48.6	48.6	48.6
38	47.6	47.6	47.6	47.6	47.6	47.6	47.6	47.6	47.6
39	46.7	46.7	46.7	46.7	46.7	46.7	46.7	46.7	46.7
40	45.7	45.7	45.7	45.7	45.7	45.7	45.7	45.7	45.7
41	44.8	44.7	44.7	44.7	44.7	44.7	44.7	44.7	44.7
42	43.8	43.8	43.8	43.8	43.8	43.8	43.8	43.8	43.8

Ages	90	91	92	93	94	95	96	97	98
43	42.8	42.8	42.8	42.8	42.8	42.8	42.8	42.8	42.8
44	41.9	41.9	41.9	41.9	41.9	41.9	41.9	41.9	41.9
45	40.9	40.9	40.9	40.9	40.9	40.9	40.9	40.9	40.9
46	40.0	40.0	40.0	40.0	40.0	40.0	39.9	39.9	39.9
47	39.0	39.0	39.0	39.0	39.0	39.0	39.0	39.0	39.0
48	38.1	38.1	38.1	38.1	38.1	38.0	38.0	38.0	38.0
49	37.1	37.1	37.1	37.1	37.1	37.1	37.1	37.1	37.1
50	36.2	36.2	36.2	36.2	36.2	36.2	36.2	36.2	36.1
51	35.3	35.2	35.2	35.2	35.2	35.2	35.2	35.2	35.2
52	34.3	34.3	34.3	34.3	34.3	34.3	34.3	34.3	34.3
53	33.4	33.4	33.4	33.4	33.4	33.4	33.4	33.4	33.4
54	32.5	32.5	32.5	32.5	32.5	32.5	32.4	32.4	32.4
55	31.6	31.6	31.6	31.6	31.6	31.5	31.5	31.5	31.5
56	30.7	30.7	30.7	30.7	30.7	30.6	30.6	30.6	30.6
57	29.8	29.8	29.8	29.8	29.8	29.8	29.7	29.7	29.7
58	28.9	28.9	28.9	28.9	28.9	28.9	28.9	28.9	28.8
59	28.1	28.1	28.0	28.0	28.0	28.0	28.0	28.0	28.0
60	27.2	27.2	27.2	27.2	27.1	27.1	27.1	27.1	27.1
61	26.4	26.3	26.3	26.3	26.3	26.3	26.3	26.3	26.2
62	25.5	25.5	25.5	25.5	25.4	25.4	25.4	25.4	25.4
63	24.7	24.7	24.6	24.6	24.6	24.6	24.6	24.6	24.6
64	23.9	23.8	23.8	23.8	23.8	23.8	23.7	23.7	23.7
65	23.0	23.0	23.0	23.0	22.9	22.9	22.9	22.9	22.9
66	22.2	22.2	22.2	22.2	22.1	22.1	22.1	22.1	22.1
67	21.4	21.4	21.4	21.3	21.3	21.3	21.3	21.3	21.3
68	20.6	20.6	20.6	20.5	20.5	20.5	20.5	20.5	20.4
69	19.9	19.8	19.8	19.7	19.7	19.7	19.7	19.7	19.6
70	19.1	19.0	19.0	18.9	18.9	18.9	18.9	18.9	18.8
71	18.3	18.3	18.2	18.2	18.1	18.1	18.1	18.1	18.0
72	17.5	17.5	17.4	17.4	17.4	17.3	17.3	17.3	17.3
73	16.8	16.7	16.7	16.6	16.6	16.6	16.5	16.5	16.5
74	16.1	16.0	15.9	15.9	15.8	15.8	15.8	15.7	15.7
75	15.4	15.3	15.2	15.2	15.1	15.1	15.0	15.0	15.0
76	14.7	14.6	14.5	14.4	14.4	14.3	14.3	14.3	14.2
77	14.0	13.9	13.8	13.7	13.7	13.6	13.6	13.5	13.5
78	13.4	13.2	13.2	13.1	13.0	12.9	12.9	12.9	12.8
79	12.7	12.6	12.5	12.4	12.4	12.3	12.2	12.2	12.1
80	12.1	12.0	11.9	11.8	11.7	11.6	11.6	11.5	11.5
81	11.6	11.4	11.3	11.2	11.1	11.0	11.0	10.9	10.9
82	11.0	10.9	10.8	10.6	10.5	10.5	10.4	10.3	10.3
83	10.5	10.4	10.2	10.1	10.0	9.9	9.8	9.7	9.7
84	10.1	9.9	9.7	9.6	9.5	9.4	9.3	9.2	9.1
85	9.6	9.5	9.3	9.1	9.0	8.9	8.8	8.7	8.6
86	9.2	9.0	8.9	8.7	8.6	8.4	8.3	8.2	8.1
87	8.9	8.7	8.5	8.3	8.1	8.0	7.9	7.8	7.7
88	8.5	8.3	8.1	7.9	7.7	7.6	7.5	7.4	7.3
89	8.2	8.0	7.8	7.6	7.4	7.2	7.1	7.0	6.9
90	7.9	7.7	7.5	7.3	7.1	6.9	6.8	6.6	6.5
91	7.7	7.4	7.2	7.0	6.8	6.6	6.5	6.3	6.2
92	7.5	7.2	6.9	6.7	6.5	6.3	6.2	6.0	5.9
93	7.3	7.0	6.7	6.5	6.3	6.1	5.9	5.8	5.6
94	7.1	6.8	6.5	6.3	6.0	5.8	5.7	5.5	5.4
95	6.9	6.6	6.3	6.1	5.8	5.6	5.5	5.3	5.1
96	6.8	6.5	6.2	5.9	5.7	5.5	5.3	5.1	4.9
97	6.6	6.3	6.0	5.8	5.5	5.3	5.1	4.9	4.8
98	6.5	6.2	5.9	5.6	5.4	5.1	4.9	4.8	4.6
99	6.4	6.1	5.8	5.5	5.3	5.0	4.8	4.6	4.5
100	6.4	6.0	5.7	5.4	5.1	4.9	4.7	4.5	4.3
101	6.3	5.9	5.6	5.3	5.1	4.8	4.6	4.4	4.2
102	6.2	5.9	5.6	5.3	5.0	4.7	4.5	4.3	4.1
103	6.2	5.8	5.5	5.2	4.9	4.7	4.4	4.2	4.0
104	6.1	5.8	5.5	5.1	4.9	4.6	4.4	4.2	4.0

Ages	90	91	92	93	94	95	96	97	98
105	6.1	5.8	5.4	5.1	4.8	4.6	4.3	4.1	3.9
106	6.1	5.7	5.4	5.1	4.8	4.6	4.3	4.1	3.9
107	6.1	5.7	5.4	5.1	4.8	4.5	4.3	4.1	3.9
108	6.1	5.7	5.4	5.1	4.8	4.5	4.3	4.1	3.9
109	6.1	5.7	5.4	5.1	4.8	4.5	4.3	4.1	3.9
110	6.1	5.7	5.4	5.1	4.8	4.5	4.3	4.1	3.9
111	6.1	5.7	5.4	5.0	4.8	4.5	4.3	4.0	3.9
112	6.0	5.7	5.3	5.0	4.7	4.5	4.2	4.0	3.8
113	6.0	5.7	5.3	5.0	4.7	4.5	4.2	4.0	3.8
114	6.0	5.6	5.3	5.0	4.7	4.4	4.2	4.0	3.8
115	6.0	5.6	5.3	5.0	4.7	4.4	4.2	3.9	3.7
116	5.9	5.6	5.2	4.9	4.6	4.3	4.1	3.9	3.7
117	5.9	5.5	5.2	4.8	4.5	4.3	4.0	3.8	3.6
118	5.8	5.4	5.1	4.8	4.4	4.2	3.9	3.7	3.5
119	5.7	5.4	5.0	4.7	4.3	4.0	3.8	3.5	3.3
120+	5.7	5.3	4.9	4.6	4.2	3.9	3.7	3.4	3.2

Ages	99	100	101	102	103	104	105	106	107
0	84.5	84.5	84.5	84.5	84.5	84.5	84.5	84.5	84.5
1	83.7	83.7	83.7	83.7	83.7	83.7	83.7	83.7	83.7
2	82.7	82.7	82.7	82.7	82.7	82.7	82.7	82.7	82.7
3	81.7	81.7	81.7	81.7	81.7	81.7	81.7	81.7	81.7
4	80.8	80.8	80.8	80.8	80.8	80.8	80.8	80.8	80.8
5	79.8	79.8	79.8	79.8	79.8	79.8	79.8	79.8	79.8
6	78.8	78.8	78.8	78.8	78.8	78.8	78.8	78.8	78.8
7	77.8	77.8	77.8	77.8	77.8	77.8	77.8	77.8	77.8
8	76.8	76.8	76.8	76.8	76.8	76.8	76.8	76.8	76.8
9	75.8	75.8	75.8	75.8	75.8	75.8	75.8	75.8	75.8
10	74.8	74.8	74.8	74.8	74.8	74.8	74.8	74.8	74.8
11	73.8	73.8	73.8	73.8	73.8	73.8	73.8	73.8	73.8
12	72.8	72.8	72.8	72.8	72.8	72.8	72.8	72.8	72.8
13	71.9	71.9	71.9	71.9	71.9	71.9	71.9	71.9	71.9
14	70.9	70.9	70.9	70.9	70.9	70.9	70.9	70.9	70.9
15	69.9	69.9	69.9	69.9	69.9	69.9	69.9	69.9	69.9
16	68.9	68.9	68.9	68.9	68.9	68.9	68.9	68.9	68.9
17	67.9	67.9	67.9	67.9	67.9	67.9	67.9	67.9	67.9
18	66.9	66.9	66.9	66.9	66.9	66.9	66.9	66.9	66.9
19	66.0	66.0	66.0	66.0	66.0	66.0	66.0	66.0	66.0
20	65.0	65.0	65.0	65.0	65.0	65.0	65.0	65.0	65.0
21	64.0	64.0	64.0	64.0	64.0	64.0	64.0	64.0	64.0
22	63.0	63.0	63.0	63.0	63.0	63.0	63.0	63.0	63.0
23	62.0	62.0	62.0	62.0	62.0	62.0	62.0	62.0	62.0
24	61.1	61.1	61.1	61.1	61.1	61.1	61.1	61.1	61.1
25	60.1	60.1	60.1	60.1	60.1	60.1	60.1	60.1	60.1
26	59.1	59.1	59.1	59.1	59.1	59.1	59.1	59.1	59.1
27	58.2	58.2	58.2	58.2	58.2	58.2	58.2	58.2	58.2
28	57.2	57.2	57.2	57.2	57.2	57.2	57.2	57.2	57.2
29	56.2	56.2	56.2	56.2	56.2	56.2	56.2	56.2	56.2
30	55.3	55.3	55.3	55.3	55.3	55.3	55.3	55.3	55.3
31	54.3	54.3	54.3	54.3	54.3	54.3	54.3	54.3	54.3
32	53.4	53.4	53.4	53.4	53.4	53.4	53.4	53.4	53.4
33	52.4	52.4	52.4	52.4	52.4	52.4	52.4	52.4	52.4
34	51.5	51.5	51.4	51.4	51.4	51.4	51.4	51.4	51.4
35	50.5	50.5	50.5	50.5	50.5	50.5	50.5	50.5	50.5
36	49.5	49.5	49.5	49.5	49.5	49.5	49.5	49.5	49.5
37	48.6	48.6	48.6	48.6	48.6	48.6	48.6	48.6	48.6
38	47.6	47.6	47.6	47.6	47.6	47.6	47.6	47.6	47.6
39	46.7	46.7	46.7	46.7	46.7	46.7	46.7	46.7	46.7
40	45.7	45.7	45.7	45.7	45.7	45.7	45.7	45.7	45.7
41	44.7	44.7	44.7	44.7	44.7	44.7	44.7	44.7	44.7
42	43.8	43.8	43.8	43.8	43.8	43.8	43.8	43.8	43.8

Ages	99	100	101	102	103	104	105	106	107
43	42.8	42.8	42.8	42.8	42.8	42.8	42.8	42.8	42.8
44	41.9	41.9	41.9	41.9	41.9	41.9	41.9	41.9	41.9
45	40.9	40.9	40.9	40.9	40.9	40.9	40.9	40.9	40.9
46	39.9	39.9	39.9	39.9	39.9	39.9	39.9	39.9	39.9
47	39.0	39.0	39.0	39.0	39.0	39.0	39.0	39.0	39.0
48	38.0	38.0	38.0	38.0	38.0	38.0	38.0	38.0	38.0
49	37.1	37.1	37.1	37.1	37.1	37.1	37.1	37.1	37.1
50	36.1	36.1	36.1	36.1	36.1	36.1	36.1	36.1	36.1
51	35.2	35.2	35.2	35.2	35.2	35.2	35.2	35.2	35.2
52	34.3	34.3	34.3	34.3	34.3	34.3	34.3	34.3	34.3
53	33.3	33.3	33.3	33.3	33.3	33.3	33.3	33.3	33.3
54	32.4	32.4	32.4	32.4	32.4	32.4	32.4	32.4	32.4
55	31.5	31.5	31.5	31.5	31.5	31.5	31.5	31.5	31.5
56	30.6	30.6	30.6	30.6	30.6	30.6	30.6	30.6	30.6
57	29.7	29.7	29.7	29.7	29.7	29.7	29.7	29.7	29.7
58	28.8	28.8	28.8	28.8	28.8	28.8	28.8	28.8	28.8
59	28.0	28.0	28.0	28.0	27.9	27.9	27.9	27.9	27.9
60	27.1	27.1	27.1	27.1	27.1	27.1	27.1	27.1	27.1
61	26.2	26.2	26.2	26.2	26.2	26.2	26.2	26.2	26.2
62	25.4	25.4	25.4	25.4	25.4	25.4	25.4	25.4	25.4
63	24.5	24.5	24.5	24.5	24.5	24.5	24.5	24.5	24.5
64	23.7	23.7	23.7	23.7	23.7	23.7	23.7	23.7	23.7
65	22.9	22.9	22.9	22.9	22.9	22.9	22.9	22.9	22.8
66	22.1	22.1	22.0	22.0	22.0	22.0	22.0	22.0	22.0
67	21.2	21.2	21.2	21.2	21.2	21.2	21.2	21.2	21.2
68	20.4	20.4	20.4	20.4	20.4	20.4	20.4	20.4	20.4
69	19.6	19.6	19.6	19.6	19.6	19.6	19.6	19.6	19.6
70	18.8	18.8	18.8	18.8	18.8	18.8	18.8	18.8	18.8
71	18.0	18.0	18.0	18.0	18.0	18.0	18.0	18.0	18.0
72	17.2	17.2	17.2	17.2	17.2	17.2	17.2	17.2	17.2
73	16.5	16.4	16.4	16.4	16.4	16.4	16.4	16.4	16.4
74	15.7	15.7	15.7	15.7	15.6	15.6	15.6	15.6	15.6
75	14.9	14.9	14.9	14.9	14.9	14.9	14.9	14.9	14.9
76	14.2	14.2	14.2	14.2	14.1	14.1	14.1	14.1	14.1
77	13.5	13.5	13.4	13.4	13.4	13.4	13.4	13.4	13.4
78	12.8	12.8	12.7	12.7	12.7	12.7	12.7	12.7	12.7
79	12.1	12.1	12.0	12.0	12.0	12.0	12.0	12.0	12.0
80	11.4	11.4	11.4	11.4	11.3	11.3	11.3	11.3	11.3
81	10.8	10.8	10.7	10.7	10.7	10.7	10.7	10.7	10.7
82	10.2	10.2	10.1	10.1	10.1	10.1	10.0	10.0	10.0
83	9.6	9.6	9.5	9.5	9.5	9.5	9.5	9.4	9.4
84	9.1	9.0	9.0	8.9	8.9	8.9	8.9	8.9	8.9
85	8.6	8.5	8.5	8.4	8.4	8.4	8.3	8.3	8.3
86	8.1	8.0	8.0	7.9	7.9	7.9	7.8	7.8	7.8
87	7.6	7.6	7.5	7.4	7.4	7.4	7.4	7.4	7.3
88	7.2	7.1	7.1	7.0	7.0	6.9	6.9	6.9	6.9
89	6.8	6.7	6.7	6.6	6.6	6.5	6.5	6.5	6.5
90	6.4	6.4	6.3	6.2	6.2	6.1	6.1	6.1	6.1
91	6.1	6.0	5.9	5.9	5.8	5.8	5.8	5.7	5.7
92	5.8	5.7	5.6	5.6	5.5	5.5	5.4	5.4	5.4
93	5.5	5.4	5.3	5.3	5.2	5.1	5.1	5.1	5.1
94	5.3	5.1	5.1	5.0	4.9	4.9	4.8	4.8	4.8
95	5.0	4.9	4.8	4.7	4.7	4.6	4.6	4.6	4.5
96	4.8	4.7	4.6	4.5	4.4	4.4	4.3	4.3	4.3
97	4.6	4.5	4.4	4.3	4.2	4.2	4.1	4.1	4.1
98	4.5	4.3	4.2	4.1	4.0	4.0	3.9	3.9	3.9
99	4.3	4.2	4.1	4.0	3.9	3.8	3.8	3.7	3.7
100	4.2	4.0	3.9	3.8	3.7	3.7	3.6	3.6	3.6
101	4.1	3.9	3.8	3.7	3.6	3.5	3.5	3.5	3.4
102	4.0	3.8	3.7	3.6	3.5	3.4	3.4	3.3	3.3
103	3.9	3.7	3.6	3.5	3.4	3.3	3.3	3.2	3.2
104	3.8	3.7	3.5	3.4	3.3	3.2	3.2	3.2	3.1

Reg. §1.401(a)(9)-9(d)

Ages	99	100	101	102	103	104	105	106	107
105	3.8	3.6	3.5	3.4	3.3	3.2	3.1	3.1	3.1
106	3.7	3.6	3.5	3.3	3.2	3.2	3.1	3.1	3.1
107	3.7	3.6	3.4	3.3	3.2	3.1	3.1	3.1	3.0
108	3.7	3.6	3.4	3.3	3.2	3.1	3.1	3.0	3.0
109	3.7	3.5	3.4	3.3	3.2	3.1	3.1	3.0	3.0
110	3.7	3.5	3.4	3.3	3.2	3.1	3.0	3.0	3.0
111	3.7	3.5	3.4	3.3	3.2	3.1	3.0	3.0	3.0
112	3.7	3.5	3.4	3.2	3.1	3.1	3.0	3.0	3.0
113	3.6	3.5	3.3	3.2	3.1	3.0	3.0	3.0	2.9
114	3.6	3.4	3.3	3.2	3.1	3.0	3.0	2.9	2.9
115	3.6	3.4	3.3	3.1	3.0	3.0	2.9	2.9	2.9
116	3.5	3.3	3.2	3.1	3.0	2.9	2.8	2.8	2.8
117	3.4	3.2	3.1	3.0	2.9	2.8	2.7	2.7	2.7
118	3.3	3.1	3.0	2.8	2.7	2.6	2.6	2.5	2.5
119	3.1	2.9	2.8	2.6	2.5	2.4	2.3	2.3	2.3
120+	3.0	2.8	2.6	2.5	2.3	2.2	2.1	2.1	2.1

Ages	108	109	110	111	112	113	114	115	116
0	84.5	84.5	84.5	84.5	84.5	84.5	84.5	84.5	84.5
1	83.7	83.7	83.7	83.7	83.7	83.7	83.7	83.7	83.7
2	82.7	82.7	82.7	82.7	82.7	82.7	82.7	82.7	82.7
3	81.7	81.7	81.7	81.7	81.7	81.7	81.7	81.7	81.7
4	80.8	80.8	80.8	80.8	80.8	80.8	80.8	80.8	80.8
5	79.8	79.8	79.8	79.8	79.8	79.8	79.8	79.8	79.8
6	78.8	78.8	78.8	78.8	78.8	78.8	78.8	78.8	78.8
7	77.8	77.8	77.8	77.8	77.8	77.8	77.8	77.8	77.8
8	76.8	76.8	76.8	76.8	76.8	76.8	76.8	76.8	76.8
9	75.8	75.8	75.8	75.8	75.8	75.8	75.8	75.8	75.8
10	74.8	74.8	74.8	74.8	74.8	74.8	74.8	74.8	74.8
11	73.8	73.8	73.8	73.8	73.8	73.8	73.8	73.8	73.8
12	72.8	72.8	72.8	72.8	72.8	72.8	72.8	72.8	72.8
13	71.9	71.9	71.9	71.9	71.9	71.9	71.9	71.9	71.9
14	70.9	70.9	70.9	70.9	70.9	70.9	70.9	70.9	70.9
15	69.9	69.9	69.9	69.9	69.9	69.9	69.9	69.9	69.9
16	68.9	68.9	68.9	68.9	68.9	68.9	68.9	68.9	68.9
17	67.9	67.9	67.9	67.9	67.9	67.9	67.9	67.9	67.9
18	66.9	66.9	66.9	66.9	66.9	66.9	66.9	66.9	66.9
19	66.0	66.0	66.0	66.0	66.0	66.0	66.0	66.0	66.0
20	65.0	65.0	65.0	65.0	65.0	65.0	65.0	65.0	65.0
21	64.0	64.0	64.0	64.0	64.0	64.0	64.0	64.0	64.0
22	63.0	63.0	63.0	63.0	63.0	63.0	63.0	63.0	63.0
23	62.0	62.0	62.0	62.0	62.0	62.0	62.0	62.0	62.0
24	61.1	61.1	61.1	61.1	61.1	61.1	61.1	61.1	61.1
25	60.1	60.1	60.1	60.1	60.1	60.1	60.1	60.1	60.1
26	59.1	59.1	59.1	59.1	59.1	59.1	59.1	59.1	59.1
27	58.2	58.2	58.2	58.2	58.2	58.2	58.2	58.2	58.2
28	57.2	57.2	57.2	57.2	57.2	57.2	57.2	57.2	57.2
29	56.2	56.2	56.2	56.2	56.2	56.2	56.2	56.2	56.2
30	55.3	55.3	55.3	55.3	55.3	55.3	55.3	55.3	55.3
31	54.3	54.3	54.3	54.3	54.3	54.3	54.3	54.3	54.3
32	53.4	53.4	53.4	53.4	53.4	53.4	53.4	53.4	53.4
33	52.4	52.4	52.4	52.4	52.4	52.4	52.4	52.4	52.4
34	51.4	51.4	51.4	51.4	51.4	51.4	51.4	51.4	51.4
35	50.5	50.5	50.5	50.5	50.5	50.5	50.5	50.5	50.5
36	49.5	49.5	49.5	49.5	49.5	49.5	49.5	49.5	49.5
37	48.6	48.6	48.6	48.6	48.6	48.6	48.6	48.6	48.6
38	47.6	47.6	47.6	47.6	47.6	47.6	47.6	47.6	47.6
39	46.7	46.6	46.6	46.6	46.6	46.6	46.6	46.6	46.6
40	45.7	45.7	45.7	45.7	45.7	45.7	45.7	45.7	45.7
41	44.7	44.7	44.7	44.7	44.7	44.7	44.7	44.7	44.7
42	43.8	43.8	43.8	43.8	43.8	43.8	43.8	43.8	43.8

Ages	108	109	110	111	112	113	114	115	116
43	42.8	42.8	42.8	42.8	42.8	42.8	42.8	42.8	42.8
44	41.9	41.9	41.9	41.9	41.9	41.9	41.9	41.9	41.8
45	40.9	40.9	40.9	40.9	40.9	40.9	40.9	40.9	40.9
46	39.9	39.9	39.9	39.9	39.9	39.9	39.9	39.9	39.9
47	39.0	39.0	39.0	39.0	39.0	39.0	39.0	39.0	39.0
48	38.0	38.0	38.0	38.0	38.0	38.0	38.0	38.0	38.0
49	37.1	37.1	37.1	37.1	37.1	37.1	37.1	37.1	37.1
50	36.1	36.1	36.1	36.1	36.1	36.1	36.1	36.1	36.1
51	35.2	35.2	35.2	35.2	35.2	35.2	35.2	35.2	35.2
52	34.3	34.3	34.3	34.3	34.3	34.3	34.3	34.3	34.3
53	33.3	33.3	33.3	33.3	33.3	33.3	33.3	33.3	33.3
54	32.4	32.4	32.4	32.4	32.4	32.4	32.4	32.4	32.4
55	31.5	31.5	31.5	31.5	31.5	31.5	31.5	31.5	31.5
56	30.6	30.6	30.6	30.6	30.6	30.6	30.6	30.6	30.6
57	29.7	29.7	29.7	29.7	29.7	29.7	29.7	29.7	29.7
58	28.8	28.8	28.8	28.8	28.8	28.8	28.8	28.8	28.8
59	27.9	27.9	27.9	27.9	27.9	27.9	27.9	27.9	27.9
60	27.1	27.1	27.1	27.1	27.1	27.1	27.1	27.1	27.1
61	26.2	26.2	26.2	26.2	26.2	26.2	26.2	26.2	26.2
62	25.4	25.4	25.4	25.4	25.4	25.4	25.4	25.4	25.3
63	24.5	24.5	24.5	24.5	24.5	24.5	24.5	24.5	24.5
64	23.7	23.7	23.7	23.7	23.7	23.7	23.7	23.7	23.7
65	22.8	22.8	22.8	22.8	22.8	22.8	22.8	22.8	22.8
66	22.0	22.0	22.0	22.0	22.0	22.0	22.0	22.0	22.0
67	21.2	21.2	21.2	21.2	21.2	21.2	21.2	21.2	21.2
68	20.4	20.4	20.4	20.4	20.4	20.4	20.4	20.4	20.4
69	19.6	19.6	19.6	19.6	19.6	19.6	19.6	19.6	19.6
70	18.8	18.8	18.8	18.8	18.8	18.8	18.8	18.8	18.8
71	18.0	18.0	18.0	18.0	18.0	18.0	18.0	18.0	18.0
72	17.2	17.2	17.2	17.2	17.2	17.2	17.2	17.2	17.2
73	16.4	16.4	16.4	16.4	16.4	16.4	16.4	16.4	16.4
74	15.6	15.6	15.6	15.6	15.6	15.6	15.6	15.6	15.6
75	14.9	14.9	14.9	14.9	14.9	14.9	14.8	14.8	14.8
76	14.1	14.1	14.1	14.1	14.1	14.1	14.1	14.1	14.1
77	13.4	13.4	13.4	13.4	13.4	13.4	13.4	13.4	13.3
78	12.7	12.7	12.7	12.7	12.7	12.7	12.6	12.6	12.6
79	12.0	12.0	12.0	12.0	12.0	12.0	12.0	11.9	11.9
80	11.3	11.3	11.3	11.3	11.3	11.3	11.3	11.3	11.3
81	10.7	10.7	10.7	10.6	10.6	10.6	10.6	10.6	10.6
82	10.0	10.0	10.0	10.0	10.0	10.0	10.0	10.0	10.0
83	9.4	9.4	9.4	9.4	9.4	9.4	9.4	9.4	9.4
84	8.9	8.9	8.9	8.8	8.8	8.8	8.8	8.8	8.8
85	8.3	8.3	8.3	8.3	8.3	8.3	8.3	8.3	8.2
86	7.8	7.8	7.8	7.8	7.8	7.8	7.8	7.7	7.7
87	7.3	7.3	7.3	7.3	7.3	7.3	7.3	7.3	7.2
88	6.9	6.9	6.9	6.9	6.9	6.8	6.8	6.8	6.8
89	6.5	6.5	6.5	6.4	6.4	6.4	6.4	6.4	6.3
90	6.1	6.1	6.1	6.1	6.0	6.0	6.0	6.0	5.9
91	5.7	5.7	5.7	5.7	5.7	5.7	5.6	5.6	5.6
92	5.4	5.4	5.4	5.4	5.3	5.3	5.3	5.3	5.2
93	5.1	5.1	5.1	5.0	5.0	5.0	5.0	5.0	4.9
94	4.8	4.8	4.8	4.8	4.7	4.7	4.7	4.7	4.6
95	4.5	4.5	4.5	4.5	4.5	4.5	4.4	4.4	4.3
96	4.3	4.3	4.3	4.3	4.2	4.2	4.2	4.2	4.1
97	4.1	4.1	4.1	4.0	4.0	4.0	4.0	3.9	3.9
98	3.9	3.9	3.9	3.9	3.8	3.8	3.8	3.7	3.7
99	3.7	3.7	3.7	3.7	3.7	3.6	3.6	3.6	3.5
100	3.6	3.5	3.5	3.5	3.5	3.5	3.4	3.4	3.3
101	3.4	3.4	3.4	3.4	3.4	3.3	3.3	3.3	3.2
102	3.3	3.3	3.3	3.3	3.2	3.2	3.2	3.1	3.1
103	3.2	3.2	3.2	3.2	3.1	3.1	3.1	3.0	3.0
104	3.1	3.1	3.1	3.1	3.1	3.0	3.0	3.0	2.9

Reg. §1.401(a)(9)-9(d)

Ages	108	109	110	111	112	113	114	115	116
105	3.1	3.1	3.0	3.0	3.0	3.0	3.0	2.9	2.8
106	3.0	3.0	3.0	3.0	3.0	3.0	2.9	2.9	2.8
107	3.0	3.0	3.0	3.0	3.0	2.9	2.9	2.9	2.8
108	3.0	3.0	3.0	3.0	2.9	2.9	2.9	2.8	2.8
109	3.0	3.0	3.0	2.9	2.9	2.9	2.9	2.8	2.8
110	3.0	3.0	3.0	2.9	2.9	2.9	2.9	2.8	2.7
111	3.0	2.9	2.9	2.9	2.9	2.9	2.8	2.8	2.7
112	2.9	2.9	2.9	2.9	2.9	2.9	2.8	2.8	2.7
113	2.9	2.9	2.9	2.9	2.9	2.8	2.8	2.7	2.7
114	2.9	2.9	2.9	2.8	2.8	2.8	2.8	2.7	2.6
115	2.8	2.8	2.8	2.8	2.8	2.7	2.7	2.7	2.6
116	2.8	2.8	2.7	2.7	2.7	2.7	2.6	2.6	2.5
117	2.7	2.6	2.6	2.6	2.6	2.6	2.5	2.5	2.4
118	2.5	2.5	2.5	2.4	2.4	2.4	2.4	2.3	2.2
119	2.3	2.3	2.2	2.2	2.2	2.2	2.1	2.1	2.0
120+	2.0	2.0	2.0	2.0	2.0	1.9	1.9	1.8	1.8

Ages	117	118	119	120+
0	84.5	84.5	84.5	84.5
1	83.7	83.7	83.7	83.7
2	82.7	82.7	82.7	82.7
3	81.7	81.7	81.7	81.7
4	80.8	80.8	80.8	80.8
5	79.8	79.8	79.8	79.8
6	78.8	78.8	78.8	78.8
7	77.8	77.8	77.8	77.8
8	76.8	76.8	76.8	76.8
9	75.8	75.8	75.8	75.8
10	74.8	74.8	74.8	74.8
11	73.8	73.8	73.8	73.8
12	72.8	72.8	72.8	72.8
13	71.9	71.9	71.9	71.9
14	70.9	70.9	70.9	70.9
15	69.9	69.9	69.9	69.9
16	68.9	68.9	68.9	68.9
17	67.9	67.9	67.9	67.9
18	66.9	66.9	66.9	66.9
19	66.0	66.0	66.0	66.0
20	65.0	65.0	65.0	65.0
21	64.0	64.0	64.0	64.0
22	63.0	63.0	63.0	63.0
23	62.0	62.0	62.0	62.0
24	61.1	61.1	61.1	61.1
25	60.1	60.1	60.1	60.1
26	59.1	59.1	59.1	59.1
27	58.2	58.2	58.2	58.2
28	57.2	57.2	57.2	57.2
29	56.2	56.2	56.2	56.2
30	55.3	55.3	55.3	55.3
31	54.3	54.3	54.3	54.3
32	53.4	53.4	53.4	53.4
33	52.4	52.4	52.4	52.4
34	51.4	51.4	51.4	51.4
35	50.5	50.5	50.5	50.5
36	49.5	49.5	49.5	49.5
37	48.6	48.6	48.6	48.6
38	47.6	47.6	47.6	47.6
39	46.6	46.6	46.6	46.6
40	45.7	45.7	45.7	45.7
41	44.7	44.7	44.7	44.7
42	43.8	43.8	43.8	43.8

Ages	117	118	119	120+
43	42.8	42.8	42.8	42.8
44	41.8	41.8	41.8	41.8
45	40.9	40.9	40.9	40.9
46	39.9	39.9	39.9	39.9
47	39.0	39.0	39.0	39.0
48	38.0	38.0	38.0	38.0
49	37.1	37.1	37.1	37.1
50	36.1	36.1	36.1	36.1
51	35.2	35.2	35.2	35.2
52	34.3	34.3	34.3	34.3
53	33.3	33.3	33.3	33.3
54	32.4	32.4	32.4	32.4
55	31.5	31.5	31.5	31.5
56	30.6	30.6	30.6	30.6
57	29.7	29.7	29.7	29.7
58	28.8	28.8	28.8	28.8
59	27.9	27.9	27.9	27.9
60	27.1	27.1	27.1	27.1
61	26.2	26.2	26.2	26.2
62	25.3	25.3	25.3	25.3
63	24.5	24.5	24.5	24.5
64	23.7	23.7	23.6	23.6
65	22.8	22.8	22.8	22.8
66	22.0	22.0	22.0	22.0
67	21.2	21.2	21.2	21.2
68	20.4	20.4	20.4	20.4
69	19.6	19.6	19.5	19.5
70	18.7	18.7	18.7	18.7
71	17.9	17.9	17.9	17.9
72	17.1	17.1	17.1	17.1
73	16.4	16.4	16.3	16.3
74	15.6	15.6	15.6	15.6
75	14.8	14.8	14.8	14.8
76	14.1	14.1	14.0	14.0
77	13.3	13.3	13.3	13.3
78	12.6	12.6	12.6	12.6
79	11.9	11.9	11.9	11.9
80	11.2	11.2	11.2	11.2
81	10.6	10.5	10.5	10.5
82	9.9	9.9	9.9	9.9
83	9.3	9.3	9.3	9.2
84	8.7	8.7	8.7	8.6
85	8.2	8.2	8.1	8.1
86	7.7	7.6	7.6	7.5
87	7.2	7.1	7.1	7.0
88	6.7	6.7	6.6	6.6
89	6.3	6.2	6.2	6.1
90	5.9	5.8	5.7	5.7
91	5.5	5.4	5.4	5.3
92	5.2	5.1	5.0	4.9
93	4.8	4.8	4.7	4.6
94	4.5	4.4	4.3	4.2
95	4.3	4.2	4.0	3.9
96	4.0	3.9	3.8	3.7
97	3.8	3.7	3.5	3.4
98	3.6	3.5	3.3	3.2
99	3.4	3.3	3.1	3.0
100	3.2	3.1	2.9	2.8
101	3.1	3.0	2.8	2.6
102	3.0	2.8	2.6	2.5
103	2.9	2.7	2.5	2.3
104	2.8	2.6	2.4	2.2

Reg. §1.401(a)(9)-9(d)

Ages	117	118	119	120+
105	2.7	2.6	2.3	2.1
106	2.7	2.5	2.3	2.1
107	2.7	2.5	2.3	2.1
108	2.7	2.5	2.3	2.0
109	2.6	2.5	2.3	2.0
110	2.6	2.5	2.2	2.0
111	2.6	2.4	2.2	2.0
112	2.6	2.4	2.2	2.0
113	2.6	2.4	2.2	1.9
114	2.5	2.4	2.1	1.9
115	2.5	2.3	2.1	1.8
116	2.4	2.2	2.0	1.8
117	2.3	2.1	1.9	1.6
118	2.1	1.9	1.7	1.4
119	1.9	1.7	1.3	1.1
120+	1.6	1.4	1.1	1.0

(e) *Mortality rates.*—The following are the mortality rates used to calculate the tables set forth in paragraphs (b), (c) and (d) of this section.

Table 4 to paragraph (e)

Age	Probability of Death
0	0.001765
1	0.000442
2	0.000293
3	0.000232
4	0.000177
5	0.000162
6	0.000153
7	0.000145
8	0.000132
9	0.000127
10	0.000128
11	0.000135
12	0.000146
13	0.000165
14	0.000192
15	0.000224
16	0.000253
17	0.000277
18	0.000293
19	0.000305
20	0.000314
21	0.000344
22	0.000378
23	0.000421
24	0.000467
25	0.000520
26	0.000581
27	0.000630
28	0.000677
29	0.000720
30	0.000762
31	0.000797
32	0.000822
33	0.000830
34	0.000826
35	0.000818
36	0.000813
37	0.000818
38	0.000830
39	0.000847

Age	Probability of Death
40	0.000872
41	0.000902
42	0.000938
43	0.000974
44	0.001012
45	0.001061
46	0.001128
47	0.001223
48	0.001345
49	0.001488
50	0.001661
51	0.001883
52	0.002134
53	0.002413
54	0.002722
55	0.003057
56	0.003418
57	0.003805
58	0.004213
59	0.004646
60	0.005104
61	0.005587
62	0.006102
63	0.006655
64	0.007255
65	0.007913
66	0.008265
67	0.008687
68	0.009194
69	0.009804
70	0.010535
71	0.011413
72	0.012454
73	0.013684
74	0.015121
75	0.016798
76	0.018740
77	0.020993
78	0.023598
79	0.026624
80	0.030122
81	0.034190
82	0.038892

Age	Probability of Death
83	0.044271
84	0.050391
85	0.057285
86	0.064967
87	0.073466
88	0.082774
89	0.092864
90	0.103667
91	0.115152
92	0.127474
93	0.140876
94	0.155859
95	0.173011
96	0.188348
97	0.205840
98	0.224127
99	0.243120
100	0.262731
101	0.282787
102	0.303096
103	0.323605
104	0.344149
105	0.362406
106	0.373952
107	0.382053
108	0.384203
109	0.386443
110	0.388694
111	0.390860
112	0.393195
113	0.395445
114	0.397687
115	0.400000
116	0.400000

Age	Probability of Death
117	0.400000
118	0.400000
119	0.400000
120	1.000000

(f) *Applicability dates.*—(1) *In General.*—The life expectancy tables and Uniform Lifetime Table set forth in this section apply for distribution calendar years beginning on or after January 1, 2021. For life expectancy tables and the Uniform Lifetime Table applicable for earlier distribution calendar years, see § 1.401(a)(9)-9, as set forth in 26 CFR Part 1 revised April 1, 2019 (formerly applicable § 1.401(a)(9)-9).

(2) *Application to life expectancies that may not be recalculated.*—(i) *Applicability of current tables.*—If an employee died before January 1, 2021, and, under the rules of § 1.401(a)(9)-5, the distribution period that applies for a calendar year following the calendar year of the employee's death is equal to a single life expectancy calculated as of the calendar year of the employee's death (or, if applicable, the following calendar year), reduced by 1 for each subsequent year, then that life expectancy is reset as provided in paragraph (f)(2)(ii) of this section. Similarly, if an employee's sole beneficiary is the employee's surviving spouse, and the spouse dies before January 1, 2021, then the spouse's life expectancy for the calendar year of the spouse's death (which is used to determine the applicable distribution period for later years) is reset as provided in paragraph (f)(2)(ii) of this section.

(ii) *Determination of applicable distribution period.*—With respect to a life expectancy described in paragraph (f)(2)(i) of this section, the distribution period that applies for a distribution calendar year beginning on or after January 1, 2021, is determined by using the Single Life Table in paragraph (b) of this section to determine initial life expectancy for the age of the relevant individual in the relevant calendar year and then reducing the resulting distribution period by 1 for each subsequent year. For example, assume that an employee died at age 80 in 2018 and the employee's designated beneficiary (who was not the employee's spouse) was age 75 in the year of the employee's death. For 2019, the distribution period that would have applied for the beneficiary was 12.7 years (the period applicable for a 76 year old under the Single Life Table in formerly applicable § 1.401(a)(9)-9), and for 2020, it would have been 11.7 years (the original distribution period, reduced by 1 year). For 2021, the applicable distribution period would be 12.0 years (the 14.0 year life expectancy for a 76 year old under the Single Life Table in paragraph (b) of this section, reduced by 2 years).

Beneficiaries

Beneficiaries: Taxability of: Sec. 401(a) Trust.—Amendments to Reg. § 1.402(a)-1, relating to the taxability of beneficiaries under a trust meeting the requirements of section 401(a), are proposed (published in the Federal Register of April 30, 1975). [*Note:* Proposed Reg. § 1.402(a)-1(a)(1)(iii) and (a)(2) were adopted by T.D. 9223 on August 26, 2005.]

☐ Section 1.402(a)-1 is amended by revising paragraphs (a)(1)(ii), (a)(1)(iii), (a)(2), (a)(5), (a)(6), (a)(7), (a)(9), and (b)(1) to read as follows:

§ 1.402(a)-1. Taxability of beneficiary under a trust which meets the requirements of section 401(a).—(a) *In general.*—(1) * * *

(ii) The provisions of section 402(a) relate only to a distribution by a trust which is described in section 401(a) and which is exempt under section 501(a) for the taxable year of the trust in which the distribution is made. With three exceptions, the distribution from such an exempt trust when received or made available is taxable to the distributee or recipient to the extent provided in section 72 (relating to annuities). First, for taxable years beginning before January 1, 1964, section 72(e)(3) (relating to the treatment of certain lump sums), as in effect before such date, shall not apply to such distributions. For taxable years beginning after December 31, 1963, such distributions may be taken into account in computations under sections 1301 through 1305 (relating to income averaging). For treatment of such total distributions, see paragraph (a)(6) of this section. Secondly, if the taxable year ends after December 31, 1969 and begins before January 1, 1974, the portion of the distribution treated as long-term capital gain is subject to the limitation under section 402(a)(5), as in effect on December 31, 1973. Thirdly, for taxable years beginning after December 31, 1973, a certain portion, described in section 402(a)(2), of a lump sum distribution, as defined in section 402(e)(4)(A) is taxable as long-term capital gain and a certain portion, described in section 402(e)(4)(E), may be taxable under section 402(e). For the treatment of such lump sum distributions, see paragraph (a)(9) of this section. Under certain circumstances, an amount representing the unrealized appreciation in the value of the securities of the employer is excludable from gross income for the year of distribution. For the rules relating to such exclusion, see paragraph (b) of this section. Furthermore, the exclusion provided by section 105(d) is applicable to a distribution from a trust described in section 401(a) and exempt under section 501(a) if such distribution constitutes wages or payments in lieu of wages for a period during which an employee is absent from work on account of a personal injury or sickness. See § 1.72-15 for the rules relating to the tax treatment of accident or health benefits received under a plan to which section 72 applies.

(iii) [This proposed amendment was adopted by T.D. 9223, 8-26-2005.]

* * *

(2) [This proposed amendment was adopted by T.D. 9223, 8-26-2005.]

* * *

(5) If pension or annuity payments or other benefits are paid or made available to the beneficiary of a deceased employee or a deceased retired employee by a trust described in section 401(a) which is exempt under section 501(a), such amounts are taxable in accordance with the rules of section 402(a) and this section. In case such amounts are taxable under section 72, the "investment in the contract" shall be determined by reference to the amount contributed by the employee and by applying the applicable rules of sections 72 and 101(b)(2)(D). In case the amounts paid to, or includible in the gross income of, the beneficiaries of the deceased employee or deceased retired employee constitute a distribution to which paragraph (a)(6) or (9) (whichever applies) of this section is applicable, the extent to which the distribution is taxable is determined by reference to the contributions of the employee, by reference to any prior distributions which were excludable from gross income as a return of

employee contributions, and by applying the applicable rules of sections 72 and 101(b).

(6) This subparagraph applies in the case of a total distribution made in a taxable year of the distributee or payee ending before January 1, 1970.

(i) If the total distributions payable with respect to any employee under a trust described in section 401(a) which in the year of distribution is exempt under section 501(a) are paid to, or includible in the gross income of, the distributee within one taxable year of the distributee on account of the employee's death or other separation from the service, or death after such separation from service, the amount of such distribution, to the extent it exceeds the net amount contributed by the employee, shall be considered a gain from the sale or exchange of a capital asset held for more than six months. The total distributions payable are includible in the gross income of the distributee within one taxable year if they are made available to such distributee and the distributee fails to make a timely election under section 72(h) to receive an annuity in lieu of such total distributions. The "net amount contributed by the employee" is the amount actually contributed by the employee plus any amounts considered to be contributed by the employee under the rules of section 72(f), 101(b), and paragraph (a)(3) of this section, reduced by any amounts theretofore distributed to him which were excludable from gross income as a return of employee contributions. See, however, paragraph (b) of this section for rules relating to the exclusion of amounts representing net unrealized appreciation in the value of securities of the employer corporation. In addition, all or part of the amount otherwise includible in gross income under this paragraph by a nonresident alien individual in respect of a distribution by the United States under a qualified pension plan may be excludable from gross income under section 402(a)(4). For rules relating to such exclusion, see paragraph (c) of this section. For additional rules relating to the treatment of total distributions described in this subdivision in the case of a nonresident alien individual, see sections 871 and 1441 and the regulations thereunder.

* * *

(7) The capital gains treatment provided by section 102(a)(2), as in effect for taxable years beginning before January 1, 1974, and paragraph (a)(6) of this section is not applicable to distributions paid during such years to a distributee to the extent such distributions are attributable to contributions made on behalf of an employee while he was a self-employed individual in the business with respect to which the plan was maintained. For the taxation of such amounts, see §1.72-18. For the rules for determining the amount attributable to contributions on behalf of an employee while he was self-employed, see paragraphs (b)(4) and (c)(2) of such section.

* * *

(9) For taxable years beginning after December 31, 1973, in the case of a lump sum distribution (as defined in section 402(e)(4)(A)) made to a recipient which is an individual, estate, or trust, so much of the total taxable amount (as defined in section 402(e)(4)(D) and §1.402(e)-2(d)(2)) of such lump sum distribution as is equal to the product of such total taxable amount multiplied by a fraction—

(i) The numerator of which is the number of calendar years of active participation (as determined under §1.402(e)-2(d)(3)(ii)) by the employee in such plan before January 1, 1974, and

(ii) The denominator of which is the number of calendar years of active participation (as determined under §1.402(e)-2(d)(3)(ii)) by the employee in such plan,

shall be treated as gain from the sale or exchange of a capital asset held for more than six months. For purposes of this subparagraph, in the case of an individual who at no time during his participation under the plan is an employee within the meaning of section 401(c)(1), determination of whether any distribution is a lump sum distribution shall be made without regard to the requirement that an election be made under section 402(e)(4)(B) and §1.402(e)-3.

(b) *Distributions including securities of the employer corporation.—* (1) *In general.—*(i) If a trust described in section 401(a) which is exempt under section 501(a) makes a distribution to a distributee, and such distribution includes securities of the employer corporation, the amount of any net unrealized appreciation in such securities shall be excluded from the distributee's income in the year of such distribution to the following extent:

(A) If the distribution constitutes a total distribution to which the regulations of paragraph (a)(6) of this section are applicable, or if the distribution would constitute a lump sum distribution as defined in section 402(e)(4)(A) (without regard to section 402(e)(4)(H)), the amount to be excluded is the entire net unrealized appreciation attributable to that part of the distribution which consists of securities of the employer corporation; and

(B) If the distribution is other than a total distribution to which paragraph (a)(6) of this section is applicable, or if the distribution is other than a lump sum distribution as defined in section 402(e)(4)(A) (without regard to section 402(e)(4)(H)), the amount to be excluded is that portion of the net unrealized appreciation in the securities of the employer corporation which is attributable to the amount considered to be contributed by the employee to the purchase of such securities.

The amount of net unrealized appreciation which is excludable under the regulations of (b)(1)(i)(A) and (B) of this section shall not be included in the basis of the securities in the hands of the distributee at the time of distribution for purposes of determining gain or loss on their subsequent disposition. Further, the amount of net unrealized appreciation which is not included in the basis of the securities in the hands of the distributee at the time of distribution shall be considered as a gain from the sale or exchange of a capital asset held for more than six months to the extent that such appreciation is realized in a subsequent taxable transaction. However, if the net gain realized by the distributee in a subsequent taxable transaction exceeds the amount of the net unrealized appreciation at the time of distribution, such excess shall constitute a long-term or short-term capital gain depending upon the holding period of the securities in the hands of the distributee.

(ii)(A) For purposes of section 402(a) and of this section, the term "securities" means only shares of stock and bonds or debentures issued by a corporation with interest coupons or in registered form, and the term "securities of the employer corporation" includes securities of a parent or subsidiary corporation (as defined in subsections (e) and (f) of section 425) of the employer corporation.

(B) For purposes of this paragraph, for taxable years beginning after December 31, 1973, the term "distributee" means "recipient".

* * *

Lump-Sum Distributions

Employee Plans: Lump-Sum Distributions.—Reproduced below is the text of a proposed amendment to Reg. §1.402(a)-1, relating to the election to treat no portion of a lump-sum distribution from an employee plan as long-term capital gain (published in the Federal Register on May 31, 1979).

☐ Paragraph 1. Section 1.402(a)-1(a)(9), as set forth in paragraph 10 of the appendix to the notice of proposed rulemaking of April 30, 1975, is revised by adding a new sentence at the end thereof to read as follows:

§1.402(a)-1. Taxability of beneficiary under a trust which meets the requirements of section 401(a).—(a) *In general.*—* * *

(9) * * * In the case of a lump sum distribution received by or made available to a recipient in a taxable year of the recipient beginning after December 31, 1975, the recipient may elect, in accordance with section 402(e)(4)(L) and §1.402(e)-14, to treat all calendar years of an employee's active participation in all plans in which the employee has been an active participant as years of active participation after December 31, 1973. If a recipient makes the election, no portion of any distribution received by or made available to the recipient with respect to the employee (whether in the recipient's taxable year for which the election is made, or thereafter) is taxable to the recipient as long-term capital gain under section 402(a)(2) and this subparagraph.

Employee Trusts: Effective Dates

Employee Trusts: Tax Reform Act of 1984: Effective Dates.—Temporary Reg. §1.402(a)(5)-1T is also proposed as a final regulation and, when adopted, would become Reg. §1.402(a)(5)-1 (published in the Federal Register on February 4, 1986).

§1.402(a)(5)-1. Rollovers of partial distributions from qualified trusts and annuities.

Lump-Sum Distributions: Treatment After 1973

Lump-Sum Distributions: Treatment of.—Reproduced below is the text of proposed Reg. §1.402(e)-2, relating to the treatment of lump-sum distributions (published in the Federal Register on April 30, 1975).

☐ There are added immediately after §1.402(e)-1 the following new sections:

§1.402(e)-2. Treatment of certain lump sum distributions made after 1973.—(a) *In general.*—(1) *Tax imposed; deduction allowed.*—For a taxable year, at the election of the recipient of a lump sum distribution, the ordinary income portion of such distribution is subject to the tax imposed by section 402(e)(1)(A) (hereinafter referred to as the "separate tax") and, under section 402(e)(3), an amount equal to such portion is allowable as a deduction from gross income (see section 62(11), as added by sec. 2005(c)(9) of Pub. L. No. 93-406, and the regulations thereunder) to the extent such portion is included in the gross income of the taxpayer for such year. The separate tax imposed by section 402(e)(1)(A) is an addition to the tax otherwise imposed under chapter 1 of the Code and may be elected whether or not the tax otherwise imposed by such chapter is computed under part I of subchapter Q of such chapter (relating to income averaging). This section applies with respect to distributions or payments made, or made available, to a recipient after December 31, 1973, in taxable years of the recipient beginning after that date.

(2) *Cross references.*—(i) *Computation; ordinary method.*—Paragraph (b) of this section provides rules with respect to a distribution which is not a multiple distribution, and does not include an annuity contract.

(ii) *Computation; special method (distribution including an annuity contract).*—Paragraph (c)(1) of this section provides rules with respect to a distribution which is not a multiple distribution and which includes an annuity contract.

(iii) *Computation; special method (multiple distribution).*—Paragraph (c)(2) of this section provides rules with respect to a distribution which is a multiple distribution.

(iv) *Lump sum distribution.*—For the definition of the term "lump sum distribution", see paragraph (d)(1) of this section.

(v) *Total taxable amount.*—For the definition of the term "total taxable amount", see paragraph (d)(2) of this section.

(vi) *Ordinary income portion.*—For the definition of the term "ordinary income portion", see paragraph (d)(3) of this section.

(vii) *Multiple distribution.*—For the definition of the term "multiple distribution", see paragraph (c)(2)(ii)(E) of this section.

(viii) *Election.*—For rules relating to the election of lump sum distribution treatment under this section, see §1.402(e)-3.

(b) *Ordinary method.*—(1) *In general.*—In the case of a distribution which is not included in a multiple distribution, and which does not include an annuity contract, if the recipient elects (under §1.402(e)-3) to treat such distribution as a lump sum distribution under this section, the tax imposed by section 402(e)(1)(A) for the recipient's taxable year is an amount equal to the initial separate tax (determined under paragraph (b)(2) of this section) for such taxable year, multiplied by a fraction—

(i) The numerator of which is the ordinary income portion (determined under paragraph (d)(3) of this section) of such lump sum distribution for such taxable year, and

(ii) The denominator of which is the total taxable amount (determined under paragraph (d)(2) of this section) of such lump sum distribution for such taxable year.

(2) *Computation of initial separate tax.*—For purposes of subparagraph (1) of this paragraph, the initial separate tax is an amount equal to 10 times the tax which would be imposed by section 1(c) (relating to unmarried individuals (other than surviving spouses and heads of households)) if the recipient were an individual referred to in such section and the taxable income referred to in such section were an amount equal to one-tenth of the excess of—

(i) The total taxable amount (determined under paragraph (d)(2) of this section) of the lump sum distribution, over

(ii) The minimum distribution allowance (determined under paragraph (b)(3) of this section).

(3) *Computation of minimum distribution allowance.*—For purposes of paragraph (b)(2)(ii) of this section, the minimum distribution allowance is the lesser of—

(i) $10,000, or

(ii) One-half of the total taxable amount of the lump sum distribution for the taxable year, reduced (but not below zero) by 20 percent of the excess (if any) of such total taxable amount over $20,000.

(4) *Example.*—The application of this paragraph is illustrated by the following example:

Example. (i) On December 22, 1975, A separates from the service of the M Corporation and receives a lump sum distribution of $65,000 from the M Corporation's contributory qualified plan. A's contributions to the plan as an employee were $15,000. A has been an active participant in the plan since February 20, 1966. A and his wife, B, are each age 50. Neither received an annuity contract from a qualified plan in 1974 or 1975. Neither received a lump sum distribution in 1974. A and B file a joint return for the calendar year 1975. Their income for 1975 consists of A's salary of $15,000 from the M Corporation and of $5,000 from the N Corporation. Their deductions for 1975 (other than deductions attributable to the distribution) consist of itemized deductions of $3,000. Their average base period income (determined under section 1302(b)(1)) for the four preceding taxable years (1971 through 1974) is $14,000. Assuming there are no changes in the applicable tax law after 1974, A and B's income tax liability for 1975 is computed as follows.

(ii) A and B's gross income for 1975 is $70,000, computed by adding the total taxable amount of the lump sum distribution (determined under paragraph (d)(2) of this section) to their otherwise computed gross income [$15,000 + $5,000 + $65,000 − $15,000]. Their adjusted gross income for 1975 is $40,000 [$70,000 − ($10,000 + $20,000)]computed by reducing their gross income by the sum of the lump sum distribution deduction allowed by section 402(e)(3) with respect to the ordinary income portion of the distribution [$50,000 × 24/120]and the deduction allowed by section 1202 with respect to the capital gains portion of the distribution [($50,000 × 96/120) × 0.5]. A and B's joint taxable income is $35,500 (their itemized deductions are $3,000 and their personal exemptions total $1,500). A and B choose to apply the income averaging rules of section 1301 for 1975. Thus, A and B's income tax liability not including the separate tax on the ordinary income portion of the distribution is $8,828.

(iii) The minimum distribution allowance with respect to A's distribution is $4,000 [$10,000 − (($50,000 − $20,000) × 0.2)]. The initial separate tax on A's distribution is 10 times the tax imposed by section 1(c), computed as if the taxable income therein described were $4,600

$$\frac{[\$50,000 - \$4,000]}{10}$$

Thus, A's initial separate tax is $8,160. The separate tax on A's distribution is computed by multiplying the initial separate tax and the quotient of the ordinary income portion divided by the total taxable amount. Thus, the separate tax on A's distribution is $1,632 [$8,160 × $10,000/$50,000].

(iv) A and B's total income tax liability for 1975 is the sum of the income tax as otherwise determined and the separate tax. Thus, A and B's total income tax liability for 1975 is $10,460 [$8,828 + $1,632].

(c) *Special method.*—(1) *Computation of separate tax on distribution including annuity contract and lump sum distribution.*—(i) *Computation.*—In the case of a distribution which is not included in a multiple distribution and which includes an annuity contract, if the recipient elects (under §1.402(e)-3) to treat the portion of such distribution not consisting of an annuity contract as a lump sum distribution under this section, the separate tax imposed by section 402(e)(1)(A) of the recipient's taxable year is the excess (if any) of the adjusted separate tax over the tax attributable to the annuity contract (determined under paragraph (c)(1)(iii) of this section).

(ii) *Definitions.*—For purposes of this section—

(A) *Adjusted separate tax.*—The adjusted separate tax is an amount equal to the adjusted initial separate tax multiplied by a fraction—

(1) The numerator of which is the ordinary income portion of the distribution, and

(2) The denominator of which is the total taxable amount (determined under paragraph (d)(2) of this section) of the lump sum distribution.

(B) *Adjusted initial separate tax.*—The adjusted initial separate tax is an amount equal to 10 times the tax which would be imposed by section 1(c) (relating to unmarried individuals (other than surviving spouses and heads of households)) if the recipient were an individual referred to in such section and the taxable income referred to in such section were an amount equal to one-tenth of the excess of—

(1) The adjusted total taxable amount of the lump sum distribution, over

(2) The adjusted minimum distribution allowance.

(C) *Adjusted total taxable amount.*—*(1)* For taxable years beginning before January 1, 1975, the adjusted total taxable amount is the sum of—

(i) The excess (if any) of the current actuarial value of annuity contracts distributed to the recipient, over the portion of the net amount contributed by the employee which is allocable to the contract, and

(ii) The total taxable amount (determined under paragraph (d)(2) of this section) of the lump sum distribution for the taxable year.

For purposes of (c)(1)(ii)(C)(1)(i) of this section, the net amount contributed by the employee which is allocable to the contract is an amount equal to the amounts considered contributed by the employee under the plan (determined by applying sections 72(f) and 101(b), and paragraph (b) of §1.72-16) reduced by any amount theretofore distributed to the employee which were not includible in his gross income multiplied by a fraction, the numerator of which is the current actuarial value of the contract, and the denominator of which is the sum of such current actuarial value and the value of other property (including cash) distributed.

(2) For taxable years beginning after December 31, 1974, the adjusted total taxable amount is the sum of—

(i) The current actuarial value of annuity contracts distributed to the recipient, reduced by the excess, if any, of the net amount contributed by the employee (as defined in paragraph (d)(2)(ii)(A) of this section) over the cash and other property distributed, and

(ii) The total taxable amount (determined under paragraph (d)(2) of this section) of the lump sum distribution for the taxable year.

(D) *Adjusted ordinary income portion.*—The adjusted ordinary income portion of a lump sum distribution is the amount which would be computed under paragraph (d)(3) of this section if "adjusted total taxable amount" is substituted for "total taxable amount" in such subparagraph.

(E) *Adjusted minimum distribution allowance.*—The adjusted minimum distribution allowance is the lesser of—

(1) $10,000, or

(2) one-half of the adjusted total taxable amount of the lump sum distribution for the taxable year,

reduced (but not below zero) by 20 percent of the excess (if any) of the adjusted total taxable amount over $20,000.

(F) *Current actuarial value.*—The current actuarial value of an annuity contract is the greater of—

(1) The cash value of the annuity contract (determined without regard to any loans under the contract) on the date of distribution, or

(2) The amount determined under the appropriate tables contained in publication No. 861, entitled "Annuity Factors for Lump Sum Distributions".

(iii) *Tax attributable to an annuity contract.*—For purposes of subdivision (i) of this subparagraph, the tax attributable to an annuity contract is the product of—

(A) The quotient of the adjusted ordinary income portion (determined under paragraph (c)(1)(ii)(D) of this section) of the lump sum distribution divided by the adjusted total taxable amount (determined under paragraph (c)(1)(ii)(C) of this section), and

(B) 10 times the tax which would be imposed by section 1(c) (relating to unmarried individuals (other than surviving spouses and heads of households)) if the recipient were an individual referred to in such section and the taxable income were an amount equal to one-tenth of the excess of—

(1) The current actuarial value of the annuity contract, over

(2) The adjusted minimum distribution allowance multiplied by a fraction—

(i) The numerator of which is the current actuarial value of the annuity contract, and

(ii) The denominator of which is the adjusted total taxable amount (determined under paragraph (c)(1)(ii) of this section).

(iv) *Examples.*—The application of this subparagraph is illustrated by the following examples:

Example (1). (i) On December 29, 1975, A separates from the service of the M Corporation and receives a distribution of the balance to the credit of his account under the M Corporation's noncontributory qualified plan. The distribution consists of cash of $44,000, and an annuity contract with a current actuarial value of $6,000. A has been a participant in the plan since March 26, 1966. A and his wife, B, are each age 50. Neither received a previous distribu-

tion from a qualified plan. A and B file a joint return for 1975. Their income for 1975, other than the distribution, consists of A's salary from the M Corporation of $15,000 and of $5,000 from the N Corporation. Their deductions (other than deductions attributable to the distribution) consist of itemized deductions of $3,000. They are not otherwise permitted to use income averaging for 1975 under section 1301. Assuming there are no changes in the applicable tax law after 1974, A and B's income tax liability for 1975 is computed as follows.

(ii) A and B's gross income for 1975 is $64,000, computed by adding the total taxable amount (determined under paragraph (d)(2) of this section) of the lump sum distribution to their otherwise computed gross income [$15,000 + $5,000 + $44,000]. Their adjusted gross income for 1975 is $37,600 [$64,000—($8,800 + $17,600)], computed by reducing their gross income by the sum of the lump sum distribution deduction allowed by section 402(e)(3) with respect to the ordinary income portion of the distribution [$44,000 × 24/120] and the deduction allowed by section 1202 with respect to the capital gains portion of the distribution [($44,000 × 96/120) × 0.5]. A and B's taxable income for 1975 is $33,100 (their itemized deductions are $3,000 and their personal exemptions total $1,500). Thus, A and B's income tax liability not including the separate tax on the ordinary income portion of the distribution is $9,122.

(iii) The adjusted total taxable amount of A's distribution is the sum of the current actuarial value of the annuity contract distributed and the total taxable amount of the lump sum distribution. Thus, the adjusted total taxable amount of A's distribution is $50,000 [$6,000 + $44,000]. The adjusted minimum distribution allowance with respect to A's distribution is the lesser of $10,000 or 1/2 of the adjusted total taxable amount, reduced by 20 percent of the excess (if any) of the adjusted total taxable amount over $20,000. Thus, the adjusted minimum distribution allowance with respect to A's distribution is $4,000 [$10,000 − (($50,000 − $20,000) × 0.2)]. The adjusted initial separate tax on A's distribution is computed by multiplying 10 times the tax imposed by section 1(c) computed as if the taxable income therein described were $4,600 [($50,000 − $4,000)/10]. Thus, A's adjusted initial separate tax is $8,160. The adjusted separate tax on A's distribution is computed by multiplying the adjusted initial separate tax by the quotient of the ordinary income portion divided by the total taxable amount. Thus, the adjusted separate tax on A's distribution is $1,632 ($8,160 × $8,800/$44,000). The tax attributable to the annuity contract is 10 times the tax that would be imposed by section 1(c) computed as if the taxable income of a person described there in were $552

$$\frac{[\,\$6,000 - (\$4,000 \times (\$6,000/\$50,000))\,]}{10}$$

multiplied by the quotient described in the second preceding sentence. Thus, the tax attributable to the annuity contract is $156 [$778 × $8,800/$44,000]. The separate tax on A's distribution is computed by reducing the adjusted separate tax by the tax attributable to the annuity contract. Thus, the separate tax on A's distribution is $1,476 [$1,632 − $156].

(iv) A and B's total income tax liability for 1975 is the sum of their income tax liability, as otherwise determined, and the separate tax. Thus A and B's total income tax liability for 1975 is $10,598 [$9,122 + $1,476].

Example (2). (i) Assume the same facts as in example (1) except that the M Corporation's qualifed plan is contributory and that A's contributions under the plan as an employee were $1,760, and the current actuarial value of the annuity contract which is distributed is $5,760.

(ii) A and B's gross income for 1975 is $62,240, computed by adding the total taxable amount (determined under paragraph (d)(2) of this section) of the lump sum distribution to their otherwise computed gross income [$15,000 + $5,000 + ($44,000 − $1,760)]. Their adjusted gross income for 1975 is $36,896 [$62,240 − ($8,448 + $16,896)], computed by reducing their gross income by the sum of the lump sum distribution deduction allowed by section 402(e)(3) with respect to the ordinary income portion of the distribution [$42,240 × 24/120] and the deduction allowed by section 1202 with respect to the capital gains portion of the distribution. [($42,240 × 96/120) × 0.5]. A and B's taxable income for 1975 is $32,396 (their itemized deductions are $3,000 and their personal exemption total $1,500). Thus A and B's income tax liability not including the separate tax on the ordinary income portion of the distribution is $8,826.

(iii) The adjusted total taxable amount of A's distribution is the sum of the current actuarial value of the annuity contract distributed and the total taxable amount of the lump sum distribution. Thus, the adjusted total taxable amount of A's distribution is $48,000 [$5,760 + ($44,000 − $1,760)]. The adjusted minimum distribution allowance with respect to A's distribution is the lesser of $10,000 or 1/2 of the adjusted total taxable amount, reduced by 20 percent of the excess of the adjusted total taxable amount over $20,000. Thus, the adjusted minimum distribution allowance with respect to A's distribution is $4,400 [$10,000 − (($48,000 − $20,000) × 0.2)]. The adjusted initial separate tax on A's distribution is 10 times the tax imposed by section 1(c) computed as if the taxable income therein described were $4,360

$$\frac{[\,(\$48,000 - \$4,400)\,]}{10}$$

Thus, A's adjusted initial separate tax is $7,656. The adjusted separate tax on A's distribution is computed by multiplying the adjusted initial separate tax by the quotient of the ordinary income portion divided by the total taxable amount. Thus, the adjusted separate tax on A's distribution is $1,531 [$7,656 × $8,448/$42,240]. The tax attributable to the annuity contract is 10 times the tax that would be imposed by section 1 (c) computed as if the taxable income of a person therein described were $523

$$\frac{[\,\$5,760 - (\$4,400 \times (\$5,760/\$48,000))\,]}{10}$$

multiplied by the quotient described in the second preceding sentence. Thus, the tax attributable to the annuity contract is $147 [$735 × $8,448/$42,240]. The separate tax on A's distribution is computed by reducing the adjusted separate tax by the tax attributable to the annuity contract. Thus, the separate tax on A's distribution is $1,384 [$1,531 – $147].

(iv) A and B's total income tax liability for 1975 is the sum of their income tax liability, as otherwise determined, and the separate tax. Thus A and B's total income tax liability for 1975 is $10,210 [$1,384 + $8,826].

Example (3). (i) On December 7, 1974, C separates from the service of P Corporation and receives a distribution of the balance to the credit of his account under the P Corporation's contributory qualified plan. The distribution consists of cash of $44,000, and an annuity contract with a current actuarial value of $6,000. C has been a participant in the plan since February 20, 1965. C's contributions under the plan as an employee were $2,000. C and his wife, D, are each age 50. Neither received a previous distribution from a qualifed plan. C and D file a joint return for 1974. Their income for 1974, other than the distribution, consists of C's salary from the P Corporation of $20,000. Their deductions (other than deductions attributable to the distribution) consist of itemized deductions of $3,000. They are not otherwise permitted to use income averaging for 1974 under section 1301. C and D's income tax liability for 1974 is computed as follows.

(ii) C and D's gross income for 1974 is $62,240, computed by adding the total taxable amount (determined under paragraph (d)(2) of this section) of the lump sum distribution to their otherwise computed gross income [$20,000 + ($44,000 – $1,760)]. Their adjusted gross income for 1974 is $39,008 [$62,240 – ($4,224 + $19,008)], computed by reducing their gross income by the sum of the lump sum distribution deduction allowed by section 402(e)(3) with respect to the ordinary income portion of the distribution [$42,240 × 12/120]and the deduction allowed by section 1202 with respect to the capital gains portion of the distribution ($42,240 × 108/120) × 0.5]. C and D's taxable income for 1974 is $34,508 (their itemized deductions are $3,000 and their personal exemptions total $1,500). C and D's income tax liability for 1974 not including the separate tax on the ordinary income portion of the distribution is $9,713.

(iii) The adjusted total taxable amount of C's distribution is the sum of the current actuarial value of the annuity contract distributed and the total taxable amount of the lump sum distribution. Thus, the adjusted total taxable amount of C's distribution is $48,000 [($6,000 – $240) + ($44,000 – $1,760)]. The adjusted minimum distribution allowance with respect to C's distribution is the lesser of $10,000 or ½ of the adjusted total taxable amount, reduced by 20 percent of the excess of the adjusted total taxable amount over $20,000. Thus, the adjusted minimum distribution allowance with respect to C's distribution is $4,400 [$10,000 – (($48,000 – $20,000) × 0.2)]. The adjusted initial separate tax on C's distribution is 10 times the tax imposed by section 1(c) computed as if the taxable income therein described were $4,360

$$\frac{[\,(\$48,000 - \$4,400)\,]}{10}$$

Thus, C's adjusted initial separate tax is $7,656. The adjusted separate tax on C's distribution is computed by multiplying the adjusted initial separate tax by the quotient of the ordinary income portion divided by the total taxable amount. Thus, the adjusted separate tax on C's distribution is $766 ($7,656 × $4,224/$42,240). The tax attributable to the annuity contract is 10 times the tax imposed by section 1(c) computed as if the taxable income therein described were $523

$$\frac{[\,\$5,760 - (\$4,400 \times (\$5,760/\$48,000))\,]}{10}$$

multiplied by the quotient described in the second preceding sentence. Thus, the amount attributable to the annuity contract is $74 [$735 × ($4,224/$42,240)]. The separate tax on C's distribution is computed by reducing the adjusted separate tax by the tax attributable to the annuity contract. Thus, the separate tax on C's distribution is $692 ($766 –$74).

(iv) C and D's total income tax liability for 1974 is the sum of their income tax liability, as otherwise determined, and the sepa-

rate tax. Thus, C and D's total income tax liability for 1974 is $10,405 [$9,713 + $692].

(2) *Computation of separate tax in case of multiple distribution.*— (i) *Computation.*—In the case of a payment or distribution which is included in a multiple distribution, the separate tax imposed on such multiple distribution by section 402(e)(1)(A) for the recipient's taxable year is the excess (if any) of the modified separate tax, over the sum of—

(A) The aggregate amount of the separate tax imposed by section 402(e)(1)(A) paid during the lookback period, and

(B) The modified tax attributable to the annuity contract.

(ii) *Definitions.*—For purposes of this section—

(A) *Modified separate tax.*—The term "modified separate tax" means an amount equal to the modified initial separate tax multiplied by a fraction—

(1) The numerator of which is the sum of the ordinary income portions of the lump sum distributions made within the lookback period, and

(2) The denominator of which is the sum of the total taxable amounts of the lump sum distributions made within the lookback period.

(B) *Modified initial separate tax.*—The modified initial separate tax is an amount equal to 10 times the tax which would be imposed by section 1(c) (relating to unmarried individuals (other than surviving spouses and heads of households)) if the recipient were an individual referred to in such section and the taxable income referred to in such section were an amount equal to one-tenth of the excess of

(1) The modified total taxable amount of the lump sum distribution, over

(2) The modified minimum distribution allowance.

(C) *Modified total taxable amount.*—The modified total taxable amount is the sum of the total taxable amounts (determined under paragraph (d)(2) of this section) of the distributions made during the lookback period and, in the case of a distribution made during such period to which paragraph (c)(1) of this section applied, the amount specified in paragraph (c)(1)(ii)(C)(1)(i) or (2)(i) of this section, whichever is applicable.

(D) *Modified minimum distribution allowance.*—The modified minimum distribution allowance is the lesser of—

(1) $10,000, or

(2) one-half of the modified total taxable amount,

reduced (but not below zero) by 20 percent of the excess of the modified total taxable amount over $20,000.

(E) *Multiple distributions.*—A distribution or payment received during a taxable year of the recipient which begins with or within a lookback period and after December 31, 1973, is included in a multiple distribution for such lookback period if—

(1) Any part of such distribution or payment (i) is treated as a lump sum distribution under this section or (ii) consists of a contract which would constitute all or a part of a lump sum distribution (determined without regard to section 402(e)(4)(B) and § 1.402(e)-3), except for the fact that it is an annuity contract, and

(2) a distribution or payment received in another such taxable year is treated as a lump sum distribution under this section. For purposes of this subdivision (E), if the recipient of a lump sum distribution is a trust and if a beneficiary of such trust is an employee with respect to the plan under which the distribution is made, or treated as the owner of such trust for purposes of subpart E of part I of subchapter J of chapter 1 of the Code (relating to grantors and others treated as substantial owners), then such employee or owner shall be treated as the sole recipient of the lump sum distribution. For purposes of this subdivision (E), the term "an employee with respect to the plan under which the distribution is made" means an individual who, immediately before the distribution is made, is a participant in the plan under which the distribution is made.

(F) *Lookback period.*—The lookback period with respect to any recipient is a period of 6 consecutive taxable years ending on the last day of the taxable year of the recipient in which a payment or distribution which is a multiple distribution is made.

(iii) *Modified tax attributable to an annuity contract.*—For purposes of subdivision (i) of this subparagraph, the modified tax attributable to an annuity contract is equal to the product of—

(A) The quotient of the sum of the ordinary income portions (determined under paragraph (d)(3)) of the lump sum distributions received during the lookback period divided by the sum of the total taxable amounts (determined under paragraph (d)(2) of the distributions made during the lookback period, and

(B) 10 times the tax which would be imposed by section 1(c) (relating to unmarried individuals (other than surviving spouses and heads of households)) if the recipient were an individual referred to in such section and the taxable income were an amount equal to one-tenth of the excess of—

(1) The sum of the amounts described in paragraph (c)(1)(ii)(C)(1)(i) or (2)(i) of this section in respect of the annuity contracts distributed during the lookback period, over

(2) The modified minimum distribution allowance multiplied by a fraction—

(i) The numerator of which is the sum of the amounts described in paragraph (c)(2)(iii)(B) in (1) of this section, and

(ii) The denominator of which is the modified total taxable amount (determined under paragraph (c)(2)(ii)(C) of this section).

(iv) The application of this subparagraph is illustrated by the following examples:

Example (1). (i) On December 7, 1976, A separates from the service of N Corporation and receives a distribution of the balance to the credit of his account under the N Corporation's noncontributory qualified plan. The distribution consists of cash of $4,000 and an annuity contract with a current actuarial value of $6,000. A has been a participant in the plan since October 13, 1967. A and his wife, B, are each age 50. A and B file a joint return for 1976. Their income for 1976, other than the distribution, consists of A's salary from N Corporation of $25,000 and interest income of $3,000. Their deductions (other than deductions attributable to the distribution) consist of itemized deductions of $2,100. They are not otherwise permitted to use income averaging for 1976 under section 1301. A received a distribution in 1975 from the M Corporation and elected lump sum treatment for such distribution. The ordinary income portion of such distribution was $10,000; the total taxable amount of such distribution was $50,000; the adjusted ordinary income portion and the adjusted total taxable amount of such distribution are the same as the ordinary income portion and the total taxable amount; and they paid a separate tax on such distribution of $1,632. Assuming there are no changes in the applicable tax law after 1974, A and B's income tax liability for 1976 is computed as follows:

(ii) A and B's gross income for 1976 is $32,000, computed by adding the total taxable amount (determined under paragraph (d)(2) of this section) of the lump sum distribution to their otherwise computed gross income [$25,000 + $3,000 + $4,000]. Their adjusted gross income for 1976 is $29,400 [$32,000 − ($1,200 + $1,400)], computed by reducing their gross income by the sum of the lump sum distribution deduction allowed by section 402(e)(3) with respect to the ordinary income portion of the distribution [$4,000 × $^{36}/_{120}$] and the deduction allowed by section 1202 with respect to the capital gains portion of the distribution [($4,000 × ($^{84}/_{120}$)) × 0.5]. A and B's taxable income for 1976 is $25,800 (their itemized deductions are $2,100 and their personal exemptions total $1,500). Thus, A and B's income tax liability for 1976, not including the separate tax on the ordinary income portion of the distribution is $6,308.

(iii) The adjusted total taxable amount of A's distribution for 1976 is the sum of the current actuarial value of the annuity contract distributed and the total taxable amount of the lump sum distribution. Thus, the adjusted total taxable amount of A's 1976 distribution is $10,000 [$6,000 + $4,000]. The modified total taxable amount is $60,000 [$50,000 + $10,000]. The modified minimum distribution allowance with respect to A's 1976 distribution is the lesser of $10,000 or $^1/_2$ of the modified total taxable amount, reduced by 20 percent of the excess (if any) of the modified total taxable amount over $20,000. Thus, the modified minimum distribution allowance with respect to A's 1976 distribution is $2,000 [$10,000 − (($60,000 − $20,000) × 0.2)]. The modified initial separate tax on A's 1976 distribution is computed by multiplying 10 times the tax imposed by section 1(c) computed as if the taxable income therein described were $5,800

$$\frac{[(\$60,000 - \$2,000)]}{10}$$

Thus, A's modified initial separate tax is $10,680. The modified separate tax on A's 1976 distribution is computed by multiplying the modified initial separate tax by the quotient of the sum of the ordinary income portions of the lump sum distributions received during the lookback period divided by the sum of the total taxable amounts of each lump sum distribution made during such period. Thus, the modified separate tax on A's 1976 distribution is $2,215 [$10,680 × ($10,000 + $1,200)/($50,000 + $4,000)]. The modified tax attributable to the annuity contract is 10 times the tax imposed by section 1(c) computed as if the taxable income of a person described therein were $580

$$\frac{[(\$6,000 - ((\$6,000/\$60,000) \times \$2,000)]}{10}$$

multiplied by the quotient described in the second preceding sentence. Thus, the modified tax attributable to the annuity contract is

$170 [$820 × ($10,000 + $1,200)/($50,000 + $4,000)]. The separate tax on A's 1976 distribution is computed by reducing the modified separate tax by the sum of the separate tax paid during the lookback period, and the modified tax attributable to the annuity contract. Thus, the separate tax on A's 1976 distribution is $413 [$2,215 − ($1,632 + $170)].

(iv) A and B's total income tax liability for 1976 is the sum of their income tax liability as otherwise determined, and the separate tax. Thus, A and B's total income tax liability for 1976 is $6,721 [$6,308 + $413].

Example (2). (i) Assume the same facts as in example (1) except that the N Corporation's qualified plan was contributory and that A's contributions under the plan as an employee were $800, and the current actuarial value of the annuity contract which is distributed is $4,800.

(ii) A and B's gross income for 1976 is $31,200, computed by adding the total taxable amount (determined under paragraph (d)(2) of this section) of the lump sum distribution to their otherwise computed gross income [$25,000 + $3,000 + ($4,000 − $800)]. Their adjusted gross income for 1976 is $29,120 [$31,200 − ($900 + $1,120)]computed by reducing their gross income by the sum of the lump sum distribution deduction allowed by section 402(e)(3) with respect to the ordinary income portion of the distribution [$3,200 × $^{36}/_{120}$] and the deduction allowed by section 1202 with respect to the capital gains portion of the distribution [($3,200 × $^{84}/_{120}$) × 0.5]. A and B's taxable income for 1976 is $25,520 (their itemized deductions are $2,100 and their personal exemptions total $1,500). Thus, A and B's income tax liability for 1976, not including the separate tax on the ordinary income portion of the distribution, is $6,207.

(iii) The adjusted total taxable amount of A's distribution for 1976 is the sum of the current actuarial value of the annuity contract distributed and the total taxable amount of the lump sum distribution. Thus, the adjusted total taxable amount of A's 1976 distribution is $8,000 [($4,800 + ($4,000 − $800)]. The modified total taxable amount is $58,000 [$50,000 + $8,000]. The modified minimum distribution allowance with respect to A's 1976 distribution is the lesser of $10,000 or $^1/_2$ of the modified total taxable amount reduced by the excess, if any, of such modified total taxable amount over $20,000. Thus, the modified minimum distribution allowance with respect to A's 1976 distribution is $2,400 [$10,000 − [(($8,000 + $50,000) − $20,000 × 0.2)]]. The modified initial separate tax on A's 1976 distribution is 10 times the tax imposed by section 1(c) computed as if the taxable income therein described were $5,560

$$\frac{[(\$58,000 - \$2,400)]}{10}$$

Thus, A's modified initial separate tax to $10,176. The modified separate tax on A's 1976 distribution is computed by multiplying the modified initial separate tax by the quotient of the sum of the ordinary income portions of each lump sum distribution received during the lookback period divided by the sum of the total taxable amounts of each lump sum distribution made during such period. Thus, the modified separate tax on A's 1976 distribution is $2,096 [$10,176 × ($10,000 + $960) / ($50,000 + $3,200)]. The modified tax attributable to the annuity contract is 10 times the tax imposed by section 1(c) computed as if the taxable income therein described were $460

$$\frac{[(\$4,800 - (\$2,400 \times (\$4,800/\$58,000)))]}{10}$$

multiplied by the quotient described in the second preceding sentence. Thus, the modified tax attributable to the annuity contract is $133 [$644 × ($10,000 + $960)/($50,000 + $3,200)]. The separate tax on A's 1976 distribution is computed by reducing the modified separate tax by the sum of the separate tax paid during the lookback period, and the modified tax attributable to the annuity contract. Thus, the separate tax on A's 1976 distribution is $331 [$2,096 − ($1,632 + $133)].

(iv) A and B's total income tax liability for 1976 is the sum of their income tax liability as otherwise determined, and the separate tax. Thus, A and B's total income tax liability for 1976 is $6,538 [$6,207 + $331].

Example (3). (i) Assume the same facts as in example (1) except that the distribution on December 7, 1976, from the N Corporation's noncontributory qualified plan consists only of an annuity contract with a current actuarial value of $6,000.

(ii) A and B's gross income for 1976 is $28,000, computed by adding the total taxable amount (determined under paragraph (d)(2) of this section) of the lump sum distribution to their otherwise computed gross income [$25,000 + $3,000 + 0]. Their adjusted gross income for 1976 is $28,000 [$28,000 − ($0 + $0)], computed by reducing their gross income by the sum of the lump sum distribution deduction allowed by section 402(e)(3) with respect to the ordinary income portion of the distribution [$0 × 36/120] and the deduction allowed by section 1202 with respect to the capital gains portion of the distribution [$0 × 84/120] × 0.5]. Their taxable income for 1976 is $24,000 (their itemized deductions are $2,100 and their personal exemptions total $1,500). Thus, A and B's income tax liability for 1976, not including the separate tax on the distribution is $5,804.

(iii) The adjusted total taxable amount of the A's distribution for 1976 is the sum of the current actuarial value of the annuity contract distributed and the total taxable amount of the lump sum distribution. Thus, the adjusted total taxable amount of A's 1976 distribution is $6,000 [$6,000 + $0]. The modified total taxable amount is $56,000 [$6,000 + $50,000]. The modified minimum distribution allowance with respect to A's 1976 distribution is the lesser of $10,000 or $1/2$ of the modified total taxable amount, reduced by 20 percent of the excess (if any) of the modified total taxable amount over $20,000. Thus, the modified minimum distribution allowance with respect to A's 1976 distribution is $2,800 [$10,000 − (($56,000 − $20,000) × 0.2)]. The modified initial separate tax on A's 1976 distribution is computed by multiplying 10 times the tax imposed by section 1(c) computed as if the taxable income therein described were $5,320.

$$\frac{[\$56,000 - \$2,800]}{10}$$

Thus, A's modified initial separate tax is $9,672. The modified separate tax on A's 1976 distribution is computed by multiplying the modified initial separate tax by the quotient of the sum of the ordinary income portions of the lump sum distributions received during the lookback period divided by the sum of the total taxable amounts of each lump sum distribution made during such period. Thus, the modified separate tax on A's 1976 distribution is $1,934 [$9,672 × ($10,000 + $0)/($50,000 + $0)]. The modified tax attributable to the annuity contract is 10 times the tax imposed by section 1(c) computed as if the taxable income of a person described therein were $570

$$\frac{[(\$6,000 - ((\$6,000/\$56,000) \times \$2,800))]}{10}$$

multiplied by the quotient described in the second preceding sentence. Thus, the modified tax attributable to the annuity contract is $161 [$805 × ($10,000 + $0)/($50,000 + $0)]. The separate tax on A's 1976 distribution is computed by reducing the modified separate tax by the sum of the separate tax paid during the lookback period, and the modified tax attributable to the annuity contract. Thus, the separate tax on A's 1976 distribution is $141 [$1,934 − ($1,632 + $161)].

(iv) A and B's total income tax liability for 1976 is the sum of their income tax liability as otherwise determined, and the separate tax. Thus, A and B's total income tax liability for 1976 is $5,945 [$5,804 + $141].

Example (4). (i) Assume the same facts as in example (3) except that the N Corporation's qualified plan was contributory and that A's contributions under the plan as an employee were $2,000.

(ii) A and B's gross income for 1976 is $28,000, computed by adding the total taxable amount (determined under paragraph (d)(2) of this section) of the lump sum distribution to their otherwise computed gross income [$25,000 + $3,000 + 0]. Their adjusted gross income for 1976 is $28,000 [$28,000 − ($0 + $0)], computed by reducing their gross income by the sum of the lump sum distribution deduction allowed by section 402(e)(3) with respect to the ordinary income portion of the distribution [$0 × 36/120] and the deduction allowed by section 1202 with respect to the capital gains portion of the distribution [($0 × 84/120) × 0.5]. Their taxable income for 1976 is $24,400 (their itemized deductions are $2,100 and their personal exemptions total $1,500). Thus, A and B's income tax liability for 1976, not including the separate tax on the distribution is $5,804.

(iii) The adjusted total taxable amount of A's distribution for 1976 is the sum of the current actuarial value of the annuity contract distributed, reduced by the excess of the net amount contributed by the employee over the cash and other property distributed, and the total taxable amount of the lump sum distribution. Thus, the adjusted total taxable amount of A's 1976 distribution is $4,000 [($6,000 − $2,000) + $0]. The modified total taxable amount is $54,000 [$50,000 + $4,000]. The modified minimum distribution total taxable amount is $54,000. [$50,000] allowance with respect to A's 1976 distributions is the lesser of $10,000 or $1/2$ of the modified total taxable amount, reduced by 20 percent of the excess (if any) of the modified total taxable amount over $20,000. Thus, the modified minimum distribution allowance with respect to A's 1976 distribution is $3,200 [$10,000 − (($54,000 − $20,000) × 0.2)]. The modified initial separate tax on A's 1976 distribution is computed by multiplying 10 times the tax imposed by section 1(c) computed as if the taxable income therein described were $5,080

$$\frac{[\$54,000 - \$3,200]}{10}$$

Thus, A's modified initial separate tax is $9,168. The modified separate tax on A's 1976 distribution is computed by multiplying the modified initial separate tax by the quotient of the sum of the ordinary income portions of the lump sum distribution received during the lookback period divided by the sum of the total taxable amounts of each lump sum distribution made during such period.

Thus, the modified separate tax on A's 1976 distribution is $1,833 [$9,168 × ($10,000 + $0)/($50,000 + $0)]. The modified tax attributable to the annuity contract is 10 times the tax imposed by section 1(c) computed as if the taxable income therein described were $376

$$\frac{[\$4,000 - ((\$4,000/\$54,000) \times \$3,200)]}{10}$$

multipled by the quotient described in the second preceding sentence. Thus, the modified tax attributable to the annuity contract is $105 [$526 × ($10,000 + $0)/($50,000 + $0)]. The separate tax on A's 1976 distribution is computed by reducing the modified separate tax by the sum of the separate tax paid during the lookback period, and the modified tax attributable to the annuity contract. Thus, the separate tax on A's 1976 distribution is $96 [$1,833 − ($1,632 + $105)].

(iv) A and B's total income tax liability for 1976 is the sum of their income tax liability as otherwise determined, and the separate tax. Thus, A and B's total income tax liability for 1976 is $5,900 [$5,804 + $96].

(d) *Definitions.*—For purposes of this section and § 1.402(e)-3—

(1) *Lump sum distribution.*—(i) For taxable years of a recipient beginning after December 31, 1973, the term "lump sum distribution" means the distribution or payment within one taxable year of the recipient of the balance under the plan to the credit of an employee which becomes payable, or is made available, to the recipient—

(A) On account of the employee's death,

(B) After the employee attains age 59$1/2$,

(C) In the case of an employee who at no time during his participation in the plan was an employee within the meaning of section 401(c)(1), on account of the employee's separation from the service, or

(D) In the case of an employee within the meaning of section 401(c)(1), after the employee has become disabled within the meaning of section 72(m)(7) and paragraph (f) of § 1.72-17,

from a trust forming part of a plan described in section 401(a) and which is exempt from tax under section 501(a) or from a plan described in section 403(a). Although periodic payments made under an annuity contract distributed under a plan described in the preceding sentence are taxed under section 72, solely for purposes of determining the adjusted total taxable amount or the modified total taxable amount, an annuity contract distributed from a plan described in the preceding sentence shall be treated as a lump sum distribution.

(ii)(A) A distribution or payment is not a lump sum distribution unless it constitutes the balance to the credit of the employee at the time the distribution or payment commences. For purposes of the preceding sentence, the time at which a distribution or payment commences shall be the date on which the requirements of subdivision (A), (B), (C), or (D) (whichever is applicable) of paragraph (d)(1)(i) of this section are satisfied, disregarding any previous distribution which constituted the balance to the credit of the employee.

(B) A distribution made before the death of an employee (for example, annuity payments received by the employee after retirement) will not preclude an amount paid on account of the death of the employee from being treated as a lump sum distribution by the recipient. Further, if a distribution or payment constitutes the balance to the credit of the employee, such distribution or payment shall not be treated as other than a lump sum distribution merely because an additional amount, attributable to the last or a subsequent year of service, is credited to the account of the employee and distributed.

(C) The application of this subdivision may be illustrated by the following example:

Example: A, an individual who is a calendar year taxpayer, retires from service with the M Corporation on October 31, 1975 after attaining age 59$1/2$. A begins to receive monthly annuity payments under the M Corporation's qualified plan on November 1, 1975. On February 3, 1976, A takes the balance to his credit under the M Corporation's plan in lieu of any future annuity payments. The balance to the credit of A under the M Corporation's plan is distributed to him on February 3, 1976, and as of such date he had not previously received any amount constituting a lump sum distribution. Such payments and distributions are not to be treated as a lump sum distribution because they are not paid within 1 taxable year of the recipient.

(iii) A payment or distribution described in paragraph (d)(1)(i) of this section which is made to more than one person (except a payment or distribution made solely to two or more trusts), shall not be treated as a lump sum distribution, unless the entire amount paid or distributed is included in the income of the employee in respect of whom the payment or distribution is made. Thus, for example, a distribution of the balance to the credit of the employee after the death of the employee made to the surviving spouse and his children cannot be treated as a lump sum distribution by the surviving spouse and children. However, a distribution to the employee's estate can be treated as a lump sum distribution even though the estate subsequently distributes the amount received to the surviving spouse and children.

(iv) The term "balance to the credit of the employee" does not include United States Retirement Plan Bonds held by a trust to the credit of an employee. Thus, a distribution or payment by a plan described in subdivision (i) of this subparagraph may constitute a lump sum distribution with respect to an employee even though the trust retains retirement plan bonds registered in the name of such employee. Similarly, the proceeds of a retirement plan bond received as a part of the balance to the credit of an employee will not be entitled to be treated as a lump sum distribution. See section 405(e) and paragraph (a)(4) of § 1.405-3.

(v) The term "balance to the credit of the employee" includes any amount to the credit of the employee under any plan which is required to be aggregated under the provisions of section 402(e)(4)(C) and paragraph (e)(1) of this section.

(vi) The term "balance to the credit of the employee" does not include any amount which has been placed in a separate account for the funding of medical benefits described in section 401(h) as defined in paragraph (a) of § 1.401-14. Thus, a distribution or payment by a plan described in subdivision (i) of this subparagraph may constitute the "balance to the credit of the employee" with respect to an employee even though the trust retains amounts attributable to the funding of medical benefits described in section 401(h).

(vii) The term "balance to the credit of the employee" includes any amount which is not forfeited under the plan as of the close of the taxable year of the recipient within which the distribution is made except that in the case of an employee who has separated from the service and incurs a break in service (within the meaning of section 411), such terms does not include an amount which is forfeited at the close of the plan year, beginning with or within such taxable year, by reason of such break in service.

(viii) The balance to the credit of the employee is includible in the gross income of the recipient if the recipient fails to make a timely election under section 72(h) to receive an annuity in lieu of such balance.

(2) *Total taxable amount.*—(i) The term "total taxable amount" means, with respect to a lump sum distribution described in the first sentence of paragraph (d)(1)(i) of this section, the amount of such lump sum distribution which exceeds the sum of—

(A) The net amount contributed by the employee, and

(B) The net unrealized appreciation attributable to that part of the distribution which consists of the securities of the employer corporation so distributed.

(ii) For purposes of paragraph (d)(2)(i)(A) of this section, the term "net amount contributed by the employee" means—

(A) For taxable years beginning after December 31, 1974, the amount actually contributed by the employee plus any amounts considered to be contributed by the employee under the rules of sections 72(f) and 101(b), and paragraph (b) of § 1.72-16, reduced by any amounts theretofore distributed to him which were excludable from gross income as a return of employee contributions.

(B) For taxable years beginning before January 1, 1975, an amount equal to the product of the amounts considered contributed by the employee under the plan (determined by applying sections 72 (f) and 101(b), and paragraph (b) of § 1.72-16) reduced by any amount theretofore distributed to the employee which were not includible in his gross income, multiplied by a fraction—

(i) The numerator of which is the excess, if any, of the sum of the current actuarial value of the annuity contract distributed and the value of the other property (including cash) distributed, over such current actuarial value, and

(ii) The denominator of which is the sum of the current actuarial value of the annuity contract distributed and the value of other property (including cash) distributed.

(iii) The provisions of this subparagraph may be illustrated by the following examples:

Example (1). A, age 60, receives a lump sum distribution from the M Corporation's noncontributory qualified plan on November 24, 1975. The distribution of $25,000 consists of cash and M Corporation securities with net unrealized appreciation of $15,000. The total taxable amount of the distribution to A is $10,000.

Example (2). B, age 60, receives a lump sum distribution from the N Corporation's contributory qualified plan on December 29, 1975. The distribution consists of $25,000 in cash. B's contributions under the plan as an employee are $5,000. The total taxable amount of the distribution to B is $20,000.

Example (3). W receives a lump sum distribution on April 1, 1975, from the M Corporation's noncontributory qualified plan as beneficiary of H on account of H's death. The distribution consists of $25,000 in cash. The total taxable amount of distribution to W is $20,000 if W is otherwise allowed a $5,000 exclusion under section 101(b).

(3) *Ordinary income portion.*—(i) The ordinary income portion of a lump sum distribution is the product of the total taxable amount of the lump sum distribution, multiplied by a fraction—

(A) the numerator of which is the number of calendar years of active participation by the employee in the plan after December 31, 1973, under which the lump sum distribution is made, and

(B) the denominator of which is the total number of calendar years of active participation by the employee in such plan.

(ii) For purposes of computing the fraction described in subdivision (i) of this subparagraph, the number of calendar years of active participation shall be the number of calendar months during the period beginning with the first month in which the employee became a participant under the plan and ending with the earliest of—

(A) The month in which the employee receives a lump sum distribution under the plan,

(B) In the case of an employee who is not an employee within the meaning of section 401(c)(1), the month in which the employee separates from the service,

(C) The month in which the employee dies, or

(D) In the case of an employee within the meaning of section 401(c)(1) who receives a lump sum distribution on account of disability, the first month in which he becomes disabled within the meaning of section 72(m)(7) and paragraph (f) of § 1.72-17.

In computing the months of active participation, in the case of active participation before January 1, 1974, a part of a calendar year in which the employee was an active participant under the plan shall be counted as 12 months, and in the case of active participation after December 31, 1973, a part of a calendar month in which an individual is an active participant under the plan shall be counted as 1 month. Thus, for example, if A, an individual, became an active participant under a plan on December 31, 1965, and continued to be an active participant under the plan until May 7, 1976, A has 108 (12 × 9) months of active participation under the plan before January 1, 1974, and A has 29 (12 + 12 + 5) months of active participation after December 31, 1973. For special rule in case of aggregation of plans, see paragraph (e)(1)(ii) of this section.

(4) *Employee; employer.*—The term "employee" includes an employee within the meaning of section 401(c)(1) and the employer of such individual is the person treated as his employer under section 401(c)(4).

(5) *Securities.*—The terms "securities" and "securities of the employer corporation" shall have the meanings provided in sections 402(a)(3)(A) and 402(a)(3)(B), respectively.

(e) *Special rules.*—(1) *Aggregation.*—(i) *Aggregation of trusts and plans.*—(A) For purposes of determining the balance to the credit of an employee, all trusts described in section 401(a) and which are exempt from tax under section 501(a) and which are part of a plan shall be treated as a single trust; all pension plans described in section 401(a) maintained by an employer shall be treated as a single plan; all profit-sharing plans described in section 401(a) maintained by an employer shall be treated as a single plan; and all stock bonus plans described in section 401(a) maintained by an employer shall be treated as a single plan. For purposes of this subdivision (i), an annuity contract shall be considered to be a trust.

(B) Trusts which are not described in section 401(a) or which are not exempt from tax under section 501(a), and annuity contracts which do not satisfy the requirements of section 404(a)(2) shall not be taken into account for purposes of subdivision (i) of this subparagraph.

(ii) *Computation of ordinary income portion.*—The ordinary income portion of a distribution from two or more plans (which are treated as a single plan under subdivision (i) of this subparagraph) shall be computed by aggregating all of the amounts which would constitute the ordinary income portion of a lump sum distribution if each plan maintained by the employer were not subject to the application of subdivision (i) of this subparagraph.

(iii) *Examples.*—The application of this subparagraph is illustrated by the following examples:

Example (1). M Corporation maintains a qualified profit-sharing plan and a qualified defined benefit pension plan. A, who has participated in each plan for 5 years and is age 55, separates from the service on December 5, 1975. On December 5, 1975, A receives a distribution of the balance to the credit of his account under the profit-sharing plan. Payment of his pension benefits, however, will not commence until he attains age 65. A is entitled to treat his profit-sharing distribution as a lump sum distribution.

Example (2). Assume the same facts as in example (1) except that instead of a profit-sharing plan, M Corporation maintains a qualified money purchase pension plan. A is not entitled to have the amount received from the money purchase pension plan treated as a lump sum distribution

Reg. §1.402(e)-2(e)(1)(iii)

Example (3). Assume the same facts as in example (2) except that the trust forming part of the defined benefit pension maintained by M Corporation is not a qualified trust. A is entitled to have the amount received from the money purchase plan treated as a lump sum distribution.

Example (4). N Corporation maintains profit-sharing plan X and profit-sharing plan Y which plans are qualified and are noncontributory. A is a participant in each plan. A has been a participant in the profit-sharing plan X since October 13, 1966 and a participant in profit-sharing plan Y since its inception on May 9, 1968. A, at age 55, separates from the service on December 5, 1975. He receives the balance to his credit from each plan upon separation. He receives $50,000 from profit-sharing plan X and $60,000 from profit-sharing plan Y. The ordinary income portion of his distribution from the N Corporation plans is $25,000 [($50,000 × ($^{24}/_{120}$)) + ($60,000 × ($^{24}/_{96}$))].

(2) *Community property laws.*—(i) Except as provided in paragraph (e)(2)(ii) of this section, the provisions of this section shall be applied without regard to community property laws.

(ii) In applying the provisions of section 402(e)(3), relating to the allowance of a deduction from gross income of the ordinary income portion of a lump sum distribution, community property laws shall not be disregarded. Thus, for example, if A, a married individual subject to the community property laws of a jurisdiction, receives a lump sum distribution of which the ordinary income portion is $10,000, and he and his wife, B, file separate returns for the taxable year, generally, one half of the total taxable amount of the lump sum distribution is includible in A's gross income, and he will be entitled to a deduction under section 402(e)(3) of $5,000. In this case, the other half of the total taxable amount is includible in B's gross income, and she will be entitled to a deduction of $5,000. The entire amount of the lump sum distribution, however, must be taken into account by A in computing the separate tax imposed by section 402(e)(1)(A).

(3) *Minimum period of service.*—For purposes of computing the separate tax imposed by section 402(e)(1)(A), no amount distributed or paid to an employee may be treated as a lump sum distribution under section 402(e)(4)(A) and this section unless he has been a participant in the plan for at least 5 full taxable years of such employee (preceding his taxable year in which such amount is distributed or paid). Thus, for example, if an amount, which would otherwise be a lump sum distribution, is distributed to A, an employee who has completed only 4 of his taxable years of participation in the plan before the first day of the taxable year in which the amount is distributed, A is not entitled to use the provisions of section 402(e) to compute the tax on the ordinary income portion of the amount distributed. If the amount were distributed to A's beneficiary on account of A's death, however, A's beneficiary could treat the distribution as a lump sum distribution under section 402(e) and this section.

(4) *Amounts subject to penalty.*—Section 402(e) and this section do not apply to an amount described in section 72(m)(5)(A)(ii) and §1.72-17(e)(1)(i)(*b*) to the extent the provisions of section 72(m)(5) apply to such amount.

(5) *Distributions including securities of the employer corporation.*—For rules relating to distributions including securities of the employer corporation, see §1.402(a)-1(b).

(6) *Liability for tax.*—(i) Except as provided in subdivision (ii) of this subparagraph the recipient shall be liable for the tax imposed by section 402(e)(1)(A).

(ii)(A) In any case in which the recipient of a lump sum distribution is a trust, if a beneficiary of such trust, is—

(1) An employee with respect to the plan under which the distribution is made, or

(2) Treated as the owner of such trust for purposes of subpart E of part I of subchapter J of chapter 1 of the Code (relating to grantors and others treated as substantial owners),

then such employee or the owner shall be treated as the sole recipient of the lump sum distribution. For purposes of (1) of this subdivision, the term "an employee with respect to the plan under which the

distribution is made" means an individual who, immediately before the distribution is made, is a participant in the plan under which the distribution is made.

(B)(1) In any case in which a lump sum distribution is made within a taxable year with respect to an individual only to two or more trusts, if a beneficiary of any one of such trusts is not treated as the sole recipient of the distribution by reason of the application of (A) of this subdivision (ii), the separate tax imposed by section 402(e)(1)(A) shall be computed as if the distribution were made to a single recipient consisting of all of such trusts but the liability for such separate tax shall be allocated among the trusts according to the relative portions of the total taxable amount of the distribution received by each trust.

(2) In any case in which a lump sum distribution is made in a succeeding taxable year in a lookback period with respect to a trust described in (1) of this subdivision (B), the separate tax imposed by section 402(1)(A) shall be computed as if the amount described in section 402(e)(2)(A) (relating to the amount of tax imposed by section 402(e)(1)(A) paid with respect to other distributions in a lookback period) includes the separate tax determined in (1) of this subdivision (B) (without regard to the allocation described therein).

(7) *Change in exempt status of trust.*—For principles applicable in making appropriate adjustments if the trust was not exempt for one or more years before the year of distribution, see §1.402(a)-1(a)(1)(iv).

(f) *Reporting.*—(1) *Information required.*—An employer who maintains a plan described in section 401(a) or 403(a), under which a distribution or payment which may be treated as a lump sum distribution is made in a taxable year of the recipient beginning after December 31, 1973, shall communicate (or cause to be communicated) in writing, to the recipient on Form 1099R the following information (where applicable):

(i) The gross amount of such distribution (including the value of any United States retirement plan bonds distributed to or held for the recipient);

(ii) The total taxable amount of such distribution;

(iii) The ordinary income portion and capital gain element of such distribution;

(iv) The net amount contributed by the employee (within the meaning of paragraph (d)(2)(ii) of this section);

(v) The portions of such distribution excludable from the gross income of the recipient under paragraph (c) of §1.72-16 and paragraph (b) of §1.402(a)-1;

(vi) The value of any United States retirement plan bonds distributed to or held for the recipient in excess of the net amount contributed by the employee (within the meaning of paragraph (d)(2)(ii) of this section) included in the basis of such bonds;

(vii) The current actuarial value of any annuity contract distributed as part of the balance to the credit of the employee in excess of the net amount contributed by the employee (within the meaning of paragraph (d)(2)(ii) of this section) considered to be an investment in the contract;

(viii) The net unrealized appreciation on any securities of the employer corporation.

(2) *Alternate method of communication.*—The obligation of the employer to communicate the information described in subparagraph (1) of this paragraph to the recipient shall be satisfied if the fiduciary of the trust or the payer of such distribution communicates the information to the recipient.

(3) *Taxable year of recipient.*—The report required by this paragraph may be prepared, at the option of the employer as if the taxable year of each employee were the calendar year.

(4) *Failure to satisfy requirements.*—In the event that the requirements of this paragraph are not satisfied, the information required to be furnished under this paragraph shall be furnished as part of the return required to be filed under section 6058 and the regulations thereunder.

Lump-Sum Distributions: Capital Gain Election

Employee Plans: Lump-Sum Distributions.—Reproduced below is the text of a proposed amendment of Reg. §1.402(e)-2, relating to the election to treat no portion of a lump-sum distribution from an employee plan as long-term capital gain (published in the Federal Register on May 31, 1979).

☐ Par. 2. Section 1.402(e)-2(d)(3) as set forth in paragraph 12 of the appendix to the notice of proposed rulemaking of April 30, 1975, is revised by adding a new subdivision (iii) to read as follows:

§1.402(e)-2. Treatment of certain lump sum distributions made after 1973.—

* * *

(d) *Definitions.*—* * *

(3) *Ordinary income portion.*—* * *

(iii) In the case of a lump sum distribution received in a taxable year of the recipient beginning after December 31, 1975, the recipient may elect, in accordance with section 402(e)(4)(L) and §1.402(e)-14, to treat all calendar years of an employee's active participation in all plans in which the employee has been an active participant as years of active participation after December 31, 1973. If a recipient makes the election, the ordinary income portion of any lump sum distribution received by the recipient with respect to the employee (whether in the recipient's taxable year for which the election is made, or thereafter) is equal to the total taxable amount of the distribution.

* * *

Lump-Sum Distributions: Election

Lump-Sum Distributions: Treatment of.—Reproduced below is the text of proposed Reg. §1.402(e)-3, relating to the treatment of lump-sum distributions (published in the Federal Register on April 30, 1975).

§1.402(e)-3. Election to treat an amount as a lump sum distribution.—(a) *In general.*—For purposes of sections 402, 403, and this section, an amount which is described in section 402(e)(4)(A) and which is not an annuity contract may be treated as a lump sum distribution under section 402(e)(4)(A) only if the taxpayer elects for the taxable year to have all such amounts received during such year so treated. Not more than one election may be made under this section with respect to an employee after such employee has attained age 59¹/₂.

(b) *Taxpayers eligible to make the election.*—Individuals, estates, and trusts are the only taxpayers eligible to make the election provided by this section. In the case of a lump sum distribution made with respect to an employee to 2 or more trusts, the election provided by this section shall be made by the employee or by the personal representative of a deceased employee.

(c) *Procedure for making election.*—(1) *Time and scope of election.*—An election under this section shall be made for each taxable year to which such election is to apply. The election shall be made before the expiration of the period (including extensions thereof) prescribed in section 6511 for making a claim for credit or refund of the assessed tax imposed by chapter 1 of subtitle A of the Code for such taxable year.

(2) *Manner of making election.*—An election by the taxpayer with respect to a taxable year shall be made by filing Form 4972 as a part of the taxpayer's income tax return or amended return for the taxable year.

(3) *Revocation of election.*—An election made pursuant to this section may be revoked within the time prescribed in subparagraph (1) of this paragraph for making an election, only if there is filed, within such time, an amended income tax return for such taxable year, which includes a statement revoking the election and is accompanied by payment of any tax attributable to the revocation. If an election for a taxable year is revoked, another election may be made for that taxable year under paragraphs (c)(1) and (2) of this section.

(4) *Effect of election on subsequent distribution.*—An election made pursuant to this section shall be an election to treat an annuity contract distributed after December 31, 1973, in a lookback period (as defined in §1.402(e)-2(c)(2)(iii)(F)) beginning after such date as a lump sum distribution in the taxable year of the recipient in which such contract is distributed. [Reg. §1.402(e)-3.]

Lump-Sum Distributions: Employee Plans

Employee Plans: Lump-Sum Distributions.—Reproduced below is the text of proposed Reg. §1.402(e)-14, relating to the election to treat no portion of a lump-sum distribution from an employee plan as long-term capital gain (published in the Federal Register on May 31, 1979).

☐ Par. 3. The following new section is added in the appropriate place:

§1.402(e)-14. Election to treat pre-1974 participation as post-1973 participation (the "402(e)(4)(L) election").—(a) *In general.*—Under section 402(e)(4)(L) and this section, the recipient of a lump sum distribution may elect to treat all calendar years of an employee's active participation in all plans in which the employee has been an active participant as years of active participation after December 31, 1973. This election is the "402(e)(4)(L) election." For rules relating to the treatment of distributions made on behalf of an employee with respect to whom the election is made, see §1.402(a)-1(a)(9) (relating to the capital gains portion of a lump sum distribution) and §1.402(e)-2(d)(3)(iii) (relating to the ordinary income portion of a lump sum distribution). For purposes of this section the term "lump sum distribution" means a lump sum distribution as defined in section 402(e)(4)(A), without regard to section 402(e)(4)(B).

(b) *Taxpayers not eligible to make the election.*—A taxpayer may not make the 402(e)(4)(L) election with respect to a lump sum distribution made on behalf of an employee, if—

(1) The taxpayer received a prior lump sum distribution made on behalf of the employee in a taxable year of the employee (or in a year that would have been a taxable year of the employee, but for the death of the employee) beginning after December 31, 1975, and

(2) A portion of that prior lump sum distribution was treated as long-term capital gain under section 402(a)(2) or 403(a)(2).

(c) *Time and scope of election.*—(1) *In general.*—The 402(e)(4)(L) election shall be made for the first lump sum distribution made with respect to an employee to which the election is to apply. The election does not apply to a lump sum distribution received by the recipient with respect to another employee. The 402(e)(4)(L) election is irrevocable. A revocation under §1.402(e)-3 of the election to apply the separate tax to a lump sum distribution will not revoke a 402(e)(4)(L) election.

(2) *Application of separate tax.*—Nothing in section 402(e)(4)(L) and this section changes the requirements which must be satisfied in order for a lump sum distribution to be eligible for application of the separate tax under section 402(e). Accordingly, a lump sum distribution is not taxable under section 402(e) merely because the 402(e)(4)(L) election is made with respect to, or otherwise applies to, the distribution.

(3) *Example.*—The provisions of subparagraph (2) of this paragraph may be illustrated by the following example:

Example. (i) A, a calendar year taxpayer aged 59¹/₂, separates from the service of A's employer, the M Corporation, on October 31, 1976. On December 15, 1976, A receives a distribution of the balance to A's credit under the M Corporation qualified profit sharing plan. A has been an active participant in the plan since January 1, 1971. The distribution is a lump sum distribution within the meaning of section 402(e)(4)(A) which satisfies the requirements of section 402(e)(4)(C), relating to the aggregation of certain trusts and plans, and section 402(e)(4)(H), relating to a minimum period of participation in the plan.

(ii) A makes the 402(e)(4)(L) election with respect to the distribution. Under section 402(e)(4)(L), all years of A's active participation in all plans in which A has been an active participant are treated as years of active participation after December 31, 1973. Accordingly, no portion of the distribution is taxable as long term capital gain under section 402(a)(2), and the total taxable amount of the distribution is "ordinary income" for purposes of section 402(e). A also makes the section 402(e)(4)(B) election for A's taxable year in which A receives the distribution. Accordingly, the total taxable amount of the distribution is taxable under the 10-year averaging provisions of section 402(e) (the separate tax).

(iii) On January 15, 1977, A receives a distribution of the balance of A's credit under the M Corporation qualified pension plan. A has been an active participant in the plan since January 1, 1958. The distribution is a lump sum distribution within the meaning of section 402(e)(4)(A) which satisfies the requirements of section 402(e)(4)(C), relating to the aggregation of certain trusts and plans, and section 402(e)(4)(H), relating to a minimum period of participation in the plan. No portion of the distribution is taxable as long-term capital gain under section 402(a)(2) because A made the 402(e)(4)(L) election with respect to A's 1976 distribution. In addition, no portion of the distribution is taxable under the 10-year averaging provisions of section 402(e) because A made a prior election under section 402(e)(4)(B) with respect to a distribution made on A's behalf and after A was age 59¹/₂ (the 1976 distribution).

(d) *Manner of making election.*—The 402(e)(4)(L) election shall be made in the manner indicated on the form filed pursuant to section 402(e)(4)(B) and §1.402(e)-3(c)(2) before the expiration of the period prescribed in §1.402(e)-3 for making the election to apply the separate tax to the ordinary income portion of a lump sum distribution.

(e) *Effective date.*—Taxpayers eligible under this section to make the 402(e)(4)(L) election may make the election with respect to a lump sum distribution received after December 31, 1975, and in a taxable year of the recipient beginning after that date. [Reg. §1.402(e)-14.]

Retirement Plans: Distributions: Deferral of Receipt: Notification of Consequences

Retirement Plans: Distributions: Deferral of Receipt: Notification of Consequences.—An amendment to Reg. §1.402(f)-1, specifying that the notice required under Code Sec. 411(a)(11) to be provided to a participant of his or her right, if any, to defer receipt of an immediately distributable benefit must also describe the consequences of failing to defer receipt of the distribution, is proposed (published in the Federal Register on October 9, 2008) (REG-107318-08).

Par. 2. For each entry listed in the "Location" column, remove the language in the "Remove" column and add the language in the "Add" column in its place.

§1.402(f)-1. Required explanation of eligible rollover distributions; questions and answers.

Location	Remove	Add
1.402(f)-1, A-2(a), first sentence	90 days	180 days

Lump-Sum Distributions: Taxability of Beneficiary

Lump-Sum Distributions: Treatment of.—Reproduced below is the text of proposed amendments of Reg. §1.403(a)-1, relating to the treatment of lump-sum distributions (published in the Federal Register on April 30, 1975).

☐ Section 1.403(a)-1(b) and (2) are amended to read as follows:

§1.403(a)-1. Taxability of beneficiary under a qualified annuity plan.—

* * *

(b) The amounts received by or made available to any employee referred to in paragraph (a) of this section under an annuity contract shall be included in the gross income of the employee for the taxable year in which received or made available, as provided in section 72 (relating to annuities), except that—

(1) For taxable years beginning before January 1, 1970, certain total distributions described in section 403(a)(2) (as in effect for such years) are taxable as long-term capital gains (see §1.403(a)-2 for rules applicable to such amounts), and

(2) For taxable years beginning after December 31, 1973, a portion of a lump sum distribution (as defined by section 402(e)(4)(A)) is treated as long-term capital gains (see paragraph (d) of §1.403(a)-2 for rules applicable to such portion and see §1.402(e)-2 for the computation of the separate tax on the portion of a lump sum distribution not treated as long-term capital gains).

For taxable years beginning before January 1, 1964, section 72(e)(3) (relating to treatment of certain lump sums), as in effect before such date, shall not apply to an amount described in this paragraph. For taxable years beginning after December 31, 1963, such amounts may be taken into account in computations under section 1301 through 1305 (relating to income averaging).

Lump-Sum Distributions: Certain Distributions

Lump-Sum Distributions: Treatment of.—Reproduced below are the texts of proposed amendments of Reg. §1.403(a)-2, relating to the treatment of lump-sum distributions (published in the Federal Register on April 30, 1975).

☐ Section 1.403(a)-2(a)(1) and (b) are amended; (c) is revised, (d) and (e) are added to read as follows:

§1.403(a)-2. Capital gains treatment for certain distributions.—

(a) For taxable years beginning before January 1, 1970, if the total amounts payable with respect to any employee for whom an annuity contract has been purchased by an employer under a plan which—

(1) Is a plan described in section 403(a)(1) and §1.403(a)-1, and

* * *

(b) For taxable years begining before January 1, 1970—

(1) The term "total amounts" means the balance to the credit of an employee with respect to all annuities under the annuity plan which becomes payable to the payee by reason of the employee's death or other separation from the service, or by reason of his death after separation from the service. If an employee commences to receive annuity payments on retirement and then a lump sum payment is made to his widow upon his death, the capital gains treatment applies to the lump sum payment, but it does not apply to amounts received before the time the "total amounts" become payable. However, if the total amount to the credit of the employee at the time of his death or other separation from the service or death after separation from the service is paid or includible in the gross income of the payee within one taxable year of the payee, such amount is entitled to the capital gains treatment notwithstanding that in a later taxable year an additional amount is credited to the employee and paid to the payee.

* * *

(c) For taxable years beginning before January 1, 1970, the provisions of this section are not applicable to any amounts paid to a payee to the extent such amounts are attributable to contributions made on behalf of an employee while he was a self-employed individual in the business with respect to which the plan was established. For the taxation of such amounts, see §1.72-18. For such years for the rules for determining the amount attributable to contributions on behalf of an employee while he was self-employed, see paragraphs (b)(4) and (c)(2) of such section.

(d) For taxable years ending after December 31, 1969, and beginning before January 1, 1974, the portion of the total amounts described in paragraph (b)(1) of this section treated as gain from the sale or exchange of a capital asset held for more than six months is subject to the limitation of section 403(a)(2)(C), as in effect on December 31, 1973.

(e) For taxable years beginning after December 31, 1973—

(1) If a lump sum distribution (as defined in section 402(e)(4)(A) and the regulations thereunder) is received by, or made available to, the recipient under an annuity contract described in subparagraph (2)(i) of this paragraph, the ordinary income portion (as defined in section 402(e)(4)(E) and the regulations thereunder) of such distribution shall be taxable in accordance with the provisions of section 402(e) and the regulations thereunder and the portion of such distribution determined under paragraph (3) of this section shall be treated in accordance with the provisions of paragraph (2) of this section.

(2) If—

(i) An annuity contract is purchased by an employer for an employee under a plan described in section 403(a)(1) and §1.403(a)-1,

(ii) Such plan requires that refunds of contributions with respect to annuity contracts purchased under the plan be used to reduce subsequent premiums on the contracts under the plan, and

(iii) A lump sum distribution (as defined in section 402(e)(4)(A) and the regulations thereunder) is paid to the recipient, the amount described in paragraph (e)(3) of this section shall be treated as gain from the sale or exchange of a capital asset held for more than 6 months.

(3) For purposes of paragraph (e)(2) of this section, the portion of a lump sum distribution treated as gain from the sale or exchange of a capital asset held for more than 6 months is an amount equal to the total taxable amount of the lump sum distribution (as defined in section 402(e)(4)(D) and the regulations thereunder) multiplied by a fraction—

(i) The numerator of which is the number of calendar years of active participation (as determined under §1.402(e)-2(d)(3)(ii)) by the employee in such plan before January 1, 1974, and

(ii) The denominator of which is the number of calendar years of active participation (as determined under §1.402(e)-2(d)(3)(ii)) by the employee in such plan.

(4) For purposes of this paragraph—

(i) In the case of an employee who is an employee without regard to section 401(c)(1), the determination of whether or not an amount is a lump sum distribution shall be made without regard to the requirements of section 402(e)(4)(B) and §1.402(e)-3.

(ii) No distribution to any taxpayer other than an individual, estate, or trust may be treated as a lump sum distribution under this section.

Lump-Sum Distributions: All Calendar-Year Treatment

Employee Plans: Lump-Sum Distributions.—Reproduced below is a proposed amendment of Reg. §1.403(a)-2, relating to the election to treat no portion of a lump-sum distribution from an employee plan as long-term capital gain (published in the Federal Register on May 31, 1979).

* * *

☐ Par. 4. Section 1.403(a)-2(e)(3), as set forth in paragraph 15 of the appendix to the notice of proposed rulemaking of April 30, 1975, is revised by adding, immediately after subdivision (ii) thereof, a new sentence to read as follows:

§1.403(a)-2. Capital gains treatment for certain distributions.—
(e) * * *
(3) * * *
(i) * * *
(ii) * * *

In the case of a lump sum distribution received by or made available to a recipient in a taxable year of the recipient beginning after December 31, 1975, the recipient may elect, in accordance with sec-tion 402(e)(4)(L) and §1.402(e)-14, to treat all calendar years of an employee's active participation in all plans in which the employee has been an active particpant as years of active participation after December 31, 1973. If a recipient makes the election, no portion of any distribution received by or made available to the recipient with respect to the employee (whether in the recipient's taxable year for which the election is made, or thereafter) is taxable to the recipient as long-term capital gain under section 403(a)(2) and this subparagraph.

* * *

Employee Trusts: Effective Dates

Employee Trusts: Tax Reform Act of 1984: Effective Dates.—Temporary Reg. §§1.404(a)-1T, 1.404(b)-1T, 1.404(d)-1T and 1.404(k)-1T are also proposed as final regulations and, when adopted, would become Reg. §§1.404(a)-1, 1.404(b)-1, 1.404(d)-1 and 1.404(k)-1 (published in the Federal Register on February 4, 1986).

§1.404(a)-1. Questions and answers relating to deductibility of deferred compensation and deferred benefits for employees.

§1.404(b)-1. Method or arrangement of contributions, etc., deferring the receipt of compensation or providing for deferred benefits.

§1.404(d)-1. Questions and answers relating to deductibility of deferred compensation and deferred benefits for independent contractors.

§1.404(k)-1. Questions and answers relating to deductibility of certain dividend distributions.

Individual Retirement Plans: Simplified Employee Pensions

Individual Retirement Plans: Simplified Employee Pensions.—Reproduced below is the text of proposed Reg. §1.404(h)-1, relating to individual retirement plans and simplified employee pensions (published in the Federal Register on July 14, 1981).

☐ Par. 5. There is added after §1.404(e)-1A the following new section:

§1.404(h)-1. Special rules for simplified employee pensions.—
(a) *In general.*—(1) Employer contributions to a simplified employee pension shall be treated as if they are made to a plan subject to the requirements of section 404. Employer contributions to a simplified employee pension are subject to the limitations of subparagraphs (2), (3), (4) and (5). For purposes of this paragraph, participants means those employees who satisfy the age, service and other requirements to participate in a simplified employee pension. For purposes of this paragraph, "compensation" means all of the compensation paid by the employer except either that for which a deduction is allowable under section 404(h) for simplified employee pensions or that for which a deduction is allowable under a plan that qualifies under section 401(a), including a plan that qualifies under section 404(a)(2) or 405.

(2) Employer contributions made for a calendar year are deductible for the taxable year of the employer with which or within which the calendar year ends.

(3) Contributions made within 3½ months after the close of a calendar year are treated as if they were made on the last day of such calendar year if they are made on account of such calendar year.

(4) The amount deductible for a taxable year for a simplified employee pension shall not exceed 15 percent of the compensation paid to the employees who are participants during the calendar year ending with or within the taxable year.

(5) The excess of the amount contributed over the amount deductible for a taxable year shall be deductible in the succeeding taxable years in order of time subject to the 15 percent limit of subparagraph (4).

(b) *Effect on stock bonus and profit-sharing trust.*—For any taxable year for which the employer has a deduction under section 404(h)(1), the otherwise applicable limitations in section 404(a)(3)(A) shall be reduced by the amount of the allowable deductions under section 404(h)(1) with respect to participants in the stock bonus or profit-sharing trust.

(c) *Effect on limit on deductions.*—For any taxable year for which the employer has an allowable deduction under section 404(h)(1), the otherwise applicable 25 percent limitations in section 404(a)(7) shall be reduced by the amount of the allowable deductions under section 404(h)(1) with respect to participants in the stock bonus or profit-sharing trust.

(d) *Effect on self-employed individuals or shareholder-employee.*—The limitations described in paragraphs (1), (2)(A), and (4) of section 404(e) or described in section 1379(b)(1) for any taxable year shall be reduced by the amount of the allowable deductions under section 404(h)(1) with respect to an employee within the meaning of section 401(c)(1) or a shareholder-employee (as defined in section 1379(d)).

(e) *Examples:.*—The provisions of this section may be illustrated by the following examples:

Example (1). Corporation X is a calendar-year taxpayer. On January 2, 1980, it adopts a simplified employee pension arrangement. At the end of 1980, it determines that it has paid $230,000 to all of its employees. Eight of its employees met its eligibility provisions for contributions to simplified employee pensions and their compensation totaled $140,000 before any contributions were made to their simplified employee pensions. Corporation X will be allowed to deduct its contributions to its employees' simplified employee pensions, not to exceed 15% of $140,000 or $21,000.

Example (2). Corporation Y is a calendar-year taxpayer which maintains a simplified employee pension agreement and a profit-sharing plan. The corporation has 100 employees. For the taxable year of 1980, it makes contributions to the simplified employee pensions of 75 of its employees. These contributions are 10 percent of compensation received in 1980. These same 75 employees are also participants in the corporation's profit-sharing plan. These 75 employees had total compensation paid during 1980 of $1,125,000. The corporation can deduct $112,500 under section 404(h) as its contributions to the simplified employee pension agreement. The corporation must reduce the otherwise applicable allowable deduction for contributions to the profit-sharing plan on behalf of these employees by the $112,500.

Example (3). Corporation Z is a calendar-year taxpayer which maintains a simplified employee pension arrangement and a profit-sharing plan. The corporation has 100 employees. For the taxable year of 1980, it makes contributions to the simplified employee pensions of 75 of its employees. These contributions are 10 percent of compensation received in 1980. Twenty-five of these employees are also participants in the corporation's profit-sharing plan. Each of these 75 employees had compensation for the year of $15,000, or total compensation of $1,125,000. The corporation deducts $112,500 under section 404(h) as its contribution to the simplified employee pension arrangement. The corporation must reduce the otherwise applicable allowable deduction for contributions to the profit-sharing plan on behalf of the 25 employees by $37,500, the amount contributed to the simplified employee pensions on behalf of employees covered by the profit-sharing plan.

Example (4). Corporation K is a taxpayer with a taxable year of December 1—November 30. On December 15, 1979, it adopts a simplified employee pension arrangement for its employees. It would like to make contributions to the plan on behalf of its employees for calendar year 1979. In order to make contributions to its employees' simplified employee pensions for calendar year 1979, the corporation must make the contributions by April 15, 1980. In order to receive a deduction for its taxable year ending November 30, 1980, for the contributions for calendar year 1979, the corporation must make the contributions by April 15, 1980. [Reg. § 1.404(h)-1.]

ESOPs: Stock: Dividends Paid Deduction

ESOPs: Stock: Dividends Paid Deduction.—Reg. § 1.404(k)-2, relating to employee stock ownership plans (ESOPs) by providing guidance concerning which corporation is entitled to the deduction for applicable dividends under Code Sec. 404(k) and by clarifying that a payment in redemption of employer securities held by an ESOP is not deductible, is proposed (published in the Federal Register on August 25, 2005) (REG-133578-05).

☐ Par. 3. Section 1.404(k)-2 is added to read as follows:

§ 1.404(k)-2. Dividends paid by corporation not maintaining ESOP.—

Q-1: What corporation is entitled to the deduction provided under section 404(k) for applicable dividends paid on applicable employer securities of a C corporation held by an ESOP if the ESOP benefits employees of more than one corporation or if the corporation paying the dividend is not the corporation maintaining the plan?

A-1: (a) *In general*. Under section 404(k), only the corporation paying the dividend is entitled to the deduction with respect to applicable employer securities held by an ESOP. Thus, no deduction is permitted to a corporation maintaining the ESOP if that corporation does not pay the dividend.

(b) *Example*. (i) *Facts*. S is a U.S. corporation that is wholly owned by P, an entity organized under the laws of Country A that is classified as a corporation for Federal income tax purposes. P is not engaged in a U.S. trade or business. P has a single class of common stock that is listed on a stock exchange in a foreign country. In addition, these shares are listed on the New York Stock Exchange, in the form of American Depositary Shares, and are actively traded through American Depositary Receipts (ADRs) meeting the requirements of section 409(l). S maintains an ESOP for its employees. The ESOP holds ADRs of P on Date X and receives a dividend with respect to those employer securities. The dividends received by the ESOP constitute applicable dividends as described in section 404(k)(2).

(ii) *Conclusion*. P, as the payor of the dividend, is entitled to a deduction under section 404(k) with respect to the dividends, although as a foreign corporation P does not obtain a U.S. tax benefit from the deduction. No corporation other than the corporation paying the dividend is entitled to the deduction under section 404(k). Thus, because S did not pay the dividends, S is not entitled to a deduction under section 404(k). The answer would be the same if P is a U.S. C corporation.

Q-2: What is the effective date of this section?

A-2: This section applies with respect to dividends paid on or after the date these regulations are published as final regulations in the Federal Register.

[Reg. § 1.404(k)-2.]

Foreign Deferred Compensation Plans: Limitations: Deductions: Adjustments: Earnings and Profits

Foreign Deferred Compensation Plans: Limitations: Deductions: Adjustments: Earnings and Profits.—Reproduced below are the texts of proposed Reg. §§ 1.404A-0—1.404A-7, relating to the limitations on deductions and adjustments to earnings and profits with respect to certain foreign deferred compensation plans (published in the Federal Register on May 7, 1993).

☐ Par. 2. Sections 1.404A-0 through 1.404A-7 are added as follows:

§ 1.404A-0. Table of Contents.—This section 1.404A-0 lists the major headings that appear in §§ 1.404A-1 through 1.404A-7.

Short taxable year.
Single plan.
Substantial risk of forfeiture.
Substantiation quality data.
Taxable year of a controlled foreign corporation.
Taxable year of a noncontrolled foreign corporation.
Taxpayer.
Termination of election.
Transition period.
Trust.
Unit credit method.
United States tax significance.
Written plan.
  (f) Application of other Code requirements.
    (1) Deductibility requirement.
    (2) Section 461 requirements.

§ 1.404A-2. Rules for qualified funded plans.
  (a) In general.
  (b) Payment to a trust.
    (1) Contribution requirements.
    (2) Trust requirements.
    (3) Retirement annuity.
    (4) Effect of reversion of overfunded contributions.
    (5) Example.
  (c) Contribution deemed made before payment.
    (1) Time of payment to trust.
    (2) Time of designation.
    (3) Irrevocable designation.
  (d) Limitation for qualified funded plans.
    (1) Plans with fixed or determinable benefits.
    (2) Plans without fixed or determinable benefits.
    (3) Limitations where more than one type of plan is maintained.
    (4) Carryover contributions.
    (5) Additional rules.
  (e) Examples.

§ 1.404A-3. Rules for qualified reserve plans.
  (a) Amounts taken into account with respect to qualified reserve plans.
    (1) General rule.
    (2) Amounts less than zero.
    (3) Exclusive rules for qualified reserve plans.
  (b) Reasonable addition to a reserve for liabilities.
    (1) General rule.
    (2) Unit credit method required.
    (3) Timing of valuation.
    (4) Permissible actuarial assumptions.
  (c) Ten-year amortization for certain changes in reserves.
    (1) Actuarial valuation.
    (2) Expected value of reserve.
    (3) Special rule for certain cost of living adjustments.
    (4) Anti-abuse rule.
  (d) Examples.

§ 1.404A-4. United States and foreign law limitations on amounts taken into account for qualified foreign plans.
  (a) In general.
  (b) Cumulative limitation.
  (c) Special rule for foreign corporations in pre-pooling years.
  (d) Rules relating to foreign currency.
    (1) Taxable years beginning after December 31, 1986.
    (2) Taxable years beginning before January 1, 1987.
    (3) Special rules for the net worth method of accounting.
  (e) Maintenance of more than one type of qualified foreign plan by an employer.
  (f) United States and foreign law limitations not applicable.
  (g) Definitions.
    (1) Cumulative United States amount.
    (2) Cumulative foreign amount.
    (3) Appropriate foreign tax law.
    (4) Aggregate amount.
  (h) Examples.

§ 1.404A-5. Additional limitations on amounts taken into account for qualified foreign plans.
  (a) Restrictions for nonqualified individuals.
    (1) General rule.
    (2) Determination of service attribution.
  (b) Records to be provided by taxpayer.
    (1) In general.

    (2) Primary evidence.
    (3) Additional requirements.
    (4) Secondary evidence.
    (5) Foreign language.
    (6) Additional information required by District Director.
    (7) Authorized officer to complete documents.
    (8) Transitional rules.
  (c) Actuarial requirements.
    (1) Reasonable actuarial assumptions.
    (2) Full funding limitation.

§ 1.404A-6. Elections under section 404A and changes in methods of accounting.
  (a) Elections, changes in accounting methods, and changes in plan years.
    (1) In general.
    (2) Single plan.
  (b) Initial elections under section 404A.
    (1) In general.
    (2) Time for making election.
    (3) Manner in which election is to be made.
    (4) Other requirements for election.
  (c) Termination of election when a plan ceases to be a qualified foreign plan.
    (1) In general.
    (2) Rules for changing method of accounting upon termination of election.
  (d) Other changes in methods of accounting and changes in plan year.
    (1) Application for consent.
    (2) Procedures for other changes in method of accounting.
    (3) Plan year.
  (e) Application of section 481.
    (1) In general.
    (2) Period of adjustment.
    (3) Allocation and source.
    (4) Example.
  (f) Computation of section 481(a) adjustment.
    (1) In general.
    (2) Old Method Closing Amount.
    (3) New Method Opening Amount.
    (4) Definitions and special rules.
    (5) Examples.
  (g) Initial section 404A (d) amounts.
    (1) In general.
    (2) Computation of amounts.
    (3) Example.

§ 1.404A-7. Effective date, retroactive elections, and transition rules.
  (a) In general.
    (1) Effective date.
    (2) Overview of retroactive elections for taxable years beginning before January 1, 1980.
    (3) Overview of special transition rules for election, revocation, and re-election.
  (b) Retroactive effective date elections for foreign subsidiaries.
    (1) In general.
    (2) Time and manner to make, perfect, or revoke election.
    (3) Requirement to amend returns.
  (c) Retroactive plan-by-plan elections for foreign subsidiaries.
    (1) In general.
    (2) Time and manner to make, perfect, or revoke election.
    (3) Requirement to amend returns.
    (4) Revocation after initial election and re-election permitted.
    (5) Examples.
  (d) Retroactive plan-by-plan qualified funded plan elections for plans of foreign branches.
    (1) In general.
    (2) Amounts allowed as a deduction.
    (3) Definitions.
    (4) Time and manner to make, perfect, or revoke election.
    (5) Examples.
  (e) Special transition rules for election, revocation and re-election.
    (1) In general.
    (2) Time and manner initially to elect, revoke and re-elect.
    (3) Revocation after initial election and re-election permitted.
    (4) Example.
  (f) Special data rules for retroactive elections.
    (1) Retroactive calculation of section 481(a) adjustments.

(2) Determination of reasonable addition to a reserve in interim years.

(3) Protective elections.

(g) Definitions and special rules.

(1) Method (1) election.

(2) Protective or Method (2) election.

(3) Open years of the taxpayer.

(4) Retroactive period.

(5) Transition period.

(6) Open period.

[Reg. § 1.404A-0.]

§1.404A-1. General rules concerning deductions and adjustments to earnings and profits for foreign deferred compensation plans.—(a) *In general.*—Section 404A provides the exclusive means by which an employer may take a deduction or reduce earnings and profits for deferred compensation in situations other than those in which a deduction or reduction of earnings and profits is permitted under section 404. A deduction or reduction of earnings and profits is permitted under section 404A for amounts paid or accrued by an employer under a foreign deferred compensation plan, in the taxable year in which the amounts are properly taken into account under §§ 1.404A-1 through 1.404A-7, if each of the following requirements is satisfied:

(1) The plan is a written plan maintained by the employer that provides deferred compensation.

(2) The plan is maintained for the exclusive benefit of the employer's employees or their beneficiaries.

(3) 90 percent or more of the amounts taken into account under the plan are attributable to services performed by nonresident aliens, the compensation for which is not subject to United States federal income tax.

(4) An election under §1.404A-6 or 1.404A-7 is made to treat the plan as either a qualified funded plan or a qualified reserve plan and to select a plan year.

(b) *90-percent test.*—(1) *Reserve plans.*—Paragraph (a)(3) of this section is not satisfied by a reserve plan unless 90 percent or more of the actuarial present value of the total vested benefits (i.e., benefits not subject to substantial risk of forfeiture) accrued under the plan is attributable to services performed by nonresident aliens, the compensation for which is not subject to United States federal income tax.

(2) *Funded plans.*—(i) *Individual account plans.*—Paragraph (a)(3) of this section is not satisfied by a funded plan with individual accounts unless 90 percent or more of the amounts allocated to individual accounts (as described in section 414(i)) under the plan are allocated to the accounts of nonresident aliens and are attributable to services the compensation for which is not subject to United States federal income tax.

(ii) *Plans without individual accounts.*—Paragraph (a)(3) of this section is not satisfied by a funded plan not described in paragraph (b)(2)(i) of this section unless 90 percent or more of the actuarial present value of the total benefits accrued under the plan is attributable to services performed by nonresident aliens the compensation for which is not subject to United States federal income tax.

(c) *Calculation of 90 percent amounts.*—(1) *In general.*—In determining whether the tests described in paragraphs (b)(1) and (b)(2)(ii) of this section are satisfied, accrued benefits and the actuarial present values of accrued benefits may be calculated under any reasonable method. See §1.404A-5(a) for rules describing the calculation of accrued benefits attributable to services for which the compensation is subject to United States federal income tax.

(2) *Safe harbor.*—The requirement of paragraph (a)(3) of this section will be deemed satisfied with respect to a plan if—

(i) The participants' benefits under the plan increase generally in proportion to their compensation taken into account under the plan; and

(ii) The sum of the following amounts does not exceed five percent of all compensation taken into account under the plan for the plan year—

(A) The compensation of United States citizens and residents taken into account under the plan; and

(B) Any other compensation subject to United States federal income tax taken into account under the plan.

(3) *Anti-abuse rule.*—Notwithstanding paragraph (c)(2) of this section, the requirement of paragraph (a)(3) of this section will not be deemed satisfied under paragraph (c)(2) of this section if the Commissioner determines that a significant purpose of the plan is to secure benefits not otherwise eligible for tax benefits under the Internal Revenue Code to participants who are United States citizens or residents.

(4) *Example.*—The principles of paragraphs (c)(2) and (c)(3) of this section are illustrated by the following example:

Example. A foreign branch of a domestic corporation maintains a deferred compensation plan under which benefits are based upon a participant's average compensation for the last five consecutive years of employment. The significant purposes of the plan do not include the provision of benefits otherwise unavailable under the Code to participants who are United States citizens or residents. The foreign branch maintains its books and records in its functional currency (FC). The taxpayer's taxable year and the plan year are coterminous with the calendar year. During the plan year in question, the compensation taken into account under the plan for all plan participants totals FC200 million. Of the FC200 million, FC6 million of the compensation taken into account under the plan is compensation for United States citizens and residents or otherwise subject to United States federal income tax. Because the FC6 million is less than five percent of all compensation taken into account under the plan for the plan year, the 90-percent requirement of paragraph (a)(3) of this section is deemed satisfied for this taxable year.

(d) *Deductions and reductions of earnings and profits.*—Deductions and reductions of earnings and profits for amounts paid by an employer to a plan that provides deferred compensation that does not meet the requirements of paragraph (a) of this section are governed exclusively by section 404, without regard to whether the plan benefits foreign employees.

(e) *Definitions.*—The following definitions apply for purposes of section 404A and §§ 1.404A-1 through 1.404A-7:

Actuarial present value. "Actuarial present value" is defined in §1.401(a)(4)-12.

Aggregate amount. "Aggregate amount" is defined in §1.404A-4(g)(4).

Appropriate foreign tax law. "Appropriate foreign tax law" is defined in §1.404A-4(g)(3).

Authorized officer. "Authorized officer" is defined in §1.404A-5(b)(7).

Carryover contributions. "Carryover contributions" are defined in §1.404A-2(d)(4).

Change in method of accounting. "Change in method of accounting" is defined in §1.404A-6(a).

Closing year. "Closing year" is defined in §1.404A-6(f)(4)(ii).

Contributions accumulated to pay deferred compensation. "Contributions accumulated to pay deferred compensation" are defined in §1.404A-2(b)(2).

Contributions to a trust. "Contributions to a trust" are defined in §1.404A-2(b)(1).

Controlled foreign corporation. "Controlled foreign corporation" means a controlled foreign corporation as defined in sections 953(c)(1)(B) and 957.

Cumulative foreign amount. "Cumulative foreign amount" is defined in §1.404A-4(g)(2).

Cumulative limitation. "Cumulative limitation" is defined in §1.404A-4(b).

Cumulative United States amount. "Cumulative United States amount" is defined in §1.404A-4(g)(1).

Deductible limit. "Deductible limit" is defined in §1.404A-2(d)(1)(i).

Deductions. "Deductions" are defined in §1.404A-1(f)(1).

Deferred compensation.—(i) *In general.*—"Deferred compensation" means any item the deductibility of which is determined by reference to section 404, without regard to whether section 404 permits a deduction and without regard to whether elections are made under §1.404A-6 or 1.404A-7. Deferred compensation, as described in the preceding sentence, does not include deferred benefits described in section 404(b)(2)(B).

(ii) *Social security.*—A plan under which a foreign government (including a political subdivision, agency or instrumentality thereof) makes a contribution or a direct payment to a participant (or the participant's beneficiary) does not provide deferred compensation to the extent of such contributions or payments. Thus, for example, a foreign country's social security system generally will not be considered as providing deferred compensation. However, the fact that employers are required to maintain the plan by reason of foreign law, or the fact that the plan supplements social security benefits provided by a foreign country, or provides benefits in lieu of such social security benefits, does not prevent a plan from providing deferred compensation.

(iii) *Termination indemnity plans.*—The determination of whether a plan (including a termination indemnity plan) provides deferred compensation must generally be made under paragraph (i) of this definition in light of all of the facts and circumstances. Benefits paid under a plan, including a plan denominated a termination indemnity plan will generally be treated as deferred compensation if—

(A) A major purpose of the plan is to provide for the payment of retirement benefits;

(B) The plan has a benefit formula providing for payment based at least in part upon length of service;

(C) The plan provides for the payment of benefits to employees (or their beneficiaries) after the employee's retirement, death or other termination of employment; and

(D) It meets such other requirements as may be prescribed by the Commissioner in guidance of general applicability with respect to termination indemnity plans.

(iv) *Example.*—The definition of deferred compensation is illustrated by the following example:

Example. A domestic corporation maintains a branch operation in foreign country *F*. *F* requires that all employers doing business in its country provide benefits to employees under a termination indemnity plan insured by *F*'s government. The plan provides for payments to employees who terminate employment for any reason, including retirement, death, voluntary resignation and discharge for cause (other than for gross misconduct) and permits withdrawals for certain hardship conditions. Upon separation, the employee (or his or her beneficiary) receives an amount equal to the accumulation on the employer's books of one-thirteenth of his or her annual salary for each year of employment, with specified adjustments for interest and inflation. This termination indemnity plan provides deferred compensation as described in paragraph (e) of this section.

Earnings and profits. "Earnings and profits" means earnings and profits computed in accordance with sections 312 and 964(a) and, for taxable years beginning after December 31, 1986, section 986 and the regulations thereunder; and for purposes of section 902 in taxable years beginning before January 1, 1987, accumulated profits within the meaning of section 902(c) as in effect on the day before the enactment of the Tax Reform Act of 1986.

Employer. "Employer" means a person that maintains a plan for the payment of deferred compensation for services provided to it by its employees. "Employer" for purposes of the acceleration of the section 481(a) adjustment is defined in § 1.404A-6(e)(2)(iv).

Equivalent of a trust. "Equivalent of a trust" means a fund—

(i) The corpus and income of which is separately identifiable and segregated, through a separate legal entity, from the general assets of the employer;

(ii) The corpus and income of which is not subject, under the applicable foreign law, to the claims of the employer's creditors prior to the claims of employees and their beneficiaries under the plan;

(iii) The corpus and income of which, by law or by contract, cannot at any time prior to the satisfaction of all liabilities with respect to employees under the plan be used for, or diverted to, any purpose other than providing benefits under the plan; and

(iv) The corpus and income of which is held by a person who has a legally enforceable duty to operate the fund prudently.

Erroneous deduction. "Erroneous deduction" is defined in § 1.404A-7(d)(3)(ii).

Exclusive benefit. "Exclusive benefit" has the same meaning as in §§ 1.401-2 and 1.413-1(d).

Fixed or determinable benefits. "Fixed or determinable benefits" are defined in § 1.404A-2(d)(1)(i).

Full funding limitation. "Full funding limitation" is defined in § 1.404A-5(c)(2).

Functional currency. "Functional currency" (abbreviated as FC) means the functional currency of a taxpayer or a qualified business unit determined in accordance with section 985(b) and the regulations thereunder, or, for taxable years beginning before January 1, 1987, the currency in which the employer's books and records were maintained for United States tax purposes.

Funded method. "Funded method" is defined in § 1.404A-6(f)(2)(iv).

Initial aggregate amount. "Initial aggregate amount" is defined in § 1.404A-6(g)(2)(iii).

Initial Cumulative foreign amount. "Initial Cumulative foreign amount" is defined in § 1.404A-6(g)(2)(ii).

Initial Cumulative United States amount. "Initial Cumulative United States amount" is defined in § 1.404A-6(g)(2)(i).

Initial section 404A(d) amounts. "Initial section 404A(d) amounts" are defined in § 1.404A-6(g).

Liability. "Liability" is defined in § 1.404A-1(f)(2).

Majority domestic corporate shareholders. "Majority domestic corporate shareholders" are defined in § 1.404A-6(c)(2)(ii)(C).

Method of accounting. "Method of accounting" is defined in § 1.404A-6(a)(1).

Method (1) election. "Method (1) election" is defined in § 1.404A-7(g)(1).

Method (2) election. "Method (2) election" is defined in § 1.404A-7(g)(2).

New Method Opening Amount. "New Method Opening Amount" is defined in § 1.404A-6(f)(3).

Noncontrolled foreign corporation. "Noncontrolled foreign corporation" means a foreign corporation other than a controlled foreign corporation.

Nonqualified individual. "Nonqualified individual" is defined in § 1.404A-5(a)(1).

Nonqualified plan. "Nonqualified plan" is defined in § 1.404A-6(f)(3)(iii).

Old Method Closing Amount. "Old Method Closing Amount" is defined in § 1.404A-6(f)(2).

Open period. "Open period" is defined in § 1.404A-7(g)(6).

Open years. "Open years" are defined in § 1.404A-7(g)(3).

Opening reserve. "Opening reserve" is defined in § 1.404A-6(f)(3)(i).

Opening year. "Opening year" is defined in § 1.404A-6(f)(4)(i).

Pay-as-you-go method. "Pay-as-you-go method" is defined in § 1.404A-6(f)(2)(iii).

Period of adjustment. "Period of adjustment" is defined in § 1.404A-6(e)(2).

Permitted plan year. "Permitted plan year" means the plan year of a plan providing deferred compensation ending with or within the employer's taxable year.

Plan year. "Plan year" means the annual accounting period of a plan providing deferred compensation.

Primary evidence. "Primary evidence" is defined in § 1.404A-5(b)(2).

Prior deduction. "Prior deduction" is defined in § 1.404A-7(d)(3)(i).

Protective election. "Protective election" is defined in § 1.404A-7(g)(2).

Qualified business unit. "Qualified business unit" is defined in section 989(a).

Qualified foreign plan. "Qualified foreign plan" means a plan that meets the requirements of paragraph (a) of this section.

Qualified funded plan. "Qualified funded plan" means a qualified foreign plan for which an election has been made under § 1.404A-6 or 1.404A-7 by the taxpayer to treat the plan as a qualified funded plan.

Qualified reserve plan. "Qualified reserve plan" means a qualified foreign plan for which an election has been made by the taxpayer under § 1.404A-6 or 1.404A-7 to treat the plan as a qualified reserve plan.

Reasonable actuarial assumptions. "Reasonable actuarial assumptions" are defined in § 1.404A-5(c).

Reductions in earnings and profits. "Reductions in earnings and profits" are defined in § 1.404A-1(f)(1).

Reserve method. "Reserve method" is defined in § 1.404A-6(f)(2)(ii).

Retirement annuity. "Retirement annuity" is defined in § 1.404A-2(b)(3).

Retroactive effective date election. "Retroactive effective date election" is defined in § 1.404A-7(b)(1).

Retroactive period. "Retroactive period" is defined in § 1.404A-7(g)(4).

Retroactive plan-by-plan election. "Retroactive plan-by-plan election" is defined in § 1.404A-7(c)(1) and (d)(1).

Revocation of election. "Revocation of election" is defined in § 1.404A-6(d)(1).

Secondary evidence. "Secondary evidence" is defined in § 1.404A-5(b)(4).

Separate funding entity. "Separate funding entity" is defined in § 1.404A-6(f)(4)(iii).

Short taxable year. "Short taxable year" is defined in § 1.404A-7(d)(2).

Single plan. "Single plan" is defined in § 1.404A-6(a)(2).

Substantial risk of forfeiture. "Substantial risk of forfeiture" is defined in § 1.404A-3(b)(2).

Substantiation quality data. "Substantiation quality data" means less than precise data that is nevertheless the best data available for the plan year at reasonable expense.

Taxable year of a controlled foreign corporation. "Taxable year of a controlled foreign corporation" means the taxable year as defined in sections 441(b) and 7701(a)(23), subject to section 898.

Taxable year of a noncontrolled foreign corporation. "Taxable year of a noncontrolled foreign corporation" means the taxable year as defined in sections 441(b) and 7701(a)(23).

Taxpayer. "Taxpayer" is defined in section 7701(a)(14).

Termination of election. "Termination of election" is defined in § 1.404A-6(c)(1).

Transition period. "Transition period" is defined in § 1.404A-7(g)(5).

Trust. "Trust" means a trust (as defined in § 301.7701-4(a) of this chapter) or the equivalent of a trust.

Unit credit method. "Unit credit method" is defined in § 1.404A-3(b)(2).

United States tax significance. "United States tax significance" is defined in §1.404A-6(b)(2)(ii).

Written plan. "Written plan" means a plan that is defined by plan instruments or required under the law of a foreign country, or both. An insurance contract can constitute a written plan.

(f) *Application of other Code requirements.*—(1) *Deductibility requirement.*—(i) *In general.*—In order to deduct amounts under section 404A, amounts contributed to a qualified funded plan or properly added to a reserve with respect to a qualified reserve plan must otherwise be deductible. The standards under section 404 are to be used in determining whether an amount would otherwise be deductible for this purpose. Thus, amounts may be taken into account under section 404A only to the extent that they are ordinary and necessary expenses during the taxable year in carrying on a trade or business and are compensation for personal services actually rendered before the end of the year. Similarly, in order to reduce earnings and profits under section 404A by amounts contributed to a qualified funded plan or properly added to a reserve with respect to a qualified reserve plan, earnings and profits must otherwise be able to be reduced by such amounts under the general principles of sections 312, 901, 902, 960, and 964.

(ii) *Capitalization requirements.*—In determining if an amount would otherwise be deductible (or able to be used to reduce earnings and profits) for purposes of paragraph (g)(1)(i) of this section, the fact that the amount is required to be capitalized (e.g., under section 263A) is ignored. Additionally, while section 404A and §§1.404A-1 through 1.404A-7 refer generally to permissible deductions or reductions of earnings and profits for deferred compensation, those references are intended to refer both to situations under which amounts may be taken into account as deductions or reductions of earnings and profits and to situations under which amounts may be taken into account through inclusion in the basis of inventory or through capitalization.

(2) *Section 461 requirements.*—In determining whether any amount of deferred compensation may be taken into account under section 404A by an accrual method taxpayer, the conditions for accrual under section 461 must be met with respect to the amount by the last day of the taxable year. For this purpose, an amount determined under §§1.404A-1 through 1.404A-7 establishes the fact of the liability and determines the amount of the liability with reasonable accuracy. See §1.461-4(d)(2)(iii), which generally provides that the economic performance requirement of section 461(h) is satisfied to the extent that any amount is otherwise properly taken into account under §§1.404A-1 through 1.404A-7. [Reg. §1.404A-1.]

§1.404A-2. Rules for qualified funded plans.—(a) *In general.*—Except as provided in this section and in §§1.404A-4 and 1.404A-5, the amount taken into account for a taxable year with respect to a qualified funded plan is the amount of the contributions paid by the employer to the trust in that year (regardless of whether the employer uses an accrual method of accounting). Accretions in a trust are not considered contributions to a plan.

(b) *Payment to a trust.*—(1) *Contribution requirements.*—Contributions paid under a qualified funded plan may not be taken into account unless they are—

(i) Paid to a trust which is operated in accordance with the requirements of section 401(a)(2);

(ii) Paid for a retirement annuity under which retirement benefits are provided and which is for the exclusive benefit of the employer's employees or their beneficiaries; or

(iii) Paid directly to a participant or beneficiary (rather than a trust).

(2) *Trust requirements.*—(i) *General rule.*—A contribution does not satisfy paragraph (b)(1)(i) of this section unless it is accumulated in the trust for the purpose of being distributed as deferred compensation. Whether a contribution is being accumulated in the trust for the purpose of being distributed as deferred compensation depends on the facts and circumstances. For purposes of paragraph (b)(1)(i) of this section, the fact that a trust has been (or has not been) involved in transactions that would be described in section 4975(c)(1) (and not exempted under section 4975(c)(2) or 4975(d)), e.g., contributions made in the form of a promissory note, if the plan were subject to section 4975(c)(1), is an important factor in determining whether the trust is not (or is) considered to be operated in accordance with the requirements of section 401(a)(2). In addition, a contribution to a trust does not satisfy paragraph (b)(1)(i) of this section unless it has substance.

(ii) *Effective date.*—The section 4975(c)(1) factor in determining compliance with section 401(a)(2) provided in this paragraph (b)(2) is taken into account for all transactions entered into after May 6, 1993.

(3) *Retirement annuity.*—A retirement annuity means a retirement annuity (as defined in section 404(a)(2)) except that the retirement annuity need not be part of a plan that meets the requirements of section 401(a) or 401(d). Notwithstanding the preceding sentence, the retirement annuity described therein need not be issued by an insurance company qualified to do business in a State in the United States if the taxpayer(s) and/or sponsoring employer(s) of the plan have shifted the risk of making payments under the plan to an entity that is qualified to do business in the country (or countries) where the plan is maintained.

(4) *Effect of reversion of overfunded contributions.*—If any portion of a contribution to a trust may revert to the benefit of the employer before the satisfaction of all liabilities to employees or their beneficiaries covered by the trust, no amount of the contribution may be taken into account under this section.

(5) *Example.*—The principles of paragraph (b) of this section are illustrated by the following example:

Example. A foreign subsidiary of a domestic corporation maintains a deferred compensation plan for its employees. The foreign subsidiary makes annual contributions under the plan to a trust. Each year after the contribution is made to the trust, the trustee lends the contribution back to the foreign subsidiary maintaining the plan. The foreign subsidiary executes promissory notes obligating it to repay the borrowed funds (at a reasonable rate of interest) to the trust and to pay any benefits due under the plan. Notwithstanding that the taxpayer may have designated the plan as a qualified funded plan, amounts may not be taken into account under section 404A with respect to contributions to the trust because the loans cause the trust to fail the requirements of section 401(a)(2). Even if the loans do not cause the trust to violate section 401(a)(2), the portion of any contribution that is loaned to the foreign subsidiary could not be taken into account because, to the extent of the loan (or loans), the contribution lacks substance and is not accumulated in the trust.

(c) *Contribution deemed made before payment.*—(1) *Time of payment to trust.*—Regardless of whether an employer uses the cash or an accrual method of accounting, for purposes of this section, a contribution to a trust that is paid after the close of an employer's taxable year is deemed to have been paid on the last day of that taxable year if—

(i) The payment is made on account of the taxable year and is made not later than the 15th day of the ninth month after the close of the taxable year;

(ii) The payment is treated by the plan in the same manner that the plan would treat a payment actually received on the last day of the taxable year; and

(iii) Either—

(A) The employer notifies the plan administrator or trustee in writing that the payment to the plan is designated on account of the taxable year;

(B) The taxpayer claims the payment as a deduction on its tax return for the taxable year; or

(C) The employer reduces earnings and profits with respect to the payment.

(2) *Time of designation.*—Any designation of a payment pursuant to paragraph (c)(1)(iii)(A) of this section must occur not later than the time described in paragraph (c)(1)(i) of this section.

(3) *Irrevocable designation.*—After a payment has been designated or claimed on a return in the manner provided in paragraph (c)(1)(iii)(A) of this section as being on account of a taxable year, the designation or claim may not be retracted or changed.

(d) *Limitation for qualified funded plans.*—(1) *Plans with fixed or determinable benefits.*—(i) *Limit on amount taken into account.*—Contributions made to a qualified funded plan under which the benefits are fixed or determinable are not taken into account under this section to the extent they exceed the amount that would be taken into account under section 404(a)(1)(A)(ii) and (iii) (determined without regard to the last sentence of paragraph (A) of section 404(a)(1) and without regard to whether the trust is exempt under section 501(a)). Benefits are considered fixed or determinable for this purpose if either benefits under or contributions to the plan are definitely determinable within the meaning of §1.401-1(b)(1)(i). The limit described in the first sentence of this paragraph (d)(1)(i) is determined on the basis of the permitted plan year of the qualified foreign plan. Thus, the limit for the employer's taxable year is the limit for the plan year ending with or within the employer's taxable year.

(ii) *Actuarial valuation requirements.*—In determining the amount to be taken into account under this section, an actuarial valuation must be made not less frequently than once every three years. However, an actuarial valuation must be made for the first plan year of the plan for which an election under §1.404A-6 is in effect. For interim years, a reasonable actuarial determination of whether the full funding limit in §1.404A-5(c)(2) applies to the qualified funded plan must be made. The Commissioner may require a full actuarial valuation in an interim year under appropriate circumstances. See §1.404A-6 for rules on changes in methods of accounting.

(2) *Plans without fixed or determinable benefits.*—Contributions made to a qualified funded plan under which the benefits are not fixed or determinable may not be taken into account under this section to the extent they exceed the limitations of section 404(a)(3) (determined without regard to whether the payment is made to a trust that is exempt under section 501(a)).

(3) *Limitations where more than one type of plan is maintained.*— Where payments are made for a taxable year to more than one type of qualified funded plan, the amounts that may be taken into account for the taxable year with respect to the payments are subject to the limitations of section 404(a)(7). The amount that is taken into account under this paragraph (d)(3) is determined without regard to whether the payment satisfies the minimum funding standard described in section 412.

(4) *Carryover contributions.*—In the event that the aggregate amount of contributions paid during an employer's taxable year in which an election under section 404A is in effect (reduced by an amount described in section 404A(g)(1)) exceeds the amount that may be taken into account under section 404A(a) and this section (computed without regard to section 404A(d) and §1.404A-4), the excess contributions are treated as an amount paid in the succeeding taxable year with respect to that qualified foreign plan. A carryover contribution is also taken into account in determining whether a carryover contribution exists for a succeeding taxable year.

(5) *Additional rules.*—The Commissioner may prescribe additional rules for determining the amount that may be taken into account under this paragraph (d) in guidance of general applicability.

(e) *Examples.*—The principles of this section are illustrated by the following examples:

Example 1. A qualified funded plan under which benefits are not fixed or determinable is maintained by a foreign branch of a domestic corporation. The foreign branch computes its income in units of local currency, the FC. The taxpayer's taxable year and the plan year are coterminous with the calendar year. The plan was established in 1985, and the taxpayer made an election to apply section 404A, a qualified funded plan election as described in §1.404A-6. For the 1985 taxable year, the employer made a FC25,000 contribution under the plan, and FC15,000 of that contribution could be taken into account under paragraph (d)(2) of this section. The cumulative foreign amount for the 1985 taxable year was FC20,000. The amount of the excess contribution carried forward was FC10,000 (FC25,000–FC15,000), because the amount of the carryover contribution is determined without regard to section 404A(d) and §1.404A-4.

Example 2. Assume the same facts as in *Example 1*, except that the entire FC25,000 contribution made under the plan may be taken into account under paragraph (d)(2) of this section. The amount of the excess contribution carried forward was zero, even though the cumulative United States amount may have exceeded the cumulative foreign amount for the taxable year, because the amount of the excess contribution is determined without regard to section 404A(d) and §1.404A-4.

Example 3. P, a domestic corporation, owns all of the one class of stock of foreign corporation S. The taxable year for P is the calendar year. The taxable year for S is the fiscal year beginning on June 1. S made a contribution to its qualified funded plan on February 15, 1983, and notified the plan's trustee in writing that S designated the contribution as a payment on account of S's preceding taxable year (ending May 31, 1982). The contribution is taken into account in computing S's earnings and profits for S's taxable year ending May 31, 1982. [Reg. §1.404A-2.]

§1.404A-3. Rules for qualified reserve plans.—(a) *Amounts taken into account with respect to qualified reserve plans.*—(1) *General rule.*— Except as provided in §§1.404A-4 and 1.404A-5, the amount taken into account for a taxable year with respect to a qualified reserve plan equals the sum of—

(i) The reasonable addition during the permitted plan year to a reserve for liabilities under the plan as described in paragraph (b) of this section; and

(ii) The amortization of certain increases or decreases in the plan reserve over ten years, as described in paragraph (c) of this section.

(2) *Amounts less than zero.*—If the amount to be taken into account under this section is less than zero, that amount must be treated as an increase in income and earnings and profits for the taxable year.

(3) *Exclusive rules for qualified reserve plans.*—No amounts may be taken into account with respect to a qualified reserve plan except as provided for in this section. Thus, for example, no deduction is allowed for benefit payments from the reserve. Similarly, no amount may be taken into account for any payments made by the employer that are used either to reinsure the liabilities or benefits under a qualified reserve plan or to fund separately all or a portion of the benefits under a qualified reserve plan. These amounts may, however, be taken into account as contributions to a qualified funded plan to the extent the requirements of §1.404A-2 are satisfied.

(b) *Reasonable addition to a reserve for liabilities.*—(1) *General rule.*—Except as provided in §1.404A-7(f)(2), the reasonable addition to a reserve for a plan year equals the increase in the reserve, determined under the unit credit method as described in paragraph (b)(2) of this section, that arises from the passage of time and from additional service and expected changes in compensation in the current plan year for employees who were included in the reserve as of the end of the prior plan year. Thus, the reasonable addition to the reserve includes an element of interest on the reserve as of the beginning of the plan year (less the interest on the benefit payments during the plan year) and the actuarial present value of the expected increase in vested benefits accrued during the current plan year for employees who were included in the reserve as of the end of the prior plan year, determined without reference to any plan amendment during the plan year.

(2) *Unit credit method required.*—The reserve for the employer's liability must be determined under the unit credit method. Thus, the reserve must be the actuarial present value of the employer's liability, taking into account service and compensation only through the valuation date. In determining the reserve under this section, benefits that are subject to a substantial risk of forfeiture may not be taken into account. The term "substantial risk of forfeiture" has the meaning stated in section 83, except that the term "property" in all events includes benefits accrued under a qualified reserve plan.

(3) *Timing of valuation.*—The determination of the reserve and the reasonable addition to the reserve must be made as of the last day of the plan year.

(4) *Permissible actuarial assumptions.*—(i) *Interest rates.*—(A) *In general.*—Notwithstanding any other provision of §§1.404A-1 through 1.404A-7, no amount may be taken into account under section 404A with respect to a qualified reserve plan unless the rate (or rates) of interest for the plan that are selected by the employer are within the permissible range. The interest rate selected by the employer for the plan under this paragraph must remain in effect for that plan until the first plan year for which that rate is no longer within the permissible range. At that time, a new rate of interest must be selected by the employer from within the permissible range applicable at that time.

(B) *Permissible range.*—For purposes of this paragraph (b)(4), the term "permissible range" means a rate of interest that is not more than 1.2 and not less than the product of 0.8 multiplied by the average rate of interest for the highest quality long-term corporate bonds denominated in the functional currency of the qualified business unit of the employer whose books reflect the plan's liabilities for the 15-year period ending on the last day before the beginning of the employer's taxable year. If there is no market in long-term corporate bonds denominated in the relevant functional currency, or if the qualified business unit computes its income or earnings and profits in dollars under §1.985-3, the employer must use a rate that can be demonstrated clearly to reflect income, based on all relevant facts and circumstances, including appropriate rates of inflation and commercial practices.

(ii) *Plan benefits.*—Except as otherwise provided by the Commissioner, changes in plan benefits or applicable foreign law that become effective (whether or not retroactively) in a future plan year may not be taken into account until the plan year the change is effective. Notwithstanding the above, the reserve calculation may take into account cost-of-living adjustments that are part of the employee's vested accrued benefit, using assumptions regarding cost-of-living adjustments that are consistent with the interest rate assumptions described in paragraph (b)(4)(i) of this section and the terms of the plan. Thus, for example, a cost-of-living adjustment that does not require any future service on the part of the employee and is not subject to employer discretion may be taken into account.

(c) *Ten-year amortization for certain changes in reserves.*—(1) *Actuarial valuation.*—Each plan year an actuarial valuation must be made as of the end of the plan year, comparing the actual reserve with the expected value of the reserve. Any difference between the actual reserve determined as of the end of the plan year and the expected value of the reserve as of that date must be amortized in level amounts of principal over ten years, beginning in the plan year of the actuarial valuation. This amortization applies regardless of whether the difference is attributable to changes in employee population, changes in plan provisions, or changes in actuarial assumptions.

(2) *Expected value of reserve.*—The expected value of the reserve as of the end of the plan year is equal to the sum of the reserve as of the end of the prior plan year plus the reasonable addition to the reserve for the plan year described in paragraph (b) of this section less the benefit payments during the plan year. Thus, the expected value of the reserve is generally determined on the basis of the plan in effect and the actuarial assumptions used as of the end of the prior plan year, but, because it includes the reasonable addition to the reserve, includes the effect of expected changes in compensation, service and vesting during the current plan year.

(3) *Special rule for certain cost of living adjustments.*—Notwithstanding the general rule that the increase in liability from a plan amendment is amortized over ten years, if under foreign law a shorter period for amortization is required, that shorter period shall be substituted for ten years in this paragraph (c) if the amendment is a cost of living adjustment that either—

(i) Relates primarily to retirees; or

(ii) Is for employees of a foreign corporation in a taxable year beginning before [INSERT DATE THAT IS 90 DAYS AFTER THE DATE OF PUBLICATION OF FINAL REGULATIONS IN THE FEDERAL REGISTER].

(4) *Anti-abuse rule.*—The Commissioner may reclassify any item included by a taxpayer as a reasonable addition to a reserve as instead subject to amortization over ten years if the Commissioner determines that the taxpayer's classification of that item circumvents the intent of section 404A(c)(4). Thus, for example, if the Commissioner determines that the vesting provisions of the plan cause the increase in vested benefits to be unreasonably large in a single plan year, the reasonable addition under paragraph (b) of this section must be calculated without recognizing any changes in vesting for the plan year.

Year	End of Year Age
1980	41
1981	42
1982	43
1983	44
1984	45

Year	Compensation for Each Employee
1980	10,000
1981	10,000
1982	10,000
1983	12,000
1984	12,000

Year	Benefit Payments
1980	0
1981	0
1982	0
1983	369
1984	6,396

(b) *Computation of amounts taken into account for 1980.* The amount taken into account for 1980 was zero because there was no reasonable addition to the reserve (i.e., no increase in the reserve on account of the passage of time, additional service or expected changes in compensation for employees who were included in the reserve at the end of the prior year) and there were no amounts that are subject to ten-year amortization under paragraph (c) of this section.

(c) *Computation of amounts taken into account for 1981.* There was no amount taken into account for 1981 for the same reason as in 1980.

(d) *Computation of amount taken into account for 1982.* The amount taken into account in 1982 was the sum of the reasonable addition to the reserve determined under paragraph (b) of this section and the amortization of certain increases in the plan reserve over ten years determined under paragraph (c) of this section. There was no reasonable addition to the reserve (i.e., no increase in the reserve on account of the passage of time, additional service or expected changes in compensation for employees who were included in the reserve at the end of the prior year) for the 1982 year because no employee was included in the reserve as of the end of 1981. There were no benefits paid during 1981. Thus, the expected value of the reserve at the end of 1982 was zero. However, the actual value of the reserve at the end of 1982 was FC733,134 (9,931 employees x 60 x 1.230380). The difference between the expected and actual values of the reserve was taken into account over ten years beginning in 1982. Thus, the total amount taken into account for 1982 was FC73,313.

(e) *Computation of amount taken into account for 1983.* Using the employee data as of the end of 1982 and the expected rate of compensation increase for 1983, each employee's accrued benefit was

(d) *Examples.*—The principles of this section are illustrated by the following examples:

Example 1. S, a foreign subsidiary of P, a domestic corporation, contributes funds to an irrevocable trust which is used to pay benefits provided under S's reserve plan. The trust does not satisfy the requirements of section 401(a), 404(a)(4), or 404(a)(5). The funds are not used to provide benefits in addition to those provided by the reserve plan. In 1984, the year the plan was adopted, S elected to treat the plan as a qualified reserve plan. In 1984, S also contributed an amount to the irrevocable trust. The fact that S contributed an amount to the trust has no effect on the computation of the amount that S is entitled to take into account under this section in 1984 (or in any other year). Furthermore, no additional amount may be taken into account for the amount of the contribution to the trust beyond the amount permitted to be taken into account under this section.

Example 2. (a) Employer Y hired 10,000 employees in 1980, each of whom was age 40 at the beginning of the year and earned FC10,000. The employees immediately commenced participation in the plan. The plan provided that the accrued benefit at the end of X years equaled: (X multiplied by one percent) multiplied by the highest one year's compensation. The plan vesting was 20 percent per year starting after two years of service with the employer. Under the plan, once an employee was vested in a benefit, the benefit could not be forfeited for any reason other than the death of the employee. Employees who terminate employment for reasons other than death or retirement receive an immediate single sum distribution in an amount equal to the actuarial present value (calculated at eight percent interest) of the vested accrued benefit (where the actuarial present value and the vested accrued benefit are determined as of the end of the prior plan year). Reserves and expected increases in the reserve were determined using eight percent interest, five percent assumed compensation increases, the UP-84 mortality table and assuming no pre-retirement terminations other than death. However as set forth in the relevant data below, the actual experience differed from these assumptions (e.g., the actual compensation did not increase five percent each year and the mortality and termination experience were different than assumed).

Number of Deaths	Number of Terminations	Number of Employees Remaining
16	5	9,979
18	5	9,956
20	5	9,931
25	5	9,901
30	25	9,846

End of Year Accrued Benefit for Each Employee	End of Year Vested Accrued Benefit for Each Employee
100	0
200	0
300	60
480	192
600	360

End of Year Actuarial Factor	End of Year Reserve for Vested Benefits
1.049706	0
1.136328	0
1.230380	733,134
1.332564	2,533,194
1.443638	5,117,062

expected to be 420 (10,500 × 4 years × .01) as of the end of 1983. 40 percent of this accrued benefit, or 168, was expected to be vested. Thus, the expected increase in each employee's vested accrued benefit was 108 (the difference between 168 and the vested accrued benefit as of the end of the prior year (60) for those employees who were included in the reserve as of the end of the prior year). There were 9,931 employees included in the reserve as of the end of the prior year and 9,931 × p_{43} were expected to be in the reserve as of the end of 1983. The actuarial present value factor for a deferred annuity of FC1 commencing at age 65 payable monthly is 1.332564. Thus, the actuarial present value of the expected increase in vested accrued benefits as of the end of the year was FC1,425,212 (9,931 employees × p_{43} × 108 × 1.332564). The reasonable addition to the reserve also included an element of interest on the reserve as of the end of the prior year equal to FC58,651 (8 percent × 733,134) that is offset by the interest attributable to the actual benefits paid during the year (FC15, which is interest on the benefits paid during the year (FC369) from the date of payment through the end of the year). Thus, the reasonable addition to the reserve for 1983 was FC1,483,848 (1,425,212 + 58,651 – 15) and the expected reserve at the end of the year was FC2,216,613 (733,134 + 1,483,848 – 369). The actual reserve at the end of 1983 is FC2,533,194, so there was an actuarial loss of FC316,581 (2,533,194 – 2,216,613) which was amortized over 10 years beginning in 1983. Thus, the total amount taken into account in 1983 was FC1,588,819 (1,483,848 + 73,313 + 10 percent of 316,581).

(f) *Computation of amount taken into account for 1984.* Using the employee data as of the end of 1983 and the expected rate of compensation increase for 1984, each employee's accrued benefit was expected to be 630 (12,600 × 5 years × .01) as of the end of 1984. 60

percent of this accrued benefit, or 378, was expected to be vested. Thus, the expected increase in each employee's vested accrued benefit was 186 (the difference between 378 and the vested accrued benefit as of the end of the prior year (192) for those employees who were included in the reserve as of the end of the prior year). There were 9,901 employees included in the reserve as of the end of the prior year and $9,901 \times p_{44}$ were expected to be in the reserve as of the end of 1984. The actuarial present value factor for a deferred annuity of FC1 commencing at age 65 payable monthly is 1.443638. Thus, the actuarial present value of the expected increase in vested accrued benefits as of the end of the year was FC2,650,355 (9,901 employees $\times p_{44} \times 186 \times 1.443638$). The reasonable addition to the reserve also included an element of interest on the reserve as of the end of the

prior year equal to FC202,656 (8 percent $\times$ 2,533,194), offset by interest attributable to the actual benefits paid during the year (FC256, which is interest on the benefits paid during the year (FC6,396) from the date of payment through the end of the year). Thus, the reasonable addition to the reserve for 1984 was FC2,852,755 (2,650,355 + 202,656 − 256) and the expected reserve at the end of the year is FC5,379,553 (2,533,194 + 2,852,755 − 6,396). The actual reserve at the end of 1984 was FC5,117,062, so there was an actuarial gain of FC262,491 (5,379,553 − 5,117,062) which was amortized over 10 years beginning in 1984. Thus, the total amount taken into account in 1984 was FC2,931,477 (2,852,755 + 73,313 + 31,658 − 10 percent of 262,491).

(g) *Alternative computation method.* The amounts taken into account for 1982, 1983 and 1984 may also be illustrated as follows—

1982
Worksheet For Calculating Amount Taken Into Account For Qualified Reserve Plans Under § 404A

(1)	Reserve at end of Prior Year	0
(2)	Interest on (1) to end of Current Year	0
(3)	Present Value of the Expected Increase in Vested Accrued Benefits for employees who were included in the reserve as of the end of the prior year.	0
(4)	Benefit Payments during current year	0
(5)	Interest on (4) from date of payment through end of Current year	0
(6)	Reasonable addition to the reserve (2) + (3) − (5)	0
(7)	Expected value of reserve (1) + (6) − (4)	0
(8)	Actual value of reserve	733,134
(9)	Amount to be amortized (8) − (7)	733,134
(10)	Remaining 10 Percent Bases from Prior Years (original amounts) (Item 12 from Prior Year)	0
(11)	10 percent Bases whose 10 years ended last year	0
(12)	(9) + (10) − (11)	733,134
(13)	10 percent of (12)	73,313
(14)	Amount Taken Into Account for Current Year [(6) + (13)]	73,313

1983
Worksheet For Calculating Amount Taken Into Account For Qualified Reserve Plans Under § 404A

(1)	Reserve at end of Prior Year	733,134
(2)	Interest on (1) to end of Current Year	58,651
(3)	Present Value of the Expected Increase in Vested Accrued Benefits for employees who were included in the reserve as of the end of the prior year	1,425,212
(4)	Benefit Payments during current year	369
(5)	Interest on (4) from date of payment through end of Current year	15
(6)	Reasonable addition to the reserve (2) + (3) − (5)	1,483,848
(7)	Expected value of reserve (1) + (6) − (4)	2,216,613
(8)	Actual value of reserve	2,533,194
(9)	Amount to be amortized (8) − (7)	316,581
(10)	Remaining 10 Percent Bases from Prior Years (original amounts) (Item 12 from Prior Year)	733,134
(11)	10 percent Bases whose 10 years ended last year	0
(12)	(9) + (10) − (11)	1,049,715
(13)	10 percent of (12)	104,971
(14)	Amount Taken Into Account for Current Year [(6) + (13)]	1,588,819

1984
Worksheet For Calculating Amount Taken Into Account For Qualified Reserve Plans Under § 404A

(1)	Reserve at end of Prior Year	2,533,194
(2)	Interest on (1) to end of Current Year	202,656
(3)	Present Value of the Expected Increase in Vested Accrued Benefits for employees who were included in the reserve as of the end of the prior year.	2,650,355
(4)	Benefit Payments during current year	6,396
(5)	Interest on (4) from date of payment through end of Current year	256
(6)	Reasonable addition to the reserve (2) + (3) − (5)	2,852,755
(7)	Expected value of reserve (1) + (6) − (4)	5,379,553
(8)	Actual value of reserve	5,117,062
(9)	Amount to be amortized (8) − (7)	(262,491)
(10)	Remaining 10 Percent Bases from Prior Years (original amounts) (Item 12 from Prior Year)	1,049,715
(11)	10 percent Bases whose 10 years ended last year	0
(12)	(9) + (10) − (11)	787,224
(13)	10 percent of (12)	78,722
(14)	Amount Taken Into Account for Current Year [(6) + (13)]	2,931,477

Example 3. (a) The facts are the same as in *Example 2*, except that the interest rate used to determine the reserve as of the end of 1984 has been decreased to 7%.

(b) The amount taken into account for 1984 under the alternative calculation method is determined as follows:

1984
Worksheet For Calculating Amount Taken Into Account For Qualified Reserve Plans Under § 404A

(1)	Reserve at end of Prior Year	2,533,194

Reg. § 1.404A-3(d)

(2)	Interest on (1) to end of Current Year	202,656
(3)	Present Value of the Expected Increase in Vested Accrued Benefits for employees who were included in the reserve as of the end of the prior year.	3,402,637
(4)	Benefit Payments during current year	6,396
(5)	Interest on (4) from date of payment through end of Current year	256
(6)	Reasonable addition to the reserve (2) + (3) − (5)	3,605,037
(7)	Expected value of reserve (1) + (6) − (4)	6,131,835
(8)	Actual value of reserve	6,569,498
(9)	Amount to be amortized (8) − (7)	437,663
(10)	Remaining 10 Percent Bases from Prior Years (original amounts) (Item 12 from Prior Year)	1,049,715
(11)	10 percent Bases whose 10 years ended last year	0
(12)	(9) + (10) − (11)	1,487,378
(13)	10 percent of (12)	148,738
(14)	Amount Taken Into Account for Current Year [(6) + (13)]	3,753,775

[Reg. § 1.404A-3.]

§1.404A-4. United States and foreign law limitations on amounts taken into account for qualified foreign plans.—(a) *In general.*—Section 404A(d) and this section place two limits on the amount taken into account for a taxable year with respect to a qualified foreign plan under section 404A(b) and (c) and §§ 1.404A-2 and 1.404A-3. First, as set forth in paragraph (b) of this section, the cumulative amounts that are or have been taken into account under section 404A through the end of the current year may not exceed the cumulative amounts deductible under foreign law in that period. Because the foreign law deduction is cumulative, however, amounts previously disallowed under this rule are taken into account in later years as the amount deductible under foreign law increases. Second, for taxable years beginning before January 1, 1987, or such later year determined under section 902(c)(3)(A), the rule in paragraph (c) of this section further limits the amount taken into account during those taxable years. Because section 404A(d) and this section apply solely to amounts that would otherwise be taken into account under § 1.404A-2 or 1.404A-3, these limitations are applied without regard to amounts taken into account under section 481 (i.e., without regard to the portion of a section 481(a) adjustment that is taken into account during any taxable year within the section 481(a) adjustment period, as defined in § 1.404A-6(e)(2)). See § 1.404A-6, however, for rules applying the section 404A(d) limitations to the calculation of the section 481(a) adjustment.

(b) *Cumulative limitation.*—The amount taken into account with respect to a qualified foreign plan for any taxable year equals—

(1) The lesser of—

(i) The cumulative United States amount; or

(ii) The cumulative foreign amount;

(2) Reduced by the aggregate amount.

(c) *Special rule for foreign corporations in pre-pooling years.*—For a taxable year of a foreign corporation beginning before January 1, 1987, or such later year determined under section 902(c)(3)(A), the reduction in earnings and profits determined under paragraph (b) of this section with respect to a qualified foreign plan may not exceed the amount allowed as a deduction under the appropriate foreign tax laws for such taxable year. See *Example 3* of paragraph (h) of this section for an illustration of this rule.

(d) *Rules relating to foreign currency.*—(1) *Taxable years beginning after December 31, 1986.*—For taxable years beginning after December 31, 1986, the cumulative United States amount, the cumulative foreign amount, and the aggregate amount must be computed in the employer's functional currency. See generally section 964 and sections 985 through 989 for rules applicable to determining and translating into dollars the amount of income or loss of foreign branches and earnings and profits (or deficits in earnings and profits) of foreign corporations.

(2) *Taxable years beginning before January 1, 1987.*—For taxable years beginning before January 1, 1987, the cumulative United States amount, the cumulative foreign amount, and the aggregate amount must be computed in the currency in which the foreign branch or foreign subsidiary kept its books and records. See Rev. Rul. 75-106, 1975-1 C.B. 31 (see § 601.601(d)(2)(ii)(*b*) of this chapter), for rules for determining the amount of income or loss of foreign branches using a net worth method of accounting. See Rev. Rul. 75-107, 1975-1 C.B. 32 (see § 601.601(d)(2)(ii)(*b*) of this chapter), for rules for determining the amount of income or loss of foreign branches using a profit and loss method of accounting. See sections 312, 902, and 1248 and the regulations thereunder for rules for determining the earnings and profits of noncontrolled foreign corporations. See section 964 and the regula-

tions thereunder for rules for determining the earnings and profits of foreign corporations for purposes of subpart F.

(3) *Special rules for the net worth method of accounting.*—For purposes of § 1.964-1(e)(4), an amount of deduction that is accrued but not paid at the end of the employer's taxable year with respect to a qualified funded plan must be treated as a short-term liability. In the case of a qualified reserve plan, for purposes of § 1.964-1(e), the amount of the reserve taken into account as a liability on the balance sheet as of the beginning of the taxable year must be limited to the aggregate amount, and the amount of the reserve taken into account as a liability on the balance sheet as of the close of the taxable year must be limited to the sum of the aggregate amount and the amount taken into account for the taxable year. For purposes of § 1.964-1(e)(4), each annual increase in the aggregate amount must be treated as a long-term liability incurred on the last day of the employer's taxable year to which the increase relates. As of the close of each taxable year, a portion of the aggregate amount equal to the amount of benefits expected to be paid during the succeeding taxable year must be reclassified as a short-term liability. The reclassified amount must be allocated to the annual increases in the aggregate amount on a first-in-first-out basis. Similar rules apply for purposes of determining the amount of reserve taken into account by a foreign branch using the net worth method of accounting for taxable years beginning before January 1, 1987, and by a qualified business unit that uses the United States dollar approximate separate transactions method of accounting under § 1.985-3 in a taxable year beginning after December 31, 1986.

(e) *Maintenance of more than one type of qualified foreign plan by an employer.*—In determining the deduction or reduction in earnings and profits when an employer maintains one plan for purposes of foreign law that is treated as two separate plans for purposes of § 1.404A-6(a)(2), the cumulative United States amount for each plan must be combined for purposes of paragraphs (a) and (b) of this section. See *Example 5* of paragraph (h) of this section for an illustration of this rule.

(f) *United States and foreign law limitations not applicable.*—The limitations set forth in this section do not apply to the adjustments required by section 481, section 446(e) and section 2(e)(3)(A) of Public Law 96-603.

(g) *Definitions.*—(1) *Cumulative United States amount.*—The term "cumulative United States amount" means (with respect to a qualified foreign plan) the amount determined under section 404A (without regard to section 404A(d)) for the taxable year of the employer and for all consecutive prior taxable years for which an election under section 404A was in effect for the plan plus the "initial section 404A amount" within the meaning of § 1.404A-6(g)(2)(i).

(2) *Cumulative foreign amount.*—The term "cumulative foreign amount" means (with respect to a qualified foreign plan) the cumulative amount allowed as a deduction under the appropriate foreign tax law for the taxable year of the employer and for all consecutive prior taxable years for which an election under section 404A was in effect for the plan plus the initial section 404A amount within the meaning of § 1.404A-6(g)(2)(ii).

(3) *Appropriate foreign tax law.*—The appropriate foreign tax law is the income tax law of the country (other than the United States) that is the principal place of business of the qualified business unit of the employer whose books reflect the plan liabilities.

(4) *Aggregate amount.*—The term "aggregate amount" means (with respect to a qualified foreign plan) amounts permitted to be

taken into account under section 404A(d)(1) for all consecutive prior taxable years for which an election under section 404A was in effect for the plan plus the initial section 404A amount required by §1.404A-6(g)(2)(iii).

(h) *Examples.*—The principles of this section are illustrated by the following examples:

Example 1. X, a foreign subsidiary of a domestic corporation, maintains its main office in foreign country *A*, and a branch, *Y*, in foreign country *B*. The functional currency of *X* is the FC. *Y*'s functional currency is the local currency, LC. *X* maintains a qualified foreign plan for the benefit of *X*'s employees in *B*. In the year the plan was adopted, a section 404A election was made for the plan. The appropriate foreign tax law is the tax law of *B* because all the employees covered by the plan are in *B* and plan liabilities are accounted for on *Y*'s books. The tax law of *B* permits *X* to deduct contributions to the plan. The cumulative amount allowed as a deduction under the tax law of *B* is LC80. The cumulative United States amount with respect to the plan is LC100. Therefore, the cumulative limitation is LC80. The earnings and profits of *X* include the profit and loss for *Y* (reflecting a reduction for contributions to the plan, computed in LC and translated into FC under the principles of section 987).

Example 2. A qualified reserve plan is maintained by a foreign branch of a domestic corporation. The foreign branch computes its income under the profit and loss method of Rev. Rul. 75-107, 1975-1 C.B. 32 (see §601.601(d)(2)(ii)(*b*) of this chapter), in units of the local currency, the FC. The foreign branch established the qualified reserve plan in 1985 and the taxpayer made the elections described in §1.404A-6. The taxpayer's taxable year and the plan year is the calendar year. The assumed amounts taken into account under section 404A and appropriate foreign tax law for selected years and the computations under this section which follow from the amounts, in units of FC, are shown in the following table—

		1985	1986	1987	1988
(1)	Amount determined with respect to the plan under section 404A for the taxable year without regard to section 404A(d)	800,000	900,000	300,000	1,000,000
(2)	Cumulative United States amount	800,000	1,700,000	2,000,000	3,000,000
(3)	Cumulative foreign amount	1,000,000	1,600,000	2,000,000	2,200,000
(4)	Lesser of cumulative United States or cumulative foreign amount	800,000	1,600,000	2,000,000	2,200,000
(5)	Reduced by aggregate amount (cumulative sum of (6) for prior years)	(0)	(800,000)	(1,600,000)	(2,000,000)
		800,000	800,000	400,000	200,000
(6)	Amount taken into account for the taxable year	800,000	800,000	400,000	200,000

Example 3. Assume the same facts as in *Example 2* for all taxable years, except that the qualified reserve plan is maintained by a foreign subsidiary of a domestic corporation. The foreign subsidiary computes its earnings and profits in units of the local currency, the FC. The foreign subsidiary's taxable year and the plan year are calendar years. The assumed amounts taken into account under section 404A and appropriate foreign law for selected years, and the computations under this section which follow from the amounts, in units of FC, are shown in the following table—

		1985	1986	1987	1988
(1)	Amount determined with respect to the plan under section 404A for the taxable year without regard to section 404A(d)	800,000	900,000	300,000	1,000,000
(2)	Amount allowed as a deduction under the appropriate foreign tax laws for the taxable year	1,000,000	600,000	400,000	200,000
(3)	Cumulative United States amount	800,000	1,700,000	2,000,000	3,000,000
(4)	Cumulative foreign amount	1,000,000	1,600,000	2,000,000	2,200,000
(5)	Lesser of cumulative United States or cumulative foreign amount	800,000	1,600,000	2,000,000	2,200,000
(6)	Reduced by aggregate amount (cumulative sum of (7) or (8), whichever is applicable, for prior years)	(0)	(800,000)	(1,400,000)	(2,000,000)
		800,000	800,000	600,000	200,000
(7)	Amount taken into account for taxable years before 1987 (lesser of (2) and (6))	800,000	600,000	n/a	n/a
(8)	Amount taken into account for taxable years after 1986 (same as (6))	n/a	n/a	600,000	200,000

Example 4. Z, a domestic corporation, maintains a retirement plan for employees employed in its foreign branch office. The foreign branch computes its income under the profit and loss method Rev. Rul. 75-107, 1975-1 C.B. 32 (see §601.601(d)(2)(ii)(*b*) of this chapter), in units of local currency, the FC. The plan is a combination book reserve and funded plan, but is considered a single plan under foreign law. The total retirement benefits that a participant is eligible to receive is the sum of the benefits provided by the qualified reserve plan and the qualified funded plan. Pursuant to §1.404A-6, in the year the plan was adopted, *Z* made a separate qualified reserve plan and funded plan election with respect to each portion of the foreign plan. The assumed deductions under section 404A and appropriate foreign law for selected years, and the computations under this section which follow from the deductions, are shown in the following table—

		Qualified funded plan		Qualified reserve plan		Combined amount—qualified foreign plans	
		1984	1985	1984	1985	1984	1985
(1)	Amount determined with respect to the qualified foreign plans under section 404A for the taxable year without regard to section 404A(d)	40,000	90,000	30,000	80,000		
(2)	Amount allowed as a deduction under the appropriate foreign tax laws for the taxable year					60,000	185,000
(3)	Cumulative United States amount	40,000	130,000	30,000	110,000		
(4)	Combined cumulative United States amount (cumulative sum of (3))					70,000	240,000
(5)	Cumulative foreign amount (cumulative sum of (2))					60,000	245,000
(6)	Aggregate amount					0	60,000
(7)	Lesser of combined cumulative United States amount or cumulative foreign amount ((4) or (5))					60,000	210,000

	Qualified funded plan		Qualified reserve plan		Combined amount—qualified foreign plans	
	1984	1985	1984	1985	1984	1985
(9) Reduced by the aggregate amount for the qualified funded and reserve plan (cumulative sum of (10) for prior years)					(0)	(60,000)
(10) Amount taken into account for taxable year					60,000	180,000

Example 5. A qualified reserve plan is maintained by M, the foreign subsidiary of N, a domestic corporation. M computes its earnings and profits in units of the local currency, the FC. The taxable years of M and N and the plan year are the calendar year. M established the qualified reserve plan in 1984 and N made the elections described in §1.404A-6. In that year, the reasonable addition to the plan reserve under §1.404A-3 was FC750,000. However, the amount allowed as a deduction under the appropriate foreign tax laws for the taxable year was FC650,000. The difference between the amount taken into account under §1.404A-3 and the deduction under the appropriate foreign tax laws, FC100,000, could not be taken into account for any succeeding taxable year under §1.404A-3, but it may later reduce M's earnings and profits pursuant to paragraph (a) of this section. [Reg. §1.404A-4.]

§1.404A-5. Additional limitations on amounts taken into account for qualified foreign plans.—(a) *Restrictions for nonqualified individuals.*—(1) *General rule.*—Notwithstanding any other provisions of §§1.404A-1 through 1.404A-7, no amount may be taken into account under section 404A for any contribution or amount accrued that is attributable to services performed either in the current or in a prior taxable year—

(i) By a citizen or resident of the United States who is a highly compensated [employee] (within the meaning of section 414(q)) (or, for taxable years beginning before January 1, 1989, by a citizen or resident of the United States who is an officer, shareholder, or highly compensated (within the meaning of §1.410(b)-1(d)); or

(ii) In the United States, the compensation for which is subject to tax under chapter 1 of subtitle A of the Internal Revenue Code.

(2) *Determination of service attribution.*—(i) *Not limited to actual service.*—Service performed by individuals described in paragraph (a)(1)(i) of this section includes service credited to those individuals. Service performed in the United States includes service credited in relation (directly or indirectly) to any United States service.

(ii) *Amounts attributable to service performed in the United States.*—The accrued benefit attributable to services described in this paragraph (a) is the excess, if any, of the total accrued benefit over the accrued benefit determined without credit for time spent performing services described in this paragraph (a) and without regard to the compensation levels for that time.

(b) *Records to be provided by taxpayer.*—(1) *In general.*—Notwithstanding any other provisions of §§1.404A-1 through 1.404A-7, no amount may be taken into account under section 404A for any contribution or amount accrued unless the taxpayer attaches a statement to its United States income tax return for any taxable year for which a qualified foreign plan maintained by an employer has United States tax significance. This statement must specify the name and type of qualified foreign plan; the cumulative United States amount, the cumulative foreign amount, and the aggregate amount with respect to the plan; the name and country of organization of the employer; and any other information the Commissioner may prescribe by forms and accompanying instructions or by revenue procedure.

(2) *Primary evidence.*—The statement described in paragraph (b)(1) of this section and any required forms must be completed in good faith with all of the information called for and with the calculations referenced in paragraph (b)(1) of this section. Except as provided in paragraph (b)(4) of this section, one of the following documents must be attached to the United States income tax return—

(i) A statement from the foreign tax authorities specifying the amount of the deduction allowed in computing taxable income under the appropriate foreign tax law for the relevant year or years with respect to the qualified foreign plan; or

(ii) If the return under the appropriate foreign tax law shows the deduction for plan contributions or plan reserves as a separate identifiable item, a copy of the foreign tax return for the relevant year or years with respect to the qualified foreign plan.

(3) *Additional requirements.*—The statement or return attached pursuant to paragraph (b)(2) of this section may be either the original, a duplicate original, a duly certified or authenticated copy, or a sworn copy. If only a sworn copy of a receipt or return is attached, there must be kept readily available for comparison on request the

original, a duplicate original, or a duly certified or authenticated copy.

(4) *Secondary evidence.*—Where the statement or return described in paragraph (b)(2)(i) or (b)(2)(ii) of this section is not available, all of the following information must be attached to the United States income tax return—

(i) A certified statement setting forth the cumulative foreign amount for each taxable year to which section 404A applies;

(ii) The excerpts from the employer's books and records showing either the change in the reserve or contributions made with respect to the plan for the taxable year to which section 404A applies; and

(iii) The computations of the foreign deduction relating to the plan to be established by data such as excerpts from the foreign law, assessment notices, or other documentary evidence.

(5) *Foreign language.*—If the relevant returns, books, records or computations are not maintained in the English language, the taxpayer must furnish, upon request, a certified translation that is satisfactory to the District Director.

(6) *Additional information required by District Director.*—If the taxpayer upon request of the District Director fails, without justification, to furnish any additional information that is significant, the provisions of section 982 will apply.

(7) *Authorized officer to complete documents.*—The documents required by this section and by §§1.404A-6 and 1.404A-7 must be signed by an authorized officer of the taxpayer (as defined in section 6062 or 6063) who must verify under penalty of perjury that the statement and all other documents submitted are true and correct to his knowledge and belief.

(8) *Transitional rule—good faith effort.*—For taxable years ending before [INSERT DATE THAT IS 90 DAYS AFTER THE DATE OF PUBLICATION OF FINAL REGULATIONS IN THE FEDERAL REGISTER] a taxpayer will be treated as satisfying this paragraph (b) if it makes a good faith effort to provide reasonable documentation.

(c) *Actuarial requirements.*—(1) *Reasonable actuarial assumptions.*—Except as otherwise specifically provided in §§1.404A-2 and 1.404A-3 and this paragraph (c), in the case of a qualified reserve plan or a qualified funded plan under which benefits are fixed or determinable, no amount may be taken into account under section 404A unless costs, liabilities, rates of interest, and other factors under the plan are determined on the basis of actuarial assumptions and methods each of which is reasonable (taking into account the experience of the plan and reasonable expectations), or which, in the aggregate, result in an amount being taken into account that is equivalent to that which would be determined if each such assumption and method were reasonable, and that, in combination, offer the actuary's best estimate of anticipated experience under the plan. For plan years beginning before January 1, 1988, the preceding sentence is satisfied if costs, liabilities, rates of interest, and other factors under the plan are determined on the basis of actuarial assumptions and methods that are reasonable in the aggregate (taking into account the experience of the plan and reasonable expectations) and that, in combination, offer the actuary's best estimate of anticipated experience under the plan. Except to the extent required under that paragraph, the interest rate determined under §1.404A-3(b)(4) may not be considered in determining whether other actuarial assumptions are reasonable in the aggregate for this purpose.

(2) *Full funding limitation.*—Notwithstanding any other provisions of §§1.404A-1 through 1.404A-7, no amount may be taken into account under section 404A if the amount causes the assets in the trust (in the case of a qualified funded plan) or if taking into account the amount causes the amount of the reserve (in the case of a qualified reserve plan) to exceed the amount described in section 412(c)(7)(A)(i). [Reg. §1.404A-5.]

§1.404A-6. Elections under section 404A and changes in methods of accounting.—(a) *Elections, changes in accounting methods, and changes in plan years.*—(1) *In general.*—(i) *Methods of accounting.*—An election under section 404A with respect to a qualified foreign plan constitutes the adoption of a method of accounting if the election is made in the taxable year in which the plan is adopted. Any election under section 404A with respect to a pre-existing plan, however, constitutes a change in method of accounting requiring the Commissioner's consent under section 446 (e) and an adjustment under section 481(a). Additionally, any other change in the method used to determine the amount taken into account under section 404A(a), as well as the revocation of any election under section 404A, constitutes a change in accounting method subject to the consent and adjustment requirements of sections 446(e) and 481(a). This section provides procedures for obtaining the Commissioner's consent to make certain changes in methods of accounting under section 404A. Additionally, §1.404A-7 provides special procedural rules applicable (along with the rules under this section) for retroactive and transition-period elections under section 404A.

(ii) *Changes not involving accounting methods.*—Any change in treatment, adjustment, or correction described in §1.446-1(e)(2)(ii)(b) (e.g., correction of computational errors) is not a change in accounting method. While a retroactive qualified funded plan election under §1.404A-7(c) constitutes a change in method of accounting, a mere election to apply the effective date of section 404A under §1.404A-7(b) retroactively does not necessarily result in a change in accounting method. Additionally, a retroactive election for funded foreign branch plans under §1.404A-7(d) will not be treated as a change in method of accounting, except to the extent that the taxpayer took erroneous deductions under its method of accounting prior to the beginning of its open period. Finally, a change of actuarial assumptions will not be treated as a change in method of accounting for purposes of this section.

(2) *Single plan.*—(i) *General rule.*—Except as otherwise provided, the rules of this section regarding elections, revocations, and re-elections, and the adoption or change of a plan year, apply separately (i.e., on a plan-by-plan basis) to each plan that qualifies as a single plan (as defined in §1.414(l)-1(b)). For purposes of this definition, a separate reserve maintained by an employer exclusively for its liability under a plan is considered a plan asset that is available exclusively to pay benefits to employees who are covered by the plan and to their beneficiaries. Although a plan may be treated as a reserve plan under foreign law, this treatment is not binding for purposes of section 404A and this section.

(ii) *Example.*—The principles of this paragraph (a)(2) are illustrated by the following example:

Example. S is a wholly-owned foreign subsidiary of *P*, a domestic corporation. *S* maintains a deferred compensation plan under local law to provide benefits to its employees upon retirement based upon years of service and the highest five-year average salary. *S* decided to account for 70 percent of its deferred compensation liabilities through an unfunded book reserve (Plan One), and to account for the remaining 30 percent through a trust equivalent (Plan Two). All of the assets of Plan One and Plan Two were available for payment of liabilities under their respective plans, and were only available for payment of liabilities under their respective plans. Thus, when deferred compensation was paid to *S*'s employees, within the meaning of this paragraph (a)(2), 70 percent of the amount was paid by check drawn against the general assets of *S* and 30 percent of the amount paid was paid by check drawn on the assets of the trust equivalent. Pursuant to this section, *P* made a qualified reserve plan election for Plan One, which it defined as a plan of deferred compensation with liability for 70 percent of the amount of deferred compensation owing to each employee under *S*'s deferred compensation plan. In addition, it made a qualified funded plan election for Plan Two, which it defined as a plan of deferred compensation with liability for the remaining 30 percent. Because *S*'s reserve for its liability was treated as a plan asset with respect to 70 percent of the liability and the assets of the trust, Plan One met the requirements of a "single plan" under §1.414(l)-1(b), and Plan Two was a separate "single plan". Thus, *S* could take into account only 70 percent of its liability to each employee under its deferred compensation plan when calculating the reasonable additions to the reserve under section 404A(c) for Plan One. Similarly, the full funding limitation and other calculations with respect to Plan Two may only be made with respect to 30 percent of *S*'s liability to each employee under the foreign deferred compensation plan.

(b) *Initial elections under section 404A.*—(1) *In general.*—The Commissioner's consent to elect initially under section 404A to treat a single plan as a qualified funded plan or as a qualified reserve plan is granted automatically if the taxpayer complies with the requirements of this paragraph (b). Except as provided in §1.404A-7, an initial election under this section with respect to any qualified foreign plan may be made only for a taxable year beginning after December 31, 1979.

(2) *Time for making election.*—(i) *Foreign branch plans.*—Except as provided in §1.404A-7, the initial election for a qualified foreign plan maintained by a foreign branch must be made no later than the time prescribed by law for filing the United States return (including extensions) for the first taxable year for which the election is to be effective.

(ii) *Foreign corporation plans.*—Except as provided in §1.404A-7, the initial election for a qualified foreign plan maintained by a foreign corporation must be made no later than the time allowed for making elections under §§1.964-1 and 1.964-1T. Thus, the election under section 404A may be deferred until the earnings and profits of the foreign corporation have United States tax significance, as defined in §§1.964-1 and 1.964-1T. United States tax significance may occur in a number of ways, including, for example, a dividend distribution, an income inclusion under section 951(a), a section 1248 transaction, a step-up of basis by earnings and profits for purposes of valuing assets for interest allocation purposes under section 864(e), or an inclusion in income of the earnings of a qualified electing fund under section 1293(a)(1).

(3) *Manner in which election is to be made.*—(i) *Foreign branch plans.*—In the case of a qualified foreign plan maintained by a domestic corporation, the initial election must be made by the taxpayer by attaching a list of plans for which section 404A treatment is desired to a return filed within the time prescribed in paragraph (b)(2)(i) of this section.

(ii) *Controlled foreign corporation plans.*—If a qualified foreign plan is maintained by a controlled foreign corporation, the initial election under this section must be made in the manner prescribed by §§1.964-1 and 1.964-1T and must include a list of all plans for which the election is made.

(iii) *Noncontrolled foreign corporation plans.*—If a qualified foreign plan is maintained by a noncontrolled foreign corporation, the initial election under this section must be made in the manner prescribed by §§1.964-1 and 1.964-1T and must include a list of all plans for which the election is made, as if the noncontrolled foreign corporation were a controlled foreign corporation. In applying the rules of §§1.964-1 and 1.964-1T, the term "majority domestic corporate shareholders" is substituted for the term "controlling United States shareholders" wherever it appears in §§1.964-1 and 1.964-1T. The term "majority domestic corporate shareholders" has the meaning set forth in §1.985-2(c)(3)(i).

(4) *Other requirements for election.*—For each plan listed, pursuant to paragraph (b)(3) of this section, the taxpayer must designate whether it elects to treat the plan as a qualified funded plan or qualified reserve plan, and must designate a plan year. Additionally, for each plan listed, the taxpayer must disclose the amount of any section 481(a) adjustment, as well as the initial cumulative United States amount, the initial cumulative foreign amount, and the initial aggregate amount defined in paragraph (g) of this section. See §1.404A-5(b) for rules on additional information required, signing and verifying required statements, and notices and forms necessary to elect under section 404A. Additionally, see §1.404A-7(d)(1) for required agreement to assessment of tax for retroactive elections for funded foreign branch plans.

(c) *Termination of election when a plan ceases to be a qualified foreign plan.*—(1) *In general.*—An election under section 404A with respect to a foreign deferred compensation plan is terminated if at any time on or after the first day of the first taxable year for which the election is effective the plan ceases to be a qualified foreign plan by reason of a failure to satisfy the conditions of section 404A(e)(1) or (2). Thus, for example, the election is terminated (subject to the consent of the Commissioner) if more than 10 percent of the amounts taken into account under the plan are attributable to services performed by employees subject to United States federal income tax. As used in this section, the term "termination" refers only to situations under which a plan ceases to be a qualified foreign plan by reason of a failure to satisfy the conditions of section 404(e)(1) or (2). Thus, the term is distinguished from a voluntary revocation of an election (i.e., under paragraph (d)(1) of this section), which also causes a plan to cease to be a qualified foreign plan. Upon termination of an election under section 404A, a change in method of accounting is required. The conditional advance consent of the Commissioner is granted for this change in method of accounting. This conditional consent may be withdrawn, however, if the District Director determines that tax avoidance was a purpose of the termination or if the procedures in paragraph (c)(2) of this section are not satisfied.

(2) *Rules for changing method of accounting upon termination of election.*—(i) *Time for making change.*—(A) *Foreign branch plans.*—Except as provided in §1.404A-7, in the case of a plan of a foreign branch the change in method of accounting required upon termination of a section 404A election must be made no later than the time prescribed by law for filing the United States return (including extensions) for the taxable year in which the plan ceases to satisfy the requirements of section 404A(e)(1) or (2)

(B) *Foreign corporation plans.*—Except as provided in §1.404A-7, in the case of a plan of a foreign corporation the change in method of accounting required upon termination of a section 404A election shall be made no later than the first year after the termination in which the earnings and profits of the foreign corporation have United States tax significance, as defined in §§1.964-1 and 1.964-1T. See paragraph (b)(2)(ii) of this section for United States tax significance examples.

(ii) *Procedures for changing method of accounting upon termination of election.*—(A) *Foreign branch plans.*—The change in method of accounting required upon termination of a section 404A election with respect to a foreign branch plan must be made by attaching a statement to the return described in paragraph (c)(2)(i)(A) of this section disclosing the amount of any section 481(a) adjustment (required under paragraph (e) of this section and computed in accordance with paragraph (f) of this section) arising upon the change.

(B) *Controlled foreign corporation plans.*—The change in method of accounting required upon termination of a section 404A election with respect to a controlled foreign corporation plan must be made in the manner prescribed by §§1.964-1 and 1.964-1T and must include disclosure of the amount of any section 481(a) adjustment (required under paragraph (e) of this section and computed in accordance with paragraph (f) of this section) arising upon the change.

(C) *Noncontrolled foreign corporation plans.*—The change in method of accounting required upon termination of a section 404A election with respect to a noncontrolled foreign corporation plan must be made in the manner prescribed by §§1.964-1 and 1.964-1T and must include disclosure of the amount of any section 481(a) adjustment (required under paragraph (e) of this section and computed in accordance with paragraph (f) of this section) arising upon the change. In applying the rules of §§1.964-1 and 1.964-1T, the term "majority domestic corporate shareholders" is substituted for the term "controlling United States shareholders" wherever it appears in §§1.964-1 and 1.964-1T. The term "majority domestic corporate shareholders" has the meaning set forth in §1.985-2(c)(3)(i).

(d) *Other changes in methods of accounting and changes in plan year.*—(1) *Application for consent.*—Except as provided in paragraph (c) of this section or in §1.404A-7, once an initial election under section 404A is effective with respect to a plan, the taxpayer must separately apply to obtain the express consent of the Commissioner prior to changing any method of accounting with respect to a foreign deferred compensation plan. Application for the consent of the Commissioner is required whether or not the method being changed is proper or permitted under the Internal Revenue Code and regulations thereunder. Any change in method of accounting not described in this paragraph (d)(1) must be made in accordance with the requirements of section 446(e) and the regulations thereunder. The procedures prescribed in this paragraph (d), however, are the exclusive procedures for making the following changes in method of accounting—

(i) Revocation of a section 404A election;

(ii) Re-election under section 404A following termination or revocation of a section 404A election;

(iii) Changing the treatment of a plan from a qualified funded plan to a qualified reserve plan (or the converse); or

(iv) Changing the actuarial funding method used to determine costs under a qualified funded plan.

(2) *Procedures for other changes in method of accounting.*—(i) *Foreign branch plans.*—To request consent to a change in method of accounting described in paragraph (d)(1) of this section, the taxpayer must file an application on Form 3115 with the Commissioner generally within 180 days after the beginning of the taxable year in which the change is requested to be effective. In the case of a revocation of an election under section 404A, however, the 180-day period in the preceding sentence is extended to the time prescribed by law for filing the United States return for the taxable year of the change.

(ii) *Foreign corporation plans.*—For a controlled corporation or a noncontrolled foreign corporation, a request for consent to revocation or to another change in method of accounting must be made in accordance with the rules of §§1.964-1 and 1.964-1T.

(3) *Plan year.*—A taxpayer must secure the consent of the Commissioner to change the plan year of a qualified foreign plan. Termination or revocation of a section 404A election will not effect a change in the plan year of the plan.

(e) *Application of section 481.*—(1) *In general.*—A change in method described in this section constitutes a change in method of accounting to which section 481 applies. Except as otherwise provided in this paragraph and in paragraph (f) of this section, this adjustment must be made in accordance with section 481 and the regulations thereunder in those circumstances. For purposes of section 481(a)(2), any change in method described in this section is considered a change in method of accounting initiated by the taxpayer.

(2) *Period of adjustment.*—(i) *In general.*—The section 481(a) adjustment period is determined under the rules of this paragraph (e)(2).

(ii) *Election or re-election.*—In the case of an election or a re-election following termination or revocation, the section 481(a) adjustment required by paragraph (e)(1) of this section must be taken into account ratably over a 15-year period, beginning with the first taxable year for which the election or re-election is effective. This section 481(a) adjustment period also applies to a change from a qualified funded plan to a qualified reserve plan.

(iii) *Termination or revocation of election and all other changes in method.*—The adjustment required by paragraph (e)(1) of this section for all changes in method (other than those described in paragraph (e)(2)(ii) of this section), including changes in election from a qualified reserve plan to a qualified funded plan, must be taken into account ratably over a six-year period, beginning with the first taxable year for which the change is effective. If an unamortized section 481(a) adjustment amount (e.g., from a previous change) remains at the end of a change in method of accounting to which this paragraph (e)(2)(iii) applies, the net amount of all of the section 481(a) adjustments must be taken into account ratably over this six-year section 481(a) adjustment period.

(iv) *Acceleration of section 481(a) adjustment.*—If the employer ceases to engage in the relevant trade or business at any time prior to the expiration of the applicable section 481(a) adjustment period provided in paragraph (e)(2)(ii) or (e)(2)(iii) of this section, the employer must take into account, in the taxable year of cessation, the balance of any section 481(a) adjustment not previously taken into account in computing taxable income (in the case of a branch) or earnings and profits (in the case of a foreign corporation). For purposes of this paragraph (e)(2)(iv), whether or not an employer ceases to engage in the trade or business is to be determined under administrative procedures issued under §1.446-1(e). In applying those procedures, "employer" is to be defined in the same manner as "taxpayer" is defined under those procedures.

(3) *Allocation and source.*—The amount of any net negative section 481(a) adjustment determined under this section and taken into account for a taxable year must be allocated and apportioned under §1.861-8 in the same manner as a deduction or reduction in earnings and profits under section 404A. Any net positive section 481(a) adjustment that is taken into account for a taxable year first must be reduced by directly allocating to such adjustment the employer's section 404A expense that is subject to apportionment (including any amount that otherwise would be capitalized); to the extent a net positive section 481(a) adjustment exceeds the amount of the employer's section 404A expense for the taxable year, such excess must be sourced or otherwise classified in the same manner as section 404A deductions or reductions in earnings and profits are allocated and apportioned.

(4) *Example.*—The principles of this paragraph (e) are illustrated by the following example:

Example. X, a domestic corporation, made an initial election under section 404A to treat an existing deferred compensation plan maintained by its foreign branch as a qualified reserve plan, effective beginning in X's 1985 taxable year. X's foreign branch maintains its books and records in FC, the functional currency. Previously, X had consistently used a permissible method of accounting with respect to the plan. The section 481(a) adjustment arising from X's change in accounting method upon its section 404A election was a negative FC150,000. Beginning with its 1985 taxable year, X took into account a negative FC10,000 each year (FC150,000/15). Effective beginning in X's 1988 taxable year, X received the Commissioner's express consent to change from a qualified reserve plan to a qualified funded plan. The section 481(a) adjustment attributable solely to the 1988 change was a positive FC132,000. Beginning with its 1988 taxable year, and for each of the five succeeding taxable years, X took into account a positive FC2,000, as computed below.

Negative 1985 section 481(a) adjustment	(FC150,000)
Less: 1985, 1986 & 1987 amounts taken into account	30,000
Subtotal	(120,000)
Positive 1988 section 481(a) adjustment	132,000

Net positive section 481(a) adjustment	12,000
Section 481(a) adjustment period	÷ 6
Net amount taken into account annually during section 481(a) adjustment period	FC2,000

(f) *Computation of section 481(a) adjustment.*—(1) *In general.*—For purposes of section 404A, except as provided in § 1.404A-7(f)(1)(ii)(C), the amount of the section 481(a) adjustment required under paragraph (e)(1) of this section equals—

    (i) The Old Method Closing Amount; less

    (ii) The New Method Opening Amount.

(2) *Old Method Closing Amount.*—(i) *In general.*—Except as otherwise provided in paragraph (f)(2)(ii), (iii), or (iv) of this section (or as otherwise prescribed by the Commissioner), the Old Method Closing Amount equals—

    (A) The total of all past deductions taken with respect to liabilities under the plan; plus

    (B) The net income earned directly or indirectly by any separate funding entity (e.g., account or trust) with respect to the plan, but only to the extent that such net income has not previously been taken into account in determining taxable income (in the case of a foreign branch) or earnings and profits (in the case of a foreign corporation); minus

    (C) The total of all past payments under the plan made to plan participants and beneficiaries by the employer, the trust, or the separate funding entity.

(ii) *Taxpayer formerly using a reserve method.*—(A) *In general.*—If a taxpayer has consistently taken amounts with respect to the plan into account under a reserve method, the Old Method Closing Amount equals the closing reserve balance at the end of the closing year calculated under the taxpayer's reserve method. For purposes of the preceding sentence, a reserve method means a method of accrual based on the actuarial present value of expected future plan benefits.

(B) *Former qualified reserve plan.*—To request the Commissioner's consent in the case of a former qualified reserve plan, the closing reserve balance must be adjusted for any unamortized increases or decreases to the reserve described in § 1.404A-3(c) that have not yet been taken into account. For example, if the closing reserve balance is FC100,000, but FC10,000 of the closing reserve balance consists of an unamortized increase in the reserve that has not previously been taken into account due to the ten-year amortization requirements of § 1.404A-3(c), the Old Method Closing Amount is FC90,000.

(iii) *Taxpayer formerly using pay-as-you-go method.*—If the taxpayer has consistently taken amounts into account with respect to the plan based only on actual payments of plan benefits to participants and beneficiaries, the Old Method Closing Amount equals zero.

(iv) *Taxpayer formerly using a funded method.*—(A) *Payment to separate funding entity.*—If the taxpayer has consistently taken amounts into account with respect to the plan based only on actual payments to a separate funding entity and on payments by the employer (but not by the funding entity) to plan participants or beneficiaries, the Old Method Closing Amount equals the balance in the separate funding entity at the end of the closing year, including amounts attributable, directly or indirectly, to net investment income that has not previously been taken into account in determining taxable income (in the case of a foreign branch) or earnings and profits (in the case of a foreign corporation).

(B) *Former qualified funded plan.*—In the case of a former qualified funded plan, the Old Method Closing Amount generally equals the amount described in paragraph (f)(2)(iv)(A) of this section, adjusted, however, by—

    (1) Reducing the amount properly to reflect any net limitations under section 404A(b) and (g) (e.g., the full funding limitation for a qualified funded plan) that were applied in determining amounts taken into account under the former section 404A method of accounting; and

    (2) Increasing the amount properly to reflect any amounts that are not paid during the closing year but that are permitted to be taken into account in the closing year under section 404A(b)(2) (relating to payments made after the close of the taxable year).

(v) *Section 404A(d) limitation.*—In computing the Old Method Closing Amount upon the termination or revocation of an election under section 404A, the limitations of section 404A(d) and § 1.404A-4 must be taken into account. Thus, if the Old Method Closing Amount is determined under paragraph (f)(2)(ii)(B) or (f)(2)(iv)(B) of this section, the amount otherwise determined under those paragraphs shall be reduced by applying the section 404A(d) and § 1.404A-4 limitations to the extent the cumulative United States

amount under § 1.404A-4 exceeds the cumulative foreign amount under § 1.404A-4.

(3) *New Method Opening Amount.*—(i) *Qualified reserve plan.*—In the case of an election to treat a plan as a qualified reserve plan, the New Method Opening Amount equals the balance of the reserve as of the end of the last day of the closing year, calculated under the rules of section 404A(c) and § 1.404A-3 based on plan information and data as of that date. The New Method Opening Amount must be reduced (or increased) for any unamortized increases (or decreases) to the reserve described in section 404A(c)(4) and § 1.404A-3(c).

(ii) *Qualified funded plan.*—In the case of an election to be treated as a qualified funded plan, the New Method Opening Amount equals the amount of funds in the trust as of the beginning of the first day of the opening year, adjusted as necessary to take into account the rules of section 404A(b) and (g). If the separate funding entity does not qualify as a trust under § 1.404A-1(e), the New Method Opening Amount in the case of a qualified funded plan is zero because there is no balance in a trust as defined in § 1.404A-1(e).

(iii) *Nonqualified plan.*—In the case of any plan that ceases to be a qualified foreign plan (either by reason of the termination or revocation of a section 404A election), the New Method Opening Amount is zero.

(iv) *Section 404A(d) limitation.*—In computing the New Method Opening Amount upon an election under section 404A, the limitation on deductions of section 404A(d) and § 1.404A-4 must be taken into account. Thus, if the New Method Opening Amount is determined under paragraph (f)(2)(i) or (f)(2)(ii) of this section, the amount otherwise determined must be reduced to the extent the cumulative United States amount computed under § 1.404A-4 exceeds the cumulative foreign amount computed under § 1.404A-4. See paragraph (g) of this section for initialization of amounts taken into account under section 404A(d).

(4) *Definitions and special rules.*—(i) *Opening year.*—For purposes of this section, the opening year is the first taxable year for which the new method of accounting is effective with respect to a plan. For example, in the case of an election to treat a foreign corporation plan as a qualified reserve plan beginning in 1989, the opening year is 1989, even though the election may not be made until 1994 pursuant to paragraph (b)(2)(ii) of this section.

(ii) *Closing year.*—For purposes of this section, the closing year is the taxable year immediately preceding the opening year.

(iii) *Separate funding entity.*—A separate funding entity described in paragraphs (f)(2)(i)(B) and (f)(2)(iv) of this section is any entity that satisfies the first requirement in the definition of the equivalent of a trust in § 1.404A-1(e) (segregation in a separate legal entity) and, in practice, also satisfies the third requirement in that definition (dedication to payment of plan benefits) with respect to benefits under the relevant plan.

(iv) *Special rules for certain foreign corporation plans.*—In the case of a foreign corporation's plan for which no method has been used for some or all prior taxable years because no calculation of earnings and profits has been necessary for those years (see, e.g., paragraph (b)(2)(ii) of this section), the employer may assume that the old method has been consistent with any method actually used consistently in immediately prior years. If no calculation of earnings and profits has been made for prior years, in determining the Old Method Closing Amount, the taxpayer may assume the method used was a method described in paragraph (f)(2)(iii) of this section. This assumed method used in the calculation of the Old Method Closing Amount must actually be used by the taxpayer for all the prior taxable years to the extent reductions of earnings and profits for those years are ever determined with respect to the plan.

(v) *Reference to rules applicable in the case of failure to consider net investment income in computing section 481(a) adjustment.*—The treatment of net investment income earned by a funding vehicle that has not previously taken into account by the taxpayer in determining taxable income (in the case of a foreign branch) or earnings and profits (in the case of a foreign corporation), and that is not properly considered (as required under paragraphs (f)(2)(i)(B) and (f)(2)(iv)(A) of this section) in determining the amount of the section 481(a) adjustment for purposes of section 404A, is determined under other applicable provisions, which may include sections 61, 671 through 679, and 1001.

(vi) *Certain section 481(a) adjustments treated as carryover contributions.*—In the case of an election for a plan to be treated as a qualified funded plan, any net positive section 481(a) adjustment is treated as a carryover contribution (within the meaning of § 1.404A-2(d)(4)) to the extent that the adjustment is attributable to limits (that would be taken into account under § 1.404A-2(d)(4)) on the amounts previously contributed to the trust under the plan that could be taken into account under section 404A.

(5) *Examples.*—The principles of paragraph (f) of this section are illustrated by the following examples:

Example 1. Nonqualified reserve plan to qualified reserve plan. A foreign subsidiary of a domestic corporation established an irrevocable balance sheet reserve for pension expenses in 1981. The subsidiary maintains its books and records in FC, the functional currency. From 1981 through 1987, the taxpayer reduced earnings and profits of the foreign subsidiary by FC150,000, the amount of the pension liability which had accrued under the plan. This method of accounting was never challenged or changed by the District Director prior to the expiration of the statute of limitations for the 1981 through 1987 taxable years. Through December 31, 1987, the last day of the closing year, actual pension payments totalled FC15,000. For the 1988 taxable year, the taxpayer made an election for the plan to be treated as a qualified reserve plan. The reserve calculated under section 404A as of the first day of the 1988 taxable year, the opening year, and based upon employee census data as of that date, was FC175,000. The Old Method Closing Amount was FC135,000 (FC150,000 less FC15,000). The New Method Opening Amount was FC175,000. The section 481(a) adjustment was a negative FC40,000 (FC135,000 less FC175,000). This adjustment is to be taken into account over the 15-year section 481(a) adjustment period prescribed in paragraph (e)(2)(ii) of this section.

Example 2. Nonqualified reserve plan to qualified reserve plan. Assume the same facts as in *Example 1*, except that the reserve calculated under section 404A as of the first day of the 1988 taxable year and based upon employee census data as of that date was FC75,000. The Old Method Closing Amount was FC135,000 (FC150,000 less FC15,000). The New Method Opening Amount was FC75,000. The section 481(a) adjustment was a positive FC60,000 (FC135,000 less FC75,000). This adjustment is to be taken into account over the 15-year section 481(a) adjustment period prescribed in paragraph (e)(2)(ii) of this section.

Example 3. Nonqualified funded plan to qualified reserve plan. M, a domestic corporation, wholly owns N, a foreign corporation. N maintains its books and records in FC, the local currency. From 1981 through 1988, N maintained a nonqualified funded plan. During this period, N contributed FC55,000 to the separate funding entity administering the plan and reduced earnings and profits by FC55,000. The separate funding entity realized net income of FC17,000 from investment of plan assets and paid nothing to participants. None of the FC17,000 net investment income earned in the separate funding entity was taken into account in computing N's earnings and profits. As of the last day of N's 1988 taxable year, the closing year, the plan's fund balance was FC72,000, comprised of FC55,000 (excess contributions) and FC17,000 (investment income). The reserve calculated under section 404A as of the first day of the 1989 taxable year, the opening year, was FC100,000. Effective for M's 1989 taxable year, M elected under section 404A to treat N's funded plan as a qualified reserve plan. The Old Method Closing Amount was FC72,000. The New Method Opening Amount was FC100,000; thus, if, in the future,

N pays FC100,000 to plan participants or beneficiaries, that FC100,000 will not again reduce N's earnings and profits. The section 481(a) adjustment was a negative FC28,000 (FC72,000 less FC100,000). However, if the District Director later challenges and requires N to change its method of accounting for foreign deferred compensation used in determining its 1981 through 1988 earnings and profits in a taxable year prior to the 1989 taxable year, the section 481(a) adjustment could be changed from a negative FC28,000 to a negative FC100,000. Pursuant to the administrative procedures under section 446(e), the District Director, upon challenging the treatment of foreign deferred compensation in years prior to 1989, could require any necessary positive section 481(a) adjustment to be taken into account in one taxable year.

Example 4. Nonqualified funded plan to qualified funded plan. Y, a domestic corporation, wholly owns X, a foreign corporation. X maintains its books and records in FC, the local currency. From 1981 through 1988, X maintained a nonqualified funded plan. During this period, X reduced earnings and profits by contributions of FC55,000 to the plan. The plan paid participants FC30,000. As of the last day of Y's 1988 taxable year, the plan's fund balance was FC29,000, comprised of FC25,000 (net contributions) and FC4,000 (interest income that was never previously taken into account in determining earnings and profits). Effective for Y's 1989 taxable year, Y elected under section 404A to treat X's funded plan as a qualified funded plan. The Old Method Closing Amount was FC29,000. The New Method Opening Amount was FC29,000. The section 481(a) adjustment was zero (FC29,000 less FC29,000). See *Example 3*, however, for the effects on the section 481(a) adjustment of a successful challenge to X's method of accounting for foreign deferred compensation in years prior to 1989 by the District Director.

Example 5. Z, the wholly owned foreign subsidiary of Y, a domestic corporation, has maintained a reserve plan for its employees, beginning in 1981. Z maintains its books and records in FC, the local currency. Effective for 1984, Y elected under section 404A to treat the plan as a qualified reserve plan. The only section 481(a) adjustment required was to take into account the limitation under section 404A(d). In 1981 through 1983, prior to the section 404A election, Z's earnings and profits were reduced by additions to the reserve. This method of accounting was never challenged or changed by the District Director prior to the expiration of the statute of limitations for the 1981 through 1983 taxable years. Thus, the Old Method Closing Amount equaled the balance in the reserve, which was FC300. To compute the New Method Opening Amount, the opening reserve took into account the lesser of the cumulative United States amount (FC300) or the cumulative foreign amount (FC90) as of the first day of 1984, the opening year. Thus, the New Method Opening Amount was FC90. The section 481(a) adjustment was therefore a positive FC210 (FC300—FC90); 1/15 of this amount, FC14 (FC210/15), is being taken into account as an increase in earnings and profits each year over the 15-year section 481(a) adjustment period that began in 1984.

Example 6. Nonqualified reserve plan to qualified reserve plan. Assume the same facts as in *Example 5* for all taxable years and the annual United States reduction, foreign reduction, cumulative United States amount, cumulative foreign amount and the section 481(a) adjustment shown below. The total annual reduction (or increase) in Z's earnings and profits was as follows—

	1984	1985	1986	1987	1988	1989	1990
Amount determined under U.S. law with respect to the plan under section 404A for the taxable year without regard to section 404A(d)	FC(40)	FC(50)	FC(60)	FC(70)	FC(80)	FC(90)	FC(100)
Amount allowed as a deduction for the taxable year under the appropriate foreign tax laws . . .	(70)	(260)	(50)	(40)	(30)	(20)	(10)
Cumulative U.S. amount	(340)	(390)	(450)	(520)	(600)	(690)	(790)
Cumulative foreign amount	(160)	(420)	(470)	(510)	(540)	(560)	(570)
Lesser of cumulative U.S. or foreign amount	(160)	(390)	(450)	(510)	(540)	(560)	(570)
Reduced by the aggregate amount	90	160	390	440	510	540	560
	(70)	(230)	(60)	(70)	(30)	(20)	(10)
Amount taken into account for the taxable year*	(70)	(230)	(50)	(70)	(30)	(20)	(10)
Positive section 481 adjustment	14	14	14	14	14	14	14
Total increase (reduction) in earnings and profits taken into account for the taxable year	FC(56)	FC(216)	FC(36)	FC(56)	FC(16)	FC(6)	FC(4)

* The limitation in § 1.404A-4(c) applies to taxable years 1984, 1985 and 1986. In 1986, the amount deductible under the appropriate foreign tax law was less than the lower of (1) the cumulative U.S. amount, or, (2) the cumulative foreign amount (then reduced by the aggregate amount).

(g) *Initial section 404A(d) amounts.*—(1) *In general.*—By making an election under section 404A, a taxpayer adopts section 404A(d) as part of its method of accounting. Section 1.404A-4 provides rules to

apply the limitations of section 404A(d) in taxable years when an election under section 404A is in effect. This paragraph (g) provides rules to compute initial amounts under section 404A(d) in the opening year. These rules are based on the rules to compute the New Method Opening Amount in paragraph (f)(3) of this section.

(2) *Computation of amounts.*—As of the first day of the opening year, the initial section 404A(d) amounts are as follows:

(i) The initial cumulative United States amount equals the New Method Opening Amount without regard to any reduction under paragraph (f)(3)(iv) of this section.

(ii) The initial cumulative foreign amount equals the New Method Opening Amount computed as though the appropriate foreign tax law were the new method of accounting and without regard to paragraph (f)(3)(iv) of this section.

(iii) The initial aggregate amount equals the lesser of—

(A) The initial cumulative United States amount; and

(B) The initial cumulative foreign amount.

(3) *Example.*—The principles of paragraph (g) of this section are illustrated by the following example:

Example. A foreign subsidiary of a domestic corporation maintains its books and records in FC, the local currency. The subsidiary established a funded deferred compensation plan in 1983 but reduced earnings and profits on a pay-as-you-go basis. The plan year and the taxable year of the domestic corporation and the subsidiary are the calendar year. For the 1990 taxable year, the domestic corporation elected to treat the plan as a qualified reserve plan. The balance in the separate funding entity as of January 1, 1990, the first day of the opening year, was FC90,000. The initial United States cumulative amount (the opening reserve) was FC150,000. The initial foreign cumulative amount (the balance in the separate funding entity) was FC90,000. The initial aggregate amount was FC90,000 (the lesser of FC90,000 or FC150,000). Since the subsidiary reduced earnings and profits on the pay-as-you-go method, the Old Method Closing Amount was zero. The section 481(a) adjustment was a negative FC90,000 (zero less FC90,000 (the lesser of FC150,000 or FC90,000)). [Reg. §1.404A-6.]

§1.404A-7. Effective date, retroactive elections, and transition rules.—(a) *In general.*—(1) *Effective date.*—Except as otherwise provided in this section, section 404A applies to taxable years beginning after December 31, 1979.

(2) *Overview of retroactive elections for taxable years beginning before January 1, 1980.*—(i) *Plans of foreign subsidiaries.*—Section 2(e)(2) of Public Law 96-603 permitted a taxpayer to make section 404A apply retroactively for all of its foreign subsidiaries. Paragraph (b) of this section describes and provides the time and manner to make, perfect, or revoke this retroactive effective date election. If a retroactive effective date election was made, the taxpayer was also eligible to make a qualified funded plan election or a qualified reserve plan election effective retroactively for any of its subsidiaries' plans that met the requirements of §1.404A-1(a) (other than paragraph (4) thereof) for the relevant period. Paragraph (c) of this section describes and provides the time and manner to make, perfect, or revoke these retroactive plan-by-plan elections for foreign subsidiaries.

(ii) *Plans of foreign branches.*—Section 2(e)(3) of Public Law 96-603 permitted a taxpayer to make a qualified funded plan election retroactively for any plans maintained by a foreign branch that met the requirements of §1.404A-1(a) (other than paragraph (4) thereof) for the relevant period. Paragraph (d) of this section describes and provides the time and manner to make this retroactive plan-by-plan qualified funded plan election for plans maintained by foreign branches.

(3) *Overview of special transition rules for election, revocation, and re-election.*—Paragraph (e) of this section provides the time and manner to make and revoke qualified funded plan and qualified reserve plan elections for a taxpayer's transition period.

(b) *Retroactive effective date elections for foreign subsidiaries.*—(1) *In general.*—Section 2(e)(2) of Public Law 96-603 permitted a taxpayer to make section 404A effective during the taxpayer's open period. If the election was made, the taxpayer accepted section 404A (including, for example, §1.404A-1(d)) as the operative law for all foreign subsidiaries (whether or not controlled foreign corporations) during the taxpayer's entire open period. If the election was made, section 404A applies to all distributions from accumulated profits (or earnings and profits) earned after December 31, 1970 (unless the election is revoked pursuant to paragraph (b)(3) of this section, if applicable). If accumulated profits were earned prior to January 1, 1971, a change in method of accounting is required for the foreign subsidiary's taxable year that ends with or within the first taxable year in the taxpayer's open period. A section 481(a) adjustment is required for amounts taken into account prior to the beginning of the foreign subsidiary's year of change and must be computed applying the rules of §1.404A-6(f).

(2) *Time and manner to make, perfect, or revoke election.*—The retroactive effective date election described in paragraph (b)(1) of this section is not effective unless the election was actually made no later than the time prescribed by law for filing the United States return for the first taxable year ending on or after December 31, 1980, including extensions (whether or not the time was actually extended for filing the taxpayer's return), and unless the taxpayer perfects the election by filing a statement indicating the taxpayer's agreement to perfect the election with an amended return for the first taxable year ending on or after December 31, 1980, on or before [*INSERT DATE THAT IS 365 DAYS AFTER THE DATE OF PUBLICATION OF FINAL REGULATIONS IN THE* FEDERAL REGISTER]. In order to be effective, the perfection must be made in the manner provided in §1.404A-6(b)(3)(ii) or (iii). An election that is not perfected is considered retroactively revoked.

(3) *Requirement to amend returns.*—(i) *In general.*—In addition to the amended return required by paragraph (b)(2) of this section, the taxpayer must file any other amended United States returns that are necessary to conform the treatment of all items affected by the election or revocation to the treatment consistent with the election or revocation within the time period described in paragraph (b)(2) of this section. If no adjustments are necessary, the amended return required by paragraph (b)(2) of this section must contain a statement to that effect.

(ii) *Required statements.*—All amended returns required by this paragraph (b)(3) must be accompanied by a statement containing—

(A) The open years, open period and retroactive period of the taxpayer;

(B) The taxable year for which the election is perfected or revoked;

(C) A statement that the election (or elections) are perfected or revoked pursuant to the authority contained in §1.404A-7; and

(D) A signature and verification as provided in §1.404A-5(b)(7).

(c) *Retroactive plan-by-plan elections for foreign subsidiaries.*—(1) *In general.*—Any taxpayer that makes a retroactive effective date election described in paragraph (a)(2)(i) of this section under the rules of paragraph (b) of this section may, at its option, also elect to treat any foreign plan of a subsidiary that met the requirements of §1.404A-1(a) (other than paragraph (4) thereof) for the relevant period as a qualified funded plan or as a qualified reserve plan under section 404A, beginning in any taxable year of the foreign subsidiary that ends with or within the taxpayer's open period (or for any earlier taxable year beginning after December 31, 1971, for which earnings and profits of the subsidiary had no United States tax significance). Alternatively, the taxpayer may decide to make no such plan-by-plan election with respect to any particular plan or plans of any of its foreign subsidiaries. Rules similar to those contained in §1.404A-6 (including, where applicable, the requirement to obtain the consent of the Commissioner) are used to effect such plan-by-plan elections. If the plan existed in a taxable year beginning prior to the first year for which the election was effective, a change in method of accounting is required for the year of the election. The year of change for purposes of computing the section 481(a) adjustment is the first year that the election is effective.

(2) *Time and manner to make, perfect, or revoke election.*—A taxpayer that is eligible to make a plan-by-plan election described in paragraph (c)(1) of this section may make or perfect such an election by attaching a statement to that effect on an amended return for the year that the election is to be effective on or before [*INSERT DATE THAT IS 365 DAYS AFTER THE DATE OF PUBLICATION OF FINAL REGULATIONS IN THE* FEDERAL REGISTER]. In order to be effective, the perfection of a plan-by-plan election must be made in the manner provided in §1.404A-6(b)(3)(ii) or (iii). An election that is not perfected is considered retroactively revoked. Any election made or perfected under this paragraph (c) will continue in effect for taxable years beginning after the taxpayer's open period, unless revoked under paragraph (c)(4) or (e) of this section or §1.404A-6.

(3) *Requirement to amend returns.*—In addition to the amended return required by paragraph (c)(2) of this section, the taxpayer must file any other amended United States returns that are necessary to conform the treatment of all items affected by the election or revocation to the treatment consistent with the election or revocation. All amended returns must be accompanied by the statement described in paragraph (b)(3)(ii) of this section (substituting "made, perfected, or revoked" for "perfected or revoked" where applicable) and all of the information required by §1.404A-6(b)(4) (and §1.404A-6(c)(2)(ii), if applicable, in the case of a termination). If no adjustments are necessary, the amended return required by paragraph (c)(2) of this section must contain a statement to that effect.

(4) *Revocation after initial election and re-election permitted.*—Any taxpayer that makes an initial election for any plan under paragraph (c)(2) of this section may, under the rules of that paragraph, revoke the election for any taxable year after the sixth consecutive taxable year for which the election is effective, and may re-elect for any taxable year after the sixth consecutive taxable year for which the election is not in effect (regardless of whether the election is not in effect due to revocation or termination of the election as defined in §1.404A-6(c)(1)). The consecutive changes in method of accounting described in the first sentence of this paragraph (c)(3) must be made under the rules in §1.404A-6 regarding the section 481(a) adjustment period. The Commissioner may approve a letter ruling request (see §601.201 of this chapter) to shorten the six-year waiting period upon a showing of extraordinary circumstances.

(5) *Examples.*—The principles of paragraphs (b) and (c) of this section are illustrated by the following examples:

Example 1. P, a domestic corporation, wholly owns two foreign subsidiaries, *S* and *T. S* and *T* maintain their books and records in FC, the local currency. Since 1978, *S* and *T* have maintained unfunded pension plans for their respective employees. *S* maintained two plans, Plan 1 and Plan 2, and *T* maintained one plan. The plan years and the taxable years of all three corporations are the calendar year.

(i) For 1978 and 1979, *P* reduced the earnings and profits of *S* and *T* by the amount of the pension liability that had accrued under the plans as follows—

Taxable year	S's Plan 1	S's Plan 2	T's plan
1978	FC30,000	FC5,000	FC70,000
1979	50,000	15,000	80,000
Total reduction in earnings and profits	FC80,000	FC20,000	FC150,000

Total reduction in earnings and profits	
S	FC100,000
T	FC150,000

(ii) In 1981, *P* made a retroactive effective date election pursuant to section 2(e)(2) of Public Law 96-603 and paragraph (b) of this section for taxable years beginning after December 31, 1977, and ending before January 1, 1980, *P*'s open period. Thus, with respect to its open period, *P* has made section 404A the operative law for all distributions of earnings and profits (or accumulated profits) earned after December 31, 1970 for *S* and *T*. The consequences of making or not making the retroactive plan-by-plan election under section 404A for each foreign plan will be determined as though section 404A had been in effect for those years. Accordingly, earnings and profits of *S* and *T* may not be reduced with respect to amounts accrued under their respective plans unless the plans met the requirements of §1.404A-1(a) for those years in the open period.

(iii) *P* made a retroactive plan-by-plan election to treat *S*'s Plan 1 as a qualified reserve plan for *P*'s retroactive period. The amount taken into account under §1.404A-3 for *S*'s Plan 1 calculated under section 404A was FC25,000 for 1978 and FC35,000 for 1979. No election under section 404A was made for *S*'s Plan 2 or for *T*'s plan.

Taxable year	Earnings and profits	Distribution of earnings and profits
1968	FC10,000	
1969	20,000	
1970	20,000	
Subtotal		50,000
1971	30,000	
1972	30,000	
1973	30,000	
1974	30,000	
1975	30,000	FC200,000
Subtotal		150,000
1976	40,000	
1977	40,000	
1978	40,000	
1979	40,000	
1980	40,000	
1981	50,000	
Subtotal		250,000
Total	FC450,000	

(ii) In 1981, *Q* made a retroactive effective date election pursuant to section 2(e)(2) of Public Law 96-603 and paragraph (b)(1) of this section for its open period. As of December 31, 1980, *Q*'s open period included the taxable years 1975 through 1979. Thus, with respect to those taxable years, *Q* has made section 404A the operative law for *R*. The consequences of making or not making the retroactive plan-by-plan election under section 404A for *R*'s foreign plan will be determined as though section 404A had been in effect for those taxable years. Thus, the earnings and profits of *R* may not be reduced with respect to amounts accrued under *R*'s plan, unless the plan met the requirements of §1.404A-1(a) for those taxable years.

Q made a retroactive plan-by-plan election to treat *R*'s plan as a qualified reserve plan effective beginning in 1971. Of the distribution of FC200,000 to *Q* in 1975, section 404A applies to FC150,000, because these accumulated profits (or earnings and profits) were earned in taxable years beginning after December 31, 1970 and were also distributed in 1975, within *Q*'s open period. However, section 404A does not apply to the FC50,000 distribution made from accumulated profits earned before December 31, 1970. Since *R*'s plan was established before *Q*'s open period, a section 481(a) adjustment is required. This section 481(a) adjustment must be taken into account in determining earnings and profits beginning with the 1971 year of change.

Thus, no amount of the accrued but unpaid pension liability attributable to *S*'s Plan 2 or to *T*'s plan may reduce *S*'s or *T*'s respective 1978 and 1979 earnings and profits. *P* amended its tax returns for 1978 and 1979 to reflect the correct reduction of earnings and profits of FC25,000 and FC35,000 with respect to *S*'s Plan 1 and no reduction for those years with respect to *S*'s Plan 2 or *T*'s plan. Since *S*'s and *T*'s plans were established during the open period, no section 481(a) adjustment is required.

Example 2. Q, a domestic corporation, has wholly owned *R*, a foreign subsidiary, since *R*'s formation in 1968. *R* maintains its books and records in FC, the local currency. Since 1968, *R* maintained an unfunded pension plan for its employees. The plan year and the taxable year of both corporations is the calendar year. *R*, since 1968, used a method of accounting under which it reduced earnings and profits by its accrued pension liability.

(i) *R*'s earnings and profits were earned and distributed to *Q* as follows—

(d) *Retroactive plan-by-plan qualified funded plan elections for certain plans of foreign branches.*—(1) *In general.*—Section 2(e)(3) of Public Law 96-603 permitted a taxpayer to make a qualified funded plan election retroactively for any plans maintained by a foreign branch that met the requirements of §1.404A-1(a) (other than paragraph (4) thereof) for the relevant period. As a condition of making this election, a taxpayer is required to agree to the assessment of all deficiencies (including interest thereon) arising during those taxable years within the open period (even those taxable years that are not open years as defined in paragraph (g)(4) of this section) to the extent that the deficiencies arise from erroneous deductions claimed by the taxpayer with respect to all of the taxpayer's foreign branches that maintained a deferred compensation plan. For a taxpayer that agrees to the assessment of tax in an election under this paragraph (d), a change in method of accounting is necessary (and a section 481(a) adjustment is required in accordance with the provisions of §1.404A-6) with respect to any erroneous deductions claimed by the taxpayer under its method of accounting in taxable years ending prior to the beginning of the open period. For such a change in method of accounting, the year of change is the first taxable year in the open period, and the method of accounting to which the taxpayer is required to change is the method permitted during the open period under this paragraph (d).

(2) *Amounts allowed as a deduction.*—If an election under section 2(e)(3) of Public Law 96-603 was made under the rules of this paragraph (d), the aggregate of the taxpayer's prior deductions is allowed as a deduction ratably over a 15-year period, beginning with the taxpayer's first taxable year beginning after December 31, 1979. A fractional part of a year which is a taxable year (as defined in sections 441(b) and 7701(a)(23)) is a taxable year for purposes of the 15-year period.

(3) *Definitions.*—(i) *Prior deduction.*—(A) *In general.*—The term "prior deduction" means a deduction with respect to a qualified funded plan (i.e., a plan that met the requirements of §1.404A-1(a) for the relevant period, and with respect to which a qualified funded plan election was made under the rules of this paragraph (d)) maintained by a foreign branch of a taxpayer for a taxable year beginning before January 1, 1980—

(1) That the taxpayer claimed;

(2) That was not allowable under the law in effect prior to the enactment of section 404A;

(3) With respect to which, on December 1, 1980, the assessment of a deficiency was not barred by any law or rule of law; and

(4) That would have been allowable if section 404A applied to taxable years beginning before January 1, 1980.

(B) *Application of section 404A(d).*—Because the prior deductions are limited by the amounts that may be taken into account under section 404A, the computation of those prior deductions for the relevant taxable years is subject to the limitations described in section 404A(d) and §1.404A-4. However, once the aggregate of prior deductions is calculated, the aggregate, or any portion thereof permitted to be taken into account over the 15-year period of paragraph (d)(2) of this section, is not subject to the limitations prescribed by section 404A(d) and §1.404A-4.

(ii) *Erroneous deduction.*—The term "erroneous deduction" means an amount that is not deductible under section 404(a) (including section 404(a)(5)), that was deducted on a taxpayer's income tax return with respect to a foreign deferred compensation plan.

	1977
Amount deducted on tax return	FC100
Amount deductible under section 404(a)	20
Amount deductible under section 404A	90

(ii) The assessment (including interest) for the open years 1977 through 1979 is based on adjustments to the erroneous deductions of FC240 (FC300 less FC60).

(iii) The amount of the prior deductions taken into account ratably over 15 years as provided in paragraph (d)(2) of this section, beginning in 1981, is a negative FC210 (FC60 less FC270).

(iv) No section 481(a) adjustment is required because X took no deductions with respect to the plan prior to the beginning of its open period.

Amount deducted on tax return	
Amount deductible under section 404(a)	
Amount deductible under section 404A	

(ii) Under paragraph (d)(1) of this section, Z agreed to an assessment of deficiencies for its 1978 taxable year based on its FC74 (FC80 - FC6) of erroneous deductions as defined in paragraph (d)(3)(ii) of this section.

(iii) The FC34 (FC40—FC6) of prior deductions is permitted to be taken into account as a deduction over the 15-year period beginning with its 1980 taxable year as provided in paragraph (d)(2) of this section.

(iv) Additionally, because Z took erroneous deductions under its method of accounting prior to the beginning of its open period, it is required to change to the method of accounting permitted during the open period, and must take a section 481(a) adjustment (determined under the snapshot method of §1.404A-6(f)) into account over the 15-year section 481(a) adjustment period of §1.404A-6(e)(2)(ii) beginning in its 1978 year of change. See paragraph (d)(1) of this section.

Example 3. A foreign branch which computes its income under the profit and loss method of Rev. Rul. 75-107, 1975-1 C.B. 32 (see §601.601(d)(2)(ii)(b) of this chapter), in units of local currency, the FC, maintains a qualified funded plan. In 1980, the taxpayer was eligible to make the elections described in this section, and did so during the 1980 taxable year. The amount determined under paragraph (d)(3)(i) of this section after taking into account the limitations prescribed [by] §1.404A-4(a) for the open period was FC1,500,000. For the 1980 taxable year, and as provided in paragraph (d) of this section,

(4) *Time and manner to make, perfect, or revoke election.*—(i) *In general.*—A plan-by-plan election described in paragraph (d)(1) of this section is not effective unless the election was actually made no later than the time prescribed by law for filing the United States return for the first taxable year ending on or after December 31, 1980, including extensions (whether or not the time was actually extended for filing the taxpayer's return), and unless the taxpayer perfects the election by filing a statement indicating the taxpayer's agreement to perfect the election with an amended return for the first taxable year ending on or after December 31, 1980, on or before [*INSERT DATE THAT IS 365 DAYS AFTER THE DATE OF PUBLICATION OF FINAL REGULATIONS IN THE FEDERAL REGISTER*]. In order to be effective, the perfection must be made in the manner provided in §1.404A-6(b)(3)(ii) or (iii). An election that is not perfected is considered retroactively revoked. Any election under this paragraph (d) will continue in effect for taxable years beginning after the taxpayer's open period, unless revoked under paragraph (e) of this section or §1.404A-6.

(ii) *Requirement to amend returns.*—In addition to the amended return required by paragraph (d)(4)(i) of this section, the taxpayer must file any other amended United States returns that are necessary to conform the treatment of all items affected by the election or revocation to the treatment consistent with the election or revocation under this paragraph (d) within the time period described in paragraph (d)(4)(i) of this section. All amended returns must be accompanied by the statement described in paragraph (b)(3)(ii) of this section and all of the information required by §1.404A-6(b)(4) (and §1.404A-6(c)(2)(ii), if applicable, in the case of a termination). If no adjustments are necessary, the amended return required by paragraph (d)(4)(i) of this section must contain a statement to that effect.

(5) *Examples.*—The principles of this paragraph (d) are illustrated by the following examples:

Example 1. (i) During its open taxable years 1977 through 1979, X, a domestic corporation, maintained a nonqualified funded plan for the employees of its foreign branch. In 1981, X made a retroactive effective date election and a retroactive plan-by-plan election to treat this plan as a qualified funded plan. The amounts deducted on X's tax returns, the amount deductible under sections 404(a) and 404A (expressed in FC, the local currency) are as follows—

1978	1979	Total
FC100	FC100	FC300
20	20	FC60
90	90	FC270

Example 2. (i) Z, a domestic corporation, maintained a nonqualified funded foreign branch plan for its foreign employees, beginning in its 1965 (calendar) taxable year. In 1981, Z made a retroactive effective date election and a retroactive plan-by-plan election to treat this plan as a qualified funded plan. As of December 31, 1980, Z's 1965 taxable year was closed, but its 1978 taxable year was open. The amounts deducted on Z's tax returns, the amount deductible under sections 404(a) and 404A (expressed in FC, the local currency) are as follows—

1965	1978	Total
FC20	FC80	FC100
5	6	FC11
10	40	FC60

FC100,000 of the prior deductions were deductible. The prior deductions allowed to be taken into account in the 1980 through 1994 taxable years are determined without regard to, and thus are not subject to, the limitations prescribed by §1.404A-4(a).

(e) *Special transition rules for election, revocation and re-election.*—(1) *In general.*—This paragraph (e) provides the time and manner for making and revoking qualified funded plan and qualified reserve plan elections for a taxpayer's transition period. A taxpayer may make an election, revoke an election, and re-elect to treat any plan that met the requirements of §1.404A-1(a) (other than paragraph (4) thereof) for the relevant period as a qualified funded plan or a qualified reserve plan under this paragraph (e) for the transition period without regard to whether a retroactive election is made under paragraph (b), (c), or (d) of this section. However, an election made under paragraph (c) or (d) of this section is deemed to continue in effect for taxable years beginning after December 31, 1979, unless revoked under paragraph (c)(4) of this section or this paragraph (e) or terminated or revoked under §1.404A-6(f). See paragraphs (c)(2) and (d)(4)(i) of this section.

(2) *Time and manner initially to elect and revoke.*—(i) *In general.*—Taxpayers that wish to make an election under this paragraph (e) may have, but were not required to have, made a Method (1) or Method (2) election for the taxable year for which an election is made under this paragraph. Those taxpayers that wish to make (or perfect)

an election under this paragraph (e) must attach a statement to that effect on an amended return for the year the election is to be effective on or before [*INSERT DATE THAT IS 365 DAYS AFTER THE DATE OF PUBLICATION OF FINAL REGULATIONS IN THE FEDERAL REGISTER*]. An election previously made that is not perfected is considered retroactively revoked.

(ii) *Requirement to amend returns.*—In addition to the amended return required by paragraph (e)(2)(i) of this section, the taxpayer must file any other amended United States returns that are necessary to conform the treatment of all items affected by the election or revocation to the treatment consistent with the election or revocation under this paragraph (e) within the time period described in paragraph (e)(2)(i) of this section. All amended returns must be accompanied by the statement described in paragraph (b)(3)(ii) of this section (substituting "made, perfected, or revoked" for "perfected or revoked" where applicable) and all of the information required by § 1.404A-6(b)(4) (and § 1.404A-6(c)(2)(ii), if applicable, in the case of a termination). If no adjustments are necessary, the amended return required by paragraph (e)(2)(i) of this section must contain a statement to that effect.

(3) *Revocation after initial election and re-election permitted.*—Any taxpayer that makes an initial election for any plan under paragraph (e)(2) of this section may, under the rules of that paragraph, revoke

> Plan-by-plan election
> effective
> 1971—1974
> 1982—1987

(ii) A section 481(a) adjustment is required for the years of change 1975, 1982 and 1988.

(f) *Special data rules for retroactive elections.*—(1) *Retroactive calculation of section 481(a) adjustments.*—(i) *General rule.*—Retroactive elections may be made only if the taxpayer calculates the section 481(a) adjustment required by § 1.404A-6 based on substantiation quality data. Substantiation quality data generally must be current as of the date of the change in method of accounting. Nevertheless, if contemporaneous substantiation quality data is not readily available, the taxpayer may calculate the section 481(a) adjustment based on backward projections to earlier years from the first taxable year beginning before January 1, 1980, for which sufficient contemporaneous substantiation quality data is readily available. However, such projections must satisfy the substantiation requirements in paragraph (f)(1)(ii) of this section. Furthermore, the taxpayer may not use any of the approaches provided for under this paragraph (f) if circumstances indicate that the overall result is a material distortion of the amounts allowable.

(ii) *Substantiation requirement for retroactive reserves.*—(A) *In general.*—Although reasonable actuarial estimates and projections may be used, the calculation of the opening balance of the reserve for the first year for which a qualified reserve plan election under paragraph (c)(1) of this section is effective must nonetheless be based on some actual contemporaneous evidence. Thus, the opening balance may be based on actual aggregate covered payroll, the actual number of covered employees, or a contemporaneous actuarial valuation that used reasonable actuarial methods. For example, if the taxpayer has contemporaneous records of the number of covered employees and the aggregate covered payroll, it may estimate other actuarial information, such as average age and marital status, based on reasonable actuarial methods (e.g., using substantiation quality data as of another date and adjusting for actual or expected changes for the interim years). The resulting combination of actual contemporaneous evidence and reasonably estimated data may be used to calculate the opening reserve. If a contemporaneous actuarial valuation is used as the basis of an opening reserve, the results of the valuation must be adjusted to reflect any difference between the actuarial method used in that actuarial valuation and the unit credit method, as required by section 404A(c) and § 1.404A-3(b).

(B) *Interpolation.*—In cases where a taxpayer can meet the substantiation requirement of paragraph (f)(1)(ii)(A) of this section for some years, but cannot meet that requirement in intervening years (including the year of the change in method of accounting), the taxpayer may interpolate a reserve balance for the intervening years based on reasonable actuarial methods. In the absence of evidence to the contrary, it is assumed that a pro rata allocation of amounts to those intervening years is a reasonable actuarial method. This paragraph (f)(1)(ii)(B) does not authorize any interpolation for years in which other evidence indicates that it would cause a material distortion (such as a year during which the work force was on strike and no deferred compensation benefits were accrued). In addition, this paragraph (f)(1)(ii)(B) does not authorize extrapolation of reserve balances to years that are not intervening years between years that meet the substantiation requirements of paragraph (f)(1)(ii)(A) of this section.

the election for any taxable year after the sixth consecutive taxable year for which the election is effective, and may re-elect for any taxable year after the sixth consecutive taxable year for which the election is not in effect (whether the election is not in effect due to either revocation or termination of the election as defined in § 1.404A-6(c)(1)). The consecutive changes in method of accounting described in the first sentence of this paragraph (e)(3) must be made under the rules in § 1.404A-6 regarding the section 481(a) adjustment period. The Commissioner may approve a letter ruling request to shorten the six-year waiting period upon a showing of extraordinary circumstances.

(4) *Example.*—The principles of paragraph (e)(3) of this section are illustrated by the following example:

Example. (i) *L*, a domestic corporation, has wholly owned foreign subsidiary *M*, since *M*'s formation in 1971. *M* maintained a funded plan for its employees from 1971 through 1991. The taxable year of *L* and *M* is the calendar year. In 1981, *L* made a Method (2) election. Within 365 days after the publication of the final regulations in the Federal Register, *L* perfected its retroactive effective date election for all its foreign subsidiaries. *L*'s election terminated in 1975 due to its plan's violation of the requirements of section 404A(e)(2). Additionally, *L* perfected, revoked and re-elected on a plan-by-plan basis its election for *M*'s plan, as follows—

> Plan-by-plan election
> terminated or revoked
> 1975—1981
> 1988—1993

(C) *Extrapolation.*—If the first year for which the taxpayer is able to meet the substantiation requirements of paragraph (f)(1)(ii)(A) of this section ("the substantiation year") is later than the year of the change in method of accounting, a taxpayer may use the approach described in this paragraph (f)(1)(ii)(C) to determine the section 481(a) adjustments described in § 1.404A-6(f) in years prior to the substantiation year. Under this approach, the taxpayer's closing balance under its prior method as of the date of the change in the method of accounting is compared with the opening balance in the substantiation year. If the closing balance exceeds the opening balance, the excess is the amount to be used in calculating the adjustment under section 481, as required by § 1.404A-6. However, if the closing balance of the taxpayer's reserve under its method used for years prior to the election under section 404A is less than the opening balance for the substantiation year, the opening balance as of the date of the change in method in accounting is assumed to be equal to the closing balance. Thus, if the closing balance is less than the opening balance for the substantiation year, there is no adjustment under section 481. In such a case, the difference between the opening balance as of the date of the change in method of accounting and the opening balance for the substantiation year is allocated to the years prior to the substantiation year based on reasonable actuarial methods using all available information.

(2) *Determination of reasonable addition to a reserve in interim years.*—In the case of a qualified reserve plan that is using the interpolation option of paragraph (f)(1)(ii)(B) of this section or that is described in the last sentence in paragraph (f)(1)(ii)(C) of this section, none of the increase in the reserve in the intervening year is considered a reasonable addition to the reserve under § 1.404A-3(b). Thus, the entire amount of the increase must be considered an amount to be amortized over ten years under § 1.404A-3(c).

(3) *Protective elections.*—For those taxpayers that relied on the prior position of the Internal Revenue Service by making a Method (1) election under which the section 481(a) adjustment was computed in a manner inconsistent with this section or by making a Method (2) election under which no section 481(a) adjustment was reflected in the original return, appropriate adjustments required by section 404A and its underlying regulations must be made on an amended return filed no later than [*INSERT DATE THAT IS 365 DAYS AFTER THE DATE OF PUBLICATION OF FINAL REGULATIONS IN THE FEDERAL REGISTER*] for the first year the election is effective and for all subsequent affected years for which a return has been filed. If no adjustments are necessary, an amended return should be filed for the first year stating that no adjustments are necessary.

(g) *Definitions and special rules.*—(1) *Method (1) election.*—The term "Method (1) election" means an election that was made under Method (1) (as defined in Ann. 81-114, 1981-28 I.R.B. 21) (see § 601.601(d)(2)(ii)(*b*) of this chapter) by claiming the deduction or credit allowable under section 404A on the taxpayer's income tax return for the first taxable year ending on or after December 31, 1980, including extensions (or an amended return filed no later than the end of the extended time period prescribed in section 6081, whether or not such time was actually extended for filing the taxpayer's return).

(2) *Protective or Method (2) election.*—The term "protective election" or "Method (2) election" means an election that was made under Method (2) (as defined in Ann. 81-114, 1981-28 I.R.B. 21) (see § 601.601(d)(2)(ii)(*b*) of this chapter) without claiming deductions attributable to a qualified foreign plan on the taxpayer's income tax return (or, in the case of foreign subsidiaries, without taking into account reductions of earnings and profits).

(3) *Open years of the taxpayer.*—The term "open years of the taxpayer" means open taxable years beginning after December 31, 1971, and for which, on December 31, 1980, the making of a refund, or the assessment of a deficiency, was not barred by any law or rule of law.

(4) *Retroactive period.*—The term "retroactive period" means a taxpayer's taxable years (whether or not the making of a refund, or the assessment of a deficiency, was barred by any law or rule of law for any taxable year) in the following range—

(i) Any taxable year selected by the taxpayer between taxable years beginning after December 31, 1970 and before January 1, 1980 (the beginning taxable year); and

(ii) The last taxable year beginning before January 1, 1980 (the ending taxable year).

(5) *Transition period.*—The term "transition period" means taxable years beginning after December 31, 1979, and before [*INSERT THE DATE OF PUBLICATION OF FINAL REGULATIONS IN THE FEDERAL REGISTER*].

(6) *Open period.*—For purposes of this section, the term "open period" means, with respect to any taxpayer, all taxable years beginning after December 31, 1971, and beginning before January 1, 1980, and for which, on December 31, 1980, the making of a refund, or the assessment of a deficiency, was not barred by any law or rule of law. [Reg. § 1.404A-7.]

IRAs: SEPs: Special Requirements

Individual Retirement Plans: Simplified Employee Pensions.—Reproduced below is the text of a proposed amendment of Reg. § 1.408-2, relating to individual retirement plans and simplified employee pensions (published in the Federal Register on July 14, 1981).

* * *

☐ Par. 6. Section 1.408-2 is amended by revising paragraph (c)(3) to read as follows:

§ 1.408-2. Individual retirement accounts.—

* * *

(c) * * *

(3) *Special requirement.*—There must be a separate accounting for the interest of each employee or member (or spouse of an employee or member).

* * *

IRAs: SEPs: Acceptable Contributions

Individual Retirement Plans: Simplified Employee Pensions: Qualified Voluntary Employee Contributions.—Reproduced below is the text of a proposed amendment of Reg. § 1.408-2, relating to individual retirement plans, simplified employee pensions and qualified voluntary employee contributions (published in the Federal Register on January 23, 1984).

* * *

☐ Par. 2. Section 1.408-2 is amended by revising paragraph (b)(1) to read as follows:

§ 1.408-2. Individual retirement accounts.—

* * *

(b) * * *

(1) *Amount of acceptable contributions.*—Except in the case of a contribution to a simplified employee pension described in section 408(k) and a rollover contribution described in section 408(d)(3),

402(a)(5), 402(a)(7), 403(a)(4), 403(b)(8), 405(d)(3), or 409(b)(3)(C), the trust instrument must provide that contributions may not be accepted by the trustee for the taxable year in excess of $2,000 on behalf of any individual for whom the trust is maintained. An individual retirement account maintained as a simplified employee pension may provide for the receipt of up to the limits specified in section 408(j) for a calendar year.

IRAs: SEPs: Flexible Premiums

Individual Retirement Plans: Simplified Employee Pensions.—Reproduced below is the text of a proposed amendment of Reg. § 1.408-3, relating to individual retirement plans and simplified employee pensions (published in the Federal Register on July 14, 1981).

☐ Par. 7. Section 1.408-3 is revised by adding new paragraphs (b)(6) and (f). These added provisions read as follows:

§ 1.408-3. Individual retirement annuities.—

* * *

(b) * * *

(6) *Flexible premium.*—(i) In the case of annuity contracts issued after November 6, 1978, the premiums under such contracts are not fixed. See paragraph (f) for the definition of an annuity contract under which "the premiums are not fixed."

(ii) In the case of a fixed premium individual retirement annuity or individual retirement endowment contract issued before November 7, 1978, the issuer of such contract may offer the holder of the contract the option of exchanging such contract for a flexible premium contract. If such an exchange is made before January 1, 1981, the exchange shall not constitute a distribution and shall be nontaxable.

* * *

(f) *Flexible premium annuity contract.*—(1) *In general.*—A flexible premium retirement annuity contract shall be considered a contract under which "the premiums are not fixed" if it provides the following:

(i) At no time after the initial premium for the contract has been paid is there a specified renewal premium required.

(ii) The contract must allow for the continuance of the contract (as a paid-up annuity) under its nonforfeiture provision if premium payments cease altogether.

(iii) The contract, if being continued on a paid-up basis (*i.e.*, if it has not been terminated by a payment in cash), will be reinstated

at any date prior to its maturity date upon payment of a premium to the insurer.

(2) *Exceptions.*—(i) The insurer may require that if a premium is remitted, it will be accepted only if the amount remitted is some stated amount, not in excess of $50.

(ii) The contract may provide that if no premiums have been received under the contract for two (2) full years and the paid-up annuity benefit at maturity of the plan stipulated in the contract arising from the premium paid prior to such two-year period would be less than $20 a month, the insurer may, at its option, terminate the contract by payment in cash of the then present value of the paid-up benefit (computed on the same basis specified in the contract for determining the paid-up benefit).

(3) *Permissible provisions.*—A flexible premium contract will not be considered to have fixed premiums merely because—

(i) A maximum limit (which may be expressed as a multiple of the premium paid in the first year of the contract) is placed on the amount of the premium that the insurer will accept in any year,

(ii) An annual charge is made against the policy value,

(iii) A fee (which may be composed of a flat dollar amount plus an amount equal to the required premium tax imposed by the state government) is charged upon the acceptance of each premium by the insurer, or

(iv) The contract requires a level annual premium for a supplementary benefit, such as a waiver of premium benefit.

IRAs: SEPs: Annual Premiums

Individual Retirement Plans: Simplified Employee Pensions: Qualified Voluntary Employee Contributions.—Reproduced below is the text of a proposed amendment of Reg. §1.408-3, relating to individual retirement plans, simplified employee pensions and qualified voluntary employee contributions (published in the Federal Register on January 23, 1984).

☐ Par. 3. Section 1.408-3 is amended by revising paragraph (b)(2) to read as follows:

§1.408-3. Individual retirement annuities.—

* * *

(b) * * *

(2) *Annual premium.*—Except in the case of a contribution to a simplified employee pension described in section 408(k), the annual premium on behalf of any individual for the annuity cannot exceed

$2,000. Any refund of premiums must be applied before the close of the calendar year following the year of the refund toward the payment of future premiums or the purchase of additional benefits. An individual retirement annuity maintained as a simplified employee pension may provide for an annual premium of up to the limits specified in section 408(j).

* * *

IRAs: SEPs: Rollover Contributions

Individual Retirement Plans: Simplified Employee Pensions.—Reproduced below is the text of a proposed amendment of Reg. §1.408-4, relating to individual retirement plans and simplified employee pensions (published in the Federal Register on July 14, 1981). Proposed amendments to Reg. §1.408-4(b)(4)(ii) withdrawn by REG-209459-78 on July 11, 2014.

☐ Par. 8. Section 1.408-4 is amended by: (1) adding new paragraphs (b)(3), (b)(4)(ii), and (c)(3)(ii); and (2) adding a new paragraph (h). These added provisions read as follows:

§1.408-4. Treatment of distributions from individual retirement arrangements.—

* * *

(b) *Rollover Contribution.*—* * *

(3) *To section 403(b) contract.*—Paragraph (a)(1) of this section does not apply to any amount paid or distributed from an individual retirement account or individual retirement annuity to the individual for whose benefit the account or annuity is maintained if—

(i) The entire amount received (including money and other property) represents the entire interest in the account or the entire value of the annuity,

(ii) No amount in the account and no part of the value of the annuity is attributable to any source other than a rollover contribution from an annuity contract described in section 403(b) and any earnings on such rollover,

(iii) The entire amount thereof is paid into an annuity contract described in section 403(b) (for the benefit of such individual) not later than the 60th day after the receipt of the payment or distribution, and

(iv) The distribution or transfer is made in a taxable year beginning after December 31, 1978.

(4) * * *

(ii) [Withdrawn by REG-209459-78 on July 11, 2014.]

(c) * * *

(3) *Time of inclusion.*—* * *

(ii) For taxable years beginning after December 31, 1976, the amount of net income determined under subparagraph (2) is includible in the gross income of the individual in the taxable year in which such excess contribution is made. The amount of net income thus distributed is subject to the tax imposed by section 408(f)(1) for the year includible in gross income.

* * *

(h) *Certain distributions of excess contributions after due date of return for taxable year.*—(1) *General rule.*—In the case of any individual, if the aggregate contributions (other than valid rollover contributions) paid for any taxable year to an individual retirement account or for an individual retirement annuity do not exceed $1,750, section 408(d)(1) shall not apply to the distribution of any such contribution to the extent that such contribution exceeds the amount allowable as a deduction under section 219 or 220 for the taxable year for which the contribution was paid—

(i) If such distribution is received after the date described in section 408(d)(4),

(ii) But only to the extent that no deduction has been allowed under section 219 or 220 with respect to such excess contribution.

(2) *Excess rollover contribution attributable to erroneous information.*—If the taxpayer reasonably relies on information supplied pursuant to subtitle F of the Internal Revenue Code of 1954 for determining the amount of a rollover contribution, but such information was erroneous, subparagraph (1) of this paragraph shall be applied by increasing the dollar limit set forth therein by that portion of the excess contribution which was attributable to such information.

(3) *Special rule for contributions to simplified employee pension.*— If employer contributions on behalf of the individual are paid for the taxable year to a simplified employee pension, the dollar limitation

of subparagraph (1) shall be the lesser of the amount of such contributions or $7,500. See §1.219-3(a)(3)(iv) for a special rule where there is more than one employer.

(4) *Effective date.*—(1)[i] Subparagraphs (1) and (2) of this paragraph shall apply to distributions in taxable years beginning after December 31, 1975.

(ii) In the case of contributions for taxable years beginning before January 1, 1978, paragraph (5) of section 408(d) of the Internal Revenue Code of 1954 shall be applied as if such paragraph did not contain any dollar limitation.

(4)[5] *Examples.*—The provisions of this paragraph may be illustrated by the following examples:

Example (1). T, a calendar-year taxpayer, had been a participant in a government pension plan for 6 years prior to separation from service on July 31, 1976. The plan required T to make mandatory contributions and as of July 31, 1976, these mandatory contributions totaled $6,000. Upon T's separation from service, she was given the option of receiving back all of her mandatory contributions or leaving them with the plan. T elected to receive her mandatory contributions and attempted to roll over these amounts into an individual retirement account (IRA) in August of 1976. The trustee of the IRA accepted these funds and an IRA was established. In March of 1977, T discovered that the funds she received from the government plan did not qualify for rollover treatment because they were employee contributions and withdrew all of the money from her IRA. T will not have to include any of the money withdrawn from the IRA in gross income for 1977 because the transitional rule of paragraph (h)(3)(ii) permits the withdrawal of all contributions which have not been allowed as deductions under section 219 or 220 made to IRA's for taxable years beginning before January 1, 1978, regardless of the amount of the contribution.

Example (2). (i) On April 1, 1980, A, a calendar-year taxpayer, receives a lump sum distribution satisfying the requirements of section 402(e)(4)(A) and (C) under the plan of A's employer. The distribution consists of $50,000 cash. A made contributions under the plan totaling $8,000, and has received no prior distributions under the plan. However, on the form furnished to A by the employer on account of the distribution, A's contributions under the plan are listed as totaling only $4,500. A reasonably relied on this information.

(ii) A desires to establish an individual retirement account (as described in section 408(a)) with the cash received in the distribution. A desires to contribute the maximum amount permitted under the rollover rules. Under sections 402(a)(5)(B) and 402(a)(5)(D)(ii), A determines that the maximum rollover amount is $45,500, the total of the distribution ($50,000), less the amount listed as A's contributions under the plan ($4,500). The actual maximum rollover amount is $42,000, the total of the distribution ($5,000), less A's actual contribution under the plan ($8,000).

(iii) On May 23, 1980, A contributes $45,500 to an individual retirement account as a rollover contribution.

(iv) On May 1, 1981, A's employer furnishes A a corrected statement indicating that A's contributions under the plan were $8,000. On June 1, 1981, A withdraws $3,500 from the individual retirement account to correct the mistaken contribution. A will not have to include the $3,500 withdrawn from the individual retirement account in gross income for 1981 because the money was placed in the individual retirement account due to erroneous information furnished by the employer and reasonably relied upon by A and thus falls under the exception provided in section 408(d)(5)(B) to section 408(d)(1).

IRAs: SEPs: Annual Reports

Individual Retirement Accounts: Annual Information Report: Trustees and Issuers.— Reproduced below is the text of proposed Reg. §1.408-5, requiring annual reporting of information relating to individual retirement plans (published in the Federal Register on November 16, 1984).

☐ Section 1.408-5 is revised to read as follows:

§1.408-5. Annual reports by trustees and issuers.—
(a) *Requirement and form of report.*—The trustee of an individual retirement account or the issuer of an individual retirement annuity (including an account or annuity that is a simplified employee pension) shall make annual calendar year reports on Form 5498 concerning the status of the account or annuity. The report shall contain the following information for transactions occurring during or after the calendar year that relate to such calendar year:

(1) The name, address, and identifying number of the trustee or issuer;

(2) The name, address, and identifying number of the participant (the individual on whose behalf the account is established or in whose name the annuity is purchased (or the beneficiary of the individual or owner));

(3) The amount of contributions (exclusive of rollover contributions) made during or after the calendar year that relate to such calendar year;

(4) The amount of rollover contributions made during the calendar year;

(5) In the case of an endowment contract, the amount of the premium allocable to the cost of life insurance paid either during or after the calendar year that relates to such calendar year; and

(6) Such other information as the Commissioner may require.

(b) *Manner and time for filing.*—The report on Form 5498 shall be filed, accompanied by transmittal Form 1096, with the appropriate Internal Revenue Service Center. The report shall be filed on or before May 31 following the calendar year for which the report is required.

(c) *Statement to participants.*—(1) Each trustee or issuer required to file Form 5498 under this section shall furnish the participant a statement containing the information required to be furnished on Form 5498 plus the value of the account or annuity at the end of the calendar year. A copy of Form 5498, containing the additional information specified in the previous sentence, may be used to satisfy the statement requirement of this paragraph. If a copy of Form 5498 is not used to satisfy the statement requirement of this paragraph, the statement shall contain the following language: "This information is being furnished to the Internal Revenue Service."

(2) Each statement required by this paragraph to be furnished to participants shall be furnished to such person on or before May 31 following the calendar year for which the report on Form 5498 is required.

(d) *Penalties.*—Section 6693 prescribes penalties for failure to file an annual report required by this section.

(e) *Effective date.*—In general, this section applies to reports for calendar years beginning with 1983. For additional requirements relating to the 1985 calendar year reports, see paragraph (f) of this section. For special requirements relating to the 1983 and 1984 calendar year reports, see paragraph (g) of this section. For requirements relating to pre-1983 calendar year reports, see 26 C.F.R. §1.408-5 (1983).

(f) *Reports for calendar year 1985.*—For calendar year 1985, both Form 5498 and the statement to the participant must report, as a separate entry, the amount of contributions made during the 1985 calendar year that relate to the 1984 calendar year. This also applies, in the case of the statement to the participant, to endowment contract premiums allocable to the cost of life insurance that are paid during the 1985 calendar year but that relate to the 1984 calendar year.

(g) *Reports for calendar years 1983 and 1984.*—(1) For calendar years 1983 and 1984, neither Form 5498 nor the statement to the participant need identify the calendar year to which a contribution relates. The form and statement need only report the amount of contributions actually made during the calendar year. This also applies to endowment contract premiums allocable to the cost of life insurance and paid during the calendar year.

(2) For calendar years 1983 and 1984, Form 5498 need not report (but the statement to the participant must report), in the case of an endowment contract, the amount of the premium allocable to the cost of life insurance paid during the calendar year.

(3) For calendar year 1983, neither Form 5498 nor the statement to the participant need separately report rollover contributions made during the calendar year. Rollover contributions are to be aggregated with the amount of other contributions made during the calendar year.

(4) For calendar year 1983, the statement to the participant need not contain the language required by paragraph (c)(1) of this section.

(5) For calendar year 1983, Form 5498 shall be filed, and the statement to the participant shall be furnished, on or before June 30, 1984.

(h) *Related reports by trustees and issuers.*—See §1.408-7 for reports relating to distributions from individual retirement plans.

IRAs: SEPs: Disclosure: Nondiscrimination

Individual Retirement Plans: Simplified Employee Pensions.—Reproduced below are the texts of proposed Reg. §§1.408-7 and 1.408-8 and a proposed amendment of Reg. §1.408-6, relating to individual retirement plans and simplified employee pensions (published in the Federal Register on July 14, 1981.)

* * *

☐ Par. 9. Section 1.408-6 is amended by deleting paragraph (d)(4)(xi) and adding a new paragraph (b) to read as follows:

§1.408-6. Disclosure statements for individual retirement arrangements.—

* * *

(b) *Disclosure statements for spousal individual retirement arrangements.*—The trustee of an individual retirement account and the issuer of an individual retirement annuity shall furnish to the benefited individual of a spousal individual retirement arrangement a disclosure statement in accordance with paragraph (d). In the case of a spousal individual retirement arrangement that uses subaccounts, the benefited individual includes both the working and non-working spouse.

☐ Par. 10. There are added after §1.408-6 the following new sections:

§1.408-7. Simplified employee pension.—(a) *In general.*—The term "simplified employee pension" means an individual retirement account or individual retirement annuity described in section 408(a), (b) or (c) with respect to which the requirements of paragraphs (b), (d), (e), (g) and (h) of this section are met and the requirements of §1.408-8 are met with respect to any calendar year.

(b) *Establishment of simplified employee pension.*—In order to establish a simplified employee pension, the employer must execute a written instrument (hereafter referred to as the simplified employee pension arrangement) within the time prescribed for making deductible contributions. This instrument shall include: the name of the employer, the requirements for employee participation, the signature of a responsible official, and the definite allocation formula specified in section 408(k)(5) and paragraph (f) of this section.

(c) *Variation in contribution.*—(1) *Permitted variations.*—An employer's total contributions to its employees' simplified employee pensions may vary annually at the employer's discretion.

(2) *Salary reduction.*—Contributions made to a simplified employee pension under an arrangement under which the contribution will be made only if the employee receives a reduction in compensation or forgoes a compensation increase shall be treated as employer contributions to a simplified employee pension only if the arrangement precludes an individual election by the employee. If there is an individual election, then the contribution shall be treated as an employee contribution.

(d) *Participation requirements.*—(1) *Age and service requirements.*—This paragraph is satisfied with respect to a simplified employee pension arrangement for a calendar year only if for such year the employer contributes to the simplified employee pension on behalf of each individual who is an employee at any time during the calendar year who has—

    (i) Attained age 25,

    (ii) Performed service for the employer during at least 3 of the immediately preceding 5 calendar years, and

    (iii) Received at least $200 compensation from the employer for the calendar year.

    (2) *Execution of documents.*—The employer may execute any necessary documents on behalf of an employee who is entitled to a contribution to a simplified employee pension if the employee is unable or unwilling to execute such documents or the employer is unable to locate the employee.

    (3) *Required employment.*—An employer may not require that an employee be employed as of a particular date in order to receive a contribution for a calendar year.

    (4) *Nonresident aliens and employees covered by collective-bargaining agreements.*—An employer may exclude from participation in the simplified employee pension arrangement employees described in section 410(b)(2)(A) or 410(b)(2)(C).

    (5) *Example.*—The provisions of this paragraph may be illustrated by the following example:

    Example. Corporation X maintains a simplified employee pension arrangement for its employees. Individual J worked for Corporation X while in graduate school in 1976, 1977, and 1978. J never worked more than 25 days in any particular year. In October of 1979, J began to work for Corporation X on a full-time basis. J earned $5,000 from Corporation X for 1979. J became 25 on December 31, 1979. Corporation X must make a contribution to a simplified employee pension maintained on behalf of J for 1979 because as of December 31, 1979, J had met the minimum age requirement of section 408(k)(2), had performed service for Corporation X in 3 of the 5 calendar years preceding 1979, and met the minimum compensation requirements of paragraph (d)(1)(iii).

Employee	Gross Income
A	$11,000
C	57,500
Totals:	$80,000

    (ii) Under the special rule of this paragraph, because only 10 percent of compensation was allocated to A, and the allocation formula provides that the same percentage will be allocated to each participant, a certain portion of the contribution to B and C under the SEP shall be deemed made to IRA's that are not part of the SEP Arrangement.

Employee	Gross Income	Allocation Compensation*	SEP-IRA Contribution	Deemed IRA Contribution**
A	$11,000	$10,000	$1,000	$ 0
B	11,500	10,455	1,045	455
C	57,500	52,273	5,227	2,273
Totals:	$80,000	$72,728	$7,272	$2,728

* Gross Income divided by 1.10.
** Also included in Allocation Compensation.

    (iv) Under section 404(h) for purposes of computing Corporation X's deduction, only the $7,272 is considered as a contribution to a SEP Arrangement described in section 408(k) under the special rule. The allowable 404(h) deduction equals $10,909 (15% of the excess of total compensation of $80,000 over the SEP contribution of $7,272 or 15% of $72,728). The other $2,728 is payment of compensation and subject to the deduction rules of section 162 or 212. Similarly, the $2,728 would not be considered as an employer SEP contribution for purposes of exemption from FICA and FUTA taxes under section 3121 and 3306.

    (v) The effect of treating the $2,273 as a contribution to SEP's for purposes of section 408(a)(1), (b)(2)(B) and (d)(5) is to not disqualify the individual retirement arrangement of C for accepting non-SEP contributions in excess of $1,500 and to allow C to withdraw the excess contribution of $2,273 without including that amount in income under section 408(d)(1).

    (g) *Permitted withdrawals.*—A simplified employee pension meets the requirements of this paragraph only if—

    (1) Employer contributions thereto are not conditioned on the retention in such pension of any portion of the amount contributed, and

    (2) There is no prohibition imposed by the employer on withdrawals from the simplified employee pension.
See section 408(d) for rules concerning the taxation of withdrawals from individual retirement accounts and annuities. See section

    (e) *Requirement of written allocation formula.*—(1) *Requirement of definite written allocation formula.*—Employer contributions to a simplified employee pension must be made under a definite written allocation formula which specifies—

    (i) The requirements which an employee must satisfy to share in an allocation, and

    (ii) The manner in which the amount allocated to each employee's account is computed.

    (2) *Employer may vary formula.*—An employer may vary the definite written allocation formula from year to year provided the simplified employee pension arrangement is amended by the permissible date for making contributions to indicate the new formula.

    (f) *Treatment of contributions which exceed the written allocation formula.*—(1) *General rule.*—To the extent that employer contributions do not satisfy § 1.408-7(e)(1), the contributions shall be deemed to be contributions which are not made under a simplified employee pension arrangement except for purposes of section 408(a)(1), (b)(2)(B) and (d)(5). These contributions shall be deemed made to an individual retirement account or individual retirement annuity not maintained as part of a simplified employee pension arrangement.

    (2) *Example.*—This paragraph is illustrated by the following example:

    Example. (i) Assume that in 1979 Corporation X adopts a simplified employee pension arrangement ("SEP Arrangement"). The arrangement calls for Corporation X to contribute the same percentage of each participant's compensation exclusive of SEP contributions to a simplified employee pension (Allocation Compensation). X has three employees, A, B, and C, who satisfy the participation requirements of the SEP Arrangement. The compensation, the contributions to the individual simplified employee pension ("SEP") for A, B and C and the varying treatment of the contributions are set forth as follows:

Net Compensation Before Contribution	SEP-IRA Contribution	Ratio of SEP-IRA Contributions to Net Compensation
$10,000	$1,000	10%
50,000	7,500	15%
$70,000	$10,000	

    (iii) To determine A's and B's Allocation Compensation the respective total compensation included in A's and B's gross income must be divided by 1.10 (1 plus the percentage of Allocation Compensation contributed to A under the SEP Arrangement). The excess of compensation included in gross income over Allocation Compensation is considered as a contribution under the SEP. The following table shows the result of this calculation:

408(f)(1) for penalties for premature withdrawals from individual retirement accounts and annuities.

    (h) *Section 401(j) plan.*—The requirements of this paragraph are met with respect to a simplified employee pension for a calendar year unless the employer maintains during any part of such year a plan—

    (1) Some or all of the active participants in which are employees (within the meaning of section 401(c)(1)) or shareholder-employees (as defined in section 1379(d)), and

    (2) To which section 401(j) applies. [Reg. § 1.408-7.]

§ 1.408-8. Nondiscrimination requirements for simplified employee pensions.—(a) *In general.*—The requirements of this section are met with respect to a simplified employee pension for a calendar year if for such year the contributions made by the employer to simplified employee pensions of its employees do not discriminate in favor of any employee who is—

    (1) An officer,

    (2) A shareholder, within the meaning of paragraph (b)(2),

    (3) A self-employed individual, or

    (4) Highly compensated.

    (b) *Special rules.*—(1) For purposes of this section, employees described in subparagraph (A) or (C) of section 410(b)(2) shall be excluded from consideration.

(2) An individual shall be considered a shareholder if he owns (with the application of section 318) more than 10 percent of the value of the stock of the employer.

(c) *Contributions must bear a uniform relationship to total compensation.*—(1) *General rule.*—Contributions shall be considered discriminatory unless employer contributions to its employees' simplified employee pensions bear a uniform relationship to the total compensation (not in excess of the first $100,000) of each employee maintaining a simplified employee pension. A rate of contribution which decreases as compensation increases shall be considered uniform.

(2) *Definition of compensation.*—For purposes of this section, the term "compensation" has the meaning set forth in §1.219-1, and

Participant	Compensation 1/1/80— 6/30/80
A	10,000
B	10,000
C	10,000

For 1980, A, B, and C received allocations equal to 7.5 percent, 5.45 percent, and 8 percent of compensation, respectively. These contributions are discriminatory because they do not bear a uniform relationship to total compensation.

(d) *Treatment of certain contributions and taxes.*—(1) *General rule.*—(i) Except as provided in this paragraph, employer contributions do not meet the requirements of this section unless such contributions meet the requirements of this section without taking into account contributions or benefits under Chapter 2 of the Internal Revenue Code (relating to tax on self-employment income), Chapter 21 (relating to Federal Insurance Contribution Act), Title II of the Social Security Act, or any other Federal or State law ("Social Security Taxes"). If the employer does not maintain an integrated plan at any time during the taxable year, taxes paid under section 3111(a) (relating to tax on employers) with respect to an employee may, for purposes of this section, be taken into account as a contribution by the employer to an employee's simplified employee pension. If contributions are made to the simplified employee pension of an owner-employee, the preceding sentence shall not apply unless taxes paid by all such owner-employees under section 1401(a) and the taxes which would be payable under section 1401(a) by such owner-employees but for paragraphs (4) and (5) of section 1402(c), are taken into account as contributions by the employer on behalf of such owner-employees. The amount of such taxes shall be determined in a manner consistent with §1.401-12(h)(3).

(ii) If contributions are made to the simplified employee pension of a self-employed individual who is not an owner-employee, the arrangement may be integrated. In such a case, the portion of the earned income of such individual which does not exceed the maximum amount which may be treated as self-employment income under section 1402(b)(1) shall be treated as "wages" under section 3121(a)(1) subject to the tax imposed by section 3111(a) and such tax shall be taken into account as employer contributions.

is determined without regard to the employer contributions to the simplified employee pension arrangement.

(3) *Example.*—The provisions of this paragraph may be illustrated by the following example:

Example. Corporation X maintains a simplified employee pension arrangement which allocates employer contributions in the manner described below. First, contributions made by June 30 of each year are allocated in proportion to compensation paid from January 1 to June 30. Second, contributions made between July 1 and December 31 are allocated in proportion to compensation paid during the same period.

In 1980, the salaries paid, and contributions allocated, are shown below:

6/30/80 Allocation	Compensation 7/1/80— 12/31/80	12/31/80 Allocation
500	10,000	1,000
500	1,000	100
500	15,000	1,500

(iii) An employer may take into account as contributions accounts not in excess of such Social Security taxes. Thus, an employer may integrate using a rate less than the maximum rate of tax under section 3111(a) or compensation less than the maximum amount specified as wages under section 3121(a).

(2) *Integrated plan defined.*—For purposes of subparagraph (1), the term "integrated plan" means a plan which meets the requirements of section 401(a), 403(a), or 405(a) but would not meet such requirements if contributions or benefits under Chapter 2 (relating to tax on self-employment income), Chapter 21 (relating to Federal Insurance Contributions Act), Title II of the Social Security Act, or any other Federal or State law were not taken into account.

(e) *Examples.*—The provisions of this section may be illustrated by the following examples:

Example (1). Corporation M adopts a simplified employee pension arrangement. The corporation would like to contribute 7.5% of an employee's first $10,000 in compensation and 5% of all compensation above $10,000. The simplified employee pension arrangement which Corporation M adopts will not be considered discriminatory within the meaning of paragraph (c) of this section because the rate of contribution decreases as compensation increases.

Example (2). Corporation L adopts a simplified employee pension plan. It wishes to contribute to the simplified employee pension of each employee who is currently performing service. The corporation would like to contribute to the simplified employee pensions 5% of the total compensation of each employee who has completed up to 5 years of service and 7% of the total compensation of each employee who has completed more than 5 years of service. The simplified employee pension plan which Corporation L adopts will be considered discriminatory within the meaning of paragraph (c) of this section because the employer contributions do not bear a uniform relationship to each employee's total compensation. [Reg. §1.408-8.]

IRAs: SEPs: Reports and Information

Individual Retirement Plans: Simplified Employee Plans.—Reproduced below is the text of proposed Reg. §1.408-9, relating to individual retirement plans and simplified employee pensions (published in the Federal Register on July 14, 1981).

§1.408-9. Reports for simplified employee pensions.—(a) *Information to be furnished upon adoption of plan.*—(1) An employer who adopts a definite written allocation formula for making contributions to an employee's simplified employee pension shall furnish the employee in writing the following information:

(i) A notice that the simplified employee pension arrangement has been adopted,

(ii) The requirements which an employee must meet in order to receive a contribution under the agreement,

(iii) The basis upon which the employer's contribution will be allocated to employees, and

(iv) Such other information that the Commissioner may require.

(2) The information in subparagraph (1) must be furnished to an employee no later than a reasonable time after the later of the time the employee becomes employed or the time of the adoption of the simplified employee pension arrangement.

(3) The Commissioner may relieve employers from furnishing any or all of the information specified in subparagraph (1).

(b) *Information to be furnished for a calendar year.*—(1) For each calendar year, the employer shall furnish to the employee a written statement indicating the amount of employer contributions made to the employee's individual retirement account or individual retirement annuity under the simplified employee pension arrangement. This requirement is satisfied if the information is on the employee's W-2 for the calendar year for which the contribution is made. Amounts described in §1.408-7(f)(1) which are not considered made under the simplified employee pension arrangement should not be included.

(2) The information required to be furnished by subparagraph (1) shall be furnished to the employee no later than the later of 30 days after the contribution or January 31 following the calendar year for which the contribution was made.

(c) The Internal Revenue Service may require reports to be filed with the Service with respect to employees who cannot be located by the employer (see §1.408-7(d)(2)). Such reports shall include such information and shall be filed in the time and manner as the Commissioner specifies.

(d) *Effective date.*—The provisions of this section are effective for calendar years beginning after December 31, 1978. [Reg. §1.408-9.]

IRAs: SEPs: Investment in Collectibles

Individual Retirement Plans: Simplified Employee Pensions: Qualified Voluntary Employee Contributions.—Reproduced below is the text of proposed Reg. §1.408-10, relating to individual retirement plans, simplified employee pensions and qualified voluntary employee contributions (published in the Federal Register on January 23, 1984).

☐ Par. 4. There is added after proposed §1.408-9, 46 Fed. Reg. 36209 (1981), the following new section:

§1.408-10. Investment in collectibles.—(a) *In general.*—The acquisition by an individual retirement account or by an individually-directed account under a plan described in section 401(a) of any collectible shall be treated (for purposes of section 402 and 408) as a distribution from such account in an amount equal to the cost to such account of such collectible.

(b) *Collectible defined.*—For purposes of this section, the term "collectible" means—

(1) Any work of art,

(2) Any rug or antique,

(3) Any metal or gem,

(4) Any stamp or coin,

(5) Any alcoholic beverage,

(6) Any musical instrument,

(7) Any historical objects (documents, clothes, etc.), or

(8) Any other tangible personal property which the Commissioner determines is a "collectible" for purposes of this section.

(c) *Individually-directed account.*—For purposes of this section, the term "individually-directed account" means an account under a plan that provides for individual accounts and that has the effect of permitting a plan participant to invest or control the manner in which the account will be invested.

(d) *Acquisition.*—For purposes of this section, the term acquisition includes purchase, exchange, contribution, or any method by which an individual retirement account or individually-directed account may directly or indirectly acquire a collectible.

(e) *Cost.*—For purposes of this section, cost means fair market value.

(f) *Premature withdrawal penalty.*—The ten percent penalty described in section 72(m)(5) and 408(f)(1) shall apply in the case of a deemed distribution from an individual retirement account described in paragraph (a) of this section.

(g) *Amounts subsequently distributed.*—When a collectible is actually distributed from an individual retirement account or an individually-directed account, any amounts included in gross income because of this section shall not be included in gross income at the time when the collectible is actually distributed.

(h) *Effective date.*—This section applies to property acquired after December 31, 1981, in taxable years ending after such date. [Reg. §1.408-10.]

Deferred Compensation Plans: Service Providers

Deferred Compensation Plans: Service Providers.—Reg. §1.409A-4 and amendments to Reg. §1.409A-0, relating to the calculation of amounts includible in income under Code Sec. 409A(a) and the additional taxes imposed by such section with respect to service providers participating in certain nonqualified deferred compensation plans, are proposed (published in the Federal Register on December 8, 2008) (REG-148326-05). Proposed Reg. §1.409A-4(a)(1)(ii)(B) withdrawn by REG-123854-12 on June 22, 2016.

Par. 2. Section 1.409A-0 is amended by adding entries for §1.409A-4 to read as follows:

Par. 3. Section 1.409A-4 is added to read as follows:

§1.409A-4. Calculation of amount includible in income and additional income taxes.—(a) *Amount includible in income due to failure to meet the requirements of section 409A(a).*—(1) *In general.*—(i) *Calculation formula.*—The amount includible in income for a service provider's taxable year due to a failure to meet the requirements of section 409A(a) with respect to a plan is the excess (if any) of—

(A) The service provider's total amount deferred under the plan for the taxable year, including the amount of any payments of amounts deferred under the plan to (or on behalf of) the service provider during such taxable year; over

(B) The portion of such amount, if any, that is either subject to a substantial risk of forfeiture (as defined in §1.409A-1(d) and applying paragraph (a)(1)(ii)(B) of this section) or has been previously included in income (as defined in §1.409A-4(a)(3)).

(ii) *Each taxable year analyzed independently.*—(A) *In general.*—An amount is includible in income under section 409A(a) for a taxable year only if a plan fails to meet the requirements of section 409A(a) during such taxable year. Whether an amount is includible in income for a taxable year due to a failure to meet the requirements of section 409A(a) during such taxable year is determined independently of whether such amounts are also includible in income due to a failure to meet the requirements of section 409A(a) in a previous or subsequent taxable year. Accordingly, an amount may be includible in income for a taxable year during which a plan fails to meet the requirements of section 409A(a), even if the same amount was includible in income in a previous taxable year, except to the extent provided in §1.409A-4(a)(3) (identification of amount previously included in income).

(B) [Reg. §1.409A-4(a)(1)(ii)(B) was withdrawn and re-proposed by REG-123854-12 on June 22, 2016.]

(iii) *Examples.*—The following examples illustrate the provisions of this paragraph (a)(1). For each of the examples, Employee A is an individual taxpayer with a calendar year taxable year. Employee A has a total amount deferred under a nonqualified deferred compensation plan of $0 in 2010, $100,000 in 2011, and $250,000 in 2012. No payments are made under the plan. The plan under which the amounts are deferred fails to meet the requirements of section 409A(a) during 2011 and 2012. The examples read as follows:

Example 1. With respect to Employee A, at no time is any deferred amount subject to a substantial risk of forfeiture. Employee A has $100,000 includible in income under section 409A(a) for 2011, because no portion of the total deferred amount for 2011 is subject to a substantial risk of forfeiture or has previously been included in income. If that $100,000 is included in income for 2011, Employee A has $150,000 includible in income under section 409A(a) for 2012 because for the taxable year 2012 the $100,000 is previously included in income (see paragraphs (a)(1)(i)(B) and (a)(3) of this section). If that $100,000 is not included in income for 2011, Employee A has $250,000 includible in income under section 409A(a) for 2012. Employee A does not avoid the requirement to include $100,000 in income under section 409A(a) for 2011 by including $250,000 in income under section 409A(a) for 2012.

Example 2. The same facts as *Example 1*, except that, with respect to Employee A, the statute of limitations on assessments has expired for 2011, but has not expired for 2012. Employee A has $250,000 includible in income under section 409A(a) for 2012, because no portion of the total deferred amount for 2012 is subject to a substantial risk of forfeiture or has previously been included in income.

(2) *Identification of the portion of the total amount deferred for a taxable year that is subject to a substantial risk of forfeiture.*—(i) *In general.*—The portion of the total amount deferred for a taxable year that is subject to a substantial risk of forfeiture (as defined in §1.409A-1(d)) is determined as of the last day of the service provider's taxable year. Accordingly, an amount may be includible in income under section 409A(a) for a taxable year even if such amount is subject to a substantial risk of forfeiture during the taxable year if the substantial risk of forfeiture lapses during such taxable year, including if the substantial risk of forfeiture lapses after the date the nonqualified deferred compensation plan under which the amount is deferred first fails to meet the requirements of section 409A(a).

(ii) *Example.*—The following example illustrates the provisions of this paragraph (a)(2): Employee B is an individual taxpayer with a calendar year taxable year. Employee B has a total amount deferred under a nonqualified deferred compensation plan of $0 for 2010, $100,000 for 2011, and $250,000 for 2012. No payments are made under the plan. Under the terms of the plan, if Employee B voluntarily separates from service before July 1, 2012, Employee B will forfeit 50 percent of the Employee B's total amount deferred under the plan. If Employee B voluntarily separates from service after June 30, 2012 but before July 1, 2013, Employee B will forfeit 20

percent of the total amount deferred under the plan. If Employee B voluntarily separates from service after June 30, 2013, Employee B will not forfeit any amount deferred under the plan. As of December 31, 2011, 50 percent of the total amount deferred under the plan ($50,000) is subject to a substantial risk of forfeiture, and the remaining amount deferred under the plan ($50,000) is not subject to a substantial risk of forfeiture. As of December 31, 2012, 20 percent of the total amount deferred under the plan ($50,000) is subject to a substantial risk of forfeiture, and the remaining amount deferred under the plan ($200,000) is not subject to a substantial risk of forfeiture. At all times the terms of the plan meet the requirements of section 409A(a) and the applicable regulations, and through May 31, 2012, the plan is operated in a manner that complies with the terms of the plan. On June 1, 2012, the plan is operated in a manner that fails to meet the requirements of section 409A(a). For purposes of determining the amount includible in income under section 409A(a), except as provided in paragraph (a)(1)(ii)(B) of this section, the portion of the total amount deferred for 2012 that is subject to a substantial risk of forfeiture is $50,000 (20 percent of $250,000).

(3) *Identification of amount previously included in income.*—(i) *In general.*—For purposes of this section, an amount is previously included in income only if the service provider has included the amount in income under an applicable provision of the Internal Revenue Code for a previous taxable year. An amount is treated as included in income for a taxable year only to the extent that the amount was properly includible in income and the service provider actually included the amount in income (including on an original or amended return or as a result of an IRS examination or a final decision of a court of competent jurisdiction). For future taxable years, the amount previously included in income is reduced to reflect any amount that was paid during the taxable year for which the amount was included in income, any amount allocated to a payment made under the plan under paragraph (f) of this section, and any amount deductible under paragraph (g) of this section.

(ii) *Examples.*—The following examples illustrate the provisions of this paragraph (a)(3). For all of the examples, Employee C is an individual taxpayer with a calendar year taxable year. Employee C has a total amount deferred under a nonqualified deferred compensation plan of $0 in 2010, $100,000 in 2011, and $250,000 in 2012. With respect to Employee C, the statute of limitations on assessments has not expired for 2011 or 2012. Except as otherwise explicitly provided in the following examples, Employee C has not included in income for 2011 on any original or amended tax return any amount deferred under the plan, none of the $250,000 total amount deferred for 2012 has previously been included in income, no payments are made under the plan, and at no time is any deferred amount subject to a substantial risk of forfeiture. The plan under which the amounts are deferred fails to meet the requirements of section 409A(a) during 2011 and 2012. The examples read as follows:

Example 1. After filing an original Federal income tax return for 2011 that did not include any amount in income under section 409A(a), on April 1, 2013, Employee C files an amended Federal income tax return for 2011 and properly includes $100,000 in income under section 409A(a) for 2011. For purposes of determining the amount includible in income under section 409A(a) for 2012, $100,000 of the $250,000 total amount deferred for 2012 has previously been included in income with respect to the plan. For 2012, Employee C includes in income $150,000 under section 409A(a) on Employee C's original Federal income tax return. As of January 1, 2013, the amount that Employee C has previously included in income under section 409A(a) with respect to the plan is $250,000.

Example 2. The facts are the same as in *Example 1*, except that Employee C receives a $10,000 payment in 2011 so that the total amount deferred for 2012 is $240,000. For purposes of determining the amount includible in income under section 409A(a) for 2012, the $100,000 previously included in income is reduced by the $10,000 payment so that $90,000 of the $240,000 total amount deferred for 2012 has previously been included in income. For 2012, Employee C includes in income $150,000 under section 409A(a) on Employee C's original Federal income tax return. As of January 1, 2013, the amount that Employee C has previously included in income under section 409A(a) with respect to the plan is $240,000.

Example 3. The facts are the same as in *Example 2*. Due to deemed investment losses during 2013, Employee C has an $80,000 total amount deferred under the plan for 2013. On December 31, 2013, Employee C's total amount deferred ($80,000) is paid to Employee C as a single sum payment. Pursuant to paragraph (f) of this section, $80,000 of the $240,000 amount previously included in income is allocated to the $80,000 payment so that none of the $80,000 is includible in income. In addition, pursuant to paragraph (g) of this section, Employee C is entitled to deduct $160,000 for 2013 equal to the remaining amount previously included in income the right to which is permanently lost. Because the entire $240,000 amount previously included in income has been allocated to a payment under paragraph (f) of this section or was deductible under paragraph (g) of this section, no portion of such amount is treated as previously included in income for 2014 or any subsequent taxable year. As of January 1, 2014, the amount that Employee C has previously included in income under section 409A(a) with respect to the plan is $0.

(b) *The total amount deferred under a plan for a taxable year.*—(1) *Application of general rules and specific rules for specific types of plans.*—Paragraph (b)(2) of this section provides general rules governing the determination of the total amount deferred under a plan for a taxable year, including the treatment of plans providing for alternative times and forms of payment and plans providing for certain payments the amount of which is determined by a formula that includes one or more variables dependent upon future events (formula amounts). Paragraphs (b)(3) through (b)(6) of this section provide specific rules governing the determination of the total amount deferred under certain types of plans. Except as otherwise provided, any applicable rules of paragraphs (b)(3) through (b)(6) of this section are applied in conjunction with the general rules provided in paragraph (b)(2) of this section.

(2) *General definition of total amount deferred.*—(i) *General calculation rules.*—Except as otherwise provided, the total amount deferred for a taxable year equals the present value of the future payments to which the service provider has a legally binding right under the plan as of the last day of the taxable year, plus the amount of any payments of amounts deferred under the plan to (or on behalf of) the service provider during such taxable year. For purposes of this section, present value means the value, as of a specified date, of an amount or series of amounts due thereafter, determined in accordance with the rules and assumptions of this paragraph (b)(2), as applicable, where each amount is multiplied by the probability that the condition or conditions on which payment of the amount is contingent will be satisfied, also determined in accordance with the rules and assumptions set forth in this paragraph (b)(2), as applicable, discounted according to an assumed rate of interest to reflect the time value of money. For this purpose, a discount for the probability that an employee will die before commencement of benefit payments is permitted, but only to the extent that benefits will be forfeited upon death. In addition, the present value cannot be discounted for the probability that payments will not be made (or will be reduced) because of the unfunded status of the plan, the risk associated with any deemed or actual investment of amounts deferred under the plan, the risk that the service recipient, the trustee, or another party will be unwilling or unable to pay, the possibility of future plan amendments, the possibility of a future change in the law, or similar risks or contingencies. If the amount payable under a plan or the value of a benefit under a plan is expressed in a currency other than the U.S. dollar, the total amount deferred is translated from foreign currency into U.S. dollars at the spot exchange rate on the last day of the service provider's taxable year. No adjustment is made to the total amount deferred to reflect the risk that the currency in which the amount payable or the value of the benefit is expressed may in the future increase or decrease in value with respect to the U.S. dollar or any other currency.

(ii) *Actuarial assumptions and methods.*—(A) *Requirement of reasonable actuarial assumptions and methods.*—For purposes of this section, the present value must be determined as of the last day of the service provider's taxable year using actuarial assumptions and methods that are reasonable as of that date, including an interest rate for purposes of discounting for present value that is reasonable as of that date.

(B) *Use of an unreasonable actuarial assumption or method.*— If any actuarial assumption or method used to determine the total amount deferred for a taxable year under a plan is not reasonable, as determined by the Commissioner, then the total amount deferred is determined by the application of the AFR and, if applicable, the applicable mortality table under section 417(e)(3)(A)(ii)(I) (the 417(e) mortality table), both determined as of the last month of the taxable year for which the amount deferred is being determined. For purposes of this section, AFR means the appropriate applicable Federal rate (as defined pursuant to section 1274(d)) based on annual compounding, for the last month of the taxable year for which the amount includible in income is being determined. The period for which excess interest will be credited, beginning with the last day of the taxable year and ending with the date the excess interest will no longer be credited (determined in accordance with the payment timing assumptions set forth in paragraph (b)(2)(vi) and (vii) of this section) is used to determine the appropriate AFR (short-term, mid-term, or long term).

(iii) *Crediting of earnings and losses.*—The earnings and losses credited under a plan as of the last day of the service provider's taxable year pursuant to the plan are given effect only to the extent the plan's terms reasonably reflect the value of the service provider's rights under the plan. For example, a plan's method of determining the amount of such earnings or losses generally will be respected for purposes of determining the total amount deferred for the taxable year, provided that the earnings and losses are credited at least once per taxable year. If earnings and losses are not credited at least annually, the total amount deferred is calculated as if the earnings or losses were credited as of the last day of the taxable year. In addition, any change in the schedule for crediting earnings during the taxable year for which the total amount deferred is calculated that would reduce the earnings credited for a taxable year in which an amount is required to be included in income under section 409A(a) is disregarded for such taxable year. For example, if a plan is amended during a taxable year that is a calendar year to change the date for crediting earnings from December 31 to July 1 of that year and the plan fails to meet the requirements of section 409A(a) during that year, the amendment is disregarded for purposes of determining the total amount deferred for the year and December 31 is treated as the date for crediting earnings and losses. If no further changes are made to the plan with respect to the crediting of earnings and losses, for subsequent taxable years, July 1 is treated as the date for crediting earnings and losses.

(iv) *Application of the general calculation rules to formula amounts.*—(A) *In general.*—With respect to a right to a payment to which this paragraph applies, the amount payable for purposes of determining the total amount deferred for the taxable year must be determined based on all of the facts and circumstances existing as of the close of the last day of the taxable year. Such determination must reflect reasonable, good faith assumptions with respect to any contingencies as to the amount of the payment, both with respect to each contingency and with respect to all contingencies in the aggregate. An assumption based on the facts and circumstances as of the close of the last day of a taxable year may be reasonable even if the facts and circumstances change in a subsequent year so that if the amount payable were determined for such subsequent year, the amount payable would be a greater (or lesser) amount. In such a case, the increase (or decrease) due to the change in the facts and circumstances is treated as earnings (or losses). This paragraph (b)(2)(iv) applies to the extent that the amount payable in a future taxable year is a formula amount to the extent that the amount payable in a future taxable year is dependent upon factors that, after applying the assumptions and other rules set out in this section, are not determinable as of the end of the taxable year for which the total amount deferred is being calculated, so that the amount payable may not readily be determined as of the end of such taxable year under the other provisions of this section. If a portion of a deferred amount is determinable under the other rules of this paragraph (b)(2), the determination of the amount deferred with respect to such portion must be determined under the rules applicable to amounts that are not formula amounts, and only the balance of the deferred amount is determined under this paragraph.

(B) *Examples.*—The following examples illustrate the provisions of this paragraph (b)(2)(iv):

Example 1. On January 1, 2020, a service provider receives a legally binding right to a payment of one percent of the service recipient's net profits for the calendar years 2020, 2021, and 2022, payable on the later of January 1, 2024 or the service provider's separation from service. The amount payable is a formula amount and this paragraph (b)(2)(iv) applies.

Example 2. On January 1, 2020, a service provider receives a legally binding right to a payment of the greater of one percent of the service recipient's net profits for the calendar years 2020, 2021, and 2022 or $10,000, payable on the later of January 1, 2024 or the service provider's separation from service. The portion of the amount payable that is a $10,000 payment, payable at the later of January 1, 2024 or the service provider's separation from service, is not a formula amount. The portion of the amount payable that is the excess, if any, of one percent of the service recipient's net profits for the calendar years 2020, 2021, and 2022 over $10,000 is a formula amount and this paragraph (b)(2)(iv) applies.

Example 3. On January 1, 2020, a service provider receives a legally binding right to payment equal to the value of 10,000 shares of service recipient stock, payable on the later of January 1, 2024 or the service provider's separation from service. Because the amount payable may increase or decrease only due to a change in value of a predetermined actual investment (10,000 shares of service recipient stock), the amount payable is not treated as a formula amount and this paragraph (b)(2)(iv) does not apply.

(v) *Treatment of payment restrictions.*—Except as specifically provided, a restriction on the payment of all or part of a deferred amount that will or may lapse under the terms of the plan, including a risk of forfeiture that is not a substantial risk of forfeiture as defined in §1.409A-1(d) or is disregarded under §1.409A-4(a)(1)(ii)(B), is ignored for purposes of determining the total amount deferred under the plan. Accordingly, in calculating the total amount deferred, there is no reduction to account for a risk that the amount may be forfeited if the risk of forfeiture is not a substantial risk of forfeiture. For example, if an amount deferred is subject to forfeiture under a noncompetition provision applicable for a prescribed period, the forfeiture provision is disregarded for purposes of determining the total amount deferred for the taxable year.

(vi) *Treatment of alternative times and forms of a future payment.*—(A) *In general.*—For purposes of determining the total amount deferred for a taxable year, if payment of a deferred amount may be made at alternative times or in alternative forms, each amount deferred under the plan is treated as payable at the time and under the form of payment for which the present value is highest. A time and form of payment is available to the extent a deferred amount under the plan may be payable in such time and form of payment under the plan's terms. If the service recipient has commenced payment of a deferred amount in a time and form of payment under the plan, or the service provider or service recipient has elected a time and form of payment under the plan, and under the plan's terms neither party can change such time and form of payment without the consent of the other party (and such consent requirement has substantive significance), the time and form of payment elected or the time and form of payment in which payments have commenced is treated as the sole available time and form of payment for such amount. If an alternative time and form of payment is available only at the service recipient's discretion, the time and form of payment is not available unless the service provider has a legally binding right under the principles of § 1.409A-1(b)(1) to any additional value that would be generated by the service recipient's exercise of such discretion. For purposes of determining the value of each available time and form of payment, the assumptions and methods described in this paragraph (b)(2)(vi) are applied, and then the value of each available time and form of payment is determined in accordance with the other applicable rules provided in paragraph (b) of this section.

(B) *Effect of status of service provider on available times and forms of payment.*—For purposes of determining whether a time and form of payment is available, if eligibility for a time and form of payment depends upon the service provider's status as of a future date, the service provider is assumed to continue in the service provider's status as of the last day of the taxable year. However, if the eligibility requirement is not bona fide and does not serve a bona fide business purpose, the eligibility requirement will be disregarded and the service provider will be treated as eligible for the alternative time and form of payment. For this purpose, an eligibility condition based upon the service provider's marital status (including status as a registered domestic partner or similar requirement), parental status, or status as a U.S. citizen or lawful permanent resident under section 7701(b)(6) is presumed to be bona fide and serve a bona fide business purpose. Notwithstanding the foregoing, if eligibility for a certain time or form of payment includes a bona fide requirement that the service provider provide additional services after the end of the taxable year, the time and form of payment is not treated as an available time and form of payment. The rules of this paragraph (b)(2)(vi)(B) apply regardless of whether the service provider's status changes during a subsequent taxable year.

(vii) *Treatment of payment triggers based upon events.*—(A) *In general.*—For purposes of determining the total amount deferred for a taxable year, if a payment trigger has occurred on or before the last day of the taxable year, a deferred amount payable upon such trigger is treated as payable at the time the payment is scheduled to be made under the terms of the plan. If the payment trigger has not occurred on or before the last day of the taxable year, the trigger is treated as occurring on the earliest possible date the trigger reasonably could occur based on the facts and circumstances as of the last day of the taxable year, and the deferred amount is treated as payable based upon the schedule of payments that would be triggered by such occurrence. Notwithstanding the foregoing, if the payment trigger requires a separation from service, a termination of employment, or other similar reduction or cessation of services, the service provider is treated as meeting such requirement as of the last day of the taxable year. For purposes of determining the earliest date the payment trigger reasonably could occur, whether the payment trigger actually occurs in a subsequent taxable year is disregarded. For purposes of this paragraph (b)(2)(vii), a payment trigger means an event (not including the mere passage of time) upon which an amount may become payable. Generally if an amount would be payable in a different time and form of payment depending upon some characteristic of an event, each type of event upon which an amount would become payable is treated as a separate payment trigger. For example, if an amount would be payable as a single sum payment if one subsidiary corporation of a service recipient that consists of multiple corporations is sold, but as an installment payment if another subsidiary corporation of the same service recipient

is sold, then the sale of the one subsidiary corporation is treated as a separate payment trigger from the sale of the other subsidiary corporation.

(B) *Certain payment triggers disregarded.*—The possibility that the following payment triggers will occur in the future is disregarded for purposes of determining the total amount deferred (but not for purposes of determining whether the plan otherwise complies with the requirements of section 409A(a)):

(1) A payment trigger that, if the trigger were the sole trigger determining when the amount would become payable, would cause the amount to be subject to a substantial risk of forfeiture, provided that if there is more than one payment trigger applicable to an amount that otherwise would be disregarded under this paragraph (b)(2)(vii)(B)(1), none of such payment triggers will be disregarded unless all such payment triggers, if applied in combination as the only payment triggers, would also cause the amount to be subject to a substantial risk of forfeiture.

(2) An unforeseeable emergency (as defined in § 1.409A-3(i)(3)).

(viii) *Treatment of amounts that may qualify as short-term deferrals.*—For purposes of calculating the total amount deferred for a taxable year, the right to a payment that, under the terms of the arrangement and the facts and circumstances as of the last day of the taxable year, may be a short-term deferral as defined under § 1.409A-1(b)(4), is not included in the total amount deferred. In addition, even if such amount is not paid by the end of the applicable 2 1/2 month period so that the amount is deferred compensation, the amount is not includible in the total amount deferred until the service provider's taxable year in which the applicable 2 1/2 month period expires.

(ix) *Examples.*—The following examples illustrate the provisions of paragraphs (b)(2)(vi) through (viii) of this section. For all of the examples, the service provider is an individual taxpayer who is an employee of the service recipient, the service provider has a calendar year taxable year, and the total amount deferred is being calculated for the 68 taxable year ending December 31, 2010. In each case, the service provider is not entitled to earnings on the amount deferred. The examples read as follows:

Example 1. Employee D, who is employed by Employer Z, is entitled to commence receiving payments at age 65. The plan provides that Employee D will receive a single sum payment, except that, after Employee D attains age 62 but before Employee D attains age 64 (whether or not Employee D is then employed by Employer Z), Employee D can elect to receive payments as a single life annuity. Employee D is age 54 as of December 31, 2010. For purposes of determining the available times and forms of payment, Employee D is assumed to survive to age 62 and be eligible to elect a single life annuity. Accordingly, for purposes of determining the total amount deferred for 2010, the amount is treated as payable as either a single sum payment or a single life annuity, whichever is more valuable.

Example 2. Employee E is entitled to a single life annuity commencing on January 1, 2020 if Employee E is not married as of January 1, 2020. Employee E is entitled to either a single life annuity or a subsidized joint and survivor annuity commencing on January 1, 2020 if Employee E is married as of January 1, 2020. Employee E is not married as of December 31, 2010. For purposes of determining the total amount deferred for 2010, Employee E is assumed to remain unmarried indefinitely, so that the subsidized joint and survivor annuity is not an available form of payment. Accordingly, for purposes of determining the total amount deferred for 2010, the amount is treated as payable as a single life annuity commencing January 1, 2020.

Example 3. Employee F is entitled to a series of three payments of $1,000 due on January 1, 2020, January 1, 2021, and January 1, 2022. Under the plan's terms, Employer X has the discretion to accelerate one or more of the payments, provided that no payment may be made before January 1, 2020. Because there is no reduction in the amount payable if a payment is accelerated, an accelerated payment is more valuable than a payment made in accordance with the three-year schedule of payments. If Employee F does not have a legally binding right to a single sum payment on January 1, 2020 (or any other form of accelerated payment), then an accelerated payment is not an available time and form of payment and, for purposes of determining the total amount deferred for 2010, the amount is treated as payable as a series of three payments of $1,000 on January 1, 2020, January 1, 2021, and January 1, 2022.

Example 4. The facts are the same as in *Example 3*, except that Employer X has no discretion to accelerate one or more of the payments. Rather, Employee F has the right to accelerate one or more of the payments provided that a payment may not be paid at any date before the later of January 1, 2020 or the date 12 months after the date of such election. As of December 31, 2010, the earliest date upon which Employee F may elect to have a payment made is January 1, 2020. Because there is no reduction in the amount payable if a payment is accelerated, the earliest possible date of payment is the most valuable time and form of payment. Accordingly, for purposes of determining the total amount deferred for 2010, the amount is treated as payable as a single sum payment of $3,000 on January 1, 2020.

Example 5. Employee G is entitled to a single sum payment upon separation from service if Employee G separates from service before January 1, 2020 and a single life annuity if Employee G separates from service after December 31, 2019. As of December 31, 2010, Employee G has not separated from service. Under paragraph (b)(2)(vi)(A) of this section, the total amount deferred is determined based upon the amount that would be payable if Employee G separated from service on December 31, 2010. Accordingly, the single life annuity is not treated as an available time and form of payment, so that the amount is treated as payable as a single sum payment upon separation from service.

Example 6. Employee H is entitled to a single sum payment of deferred compensation upon the earlier of January 1, 2020 or an unforeseeable emergency. Because the payment upon an unforeseeable emergency is disregarded, for purposes of determining the total amount deferred, the deferred amount is treated as payable only on January 1, 2020.

Example 7. Employee I is entitled to a single sum payment of deferred compensation upon the earlier of January 1, 2020 or Employee I's involuntary separation from service. Under the facts and circumstances existing at the time the right to the payment was granted, if the deferred amount had been payable only upon Employee I's involuntary separation from service, the amount would have been subject to a substantial risk of forfeiture. Under paragraph (b)(2)(iv)(B) of this section, the right to a payment upon the Employee I's involuntary separation from service is disregarded, and the amount is treated as payable only on January 1, 2020.

Example 8. Employee J is entitled to a single sum payment of deferred compensation upon the earlier of January 1, 2020 or Employee J's separation from service. As of December 31, 2010, Employee J has not separated from service. Under paragraph (b)(2)(vi)(A) of this section, the total amount deferred is determined based upon the amount that would be payable if Employee J separated from service on December 31, 2010 and therefore had the right to receive the payment on December 31, 2010. The total amount deferred for 2010 is the greater of the amount that would be payable on December 31, 2010 or the present value of the amount that would be payable on January 1, 2020.

Example 9. Employee K is entitled to a single sum payment of deferred compensation upon the earlier of January 1, 2020 or the first day of the third month following Employee K's separation from service. As of December 31, 2010, Employee K has not separated from service. Under paragraph (b)(2)(vi)(A) of this section, the total amount deferred is determined based upon the amount that would be payable if Employee K separated from service on December 31, 2010, and therefore had a right to a payment on March 1, 2011. The total amount deferred for 2010 is the greater of the present value as of December 31, 2010 of the amount that would be payable on March 1, 2011 or the present value as of December 31, 2010 of the amount that would be payable on January 1, 2020.

Example 10. Employee L is entitled to a single sum payment of deferred compensation upon the earlier of January 1, 2020 or a separation from service that occurs on or before July 1, 2010. As of December 31, 2010, Employee L has not separated from service. For purposes of determining the total amount deferred, the right to be paid upon a separation from service on or before July 1, 2010 is ignored because it is no longer a possible payment trigger, and the amount is treated as payable only on January 1, 2020.

Example 11. Employee M is entitled to a single sum payment of deferred compensation upon the earliest of the date Employee M dies, Employee M attains age 65, or a child of Employee M becomes a full-time student at an accredited college or university (whether or not Employee M continues to be employed on such date). As of December 31, 2010, Employee M has a 10-year old child who is in the fifth grade. For purposes of determining the total amount deferred, the earliest time that the payment reasonably could be due upon Employee M's child entering a college or university is August 1, 2018. Thus, the total amount deferred for 2010 is the more valuable of the amount that would be payable on the Employee M's 65th birthday and the amount that would be payable on August 1, 2018. Because any additional value that would be payable upon Employee M's death is a death benefit excluded from the definition of deferred compensation under section 409A(d)(1)(B) and § 1.409A-1(a)(5), that additional value, if any, is not required to be calculated.

(3) *Account balance plans.*—(i) *In general.*—For purposes of this section, if benefits are provided under a nonqualified deferred compensation plan that is described in § 1.409A-1(c)(2)(i)(A) or (B) (an account balance plan), the present value of the amount payable equals the amount credited to the service provider's account as of the last day of the taxable year, including both the principal amount

credited to the account, and any earnings or losses attributable to the principal amounts credited to the account through the last day of the taxable year. For purposes of this section, earnings or losses means any increase or decrease in the amount credited to a service provider's account that is attributable to amounts previously credited to the service provider's account, regardless of whether the plan denominates that increase or decrease as earnings or losses. For rules related to the crediting of earnings, see paragraph (b)(2)(iii) of this section. For rules relating to earnings based on an unreasonable interest rate or a rate of return based on an investment other than a single predetermined actual investment or a single reasonable interest rate, see paragraph (b)(3)(ii) of this section.

(ii) *Unreasonable rate of return.*—(A) *Application.*—This paragraph (b)(3)(ii) applies to an account balance plan under which the amount of earnings or losses credited is not based on either a predetermined actual investment, within the meaning of § 31.3121(v)(2)-1(d)(2)(i)(B) of this chapter, or a rate of interest that is not higher than a reasonable rate of interest, within the meaning of § 31.3121(v)(2)-1(d)(2)(i)(C) of this chapter, as determined by the Commissioner.

(B) *Unreasonably high interest rate.*—If the earnings or losses to be credited under a plan are based on an unreasonably high rate of interest, the amount deferred under the plan is equal to the present value as of the end of the taxable year (using a reasonable interest rate) of the amount that will be credited to the service recipient's account using the unreasonably high rate for the entire period for which the unreasonably high interest will be credited under the plan, beginning with the last day of such taxable year and ending with the date the unreasonably high interest will no longer be credited (determined in accordance with the payment timing assumptions set forth in paragraph (b)(2)(vi) and (vii) of this section). If the service recipient fails to use a reasonable interest rate to determine the amount includible in income, AFR will be used. For purposes of this section, *AFR* means the appropriate applicable Federal rate (as defined pursuant to section 1274(d)) based on annual compounding, for the last month of the taxable year for which the amount includible in income is being determined. The period described in the first sentence of this paragraph (b)(3)(ii)(B) is used to determine the appropriate AFR (short-term, mid-term, or long-term). For purposes of this paragraph (b)(3)(ii)(B), an unreasonably high interest rate includes a fixed interest rate that exceeds an interest rate that is reasonable, within the meaning of § 31.3121(v)(2)-1(d)(2)(i)(C) of this chapter.

(C) *Other rates of return.*—If the amount of earnings or losses credited is based on a rate of return that is not an unreasonably high interest rate, within the meaning of paragraph (b)(3)(ii)(B) of this section, but is also not a predetermined actual investment, within the meaning of § 31.3121(v)(2)-1(d)(2)(i)(B) of this chapter or a rate of interest that is no more than a reasonable rate of interest, within the meaning of § 31.3121(v)(2)-1(d)(2)(i)(C) of this chapter, the amount payable is a formula amount.

(4) *Reimbursement and in-kind benefit arrangements.*—For purposes of this section, if benefits for a service provider are provided under a nonqualified deferred compensation plan described in § 1.409A-1(c)(2)(i)(E) (a reimbursement arrangement), or under a nonqualified deferred compensation plan that would be described in § 1.409A-1(c)(2)(i)(E) except that the amounts, separately or in the aggregate, constitute a substantial portion of either the overall compensation earned by the service provider for performing services for the service recipient or the overall compensation received due to a separation from service, the arrangement is treated as providing for a formula amount to the extent that the expenses to be reimbursed are not explicitly identified to be a specific amount. Notwithstanding the foregoing, if the expenses eligible for reimbursement are limited, it is presumed that the limit reflects the reasonable amount of eligible expenses that the service provider will incur at the earliest possible date during the time period to which the limit applies, and for which the service provider will request reimbursement at the earliest possible date that the service provider may request reimbursement. This presumption may be rebutted only by demonstrating by clear and convincing evidence that it is unreasonable to assume that a service provider would incur such amount of expenses during the applicable time period. This presumption is not applicable to any reimbursement arrangement to which § 1.409A-3(i)(1)(iv)(B) applies (certain medical reimbursement arrangements). In addition, this paragraph (b)(4) also applies to an arrangement providing a service provider a right to in-kind benefits from the service recipient, or a payment by the service recipient directly to the person providing the goods or services to the service provider.

(5) *Split-dollar life insurance arrangements.*—For purposes of this section, if benefits for a service provider are provided under a nonqualified deferred compensation plan described in § 1.409A-1(c)(2)(i)(F) (a split-dollar life insurance arrangement), the

amount of the future payment to which the service provider is entitled is treated as the amount that would be includible in income under §1.61-22 or §1.7872-15 (as applicable) or, if those regulations are not applicable, the amount that would be includible in income under any other applicable guidance. For this purpose, the payment timing assumptions set forth in paragraph (b)(2)(vi) and (vii) of this section generally apply. However, in the case of an arrangement subject to §1.7872-15, to the extent the assumptions set forth in paragraph (b)(2)(vi) and (vii) of this section conflict with the provisions of §1.7872-15, the provisions of §1.7872-15 apply, and the conflicting assumptions set forth in paragraph (b)(2)(vi) and (vii) of this section do not apply. In either case, for purposes of determining the total amount deferred under the plan for the taxable year, the benefits under the split-dollar life insurance arrangement are included only to the extent that the right to such benefits constitutes a right to deferred compensation under §1.409A-1(b).

(6) *Stock rights.*—If a stock right has not been exercised during the service recipient's taxable year, and remains outstanding as of the last day of the service provider's taxable year for which the total amount deferred is being calculated, the total amount deferred under the stock right for such taxable year is the excess of the fair market value of the underlying stock on the last day of the service provider's taxable year (determined in accordance with §1.409A-1(b)(5)(iv)) over the sum of the stock right's exercise price plus any amount paid for the stock right. If a stock right has been exercised during the service provider's taxable year, the payment amount for purposes of calculating the total amount deferred for the taxable year under the stock right is the excess of the fair market value of the underlying stock (as determined in accordance with §1.409A-1(b)(5)(iv)) on the date of exercise over the sum of the exercise price of the stock right and any amount paid for the stock right.

(7) *Anti-abuse provision.*—The Commissioner may disregard all or part of the rules of paragraphs (b)(2) through (b)(6) of this section or all or part of the plan's terms if the Commissioner determines based on all of the facts and circumstances that the plan terms have been established to eliminate or minimize the total amount deferred under the plan determined in accordance with the rules of paragraphs (b)(2) through (b)(6) of this section and if the rules of paragraphs (b)(2) through (b)(6) of this section were applied or such plan terms were given effect, the total amount deferred would not reasonably reflect the present value of the right. For example, if a plan provides that a deferred amount is payable upon a separation from service but also contains a provision that the amount will be forfeited upon a separation from service occurring on the last day of the service provider's taxable year (so that the application of paragraph (b)(2)(vii)(A) of this section treating the service provider as separating from service on the last day of the taxable year for purposes of determining the timing of the payment in calculating the total amount deferred would result in a zero amount deferred), the latter provision will be disregarded.

(c) *Additional 20 percent tax under section 409A(a)(1)(B)(i)(II).*—With respect to an amount required to be included in income under section 409A(a) for a taxable year, the amount is subject to an additional income tax equal to 20 percent of the amount required to be included in income under section 409A(a).

(d) *Premium interest tax under section 409A(a)(1)(B)(i)(I).*—(1) *In general.*—With respect to an amount required to be included in income under section 409A(a) for a taxable year, the amount is subject to an additional income tax equal to the amount of interest at the underpayment rate plus one percentage point on the underpayments that would have occurred had the deferred compensation been includible in the service provider's gross income for the taxable year in which first deferred or, if later, the first taxable year in which such deferred compensation is not subject to a substantial risk of forfeiture. The amount required to be allocated to determine the additional tax described in this paragraph (d) is the amount required to be included in income under section 409A(a) for the taxable year, regardless of whether additional amounts were deferred under the plan in previous years.

(2) *Identification of taxable year deferred amount was first deferred or vested.*—(i) *Method of identification.*—The following method is applied for purposes of determining the taxable year or years in which

an amount required to be included in income under section 409A(a) was first deferred and not subject to a substantial risk of forfeiture.

(A) For each taxable year preceding the taxable year for which the deferred amount is includible in income (the current taxable year) in which the service provider had an amount deferred under the plan that was not subject to a substantial risk of forfeiture (vested), ending with the later of the first taxable year in which the service provider had no vested amount deferred or the first taxable year beginning after December 31, 2004, calculate the vested total amount deferred for such year. For each year, include any deferred amount that was previously included in income under paragraph (a)(3) of this section but has not been paid, but exclude any amount paid to (or on behalf of) the service provider during such taxable year.

(B) Identify any payments made under the plan to (or on behalf of) the service provider for each taxable year identified in paragraph (d)(2)(i)(A) of this section.

(C) Identify any deemed net investment losses or other net decreases in the amount deferred (other than as a result of a payment) applicable to amounts that are vested for the current taxable year and each preceding taxable year identified in paragraph (d)(2)(i)(A) of this section.

(D) Starting with the first taxable year during which there was a payment identified under paragraph (d)(2)(i)(B) of this section or a loss identified under paragraph (d)(2)(i)(C) of this section (or both), subtract the total payments and loss for such taxable year from the amount determined under paragraph (d)(2)(i)(A) of this section for the earliest taxable year before such year in which there is such an amount, and from the amount determined under paragraph (d)(2)(i)(A) of this section for each subsequent taxable year ending before the taxable year in which the payment was made or the loss incurred. Do not reduce any taxable year-end balance below zero.

(E) Repeat this process for each subsequent taxable year during which there was a payment identified under paragraph (d)(2)(i)(B) of this section or a loss identified under paragraph (d)(2)(i)(C) of this section (or both).

(F) For each taxable year identified in paragraph (d)(2)(i)(A) of this section, determine the excess (if any) of the remaining amount deferred for the taxable year over the remaining amount deferred for the previous taxable year. Treat the amount deferred in taxable years beginning before January 1, 2005 as zero.

(G) Determine how much of the total amount deferred for the current taxable year was previously included in income in accordance with paragraph (a)(3) of this section.

(H) Subtract the amount determined in paragraph (d)(2)(i)(G) of this section from the excess amount determined in paragraph (d)(2)(i)(F) of this section for the earliest taxable year in which there is any such excess amount, but do not reduce the balance below zero. If the amount determined in paragraph (d)(2)(i)(G) of this section exceeds the amount determined in paragraph (d)(2)(i)(F) of this section for that earliest taxable year, subtract the excess from the amount determined in paragraph (d)(2)(i)(F) of this section for the next succeeding taxable year, but do not reduce the balance below zero. Repeat this process until the excess has been reduced to zero. The balance remaining with respect to each taxable year identified in paragraph (d)(2)(i)(A) of this section is the portion of the amount includible in income under section 409A(a) in the current taxable year that was first deferred and vested in that taxable year.

(ii) *Examples.*—The following examples illustrate the provisions of paragraph (d)(2) of this section. In all of the following examples, the service provider is an individual taxpayer with a calendar year taxable year who elects to defer a portion of the bonus that would otherwise be payable to the service provider in each of Year 1 through Year 4. All amounts deferred are deferred under the same plan, and no amount deferred under the plan is ever subject to a substantial risk of forfeiture. The plan does not fail to meet the requirements of section 409A(a) in any year prior to Year 4, and no amounts deferred under the plan are otherwise includible in income until Year 4, except for payments actually made to the service provider. The service provider had no amount deferred under the plan prior to Year 1. The plan fails to meet the requirements of section 409A(a) in Year 4. The examples read as follows:

Example 1.

	Year 1	Year 2	Year 3	Year 4
Opening Total Amount	0	110	275	495
Bonus Deferral	100	150	200	250
Net Gains (Losses)	10	15	20	25
Payments	0	0	0	0
Closing Total Amount	110	275	495	770

Reg. §1.409A-4(d)(2)(ii)

(i) The amount required to be included in income under section 409A is 770. To calculate the premium interest tax, the 770 must be allocated to the year or years in which the amount was first deferred and vested.

Year 1	Year 2	Year 3
110	275	495

(ii) *Step A.* Identification of vested total amount deferred excluding payments and including deferred amounts previously included in income.

(iii) *Step B.* Identification of any payments for each year other than Year 4.

Year 1	Year 2	Year 3
0	0	0

(iv) *Step C.* Identification of any other decreases attributable to vested amounts.

Year 1	Year 2	Year 3	Year 4
0	0	0	0

(v) *Steps D and E.* Subtraction of payments and decreases from amounts deferred.

Year 1	Year 2	Year 3
110	275	495
-0	-0	-0
110	275	495

(vi) *Step F.* Subtraction of previous year total from each year's total.

Year 1	Year 2	Year 3
110	275	495
-0	-110	-275
110	165	220

(viii) Because no amount was previously included in income, Step G does not apply. Accordingly, the 770 is allocated such that 110 is treated as first deferred and vested in Year 1, 165 in Year 2, 220 in Year 3. The remainder (275) is treated as first deferred in Year 4, but is not required to be allocated for purposes of the premium interest tax because there is no hypothetical underpayment for such year.

Example 2.

	Year 1	Year 2	Year 3	Year 4
Opening Total Amount	0	110	235	365
Bonus Deferral	100	150	200	250
Net Gains (Losses)	10	(25)	(30)	25
Payments	0	0	(40)	(50)
Closing Total Amount	110	235	365	590

(i) The amount that is includible in income under section 409A(a) for Year 4 is the closing total amount (590), plus the amounts paid during Year 4 that were includible in income (50) or 640. To calculate the premium interest tax, the 640 must be allocated to the year or years in which the amount was first deferred and vested.

Year 1	Year 2
110	235

(ii) *Step A.* Identification of vested total amount deferred excluding payments and including deferred amounts previously included in income.

Year 3
365

(iii) *Step B.* Identification of any payments for each year other than Year 4.

Year 1	Year 2
0	0

Year 3
(40)

(iv) *Step C.* Identification of any other decreases attributable to vested amounts.

Year 1	Year 2
0	(25)

Year 3	Year 4
(30)	0

(v) *Steps D and E.* Subtraction of payments and decreases from amounts deferred.

Year 1	Year 2	Year 3
110	235	365
-25(Year 2)	-40(Year 3)	
-40(Year 3)	-30(Year 3)	
-30(Year 3)		
15	165	365

(vi) *Step F.* Subtraction of previous year total from each year's total.

Year 1	Year 2	Year 3
15	165	365
-0	-15	-165
15	150	200

(vii) Because no amount was previously included in income, Step G does not apply. Accordingly, the 640 is allocated such that 15 is treated as first deferred and vested in Year 1, 150 in Year 2, and 200 in Year 3. The remaining amount includible in income under section 409A for Year 4 (275) is treated as first deferred in Year 4, but is not required to be allocated for purposes of the premium interest tax because there is no hypothetical underpayment for Year 4.

Example 3. (i) The facts are the same as in *Example 2* except 125 was previously included in income under paragraph (a)(3) of this section. Accordingly, of the 590 closing total amount for Year 4 plus the 50 payment during Year 4, or 640, only 515 (640 - 125) must be included in income under section 409A(a). To calculate the premium

Year 1	Year 2	Year 3
15	150	200
-15	-110	-0
0	40	200

(iii) Accordingly, for purposes of calculating the premium interest tax, the 125 previously included in income is allocated so that of the 515 includible in income under section 409A(a), 0 is treated as first deferred and vested in Year 1, 40 in Year 2, and 200 in Year 3.

(3) *Calculation of hypothetical underpayment for the taxable year during which a deferred amount was first deferred and vested.*— (i) *Calculation method.*—The hypothetical underpayment for a taxable year is determined by treating as an additional cash payment of compensation to the service provider for such taxable year, the amount determined pursuant to paragraph (d)(2) of this section to be the portion of the amount includible in income under section 409A(a) that was first deferred and vested during such taxable year. The hypothetical underpayment is calculated based on the service provider's taxable income, credits, filing status, and other tax information for the year, based on the service provider's original return filed for such year, as adjusted by any examination for such year or any amended return the service provider filed for such 82 year that was accepted by the Commissioner. The hypothetical underpayment must reflect the effect that such additional compensation would have had on the service provider's Federal income tax liability for such year, including the continued availability of any deductions taken, and the use of any carryovers such as carryover losses. For purposes of calculating a hypothetical underpayment in a subsequent year (whether or not a portion of the amount includible in income under section 409A(a) was first deferred and vested in the subsequent year), any changes to the service provider's Federal income tax liability for the subsequent year that would have occurred if the portion of the amount that was first deferred and vested during the previous taxable year had been included in the service provider's income for the previous year must be taken into account. Assumptions not based on the service provider's taxable income, credits, filing status, and other tax information for the year, based on the service provider's original return for such year, as adjusted by any examination for such year or any amended return the service provider filed for such year that was accepted by the Commissioner, may not be applied. For example, the service provider may not assume that some of the additional compensation would have been deferred under the terms of a qualified plan. If the service provider's Federal income tax liability for the taxable year in which an amount required to be included in income under section 409A(a) was first deferred and vested is adjusted (for example, by an amended return or IRS examination), and the adjustment affects the amount of the hypothetical underpayment, the service provider must recalculate the hypothetical underpayment and adjust the amount of premium interest tax due with respect to such inclusion in income under section 409A(a), as appropriate.

(ii) *Examples.*—The following examples illustrate the provisions of paragraph (d)(3)(i) of this section. In all of the following examples, Employee N is an individual taxpayer with a calendar year taxable year. For the year 2020, Employee N has a total amount deferred of $100,000 which is includible in income under section 409A(a). For purposes of determining the premium interest tax, assume that $30,000 was first deferred and vested in 2018, $35,000 was first deferred and vested in 2019, and $35,000 was first deferred and vested in 2020. The first year that Employee N had a vested deferred amount under the plan was 2018. The examples read as follows:

Example 1. For the taxable years 2018 and 2019, Employee N has no carryover losses or other items a change in which could affect the adjusted gross income for a subsequent taxable year. Employee N determines the hypothetical underpayment for 2018 by assuming an additional cash compensation payment of $30,000 for 2018, and determining the hypothetical underpayment of Federal income tax that would result. Employee N determines the hypothetical underpayment for 2019 by assuming an additional cash compensation payment of $35,000 in 2019, and determining the hypothetical underpayment of Federal income tax for 2019 that would result. There is no hypothetical underpayment with respect to hypothetical income in 2020 because the tax payment would not have been due until 2021. Therefore, Employee N is not required to determine a hypothetical underpayment for 2020.

Example 2. The facts are the same as in *Example 1*, except that in 2018, Employee N had an excess charitable contribution the deduction of which was not permitted under section 170(b), and which was carried over to subsequent taxable years under section 170(d).

interest tax, the 125 must be allocated to the year or years in which such amount was first deferred.

(ii) *Step G.* Allocation of amounts previously included in income.

For purposes of determining the hypothetical underpayment for 2018, Employee N uses the charitable contribution deduction that otherwise would have been available if the $30,000 compensation payment had actually been made. Employee N must then calculate the hypothetical underpayment for all subsequent years in a manner that eliminates the portion of any carryovers of excess contributions under section 170(d) related to the charitable contribution in 2018 that would not have been available in such subsequent years as a result of having been deducted in 2018.

Example 3. The facts are the same as in *Example 2*, except that in 2021 the IRS examines Employee N's 2018 return and determines that Employee N had $20,000 in unreported income for that year. In addition to paying the tax deficiency owed for 2018, Employee N must redetermine the hypothetical underpayment for 2018 and recalculate the premium interest tax owed for 2020.

(4) *Calculation of hypothetical premium underpayment interest.*— (i) *Calculation method.*—The amount of hypothetical premium underpayment interest is determined for any taxable year by applying the applicable rate of interest under section 6621 plus one percentage point to determine the underpayment interest under section 6601 that would be due for such underpayment as of the last day of the taxable year for which the amount deferred is includible in income under section 409A(a). The amount of additional income tax under paragraph (d)(2) of this section with respect to an amount required to be included in income under section 409A(a) is the sum of all of the hypothetical premium underpayment interest for all years in which there was determined a hypothetical underpayment.

(ii) *Examples.*—The following examples illustrate the provisions of this paragraph (d)(4). In each of these examples, the service provider is an individual taxpayer with a calendar year taxable year. At all times the total amount deferred under the nonqualified deferred compensation plan is not subject to a substantial risk of forfeiture. The examples read as follows:

Example 1. Employee O has a total amount deferred under a nonqualified deferred compensation plan for 2010 of $100,000. The entire deferred amount was first deferred in 2006. For purposes of calculating the hypothetical premium underpayment interest tax, Employee O first must determine the hypothetical underpayment for taxable years 2006 through 2009 under the rules of paragraph (d)(3) of this section. Then Employee O must determine the underpayment interest under section 6601 that would have accrued, calculated using the applicable underpayment interest rate under section 6621 increased by one percentage point, applied through December 31, 2010. That amount is the premium interest tax that is due for 2010.

Example 2. Employee P has a total amount deferred under a nonqualified deferred compensation plan for 2010 of $100,000. $60,000 of that deferred amount was first deferred in 2006. $30,000 of that amount was first deferred in 2008. $10,000 of that amount was first deferred in 2010. For purposes of calculating the hypothetical premium underpayment interest tax, Employee P first must determine the hypothetical underpayment for taxable years 2006 through 2009 under the rules of paragraph (d)(3) of this section applying $60,000 of hypothetical additional compensation for 2006, and applying $30,000 of hypothetical additional compensation for 2008. The $10,000 of hypothetical additional compensation in 2010 would not result in a hypothetical underpayment because the Federal income tax applicable to that hypothetical additional compensation would not yet be due. Second, Employee P must determine the underpayment interest under section 6601 that would have accrued, calculated using the applicable underpayment interest rate under section 6621 increased by one percentage point, applied through December 31, 2010, for both the hypothetical underpayment occurring in 2006 and the hypothetical underpayment occurring in 2008. The sum of those two amounts is the premium interest tax that is due for 2010.

(e) *Amounts includible in income under section 409A(b).*— [Reserved].

(f) *Application of amounts included in income under section 409A to payments of amounts deferred.*—(1) *In general.*—Section 409A(c) provides that any amount included in gross income under section 409A is not required to be included in gross income under any other provision of this chapter or any other rule of law later than the time provided in this section. An amount included in income under section 409A that has neither been paid in the taxable year the amount was included in income under section 409A nor served as the basis for a deduction under paragraph (g) of this section is allocated to the first payment of an amount deferred under the plan in any year subsequent to the year the amount was included in income under section 409A. To the extent the amount included in income under section 409A exceeds such payment, the excess is allocated to the next payment of an amount deferred under the plan. This process is repeated until the entire amount included in income under section 409A has been paid or the service provider has become entitled to a deduction under paragraph (g) of this section.

(2) *Application of the plan aggregation rules.*—The plan aggregation rules of § 1.409A-1(c)(2) apply to the allocation of amounts previously included in income under section 409A to payments made under the plan. Accordingly, references to an amount deferred under a plan, or a payment of an amount deferred under a plan, refer to an amount deferred or a payment made under all arrangements in which a service provider participates that together are treated as a single plan under § 1.409A-1(c)(2).

(3) *Examples.*—The following examples illustrate the provisions of this section. In each of these examples, the service provider is an individual taxpayer with a calendar year taxable year. Each service provider has a total amount deferred under a nonqualified deferred compensation plan of $0 for 2010, a total amount deferred under the plan of $100,000 for 2011, a total amount deferred under the plan of $250,000 for 2012, and a total amount deferred under the plan of $400,000 for 2013. At all times the total amount deferred under the plan is not subject to a substantial risk of forfeiture. During 2011, the plan fails to comply with section 409A(a) and each service provider includes $100,000 in income under section 409A. Except as otherwise provided in the following examples, the service provider does not receive any payments of amounts deferred under the plan. The examples read as follows:

Example 1. During 2012, Employee Q receives a $10,000 payment under the plan. During 2013, Employee Q receives a $150,000 payment under the plan. For 2012, $10,000 of the $100,000 included in income under section 409A(a) is allocated under paragraph (f)(1) of this section to the $10,000 payment, so that no amount is includible in gross income as a result of such payment and Employee Q retains $90,000 of amounts previously included in income under the plan to allocate to future plan payments. For 2013, the remaining $90,000 included in income under section 409A(a) is allocated to the $150,000 payment, so that only $60,000 is includible in income as a result of such payment.

Example 2. During 2012, Employee R receives a $10,000 payment under the plan. During 2014, Employee R receives a $50,000 payment, equaling the entire amount deferred under the plan. For 2012, $10,000 of the $100,000 previously included in income is allocated pursuant to paragraph (f)(1) of this section to the $10,000 payment, so that no amount is includible in gross income as a result of such payment. For 2014, $50,000 of the $90,000 remaining amount previously included in income is allocated pursuant to paragraph (f)(1) of this section to the $50,000 payment, so that no amount is includible in gross income as a result of such payment. Provided that the requirements of paragraph (g) of this section are otherwise met, Employee R is entitled to a deduction for 2014 equal to the remaining amount ($40,000) that was previously included in income under section 409A(a) that has not been allocated to a payment under the plan.

(g) *Forfeiture or other permanent loss of right to deferred compensation.*—(1) *Availability of deduction to the service provider.*—If a service provider has included a deferred amount in income under section 409A, but has not actually received payment of such deferred amount or otherwise allocated the amount included in income under paragraph (f) of this section, the service provider is entitled to a deduction for the taxable year in which the right to that amount of deferred compensation is permanently forfeited under the plan's terms or the right to the payment of the amount is otherwise permanently lost. The deduction to which the service provider is entitled equals the deferred amount included in income under section 409A in a previous year, less any portion of such deferred amount previously included in income under section 409A that was allocated under paragraph (f) of this section to amounts paid under the plan, including any deferred amount paid in the year the right to any remaining deferred compensation is permanently forfeited or otherwise lost. For this purpose, a mere diminution in the deferred amount under the plan due to deemed investment loss, actuarial

reduction, or other decrease in the amount deferred is not treated as a permanent forfeiture or loss of the right if the service provider retains the right to an amount deferred under the plan (whether or not such right is subject to a substantial risk of forfeiture as defined in § 1.409A-1(d)). In addition, a deferred amount is not treated as permanently forfeited or otherwise lost if the obligation to make the payment of such deferred amount is substituted for another deferred amount or obligation to make a payment in a future year. However, a deferred amount is treated as permanently lost if the service provider's right to receive the payment of the deferred amount becomes wholly worthless during the taxable year. Whether the right to the payment of a deferred amount has become wholly worthless is determined based on all the facts and circumstances existing as of the last day of the relevant service provider taxable year.

(2) *Application of the plan aggregation rules.*—For purposes of determining whether the right to a deferred amount is permanently forfeited or otherwise lost, the plan aggregation rules of § 1.409A-1(c) apply. Accordingly, if the right to an identified deferred amount under a plan is permanently forfeited or otherwise lost, but an additional amount remains deferred under the plan, the service provider is not entitled to a deduction.

(3) *Examples.*—The following examples illustrate the provisions of this paragraph (g). In each example, the service provider is an individual taxpayer who has a calendar year taxable year and the service recipient does not experience bankruptcy at any time or otherwise discharge any obligation to make a payment of a deferred amount, except as expressly provided in the example. The examples read as follows:

Example 1. For 2010, Employee S has a total amount deferred under an elective account balance plan of $1,000,000. The plan fails to meet the requirements of section 409A(a) during 2010 and Employee S includes $1,000,000 in income under section 409A(a) for the year 2010. In 2011, Employee S experiences investment losses but no payments before July 1, 2011, such that Employee S's account balance under the plan is $500,000. On July 1, 2011, Employee S separates from service and receives a $500,000 payment equal to the entire amount deferred under the plan, and retains no other right to deferred compensation under the plan (including all arrangements aggregated with the arrangement under which the payment was made). For 2011, Employee S is entitled to deduct $500,000 (which is the amount Employee S previously included in income under section 409A(a) ($1,000,000) less the amount actually received by Employee S ($500,000)).

Example 2. For 2010, Employee T has a total amount deferred under an elective account balance plan of $1,000,000. The plan fails to meet the requirements of section 409A(a) for 2010 and Employee T includes $1,000,000 in income under section 409A(a) for 2010. For 2011, Employee T has a total amount deferred under the plan of $500,000, due solely to the deemed investment losses attributable to Employee T's account balance (with no payments being made during 2011). Because Employee T retains the right to an amount deferred under the plan, Employee T is not entitled to a deduction for 2011 as a result of the deemed investment losses.

Example 3. For 2010, Employee U has a total amount deferred under an elective account balance plan of $1,000,000. The elective account balance plan consists of one arrangement providing for salary deferrals with an amount deferred for 2010 of $600,000, and another arrangement providing for bonus deferrals with an amount deferred for 2010 of $400,000. The plan fails to meet the requirements of section 409A(a) during 2010 and Employee U includes $1,000,000 in income under section 409A(a) for 2010. On July 1, 2011, Employee U's account balance attributable to the salary deferral arrangement is $500,000, the reduction of which is due solely to deemed investment losses in 2011 and not any payments. On July 1, 2011, Employee U is paid the $500,000 equaling the entire account balance attributable to the salary deferral arrangement. On December 31, 2011, Employee U has an account balance attributable to the bonus deferral arrangement equal to $300,000. Because Employee U retains an amount deferred under the elective account balance plan, Employee U is not entitled to a deduction for 2011 as a result of the deemed investment losses.

(h) *Effective/applicability date.*—The rules of this section apply to taxable years ending on or after the date of publication of the Treasury decision adopting these rules as final regulation in the **Federal Register**. [Reg. § 1.409A-4.]

Nonqualified Deferred Compensation Plans: Section 409A

Nonqualified Deferred Compensation Plans: Section 409A.—Amendments to Reg. §§ 1.409A-0—1.409A-4 and 1.409A-6, affecting participants, beneficiaries, sponsors, and administrators of nonqualified deferred compensation plans, are proposed (published in the Federal Register on June 22, 2016) (corrected August 4, 2016) (REG-123854-12).

Par. 2. Section 1.409A-0 is amended by:

1. Revising the entry for § 1.409A-1 by adding paragraph (b)(13).

2. Redesignating paragraph (q) as paragraph (r), and revising paragraph (q) in §1.409A-1.
3. Revising the entry to paragraph (d) in §1.409A-3.
4. Revising the entry to u)(4)(xiii) in §1.409A-3.
The revisions and addition read as follows:

§1.409A-0. Table of contents.
* * *

§1.409A-1 Definitions and covered plans.
* * *

(b) * * *
    (13) Recurring part-year compensation.
* * *

(q) References to a payment being made.
(r) Application of definitions and rules.
* * *

§1.409A-3 Permissible Payments.

Par. 3. Section 1.409A-1 is amended by:
1. Revising paragraph (a)(4).
2. Revising the first sentence of paragraph (b)(1).
3. Revising paragraphs (b)(3) and (b)(4)(i)(B).
4. Revising paragraph (b)(4)(ii).
5. Adding a last sentence to paragraph (b)(5)(iii)(A).
6. Revising paragraph (b)(5)(iii)(E)(*1*).
7. Revising the first sentence of paragraph (b)(5)(vi)(A).
8. Revising paragraphs (b)(5)(vi)(E) and (b)(5)(vi)(F).
9. Revising paragraph (b)(9)(iii)(A).
10. Adding a last sentence to paragraph (b)(11).
11. Adding paragraph (b)(13).
12. Revising paragraphs (h)(4) and (h)(5).
13. Redesignating paragraph (q) as paragraph (r) and revising paragraphs (q) and (r).
The revisions and additions read as follows:

§1.409A-1. Definitions and covered plans.
* * *

(a) * * *

(4) *Section 457(f) and section 457A plans.*—A deferred compensation plan under section 457(f) or a nonqualified deferred compensation plan under section 457A may be a nonqualified deferred compensation plan for purposes of this paragraph (a). The rules of section 409A apply to nonqualified deferred compensation plans separately and in addition to any requirements applicable to such plans under section 457(f) or section 457A. In addition, nonelective deferred compensation of non-employees described in section 457(e)(12) and a grandfathered plan or arrangement described in §1.457-2(k)(4) may be a nonqualified deferred compensation plan for purposes of this paragraph (a). The term *nonqualified deferred compensation plan* does not include a length of service award to a *bona fide* volunteer under section 457(e)(11)(A)(ii).
* * *

(b) * * *

(1) * * * Except as otherwise provided in paragraphs (b)(3) through (b)(13) of this section, a plan provides for the deferral of compensation if, under the terms of the plan and the relevant facts and circumstances, the service provider has a legally binding right during a taxable year to compensation that, pursuant to the terms of the plan, is or may be payable to (or on behalf of) the service provider in a later taxable year. * * *
* * *

(3) *Compensation payable pursuant to the service recipient's customary payment timing arrangement.*—A deferral of compensation does not occur solely because compensation is paid after the last day of the service provider's taxable year pursuant to the timing arrangement under which the service recipient normally compensates service providers for services performed during a payroll period described in section 3401(b), or with respect to a non-employee service provider, a period not longer than the payroll period described in section 3401(b) or if no such payroll period exists, a period not longer than the earlier of the normal timing arrangement under which the service recipient normally compensates non-employee service providers or 30 days after the end of the service provider's taxable year.

(4) * * *
(i) * * *

(B) A payment is treated as actually or constructively received for purposes of this paragraph (b)(4) if it is made in accordance with the rules in §1.409A-1(q).
* * *

(ii) *Certain delayed payments.*—A payment that otherwise qualifies as a short-term deferral under paragraph (b)(4)(i) of this section but is made after the applicable 2½ month period may continue to qualify as a short-term deferral if a taxpayer establishes that it was administratively impracticable for the service recipient to make the payment by the end of the applicable 2½ month period and, as of the date upon which the legally binding right to the compensation arose, such impracticability was unforeseeable, or the taxpayer establishes that making the payment by the end of the applicable 2½ month period would have jeopardized the ability of the service recipient to continue as a going concern, and provided further that the payment is made as soon as administratively practicable or as soon as the payment would no longer have such effect. For purposes of this paragraph (b)(4)(ii), an action or failure to act of the service provider or a person under the service provider's control, such as a failure to provide necessary information or documentation, is not an unforeseeable event. In addition, a payment that otherwise qualifies as a short-term deferral under paragraph (b)(4)(i) of this section but is made after the applicable 2½ month period may continue to qualify as a short-term deferral if the taxpayer establishes that the service recipient reasonably anticipated that the service recipient's deduction with respect to such payment otherwise would not be permitted by application of section 162(m), and, as of the date the legally binding right to the payment arose, a reasonable person would not have anticipated the application of section 162(m) at the time of the payment, and provided further that the payment is made as soon as reasonably practicable following the first date on which the service recipient anticipates or reasonably should anticipate that, if the payment were made on such date, the service recipient's deduction with respect to such payment would no longer be restricted due to the application of section 162(m). Further, a payment that otherwise qualifies as a short-term deferral under paragraph (b)(4)(i) of this section but is made after the applicable 2½ month period may continue to qualify as a short-term deferral if the taxpayer establishes that the service recipient reasonably anticipated that making the payment by the end of the applicable 2½ month period would have violated Federal securities laws or other applicable law, provided that the payment is made as soon as reasonably practicable following the first date on which the service recipient anticipates or reasonably should anticipate that making the payment would not cause such violation. The making of a payment that would cause inclusion in gross income or the application of any penalty provision or other provision of the Internal Revenue Code is not treated as a violation of applicable law. For additional rules applicable to certain transaction-based compensation, see §1.409A–3(i)(5)(iv)(A).

* * *

(5) * * *
(iii) * * *

(A) * * * The stock price will not be treated as based on a measure other than the fair market value to the extent that the amount payable upon the service provider's involuntary separation

* * *

(d) ***
(1) In general.
(2) Payments due following death.
* * *

(j) * * *
(4) * * *
    (xiii) Certain offsets.
      (A) De minimis offset.
      (B) Compliance with Federal debt collection laws.
* * *

from service for cause, or the occurrence of a condition within the service provider's control such as noncompliance with a noncompetition or nondisclosure agreement (whether or not the condition is specified at the time the stock right is granted), is based on a measure that results in a payment of less than fair market value.

* * *

(E) *Eligible issuer of service recipient stock.—(1) In general.—* The term *eligible issuer of service recipient stock* means the corporation or other entity for which the service provider provides direct services on the date of grant of the stock right or a corporation or other entity for which it is reasonably anticipated that the service provider will begin providing direct services within 12 months after the date of grant, and any corporation or other entity (a related corporation or other entity) in a chain of corporations or other entities in which each corporation or other entity has a controlling interest in another corporation or other entity in the chain, ending with the corporation or other entity that has a controlling interest in the corporation or other entity for which the service provider provides direct services on the date of grant of the stock right or the corporation or other entity for which it is reasonably anticipated that the service provider will begin providing direct services within 12 months after the date of grant. If it is reasonably anticipated that a service provider will begin providing services for a corporation or other entity within 12 months after the date of grant, that corporation or other entity (or a related corporation or other entity) will be an eligible issuer of service recipient stock only if the services in fact commence within 12 months after the date of grant and the stock otherwise is service recipient stock at the time the services begin or, if services do not commence within that 12 month period, the right is forfeited. For this purpose, the term *controlling interest* has the same meaning as provided in § 1.414(c)-2(b)(2)(i), substituting the language "at least 50 percent" for "at least 80 percent" each place it appears in § 1.414(c)-2(b)(2)(i). In addition, if the use of such stock with respect to the grant of a stock right to a service provider is based upon legitimate business criteria, the term *controlling interest* has the same meaning as provided in § 1.414(c)-2(b)(2)(i), substituting the language "at least 20 percent" for "at least 80 percent" each place it appears in § 1.414(c)-2(b)(2)(i). For purposes of determining ownership of an interest in an organization, the rules of § § 1.414(c)-3 and 1.414(c)-4 apply. The determination of whether a grant is based on legitimate business criteria is based on the facts and circumstances, focusing primarily on whether there is a sufficient nexus between the service provider and the issuer of the stock right so that the grant serves a legitimate non-tax business purpose other than simply providing compensation to the service provider that is excluded from the requirements of section 409A. For example, when stock of a corporation that owns an interest in a joint venture involving an operating business is granted to service providers of the joint venture who are former service providers of such corporation, that use is generally based upon legitimate business criteria, and therefore could be service recipient stock with respect to such service providers if the corporation owns at least 20 percent of the joint venture and the other requirements of this paragraph (b)(5)(iii) are met. Similarly, the legitimate business criteria requirement generally would be met if the corporate venturer issued such a right to a service provider of the joint venture who it reasonably expected would become a service provider of the corporate venturer. However, if a service provider has no real nexus with a corporate venturer, such as generally happens when the corporate venturer is a passive investor in the service recipient joint venture, a stock right issued to the service provider on the investor corporation's stock generally would not be based upon legitimate business criteria. Similarly, if a corporation holds only a minority interest in an entity that in turn holds a minority interest in the entity for which the service provider performs services, such that the corporation holds only an insubstantial indirect interest in the entity receiving the services, legitimate business criteria generally would not exist for issuing a stock right on the corporation's stock to the service provider.

* * *

(vi) * * *

(A) * * * The term *option* means the right or privilege of a person to purchase stock from a corporation by virtue of an offer of the corporation continuing for a stated period of time, whether or not irrevocable, to sell such stock at a price determined under paragraph (b)(5)(vi)(D) of this section, such person being under no obligation to purchase.

* * *

(E) *Exercise.—*The term *exercise,* when used in reference to an option, means the act of acceptance by the holder of the option of the offer to sell contained in the option. In general, the time of exercise is the time when there is a sale or a contract to sell between the corporation and the holder. A promise to pay the exercise price is not an exercise of the option unless the holder of the option is subject to personal liability on such promise. An agreement or undertaking

by the service provider to make payments under a stock purchase plan is not the exercise of an option to the extent the payments made remain subject to the withdrawal by or refund to the service provider.

(F) *Transfer.—*The term *transfer,* when used in reference to the transfer to a person of a share of stock pursuant to the exercise of an option, means the transfer of ownership of such share, or the transfer of substantially all the rights of ownership. Such transfer must, within a reasonable time, be evidenced on the books of the corporation. A transfer may occur even if a share of stock is subject to a substantial risk of forfeiture or is not otherwise transferable immediately after the date of exercise. A transfer does not fail to occur merely because, under the terms of the arrangement, the person may not dispose of the share for a specified period of time, or the share is subject to a right of first refusal or a right to acquire the share at the share's fair market value at the time of the sale.

* * *

(9) * * *

(iii) * * *

(A) The separation pay (other than amounts described in paragraphs (b)(9)(iv) and (v) of this section) does not exceed two times the lesser of —

(1) The service provider's annualized compensation based upon the annual rate of pay for services provided to the service recipient for the service provider's taxable year preceding the taxable year in which the service provider has a separation from service with such service recipient (or for the taxable year in which the service provider has a separation from service if the service provider had no compensation from the service recipient in the preceding taxable year), adjusted for any increase during that year that was expected to continue indefinitely if the service provider had not separated from service; or

(2) The maximum amount that may be taken into account under a qualified retirement plan pursuant to section 401(a)(17) for the calendar year in which the service provider has a separation from service.

* * *

(11) * * * In addition, a plan does not provide for a deferral of compensation for purposes of this paragraph (b) to the extent it provides for a payment of reasonable attorneys' fees or other reasonable expenses incurred by the service provider to enforce any *bona fide* legal claim against the service recipient with respect to the service relationship between the service provider and the service recipient.

* * *

(13) *Recurring part-year compensation.—*A plan in which a service provider participates that provides for the payment of recurring part-year compensation (as defined in § 1.409A-2(a)(14)), whether or not at the service provider's election, does not provide for a deferral of compensation for purposes of this paragraph (b) if the plan does not defer payment of any of the recurring part-year compensation to a date beyond the last day of the 13th month following the first day of the service period for which the recurring part-year compensation is paid, and the amount of the service provider's recurring part-year compensation does not exceed the annual compensation limit under section 401(a)(17) for the calendar year in which the service period commences.

* * *

(h) * * *

(4) *Asset purchase transactions.—*If as part of a sale or other disposition of assets by one service recipient (seller) to an unrelated service recipient (buyer), a service provider of the seller would otherwise experience a separation from service with the seller, the seller and the buyer may retain the discretion to specify, and may specify, whether a service provider providing services to the seller immediately before the asset purchase transaction and providing services to the buyer after and as a result of the asset purchase transaction has experienced a separation from service for purposes of this paragraph (h), provided that the asset purchase transaction results from *bona fide,* arm's length negotiations, all service providers providing services to the seller immediately before the asset purchase transaction and providing services to the buyer after and as a result of the asset purchase transaction are treated consistently (regardless of position at the seller) for purposes of applying the provisions of any nonqualified deferred compensation plan, and such treatment is specified in writing no later than the closing date of the asset purchase transaction. For purposes of this paragraph (h)(4), references to a sale or other disposition of assets, or an asset purchase transaction, refer only to a transfer of substantial assets, such as a plant or division or substantially all of the assets of a trade or business, and do not refer to a stock purchase treated as a deemed asset sale under section 338. For purposes of this paragraph (h)(4), whether a service recipient is related to another service recipient is

determined under the rules provided in paragraph (f)(2)(ii) of this section.

(5) *Dual status.*—If a service provider provides services both as an employee of a service recipient and as an independent contractor of the service recipient, the service provider must separate from service both as an employee and as an independent contractor to be treated as having separated from service. Notwithstanding the foregoing, if a service provider provides services as an employee of a service recipient and as a member of the board of directors of a corporate service recipient (or an analogous position with respect to a non-corporate service recipient), the services provided as a director are not taken into account in determining whether the service provider has a separation from service as an employee for purposes of a nonqualified deferred compensation plan in which the service provider participates as an employee that is not aggregated with any plan in which the service provider participates as a director under paragraph (c)(2)(ii) of this section. In addition, if a service provider provides services both as an employee of a service recipient and as a member of the board of directors of a corporate service recipient (or an analogous position with respect to a non-corporate service recipient), the services provided as an employee are not taken into account in determining whether the service provider has a separation from service as a director for purposes of a nonqualified deferred compensation plan in which the service provider participates as a director that is not aggregated with any plan in which the service provider participates as an employee under paragraph (c)(2)(ii) of this section.

* * *

(q) *References to a payment being made.*—A payment is made or an amount is paid or received when any taxable benefit is actually or constructively received, which includes a transfer of cash, a transfer of property includible in income under section 83, any other event that results in the inclusion in income under the economic benefit doctrine, a contribution to a trust described in section 402(b) at the time includible in income under section 402(b), a transfer or creation of a beneficial interest in a section 402(b) trust at the time includible in income under section 402(b), and the inclusion of an amount in income under 457(f)(1)(A). In addition, a payment is made or an amount is paid or received upon the transfer, cancellation, or reduction of an amount of deferred compensation in exchange for benefits under a welfare benefit plan, a fringe benefit excludible under section 119 or section 132, or any other benefit that is excludible from gross income. Notwithstanding the foregoing, the occurrence of any of the following events is not a payment:

(1) a grant of an option that does not have a readily ascertainable fair market value (as defined under §1.83-7(b));

(2) a transfer of property (including an option that has a readily ascertainable fair market value) that is substantially nonvested (as defined under §1.83-3(b)) with respect to which the service provider does not make a valid election under section 83(b); or

(3) a contribution to a trust described in section 402(b) or a transfer or creation of a beneficial interest in a section 402(b) trust unless and until the amount is includible in income under section 402(b).

(r) *Application of definitions and rules.*—The definitions and rules set forth in paragraphs (a) through (q) of this section apply for purposes of section 409A, this section, and §§1.409A-2 through 1.409A-6.

Par. 4. Section 1.409A-2 is amended by revising paragraph (b)(2)(i) to read as follows:

§1.409A-2. Deferral elections.

* * *

(b) * * *

(2) *Definitions of payments for purposes of subsequent changes in the time or form of payment.*—(i) *In general.*—Except as provided in paragraphs (b)(2)(ii) and (iii) of this section, the term *payment* refers to each separately identified amount to which a service provider is entitled to payment under a plan on a determinable date, and includes amounts applied for the benefit of the service provider. An amount is separately identified only if the amount may be objectively determined under a nondiscretionary formula. For example, an amount identified as 10 percent of the account balance as of a specified payment date would be a separately identified amount. The determination of whether a payment is or has been made for purposes of this paragraph (b) is made in accordance with the rules in §1.409A-1(q). For additional rules relating to the application of this paragraph (b) to amounts payable at a fixed time or pursuant to a fixed schedule, see §1.409A-3(i)(1).

* * *

Par. 5. Section 1.409A-3 is amended by:
1. Revising paragraph (b).
2. Redesignating paragraph (d) as paragraph (d)(1) and revising the heading of paragraph (d)(1).
3. Adding paragraph (d)(2).
4. Revising paragraphs (i)(5)(iii) and (i)(5)(iv)(A).
5. Revising paragraphs (j)(1) and (j)(2).
6. Revising paragraph (j)(4)(iii)(B).
7. Revising paragraphs (j)(4)(ix)(A) and (j)(4)(ix)(C).
8. Revising paragraph (j)(4)(xiii).
The revisions and additions read as follows:

§1.409A-3. Permissible payments.

* * *

(b) *Designation of payment upon a permissible payment event.*—Except as otherwise specified in this section, a plan provides for the payment upon an event described in paragraph (a)(1), (2), (3), (5), or (6) of this section if the plan provides the date of the event is the payment date, or specifies another payment date that is objectively determinable and nondiscretionary at the time the event occurs. A plan may also provide that a payment upon an event described in paragraph (a)(1), (2), (3), (5), or (6) of this section is to be made in accordance with a schedule that is objectively determinable and nondiscretionary based on the date the event occurs and that would qualify as a fixed schedule under paragraph (i)(1) of this section if the payment event were instead a fixed date, provided that the schedule must be fixed at the time the permissible payment event is designated. In addition, a plan may provide that a payment, including a payment that is part of a schedule, is to be made during a designated taxable year of the service provider that is objectively determinable and nondiscretionary at the time the payment event occurs such as, for example, a schedule of three substantially equal payments payable during the first three taxable years following the taxable year in which a separation from service occurs. A plan may also provide that a payment, including a payment that is part of a schedule, is to be made during a designated period objectively determinable and nondiscretionary at the time the payment event occurs, but only if the designated period both begins and ends within one taxable year of the service provider or the designated period is not more than 90 days and the service provider does not have a right to designate the taxable year of the payment (other than an election that complies with the subsequent deferral election rules of §1.409A-2(b)). However, in the case of a payment to be made following the death of the service provider or a beneficiary who has become entitled to payment due to the service provider's death, in addition to the permitted designated periods described in the previous sentence, the designated period may begin on the date of death and end on December 31 of the first calendar year following the calendar year during which the death occurs, and the payment recipient may have the right to designate the taxable year of payment. If a plan provides for a period of more than one day following a payment event during which a payment may be made, such as permitting payment within 90 days following the date of the event, the payment date for purposes of the subsequent deferral rules under §1.409A-2(b) is treated as the first possible date upon which a payment could be made under the terms of the plan. A plan may provide for payment upon the earliest or latest of more than one event or time, provided that each event or time is described in paragraphs (a)(1) through (6) of this section. For examples illustrating the provisions of this paragraph, see paragraph (i)(1)(vi) of this section.

* * *

(d) *When a payment is treated as made upon the designated payment date.*—(1) *In general.*—* * *

(2) *Payments due following death.*—A payment specified to be made under the plan on any date within the period beginning on the date of the death of the service provider, or of a beneficiary who has become entitled to payment due to the service provider's death, and

ending on December 31 of the first calendar year following the calendar year during which the death occurs (including a payment specified to be made upon death) is treated as made on the date specified under the plan if the payment is made on any date during this period, regardless of whether the payment recipient designates the taxable year of payment. Further, any change to the time or form of a payment that is specified to be made under the plan during this period to provide that the payment will be made on any other date during this period will not be treated as a subsequent deferral election for purposes of §1.409A-2(b)(1) or an impermissible acceleration for purposes of §1.409A-3(j)(1).

* * *

(i) * * *

(5) * * *

(iii) *Attribution of stock ownership.*—For purposes of paragraph (i)(5) of this section, section 318(a) applies to determine stock ownership. Stock underlying a vested option is considered owned by the person who holds the vested option (and the stock underlying a nonvested option is not considered owned by the person who holds the nonvested option). For purposes of the preceding sentence, however, if a vested option is exercisable for stock that is not substantially vested (as defined by §1.83-3(b) and (j)), the stock underlying the option is not treated as owned by the person who holds the option.

* * *

(iv) *Special rules for certain delayed payments pursuant to a change in control event.*—(A) *Certain transaction-based compensation.*—Payments of compensation related to a change in control event described in paragraph (i)(5)(v) of this section (change in the ownership of a corporation) or paragraph (i)(5)(vii) of this section (change in the ownership of a substantial portion of a corporation's assets) that occur because a service recipient purchases its stock held by the service provider or because the service recipient or a third party purchases a stock right or a statutory stock option described in §1.409A-1(b)(5)(ii) held by a service provider, or that are calculated by reference to the value of stock of the service recipient (collectively, transaction-based compensation), may be treated as paid on a designated date or pursuant to a payment schedule that complies with the requirements of section 409A if the transaction-based compensation is paid on the same schedule and under the same terms and conditions as apply to payments to shareholders generally with respect to stock of the service recipient pursuant to a change in control event described in paragraph (i)(5)(v) of this section (change in the ownership of a corporation) or as apply to payments to the service recipient pursuant to a change in control event described in paragraph (i)(5)(vii) of this section (change in the ownership of a substantial portion of a corporation's assets). In addition, to the extent that the transaction-based compensation is paid not later than five years after the change in control event, the payment of such compensation will not violate the initial or subsequent deferral election rules set out in §1.409A-2(a) and (b) solely as a result of such transaction-based compensation being paid pursuant to such schedule and terms and conditions. The payment or agreement to pay transaction-based compensation payable with respect to a stock right described in §1.409A-1(b)(5)(i)(A) or (B) or a statutory stock option described in §1.409A-1(b)(5)(ii) also will not cause the stock right or statutory stock option to be treated as having provided for the deferral of compensation from the original grant date solely as a result of the transaction-based compensation being paid on the same schedule and under the same terms and conditions as apply to payments to shareholders generally with respect to stock of the service recipient pursuant to the change in control event described in paragraph (i)(5)(v) of this section (change in the ownership of a corporation) or as apply to payments to the service recipient pursuant to the change in control event described in paragraph (i)(5)(vii) of this section (change in the ownership of a substantial portion of a corporation's assets) and the transaction-based compensation is paid not later than five years after the change in control event. If before and in connection with a change in control event described in paragraph (i)(5)(v) or (i)(5)(vii) of this section, transaction-based compensation that would otherwise be payable as a result of such event is made subject to a condition on payment that is a substantial risk of forfeiture (as defined in §1.409A-1(d), without regard to the provisions of that section under which additions or extensions of forfeiture conditions are disregarded) and the transaction-based compensation is payable under the same terms and conditions as apply to payments made to shareholders generally with respect to stock of the service recipient pursuant to a change in control event described in paragraph (i)(5)(v) of this section or to payments to the service recipient pursuant to a change in control event described in paragraph (i)(5)(vii) of this section, for purposes of determining whether such transaction-based compensation is a short-term deferral the requirements of §1.409A– 1(b)(1) are applied as if the legally binding right to such transaction-

based compensation arose on the date that it became subject to such substantial risk of forfeiture.

* * *

(j) *Prohibition on acceleration of payments.*—(1) *In general.*—Except as provided in paragraph (j)(4) of this section, a nonqualified deferred compensation plan may not permit the acceleration of the time or schedule of any payment or amount scheduled to be paid pursuant to the terms of the plan, and no such accelerated payment may be made whether or not provided for under the terms of such plan. For purposes of determining whether a payment of deferred compensation has been made, the rules of paragraph (f) of this section (on substituted payments) apply. For purposes of this paragraph (j), an impermissible acceleration does not occur if payment is made in accordance with plan provisions or an election as to the time and form of payment in effect at the time of initial deferral (or added in accordance with the rules applicable to subsequent deferral elections under §1.409A-2(b)) pursuant to which payment is required to be made on an accelerated schedule as a result of an intervening payment event that is an event described in paragraph (a)(1), (2), (3), (5) or (6) of this section. For such purpose, the intervening payment event may apply with respect to either the service provider or, following the service provider's death, a beneficiary who becomes entitled to payment due to the service provider's death (substituting such beneficiary for the service provider in the definitions of *disability* in paragraph (i)(4) of this section and *unforeseeable emergency* in paragraph (i)(3) of this section, as applicable). For example, a plan may provide that a participant will receive six installment payments commencing at separation from service, and also provide that if the participant dies after such payments commence but before all payments have been made, all remaining amounts will be paid in a lump sum payment. Additionally, it is not an acceleration of the time or schedule of payment of a deferral of compensation if a service recipient waives or accelerates the satisfaction of a condition constituting a substantial risk of forfeiture applicable to such deferral of compensation, provided that the requirements of section 409A (including the requirement that the payment be made upon a permissible payment event) are otherwise satisfied with respect to such deferral of compensation. For example, if a nonqualified deferred compensation plan provides for a lump sum payment of the vested benefit upon separation from service, and the benefit vests under the plan only after 10 years of service, it is not a violation of the requirements of section 409A if the service recipient reduces the vesting requirement to five years of service, even if a service provider becomes vested as a result and receives a payment in connection with a separation from service before the service provider would have completed 10 years of service. However, if the plan in this example had provided for a payment on a fixed date, rather than at separation from service, the date of payment could not be accelerated due to the accelerated vesting. For the definition of a payment for purposes of this paragraph (j), see §1.409A–2(b)(5) (coordination of the subsequent deferral election rules with the prohibition on acceleration of payments). For other permissible payments, see §1.409A–2(b)(2)(iii) (certain immediate payments of remaining installments) and paragraph (d) of this section (certain payments made no more than 30 days before the designated payment date).

(2) *Application to multiple payment events.*—The addition of a permissible payment event, the deletion of a permissible payment event, or the substitution of one permissible payment event for another permissible payment event, results in an acceleration of a payment if the addition, deletion, or substitution could result in the payment being made on an earlier date than such payment would have been made absent such addition, deletion, or substitution. Notwithstanding the previous sentence, the addition of death, disability (as defined in paragraph (i)(4) of this section), or an unforeseeable emergency (as defined in paragraph (i)(3) of this section), as a potentially earlier alternative or intervening payment event to an amount previously deferred will not be treated as resulting in an acceleration of a payment, even if such addition results in the payment being paid at an earlier time than such payment would have been made absent the addition of the payment event. For such purpose, the earlier alternative or intervening payment event may apply with respect to either the service provider or, following the service provider's death, a beneficiary who becomes entitled to payment due to the service provider's death (substituting such beneficiary for the service provider in the definitions of *disability* in paragraph (i)(4) of this section and *unforeseeable emergency* in paragraph (i)(3) of this section, as applicable). However, the addition of such a payment event as a potentially later alternative payment event generally is subject to the rules governing changes in the time and form of payment (see §1.409A–2(b)).

* * *

(4) * * *

(iii) * * *

(B) *Compliance with ethics laws or conflicts of interest laws.*— A plan may provide for acceleration of the time or schedule of a payment under the plan, or a payment may be made under a plan, to the extent reasonably necessary to avoid the violation of an applicable Federal, state, local, or *bona fide* foreign ethics law or conflicts of interest law (including under circumstances in which such payment is reasonably necessary to permit the service provider to participate in activities in the normal course of his or her position in which the service provider would otherwise not be able to participate under an applicable rule). A payment is reasonably necessary to avoid the violation of a Federal, state, local, or *bona fide* foreign ethics law or conflicts of interest law if the payment is a necessary part of a course of action that results in compliance with a Federal, state, local, or *bona fide* foreign ethics law or conflicts of interest law that would be violated absent such course of action, regardless of whether other actions would also result in compliance with the Federal, state, local, or *bona fide* foreign ethics law or conflicts of interest law.

* * *

(ix) * * *

(A) The service recipient's termination and liquidation of the plan within 12 months of a corporate dissolution taxed under section 331, or with the approval of a U.S. bankruptcy court, provided that the amounts deferred under the plan are included in the participants' gross incomes in the latest of the following years (or, if earlier, the taxable year in which the amount is actually or constructively received).

(1) The calendar year in which the plan termination and liquidation occurs;

(2) The first calendar year in which the amount is no longer subject to a substantial risk of forfeiture; or

(3) The first calendar year in which the payment is administratively practicable.

* * *

(C) The service recipient's termination and liquidation of the plan, provided that—

(1) The termination and liquidation does not occur proximate to a downturn in the financial health of the service recipient;

(2) The service recipient terminates and liquidates all agreements, methods, programs, and other arrangements sponsored by the service recipient that would be aggregated with any terminated and liquidated agreements, methods, programs, and other

arrangements under §1.409A-1(c) as if there were one service provider that had deferrals of compensation under every such agreement, method, program, and other arrangement sponsored by the service recipient (for example, all elective account balance plans that the service recipient sponsors);

(3) No payments in liquidation of the plan are made within 12 months of the date the service recipient takes all necessary action to irrevocably terminate and liquidate the plan other than payments that would be payable under the terms of the plan if the action to terminate and liquidate the plan had not occurred;

(4) All payments are made within 24 months of the date the service recipient takes all necessary action to irrevocably terminate and liquidate the plan; and

(5) The service recipient does not adopt any new agreement, method, program, or other arrangement described in paragraph (C)(2) of this subsection, at any time within three years following the date the service recipient takes all necessary action to irrevocably terminate and liquidate the plan.

* * *

(xiii) *Certain offsets.*—(A) *De minimis offset.*—A plan may provide for the acceleration of the time or schedule of a payment, or a payment may be made under such plan, as satisfaction of a debt of the service provider to the service recipient, if such debt is incurred in the ordinary course of the service relationship between the service recipient and the service provider, the entire amount of reduction in any of the service recipient's taxable years does not exceed $5,000, and the reduction is made at the same time and in the same amount as the debt otherwise would have been due and collected from the service provider.

(B) *Compliance with Federal debt collection laws.*—A plan may provide for the acceleration of the time or schedule of a payment, or a payment may be made under such plan, as satisfaction of a debt of the service provider to the service recipient, to the extent reasonably necessary to comply with 31 U.S.C. sections 3711 et. seq. or similar Federal nontax law regarding debt collection relating to claims of the Federal government. A payment is reasonably necessary to comply with such a Federal debt collection law if the payment is a necessary part of a course of action that results in compliance with the Federal debt collection law that would be violated absent such course of action, regardless of whether other actions would also result in compliance with the Federal debt collection law.

* * *

Par. 6. Section 1.409A-4 (REG-148326-05), as proposed at 73 FR 74380 (December 8, 2008), is proposed to be amended by revising paragraph (a)(1)(ii)(B) to read as follows:

§1.409A-4. Calculation of amount includible in income and additional income taxes.

* * *

(a)(1)(ii)(B) *Treatment of certain deferred amounts otherwise subject to a substantial risk of forfeiture.*—For purposes of determining the amount includible in income under section 409A(a)(1) and paragraph (a)(1)(i) of this section, an amount deferred under a plan that is otherwise subject to a substantial risk of forfeiture for a taxable year is treated as not subject to a substantial risk of forfeiture for the taxable year, if during the taxable year any of the following occur:

(1) A change (including an initial deferral election) that is not authorized under §1.409A-1, §1.409A-2, or §1.409A-3 is made to a provision of the plan providing for the time or form of payment of the deferred amount; if the service recipient has not made a reasonable, good faith determination that, absent the change, the provision fails to comply with the requirements of section 409A(a).

(2) The service recipient has engaged in a pattern or practice of permitting substantially similar failures to comply with section 409A(a) under one or more nonqualified deferred compensation plans while amounts deferred under the plans are nonvested, and the facts and circumstances indicate that the deferred amount would be

affected by the pattern or practice. Whether such a pattern or practice exists will depend on the facts and circumstances, including, but not limited to, whether the service recipient has taken commercially reasonable measures to identify and correct the substantially similar failures promptly upon discovery, whether the failures have affected nonvested deferred amounts with greater frequency than vested deferred amounts, whether the failures have occurred more frequently under newly adopted plans, and whether the failures appear intentional, are numerous, or repeat one or more similar past failures that were previously identified and corrected.

(3) The correction of a failure to comply with section 409A(a) affecting the deferred amount is not consistent with an applicable correction method (if one exists) set forth in applicable guidance issued by the Treasury Department and the IRS for correcting failures under section 409A(a), or the failure is not corrected in substantially the same manner as a substantially similar failure affecting a nonvested deferred amount under another plan sponsored by the service recipient. Solely with respect to the deferred amount, the requirements under applicable correction guidance with respect to eligibility, income inclusion, additional taxes, premium interest, and information reporting by the service recipient or service provider do not apply.

Par. 7. Section 1.409A-6 is amended by revising paragraph (b) to read as follows:

§1.409A-6. Application of section 409A and effective dates.

* * *

(b) *Regulatory applicability date.*—Section 1.409A-0, §1.409A-1, §1.409A-2, §1.409A-3 and this section, as amended, apply for taxable years beginning on or after publication of the Treasury decision

adopting these rules as final regulations in the *Federal Register*. Section 1.409A-0, §1.409A-1, §1.409A-2, §1.409A-3 and this section as they appeared in the April 2009 edition of 26 CFR part 1 apply for taxable years beginning on or after January 1, 2009 and before publication of the Treasury decision adopting these rules as final regulations in the *Federal Register*.

Employee Plans: Vesting Standards

Qualified Employee Plans: Minimum Vesting Standards.—Temporary Reg. §1.410(a)-3T, relating to minimum vesting standards for qualified employee plans, is also proposed as a final regulation and, when adopted, would become Reg. §1.410(a)-3 (published in the Federal Register on January 6, 1988).

§1.410(a)-3. Minimum age and service conditions.

Pension Plans: Accruals: Retirement Age

Pension Plans: Accruals: Retirement Age.—Reproduced below is the text of proposed Reg. §1.410(a)-4A, relating to the requirement for continued accruals beyond normal retirement age under employee pension plans (published in the Federal Register on April 11, 1988).

☐ Par. 2. A new §1.410(a)-4A is added immediately after §1.410(a)-4 to read as follows:

§1.410(a)-4A. Maximum age conditions after 1987.— (a) *Maximum age conditions.*—Under section 410(a)(2), a plan is not a qualified plan (and a trust forming a part of such plan is not a qualified trust) if the plan, either directly or indirectly, excludes any employee from participation on the basis of attaining a maximum age.

(b) *Effective date and transitional rule.*—If a plan contains a provision that excludes an employee from participation on the basis of attaining a maximum age, the provision may not be applied in a plan year beginning on or after January 1, 1988, to any employee (regardless of when the employee first performed an hour of service for the employer) who is credited with at least 1 hour of service on or after January 1, 1988. For purposes of determining when such an employee (who is not otherwise ineligible to participate in the plan) must become eligible to participate in the plan under section 410(a)(1)(A)(ii), section 410(a)(1)(B) and the provisions of the plan, hours of service and years of service credited to the employee before the first plan year beginning on or after January 1, 1988, are taken into account in accordance with section 410 and the regulations thereunder and in accordance with 29 CFR Part 2530. Any employee who would be eligible to participate in the plan taking such service into account and whose entry date would be prior to the first day of the first plan year beginning on or after January 1, 1988, must participate in the plan as of the first day of such plan year.

(c) *Examples.*—The provisions of this section may be illustrated by the following examples:

Example (1). Employer X maintains a defined benefit plan that uses a 12-month period beginning July 1 and ending June 30 as its plan year and that specifies a normal retirement age of 65. The plan provides that each employee of X is eligible to become a participant in the plan on the first entry date on or after the employee completes 1 year of service for X. The plan has 2 entry dates, July 1 and January 1. However, prior to the plan year beginning July 1, 1988, the plan contained a provision that excluded from participation any employee first hired within 5 years of attaining the plan's specified normal retirement age of 65. Employee A was hired by X on August 1, 1986 at age 62. A completes 1 year of service for X by August 1, 1987. If A performs at least one hour of service for X on or after January 1, 1988, the plan, in order to meet the requirements of section 410(a)(2), may not apply the maximum age provision to A on or after July 1, 1988, and A must be eligible to become a participant in the plan in accordance with the other eligibility rules contained in the plan, taking into account A's service with X performed prior to July 1, 1988 to the extent required under the terms of the plan or under section 410 and the regulations thereunder and under regulations in 29 CFR Part 2530. Accordingly, if A is still employed by X on July 1, 1988, A must become a participant in the plan on that date.

Example (2). Employer Y maintains a defined benefit plan that uses the calendar year as its plan year and that specifies a normal retirement age of 65. Employee B is first hired by Y in 1988 when B is age 66. In order for the plan to meet the requirements of section 410(a)(2), B may not be excluded from plan participation on the basis of B having attained a specified age. [Reg. §1.410(a)-4A.]

Qualified Employee Plans: Minimum Vesting Standards

Qualified Employee Plans: Minimum Vesting Standards.—Temporary Reg. §§1.410(a)-8T and 1.410(a)-9T, relating to minimum vesting standards for qualified employee plans, are also proposed as final regulations and, when adopted, would become Reg. §§1.410(a)-8 and 1.410(a)-9, respectively (published in the Federal Register on January 6, 1988).

§1.410(a)-8. Year of service; break in service.

§1.410(a)-9. Elapsed time.

Pension Plans: Continued Accruals Beyond Retirement Age

Pension Plans: Accruals: Retirement Age.—Reproduced below is the text of a proposed amendment of Reg. §1.411(a)-1, relating to the requirement for continued accruals beyond normal retirement age under employee pension plans (published in the Federal Register on April 11, 1988).

☐ Par. 3. Section 1.411(a)-1 is amended by revising paragraph (a)(3) to read as follows:

§1.411(a)-1. Minimum vesting standards; general rules.—(a) *In general.*—* * *

(3) The plan satisfies the requirements of—

(A) Section 411(a)(2) and §1.411(a)-3 (relating to vesting in accrued benefit derived from employer contributions),

(B) In the case of a defined benefit plan, section 411(b)(1) and (3) (see §§1.411(b)-1 and 1.411(b)-2, relating to accrued benefit

requirements, separate accounting and accruals and allocations after a specified age), and

(C) In the case of a defined contribution plan, section 411(b)(2) and (3) (see §§1.411(b)-1(e)(2) and 1.411(b)-2, relating to accruals and allocations after a specified age and separate accounting).

* * *

Employee Plans: Vesting Standards

Qualified Employee Plans: Minimum Vesting Standards.—Temporary Reg. §§1.411(a)-3T and 1.411(a)-4T, relating to minimum vesting standards for qualified employee plans, are also proposed as final regulations and, when adopted, would become Reg. §§1.411(a)-3 and 1.411(a)-4 (published in the Federal Register on January 6, 1988).

§1.411(a)-3. Vesting in employer-derived benefits.

§1.411(a)-4. Forfeitures, suspensions, etc.

Pension Plans: Accruals: Definitions: Special Rules

Pension Plans: Accruals: Retirement Age.—Reproduced below is the text of a proposed amendment of Reg. §1.411(a)-7, relating to the requirement for continued accruals beyond normal retirement age under employee pension plans (published in the Federal Register on April 11, 1988).

☐ Par. 4. Section 1.411(a)-7 is amended by adding a new subparagraph (b)(3) to read as follows:

§1.411(a)-7. Definitions and special rules.—
* * *

(b) *Normal retirement age.* * * *

(3) *Effect of Omnibus Budget Reconciliation Act of 1986 (OBRA).*—[RESERVED]

* * *

Employee Plans: Vesting Standards

Qualified Employee Plans: Minimum Vesting Standards.—Temporary Reg. §1.411(a)-8T, relating to minimum vesting standards for qualified employee plans, is also proposed as a final regulation and, when adopted, would become Reg. §1.411(a)-8 (published in the Federal Register on January 6, 1988).

§1.411(a)-8. Changes in vesting schedule.

Retirement Plans: Distributions: Deferral of Receipt: Notification of Consequences

Retirement Plans: Distributions: Deferral of Receipt: Notification of Consequences.—Amendments to Reg. §1.411(a)-11, specifying that the notice required under Code Sec. 411(a)(11) to be provided to a participant of his or her right, if any, to defer receipt of an immediately distributable benefit must also describe the consequences of failing to defer receipt of the distribution, are proposed (published in the Federal Register on October 9, 2008) (REG-107318-08).

Par. 2. For each entry listed in the "Location" column, remove the language in the "Remove" column and add the language in the "Add" column in its place.

Location	Remove	Add
1.411(a)-11(c)(2)(ii)	90 days	180 days
1.411(a)-11(c)(2)(iii)(A), first sentence	90 days	180 days

Par. 3. Section 1.411(a)-11 is amended as follows:

1. The second sentence of paragraph (c)(2)(i) is revised.
2. The second sentence of paragraph (c)(2)(iii)(B)(3) is revised.
3. Paragraphs (c)(2)(vi) and (h) are added.

The additions and revisions read as follows:

§1.411(a)-11. Restriction and valuation of distributions.

* * *

(c) * * *

(2) *Consent.*—(i) * * * In addition, so long as a benefit is immediately distributable, a participant must be informed of the right, if any, to defer receipt of the distribution and of the consequences of failing to defer such receipt. * * *

* * *

(iii) * * *

(B) * * *

(3) * * * The summary described in paragraph (c)(2)(iii)(B)(2) of this section must advise the participant of the right, if any, to defer receipt of the distribution and of the consequences of failing to defer such receipt, must set forth a summary of the distribution options under the plan, must refer the participant to the most recent version of the notice (and, in the case of a notice provided in any document containing information in addition to the notice, must identify that document and must provide a reasonable indication of where the notice may be found in that document, such as by index reference or by section heading), and must advise the participant that, upon request, a copy of the notice will be provided without charge.

* * *

(vi) *Consequences of failing to defer.*—(A) A notice under this paragraph (c)(2) that is required to describe the consequences of failing to defer receipt of a distribution until it is no longer immediately distributable must, to the extent applicable under the plan and in a manner designed to be easily understood, provide the participant with the information set out in paragraphs (c)(2)(vi)(A)(1) through (5) of this section and explain why it is relevant to a decision whether to defer.

(1) A description of the following federal tax implications of failing to defer: differences in the timing of inclusion in taxable income of an immediately commencing distribution that is not rolled over (or not eligible to be rolled over) and a distribution that is deferred until it is no longer immediately distributable (including, as applicable, differences in the taxation of distributions of designated Roth contributions within the meaning of section 402A); application of the 10% additional tax on certain distributions before age 59½ under section 72(t); and, in the case of a defined contribution plan, loss of the opportunity upon immediate commencement for future tax-favored treatment of earnings if the distribution is not rolled over (or not eligible to be rolled over) to an eligible retirement plan described in section 402(c)(8)(B).

(2) In the case of a defined benefit plan, a statement of the amount payable to the participant under the normal form of benefit both upon immediate commencement and upon commencement when the benefit is no longer immediately distributable (assuming no future benefit accruals). The statement need not vary based on the participant's marital status if the plan is permitted, pursuant to §1.417(a)(3)-1(c)(2)(ii), to provide a QJSA explanation that does not vary based on the participant's marital status.

(3) In the case of a defined contribution plan, a statement that some currently available investment options in the plan may not be generally available on similar terms outside the plan and contact information for obtaining additional information on the general availability outside the plan of currently available investment options in the plan.

(4) In the case of a defined contribution plan, a statement that fees and expenses (including administrative or investment-related fees) outside the plan may be different from fees and expenses that apply to the participant's account and contact information for obtaining additional information on the fees and expenses that apply to the participant's account.

(5) An explanation of any provisions of the plan (and provisions of an accident or health plan maintained by the employer) that could reasonably be expected to materially affect a participant's decision whether to defer receipt of the distribution. Such provisions would include, for example: plan terms under which a participant who fails to defer may lose eligibility for retiree health coverage or eligibility for early retirement subsidies or social security supplements; plan terms under which the benefit of a rehired participant who failed to defer may be adversely affected by the decision not to defer; and, in the case of a defined contribution plan, plan terms under which undistributed benefits that otherwise are nonforfeitable become forfeitable upon the participant's death.

(B) *Location of information; incorporation by reference.*—In general, the information required to be provided in a notice under this paragraph (c)(2)(vi) must appear together (for example, in a list of consequences of failing to defer). However, the notice will not be treated as failing to satisfy the requirements of this paragraph (c)(2)(vi) merely because the notice includes a cross-reference to where the required information may be found in notices or other information provided or made available to the participant, as long as the notice of consequences of failing to defer includes a statement of how the referenced information may be obtained without charge and explains why the referenced information is relevant to a decision whether to defer. * * *

(h) *Consequences of Failing to Defer Effective/Applicability Date.*—The provisions in paragraph (c) of this section that describe the requirement to notify participants of the consequences of failing to defer are effective for notices provided on or after the first day of the first plan year beginning on or after January 1, 2010.

Defined Benefit Plans: Accrual Rules

Defined Benefit Plans: Accrual Rules.—Amendments to Reg. §1.411(b)-1, providing guidance on the application of the accrual rule for defined benefit plans under Code Sec. 411(b)(1)(B) in cases where plan benefits are determined on the basis of the greatest of two or more separate formulas, are proposed (published in the Federal Register on June 18, 2008) (REG-100464-08).

☐ Par. 2. Section 1.411(b)-1 is amended by adding new paragraph (b)(2)(ii)(G) to read as follows:

§1.411(b)-1. Accrued benefit requirements.

* * *

(b) * * *

(2) * * *

(ii) * * *

(G) *Special rule for multiple formulas.*—*(1) In general.*—Notwithstanding paragraph (a)(1) of this section, a plan that determines a participant's accrued benefit as the greatest of the benefits determined under two or more separate formulas is permitted, to the extent provided under this paragraph (b)(2)(ii)(G), to demonstrate satisfaction of section 411(b)(1)(B) and this paragraph (b) by demonstrating that each separate formula satisfies the requirements of section 411(b)(1)(B) and this paragraph (b).

(2) *Separate bases requirement.*—A plan is eligible for separate testing under this paragraph (b)(2)(ii)(G) if each of the separate formulas uses a different basis for determining benefits. For example, a plan is eligible for this special rule if it provides an accrued benefit equal to the greater of the benefits under two formulas, one of which determines accrued benefits on the basis of highest average compensation and the other of which determines accrued benefits on the basis of career average compensation. As another example, a defined benefit plan that bases benefits on highest average compensation and that is amended to add a statutory hybrid benefit formula (as defined in §1.411(a)(13)-1(d)(3)) that provides for pay credits to be made based on each year's compensation is eligible

for this separate testing exception if the plan provides that one or more participants are entitled to the greater of the benefit determined under the statutory hybrid benefit formula and the benefit determined under the original formula.

(3) *Plans with three or more formulas.*—If a plan determines a participant's benefits as the greatest of the benefits determined under three or more separate formulas, but two or more of the formulas use the same basis for determining benefits, then the plan may nonetheless apply paragraphs (b)(2)(ii)(G)(1) and (2) of this section by aggregating all benefit formulas that have the same basis and treating those aggregated formulas as a single formula for purposes of paragraphs (b)(2)(ii)(G)(1) and (2) of this section.

(4) *Anti-abuse rule.*—A plan is not eligible for separate testing under this paragraph (b)(2)(ii)(G) if the Commissioner determines that the plan's use of separate formulas with different bases is structured to evade the requirement to aggregate formulas under paragraph (a)(1) of this section (for example, if the differences between the bases of the separate formulas are minor).

(5) *Effective/applicability date.*—This paragraph (b)(2)(ii)(G) is applicable for plan years beginning on or after January 1, 2009.

Pension Plans: Accruals

Pension Plans: Accruals: Retirement Age.—Reproduced below are the texts of proposed Reg. §1.411(b)-2 and a proposed amendment of Reg. §1.411(c)-1, relating to the requirement for continued accruals beyond normal retirement age under employee pension plans (published in the Federal Register on April 11, 1988). *Note: Taxpayers may rely on these proposed regulations pending the issuance of final regulations. The IRS will apply them in issuing rulings and in examining returns. If final regulations are less favorable, they will not be applied retroactively.*

☐ Par. 5. A new section 1.411(b)-2 is added after §1.411(b)-1 to read as follows:

§1.411(b)-2. Accruals and allocations after a specified age.—(a) *In general.*—Section 411(b)(1)(H) provides that a defined benefit plan does not satisfy the minimum vesting standards of section 411(a) if, under the plan, benefit accruals on behalf of a participant are discontinued or the rate of benefit accrual on behalf of a participant is reduced because of the participant's attainment of any age. Section 411(b)(2) provides that a defined contribution plan does not satisfy the minimum vesting standards of section 411(a) if, under the plan, allocations to a participant's account are reduced or discontinued or the rate of allocations to a participant's account is reduced because of the participant's attainment of any age. A defined benefit plan is not considered to discontinue benefit accruals or reduce the rate of benefit accrual on behalf of a participant because of the attainment of any age in violation of section 411(b)(1)(H) and a defined contribution plan is not considered to reduce or discontinue allocations to a participant's account or reduce the rate of allocations to a participant's account because of the attainment of any age in violation of section 411(b)(2) solely because of a positive correlation between increased age and a reduction or discontinuance in benefit accruals or account allocations under a plan. Thus, for example, if a defined benefit plan or a defined contribution plan provides for reduced or discontinued benefit accruals or account allocations on behalf of participants who have completed a specified number of years of credited service, the plan will not thereby fail to satisfy section 411(b)(1)(H) or (b)(2) solely because of a positive correlation between increased age and completion of the specified number of years of credited service. See paragraph (b)(2) of this section for rules relating to benefit and service limitations under defined benefit plans and paragraph (c)(2) of this section for rules relating to limitations on allocations under defined contribution plans. Also, if benefit accruals or the rate of benefit accrual on behalf of a participant in a defined benefit plan or allocations or the rate of allocations to the account of a participant in a defined contribution plan are reduced or discontinued under the plan and the reason for the reduction or discontinuance is neither directly nor indirectly related to the participant's attainment of a specified age, the plan does not thereby fail to satisfy the requirements of section 411(b)(1)(H) or (b)(2). Thus, for example, if a defined benefit plan is amended to cease or reduce the rate of benefit accrual for all plan participants, such cessation or reduction does not fail to satisfy the requirements of section 411(b)(1)(H).

(b) *Defined benefit plans.*—(1) *In general.*—(i) A defined benefit plan does not satisfy the minimum vesting standards of section 411(a) if, either directly or indirectly, because of the attainment of any age—

(A) A participant's accrual of benefits is discontinued or the rate of a participant's accrual of benefits is decreased, or

(B) A participant's compensation after the attainment of such age is not taken into account in determining the participant's accrual of benefits.

(ii) In determining whether a defined benefit plan satisfies paragraph (b)(1)(i) of this section, the subsidized portion of an early retirement benefit (whether provided on a temporary or permanent basis), a social security supplement (as defined in

§1.411(a)-7(c)(4)(ii)) and a qualified disability benefit (as defined in §1.411(a)-7(c)(3)) are disregarded in determining the rate of a participant's accrual of benefits under the plan.

(iii) The provisions of paragraph (b)(1)(i) of this section may be illustrated by the following example. In the example, assume that the participant completes the hours of service in a plan year required under the plan to accrue a full benefit for the plan year.

Example. Employer X maintains a defined benefit plan that provides a normal retirement benefit of 1% of a participant's average annual compensation, multiplied by the participant's years of credited service under the plan. Normal retirement age under the plan is age 65. The plan contains no limitations (other than the limitations imposed by section 415) on the maximum amount of benefits the plan will pay to any participant or on the maximum number of years of credited service taken into account under the plan for purposes of determining the amount of any participant's normal retirement benefit. Participant A became a participant in the plan at age 25 and worked continuously for X until A retires at age 70. The plan will satisfy the requirements of section 411(b)(1)(H) and paragraph (b)(2) of this section if, under the plan's benefit formula, upon A's retirement, A has an accrued normal retirement benefit of at least 45% of A's average annual compensation (1% per year × 45 years).

(2) *Benefit and service limitations.*—(i) *In general.*—A defined benefit plan does not fail to satisfy section 411(b)(1)(H) and paragraph (b) of this section solely because the plan limits the amount of benefits a participant may accrue under the plan or limits the number of years of service or years of participation taken into account for purposes of determining the accrual of benefits under the plan (credited service). For this purpose, a limitation that is expressed as a percentage of compensation (whether averaged over a participant's total years of credited service for the employer or over a shorter period) and a limitation of the type described in section 401(a)(5)(D) are treated as permissible limitations on the amount of benefits a participant may accrue under the plan. However, in applying a limitation on the number of years of credited service that are taken into account under a plan, the plan may not take into account any year of service that is disregarded in determining the accrual of benefits under the plan (prior to the effective date of section 411(b)(1)(H) and this section) because of the attainment of any age.

(ii) *Limitation not based on age.*—Any limitation on the amount of benefits a participant may accrue under the plan and any limitation on the number of years of credited service taken into account under the plan may not be based, directly or indirectly, on the attainment of any age. A limitation that is determined by reference to age or that is not determinable except by reference to age is considered a limitation directly based on age. Thus, a plan provision that, for purposes of benefit accrual, disregards years of service completed after a participant becomes eligible to receive social security benefits is considered a limitation directly based on age. Similarly, a plan provision that, for purposes of benefit accrual, disregards years of service completed after the sum of a participant's age and the participant's number of years of credited service equals a specified number, is considered a limitation directly based on age. Whether a limitation is indirectly based on age is determined with reference to all the facts and circumstances.

(iii) *Examples.*—The provisions of paragraph (b)(2) of this section may be illustrated by the following examples. In each example, assume that the participant completes the hours of service in a plan year required under the plan to accrue a full benefit for the plan year.

Example (1). Assume the same facts as in the *Example* set forth in paragraph (b)(1)(ii) of this section, except that the plan provides that not more than 35 years of credited service will be taken into account in determining a participant's normal retirement benefit under the plan. Upon A's retirement at age 70, A will have a normal retirement benefit under the plan's benefit formula of 35% of A's average annual compensation (1% per year × 35 years). The plan will not fail to satisfy the requirements of section 411(b)(1)(H) and this paragraph (b) merely because the plan provides that the final 10 years of A's service under the plan is not taken into account in determining A's normal retirement benefit. The result would be the same if the plan provided that no participant could accrue a normal retirement benefit in excess of 35% of the participant's average annual compensation.

Example (2). Employer Y maintains a defined benefit plan that provides a normal retirement benefit of 50% of a participant's final average compensation. Normal retirement age under the plan is age 65. Other than the limitations imposed by section 415, the plan contains no provision that limits the accrual of the benefit payable to a participant who has less than a specified number of years of credited service for Y. Participant A is hired by Y at age 66 and commences participation in the plan at age 67. Under the plan's benefit formula, if A completes one year of credited service under the plan, A will be entitled to receive (subject to the limitations of section 415) a normal retirement benefit equal to 50% of A's final average compensation.

(3) *Different rates of benefit accrual.*—(i) *In general.*—A defined benefit plan does not fail to satisfy the requirements of section 411(b)(1)(H) and paragraph (b) of this section solely because the plan provides for the accrual of benefits at different rates with respect to participants under the plan. Accordingly, a plan under which a participant's accrued benefit is determined in accordance with the fractional rule described in section 411(b)(1)(C) and §1.411(b)-1(b)(3) will not fail to satisfy the requirements of section 411(b)(1)(H) and paragraph (b) of this section solely because the rate at which a participant's normal retirement benefit accrues differs depending on the number of years of credited service a participant would have between the date of commencement of participation and the attainment of normal retirement age. In addition, a plan will not be treated as failing to satisfy section 411(b)(1)(H) and paragraph (b) of this section solely because the plan's benefit formula provides, on a uniform and consistent basis, a normal retirement benefit equal to, for example, 2% of average annual compensation multiplied by a participant's first 15 years of credited service and 1% of average annual compensation multiplied by a participant's years of credited service in excess of 15 years. The preceding sentence applies regardless of when the participant's normal retirement age occurs.

(ii) *Differences not based on age.*—Any differences in the rate of benefit accrual described in paragraph (b)(3)(i) of this section may not be based, directly or indirectly, on the attainment of any age.

(4) *Certain adjustments for delayed retirement.*—(i) *In general.*—Under section 411(b)(1)(H)(iii), a plan may provide that benefit accruals that would otherwise be required under section 411(b)(1)(H)(i) and paragraph (b) of this section for a plan year are reduced (but not below zero) as set forth in paragraph (b)(4)(ii) and (iii) of this section. This paragraph (b)(4) applies for a plan year to a participant who, as of the end of the plan year, has attained normal retirement age under the plan.

(ii) *Distribution of benefits.*—(A) A plan may provide that the benefit accrual otherwise required under section 411(b)(1)(H)(i) and paragraph (b) of this section for a plan year is reduced (but not below zero) by the actuarial equivalent of total plan benefit distributions (as determined under this paragraph (b)(4)(ii)) made to the participant by the close of the plan year.

(B) The plan benefit distributions described in this paragraph (b)(4)(ii) are limited to distributions made to the participant during plan years and periods with respect to which section 411(b)(1)(H)(i) and this section apply (including plan years and periods beginning before January 1, 1988) for which the plan could (without regard to section 401(a)(9) and the regulations thereunder) provide for the suspension of the participant's plan benefits in accordance with section 203(a)(3)(B) of the Employee Retirement Income Security Act of 1974 (ERISA) and regulations issued thereunder by the Department of Labor.

(C) For purposes of determining the total amount of plan benefit distributions that may be taken into account under this paragraph (b)(4)(ii) as of the close of a plan year, distributions shall be disregarded to the extent the total amount of distributions made to the participant by the close of the plan year exceeds the total amount of the distributions the participant would have received by the close of the plan year if the distributions had been made in accordance with the plan's normal form of benefit distribution. Accordingly, the plan is required to accrue a benefit for the plan year on behalf of a participant in accordance with the plan's benefit formula, taking into account all of the participant's years of credited service, reduced (but not below the participant's normal retirement benefit for the prior plan year) by the actuarial equivalent of total benefit distributions (taken into account under this paragraph (b)(4)(ii)) made to the participant by the close of the plan year. If, by the close of the plan year, the actuarial equivalent of total plan benefit distributions made to the participant and taken into account under this paragraph (b)(4)(ii) is greater than the total benefit accruals required under section 411(b)(1)(H)(i) and paragraph (b) of this section for the plan years during which such distributions were made, the plan is not required under section 411(b)(1)(H)(i) and paragraph (b) of this section to accrue any benefit on behalf of the participant for the plan year.

(iii) *Adjustment in benefits payable.*—(A) A plan may provide that the benefit accrual otherwise required under section 411(b)(1)(H)(i) and paragraph (b) of this section for the plan year is reduced (but not below zero) by the amount of any actuarial adjustment under the plan in the benefit payable for the plan year with respect to the participant because of a delay in the payment of plan benefits after the participant's attainment of normal retirement age.

(B) For purposes of subdivision (iii)(A), the actuarial adjustment may be taken into account for a plan year only to the extent it is made to the greater of (1) the participant's retirement benefit as of the close of the prior plan year, including any actuarial adjustment made under the plan for the prior plan year, and (2) the participant's normal retirement benefit as of the close of the prior plan year determined by including benefit accruals required by section 411(b)(1)(H)(i) and paragraph (b) of this section. If the retirement benefit, as actuarially adjusted for the plan year in accordance with this paragraph (b)(4)(iii) for delayed payment, exceeds the normal retirement benefit, as determined by including benefit accruals required for the plan year by section 411(b)(1)(H)(i) and paragraph (b) of this section, the plan shall be required to provide the retirement benefit, as actuarially adjusted in accordance with this paragraph (b)(4)(iii) under the plan. Notwithstanding the provisions of this subdivision (iii)(B), in the case of a plan that suspends benefit payments in accordance with section 203(a)(3)(B) of the Employee Retirement Income Security Act of 1974 and the regulations issued thereunder by the Department of Labor, the plan does not fail to satisfy the requirements of section 411(b)(1)(H) and paragraph (b) of this section solely because the plan provides that the retirement benefit to which a participant is entitled as of the close of a plan year ending after the participant attains normal retirement age under the plan is the greater of (1) the benefit payable at normal retirement age (not including benefit accruals otherwise required by section 411(b)(1)(H) and paragraph (b) of this section) actuarially adjusted under the plan to the close of the plan year for delayed payment, and (2) the retirement benefit determined under the plan as of the close of the plan year determined by including benefit accruals required by section 411(b)(1)(H) and paragraph (b) of this section and determined without regard to any offset that would otherwise be applicable under this paragraph (b)(4)(iii).

(iv) *Examples.*—The provisions of paragraph (b)(4) of this section may be illustrated by the following examples. In each example, assume that the participant completes the hours of service in a plan year required under the plan to accrue a full benefit for the plan year and assume that the participant is not married unless otherwise specified.

Example (1). Employer Y maintains a defined benefit plan that provides a normal retirement benefit of $20 per month multiplied by the participant's years of credited service. The plan contains no limit on the number of years of credited service taken into account for purposes of determining the normal retirement benefit provided by the plan. Participant A attains normal retirement age of 65 and continues in the full time service of Y. At age 65, A has 30 years of credited service under the plan and could receive a normal retirement benefit of $600 per month ($20 × 30 years) if A retires. The plan provides for the suspension of A's normal retirement benefit (in accordance with section 203(a)(3)(B) of the Employee Retirement Income Security Act of 1974 (ERISA) and regulations thereunder issued by the Department of Labor) during the period of A's continued employment with Y. Accordingly, the plan does not provide for an actuarial adjustment of A's normal retirement benefit because of delayed payment and the plan does not pay A's normal retirement benefit while A remains in the full time service of Y. If A retires at age 67, after completing two additional years of credited service for Y, A must receive additional accruals for the two years of credited service completed after attaining normal retirement age in order for the plan to satisfy section 411(b)(1)(H)(i). Accordingly, A is entitled to receive a normal retirement benefit of $640 per month ($20 × 32 years).

Example (2). Assume the same facts as in *Example (1),* except that the plan provides that at the time A's normal retirement benefit becomes payable, the amount of A's normal retirement benefit (determined as of A's normal retirement age and each year thereafter) will be actuarially increased for delayed retirement. The plan offsets this actuarial increase against benefit accruals in plan years ending after A's attainment of normal retirement age, as permitted by paragraph (b)(4)(iii) of this section. Accordingly, the plan does not provide for the suspension of normal retirement benefits (in accordance with section 203(a)(3)(B) of ERISA and regulations thereunder issued by the Department of Labor). Under section 411(b)(1)(H), the plan must provide A with a benefit of at least $620 per month after A completes 31 years of credited service for Y. However, under paragraph (b)(4)(iii) of this section, the plan is not required to provide A with a benefit accrual for A's additional year of credited service for Y because, under the plan, A will be entitled to receive, upon retirement at age 66 after completing 1 additional year of credited service for Y, an actuarially increased benefit of $672 per month. This monthly benefit of $672 is the greater of A's normal retirement benefit at normal retirement age ($20 × 30 years = $600) actuarially adjusted for delayed payment and A's normal retirement benefit ($20 × 31 years = $620) determined by taking into account A's year of credited service after attaining normal retirement age. Under the plan, A will be entitled to receive, upon retirement at age 67 after completing 2 additional years of credited service for Y after attaining normal retirement age, an actuarially increased benefit of $756 per month. This monthly benefit of $756 is the greater of A's actuarially adjusted normal retirement benefit at age 66 ($672) actuarially adjusted to $756 for delayed payment to age 67 and A's normal retirement benefit ($20 × 32 years = $640) determined by taking into account A's years of credited service after attaining normal retirement age.

Example (3). Assume the same facts as in *Example (1),* except that the plan neither provides for the suspension of normal retirement benefit payments (in accordance with section 203(a)(3)(B) of ERISA and regulations thereunder issued by the Department of Labor) nor provides for an actuarial increase in benefit payments because of delayed payment of benefits. Consequently, the plan provides that the normal retirement benefit will be paid to a participant, beginning at age 65 (normal retirement age) even though the participant remains in the service of Y and offsets the value of the benefit distributions against benefit accruals in plan years ending after the participant's attainment of normal retirement age, as permitted by paragraph (b)(4)(ii) of this section. Participant B (who remains in the full time service of Y) receives 12 monthly benefit payments prior to attainment of age 66. The total monthly benefit payments of $7,200 ($600 × 12 payments) have an actuarial value at age 66 of $7,559 (reflecting interest and mortality) which would produce a monthly benefit of $72 commencing at age 66. The benefit accrual for the year of credited service B completed after attaining normal retirement age is $20 per month ($20 × 1 year). Because the actuarial value (determined as a monthly benefit of $72) of the benefit payments made during the one year of credited service after B's attainment of normal retirement age exceeds the benefit accrual for the one year of credited service after B's attainment of normal retirement age, the plan is not required to accrue benefits on behalf of B for the one year of credited service after B's attainment of normal retirement age and the plan is not required to increase B's monthly benefit payment of $600 at age 66. Assume B receives 24 monthly benefit payments prior to B's retirement at age 67. The total monthly benefit payments of

$14,400 ($600 × 24 payments) have an actuarial value at age 67 of $15,839 (reflecting interest and mortality) which would produce a monthly benefit payment of $156 commencing at age 67. The benefit accrual for the two years of credited service after attaining normal retirement age is $40 per month ($20 × 2 years). Because the actuarial value (determined as a monthly benefit of $156) of the benefit payments made during the two years of credited service after B's normal retirement age exceeds the benefit accrual for the two years of credited service after B's normal retirement age ($20 × 2 years = $40), the plan is not required to accrue benefits on behalf of B for the second year of credited service B completed after attaining normal retirement age and the plan is not required to increase B's monthly benefit payment of $600.

Example (4). Assume that Employer Z maintains a defined benefit plan that provides a normal retirement benefit of 2% of the average of a participant's high three consecutive years of compensation multiplied by the participant's years of credited service under the plan. The plan contains no limit on the number of years of credited service taken into account for purposes of determining the normal retirement benefit provided by the plan. Participant C, who has attained normal retirement age (age 65) under the plan, continues in the full time service of Z. At normal retirement age, C has average compensation of $20,000 for C's high three consecutive years and has 10 years of credited service under the plan. Thus, at normal retirement age, C is entitled to receive an annual normal retirement benefit of $4,000 ($20,000 × .02 × 10 years). Assume further that the plan provides for the suspension of N's normal retirement benefit (in accordance with section 203(a)(3)(B) of ERISA and regulations issued thereunder by the Department of Labor) during the period of C's continued employment with Z. Accordingly, the plan does not provide for the actuarial increase of C's normal retirement benefit because of delayed payment and the plan does not pay C's normal retirement benefit while C remains in the full time service of Z. At age 70, when C retires, C has average annual compensation for C's high three consecutive years of $35,000. Under section 411(b)(1)(H), C must be credited with 15 years of credited service for Z and C's increased compensation after attaining normal retirement age must be taken into account for purposes of determining C's normal retirement benefit. At age 70, C is entitled to receive an annual normal retirement benefit of $10,500 ($35,000 × .02 × 15 years).

Example (5). Assume the same facts as in *Example (4),* except that the payment of C's retirement benefit is not suspended (in accordance with section 203(a)(3)(B) of ERISA and regulations issued thereunder by the Department of Labor) and, accordingly, the plan provides that retirement benefits that commence after a participant's normal retirement age will be actuarially increased for late retirement. The plan offsets this actuarial increase against benefit accruals in plan years ending after C's attainment of normal retirement age, as permitted by paragraph (b)(4)(iii) of this section. Under this provision, at the close of each plan year after C's attainment of normal retirement age, C's retirement benefit is actuarially increased. Under this provision, the actuarial increase for the plan year is made to the greater of C's normal retirement benefit at the close of the prior plan year (including previous actuarial adjustments) and C's normal retirement benefit at the close of the prior plan year determined by including all benefit accruals. Accordingly, at the close of each plan year, C is entitled to receive an annual normal retirement benefit equal to the greater of C's normal retirement benefit (adjusted actuarially under the plan from the benefit to which C was entitled at the close of the prior plan year) determined at the close of the plan year and C's normal retirement benefit determined at the close of the plan year by taking into account C's years of credited service and benefit accruals after C's attainment of normal retirement age. The foregoing is illustrated in the following table with respect to certain years of credited service performed by C after attaining normal retirement age 65.

1	2	3	4	5	6
Age	Years of credited service	Average compensation for high three consecutive years	Normal retirement benefit with additional accruals (.02 × Column 2 × Column 3)	Retirement benefit, as actuarially increased under the plan from the benefit at prior age (Column 6)	Normal retirement benefit to which C is entitled (greater of Column 4 and Column 5)
65	10	$20,000	$4,000	N/A	$4,000
66	11	$21,000	$4,620	$4,482	$4,620
67	12	$29,000	$6,960	$5,192	$6,960
68	13	$30,000	$7,800	$7,848	$7,848
69	14	$33,000	$9,240	$8,880	$9,240
70	15	$35,000	$10,500	$10,494	$10,500

Example (6). Assume the same facts as in *Example (4),* except that C does not retire at age 70, but continues in the full time service of Z. Upon C's attainment of age 70, the plan commences benefit payments to C. The annual benefit paid to C in the first plan year is $10,500 ($35,000 × .02 × 15 years). In determining the annual benefit payable to C in each subsequent plan year, the plan offsets the value of benefit distributions made to the participant by the close of the prior plan year against benefit accruals in plan years during which such distributions were made, as permitted by paragraph (b)(4)(ii) of

this section. Accordingly, for each subsequent plan year, C is entitled under the plan to receive benefit payments based on C's benefit (at the close of the prior plan year) determined under the plan formula by taking into account all of C's years of credited service, reduced (but not below C's normal retirement benefit for the prior plan year) by the value of total benefit distributions made to C by the close of the prior plan year. The foregoing is illustrated in the following table with respect to certain years of credited service performed by C while benefits were being distributed to C.

1 Years of benefit distributions	2 Years of credited service (as of close of the year)	3 Average compensation for high three years	4 Normal retirement benefit with additional accruals (.02 × Column 2 × Column 3)	5 Suspendible benefit distributions made during the year	6 Cumulative suspendible benefit distributions made as of close of the year	7 Annual benefit that is actuarial equivalent of cumulative suspendible benefit distributions made as of close of the year	8 Retirement benefit to which C is entitled at close of the year (Column 4 – Column 7, but not less than Column 8 for prior year)
N/A	15	$35,000	$10,500	N/A	N/A	N/A	$10,500
1	16	$35,000	$11,200	$10,500	$10,500	$1,472	$10,500
2	17	$45,000	$15,300	$10,500	$21,000	$3,209	$12,091
3	18	$50,000	$18,000	$12,091	$33,091	$5,510	$12,490

(c) *Defined contribution plans.*—(1) *In general.*—A defined contribution plan (including a target benefit plan described in § 1.410(a)-4(a)(1)) does not satisfy the minimum vesting standards of section 411(a) if, either directly or indirectly, because of the attainment of any age—

    (i) The allocation of employer contributions or forfeitures to the accounts of participants is discontinued, or

    (ii) The rate at which the allocation of employer contributions or forfeitures is made to the accounts of participants is decreased.

    (2) *Limitations on allocations.*—(i) A defined contribution plan (including a target benefit plan described in § 1.410(a)-4(a)(1)) does not fail to satisfy the minimum vesting standards of section 411(a) solely because the plan limits the total amount of employer contributions and forfeitures that may be allocated to a participant's account (for a particular plan year or for the participant's total years of credited service under the plan) or solely because the plan limits the total number of years of credited service for which a participant's account may receive allocations of employer contributions and forfeitures. The limitations described in the preceding sentence may not be applied with respect to the allocation of gains, losses or income of the trust to the account of a participant. Furthermore, a defined contribution plan (including a target benefit plan) does not fail to satisfy section 411(a) solely because the plan limits the number of years of credited service that may be taken into account for purposes of determining the amount of, or the rate at which, employer contributions and forfeitures are allocated to a participant's account for a particular plan year. However, in applying a credited service limitation described in this paragraph (c)(2)(i), the plan may not take into account any year of service (prior to the effective date of section 411(b)(2) and paragraph (c) of this section) that is disregarded in determining allocations to a participant's account because of the participant's attainment of any age.

    (ii) Any limitation described in paragraph (c)(2)(i) of this section may not be based, directly or indirectly, on the attainment of any age. The provisions of paragraph (b)(2)(ii) of this section shall also apply for purposes of this paragraph (c).

    (iii) The Commissioner shall provide such additional rules as may be necessary or appropriate with respect to the application of section 411(b)(2) and this section to target benefit plans.

(d) *Benefits and forms of benefits subject to requirements.*—(1) *General rule.*—Except as provided in paragraph (d)(2) of this section, section 411(b)(1)(H) and (b)(2) and paragraphs (b) and (c) of this section apply to all benefits (and forms of benefits) provided under a defined benefit plan and a defined contribution plan, including accrued benefits, benefits described in section 411(d)(6), ancillary benefits and other rights and features provided under the plan. Accordingly, except as provided in paragraph (d)(2) of this section, benefit accruals under a defined benefit plan and allocations under a defined contribution plan will be considered to be reduced on account of the attainment of a specified age if optional forms of benefits, ancillary benefits, or other rights or features under the plan provided with respect to benefits or allocations attributable to credited service prior to the attainment of such age are not provided (on at least as favorable a basis to participants) with respect to benefits or allocations attributable to credited service after such age. Thus, for example, a plan may not provide a lump sum payment only with respect to benefits attributable to years of credited service before the attainment of a specified age. Similarly, except as provided in paragraph (d)(2) of this section, if an optional form of benefit is available under the plan at a specified age, the availability of such form of benefit, or the method for determining the manner in which such benefit is paid, may not, directly or indirectly, be denied or provided on terms less favorable to participants because of the attainment of any higher age. Similarly, if the method for determining the amount or the rate of the subsidized portion of a joint and survivor annuity or the subsidized portion of a joint and survivor annuity or the substantial portion of a preretirement survivor annuity is less favorable with respect to participants who have attained a specified age than with respect to participants who have not attained such age, benefit accruals or account allocations under the plan will be considered to be reduced on account of the attainment of such age.

    (2) *Special rule for certain benefits.*—A plan will not fail to satisfy section 411(b)(1)(H) or paragraph (b) of this section merely because the following benefits, or the manner in which such benefits are provided under the plan, vary because of the attainment of any higher age.

    (i) The subsidized portion of an early retirement benefit (whether provided on a temporary or permanent basis),

    (ii) A qualified disability benefit (as defined in § 1.411(a)-7(c)(3)); and

    (iii) A social security supplement (as defined in § 1.411(a)-7(c)(4)(ii)).

(e) *Coordination with certain provisions.*—Notwithstanding section 411(b)(1)(H), (b)(2) and the preceding paragraphs of this section, the following rules shall apply.

    (1) *Section 415 limitations.*—No allocation to the account of a participant in a defined contribution plan (including a target benefit plan described in § 1.410(a)-4(a)(1)) shall be required for a limitation year by section 411(b)(2) and no benefit accrual with respect to a participant in a defined benefit plan shall be required for a limitation year by section 411(b)(1)(H)(i) to the extent that the allocation or accrual would cause the plan to exceed the limitations of section 415(b), (c) or (e) applicable to the participant for the limitation year.

    (2) *Prohibited discrimination.*—(i) No allocation to the account of a highly compensated employee in a defined contribution plan (including a target benefit plan) shall be required for a plan year by section 411(b)(2) to the extent the allocation would cause the plan to discriminate in favor of highly compensated employees within the meaning of section 401(a)(4).

    (ii) No benefit accrual on behalf of a highly compensated employee in a defined benefit plan shall be required for a plan year by section 411(b)(1)(H)(i) to the extent such benefit accrual would cause the plan to discriminate in favor of highly compensated employees within the meaning of section 401(a)(4).

    (iii) The Commissioner may provide additional rules relating to prohibited discrimination in favor of highly compensated employees.

    (3) *Permitted disparity.*—In the case of a plan that would fail to satisfy section 401(a)(4) except for the application of section 401(l), no allocation to the account of a participant in a defined contribution plan and no benefit accrual on behalf of a participant in a defined benefit plan shall be required under section 411(b)(1)(H) or (b)(2) for a plan year to the extent such allocation or accrual would cause the plan to fail to satisfy the requirements of section 401(l) and the regulations thereunder for the plan year.

(f) *Effective dates.*—(1) *Noncollectively bargained plans.*—(i) *In general.*—Except as otherwise provided in paragraph (f)(2) of this section, section 411(b)(1)(H) and (b)(2) and paragraphs (b) and (c) of this section are effective for plan years beginning on or after January 1, 1988, with respect to a participant who is credited with at least 1 hour of service in a plan year beginning on or after January 1, 1988. Section 411(b)(1)(H) and (b)(2) and paragraphs (b) and (c) of this section are not effective with respect to a participant who is not credited with at least 1 hour of service in a plan year beginning on or after January 1, 1988.

    (ii) *Defined benefit plans.*—In the case of a participant who is credited with at least 1 hour of service in a plan year beginning on or after January 1, 1988, section 411(b)(1)(H) and paragraph (b) of this section are effective with respect to all years of service completed by the participant, including years of service completed before the first plan year beginning on or after January 1, 1988. Accordingly, in the case of a participant described in the preceding sentence, a defined benefit plan does not satisfy section 411(b)(1)(H) and paragraph (b) of this section for a plan year beginning on or after January 1, 1988, if the plan disregards, because of the participant's attainment of any age, any year of service completed by the participant or any compensation earned by the participant after attaining such age. However, a defined benefit plan is not required under section 411(b)(1)(H) and paragraph (b) of this section to take into account for benefit accrual purposes any year of service completed before an employee becomes a participant in the plan. See paragraph (b)(2) of this section for rules relating to benefit and service limitations that may be imposed by a defined benefit plan.

    (iii) *Defined contribution plans.*—Section 411(b)(2) and paragraph (c) of this section are not applicable with respect to allocations of employer contributions or forfeitures to the accounts of participants under a defined contribution plan for a plan year beginning before January 1, 1988. However, in the case of a defined contribution plan under which allocations to the accounts of participants for a plan year are determined on the basis of an allocation formula that takes into account service or compensation for the employer during prior plan years, section 411(b)(2) and paragraph (c) of this section are effective for plan years beginning on or after January 1, 1988, with respect to all years of service completed by the participant, including years of service completed before the first plan year beginning on or after January 1, 1988. Accordingly, in the case of a participant who has at least 1 hour of service in a plan year beginning on or after January 1, 1988, a defined contribution plan containing an allocation formula described in the preceding sentence does not satisfy section 411(b)(2) and paragraph (c) of this section with respect to allocations for a plan year beginning on or after January 1, 1988, if the plan disregards, because of the participant's attainment of any age, any year of service completed by the participant. See paragraph (c)(2) of this section for rules relating to limitations on allocations to the accounts of participants that may be imposed by a defined contribution plan.

(iv) *Employee contributions.*—In applying paragraph (f)(1)(i), (ii) and (iii) of this section to plan years beginning on or after January 1, 1988, a year of service completed before the first plan year beginning on or after January 1, 1988, will not be treated as being disregarded under a plan on account of a participant's attainment of a specified age solely because such year of service is disregarded under the plan because the participant was not eligible to make voluntary or mandatory employee contributions (as well as contributions under a cash or deferred arrangement described in section 401(k)) under the plan for such year. A plan is not required to permit a participant to make voluntary or mandatory employee contributions (as well as contributions under a cash or deferred arrangement described in section 401(k)) for a plan year beginning before January 1, 1988, in order to satisfy section 411(b)(1)(H) or (b)(2) or paragraph (b) or (c) of this section for a plan year beginning on or after January 1, 1988.

(v) *Hour of service.*—For purposes of this paragraph (f)(1), one hour of service means one hour of service recognized under the plan or required to be recognized under the plan by section 410 (relating to minimum participation standards) or section 411 (relating to minimum vesting standards). In the case of a plan that does not determine service on the basis of hours of service, one hour of service means any service recognized under the plan or required to be recognized under the plan by section 410 (relating to minimum participation standards) or section 411 (relating to minimum vesting standards).

(vi) *Examples.*—The provisions of paragraph (f)(1) of this section may be illustrated by the following examples. In each example, assume that the participant completes the hours of service in a plan year required under the plan to accrue a full benefit or receive an allocation for the plan year.

Example (1). Employer X maintains a noncontributory defined benefit plan (that is not a collectively bargained plan) that provides a normal retirement benefit equal to 1% of a participant's average annual compensation for the participant's three consecutive years of highest compensation, multiplied by the participant's years of credited service under the plan. The plan contains no limit on the number of years of credited service taken into account for purposes of determining the normal retirement benefit provided by the plan. The plan uses the calendar year as its plan year. The plan specifies a normal retirement age of 65 and provides (prior to January 1, 1988) that no compensation earned and no service performed by a participant after attainment of normal retirement age will be taken into account in determining the participant's normal retirement benefit. Participant A attains normal retirement age on December 15, 1985. A continues in the full time service of X and has at least 1 hour of service for X during the plan year beginning on January 1, 1988. As of the plan year ending December 31, 1985, A had 35 years of credited service under the plan. In accordance with the plan provisions in effect prior to January 1, 1988, A's service and compensation during the 1986 and 1987 plan years is not taken into account in determining A's normal retirement benefit for those plan years. Beginning on January 1, 1988, the plan provisions that compensation earned and years of service completed after normal retirement age are not taken into account in determining a participant's normal retirement benefit may not be applied to A. Thus, as of the plan year beginning January 1, 1988, A's normal retirement benefit under the plan must be determined without regard to those provisions. Accordingly, beginning on January 1, 1988, the plan is required to take into account A's service for X and A's compensation from X during the 1986 and 1987 plan years for purposes of determining A's normal retirement benefit in order to satisfy section 411(b)(1)(H) and paragraph (b) of this section.

Example (2). Assume the same facts as in *Example (1)*, except that the plan provides that, in determining a participant's normal retirement benefit under the plan (a) not more than 35 years of credited service will be taken into account and (b) no compensation earned after 35 years of credited service have been completed are taken into account. Accordingly, the plan is not required to take into account A's service for X or A's compensation from X during the 1986 and 1987 plan years for purposes of determining A's normal retirement benefit in order to satisfy section 411(b)(1)(H) and paragraph (b) of this section.

Example (3). Assume the same facts as in *Example (1)*, except that A retires on December 5, 1987 and does not perform any hours of service for X after A's retirement. Accordingly, the plan is not required to take into account A's service for X and A's compensation from X during the 1986 and 1987 plan years for purposes of determining A's normal retirement benefit in order to satisfy section 411(b)(1)(H) and paragraph (b) of this section.

Example (4). Assume the same facts as in *Example (1)*, except that the plan requires, as a condition to accruing benefits attributable to employer contributions under the plan, that a participant make employee contributions under the plan. The plan provides that a participant is not eligible to make employee contributions in a plan year beginning after the plan year in which the participant attains normal retirement age under the plan. Accordingly, A does not make employee contributions during the 1986 and 1987 plan years and, therefore, does not accrue in those plan years a benefit attributable to employer contributions. The plan is not required to take into account A's service for X and A's compensation from X during the 1986 and 1987 plan years in order to satisfy section 411(b)(1)(H) and paragraph (b) of this section. In addition, the plan is not required to permit A to make employee contributions to the plan for the 1986 and 1987 plan years in order to satisfy section 411(b)(1)(H) and paragraph (b) of this section.

Example (5). Employer Y maintains a profit-sharing plan (that is not a collectively bargained plan). The plan is the only qualified plan maintained by Y and uses the calendar year as its plan year. The formula under the plan for allocating employer contributions and forfeitures to the accounts of participants contains a years of service factor. Pursuant to the allocation formula containing the years of service factor, employer contributions and forfeitures for the plan year are allocated among the accounts of participants on the basis of one unit for each full $200 of compensation of the participant for the plan year and one unit for each year of credited service for Y completed by the participant. The plan contains no limit on the number of years of credited service taken into account for purposes of determining the allocation to the account of a participant for the plan year under the plan's allocation formula. The plan specifies a normal retirement age of 65 and provides (prior to January 1, 1988) that no service performed by a participant in a plan year beginning after attainment of normal retirement age will be taken into account in determining the allocation to the participant's account for a plan year. Participant B attains normal retirement age on December 15, 1985. B continues in the full time service of Y and has at least 1 hour of service for Y during the plan year beginning January 1, 1988. As of the plan year ending December 31, 1985, B had 35 years of credited service under the plan. In accordance with the plan provisions in effect prior to January 1, 1988, B's service during the 1986 and 1987 plan years is not taken into account in determining the allocation of employer contributions and forfeitures to B's account for the 1986 and 1987 plan years. As of the plan year beginning January 1, 1988, the plan provision that years of service in plan years beginning after attainment of normal retirement age are not taken into account in determining the allocation of employer contributions and forfeitures to the accounts of participants may not be applied to B. Thus, the allocation of employer contributions and forfeitures to B's account for the 1988 plan year must be determined under the allocation formula contained in the plan without regard to that provision. Accordingly, the plan is required to take into account B's service for Y during the 1986 and 1987 plan years for purposes of determining the allocation of employer contributions and forfeitures to B's account for the 1988 plan year in order to satisfy section 411(b)(2) and paragraph (c) of this section. However, the plan is not required to provide any additional allocations to B's account under the plan for the 1986 or 1987 plan year in order to satisfy section 411 (b)(2) and paragraph (c) of this section.

Example (6). Assume the same facts as in *Example (5)*, except that the plan provides that, in determining the allocation of employer contributions and forfeitures to the account of a participant for a plan year, not more than 35 years of credited service for Y will be taken into account. Accordingly, the plan is not required to take into account B's service for Y during the 1986 or 1987 plan years for purposes of determining the allocation of employer contributions and forfeitures to B's account for the 1988 plan year under the allocation formula contained in the plan.

(2) *Collectively bargained plans.*—(i) In the case of a plan maintained pursuant to 1 or more collective bargaining agreements between employee representatives and 1 or more employers, ratified before March 1, 1986, section 411(b)(1)(H) and (b)(2) is effective for benefits provided under, and employees covered by, any such agreement with respect to plan years beginning on or after the later of—

(A) January 1, 1988, or

(B) The date on which the last of such collective bargaining agreements terminates (determined without regard to any extension of any such agreement occurring on or after March 1, 1986). However, notwithstanding the preceding sentence, section 411(b)(1)(H) and (b)(2) shall be effective for benefits provided under, and employees covered by, any agreement described in this paragraph (f)(2)(i) no later than with respect to the first plan year beginning on or after January 1, 1990.

(ii) The effective date provisions of paragragh (f)(1) of this section shall apply in the same manner to plans described in paragraph (f)(2)(i) of this section, except that the effective date determined under paragraph (f)(2)(i) of this section shall be substituted for the effective date determined under paragraph (f)(1) of this section.

(iii) In accordance with the provisions of paragraph (f)(?)(i) of this section, a plan described therein may be subject to different effective dates under section 411(b)(1)(H) and (b)(2) for employees who are covered by a collective bargaining agreement and employees who are not covered by a collective bargaining agreement.

(iv) For purposes of paragraph (f)(2)(i) of this section, the service crediting rules of paragraph (f)(1) of this section shall apply to a plan described in paragraph (f)(2)(i) of this section, except that in applying such rules the effective date determined under paragraph (f)(2)(i) of this section shall be substituted for the effective date determined under paragraph (f)(1) of this section. See paragraph (f)(1)(v) of this section for rules relating to the recognition of an hour of service.

(3) *Amendments to plans.*—(i) Except as provided in paragraph (f)(3)(ii) of this section, plan amendments required by section 411(b)(1)(H) and (b)(2) (the applicable sections) shall not be required to be made before the first plan year beginning on or after January 1, 1989, if the following requirements are met—

(A) The plan is operated in accordance with the requirements of the applicable section for all periods before the first plan

☐ Par. 6. Section 1.411(c)-1 is amended by revising paragraph (f)(2) to read as follows:

§ 1.411(c)-1. Allocation of accrued benefits between employer and employee contributions.—

* * *

(f) *Suspension of benefits, etc.*—* * *

year beginning on or after January 1, 1989, for which such section is effective with respect to the plan; and

(B) Such plan amendments are adopted no later than the last day of the first plan year beginning on or after January 1, 1989, and are made effective retroactively for all periods for which the applicable section is effective with respect to the plan.

(ii) In the case of a collectively bargained plan described in paragraph (f)(2)(i) of this section that satisfies the requirements of paragraph (f)(3)(i) of this section (as modified by this paragraph (f)(3)(ii)), paragraph (f)(3)(i) shall be applied by substituting for "the first plan year beginning on or after January 1, 1989," the first plan year beginning on or after the later of—

(A) January 1, 1989, or

(B) The date on which the last of such collective bargaining agreements terminates (determined without regard to any extension of any such agreement occurring on or after March 1, 1986). However, notwithstanding the preceding sentence, section 411(b)(1)(H) and (b)(2) shall be applicable to plans described in this paragraph (f)(3)(ii) no later than the first plan year beginning on or after January 1, 1990. [Reg. § 1.411(b)-2.]

(2) *Employment after retirement.*—Except as permitted by paragraph (f)(1) of this section, a defined benefit plan must make an actuarial adjustment to an accrued benefit the payment of which is deferred past normal retirement age. See, also, section 411(b)(1)(H) (relating to continued accruals after normal retirement age) and § 1.411(b)-2.

Employers-Employees: Retirement Plans: Contributions: Allocation: Accrued Benefits

Employers-Employees: Retirement Plans: Contributions: Allocation: Accrued Benefits.— An amendment to Reg. § 1.411(c)-1, relating to guidance on calculation of an employee's accrued benefit derived from the employee's contributions to a qualified defined benefit pension plan, is proposed (published in the Federal Register on December 22, 1995).

☐ Par. 2. Section 1.411(c)-1 is amended by:

1. Revising paragraphs (c)(1), (c)(2), (c)(3), (c)(5) and (c)(6).
2. Revising paragraph (d).
3. Adding paragraph (g).

The additions and revisions read as follows:

§ 1.411(c)-1. Allocation of accrued benefits between employer and employee contributions.—

* * *

(c) *Accrued benefit derived from mandatory employee contributions to a defined benefit plan.*—(1) *General Rule.*—In the case of a defined benefit plan (as defined in section 414(j)), the accrued benefit derived from contributions made by an employee under the plan as of any applicable date in the form of an annual benefit commencing at normal retirement age and nondecreasing for the life of the participant is equal to the amount of the employee's accumulated contributions (determined under paragraph (c)(3) of this section) divided by the appropriate conversion factor with respect to that form of benefit (determined under paragraph (c)(2) of this section). Paragraph (e) of this section provides rules for actuarial adjustments where the benefit is to be determined in a form other than the form described in this paragraph (c)(1).

(2) *Appropriate conversion factor.*—For purposes of this paragraph, with respect to a form of annual benefit commencing at normal retirement age described in paragraph (c)(1), the term *appropriate conversion factor* means the present value of an annuity in the form of that annual benefit commencing at normal retirement age at a rate of $1 per year, computed using an interest rate and mortality table which would be used under the plan under section 417(e)(3) and § 1.417(e)-1T (as of the determination date).

(3) *Accumulated contributions.*—For purposes of section 411(c) and this section, the term *accumulated contributions* means the total of—

(i) All mandatory contributions made by the employee (determined under paragraph (c)(4) of this section);

(ii) Interest (if any) on such contributions, computed at the rate provided by the plan to the end of the last plan year to which section 411(a)(2) does not apply (by reason of the applicable effective dates);

(iii) Interest on the sum of the amounts determined under paragraphs (c)(3)(i) and (ii) of this section compounded annually at the rate of 5 percent per annum from the beginning of the first plan year to which section 411(a)(2) applies (by reason of the applicable effective date) to the beginning of the first plan year beginning after December 31, 1987;

(iv) Interest on the sum of the amounts determined under paragraphs (c)(3)(i) through (iii) of this section compounded annu-

ally at 120 percent of the Federal mid-term rate(s) (as in effect under section 1274(d) of the Internal Revenue Code for the first month of a plan year) for the period beginning with the first plan year beginning after December 31, 1987 and ending on the determination date; and

(v) Interest on the sum of the amounts determined under paragraphs (c)(3)(i) through (iv) of this section compounded annually, using an interest rate which would be used under the plan under section 417(e)(3) and § 1.417(e)-1T (as of the determination date), from the determination date to the date on which the employee would attain normal retirement age.

* * *

(5) *Determination date.*—(i) For purposes of section 411(c) and this section, in a case in which a participant will receive his or her entire accrued benefit derived from employee contributions in any one of the forms described in paragraph (c)(5)(ii), the term *determination date* means the date on which distribution of such benefit commences. Alternatively, in such a case, the plan may provide that the determination date is the annuity starting date with respect to that benefit, as defined in § 1.401(a)-20, Q&A-10.

(ii) Paragraph (c)(5)(i) applies to the following forms: an annuity that is substantially nonincreasing (e.g., an annuity that is nonincreasing except for automatic increases to reflect increases in the consumer price index), substantially nonincreasing installment payments for a fixed number of years, or a single sum distribution.

(iii) In a case in which a participant will receive a distribution that is not described in paragraph (c)(5)(i), the determination date will be as provided by the Commissioner.

(6) *Examples.*

(i) *Facts.* (A) In the following examples, Employer X maintains a qualified defined benefit plan that required mandatory employee contributions for 1987 and prior years, but not for years after 1987. The plan year is the calendar year. The plan provides for a normal retirement age of 65 and for 100 percent vesting in the employer-derived portion of a participant's accrued benefit after 5 years of service.

(B) The terms of the plan provide that the normal form of benefit is a level monthly amount commencing at normal retirement age and payable for the life of the participant. A plan participant who elects not to receive benefits in the form of the qualified joint and survivor annuity provided by the plan may elect to receive a single-sum distribution of the present value of his or her accrued benefit upon termination of employment.

(C) As of January 1, 1995, the plan was amended to provide that, for purposes of computing actuarially equivalent benefits, the single sum is calculated using the unisex version of the 1983 GAM mortality table (as provided in Revenue Ruling 95-6 (1995-1 C.B. 80)), and interest at the rate equal to the annual rate of interest on 30-year Treasury securities for the first calendar month preceding the first day of the plan year during which the annuity starting date occurs.

(D) Under the plan, employee contributions are accumulated at 3 percent interest for plan years beginning before 1976, 5 percent interest for plan years beginning after 1975 and before 1988, and interest at 120 percent of the Federal mid-term rate (as in effect under section 1274(d) for the first month of the plan year) for plan years beginning after 1987 until the determination date. Under the plan, the determination date is defined as the annuity starting date. For the period from the determination date until the date on which the employee attains normal retirement age, interest is credited at the interest rate which would be used under the plan under section 417(e)(3) as of the determination date.

(E) A, an unmarried participant, terminates employment with X on January 1, 1997 at age 56 with 15 years of service. As of December 31, 1987, A's total accumulated mandatory employee contributions to the plan, including interest compounded annually at 5 percent for plan years beginning after 1975 and before 1988, equaled $3,021. A receives his or her accrued benefit in the form of an annual single life annuity commencing at normal retirement age. A's annuity starting date is January 1, 2006, and therefore the determination date is January 1, 2006.

(ii) *Annuity at Normal Retirement Age—Determination of Employee-Derived and Total Plan Vested Accrued Benefit.*

Example 1.

For purposes of this example, it is assumed that A's total accrued benefit under the plan in the normal form of benefit commencing at normal retirement age is $2,949 per year. A's benefit, as of January 1, 2006, would be determined as follows:

(A) Determine A's total accrued benefit in the form of an annual single life annuity commencing at normal retirement age under the plan's formula ($2,949 per year payable at age 65).

(B) Determine A's accumulated contributions with interest to January 1, 1997. As of December 31, 1987, A's accumulated contributions with interest under the plan provisions were $3,021. A's employee contributions are accumulated from December 31, 1987 to January 1, 1997 using 120 percent of the Federal mid-term rate under section 1274(d). This rate is 10.61 percent for 1988, 11.11 percent for 1989, 9.57 percent for 1990, 9.78 percent for 1991, 8.10 percent for 1992, 7.63 percent for 1993, 6.40 percent for 1994, and 9.54 percent for 1995. It is assumed for purposes of this example that 120 percent of the Federal mid-term rate is 7.00 percent for each year between 1996 and 2006, and that the 30-year Treasury rate for December 2005 is 8.00 percent. Thus, A's contributions accumulated to January 1, 1997, equal $6,480.

(C) Determine A's accumulated contributions with interest to normal retirement age (January 1, 2006) using, for the 1996 plan year and for years until normal retirement age, 120 percent of the Federal mid-term rate under section 1274(d), which is assumed to be 7.00 percent ($11,913).

(D) Determine the accrued annual annuity benefit derived from A's contributions by dividing A's accumulated contributions

determined in paragraph (C) of this *Example 1* by the plan's appropriate conversion factor. The plan's appropriate conversion factor at age 65 is 9.196, and the accrued benefit derived from A's contributions would be $11,913 ÷ 9.196 = $1,295.

(E) Determine the accrued benefit derived from employer contributions as the excess, if any, of the employee's accrued benefit under the plan over the accrued benefit derived from employee contributions ($2,949 – $1,295 = $1,654 per year).

(F) Determine the vested percentage of the accrued benefit derived from employer contributions under the plan's vesting schedule (100 percent).

(G) Determine the vested accrued benefit derived from employer contributions by multiplying the accrued benefit derived from employer contributions by the vested percentage ($1,654 × 100 percent = $1,654 per year).

(H) Determine A's vested accrued benefit in the form of an annual single life annuity commencing at normal retirement age by adding the accrued benefit derived from employee contributions and the vested accrued benefit derived from employer contributions, the sum of paragraphs (D) and (G) of this *Example 1* ($1,295 + $1,654 = $2,949 per year).

Example 2.

This example assumes the same facts as *Example 1* except that A's total accrued benefit under the plan in the normal form of benefit commencing at normal retirement age is $1,000 per year. A's benefit, as of January 1, 2006, would be determined as follows:

(A) Determine A's total accrued benefit in the form of an annual single life annuity commencing at normal retirement age under the plan's formula ($1,000 per year payable at age 65).

(B) Determine A's accumulated contributions with interest to January 1, 1997 ($6,480 from paragraph (B) of *Example 1*).

(C) Determine A's accumulated contributions with interest to normal retirement age (January 1, 2006) ($11,913 from paragraph (C) of *Example 1*).

(D) Determine the accrued annual annuity benefit derived from A's contributions by dividing A's accumulated contributions determined in paragraph (C) of this *Example 2* by the plan's appropriate conversion factor ($1,295 from paragraph (D) of *Example 1*).

(E) Determine the accrued benefit derived from employer contributions as the excess, if any, of the employee's accrued benefit under the plan over the accrued benefit derived from employee contributions. Because the accrued benefit derived from employee contributions ($1,295) is greater than the employee's accrued benefit under the plan ($1,000), the accrued benefit derived from employer contributions is zero, and A's vested accrued benefit in the form of an annual single life annuity commencing at normal retirement age is $1,295 per year.

(d) *Delegation to Commissioner.*—The Commissioner may prescribe additional guidance on calculating the accrued benefit derived from employee contributions under a defined benefit plan through publication in the Internal Revenue Bulletin of revenue rulings, notices, or other documents (see § 601.601(d)(2) of this chapter).

(e) * * *

(f) * * *

(g) *Effective date.*—Paragraphs (c)(1), (c)(2), (c)(3), (c)(5), (c)(6) and (d) of this section are effective for plan years beginning on or after January 1, 1997.

Employee Trusts: Discrimination

Employee Trusts: Vesting Schedule: Discrimination.—Reproduced below is the text of proposed Reg. §1.411(d)-1, relating to a determination if the vesting schedule of a qualified plan discriminates in favor of employees who are officers, shareholders, or highly compensated (published in the Federal Register on April 9, 1980); modifications to proposed regulations (published in the Federal Register on June 12, 1980).

§1.411(d)-1. Coordination of vesting and discrimination requirements.—(a) *General rule.*—A plan which satisfies the requirements of section 411(a)(2) shall be treated as satisfying any vesting schedule requirements resulting from the application of section 401(a)(4) unless the plan is discriminatory within the meaning of section 411(d)(1) and this section. A plan is discriminatory if there is a pattern of abuse or there is discriminatory vesting as determined under paragraphs (b) and (c) of this section, respectively. Under section 401(a)(4), a plan which discriminates in favor of employees who are officers, shareholders, or highly compensated (hereinafter referred to as "prohibited group"), is not a qualified plan under section 401(a).

(b) *Pattern of abuse.*—(1) *Definition.*—A plan is discriminatory under section 411(d)(1)(A) and shall not be considered to satisfy the requirements of section 401(a)(4) if there has been a pattern of abuse under the plan tending to discriminate in favor of the prohibited group (hereinafter referred to as "pattern of abuse").

(2) *Test for pattern of abuse.*—The determination of whether there has been a pattern of abuse shall be made on the basis of the facts and circumstances of each case. An example of a pattern of abuse is the systematic dismissal of employees before their accrued benefits vest.

(c) *Discriminatory vesting.*—(1) *Definition.*—A plan is discriminatory under section 411(d)(1)(B) and shall not be considered to satisfy the requirements of section 401(a)(4) if there have been, or there is reason to believe there will be, an accrual of benefits or forfeitures tending to discriminate in favor of the prohibited group by operation of the vesting schedule (hereinafter referred to as "discriminatory vesting").

(2) *Test for discriminatory vesting.*—The determination of whether there is, or there is reason to believe there will be, discriminatory vesting shall be made on the basis of the facts and circumstances of each case. A reasonable disparity between the vested benefits paid to or accrued by the prohibited group and the vested

benefits paid to or accrued by other employees will not result in a finding that there is discriminatory vesting.

(d) [Withdrawn.]

(e) *Defined benefit plans.*—A defined benefit plan which satisfies the benefit accrual requirements of section 411(b) shall still be subject to the nondiscrimination requirements of section 401(a)(4) with re-

gard to its benefit accrual rates. Thus, even though a plan satisfies the section 411(b) requirements, the plan may still be discriminatory under section 401(a)(4) with respect to its benefit accruals.

(f) *Effective date.*—This section shall apply to plan years beginning 30 days after the publication of this section in the FEDERAL REGISTER as a Treasury decision. [Reg. §1.411(d)-1.]

Employees' Trusts: Minimum Funding Requirements

Employees' Trusts: Minimum Funding Requirements: Minimum Funding Excise Taxes.— Reproduced below are the texts of proposed Reg. §§1.412(a)-1, 1.412(b)-1 and 1.412(b)-4, 1.412(c)(2)-2, 1.412(c)(4)-1—1.412(c)(10)-1, 1.412(g)-1, proposed amendments to Reg. §§1.413-1 and 1.413-2, and the proposed deletions of Temporary Reg. §§11.412(c)-7, 11.412(c)-11 and 11.412(c)-12, relating to the minimum funding requirements for employee pension benefit plans, and to excise taxes for failure to meet the minimum funding standards (published in the Federal Register on December 1, 1982).

☐ Paragraph 1. The Income Tax Regulations, 26 CFR Part 1, are amended by adding the following new sections immediately after §1.411(d)-3:

§1.412(a)-1. General scope of minimum funding standard requirements.—(a) *General rule.*—Section 412 of the Code provides minimum funding requirements for plans that include a trust qualified under section 401(a) and for plans that meet the requirements of section 403(a) or section 405(a). Generally, such plans include defined benefit pension plans, money purchase pension plans (including target benefit plans), qualified annuity plans, and qualified bond purchase plans. The minimum funding requirements continue to apply to any plan that was qualified under, or was determined to have met the requirements of, these sections for any plan year beginning on or after the effective date described in paragraph (d) of this section for the plan. Also, under section 302 of the Employee Retirement Income Security Act of 1974 ("ERISA"), the minimum funding requirements apply to employee pension benefit plans described in section 301(a) of that Act. The regulations prescribed under this section and the following sections with respect to section 412 also apply for purposes of sections 302 and 305 of ERISA. These topics are among those discussed in the following sections: maintenance of a funding standard account (including rules for combining and off-setting amounts to be amortized, rules for computing interest on amounts charged and credited to the account, rules relating to the treatment of gains and losses, and rules relating to retroactive changes in the funding standard account required by the Commissioner), §1.412(b)-1; amortization of experience gains in connection with group deferred annuity contracts, §1.412(b)-2; funding standard account adjustments for plan mergers and spinoffs, §1.412(b)-3; plan terminations, §1.412(b)-4; election of the alternative amortization method of funding, §1.412(b)-5; determinations to be made under funding method, §1.412(c)(1)-1; shortfall method, §1.412(c)(1)-2; valuation of plan assets and reasonable valuation methods, §1.412(c)(2)-1; bond valuation election, §1.412(c)(2)-2; reasonable funding methods, §1.412(c)(3)-1 and -2; certain changes in accrued liability, §1.412(c)(4)-1; changes in funding method or plan year, §1.412(c)(5)-1; full funding and the full funding limitation, §1.412(c)(6)-1 and §1.412(c)(7)-1; retroactive plan amendment §1.412(c)(8)-1; frequency of actuarial valuations, §1.412(c)(9)-1; time for making contributions to satisfy section 412, §1.412(c)(10)-1; and maintenance of an alternative funding standard account, §1.412(g)-1.

(b) *Exceptions.*—See section 412(h) for a list of plans not subject to the requirements of section 412. These excepted plans include profit-sharing or stock bonus plans; certain insurance contract, government, and church plans; and certain plans that do not provide for employer contributions.

(c) *Failure to meet minimum funding standards.*—A plan fails to meet the minimum funding standards for a plan year if, as of the end of that plan year, there is an accumulated funding deficiency as defined in section 412(a) and §54.4971-1(d). See regulations under section 4971 for rules relating to taxes for failure to meet the minimum funding standards.

(d) *Effective date.*—(1) *In general.*—Unless otherwise provided, this section and the following sections providing regulations under section 412 apply to any plan year to which section 412 applies. For a plan in existence on January 1, 1974, section 412 generally applies to plan years beginning in 1976. However, this time is extended by special transitional rules under section 1017(c)(2) of ERISA for such existing plans under collective bargaining agreements. For a plan not in existence on January 1, 1974, section 412 generally applies for plan years beginning after September 2, 1974.

(2) *Date when plan is in existence.*—See §1.410(a)-2(c) for rules concerning the date when a plan is considered to be in existence.

(3) *Early application of section 412.*—See §1.410(a)-2(d) for rules permitting plans in existence on January 1, 1974, to elect to have section 412, as well as other provisions added by section 1013 of ERISA, apply to a plan year beginning after September 4, 1974, and before the effective date of the provision otherwise applicable to the plan.

(4) *Transitional rule.*—The regulations issued under sections §1.412(b)-1, §1.412(b)-3, §1.412(b)-4, §1.412(c)(2)-2, §1.412(c)(4)-1, §1.412(c)(5)-1, §1.412(c)(6)-1, §1.412(c)(7)-1, §1.412(c)(8)-1, §1.412(c)(9)-1, §1.412(c) (10)-1, and §1.412(g)-1, unless otherwise indicated, are effective with respect to a particular plan when section 412 first applies to that plan. However, for plan years beginning on or before [INSERT DATE 60 DAYS AFTER PUBLICATION OF THESE REGULATIONS AS A TREASURY DECISION IN THE FEDERAL REGISTER], the plan may rely on the prior published position of the Internal Revenue Service with respect to the application of section 412. Other effective dates are included in §1.412(b)-2, §1.412(c)(1)-2, §1.412(c)(2)-1, §1.412(c)(3)-2 and §1.412(i)-1. [Reg. §1.412(a)-1.]

§1.412(b)-1. Funding standard account.—(a) *General rule.*—Generally, for each single plan subject to the minimum funding standards there must be maintained a funding standard account as prescribed by section 412(b). (See §1.414(1)-1(b)(1) for definition of "single plan".) Such an account for a money purchase pension plan reflects charges for contributions required under the plan, credits for amounts contributed, and charges and credits for amortization bases described in paragraph (b)(3) of this section.

(b) *Definitions and special rules.*—(1) *Accounting date.*—(i) *In general.*—Each charge or credit to the funding standard account is charged or credited as of an accounting date. The accounting date for an item depends on the nature of the item and must be consistent with the computation of the amount of that item.

(ii) *Specific accounting dates.*—The accounting date for each individual charge for normal cost or any charge or credit for the amortization of an amortization base is the date as of which the charge or credit is computed as due during the plan year. The last day of the plan year is the accounting date for any credit described in section 412(b)(3)(C). The first day of the plan year is the accounting date for any credit described in section 412(b)(3)(D) or for any accumulated funding deficiency or credit balance existing as of the end of the prior plan year. The accounting date for each contribution is the date the contribution is made or, if made during the period described in section 412(c)(10), the last day of the plan year. Further, any contribution made must be credited as of the accounting date.

(2) *Valuation rate.*—The term "valuation rate" means the assumed interest rate used to value plan liabilities.

(3) *Amortization base.*—For purposes of this section, the term "amortization base" means any amount established under section 412(b)(2)(B), (C), or (D) to be amortized as a charge to the funding standard account, under section 412(b)(3)(B) to be amortized as a credit to the funding standard account, any other base resulting from a combination or offset of bases or any shortfall gain or loss base under §1.412(c)(1)-2. Any base required by the Commissioner to be established pursuant to an approved change in funding method is also an amortization base. Each amortization base established under one of the provisions enumerated above with respect to a particular year is referred to as an "individual base".

(4) *Amortization period.*—The amortization period for a base is the period of years stated in section 412(b)(2) or (3) over which a particular base is to be amortized. See §1.412(c)(1)-2(g)(2) and (h)(2) for amortization periods under the shortfall method. See section 412(b)(2) and (3) for amortization periods for bases described in those sections. See paragraph (d) of this section for amortization periods of bases resulting from a combination or offset of bases. If the number of years in the amortization period is not an integer, the charge or credit in the last year will not be for the entire amortization amount but will be for the outstanding balance of the base at the time of the charge or credit.

(5) *Outstanding balance.*—The outstanding balance of a base as of the end of a plan year equals the difference between two amounts:

(i) The first amount is the outstanding balance of the base as of the beginning of the plan year (or, if later, the date as of which the base is required to be established) increased by interest at the valuation rate.

(ii) The second amount is the charge (or credit) for that year for the base increased by interest at the valuation rate.

For purposes of testing the basic funding formula in §1.412(c)(3)-1(b)(1) the outstanding balance of amortizable bases must be computed as of the valuation date (the same date as of which the present value of future benefits and the present value of normal costs over the future working lifetime of participants are determined), rather than as of the end of the plan year. In testing the basic funding formula, the outstanding balance as of a valuation date equals the difference between two amounts. The first amount is the outstanding balance as of the preceding valuation date (or, if later, the date as of which the base is required to be established) increased by interest at the valuation rate. The second amount is the charge (or credit) for the plan year preceding the plan year to which the current valuation refers increased by interest at the valuation rate.

(6) *Remaining amortization period.*—The remaining amortization period for an amortization base is the difference between the amortization period and the number of years (including whole and fractional years) for which the base has been reduced by charging or crediting the funding standard account, as the case may be, with the amortization payment for each year.

(7) *Amortization amount.*—The amortization amount is the amount of the charge or credit to the funding standard account required with respect to an amortization base for a plan year.

(8) *True and absolute values.*—See §1.404(a)-14(b)(4) for a definition of the terms "true value" and "absolute value."

(9) *Immediate gain type funding method.*—A funding method is an immediate gain type method if, under the method—

(i) The accrued liability may be determined solely from the computations with respect to the liabilities;

(ii) The accrued liability is an integral part of the funding method; and

(iii) The accrued liability is the excess of the present value, as of any valuation date, of the projected future benefit costs for all plan participants and beneficiaries over the present value of future contributions for the normal cost of all current plan participants. Examples of the immediate gain type of funding method are the unit credit method, the entry-age normal cost method, and the individual level premium method.

(10) *Spread gain type funding method.*—A funding method is a spread gain type method if it is not an immediate gain type method. Examples of the spread gain type of funding method are the aggregate cost method, the frozen initial liability cost method and the attained age normal cost method.

(11) *Actual unfunded liability for immediate gain funding methods.*—(i) *In general.*—For a funding method of the immediate gain type, the actual unfunded liability as of any valuation date is the excess, if any, of the accrued liability over the actuarial value of assets as of that date.

(ii) *Accrued liability.*—The accrued liability is equal to the present value of future benefits less the present value of future normal costs. Generally, for purposes of computing costs for a plan year and gains and losses for a plan year, the normal cost for the plan year to which the valuation refers is considered to be a future normal cost and is not included in the accrued liability.

(iii) *Actuarial value of assets.*—The value of assets must be determined in a manner consistent with section 412(c)(2) of the Code and §1.412(c)(2)-1. Furthermore, for purposes of computing costs for a plan year and gains and losses for a plan year, the assets must be treated in a manner that is consistent with the method of calculation of the accrued liability. If, in determining the accrued liability, the normal cost for the plan year to which the valuation refers is treated as a future normal cost, then the assets used to compute the unfunded accrued liability should not include contributions that are credited to the funding standard account for the plan year to which the valuation refers or for any plan year thereafter.

(12) *Actual unfunded liability for spread gain funding methods.*—For a funding method of the spread gain type that maintains an unfunded liability, the actual unfunded liability equals the expected unfunded liability.

(13) *Expected unfunded liability.*—The expected unfunded liability as of any valuation date is determined as:

(i) The actual unfunded liability as of the prior valuation date increased with interest at the valuation rate of this later valuation date, plus

(ii) Normal costs representing accrued liabilities that were not included in determining the accrued liability as of the prior valuation date (*i.e.,* such costs were considered future normal costs as of the prior valuation date) but that are included (*i.e.,* are not considered future normal costs) in determining the accrued liability as of this later valuation date, plus interest at the valuation rate from the date as of which the normal costs were assumed payable to this valuation date, minus

(iii) The amount considered contributed by the employer to or under the plan for the plan year that was included in the calculation of the actual unfunded liability as of the prior valuation date and was included in the calculation of the actual unfunded liability as of this later valuation date, plus interest at the valuation rate from the date on which the contribution was made if made during the plan year, or under section 412(c)(10) was deemed to have been made if made after the plan year, to this later valuation date.

(14) *Plan year to which a valuation refers.*—The plan year for which the funding standard account is charged with the first normal cost determined by a valuation is the plan year to which the valuation refers. See also §1.412(c)(9)-1(b) concerning the date of a valuation.

(c) *Establishment and maintenance of amortization bases.*—(1) *Immediate gain type funding methods.*—Under a plan using an immediate gain type funding method, a new amortization base must be established to reflect each change in unfunded past service liability arising from a plan amendment, net experience gain or loss, and change in unfunded past service liability arising from a change in funding method or actuarial assumptions.

(2) *Spread gain type funding methods.*—(i) *In general.*—Under a plan using a spread gain type funding method, amortization bases may be established to reflect changes in unfunded past service liability arising from plan amendments or changes in actuarial assumptions. Alternatively, these changes in unfunded liability may be reflected in the normal cost. Whether these changes are reflected in amortization bases or in the normal cost is part of the funding method. Thus, any change from past practice constitutes a change in funding method and must be approved under section 412(c)(5). Furthermore, the method must treat increases and decreases due to any type of event consistently.

(ii) *Experience gain or loss.*—An amortization base may not be established to reflect a net experience gain or loss under a plan using a spread gain type funding method.

(3) *Special amortization bases.*—Any amortization base established to amortize a waived funding deficiency under section 412(b)(2)(C) must continue to be maintained regardless of the type of funding method used by the plan. Also see §1.412(b)-1(d)(1).

(d) *Combining and offsetting amounts to be amortized.*—(1) *In general.*—Under section 412(b)(4), individual bases, with the exception of bases under section 412(b)(2)(C), may be combined and offset to form a single base. This single base is computed under the provisions of paragraph (d) that follow. However, any number of amortization bases having the same remaining amortization period may be combined and offset simply by adding the outstanding balances of the individual bases, using true rather than absolute values, without regard to the computations under paragraph (d) of this section that follow. Bases under section 412(b)(2)(C) may not be combined with any bases not established under section 412(b)(2)(C).

(2) *Combined outstanding balances of bases for charges and for credits.*—Except as provided in subparagraph (1), the outstanding balances of any individual bases established for the purpose of charging the funding standard account may be combined as of any date by adding the outstanding balance of each base to be combined as of that date. Likewise, the outstanding balances of any bases for crediting the account may be combined.

(3) *Determine remaining amortization period of each combined base.*—The remaining amortization period of a combined base is determined as follows:

(i) Add the amortization amounts, based on the same mode of payment, for the individual bases being combined. Amortization amounts are of the same mode of payment if they are charged or credited on the same day of the plan year, or on the same days if charged or credited in installments during the plan year.

(ii) Divide the outstanding balance of the combined base by the combined amortization amount determined under subdivision (i).

(iii) Compute the period of years for which the amount determined under subdivision (ii) provides an annuity certain of $1 per year at the valuation rate. This number, the remaining amortization period, must be computed in terms of fractional years, if necessary. Standard present value tables may be used together with linear interpolation.

(iv) As an alternative, the amortization period may be rounded to the next lowest integer (if charge bases) or next highest integer (if credit bases) and the amortization amount must then be recomputed by dividing the outstanding balance of the combined base by the present value of an annuity certain of $1 per year at the valuation rate for the rounded amortization period.

(4) *Offset.*—Combined bases may be offset only if all charge and credit bases have been combined (except those that may not be combined pursuant to subparagraph (1)). The combined charge base and the combined credit base are offset by subtracting the lesser outstanding balance from the greater outstanding balance. The difference between these two outstanding balances is amortized over the remaining amortization period for the greater of the two outstanding balances, whether for charges or for credits. The amortization

Base	Outstanding balance (beginning of year)
(i) *Individual bases.*	
A	$165,468
B	8,863
C	(4,153)
D	(30,745)
(ii) *Combined bases.*	
AB	$174,331
CD	(34,898)
(iii) *Offset base.*	
ABCD	$139,433

(iv) The outstanding balances of the charge and credit bases were combined in step (ii) by adding outstanding balances of the like bases (165,468 + 8,863 = 174,331 and 4,153 + 30,745 = 34,898). The charge and credit base amortization amounts were similarly computed (10,000 + 1,000 = 11,000 and 500 + 2,000 = 2,500). The remaining amortization periods were derived from standard present value tables and linear interpolation as the amount having a present value at the 5 percent valuation rate for a $1 per year annuity certain equal to the ratio of the outstanding balance to the amortization amount.

(v) The combined bases were offset in step (iii) by subtracting base CD from AB to obtain the $139,433 outstanding balance, using the 32.23 remaining amortization period for base AB, and computing the $8,798 amortization amount as the level annual amount necessary to amortize the base fully over 32.23 years. (Alternatively, the amortization period may be rounded to 32 years. The amortization charge corresponding to that amortization period is $8,823.)

(e) *Interest.*—(1) *General rule.*—The funding standard account is charged or credited with interest at the valuation rate for the time between the accounting date for the item giving rise to the interest charge or credit and the end of the plan year.

(2) *Change of interest rate.*—A change of the assumed interest rate under a plan does not affect the outstanding balance or the remaining amortization period of any existing base. However, the amortization amount for each base is increased to reflect an increase in interest and decreased to reflect a decrease in interest so that the present value of future amortization amounts equals the outstanding balance of the base. This change is made in addition to creating any new base required by § 1.412(b)-1(c).

(f) *Gains and losses.*—(1) *Amortization requirements.*—(i) *Immediate gain type funding method.*—A plan that uses an immediate gain type of funding method separately amortizes experience gains and losses over the period prescribed in section 412(b)(2)(B)(iv) and (3)(B)(ii). The first year of the amortization of an experience gain or loss determined as of a particular valuation date is the plan year to which the valuation refers.

(ii) *Spread gain type funding method.*—A plan that uses a spread gain type of funding method spreads experience gains and losses over future periods as a part of the plan's normal cost. These gains and losses are reflected in the amount charged to the funding standard account under section 412(b)(2)(A) and are not separately amortized.

(2) *Amount of experience gain or loss.*—(i) *In general.*—For an immediate gain type of funding method the experience gain determined as of a valuation date is the excess of the expected unfunded liability described in § 1.412(b)-1(b)(13) over the actual unfunded liability described in § 1.412(b)-1(b)(11). The experience loss is the excess of the actual unfunded liability described in § 1.412(b)-1(b)(11) over the expected unfunded liability described in § 1.412(b)-1(b)(13).

(ii) *Special rule.*—Paragraph (f)(2)(ii) of this section applies to an immediate gain funding method if there are no other amortization charges (under section 412(b)(2)(B), (C), or (D)) or credits (under

amount (charge or credit) for this offset base is the level amount payable for each plan year to reduce the outstanding balance of the base to zero over the remaining amortization period at the valuation rate. However, see paragraph (d)(3)(iv) of this section concerning an alternative method of computing the remaining amortization period.

(5) *Example.*—The principles of paragraph (d) of this section are illustrated by the following example.

Example. Assume that at the beginning of a plan year the actuary for a plan decides to combine and offset the amortization bases as reflected in the plan's funding standard account. No funding deficiency of the plan has been waived. All amortization amounts are due at the end of the plan year. The valuation rate is 5 percent. Based on pertinent information from the plan records, all amortization bases, A and B for charges and C and D for credits, are combined and offset as follows:

Amortization amount (due end of year)	Remaining amortization period
$10,000	36
1,000	12
(500)	11
(2,000)	30
$11,000	32.23
(2,500)	24.53
$8,798	32.23

section 412(b)(3)(B)) for the first plan year in which the loss will be amortized. The experience loss as of the valuation date is the sum of—

(A) The actual unfunded liability as of the valuation date, plus

(B) Any credit balance (or minus any funding deficiency) in the funding standard account as of the first day of the first plan year in which the loss will be amortized adjusted with interest at the valuation rate to the valuation date.

(g) *Certain retroactive changes required by Commissioner.*—Under section 412(c)(3), all costs, liabilities, rates of interest, and other factors under the plan must be determined on the basis of actuarial assumptions and methods which, in the aggregate, are reasonable. Assumptions and methods are established in the first Schedule B (Form 5500) that is filed with respect to a plan year and may not be changed for that plan year. However, upon a determination by the Commissioner that the actuarial assumptions and methods used by a plan are not reasonable in the aggregate, the Commissioner may require certain retroactive adjustments to the funding standard account of the plan. The funding standard account must reflect these changes, as required by the Commissioner.

(h) *Reasonable actuarial assumptions.*—(1) *In general.*—The determination whether actuarial assumptions are reasonable in the aggregate is generally based upon the experience under the plan, unless it is established that past experience is not likely to recur and thus is not a good indication of future experience. In addition, assumptions may be considered unreasonable in the circumstances described in paragraphs (h)(2)-(4) of this section.

(2) *No counterbalancing assumptions.*—Assumptions may be considered unreasonable if an assumption used by the plan is not yet reflected in the experience of the plan, is not reasonable under the circumstances of the plan, and is not counterbalanced by another assumption. For example, if a plan with one participant who has not yet attained the normal retirement age, an assumption of an unreasonable annuity purchase rate at normal retirement age may cause assumptions to be unreasonable in the aggregate. In contrast, an unreasonable annuity purchase rate could be counterbalanced by a change in the plan interest rate.

(3) *Inconsistent with benefit structure.*—Assumptions may be unreasonable if use of an assumption is inconsistent with the benefit structure of the plan. For example, a plan which provides benefits not based on compensation may not assume a salary increase if it spreads the present value of future normal costs over the present value of future compensation.

(4) *Inconsistent assumptions.*—Assumptions may be considered unreasonable in the aggregate if one plan assumption is inconsistent with other assumptions used by the plan. For example, an assumption which projects benefits based on a salary increase of 5-percent per year may cause assumptions to be unreasonable in the aggregate in a plan which spreads normal costs over future years' compensation using an assumption of 8-percent annual compensation increases. [Reg. § 1.412(b)-1.]

□ Par. 2. The Income Tax Regulations, 26 CFR Part 1, are amended by adding the following new sections after § 1.412(b)-2:

§ 1.412(b)-3. Funding standard account adjustments for plan mergers and spinoffs.—[RESERVED]

§ 1.412(b)-4. Plan termination and plan years of less than twelve months.—(a) *General rules.*—The minimum funding standard under section 412 applies to a plan until the end of the plan year in which the plan terminates. Therefore, the funding standard account (or the alternative funding standard account, as the case may be) must be maintained until the end of the plan year in which the plan terminates even though the plan terminates before the last day of the plan year.

(b) *Defined benefit plans.*—In the case of a defined benefit plan, the charges and credits to the funding standard account are adjusted ratably to reflect the portion of the plan year before the day of plan termination. Similarly, annual charges and credits to the funding standard account are adjusted for a short plan year. However, this ratable adjustment is not made for charges described in section 412(b)(2)(C), credits under section 412(b)(3)(A), (C), and (D), for interest charges and credits under section 412(b)(5), and for credits under section 412(c)(6).

(c) *Money purchase pension plans.*—(1) *General rule for termination.*—In the case of a money purchase pension plan, the minimum funding standard requires the funding standard account to be charged with the entire amount of any contribution due on or before the date of plan termination. However, it does not require a charge for contributions due after that date.

(2) *General rule for short plan year.*—In the case of a money purchase pension plan, the minimum funding standard requires the funding standard account to be charged with the entire amount of any contribution due as of a date within a short plan year.

(3) *Due date of contributions.*—For purposes of paragraphs (c)(1) and (2) of this section, a contribution is due as of the earlier of—

(i) The date specified in the plan, or

(ii) The date as of which the contribution is required to be allocated.

(4) *Date for allocation of contribution.*—For purposes of paragraph (c)(3)(ii) of this section, a contribution is required to be allocated as of a date if all the requirements for the allocation have been satisfied as of that date.

(d) *Date of plan termination.*—(1) *Title IV plans.*—In the case of a plan subject to Title IV of ERISA, the date of plan termination is generally the date described in section 4048 of ERISA. However, if that date precedes the tenth day after the date on which notice of intent to terminate is filed, and if any contributions made or required by Code section 412 to avoid an accumulated funding deficiency for the period ending on such tenth day would increase any participant's benefits upon termination (taking benefits guaranteed by the Pension Benefit Guaranty Corporation into account), the date of termination will be the tenth day after the date on which notice of intent to terminate is filed.

(2) *Other plans.*—In the case of a plan not subject to Title IV of ERISA, the date of plan termination occurs no earlier than the date on which the actions necessary to effect the plan termination are taken. The determination of this date is based on the facts and circumstances of each case.

(e) *Partial terminations.*—This section does not apply to a partial plan termination within the meaning of section 411(d)(3)(A).

(f) *Funding excise taxes.*—See § 54.4971-3(d) of the Pension Excise Tax Regulations (26 CFR Part 54) for the effect of plan termination on an employer's liability for taxes imposed by section 4971(a) and (b). [Reg. § 1.412(b)-4.]

□ Par. 3. The Income Tax Regulations, 26 CFR Part 1, are amended by adding the following new section after § 1.412(c)(2)-1:

§ 1.412(c)(2)-2. Bond valuation election.—(a) *Scope of election.*—(1) *In general.*—The election described in section 412(c)(2)(B) with respect to bonds generally applies to all bonds and evidences of indebtedness including those acquired by merger. The election applies only to defined benefit plans. A defined contribution plan must value bonds and other evidences of indebtedness on the basis of fair market value.

(2) *Exception.*—The election does not apply to bonds or evidences of indebtedness at any time that they are in default as to principal or interest.

(3) *Convertible debt.*—For purposes of this section, a debt instrument which is convertible into an equity security and acquired after [THE DATE 90 DAYS AFTER THE DATE ON WHICH § 1.412(c)(2)-2 IS ADOPTED AS A TREASURY DECISION]is treated as an evidence of indebtedness until the conversion occurs.

(b) *Effect of election.*—(1) *In general.*—The effect of the election is that bonds and other evidences of indebtedness included among the plan assets are valued on an amortized basis rather than on a fair market value basis.

(2) *Amount amortized.*—(i) *In general.*—The amount amortized with respect to a bond or other evidence of indebtedness is generally the difference between its initial cost when acquired by the plan and its redemption value at the end of the amortization period. In the case of a bond or other evidence of indebtedness that was acquired by the plan in a plan year before the plan year for which the election was made, the amortized value for each year must be determined as though the election had always been in effect with respect to the bond or other evidence of indebtedness.

(ii) *Spinoffs.*—The amount amortized after a spinoff is based on the initial cost to the plan which acquired the bond or other evidence of indebtedness and not the value to the plan after the spinoff.

(iii) *Mergers.*—The amount amortized after a merger is based on the cost to the plan which first elected to value the bonds and other evidences of indebtedness on an amortized basis. In the case of a bond or other evidence of indebtedness that was acquired by any merging plan before the election was first made with respect to the bond or other evidence of indebtedness, the premium or discount shall be amortized as provided in paragraph (b)(2)(i).

(3) *Amortization period.*—The amortization period is the time from the date on which the plan acquires the bond or other evidence of indebtedness to its maturity date (or, in the case of a debt instrument that is callable prior to maturity, the earliest call date).

(c) *Effect of default.*—Once the election is made, it applies to each debt instrument held or acquired that is not in default as to principal or interest. While in default, the instrument is subject to the fair market value requirements of section 412(c)(2)(A).

(d) *Manner of making election.*—The plan administrator makes the election by preparing a statement that the election described in section 412(c)(2)(B) is being made and by filing the statement attached to the annual return required under section 6058 for the first plan year for which the election is to apply.

(e) *Revocation of election.*—(1) *Effect.*—Once consent to the revocation of the election is obtained as prescribed in paragraph (e)(2) of this section, all plan assets are valued under section 412(c)(2)(A).

(2) *Consent.*—Consent for the revocation of the election must be obtained in the manner prescribed by the Commissioner for obtaining permission to change funding methods under section 412(c)(5) and § 1.412(c)(5)-1.

(3) *Mergers.*—A plan which has acquired a bond or other evidence of indebtedness by merger must obtain the consent of the Commissioner to value bonds and other evidences of indebtedness on a basis other than amortized value if an election under section 412(c)(2)(B) with respect to the asset acquired had been made prior to the merger. [Reg. § 1.412(c)(2)-2.]

□ Par. 4. The Income Tax Regulations, 26 CFR Part 1, are amended by adding the following new sections after § 1.412(c)(3)-2:

§ 1.412(c)(4)-1. Certain changes in accrued liability.—(a) *In general.*—In the case of immediate gain type funding methods, section 412(c)(4) treats certain increases and decreases in the accrued liability under a plan as an experience gain or loss. Plans using a spread gain

type of funding method will reflect the gain or loss in determining the normal cost under the plan. Under section 412(b)(2) and (3), plans which are valued using a funding method of the immediate gain type will amortize the amount treated as an experience gain or loss in equal amounts over the period described in section 412(b). See §1.412(b)-1(b) (9) and (10) for examples of spread gain type and immediate gain type funding methods.

(b) *Applicable changes.*—A change treated as an experience gain or loss under section 412(c)(4) includes an increase or decrease in accrued liability caused by:

(1) A change in benefits under the Social Security Act,

(2) A change in other retirement benefits created under Federal or State law,

(3) A change in the definition of "wages" under section 3121, or

(4) A change in the amount of wages under section 3121 that are taken into account for purposes of section 401(a)(5) and the regulations thereunder. [Reg. §1.412(c)(4)-1.]

§1.412(c)(5)-1. Change in plan year or funding method.—Approval given under section 412(c)(5) authorizes a change in plan year or funding method. Written requests for approval are to be submitted, as directed by the Commissioner, to Commissioner of Internal Revenue, Attention: OP:E:A:P, 1111 Constitution Avenue, N.W., Washington, D.C. 20224. Such a request must be submitted before the close of the plan year for which the change is to be effective unless an extension of time for filing the request is granted. [Reg. §1.412(c)(5)-1.]

§1.412(c)(6)-1. Full funding and full funding limitation.—(a) *In general.*—This section provides rules relating to full funding and the full funding limitation under section 412(c)(6) and (7). The full funding limitation for a plan year is the excess, if any, of the accrued liability under the plan plus the normal cost for the plan year over the value of the plan's assets.

(b) *Valuation.*—(1) *Timing rule.*—For purposes of this section, assets and accrued liabilities are to be valued at the usual time used by the plan for valuations.

(2) *Interest adjustments.*—If the valuation is performed before the end of the plan year, the assets and accrued liabilities (including normal cost) are projected to the end of the plan year. The projection is based on the valuation rate.

(c) *Calculation of accrued liability.*—The accrued liability of a plan is determined under the funding method used by the plan. However, if the funding method used by the plan is not an immediate gain method and, thus, does not directly calculate an accrued liability, the calculation of the accrued liability is made under the entry age normal funding method.

(d) *Calculation of normal cost.*—In general, the normal cost is the normal cost determined under the funding method used by the plan. However, if under paragraph (c) accrued liability is calculated under the entry age normal cost method, then the normal cost is also calculated under the entry age normal cost method.

(e) *Calculation of assets.*—The value of plan assets used to determine the full funding limitation is the lesser of the fair market value of the assets or the actuarial value of the assets, if different. The value of plan assets must be reduced by any credit balance existing on the first day of the plan year.

(f) *Effect of full funding on deduction limits.*—See §1.404(a)-14(k) for provisions relating to the effect of the full funding limitation on the maximum deductible contribution limitations and 10-year amortization bases under section 404(a).

(g) *Effect of the full funding limitation on the funding standard account.*—(1) *General rule.*—If, as of the end of any plan year, the accumulated funding deficiency (calculated without regard to any credit balance for the plan year or any contributions made for that plan year) exceeds the full funding limitation of section 412(c)(7) calculated as of the valuation date and projected, if necessary, to the end of the plan year, then the following adjustments are made:

(i) The amount of such excess is credited to the funding standard account for that plan year.

(ii) As of the end of that plan year, all the amounts described in paragraphs (2)(B), (C), (D), and (3)(B) of section 412(b) which are required to be amortized shall be considered fully amortized.

(2) *Example.*—The principles of section 412(c)(6) and of paragraph (e) of this section are illustrated in the following example:

Example. Assume that a single employer plan is established on January 1, 1976, with a calendar plan year. The funding method is the accrued benefit cost method (unit credit method), the interest assumption is 5 percent, and both the normal cost and the amortization charges and credits are calculated on the basis of payment at the beginning of the year. The annual charge to the funding standard

account due to the amortization (over 30 years) of the initial past service liability is $200, and the annual credit due to the amortization (over 15 years) of a 1979 experience gain is $10. A valuation is performed as of January 1, 1985, to determine costs for the 1985 plan year. There was a credit balance of $100 in the funding standard account on December 31, 1984. As of January 1, 1985, plan assets (determined in accordance with section 412(c)(7)(B) and reduced by the $100 credit balance as of January 1, 1985) were $10,400; the accrued liability under the plan was $10,000; the normal cost (for the 1985 plan year) was $1,200; and the 1985 employer contribution (made as of January 1, 1985) was $1,000. The accumulated funding deficiency (calculated ignoring the credit balance and employer contribution) as of December 31, 1985, is $1,459.50, determined as the excess of charges of $1,470 ($1,200 normal cost, plus $200 amortization charge, plus $70 interest) over the credits of $10.50 ($10 amortization credit, plus $.50 interest). The full funding limitation as of the valuation date (January 1, 1985) is $800, determined as the excess of the sum of the accrued liability ($10,000) plus normal cost ($1,200) over the adjusted plan assets ($10,400). The value of this $800 as of the end of the year (i.e., December 31, 1985) is $800 plus $40 interest, or $840.00. The excess, as of the end of the 1985 plan year, of the accumulated funding deficiency over the full funding limitation is thus $1,459.50 minus $840.00, or $619.50. The funding standard account is charged and credited as follows:

Charges

Normal cost	$1,200.00
Amortization charge	200.00
Interest	70.00
Total	$1,470.00

Credits

Credit balance	$100.00
Contribution	1,000.00
Amortization credit	10.00
Interest	55.50
Sec. 412(c)(6) credit	619.50
Total	$1,784.50
Credit balance December 31, 1985	$314.50

[Reg. §1.412(c)(6)-1.]

§1.412(c)(7)-1. Full funding limitation.—See §1.412(c)(6)-1 for rules relating both to full funding under section 412(c)(6) and to the full funding limitation under section 412(c)(7). [Reg. §1.412(c)(7)-1.]

§1.412(c)(8)-1. Election to treat certain retroactive plan amendments as made on first day of a plan year.—The function of the Secretary of Labor described in section 412(c)(8) was transferred to the Secretary of Treasury as of December 31, 1978, by Reorganization Plan No. 4 of 1978, 1979-1 C.B. 480. Therefore, the material described in section 412(c)(8) now must be filed as directed by the Secretary of Treasury. [Reg. §1.412(c)(8)-1.]

§1.412(c)(9)-1. Frequency of actuarial valuations.—(a) *Required valuation.*—Section 412(c)(9) requires an actuarial valuation not less frequently than once every three years. Paragraph (b) of this section provides general rules for performing valuations. Paragraph (d) describes certain situations in which the Commissioner may require an actuarial valuation more frequently than once every three years. These rules may be waived at the discretion of the Commissioner and do not apply to multiemployer plans within the meaning of section 414(f).

(b) *General rules for valuations.*—(1) *Date of valuation.*—Except as provided by the Commissioner, the valuation must be as of a date within the plan year to which the valuation refers or within the one month prior to that year. All assets and liabilities must be valued as of the same date. The valuation must use data as of the valuation date; it is not permissible to use adjusted data from a prior or subsequent year.

(2) *Use of prior valuations.*—A plan may not use a valuation for any subsequent plan year if that valuation was not also used for the year to which it refers. Also, a prior valuation may not be used if the plan has used any subsequent valuation for another plan year.

(c) *Funding standard account rules for years when there is no valuation.*—(1) *Amortization of bases.*—After an amortization base is established, the amortization amount of that base is charged or credited in each plan year, whether or not a valuation is performed for the year, until the outstanding balance of the base is zero. However, see §1.412(c)(6)-1 for rules for years after a full funding limitation credit and §1.412(b)-1 for combining and offsetting bases.

(2) *Normal cost.*—If valuations are performed less frequently than every year, then any valuation computes the normal cost for the year to which the valuation refers and for subsequent years until another valuation applies. In those subsequent years, the normal cost is—

(i) If the funding method computes normal cost as a level dollar amount, the same dollar amount as for the year to which the valuation refers;

(ii) If the funding method computes normal cost as a level percentage of pay, the same percentage of current pay as for the year to which the valuation refers, or

(iii) If the funding method computes normal cost as an amount equal to the present value of benefits accruing under the method for the year, under any reasonable method.

The rules in subdivisions (i) and (ii) apply whether the funding method computes normal cost on either an individual or an aggregate basis.

(d) *Situations when more frequent valuations are required.*—(1) *Amendments increasing actuarial costs.*—(i) *General rule.*—A valuation is required for any plan year when a plan amendment first increases the actuarial costs of a plan. For this purpose, actuarial costs consist of the plan's normal cost under section 412(b)(2)(A), amortization charges under section 412(b)(2)(B), and amortization credits under section 412(b)(3)(B).

(ii) *Exception.*—No valuation will be required under paragraph (d)(1)(i) of this section if two conditions are met: first, the plan actuary estimates that the cost increase attributable to the amendment is less than 5 percent of the actuarial cost determined without regard to the amendment; and second, the actuary files a signed statement to that effect with the annual return required under section 6058 for the year of the amendment.

(2) *Certain changes in number of participants.*—(i) *General rule.*—A valuation is required for a plan year when the actual number of plan participants that would be considered in the current valuation differs from the number of participants that were considered in the prior valuation by more than 20 percent of that number.

(ii) *Exception.*—Notwithstanding subdivision (i), no valuation will be required merely because of a change in the number of estimated participants under a plan that determines normal cost as a level percentage of payroll (on either an individual or aggregate basis) or as a level dollar amount per individual.

(iii) *Plans using shortfall method.*—No valuation will be required merely because of a change in the number of estimated participants under a plan which uses the shortfall method described in §1.412(c)(1)-2. However, a valuation is required for a plan year if the estimated units of service or production ("estimated base units" under §1.412(c)(1)-2(e)) for the prior plan year exceeds the actual number of units of service or production for that plan year by more than 20 percent.

(3) *Change in actuarial funding method or assumptions.*—A valuation is required for any plan year with respect to which a change in the funding method or actuarial assumptions of a plan is made.

(4) *Mergers and spinoffs.*—(i) *General rule.*—A valuation is required for any plan year in which a plan merger or spinoff occurs.

(ii) *Safe harbor for mergers.*—In the case of a merger, no valuation will be required under paragraph (d)(4) of this section if the de minimis rule in §1.414(1)-1(h) is satisfied.

(iii) *Safe harbor for spinoffs.*—In the case of a spinoff, no valuation will be required under paragraph (d)(4) of this section if the present value of all the benefits being spun off from the plan during the plan year is less than 3 percent of the plan's assets as of the beginning of the year.

(5) *Change in average age of participants.*—(i) *General rule.*—A valuation is required for any plan year with respect to which the average age of plan participants changes significantly, within the meaning of subdivisions (ii) and (iii), from the average age of plan participants at the last valuation.

(ii) *Rule for large plans.*—For a plan with 100 or more participants, an increase or decrease in average age of more than two years is a significant change.

(iii) *Rule for small plans.*—For a plan with fewer than 100 participants, an increase or decrease in average age of more than four years is a significant change.

(6) *Alternative minimum funding standard account.*—A valuation is required for each year for which the plan uses the alternative minimum funding standard account.

(7) *Deductibility considerations.*—A valuation is required when it appears that the full funding limitation has been reached for purposes of determining the maximum deductible contribution limitations of section 404(a).

(8) *Other situations.*—The Commissioner may require valuations in other situations as the facts and circumstances warrant. [Reg. §1.412(c)(9)-1.]

§1.412(c)(10)-1. Time for making contributions to satisfy section 412.—(a) *General rule.*—Under section 412(c)(10), a contribution made after the end of a plan year but no later than two and one-half months after the end of that year is deemed to have been made on the last day of that year.

(b) *Extension of general rule.*—(1) *Plan years ending before* [90 DAYS AFTER PUBLICATION DATE OF FINAL REGULATIONS].—For plan years ending before [90 DAYS AFTER PUBLICATION OF FINAL REGULATIONS], for purposes of section 412 a contribution for such a plan year that is made not later than eight and one-half months after the end of that plan year is deemed to have been made on the last day of that year.

(2) *Plan years ending on or after* [90 DAYS AFTER PUBLICATION OF FINAL REGULATIONS].—(i) *Transitional rule.*—The two and one-half month period provided in section 412(c)(10) and §1.410(c)(10)-1(a) is extended for each of the first three plan years ending after [90 DAYS AFTER PUBLICATION OF FINAL REGULATIONS]. For the first plan year ending after [90 DAYS AFTER PUBLICATION OF FINAL REGULATIONS], a contribution made not later than eight and one-half months after the end of that plan year is deemed to have been made on the last day of that year. For the second year, the two and one-half month period is extended to six and one-half months, and for the third year, the two and one-half month period is extended to four and one-half months.

(ii) *Extensions of general and transitional periods.*—The time for making contributions under the general rule described in paragraph (a) and transitional rule of paragraph (b)(2)(i) of this section may be extended to a date not beyond eight and one-half months after the end of the plan year. Extensions of the two and one-half month period and transitional years' periods are granted on an individual basis by the Commissioner. A request for extension should be submitted to the Commissioner of Internal Revenue, 1111 Constitution Avenue, N.W., Washington, D.C. 20224 (Attention OP:E:A).

(c) *Effect on section 404.*—The rules of this section, relating to the timing of contributions for purposes of section 412, operate independently from the rules under section 404(a)(6), relating to the timing of contributions for purposes of claiming a deduction under section 404. [Reg. §1.412(c)(10)-1.]

§1.412(g)-1. Alternative minimum funding standard account.—(a) *In general.*—A plan that maintains an alternative minimum funding standard account ("ASA") for any plan year under section 412(g) must satisfy the requirements of this section. To use the ASA, a plan must use a funding method that requires contributions for all years that are not less than those required under the entry age normal cost method of funding. A funding method does not affect the actual cost of plan benefits but only the incidence of contributions in different years. Thus, any funding method that requires a contribution in one year that exceeds that required by the entry age normal method (EAN) for that year must require a lesser contribution in another year. Hence, only a plan which uses the EAN cost method may use the ASA.

(b) *Special rules.*—(1) *Dual accounting.*—While maintaining an ASA, a plan must maintain the funding standard account under section 412(b) for each plan year.

(2) *Change of method.*—For any plan year, the choice of whether to use the ASA is independent of whether the ASA or funding standard account was used in the prior year. Any change from the choice made in the prior year does not require approval of the Commissioner. Further, a plan which has filed for a plan year the actuarial report described in section 6059(b) using the ASA to determine its minimum funding requirement may change to use the funding standard account to determine the funding requirement for that year. However, a plan may not switch to the ASA for a plan year after having filed the actuarial report for that year using the funding standard account.

(3) *PBGC Valuation.*—In determining charges and credits to the ASA under paragraphs (b) and (c) of this section (other than the amount in paragraph (c)(2)(i)), a plan must value its assets and liabilities on a termination basis as provided in regulations issued by the Pension Benefit Guaranty Corporation (PBGC) under sections 4041 and 4062 of the Employee Retirement Income Security Act of 1974 ("ERISA") for plans placed in trusteeship by PBGC.

(4) *Cumulative nature of account.*—When the ASA is used for a plan year after a plan year for which the ASA was not used, the credit balance and charge balance as of the first day of the year equal

zero. However, during any continuous period of years for which the ASA is used, the credit or charge balance as of the end of any ASA year are carried forward as beginning balances in the next ASA year.

(c) *Charges.*—(1) *In general.*—The ASA is charged with the amounts described in paragraph (c) of this section.

(2) *Normal cost.*—The ASA is charged with the normal cost of the plan for a plan year. This amount is the normal cost for that plan year computed—

(i) Under the method of funding and actuarial assumptions used for purposes of maintaining the plan's funding standard account or, if less,

(ii) As the present value of benefits expected, on a termination basis, to accrue during the plan year.

(3) *Unfunded accrued benefits.*—The ASA is charged with the unfunded accrued benefits of the plan for a plan year. This amount is the excess of—

(i) The present value of accrued benefits under the plan, determined as of the valuation date for the plan year, over

(ii) The fair market value of plan assets, determined as of the valuation date for the plan year.

Because fair market value is used, any election to value evidences of indebtedness at amortized value does not apply in computing this value.

(4) *Credit balance from prior plan year.*—The ASA is charged as of the first day of a plan year with any ASA credit balance carried forward from the prior plan year.

☐ Par. 6. The Income Tax Regulations, 26 CFR Part 1, are further amended by adding new paragraphs (e) and (f) of §1.413-2 to read as follows:

§1.413-2. Special rules for plans maintained by more than one employer.

* * *

(e) *Minimum funding standard.*—The minimum funding standard for a plan maintained by more than one employer shall be deter-

(5) *Interest.*—The ASA is charged with interest on the amounts charged to the ASA under paragraph (b)(2), (b)(3) and (b)(4) of this section, as generally prescribed for the funding standard account under §1.412(b)-1(e).

(d) *Credits.*—(1) *In general.*—The ASA is credited with the amounts described in paragraph (d) of this section.

(2) *Employer contributions.*—The ASA is credited with the amount of contributions made by the employer to the plan for the plan year.

(3) *Interest.*—The ASA is credited with the interest on the amount credited under paragraph (d)(2) of this section, determined as of the end of the plan year as generally prescribed for the funding standard account under §1.412(b)-1(e). [Reg. §1.412(g)-1.]

§1.413-1. Special rules for collectively bargained plans.—

* * *

(f) *Minimum funding standard.*—The minimum funding standard for a collectively bargained plan shall be determined as if all participants in the plan were employed by a single employer.

(g) *Liability for funding tax.*—See §54.4971-3 of the Pension Excise Tax Regulations, 26 CFR Part 54, for rules under section 413(b)(6), relating to liability for excise tax on failure to meet minimum funding standards with respect to collectively bargained plans.

* * *

mined as if all participants in the plan were employed by a single employer.

(f) *Liability for funding tax.*—See §54.4971-3 of the Pension Excise Tax Regulations, 26 CFR Part 54, for rules under section 413(c)(5), relating to liability for excise tax on failure to meet minimum funding standards with respect to plans maintained by more than one employer.

☐ Par. 7. The Temporary Regulations under the Employee Retirement Income Security Act of 1974, 26 CFR Part 11, are amended by removing §11.412(c)-7.

§11.412(c)-7. Election to treat certain retroactive plan amendments as made on the first day of the plan year.

☐ Par. 7. The Temporary Regulations under the Employee Retirement Income Security Act of 1974, 26 CFR Part 11, are amended by removing §11.412(c)-11.

§11.412(c)-11. Election with respect to bonds.

☐ Par. 7. The Temporary Regulations under the Employee Retirement Income Security Act of 1974, 26 CFR Part 11, are amended by removing §11.412(c)-12.

§11.412(c)-12. Extension of time to make contributions to satisfy requirements of section 412.

Multiple Employer Plans: Unified Plan Rule: Exception

Multiple Employer Plans: Unified Plan Rule: Exception.—Amendments to Reg. §1.413-2, relating to the tax qualification of plans maintained by more than one employer, are proposed (published in the Federal Register on July 3, 2019) (corrected August 21, 2019) (REG-121508-18).

Par. 2. Section 1.413-2 is amended by:
1. Removing paragraph (a)(3)(iv).
2. Adding and reserving paragraphs (e) and (f).
3. Adding paragraph (g).
The additions read as follows:

§1.413-2. Special rules for plans maintained by more than one employer.

* * *

(e) [Reserved]
(f) [Reserved]

(g) *Qualification of a section 413(c) plan.*—(1) *General rule.*—Except as provided in paragraph (g)(2) of this section, the qualification of a section 413(c) plan under section 401(a) or 403(a), taking into account the rules of section 413(c) and this section, is determined with respect to all participating employers. Consequently, the failure by one participating employer (or by the plan itself) to satisfy an applicable qualification requirement will result in the disqualification of the section 413(c) plan for all participating employers.

(2) *Exception to general rule for participating employer failures.*—(i) *In general.*—A section 413(c) plan that is a defined contribution plan will not be disqualified on account of a participating employer failure, provided that the following conditions are satisfied—

(A) The section 413(c) plan satisfies the eligibility requirements of paragraph (g)(3) of this section;

(B) The section 413(c) plan administrator satisfies the notice requirements described in paragraph (g)(4) of this section;

(C) If the unresponsive participating employer fails to take appropriate remedial action with respect to the participating employer failure, as described in paragraph (g)(5)(ii) of this section, the section 413(c) plan administrator implements a spinoff described in paragraph (g)(2)(ii) of this section; and

(D) The section 413(c) plan administrator complies with any information request that the IRS or a representative of the spun-off plan makes in connection with an IRS examination of the spun-off plan, including any information request related to the participation of the unresponsive participating employer in the section 413(c) plan for years prior to the spinoff.

(ii) *Spinoff.*—A spinoff is described in this paragraph (g)(2)(ii) if it satisfies either of the following requirements—

(A) The spinoff is initiated by the unresponsive participating employer, as described in paragraph (g)(5)(iii) of this section, and implemented by the section 413(c) plan administrator, as described in paragraph (g)(6)(ii) of this section; or

(B) The spinoff is a spinoff-termination pursuant to plan terms, as described in paragraph (g)(7) of this section.

(iii) *Definitions.*—The following definitions apply for purposes of this paragraph (g):

(A) *Employee.*—An employee is a current or former employee of a participating employer.

(B) *Known qualification failure.*—A known qualification failure is a failure to satisfy a qualification requirement with respect to a section 413(c) plan that is identified by the section 413(c) plan administrator and is attributable solely to an unresponsive participating employer. For purposes of this paragraph (g)(2)(iii)(B), an unresponsive participating employer includes any employer that is treated as a single employer with that unresponsive participating employer under section 414(b), (c), (m), or (o)).

(C) *Participating employer.*—A participating employer is one of the employers maintaining a section 413(c) plan.

(D) *Participating employer failure.*—A participating employer failure is a known qualification failure or a potential qualification failure.

(E) *Potential qualification failure.*—A potential qualification failure is a failure to satisfy a qualification requirement with respect to a section 413(c) plan that the section 413(c) plan administrator reasonably believes might exist, but the section 413(c) plan administrator is unable to determine whether the qualification requirement is satisfied solely due to an unresponsive participating employer's failure to provide data, documents, or any other information necessary to determine whether the section 413(c) plan is in compliance with the qualification requirement as it relates to the participating employer. For purposes of this paragraph (g)(2)(iii)(E), an unresponsive participating employer includes any employer that is treated as a single employer with that unresponsive participating employer under section 414(b), (c), (m), or (o)).

(F) *Section 413(c) plan administrator.*—A section 413(c) plan administrator is the plan administrator of a section 413(c) plan, determined under the rules of section 414(g).

(G) *Unresponsive participating employer.*—An unresponsive participating employer is a participating employer in a section 413(c) plan that fails to comply with reasonable and timely requests from the section 413(c) plan administrator for information needed to determine compliance with a qualification requirement or fails to comply with reasonable and timely requests from the section 413(c) plan administrator to take actions that are needed to correct a failure to satisfy a qualification requirement as it relates to the participating employer.

(3) *Eligibility for exception to general rule.*—(i) *In general.*—To be eligible for the exception described in paragraph (g)(2) of this section, a section 413(c) plan must satisfy the following requirements—

(A) *Practices and procedures.*—The section 413(c) plan administrator has established practices and procedures (formal or informal) that are reasonably designed to promote and facilitate overall compliance with applicable Code requirements, including procedures for obtaining information from participating employers.

(B) *Plan language.*—The section 413(c) plan document describes the procedures that would be followed to address participating employer failures, including the procedures that the section 413(c) plan administrator would follow if the unresponsive participating employer does not take appropriate remedial action or initiate a spinoff pursuant to paragraph (g)(5) of this section.

(C) *Not under examination.*—At the time the first notice described in paragraph (g)(4)(i) of this section is provided to the unresponsive participating employer, the section 413(c) plan is not under examination under the rules of paragraph (g)(3)(ii) of this section.

(ii) *Under examination.*—For purposes of this section, a plan is under examination if—

(A) The plan is under an Employee Plans examination (that is, an examination of a Form 5500 series or other examination by the Employee Plans Office of the Tax Exempt and Government Entities Division of the IRS (Employee Plans) (or any successor IRS office that has jurisdiction over qualified retirement plans));

(B) The plan is under investigation by the Criminal Investigation Division of the IRS (or its successor); or

(C) The plan is treated as under an Employee Plans examination under the rules of paragraph (g)(3)(iii) of this section.

(iii) *Certain plans treated as under an Employee Plans examination.*—(A) *Notification of pending examination.*—For purposes of this section, a plan is treated as under an Employee Plans examination if the section 413(c) plan administrator, or an authorized representative, has received verbal or written notification from Employee Plans of an impending Employee Plans examination, or of an impending referral for an Employee Plans examination. A plan is also treated as under an Employee Plans examination if it has been under an Employee Plans examination and the plan has an appeal pending with the IRS Office of Appeals (or its successor), or is in litigation with the IRS, regarding issues raised in an Employee Plans examination.

(B) *Pending determination letter application.*—(1) *Possible failures identified by IRS.*—For purposes of this section, a section 413(c) plan is treated as under an Employee Plans examination if a Form 5300, "Application for Determination for Employee Benefit Plan," Form 5307, "Application for Determination for Adopters of Modified Volume Submitter Plans," or Form 5310, "Application for Determination for Terminating Plan" (or any successor form for one or more of these forms) has been submitted with respect to the plan and the IRS agent notifies the applicant of possible qualification failures, whether or not the applicant is officially notified of an examination. This includes a case in which, for example, a determination letter on plan termination had been submitted with respect to the plan, and an IRS agent notifies the applicant that there are partial termination concerns. In addition, if, during the review process, the IRS agent requests additional information that indicates the existence of a failure not previously identified by the applicant, then the plan is treated as under an Employee Plans examination (even if the determination letter application is subsequently withdrawn).

(2) *Failures identified by determination letter applicant.*—For purposes of paragraph (g)(3)(iii)(B)(1) of this section, an IRS agent is not treated as notifying a determination letter applicant of a possible qualification failure if the applicant (or the authorized representative) has identified the failure, in writing, to the reviewing IRS agent before the agent recognizes the existence of the failure or addresses the failure in communications with the applicant. For purposes of this paragraph (g)(3)(iii)(B)(2), submission of a determination letter application does not constitute an identification of a failure to the IRS.

(C) *Aggregated plans.*—For purposes of this section, a plan is treated as under an Employee Plans examination if it is aggregated for purposes of satisfying the nondiscrimination requirements of section 401(a)(4), the minimum participation requirements of section 401(a)(26), the minimum coverage requirements of section 410(b), or the requirements of section 403(b)(12)(A)(i), with any plan that is under an Employee Plans examination. In addition, a plan is treated as under an Employee Plans examination with respect to a failure of a qualification requirement (other than those described in the preceding sentence) if the plan is aggregated with another plan for purposes of satisfying that qualification requirement (for example, section 401(a)(30), 415, or 416) and that other plan is under an Employee Plans examination. For purposes of this paragraph (g)(3)(iii)(C), the term aggregation does not include consideration of benefits provided by various plans for purposes of the average benefits test set forth in section 410(b)(2).

(4) *Notice requirements.*—The section 413(c) plan administrator satisfies the notice requirements with respect to a participating employer failure if it satisfies the requirements of this paragraph (g)(4).

(i) *First notice.*—The section 413(c) plan administrator must provide notice to the unresponsive participating employer describing the participating employer failure, the remedial actions the employer would need to take to remedy the failure, and the employer's option to initiate a spinoff of plan assets and account balances attributable to participants who are employees of that employer. In addition, the notice must explain the consequences under plan terms if the unresponsive participating employer neither takes appropriate remedial action with respect to the participating employer failure nor initiates a spinoff, including the possibility that a spinoff of assets and account balances attributable to participants who are employees of that employer would occur, followed by a termination of that plan.

(ii) *Second notice.*—If, by the end of the 90-day period following the date the first notice described in paragraph (g)(4)(i) of this section is provided, the unresponsive participating employer neither takes appropriate remedial action with respect to the participating employer failure nor initiates a spinoff, then the section 413(c) plan administrator must provide a second notice to the employer. The second notice must be provided no later than 30 days after the expiration of the 90-day period described in the preceding sentence. The second notice must include the information required to be included in the first notice and must also specify that if, within 90 days following the date the second notice is provided, the employer neither takes appropriate remedial action with respect to the participating employer failure nor initiates a spinoff, a notice describing the participating employer failure and the consequences of not correcting that failure will be provided to participants who are employees of the unresponsive participating employer (and their beneficiaries) and to the Department of Labor.

(iii) *Third notice.*—If, by the end of the 90-day period following the date the second notice described in paragraph (g)(4)(ii) of this section is provided, the unresponsive participating employer neither takes appropriate remedial action with respect to the participating employer failure nor initiates a spinoff, then the section 413(c) plan administrator must provide a third notice to that employer. The third notice must be provided no later than 30 days after the expiration of the 90-day period described in the preceding sentence. Within this time period, the third notice must also be provided to participants who are employees of that employer (and their beneficiaries) and to the Office of Enforcement of the Employee Benefits Security Administration in the Department of Labor (or its successor office). The third notice must include the information required to be included in the first notice, the deadline for employer action, and an explanation of any adverse consequences to participants in the event that a spinoff-termination occurs, and state that the notice is being provided to participants who are employees of the unresponsive participating employer (and their beneficiaries) and to the Department of Labor.

(5) *Actions by unresponsive participating employer.*—(i) *In general.*—An unresponsive participating employer takes appropriate remedial action with respect to a participating employer failure for purposes of paragraph (g)(2)(i)(C) of this section if it satisfies the requirements of paragraph (g)(5)(ii) of this section. Alternatively, an unresponsive participating employer initiates a spinoff with respect to a participating employer failure for purposes of paragraph (g)(2)(ii)(A) of this section if the employer satisfies the requirements of paragraph (g)(5)(iii) of this section. The final deadline for an unresponsive participating employer to take one of these actions is 90 days after the third notice is provided. See paragraph (g)(7) of this section for the consequences of the employer's failure to meet this deadline.

(ii) *Appropriate remedial action.*—(A) *Appropriate remedial action with respect to potential qualification failure.*—An unresponsive participating employer takes appropriate remedial action with respect to a potential qualification failure if the employer provides data, documents, or any other information necessary for the section 413(c) plan administrator to determine whether a qualification failure exists. If the unresponsive participating employer provides this information, the section 413(c) plan administrator determines that, based on this information, a qualification failure exists that is attributable solely to that employer, and the participating employer fails to comply with reasonable and timely requests from the section 413(c) plan administrator to take actions that are needed to correct that qualification failure, then the qualification failure becomes a known qualification failure. In that case, the section 413(c) plan will be eligible for the exception in paragraph (g)(2) of this section with respect to the known qualification failure by satisfying the conditions set forth in paragraph (g)(2) of this section with respect to that known qualification failure, taking into account the rules of paragraph (g)(6)(i) of this section.

(B) *Appropriate remedial action with respect to known qualification failure.*—An unresponsive participating employer takes appropriate remedial action with respect to a known qualification failure if the employer takes action, such as making corrective contributions, that corrects, or enables the section 413(c) plan administrator to correct, the known qualification failure.

(iii) *Employer-initiated spinoff.*—An unresponsive participating employer initiates a spinoff pursuant to this paragraph (g)(5)(iii) if, after receiving a notice described in paragraph (g)(4) of this section, the employer directs the section 413(c) plan administrator to spin off plan assets and account balances held on behalf of its employees to a separate single-employer plan established and maintained by that employer in a manner consistent with plan terms.

(6) *Actions by section 413(c) plan administrator.*—(i) *Rules for a potential qualification failure that becomes a known qualification failure.*—

For purposes of applying paragraph (g)(2) of this section to a potential qualification failure that becomes a known qualification failure, actions taken (including notices provided) when the failure was a potential qualification failure are not taken into account. For example, a notice that the section 413(c) plan administrator provided in connection with the potential qualification failure would not satisfy the notice requirements for the known qualification failure. However, in determining whether the section 413(c) plan is under examination, as described in paragraph (g)(3)(iii) of this section, as of the date of the first notice describing the known qualification failure, the section 413(c) plan administrator will be treated as providing that notice on the date the first notice was provided with respect to the related potential qualification failure, but only if the following conditions are satisfied—

(A) After determining that a qualification failure exists, the section 413(c) plan administrator makes a reasonable and timely request to the participating employer to take actions that are needed to correct the failure, and

(B) As soon as reasonably practicable after the participating employer fails to respond to that request, the section 413(c) plan administrator provides the first notice described in paragraph (g)(4)(i) of this section with respect to the known qualification failure.

(ii) *Implementing employer-initiated spinoff.*—If an unresponsive participating employer initiates a spinoff pursuant to paragraph (g)(5)(iii) of this section by directing the section 413(c) plan administrator to spin off the assets and account balances held on behalf of its employees to a separate single-employer plan established and maintained by the employer, the section 413(c) plan administrator must implement and complete a spinoff of the assets and account balances held on behalf of the employees of the employer that are attributable to their employment by the employer within 180 days of the date on which the unresponsive participating employer initiates the spinoff. The section 413(c) plan administrator must report the spinoff to the IRS (in the manner prescribed by the IRS in forms, instructions, and other guidance).

(7) *Spinoff-termination.*—(i) *Spinoff.*—If the unresponsive participating employer neither takes appropriate remedial action described in paragraph (g)(5)(ii) of this section nor initiates a spinoff pursuant to paragraph (g)(5)(iii) of this section, then, in accordance with plan language, the section 413(c) plan administrator must take the following steps as soon as reasonably practicable after the deadline described in paragraph (g)(5)(i) of this section—

(A) Send notification of spinoff-termination to participants who are employees of the unresponsive participating employer (and their beneficiaries) as described in paragraph (g)(7)(iii) of this section;

(B) Stop accepting contributions from the unresponsive participating employer;

(C) Implement a spinoff, in accordance with the transfer requirements of section 414(l) and the anti-cutback requirements of section 411(d)(6), of the plan assets and account balances held on behalf of employees of the unresponsive participating employer that are attributable to their employment by that employer to a separate single-employer plan and trust that has the same plan administrator, trustee, and substantive plan terms as the section 413(c) plan; and

(D) Terminate the spun-off plan and distribute assets of the spun-off plan to plan participants (and their beneficiaries) as soon as reasonably practicable after the plan termination date.

(ii) *Termination of spun-off plan.*—In terminating the spun-off plan, the section 413(c) plan administrator must—

(A) Reasonably determine whether, and to what extent, the survivor annuity requirements of sections 401(a)(11) and 417 apply to any benefit payable under the plan and take reasonable steps to comply with those requirements (if applicable);

(B) Provide each participant and beneficiary with a nonforfeitable right to his or her accrued benefits as of the date of plan termination, subject to income, expenses, gains, and losses between that date and the date of distribution; and

(C) Notify the participants and beneficiaries of their rights under section 402(f).

(iii) *Contents of the notification of spinoff-termination.*—For the notice required to be provided in paragraph (g)(7)(i)(A), the section 413(c) plan administrator must provide information relating to the spinoff-termination to participants who are employees of the unresponsive participating employer (and their beneficiaries), including the following—

(A) Identification of the section 413(c) plan and contact information for the section 413(c) plan administrator;

(B) The effective date of the spinoff-termination;

(C) A statement that no more contributions will be made to the section 413(c) plan;

(D) A statement that as soon as practicable after the spinoff-termination, participants and beneficiaries will receive a distribution from the spun-off plan; and

(E) A statement that before the distribution occurs, participants and beneficiaries will receive additional information about their options with respect to that distribution.

(iv) *Reporting spinoff-termination.*—The section 413(c) plan administrator must report a spinoff-termination pursuant to this paragraph (g)(7) to the IRS (in the manner prescribed by the IRS in forms, instructions, and other guidance).

(8) *Other rules.*—(i) *Form of notices.*—Any notice provided pursuant to paragraph (g)(4) or (g)(7)(i)(A) of this section may be provided in writing or in electronic form. For notices provided to participants and beneficiaries, see generally § 1.401(a)-21 for rules permitting the use of electronic media to provide applicable notices to recipients with respect to retirement plans.

(ii) *Qualification of spun-off plan.*—(A) *In general.*—In the case of any plan that is spun off in accordance with paragraph (g)(6)(ii) or (g)(7) of this section, any participating employer failure that would have affected the qualification of the section 413(c) plan, but for the application of the exception set forth in paragraph (g)(2) of this section, will be a qualification failure with respect to the spun-off plan.

(B) *Favorable tax treatment upon termination.*—Notwithstanding paragraph (g)(8)(ii)(A) of this section, distributions made

from a spun-off plan that is terminated in accordance with paragraph (g)(7) of this section will not, solely because of the participating employer failure, fail to be eligible for favorable tax treatment accorded to distributions from qualified plans (including that the distributions will be treated as eligible rollover distributions under section 402(c)(4)), except as provided in paragraph (g)(8)(ii)(C) of this section.

(C) *Exception for responsible parties.*—The IRS reserves the right to pursue appropriate remedies under the Code against any party (such as the owner of the participating employer) who is responsible for the participating employer failure. The IRS may pursue appropriate remedies against a responsible party even in the party's capacity as a participant or beneficiary under the spun-off plan that is terminated in accordance with paragraph (g)(7) of this section (such as by not treating a plan distribution made to the responsible party as an eligible rollover distribution).

(iii) *Additional guidance.*—The Commissioner may provide additional guidance in revenue rulings, notices, or other guidance published in the Internal Revenue Bulletin, or in forms and instructions, that the Commissioner determines to be necessary or appropriate with respect to the requirements of this paragraph (g).

(9) *Applicability date.*—This paragraph (g) applies on or after the date of publication of the Treasury decision adopting these rules as final regulations in the **Federal Register**.

Affiliated Service Groups: Separate Service Organizations

Employees' Trusts: Affiliated Service Groups.—Reproduced below are the texts of proposed Reg. §§1.414(m)-1—1.414(m)-4, which prescribe rules for determining whether two or more separate service organizations constitute an affiliated group and which detail how certain requirements are satisfied by a qualified retirement plan maintained by a member of an affiliated service group (published in the Federal Register on February 28, 1983).

☐ Par. 2. The following new sections are added at the appropriate place:

§1.414(m)-1. Affiliated service groups.—(a) *In general.*—Section 414(m) provides rules that require, in some circumstances, employees of separate organizations to be treated as if they were employed by a single employer for purposes of certain employee benefit requirements. For other rules requiring aggregation of employees of different organizations, see section 414(b) (relating to controlled groups of corporations) and section 414(c) (relating to trades or businesses under common control). If aggregation is required under either of the preceding provisions and also under section 414(m), the requirements with respect to all of the applicable provisions must be satisfied.

(b) *Aggregation.*—Except as provided in paragraph (c), all the employees of the members of an affiliated service group shall be treated as if they were employed by a single employer for purposes of the employee benefit requirements listed in § 1.414(m)-3.

(c) *Aggregation not required.*—Pursuant to the authority contained in section 414(m)(1), a corporation, other than a professional service corporation, shall not be treated as a First Service Organization (see § 1.414(m)-2) for purposes of section 414(m)(2)(A). Also, a special rule is provided in §1.414(m)-2(c)(4) for determining ownership under section 414(m)(2)(B). For purposes of this paragraph, a professional service corporation is a corporation that is organized under state law for the principal purpose of providing professional services and has at least one shareholder who is licensed or otherwise legally authorized to render the type of services for which the corporation is organized. "Professional services" means the services performed by certified or other public accountants, actuaries, architects, attorneys, chiropodists, chiropractors, medical doctors, dentists, professional engineers, optometrists, osteopaths, podiatrists, psychologists, and veterinarians. The Commissioner may expand the list of services in the preceding sentence. However, no such expansion will be effective with respect to any organization until the first day of the first plan year beginning at least 180 days after the publication of such change. [Reg. § 1.414(m)-1.]

§1.414(m)-2. Definitions.—(a) *Affiliated service group.*—"Affiliated service group" means a group consisting of a service organization (First Service Organization) and

(1) One or more A Organizations described in paragraph (b), or

(2) One or more B Organizations described in paragraph (c), or

(3) One or more A Organizations described in paragraph (b) and one or more B Organizations described in paragraph (c).

(b) *A Organizations.*—(1) *General rule.*—A service organization is an A Organization if it:

(i) Is a partner or shareholder in the First Service Organization (regardless of the percentage interest it owns in the First Service Organization but determined with regard to the constructive ownership rules of paragraph (d)); and

(ii) Regularly performs services for the First Service Organization, or is regularly associated with the First Service Organization in performing services for third persons.

It is not necessary that any of the employees of the organization directly perform services for the First Service Organization; it is sufficient that the organization is regularly associated with the First Service Organization in performing services for third persons.

(2) *Regularly performs services for.*—The determination of whether a service organization regularly performs services for the First Service Organization or is regularly associated with the First Service Organization in performing services for third persons shall be made on the basis of the facts and circumstances. One factor that is relevant in making this determination is the amount of the earned income that the organization derives from performing services for the First Service Organization, or from performing services for third persons in association with the First Service Organization.

(3) *Examples.*—The provisions of this paragraph may be illustrated by the following examples.

Example (1). A Organization. (i) Attorney N is incorporated, and the corporation is a partner in a law firm. Attorney N and his corporation are regularly associated with the law firm in performing services for third persons.

(ii) Considering the law firm as a First Service Organization, the corporation is an A Organization because it is a partner in the law firm and it is regularly associated with the law firm in performing services for third persons. Accordingly, the corporation and the law firm constitute an affiliated service group.

Example (2). Corporation. (i) Corporation F is a service organization that is a shareholder in Corporation G, another service organization. F regularly provides services for G. Neither corporation is a professional service corporation within the meaning of subsection (1)(c).

(ii) Neither corporation may be considered a First Service Organization for purposes of this paragraph and, thus, aggregation will not be required by operation of the A Organization test. However, G or F may be treated as a First Service Organization and the other organization may be a B Organization under the rules of subsection (2)(c).

Example (3). Regularly associated with. (i) R, S & T is a law partnership with offices in numerous cities. The office in the city of D is incorporated, and the corporation is a partner in the law firm. All of the employees of the corporation work directly for the corporation, and none of them work directly for any of the other offices of the law firm.

(ii) Considering the law firm as a First Service Organization, the corporation is an A Organization because it is a partner in the First Service Organization and is regularly associated with the law firm in performing services for third persons. Accordingly, the corporation and the law firm constitute an affiliated service group.

(c) *B Organizations.*—(1) *General rule.*—An organization is a B Organization if:

(i) A significant portion of the business of the organization is the performance of services for the First Service Organization, for one or more A Organizations determined with respect to the First Service Organization, or for both,

(ii) Those services are of a type historically performed by employees in the service field of the First Service Organization or the A Organizations, and

(iii) Ten percent or more of the interests in the organization is held, in the aggregate, by persons who are designated group members (as defined in subparagraph (4)) of the First Service Organization or of the A Organizations, determined using the constructive ownership rules of paragraph (d).

(2) *Significant portion.*—(i) *General rule.*—Except as provided in subdivisions (ii) and (iii), the determination of whether providing services for the First Service Organization, for one or more A Organizations, or for both, is a significant portion of the business of an organization will be based on the facts and circumstances. Wherever it appears in this paragraph (2), "one or more A Organizations" means one or more A Organizations determined with respect to the First Service Organization.

(ii) *Service Receipts safe harbor.*—The performance of services for the First Service Organizations, for one or more A Organizations, or for both, will not be considered a significant portion of the business of an organization if the Service Receipts Percentage is less than five percent.

(iii) *Total Receipts threshold test.*—The performance of services for the First Service Organization, for one or more A Organizations, or for both, will be considered a significant portion of the business of an organization if the Total Receipts Percentage is ten percent or more.

(iv) *Service Receipts Percentage.*—The Service Receipts Percentage is the ratio of the gross receipts of the organization derived from performing services for the First Service Organization, for one or more A Organizations, or for both, to the total gross receipts of the organization derived from performing services. This ratio is the greater of the ratio for the year for which the determination is being made or for the three year period including that year and the two preceding years (or the period of the organization's existence, if less).

(v) *Total Receipts Percentage.*—The Total Receipts Percentage is calculated in the same manner as the Service Receipts Percentage, except that gross receipts in the denominator are determined without regard to whether they were derived from performing services.

(3) *Historically performed.*—Services will be considered of a type historically performed by employees in a particular service field if it was not unusual for the services to be performed by employees of organizations in that service field (in the United States) on December 13, 1980.

(4) *Designated group.*—(i) *Definition.*—"Designated group" members are the officers, the highly compensated employees, and the common owners of an organization (as defined in subdivision (ii)). However, even though a person is not a common owner, the interests the person holds in the potential B Organization will be taken into account if the person is an officer or a highly compensated employee of the First Service Organization or of an A Organization.

(ii) *Common owner.*—A person who is an owner of a First Service Organization or of an A Organization is a common owner if at least three percent of the interests in the organization is, in the aggregate, held by persons who are owners of the potential B Organization (determined using the constructive ownership rules of paragraph (d)).

(5) *Owner.*—The term "owner" includes organizations that have an ownership interest described in paragraph (e).

(6) *Aggregation of ownership interests.*—It is not necessary that a single designated group member of the First Service Organization or of an A Organization own ten percent or more of the interests, determined using the constructive ownership rules of paragraph (d), in the organization for the organization to be a B Organization. It is sufficient that the sum of the interests, determined using the constructive ownership rules of paragraph (d), held by all of the desig-

nated group members of the First Service Organization, and the designated group members of the A Organizations, is ten percent or more of the interests in the organization.

(7) *Non-service organization.*—An organization may be a B Organization even though it does not qualify as a service organization under paragraph (f).

(8) *Examples.*—The provisions of this paragraph may be illustrated by the following examples.

Example (1). B Organization. (i) R is a service organization that has 11 partners. Each partner of R owns one percent of the stock in Corporation D. The corporation provides services to the partnership of a type historically performed by employees in the service field of the partnership. A significant portion of the business of the corporation consists of providing services to the partnership.

(ii) Considering the partnership as a First Service Organization, the corporation is a B Organization because a significant portion of the business of the corporation is the performance of services for the partnership of a type historically performed by employees in the service field of the partnership, and more than ten percent of the interests in the corporation is held, in the aggregate, by the designated group members (consisting of the 11 common owners of the partnership). Accordingly, the corporation and the partnership constitute an affiliated service group.

(iii) A similar result would be obtained if no more than 8 percent of the 11 percent ownership in Corporation D were held by highly compensated employees of R who were not owners of R (even though no one group of the three preceding groups held 10 percent or more of the stock of Corporation D).

Example (2). Other aggregation rules. (i) C, an individual, is a 60 percent partner in D, a service organization, and regularly performs services for D. C is also an 80 percent partner in F. A significant portion of the gross receipts of F are derived from providing services to D of a type historically performed by employees in the service field of D.

(ii) Viewing D as a First Service Organization, F is a B Organization because a significant portion of gross receipts of F are derived from performing services for D of a type historically performed by employees in that service field, and more than ten percent of the interests in F is held by the designated group member C (who is a common owner of D). Accordingly, D and F constitute an affiliated service group. Additionally, the employees of D and F are aggregated under the rules of section 414(c). Thus, any plan maintained by a member of the affiliated service group must satisfy the aggregation rules of sections 414(c) and 414(m).

Example (3). Common owner. (i) Corporation T is a service organization. The sole function of Corporation W is to provide services to Corporation T of a type historically performed by employees in the service field of Corporation T. Individual C owns all of the stock of Corporation W and two percent of the stock of Corporation T. C is not an officer or a highly compensated employee of Corporation T.

(ii) Considering Corporation T as a First Service Organization, Corporation W is not a B Organization because it is not 10 percent owned by designated group members. Because C owns less than 3 percent of Corporation T, C is not a common owner of T.

Example (4). B Organization. (i) Individual M owns one-third of an employee benefit consulting firm. M also owns one-third of an insurance agency. A significant portion of the business of the consulting firm consists of assisting the insurance agency in developing employee benefit packages for sale to third persons and providing services to the insurance company in connection with employee benefit programs sold to other clients of the insurance agency. Additionally, the consulting firm frequently provides services to clients who have purchased insurance arrangements from the insurance company for the employee benefit plans they maintain. The insurance company frequently refers clients to the consulting firm to assist them in the design of their employee benefit plans. The percentage of the total gross receipts of the consulting firm that represent gross receipts from the performance of these services for the insurance agency is 20 percent.

(ii) Considering the insurance agency as a First Service Organization, the consulting firm is a B Organization because a significant portion of the business of the consulting firm (as determined under the Total Receipts Percentage Test) is the performance of services for the insurance agency of a type historically performed by employees in the service field of insurance, and more than 10 percent of the interests in the consulting firm is held by owners of the insurance agency. Thus, the insurance agency and the consulting firm constitute an affiliated service group.

Example (5). B Organization. (i) Attorney T is incorporated, and the corporation is a 6% shareholder in a law firm (which is also incorporated). All of the work of Corporation T is performed for the law firm.

(ii) Under the principles of section 267(c), T is deemed to own the shares of the law firm owned by T Corporation. Thus, T is a common owner of the law firm. Considering the law firm as a First Service Organization, Corporation T is a B Organization because a significant portion of the business of Corporation T consists of performing services for the law firm of a type historically performed by

	Origin of income
Year 1	Services
	Total
Year 2	Services
	Total
Year 3	Services
	Total

(ii) In year 1 (the first year of existence of Corporation X), the Services Receipts Percentage for Corporation X (for its business with Corporation Z) is less than five percent ($4/$100, or 4%). Thus performing services for Corporation Z will not be considered a significant portion of the business of Corporation X.

(iii) In year 2, the Services Receipts Percentage is the greater of the ratio for that year ($9/$150, or 6%) or for years 1 and 2 combined ($13/$250, or 5.2%), which is six percent. The Total Receipts Percentage is the greater of the ratio for that year ($9/$180, or 5%) or for years 1 and 2 combined ($13/$300, or 4.3%), which is five percent. Because the Services Receipts Percentage is greater than five percent and the Total Receipts Percentage is less than ten percent, whether performing services for Corporation Z constitutes a significant portion of the business of Corporation X is determined by the facts and circumstances.

(iv) In year 3, the Services Receipts Percentage is the greater of the ratio for that year ($42/$200, or 21%) or for years, 1, 2, and 3 combined ($55/$450, or 12.2%), which is 21 percent. The Total Receipts Percentage is the greater of the ratio for that year ($42/$240, or 17.5%) or for years 1, 2, and 3 combined ($55/$540, or 10.1%), which is 17.5 percent. Because the Total Receipts Percentage is greater than ten percent and the Services Receipts Percentage is not less than five percent, a significant portion of the business of Corporation X is considered to be the performances of services for Corporation Z.

(d) *Ownership.*—(1) *Constructive ownership.*—Except as otherwise provided in the regulations under section 414(m), the principles of section 267(c) (relating to constructive ownership of stock) shall apply in determining ownership for purposes of section 414(m). Accordingly, the rules of section 267(c) shall apply to partnership interests as well as to stock.

(2) *Qualified plans.*—In determining ownership for purposes of section 414(m), an individual's interest under a plan that qualifies under section 401(a) will be taken into account.

(3) *Special rules.*—For purposes of section 414(m):

(i) Stock or partnership interests owned, directly or indirectly, by or for a corporation, partnership, estate, or trust shall be considered as being owned proportionately by or for its shareholders, partners, or beneficiaries;

(ii) An individual shall be considered as owning the stock or partnership interests owned, directly or indirectly, by or for his family;

(iii) An individual owning (otherwise than by the application of subdivision (ii)) any stock in a corporation or interest in a partnership shall be considered as owning the stock or partnership interests owned, directly or indirectly, by or for his partner;

(iv) The family of an individual shall include only his brothers and sisters (whether by the whole or half blood), spouse, ancestors, and lineal descendants; and

(v) Stock or partnership interests constructively owned by a person by reason of the application of subdivision (i) shall, for the purpose of applying subdivision (i), (ii), or (iii), be treated as actually owned by such person, but stock or partnership interests constructively owned by an individual by reason of the application of subdivision (ii) or (iii) shall not be treated as owned by him for the purpose of again applying either of such subdivisions in order to make another the constructive owner of such stock or partnership interests.

(4) *Examples.*—The provisions of this paragraph may be illustrated by the following examples.

Example (1). Constructive ownership. (i) Individual K is incorporated as K Corporation, and K Corporation is a partner in a management consulting firm K & F. K regularly performs services for the management consulting firm K & F. The secretarial services for the consulting firm are performed by Corporation M. A significant portion of the business of the secretarial corporation, M, consists of providing services to the consulting firm. All of the stock of the secretarial corporation, M, is owned by individual K.

(ii) Considering the consulting firm as a First Service Organization, Corporation K is an A Organization because it is a partner in the consulting firm and regularly performs services for the firm or is

employees, and 100 percent of Corporation T is owned by a common owner of the law firm.

Example (6). Significant portion. (i) The income of Corporation X is derived from both performing services and other business activities. The amount of its receipts derived from performing services for, and its total receipts derived from, Corporation Z and the total for all other customers is set forth below:

Corporation Z	All customers
$4	$100
	$120
$9	$150
	$180
$42	$200
	$240

regularly associated with the firm in performing services for third persons.

(iii) Under the principles of section 267(c), individual K is deemed to own the partnership interest in the consulting firm that is held by K Corporation. Thus, K is considered to be an owner of the consulting firm.

(iv) Considering the consulting firm as a First Service Organization, the secretarial corporation is a B Organization because a significant portion of its business consists of performing services for the consulting firm or for Corporation K of a type historically performed by employees in the service field of management consulting, and at least ten percent of the interests in the secretarial corporation, M, is held by individual K, an owner of the consulting firm.

Example (2). Constructive ownership. (i) J is the office manager and a highly compensated employee of an accounting partnership H & H. The secretarial services for the partnership are provided by Corporation W. J owns fifty percent of the stock of the secretarial corporation. A significant portion of the business of the secretarial corporation consists of providing services to the partnership.

(ii) Considering the partnership as a First Service Organization, the secretarial corporation is a B Organization because a significant portion of the business of the secretarial corporation is the performance of services for the partnership of a type historically performed by employees of accounting firms, and more than ten percent of the interest in the corporation is held by a highly compensated employee of the partnership.

(iii) Under the principles of section 267(c), the result would be the same, for example, if the stock were held (instead of by J) by the spouse of J, the children of J, the parents or grandparents of J, a trust for the benefit of J's children, or by a combination of such relatives.

Example (3). Qualified plan. (i) T is the chief executive officer of W Corporation, which is a consulting firm. T is also a participant in the W Corporation Profit-Sharing Plan, which qualifies under section 401(a). T's account balance in the plan is $150,000, and it consists of 25 percent of the stock of X Corporation. The sole function of X Corporation is to provide secretarial services to W Corporation.

(ii) Considering W Corporation as a First Service Organization, X Corporation is a B Organization because a significant portion of the business of X Corporation consists of providing secretarial services to W Corporation, secretarial services are of a type historically performed by employees in the field of consulting, and 25 percent of the stock of X Corporation is considered to be owned by T, a highly compensated employee of W Corporation, using the principles of section 267(c). Accordingly, W Corporation and X Corporation constitute an affiliated service group.

(e) *Organization.*—(1) *General rule.*—The term "organization" includes a sole proprietorship, partnership, corporation, or any other type of entity regardless of its ownership format.

(2) *Special rule.*—[Reserved.]

(f) *Service organization.*—(1) *Non-capital intensive organizations.*—The principal business of an organization will be considered the performance of services if capital is not a material income-producing factor for the organization, even though the organization is not engaged in a field listed in subparagraph (2). Whether capital is a material income-producing factor must be determined by reference to all the facts and circumstances of each case. In general, capital is a material income-producing factor if a substantial portion of the gross income of the business is attributable to the employment of capital in the business, as reflected, for example, by a substantial investment in inventories, plant, machinery, or other equipment. Additionally, capital is a material income-producing factor for banks and similar institutions. However, capital is not a material income-producing factor if the gross income of the business consists principally of fees, commissions, or other compensation for personal services performed by an individual.

(2) *Specific fields.*—Regardless of whether subparagraph (1) applies, an organization engaged in any one or more of the following fields is a service organization:

(i) Health;

(ii) Law;

(iii) Engineering;

(iv) Architecture;

(v) Accounting;

(vi) Actuarial science;

(vii) Performing arts;

(viii) Consulting; and

(ix) Insurance.

Notwithstanding the preceding sentence, an organization will not be considered to be performing services merely because it is engaged in the manufacture or sale of equipment or supplies used in the above fields, or merely because it is engaged in performing research or publishing in the above fields. An organization will not be considered to be a service organization under this subparagraph (2) merely because an employee provides one of the enumerated services to the organization or to other employees of the organization unless the organization is also engaged in the performance of the same services for third parties.

(3) *Other organizations.*—Organizations engaged in performing services and that are not described in subparagraph (1) or (2) shall not be considered to be service organizations. The Commissioner may expand the list of fields contained in subparagraph (2). However, no such expansion will be effective until the first day of the first plan year beginning at least 180 days after the publication of such change.

(4) *Exempted organizations.*—The Commissioner may determine that certain organizations, or types of organizations, should not be considered as subject to the requirements of section 414(m), even though the organizations are described in subparagraph (1) or (2).

(g) *Multiple affiliated service groups.*—(1) *Multiple First Service Organizations.*—Two or more affiliated service groups will not be aggregated simply because an organization is an A Organization or a B Organization with respect to each affiliated service group.

(2) *Multiple A or B Organizations.*—If an organization is a First Service Organization with respect to two or more A Organizations or two or more B Organizations, or both, all of the organizations shall be considered to constitute a single affiliated service group.

(3) The provisions of this paragraph may be illustrated by the following examples.

Example (1). Multiple First Service Organizations. (i) Corporation P provides secretarial service to numerous dentists in a medical building, each of whom maintains his own separate unincorporated practice. Dentist T owns 20 percent of the secretarial corporation and accounts for 20 percent of its gross receipts. Dentist W owns 25 percent of the corporation and accounts for 25 percent of its gross receipts.

(ii) Considering Dentist T as a First Service Organization, the secretarial corporation, P, is a B Organization because 20 percent of the gross receipts of the corporation are derived from performing services for Dentist T of a type historically performed by employees of dentists, and 20 percent of the interests in the corporation is owned by Dentist T. Accordingly, Dentist T and the corporation constitute an affiliated service group.

(iii) Considering Dentist W as a First Service Organization, the secretarial corporation, P, is a B Organization because 25 percent of the gross receipts of the corporation are derived from performing services for Dentist W of a type historically performed by employees of dentists, and 25 percent of the interests in the corporation is owned by Dentist W. Accordingly, Dentist W and the corporation constitute an affiliated service group. However, this affiliated service group does not include Dentist T even though the secretarial corporation, P, is a B Organization with respect to both dentists. Thus, there are two affiliated service groups.

Example (2). Multiple B Organizations. (i) Doctor N is incorporated as Corporation N. Secretarial services are provided to Corporation N by Corporation Q. Corporation N owns 20 percent of the interests in the secretarial corporation and provides 20 percent of its gross receipts. Nursing services are provided to Corporation N by Corporation R. Corporation N owns 25 percent of the interests in the nursing corporation and provides 25 percent of its gross receipts.

(ii) Considering Corporation N as a First Service Organization, the secretarial corporation, Q, is a B Organization because 20 percent of the gross receipts of the secretarial corporation, Q, are derived from performing services for Corporation N of a type historically performed by employees of doctors, and 20 percent of the secretarial corporation is owned by the owner of Corporation N. Accordingly, Corporation N and the secretarial corporation, Q, constitute an affiliated service group.

(iii) Considering Corporation N as a First Service Organization, the nursing corporation, R, is a B Organization because 25 percent of the gross receipts of the nursing corporation, R, are derived from performing services for Corporation N of a type histori-

cally performed by employees of doctors, and 25 percent of the nursing corporation is owned by the owner of Corporation N. Accordingly, Corporation N and the nursing corporation constitute an affiliated service group.

(iv) For purposes of section 414(m), there will be considered to be one affiliated service group consisting of Corporation N, the secretarial corporation, Q, and the nursing corporation, R. [Reg. § 1.414(m)-2.]

§ 1.414(m)-3. Employee benefit requirements.—(a) *Employee benefit requirements affected.*—All of the employees of the members of an affiliated service group shall be treated as employed by a single employer for purposes of the following employee benefit requirements:

(1) Sections 401(a)(3) and 410 (relating to minimum participation requirements);

(2) Section 401(a)(4) (requiring that contributions or benefits do not discriminate in favor of employees who are officers, shareholders, or highly compensated);

(3) Sections 401(a)(7) and 411 (relating to minimum vesting standards);

(4) Sections 401(a)(16) and 415 (relating to limitations on contributions and benefits);

(5) Section 408(k) (relating to simplified employee pensions);

(6) Section 105(h) (relating to self-insured medical reimbursement plans);

(7) Section 125 (relating to cafeteria plans); and

(8) Pursuant to the authority granted in section 414(m)(6), section (a)(10) (relating to plans providing contributions or benefits to owner-employees).

(b) *Special requirements.*—If a plan maintained by a member of an affiliated service group covers an employee described in section 401(c)(1) (self-employed individual), an owner-employee within the meaning of section 401(c)(3), or a shareholder-employee within the meaning of section 1379(d), the plan must also satisfy the following requirements to the extent they apply:

(1) Section 401(a)(9) (relating to special distribution requirements for plans benefiting self-employed individuals);

(2) Section 401(a)(17) (relating to a limitation on the compensation base of plans benefiting self-employed individuals or shareholder-employees); and

(3) Section 401(a)(18) (relating to special requirements for defined benefit plans benefiting self-employed individuals or shareholder-employees). Pursuant to the authority granted in section 414(m)(6), a plan that covers a self-employed individual, an owner-employee, or a shareholder-employee will be subject to the preceding requirements, even though that individual is not employed by the member of the affiliated service group maintaining the plan. These requirements apply only if the earned income of the self-employed individual or owner-employee or the compensation received as a shareholder-employee is taken into account in computing contributions or benefits under the plan.

(c) *Multiple employer plans.*—(1) *General rule.*—If a plan maintained by a member of an affiliated service group covers an individual who is not an employee of the member, but who is an employee of another member of that affiliated service group, the plan will be considered to be maintained by the member that does employ that individual. Thus, the plan will be considered to be maintained by more than one employer for purposes of section 413(c)(2) (relating to the exclusive benefit rule), (4) (relating to funding), (5) (relating to liability for funding tax), and (6) (relating to deductions). Therefore, a member of an affiliated service group may deduct contributions on behalf of individuals who are not employees of that member, if the individuals are employed by another member of that affiliated service group.

(2) *Special rule.*—The multiple employer plan rule contained in subparagraph (1) shall not apply in the case of a controlled group of corporations (as described in section 414(b)) or a group of trades or businesses under common control (as described in section 414(c)).

(d) *Discrimination.*—In testing for discrimination under section 401(a)(4) (requiring that contributions or benefits do not discriminate in favor of employees who are officers, shareholders, or highly compensated), all of the compensation paid to an employee must be considered in determining the contributions or benefits under a plan maintained by a member of an affiliated service group, without regard to the percentage of the organization employing the individual owned by the member maintaining the plan.

(e) *Example.*—The provisions of this section may be illustrated by the following example:

(1) T is incorporated and Corporation T is a partner in a service organization. Corporation T employs only its sole shareholder and maintains a retirement plan. W and Z, the other partners in the

service organization, are not incorporated. Each partner has a one-third interest, in the service organization. The partnership has eight common law employees.

(2) Considering the partnership as a First Service Organization, Corporation T is an A Organization because it is a partner in the First Service Organization and regularly performs services for the partnership or is regularly associated with the partnership in performing services for third persons. Accordingly, the partnership and Corporation T constitute an affiliated service group.

(3) If the retirement plan maintained by Corporation T covers any of the common law employees of the partnership, it will be benefiting individuals who are not employees of the member of the affiliated service group maintaining the plan (Corporation T). As such, the plan will be considered to be maintained by more than one employer, and will be subject to the rules of section 413(c)(2), (4), (5), and (6) and the regulations thereunder. Thus, contributions by Corporation T on behalf of these individuals will not fail to be deductible under section 404 merely because they are not employees of Corporation T. In testing for discrimination under section 401(a)(4), all of the compensation paid to the employees of the partnership must be taken into account in determining their contributions or benefits under the plan, without regard to the percentage of the partnership owned by Corporation T.

(4) If the plan maintained by Corporation T covers partners W and Z, the plan must also satisfy the requirements listed in paragraph (b), to the extent they are applicable. [Reg. § 1.414(m)-3.]

§ 1.414(m)-4. Effective dates.—(a) *Effective dates.*—(1) *New plans.*—In the case of a plan that was not in existence on November 30, 1980, section 414(m) and the regulations thereunder apply to plan years ending after November 30, 1980.

(2) *Existing plans.*—In the case of a plan in existence on November 30, 1980, section 414(m) and the regulations thereunder shall apply to plan years beginning after November 30, 1980.

(b) *Frozen plan.*—(1) *Defined contribution plans.*—In the case of a defined contribution plan in existence on November 30, 1980, that fails to satisfy the requirements of section 401(a) solely because of the application of section 414(m), the trust shall be treated as continuing to satisfy the requirements of section 401(a) after the effective date of section 414(m) if the plan is terminated and all amounts are distributed to the participants within 180 days after the latest of:

(i) [insert the date of publication of this regulation in the Federal Register as a Treasury decision],

(ii) The date on which notice of the final determination with respect to a request for a determination letter is issued by the Internal Revenue Service, such request is withdrawn, or such request is finally disposed of by the Internal Revenue Service, provided the request for a determination letter was pending on [insert the date of the publication of this regulation in the Federal Register as a Treasury decision] or, in the case of a request for a determination letter on the plan termination, was made within 60 days after [insert the date of the publication of this regulation in the Federal Register as a Treasury decision].

(iii) If a petition is timely filed with the United States Tax Court for a declaratory judgment under section 7476 with respect to the final determination (or the failure of the Internal Revenue Service to make a final determination) in response to such request, the date on which the decision of the United States Tax Court in such proceeding becomes final.

(2) *Defined benefit plans.*—In the case of a defined benefit plan in existence on November 30, 1980, that fails to satisfy the requirements of section 401(a) solely because of the application of section 414(m), the trust shall be treated as continuing to satisfy the requirements of section 414(m) if the plan is terminated within 180 days after the latest of the dates determined in a manner consistent with paragraph (b)(1). However, deductions for contributions to the plan for plan years after the effective date of section 414(m) are limited to those necessary to satisfy the minimum funding standards of section 412. [Reg. § 1.414(m)-4.]

Affiliated Service Groups: Employee Leasing, Etc.

Employee Trusts: Affiliated Service Groups, Employee Leasing and Other Arrangements.—Reproduced below is the text of proposed Reg. § 1.414(o)-1, relating to affiliated service groups, employee leasing and other arrangements (published in the Federal Register on August 27, 1987).

☐ Par. 2. The following new section is added immediately following § 1.414(m)-4 and reads as follows:

§ 1.414(o)-1. Avoidance of employee benefit requirements through the use of separate organizations, employee leasing, or other arrangements.—(a) *In general.*—(1) Pursuant to section 414(o), this section provides rules, in addition to the rules contained in sections 414(m) and 414(n) and the regulations thereunder, to prevent the avoidance of any employee benefit requirement listed in either § 1.414(m)-3 or § 1.414(n)-3, through the use of separate organizations, employee leasing, or other arrangements.

(2) For the definition of the terms "person" and "leased employee", see § 1.414(n)-1(b). For the definition of the term "organization", see § 1.414(m)-5(a)(2). For the definition of the terms "management functions" and "management activities or services", see § 1.414(m)-5(c).

(3) For purposes of this section, the term "plan" means a stock bonus, pension, or profit-sharing plan qualified under section 401(a) or a simplified employee pension under section 408(k).

(4) For purposes of this section, the term "employee" includes a "self-employed individual" as defined in section 401(c)(1).

(5) For purposes of this section, the term "maintained", when used in the context of a plan maintained by any person, means "maintained at any time".

(6) For purposes of this section, services performed for a person other than as an employee of such person means services performed directly or indirectly for such person.

(b) *Services performed by leased owners.*—(1) *In general.*—(i) If an individual is a leased owner with respect to a recipient, then for purposes of determining whether any qualified plan actually maintained by the recipient and whether any qualified plan maintained by a leasing organization in which the leased owner is a participant (or in which the leased owner has or had an accrued benefit) satisfies the employee benefit requirements of section 1.414(n)-3(a) (except for paragraph (a)(6) of that section) for a plan year, the leased owner's interest in the leasing organization's qualified plan attributable to services performed by the leased owner for the recipient is to be treated as provided under a separate qualified plan maintained by the recipient covering only the leased owner and the leased owner is to be treated as an employee of the recipient. If a separate qualified plan is treated as maintained by the recipient with respect to a leased owner and such leased owner also participates in a qualified plan actually maintained by the recipient, the leased owner's interest in the leasing organization's qualified plan attributable to the leased

owner's performance of services for the recipient that is treated as provided to the leased owner under a separate qualified plan of the recipient is to be treated as provided to the leased owner under the qualified plan actually maintained by the recipient for purposes of determining whether such qualified plan satisfies the applicable employee benefit requirements. If either the separate qualified plan for the leased owner that is treated as maintained by the recipient or any qualified plan that is actually maintained by the recipient fails to satisfy any of the applicable employee benefit requirements, then except as provided in paragraphs (b)(1)(ii) and (b)(1)(iii) of this section, the following qualified plans shall be treated as not satisfying such requirements: any qualified plan actually maintained by the recipient in which the leased owner is a participant (or has or had an accrued benefit) and any qualified plan that is actually maintained by a leasing organization in which the leased owner has an interest that is attributable to the leased owner's performance of services for the recipient.

(ii) The Commissioner will not apply paragraph (b)(1)(i) of this section so as to disqualify a plan actually maintained by a recipient unless the Commissioner determines that, taking into account all the facts and circumstances, the disqualification of a leasing organization's plan would be ineffective as a means of securing compliance with the applicable employee benefit requirements. For example, it may be appropriate to disqualify the recipient's plan where a leasing organization's plan was terminated or substantial assets were removed therefrom in a year for which the statute of limitations has run with respect to the employer, employee, or trust.

(iii) If pursuant to paragraph (b)(1)(i) of this section, more than one leasing organization plan is subject to disqualification and at least one of the plans would not be disqualified if another plan or plans were disqualified first, all affected plan sponsors may, by agreement, elect the plan or plans subject to disqualification, provided that such election is not inconsistent with the purposes of this paragraph (b), such as where the plan or plans elected were terminated or substantial assets were removed therefrom in a year for which the statute of limitations has run with respect to the employer, employee, or trust. In the absence of such an election, the Commissioner, taking into account all the facts and circumstances, shall have the discretion to determine which plan or plans shall be disqualified.

(2) *Leased owner.*—(i) For purposes of this paragraph (b), an individual is a "leased owner" with respect to a recipient if during

the plan year of a plan maintained by a leasing organization the individual (A) performs any services for a recipient other than as an employee of the recipient and (B) is, at the time such services are performed, a five-percent owner of the recipient. The fact that an individual may also perform services as an employee of the recipient does not affect his status as a leased owner. If an individual becomes a leased owner with respect to a recipient, such individual is from that point on always to be considered a leased owner with respect to the recipient, notwithstanding anything in this paragraph (b) to the contrary, even if subsequently all services performed by the individual for the recipient are performed as an employee of the recipient.

(ii) Except as provided in paragraph (b)(2)(iii) of this section, and notwithstanding the first sentence of paragraph (b)(2)(i) of this section to the contrary, an individual is not a leased owner with respect to a recipient for purposes of a plan year of a plan maintained by a leasing organization if, during each calendar year containing at least one day of such plan year, less than 25 percent of his total hours actually worked for substantial compensation are for all recipients with respect to which he is a leased owner (but for the application of this paragraph (b)(2)(ii)) and less than 25 percent of his total compensation is derived from performing services for all such recipients. For purposes of this paragraph (b)(2)(ii), performing services for the recipient includes services performed as an employee of the recipient and in any other capacity. For purposes of this paragraph (b)(2)(ii), the term "compensation" means (A) with respect to services performed as a common-law employee, compensation reportable on Form W-2, and (B) with respect to services performed other than as a common-law employee, earned income as defined in section 401(c)(2). See section 414(s) for the definition of "compensation" for years beginning after December 31, 1986.

(iii) Paragraph (b)(2)(ii) of this section does not apply to an individual who (A) is a leased owner with respect to a recipient pursuant to the application of the first sentence of paragraph (b)(2)(i) of this section, and (B) performs professional services (as defined in §1.414(m)-1(c)) for the recipient, whether or not as an employee of the recipient, during the plan year of the plan maintained by the leasing organization, of the same type as the professional services performed by the recipient for third parties.

(3) *Recipient.*—For purposes of this paragraph (b), the term "recipient" has the same meaning as in paragraphs (b)(2) and (b)(6) of §1.414(n)-1, except that "leased owner" is substituted for "leased employee".

(4) *Leasing organization.*—For purposes of this paragraph (b), the term "leasing organization" has the same meaning as in §1.414(n)-1(b)(1), except that "leased owner" is substituted for "leased employee" and that "or provided" is added after "provides".

(5) *Five-percent owner.*—For purposes of this paragraph (b), an individual is a five-percent owner of a recipient if such individual is a 5-percent owner (as defined in section 416(i)) of any person included in the recipient.

(6) *Contributions, benefit, etc., provided to a leased owner.*—For purposes of this paragraph (b), a leased owner's interest in a leasing organization (as defined in §1.414(n)-2(b)(1)(i)) and in a leasing organization's qualified plan (as defined in §1.414(n)-2(b)(1)(i)), to the extent attributable to services for the recipient by the leased owner, is, for purposes of the applicable employee benefit requirements, treated as provided by the recipient or under a plan of the recipient. For rules relating to the application of this requirement, see paragraph (b)(2) of §1.414(n)-2.

(7) *Effect on employee rules.*—To the extent that a leased owner performs services for a recipient other than in the capacity of an employee, a leased owner is not an employee of the recipient and may not be actually covered by a plan of the recipient. Such leased owner may, however, qualify as a leased employee under section 414(n) and the regulations thereunder.

(c) [(c) through (j) withdrawn: 4/27/93]

(k) *Effective dates.*—(1) [(k)(1) withdrawn: 4/27/93]

(2) The provisions of paragraph (b) of this section are effective for tax years of recipients beginning after December 31, 1983. Therefore, the provisions of paragraph (b) apply to plan years beginning during and after the first tax year of a recipient beginning after December 31, 1983. For purposes of applying paragraph (b) to plan years beginning during and after the first tax year of a recipient beginning after December 31, 1983, contributions, forfeitures and benefits provided during any plan year beginning prior to the first tax year of a recipient beginning after December 31, 1983, shall be taken into account if they would have been taken into account had paragraph (b) been effective for such prior plan year.

(3) [(k)(3) withdrawn: 4/27/93]

(4) [(k)(4) withdrawn: 4/27/93]

[Reg. §1.414(o)-1.]

Employee Trusts: Highly Compensated Employees

Employee Benefit Plans: Highly Compensated Employees: Compensation: Definition.— Temporary Reg. §1.414(q)-1T, relating to the scope and meaning of the terms "highly compensated employee" and "compensation", is also proposed as a final regulation and, when adopted, would become Reg. §1.414(q)-1 (published in the Federal Register on February 19, 1988).

§1.414(q)-1. Highly compensated employee.

Qualified Plans: Automatic Contribution Arrangements

Qualified Plans: Automatic Contribution Arrangements.—Reg. §1.414(w)-1, relating to automatic contribution arrangements allowed by certain qualified plans, was adopted by T.D. 9447 on February 23, 2009 (published in the Federal Register on November 8, 2007) (REG-133300-07).

⧳→ *Caution: Proposed Reg. §1.414(w)-1, below, was adopted by T.D. 9447 on February 23, 2009. Final Reg. §1.414(w)-1 applies for plan years beginning on or after January 1, 2010. For plan years beginning prior to January 1, 2010, a plan that operates in accordance with this proposed Reg. §1.414(w)-1 or final Reg. §1.414(w)-1 will be treated as operating in accordance with a good faith interpretation of Code Sec. 414(w).*

☐ Par. 13. Section 1.414(w)-1 is added to read as follows:

§1.414(w)-1. Permissible withdrawals from eligible automatic contribution arrangements.—(a) *Overview.*—Section 414(w) provides rules under which certain employees are permitted to elect to make a withdrawal from an eligible automatic contribution arrangement. This section sets forth the rules applicable to permissible withdrawals from an eligible automatic contribution arrangement within the meaning of section 414(w). Paragraph (b) of this section defines an eligible automatic contribution arrangement. Paragraph (c) of this section describes a permissible withdrawal and addresses which employees are eligible to elect a withdrawal, the timing of the withdrawal election, and the amount of the withdrawal. Paragraph (d) of this section describes the tax and other consequences of the withdrawal. Paragraph (e) of this section includes the definitions applicable to this section.

(b) *Eligible automatic contribution arrangement.*—(1) *In general.*—An eligible automatic contribution arrangement is an automatic contribution arrangement under an applicable employer plan that, for the plan year, satisfies the uniformity requirement under paragraph (b)(2) of this section, the notice requirement under paragraph (b)(3) of this section, and the default investment requirement under (b)(4) of this section.

(2) *Uniformity requirement.*—An eligible automatic contribution arrangement must provide that the default elective contribution is a uniform percentage of compensation. An arrangement does not violate the uniformity requirement of this paragraph (b)(2) merely because the percentage varies in a manner that is permitted under §1.401(k)-3(j)(2)(iii), except that the rules of §§1.401(k)-3(j)(2)(iii)(A) and 1.401(k)-3(j)(2)(iii)(B) are applied without regard to whether the arrangement is intended to be a qualified automatic contribution arrangement.

(3) *Notice requirement.*—(i) *General rule.*—The notice requirement of this paragraph (b)(3) is satisfied for a plan year if each eligible employee is given notice of the employee's rights and obligations under the arrangement. The notice must be sufficiently accurate and comprehensive to apprise the employee of such rights and obligations, and be written in a manner calculated to be understood by the average employee to whom the arrangement applies. The notice must be in writing, however, see §1.401(a)-21 for rules permitting the use of electronic media to provide applicable notices.

(ii) *Content requirement.*—The notice must include the provisions found in §1.401(k)-3(d)(2)(ii) to the extent those provisions apply to the arrangement. A notice is not considered sufficiently accurate and comprehensive unless the notice accurately describes—

(A) The level of elective contributions which will be made on the employee's behalf if the employee does not make an affirmative election;

(B) The employee's rights to elect not to have default elective contributions made to the plan on his or her behalf or to have a different percentage of compensation or amount of elective contributions made to the plan on his or her behalf;

(C) How contributions made under the arrangement will be invested in the absence of any investment election by the employee; and

(D) The employee's rights to make a permissible withdrawal, if applicable, and the procedures to elect such a withdrawal.

(iii) *Timing.*—(A) *General rule.*—The timing requirement of this paragraph (b)(3)(iii) is satisfied if the notice is provided within a reasonable period before the beginning of each plan year (or, in the year an employee becomes an eligible employee, within a reasonable period before the employee becomes an eligible employee). In addition, a notice satisfies the timing requirements of paragraph (b)(3) of this section only if it is provided sufficiently early so that the employee has a reasonable period of time after receipt of the notice and before the first elective contribution is made under the arrangement to make the election described under paragraph (b)(ii)(A) of this section.

(B) *Deemed satisfaction of timing requirement.*—The timing requirement of this paragraph (b)(3)(iii) is satisfied if at least 30 days (and no more than 90 days) before the beginning of each plan year, the notice is given to each eligible employee for the plan year. In the case of an employee who does not receive the notice within the period described in the previous sentence because the employee becomes an eligible employee after the 90th day before the beginning of the plan year, the timing requirement is deemed to be satisfied if the notice is provided no more than 90 days before the employee becomes an eligible employee (and no later than the date the employee becomes an eligible employee).

(4) *Default investment requirement.*—To the extent the plan is subject to Title I of ERISA, default elective contributions under an eligible automatic contribution arrangement must be invested in accordance with regulations prescribed by the Secretary of Labor under section 404(c)(5) of ERISA.

(c) *Permissible withdrawal.*—(1) *In general.*—If the plan provides, any employee who has default elective contributions made under the eligible automatic contribution arrangement may elect to make a withdrawal of such contributions (and earnings attributable thereto) in accordance with the requirements of this paragraph (c). An applicable employer plan that includes an eligible automatic contribution arrangement will not fail to satisfy the prohibition on in-service withdrawals under sections 401(k)(2)(B), 403(b)(7), 403(b)(11), or 457(d)(1) merely because it permits withdrawals that satisfy the timing requirement of paragraph (c)(2) of this section and the amount requirement of paragraph (c)(3) of this section.

(2) *Timing.*—The election to withdraw default elective contributions must be made no later than 90 days after the date of the first default elective contribution under the eligible automatic contribution arrangement. The date of the first default elective contribution is the date that the compensation that is subject to the cash or deferred election would otherwise have been included in gross income. The effective date of an election described in this paragraph (c)(2) cannot be later than the last day of the payroll period that begins after the date the election is made.

(3) *Amount of distributions.*—(i) *In general.*—A distribution satisfies the requirement of this paragraph (c)(3) if the distribution is equal to the amount of default elective contributions made under the eligible automatic contribution arrangement through the effective date of the election described in paragraph (c)(2) of this section (adjusted for allocable gains and losses to the date of distribution). If default elective contributions are separately accounted for in the participant's account, the amount of the distribution will be the total amount in that account. However, if default elective contributions

are not separately accounted for under the plan, the amount of the allocable gains and losses will be determined under rules similar to those provided under § 1.401(k)-2(b)(2)(iv) for the distribution of excess contributions.

(ii) *Fees.*—The distribution amount as determined under this paragraph (c)(3) may be reduced by any generally applicable fees. However, the plan may not charge a different fee for a distribution under section 414(w) than applies to other distributions.

(d) *Consequences of the withdrawal.*—(1) *Income tax consequences.*—(i) *Year of inclusion.*—The amount of the withdrawal is includible in the eligible employee's gross income for the taxable year in which the distribution is made. However, the portion of the distribution consisting of designated Roth contributions is not included in an employee's gross income a second time. The portion of the withdrawal that is treated as an investment in the contract is determined without regard to any plan contributions other than those distributed as withdrawal default elective contributions.

(ii) *No additional tax on early distributions from qualified retirement plans.*—The withdrawal is not subject to the additional tax under section 72(t).

(iii) *Reporting.*—The amount of the withdrawal is reported on Form 1099-R, Distributions From Pensions, Annuities, Retirement or Profit-Sharing Plans, IRAs, Insurance Contracts, etc., as described in the applicable instructions.

(2) *Forfeiture of matching contributions.*—In the case of any withdrawal made under paragraph (c) of this section, employer matching contributions with respect to the amount withdrawn must be forfeited.

(3) *Consent rules.*—A withdrawal made under paragraph (c) of this section may be made without regard to any notice or consent otherwise required under section 401(a)(11) or 417.

(e) *Definitions.*—Unless indicated otherwise, the following definitions apply for purposes of section 414(w) and this section.

(1) *Applicable employer plan.*—An applicable employer plan means a plan that—

(i) Is qualified under section 401(a);

(ii) Satisfies the requirements of section 403(b); or

(iii) Is a section 457(b) eligible governmental plan described in § 1.457-2(f).

(2) *Automatic contribution arrangement.*—An automatic contribution arrangement means an arrangement that provides for a cash or deferred election that provides that in the absence of an eligible employee's affirmative election, a default election applies under which the employee is treated as having elected to have default elective contributions made on his or her behalf under the plan. This default election ceases to apply with respect to an employee if the employee makes an affirmative election (that remains in effect) to—

(i) Not have any default elective contributions made on his or her behalf; or

(ii) Have default elective contributions made in a different amount or percentage of compensation.

(3) *Default elective contributions.*—Default elective contributions means contributions made at a specified level or amount under an automatic contribution arrangement that are—

(i) Contributions described in section 402(g)(3)(A) or 402(g)(3)(C); or

(ii) Contributions made pursuant to a cash or deferred election within the meaning of section 457(b)(4) where the contributions are under a section 457(b) eligible governmental plan.

(4) *Eligible employee.*—An eligible employee means an employee who is eligible to make a cash or deferred election under the plan.

(f) *Effective date.*—Section 414(w) and this section apply to plan years beginning on or after January 1, 2008. [Reg. § 1.414(w)-1.]

Qualified Plans: Compensation: Treatment of Income from Indian Fishing Rights-Related Activity

Qualified Plans: Compensation: Treatment of Income from Indian Fishing Rights-Related Activity.—Amendments to Reg. § 1.415(c)-2, clarifying that amounts paid to an Indian tribe member as remuneration for services performed in a fishing rights-related activity may be treated as compensation for purposes of applying the limits on qualified plan benefits and contributions, are proposed (published in the Federal Register on November 15, 2013) (REG-120927-13).

☐ Par. 2. Section 1.415(c)-2 is amended by adding paragraphs (g)(9) and (h) to read as follows:

§1.415(c)-2. Compensation.

* * *

(g) * * *

(9) *Income derived by Indians from exercise of fishing rights.*—Amounts paid to a member of an Indian tribe directly or through a qualified Indian entity (within the meaning of section 7873(b)(3)) as compensation for services performed in a fishing rights-related activ-

ity (as defined in section 7873(b)(1)) of the tribe do not fail to constitute compensation under paragraphs (b)(1) and (b)(2) of this section and are not excluded from the definition of compensation pursuant to paragraph (c)(4) of this section merely because those amounts are not subject to income or employment taxes as a result of section 7873(a)(1) and (2). Thus, the determination of whether an amount constitutes wages, salaries, or earned income for purposes of

paragraph (b)(1) or (a)(2) of this section is made without regard to the exemption from taxation under section 7873(a)(1) and (2).

(h) *Effective/applicability date.*—Section 1.415(c)-2(g)(9) shall apply for plan years ending on or after the date of publication of the Treasury decision adopting these rules as final regulations in the **Federal Register**.

Retirement Plans: Distributions: Deferral of Receipt: Notification of Consequences

Retirement Plans: Distributions: Deferral of Receipt: Notification of Consequences.—Amendments to Reg. §1.417(e)-1, specifying that the notice required under Code Sec. 411(a)(11) to be provided to a participant of his or her right, if any, to defer receipt of an immediately distributable benefit must also describe the consequences of failing to defer receipt of the distribution, are proposed (published in the Federal Register on October 9, 2008) (REG-107318-08).

Par. 2. For each entry listed in the "Location" column, remove the language in the "Remove" column and add the language in the "Add" column in its place.

§1.417(e)-1. Restrictions and valuations of distributions from plans subject to sections 401(a)(11) and 417.

Location	Remove	Add
1.417(e)-1(b)(3)(i)	90 days	180 days
1.417(e)-1(b)(3)(ii), first sentence	90 days	180 days
1.417(e)-1 (b)(3)(iii)	90 days	180 days
1.417(e)-1 (b)(3)(vi), second sentence	90 days	180 days
1.417(e)-1(b)(3)(vii)	90 days	180 days
1.417(e)-1(b)(3)(vii)	90-day	180-day

Minimum Present Value Requirements: Benefit Plan Distributions: Update

Minimum Present Value Requirements: Benefit Plan Distributions: Update.—Amendments to Reg. §1.417(e)-1, relating to the minimum present value requirements applicable to certain defined benefit pension plans, are proposed (published in the Federal Register on November 25, 2016) (REG-107424-12).

Par. 2. Section 1.417(e)-1 is amended by:

1. Revising paragraphs (d)(1)(i), (d)(2), (d)(3), (d)(4), and (d)(6).
2. Adding paragraph (d)(8)(vi).
3. Revising paragraph (d)(9).
4. Removing paragraph (d)(10).

The addition and revisions read as follows:

§1.417(e)-1. Restrictions and valuations of distributions from plans subject to sections 401(a)(11) and 417.

* * *

(d) *Present value requirement.*—(1) *General rule.*—(i) *Defined benefit plans.*—(A) *In general.*—A defined benefit plan must provide that the present value of any accrued benefit and the amount (subject to sections 411(c)(3) and 415) of any distribution, including a single sum, must not be less than the amount calculated using the applicable mortality table described in paragraph (d)(2) of this section and the applicable interest rate described in paragraph (d)(3) of this section, as determined for the month described in paragraph (d)(4) of this section. The present value of any optional form of benefit, determined in accordance with the preceding sentence, cannot be less than the present value of the accrued benefit payable at normal retirement age, except to the extent that, for an optional form of benefit payable after normal retirement age, the requirements for suspension of benefits under section 411(a)(3)(B) are satisfied. The same rules used for the plan under this paragraph (d) must also be used to compute the present value of the benefit for purposes of determining whether consent for a distribution is required under paragraph (b) of this section.

(B) *Payment of a portion of a participant's benefit.*—The rules of this paragraph (d)(1) apply with respect to a payment of only a portion of the accrued benefit in the same manner as these rules would apply to a distribution of the entire accrued benefit. See paragraph (d)(7) of this section.

(C) *Special rules for applicable defined benefit plans.*—See section 411(a)(13) and the regulations thereunder for an exception from the rules of section 417(e)(3) and this paragraph (d) that applies to certain distributions from certain applicable defined benefit plans.

* * *

(2) *Applicable mortality table.*—(i) *In general.*—The applicable mortality table for a calendar year is the mortality table that is prescribed by the Commissioner in guidance published in the Internal Revenue Bulletin. See §601.601(d)(2) of this chapter. This mortality table is to be based on the table specified under section 430(h)(3)(A), but without regard to section 430(h)(3)(C) or (D)

(ii) *Mortality discounts.*—(A) *In general.*—Except as provided under paragraph (d)(2)(ii)(B) of this section, the probability of

death under the applicable mortality table is taken into account for purposes of determining the present value under this paragraph (d) without regard to the death benefits provided under the plan (other than a death benefit that is part of the normal form of benefit or part of another optional form of benefit, as described in §1.411(d)-3(g)(6)(ii)(B), for which present value is determined).

(B) *Special rule for employee-provided benefit.*—For purposes of determining the present value under this paragraph (d) with respect to the accrued benefit derived from employee contributions (that is determined in accordance with the requirements of section 411(c)(3)), the probability of death during the assumed deferral period, if any, is not taken into account. For purposes of the preceding sentence, the assumed deferral period is the period between the date of the present value determination and the assumed commencement date for the annuity attributable to contributions made by an employee.

(3) *Applicable interest rate.*—(i) *In general.*—The applicable interest rate for a month is determined using the first, second, and third segment rates for that month under section 430(h)(2)(C), as modified pursuant to section 417(e)(3)(D) (and without regard to the segment rate stabilization rules of section 430(h)(2)(C)(iv)). The applicable interest rate is specified by the Commissioner in revenue rulings, notices, or other guidance published in the Internal Revenue Bulletin, and is applied under rules similar to the rules under §1.430(h)(2)-1(b). Thus, for example, in determining the present value of a straight life annuity, the first segment is applied with respect to payments expected to be made during the 5-year period beginning on the annuity starting date, the second segment rate is applied with respect to payments expected to be made during the 15-year period following the end of that 5-year period, and the third segment rate is applied with respect to payments expected to be made after the end of that 15-year period. The interest rates that are published by the Commissioner are to be used for this purpose without further adjustment.

(ii) *Examples.*—The following examples illustrate the rules of paragraphs (d)(2) and (3) of this section.

Example 1. (i) Plan A is a non-contributory single-employer defined benefit plan with a calendar-year plan year, a one-year stability period coinciding with the calendar year, and a two-month lookback used for determining the applicable interest rate. The normal retirement age is 65, and all participant elections are made with proper spousal consent. Plan A provides for optional single sum payments equal to the present value of the participant's accrued benefit. Plan A provides that the applicable interest rates are the segment rates as specified by the Commissioner for the second full calendar month preceding the calendar year that contains the annuity starting date. The applicable mortality table is the table specified by the Commissioner for the calendar year that contains the annuity starting date.

(ii) Participant P retires in May 2017 at age 60 and elects (with spousal consent) to receive a single-sum payment. P has an accrued benefit of $2,000 per month payable as a life annuity beginning at the plan's normal retirement age of 65. The applicable mortality rates for 2017 apply. The applicable interest rates published by the Commissioner for November 2016 are 1.57%, 3.45%, and 4.39% for the first, second, and third segment rates, respectively. The deferred annuity factor calculated based on these interest rates and the applicable mortality table for 2017 is 10.931 for a participant age 60. To satisfy the requirements of section 417(e)(3) and this paragraph (d), the single-sum payment received by P cannot be less than $262,344 (that is, $2,000 x 12 x 10.931).

Example 2. (i) The facts are the same as for *Example 1* of this paragraph (d)(3)(ii), except that Plan A provides for mandatory employee contributions. Participant Q retires in May 2017 at age 60 and elects (with spousal consent) to receive a single-sum payment of Q's entire accrued benefit. Q has an accrued benefit of $2,000 per month payable as a life annuity beginning at Plan A's normal retirement age of 65, consisting of an accrued benefit derived from employee contributions determined in accordance with section 411(c)(2) (Q's employee-provided accrued benefit) of $500 per month and an accrued benefit derived from employer contributions (Q's employer-provided accrued benefit) of $1,500 per month.

(ii) Pursuant to paragraph (d)(2)(ii)(B) of this section, the single-sum payment used to settle Q's employee-provided accrued benefit cannot be less than the present value of that portion of Q's accrued benefit determined using the applicable interest and mortality rates described in paragraphs (d)(3)(i) and (d)(2)(ii) of this section, determined without taking the probability of death during the assumed deferral period into account. The deferred annuity factor calculated based on the interest and mortality rates specified in *Example 1* of this paragraph (d)(3)(ii) (taking the probability of death only after age 65 into account) is 11.266 for a participant age 60. To satisfy the requirement of section 417(e)(3) and this paragraph (d), the single-sum payment received by Q with respect to the employee-provided portion of the accrued benefit cannot be less than the minimum present value of $67,596 (that is, $500 x 12 x 11.266).

(iii) The single-sum payment used to settle Q's employer-provided accrued benefit cannot be less than the present value of that portion of Q's accrued benefit determined using the applicable interest and mortality rates. However, for this purpose, Plan A is permitted to take the probability of death during the assumed deferral period into account. The single-sum payment received by Q with respect to the employer-provided portion of the accrued benefit cannot be less than $196,758 (that is, $1,500 x 12 x 10.931).

(iv) The total single-sum payment received by Q cannot be less than the sum of the minimum present value of Q's employee- and employer-provided accrued benefits, or $264,354 ($67,596 + $196,758).

(4) *Time for determining interest rate and mortality table.*— (i) *Interest rate general rule.*—Except as provided in paragraph (d)(4)(v) or (vi) of this section, the applicable interest rate to be used for a distribution is the applicable interest rate determined under paragraph (d)(3) of this section for the applicable lookback month. The applicable lookback month for a distribution is the lookback month (as described in paragraph (d)(4)(iv) of this section) for the stability period (as described in paragraph (d)(4)(iii) of this section) that contains the annuity starting date for the distribution. The time and method for determining the applicable interest rate for each participant's distribution must be determined in a consistent manner that is applied uniformly to all participants in the plan.

(ii) *Mortality table general rule.*—The applicable mortality table to be used for a distribution is the mortality table that is published for the calendar year during which the stability period containing the annuity starting date begins.

(iii) *Stability period.*—A plan must specify the period for which the applicable interest rate remains constant (the stability period). This stability period may be one calendar month, one plan quarter, one calendar quarter, one plan year, or one calendar year. This same stability period also applies to the applicable mortality table.

(iv) *Lookback month.*—A plan must specify the lookback month that is used to determine the applicable interest rate with respect to a stability period. The lookback month may be the first,

second, third, fourth, or fifth full calendar month preceding the first day of the stability period.

(v) *Permitted average interest rate.*—A plan may apply the rules of paragraph (d)(4)(i) of this section by substituting a permitted average applicable interest rate with respect to the plan's stability period for the applicable interest rate determined under paragraph (d)(3) of this section for the applicable lookback month for the stability period. For this purpose, a permitted average applicable interest rate with respect to a stability period is the applicable interest rate that is computed by averaging the applicable interest rates determined under paragraph (d)(3) of this section for two or more consecutive months from among the first, second, third, fourth, and fifth calendar months preceding the first day of the stability period. For this paragraph (d)(4)(v) to apply, a plan must specify the manner in which the permitted average interest rate is computed.

(vi) *Additional determination dates.*—The Commissioner may prescribe, in guidance published in the Internal Revenue Bulletin, other times that a plan may provide for determining the applicable interest rate.

(vii) *Example.*—The following example illustrates the rules of this paragraph (d)(4):

Example. (i) The facts are the same as *Example 1* of paragraph (d)(3)(ii) of this section, except that Plan A provides that the applicable interest rates are the rates for the third full calendar month preceding the beginning of the plan quarter that contains the annuity starting date. Plan A also provides that the applicable mortality table is the table specified by the Commissioner for the calendar year that contains the beginning of the stability period.

(ii) The segment interest rates that apply for annuity starting dates during the period beginning April 1, 2017 and ending June 30, 2017 are the segment rates for January 2017. This plan design permits the applicable interest rate to be fixed for each plan quarter and for the applicable interest rate for all distributions made during each plan quarter to be determined before the beginning of the plan quarter.

* * *

(6) *Exceptions.*—(i) *In general.*—This paragraph (d) (other than the provisions relating to section 411(d)(6) requirements in paragraph (d)(9) of this section) does not apply to the amount of a distribution paid in the form of an annual benefit that—

(A) Does not decrease during the life of the participant, or, in the case of a QPSA, the life of the participant's spouse; or

(B) Decreases during the life of the participant merely because of—

(1) The death of the survivor annuitant (but only if the reduction is to a level not below 50 percent of the annual benefit payable before the death of the survivor annuitant): or

(2) The cessation or reduction of a social security supplement or qualified disability benefit (as defined in section 411(a)(9)).

(ii) *Example.*—The following example illustrates the rules of this paragraph (d)(6).

Example. (i) The facts are the same as *Example 1* of paragraph (d)(3)(ii) of this section. Plan A also provides an optional distribution in the form of a Social Security level income option. Under this provision, the participant's benefit is adjusted so that a larger amount is payable until age 65, at which time it is reduced to provide a level income in combination with the participant's estimated social security benefit beginning at age 65. Participant R's reduced early retirement benefit payable as a straight life annuity benefit commencing at age 60 is $1,300 per month (which is less than the actuarially equivalent benefit that would have been determined using the applicable interest and mortality rates under section 417(e)(3)) and R's estimated social security benefit is $1,000 per month beginning at age 65.

(ii) Because the benefit payable under the social security level income option decreases at age 65 and the decrease is not on account of the death of the participant or a beneficiary or the cessation or reduction of social security supplements or qualified disability benefits, the benefits payable under the social security level income option are subject to the minimum present value requirements of section 417(e)(3). As illustrated in *Example 1* of paragraph (d)(3)(ii) of this section, the minimum present value of Participant R's benefits under section 417(e)(3) is $262,344, which is based on the present value of R's accrued benefit, not R's benefit that would be payable as a straight life annuity at the annuity starting date.

(iii) The deferred annuity factor for a participant age 60 with lifetime benefits commencing at age 65, based on the November 2016 segment rates and the applicable mortality table for 2017, is 10.931. The corresponding temporary annuity factor to age 65 is 4.752. The minimum benefits payable to Participant R in the form of a social security level income option (with a decrease of $1,000 – equal to the participant's estimated social security benefit – occurring at age 65) are $2,090.99 per month until age 65 and $1,090.99 per month thereafter. Any amounts less than this would have a present value smaller than the required amount of $262,344, and thus would fail to satisfy the minimum present value requirement of section 417(e)(3).

* * *

(8) * * *

(vi) *Applicability date for provisions reflecting PPA '06 updates and other rules.*—Paragraphs (d)(1) through (4) of this section apply to distributions with annuity starting dates in plan years beginning on or after the date regulations that finalize these proposed regulations are published in the **Federal Register**. Prior to this applicability date, taxpayers must continue to apply the provisions of § 1.417(e)-1(d) as contained in 26 CFR part 1 as in effect immediately before publication of those final regulations, except to the extent superseded by statutory changes and guidance of general applicability relating to those statutory changes.

(9) *Relationship with section 411(d)(6).*—(i) *In general.*—A plan amendment that changes the interest rate or the mortality assumptions used for the purposes described in paragraph (d)(1) of this section (including a plan amendment that changes the time for determining those assumptions) is generally subject to section 411(d)(6). However, for certain exceptions to the rule in the preceding sentence, see paragraph (d)(7)(iv) of this section, § 1.411(d)-4, Q&A-2(b)(2)(v) (with respect to plan amendments relating to involuntary distributions), and section 1107(a)(2) of the Pension Protection Act of 2006, Public Law 109-280, 120 Stat. 780 (2006) (PPA '06) (with respect to certain plan amendments that were made pursuant to a change to the Internal Revenue Code by PPA '06 or regulations issued thereunder).

(ii) *Section 411(d)(6) relief for change in time for determining interest rate and mortality table.*—Notwithstanding the general rule of paragraph (d)(9)(i) of this section, if a plan amendment changes the time for determining the applicable interest rate (and, if the amendment changes the stability period described in paragraph (d)(4)(iii) of this section, the time for determining the applicable mortality table), including an indirect change as a result of a change in plan year, the amendment will not be treated as reducing accrued benefits in violation of section 411(d)(6) merely on account of this change if the conditions of this paragraph (d)(9)(ii) are satisfied. If the plan amendment is effective on or after the date the amendment is adopted, any distribution for which the annuity starting date occurs in the one-year period commencing at the time the amendment is effective must be determined using the interest rate and mortality table provided under the plan determined at either the date for determining the interest rate and mortality table before the amendment or the date for determining the interest rate and mortality table after the amendment, whichever results in the larger distribution. If the plan amendment is adopted retroactively (that is, the amendment is effective prior to the adoption date), the plan must use the interest rate and mortality table determination dates resulting in the larger distribution for distributions with annuity starting dates occurring during the period beginning with the effective date and ending one year after the adoption date.

* * *

Employee Trusts: Effective Dates

Employee Trusts: Tax Reform Act of 1984: Effective Dates.—Temporary Reg. §§1.419-1T and 1.419A-1T are also proposed as final regulations and, when adopted, would become Reg. §§1.419-1 and 1.419A-1, respectively (published in the Federal Register on February 4, 1986).

§1.419-1. Treatment of welfare benefit funds.

§1.419A-1. Qualified asset account limitation of additions to account.

Welfare Benefit Funds: Collective Bargaining

Welfare Benefit Fund: Collective Bargaining: Limits on Contributions and Reserves.— Temporary Reg. §1.419A-2T, relating to welfare benefit funds maintained pursuant to collective bargaining agreements, is also proposed as a final regulation and, when adopted, would become Reg. §1.419A-2 (published in the Federal Register on July 3, 1985).

§1.419A-2. Qualified asset account limitation for collectively bargained funds.

Defined Benefit Plans: Multiemployer Plan Funding Guidance

Defined Benefit Plans: Multiemployer Plan Funding Guidance.—Reg. §§1.432(a)-1 and 1.432(b)-1, providing additional rules for certain multiemployer defined benefit plans that are in effect on July 16, 2006 and affecting multiemployer plans that are either endangered or critical status, are proposed (published in the Federal Register on March 18, 2008) (REG-151135-07).

☐ Par. 2. Section 1.432(a)-1 is added to read as follows:

§1.432(a)-1. General rules relating to section 432.—(a) *In general.*—(1) *Overview.*—This section provides rules relating to multiemployer plans (within the meaning of section 414(f)) that are in endangered status or critical status under section 432. Section 432 and this section only apply to multiemployer plans that are in effect on July 16, 2006. Paragraph (b) of this section sets forth definitions of terms that apply for purposes of section 432. Paragraph (c) of this section sets forth special rules for plans described in section 404(c) and for the treatment of nonbargained participation.

(2) *Plans in endangered status.*—(i) *Plan sponsor must adopt funding improvement plan.*—If a plan is in endangered status, the plan sponsor must adopt and implement a funding improvement plan that satisfies the requirements of section 432(c).

(ii) *Restrictions applicable to plans in endangered status.*—If a plan is in endangered status, the plan and plan sponsor must satisfy the requirements of section 432(d)(1) during the funding plan adoption period specified in section 432(c)(8).

(iii) *Restrictions applicable after the adoption of funding improvement plan.*—In the case of a plan that is in endangered status after adoption of the funding improvement plan, the plan and the plan sponsor must satisfy the requirements of section 432(d)(2) until the end of the funding improvement period.

(3) *Plans in critical status.*—(i) *Plan sponsor must adopt rehabilitation plan.*—If a plan is in critical status, the plan sponsor must adopt and implement a rehabilitation plan that satisfies the requirements of section 432(e).

(ii) *Restrictions applicable to plans in critical status.*—If a plan is in critical status, the plan and the plan sponsor must satisfy the requirements of section 432(f)(4) during the rehabilitation plan adoption period as defined in section 432(e)(5). The plan must also apply the restrictions on single sum and other accelerated benefits set forth in paragraph (a)(3)(iii) of this section.

(iii) *Restrictions on single sums and other accelerated benefits.*— (A) *In general.*—A plan in critical status is required to provide that, effective on the date the notice of certification of the plan's critical status for the initial critical year under § 1.432(b)-1(e) is sent, no payment in excess of the monthly amount payable under a single life annuity (plus any social security supplements described in the last sentence of section 411(a)(9)), and no payment for the purchase of an irrevocable commitment from an insurer to pay benefits, may be made except as provided in section 432(f)(2). A plan amendment that provides for these restrictions does not violate section 411(d)(6).

(B) *Exceptions.*—Pursuant to section 432(f)(2)(B), the restrictions under this paragraph (a)(3)(iii) do not apply to a benefit which under section 411 (a)(11) may be immediately distributed without the consent of the participant or to any makeup payment in the case of a retroactive annuity starting date or any similar payment of benefits owed with respect to a prior period.

(C) [Reserved.]

(D) *Correction of erroneous restrictions.*—If the notice described in § 1.432(b)-1(e) has been sent and the restrictions provided under this paragraph (a)(3)(iii) have been applied, and it is later determined that the restrictions should not have been applied, then the plan must correct any benefit payments that were restricted in error. Thus, for example, if pursuant to section 212(e)(2) of the Pension Protection Act of 2006, Public Law 109-280, 120 Stat. 780 the enrolled actuary for the plan certified that it was reasonably expected that the plan would be in critical status with respect to the first plan year beginning after 2007, and the notice described in § 1.432(b)-1(e)(3)(i) was sent, but the plan is not later certified to be in critical status for that plan year, then the plan must correct any benefit payments that were restricted after the notice was sent. Similarly, if the enrolled actuary for the plan certified that it was reasonably expected that the plan would be in critical status with respect to the first plan year beginning after 2007, and the notice described in § 1.432(b)-1(e)(3)(i) was sent before the first day of that plan year, the restriction on benefits under section 432(f)(2) first applies beginning on the first day of the first plan year beginning after 2007. If the plan restricts benefits before that date, then the plan must correct any improperly restricted benefits.

(iv) *Restrictions applicable after the adoption of rehabilitation plan.*—In the case of a plan that is in critical status after the adoption of the rehabilitation plan, the plan and the plan sponsor must satisfy the requirements of section 432(f)(1) until the end of the rehabilitation period.

(b) *Definitions.*—The following definitions apply for purposes of section 432 and the regulations:

(1) *Accumulated funding deficiency.*—The term accumulated funding deficiency has the same meaning as the term accumulated funding deficiency under section 431(a).

(2) *Active participant.*—The term active participant means a participant who is in covered service under the plan.

(3) *Bargaining party.*—Except as provided in paragraph (c)(1) of this section, the term bargaining party means an employer who has an obligation to contribute under the plan and an employee organization which, for purposes of collective bargaining, represents plan participants employed by an employer which has an obligation to contribute under the plan.

(4) *Benefit commencement date.*—The term benefit commencement date means the annuity starting date (or in the case of a retroactive annuity starting date, the date on which benefit payments begin).

(5) *Critical status.*—A multiemployer plan is in critical status if the plan meets one of the tests set forth in § 1.432(b)-1(c).

(6) *Endangered status.*—A plan is in endangered status if the plan meets one of the tests set forth in § 1.432(b)-1(b).

(7) *Funded percentage.*—The term funded percentage means a fraction (expressed as a percentage) the numerator of which is the actuarial value of the plan's assets as determined under section 431(c)(2) and the denominator of which is the accrued liability of the plan, determined using the actuarial assumptions described in section 431(c)(3) and the unit credit funding method.

(8) *Funding improvement period for endangered or seriously endangered plans.*—The term funding improvement period means the period that begins on the first day of the first plan year beginning after the earlier of the second anniversary of the date of the adoption of the funding improvement plan, or the expiration of the collective bargaining agreements that are in effect on the due date for the actuarial certification of endangered status for the initial endangered year and which cover, as of such due date, at least 75 percent of the active participants in the plan. The funding improvement period ends on the last day of the 10th year (15 years for seriously endangered plans, except as provided in section 432(c)(5)) after it begins or, if earlier, the date of the change in status described in section 432(c)(4)(C).

(9) *Funding plan adoption period.*—The term funding plan adoption period means the period that begins on the date of the actuarial certification for the initial endangered year and ends on the day before the first day of the funding improvement period.

(10) *Inactive participant.*—The term inactive participant means —

(i) A participant who is not an active participant,
(ii) A beneficiary under the plan, or
(iii) An alternate payee under the plan.

☐ Par. 3. Section 1.432(b)-1 is added to read as follows:

§ 1.432(b)-1. Determination of status and adoption of a plan.—(a) *In general.*—This section provides rules relating to multiemployer

(11) *Initial critical year.*—The term initial critical year means the first year for which the enrolled actuary for the plan has certified that the plan is or will be in critical status. If a plan is in critical status in one year, emerges from critical status in a subsequent year and then returns to critical status, the year of reentry into critical status is treated as the initial critical year with respect to subsequent years.

(12) *Initial endangered year.*—The term initial endangered year means the first year for which the enrolled actuary for the plan has certified that the plan is in endangered status. If a plan is in endangered status in one year, changes from endangered status in a subsequent year and then returns to endangered status, the year of reentry into endangered status is treated as the initial endangered year with respect to subsequent years.

(13) *Nonbargained participant.*—The term nonbargained participant means a participant in the plan whose participation is other than pursuant to a collective bargaining agreement within the meaning of section 7701(a)(46). A participant will not be treated as a nonbargained participant merely because the participant is no longer covered by the collective bargaining agreement solely as a result of retirement or severance from employment.

(14) *Obligation to contribute.*—The term obligation to contribute means an obligation to contribute arising under one or more collective bargaining (or related) agreements or as a result of a duty under applicable labor-management relations law.

(15) *Plan sponsor.*—Except as provided in paragraph (c)(1) of this section, the term plan sponsor means the association, committee, joint board of trustees, or other similar group of representatives of the parties who establish or maintain the plan.

(16) *Rehabilitation period.*—The term rehabilitation period means the period that begins on the first day of the first plan year beginning after the earlier of the second anniversary of the date of the adoption of the rehabilitation plan, or the expiration of the collective bargaining agreements that are in effect on the due date for the actuarial certification of critical status for the initial critical year and which cover, as of such due date, at least 75 percent of the active participants in the plan. The rehabilitation period ends on the last day of the 10th year after it begins or, if earlier, the plan year preceding the plan year in which the plan has emerged from critical status as described in section 432(e)(4)(B).

(17) *Rehabilitation plan adoption period.*—The term rehabilitation plan adoption period means the period that begins on the date of the actuarial certification for the initial critical year and ends on the day before the first day of the rehabilitation period.

(18) *Seriously endangered status.*—A plan is in seriously endangered status if the plan is in endangered status and is described in both § 1.432(b)-1(b)(2) and (3).

(c) *Special rules.*—(1) *Plan described in section 404(c).*—In the case of a plan described in section 404(c), or a continuation of such a plan, the association of employers that is the employer settlor of the plan is treated as a bargaining party and is treated as the plan sponsor for purposes of section 432.

(2) *Plans covering both bargained and nonbargained participants.*—In the case of an employer that contributes to a plan with respect to both employees who are covered by one or more collective bargaining agreements and employees who are nonbargained participants, if the plan is in endangered status or critical status, benefits of and contributions for the nonbargained participants (including surcharges on those contributions) are determined as if those nonbargained participants were covered under the employer's collective bargaining agreement in effect when the plan entered endangered or critical status that is the first to expire.

(3) *Plans covering nonbargained participants only.*—In the case of an employer that contributes to a multiemployer plan only with respect to employees who are not covered by a collective bargaining agreement, section 432 and the regulations thereunder are applied as if the employer were the bargaining party, and its participation agreement with the plan were a collective bargaining agreement with a term ending on the first day of the plan year beginning after the employer is provided the schedules described in sections 432(c) and (e).

(d) *Effective/applicability date.*—These regulations apply to plan years ending after March 18, 2008, but only with respect to plan years that begin on or after January 1, 2008. [Reg. § 1.432(a)-1.]

plans (within the meaning of section 414(f)) that are in endangered status or critical status under section 432. Section 432 and this section only apply to multiemployer plans that are in effect on July 16, 2006. Paragraph (b) of this section sets forth the factors for determining whether a plan is in endangered status. Paragraph (c) of this section sets forth the factors for determining whether a plan is in critical status. Paragraph (d) sets forth the requirements for the annual certification by the plan's enrolled actuary. Paragraph (e) of this section describes the notice to employees that is required for plans that are in endangered or critical status.

(b) *Determination of endangered status.*—(1) *In general.*—A plan is in endangered status for a plan year if, as determined by the enrolled actuary for the plan, the plan is not in critical status for the plan year and if, as of the beginning of the plan year, the plan is described either in paragraph (b)(2) of this section or paragraph (b)(3) of this section. The enrolled actuary's determination of whether a plan is in endangered status is made under the rules of paragraph (d)(5) of this section.

(2) *Endangered status based on funding percentage.*—A plan is described in this paragraph (b)(2) for a plan year if the plan's funded percentage for such plan year is less than 80 percent.

(3) *Endangered status based on projection of funding deficiency.*— A plan is described in this paragraph (b)(3) for a plan year if the plan has an accumulated funding deficiency for such plan year (or is projected to have such an accumulated funding deficiency for any of the 6 succeeding plan years), taking into account any extension of amortization periods under section 431(d).

(c) *Critical Status.*—(1) *In general.*—A multiemployer plan is in critical status for a plan year if, as determined by the enrolled actuary for the plan, the plan is described in one or more of paragraphs (c)(2) through (c)(6) of this section as of the beginning of the plan year. The enrolled actuary's determination of critical status must be made in accordance with the rules of paragraph (d)(5) of this section. Notwithstanding paragraph (d)(5)(iii) of this section, for purposes of applying the critical status tests described in paragraphs (c)(2) and (c)(5) of this section, the actuary must assume that the terms of all collective bargaining agreements pursuant to which the plan is maintained for the current plan year continue in effect for succeeding plan years.

(2) *Critical status based on 6-year projection of benefit payments.*— A plan is described in this paragraph (c)(2) if the funded percentage of the plan is less than 65 percent, and the present value of all nonforfeitable benefits projected to be payable under the plan during the current plan year and each of the 6 succeeding plan years (plus administrative expenses for such plan years) is greater than the sum of—

(i) The fair market value of plan assets, plus

(ii) The present value of the reasonably anticipated employer contributions for the current plan year and the 6 succeeding plan years.

(3) *Critical status based on short term funding deficiency.*—A plan is described in this paragraph (c)(3) if—

(i) The plan has an accumulated funding deficiency for the current plan year, not taking into account any extension of amortization periods under section 431(d), or

(ii) The plan is projected to have an accumulated funding deficiency for any of the 3 succeeding plan years (4 succeeding plan years if the funded percentage of the plan is 65 percent or less), not taking into account any extension of amortization periods under section 431(d).

(4) *Critical status based on contributions less than normal cost plus interest.*—A plan is described in this paragraph (c)(4) if—

(i) The present value of the reasonably anticipated employer and employee contributions for the current plan year is less than the sum of—

(A) The plan's normal cost (determined under the unit credit funding method), and

(B) Interest (determined at the rate used for determining costs under the plan) on the excess if any of—

(1) The accrued liability of the plan (determined using the actuarial assumptions described in section 431(c)(3) and the unit credit funding method) over

(2) The actuarial value of assets determined under section 431(c)(2),

(ii) The present value, as of the beginning of the current plan year, of nonforfeitable benefits of inactive participants is greater than the present value of nonforfeitable benefits of active participants, and

(iii) The plan has an accumulated funding deficiency for the current plan year (or is projected to have such a deficiency for any of the 4 succeeding plan years), not taking into account any extension of amortization periods under section 431(d).

(5) *Critical status based on 4-year projection of benefit payments.*— A plan is described in this paragraph (c)(5) if the present value of all benefits projected to be payable under the plan during the current plan year or any of the 4 succeeding plan years (plus administrative expenses for such plan years) is greater than the sum of—

(i) The fair market value of plan assets, plus

(ii) The present value of the reasonably anticipated employer contributions for the current plan year and each of the 4 succeeding plan years.

(6) *Critical status based on failure to meet emergence criteria.*—A plan is described in this paragraph (c)(6) if—

(i) The plan was in critical status for the immediately preceding plan year, and

(ii) The enrolled actuary for the plan has certified that the plan is projected to have an accumulated funding deficiency for the plan year or any of the 9 succeeding plan years, without regard to the use of the shortfall funding method but taking into account any extensions of the amortization periods under section 431(d).

(d) *Annual certification by the plan's enrolled actuary.*—(1) *In general.*—Not later than the 90th day of each plan year of a multiemployer plan, the enrolled actuary for the plan must certify to the Secretary of the Treasury and to the plan sponsor—

(i) Whether or not the plan is in endangered status for such plan year;

(ii) Whether or not the plan is or will be in critical status for such plan year, and

(iii) In the case of a plan which is in a funding improvement or rehabilitation period, whether or not the plan is making the scheduled progress in meeting the requirements of its funding improvement or rehabilitation plan.

(2) *Transmittal of certification.*—(i) *Transmittal to the plan sponsor.*—The certification of plan status described in paragraph (d)(1) must be submitted to the plan sponsor at the address stated by the plan sponsor on their Annual Report (Form 5500) or such other address as the plan sponsor may designate in writing for receipt of this certification.

(ii) *Transmittal to the Secretary of the Treasury.*—Except as provided in guidance of general applicability to be published in the Internal Revenue Bulletin, the annual certification of plan status described in paragraph (d)(1) must be transmitted to the Secretary of the Treasury by mailing the certification to:

Internal Revenue Service
Employee Plans Compliance Unit
Group 7602 (SE:TEGE:EP)
Room 1700 - 17th Floor
230 S. Dearborn Street
Chicago, IL 60604

(3) *Content of annual certification.*—(i) *In general.*—The annual certification must contain the information described in this paragraph (d)(3). The Secretary may add to or otherwise modify the requirements in this paragraph (d)(3) in guidance of general applicability to be published in the Internal Revenue Bulletin.

(ii) *Plan identification.*—The annual certification must include the name of the plan; the plan number; the name, address, and telephone number of the plan sponsor; and the plan year for which the certification is being made.

(iii) *Enrolled actuary identification.*—The annual certification must include the name, address and telephone number of the enrolled actuary signing the certification; the actuary's enrollment identification number; the actuary's signature, and the date of the signature.

(iv) *Information on plan status.*—The annual certification must state whether the plan is in endangered status (which includes seriously endangered status); critical status, or neither endangered nor critical status.

(v) *Information on scheduled progress.*—If the annual certification is made with respect to a plan year that is within the plan's funding improvement period or rehabilitation period arising from a prior certification of endangered or critical status, the actuary must also certify whether or not the plan is making scheduled progress in meeting the requirements of its funding improvement or rehabilitation plan.

(4) *Penalty for failure to secure timely actuarial certification.*—A failure of a plan's actuary to certify the plan's status under this paragraph (d) by the date specified in paragraph (d)(1) of this section is treated as a failure or refusal by the plan administrator to file the annual report required to be filed with the Secretary of Labor under

section 101(b)(4) of the Employee Retirement Income Security Act of 1974.

(5) *Actuarial projections of assets and liabilities.*—(i) *In general.*— In making the determinations and projections under section 432(b) and this section, the enrolled actuary for the plan must make projections required for the current and succeeding plan years of the current value of the assets of the plan and the present value of all liabilities to participants and beneficiaries under the plan for the current plan year as of the beginning of such year. These projections must be based on reasonable actuarial estimates, assumptions, and methods in accordance with section 431(c)(3) and that offer the actuary's best estimate of anticipated experience under the plan. Notwithstanding the previous sentence, the actuary is permitted to rely on the plan sponsor's projection of activity in the industry provided under paragraph (d)(5)(iii) of this section. The projected present value of liabilities as of the beginning of such year must be determined based on the most recent information reported on the most recent of either—

(A) The actuarial statement required under section 103(d) of the Employee Retirement Income Security Act of 1974 that has been filed with respect to the most recent year, or

(B) The actuarial valuation for the preceding plan year.

(ii) *Determinations of future contributions.*—Any actuarial projection of plan assets shall assume either—

(A) Reasonably anticipated employer contributions for the current and succeeding plan years, assuming that the terms of the one or more collective bargaining agreements pursuant to which the plan is maintained for the current plan year continue in effect for succeeding plan years, or

(B) That employer contributions for the most recent plan year will continue indefinitely, but only if the enrolled actuary for the plan determines there have been no significant demographic changes that would make such assumption unreasonable.

(iii) *Projected industry activity.*—The plan sponsor shall provide any necessary projection of activity in the industry, including future covered employment, to the plan actuary. For this purpose, the plan sponsor must act reasonably and in good faith.

(6) *Treatment of amortization extensions under section 412(e).*— For purposes of section 432, if the plan received an extension of any amortization period under section 412(e), the extension is treated the same as an extension under section 431(d). Thus, such an extension is not taken into account in determining whether a plan has or will have an accumulated funding deficiency under paragraph (c)(3) and (c)(4) of this section, but it is taken into account in determining whether a plan has or will have an accumulated funding deficiency under paragraph (b)(3) of this section.

(e) *Notice of endangered or critical status.*—(1) *In general.*—In any case in which the enrolled actuary for the plan certifies that a multiemployer plan is or will be in endangered or critical status for a plan year, the plan sponsor must, not later than 30 days after the date of the certification, provide notification of the endangered or critical status to the participants and beneficiaries, the Pension Benefit Guaranty Corporation, and the Secretary of Labor.

(2) *Plans in critical status.*—If it is certified that a multiemployer plan is or will be in critical status for a plan year, the plan sponsor must include in the notice an explanation of the possibility that adjustable benefits (as defined in section 432(e)(8)) may be reduced, and such reductions may apply to participants and beneficiaries whose benefit commencement date is on or after the date such notice is provided for the first plan year in which the plan is in critical status. If the plan provides benefits that are restricted under section 432(f)(2), the notice must also include an explanation that the plan cannot pay single sums and similar benefits described in section 432(f)(2) that are greater than the monthly amount due under a single life annuity. A plan sponsor that sends the model notice issued by the Secretary of Labor pursuant to section 432(b)(3)(D)(iii) satisfies this requirement.

(3) *Transition rules.*—(i) *Early notice permitted.*—If, after August 17, 2006, the enrolled actuary for the plan certifies that a plan is reasonably expected to be in critical status with respect to the first plan year beginning after 2007, then the notice described in this paragraph (e) may be provided before the date the actuary certifies the plan is in critical status for that plan year. The ability to provide early notice does not extend the otherwise applicable deadline for providing the notice under paragraph (e)(1) of this section.

(ii) *Reformation of prior notice.*—If notice has been provided prior to the date required under paragraph (e)(1) of this section, but the notice did not include all of the information described in paragraph (e)(2) of this section, then that notice will not satisfy the requirements for notice under section 432(b)(3)(D). Accordingly, the restrictions under section 432(f)(2) will not apply as a result of the issuance of such a notice. However, if prior to the date notice is required to be provided under paragraph (e)(1) of this section additional notice is provided that includes all of the information required under paragraph (e)(2) of this section, then the notice requirements of section 432(b)(3)(D) are satisfied as of the date of that additional notice and the restrictions of section 432(f)(2) will apply beginning on that date. In such a case, the date of the earlier notice will still apply for purposes of section 432(e)(8)(A)(ii) provided that the earlier notice included all of the information required under section 432(b)(3)(D)(ii).

(f) *Effective/applicability date.*—These regulations apply to plan years ending after March 18, 2008, but only with respect to plan years that begin on or after January 1, 2008. [Reg. § 1.432(b)-1.]

ACCOUNTING PERIODS AND METHODS OF ACCOUNTING

Foreign Corporations: Tax Years

Foreign Corporations: Tax Years.—Amendments to Reg. § 1.442-1, relating to the required taxable year of those foreign corporations beginning after July 10, 1989, are proposed (published in the Federal Register on January 5, 1993).

☐ Par. 3. Section 1.442-1 is amended by adding a sentence to the end of paragraphs (a)(1), (b)(3) and (c)(5), to read as follows:

§ 1.442-1. Change of annual accounting period.—(a) * * *

(1) * * * For special rules relating to controlled foreign corporations and foreign personal holding companies that are specified foreign corporations, within the meaning of section 898 and § 1.898-2, see section 898 and the regulations under that section.

* * *

(b) * * *

(3) * * * For special rules relating to controlled foreign corporations and foreign personal holding companies that are specified

foreign corporations, within the meaning of section 898 and § 1.898-2, see section 898 and the regulations under that section.

* * *

(c) * * *

(5) * * * For special rules relating to controlled foreign corporations and foreign personal holding companies that are specified foreign corporations, within the meaning of section 898 and § 1.898-2, see section 898 and the regulations under that section.

* * *

Taxable Year: Partnerships, S Corporations, Personal Service Corporations

Taxable Year: Election: Partnership: S Corporation: Personal Service Corporation.— Temporary Reg. §§ 1.444-0T—1.444-3T, relating to the election of a taxable year by a partnership, S corporation or personal service corporation, are also proposed as final regulations and, when adopted, would become Reg. §§ 1.444-0—1.444-3 (published in the Federal Register on May 27, 1988).

§ 1.444-0. Table of contents.

§ 1.444-1. Election to use a taxable year other than the required taxable year.

§ 1.444-2. Tiered structure.

§ 1.444-3. Manner and time of making section 444 election.

Commodities: Securities: Mark-to-Market Accounting

Commodities: Securities: Mark-to-Market Accounting.—Amendments to Reg. §1.446-1, regarding the election to use the mark-to-market method of accounting for dealers in commodities and traders in securities or commodities, are proposed (published in the Federal Register on January 28, 1999) (REG-104924-98).

☐ Par. 2. In §1.446-1, paragraph (c)(2)(iii) is added to read as follows:

§1.446-1. General rule for methods of accounting.

* * *

(c) * * *

(2) * * *

(iii) Section 475 is the exclusive authority on which a taxpayer may rely to use the mark-to-market method of accounting for nonfinancial customer paper, as defined in section 475(c)(4)(B). Thus,

except to the extent provided in §1.475(c)-2(d), the mark-to-market method of accounting is not a permissible method of accounting for nonfinancial customer paper. In addition, the lower-of-cost-or-market method of accounting is not a permissible method of accounting for these assets. See §1.471-12. This paragraph (c)(2)(iii) applies to all tax years ending on or after January 28, 1999.

* * *

Debt Instruments: Allocation of Interest: Certain Small Transactions

Debt Instruments: Allocation of Interest: Certain Small Transactions.—An amendment to Reg. §1.446-2, relating to the tax treatment of debt instruments with original issue discount and the imputation of interest on deferred payments under certain contracts for the sale or exchange of property, is proposed (published in the Federal Register on December 22, 1992) (FI-189-84). (Reg. §1.446-2 was adopted by T.D. 8517 on January 27, 1994. T.D. 8517, however, states that Reg. §1.446-2(e)(3) of the proposed regulations issued on December 22, 1992, remains in proposed form.)

§1.446-2. Method of accounting for interest.

* * *

(e) *Allocation of interest to payments.*—* * *

(3) *Allocation respected in certain small transactions.*—(i) *In general.*—If the aggregate amount of interest and principal payable under a contract does not exceed $250,000 and section 483 does not apply to the loan, an express allocation of the payments between interest and principal by the parties is respected. Similarly, if section 483 applies to a contract under which the aggregate amount payable does not exceed $250,000, but does not apply to a party to the contract (as, for example, in the case of an obligor under a debt instrument given in consideration for the sale or exchange of personal use property), an express allocation of the payments between interest and principal by the parties is respected for purposes of determining the tax liability of the party not subject to section 483.

(ii) *Prepaid interest.*—The amount of interest allocated to any payment under this paragraph (e)(3) is treated as prepaid interest to the extent the amount exceeds—

(A) The aggregate amount of accrued interest as of the date the payment becomes due; reduced (but not below zero) by

(B) The aggregate amount of interest allocated to prior payments under this paragraph (e)(3).

(iii) *Accounting for prepaid interest.*—Prepaid interest must be included in income by a lender when received, regardless of the lender's method of accounting. Except as otherwise provided in section 461(g)(2), prepaid interest is not deductible before such interest accrues (as determined under paragraph (c) of this section).

* * *

Accrual Method of Accounting: Income Inclusion

Accrual Method of Accounting: Income Inclusion.—Amendments to Reg. §§1.446-1 and 1.446-2, regarding the timing of income inclusion under section 451 of the Internal Revenue Code, are proposed (published in the Federal Register on September 9, 2019) (REG-104870-18).

Par. 2. Section 1.446-1 is amended by adding "(See §1.451-1 for rules relating to the taxable year of inclusion.)" between the first and second sentences of paragraph (c)(1)(ii)(A).

§1.446-1. General rule for methods of accounting.

Par. 3. Section 1.446-2 is amended by removing "or" at the end of paragraph (a)(2)(i)(E), removing the period at the end of paragraph (a)(2)(i)(F) and adding in its place "; or" and adding paragraph (a)(2)(i)(G).

The addition reads as follows:

§1.446-2. Method of accounting for interest.—(a) * * *

(2) * * *

(i) * * *

(G) Section 1.451-3(i) (special ordering rule for specified fees).

* * *

Notional Principal Contracts: Timing of Income and Deductions

Notional Principal Contracts: Timing of Income and Deductions.—An amendment to Reg. §1.446-3, relating to notional principal contracts, is proposed (published in the Federal Register on July 10, 1991). (Reg. §1.446-3 was adopted by T.D. 8491 on October 8, 1993. T.D. 8491, however, states that the special rules found in Reg. §1.446-3(e)(4)(iv) of the proposed regulations issued on July 10, 1991, remain in proposed form.)

§1.446-3. Notional principal contracts.

* * *

(e) *Taxable year of inclusion and deduction.*—

* * *

(4) *Special rules.*—(i) *Compound and disguised notional principal contracts.*—* * *

(iv) *Caps and floors that are significantly in-the-money.*—If, on the date that a cap or floor is entered into, the current value of the specified index in a cap agreement exceeds the cap rate by a significant amount, or the floor rate exceeds the current value of the specified index in a floor agreement by a significant amount, then the cap or floor is treated as including one or more loans. The time value component of a cap or floor that is significantly in-the-money is recognized as interest for all purposes of the Code. For any taxable year during the term of the agreement, this time value component is deemed to be the lesser of:

(A) the ratable daily portion of the cap or floor premium that is recognized for the taxable year under paragraph (a)(3)(ii) (C) of this section, multiplied by the discount rate used by the parties to determine the amount paid for the cap or floor compounded from the date the premium is paid to the earlier of the date such option contracts expire or the end of the taxable year; or

(B) the net income or deduction from the cap or floor for the taxable year under paragraph (e)(1) of this section, computed without regard to this paragraph (e)(4)(iv).

In the case of an interest rate cap or an interest rate floor, a significant amount for purposes of this paragraph (e)(4)(iv) is more than 25 basis points. Interest recognized under this paragraph (e)(4)(iv) is not included in the net income or deduction from the cap or floor under paragraph (e)(1) of this section.

* * *

Notional Principal Contracts: Contingent Nonperiodic Payments

Notional Principal Contracts: Contingent Nonperiodic Payments.—Amendments to Reg. §1.446-3, relating to the inclusion into income or deduction of a contingent nonperiodic payment provided for under a notional principal contract, are proposed (published in the Federal Register on February 26, 2004) (corrected March 23, 2004) (REG-166012-02).

☐ Par. 4. Section 1.446-3 is amended by:

1. Revising the introductory text of paragraph (a) and the table of contents in paragraph (a).
2. Adding paragraph (c)(5).
3. Revising paragraphs (d), (f)(2)(i), (f)(2)(iii)(A), and (g)(4).
4. Redesignating the text of paragraph (g)(6) as paragraph (g)(7).
5. Adding new paragraph (g)(6).
6. Amending the newly designated text of paragraph (g)(7) by:
    (a) Revising the heading for *Example 3.*
    (b) Adding *Example 5* through *Example 9.*
7. Revising paragraphs (i) and (j).

The revisions and additions read as follows:

§1.446-3. Notional principal contracts.—(a) *Table of contents.*—This paragraph (a) lists captioned paragraphs contained in this section.

§1.446-3 Notional principal contracts
   (a) Table of contents.
   (b) Purpose.
   (c) Definitions and scope.
      (1) Notional principal contract.
         (i) In general.
         (ii) Excluded contracts.
         (iii) Transactions within section 475.
         (iv) Transactions within section 988.
      (2) Specified index.
      (3) Notional principal amount.
      (4) Special definitions.
         (i) Related person and party to the contract.
         (ii) Objective financial information.
         (iii) Dealer in notional principal contracts.
      (5) Risk-free interest rate and determination date.
         (i) Risk-free interest rate.
         (ii) Determination date.
   (d) Taxable year of inclusion and deduction; adjustment of gain or loss.
      (1) Inclusion and deduction.
      (2) Adjustment of gain or loss.
   (e) Periodic payments.
      (1) Definition.
      (2) Recognition rules.
         (i) In general.
         (ii) Rate set in arrears.
         (iii) Notional principal amount set in arrears.
      (3) Examples.
   (f) Nonperiodic payments.
      (1) Definition.
      (2) Recognition rules.
         (i) In general.
         (ii) General rule for swaps.
         (iii) Alternative methods for swaps.
            (A) Prepaid swaps.
            (B) Other nonperiodic swap payments.
         (iv) General rule for caps and floors.
         (v) Alternative methods for caps and floors that hedge debt instruments.
            (A) Prepaid caps and floors.
            (B) Other caps and floors.
            (C) Special method for collars.
         (vi) Additional methods.
      (3) Term of extendible or terminable contracts.
      (4) Examples.
   (g) Special rules.
      (1) Disguised notional principal contracts.
      (2) Hedged notional principal contracts.
      (3) Options and forwards to enter into notional principal contracts.
      (4) Swaps with significant nonperiodic payments.
      (5) Caps and floors that are significantly in-the-money. [Reserved]
      (6) Notional principal contracts with contingent nonperiodic payments.
         (i) Definitions.
            (A) Noncontingent nonperiodic payments.
            (B) Contingent nonperiodic payments.
         (ii) Noncontingent swap method.

            (iii) Determining projected amount of contingent payment.
               (A) Payment based on actively traded futures or forward contracts.
               (B) Payment based on extrapolation from current market prices.
               (C) Payment based on reasonable estimate.
            (iv) Redeterminations of projected payments and level payment amounts.
               (A) General rule.
               (B) Special rule for fixed but deferred contingent nonperiodic payments.
            (v) Adjustments following redeterminations.
            (vi) Adjustments for differences between projected and actual payments.
            (vii) Recordkeeping requirements.
         (7) Examples.
   (h) Termination payments.
      (1) Definition.
      (2) Taxable year of inclusion and deduction by original parties.
      (3) Taxable year of inclusion and deduction by assignees.
      (4) Special rules.
         (i) Assignment of one leg of a contract.
         (ii) Substance over form.
      (5) Examples.
   (i) Election to mark to market.
      (1) General rule.
      (2) Scope of election.
      (3) Determination of fair market value.
         (i) Determination based on readily ascertainable value.
         (ii) Determination based on value used for financial statements.
         (iii) Determination based on counterparty's mark-to-market value.
         (iv) Determination based on value used in determining net asset value.
      (4) Requirements for use of financial statement values. [Reserved]
      (5) Notional principal contracts accruing interest on significant nonperiodic payments.
         (i) General rule.
         (ii) Special rules for significant contingent nonperiodic payments.
         (iii) Nonapplicability to regulated investment companies.
      (6) Election.
   (j) Effective dates.
      (1) General rule.
      (2) Exception.

* * *

(c) * * *

(5) *Risk-free interest rate and determination date.*—(i) *Risk-free interest rate.*—The risk-free interest rate is the applicable Federal rate determined in accordance with section 1274(d)(1) for a determination date and the period remaining in the term of the contract on the determination date.

(ii) *Determination date.*—A determination date is the commencement date of the swap, each redetermination date as defined in paragraph (g)(6)(ii) of this section, and each special redetermination date as defined in paragraph (g)(6)(iv)(B) of this section.

(d) *Taxable year of inclusion and deduction; adjustment of gain or loss.*—(1) *Inclusion and deduction.*—For all purposes of the Internal

Reg. §1.446-3(d)(1)

Revenue Code, the net income or net deduction from a notional principal contract for a taxable year is taken into account for that taxable year. The net income or net deduction from a notional principal contract for a taxable year equals the total of all of the periodic payments that are recognized from that contract for the taxable year under paragraph (e) of this section, all of the nonperiodic payments that are recognized from that contract for the taxable year under paragraph (f) of this section, and the mark-to-market income inclusions and deductions recognized from that contract under paragraph (i) of this section.

(2) *Adjustment of gain or loss.*—Proper adjustment shall be made in the amount of any gain or loss realized on a sale, exchange, or termination of a notional principal contract for inclusions or deductions pursuant to paragraphs (d)(1) and (g)(4) of this section and for payments or receipts with respect to the notional principal contract.

* * *

(f) * * *

(2) *Recognition rules.*—(i) *In general.*—All taxpayers, regardless of their method of accounting, must recognize the ratable daily portion of a nonperiodic payment for the taxable year to which that portion relates. Generally, a nonperiodic payment must be recognized over the term of a notional principal contract in a manner that reflects the economic substance of the contract. See paragraph (g)(6) of this section for additional rules for contingent nonperiodic payments.

* * *

(iii) * * *

(A) *Prepaid swaps.*—An upfront payment on a swap may be amortized by assuming that the nonperiodic payment represents the present value of a series of equal payments made throughout the term of the swap contract (the level payment method), adjusted as appropriate to take account of increases or decreases in the notional principal amount. The discount rate used in this calculation must be the rate (or rates) used by the parties to determine the amount of the nonperiodic payment. If that rate is not readily ascertainable, the discount rate used must be a rate that is reasonable under the circumstances. Under this method, an upfront payment is allocated by dividing each equal payment into its principal recovery and time value components. The principal recovery components of the equal payments are treated as periodic payments that are deemed to be made on each of the dates that the swap contract provides for periodic payments by the payor of the nonperiodic payment or, if none, on each of the dates that the swap contract provides for periodic payments by the recipient of the nonperiodic payment. The sum of the principal recovery components equals the amount of the upfront payment. The time value component is used to compute the amortization of the nonperiodic payment but is otherwise disregarded. See paragraph (f)(4) *Example 5* of this section.

* * *

(g) * * *

(4) *Swaps with significant nonperiodic payments.*—The parties to a swap with one or more significant nonperiodic payments must treat the contract as two or more separate transactions consisting of an on-market swap and one or more loans. The parties must account for the loans separately from the swap. The payments associated with the on-market swap are included in the net income or net deduction from the swap under paragraph (d) of this section. The time value components associated with the loans are not included in the net income or net deduction from the swap under paragraph (d) of this section but are recognized as interest for all purposes of the Internal Revenue Code. The on-market swap must result in recognition of the payments associated with the swap in a manner that complies with the principles set forth in paragraph (f)(2)(i) of this section. See paragraph (g)(7) *Example 3* of this section for a situation in which the on-market swap payments for a party making a significant nonperiodic upfront payment will be level payments that may be constructed through a combination of the actual payments on the swap and level payments computed under the level payment method provided by paragraph (f)(2)(iii)(A) of this section. In certain cases, a swap with significant nonperiodic payments other than an upfront payment may be treated as if the swap provided for a series of level payment loan advances having a present value equal to the present value of the nonperiodic payments, with the amount of each loan advance being immediately returned as a level payment on the swap. See paragraph (g)(7) *Example 5* of this section. For purposes of section 956, the Commissioner may treat any nonperiodic swap payment, whether or not it is significant, as one or more loans.

* * *

(6) *Notional principal contracts with contingent nonperiodic payments.*—(i) *Definitions.*—(A) *Noncontingent nonperiodic payments.*—A noncontingent nonperiodic payment is a nonperiodic payment that

either is fixed on or before the end of the taxable year in which a contract commences or is equal to the sum of amounts that would be periodic payments if they are paid when they become fixed (including amounts determined as interest accruals).

(B) *Contingent nonperiodic payments.*—A contingent nonperiodic payment is any nonperiodic payment other than a noncontingent nonperiodic payment.

(ii) *Noncontingent swap method.*—Under the noncontingent swap method, a taxpayer, regardless of its method of accounting, recognizes each contingent nonperiodic payment with respect to a notional principal contract by determining the projected amount of the payment and by applying to that projected amount the level payment method described in paragraphs (f)(2)(iii)(A) and (B) of this section. The projected amount of a contingent nonperiodic payment is the reasonably expected amount of the payment, which is determined by using one of the methods described in paragraph (g)(6)(iii) of this section and by using the risk-free interest rate in applying the level payment method. On each successive anniversary date for the notional principal contract (a redetermination date) and each special redetermination date (as defined in paragraph (g)(6)(iv)(B) of this section), the taxpayer must redetermine the projected amount of each contingent nonperiodic payment, reapply the level payment method as provided in paragraph (g)(6)(iv) of this section, and make the adjustments specified in paragraph (g)(6)(v) of this section. If paragraph (g)(4) of this section applies to the notional principal contract, redeterminations and adjustments must also be made to account for the time value components of the transaction as interest in accordance with that paragraph. Except for contingent nonperiodic payments governed by paragraph (g)(6)(iv)(B) of this section, in the taxable year in which a contingent payment is made or received, the parties must make appropriate adjustments to the amount of income or deductions attributable to the notional principal contract for any differences between projected and actual contingent nonperiodic payments as provided in paragraph (g)(6)(vi) of this section.

(iii) *Determining projected amount of contingent payment.*—(A) *Payment based on actively traded futures or forward contracts.*—If a contingent nonperiodic payment is determined under the contract by reference to the value of a specified index on a designated future date, the projected amount of the payment may be determined on the basis of the future value for the specified index in actively traded futures or forward contracts, if any, providing for delivery or settlement on the designated future date. If no actively traded contract exists for the designated future date, a determination from the future values for the specified index in actively traded futures or forward contracts, if any, providing for delivery or settlement on dates within three months of the designated future date may be used.

(B) *Payment based on extrapolation from current market prices.*—If a contingent nonperiodic payment is determined under the contract by reference to the value of a specified index on a designated future date, the projected amount of the payment may be determined on the basis of the current value of the specified index as established by objective financial information adjusted to convert the current value to a future value for the specified index on the designated future date. The current value is converted to a future value by adding to the current value an amount equal to the accrual of interest on the current value under a constant yield method at the risk-free interest rate with appropriate compounding and by making appropriate adjustments for expected cash payments on the property underlying the specified index.

(C) *Payment based on reasonable estimate.*—If the methods provided in paragraphs (g)(6)(iii)(A) and (B) of this section do not result in a reasonable estimate of the amount of the contingent payment, the taxpayer must use another method that does result in a reasonable estimate of the amount of the contingent payment and that is based on objective financial information.

(iv) *Redeterminations of projected payments and level payment amounts.*—(A) *General rule.*—On each redetermination date, the taxpayer must redetermine the projected amount using current values on the redetermination date and the same method that was used on the commencement date of the notional principal contract, and must reapply the level payment method as of the commencement date of the notional principal contract on the basis of the new projected payment amount and the risk-free interest rate in effect on the redetermination date.

(B) *Special rule for fixed but deferred contingent nonperiodic payments.*—If a contingent nonperiodic payment is fixed more than six months before it is due, and if the date the payment is fixed is in a different taxable year from the date the payment is due, the date on which the payment is fixed is a special redetermination date. As of that date, the taxpayer must treat the fixed amount as the projected amount for that contingent nonperiodic payment and apply paragraphs (g)(6)(iv) and (v) of this section as if the special redetermination date were a redetermination date.

(v) *Adjustments following redeterminations.*—Following each redetermination of projected payments and level payment amounts, the taxpayer must apply the new schedule of level payments for purposes of determining amounts to be recognized in the current and subsequent taxable years with respect to the contingent nonperiodic payments. Any difference between the amounts recognized in prior taxable years and the amounts that would have been recognized in those years had the new level payment schedule been in effect for those years is taken into account as additional payments or receipts with respect to the contract ratably over the one-year period beginning with the redetermination date and, to the extent attributable to a difference in the interest amounts calculated under paragraph (g)(4) of this section, is recognized as interest for all purposes of the Internal Revenue Code.

(vi) *Adjustments for differences between projected and actual payments.*—Any difference between the amounts taken into account under paragraph (f) and this paragraph (g)(6) on the one hand and the amount of the actual payment under the contract on the other hand is taken into account as an adjustment to the net income or net deduction from the notional principal contract for the taxable year during which the payment occurs, and not as an adjustment to interest income or expense.

(vii) *Recordkeeping requirements.*—The books and records maintained by a taxpayer must contain a description of the method used to determine the projected amount of a contingent payment, projected payment schedules, any adjustments following redeterminations, and any adjustments for differences between projected and actual contingent payments.

(7) * * *

Example 3. Upfront significant nonperiodic payment. * * *

* * *

Example 5. Backloaded significant nonperiodic payment. (i) On January 1, 2003, unrelated parties *P* and *Q* enter into an interest rate swap contract. Under the terms of the contract, *P* agrees to make five annual payments to *Q* equal to LIBOR times a notional principal amount of $100,000,000. In return, *Q* agrees to pay *P* 6% of $100,000,000 annually, plus $24,420,400 on December 31, 2007. At the time *P* and *Q* enter into this swap agreement the rate for similar on-market swaps is LIBOR to 10%. Assume that on January 1, 2003, the risk-free rate is 10%.

(ii) The $24,420,400 payment from *Q* to *P* is significant when compared to the present value of the total payments due from *Q* under the contract. Accordingly, pursuant to paragraph (g)(4) of this section, the transaction is recharacterized as two separate transactions. First, *P* is treated as paying to *Q* a series of $4,000,000 level payment loan advances. The present value of the level payment loan advances equals the present value of $24,420,400, the significant nonperiodic payment. Stated differently, the sum of the level payment loan advances and accrued interest on those advances equals the significant nonperiodic payment.

(iii) Next, *Q* is treated as using each loan advance to fund five annual level swap payments of $4,000,000. The level payment loan advances and accrued interest on the advances computed with annual compounding at 10% are as follows:

	Level Payment	Accrued Interest
2003	$ 4,000,000	$ 0
2004	4,000,000	400,000
2005	4,000,000	840,000
2006	4,000,000	1,324,000
2007	4,000,000	1,856,400
	$20,000,000	$4,420,400

(iv) *P* recognizes interest income, and *Q* accrues interest expense, each taxable year equal to the interest accruals on the deemed level payment loan advances. These interest amounts are not included in the parties' net income or net deduction from the swap contract under paragraph (d) of this section.

(v) The level payment amounts of $4,000,000 are taken into account in determining the parties' net income and deductions on the swap pursuant to paragraph (d) of this section.

Example 6. Contingent nonperiodic payment on an equity swap. (i) On January 1, 2005, unrelated parties *V* and *W* enter into an equity swap contract. Under the terms of the contract, *V* agrees to make three annual payments to *W* equal to 1-year LIBOR times a notional principal amount of $50,000,000. In return, *W* agrees to make a single payment on December 31, 2007, equal to the appreciation, if any, of a $50,000,000 investment in a basket of equity securities over the term of the swap. *V* is obligated to make a single payment on December 31, 2007, equal to the depreciation, if any, in the same $50,000,000 investment in the basket of equity securities. Assume that on January 1, 2005, 1-year LIBOR is 9.5%, and the risk-free rate is 10.0%.

(ii) This contract is a notional principal contract as defined in paragraph (c)(1) of this section. The annual LIBOR-based payments from *V* to *W* are periodic payments and the single payment on December 31, 2007, is a contingent nonperiodic payment.

(iii) Pursuant to the method described in (g)(6)(iii)(B) of this section, the parties determine that the projected amount of the contingent nonperiodic payment that *W* will pay *V* on December 31, 2007, is $16,550,000. The present value of this projected fixed payment is significant when compared to the present value of the total payments due from *W* under the contract. Accordingly, pursuant to paragraph (g)(4) of this section, the transaction is recharacterized as two separate transactions.

(iv) As a preliminary step, using the risk-free rate of 10.0% as the discount rate, the parties determine the level payment amounts that have a present value equal to the present value of $16,550,000, the projected significant nonperiodic payment. Stated differently, the sum of the level payment amounts and accrued interest at 10.0% on those amounts must equal the projected significant nonperiodic payment. The level payment amounts thus determined are $5,000,000.

(v) Next, *V* is treated as paying to *W* a series of $5,000,000 loan advances.

(vi) Then, *W* is treated as using each loan advance to fund one of the three annual level swap payments of $5,000,000. The level payment loan advances and accrued interest on the advances computed with annual compounding at 10.0% are as follows:

	Level Payment	Accrued Interest
2005	$ 5,000,000	$ 0
2006	5,000,000	500,000
2007	5,000,000	1,050,000
	$15,000,000	$1,550,000

(vii) No interest amount is taken into account for the contract year 2005.

(viii) The level payment amount of $5,000,000 is taken into account for the contract year 2005 in determining the parties' net income and deductions on the swap pursuant to paragraph (d) of this section.

(ix) For the contract year 2005, *V* makes a swap payment to *W* equal to 1-year LIBOR at 9.5% times $50,000,000, or $4,750,000, and *W* is deemed to make a swap payment to *V* equal to the annual level payment of $5,000,000. The net of the ratable daily portions of these payments determines the annual net income or deduction from the contract for both *V* and *W*.

Example 7. Initial Adjustment. (i) The terms of the equity swap agreement are the same as in *Example 6*. In addition, assume that on January 1, 2006, the first redetermination date, 1-year LIBOR is 10.0%, and the risk-free rate is 10.5%. On that date, the parties redetermine the projected amount of the contingent nonperiodic payment using current values in effect on that date. Under the method described in (g)(6)(iii)(B) of this section, the parties determine that the reprojected amount of the contingent nonperiodic payment that *W* will pay *V* on December 31, 2007, is $23,261,500. The present value as of January 1, 2005, of this projected fixed payment is significant when compared to the present value of the total payments due from *W* under the contract. Accordingly, pursuant to paragraph (g)(4) of this section, the transaction is recharacterized as two separate transactions.

(ii) The parties use the redetermined projected amount of $23,261,500, to reapply the method provided by paragraph (g)(4) of this section effective as of the commencement date of the swap. As a preliminary step, using the risk-free rate of 10.5% as the discount rate, the parties determine the level payment amounts that have a present value equal to the present value of $23,261,500, the reprojected significant nonperiodic payment. Stated differently, the sum of the level payment amounts and accrued interest at 10.5% on those amounts must equal the reprojected significant nonperiodic payment. The level payment amounts thus determined are $6,993,784.

(iii) Next, *V* is treated as paying to *W* a series of $6,993,784 loan advances.

(iv) Then, *W* is treated as using each loan advance to fund one of the three annual level swap payments of $6,993,784. The level payment loan advances and accrued interest on the advances computed with annual compounding at 10.5%, are as follows:

	Level Payment	Accrued Interest
2005	$ 6,993,784	$ 0
2006	6,993,784	734,347
2007	6,993,784	1,545,801
	$20,981,352	$2,280,148

(v) For the contract year 2006, *V* recognizes interest income, and *W* accrues interest expense equal to the accrued interest of

$734,347 on the deemed level payment loan advance. These interest amounts are not included in the parties' net income or net deduction from the swap contract under paragraph (d) of this section.

(vi) The level payment amount of $6,993,784 is taken into account for the contract year 2006 in determining the parties' net income and deductions on the swap pursuant to paragraph (d) of this section.

(vii) The parties also take into account for the contract year 2006 the difference between the amount recognized for 2005 and the amount that would have been recognized in 2005 had the new level payment schedule in this *Example 7* been in effect in 2005. Thus, for purposes of paragraph (d) of this section, W is treated as making a swap payment, and V is treated as receiving a swap payment of $1,993,784 ($6,993,784 – $5,000,000) for purposes of paragraph (d) of this section.

(viii) For the contract year 2006, V makes a swap payment to W equal to 1-year LIBOR at 10.0% times $50,000,000, or $5,000,000, and W is deemed to make a swap payment to V equal to the annual level payment of $6,993,784 and the adjustment amount of $1,993,784. The net of the ratable daily portions of these payments determines the annual net income or deduction from the contract for both V and W.

Example 8. Subsequent Adjustment. (i) The terms of the equity swap agreement are the same as in *Example 7*. In addition, assume that on January 1, 2007, the second redetermination date, 1-year LIBOR is 11.0%, and the risk-free rate is also 11.0%. On that date, the parties redetermine the projected amount of the contingent nonperiodic payment using current values in effect on that date. The parties determine that the reprojected amount of the contingent nonperiodic payment that W will pay V on December 31, 2007, is $11,050,000. The present value as of January 1, 2005, of this projected fixed payment is significant when compared to the present value of the total payments due from W under the contract. Accordingly, pursuant to paragraph (g)(4) of this section, the transaction is recharacterized as two separate transactions.

(ii) The parties use the redetermined projected amount of $11,050,000, to reapply the method provided by paragraph (g)(4) effective as of the commencement date of the swap. As a preliminary step, using the risk-free rate of 11.0% as the discount rate, the parties determine the level payment amounts that have a present value equal to the present value of $11,050,000, the reprojected significant nonperiodic payment. Stated differently, the sum of the level payment amounts and accrued interest at 11.0% on those amounts must equal the reprojected significant nonperiodic payment. The level payment amounts thus determined are $3,306,304.

(iii) Next, V is treated as paying to W a series of $3,306,304 loan advances.

(iv) Then, W is treated as using each loan advance to fund one of the three annual level swap payments of $3,306,304. The level payment loan advances and accrued interest on the loan advances computed with annual compounding at 11.0% are as follows:

	Level Payment	Accrued Interest
2005	$3,306,304	$ 0
2006	3,306,304	363,693
2007	3,306,304	767,393
	$9,918,912	$1,131,086

(v) For 2007, V recognizes interest income, and W accrues interest expense equal to the $767,393 accrued interest amount for 2007 on the deemed loan advances. In addition, V has a net interest expense item and W has a net interest income item equal to $370,654 ($734,347 – $363,693), the difference between the interest accrual taken into account for 2006 and the amount that would have been taken into account for 2006 had the new level payment schedule in this *Example 8* been in effect for 2006. As a result, V has net interest income and W has net interest expense in the amount of $396,739 for 2007. These interest amounts are not included in the parties' net income or net deduction from the swap contract under paragraph (d) of this section.

(vi) The level payment amount of $3,306,304 is taken into account for the contract year 2007 in determining the parties' net income and deductions on the swap pursuant to paragraph (d) of this section.

(vii) For 2007, the parties also take into account for 2007 the difference between the amounts previously recognized for 2005 and 2006 and the amounts that would have been recognized for those years had the new level payment schedule in this *Example 8* been in effect in 2005 and 2006. The amounts previously recognized were: a total of $6,993,784 for 2005, which is the sum of $5,000,000 (in 2005) and $1,993,784 (in 2006), and a total of $6,993,784 for 2006 (in 2006).

The adjustment amount, therefore, equals two times $3,687,480 ($6,993,784 – $3,306,304), or $7,374,960. This amount is taken into account as a payment for purposes of paragraph (d) of this section.

(viii) For the contract year 2007, V makes a swap payment to W equal to 1-year LIBOR at 11.0% times $50,000,000, or $5,500,000. W is deemed to make a swap payment to V equal to the annual level payment for 2007 of $3,306,304, and V is deemed to make a swap payment to W equal to the adjustment amount of $7,374,960. The net of the ratable daily portions of these payments determines the annual net income or deduction from the contract for both V and W.

Example 9. Adjustment for actual payment. (i) The terms of the equity swap agreement are the same as in *Example 8*. In addition, on December 31, 2007, W makes a payment to V of $25,000,000, an amount equal to the appreciation of a $50,000,000 investment in the basket of equity securities.

(ii) For 2007, $13,950,000, the difference between $25,000,000 and $11,050,000, the projected amount of the contingent payment as of January 1, 2007, is taken into account as an adjustment to the parties' net income or deductions for each party's taxable year that contains December 31, 2007, pursuant to paragraph (d) of this section.

* * *

(i) *Election to mark to market.*—A taxpayer may elect to mark to market notional principal contracts providing for nonperiodic payments. The rules of paragraphs (f) (other than (f)(2)(i)), (g)(6)(ii) through (vii), and (h) of this section do not apply to contracts to which this paragraph (i) applies. See paragraph (i)(5) of this section for rules respecting interest accruals under paragraph (g)(4) of this section for contracts providing for significant nonperiodic payments to which this paragraph (i) applies.

(1) *General rule.*—In the case of any contract held at the close of the taxable year to which this paragraph (i) applies, the taxpayer shall determine income inclusions and deductions by reference to the gain or loss that would be realized if the contract were sold for its fair market value on the last business day of the taxable year. Proper adjustment shall be made in the amount of any gain or loss subsequently realized (or calculated) for the income inclusions and deductions taken into account by reason of this paragraph (i)(1) as provided in paragraph (d)(2) of this section.

(2) *Scope of election.*—The election provided by this paragraph is available for notional principal contracts that are—

(i) Of a type that is actively traded within the meaning of § 1.1092(d)-1(c) (determined without regard to the limitation in § 1.1092(d)-1(c)(2));

(ii) Marked to market by the taxpayer for purposes of determining the taxpayer's financial income provided the taxpayer satisfies the requirements in paragraph (i)(4) of this section;

(iii) Subject to an agreement by a party to the contract that is subject to section 475 to supply to the taxpayer the value that it uses in applying section 475(a)(2); or

(iv) Marked to market by a regulated investment company described in section 1296(e)(2).

(3) *Determination of fair market value.*—For purposes of paragraph (i)(1) of this section, fair market value is determined by applying the rules set forth in paragraphs (i)(3)(i) through (iv) of this section.

(i) *Determination based on readily ascertainable value.*—For a contract described in paragraph (i)(2)(i) of this section, fair market value is determined based on the mean between the bid and asked prices quoted for the contract on an established financial market as defined in § 1.1092(d)-1(b)(1), or, if bid and asked prices are not available, comparable prices determined on the basis of recent price quotations described in § 1.1092(d)-1(b)(2).

(ii) *Determination based on value used for financial statements.*—For a contract described in paragraph (i)(2)(ii) of this section that is not described in paragraph (i)(2)(i) of this section, fair market value is the value used by the taxpayer for purposes of preparing its financial statements under paragraph (i)(4) of this section.

(iii) *Determination based on counterparty's mark-to-market value.*—For a contract described in paragraph (i)(2)(iii) of this section that is not described in paragraph (i)(2)(i) of this section, fair market value is the mark-to-market value provided by a counterparty as being the value the counterparty used for purposes of section 475(a)(2).

(iv) *Determination based on value used in determining net asset value.*—Notwithstanding paragraphs (i)(3)(i) through (iii) of this section, for a contract described in paragraph (i)(2)(iv) of this section, fair market value is the value used by the taxpayer in determining its net asset value.

(4) *Requirements for use of financial statement values.*—[Reserved].

(5) *Notional principal contracts accruing interest on significant nonperiodic payments.*—(i) *General rule.*—If a notional principal contract that is marked to market under this paragraph (i) provides for one or more significant nonperiodic payments, paragraph (g)(4) of this section applies to the contract (computed with regard to the rule in paragraph (i)(5)(ii) of this section). Proper adjustment shall be made in the amount of any income inclusions or deductions recognized under paragraph (i)(1) of this section to take into account amounts recognized as interest under paragraph (g)(4) of this section and the payment or receipt of the nonperiodic payment or payments.

(ii) *Special rules for significant contingent nonperiodic payments.*—In the case of a contract providing for a significant contingent nonperiodic payment, the projected amount of the payment is determined by applying one of the methods described in paragraph (g)(6)(iii) of this section or by applying the deemed equivalent value method described in this paragraph (i)(5)(ii). The amount of the payment is not redetermined except as provided in paragraph (g)(6)(iv)(B) of this section. The deemed equivalent value method may be applied if the contract fixes the timing and amount of all of the payments under the contract, except for a sole significant contingent nonperiodic payment. Under the deemed equivalent value

method, the amount of the significant contingent nonperiodic payment is the amount that, as of the date the terms of the contract are fixed, causes the present value of all of the payments by the taxpayer to equal the present value of all of the payments of the counterparty to the contract. The present value of each payment of the contract is determined by applying the risk-free interest rate.

(iii) *Nonapplicability to regulated investment companies.*—Paragraphs (i)(5)(i) and (ii) of this section do not apply to a regulated investment company described in paragraph (i)(2)(iv) of this section that makes an election under paragraph (i) of this section.

(6) *Election.*—An election to apply this paragraph (i) must be made with respect to all notional principal contracts described in paragraph (i)(2) of this section to which the taxpayer is a party. The election must be made in the time and manner prescribed by the Commissioner and is effective for the taxable year for which made and all subsequent taxable years, unless revoked with the consent of the Commissioner.

(j) *Effective dates.*—(1) *General rule.*—Except as provided in paragraph (j)(2) of this section, this section is applicable for notional principal contracts entered into on or after December 13, 1993.

(2) *Exception.*—Paragraphs (g)(6) (other than (g)(6)(i)) and (i) of this section are applicable for notional principal contracts entered into on or after 30 days after the date a Treasury decision based on these proposed regulations is published in the Federal Register.

Section 1256 Contracts: Swap Exclusions

Section 1256 Contracts: Swap Exclusions.—Amendment to Reg. §1.446-3, providing guidance on the category of swaps and similar agreements that are within the scope of Code Sec. 1256(b)(2)(B), are proposed (published in the Federal Register on September 16, 2011) (REG-111283-11).

☐ Par. 2. Section 1.446-3 is amended by:
1. Revising the entries for the table of contents in §1.446-3(a) for paragraphs (c) and (j).
2. Revising paragraphs (c)(1), (c)(2), and (c)(3).
3. Adding and reserving paragraph (c)(5).
4. Adding paragraph (c)(6).
5. Adding two sentences to the end of paragraph (j).
The revisions and additions read as follows:

§1.446-3. Notional principal contracts.

* * *

(c) Definitions and scope.
  (1) Notional principal contract.
    (i) In general.
    (ii) Payment defined.
    (iii) Included contracts.
      (A) Special rule for credit default swaps.
      (B) Special rule for nonfunctional currency notional principal contracts.
    (iv) Excluded contracts.
    (v) Transactions within section 475.
    (vi) Transactions within section 988.
  (2) Specified index.
    (i) Specified financial index.
    (ii) Specified non-financial index.
  (3) Notional principal amount.
  (4) Special definitions.
    (i) Related person and party to the contract.
    (ii) Objective financial information.
    (iii) Dealer in notional principal contracts.
  (5) [Reserved]
  (6) Examples.

* * *

(j) Effective/applicability date.

* * *

(c) *Definitions and scope.*—(1) *Notional principal contract.*—(i) *In general.*—A notional principal contract is a financial instrument that requires one party to make two or more payments to the counterparty at specified intervals calculated by reference to a specified index upon a notional principal amount in exchange for specified consideration or a promise to pay similar amounts. An agreement between a taxpayer and a qualified business unit (as defined in section 989(a)) of the taxpayer, or among qualified business units of the same taxpayer, is not a notional principal contract because a taxpayer cannot enter into a contract with itself.

(ii) *Payment defined.*—For purposes of paragraph (c)(1)(i) of this section, a payment includes an amount that is fixed on one date and paid or otherwise taken into account on a later date. Thus, for example, a contract that provides for a settlement payment referenced to the appreciation or depreciation on a specified number of

shares of common stock, adjusted for actual dividends paid during the term of the contract, is treated as a contract with more than one payment with respect to that leg of the contract. See *Example 2* of this paragraph (c).

(iii) *Included contracts.*—Notional principal contracts governed by this section include contracts commonly referred to as interest rate swaps, currency swaps, basis swaps, interest rate caps, interest rate floors, commodity swaps, equity swaps, equity index swaps, credit default swaps, weather-related swaps, and similar agreements that satisfy the requirements of paragraph (c)(1)(i). A collar is not itself a notional principal contract, but a cap and a floor that comprise a collar may be treated as a single notional principal contract under paragraph (f)(2)(v)(C) of this section. A contract may be a notional principal contract governed by this section even though the term of the contract is subject to termination or extension. Each confirmation under a master agreement to enter into an agreement covered by this section is treated as a separate notional principal contract (or as more than one notional principal contract if the confirmation creates more than one notional principal contract). Notwithstanding the rule under paragraph (c)(3) of this section—

(A) *Special rule for credit default swaps.*—A credit default swap contract that permits or requires the delivery of specified debt instruments in satisfaction of one leg of the contract is a notional principal contract if it otherwise satisfies the requirements of paragraph (c)(1)(i) of this section.

(B) *Special rule for nonfunctional currency notional principal contracts.*—A notional principal contract that permits or requires the delivery of specified currency in satisfaction of one or both legs of the contract but that otherwise qualifies as a nonfunctional currency notional principal contract under §1.988-1(a)(2)(iii)(B) is a notional principal contract.

(iv) *Excluded contracts.*—A forward contract, an option, and a guarantee are not notional principal contracts. An instrument or contract that constitutes indebtedness under general Federal income tax law is not a notional principal contract. An option or forward contract that entitles or obligates a person to enter into a notional principal contract is not a notional principal contract, but payments made under such an option or forward contract may be governed by paragraph (g)(3) of this section.

(v) *Transactions within section 475.*—To the extent that the rules provided in paragraphs (e) and (f) of this section are inconsistent with the rules that apply to any notional principal contract that is governed by section 475 and the regulations thereunder, the rules of section 475 and the regulations thereunder govern.

(vi) *Transactions within section 988.*—To the extent that the rules provided in this section are inconsistent with the rules that apply to any notional principal contract that is also a section 988 transaction or that is integrated with other property or debt pursuant to section 988(d), the rules of section 988 and the regulations thereunder govern. The rules of § 1.446-3(g)(4) are not considered to be inconsistent with the rules of section 988. See § 1.988-2(e)(3)(iv).

(2) *Specified index.*—A specified index may be either a specified financial index or a specified non-financial index.

(i) *Specified financial index.*—A specified financial index is—
(A) A fixed rate, price, or amount;
(B) A fixed rate, price, or amount applicable in one or more specified periods followed by one or more different fixed rates, prices, or amounts applicable in other periods;
(C) An index that is based on objective financial information (as defined in paragraph (c)(4)(ii) of this section); and
(D) An interest rate index that is regularly used in normal lending transactions between a party to the contract and unrelated persons.

(ii) *Specified non-financial index.*—A specified non-financial index is any objectively determinable information that—
(A) Is not within the control of any of the parties to the contract and is not unique to one of the parties' circumstances;
(B) Is not financial information; and
(C) Cannot be reasonably expected to front-load or back-load payments accruing under the contract.

(3) *Notional principal amount.*—For purposes of this section, a notional principal amount is any specified amount of money or property that, when multiplied by either a specified financial index or a specified non-financial index, measures a party's rights and obligations under the contract, but is not borrowed, loaned, or sold between the parties as part of the contract. The notional principal amount may vary over the term of the contract, provided that it is set in advance or varies based on objective financial information (as defined in paragraph (c)(4)(ii) of this section). If a notional principal contract references a notional principal amount that varies, or that references a different notional principal amount for each party, and a principal purpose for entering into the contract is to avoid the application of the rules in this section, the Commissioner may recharacterize the contract according to its substance, including by separating the contract into a series of notional principal contracts for purposes of applying the rules of this section or by treating the contract, in whole or in part, as a loan.

* * *

(5) [Reserved]

(6) *Examples.*—The following examples illustrate the application of paragraph (c) of this section.

Example 1. Forward rate agreement. (i) On January 1, 2012, A enters into a contract with unrelated counterparty B under which on December 31, 2013, A will pay or receive from B, as the case may be, an amount determined by subtracting 6% multiplied by a notional amount of $10 million from 3 month LIBOR on December 31, 2013 multiplied by the same notional amount ((3 month LIBOR × $10,000,000) - (6% × $10,000,000)). The contract provides for no other payments.

(ii) Because this contract provides for a single net payment between A and B determined by interest rates in effect on the settlement date of the contract, the contract is not a notional principal contract defined in § 1.446-3(c)(1)(i).

Example 2. Equity total return contract with dividend adjustments. (i) On January 1, 2012, A enters into a contract with unrelated counterparty B under which on December 31, 2013, A will receive from B an amount equal to the appreciation (if any) on a notional amount of 1 million shares of XYZ common stock, plus any dividends or other distributions that are paid on 1 million shares of XYZ common stock during the term of the contract. In return, on December 31, 2013 A will pay B an amount equal to any depreciation on 1 million shares of XYZ common stock, and an amount equal to 3 month LIBOR multiplied by the notional value of 1 million shares of XYZ stock on January 1, 2012 compounded over the term of the contract. All payments are netted such that A and B are only liable for the net payment due under the contract on December 31, 2013.

(ii) Because both legs of this contract provide for payments that become fixed during the term of the contract (the dividend payments and the LIBOR-based payments), each leg of the contract is treated as providing for more than one payment. In addition, since the indices referenced in the contract are specified indices described in paragraph (c)(2)(i) of this section, and the 1 million shares of XYZ common stock are a notional principal amount described in paragraph (c)(3) of this section, the contract is a notional principal contract defined in § 1.446-3(c)(1)(i).

* * *

(j) *Effective/applicability date.*—* * * The rules of paragraph (c) of this section apply to notional principal contracts entered into on or after the date of publication of a Treasury decision adopting these rules as final regulations in the **Federal Register**. Section 1.446-3(c) as contained in 26 CFR part 1 revised April 1, 2011, continues to apply to notional principal contracts entered into before the date of publication of a Treasury decision adopting these rules as final regulations in the **Federal Register**.

Notional Principal Contracts: Nonperiodic Payments: Swaps

Notional Principal Contracts: Nonperiodic Payments: Swaps.—Amendments to Reg. § 1.446-3, providing that, subject to certain exceptions, a notional principal contract with a nonperiodic payment, regardless of whether it is significant, must be treated as two separate transactions consisting of one or more loans and an on-market, level payment swap, are proposed (published in the Federal Register on May 8, 2015) (REG-102656-15; REG-107548-11).

Par. 2. Section 1.446-3 is amended by:
1. Revising paragraph (g)(4).
2. Revising paragraph (g)(6), *Examples* 2, 3 and 4.
3. Revising paragraph (j)(2).
The revisions read as follows:

§1.446-3. Notional principal contracts.
* * *

(g) * * *
(4) [The text of the proposed amendment to § 1.446-3(g)(4) is the same as the text of § 1.446-3T(g)(4) as added by T.D. 9719].

* * *

(6) * * *
Example 2. [The text of proposed amendment to § 1.446-3(g)(6) *Example 2* is the same as the text of § 1.446-3T(g)(6) *Example 2* as added by T.D. 9719].

Example 3. [The text of proposed amendment to § 1.446-3(g)(6) *Example 3* is the same as the text of § 1.446-3T(g)(6) *Example 3* as added by T.D. 9719].

Example 4. [The text of proposed amendment to § 1.446-3(g)(6) *Example 4* is the same as the text of § 1.446-3T(g)(6) *Example 4* as added by T.D. 9719].

* * *

(j) * * *
(2) [The text of the proposed amendment to § 1.446-3(j)(2) is the same as the text of § 1.446-3T(j)(2) as added by T.D. 9719].

Deduction for Business Interest Expense: Limitation

Deduction for Business Interest Expense: Limitation.—Amendments to Reg. § 1.446-3, regarding the limitation on the deduction for business interest expense after the enactment of recent tax legislation, are proposed (published in the Federal Register on December 28, 2018) (REG-106089-18).

Par. 12. Section 1.446-3 is amended by revising paragraphs (g)(4) and (j)(2) to read as follows:

§1.446-3. Notional principal contracts.
* * *

(g) * * *

(4) *Swaps with significant nonperiodic payments.*—For swaps with significant nonperiodic payments, see § 1.163(j)-1(b)(20)(ii).
* * *

(j) * * *

(2) The rules provided in paragraph (g)(4) of this section apply to notional principal contracts entered into on or after the date of publication of a Treasury decision adopting these rules as final regulations in the **Federal Register**. Taxpayers may apply the rules provided in paragraph (g)(4) of this section to notional principal contracts entered into before the date of publication of a Treasury decision adopting these rules as final regulations in the **Federal Register**.

Foreign Personal Holding Company Income: Foreign Currency Gain or Loss: Exclusion

Foreign Personal Holding Company Income: Foreign Currency Gain or Loss: Exclusion—Amendments to Reg. §1.446-4, providing guidance on the treatment of foreign currency gain or loss of a controlled foreign corporation under the business needs exclusion from foreign personal holding company income, are proposed (published in the Federal Register on December 19, 2017) (REG-119514-15).

Par. 2. Section 1.446-4 is amended by:

1. Revising the first sentence of paragraph (a).

2. Revising the heading of paragraph (g) and adding a sentence at the end of paragraph (g).

3. Removing paragraph (h).

The revisions and addition read as follows:

§1.446-4. Hedging transactions.—(a) *In general.*—Except as provided in this paragraph (a), a hedging transaction as defined in §1.1221-2(b) (whether or not the character of gain or loss from the transaction is determined under §1.1221-2) and a bona fide hedging transaction as defined in §1.954-2(a)(4)(ii) must be accounted for under the rules of this section. * * *

* * *

(g) *Applicability date.*—* * * This section applies to a bona fide hedging transaction (as defined in §1.954-2(a)(4)(ii)) entered into on or after the date that these regulations are published as final regulations in the *Federal Register*.

Limitation on Cash Method of Accounting

Accounting Methods: Cash Method: Limitations.—Temporary Reg. §1.448-1T, relating to the limitation on the use of the cash method of accounting, is proposed and, when adopted, would become Reg. §1.448-1 (published in the Federal Register on June 16, 1987).

§1.448-1. Limitation on the use of the cash receipts and disbursements method of accounting.

Imputed Interest: Original Issue Discount

Imputed Interest: Original Issue Discount: Safe Haven Interest Rates.—Reproduced below is the text of a proposed amendment to Reg. §1.451-1, relating to (1) the tax treatment of debt instruments issued after July 1, 1982, that contain original issue discount, (2) the imputation of and the accounting for interest with respect to sales and exchanges of property occurring after December 31, 1984, and (3) safe haven interest rates for loans or advances between commonly or controlled taxpayers and safe haven leases between such taxpayers (published in the Federal Register on April 8, 1986).

☐ Par. 9. In paragraph (d) of §1.451-1 the heading and text are revised to read as follows:

§1.451-1. General rule for taxable year of inclusion.—

* * *

(d) *Special rule for inclusion of original issue discount.*—For inclusion of original issue discount in respect of certain debt instruments issued after May 27, 1969, see section 1272.

* * *

Accrual Method of Accounting: Income Inclusion

Accrual Method of Accounting: Income Inclusion.—Amendments to Reg. §1.451-1, regarding the timing of income inclusion under section 451 of the Internal Revenue Code, are proposed (published in the Federal Register on September 9, 2019) (REG-104870-18).

Par. 4. Section 1.451-1 is amended by:

a. Adding "(the all events test)" to the end of the second sentence of paragraph (a);

b. Redesignating paragraphs (b) through (g) as (d) through (i); and

c. Adding new paragraphs (b) and reserved (c).

The additions read as follows:

§1.451-1. General rule for taxable year of inclusion.

* * *

(b) *Special rule for timing of income inclusion for taxpayers with an applicable financial statement using an accrual method of accounting.*—For the timing of income inclusion with respect to taxpayers with an applicable financial statement using an accrual method of accounting, see also §1.451-3.

(c) [Reserved]

* * *

Imputed Interest: Original Issue Discount

Imputed Interest: Original Issue Discount: Safe Haven Interest Rates.—Reproduced below is the text of a proposed amendment to Reg. §1.451-2, relating to (1) the tax treatment of debt instruments issued after July 1, 1982, that contain original issue discount, (2) the imputation of and the accounting for interest with respect to sales and exchanges of property occurring after December 31, 1984, and (3) safe haven interest rates for loans or advances between commonly or controlled taxpayers and safe haven leases between such taxpayers (published in the Federal Register on April 8, 1986).

☐ Par. 10. Paragraph (b) of §1.451-2 is amended by removing the eighth and ninth sentences and adding in their place new sentences to read as follows:

§1.451-2. Constructive receipt of income.—

* * *

(b) *Examples of constructive receipt.*—* * * However, in the case of certain deposits made after December 31, 1970, in banks, domestic building and loan associations, and similar financial institutions, the inclusion rules of section 1272 apply. See §§1.1232-3A and 1.1272-1. * * *

* * *

Accrual Method of Accounting: Income Inclusion

Accrual Method of Accounting: Income Inclusion.—Reg. §1.451-3, regarding the timing of income inclusion under section 451 of the Internal Revenue Code, is proposed (published in the Federal Register on September 9, 2019) (corrected October 9, 2019) (REG-104870-18).

Par. 5. Section 1.451-3 is added to read as follows:

§1.451-3. Timing of income inclusion for taxpayers with an applicable financial statement using an accrual method of accounting.—(a) *Table of contents.*—This paragraph (a) lists captioned paragraphs contained in §1.451-3.

§1.451-3 Timing of income inclusion for taxpayers with an applicable financial statement using an accrual method of accounting.

(b) *General rule.*—If a taxpayer has an applicable financial statement (AFS), the all events test under § 1.451 1(a) with respect to any item of gross income, or portion thereof, is met no later than when that item, or portion thereof, is taken into account as revenue in the taxpayer's AFS (the AFS income inclusion rule). Except as provided in paragraph (i) of this section for certain items of income with respect to debt instruments, the AFS income inclusion rule does not apply to any item of gross income, or portion thereof, when the timing of income for that item, or portion thereof, is determined using a special method of accounting, as defined in paragraph (c)(5) of this section. If a special method of accounting is used, income is taken into account as prescribed by that special method of accounting. See, however, paragraph (d) of this section for exceptions for taxpayers without an AFS and income in connection with a mortgage servicing contract.

(c) *Definitions.*—For purposes of this section, the following definitions apply:

(1) *Applicable financial statement.*—Subject to the rules in paragraph (c)(1)(iv) of this section, *applicable financial statement* (AFS) means the taxpayer's financial statement listed in paragraphs (c)(1)(i) through (iii) of this section that has the highest priority, including priority within paragraphs (c)(1)(i)(B) and (c)(1)(ii)(B) of this section. The financial statements are, in order of descending priority:

(i) *GAAP Statements.*—A financial statement that is certified as being prepared in accordance with generally accepted accounting principles (GAAP) and is:

(A) A Form 10-K (or successor form), or annual statement to shareholders, filed with the United States Securities and Exchange Commission (SEC);

(B) An audited financial statement of the taxpayer that is used for:

(1) Credit purposes;

(2) Reporting to shareholders, partners, or other proprietors, or to beneficiaries; or

(3) Any other substantial non-tax purpose; or

(C) A financial statement, other than a tax return, filed with the Federal government or any Federal agency, other than the SEC or the Internal Revenue Service;

(ii) *IFRS Statements.*—A financial statement that is certified as being prepared in accordance with international financial reporting standards (IFRS) and is:

(A) Filed by the taxpayer with an agency of a foreign government that is equivalent to the SEC, and has reporting standards not less stringent than the standards required by the SEC;

(B) An audited financial statement of the taxpayer that is used for:

(1) Credit purposes;

(2) Reporting to shareholders, partners, or other proprietors, or to beneficiaries; or

(3) Any other substantial non-tax purpose; or

(C) A financial statement, other than a tax return, filed with the Federal government or any Federal agency, other than the SEC or the Internal Revenue Service, or a foreign government or agency of a foreign government, other than an agency that is equivalent to the SEC or the Internal Revenue Service; or

(iii) *Other Statements.*—A financial statement, other than a tax return, filed with the Federal government or any Federal agency, a state government or state agency, or a self-regulatory organization (for example, a financial statement filed with a state agency that regulates insurance companies or the Financial Industry Regulatory Authority). Additional financial statements included in this paragraph (c)(1)(iii) may be provided in guidance published in the Internal Revenue Bulletin (see § 601.601(d) of this chapter).

(iv) *Additional rules for determining priority.*—If a taxpayer restates revenue in an AFS prior to the date that the taxpayer files its Federal income tax return for such taxable year, for purposes of determining priority, the restated AFS must be used instead of the original AFS. A taxpayer with different financial accounting and taxable years that is required to file both annual financial statements and periodic financial statements covering less than a year with a government agency must use the annual statement filed with the agency to determine priority.

(2) *Equity method.*—*Equity method* means a method of accounting for financial accounting purposes under which an investment is initially recorded at cost and subsequently increased or decreased in carrying value by the investor's proportionate share of income and losses and such income or losses are reported as separate items on the investor's statement of income.

(3) *Performance obligation.*—*Performance obligation* means a promise in a contract with a customer to transfer to the customer either a good or service, or a combination of both, that is distinct; or a series of distinct goods or services, or a combination of both, that are substantially the same and that have the same pattern of transfer to the customer.

(4) *Revenue.*—*Revenue* means all transaction price amounts includible in gross income under section 61. The characterization of a transaction price in the AFS is not determinative of whether it is taken into account as revenue in a taxpayer's AFS. For example, any transaction price amount that is reported as other comprehensive income in an AFS is taken into account as revenue in an AFS.

(5) *Special method of accounting.*—*Special method of accounting* means a method of accounting permitted or required under any provision of the Code, the Income Tax Regulations, or other guidance published in the Internal Revenue Bulletin (see § 601.601(d) of this chapter) under which an item of income is taken into account in a taxable year other than the taxable year in which the all events test is met. See, however, paragraph (i) of this section relating to certain items of income with respect to debt instruments. The following are examples of special methods of accounting to which the AFS income inclusion rule generally does not apply:

(i) The crop method of accounting under sections 61 and 162;

(ii) Methods of accounting provided in sections 453 through 460;

(iii) Methods of accounting for hedging transactions under § 1.446-4;

(iv) Methods of accounting for REMIC inducement fees under § 1.446-6;

(v) Methods of accounting for gain on shares in a money market fund under § 1.446-7;

(vi) Methods of accounting for certain rental payments under section 467;

(vii) The mark-to-market method of accounting under section 475;

(viii) Timing rules for income and gain associated with a transaction that is integrated under § 1.988-5, and income and gain under the nonfunctional currency contingent payment debt instrument rules in § 1.988-6;

(ix) Except as otherwise provided in paragraph (i) of this section, timing rules for original issue discount (OID) under section 811(b)(3) or 1272 (and the regulations under section 1272), income under the contingent payment debt instrument rules in § 1.1275-4, income under the variable rate debt instrument rules in § 1.1275-5, income and gain associated with a transaction that is integrated under § 1.1275-6, and income under the inflation-indexed debt instrument rules in § 1.1275-7;

(x) Timing rules for de minimis OID under § 1.1273-1(d) and for de minimis market discount (as defined in section 1278(a)(2)(C));

(xi) Timing rules for accrued market discount under sections 1276 and 1278(b); and

(xii) Methods of accounting provided in sections 1502 and 1503 and the regulations thereunder, including the method of accounting relating to intercompany transactions under § 1.1502-13.

(6) *Transaction price.*—The transaction price means the gross amount of consideration to which a taxpayer expects to be entitled for AFS purposes in exchange for transferring promised goods, services, or other property, including amounts referred to in paragraph (i) of this section, but not including:

(i) Amounts collected on behalf of third parties (for example, some sales taxes) that are otherwise not income to the taxpayer;

(ii) Increases in consideration to which a taxpayer's entitlement is contingent on the occurrence or nonoccurrence of a future event (for example, bonuses contingent on performance and insurance contract commissions contingent on renewal) for the period in which the amount is contingent. Amounts included in the transaction price for AFS purposes are presumed to not be contingent on the occurrence or nonoccurrence of a future event, unless, upon examination of all the facts and circumstances existing at the end of the taxable year, it can be established to the satisfaction of the Commissioner that the amount is contingent on the occurrence or nonoccurrence of a future event. An amount included in the transaction price for AFS purposes that is actually or constructively received, that is due and payable, or for which the taxpayer has an enforceable right to payment for performance completed to date, however, will not be treated as contingent on the occurrence or nonoccurrence of a future event; or

(iii) Reductions for amounts subject to section 461, including allowances, adjustments, rebates, chargebacks, refunds, rewards (for example, estimated redemption costs associated with loyalty programs), and amounts included in costs of goods sold.

(d) *Exceptions to the AFS income inclusion rule.*—The AFS income inclusion rule does not apply unless all of the taxpayer's taxable year is covered by an AFS. In addition, the AFS income inclusion rule does not apply to any item of income in connection with a mortgage servicing contract.

(e) *No change in the treatment of a transaction.*—Except as provided in paragraph (i)(2) of this section, the AFS income inclusion rule does not change the treatment of a transaction for Federal income tax purposes. The following are examples of transactions where the treatment for AFS purposes does not change the treatment of the transaction for Federal income tax purposes:

(1) A transaction treated as a lease, license, or similar transaction for Federal income tax purposes that is treated as a sale or financing for AFS purposes, and vice versa;

(2) A transaction that is not required to be marked-to-market for Federal income tax purposes but that is marked-to-market for AFS purposes;

(3) Asset sale and liquidation treatment under section 336(e) or 338(h)(10);

(4) A distribution of a corporation or the allocable share of partnership items or an income inclusion under section 951, 951A, or 1293(a) for Federal income tax purposes that is accounted for under the equity method for AFS purposes;

(5) A distribution of previously taxed earnings and profits of a foreign corporation; and

(6) A deposit or conduit payment for Federal income tax purposes that is treated as revenue for AFS purposes.

(f) *No change to exclusion provisions and the treatment of non-recognition transactions.*—The AFS income inclusion rule does not change the applicability of any exclusion provision, or the treatment of non-recognition transactions, in the Code, the Income Tax Regulations, or other guidance published in the Internal Revenue Bulletin (see § 601.601(d) of this chapter). The following are examples of exclusion provisions and non-recognition transactions that are not affected by the AFS income inclusion rule:

(1) Any non-recognition transaction, within the meaning of section 7701(a)(45), (for example, a liquidation described in sections 332 and 337, an exchange described in section 351, a distribution described in section 355, a reorganization described in section 368, a contribution described in section 721, or transactions described in sections 1031 through 1045); and

(2) Items specifically excluded from income under sections 101 through 140.

(g) *Contracts with multiple performance obligations.*—(1) *In general.*—For purposes of this section, if a taxpayer's contract with a customer has more than one performance obligation, transaction price is allocated to performance obligations as transaction price is allocated to performance obligations in the taxpayer's AFS.

(2) *Example.*—Taxpayer A, a manufacturer and servicer of airplane parts, is a calendar-year accrual method taxpayer with an AFS. In 2018, A enters into a $100x contract to sell airplane parts and to service those parts, as necessary, in 2018, 2019, and 2020. For AFS purposes, A allocates $40x of the total contract price to the delivery of parts in 2018, $10x to the provision of services in 2018, $20x to the provision of services in 2019, and $30x to the provision of services in 2020. In 2018, A delivers parts and provides services. On its 2018 AFS, A includes the $40x for the delivery of parts and the $10x for the provision of services in revenue. Under paragraph (g)(1) of this section, because the contract involves multiple performance obligations, A must use its transaction price AFS allocation to determine whether income from the sale of airplane parts and services are included in revenue in its AFS for purposes of this section. Accordingly, under the AFS income inclusion rule in paragraph (b) of this section, for the $40x sale of airplane parts and the $10x provision of services in 2018 the all events test is not met any later than A's 2018 taxable year.

(h) *Additional AFS issues.*—(1) *AFS covering groups of entities.*—(i) *In general.*—For purposes of this section, if a taxpayer's financial results are reported on the AFS for a group of entities, the taxpayer's AFS is the group's AFS. However, if the taxpayer's financial results are also reported on a separate AFS that is of equal or higher priority to the group's AFS under paragraph (c)(1) of this section, then the taxpayer's AFS is the separate AFS.

(ii) *Example.*—Taxpayer B, a reseller of computers and electronics, is a calendar-year accrual method taxpayer. In 2018, B's financial results are included in its parent corporation's consolidated Form 10-K filed with the SEC, but it files a separate Federal income tax return. Under paragraph (h)(1) of this section, because its financial results are reported on the AFS for its parent corporation, B must use its parent corporation's consolidated Form 10-K as its AFS. Accordingly, under the AFS income inclusion rule in paragraph (b) of this section, for the sale of computers and electronics the all events test is not met any later than when the sale is included in its parent corporation's consolidated Form 10-K.

(2) *Separately stated items.*—If a group's AFS is treated as the taxpayer's AFS, the taxpayer must look to any separately stated items to determine the amount of revenue allocated to the taxpayer.

(3) *Non-separately stated items.*—If a group's AFS does not separately state items, the portion of the revenue allocable to the taxpayer is determined by relying on the source documents that were used to create the group's AFS.

(4) *Computation of revenue when the AFS covers mismatched reportable periods.*—(i) *In general.*—If a taxpayer's AFS is prepared on the basis of a financial accounting year that differs from the taxpayer's taxable year, the taxpayer must use one of the permissible methods listed in paragraph (h)(4)(ii) of this section to determine revenue for purposes of the AFS income inclusion rule.

(ii) *Permissible methods to determine revenue.*—For purposes of paragraph (h)(4)(i) of this section, a taxpayer must use one of the following methods to determine revenue for the taxable year in order to apply the AFS income inclusion rule:

(A) The taxpayer computes revenue by using the accounting principles used to create its AFS to determine whether an item would be included in revenue in an AFS for the taxable year as if its financial reporting period was the same as its taxable year, for example, by conducting an interim closing of its books.

(B) The taxpayer computes revenue by including a pro rata portion of the revenue for each financial accounting year that includes any part of the taxpayer's taxable year. If the taxpayer's AFS for part of the taxable year is not available by the due date of the return (with extension), the taxpayer must make a reasonable estimate of revenue for the pro rata portion of the taxable year for which an AFS is not yet available. See §1.451-1(a) for adjustments after actual amounts are determined.

(C) If a taxpayer's financial accounting year ends five or more months after the end of its taxable year, the taxpayer computes revenue for Federal income tax purposes based on the revenue reported on the AFS prepared for the financial accounting year ending within the taxpayer's taxable year. For purposes of this paragraph (h)(4)(ii)(C), if a taxpayer uses a 52-53 week year for financial accounting or Federal income tax purposes, the last day of such year shall be deemed to occur on the last day of the calendar month ending closest to the end of such year.

(iii) *Method of accounting.*—A change in the method of computing revenue under this paragraph (h)(4) is a change in method of accounting under section 446. A taxpayer may change its method of accounting only with the consent of the Commissioner as required under section 446(e) and the corresponding regulations.

(5) *Restatement of AFS.*—If a taxpayer restates revenue on an AFS and such restatement changes the timing of when an item of income, or a portion thereof, is taken into account as revenue on the AFS, the change constitutes a change in method of accounting under section 446. A taxpayer may change its method of accounting only with the consent of the Commissioner as required under section 446(e) and the corresponding regulations. If a taxpayer restates revenue on an AFS to correct an error or the restatement results in a change in the estimate of the taxpayer's pro rata portion of revenue under paragraph (h)(4)(ii)(B) of this section, see §1.451-1(a).

(i) *Special ordering rule for certain items of income with respect to debt instruments.*—(1) *In general.*—If an item of income, or portion thereof, with respect to a debt instrument is described in paragraph (i)(2) of this section, the rules of this section apply before the rules in sections 1271 through 1275 and §§1.1271-1 through 1.1275-7 (OID rules). Therefore, an item of income, or portion thereof, described in paragraph (i)(2) of this section may not be taken into income later than when that item, or portion thereof, is taken into account as revenue in the taxpayer's AFS, regardless of whether the timing of income inclusion for that item is normally determined using a special method of accounting. See also §1.1275-2(l) for the treatment of the items described in paragraph (i)(2) of this section under the OID rules.

(2) *Specified fees.*—Paragraph (i)(1) of this section applies to fees (specified fees) that are not treated as discount or as an adjustment to the yield of a debt instrument over the life of the instrument (such as points) in the taxpayer's AFS and, but for paragraph (i) of this section and §1.1275-2(l), would be treated as creating or increasing OID for Federal income tax purposes. For example, the following specified fees (specified credit card fees) are described in this paragraph (i)(2):

(i) A payment of additional interest or a similar charge provided with respect to amounts that are not paid when due on a credit card account (for example, credit card late fees);

(ii) Amounts charged under a credit card agreement when the cardholder uses the credit card to conduct a cash advance transaction (for example, credit card cash advance fees); and

(iii) Amounts a credit or debit card issuer is entitled to upon a purchase of goods or services by one of its cardholders (for example, interchange fees, which are sometimes labeled merchant discount in certain private label credit card transactions).

(3) *Example.*—Taxpayer C, a credit card issuer, is a calendar-year accrual method taxpayer with an AFS. In 2019, a cardholder uses C's credit card to purchase $100 of merchandise from a merchant and the cardholder earns a reward of 1% of the purchase price of $100 ($1) as part of C's cardholder loyalty program. Upon purchase, C becomes entitled to an interchange fee equal to 2% of the purchase price of $100 ($2). In 2019, C reports the $2 of interchange fees as revenue in its AFS. C's $2 of interchange fees is described in paragraph (i)(2)(iii) of this section. Under paragraph (i)(1) of this section, C must apply the rules in this section before applying the OID rules. See also §1.1275-2(l). Therefore, C's $2 of interchange fees is included in taxable income in 2019, the year it is included as revenue in C's AFS. Under paragraph (c)(6)(iii) of this section, the $2 of interchange revenue is not reduced by the $1 reward. Even if C reports interchange fees net of rewards in its AFS for 2019 ($2 of interchange fee minus $1 reward liability), under paragraph (c)(6) of this section, C includes $2 of interchange revenue in taxable income in 2019. See §§162 and 461(h) for the treatment of the reward by C.

(j) *Treatment of adjustments to deferred revenue in an AFS.*—(1) *In general.*—For purposes of this section, if a taxpayer treats an item of income as deferred revenue in its AFS and writes down or adjusts that item, or portion thereof, to an equity account (for example, retained earnings) or otherwise writes down or adjusts that item of deferred revenue in a subsequent taxable year, revenue for that subsequent taxable year includes that item, or portion thereof, that is written down or adjusted.

(2) *Example.*—Taxpayer D, a remanufacturer of industrial equipment, is a calendar-year accrual method taxpayer with an AFS. In 2018, D enters into a contract with a customer to remanufacture equipment in 2019 and 2020 for $100x. The contract is not a long-term contract under section 460. In its 2018 AFS, D treats the $100x as deferred revenue. In 2019, all the stock of D is acquired by an unrelated third party. In its 2019 AFS, D adjusts deferred revenue to $90x (the expected cost to provide the services) by charging $10x ($100x - $90x = $10x) to retained earnings. In its 2019 AFS, D includes $50x of the $90x of deferred revenue in revenue. Under paragraph (j)(1) of this section, D's adjustment to deferred revenue in 2019 is treated as revenue under paragraph (c)(4) of this section in 2019. Therefore, under the AFS income inclusion rule in paragraph (b) of this section, D is treated as including $60x ($50x + $10x = $60x) in revenue in its 2019 AFS, and the all events test is met for that $60x no later than D's 2019 taxable year.

(k) *Cumulative rule for multi-year contracts.*—In the case of a multi-year contract, a taxpayer must take into account the cumulative amounts included in income in prior taxable years on the contract, if any, in order to determine the amount to be included for the taxable years remaining in the contract. For purposes of this paragraph (k), multiyear contract means a contract that spans more than one taxable year.

(l) *Methods of accounting.*—(1) *In general.*—A change in the method of recognizing revenue in an AFS that changes or could change the timing of the recognition of income for Federal income tax purposes is a change in method of accounting under section 446. A taxpayer may change its method of accounting only with the consent of the Commissioner as required under section 446(e) and the corresponding regulations. Accordingly, a taxpayer that changes the method of accounting used to recognize revenue in its AFS is required to secure consent of the Commissioner before computing income using this new method for Federal income tax purposes.

(2) *Transition rule for changes in method of accounting.*—(i) *In general.*—Except as provided in paragraph (l)(2)(ii) of this section, a taxpayer that makes a qualified change in method of accounting for the taxpayer's first taxable year beginning after December 31, 2017, is treated as making a change in method initiated by the taxpayer for purposes of section 481(a)(2). A taxpayer obtains the consent of the Commissioner to make a qualified change in method of accounting by using the applicable administrative procedures that govern voluntary automatic changes in method of accounting under section 446(e). See section §1.446-1(e)(3).

(ii) *Special rules for OID and specified fees.*—The rules of paragraph (l)(2)(i) of this section apply to a qualified change in method of accounting required under section 451(b) and paragraph (i) of this section for the taxpayer's first taxable year beginning after December 31, 2018, if the change relates to a specified credit card fee (as defined in paragraph (i)(2) of this section). The rules of paragraph (l)(2)(i) of this section apply to a qualified change in method of accounting required under section 451(b) and paragraph (i) of this section for the taxpayer's first taxable year beginning one year after the date the Treasury decision adopting these regulations as final is published in the **Federal Register**, if the change relates to a specified fee (as defined in paragraph (i)(2) of this section) other than a specified credit card fee. For purposes of this paragraph (l)(2)(ii), the section

481(a) adjustment period for any adjustment under section 481(a) for a qualified change in method of accounting required under section 451(b) and paragraph (i) of this section is six taxable years.

(iii) *Qualified change in method of accounting.*—For purposes of paragraph (l)(2) of this section, a qualified change in method of accounting means any change in method of accounting that is required by section 13221 of the Tax Cuts and Jobs Act, Public Law No. 115-97 (131 Stat. 2054) (TCJA), or was prohibited under the Internal Revenue Code of 1986 prior to TCJA section 13221 and is now permitted as a result of TCJA section 13221.

(m) *Examples.*—The following examples illustrate the provisions of this section:

(1) *Example 1. Mismatched reportable periods.* Taxpayer A is a calendar-year accrual method taxpayer with an AFS. For AFS purposes, A's financial results are reported on a June 30 fiscal year. Using the method described in paragraph (h)(4)(ii)(A) of this section, for the taxable year 2018, A uses the financial results reported on its June 30, 2018, AFS to determine whether an item of income was taken into account as revenue in A's AFS from January 1, 2018, through June 30, 2018, and uses its June 30, 2019, AFS to determine whether an item of income is taken into account as revenue in A's AFS from July 1, 2018, through December 31, 2018.

(2) *Example 2. Provision of installation services.* Taxpayer B is a calendar-year accrual method taxpayer with an AFS. In 2018, B enters into a contract with a customer to provide manufacturing equipment installation services for $100,000. Throughout the contract, the customer retains control of the equipment. B has an enforceable right to payment for services partially performed. The contract is not a long-term contract under section 460. B begins providing the installation services in 2018 and completes the installation services in 2019. Under the contract, B bills the customer $50,000 in 2018 when installation begins. B includes $60,000 in revenue in its 2018 AFS and $40,000 in revenue in its 2019 AFS. Under the AFS income inclusion rule in paragraph (b) of this section, because $60,000 of revenue from the installation services is included in B's 2018 AFS, the all events test for that $60,000 of income is met in B's 2018 taxable year.

(3) *Example 3. Provision of goods.* Taxpayer C is a calendar-year accrual method taxpayer with an AFS. In 2018, C enters into a

contract with a customer to provide 50 customized computers for $80,000. Under the contract, C can bill $80,000 after the customer accepts delivery of the computers. However, because of the customization, the contract provides that C can be paid for work performed to date, even if the contract is not completed for reasons other than C's failure to perform. C delivers all of the computers in 2018. Customer accepts delivery of the computers and C bills the customer in 2019. C includes all $80,000 in revenue in its 2018 AFS. Under the AFS income inclusion rule in paragraph (b) of this section, because $80,000 of revenue from the provision of goods is included in C's 2018 AFS, the all events test for that $80,000 of income is met in C's 2018 taxable year. Under paragraph (c)(6)(ii) of this section, the limitation on C's ability to bill until after the customer accepts delivery of the computers is not a future event that restricts C's enforceable right to payment for the goods.

(4) *Example 4. Provision of services included in AFS without deferral of advance payments under section 451(c)(1)(B).* Taxpayer D, an engineering services provider, is a calendar-year accrual method taxpayer with an AFS. In 2018, D enters into a contract with a customer to provide services for four years for a total of $100x. Under the contract, D receives $25x each year of the contract. D does not elect to defer advance payments under section 451(c)(1)(B). For AFS purposes, D reports $50x, $0, $20x, and $30x of revenue from the contract in 2018, 2019, 2020, and 2021, respectively. Under paragraph (g)(1) of this section, the allocation of the transaction price in D's AFS is used to determine when all or part of that item is taken into account for purposes of paragraph (b) of this section. In 2018, D includes all of the $25x payment in income from the contract under the all events test. In addition, under paragraph (b) of this section, because $50x of revenue from the provision of services is included in D's 2018 AFS, the all events test for that portion of the provision of services is not met later than D's 2018 taxable year. Therefore, D must include the additional $25x ($50x − $25x = $25x) reported on the AFS as income in 2018. In 2019, under paragraph (k) of this section, D includes $0 of the $25x payment in income from the contract because the payment received in 2019 relates to income included in 2018. In 2020, D includes all of the $25x payment in income from the contract under the all events test. In 2021, D includes the remaining $25x payment in income under the contract under the all events test. This example is summarized in the table below:

	2018	2019	2020	2021	Total
Payments	$25x	$25x	$25x	$25x	$100x
AFS Revenue	$50x	$0	$20x	$30x	$100x
Income	$50x	$0	$25x	$25x	$100x

(5) *Example 5. Provision of services included in AFS with deferral of advance payments under section 451(c)(1)(B).* The facts are the same as in *Example 4* in paragraph (m)(4) of this section, except D elects to defer advance payments under section 451(c)(1)(B). Under paragraph (g)(1) of this section, the allocation of the transaction price in D's AFS is used to determine when all or part of that item is taken into account for purposes of paragraph (b) of this section. In 2018, D includes all of the $25x payment in income from the contract under the all events test. In addition, under paragraph (b) of this section, because $50x of revenue from the provision of services is included in D's 2018 AFS, the all events test for that portion of the provision of

services is not met later than D's 2018 taxable year. Therefore, D must include an additional $25x ($50x − $25x = $25x) of income in 2018. In 2019, under paragraph (k) of this section, D includes $0 of the $25x payment in income from the contract because the payment received in 2019 relates to income included in 2018. In 2020, D includes $20x of the $25x payment in income from the contract under the deferral method for advance payments under section 451(c)(1)(B). In 2021, D includes the $5x that was deferred in 2020 under the deferral method for advance payments under section 451(c)(1)(B) and the remaining $25x payment in income under the contract under the all events test. This example is summarized in the table below:

	2018	2019	2020	2021	Total
Payments	$25x	$25x	$25x	$25x	$100x
AFS Revenue	$50x	$0	$20x	$30x	$100x
Income	$50x	$0	$20x	$30x	$100x

(6) *Example 6. Sale of goods with AFS revenue adjustments.* Taxpayer E, a manufacturer of automobile parts, is a calendar-year accrual method taxpayer with an AFS. E normally sells parts for $10 per part with a 2% bonus if the parts are delivered on time. Traditionally, 5% of parts sold are returned. In 2018, E enters a contract to sell 1,000 parts to a customer for $10 per part, for a total of $10,000 (1,000 x $10 = $10,000). The contract also provides that E will receive a 2% bonus if it delivers all the parts to the customer by February 1, 2019. E delivers 500 parts to the customer on December 31, 2018. On December 31, 2018, the additional 500 parts were scheduled for shipment to the customer on January 4, 2019. For AFS purposes, E expects to earn the 2% bonus and to have 5% of the parts returned. In its 2018 AFS, E reports $4,850 ($5,000 + $100 - $250 = $4,850) of revenue from the contract, including a $100 (2% x $5,000 = $100) adjustment for the expected bonus and a $250 (5% x $5,000 = $250) adjustment for anticipated returns. Under paragraph (c)(6)(iii) of this section, E's transaction price does not include anticipated returns. See §1.461-4(g)(3) for rules on when the return liability is incurred. Under paragraph (c)(6)(ii) of this section, the performance bonus is presumed not to be contingent on the occurrence or nonoccurrence of a future event. However, at the end of the year, all parts have yet to be delivered within the February 1, 2019 deadline. Under the contract, E has no right to payment of the bonus at the end of the year. Therefore, the presumption is rebutted. In addition, under paragraph

(g)(1) of this section, the allocation of the transaction price in E's AFS is used to determine when all or part of that item is taken into account for purposes of paragraph (b) of this section. Accordingly, under paragraph (b) of this section, because $5,000 of revenue from the sale of parts is taken into account in E's 2018 AFS, the all events test for $5,000 of income allocated to those parts is met in E's 2018 taxable year.

(7) *Example 7. Chargebacks.* Taxpayer F, a manufacturer of pharmaceuticals, is a calendar-year accrual method taxpayer with an AFS. In addition to billing the wholesaler for the sale of the pharmaceutical at the wholesale acquisition cost under the contract, F generally credits or pays wholesalers a chargeback of 40% of the wholesale acquisition cost for sales made by those wholesalers to qualifying customers. In 2018, F enters into a contract to sell 1,000 units to W, a wholesaler, for $10 per unit, totaling $10,000 (1,000 x $10 = $10,000). The contract also provides that F will issue a 40% chargeback for sales by W to certain qualifying customers. F delivers 600 units to W on December 31, 2018, and bills W $6,000 under the contract. For AFS purposes, F adjusts its revenue by 40% for all sales to W for anticipated chargebacks. As such, in its 2018 AFS, F reports $3,600 ($6,000 - $2,400 = $3,600) of revenue from the contract with W, decreasing revenue by $2,400 (40% x $6,000 = $2,400) for anticipated chargeback claims. For Federal income tax purposes, under paragraph (c)(6)(iii)

of this section, F's 2018 revenue is $6,000 because F's revenue is not reduced for anticipated chargebacks.

(8) *Example 8. Sale of property using a special method of accounting.* Taxpayer G, a provider of financial services, is a calendar-year accrual method taxpayer with an AFS. In 2018, G sells a building for $100x, payable in five annual payments of $20x starting in 2018. In its 2018 AFS, G reports all $100x of revenue from the sale of the building. For Federal income tax purposes, G uses the installment method under section 453 for the sale of the building. Under paragraph (c)(5) of this section, the installment method under section 453 is a special method of accounting because it requires income to be taken into account in a taxable year other than the taxable year in which the all events test is met. Therefore, under paragraph (b) of this section, this section does not apply to G's sale of the building because it is using a special method of accounting and the income is taken into account as prescribed in section 453.

(9) *Example 9. Non-recognition provisions not changed for Federal income tax purposes.* Taxpayer H (Distributing) is a calendar-year accrual method C corporation with an AFS. On December 31, 2018, Distributing (i) contributes assets to a wholly owned subsidiary (Controlled) in exchange for Controlled stock and $100x, and (ii) distributes all of Controlled's stock pro rata to its shareholders. The transaction qualifies as a reorganization under section 368(a)(1)(D) and a distribution to which section 355 applies (D reorganization). Distributing's realized gain on the transferred assets for book and tax purposes is $150x. On January 15, 2019, in pursuance of the plan of reorganization, Distributing distributes the $100x to its shareholders. Consequently, no gain to Distributing is recognized under section 361(b)(1)(A). On Distributing's 2018 AFS, Distributing recognizes revenue of $150x related to the D reorganization. Under paragraph (f) of this section, nothing in section 451(b) or this section changes the applicability of any deferral, non-recognition, or exclusion provision of the Code, the Income Tax Regulations, or other guidance published in the Internal Revenue Bulletin. Section 361 provides that Distributing does not recognize any gain from the D reorganization. Pursuant to paragraph (f) of this section, nothing in section 451(b) or this section would change the result that Distributing does not recognize gain on Distributing's (i) contribution of assets to Controlled, (ii) receipt of Controlled stock and cash, and (iii) distribution of Controlled stock and cash to Distributing's shareholders.

(10) *Example 10. Insurance contract renewals.* The taxpayer, an insurance agent, is engaged by an insurance carrier to sell insurance. By written binding contract between the taxpayer and the insurance carrier, the taxpayer is entitled to receive a $50 commission from the insurance carrier at the time a policy is sold to a customer. The written binding contract also provides that the taxpayer is entitled to receive an additional $25 commission each time a policy is renewed. The taxpayer sells 1,000 one-year policies in year one, of which 800 are renewed in year two and 700 are renewed in year three. The taxpayer does not have any ongoing obligation to provide additional services to the insurance carrier or the customers after the initial sale of the policy. The taxpayer includes $86,000 in revenue in its AFS for year one, which includes $50,000 of consideration for policies sold in year one and an estimate of $36,000 of consideration for the policies expected to be renewed in years two and three. Under paragraph (c)(6)(ii) of this section, because the taxpayer is able to demonstrate by written binding contract that the amounts related to future insurance contract renewals are contingent on the occurrence of a future event (that is the customer contract renewal), the taxpayer's transaction price from commissions is $50,000 ($50 * 1,000) in year one, $20,000 ($25 * 800) in year two, and $17,500 ($25 * 700) in year three.

(n) *Applicability date.*—(1) *In general.*—Except as provided in paragraph (n)(2) of this section, these regulations are proposed to apply for taxable years beginning after the date the Treasury decision adopting these regulations as final is published in the **Federal Register**.

(2) *Delayed application with respect to certain fees.*—Notwithstanding paragraph (n)(1) of this section, paragraph (i)(2) of this section is proposed to apply to specified fees (as defined in paragraph (i)(2) of this section) other than specified credit card fees (as defined in paragraph (i)(2) of this section) for taxable years beginning one year after the date the Treasury decision adopting these regulations as final is published in the **Federal Register**.

(3) *Early application of this section.*—(i) *In general.*—Except as provided in paragraph (n)(3)(ii) of this section, until the date the Treasury decision adopting these regulations as final regulations is published in the **Federal Register**, a taxpayer may rely on these proposed regulations for taxable years beginning after December 31, 2017, if the taxpayer applies all the applicable rules contained in these proposed regulations (other than those applicable to specified fees), and consistently applies these proposed regulations to all items of income during the taxable year (other than specified fees).

(ii) *Certain fees.*—(A) *Specified credit card fees.*—Until the date the Treasury decision adopting these regulations as final regulations is published in the **Federal Register**, in the case of a specified credit card fee, a taxpayer may rely on these proposed regulations for taxable years beginning after December 31, 2018, if the taxpayer applies all the applicable rules contained in these proposed regulations for a specified credit card fee, and consistently applies these proposed regulations to all items of income during the taxable year (other than specified fees that are not specified credit card fees).

(B) *Specified fees.*—Paragraph (n)(3)(i) of this section does not apply to specified fees that are not specified credit card fees. [Reg. §1.451-3.]

Goods, Services, and Other Items: Advance Payments

Goods, Services, and Other Items: Advance Payments.—Reg. §1.451-8, regarding the timing of income inclusion under section 451 of the Internal Revenue Code of advance payments for goods, services, and certain other items, is proposed (published in the Federal Register on September 9, 2019) (REG-104554-18).

Par. 2. Section 1.451-8 is added to read as follows:

§1.451-8. Advance payments for goods, services, and certain other items.—(a) *In general.*—Except as provided in paragraph (c) or (d) of this section, an accrual method taxpayer shall include an advance payment in gross income no later than in the taxable year in which the taxpayer receives the advance payment as provided under §1.451-1(a).

(b) *Definitions.*—Except as otherwise provided in this section, the following definitions apply for purposes of this section:

(1) *Advance payment.*—(i) *In general.*—An advance payment is a payment received by a taxpayer if:

(A) The full inclusion of the payment in the gross income of the taxpayer for the taxable year of receipt is a permissible method of accounting, without regard to this section;

(B) Any portion of the payment is included in revenue by the taxpayer in an applicable financial statement for a subsequent taxable year;

(C) The payment is for:
(1) Services;
(2) The sale of goods;
(3) The use, including by license or lease, of intellectual property, including copyrights, patents, trademarks, service marks, trade names, and similar intangible property rights, such as franchise rights and arena naming rights;
(4) The occupancy or use of property if the occupancy or use is ancillary to the provision of services, for example, advance payments for the use of rooms or other quarters in a hotel, booth space at a trade show, campsite space at a mobile home park, and recreational or banquet facilities, or other uses of property, so long as the use is ancillary to the provision of services to the property user;
(5) The sale, lease, or license of computer software;
(6) Guaranty or warranty contracts ancillary to an item or items described in paragraph (b)(1)(i)(C)(1), (2), (3), (4), or (5) of this section;
(7) Subscriptions in tangible or intangible format. Subscriptions for which an election under section 455 is in effect is not included in this paragraph (b)(1)(i)(C)(7);
(8) Memberships in an organization. Memberships for which an election under section 456 is in effect are not included in this paragraph (b)(1)(i)(C)(8);
(9) An eligible gift card sale;
(10) Any other payment specified by the Secretary in other guidance published in the Internal Revenue Bulletin (see §601.601(d)(2)); or
(11) Any combination of items described in paragraphs (b)(1)(i)(C)(1) through (10) of this section.

(ii) *Exclusions from the definition of advance payment.*—An advance payment does not include:
(A) Rent, except for amounts paid with respect to an item or items described in paragraph (b)(1)(i)(C)(3), (4) or (5) of this section;
(B) Insurance premiums, to the extent the inclusion of those premiums is governed by subchapter L;
(C) Payments with respect to financial instruments (for example, debt instruments, deposits, letters of credit, notional princi-

pal contracts, options, forward contracts, futures contracts, foreign currency contracts, credit card agreements (including rewards or loyalty points under such agreements), financial derivatives, or similar items), including purported prepayments of interest;

(D) Payments with respect to service warranty contracts for which the taxpayer uses the accounting method provided in Revenue Procedure 97-38 (1997-2 CB 479);

(E) Payments with respect to warranty and guaranty contracts under which a third party is the primary obligor;

(F) Payments subject to section 871(a), 881, 1441, or 1442;

(G) Payments in property to which section 83 applies; and

(H) Payments received in a taxable year earlier than the taxable year immediately preceding the taxable year of the contractual delivery date for a specified good.

(2) *Applicable financial statement.*—Applicable financial statement has the same meaning as provided in proposed § 1.451-3(c)(1).

(3) *Eligible gift card sale.*—Eligible gift card sale means the sale of a gift card or gift certificate if:

(i) The taxpayer is primarily liable to the customer, or holder of the gift card, for the value of the card until redemption or expiration; and

(ii) The gift card is redeemable by the taxpayer or by any other entity that is legally obligated to the taxpayer to accept the gift card from a customer as payment for items listed in paragraphs (b)(1)(i)(C)(*1*) through (*11*) of this section.

(4) *Performance obligation.*—Performance obligation has the same meaning as provided in proposed § 1.451-3(c)(3).

(5) *Received.*—An item of gross income is received by the taxpayer if it is actually or constructively received, or if it is due and payable to the taxpayer.

(6) *Revenue.*—Revenue has the same meaning as provided in proposed § 1.451-3(c)(4) and is determined under the rules provided in proposed § 1.451-3.

(7) *Transaction price.*—Transaction price has the same meaning as provided in proposed § 1.451-3(c)(6).

(8) *Contractual delivery date.*—Contractual delivery date means the month and year of delivery listed in the written contract to the transaction.

(9) *Specified good.*—A specified good means a good for which:

(i) During the taxable year a payment is received, the taxpayer does not have on hand (or available to it in such year through its normal source of supply) goods of a substantially similar kind and in a sufficient quantity to satisfy the contract to transfer the good to the customer; and

(ii) All the revenue from the sale of the good is recognized in the taxpayer's AFS in the year of delivery.

(c) *Deferral method for taxpayers with an applicable financial statement (AFS).*—(1) *In general.*—An accrual method taxpayer with an AFS that receives an advance payment may elect the deferral method described in this paragraph (c) if the taxpayer is able to determine the extent to which advance payments are included in revenue in its AFS in the taxable year received, including a short taxable year (if applicable). A taxpayer that uses the deferral method must:

(i) Include the advance payment, or any portion thereof, in gross income in the taxable year of receipt to the extent included in revenue in its AFS; and

(ii) Include the remaining portion of such advance payment in gross income in the taxable year following the taxable year in which such advance payment is received.

(2) *Acceleration of advance payments.*—(i) *In general.*—A taxpayer that uses the deferral method described in this paragraph (c) must include in gross income for the taxable year of receipt or, if applicable, for a short taxable year described in paragraph (c)(4) of this section, all advance payments not previously included in gross income:

(A) If, in that taxable year, the taxpayer either dies or ceases to exist in a transaction other than a transaction to which section 381(a) applies; or

(B) If, and to the extent that, in that taxable year, the taxpayer's obligation with respect to the advance payments is satisfied or otherwise ends other than in:

(*1*) A transaction to which section 381(a) applies; or

(*2*) A section 351(a) transfer that is part of a section 351 transaction in which:

(*i*) Substantially all assets of the trade or business (including advance payments) are transferred;

(*ii*) The transferee adopts or uses the deferral method in the year of transfer; and

(*iii*) The transferee and the transferor are members of the same consolidated group, as defined in § 1.1502-1(h).

(ii) *Example. Ceasing to exist.*—A is a calendar year taxpayer and is in the business of selling and licensing computer software (off the shelf, fully customized, and semi-customized) and providing customer support. On July 1, 2018, A enters into a 2-year software maintenance contract and receives an advance payment. Under the contract, A will provide software updates if it develops an update within the contract period, as well as online and telephone customer support. A ceases to exist on December 1, 2018, in a transaction that does not involve a section 351(a) transfer described in paragraph (c)(2)(i)(B)(2) of this section and is not a transaction to which section 381(a) applies. For federal income tax purposes, A must include the entire advance payment in gross income in its 2018 taxable year.

(3) *Financial statement adjustments.*—(i) *In general.*—Notwithstanding section 451(c)(4)(A)(ii), if a taxpayer treats an advance payment as an item of deferred revenue in its AFS and writes-down or adjusts that item, or portion thereof, to an equity account (for example, retained earnings) or otherwise writes-down or adjusts that item of deferred revenue in a subsequent taxable year, revenue for that subsequent taxable year includes that item, or portion thereof, that is written down or adjusted.

(ii) *Examples.*—(A) *Example 1.* On May 1, 2018, A, a corporation that files its federal income tax return on a calendar year basis, received $100 as an advance payment for a 2-year contract to provide services. For financial accounting purposes, A recorded $100 as a deferred revenue liability in its AFS, expecting to report 1/4 of the advance payment in revenue in its AFS for 2018, 1/2 for 2019, and 1/4 for 2020. On August 31, 2018, C, an unrelated corporation that files its federal income tax return on a calendar year basis, acquired all of the stock of A, and A joined C's consolidated group. A's short taxable year ended on August 31, 2018, and, as of that date, A had included only 1/4 ($25) of the advance payment in revenue in its AFS. On September 1, 2018, after the stock acquisition, and in accordance with purchase accounting rules, C wrote down A's deferred revenue liability to its fair value of $10 as of the date of the acquisition. The $10 will be included in revenue on A's AFS in accordance with the method of accounting A uses for financial accounting purposes. For federal income tax purposes, A uses the deferral method. For federal income tax purposes, A must take 1/4 ($25) of the advance payment into income for its short taxable year ending August 31, 2018, and the remainder of the advance payment ($75) ($65 write down + $10 future financial statement revenue) must be included in income for A's next succeeding taxable year.

(B) *Example 2.* On May 1, 2018, B, a corporation that files its federal income tax return on a calendar year basis, received $100 advance payment for a contract to be performed in 2018, 2019, and 2020. On August 31, 2018, D, a corporation that is not consolidated for federal income tax purposes, acquired all of the stock of B. Before the stock acquisition, on its AFS for 2018, B included $40 of the advance payment in revenue, and $60 as a deferred revenue liability. On September 1, 2018, after the stock acquisition and in accordance with purchase accounting rules, D wrote down its $60 deferred revenue liability to $10 (its fair value) as of the date of the acquisition. After the acquisition, B does not include in revenue any of the $10 deferred revenue liability in its 2018 AFS. B does include $5 in revenue in 2019, and $5 in revenue in 2020. For federal income tax purposes, B uses the deferral method. For federal income tax purposes, B must take $40 of the advance payment into income in 2018, and the remainder of the advance payment ($60) ($50 write down + $10 future financial statement revenue) must be included in income for B's next succeeding taxable year, 2019.

(4) *Short taxable year rule.*—(i) *In general.*—If the taxpayer's next succeeding taxable year is a short taxable year, other than a taxable year in which the taxpayer dies or ceases to exist in a transaction other than a transaction to which section 381(a) applies, and the short taxable year consists of 92 days or less, a taxpayer using the deferral method must include the portion of the advance payment not included in the taxable year of receipt in gross income for the short taxable year to the extent included in revenue in an AFS. Any amount of the advance payment not included in the taxable year of receipt and the short taxable year must be included in gross income for the taxable year immediately following the short taxable year.

(ii) *Example.*—A is a calendar year taxpayer and is in the business of selling and licensing computer software (off the shelf, fully customized, and semi-customized) and providing customer support. On July 1, 2018, A receives an advance payment for a 2-year software maintenance contract. Under the contract, A will provide software updates if it develops an update within the contract period, as well as online and telephone customer support. A changes its taxable period to a fiscal year ending March 31 so that A has a short taxable year beginning January 1, 2019, and ending March 31, 2019. In its AFS, A includes 1/4 of the payment in revenue for the taxable year ending December 31, 2018; 1/6 in revenue for the short taxable year ending March 31, 2019; 1/4 in revenue for the taxable year ending March 31, 2020; and 1/4 in revenue for the taxable year ending March 31, 2021. Because the taxable year ending March 31, 2019, is 92 days or less, A must include 1/4 of the payment in gross income for the taxable year ending December 31, 2018, 1/6 in gross income for the short taxable year ending March 31, 2019, and the remaining amount in gross income for the taxable year ending March 31, 2020.

(5) *Financial statement conformity requirement.*—A taxpayer that uses the deferral method under this paragraph (c) must use the same financial statement that is used to apply the rules in section 451(b) and the accompanying regulations when applying the deferral method provided in section 451(c) and these regulations.

(6) *Allocation of transaction price.*—A taxpayer using the deferral method under this paragraph (c) must use the allocation rules provided in proposed § 1.451-3(g).

(7) *Rules relating to eligible gift card sales.*—For purposes of paragraphs (b)(1)(i)(B) and (c)(1) of this section, if an eligible gift card is redeemable by an entity described in paragraph (b)(3)(ii) of this section whose financial results are not included in the taxpayer's AFS, a payment will be treated as included by the taxpayer in revenue in its AFS to the extent the gift card is redeemed by the entity during the taxable year.

(8) *Examples.*—The following examples illustrate the rules of this paragraph (c). In each example in paragraphs (c)(8)(i) through (xxv) of this section, the taxpayer uses an accrual method of accounting for federal income tax purposes and files its returns on a calendar year basis. Except as stated otherwise, the taxpayer in each example has an AFS.

(i) *Example 1. Services.* On November 1, 2018, A, in the business of giving dancing lessons, receives an advance payment for a 1-year contract commencing on that date and providing for up to 48 individual, 1-hour lessons. A provides eight lessons in 2018 and another 35 lessons in 2019. In its AFS, A includes 1/6 of the payment in revenue for 2018, and 5/6 of the payment in revenue for 2019. A uses the deferral method. For federal income tax purposes, A must include 1/6 of the payment in gross income for 2018, and the remaining 5/6 of the payment in gross income for 2019.

(ii) *Example 2. Services.* Assume the same facts as in Example 1 in paragraph (c)(8)(i) of this section, except that the advance payment is received for a 3-year contract under which up to 96 lessons are provided. A provides eight lessons in 2018, 48 lessons in 2019, and 40 lessons in 2020. In its AFS, A includes 1/12 of the payment in revenue for 2018, 1/2 of the payment in revenue for 2019, and 5/12 of the payment in gross revenue for 2020. For federal income tax purposes, A must include 1/12 of the payment in gross income for 2018, and the remaining 11/12 of the payment in gross income for 2019.

(iii) *Example 3. Goods and Services.* On June 1, 2018, B, a landscape architecture firm, receives an advance payment for goods and services that, under the terms of the agreement, must be provided by December 2019. On December 31, 2018, B estimates that 3/4 of the work under the agreement has been completed. In its AFS, B includes 3/4 of the payment in revenue for 2018 and 1/4 of the payment in revenue for 2019. B uses the deferral method. For federal income tax purposes, B must include 3/4 of the payment in gross income for 2018, and the remaining 1/4 of the payment in gross income for 2019, regardless of whether B completes the job in 2019.

(iv) *Example 4. Repair Contracts.* On July 1, 2018, C, in the business of selling and repairing television sets, receives an advance payment for a 2-year contract under which C agrees to repair or replace, or authorizes a representative to repair or replace, certain parts in the customer's television set if those parts fail to function properly. In its AFS, C includes 1/4 of the payment in revenue for 2018, 1/2 of the payment in revenue for 2019, and 1/4 of the payment in revenue for 2020. C uses the deferral method. For federal income tax purposes, C must include 1/4 of the payment in gross income for 2018 and the remaining 3/4 of the payment in gross income for 2019.

(v) *Example 5. Online Website Design.* D, in the business of building and designing websites, receives advance payments that oblige D to build and design various websites. D tracks each request for a website with unique identifying numbers. On July 20, 2018, D receives online payments for 2 websites. One of the website requests is submitted and processed on September 1, 2018, and the other is submitted and processed on February 1, 2020. In its AFS, D includes the payment for the September 1, 2018, website in revenue for 2018 and the payment for the February 1, 2020, website in revenue for 2020. D uses the deferral method. For federal income tax purposes, D must include the payment for the September 1, 2018, website in gross income for 2018 and the payment for the February 1, 2020, website in gross income for 2019.

(vi) *Example 6. Gift Cards.* E, a hair styling salon, receives advance payments for gift cards that may later be redeemed at the salon for hair styling services or hair care products at the face value of the gift card. The gift cards look like standard credit cards, and each gift card has a magnetic strip that, in connection with E's computer system, identifies the available balance. The gift cards may not be redeemed for cash and have no expiration date. In its AFS, E includes advance payments for gift cards in revenue when redeemed. E is not able to determine the extent to which advance payments are included in revenue in its AFS for the taxable year of receipt and therefore does not meet this requirement of paragraph (c)(1) of this section. Therefore, E may not use the deferral method for these advance payments.

(vii) *Example 7. Gift Cards.* Assume the same facts as in Example 6 in paragraph (c)(8)(vi) of this section, except that the gift cards have an expiration date 12 months from the date of sale, E does not accept expired gift cards, and E includes unredeemed gift cards in revenue in its AFS for the taxable year in which the cards expire. Because E tracks the sale date and the expiration date of the gift cards for purposes of its AFS, E is able to determine the extent to which advance payments are included in revenue for the taxable year of receipt. Therefore, E meets this requirement of paragraph (c)(1) of this section and may use the deferral method for these advance payments.

(viii) *Example 8. Online Subscriptions.* G is in the business of compiling and providing business information for a particular industry in an online format accessible over the internet. On September 1, 2018, G receives an advance payment from a subscriber for 1 year of access to its online database, beginning on that date. In its AFS, G includes 1/3 of the payment in revenue for 2018 and the remaining 2/3 in revenue for 2019. G uses the deferral method. For federal income tax purposes, G must include 1/3 of the payment in gross income for 2018 and the remaining 2/3 of the payment in gross income for 2019.

(ix) *Example 9. Membership Fees.* On December 1, 2018, H, in the business of operating a chain of "shopping club" retail stores, receives advance payments for membership fees. Upon payment of the fee, a member is allowed access for a 1-year period to H's stores, which offer discounted merchandise and services. In its AFS, H includes 1/12 of the payment in revenue for 2018 and 11/12 of the payment in revenue for 2019. H uses the deferral method. For federal income tax purposes, H must include 1/12 of the payment in gross income for 2018, and the remaining 11/12 of the payment in gross income for 2019.

(x) *Example 10. Cruise.* In 2018, I, in the business of operating tours, receives payments from customers for a 10-day cruise that will take place in April 2019. Under the agreement, I charters a cruise ship, hires a crew and a tour guide, and arranges for entertainment and shore trips for the customers. In its AFS, I includes the payments in revenue for 2019. I uses the deferral method. For federal income tax purposes, I must include the payments in gross income for 2019.

(xi) *Example 11. Travel agent services.* On November 1, 2018, J, a travel agent, receives payment from a customer for an airline flight that will take place in April 2019. J purchases and delivers the airline ticket to the customer on November 14, 2018. J retains a portion of the customer's payment (the excess of the customer's payment over the cost of the airline ticket) as its commission. Because J is not required to provide any services after the ticket is delivered to the customer, J earns its commission when the airline ticket is delivered. The customer may cancel the flight and receive a refund from J only to the extent the airline itself provides refunds. In its AFS, J includes its commission in revenue for 2019. The commission is not an advance payment because the payment is not earned by J, in whole or in part, in a subsequent taxable year. Thus, J may not use the deferral method for this payment.

(xii) *Example 12. Broadcasting Rights.* K, a professional sports franchise, is a member of a sports league that enters into contracts with television networks for the right to broadcast games to be played between teams in the league. The money received by the sports league under the contracts is divided equally among the member teams. The league entered into a 3-year broadcasting contract beginning October 1, 2018. K receives three equal installment payments on October 1 of each contract year, beginning in 2018. In its AFS, K includes 1/4 of the first installment payment in revenue for 2018 and 3/4 in revenue for 2019; K includes 1/4 of the second installment in revenue for 2019 and 3/4 in revenue for 2020; K includes 1/4 of the third installment in revenue for 2020 and 3/4 in revenue for 2021. K uses the deferral method. Each installment payment constitutes an advance payment under paragraph (b)(1) of this section. For federal income tax purposes, K must include 1/4 of the first installment payment in gross income for 2018 and 3/4 in gross income for 2019; 1/4 of the second installment in gross income for 2019 and 3/4 in gross income for 2020; and 1/4 of the third installment in gross income for 2020 and 3/4 in gross income for 2021.

(xiii) *Example 13. Insurance Claims Administration.* L is in the business of negotiating, placing, and servicing insurance coverage and administering claims for insurance companies. On December 1, 2018, L enters into a contract with an insurance company to provide property and casualty claims administration services for a 4-year period beginning January 1, 2019. Pursuant to the contract, the insurance company makes four equal annual payments to L; each payment relates to a year of service and is made during the month prior to the service year (for example, L is paid on December 1, 2018, for the service year beginning January 1, 2019). In its AFS, L includes the first payment in revenue for 2019; the second payment in revenue for 2020; the third payment in revenue for 2021; and the fourth payment in revenue for 2022. L uses the deferral method. Each annual payment constitutes an advance payment under paragraph (b)(1) of this section. For federal income tax purposes, L must include the first payment in gross income for 2019; the second payment in gross income for 2020; the third payment in gross income for 2021; and the fourth payment in gross income for 2022.

(xiv) *Example 14. Internet Services.* M is a cable internet service provider that enters into contracts with subscribers to provide internet services for a monthly fee (paid prior to the service month). For those subscribers who do not own a compatible modem, M provides a rental cable modem for an additional monthly charge (also paid prior to the service month). Pursuant to the contract, M will replace or repair the cable modem if it proves defective during the contract period. In December 2018, M receives payments from subscribers for January 2019 internet service and cable modem use. In its AFS, M includes the entire amount of these payments in revenue for 2019. M uses the deferral method. Because a subscriber's use of a cable modem is ancillary to the provision of internet services by M, and because the cable modem warranty is ancillary to the use of the cable modem, the payments are advance payments. For federal income tax purposes, M must include the advance payments in gross income for 2019.

(xv) *Example 15. License Agreement.* On January 1, 2019, N enters into, and receives advance payments pursuant to, a 5-year license agreement for the use of N's trademark. Under the contract, the licensee pays N both the first-year (2019) license fee and the fifth-year (2023) license fee upon commencement of the agreement. The fees for the second, third, and fourth years are payable on January 1 of each license year. The contract provides the customer with access to N's trademark throughout the term of the agreement. In its AFS, N includes the fees in revenue for the respective license year. N uses the deferral method. For federal income tax purposes, N must include the first-year license fee in gross income for 2019, the second-year and the fifth-year license fee in gross income for 2020, the third-year license fee in gross income for 2021, and the fourth-year license fee in gross income for 2022.

(xvi) *Example 16. Computer Software Subscription.* On July 1, 2018, O, in the business of licensing computer software (off the shelf, fully customized, and semi-customized) and providing customer support, receives an advance payment for a 2-year "software subscription contract" under which O will provide software updates if it develops an update within the contract period, as well as online and telephone customer support. In its AFS, O includes 1/4 of the payment in revenue for 2018, 1/2 in revenue for 2019, and the remaining 1/4 in revenue for 2020, regardless of when O provides updates or customer support. O uses the deferral method. For federal income tax purposes, O must include 1/4 of the payment in gross income for 2018 and 3/4 in gross income for 2019.

(xvii) *Example 17. Performance Obligation.* P is in the business of licensing computer software (off the shelf, fully customized, and semi-customized) and providing customer support. On July 1, 2018, P receives an advance payment of $100 for a 2-year software subscription that includes a 1-year "software maintenance contract" under which P will provide integral software updates within the contract period, as well as a "customer support agreement" for online and telephone customer support. In its AFS, P allocates $80 of the payment to the subscription agreement and $20 to the customer support agreement. With respect to the $80 allocable to the subscription agreement, P includes 1/4 ($20) in revenue for 2018, 1/2 ($40) in revenue for 2019, and the remaining 1/4 ($20) in revenue for 2020. With respect to the $20 allocable to the customer support agreement, P includes 1/2 ($10) in revenue for 2018, and the remaining 1/2 ($10) in revenue for 2019 regardless of when P provides the customer support. For federal income tax purposes, P must include $30 in gross income for 2018 ($20 allocable to the subscription agreement and $10 allocable to the customer support agreement) and the remaining $70 in gross income for 2019.

(xviii) *Example 18. Gift Cards Administered by Another.* Q corporation operates department stores. U corporation, V corporation, and W corporation are wholly owned domestic subsidiaries of Q that file a consolidated federal income tax return with Q. X corporation is a controlled foreign subsidiary of Q that is prohibited from filing a consolidated return with Q. U sells Brand A goods, V sells Brand B goods, X sells Brand C goods, and Z is an unrelated entity that sells Brand D goods. W administers a gift card program for the Q consolidated group, X, and Z. Pursuant to the underlying agreements, W issues gift cards that are redeemable for goods or services offered by U, V, X, and Z. In addition, U, V, X, and Z sell gift cards to customers on behalf of W and remit amounts received to W. The agreements provide that W is primarily liable to the customer for the value of the gift card until redemption, and U, V, X, and Z are obligated to accept the gift card as payment for goods or services. When a customer purchases goods or services with a gift card at U, V, X, or Z, W reimburses that entity for the sales price of the goods or services purchased with the gift card, up to the total gift card value. In 2018, W sells gift cards with a total value of $900,000, and, at the end of 2018, the unredeemed balance of the gift cards is $100,000. In the consolidated group's AFS, the group includes revenue from the sale of a gift card when the gift card is redeemed. W tracks sales and redemptions of gift cards electronically, is able to determine the extent to which advance payments are included in revenue in its consolidated AFS for the taxable year of receipt, and meets the requirements of paragraph (c)(1) of this section. The payments W receives from the sale of gift cards are advance payments because they are payments for eligible gift cards. Thus, W is eligible to use the deferral method. At the end of 2018, W includes $800,000 in income in its consolidated AFS. Under the deferral method, W must include $800,000 of the payments from gift card sales in gross income in 2018 and the remaining $100,000 of the payments in gross income in 2019.

(xix) *Example 19. Gift Cards of Affiliates.* R is a Subchapter S corporation that operates an affiliated restaurant corporation and manages other affiliated restaurants. These other restaurants are owned by other Subchapter S corporations, partnerships, and limited liability companies. R has a partnership interest or an equity interest in some of the restaurants. R administers a gift card program for participating restaurants. Each participating restaurant operates under a different trade name. Under the gift card program, R and each of the participating restaurants sell gift cards, which are issued with R's brand name and are redeemable at all participating restaurants. Participating restaurants sell the gift cards to customers and remit the proceeds to R, R is primarily liable to the customer for the value of the gift card until redemption, and the participating restaurants are obligated under an agreement with R to accept the gift card as payment for food, beverages, taxes, and gratuities. When a customer uses a gift card to make a purchase at a participating restaurant, R is obligated to reimburse that restaurant for the amount of the purchase, up to the total gift card value. In R's AFS, R includes revenue from the sale of a gift card when a gift card is redeemed at a participating restaurant. R tracks sales and redemptions of gift cards electronically, is able to determine the extent to which advance payments are included in revenue in its AFS for the taxable year of receipt, and meets the requirements of paragraph (c)(1) of this section. The payments R receives from the sale of gift cards are advance payments because they are payments for eligible gift card sales. Thus, for federal income tax purposes, R is eligible to use the deferral method. In the taxable year of receipt, R must include the advance payment in income to the extent included in its AFS, and must include any remaining amount in income in the taxable year following the taxable year of receipt.

(xx) *Example 20. Gift Cards for Domestic and International Hotels.* S is a corporation that operates for the benefit of its franchisee members, who own and operate domestic and international individual member hotels. S collects membership fees from the member hotels in exchange for providing a wide variety of management support services, which include making reservations for customers at the various member hotels. S also administers a gift card program for its members by selling gift cards that may be redeemed for hotel rooms and food or beverages provided by any member hotel. The agreements underlying the gift card program provide that S is entitled to the proceeds from the sale of the gift cards, must reimburse the member hotel for the value of a gift card redeemed, and until redemption remains primarily liable to the customer for the value of the card. In S's AFS, S includes payments from the sale of a gift card when the card is redeemed. S tracks sales and redemptions of gift cards electronically, is able to determine the extent to which advance payments are included in revenue in its AFS for the taxable year of receipt, and meets the requirements of paragraph (c)(1) of this section. The payments S receives from the sale of gift cards are advance payments because they are payments for eligible gift card sales. Thus, for federal income tax purposes, S is eligible to use the deferral method. In the taxable year of receipt, S must include in income the advance payment to the extent included in its AFS, and must include any remaining amount in income in the taxable year following the taxable year of receipt.

(xxi) *Example 21. Discount Voucher.* On December 10, 2018, T, in the business of selling home appliances, sells a washing machine for $500. As part of the sale, T gives the customer a 40 percent discount voucher for any future purchases of T's goods up to $100 in the next

60 days. In its AFS, T treats the discount voucher as a separate performance obligation and allocates $30 of the $500 sales price to the discount voucher. T includes $12 of the amount allocated to the discount voucher in revenue for 2018 and includes $18 of the discount voucher in revenue for 2019. T uses the deferral method. For federal income tax purposes, T must include the $12 allocable to the discount voucher in gross income in 2018 and the remaining $18 allocated to the discount voucher in gross income in 2019.

(xxii) *Example 22. Rewards.* On December 31, 2018, U, in the business of selling consumer electronics, sells a new TV for $1,000 and gives the customer 50 reward points. Each reward point is redeemable for a $1 discount on any future purchase of U's products. The reward points are not redeemable for cash and have a 2-year expiration date. U tracks each customer's reward points and does not sell reward points separately. In its AFS, U treats the rewards points as a separate performance obligation and allocates $45 of the $1,000 sales price to the rewards points. U does not include any of the amount allocated to the reward points in revenue for 2018. U includes $25 of the reward points in revenue for 2019 and $20 of the reward points in revenue for 2020. U uses the deferral method. For federal income tax purposes, U does not include any amount of the reward points in gross income in 2018, and includes the entire $45 allocated to the reward points in gross income in 2019.

(xxiii) *Example 23. Credit Card Rewards.* V, a wholly owned credit card company, issues credit cards. V also has a loyalty program in which cardholders earn reward points for the use of its credit card to make purchases. Each reward point is redeemable for a $1 on any future purchases. V may not use the deferral method because payments under credit card agreements including rewards for credit card purchases are excluded from the definition of an advance payment under paragraph (b)(1)(ii)(C) of this section.

(xxiv) *Example 24. Airline Reward Miles.* On January 1, 2018, W, in the business of transporting passengers on airplanes, sells a customer a $700 airline ticket to fly roundtrip in 2018. As part of the purchase, the customer also receives 7,000 points (air miles) from W to be used for future air travel. In its AFS, W allocates $665 to the roundtrip airfare and $35 to the air miles. In its AFS, the $665 allocated to the airfare is included in Year 1 when the customer takes the roundtrip flight. The $35 allocated to the air miles is deferred and included in Year 3 when the customer redeems the air miles. W uses the deferral method described in paragraph (c) of this section. For federal income tax purposes, the $665 is included in gross income in Year 1 and the $35 allocated to the air miles is included in gross income in Year 2.

(xxv) *Example 25. Chargebacks.* Taxpayer X, a manufacturer of pharmaceuticals, is a calendar-year accrual method taxpayer with an AFS. In addition to billing the wholesaler for the sale of the pharmaceuticals at the wholesale acquisition cost under the contract, X generally credits or pays wholesalers a chargeback of 40% of the wholesale acquisition cost for sales made by those wholesalers to qualifying customers. In 2018, X enters into a contract to sell 1,000 units to W, a wholesaler, for $10 per unit, totaling $10,000 (1,000 x $10 = $10,000). The contract also provides that X will issue a 40% chargeback for sales by W to certain qualifying customers. X delivers 600 units to W on December 31, 2018, and bills W $6,000 under the contract. For AFS purposes, X adjusts its revenue by 40% for all sales to W for anticipated chargebacks. As such, in its 2018 AFS, X reports $3,600 ($6,000 - $2,400 = $3,600) of revenue from the contract with W, decreasing revenue by $2,400 (40% x $6,000 = $2,400) for anticipated chargeback claims. For federal income tax purposes, under proposed §1.451-3(c)(4), X's 2018 revenue is $6,000 because revenue is not reduced for anticipated chargebacks. Because no portion of the $6,000 is included in revenue on an AFS in a subsequent taxable year (that is, on an AFS after 2018), none of the $6,000 is an advance payment under paragraph (b)(1)(i) of this section.

(d) *Deferral method for taxpayers without an AFS (non-AFS deferral method).*—(1) *In general.*—Only a taxpayer described in paragraph (d)(2) of this section may elect to use the non-AFS deferral method described in paragraph (d)(4) of this section.

(2) *Taxpayers eligible to use the non-AFS deferral method.*—A taxpayer is eligible to use the non-AFS deferral method if the taxpayer does not have an applicable financial statement as defined in proposed §1.451-3(c)(1) and is able to determine the extent to which advance payments are earned in the taxable year of receipt, or a short taxable year, if applicable.

(3) *Advance payment.*—For purposes of the non-AFS deferral method, in applying paragraph (b)(1)(i)(B) of this section, an advance payment is any portion of the payment received that is earned by the taxpayer, in whole or in part, in a subsequent taxable year.

(4) *Deferral of advance payments based on when payment is earned.*—(i) *In general.*—The non-AFS deferral method described in this paragraph (d) is a permissible method of accounting that may be used only by a taxpayer described in paragraph (d)(2) of this section.

Under the non-AFS deferral method of accounting, a taxpayer includes the advance payment in gross income for the taxable year of receipt, including, if applicable, a short taxable year described in paragraph (d)(8) of this section, to the extent that it is earned in that taxable year and includes the remaining portion of the advance payment in gross income in the next succeeding taxable year.

(ii) *When payment is earned.*—A payment is earned when the all events test described in §1.451-1(a) is met, without regard to when the amount is received, as defined under paragraph (b)(5) of this section, by the taxpayer. If a taxpayer is unable to determine the extent to which a payment is earned in the taxable year of receipt, the taxpayer may determine that amount:

(A) On a statistical basis if adequate data are available to the taxpayer;

(B) On a straight line ratable basis over the term of the agreement if the taxpayer receives advance payments under a fixed term agreement and if it is not unreasonable to anticipate at the end of the taxable year of receipt that the advance payment will be earned ratably over the term of the agreement; or

(C) By the use of any other basis that in the opinion of the Commissioner results in a clear reflection of income.

(5) *Contracts with multiple obligations.*—(i) *In general.*—If a taxpayer receives a payment that is attributable to more than one item described in paragraph (b)(1)(i)(C) of this section, the taxpayer must allocate the payment to such items in a manner that is based on objective criteria.

(ii) *Objective criteria.*—A taxpayer's allocation method with respect to a payment described in paragraph (d)(5)(i) of this section is based on objective criteria if the allocation method is based on payments the taxpayer regularly receives for an item or items it regularly sells or provides separately or any method that may be provided in guidance published in the Internal Revenue Bulletin (*see* §601.601(d) of this chapter).

(6) *Acceleration of advance payments.*—For purposes of this paragraph (d), the acceleration rules provided in paragraph (c)(2) of this section apply to a taxpayer that uses the non-AFS deferral method.

(7) *Advance payments in certain acquisitions and other financial statement adjustments.*—For purposes of this paragraph (d), the rules provided in paragraph (c)(3) of this section apply to a taxpayer that uses the non-AFS deferral method.

(8) *Short taxable year rule.*—For purposes of this paragraph (d), the short taxable year rule provided in paragraph (c)(4) of this section applies to a taxpayer that uses the non-AFS deferral method.

(9) *Eligible gift card sale.*—For purposes of paragraphs (b)(1)(i)(B) and (d)(4) of this section, if an eligible gift card is redeemable by an entity described in paragraph (b)(3)(ii), including an entity whose financial results are not included in the taxpayer's financial statement, a payment will be treated as earned by the taxpayer to the extent the gift card is redeemed by the entity during the taxable year.

(10) *Examples.*—The rules of this paragraph (d) are illustrated by the examples in paragraphs (d)(10)(i) and (ii). In each of these examples, the taxpayer uses the non-AFS deferral method described in this paragraph (d).

(i) *Example 1.* A, a video arcade operator, receives payments in 2018 for game tokens that are used by customers to play the video games offered by A. The tokens cannot be redeemed for cash. The tokens are imprinted with the name of the video arcade, but they are not individually marked for identification. A completed a study on a statistical basis, based on adequate data available to A, and concluded that for payments received in the current year, x percent of tokens are expected to be used in the current year, y percent of tokens are expected to be used in the next year, and the remaining z percent of tokens are expected to never be used. Based on the study, A treats as earned for 2018 x percent (for tokens expected to be used in that year) as well as z percent (for tokens that are expected to never be used). Using the study, A determines the extent to which advance payments are earned in the taxable year of receipt. A may determine the extent to which a payment is earned in the taxable year of receipt on a statistical basis provided that any portion that is not included in the taxable year of receipt is included in the next succeeding taxable year. Thus, for federal income tax purposes, A must include x percent and z percent of the advance payments in gross income for 2018 and y percent of the advance payments in gross income for 2019.

(ii) *Example 2.* B is in the business of providing internet services. On September 1, 2018, B receives an advance payment from a customer for a 2-year term for access to its internet services, beginning on that date. B does not have an AFS. B is unable to determine the extent to which the payment is earned in the taxable year of receipt. For federal income tax purposes, B may determine the extent to which the payment is earned in the year of receipt on a straight line ratable basis over the term of the agreement if it is not unreasonable to anticipate at the end of the taxable year of receipt that the advance payment will be earned ratably over the term of the agreement.

(e) *Method of accounting.*—The use of the deferral method under paragraph (c) of this section or the non-AFS deferral method under paragraph (d) of this section is the adoption of, or a change in, a method of accounting under section 446 of the Internal Revenue Code or the accompanying regulations. In addition, a change in the manner of recognizing advance payments in revenue in an AFS that changes or could change the timing of the inclusion of income for federal income tax purposes is a change in method of accounting under section 446 and the accompanying regulations. A taxpayer may change its method of accounting to use the methods described in paragraphs (c) or (d) of this section, or change its manner of recognizing advance payments in revenue in an AFS only with the consent of the Commissioner as required under section 446(e) and the corresponding regulations.

(f) *Applicability date.*—The rules of this section are applicable for taxable years beginning on or after the date of publication of the Treasury decision adopting these rules as final regulations in the **Federal Register**. Until the date the Treasury decision adopting these regulations as final regulations is published in the **Federal Register**, a taxpayer may rely on these proposed regulations for taxable years beginning after December 31, 2017, provided that the taxpayer applies all the applicable rules contained in these proposed regulations, and consistently applies these proposed regulations to all advance payments. See section 7805(b)(7). [Reg. § 1.451-8.]

Installment Sales Reporting

Installment Sales Reporting: Sales Occurring After October 19, 1980: General Rules.— Temporary Reg. §§ 15A.453-0 and 15A.453-1, relating to installment sales or reporting of gain for sales occurring after October 19, 1980, have also been proposed as final regulations and, when adopted, would become Reg. §§ 1.453-0 and 1.453-1 (published in the Federal Register on February 4, 1981).

§ 15A.453-0. Taxable years affected.

§ 15A.453-1. Installment method reporting for sales of real proerty and casual sales of personal property.

Installment Obligations

Installment Obligations: Nonrecognition Transactions.—Reproduced below is the text of a proposed amendment of Reg. § 1.453-1, relating to installment obligations received in certain nonrecognition transactions (published in the Federal Register on May 3, 1984).

☐ Paragraph. Section 1.453-1 is amended by revising paragraph (f) to read as follows:

§ 1.453-1. Installment method reporting for sales of real property and casual sales of personal property.

* * *

(f) *Installment obligations received in certain nonrecognition exchanges.*—(1) *Exchanges described in section 1031(b).*—(i) *In general.*— The provisions of paragraph (f)(1) of this section apply to exchanges described in section 1031(b) ("section 1031(b) exchanges") in which the taxpayer receives as boot (property which is "other property" under section 1031(b)) an installment obligation issued by the other party to the exchange, as well as property with respect to which no gain or loss is recognized ("permitted property" for purposes of paragraph (f)(1) of this section). However, an exchange otherwise described in section 1036 in which the receipt of an installment obligation is treated as a dividend (or would be treated as a dividend if the issuing corporation had adequate earnings and profits) is not a section 1031(b) exchange for purposes of this section.

(ii) *Exclusion from payment.*—Receipt of permitted property will not be considered payment for purposes of paragraph (c) of this section.

(iii) *Installment method determinations.*—In a section 1031(b) exchange, the taxpayer's basis in the property transferred by the taxpayer, including nondeductible expenses of the exchange, will first be allocated to the permitted property received by the taxpayer up to, but not in excess of, the fair market value of such property. If the taxpayer's basis exceeds the fair market value of the permitted property, that excess amount of basis is "excess basis." In making all required installment method determinations, the exchange is treated as if the taxpayer had made an installment sale of appreciated property (with a basis equal to the amount of excess basis) in which the consideration received was the installment obligation and any other boot. In a section 1031(b) exchange, only net qualifying indebtedness is taken into account in determining the amount of qualifying indebtedness (as defined in § 1.453-1A(b)(2)(iv)). For this purpose, net qualifying indebtedness is the excess of—

(A) Liabilities of the taxpayer (or liabilities encumbering the property) assumed or taken subject to by the other party to the exchange as part of the consideration to the taxpayer, over

(B) The sum of any net cash paid (cash paid less any cash received) by the taxpayer in the exchange and any liability assumed or taken subject to by the taxpayer in the exchange.

Therefore, for purposes of installment method determinations, the selling price is the sum of the face value of the installment obligation (reduced by any portion of the obligation characterized as interest by section 483 or 1232), any net qualifying indebtedness, any cash received (in excess of any cash paid) by the taxpayer, and the fair market value of any other boot. The basis is the excess basis. The total contract price is the selling price less any net qualifying indebtedness that does not exceed the excess basis. Finally, payment in the year of exchange includes any net qualifying indebtedness that exceeds the excess basis.

(iv) *Examples.*—The provisions of paragraph (f)(1) of this section are illustrated by the following examples:

Example (1). In 1981, A makes a section 1031(b) exchange of real property held for investment (basis $400,000) for permitted property worth $200,000, and an $800,000 installment obligation issued by the other party to the exchange bearing adequate stated interest. Neither the property transferred by A nor the property received in the exchange is mortgaged property. A's basis of $400,000 is allocated first to the permitted property received, up to the fair market value of $200,000. A's excess basis is $200,000 ($400,000 – $200,000). Since the installment obligation is the only boot received by A in the exchange, A's entire excess basis of $200,000 is allocable to it. Under the installment method, the selling price is $800,000 (the face amount of the installment obligation), and the contract price is also $800,000 (selling price less qualifying indebtedness, $800,000 – 0). The gross profit is $600,000 (selling price less excess basis allocated to the installment obligation, $800,000 – $200,000), and the gross profit ratio is 75% ($600,000/$800,000). A recognizes no gain until payments are received on the installment obligation. As A receives payments (exclusive of interest) on the installment obligation, 75% of each payment will be gain attributable to the exchange and 25% of each payment will be recovery of basis. A will hold the permitted property received in the exchange with a basis of $200,000.

Example (2). The facts are the same as in example (1), except that in the exchange A receives permitted property worth $200,000, a $600,000 installment obligation, and $200,000 in cash. A is treated as having sold appreciated property (basis equal to the $200,000 excess basis) for $200,000 cash and a $600,000 installment obligation. As in example (1), the contract price and the selling price are $800,000, the gross profit is $600,000, and the gross profit ratio is 75%. Accordingly, A will recognize gain of $150,000 on receipt of the cash (75% of the $200,000 payment). A holds the permitted property with a basis of $200,000.

Example (3). The facts are the same as in example (2), except that A does not receive $200,000 in cash. Instead, the property transferred by A in the exchange was subject to a mortgage (meeting the definition of qualifying indebtedness) of $200,000 to which the other party to the exchange took subject. The permitted property received by A in the exchange was not subject to a mortgage. A is treated as having sold appreciated property (basis equal to $200,000 excess basis) for $600,000 cash and $200,000 net relief of mortgage liability. The mortgage liability of which A is deemed relieved ($200,000), reduced by any cash paid by A and any mortgage liability encumbering the like-kind property received by A in the simultaneous exchange ($0), is treated as qualifying indebtedness. Since the qualifying indebtedness ($200,000) does not exceed A's excess basis ($200,000), B's taking subject to such indebtedness does not constitute payment to A in the year of exchange. Under the installment method, the selling price is $800,000 and the total contract price is $600,000 (selling price of $800,000 less $200,000 of qualifying indebtedness that does not exceed A's excess basis). Gross profit is also $600,000 (800,000 selling price less $200,000 excess basis), and the gross profit ratio is 1 ($600,000/600,000). A recognizes no gain until payments are received on the installment obligation. As A receives payment (exclusive of interest) in the $600,000 installment obligation, the full amount received will be gain attributable to the exchange. A holds the permitted property with a basis of $200,000.

Example (4). The facts are the same as in example (2), except that A's basis in the property transferred by A was only $160,000. Since A's basis first must be allocated to permitted property received in the exchange up to the fair market value ($200,000) of that permitted property, there is no excess basis. Accordingly, A will recognize gain equal to the full amount of cash received ($200,000), and will hold the installment obligation at a basis of zero. A will hold the permitted property at a basis of $160,000.

(2) *Certain exchanges described in section 356(a).—(i) In general.*—The provisions of paragraph (f)(2) of this section apply to exchanges described in section 356(a)(1) ("section 356(a)(1) exchanges") in which the taxpayer receives as boot (property which is "other property" under section 356(a)(1)(B)) an installment obligation issued by a qualifying corporation which is not treated as a dividend to the taxpayer. For purposes of section 453(f)(6) and paragraph (f)(2) of this section, any such section 356(a)(1) exchange shall be treated as a disposition of property by the taxpayer to the qualifying corporation and an acquisition of such property by the qualifying corporation from the taxpayer. If section 354 would apply to the exchange but for the receipt of boot, the term "qualifying corporation" means a corpoation the stock of which could be received by the taxpayer in the exchange without recognition of gain or loss. If section 355 would apply to the exchange but for the receipt of boot, the term "qualifying corporation" means the distributing corporation (referred to in section 355(a)(1)(A)). Receipt of an installment obligation is treated as a dividend if section 356(a)(2) applies (determined without regard to the presence or absence of accumulated earnings and profits), or if section 356(e) (relating to certain exchanges for section 306 stock) applies to the taxpayer's receipt of the installment obligation.

(ii) *Exclusion from payment.*—Receipt of permitted property shall not be considered payment for purposes of paragraph (c) of this section. For purposes of paragraph (f)(1) of this section, "permitted property" means property, the receipt of which does not result in recognition of gain under section 356(a)(1) (i.e., stock of a qualifying corporation).

(iii) *Installment method determinations.*—Installment method determinations with respect to an installment obligation received in an exchange to which paragraph (f)(2) of this section applies shall be made in accordance with the rules prescribed in paragraph (f)(1)(iii) of this section. In applying such rules, a section 356(a)(1) exchange shall be treated as a section 1031(b) exchange and permitted property shall mean permitted property described in paragraph (f)(2) of this section.

(iv) *Examples.*—The provisions of paragraph (f)(2) of this section are illustrated by the following examples:

Example (1). T corporation and P corporation are unrelated closely held corporations. A owns 10% of the stock of T. A is not related to any other T stockholder or to any P stockholder. S corporation is a wholly-owned subsidiary of P. Pursuant to a plan of reorganization, T merges with and into S. In the merger, the T shares held by A are exchanged for shares of P worth $100,000 and a $300,000 installment obligation (bearing adequate interest) issued by P. In the merger the other stockholders of T exchange their T shares solely for P shares worth in the aggregate, $3,600,000. The merger is a reorganization described in sections 368(a)(1)(A) and (a)(2)(D), and T, S, and P each is a party to the reorganization under section 368(b). P is a qualifying corporation and A is party to a section 356(a)(1) exchange in which receipt by A of the installment obligation will not be treated as a dividend to A. Because, for purposes of section 453(f)(6), this transaction is treated as a direct exchange between P and A, no gain or loss is recognized by S with respect to the P obligation. Assume A's basis in the T shares exchanged by A was $150,000. A's basis is allocated first to the permitted property (P shares) received, up to the fair market value of $100,000. A's excess basis is $50,000 ($150,000 – $100,000). Since the installment obligation is the only boot received by A in the exchange, the entire excess basis of $50,000 is allocable to it. Under the installment method, the contract price is $300,000 (face amount of the installment obligation), the gross profit is $250,000 (contract price less $50,000 excess basis allocated to the installment obligation), and the gross profit ratio is 5/6 ($250,000/$300,000). A recognizes no gain until payments are received on the installment obligation. As A receives payments (exclusive of interest) on the installment obligation, 5/6ths of each payment will be gain attributable to the exchange and 1/6th of each payment will be recovery of basis. A will hold the permitted property (P stock) received in the exchange at a basis of $100,000.

Example (2). The facts are the same as in exmaple (1). B, who also owns 10% of the stock of T directly and owns no other stock by T

by attribution within the meaning of 318(a), exchanges the T shares in the merger for $400,000 installment obligation issued by P (bearing adequate interest). Although section 356(a)(1) will not apply to this exchange becasue B receives no P stock in the transaction and the character of the gain is determined under section 302(a), for purposes of section 453 and paragraph (a) of this section, B is treated as having sold the T shares to P in exchange for P's installment obligation. B will report the installment sale on the installment method unless B elects under paragraph (e) of this section not to report the transaction on the installment method. If, by reason of constructive ownership of T shares under section 381(a) and failure to meet the requirements of section 302(c)(2), the character of the transaction as to B were determined under section 302(d), section 453 would not apply to the exchange by B.

Example (3). The facts are the same as in examples (1) and (2), except that the P stock is voting stock and S merges into T in a reorganization described in section 368(a)(2)(E). The results are the same as in examples (1) and (2).

Example (4) (i). T Corporation and larger P Corporation are unrelated public corporations the stock of each of which is widely held. A is a stockholder of T. S Corporation is a wholly owned subsidiary of P. On December 31, 1981, pursuant to a plan of reorganization which provides for a "note option" election, T merges with and into S. In the merger, A exercises the note option and the T shares held by A are exchanged for a $30,000 installment obligation (bearing adequate interest) issued by P, 1,000 P shares (worth $10 per share on the date of merger), and a non-negotiable certificate evidencing a right to receive (within 5 years from the date of merger) up to 1,000 additional P shares (plus adequate interest) if certain earnings conditions are satisfied. Neither the installment obligation nor the certificate evidencing the right to receive additional P shares is readily tradable within the meaning of § 1.453-1A(c)(4)(iv)(C). There is a valid business reason for not issuing all of the P shares immediately. Certain of the other T shareholders exercise the note option and exchange their T shares for a similar package. Other T shareholders do not exercise the note option and receive in the merger P shares plus a non-negotiable right to receive up to an equal number of additional P shares (plus adequate interest) within 5 years. In the aggregate, the total outstanding T shares are exchanged for 20% P installment obligations, 40% P shares, and rights to receive an equal number of additional P shares within 5 years. The merger of T into S qualifies as a reorganization under section 368(a)(1)(A) and (a)(2)(D). P is a qualifying corporation, the P shares received and which may subsequently be received by A are permitted property, and the exchange to which A is a party is a section 356(a)(1) exchange.

(ii) Assume A's basis in the T shares exchanged by A was $25,000. A's basis is allocated first to permitted property (P shares) up to fair market value. In the exchange A has received 1,000 P shares (worth $10,000) and may receive up to an additional 1,000 P shares in the future. In allocating A's basis, it is assumed that all contingencies contemplated by the merger agreement will be met or otherwise resolved in a manner that will maximize the consideration A will receive. It is further assumed that each P share, when received, will have a fair market value equal to the fair market value ($10) of a P share at the date of merger. Accordingly, since A may receive a maximum of 2,000 P shares, $20,000 (2,000 × $10) of A's basis will be allocated to the 1,000 P shares A has received ($10 per share) and to A's right to receive up to an additional 1,000 P shares (at $10 per share). A's excess basis of $5,000 ($25,000 – $20,000) is allocated to the $30,000 P installment obligation.

(iii) In 1983 the earnings condition is fully satisfied and A receives an additional 1,000 P shares (plus adequate interest). Each P share held by A has a basis of $10.

(iv) Assume instead that the earnings condition is only partly satisfied and, by the close of 1986, A has received only an additional 600 P shares and is not entitled to receive any further P shares. Initially, each P share received by A was assigned a basis of $10. Of A's $25,000 basis in the T shares exchanged, $4,000 ($20,000 initially allocated to P shares received and to be received less $16,000 (1,600 P shares × $10)) now must be accounted for. The $4,000 of remaining basis will be assigned to the P shares than held by A. Thus, if A continues to hold all 1,600 P shares, A's basis in each P share will be increased by $2.50 ($4,000 divided by 1,600 P shares), If A previously sold 800 P shares and retains only 800 P shares, A's basis in each retained P share will be increased by $5 ($4,000 divided by 800 P shares). If A retains no P shares, and if all of the additional 600 P shares were issued to A and sold by A before the final year of the five year earn-out term (i.e., by the end of 1985), A's remaining basis of $4,000 will be added to the basis at which A holds the unpaid portion of the P installment obligation (up to but not in excess of the maximum amount remaining payable under that obligation less A's remaining basis in the installment obligation determined immediately before the addition to basis). If A has previously disposed of the P installment obligation, so that A holds neither P shares nor the P installment obligation to which the remaining $4,000 of A's basis can be allocated, A will be allowed a $4,000 loss in 1986. Similarly, if A continues to hold the P installment obligation but the facts are such that the maximum amount thereafter payable under the obligation is only $3,000 in excess of A's basis in the obligation determined immediately before assignment of A's remaining $4,000 basis, $3,000 of that remaining basis would be assigned to the installment obligation and P would be allowed a $1,000 loss in 1986.

Example (5). Pursuant to a plan to acquire all the stock of T corporation, P purchases 90% of the T stock for cash. To acquire the remaining 10% of T stock P creates S corporation and transfers P stock and P's newly issued installment notes to S in exchange for all of S's stock. The P notes are not readily tradable. Thereafter S merges into T, and P stock and P's installment notes are distributed to the T minority shareholders, and the S stock held by P is automatically converted into T stock. Assume that for federal tax purposes the existence of S is disregarded and the transaction is treated as a sale of T stock to P in exchange for P stock and P's installment notes. The minority shareholders will report the gain realized on the receipt of the P installment notes on the installment method unless they elect otherwise. The receipt of P stock will be treated as a payment in the year of sale.

Example (6). The facts are the same as example (5) except P transferred only P's installment notes to S and only these notes were distributed to T minority shareholders. As in example (5) the transaction is treated as a sale of T stock to P in exchange for P's installment notes. Each minority shareholder realizing gain on the receipt of the installment notes will report the gain on the installment method unless electing otherwise.

(3) *Other partial recognition exchanges.*—(i) *In general.*—The provisions of paragraph (f)(3) of this section apply to exchanges not described in paragraph (f)(1) or (2) of this section in which a taxpayer, in exchange for appreciated property, receives both permitted property (*i.e.*, property with respect to which no gain or loss would be recognized but which, in the hands of the taxpayer, would have as basis for determining gain or loss the same basis in whole or in part as the property exchanged) and boot that includes an installment obligation issued by the other party to the exchange. Ordinarily, the installment method rules set forth in paragraph (f)(1)(ii) and (iii) of this section will apply to an exchange described in paragraph (f)(3) of this section subject to such variations, if any, as may be required under the applicable provisions of the Code.

(ii) *Exchanges to which section 351 applies.*—If a taxpayer receives, in an exchange to which section 351(b) applies (a "section 351(b) exchange"), an installment obligation that is not a security within the meaning of section 351(a), the installment obligation is boot and the stock and securities (within the meaning of section 351(a)) are permitted property (within the meaning of paragraph (f)(1)(ii) of this section). The taxpayer will report the installment obligation on the installment method and any other boot received will be treated as a payment made in the year of the exchange. In applying the rules of paragraph (f)(1)(iii) of this section to a section 351(b) exchange the excess basis is the amount, if any, by which the taxpayer's basis in the property transferred (plus any cash transferred) by the taxpayer exceeds the sum of the transferred liabilities which are not treated as money received under section 357 plus the fair market value of permitted property received by the taxpayer. In determining selling price and total contract price, transferred liabilities which are not treated as money received under section 357 shall be disregarded. For purposes of paragraph (f)(3)(ii) of this section, transferred liabilities are liabilities described in section 357(a)(2). Solely for the purpose of applying section 358(a)(1), the taxpayer shall be treated as if the taxpayer elected not to report receipt of the installment obligation on the installment method. Under section 362(a)(1) the corporation's basis in the property received from the taxpayer is the taxpayer's basis in the property increased by the gain recognized by the taxpayer at the time of the exchange. As the taxpayer recognizes gain on the installment method, the corporation will increase its basis in the property by an amount equal to the amount of gain recognized by the taxpayer.

(iii) *Examples.*—The provisions of paragraph (f)(3) of this section are illustrated by the following examples. In each example, assume that adequate stated interest means both a reasonable rate of interest within the meaning of any applicable regulation promulgated under section 385 and a rate of interest not less than the test rate prescribed in the regulations under section 483, and that the debt to equity ratio of the issuing corporation is a permissible ratio under any applicable regulation promulgated under section 385.

Example (1). A owns Blackacre, unimproved real property, with a basis of $300,000. The fair market value of Blackacre is $700,000. Blackacre is encumbered by a longstanding mortgage of $200,000. A transfers Blackacre, subject to the mortgage, to a newly organized X corporation. A receives in exchange all of the stock of X, worth $400,000, and a $100,000 installment obligation (bearing adequate stated interest) issued by X. A realizes $400,000 of gain on the exchange. The installment obligation calls for a single payment of the full $100,000 face amount three years following the date of issue. The installment obligation is not a "security" within the meaning of section 351(a), and thus the exchange by A is a transaction described in section 351(b). The installment obligation is boot received by A in the exchange and the X stock is permitted property received by A in exchange. In applying the provisions of paragraph (f)(1)(ii) and (iii) of this section to a section 351(b) exchange, reference is required to section 357(a) under which the $200,000 mortgage liability is not treated as money or other property received by A in the exchange, and to section 358(a)(1) under which the basis of the X stock in the hands of A will be determined. These rules apply as follows: Neither receipt of the X stock nor relief of the mortgage encumbrance is treated as payment to A and thus A will recognize no gain in the year of the exchange. A's basis of $300,000 in Blackacre is reduced by the $200,000 mortgage from which A is deemed relieved in the exchange. The remaining basis of $100,000 is allocated to the X stock (but not in excess of the fair market value of the X stock); since the fair market value of the X stock is $400,000, the basis of the X stock in the hands of A is $100,000. Accordingly, in A's hands the installment obligation has a basis of zero. In the hands of X, the initial basis of Blackacre, determined under section 362(a), is $300,000 (the basis of the property in the hands of A), increased by the amount of gain recognized by A at the time of the transfer ($0)). As A receives payments on the installment obligation and recognizes gain, X's basis in Blackacre will be increased, at that time, in an amount equal to the gain recognized by A. Thus, if the $100,000 installment obligation is paid in full on the third anniversary date, A will recognize gain of $100,000 (because A's basis in the installment obligation is zero) and X at that time will increase the basis at which it holds Blackacre by $100,000. If in the third year X had sold the property for cash before making payment on the installment obligation, X would recognize a loss of $100,000 when X paid the obligation in that amount to A on the third anniversary date.

Example (2). B owns Whiteacre, unencumbered, unimproved real property, with a basis of $250,000. The fair market value of Whiteacre is $300,000. A transfers Whiteacre to newly organized Y corporation in exchange for all of the stock of Y corporation (worth $200,000) and a $100,000 installment obligation (bearing adequate interest). The installment obligation is payable in full on the second anniversary of the date of issue. The installment obligation is not a "security" within the meaning of section 351(a), and thus the transaction is a section 351(b) exchange. Applying the rules summarized in example (1) to the facts of this case, receipt of the installment obligation is not treated as payment to A, $200,000 of A's basis of $250,000 in Whiteacre is allocated to the Y stock (equal to the fair market value of the Y stock), and the excess basis of $50,000 is allocated to the installment obligation. In the hands of Y, the basis of Whiteacre initially is $250,000, and will be increased by $50,000 when the installment obligation is paid and A recognizes gain of $50,000.

Example (3). D owns a machine which is unencumbered 5-year recovery property with an adjusted basis of $500,000. The recomputed basis (as defined in section 1245(a)(2)) of the machine in the hands of D is $1 million. The fair market value of the machine also is $1 million. D transfers the machine to newly organized X corporation, and E, an unrelated individual, simultaneously transfers property worth $1 million to X corporation. D receives in exchange 400 shares of X common stock worth $400,000, a $400,000 15-year debenture issued by X (worth its face amount), and a $200,000 installment obligation (bearing adequate interest) issued by X. The installment obligation calls for a single payment of the full $200,000 face amount two years following the date of issue. E receives in the exchange 1,000 shares of X common stock worth $1 million. D and E are in control (as defined in section 368(c)) of X immediately after the exchange. The debenture received by D is a "security" within the meaning of section 351(a), but the installment obligation received by D is not a "security" within the meaning of that section and thus the exchange by D is a transaction described in section 351(b). The installment obligation is boot received by D in the exchange and the X stock and X debenture are permitted property received by D in the exchange. Since the aggregate fair market value ($800,000) of X stock ($400,000) and the X debenture ($400,000) received by D exceeds D's $500,000 adjusted basis in the machine, all of that basis is allocated proportionately among the items of permitted property. Thus, D will hold the X stock with a basis of $250,000 and the X debenture with a basis of $250,000. Since there is no excess basis, in the hands of D the installment obligation has a basis of zero. In the hands of X, the adjusted basis of the machine remains $500,000. When D receives payment from X on the $200,000 installment obligation, D will recognize gain of $200,000, all of which gain will be treated as ordinary income. See sections 1245(a)(1) and 453B(a). At that time, X's adjusted basis in the machine will be increased in an amount equal to the $200,000 gain recognized by D.

Example (4). In 1976 H and W purchased Blackacre as their principal residence for $50,000. In 1981 H and W, both of whom are less than 55 years of age, sold Blackacre to A for $90,000: $15,000 cash, A's assumption of the $40,000 mortgage, and A's promise to pay H and W $7,000 (with adequate stated interest) in each of the next 5 years. Within 2 years of the sale of Blackacre, H and W acquire Whiteacre, an unencumbered property, which will be their principal residence, for $80,000. Of the $40,000 gain that H and W realized upon the sale of Whiteacre, $30,000 will not be recognized pursuant to the provisions of section 1034. Unless H and W elect not to report the transaction on the installment method, they will treat the $10,000 gain to be recognized as the gross profit for purposes of calculating the gross profit ratio. Accordingly the gross profit ratio is $^1/_5$ ($10,000 gross profit/$50,000 contract price) and H and W will report as gain $3,000 ($^1/_5 \times$ $15,000) in the year of the sale and $1,400 ($^1/_5 \times$ $7,000) in each of the next five years.

(4) *Installment obligations received as distributions in redemptions of stock pursuant to section 302(a).*—If a corporation redeems its stock

and the redemption is treated as a distribution in part or full payment in exchange for the stock under section 302(a), then an installment obligation which meets the requirements of section 453 and is distributed in the redemption shall be reported on the installment method unless the taxpayer elects otherwise.

Example. A owns 10% of the stock of X corporation and is not considered as owning (under section 318(a)) any other shares of X corporation. X redeems all of A's X shares and distributes its installment obligation to A in full payment. The reduction is treated as a sale of the X shares by A under section 302(b)(3). A will report any gain realized in the redemption on the installment method unless A elects otherwise.

* * *

Installment Obligations: Dispositions: Nonrecognition of Gain or Loss

Installment Obligations: Dispositions: Nonrecognition of Gain or Loss—Reg. §1.453B-1, relating to the nonrecognition of gain or loss on certain dispositions of an installment obligation, is proposed (published in the Federal Register on December 23, 2014) (REG-109187-11).

☐ Par. 4. Section 1.453B-1 is added to read as follows:

§1.453B-1. Gain or loss on disposition of installment obligations.—(a) *General rule.*—[Reserved].

(b) *Basis of obligation.*—[Reserved].

(c) *Dispositions on which no gain or loss is recognized.*—(1) *Certain nonrecognition transactions.*—(i) *In general.*—If the Internal Revenue Code provides an exception to the recognition of gain or loss for certain dispositions, no gain or loss shall be recognized under section 453B on the disposition of an installment obligation within that exception. These exceptions include—

(A) Certain transfers to corporations under sections 351 and 361;

(B) Contributions to a partnership under section 721; and

(C) Distributions by a partnership to a partner under section 731 (except as provided by sections 704(c)(1)(B), 736, 737, and 751(b)).

(ii) *Transactions resulting in a satisfaction of installment obligations.*—Paragraph (c)(1)(i) of this section does not apply to a disposition that results in a satisfaction of an installment obligation, regardless of whether the disposition occurs as part of a transaction for which the Internal Revenue Code provides an exception to the recognition of gain or loss. These dispositions include, but are not limited to—

(A) The receipt of stock of a corporation from the corporation in satisfaction of an installment obligation of the corporation; and

(B) The receipt of an interest in a partnership from the partnership in satisfaction of an installment obligation of the partnership.

(2) *Effective/applicability date.*—This paragraph (c) applies to satisfactions, distributions, transmissions, sales, or other dispositions of installment obligations after the date these regulations are published as final regulations in the **Federal Register**. [Reg. §1.453B-1.]

Imputed Interest: Original Issue Discount: Safe Haven Rates

Imputed Interest: Original Issue Discount: Safe Haven Interest Rates.—Reproduced below is the text of a proposed amendment of Reg. §1.454-1, relating to (1) the tax treatment of debt instruments issued after July 1, 1982, that contain original issue discount, (2) the imputation of and the accounting for interest with respect to sales and exchanges of property occurring after December 31, 1984, and (3) safe haven interest rates for loans or advances between commonly controlled taxpayers and safe haven leases between such taxpayers (published in the Federal Register on April 8, 1986).

☐ Par. 11. Paragraph (a)(1)(i) of §1.454-1 is revised to read as follows:

§1.454-1. Obligations issued at discount.—

(a) *Certain non-interest bearing obligations issued at discount.*—(1) *Election to include increase in income currently.*—If a taxpayer owns—

(i) A non-interest bearing obligation issued at a discount and redeemable for fixed amounts increasing at stated intervals (other than a debt instrument issued after May 27, 1969, as to which inclusion of original issue discount is required under section 1272), or

* * *

Deferred Compensation Plans: State and Local Governments: Tax-Exempt Entities

Deferred Compensation Plans: State and Local Governments: Tax-Exempt Entities.—Reg. §1.457-11 and amendments to Reg. §§1.457-1, 1.457-2, 1.457-4, 1.457-6, 1.457-7, 1.457-9 and 1.457-10—1.457-13, prescribing rules under section 457 of the Internal Revenue Code for the taxation of compensation deferred under plans established and maintained by State or local governments or other tax exempt organizations, are proposed (published in the Federal Register on June 22, 2016) (REG-147196-07).

Par. 2. Section 1.457-1 is revised to read as follows:

§1.457-1. General overview of section 457.—Section 457 provides rules for nonqualified deferred compensation plans established by eligible employers as defined under §1.457-2(d). Eligible employers may establish either deferred compensation plans that are eligible plans that meet the requirements of section 457(b) and §§1.457-3 through 1.457-10, or deferred compensation plans that do not meet the requirements of section 457(b) and §§1.457-3 through 1.457-10

(and therefore are ineligible plans which are generally subject to federal income tax treatment under section 457(f) and §1.457-12(a)). Plans described in §1.457-11 are not subject to section 457 or are treated as not providing for a deferral of compensation for purposes of section 457 (and, accordingly, the rules under §§1.457-3 through 1.457-10 and §1.457-12(a) do not apply to these plans).

Par. 3. Section 1.457-2 is amended by:
1. Revising the introductory text.
2. Revising the second sentence of paragraph (f).
3. Revising the last sentence of paragraph (i).
4. Revising paragraph (k).
The revisions read as follows:

§1.457-2. Definitions.—This section sets forth the definitions that are used under §§1.457-1 through 1.457-12.

* * *

(f) * * * An eligible governmental plan is an eligible plan that is established and maintained by a State as defined in paragraph (l) of this section and that meets the requirements of section 401(a)(37). * * *

* * *

(i) * * * Solely for purposes of section 457 and §§1.457-2 through 1.457-12, the term *nonelective employer contribution* includes employer contributions that would be described in section 401(m) if they were contributions to a qualified plan.

* * *

(k) *Plan.*—*Plan* includes any agreement, method, program, or other arrangement (including an individual employment agreement) under which the payment of compensation for services rendered to an eligible employer is deferred (whether by salary reduction, nonelective employer contribution, or otherwise). However, the

Par. 4. Section 1.457-4 is amended by:

1. Revising paragraphs (a), (b), and the last sentence of (e)(1).

2. Removing the language "§1.457-11" wherever it appears in paragraphs (e)(1), (e)(2), (e)(3), and (e)(5) *Example 1* and adding the language "§1.457-12" in its place.

The revisions read as follows:

§1.457-4. Annual deferrals, deferral limitations, and deferral agreements under eligible plans.—(a) *Taxation of annual deferrals.*—With the exception of designated Roth contributions (which are not excludable from gross income), annual deferrals that satisfy the requirements of paragraphs (b) and (c) of this section are excluded from the gross income of a participant in the year deferred or contributed and are not includible in gross income until paid to the participant in the case of an eligible governmental plan, or until paid or otherwise made available to the participant in the case of an eligible plan of a tax-exempt entity. See §1.457-7.

(b) *Agreement for deferral.*—(1) *In general.*—To be an eligible plan, the plan must provide that compensation for any calendar month may be deferred by salary reduction only if an agreement providing for the deferral has been entered into before the first day of the month in which the compensation to be deferred under the agreement would otherwise be paid or made available, and any modification or revocation of such an agreement may not become effective before the first day of the month following the month in which the modification or revocation occurs. However, a new employee may defer compensation in the first calendar month of employment if an agreement providing for the deferral is entered into on or before the first day the participant performs services for the eligible employer. An eligible plan may provide that if a participant enters into an agreement providing for deferral by salary reduction under the plan, the agreement will remain in effect until the participant revokes or alters the terms of the agreement. Nonelective employer contributions to an eligible plan are not subject to the timing rules for salary reduction agreements described in this paragraph (b)(1).

(2) *Designated Roth contributions in plans maintained by eligible governmental employers.*—(i) *Elections.*—An election by a participant to make a designated Roth contribution (as defined in section 402A(c)(1)) to an eligible governmental plan in lieu of all or a portion

plans described in §1.457-11 are either not subject to section 457 or are treated as not providing for a deferral of compensation for purposes of section 457, even if the payment of compensation is deferred under the plan.

* * *

of the amount that the participant could elect to contribute to the plan on a pre-tax basis must be irrevocably designated as an elective deferral that is not excludable from gross income in accordance with the timing rules under paragraph (b)(1) of this section. Designated Roth contributions are treated the same as pre-tax contributions for purposes of §§1.457-1 through 1.457-10, except as otherwise specifically provided in those sections.

(ii) *Separate accounting.*—Contributions and withdrawals of a participant's designated Roth contributions must be credited and debited to a designated Roth account maintained for the participant, and the plan must maintain a record of the participant's investment in the contract (that is, designated Roth contributions that have not been distributed) with respect to the participant's designated Roth account. In addition, gains, losses, and other credits or charges must be separately allocated on a reasonable and consistent basis to the designated Roth account and other accounts under the plan. However, forfeitures may not be allocated to the designated Roth account, and no contributions other than designated Roth contributions and rollover contributions described in section 402A(c)(3)(B) may be allocated to such account. The separate accounting requirement described in this paragraph applies to a plan at the time a designated Roth contribution is contributed to the plan and continues to apply until all designated Roth contributions (and the earnings attributable thereto) are distributed from the plan. See A-13 of §1.402A-1 for additional requirements for separate accounting.

* * *

(e) * * *

(1) * * * Thus, an excess deferral is includible in gross income when deferred or, if later, when the excess deferral first ceases to be subject to a substantial risk of forfeiture, under the rules described in §1.457-12(e).

* * *

Par. 5. Section 1.457-6 is amended by revising the first sentence of paragraph (b)(1) to read as follows:

§1.457-6. Timing of distributions under eligible plans.

* * *

(b) * * *

(1) * * * An employee has a severance from employment with the eligible employer if the employee dies, retires, or otherwise has a severance from employment (including as described in section 414(u)(12)(B)) with the eligible employer.* * *

* * *

Par. 6. Section 1.457-7 is amended by revising the section heading and paragraph (b)(1), redesignating paragraph (b)(4) as (b)(5), and adding a new paragraph (b)(4) to read as follows:

§1.457-7. Taxation of distributions under eligible plans.

* * *

(b) * * *

(1) *Amounts included in gross income in year paid under an eligible governmental plan.*—Except as provided in paragraphs (b)(2), (3), and (4) of this section (or in §1.457-10(c) relating to payments to a spouse or former spouse pursuant to a qualified domestic relations order), amounts deferred under an eligible governmental plan are includible in the gross income of a participant or beneficiary for the taxable year in which paid to the participant or beneficiary under the plan.

Distributions from designated Roth accounts are excludable from gross income to the extent provided in section 402A and §§1.402A-1 and 1.402A-2.

* * *

(4) *Certain amounts from an eligible governmental plan not in excess of the amount paid for qualified health insurance premiums.*—Amounts paid to a participant who is an eligible retired public safety officer from an eligible governmental plan are excludible from gross income to the extent provided in section 402(l).

* * *

Par. 7. Section 1.457-9 is amended by revising the third sentence of paragraph (a) and the last sentence of paragraph (b) to read as follows:

§1.457-9. Effect on eligible plans when not administered in accordance with eligibility requirements.—(a) * * * If a plan ceases to be an eligible governmental plan, amounts subsequently deferred by participants are includible in gross income when deferred, or, if later,

when the amounts deferred first cease to be subject to a substantial risk of forfeiture, under the rules described in §1.457-12(e). * * *

(b) * * * See §1.457-12 for rules regarding the treatment of an ineligible plan.

Par. 8. Section 1.457-10 is amended by removing the language "§1.457-11" wherever it appears in paragraphs (a)(2)(i), (a)(3) *Example 2* (ii), (c)(2) *Example 1* (ii) and *Example 2* (ii) and adding the language "§1.457-12" in its place.

§1.457-10. Miscellaneous provisions.

Par. 10. Add a new §1.457-11 to read as follows:

§1.457-11. Exclusions and exceptions for certain plans.—(a) *In general.*—The plans described in paragraphs (b) and (c) of this section either are not subject to section 457 or are treated as not providing for a deferral of compensation for purposes of section 457, and, accordingly, the provisions of §§1.457-3 through 1.457-10 and 1.457-12(a) do not apply to these plans.

(b) *Plans not subject to section 457.*—The following plans are not subject to section 457:

(1) Any plan satisfying the conditions in section 1107(c)(4) of the Tax Reform Act of 1986, Public Law 99-514 (100 Stat. 2494) (TRA '86) (relating to certain plans for State judges);

(2) Any of the following plans (to which specific transitional statutory exclusions apply):

(i) A plan of a tax-exempt entity in existence prior to January 1, 1987, if the conditions of section 1107(c)(3)(B) of the TRA '86, as amended by section 1011(e)(6) of the Technical and Miscellaneous Revenue Act of 1988, Public Law 100-647 (102 Stat. 3342) (TAMRA), are satisfied (see §1.457-2(b)(4) for a different rule that may apply to the annual deferrals permitted under this type of plan);

(ii) A collectively bargained nonelective deferred compensation plan in effect on December 31, 1987, if the conditions of section 6064(d)(2) of TAMRA are satisfied;

(iii) Amounts deferred under plans described in section 6064(d)(3) of TAMRA (relating to amounts deferred under certain nonelective deferred compensation plans in effect before 1989); and

(iv) Any plan satisfying the conditions in section 1107(c)(4) and (5) of TRA '86 (relating to certain plans for certain individuals with respect to which the IRS issued guidance before 1977); and

(3) Any plan described in section 457(e)(12) that provides only nonelective deferred compensation attributable to services not performed as an employee (for example, a plan providing nonelective deferred compensation attributable to services performed by independent contractors). For this purpose, deferred compensation is nonelective only if all individuals, other than those who have not satisfied any applicable initial service requirement, with the same relationship to the payor are covered under the same plan with no individual variations or options under the plan.

(c) *Plans treated as not providing for a deferral of compensation.*—The following plans are treated as not providing for a deferral of compensation for purposes of section 457, §§1.457-1 through 1.457-10, and §1.457-12:

(1) A bona fide vacation leave, sick leave, compensatory time, severance pay, disability pay, or death benefit plan, as described in section 457(e)(11)(A)(i) (see paragraph (d) of this section for the definition of a bona fide severance pay plan, paragraph (e) of this section for the definitions of a bona fide death benefit plan and a bona fide disability pay plan, and paragraph (f) of this section for the requirements for a bona fide sick or vacation leave plan); and

(2) A plan described in section 457(e)(11)(A)(ii) paying solely length of service awards that are based on service accrued after December 31, 1996, to bona fide volunteers (and their beneficiaries) on account of qualified services performed by those volunteers.

(d) *Definition of bona fide severance pay plan.*—(1) *In general.*—A bona fide severance pay plan is an arrangement that meets the following requirements:

(i) Except as provided in paragraph (d)(3) of this section, benefits are payable only upon involuntary severance from employment, as defined in paragraph (d)(2) of this section (see §1.457-6(b) for the meaning of severance from employment);

(ii) The amount payable does not exceed two times the participant's annualized compensation based upon the annual rate of pay for services provided to the eligible employer for the calendar year preceding the calendar year in which the participant has a severance from employment with the eligible employer (or the current calendar year if the participant had no compensation for services provided to the eligible employer in the preceding calendar year), adjusted for any increase during the year used to measure the rate of pay that was expected to continue indefinitely if the participant had not had a severance from employment; and

(iii) The entire severance benefit must be paid to the participant no later than the last day of the second calendar year following the calendar year in which the severance from employment occurs, pursuant to a requirement contained in a written plan document.

(2) *Involuntary severance from employment.*—(i) *In general.*—For purposes of paragraph (d)(1)(i) of this section, an *involuntary severance from employment* means a severance from employment due to the independent exercise of the eligible employer's unilateral authority to terminate the participant's services, other than due to the participant's implicit or explicit request, if the participant was willing and able to continue performing services. An involuntary severance from employment may include an eligible employer's failure to renew a contract at the time the contract expires, provided that the employee was willing and able to execute a new contract providing terms and

conditions substantially similar to those in the expiring contract and to continue providing such services. The determination of whether a severance from employment is involuntary is based on all the facts and circumstances without regard to any characterization of the reason for the payment by the employer or participant.

(ii) *Severance from employment for good reason.*—(A) *In general.*—Notwithstanding paragraph (d)(2)(i) of this section, a participant's voluntary severance from employment will be treated as an involuntary severance from employment, for purposes of paragraph (d)(1)(i) of this section, if the severance occurs under certain bona fide conditions that are pre-specified in writing (referred to herein as a severance from employment for good reason), provided that the avoidance of the requirements of section 457 is not the primary purpose of the inclusion of the conditions or of the actions by the employer in connection with the satisfaction of the conditions, and a voluntary severance from employment under such conditions effectively constitutes an involuntary severance from employment. Notwithstanding the previous sentence, once the bona fide conditions have been established, the elimination of one or more of the conditions may result in the extension of a substantial risk of forfeiture, the recognition of which would be subject to the rules discussed in §1.457-12(e)(2).

(B) *Material negative change required.*—A severance from employment for good reason will be treated as an involuntary severance from employment only if the relevant facts and circumstances demonstrate that it was the result of unilateral employer action that caused a material negative change to the participant's relationship with the eligible employer. Some factors that may provide evidence of such a material negative change include a material reduction in the duties to be performed, a material negative change in the conditions under which the duties are to be performed, or a material reduction in the compensation to be received for performing such services. Other factors to be considered in determining whether a severance from employment due to good reason will be treated as an involuntary severance from employment include the extent to which the payments upon a severance from employment for good reason are in the same amount and made at the same time and in the same form as payments that would be made upon an actual involuntary severance from employment, and whether the employee is required to give the employer notice of the existence of the condition that would result in the treatment of a severance from employment as being for good reason and a reasonable opportunity to remedy the condition.

(C) *Safe harbor.*—The requirements of paragraph (d)(2)(ii)(B) of this section are deemed to be satisfied if a severance from employment occurs under the conditions described in paragraph (d)(2)(ii)(C)(1) of this section, those conditions are specified in writing by the time the legally binding right to the payment arises, and the plan also satisfies the requirements in paragraphs (d)(2)(ii)(C)(2) and (3) of this section.

(1) The severance from employment occurs during a limited period of time not to exceed two years following the initial existence of one or more of the following conditions arising without the consent of the participant:

(i) A material diminution in the participant's base compensation;

(ii) A material diminution in the participant's authority, duties, or responsibilities;

(iii) A material diminution in the authority, duties, or responsibilities of the supervisor to whom the participant is required to report, including a requirement that a participant report to a corporate officer or employee instead of reporting directly to the board of directors (or similar governing body) of an organization;

(iv) A material diminution in the budget over which the participant retains authority;

(v) A material change in the geographic location at which the participant must perform services; or

(vi) Any other action or inaction that constitutes a material breach by the eligible employer of the agreement under which the participant provides services.

(2) The amount, time, and form of payment upon the severance from employment is substantially the same as the amount, time, and form of payment that would have been made upon an actual involuntary severance from employment, to the extent such right to payment exists.

(3) The participant is required to provide notice to the eligible employer of the existence of the applicable condition(s) described in paragraph (d)(2)(ii)(C)(1) of this section within a period not to exceed 90 days after the initial existence of the condition(s), upon the notice of which, the employer must be provided a period of at least 30 days during which it may remedy the condition(s) and not be required to pay the amount.

(3) *Window programs.*—The requirement in paragraph (d)(1)(i) of this section that benefits be payable only upon involuntary sever-

ance from employment does not apply to a bona fide severance pay plan that provides benefits upon a severance from employment pursuant to a window program. For this purpose, a *window program* means a program established by an employer to provide separation pay in connection with an impending severance from employment, if the program is made available by the employer for a limited period of time (typically no longer than 12 months) to participants who have a severance from employment during that period or to participants who have a severance from employment during that period under specified circumstances. A program is not considered a window program for purposes of this paragraph if it is part of a pattern of multiple similar programs that, if offered as a single program, would not be a window program under this paragraph. Whether multiple programs constitute a pattern of similar programs is determined based on the relevant facts and circumstances. Although no one factor is determinative, relevant factors include whether the benefits are on account of a specific reduction in workforce (or some other entity-related operational condition), the degree to which the separation pay relates to an event or condition, and whether the event or condition is temporary or discrete or is a permanent aspect of the employer's practices.

(4) *Voluntary early retirement incentive plans.*—(i) *In general.*—Notwithstanding paragraph (d)(1) of this section, an applicable voluntary early retirement incentive plan (as defined in section 457(e)(11)(D)(ii)) is treated as a bona fide severance pay plan for purposes of this section with respect to payments or supplements made as an early retirement benefit, a retirement-type subsidy, or an early retirement benefit described in the last sentence of section 411(a)(9), if the payments or supplements are made in coordination with a defined benefit pension plan that is qualified under section 401(a) maintained by an eligible employer described in section 457(e)(1)(A) or by an education association described in section 457(e)(11)(D)(ii)(II). See section 1104(d)(4) of the Pension Protection Act of 2006, Public Law 109-280 (120 Stat. 780), regarding the application of the Internal Revenue Code and certain other laws to any plan, arrangement, or conduct to which section 457(e)(11)(D) does not apply.

(ii) *Definitions.*—The definitions in § 1.411(d)-3(g)(6)(i) and (iv) apply for purposes of determining whether payments or supplements are an early retirement benefit or a retirement-type subsidy, and the definition in § 1.411(a)-7(c)(4) applies for purposes of determining whether payments or supplements are an early retirement benefit described in the last sentence of section 411(a)(9).

(e) *Bona fide death benefit or disability pay plans.*—(1) *Bona fide death benefit plan.*—For purposes of section 457(e)(11)(A)(i) and this section, a *bona fide death benefit plan* is a plan providing death benefits as defined in § 31.3121(v)(2)-1(b)(4)(iv)(C) of this chapter, provided that, for purposes of this paragraph (e)(1), the death benefits may be provided through insurance and the lifetime benefits payable under the plan are not treated as including the value of any term life insurance coverage provided under the plan that is includible in gross income.

(2) *Bona fide disability pay plan.*—For purposes of section 457(e)(11)(A)(i) and this section, a *bona fide disability pay plan* is a plan that pays benefits (whether or not insured) only in the event that a participant is disabled, provided that, for purposes of this paragraph (e)(2), the value of any disability insurance coverage provided under the plan that is included in gross income is disregarded. For this purpose, a participant is considered disabled only if the participant meets one of the following conditions:

(i) The participant is unable to engage in any substantial gainful activity by reason of any medically determinable physical or mental impairment that can be expected to result in death or last for a continuous period of not less than 12 months;

(ii) The participant is, by reason of any medically determinable physical or mental impairment that can be expected to result in death or last for a continuous period of not less than 12 months, receiving income replacement benefits for a period of not less than three months under an accident and health plan covering employees of the eligible employer; or

(iii) The participant is determined to be totally disabled by the Social Security Administration or Railroad Retirement Board.

(f) *Bona fide sick and vacation leave plans.*—(1) *In general.*—For purposes of section 457(e)(11)(A)(i) and this section, the determination of whether a sick or vacation leave plan is a bona fide sick or vacation leave plan is made based on the relevant facts and circumstances. In general, a plan is treated as a bona fide sick or vacation leave plan, and not an arrangement to defer compensation, if the facts and circumstances demonstrate that the primary purpose of the plan is to provide participants with paid time off from work because of sickness, vacation, or other personal reasons. Factors used in determining whether a plan is a bona fide sick or vacation leave plan include whether the amount of leave provided could reasonably be expected to be used in the normal course by an employee (before the employee ceases to provide services to the eligible employer) absent unusual circumstances, the ability to exchange unused accumulated leave for cash or other benefits (including nontaxable benefits and the use of leave to postpone the date of termination of employment), the applicable restraints (if any) on the ability to accumulate unused leave and carry it forward to subsequent years in circumstances in which the accumulated leave may be exchanged for cash or other benefits, the amount and frequency of any in-service distributions of cash or other benefits offered in exchange for accumulated and unused leave, whether any payment of unused leave is made promptly upon severance from employment (or instead is paid over a period after severance from employment), and whether the program (or a particular feature of the program) is available only to a limited number of employees.

(2) *Delegation of authority to Commissioner.*—The Commissioner may provide additional rules regarding the requirements of a bona fide sick or vacation leave plan under section 457, in revenue rulings, notices, or other guidance published in the Internal Revenue Bulletin (see § 601.601(d)(2)(ii)(b) of this chapter), as the Commissioner determines to be necessary or appropriate.

Pars. 9 and 11. Redesignate § 1.457-11 as § 1.457-12 and revise newly-redesignated § 1.457-12 to read as follows:

§ 1.457-12. Tax treatment of participants if plan is not an eligible plan.—(a) *Tax treatment of an ineligible plan under section 457(f).*—(1) *In general.*—Pursuant to section 457(f)(1), if an eligible employer provides for a deferral of compensation under an ineligible plan, amounts will be included in income in accordance with paragraphs (a)(2) through (4) of this section, except as otherwise provided in this paragraph (a) or paragraph (b) of this section. See § 1.457-11 for plans that are not subject to section 457 or are not treated as providing for a deferral of compensation for purposes of section 457.

(2) *Income inclusion.*—The present value of compensation deferred under an ineligible plan is includible in the gross income of a participant or beneficiary under section 457(f) on the applicable date. For this purpose, the applicable date is the later of the first date on which there is a legally binding right to the compensation or, if the compensation is subject to a substantial risk of forfeiture, the first date on which the substantial risk of forfeiture (within the meaning of section 457(f)(3)(B) and paragraph (e) of this section) lapses. Paragraph (c) of this section provides rules for determining the present value of the compensation deferred under the plan, including a requirement that the amount of compensation deferred under an ineligible plan as of an applicable date includes any earnings on the compensation as of that date.

(3) *Treatment of earnings after income inclusion.*—Earnings credited on compensation deferred under an ineligible plan after the date on which the compensation is includible in gross income under section 457(f)(1) pursuant to paragraph (a)(2) of this section are

includible in the gross income of a participant or beneficiary when paid or made available to the participant or beneficiary.

(4) *Income inclusion when compensation is paid or made available.*—Amounts paid or made available to a participant or beneficiary under an ineligible plan are includible in the gross income of the participant or beneficiary under section 72, relating to annuities. For this purpose, an amount is paid or made available if there is actual or constructive receipt (within the meaning of § 1.451-2) of any taxable or nontaxable benefit, including a transfer of cash, a transfer of property includible in income under section 83, any other event that results in the inclusion in income under the economic benefit doctrine, a contribution to (or transfer or creation of a beneficial interest in) a trust described in section 402(b) at a time when contributions to the trust are includible in income under section 402(b), or inclusion of an amount in income under section 457A. An amount is also paid or made available for this purpose if there is a transfer, cancellation, or reduction of an amount of deferred compensation in exchange for benefits under a welfare benefit plan, a fringe benefit excludible under section 119 or section 132, or any other benefit that is excludible from gross income.

(5) *Investment in the contract.*—For purposes of applying section 72 to amounts that are paid or made available as described in paragraph (a)(4) of this section, a participant is treated as having an investment in the contract to the extent that compensation has been included in gross income by the participant in accordance with paragraph (a)(2) of this section. An amount is treated as included in income for a taxable year only to the extent that the amount was

properly includible in income and the participant actually included the amount in income (including on an original or amended federal income tax return or as a result of an IRS examination or a final decision of a court of competent jurisdiction).

(b) *Exceptions.*—(1) *In general.*—Section 457(f)(1) and paragraph (a) of this section do not apply to a plan or a portion of a plan described in this paragraph (b). The determination of whether a plan or a portion of a plan is described in this paragraph (b) is made as of the date on which the legally binding right to an amount arises. However, a plan or portion of a plan will cease to be a plan that is described in this paragraph (b) on the first date that it no longer meets the requirements described in this paragraph (b).

(2) *Certain retirement plans.*—Annuity plans and contracts described in section 403 and plans described in section 401(a) are not subject to the provisions of section 457(f)(1) and paragraph (a) of this section.

(3) *Section 402(b) trusts.*—(i) *Section 402(b).*—The portion of a plan that consists of a trust to which section 402(b) applies is not subject to the provisions of section 457(f)(1) and paragraph (a) of this section.

(ii) *Example.*—The provisions of this paragraph (b)(3) are illustrated in the following example:

Example. (i) *Facts.* On October 1, 2017, an eligible employer establishes an ineligible plan covering only one participant (a highly compensated employee under section 414(q)) under which the participant obtains an unconditional right to be paid $150,000 (plus interest at a specified reasonable rate) on October 1, 2021. As part of the plan, the employer simultaneously establishes a trust described in section 402(b) in the United States for the sole benefit of the participant. Under the terms of the plan and trust, the assets of the trust are also payable to the participant on October 1, 2021, and the amount that the employer is otherwise obligated to pay under the plan will be reduced (offset) by the amount paid to the participant from the trust. Section 402(b)(4) applies to the trust, and the trust has assets of $98,000 on October 1, 2017 and $100,000 on December 31, 2017.

(ii) *Conclusion.* Section 457(f) and this section apply only to the portion of the plan that is not funded through the section 402(b) trust. Thus, the participant has income under section 457(f) equal to the present value of the portion of the compensation deferred under the plan that is not funded through the section 402(b) trust on the date on which there is a legally binding right to the compensation (October 1, 2017). This present value is equal to $52,000 ($150,000 - $98,000), which is included in the participant's gross income on October 1, 2017. The participant must also include $100,000 in gross income on December 31, 2017 pursuant to section 402(b)(4)(A).

(4) *Qualified governmental excess benefit arrangements under section 415(m).*—A qualified governmental excess benefit arrangement described in section 415(m) is not subject to the provisions of section 457(f)(1) and paragraph (a) of this section.

(5) *Nonqualified annuities under section 403(c).*—(i) *Section 403(c) annuities.*—The portion of a plan in which premiums are paid by an employer for an annuity contract to which section 403(c) applies is not subject to the provisions of section 457(f)(1) and paragraph (a) of this section.

(ii) *Examples.*—The provisions of this paragraph (b)(5) are illustrated by the following examples:

Example 1. (i) *Facts.* A tax-exempt entity pays a premium for an annuity contract (described in section 403(c)) for the benefit of a participant. The annuity contract has a value of $135,000, and the participant is substantially vested (as defined in §1.83-3(b)) at the time the premium is paid. The participant includes the full value ($135,000) in income under section 403(c) in the year the employer pays the premium.

(ii) *Conclusion.* Although the participant has a legally binding right to payments under the annuity contract that will be made in a subsequent taxable year, the participant's interest in the annuity contract is not subject to section 457(f)(1) and paragraph (a) of this section.

Example 2. (i) *Facts.* The facts are the same as in *Example 1 of this paragraph (b)(5)*, except the participant's rights in the annuity contract are not substantially vested (as defined in §1.83-3(b)) at the time the premium is paid and do not become substantially vested until a future taxable year. The participant does not include the full value of the contract in income under section 403(c) in the year the employer pays the premium.

(ii) *Conclusion.* Neither the payment of the premium nor the participant's interest in the annuity contract is subject to section 457(f)(1) or paragraph (a) of this section.

(6) *Transfer of property under section 83.*—(i) *Section 83.*—The portion of a plan that consists of a transfer of property to which section 83 applies is not subject to the provisions of section 457(f)(1) and paragraph (a) of this section. Specifically, section 457(f)(1) and paragraph (a) of this section do not apply if, on or before the first date on which compensation deferred under a plan is not subject to a substantial risk of forfeiture (within the meaning of section 457(f)(3)(B) and paragraph (e) of this section), the amount is paid through a transfer of property described in section 83. However, section 457(f)(1) and paragraph (a) of this section do apply if the first date on which compensation deferred under a plan is not subject to a substantial risk of forfeiture (as defined in section 457(f)(3)(B) and paragraph (e) of this section) precedes the date on which the amount is paid through a transfer of property described in section 83. If deferred compensation payable in property is includible in gross income under section 457(f)(1)(A), then, as provided in section 72, the amount includible in gross income when that property is later transferred or made available to the participant or beneficiary is the excess of the value of the property at that time over the amount previously included in gross income under section 457(f)(1)(A).

(ii) *Examples.*—The provisions of this paragraph (b)(6) are illustrated by the following examples:

Example 1. (i) *Facts.* On December 1, 2017, an eligible employer agrees to transfer property that is substantially vested (within the meaning of §1.83-3(b)) and has a fair market value equal to a specified dollar amount, to a participant on January 15, 2020. The participant's rights under the agreement are not subject to a substantial risk of forfeiture (within the meaning of section 457(f)(3)(B) and paragraph (e) of this section).

(ii) *Conclusion.* Because there is no substantial risk of forfeiture (within the meaning of section 457(f)(3)(B) and paragraph (e) of this section) with respect to the agreement to transfer property in 2020, the present value of the amount on the applicable date (December 1, 2017) is includible in the participant's gross income under section 457(f)(1)(A). Under paragraph (a)(4) of this section, when the substantially vested property is transferred to the participant on January 15, 2020, the amount includible in the participant's gross income is equal to the excess of the fair market value of the property on that date over the amount that was included in gross income for 2017.

Example 2. (i) *Facts.* Under a bonus plan, an eligible employer agrees in 2021 to transfer property that is substantially nonvested (within the meaning of §1.83-3(b)) to Participants A and B in 2023 if they are continuously employed by the eligible employer through the date of the transfer (which condition constitutes a substantial risk of forfeiture within the meaning of section 457(f)(3)(B) and paragraph (e) of this section). In 2023, the eligible employer transfers the property to Participants A and B, subject to a substantial risk of forfeiture (within the meaning of §1.83-3(c)), that lapses in 2025. Participant A makes a timely election to include the fair market value of the property in gross income under section 83(b). Participant B does not make this election.

(ii) *Conclusion.* The compensation deferred for both Participants A and B is not subject to section 457(f)(1) or paragraph (a) of this section because section 83 applies to the transfer of property on or before the date on which the property is not subject to a substantial risk of forfeiture (within the meaning of section 457(f)(3)(B) and paragraph (e) of this section). Because of the section 83(b) election, Participant A includes the fair market value of the property (disregarding lapse restrictions) in gross income for 2023 under section 83(b)(1). Participant B includes the value of the property in gross income when the substantial risk of forfeiture lapses in 2025 under section 83(a).

(7) *Applicable employment retention plan.*—The portion of a plan that is an applicable employment retention plan as described in section 457(f)(4) with respect to any participant is not subject to the provisions of section 457(f)(1) and paragraph (a) of this section. See also section 1104(d)(4) of the Pension Protection Act of 2006, Public Law 109-280 (120 Stat. 780), regarding the application of the Internal Revenue Code and certain other laws to any plan, arrangement, or conduct to which section 457(f)(2)(F) does not apply.

(c) *Amount included in income.*—(1) *Calculation of present value.*— (i) *In general.*—Except as otherwise provided in this paragraph (c), the present value of compensation deferred under an ineligible plan as of an applicable date equals the present value of the future payments to which the participant has a legally binding right (as described in paragraph (d) of this section). For this purpose, present value is determined in accordance with the provisions of this paragraph (c)(1)(i) by multiplying the amount of a payment (or the amount of each payment in a series of payments) by the probability that any condition or conditions on which the payment is contingent will be satisfied and discounting the amount using an assumed rate of interest to reflect the time value of money.

(ii) *Actuarial assumptions.*—(A) *In general.*—(1) *Reasonable actuarial assumptions.*—For purposes of paragraph (c)(1)(i) of this section, present value is determined using actuarial assumptions and methods that, based on all of the facts and circumstances, are reasonable as of the applicable date, including an interest rate that is reasonable as of that date and other assumptions necessary to determine the present value (without regard to whether the present value of the compensation deferred under the plan is reasonably ascertainable as described in § 31.3121(v)(2)-1(e)(4)(i)(B) of this chapter).

(2) *Probability of death before the payment of benefits.*—For purposes of paragraph (c)(1)(i) of this section, the probability that a participant will die before a payment is made is permitted to be taken into account only to the extent that the payment is forfeitable upon death.

(3) *Probability that the payment will not be made.*—For purposes of paragraph (c)(1)(i) of this section, the probability that payments will not be made (or will be reduced) because of the unfunded status of a plan, the risk associated with any deemed or actual investment of compensation deferred under the plan, the risk that the eligible employer or another party will be unwilling or unable to pay, the possibility of future plan amendments, the possibility of a future change in the law, or similar risks or contingencies are not taken into account.

(B) *Payments made in foreign currency.*—The rules in § 1.409A-4(b)(2)(i) apply for purposes of determining the treatment of payments in foreign currency.

(C) *Treatment of payment triggers based upon events.*—(1) *In general.*—Except as provided in paragraph (c)(1)(ii)(C)(2) of this section, the rules in § 1.409A-4(b)(2)(vii) apply for purposes of determining the treatment of payment triggers based upon events.

(2) *Treatment of severance from employment.*—If the date on which a payment will be made depends on the date the participant has a severance from employment (as described in § 1.457-6(b)) and the participant has not had a severance from employment by the applicable date, then for purposes of paragraph (c)(1)(ii)(A)(1) of this section, the severance from employment may be treated as occurring on any date that is not later than the fifth anniversary of the applicable date, unless this assumption would be unreasonable under the facts and circumstances.

(iii) *Unreasonable assumptions.*—If any actuarial assumption or method used to determine the present value of compensation deferred under the plan is not reasonable, as determined by the Commissioner, then the Commissioner will determine the present value using actuarial assumptions and methods that the Commissioner determines to be reasonable, including the AFR and the applicable mortality table under section 417(e)(3)(B) as of the applicable date. For purposes of this section, *AFR* means the mid-term applicable federal rate (as defined pursuant to section 1274(d)) for January 1 of the relevant calendar year, compounded annually.

(iv) *Account balance plans.*—(A) *In general.*—To the extent benefits are provided under an account balance plan, as defined in § 31.3121(v)(2)-1(c)(1)(ii) and (iii) of this chapter, to which earnings (or losses, if applicable) are credited at least annually, the present value of compensation deferred under the plan as of an applicable date is the amount credited to the participant's account, including both the principal amount credited to the account and any earnings or losses attributable to the principal amount that have been credited to the account, as of that date.

(B) *Unreasonable rates of return.*—This paragraph (c)(1)(iv)(B) applies to an account balance plan under which the income credited is based on neither a predetermined actual investment, within the meaning of § 31.3121(v)(2)-1(d)(2)(i)(B) of this chapter, nor a rate of interest that is reasonable, within the meaning of § 31.3121(v)(2)-1(d)(2)(i)(C) of this chapter, as determined by the Commissioner. The present value of compensation deferred under that type of plan as of an applicable date is equal to the amount credited to the participant's account as of that date, plus the present value of the excess (if any) of the earnings to be credited under the plan over the earnings that would be credited through the projected payment date using a reasonable rate of interest. If the present value of compensation deferred under the plan is not determined and is not taken into account by the taxpayer in this manner, the present value of the compensation deferred under the plan will be treated as equal to the amount credited to the participant's account as of the applicable date, plus the present value of the excess (if any) of the earnings to be credited under the plan through the projected payment date over the earnings that would be credited using the AFR.

(C) *Combinations of predetermined actual investments or interest rates.*—If the amount of earnings or losses credited under an account balance plan is based on the greater of two or more rates of return (each of which would be a predetermined actual investment or a reasonable interest rate if the earnings or losses credited were based on only one of those rates of return), then the amount included in income on the applicable date is the sum of the amount credited to the participant's account as of the applicable date and the present value (determined under paragraph (c)(1)(i) of this section) of the right to future earnings.

(D) *Examples.*—The following examples illustrate the provisions of paragraphs (c)(1)(i) through (iv) of this section. For purposes of these examples, assume that the arrangements are either not subject to section 409A or 457A or otherwise comply with the requirements of those provisions, and that the parties are not under examination for any of the tax years in question.

Example 1. (i) *Facts.* On October 1, 2017, an eligible employer agrees to pay $100,000 to a participant on January 1, 2024, if the participant is alive on that date. The employer determines that the October 1, 2017 present value of that payment is $75,000 based on the second segment rate used for purposes of section 417(e)(3)(C) on October 1, 2017, and using the mortality table applicable under section 417(e)(3)(B) on October 1, 2017.

(ii) *Conclusion.* The present value has been determined in accordance with paragraph (c)(1)(i) of this section.

Example 2. (i) *Facts.* On October 1, 2018, an eligible employer agrees to pay $100,000 to a participant at severance from employment. The assumptions that the employer uses to determine the present value are that the participant will have a severance from employment on October 1, 2023 (the fifth anniversary of the date the participant obtains the right to the payment in accordance with paragraph (c)(1)(ii)(C)(2) of this section) and that the present value will be determined using a rate of 4.5% compounded monthly.

(ii) *Conclusion.* Assuming, solely for purposes of this example, that the employer's severance from employment date and interest rate assumptions are reasonable, the value included in income on the applicable date (October 1, 2018) is $79,885.

Example 3. (i) *Facts.* On October 1, 2017, an eligible employer agrees to pay $100,000 to a participant at severance from employment, but no payment will be made if the severance from employment occurs on or after October 1, 2021.

(ii) *Conclusion.* Although paragraph (c)(1)(ii)(C)(2) of this section provides that for purposes of determining when a payment will be made, severance may be treated as if it occurred on the fifth anniversary of the applicable date, that assumption would be unreasonable under these facts and circumstances and would not be permitted under paragraph (c)(1)(ii)(C)(2) of this section. Accordingly, for purposes of determining the present value, an assumption that severance from employment would occur after September 30, 2021 would be unreasonable.

Example 4. (i) *Facts.* An eligible employer maintains a supplemental executive retirement plan that provides a subsidized early retirement benefit payable to participants between age 60 and 65. A 60 year old participant becomes vested in the right to the subsidized early retirement benefit on December 31, 2017.

(ii) *Conclusion.* The assumption under paragraph (c)(1)(ii)(C)(2) of this section would not be permitted for purposes of determining the amount to be included in income because the nature of the subsidized early retirement benefit causes it to decline in value until it becomes worthless upon attainment of age 65. In other words, the value of the subsidized early retirement benefit using the assumption permitted in paragraph (c)(1)(ii)(C)(2) of this section would result in a value of $0 and would be unreasonable under the facts and circumstances.

Example 5. (i) *Facts.* On October 1, 2017, an eligible employer agrees to provide compensation to an employee for prior services in an amount equal to $100,000, plus interest at a reasonable rate, with payment to be made at the time of the employee's severance from employment. The participant's right to the compensation is not subject to a substantial risk of forfeiture at any time.

(ii) *Conclusion.* Because the agreement provides for a reasonable rate of interest, the amount included in income on the applicable date (October 1, 2017) is $100,000.

Example 6. (i) *Facts.* The facts are the same as in *Example 5* of this paragraph (c)(1)(iv)(D), except that the right is subject to a requirement that the participant continue to provide substantial services for three additional years (which constitutes a substantial risk of forfeiture as described in paragraph (e) of this section). On October 1, 2020, when the substantial risk of forfeiture lapses, the account balance is $116,147.

(ii) *Conclusion.* The amount included in income on the applicable date (October 1, 2020) is $116,147.

Example 7. (i) *Facts.* The facts are the same as in *Example 5* of this paragraph (c)(1)(iv)(D), except that the rate of interest credited on the account is 5% above a reasonable rate of interest. On October 1, 2017, the sum of the $100,000 account balance, plus the present value of the right to receive the difference between a reasonable rate of return and the rate of return being credited on the account (from October 1, 2017 until October 1, 2022) is $128,336. The participant has a severance from employment on October 16, 2020, and is paid $135,379 on that date.

(ii) *Conclusion.* The amount included in income on the applicable date (October 1, 2017) is $128,336. Pursuant to paragraph (a)(5) of this section, the $128,336 is treated as investment in the contract for purposes of section 72 and, pursuant to paragraph (a)(4) of this section, the participant recognizes an additional $7,043 ($135,379, minus the $128,336 that was previously included in gross income for 2017) in income attributable to the payment on October 16, 2020.

Example 8. (i) *Facts.* The facts are the same as in *Example 5* of this paragraph (c)(1)(iv)(D), except that the employer also agrees to pay the participant an amount that is estimated to be equal to the federal, state, and local income taxes due (based on a fixed percentage that is pre-specified in the agreement) attributable to the amount included in income on the applicable date (October 1, 2017). In exchange for that tax payment, the amount payable upon severance from employment is to be reduced by an amount equal to the federal, state, and local income taxes for the taxable year of payment that the employer estimates would otherwise have been due but for the income inclusion in 2017. In satisfaction of this obligation to make the tax payment, the employer pays the participant $66,667 on April 15, 2018.

(ii) *Conclusion.* The present value on the applicable date (October 1, 2017) is $100,000, plus the present value of the $66,667 payment to be made on April 15, 2018, minus the present value of the reduction that will be applied at the time of payment (which, if reasonable, may be assumed to be October 1, 2022 in accordance with paragraph (c)(1)(ii)(C)(2) of this section).

Example 9. (i) *Facts.* An eligible employer credits $100,000 on December 31, 2017, to the account of a participant under an ineligible plan, subject to the condition that the amount will be forfeited if the participant voluntarily terminates employment before December 31, 2019. The account balance will be credited with notional annual earnings based on the greater of the return of a designated S&P 500 index fund or a specified rate of interest and will be paid on December 31, 2025.

(ii) *Conclusion.* Under paragraph (c)(1)(iv)(C) of this section, the sum of the amount credited to the participant's account as of the applicable date (December 31, 2019) and the present value (determined under paragraph (c)(1)(i) of this section) of the right to future earnings based on the greater of the return of the designated S&P 500 index fund or the specified rate of interest must be included in the participant's gross income on the applicable date.

(v) *Application of the general calculation rules to formula amounts.*—With respect to a right to receive a formula amount, the amount or amounts of future payments under the plan, for purposes of determining the present value as of an applicable date, is determined based on all of the facts and circumstances existing as of that date. This determination must reflect reasonable, good faith assumptions with respect to any contingencies as to the amount of the payment, both with respect to each contingency and with respect to all contingencies in the aggregate. An assumption based on the facts and circumstances as of the applicable date may be reasonable even if the facts and circumstances change in the future so that when the amount payable is determined in a subsequent year, the amount payable is a greater (or lesser) amount. In such a case, the increase (or decrease) due to the change in the facts and circumstances is treated as earnings (or losses). For purposes of this paragraph (c)(1)(v), an amount payable is a formula amount to the extent that the amount payable in a future taxable year is dependent upon factors that, after applying the assumptions and other rules set forth in this section, are not determinable as of the applicable date, such that the amount payable may not be readily determined as of that date under the other provisions of this section. If some portion of an amount payable is not a formula amount, the amount payable with respect to such portion is determined under the rules applicable to amounts that are not formula amounts, and only the balance of the amount payable is determined under the rules applicable to formula amounts.

(vi) *Treatment of payment restrictions.*—The rules in § 1.409A-4(b)(2)(v) apply for purposes of determining the treatment of payment restrictions.

(vii) *Treatment of alternative times and forms of a future payment.*—The rules in § 1.409A-4(b)(2)(vi) apply for purposes of determining the treatment of alternative times and forms of a future payment.

(viii) *Reimbursement and in-kind benefit arrangements.*—The rules in § 1.409A-4(b)(4) apply for purposes of determining the present value of reimbursement and in-kind benefit arrangements.

(ix) *Split-dollar life insurance arrangements.*—The rules in § 1.409A-4(b)(5) apply for purposes of determining the present value of benefits provided under a split-dollar life insurance arrangement.

(2) *Forfeiture or other permanent loss of right to compensation previously included in income.*—(i) *In general.*—If a participant has included compensation under a plan in income pursuant to paragraph (a)(2) or (4) of this section, but all or a portion of that compensation is never paid under the plan, the participant is entitled to a deduction for the taxable year in which the entire remaining right to the payment of the compensation is permanently forfeited under the plan's terms or otherwise permanently lost. The deduction to which the participant is entitled equals the excess of the amounts included in income under paragraphs (a)(2) and (4) of this section with respect to the compensation over the total amount of the compensation actually received that constitutes investment in the contract under paragraph (a)(5) of this section.

(ii) *Forfeiture or permanent loss of right.*—For purposes of this paragraph (c)(2), a mere diminution in the amount payable under the plan due to a deemed investment loss, an actuarial reduction, or any other decrease in the amount deferred under the plan is not treated as a forfeiture or permanent loss of the right if the participant retains the right to any payment under the plan (whether or not such right is subject to a substantial risk of forfeiture as described in paragraph (e) of this section). In addition, an amount payable under a plan is not treated as forfeited or otherwise permanently lost if another amount or an obligation to make a payment in a future year is substituted for the original amount. However, an amount payable under a plan is treated as permanently lost if the participant's right to receive payment of the amount becomes wholly worthless during the taxable year. Whether the right to receive payment has become wholly worthless is determined based on the relevant facts and circumstances existing as of the last day of the relevant taxable year.

(iii) *Examples.*—The provisions of this paragraph (c)(2) are illustrated in the following examples:

Example 1. (i) *Facts.* On October 1, 2017, an eligible employer establishes an ineligible plan for a participant under which the employer agrees to pay the amount credited to the participant's account when the participant has a severance from employment. The obligation to make the payment is not subject to a substantial risk of forfeiture. The account balance on October 1, 2017 is $125,000, and the participant includes $125,000 in income in 2017. The plan subsequently experiences notional investment losses, and the participant receives $75,000 from the plan in a lump-sum distribution in 2024, when the participant has a severance from employment. The $75,000 lump-sum distribution represents all amounts due to the participant under the plan.

(ii) *Conclusion.* For 2024, the participant is entitled to deduct $50,000 (the excess of the amount included in income under paragraph (a)(2) of this section ($125,000) over the amount actually received that constitutes investment in the contract under paragraph (a)(5) of this section ($75,000)).

Example 2. (i) *Facts.* The facts are the same facts as in *Example 1* of this paragraph (c)(2)(iii), except that the plan provides that the participant will receive the deferred compensation in three installments (1/3 of the account balance in 2024, 1/2 of the then remaining account balance in 2025, and the remaining balance in 2026), and that the sum of all three installments is $75,000.

(ii) *Conclusion.* The participant is entitled to deduct $50,000 in the taxable year of the last installment payment (2026) ($125,000, reduced by the sum of the amounts received in 2024, 2025, and 2026 ($75,000)).

(d) *Definition of deferral of compensation.*—(1) *In general.*—(i) *Legally binding right.*—A plan provides for the deferral of compensation with respect to a participant for purposes of section 457(f) and this section if, under the terms of the plan and the relevant facts and circumstances, the participant has a legally binding right during a calendar year to compensation that, pursuant to the terms of the plan, is or may be payable to (or on behalf of) the participant in a later calendar year. Whether a plan provides for the deferral of compensation for purposes of section 457(f) and this section is determined based on the relevant facts and circumstances at the time that the participant obtains a legally binding right to the compensation, or, if later, when a plan is amended to convert a right that does not provide for a deferral of compensation into a right that does provide for a deferral of compensation. For example, if a plan providing for retiree health care does not initially provide for a deferral of compensation but is later amended to provide the ability to receive future cash payments instead of health benefits, it may become a plan that provides for the deferral of compensation at the time of the amendment. An amount of compensation deferred under a plan that provides for the deferral of compensation within the meaning of section 457(f) and this section does not cease to be an amount subject to section 457(f) and this section by reason of any change to the plan that would otherwise recharacterize the right to the amount as a right that does not provide for the deferral of compensation with respect to such amount. In addition, any change under the plan that results in an exchange of an amount deferred under the plan for some other right or benefit that would otherwise be excluded from the participant's gross income does not affect the characterization of the plan as one that provides for a deferral of compensation.

(ii) *Discretion to reduce or eliminate compensation.*—A participant does not have a legally binding right to compensation to the extent that the compensation may be reduced or eliminated unilaterally by the employer or another person after the services creating the right to the compensation have been performed. However, if the facts and circumstances indicate that the discretion to reduce or eliminate the compensation is available or exercisable only upon a condition, or the discretion to reduce or eliminate the compensation lacks substantive significance, a participant is considered to have a legally binding right to the compensation. Whether the discretion to reduce or eliminate compensation lacks substantive significance depends on all the relevant facts and circumstances. However, if the participant to whom the compensation may be paid has effective control of the person retaining the discretion to reduce or eliminate the compensation, or has effective control over any portion of the compensation of the person retaining the discretion to reduce or eliminate the compensation, or is a member of the family (as defined in section 267(c)(4) but also including the spouse of any member of the family) of the person retaining the discretion to reduce or eliminate the compensation, the discretion to reduce or eliminate the compensation is not treated as having substantive significance. Compensation is not considered subject to unilateral reduction or elimination merely because it may be reduced or eliminated by operation of the objective terms of the plan, such as the application of a nondiscretionary, objective provision creating a substantial risk of forfeiture or the application of a formula that provides for benefits to be offset by benefits provided under another plan (such as a plan that is qualified under section 401(a)).

(2) *Short-term deferrals.*—For purposes of section 457(f) and this section, a deferral of compensation does not occur under a plan with respect to any payment for which a deferral of compensation does not occur under section 409A pursuant to § 1.409A-1(b)(4) (short-term deferrals), except that, for purposes of this paragraph, in applying the rules provided in § 1.409A-1(b)(4) the meaning of *substantial risk of forfeiture* under § 1.457-12(e) applies in each place that term is used (and not the meaning of *substantial risk of forfeiture* provided under § 1.409A-1(d)).

(3) *Recurring part-year compensation.*—For purposes of section 457(f) and this section and notwithstanding paragraph (d)(2) of this section, a deferral of compensation does not occur under a plan with respect to an amount that is recurring part-year compensation (as defined in § 1.409A-2(a)(14)), if the plan does not defer payment of any of the recurring part-year compensation to a date beyond the last day of the 13th month following the first day of the service period for which the recurring part-year compensation is paid, and the amount of the recurring part-year compensation does not exceed the annual compensation limit under section 401(a)(17) for the calendar year in which the service period commences.

(4) *Certain other exceptions.*—For purposes of section 457(f) and this section, a deferral of compensation does not occur to the extent that a plan provides for:

(i) The payment of expense reimbursements, medical benefits, or in-kind benefits, as described in § 1.409A-1(b)(9)(v)(A), (B), or (C);

(ii) Certain indemnification rights, liability insurance, or legal settlements, as described in § 1.409A-1(b)(10), or (11); or

(iii) Taxable educational benefits for an employee (which, for this purpose, means solely benefits consisting of educational assistance, as defined in section 127(c)(1) and the regulations thereunder, attributable to the education of an employee, and does not include any benefits provided for the education of any other person, including any spouse, child, or other family member of the employee).

(5) *Interaction with section 409A.*—(i) *In general.*—The rules of section 457(f) apply to an ineligible plan separately and in addition to any requirements applicable to the plan under section 409A.

(ii) *Acceleration of the time or schedule of a payment.*—Although section 457(f) and this section do not preclude the acceleration of payments, see § 1.409A-3(a) for the general rules and exceptions relating to the acceleration of payments that are subject to section 409A.

(iii) *Example.*—The provisions of this paragraph (d)(5) are illustrated in the following example:

Example. (i) *Facts.* On December 1, 2017, an eligible employer establishes an account balance plan for an employee that is subject to section 457(f), under which an initial amount is credited to the account and is increased periodically by earnings based on a reasonable specified rate of interest. The entire account balance is subject to a substantial risk of forfeiture until December 1, 2021. Under the terms of the plan, the account balance will be paid in three annual installments on each January 15, beginning in 2024 (one third of the balance for the first installment, one half of the then remaining balance for the second installment, and the remaining balance for the third installment). However, in 2022, the plan is amended to provide for payments to begin in 2023, such that the plan fails to comply with the requirements of section 409A during 2022. The account balance is: $100,000 on December 1, 2021; $118,000 on December 31, 2022; $120,000 on January 15, 2023 (so that the payment made that day is $40,000 ($120,000/3)); $88,000 on January 15, 2024 (so that the payment made that day is $44,000 ($88,000/2)); and $50,000 on January 15, 2025 (so that the payment made that day is $50,000).

(ii) *Conclusion: Federal income tax treatment in 2021.* The plan provides for a deferral of compensation to which section 457(f) applies. Under section 457(f) and paragraph (a)(2) of this section, the $100,000 amount of the account balance on December 1, 2021, when the benefits cease to be subject to a substantial risk of forfeiture, is included in the employee's gross income on that date.

(iii) *Conclusion: Federal income tax treatment after 2021*—(1) *Treatment in 2022 under section 409A.* Because the arrangement fails to meet the requirements of section 409A in 2022, the employee has gross income under section 409A equal to the account balance on December 31, 2022, reduced by the amount previously included in income. Accordingly, the amount included in gross income under section 409A is equal to $18,000 (the $118,000 account balance on December 31, 2022, reduced by the $100,000 previously included in income under section 457(f) for 2021). The amount included in gross income under section 409A is subject to an additional 20 percent tax under section 409A(a)(1)(B)(i)(II) and a premium interest tax under section 409A(a)(1)(B)(i)(I).

(2) *Federal income tax treatment of first installment payment in 2023*—(i) *Earnings previously included under section 409A.* The first $18,000 of the $40,000 payment in 2023 is excluded from gross income under section 409A as a result of the earlier inclusion of that amount in income in 2022 due to the section 409A violation. See § 1.409A-4(f).

(ii) *Deferral of compensation under section 457(f).* The amount of the investment in the contract (described in paragraph (a)(5) of this section) allocated to the remaining $22,000 of the installment paid in 2023 is $33,333 ($100,000/3), so no amount is included in gross income for 2023.

(3) *Federal income tax treatment of second installment payment in 2024.* The employee has unused investment in the contract from 2023 in the amount of $11,333 ($33,333 - $22,000). Assuming that the employee elects to redetermine the amount recognized for the current and subsequent years in 2024 pursuant to § 1.72-4(d)(3)(ii), the amount included in gross income for 2024 is $5,000 (the payment of $44,000, reduced by the portion of the remaining investment in the contract that is allocable to the installment, which is $39,000 (($100,000 – $22,000)/2)).

(4) *Federal income tax treatment of third installment payment in 2025.* The amount included in gross income for 2025 is $11,000 (the payment of $50,000, reduced by the remaining investment in the contract of $39,000).

(e) *Rules relating to substantial risk of forfeiture.*—(1) *Substantial risk of forfeiture.*—(i) *In general.*—An amount of compensation is subject to a substantial risk of forfeiture only if entitlement to the amount is conditioned on the future performance of substantial services, or upon the occurrence of a condition that is related to a purpose of the compensation if the possibility of forfeiture is substantial. An amount is not subject to a substantial risk of forfeiture if the facts and circumstances demonstrate that the forfeiture condition is unlikely to be enforced (see paragraph (e)(1)(v) of this section). If a plan provides that entitlement to an amount is conditioned on involuntary severance from employment without cause (which includes, for this purpose, a voluntary severance from employment that is treated as involuntary under § 1.457-11(d)(2)(ii)), the right is subject to a substantial risk of forfeiture if the possibility of forfeiture is substantial.

(ii) *Substantial future services.*—For purposes of paragraph (e)(1)(i) of this section, the determination of whether an amount of compensation is conditioned on the future performance of substantial services is based on the relevant facts and circumstances, such as whether the hours required to be performed during the relevant period are substantial in relation to the amount of compensation.

(iii) *Condition related to a purpose of the compensation.*—For purposes of paragraph (e)(1)(i) of this section, a condition related to a purpose of the compensation must relate to the participant's performance of services for the employer or to the employer's government-mental or tax-exempt activities (as applicable) or organizational goals.

(iv) *Noncompetition conditions.*—For purposes of paragraph (e)(1)(i) of this section, an amount of compensation will not be treated as subject to a substantial risk of forfeiture merely because the right to payment of the amount is conditioned, directly or indirectly, upon the employee refraining from the future performance of certain services, unless each of the of the following conditions is satisfied:

(A) The right to payment of the amount is expressly conditioned upon the employee refraining from the future performance of services pursuant to an enforceable written agreement.

(B) The employer makes reasonable ongoing efforts to verify compliance with noncompetition agreements (including the noncompetition agreement applicable to the employee).

(C) At the time that the enforceable written agreement becomes binding, the facts and circumstances demonstrate that the employer has a substantial and bona fide interest in preventing the employee from performing the prohibited services and that the employee has bona fide interest in, and ability to, engage in the prohibited competition. Factors taken into account for this purpose include the employer's ability to show significant adverse economic consequences that would likely result from the prohibited services; the marketability of the employee based on specialized skills, reputation, or other factors; and the employee's interest, financial need, and ability to engage in the prohibited services.

(v) *Enforcement of forfeiture condition.*—To constitute a substantial risk of forfeiture, the possibility of actual forfeiture in the event that the forfeiture condition occurs must be substantial based on the relevant facts and circumstances. Factors to be considered for this purpose include, but are not limited to, the extent to which the employer has enforced forfeiture conditions in the past, the level of control or influence of the employee with respect to the organization and the individual(s) who would be responsible for enforcing the forfeiture condition, and the likelihood that such provisions would be enforceable under applicable law.

(2) *Addition or extension of risk of forfeiture.*—(i) *General rule.*—The initial addition or extension of any risk of forfeiture after a legally binding right to compensation arises, including the application of a risk of forfeiture to a plan providing for deferrals of current compensation (an additional or extended risk of forfeiture), will be disregarded unless the plan meets the requirements of paragraphs (e)(2)(ii) through (v) of this section.

(ii) *Benefit must be materially greater.*—A deferred amount will not be subject to a substantial risk of forfeiture for purposes of section 457 and this section after the date on which an employee could have received the amount, unless the present value of the amount made subject to the additional or extended substantial risk of forfeiture (disregarding the risk of forfeiture in determining the present value of the amount) is materially greater than the present value of the amount the employee otherwise would have received absent the initial or extended risk of forfeiture. For purposes of this paragraph (e)(2)(ii), present value is determined in accordance with the rules described in paragraph (c) of this section as of the applicable date for the amount the employee otherwise would have received absent the initial or extended risk of forfeiture. In addition, an amount is materially greater for purposes of this paragraph (e)(2)(ii) only if the present value of the amount subject to the additional or extended substantial risk of forfeiture is more than 125 percent of the present value of the amount that the employee would have received absent the additional or extended risk of forfeiture. For this purpose, compensation that the participant would receive for continuing to perform services, regardless of whether the deferred amount is subjected to an additional or extended substantial risk of forfeiture, is not taken into account.

(iii) *Minimum two years of substantial future services.*—The employee must be required to perform substantial services in the future, or refrain from competing pursuant to an agreement that meets the requirements of paragraph (e)(1)(iv) of this section, for a minimum of two years after the date that the employee could have received the compensation in the absence of the additional or extended substantial risk of forfeiture. For example, if an employee elects to defer a fixed percentage from each semi-monthly payroll, the two year minimum applies to each semi-monthly payroll amount that would otherwise have been paid. Notwithstanding the two year minimum, a plan may provide that that the substantial future service condition will lapse upon death, disability, or involuntary severance from employment without cause.

(iv) *Timing.*—The parties must agree in writing to any addition or extension of a substantial risk of forfeiture under this paragraph (e)(2). In the case of an initial addition of a substantial risk of forfeiture if none previously existed (for example, in the case of a deferral of current compensation), this written agreement must be entered into before the beginning of the calendar year in which any services that give rise to the compensation are performed, and, in the case of an extension of a substantial risk of forfeiture, the written agreement must be entered into at least 90 days before an existing substantial risk of forfeiture would have lapsed. If an employee with respect to whom compensation is made subject to an initial or extended substantial risk of forfeiture was not providing services to the employer at least 90 days before the addition or extension, the addition or extension may be agreed to in writing within 30 days after commencement of employment but only with respect to amounts attributable to services rendered after the addition or extension is agreed to in writing.

(v) *Substitutions.*—For purposes of paragraph (e)(2) of this section, if an amount is forfeited or relinquished and replaced, in whole or part, with a right to another amount (or benefit) that is a substitute for the amount that was forfeited or relinquished and that is subject to a risk of forfeiture, the risk of forfeiture will be disregarded unless the requirements of paragraphs (e)(2)(ii) through (iv) of this section are satisfied.

(3) *Examples.*—The provisions of this paragraph (e) are illustrated in the following examples:

Example 1. (i) *Facts.* On January 15, 2017, an employee has a severance from employment with an eligible employer and enters into an agreement with the eligible employer under which the eligible employer agrees to pay the employee $250,000 on January 15, 2018, if the employee provides consulting services to the employer until that date. The consulting services required are insubstantial in relation to the payment. The employee provides the required consulting services for the employer through January 15, 2018.

(ii) *Conclusion.* The consulting services provided by the former employee do not constitute substantial services because they are insubstantial in relation to the payment. Accordingly, the present value of $250,000 payable on January 15, 2018 is includible in the employee's gross income on January 15, 2017.

Example 2. (i) *Facts.* On January 27, 2020, an eligible employer agrees to pay an employee an amount equal to $120,000 on January 1, 2023, provided that the employee continues to provide substantial services to the employer through that date. In 2021, the parties enter into a written agreement to extend the date through which substantial services must be performed to January 1, 2025, in which event, the employer will pay an amount that has a present value of $145,000 on January 1, 2023.

(ii) *Conclusion.* As of the date the initial risk of forfeiture would have lapsed, the present value of the compensation subject to the extended substantial risk of forfeiture is not materially greater than the present value of the amount previously deferred under the plan ($145,000 is not more than 125% of $120,000) and, therefore, the intended extension of the substantial risk of forfeiture is disregarded under the provisions of paragraph (e)(2) of this section. Accordingly, the employee will recognize income, on the applicable date (January 1, 2023) in an amount equal to $120,000 (the amount that is not subject to a substantial risk of forfeiture on that date, disregarding the intended extension). With respect to the amount that is ultimately paid under the plan on January 1, 2025, the employee is treated as having investment in the contract of $120,000 (pursuant to paragraph (a)(5) of this section).

Example 3. (i) *Facts.* On December 31, 2017, a participant enters into an agreement to defer $15,000 of the participant's current compensation that would otherwise be paid during 2018, with payment of the deferred amounts to be made on December 31, 2024, but only if the participant continues to provide substantial services until December 31, 2024. Under the terms of the agreement, the participant's periodic payments of current compensation are reduced, and a corresponding amount is credited (with a 30% employer match) to an account earning a reasonable rate of interest. The present value of the amount payable on December 31, 2024 is 130% of the present value of the amount deferred.

(ii) *Conclusion.* The amounts deferred are subject to a substantial risk of forfeiture because the plan satisfies the requirements of paragraphs (e)(2)(ii) through (v) of this section.

Example 4. (i) *Facts.* Employee A is a well-known college sports coach with a long history of success in a sports program at University X. University X reasonably expects that the loss of Employee A would be substantially detrimental to its sports program and would result in significant financial losses. Employee A has bona fide interest in continuing to work as a college sports coach and is highly marketable. On June 1, 2020, Employee A and University X enter into a written agreement under which Employee A agrees to provide substantial services to University X until June 1, 2023. The parties further agree that University X will pay $500,000 to Employee A on June 1, 2025 if Employee A has not performed services as a sports coach before that date for any other college or university with a sports program similar to that of University X. The agreement is enforceable under applicable law and University X would be reasonably expected to enforce it.

Pars. 9 and 12. Redesignate § 1.457-12 as § 1.457-13 and revise newly-redesignated § 1.457-13 to read as follows:

§1.457-13. Applicability dates.—(a) *General applicability date.*—Except as otherwise provided in paragraph (b) of this section, § § 1.457-1 through 1.457-12 apply to compensation deferred under a plan for calendar years beginning after the date of publication of the Treasury decision adopting these rules as final regulations in the **Federal Register,** including deferred amounts to which the legally binding right arose during prior calendar years that were not previously included in income during one or more prior calendar years.

(b) *Special applicability dates.*—(1) *Plans maintained pursuant to collective bargaining agreements.*—In the case of a plan maintained pursuant to one or more collective bargaining agreements that have been ratified and are in effect on the date of publication of the Treasury decision adopting these rules as final regulations in the **Federal Register,** these regulations will not apply with respect to compensation deferred under the plan before the earlier of:

(ii) *Conclusion.* The $500,000 payable under the agreement is subject to a substantial risk of forfeiture until June 1, 2025, and includible in Employee A's gross income on that date

(i) The date on which the last of the collective bargaining agreements terminates (determined without regard to any extension thereof after the date of publication of the Treasury decision adopting these rules as final regulations in the **Federal Register**); or

(ii) The first day of the third calendar year beginning after the date of publication of the Treasury decision adopting these rules as final regulations in the **Federal Register**.

(2) *Governmental plans.*—If legislation is required to amend a governmental plan, these regulations will not apply to compensation deferred under that plan in taxable years ending before the day following the end of the second legislative session of the legislative body with the authority to amend the plan that begins after the date of publication of the Treasury decision adopting these rules as final regulations in the **Federal Register**.

Long-Term Contracts: Home Construction Contracts: Rules

Long-Term Contracts: Home Construction Contracts: Rules.—Amendments to Reg. § §1.460-3, 1.460-4, 1.460-5 and 1.460-6, regarding accounting for certain long-term construction contracts that qualify as home construction contracts, are proposed (published in the Federal Register on August 4, 2008) (REG-120844-07).

Par. 2. Section 1.460-3 is amended by:
1. Revising paragraph (b)(1)(ii).
2. Redesignating paragraphs (b)(2)(ii), (b)(2)(iii) and (b)(2)(iv) as paragraphs (b)(2)(iii), (b)(2)(iv) and (b)(2)(v), respectively, and revising them.
3. Adding a new paragraph (b)(2)(ii).
The revisions and addition read as follows:

§1.460-3. Long-term construction contracts.

* * *

(b) * * *

(1) * * *

(ii) Construction contract, other than a home construction contract, that a taxpayer estimates (when entering into the contract) will be completed within 2 years of the contract commencement date, provided the taxpayer satisfies the $10,000,000 gross receipts test described in paragraph (b)(3) of this section.

(2) * * *

(ii) *Land improvements.*—For purposes of paragraph (b)(2)(i)(B) of this section, improvements to real property directly related to, and located on the site of, the dwelling units consist of improvements to land on which dwelling units (as described in paragraph (b)(2)(i)(A) of this section) are constructed, and common improvements as defined in paragraph (b)(2)(iv) of this section. A long-term construction contract is a home construction contract if a taxpayer (including a subcontractor working for a general contractor) meets the 80% test in paragraph (b)(2)(i) of this section as applied to either paragraph (b)(2)(i)(A) of this section or paragraph (b)(2)(i)(B) of this section, or both paragraphs (b)(2)(i)(A) and (b)(2)(i)(B) of this section, collectively.

(iii) *Townhouses and rowhouses.*—For purposes of determining whether a long-term construction contract is a home construction contract under paragraph (b)(2) of this section, each townhouse or

rowhouse is a separate building. For this purpose, the term townhouse and rowhouse includes an individual condominium unit.

(iv) *Common improvements.*—(A) *In general.*—A taxpayer includes in the cost of a dwelling unit or land its allocable share of the cost that the taxpayer incurs for any common improvements that benefit the dwelling unit or land.

(B) *Definition.*—For purposes of this section, a *common improvement* is an improvement that the taxpayer is contractually obligated, or required by law, to construct within the tract or tracts of land containing the dwelling units (or the land on which dwelling units are to be constructed) and that benefits the dwelling units (or the land on which dwelling units are to be constructed). In general, a common improvement does not solely benefit any particular dwelling unit or any particular lot on which a dwelling unit is constructed. However, land clearing and grading are common improvements, even when performed on a particular lot. Other examples of common improvements are sidewalks, sewers, roads and clubhouses.

(v) *Mixed use costs.*—If a contract involves the construction of both commercial units and dwelling units, a taxpayer must allocate the costs among the commercial units and dwelling units using a reasonable method or combination of reasonable methods. In general, the reasonableness of an allocation method will be based on facts and circumstances. Examples of methods that may be reasonable are specific identification, square footage, or fair market value.

* * *

Par. 3. Section 1.460-4 is amended by:
1. Revising the third sentence in paragraph (c)(1).
2. Redesignating paragraph (g) as paragraph (g)(1) and revising newly redesignated paragraph (g)(1).
3. Adding a paragraph (g)(2).
4. Revising *Example 5.* of paragraph (h).
The revisions and additions read as follows:

§1.460-4. Methods of accounting for long-term contracts.

* * *

(c) * * *

(1) * * * Permissible exempt contract methods are the PCM, the EPCM described in paragraph (c)(2) of this section, the CCM described in paragraph (d) of this section, the accrual method, and any other permissible method. * * *

* * *

(g) *Method of accounting.*—(1) *In general.*—A taxpayer must apply its method(s) of accounting for long-term contracts consistently for all similarly classified long-term contracts until the taxpayer obtains the Commissioner's consent under section 446(e) to change to another method of accounting.

(2) *Taxpayer-initiated change in method of accounting.*—(i) *Change to PCM for long-term contracts for which PCM is required.*—A taxpayer-initiated change in method of accounting for long-term contracts (or portion thereof) for which income must be determined using the PCM described in paragraph (b) of this section and the costs allocation rules described in § 1.460-5(b) or (c) (required PCM contracts) from a method of accounting that does not comply with paragraph (b) of this section and § 1.460-5(b) or (c) to a method that complies with paragraph (b) of this section and § 1.460-5(b) or (c) must be applied to all required PCM contracts entered into before the year of change and not reported as completed as of the beginning of the year of change. Accordingly, a section 481(a) adjustment will be required.

(ii) *Change from a permissible PCM method to another permissible PCM method for long-term contracts for which PCM is required.*—A taxpayer initiated change in method of accounting for required PCM contracts, as defined in paragraph (g)(2)(i) of this section (or a portion thereof), from a method of accounting that complies with paragraph (b) of this section and §1.460-5(b) or (c) to another method of accounting that complies with paragraph (b) of this section and §1.460-5(b) or (c) must be made on a cut-off basis and applied only to contracts entered into during and after the year of change. Accordingly, a section 481(a) adjustment will be neither permitted nor required.

(iii) *Change to an exempt contract method for home construction contracts.*—A taxpayer-initiated change in method of accounting for home construction contracts, as defined in §1.460-3(b)(2), to a permissible exempt contract method, as described in paragraph (c)(1) of this section, must be applied to all home construction contracts entered into before the year of change and not reported as completed as of the beginning of the year of change. Accordingly, a section 481(a) adjustment will be required.

(iv) *Change to an exempt contract method for exempt contracts other than home construction contracts.*—A taxpayer-initiated change in method of accounting for long-term contracts (or portion thereof) not described in paragraphs (g)(2)(i), (ii) and (iii) of this section to a permissible exempt contract method as described in paragraph (c)(1) of this section must be applied to all contracts that are eligible to use the exempt contract method entered into before the year of change

Par. 4. Section 1.460-5 is amended by:
1. Adding a new sentence to the end of paragraph (c)(2).
2. Revising paragraph (g).
The revision and addition read as follows:

§1.460-5. Cost allocation rules.

* * *

(c) * * *

(2) * * * Further, this election is not available if a taxpayer is changing from a cost allocation method other than as prescribed in paragraph (b) of this section, in which case the taxpayer must follow the procedures under §1.446-1(e) for obtaining the Commissioner's consent for the change in method of accounting.

* * *

(g) *Method of accounting.*—A taxpayer that adopts, elects, or otherwise changes to a cost allocation method of accounting (or changes to another cost allocation method of accounting with the Commissioner's consent) must apply that method consistently for all

Par. 5. Section 1.460-6 is amended by:
1. Adding paragraph (c)(3)(vii).
2. Redesignating paragraph (d)(2)(iv) as paragraph (d)(2)(v).
3. Adding a new paragraph (d)(2)(iv).
The additions and revision read as follows:

§1.460-6. Look-back method.

* * *

(c) * * *

(3) * * *

(vii) *Section 481(a) adjustments.*—For purposes of determining the hypothetical underpayment or overpayment of tax for any year, amounts reported as section 481(a) adjustments shall be taken into account in the tax year or years they are reported. However, any portion of a section 481(a) adjustment not yet reported as of the tax year in which the contract is completed shall be taken into account in the tax year the contract is completed for purposes of determining the hypothetical underpayment or overpayment of tax.

and not reported as completed as of the beginning of the year of change. Accordingly, a section 481(a) adjustment will be required.

(h) * * *

* * *

Example 5. PCM—contract terminated. C, whose taxable year ends December 31, determines the income from long-term contracts using the PCM. During 2001, C buys land and begins constructing a building that will contain 50 apartment units on that land. C enters into a contract to sell the building to B for $2,400,000. B gives C a $50,000 deposit toward the purchase price. By the end of 2001, C has incurred $500,000 of allocable contract costs on the building and estimates that the total allocable contract costs on the building will be $1,500,000. Thus, for 2001, C reports gross receipts of $800,000 ($500,000 / $1,500,000 × $2,400,000), current-year costs of $500,000, and gross income of $300,000 ($800,000 – $500,000). In 2002, after C has incurred an additional $250,000 of allocable contract costs on the building, B files for bankruptcy protection and defaults on the contract with C, who is permitted to keep B's $50,000 deposit as liquidated damages. In 2002, C reverses the transaction with B under paragraph (b)(7) of this section and reports a loss of $300,000 ($500,000 – $800,000). In addition, C obtains an adjusted basis in the building sold to B of $700,000 ($500,000 (current-year costs deducted in 2001) – $50,000 (B's forfeited deposit) + $250,000 (current-year costs incurred in 2002). C may not apply the look-back method to this contract in 2002.

* * *

similarly classified contracts, until the taxpayer obtains the Commissioner's consent under section 446 to change to another cost allocation method. A taxpayer-initiated change in cost allocation method from a method that does not comply with the cost allocation rules of this section to a method that complies with the cost allocation rules of this section must be applied to all long-term contracts to which the rules of this section apply, including contracts entered into before the year of change and not reported as completed as of the beginning of the year of change. Accordingly, a section 481(a) adjustment is required. Any other taxpayer-initiated change in cost allocation method to a method permitted under the rules of this section must be made on a cut-off basis and applied only to contracts entered into during and after the year of change, in which case a section 481(a) adjustment will be neither permitted nor required.

* * *

(d) * * *

(2) * * *

(iv) *Section 481(a) adjustments.*—For purposes of determining the hypothetical underpayment or overpayment of tax for any year under the simplified marginal impact method, amounts reported as section 481(a) adjustments shall be taken into account in the tax year or years they are reported. However, any portion of a section 481(a) adjustment not yet reported as of the tax year in which the contract is completed shall be taken into account in the tax year the contract is completed for purposes of determining the hypothetical underpayment or overpayment of tax.

* * *

Deduction Limited to Amount at Risk

Deduction Limited to Amount at Risk.—Reproduced below are the texts of proposed Reg. §§1.465-1—1.465-7, 1.465-9—1.465-13 and 1.465-22—1.465-26, relating to the determination of amounts at risk with respect to certain activities (published in the Federal Register on June 5, 1979). Proposed Reg. §§1.465-8 and 1.465-20 were adopted by T.D. 9124 on April 30, 2004.

§1.465-1. General rules; limitation of deductions to amount at risk.—(a) *In general.*—For taxable years beginning after December 31, 1975, section 465 generally limits the amount of any loss described in section 465(d) that is otherwise deductible in connection with an activity described in section 465(c)(1). Under section 465 the amount of the loss is allowed as a deduction only to the extent that the taxpayer is at risk with respect to the activity at the close of the taxable year. The determination of the amount the taxpayer is at risk in cases where the activity is engaged in by an entity separate from the taxpayer is made as of the close of the taxable year of the entity

engaging in the activity (for example, a partnership). For the purposes of these regulations, in cases where the activity is engaged in by an entity separate from the taxpayer references to a taxable year shall apply to the taxable year of the entity unless otherwise stated. For rules determining the amount at risk and for more specific rules regarding the effective dates, see §§1.465-20 through 1.465-25 and 1.465-95.

(b) *Substance over form.*—In applying section 465 and these regulations, substance will prevail over form. Regardless of the form a transaction may take, the taxpayer's amount at risk will not be increased if the transaction is inconsistent with normal commercial practices or is, in essence, a device to avoid section 465. See § 1.465-4 for rules regarding attempts to avoid the at risk provisions.

(c) *Activities.*—See sections 465(c)(1)(A) through (D) and §§ 1.465-42 through 1.465-45 for the activities to which section 465 applies for taxable years beginning generally after December 31, 1975. These activities are holding, producing, or distributing movies and video tapes, farming, leasing of personal property, and exploring for or exploiting oil and gas resources. See section 465(c)(3) and section 465(c)(1)(E) for additional activities to which section 465 applies for taxable years beginning generally after December 31, 1978.

(d) *Taxpayers affected by at risk provisions.*—(1) For taxable years beginning generally after December 31, 1975, section 465 applies to all noncorporate taxpayers, to electing small business corporations (as defined in section 1371(b)), and to personal holding companies (as defined in section 542). For special rules relating to electing small business corporations, see § 1.465-10.

(2) See section 465(a)(1)(C) for additional taxpayers to whom section 465 applies for taxable years beginning generally after December 31, 1978.

(e) *Basis.*—The provisions of section 465 and the regulations thereunder are only intended to limit the extent to which certain losses in connection with covered activities may be deducted in a given year by a taxpayer. Section 465 does not apply for other purposes, such as determining adjusted basis. Thus, for example, the adjusted basis of a partner in a partnership interest is not affected by section 465. [Reg. § 1.465-1.]

§ 1.465-2. General rules; allowance of deductions.—(a) *In general.*—In any taxable year, there are two ways in which deductions allocable to an activity to which section 465 applies will be allowable under section 465. First, deductions allocable to an activity and otherwise allowable will be allowable in a taxable year to the extent of income received or accrued from the activity in that taxable year. See the example at § 1.465-11(c)(2). Thus, to the extent there is income from the activity in a taxable year, deductions allocable to that activity will be allowable without regard to the amount at risk. Second, losses from the activity (that is, the excess of deductions allocable to the activity over the income received or accrued from the activity) will be allowable to the extent the taxpayer is at risk with respect to that activity at the close of the taxable year. See the example at § 1.465-11(a)(2). Also see §§ 1.465-11 through 1.465-13 for the definition of loss.

(b) *Carryover of loss.*—A loss which is disallowed by reason of section 465(a) shall be treated as a deduction for the succeeding taxable year with respect to the same activity to which it is allocable. In the succeeding taxable year there will again be two ways for the deduction to be allowable. There is no limit to the number of years to which a taxpayer may carry over a loss disallowed solely by reason of section 465(a). [Reg. § 1.465-2.]

§ 1.465-3. General rules; amount at risk below zero.—(a) *Loss deductions.*—The amount of loss which is allowed for a taxable year cannot reduce a taxpayer's amount at risk below zero. Otherwise allowable losses for a taxable year which exceed a taxpayer's amount at risk shall be treated in accordance with § 1.465-2.

(b) *Negative at risk.*—A taxpayer's amount at risk may be reduced below zero. For example, if a taxpayer's amount at risk in an activity is $100 and if $120 is distributed to the taxpayer from the activity, (or if a $120 recourse loan is converted to nonrecourse), the taxpayer's amount at risk is reduced to negative $20. In that event for the taxpayer to restore the amount the taxpayer is at risk in the activity to zero, the amount at risk must be increased by $20. Thus, in such a case if in the succeeding taxable year the taxpayer incurs a loss described in section 465(d) of $40, the amount at risk must be increased by $60 ($40 + $20) in order for the full $40 to be allowed under section 465.

(c) *Recapture of certain loss deductions.*—For taxable years beginning after December 31, 1978 see section 465(e) for rules relating to the recapture of certain loss deductions. [Reg. § 1.465-3.]

§ 1.465-4. General rules; rules regarding attempts to avoid the at risk provisions.—(a) *General rule.*—If a taxpayer engages in a pattern of conduct which is not within normal commercial practice or has the effect of avoiding the provisions of section 465, the taxpayer's amount at risk may be adjusted to reflect more accurately the amount which is actually at risk. For example, increases in the amount at risk occurring toward the close of a taxable year which have the effect of increasing the amount of losses which will be allowed to the taxpayer under section 465 for the taxable year will be examined closely. If, considering all the facts and circumstances, it appears that the event

which increases the amount at risk at the close of the taxable year will be accompanied by an event which decreases the amount at risk after the close of the taxable year, these amounts will be disregarded in determining the amount at risk unless the taxpayer can establish—

(1) The existence of a valid business purpose for increasing and then decreasing the amount at risk; and

(2) That the increases and decreases are not a device for avoiding section 465.

(b) *Facts and circumstances.*—The facts and circumstances to be considered include—

(1) The length of time between the increase and decrease in the amount at risk;

(2) The nature of the activity and deviations from normal business practice in the conduct of that activity;

(3) The use of those amounts which increased the amount at risk toward the close of the taxable year;

(4) Contractual arrangements between parties to the activity; and

(5) The occurrence of unanticipated events which make the decrease in the amount at risk necessary. [Reg. § 1.465-4.]

§ 1.465-5. General rules; recourse liabilities which become nonrecourse upon the occurrence of an event.—In the case of liabilities which are recourse for a period of time and then after the occurrence of an event or lapse of a period of time become nonrecourse, a taxpayer shall be considered at risk during the period of recourse liability if—

(a) On the basis of all the facts and circumstances, the reasons for entering into such a borrowing arrangement are primarily business motivated and not primarily related to Federal income tax consequences; and

(b) Such a borrowing arrangement is consistent with the normal commercial practice of financing the activity for which the money is being borrowed. [Reg. § 1.465-5.]

§ 1.465-6. General rules; amounts protected against loss.—(a) *In general.*—Notwithstanding any other provision in any regulation under section 465, assets of a taxpayer (including money) contributed to an activity shall not be treated as increasing the taxpayer's amount at risk to the extent the taxpayer is protected against loss of such assets. In addition, amounts borrowed by a taxpayer shall not be considered at risk to the extent the taxpayer is protected against loss of the borrowed amount. Similarly, such amounts shall not be considered at risk if the taxpayer is protected against loss of the property pledged as security and the taxpayer is not personally liable for repayment.

(b) *Contributions from other partners.*—A partner shall not be at risk with respect to any partnership liability to the extent the partner would be entitled to contributions from other partners if the partner were called upon to pay the partnership's creditor, because to that extent the partner is protected against loss. See § 1.465-24(a)(2)(ii) for an example relating to the treatment of contributions by partners.

(c) *Contingent liabilities.*—If a taxpayer is liable for repayment of an amount borrowed only upon the occurrence of a contingency, the taxpayer shall not be considered at risk with respect to such amount if the likelihood of the contingency occurring is such that the taxpayer is effectively protected against loss. Conversely, the taxpayer will be considered at risk if the likelihood of the contingency occurring is such that the taxpayer is not effectively protected against loss, or if the protection against loss does not cover all likely possibilities. For example, a taxpayer who obtains casualty insurance or insurance protection against tort liability will not ordinarily be considered "not at risk" solely because of such hazard insurance protection.

(d) *Guarantors.*—If a taxpayer guarantees repayment of an amount borrowed by another person (primary obligor) for use in an activity, the guarantee shall not increase the taxpayer's amount at risk. If the taxpayer repays to the creditor the amount borrowed by the primary obligor, the taxpayer's amount at risk shall be increased at such time as the taxpayer has no remaining legal rights against the primary obligor.

(e) *Examples.*—The provisions of this section may be illustrated by the following examples:

Example (1). A, an individual, borrows $6,000 from a bank for use in an activity described in section 465(c)(1). A is not personally liable for repayment of the loan but instead pledges as security assets not used in the activity with a net fair market value of $6,000. However B, a third party, guarantees A that A's entire loss from the activity will be repaid to A by B. Since A is protected against loss on the loan, A's amount at risk is not increased as a result of the entire transaction.

Example (2). Assume the same facts as in example (1) except that B, instead of guaranteeing A's entire loss from the activity, guarantees A against loss of A's security in excess of $2,000. Accordingly, A is considered as having pledged as security assets with a net fair market value of $2,000. Under §1.465-25(a)(1), A's amount at risk is increased by $2,000.

Example (3). C, an individual, is engaged in the activity of farming. C borrows $10,000 for use on the farm from an unrelated third party. As security C pledges future crops. Under the general terms of the loan agreement, C is not personally liable for repayment of the $10,000. There is, however, one exception to this general provision. C will be personally liable if the crops are destroyed as the result of flooding. While drought is a constant concern for farmers in the area, flooding is not. Accordingly, although C is personally liable in the event of flooding, C's amount at risk will not be increased unless flooding actually occurs and destroys the crops, because the likelihood of flooding is such that C is effectively protected against loss. If the contingency does occur, C's amount at risk is increased at the end of the year in which it occurs.

Example (4). D, an individual calendar year taxpayer, is engaged in the activity or producing motion picture films. In 1979 D borrows $100,000 for use in the activity from E, the promoter. D is personally liable for repayment of the loan. E has neither a capital interest in the activity nor an interest in the net profits of the activity. Therefore, E is not considered a person with an interest in the activity other than that of a creditor. See §1.465-8(b). However, E agrees to protect D against loss of up to the first $40,000 of losses from the activity. Thus, under the agreement D will not bear the economic burden of any loss until the total losses exceed $40,000. All of the losses in excess of $40,000 will be borne by D. As a result of this protection-against-loss agreement, the $100,000 borrowed for use in the activity will increase D's amount at risk by $60,000. At the close of 1979, D's losses from the activity amount to $70,000. However, because D's amount at risk is only $60,000, D will only be permitted to deduct $60,000. The remaining $10,000 of deductions shall be treated in accordance with §1.465-2(b). [Reg. §1.465-6.]

§1.465-7. General rules; amounts loaned to the activity by the taxpayer.—(a) *Partners.*—The amount at risk in an activity of a partner who lends the partnership money for use in the activity shall be increased by the amount by which that partner's basis in the partnership is increased under §1.752-1(e) due to the incurrence by the partnership of that liability. The amount at risk of any other partners shall not be increased as a result of the loan.

(b) *Shareholders of electing small business corporations.*—For rules relating to amounts loaned by a shareholder to an electing small business corporation, see §1.465-10(c).

(c) *Special rules.*—For special rules relating to amounts borrowed from persons with an interest in the activity other than that of creditor and amounts borrowed from persons with a special relationship to the taxpayer, see section 465(b)(3) and §§1.465-8 and 1.465-20. [Reg. §1.465-7.]

§1.465-9. General rules; rules of construction.—(a) *Amounts protected against loss.*—Section 465(b)(4) and §1.465-6 provide special rules relating to amounts protected against loss which override the other rules contained in section 465. Where the regulations under section 465 refer to cash or property contributed to an activity and amounts borrowed for use in an activity, it may be assumed that such cash, property, or amounts are not protected against loss under section 465(b)(4) unless expressly provided otherwise.

(b) *Amounts borrowed for use in an activity.*—Section 465(b)(3) and §1.465-20 contain special rules relating to treatment of amounts borrowed from certain persons. Where the regulations under section 465 refer to amounts borrowed for use in an activity, it may be assumed that such amounts are borrowed neither from a person with an interest (other than an interest as a creditor) in the activity nor from a person who has a special relationship to the taxpayer specified within any one of the paragraphs of section 267(b), unless expressly provided otherwise.

(c) *Use of the term "activity".*—For the purposes of the regulations under section 465, unless expressly provided otherwise, use of the term "activity" shall refer to an activity which is described in section 465(c)(1).

(d) *Single activity.*—For the purposes of the regulations under section 465, unless otherwise stated, it is assumed that an entity conducting an activity is engaged only in that one activity.

(e) *Double counting of additions and reductions to amount at risk.*—An amount, or portion of an amount (which is contributed, borrowed, etc.), can only increase or decrease a taxpayer's amount at risk one time. Thus, if a portion of an amount increases a taxpayer's amount at risk under more than one section of the regulations, that portion can increase the taxpayer's amount at risk in the activity only once.

(f) *Personal funds or personal assets.*—For the purposes of the regulations under section 465, unless otherwise stated, the terms "personal funds" and "personal assets" of a taxpayer refer to funds and assets which—

(1) Are owned by the taxpayer;

(2) Are not acquired through borrowing; and

(3) Have a basis equal to their fair market value.

(g) *Foreclosure.*—If a foreclosure occurs within an activity, it will be treated as a disposition of the asset which is the subject of the foreclosure. For rules relating to dispositions, see §1.465-66. [Reg. §1.465-9.]

§1.465-10. General rules; rules relating to subchapter S corporations and their shareholders.—(a) *In general.*—In the case of electing small business corporations (as defined in section 1371(b)) the at risk rules of section 465 apply at both the corporate level and the shareholder level. Therefore, losses from an activity can be deducted by the corporation only to the extent that the corporation is at risk in the activity. In addition, each shareholder will be allowed a loss in the activity only to the extent that the shareholder is at risk in the activity.

(b) *Determination of corporation's amount at risk.*—(1) *General rule.*—Except as provided in paragraph (b)(2) of this section, an electing small business corporation's amount at risk in an activity is determined in the same manner as that of any other taxpayer.

(2) *Special rule for certain borrowed amounts.*—Amounts borrowed by an electing small business corporation from one or more of its shareholders may increase the corporation's amount at risk, notwithstanding the fact that the shareholders have an interest in the activity other than that of a creditor.

(c) *Determination of shareholder's amount at risk.*—The amount at risk of a shareholder of an electing small business corporation (as described in section 1371(b)) shall be adjusted to reflect any increase or decrease in the adjusted basis of any indebtedness of the corporation to the shareholder described in section 1374(c)(2)(B).

(d) *Example.*—The provisions of this section may be illustrated by the following example:

Example. A is the single shareholder in X, an electing small business corporation engaged in an activity described in section 465(c)(1). A contributed $50,000 to X in exchange for its stock under section 351. In addition, A borrowed $40,000 for which A assumed personal liability A then loaned the entire amount to X for use in the activity. During its taxable year, X had a net operating loss of $75,000. At the close of the taxable year (without reduction for any losses of X) A's amount at risk is $90,000 ($50,000 + $40,000). However, it is also necessary to determine X's amount at risk in the activity. X is also at risk for the $40,000 borrowed from A and expended in the activity. Therefore, X's amount at risk in the activity is $90,000 ($50,000 + $40,000). Because X's amount at risk in the activity ($90,000) exceeds the net operating loss ($75,000), the entire loss is allowed to the corporation and allocated to A. Since A's amount at risk ($90,000) also exceeds the loss ($75,000) A will be allowed the entire loss deduction. [Reg. §1.465-10.]

§1.465-11. Definition of loss; in general.—(a) *In general.*—(1) *Loss.*—A taxpayer has a loss described in section 465(d) in a taxable year in an amount equal to the excess of allowable deductions allocable to an activity over the income received or accrued from the activity by the taxpayer for the taxable year. Such loss is referred to as a section 465(d) loss in the regulations under section 465. See §1.465-13 for the definition of allowable deductions allocable to an activity and §1.465-12 for a definition of income from the activity.

(2) *Example.*—The application of this paragraph may be illustrated by the following example:

Example. In 1977 B, a calendar year individual, contributes $15,000 to an activity described in section 465(c)(1). During 1977 B has income of $20,000 from the activity and has allowable deductions of $45,000 from the activity. From this $45,000 of allowable deductions, B must first take a deduction of $20,000 to reflect the income received by B from the activity in 1977. The remaining $25,000 ($45,000 – $20,000) is B's section 465(d) loss. Assuming B's amount at risk in the activity is $15,000 at the close of 1977, B is also allowed to deduct $15,000 of the $25,000 section 465(d) loss for 1977. The remaining $10,000 ($25,000 – $15,000) of the section 465(d) loss which is not allowed as a deduction for 1977 will be treated as a deduction allocable to the activity for 1978.

(b) *Carryover loss.*—For the carryover of losses disallowed by section 465, see §1.465-2(b).

(c) *Loss with no amount at risk.*—(1) *In general.*—A section 465(d) loss is determined without regard to the amount at risk. Thus, even if the taxpayer has no amount at risk in the activity, deductions are allowable under section 465 for a taxable year to the extent there is income from the activity in that taxable year.

(2) *Example.*—The provisions of this paragraph may be illustrated by the following example:

Example. Before taking into account any gain or loss during 1978, the amount that C, a calendar year taxpayer, is at risk in an activity described in section 465(c)(1) is equal to minus $20,000. During 1978 C has deductions of $10,000 allocable to the activity and income of $15,000 from the activity. Because the income from the activity exceeds the amount of allocable deductions from the activity, there is no section 465(d) loss in 1978 to be disallowed under section 465(a). Thus, although C has a negative amount at risk, C is permitted to take deductions in the amount of $10,000 for 1978. [Reg. § 1.465-11.]

§1.465-12. Definition of loss; income from the activity.—(a) *In general.*—Income received or accrued from an activity includes gain recognized upon the disposition of the activity or an interest in the activity in accordance with §1.465-66. For the purposes of this section and the determinations made under section 465(d), the character of any gain is irrelevant. Thus, all short-term capital gains and long-term capital gains attributable to the activity shall be included as income from the activity. For more rules relating to income from an activity see §§1.465-42 through 1.465-45.

(b) *Example.*—The provisions of this section may be illustrated by the following example:

Example. On February 1, 1977, A, an individual on a calendar year, purchases a piece of equipment to be used in an activity described in section 465(c)(1)(C). A bought the equipment for $50,000, paying $5,000 from personal assets and borrowing $45,000 from a bank on a nonrecourse basis secured only by the newly purchased equipment. On February 1, 1977, A has a basis in the activity of $50,000 and an initial amount at risk of $5,000. At the close of 1977 after the application of section 465, A's basis has been reduced to $35,000, A's amount at risk has been reduced to zero, and A has a loss of $10,000 disallowed by reason of section 465(a). In 1978, the bank forecloses on the equipment when it is still encumbered by the $45,000 loan. Assuming there were no other transactions relating to this activity, A recognizes a $10,000 gain ($45,000 – $35,000) on this disposition. For purposes of section 465(d), this $10,000 of gain is income from the activity, and the $10,000 of disallowed loss in 1977 is treated as a deduction for 1978. Since the income from the activity for 1978 ($10,000) is equal to the deductions attributable to the activity for 1978 ($10,000), there is no section 465(d) loss for 1978. Therefore, the $10,000 of gain is included in the gross income in 1978 and the $10,000 of disallowed loss is allowed as a deduction for 1978. [Reg. § 1.465-12.]

§1.465-13. Definition of loss; deductions from the activity.—(a) *General rule.*—For the purposes of section 465 allowable deductions allocable to an activity are those otherwise allowable deductions incurred in a trade or business or for the production of income from the activity. For the purposes of this section capital losses shall be treated as deductions without regard to section 1211. See § 1.465-38 for rules relating to the order in which deductions are to be allowed and §1.465-2(b) for the treatment of loss deductions which are disallowed by section 465.

(b) *Capital gain.*—(1) *In general.*—For the purposes of section 465 the deduction for capital gains provided for in section 1202 shall not be treated as a deduction allocable to an activity. Therefore, the capital gain deduction described in section 1202 will not be subject to the limitations of section 465(a) and has no effect on the amount at risk.

(2) *Example.*—The provision of paragraph (b)(1) of this section may be illustrated by the following example:

Example. At the close of 1976 A, an individual and a calendar year taxpayer, has $1,000 of section 465(d) losses disallowed under section 465(a) for an activity described in section 465(c)(1). Before A has any other deductions allocable to the activity, A sells the entire activity, realizing $1,900 of long term capital gain. For 1977 A is allowed a deduction of $950 under section 1202. Other than the disallowed loss of $1,000 and the section 1202 deduction, A has no other deductions. In accordance with §1.465-66 A has received $1,900 income from the activity. Since the $950 deduction under section 1202 is not allocable to the activity, the only deduction allocable to the activity for 1977 is the $1,000 disallowed in 1976. Therefore, for 1977 $1,900 will be included in gross income, $950 is allowed as a deduction, and in addition the full disallowed loss of $1,000 is allowed as a deduction since it is not in excess of the income from the activity ($1,900).

(c) *Dual use of assets or personnel.*—Proper allocation rules are necessary if assets or personnel are used either in two or more

separate activities referred to in section 465(c)(2), or in one or more activities referred to in section 465(c)(2) and an activity to which section 465 does not apply. In such a case the deductions attributable to the use of these assets or personnel must be allocated between the activities on a reasonable basis. [Reg. § 1.465-13].

§1.465-22. Effect on amount at risk of money transactions.—(a) *Money contributed to activity.*—A taxpayer's amount at risk in an activity shall be increased by the amount of personal funds the taxpayer contributes to the activity. For this purpose a contribution by a partner to a partnership conducting only one activity is a contribution to the activity. However, a partner's amount at risk shall not be increased by the amount which the partner is required under the partnership agreement to contribute until such time as the contribution is actually made. Neither shall a partner's amount at risk be increased in the case of a note payable to the partnership for which a partner is personally liable until such time as the proceeds of the note are actually devoted to the activity. See §1.465-10 for rules relating to amounts loaned by a shareholder to an electing small business corporation. See §1.465-7(a) for the treatment of a loan by a partner to the partnership.

(b) *Withdrawal of money from the activity.*—A taxpayer's amount at risk in an activity shall be decreased by the amount of money withdrawn from the activity by or on behalf of the taxpayer. Amounts withdrawn from an activity include distributions from a partnership or an electing small business corporation (as defined in section 1371(b)). In the case of a taxpayer who is a shareholder of an electing small business corporation (as defined in section 1371(b)), withdrawals shall include repayments of any indebtedness of the corporation to the shareholder described in section 1374(c)(2)(B) to the extent of any decrease in the shareholder's adjusted basis of such indebtedness. For the treatment of amounts already used in an activity which are used to repay a loan, see §§1.465-24(b)(2)(i) and 1.465-25(b)(2).

(c) *Effect of income and loss from activity on amount of risk.*—(1) *Income.*—A taxpayer's amount at risk in an activity shall be increased by an amount equal to the excess of the taxpayer's share of all items of income received or accrued from the activity during the taxable year over the taxpayer's share of allowable deductions which are allocable to the activity for the taxable year. A taxpayer's amount at risk in an activity shall also be increased by the taxpayer's share of tax-exempt receipts of the activity.

(2) *Loss.*—A taxpayer's amount at risk in an activity shall be decreased by the amount of loss from the activity allowed as a deduction to the taxpayer under section 465(a). A loss shall reduce a taxpayer's amount at risk in the activity at the close of the taxable year after the taxable year for which the loss is allowable. A taxpayer's amount at risk in an activity shall be decreased by the taxpayer's share of expenses relating to the production of tax-exempt receipts of the activity which are not deductible in determining taxable income from the activity.

(3) *Cross references.*—For the definition of income from the activity, see §1.465-12. For definition of loss from the activity, see section 465(d) and §1.465-11. For the timing of increases and decreases to the amount at risk, see §1.465-39.

(d) *Payment to seller.*—Payment by a purchaser to the seller for an interest in an activity shall be treated by the purchaser as if the payment to the seller were a contribution to the activity. For rules relating to the contribution of borrowed amounts see §§1.465-20, 1.465-24, and 1.465-25. [Reg. §1.465-22.]

§1.465-23. Effect on amount at risk of property transactions.—(a) *Contributions of property.*—(1) *Contribution of unencumbered property.*—When a taxpayer contributes unencumbered property to an activity, the taxpayer's amount at risk in the activity shall be increased by the adjusted basis of the contributed property. However, see §§1.465-20, 1.465-24, and 1.465-25 for rules relating to the contribution to the activity of property that has been purchased with borrowed funds.

(2) *Contribution of encumbered property.*—(i) Except as may otherwise result due to the application of §1.465-20, when a taxpayer contributes to an activity property that is subject only to liabilities for which the taxpayer is personally liable for repayment, the taxpayer's amount at risk in the activity shall be increased by the adjusted basis of the contributed property.

(ii) Except as may otherwise result due to the application of §1.465-20, when a taxpayer contributes to an activity property that is subject to a liability for which the taxpayer is not personally liable for repayment, the taxpayer's amount at risk is increased by the adjusted basis in the property and is decreased by the amount of encumbrances to which the property is subject which would not have increased the taxpayer's amount at risk if incurred for use in the activity. If after contribution of the property to the activity such an encumbrance is reduced, it shall be treated as the repayment of a loan used in the activity for which the taxpayer is not personally liable and for which there is no property used outside the activity pledged as security. See § 1.465-25(b)(2)(i).

If the basis of such property is decreased (for example, due to depreciation) prior to contribution to the activity, the portion of the basis consisting of amounts which would have increased the taxpayer's amount at risk if contributed directly to the activity will be decreased first.

(iii) The provisions of this paragraph may be illustrated by the following examples.

Example (1). In 1976 A, a calendar year individual taxpayer, purchases an asset for $5,000 financed in part by a $3,000 nonrecourse loan secured only by the asset and in part by $2,000 of cash from personal funds. Thereafter, in 1976 A contributes the asset to an activity before any of the nonrecourse debt has been repaid. Under § 1.465-23(a)(2)(ii), A's amount at risk in the activity will be increased to the extent the taxpayer's adjusted basis in the asset consists of amounts which would have increased the taxpayer's amount at risk if contributed directly to the activity. In this instance the $3,000 nonrecourse loan is secured by an asset used in the activity. Because these loan proceeds would not increase the amount at risk if contributed directly to the activity, they will not increase the amount at risk in this case. However, the $2,000 of personal funds used for part payment of the asset would have increased A's amount at risk in the activity by $2,000 if contributed directly to the activity. Consequently, A's amount at risk in the activity is increased by $2,000 as a result of the contribution of the asset to the activity.

Example (2). In 1976 B, a calendar year individual taxpayer, purchases an asset for $5,000 financed in part by a $3,000 nonrecourse loan secured only by the asset and in part by $2,000 of cash from personal funds. B uses the asset in an activity to which section 465 does not apply and takes $1,000 of depreciation. Thereafter, B contributes the asset to an activity described in section 465(c)(1). None of the nonrecourse debt had been repaid at the time of the contribution. Under § 1.465-23(a)(2)(ii) the $1,000 of depreciation will be deducted first from the portion of the basis that consists of amounts which would have increased the taxpayer's amount at risk in the activity if contributed directly to the activity. This means that at the time of contribution to the activity the asset has an adjusted basis of $4,000, consisting in part of a $3,000 nonrecourse loan and in part of $1,000 of personal funds which would have increased B's amount at risk in the activity if contributed directly to the activity. Consequently, B's amount at risk in the activity is increased by $1,000 as a result of the contribution of the asset to the activity.

(b) *Adjusted basis.*—(1) For the purpose of this section the adjusted basis is that adjusted basis which would have been used in determining the amount of loss if the property were sold immediately after being contributed to the activity.

(2) The provisions of this paragraph may be illustrated by the following examples:

Example (1). In 1972 A, an individual calendar year taxpayer, purchases a car for $5,000 using personal assets to pay the seller. From 1972 through 1975 the car is used solely for A's personal nonbusiness needs. On January 1, 1976, A converts the use of the car and begins using the car solely for business purposes. On January 1, 1976, the fair market value of the car is $2,400. For 1976 A is allowed a deduction of $600 for depreciation of the car. On January 1, 1977, A contributes the car to an activity described in section 465(c)(1). If on January 1, 1977, the car had been sold the allowable loss would have been the excess (if any) of $1,800 ($2,400 – $600) over the amount realized on the sale (see § 1.165-7(a)(5)). As a result of contributing the car, A's amount at risk in the activity is increased by $1,800.

Example (2). Assume the same facts as in example (1) except that A contributes the car to the activity described in section 465(c)(1) on January 1, 1976. On that date the car is converted from personal use to use in a trade or business or for the production of income. If the car were to be sold thereafter, the loss would be determined with reference to an adjusted basis of $2,400. Accordingly, A's amount at risk is increased by $2,400.

(c) *Distribution of property.*—A taxpayer's amount at risk in an activity shall be decreased by—

(1) The adjusted basis in the hands of the taxpayer of property (other than money) which is withdrawn by or on behalf of the taxpayer from the activity; less

(2) The amount of liabilities to which the property is subject to for which the taxpayer is not personally liable.

If a taxpayer is distributed property described in this paragraph, repayment of the liability by the taxpayer after the distribution shall not increase the taxpayer's amount at risk.

(d) *Use of property as security for a nonrecourse loan.*—For rules relating to the treatment of a taxpayer's amount at risk when the

taxpayer pledges property as security for a nonrecourse loan, see § 1.465-25.

(e) *Contribution of property previously serving as security for a nonrecourse loan.*—For rules relating to the treatment of a taxpayer's amount at risk when the taxpayer contributes to an activity property that had served as security for a nonrecourse loan used in the activity, see § 1.465-25(a)(3). [Reg. § 1.465-23.]

§ 1.465-24. Effect on amount at risk of loans for which borrower is personally liable for repayment.—(a) *Creation of loan.*—(1) *General rule.*—A taxpayer's amount at risk in an activity is increased by the amount of any liability incurred in the conduct of an activity for use in the activity to the extent the taxpayer is personally liable for repayment of the liability.

(2) *Partnerships.*—(i) When a partnership incurs a liability in the conduct of an activity and under state law members of the partnership may be held personally liable for repayment of the liability, each partner's amount at risk is increased to the extent the partner is not protected against loss. To the extent the partner is protected against loss (such as through a right of contribution), the liability shall be treated in the same manner as amounts borrowed for which the taxpayer has no personal liability and for which no security is pledged. See § 1.465-25.

(ii) The application of this paragraph may be illustrated by the following example:

Example. A and B are equal general partners in partnership AB, which is engaged solely in an activity described in section 465(c)(1). AB borrows $25,000 from a bank to purchase equipment to be used in the activity. In addition to giving the bank a security interest in the newly purchased equipment, A and B each assumes personal liability for the loan. Although either A or B could be called upon by the bank to repay the entire $25,000, in such instance the partner who paid would be entitled to $12,500 from the other partner. Thus, although each is personally liable for $25,000, each is protected against loss in excess of $12,500. Accordingly, the loan increases the amount each is at risk with respect to the activity by $12,500.

(3) *Small business corporations.*—The amount at risk of a shareholder of an electing small business corporation (as defined in section 1371(b)) shall not be increased by indebtedness incurred by the corporation from persons other than that shareholder. For treatment of indebtedness described in section 1374(c)(2)(B) (relating to loans by shareholders to electing small business corporations), see § 1.465-10(c).

(b) *Repayment of loan.*—(1) *General rule.*—(i) Except as otherwise provided in this paragraph, the repayment by the taxpayer of a liability for which the taxpayer is personally liable does not affect the taxpayer's amount at risk. For this purpose, whether a taxpayer is considered personally liable for repayment of a liability is determined at the time of repayment.

(ii) The provisions of paragraph (b)(1) of this section, may be illustrated by the following examples:

Example (1). In 1977 A, an individual calendar year taxpayer, borrows $10,000 from a bank, assuming personal liability for repayment, for use in partnership AB, which is engaged solely in an activity. At the close of 1977 A's amount at risk is $10,000. In December of 1978 A takes $3,000 of personal funds and uses these funds to repay the bank. If no other factors occur during the year to affect A's amount at risk in the activity, A's amount at risk will be $10,000 at the close of 1978 because the repayment with personal assets of a liability for which A was personally liable does not affect A's amount at risk in the activity.

Example (2). In 1977 B, a calendar year taxpayer borrows $5,000 for use in an activity. B is personally liable for the repayment of the loan. At the end of 1977 B's amount at risk in the activity is $5,000. In 1978 when the amount of the loan is still $5,000, the loan obligation is purchased by C, a person who has an interest (other than interest as a creditor) in the activity. As a result of C's interest in the activity the loan is not treated in the same manner as a loan for which B is personally liable for repayment as long as C is the holder of the note. See § 1.465-20. Accordingly, B's amount at risk in the activity is decreased by $5,000, and repayments on the note made by B to C are not governed by this section. See § 1.465-5 for the effect on the amount at risk of loans which convert from recourse to nonrecourse. See § 1.465-25 for the effect on the amount at risk of repayments of a loan for which the borrower is not personally liable for repayment.

(2) *Repayments using amounts which would not increase the taxpayer's amount at risk if contributed to the activity.*—(i) If a taxpayer repays a loan for which the taxpayer is personally liable with assets already in the activity, the taxpayer's amount at risk in the activity will be decreased by the adjusted basis (as defined in § 1.465-23(b)(1)) of such assets. If the taxpayer repays a loan for which the taxpayer is

personally liable with funds which, if contributed to the activity, would not increase the taxpayer's amount at risk, the taxpayer's amount at risk shall be decreased to the extent of the repayment. Thus, for example, if a taxpayer repays a loan for which the taxpayer is personally liable with funds received from a nonrecourse loan secured by property used in the activity, the taxpayer's amount at risk shall be decreased to the extent of the repayment. The payment by a partnership of a liability which, pursuant to paragraph (a)(2) of this section, is deemed to be incurred by a partner in the conduct of the activity shall decrease the partner's amount at risk in the activity to the extent such partner's basis in the partnership is decreased due to the payment of the liability by the partnership.

(ii) The provisions of paragraph (b)(2) of this section may be illustrated by the following example:

Example. In 1977 A, an individual calendar year taxpayer, borrows $10,000 from a bank, assuming personal liability for repayment, for use in partnership AB, which is engaged solely in an activity described in section 465(c)(1). At the close of 1977 A's amount at risk in the activity is $10,000. In December of 1978 A borrows $3,000 for which A is not personally liable and which is secured by property used in the activity, and uses the funds to pay the bank. If no other factors occur during the year to affect A's amount at risk in the activity, A's amount at risk will be decreased by the amount of the repayment, because A used funds for the repayment which would not have increased A's amount at risk had they been contributed to the activity. Therefore, at the close of 1978 A's amount at risk is $7,000. The result would be the same if the $3,000 used for the repayment of the loan were withdrawn from AB. See § 1.465-22.

(3) *Repayment of a loan for which others are personally liable.*— Where more than one person is personally liable for repayment of a loan, repayment of that portion of the loan for which the taxpayer is personally liable and not protected against loss shall be treated in accordance with § 1.465-24(b). Repayment of that portion of the loan for which the taxpayer is protected against loss (such as through a right of contribution) shall be treated as a repayment of a loan for which the taxpayer has no personal liability and for which no security is pledged. See § 1.465-25. Also, see the example at paragraph (a)(2) of this section. [Reg. § 1.465-24.]

§ 1.465-25. Effect on amount at risk of loan for which borrower is not personally liable for repayment.—(a) *Nonrecourse loan for which taxpayer pledges property not used in the activity.*—(1) *In general.*—A taxpayer's amount at risk in an activity is increased by amounts borrowed for use in the activity when the taxpayer is not personally liable for repayment of the loan if the taxpayer pledges as security property not used in the activity. However, the amount of the increase shall not exceed the net fair market value (as defined in paragraph (a)(4) of this section) of the pledged property. If the net fair market value of the security changes (in accordance with paragraph (a)(4) of this section) after the loan is made, a redetermination shall be made of the taxpayer's amount at risk in the activity using the new net fair market value.

(2) *Repayment of loan.*—To the extent a taxpayer's amount at risk is increased by a portion of a liability described in paragraph (a)(1) of this section, the taxpayer's repayment of that portion of the liability will be treated in the same manner as the repayment of a loan for which the taxpayer is personally liable in accordance with § 1.465-24(b). However, to the extent the amount of the liability exceeds the net fair market value of property not used in the activity which secures the loan, repayment of that portion of the liability is considered as the repayment of a loan for which the taxpayer is not personally liable and has not pledged property used outside the activity in accordance with paragraph (b)(2)(i) of this section. Repayments of the loan are considered to be made first in respect of that portion of the loan which exceeds the net fair market value of property not used in the activity which secures the loan. If a portion of an amount borrowed is used in the activity and a portion is used outside the activity, repayment will be considered made first in respect of the portion used outside the activity.

(3) *Contribution of security to activity.*—If property which is pledged as security for an amount borrowed for use in an activity is subsequently contributed to the activity, the amount at risk shall be redetermined in accordance with this section as though the net fair market value of the security had been reduced to zero. This will reduce the amount at risk in accordance with § 1.465-25(a)(1). Furthermore, the contribution of the property to the activity will be treated as a contribution of unencumbered property and will increase the amount at risk in accordance with § 1.465-23(a)(1).

(4) *Net fair market value; changes in net fair market value.*—The net fair market value of property is the amount by which the property's fair market value at the date it is pledged as security exceeds the total amount of superior liens to which it is subject. Subsequent changes in the fair market value of the property are not taken into account for purposes of determining net fair market value. However, to the extent the amount of superior liens changes during a taxable year the net fair market value shall be adjusted at the close of the taxable year. Thus, the net fair market value of property will be reduced to the extent of increases in superior liens to which the property is subject and will be increased to the extent of decreases in superior liens of which the property is relieved. For purposes of determining the effect of superior liens on the calculations described in this paragraph, it is not relevant that other property is also subject to any such superior lien. If a portion of an amount borrowed which is secured by property described in this section is not contributed to an activity, that portion shall be treated as a superior lien on such property, thus reducing its net fair market value in accordance with § 1.465-25(a)(4).

(b) *Nonrecourse loan for which a taxpayer pledges assets used in the activity.*—(1) *In general.*—(i) *Borrowed funds used in the activity.*—A taxpayer's amount at risk is unaffected by amounts borrowed for use in an activity where the taxpayer is not personally liable for repayment of the loan and has not pledged as security property used outside the activity. Thus, a taxpayer's amount at risk in a partnership activity is unaffected to the extent the taxpayer borrows for use in the partnership money secured only by the partnership interest. Where a partnership borrows amounts for use in the activity pledging only property used in the activity for repayment of the loan, and neither the partnership nor any partner is personally liable for repayment of the loan, the loan shall be treated by each partner as a loan which is described in this paragraph.

(ii) *Borrowed funds used outside the activity.*—A taxpayer's amount at risk is affected by amounts borrowed for use outside the activity where the taxpayer is not personally liable for repayment of the loan and has pledged as security only property used in the activity. In such a case, the taxpayer's amount at risk in the activity is decreased by an amount equal to the amount borrowed for use outside the activity. This result is unchanged if the only security for the loan is the taxpayer's interest in the activity. If the taxpayer has pledged as security property, some of which is used in the activity (including for this purpose the taxpayer's interest in the activity) and some of which is not, the taxpayer's amount at risk in the activity shall be reduced by the excess, if any, of amounts borrowed for use outside the activity over the net fair market value of the security not used in the activity.

(2) *Repayment of loan.*—(i) *Borrowed funds used in the activity.*— Where a taxpayer's amount at risk was not increased as a result of the rule contained in paragraph (b)(1)(i) of this section, a subsequent repayment of the loan by the taxpayer will increase the taxpayer's amount at risk to the extent of the repayment. However, if the amount used to repay the loan would not have increased the taxpayer's amount at risk in the activity if the amount had been contributed to the activity, the repayment will not increase the taxpayer's amount at risk. Thus, for example, if a nonrecourse loan (the proceeds of which were used in the activity) which did not increase the taxpayer's amount at risk is repaid with money borrowed by the taxpayer with a second nonrecourse loan secured only by property used in the activity, the taxpayer's amount at risk will not be increased by the repayment. When a liability described in paragraph (b)(1)(i) of this section is repaid with assets already used in the activity, the taxpayer's amount at risk will not be affected as a result of the repayment. Therefore, when a partnership incurs such a liability and thereafter repays it with assets used in the activity, no partner's amount at risk is affected upon the incurrence of the liability or upon repayment.

(ii) *Borrowed funds not used in the activity.*—A taxpayer's amount at risk is affected by the repayment by the taxpayer of amounts borrowed for use outside the activity where the taxpayer is not personally liable for repayment of the loan and has pledged as security only property used in the activity (including for this purpose the taxpayer's interest in the activity). In such a case the taxpayer's amount at risk in the activity is increased by the amount of the repayment. If the taxpayer has pledged as security property, some of which is used in the activity and some of which is not, upon repayment the taxpayer's amount at risk in the activity will be increased by the lesser of the amount of the repayment made by the taxpayer or the amount (if any) by which the outstanding liability (immediately before repayment) exceeds the net fair market value of the property not used in the activity which is pledged as security. However, if the amount used to repay the loan would not have increased the taxpayer's amount at risk in the activity if the amount had been contributed to the activity, the repayment will not increase the amount at risk. Thus, if the repayment is made using assets already in the activity, the repayment will not increase the taxpayer's amount at risk.

(3) *Examples.*—The provisions of this section may be illustrated by the following examples:

Example (1). (i) In 1977 A, a calendar year individual, pledges A's house (which is not used in the activity) as well as an asset used in the activity as security to borrow $8,000 on a nonrecourse basis to be used in an activity. On the day the house is pledged as security, its fair market value is $60,000, and it is subject to a superior lien of $54,000. If the amount of the superior lien is not reduced during the balance of the year, at the close of 1977 the net fair market value of the house is $6,000 ($60,000 – $54,000), since the net fair market value of the security ($6,000) is less than the amount borrowed ($8,000), the increase in A's amount at risk is limited to $6,000.

(ii) In 1978 A reduces the amount of the superior lien on the house to $53,000. Accordingly, the house's net fair market value at the close of 1978 is $7,000 ($60,000 – $53,000). In accordance with paragraph (a)(4) of this section, a redetermination of the amount at risk is made using the new net fair market value. Using the new value, the amount borrowed ($8,000) is still more than the net fair market value ($7,000). Therefore, the new net fair market value would be used to measure the increase in A's amount at risk in the activity. The new amount determined under paragraph (a)(4) of this section ($7,000) exceeds the earlier amount determined under this section ($6,000) by $1,000. Thus, A's amount at risk is increased by $1,000.

(iii) In 1979 the fair market value of A's house increases to $75,000. On December 31, 1979, A obtains a $10,000 second mortgage on the house. The second mortgage is made superior to the lien for the $8,000 loan made in 1977. At the close of 1979 the original lien on the house has been reduced to $52,000 and the second mortgage is $10,000. Since changes in the fair market value of security are ignored for purposes of determining net fair market value, the net fair market value of the house at the end of 1979 is determined by comparing its fair market value at the time the $8,000 was borrowed in 1977, $60,000, with the amount of superior liens outstanding at the end of 1979, $62,000 ($52,000 + $10,000). Since the fair market value of the house as so determined is less than the total of the superior liens to which the house is subject at the end of 1979, the net fair market value of the house at that time is 0. In accordance with paragraph (a)(4) of this section a redetermination of the amount at risk is made using the new net fair market value. Using the new value the amount borrowed ($8,000) is still more than the net fair market value (0). Therefore, the new net fair market value would be used to measure the increase in A's amount at risk in the activity. The new amount determined under paragraph (a)(4) of this section (0) is less than the earlier amount determined under this section ($7,000) by $7,000. Thus, A's amount at risk is decreased by $7,000.

Example (2). (i) In 1977 B, a calendar year individual, pledges shares of stock that are not used in the activity as security to borrow $20,000 on a nonrecourse basis to be used in an activity. On the day the shares are pledged, they are worth $40,000 and are not subject to any superior liens. At the close of 1977 the fair market value of the shares is $30,000. Nevertheless, at the close of 1977 the net fair market value of the shares is $40,000, because changes in the fair market value of security are ignored for purposes of determining net fair market value. Since the net fair market value of the shares ($40,000) is greater than the amount borrowed ($20,000), B's amount at risk in the activity is increased by $20,000.

(ii) In 1978, B, using personal assets, repays $4,000 of the loan secured by the shares of stock. In accordance with paragraph (a)(2) of this section, repayments of such a loan are treated like repayments of a loan for which the taxpayer is personally liable. Thus, B's amount at risk is not affected by the repayment.

(iii) In 1979 the shares of stock are made subject to a $30,000 lien superior to the previous lien. At the close of 1979 the net fair market value of the shares of stock is $10,000 ($40,000 fair market value minus $30,000 superior lien). Accordingly, a redetermination must be made of B's amount at risk. Since the new net fair market value of the shares of stock ($10,000) is less than the amount of the loan outstanding ($16,000), the net fair market value is used to measure any change in A's amount at risk. The new amount determined under this section ($10,000) is less than the earlier amount determined under this section ($16,000) by $6,000. Thus, in accordance with paragraph (a) of this section B's amount at risk is decreased under this section by $6,000.

(iv) In 1980 B repays $7,000 of the loan secured by the shares of stock. In accordance with paragraph (a)(2) of this section, the repayment is first deemed to be made in respect of that portion of the loan, $6,000, which exceeds the net fair market value of property not used in the activity which secures the loan. Pursuant to paragraph (b)(2)(i) of this section the repayment will result in a corresponding increase of $6,000 in the amount at risk. The remaining $1,000 repayment is treated under paragraph (a)(2) of this section in the same manner as the repayment of a loan for which the taxpayer is personally liable. Repayment of such a loan results in no change in the amount at risk. Accordingly, as a result of the $7,000 repayment, B's amount at risk is increased by $6,000.

Example (3). (i) In 1977 C, a calendar year individual, purchases an asset for $10,000 for use in an activity. C pays for the asset with $2,000 of personal funds and a purchase money mortgage of $8,000 on which C is not personally liable. At the end of 1977 C still owes $8,000 on the purchase money mortgage. As a result of this transaction C's amount at risk in the activity is increased by $2,000.

(ii) In 1978 C repays $3,000 of the purchase money mortgage, $2,000 with personal funds from outside the activity and $1,000 with funds from within the activity. Since the $2,000 of funds from outside the activity can increase C's amount at risk if contributed to the activity, their use to repay the loan will increase C's amount at risk by $2,000. The additional $1,000 of repayment is from funds already within the activity. Accordingly, the use of those funds to repay the loan does not increase C's amount at risk in the activity.

Example (4). (i) In 1977 D, a calendar year individual, borrows $5,000 for use in a farming activity described in section 465(c)(1)(B). D is personally liable on the loan. At the end of 1977 the $5,000 loan remains outstanding. Accordingly, D's amount at risk in the activity is increased by $5,000.

(ii) In 1979 D requests the lender to convert the $5,000 loan into a nonrecourse loan secured by assets in the farming activity. The lender agrees to the request. Assuming that § 1.465-5 applies and the recourse loan increases D's amount at risk prior to conversion, the conversion of the loan from recourse to nonrecourse reduces D's amount at risk by $5,000 at the close of 1979.

(iii) In 1980 D repays $1,000 of the $5,000 loan with personal funds from outside the activity and $2,000 with money from the activity. The repayment of $3,000 of the loan increases D's amount at risk to the extent a contribution of amounts used to repay the loan would have increased the taxpayer's amount at risk in the activity. Since $2,000 from the activity was used to repay the loan, D's amount at risk in the activity is not increased to the extent of that $2,000. However, the $1,000 from outside the activity would have increased the amount at risk if it were contributed to the activity. Therefore, at the end of 1980 D's amount at risk will be increased by $1,000.

Example (5). E and F form partnership EF to engage in an activity described in section 465(c)(1). Partnership EF borrows $20,000 secured by a purchase money mortgage for which neither of the partners is personally liable and uses the funds to purchase an asset for use in the activity. This transaction does not increase the amount E and F are at risk in the activity. Thereafter, EF repays $5,000 of the purchase money mortgage with funds from the activity. Pursuant to paragraph (c) of this section the repayment by EF has no effect on the amount E and F are at risk in the activity.

Example (6). A, an individual calendar year taxpayer, is engaged in a farming activity described in section 465(c)(1)(B). On January 6, 1978, A borrows $8,000 using machinery from the activity as security. A is not personally liable for repayment of the loan. A uses the $8,000 (along with $2,000 from personal funds) to purchase an automobile for use outside the activity. Subsequently, A pledges the automobile as security to borrow $8,000. A uses this $8,000 to purchase a truck which is contributed to the farming activity in August of 1978. Section 465(b)(2) provides that no property shall be taken into account as security if it is directly or indirectly financed by indebtedness which is secured by property used in the activity. Accordingly, if no other events affecting A's amount at risk occur in 1978, A's amount at risk in the farming activity at the close of 1978 will be the same as it was at the close of 1977.

(c) *Repayment of nonrecourse liability by a partnership.*—The repayment by a partnership of a liability for which a taxpayer is not personally liable and for which that taxpayer has not pledged as security assets used outside the activity shall not affect the taxpayer's amount at risk. [Reg. § 1.465-25.]

§ 1.465-26. Effect of transfers by gift or at death on amount at risk; cross reference.—For rules relating to the effect on the amount at risk of transfers by gift or at death, see §§ 1.465-57 through 1.465-59. [Reg. § 1.465-26.]

Deduction Limited to Amount at Risk

Deduction Limited to Amount at Risk.—Reproduced below are the texts of proposed Reg. §§ 1.465-38, 1.465-39, 1.465-41—1.465-45, 1.465-66—1.465-69, 1.465-75—1.465-79 and 1.465-95, relating to the determination of amounts at risk with respect to certain activities (published in the Federal Register on June 5, 1979).

§ 1.465-38. Ordering rules.—(a) *In general.*—In determining which items of deductions otherwise allowable are to be allowed under section 465(a), the following ordering system shall be used:

(1) First, all capital losses shall be allowed.

(2) Second, all items of deduction entering into the computation under section 1231 shall be allowed.

(3) Third, all items of deduction to the extent they do not constitute items of tax preference under section 57 and are not described in paragraph (a)(1) or (2) of this section shall be allowed.

(4) Fourth, all items of tax preference under section 57 not described in paragraph (a)(1) or (2) of this section shall be allowed.

(b) *Retention of identity.*—When treated as deductions in succeeding taxable years, deductions which are disallowed under section 465(a) shall retain their identity according to the classifications enumerated in paragraph (a) of this section.

(c) *Special rule.*—Deductions described in paragraph (a)(4) of this section (relating to tax preference items) which are disallowed by section 465(a) shall be further subdivided according to the taxable year in which they were originally paid or accrued. When such deductions are allowed, those deductions paid or accrued in the earliest taxable years shall be allowed first.

(d) *Examples.*—The provisions of this section may be illustrated by the following examples:

Example (1). A, an individual calendar year taxpayer, is engaged in an activity described in section 465(c)(1). At the close of 1977 A is at risk $1000 in the activity. During 1978 A had $3000 of income from the activity and $7500 of deductions allocated to the activity. Of the $7500 of deductions $2500 are of the type described in § 1.465-38(a)(3) and $5000 are of the type described in § 1.465-38(a)(4). Assuming nothing else has occurred during 1978 to affect A's amount at risk, A will be allowed $4000 of deductions and $3500 of deductions will be disallowed. Since A has no deductions described in § 1.465-38(a)(1) or § 1.465-38(a)(2), the $4000 of allowed deductions will consist of the entire $2500 described in § 1.465-38(a)(3) and $1500 of the $5000 deductions described in § 1.465-38(a)(4). The $3500 deductions disallowed will consist of deductions in § 1.465-38(a)(4).

Example (2). Assume the same facts as in example (1), and in addition during 1979 A has income from the activity of $10,000. During 1979 A incurred $14,000 of deductions of which $4,000 are described in § 1.465-38(a)(3) and $10,000 are described in § 1.465-38(a)(4). When A's current deductions are added to the deductions which were not allowed and therefore carried over from 1978, A's total deductions from the activity for 1979 are $17,500 ($14,000 + $3,500), of which $4,000 are described in § 1.465-38(a)(3) and $13,500 are described in § 1.465-38(a)(4) ($10,000 + $3,500). Of the $13,500 of deductions described in § 1.465-38(a)(4), $3,500 are from 1978 and $10,000 are from 1979. Assuming nothing occurs during 1979 to affect A's amount at risk, A will be allowed deductions from the activity in the amount of $10,000 (see § 1.465-2(a)). Since A has no

deductions described in § 1.465-38(a)(1) or § 1.465-38(a)(2), the entire $10,000 of deductions will come from those deductions described in § 1.465-38(a)(3) and § 1.465-38(a)(4). Of A's $17,500 of deductions from the activity the entire $4,000 described in § 1.465-38(a)(3) will be allowed. Of the $13,500 deductions described in § 1.465-38(a)(4), $6,000 will be allowed. Pursuant to § 1.465-38(c) deductions described in § 1.465-38(a)(4) and occurring in the earliest years shall be allowed first. Accordingly, the $6,000 deductions described in § 1.465-38(a)(4) which are to be allowed shall consist of the entire $3,500 attributable to 1978 and $2,500 of the $10,000 deductions described in § 1.465-38(a)(4) attributable to 1979. The remaining $7,500 of deductions described in § 1.465-38(a)(4) and attributable to 1979 will be carried over and treated as deductions from the activity for 1980. [Reg. § 1.465-38.]

§ 1.465-39. Timing of increases and decreases to the amount at risk.—(a) *General rule.*—Except as provided in paragraph (b) of this section, factors which increase or decrease the amount a taxpayer is at risk in a taxable year shall so increase or decrease the amount at risk before determining the amount of section 465(d) loss which is allowed for the year.

(b) *Exception.*—Section 465(d) losses which are allowed as deductions for a taxable year under section 465 reduce the amount a taxpayer is at risk with respect to that activity at the close of the immediately succeeding taxable year of the taxpayer.

(c) *Procedure.*—The amount a taxpayer is at risk in an activity at the close of a taxable year of the taxpayer is determined by—

(1) Reducing the amount at risk in the activity at the close of the preceding taxable year by the amount of the section 465(d) loss which was allowed as a deduction in the preceding taxable year;

(2) Increasing the amount at risk in the activity (determined after the application of paragraph (c)(1) of this section) by all factors occurring during the taxable year which increase the amount at risk; and

(3) Decreasing the amount at risk in the activity (determined after the application of paragraph (c)(2) of this section) by all factors occurring during the taxable year which decrease the amount at risk.

See § 1.465-41 for illustrations of the operation of this section. [Reg. § 1.465-39.]

§ 1.465-41. Examples.—The provisions of §§ 1.465-1 through 1.465-40 may be illustrated by the following examples:

Example (1). On January 1, 1976, A and B as equal partners form partnership AB. Both A and B, as well as partnership AB, are calendar year taxpayers. On January 1, 1976, A and B each contributes $5,000 from personal assets to AB. On August 1, 1976, AB borrows $6,000 from a bank with A and B each assuming personal liability. On December 31, 1976, AB reduces the amount outstanding on the loan to $4,500. AB has neither loss nor income for 1976. As of December 31, 1976, A's amount at risk in the activity engaged in by AB is determined as follows:

Amount at risk in activity as of 1/1/76	$0
Plus:	
Contributions	5,000
Allocable share of loan for which personal liability was assumed ($6,000) ÷ 2	3,000
	$8,000
Less:	
Allocable share of net reduction in personal liability (See § 1.465-24(b)(2)(i))	
$$\left(\frac{\$6,000 - \$4,500}{2} \right) \quad \ldots\ldots\ldots\ldots\ldots\ldots\ldots\ldots\ldots\ldots$$	750
Amount at risk in activity as of 12/31/76	$7,250

Example (2). Assume the same facts as in example (1) and in addition on February 1, 1977, AB borrows $20,000 under a nonrecourse financing arrangement with the lender taking as security equipment purchased with the newly acquired funds. On May 1, 1977 AB reduces the amount outstanding on the loan on which A and B have assumed personal liability to $4,000 ($4,500 − $500). On August 1, 1977 AB reduces the principal amount due on the nonre-

course loan to $19,000. On October 1, 1977 AB distributes $2,000 each to both A and B. On December 1, 1977 AB reduces the amount outstanding on the loan on which A and B have assumed personal liability to $2,500 ($4,000 − $1,500). A and B are each allocated $3,000 as their distributive share of partnership income for its taxable year ending December 31, 1977. As of December 31, 1977, A's amount at risk in the activity engaged in by AB is determined as follows:

Amount at risk in activity as of 1/1/77		$7,250
Plus:		
Income from the activity		3,000
		$10,250
Less:		
Allocable share of net reduction in personal liability—5/1/77 ($500 ÷ 2)	$250	
Allocable share of net reduction in personal liability—12/1/77 ($1,500 ÷ 2)	750	
Distribution	2,000	3,000
Amount at risk in activity as of 12/31/77		$7,250

The $20,000 nonrecourse loan does not affect the amount at risk of either A or B because neither of them assumed personal liability and neither of them pledged property not used in the activity as security. Under § 1.465-25(b)(2) the reduction in the nonrecourse liability did not reduce either partner's amount at risk, because the loan was

repaid with amounts already in the activity. Under § 1.465-24(b)(2) the reduction in personal liability did reduce the amount at risk, because the repayment was made with amounts already in the activity.

Example (3). Assume the same facts as in example (2) and in addition on March 1, 1978, A and B each contributes $1,000 to AB. On September 1, 1978 A and B each contributes $1,500 to AB and on the same date AB reduces the outstanding amount due on the loan for which A and B are personally liable to zero, and also repays $500 on

Amount at risk in activity as of 1/1/78	
Plus:	
Contribution—3/1/78	1,000
Contribution—9/1/78	1,500
	$9,750
Less:	
Allocable share of net reduction in personal liability ($2,500 ÷ 2)	1,250
Amount at risk in activity as of 12/31/78	$8,500

A was allocated $10,500 in partnership losses. Since A's amount at risk as of December 31, 1978 is only $8,500, A's loss deduction for the activity will also be so limited. Thus, A may take a loss deduction of $8,500 for 1978. This deduction will decrease A's amount at risk at the close of 1979. The $2,000 not allowed as a loss deduction for 1978 will be treated as a deduction in 1979. Under §1.465-25(b)(2)(i) the reduction in nonrecourse liability did not reduce either partner's amount at risk, because the loan was repaid with amounts already in the activity.

Amount at risk in activity as of 1/1/79	
Less:	
Loss allowed in 1978	8,500
	$0
Plus: Contribution	1,000
Amount at risk in activity as of 12/31/79	$1,000

A had a $2,000 loss deduction which was not allowed in 1978 and is treated as a deduction for 1979. Since $500 is A's distributive share of partnership income (which is calculated without regard to such deduction), A's section 465(d) loss for 1979 is $1,500 ($2,000 – $500). Since A is at risk $1,000 as of December 31, 1979, only $1,000 is allowable as loss deduction for 1979. The remaining $500 is treated as a deduction for 1980. Therefore, of the $2,000 disallowed loss deduction for 1978 treated as a deduction for 1979, $500 is deductible by reason of A's share of partnership income, $1,000 is deductible because A was at risk $1,000, and the remaining $500 is not deductible for 1979 but is treated as a deduction allocable to the activity for 1980.

Example (5). On July 1, 1976, C, along with many other persons, forms partnership W. C is a calendar year taxpayer and partnership W is on a taxable year ending June 30. On July 1, 1976, C contributes

Amount at risk in activity as of 7/1/76 (prior to contribution)	
Plus:	
Contribution—7/1/76	3,000
Allocable share of loan for which personal liability was assumed	7,500
	$10,500
Less:	
Allocable share of net reduction in personal liability	$1,500
Amount at risk in activity as of 6/30/77	$9,000

Although C's allocable share of W's losses for the taxable year ending June 30, 1977, is $13,000, C's allowable loss deduction is limited to the amount at risk as of the close of the partnership's taxable year. Thus, C's loss deduction for the taxable year ending December 31, 1977, is $9,000. The $4,000 not allowed as a loss deduction in 1977 will be treated as a deduction in 1978. The fact that prior to December 31, 1977, but after the close of W's taxable year on June 30, 1977, C made a contribution to W does not increase the amount of loss which C

Amount at risk in activity as of 7/1/77	$9,000
Less:	
Loss allowed in 1977	9,000
	$0
Plus:	
Contribution—9/1/77	6,000
Less:	
Net reduction in personal liability 11/1/77	1,000
Amount at risk in activity as of 6/30/78	$5,000

C has $4,000 of deductions which were not allowed in 1977 as well as $250 of current loss for W's taxable year ending June 30, 1978. Since $4,250, the entire amount of section 465(d) loss ($4,000 + $250), is less than the amount at risk as of the close of W's taxable year, the entire amount is allowable as a deduction for C's taxable year ending December 31, 1978. The fact that prior to December 31, 1978, but after the close of W's taxable year on June 30, 1978, W made a distribution

Amount at risk in activity as of 7/1/78	
Less:	
Loss allowed in 1978	4,250
	$750
Plus:	
Income from the activity	1,000

the loan for which A and B had not assumed personal liability. For AB's taxable year ending December 1978 A and B each has $10,500 of section 465(d) losses. As of December 31, 1978, A's amount at risk for the activity engaged in by AB is determined as follows:

	$7,250
Plus:	
Contribution—3/1/78	1,000
Contribution—9/1/78	1,500
	$9,750
Less:	
Allocable share of net reduction in personal liability ($2,500 ÷ 2)	1,250
Amount at risk in activity as of 12/31/78	$8,500

Example (4). Assume the facts as in example (3) and in addition on March 1, 1979, A and B each contributes $1,000 to AB. For AB's taxable year ending December 31, 1979, A and B are each allocated $500 as their share of partnership income (which is calculated without regard to the $2,000 loss deduction disallowed in 1978). As of December 31, 1979, A's amount at risk in the activity engaged in by AB is determined as follows:

	$8,500
Less:	
Loss allowed in 1978	8,500
	$0
Plus: Contribution	1,000
Amount at risk in activity as of 12/31/79	$1,000

$3,000 to W. On August 1, 1976, W borrows a sum of money for which C's allocable share of personal liability is $7,500. On October 1, 1976, W borrows a sum of money under a nonrecourse financing arrangement with respect to which C's allocable share is $10,000. On March 1, 1977, W repays a portion of the loan for which C is personally liable, thereby reducing C's personal liability to $6,000. C's allocable share of W's losses for the taxable year ending June 30, 1977, is $13,000. On September 1, 1977, C contributes unencumbered personal assets with an adjusted basis of $6,000 to W. On November 1, 1977, W repays another portion of the loan for which C is personally liable, reducing C's personal liability to $5,000. On December 1, 1977, W repays part of the nonrecourse loan thereby reducing C's allocable portion of the amount outstanding to $8,000. The amount of loss deduction which C is allowed for 1977 is determined as follows:

	$0
	3,000
	7,500
	$10,500
	$1,500
	$9,000

may deduct for 1977. That amount is limited to the amount C was at risk in the activity as of the close of W's taxable year.

Example (6). Assume the same facts as in example (5), and in addition for the taxable year ending June 30, 1978, C's allocable share of W's losses is $250 (which is calculated without regard to the $4,000 loss deduction carryover from 1977). On October 1, 1978, W distributes $2,000 to C. The amount of loss deduction which C is allowed for 1978 is determined as follows:

	$9,000
	9,000
	$0
	6,000
	1,000
	$5,000

to C does not decrease the amount of allowable loss which C may deduct in 1978 unless §1.465-4 is found to apply.

Example (7). Assume the facts as in example (6), and in addition for W's taxable year ending June 30, 1979, C's allocable share of income is $1,000. No other events occur which affect C's amount at risk. C's amount at risk as of June 30, 1979, is determined as follows:

	$5,000
Less:	
	4,250
	$750
Plus:	
	1,000

	$1,750
Less:	
Distribution—10/1/78	2,000
Amount at risk in activity as of 6/30/79	$(250)

For the recapture of certain losses where the amount at risk is less than zero, see section 465(e). [Reg. § 1.465-41.]

§ 1.465-42. Activities to which section 465 applies; holding, producing, or distributing motion picture films or video tapes.—(a) *In general.*—Section 465 applies to any taxpayer described in § 1.465-1(d) who is engaged in the activity of holding, producing, or distributing motion picture films or video tapes either as a trade or business or for the production of income.

(b) *Loss.*—All receipts related to holding, producing, or distributing motion picture films or video tapes and all items of deduction incurred with respect to such receipts are to be taken into account in determining whether there is a section 465(d) loss.

(c) *Separate activities.*—(1) *General rule.*—Except in the case of a partner's interest in a partnership or a shareholder's interest in an electing small business corporation, a taxpayer's interest in each different film or video tape shall be considered a separate activity. Thus, if an individual has an interest in four different films, each film represents a separate activity to that individual and that individual has a separate section 465(d) loss and a separate amount at risk with respect to each film.

(2) *Partners and shareholders.*—In the case of a partner's interest in a partnership or a shareholder's interest in an electing small business corporation, all films and video tapes in which the partnership or corporation has an interest shall be treated as one activity of the partner or shareholder. Thus, if a partnership has an interest in three different films and two different video tapes, the five films and video tapes will constitute one activity for each partner. This means that all items of income allocated to a partner from the films and video tapes shall be aggregated with all items of deductions allocated to that partner from the films and video tapes so as to result in one amount at risk and one section 465(d) loss (if any) for each partner.

(d) *Different film or video tape.*—(1) *General rule.*—For the purposes of paragraph (c) of this section, a different film or video tape is one—

(i) In which the finished product is viewed as a single work; and

(ii) Which is of a length such that individuals could normally be expected to view it in one sitting.

For the purposes of paragraph (c) of this section, a movie or video tape can consist of more than one reel.

(2) *Special rule.*—In cases where more than one film or video tape exists as a result of applying paragraph (d)(1)(ii) of this section, each portion of the film or video tape which is intended to be viewed in a separate sitting shall be a different film or video tape. [Reg. § 1.465-42.]

§ 1.465-43. Activities to which section 465 applies; farming.—(a) *In general.*—Section 465 applies to any taxpayer described in § 1.465-1(d) who is engaged in farming (as defined in section 464(e)) as a trade or business or for the production of income.

(b) *Loss.*—All receipts related to the farming activity and all items of deduction incurred with respect to such receipts are to be taken into account in determining whether there is a section 465(d) loss.

(c) *Separate activities.*—For each farm rules similar to those found in § 1.465-42(c) shall apply for purposes of determining what constitutes a separate activity.

(d) *Farm.*—As used in this section, the term "farm" includes all property where the cultivation of land or the raising or harvesting of any agricultural or horticultural commodity occurs, including the raising, shearing, feeding, caring for, training, and management of animals. For purposes of the preceding sentence, trees (other than trees bearing fruit or nuts) shall not be treated as an agricultural or horticultural commodity.

(e) *Farm activity.*—When a procedure for the processing of products grown or animals raised on a farm is carried on within the physical boundaries of a farm, it is necessary to determine whether such activity constitutes a farm activity. In such event, the facts and circumstances of each case must be evaluated. Generally, the most significant facts and circumstances in making this determination include—

(1) The similarity of the product as processed to the product as it is being grown or raised;

(2) The consistency with normal commercial practice of conducting the procedure within the physical boundaries of a farm; and

(3) The necessity of the procedure to obtain a marketable product.

If it is determined that the processing procedure is a nonfarm activity, receipts and expenditures from the farm activity and the nonfarm activity cannot be aggregated, and section 465 shall apply only to the receipts and expenditures from the farm activity.

(f) *Examples.*—The provisions of paragraph (e) of this section may be illustrated by the following examples:

Example (1). A operates a farm where A plants and harvests potatoes. On one portion of the farm A also operates a plant in which the potatoes are processed into potato chips. These potato chips are then shipped to various distributors who bag and sell the potato chips to retailers. The processing of potato chips by A shall not be considered a farm activity. The processing neither results in a final product (potato chip) similar to the product as grown (potato) nor is it necessary to obtain a marketable product.

Example (2). B is engaged in the farm activity of growing tobacco. Among the steps B takes to produce a product that is marketable is to maintain a warehouse within the physical boundaries of the farm for the purpose of curing and packing the tobacco that B has grown on the farm. There is no market for the tobacco in the form it takes when harvested. The curing and packing aspect of B's operations is a farm activity, because the final product as processed is similar to the product as grown, and the procedure is necessary to obtain a marketable product.

Example (3). C is engaged in growing wine grapes. In addition, C operates a winery within the boundaries of the farm. The capacity of C's winery is such that C purchases grapes from neighboring farms for use in making the wine in addition to using grapes grown in C's own vineyard. Most of the grape growers in the region of C's vineyard do not operate their own wineries but, instead, sell their grapes to a winery. Therefore the operation of the winery on the farm is not consistent with normal commercial practice. Thus, the operation of the winery is not a farm activity. The end product of the winery (wine) is not similar to the product as grown (grapes). In addition, harvested grapes are a marketable commodity without further processing. The result is the same even if the size of C's winery is such that it can only accommodate the grapes grown by C.

Example (4). D operates a farm on which D raises Black Angus steers. In addition, D maintains facilities on the farm to slaughter the steers. D has a contract with several grocery stores and restaurants in the area to provide them with this meat. Under these circumstances the slaughtering facilities will not be considered a farm activity. [Reg. § 1.465-43.]

§ 1.465-44. Activities to which section 465 applies; leasing section 1245 property.—(a) *In general.*—Section 465 applies to any taxpayer described in § 1.465-1(d)(1) who is engaged in the leasing of any section 1245 property (as defined in section 1245(a)(3)) as a trade or business or for the production of income. However, see section 465(c)(3)(D)(ii) for special exceptions relating to certain corporations engaged in equipment leasing.

(b) *Loss.*—All receipts related to the leasing of section 1245 property and all items of deduction incurred with respect to such receipts are to be taken into account in determining whether there is a section 465(d) loss.

(c) *Separate activities.*—(1) *General rule.*—For each section 1245 property which is leased or held for leasing, rules similar to those found in § 1.465-42(c) shall apply for purposes of determining what constitutes a separate activity.

(2) *Section 1245 property.*—For the purposes of section 465 where several section 1245 properties, such as parts of a computer system, comprise one unit under the same lease agreement and are neither separately financed nor subject to different lease terms, the properties will be considered one section 1245 property.

(d) *Lease.*—For the purposes of section 465, a lease is any arrangement or agreement, formal or informal, written or oral, whereby the owner of property receives consideration in any form for the use of the property by another party. Whether a specific transaction constitutes a lease or sale shall be determined on the basis of the particular facts and circumstances.

(e) *Ancillary leasing of section 1245 property.*—Section 465 shall not apply to amounts received or accrued where the leasing of section 1245 property is incidental to making real property available as living accommodations (such as where an unfurnished rental apartment is equipped with a stove or refrigerator). Section 465 shall also not apply to amounts received or accrued where the leasing of section 1245 property is incidental to the furnishing of services. [Reg. § 1.465-44.]

§ 1.465-45. Activities to which section 465 applies; exploring for, or exploiting, oil and gas resources.—(a) *In general.*—Section 465 applies to any taxpayer described in § 1.465-1(d) who is engaged in exploring for, or exploiting, oil and gas resources as a trade or business or for the production of income.

(b) *Loss.*—All receipts related to exploring for, or exploiting, oil and gas resources and which constitute gross income from the property within the meaning of section 613, and all items of deduction incurred with respect to such receipts, are to be taken into account in determining whether there is a section 465(d) loss.

(c) *Separate activities.*—For each separate oil and gas property (as defined under section 614) rules similar to those found in § 1.465-42(c) shall apply for purposes of determining what constitutes a separate activity.

(d) *Depletion.*—In the case of exploring for, or exploiting, oil and gas resources a taxpayer's allowable deduction under section 611 (relating to an allowance for depletion) shall be considered a deduction incurred in the production of income from the activity. Therefore, it must be taken into account in determining the taxpayer's section 465(d) loss. A taxpayer's amount at risk in an activity shall be increased by the excess of the deductions for depletion over the basis of the property (used within the activity) subject to depletion. [Reg. § 1.465-45.]

§ 1.465-66. Transfers and dispositions; general rule.—(a) *General rule.*—In the case of a transfer or other disposition of all or part of either an activity or an interest in an activity during a taxable year, any gain recognized on the transfer or disposition shall be treated as income from the activity in accordance with § 1.465-12. In the case of a liquidation by a partnership of a partner's interest in that partnership, or complete redemption by an electing small business corporation of a shareholder's stock in that corporation, the provisions of this section shall apply. In general, this section will cause amounts disallowed by section 465 in previous taxable years to be allowed for the taxable year of transfer or disposition. In addition, any gain recognized as the result of a transfer or disposition of an asset which was at one time used in an activity shall be treated as income from the activity, notwithstanding the fact that the taxpayer's participation in the activity ended prior to the transfer or disposition.

(b) *Examples.*—The provisions of this section may be illustrated by the following examples:

Example (1). On January 1, 1976, A and B as equal partners form partnership AB. A and B, as well as AB, are calendar year taxpayers. After the close of taxable year 1978 A's basis in AB is $3,000, A's amount at risk is zero, and A has $7,000 of losses from the activity which would have been allowed but for section 465(a). AB's assets are subject to a nonrecourse loan of $20,000, of which A's share is $10,000. On January 1, 1979, C purchases A's interest in AB for $11,000. C pays A $1,000 in cash and takes a 50 percent interest in the partnership, which is renamed BC. BC's assets are still encumbered to the extent of $20,000. A's amount realized is $11,000, which includes $1,000 cash as well as the amount of the encumbrance on A's share of AB's assets ($10,000). Therefore, A's gain is $8,000 ($11,000 – $3,000). This $8,000 is income from the activity. Assuming A is entitled to no deductions allocable to the activity for 1979 other than those disallowed in 1978 under section 465(a), income allocable to the activity for 1979 ($8,000) will exceed the deductions ($7,000). Consequently, A will not have a section 465(d) loss from the activity in 1979 because $7,000 is less than the amount of income from the activity for 1979 ($8,000). The $7,000 of deductions will be allowed for 1979.

Example (2). On January 1, 1978, D, an individual, purchases a piece of equipment to be used in an activity described in section 465(c)(1)(C). D purchases the equipment for $10,000, paying $1,000 from personal assets and borrowing $9,000 from a bank. The loan from the bank is a nonrecourse loan secured by the equipment. After the close of 1980 D's basis in the equipment is $2,000 and the amount at risk in the activity is zero. As of the beginning of 1981 D has $7,000 of losses which would be allowed but for section 465(a). The equipment is still encumbered by the $9,000 loan. On January 1, 1981, D gives the piece of equipment to a relative, E. The fair market value of the equipment at the time of the transfer is $9,500. E pays no cash to D but takes the equipment still subject to the nonrecourse loan. D's amount realized on the transfer is $9,000, attributable to the liabilities to which the equipment is subject. D must recognize $7,000 ($9,000 – $2,000) of income on the disposition. This $7,000 is income from the activity. Assuming D is entitled to no deductions allocable to the activity for 1981 other than those disallowed in 1980 under section 465(a) the income allocable from the activity for 1981 ($7,000) will equal the deductions allocable to the activity for 1981 ($7,000). Consequently, D will not have a section 465(d) loss from the activity in 1981

and the $7,000 of deductions will be allowed for 1981, because there is an equal amount of income from the activity in that year.

Example (3). E, an individual calendar year taxpayer, is a partner in partnership EFGH, which is also a calendar year taxpayer. At the close of 1978 E's amount at risk is zero, E's adjusted basis is $350, and E has deductions disallowed by section 465 in the amount of $50. E's share of nonrecourse liabilities of the partnership is $400. At the close of 1979 none of the figures has changed and EFGH distributes property (which is not described in section 751) to E in complete liquidation of E's interest in EFGH. Under section 752(b) E is treated as receiving $400. Under section 732(b), E's basis of $350 is reduced to zero. E must recognize $50 of gain ($400 – $350). Under this section, E has income from the activity in the amount of the gain recognized ($50). This will allow E to deduct the $50 deductions previously suspended. In 1979 E will not have a section 465(d) loss from the activity [Reg. § 1.465-66.]

§ 1.465-67. Transfers and dispositions; pass through of losses suspended under section 465(a).—(a) *Applicability.*—This section shall apply to any transfer or disposition in which—

(1) The taxpayer transfers or disposes of such taxpayer's entire interest in the activity or the entity conducting the activity,

(2) The basis of the transferee is determined in whole or in part by reference to the basis of the transferor; and

(3) The transferor has suspended losses under section 465(a) at the time of the transfer or disposition.

For the treatment of any gain recognized by the transferor, see § 1.465-66.

(b) *Pass through of suspended losses.*—If at the close of the taxable year in which the transfer or disposition occurs, the amount of the transferor's section 465(d) loss from the activity is in excess of the transferor's amount at risk in the activity, such excess shall be added to the transferor's basis in the activity. The preceding sentence is to be applied after the determination of any gain to the transferor and is to be used solely for the purpose of determining the basis of the property in the hands of the transferee. [Reg. § 1.465-67.]

§ 1.465-68. Transfers and dispositions; amounts at risk in excess of losses disallowed.—(a) *Applicability.*—This section shall apply to any transfer or disposition (except a transfer at death) in which—

(1) The taxpayer transfers or disposes of such taxpayer's entire interest in the activity or the entity conducting the activity;

(2) The basis of the transferee is determined in whole or in part by reference to the basis of the transferor; and

(3) The transferor has an amount at risk which is in excess of losses from the activity.

(b) *General rule.*—At the close of the transferor's taxable year in which the transfer or disposition occurs, the transferor's amount at risk in the activity (after being reduced by the transferor's losses from that activity for that taxable year) shall be added to the transferee's amount at risk. In addition, the transferee's amount at risk shall be increased by the amount that the transferee's basis is increased under section 1015(d) (relating to gift tax paid by the transferor).

(c) *Limitation.*—The amount by which the transferee's amount at risk is increased under paragraph (b) of this section shall be limited to the amount of the transferee's basis which exceeds the amount considered paid by the transferee at the time of the transfer. For the purposes of this section the amount considered paid by the transferee includes the amount of liabilities to which the transferred property is subject.

(d) *Examples.*—The provisions of this section may be illustrated by the following examples:

Example (1). On December 31, 1978, F, an individual, makes a gift to G of F's entire interest in an activity described in section 465(c)(1). F had engaged in the activity as an individual. As of the close of 1978 F's amount at risk in the activity is $500, F's adjusted basis in the activity is $9,500, the fair market value of the activity is $20,000, and the activity is subject to a nonrecourse liability of $9,000. G does not pay any cash to F but takes the gift subject to the $9,000 liability. Since F's amount at risk in the activity is $500 at the close of the year, this amount shall be added to G's amount at risk. This amount is not limited by paragraph (c) of this section, because the amount of G's adjusted basis which exceeds the amount G is considered to have paid at the time of the transfer is also $500 ($9,500 – $9,000). Therefore, G is at risk in the amount of $500.

Example (2). Assume the same facts as in example (1), except that in addition to G taking the gift subject to the $9,000 liability, G also pays F $1,500 in cash. Regardless of how much F is at risk, G's amount at risk will not be increased as the result of this section. This is because the amount of increase is limited to the excess of G's basis ($10,500, consisting of the $9,000 liability, plus the $1,500 cash paid to F) over the amount G is considered to have paid F ($9,000 + $1,500 = $10,500). Since the excess is zero ($10,500 – $10,500), the amount of increase under §1.465-68(b) is also zero. G's amount at risk will be increased, however, under §1.465-22(d) by the $1,500 cash paid to F, and therefore, G's amount at risk is $1,500. [Reg. §1.465-68.]

§1.465-69. Transfers and dispositions; amounts at risk in excess of losses disallowed with respect to transfers at death.— (a) *Applicability.—*If after the close of the taxable year in which a decedent dies, the decedent's amount at risk in the activity (after being reduced by losses previously suspended under section 465(a)) is greater than zero, such amount shall be added to the successor's amount at risk. However, this amount must be adjusted to reflect changes, if any, in the amount at risk occurring as the result of the decedent's death. The successor's amount at risk shall also be increased by the amount which the successor's basis in the activity is increased under section 1014 or 1023(h), (c), (d), and (e).

(b) *Example.—*The provisions of this section may be illustrated by the following example:

Example. H, an individual, is engaged in an activity described in section 465(c)(1) for a taxable year in which section 1023 applies. On December 31 of such year, H dies. On that date H's basis in the activity is $6,000, H's amount at risk in the activity is $2,500, and the fair market value of the activity is $12,500. Under H's will, J is the sole beneficiary of H's interest in the activity. During the period between H's death and the time J succeeded to the activity nothing occurred which affected the amount at risk. Under sections 1023(h), (c), (d), and (e), the basis of the activity in the hands of J is increased by $5,000, which when added to H's basis of $6,000, gives J a basis in the activity of $11,000. To determine J's amount at risk in the activity, H's amount at risk in the activity ($2,500) is added to the amount by which J's basis in the activity is increased under sections 1023(h), (c), (d), and (e) ($5,000). Therefore, J's amount at risk in the activity is $7,500 ($2,500 + $5,000). [Reg. §1.465-69.]

§1.465-75. Amounts at risk with respect to activities begun prior to effective date; in general.—Section 465 generally applies to losses attributable to amounts paid or incurred in taxable years beginning after December 31, 1975. For the purposes of applying the at risk limitation to activities begun before the effective date of the provision (and which were not excepted from application of the provision), it is necessary to determine the amount at risk as of the first day of the first taxable year beginning after December 31, 1975. The amount at risk in an activity as of the first day of the first taxable year of the taxpayer beginning after December 31, 1975 (for the purposes of §§1.465-75 through 1.465-79, such first day shall be referred to as the effective date) shall be determined according to the rules provided in §§1.465-76 through 1.465-79. [Reg. §1.465-75.]

§1.465-76. Amounts at risk with respect to activities begun prior to effective date; determination of amount at risk.—(a) *Initial amount.—*The amount a taxpayer is at risk on the effective date with respect to an activity to which section 465 applies shall be determined in accordance with this section. The initial amount the taxpayer is at risk in the activity shall be the taxpayer's initial basis in the activity as modified by disregarding amounts described in section 465(b)(3) or (4) (relating generally to amounts protected against loss or borrowed from related persons).

(b) *Succeeding adjustments.—*For each taxable year ending before the effective date, the initial amount at risk shall be increased and decreased by the items which increased and decreased the taxpayer's basis in the activity in that year as modified by disregarding the amounts described in section 465(b)(3) or (4).

Initial amount at risk	$10,000
Plus:	
Items which increased basis other than amounts described in section 465 (b)(3) or (4)	$0
	$10,000
Less:	
Distribution	3,000
J's amount at risk on effective date	$7,000

Example (2). Assume the same facts as in example (1) except that JK has a section 465(d) loss for 1975, of which J's share is $12,000. Although J's basis in the activity is $13,000 ($10,000 + $18,000 –

Initial amount at risk	$10,000
Plus:	
Items which increased basis other than amounts described in section 465 (b)(3) or (4)	0
	$10,000
Less:	
Distribution plus	
Portion of loss ($12,000) in excess of portion of basis not at risk ($18,000) ($3,000 + 0)	3,000
J's amount at risk on effective date	$7,000

Example (3). Assume the same facts as in example (1) except that JK has a section 465(d) loss for 1975, and J's share is $23,000. J's basis in

Initial amount at risk	$10,000
Plus:	
Items which increased basis other than amounts described in section 465(b)(3) or (4)	0
	$10,000

(c) *Application of losses and withdrawals.—*(1) Losses described in section 465(d) which are incurred in taxable years beginning prior to January 1, 1976 and deducted in such taxable years will be treated as reducing first that portion of the taxpayer's basis which is attributable to amounts not at risk. On the other hand, withdrawals made in taxable years beginning before January 1, 1976 will be treated as reducing the amount which the taxpayer is at risk.

(2) Therefore, if in a taxable year beginning prior to January 1, 1976 there is a loss described in section 465(d), it shall reduce the amount at risk only to the extent it exceeds the amount of the taxpayer's basis which is not at risk. For the purposes of this paragraph the taxpayer's basis which is not at risk is that portion of the taxpayer's basis in the activity (as of the close of the taxable year and prior to reduction for the loss) which is attributable to amounts described in section 465(b)(3) or (4).

(d) *Amount at risk shall not be less than zero.—*If, after determining the amount described in paragraph (a), (b), and (c) of this section, the amount at risk (but for this paragraph) would be less than zero, the amount at risk on the effective date shall be zero. [Reg. §1.465-76.]

§1.465-77. Amounts at risk with respect to activities begun prior to effective date; allocation of loss for different taxable years.—If the taxable year of the entity conducting the activity differs from that of the taxpayer, the loss attributable to the activity for the first taxable year of the entity ending after the beginning of the first taxable year of the taxpayer beginning after December 31, 1975, shall be allocated in the following manner: That portion of the loss from the activity for such taxable year of the entity which is attributable to taxable years of the taxpayer beginning before January 1, 1976, is that portion which bears the same ratio to the total loss as the number of days in such taxable year before January 1, 1976, bears to the total number of days in the entire taxable year. Consequently, that portion shall be treated in accordance with §1.465-76. [Reg. §1.465-77.]

§1.465-78. Amounts at risk with respect to activities begun prior to effective date; insufficient records.—If sufficient records do not exist to accurately determine under §1.465-76 the amount which a taxpayer is at risk on the effective date, the amount at risk shall be the taxpayer's basis in the activity reduced (but not below zero) by the taxpayer's share of amounts described in section 465(b)(3) or (4) with respect to the activity on the day before the effective date [Reg. §1.465-78.]

§1.465-79. Amounts at risk with respect to activities begun prior to effective date; examples.—The provisions of §1.465-75 and §1.465-76 may be illustrated by the following examples:

Example (1). J and K, as equal partners, form partnership JK on January 1, 1975 to engage in an activity described in section 465(c)(1). Both J and K, as well as JK, are calendar year taxpayers. On January 1, 1975, each partner contributes $10,000 in cash from personal assets to JK. On July 1, 1975, JK borrows $40,000 (of which J's share is $20,000) from a bank under a nonrecourse financing arrangement secured only by the new equipment purchased with the $40,000 for use in the activity. On September 1, 1975, JK reduces the amount due on the loan to $36,000 (of which J's share is $18,000). On October 1, 1975, JK distributes $3,000 to each partner. For taxable year 1975, JK has no income or loss. Although J's basis in the activity is $25,000 ($10,000 + $18,000 – $3,000), J's amount at risk on the effective date is $7,000, determined as follows:

($3,000 + $12,000)), J's amount at risk on the effective date is $7,000, determined as follows:

the activity is $2,000 ($10,000 + $18,000 – ($3,000 + $23,000)). The amount at risk on the effective date is determined as follows:

Less:

Distribution	$3,000		
Portion of loss ($23,000) in excess of portion of basis not at risk ($18,000)	5,000		8,000
J's amount at risk on the effective date			$2,000

[Reg. §1.465-79.]

§1.465-95. Effective date.—(a) *In general.*—Except as otherwise provided, the regulations under section 465 shall apply to losses attributable to amounts paid or incurred in taxable years beginning after December 31, 1975. For purposes of this paragraph, any amount allowed or allowable for depreciation, amortization, or depletion for any period shall be treated as an amount paid or incurred in such period.

(b) *Special rules.*—For special rules relating to the effective date of section 465 with respect to certain leasing activities and certain movie and video tape activities, see section 204(c)(2) and (3) of the Tax Reform Act of 1976 (90 Stat. 1532). [Reg. §1.465-95.]

Deduction Limited to Amount at Risk

Deduction Limited to Amount at Risk.—Amendments to Reg. §§7.465-1—7.465-5, relating to the determination of amounts at risk with respect to certain activities, are proposed (published in the Federal Register on June 5, 1979).

☐ Par. 2. Sections 7.465-1 through 7.465-5 of this chapter (26 CFR Part 7), promulgated by Treasury Decision 7504, are hereby revoked.

§7.465-1. Amounts at risk with respect to activities begun prior to effective date; in general (Temporary).

§7.465-2. Determination of amount at risk (Temporary).

§7.465-3. Allocation of loss for different taxable years (Temporary).

§7.465-4. Insufficient records (Temporary).

§7.465-5. Examples (Temporary).

Nuclear Decommissioning Funds: Contributions to Trusts: Deductions

Nuclear Decommissioning Funds: Contributions to Trusts: Deductions.—Amendments to Reg. §1.468A-1, relating to deductions for contributions to trusts maintained for decommissioning nuclear power plants and the use of the amounts in those trusts to decommission nuclear plants, are proposed (published in the Federal Register on December 29, 2016) (REG-112800-16).

Par. 2. Section §1.468A-1 is amended by revising paragraph (b)(6) to read as follows:

§1.468A-1. Nuclear decommissioning costs; general rules.

* * *

(b) * * *

(6)(i) The term *nuclear decommissioning costs* or *decommissioning costs* includes all otherwise deductible expenses to be incurred in connection with the entombment, decontamination, dismantlement, removal and disposal of the structures, systems and components of a nuclear power plant, whether that nuclear power plant will continue to produce electric energy or has permanently ceased to produce electric energy. Such term includes all otherwise deductible expenses to be incurred in connection with the preparation for decommissioning, such as engineering and other planning expenses, and all otherwise deductible expenses to be incurred with respect to the plant after the actual decommissioning occurs, such as physical security and radiation monitoring expenses. An expense is otherwise deductible for purposes of this paragraph (b)(6) if it would be deductible or recoverable through depreciation or amortization under chapter 1 of the Internal Revenue Code without regard to section 280B.

(ii) The term nuclear decommissioning costs or decommissioning costs also includes costs incurred in connection with the construction, operation, and ultimate decommissioning of a facility used solely to store, pending delivery to a permanent repository or disposal, spent nuclear fuel generated by the nuclear power plant or plants located on the same site as the storage facility (for example, an Independent Spent Fuel Storage Installation). Such term does not include otherwise deductible expenses to be incurred in connection with the disposal of spent nuclear fuel under the Nuclear Waste Policy Act of 1982 (Public Law 97-425).

* * *

Nuclear Decommissioning Funds: Contributions to Trusts: Deductions

Nuclear Decommissioning Funds: Contributions to Trusts: Deductions.—Amendments to Reg. §1.468A-5, relating to deductions for contributions to trusts maintained for decommissioning nuclear power plants and the use of the amounts in those trusts to decommission nuclear plants, are proposed (published in the Federal Register on December 29, 2016) (REG-112800-16).

Par. 3. Paragraph §1.468A-5 is amended by revising the heading and paragraphs (b)(2)(i) and (d)(3)(i) to read as follows:

§1.468A-5. Nuclear decommissioning fund—miscellaneous provisions.

* * *

(b) * * *

(2) * * *

(i) A payment by a nuclear decommissioning fund for the purpose of satisfying, in whole or in part, the liability of the electing taxpayer for decommissioning costs of the nuclear power plant to which the nuclear decommissioning fund relates, whether such payment is made to an unrelated party in satisfaction of the decommissioning liability or to the plant operator or other otherwise disqualified person as reimbursement solely for actual expenses paid by such person in satisfaction of the decommissioning liability;

* * *

(d) * * *

(3) * * *

(i) The substantial completion of the decommissioning of a nuclear power plant occurs on the date on which all Federal, state, local, and contractual decommissioning requirements are fully satisfied (the substantial completion date). Except as otherwise provided in paragraph (d)(3)(ii) of this section, the substantial completion date is also the termination date.

* * *

Escrow Funds: Reporting of Income: Qualified Settlement Funds

Escrow Funds: Reporting of Income: Qualified Settlement Funds: Qualified Trusts: Escrow Accounts—Reg. §§1.468B-8, relating to the designation of the person required to report the income earned on qualified settlement funds and certain other funds, trusts, and escrow accounts, and other related rules, is proposed (published in the Federal Register on February 1, 1999) (REG-209619-93). Proposed Reg. §§1.468B-7 and 1.468B-9 and proposed amendments to Reg. §§1.468B-0, 1.468B-1 and 1.468B-5 were adopted by T.D. 9249 on February 3, 2006. Proposed Reg. §1.468D-6 was withdrawn on February 7, 2006.

☐ Par. 5. [Section 1.468B-8 is] added to read as follows:

§1.468B-8. Contingent at-closing escrows.—(a) *Scope.*—This section provides rules under section 468B(g) for the taxation of income earned on a contingent at-closing escrow, which is defined in paragraph (b) of this section. No inference should be drawn from this section concerning the tax treatment of a contingent at-closing escrow, or of parties to the escrow, under sections of the Internal Revenue Code other than section 468B. See also paragraph (d) of this section.

(b) *Definitions.*—For purposes of this section, the following definitions apply—

Administrator means an escrow agent, escrow holder, trustee, or other person responsible for administering an escrow account, trust, or fund (the purchaser or the seller may be the administrator);

Contingent at-closing escrow means an escrow account, trust, or fund that satisfies the following requirements—

(1) The escrow is established in connection with the sale or exchange (other than an exchange to which section 354, 355, or 356 applies) of real or personal property used in a trade or business or held for investment (including stock in a corporation or an interest in a partnership);

(2) Depending on whether events specified in the agreement between the purchaser and the seller that are subject to bona fide contingencies (not including events that are certain, or reasonably certain, to occur, such as the passage of time, or that are certain, or reasonably certain, not to occur) either occur or fail to occur, the escrow's assets (except for assets set aside for taxes or expenses) will be distributable—

(i) Entirely to the purchaser;

(ii) Entirely to the seller; or

(iii) In part, to the purchaser with the remainder to the seller; and

(3) The escrow is not a qualified escrow account or qualified trust established in connection with a deferred exchange under section 1031(a)(3);

Determination date means the date on which (or by which) the last of the events subject to a bona fide contingency specified in the agreement between the purchaser and the seller (referred to in the definition of *contingent at-closing escrow*) has either occurred or failed to occur;

Purchaser means, in the case of an exchange of property, the transferee of the property; and

Seller means, in the case of an exchange of property, the transferor of the property.

(c) *Tax liability of purchaser and seller for the period prior to the determination date.*—For the period prior to the determination date, the purchaser is treated as owning the assets of the contingent at-closing escrow for federal income tax purposes. Thus, in computing the purchaser's income tax liability, the purchaser must take into account all items of income, deduction, and credit (including capital gains and losses) of the escrow until the determination date.

(d) *Transfer of interest in the assets of the escrow on the determination date.*—No inference should be drawn from this section whether, for purposes of Internal Revenue Code sections other than 468B, there is a transfer of ownership of the assets of a contingent at-closing escrow on the determination date from the purchaser to the seller or from the seller to the purchaser, or the tax consequences of such a transfer. Thus, for example, if there is a transfer of ownership of the assets of the escrow from the purchaser to the seller on the determination date for purposes of other Code sections, no inference should be drawn from this section whether any portion of the amount transferred is unstated interest. See § 1.483-4.

(e) *Tax liability of purchaser and seller for the period beginning on the determination date.*—For the period beginning on the determination date, the purchaser and the seller must each take into account in determining their income tax liabilities the income, deductions, and credits (including capital gains and losses) corresponding to their ownership interests in the assets of the escrow.

(f) *Statement required to be provided to administrator within 30 days after the determination date.*—Within 30 days after the determination date, the purchaser and the seller must provide the administrator with a written statement that—

(1) Is signed by the purchaser and the seller;

(2) Specifies the determination date; and

(3) Specifies the purchaser's and seller's ownership interests in each asset of the escrow.

(g) *Reporting obligations of the administrator.*—(1) *In general.*—The administrator of a contingent at-closing escrow must, for each calendar year (or portion thereof) that the escrow is in existence, report the income of the escrow on Forms 1099 in accordance with the informa-

tion reporting requirements of subpart B, Part III, subchapter A, chapter 61, Subtitle F of the Internal Revenue Code. The Forms 1099 must show as payor the administrator of the escrow and as payee the person (or persons) treated as the payee (or payees) under paragraph (g)(2) of this section.

(2) *Person treated as payee.*—In satisfying the reporting obligations of paragraph (g)(1) of this section, the following rules apply to the administrator—

(i) For the period prior to the determination date, the administrator must treat the purchaser as the payee of the income of the escrow;

(ii) For the period beginning on the determination date, if the written statement described in paragraph (f) of this section is timely provided to the administrator, the administrator must treat as the payee (or payees) of the income of the escrow the purchaser or seller (or both) in accordance with their respective ownership interests as shown on the statement; and

(iii) If the written statement described in paragraph (f) of this section is not provided to the administrator, the administrator must continue to treat the purchaser as the payee of the income of the escrow.

(3) *Relief from penalties for filing incorrect information return or payee statement.*—For purposes of sections 6721 and 6722, the administrator will not be treated as failing to file or furnish a correct information return or payee statement solely because, in preparing a Form 1099, the administrator relies on a statement described in paragraph (f) of this section and therefore treats the purchaser or seller (or both) as the payee (or payees) of the income of the escrow in accordance with their respective ownership interests in the assets of the escrow as shown on the statement. If a statement described in paragraph (f) of this section is not provided to the administrator, the administrator will not be treated as failing to file or furnish a correct information return or payee statement solely because, in preparing a Form 1099, the administrator relies on the absence of the statement and therefore treats the purchaser as the payee.

(h) *Effective date.*—(1) *In general.*—The provisions of this section apply to contingent at-closing escrows that are established after the date of publication of final regulations in the Federal Register.

(2) *Transition rule.*—With respect to a contingent at-closing escrow established after August 16, 1986, but on or before the date of publication of final regulations in the Federal Register, the Internal Revenue Service will not challenge a reasonable, consistently applied method of taxation for income earned by the escrow. The Internal Revenue Service will also not challenge a reasonable, consistently applied method for reporting such income.

(i) [Reserved]

(j) *Example.*—The provisions of this section may be illustrated by the following example:

Example. (i) P and S are corporations. In 1999, P enters into a contract with S for the purchase of rental real estate. On October 1, 1999, the date of sale, S transfers the real estate to P, and P pays S a portion of the purchase price, $9,000,000. P deposits the remaining portion of the purchase price, $850,000, into an escrow account as required by the contract. H is the escrow holder.

(ii) The contract provides that the escrow balance as of November 1, 2000, is payable entirely to P, entirely to S, or partially to P and partially to S depending on the amount, if any, by which the average rental income from the real estate during a specified testing period ending on September 30, 2000, exceeds one or more specified earnings targets.

(iii) According to the terms of the contract, the income earned on the escrow must be accumulated and is not currently distributable to P or S during the period prior to November 1, 2000.

(iv) During the testing period specified in the contract between P and S, the average rental income earned on the property exceeds one (but not all) of the specified earnings targets. As a result, on September 30, 2000, the end of the testing period, P became entitled to 40% of the escrow assets and S became entitled to 60% of the escrow assets.

(v) On October 30, 2000, P and S provide H with the written statement described in paragraph (f) of this section. The written statement is thus provided within 30 days of September 30, 2000. The statement indicates that P's ownership interest in each asset of the escrow is 40 percent and S's ownership interest in each asset is 60 percent.

(vi) The escrow is a contingent at-closing escrow. September 30, 2000, is the determination date because this is the date on which the testing period ends. As of this date, all contingencies specified in the contract are resolved.

(vii) P must take into account all of the income, deductions, and credits (including capital gains and losses) of the escrow in computing P's income tax liability for the period prior to September 30, 2000. See paragraph (c) of this section.

(viii) For the period beginning on September 30, 2000, P must take into account in computing P's income tax liability 40 percent of each item of income, deduction, and credit of the escrow (including capital gains and losses), and S must take into account in computing S's income tax liability 60 percent of these items. See paragraph (e) of this section.

(ix) H is subject to the information reporting requirements of paragraph (g)(1) of this section. H must file Forms 1099 and furnish payee statements to reflect the fact that prior to September 30, 2000, P is the payee of all the income of the escrow, and for the period beginning on September 30, 2000, P is the payee of 40 percent of the income, and S is the payee of 60 percent of the income.

[Reg. § 1.468B-8.]

Passive Activity Losses and Credits: Limitations

Passive Activity Losses and Credits: Limitations.— Reg. §§1.469–1T, 1.469–2T, 1.469–3T and 1.469–5T, relating to the limitations on passive activity losses and credits, are proposed (published in the Federal Register on February 24, 1988) (LR-14-88). Reg. §1.469–11T was adopted by T.D. 8417 on May 11, 1992.

§1.469–1T. General rules (temporary).

§1.469–2T. Passive activity loss (temporary).

§1.469–3T. Passive activity credit (temporary).

§1.469–5T. Material participation (temporary).

Passive Activity Losses and Credits: Limitations

Passive Activity Losses and Credits: Limitations.—Amendments to Reg. §§1.469–0, 1.469–5, 1.469–5T and 1.469–9, regarding the definition of an "interest in a limited partnership as a limited partner" for purposes of determining whether a taxpayer materially participates in an activity under section 469 of the Internal Revenue Code, are proposed (published in the Federal Register on November 28, 2011) (REG-109369-10).

☐ Par. 2. Section 1.469–0 is amended by:
1. Revising the entries for § 1.469–5(a), (b), (c), (d), and (e).
2. Removing the entries for § 1.469–5T(e)(1), (e)(2), and (e)(3).
The revisions read as follows:

§1.469–0. Table of contents.

* * *

§1.469–5. Material participation.
(a) through (d) [Reserved].
(e) Treatment of an interest in a limited partnership as a limited partner.
(1) In general.

(2) Exceptions.
(3) Interest in a limited partnership as a limited partner.
(i) In general.
(ii) Individual holding an interest other than an interest in a limited partnership as a limited partner.
(4) Effective/applicability date.

* * *

☐ Par. 3. In §1.469–5, paragraphs (a), (b), (c), (d), and (e) are revised to read as follows:

§1.469–5. Material participation.—(a) through (d) [Reserved].

(e) *Treatment of an interest in a limited partnership as a limited partner.*—(1) *In general.*—Except as otherwise provided in this paragraph (e), an individual shall not be treated as materially participating in any activity in which the individual owns an interest in a limited partnership as a limited partner (as defined in paragraph (e)(3)(i) of this section) for purposes of applying section 469 and the regulations thereunder to—

(i) The individual's share of any income, gain, loss, deduction, or credit from such activity that is attributable to an interest in a limited partnership as a limited partner; and

(ii) Any gain or loss from such activity recognized upon a sale or exchange of such an interest.

(2) *Exceptions.*—Paragraph (e)(1) of this section shall not apply to an individual's share of income, gain, loss, deduction, and credit for a taxable year from any activity in which the individual would be treated as materially participating for the taxable year under paragraphs (a)(1), (a)(5), or (a)(6) of § 1.469–5T if the individual did not own an interest in a limited partnership as a limited partner (as defined in paragraph (e)(3)(i) of this section) for such taxable year.

(3) *Interest in a limited partnership as a limited partner.*—(i) *In general.*—Except as provided in paragraph (e)(3)(ii) of this section, for purposes of section 469(h)(2) and this paragraph (e), an interest in an

entity shall be treated as an interest in a limited partnership as a limited partner if—

(A) The entity in which such interest is held is classified as a partnership for Federal income tax purposes under § 301.7701-3; and

(B) The holder of such interest does not have rights to manage the entity at all times during the entity's taxable year under the law of the jurisdiction in which the entity is organized and under the governing agreement.

(ii) *Individual holding an interest other than an interest in a limited partnership as a limited partner.*—An individual shall not be treated as holding an interest in a limited partnership as a limited partner for the individual's taxable year if such individual also holds an interest in the partnership that is not an interest in a limited partnership as a limited partner (as defined in paragraph (e)(3)(i) of this section), such as a state-law general partnership interest, at all times during the entity's taxable year ending with or within the individual's taxable year (or the portion of the entity's taxable year during which the individual (directly or indirectly) owns such interest in a limited partnership as a limited partner).

(4) *Effective/applicability date.*—This section applies to taxable years beginning on or after the date of publication of the Treasury decision adopting these rules as a final regulation in the **Federal Register.**

* * *

☐ Par. 4. Section 1.469–5T paragraph (e) is revised to read as follows:

§1.469–5T. Material participation (Temporary).

* * *

☐ Par. 5. Section 1.469–9 paragraph (f)(1) is revised to read as follows:

§1.469–9. Rules for certain rental real estate activities.

* * *

(e) *Treatment of Limited Partners.*—[Reserved]. See § 1.469-5(e) for rules relating to this paragraph (e).

* * *

(f) *Limited partnership interests in rental real estate activities.*— (1) *In general.*—If a taxpayer elects under paragraph (g) of this section to treat all interests in rental real estate as a single rental real estate activity, and at least one interest in rental real estate is held by the taxpayer as an interest in a limited partnership as a limited partner (within the meaning of § 1.469-5(e)(3)), the combined rental real estate activity of the taxpayer will be treated as an interest in a limited partnership as a limited partner for purposes of determining material participation. Accordingly, the taxpayer will not be treated under this section as materially participating in the combined rental real estate activity unless the taxpayer materially participates in the activity under the tests listed in § 1.469-5(e)(2) (dealing with the tests for determining the material participation of a limited partner).

* * *

Deduction for Business Interest Expense: Limitation

Deduction for Business Interest Expense: Limitation.—Amendments to Reg. §1.469-9, regarding the limitation on the deduction for business interest expense after the enactment of recent tax legislation, are proposed (published in the Federal Register on December 28, 2018) (REG-106089-18).

Par. 13. Section 1.469-9 is amended by revising paragraph (b)(2) to read as follows:

§1.469-9. Rules for certain rental real estate activities.

* * *

(b) * * *

(2) *Real property trade or business.*—The following terms have the following meanings in determining whether a trade or business is a real property trade or business for purposes of section 469(c)(7)(C) and this section.

(i) *Real property.*—(A) *In general.*—The term *real property* includes land, buildings, and other inherently permanent structures that are permanently affixed to land. Any interest in real property, including fee ownership, co-ownership, a leasehold, an option, or a similar interest is real property under this section. Tenant improvements to land, buildings, or other structures that are inherently permanent or otherwise classified as real property within the meaning of this section are real property for purposes of section 469(c)(7)(C). However, property produced for sale that is not real property in the hands of the producing taxpayer or a related person, but that may be incorporated into real property by an unrelated person, is not treated as real property of the producing taxpayer for purposes of section 469(c)(7)(C) and this section (for example, bricks, nails, paint, and windowpanes).

(B) *Land.*—The term *land* includes water and air space superjacent to land and natural products and deposits that are unsevered from the land. Natural products and deposits, such as plants, crops, trees, water, ores, and minerals, cease to be real property when they are harvested, severed, extracted, or removed from the land. Accordingly, any trade or business that involves the cultivation and harvesting of plants, crops, or trees, or severing, extracting, or removing natural products or deposits from land is not a real property trade or business for purposes of section 469(c)(7)(C) and this section. The storage or maintenance of severed or extracted natural products or deposits, such as plants, crops, trees, water, ores, and minerals, in or upon real property does not cause the stored property to be recharacterized as real property, and any trade or business relating to or involving such storage or maintenance of severed or extracted natural products or deposits is not a real property trade or business, even though such storage or maintenance otherwise may occur upon or within real property.

(C) *Inherently permanent structure.*—The term *inherently permanent structure* means any permanently affixed building or other permanently affixed structure. If the affixation is reasonably expected to last indefinitely, based on all the facts and circumstances, the affixation is considered permanent. However, an asset that serves an active function, such as an item of machinery or equipment (for example, HVAC system, elevator or escalator), is not a building or other inherently permanent structure, and therefore is not real property for purposes of section 469(c)(7)(C) and this section, even if such item of machinery or equipment is permanently affixed to or becomes incorporated within a building or other inherently permanent structure. Accordingly, a trade or business that involves the manufacture, installation, operation, maintenance, or repair of any asset that serves an active function will not be a real property trade or business, or a unit or component of another real property trade or business, for purposes of section 469(c)(7)(C) and this section.

(D) *Building.*—(1) *In general.*—A *building* encloses a space within its walls and is generally covered by a roof or other external upper covering that protects the walls and inner space from the elements.

(2) *Types of buildings.*—Buildings include the following assets if permanently affixed to land: houses; townhouses; apartments; condominiums; hotels; motels; stadiums; arenas; shopping malls; factory and office buildings; warehouses; barns; enclosed garages; enclosed transportation stations and terminals; and stores.

(E) *Other inherently permanent structures.*—(1) *In general.*—Other inherently permanent structures include the following assets if permanently affixed to land: parking facilities; bridges; tunnels; roadbeds; railroad tracks; pipelines; storage structures such as silos and oil and gas storage tanks; and stationary wharves and docks.

(2) *Facts and circumstances determination.*—The determination of whether an asset is an inherently permanent structure is based on all the facts and circumstances. In particular, the following factors must be taken into account:

(i) The manner in which the asset is affixed to land and whether such manner of affixation allows the asset to be easily removed from the land;

(ii) Whether the asset is designed to be removed or to remain in place indefinitely on the land;

(iii) The damage that removal of the asset would cause to the asset itself or to the land to which it is affixed;

(iv) Any circumstances that suggest the expected period of affixation is not indefinite (for example, a lease that requires or permits removal of the asset from the land upon the expiration of the lease); and

(v) The time and expense required to move the asset from the land.

(ii) *Other definitions.*—(A) through (G) [Reserved]

(H) *Real property operation.*—The term *real property operation* means handling, by a direct or indirect owner of the real property, the day-to-day operations of a trade or business, within the meaning of paragraph (b)(1) of this section, relating to the maintenance and occupancy of the real property that affect the availability and functionality of that real property used, or held out for use, by customers where payments received from customers are principally for the customers' use of the real property. The principal purpose of such business operations must be the provision of the use of the real property, or physical space accorded by or within the real property, to one or more customers, and not the provision of other significant or extraordinary personal services, within the meaning of §1.469-1T(e)(3)(iv) and (v), to customers in conjunction with the customers' incidental use of the real property or physical space. If the real property or physical space is provided to a customer to be used to carry on the customer's trade or business, the principal purpose of the business operations must be to provide the customer with exclusive use of the real property or physical space in furtherance of the customer's trade or business, and not to provide other significant or extraordinary personal services to the customer in addition to or in conjunction with the use of the real property or physical space, regardless of whether the customer pays for the services separately. However, other incidental personal services may be provided to the customer in conjunction with the use of real property or physical space, as long as such services are insubstantial in relation to the customer's use of the real property or physical space and the receipt of such services is not a significant factor in the customer's decision to use the real property or physical space.

(I) *Real property management.*—The term *real property management* means handling, by a professional manager, the day-to-day operations of a trade or business, within the meaning of paragraph (b)(1) of this section, relating to the maintenance and occupancy of real property that affect the availability and functionality of that property used, or held out for use, by customers where payments received from customers are principally for the customers' use of the real property. The principal purpose of such business operations must be the provision of the use of the real property, or physical space accorded by or within the real property, to one or more customers, and not the provision of other significant or extraordinary personal services, within the meaning of §1.469-1T(e)(3)(iv) and (v), to customers in conjunction with the customers' incidental use of the real property or physical space. If the real property or physical space is provided to a customer to be used to carry on the customer's trade or business, the principal purpose of the business operations must be to provide the customer with exclusive use of the real property or physical space in furtherance of the customer's trade or business, and not to provide other significant or extraordinary personal services to the customer in addition to or in conjunction with the use of the real property or physical space, regardless of whether the customer pays for the services separately. However, other incidental personal services may be provided to the customer in conjunction with the use of real property or physical space, as long as such services are insubstantial in relation to the customer's use of the real property or physical space and the receipt of such services is not a significant factor in the customer's decision to use the real property or physical space. A professional manager is a person responsible, on a full-time basis, for the overall management and oversight of the real property or properties and who is not a direct or indirect owner of the real property or properties.

(J) and (K) [Reserved]

(iii) *Examples.*—The following examples illustrate the operation of this paragraph (b)(2):

(A) *Example 1.* A owns farmland and uses the land in A's farming business to grow and harvest crops of various kinds. As part of this farming business, A utilizes a greenhouse that is an inherently permanent structure to grow certain crops during the winter months. Under the rules of this section, any trade or business that involves the cultivation and harvesting of plants, crops, or trees is not a real property trade or business for purposes of section 469(c)(7)(C) and this section, even though the cultivation and harvesting of crops occurs upon or within real property. Accordingly, under these facts, A is not engaged in a real property trade or business for purposes of section 469(c)(7)(C) and this section.

(B) *Example 2.* B is a retired farmer and owns farmland that B rents exclusively to C to operate a farm. The arrangement between B and C is a trade or business (within the meaning of paragraph (b)(1) of this section) where payments by C are principally for C's use of B's real property. B also provides certain farm equipment for C's use. However, C is solely responsible for the maintenance and repair of the farm equipment along with any costs associated with operating the equipment. B also occasionally provides oral advice to C regarding various aspects of the farm operation, based on B's prior experience as a farmer. Other than the provision of this occasional advice, B does not provide any significant or extraordinary personal services to C in connection with the rental of the farmland to C. Under these facts, B is engaged in a real property trade or business (which does not include the use or deemed rental of any farm equipment) for purposes of section 469(c)(7)(C) and this section, and B's oral advice is an incidental personal service that B provides in conjunction with C's use of the real property. Nevertheless, under these facts, C is not engaged in a real property trade or business for purposes of section 469(c)(7)(C) and this section because C is engaged in the business of farming.

(C) *Example 3.* D owns a building in which D operates a restaurant and bar. Even though D provides customers with use of the physical space inside the building, D is not engaged in a trade or business where payments by customers are principally for the use of real property or physical space. Instead, the payments by D's customers are principally for the receipt of significant or extraordinary personal services (within the meaning of §1.469-1T(e)(3)(iv) and (v)), mainly food and beverage preparation and presentation services, and the use of the physical space by customers is incidental to the receipt of these personal services. Under the rules of this section, any trade or business that involves the provision of significant or extraordinary personal services to customers in conjunction with the customers' incidental use of real property or physical space is not a real property trade or business, even though the business operations occur upon or within real property. Accordingly, under these facts, D is not engaged in a real property trade or business for purposes of section 469(c)(7)(C) and this section.

(D) *Example 4.* E owns a majority interest in an S corporation, X, that is engaged in the trade or business of manufacturing industrial cooling systems for installation in commercial buildings and for other uses. E also owns a majority interest in an S corporation, Y, that purchases the industrial cooling systems from X and that installs, maintains, and repairs those systems in both existing commercial buildings and commercial buildings under construction. Under the rules of this section, any trade or business that involves the manufacture, installation, operation, maintenance, or repair of any machinery or equipment that serves an active function will not be a real property trade or business (or a unit or component of another real property trade or business) for purposes of section 469(c)(7)(C) and this section, even though the machinery or equipment will be permanently affixed to real property once it is installed. In this case, the industrial cooling systems are machinery or equipment that serves an active function. Accordingly, under these facts, E, X and Y will not be treated as engaged in one or more real property trades or businesses for purposes of section 469(c)(7)(C) and this section.

(E) *Example 5.* (1) F owns an interest in P, a limited partnership. P owns and operates a luxury hotel. In addition to providing rooms and suites for use by customers, the hotel offers many additional amenities such as in-room food and beverage service, maid and linen service, parking valet service, concierge service, front desk and bellhop service, dry cleaning and laundry service, and in-room barber and hairdresser service. P contracted with M to provide maid and janitorial services to P's hotel. M is an S corporation principally engaged in the trade or business of providing maid and janitorial services to various types of businesses, including hotels. G is a professional manager employed by M who handles the day-to-day business operations relating to M's provision of maid and janitorial services to M's various customers, including P.

(2) Even though the personal services that P provides to the customers of its hotel are significant personal services within the meaning of §1.469-1T(e)(3)(iv), the principal purpose of P's hotel business operations is the provision of use of the hotel's rooms and suites to customers, and not the provision of the significant personal services to P's customers in conjunction with the customers' incidental use of those rooms or suites. The provision of these significant personal services by P to P's customers is incidental to the customers' use of the hotel's real property. Accordingly, under these facts, F and P are treated as engaged in a real property trade or business for purposes of section 469(c)(7)(C) and this section.

(3) With respect to the maid and janitorial services provided by M, M's operations affect the availability and functionality of real property used, or held out for use, by customers in a trade or business where payments by customers are principally for the use of real property (in this case, P's hotel). However, M does not operate or manage real property. Instead, M is engaged in a trade or business of providing maid and janitorial services to customers, such as P, that are engaged in real property trades or businesses. Thus, M's business operations are merely ancillary to real property trades or businesses. Therefore, M is not engaged in real property operations or management as defined in this section. Accordingly, under these facts, M is not engaged in a real property trade or business within the meaning of section 469(c)(7)(C) and this section.

(4) With respect to the day-to-day business operations that G handles as a professional manager of M, the business operations that G manages is not the provision of use of P's hotel rooms and suites to customers. G does not operate or manage real property. Instead, G manages the provision of maid and janitorial services to customers, including P's hotel. Therefore, G is not engaged in real property management as defined in this section. Accordingly, under these facts, G is not engaged in a real property trade or business within the meaning of section 469(c)(7)(C) and this section.

* * *

Deduction for Business Interest Expense: Limitation

Deduction for Business Interest Expense: Limitation.—Amendments to Reg. §1.469-11, regarding the limitation on the deduction for business interest expense after the enactment of recent tax legislation, are proposed (published in the Federal Register on December 28, 2018) (REG-106089-18).

Par. 14. Section 1.469-11 is amended by:

1. Removing the period at the end of paragraph (a)(1) and adding a semicolon in its place;

2. Revising paragraph (a)(3);

3. Redesignating paragraphs (a)(4) and (5) as paragraphs (a)(5) and (6), respectively; and

4. Adding a new paragraph (a)(4).

The revision and addition read as follows:

§1.469-11.   Effective date and transition rules.—(a) * * *

(3) The rules contained in §1.469-9, other than paragraph (a)(4) of this section, apply for taxable years beginning on or after January 1, 1995, and to elections made under §1.469-9(g) with returns filed on or after January 1, 1995, and the rules contained in §1.469-11(a)(4) apply for taxable years beginning on or after the date of the Treasury decision adopting these regulations as final regulations is published in the **Federal Register**;

(4) The rules contained in §1.469-9(b)(2) apply to taxable years beginning after December 31, 2018. Paragraph (b) of this section applies to loss corporations that have undergone an ownership change during a taxable year ending after the date of the Treasury decision adopting these regulations as final regulations is published in the **Federal Register**. However, taxpayers and their related parties, within the meaning of sections 267(b) and 707(b)(1), may rely on the rules of this section if applied consistently by the taxpayers and their

related parties, until the date the Treasury decision adopting these regulations as final regulations is published in the **Federal Register;**

* * *

Commodities: Securities: Mark-to-Market Accounting

Commodities: Securities: Mark-to-Market Accounting.—Reg. §1.471-12, regarding the election to use the mark-to-market method of accounting for dealers in commodities and traders in securities or commodities, is proposed (published in the Federal Register on January 28, 1999) (REG-104924-98).

☐ Par. 3. Section 1.471-12 is added as follows:

§1.471-12. Nonfinancial customer paper.—Nonfinancial customer paper, as defined in section 475(c)(4)(B), may not be treated as

inventory except as provided in §1.475(c)-2(d). This section applies to taxable years ending on or after January 28, 1999. [Reg. §1.471-12.]

Last-In, First-Out Rule: Increase in Value of Inventories

Inventories: Last-In, First-Out Rule: Increase in Value: Three-Year Averaging Method.— Reproduced below is the text of a proposed amendment to Reg. §1.472-2, relating to 3-year averaging for increases in inventory value (published in the Federal Register on February 10, 1983).

☐ Paragraph. Section 1.472-2 is amended as follows:

1. Paragraph (c) is revised to read as set forth below.
2. Paragraph (f) is deleted.

§1.472-2. Requirements incident to the adoption and use of LIFO inventory method.—

* * *

(c)(1) Goods of the specified type included in the opening inventory of the taxable year for which the method is first used shall be considered as having been acquired at the same time and at a unit cost equal to the actual cost of the aggregate divided by the number of units on hand. The actual cost of the aggregate shall be determined pursuant to the inventory method employed by the taxpayer under the regulations applicable to the prior taxable year with the exception that restoration to the opening inventory of the taxable year for which the LIFO method is first used shall be made with respect to any writedown to market values resulting from the pricing of former inventories.

(2) In the case of a taxpayer first using the LIFO method before January 1, 1982, goods of the specified type on hand as of the close of the taxable year preceding the taxable year for which this inventory method is first used shall be included in the taxpayer's

closing inventory for such preceding taxable year at a cost determined in the manner prescribed in paragraph (c)(1) of this section.

(3) In the case of a taxpayer first using the LIFO method after December 31, 1981—

(i) The amount arising from the restoration referred to in paragraph (c)(1) of this section shall be included in the taxpayer's gross income ratably in each of the three taxable years beginning with the taxable year for which the LIFO method is first used.

(ii) Neither an adjustment to the closing inventory nor an amended return shall be required for the taxable year preceding the taxable year for which the LIFO method is first used.

(iii) The provisions of paragraph (c)(3) of this section may be illustrated by the following example:

Example. X, a calendar year taxpayer, first adopts the LIFO method for 1982 and the closing inventory for 1981 included a writedown to market values of $9,000. Such writedown amount shall be restored to the 1982 opening inventory and $3,000 shall be included in X's gross income in each of the taxable years 1982, 1983, and 1984.

LIFO Inventories: Inventory Price Index Computation Method Pools

LIFO Inventories: Inventory Price Index Computation Method Pools.—Amendments to Reg. §1.472-8, relating to the establishment of dollar-value last-in, first-out (LIFO) inventory pools by certain taxpayers that use the inventory price index computation (IPIC) pooling method, are proposed (published in the Federal Register on November 28, 2016) (REG-125946-10).

Par. 2. Section 1.472-8 is amended as follows:

1. Paragraph (b)(4) is revised.
2. Paragraph (c)(2) is revised.
3. Paragraph (e)(3)(ii) is revised.
4. Paragraph (e)(3)(iii)(B)(2) is amended by removing "Table 6 (Producer price indexes and percent changes for commodity groupings and individual items, not seasonally adjusted)" and adding in its place "Table 9 (formerly Table 6) (Producer price indexes and percent changes for commodity and service groupings and individual items, not seasonally adjusted)" in the first sentence; and removing "Table 6" and adding in its place "Table 9" in the second sentence.
5. Paragraphs (e)(3)(iii)(C)(*1*) and (2) are amended by removing "Table 6" and adding in its place "Table 9".
6. Paragraph (e)(3)(v) is revised.

The revisions read as follows:

§1.472-8. Dollar-value method of pricing LIFO inventories.

* * *

(b) * * *

(4) *IPIC method pools.*—(i) *In general.*—A manufacturer or processor that elects to use the inventory price index computation method described in paragraph (e)(3) of this section (IPIC method) for a trade or business may elect to establish dollar-value pools for those manufactured or processed items accounted for using the IPIC method as provided in this paragraph (b)(4)(i) based on the 2-digit commodity codes (that is, major commodity groups) in Table 9 (formerly Table 6) (Producer price indexes and percent changes for commodity and service groupings and individual items, not seasonally adjusted) of the "PPI Detailed Report" published monthly by the United States Bureau of Labor Statistics (available at http://www.bls.gov). A taxpayer electing to establish dollar-value pools under this paragraph (b)(4)(i) may combine IPIC pools of manufactured or processed goods that comprise less than 5 percent of the total current-year cost of all dollar-value pools for that trade or business to form a single miscellaneous manufactured or processed IPIC pool. A taxpayer electing to establish dollar-value pools under this paragraph (b)(4)(i) may combine a miscellaneous manufactured or processed IPIC pool that comprises less than 5 percent of the total current-year cost of all dollar-value pools with the largest manufactured or processed IPIC pool. Each of these 5-percent rules is a

method of accounting. A taxpayer may not change to, or cease using, either 5-percent rule without obtaining the Commissioner's prior consent. Whether a specific manufactured or processed IPIC pool or the miscellaneous manufactured or processed IPIC pool satisfies the applicable 5-percent rule must be determined in the year of adoption or year of change, whichever is applicable, and redetermined every third taxable year. Any change in pooling required or permitted as a result of a 5-percent rule is a change in method of accounting. A taxpayer must secure the consent of the Commissioner pursuant to §1.446-1(e) before combining or separating manufactured or processed IPIC pools and must combine or separate its manufactured or processed IPIC pools in accordance with paragraph (g)(2) of this section.

(ii) *Pooling of goods a manufacturer or processor purchased for resale.*—A manufacturer or processor electing to establish dollar-value pools under paragraph (b)(4)(i) of this section and that is also engaged, within the same trade or business, in wholesaling or retailing goods purchased from others (resale), must establish pools for its resale goods in accordance with paragraph (c)(2)(i) of this section. A manufacturer or processor that must establish dollar-value pools for resale goods under this paragraph (b)(4)(ii) may combine IPIC pools of resale goods that comprise less than 5 percent of the total current-year cost of all dollar-value pools for that trade or business to form a single miscellaneous resale IPIC pool. The single miscellaneous resale

IPIC pool established pursuant to this paragraph (b)(4)(ii) may not be combined with any other IPIC pool. This 5-percent rule is a method of accounting. A taxpayer may not change to, or cease using, this 5-percent rule without obtaining the Commissioner's prior consent. Whether a specific resale IPIC pool satisfies the 5-percent rule must be determined in the year of adoption or year of change, whichever is applicable, and redetermined every third taxable year. Any change in pooling required or permitted as a result of this 5-percent rule is a change in method of accounting. A taxpayer must secure the consent of the Commissioner pursuant to §1.446-1(e) before combining or separating resale IPIC pools and must combine or separate its resale IPIC pools in accordance with paragraph (g)(2) of this section.

(iii) *No commingling of manufactured goods and resale goods within a pool.*—Notwithstanding any other rule provided in paragraph (b) or (c) of this section, a manufacturer or processor electing to establish dollar-value pools under paragraph (b)(4)(i) of this section and that is also engaged in retailing or wholesaling may not include manufactured or processed goods in the same IPIC pool as goods purchased for resale. Further, in applying the 5-percent rules described in paragraphs (b)(4)(i) and (ii) of this section, a taxpayer may not combine an IPIC pool of manufactured or processed goods that comprises less than 5 percent of the total current-year cost of all dollar-value pools for that trade or business with a resale IPIC pool that comprises less than 5 percent of the total current-year cost of all dollar-value pools for the purpose of forming a single miscellaneous IPIC pool.

(iv) *Examples.*—The rules of paragraph (b)(4) of this section may be illustrated by the following examples:

Example 1. (i) Taxpayer is engaged in the trade or business of manufacturing products A, B, and C. In order to cover temporary shortages, Taxpayer also purchases a small quantity of identical products for resale to customers. Taxpayer treats its manufacturing and resale activities as a single trade or business. Taxpayer uses the IPIC method described in paragraph (e)(3) of this section. Pursuant to its election, Taxpayer establishes dollar-value pools for the manufactured items under paragraph (b)(4)(i) of this section, based on the 2-digit commodity codes in Table 9 of the PPI Detailed Report. Taxpayer also establishes dollar-value pools for the items purchased for resale under paragraph (b)(4)(ii) of this section, based on the 2-digit commodity codes in Table 9 of the PPI Detailed Report. Taxpayer does not choose to use the 5-percent rules under paragraphs (b)(4)(i) and (ii) of this section.

(ii) Even though Taxpayer has manufactured items and resale items that share the same 2-digit commodity codes, under paragraph (b)(4)(iii) of this section, Taxpayer's manufactured goods may not be included in the same IPIC pool as its goods purchased for resale.

Example 2. (i) The facts are the same as in *Example 1*, except Taxpayer establishes three IPIC pools for its manufacturing activities and three IPIC pools for its resale activities. Further, Taxpayer chooses to use the 5-percent rules of paragraphs (b)(4)(i) and (ii) of this section. The percentage of total current-year cost of each IPIC pool to the current-year cost of all dollar-value pools for the trade or business is as follows:

	Percentage of total current-year cost of IPIC pool to current-year cost of all dollar-value pools
Manufacturing Pools:	
Pool A	90%
Pool B	1%
Pool C	1%
Resale Pools:	
Pool D	6%
Pool E	1%
Pool F	1%
	100%

(ii) For purposes of applying the 5-percent rules to Taxpayer's manufacturing operations under paragraph (b)(4)(i) of this section, because Pools B and C each comprise less than 5 percent of the total current-year cost of all dollar-value pools, Pools B and C may be combined to form a single miscellaneous pool of manufactured or processed goods (new Pool G).

(iii) For purposes of applying the 5-percent rules to Taxpayer's resale operations under paragraph (b)(4)(ii) of this section, because Pools E and F each comprise less than 5 percent of the total current-year cost of all dollar-value pools, Pools E and F may be combined to form a single miscellaneous pool of resale goods (new Pool H).

(iv) Because Pool G comprises less than 5 percent of the total current-year cost of all dollar-value pools, under paragraph (b)(4)(i) of this section, Pool G may be combined with Pool A, the largest IPIC pool of manufactured goods.

(v) Although Pool H also comprises less than 5 percent of the total current-year cost of all dollar-value pools, under paragraph (b)(4)(ii) of this section, Pool H may not be combined with Pool A, the largest pool of manufactured goods, or Pool D, the largest pool of resale goods.

* * *

(c) * * *

(2) *IPIC method pools.*—(i) *In general.*—A retailer that elects to use the inventory price index computation method described in paragraph (e)(3) of this section (IPIC method) for a trade or business may elect to establish dollar-value pools for those purchased items accounted for using the IPIC method as provided in this paragraph (c)(2)(i) based on either the general expenditure categories (that is, major groups) in Table 3 (Consumer Price Index for all Urban Consumers (CPI-U): U.S. city average, detailed expenditure categories) of the "CPI Detailed Report" or the 2-digit commodity codes (that is, major commodity groups) in Table 9 (formerly Table 6) (Producer price indexes and percent changes for commodity and service groupings and individual items, not seasonally adjusted) of the "PPI Detailed Report." A wholesaler, jobber, or distributor that elects to use the IPIC method for a trade or business may elect to establish dollar-value pools for any group of resale goods accounted for using the IPIC method based on the 2-digit commodity codes (that is, major commodity groups) in Table 9 (Producer price indexes and percent changes for commodity and service groupings and individual items, not seasonally adjusted) of the "PPI Detailed Report." The "CPI Detailed Report" and the "PPI Detailed Report" are published monthly by the United States Bureau of Labor Statistics (BLS) (available at http://www.bls.gov). A taxpayer electing to establish dollar-value pools under this paragraph (c)(2)(i) may combine IPIC pools of resale goods that comprise less than 5 percent of the total current-year cost of all dollar-value pools for that trade or business to form a single miscellaneous resale IPIC pool. A taxpayer electing to establish pools under this paragraph (c)(2)(i) may combine a miscellaneous resale IPIC pool that comprises less than 5 percent of the total current-year cost of all dollar-value pools with the largest resale IPIC pool. Each of these 5-percent rules is a method of accounting. A taxpayer may not change to, or cease using, either 5-percent rule without obtaining the Commissioner's prior consent. Whether a specific resale IPIC pool or the miscellaneous resale IPIC pool satisfies the applicable 5-percent rule must be determined in the year of adoption or year of change, whichever is applicable, and redetermined every third taxable year. Any change in pooling required or permitted under a 5-percent rule is a change in method of accounting. A taxpayer must secure the consent of the Commissioner pursuant to §1.446-1(e) before combining or separating resale IPIC pools and must combine or separate its resale IPIC pools in accordance with paragraph (g)(2) of this section.

(ii) *Pooling of manufactured or processed goods of a wholesaler, retailer, jobber, or distributor.*—A wholesaler, retailer, jobber, or distributor electing to establish dollar-value pools under paragraph (c)(2)(i) of this section and that is also engaged, within the same trade or business, in manufacturing or processing, must establish pools for its manufactured or processed goods in accordance with paragraph (b)(4)(i) of this section. A wholesaler, retailer, jobber, or distributor that must establish dollar-value pools for manufactured or processed goods under this paragraph (c)(2)(ii) may combine IPIC pools of manufactured or processed goods that comprise less than 5 percent of the total current-year cost of all dollar-value pools for that trade or business to form a single miscellaneous manufactured or processed IPIC pool. The single miscellaneous manufactured or processed IPIC pool established pursuant to this paragraph (c)(2)(ii) may not be combined with any other IPIC pool. This 5-percent rule is a method of accounting. A taxpayer may not change to, or cease using, this 5-percent rule without obtaining the Commissioner's prior consent. Whether a specific manufactured or processed IPIC pool satisfies the 5-percent rule must be determined in the year of adoption or year of change, whichever is applicable, and redetermined every third taxable year. Any change in pooling required or permitted as a result of a 5-percent rule is a change in method of accounting. A taxpayer must secure the consent of the Commissioner pursuant to § 1.446-1(e) before combining or separating manufactured or processed IPIC pools and must combine or separate its manufactured or processed IPIC pools in accordance with paragraph (g)(2) of this section.

(iii) *No commingling of manufactured goods and purchased goods within a pool.*—Notwithstanding any other rule provided in paragraph (b) or (c) of this section, a wholesaler, retailer, jobber, or distributor electing to establish dollar-value pools under paragraph (c)(2)(i) of this section and that is also engaged in manufacturing or processing may not include manufactured or processed goods in the same IPIC pool as goods purchased for resale. Further, in applying the 5-percent rules described in paragraphs (c)(2)(i) and (ii) of this section, a taxpayer may not combine an IPIC pool of manufactured or processed goods that comprises less than 5 percent of the total current-year cost of all dollar-value pools with a resale IPIC pool that comprises less than 5 percent of the total current-year cost of all dollar-value pools for purposes of forming a single miscellaneous IPIC pool.

(iv) *Examples.*—The rules of paragraph (c)(2) of this section may be illustrated by the following examples:

Example 1. (i) Taxpayer is engaged in the trade or business of wholesaling products A, B, and C. Taxpayer also manufactures a small quantity of identical products for sale to customers. Taxpayer treats its wholesaling and manufacturing activities as a single trade or business. Taxpayer uses the IPIC method described in paragraph (e)(3) of this section. Pursuant to its election, Taxpayer establishes dollar-value pools for the wholesale items purchased for resale under paragraph (c)(2)(i) of this section, based on the 2-digit commodity codes in Table 9 of the PPI Detailed Report. Taxpayer also establishes dollar-value pools for the manufactured items under paragraph (c)(2)(ii) of this section, based on the 2-digit commodity codes in Table 9 of the PPI Detailed Report. Taxpayer does not choose to use the 5-percent rules under paragraphs (c)(2)(i) and (ii) of this section.

(ii) Even though Taxpayer has resale and manufactured items that share the same 2-digit commodity codes, under paragraph (c)(2)(iii) of this section, Taxpayer's resale goods may not be included in the same IPIC pool as its manufactured goods.

Example 2. (i) The facts are the same as in *Example 1*, except Taxpayer establishes three IPIC pools for its wholesale activities and three IPIC pools for its manufacturing activities. Further, Taxpayer chooses to use the 5-percent rules of paragraphs (c)(2)(i) and (ii) of this section. The percentage of total current-year cost of each IPIC pool to the current-year cost of all dollar-value pools for the trade or business is as follows:

	Percentage of total current-year cost of IPIC pool to current-year cost of all dollar-value pools
Wholesaling Pools:	
Pool J	90%
Pool K	1%
Pool L	1%
Manufacturing Pools:	
Pool M	6%
Pool N	1%
Pool O	1%
	100%

(ii) For purposes of applying the 5-percent rules to Taxpayer's wholesaling operations under paragraph (c)(2)(i) of this section, because Pools K and Pool L each comprise less than 5 percent of the total current-year cost of all dollar-value pools, Pools K and L may be combined to form a single miscellaneous pool of wholesale goods (new Pool P).

(iii) For purposes of applying the 5-percent rules to Taxpayer's manufacturing operations under paragraph (c)(2)(ii) of this section, because Pools N and O each comprise less than 5 percent of the total current-year cost of all dollar-value pools, Pools N and O may be combined to form a single miscellaneous pool of manufactured goods (new Pool Q).

(iv) Because Pool P comprises less than 5 percent of the total current-year cost of all dollar-value pools, under paragraph (c)(2)(i) of this section, Pool P may be combined with Pool J, the largest IPIC pool of resale goods.

(v) Although Pool Q also comprises less than 5 percent of the total current-year cost of all dollar-value pools, under paragraph (c)(2)(ii) of this section, Pool Q may not be combined with Pool J, the largest pool of resale goods, or Pool M, the largest pool of manufactured goods.

* * *

(e) * * *

(3) * * *

(ii) *Eligibility.*—Any taxpayer electing to use the dollar-value LIFO method may elect to use the IPIC method. Except as provided in other published guidance, a taxpayer that elects to use the IPIC method for a specific trade or business must use that method to account for all items of dollar-value LIFO inventory.

* * *

(v) *Effective/applicability date.*—The rules of this paragraph (e)(3) and paragraphs (b)(4) and (c)(2) of this section are applicable for taxable years ending on or after the date the Treasury decision adopting these rules as final regulations is published in the **Federal Register**.

* * *

Methods of Accounting: Mark-to-Market Method: Dealers in Securities

Methods of Accounting: Mark-to-Market Method: Dealers in Securities.—Reproduced below are the texts of proposed Reg. §§ 1.475(a)-1, 1.475(a)-2 and 1.475(b)-3, relating to the mark-to-market method of accounting for securities that is required to be used by a dealer in securities (published in the Federal Register on January 4, 1995) (FI-42-94). Reg. §§ 1.475-0, 1.475(a)-3 and 1.475(b)-4 and amendments to Reg. §§ 1.475(c)-1, 1.475(c)-2 and 1.475(e)-1 were adopted by T.D. 8700 on December 23, 1996.

☐ Par. 3. Section 1.475(a)-1 is added as follows:

§ 1.475(a)-1. Mark to market of debt instruments.— (a) *Overview.*—This section provides rules for taking into account interest accruals and gain and loss on a debt instrument to which section 475(a) applies. Paragraph (b) of this section clarifies that the mark-to-market computation affects neither the amount treated as interest earned from a debt instrument nor the taxable year in which that interest is taken into account. Paragraph (c) of this section prescribes general rules. Paragraph (d) of this section prescribes additional rules for instruments acquired with market discount. Paragraph (e) of this section provides rules for taking into account

market discount that accrued on a bond before the bond became subject to the mark-to-market requirements. Paragraph (f) of this section prescribes rules for computing the mark-to-market gain or loss on partially or wholly worthless debts, and paragraph (g) provides rules for dealers accounting for bad debts using a reserve method of accounting.

(b) *No effect on amount of market discount, acquisition premium, or bond premium.*—Marking a debt instrument to market does not create, increase, or reduce market discount, acquisition premium, or bond premium, nor does it affect the adjusted issue price of, or accruals of original issue discount (OID) on, a bond issued with OID.

(c) *Accrual of interest, discount, and premium.*—In general, the amount of gain or loss from marking a debt instrument to market is computed after adjustments to basis for accruals of stated interest, discount, and premium.

(1) *Qualified stated interest.*—Immediately before a debt instrument is marked to market under section 475(a), the holder of the instrument must take any unpaid accrued qualified stated interest into account and must correspondingly increase the basis of the instrument. The holder must later decrease the basis of the instrument when accrued qualified stated interest is actually received. (See § 1.1273-1(c) for the definition of qualified stated interest and § 1.446-2(b) for the rule governing its accrual.)

(2) *General rule regarding accrual of discount.*—If a bond that was acquired with OID or market discount is marked to market under section 475(a), then, immediately before the bond is marked to market, the discount accrued through that date (determined under section 1272, 1275(d), or 1276, as applicable) is included in gross income, to the extent not previously included, and the bond's basis is correspondingly increased for amounts so included. (Because accrued OID is determined under all of the rules of section 1272 and the regulations thereunder, it is computed taking into account the reduction for acquisition premium that is required by section 1272(a)(7).) See paragraph (d) of this section, which requires the current inclusion in income of market discount on bonds marked to market. See paragraph (e) of this section for exceptions, and additional rules, for market discount bonds that become subject to section 475(a) after acquisition.

(3) *Bond premium.*—If a debt instrument that is subject to the basis adjustment required by section 1016(a)(5) or (6) is marked to market under section 475(a), then, immediately before the debt instrument is marked to market, the required basis adjustment must be made. Accordingly, the mark-to-market adjustment is computed after the basis of the debt instrument has been adjusted under section 1016(a)(5) or (6) for disallowed amortizable bond premium (in the case of tax-exempt bonds) or deductible bond premium (in the case of taxable bonds). If an election under section 171(c) is made after the first taxable year in which section 475(a) applies to the bond, the amount of bond premium is determined under section 171(b)(1) without regard to any basis adjustments that may have been required as a result of the bond being marked to market in prior taxable years. See paragraph (b) of this section for the rule that marking a debt instrument to market does not affect bond premium.

(d) *Mandatory current inclusion of market discount.*—(1) *General rule.*—If section 475(a) applies to a bond during any portion of a taxable year, gross income for that taxable year includes the market discount attributable to the portion of the year to which section 475(a) applies (as determined under section 1276(b)). Section 1276 does not apply to the bond except with respect to market discount, if any, that accrued before the bond became subject to section 475(a). Similarly, section 1277 does not apply to the bond except with respect to any net direct interest expense (as defined in section 1277(c)) that accrued before the bond became subject to section 475(a). See paragraph (e) of this section for additional rules governing this situation. For purposes of the Code other than the purposes described in the last sentence of section 1278(b)(1), any amount included in gross income under this paragraph (d)(1) is treated as interest. The bond's basis is correspondingly increased for any amount so included in gross income.

(2) *Interaction with section 1278(b).*—Paragraph (d)(1) of this section applies to a dealer, even if the dealer has not elected under section 1278(b) to include market discount currently. If the dealer has not made that election, however, this paragraph (d) does not require current inclusion of market discount on any bond to which section 475(a) does not apply.

(e) *Recognition of market discount that accrued before section 475(a) applies to a market discount bond.*—(1) *General rule.*—In the case of a debt instrument that is acquired with market discount, that is not subject to an election under section 1278(b), and that first becomes subject to section 475(a) in the taxpayer's hands on a date after its acquisition, this paragraph (e) governs the recognition of market discount that is attributable (as determined under section 1276(b)) to any period before section 475(a) applies to the debt instrument. To the extent that the market discount described in the preceding sentence is greater than the excess, if any, of the fair market value of the debt instrument at the time it became subject to section 475(a) over its adjusted basis at that time, section 1276(a)(1) applies to any gain recognized under section 475(a). To the extent of any remaining market discount that had accrued before section 475(a) became applicable, section 1276(a) applies no later than it would have applied if

section 475(a) did not apply to the bond. For example, section 1276(a) applies to the previously accrued market discount as partial principal payments are made. Except as provided in the preceding sentences, gain recognized under section 475(a) is not recharacterized as interest by section 1276(a).

(2) *Examples.*—The rules of paragraphs (d) and (e) of this section are illustrated by the following examples:

Example 1.

(i) *Facts.* Bond X was issued on January 1, 1996, for $1,000. Bond X matures on December 31, 2005, provides for a principal payment of $1,000 on the maturity date, and provides for interest payments at a rate of 8%, compounded annually, on December 31 of each year. D is a dealer in securities within the meaning of section 475(c)(1). On January 1, 1997, D purchased bond X for $955. D had not elected under section 1278(b) to include market discount in gross income currently. Under section 475(b), section 475(a) did not apply to bond X until January 1, 1999, at which time bond X had a fair market value of $961. On December 31, 1999, bond X had a fair market value of $980.

(ii) *Holdings.* In the absence of an election under section 1276(b)(2), market discount on bond X accrues under section 1276(b)(1) at the rate of $5 per year. On January 1, 1999, when bond X became subject to section 475(a), $10 of market discount had accrued, but the excess of the bond's fair market value on January 1, 1999, over its adjusted basis on that date (the built-in gain) was only $6 ($961 – $955). During 1999, D is required to include as interest income the $5 of market discount that accrues during that year, and D increases by that amount its basis in the bond and the amount to be used in computing mark-to-market gain or loss. On December 31, 1999, B must mark bond X to market and recognize a gain of $14 ($980 – [$961 + $5]). Under section 1276(a)(1) and (4) and paragraph (e)(1) of this section, $4 of that $14 gain is treated as interest income. The $4 is the amount by which the market discount of $10 that had accrued on January 1, 1999, exceeded the $6 built-in gain on that date.

Example 2.

(i) *Facts.* The facts are the same as in *Example 1*, except that, in addition, D sells bond X for its fair market value of $1,000 on June 30, 2000.

(ii) *Holdings.* Immediately before the sale, D is required to include as interest income the $2.50 of market discount that accrued during the portion of the year through June 30, and D increases by that amount its basis in the bond and the amount to be used in computing mark-to-market gain or loss. Also, under § 1.475(a)-2, immediately before the sale, D recognizes $17.50 of mark-to-market gain (the increase in value since the preceding mark to market less the basis increase of $2.50 from the market discount accrual. See § 1.475(a)-2). On the sale, D also recognizes the $6 of built-in gain, all of which is recharacterized as ordinary interest income under section 1276(a)(4).

Example 3.

(i) *Facts.* The facts are the same as in *Example 1*, except that, during 2001, the issuer of bond X made a partial principal payment in the amount of $20.

(ii) *Holdings.* Under paragraph (e)(1) of this section and section 1276(a)(4), $6 of the partial principal payment is included in D's 2001 income as interest income. The $6 is the portion of the $10 of market discount that had accrued at the time bond X became subject to section 475(a) and that had not previously caused gain or a partial principal payment to be treated as interest income.

(f) *Worthless debts.*—(1) *Computation of mark-to-market gain or loss.*—This paragraph (f) applies to any dealer that, under section 475(a)(2), marks to market either a debt that was charged off during the year because it became partially worthless or a debt that became wholly worthless during the taxable year (without regard to whether the debt was charged off). Any gain or loss attributable to marking a debt to market is determined by deeming the debt's adjusted basis to be the debt's adjusted basis under § 1.1011-1, less the amount charged off during the taxable year or during any prior taxable year, to the extent that amount has not previously reduced tax basis. A debt that becomes wholly worthless is deemed to have an adjusted basis of zero. The deemed adjusted basis, however, is used solely for this paragraph (f). Thus, any portion of a loss attributable to a bad debt continues to be accounted for under the bad debt provisions of the Code, and the basis of the debt continues to be adjusted as otherwise required under the Code.

(2) *Treatment of mark-to-market gain or loss.*—To the extent that a debt has been previously charged off, mark-to-market gain is treated as a recovery. Thus, for example, a dealer using the section 585 reserve method of accounting for bad debts must credit to the reserve any portion of mark-to-market gain that is treated as a recovery of a bad debt previously charged to the reserve account, and the dealer must include any excess in gross income as required by

§ 1.585-3(a). Similarly, if a dealer is a large bank that changed to the specific charge-off method of accounting for bad debts using the elective cut-off procedures described in § 1.585-7, the dealer must charge to the reserve for pre-disqualification loans all losses recognized as a result of marking to market a debt that is a pre-disqualification loan within the meaning of § 1.585-7(b)(2). Marking a pre-disqualification loan to market, however, is not a disposition of that loan under § 1.585-7(d).

(g) *Additional rules applicable to reserve-method taxpayers.*—If a dealer accounts for bad debts using the reserve method of accounting under section 585 or 593, the following additional rules apply in computing a reasonable addition to a reserve—

(1) To determine the amount of total loans outstanding, the outstanding balance on a debt that is marked to market is increased or decreased by the amount of any mark-to-market gain or loss recognized, except that the outstanding balance of the debt may never exceed the actual balance currently due; and

(2) If the reasonable addition to the reserve is computed based on a percentage of taxable income, any gain or loss attributable to marking a debt to market must be taken into account in computing taxable income.

(h) *Example.*—This example illustrates paragraphs (f) and (g) of this section.

Example.

(i) B, a calendar year taxpayer, is a dealer that marks some of its debts to market under section 475(a)(2). Additionally, B is a bank that accounts for bad debts using the section 585 reserve method of accounting. B has not made an election to use the conformity method of accounting described in § 1.166-2(d)(3).

(ii) On December 31, 1995, B has total loans outstanding of $1,000,000 and a bad debt reserve balance of $1000. Among the loans that B marks to market is loan X. On January 1, 1995, loan X had a

book and tax basis of $100. During the taxable year, loan X became partially worthless, and B charged off the loan by $5. Thus, loan X had a book basis of $95 and a tax basis of $100. The fair market value of loan X was $94 on December 31, 1995.

(iii) B computes the amount of gain or loss to be taken into account under section 475(a)(2) with respect to loan X using the rules of paragraph (f) of this section. Under paragraph (f)(1) of this section, B treats the adjusted tax basis of loan X as having been reduced by the $5 charge-off. Thus, B determines that it is required to take into account a $1 mark-to-market loss based on the difference between B's adjusted basis in loan X of $95, as determined under paragraph (f)(1) of this section, and loan X's fair market value of $94.

(iv) Further, B decides to claim a bad debt deduction with respect to loan X in 1995, rather than waiting until loan X becomes totally worthless. Thus, B charges the $5 of partial worthlessness to its reserve for bad debts. In computing a reasonable addition to the reserve under section 585(b), B reduces the amount of its total loans outstanding by $6 ($5 charged to the reserve for bad debts, plus $1 mark-to-market loss).

(v) On December 31, 1997, loan X has a fair market value of $93 and an adjusted basis (and outstanding principal balance) of $90. No additional worthlessness occurred with respect to loan X in 1996 or 1997. X determines that it is required to recognize a $3 mark-to-market gain with respect to loan X. Because B previously charged $5 to the bad debt reserve with respect to loan X, the entire $3 is a recovery item and must be credited to the bad debt reserve. See paragraph (f)(2) of this section. In computing a reasonable addition to the reserve for 1997, B does not increase the balance of its total loans outstanding by the $3 mark-to-market gain, because that adjustment would increase the balance to an amount in excess of the actual outstanding principal balance of $90. See paragraph (g)(1) of this section.

[Reg. § 1.475(a)-1.]

☐ Par. 4. Section 1.475(a)-2 is added as follows:

§ 1.475(a)-2. Mark to market upon disposition of security by a dealer.—

(a) *General rule.*—If a dealer in securities ceases to be the owner of a security for federal income tax purposes and if the security would have been marked to market under section 475(a) if the dealer's taxable year had ended immediately before the dealer ceases to own it, then (whether or not the security is inventory in the hands of the dealer) the dealer must recognize gain or loss on the security as if it were sold for its fair market value immediately before the dealer ceases to own it, and gain or loss is taken into account at that time. The amount of any gain or loss subsequently realized must be properly adjusted, in the form of a basis adjustment or otherwise, for gain or loss taken into account under this paragraph (a). See § 1.475(b)-4(b) for the rule governing when a security with substituted basis must be identified if it is to be exempted from the application of section 475(a).

☐ Par. 6. Section 1.475(b)-3 is added as follows:

§ 1.475(b)-3. Exemption of securities in certain securitization transactions.—

(a) *Exemption of contributed assets.*—If a taxpayer expects to contribute securities (for example, mortgages) to a trust or other entity, including a REMIC, in exchange for interests therein (including ownership interests or debt issued by the trust or other entity), the contributed securities qualify as held for investment (within the meaning of section 475(b)(1)(A)) or not held for sale (within the meaning of section 475(b)(1)(B)) only if the taxpayer expects each of the interests received (whether or not a security within the meaning of section 475(c)(2)) to be either held for investment or not held for sale to customers in the ordinary course of the taxpayer's trade or business.

(b) *Exemption of resulting interests.*—(1) *General rule.*—If a taxpayer contributes securities to a trust or other entity in exchange for interests therein (including ownership interests or debt issued by the trust or other entity) and if, for federal income tax purposes, the ownership of the interests received is not treated as ownership of the securities contributed, the interests received may be identified as being described in section 475(b)(1), even if some or all of the contributed securities were not so described and could not have been

(b) *Example.*—The rule of paragraph (a) of this section is illustrated by the following example.

Example.

(i) *Facts.* D is a dealer in securities within the meaning of section 475(c)(1) and is a member of a consolidated group that uses the calendar year as its taxable year. On February 1, 1995, D acquired for $100 a debt instrument issued by an unrelated party. On June 1, 1995, D sold the debt instrument to another member of the group, M1, for $110, which was the fair market value of the security on that date. D would have been required to mark the debt instrument to market under section 475(a) if its taxable year had ended immediately before it sold the debt instrument to M1.

(ii) *Holding.* Under paragraph (a) of this section, D marks the debt instrument to market immediately before the sale to M1 and takes into account $10 of gain. The gain is not deferred intercompany gain. As a result, D's basis in the debt instrument increases to $110 immediately before the sale. Accordingly, there is no gain or loss on the sale, and M1's basis in the debt instrument is $110.

[Reg. § 1.475(a)-2.]

so identified. For purposes of determining the timeliness of an identification of an interest received, the interest is treated as acquired on the day of its receipt.

(2) *Examples.*—The following examples illustrate the principles of paragraph (b)(1) of this section.

Example 1. Identification of REMIC regular interests. If a taxpayer holds mortgages that are marked to market under section 475 and the taxpayer contributes the mortgages to a REMIC in exchange for REMIC regular interests that are described in section 475(b)(1), the taxpayer may identify the regular interests as exempt from mark-to-market treatment. This is permissible because REMIC regular interests are debt securities issued by the REMIC and do not represent continued ownership of the contributed mortgages.

Example 2. Identification of interests in a grantor trust. If a taxpayer contributes securities to a grantor trust and receives beneficial interests therein and if the taxpayer marked the contributed securities to market under section 475, the taxpayer cannot identify the beneficial interests in the grantor trust as exempt from mark-to-market treatment. Because ownership of a beneficial interest in a grantor trust represents continued ownership of an undivided interest in the contributed assets, no new security has been acquired.

[Reg. § 1.475(b)-3.]

Commodities: Securities: Mark-to-Market Accounting

Commodities: Securities: Mark-to-Market Accounting.—Reg. §§1.475(e)-1, 1.475(f)-1 and 1.475(f)-2 and amendments to Reg. §§1.475(c)-1, 1.475(c)-2 and redesignated 1.475(g)-1, regarding the election to use the mark-to-market method of accounting for dealers in commodities and traders in securities or commodities, are proposed (published in the Federal Register on January 28, 1999) (REG-104924-98).

☐ Par. 4. In §1.475(c)-1, paragraphs (b)(3)(i) and (b)(4)(ii) are revised to read as follows:

§1.475(c)-1. Definitions—dealer in securities.

* * *

(b) * * *

(3) * * *

(i) For purposes of section 471, the taxpayer accounts for any security (as defined in section 475(c)) as inventory;

* * *

(4) * * *

☐ Par. 5. In §1.475(c)-2, paragraph (d) is added to read as follows:

§1.475(c)-2. Definitions—security.

* * *

(d) *Inventory.*—(1) *Nonfinancial customer paper is generally not marked to market under section 475.*—Except as provided in paragraph (d)(3) of this section, nonfinancial customer paper (as defined in section 475(c)(4)(B)) is not a security even if it is inventory.

☐ Par. 7. New §1.475(e)-1 and §§1.475(f)-1 and 1.475(f)-2 are added to read as follows:

§1.475(e)-1. Election of mark-to-market accounting for dealers in commodities.—(a) *Time and manner of making election.*—An election under section 475(e)(1) must be made in the time and manner prescribed by the Commissioner.

(b) *Application of securities dealer rules to electing commodities dealers.*—Except as otherwise provided in this section or in other guidance prescribed by the Commissioner, the rules and administrative interpretations under section 475 for dealers in securities apply to dealers in commodities that make an election under section 475(e)(1).

(c) *Commodity derivatives deemed not held for investment.*—(1) *In general.*—Except as otherwise determined by the Commissioner in a revenue ruling, revenue procedure, or letter ruling, if a dealer in commodities that made an election under section 475(e)(1) holds a commodity described in section 475(e)(2)(B) or (C) (describing certain notional principal contracts and commodity derivatives), section 475(b)(1)(A) (exempting from mark-to-market accounting certain positions that are held for investment) does not apply to that commodity.

(2) *Character of commodity derivatives required to be marked to market.*—If a commodity is required to be marked to market because of the application of paragraph (c)(1) of this section, the gain or loss with respect to that commodity is ordinary.

(d) *Same day identification.*—An identification of a commodity as exempt from mark-to-market accounting under section 475(b)(2) is not effective unless it is made before the close of the day on which the commodity was acquired, originated, or entered into. [Reg. §1.475(e)-1.]

§1.475(f)-1. Procedures for electing mark-to-market accounting for traders.—(a) *Time and manner of making election.*—An election under section 475(f)(1) or (2) must be made in the time and manner prescribed by the Commissioner.

(b) *Coordination with section 475(a).*—If a dealer in securities also has a securities or commodities trading business or a commodities dealing business, the dealer may make an election under section 475(e)(1), (f)(1), or (f)(2) for that business. [Reg. §1.475(f)-1.]

§1.475(f)-2. Election of mark-to-market accounting for traders in securities or commodities.—(a) *Securities not held in connection with trading activities.*—(1) *Taxpayer identification of investment securities.*—If a trader in securities makes an election under section 475(f)(1)(A) (electing trader) and holds a security other than in connection with that trading business, the electing trader must identify that security in accordance with section 475(f)(1)(B)(ii). If the electing trader is also a dealer in securities, however, the preceding sentence applies only to securities described in section 475(b)(1) (without regard to section 475(b)(2)).

(ii) *Continued applicability of an election.*—(A) *In general.*—Except as provided in paragraph (b)(4)(ii)(B) of this section, an election under this paragraph (b)(4) continues in effect for subsequent taxable years until revoked. The election may be revoked only with the consent of the Commissioner.

(B) *Taxable years ending after July 22, 1998.*—An election under this paragraph (b)(4) is ineffective for taxable years ending after July 22, 1998.

* * *

(2) *Treatment of nonfinancial customer paper under other sections of the Internal Revenue Code.*—For nonfinancial customer paper that is not a security, the mark-to-market method of accounting and the lower-of-cost-or-market method of accounting are not permissible methods of accounting. See §§1.446-1(c)(2)(iii) and 1.471-12.

(3) *Nonfinancial customer paper treated as inventory.*—[Reserved].

(2) *Satisfaction of Commissioner.*—In no event is the requirement of section 475(f)(1)(B)(i) satisfied unless the electing trader demonstrates by clear and convincing evidence that a security has no connection to its trading activities.

(3) *Substantially similar securities held for trading and investment.*—An electing trader that holds a security other than in connection with its trading business and also trades the same or substantially similar securities in no event satisfies the requirement of section 475(f)(1)(B)(i) unless the security is held in a separate, nontrading account maintained with a third party.

(4) *Consequences of failure to identify investment securities.*—If an electing trader holds a security that is not held in connection with its trading business and fails to identify the security in a manner that satisfies the requirements of section 475(f)(1)(B)(ii)—

(i) The consequences described in section 475(d)(2) apply to the security; and

(ii) The character of the gain or loss with respect to the security is ordinary.

(5) *Commissioner identification of investment securities.*—Notwithstanding paragraph (a)(4) of this section, the Commissioner may treat a security described in that paragraph as meeting the requirements of section 475(f)(1)(B)(i) and (ii).

(b) *Character of securities marked to market.*—The gain or loss with respect to a security that is marked to market under section 475(f)(1)(A) is ordinary.

(c) *Application of securities dealer rules to electing traders.*—Except as otherwise provided in this section or in other guidance prescribed by the Commissioner, the principles of the rules and administrative interpretations under section 475 for dealers in securities apply to traders in securities that make an election under section 475(f)(1).

(d) *Same day identification.*—An identification of a security as exempt from mark-to-market accounting under section 475(f)(1)(B) is not effective unless it is made before the close of the day on which the security was acquired, originated, or entered into.

(e) *Application to traders in commodities.*—(1) *General rule.*—If a trader in commodities makes an election under section 475(f)(2), paragraphs (a), (b), (c), and (d) of this section apply to the trader in the same manner that they apply to a trader in securities who makes an election under section 475(f)(1).

(2) *Coordination with section 1256.*—If a trader in commodities makes an election under section 475(f)(2) and trades section 1256 contracts that are commodities as defined in section 475(e)(2), then the rules of section 475(f) and paragraph (e)(1) of this section apply to those contracts, and not the capital character rules of section 1256. [Reg. §1.475(f)-2.]

☐ Par. 6. Section 1.475(e)-1 is redesignated as §1.475(g)-1. [*NOTE: Reg. §1.475(e)-1 was redesignated as Reg. §1.475(g)-1 by T.D. 9328 on June 11, 2007.*]

☐ Par. 8. Newly designated §1.475(g)-1 is amended by revising paragraphs (h)(2) and (i) and adding paragraphs (k), (l), and (m) to read as follows:

§1.475(g)-1. Effective dates.

* * *

(h) * * *

(2) Section 1.475(c)-1(b) (concerning sellers of nonfinancial goods and services) applies as follows:

(i) Except as otherwise provided in this paragraph (h)(2), §1.475(c)-1(b) applies to taxable years ending on or after December 31, 1993.

(ii) Section 1.475(c)-1(b)(4)(ii)(B) applies to taxable years ending after July 22, 1998.

* * *

(i) Section 1.475(c)-2 (concerning the definition of security) applies as follows:

(1) Section 1.475(c)-2(a), (b), and (c) (concerning the definition of security) applies to taxable years ending on or after December 31, 1993. By its terms, however, §1.475(c)-2(a)(3) applies only to residual interests or to interests or arrangements acquired on or after January 4, 1995; and the integrated transactions that are referred to in

§1.475(c)-2(a)(2) and (b) exist only after August 13, 1996 (the effective date of §1.1275-6).

(2) Section 1.475(c)-2(d) applies as follows:

(i) Section 1.475(c)-2(d)(1) applies to taxable years ending after July 22, 1998.

(ii) Section 1.475(c)-2(d)(2) applies to taxable years ending on or after January 28, 1999.

* * *

(k) Section 1.475(e)-1(a) (concerning the time and manner for making the mark-to-market election for dealers in commodities) applies to taxable years ending on or after January 28, 1999. Section 1.475(e)-1(b), (c) and (d) applies to commodities acquired on or after March 1, 1999.

(l) Section 1.475(f)-1 (procedures for electing mark-to-market accounting for traders in securities or commodities) applies to taxable years ending on or after January 28, 1999.

(m) Section 1.475(f)-2 (concerning the mark-to-market rules for traders in securities or commodities) applies to securities or commodities acquired on or after March 1, 1999.

Global Dealing Operations: Allocation and Sourcing of Income and Deductions

Global Dealing Operations: Allocation and Sourcing of Income and Deductions.—Reg. §1.475(g)-2 and amendments to Reg. §§1.482-0 and 1.482-1, relating to the allocation and sourcing of income, deductions, gains and losses from a global dealing operation, are proposed (published in the Federal Register on March 6, 1998) (REG-208299-90).

☐ Par. 2. Section 1.475(g)-2 is added as follows:

§1.475(g)-2. Risk transfer agreements in a global dealing operation.—(a) *In general.*—This section provides computational rules to coordinate the application of section 475 and §1.446-4 with rules for allocation and sourcing under the global dealing regulations. If the requirements in paragraph (c) of this section are met, a risk transfer agreement (RTA) (as defined in paragraph (b) of this section) is accounted for under the rules of paragraph (d) of this section.

(b) *Definition of risk transfer agreement.*—For purposes of this section, a risk transfer agreement (RTA) is a transfer of risk between two qualified business units (QBUs) (as defined in §1.989(a)-1(b)) of the same taxpayer such that—

(1) The transfer is consistent with the business practices and risk management policies of each QBU;

(2) The transfer is evidenced in each QBU's books and records;

(3) Each QBU records the RTA on its books and records at a time no later than the time the RTA is effective; and

(4) Except to the extent required by paragraph (b)(3) of this section, the entry in the books and records of each QBU is consistent with that QBU's normal accounting practices.

(c) *Requirements for application of operational rule.*—(1) The position in the RTA of one QBU (the hedging QBU) would qualify as a hedging transaction (within the meaning of §1.1221-2(b)) with respect to that QBU if—

(i) The RTA were a transaction entered into with an unrelated party; and

(ii) For purposes of determining whether the hedging QBU's position satisfies the risk reduction requirement in §1.1221-2(b), the only risks taken into account are the risks of the hedging QBU (that is, the risks that would be taken into account if the hedging QBU were a separate corporation that had made a separate-entity election under §1.1221-2(d)(2));

(2) The other QBU (the marking QBU) is a regular dealer in securities (within the meaning of §1.482-8(a)(2)(iii));

(3) The marking QBU would mark to market its position in the RTA under section 475 if the RTA were a transaction entered into with an unrelated party; and

(4) Income of the marking QBU is subject to allocation under §1.482-8 to two or more jurisdictions or is sourced under §1.863-3(h) to two or more jurisdictions.

(d) *Operational rule.*—If the requirements in paragraph (c) of this section are met, each QBU that is a party to a RTA (as defined in paragraph (b) of this section) takes its position in the RTA into account as if that QBU had entered into the RTA with an unrelated party. Thus, the marking QBU marks its position to market, and the hedging QBU accounts for its position under §1.446-4. Because this section only effects coordination with the allocation and sourcing rules, it does not affect factors such as the determination of the amount of interest expense that is incurred by either QBU and that is subject to allocation and apportionment under section 864(e) or 882(c). [Reg. §1.475(g)-2.]

☐ Par. 3. Section 1.482-0 is amended as follows: 1. The introductory text is revised. 2. The section heading and entries for §1.482-8 are redesignated as the section heading and entries for §1.482-9. 3. A new section heading and entries for §1.482-8 are added. The addition and revision read as follows:

§1.482-0. Outline of regulations under section 482.—This section contains major captions for §§1.482-1 through 1.482-9.

* * *

§1.482-8. Allocation of income earned in a global dealing operation.

(a) General requirements and definitions.

(1) In general.

(2) Definitions.

(i) Global dealing operation.

(ii) Participant.

(iii) Regular dealer in securities.

(iv) Security.

(3) Factors for determining comparability for a global dealing operation.

(i) Functional analysis.

(ii) Contractual terms.

(iii) Risk.

(iv) Economic conditions.

(4) Arm's length range.

(i) General rule.

(ii) Reliability.

(iii) Authority to make adjustments.

(5) Examples.

(b) Comparable uncontrolled financial transaction method.

(1) General rule.

(2) Comparability and reliability.

(i) In general.

(ii) Adjustments for differences between controlled and uncontrolled transactions.

(iii) Data and assumptions.

(3) Indirect evidence of the price of a comparable uncontrolled financial transaction.

(i) In general.

(ii) Public exchanges or quotation media.

(iii) Limitation on use of public exchanges or quotation media.

(4) Arm's length range.

(5) Examples.

(c) Gross margin method.

(1) General rule.

(2) Determination of an arm's length price.

(i) In general.

(ii) Applicable resale price.

(iii) Appropriate gross profit.

(3) Comparability.

(i) In general.

(ii) Adjustments for differences between controlled and uncontrolled transactions.

(iii) Reliability.

(iv) Data and assumptions.

(A) In general.

(B) Consistency in accounting.

(4) Arm's length range.

(5) Example.

(d) Gross markup method.

(1) General rule.

(2) Determination of an arm's length price.

(i) In general.

(ii) Appropriate gross profit.

(3) Comparability and reliability.

(i) In general.

(ii) Adjustments for differences between controlled and uncontrolled transactions.

(iii) Reliability.

(iv) Data and assumptions.

(A) In general.

(B) Consistency in accounting.

(4) Arm's length range.

(e) Profit split method.

(1) General rule.

(2) Appropriate share of profit and loss.

(i) In general.

(ii) Adjustment of factors to measure contribution clearly.

(3) Definitions.

(4) Application.

(5) Total profit split.

(i) In general.

(ii) Comparability.

(iii) Reliability.

(iv) Data and assumptions.

(A) In general.

(B) Consistency in accounting.

(6) Residual profit split.

(i) In general.

(ii) Allocate income to routine contributions.

(iii) Allocate residual profit.

(iv) Comparability.

(v) Reliability.

(vi) Data and assumptions.

(A) General rule.

(B) Consistency in accounting.

(7) Arm's length range.

(8) Examples.

(f) Unspecified methods.

(g) Source rule for qualified business units.

□ Par. 4. Section 1.482-1 is amended as follows: 1. In paragraph (a)(1), remove the last sentence and add two new sentences in its place. 2. Revise paragraph (b)(2)(i). 3. In paragraph (c)(1), revise the last sentence. 4. In paragraph (d)(3)(v), revise the last sentence. 5. In paragraph (i), revise the introductory text. The additions and revisions read as follows:

§1.482-1. Allocation of income and deductions among taxpayers.—(a) *In general.*—(1) *Purpose and scope.*—* * * Section 1.482-8 elaborates on the rules that apply to controlled entities engaged in a global securities dealing operation. Finally, §1.482-9 provides examples illustrating the application of the best method rule.

* * *

(b) * * *

(2) * * *

(i) *Methods.*—Sections 1.482-2 through 1.482-6 and §1.482-8 provide specific methods to be used to evaluate whether transactions between or among members of the controlled group satisfy the arm's length standard, and if they do not, to determine the arm's length result.

(c) *Best method rule.*—(1) *In general.*—* * * See §1.482-9 for examples of the application of the best method rule.

* * *

(d) * * *

(3) * * *

(v) *Property or services.*—* * * For guidance concerning the specific comparability considerations applicable to transfers of tangible and intangible property, see §§1.482-3 through 1.482-6 and §1.482-8; see also §1.482-3(f), dealing with the coordination of the intangible and tangible property rules.

* * *

(i) *Definitions.*—The definitions set forth in paragraphs (i)(1) through (10) of this section apply to §§1.482-1 through 1.482-9.

* * *

Eligible Terminated S Corporations: Definition: Distributions of Money

Eligible Terminated S Corporations: Definition: Distributions of Money.—Reg. §1.481-5 and amendments to Reg. §§1.481-5 and 1.481-6, regarding the definition of an eligible terminated S corporation (ETSC) and providing rules relating to distributions of money by an ETSC after the post-termination transition period, are proposed (published in the Federal Register on November 7, 2019) (REG-131071-18).

Par. 3. Section 1.481-5 is redesignated as §1.481-6.

§1.481-5. Eligible terminated S corporation.

Par. 4. Add new §1.481-5 to read as follows:

§1.481-5. Eligible terminated S corporation.—(a) *Scope.*—Section 481(d)(2) and this section provide rules relating to the qualification of a corporation as an eligible terminated S corporation (ETSC). Paragraph (b) of this section sets forth the requirements a corporation must meet to qualify as an ETSC. Paragraph (c) of this section describes certain transfers and other events that are disregarded for purposes of determining whether a corporation qualifies as an ETSC. Paragraph (d) of this section contains examples illustrating the rules of this section.

(b) *ETSC qualification.*—For a C corporation to qualify as an ETSC, it must satisfy the following requirements:

(1) The corporation must have been an S corporation on December 21, 2017;

(2) During the 2-year period beginning on December 22, 2017, the corporation must have made a valid revocation of its S election under section 1362(d)(1) and the regulatory provisions in this part under section 1362 of the Code (Revocation); and

(3) Except as provided in paragraph (c) of this section, the owners of the shares of stock of the corporation must be the same (and in identical proportions) on both:

(i) December 22, 2017; and

(ii) The day on which the Revocation is made.

(c) *Certain disregarded events.*—The following events are disregarded for purposes of determining whether the requirement in paragraph (b)(3) of this section is satisfied:

(1) Transfers of stock between a shareholder and that shareholder's trust treated as wholly owned by that shareholder under subpart E of subchapter J of chapter 1 of the Code;

(2) Transfers of stock between a shareholder and an entity owned by that shareholder which is disregarded as separate from its owner under §301.7701-2(c)(2)(i) of this chapter;

(3) An election by a shareholder trust to be treated as part of a decedent's estate under section 645 or the termination of an election under that section;

(4) A change in the status of a shareholder trust from one type of eligible S corporation shareholder trust described in section 1361(c)(2)(A) to another type of eligible S corporation shareholder trust; for example, a trust to which the shares of stock were transferred pursuant to the terms of a will (testamentary trust) described in section 1361(c)(2)(A)(iii) which elects to become an electing small business trust described in section 1361(c)(2)(A)(v) and (e); and

(5) A transaction that includes more than one of the events described in this paragraph (c).

(d) *Examples.*—The following examples illustrate the rules of this section. For purposes of the examples in this paragraph (d), as of December 1, 2017, X is a calendar year S corporation with 100 shares of stock outstanding that is owned equally by unrelated individuals A and B. Pursuant to section 1362(d)(1) and §§1.1362-2 and 1.1362-6, X made a valid revocation of its S election on March 15, 2019, effective on January 1, 2019. At all times, X has a single class of stock outstanding. The examples describe all relevant transactions involving the X stock from December 1, 2017 until March 15, 2019.

(1) *Example 1*—(i) *Facts.* On June 5, 2018, A contributed 20 of its shares of X stock to Y, a wholly owned limited liability company that is disregarded as an entity separate from A pursuant to §301.7701-2(c)(2)(i) of this chapter. On June 14, 2018, A contributed all of its interest in Y to Trust, which was a revocable trust treated as a wholly owned grantor trust of A pursuant to sections 671 and 676. On December 27, 2018, B sold 10 shares of its X stock to C, an unrelated person.

(ii) *Analysis.* X is an ETSC if it satisfies the requirements of paragraph (b) of this section.

(A) *S corporation.* X was an S corporation on December 21, 2017. Therefore, X satisfies the requirement of paragraph (b)(1) of this section.

(B) *Date of revocation.* X made a valid revocation of its S election pursuant to section 1362(d)(1) on March 15, 2019, which is within the 2-year period specified in paragraph (b)(2) of this section. Therefore, X satisfies the requirement of paragraph (b)(2) of this section.

(C) *Ownership.* For purposes of the requirement in paragraph (b)(3) of this section, the relevant dates are: December 22, 2017, and March 15, 2019 (the date X made a revocation of its S corporation status).

(1) *A's ownership interest.* As of December 22, 2017, A owned 50 shares of the outstanding shares of X stock. On June 5, 2018, A contributed 20 of its shares of X stock to Y (Transfer). On June 14, 2018, A contributed all of its interest in Y to Trust (Contribution). Both the Transfer and the Contribution are disregarded for purposes of determining whether the requirement of paragraph (b)(3) of this section is satisfied. See paragraphs (c)(2) and (1) of this section, respectively. Therefore, A owns 50 shares of the outstanding stock of X on March 15, 2019.

(2) *B's ownership interest.* As of December 22, 2017, B owned 50 shares of the outstanding shares of X stock. On December 27, 2018, B sold 10 shares to C. Therefore, B owns 40 shares of the outstanding stock of X on March 15, 2019.

(3) *C's ownership interest.* As of December 22, 2017, C owned no shares of X stock. On December 27, 2018, C purchased 10 shares from

B. Therefore, C owns 10 shares of the outstanding stock of X on March 15, 2019.

(4) *Failure to satisfy the requirement in paragraph (b)(3) of this section.* As described in paragraphs (d)(1)(ii)(C)(2) and (3) of this section, B's and C's interest in X were not in the same proportions on December 22, 2017, and March 15, 2019. Therefore, X does not satisfy the requirement of paragraph (b)(3) of this section and does not qualify as an ETSC.

(iii) *Restoration of interests prior to end of PTTP.* If C transferred its shares of X stock back to B on February 1, 2019, then on December 22, 2017, and March 15, 2019, A and B will have owned 50 shares of the outstanding stock of X. Therefore, X satisfies the requirement of paragraph (b)(3) of this section and qualifies as an ETSC.

(2) *Example 2*—(i) *Facts.* The facts are the same as in paragraph (d)(1)(i) of this section (the facts in *Example 1*), except that B sold 10 shares of its X stock to C on December 18, 2017, in addition to the sale of 10 shares of X stock on December 27, 2018.

(ii) *Analysis.* The analysis in paragraphs (d)(1)(ii)(A) and (B) of this section remains the same regarding the requirements of paragraphs (b)(1) and (2) of this section. With respect to the requirement of paragraph (b)(3) of this section, on December 22, 2017, A owned 50%, B owned 40%, and C owned 10% of the outstanding stock of X. As in paragraph (d)(1)(ii)(C)(1) of this section, the Transfer and the Contribution are disregarded for purposes of determining whether the requirement of paragraph (b)(3) of this section is satisfied. Therefore, on March 15, 2019, A owned 50% (50 shares), B owned 30% (30 shares), and C owned 20% (20 shares) of the outstanding shares of X. Even though A, B, and C owned shares of X on December 22, 2017, B's and C's proportionate ownership interest of X stock was not the same on December 22, 2017 and March 15, 2019. Therefore, X does not satisfy the requirement of paragraph (b)(3) of this section and does not qualify as an ETSC.

(3) *Example 3*—(i) *Facts.* The facts are the same as in paragraph (d)(1)(i) of this section (the facts in *Example 1*), except that X made a valid revocation of its S election on November 1, 2019, effective on January 1, 2020.

(ii) *Analysis.* The analysis in paragraphs (d)(1)(ii)(A) through (C) of this section remains the same regarding the requirements of paragraphs (b)(1) through (3) of this section, except that the relevant dates are: December 22, 2017, and November 1, 2019 (the date X made a revocation of its S corporation status). Although the effective date of X's revocation of its S election (January 1, 2020) occurs after the conclusion of the 2-year period specified in paragraph (b)(2) of this section, it is irrelevant for purposes of determining whether the requirements of paragraphs (b)(2) and (3) of this section are satisfied. [Reg. §1.481-5.]

Par. 5. Newly redesignated §1.481-6 is amended by revising the section heading and adding three sentences at the end of the paragraph to read as follows:

§1.481-6. Applicability date.—* * * The rules of §1.481-5 generally apply to taxable years beginning after [DATE OF PUBLICATION OF THE FINAL RULES IN THE **FEDERAL REGISTER**]. However, corporations may choose to apply the rules in §§1.316-2, 1.481-5, 1.1371-1, 1.1371-2, and 1.1377-2 in their entirety, to the extent applicable, to taxable years that began on or before [DATE OF PUBLICA-

TION OF THE FINAL RULES IN THE **FEDERAL REGISTER**] and with respect to which the period described in section 6511(a) has not expired. If the corporation makes the choice described in the previous sentence, all shareholders of the corporation must report consistently.

Foreign Corporations: Certain Transfers of Property

Foreign Corporations: Certain Transfers of Property.—Amendments to Reg. §1.482-1, relating to certain transfers of property by United States persons to foreign corporations and affecting United States persons that transfer certain property, including foreign goodwill and going concern value, to foreign corporations in nonrecognition transactions described in section 367 of the Internal Revenue Code, are proposed (published in the Federal Register on September 16, 2015) (REG-139483-13).

Par. 14. Section 1.482-1 is amended by revising paragraphs (f)(2)(i) and (f)(2)(ii)(B) and adding paragraph (j)(7) to read as follows:

§1.482-1. Allocation of income and deductions among taxpayers.—[The text of the proposed amendments to §1.482-1 is the same

as the text of §1.482-1T(f)(2)(i), (f)(2)(ii)(B), and (j)(7) as added by T.D. 9738].

Global Dealing Operations: Allocation and Sourcing of Income and Deductions

Global Dealing Operations: Allocation and Sourcing of Income and Deductions.—Amendments to Reg. §1.482-2, relating to the allocation and sourcing of income, deductions, gains and losses from a global dealing operation, are proposed (published in the Federal Register on March 6, 1998) (REG-208299-90).

☐ Par. 5. Section 1.482-2 is amended as follows:

1. In paragraph (a)(3)(iv), revise the first sentence.
2. Revise paragraph (d).

The revisions read as follows:

§1.482-2. Determination of taxable income in specific situations.—(a) * * *

   (3) * * *

     (iv) Fourth, section 482 and paragraphs (b) through (d) of this section and §§1.482-3 through 1.482-8, if applicable, may be applied by the district director to make any appropriate allocations,

other than an interest rate adjustment, to reflect an arm's length transaction based upon the principal amount of the loan or advance and the interest rate as adjusted under paragraph (a)(3)(i), (ii), or (iii) of this section. * * *

       * * *

(d) *Transfer of property.*—For rules governing allocations under section 482 to reflect an arm's length consideration for controlled transactions involving the transfer of property, see §§ 1.482-3 through 1.482-6 and § 1.482-8.

Global Dealing Operations: Allocation and Sourcing of Income and Deductions

Global Dealing Operations: Allocation and Sourcing of Income and Deductions.—Reg. § 1.482-8 and an amendment to Reg. § 1.482-8, relating to the allocation and sourcing of income, deductions, gains and losses from a global dealing operation, are proposed (published in the Federal Register on March 6, 1998) (REG-208299-90).

□ Par. 6. Section 1.482-8 is redesignated as § 1.482-9 and a new § 1.482-8 is added to read as follows:

§ 1.482-8. Allocation of income earned in a global securities dealing operation.—(a) *General requirements and definitions.*—(1) *In general.*—Where two or more controlled taxpayers are participants in a global dealing operation, the allocation of income, gains, losses, deductions, credits and allowances (referred to herein as income and deductions) from the global dealing operation is determined under this section. The arm's length allocation of income and deductions related to a global dealing operation must be determined under one of the methods listed in paragraphs (b) through (f) of this section. Each of the methods must be applied in accordance with all of the provisions of § 1.482-1, including the best method rule of § 1.482-1(c), the comparability analysis of § 1.482-1(d), and the arm's length range of § 1.482-1(e), as those sections are supplemented or modified in paragraphs (a)(3) and (a)(4) of this section. The available methods are—

(i) The comparable uncontrolled financial transaction method, described in paragraph (b) of this section;

(ii) The gross margin method, described in paragraph (c) of this section;

(iii) The gross markup method, described in paragraph (d) of this section;

(iv) The profit split method, described in paragraph (e) of this section; and

(v) Unspecified methods, described in paragraph (f) of this section.

(2) *Definitions.*—(i) *Global dealing operation.*—A global dealing operation consists of the execution of customer transactions, including marketing, sales, pricing and risk management activities, in a particular financial product or line of financial products, in multiple tax jurisdictions and/or through multiple participants, as defined in paragraph (a)(2)(ii) of this section. The taking of proprietary positions is not included within the definition of a global dealing operation unless the proprietary positions are entered into by a regular dealer in securities in its capacity as such a dealer under paragraph (a)(2)(iii) of this section. Lending activities are not included within the definition of a global dealing operation. Therefore, income earned from such lending activities or from securities held for investment is not income from a global dealing operation and is not governed by this section. A global dealing operation may consist of several different business activities engaged in by participants. Whether a separate business activity is a global dealing operation shall be determined with respect to each type of financial product entered on the taxpayer's books and records.

(ii) *Participant.*—(A) A participant is a controlled taxpayer, as defined in § 1.482-1(i)(5), that is—

(1) A regular dealer in securities as defined in paragraph (a)(2)(iii) of this section; or

(2) A member of a group of controlled taxpayers which includes a regular dealer in securities, but only if that member conducts one or more activities related to the activities of such dealer.

(B) For purposes of paragraph (a)(2)(ii)(A)(2) of this section, such related activities are marketing, sales, pricing, risk management or brokering activities. Such related activities do not include credit analysis, accounting services, back office services, general supervision and control over the policies of the controlled taxpayer, or the provision of a guarantee of one or more transactions entered into by a regular dealer in securities or other participant.

(iii) *Regular dealer in securities.*—For purposes of this section, a regular dealer in securities is a taxpayer that—

(A) Regularly and actively offers to, and in fact does, purchase securities from and sell securities to customers who are not controlled taxpayers in the ordinary course of a trade or business; or

(B) Regularly and actively offers to, and in fact does, enter into, assume, offset, assign or otherwise terminate positions in securities with customers who are not controlled entities in the ordinary course of a trade or business.

(iv) *Security.*—For purposes of this section, a security is a security as defined in section 475(c)(2) or foreign currency.

(3) *Factors for determining comparability for a global dealing operation.*—The comparability factors set out in this paragraph (a)(3) must be applied in place of the comparability factors described in § 1.482-1(d)(3) for purposes of evaluating a global dealing operation.

(i) *Functional analysis.*—In lieu of the list set forth in § 1.482-1(d)(3)(i)(A) through (H), functions that may need to be accounted for in determining the comparability of two transactions are—

(A) Product research and development;

(B) Marketing;

(C) Pricing;

(D) Brokering; and

(E) Risk management.

(ii) *Contractual terms.*—In addition to the terms set forth in § 1.482-1(d)(3)(ii)(A), and subject to § 1.482-1(d)(3)(ii)(B), significant contractual terms for financial products transactions include—

(A) Sales or purchase volume;

(B) Rights to modify or transfer the contract;

(C) Contingencies to which the contract is subject or that are embedded in the contract;

(D) Length of the contract;

(E) Settlement date;

(F) Place of settlement (or delivery);

(G) Notional principal amount;

(H) Specified indices;

(I) The currency or currencies in which the contract is denominated;

(J) Choice of law and jurisdiction governing the contract to the extent chosen by the parties; and

(K) Dispute resolution, including binding arbitration.

(iii) *Risk.*—In lieu of the list set forth in § 1.482-1(d)(3), significant risks that could affect the prices or profitability include—

(A) Market risks, including the volatility of the price of the underlying property;

(B) Liquidity risks, including the fact that the property (or the hedges of the property) trades in a thinly traded market;

(C) Hedging risks;

(D) Creditworthiness of the counterparty; and

(E) Country and transfer risk.

(iv) *Economic conditions.*—In lieu of the list set forth in § 1.482-1(d)(3)(iv)(A) through (H), significant economic conditions that could affect the prices or profitability include—

(A) The similarity of geographic markets;

(B) The relative size and sophistication of the markets;

(C) The alternatives reasonably available to the buyer and seller;

(D) The volatility of the market; and

(E) The time the particular transaction is entered into.

(4) *Arm's length range.*—(i) *General rule.*—Except as modified in this paragraph (a)(4), § 1.482-1(e) will apply to determine the arm's length range of transactions entered into by a global dealing operation as defined in paragraph (a)(2)(i) of this section. In determining the arm's length range, whether the participant is a buyer or seller is a relevant factor.

(ii) *Reliability.*—In determining the reliability of an arm's length range, it is necessary to consider the fact that the market for financial products is highly volatile and participants in a global dealing operation frequently earn only thin profit margins. The reliability of using a statistical range in establishing a comparable price of a financial product in a global dealing operation is based on facts and circumstances. In a global dealing operation, close proximity in time between a controlled transaction and an uncontrolled transaction may be a relevant factor in determining the reliability of the uncontrolled transaction as a measure of the arm's length price. The relevant time period will depend on the price volatility of the particular product.

(iii) *Authority to make adjustments.*—The district director may, notwithstanding § 1.482-1(e)(1), adjust a taxpayer's results under a method applied on a transaction by transaction basis if a valid statistical analysis demonstrates that the taxpayer's controlled prices, when analyzed on an aggregate basis, provide results that are not arm's length. See § 1.482-1(f)(2)(iv). This may occur, for example, when there is a pattern of prices in controlled transactions that are higher or lower than the prices of comparable uncontrolled transactions.

(5) *Examples.*—The following examples illustrate the principles of this paragraph (a).

Example 1. Identification of participants. (i) B is a foreign bank that acts as a market maker in foreign currency in country X, the country of which it is a resident. C, a country Y resident corporation, D, a country Z resident corporation, and USFX, a U.S. resident corporation are all members of a controlled group of taxpayers with B, and each acts as a market maker in foreign currency. In addition to market-making activities conducted in their respective countries, C, D, and USFX each employ marketers and traders, who also perform risk management with respect to their foreign currency operations. In a typical business day, B, C, D, and USFX each enter into several hundred spot and forward contracts to purchase and sell Deutsche marks (DM) with unrelated third parties on the interbank market. In the ordinary course of business, B, C, D, and USFX also enter into contracts to purchase and sell DM with each other.

(ii) Under § 1.482-8(a)(2)(iii), B, C, D, and USFX are each regular dealers in securities because they each regularly and actively offer to, and in fact do, purchase and sell currencies to customers who are not controlled taxpayers, in the ordinary course of their trade or business. Consequently, each controlled taxpayer is also a participant. Together, B, C, D, and USFX conduct a global dealing operation within the meaning of § 1.482-8(a)(2)(i) because they execute customer transactions in multiple tax jurisdictions. Accordingly, the controlled transactions between B, C, D, and USFX are evaluated under the rules of § 1.482-8.

Example 2. Identification of participants. (i) The facts are the same as in Example 1, except that USFX is the only member of the group of controlled taxpayers that buys from and sells foreign currency to customers. C performs marketing and pricing activities with respect to the controlled group's foreign currency operation. D performs accounting and back office services for B, C, and USFX, but does not perform any marketing, sales, pricing, risk management or brokering activities with respect to the controlled group's foreign currency operation. B provides guarantees for all transactions entered into by USFX.

(ii) Under § 1.482-8(a)(2)(iii), USFX is a regular dealer in securities and therefore is a participant. C also is a participant because it performs activities related to USFX's foreign currency dealing activities. USFX's and C's controlled transactions relating to their DM activities are evaluated under § 1.482-8. D is not a participant in a global dealing operation because its accounting and back office services are not related activities within the meaning of § 1.482-8(a)(2)(ii)(B). B also is not a participant in a global dealing operation because its guarantee function is not a related activity

10:00 a.m.	1.827DM: $1
10:04 a.m.	1.827DM: $1
10:06 a.m.	1.826DM: $1
10:08 a.m.	1.825DM: $1
10:10 a.m.	1.827DM: $1
10:12 a.m.	1.824DM: $1
10:15 a.m.	1.825DM: $1
10:18 a.m.	1.826DM: $1
10:20 a.m.	1.824DM: $1
10:23 a.m.	1.825DM: $1
10:25 a.m.	1.825DM: $1
10:27 a.m.	1.827DM: $1
10:30 a.m.	1.824DM: $1
10:45 a.m.	1.822DM: $1
10:50 a.m.	1.821DM: $1
10:55 a.m.	1.822DM: $1
11:00 a.m.	1.819DM: $1

(ii) USFX and C are participants in a global dealing operation under § 1.482-8(a)(2)(i). Therefore, USFX determines its arm's length price for its controlled DM contracts under § 1.482-8(a)(4). Under § 1.482-8(a)(4), the relevant arm's length range for setting the prices of USFX's controlled DM transactions occurs between 10:00 a.m. and 10:30 a.m. Because USFX has no controlled transactions between 10:45 a.m. and 11:00 a.m., and the price movement during this later time period continued to decrease, the 10:45 a.m. to 11:00 a.m. time period is not part of the relevant arm's length range for pricing USFX's controlled transactions.

(b) *Comparable uncontrolled financial transaction method.*—(1) *General rule.*—The comparable uncontrolled financial transaction (CUFT) method evaluates whether the amount charged in a controlled financial transaction is arm's length by reference to the amount charged in a comparable uncontrolled financial transaction.

(2) *Comparability and reliability.*—(i) *In general.*—The provisions of § 1.482-1(d), as modified by paragraph (a)(3) of this section, apply in determining whether a controlled financial transaction is comparable to a particular uncontrolled financial transaction. All of

within the meaning of § 1.482-8(a)(2)(ii)(B). Accordingly, the determination of whether transactions between B and D and other members of the controlled group are at arm's length is not determined under § 1.482-8.

Example 3. Scope of a global dealing operation. (i) C, a U.S. resident commercial bank, conducts a banking business in the United States and in countries X and Y through foreign branches. C regularly and actively offers to, and in fact does, purchase from and sell foreign currency to customers who are not controlled taxpayers in the ordinary course of its trade or business in the United States and countries X and Y. In all the same jurisdictions, C also regularly and actively offers to, and in fact does, enter into, assume, offset, assign, or otherwise terminate positions in interest rate and cross-currency swaps with customers who are not controlled taxpayers. In addition, C regularly makes loans to customers through its U.S. and foreign branches. C regularly sells these loans to a financial institution that repackages the loans into securities.

(ii) C is a regular dealer in securities within the meaning of § 1.482-8(a)(2)(ii) because it purchases and sells foreign currency and enters into interest rate and cross-currency swaps with customers. Because C conducts these activities through U.S. and foreign branches, these activities constitute a global dealing operation within the meaning of § 1.482-8(a)(2)(i). The income, expense, gain or loss from C's global dealing operation is sourced under § § 1.863-3(h) and 1.988-4(h). Under § 1.482-8(a)(2)(i), C's lending activities are not, however, part of a global dealing operation.

Example 4. Dissimilar products. The facts are the same as in Example 1, but B, C, D, and USFX also act as a market maker in Malaysian ringgit-U.S. dollar cross-currency options in the United States and countries X, Y, and Z. The ringgit is not widely traded throughout the world and is considered a thinly traded currency. The functional analysis required by § 1.482-8(a)(3)(i) shows that the development, marketing, pricing, and risk management of ringgit-U.S. dollar cross-currency option contracts are different than that of other foreign currency contracts, including option contracts. Moreover, the contractual terms, risks, and economic conditions of ringgit-U.S. dollar cross-currency option contracts differ considerably from that of other foreign currency contracts, including option contracts. See § 1.482-8(a)(3)(ii) through (iv). Accordingly, the ringgit-U.S. dollar cross-currency option contracts are not comparable to contracts in other foreign currencies.

Example 5. Relevant time period. (i) USFX is a U.S. resident corporation that is a regular dealer in securities acting as a market maker in foreign currency by buying from and selling currencies to customers. C performs marketing and pricing activities with respect to USFX's foreign currency operation. Trading in Deutsche marks (DM) is conducted between 10:00 a.m. and 10:30 a.m. and between 10:45 a.m. and 11:00 a.m. under the following circumstances.

Uncontrolled Transaction
Controlled Transaction
Uncontrolled Transaction
Uncontrolled Transaction
Controlled Transaction
Uncontrolled Transaction
Uncontrolled Transaction
Controlled Transaction
Uncontrolled Transaction
Uncontrolled Transaction
Uncontrolled Transaction
Controlled Transaction
Uncontrolled Transaction
Uncontrolled Transaction
Uncontrolled Transaction
Uncontrolled Transaction
Uncontrolled Transaction

the relevant factors in paragraph (a)(3) of this section must be considered in determining the comparability of the two financial transactions. Comparability under this method depends on close similarity with respect to these factors, or adjustments to account for any differences. Accordingly, unless the controlled taxpayer can demonstrate that the relevant aspects of the controlled and uncontrolled financial transactions are comparable, the reliability of the results as a measure of an arm's length price is substantially reduced.

(ii) *Adjustments for differences between controlled and uncontrolled transactions.* If there are differences between controlled and uncontrolled transactions that would affect price, adjustments should be made to the price of the uncontrolled transaction according to the comparability provisions of § 1.482-1(d)(2) and paragraph (a)(3) of this section.

(iii) *Data and assumptions.*—The reliability of the results derived from the CUFT method is affected by the completeness and accuracy of the data used and the reliability of the assumptions made to apply the method. See § 1.482-1(c)(2)(ii). In the case of a global dealing operation in which the CUFT is set through the use of indirect evidence, participants generally must establish data from a public exchange or quotation media contemporaneously to the time of the transaction, retain records of such data, and upon request furnish to the district director any pricing model used to establish indirect evidence of a CUFT, in order for this method to be a reliable means of evaluating the arm's length nature of the controlled transactions.

(3) *Indirect evidence of the price of a comparable uncontrolled financial transaction.*—(i) *In general.*—The price of a CUFT may be derived from data from public exchanges or quotation media if the following requirements are met—

(A) The data is widely and routinely used in the ordinary course of business in the industry to negotiate prices for uncontrolled sales;

(B) The data derived from public exchanges or quotation media is used to set prices in the controlled transaction in the same way it is used for uncontrolled transactions of the taxpayer, or the same way it is used by uncontrolled taxpayers; and

(C) The amount charged in the controlled transaction is adjusted to reflect differences in quantity, contractual terms, counterparties, and other factors that affect the price to which uncontrolled taxpayers would agree.

(ii) *Public exchanges or quotation media.*—For purposes of paragraph (b)(3)(i) of this section, an established financial market, as defined in § 1.1092(d)-1(b), qualifies as a public exchange or a quotation media.

(iii) *Limitation on use of data from public exchanges or quotation media.*—Use of data from public exchanges or quotation media is not appropriate under extraordinary market conditions. For example, under circumstances where the trading or transfer of a particular country's currency has been suspended or blocked by another country, causing significant instability in the prices of foreign currency contracts in the suspended or blocked currency, the prices listed on a quotation medium may not reflect a reliable measure of an arm's length result.

(4) *Arm's length range.*—See § 1.482-1(e)(2) and paragraph (a)(4) of this section for the determination of an arm's length range.

(5) *Examples.*—The following examples illustrate the principles of this paragraph (b).

Example 1. Comparable uncontrolled financial transactions. (i) B is a foreign bank resident in country X that acts as a market maker in foreign currency in country X. C, a country Y resident corporation, D, a country Z resident corporation, and USFX, a U.S. resident corporation are all members of a controlled group of taxpayers with B, and each acts as a market maker in foreign currency. In addition to market marking activities conducted in their respective countries, C, D, and USFX each employ marketers and traders, who also perform risk management with respect to their foreign currency operations. In a typical business day, B, C, D, and USFX each enter into several hundred spot and forward contracts to purchase and sell Deutsche marks (DM) with unrelated third parties on the interbank market. In the ordinary course of business, B, C, D, and USFX also each enter into contracts to purchase and sell DM with each other. On a typical day, no more than 10% of USFX's DM trades are with controlled taxpayers. USFX's DM-denominated spot and forward contracts do not vary in their terms, except as to the volume of DM purchased or sold. The differences in volume of DM purchased and sold by USFX do not affect the pricing of the DM. USFX maintains contemporaneous records of its trades, accounted for by type of trade and counterparty. The daily volume of USFX's DM-denominated spot and forward contracts consistently provides USFX with third party transactions that are contemporaneous with the transactions between controlled taxpayers.

(ii) Under § 1.482-8(a)(2)(iii), B, C, D, and USFX each are regular dealers in securities because they each regularly and actively offer to, and in fact do, purchase and sell currencies to customers who are not controlled taxpayers, in the ordinary course of their trade or business. Consequently, each controlled taxpayer is also a participant. Together, B, C, D, and USFX conduct a global dealing operation within the meaning of § 1.482-8(a)(2)(i) because they execute customer transactions in multiple tax jurisdictions. To determine the comparability of USFX's controlled and uncontrolled DM-denominated spot and forward transactions, the factors in § 1.482-8(a)(3) must be considered. USFX performs the same functions with respect to controlled and uncontrolled DM-denominated spot and forward transactions. See § 1.482-8(a)(3)(i). In evaluating the contractual terms under § 1.482-8(a)(3)(ii), it is determined that the volume of DM transactions varies, but these variances do not affect the pricing of USFX's uncontrolled DM transactions. Taking into account the risk factors of § 1.482-8(a)(3)(iii), USFX's risk associated with both the controlled and uncontrolled DM transactions does not vary in any material respect. In applying the significant factors for evaluating the economic conditions under § 1.482-8(a)(3)(iv), USFX

has sufficient third party DM transactions to establish comparable economic conditions for evaluating an arm's length price. Accordingly, USFX's uncontrolled transactions are comparable to its controlled transactions in DM spot and forward contracts.

Example 2. Lack of comparable uncontrolled financial transactions. The facts are the same as in Example 1, except that USFX trades Italian lira (lira) instead of DM. USFX enters into few uncontrolled and controlled lira-denominated forward contracts each day. The daily volume of USFX's lira forward purchases and sales does not provide USFX with sufficient third party transactions to establish that uncontrolled transactions are sufficiently contemporaneous with controlled transactions to be comparable within the meaning of § 1.482-8(a)(3). In applying the comparability factors of § 1.482-8(a)(3), and of paragraph (a)(3)(iv) of this section in particular, USFX's controlled and uncontrolled lira forward purchases and sales are not entered into under comparable economic conditions. Accordingly, USFX's uncontrolled transactions in lira forward contracts are not comparable to its controlled lira forward transactions.

Example 3. Indirect evidence of the price of a comparable uncontrolled financial transaction. (i) The facts are the same as in Example 2, except that USFX uses a computer quotation system (CQS) that is an interdealer market, as described in § 1.1092(d)-1(b)(2), to set its price on lira forward contracts with controlled and uncontrolled taxpayers. Other financial institutions also use CQS to set their prices on lira forward contracts. CQS is an established financial market within the meaning of § 1.1092(d)-1(b).

(ii) Because CQS is an established financial market, it is a public exchange or quotation media within the meaning of § 1.482-8(b)(3)(i). Because other financial institutions use prices from CQS in the same manner as USFX, prices derived from CQS are deemed to be widely and routinely used in the ordinary course of business in the industry to negotiate prices for uncontrolled sales. See § 1.482-8(b)(3)(i)(A) and (B). If USFX adjusts the price quoted by CQS under the criteria specified in § 1.482-8(b)(2)(ii)(A)(3), the controlled price derived by USFX from CQS qualifies as indirect evidence of the price of a comparable uncontrolled financial transaction.

Example 4. Indirect evidence of the price of a comparable uncontrolled financial transaction—internal pricing models. (i) T is a U.S. resident corporation that acts as a market maker in U.S. dollar-denominated notional principal contracts. T's marketers and traders work together to sell notional principal contracts (NPCs), primarily to T's North and South American customers. T typically earns 4 basis points at the inception of each standard 3 year U.S. dollar-denominated interest rate swap that is entered into with an unrelated, financially sophisticated, creditworthy counterparty. TS, T's wholly owned U.K. subsidiary, also acts as a market maker in U.S. dollar-denominated NPCs, employing several traders and marketers who initiate contracts primarily with European customers. On occasion, for various business reasons, TS enters into a U.S. dollar-denominated NPC with T. The U.S. dollar-denominated NPCs that T enters into with unrelated parties are comparable in all material respects to the transactions that T enters into with TS. TS prices all transactions with T using the same pricing models that TS uses to price transactions with third parties. The pricing models analyze relevant data, such as interest rates and volatilities, derived from public exchanges. TS records the data that were used to determine the price of each transaction at the time the transaction was entered into. Because the price produced by the pricing models is a mid-market price, TS adjusts the price so that it receives the same 4 basis point spread on its transaction with T that it would earn on comparable transactions with comparable counterparties during the same relevant time period.

(ii) Under § 1.482-8(a)(2), T and TS are participants in a global dealing operation that deals in U.S. dollar-denominated NPCs. Because the prices produced by TS's pricing model are derived from information on public exchanges and TS uses the same pricing model to set prices for controlled and uncontrolled transactions, the requirements of § 1.482-8(b)(3)(i)(A) and (B) are met. Because the U.S. dollar-denominated NPCs that T enters into with customers (uncontrolled transactions) are comparable to the transactions between T and TS within the meaning of § 1.482-8(a)(3) and TS earns 4 basis points at inception of its uncontrolled transactions that are comparable to its controlled transactions, TS has also satisfied the requirements of § 1.482-8(b)(3)(i)(C). Accordingly, the price produced by TS's pricing model constitutes indirect evidence of the price of a comparable uncontrolled financial transaction.

(c) *Gross margin method.*—(1) *General rule.*—The gross margin method evaluates whether the amount allocated to a participant in a global dealing operation is arm's length by reference to the gross profit margin realized on the sale of financial products in comparable uncontrolled transactions. The gross margin method may be used to establish an arm's length price for a transaction where a participant resells a financial product to an unrelated party that the participant purchased from a related party. The gross margin method may apply to transactions involving the purchase and resale of debt and equity instruments. The method may also be used to evaluate whether a participant has received an arm's length commission for its activities in a global dealing operation when the participant has not taken title to a security or has not become a party to a derivative financial product. To meet the arm's length standard, the gross profit margin on controlled transactions should be similar to that of comparable uncontrolled transactions.

(2) *Determination of an arm's length price.*—(i) *In general.*—The gross margin method measures an arm's length price by subtracting the appropriate gross profit from the applicable resale price for the financial product involved in the controlled transaction under review.

(ii) *Applicable resale price.*—The applicable resale price is equal to either the price at which the financial product involved is sold in an uncontrolled sale or the price at which contemporaneous resales of the same product are made. If the product purchased in the controlled sale is resold to one or more related parties in a series of controlled sales before being resold in an uncontrolled sale, the applicable resale price is the price at which the product is resold to an uncontrolled party, or the price at which contemporaneous resales of the same product are made. In such case, the determination of the appropriate gross profit will take into account the functions of all members of the controlled group participating in the series of controlled sales and final uncontrolled resales, as well as any other relevant factors described in paragraph (a)(3) of this section.

(iii) *Appropriate gross profit.*—The appropriate gross profit is computed by multiplying the applicable resale price by the gross profit margin, expressed as a percentage of total revenue derived from sales, earned in comparable uncontrolled transactions.

(3) *Comparability and reliability.*—(i) *In general.*—The provisions of § 1.482-1(d), as modified by paragraph (a)(3) of this section, apply in determining whether a controlled transaction is comparable to a particular uncontrolled transaction. All of the factors described in paragraph (a)(3) of this section must be considered in determining the comparability of two financial products transactions, including the functions performed. The gross margin method considers whether a participant has earned a sufficient gross profit margin on the resale of a financial product (or line of products) given the functions performed by the participant. A reseller's gross profit margin provides compensation for performing resale functions related to the product or products under review, including an operating profit in return for the reseller's investment of capital and the assumption of risks. Accordingly, where a participant does not take title, or does not become a party to a financial product, the reseller's return to capital and assumption of risk are additional factors that must be considered in determining an appropriate gross profit margin. An appropriate gross profit margin primarily should be derived from comparable uncontrolled purchases and resales of the reseller involved in the controlled sale. This is because similar characteristics are more likely to be found among different resales of a financial product or products made by the same reseller than among sales made by other resellers. In the absence of comparable uncontrolled transactions involving the same reseller, an appropriate gross profit margin may be derived from comparable uncontrolled transactions of other resellers.

(ii) *Adjustments for differences between controlled and uncontrolled transactions.*—If there are material differences between controlled and uncontrolled transactions that would affect the gross profit margin, adjustments should be made to the gross profit margin earned in the uncontrolled transaction according to the comparability provisions of § 1.482-1(d)(2) and paragraph (a)(3) of this section. For this purpose, consideration of operating expenses associated with functions performed and risks assumed may be necessary because differences in functions performed are often reflected in operating expenses. The effect of a difference in functions performed on gross profit, however, is not necessarily equal to the difference in the amount of related operating expenses.

(iii) *Reliability.*—In order for the gross margin method to be considered a reliable measure of an arm's length price, the gross profit should ordinarily represent an amount that would allow the participant who resells the product to recover its expenses (whether directly related to selling the product or more generally related to maintaining its operations) and to earn a profit commensurate with the functions it performed. The gross margin method may be a reliable means of establishing an arm's length price where there is a purchase and resale of a financial product and the participant who resells the property does not substantially participate in developing a product or in tailoring the product to the unique requirements of a customer prior to the resale.

(iv) *Data and assumptions.*—(A) *In general.*—The reliability of the results derived from the gross margin method is affected by

the completeness and accuracy of the data used and the reliability of the assumptions made to apply the method. See § 1.482-1(c)(2)(ii). A participant may establish the gross margin by comparing the bid and offer prices on a public exchange or quotation media. In such case, the prices must be contemporaneous to the controlled transaction, and the participant must retain records of such data.

(B) *Consistency in accounting.*—The degree of consistency in accounting practices between the controlled transaction and the uncontrolled transactions may affect the reliability of the gross margin method. For example, differences as between controlled and uncontrolled transactions in the method used to value similar financial products (including methods of accounting, methods of estimation, and the timing for changes of such methods) could affect the gross profit. The ability to make reliable adjustments for such differences could affect the reliability of the results.

(4) *Arm's length range.*—See § 1.482-1(e)(2) and paragraph (a)(4) of this section for the determination of an arm's length range.

(5) *Example.*—The following example illustrates the principles of this paragraph (c).

Example 1. Gross margin method. (i) T is a U.S. resident financial institution that acts as a market maker in debt and equity instruments issued by U.S. corporations. Most of T's sales are to U.S.-based customers. TS, T's U.K. subsidiary, acts as a market maker in debt and equity instruments issued by European corporations and conducts most of its business with European-based customers. On occasion, however, a customer of TS wishes to purchase a security that is either held by or more readily accessible to T. To facilitate this transaction, T sells the security it owns or acquires to TS, who then promptly sells it to the customer. T and TS generally derive the majority of their profit on the difference between the price at which they purchase and the price at which they sell securities (the bid/offer spread). On average, TS's gross profit margin on its purchases and sales of securities from unrelated persons is 2%. Applying the comparability factors specified in § 1.482-8(a)(3), T's purchases and sales with unrelated persons are comparable to the purchases and sales between T and TS.

(ii) Under § 1.482-8(a)(2), T and TS are participants in a global dealing operation that deals in debt and equity securities. Since T's related purchases and sales are comparable to its unrelated purchases and sales, if TS's gross profit margin on purchases and sales of comparable securities from unrelated persons is 2%, TS should also typically earn a 2% gross profit on the securities it purchases from T. Thus, when TS resells for $100 a security that it purchased from T, the arm's length price at which TS would have purchased the security from T would normally be $98 ($100 sales price minus (2% gross profit margin × $100)).

(d) *Gross markup method.*—(1) *General rule.*—The gross markup method evaluates whether the amount allocated to a participant in a global dealing operation is arm's length by reference to the gross profit markup realized in comparable uncontrolled transactions. The gross markup method may be used to establish an arm's length price for a transaction where a participant purchases a financial product from an unrelated party that the participant sells to a related party. This method may apply to transactions involving the purchase and resale of debt and equity instruments. The method may also be used to evaluate whether a participant has received an arm's length commission for its role in a global dealing operation when the participant has not taken title to a security or has not become a party to a derivative financial product. To meet the arm's length standard, the gross profit markup on controlled transactions should be similar to that of comparable uncontrolled transactions.

(2) *Determination of an arm's length price.*—(i) *In general.*—The gross markup method measures an arm's length price by adding the appropriate gross profit to the participant's cost or anticipated cost, of purchasing, holding, or structuring the financial product involved in the controlled transaction under review (or in the case of a derivative financial product, the initial net present value, measured by the anticipated cost of purchasing, holding, or structuring the product).

(ii) *Appropriate gross profit.*—The appropriate gross profit is computed by multiplying the participant's cost or anticipated cost of purchasing, holding, or structuring a transaction by the gross profit markup, expressed as a percentage of cost, earned in comparable uncontrolled transactions.

(3) *Comparability and reliability.*—(i) *In general.*—The provisions of § 1.482-1(d), as modified by paragraph (a)(3) of this section, apply in determining whether a controlled transaction is comparable to a particular uncontrolled transaction. All of the factors described in paragraph (a)(3) of this section must be considered in determining the comparability of two financial products transactions, including the functions performed. The gross markup method considers whether a participant has earned a sufficient gross markup on the

sale of a financial product, or line of products, given the functions it has performed. A participant's gross profit markup provides compensation for purchasing, hedging, and transactional structuring functions related to the transaction under review, including an operating profit in return for the investment of capital and the assumption of risks. Accordingly, where a participant does not take title, or does not become a party to a financial product, the reseller's return to capital and assumption of risk are additional factors that must be considered in determining the gross profit markup. An appropriate gross profit markup primarily should be derived from comparable uncontrolled purchases and sales of the participant involved in the controlled sale. This is because similar characteristics are more likely to be found among different sales of property made by the same participant than among sales made by other resellers. In the absence of comparable uncontrolled transactions involving the same participant, an appropriate gross profit markup may be derived from comparable uncontrolled transactions of other parties whether or not such parties are members of the same controlled group.

(ii) *Adjustments for differences between controlled and uncontrolled transactions.*—If there are material differences between controlled and uncontrolled transactions that would affect the gross profit markup, adjustments should be made to the gross profit markup earned in the uncontrolled transaction according to the comparability provisions of §1.482-1(d)(2) and paragraph (a)(3) of this section. For this purpose, consideration of operating expenses associated with the functions performed and risks assumed may be necessary, because differences in functions performed are often reflected in operating expenses. The effect of a difference in functions on gross profit, however, is not necessarily equal to the difference in the amount of related operating expenses.

(iii) *Reliability.*—In order for the gross markup method to be considered a reliable measure of an arm's length price, the gross profit should ordinarily represent an amount that would allow the participant who purchases the product to recover its expenses (whether directly related to selling the product or more generally related to maintaining its operations) and to earn a profit commensurate with the functions it performed. As with the gross margin method, the gross markup method may be a reliable means of establishing an arm's length price where there is a purchase and resale of a financial product and the participant who resells the property does not substantially participate in developing a product or in tailoring the product to the unique requirements of a customer prior to the resale.

(iv) *Data and assumptions.*—(A) *In general.*—The reliability of the results derived from the gross markup method is affected by the completeness and accuracy of the data used and the reliability of the assumptions made to apply the method. See §1.482-1(c)(2)(ii). A participant may establish the gross markup by comparing the bid and offer prices on a public exchange or quotation media. In such case, the prices must be contemporaneous with the controlled transaction, and the participant must retain records of such data.

(B) *Consistency in accounting.*—The degree of consistency in accounting practices between the controlled transaction and the uncontrolled transactions may affect the reliability of the gross markup method. For example, differences as between controlled and uncontrolled transactions in the method used to value similar financial products (including methods in accounting, methods of estimation, and the timing for changes of such methods) could affect the gross profit. The ability to make reliable adjustments for such differences could affect the reliability of the results.

(4) *Arm's length range.*—See §1.482-1(e)(2) and paragraph (a)(4) of this section for the determination of an arm's length range.

(e) *Profit split method.*—(1) *General rule.*—The profit split method evaluates whether the allocation of the combined operating profit or loss of a global dealing operation to one or more participants is at arm's length by reference to the relative value of each participant's contribution to that combined operating profit or loss. The combined operating profit or loss must be derived from the most narrowly identifiable business activity of the participants for which data is available that includes the controlled transactions (relevant business activity).

(2) *Appropriate share of profit and loss.*—(i) *In general.*—The relative value of each participant's contribution to the global dealing activity must be determined in a manner that reflects the functions performed, risks assumed, and resources employed by each participant in the activity, consistent with the comparability provisions of §1.482-1(d), as modified by paragraph (a)(3) of this section. Such an allocation is intended to correspond to the division of profit or loss that would result from an arrangement between uncontrolled taxpayers, each performing functions similar to those of the various controlled taxpayers engaged in the relevant business activity. The

relative value of the contributions of each participant in the global dealing operation should be measured in a manner that most reliably reflects each contribution made to the global dealing operation and each participant's role in that contribution. In appropriate cases, the participants may find that a multi-factor formula most reliably measures the relative value of the contributions to the profitability of the global dealing operation. The profit allocated to any particular participant using a profit split method is not necessarily limited to the total operating profit from the global dealing operation. For example, in a given year, one participant may earn a profit while another participant incurs a loss, so long as the arrangement is comparable to an arrangement to which two uncontrolled parties would agree. In addition, it may not be assumed that the combined operating profit or loss from the relevant business activity should be shared equally or in any other arbitrary proportion. The specific method must be determined under paragraph (e)(4) of this section.

(ii) *Adjustment of factors to measure contribution clearly.*—In order to reliably measure the value of a participant's contribution, the factors, for example, those used in a multi-factor formula, must be expressed in units of measure that reliably quantify the relative contribution of the participant. If the data or information is influenced by factors other than the value of the contribution, adjustments must be made for such differences so that the factors used in the formula only measure the relative value of each participant's contribution. For example, if trader compensation is used as a factor to measure the value added by the participants' trading expertise, adjustments must be made for variances in compensation paid to traders due solely to differences in the cost of living.

(3) *Definitions.*—The definitions in this paragraph (e)(3) apply for purposes of applying the profit split methods in this paragraph (e).

Gross profit is gross income earned by the global dealing operation.

Operating expenses includes all expenses not included in the computation of gross profit, except for interest, foreign income taxes as defined in §1.901-2(a), domestic income taxes, and any expenses not related to the global dealing activity that is evaluated under the profit split method. With respect to interest expense, see section 864(e) and the regulations thereunder and §1.882-5.

Operating profit or loss is gross profit less operating expenses, and includes all income, expense, gain, loss, credits or allowances attributable to each global dealing activity that is evaluated under the profit split method. It does not include income, expense, gain, loss, credits or allowances from activities that are not evaluated under the profit split method, nor does it include extraordinary gains or losses that do not relate to the continuing global dealing activities of the participant.

(4) *Application.*—Profit or loss shall be allocated under the profit split method using either the total profit split, described in paragraph (e)(5) of this section, or the residual profit split, described in paragraph (e)(6) of this section.

(5) *Total profit split.*—(i) *In general.*—The total profit split derives the percentage of the combined operating profit of the participants in a global dealing operation allocable to a participant in the global dealing operation by evaluating whether uncontrolled taxpayers who perform similar functions, assume similar risks, and employ similar resources would allocate their combined operating profits in the same manner.

(ii) *Comparability.*—The total profit split evaluates the manner by which comparable uncontrolled taxpayers divide the combined operating profit of a particular global dealing activity. The degree of comparability between the controlled and uncontrolled taxpayers is determined by applying the comparability standards of §1.482-1(d), as modified by paragraph (a)(3) of this section. In particular, the functional analysis required by §1.482-1(d)(3)(i) and paragraph (a)(3)(i) of this section is essential to determine whether two situations are comparable. Nevertheless, in certain cases, no comparable ventures between uncontrolled taxpayers may exist. In this situation, it is necessary to analyze the remaining factors set forth in paragraph (a)(3) of this section that could affect the division of operating profits between parties. If there are differences between the controlled and uncontrolled taxpayers that would materially affect the division of operating profit, adjustments must be made according to the provisions of §1.482-1(d)(2) and paragraph (a)(3) of this section.

(iii) *Reliability.*—As indicated in §1.482-1(c)(2)(i), as the degree of comparability between the controlled and uncontrolled transactions increases, the reliability of a total profit split also increases. In a global dealing operation, however, the absence of external market benchmarks (for example, joint ventures between uncontrolled taxpayers) on which to base the allocation of operating profits does not preclude use of this method if the allocation of the operating profit takes into account the relative contribution of each participant. The reliability of this method is increased to the extent that the allocation has economic significance for purposes other than tax (for example, satisfying regulatory standards and reporting, or determining bonuses paid to management or traders). The reliability of the analysis under this method may also be enhanced by the fact that all parties to the controlled transaction are evaluated under this method. The reliability of the results, however, of an analysis based on information from all parties to a transaction is affected by the reliability of the data and assumptions pertaining to each party to the controlled transaction. Thus, if the data and assumptions are significantly more reliable with respect to one of the parties than with respect to the others, a different method, focusing solely on the results of that party, may yield more reliable results.

(iv) *Data and assumptions.*—(A) *In general.*—The reliability of the results derived from the total profit split method is affected by the quality of the data used and the assumptions used to apply the method. See §1.482-1(c)(2)(ii). The reliability of the allocation of income, expense, or other attributes between the participants' relevant business activities and the participants' other activities will affect the reliability of the determination of the combined operating profit and its allocation among the participants. If it is not possible to allocate income, expense, or other attributes directly based on factual relationships, a reasonable allocation formula may be used. To the extent direct allocations are not made, the reliability of the results derived from application of this method is reduced relative to the results of a method that requires fewer allocations of income, expense, and other attributes. Similarly, the reliability of the results derived from application of this method is affected by the extent to which it is possible to apply the method to the participants' financial data that is related solely to the controlled transactions. For example, if the relevant business activity is entering into interest rate swaps with both controlled and uncontrolled taxpayers, it may not be possible to apply the method solely to financial data related to the controlled transactions. In such case, the reliability of the results derived from application of this method will be reduced.

(B) *Consistency in accounting.*—The degree of consistency between the controlled and uncontrolled taxpayers in accounting practices that materially affect the items that determine the amount and allocation of operating profit affects the reliability of the result. Thus, for example, if differences in financial product valuation or in cost allocation practices would materially affect operating profit, the ability to make reliable adjustments for such differences would affect the reliability of the results.

(6) *Residual profit split.*—(i) *In general.*—The residual profit split allocates the combined operating profit or loss between participants following the two-step process set forth in paragraphs (e)(6)(ii) and (iii) of this section.

(ii) *Allocate income to routine contributions.*—The first step allocates operating income to each participant to provide an arm's length return for its routine contributions to the global dealing operation. Routine contributions are contributions of the same or similar kind as those made by uncontrolled taxpayers involved in similar business activities for which it is possible to identify market returns. Routine contributions ordinarily include contributions of tangible property, services, and intangibles that are generally owned or performed by uncontrolled taxpayers engaged in similar activities. For example, transactions processing and credit analysis are typically routine contributions. In addition, a participant that guarantees obligations of or otherwise provides credit support to another controlled taxpayer in a global dealing operation is regarded as making a routine contribution. A functional analysis is required to identify the routine contributions according to the functions performed, risks assumed, and resources employed by each of the participants. Market returns for the routine contributions should be determined by reference to the returns achieved by uncontrolled taxpayers engaged in similar activities, consistent with the methods described in §§1.482-2 through 1.482-4 and this §1.482-8.

(iii) *Allocate residual profit.*—The allocation of income to the participant's routine contributions will not reflect profits attributable to each participant's valuable nonroutine contributions to the global dealing operation. Thus, in cases where valuable nonroutine contributions are present, there normally will be an unallocated residual profit after the allocation of income described in paragraph (e)(6)(ii) of this section. Under this second step, the residual profit generally should be divided among the participants based upon the relative value of each of their nonroutine contributions. Nonroutine contributions are contributions so integral to the global dealing operation that it is impossible to segregate them from the operation and find a separate market return for the contribution. Pricing and risk managing financial products almost invariably involve nonroutine contributions. Similarly, product development and information technology are generally nonroutine contributions. Marketing may be a nonrou-

tine contribution if the marketer substantially participates in developing a product or in tailoring the product to the unique requirements of a customer. The relative value of the nonroutine contributions of each participant in the global dealing operation should be measured in a manner that most reliably reflects each nonroutine contribution made to the global dealing operation and each participant's role in the nonroutine contributions.

(iv) *Comparability.*—The first step of the residual profit split relies on external market benchmarks of profitability. Thus, the comparability considerations that are relevant for the first step of the residual profit split are those that are relevant for the methods that are used to determine market returns for routine contributions. In the second step of the residual profit split, however, it may not be possible to rely as heavily on external market benchmarks. Nevertheless, in order to divide the residual profits of a global dealing operation in accordance with each participant's nonroutine contributions, it is necessary to apply the comparability standards of §1.482-1(d), as modified by paragraph (a)(3) of this section. In particular, the functional analysis required by §1.482-1(d)(3)(i) and paragraph (a)(3)(i) of this section is essential to determine whether two situations are comparable. Nevertheless, in certain cases, no comparable ventures between uncontrolled taxpayers may exist. In this situation, it is necessary to analyze the remaining factors set forth in paragraph (a)(3) of this section that could affect the division of operating profits between parties. If there are differences between the controlled and uncontrolled taxpayers that would materially affect the division of operating profit, adjustments must be made according to the provisions of §1.482-1(d)(2) and paragraph (a)(3) of this section.

(v) *Reliability.*—As indicated in §1.482-1(c)(2)(i), as the degree of comparability between the controlled and uncontrolled transactions increases, the reliability of a residual profit split also increases. In a global dealing operation, however, the absence of external market benchmarks (for example, joint ventures between uncontrolled taxpayers) on which to base the allocation of operating profits does not preclude use of this method if the allocation of the residual profit takes into account the relative contribution of each participant. The reliability of this method is increased to the extent that the allocation has economic significance for purposes other than tax (for example, satisfying regulatory standards and reporting, or determining bonuses paid to management or traders). The reliability of the analysis under this method may also be enhanced by the fact that all parties to the controlled transaction are evaluated under this method. The reliability of the results, however, of an analysis based on information from all parties to a transaction is affected by the reliability of the data and assumptions pertaining to each party to the controlled transaction. Thus, if the data and assumptions are significantly more reliable with respect to one of the parties than with respect to the others, a different method, focusing solely on the results of that party, may yield more reliable results.

(vi) *Data and assumptions.*—(A) *General rule.*—The reliability of the results derived from the residual profit split is measured under the standards set forth in paragraph (e)(5)(iv)(A) of this section.

(B) *Consistency in accounting.*—The degree of accounting consistency between controlled and uncontrolled taxpayers is measured under the standards set forth in paragraph (e)(5)(iv)(B) of this section.

(7) *Arm's length range.*—See §1.482-1(e)(2) and paragraph (a)(4) of this section for the determination of an arm's length range.

(8) *Examples.*—The following examples illustrate the principles of this paragraph (e).

Example 1. Total profit split. (i) P, a U.S. corporation, establishes a separate U.S. subsidiary (USsub) to conduct a global dealing operation in over-the-counter derivatives. USsub in turn establishes subsidiaries incorporated and doing business in the U.K. (UKsub) and Japan (Jsub). USsub, UKsub, and Jsub each employ marketers and traders who work closely together to design and sell derivative products to meet the particular needs of customers. Each also employs personnel who process and confirm trades, reconcile trade tickets and provide ongoing administrative support (back office services) for the global dealing operation. The global dealing operation maintains a single common book for each type of risk, and the book is maintained where the head trader for that type of risk is located. Thus, notional principal contracts denominated in North and South American currencies are booked in USsub, notional principal contracts denominated in European currencies are booked in UKsub, and notional principal contracts denominated in Japanese yen are booked in Jsub. However, each of the affiliates has authorized a trader located in each of the other affiliates to risk manage its books during periods when the booking location is closed. This grant of authority is necessary because marketers, regardless of their location, are expected to sell all of the group's products, and need to receive pricing information with respect to products during their clients' business hours, even if the booking location is closed. Moreover, P is known for making a substantial amount of its profits from trading activities, and frequently does not hedge the positions arising from its customer transactions in an attempt to profit from market changes. As a result, the traders in "off-hours" locations must have a substantial amount of trading authority in order to react to market changes.

(ii) Under §1.482-8(a)(2), USsub, UKsub and Jsub are participants in a global dealing operation in over-the-counter derivatives. P determines that the total profit split method is the best method to allocate an arm's length amount of income to each participant. P allocates the operating profit from the global dealing operation between USsub, UKsub and Jsub on the basis of the relative compensation paid to marketers and traders in each location. In making the allocation, P adjusts the compensation amounts to account for factors unrelated to job performance, such as the higher cost of living in certain jurisdictions. Because the traders receive significantly greater compensation than marketers in order to account for their greater contribution to the profits of the global dealing operation, P need not make additional adjustments or weight the compensation of the traders more heavily in allocating the operating profit between the affiliates. For rules concerning the source of income allocated to USsub, UKsub and Jsub (and any U.S. trade or business of the participants), see §1.863-3(h).

Example 2. Total profit split. The facts are the same as in Example 1, except that the labor market in Japan is such that traders paid by Jsub are paid the same as marketers paid by Jsub at the same seniority level, even though the traders contribute substantially more to the profitability of the global dealing operation. As a result, the allocation method used by P is unlikely to compensate the functions provided by each affiliate so as to be a reliable measure of an arm's length result under §§1.482-8(e)(2) and 1.482-1(c)(1), unless P weights the compensation of traders more heavily than the compensation of marketers or develops another method of measuring the contribution of traders to the profitability of the global dealing operation.

Example 3. Total profit split. The facts are the same as in Example 2, except that, in P's annual report to shareholders, P divides its operating profit from customer business into "dealing profit" and "trading profit." Because both marketers and traders are involved in the dealing function, P divides the "dealing profit" between the affiliates on the basis of the relative compensation of marketers and traders. However, because only the traders contribute to the trading profit, P divides the trading profit between the affiliates on the basis of the relative compensation only of the traders. In making that allocation, P must adjust the compensation of traders in Jsub in order to account for factors not related to job performance.

Example 4. Total profit split. The facts are the same as in Example 1, except that P is required by its regulators to hedge its customer positions as much as possible and therefore does not earn any "trading profit." As a result, the marketing intangibles, such as customer relationships, are relatively more important than the intangibles used by traders. Accordingly, P must weight the compensation of marketers more heavily than the compensation of traders in order to take into account accurately the contribution each function makes to the profitability of the business.

Example 5. Residual profit split. (i) P is a U.S. corporation that engages in a global dealing operation in foreign currency options directly and through controlled taxpayers that are incorporated and operate in the United Kingdom (UKsub) and Japan (Jsub). Each controlled taxpayer is a participant in a global dealing operation. Each participant employs marketers and traders who work closely together to design and sell foreign currency options that meet the particular needs of customers. Each participant also employs salespeople who sell foreign currency options with standardized terms and conditions, as well as other financial products offered by the controlled group. The traders in each location risk manage a common book of transactions during the relevant business hours of each location. P has a AAA credit rating and is the legal counterparty to all third party transactions. The traders in each location have discretion to execute contracts in the name of P. UKsub employs personnel who process and confirm trades, reconcile trade tickets, and provide ongoing administrative support (back office services) for all the participants in the global dealing operation. The global dealing operation has generated $192 of operating profit for the period.

(ii) After analyzing the foreign currency options business, P has determined that the residual profit split method is the best method to allocate the operating profit of the global dealing operation and to determine an arm's length amount of compensation allocable to each participant in the global dealing operation.

(iii) The first step of the residual profit split method (§1.482-8(e)(6)(ii)) requires P to identify the routine contributions performed by each participant. P determines that the functions performed by the salespeople are routine. P determines that the arm's length compensation for salespeople is $3, $4, and $5 in the United States, the United Kingdom, and Japan, respectively. Thus, P allocates $3, $4, and $5 to P, UKsub, and Jsub, respectively.

(iv) Although the back office function would not give rise to participant status, in the context of a residual profit split allocation, the back office function is relevant for purposes of receiving remuneration for routine contributions to a global dealing operation. P determines that an arm's length compensation for the back office is $20. Since the back office services constitute routine contributions, $20 of income is allocated to UKsub under step 1 of the residual profit split method. In addition, P determines that the comparable arm's length compensation for the risk to which P is subject as counterparty is $40. Accordingly, $40 is allocated to P as compensation for acting as counterparty to the transactions entered into in P's name by Jsub and UKsub.

(v) The second step of the residual profit split method (§1.482-8(e)(6)(iii)) requires that the residual profit be allocated to participants according to the relative value of their nonroutine contributions. Under P's transfer pricing method, P allocates the residual profit of $120 ($192 gross income minus $12 salesperson commissions minus $20 payment for back office services minus $40 compensation for the routine contribution of acting as counterparty) using a multifactor formula that reflects the relative value of the nonroutine contributions. Applying the comparability factors set out in §1.482-8(a)(3), P allocates 40% of the residual profit to UKsub, 35% of the residual profit to P, and the remaining 25% of residual profit to Jsub. Accordingly, under step 2, $48 is allocated to UKsub, $42 is allocated to P, and $30 is allocated to Jsub. See §1.863-3(h) for the source of income allocated to P with respect to its counterparty function.

(f) *Unspecified methods.*—Methods not specified in paragraphs (b), (c), (d), or (e) of this section may be used to evaluate whether the amount charged in a controlled transaction is at arm's length. Any method used under this paragraph (f) must be applied in accordance with the provisions of §1.482-1 as modified by paragraph (a)(3) of this section.

(g) *Source rule for qualified business units.*—See §1.863-3(h) for application of the rules of this section for purposes of determining the source of income, gain or loss from a global dealing operation among qualified business units (as defined in section 989(c) and §§1.863-3(h)(3)(iv) and 1.989(a)-1). [Reg. §1.482-8.]

EXEMPT ORGANIZATIONS

Exemption from Tax: Social Welfare Organizations: Guidance on Candidate-Related Political Activities

Exemption from Tax: Social Welfare Organizations: Guidance on Candidate-Related Political Activities.—Amendments to Reg. §1.501(c)(4)-1, providing guidance to tax-exempt social welfare organizations on political activities related to candidates that will not be considered to promote social welfare, are proposed (published in the Federal Register on November 29, 2013) (REG-134417-13).

☐ Par. 2. Section 1.501(c)(4)-1 is proposed to be amended by revising the first sentence of paragraph (a)(2)(ii) and adding paragraphs (a)(2)(iii) and (c) to read as follows:

§1.501(c)(4)-1. Civic organizations and local associations of employees.—(a) * * *

(2) * * *

(ii) * * * The promotion of social welfare does not include direct or indirect candidate-related political activity, as defined in paragraph (a)(2)(iii) of this section. * * *

(iii) *Definition of candidate-related political activity.*—(A) *In general.*—For purposes of this section, candidate-related political activity means:

(1) Any communication (as defined in paragraph (a)(2)(iii)(B)(3) of this section) expressing a view on, whether for or against, the selection, nomination, election, or appointment of one or more clearly identified candidates or of candidates of a political party that—

(i) Contains words that expressly advocate, such as "vote," "oppose," "support," "elect," "defeat," or "reject;" or

(ii) Is susceptible of no reasonable interpretation other than a call for or against the selection, nomination, election, or appointment of one or more candidates or of candidates of a political party;

(2) Any public communication (defined in paragraph (a)(2)(iii)(B)(5) of this section) within 30 days of a primary election or 60 days of a general election that refers to one or more clearly identified candidates in that election or, in the case of a general election, refers to one or more political parties represented in that election;

(3) Any communication the expenditures for which are reported to the Federal Election Commission, including independent expenditures and electioneering communications;

(4) A contribution (including a gift, grant, subscription, loan, advance, or deposit) of money or anything of value to or the solicitation of contributions on behalf of—

(i) Any person, if the transfer is recognized under applicable federal, state, or local campaign finance law as a reportable contribution to a candidate for elective office;

(ii) Any section 527 organization; or

(iii) Any organization described in section 501(c) that engages in candidate-related political activity within the meaning of this paragraph (a)(2)(iii) (see special rule in paragraph (a)(2)(iii)(D) of this section);

(5) Conduct of a voter registration drive or "get-out-the-vote" drive;

(6) Distribution of any material prepared by or on behalf of a candidate or by a section 527 organization including, without limitation, written materials, and audio and video recordings;

(7) Preparation or distribution of a voter guide that refers to one or more clearly identified candidates or, in the case of a general election, to one or more political parties (including material accompanying the voter guide); or

(8) Hosting or conducting an event within 30 days of a primary election or 60 days of a general election at which one or more candidates in such election appear as part of the program.

(B) Related definitions.—The following terms are defined for purposes of this paragraph (a)(2)(iii) only:

(1) "Candidate" means an individual who publicly offers himself, or is proposed by another, for selection, nomination, election, or appointment to any federal, state, or local public office or office in a political organization, or to be a Presidential or Vice-Presidential elector, whether or not such individual is ultimately selected, nominated, elected, or appointed. Any officeholder who is the subject of a recall election shall be treated as a candidate in the recall election.

(2) "Clearly identified" means the name of the candidate involved appears, a photograph or drawing of the candidate appears, or the identity of the candidate is apparent by reference, such as by use of the candidate's recorded voice or of terms such as "the Mayor," "your Congressman," "the incumbent," "the Democratic nominee," or "the Republican candidate for County Supervisor." In addition, a candidate may be "clearly identified" by reference to an issue or characteristic used to distinguish the candidate from other candidates.

(3) "Communication" means any communication by whatever means, including written, printed, electronic (including Internet), video, or oral communications.

(4) "Election" means a general, special, primary, or run-off election for federal, state, or local office; a convention or caucus of a political party that has authority to nominate a candidate for federal, state or local office; a primary election held for the selection of delegates to a national nominating convention of a political party; or a primary election held for the expression of a preference for the nomination of individuals for election to the office of President. A special election or a runoff election is treated as a primary election if held to nominate a candidate. A convention or caucus of a political party that has authority to nominate a candidate is also treated as a primary election. A special election or a runoff election is treated as a general election if held to elect a candidate. Any election or ballot measure to recall an individual who holds state or local elective public office is also treated as a general election.

(5) "Public communication" means any communication (as defined in paragraph (a)(2)(iii)(B)(3) of this section)—

(i) By broadcast, cable, or satellite;

(ii) On an Internet Web site;

(iii) In a newspaper, magazine, or other periodical;

(iv) In the form of paid advertising; or

(v) That otherwise reaches, or is intended to reach, more than 500 persons.

(6) "Section 527 organization" means an organization described in section 527(e)(1) (including a separate segregated fund described in section 527(f)(3)), whether or not the organization has filed notice under section 527(i).

(C) Attribution.—For purposes of this section, activities conducted by an organization include activities paid for by the organization or conducted by an officer, director, or employee acting in that capacity or by volunteers acting under the organization's direction or supervision. Communications made by an organization include communications the creation or distribution of which is paid for by the organization or that are made in an official publication of the organization (including statements or material posted by the organization on its Web site), as part of the program at an official function of the organization, by an officer or director acting in that capacity, or by an employee, volunteer, or other representative authorized to communicate on behalf of the organization and acting in that capacity.

(D) Special rule regarding contributions to section 501(c) organizations.—For purposes of paragraph (a)(2)(iii)(A)(4) of this section, a contribution to an organization described in section 501(c) will not be treated as a contribution to an organization engaged in candidate-related political activity if—

(1) The contributor organization obtains a written representation from an authorized officer of the recipient organization stating that the recipient organization does not engage in such activity (and the contributor organization does not know or have reason to know that the representation is inaccurate or unreliable); and

(2) The contribution is subject to a written restriction that it not be used for candidate-related political activity within the meaning of this paragraph (a)(2)(iii).

(c) Effective/applicability date.—Paragraphs (a)(2)(ii) and (iii) of this section apply on and after the date of publication of the Treasury decision adopting these rules as final regulations in the **Federal Register**.

Exemption from Tax: VEBA: Geographic Locale Restriction

Exemption from Tax: VEBA: Geographic Locale Restriction.—Reproduced below is the text of a proposed amendment to Reg. §1.501(c)(9)-2, relating to the qualification of voluntary employees' beneficiary associations under Code Sec. 501(c)(9) (published in the Federal Register on August 7, 1992).

☐ Par. 2. In §1.501(c)(9)-2, paragraph (a)(1) is amended by adding a sentence between the fourth and fifth sentences, and a new paragraph (d) is added, to read as follows:

§1.501(c)(9)-2. Membership in a voluntary employees' beneficiary association; employees; voluntary association of employees.— (a) * * *

(1) In general.—* * * (See paragraph (d) of this section for the meaning of geographic locale.) * * *

* * *

(d) Meaning of geographic locale.—*(1) Three-state safe harbor.*—An area is a single geographic locale for purposes of paragraph (a)(1) of this section if it does not exceed the boundaries of three contiguous states, *i.e.,* three states each of which shares a land or river border with at least one of the others. For this purposes, Alaska and Hawaii are deemed to be contiguous with each other and with each of the following states: Washington, Oregon, and California.

(2) Discretionary authority to recognize larger areas as geographic locales.—In determining whether an organization covering employees of employers engaged in the same line of business is a voluntary employees' beneficiary association (VEBA) described in section 501(c)(9), the Commissioner may recognize an area that does not satisfy the three-state safe harbor in paragraph (d)(1) of this section as a single geographic locale if—

(i) It would not be economically feasible to cover employees of employers engaged in that line of business in that area under two or more separate VEBAs each extending over fewer states; and

(ii) Employment characteristics in that line of business, population characteristics, or other regional factors support the particular states included. This paragraph (d)(2)(ii) is deemed satisfied if the states included are contiguous.

(3) *Examples.*—The following examples illustrate this paragraph (d).

Example 1. The membership of the W Association is made up of employers whose business consists of the distribution of produce in Virginia, North Carolina, and South Carolina. Because Virginia and South Carolina each share a land border with North Carolina, the three states are contiguous states and form a single geographic locale.

Example 2. The membership of the X Association is made up of employers whose business consists of the retail sale of computer software in Montana, Wyoming, North Dakota, South Dakota, and Nebraska, which are contiguous states. X establishes the X Trust to provide life, sick, accident, or other benefits for the employees of its members. The X Trust applies for recognition of exemption as a VEBA, stating that it intends to permit employees of any employer that is a member of X to join the proposed VEBA. In its application, the X Trust provides summaries of employer data and economic analyses showing that no division of the region into smaller groups of states would enable X to establish two or more separate VEBAs each with enough members to make the formation of those separate VEBAs economically feasible. Furthermore, although some possible divisions of the region into three-state or four-state areas could form an economically feasible VEBA, any such division of the five-state region covered by X would leave employees of X's employer-members located in at least one state without a VEBA. The Commissioner may, as a matter of administrative discretion, recognize the X Trust as a VEBA described in section 501(c)(9) based on its showing that the limited number of employees in each state would make any division of the region into two or more VEBAs economically infeasible.

Example 3. The membership of the Y Association is made up of employers whose business consists of shipping freight by barge on the Mississippi and Ohio Rivers. Some of the members of Y conduct their business out of ports in Louisiana, while other operate out of ports in Arkansas, Missouri, and Ohio. Y establishes the Y Trust to provide life, sick, accident, or other benefits to the employees of its members. The Y Trust applies for recognition of exemption as a VEBA, stating that it intends to permit the employees of any employer that is a member of Y to join the proposed VEBA. In its application, the Y Trust sets forth facts tending to show that there are so few members of Y in each of the four states that any division of

those states into two or more separate regions would result in creating VEBAs that would be too small to be economically feasible, that all of the members of Y are engaged in river shipping between inland and Gulf ports that are united by the existence of a natural waterway, and that the labor force engaged in providing transportation by river barge is distinct from that engaged in providing other means of transportation. Even though Ohio, Louisiana, Arkansas, and Missouri are not contiguous, because Ohio does not share a land or river border with any of the other three states, the Commissioner may, as a matter of administrative discretion, recognize the Y Trust as a VEBA described in section 501(c)(9) based on its showing that the establishment of separate characteristics of the river shipping business justify permitting a VEBA to cover the scattered concentrations of employees in that business located in Louisiana, Arkansas, Missouri, and Ohio.

Example 4. The membership of the Z Association is made up of employers whose business consists of the retail sale of agricultural implements in the states west of the Mississippi River except California, Alaska, and Hawaii. There are 21 states in the region covered by Z. Z established the Z1 Trust, the Z2 Trust, and the Z3 Trust to provide life, sick, accident or other benefits to the employees of its members. The trusts cover different subregions which were formed by dividing the Z region into three areas each consisting of seven contiguous states. Each trust applies for recognition of exemption as a VEBA, stating that it intends to permit the employees of any employer that is member of Z located within its subregion to join its proposed VEBA. Each trust sets forth facts in its application tending to show that four states within its particular subregion would be needed to create a VEBA large enough to be economically feasible, so that any further division of its seven-state subregion would leave employees of at least some of Z's employer-members located in the subregion in an area too small to support an economically feasible VEBA. The applications contain no justification for the choice of three seven-state subregions. Since the applicants have not shown that it would not be economically feasible to divide the Z region into smaller subregions (*e.g.*, four containing four states and one containing five states), the applicants have not satisifed paragraph (d)(2)(i) of this section, and the Commissioner does not have the discretion to recognize the Z1, Z2, and Z3 Trusts as VEBAs described in section 501(c)(9).

Qualified Group Legal Services Plans

Qualified Group Legal Services Plans.—Reproduced below is the text of proposed Reg. §1.501(c)(20)-1, relating to qualified group legal services plans (published in the Federal Register on April 29, 1980).

☐ Par. 3. There is added in the appropriate place the following new section:

§1.501(c)(20)-1. Qualified group legal services plan trust.— (a) *Qualified group legal services plan.*—For purposes of this section, a "qualified group legal services plan" is a plan that satisfies the requirements of section 120(b) and §1.120-2.

(b) *General requirements for exemption.*—Under section 501(c)(20), an organization or trust created or organized in the United States is exempt as provided in section 501(a) if the exclusive function of the organization or trust is to form part of a qualified group legal services plan or plans.

(c) *Exception for trust associated with section 501(c) organization.*— As described in section 120(c)(5)(C), employer contributions under a qualified group legal services plan may be paid to an organization described in section 501(c) if that organization is permitted by section 501(c) to receive payments from an employer for support of a qualified group legal services plan. However, that organization must, in turn, pay or credit the contributions to an organization or trust

described in section 501(c)(20). In such a case, the organization or trust to which the contributions are finally paid or credited is considered to satisfy the requirement that the *exclusive* function of the organization or trust be to form part of a qualified group legal services plan or plans, notwithstanding that the organization or trust provides legal services or indemnification against the cost of legal services unassociated with such a qualified plan. This exception applies, however, only if any such legal service or indemnification is provided under a program established and maintained by the organization described in section 501(c) to which the employer contributions under a qualified group legal services plan are first paid under section 120(c)(5)(C). Whether providing legal services or indemnification against the cost of legal services unassociated with a qualified group legal services plan is a permissible activity of an organization described in section 501(c) is determined under the rules under that paragraph of section 501(c) in which the organization is described. [Reg. §1.501(c)(20)-1.]

Charitable Hospitals: Additional Requirements

Charitable Hospitals: Additional Requirements.—Reg. §§1.501(r)-0—1.501(r)-7, providing guidance regarding the requirements for charitable hospital organizations relating to financial assistance and emergency medical care policies, charges for certain care provided to individuals eligible for financial assistance, and billing and collections, are proposed (published in the Federal Register on June 26, 2012) (REG-130266-11) (corrected August 10, 2012).

Proposed Reg. §§1.501(r)-0—1.501(r)-7 were adopted by T.D. 9708 on December 29, 2014. However, for tax years beginning on or before December 29, 2015, a hospital may rely on the final regulations or the 2012 and/or 2013 proposed regulations (REG-130266-11 and/or REG-106499-12).

☐ Par. 2. Section 1.501(r)-0 is added to read as follows:

§1.501(r)-0. Outline of regulations.—This section lists the table of contents for §§1.501(r)-1 through 1.501(r)-7.

§1.501(r)-1. Definitions.
  (a) Application.
  (b) Definitions.
    (1) Amounts generally billed (AGB).
    (2) AGB percentage.
    (3) Application period.
    (4) Billing and collections policy.

    (5) Completion deadline.
    (6) Disregarded entity.
    (7) Emergency medical care.
    (8) Emergency medical conditions.
    (9) Extraordinary collection action (ECA).
    (10) Financial assistance policy (FAP).
    (11) FAP application.
    (12) FAP application form.
    (13) FAP-eligible individual.

(14) Gross charges.

(15) Hospital facility.

(16) Hospital organization.

(17) Medicare fee-for-service.

(18) Notification period.

(19) Plain language summary.

(20) Primary payer.

(21) Private health insurer.

(22) Referring.

§1.501(r)-2. Failures to satisfy section 501(r) requirements. [Reserved]

§1.501(r)-3. Community health needs assessments. [Reserved]

§1.501(r)-4. Financial assistance policy and emergency medical care policy.

(a) In general.

(b) Financial assistance policy.

(1) In general.

(2) Eligibility criteria and basis for calculating amounts charged to patients.

(3) Method for applying for financial assistance.

(4) Actions that may be taken in the event of nonpayment.

(5) Widely publicizing the FAP.

(6) Readily obtainable information.

(c) Emergency medical care policy.

(1) In general.

(2) Interference with provision of emergency medical care.

(3) Relation to federal law governing emergency care.

(4) Examples.

(d) Establishing the FAP and other policies.

(1) In general.

(2) Authorized body.

☐ Par. 3. Section 1.501(r)-1 is added to read as follows:

§1.501(r)-1. Definitions.—(a) *Application.*—The definitions set forth in this section apply to §§1.501(r)-2 through 1.501(r)-7.

(b) *Definitions.*—(1) *Amounts generally billed (AGB)* means the amounts generally billed for emergency or other medically necessary care to individuals who have insurance covering such care, determined in accordance with §1.501(r)-5(b).

(2) *AGB percentage* means a percentage of gross charges that a hospital facility uses under §1.501(r)-5(b)(1) to determine the AGB for any emergency or other medically necessary care it provides to a FAP-eligible individual.

(3) *Application period* means the period during which a hospital facility must accept and process an application for assistance under its financial assistance policy (FAP) submitted by an individual in order to have made reasonable efforts to determine whether the individual is FAP-eligible. With respect to any care provided by a hospital facility to an individual, the application period begins on the date the care is provided to the individual and ends on the 240th day after the hospital facility provides the individual with the first billing statement for the care.

(4) *Billing and collections policy* means a written policy that includes all of the elements described in §1.501(r)-4(b)(4).

(5) *Completion deadline* means the date after which a hospital facility may initiate or resume extraordinary collection actions against an individual who has submitted an incomplete FAP application if that individual has not provided the hospital facility with the missing information and/or documentation necessary to complete the application. The completion deadline must be specified in a written notice (as described in §1.501(r)-6(c)(3)(i)(C)) and must be no earlier than the later of—

(i) 30 days after the hospital facility provides the individual with this written notice; or

(ii) The last day of the application period described in paragraph (b)(3) of this section.

(6) *Disregarded entity* means an entity that is generally disregarded as separate from its owner for federal tax purposes under §301.7701-3 of this chapter. One example of a disregarded entity is a domestic single member limited liability company that does not elect to be classified as an association taxable as a corporation for federal tax purposes.

(7) *Emergency medical care* means care provided by a hospital facility for emergency medical conditions.

(8) *Emergency medical conditions* means emergency medical conditions as defined in section 1867 of the Social Security Act (42 U.S.C. 1395dd).

(9) *Extraordinary collection action (ECA)* means an action described in §1.501(r)-6(b).

(10) *Financial assistance policy (FAP)* means a written policy that meets the requirements described in §1.501(r)-4(b).

(11) *FAP application* means the information and accompanying documentation that a hospital facility requires an individual to sub-

mit to apply for financial assistance under the facility's FAP. A FAP application is considered complete if it contains information and documentation sufficient for the hospital facility to determine whether the applicant is FAP-eligible and incomplete if it does not contain such information and documentation.

(12) *FAP application form* means the application form (and any accompanying instructions) that a hospital facility requires an individual to submit as part of his or her FAP application.

(13) *FAP-eligible individual* means an individual eligible for financial assistance under a hospital facility's FAP, without regard to whether the individual has applied for assistance under the FAP.

(14) *Gross charges*, or the *chargemaster rate*, means a hospital facility's full, established price for medical care that the hospital facility consistently and uniformly charges all patients before applying any contractual allowances, discounts, or deductions.

(15) *Hospital facility* means a facility that is required by a state to be licensed, registered, or similarly recognized as a hospital. Except as otherwise provided in published guidance, a hospital organization may treat multiple buildings operated under a single state license as a single hospital facility. For purposes of this paragraph (b)(15), the term "state" includes only the 50 states and the District of Columbia and not any U.S. territory or foreign country. References to a hospital facility taking actions include instances in which the hospital organization operating the hospital facility takes action through or on behalf of the hospital facility.

(16) *Hospital organization* means an organization recognized (or seeking to be recognized) as described in section 501(c)(3) that operates one or more hospital facilities, including a hospital facility operated through a disregarded entity.

(17) *Medicare fee-for-service* means health insurance available under Medicare Part A and Part B of Title XVIII of the Social Security Act.

(18) *Notification period* means the period during which a hospital facility must notify an individual about its FAP in accordance with §1.501(r)-6(c)(2) in order to have made reasonable efforts to determine whether the individual is FAP-eligible. With respect to any care provided by a hospital facility to an individual, the notification period begins on the first date care is provided to the individual and ends on the 120th day after the hospital facility provides the individual with the first billing statement for the care.

(19) *Plain language summary* means a written statement that notifies an individual that the hospital facility offers financial assistance under a FAP and provides the following additional information in language that is clear, concise, and easy to understand—

(i) A brief description of the eligibility requirements and assistance offered under the FAP;

(ii) The direct website address (or URL) and physical location(s) (including a room number, if applicable) where the individual can obtain copies of the FAP and FAP application form;

(iii) Instructions on how the individual can obtain a free copy of the FAP and FAP application form by mail;

---

(3) Implementing a policy.

(4) Establishing a policy for more than one hospital facility.

§1.501(r)-5. Limitation on charges.

(a) In general.

(b) Amounts generally billed.

(1) Look-back method.

(2) Prospective Medicare method.

(3) Examples.

(c) Gross charges.

(d) Safe harbor for certain charges in excess of AGB.

§1.501(r)-6. Billing and collection.

(a) In general.

(b) Extraordinary collection actions.

(c) Reasonable efforts.

(1) In general.

(2) Notification.

(3) Incomplete FAP applications.

(4) Complete FAP applications.

(5) Suspending ECAs while a FAP application is pending.

(6) Waiver does not constitute reasonable efforts.

(7) Agreements with other parties.

(8) Clear and conspicuous placement.

§1.501(r)-7. Effective/applicability dates.

(a) Statutory effective/applicability date.

(1) In general.

(2) Community health needs assessment.

(b) Effective/applicability date of regulations.

[Reg. §1.501(r)-0.]

(iv) The contact information, including the telephone number(s) and physical location (including a room number, if applicable), of hospital facility staff who can provide an individual with information about the FAP and the FAP application process, as well as of the nonprofit organizations or government agencies, if any, that the hospital facility has identified as available sources of assistance with FAP applications;

(v) A statement of the availability of translations of the FAP, FAP application form, and plain language summary in other languages, if applicable; and

(vi) A statement that no FAP-eligible individual will be charged more for emergency or other medically necessary care than AGB.

(20) *Primary payer* means a health insurer (whether a private health insurer or a public payer such as Medicare) that pays first on a claim for medical care (usually after a deductible has been paid by the insured) up to the limits of the policy or program, regardless of other insurance coverage the insured may have. Primary payers are distinguished from secondary payers that pay second on a claim for medical care to the extent payment has not been made by the primary payer.

(21) *Private health insurer* means any organization that offers insurance for medical care that is not a governmental unit described in section 170(c)(1). For purposes of § 1.501(r)-5(b), claims paid under Medicare Advantage (Part C of Title XVIII of the Social Security Act) are treated as claims paid by a private health insurer.

(22) *Referring* an individual's debt to a debt collection agency or other party includes contracting with, delegating, or otherwise using the debt collection agency or other party to collect amounts owed by the individual to the hospital facility while still maintaining ownership of the debt. [Reg. § 1.501(r)-1.]

☐ Par. 4. Sections 1.501(r)-2 and 1.501(r)-3 are added and reserved to read as follows:

§ 1.501(r)-2. Failures to satisfy section 501(r) requirements.— [Reserved].

§ 1.501(r)-3. Community health needs assessments.—[Reserved].

☐ Par. 5. Sections 1.501(r)-4, 1.501(r)-5, 1.501(r)-6, and 1.501(r)-7 are added to read as follows:

§ 1.501(r)-4. Financial assistance policy and emergency medical care policy.—(a) *In general.*—A hospital organization meets the requirements of section 501(r)(4) with respect to a hospital facility it operates if the hospital organization establishes for that hospital facility—

(1) A written financial assistance policy (FAP) that meets the requirements described in paragraph (b) of this section; and

(2) A written emergency medical care policy that meets the requirements described in paragraph (c) of this section.

(b) *Financial assistance policy.*—(1) *In general.*—To satisfy paragraph (a)(1) of this section, a hospital facility's FAP must apply to all emergency and other medically necessary care provided by the hospital facility and include—

(i) Eligibility criteria for financial assistance and whether such assistance includes free or discounted care;

(ii) The basis for calculating amounts charged to patients;

(iii) The method for applying for financial assistance;

(iv) In the case of a hospital facility that does not have a separate billing and collections policy, the actions that may be taken in the event of nonpayment; and

(v) Measures to widely publicize the FAP within the community served by the hospital facility.

(2) *Eligibility criteria and basis for calculating amounts charged to patients.*—(i) *In general.*—To satisfy paragraphs (b)(1)(i) and (b)(1)(ii) of this section, the FAP must—

(A) Specify all financial assistance available under the FAP, including all discount(s) and free care and, if applicable, the amount(s) (for example, gross charges) to which any discount percentages will be applied;

(B) Specify all of the eligibility criteria that an individual must satisfy to receive each such discount, free care, or other level of assistance;

(C) State that following a determination of FAP-eligibility, a FAP-eligible individual will not be charged more for emergency or other medically necessary care than the amounts generally billed to individuals who have insurance covering such care (AGB);

(D) Describe which method under § 1.501(r)-5(b) the hospital facility uses to determine AGB; and

(E) If the hospital facility uses the look-back method described in § 1.501(r)-5(b)(1) to determine AGB, either state the hospital facility's AGB percentage(s) and describe how the hospital facility calculated such percentage(s) or explain how members of the public may readily obtain this information in writing and free of charge.

(ii) *Examples.*—The following examples illustrate this paragraph (b)(2):

Example 1. Q is a hospital facility that establishes a FAP that provides assistance to all uninsured and underinsured individuals whose family income is less than or equal to x% of the Federal Poverty Level (FPL), with the level of discount for which an individual is eligible under Q's FAP determined based upon the individual's family income as a percentage of FPL. Q's FAP defines the meaning of "uninsured," "underinsured," "family income," and "Federal Poverty Level" and specifies that all emergency and other medically necessary care provided by Q is covered under the FAP. Q's FAP also states that Q determines AGB by multiplying the gross charges for any emergency or other medically necessary care it provides to a FAP-eligible individual by 50 percent. The FAP states, further, that Q calculated the AGB percentage of 50 percent based on all claims paid in full to Q by Medicare and private health insurers and the individuals they insured over a specified 12-month period, divided by the associated gross charges for those claims. Q's FAP contains the following chart, specifying each discount available under the FAP, the amounts (gross charges) to which these discounts will be applied, and the specific eligibility criteria for each such discount:

Family income as % of FPL	Discount off of gross charges
>y% - x%	50%
>z% - y%	75%
≤z%	Free

Q's FAP also contains a statement that no FAP-eligible individual will be charged more for emergency or other medically necessary care than AGB because Q's AGB percentage is 50 percent of gross charges and the most a FAP-eligible individual will be charged is 50 percent of gross charges. Q's FAP satisfies the requirements of this paragraph (b)(2).

Example 2. R is a hospital facility that establishes a FAP that provides assistance based on household income. R's FAP defines the meaning of "household income" and specifies that all emergency and other medically necessary care provided by R is covered under the FAP. R's FAP contains the following chart, specifying the assistance available under the FAP and the specific eligibility criteria for each level of assistance offered, which R updates occasionally to account for inflation:

Household income	Maximum amount individual will be responsible for paying
>$b - $a	40% of gross charges, up to the lesser of AGB or x% of annual household income
>$c - $b	20% of gross charges, up to the lesser of AGB or y% of annual household income
≤$c	$0 (free)

R's FAP contains a statement that no FAP-eligible individual will be charged more for emergency or other medically necessary care than AGB. R's FAP also states that R determines AGB by multiplying the gross charges for any emergency or other medically necessary care it provides by AGB percentages, which are based on claims paid under Medicare. In addition, the FAP provides a web address individuals can visit, and a telephone number they can call, if they would like to obtain an information sheet stating R's AGB percentages and explaining how these AGB percentages were calculated. This information sheet, which R makes available on its website and provides to any individual who requests it, states that R's AGB percentages are 35 percent of gross charges for inpatient care and 60 percent of gross charges for outpatient care. It also states that these percentages were based on all claims paid to R for emergency or other medically necessary inpatient and outpatient care by Medicare and Medicare beneficiaries over a specified 12-month period, divided by the associated gross charges for those claims. R's FAP satisfies the requirements of this paragraph (b)(2).

(3) *Method for applying for financial assistance.*—(i) *In general.*— To satisfy paragraph (b)(1)(iii) of this section, a hospital facility's FAP must describe how an individual applies for financial assistance under the FAP. In addition, either the hospital facility's FAP or FAP application form (including accompanying instructions) must describe the information and documentation the hospital facility may require an individual to submit as part of his or her FAP application and provide the contact information described in §1.501(r)-1(b)(19)(iv). The hospital facility may not deny financial assistance under the FAP based on an applicant's failure to provide information or documentation that the hospital facility's FAP or FAP application form does not require an individual to submit as part of a FAP application.

(ii) *Example.*—The following example illustrates this paragraph (b)(3):

Example. S is a hospital facility with a FAP that bases eligibility solely on an individual's household income. S's FAP provides that an individual may apply for financial assistance by completing and submitting S's FAP application form. S's FAP also describes how individuals can obtain copies of the FAP application form. S's FAP application form contains lines on which the applicant lists all items of household income received by the applicant's household over the last three months and the names of the applicant's household members. The instructions to S's FAP application form tell applicants where to submit the application and provide that an applicant must attach to his or her FAP application form proof of household income in the form of the applicant's most recent federal tax return, payroll check stubs from the last three months, documentation of the applicant's qualification for certain specified state meanstested programs, or other reliable evidence of the applicant's earned and unearned household income. S does not require FAP applicants to submit any information or documentation not mentioned in the FAP application form instructions. S's FAP application form instructions also provide the contact information of hospital facility staff who can provide an applicant with information about the FAP and FAP application process. S's FAP satisfies the requirements of this paragraph (b)(3).

(4) *Actions that may be taken in the event of nonpayment.*—(i) *In general.*—To satisfy paragraph (b)(1)(iv) of this section, either a hospital facility's FAP or a separate written billing and collections policy established by the hospital facility must describe—

(A) Any actions that the hospital facility (or other authorized party) may take relating to obtaining payment of a bill for medical care, including, but not limited to, any extraordinary collection actions described in §1.501(r)-6(b);

(B) The process and time frames the hospital facility (or other authorized party) uses in taking the actions described in paragraph (b)(4)(i)(A) of this section, including, but not limited to, the reasonable efforts it will make to determine whether an individual is FAP-eligible before engaging in any extraordinary collection actions, as described in §1.501(r)-6(c); and

(C) The office, department, committee, or other body with the final authority or responsibility for determining that the hospital facility has made reasonable efforts to determine whether an individual is FAP-eligible and may therefore engage in extraordinary collection actions against the individual.

(ii) *Separate billing and collections policy.*—In the case of a hospital facility that satisfies paragraph (b)(1)(iv) of this section by establishing a separate written billing and collections policy, the hospital facility's FAP must state that the actions the hospital facility may take in the event of nonpayment are described in a separate billing and collections policy and explain how members of the public may readily obtain a free copy of this separate policy.

(5) *Widely publicizing the FAP.*—(i) *In general.*—To satisfy paragraph (b)(1)(v) of this section, a FAP must include, or explain how members of the public may readily obtain a free written description of, measures taken by the hospital facility to—

(A) Make the FAP, FAP application form, and a plain language summary of the FAP (as defined in §1.501(r)-1(b)(19)) widely available on a website, as described in paragraph (b)(5)(iv) of this section;

(B) Make paper copies of the FAP, FAP application form, and plain language summary of the FAP available upon request and without charge, both in public locations in the hospital facility and by mail, in English and in the primary language of any populations with limited proficiency in English that constitute more than 10 percent of the residents of the community served by the hospital facility;

(C) Inform and notify visitors to the hospital facility about the FAP through conspicuous public displays or other measures reasonably calculated to attract visitors' attention; and

(D) Inform and notify residents of the community served by the hospital facility about the FAP in a manner reasonably calculated to reach those members of the community who are most likely to require financial assistance.

(ii) *Meaning of inform and notify.*—For purposes of paragraphs (b)(5)(i)(C) and (b)(5)(i)(D) of this section, a measure will inform and notify visitors to a hospital facility or residents of a community about the hospital facility's FAP if the measure, at a minimum, notifies the reader or listener that the hospital facility offers financial assistance under a FAP and informs him or her about how or where to obtain more information about the FAP.

(iii) *Meaning of reasonably calculated.*—Whether one or more measures to widely publicize a hospital facility's FAP are reasonably calculated to inform and notify visitors to a hospital facility or residents of a community about the hospital facility's FAP in the manner described in paragraphs (b)(5)(i)(C) and (b)(5)(i)(D) of this section will depend on all of the facts and circumstances, including the primary language(s) spoken by the residents of the community served by the hospital facility and other attributes of the community and the hospital facility.

(iv) *Widely available on a website.*—For purposes of paragraph (b)(5)(i)(A) of this section, a hospital facility makes its FAP, FAP application form, and plain language summary of the FAP widely available on a website only if—

(A) The hospital facility conspicuously posts complete and current versions of these documents in English and in the primary language of any populations with limited proficiency in English that constitute more than 10 percent of the residents of the community served by the hospital facility on—

(1) The hospital facility's website;

(2) If the hospital facility does not have its own website separate from the hospital organization that operates it, the hospital organization's website; or

(3) A website established and maintained by another entity, but only if the website of the hospital facility or hospital organization (if the facility or organization has a website) provides a conspicuously-displayed link to the web page on which the document is posted, along with clear instructions for accessing the document on that website;

(B) Any individual with access to the Internet can access, download, view, and print a hard copy of these documents without requiring special computer hardware or software (other than software that is readily available to members of the public without payment of any fee) and without payment of a fee to the hospital facility, hospital organization, or other entity maintaining the website; and

(C) The hospital facility provides any individual who asks how to access a copy of the FAP, FAP application form, or plain language summary of the FAP online with the direct website address, or URL, of the web page on which these documents are posted.

(v) *Limited English proficient populations.*—For purposes of paragraphs (b)(5)(i)(B) and (b)(5)(iv)(A) of this section, a hospital facility may determine whether any language minority with limited proficiency in English constitutes more than 10 percent of the residents of the community served by the hospital facility based on the latest data available from the U.S. Census Bureau or other similarly reliable data.

(vi) *Examples.*—The following examples illustrate this paragraph (b)(5):

Example 1. (i) Z is a hospital facility whose FAP states that Z will make its FAP, FAP application form, and a plain language summary of its FAP widely available through its website. In accordance with its FAP, the home page and main billing page of Z's website conspicuously display the following message: "Need help paying your bill? You may be eligible for financial assistance. Click *here* for more information." When readers click on the link, they are taken to a web page that explains the various discounts available under Z's FAP and the specific eligibility criteria for each such discount. This web page also provides a telephone number and room number of Z that individuals can call or visit for more information about the FAP, as well as the name and contact information of a few nonprofit organizations and government agencies that Z has identified as capable and available sources of assistance with FAP applications. In addition, the web page contains prominently-displayed links that allow readers to download PDF files of the FAP and the FAP application form, free of charge. Z provides any individual who asks how to access a copy of the FAP, FAP application form, or plain language summary of the FAP online with the URL of this web page. Z's FAP includes measures to make the FAP widely available on a website within the meaning of paragraph (b)(5)(i)(A) of this section.

(ii) Z's FAP also states that Z will make paper copies of the FAP, FAP application form, and plain language summary of the FAP available upon request and without charge, both by mail and in its billing office, admissions and registrations areas, and emergency room, and will inform and notify visitors to the hospital facility about the FAP in these same locations using signs and brochures. In accordance with its FAP, Z conspicuously displays a sign in large font regarding the FAP in its billing office, admissions and registrations areas, and emergency room. The sign says: "Uninsured? Having trouble paying your hospital bill? You may be eligible for financial assistance." The sign also provides the URL of the web page where Z's FAP and FAP application form can be accessed. In addition, the sign provides a telephone number and room number of Z that individuals can call or visit with questions about the FAP or the FAP application process. Underneath each sign, Z conspicuously displays copies of a brochure that contains all of the information required to be included in a plain language summary of the FAP (as defined in §1.501(r)-1(b)(19)). Z makes these brochures available in quantities sufficient to meet visitor demand. Z also makes paper copies of its FAP and FAP application form available upon request and without charge in these same locations and by mail. Z's FAP includes measures to widely publicize the FAP within the meaning of paragraphs (b)(5)(i)(B) and (b)(5)(i)(C) of this section.

(iii) In addition, Z's FAP states that Z will inform and notify members of the community served by the hospital facility about the FAP through its quarterly newsletter and by distributing copies of its FAP brochures to physicians and local nonprofit organizations and public agencies that address the health needs of lowincome people. In accordance with its FAP, Z distributes copies of the brochure and its FAP application form to all of its referring staff physicians and to the community health centers serving its community. Z also distributes copies of these documents to the local health department and to numerous public agencies and nonprofit organizations in its community that address the health issues and other needs of low-income populations, in quantities sufficient to meet demand. In addition, every issue of the quarterly newsletter that Z mails to the individuals in its customer database contains a prominently-displayed advertisement informing readers that Z offers financial assistance and that people having trouble paying their hospital bills may be eligible for financial assistance. The advertisement also provides readers with the URL of the web page where Z's FAP and FAP application form can be accessed and a telephone number and room number of Z that individuals can call or visit with questions about the FAP or the FAP application process. Z's FAP includes measures to widely publicize its FAP within the meaning of paragraph (b)(5)(i)(D) of this section.

(iv) Because Z's FAP includes measures to widely publicize the FAP described in paragraphs (b)(5)(i)(A), (b)(5)(i)(B), (b)(5)(i)(C), and (b)(5)(i)(D) of this section, Z's FAP meets the requirements of this paragraph (b)(5).

Example 2. Assume the same facts as *Example 1*, except that Z serves a community in which 11 percent of the residents speak Spanish and have limited proficiency in English. Z's FAP states that Z will provide all of the information described in *Example 1*, including the FAP itself, in both Spanish and English. In accordance with its FAP, Z translates its FAP, FAP application form, and FAP brochure (which constitutes a plain language summary of the FAP) into Spanish, and displays and distributes Spanish versions of these documents in its hospital facility and in the Spanish-speaking portions of the community it serves, using all of the measures described in *Example 1*. Moreover, the home page and main billing page of Z's website conspicuously display an "¿Habla Español?" link that takes readers to a web page that summarizes the FAP in Spanish and contains links that allow readers to download PDF files of the Spanish versions of the FAP and FAP application form, free of charge. Z's FAP meets the requirements of this paragraph (b)(5) by including measures to widely publicize the FAP within the community served by Z.

Example 3. Assume the same facts as *Example 1*, except that instead of including generalized summaries of the measures Z will take to widely publicize its FAP in the FAP itself, Z's FAP states that a task force established by Z with control over a set budget will meet at least annually to develop and adopt a plan to widely publicize Z's FAP. The FAP further states that the task force will summarize this plan in a one-page information sheet that will be made available upon request in Z's billing office and posted on the web page through which Z makes its FAP and FAP application form widely

available. In year 1, the task force considers the needs of Z's patients and the surrounding community and adopts and implements a plan to take all of the measures described in *Example 1*. The task force prepares a one-page information sheet summarizing this plan that is made available as described in the FAP. Z's FAP meets the requirements of this paragraph (b)(5) in year 1 by including measures to widely publicize the FAP within the community served by Z.

(6) *Readily obtainable information.*—For purposes of this paragraph (b), members of the public may readily obtain information if a hospital facility makes the information available free of charge both on a website and in writing upon request in a manner similar to that described in paragraphs (b)(5)(i)(A) and (b)(5)(i)(B) of this section.

(c) *Emergency medical care policy.*—(1) *In general.*—To satisfy paragraph (a)(2) of this section, a hospital facility must establish a written policy that requires the hospital facility to provide, without discrimination, care for emergency medical conditions to individuals regardless of whether they are FAP-eligible.

(2) *Interference with provision of emergency medical care.*—A hospital facility's emergency medical care policy will not be described in paragraph (c)(1) of this section unless it prohibits the hospital facility from engaging in actions that discourage individuals from seeking emergency medical care, such as by demanding that emergency department patients pay before receiving treatment for emergency medical conditions or by permitting debt collection activities in the emergency department or in other areas of the hospital facility where such activities could interfere with the provision, without discrimination, of emergency medical care.

(3) *Relation to federal law governing emergency medical care.*—Subject to paragraph (c)(2) of this section, a hospital facility's emergency medical care policy will be described in paragraph (c)(1) of this section if it requires the hospital facility to provide the care for emergency medical conditions that the hospital facility is required to provide under Subchapter G of Chapter IV of Title 42 of the Code of Federal Regulations (or any successor regulations).

(4) *Examples.*—The following examples illustrate this paragraph (c):

Example 1. F is a hospital facility with a dedicated emergency department that is subject to the Emergency Medical Treatment and Labor Act (EMTALA) and is not a critical access hospital. F establishes a written emergency medical care policy requiring F to comply with EMTALA by providing medical screening examinations and stabilizing treatment and referring or transferring an individual to another facility, when appropriate, and to provide emergency services in accordance with 42 CFR §482.55 (or any successor regulation). F's emergency medical care policy also states that F prohibits any actions that would discourage individuals from seeking emergency medical care, such as by demanding that emergency department patients pay before receiving treatment for emergency medical conditions or permitting debt collection activities in the emergency department or in other areas of the hospital facility where such activities could interfere with the provision, without discrimination, of emergency medical care. F's emergency medical care policy is described in paragraph (c)(1) of this section.

Example 2. G is a rehabilitation hospital facility. G does not have a dedicated emergency department, nor does it have specialized capabilities that would make it appropriate to accept transfers of individuals who need stabilizing treatment for an emergency medical condition. G establishes a written emergency medical care policy that addresses how it appraises emergencies, provides initial treatment, and refers or transfers an individual to another facility, when appropriate, in a manner that complies with 42 CFR §482.12(f)(2) (or any successor regulation). G's emergency medical care policy also states that G prohibits any actions that would discourage individuals from seeking emergency medical care, such as by permitting debt collection activities in any areas of the hospital facility where such activities could interfere with the provision, without discrimination, of emergency medical care. G's emergency medical care policy is described in paragraph (c)(1) of this section.

(d) *Establishing the FAP and other policies.*—(1) *In general.*—A hospital organization has established a FAP, a billing and collections policy, or an emergency medical care policy for a hospital facility only if an authorized body of the hospital organization has adopted the policy for the hospital facility and the hospital facility has implemented the policy.

(2) *Authorized body.*—For purposes of this paragraph (d), an authorized body of a hospital organization means—

(i) The governing body (that is, the board of directors, board of trustees, or equivalent controlling body) of the hospital organization;

(ii) A committee of the governing body, which may be composed of any individuals permitted under state law to serve on such a committee, to the extent that the committee is permitted by state law to act on behalf of the governing body;

(iii) To the extent permitted under state law, other parties authorized by the governing body of the hospital organization to act on its behalf; or

(iv) In the case of a hospital facility (operated by the hospital organization) that has its own governing body and is recognized as an entity under state law but is a disregarded entity for federal tax purposes, the governing body of that disregarded entity (or a committee of or other parties authorized by that governing body as described in paragraphs (d)(2)(ii) or (d)(2)(iii) of this section).

(3) *Implementing a policy.*—For purposes of this paragraph (d), a hospital facility has implemented a policy if the hospital facility has consistently carried out the policy.

(4) *Establishing a policy for more than one hospital facility.*—Although a hospital organization operating more than one hospital facility must separately establish a FAP and emergency medical care policy for each hospital facility it operates, such policies may contain the same operative terms. However, different AGB percentages and methods of determining AGB and the unique attributes of the communities that different hospital facilities serve may require the hospital facilities to include in their FAPs (or otherwise make available) different information regarding AGB and different measures to widely publicize the FAP in order to meet the requirements of paragraphs (b)(2) and/or (b)(5) of this section. [Reg. § 1.501(r)-4.]

§1.501(r)-5. Limitation on charges.—(a) *In general.*—A hospital organization meets the requirements of section 501(r)(5) with respect to a hospital facility it operates if the hospital facility limits the amount charged for care it provides to any individual who is eligible for assistance under its financial assistance policy (FAP) to—

(1) In the case of emergency or other medically necessary care, not more than the amounts generally billed to individuals who have insurance covering such care (AGB), as determined under paragraph (b) of this section; and

(2) In the case of all other medical care, less than the gross charges for such care, as described in paragraph (c) of this section.

(b) *Amounts generally billed.*—In order to meet the requirements of paragraph (b)(1) of this section, a hospital facility must determine AGB for emergency or other medically necessary care using a method described in either paragraph (b)(1) or (b)(2) of this section. A hospital facility may use only one of these methods to determine AGB. After choosing a particular method, a hospital facility must continue to use that method.

(1) *Look-back method.*—(i) *In general.*—A hospital facility may determine AGB for any emergency or other medically necessary care it provides to a FAP-eligible individual by multiplying the hospital facility's gross charges for the care provided to the individual by one or more percentages of gross charges (AGB percentages). The hospital facility must calculate its AGB percentage(s) at least annually by dividing the sum of all claims for emergency and other medically necessary care described in either paragraph (b)(1)(i)(A) or (b)(1)(i)(B) of this section that have been paid in full to the hospital facility during a prior 12-month period by the sum of the associated gross charges for those claims:

(A) Claims paid by Medicare fee-for-service as the primary payer, including any associated portions of the claims paid by Medicare beneficiaries in the form of co-insurance or deductibles; or

(B) Claims paid by both Medicare fee-for-service and all private health insurers as primary payers, together with any associated portions of these claims paid by Medicare beneficiaries or insured individuals in the form of co-payments, co-insurance, or deductibles.

(ii) *One or multiple AGB percentages.*—A hospital facility's AGB percentage that is calculated using the method described in this paragraph (b)(1) may be one average percentage of gross charges for all emergency and other medically necessary care provided by the hospital facility. Alternatively, a hospital facility may calculate multiple AGB percentages for separate categories of care (such as inpatient and outpatient care or care provided by different departments) or for separate items or services, as long as the hospital facility calculates AGB percentages for all emergency and other medically necessary care provided by the hospital facility.

(iii) *Start date for applying AGB percentages.*—For purposes of determining AGB under this paragraph (b)(1), with respect to any AGB percentage that a hospital facility has calculated, the hospital facility must begin applying the AGB percentage by the 45th day after the end of the 12-month period the hospital facility used in calculating the AGB percentage.

(2) *Prospective Medicare method.*—As an alternative to the method described in paragraph (b)(1) of this section, a hospital

facility may determine AGB for any emergency or other medically necessary care provided to a FAP-eligible individual by using the billing and coding process the hospital facility would use if the FAP-eligible individual were a Medicare fee-for-service beneficiary and setting AGB for the care at the amount the hospital facility determines would be the amount Medicare and the Medicare beneficiary together would be expected to pay for the care.

(3) *Examples.*—The following examples illustrate this paragraph (b):

Example 1. On January 15 of year 1, Y, a hospital facility, generates data on all claims paid to it in full for emergency or other medically necessary care by all private health insurers and Medicare fee-for-service as primary payers over the immediately preceding calendar year. Y determines that it received a total of $360 million on these claims from the private health insurers and Medicare and another $40 million from their insured patients and Medicare beneficiaries in the form of deductibles, co-insurance, and co-payments. Y's gross charges for these claims totaled $800 million. Y calculates that its AGB percentage is 50 percent of gross charges ($400 million/$800 million × 100). Y determines AGB for any emergency or other medically necessary care it provides to a FAP-eligible individual between February 1 of year 1 (less than 45 days after the end of the 12-month claim period) and January 31 of year 2 by multiplying the gross charges for the care provided to the individual by 50%. Y has determined AGB in accordance with this paragraph (b).

Example 2. On September 20 of year 1, X, a hospital facility, generates data on all claims paid to it in full for emergency or other medically necessary care by Medicare fee-for-service as the primary payer over the 12 months ending on August 31 of year 1. X determines that, of these claims for inpatient services, it received a total of $80 million from Medicare and another $20 million from Medicare beneficiaries in the form of co-insurance or deductibles. X's gross charges for these inpatient claims totaled $250 million. Of the claims for outpatient services, X received a total of $100 million from Medicare and another $25 million from Medicare beneficiaries. X's gross charges for these outpatient claims totaled $200 million. X calculates that its AGB percentage for inpatient services is 40 percent of gross charges ($100 million/$250 million × 100) and its AGB percentage for outpatient services is 62.5 percent of gross charges ($125 million/$200 million × 100). Between October 15 of year 1 (45 days after the end of the 12-month claim period) and October 14 of year 2, X determines AGB for any emergency or other medically necessary inpatient care it provides to a FAP-eligible individual by multiplying the gross charges for the inpatient care it provides to the individual by 40% and AGB for any emergency or other medically necessary outpatient care it provides to a FAP-eligible individual by multiplying the gross charges for the outpatient care it provides to the individual by 62.5%. X has determined AGB in accordance with this paragraph (b).

Example 3. Z is a hospital facility. Whenever Z provides emergency or other medically necessary care to a FAP-eligible individual, Z determines the AGB for the care by using the billing and coding process it would use if the individual were a Medicare fee-for-service beneficiary and setting AGB for the care at the amount it determines Medicare and the Medicare beneficiary together would be expected to pay for the care. Z determines AGB in accordance with this paragraph (b).

(c) *Gross charges.*—A hospital facility must charge a FAP-eligible individual less than the gross charges for any medical care provided to that individual. However, a billing statement issued to a FAP-eligible individual for medical care provided by a hospital facility may state the gross charges for such care as the starting point to which various contractual allowances, discounts, or deductions are applied, as long as the actual amount the individual is expected to pay is less than the gross charges for such care.

(d) *Safe harbor for certain charges in excess of AGB.*—A hospital facility will be deemed to meet the requirements of paragraph (a) of this section, even if it charges more than AGB for emergency or other medically necessary care (or gross charges for any medical care) provided to a FAP-eligible individual if—

(1) The FAP-eligible individual has not submitted a complete FAP application to the hospital facility as of the time of the charge; and

(2) The hospital facility has made and continues to make reasonable efforts to determine whether the individual is FAP-eligible, as described in § 1.501(r)-6(c), during the applicable time periods described in that section (including by correcting the amount charged if the individual is subsequently found to be FAP-eligible). [Reg. § 1.501(r)-5.]

§1.501(r)-6. Billing and collection.—(a) *In general.*—A hospital organization meets the requirements of section 501(r)(6) with respect to a hospital facility it operates if the hospital facility does not engage in extraordinary collection actions (ECAs), as defined in paragraph

(b) of this section, against an individual before the hospital facility has, consistent with paragraph (c) of this section, made reasonable efforts to determine whether the individual is eligible for assistance under its financial assistance policy (FAP). For purposes of this section, with respect to any debt owed by an individual for care provided by a hospital facility—

(1) ECAs against the individual include ECAs against any other individual who has accepted or is required to accept responsibility for the individual's hospital bills; and

(2) The hospital facility will be deemed to have engaged in an ECA against the individual if any purchaser of the individual's debt or any debt collection agency or other party to which the hospital facility has referred the individual's debt has engaged in an ECA against the individual.

(b) *Extraordinary collection actions.*—ECAs are actions taken by a hospital facility against an individual related to obtaining payment of a bill for care covered under the hospital facility's FAP that require a legal or judicial process or involve selling an individuals' debt to another party or reporting adverse information about the individual to consumer credit reporting agencies or credit bureaus. For purposes of this paragraph (b), actions that require a legal or judicial process include, but are not limited to, actions to—

(1) Place a lien on an individual's property;

(2) Foreclose on an individual's real property;

(3) Attach or seize an individual's bank account or any other personal property;

(4) Commence a civil action against an individual;

(5) Cause an individual's arrest;

(6) Cause an individual to be subject to a writ of body attachment; and

(7) Garnish an individual's wages.

(c) *Reasonable efforts.*—(1) *In general.*—With respect to any care provided by a hospital facility to an individual, the hospital facility will have made reasonable efforts to determine whether the individual is FAP-eligible only if the hospital facility—

(i) Notifies the individual about its FAP during the notification period (as defined in §1.501(r)-1(b)(18)), as described in paragraph (c)(2) of this section;

(ii) In the case of an individual who submits an incomplete FAP application during the application period (as defined in §1.501(r)-1(b)(3)), meets the requirements described in paragraph (c)(3) of this section; and

(iii) In the case of an individual who submits a complete FAP application during the application period, meets the requirements described in paragraph (c)(4) of this section.

(2) *Notification.*—(i) *In general.*—Except as provided in paragraph (c)(2)(ii) of this section, with respect to any care provided by a hospital facility to an individual, a hospital facility will have notified the individual about its FAP for purposes of paragraph (c)(1)(i) of this section only if the hospital facility—

(A) Distributes a plain language summary of the FAP (as defined in §1.501(r)-1(b)(19)) and offers a FAP application form to the individual before discharge from the hospital facility;

(B) Includes a plain language summary of the FAP with all (and at least three) billing statements for the care and all other written communications regarding the bill provided to the individual during the notification period;

(C) Informs the individual about the FAP in all oral communications with the individual regarding the amount due for the care that occur during the notification period; and

(D) Provides the individual with at least one written notice that—

(1) Informs the individual about the ECAs the hospital facility or other authorized party may take if the individual does not submit a FAP application or pay the amount due by a deadline (specified in the notice) that is no earlier than the last day of the notification period; and

(2) Is provided to the individual at least 30 days before the deadline specified in the written notice.

(ii) *Notification when FAP application is submitted.*—If an individual submits a complete or incomplete FAP application to a hospital facility during the application period, the hospital facility will be deemed to have notified the individual about its FAP for purposes of paragraph (c)(1)(i) of this section as of the day the application is submitted. However, to have made reasonable efforts to determine whether such an individual is FAP-eligible, the hospital facility must meet the requirements of paragraphs (c)(3) and (c)(4) of this section, as applicable.

(iii) *When no FAP application is submitted.*—If an individual fails to submit a FAP application during the notification period (or, if later, by the deadline specified in the written notice described in

paragraph (c)(2)(i)(D) of this section) and the hospital facility has notified (and documented that it has notified) the individual as described in paragraph (c)(2)(i) of this section, the hospital facility will have satisfied paragraph (c)(1)(i) of this section. Until and unless the individual subsequently submits a FAP application during the remainder of the application period, paragraphs (c)(1)(ii) and (c)(1)(iii) do not apply. As a result, the hospital facility will have made reasonable efforts to determine whether the individual is FAP-eligible and may engage in one or more ECAs against the individual.

(iv) *Example.*—The following example illustrates this paragraph (c)(2):

Example. Individual A receives care from hospital facility T on February 1 and February 2. When A is discharged from T on February 2, T gives A its FAP application form and a plain language summary of its FAP. On March 1, April 15, and May 30, T sends A billing statements that include a one-page insert that provides a plain language summary of the FAP. With the May 30 billing statement, T also includes a letter that informs A that if she does not pay the amount owed or submit a FAP application form by June 29 (120 days after the first billing statement was provided on March 1), T may report A's delinquency to credit reporting agencies, seek to obtain a judgment against A, and, if such a judgment is obtained, seek to attach and seize A's bank account or other personal property, which are the only ECAs that T (or any party to which T refers A's debt) may take in accordance with T's billing and collections policy. T does not have any other written or oral communications with A about her bill before June 29. T keeps electronic records showing that it provided a plain language summary and FAP application to A on discharge and included the letter regarding ECAs and the plain language summaries with the billing statements sent to A. A does not submit a FAP application form by June 29. T has made reasonable efforts to determine whether A is FAP-eligible, and thus may engage in ECAs against A, as of June 30.

(3) *Incomplete FAP applications.*—(i) *In general.*—With respect to any care provided by a hospital facility to an individual, if the individual submits an incomplete FAP application during the application period, the hospital facility will have made reasonable efforts to determine whether the individual is FAP-eligible only if the hospital facility—

(A) Suspends any ECAs against the individual as described in paragraph (c)(5) of this section;

(B) Provides the individual with a written notice that describes the additional information and/or documentation required under the FAP or FAP application form that the individual must submit to the hospital facility to complete his or her FAP application and includes a plain language summary of the FAP with this notice; and

(C) Provides the individual with at least one written notice that—

(1) Informs the individual about the ECAs the hospital facility or other authorized party may initiate or resume if the individual does not complete the FAP application or pay the amount due by a completion deadline (specified in the notice) that is no earlier than the later of the last day of the application period or 30 days after the hospital facility provides the individual with the written notice; and

(2) Is provided to the individual at least 30 days before the completion deadline.

(ii) *FAP application completed by the completion deadline.*—If an individual who has submitted an incomplete FAP application during the application period completes the FAP application by the completion deadline, the individual will be considered to have submitted a complete FAP application during the application period, and the hospital facility will therefore only have made reasonable efforts to determine whether the individual is FAP-eligible if it meets the requirements for complete FAP applications described in paragraph (c)(4) of this section.

(iii) *FAP application not completed by the completion deadline.*—If an individual who submits an incomplete FAP application to a hospital facility during the application period fails to complete the FAP application by the completion deadline and the hospital facility has met the requirements described in paragraph (c)(3)(i) of this section, the hospital facility will have made reasonable efforts to determine whether the individual is FAP-eligible and may initiate or resume ECAs against the individual after the completion deadline.

(iv) *Examples.*—The following examples illustrate this paragraph (c)(3):

Example 1. (i) Assume the same facts as the example in paragraph (c)(2)(iv) of this section and the following additional facts: A submits an incomplete FAP application to T on October 13, two weeks before the last day of the application period on October 27 (240 days after the first billing statement was provided on March 1).

Eligibility for assistance under T's FAP is based solely on an individual's family income and the instructions to T's FAP application form require applicants to attach certain documentation verifying family income to their application forms. The FAP application form that A submits to T on October 13 includes all of the required income information, but A fails to attach the required documentation verifying her family income. After receiving A's incomplete FAP application on October 13, T does not initiate any new ECAs against A and does not take any further action on the ECAs T previously initiated against A. On October 15, a member of T's staff calls A to inform her that she failed to attach any of the required documentation of her family income and explain what kind of documentation A needs to submit and how she can submit it. On October 16, T sends a letter to A explaining the kind of documentation of family income that A must provide to T to complete her application and informing A about the ECAs that T (or any other authorized party) may initiate or resume against A if A does not submit the missing documentation or pay the amount due by November 15 (30 days after October 16). T includes a plain language summary of the FAP with the letter. T has met the requirements of this paragraph (c)(3).

(ii) On November 15, A provides T with the missing documentation. Because A provides the missing documentation by the completion deadline, she has submitted a complete FAP application during the application period. As a result, to have made reasonable efforts to determine whether A is FAP-eligible, T must assess the documentation to determine whether A is FAP-eligible and otherwise meet the requirements for complete FAP applications described in paragraph (c)(4) of this section.

Example 2. Individual B receives care from hospital facility U on January 10. U has established a FAP that provides assistance to all individuals whose household income is less than $y, and the instructions to U's FAP application form specify the documentation that applicants must provide to verify their household income. Upon discharge, U's staff gives B a plain language summary of the FAP and a copy of its FAP application form. On January 20, B submits a FAP application form to U indicating that he has household income of less than $y. The FAP application form includes all of the required income information, but B fails to attach the required documentation verifying household income. On February 1, U sends B the first billing statement for the care and includes with the statement another plain language summary of the FAP. U also includes with the billing statement a letter informing B that the income information he provided on his FAP application form indicates that he may be eligible to pay only x% of the amount stated on the billing statement if he can provide documentation that verifies his household income. In addition, this letter describes the type of documentation (also described in the instructions to U's FAP application form) that B needs to provide to complete his FAP application. By August 30, B has not provided the missing documentation. U sends B a written notice on August 30 informing him about the ECAs U (or any other authorized party) may initiate against B if B does not submit the missing documentation or pay the amount due by September 29 (240 days after the first billing statement was provided on February 1 and the last day of the application period). B fails to provide the missing documentation by September 29. U has made reasonable efforts to determine whether B is FAP-eligible, and thus may engage in ECA's against B, as of September 30.

(4) *Complete FAP applications.*—(i) *In general.*—With respect to any care provided by a hospital facility to an individual, if the individual submits a complete FAP application during the application period, the hospital facility will have made reasonable efforts to determine whether the individual is FAP-eligible only if the hospital facility does the following in a timely manner—

(A) Suspends any ECAs against the individual as described in paragraph (c)(5) of this section;

(B) Makes and documents a determination as to whether the individual is FAP-eligible;

(C) Notifies the individual in writing of the eligibility determination (including, if applicable, the assistance for which the individual is eligible) and the basis for this determination;

(D) If the hospital facility determines the individual is FAP-eligible, does the following—

(1) Provides the individual with a billing statement that indicates the amount the individual owes as a FAP-eligible individual and shows, or describes how the individual can get information regarding, the AGB for the care and how the hospital facility determined the amount the individual owes as a FAP-eligible individual;

(2) If the individual has made payments to the hospital facility (or any other party) for the care in excess of the amount he or she is determined to owe as a FAP-eligible individual, refunds those excess payments; and

(3) Takes all reasonably available measures to reverse any ECA (with the exception of a sale of debt) taken against the

individual to collect the debt at issue; such reasonably available measures generally include, but are not limited to, measures to vacate any judgment against the individual, lift any lien or levy on the individual's property, and remove from the individual's credit report any adverse information that was reported to a consumer reporting agency or credit bureau.

(ii) *Determination based on complete FAP applications.*—If a hospital facility has met the requirements described in paragraph (c)(4)(i) of this section and not violated the anti-abuse rule described in paragraph (c)(4)(iii) of this section, the hospital facility has made reasonable efforts to determine whether the individual is FAP-eligible and may initiate or resume ECAs against the individual. To have made reasonable efforts to determine the FAP-eligibility of an individual who has submitted a complete FAP application during the application period, the hospital facility must meet the requirements described in this paragraph (c)(4) regardless of whether the hospital facility has previously made such reasonable efforts under paragraphs (c)(2)(iii) or (c)(3)(iii) of this section.

(iii) *Anti-abuse rule for complete FAP applications.*—A hospital facility will not have made reasonable efforts to determine whether an individual is FAP-eligible if the hospital facility bases its determination that the individual is not FAP-eligible on information that the hospital facility has reason to believe is unreliable or incorrect or on information obtained from the individual under duress or through the use of coercive practices. For purposes of this paragraph (c)(4)(iii), a coercive practice includes delaying or denying emergency medical care to an individual until the individual has provided the requested information.

(iv) *Presumptive eligibility permitted.*—A hospital facility will have made reasonable efforts to determine whether an individual is FAP-eligible if the hospital facility determines that the individual is eligible for the most generous assistance (including free care) available under the FAP based on information other than that provided by the individual as part of a complete FAP application and the hospital facility meets the requirements described in paragraph (c)(4)(i) of this section.

(v) *Examples.*—The following examples illustrate this paragraph (c)(4):

Example 1. V is a hospital facility with a FAP under which the specific assistance for which an individual is eligible depends exclusively upon that individual's household income. The most generous assistance offered for care under V's FAP is 90 percent off of gross charges up to a maximum amount due of $1,000. On March 3, D, an individual, receives care from V, the gross charges for which are $500. Although D does not submit a FAP application to V, V learns that D is eligible for certain benefits under a state program that bases eligibility on household income. Based on this knowledge, V determines that D is eligible under V's FAP to receive the most generous assistance under the FAP, resulting in D owing $50 (90 percent off of the $500 in gross charges) for the March 3 care. V documents this determination, and, on March 21, sends D a billing statement that informs him that V determined he was eligible for the 90% discount based on his eligibility for the benefits under the state program and the fact that his bill, after the discount, was not more than $1,000. This billing statement indicates an amount owed of $50, shows that V arrived at $50 by applying a 90 percent discount to the gross charges for the care, and provides a telephone number D can call to obtain the AGB for the care he received. V has made reasonable efforts to determine whether D is FAP-eligible as of March 21.

Example 2. Individual C receives care from hospital facility W on September 1. W has established a FAP that provides assistance only to individuals whose family income is less than or equal to x% of the Federal Poverty Level (FPL), which, in the case of C's family size, is $y. Upon discharge, W's staff gives C a plain language summary of the FAP and a FAP application form and informs C that if she needs assistance in filling out the form, W has a social worker on staff who can assist her. C expresses interest in getting assistance with a FAP application while she is still on site and is directed to K, one of W's social workers. K explains the eligibility criteria in W's FAP to C, and C realizes that to determine her family income as a percentage of FPL she needs to look at her prior year's tax returns. On September 20, after returning home and obtaining the necessary information, C submits a FAP application to W that contains all of the information and documentation required in the FAP application form instructions. W's staff promptly examines C's FAP application and, based on the information and documentation therein, determines that C's family income is well in excess of $y. On October 1, W sends C her first billing statement for the care she received on September 1. With the billing statement, W includes a letter informing C that she is not eligible for financial assistance because her FAP application indicates that she has family income in excess of x% of FPL ($y for a family the size of C's family) and W only provides financial assistance to individuals with family income that is less than x% of FPL.

W has made reasonable efforts to determine whether C is FAP-eligible as of October 1.

Example 3. E, an individual, receives care from P, a hospital facility, in February. P provides E with the first billing statement for the care on March 1. P notifies E about its FAP as described in paragraph (c)(2)(i) of this section, but E fails to submit a FAP application by P's specified deadline of June 30 (120 days after the initial March 1 billing statement and the last day of the notification period). In September, P seeks and obtains a judgment against E, in which the court determines that E owes P $1,200 for the care P provided and states that E has 30 days to pay this amount. E does not pay any of the $1,200 in 30 days. By October 20, P has seized E's bank account and obtained a total of $450 in funds from the account. E submits a complete FAP application to P on October 20, before the last day of the application period on October 27 (240 days after the initial March 1 billing statement). Upon receiving this application, P does not seize any additional funds from E's bank account and also does not initiate any additional ECAs against E. P promptly examines the application and determines that E is eligible under P's FAP to receive a discount that results in E only owing $150 for the care she received. P also determines that the AGB for the care is $500. P documents this determination, seeks to vacate the judgment against E, lifts the levy on E's bank account, and sends E a letter that informs her about the FAP discount for which she is eligible and explains the basis for this eligibility determination. P includes with this letter a check for $300 (the $450 that P seized from E's bank account minus the $150 that E owes as a FAP-eligible individual) and a billing statement that indicates a $300 refund, shows how P applied the FAP discount for which E is eligible to arrive at an amount owed of $150, and states that the AGB for the care is $500. P has made reasonable efforts to determine whether E is FAP-eligible.

Example 4. R, a hospital facility, has established a FAP that provides financial assistance only to individuals whose family income is less than or equal to x% of the Federal Poverty Level (FPL), as based on their prior year's federal tax return. Individual L receives care from R. While L is being discharged from R, she is approached by M, an employee of a debt collection company that has a contract with R to handle all of R's patient billing. M asks L for her family income information, telling L that this information is needed to determine whether L is eligible for financial assistance. L tells M that she does not know what her family income is and would need to consult her tax returns to determine it. M tells L that she can just provide a "rough estimate" of her family income. L states that her family income may be around $y, an amount slightly above the amount that would allow her to qualify for financial assistance. M enters $y on the income line of a FAP application form with L's name on it and marks L as not FAP-eligible. Based on M's information collection, R determines that L is not FAP-eligible and notifies L of this determination with her first billing statement. Because M had reason to believe that the income estimate provided by L was unreliable, R has violated the anti-abuse rule described in paragraph (c)(4)(iii) of this section. Thus, R has not made reasonable efforts to determine whether L is FAP-eligible.

(5) *Suspending ECAs while a FAP application is pending.*—If an individual submits a complete or incomplete FAP application during the application period, the hospital facility will have made reasonable efforts to determine whether the individual is FAP-eligible only if the hospital facility does not initiate any ECAs, or take further action on any previously-initiated ECAs, against the individual after receiving the application and until either—

(i) The hospital facility has met the requirements described in paragraph (c)(4) of this section; or

(ii) In the case of an incomplete FAP application, the completion deadline has passed without the individual having completed the FAP application.

(6) *Waiver does not constitute reasonable efforts.*—For purposes of this paragraph (c), obtaining a signed waiver from an individual, such as a signed statement that the individual does not wish to apply for assistance under the FAP or receive the information described in paragraphs (c)(2) or (c)(3) of this section, will not constitute a determination of FAP-eligibility and will not satisfy the requirement to make reasonable efforts to determine whether the individual is FAP-eligible before engaging in ECAs against the individual.

(7) *Agreements with other parties.*—If a hospital facility refers or sells an individual's debt to another party during the application period, the hospital facility will have made reasonable efforts to determine whether the individual is FAP-eligible only if it first obtains (and, to the extent applicable, enforces) a legally binding written agreement from the party that—

(i) In the case of any debt referred to the party during the notification period, the party will refrain from engaging in ECAs against the individual until the hospital facility has met (and documented that it has met) the requirements necessary to have made reasonable efforts under paragraph (c)(2)(iii), (c)(3)(iii), or (c)(4)(ii) of this section;

(ii) If the individual submits a FAP application during the application period, the party will suspend any ECAs against the individual as described in paragraph (c)(5) of this section;

(iii) If the individual submits a FAP application during the application period and the hospital facility determines the individual to be FAP-eligible, the party will do the following in a timely manner—

(A) Adhere to procedures specified in the agreement that ensure that the individual does not pay, and has no obligation to pay, the party and the hospital facility together more than he or she is required to pay as a FAP-eligible individual; and

(B) If applicable and if the party (rather than the hospital facility) has the authority to do so, takes all reasonably available measures to reverse any ECA (other than the sale of a debt) taken against the individual as described in paragraph (c)(4)(i)(D)(3) of this section; and

(iv) If the party refers or sells the debt to yet another party during the application period, the party will obtain a written agreement from that other party including all of the elements described in this paragraph (c)(7).

(8) *Clear and conspicuous placement.*—A hospital facility may print any written notice or communication described in this paragraph (c), including any plain language summary of the FAP, on a billing statement or along with other descriptive or explanatory matter, as long as the required information is conspicuously placed and of sufficient size to be clearly readable. [Reg. §1.501(r)-6.]

§1.501(r)-7. **Effective/applicability dates.**—(a) *Statutory effective/ applicability date.*—(1) *In general.*—Except as provided in paragraph (a)(2) of this section, section 501(r) applies to taxable years beginning after March 23, 2010.

(2) *Community health needs assessment.*—The requirements of section 501(r)(3) apply to taxable years beginning after March 23, 2012.

(b) *Effective/applicability date of regulations.*—The rules of §1.501(r)-1 and §§1.501(r)-4 through 1.501(r)-6 apply to taxable years beginning on or after the date these regulations are published as final regulations in the **Federal Register**. [Reg. §1.501(r)-7.]

Charitable Hospitals: Community Health Needs Assessments

Charitable Hospitals: Community Health Needs Assessments.—Reg. §§1.501(r)-2 and 1.501(r)-3, and amendments to Reg. §§1.501(r)-0, 1.501(r)-1 and 1.501(r)-7, providing guidance to charitable hospital organizations on the community health needs assessment (CHNA) requirements, and related excise tax and reporting obligations, enacted as part of the Patient Protection and Affordable Care Act of 2010, are proposed (published in the Federal Register on April 5, 2013) (REG-106499-12) (corrected May 21, 2013).

Proposed Reg. §§1.501(r)-2 and 1.501(r)-3 and proposed amendments to Reg. §§1.501(r)-0, 1.501(r)-1 and 1.501(r)-7 were adopted by T.D. 9708 on December 29, 2014. However, for tax years beginning on or before December 29, 2015, a hospital may rely on the final regulations or the 2012 and/or 2013 proposed regulations (REG-130266-11 and/or REG-106499-12).

☐ Par. 2. Section 1.501(r)-0 as proposed to be amended at 77 FR 38160 (June 26, 2012) is proposed to be further amended as follows:

1. Adding a new entry to §1.501(r)-1, paragraph (c).
2. Adding new entries to §1.501(r)-2 and §1.501(r)-3.
3. Revising the entry to §1.501(r)-7.

The revision and additions to read as follows:

§1.501(r)-0. **Outline of regulations.**

* * *

§1.501(r)-1 *Definitions.*

* * *

(c) Additional definitions.

(1) Authorized body of a hospital facility.
(2) Operating a hospital facility.
(3) Partnership agreement.
(4) Widely available on a Web site.

§1.501(r)-2 *Failures to satisfy section 501(r).*

(a) Revocation of section 501(c)(3) status.

(b) Minor and inadvertent omissions and errors.

(c) Excusing certain failures if hospital facility corrects and discloses.

(d) Taxation of noncompliant hospital facilities.

   (1) In general.

   (2) Noncompliant facility income.

   (3) No aggregation.

   (4) Interaction with other Code provisions.

§1.501(r)-3 Community health needs assessments.

(a) In general.

(b) Conducting a CHNA.

   (1) In general.

   (2) Date a CHNA is conducted.

   (3) Community served by the hospital facility.

   (4) Assessing community health needs.

   (5) Persons representing the broad interests of the community.

   (6) Medically underserved populations.

   (7) Documentation of a CHNA.

   (8) Making the CHNA report widely available to the public.

(c) Implementation strategy.

   (1) In general.

   (2) Description of how the hospital facility plans to address a significant health need.

   (3) Description of why a hospital facility is not addressing a significant health need.

   (4) Joint implementation strategies.

   (5) When the implementation strategy must be adopted.

(d) New hospital facilities.

(e) Transition rules.

   (1) CHNA conducted in taxable year beginning before March 23, 2012.

   (2) CHNA conducted in first taxable year beginning after March 23, 2012.

*   *   *

§1.501(r)-7 Effective/applicability dates.

(a) Effective/applicability date.

(b) Reliance and transition period.

☐ Par. 3. Section 1.501(r)-1 as proposed to be amended at 77 FR 38160 (June 26, 2012) is proposed to be further amended by revising paragraphs (b)(15) and (b)(16) and adding new paragraph (c) to read as follows:

§1.501(r)-1. Definitions.

*   *   *

(b) * * *

(15) *Hospital facility* means a facility that is required by a state to be licensed, registered, or similarly recognized as a hospital. Multiple buildings operated under a single state license are considered to be a single hospital facility. For purposes of this paragraph (b)(15), the term "state" includes only the 50 states and the District of Columbia and not any U.S. territory or foreign country. References to a hospital facility taking actions include instances in which the hospital organization operating the hospital facility takes actions through or on behalf of the hospital facility.

(16) *Hospital organization* means an organization recognized (or seeking to be recognized) as described in section 501(c)(3) that operates one or more hospital facilities. If the section 501(c)(3) status of such an organization is revoked, the organization will, for purposes of section 4959, continue to be treated as a hospital organization during the taxable year in which such revocation becomes effective.

*   *   *

(c) *Additional definitions.*—(1) *Authorized body of a hospital facility* means

   (i) The governing body (that is, the board of directors, board of trustees, or equivalent controlling body) of the hospital organization that operates the hospital facility, or a committee of, or other party authorized by, that governing body to the extent such committee or other party is permitted under state law to act on behalf of the governing body; or

   (ii) If the hospital facility has its own governing body and is recognized as an entity under state law but is a disregarded entity for federal tax purposes, the governing body of that hospital facility, or a committee of, or other party authorized by, that governing body to the extent such committee or other party is permitted under state law to act on behalf of the governing body.

(2) *Operating a hospital facility* includes operating the facility through the organization's own employees or contracting out to another organization to operate the facility. For example, if an organization hires a management company to operate the facility, the hiring organization is considered to operate the facility. An organization also operates a hospital facility if it is the sole member or owner of a disregarded entity that operates the hospital facility. In addition, an organization operates a hospital facility if it owns a capital or profits interest in, or is a member of, a joint venture, limited liability company, or other entity treated as a partnership for federal income tax purposes that operates the hospital facility unless either—

   (i) The organization does not have control over the operation of the hospital facility sufficient to ensure that the operation of the hospital facility furthers an exempt purpose described in section 501(c)(3) and thus treats the operation of the hospital facility, including the facility's provision of medical care, as an unrelated trade or business described in section 513(a) with respect to the hospital organization; or

   (ii) At all times since March 23, 2010, the organization has been organized and operated primarily for educational or scientific purposes and has not engaged primarily in the operation of one or more hospital facilities and, pursuant to a partnership agreement entered into prior to March 23, 2010,—

     (A) Does not own more than 35 percent of the capital or profits interest in the partnership (determined in accordance with section 707(b)(3));

     (B) Does not own a general partner interest, managing-member interest, or similar interest in the partnership; and

     (C) Does not have control over the operation of the hospital facility sufficient to ensure that the hospital facility complies with the requirements of section 501(r).

(3) *Partnership agreement*, for purposes of paragraph (c)(2)(ii) of this section, includes all written agreements among the partners, or between one or more partners and the partnership, concerning affairs of the partnership and responsibilities of the partners, whether or not embodied in a document referred to by the partners as the partnership agreement, entered into before March 23, 2010. A partnership agreement also includes any modifications to the agreement agreed to by all partners, or adopted in any other manner provided by the partnership agreement, but no such modifications adopted on or after March 23, 2010, that affect whether or not the agreement is described in paragraph (c)(2)(ii) of this section. In addition, a partnership agreement includes provisions of federal, state, or local law, as in effect before March 23, 2010, that govern the affairs of the partnership or are considered under such law to be part of the agreement.

(4) *Widely available on a Web site* means—

   (i) The hospital facility conspicuously posts a complete and current version of the document on—

     (A) The hospital facility's Web site;

     (B) If the hospital facility does not have its own Web site separate from the hospital organization that operates it, the hospital organization's Web site; or

     (C) A Web site established and maintained by another entity, but only if the Web site of the hospital facility or hospital organization (if the facility or organization has a Web site) provides a conspicuously-displayed link to the web page on which the document is posted, along with clear instructions for accessing the document on that Web site;

   (ii) Individuals with access to the Internet can access, download, view, and print a hard copy of the document without requiring special computer hardware or software (other than software that is readily available to members of the public without payment of any fee); without payment of a fee to the hospital facility, hospital organization, or other entity maintaining the Web site; and without creating an account or being otherwise required to provide personally identifiable information; and

   (iii) The hospital facility provides individuals who ask how to access a copy of the document online with the direct Web site address, or URL, of the web page on which the document is posted.

☐ Par. 4. Sections 1.501(r)-2 and 1.501(r)-3 are added to read as follows:

§1.501(r)-2. Failures to satisfy section 501(r).

—(a) *Revocation of section 501(c)(3) status.*—Except as otherwise provided in paragraphs (b) and (c) of this section, a hospital organization failing to meet one or more of the requirements of section 501(r) separately with respect to one or more hospital facilities it operates may have its section 501(c)(3) status revoked as of the first day of the taxable year in which the failure occurs. In determining whether to continue to recognize the section 501(c)(3) status of a hospital organization that fails to meet one or more of the requirements of section 501(r) with respect to one or more hospital facilities, the Commissioner will consider all relevant facts and circumstances including, but not limited to, the following—

(1) Whether the organization has previously failed to meet the requirements of section 501(r), and, if so, whether the same type of failure previously occurred;

(2) The size, scope, nature, and significance of the organization's failure(s);

(3) In the case of an organization that operates more than one hospital facility, the number, size, and significance of the facilities that have failed to meet the section 501(r) requirements relative to those that have complied with these requirements;

(4) The reason for the failure(s);

(5) Whether the organization had, prior to the failure(s), established practices and procedures (formal or informal) reasonably designed to promote and facilitate overall compliance with the section 501(r) requirements;

(6) Whether the practices and procedures had been routinely followed and the failure(s) occurred through an oversight or mistake in applying them;

(7) Whether the organization has implemented safeguards that are reasonably calculated to prevent similar failures from occurring in the future;

(8) Whether the organization corrected the failure(s) as promptly after discovery as is reasonable given the nature of the failure(s); and

(9) Whether the organization took the measures described in paragraphs (a)(7) and (a)(8) of this section before the Commissioner discovered the failure(s).

(b) *Minor and inadvertent omissions and errors.*—A hospital facility's omission of required information from a policy or report described in §1.501(r)-3 or §1.501(r)-4, or error with respect to the implementation or operational requirements described in §1.501(r)-3 through §1.501(r)-6, will not be considered a failure to meet a requirement of section 501(r) if—

(1) Such omission or error was minor, inadvertent, and due to reasonable cause; and

(2) The hospital facility corrects such omission or error as promptly after discovery as is reasonable given the nature of the omission or error.

(c) *Excusing certain failures if hospital facility corrects and discloses.*—Pursuant to guidance set forth by revenue procedure, notice, or other guidance published in the Internal Revenue Bulletin, a hospital facility's failure to meet one or more of the requirements described in §1.501(r)-3 through §1.501(r)-6 that is neither willful nor egregious shall be excused for purposes of this section if the hospital facility corrects and makes disclosure in accordance with the rules set forth in the guidance. If a hospital facility's failure was willful or egregious, the failure will not be excused, even if the hospital facility corrects and makes disclosure in accordance with the guidance, and no presumption will be created by a hospital facility's correction and disclosure that the failure was neither willful nor egregious. For purposes of this paragraph (c), willful is to be interpreted consistent with the meaning of that term in the context of civil penalties, which would include a failure due to gross negligence, reckless disregard, or willful neglect. Furthermore, notwithstanding a hospital facility's compliance with such future guidance, a hospital facility may, in the discretion of the IRS, be subject to an excise tax under section 4959 for failures to meet the requirements of section 501(r)(3).

(d) *Taxation of noncompliant hospital facilities.*—(1) *In general.*—Except as otherwise provided in paragraphs (b) and (c) of this section, if a hospital organization that operates more than one hospital facility fails to meet one or more of the requirements of section 501(r) separately with respect to a hospital facility during a taxable year, the income derived from the noncompliant hospital facility ("noncompliant facility income") during that taxable year will be subject to tax computed as provided in section 11 (or as provided in section 1(e) if the hospital organization is a trust described in section 511(b)(2)), but substituting "noncompliant facility income" for "taxable income," if—

(i) The hospital organization continues to be recognized as described in section 501(c)(3) during the taxable year, but

(ii) The hospital organization would not continue to be recognized as described in section 501(c)(3) during the taxable year based on the facts and circumstances described in paragraph (a) of this section (but disregarding paragraph (a)(3)) if the noncompliant hospital facility were the only hospital facility operated by the organization.

(2) *Noncompliant facility income.*—(i) *In general.*—For purposes of this paragraph (d), the noncompliant facility income derived from a hospital facility during a taxable year will be the gross income

derived from that hospital facility during the taxable year, less the deductions allowed by chapter 1 of the Internal Revenue Code (Code) that are directly connected to the operation of that hospital facility during the taxable year, excluding any gross income and deductions taken into account in computing any unrelated business taxable income described in section 512 that is derived from the facility during the taxable year.

(ii) *Directly connected deductions.*—For purposes of this paragraph (d), to be directly connected with the operation of a hospital facility that has failed to meet the requirements of section 501(r), an item of deduction must have proximate and primary relationship to the operation of the hospital facility. Expenses, depreciation, and similar items attributable solely to the operation of a hospital facility are proximately and primarily related to such operation, and therefore qualify for deduction to the extent that they meet the requirements of section 162, section 167, or other relevant provisions of the Code. Where expenses, depreciation, and similar items are attributable to a noncompliant hospital facility and other hospital facilities operated by the hospital organization (and/or to other activities of the hospital organization unrelated to the operation of hospital facilities), such items shall be allocated between the hospital facilities (and/or other activities) on a reasonable basis. The portion of any such item so allocated to a noncompliant hospital facility is proximately and primarily related to the operation of that facility and shall be allowable as a deduction in computing the facility's noncompliant facility income in the manner and to the extent it would meet the requirements of section 162, section 167, or other relevant provisions of the Code.

(3) *No aggregation.*—In computing the noncompliant facility income of a hospital facility, the gross income from (and the deductions allowed with respect to) the hospital facility may not be aggregated with the gross income from (and the deductions allowed with respect to) the hospital organization's other noncompliant hospital facilities subject to tax under this paragraph (d) or its unrelated trade or business activities described in section 513.

(4) *Interaction with other Code provisions.*—(i) *Hospital organization operating a noncompliant hospital facility continues to be treated as tax-exempt.*—A hospital organization operating a noncompliant hospital facility subject to tax under this paragraph (d) shall continue to be treated as an organization that is exempt from tax under section 501(a) because it is described in section 501(c)(3) for all purposes of the Code. Thus, for example, the application of this paragraph (d) shall not, by itself, affect the tax-exempt status of bonds issued to finance the noncompliant hospital facility.

(ii) *Noncompliant hospital facility operated by a tax-exempt hospital organization is subject to tax.*—A noncompliant hospital facility described in paragraph (d)(1) of this section is subject to tax under this paragraph (d), notwithstanding the fact that the hospital organization operating the hospital facility is otherwise exempt from tax under section 501(a) and subject to tax under section 511(a) and that §1.11-1(a) of this chapter states such organizations are not liable to the tax imposed under section 11.

(iii) *Noncompliant hospital facility not a business entity.*—A noncompliant hospital facility subject to tax under this paragraph (d) is not considered a business entity for purposes of §301.7701-2(b)(7) of this chapter. [Reg. §1.501(r)-2.]

§1.501(r)-3. Community health needs assessments.—(a) *In general.*—With respect to any taxable year, a hospital organization meets the requirements of section 501(r)(3) with respect to a hospital facility it operates only if—

(1) The hospital facility has conducted a community health needs assessment (CHNA) that meets the requirements of paragraph (b) of this section in such taxable year or in either of the two taxable years immediately preceding such taxable year; and

(2) An authorized body of the hospital facility (as defined in §1.501(r)-1(c)(1)) has adopted an implementation strategy to meet the community health needs identified through the CHNA, as described in paragraph (c) of this section, by the end of the taxable year in which the hospital facility conducts the CHNA.

(b) *Conducting a CHNA.*—(1) *In general.*—To conduct a CHNA for purposes of paragraph (a) of this section, a hospital facility must complete all of the following steps—

(i) Define the community it serves;

(ii) Assess the health needs of that community;

(iii) In assessing the health needs of the community, take into account input from persons who represent the broad interests of that community, including those with special knowledge of or expertise in public health;

(iv) Document the CHNA in a written report ("CHNA report") that is adopted for the hospital facility by an authorized body of the hospital facility; and

(v) Make the CHNA report widely available to the public.

(2) *Date a CHNA is conducted.*—For purposes of this section, a hospital facility will be considered to have conducted a CHNA on the date it has completed all of the steps described in paragraph (b)(1) of this section. Solely for purposes of determining the date on which a CHNA has been conducted, a hospital facility will be considered to have made the CHNA report widely available to the public on the date it first makes the CHNA report widely available to the public as described in paragraph (b)(8)(i) of this section.

(3) *Community served by the hospital facility.*—In defining the community it serves for purposes of paragraph (b)(1)(i) of this section, a hospital facility may take into account all of the relevant facts and circumstances, including the geographic area served by the hospital facility, target populations served (for example, children, women, or the aged), and principal functions (for example, focus on a particular specialty area or targeted disease). A hospital facility may define its community to include populations in addition to its patient populations and geographic areas outside of those in which its patient populations reside. However, a hospital facility may not define its community to exclude medically underserved, low-income, or minority populations who are part of its patient populations, live in geographic areas in which its patient populations reside (unless they are not part of the hospital facility's target populations or affected by its principal functions), or otherwise should be included based on the method the hospital facility uses to define its community. In addition, if a hospital facility's method of defining its community takes into account patient populations, the hospital facility must treat as patients all individuals who receive care from the hospital facility, without regard to whether (or how much) they or their insurers pay for the care received or whether they are eligible for assistance under the hospital facility's financial assistance policy.

(4) *Assessing community health needs.*—To assess the health needs of the community it serves for purposes of paragraph (b)(1)(ii) of this section, a hospital facility must identify significant health needs of the community, prioritize those health needs, and identify potential measures and resources (such as programs, organizations, and facilities in the community) available to address the health needs. For these purposes, the health needs of a community include requisites for the improvement or maintenance of health status in both the community at large and in particular parts of the community (such as particular neighborhoods or populations experiencing health disparities). A hospital facility may determine whether a health need is significant based on all of the facts and circumstances present in the community it serves. In addition, a hospital facility may use any criteria to prioritize the significant health needs it identifies, including, but not limited to, the burden, scope, severity, or urgency of the health need; the estimated feasibility and effectiveness of possible interventions; the health disparities associated with the need; or the importance the community places on addressing the need.

(5) *Persons representing the broad interests of the community.*—To take into account input from persons who represent the broad interests of the community it serves (including those with special knowledge of or expertise in public health) for purposes of paragraph (b)(1)(iii) of this section, a hospital facility must take into account input from the sources listed in paragraphs (b)(5)(i), (b)(5)(ii), and (b)(5)(iii) of this section in assessing the health needs of its community. Input from these persons includes, but is not limited to, input on any financial and other barriers to access to care in the community. In addition, a hospital facility may take into account input from a broad range of persons located in or serving its community, including, but not limited to, health care consumers and consumer advocates, nonprofit and community-based organizations, academic experts, local government officials, local school districts, health care providers and community health centers, health insurance and managed care organizations, private businesses, and labor and workforce representatives. A hospital facility must take into account input from the following sources in assessing the health needs of its community—

(i) At least one state, local, tribal, or regional governmental public health department (or equivalent department or agency) with knowledge, information, or expertise relevant to the health needs of that community;

(ii) Members of medically underserved, low-income, and minority populations in the community served by the hospital facility, or individuals or organizations serving or representing the interests of such populations; and

(iii) Written comments received on the hospital facility's most recently conducted CHNA and most recently adopted implementation strategy.

(6) *Medically underserved populations.*—For purposes of this paragraph (b), medically underserved populations include populations experiencing health disparities or at risk of not receiving adequate medical care as a result of being uninsured or underinsured or due to geographic, language, financial, or other barriers.

(7) *Documentation of a CHNA.*—(i) *In general.*—For purposes of paragraph (b)(1)(iv) of this section, the CHNA report adopted for the hospital facility by an authorized body of the hospital facility must include—

(A) A definition of the community served by the hospital facility and a description of how the community was determined;

(B) A description of the process and methods used to conduct the CHNA;

(C) A description of how the hospital facility took into account input from persons who represent the broad interests of the community it serves;

(D) A prioritized description of the significant health needs of the community identified through the CHNA, along with a description of the process and criteria used in identifying certain health needs as significant and prioritizing such significant health needs; and

(E) A description of the potential measures and resources identified through the CHNA to address the significant health needs.

(ii) *Process and methods used to conduct the CHNA.*—A hospital facility's CHNA report will be considered to describe the process and methods used to conduct the CHNA for purposes of paragraph (b)(7)(i)(B) of this section if the CHNA report describes the data and other information used in the assessment, as well as the methods of collecting and analyzing this data and information, and identifies any parties with whom the hospital facility collaborated, or with whom it contracted for assistance, in conducting the CHNA.

(iii) *Input from persons who represent the broad interests of the community served by the hospital facility.*—A hospital facility's CHNA report will be considered to describe how the hospital facility took into account input from persons who represent the broad interests of the community it serves for purposes of paragraph (b)(7)(i)(C) of this section if the CHNA report summarizes, in general terms, the input provided by such persons and how and over what time period such input was provided (for example, whether through meetings, focus groups, interviews, surveys, or written comments and between what dates); provides the names of organizations providing input and summarizes the nature and extent of the organization's input; and describes the medically underserved, low-income, or minority populations being represented by organizations or individuals that provided input. A CHNA report does not need to name or otherwise individually identify any individuals participating in community forums, focus groups, survey samples, or similar groups.

(iv) *Separate CHNA reports.*—While a hospital facility may conduct its CHNA in collaboration with other organizations and facilities (including, but not limited to, related and unrelated hospital organizations and facilities, for-profit and government hospitals, governmental departments, and nonprofit organizations), every hospital facility must document the information described in this paragraph (b)(7) in a separate CHNA report to satisfy paragraph (b)(1)(iv) of this section unless it is eligible to adopt a joint CHNA report as described in paragraph (b)(7)(v) of this section. However, if a hospital facility is collaborating with other facilities and organizations in conducting its CHNA or if another organization has conducted a CHNA for all or part of the hospital facility's community, portions of the hospital facility's CHNA report may be substantively identical to portions of a CHNA report of a collaborating hospital facility or the other organization conducting a CHNA, if appropriate under the facts and circumstances. For example, if a hospital facility conducts a survey of the health needs of residents of homeless shelters located in the community in collaboration with other hospital facilities, the description of that survey in the hospital facility's CHNA report may be identical to the description contained in the CHNA reports for the other collaborating hospital facilities. Similarly, if the state or local public health department with jurisdiction over the community served by the hospital facility conducts an inventory of community health improvement resources available in that community, the hospital facility may include that inventory in its CHNA report.

(v) *Joint CHNA reports.*—(A) *In general.*—A hospital facility that collaborates with other hospital facilities in conducting its CHNA will satisfy paragraph (b)(1)(iv) of this section if an authorized body of the hospital facility adopts for the hospital facility a joint CHNA report produced for all of the collaborating hospital facilities, as long as all of the collaborating hospital facilities define their community to be the same and conduct a joint CHNA process, and the joint CHNA report is clearly identified as applying to the hospital facility.

(B) *Example.*—The following example illustrates this paragraph (b)(7)(v):

Example. P is one of ten hospital facilities located in and serving the populations of a particular Metropolitan Statistical Area

(MSA). P and the other nine facilities in the MSA, some of which are unrelated to P, decide to collaborate in conducting a CHNA for the MSA and to each define their community as constituting the entire MSA. The ten hospital facilities work together with the state and local health departments of jurisdictions in the MSA to assess the health needs of the MSA and collaborate in conducting surveys and holding public forums to receive input from the MSA's residents, including its medically underserved, low-income, and minority populations. The hospital facilities then work together to prepare a joint CHNA report documenting this joint CHNA process that contains all of the elements described in paragraph (b)(7)(i) of this section. The joint CHNA report identifies all of the collaborating hospital facilities, including P, by name, both within the report itself and on the cover page. The board of directors of the hospital organization operating P adopts the joint CHNA report for P. P has complied with the requirements of this paragraph (b)(7)(v) and, accordingly, has satisfied paragraph (b)(1)(iv) of this section.

(8) *Making the CHNA report widely available to the public.*—(i) *In general.*—For purposes of paragraph (b)(1)(v) of this section, a hospital facility's CHNA report is made widely available to the public only if the hospital facility—

(A) Makes the CHNA report widely available on a Web site, as defined in §1.501(r)-1(c)(4), at least until the date the hospital facility has made widely available on a Web site its two subsequent CHNA reports; and

(B) Makes a paper copy of the CHNA report available for public inspection without charge at the hospital facility at least until the date the hospital facility has made available for public inspection without charge a paper copy of its two subsequent CHNA reports.

(ii) *Making draft CHNA reports widely available.*—Notwithstanding paragraph (b)(8)(i) of this section, if a hospital facility makes widely available on a Web site (and/or for public inspection) a version of the CHNA report that is expressly marked as a draft on which the public may comment, the hospital facility will not be considered to have made the CHNA report widely available to the public for purposes of determining the date on which the hospital facility has conducted a CHNA under paragraph (a) of this section.

(c) *Implementation strategy.*—(1) *In general.*—For purposes of paragraph (a)(2) of this section, a hospital facility's implementation strategy to meet the community health needs identified through the hospital facility's CHNA is a written plan that, with respect to each significant health need identified through the CHNA, either—

(i) Describes how the hospital facility plans to address the health need; or

(ii) Identifies the health need as one the hospital facility does not intend to address and explains why the hospital facility does not intend to address the health need.

(2) *Description of how the hospital facility plans to address a significant health need.*—In describing how a hospital facility plans to address a significant health need identified through a CHNA for purposes of paragraph (c)(1)(i) of this section, the implementation strategy must describe the actions the hospital facility intends to take to address the health need, the anticipated impact of these actions, and a plan to evaluate such impact. The implementation strategy must also identify the programs and resources the hospital facility plans to commit to address the health need. Finally, the implementation strategy must describe any planned collaboration between the hospital facility and other facilities or organizations in addressing the health need.

(3) *Description of why a hospital facility is not addressing a significant health need.*—In explaining why it does not intend to address a significant health need for purposes of paragraph (c)(1)(ii) of this section, a hospital facility may provide a brief explanation of its reason for not addressing the health need, including, but not limited to, resource constraints, other facilities or organizations in the community addressing the need, relative lack of expertise or competencies to effectively address the need, a relatively low priority assigned to the need, and/or a lack of identified effective interventions to address the need.

(4) *Joint implementation strategies.*—A hospital facility may develop an implementation strategy in collaboration with other facilities and organizations, including, but not limited to, related and unrelated hospital organizations and facilities, for-profit and government hospitals, governmental departments, and nonprofit organiza-

tions. In general, a hospital facility that collaborates with other facilities and organizations in developing its implementation strategy must still document its implementation strategy in a separate written plan that is tailored to the particular hospital facility, taking into account its specific programs and resources. However, a hospital facility that adopts a joint CHNA report described in paragraph (b)(7)(v) of this section may also adopt a joint implementation strategy that, with respect to each significant health need identified through the joint CHNA, either describes how the collaborating hospital facilities plan to address the health need or identifies the health need as one the hospital facilities do not intend to address and explains why the hospital facilities do not intend to address the health need, as long as the joint implementation strategy—

(i) Is clearly identified as applying to the hospital facility;

(ii) Clearly identifies the hospital facility's particular role and responsibilities in taking the actions described in the implementation strategy and the programs and resources the hospital facility plans to commit to such actions; and

(iii) Includes a summary or other tool that helps the reader easily locate those portions of the joint implementation strategy that relate to the hospital facility.

(5) *When the implementation strategy must be adopted.*—(i) *In general.*—For purposes of paragraph (a)(2) of this section, in order to have adopted an implementation strategy to meet the health needs identified through a hospital facility's CHNA by the end of the same taxable year in which the hospital facility conducts that CHNA, an authorized body of the hospital facility must adopt the implementation strategy during the taxable year in which the hospital facility completes the final step for the CHNA described in paragraph (b)(1) of this section, regardless of whether the hospital facility began working on the CHNA in a prior taxable year.

(ii) *Example.*—The following example illustrates this paragraph (c)(5):

Example. M is a hospital facility that last conducted a CHNA and adopted an implementation strategy in Year 1. In Year 3, M defines the community it serves, assesses the health needs of that community, and takes into account input from persons who represent the broad interests of that community. In Year 4, M documents its CHNA in a CHNA report that is adopted by an authorized body of M, makes the CHNA report widely available on a Web site, and makes paper copies available for public inspection. To meet the requirements of paragraph (a)(2) of this section, an authorized body of M must adopt an implementation strategy to meet the health needs identified through that CHNA by the last day of Year 4.

(d) *New hospital facilities.*—A hospital facility that is newly acquired or placed into service, or that becomes newly subject to the requirements of section 501(r) because the hospital organization that operates it is newly recognized as described in section 501(c)(3), must meet the requirements of section 501(r)(3) by the last day of the second taxable year beginning after the date, respectively, the hospital facility is acquired; licensed, registered, or similarly recognized by its state as a hospital; or newly subject to the requirements of section 501(r) as a result of the hospital organization operating it being recognized as described in section 501(c)(3).

(e) *Transition rules.*—(1) *CHNA conducted in taxable year beginning before March 23, 2012.*—A hospital facility that conducted a CHNA described in section 501(r)(3) in either its first taxable year beginning after March 23, 2010, or its first taxable year beginning after March 23, 2011, does not need to meet the requirements of section 501(r)(3) again until the third taxable year following the taxable year in which the hospital facility conducted that CHNA, provided that the hospital facility has adopted an implementation strategy to meet the community health needs identified through that CHNA on or before the 15th day of the fifth calendar month following the close of its first taxable year beginning after March 23, 2012.

(2) *CHNA conducted in first taxable year beginning after March 23, 2012.*—A hospital facility that conducts a CHNA described in section 501(r)(3) in its first taxable year beginning after March 23, 2012, will be deemed to satisfy paragraph (a)(2) of this section during that taxable year if an authorized body of the hospital facility adopts an implementation strategy to meet the community health needs identified through that CHNA on or before the 15th day of the fifth calendar month following the close of its first taxable year beginning after March 23, 2012. [Reg. §1.501(r)-3.]

☐ Par. 5. Section 1.501(r)-7 as proposed to be amended at 77 FR 38169 (June 26, 2012) is proposed to be further amended by revising the section to read as follows:

§1.501(r)-7. Effective/applicability dates.—(a) *Effective/applicability date.*—The rules of §1.501(r)-1 through §1.501(r)-6 are effective on

the date of publication of the Treasury decision adopting these rules as final or temporary regulations.

(b) *Reliance and transition period.*—A hospital facility may rely on §1.501(r)-3 of the proposed regulations published in the **Federal Register** on April 5, 2013, for any CHNA conducted or implementa-tion strategy adopted on or before the date that is six months after these regulations are published as final or temporary regulations in the **Federal Register**. [Reg. §1.501(r)-7.]

Employee Trusts: Effective Dates

Employee Trusts: Tax Reform Act of 1984: Effective Dates.—Temporary Reg. §1.505(c)-1T is proposed as a final regulation and, when adopted, would become Reg. §1.505(c)-1 (published in the Federal Register on February 4, 1986).

§1.505(c)-1. Questions and answers relating to the notification requirement for recognition of exemption under paragraphs (9), (17) and (20) of section 501(c).

Exempt Organization: Unrelated Business Taxable Income

Exempt Organization: Unrelated Business Taxable Income.—Amendments to Reg. §1.509(a)-3, providing guidance on how an exempt organization subject to the unrelated business income tax described in section 511 of the Internal Revenue Code (Code) determines if it has more than one unrelated trade or business, and, if so, how the exempt organization calculates unrelated business taxable income, are proposed (published in the Federal Register on April 24, 2020) (REG-106864-18).

Par. 3. Section 1.509(a)-3 is proposed to be amended by:
1. Revising the first sentence of paragraph (a)(3)(i).
2. Redesignating paragraph (a)(4) as paragraph (a)(5).
3. Adding new paragraph (a)(4).
4. Revising paragraph (o).
The revisions and additions read as follows:

§1.509(a)-3. Broadly, publicly supported organizations.
(a) * * *
(3) * * *
(i) * * * An organization will meet the not-more-than-one-third support test under section 509(a)(2)(B) if it normally (within the meaning of paragraph (c) or (d) of this section) receives not more than one-third of its support in each taxable year from the sum of its gross investment income (as defined in section 509(e)) and the excess (if any) of the amount of its unrelated business taxable income (as defined in section 512, without regard to section 512(a)(6)) derived from trades or businesses that were acquired by the organization after June 30, 1975, over the amount of tax imposed on such income by section 511.

* * *

(4) *Unrelated business activities.*—The denominator of the one-third support fraction and the denominator of the not-more-than-one-third support fraction both include net income from unrelated business activities, whether or not such activities are carried on regularly as a trade or business. The term *net income from unrelated business activities* includes (but is not limited to) an organization's unrelated business taxable income (UBTI) within the meaning of section 512. However, when calculating UBTI for purposes of determining the denominator of both support fractions, section 512(a)(6) does not apply. Accordingly, in the case of an organization that derives gross income from the regular conduct of two or more unrelated business activities, support includes the aggregate of gross income from all such unrelated business activities less the aggregate of the deductions allowed with respect to all such unrelated business activities.

* * *

(o) *Applicability date.*—This section generally applies to taxable years beginning after December 31, 1969, except paragraphs (a)(3)(i) and (a)(4) of this section apply to taxable years beginning on or after [DATE OF PUBLICATION OF THE FINAL RULES IN THE **Federal Register**]. For taxable years beginning before [DATE OF PUBLICATION OF THE FINAL RULES IN THE **Federal Register**], see these paragraphs as in effect and contained in 26 CFR part 1 revised as of April 1, 2019.

Type I and Type III Supporting Organizations: Requirements

Type I and Type III Supporting Organizations: Requirements.—Amendments to Reg. §1.509(a)-4, regarding the prohibition on certain contributions to Type I and Type III supporting organizations and the requirements for Type III supporting organizations, are proposed (published in the Federal Register on February 19, 2016) (REG-118867-10).

Par. 2. Section 1.509(a)-4 is amended by:
1. Revising paragraphs (f)(5)(ii), (i)(2)(i) introductory text, (i)(2)(i)(A), (i)(2)(iii), and (i)(3)(i);
2. Adding *Example 3* to paragraph (i)(3)(iv);
3. Revising paragraphs (i)(4)(ii)(A)(1), (i)(4)(ii)(B), (i)(4)(iii) and (iv), (i)(5)(ii)(A) and (B), (i)(5)(iii)(A), *Example 4* of paragraph (i)(5)(iii)(D), the third sentence of paragraph (i)(6) introductory text, and paragraphs (i)(6)(iii) and (v) introductory text and (l).
The revisions and additions read as follows:

§1.509(a)-4. Supporting organizations.
* * *
(f) * * *
(5) * * *

(ii) *Meaning of control.*—For purposes of paragraph (f)(5)(i) of this section, the governing body of a supported organization will be considered *controlled* by a person described in paragraph (f)(5)(i)(A) of this section if that person, alone or by aggregating the person's votes or positions of authority with persons described in paragraph (f)(5)(i)(B) or (C) of this section, may require the governing body of the supported organization to perform any act that significantly affects its operations or may prevent the governing body of the supported organization from performing any such act. The governing body of a supported organization will generally be considered to be controlled directly or indirectly by one or more persons described in paragraph (f)(5)(i)(A), (B), or (C) of this section if the voting power of such persons is 50 percent or more of the total voting power of such governing body or if one or more of such persons have the right to exercise veto power over the actions of the governing body of the supported organization. However, all pertinent facts and circumstances will be taken into consideration in determining whether one or more persons do in fact directly or indirectly control the governing body of a supported organization.

* * *

(i) * * *
(2) * * *

(i) *Annual notification.*—For each taxable year (the Reporting Year), a Type III supporting organization must provide the following documents to each of its supported organizations:

(A) A written notice addressed to a principal officer of the supported organization describing the type and amount of all of the support (including all of the distributions described in paragraph (i)(6) of this section if applicable) the supporting organization provided to the supported organization during the supporting organization's taxable year immediately preceding the Reporting Year (and during any other taxable year of the supporting organization ending after December 28, 2012, for which such support information has not previously been provided);

* * *

(iii) *Due date.*—The notification documents required by this paragraph (i)(2) shall be delivered or electronically transmitted by the last day of the fifth calendar month of the Reporting Year.

* * *

(3) * * *

(i) *General rule.*—A supporting organization meets the responsiveness test only if it is responsive to the needs or demands of each of its supported organizations. Except as provided in paragraph (i)(3)(v) of this section, in order to meet this test, a supporting organization must satisfy the requirements of paragraphs (i)(3)(ii) and (iii) of this section with respect to each of its supported organizations.

* * *

(iv) * * *

Example 3. Z is described in section 501(c)(3). Z's organizational documents provide that it supports ten different organizations, each of which is described in section 509(a)(1). One of the directors of S (one of the supported organizations) is a voting member of Z's board of directors and participates in Z's regular board meetings. Officers of Z hold regular face-to-face or telephonic meetings during the year to which officers of all the supported organizations are invited. Z's meetings with the supported organizations may be held jointly or separately. Prior to the meetings, Z makes available to the supported organizations (including by email) up-to-date information about its activities including its assets and liabilities, receipts and distributions, and investment policies and returns. In the meetings, officers of each of the supported organizations have an opportunity to ask questions and discuss with officers of Z the projected needs of their organizations, as well as Z's investment and grant making policies and practices. In addition to holding these meetings with the supported organizations, Z provides the contact information of one of its officers to each of the supported organizations and encourages them to contact that officer if they have questions, or if they wish to schedule additional meetings to discuss the projected needs of their organization and how Z should distribute its income and invest its assets. Z provides the information required under paragraph (i)(2) of this section and a copy of its annual audited financial statements to the principal officers of the supported organizations. Z meets the relationship test of paragraph (i)(3)(ii)(B) or (C) of this section with respect to each of its supported organizations. Based on these facts, Z also satisfies the significant voice requirement of paragraph (i)(3)(iii) of this section, and therefore meets the responsiveness test of this paragraph (i)(3) with respect to each of its ten supported organizations.

* * *

(4) * * *

(ii) * * *

(A) * * *

(1) Directly further the exempt purposes of one or more supported organizations by performing the functions of, or carrying out the purposes of, such supported organization(s); and

* * *

(B) *Meaning of substantially all.*—For purposes of paragraph (i)(4)(ii)(A) of this section, in determining whether substantially all of a supporting organization's activities directly further the exempt purposes of one or more supported organization(s), all pertinent facts and circumstances will be taken into consideration.

* * *

(iii) *Parent of supported organization(s).*—For purposes of paragraph (i)(4)(i)(B) of this section, in order for a supporting organization to qualify as the parent of each of its supported organizations, the supporting organization and its supported organizations must be part of an integrated system (such as a hospital system), the supporting organization must engage in activities typical of the parent of an integrated system, and a majority of the officers, directors, or trustees of each supported organization must be appointed or elected, directly or indirectly, by the governing body, members of the governing body, or officers (acting in their official capacities) of the supporting organization. For purposes of this paragraph (i)(4)(iii), examples of activities typical of the parent of an integrated system of supported organizations include (but are not limited to) coordinating the activities of the supported organizations and engaging in overall planning, policy development, budgeting, and resource allocation for the supported organizations.

(iv) *Supporting a governmental supported organization.*— (A) *In general.*—A supporting organization satisfies the requirements of this paragraph (i)(4)(iv) if—

(1) The supporting organization supports only governmental supported organizations, and, if the supporting organization supports more than one governmental supported organization, all of the governmental supported organizations either—

(i) Operate within the same geographic region; or

(ii) Work in close coordination or collaboration with one another to conduct a service, program, or activity that the supporting organization supports; and

(2) A substantial part of the supporting organization's total activities are activities that directly further, as defined by paragraph (i)(4)(ii)(C) of this section, the exempt purposes of its governmental supported organization(s).

(B) *Governmental supported organization defined.*—For purposes of paragraph (i)(4)(iv)(A) of this section, the term *governmental supported organization* means a supported organization that is—

(1) A governmental unit described in section 170(c)(1); or

(2) An organization described in section 170(c)(2) and (b)(1)(A) (other than in clauses (vii) and (viii)) that is an instrumentality of one or more governmental units described in section 170(c)(1).

(C) *Geographic region defined.*—For purposes of paragraph (i)(4)(iv)(A)(1) of this section, the term *geographic region* means a city, county, or metropolitan area.

(D) *Close cooperation or coordination.*—To satisfy the close cooperation or coordination requirement of paragraph (i)(4)(iv)(A)(1) of this section, the supporting organization shall maintain on file a letter from each of the governmental supported organizations (or a joint letter from all of them) describing their collaborative or cooperative efforts with respect to the particular service, program, or activity.

(E) *Exception for organizations supporting a governmental supported organization on or before February 19, 2016.*—A Type III supporting organization in existence on or before February 19, 2016 will be treated as meeting the requirements of this paragraph (i)(4)(iv) if it met and continues to meet the following requirements—

(1) It supports one or more governmental supported organizations described in paragraph (i)(4)(iv)(B) of this section and does not support more than one supported organization that is not a governmental supported organization;

(2) Each of the supported organizations is designated by the supporting organization as provided in paragraph (d)(4) of this section on or before February 19, 2016; and

(3) A substantial part of the supporting organization's total activities are activities that directly further, as defined by paragraph (i)(4)(ii)(C) of this section, the exempt purposes of its governmental supported organization(s).

(F) *Transition rule for supporting organizations in existence on or before February 19, 2016.*—Until the earlier of the first day of the organization's first taxable year beginning after the date final regulations are published in the **Federal Register** under this paragraph (i)(4)(iv) or the first day of the organization's second taxable year beginning after February 19, 2016, a Type III supporting organization in existence on or before February 19, 2016 will be treated as meeting the requirements of this paragraph (i)(4)(iv) if it met and continues to meet the following requirements—

(1) It supports at least one supported organization that is a governmental entity to which the supporting organization is responsive within the meaning of paragraph (i)(3) of this section; and

(2) It engages in activities for or on behalf of the governmental supported organization described in paragraph (i)(4)(iv)(F)(1) of this section that perform the functions of, or carry out the purposes of, that governmental supported organization and that, but for the involvement of the supporting organization, would normally be engaged in by the governmental supported organization itself.

* * *

(5) * * *

(ii) * * *

(A) *Annual distribution.*—With respect to each taxable year, a supporting organization must make distributions described in paragraph (i)(6) of this section in a total amount equaling or exceeding the supporting organization's distributable amount for the taxable year, as defined in paragraph (i)(5)(ii)(B) of this section, on or before the last day of the taxable year.

(B) *Distributable amount.*—Except as provided in paragraphs (i)(5)(ii)(D) and (E) of this section, the distributable amount for a taxable year is an amount equal to the greater of 85 percent of the supporting organization's adjusted net income (as determined by applying the principles of section 4942(f) and § 53.4942(a)-2(d) of this chapter) for the taxable year immediately preceding the taxable year of the required distribution (immediately preceding taxable year) or its minimum asset amount (as defined in paragraph (i)(5)(ii)(C) of this section) for the immediately preceding taxable year.

* * *

(iii) * * *

(A) *General rule.*—With respect to each taxable year, a non-functionally integrated Type III supporting organization must distribute one-third or more of its distributable amount to one or more supported organizations that are attentive to the operations of the supporting organization (within the meaning of paragraph (i)(5)(iii)(B) of this section).

* * *

(D) * * *

Example 4. O is an organization described in section 501(c)(3). O is organized to support five private universities, V, W, X, Y, and Z, each of which is described in section 509(a)(1). O meets the responsiveness test described in paragraph (i)(3) of this section with respect to each of its supported organizations. Each year, O distributes an aggregate amount that equals its distributable amount described in paragraph (i)(5)(ii)(B) of this section and distributes an equal amount to each of the five universities. O distributes annually to each of V and W an amount that equals more than 10 percent of each university's total annual support received in its most recently completed taxable year. Based on these facts, O meets the requirements of paragraph (i)(5)(iii) of this section because it distributes two-fifths (more than the required one-third) of its distributable amount to supported organizations that are attentive to O.

(6) *Distributions that count toward distribution requirement.*—* * * Distributions by the supporting organization that count toward the distribution requirement imposed in paragraph (i)(5)(ii) of this section are limited to thefollowing—

* * *

(iii) Any reasonable and necessary—

(A) Administrative expenses paid to accomplish the exempt purposes of the supported organization, which do not include expenses incurred in the production of investment income or the conduct of fundraising activities, except as provided in paragraph (i)(6)(iii)(B) of this section; and

(B) Expenses incurred to solicit contributions that are received directly by a supported organization, but only to the extent the amount of such expenses does not exceed the amount of contributions actually received by the supported organization as a result of the solicitation, as substantiated in writing by the supported organization;

* * *

(v) Any amount set aside for a specific project that accomplishes the exempt purposes of a supported organization, with such set-aside counting toward the distribution requirement for the taxable year in which the amount is set aside but not in the year in which it is actually paid, if, at the time of the set-aside, the supporting organization—

* * *

(l) *Effective/applicability dates.*—(1) Paragraphs (a)(6), (f)(5), and (i) of this section are effective on December 28, 2012, except—

(i) Paragraphs (i)(4)(ii)(C), (i)(5)(ii)(C) and (D), (i)(6)(iv), (i)(7)(ii), and (i)(8) of this section are applicable on December 21, 2015; and

(ii) Paragraphs (f)(5)(ii), (i)(2)(i) and (iii), (i)(3)(i), (i)(4)(ii)(A)(1), (i)(4)(ii)(B), (i)(4)(iii) and (iv), (i)(5)(ii)(A) and (B), (i)(5)(iii)(A), (i)(6)(i), (iii) and (v) of this section, *Example 3* of paragraph (i)(3)(iv) of this section, and *Example 4* of paragraph (i)(5)(iii)(D) of this section are effective on the date the Treasury decision adopting these rules as final or temporary regulations is published in the **Federal Register**.

(2) See paragraphs (i)(5)(ii)(B) and (C) and (i)(8) of §1.509(a)–4T contained in 26 CFR part 1, revised as of April 1, 2015, for certain rules regarding non-functionally integrated Type III supporting organizations effective before December 21, 2015. See paragraphs (i)(5)(ii)(A) and (B) and (i)(5)(iii)(D) of §1.509(a)-4 (as effective December 21, 2015), for certain rules regarding non-functionally integrated Type III supporting organizations effective before the date the Treasury decision adopting these rules as final or temporary regulations is published in the Federal Register.

Guidance under Section 529A: Qualified ABLE Programs

Guidance under Section 529A: Qualified ABLE Programs.—Amendments to Reg. §1.511-2, regarding programs under The Stephen Beck, Jr., Achieving a Better Life Experience Act of 2014 and rules under which States or State agencies or instrumentalities may establish and maintain a new type of tax-favored savings program through which contributions may be made to the account of an eligible disabled individual to meet qualified disability expenses, are proposed (published in the Federal Register on June 22, 2015) (REG-102837-15).

Par. 2. Section 1.511-2 is amended by adding paragraph (e) to read as follows:

§1.511-2. Organizations subject to tax.

* * *

(e) *ABLE programs.*—(1) *Unrelated business taxable income.*—A qualified ABLE program described in section 529A generally is exempt from income taxation, but is subject to taxes imposed by section 511 relating to the imposition of tax on unrelated business income. A qualified ABLE program is required to file Form 990-T, "Exempt Organization Business Income Tax Return," if such filing would be required under the rules of §§1.6012-2(e) and 1.6012-3(a)(5) if the ABLE program were an organization described in those sections.

(2) *Effective/applicability dates.*—This paragraph (e) applies to taxable years beginning after December 31, 2014.

Exempt Organization: Unrelated Business Taxable Income

Exempt Organization: Unrelated Business Taxable Income.—Reg. §1.512(a)-6 and amendments to Reg. §1.512(a)-1, providing guidance on how an exempt organization subject to the unrelated business income tax described in section 511 of the Internal Revenue Code (Code) determines if it has more than one unrelated trade or business, and, if so, how the exempt organization calculates unrelated business taxable income, are proposed (published in the Federal Register on April 24, 2020) (REG-106864-18).

Par. 4. Section 1.512(a)-1 is proposed to be amended by:

1. Revising the first and fourth sentence of paragraph (a).
2. Revising the first and second sentence of paragraph (b).
3. Adding two sentences to the end of paragraph (c).
4. Revising paragraph (h).

The revisions and additions read as follows:

§1.512(a)-1. Definition.—(a) * * * Except as otherwise provided in §1.512(a)-3, §1.512(a)-4, or paragraph (f) of this section, section 512(a)(1) defines *unrelated business taxable income* as the gross income derived from any unrelated trade or business regularly carried on, less those deductions allowed by chapter 1 of the Internal Revenue Code (Code) which are directly connected with the carrying on of such trade or business, subject to certain modifications referred to in §1.512(b)-1. * * * In the case of an organization with more than one unrelated trade or business, unrelated business taxable income is calculated separately with respect to each such trade or business. *See* §1.512(a)-6. * * *

(b) * * * Expenses, depreciation, and similar items attributable solely to the conduct of unrelated business activities are proximately and primarily related to that business activity, and therefore qualify for deduction to the extent that they meet the requirements of section 162, section 167, or other relevant provisions of the Code. Thus, for example, salaries of personnel employed full-time in carrying on unrelated business activities are directly connected with the conduct of that activity and are deductible in computing unrelated business taxable income if they otherwise qualify for deduction under the requirements of section 162.

(c) * * * However, allocation of expenses, depreciation, and similar items using an unadjusted gross-to-gross method is not reasonable. For example, if a social club charges nonmembers a higher price than it charges members for the same good or service, it must adjust the price of the good or service provided to members for purposes of determining the allocation of indirect expenses to avoid overstating the deductions allocable to the unrelated business activity of providing goods and services to nonmembers.

* * *

(h) *Applicability date.*—This section generally applies to taxable years beginning after December 12, 1967, except as provided in paragraph (g)(2) of this section, and except that paragraphs (a) through (c) of this section apply to taxable years beginning on or [DATE OF PUBLICATION OF THE FINAL RULES IN THE **Federal Register**]. For taxable years beginning before [DATE OF PUBLICATION OF THE FINAL RULES IN THE **Federal Register**], see these paragraphs as in effect and contained in 26 CFR part 1 revised as of April 1, 2019.

Par. 5. Section 1.512(a)-6 is proposed to be added to read as follows:

§1.512(a)-6. Special rule for organizations with more than one unrelated trade or business.—(a) *More than one unrelated trade or business.*—(1) *In general.*—An organization with more than one unrelated trade or business must compute unrelated business taxable income (UBTI), including for purposes of determining any net operating loss (NOL) deduction, separately with respect to each such trade or business, without regard to the specific deduction in section 512(b)(12). An organization with more than one unrelated trade or business computes its total UBTI under paragraph (g) of this section.

(2) *Separate trades or businesses.*—For purposes of section 512(a)(6)(A) and paragraph (a)(1) of this section, an organization identifies its separate unrelated trades or businesses using the methods described in paragraphs (b) through (e) of this section.

(b) *North American Industry Classification System.*—(1) *In general.*—Except as provided in paragraphs (c) through (e) of this section, an organization will identify each of its separate unrelated trades or businesses using the first two digits of the North American Industry Classification System code (NAICS 2-digit code) that most accurately describes the trade or business. The NAICS 2-digit code chosen must identify the unrelated trade or business in which the organization engages (directly or indirectly) and not the activities the conduct of which are substantially related to the exercise or performance by such organization of its charitable, educational, or other purpose or function constituting the basis for its exemption under section 501 (or, in the case of an organization described in section 511(a)(2)(B), to the exercise or performance of any purpose or function described in section 501(c)(3)). For example, a college or university described in section 501(c)(3) cannot use the NAICS 2-digit code for educational services to identify all its separate unrelated trades or businesses, and a qualified retirement plan described in section 401(a) cannot use the NAICS 2-digit code for finance and insurance to identify all of its unrelated trades or businesses.

(2) *Codes only reported once.*—An organization will report each NAICS 2-digit code only once. For example, a hospital organization that operates several hospital facilities in a geographic area (or multiple geographic areas), all of which include pharmacies that sell goods to the general public, would include all the pharmacies under the NAICS 2-digit code for retail trade, regardless of whether the hospital organization keeps separate books and records for each pharmacy.

(3) *Erroneous codes.*—Once an organization has identified a separate unrelated trade or business using a particular NAICS 2-digit code, the organization may not change the NAICS 2-digit code describing that unrelated trade or business unless the organization can show that the NAICS 2-digit code chosen was due to an unintentional error and that another NAICS 2-digit code more accurately describes the trade or business.

(c) *Activities in the nature of investments.*—(1) *In general.*—An organization's activities in the nature of investments (investment activities) are treated collectively as a separate unrelated trade or business for purposes of section 512(a)(6)(A) and paragraph (a) of this section. Except as provided in paragraphs (c)(6) and (c)(8) of this section, an organization's investment activities are limited to its—

(i) Qualifying partnership interests (described in paragraph (c)(2) of this section);

(ii) Qualifying S corporation interests (described in paragraph (e)(2)(i) of this section); and

(iii) Debt-financed property or properties (within the meaning of section 514).

(2) *Qualifying partnership interests.*—(i) *Directly-held partnership interests.*—An interest in a partnership is a qualifying partnership interest (QPI) if the exempt organization holds a direct interest in a partnership (directly-held partnership interest) that meets the requirements of either the de minimis test (described in paragraph (c)(3) of this section) or the control test (described in paragraph (c)(4) of this section).

(ii) *Indirectly-held partnership interests.*—If an organization does not control (within the meaning of paragraph (c)(4)(iii) of this section) a partnership in which the organization holds a direct interest but that directly-held partnership interest is not a QPI because the organization holds more than 20 percent of the capital interest, any partnership in which the organization holds an indirect interest through the directly-held partnership interest (indirectly-held partnership interest) may be a QPI if the indirectly-held partnership interest meets the requirements of the de minimis test (described in paragraph (c)(3) of this section) (look-through rule). For example, if an organization directly holds 50 percent of the capital interests of a partnership that it does not control and the directly-held partnership holds 4 percent of the capital and profits interests of lower-tier partnership A, and 10 percent of the capital and profits interests of lower-tier partnership B, the organization may aggregate its interest

in lower-tier partnership A with its other QPIs because the organization indirectly holds 2 percent of the capital and profits interests of lower-tier partnership A (4 percent x 50 percent). However, the organization may not aggregate its interest in lower-tier partnership B with its QPIs because the organization indirectly holds 5 percent of the capital and profits interests of lower-tier partnership B (10 percent x 50 percent), which does not meet the requirements of the de minimis test.

(iii) *Designation.*—An organization that has a partnership interest meeting the requirements of paragraph (c)(2)(i) or (ii) of this section in a taxable year may designate that partnership interest as a QPI by including its share of partnership gross income (and directly connected deductions) with the gross income (and directly connected deductions) from its other investment activities (see paragraph (c)(1) of this section) in accordance with forms and instructions. Any partnership interest that is designated as a QPI remains a QPI unless and until it no longer meets the requirements of paragraph (c)(2)(i) or (ii) of this section. For example, if an organization designates a directly-held partnership interest that meets the requirements of the de minimis rule as a QPI in one taxable year, the organization cannot, in the next taxable year, use NAICS 2-digit codes to describe the partnership trades or businesses that are unrelated trades or businesses with respect to the organization unless the directly-held partnership interest fails to meet the requirements of both the de minimis test and the control test.

(3) *De minimis test.*—A partnership interest is a QPI that meets the requirements of the de minimis test if the organization holds directly (within the meaning of paragraph (c)(2)(i) of this section) or indirectly (within the meaning of paragraph (c)(2)(ii) of this section) no more than 2 percent of the profits interest and no more than 2 percent of the capital interest.

(4) *Control test.*—(i) *In general.*—A partnership interest is a QPI that meets the requirements of the control test if the organization holds no more than 20 percent of the capital interest and does not control the partnership within the meaning of paragraph (c)(4)(iii) of this section.

(ii) *Combining related interests.*—When determining an organization's percentage interest in a partnership for purposes of paragraph (c)(4)(i) of this section, the interests of a supporting organization (as defined in section 509(a)(3) and §1.509(a)-4) or a controlled entity (as defined in section 512(b)(13)(D) and §1.512(a)-1(l)) in the same partnership will be taken into account. For example, if an organization owns 10 percent of the capital interests in a partnership, and its supporting organization owns an additional 15 percent capital interest in that partnership, the organization would not meet the requirements of the control test because its aggregate percentage interest exceeds 20 percent (10 percent + 15 percent = 25 percent).

(iii) *Control.*—All facts and circumstances, including the partnership agreement, are relevant for determining whether an organization controls a partnership. In any case, however, an organization controls a partnership if—

(A) The organization, by itself, may require the partnership to perform, or may prevent the partnership from performing, any act that significantly affects the operations of the partnership;

(B) Any of the organization's officers, directors, trustees, or employees have rights to participate in the management of the partnership at any time;

(C) Any of the organization's officers, directors, trustees, or employees have rights to conduct the partnership's business at any time; or

(D) The organization, by itself, has the power to appoint or remove any of the partnership's officers or employees or a majority of directors.

(5) *Reliance on Schedule K-1 (Form 1065).*—(i) *In general.*—When determining the organization's percentage interest (described in paragraph (c)(5)(ii) of this section) in a partnership for purposes of the de minimis test (described in paragraph (c)(3) of this section) and the control test (described in paragraph (c)(4) of this section), an organization may rely on the Schedule K-1 (Form 1065) (or its successor) it receives from the partnership if the form lists the organization's percentage profits interest or its percentage capital interest, or both, at the beginning and end of the year. However, the organization may not rely on the form to the extent that any information about the organization's percentage interest is not specifically provided. For example, if the Schedule K-1 (Form 1065) an organization receives from a partnership lists the organization's profits interest as "variable" but lists its percentage capital interest at the beginning and end of the year, the organization may rely on the form only with respect to its percentage capital interest.

(ii) *Determining percentage interest.*—For purposes of paragraph (c)(5)(i) of this section, an organization determines its percentage interest by taking the average of the organization's percentage interest at the beginning and the end of the partnership's taxable year, or, in the case of a partnership interest held for less than a year, the percentage interest held at the beginning and end of the period of ownership within the partnership's taxable year. For example, if an organization acquires an interest in a partnership that files on a calendar year basis in May and the partnership reports on Schedule K-1 (Form 1065) that the partner held a 3 percent profits interest at the date of acquisition but held a 1 percent profits interest at the end of the calendar year, the organization will be considered to have held 2 percent of the profits interest in that partnership for that year ((3 percent + 1 percent)/2).

(6) *UBTI from the investment activities of organizations subject to section 512(a)(3).*—For purposes of paragraph (c)(1) of this section, UBTI from the investment activities of an organization subject to section 512(a)(3) includes any amount that—

(i) would be excluded from the calculation of UBTI under section 512(b)(1), (2), (3), or (5) if the organization were subject to section 512(a)(1);

(ii) is attributable to income set aside (and not in excess of the set aside limit described in section 512(a)(3)(E)), but not used, for a purpose described in section 512(a)(3)(B)(i) or (ii); or

(iii) is in excess of the set aside limit described in section 512(a)(3)(E).

(7) *Transition rule for certain partnership interests.*—(i) *In general.*—If a directly-held partnership interest acquired prior to August 21, 2018, is not a QPI, an organization may treat such partnership interest as a separate unrelated trade or business for purposes of section 512(a)(6) regardless of the number of unrelated trades or businesses directly or indirectly conducted by the partnership. For example, if an organization has a 35 percent capital interest in a partnership acquired prior to August 21, 2018, it can treat the partnership as a single trade or business even if the partnership's investments generated UBTI from lower-tier partnerships that were engaged in multiple trades or businesses. A partnership interest acquired prior to August 21, 2018, will continue to meet the requirement of this rule even if the organization's percentage interest in such partnership changes before the end of the transition period (see paragraph (c)(7)(iii) of this section).

(ii) *Exclusivity.*—An organization may apply either the transition rule in paragraph (c)(7)(i) of this section or the look-through rule in paragraph (c)(2)(ii) of this section, but not both, to a partnership interest described in paragraph (c)(7)(i) of this section that also qualifies for application of the look-through rule described in paragraph (c)(2)(ii).

(iii) *Transition period.*—An organization may rely on this transition rule until the first day of the organization's first taxable year beginning after [DATE OF PUBLICATION OF THE FINAL RULES IN THE **Federal Register**].

(8) *Limitations.*—(i) *Social clubs.*—Paragraphs (c)(2) (regarding QPIs) and (c)(7) (transition rule for certain partnership interests) of this section do not apply to social clubs described in section 501(c)(7).

(ii) *General partnership interests.*—Any partnership in which an organization is a general partner is not a QPI within the meaning of paragraph (c)(2) of this section, regardless of the organization's percentage interest.

(iii) *Application of other sections.*—This paragraph (c) will not otherwise impact application of section 512(c) and the fragmentation principle under section 513(c).

(d) *Income from certain controlled entities.*—(1) *Specified payments from controlled entities.*—If an organization (controlling organization) controls another entity (within the meaning of section 512(b)(13)(D)) (controlled entity), all specified payments (as defined in section 512(b)(13)(C)) received by a controlling organization from that controlled entity will be treated as gross income from a separate unrelated trade or business for purposes of paragraph (a) of this section. If a controlling organization receives specified payments from two different controlled entities, the payments from each controlled entity are treated as a separate unrelated trade or business. For example, a controlling organization that receives rental payments from two con-

trolled entities will have two separate unrelated trades or businesses, one for each controlled entity. The specified payments from a controlled entity will be treated as gross income from one trade or business regardless of whether the controlled entity engages in more than one unrelated trade or business or whether the controlling organization receives more than one type of specified payment from that controlled entity.

(2) *Certain amounts derived from controlled foreign corporations.*—All amounts included in UBTI under section 512(b)(17) will be treated as income derived from a separate unrelated trade or business for purposes of paragraph (a) of this section.

(e) *S corporation interests.*—(1) *In general.*—Except as provided in paragraph (e)(2) of this section, if an organization owns stock in an S corporation (S corporation interest), such S corporation interest will be treated as an interest in a separate unrelated trade or business for purposes of paragraph (a) of this section. Thus, if an organization owns two S corporation interests, neither of which is described in paragraph (e)(2) of this section, the exempt organization will report two separate unrelated trades or businesses, one for each S corporation interest. The UBTI from an S corporation interest is the amount described in section 512(e)(1)(B).

(2) *Exception.*—(i) *Qualifying S corporation interest.*—Notwithstanding paragraph (e)(1) of this section, an organization may aggregate its UBTI from an S corporation interest with its UBTI from other investment activities (described in paragraph (c)(1) of this section) if the organization's ownership interest (by percentage of stock ownership) in the S corporation meets the criteria for a QPI as described in paragraph (c)(2)(i) of this section (qualifying S corporation interest).

(ii) *Reliance on Schedule K-1 (Form 1120-S).*—When determining how much S corporation stock an organization owns for purposes of paragraph (e)(2)(i) of this section, the organization may rely on the Schedule K-1 (Form 1120-S) (or its successor) it receives from the S corporation if the form lists the organization's percentage of stock ownership for the year.

(f) *Allocation of deductions.*—An organization must allocate deductions between separate unrelated trades or businesses using the method described in § 1.512(a)-1(c).

(g) *Total UBTI.*—(1) *In general.*—The total UBTI of an organization with more than one unrelated trade or business is the sum of the UBTI computed with respect to each separate unrelated trade or business (as identified under paragraph (a)(2) of this section and subject to the limitation described in paragraph (g)(2) of this section), less a specific deduction under section 512(b)(12).

(2) *UBTI not less than zero.*—For purposes of paragraph (g)(1) of this section, the UBTI with respect to any separate unrelated trade or business identified under paragraph (a)(2) of this section cannot be less than zero.

(h) *Net operating losses.*—(1) *In general.*—For taxable years beginning after December 31, 2017, an exempt organization with more than one unrelated trade or business determines the NOL deduction allowed by sections 172(a) and 512(b)(6) separately with respect to each of its unrelated trades or businesses. Accordingly, if an exempt organization has more than one unrelated trade or business, § 1.512(b)-1(e) applies separately with respect to each such unrelated trade or business.

(2) *Coordination of pre-2018 and post-2017 NOLs.*—An organization with losses arising in a taxable year beginning before January 1, 2018 (pre-2018 NOLs), and with losses arising in a taxable year beginning after December 31, 2017 (post-2017 NOLs), deducts its pre-2018 NOLs from total UBTI before deducting any post-2017 NOLs with regard to a separate unrelated trade or business against the UBTI from such trade or business. Pre-2018 NOLs are taken against the total UBTI as determined under paragraph (g) of this section in the manner that results in maximum utilization of the pre-2018 NOLs in a taxable year.

(i) *Applicability dates.*—This section is applicable to taxable years beginning on or after [DATE OF PUBLICATION OF THE FINAL RULES IN THE **Federal Register**]. [Reg. § 1.512(a)-6.]

Section 1256 Contracts: Swap Exclusions

Section 1256 Contracts: Swap Exclusions.—Amendment to Reg. § 1.512(b)-1, providing guidance on the category of swaps and similar agreements that are within the scope of Code Sec. 1256(b)(2)(B), are proposed (published in the Federal Register on September 16, 2011) (REG-111283-11).

☐ Par. 3. Section 1.512(b)-(1) is amended by:

1. Revising paragraph (a)(1).

2. Adding two sentences to the end of paragraph (a)(3).

The revision and addition read as follows:

§1.512(b)-1. Modifications.

* * *

(a) *Certain Investment Income.*—(1) *In general.*—Dividends, interest, payments with respect to securities loans (as defined in section 512(a)(5)), annuities, income from notional principal contracts (as defined in §1.446-3(c)), other substantially similar income from ordinary and routine investments to the extent determined by the Commissioner, and all deductions directly connected with any of the foregoing items of income shall be excluded in computing unrelated business taxable income.

* * *

(3) * * * The rules of paragraph (a)(1) of this section apply to notional principal contracts as defined in §1.446-3(c) that are entered into on or after the date of publication of a Treasury decision adopting these rules as final regulations in the **Federal Register**. Section 1.512(b)-1(a)(1) as contained in 26 CFR part 1 revised April 1, 2011, continues to apply to notional principal contracts entered into before the date of publication of a Treasury decision adopting these rules as final regulations in the **Federal Register**.

* * *

Exempt Organization: Unrelated Business Taxable Income

Exempt Organization: Unrelated Business Taxable Income.—Amendments to Reg. §1.512(b)-1, providing guidance on how an exempt organization subject to the unrelated business income tax described in section 511 of the Internal Revenue Code (Code) determines if it has more than one unrelated trade or business, and, if so, how the exempt organization calculates unrelated business taxable income, are proposed (published in the Federal Register on April 24, 2020) (REG-106864-18).

Par. 6. Section 1.512(b)-1 is proposed to be amended by:

1. Revising paragraph (a)(1).
2. Adding a new sentence to the end of paragraph (a)(3).
3. Adding a new paragraph (e)(5).
4. Adding new paragraphs (g)(4) and (5).

The revisions and additions read as follows:

§1.512(b)-1. Modifications.

(a) * * *

(1) * * * Dividends (including an inclusion of subpart F income under section 951(a)(1)(A) or an inclusion of global intangible low-taxed income (GILTI) under section 951A(a), both of which are treated in the same manner as a dividend for purposes of section 512(b)(1)), interest, payments with respect to securities loans (as defined in section 512(a)(5)), annuities, income from notional principal contracts (as defined in §1.837-7 or regulations issued under section 446), other substantially similar income from ordinary and routine investments to the extent determined by the Commissioner, and all deductions directly connected with any of the foregoing items of income must be excluded in computing unrelated business taxable income.

* * *

(3) * * * The exclusion under paragraph (a)(1) of this section of an inclusion of subpart F income under section 951(a)(1)(A) or an inclusion of GILTI under section 951A(a) from income (both inclusions being treated in the same manner as dividends) is applicable to taxable years beginning on or after [DATE OF PUBLICATION OF THE FINAL RULES IN THE **Federal Register**]. However, an organization may choose to apply this exclusion to taxable years beginning before [DATE OF PUBLICATION OF THE FINAL RULES IN THE **Federal Register**].

* * *

(e) * * *

(5) See §1.512(a)-6(h) regarding the computation of the net operating loss deduction when an organization has more than one unrelated trade or business.

* * *

(g) * * *

(4) The term *unrelated business taxable income* as used in section 512(b)(10) and (11) refers to unrelated business taxable income after application of section 512(a)(6).

(5) Paragraph (g)(4) of this section is applicable to taxable years beginning on or after [DATE OF PUBLICATION OF THE FINAL RULES IN THE **Federal Register**].

* * *

Guidance under Section 529A: Qualified ABLE Programs

Guidance under Section 529A: Qualified ABLE Programs.—Amendments to Reg. §1.513-1, regarding programs under The Stephen Beck, Jr., Achieving a Better Life Experience Act of 2014 and rules under which States or State agencies or instrumentalities may establish and maintain a new type of tax-favored savings program through which contributions may be made to the account of an eligible disabled individual to meet qualified disability expenses, are proposed (published in the Federal Register on June 22, 2015) (REG-102837-15).

Par. 3. Section 1.513-1 is amended by adding *Example 4* to paragraph (d)(4)(i) to read as follows:

§1.513-1. Definition of unrelated trade or business.

* * *

(d) * * *

(4) * * *

(i) * * *

Example 4. P is a qualified ABLE program described in section 529A. P receives amounts in order to open or maintain ABLE accounts, as administrative or maintenance fees and other similar fees including service charges. Because the payment of these amounts are essential to the operation of a qualified ABLE program, the income generated from the activity does not constitute gross income from an unrelated trade or business.

* * *

Exempt Organization: Unrelated Business Taxable Income

Exempt Organization: Unrelated Business Taxable Income.—Amendments to Reg. §1.513-1, providing guidance on how an exempt organization subject to the unrelated business income tax described in section 511 of the Internal Revenue Code (Code) determines if it has more than one unrelated trade or business, and, if so, how the exempt organization calculates unrelated business taxable income, are proposed (published in the Federal Register on April 24, 2020) (REG-106864-18).

Par. 7. Section 1.513-1 is proposed to be amended by:

1. Revising the third and fourth sentence in paragraph (a).
2. Redesignating paragraphs (f) and (g) as paragraphs (g) and (h).
3. Adding new paragraph (f).
4. Adding a new sentence to the end of new paragraph (h).

The revisions and additions read as follows:

§1.513-1. Definition of unrelated trade or business..—(a) * * *
For certain exceptions from this definition, see paragraph (e) of this section. For a special definition of *unrelated trade or business* applicable to certain trusts, see paragraph (f) of this section. * * *

* * *

(f) *Special definition of "unrelated trade or business" for trusts.*—In the case of a trust computing its unrelated business taxable income under section 512 for purposes of section 681, or a trust described in section 401(a) or section 501(c)(17), which is exempt from tax under section 501(a), section 513(b) provides that the term *unrelated trade or business* means any trade or business regularly carried on by such trust or by a partnership of which it is a member. This definition also applies to an individual retirement account described in section 408 that, under section 408(e), is subject to the tax imposed by section 511.

* * *

(h) * * * Paragraph (f) of this section applies to taxable years beginning on or after [DATE OF PUBLICATION OF THE FINAL RULES IN THE **Federal Register**].

* * *

Partnerships: Tax-Exempt Organization Partners: Fractions Rule

Partnerships: Tax-Exempt Organization Partners: Fractions Rule.—Amendments to Reg. §1.514(c)-2, relating to the application of section 514(c)(9)(E) of the Internal Revenue Code (Code) to partnerships that hold debt-financed real property and have one or more (but not all) qualified tax-exempt organization partners within the meaning of section 514(c)(9)(C), are proposed (published in the Federal Register on November 23, 2016) (REG-136978-12).

Par. 2. Section 1.514(c)-2 is amended by:

1. In paragraph (a), adding entries for (d)(2)(i) through (iii), adding entries for (d)(3)(i) and (ii), revising the entry for (d)(6), removing entries for (d)(6)(i) and (ii), and (d)(7), adding entries for (k)(1)(i) through (iv), revising the entries for (k)(2)(i) and (ii), adding an entry for (k)(2)(iii), and revising the entry for (n).

2. Revising paragraphs (d)(2) and (3).

3. Removing paragraph (d)(6).

4. Redesignating paragraph (d)(7) as paragraph (d)(6).

5. Revising newly redesignated paragraph (d)(6) *Example 1* paragraph (i) and adding paragraph (iv).

6. Removing the language "(i.e., reverse)" in paragraph (e)(1)(i) and adding the language "(that is, reverse)" in its place.

7. Removing the language "other partners; and" at the end of paragraph (e)(1)(iii) and adding the language "other partners;" in its place.

8. Removing the language "of §1.704-1(b)(2)(ii)(*d*)." at the end of paragraph (e)(1)(iv) and adding the language "of §1.704-1(b)(2)(ii)(*d*);" in its place.

9. Removing the language "the regulations thereunder." at the end of paragraph (e)(1)(v) and adding the language "the regulations thereunder;" in its place.

10. Adding new paragraphs (e)(1)(vi) and (vii).

11. Adding *Example 5* to paragraph (e)(5).

12. Removing the word "and" at the end of paragraph (f)(3).

13. Redesignating paragraph (f)(4) as paragraph (f)(5) and adding new paragraph (f)(4).

14. Revising paragraph (k)(1).

15. Revising the subject heading for paragraph (k)(2)(i).

16. Revising paragraph (k)(2)(i)(A).

17. Redesignating paragraph (k)(2)(ii) as paragraph (k)(2)(iii) and adding new paragraph (k)(2)(ii).

18. Revising paragraph (k)(3)(ii)(B).

19. Removing the second sentence in paragraph (m)(1)(ii).

20. Revising *Example 3*(ii) of paragraph (m)(2).

21. Revising the subject heading for paragraph (n).

22. Adding a sentence to the end of paragraph (n)(2).

The revisions and additions read as follows:

§1.514(c)-2. Permitted allocations under section 514(c)(9)(E).—
(a) *Table of contents.—** * ***

    (d) * * *

        (2) * * *

            (i) In general.

            (ii) Limitation.

            (iii) Distributions disregarded.

        (3) * * *

            (i) In general.

            (ii) Reasonable guaranteed payments may be deducted only when paid in cash.

* * *

        (6) Examples.

* * *

    (k) * * *

        (1) * * *

            (i) In general.

            (ii) Acquisition of partnership interests after initial formation of partnership.

            (iii) Capital commitment defaults or reductions.

            (iv) Examples.

        (2) * * *

            (i) Qualified organizations.

            (ii) Non-qualified organizations.

            (iii) Example.

* * *

    (n) Effective/applicability dates.

* * *

    (d) * * *

    (2) *Preferred returns.*—(i) *In general.*—Items of income (including gross income) and gain that may be allocated to a partner with respect to a current or cumulative reasonable preferred return for capital (including allocations of minimum gain attributable to nonrecourse liability (or partner nonrecourse debt) proceeds distributed to the partner as a reasonable preferred return) are disregarded in computing overall partnership income or loss for purposes of the fractions rule. Similarly, if a partnership agreement effects a reasonable preferred return with an allocation of what would otherwise be overall partnership income, those items comprising that allocation are disregarded in computing overall partnership income for purposes of the fractions rule.

    (ii) *Limitation.*—Except as otherwise provided in paragraph (d)(2)(iii) of this section, items of income and gain (or part of what would otherwise be overall partnership income) that may be allocated to a partner in a taxable year with respect to a reasonable preferred return for capital are disregarded under paragraph (d)(2)(i) of this section for purposes of the fractions rule only if the partnership agreement requires the partnership to make distributions first to pay any accrued, cumulative, and compounding unpaid preferred return to the extent such accrued but unpaid preferred return has not otherwise been reversed by an allocation of loss prior to such distribution.

    (iii) *Distributions disregarded.*—A distribution is disregarded for purposes of paragraph (d)(2)(ii) of this section if the distribution—

    (A) Is made pursuant to a provision in the partnership agreement intended to facilitate the partners' payment of taxes imposed on their allocable shares of partnership income or gain;

    (B) Is treated as an advance against distributions to which the distributee partner would otherwise be entitled under the partnership agreement; and

    (C) Does not exceed the distributee partner's allocable share of net partnership income and gain multiplied by the sum of the highest statutory federal, state, and local tax rates applicable to such partner.

    (3) *Guaranteed payments.*—(i) *In general.*—A current or cumulative reasonable guaranteed payment to a qualified organization for capital or services is treated as an item of deduction in computing overall partnership income or loss, and the income that the qualified organization may receive or accrue from the current or cumulative reasonable guaranteed payment is not treated as an allocable share of overall partnership income or loss. The treatment of a guaranteed payment as reasonable for purposes of section 514(c)(9)(E) does not affect its possible characterization as unrelated business taxable income under other provisions of the Internal Revenue Code.

    (ii) *Reasonable guaranteed payments may be deducted only when paid in cash.*—If a partnership that avails itself of paragraph (d)(3)(i) of this section would otherwise be required (by virtue of its method of accounting) to deduct a reasonable guaranteed payment to a qualified organization earlier than the taxable year in which it is paid in cash, the partnership must delay the deduction of the guaranteed payment until the taxable year it is paid in cash. For purposes of this paragraph (d)(3)(ii), a guaranteed payment that is paid in cash on or before the due date (not including extensions) for filing the partnership's return for a taxable year may be treated as paid in that prior taxable year.

* * *

(6) * * *

Example 1. * * *

(i) The partnership agreement provides QO a 10 percent preferred return on its unreturned capital. The partnership agreement provides that the preferred return may be compounded (at 10 percent) and may be paid in future years and requires that when distributions are made, they must be made first to pay any accrued, cumulative, and compounding unpaid preferred return not previously reversed by a loss allocation. The partnership agreement also allows distributions to be made to facilitate a partner's payment of federal, state, and local taxes. Under the partnership agreement, any such distribution is treated as an advance against distributions to which the distributee partner would otherwise be entitled and must not exceed the partner's allocable share of net partnership income or gain for that taxable year multiplied by the sum of the highest statutory federal, state, and local tax rates applicable to the partner. The partnership agreement first allocates gross income and gain 100 percent to QO, to the extent of the preferred return. All remaining income or loss is allocated 50 percent to QO and 50 percent to TP.

* * *

(iv) The facts are the same as in paragraph (i) of this *Example 1*, except the partnership makes a distribution to TP of an amount computed by a formula in the partnership agreement equal to TP's allocable share of net income and gain multiplied by the sum of the highest statutory federal, state, and local tax rates applicable to TP. The partnership satisfies the fractions rule. The distribution to TP is disregarded for purposes of paragraph (d)(2)(ii) of this section because the distribution is made pursuant to a provision in the partnership agreement that provides that the distribution is treated as an advance against distributions to which TP would otherwise be entitled and the distribution did not exceed TP's allocable share of net partnership income or gain for that taxable year multiplied by the sum of the highest statutory federal, state, and local tax rates applicable to TP. The income and gain that is specially allocated to QO with respect to its preferred return is disregarded in computing overall partnership income or loss for purposes of the fractions rule because the requirements of paragraph (d) of this section are satisfied. After disregarding those allocations, QO's fractions rule percentage is 50 percent (see paragraph (c)(2) of this section), and, under the partnership agreement, QO may not be allocated more than 50 percent of overall partnership income in any taxable year.

(e) * * *

(1) * * *

(vi) Allocations of what would otherwise be overall partnership income that may be made to chargeback (that is, reverse) prior allocations of partner-specific expenditures that were disregarded in computing overall partnership income or loss for purposes of the fractions rule under paragraph (f) of this section; and

(vii) Allocations of what would otherwise be overall partnership income that may be made to chargeback (that is, reverse) prior allocations of unlikely losses and deductions that were disregarded in computing overall partnership income or loss for purposes of the fractions rule under paragraph (g) of this section.

* * *

(5) * * *

Example 5. Chargeback of prior allocations of unlikely losses and deductions. (i) Qualified organization (QO) and taxable corporation (TP) are equal partners in a partnership that holds encumbered real property. The partnership agreement generally provides that QO and TP share partnership income and deductions equally. QO contributes land to the partnership, and the partnership agreement provides that QO bears the burden of any environmental remediation required for that land, and, as such, the partnership will allocate 100 percent of the expense attributable to the environmental remediation to QO. In the unlikely event of the discovery of environmental conditions that require remediation, the partnership agreement provides that, to the extent its cumulative net income (without regard to the remediation expense) for the taxable year the partnership incurs the remediation expense and for subsequent taxable years exceeds $500x, after allocation of the $500x of cumulative net income, net income will first be allocated to QO to offset any prior allocation of the environmental remediation expense deduction. On January 1 of Year 3, the partnership incurs a $100x expense for the environmental remediation of the land. In that year, the partnership had gross income of $60x and other expenses of $30x for total net income of $30x without regard to the expense associated with the environmental remediation. The partnership allocated $15x of income to each of QO and TP and $100x of remediation expense to QO.

(ii) The partnership satisfies the fractions rule. The allocation of the expense attributable to the remediation of the land is disregarded under paragraph (g) of this section. QO's share of overall partnership income is 50 percent, which equals QO's share of overall partnership loss.

(iii) In Year 8, when the partnership's cumulative net income (without regard to the remediation expense) for the taxable year the partnership incurred the remediation expense and subsequent taxable years is $480x (the $30x from Year 3, plus $450x of cumulative net income for Years 4-7), the partnership has gross income of $170x and expenses of $50x, for total net income of $120x. The partnership's cumulative net income for all years from Year 3 to Year 8 is $600x ($480x for Years 3-7 and $120x for Year 8). Pursuant to the partnership agreement, the first $20x of net income for Year 8 is allocated equally between QO and TP because the partnership must first earn cumulative net income in excess of $500x before making the offset allocation to QO. The remaining $100x of net income for Year 8 is allocated to QO to offset the environmental remediation expense allocated to QO in Year 3.

(iv) Pursuant to paragraph (e)(1)(vii) of this section, the partnership's allocation of $100x of net income to QO in Year 8 to offset the prior environmental remediation expense is disregarded in computing overall partnership income or loss for purposes of the fractions rule. The allocation does not cause the partnership to violate the fractions rule.

(f) * * *

(4) Expenditures for management and similar fees, if such fees in the aggregate for the taxable year are not more than 2 percent of the partner's capital commitments; and * * *

* * *

(k) *Special rules.*—(1) *Changes in partnership allocations arising from a change in the partners' interests.*—(i) *In general.*—A qualified organization that acquires a partnership interest from another qualified organization is treated as a continuation of the prior qualified organization partner (to the extent of that acquired interest) for purposes of applying the fractions rule. Changes in partnership allocations that result from other transfers or shifts of partnership interests will be closely scrutinized (to determine whether the transfer or shift stems from a prior agreement, understanding, or plan or could otherwise be expected given the structure of the transaction), but generally will be taken into account only in determining whether the partnership satisfies the fractions rule in the taxable year of the change and subsequent taxable years.

(ii) *Acquisition of partnership interests after initial formation of partnership.*—Changes in partnership allocations due to an acquisition of a partnership interest by a partner (new partner) after the initial formation of a partnership will not be closely scrutinized under paragraph (k)(1)(i) of this section, but will be taken into account only in determining whether the partnership satisfies the fractions rule in the taxable year of the change and subsequent taxable years, and disproportionate allocations of income, loss, or deduction to the partners to adjust the partners' capital accounts as a result of, and to reflect, the new partner acquiring the partnership interest and the resulting changes to the other partners' interests will be disregarded in computing overall partnership income or loss for purposes of the fractions rule if such changes and disproportionate allocations are not inconsistent with the purpose of the fractions rule under paragraph (k)(4) of this section and—

(A) The new partner acquires the partnership interest no later than 18 months following the formation of the partnership (applicable period);

(B) The partnership agreement and other relevant documents anticipate the new partners acquiring the partnership interest during the applicable period, set forth the time frame in which the new partners will acquire the partnership interests, and provide for the amount of capital the partnership intends to raise;

(C) The partnership agreement and other relevant documents specifically set forth the method for determining any applicable interest factor and for allocating income, loss, or deduction to the partners to account for the economics of the arrangement in the partners' capital accounts after the new partner acquires the partnership interest; and

(D) The interest rate for any applicable interest factor is not greater than 150 percent of the highest applicable Federal rate, at the appropriate compounding period or periods, at the time the partnership was formed.

(iii) *Capital commitment defaults or reductions.*—Changes in partnership allocations that result from an unanticipated partner default on a capital contribution commitment or an unanticipated reduction in a partner's capital contribution commitment, that are effected pursuant to provisions prescribing the treatment of such events in the partnership agreement, and that are not inconsistent with the purpose of the fractions rule under paragraph (k)(4) of this section, will not be closely scrutinized under paragraph (k)(1)(i) of this section, but will be taken into account only in determining whether the partnership satisfies the fractions rule in the taxable year of the change and subsequent taxable years. In addition, partnership allocations of income, loss, or deduction to partners made pursuant to the partnership agreement to adjust partners' capital accounts as a result of unanticipated capital contribution defaults or reductions will be disregarded in computing overall partnership income or loss for purposes of the fractions rule. The adjustments may include allocations to adjust partners' capital accounts to be consistent with the partners' adjusted capital commitments.

(iv) *Examples.*—The following examples illustrate the provisions of paragraph (k)(1) of this section.

Example 1. Staged closing. (i) On July 1 of Year 1, two taxable partners (TP1 and TP2) form a partnership that will invest in debt-financed real property. The partnership agreement provides that, within an 18-month period, partners will be added so that an additional $1000x of capital can be raised. The partnership agreement sets forth the method for determining the applicable interest factor that complies with paragraph (k)(1)(ii)(D) of this section and for allocating income, loss, or deduction to the partners to account for the economics of the arrangement in the partners' capital accounts. During the partnership's Year 1 taxable year, partnership had $150x of net income. TP1 and TP2, each, is allocated $75x of net income.

(ii) On January 1 of Year 2, qualified organization (QO) joins the partnership. The partnership agreement provides that TP1, TP2, and QO will be treated as if they had been equal partners from July 1 of Year 1. Assume that the interest factor is treated as a reasonable guaranteed payment to TP1 and TP2, the expense from which is taken into account in the partnership's net income of $150x for Year 2. To balance capital accounts, the partnership allocates $100x of the income to QO ($50x, or the amount of one-third of Year 1 income that QO was not allocated during the partnership's first taxable year, plus $50x, or one-third of the partnership's income for Year 2) and the remaining income equally to TP1 and TP2. Thus, the partnership allocates $100x to QO and $25x to TP1 and TP2, each.

(iii) The partnership's allocation to QO would violate the fractions rule because QO's overall percentage of partnership income for Year 2 of 66.7 percent is greater than QO's fractions rule percentage of 33.3 percent. However, the special allocation of $100x to QO for Year 2 is disregarded in determining QO's percentage of overall partnership income for purposes of the fractions rule because the requirements in paragraph (k)(1)(ii) of this section are satisfied.

Example 2. Capital call default. (i) On January 1 of Year 1, two taxable partners, (TP1 and TP2) and a qualified organization (QO) form a partnership that will hold encumbered real property and agree to share partnership profits and losses, 60 percent, 10 percent, and 30 percent, respectively. TP1 agreed to a capital commitment of $120x, TP2 agreed to a capital commitment of $20x, and QO agreed to a capital commitment of $60x. The partners met half of their commitments upon formation of the partnership. The partnership agreement requires a partner's interest to be reduced if the partner defaults on a capital call. The agreement also allows the non-defaulting partners to make the contribution and to increase their own interests in the partnership. Following a capital call default, the partnership agreement requires allocations to adjust capital accounts to reflect the change in partnership interests as though the funded commitments represented the partner's interests from the partnership's inception.

(ii) In Year 1, partnership had income of $100x, which was allocated to the partners $60x to TP1, $10x to TP2, and $30x to QO.

(iii) In Year 2, partnership required each partner to contribute the remainder of its capital commitment, $60x from TP1, $10x from TP2, and $30x from QO. TP1 could not make its required capital contribution, and QO contributed $90x, its own capital commitment, in addition to TP1's. TP1's default was not anticipated. As a result and pursuant to the partnership agreement, TP1's interest was reduced to 30 percent and QO's interest was increased to 60 percent. Partnership had income of $60x and losses of $120x in Year 2, for a net loss of $60x. Partnership allocated to TP1 $48x of loss (special allocation of $30x of gross items of loss to adjust capital accounts and

$18x of net loss (30 percent of $60x net loss)), TP2 $6x of net loss (10 percent of $60x net loss), and QO $6x of loss (special allocation of $30x of gross items of income to adjust capital accounts - $36x of net loss (60 percent of $60x net loss)). At the end of Year 2, TP1's capital account equals $72x (capital contribution of $60x + $60x income from Year 1 - $48x loss from Year 2); TP2's capital account equals $24x (capital contributions of $20x + $10x income from Year 1 - $6x loss from Year 2); and QO's capital account equals $144x (capital contributions of $120x ($30x + $90x) + $30x income from Year 1 - $6x loss from Year 2).

(iv) The changes in partnership allocations to TP1 and QO due to TP1's unanticipated default on its capital contribution commitment were effected pursuant to provisions prescribing the treatment of such events in the partnership agreement. Therefore these changes in allocations will not be closely scrutinized under paragraph (k)(1)(i) of this section, but will be taken into account only in determining whether the partnership satisfies the fractions rule in the taxable year of the change and subsequent taxable years. In addition, pursuant to paragraph (k)(1)(iii) of this section, the special allocations of $30x additional loss to TP1 and $30x additional income to QO to adjust their capital accounts to reflect their new interests in the partnership are disregarded when calculating QO's percentage of overall partnership income and loss for purposes of the fractions rule.

(2) * * *

(i) *Qualified organizations.*—* * *

(A) Qualified organizations do not hold (directly or indirectly through a partnership), in the aggregate, interests of greater than five percent in the capital or profits of the partnership; and
* * *

(ii) *Non-qualified organizations.*—Section 514(c)(9)(B)(vi) does not apply to a partnership otherwise subject to that section if—

(A) All partners other than qualified organizations do not hold (directly or indirectly through a partnership), in the aggregate, interests of greater than five percent in the capital or profits of the partnership; and

(B) Allocations have substantial economic effect without application of the special rules in §1.704-1(b)(2)(iii)(c) (regarding the presumption that there is a reasonable possibility that allocations will affect substantially the dollar amounts to be received by the partners from the partnership if there is a strong likelihood that offsetting allocations will not be made in five years, and the presumption that the adjusted tax basis (or book value) of partnership property is equal to the fair market value of such property).
* * *

(3) * * *

(ii) * * *

(B) $1,000,000.
* * *

(m) * * *

(2) * * *

Example 3. * * *

(ii) P2 satisfies the fractions rule with respect to the P2/P1A chain. See §1.702-1(a)(8)(ii) (for rules regarding separately stating partnership items). P2 does not satisfy the fractions rule with respect to the P2/P1B chain.

(n) *Effective/applicability dates.*—* * *

(2) * * * However, paragraphs (d)(2)(ii) and (iii), (d)(6) *Example 1*(i) and (iv), (e)(1)(vi) and (vii), (e)(5) *Example 5*, (f)(4), (k)(1)(ii) through (iv), (k)(2)(i)(A), (k)(2)(ii), (k)(3)(ii)(B), (m)(1)(ii), and (m)(2) *Example 3*(ii) of this section apply to taxable years ending on or after the date these regulations are published as final regulations in the **Federal Register**.
* * *

Exempt Organizations

Exempt Organizations: Unrelated Trade or Business: Bingo Games.—Reproduced below is the text of a proposed amendment of Reg. §1.527-3, relating to the treatment of proceeds from bingo games (published in the Federal Register on August 28, 1979).

☐ Par. 2. Section 1.527-3(b)[(a)](1) is revised to read as follows:

§1.527-3. Political organization taxable income.—
* * *

(b)[a] *Exempt function income defined.*—(1) *In general.*—For purposes of section 527 and these regulations the term "exempt function income" means any amount received as—

(i) A contribution of money or other property;

(ii) Membership dues, fees, or assessments from a member of a political organization;

(iii) Proceeds from a political fund raising or entertainment event, or proceeds from the sale of political campaign materials,

which are not received in the ordinary course of any trade or business; and

(iv) Proceeds from the conduct of any bingo game (as defined in section 513(f)(2)) unless the proceeds were held on October 21, 1978, by the political organization that conducted the bingo games and thereafter were used by that organization to make a contribution or expenditure (as defined in section 301(e) and (f) of the Federal Election Campaign Act of 1971; 2 U.S.C. 431(e), (f)) in connection with an election held before January 1, 1979, to the extent such amount is segregated for use only for the exempt function of the political organization. (See also §1.527-4 regarding the treatment of expenditures for a judicially determined illegal activity.)

* * *

Qualified State Tuition Programs: Distributions: Reporting Requirements

Qualified State Tuition Programs: Distributions: Reporting Requirements.—Reg. §§1.529-0—1.529-6, relating to qualified state tuition programs (QSTPs) and affecting QSTPs established and maintained by a state, or an agency or instrumentality of a state, and individuals receiving distributions from QSTPs, are proposed (published in the Federal Register on August 24, 1998) (REG-106177-97).

☐ Par. 2. An undesignated center heading [Qualified State Tuition Programs] and §§1.529-0 through 1.529-6 are added to read as follows:

§1.529-0. Table of contents.—This section lists the following captions contained in §§1.529-1 through 1.529-6:

§1.529-1. Qualified State tuition program, unrelated business income tax and definitions.—(a) *In general.*—A qualified State tuition program (QSTP) described in section 529 is exempt from income tax, except for the tax imposed under section 511 on the QSTP's unrelated business taxable income. A QSTP is not required to file Form 990, Return of Organization Exempt From Income Tax, Form 1041, U.S. Income Tax Return for Estates and Trusts, or Form 1120, U.S. Corporation Income Tax Return. A QSTP may be required to file Form 990-T, Exempt Organization Business Income Tax Return. See §§1.6012-2(e) and 1.6012-3(a)(5) for requirements for filing Form 990-T.

(b) *Unrelated business income tax rules.*—For purposes of section 529, this section and §§1.529-2 through 1.529-6:

(1) *Application of section 514.*—An interest in a QSTP shall not be treated as debt for purposes of section 514. Consequently, a QSTP's investment income will not constitute debt-financed income subject to the unrelated business income tax merely because the program accepts contributions and is obligated to pay out or refund such contributions and certain earnings attributable thereto to designated beneficiaries or to account owners. However, investment income of a QSTP shall be subject to the unrelated business income tax as debt-financed income to the extent the program incurs indebtedness when acquiring or improving income-producing property.

(2) *Penalties and forfeitures.*—Earnings forfeited on prepaid educational arrangements or contracts and educational savings accounts and retained by a QSTP, or amounts collected by a QSTP as penalties on refunds or excess contributions are not unrelated business income to the QSTP.

(3) *Administrative and other fees.*—Amounts paid, in order to open or maintain prepaid educational arrangements or contracts and educational savings accounts, as administrative or maintenance fees, and other similar fees including late fees, service charges, and finance charges, are not unrelated business income to the QSTP.

(c) *Definitions.*—For purposes of section 529, this section and §§ 1.529-2 through 1.529-6:

Account means the formal record of transactions relating to a particular designated beneficiary when it is used alone without further modification in these regulations. The term includes prepaid educational arrangements or contracts described in section 529(b)(1)(A)(i) and educational savings accounts described in section 529(b)(1)(A)(ii).

Account owner means the person who, under the terms of the QSTP or any contract setting forth the terms under which contributions may be made to an account for the benefit of a designated beneficiary, is entitled to select or change the designated beneficiary of an account, to designate any person other than the designated beneficiary to whom funds may be paid from the account, or to receive distributions from the account if no such other person is designated.

Contribution means any payment directly allocated to an account for the benefit of a designated beneficiary or used to pay late fees or administrative fees associated with the account. In the case of a tax-free *rollover*, within the meaning of this paragraph (c), into a QSTP account, only the portion of the rollover amount that constituted *investment in the account*, within the meaning of this paragraph (c), is treated as a contribution to the account as required by § 1.529-3(a)(2).

Designated beneficiary means—

(1) The individual designated as the beneficiary of the account at the time an account is established with the QSTP;

(2) The individual who is designated as the new beneficiary when beneficiaries are changed; and

(3) The individual receiving the benefits accumulated in the account as a scholarship in the case of a QSTP account established by a State or local government or an organization described in section 501(c)(3) and exempt from taxation under section 501(a) as part of a scholarship program operated by such government or organization.

Distributee means the designated beneficiary or the account owner who receives or is treated as receiving a distribution from a QSTP. For example, if a QSTP makes a distribution directly to an eligible educational institution to pay tuition and fees for a designated beneficiary or a QSTP makes a distribution in the form of a check payable to both a designated beneficiary and an eligible educational institution, the distribution shall be treated as having been made in full to the designated beneficiary.

Distribution means any disbursement, whether in cash or in-kind, from a QSTP. Distributions include, but are not limited to, tuition credits or certificates, payment vouchers, tuition waivers or other similar items. Distributions also include, but are not limited to, a refund to the account owner, the designated beneficiary or the designated beneficiary's estate.

Earnings attributable to an account are the total account balance on a particular date minus the investment in the account as of that date.

Earnings ratio means the amount of earnings allocable to the account on the last day of the calendar year divided by the total account balance on the last day of that calendar year. The earnings ratio is applied to any distribution made during the calendar year. For purposes of computing the earnings ratio, the earnings allocable to the account on the last day of the calendar year and the total account balance on the last day of the calendar year include all distributions made during the calendar year and any amounts that have been forfeited from the account during the calendar year.

Eligible educational institution means an institution which is described in section 481 of the Higher Education Act of 1965 (20 U.S.C 1088) as in effect on August 5, 1997, and which is eligible to participate in a program under title IV of such Act. Such institutions generally are accredited post-secondary educational institutions offering credit toward a bachelor's degree, an associate's degree, a graduate level or professional degree, or another recognized post-secondary credential. Certain proprietary institutions and post-secondary vocational institutions also are eligible institutions. The institution must be eligible to participate in Department of Education student aid programs.

Final distribution means the distribution from a QSTP account that reduces the total account balance to zero.

Forfeit means that earnings and contributions allocable to a QSTP account are withdrawn by the QSTP from the account or deducted by the QSTP from a distribution to pay a penalty as required by § 1.529-2(e).

Investment in the account means the sum of all contributions made to the account on or before a particular date less the aggregate amount of contributions included in distributions, if any, made from the account on or before that date.

Member of the family means an individual who is related to the designated beneficiary as described in paragraphs (1) through (9) of this definition. For purposes of determining who is a member of the family, a legally adopted child of an individual shall be treated as the child of such individual by blood. The terms brother and sister

include a brother or sister by the halfblood. Member of the family means—

(1) A son or daughter, or a descendant of either;

(2) A stepson or stepdaughter;

(3) A brother, sister, stepbrother, or stepsister;

(4) The father or mother, or an ancestor of either;

(5) A stepfather or stepmother;

(6) A son or daughter of a brother or sister;

(7) A brother or sister of the father or mother;

(8) A son-in-law, daughter-in-law, father-in-law, mother-in-law, brother-in-law, or sister-in-law; or

(9) The spouse of the designated beneficiary or the spouse of any individual described in paragraphs (1) through (8) of this definition.

Person has the same meaning as under section 7701(a)(1).

Qualified higher education expenses means—

(1) Tuition, fees, and the costs of books, supplies, and equipment required for the enrollment or attendance of a designated beneficiary at an eligible educational institution; and

(2) The costs of room and board (as limited by paragraph (2)(i) of this definition) of a designated beneficiary (who meets requirements of paragraph (2)(ii) of this definition) incurred while attending an eligible educational institution:

(i) The amount of room and board treated as qualified higher education expenses shall not exceed the minimum room and board allowance determined in calculating costs of attendance for Federal financial aid programs under section 472 of the Higher Education Act of 1965 (20 U.S.C. 1087ll) as in effect on August 5, 1997. For purposes of these regulations, room and board costs shall not exceed $1,500 per academic year for a designated beneficiary residing at home with parents or guardians. For a designated beneficiary residing in institutionally owned or operated housing, room and board costs shall not exceed the amount normally assessed most residents for room and board at the institution. For all other designated beneficiaries the amount shall not exceed $2,500 per academic year. For this purpose the term academic year has the same meaning as that term is given in 20 U.S.C. 1088(d) as in effect on August 5, 1997.

(ii) Room and board shall be treated as qualified higher education expenses for a designated beneficiary if they are incurred during any academic period during which the designated beneficiary is enrolled or accepted for enrollment in a degree, certificate, or other program (including a program of study abroad approved for credit by the eligible educational institution) that leads to a recognized educational credential awarded by an eligible educational institution. In addition, the designated beneficiary must be enrolled at least half-time. A student will be considered to be enrolled at least half-time if the student is enrolled for at least half the full-time academic workload for the course of study the student is pursuing as determined under the standards of the institution where the student is enrolled. The institution's standard for a full-time workload must equal or exceed the standard established by the Department of Education under the Higher Education Act and set forth in 34 CFR 674.2(b).

Rollover distribution means a distribution or transfer from an account of a designated beneficiary that is transferred to or deposited within 60 days of the distribution into an account of another individual who is a member of the family of the designated beneficiary. A distribution is not a rollover distribution unless there is a change in beneficiary. The new designated beneficiary's account may be in a QSTP in either the same State or a QSTP in another State.

Total account balance means the total amount or the total fair market value of tuition credits or certificates or similar benefits allocable to the account on a particular date. For purposes of computing the *earnings ratio*, the total account balance is adjusted as described in this paragraph (c).

[Reg. § 1.529-1.]

§ 1.529-2. Qualified State tuition program described.—(a) *In general.*—To be a QSTP, a program must satisfy the requirements described in paragraphs (a) through (i) of this section. A QSTP is a program established and maintained by a State or an agency or instrumentality of a State under which a person—

(1) May purchase tuition credits or certificates on behalf of a designated beneficiary that entitle the beneficiary to the waiver or payment of qualified higher education expenses of the beneficiary; or

(2) May make contributions to an account that is established for the purpose of meeting the qualified higher education expenses of the designated beneficiary of the account.

(b) *Established and maintained by a State or agency or instrumentality of a State.*—(1) *Established.*—A program is established by a State or an agency or instrumentality of a State if the program is initiated by State statute or regulation, or by an act of a State official or agency with the authority to act on behalf of the State.

(2) *Maintained.*—A program is maintained by a State or an agency or instrumentality of a State if

(i) The State or agency or instrumentality sets all of the terms and conditions of the program, including but not limited to who may contribute to the program, who may be a designated beneficiary of the program, what benefits the program may provide, when penalties will apply to refunds and what those penalties will be; and

(ii) The State or agency or instrumentality is actively involved on an ongoing basis in the administration of the program, including supervising all decisions relating to the investment of assets contributed to the program.

(3) *Actively involved.*—Factors that are relevant in determining whether a State, agency or instrumentality is actively involved include, but are not limited to: whether the State provides services or benefits (such as tax, student aid or other financial benefits) to account owners or designated beneficiaries that are not provided to persons who are not account owners or designated beneficiaries; whether the State or agency or instrumentality establishes detailed operating rules for administering the program; whether officials of the State or agency or instrumentality play a substantial role in the operation of the program, including selecting, supervising, monitoring, auditing, and terminating any private contractors that provide services under the program; whether the State or agency or instrumentality holds the private contractors that provide services under the program to the same standards and requirements that apply when private contractors handle funds that belong to the State or provide services to the State; whether the State provides funding for the program; and, whether the State or agency or instrumentality acts as trustee or holds program assets directly or for the benefit of the account owners or designated beneficiaries. If the State or an agency or instrumentality thereof exercises the same authority over the funds invested in the program as it does over the investments in or pool of funds of a State employees' defined benefit pension plan, then the State or agency or instrumentality will be considered actively involved on an ongoing basis in the administration of the program.

(c) *Permissible uses of contributions.*—Contributions to a QSTP can be placed into either a prepaid educational arrangement or contract described in section 529(b)(1)(A)(i) or an educational savings account described in section 529(b)(1)(A)(ii), or both, but cannot be placed into any other type of account.

(1) A prepaid educational services arrangement or contract is an account through which tuition credits or certificates or other rights are acquired that entitle the designated beneficiary of the account to the waiver or payment of qualified higher education expenses.

(2) An educational savings account is an account that is established exclusively for the purpose of meeting the qualified higher education expenses of a designated beneficiary.

(d) *Cash contributions.*—A program shall not be treated as a QSTP unless it provides that contributions may be made only in cash and not in property. A QSTP may accept payment, however, in cash, or by check, money order, credit card, or similar methods.

(e) *Penalties on refunds.*—(1) *General rule.*—A program shall not be treated as a QSTP unless it imposes a more than de minimis penalty on the earnings portion of any distribution from the program that is not—

(i) Used exclusively for qualified higher education expenses of the designated beneficiary;

(ii) Made on account of the death or disability of the designated beneficiary;

(iii) Made on account of the receipt of a scholarship (or allowance or payment described in section 135(d)(1)(B) or (C)) by the designated beneficiary to the extent the amount of the distribution does not exceed the amount of the scholarship, allowance, or payment; or

(iv) A rollover distribution.

(2) *More than de minimis penalty.*—(i) *In general.*—A penalty is more than de minimis if it is consistent with a program intended to assist individuals in saving exclusively for qualified higher education expenses. Except as provided in paragraph (e)(2)(ii) of this section, whether any particular penalty is more than de minimis depends on the facts and circumstances of the particular program, including the extent to which the penalty offsets the federal income tax benefit from having deferred income tax liability on the earnings portion of any distribution.

(ii) *Safe harbor.*—A penalty imposed on the earnings portion of a distribution is more than de minimis if it is equal to or greater than 10 percent of the earnings.

(3) *Separate distributions.*—For purposes of applying the penalty, any single distribution described in paragraph (e)(1) of this section will be treated as a separate distribution and not part of a single aggregated annual distribution by the program, notwithstanding the rules under § 1.529-3 and § 1.529-4.

(4) *Procedures for verifying use of distributions and imposing and collecting penalties.*—(i) *In general.*—To be treated as imposing a more than de minimis penalty as required in paragraph (e)(1) of this section, a program must implement practices and procedures to identify whether a distribution is subject to a penalty and collect any penalty that is due.

(ii) *Safe harbor.*—A program that falls within the safe harbor described in paragraphs (e)(4)(ii)(A) through (E) of this section will be treated as implementing practices and procedures to identify whether a more than de minimis penalty must be imposed as required in paragraph (e)(1) of this section.

(A) *Distributions treated as payments of qualified higher education expenses.*—The program treats distributions as being used to pay for qualified higher education expenses only if—

(1) The distribution is made directly to an eligible educational institution;

(2) The distribution is made in the form of a check payable to both the designated beneficiary and the eligible educational institution;

(3) The distribution is made after the designated beneficiary submits substantiation to show that the distribution is a reimbursement for qualified higher education expenses that the designated beneficiary has already paid and the program has a process for reviewing the validity of the substantiation prior to the distribution; or

(4) The designated beneficiary certifies prior to the distribution that the distribution will be expended for his or her qualified higher education expenses within a reasonable time after the distribution; the program requires the designated beneficiary to provide substantiation of payment of qualified higher education expenses within 30 days after making the distribution and has a process for reviewing the substantiation; and the program retains an account balance that is large enough to collect any penalty owed on the distribution if valid substantiation is not produced.

(B) *Treatment of all other distributions.*—The program collects a penalty on all distributions not treated as made to pay qualified higher education expenses except where—

(1) Prior to the distribution the program receives written third party confirmation that the designated beneficiary has died or become disabled or has received a scholarship (or allowance or payment described in section 135(d)(1)(B) or (C)) in an amount equal to the distribution; or

(2) Prior to the distribution the program receives a certification from the account owner that the distribution is being made because the designated beneficiary has died or become disabled or has received a scholarship (or allowance or payment described in section 135(d)(1)(B) or (C)) received by the designated beneficiary (and the distribution is equal to the amount of the scholarship, allowance, or payment) and the program withholds and reserves a portion of the distribution as a penalty. Any penalty withheld by the program may be refunded after the program receives third party confirmation that the designated beneficiary has died or become disabled or has received a scholarship or allowance (or payment described in section 135(d)(1)(B) or (C)).

(C) *Refunds of penalties.*—The program will refund a penalty collected on a distribution only after the designated beneficiary substantiates that he or she had qualified higher education expenses greater than or equal to the distribution, and the program has reviewed the substantiation.

(D) *Documentation of amounts refunded and not used for qualified higher education expenses.*—The program requires the distributee, defined in § 1.529-1(c), to provide a signed statement identifying the amount of any refunds received from eligible educational institutions at the end of each year in which distributions for qualified higher education expenses were made and of the next year.

(E) *Procedures to collect penalty.*—The program collects required penalties by retaining a sufficient balance in the account to pay the amount of penalty, withholding an amount equal to the penalty from a distribution, or collecting the penalty on a State income tax return.

(f) *Separate accounting.*—A program shall not be treated as a QSTP unless it provides separate accounting for each designated beneficiary. Separate accounting requires that contributions for the benefit of a designated beneficiary and any earnings attributable thereto must be allocated to the appropriate account. If a program does not ordinarily provide each account owner an annual account statement showing the total account balance, the investment in the account, earnings, and distributions from the account, the program must give this information to the account owner or designated beneficiary upon request. In the case of a prepaid educational arrangement or contract described in section 529(b)(1)(A)(i) the total account balance may be shown as credits or units of benefits instead of fair market value.

(g) *No investment direction.*—A program shall not be treated as a QSTP unless it provides that any account owner in, or contributor to, or designated beneficiary under, such program may not directly or indirectly direct the investment of any contribution to the program or directly or indirectly direct the investment of any earnings attributable to contributions. A program does not violate this requirement if a person who establishes an account with the program is permitted to select among different investment strategies designed exclusively by the program, only at the time the initial contribution is made establishing the account. A program will not violate the requirement of this paragraph (g) if it permits a person who establishes an account to select between a prepaid educational services account and an educational savings account. A program also will not violate the requirement of this paragraph (g) merely because it permits its board members, its employees, or the board members or employees of a contractor it hires to perform administrative services to purchase tuition credits or certificates or make contributions as described in paragraph (c) of this section.

(h) *No pledging of interest as security.*—A program shall not be treated as a QSTP unless the terms of the program or a state statute or regulation that governs the program prohibit any interest in the program or any portion thereof from being used as security for a loan. This restriction includes, but is not limited to, a prohibition on the use of any interest in the program as security for a loan used to purchase such interest in the program.

(i) *Prohibition on excess contributions.*—(1) *In general.*—A program shall not be treated as a QSTP unless it provides adequate safeguards to prevent contributions for the benefit of a designated beneficiary in excess of those necessary to provide for the qualified higher education expenses of the designated beneficiary.

(2) *Safe harbor.*—A program satisfies this requirement if it will bar any additional contributions to an account as soon as the account reaches a specified account balance limit applicable to all accounts of designated beneficiaries with the same expected year of enrollment. The total contributions may not exceed the amount determined by actuarial estimates that is necessary to pay tuition, required fees, and room and board expenses of the designated beneficiary for five years of undergraduate enrollment at the highest cost institution allowed by the program. [Reg. § 1.529-2.]

§ 1.529-3. Income tax treatment of distributees.—(a) *Taxation of distributions.*—(1) *In general.*—Any distribution, other than a rollover distribution, from a QSTP account must be included in the gross income of the distributee to the extent of the earnings portion of the distribution and to the extent not excluded from gross income under any other provision of chapter 1 of the Internal Revenue Code. If any amount of a distribution is forfeited under a QSTP as required by § 1.529-2(e), this amount is neither included in the gross income of the distributee nor deductible by the distributee.

(2) *Rollover distributions.*—No part of a rollover distribution is included in the income of the distributee. Following the rollover distribution, that portion of the rollover amount that constituted investment in the account, defined in § 1.529-1(c), of the account from which the distribution was made is added to the investment in the account of the account that received the distribution. That portion of the rollover amount that constituted earnings of the account that made the distribution is added to the earnings of the account that received the distribution.

(b) *Computing taxable earnings.*—(1) *Amount of taxable earnings in a distribution.*—(i) *Educational savings account.*—In the case of an educational savings account, the earnings portion of a distribution is equal to the product of the amount of the distribution and the earnings ratio, defined in § 1.529-1(c). The return of investment portion of the distribution is equal to the amount of the distribution minus the earnings portion of the distribution.

(ii) *Prepaid educational services account.*—In the case of a prepaid educational services account, the earnings portion of a distribution is equal to the value of the credits, hours, or other units of education distributed at the time of distribution minus the return of investment portion of the distribution. The value of the credits, hours, or other units of education may be based on the tuition waived or the cash distributed. The return of investment portion of the distribution is determined by dividing the investment in the account at the end of the year in which the distribution is made by the number of credits, hours, or other units of education in the account at the end of the calendar year (including all credits, hours, or other units of education distributed during the calendar year), and multiplying that amount by the number of credits, hours, or other units of education distributed during the current calendar year.

(2) *Adjustment for programs that treated distributions and earnings in a different manner for years beginning before January 1, 1999.*—For calendar years beginning after December 31, 1998, a QSTP must treat taxpayers as recovering investment in the account and earnings ratably with each distribution. Prior to January 1, 1999, a program may have treated distributions in a different manner and reported them to taxpayers accordingly. In order to adjust to the method described in this section, if distributions were treated as coming first from the investment in the account, the QSTP must adjust the investment in the account by subtracting the amount of the investment in the account previously treated as distributed. If distributions were treated as coming first from earnings, the QSTP must adjust the earnings portion of the account by subtracting the amount of earnings previously treated as distributed. After the adjustment is made, the investment in the account is recovered ratably in accordance with this section. If no previous distribution was made but earnings were treated as taxable to the taxpayer in the year they were allocated to the account, the earnings treated as already taxable are treated as additional contributions and added to the investment in the account.

(3) *Examples.*—The application of this paragraph (b) is illustrated by the following examples. The rounding convention used (rounding to three decimal places) in these examples is for purposes of illustration only. A QSTP may use another rounding convention as long as it consistently applies the convention. The examples are as follows:

Example 1. (i) In 1998, an individual, A, opens a prepaid educational services account with a QSTP on behalf of a designated beneficiary. Through the account A purchases units of education equivalent to eight semesters of tuition for full-time attendance at a public four-year university covered by the QSTP. A contributes $16,000 that includes payment of processing fees to the QSTP. In 2011 the designated beneficiary enrolls at a public four-year university. The QSTP makes distributions on behalf of the designated beneficiary to the university in August for the fall semester and in December for the spring semester. Tuition for full-time attendance at the university is $7,500 per academic year in 2011 and 2012, $7,875 for the academic year in 2013, and $8,200 for the academic year in 2014. The only expense covered by the QSTP distribution is tuition for four academic years. The calculations are as follows:

2011

Investment in the account as of 12/31/2011	=	$16,000
Units in account	=	8
Per unit investment	=	$2,000
Units distributed in 2011	=	2
Investment portion of distribution in 2011 ($2,000 per unit × 2 units)	=	$4,000
Current value of two units distributed in 2011	=	$7,500
Earnings portion of distribution in 2011 ($7,500 - $4,000)	=	$3,500

2012

Investment in the account as of 12/31/2012 ($16,000-$4,000)	=	$12,000
Units in account	=	6
Per unit investment	=	$2,000
Units distributed in 2012	=	2
Investment portion of distribution in 2012 ($2,000 per unit × 2 units)	=	$4,000
Current value of two units		

distributed in 2012	=	$7,500
Earnings portion of distribution in 2012 ($7,500 - $4,000)	=	$3,500

2013

Investment in the account as of 12/31/2013 ($12,000-$4000)	=	$8,000
Units in account	=	4
Per unit investment	=	$2,000
Units distributed in 2013	=	2
Investment portion of distribution in 2013 ($2,000 per unit × 2 units)	=	$4,000
Current value of two units distributed in 2013	=	$7,875
Earnings portion of distribution in 2013 ($7,875 - $4,000)	=	$3,875

2014

Investment in the account as of 12/31/2014 ($8,000-$4000)	=	$4,000
Units in account	=	2
Per unit investment	=	$2,000
Units distributed in 2014	=	2
Investment portion of distribution in 2014 ($4,000 per unit × 2 units)	=	$4,000
Current value of two units distributed in 2014	=	$8,200
Earnings portion of distribution in 2014 ($8,200 - $4,000)	=	$4,200

12/31/2014 (after distributions)

Investment in the account as of 12/31/2014 ($4,000-$4000)	=	0

(ii) In each year the designated beneficiary includes in his or her gross income the earnings portion of the distribution for tuition.

Example 2. (i) In 1998, an individual, B, opens a college savings account with a QSTP on behalf of a designated beneficiary. B contributes $18,000 to the account that includes payment of processing fees to the QSTP. On December 31, 2011, the total balance in the account for the benefit of the designated beneficiary is $30,000 (including distributions made during the year 2011). In 2011 the designated beneficiary enrolls at a four-year university. The QSTP makes distributions on behalf of the designated beneficiary to the university in August for the fall semester and in December for the spring semester. Tuition for full-time attendance at the university is $7,500 per academic year in 2011 and 2012, $7,875 for the academic year in 2013, and $8,200 for the academic year in 2014. The only expense covered by the QSTP distributions is tuition for four academic years. On the last day of the calendar year the account is allocated earnings of 5% on the total account balance on that day. Under the terms of the QSTP, a penalty of 15% is applied to the earnings not used to pay tuition. The calculations are as follows:

2011

Investment in the account	=	$18,000
Total account balance as of 12/31/2011	=	$30,000
Earnings as of 12/31/2011	=	$12,000
Distributions in 2011	=	$7,500
Earnings ratio for 2011 ($12,000 ÷ $30,000)	=	40%
Earnings portion of distributions in 2011 ($7,500 × .4)	=	$3,000
Return of investment portion of distributions in 2011 ($7,500 - $3,000)	=	$4,500

2012

Investment in the account as of 12/31/2012 ($18,000 - $4,500)	=	$13,500
Total account balance as of 12/31/12 [($30,000-$7,500) × 105%]	=	$23,625
Earnings as of 12/31/2012	=	$10,125
Distributions in 2012	=	$7,500
Earnings ratio for 2012 ($10,125 ÷ $23,625)	=	42.9%
Earnings portion of distributions in 2012 ($7,500 × .429)	=	$3,217.50
Return of investment portion of distributions in 2012 ($7,500 - $3,217.50)	=	$4,282.50

2013

Investment in the account as of 12/31/2013 ($13,500 - $4,282.50)	=	$9,217.50
Total account balance as of 12/31/13 [($23,625-$7,500) × 105%]	=	$16,931.25
Earnings as of 12/31/2013	=	$7,713.75
Distributions in 2013	=	$7,875
Earnings ratio for 2013 ($7,713.75 ÷ $16,931.25)	=	45.6%
Earnings portion of distributions in 2013 ($7,875 × .456)	=	$3,591
Return of investment portion of distributions in 2013 ($7,875 - $3,591)	=	$4,284

2014

Investment in the account as of 12/31/2014 ($9,217.50 - $4,284)	=	$4,933.50

Total account balance as of 12/31/14		
[($16,931.25 - $7,875) × 105%]	=	$9,509.06
Earnings as of 12/31/2014	=	$4,575.56
Distributions in 2014 for qualified higher education expenses (QHEE)	=	$8,200
Distributions in 2014 not for qualified higher education expenses (Non-QHEE)	=	$1,309.06
Total distributions	=	$9,509.06
Earnings portion of QHEE distribution in 2014 [($8,200 ÷ $9,509.06) × $4,575.56]	=	$3,945.68
Return of investment portion of QHEE distribution in 2014	=	$4,254.32
Earnings portion of Non-QHEE distribution subject to penalty [($1,309.06 ÷ $9,509.06) × $4,575.56)]	=	$629.89
Return of investment portion of non-QHEE distribution in 2014	=	$679.17

(ii) In years 2011 through 2013 the designated beneficiary includes in gross income the earnings portion of the distributions for tuition. In year 2014 the designated beneficiary includes in gross income the earnings portion of the distribution for tuition, $3,945.68, plus the earnings portion of the distribution that was not used for tuition after reduction for the penalty, i.e. $535.41 ($629.89 minus a 15% penalty of $94.48).

(c) *Change in designated beneficiaries.*—(1) *General rule.*—A change in the designated beneficiary of a QSTP account is not treated as a distribution if the new designated beneficiary is a member of the family of the transferor designated beneficiary. However, any change of designated beneficiary not described in the preceding sentence is treated as a distribution to the account owner, provided the account owner has the authority to change the designated beneficiary. For rules related to a change in the designated beneficiary pursuant to a rollover distribution see §§ 1.529-1(c) and 1.529-3(a)(2).

(2) *Scholarship program.*—Notwithstanding paragraph (c)(1) of this section, the requirement that the new beneficiary be a member of the family of the transferor beneficiary shall not apply to a change in designated beneficiary of an interest in a QSTP account purchased by a State or local government or an organization described in section 501(c)(3) as part of a scholarship program.

(d) *Aggregation of accounts.*—If an individual is a designated beneficiary of more than one account under a QSTP, the QSTP shall treat all contributions and earnings as allocable to a single account for purposes of calculating the earnings portion of any distribution from that QSTP. For purposes of determining the effect of the distribution on each account, the earnings portion and return of investment in the account portion of the distribution shall be allocated pro rata among the accounts based on total account value as of the close of the current calendar year. [Reg. § 1.529-3.]

§ 1.529-4. Time, form, and manner of reporting distributions from QSTPs and backup withholding.—(a) *Taxable distributions.*—The portion of any distribution made during the calendar year by a QSTP that represents earnings shall be reported by the payor as described in this section.

(b) *Requirement to file return.*—(1) *Form of return.*—A payor must file a return required by this section on Form 1099-G. A payor may use forms containing provisions similar to Form 1099-G if it complies with applicable revenue procedures relating to substitute Forms 1099. A payor must file a separate return for each distributee who receives a taxable distribution.

(2) *Payor.*—For purposes of this section, the term "payor" means the officer or employee having control of the program, or their designee.

(3) *Information included on return.*—A payor must include on Form 1099-G—

(i) The name, address, and taxpayer identifying number (TIN) (as defined in section 7701(a)(41)) of the payor;

(ii) The name, address, and TIN of the distributee;

(iii) The amount of earnings distributed to the distributee in the calendar year; and

(iv) Any other information required by Form 1099-G or its instructions.

(4) *Time and place for filing return.*—A payor must file any return required by this paragraph (b) on or before February 28 of the year following the calendar year in which the distribution is made. A payor must file the return with the IRS office designated in the instructions for Form 1099-G.

(5) *Returns required on magnetic media.*—If a payor is required to file at least 250 returns during the calendar year, the returns must be filed on magnetic media. If a payor is required to file fewer than 250 returns, the prescribed paper form may be used.

(6) *Extension of time to file return.*—For good cause, the Commissioner may grant an extension of time in which to file Form 1099-G for reporting taxable earnings under section 529. The application for extension of time must be submitted in the manner prescribed by the Commissioner.

(c) *Requirement to furnish statement to the distributee.*—(1) *In general.*—A payor that must file a return under paragraph (b) of this section must furnish a statement to the distributee. The requirement to furnish a statement to the distributee will be satisfied if the payor provides the distributee with a copy of the Form 1099-G (or a substitute statement that complies with applicable revenue procedures) containing all the information filed with the Internal Revenue Service and all the legends required by paragraph (c)(2) of this section by the time required by paragraph (c)(3) of this section.

(2) *Information included on statement.*—A payor must include on the statement that it must furnish to the distributee—

(i) The information required under paragraph (b)(3) of this section;

(ii) The telephone number of a person to contact about questions pertaining to the statement; and

(iii) A legend as required on the official Internal Revenue Service Form 1099-G.

(3) *Time for furnishing statement.*—A payor must furnish the statement required by paragraph (c)(1) of this section to the distributee on or before January 31 of the year following the calendar year in which the distribution was made. The statement will be considered furnished to the distributee if it is mailed to the distributee's last known address.

(4) *Extension of time to furnish statement.*—For good cause, the Commissioner may grant an extension of time to furnish statements to distributees of taxable earnings under section 529. The application for extension of time must be submitted in the manner prescribed by the Commissioner.

(d) *Backup withholding.*—Distributions from a QSTP are not subject to backup withholding.

(e) *Effective date.*—The reporting requirements set forth in this section apply to distributions made after December 31, 1998. [Reg. § 1.529-4.]

§ 1.529-5. Estate, gift, and generation-skipping transfer tax rules relating to qualified State tuition programs.—(a) *Gift and generation-skipping transfer tax treatment of contributions after August 20, 1996, and before August 6, 1997.*—A contribution on behalf of a designated beneficiary to a QSTP (or to a program that meets the transitional rule requirements under § 1.529-6(b)) after August 20, 1996, and before August 6, 1997, is not treated as a taxable gift. The subsequent waiver of qualified higher education expenses of a designated beneficiary by an educational institution (or the subsequent payment of higher education expenses of a designated beneficiary to an educational institution) under a QSTP is treated as a qualified transfer under section 2503(e) and is not treated as a transfer of property by gift for purposes of section 2501. As such, the contribution is not subject to the generation-skipping transfer tax imposed by section 2601.

(b) *Gift and generation-skipping transfer tax treatment of contributions after August 5, 1997.*—(1) *In general.*—A contribution on behalf of a designated beneficiary to a QSTP (or to a program that meets the transitional rule requirements under § 1.529-6(b)) after August 5, 1997, is a completed gift of a present interest in property under section 2503(b) from the person making the contribution to the designated beneficiary. As such, the contribution is eligible for the annual gift tax exclusion provided under section 2503(b). The portion of a contribution excludible from taxable gifts under section 2503(b) also satisfies the requirements of section 2642(c)(2) and, therefore, is also excludible for purposes of the generation-skipping transfer tax imposed under section 2601. A contribution to a QSTP after August 5, 1997, is not treated as a qualified transfer within the meaning of section 2503(e).

(2) *Contributions that exceed the annual exclusion amount.*— (i) Under section 529(c)(2)(B) a donor may elect to take certain contributions to a QSTP into account ratably over a five year period in determining the amount of gifts made during the calendar year. The provision is applicable only with respect to contributions not in excess of five times the section 2503(b) exclusion amount available in the calendar year of the contribution. Any excess may not be taken into account ratably and is treated as a taxable gift in the calendar year of the contribution.

(ii) The election under section 529(c)(2)(B) may be made by a donor and his or her spouse with respect to a gift considered to be made one-half by each spouse under section 2513.

(iii) The election is made on Form 709, Federal Gift Tax Return, for the calendar year in which the contribution is made.

(iv) If in any year after the first year of the five year period described in section 529(c)(2)(B), the amount excludible under section 2503(b) is increased as provided in section 2503(b)(2), the donor may make an additional contribution in any one or more of the four remaining years up to the difference between the exclusion amount as increased and the original exclusion amount for the year or years in which the original contribution was made.

(v) *Example.*—The application of this paragraph (b)(2) is illustrated by the following example:

Example. In Year 1, when the annual exclusion under section 2503(b) is $10,000, P makes a contribution of $60,000 to a QSTP for the benefit of P's child, C. P elects under section 529(c)(2)(B) to account for the gift ratably over a five year period beginning with the calendar year of contribution. P is treated as making an excludible gift of $10,000 in each of Years 1 through 5 and a taxable gift of $10,000 in Year 1. In Year 3, when the annual exclusion is increased to $12,000, P makes an additional contribution for the benefit of C in the amount of $8,000. P is treated as making an excludible gift of $2,000 under section 2503(b); the remaining $6,000 is a taxable gift in Year 3.

(3) *Change of designated beneficiary or rollover.*—(i) A transfer which occurs by reason of a change in the designated beneficiary, or a rollover of credits or account balances from the account of one beneficiary to the account of another beneficiary, is not a taxable gift and is not subject to the generation-skipping transfer tax if the new beneficiary is a member of the family of the old beneficiary, as defined in §1.529-1(c), and is assigned to the same generation as the old beneficiary, as defined in section 2651.

(ii) A transfer which occurs by reason of a change in the designated beneficiary, or a rollover of credits or account balances from the account of one beneficiary to the account of another beneficiary, will be treated as a taxable gift by the old beneficiary to the new beneficiary if the new beneficiary is assigned to a lower generation than the old beneficiary, as defined in section 2651, regardless of whether the new beneficiary is a member of the family of the old beneficiary. The transfer will be subject to the generation-skipping transfer tax if the new beneficiary is assigned to a generation which is two or more levels lower than the generation assignment of the old beneficiary. The five year averaging rule described in paragraph (b)(2) of this section may be applied to the transfer.

(iii) *Example.*—The application of this paragraph (b)(3) is illustrated by the following example:

Example. In Year 1, P makes a contribution to a QSTP on behalf of P's child, C. In Year 4, P directs that a distribution from the account for the benefit of C be made to an account for the benefit of P's grandchild, G. The rollover distribution is treated as a taxable gift by C to G, because, under section 2651, G is assigned to a generation below the generation assignment of C.

(c) *Estate tax treatment for estates of decedents dying after August 20, 1996, and before June 9, 1997.*—The gross estate of a decedent dying after August 20, 1996, and before June 9, 1997, includes the value of any interest in any QSTP which is attributable to contributions made by the decedent to such program on behalf of a designated beneficiary.

(d) *Estate tax treatment for estates of decedents dying after June 8, 1997.*—(1) *In general.*—Except as provided in paragraph (d)(2) of this section, the gross estate of a decedent dying after June 8, 1997, does not include the value of any interest in a QSTP which is attributable to contributions made by the decedent to such program on behalf of any designated beneficiary.

(2) *Excess contributions.*—In the case of a decedent who made the election under section 529(c)(2)(B) and paragraph (b)(3)(i) of this section who dies before the close of the five year period, that portion of the contribution allocable to calendar years beginning after the date of death of the decedent is includible in the decedent's gross estate.

(3) *Designated beneficiary decedents.*—The gross estate of a designated beneficiary of a QSTP includes the value of any interest in the QSTP. [Reg. §1.529-5.]

§1.529-6. Transition rules.—(a) *Effective date.*—Section 529 is effective for taxable years ending after August 20, 1996, and applies to all contracts entered into or accounts opened on August 20, 1996, or later.

(b) *Programs maintained on August 20, 1996.*—Transition relief is available to a program maintained by a State under which persons could purchase tuition credits, certification or similar rights on behalf of, or make contributions for educational expenses of, a designated beneficiary if the program was in existence on August 20, 1996. Such program must meet the requirements of a QSTP before the later of August 20, 1997, or the first day of the first calendar quarter after the close of the first regular session of the State legislature that begins after August 20, 1996. If a State has a two-year legislative session, each year of such session shall be deemed to be a separate regular session of the State legislature. The program, as in effect on August 20, 1996, shall be treated as a QSTP with respect to contributions (and earnings allocable thereto) pursuant to contracts entered into under the program. This relief is available for contributions (and earnings allocable thereto) made before, and the contracts entered into before, the first date on which the program becomes a QSTP. The provisions of the program, as in effect on August 20, 1996, shall apply in lieu of section 529(b) with respect to such contributions and earnings. A program shall be treated as meeting the transition rule if it conforms to the requirements of section 529, §§1.529-1 through 1.529-5 and this section by the date this document is published as final regulations in the Federal Register.

(c) *Retroactive effect.*—No income tax liability will be asserted against a QSTP for any period before the program meets the requirements of section 529, §§1.529-1 through 1.529-5 and this section if the program qualifies for the transition relief described in paragraph (b) of this section.

(d) *Contracts entered into and accounts opened before August 20, 1996.*—(1) *In general.*—A QSTP may continue to maintain agreements in connection with contracts entered into and accounts opened before August 20, 1996, without jeopardizing its tax exempt status even if maintaining the agreements is contrary to section 529(b) provided that the QSTP operates in accordance with the restrictions contained in this paragraph (d). However, distributions made by the QSTP, regardless of the terms of any agreement executed before August 20, 1996, are subject to tax according to the rules of §1.529-3 and subject to the reporting requirements of §1.529-4.

(2) *Interest in program pledged as security for a loan.*—An interest in the program, or a portion of an interest in the program, may be used as security for a loan if the contract giving rise to the interest was entered into or account was opened prior to August 20, 1996 and the agreement permitted such a pledge.

(3) *Member of the family.*—In the case of an account opened or a contract entered into before August 20, 1996, the rules regarding a change in beneficiary, including the rollover rule in §1.529-3(a) and the gift tax rule in §1.529-5(b)(3), shall be applied by treating any transferee beneficiary permitted under the terms of the account or contract as a member of the family of the transferor beneficiary.

(4) *Eligible educational institution.*—In the case of an account opened or contract entered into before August 20, 1996, an eligible educational institution is an educational institution in which the beneficiary may enroll under the terms of the account or contract. [Reg. §1.529-6.]

ABLE Accounts: Contribution Limits

ABLE Accounts: Contribution Limits.—Amendments to Reg. §§1.529A-0 and 1.529A-1, containing proposed regulations related to the Internal Revenue Code, which allows a State (or its agency or instrumentality) to establish and maintain a tax-advantaged savings program under which contributions may be made to an ABLE account for the purpose of paying for the qualified disability expenses of the designated beneficiary of the account, are proposed (published in the Federal Register on October 10, 2019) (REG-128246-18).

Par. 2. Section 1.529A-0, as proposed to be added at 80 FR 35602, June 22, 2015, is further amended by adding an entry for §1.529A-8 in numerical order to read as follows:

§1.529A-0. Table of contents.

* * *

§1.529A-8 Additional contributions to ABLE accounts made by an employed designated beneficiary.

(a) Additional contributions to ABLE accounts made by an employed designated beneficiary.

(1) In general.

(2) Amount of additional contribution.

(b) Additional definitions.

(1) Employed designated beneficiary.

(2) Applicable poverty line.

(3) Excess compensation contribution.

(c) Example.

(d) Responsibility for ensuring contribution limit is met.

(e) Return of excess compensation contributions.

(f) Applicability date.

Par.3. Section 1.529A-1, as proposed to be added at 80 FR 35602, June 22, 2015, is further amended by revising paragraph (b)(3) to read as follows:

§1.529A-1. Exempt status of qualified ABLE program and definitions.

* * *

(b) * * *

(3) *Contribution* means any payment directly allocated to an ABLE account for the benefit of the designated beneficiary, including amounts transferred from a qualified tuition program under section 529 after December 22, 2017 and before January 1, 2026. * * *

Guidance under Section 529A: Qualified ABLE Programs

Guidance under Section 529A: Qualified ABLE Programs.—Reg. §§1.529A-0—1.529A-7, regarding programs under The Stephen Beck, Jr., Achieving a Better Life Experience Act of 2014 and rules under which States or State agencies or instrumentalities may establish and maintain a new type of tax-favored savings program through which contributions may be made to the account of an eligible disabled individual to meet qualified disability expenses, are proposed (published in the Federal Register on June 22, 2015) (corrected August 7, 2015) (REG-102837-15).

Par. 4. An undesignated center heading [Qualified ABLE Programs] is added immediately following §1.528-10 and §§1.529A-0 through 1.529A-7 are added to read as follows:

§1.529A-0. Table of contents.—This section lists the following captions contained in §§1.529A-1 through 1.529A-7.

§1.529A-1 Exempt status of qualified ABLE program and definitions.

(a) In general.

(b) Definitions.

(1) ABLE account.

(2) Contracting State.

(3) Contribution.

(4) Designated beneficiary.

(5) Disability certification.

(6) Distribution.

(7) Earnings.

(8) Earnings ratio.

(9) Eligible individual.

(10) Excess contribution.

(11) Excess aggregate contribution.

(12) Investment in the account.

(13) Member of the family.

(14) Program-to-program transfer.

(15) Qualified ABLE program.

(16) Qualified disability expenses.

(17) Rollover.

(c) Effective/applicability date.

§1.529A-2 Qualified ABLE program.

(a) In general.

(b) Established and maintained by a State or agency or instrumentality of a State. 36

(1) Established.

(2) Maintained.

(3) Community Development Financial Institutions (CDFIs).

(c) Establishment of an ABLE account.

(1) In general.

(2) Only one ABLE account.

(3) Beneficial interest.

(d) Eligible individual.

(1) In general.

(2) Frequency of recertification.

(3) Loss of qualification as an eligible individual.

(e) Disability certification.

(1) In general.

(2) Marked and severe functional limitations.

(3) Compassionate allowance list.

(4) Additional guidance.

(5) Restriction on use of certification.

(f) Change of designated beneficiary.

(g) Contributions.

(1) Permissible property.

(2) Annual contributions limit.

(3) Cumulative limit.

(4) Return of excess contributions and excess aggregate contributions.

(h) Qualified disability expenses.

(1) In general.

(2) Example.

(i) Separate accounting.

(j) Program-to-program transfers.

(k) Carryover of attributes.

(l) Investment direction.

(m) No pledging of interest as security.

(n) No sale or exchange.

(o) Change of residence.

(p) Post-death payments.

(q) Reporting requirements.

(r) Effective/applicability date.

§1.529A-3 Tax treatment.

(a) Taxation of distributions.

(b) Additional exclusions from gross income.

(1) Rollover.

(2) Program-to-program transfers.

(3) Change in designated beneficiary.

(4) Payments to creditors post-death.

(c) Computation of earnings.

(d) Additional tax on amounts includible in gross income.

(1) In general.

(2) Exceptions.

(e) Tax on excess contributions.

(f) Filing requirements.

(g) Effective/applicability date.

§1.529A-4 Gift, estate, and generation-skipping transfer taxes.

(a) Contributions.

(1) In general.

(2) Generation-skipping transfer (GST) tax.

(3) Designated beneficiary as contributor.

(b) Distributions.

(c) Change of designated beneficiary.

(d) Transfer tax on death of designated beneficiary.

(e) Effective/applicability date.

§1.529A-5 Reporting of the establishment of and contributions to an ABLE account.

(a) In general.

(b) Additional definitions.

(1) Filer.

(2) TIN.

(c) Requirement to file return.

(1) Form of return.

(2) Information included on return.

(3) Time and manner of filing return.

(d) Requirement to furnish statement.

(1) In general.

(2) Time and manner of furnishing statement.

(3) Copy of Form 5498-QA.

(e) Request for TIN of designated beneficiary.

(f) Penalties.

    (1) Failure to file return.

    (2) Failure to furnish TIN.

(g) Effective/applicability date.

§1.529A-6 *Reporting of distributions from and termination of an ABLE account.*

(a) In general.

(b) Requirement to file return.

    (1) Form of return.

    (2) Information included on return.

    (3) Time and manner of filing return.

(c) Requirement to furnish statement.

    (1) In general.

    (2) Time and manner of furnishing statement.

    (3) Copy of Form 1099-QA.

(d) Request for TIN of contributor(s).

(e) Penalties.

    (1) Failure to file return.

    (2) Failure to furnish TIN.

(f) Effective/applicability date.

§1.529A-7 *Electronic furnishing of statements to designated beneficiaries and contributors.*

(a) Electronic furnishing of statements.

    (1) In general.

    (2) Consent.

    (3) Required disclosures.

    (4) Format.

    (5) Notice.

    (6) Access period.

(b) Effective/applicability date.

[Reg. §1.529A-0.]

§1.529A-1. Exempt status of qualified ABLE program and definitions.—(a) *In general.*—A qualified ABLE program described in section 529A is exempt from income tax, except for the tax imposed under section 511 on the unrelated business taxable income of that program.

(b) *Definitions.*—For purposes of section 529A, this section and §§1.529A-2 through 1.529A-7—

(1) *ABLE account* means an account established under a qualified ABLE program and owned by the designated beneficiary of that account.

(2) *Contracting State* means a State without a qualified ABLE program of its own, which, in order to make ABLE accounts available to its residents who are eligible individuals, contracts with another State having such a program.

(3) *Contribution* means any payment directly allocated to an ABLE account for the benefit of a designated beneficiary.

(4) *Designated beneficiary* means the individual who is the owner of the ABLE account and who either established the account at a time when he or she was an eligible individual or who has succeeded the former designated beneficiary in that capacity (successor designated beneficiary). If the designated beneficiary is not able to exercise signature authority over his or her ABLE account or chooses to establish an ABLE account but not exercise signature authority, references to the designated beneficiary with respect to his or her actions include actions by the designated beneficiary's agent under a power of attorney or, if none, a parent or legal guardian of the designated beneficiary.

(5) *Disability certification* means a certification deemed sufficient by the Secretary to establish a certain level of physical or mental impairment that meets the requirements described in §1.529A-2(e).

(6) *Distribution* means any payment from an ABLE account. A *program-to-program transfer* is not a distribution.

(7) *Earnings* attributable to an account are the excess of the total account balance on a particular date over the *investment in the account* as of that date.

(8) *Earnings ratio* means the amount of earnings attributable to the account as of the last day of the calendar year in which the designated beneficiary's taxable year begins, divided by the total account balance on that same date, after taking into account all distributions made during that calendar year and all contributions received during that same year other than those (if any) returned in accordance with §1.529A-2(g)(4).

(9) *Eligible individual* for a taxable year means an individual who either:

    (i) Is entitled during that taxable year to benefits based on blindness or disability under title II or XVI of the Social Security Act, provided that such blindness or disability occurred before the date on which the individual attained age 26 (and, for this purpose, an individual is deemed to attain age 26 on his or her 26th birthday); or

    (ii) Is the subject of a disability certification filed with the Secretary for that taxable year.

(10) *Excess contribution* means the amount by which the amount contributed during the taxable year of the designated beneficiary to an ABLE account exceeds the limit in effect under section 2503(b) for the calendar year in which the taxable year of the designated beneficiary begins.

(11) *Excess aggregate contribution* means the amount contributed during the taxable year of the designated beneficiary that causes the total of amounts contributed since the establishment of the ABLE account (or of an ABLE account for the same designated beneficiary that was rolled into the current ABLE account) to exceed the limit in effect under section 529(b)(6). In the context of the safe harbor in §1.529A-2(g)(3), however, excess aggregate contribution means a contribution that causes the account balance to exceed the limit in effect under section 529(b)(6).

(12) *Investment in the account* means the sum of all contributions made to the account, reduced by the aggregate amount of contributions included in distributions, if any, made from the account. In the case of a rollover into an ABLE account the amount included as investment in the recipient account is not the full amount of the rollover contribution, but instead is equal to the amount of the rollover contribution that constituted the investment in the account from which the rollover was made.

(13) *Member of the family* means a sibling, whether by blood or by adoption. Such term includes a brother, sister, stepbrother, stepsister, half-brother, and half-sister.

(14) *Program-to-program transfer* means the direct transfer of the entire balance of an ABLE account into an ABLE account of the same designated beneficiary in which the transferor ABLE account is closed upon completion of the transfer, or of part or all of the balance to an ABLE account of another eligible individual who is a member of the family of the former designated beneficiary, without any intervening distribution or deemed distribution to the designated beneficiary.

(15) *Qualified ABLE program* means a program established and maintained by a State, or agency or instrumentality of a State, under which an ABLE account may be established by and for the benefit of the account's designated beneficiary who is an eligible individual, and that meets the requirements described in §1.529A-2.

(16) *Qualified disability expenses* means any expenses incurred at a time when the designated beneficiary is an eligible individual that relate to the blindness or disability of the designated beneficiary of an ABLE account, including expenses that are for the benefit of the designated beneficiary in maintaining or improving his or her health, independence, or quality of life. *See* §1.529A-2(h). Any expenses incurred at a time when a designated beneficiary is neither disabled nor blind within the meaning of §1.529A-1(b)(9)(i) or §1.529A-2(e)(1)(i) are not qualified disability expenses.

(17) *Rollover* means a contribution to an ABLE account of a designated beneficiary (or of an eligible individual who is a member of the family of the designated beneficiary) of all or a portion of an amount withdrawn from the designated beneficiary's ABLE account, provided the contribution is made within 60 days of the date of the withdrawal and, in the case of a rollover to the designated beneficiary's ABLE account, no rollover has been made to an ABLE account of the designated beneficiary within the prior 12 months.

(c) *Effective/applicability date.*—This section applies to taxable years beginning after December 31, 2014. [Reg. §1.529A-1.]

§1.529A-2. Qualified ABLE program.—(a) *In general.*—A qualified ABLE program is a program established and maintained by a State, or an agency or instrumentality of a State, that satisfies all of the requirements of this section and under which—

(1) An ABLE account may be established for the purpose of meeting the qualified disability expenses of the designated beneficiary of the account;

(2) The designated beneficiary must be a resident of such State or a resident of a Contracting State (as residence is determined under the law of the State of the designated beneficiary's residence);

(3) A designated beneficiary is limited to only one ABLE account at a time except as otherwise provided with respect to program-to-program transfers and rollovers;

(4) Any person may make contributions to such an ABLE account, subject to the limitations described in paragraph (g) of this section; and

(5) Distributions (other than rollovers and returns of contributions as described in paragraph (g)(4) of this section) may be made only to or for the benefit of the designated beneficiary of the ABLE account.

(b) *Established and maintained by a State or agency or instrumentality of a State*—(1) *Established.*—A program is established by a State or its agency or instrumentality if the program is initiated by State statute or regulation or by an act of a State official or agency with the authority to act on behalf of the State.

(2) *Maintained.*—A program is maintained by a State or an agency or instrumentality of a State if—

(i) The State or its agency or instrumentality sets all of the terms and conditions of the program, including but not limited to who may contribute to the program, who may be a designated beneficiary of the program, and what benefits the program may provide; and

(ii) The State or its agency or instrumentality is actively involved on an ongoing basis in the administration of the program, including supervising the implementation of decisions relating to the investment of assets contributed under the program. Factors that are relevant in determining whether a State or its agency or instrumentality is actively involved in the administration of the program include, but are not limited to: whether the State or its agency or instrumentality provides services to designated beneficiaries that are not provided to persons who are not designated beneficiaries; whether the State or its agency or instrumentality establishes detailed operating rules for administering the program; whether officials of the State or its agency or instrumentality play a substantial role in the operation of the program, including selecting, supervising, monitoring, auditing, and terminating the relationship with any private contractors that provide services under the program; whether the State or its agency or instrumentality holds the private contractors that provide services under the program to the same standards and requirements that apply when private contractors handle funds that belong to the State or its agency or instrumentality or provide services to the State or its agency or instrumentality; whether the State or its agency or instrumentality provides funding for the program; and whether the State or its agency or instrumentality acts as trustee or holds program assets directly or for the benefit of the designated beneficiaries. For example, if the State or its agency or instrumentality thereof exercises the same authority over the funds invested in the program as it does over the investments in or pool of funds of a State employees' defined benefit pension plan, then the State or its agency or instrumentality will be considered actively involved on an ongoing basis in the administration of the program.

(3) *Community Development Financial Institutions (CDFIs).*—Some or all of the services described in paragraphs (b)(2)(i) and (ii) of this section may be performed by one or more Community Development Financial Institutions (CDFIs) with whom the State (or its agency or instrumentality) contracts for that purpose.

(c) *Establishment of an ABLE account.*—(1) *In general.*—Except as otherwise provided in this paragraph (c), a qualified ABLE program must provide that an ABLE account may be established only for an eligible individual under a qualified ABLE program of the State in which the eligible individual is a resident. The qualified ABLE program also may allow the establishment of an ABLE account for an eligible individual who is a resident of a *Contracting State* as defined in §1.529A-1(b)(2). If an eligible individual is unable to establish an ABLE account on his or her own behalf, the ABLE account may be established on behalf of the eligible individual by the eligible individual's agent under a power of attorney or, if none, by a parent or legal guardian of the eligible individual.

(2) *Only one ABLE account.*—(i) *In general.*—Except in the case of rollovers or program-to-program transfers, a designated beneficiary is limited to one ABLE account at a time, regardless of where located. To ensure that this requirement is met, a qualified ABLE program must obtain a verification, signed under penalties of perjury, that the eligible individual has no other existing ABLE account (other than an ABLE account that will terminate with the rollover or program-to-program transfer into the new ABLE account) before that program can permit the establishment of an ABLE account for that eligible individual. In the case of a rollover, the ABLE account from which amounts were rolled must be closed as of the 60th day after the amount was distributed from the ABLE account in order for the account that received the rollover to be treated as an ABLE account.

(ii) *Treatment of additional accounts.*—Except in the case of rollovers or program-to-program transfers, if an ABLE account is established for a designated beneficiary who already has an ABLE account in existence, an additional account will not be treated as an ABLE account. However, if all contributions made to that account are returned in accordance with the rules that apply to excess contributions and excess aggregate contributions under paragraph (g)(4) of this section, the additional account will be treated as never having been established.

(3) *Beneficial interest.*—The eligible individual for whose benefit an ABLE account is established is the designated beneficiary of the account. A person other than the designated beneficiary with signature authority over the account of the designated beneficiary may neither have nor acquire any beneficial interest in the account during the lifetime of the designated beneficiary and must administer the account for the benefit of the designated beneficiary of the account.

(d) *Eligible individual.*—(1) *In general.*—Whether an individual is an eligible individual (as defined in §1.529A-1(b)(9)) is determined for each taxable year, and that determination applies for the entire year. A qualified ABLE program must specify the documentation that an individual must provide, both at the time an ABLE account is established for that individual and thereafter, in order to ensure that the designated beneficiary of the ABLE account is, and continues to be, an eligible individual. For purposes of determining whether an individual is an eligible individual, a disability certification will be deemed to be filed with the Secretary once the qualified ABLE program has received the disability certification (as described in paragraph (e) of this section) or a disability certification has been deemed to have been received under the rules of the qualified ABLE program, which information the qualified ABLE program will file in accordance with the filing requirements under §1.529A-5(c)(2)(iv).

(2) *Frequency of recertification.*—(i) *In general.*—A qualified ABLE program may choose different methods of ensuring a designated beneficiary's status as an eligible individual and may impose different periodic recertification requirements for different types of impairments.

(ii) *Considerations.*—In developing its rules on recertification, a qualified ABLE program may take into consideration whether an impairment is incurable and, if so, the likelihood that a cure may be found in the future. For example, a qualified ABLE program may provide that the initial certification will be deemed to be valid for a stated number of years, which may vary with the type of impairment. If the qualified ABLE program imposes an enforceable obligation on the designated beneficiary or other person with signature authority over the ABLE account to promptly report changes in the designated beneficiary's condition that would result in the designated beneficiary's failing to satisfy the definition of eligible individual, the program also may provide that a certification is valid until the end of the taxable year in which the change in the designated beneficiary's condition occurred.

(3) *Loss of qualification as an eligible individual.*—If the designated beneficiary of an ABLE account ceases to be an eligible individual, then for each taxable year in which the designated beneficiary is not an eligible individual, the account will continue to be an ABLE account, the designated beneficiary will continue to be the designated beneficiary of the ABLE account (and will be referred to as such), and the ABLE account will not be deemed to have been distributed. However, beginning on the first day of the designated beneficiary's first taxable year for which the designated beneficiary does not satisfy the definition of an eligible individual, additional contributions to the designated beneficiary's ABLE account must not be accepted by the qualified ABLE program. Additionally, no amounts incurred during that year and each subsequent year in which the designated beneficiary does not satisfy the definition of an eligible individual will be qualified disability expenses. If the designated beneficiary subsequently again becomes an eligible individual, contributions to the designated beneficiary's ABLE account again may be accepted subject to the contribution limits under section 529A, and expenses incurred that meet the definition of a qualified disability expense will be qualified disability expenses

(e) *Disability certification.*—(1) *In general.*—Except as provided in paragraph (e)(3) of this section or additional guidance described in paragraph (e)(4) of this section, a disability certification with respect to an individual is a certification signed under penalties of perjury by the individual, or by the other individual establishing (or with signature authority over) the ABLE account for the individual, that—

(i) The individual—

(A) Has a medically determinable physical or mental impairment that results in marked and severe functional limitations (as defined in paragraph (e)(2) of this section), and that—

(1) Can be expected to result in death; or

(2) Has lasted or can be expected to last for a continuous period of not less than 12 months; or

(B) Is blind (within the meaning of section 1614(a)(2) of the Social Security Act);

(ii) Such blindness or disability occurred before the date on which the individual attained age 26 (and, for this purpose, an individual is deemed to attain age 26 on his or her 26th birthday); and

(iii) Includes a copy of the individual's diagnosis relating to the individual's relevant impairment or impairments, signed by a physician meeting the criteria of section 1861(r)(1) of the Social Security Act (42 U.S.C. 1395x(r)).

(2) *Marked and severe functional limitations.*—For purposes of paragraph (e)(1) of this section, the phrase "marked and severe functional limitations" means the standard of disability in the Social Security Act for children claiming Supplemental Security Income for the Aged, Blind, and Disabled (SSI) benefits based on disability (*see*

20 CFR 416.906). Specifically, this is a level of severity that meets, medically equals, or functionally equals the severity of any listing in appendix 1 of subpart P of 20 CFR part 404, but without regard to age. (*See* 20 CFR 416.906, 416.924 and 416.926a.) Such phrase also includes any impairment or standard of disability identified in future guidance published in the Internal Revenue Bulletin (*see* § 601.601(d)(2) of this chapter). Consistent with the regulations of the Social Security Administration, the level of severity is determined by taking into account the effect of the individual's prescribed treatment. (*See* 20 CFR 416.930.)

(3) *Compassionate allowance list.*—Conditions listed in the "List of Compassionate Allowances Conditions" maintained by the Social Security Administration (at *www.socialsecurity.gov/compassionateallowances/conditions.htm*) are deemed to meet the requirements of section 529A(e)(1)(B) regarding the filing of a disability certification, if the condition was present before the date on which the individual attained age 26. To establish that an individual with such a condition meets the definition of an eligible individual, the individual must identify the condition and certify to the qualified ABLE program both the presence of the condition and its onset prior to age 26, in a manner specified by the qualified ABLE program.

(4) *Additional guidance.*—Additional guidance on conditions deemed to meet the requirements of section 529A(e)(1)(B) may be identified in future guidance published in the Internal Revenue Bulletin. *See* § 601.601(d)(2) of this chapter.

(5) *Restriction on use of certification.*—No inference may be drawn from a disability certification described in this paragraph (e) for purposes of establishing eligibility for benefits under title II, XVI, or XIX of the Social Security Act.

(f) *Change of designated beneficiary.*—A qualified ABLE program must permit a change in the designated beneficiary of an ABLE account, but only during the life of the designated beneficiary. At the time of the change, the successor designated beneficiary must be an eligible individual.

(g) *Contributions.*—(1) *Permissible property.*—Except in the case of program-to-program transfers, contributions to an ABLE account may only be made in cash. A qualified ABLE program may allow cash contributions to be made in the form of a check, money order, credit card, electronic transfer, or similar method.

(2) *Annual contributions limit.*—A qualified ABLE program must provide that no contribution to an ABLE account will be accepted to the extent such contribution, when added to all other contributions (whether from the designated beneficiary or one or more other persons) to that ABLE account made during the designated beneficiary's taxable year causes the total of such contributions to exceed the amount in effect under section 2503(b) for the calendar year in which the designated beneficiary's taxable year begins. For this purpose, contributions do not include rollovers or program-to-program transfers.

(3) *Cumulative limit.*—(i) *In general.*—A qualified ABLE program maintained by a State or its agency or instrumentality must provide adequate safeguards to prevent aggregate contributions on behalf of a designated beneficiary in excess of the limit established by that State under section 529(b)(6). For purposes of the preceding sentence, aggregate contributions include contributions to any prior ABLE account maintained by any State or its agency or instrumentality for the same designated beneficiary or any prior designated beneficiary.

(ii) *Safe harbor.*—A qualified ABLE program maintained by a State or its agency or instrumentality satisfies the requirement in paragraph (g)(3)(i) of this section if it refuses to accept any additional contribution to an ABLE account once the balance in that account reaches the limit established by that State under section 529(b)(6). Once the account balance falls below such limit, additional contributions again may be accepted, subject to the limits under this paragraph (g)(3)(i) of this section.

(4) *Return of excess contributions and excess aggregate contributions.*—If an excess contribution as defined in § 1.529A-1(b)(10) or an excess aggregate contribution as defined in § 1.529A-1(b)(11) is allocated to or deposited into the ABLE account of a designated beneficiary, a qualified ABLE program must return that excess contribution or excess aggregate contribution, including all net income attributable to that excess contribution or excess aggregate contribution, as determined under the rules set forth in § 1.408-11 (treating an IRA as an ABLE account and returned contributions under section 408(d)(4) as excess contributions or excess aggregate contributions), to the person or persons who made that contribution. An excess contribution or excess aggregate contribution must be returned to its contributor(s) on a last-in-first-out basis until the entire excess contribution or excess aggregate contribution, along with all net income attributa-

ble to such contribution, has been returned. Returned contributions must be received by the contributor(s) on or before the due date (including extensions) for the Federal income tax return of the designated beneficiary for the taxable year in which the excess contribution or excess aggregate contribution was made. *See* § 1.529A-3(e) for income tax considerations for the contributor(s). If an excess contribution or excess aggregate contribution and the net income attributable to the excess contribution or excess aggregate contribution are returned to a contributor other than the designated beneficiary, the qualified ABLE program must notify the designated beneficiary of such return at the time of the return.

(h) *Qualified disability expenses.*—(1) *In general.*—Qualified disability expenses, as defined in § 1.529A-1(b)(16), are expenses incurred that relate to the blindness or disability of the designated beneficiary of the ABLE account and are for the benefit of that designated beneficiary in maintaining or improving his or her health, independence, or quality of life. Such expenses include, but are not limited to, expenses related to the designated beneficiary's education, housing, transportation, employment training and support, assistive technology and related services, personal support services, health, prevention and wellness, financial management and administrative services, legal fees, expenses for oversight and monitoring, and funeral and burial expenses, as well as other expenses that may be identified from time to time in future guidance published in the Internal Revenue Bulletin. *See* § 601.601(d)(2) of this chapter. Qualified disability expenses include basic living expenses and are not limited to items for which there is a medical necessity or which solely benefit a disabled individual. A qualified ABLE program must establish safeguards to distinguish between distributions used for the payment of qualified disability expenses and other distributions, and to permit the identification of the amounts distributed for housing expenses as that term is defined for purposes of the Supplemental Security Income program of the Social Security Administration.

(2) *Example.*—The following example illustrates this paragraph (h):

Example. B, an individual, has a medically determined mental impairment that causes marked and severe limitations on her ability to navigate and communicate. A smart phone would enable B to navigate and communicate more safely and effectively, thereby helping her to maintain her independence and to improve her quality of life. Therefore, the expense of buying, using, and maintaining a smart phone that is used by B would be considered a qualified disability expense.

(i) *Separate accounting.*—A program will not be treated as a qualified ABLE program unless it provides separate accounting for each ABLE account. Separate accounting requires that contributions for the benefit of a designated beneficiary and any earnings attributable thereto must be allocated to that designated beneficiary's account. Whether or not a program provides each designated beneficiary an annual account statement showing the total account balance, the investment in the account, the accrued earnings, and the distributions from the account, the program must give this information to the designated beneficiary upon request.

(j) *Program-to-program transfers.*—A qualified ABLE program may permit a change of qualified ABLE program or a change of designated beneficiary by means of a program-to-program transfer as defined in § 1.529A-1(b)(14). In that event, subject to any contrary provisions or limitations adopted by the qualified ABLE program, rules similar to the rules of § 1.401(a)(31)-1, Q&A-3 and 4 (which apply for purposes of a direct rollover from a qualified plan to an eligible retirement plan) apply for purposes of determining whether an amount is paid in the form of a program-to-program transfer.

(k) *Carryover of attributes.*—Upon a rollover or program-to-program transfer, all of the attributes of the former ABLE account relevant for purposes of calculating the investment in the account and applying the annual and cumulative limits on contributions are applicable to the recipient ABLE account. The portion of the rollover or transfer amount that constituted investment in the account from which the distribution or transfer was made is added to investment in the recipient ABLE account. Similarly, the portion of the rollover or transfer amount that constituted earnings of the account from which the distribution or transfer was made is added to the earnings of the recipient ABLE account.

(l) *Investment direction.*—A program will not be treated as a qualified ABLE program unless it provides that the designated beneficiary of an ABLE account established under such program may direct, whether directly or indirectly, the investment of any contributions to the program (or any earnings thereon) no more than two times in any calendar year.

(m) *No pledging of interest as security.*—A program will not be treated as a qualified ABLE program unless the terms of the program, or a state statute or regulation that governs the program, prohibit any interest in the program or any portion thereof from being used as security for a loan. This restriction includes, but is not limited to, a prohibition on the use of any interest in the ABLE program as security for a loan used to purchase such interest in the program.

(n) *No sale or exchange.*—A qualified ABLE program must ensure that no interest in an ABLE account may be sold or exchanged.

(o) *Change of residence.*—A qualified ABLE program may continue to maintain the ABLE account of a designated beneficiary after that designated beneficiary changes his or her residence to another State.

(p) *Post-death payments.*—A qualified ABLE program must provide that a portion or all of the balance remaining in the ABLE account of a deceased designated beneficiary must be distributed to a State that files a claim against the designated beneficiary or the ABLE account itself with respect to benefits provided to the designated beneficiary under that State's Medicaid plan established under title XIX of the Social Security Act. The payment of such claim (if any) will be made only after providing for the payment from the designated beneficiary's ABLE account of all outstanding payments due for his or her qualified disability expenses, and will be limited to the amount of the total medical assistance paid for the designated beneficiary after the establishment of the ABLE account (the date on which the ABLE account, or any ABLE account from which amounts were rolled or transferred to the ABLE account of the same designated beneficiary, was opened) over the amount of any premiums paid, whether from the ABLE account or otherwise by or on behalf of the designated beneficiary, to a Medicaid Buy-In program under any such State Medicaid plan.

(q) *Reporting requirements.*—A qualified ABLE program must comply with all applicable reporting requirements, including without limitation those described in §§1.529A-5 through 1.529A-7.

(r) *Effective/applicability dates.*—This section applies to taxable years beginning after December 31, 2014. [Reg. §1.529A-2.]

§1.529A-3. Tax treatment.—(a) *Taxation of distributions.*—Each distribution from an ABLE account consists of earnings (computed in accordance with paragraph (c) of this section) and investment in the account. If the total amount distributed from an ABLE account to or for the benefit of the designated beneficiary of that ABLE account during his or her taxable year does not exceed the qualified disability expenses of the designated beneficiary for that year, no amount distributed is includible in the gross income of the designated beneficiary for that year. If the total amount distributed from an ABLE account to or for the benefit of the designated beneficiary of that ABLE account during his or her taxable year exceeds the qualified disability expenses of the designated beneficiary for that year, the distributions from the ABLE account, except to the extent excluded from gross income under this section or any other provision of chapter 1 of the Internal Revenue Code, must be included in the gross income of the designated beneficiary in the manner provided under this section and section 72. In such a case, the earnings portion of the distribution includible in gross income is equal to the earnings portion of the distribution reduced by an amount that bears the same ratio to the earnings portion as the amount of qualified disability expenses during the year bears to the total distributions during the year. For this purpose, all amounts relevant under section 72 are determined as of December 31 of the year in which the designated beneficiary's taxable year begins, and all amounts distributed from an ABLE account to or for the benefit of the designated beneficiary during his or her taxable year are treated as one distribution. If an excess contribution or excess aggregate contribution is returned within the time period required in §1.529A-2(g)(4), any net income distributed is includible in the gross income of the contributor(s) in the taxable year in which the excess contribution or excess aggregate contribution was made.

(b) *Additional exclusions from gross income.*—(1) *Rollover.*—A rollover as defined in §1.529A-1(b)(17) is not includible in gross income under paragraph (a) of this section.

(2) *Program-to-program transfers.*—A program-to-program transfer as defined in §1.529A-1(b)(14) is not a distribution and is not includible in gross income under paragraph (a) of this section.

(3) *Change of designated beneficiary.*—(i) *In general.*—A change of designated beneficiary of an ABLE account is not treated as a distribution for purposes of section 529A, and is not includible in gross income under paragraph (a) of this section, if the successor designated beneficiary is—

(A) An eligible individual for such calendar year; and

(B) A member of the family of the former designated beneficiary 58

(ii) *Other designated beneficiary changes.*—In the case of any change of designated beneficiary not described in paragraph (b)(3)(i) of this section, the former designated beneficiary of that ABLE account will be treated as having received a distribution of the fair market value of the assets in that ABLE account on the date on which the change is made to the new designated beneficiary.

(4) *Payments to creditors post-death.*—Distributions made after the death of the designated beneficiary in payment of outstanding obligations due for qualified disability expenses of the designated beneficiary are not includible in the gross income of the designated beneficiary or his or her estate. Included among these obligations is the post-death payment of any part of a claim filed against the designated beneficiary or the ABLE account by a State under a State Medicaid plan.

(c) *Computation of earnings.*—The earnings portion of a distribution is equal to the product of the amount of the distribution and the earnings ratio, as defined in §1.529A-1(b)(8). The balance of the distribution (the amount of the distribution minus the earnings portion of that distribution) is the portion of that distribution that constitutes the return of investment in the account.

(d) *Additional tax on amounts includible in gross income.*—(1) *In general.*—If any amount of a distribution from an ABLE account is includible in the gross income of a person for any taxable year under paragraph (a) of this section (the "includible amount"), the tax imposed on that person by Chapter 1 of the Internal Revenue Code shall be increased by an amount equal to 10 percent of the includible amount.

(2) *Exceptions.*—(i) *Distributions on or after the death of the designated beneficiary.*—Paragraph (d)(1) of this section does not apply to any distribution made from the ABLE account on or after the death of the designated beneficiary to the estate of the designated beneficiary, to an heir or legatee of the designated beneficiary, or to a creditor described in paragraph (b)(4) of this section.

(ii) *Returned excess contributions and additional accounts.*—Paragraph (d)(1) of this section does not apply to any return made in accordance with §1.529A-2(g)(4) of an excess contribution, excess aggregate contribution, or additional account.

(e) *Tax on excess contributions.*—Under section 4973(h), a contribution to an ABLE account in excess of the annual contributions limit described in §1.529A-2(g)(2) is subject to an excise tax in an amount equal to 6 percent of the excess contribution. However, if the excess contribution is returned in accordance with the provisions of §1.529A-2(g)(4), it is treated as an amount not contributed.

(f) *Filing requirements.*—A qualified ABLE program is not required to file Form 990, "Return of Organization Exempt From Income Tax," Form 1041, "U.S. Income Tax Return for Estates and Trusts," or Form 1120, "U.S. Corporation Income Tax Return." However, a qualified ABLE program is required to file Form 990-T, "Exempt Organization Business Income Tax Return," if such filing would be required under the rules of §§1.6012-2(e) and 1.6012-3(a)(5) if the ABLE program were an organization described in those sections.

(g) *Effective/applicability dates.*—This section applies to taxable years beginning after December 31, 2014. [Reg. §1.529A-3.]

§1.529A-4. Gift, estate, and generation-skipping transfer taxes.—(a) *Contributions.*—(1) *In general.*—Each contribution by a person to an ABLE account other than by the designated beneficiary of that account is treated as a completed gift to the designated beneficiary of the account for gift tax purposes. Under the applicable gift tax rules, a contribution from a corporation, partnership, trust, estate, or other entity is treated as a gift by the shareholders, partners, or other beneficial owners in proportion to their respective ownership interests in the entity. *See* §25.2511-1(c) and (h). A gift into an ABLE account is not treated as either a gift of a future interest in property, or a qualified transfer under section 2503(e). To the extent a contributor's gifts to the designated beneficiary, including gifts paid into the designated beneficiary's ABLE account, do not exceed the annual limit in section 2503(b), the contribution is not subject to gift tax. This provision, however, does not change any other provision applicable to the transfer. For example, a contribution by the employer of the designated beneficiary's parent continues to constitute earned income to the parent and then a gift by the parent to the designated beneficiary.

(2) *Generation-skipping transfer (GST) tax.*—To the extent the contribution into an ABLE account is a nontaxable gift for gift tax purposes, the inclusion ratio for purposes of the GST tax will be zero pursuant to section 2642(c)(1).

(3) *Designated beneficiary as contributor.*—A designated beneficiary may make a contribution to fund his or her own ABLE account.

That contribution is not a gift. However, in the event of any change of designated beneficiary, the portion of the then fair market value of the ABLE account attributable to that contribution and any earnings attributable to that contribution will constitute a gift by the designated beneficiary to the successor designated beneficiary, and the usual gift and GST tax rules will apply.

(b) *Distributions.*—No distribution from an ABLE account to or for the benefit of the designated beneficiary is treated as a taxable gift to that designated beneficiary.

(c) *Change of designated beneficiary.*—Neither gift tax nor generation-skipping transfer tax applies to a change of designated beneficiary if the successor designated beneficiary is both an eligible individual and a member of the family (as described in §1.529A-1(b)(13)) of the designated beneficiary. The previous sentence does not apply to any other change of designated beneficiary.

(d) *Transfer tax on death of designated beneficiary.*—Upon the death of the designated beneficiary, the designated beneficiary's ABLE account is includible in his or her gross estate for estate tax purposes under section 2031. The payment of outstanding qualified disability expenses and the payment of certain claims made by a State under its Medicaid plan may be deductible for estate tax purposes if the requirements of section 2053 are satisfied.

(e) *Effective/applicability date.*—This section applies to taxable years beginning after December 31, 2014. [Reg. §1.529A-4.]

§1.529A-5. Reporting of the establishment of and contributions to an ABLE account.—(a) *In general.*—A filer defined in paragraph (b)(1) of this section must, with respect to each ABLE account—

(1) File an annual information return, as described in paragraph (c) of this section, with the Internal Revenue Service; and

(2) Furnish an annual statement, as described in paragraph (d) of this section, to the designated beneficiary of the ABLE account.

(b) *Additional definitions.*—In addition to the definitions in §1.529A-1(b), the following definitions also apply for purposes of this section—

(1) *Filer* means the State or its agency or instrumentality that establishes and maintains the qualified ABLE program under which an ABLE account is established. The filing may be done by either an officer or employee of the State or its agency or instrumentality having control of the qualified ABLE program, or the officer's or employee's designee.

(2) *TIN* means taxpayer identification number as defined in section 7701(a)(41).

(c) *Requirement to file return.*—(1) *Form of return.*—For purposes of reporting the information described in paragraph (c)(2) of this section, the filer must file Form 5498-QA, "ABLE Account Contribution Information," or any successor form, together with Form 1096, "Annual Summary and Transmittal of U.S. Information Returns."

(2) *Information included on return.*—With respect to each ABLE account, the filer must include on the return—

(i) The name, address, and TIN of the designated beneficiary of the ABLE account;

(ii) The name, address, and TIN of the filer;

(iii) Information regarding the establishment of the ABLE account, as required by the form and its instructions;

(iv) Information regarding the disability certification or other basis for eligibility of the designated beneficiary, as required by the form and its instructions. For further information regarding eligibility and disability certification, *see* §1.529A-2(d) and (e), respectively;

(v) The total amount of any contributions made with respect to the ABLE account during the calendar year;

(vi) The fair market value of the ABLE account as of the last day of the calendar year; and

(vii) Any other information required by the form, its instructions, or published guidance. *See* §§601.601(d) and 601.602 of this chapter.

(3) *Time and manner of filing return.*—(i) *In general.*—Except as provided in paragraph (c)(3)(ii) of this section, the information returns required under this paragraph must be filed on or before May 31 of the year following the calendar year with respect to which the return is being filed, in accordance with the forms and their instructions.

(ii) *Extensions of time.*—See §§1.6081-1 and 1.6081-8 of this chapter for rules relating to extensions of time to file information returns required in this section.

(iii) *Electronic filing.*—See §301.6011-2 of this chapter for rules relating to electronic filing.

(iv) *Substitute forms.*—The filer may file the returns required under this paragraph (c) on a substitute form. A substitute form must comply with applicable revenue procedures (*see* §601.601(d)(2) of this chapter) or other guidance published by the IRS, including Publication 1179, "General Rules and Specifications for Substitute Forms 1096, 1098, 1099, 5498, and Certain Other Information Returns."

(d) *Requirement to furnish statement.*—(1) *In general.*—The filer must furnish a statement to the designated beneficiary of the ABLE account for which it is required to file a Form 5498-QA (or any successor form). The statement must include—

(i) The information required under paragraph (c)(2) of this section;

(ii) A legend that identifies the statement as important tax information that is being furnished to the Internal Revenue Service; and

(iii) The name and address of the office or department of the filer that is the information contact for questions regarding the ABLE account to which the Form 5498-QA relates.

(2) *Time and manner of furnishing statement.*—(i) *In general.*—Except as provided in paragraph (d)(2)(ii) of this section, the filer must furnish the statement described in paragraph (d)(1) of this section to the designated beneficiary on or before March 15 of the year following the calendar year with respect to which the statement is being furnished. If mailed, the statement must be sent to the designated beneficiary's last known address. The statement may be furnished electronically, as provided in §1.529A-7.

(ii) *Extensions of time.*—The Internal Revenue Service may grant an extension of time to furnish statements required in this section upon a showing of good cause. *See* the instructions to Form 5498-QA.

(3) *Copy of Form 5498-QA.*—The filer may satisfy the requirement of this paragraph (d) by furnishing either a copy of Form 5498-QA (or successor form) or another document that contains the information required by paragraph (d)(1) of this section, if the document complies with applicable revenue procedures (*see* §601.601(d)(2) of this chapter) or other guidance published by the IRS relating to substitute statements, including Publication 1179, "General Rules and Specifications for Substitute Forms 1096, 1098, 1099, 5498, and Certain Other Information Returns."

(e) *Request for TIN of designated beneficiary.*—The filer must request the TIN of the designated beneficiary at the time the ABLE account is opened if the filer does not already have a record of the designated beneficiary's correct TIN. The filer must clearly notify the designated beneficiary that the law requires the designated beneficiary to furnish a TIN so that it may be included on an information return to be filed by the filer. The designated beneficiary may provide his or her TIN in any manner including orally, in writing, or electronically. If the TIN is furnished in writing, no particular form is required. Form W-9, "Request for Taxpayer Identification Number and Certification," may be used, or the request may be incorporated into the forms related to the establishment of the ABLE account.

(f) *Penalties.*—(1) *Failure to file return.*—The section 6693 penalty may apply to the filer that fails to file information returns at the time and in the manner required by this section, unless it is shown that such failure is due to reasonable cause. *See* section 6693 and the regulations thereunder.

(2) *Failure to furnish TIN.*—The section 6723 penalty may apply to any designated beneficiary who fails to furnish his or her TIN to the filer. *See* section 6723, and the regulations thereunder, for rules relating to the penalty for failure to furnish a TIN.

(g) *Effective/applicability date.*—The rules of this section apply to information returns required to be filed, and payee statements required to be furnished, after December 31, 2015. [Reg. §1.529A-5.]

§1.529A-6. Reporting of distributions from and termination of an ABLE account.—(a) *In general.*—The filer as defined in §1.529A-5(b)(1) must, with respect to each ABLE account from which any distribution is made or which is terminated during the calendar year—

(1) File an annual information return, as described paragraph (b) of this section, with the Internal Revenue Service; and

(2) Furnish an annual statement, as described in paragraph (c) of this section, to the designated beneficiary of the ABLE account and to each contributor who received a returned contribution in accordance with §1.529A-2(g)(4) attributable to the calendar year.

(b) *Requirement to file return.*—(1) *Form of return.*—For purposes of reporting the information in paragraph (b)(2) of this section, the filer must file Form 1099-QA, "Distributions from ABLE Accounts," or any successor form, together with Form 1096, "Annual Summary and Transmittal of U.S. Information Returns."

(2) *Information included on return.*—The filer must include on the return—

(i) The name, address, and TIN of the designated beneficiary of the ABLE account or of any contributor who received a returned contribution in accordance with §1.529A-2(g)(4) attributable to the calendar year, as applicable;

(ii) The name, address, and TIN of the filer;

(iii) The aggregate amount of distributions from the ABLE account during the calendar year;

(iv) Information as to basis and earnings with respect to such distributions or returns of contributions;

(v) Information regarding termination (if any) of the ABLE account;

(vi) Information regarding each rollover and any program-to-program transfer to or from the ABLE account during the designated beneficiary's taxable year;

(vii) Whether the return is being furnished to the designated beneficiary or to a contributor; and

(viii) Any other information required by the form, its instructions, or published guidance. See §§601.601(d) and 601.602 of this chapter.

(3) *Time and manner of filing return.*—(i) *In general.*—Except as provided in paragraph (b)(3)(ii) of this section, the Forms 1099-QA and 1096 must be filed on or before February 28 (March 31 if filing electronically) of the year following the calendar year with respect to which the return is being filed, in accordance with the forms and their instructions.

(ii) *Extensions of time.*—See §§1.6081-1 and 1.6081-8 of this chapter for rules relating to extensions of time to file information returns required in this section.

(iii) *Electronic filing.*—See §301.6011-2 of this chapter for rules relating to electronic filing.

(iv) *Substitute forms.*—The filer may file the return required under this paragraph (b) on a substitute form. A substitute form must comply with applicable revenue procedures (see §601.601(d)(2) of this chapter) or other guidance published by the IRS, including Publication 1179, "General Rules and Specifications for Substitute Forms 1096, 1098, 1099, 5498, and Certain Other Information Returns."

(c) *Requirement to furnish statement.*—(1) *In general.*—The filer must furnish a statement to the designated beneficiary and each contributor (if any) of the ABLE account for which it is required to file a Form 1099-QA (or any successor form). The statement must include—

(i) The information required under paragraph (b)(2) of this section.

(ii) A legend that identifies the statement as important tax information that is being furnished to the Internal Revenue Service;

(iii) The name and address of the office or department of the filer that is the information contact for questions regarding the ABLE account to which the Form 1099-QA relates.

(2) *Time and manner of furnishing statement.*—(i) *In general.*—Except as provided in paragraph (c)(2)(ii) of this section, a filer must furnish the statement described in paragraph (c)(1) of this section to the designated beneficiary on or before January 31 of the year following the calendar year with respect to which the statement is being furnished. If mailed, the statement must be sent to the recipient's last known address. The statement may be furnished electronically, as provided in §1.529A-7.

(ii) *Extensions of time.*—The Internal Revenue Service may grant an extension of time to furnish statements required in this section upon a showing of good cause. See the instructions to Form 1099-QA.

(3) *Copy of Form 1099-QA.*—A filer may satisfy the requirement of this paragraph (c) by furnishing either a copy of Form 1099-QA (or successor form) or another document that contains the information required by paragraph (c)(1) of this section and that complies with applicable revenue procedures (see §601.601(d)(2) of this chapter) or other guidance published by the IRS relating to substitute statements, including Publication 1179, "General Rules and Specifications for Substitute Forms 1096, 1098, 1099, 5498, and Certain Other Information Returns."

(d) *Request for TIN of contributor(s).*—A filer must request the TIN for each contributor to the ABLE account at the time a contribution is made, if the filer does not already have a record of that person's correct TIN. The filer must clearly notify each contributor to the account that the law requires that person to furnish a TIN so that

it may be included on an information return to be filed by the filer. The contributor may provide his or her TIN in any manner including orally, in writing, or electronically. If the TIN is furnished in writing, no particular form is required. Form W-9, "Request for Taxpayer Identification Number and Certification," may be used, or the request may be incorporated into the forms related to the establishment of the ABLE account.

(e) *Penalties.*—(1) *Failure to file return.*—The section 6693 penalty may apply to a filer that fails to file information returns at the time and in the manner required by this section, unless it is shown that such failure is due to reasonable cause. See section 6693 and the regulations thereunder.

(2) *Failure to furnish TIN.*—The section 6723 penalty may apply to any contributor who fails to furnish his or her TIN to the filer. See section 6723, and the regulations thereunder, for rules relating to the penalty for failure to furnish a TIN.

(f) *Effective/applicability date.*—The rules of this section apply to information returns required to be filed, and payee statements required to be furnished, after December 31, 2015. [Reg. §1.529A-6.]

§1.529A-7. Electronic furnishing of statements to designated beneficiaries and contributors.—(a) *Electronic furnishing of statements.*—(1) *In general.*—A filer required under §1.529A-5 or §1.529A-6 of this chapter to furnish a written statement to a designated beneficiary of or contributor to an ABLE account may furnish the statement in an electronic format in lieu of a paper format. A filer who meets the requirements of paragraphs (a)(2) through (6) of this section is treated as furnishing the required statement.

(2) *Consent.*—(i) *In general.*—The recipient of the statement must have affirmatively consented to receive the statement in an electronic format. The consent may be made electronically in any manner that reasonably demonstrates that the recipient can access the statement in the electronic format in which it will be furnished to the recipient. Alternatively, the consent may be made in a paper document if it is confirmed electronically.

(ii) *Withdrawal of consent.*—The consent requirement of this paragraph (a)(2) is not satisfied if the recipient withdraws the consent and the withdrawal takes effect before the statement is furnished. The filer may provide that a withdrawal of consent takes effect either on the date it is received by the filer or on another date no more than 60 days later. The filer also may provide that a request for a paper statement will be treated as a withdrawal of consent.

(iii) *Change in hardware or software requirements.*—If a change in the hardware or software required to access the statement creates a material risk that the recipient will not be able to access the statement, the filer must, prior to changing the hardware or software, provide the recipient with a notice. The notice must describe the revised hardware and software required to access the statement and inform the recipient that a new consent to receive the statement in the revised electronic format must be provided to the filer if the recipient does not want to withdraw the consent. After implementing the revised hardware and software, the filer must obtain from the recipient, in the manner described in paragraph (a)(2)(i) of this section, a new consent or confirmation of consent to receive the statement electronically.

(iv) *Examples.*—For purposes of the following examples that illustrate the rules of this paragraph (a)(2), assume that the requirements of §1.529A-7(a)(3) have been met:

Example 1. Filer F sends Recipient R a letter stating that R may consent to receive statements required under §1.529A-5 or §1.529A-6 electronically on a Web site instead of in a paper format. The letter contains instructions explaining how to consent to receive the statements electronically by accessing the Web site, downloading the consent document, completing the consent document, and e-mailing the completed consent back to F. The consent document posted on the Web site uses the same electronic format that F will use for the electronically furnished statements. R reads the instructions and submits the consent in the manner provided in the instructions. R has consented to receive the statements electronically in the manner described in paragraph (a)(2)(i) of this section.

Example 2. Filer F sends Recipient R an e-mail stating that R may consent to receive statements required under §1.529A-5 or §1.529A-6 electronically instead of in a paper format. The e-mail contains an attachment instructing R how to consent to receive the statements electronically. The e-mail attachment uses the same electronic format that F will use for the electronically furnished statements. R opens the attachment, reads the instructions, and submits the consent in the manner provided in the instructions. R has consented to receive the statements electronically in the manner described in paragraph (a)(2)(i) of this section.

Example 3. Filer F posts a notice on its Web site stating that Recipient R may receive statements required under §1.529A-5 or

§1.529A-6 electronically instead of in a paper format. The Web site contains instructions on how R may access a secure Web page and consent to receive the statements electronically. By accessing the secure Web page and giving consent, R has consented to receive the statements electronically in the manner described in paragraph (a)(2)(i) of this section.

(3) *Required disclosures.*—(i) *In general.*—Prior to, or at the time of, a recipient's consent, the filer must provide to the recipient a clear and conspicuous disclosure statement containing each of the disclosures described in paragraphs (a)(3)(ii) through (viii) of this section.

(ii) *Paper statement.*—The recipient must be informed that the statement will be furnished on paper if the recipient does not consent to receive it electronically.

(iii) *Scope and duration of consent.*—The recipient must be informed of the scope and duration of the consent. For example, the recipient must be informed whether the consent applies to statements furnished every year after the consent is given until it is withdrawn in the manner described in paragraph (a)(3)(v)(A) of this section, or only to the statement required to be furnished on or before the due date immediately following the date on which the consent is given.

(iv) *Post-consent request for a paper statement.*—The recipient must be informed of any procedure for obtaining a paper copy of the recipient's statement after giving the consent and whether a request for a paper statement will be treated as a withdrawal of consent.

(v) *Withdrawal of consent.*—The recipient must be informed that—

(A) The recipient may withdraw a consent by writing (electronically or on paper) to the person or department whose name, mailing address, and e-mail address is provided in the disclosure statement;

(B) The filer will confirm, in writing (either electronically or on paper), the withdrawal and the date on which it takes effect; and

(C) A withdrawal of consent does not apply to a statement that was furnished electronically in the manner described in this paragraph (a) before the date on which the withdrawal of consent takes effect.

(vi) *Notice of termination.*—The recipient must be informed of the conditions under which a filer will cease furnishing statements electronically to the recipient.

(vii) *Updating information.*—The recipient must be informed of the procedures for updating the information needed by the filer to contact the recipient. The filer must inform the recipient of any change in the filer's contact information.

(viii) *Hardware and software requirements.*—The recipient must be provided with a description of the hardware and software

required to access, print, and retain the statement, and the date when the statement will no longer be available on the Web site.

(4) *Format.*—The electronic version of the statement must contain all required information and comply with applicable revenue procedures or other guidance published by the IRS relating to substitute statements to recipients, including Publication 1179, "General Rules and Specifications for Substitute Forms 1096, 1098, 1099, 5498, and Certain Other Information Returns."

(5) *Notice.*—(i) *In general.*—If the statement is furnished on a Web site, the filer must notify the recipient that the statement is posted on a Web site. The notice may be delivered by mail, electronic mail, or in person. The notice must provide instructions on how to access and print the statement. The notice must include the following statement in capital letters, "IMPORTANT TAX RETURN DOCUMENT AVAILABLE." If the notice is provided by electronic mail, the foregoing statement must be on the subject line of the electronic mail.

(ii) *Undeliverable electronic address.*—If an electronic notice described in paragraph (a)(5)(i) of this section is returned as undeliverable, and the correct electronic address cannot be obtained from the filer's records or from the recipient, then the filer must furnish the notice by mail or in person within 30 days after the electronic notice is returned.

(iii) *Corrected statements.*—If the filer has corrected a recipient's statement that was furnished electronically, the filer must furnish the corrected statement to the recipient electronically. If the recipient's statement was furnished through a Web site posting and the filer has corrected the statement, the filer must notify the recipient that it has posted the corrected statement on the Web site within 30 days of such posting in the manner described in paragraph (a)(5)(i) of this section. The corrected statement or the notice must be furnished by mail or in person if—

(A) An electronic notice of the Web site posting of an original statement or the corrected statement was returned as undeliverable; and

(B) The recipient has not provided a new e-mail address.

(6) *Access period.*—Statements furnished on a Web site must be retained on the Web site through October 15 of the year following the calendar year to which the statements relate (or the first business day after such October 15 if October 15 falls on a Saturday, Sunday, or legal holiday). The filer must maintain access to corrected statements that are posted on the Web site through October 15 of the year following the calendar year to which the statements relate (or the first business day after such October 15 if October 15 falls on a Saturday, Sunday, or legal holiday) or the date 90 days after the corrected statements are posted, whichever is later. The rules in this paragraph (a)(6) do not replace the filer's obligation to keep records under section 6001 and §1.6001-1(a) of this chapter.

(b) *Effective/applicability date.*—This section applies to statements required to be furnished after December 31, 2015. [Reg. §1.529A-7.]

ABLE Accounts: Contribution Limits

ABLE Accounts: Contribution Limits.—Reg. §1.529A-8, containing proposed regulations related to the Internal Revenue Code, which allows a State (or its agency or instrumentality) to establish and maintain a tax-advantaged savings program under which contributions may be made to an ABLE account for the purpose of paying for the qualified disability expenses of the designated beneficiary of the account, is proposed (published in the Federal Register on October 10, 2019) (REG-128246-18).

Par. 4. Section 1.529A-8 is added to read as follows:

§1.529A-8. Additional contributions to ABLE accounts made by an employed designated beneficiary.—(a) *Additional contributions by an employed designated beneficiary.*—(1) *In general.*—An employed designated beneficiary defined in paragraph (b)(1) of this section may contribute amounts up to the limit specified in paragraph (a)(2) of this section in addition to the annual amount described in section 529A(b)(2)(B)(i).

(2) *Amount of additional permissible contribution.*—Any additional contribution made by the designated beneficiary pursuant to this section is limited to the lesser of—

(i) The designated beneficiary's compensation as defined by section 219(f)(1) for the taxable year; or

(ii) An amount equal to the applicable poverty line, as defined in paragraph (b)(2) of this section, for a one-person household for the calendar year preceding the calendar year in which the designated beneficiary's taxable year begins.

(b) *Additional definitions.*—In addition to the definitions in §1.529A-1(b), the following definitions also apply for the purposes of this section—

(1) *Employed designated beneficiary* means a designated beneficiary who is an employee (including an employee within the mean-

ing of section 401(c)), with respect to whom no contribution is made for the taxable year to—

(i) A defined contribution plan (within the meaning of section 414(i)) with respect to which the requirements of sections 401(a) or 403(a) are met;

(ii) An annuity contract described in section 403(b); and

(iii) An eligible deferred compensation plan described in section 457(b).

(2) *Applicable poverty line* means the amount provided in the poverty guidelines updated periodically in the **Federal Register** by the U.S. Department of Health and Human Services under the authority of 42 U.S.C. 9902(2) for the State of residence of the employed designated beneficiary. If the designated beneficiary lives in more than one state during the taxable year, the applicable poverty line is the poverty line for the state in which the designated beneficiary resided longer than in any other state during that year.

(3) *Excess compensation contribution* means the amount by which the amount contributed during the taxable year of an employed designated beneficiary to the designated beneficiary's ABLE account exceeds the limit in effect under section 529A(b)(2)(B)(ii) and paragraph (a)(2) of this section for the calendar year in which that taxable year of the employed designated beneficiary begins.

(c) *Example.*—The following example illustrates the principles of paragraphs (a)(2) and (b)(2) of this section. In 2019, A, the designated beneficiary of an ABLE account, lives in Hawaii. A's compensation, as defined by section 219(f)(1), for 2019 is $20,000. The poverty line for a one-person household in Hawaii was $13,960 in 2018. Because A's compensation exceeded the applicable poverty line amount, A's additional permissible contribution in 2019 is limited to $13,960, the amount of the 2018 applicable poverty line.

(d) *Responsibility for ensuring contribution limit is met.*—(1) The employed designated beneficiary, or the person acting on his or her behalf, is solely responsible for ensuring that the requirements in section 529A(b)(2)(B)(ii) and paragraph (a)(2) of this section are met and for maintaining adequate records for that purpose.

(2) A qualified ABLE program may allow a designated beneficiary (or the person acting on his or her behalf) to certify, under penalties of perjury, and in the manner specified by the qualified ABLE program that —

(i) The designated beneficiary is an employed designated beneficiary; and

(ii) The designated beneficiary's contributions of compensation are not excess compensation contributions.

(e) *Return of excess compensation contributions.*—If an excess compensation contribution is deposited into or allocated to the ABLE account of a designated beneficiary, the qualified ABLE program must return that excess contribution, including all net income attributable to the excess contribution, as determined under the rules set forth in §1.408-11 (treating references to an IRA as references to an ABLE account, and references to returned contributions under section 408(d)(4) as references to excess compensation contributions), to the employed designated beneficiary. The employed designated beneficiary, or the person acting on the employed designated beneficiary's behalf, is responsible for identifying any excess compensation contribution and for requesting the return of the excess compensation contribution. The excess compensation contribution, if requested, must be received by the employed designated beneficiary on or before the due date (including extensions) of the Federal income tax return of the employed designated beneficiary for the taxable year in which the excess compensation contribution is made.

(f) *Applicability date.*—The rules of this section apply to taxable years beginning after [DATE OF PUBLICATION OF FINAL REGULATIONS IN THE **FEDERAL REGISTER**]. [Reg. §1.529A-8.]

CORPORATIONS USED TO AVOID INCOME TAX ON SHAREHOLDERS

Foreign Corporations: Tax Years

Foreign Corporations: Tax Years.—Reproduced below are the texts of proposed Reg. §1.563-3 and a proposed amendment to Reg. §1.563-3, relating to the required taxable year of those foreign corporations beginning after July 10, 1989 (published in the Federal Register on January 5, 1993).

☐ Par. 5. Section 1.563-3 is redesignated as Reg. §1.563-4 and a new Reg. §1.563-3 is added as follows:

§1.563-3. Foreign personal holding company tax; procedure for designation of a dividend as being taken into account under section 563(c).—In determining the deduction for dividends paid under section 561, a foreign personal holding company may designate a dividend paid after the close of any taxable year beginning after July 10, 1989, and on or before the 15th day of the third month following the close of that taxable year, as being taken into account under section 563(c) and this section by making the designation on an attachment to Schedule N of Form 5471. The designation must set forth the date of the distribution and a statement indicating the extent to which the distribution is being taken into account under section 563(c), and any other information required by Form 5471 and the instructions to that form. The designation must be signed and

dated by a duly authorized corporate officer of the foreign personal holding company. If a foreign personal holding company took a dividend paid into account under section 563(c) for any taxable year beginning after July 10, 1989, and ending prior to [INSERT DATE THAT IS 120 DAYS AFTER DATE OF PUBLICATION OF FINAL REGULATIONS IN THE FEDERAL REGISTER] but did not follow the procedures set forth in this paragraph, then a designation on an attachment to Schedule N of Form 5471 setting forth the information required above should be signed in a manner set forth above and attached to the first Form 5471 and, if applicable, Form 1120F, to be filed after [INSERT DATE THAT IS 120 DAYS AFTER DATE OF PUBLICATION OF FINAL REGULATIONS IN THE FEDERAL REGISTER].[Reg. §1.563-3.]

BANKING INSTITUTIONS

Minimum Addition to Reserves for Losses: Mutual Savings Banks

Minimum Addition to Reserves for Losses: Mutual Savings Banks.—Reproduced below is the text of a proposed amendment of Reg. §1.581-2, relating to the minimum addition to reserves for losses on loans of mutual savings banks and other organizations (published in the Federal Register on December 19, 1983).

§1.581-2. Mutual savings banks, building and loan associations, and cooperative banks.

☐ Par. 2. Section 1.581-2(b) is amended by removing the phrase "See section 593 and §1.593-1" and inserting in its place "See section 593 and §§1.593-1 through 1.593-8".

Imputed Interest: Original Issue Discount: Safe Haven Rates

Imputed Interest: Original Issue Discount: Safe Haven Interest Rates.—Reproduced below is the text of a proposed amendment of Reg. §1.582-1, relating to (1) the tax treatment of debt instruments issued after July 1, 1982, that contain original issue discount, (2) the imputation of and the accounting for interest with respect to sales and exchanges of property occurring after December 31, 1984, and (3) safe haven interest rates for loans or advances between commonly controlled taxpayers and safe haven leases between such taxpayers (published in the Federal Register on April 8, 1986).

§1.582-1. Bad debts, losses, and gains with respect to securities held by financial institutions.

☐ Par. 14. In §1.582-1, paragraphs (d) and (e)(3)(i) are amended by removing the phrase "section 1232" from each place that it appears and adding in its place the phrase "sections 1271 through 1275".

Minimum Addition to Reserves for Losses: Mutual Savings Banks

Minimum Addition to Reserves for Losses: Mutual Savings Banks.—Reproduced below are the texts of proposed amendments to Reg. §§1.591-1, relating to the minimum addition to reserves for losses on loans of mutual savings banks and other organizations (published in the Federal Register on December 19, 1983).

☐ Par. 3. Section 1.591-1 is amended as follows:

1. Paragraph (a)(2) is amended by inserting "or a mutual savings bank described in section 591(b)" after "domestic building and loan association".

2. Paragraph (c)(2) is removed and paragraph (c)(1) is redesignated as paragraph (c)(2).

3. Paragraph (c)(2) as so redesignated is amended by inserting "and before the first day of the taxpayer's first taxable year ending after August 13, 1981," after "October 16, 1962," and by removing "; and" and inserting a period in lieu thereof.

4. A new paragraph (c)(1) is added which reads as follows:

§1.591-1. Deduction for dividends paid on deposits.
* * *

(c) *Effective date.*—* * *

(1) Dividends or interest paid or credited during a taxable year ending after August 13, 1981, by any taxpayer which (at the time of such payment or credit) qualifies as (i) a mutual savings bank (including a mutual savings bank which has capital stock repre-

sented by shares and which is subject to, and operates under, Federal or State laws relating to mutual savings banks), (ii) a domestic building and loan association (as defined in section 7701(a)(19)), (iii) a cooperative bank (as defined in section 7701(a)(32)), or (iv) any other savings institution chartered and supervised as a savings and loan or similar association under Federal or State law; and

* * *

NATURAL RESOURCES

Depletion: Lease of Mineral Property: Uniform Capitalization Rules: Treatment of Delay Rental

Depletion: Lease of Mineral Property: Uniform Capitalization Rules: Treatment of Delay Rental.—Amendments to Reg. §1.612-3, conforming regulations relating to delay rental to the requirements of Code Sec. 263A relating to capitalization and inclusion in inventory of costs of certain expenses, are proposed (published in the Federal Register on February 8, 2000) (REG-103882-99).

☐ Par. 2. In §1.612-3, the second sentence of paragraph (c)(2) is removed and two sentences are added in its place to read as follows:

§1.612-3. Depletion; treatment of bonus and advanced royalty.
* * *

(c) * * *

(2) * * * To the extent the delay rental is not required to be capitalized under section 263A and the regulations thereunder, the payor may at his election deduct such amount or under section 266

and the regulations thereunder, charge it to depletable capital account. The second sentence of this paragraph (c)(2) applies to delay rentals paid with respect to leasing transactions entered into on or after the date these regulations are published as final regulations in the Federal Register.

* * *

Partners and Partnerships: Sales or Exchanges: Certain Distributions

Partners and Partnerships: Sales or Exchanges: Certain Distributions.—Amendments to Reg. §1.617-4, prescribing how a partner should measure its interest in a partnership's unrealized receivables and inventory items, and that provide guidance regarding the tax consequences of a distribution that causes a reduction in that interest, are proposed (published in the Federal Register on November 3, 2014) (REG-151416-06).

☐ Par. 2. Section 1.617-4 is amended by adding a new sentence at the end of paragraph (c)(3)(ii)(*g*) to read as follows:

§1.617-4. Treatment of gain from disposition of certain mining property.
* * *

(c) * * *
(3) * * *

(ii) * * *

(*g*) * * * *See also* §§1.732-1(c)(2)(iii) and 1.755-1(c)(2)(iii) for rules governing the application of section 617 to partnership property in certain situations.

* * *

Imputed Interest: Original Issue Discount: Safe Haven Rates

Imputed Interest: Original Issue Discount: Safe Haven Interest Rates.—Reproduced below is the text of a proposed amendment of Reg. §1.636-1, relating to (1) the tax treatment of debt instruments issued after July 1, 1982, that contain original issue discount, (2) the imputation of and the accounting for interest with respect to sales and exchanges of property occurring after December 31, 1984, and (3) safe haven interest rates for loans or advances between commonly controlled taxpayers and safe haven leases between such taxpayers (published in the Federal Register on April 8, 1986).

☐ Par. 15. In §1.636-1, paragraph (a)(1)(ii) is amended by removing the phrase "section 1232" and adding in its place the phrase "section 1271".

§1.636-1. Treatment of production payments as loans.
* * *

ESTATES, TRUSTS, BENEFICIARIES, AND DECEDENTS

Charitable Contributions: Substantiation

Charitable Contributions: Substantiation Requirements.—Amendments to Reg. §1.642(c)-1, relating to deductions in excess of $5,000 claimed for charitable contributions of property, are proposed (published in the Federal Register on May 5, 1988).

* * *

☐ Par. 2. Paragraph (a)(1) of §1.642(c)-1 is amended by revising the first sentence to read as set forth below.

§1.642(c)-1. Unlimited deduction for amounts paid for charitable purpose.—(a) *In general.*—(1) Any part of the gross income of an estate or trust which, pursuant to the terms of the governing instrument, is paid (or treated under paragraph (b) of this section as paid) during the taxable year for a purpose specified in section 170(c) shall

be allowed as a deduction to such estate or trust in lieu of the limited charitable contributions deduction authorized by section 170(a) (provided that the recordkeeping and return requirements for charitable contribution deductions contained in §1.170A-13 are satisfied). * * *

Charitable Contributions: Substantiation

Charitable Contributions: Substantiation Requirements.—Amendments to Reg. §1.642(c)-2, relating to deductions in excess of $5,000 claimed for charitable contributions of property, are proposed (published in the Federal Register on May 5, 1988).

☐ Par. 3. Section 1.642(c)-2 is amended by adding a new paragraph (e) immediately after paragraph (d) to read as set forth below.

§1.642(c)-2. Unlimited deduction for amounts permanently set aside for a charitable purpose.—
* * *

(e) *Substantiation requirements.*— No deduction shall be allowed under paragraphs (a), (b)(2), or (c) of this section unless the recordkeeping and return requirements for charitable contribution deductions contained in §1.170A-13 are satisfied.

Gross Income of Beneficiary

Gross Income of Beneficiary: Character of Amounts.—Reproduced below is the text of the proposed amendment of Reg. §1.652(b)-1, relating to the character of amounts included in the gross income of a beneficiary (published in the Federal Register on April 30, 1975).

☐ Section 1.652(b)-1 is amended by deleting "72(n)" and inserting in lieu thereof "402(a)(2)". As amended § 1.652(b)-1 reads as follows:

§1.652(b)-1. Character of amounts.—In determining the gross income of a beneficiary, the amounts includible under § 1.652(a)-1 have the same character in the hands of the beneficiary as in the hands of the trust. For example, to the extent that the amounts specified in § 1.652(a)-1 consist of income exempt from tax under section 103, such amounts are not included in the beneficiary's gross income. Similarly, dividends distributed to a beneficiary retain their original character in the beneficiary's hands for purposes of determining the availability to the beneficiary of the dividends received credit under section 34 (for dividends received on or before December 31, 1964) and the dividend exclusion under section 116. Also, to the extent that the amounts specified in § 1.652(a)-1 consist of "earned income" in the hands of the trust under the provisions of section 1348 such amount shall be treated under section 1348 as "earned income" in the hands of the beneficiary. Similarly, to the extent the amounts specified in § 1.652(a)-1 consist of an amount received as a part of a lump sum distribution from a qualified plan and to which the provisions of section 402(a)(2) would apply in the hands of the trust, such amount shall be treated as subject to such section in the hands of the beneficiary except where such amount is deemed under section 666(a) to have been distributed in a preceding taxable year of the trust and the partial tax described in section 668(a)(2) is determined under section 668(b)(1)(B). The tax treatment of amounts determined under § 1.652(a)-1 depends upon the beneficiary's status with respect to them, not upon the status of the trust. Thus, if a beneficiary is deemed to have received foreign income of a foreign trust, the includibility of such income in his gross income depends upon his taxable status with respect to that income.

Estates and Trusts: Charitable Remainder Trusts

Estates and Trusts: Charitable Remainder Trusts.—Reproduced below is the text of a proposed amendment of Reg. §1.664-1, relating to transfers for public, charitable and religious uses (published in the Federal Register on December 19, 1975).

☐ Paragraph (f) of § 1.664-1 is amended by revising the heading of subparagraph (3) and by adding a new subparagraph (4) at the end thereof. These revised and added provisions read as follows:

§1.664-1. Charitable remainder trusts.

* * *

(f) *Effective date.*—* * *

(3) *Amendment of certain trusts created after July 31, 1969.*—* * *

(4) *Certain wills and trusts in existence on September 21, 1974.*—(i) In the case of a will executed before September 21, 1974, or a trust created (within the meaning of applicable local law) after July 31, 1969, and before September 21, 1974, which is amended pursuant to section 2055(e)(3) and §20.2055-2(g), a charitable remainder trust resulting from such amendment will be treated as a charitable remainder trust from the date it would be deemed created under

§1.664-1(a)(4) and (5), whether or not such date is after September 20, 1974.

(ii) Property transferred to a trust created (within the meaning of applicable local law) before August 1, 1969, whose governing instrument provides that an organization described in section 170(c) receives an irrevocable remainder interest in such trust shall be deemed transferred to a trust created on the date of such transfer, provided that the transfer occurs after July 31, 1969, and prior to October 18, 1971, and pursuant to an amendment provided in §20.2055-2(g), the transferred property and any undistributed income therefrom is severed and placed in a separate trust as of the date of the amendment.

* * *

Application of the Grantor Trust Rules to Nonexempt Employees' Trusts

Application of the Grantor Trust Rules to Nonexempt Employees' Trusts.—Amendments to Reg. §§1.671-1 and 1.671-2, relating to the application of the grantor trust rules to nonexempt employees' trusts, are proposed (published in the Federal Register on September 27, 1996) (REG-209826-96).

☐ Par. 2. Section 1.671-1 is amended by adding paragraphs (g) and (h) to read as follows:

§1.671-1. Grantors and others treated as substantial owners; scope.

* * *

(g) *Domestic nonexempt employees' trust.*—(1) *General rule.*—An employer is not treated as an owner of any portion of a nonexempt employees' trust described in section 402(b) that is part of a deferred compensation plan, and that is not a foreign trust within the meaning of section 7701(a)(31), regardless of whether the employer has a power or interest described in sections 673 through 677 over any portion of the trust. See section 402(b)(3) and § 1.402(b)-1(b)(6) for rules relating to treatment of a beneficiary of a nonexempt employees' trust as the owner of a portion of the trust.

(2) *Example.*—The following example illustrates the rules of paragraph (g)(1) of this section:

Example. Employer X provides nonqualified deferred compensation through Plan A to certain of its management employees. Employer X has created Trust T to fund the benefits under Plan A. Assets of Trust T may not be used for any purpose other than to satisfy benefits provided under Plan A until all plan liabilities have been satisfied. Trust T is classified as a trust under §301.7701-4 of this chapter, and is not a foreign trust within the meaning of section 7701(a)(31). Under §1.83-3(e), contributions to Trust T are considered transfers of property to participants within the meaning of section 83. On these facts, Trust T is a nonexempt employees' trust described in section 402(b). Because Trust T is a nonexempt employees' trust described in section 402(b) that is part of a deferred compensation plan, and that is not a foreign trust within the meaning of section 7701(a)(31), Employer X is not treated as an owner of any portion of Trust T.

(h) *Foreign employees' trust.*—(1) *General rules.*—Except as provided under section 679 or as provided under this paragraph (h)(1), an employer is not treated as an owner of any portion of a foreign employees' trust (as defined in paragraph (h)(2) of this section),

regardless of whether the employer has a power or interest described in sections 673 through 677 over any portion of the trust.

(i) *Plan of CFC employer.*—If a controlled foreign corporation (as defined in section 957) maintains a deferred compensation plan funded through a foreign employees' trust, then, with respect to the controlled foreign corporation, the provisions of subpart E apply to the portion of the trust that is the fractional interest described in paragraph (h)(3) of this section.

(ii) *Plan of U.S. employer.*—If a United States person (as defined in section 7701(a)(30)) maintains a deferred compensation plan that is funded through a foreign employees' trust, then, with respect to the U.S. person, the provisions of subpart E apply to the portion of the trust that is the fractional interest described in paragraph (h)(3) of this section.

(iii) *Plan of U.S.-related foreign partnership employer.*—(A) *General rule.*—If a U.S.-related foreign partnership (as defined in paragraph (h)(1)(iii)(B) of this section) maintains a deferred compensation plan funded through a foreign employees' trust, then, with respect to the U.S.-related foreign partnership, the provisions of subpart E apply to the portion of the trust that is the fractional interest described in paragraph (h)(3) of this section.

(B) *U.S.-related foreign partnership.*—For purposes of this paragraph (h), a U.S.-related foreign partnership is a foreign partnership in which a U.S. person or a controlled foreign corporation owns a partnership interest either directly or indirectly through one or more partnerships.

(iv) *Application of §1.1297-4 to plan of foreign non-CFC employer.*—A foreign employer that is not a controlled foreign corporation may be treated as an owner of a portion of a foreign employees' trust as provided in §1.1297-4.

(v) *Application to employer entity.*—The rules of paragraphs (h)(1)(i) through (h)(1)(iv) of this section apply to the employer whose employees benefit under the deferred compensation plan funded through a foreign employees' trust, or, in the case of a deferred compensation plan covering independent contractors, the recipient of services performed by those independent contractors, regardless of whether the plan is maintained through another entity. Thus, for example, where a deferred compensation plan benefitting employees of a controlled foreign corporation is funded through a foreign employees' trust, the controlled foreign corporation is considered to be the grantor of the foreign employees' trust for purposes of applying paragraph (h)(1)(i) of this section.

(2) *Foreign employees' trust.*—A foreign employees' trust is a nonexempt employees' trust described in section 402(b) that is part of a deferred compensation plan, and that is a foreign trust within the meaning of section 7701(a)(31).

(3) *Fractional interest for paragraph (h)(1).*—(i) *In general.*—The fractional interest for a foreign employees' trust used for purposes of paragraph (h)(1) of this section for a taxable year of the employer is an undivided fractional interest in the trust for which the fraction is equal to the relevant amount for the employer's taxable year divided by the fair market value of trust assets for the employer's taxable year.

(ii) *Relevant amount.*—(A) *In general.*—For purposes of applying paragraph (h)(3)(i) of this section, and except as provided in paragraph (h)(3)(iii) of this section, the relevant amount for the employer's taxable year is the amount, if any, by which the fair market value of trust assets, plus the fair market value of any assets available to pay plan liabilities that are held in the equivalent of a trust within the meaning of section 404A(b)(5)(A), exceed the plan's accrued liability. The following rules apply for this purpose:

(1) The plan's accrued liability is determined using a projected unit credit funding method that satisfies the requirements of §1.412(c)(3)-1, taking into account only liabilities relating to services performed through the measurement date for the employer or a predecessor employer.

(2) The plan's accrued liability is reduced (but not below zero) by any liabilities that are provided for under annuity contracts held to satisfy plan liabilities.

(3) Any amount held under an annuity contract that exceeds the amount that is needed to satisfy the liabilities provided for under the contract (e.g., the value of a participation right under a participating annuity contract) is added to the fair market value of any assets available to pay plan liabilities that are held in the equivalent of a trust.

(4) If the relevant amount as determined under this paragraph (h)(3)(ii), without regard to this paragraph (h)(3)(ii)(A)(4), is greater than the fair market value of trust assets, then the relevant amount is equal to the fair market value of trust assets.

(B) *Permissible actuarial assumptions for accrued liability.*—For purposes of paragraph (h)(3)(ii)(A) of this section, a plan's accrued liability must be calculated using an interest rate and other actuarial assumptions that the Commissioner determines to be reasonable. It is appropriate in determining this interest rate to look to available information about rates implicit in current prices of annuity contracts, and to look to rates of return on high-quality fixed-income investments currently available and expected to be available during the period prior to maturity of the plan benefits. If the qualified business unit computes its income or earnings and profits in dollars pursuant to the dollar approximate separate transactions method under §1.985-3, the employer must use an exchange rate that can be demonstrated to clearly reflect income, based on all relevant facts and circumstances, including appropriate rates of inflation and commercial practices.

(iii) *Exception for reasonable funding.*—The relevant amount does not include an amount that the taxpayer demonstrates to the Commissioner is attributable to amounts that were properly contributed to the trust pursuant to a reasonable funding method, applied using actuarial assumptions that the Commissioner determines to be reasonable, or any amount that the taxpayer demonstrates to the Commissioner is attributable to experience that is favorable relative to any actuarial assumptions used that the Commissioner determines to be reasonable. For this paragraph (h)(3)(iii) to apply to a controlled foreign corporation employer described in paragraph (h)(1)(i) of this section, the taxpayer must indicate on a statement attached to a timely filed Form 5471 that the taxpayer is relying on this rule. For purposes of this paragraph (h)(3)(iii), an amount is considered contributed pursuant to a reasonable funding method if the amount is contributed pursuant to a funding method permitted to be used under section 412 (e.g., the entry age normal funding method) that is consistently used to determine plan contributions. In addition, for purposes of this paragraph (h)(3)(iii), if there has been a change to that method from another funding method, an amount is considered contributed pursuant to a reasonable funding method only if the

prior funding method is also a funding method described in the preceding sentence that was consistently used to determine plan contributions. For purposes of this paragraph (h)(3)(iii), a funding method is considered reasonable only if the method provides for any initial unfunded liability to be amortized over a period of at least 6 years, and for any net change in accrued liability resulting from a change in funding method to be amortized over a period of at least 6 years.

(iv) *Reduction for transition amount.*—The relevant amount is reduced (but not below zero) by any transition amount described in paragraphs (h)(5), (h)(6), or (h)(7) of this section.

(v) *Fair market value of assets.*—For purposes of paragraphs (h)(3)(i) and (ii) of this section, for a taxable year of the employer, the fair market value of trust assets, and the fair market value of other assets held in the equivalent of a trust within the meaning of section 404A(b)(5)(A), equals the fair market value of those assets, as of the measurement date for the employer's taxable year, adjusted to include contributions made after the measurement date and by the end of the employer's taxable year.

(vi) *Annual valuation.*—For purposes of determining the relevant amount for a taxable year of the employer, the fair market value of plan assets, and the plan's accrued liability as described in paragraphs (h)(3)(ii) and (iii) of this section, and the normal cost as described in paragraph (h)(4) of this section, must be determined as of a consistently used annual measurement date within the employer's taxable year.

(vii) *Special rule for plan funded through multiple trusts.*—In cases in which a plan is funded through more than one foreign employees' trust, the fractional interest determined under paragraph (h)(3)(i) of this section in each trust is determined by treating all of the trusts as if their assets were held in a single trust for which the fraction is determined in accordance with the rules of this paragraph (h)(3).

(4) *De minimis exception.*—If the relevant amount is not greater than the plan's normal cost for the plan year ending with or within the employer's taxable year, computed using a funding method and actuarial assumptions as described in paragraph (h)(3)(ii) of this section or as described in paragraph (h)(3)(iii) of this section if the requirements of that paragraph are met, that are used to determine plan contributions, then the relevant amount is considered to be zero for purposes of applying paragraph (h)(3)(i) of this section.

(5) *General rule for transition amount.*—(i) *General rule.*—If paragraphs (h)(6) and (h)(7) of this section do not apply to the employer, the transition amount for purposes of paragraph (h)(3)(iv) of this section is equal to the preexisting amount multiplied by the applicable percentage for the year in which the employer's taxable year begins.

(ii) *Preexisting amount.*—The preexisting amount is equal to the relevant amount of the trust, determined without regard to paragraphs (h)(3)(iv) and (h)(4) of this section, computed as of the measurement date that immediately precedes September 27, 1996 disregarding contributions to the trust made after the measurement date.

(iii) *Applicable percentage.*—The applicable percentage is equal to 100 percent for the employer's first taxable year ending after this document is published as a final regulation in the Federal Register and prior taxable years of the employer, and is reduced (but not below zero) by 10 percentage points for each subsequent taxable year of the employer.

(6) *Transition amount for new CFCs.*—(i) *General rule.*—In the case of a new controlled foreign corporation employer, the transition amount for purposes of paragraph (h)(3)(iv) is equal to the pre-change amount multiplied by the applicable percentage for the year in which the new controlled foreign corporation employer's taxable year begins.

(ii) *Pre-change amount.*—The pre-change amount for purposes of paragraph (h)(6)(i) is equal to the relevant amount of the trust, determined without regard to paragraphs (h)(3)(iv) and (h)(4) of this section and disregarding contributions to the trust made after the measurement date, for the new controlled foreign corporation employer's last taxable year ending before the corporation becomes a new controlled foreign corporation employer.

(iii) *Applicable percentage.*—(A) *General rule.*—Except as provided in paragraph (h)(6)(iii)(B) of this section, the applicable percentage is equal to 100 percent for a new controlled foreign corporation employer's first taxable year ending after the corporation becomes a controlled foreign corporation. The applicable percentage is reduced (but not below zero) by 10 percentage points for each subsequent taxable year of the new controlled foreign corporation.

(B) *Interim rule.*—For any taxable year of a new controlled foreign corporation employer that ends on or before the date this document is published as a final regulation in the Federal Register, the applicable percentage is equal to 100 percent. The applicable percentage is reduced by 10 percentage points for each subsequent taxable year of the new controlled foreign corporation employer that ends after the date this document is published as a final regulation in the Federal Register.

(iv) *New CFC employer.*—For purposes of paragraph (h)(6) of this section, a new controlled foreign corporation employer is a corporation that first becomes a controlled foreign corporation within the meaning of section 957 after September 27, 1996. A new controlled foreign corporation employer includes a corporation that was a controlled foreign corporation prior to, but not on, September 27, 1996 and that first becomes a controlled foreign corporation again after September 27, 1996.

(v) *Anti-stuffing rule.*—Notwithstanding paragraph (h)(6)(iii) of this section, if, prior to becoming a controlled foreign corporation, a corporation contributes amounts to a foreign employees' trust with a principal purpose of obtaining tax benefits by increasing the pre-change amount, the applicable percentage with respect to those amounts is 0 percent for all taxable years of the new controlled foreign corporation employer.

(7) *Transition amount for new U.S.-related foreign partnerships.*—(i) *General rule.*—In the case of a new U.S.-related foreign partnership employer, the transition amount for purposes of paragraph (h)(3)(iv) of this section is equal to the pre-change amount multiplied by the applicable percentage for the year in which the new U.S.-related foreign partnership employer's taxable year begins.

(ii) *Pre-change amount.*—The pre-change amount for purposes of paragraph (h)(7)(i) of this section is equal to the relevant amount of the trust, determined without regard to paragraphs (h)(3)(iv) and (h)(4) of this section and disregarding contributions to the trust made after the measurement date, for the entity's last taxable year ending before the entity becomes a new U.S.-related foreign partnership employer.

(iii) *Applicable percentage.*—(A) *General rule.*—Except as provided in paragraph (h)(7)(iii)(B) of this section, the applicable percentage is equal to 100 percent for a new U.S.-related foreign partnership employer's first taxable year ending after the entity becomes a new U.S.-related foreign partnership employer. The applicable percentage is reduced (but not below zero) by 10 percentage points for each subsequent taxable year of the new U.S.-related foreign partnership employer.

(B) *Interim rule.*—For any taxable year of a new U.S.-related foreign partnership employer that ends on or before the date this document is published as a final regulation in the Federal Register, the applicable percentage is equal to 100 percent. The applicable percentage is reduced by 10 percentage points for each subsequent taxable year of the new U.S.-related foreign partnership employer that ends after the date this document is published as a final regulation in the Federal Register.

(iv) *New U.S.-related foreign partnership employer.*—For purposes of paragraph (h)(7) of this section, a new U.S.-related foreign partnership employer is an entity that was a foreign corporation other than a controlled foreign corporation, or that was a foreign partnership other than a U.S.-related foreign partnership, and that changes from this status to a U.S.-related foreign partnership after September 27, 1996. A new U.S.-related foreign partnership employer includes a corporation that was a U.S.-related foreign partnership prior to, but not on, September 27, 1996 and that first becomes a U.S.-related foreign partnership again after September 27, 1996.

(v) *Anti-stuffing rule.*—Notwithstanding paragraph (h)(7)(iii) of this section, if, prior to becoming a new U.S.-related foreign partnership employer, an entity contributes amounts to a foreign employees' trust with a principal purpose of obtaining tax benefits by increasing the pre-change amount, the applicable percentage with respect to those amounts is 0 percent for all taxable years of the new U.S.-related foreign partnership employer.

(8) *Examples.*—The following examples illustrate the rules of paragraph (h) of this section. In each example, the employer has a power or interest described in sections 673 through 677 over the foreign employees' trust, and the monetary unit is the applicable functional currency (FC) determined in accordance with section 985(b) and the regulations thereunder.

Example 1. (i) Employer X is a controlled foreign corporation (as defined in section 957). Employer X maintains a defined benefit retirement plan for its employees. Employer X's taxable year is the calendar year. Trust T, a foreign employees' trust, is the sole funding vehicle for the plan. Both the plan year of the plan and the taxable year of Trust T are the calendar year.

(ii) As of December 31, 1997, Trust T's measurement date, the fair market value (as described in paragraph (h)(3)(iv) of this section) of Trust T's assets is FC 1,000,000, and the amount of the plan's accrued liability is FC 800,000, which includes a normal cost for 1997 of FC 50,000. The preexisting amount for Trust T is FC 40,000. Thus, the relevant amount for 1997 is FC 160,000 (which is greater than the plan's normal cost for the year). Employer X's shareholder does not indicate on a statement attached to a timely filed Form 5471 that any of the relevant amount qualifies for the exception described in paragraph (h)(3)(iii) of this section. Therefore, the fractional interest for Employer X's taxable year ending on December 31, 1997, is 16 percent. Employer X is treated as the owner for federal income tax purposes of an undivided 16 percent interest in each of Trust T's assets for the period from January 1, 1997 through December 31, 1997. Employer X must take into account a 16 percent pro rata share of each item of income, deduction or credit of Trust T during this period in computing its federal income tax liability.

Example 2. Assume the same facts as in *Example 1*, except that Employer X's shareholder indicates on a statement attached to a timely filed Form 5471 and can demonstrate to the satisfaction of the Commissioner that, in reliance on paragraph (h)(3)(iii) of this section, FC 100,000 of the fair market value of Trust T's assets is attributable to favorable experience relative to reasonable actuarial assumptions used. Accordingly, the relevant amount for 1997 is FC 60,000. Because the plan's normal cost for 1997 is less than FC 60,000, the de minimis exception of paragraph (h)(4) of this section does not apply. Therefore, the fractional interest for Employer X's taxable year ending on December 31, 1997, is 6 percent. Employer X is treated as the owner for federal income tax purposes of an undivided 6 percent interest in each of Trust T's assets for the period from January 1, 1997, through December 31, 1997. Employer X must take into account a 6 percent pro rata share of each item of income, deduction or credit of Trust T during this period in computing its federal income tax liability.

(9) *Effective date.*—Paragraphs (g) and (h) of this section apply to taxable years of an employer ending after September 27, 1996.

☐ Par. 3. Section 1.671-2 is amended by adding paragraph (f) to read as follows:

§ 1.671-2. Applicable principles.

* * *

(f) For purposes of subtitle A of the Internal Revenue Code, a person that is treated as the owner of any portion of a trust under subpart E is considered to own the trust assets attributable to that portion of the trust.

CFCs: U.S. Shareholders: Ownership Attribution

CFCs: U.S. Shareholders: Ownership Attribution.—Amendments to Reg. § 1.672(f)-2, relating to the modification of section 958(b) of the Internal Revenue Code by the Tax Cuts and Jobs Act, which was enacted on December 22, 2017, are proposed (published in the Federal Register on October 2, 2019) (REG-104223-18).

Par. 5. Section 1.672(f)-2 is amended by revising paragraphs (a) and (e) to read as follows:

§ 1.672(f)-2. Certain foreign corporations.—(a) *Application of general rule in this section.*—Subject to the provisions of paragraph (b) of this section, if the owner of any portion of a trust upon application of the grantor trust rules without regard to section 672(f) is a controlled foreign corporation or a passive foreign investment company (as defined in section 1297), the corporation will be treated as a domestic corporation for purposes of applying the rules of § 1.672(f)-1. For purposes of this section, the only controlled foreign corporations taken into account are those that are controlled foreign corporations within the meaning provided in section 957, determined without applying subparagraphs (A), (B), and (C) of section 318(a)(3) so as to consider a United States person as owning stock which is owned by a person who is not a United States person.

* * *

(e) *Applicability dates.*—Except as provided in this paragraph (e), the rules of this section apply to taxable years of shareholders of controlled foreign corporations and passive foreign investment companies beginning after August 10, 1999, and taxable years of controlled foreign corporations and passive foreign investment companies ending with or within such taxable years of the shareholders. The provisions in paragraph (a) of this section relating to the controlled foreign corporations taken into account for purposes of this section apply to taxable years of foreign corporations ending on or after October 1, 2019, and taxable years of United States shareholders in which or with which such taxable years of foreign corporations

end. For taxable years of foreign corporations ending before October 1, 2019, and taxable years of United States shareholders in which or with which such taxable years of foreign corporations end, a taxpayer may apply such provisions to the last taxable year of a foreign corporation beginning before January 1, 2018, and each subsequent taxable year of the foreign corporation, and to taxable years of United States shareholders in which or with which such taxable years of the foreign corporation end, provided that the taxpayer and United States persons that are related (within the meaning of section 267 or 707) to the taxpayer consistently apply such provisions with respect to all foreign corporations.

PARTNERS AND PARTNERSHIPS

Personal Service Corporation: Taxable Years

Personal Service Corporations: Partnerships: S Corporations: Taxable Years.—Temporary Reg. §1.702-3T is also proposed as a final regulation and, when adopted, would become Reg. §1.702-3 (published in the Federal Register on December 23, 1987).

§1.702-3. 4-year spread.

Partnerships: Equity for Services

Partnerships: Equity for Services.—Amendments to Reg. §1.704-1, providing that the transfer of a partnership interest in connection with the performance of services is subject to Code Sec. 83 and providing rules for coordinating Code Sec. 83 with partnership taxation principles, are proposed (published in the Federal Register on May 24, 2005) (REG-105346-03).

☐ Par. 4. Section 1.704-1 is amended as follows:

1. In paragraph (b)(0), an entry is added to the table for §1.704-1(b)(4)(xii).
2. In paragraph (b)(1)(ii)(*a*), a sentence is added at the end of the paragraph.
3. Paragraph (b)(2)(iv)(*b*)(*1*) is revised.
4. Paragraph (b)(2)(iv)(*f*)(*5*)(*iii*) is revised.
5. Paragraph (b)(4)(xii) is added.
6. Paragraph (b)(5) *Example 29* is added.

The additions and revisions read as follows:

§1.704-1. Partner's distributive share.

***

(b) *** (0) ***

***

Substantialy nonvested interests . . . . 1.704-1(b)(4)(xii)

***

(1) ***

(ii) *** (*a*) *** In addition, paragraph (b)(4)(xii) and paragraph (b)(5) *Example 29* of this section apply to compensatory partnership interests (as defined in §1.721-1(b)(3)) that are transferred on or after the date final regulations are published in the Federal Register.

***

(2) ***

(iv) ***

(*b*) ***

(*1*) the amount of money contributed by that partner to the partnership and, in the case of a compensatory partnership interest (as defined in §1.721-1(b)(3)) that is transferred on or after the date final regulations are published in the Federal Register, the amount included on or after that date in the partner's compensation income under section 83(a), (b), or (d)(2).

***

(*f*) ***

(*5*) ***

(*iii*) In connection with the transfer or vesting of a compensatory partnership interest (as defined in §1.721-1(b)(3)) that is transferred on or after the date final regulations are published in the Federal Register, but only if the transfer or vesting results in the service provider recognizing income under section 83 (or would result in such recognition if the interest had a fair market value other than zero).

***

(4) ***

(xii) *Substantially nonvested interests.*—(*a*) *In general.*—If a section 83(b) election has been made with respect to a substantially nonvested interest, the holder of the nonvested interest may be allocated partnership income, gain, loss, deduction, or credit (or items thereof) that will later be forfeited. For this reason, allocations of partnership items while the interest is substantially nonvested cannot have economic effect.

(*b*) *Deemed Compliance with Partners' Interests in the Partnership.*—If a section 83(b) election has been made with respect to a substantially nonvested interest, allocations of partnership items while the interest is substantially nonvested will be deemed to be in accordance with the partners' interests in the partnership if—

(*1*) The partnership agreement requires that the partnership make forfeiture allocations if the interest for which the section 83(b) election is made is later forfeited; and

(*2*) All material allocations and capital account adjustments under the partnership agreement not pertaining to substantially nonvested partnership interests for which a section 83(b) election has been made are recognized under section 704(b).

(*c*) *Forfeiture allocations.*—Forfeiture allocations are allocations to the service provider (consisting of a pro rata portion of each item) of gross income and gain or gross deduction and loss (to the extent such items are available) for the taxable year of the forfeiture in a positive or negative amount equal to—

(*1*) The excess (not less than zero) of the—

(*i*) Amount of distributions (including deemed distributions under section 752(b) and the adjusted tax basis of any property so distributed) to the partner with respect to the forfeited partnership interest (to the extent such distributions are not taxable under section 731); over

(*ii*) Amounts paid for the interest and the adjusted tax basis of property contributed by the partner (including deemed contributions under section 752(a)) to the partnership with respect to the forfeited partnership interest; minus

(*2*) The cumulative net income (or loss) allocated to the partner with respect to the forfeited partnership interest.

(*d*) *Positive and negative amounts.*—For purposes of paragraph (b)(4)(xii)(*c*) of this section, items of income and gain are reflected as positive amounts, and items of deduction and loss are reflected as negative amounts.

(*e*) *Exception.*—Paragraph (b)(4)(xii)(*b*) of this section shall not apply to allocations of partnership items made with respect to a substantially nonvested interest for which the holder has made a section 83(b) election if, at the time of the section 83(b) election, there is a plan that the interest will be forfeited. In such a case, the partners' distributive shares of partnership items shall be determined in accordance with the partners' interests in the partnership under paragraph (b)(3) of this section. In determining whether there is a plan that the interest will be forfeited, the Commissioner will consider all of the facts and circumstances (including the tax status of the holder of the forfeitable compensatory partnership interest).

(*f*) *Cross references.*—Forfeiture allocations may be made out of the partnership's items for the entire taxable year of the forfeiture. See §1.706-3(b) and paragraph (b)(5) *Example 29* of this section.

***

(5) ***

Example 29. (i) In Year 1, A and B each contribute cash to LLC, a newly formed limited liability company classified as a partnership for Federal tax purposes, in exchange for equal units in LLC. Under LLC's operating agreement, each unit is entitled to participate equally in the profits and losses of LLC. The operating agreement also provides that the partners' capital accounts will be determined and maintained in accordance with paragraph (b)(2)(iv) of this section, that liquidation proceeds will be distributed in accordance with the partners' positive capital account balances, and that any partner with a deficit balance in that partner's capital account following the liquidation of the partner's interest must restore that deficit to the partnership. At the beginning of Year 3, SP agrees to perform services for LLC. In connection with the performance of SP's services and a payment of $10 by SP to LLC, LLC transfers a 10% interest in LLC to SP. SP's interest in LLC is substantially nonvested (within the meaning of §1.83-3(b)). At the time of the transfer of the LLC interest to SP, LLC's operating agreement is amended to provide that, if SP's interest is forfeited, then SP is entitled to a return of SP's $10 initial contribution, and SP's distributive share of all partnership items (other than forfeiture allocations under §1.704-1(b)(4)(xii)) will be zero with respect to that interest for the taxable year of the partnership in which the interest was forfeited. The operating agreement is also amended to require that LLC make forfeiture allocations if SP's interest is forfeited. Additionally, the operating agreement is amended to provide that no part of LLC's compensation deduction is allocated to the service provider to whom the interest is transferred. SP makes an election under section 83(b) with respect to SP's interest in LLC. Upon receipt, the fair market value of SP's interest in LLC is $100. In each of Years 3, 4, 5, and 6, LLC has operating income of $100 (consisting of $200 of gross receipts and $100 of deductible expenses), and makes no distributions. SP forfeits SP's interest in LLC at the beginning of Year 6. At the time of the transfer of the interest to SP, there is no plan that SP will forfeit the interest in LLC.

(ii) Because a section 83(b) election is made, SP recognizes compensation income in the year of the transfer of the LLC interest. Therefore, SP recognizes $90 of compensation income in the year of the transfer of the LLC interest (the excess of the fair market value of SP's interest in LLC, $100, over the amount SP paid for the interest, $10). Under paragraph (b)(2)(iv)(*b*)(*1*) of this section, in Year 3, SP's capital account is initially credited with $100, the amount paid for the interest ($10) plus the amount included in SP's compensation income upon the transfer under section 83(b) ($90). Under §§1.83-6(b) and 1.721-1(b)(2), LLC does not recognize gain on the transfer of the

interest to SP. LLC is entitled to a compensation deduction of $90 under section 83(h). Under the terms of the operating agreement, the deduction is allocated equally to A and B.

(iii) As a result of SP's election under section 83(b), SP is treated as a partner starting from the date of the transfer of the LLC interest to SP in Year 3. Section 1.761-1(b). In each of years 3, 4 and 5, SP's distributive share of partnership income is $10 (10% of $100), A's distributive share of partnership income is $45 (45% of $100), and B's distributive share of partnership income is $45 (45% of $100). In accordance with the operating agreement, SP's capital account is increased (to $130) by the end of Year 5 by the amounts allocated to SP, and A's and B's capital accounts are increased by the amounts allocated to A and B. Because LLC satisfies the requirements of paragraph (b)(4)(xii) of this section, LLC's allocations in years 3, 4 and 5 are deemed to be in accordance with the partners' interests in the partnership.

(iv) As a result of the forfeiture of the LLC interest by SP in year 6, LLC is required to recognize income ($90) equal to the amount of the allowable deduction on the transfer of the LLC interest to SP under §1.83-6(c). LLC repays SP's $10 capital contribution to SP, reducing SP's capital account to $120. Under the terms of the operating agreement, because SP forfeited SP's interest, SP's distributive share of all partnership items (other than forfeiture allocations) is zero for Year 6. To reverse SP's prior allocations of LLC income, LLC makes forfeiture allocations of $30 of deductions ($0 (the difference between the $10 distributed to SP and the $10 contributed to LLC by SP) minus $30 (the cumulative net LLC income allocated to SP) to SP in Year 6. Notwithstanding section 706(c) and (d), these allocations may be made out of LLC's partnership items for the entire taxable year of the forfeiture. Thus, in Year 6, $30 of deductions are allocated to SP, and the remaining $220 of net operating income ($200 of gross receipts and $90 of income under §1.83-6(c) less $70 of remaining deductions) are allocated to A and B equally for tax purposes. In accordance with section 83(b)(1) (last sentence), SP does not receive a deduction or capital loss for the amount ($90) that was included in SP's compensation income. Because LLC satisfies the requirements of paragraph (b)(4)(xii) of this section, LLC's allocations in year 6 are deemed to be in accordance with the partners' interests in the partnership.

* * *

Allocation and Apportionment of Deductions and Foreign Tax Credit: Guidance

Allocation and Apportionment of Deductions and Foreign Tax Credit: Guidance.—Amendments to Reg. §1.704-1, relating to the allocation and apportionment of deductions and creditable foreign taxes, the definition of financial services income, foreign tax redeterminations, availability of foreign tax credits under the transition tax, and the application of the foreign tax credit limitation to consolidated groups, are proposed (published in the Federal Register on December 17, 2019) (REG-105495-19).

Par 2. Section 1.704-1 is amended by

1. Revising the fourth sentence and adding a new fifth sentence in paragraph (b)(1)(ii)(*b*)(*1*).

2. Revising paragraph (b)(4)(viii)(*d*)(*1*).

The revisions read as follows:

§1.704-1. Partner's distributive share.

* * *

(b) * * *

(1) * * *

(ii) * * *

(*b*) * * *

(*1*) * * * Except as provided in the next sentence, the provisions of paragraphs (b)(4)(viii)(*a*)(*1*), (b)(4)(viii)(*c*)(*1*), (b)(4)(viii)(*c*)(*2*)(*ii*) and (*iii*), and (b)(4)(viii)(*c*)(*3*) and (*4*), (b)(4)(viii)(*d*)(*1*) (as in effect on July 24, 2019), and *Examples 1, 2,* and *3* in paragraphs (b)(6)(i), (ii), and (iii) of this section apply for partnership taxable years that both begin on or after January 1, 2016, and end after February 4, 2016. For partnership taxable years beginning after December 31, 2019, paragraph (b)(4)(viii)(*d*)(*1*) of this section applies. * * *

* * *

(4) * * *

(viii) * * *

(*d*) * * *

(*1*) *In general.*—CFTEs are allocated and apportioned to CFTE categories in accordance with §1.861-20 by treating each CFTE category as a statutory grouping (with no residual grouping). See *Examples 2* and *3* in paragraphs (b)(6)(ii) and (iii) of this section, which illustrate the application of this paragraph in the case of serial disregarded payments subject to withholding tax. In addition, if as described in §1.861-20(e), foreign law does not provide for the direct allocation or apportionment of expenses, losses or other deductions allowed under foreign law to a CFTE category of income, then such expenses, losses or other deductions must be allocated and apportioned to gross income as determined under foreign law in a manner that is consistent with the allocation and apportionment of such items for purposes of determining the net income in the CFTE categories for Federal income tax purposes pursuant to paragraph (b)(4)(viii)(*c*)(*3*) of this section.

* * *

Partners and Partnerships: Sales or Exchanges: Certain Distributions

Partners and Partnerships: Sales or Exchanges: Certain Distributions.—Amendments to Reg. §§1.704-1 and 1.704-3, prescribing how a partner should measure its interest in a partnership's unrealized receivables and inventory items, and that provide guidance regarding the tax consequences of a distribution that causes a reduction in that interest, are proposed (published in the Federal Register on November 3, 2014) (REG-151416-06).

☐ Par. 3. Section 1.704-1 is amended by:

a. Revising paragraph (b)(2)(iv)(*f*) introductory text.

b. Redesignating paragraph (b)(2)(iv)(*f*)(*5*)(*v*) as paragraph (b)(2)(iv)(*f*)(*5*)(*vi*).

c. Adding new paragraph (b)(2)(iv)(*f*)(*5*)(*v*).

d. Designating the undesignated text after paragraph (b)(2)(iv)(*f*)(*5*)(*vi*) as paragraph (b)(2)(iv)(*f*)(*5*)(*vii*).

The revisions and additions read as follows:

§1.704-1. Partner's distributive share.

* * *

(b) * * *

    (2) * * *

        (iv) * * *

        (f) Revaluations of property.—A partnership agreement may, upon the occurrence of certain events, and must in the circumstances described in §1.751-1(b)(2)(iv), increase or decrease the capital accounts of the partners to reflect a revaluation of partnership property (including intangible assets such as goodwill) on the partnership's books. If a partnership that revalues its property pursuant to this paragraph owns an interest in another partnership, that partnership in which it owns an interest may also revalue its property in

accordance with this section. Similarly, if an interest in a partnership that revalues its property pursuant to this paragraph is owned by another partnership, the partnership owning that interest may also revalue its property in accordance with this section. Capital accounts so adjusted will not be considered to be determined and maintained in accordance with the rules of this paragraph (b)(2)(iv) unless—

* * *

(5) * * *

        (v) In connection with an agreement to change (other than a de minimis change) the manner in which the partners share any item or class of items of income, gain, loss, deduction or credit of the partnership under the partnership agreement, or

* * *

□ Par. 4. Section 1.704-3 is amended in paragraph (a)(9) by adding a sentence immediately following the first sentence to read as follows:

§1.704-3. Contributed property.—(a) * * *

    (9) * * * If a partnership (the upper-tier partnership) owns an interest in another partnership (the lower-tier partnership), and both the upper-tier partnership and the lower-tier partnership simultane-

ously revalue partnership property pursuant to §1.704-1(b)(2)(iv)(f), the principles of this paragraph (a)(9) shall apply to any reverse section 704(c) allocations created upon the revaluation. * * *

* * *

□ Par. 18. For each section listed in the table, remove the language in the "Remove" column and add in its place the language in the "Add" column as set forth below:

Section	Remove	Add
§1.704-3, paragraph (a)(6)(ii)	§1.743-1(b) or 1.751-1(a)(2)	§1.743-1(b), 1.751-1(a)(2), or 1.751-1(b)

Partnerships: Centralized Partnership Audit Regime

Partnerships: Centralized Partnership Audit Regime.—Amendments to Reg. §1.704-1, implementing the centralized partnership audit regime that have not been finalized to reflect the changes made by the Technical Corrections Act of 2018, contained in Title II of the Consolidated Appropriations Act of 2018 (TTCA), are proposed (published in the Federal Register on August 17, 2018) (REG-136118-15; REG-119337-17; REG-118067-17; REG-120232-17 and REG-120233-17).

Par. 2. Section 1.704-1 is amended by:

1. Adding paragraph (b)(1)(viii).

2. Adding a sentence to the end of paragraph (b)(2)(iii)(*a*).

3. Adding paragraphs (b)(2)(iii)(*f*), (b)(2)(iv)(*i*)(4), and (b)(4)(xi) through (xv).

The additions read as follows:

§1.704-1. Partner's distributive share.

* * *

(b) * * *

    (1) * * *

        (viii) *Items relating to a final determination under the centralized partnership audit regime.*—(*a*) *In general.*—Certain items of income, gain, loss, deduction or credit may result from a final determination under subchapter C of chapter 63 of the Internal Revenue Code (subchapter C of chapter 63) (relating to the centralized partnership audit regime). Special rules under section 704(b) and §1.704-1(b) apply to these items that take into account that the item relates to the reviewed year (as defined in §301.6241-1(a)(8) of this chapter) but occurs in the adjustment year (as defined in §301.6241-1(a)(1) of this chapter). See paragraphs (b)(2)(iii)(*a*) and (*f*), (b)(2)(iv)(*i*)(4), and (b)(4)(xi) through (xv) of this section.

        (*b*) *Successors.*—(*1*) *In general.*—In the case of a transfer or liquidation of a partnership interest subsequent to a reviewed year, a successor has the meaning provided in paragraph (b)(1)(viii)(*b*) of this section. In the case of a subsequent transfer by a successor of a partnership interest, the principles of paragraph (b)(1)(viii)(*b*) of this section will also apply to the new successor.

        (*2*) *Identifiable transferee partner.*—Except as otherwise provided in paragraph (b)(1)(viii)(*b*)(3) of this section, in the case of a transfer of all or part of a partnership interest during or subsequent to the reviewed year, a successor is the partner to which the reviewed year transferor partner's capital account carried over (or would carry over if the partnership maintained capital accounts) under paragraph (b)(2)(iv)(*l*) of this section (an identifiable transferee partner).

        (*3*) *Unidentifiable transferee partner.*—If, after exercising reasonable diligence, the partnership cannot determine an identifiable transferee partner under paragraph (b)(1)(viii)(*b*)(2) of this section, each partner in the adjustment year that is not an identifiable transferee partner and was not a partner in the reviewed year, (an unidentifiable transferee partner) is a successor to the extent of the proportion of its interest in the partnership to the total interests of unidentifiable transferee partners in the partnership (considering all facts and circumstances).

        (*4*) *Liquidation of partnership interest.*—In the case of a liquidation of a partner's entire interest in the partnership during or subsequent to the reviewed year, the successors to the liquidated partner are certain adjustment year partners (as defined in

§301.6241-1(a)(2) of this chapter) as provided in this paragraph (b)(1)(viii)(*b*)(4). The determination of the extent to which the adjustment year partners are treated as successors under this section must be made in a manner that reflects the extent to which the adjustment year partners' interests in the partnership increased as a result of the liquidating distribution (considering all facts and circumstances).

    (2) * * *

        (iii) * * *

        (*a*) * * *Notwithstanding any other sentence of this paragraph (b)(2)(iii)(*a*), an allocation of any of the following will be substantial only if the allocation is described in paragraph (b)(2)(iii)(*f*) of this section: an expenditure for any payment required to be made by a partnership under subchapter C of chapter 63 (relating to the centralized partnership audit regime), adjustments reflected on a statement furnished to a pass-through partner (as defined in §301.6241-1(a)(5) of this chapter) under §301.6226-3(e)(4) of this chapter, or interest, penalties, additions to tax, or additional amounts described in section 6233.

* * *

        (*f*) *Certain expenditures under the centralized partnership audit regime.*—(*1*) *In general.*—The economic effect of an allocation of an expenditure for any payment required to be made by a partnership under subchapter C of chapter 63 (as described in §301.6241-4(a) of this chapter) is substantial only if the expenditure is allocated in the manner described in this paragraph (b)(2)(iii)(*f*). For partnerships with allocations that do not satisfy paragraph (b)(2)(ii) of this section, see paragraph (b)(4)(xi) of this section.

        (*2*) *Expenditures for imputed underpayments or similar amounts.*—Except as otherwise provided, an expenditure for an imputed underpayment, as defined in §301.6241-1(a)(3) of this chapter, is allocated to the reviewed year partner (or its successor, as defined in paragraph (b)(1)(viii)(*b*) of this section) in proportion to the allocation of the notional item (as described in §301.6225-4(b) of this chapter) to which the expenditure relates, taking into account modifications under §301.6225-2 of this chapter attributable to that partner.

        (*3*) *Interest, penalties, additions to tax, or additional amounts described in section 6233.*—An expenditure for interest, penalties, additions to tax, or additional amounts as determined under section 6233 (or penalties and interest described in §301.6226-3(e)(4)(iv) of this chapter) is allocated to the reviewed year partner (or its successor, as defined in paragraph (b)(1)(viii)(*b*) of this section) in proportion to the allocation of the portion of the imputed underpayment with respect to which the penalty applies or related notional item to which it relates (whichever is appropriate), taking into account modifications under § 301.6225-2 of this chapter attributable to that partner.

(4) *Imputed underpayments unrelated to notional items.*— In the case of an imputed underpayment that results from a partnership adjustment for which no notional items are created under § 301.6225-4(b)(2) of this chapter, the expenditure must be allocated to the reviewed year partner (or its successor, as defined in paragraph (b)(1)(viii)(b) of this section) that would have borne the economic benefit or burden of the partnership adjustment if the partnership and its partners had originally reported in a manner consistent with the partnership adjustment that resulted in the imputed underpayment with respect to the reviewed year.

(iv) * * *

(i) * * *

(4) *Certain expenditures under the centralized partnership audit regime.*—Notwithstanding paragraph (b)(2)(iv)(i)(1) of this section, the economic effect of an allocation of an expenditure for any payment required to be made by a partnership under subchapter C of chapter 63 (as described in § 301.6241-4(a) of this chapter) is substantial only if the expenditure is allocated in the manner described in paragraph (b)(2)(iii)(f) of this section. For partnerships with allocations that do not satisfy paragraph (b)(2)(ii) of this section, see paragraph (b)(4)(xii) of this section.

* * *

(4) * * *

(xi) *Notional items under the centralized partnership audit regime.*—An allocation of a notional item (as described in § 301.6225-4(b)(3) of this chapter) does not have substantial economic effect within the meaning of paragraph (b)(2) of this section. However, the allocation of a notional item of income or gain described in § 301.6225-4(b)(3)(ii) and (iv) of this chapter, or expense or loss described in § 301.6225-4(b)(3)(iii) and (v) of this chapter, will be deemed to be in accordance with the partners' interests in the partnership if the notional item is allocated in the manner in which the corresponding actual item would have been allocated in the reviewed year under the rules of this section, treating successors (as defined in paragraph (b)(1)(viii)(b) of this section) as reviewed year partners. Additionally, the allocation of a notional item of expense or loss described in § 301.6225-4(b)(3)(iv) of this chapter, or a notional item of income or gain described in § 301.6225-4(b)(3)(v) of this chapter, will be deemed to be in accordance with the partners' interests in the partnership if the notional item is allocated to the reviewed year partners (or their successors as defined in paragraph

(b)(1)(viii)(b) of this section) in the manner in which the excess item was allocated in the reviewed year.

(xii) *Certain section 705(a)(2)(B) expenditures under the centralized partnership audit regime.*—An allocation of an expenditure for any payment required to be made by a partnership under subchapter C of chapter 63 (relating to the centralized partnership audit regime and as described in § 301.6241-4(a) of this chapter) will be deemed to be in accordance with the partners' interests in the partnership, as provided in paragraph (b)(3) of this section, only if the expenditure is allocated in the manner described in paragraph (b)(2)(iii)(f) of this section and if the partners' distribution rights are reduced by the partners' shares of the imputed underpayment.

(xiii) *Partnership adjustments that do not result in an imputed underpayment under the centralized partnership audit regime.*—An allocation of an item arising from a partnership adjustment that does not result in an imputed underpayment (as defined in § 301.6225-1(f) of this chapter) does not have substantial economic effect within the meaning of paragraph (b)(2) of this section. However, the allocation of such an item will be deemed to be in accordance with the partners' interests in the partnership if allocated in the manner in which the item would have been allocated in the reviewed year under the rules of this section, treating successors as defined in paragraph (b)(1)(viii)(b) of this section as reviewed year partners.

(xiv) *Partnership adjustments subject to an election under section 6226.*—An allocation of an item arising from a partnership adjustment that results in an imputed underpayment for which an election is made under § 301.6226-1 of this chapter does not have substantial economic effect within the meaning of paragraph (b)(2) of this section. However, the allocation of such an item will be deemed to be in accordance with the partners' interests in the partnership if allocated in the adjustment year (as defined in § 301.6241-1(a)(1) of this chapter) in the manner in which the item would have been allocated under the rules of this section (or otherwise taken into account under subtitle A of the Code) in the reviewed year (as defined in § 301.6241-1(a)(8) of this chapter), followed by any intervening years (as defined in § 301.6226-3(b)(3) of this chapter), concluding with the reporting year (as defined in § 301.6226-3(a) of this chapter).

(xv) *Substantial economic effect under sections 168(h) and 514(c)(9)(E)(i)(ll).*—An allocation described in paragraphs (b)(4)(xi) through (xiv) of this section will be deemed to have substantial economic effect for purposes of sections 168(h) and 514(c)(9)(E)(i)(ll) if the allocation is deemed to be in accordance with the partners' interests in the partnership under the applicable rules set forth in paragraphs (b)(4)(xi) through (xiv) of this section.

* * *

Partnerships: Distribution of Property: Assets-Over Merger

Partnerships: Distribution of Property: Assets-Over Merger.—Amendments to Reg. §§ 1.704-3 and 1.704-4, providing rules concerning the application of Code Secs. 704(c)(1)(B) and 737 to distributions of property after two partnerships engage in an assets-over merger, are proposed (published in the Federal Register on August 22, 2007) (REG-143397-05) (corrected November 6, 2007).

☐ Par. 2. Section 1.704-3 is amended as follows:

1. Paragraphs (a)(9) through (a)(12) are redesignated as paragraphs (a)(10) through (a)(13), respectively.

2. New paragraph (a)(9) is added.

3. Paragraph (f) is amended by revising the paragraph heading and adding one additional sentence at the end of the paragraph.

The revisions and additions read as follows:

§ 1.704-3. Contributed Property.
(a) * * *

(9) *Section 704(c) property transferred in an assets-over merger.*— Assets transferred to a transferee partnership from the transferor partnership in an assets-over merger as defined in § 1.708-1(c)(3)(i) (the transferor partnership being the partnership considered to have been terminated under § 1.708-1(c)(1) and the transferee partnership being the partnership considered to be the resulting partnership under § 1.708-(1)(c)(1)) may have both original section 704(c) gain or loss (see § 1.704-4(c)(4)(ii)(A) for the definition of original section 704(c) gain or loss) and new section 704(c) gain or loss. The transferee partnership may continue to use the section 704(c) allocation method adopted by the transferor partnership with respect to section 704(c) property originally contributed to the transferor partnership or it may adopt another reasonable section 704(c) method. Also, the transferee partnership may continue to use the section 704(c) allocation

method adopted by the transferor partnership with respect to new section 704(c) gain or loss to account for differences between book value and adjusted tax basis as a result of a prior revaluation. In addition, the transferee partnership may adopt any reasonable section 704(c) method with respect to new section 704(c) gain or loss in excess of the amount of new section 704(c) gain or loss described in the prior sentence. With respect to both original and new section 704(c) gain or loss, the transferee partnership must use a reasonable method that is consistent with the purpose of sections 704(b) and 704(c).

* * *

(f) *Effective/applicability date.*—* * * Paragraph (a)(9) is effective for any distribution of property after January 19, 2005, if such property was contributed in a merger using the assets-over form after May 3, 2004.

☐ Par. 3. Section 1.704-4 is amended as follows:

1. Paragraph (a)(1) is amended by removing the phrase "five years" and adding in its place the phrase "seven years."

2. Paragraph (a)(4)(i) is amended by removing the phrase "five-year" and adding in its place the phrase "seven-year."

3. Paragraph (a)(4)(ii) is amended by removing the phrase "five-year" and adding in its place the phrase "seven-year."

4. Paragraphs (c)(4)(i) and (c)(4)(ii) are added.

5. Paragraph (c)(7) is redesignated as paragraph (c)(8).

6. A new paragraph (c)(7) is added.

7. Paragraphs (f)(2), *Examples (1) and (2)* are amended by removing the language "five-year" and replacing it with the language "seven-year" wherever it appears throughout both examples.

8. Paragraph (g) is amended by revising the paragraph heading and adding two sentences at the end of the paragraph.

The revisions and additions read as follows:

§1.704-4. Distribution of contributed property.

* * *

(c) * * *

(4) *Complete transfer to another partnership (Assets-Over Merger).*—(i) *In general.*—Section 704(c)(1)(B) and this section do not apply to the transfer in an assets-over merger as defined in §1.708-1(c)(3)(i) by a partnership (the transferor partnership, which is considered to be the terminated partnership as a result of the merger) of all of its assets and liabilities to another partnership (the transferee partnership, which is considered to be the resulting partnership after the merger), followed by a distribution of the interest in the transferee partnership in liquidation of the transferor partnership as part of the same plan or arrangement.

(ii) *Subsequent distributions.*—Except as provided in paragraph (c)(4)(E) below, section 704(c)(1)(B) and this section apply to the subsequent distribution by the transferee partnership of section 704(c) property contributed by the transferor partnership to the transferee partnership in an assets-over merger, as provided in paragraphs (c)(4)(ii)(A) through (D) of this section.

(A) *Original section 704(c) gain or loss.*—The seven-year period in section 704(c)(1)(B) does not restart with respect to original section 704(c) gain or loss as a result of the transfer of the section 704(c) property to the transferee partnership. For purposes of this paragraph (c)(4)(ii)(A), the amount of original section 704(c) gain or loss is the difference between the property's fair market value and the contributing partner's adjusted tax basis, at the time of contribution, to the extent such difference has not been eliminated by section 704(c) allocations, prior revaluations, or in connection with the merger. See §§1.704-4(a) and (b) for post-merger distributions of property contributed to the transferee partnership prior to the merger. A subsequent distribution by the transferee partnership of property with original section 704(c) gain or loss to a partner other than the partner that contributed such property to the transferor partnership is subject to section 704(c)(1)(B) if the distribution occurs within seven years of the contribution of the property to the transferor partnership. See §1.704-4(c)(4)(ii)(B) for rules relating to the distribution of property with new section 704(c) gain or loss. See §1.737-2(b)(1)(ii)(A) for a similar rule in the context of section 737.

(B) *New section 704(c) gain or loss.*—A subsequent distribution of property with new section 704(c) gain or loss by the transferee partnership to a partner other than the contributing partner is subject to section 704(c)(1)(B) if the distribution occurs within seven years of the contribution of the property to the transferee partnership by the transferor partnership. For these purposes, a partner of the transferor partnership is deemed to have contributed to the transferee partnership an undivided interest in the property of the transferor partnership. The determination of the partners' undivided interest for this purpose shall be determined by the transferor partnership using any reasonable method. New section 704(c) gain or loss shall be allocated among the partners of the transferor partnership in a manner consistent with the principles of §§1.704-3(a)(7) and 1.704-3(a)(10). See §1.737-2(b)(1)(ii)(B) for a similar rule in the context of section 737.

(C) *Ordering Rule.*—(1) *Post-merger revaluation.*—Revaluations after a merger that reflect a reduction in the amount of built-in gain or loss inherent in property will reduce new section 704(c) gain or loss prior to reducing original section 704(c) gain or loss.

(2) *Post-merger partial recognition.*—For purposes of this section, if less than all of a section 704(c) property is distributed, then a proportionate amount of original and new section 704(c) gain or loss must be recognized.

(D) *Subsequent Mergers.*—If the transferee partnership (first transferee partnership) is subsequently merged into another partnership (new transferee partnership) the new section 704(c) gain or loss that resulted from the merger of the transferor partnership into the first transferee partnership shall be subject to section 704(c)(1)(B) for seven years from the time of the contribution by the transferor partnership to the first transferee partnership (original merger) and new section 704(c) gain or loss that resulted from the merger of the first transferee into the new transferee (subsequent merger) shall be subject to section 704(c)(1)(B) for seven years from the time of the subsequent merger. See §1.737-2(b)(1)(ii)(D) for a similar rule in the context of section 737.

(E) *Identical Ownership or De Minimis Change in Ownership Exception.*—Section 704(c)(1)(B) and this section do not apply to new section 704(c) gain or loss in property transferred by the transferor partnership to the transferee partnership if both the transferor partnership and the transferee partnership are owned by the same owners in the same proportions or the difference in ownership is de minimis. The transferor partnership and the transferee partnership are owned by the same owners in the same proportions if each partner owns identical interests in book capital and in each item of income, gain, loss, deduction, and credit, and identical shares of distributions and liabilities in each of the transferor and transferee partnerships. A difference in ownership is de minimis if ninety seven percent of the interests in book capital and in each item of income, gain, loss, deduction and credit and shares of distributions, and liabilities of the transferor partnership and transferee partnership are owned by the same owners in the same proportions. See §1.737-2(b)(1)(ii)(E) for a similar rule in the context of section 737.

(F) *Examples.*—The following examples illustrate the rules of paragraph (c)(4)(ii) of this section.

Example (1). New section 704(c) gain. (i) *Facts* . On January 1, 2005, A contributes Asset 1, with a basis of $200x and a fair market value of $300x, to partnership PRS1 in exchange for a 50 percent interest. On the same date, B contributes $300x of cash to PRS1 in exchange for a 50 percent interest. Also on January 1, 2005, C contributes Asset 2, with a basis of $100x and a fair market value of $200x, to partnership PRS2 in exchange for a 50 percent interest. D contributes $200x of cash to PRS2 in exchange for a 50 percent interest. On January 1, 2008, PRS1 and PRS2 undertake an assets-over partnership merger in which PRS1 is the continuing partnership and PRS2 is the terminating partnership for both state law and federal tax purposes. At the time of the merger, PRS1's only assets are Asset 1, with a fair market value of $900x, and $300x in cash. PRS2's only assets are Asset 2, with a fair market value of $600x, and $200x in cash. After the merger, the partners have book capital and profits interests in PRS1 as follows: A, 30 percent; B, 30 percent; C, 20 percent; and D, 20 percent. PRS1 and PRS2 both have provisions in their respective partnership agreements requiring the revaluation of partnership property upon entry of a new partner. PRS1 would not be treated as an investment company (within the meaning of section 351) if it were incorporated. Neither partnership holds any unrealized receivables or inventory for purposes of section 751. In addition, neither partnership has a section 754 election in place. Asset 1 and Asset 2 are nondepreciable capital assets. On January 1, 2013, PRS1 has the same assets that it had after the merger. Each asset has the same value that it had at the time of the merger. On this date, PRS1 distributes Asset 2 to A in liquidation of A's interest.

(ii) *Analysis.* On the date of the merger of PRS2 into PRS1, the fair market value of Asset 2 ($600x) exceeded its adjusted tax basis ($100x). Thus, pursuant to §1.704-4(c)(4)(ii)(A), when Asset 2 was contributed to PRS1 in the merger, it was section 704(c) gain property. The total amount of the section 704(c) gain was $500x ($600x (fair market value) — $100x (adjusted basis)). The amount of original section 704(c) gain attributable to Asset 2 equals $100x, the difference between its fair market value ($200x) and adjusted tax basis ($100x) upon contribution to PRS2 by C. The amount of new section 704(c) gain attributable to Asset 2 equals $400x, the total amount of section 704(c) gain ($500x) less the amount of the original section 704(c) gain ($100x). The distribution of Asset 2 to A occurs more than seven years after the contribution by C of Asset 2 to PRS2. Therefore, pursuant to §1.704-4(c)(4)(ii)(A), section 704(c)(1)(B) does not apply to the $100x of original section 704(c) gain. The distribution of Asset 2 to A, however, occurs within seven years of the contribution in the merger of Asset 2 to PRS1 by PRS2. Pursuant to §1.704-4(c)(4)(ii)(B), section 704(c)(1)(B) applies to the new section 704(c) gain. As the transferees of PRS2's partnership interest in PRS1, C and D succeed to one-half of the $400x of the new section 704(c) gain created by the merger. Thus, as a result of the distribution of Asset 2 to A within seven years of the merger, C and D are required to recognize $200x of gain each. See §1.737-2(b)(1)(ii)(F), *Example (1)* for analysis of a similar example under section 737.

Example (2). Revaluation gain and merger gain. (i) *Facts* . The facts are the same as *Example (1)*, except that during 2005, PRS2 admitted E as a new partner in PRS2 at a time when the fair market value of Asset 2 was $300x and PRS2's only other asset was cash of $200X. In exchange for a contribution of cash of $250x, E was admitted as a one-third partner in PRS2. In accordance with the terms of PRS2's partnership agreement, the partnership revalued its assets pursuant to §1.704-1(b)(2)(iv)(f) upon admission of E so that the unrealized gain of $100X attributable to Asset 2 was allocated equally between C and D, or $50X each. On January 1, 2008, PRS2 merges into PRS1. At the time of the merger, PRS1's only assets are Asset 1, with a fair market value of $550x, and $300x in cash. PRS2's only assets are Asset 2, with a fair market value of $400x, and $400x in cash. After the merger, the partners have book capital and profits and loss interests in PRS1 as follows: A, 25.76 percent; B, 25.76 percent; C, 16.16 percent; D, 16.16 percent; and E, 16.16 percent. On January 1, 2011, Asset 2 is distributed to A when its value is still $400x.

(ii) Analysis. On the date of the merger of PRS2 into PRS1, the fair market value of Asset 2 ($400x) exceeded its adjusted tax basis ($100x). Thus, when Asset 2 was contributed to PRS1 in the merger, it was section 704(c) gain property. The total amount of the section 704(c) gain was $300x ($400x (fair market value) - $100x (adjusted basis)). The amount of the original section 704(c) gain attributable to Asset 2 equals $100x, the difference between its fair market value of $200x and adjusted tax basis $100x upon contribution to PRS2 by C. The amount of the new section 704(c) gain attributable to Asset 2 equals $200x, the total section 704(c) gain ($300x) less the amount of the original section 704(c) gain ($100x). The distribution of Asset 2 to A occurs within seven years after the contribution by C to PRS2. Therefore, pursuant to § 1.704-4(c)(4)(ii)(A), section 704(c)(1)(B) applies to the original section 704(c) gain. The distribution of Asset 2 to A also occurs within seven years of the contribution of Asset 2 to PRS1 by PRS2. Pursuant to § 1.704-4(c)(4)(ii)(B), section 704(c)(1)(B) applies to the new section 704(c) gain. As the transferees of PRS2's partnership interest in PRS1, C and D each succeed to $50x of new section 704(c) gain as a result of the revaluation of Asset 2 upon admission of E as a partner. Moreover, C, D and E each succeed to $33.33x of new section 704(c) gain as a result of the merger. C also has $100x of original section 704(c) gain as a result of the original contribution of Asset 2 to PRS2. Thus, as a result of the distribution of Asset 2 to A within seven years of the merger, C, D and E are each required to recognize gain. C will recognize a total of $183.33x of gain ($100x of original section 704(c) gain and $83.33x of new section 704(c) gain). D will recognize a total of $83.33x of gain (all new section 704(c) gain) and E will recognize $33.33x of gain (all new section 704(c) gain). See § 1.737-2(b)(1)(ii)(F), *Example (2)* for a similar example under section 737.

Example (3). Revaluation loss and merger gain. (i) *Facts.* The facts are the same as *Example (1)* except that during 2005, PRS2 admitted E as a new partner in PRS2 at a time when the fair market value of Asset 2 was $150x and PRS2's only other asset was cash of $200x. In exchange for a contribution of cash of $175x, E was admitted as a one-third partner in PRS2. In accordance with the terms of PRS2's partnership agreement, the partnership revalued its assets upon admission of E so that the unrealized loss of $50x attributable to Asset 2 was allocated equally between C and D, or $25x each. On January 1, 2008, PRS 2 merges into PRS1. At the time of the merger, PRS1's only assets are Asset 1, with a fair market value of $900x, and $300x in cash. PRS2's only assets are Asset 2, with a fair market value of $600x, and $375x in cash. After the merger, the partners have book capital and profits and loss interests in PRS1 as follows: A, 27.5 percent; B, 27.5 percent; C, 15 percent; D, 15 percent; and E, 15 percent. On January 1, 2013, Asset 2 is distributed to A when its value is still $600x.

(ii) Analysis. On the date of the merger of PRS2 into PRS1, the fair market value of Asset 2 ($600x) exceeded its adjusted tax basis ($100x). Thus, when Asset 2 was contributed to PRS1 in the merger, it was section 704(c) gain property. The total amount of the section 704(c) gain was $500x ($600x (fair market value) - $100x (adjusted basis)). The amount of the original section 704(c) gain attributable to Asset 2 equals $50x, the difference between its fair market value ($200x) and adjusted tax basis ($100x) upon contribution to PRS2 by C, less the unrealized loss ($50X) attributable to the revaluation of PRS2 on the admission of E as a partner in PRS2. The amount of the new section 704(c) gain attributable to Asset 2 equals $450x, the total section 704(c) gain ($500x) less the amount of the original section 704(c) gain ($50x). The distribution of Asset 2 to A occurs more than seven years after the contribution by C to PRS2. Therefore, pursuant to § 1.704-4(c)(4)(ii)(A), section 704(c)(1)(B) does not apply to the original section 704(c) gain. The distribution of Asset 2 to A, however, occurs within seven years of the contribution of Asset 2 to PRS1 and PRS2. Pursuant to § 1.704-4(c)(4)(ii)(B), section 704(c)(1)(B) applies to the new section 704(c) gain. As the transferees of PRS2's partnership interest in PRS1, C, D and E each succeed to $150x of new section 704(c) gain. Thus, as a result of the distribution of Asset 2 to A within seven years of the merger, C, D and E are each required to recognize $150x of gain.

Example (4). Reverse section 704(c) gain. (i) *Facts.* The facts are the same as *Example (1),* except that on January 1, 2013, PRS1 distributes Asset 1 to C in liquidation of C's interest in PRS1.

(ii) Analysis. The distribution of Asset 1 to C occurs more than seven years after the contribution of Asset 1 to PRS1. Thus, pursuant to § 1.704-4(c)(4)(ii)(A), section 704(c)(1)(B) does not apply to the original section 704(c) gain. Pursuant to § 1.704-4(c)(7), section 704(c)(1)(B) does not apply to reverse section 704(c) gain in Asset 1 resulting from a revaluation of PRS1's partnership property at the time of the merger. Accordingly, neither A nor B will recognize gain under section 704(c)(1)(B) as a result of the distribution of Asset 1 to C. See § 1.737-2(b)(1)(ii)(F), *Example (4)* for a similar example under section 737.

Example (5). Identical ownership exception. (i) *Facts.* In 1990, A, an individual, and B, a subchapter C corporation, formed PRS1, a partnership. A owned 75 percent of the interests in the book capital (as determined for purposes of § 1.704-1(b)(2)(iv)), profits, losses, distributions, and liabilities (under section 752) of PRS1. B owned the remaining 25 percent interest in the book capital, profits, losses, distributions, and liabilities of PRS1. In the same year, A and B also formed another partnership, PRS2, with A owning 75 percent of the interests in the book capital, profits, losses, distributions, and liabilities of PRS2 and B owning the remaining 25 percent of the book capital, profits, losses, distributions, and liabilities. Upon formation of the partnerships, A contributed Asset X to PRS1 and Asset Y to PRS2 and B contributed cash. Both Assets X and Y had section 704(c) built-in gain at the time of contribution to the partnerships.

(ii) In January 2005, PRS1 is merged into PRS2 in an assets-over merger in which PRS1 is the terminating partnership and PRS2 as the continuing partnership for both state law and federal income tax purposes. At the time of the merger, both Asset X and Y had increased in value from the time they were contributed to PRS1 and PRS2, respectively. As a result, a new layer of section 704(c) gain was created with respect to Asset X in PRS1, and reverse section 704(c) gain was created with respect to Asset Y in PRS2. After the merger, A had a 75 percent interest in PRS2's capital, profits, losses, distributions, liabilities, and all other items. B held the remaining 25 percent interest in PRS2's capital, profits, losses, distributions, liabilities, and all other items. In 2006, PRS2 distributes Asset X to A.

(iii) Analysis. The 2006 distribution of Asset X occurs more than seven years after the formation of the partnerships and the original contribution of both Assets X and Y to the partnerships. Therefore, the original layer of built-in gain created on the original contribution of Asset X to PRS1 is not taken into account in applying section 704(c)(1)(B) to the proposed distribution. In addition, paragraph (c)(4)(ii)(E) of this section provides that section 704(c)(1)(B) and paragraph (c)(4)(ii)(B) of this section do not apply to new section 704(c) gain or loss in property transferred by the transferor partnership to the transferee partnership if both the transferor partnership and the transferee partnership are owned by the same owners in the same proportions. The transferor partnership and the transferee partnership are owned by the same owners in the same proportions if each partner's percentage interest in the transferor partnership's book capital, profits, losses, distributions, and liabilities, is the same as the partner's percentage interest in those items of the transferee partnership. In this case, A owned 75 percent and B owned 25 percent of the interests in the book capital, and in each item of income, gain, loss and credit, and share of distributions and liabilities of PRS1 and PRS2 prior to the merger and 75 percent and 25 percent, respectively, of PRS2 after the merger. As a result, the requirements of the identical ownership exception of paragraph (c)(4)(ii)(E) of this section are satisfied. Thus, the new built-in gain created upon contribution of Asset X in connection with the partnership merger will not be taken into account in applying section 704(c)(1)(B) to the proposed distribution. See § 1.737-2(b)(1)(ii)(F), *Example (5)* for a similar example under section 737.

* * *

(7) *Reverse section 704(c) gain or loss.*—Section 704(c)(1)(B) and this section do not apply to reverse section 704(c) gain or loss as described in § 1.704-3(a)(6)(i).

* * *

(g) *Effective/applicability date.*—* * * Paragraphs (a)(1), (a)(4)(i), (a)(4)(ii), and (f)(2), *Examples (1) and (2),* are effective August 22, 2007. Paragraphs (c)(4) and (c)(7) are effective for any distributions of property after January 19, 2005, if such property was contributed in a merger using the assets-over form after May 3, 2004.

Partners and Partnerships: American Jobs Creation Act of 2004 and Taxpayer Relief Act of 1997: Guidance

Partners and Partnerships: American Jobs Creation Act of 2004 and Taxpayer Relief Act of 1997: Guidance.—Amendments to Reg. §§1.704-3 and 1.704-4, providing guidance on certain provisions of the American Jobs Creation Act of 2004, conforming the regulations to statutory changes in the Taxpayer Relief Act of 1997, modifying the basis allocation rules to prevent certain unintended consequences of the current basis allocation rules for substituted basis transactions and providing additional guidance on allocations resulting from revaluations of partnership property, are proposed (published in the Federal Register on January 16, 2014) (REG-144468-05) (corrected April 15, 2014).

☐ Par. 2. Section 1.704-3 is amended by:

1. Revising paragraph (a)(3)(ii).
2. Adding paragraph (a)(3)(iii).
3. Revising paragraph (a)(6)(i).
4. Adding paragraph (a)(6)(iii).
5. Adding paragraph (a)(6)(iv).
6. Revising paragraph (a)(7).
7. Revising the first sentence in paragraph (a)(10) by removing the word "allocation" before the word "method".
8. Redesignating paragraph (f) as paragraph (g).
9. Adding a new paragraph (f).
10. Adding a sentence at the end of newly redesignated paragraph (g).

The revisions and additions read as follows.

§1.704-3. Contributed property.—(a) * * *

(3) * * *

(ii) *Built-in gain and built-in loss.*—The built-in gain on section 704(c) property is the excess of the property's book value over the contributing partner's adjusted tax basis upon contribution. The built-in gain is thereafter reduced by decreases in the difference between the property's book value and adjusted tax basis (other than decreases to the property's book value pursuant to §1.704-1(b)(2)(iv)(*f*) or §1.704-1(b)(2)(iv)(*s*)). The built-in loss on section 704(c) property is the excess of the contributing partner's adjusted tax basis over the property's book value upon contribution. The built-in loss is thereafter reduced by decreases in the difference between the property's adjusted tax basis and book value (other than increases to the property's book value pursuant to §1.704-1(b)(2)(iv)(*f*) or §1.704-1(b)(2)(iv)(*s*)). For purposes of paragraph (a)(6)(iii) and (iv) of this section, a built-in gain or built-in loss referred to in this paragraph shall be referred to as a forward section 704(c) allocation. *See* §1.460-4(k)(3)(v)(A) for a rule relating to the amount of built-in income or built-in loss attributable to a contract accounted for under a long-term contract method of accounting.

(iii) *Effective/applicability date.*—The provisions of paragraph (a)(3)(ii) of this section apply to partnership contributions and transactions occurring on or after the date of publication of the Treasury decision adopting these rules as final regulations in the **Federal Register.** * * *

* * *

(6)(i) *Revaluations under section 704(b).*—The principles of this section apply with respect to property for which differences between book value and adjusted tax basis are created when a partnership revalues partnership property pursuant to §1.704-1(b)(2)(iv)(*f*) or §1.704-1(b)(2)(iv)(*s*) (reverse section 704(c) allocations). Each such revaluation creates a separate amount of built-in gain or built-in loss, as the case may be (a section 704(c) layer), that must be tracked separately from built-in gain or built-in loss arising from contribution (a forward section 704(c) layer) and any other revaluation (a reverse section 704(c) layer). For instance, one section 704(c) layer with respect to a particular property may be of built-in gain, and another section 704(c) layer with respect to the same property may be of built-in loss.

* * *

(iii) *Allocation method.*—A partnership may use any reasonable method to allocate the items of income, gain, loss, and deduction associated with an item of property among the property's forward and reverse section 704(c) layers.

(iv) *Effective/applicability date.*—The provisions of paragraph (a)(6)(iii) of this section apply to partnership contributions and transactions occurring on or after the date of publication of the Treasury decision adopting these rules as final regulations in the **Federal Register.**

* * *

(7) *Transfers of a partnership interest..*—If a contributing partner transfers a partnership interest, built-in gain must be allocated to the transferee partner as it would have been allocated to the transferor partner. If the contributing partner transfers a portion of the partnership interest, the share of built-in gain proportionate to the interest transferred must be allocated to the transferee partner. Rules for the allocation of built-in loss are provided in paragraph (f) of this section.

* * *

(f) *Special rules for built-in loss property.*—(1) *General principles.*—(i) *Contributing partner.*—If a partner contributes section 704(c)(1)(C) property (as defined in paragraph (f)(2)(i) of this section) to a partnership, the excess of the adjusted basis of the section 704(c)(1)(C) property (determined without regard to paragraph (f)(1)(ii) of this section) over its fair market value immediately before the contribution will be taken into account only in determining the amount of

items allocated to the section 704(c)(1)(C) partner (as defined in paragraph (f)(2)(ii) of this section) that contributed such section 704(c)(1)(C) property.

(ii) *Non-contributing partners.*—In determining the amount of items allocated to partners other than the section 704(c)(1)(C) partner, the initial basis of section 704(c)(1)(C) property in the hands of the partnership is equal to the property's fair market value at the time of contribution.

(2) *Definitions.*—For purposes of this section—

(i) *Section 704(c)(1)(C) property.*—The term *section 704(c)(1)(C) property* means section 704(c) property (as defined in paragraph (a)(3)(i) of this section) with a built-in loss at the time of contribution. Section 704(c)(1)(C) property does not include a §1.752-7 liability (within the meaning of §1.752-7(b)(3)) or property for which differences between book value and adjusted tax basis are created when a partnership revalues property pursuant to §1.704-1(b)(2)(iv)(*f*) or §1.704-1(b)(2)(iv)(*s*).

(ii) *Section 704(c)(1)(C) partner.*—The term *section 704(c)(1)(C) partner* means a partner that contributes section 704(c)(1)(C) property to a partnership.

(iii) *Section 704(c)(1)(C) basis adjustment.*—A property's section 704(c)(1)(C) basis adjustment is initially equal to the excess of the adjusted basis of section 704(c)(1)(C) property (determined without regard to paragraph (f)(1)(ii) of this section) over its fair market value immediately before the contribution, and is subsequently adjusted for the recovery of the section 704(c)(1)(C) basis adjustment under paragraph (f)(3)(ii)(D) of this section.

(3) *Operational rules.*—(i) *In general.*—Except as provided in this section, section 704(c)(1)(C) property is subject to the rules and regulations applicable to section 704(c) property. *See*, for example, §1.704-3(a)(9).

(ii) *Effect of section 704(c)(1)(C) basis adjustment.*—(A) *In general.*—The section 704(c)(1)(C) basis adjustment is an adjustment to the basis of partnership property with respect to the section 704(c)(1)(C) partner only. A section 704(c)(1)(C) basis adjustment amount is excluded from the partnership's basis of section 704(c)(1)(C) property. Thus, for purposes of calculating income, deduction, gain, and loss, the section 704(c)(1)(C) partner will have a special basis for section 704(c)(1)(C) property in which the partner has a section 704(c)(1)(C) basis adjustment. The section 704(c)(1)(C) basis adjustment has no effect on the partnership's computation of any item under section 703.

(B) *Computation of section 704(c)(1)(C) partner's distributive share of partnership items.*—The partnership first computes its items of income, deduction, gain, or loss at the partnership level under section 703. The partnership then allocates the partnership items among the partners, including the section 704(c)(1)(C) partner, in accordance with section 704, and adjusts the partners' capital accounts accordingly. The partnership then adjusts the section 704(c)(1)(C) partner's distributive share of the items of partnership income, deduction, gain, or loss in accordance with paragraphs (f)(3)(ii)(C) and (D) of this section, to reflect the effects of the section 704(c)(1)(C) partner's section 704(c)(1)(C) basis adjustment. These adjustments to the section 704(c)(1)(C) partner's distributive share must be reflected on Schedules K and K-1 of the partnership's return (Form 1065). The adjustments to the section 704(c)(1)(C) partner's distributive shares do not affect the section 704(c)(1)(C) partner's capital account.

(C) *Effect of section 704(c)(1)(C) basis adjustment in determining items of income, gain, or loss.*—The amount of a section 704(c)(1)(C) partner's income, gain, or loss from the sale or exchange of partnership property in which the section 704(c)(1)(C) partner has a section 704(c)(1)(C) basis adjustment is equal to the section 704(c)(1)(C) partner's share of the partnership's gain or loss from the sale of the property (including any remedial allocations under

§1.704-3(d)), minus the section 704(c)(1)(C) partner's section 704(c)(1)(C) basis adjustment for the partnership property.

(D) *Effect of section 704(c)(1)(C) basis adjustment in determining items of deduction.*—(1) *In general.*—If section 704(c)(1)(C) property is subject to amortization under section 197, depreciation under section 168, or other cost recovery in the hands of the section 704(c)(1)(C) partner, the section 704(c)(1)(C) basis adjustment associated with the property is recovered in accordance with section 197(f)(2), section 168(i)(7), or another applicable Internal Revenue Code section. The amount of any section 704(c)(1)(C) basis adjustment that is recovered by the section 704(c)(1)(C) partner in any year is added to the section 704(c)(1)(C) partner's distributive share of the partnership's depreciation or amortization deductions for the year. The basis adjustment is adjusted under section 1016(a)(2) to reflect the recovery of the section 704(c)(1)(C) basis adjustment.

(2) *Example.*—A contributes Property, with an adjusted basis of $12,000 and a fair market value of $5,000 on January 1 of the year of contribution, and B contributes $5,000 to PRS, a partnership. Prior to the contribution, A depreciates Property under section 168 over 10 years using the straight-line method and the half-year convention. On the contribution date, Property has 7.5 years remaining in its recovery period. Property is section 704(c)(1)(C) property, and A's section 704(c)(1)(C) basis adjustment is $7,000. PRS's basis in Property is $5,000 (fair market value) and, in accordance with section 168(i)(7), the depreciation is $667 per year ($5,000 divided by 7.5 years), which is shared equally between A and B. A's $7,000 section 704(c)(1)(C) basis adjustment is subject to depreciation of $933 per year in accordance with section 168(i)(7) ($7,000 divided by 7.5 years), which is taken into account by A.

(iii) *Transfer of section 704(c)(1)(C) partner's partnership interest.*—(A) *General rule.*—Except as provided in paragraph (f)(3)(iii)(B) of this section, if a section 704(c)(1)(C) partner transfers its partnership interest, the portion of the section 704(c)(1)(C) basis adjustment attributable to the interest transferred is eliminated and the transferee is not treated as the section 704(c)(1)(C) partner with respect to the interest transferred. The transferor remains the section 704(c)(1)(C) partner with respect to any remaining section 704(c)(1)(C) basis adjustment.

(B) *Special rules.*—(1) *General rule for transfer of partnership interest in nonrecognition transaction.*—Except as provided in paragraph (f)(3)(iii)(B)(2) of this section, paragraph (f)(3)(iii)(A) of this section does not apply to the extent a section 704(c)(1)(C) partner transfers its partnership interest in a nonrecognition transaction. Instead, the transferee of all or a portion of a section 704(c)(1)(C) partner's partnership interest succeeds to the transferor's section 704(c)(1)(C) basis adjustments in an amount attributable to the interest transferred and the transferee will be treated as the section 704(c)(1)(C) partner with respect to the transferred interest. Regardless of whether a section 754 election is in effect or a substantial built-in loss exists with respect to the transfer, the amount of any section 704(c)(1)(C) basis adjustment with respect to section 704(c)(1)(C) property to which the transferee succeeds shall be decreased by the amount of any negative section 743(b) adjustment that would be allocated to the section 704(c)(1)(C) property pursuant to the provisions of §1.755-1 if the partnership had a section 754 election in effect upon the transfer. If the nonrecognition transaction is described in section 168(i)(7)(B), then the rules in section 168(i)(7)(A) apply with respect to transferor's cost recovery deductions under section 168. If gain or loss is recognized on the transaction, appropriate adjustments must be made to the section 704(c)(1)(C) basis adjustment.

(2) *Exception for gifts.*—Paragraph (f)(3)(iii)(B)(1) of this section does not apply to the transfer of all or a portion of a section 704(c)(1)(C) partner's partnership interest by gift.

(C) *Examples.*—The following examples illustrate the principles of this paragraph (f)(3)(iii)—

Example 1. Sale of entire partnership interest. In Year 1, A contributes nondepreciable Property, with an adjusted basis of $11,000 and a fair market value of $5,000, and B and C each contribute $5,000 cash to PRS, a partnership. PRS's basis in Property is $5,000, and A's section 704(c)(1)(C) basis adjustment in Property is $6,000. In Year 3, Property's fair market value is unchanged and A's section 704(c)(1)(C) basis adjustment remains $6,000. D purchases A's interest in PRS for its fair market value of $5,000. PRS does not have a section 754 election in effect in Year 3. A recognizes a loss of $6,000 on the sale, which equals the excess of its basis in PRS ($11,000) over the amount realized on the sale ($5,000). Pursuant to paragraph (f)(3)(iii)(A) of this section, D does not succeed to A's section 704(c)(1)(C) basis adjustment, which is eliminated upon the sale.

Example 2. Sale of portion of partnership interest. Assume the same facts as *Example 1* except that D purchases 50 percent of A's interest in PRS for its fair market value of $2,500. A recognizes a loss of $3,000 on the sale, which equals the excess of its basis in the 50 percent interest in PRS ($5,500) over the amount realized on the sale ($2,500). Pursuant to paragraph (f)(3)(iii)(A) of this section, D does not succeed to A's section 704(c)(1)(C) basis adjustment, and A's section 704(c)(1)(C) basis adjustment is reduced to $3,000 upon the sale.

Example 3. Section 721 transaction—(i) Assume the same facts as *Example 1* except that instead of selling its interest in PRS to D in Year 3, A contributes its interest in PRS to UTP, a partnership, in exchange for a 50 percent interest in UTP. Following the contribution, UTP's basis in PRS is $5,000 plus a $6,000 section 704(c)(1)(C) basis adjustment solely allocable to A. Under the facts of this example, UTP's share of basis in PRS property is the same.

(ii) Under paragraph (f)(3)(iii)(B)(1) of this section, UTP succeeds to A's $6,000 section 704(c)(1)(C) basis adjustment in Property. PRS does not have a section 754 election in effect and does not have a substantial built-in loss (within the meaning of §1.743-1(a)(2)(i)) with respect to the transfer. Paragraph (f)(3)(iii)(B)(1) of this section requires PRS to reduce the amount of the section 704(c)(1)(C) basis adjustment by the amount of the negative section 743(b) adjustment that would be allocated to Property if PRS had an election under section 754 in effect. Because UTP's basis in PRS equals UTP's share of basis in PRS property, no negative section 743(b) adjustment would result from the transfer. Accordingly, UTP's section 704(c)(1)(C) basis adjustment in Property is $6,000. Pursuant to paragraph (a)(9) of this section, UTP must allocate its distributive share of PRS's items with respect to the section 704(c)(1)(C) basis adjustment solely to A.

(iii) In Year 3, PRS sells Property for its fair market value of $5,000. PRS realizes no gain or loss on the sale. Pursuant to paragraph (f)(3)(ii)(C) of this section, PRS reduces UTP's allocable gain from the sale of Property ($0) by the amount of UTP's section 704(c)(1)(C) basis adjustment for Property ($6,000). Thus, UTP is allocated a $6,000 loss. Pursuant to paragraph (a)(9) of this section, UTP must allocate the $6,000 loss with respect to the section 704(c)(1)(C) basis adjustment to A. A's basis in UTP decreases from $11,000 to $5,000 and its section 704(c)(1)(C) basis adjustment in UTP is eliminated.

Example 4. Interaction with section 362(e)(2)(A)—(i) Assume the same facts as *Example 1* except that instead of selling its interest in PRS to D in Year 3, A contributes its interest in PRS to Y Corp, a corporation, in a transfer described in section 351. PRS has a section 754 election in effect. A's basis in its Y Corp stock is $11,000 under section 358.

(ii) A and Y Corp do not elect to apply the provisions of section 362(e)(2)(C). Therefore, section 362(e)(2)(A) will apply because Y Corp's basis in PRS ($11,000) would exceed the fair market value of PRS ($5,000) immediately after the transaction. Thus, pursuant to section 362(e)(2)(B), Y Corp's basis in PRS will be $5,000. Y Corp succeeds to A's $6,000 section 704(c)(1)(C) basis adjustment in Property pursuant to paragraph (f)(3)(iii)(B)(1) of this section. Pursuant to §1.743-1, Y Corp's section 743(b) adjustment is ($6,000), or the difference between Y Corp's basis in PRS of $5,000 and Y Corp's share of the adjusted basis of PRS's property of $11,000 (which is Y Corp's cash on liquidation of $5,000, increased by the $6,000 tax loss that would be allocated to Y Corp upon a hypothetical transaction). The ($6,000) section 743(b) adjustment will be allocated to PRS's property in accordance with section 755 and the regulations thereunder.

Example 5. Gift of partnership interest. Assume the same facts as *Example 1* except that instead of selling its PRS interest to D in Year 3, A makes a gift of its PRS interest to D. Pursuant to paragraph (f)(3)(iii)(B)(2) of this section, D does not succeed to any of A's section 704(c)(1)(C) basis adjustment in Property. The $6,000 section 704(c)(1)(C) basis adjustment is eliminated upon the gift.

(iv) *Transfer of section 704(c)(1)(C) property by partnership.*—(A) *Like-kind exchange.*—(1) *General rule.*—If a partnership disposes of section 704(c)(1)(C) property in a like-kind exchange described in section 1031 and the regulations thereunder, the substituted basis property (as defined in section 7701(a)(42)) received by the partnership is treated, solely with respect to the section 704(c)(1)(C) partner, as section 704(c)(1)(C) property with the same section 704(c)(1)(C) basis adjustment as the section 704(c)(1)(C) property disposed of by the partnership (with appropriate adjustments for any portion of the section 704(c)(1)(C) basis adjustment taken into account in determining the section 704(c)(1)(C) partner's gain or loss recognized on the transfer).

(2) *Example.*—A contributes Property 1 with an adjusted basis of $12,000 and a fair market value of $10,000 and B contributes $10,000 cash to PRS, a partnership. A has a $2,000 section 704(c)(1)(C) basis adjustment in Property 1, and PRS has an adjusted basis in Property 1 of $10,000, or its fair market value. PRS subsequently engages in a like-kind exchange under section 1031 of Property 1 when the fair market value of Property 1 is $13,000 and receives Property 2 with a fair market value of $12,000 and $1,000

cash in exchange. PRS's gain on the transaction is $3,000 ($13,000 minus PRS's $10,000 adjusted basis) but is recognized only to the extent of the cash received of $1,000, of which $500 is allocable to A. As provided in paragraph (f)(3)(iv)(A)(1) of this section, Property 2 is treated as section 704(c)(1)(C) property with respect to A and has the same section 704(c)(1)(C) basis adjustment as Property 1. Because PRS recognized gain on the transaction, A must use $500 of its section 704(c)(1)(C) basis adjustment to reduce A's gain to $0. Therefore, A's $2,000 section 704(c)(1)(C) basis adjustment is reduced to $1,500.

(B) *Contribution of 704(c)(1)(C) property in section 721 transaction.*—(1) *In general.*—The rules set forth in this paragraph (f)(3)(iv)(B) apply if a section 704(c)(1)(C) partner contributes section 704(c)(1)(C) property to an upper-tier partnership, and that upper-tier partnership subsequently contributes the section 704(c)(1)(C) property to a lower-tier partnership in a transaction described in section 721(a) (whether as part of a single transaction or as separate transactions). The interest in the lower-tier partnership received by the upper-tier partnership is treated as the section 704(c)(1)(C) property with the same section 704(c)(1)(C) basis adjustment as the contributed property. The lower-tier partnership determines its basis in the contributed property by excluding the existing section 704(c)(1)(C) basis adjustment under the principles of paragraph (f)(3)(ii)(A) of this section. However, the lower-tier partnership also succeeds to the upper-tier partnership's section 704(c)(1)(C) basis adjustment. The portion of the upper-tier partnership's basis in its interest in the lower-tier partnership attributable to the section 704(c)(1)(C) basis adjustment must be segregated and allocated solely to the section 704(c)(1)(C) partner for whom the initial section 704(c)(1)(C) basis adjustment was made. Similarly, the section 704(c)(1)(C) basis adjustment to which the lower-tier partnership succeeds must be segregated and allocated solely to the uppertier partnership, and the section 704(c)(1)(C) partner for whom the initial section 704(c)(1)(C) basis adjustment was made. If gain or loss is recognized on the transaction, appropriate adjustments must be made to the section 704(c)(1)(C) basis adjustment.

(2) *Special rules.*—(a) To the extent that any section 704(c)(1)(C) basis adjustment in a tiered partnership is recovered under paragraphs (f)(3)(ii)(C) or (D) of this section, or is otherwise reduced, upper- or lower-tier partnerships in the tiered structure must make conforming reductions to related section 704(c)(1)(C) basis adjustments to prevent duplication of loss.

(b) Section 704(c)(1)(C) property that is contributed by an upper-tier partnership to a lower-tier partnership will have an additional section 704(c)(1)(C) basis adjustment if the value of the section 704(c)(1)(C) property is less than its tax basis (as adjusted under paragraph (f)(3)(ii) of this section) at the time of the transfer to the lower-tier partnership. Any additional section 704(c)(1)(C) basis adjustment determined under this paragraph will be allocated among the partners of the upper-tier partnership in a manner that reflects their relative shares of that loss.

(3) *Example 1.*—(i) In Year 1, A contributes Property with an adjusted basis of $11,000 and a fair market value of $5,000, and B contributes $5,000 cash to UTP, a partnership. Later in Year 1, when Property's basis has not changed, and Property is worth at least $5,000, UTP contributes Property to LTP in a section 721 transaction for a 50-percent interest in LTP. In Year 2, LTP sells Property for its fair market value of $29,000.

(ii) A has a $6,000 section 704(c)(1)(C) basis adjustment in Property. After the section 721 transaction, A's section 704(c)(1)(C) basis adjustment in Property becomes A's section 704(c)(1)(C) adjustment in UTP's interest in LTP. UTP has a section 704(c)(1)(C) adjustment in Property in the amount of A's section 704(c)(1)(C) adjustment in Property. This section 704(c)(1)(C) adjustment must be segregated and allocated solely to A. UTP's basis in its interest in LTP is determined without reference to the section 704(c)(1)(C) adjustment. Thus, UTP's basis in LTP is $5,000. LTP's basis in Property is determined without reference to the section 704(c)(1)(C) basis adjustment; therefore, LTP's basis in Property is $5,000.

(iii) Upon the sale of Property, LTP realizes a gain of $24,000 ($29,000 fair market value minus $5,000 adjusted basis). UTP's allocable share of the $24,000 gain from the sale of Property by LTP is $12,000, reduced by UTP's $6,000 section 704(c)(1)(C) basis adjustment in Property. Because UTP's section 704(c)(1)(C) basis adjustment must be segregated and allocated solely to A, UTP allocates the $12,000 of gain equally between A and B, but allocates the recovery of the $6,000 section 704(c)(1)(C) basis adjustment to A. Therefore, pursuant to paragraph (f)(3)(ii)(C) of this section, A recognizes no gain or loss on the sale (A's $6,000 share of UTP's gain minus the $6,000 section 704(c)(1)(C) basis adjustment). Because UTP's section 704(c)(1)(C) adjustment in Property is used, A's section 704(c)(1)(C) basis adjustment in UTP's interest in LTP is reduced to $0 to prevent duplication of loss pursuant to paragraph (f)(3)(iv)(B)(2)(a) of this section.

Example 2— Assume the same facts as *Example 1*, except that in Year 2, UTP sells its entire interest in LTP to D for its fair market value of $17,000. UTP recognizes a $12,000 gain on the sale, which equals the excess of UTP's amount realized on the sale ($17,000) over UTP's basis in LTP ($5,000). UTP allocates the $12,000 gain equally to A and B. However, A's $6,000 section 704(c)(1)(C) adjustment in UTP's interest in LTP offsets A's share of the gain. Therefore, A recognizes no gain or loss on the sale. D does not receive any of UTP's section 704(c)(1)(C) basis adjustment in Property, which is eliminated upon the sale.

Example 3—(i) Assume the same facts as *Example 1*, except that at the time UTP contributes Property to LTP, the fair market value of Property has fallen to $2,000. In Year 2, LTP sells Property for its fair market value of $2,000.

(ii) A has a $6,000 section 704(c)(1)(C) basis adjustment in Property. After the section 721 transaction, pursuant to paragraph (f)(3)(iv)(B)(1) of this section, A's section 704(c)(1)(C) basis adjustment in Property becomes A's section 704(c)(1)(C) adjustment in UTP's interest in LTP. Pursuant to paragraph (f)(3)(iv)(B)(1) of this section, UTP has a section 704(c)(1)(C) adjustment in Property in the amount of A's section 704(c)(1)(C) adjustment in Property. This section 704(c)(1)(C) adjustment must be segregated and allocated solely to A. Because UTP's basis in Property ($5,000) exceeds the fair market value of Property ($2,000) by $3,000 at the time of UTP's contribution to LTP, UTP has an additional section 704(c)(1)(C) adjustment of $3,000 in Property pursuant to paragraph (f)(3)(iv)(B)(2)(b) of this section. Partners A and B share equally in this $3,000 section 704(c)(1)(C) adjustment. UTP's basis in its interest in LTP is determined without reference to A's section 704(c)(1)(C) adjustment. Thus, UTP's basis in LTP is $5,000. Pursuant to paragraph (f)(3)(iv)(B)(1) of this section, LTP's basis in Property is determined without reference to either section 704(c)(1)(C) basis adjustment; therefore, LTP's basis in Property is $2,000.

(iii) Upon the sale of Property, LTP recognizes no gain or loss ($2,000 sales price minus $2,000 adjusted basis). However, the sale of Property triggers UTP's two separate section 704(c)(1)(C) basis adjustments. First, UTP applies the $3,000 section 704(c)(1)(C) adjustment attributable to the built-in loss in Property arising after A contributed Property to UTP. This results in an allocation of ($1,500) of loss to each of A and B. Next, UTP applies the $6,000 section 704(c)(1)(C) basis adjustment attributable to A's initial contribution of Property to UTP, resulting in an additional ($6,000) of loss allocated to A. Thus, the sale of Property by LTP results in A recognizing ($7,500) of loss, and B recognizing ($1,500) of loss. Pursuant to paragraph (f)(3)(iv)(B)(2)(a) of this section, because UTP's section 704(c)(1)(C) adjustment in Property is used, A's section 704(c)(1)(C) basis adjustment in UTP's interest in LTP is reduced to $0 to prevent duplication of loss

(C) *Section 351 transactions.*—(1) *Basis in transferred property.*—A corporation's adjusted basis in property transferred to the corporation by a partnership in a transaction described in section 351 is determined under section 362 (including for purposes of applying *section 362(e)*) by taking into account any section 704(c)(1)(C) basis adjustment for the property (other than any portion of a section 704(c)(1)(C) basis adjustment that reduces a partner's gain under paragraph (f)(3)(iv)(C)(2) of this section).

(2) *Partnership gain.*—The amount of gain, if any, recognized by the partnership on the transfer of property by the partnership to a corporation in a transfer described in section 351 is determined without regard to any section 704(c)(1)(C) basis adjustment for the transferred property. The amount of gain, if any, recognized by the partnership on the transfer that is allocated to the section 704(c)(1)(C) partner is adjusted to reflect the partner's section 704(c)(1)(C) basis adjustment in the transferred property.

(3) *Basis in stock.*—The partnership's adjusted basis in stock received from a corporation in a transfer described in section 351 is determined without regard to the section 704(c)(1)(C) basis adjustment in property transferred to the corporation in the section 351 exchange. A partner with a section 704(c)(1)(C) basis adjustment in property transferred to the corporation, however, has a basis adjustment in the stock received by the partnership in the section 351 exchange in an amount equal to the partner's section 704(c)(1)(C) basis adjustment in the transferred property, reduced by any portion of the section 704(c)(1)(C) basis adjustment that reduced the partner's gain under paragraph (f)(3)(iv)(C)(2) of this section.

(4) *Example.*—The following example illustrates the provisions of this paragraph (f)(3)(iv)(C).

Example. Section 351 transaction—(i) In Year 1, A contributes $10,000 cash and B contributes Property with an adjusted basis of $18,000 and a fair market value of $10,000 to PRS, a partnership. PRS takes Property with a basis of $10,000. B's section 704(c)(1)(C) basis adjustment for Property is $8,000. PRS contributes Property to Y Corp in a section 351 transaction. Under section 362(e)(2)(A), Y Corp takes a $10,000 basis in Property. PRS's basis in its Y Corp stock is $10,000 under section 358. Pursuant to paragraph (f)(3)(iv)(C)(3) of this section, B has a section 704(c)(1)(C) basis adjustment of $8,000 in the Y Corp stock received by PRS in the section 351 exchange.

(ii) In Year 2, Y Corp sells Property for its fair market value of $10,000. Y Corp recognizes no gain or loss on the sale of Property. Pursuant to paragraph (f)(3)(iv)(C)(1) of this section, B does not take into account its section 704(c)(1)(C) basis adjustment upon the sale by Y Corp of Property. Instead, B will take the section 704(c)(1)(C) basis adjustment into account when PRS disposes of the Y Corp stock.

(D) *Section 708(b)(1)(B) transactions.—(1) In general.—*A partner with a section 704(c)(1)(C) basis adjustment in section 704(c)(1)(C) property held by a partnership that terminates under section 708(b)(1)(B) will continue to have the same section 704(c)(1)(C) basis adjustment for section 704(c)(1)(C) property deemed contributed by the terminated partnership to the new partnership under §1.708-1(b)(4). In addition, the deemed contribution of property by a terminated partnership to a new partnership is not subject to this section and does not create a section 704(c)(1)(C) basis adjustment.

(2) *Example.—*A contributes Property with an adjusted basis of $11,000 and a fair market value of $5,000 and B contributes $5,000 cash to PRS, a partnership. B sells its entire interest in PRS to C for its fair market value of $5,000, which terminates PRS under section 708(b)(1)(B). Under §1.708-1(b)(4), PRS is deemed to contribute all of its assets and liabilities to a new partnership (New PRS) in exchange for an interest in New PRS. Immediately thereafter, PRS is deemed to distribute its interest in New PRS equally to A and C in complete liquidation of PRS. New PRS takes Property with a basis of $5,000 and A retains its $6,000 section 704(c)(1)(C) basis adjustment related to Property inside New PRS.

(E) *Disposition in an installment sale.—*If a partnership disposes of section 704(c)(1)(C) property in an installment sale (as defined in section 453(b)), the installment obligation received by the partnership is treated as the section 704(c)(1)(C) property with the same section 704(c)(1)(C) basis adjustment as the section 704(c)(1)(C) property disposed of by the partnership (with appropriate adjustments for any gain recognized on the installment sale).

(F) *Contributed contracts.—*If a partner contributes to a partnership a contract that is section 704(c)(1)(C) property, and the partnership subsequently acquires property pursuant to the contract in a transaction in which less than all of the loss is recognized, then the acquired property is treated as section 704(c)(1)(C) property with the same section 704(c)(1)(C) basis adjustment as the contract (with appropriate adjustments for any gain or loss recognized on the acquisition). For this purpose, the term *contract* includes, but is not limited to, options, forward contracts, and futures contracts.

(v) *Distributions.—(A) Current distribution of section 704(c)(1)(C) property to section 704(c)(1)(C) partner.—*If a partnership distributes property to a partner and the partner has a section 704(c)(1)(C) basis adjustment for the property, the section 704(c)(1)(C) basis adjustment is taken into account under section 732. *See* §1.732-2(a). For certain adjustments to the basis of remaining partnership property after the distribution of section 704(c)(1)(C) property to the section 704(c)(1)(C) partner, see §1.734-2(c).

(B) *Distribution of section 704(c)(1)(C) property to another partner.—*If a partner receives a distribution of property in which another partner has a section 704(c)(1)(C) basis adjustment, the distributee does not take the section 704(c)(1)(C) basis adjustment into account under section 732. If section 704(c)(1)(B) applies to treat the section 704(c)(1)(C) partner as recognizing loss on the sale of the distributed property, the section 704(c)(1)(C) basis adjustment is taken into account in determining the amount of the loss. A section 704(c)(1)(C) partner with a section 704(c)(1)(C) basis adjustment in the distributed property that is not taken into account as described in the prior sentence reallocates the section 704(c)(1)(C) basis adjustment among the remaining items of partnership property under §1.755-1(c).

(C) *Distributions in complete liquidation of a section 704(c)(1)(C) partner's interest.—*If a section 704(c)(1)(C) partner receives a distribution of property (whether or not the partner has a section 704(c)(1)(C) basis adjustment in the property) in liquidation of its interest in the partnership, the adjusted basis to the partnership of the distributed property immediately before the distribution includes the section 704(c)(1)(C) partner's section 704(c)(1)(C) basis adjustment for the property in which the section 704(c)(1)(C) partner relinquished an interest. For purposes of determining the section 704(c)(1)(C) partner's basis in distributed property under section 732, the partnership reallocates any section 704(c)(1)(C) basis adjustment from section 704(c)(1)(C) property retained by the partnership to distributed properties of like character under the principles of §1.755-1(c)(i), after applying sections 704(c)(1)(B) and 737. If section 704(c)(1)(C) property is retained by the partnership, and no property of like character is distributed, then that property's section 704(c)(1)(C) basis adjustment is not reallocated to the distributed property for purposes of applying section 732. See §1.734-2(c)(2) for rules regarding the treatment of any section 704(c)(1)(C) adjustment that is not fully utilized by the section 704(c)(1)(C) partner.

(D) *Examples.—*The following examples illustrate the principles of this paragraph (f)(3)(v).

Example 1. Current distribution of section 704(c)(1)(C) property to section 704(c)(1)(C) partner—(i) A contributes Property 1 with an adjusted basis of $15,000 and a fair market value of $10,000 and Property 2 with an adjusted basis of $5,000 and a fair market value of $20,000 and B contributes $30,000 cash to PRS, a partnership. Property 1 and Property 2 are both capital assets. When Property 1 has a fair market value of $12,000, and neither A nor B's basis in PRS has changed, PRS distributes Property 1 to A in a current distribution.

(ii) Property 1 has an adjusted basis to PRS of $10,000, and A has a section 704(c)(1)(C) basis adjustment of $5,000 in Property 1. Pursuant to §1.732-2(c) and paragraph (f)(3)(v)(A) of this section, for purposes of section 732(a)(1), the adjusted basis of Property 1 to PRS immediately before the distribution is $15,000 (PRS's $10,000 adjusted basis increased by A's $5,000 section 704(c)(1)(C) basis adjustment for Property 1) and, therefore, A takes a $15,000 adjusted basis in Property 1 upon the distribution. Accordingly, no adjustment is required to PRS's property under section 734.

Example 2. Current distribution of section 704(c)(1)(C) property to another partner. Assume the same facts as *Example 1* except PRS distributes Property 1 to B in a distribution to which section 704(c)(1)(B) does not apply. B does not take any portion of A's section 704(c)(1)(C) basis adjustment into account. Accordingly, pursuant to §1.732-1(a) and paragraph (f)(3)(v)(B) of this section, for purposes of section 732(a)(1), the adjusted basis of Property 1 to PRS immediately before the distribution is $10,000 and, therefore, B takes a $10,000 adjusted basis in Property 1 upon the distribution. Accordingly, no adjustment is required to PRS's property under section 734. A's section 704(c)(1)(C) basis adjustment in Property 1 is reallocated to Property 2 in accordance with §1.755-1(c).

Example 3. (i) *Liquidating distribution to section 704(c)(1)(C) partner.* In Year 1, A contributes Property 1 with an adjusted basis of $15,000 and a fair market value of $10,000 and Property 2 with an adjusted basis of $5,000 and a fair market value of $20,000 and B and C each contribute $30,000 cash to PRS, a partnership. Property 1 and Property 2 are both capital assets. In a later year, when the fair market value of Property 2 is still $20,000, and no partner's basis in PRS has changed, PRS distributes Property 2 and $10,000 to A in complete liquidation of A's partnership interest in a distribution to which section 737 does not apply. PRS has a section 754 election in effect for the year of the distribution.

(ii) Property 2 has an adjusted basis to PRS of $5,000, and A has a section 704(c)(1)(C) basis adjustment of $5,000 in Property 1. Pursuant to §1.732-2(c) and paragraph (f)(3)(v)(C) of this section, for purposes of section 732(b), the adjusted basis of Property 2 to PRS immediately before the distribution is $10,000 (PRS's $5,000 adjusted basis in Property 2 increased by A's $5,000 section 704(c)(1)(C) basis adjustment for Property 1), and A's adjusted basis in Property 2 upon the distribution is $10,000 (A's $20,000 basis in PRS minus the $10,000 cash distributed). Therefore, no adjustment is required to PRS's property under section 734.

(vi) *Returns.—*A partnership that owns property with a section 704(c)(1)(C) basis adjustment must attach a statement to the partnership return for the year of the contribution setting forth the name and taxpayer identification number of the section 704(c)(1)(C) partner as well as the section 704(c)(1)(C) basis adjustment and the section 704(c)(1)(C) property to which the adjustment relates.

(g) * * *. The provisions of paragraph (f) of this section apply to partnership contributions occurring on or after the date of publication of the Treasury decision adopting these rules as final regulations in the **Federal Register**.

□ Par. 3. Section 1.704-4 is amended as follows:

1. In paragraph (a)(1), by removing "five years" and adding in its place "seven years".

2. In paragraph (a)(4) by removing "five-year" and adding in its place "seven-year" each time it appears.

3. By revising paragraph (a)(4)(i).

4. In paragraph (f)(2), *Examples 1* and *2*, by removing the phrase "five-year" and adding in its place "seven-year" each time it appears and removing "2000" and adding in its place "2002" each time it appears.

5. By adding a sentence to the end of paragraph (g).
The revision and addition read as follows:

§1.704-4. Distribution of contributed property.—(a) ＊ ＊ ＊

(4) *Determination of seven-year period.*—(i) *General rule.*—The seven-year period specified in paragraph (a)(1) of this section begins on, and includes, the date of contribution and ends on, and includes, the last date that is within seven years of the contribution. For example, if a partner contributes section 704(c) property to a partner-

ship on May 15, 2016, the seven-year period with respect to the section 704(c) property ends on, and includes, May 14, 2023.

＊ ＊ ＊

(g) ＊ ＊ ＊ The provisions of this section relating to the seven-year period for determining the applicability of section 704(c)(1)(B) are applicable for partnership contributions occurring on or after the date of publication of the Treasury decision adopting these rules as final regulations in the **Federal Register**.

Partnerships: Centralized Partnership Audit Regime

Partnerships: Centralized Partnership Audit Regime.—Amendments to Reg. §1.705-1, implementing the centralized partnership audit regime that have not been finalized to reflect the changes made by the Technical Corrections Act of 2018, contained in Title II of the Consolidated Appropriations Act of 2018 (TTCA), are proposed (published in the Federal Register on August 17, 2018) (REG-136118-15; REG-119337-17; REG-118067-17; REG-120232-17 and REG-120233-17).

Par. 3. Section 1.705-1 is amended by adding paragraph (a)(10) to read as follows:

§1.705-1. Determination of basis of partner's interest.—(a) ＊ ＊ ＊

(10) For rules relating to determining the adjusted basis of a partner's interest in a partnership following a final determination under subchapter C of chapter 63 of the Internal Revenue Code

(relating to the centralized partnership audit regime), see §§301.6225-4 and 301.6226-4 of this chapter.

＊ ＊ ＊

Partnerships: Allocable Cash Basis: Tiered Partnership Items

Partnerships: Allocable Cash Basis: Tiered Partnership Items.—Amendments to Reg. §1.706-0, regarding the determination of a partner's distributive share of certain allocable cash basis items and items attributable to an interest in a lower-tier partnership during a partnership taxable year in which a partner's interest changes, are proposed (published in the Federal Register on August 3, 2015) (corrected October 29, 2015) (REG-109370-10).

Par. 2. Section 1.706-0 is amended by removing the entry for §1.706-2T and adding entries for §§1.706-2, 1.706-3, and 1.706-6 to read as follows:

§1.706-0. Table of contents.

＊ ＊ ＊

§1.706-2 Certain allocable cash basis items.
    (a) Allocable cash basis items prorated over period to which attributable.
        (1) In general.
        (2) Allocable cash basis item.
        (3) Items attributable to periods not within taxable year.
        (4) Treatment of deductible items attributable to prior periods.
    (b) Example.
    (c) De minimis exception.

    (d) Effective/applicability date.
§1.706-3 Items attributable to interest in lower-tier partnership.
    (a) General rule.
    (b) Safe harbor.
    (c) De minimis upper-tier partner exception.
    (d) Effective/applicability date.

＊ ＊ ＊

§1.706-6 Property transferred in connection with the performance of services.
    (a) Forfeiture allocations.
    (b) Effective date.

CFCs: U.S. Shareholders: Ownership Attribution

CFCs: U.S. Shareholders: Ownership Attribution.—Amendments to Reg. §1.706-1, relating to the modification of section 958(b) of the Internal Revenue Code by the Tax Cuts and Jobs Act, which was enacted on December 22, 2017, are proposed (published in the Federal Register on October 2, 2019) (REG-104223-18).

Par. 6. Section 1.706-1 is amended by:
1. Revising paragraph (b)(6)(ii).
2. Revising the heading for paragraph (b)(6)(v).
3. In paragraph (b)(6)(v)(A), revising the first sentence and adding two sentences after the first sentence.
The revisions and addition read as follows:

§1.706-1. Taxable years of partner and partnership.

＊ ＊ ＊

(b) ＊ ＊ ＊
    (6) ＊ ＊ ＊

(ii) *Definition of foreign partner.*—For purposes of this paragraph (b)(6), a foreign partner is any partner that is not a United States person (as defined in section 7701(a)(30)), except that a partner that is a controlled foreign corporation (within the meaning of section 957(a)) in which a United States shareholder (as defined in section 951(b)) owns (within the meaning of section 958(a)) stock is not treated as a foreign partner.

＊ ＊ ＊

(v) *Applicability dates.*—(A) ＊ ＊ ＊ The provisions of this paragraph (b)(6) (other than paragraph (b)(6)(iii) of this section and paragraph (b)(6)(ii) of this section to the extent described in the next sentence) apply to partnership taxable years, other than those of an

existing partnership, that begin on or after July 23, 2002. The provisions in paragraph (b)(6)(ii) of this section relating to controlled foreign corporations apply to taxable years of foreign corporations ending on or after October 1, 2019, and taxable years of United States shareholders in which or with which such taxable years of foreign corporations end. For taxable years of foreign corporations ending before October 1, 2019, and taxable years of United States shareholders in which or with which such taxable years of foreign corporations end, a taxpayer may apply such provisions to the last taxable year of a foreign corporation beginning before January 1, 2018, and each subsequent taxable year of the foreign corporation, and to taxable years of United States shareholders in which or with which such taxable years of the foreign corporation end, provided that the taxpayer and United States persons that are related (within the meaning of section 267 or 707) to the taxpayer consistently apply such provisions with respect to all foreign corporations. ＊ ＊ ＊

＊ ＊ ＊

Partnerships: Taxable Year: Related Parties

Deductions: Losses: Interest: Transactions Between Related Taxpayers.—Temporary Reg. §1.706-2T, relating to deductions, timing of deductions and losses in transactions between certain related taxpayers, is also proposed as a final regulation and, when adopted, would become Reg. §1.706-2 (published in the Federal Register on November 30, 1984).

§1.706-2. Temporary regulations; questions and answers under the Tax Reform Act of 1984.

Partnerships: Allocable Cash Basis: Tiered Partnership Items

Partnerships: Allocable Cash Basis: Tiered Partnership Items.—Reg. §1.706-2 and amendments to Temporary Reg. §1.706-2T, regarding the determination of a partner's distributive share of certain allocable cash basis items and items attributable to an interest in a lower-tier partnership during a partnership taxable year in which a partner's interest changes, are proposed (published in the Federal Register on August 3, 2015) (corrected October 29, 2015) (REG-109370-10).

Par. 3. Section 1.706-2 is added to read as follows:

§1.706-2. Certain allocable cash basis items.—(a) *Allocable cash basis items prorated over period to which attributable.*—(1) *In general.*—If during any taxable year of the partnership there is a change in any partner's interest in the partnership, then each partner's distributive share of any allocable cash basis item shall be determined—

(i) By assigning the appropriate portion of such item to each day in the period to which it is attributable; and

(ii) By allocating the portion assigned to any such day among the partners in proportion to their interests in the partnership at the close of such day.

(2) *Allocable cash basis item.*—For purposes of this section, the term *allocable cash basis item* means any of the following items of deduction, loss, income, or gain with respect to which the partnership uses the cash receipts and disbursements method of accounting:

(i) Interest;

(ii) Taxes;

(iii) Payments for the use of property or for services (other than deductions for the transfer of an interest in the partnership in connection with the performance of services; such deductions generally must be allocated under the rules for extraordinary items in §1.706-4(e));

(iv) Any allowable deduction that had been previously deferred under section 267(a)(2);

(v) Any deduction, loss, income, or gain item that accrues over time and that would, if not allocated as an allocable cash basis item, result in the significant misstatement of a partner's income.

(3) *Items attributable to periods not within taxable year.*—If any portion of any allocable cash basis item is attributable to—

(i) Any period before the beginning of the taxable year, such portion shall be assigned under paragraph (a)(1)(i) of this section to the first day of the taxable year, or

(ii) Any period after the close of the taxable year, such portion shall be assigned under paragraph (a)(1)(i) of this section to the last day of the taxable year.

(4) *Treatment of deductible items attributable to prior periods.*—If any portion of a deductible cash basis item is assigned under paragraph (a)(3)(i) of this section to the first day of any taxable year—

(i) Such portion shall be allocated among persons who are partners in the partnership during the period to which such portion is attributable in accordance with their varying interests in the partnership during such period; and

(ii) Any amount allocated under paragraph (a)(4)(i) of this section to a person who is not a partner in the partnership on such first day shall be capitalized by the partnership and allocated among partnership assets under the principles of section 755 (applying the principles of §1.755-1(b) for partners who sold or exchanged their interest, and the principles of §1.755-1(c) for partners who received a distribution from the partnership in exchange for their interest).

(b) *Example 1.* On January 1, 2015, A, B, and C are equal one-third partners in PRS, a calendar year partnership that uses the cash receipts and disbursements method of accounting. On July 1, 2015, A sells her entire interest in PRS to D. On December 1, 2015, PRS pays a $12,000 interest expense that is attributable to every day in PRS's taxable year. Assume the de minimis exception of paragraph (c) of this section does not apply, and that the $12,000 interest expense

must be allocated under the rules of paragraph (a) of this section. A was a partner in PRS for 181 days, and D was a partner in PRS for 184 days, including on July 1 pursuant to paragraph (a)(1)(ii) of this section. Under paragraph (a) of this section, A is entitled to 181/365 of her otherwise allocable share of deductions for the $12,000 interest expense, and D is entitled to 184/365 of his otherwise allocable share of deductions for the $12,000 interest expense. Thus, PRS allocates the interest expense deductions $1,983.56 to A, $2,016.44 to D, and $4,000 to each B and C.

Example 2. In 2015, E, F, and G are equal one-third partners in PRS, a calendar year partnership that uses the cash receipts and disbursements method of accounting. On December 31, 2015, E sells her entire interest in PRS to H. In November 2016, PRS makes a $6,000 payment for the use of property that is attributable to the period from January 1, 2015 to December 31, 2016. Assume the de minimis exception of paragraph (c) of this section does not apply, and that the $6,000 payment for the use of property must be allocated under the rules of paragraph (a) of this section. Under paragraph (a)(3)(i) of this section, half of the $6,000 expense is attributable to 2015 and must be assigned to January 1, 2016. Of this $3,000 assigned to January 1, 2016, one-third is allocable to each E, F, and G under paragraph (a)(4)(i) of this section. However, because E is not a partner in 2016, PRS must capitalize E's $1,000 share of the expense under paragraph (a)(4)(ii) of this section. Because E sold her interest to H, PRS must treat the capitalized $1,000 similar to a section 743(b) adjustment for H allocated among PRS's property under the principles of §1.755-1(b).

Example 3. Assume the same facts as Example 2, except that on December 31, 2015, PRS distributed property to E in complete redemption of E's interest, and H never becomes a partner in PRS. PRS must capitalize E's $1,000 share of the expense under paragraph (a)(4)(ii) of this section. However, because E was redeemed, PRS must instead treat the capitalized $1,000 similar to a section 734(b) common basis adjustment allocated among PRS's property under the principles of §1.755-1(c).

(c) *De minimis exception.*—An item described in paragraph (a)(2) of this section will not be subject to the rules of this section if, for the partnership's taxable year the total amount of the particular class of allocable cash basis items described in paragraph (a)(2)(i) through (v) of this section (but in no event counting an item more than once) is less than five percent of the partnership's gross income, including tax-exempt income described in section 705(a)(1)(B), in the case of income or gain items, or gross expenses and losses, including section 705(a)(2)(B) expenditures, in the case of losses and expense items; and the total amount of allocable cash basis items from all classes of allocable cash basis items amounting to less than five percent of the partnership's gross income, including tax-exempt income described in section 705(a)(1)(B), in the case of income or gain items, or gross expenses and losses, including section 705(a)(2)(B) expenditures, in the case of losses and expense items, does not exceed $10 million in the taxable year, determined by treating all such allocable cash basis items as positive amounts.

(d) *Effective/applicability date.*—This section applies to taxable years beginning on or after the date of publication of the Treasury decision adopting these rules as a final regulation in the **Federal Register**. [Reg. §1.706-2.]

Par. 4. Section 1.706-2T is removed.

§1.706-2T. Temporary regulations; question and answer under the Tax Reform Act of 1984 (Temporary).

Partnerships: Equity for Services

Partnerships: Equity for Services.—Reg. §1.706-3, providing that the transfer of a partnership interest in connection with the performance of services is subject to Code Sec. 83 and providing rules for coordinating Code Sec. 83 with partnership taxation principles, is proposed (published in the Federal Register on May 24, 2005) (REG-105346-03). Proposed Reg. §1.706-3(a) withdrawn by REG-109370-10 on August 3, 2015; REG-109370-10 also proposed to redesignate Reg. §1.706-3(b) and (c) as Reg. §1.706-6(a) and (b).

☐ Par. 5. Section 1.706-3 is added to read as follows:

§1.706-3. Property transferred in connection with the performance of services.—(a) [Withdrawn by REG-109370-10 on August 3, 2015.]

(b) *Forfeiture allocations.*—If an election under section 83(b) is made with respect to a partnership interest that is substantially

nonvested (within the meaning of §1.83-3(b)), and that interest is later forfeited, the partnership must make forfeiture allocations to reverse prior allocations made with respect to the forfeited interest. See §1.704-1(b)(4)(xii). Although the person forfeiting the interest may not have been a partner for the entire taxable year, forfeiture allocations may be made out of the partnership's items for the entire taxable year.

(c) *Effective date.*—This section applies to transfers of property on or after the date final regulations are published in the Federal Register. [Reg. § 1.706-3.]

Partnerships: Allocable Cash Basis: Tiered Partnership Items

Partnerships: Allocable Cash Basis: Tiered Partnership Items.—Reg. §1.706-3 and amendments to Reg. §§1.706-3 and 1.706-4, regarding the determination of a partner's distributive share of certain allocable cash basis items and items attributable to an interest in a lower-tier partnership during a partnership taxable year in which a partner's interest changes, are proposed (published in the Federal Register on August 3, 2015) (corrected October 29, 2015) (REG-109370-10).

Par. 5. Section 1.706-3 is added to read as follows:

§1.706-3. Items attributable to interest in lower-tier partnership.

—(a) *General rule.*—Except as provided in paragraphs (b) and (c) of this section, if during any taxable year of the partnership—

(1) There is a change in any partner's interest in the partnership (the upper-tier partnership); and

(2) Such partnership is a partner in another partnership (the lower-tier partnership),

then each partner's distributive share of any item of the upper-tier partnership attributable to the lower-tier partnership shall be determined by assigning the appropriate portion (determined by applying principles similar to the principles of §1.706-2(a)(3) and (4)) of each such item to the appropriate days during which the upper-tier partnership is a partner in the lower-tier partnership and by allocating the portion assigned to any such day among the partners in proportion to their interests in the upper-tier partnership at the close of such day. An upper-tier partnership's distributive share of any items of income, gain, loss, deduction, or credit from a lower-tier partnership is considered to be realized or sustained by the upper-tier partnership at the same time and in the same manner as such items were realized or sustained by the lower-tier partnership. For an additional example of the application of the principles of this paragraph (a), see Revenue Ruling 77-311, 1977-2 CB 218. *See* section 601.601(d)(2)(ii)(b).

(b) *De minimis upper-tier partnership exception.*—A de minimis upper-tier partnership is not required to, but may, apply paragraph (a) of this section. For purposes of this paragraph, a de minimis upper-tier partnership is a partnership that directly owns an interest in less than 10 percent of the profits and capital of the lower-tier partnership. This paragraph (b) only applies if all de minimis upper-tier partnerships own an interest in, in the aggregate, less than 30 percent of the profits and capital of the lower-tier partnership, and if no partnership is created with a purpose of avoiding the application of this section.

(c) *Example 1.* On January 1, 2015, A, B, and C are equal one-third partners in UTP, a calendar year partnership that uses the proration method and calendar day convention to account for variations during its taxable year. UTP is itself a partner in a lower-tier partnership, LTP, which is also a calendar year partnership. UTP owns a 15 percent interest in the profits and capital of LTP throughout 2015. On August 1, 2015, A sells her entire interest in UTP to D. During 2015, LTP incurred $100,000 of ordinary deductions, which

were attributable to the period from January 1, 2015, to July 1, 2015. None of LTP's deductions were extraordinary items within the meaning of §1.706-4(e). UTP's distributive share of LTP's deductions is $15,000. Under paragraph (a) of this section, UTP must assign the $15,000 equally among all days from January 1, 2015 to July 1, 2015, and allocate the assigned daily portions among its partners in accordance with their interests in UTP on those days. Accordingly, A, B, and C are each allocated $5,000 of the deduction, and D is not allocated any portion of the deduction.

Example 2. Assume the same facts as Example 1, except that UTP owned a 9 percent interest in the profits and capital of LTP throughout 2015, and that LTP had only one other partner, which owned the remaining 91 percent of LTP. UTP's distributive share of LTP's $100,000 ordinary deductions is $9,000. UTP qualifies as a de minimis upper-tier partnership under paragraph (b) of this section, and therefore UTP is not required to apply the rules of paragraph (a) of this section. Instead, UTP may apply the rules of §1.706-4 to the $9,000 ordinary deduction. If UTP decides to apply the rules of §1.706-4, UTP prorates the $9,000 deduction equally over its entire taxable year, and allocates it according to its partners' interests on each day. Because A was a partner in UTP for 213 days, and D was a partner in UTP for 152 days, UTP allocates the $9,000 deduction $3,000 to each of B and C, $1,750.68 to A, and $1,249.32 to D.

Example 3. Assume the same facts as Example 2, except that UTP uses the interim closing method rather than the proration method. UTP qualifies as a de minimis upper-tier partnership under paragraph (b) of this section, and therefore UTP is not required to apply the rules of paragraph (a) of this section. Instead, UTP may apply the rules of §1.706-4 to the $9,000 ordinary deduction. UTP's distributive share of LTP items is considered to have been realized or sustained by UTP at the same time and in the same manner as such items were realized or sustained by LTP. Accordingly, even if UTP decides to apply the rules of §1.706-4, UTP's application of the interim closing method of §1.706-4 to the $9,000 deduction results in UTP allocating to each of A, B, and C $3,000 of the deduction, and not allocating any portion of the deduction to D. UTP would reach the same result if it had instead chosen to apply the rules of paragraph (a) of this section.

(d) *Effective/applicability date.*—This section applies to partnership taxable years beginning on or after the date of publication of the Treasury decision adopting these rules as a final regulation in the **Federal Register**. [Reg. § 1.706-3.]

Par. 6. As proposed to be added May 24, 2005 (70 FR 29675), redesignate §1.706-3(b) and (c) as §1.706-6(a) and (b).

§1.706-3. Items attributable to interest in lower-tier partnership.

Par. 7. Section 1.706-4 is amended by:
a. Adding a new sentence to the end of paragraph (b)(2);
b. Revising paragraph (e)(1);
c. Redesignating paragraphs (e)(2)(ix), (x), and (xi) as paragraphs (e)(2)(xi), (xii), and (xiii) respectively;
d. Adding new paragraphs (e)(2)(ix) and (e)(2)(x);
e. Adding a new sentence to the end of paragraph (e)(3);
f. Revising paragraph (e)(4) Example 3; and
g. Revising the first sentence of paragraph (f).
The additions and revisions read as follows:

§1.706-4. Determination of distributive share when a partner's interest varies

* * *

(b) * * *

(2) * * * However, this paragraph (b)(2) does not apply to any deduction for the transfer of an interest in the partnership in connection with the performance of services. Instead, such deduction must be allocated under the extraordinary item rules of paragraphs (e)(1) and (2) of this section.

* * *

(e) * * *

(1) *General principles.*—Extraordinary items may not be prorated. The partnership must allocate extraordinary items among the partners in proportion to their interests in the partnership item at the

time of day on which the extraordinary item occurred, regardless of the method (interim closing or proration method) and convention (daily, semi-monthly, or monthly) otherwise used by the partnership. These rules require the allocation of extraordinary items as an exception to the proration method, which would otherwise ratably allocate the extraordinary items across the segment, and the conventions, which could otherwise inappropriately shift extraordinary items between a transferor and transferee. However, publicly traded partnerships (as defined in section 7704(b)) that are treated as partnerships may, but are not required to, apply their selected convention in determining who held publicly traded units (as described in §1.7704-1(b) or §1.7704-1(c)(1)) at the time of the occurrence of any extraordinary item except extraordinary items described in paragraph (e)(2)(ix) of this section. Publicly traded partnerships that choose to treat items described in paragraph (e)(2)(ix) of this section as extraordinary items must allocate those items among the partners in proportion to their interests in those items at the time of day on which the items are deemed to have occurred according to the special timing rules for those items in paragraph (e)(2)(ix) of this section, regardless of the method and convention otherwise used by the partnership. Extraordinary items continue to be subject to any special limitation or requirement relating to the timing or amount of income, gain, loss, deduction, or credit applicable to the entire partnership taxable year (for example, the limitation for section 179 expenses).

(2) * * *

(ix) For publicly traded partnerships (as defined in section 7704(b)), any item of income that is an amount subject to withholding as defined in §1.1441-2(a) (excluding amounts effectively connected with the conduct of a trade or business within the United States) or a withholdable payment under §1.1473-1(a) occurring during a taxable year if the partners agree (within the meaning of paragraph (e) of this section) to consistently treat all such items as extraordinary items for that taxable year. If the partners so agree, then for purposes of section 706 such items shall be treated as occurring at the next time as of which the recipients of a distribution by the partnership are determined, or, to the extent such income items arise between the final time during the taxable year as of which the recipients of a distribution by the partnership are determined and the end of the taxable year, such items shall be treated as occurring at the final time during the taxable year as of which the recipients of a distribution by the partnership are determined. This paragraph (e)(2)(ix) does not apply unless the partnership has a regular practice of making at least four distributions (other than de minimis distributions) to its partners during each taxable year.

(x) Any deduction for the transfer of an interest in the partnership in connection with the performance of services. Such an extraordinary item is treated as occurring immediately before the transfer or vesting of the partnership interest that results in compensation income for the person who performs the services, but in no case shall the item be treated as occurring prior to the beginning of the partnership's taxable year.

* * *

(3) * * * However, this paragraph (e)(3) does not apply to any deduction for the transfer of an interest in the partnership in connection with the performance of services. Instead, such deduction must be allocated under the extraordinary item rules of paragraphs (e)(1) and (2) of this section.

(4) * * *

Example 3. (i) Assume the same facts as in *Example 2*, except that PRS is a publicly traded partnership (within the meaning of section 7704(b)), A held a publicly traded unit (as described in §1.7704 1(b) or §1.7704-1(c)(1)) in PRS, and the extraordinary item recognized at 3:15 p.m. on December 7, 2016 is not described in paragraph (e)(2)(ix) of this section. Under PRS's monthly convention, the December 12 variation is deemed to have occurred for purposes of this section at the end of the day on November 30, 2016. Pursuant to paragraph (e)(1) of this section, a publicly traded partnership (as defined in section 7704(b)) may choose to respect its conventions in determining who held its publicly traded units (as described in §1.7704-1(b) or §1.7704-1(c)(1)) at the time of the occurrence of an extraordinary item, except for extraordinary items described in paragraph (e)(2)(ix) of this section. Therefore, PRS may choose to treat A as not having been a partner in PRS for purposes of this paragraph (e) at the time the extraordinary item arose, and thus PRS may choose not to allocate A any share of the extraordinary item.

(ii) Assume the same facts as in paragraph (i) of this *Example 3*, except that on November 5, 2016, PRS recognizes an item of income that is an amount subject to withholding as defined in §1.1441-2(a) (and that is not effectively connected with the conduct of a trade or business within the United States). PRS has a regular practice of making quarterly distributions to its partners each taxable year. PRS determines that the recipients of its fourth-quarter distribution will be interest holders of record at the close of business on December 15, 2016. The partners of PRS agree (within the meaning of paragraph (f) of this section) to consistently treat all such items during the taxable year as extraordinary items. Pursuant to paragraph (e)(2)(ix) of this section, the item of income that arose on November 5 is treated as an extraordinary item occurring at the next time as of which the recipients of a distribution by the partnership are determined (unless that time occurs in a different taxable year). Because December 15 occurs before the end of PRS's taxable year, the item of income is treated as occurring at the close of business on December 15, and must be allocated according to PRS's partners' interests at that time, determined without regard to PRS's applicable convention. Therefore, A will not be allocated any share of the item because A disposed of its entire interest in PRS before the close of business on December 15.

(iii) Assume the same facts as in paragraph (ii) of this *Example 3*, except that PRS determines that the recipients of its fourth-quarter distribution will be interest holders of record at the close of business on January 15, 2017, and PRS determines that the recipients of its third-quarter distribution will be interest holders of record at the close of business on October 21, 2016. Therefore, the last time during 2016 as of which the recipients of a distribution by PRS are determined is at the close of business on October 21, 2016. Pursuant to paragraph (e)(2)(ix) of this section, because the item of income subject to withholding as defined in §1.1441-2(a) which arises on November 5 arises between the final time during the taxable year as of which the recipients of a distribution are determined and the end of the taxable year, such item shall be treated as occurring at the final time during the taxable year as of which the recipients of a distribution by the partnership are determined. Therefore, the item of income subject to withholding as defined in §1.1441-2(a) which arises on November 5, 2016 is treated as occurring at the close of business on October 21, 2016, and must be allocated according to PRS's partners' interests at that time.

(f) *Agreement of the partners.*—For purposes of paragraphs (a)(3)(iii) (relating to selection of the proration method), (c)(3) (relating to selection of the semi-monthly or monthly convention), (d)(1) (relating to performance of regular semi-monthly or monthly interim closings), (e)(2)(ix) (relating to a publicly traded partnership's treatment of all amounts subject to withholding as defined in §1.1441-2(a) that are not effectively connected with the conduct of a trade or business within the United States or withholdable payments under §1.1473-1(a) as extraordinary items), and (e)(2)(xi) (relating to selection of additional extraordinary items) of this section, the term agreement of the partners means either an agreement of all the partners to select the method, convention, or extraordinary item in a dated, written statement maintained with the partnership's books and records, including, for example, a selection that is included in the partnership agreement, or a selection of the method, convention, or extraordinary item made by a person authorized to make that selection, including under a grant of general authority provided for by either state law or in the partnership agreement, if that person's selection is in a dated, written statement maintained with the partnership's books and records.

* * *

Partnerships: Centralized Partnership Audit Regime

Partnerships: Centralized Partnership Audit Regime.—Amendments to Reg. §1.706-4, implementing the centralized partnership audit regime that have not been finalized to reflect the changes made by the Technical Corrections Act of 2018, contained in Title II of the Consolidated Appropriations Act of 2018 (TTCA), are proposed (published in the Federal Register on August 17, 2018) (REG-136118-15; REG-119337-17; REG-118067-17; REG-120232-17 and REG-120233-17).

Par. 4. Section 1.706-4 is amended by redesignating paragraphs (e)(2)(viii) through (xi) as paragraphs (e)(2)(ix) through (xii), respectively, and adding a new paragraph (e)(2)(viii) to read as follows:

§1.706-4. Determination of distributive share when a partner's interest varies.

* * *

(e) * * *

(2) * * *

(viii) Any item arising from a final determination under subchapter C of chapter 63 of the Internal Revenue Code (relating to the centralized partnership audit regime) with respect to a partnership adjustment resulting in an imputed underpayment for which no election is made under §301.6226-1 of this chapter or for which a pass-through partner (as defined in §301.6241-1(a)(5)) pays an imputed underpayment under §301.6226-3(e)(4).

Partnerships: Equity for Services

Partnerships: Equity for Services.—Amendments to Reg. §1.707-1, providing that the transfer of a partnership interest in connection with the performance of services is subject to Code Sec. 83 and providing rules for coordinating Code Sec. 83 with partnership taxation principles, are proposed (published in the Federal Register on May 24, 2005) (REG-105346-03).

☐ Par. 6. In §1.707-1, paragraph (c) is amended by revising the second sentence to read as follows:

§1.707-1. Transactions between partner and partnership.

* * *

(c) *Guaranteed Payments.*—* * * However, except as otherwise provided in section 83 and the regulations thereunder, a partner must include such payments as ordinary income for that partner's taxable year within or with which ends the partnership taxable year in which the partnership deducted such payments as paid or accrued under its method of accounting. * * *

* * *

Disguised Payments: Services

Disguised Payments: Services.—Amendments to Reg. §§1.707-0 and 1.707-1, relating to disguised payments for services under section 707(a)(2)(A) of the Internal Revenue Code and providing guidance to partnerships and their partners regarding when an arrangement will be treated as a disguised payment for services, are proposed (published in the Federal Register on July 23, 2015) (REG-115452-14).

Par. 2. Section 1.707-0 is amended by revising §1.707-2 to read as follows:

§1.707-0. Table of contents.

* * *

§1.707-2. Disguised payments for services.
(a) In general.
(b) Elements necessary to characterize arrangements as disguised payments for services.
(1) In general.

(2) Application and timing.
(i) Timing and effect of the determination.
(ii) Timing of inclusion.
(3) Application of disguised payment rules.
(c) Factors considered.
(d) Examples.

* * *

Par. 3. Section 1.707-1 is amended by adding a sentence at the end of paragraph (a) and revising paragraph (c) Example 2 to read as follows.

§1.707-1. Transactions between partner and partnership.—(a) * * * For arrangements pursuant to which a purported partner performs services for a partnership and the partner receives a related direct or indirect allocation and distribution from the partnership, see §1.707-2 to determine whether the arrangement should be treated as a disguised payment for services.

(c) * * *

Example 2. Partner C in the CD partnership is to receive 30 percent of partnership income, but not less than $10,000. The income of the partnership is $60,000, and C is entitled to $18,000 (30 percent of $60,000). Of this amount, $10,000 is a guaranteed payment to C. The $10,000 guaranteed payment reduces the partnership's net income to $50,000 of which C receives $8,000 as C's distributive share.

* * *

Disguised Payments: Services

Disguised Payments: Services.—Reg. §1.707-2, relating to disguised payments for services under section 707(a)(2)(A) of the Internal Revenue Code and providing guidance to partnerships and their partners regarding when an arrangement will be treated as a disguised payment for services, is proposed (published in the Federal Register on July 23, 2015) (corrected August 19, 2015) (REG-115452-14).

Par. 4. Section 1.707-2 is added to read as follows:

§1.707-2. Disguised payments for services.—(a) *In general.*—This section prescribes rules for characterizing arrangements as disguised payments for services. Paragraph (b) of this section outlines the elements necessary to characterize an arrangement as a payment for services, and it provides operational rules regarding application and timing of this section. Paragraph (c) of this section identifies the factors that weigh in the determination of whether an arrangement includes the elements described in paragraph (b) of this section that make it appropriate to characterize the arrangement as a payment for services. Paragraph (d) of this section provides examples applying these rules to determine whether an arrangement is a payment for services.

(b) *Elements necessary to characterize arrangements as disguised payments for services.*—(1) *In general.*—An arrangement will be treated as a disguised payment for services if—

(i) A person (service provider), either in a partner capacity or in anticipation of becoming a partner, performs services (directly or through its delegate) to or for the benefit of a partnership;

(ii) There is a related direct or indirect allocation and distribution to such service provider; and

(iii) The performance of such services and the allocation and distribution, when viewed together, are properly characterized as a transaction occurring between the partnership and a person acting other than in that person's capacity as a partner.

(2) *Application and timing.*—(i) *Timing and effect of the determination.*—Whether an arrangement is properly characterized as a payment for services is determined at the time the arrangement is entered into or modified and without regard to whether the terms of the arrangement require the allocation and distribution to occur in the same taxable year. An arrangement that is treated as a payment for services under this paragraph (b) is treated as a payment for services for all purposes of the Internal Revenue Code, including for example, sections 61, 409A, and 457A (as applicable). The amount paid to a person in consideration for services under this section is treated as a payment for services provided to the partnership, and, when appropriate, the partnership must capitalize these amounts (or otherwise treat such amounts in a manner consistent with their recharacterization). The partnership must also treat the arrangement as a payment to a non-partner in determining the remaining partners' shares of taxable income or loss.

(ii) *Timing of inclusion.*—The inclusion of income by the service provider and deduction (if applicable) by the partnership of amounts paid pursuant to an arrangement that is characterized as a payment for services under paragraph (b)(1) of this section is taken into account in the taxable year as required under applicable law by applying all relevant sections of the Internal Revenue Code, including for example, sections 409A and 457A (as applicable), to the allocation and distribution when they occur (or are deemed to occur under all other provisions of the Internal Revenue Code).

(3) *Application of disguised payment rules.*—If a person purports to provide services to a partnership in a capacity as a partner or in anticipation of becoming a partner, the rules of this section apply for purposes of determining whether the services were provided in exchange for a disguised payment, even if it is determined after applying the rules of this section that the service provider is not a partner. If after applying the rules of this section, no partnership exists as a result of the service provider failing to become a partner under the arrangement, then the service provider is treated as having provided services directly to the other purported partner.

(c) *Factors considered.*—Whether an arrangement constitutes a payment for services (in whole or in part) depends on all of the facts and circumstances. Paragraphs (c)(1) through (6) of this section provide a non-exclusive list of factors that may indicate that an arrangement constitutes (in whole or in part) a payment for services. The presence or absence of a factor is based on all of the facts and circumstances at the time the parties enter into the arrangement (or if the parties modify the arrangement, at the time of the modification). The most important factor is significant entrepreneurial risk as set forth in paragraph (c)(1) of this section. An arrangement that lacks significant entrepreneurial risk constitutes a payment for services. An arrangement that has significant entrepreneurial risk will generally not constitute a payment for services unless other factors establish otherwise. For purposes of making determinations under this paragraph (c), the weight to be given to any particular factor, other than entrepreneurial risk, depends on the particular case and the absence of a factor is not necessarily indicative of whether or not an arrangement is treated as a payment for services.

(1) The arrangement lacks significant entrepreneurial risk. Whether an arrangement lacks significant entrepreneurial risk is based on the service provider's entrepreneurial risk relative to the overall entrepreneurial risk of the partnership. Paragraphs (c)(1)(i) through (v) of this section provide facts and circumstances that create a presumption that an arrangement lacks significant entrepreneurial risk and will be treated as a disguised payment for services unless other facts and circumstances establish the presence of significant entrepreneurial risk by clear and convincing evidence:

(i) Capped allocations of partnership income if the cap is reasonably expected to apply in most years;

(ii) An allocation for one or more years under which the service provider's share of income is reasonably certain;

(iii) An allocation of gross income;

(iv) An allocation (under a formula or otherwise) that is predominantly fixed in amount, is reasonably determinable under all the facts and circumstances, or is designed to assure that sufficient net profits are highly likely to be available to make the allocation to the service provider (e.g. if the partnership agreement provides for an allocation of net profits from specific transactions or accounting periods and this allocation does not depend on the long-term future success of the enterprise); or

(v) An arrangement in which a service provider waives its right to receive payment for the future performance of services in a manner that is non-binding or fails to timely notify the partnership and its partners of the waiver and its terms.

(2) The service provider holds, or is expected to hold, a transitory partnership interest or a partnership interest for only a short duration.

(3) The service provider receives an allocation and distribution in a time frame comparable to the time frame that a non-partner service provider would typically receive payment.

(4) The service provider became a partner primarily to obtain tax benefits that would not have been available if the services were rendered to the partnership in a third party capacity.

(5) The value of the service provider's interest in general and continuing partnership profits is small in relation to the allocation and distribution.

(6) The arrangement provides for different allocations or distributions with respect to different services received, the services are provided either by one person or by persons that are related under sections 707(b) or 267(b), and the terms of the differing allocations or distributions are subject to levels of entrepreneurial risk that vary significantly.

(d) *Examples.*—The following examples illustrate the application of this section:

Example 1. Partnership ABC constructed a building that is projected to generate $100,000 of gross income annually. A, an architect, performs services for partnership ABC for which A's normal fee would be $40,000 and contributes cash in an amount equal to the value of a 25 percent interest in the partnership. In exchange, A will receive a 25 percent distributive share for the life of the partnership and a special allocation of $20,000 of partnership gross income for the first two years of the partnership's operations. The ABC partnership agreement satisfies the requirements for economic effect contained in § 1.704-1(b)(2)(ii), including requiring that liquidating distributions are made in accordance with the partners' positive capital account balances. Under paragraph (c) of this section, whether the arrangement is treated as a payment for services depends on the facts and circumstances. The special allocation to A is a capped amount and the cap is reasonably expected to apply. The special allocation is also made out of gross income. Under paragraphs (c)(1)(i) and (iii) of this section, the capped allocations of income and gross income allocations described are presumed to lack significant entrepreneurial risk. No additional facts and circumstances establish otherwise by clear and convincing evidence. Thus, the allocation lacks significant entrepreneurial risk. Accordingly, the arrangement provides for a disguised payment for services as of the date that A and ABC enter into the arrangement and, pursuant to paragraph (b)(2)(ii) of this section, should be included in income by A in the time and manner required under applicable law as determined by applying all relevant sections of the Internal Revenue Code to the arrangement.

Example 2. A, a stock broker, agrees to effect trades for Partnership ABC without the normal brokerage commission. A contributes 51 percent of partnership capital and in exchange, receives a 51 percent interest in residual partnership profits and losses. In addition, A receives a special allocation of gross income that is computed in a manner which approximates its foregone commissions. The special allocation to A is computed by means of a formula similar to a normal brokerage fee and varies with the value and amount of services rendered rather than with the income of the partnership. It is reasonably expected that Partnership ABC will have sufficient gross income to make this allocation. The ABC partnership agreement satisfies the requirements for economic effect contained in § 1.704-1(b)(2)(ii), including requiring that liquidating distributions are made in accordance with the partners' positive capital account balances. Under paragraph (c) of this section, whether the arrangement is treated as a payment for services depends on the facts and circumstances. Under paragraphs (c)(1)(iii) and (iv) of this section, because the allocation is an allocation of gross income and is reasonably determinable under the facts and circumstances, it is presumed to lack significant entrepreneurial risk. No additional facts and circumstances establish otherwise by clear and convincing evidence. Thus, the allocation lacks significant entrepreneurial risk. Accordingly, the arrangement provides for a disguised payment for services as of the date that A and ABC enter into the arrangement and, pursuant to

paragraph (b)(2)(ii) of this section, should be included in income by A in the time and manner required under applicable law as determined by applying all relevant sections of the Internal Revenue Code to the arrangement.

Example 3. (i) M performs services for which a fee would normally be charged to new partnership ABC, an investment partnership that will acquire a portfolio of investment assets that are not readily tradable on an established securities market. M will also contribute $500,000 in exchange for a one percent interest in ABC's capital and profits. In addition to M's one percent interest, M is entitled to receive a priority allocation and distribution of net gain from the sale of any one or more assets during any 12-month accounting period in which the partnership has overall net gain in an amount intended to approximate the fee that would normally be charged for the services M performs. A, a company that controls M, is the general partner of ABC and directs all operations of the partnership consistent with the partnership agreement, including causing ABC to purchase or sell an asset during any accounting period. A also controls the timing of distributions to M including distributions arising from M's priority allocation. Given the nature of the assets in which ABC will invest and A's ability to control the timing of asset dispositions, the amount of partnership net income or gains that will be allocable to M under the ABC partnership agreement is highly likely to be available and reasonably determinable based on all facts and circumstances available upon formation of the partnership. A will be allocated 10 percent of any net profits or net losses of ABC earned over the life of the partnership. A undertakes an enforceable obligation to repay any amounts allocated and distributed pursuant to this interest (reduced by reasonable allowances for tax payments made on A's allocable shares of partnership income and gain) that exceed 10 percent of the overall net amount of partnership profits computed over the life of the partnership (a "clawback obligation"). It is reasonable to anticipate that A could and would comply fully with any repayment responsibilities that arise pursuant to this obligation. The ABC partnership agreement satisfies the requirements for economic effect contained in § 1.704-1(b)(2)(ii), including requiring that liquidating distributions are made in accordance with the partners' positive capital account balances.

(ii) Under paragraph (c) of this section, whether A's arrangement is treated as a payment for services in directing ABC's operations depends on the facts and circumstances. The most important factor in this facts and circumstances determination is the presence or absence of significant entrepreneurial risk. The arrangement with respect to A creates significant entrepreneurial risk under paragraph (c)(1) of this section because the allocation to A is of net profits earned over the life of the partnership, the allocation is subject to a clawback obligation and it is reasonable to anticipate that A could and would comply with this obligation, and the allocation is neither reasonably determinable nor highly likely to be available. Additionally, other relevant factors do not establish that the arrangement should be treated as a payment for services. Thus, the arrangement with respect to A does not constitute a payment for services for purposes of paragraph (b)(1) of this section.

(iii) Under paragraph (c) of this section, whether M's arrangement is treated as a payment for services depends on the facts and circumstances. The most important factor in this facts and circumstances determination is the presence or absence of entrepreneurial risk. The priority allocation to M is an allocation of net profit from any 12-month accounting period in which the partnership has net gain, and thus it does not depend on the overall success of the enterprise. Moreover, the sale of the assets by ABC, and hence the timing of recognition of gains and losses, is controlled by A, a company related to M. Taken in combination, the facts indicate that the allocation is reasonably determinable under all the facts and circumstances and that sufficient net profits are highly likely to be available to make the priority allocation to the service provider. As a result, the allocation presumptively lacks significant entrepreneurial risk. No additional facts and circumstances establish otherwise by clear and convincing evidence. Accordingly, the arrangement provides for a disguised payment for services as of the date M and ABC enter into the arrangement and, pursuant to paragraph (b)(2)(ii) of this section, should be included in income by M in the time and manner required under applicable law as determined by applying all relevant sections of the Internal Revenue Code to the arrangement.

(iv) Assume the facts are the same as paragraph (i) of this example, except that the partnership can also fund M's priority allocation and distribution of net gain from the revaluation of any partnership assets pursuant to § 1.704-1(b)(2)(iv)(f). As the general partner of ABC, A controls the timing of events that permit revaluation of partnership assets and assigns values to those assets for purposes of the revaluation. Under paragraph (c) of this section, whether M's arrangement is treated as a payment for services depends on the facts and circumstances. The most important factor in this facts and circumstances determination is the presence or absence of significant entrepreneurial risk. Under this arrangement, the valuation of the assets is controlled by A, a company related to M, and the assets of the company are difficult to value. This fact, taken in combination with the partnership's determination of M's profits by reference to a specified accounting period, causes the allocation to be reasonably determinable under all the facts and circumstances or to ensure that net profits are highly likely to be available to make the priority allocation to the service provider. No additional facts and circumstances establish otherwise by clear and convincing evidence. Accordingly, the arrangement provides for a disguised payment for services as of the date M and ABC enter into the arrangement and, pursuant to paragraph (b)(2)(ii) of this section, should be included in income by M in time and manner required under applicable law as determined by applying all relevant sections of the Internal Revenue Code to the arrangement.

Example 4. (i) The facts are the same as in *Example 3,* except that ABC's investment assets are securities that are readily tradable on an established securities market, and ABC is in the trade or business of trading in securities and has validly elected to mark-to-market under section 475(f)(1). In addition, M is entitled to receive a special allocation and distribution of partnership net gain attributable to a specified future 12-month taxable year. Although it is expected that one or more of the partnership's assets will be sold for a gain, it cannot reasonably be predicted whether the partnership will have net profits with respect to its entire portfolio in that 12-month taxable year.

(ii) Under paragraph (c) of this section, whether the arrangement is treated as a payment for services depends on the facts and circumstances. The most important factor in this facts and circumstances determination is the presence or absence of significant entrepreneurial risk. The special allocation to M is allocable out of net profits, the partnership assets have a readily ascertainable market value that is determined at the close of each taxable year, and it cannot reasonably be predicted whether the partnership will have net profits with respect to its entire portfolio for the year to which the special allocation would relate. Accordingly, the special allocation is neither reasonably determinable nor highly likely to be available because the partnership assets have a readily ascertainable fair market value that is determined at the beginning of the year and at the end of the year. Thus, the arrangement does not lack significant entrepreneurial risk under paragraph (c)(1) of this section. Additionally, the facts and circumstances do not establish the presence of other factors that would suggest that the arrangement is properly characterized as a payment for services. Accordingly, the arrangement does not constitute a payment for services under paragraph (b)(1) of this section.

Example 5. (i) A is a general partner in newly-formed partnership ABC, an investment fund. A is responsible for providing management services to ABC, but has delegated that management function to M, a company controlled by A. Funds that are comparable to ABC commonly require the general partner to contribute capital in an amount equal to one percent of the capital contributed by the limited partners, provide the general partner with an interest in 20 percent of future partnership net income and gains as measured over the life of the fund, and pay the fund manager annually an amount equal to two percent of capital committed by the partners.

(ii) Upon formation of ABC, the partners of ABC execute a partnership agreement with terms that differ from those commonly agreed upon by other comparable funds. The ABC partnership agreement provides that A will contribute nominal capital to ABC, that ABC will annually pay M an amount equal to one percent of capital committed by the partners, and that A will receive an interest in 20 percent of future partnership net income and gains as measured over the life of the fund. A will also receive an additional interest in future partnership net income and gains determined by a formula (the "Additional Interest"). The parties intend that the estimated present value of the Additional Interest approximately equals the present value of one percent of capital committed by the partners determined annually over the life of the fund. However, the amount of net profits that will be allocable to A under the Additional Interest is neither highly likely to be available nor reasonably determinable based on all facts and circumstances available upon formation of the partnership. A undertakes a clawback obligation, and it is reasonable to anticipate that A could and would comply fully with any repayment responsibilities that arise pursuant to this obligation. The ABC partnership agreement satisfies the requirements for economic effect contained in §1.704-1(b)(2)(ii), including requiring that liquidating distributions

are made in accordance with the partners' positive capital account balances.

(iii) Under paragraph (c) of this section, whether the arrangement relating to the Additional Interest is treated as a payment for services depends on the facts and circumstances. The most important factor in this facts and circumstances determination is the presence or absence of significant entrepreneurial risk. The arrangement with respect to A creates significant entrepreneurial risk under paragraph (c)(1) of this section because the allocation to A is of net profits, the allocation is subject to a clawback obligation over the life of the fund and it is reasonable to anticipate that A could and would comply with this obligation, and the allocation is neither reasonably determinable nor highly likely to be available. Additionally, the facts and circumstances do not establish the presence of other factors that would suggest that the arrangement is properly characterized as a payment for services. Accordingly, the arrangement does not constitute a payment for services under paragraph (b)(1) of this section.

Example 6. (i) A is a general partner in limited partnership ABC, an investment fund. A is responsible for providing management services to ABC, but has delegated that management function to M, a company controlled by A. The ABC partnership agreement provides that A must contribute capital in an amount equal to one percent of the capital contributed by the limited partners, that A is entitled to an interest in 20 percent of future partnership net income and gains as measured over the life of the fund, and that M is entitled to receive an annual fee in an amount equal to two percent of capital committed by the partners. The amount of partnership net income or gains that will be allocable to A under the ABC partnership agreement is neither highly likely to be available nor reasonably determinable based on all facts and circumstances available upon formation of the partnership. A also undertakes a clawback obligation, and it is reasonable to anticipate that A could and would comply fully with any repayment responsibilities that arise pursuant to this obligation.

(ii) ABC's partnership agreement also permits M (as A's appointed delegate) to waive all or a portion of its fee for any year if it provides written notice to the limited partners of ABC at least 60 days prior to the commencement of the partnership taxable year for which the fee is payable. If M elects to waive irrevocably its fee pursuant to this provision, the partnership will, immediately following the commencement of the partnership taxable year for which the fee would have been payable, issue to M an interest determined by a formula in subsequent partnership net income and gains (the "Additional Interest"). The parties intend that the estimated present value of the Additional Interest approximately equals the estimated present value of the fee that was waived. However, the amount of net income or gains that will be allocable to M is neither highly likely to be available nor reasonably determinable based on all facts and circumstances available at the time of the waiver of the fee. The ABC partnership agreement satisfies the requirements for economic effect contained in §1.704-1(b)(2)(ii), including requiring that liquidating distributions are made in accordance with the partners' positive capital account balances. The partnership agreement also requires ABC to maintain capital accounts pursuant to §1.704-1(b)(2)(iv) and to revalue partner capital accounts under §1.704-1(b)(2)(iv)(f) immediately prior to the issuance of the partnership interest to M. M undertakes a clawback obligation, and it is reasonable to anticipate that M could and would comply fully with any repayment responsibilities that arise pursuant to this obligation.

(iii) Under paragraph (c) of this section, whether the arrangements relating to A's 20 percent interest in future partnership net income and gains and M's Additional Interest are treated as payment for services depends on the facts and circumstances. The most important factor in this facts and circumstances determination is the presence or absence of significant entrepreneurial risk. The allocations to A and M do not presumptively lack significant entrepreneurial risk under paragraph (c)(1) of this section because the allocations are based on net profits, the allocations are subject to a clawback obligation over the life of the fund and it is reasonable to anticipate that A and M could and would comply with this obligation, and the allocations are neither reasonably determinable nor highly likely to be available. Additionally, the facts and circumstances do not establish the presence of other factors that would suggest that the arrangement is properly characterized as a payment for services. Accordingly, the arrangements do not constitute payment for services under paragraph (b)(1) of this section. [Reg. §1.707-2.]

Disguised Payments: Services

Disguised Payments: Services.—Amendments to Reg. §1.707-9, relating to disguised payments for services under section 707(a)(2)(A) of the Internal Revenue Code and providing guidance to partnerships and their partners regarding when an arrangement will be treated as a disguised payment for services, are proposed (published in the Federal Register on July 23, 2015) (REG-115452-14).

Par. 5. Section 1.707-9 is amended by:

a. Redesignating paragraph (b) as paragraph (c);

b. Redesignating paragraph (a) as paragraph (b); and

c. Adding new paragraph (a).

The addition reads as follows:

§1.707-9. Effective dates and transitional rules.—(a) *Section 1.707-2.*—(1) *In general.*—Section 1.707-2 applies to all arrangements entered into or modified after the date of publication of the Treasury decision adopting that section as final regulations in the **Federal Register**. To the extent that an arrangement permits a service provider to waive all or a portion of its fee for any period subsequent to the date the arrangement is created, then the arrangement is modified for purposes of this paragraph on the date or dates that the fee is waived.

(2) *Arrangements entered into or modified before final regulations are published in the Federal Register.*—In the case of any arrangement entered into or modified that occurs on or before final regulations are published in the **Federal Register**, the determination of whether the arrangement is a disguised fee for services under section 707(a)(2)(A) is to be made on the basis of the statute and the guidance provided regarding that provision in the legislative history of section 73 of the Tax Reform Act of 1984 (Pub. L. 98-369, 98 Stat. 494). See H.R. Rep. No. 861, 98th Cong., 2d Sess. 859-2 (1984); S. Prt. No. 169 (Vol. I), 98th Cong., 2d Sess. 223-32 (1984); H.R. Rep. No. 432 (Pt. 2), 98th Cong., 2d Sess. 1216-21 (1984).

* * *

Partnerships: Equity for Services

Partnerships: Equity for Services.—Amendments to Reg. §1.721-1, providing that the transfer of a partnership interest in connection with the performance of services is subject to Code Sec. 83 and providing rules for coordinating Code Sec. 83 with partnership taxation principles, are proposed (published in the Federal Register on May 24, 2005) (REG-105346-03).

☐ Par. 7. In §1.721-1, paragraph (b) is revised to read as follows:

§1.721-1. Nonrecognition of gain or loss on contribution.

* * *

(b)(1) Except as otherwise provided in this section or §1.721-2, section 721 does not apply to the transfer of a partnership interest in connection with the performance of services or in satisfaction of an obligation. The transfer of a partnership interest to a person in connection with the performance of services constitutes a transfer of property to which section 83 and the regulations thereunder apply. To the extent that a partnership interest transferred in connection with the performance of services rendered by a decedent prior to the decedent's death is transferred after the decedent's death to the decedent's successor in interest, the fair market value of such interest is an item of income in respect of a decedent under section 691.

(2) Except as provided in section 83(h) and 1.83-6(c), no gain or loss shall be recognized by a partnership upon—

(i) The transfer or substantial vesting of a compensatory partnership interest; or

(ii) The forfeiture of a compensatory partnership interest. See §1.704-1(b)(4)(xii) for rules regarding forfeiture allocations of partnership items that may be required in the taxable year of a forfeiture.

(3) For purposes of this section, a compensatory partnership interest is an interest in the transferring partnership that is transferred in connection with the performance of services for that partnership (either before or after the formation of the partnership), including an interest that is transferred on the exercise of a compensatory partnership option. A compensatory partnership option is an option to acquire an interest in the issuing partnership that is granted in connection with the performance of services for that partnership (either before or after the formation of the partnership).

(4) To the extent that a partnership interest is—

(i) Transferred to a partner in connection with the performance of services rendered to the partnership, it is a guaranteed payment for services under section 707(c);

(ii) Transferred in connection with the performance of services rendered to a partner, it is not deductible by the partnership, but is deductible only by such partner to the extent allowable under Chapter 1 of the Code.

(5) This paragraph (b) applies to interests that are transferred on or after the date final regulations are published in the Federal Register.

* * *

Installment Obligations: Dispositions: Nonrecognition of Gain or Loss

Installment Obligations: Dispositions: Nonrecognition of Gain or Loss—Amendments to Reg. §1.721-1, relating to the nonrecognition of gain or loss on certain dispositions of an installment obligation, are proposed (published in the Federal Register on December 23, 2014) (REG-109187-11).

☐ Par. 5. Section 1.721-1(a) is amended by adding new ninth and tenth sentences to read as follows:

§1.721-1. Nonrecognition of gain or loss on contribution.—(a) * * * For rules in determining a partner's gain or loss when an installment obligation of a partnership is contributed to the partnership, see section 453B and §1.453B-1(c). The preceding sentence applies to satisfactions of installment obligations after the date these regulations are published as final regulations in the **Federal Register**.

* * *

Partners and Partnerships: Sales or Exchanges: Certain Distributions

Partners and Partnerships: Sales or Exchanges: Certain Distributions.—Amendments to Reg. §1.732-1, prescribing how a partner should measure its interest in a partnership's unrealized receivables and inventory items, and that provide guidance regarding the tax consequences of a distribution that causes a reduction in that interest, are proposed (published in the Federal Register on November 3, 2014) (REG-151416-06).

☐ Par. 5. Section 1.732-1 is amended by adding paragraphs (c)(2)(iii), (iv), (v), (vi), and (vii), and revising paragraph (c)(5) to read as follows:

§1.732-1. Basis of distributed property other than money.

* * *

(c) * * *

(2) * * *

(iii) *Property subject to section 1245.*—Any increase in basis allocated to capital gain property pursuant to the second sentence in paragraph (c)(2)(ii) of this section is not taken into account in determining the recomputed or adjusted basis in the property for purposes of section 1245(a)(1). Notwithstanding the prior sentence, any depreciation or amortization of the increase in basis that is allowed or allowable is taken into account in computing the property's recomputed basis. In the case of property that is subject to section 617(d)(1), section 1250(a)(1), section 1252(a)(1), or section 1254(a)(1), rules similar to the rule in this paragraph (c)(2)(iii) shall apply. *See Examples 2 and 3 in § 1.755-1(c)(6).*

(iv) *Section 1231 property.*—Any increase in basis allocated to capital gain property pursuant to the second sentence in paragraph (c)(2)(ii) of this section is not taken into account in determining section 1231 gain and loss, as defined in section 1231(a)(3). *See Examples 2 and 3 in § 1.755-1(c)(6).*

(v) *Property subject to section 1248.*—Any increase in basis allocated to stock in a foreign corporation pursuant to the second sentence in paragraph (c)(2)(ii) of this section or any decrease in basis allocated to stock in a foreign corporation pursuant to the second sentence in paragraph (c)(2)(i) of this section is not taken into account in determining the amount of gain recognized on the sale or exchange of such stock for purposes of section 1248(a). In the case of property that is subject to section 995(c), rules similar to the rule set forth in this paragraph (c)(2)(v) shall apply. *See Examples 8 and 9 in § 1.751-1(g).*

(vi) *Special rule.*—Any basis adjustment to an asset that is not taken into account under paragraph (c)(2)(iii), (iv), or (v) of this section shall, upon a taxable disposition, be treated as gain or loss, as the case may be, from the sale or exchange of a capital asset with the same holding period as the underlying asset. *See Examples 2 and 3 in § 1.755-1(c)(6).*

(vii) *Election not to apply the provisions of paragraphs (c)(2)(iii), (iv), and (v).*—See § 1.755-1(c)(2)(vi) for rules regarding an election to have the provisions of paragraphs (c)(2)(iii), (iv), and (v) of this section, and § 1.755-1(c)(2)(iii), (iv), and (v) not apply. *See Examples 2 and 3 in § 1.755-1(c)(6).*

* * *

(5) *Effective/applicability date.*—This paragraph (c) applies to distributions of property from a partnership that occur on or after

December 15, 1999, except that paragraphs (c)(2)(iii), (iv), (v), (vi), and (vii) of this section apply to distributions of property from a partnership that occur on or after the date of publication of a Trea-

sury decision adopting these rules as final regulations in the **Federal Register**.

* * *

Partners and Partnerships: American Jobs Creation Act of 2004 and Taxpayer Relief Act of 1997: Guidance

Partners and Partnerships: American Jobs Creation Act of 2004 and Taxpayer Relief Act of 1997: Guidance.—Amendments to Reg. §1.732-2, providing guidance on certain provisions of the American Jobs Creation Act of 2004, conforming the regulations to statutory changes in the Taxpayer Relief Act of 1997, modifying the basis allocation rules to prevent certain unintended consequences of the current basis allocation rules for substituted basis transactions and providing additional guidance on allocations resulting from revaluations of partnership property, are proposed (published in the Federal Register on January 16, 2014) (REG-144468-05).

☐ Par. 4. Section 1.732-2 is amended by:

1. Redesignating paragraph (b) introductory text as (b)(1) introductory text and revising it.

2. Adding paragraph (b)(2.

3. Redesignating paragraph (c) as paragraph (d).

4. Adding a new paragraph (c).

The revisions and addition reads as follows:

§1.732-2. Special partnership basis of distributed property.

* * *

(b) *Adjustments under section 743(b).*—(1) *In general.*—In the case of a distribution of property to a partner who acquired any part of its interest in a transfer, if there was an election under section 754 in effect with respect to the transfer, or if the partnership had a substantial built-in loss (as defined in §1.743-1(a)(2)(i)) immediately after the transfer, then, for purposes of section 732 (other than subsection (d) thereof), the adjusted partnership basis of the distributed property shall take into account, in addition to any adjustments under section 734(b), the transferee's special basis adjustment for the distributed property under section 743(b). The application of this paragraph may be illustrated by the following example:

* * *

(2) *Effective/applicability date.*—Paragraph (b)(1) of this section relating to substantial built-in losses is applicable for partnership

distributions occurring on or after the date of publication of the Treasury decision adopting these rules as final regulations in the **Federal Register**.

(c) *Adjustments under section 704(c)(1)(C).*—(1) *In general.*—In the case of a distribution of property to a section 704(c)(1)(C) partner (as defined in §1.704-3(f)(2)(ii)), for purposes of section 732 (other than subsection (d) thereof), the adjusted partnership basis of the distributed property shall take into account, in addition to any adjustments under section 734(b), the distributee's section 704(c)(1)(C) basis adjustment (if any) for the distributed property.

(2) *Effective/applicability date.*—Paragraph (c)(1) of this section is applicable for partnership distributions occurring on or after the date of publication of the Treasury decision adopting these rules as final regulations in the **Federal Register**.

* * *

Partners and Partnerships: American Jobs Creation Act of 2004 and Taxpayer Relief Act of 1997: Guidance

Partners and Partnerships: American Jobs Creation Act of 2004 and Taxpayer Relief Act of 1997: Guidance.—Amendments to Reg. §§1.734-1 and 1.734-2, providing guidance on certain provisions of the American Jobs Creation Act of 2004, conforming the regulations to statutory changes in the Taxpayer Relief Act of 1997, modifying the basis allocation rules to prevent certain unintended consequences of the current basis allocation rules for substituted basis transactions and providing additional guidance on allocations resulting from revaluations of partnership property, are proposed (published in the Federal Register on January 16, 2014) (REG-144468-05) (corrected April 15, 2014).

☐ Par. 5. Section 1.734-1 is amended by:

1. Revising the section heading.

2. Revising paragraph (a).

3. Revising paragraph (b)(2)(i).

4. Adding *Example 3* following paragraph (b)(2)(ii).

5. Adding a sentence at the end of paragraph (d).

6. Adding paragraphs (f), (g), and (h).

The revisions and additions read as follows:

§1.734-1. Adjustment to basis of undistributed partnership property where partnership has a section 754 election or there is a substantial basis reduction with respect to a distribution.—

(a) *General rule.*—(1) *Adjustments to basis.*—A partnership shall not adjust the basis of partnership property as the result of a distribution of property to a partner unless the election provided in section 754 (relating to optional adjustment to basis of partnership property) is in effect or there is a substantial basis reduction (within the meaning of paragraph (a)(2)(i) of this section) with respect to the distribution.

(2) *Substantial basis reduction.*—(i) *In general.*—For purposes of this section, there is a substantial basis reduction with respect to a distribution of property or properties to a partner if the sum of the amounts described in section 734(b)(2)(A) and (b)(2)(B) exceeds $250,000. If there is a substantial basis reduction under this section, the partnership is treated as having an election under section 754 in effect solely for the distribution to which the substantial basis reduction relates.

(ii) *Special rules for tiered partnerships.*—See paragraph (f) of this section for special rules regarding tiered partnerships.

(iii) *Special rules for securitization partnerships.*—See paragraph (g) of this section for special rules regarding securitization partnerships.

(b) " " "

(2) *Decrease in basis.*—(i) When a partnership with a section 754 election in effect makes a distribution in liquidation of a partner's

entire interest in the partnership, or when there is a substantial basis reduction (within the meaning of paragraph (a)(2)(i) of this section), the partnership shall decrease the adjusted basis of the remaining partnership property by—

(ii) * * *

Example 3—(i) A, B, and C each contribute $2 million to PRS, a partnership. PRS purchases Property 1 and Property 2, both of which are capital assets, for $1 million and $5 million respectively. In Year 2, the fair market value of Property 1 increases to $3 million and the fair market value of Property 2 increases to $6 million. Also in Year 2, PRS distributes Property 1 to C in liquidation of C's interest in PRS at a time when C's basis in its PRS interest is still $2 million. PRS does not have an election under section 754 in effect.

(ii) Under section 732, the basis of Property 1 in the hands of C is $2 million. Because the excess of C's adjusted basis in Property 1 ($2 million) over PRS's adjusted basis in Property 1 ($1 million) is $1 million, the amount described in section 734(b)(2)(B) ($1 million) exceeds $250,000, and therefore, there is a substantial basis reduction with respect to the distribution. Accordingly, pursuant to paragraph (a)(2)(i) of this section, PRS is treated as having a section 754 election in effect in Year 2 and must reduce its basis in Property 2 in accordance with paragraph (b)(2)(i) of this section.

* * *

(d) * * * A partnership required to adjust the basis of partnership property following the distribution of property because there is a substantial basis reduction (within the meaning of paragraph (a)(2)(i) of this section) with respect to the distribution is subject to, and required to comply with, the provisions of this paragraph (d) solely with respect to the distribution to which the substantial basis reduction relates.

* * *

(f) *Adjustments with respect to tiered partnerships.*—(1) *In general.*—If an upper-tier partnership makes an adjustment under paragraph (b) of this section to the basis of an interest it holds in a lower-tier partnership that has an election under section 754 in effect, the lower-tier partnership must make adjustments under paragraph (b) of this section to the upper-tier partnership's share of the lower-tier partnership's assets. The amount of the lower-tier partnership's adjustment is equal to the adjustment made by the upper-tier partnership to the basis of its interest in the lower-tier partnership. The lower-tier partnership's adjustment to the upper-tier partnership's share of its assets is for the upper-tier partnership only and does not

	Adjusted basis
Property 1	$2.2 million
Property 2	$2.8 million

UTP also owns a 50 percent interest in LTP, a partnership. UTP's interest in LTP has an adjusted basis of $4 million and a fair market value of $3 million. LTP owns one asset, Property 3, a capital asset, which has an adjusted basis of $8 million and a fair market value of $6 million. Neither UTP nor LTP has an election under section 754 in effect.

(ii) *Liquidating distribution to A of Property 1.*—UTP distributes Property 1 to A in complete liquidation of A's interest in UTP. Under section 732(b), the adjusted basis of Property 1 to A is $3 million. Therefore, there is a substantial basis reduction with respect to the distribution to A because the sum of the amounts described in section 734(b)(2)(A) ($0) and section 734(b)(2)(B) (the excess of $3 million over $2.2 million, or $800,000) exceeds $250,000. Therefore, pursuant to paragraph (b)(2) of this section, UTP must decrease the basis of its property by $800,000. Under § 1.755-1(c), UTP must de-

affect the basis in the lower-tier partnership's property for the other partners of the lower-tier partnership. Additionally, if there is a substantial basis reduction (within the meaning of paragraph (a)(2)(i) of this section) with respect to a distribution by an upper-tier partnership that (either directly or indirectly through one or more partnerships) holds an interest in a lower-tier partnership, each lower-tier partnership is treated, solely with respect to the distribution, as if it had made an election under section 754 for the taxable year in which the distribution occurs. For additional examples of the application of the principles of this paragraph (f)(1), see Revenue Ruling 92-15, 1992-1 CB 215. *See* § 601.601(d)(2)(ii)(b)

(2) *Example.*—(i) *Facts.*—A, B, and C are equal partners in UTP, a partnership. Each partner's interest in UTP has an adjusted basis and fair market value of $3 million. UTP owns two capital assets with the following adjusted bases and fair market values:

	Fair market value
	$3 million
	$3 million

crease the adjusted basis of its 50 percent interest in LTP by $800,000. Likewise, pursuant to paragraph (f)(1) of this section, LTP must decrease its basis in UTP's share of Property 3 by $800,000 in accordance with § 1.755-1(c).

(g) *Securitization partnerships.*—A securitization partnership (as defined in § 1.743-1(o)(2)) shall not be treated as having a substantial basis reduction with respect to any distribution of property to a partner.

(h) *Effective/applicability date.*—The rules relating to substantial basis reductions in paragraphs (a) and (b) of this section and paragraphs (f) and (g) of this section apply to partnership distributions occurring on or after the date of publication of the Treasury decision adopting these rules as final regulations in the **Federal Register**.

☐ Par. 6. Section 1.734-2 is amended by revising the section heading and adding paragraph (c) to read as follows:

§ 1.734-2. Adjustment after distribution to transferee partner or section 704(c)(1)(C) partner.

* * *

(c)(1) Section 704(c)(1)(C) basis adjustments will be taken into account in determining the basis adjustment under section 734(b). However, section 704(c)(1)(C) basis adjustments, other than a section 704(c)(1)(C) basis adjustment applied as an adjustment to the basis of partnership property pursuant to paragraph (c)(2) of this section, will not be taken into account in making allocations under § 1.755-1(c).

(2) *Liquidating distributions.*—If a section 704(c)(1)(C) partner receives a distribution of property (including money) in liquidation of its entire partnership interest, the section 704(c)(1)(C) partner's section 704(c)(1)(C) basis adjustments that are treated as basis in the distributed property pursuant to section 732 will be taken into account in determining the basis adjustment under section 734(b), regardless of whether the distributed property is section 704(c)(1)(C) property. If any section 704(c)(1)(C) basis adjustment cannot be reallocated to distributed property in connection with the distribution, then that remaining section 704(c)(1)(C) basis adjustment shall be treated as a positive section 734(b) adjustment. If the distribution also gives rise to a negative section 734(b) adjustment without regard to the section 704(c)(1)(C) basis adjustment reallocation, then the negative section 734(b) adjustment and the section 704(c)(1)(C) basis adjustment reallocation are netted together, and the net amount is allocated under § 1.755-1(c). If the partnership does not have a section 754 election in effect at the time of the liquidating distribution, the partnership shall be treated as having made a section 754 election solely for purposes of computing any negative section 734(b) adjustment that would arise from the distribution.

(3) The following examples illustrate the provisions of this paragraph (c).

Example 1—(i) In Year 1, A contributes $5,000 cash and Property A, a capital asset, with an adjusted basis of $7,000 and a fair market value of $5,000; B contributes $8,000 cash and Property B, a capital asset, with an adjusted basis and fair market value of $2,000; and C contributes $7,000 cash and Property C, a capital asset, with an adjusted basis and fair market value of $3,000 to PRS, a partnership. In Year 3, Property B has appreciated in value to $8,000. PRS distributes Property B and $4,000 to C in complete liquidation of C's interest in PRS at a time when no partner's basis in PRS has changed. PRS revalues its property under § 1.704-1(b)(2)(iv)(f) in connection with the distribution, and makes an election under section 754. C recognizes no gain or loss on the distribution.

(ii) C receives Property B with a basis of $6,000 (C's adjusted basis in PRS of $10,000 minus the $4,000 cash distributed). Because PRS has an election under section 754 in effect, PRS must reduce its

basis in remaining partnership property under § 1.734-1(b)(2)(ii) by $4,000 (C's $6,000 basis in Property B minus PRS's $2,000 adjusted basis in Property B prior to the distribution. Under § 1.755-1(c)(2)(ii), that basis reduction must be allocated within a class first to properties with unrealized depreciation in proportion to their respective amounts of unrealized depreciation. Any remaining decrease must be allocated in proportion to the properties' adjusted bases. Because there is no unrealized depreciation in either Property A (disregarding A's section 704(c)(1)(C) basis adjustment) or Property C, the decrease must be allocated between the two properties in proportion to their adjusted bases, $2,500 ($4,000 multiplied by $5,000 divided by $8,000) to Property A and $1,500 ($4,000 multiplied by $3,000 divided by $8,000) to Property C.

(iii) In a subsequent year, PRS sells Property A for its fair market value of $7,500 and recognizes $5,000 of gain ($7,500 amount realized minus adjusted basis of $2,500). Pursuant to § 1.704-3(f)(3)(ii)(B), A's $2,500 distributive share of the $5,000 gain from the sale of Property A is reduced by A's $2,000 section 704(c)(1)(C) basis adjustment. Therefore, A recognizes a gain of $500 on the sale.

Example 2—(i) A contributes Property 1 with an adjusted basis of $15,000 and a fair market value of $10,000 and Property 2 with an adjusted basis of $15,000 and a fair market value of $20,000, and B and C each contribute $30,000 cash to PRS, a partnership. A has a section 704(c)(1)(C) basis adjustment of $5,000 with respect to Property 1. PRS's adjusted bases in Property 1 and Property 2 are $10,000 and $15,000, respectively. When the fair market value of A's interest in PRS is still $30,000, and no partner's basis in its PRS interest has changed, PRS makes a liquidating distribution to A of $30,000 cash, which results in A realizing no gain or loss. PRS has an election under section 754 in effect.

(ii) A is unable to take into account A's section 704(c)(1)(C) basis adjustment in Property 1 upon the distribution of the cash as described in paragraph (c)(2) of this section because A cannot increase the basis of cash under § 1.704-3(f)(3)(v)(C). Thus, A's $5,000 section 704(c)(1)(C) basis adjustment is treated as a positive section 734(b) adjustment to the partnership's assets retained. PRS's $5,000 section 734(b) adjustment will be allocated to Property 2, increasing its basis from $15,000 to $20,000 under § 1.755-1(c).

Example 3—(i) A contributes Property 1 with an adjusted basis of $35,000 and a fair market value of $30,000, B contributes Property 2 with an adjusted basis and fair market value of $30,000, and C contributes $30,000 cash to PRS, a partnership. Property 1 is a capital asset, and Property 2 is inventory (as defined in section 751(d)). PRS's adjusted basis in Property 1 is $30,000 under section 704(c)(1)(C)(ii), and A has a section 704(c)(1)(C) basis adjustment of $5,000 with respect to Property 1. Later, at a time when the value and bases of the properties have not changed, PRS distributes $30,000 cash to A in complete liquidation of A's interest. A recognizes a ($5,000) loss under section 731(a)(2) on the distribution. PRS has an election under section 754 in effect.

(ii) The distribution results in a negative section 734(b) adjustment to capital gain property of ($5,000) (the amount of loss A recognizes under section 731(a)(2)). Additionally, because A is unable to take into account A's section 704(c)(1)(C) basis adjustment in Property 1 upon the distribution of the cash, A's $5,000 section 704(c)(1)(C) basis adjustment is treated as a positive section 734(b) adjustment. Pursuant to paragraph (c)(2) of this section, these two adjustments are netted together, resulting in no adjustment under section 734(b). Therefore, the partnership's basis in Property 1 and Property 2 remains $30,000.

Example 4—(i) Assume the same facts as in *Example 3* except that PRS distributes Property 2 to A in complete liquidation of A's interest in a transaction to which section 704(c)(1)(B) and section 737 do not apply.

(ii) Pursuant to §1.704-3(f)(v)(C), A cannot include A's section 704(c)(1)(C) basis adjustment in the basis of the distributed property, because the section 704(c)(1)(C) property and the distributed property are not of like character. Accordingly, the basis to A of Property 2 is $30,000. A also recognizes a $5,000 capital loss under section 731(a)(2), resulting in a ($5,000) basis adjustment under section 734(b). Because the section 704(c)(1)(C) basis adjustment to Property 1 was not reallocated in connection with the distribution, that remaining $5,000 section 704(c)(1)(C) basis adjustment is treated as a positive section 734(b) adjustment. Pursuant to paragraph (c)(2) of this section, these two adjustments are netted together, resulting in no adjustment under section 734(b). Therefore, the basis of Property 1 remains $30,000.

(4) *Effective/applicability date.*—This paragraph (c) applies to partnership distributions occurring on or after the date of publication of the Treasury decision adopting these rules as final regulations in the **Federal Register.**

Partners and Partnerships: Sales or Exchanges: Certain Distributions

Partners and Partnerships: Sales or Exchanges: Certain Distributions.—Amendments to Reg. §1.736-1, prescribing how a partner should measure its interest in a partnership's unrealized receivables and inventory items, and that provide guidance regarding the tax consequences of a distribution that causes a reduction in that interest, are proposed (published in the Federal Register on November 3, 2014) (REG-151416-06).

☐ Par. 6. Section 1.736-1 is amended in paragraph (b)(4) by removing the language "paragraph (b)(3)(iii)" from the last sentence and adding the language "paragraph (b)(3)" in its place.

§1.736-1. Payments to a retiring partner or a deceased partner's successor in interest.

Disguised Payments: Services

Disguised Payments: Services.—Amendments to Reg. §1.736-1, relating to disguised payments for services under section 707(a)(2)(A) of the Internal Revenue Code and providing guidance to partnerships and their partners regarding when an arrangement will be treated as a disguised payment for services, are proposed (published in the Federal Register on July 23, 2015) (REG-115452-14).

Par. 6. Section 1.736-1 is amended by adding a sentence at the end of paragraph (a)(1)(i) to read as follows:

§1.736-1. Payments to a retiring partner or a deceased partner's successor in interest.—(a) * * *

(1)(i) * * * Section 736 does not apply to arrangements treated as disguised payments for services under §1.707-2.

* * *

Partnerships: Distribution of Property: Assets-Over Merger

Partnerships: Distribution of Property: Assets-Over Merger.—Amendments to Reg. §§1.737-1, 1.737-2 and 1.737-5, providing rules concerning the application of Code Secs. 704(c)(1)(B) and 737 to distributions of property after two partnerships engage in an assets-over merger, are proposed (published in the Federal Register on August 22, 2007) (REG-143397-05) (corrected November 6, 2007).

☐ Par. 4. Section 1.737-1(c)(1) is amended by removing the phrase "five years" and adding in its place the phrase "seven years."

§1.737-1. Recognition of precontribution gain.

☐ Par. 5. Section 1.737-2 is amended as follows:
1. Paragraph (b) is revised.
2. Paragraph (e) is redesignated as paragraph (f).
3. New paragraph (e) is added.
The additions and revisions read as follows:

§1.737-2. Exceptions and special rules.

* * *

(b) *Transfers to another partnership.*—(1) *Complete transfer to another partnership (Assets-over merger).*—(i) *In General.*—Section 737 and this section do not apply to a transfer in an assets-over merger as defined in §1.708-1(c)(3) by a partnership (the transferor partnership, which is considered to be the terminated partnership as a result of the merger) of all of its assets and liabilities to another partnership (the transferee partnership, which is considered to be the resulting partnership after the merger) followed by a distribution of the interest in the transferee partnership in liquidation of the transferor partnership as part of the same plan or arrangement.

(ii) *Subsequent distributions.*—(A) *Original section 704(c) gain.*—If, immediately before the assets-over merger, the transferor partnership holds property that has original built-in gain (as defined in §1.704-4(c)(4)(ii)(A)), the seven year period in section 737(b) does not restart with respect to such gain as a result of the transfer of such section 704(c) property to the transferee partnership. A subsequent distribution of other property by the transferee partnership to the partner who contributed the original section 704(c) gain property to the transferor partnership is only subject to section 737 with respect to the original section 704(c) gain if the distribution occurs within seven years of the time such property was contributed to the transferor partnership. See §1.704-4(c)(4)(ii)(A) for a similar provision in the context of section 704. See §1.737-1 for post-merger distribution

of property contributed to the transferee partnership prior to the merger.

(B) *New section 704(c) gain.*—Except as provided in paragraph (b)(1)(ii)(E) of this section, if new built-in gain is created upon the contribution of assets by the transferor partnership to the transferee partnership, a subsequent distribution by the transferee partnership of property to a partner of the transferee partnership (other than property deemed contributed by such partner) is subject to section 737, if such distribution occurs within seven years of the contribution by the transferor partnership to the transferee partnership. For these purposes, a partner of the transferor partnership is deemed to have contributed to the transferee partnership an undivided interest in the property of the transferor partnership. The determination of the partner's undivided interest for this purpose shall be determined by the transferor partnership using any reasonable method. See §1.704-4(c)(4)(ii)(B) for a similar provision in the context of section 704.

(C) *Ordering Rule.*—For purposes of this section, if a partner is required to recognize gain under this section, the partner shall recognize a proportionate amount of original and new section 704(c) gain.

(D) *Subsequent Mergers.*—If the transferee partnership (first transferee partnership) is subsequently merged into another partnership (new transferee partnership) the section 704(c) gain that resulted from the merger of the transferor partnership into the first transferee partnership shall be subject to section 737 for seven years from the time of the contribution by the transferor partnership to the first transferee partnership (original merger) and section 704(c) gain that resulted from the merger of the first transferee partnership into the new transferee partnership shall be subject to section 737 for seven years from the time of the contribution by the first transferee partnership to the new transferee partnership (subsequent merger). See § 1.704-4(c)(4)(ii)(D) for a similar rule in the context of section 704.

(E) *Identical Ownership or De Minimis Change In Ownership.*—For purposes of section 737(b) and this section, net precontribution gain does not include new section 704(c) gain in property transferred by the transferor partnership to the transferee partnership if both the transferor partnership and the transferee partnership are owned by the same owners in the same proportions or if the difference in ownership is de minimis. The transferor partnership and the transferee partnership are owned by the same owners in the same proportions if each partner owns identical interests in book capital and each item of income, gain, loss, deduction, and credit, and identical shares of distributions and liabilities in each of the transferor and transferee partnerships. A difference in ownership is de minimis if ninety seven percent of interests in book capital and each item of income, gain, loss, deduction and credit and shares in distributions and liabilities of the transferor partnership and transferee partnership are owned by the same owners in the same proportions. See § 1.704-4(c)(4)(ii)(E) for a similar provision in the context of section 704.

(F) *Examples.*—The following examples illustrate the rules of paragraph (b)(3) of this section.

Example (1). No net precontribution gain. (i) *Facts* . On January 1, 2005, A contributes Asset 1, with a basis of $200x and a fair market value of $300x, to partnership PRS1 in exchange for a 50 percent interest. On the same date, B contributes $300x of cash to PRS1 in exchange for a 50 percent interest. Also on January 1, 2005, C contributes Asset 2, with a basis of $100x and a fair market value of $200x, to partnership PRS2 in exchange for a 50 percent interest. D contributes $200x of cash to PRS2 in exchange for a 50 percent interest. On January 1, 2008, PRS1 and PRS2 undertake an assets-over partnership merger in which PRS1 is the continuing partnership and PRS2 is the terminating partnership for both state law and federal tax purposes. At the time of the merger, PRS1's only assets are Asset 1, with a fair market value of $900x, and $300x in cash. PRS2's only assets are Asset 2, with a fair market value of $600x and $200x in cash. After the merger, the partners have capital and profits interests in PRS1 as follows: A, 30 percent; B, 30 percent; C, 20 percent; and D, 20 percent. PRS1 and PRS2 both have provisions in their respective partnership agreements requiring the revaluation of partnership property upon entry of a new partner. PRS1 would not be treated as an investment company (within the meaning of section 351) if it were incorporated. Neither partnership holds any unrealized receivables or inventory for purposes of section 751. In addition, neither partnership has a section 754 election in place. Asset 1 and Asset 2 are nondepreciable capital assets. On January 1, 2013, PRS1 has the same assets that it had after the merger. Each asset has the same value that it had at the time of the merger. On this date, PRS1 distributes Asset 2 to A in liquidation of A's interest.

(ii) *Analysis.* Section 737(a) requires A to recognize gain when it receives a distribution of property in an amount equal to the lesser of the excess distribution or the partner's net precontribution gain. The distribution of Asset 2 to A results in an excess distribution of $400x ($600x fair market value of Asset 2 - $200x adjusted basis in A's partnership interest). However, the distribution of Asset 2 to A occurs more than seven years after the contribution by A of Asset 1 to PRS1 and A made no subsequent contributions to PRS1. Therefore, A's net precontribution gain for purposes of section 737(b) at the time of the distribution is zero. The $600x of reverse section 704(c) gain in Asset 1, resulting from a revaluation of PRS1's partnership property at the time of the merger, is not net precontribution gain (See § 1.737-2(e)). Accordingly, A will not recognize gain under section 737 as a result of the distribution of Asset 2. See § 1.704-4(c)(4)(ii)(F), *Example (1)* for a similar example under section 704.

Example (2). Revaluation gain and merger gain. (i) *Facts* . The facts are the same as *Example (1)*, except that on January 1, 2007, E joins PRS2 as a one-third partner for $250x in cash. At the time E joins the partnership, Asset 2 has a fair market value of $300x. On January 1, 2008, PRS2 merges into PRS1. At the time of the merger, Asset 1 and Asset 2 both have a fair market value of $400x. On January 1, 2011, Asset 1 is distributed to C when its value is $275x.

(ii) *Analysis.* Section 737(a) requires A to recognize gain when it receives a distribution of property in an amount equal to the lesser of the excess distribution or the partner's net precontribution gain. The distribution of Asset 1 to C results in an excess distribution of $175x ($275x fair market value of Asset 1 - $100x adjusted basis in C's partnership interest). The distribution of Asset 1 to C occurs

within seven years of the original contribution of Asset 2 by C to PRS2. Therefore, C's net precontribution gain at the time of the distribution is $183.33x, which includes C's original section 704(c) gain from the contribution of Asset 2 to PRS2 of $100x plus C's share of new section 704(c) gain of $83.33x ($50x of reverse section 704(c) gain upon the admission of E, plus $33.33x of additional section 704(c) gain upon merger). C's excess distribution is less than C's net precontribution gain. Thus, C will recognize $175x of gain upon receipt of Asset 1 in accordance with section 737(a). See § 1.704-4(c)(4)(ii)(F), *Example (2)* for a similar example under section 704.

Example (3). Fluctuations in the value of an asset. (i) *Facts*. The facts are the same as *Example (1)*, except that on January 1, 2011, Asset 1 is distributed to C when its fair market value is $300x. Immediately prior to the distribution, PRS1 revalues its property in accordance with § 1.704-1(b)(2)(iv)(f).

(ii) *Analysis.* The distribution of Asset 1 to C occurs within seven years of the original contribution of Asset 2 by C to PRS2 and within seven years of the date of the merger. Therefore, C's net precontribution gain at the time of the distribution equals $300x ($100x of original section 704(c) gain from the contribution of Asset 2 to PRS2 and $200x of new section 704(c) gain). The distribution of Asset 1 to C results in an excess distribution of $200x ($300x fair market value of Asset 1 - $100x adjusted basis in C's partnership interest). Accordingly, in accordance with section 737(a), C will recognize gain of $200x upon receipt of Asset 1.

Example (4). Reverse section 704(c) gain. (i) Facts. The facts are the same as *Example (1)*, except that on January 1, 2011, PRS1 distributes Asset 2 to A in liquidation of A's interest in PRS1. At the time of the distribution, Asset 2 has a value of $600x.

(ii) *Analysis.* Section 737(a) requires A to recognize gain when it receives a distribution of property in an amount equal to the lesser of the excess distribution or the partner's net precontribution gain. The distribution of Asset 2 to A results in an excess distribution of $400x ($600x fair market value -200x adjusted basis in A's partnership interest). The distribution of Asset 2 to A occurs within seven years after the contribution of Asset 1 to PRS1 by A. Thus, A's net precontribution gain for purposes of section 737(b) at the time of the distribution is $100x (A's original section 704(c) gain from the contribution of Asset 1 to PRS1). Under § 1.737-2(e), A's net precontribution gain does not include A's reverse section 704(c) gain upon the revaluation of the Assets of PRS1 prior to the merger. Accordingly, A will recognize $100x of gain (the lesser of the excess distribution or net precontribution gain) under section 737 as a result of the distribution of Asset 2. See § 1.704-4(c)(4)(ii)(F), *Example (4)* for a similar example under section 704.

Example (5). Identical ownership exception. (i) *Facts.* In 1990, A, an individual, and B, a subchapter C corporation, formed PRS1, a partnership. A owned 75 percent of the interests in the book capital, profits, losses, distributions, and liabilities of PRS1. B owned the remaining 25 percent interest in the book capital, profits, losses, distributions, and liabilities of PRS1. In the same year, A and B also formed another partnership, PRS2, with A owning 75 percent of the interests in PRS2 and B owning the remaining 25 percent. Upon formation of the partnerships, A contributed Asset X to PRS1 and Asset Y to PRS2 and B contributed cash. Both Assets X and Y had section 704(c) built-in gain at the time of contribution to the partnerships.

(ii) In January 2005, PRS1 is merged into PRS2 in an assets-over merger in which PRS1 is the terminating partnership and PRS2 as the continuing partnership for both state law and federal income tax purposes. At the time of the merger, both Assets X and Y had increased in value from the time they were contributed to PRS1 and PRS2, respectively. As a result, a new layer of section 704(c) gain was created with respect to Asset X in PRS1. After the merger, A had a 75 percent interest in PRS2's book capital, profits, losses, distributions, and liabilities. B held the remaining 25 percent interest in PRS2's book capital, profits, losses, distributions, and liabilities. In 2006, PRS2 distributes Asset X to A.

(iii) *Analysis.* The 2006 distribution by PRS2 occurs more than seven years after the formation of the partnerships and the original contribution of Asset X to the partnerships. Therefore, the original layer of built-in gain created on the original contribution of Asset X to the partnerships should not be taken into account in applying section 737 to the proposed liquidation. In addition, paragraph (b)(1)(ii)(E) of this section provides that section 737(a) does not apply to newly created section 704(c) gain in property transferred by the transferor partnership to the transferee partnership if both the transferor partnership and the transferee partnership are owned by the same owners in the same proportions. The transferor partnership and the transferee partnership are owned by the same owners in the same proportions if each partner's percentage interest in the transferor partnership's book capital, profits, losses, distributions, and liabilities is the same as the partner's percentage interest in those items of the transferee partnership. In this case, A owned 75 percent and B owned 25 percent of the interests in the book capital, profits, losses, distributions, and liabilities of PRS1 and PRS2 prior to the merger and 75 percent and 25 percent, respectively, of PRS2 after the merger. As a result, the requirements of the identical ownership exception of paragraph (b)(1)(ii)(E) of this section are satisfied. Thus, the new built-in gain created upon contribution of Asset X in connection with the partnership merger will not be taken into account in applying section 737 to the proposed distribution. See §1.704-4(c)(4)(ii)(F), *Example (5)* for a similar example under section 704.

(2) *Certain divisive transactions.*—(i) *In general.*—Section 737 and this section do not apply to a transfer by a partnership (transferor partnership) of all of the section 704(c) property contributed by a partner to a second partnership (transferee partnership) in an exchange described in section 721, followed by a distribution as part of the same plan or arrangement of an interest in the transferee

partnership (and no other property) in complete liquidation of the interest of the partner that originally contributed the section 704(c) property to the transferor partnership (divisive transactions).

(ii) *Subsequent distributions.*—After a divisive transaction referred to in paragraph (b)(2)(i) of this section, a subsequent distribution of property by the transferee partnership to a partner of the transferee partnership that was formerly a partner of the transferor partnership is subject to section 737 to the same extent that a distribution from the transferor partnership would have been subject to section 737.

* * *

(e) *Reverse section 704(c) gain.*—For purposes of section 737(b), net precontribution gain does not include reverse section 704(c) gain as described in §1.704-3(a)(6)(i).

□ Par. 6. Section 1.737-5 is amended by revising the section heading and adding two additional sentences at the end of the paragraph to read as follows:

§1.737-5. Effective/applicability date.
* * * Section 1.737-1(c) is effective as of August 22, 2007. Section 1.737-2(b)(1) is effective for any distribution of property after January

19, 2005, if such property was contributed in a merger using the assets-over form after May 3, 2004.

Partners and Partnerships: American Jobs Creation Act of 2004 and Taxpayer Relief Act of 1997: Guidance

Partners and Partnerships: American Jobs Creation Act of 2004 and Taxpayer Relief Act of 1997: Guidance.—Amendments to Reg. §1.737-1, providing guidance on certain provisions of the American Jobs Creation Act of 2004, conforming the regulations to statutory changes in the Taxpayer Relief Act of 1997, modifying the basis allocation rules to prevent certain unintended consequences of the current basis allocation rules for substituted basis transactions and providing additional guidance on allocations resulting from revaluations of partnership property, are proposed (published in the Federal Register on January 16, 2014) (REG-144468-05).

□ Par. 7. Section 1.737-1 is amended by revising paragraph (c)(1) and adding paragraphs (c)(3) and (4) to read as follows:

§1.737-1. Recognition of precontribution gain.

* * *

(c) *Net precontribution gain.*—(1) *General rule.*—The distributee partner's net precontribution gain is the net gain (if any) that would have been recognized by the distributee partner under section 704(c)(1)(B) and §1.704-4 if all property that had been contributed to the partnership by the distributee partner within seven years of the distribution and is held by the partnership immediately before the distribution had been distributed by the partnership to another partner other than the partner who owns, directly or indirectly, more than 50 percent of the capital or profits interest in the partnership.

* * *

(3) *Determination of seven-year period.*—(i) *General rule.*—The seven-year period specified in paragraph (c)(1) of this section begins on, and includes, the date of contribution and ends on, and includes, the last date that is within seven years of the contribution. For

example, if a partner contributes 704(c) property to a partnership on May 15, 2016, the seven-year period with respect to the section 704(c) property ends on, and includes, May 14, 2023.

(ii) *Section 708(b)(1)(B) terminations.*—A termination of the partnership under section 708(b)(1)(B) does not begin a new seven-year period for each partner with respect to built-in gain and built-in loss property that the terminated partnership is deemed to contribute to the new partnership under §1.708-1(b)(4). See §1.704-3(a)(3)(ii) for the definitions of built-in gain and built-in loss on section 704(c) property.

(4) *Effective/applicability date.*—The provisions of paragraph (c)(1) and (3) of this section relating to the seven-year period for determining the applicability of section 737(b) apply for partnership contributions occurring on or after the date of publication of the Treasury decision adopting these rules as final regulations in the **Federal Register.**

* * *

Partners and Partnerships: American Jobs Creation Act of 2004 and Taxpayer Relief Act of 1997: Guidance

Partners and Partnerships: American Jobs Creation Act of 2004 and Taxpayer Relief Act of 1997: Guidance.—Amendments to Reg. §1.743-1, providing guidance on certain provisions of the American Jobs Creation Act of 2004, conforming the regulations to statutory changes in the Taxpayer Relief Act of 1997, modifying the basis allocation rules to prevent certain unintended consequences of the current basis allocation rules for substituted basis transactions and providing additional guidance on allocations resulting from revaluations of partnership property, are proposed (published in the Federal Register on January 16, 2014) (REG-144468-05).

□ Par. 8. Section 1.743-1 is amended by:
1. Revising the section heading.
2. Revising paragraph (a).
3. Revising paragraph (b).
4. Redesignating paragraph (f) introductory text as paragraph (f)(1) introductory text and revising it.
5. Adding paragraph (f)(2).
6. In paragraph (h)(1), removing "§1.708-1(b)(1)(iv)" and adding in its place "§1.708-1(b)(4)".
7. Revising paragraph (j)(3)(ii) *Example 1*.
8. Revising paragraph (j)(3)(ii) *Example 3*.
9. Revising paragraph (k)(1)(iii).
10. Adding paragraph (k)(2)(iv).
11. Redesignating paragraph (l) as paragraph (p).
12. Adding a new paragraph (l).
13. Adding paragraphs (m), (n), and (o).
14. Revising newly redesignated paragraph (p).
The revisions and additions read as follows:

§1.743-1. Special rules where partnership has a section 754 election in effect or has a substantial built-in loss immediately after transfer of partnership interest.—(a) *Generally.*—(1) *Adjustment to basis.*—The basis of partnership property is adjusted as a result of the

transfer of an interest in a partnership by sale or exchange or on the death of a partner if the election provided by section 754 (relating to optional adjustments to the basis of partnership property) is in effect with respect to the partnership, or if the partnership has a substantial built-in loss (within the meaning of paragraph (a)(2)(i) of this section) immediately after the transfer.

(2) *Substantial built-in loss.*—(i) *In general.*—A partnership has a substantial built-in loss with respect to a transfer of an interest in a partnership if the partnership's adjusted basis in partnership property exceeds the fair market value of the property (as determined in paragraph (a)(2)(iii) of this section) by more than $250,000 immediately after the transfer.

(ii) *Impact of section 743 basis adjustments and section 704(c)(1)(C) basis adjustments.*—For purposes of paragraph (a)(2)(i) of this section, any section 743 or section 704(c)(1)(C) basis adjustments (as defined in §1.704-3(f)(2)(iii)) (other than the transferee's section 743(b) basis adjustments or section 704(c)(1)(C) basis adjustments) to partnership property are disregarded.

(iii) *Determination of fair market value in tiered situation.*—For purposes of paragraph (a)(2)(i) of this section, an upper-tier partnership's fair market value in a lower-tier partnership is equal to the sum of—

(A) The amount of cash that the upper-tier partnership would receive if the lower-tier partnership sold all of its property for cash to an unrelated person for an amount equal to the fair market value of such property, satisfied all of its liabilities (other than §1.752-7 liabilities), paid an unrelated person to assume all of its §1.752-7 liabilities in a fully taxable, arm's-length transaction, and liquidated; and

(B) The upper-tier partnership's share of the lower-tier partnership's liabilities as determined under section 752 and the regulations.

(iv) *Example.*—A and B are equal partners in PRS, a partnership. PRS owns Property 1, with an adjusted basis of $3 million and a fair market value of $2 million, and Property 2, with an adjusted basis of $1 million and a fair market value of $1 million. In Year 2, A sells 50 percent of its interest in PRS to C for its fair market value of $750,000. PRS does not have section 754 election in effect. Under paragraph (a)(2)(i) of this section, PRS has a substantial built-in loss because, immediately after the transfer, the adjusted basis of PRS's property ($4 million) exceeds the fair market value of the property ($3 million) by more than $250,000. Thus, pursuant to paragraph (a)(1) of this section, PRS must adjust the bases of its properties as if PRS had made a section 754 election for Year 2.

(b) *Determination of adjustment.*—In the case of the transfer of an interest in a partnership, either by sale or exchange or as a result of the death of a partner, a partnership that has an election under section 754 in effect or that has a substantial built-in loss (within the meaning of paragraph (a)(2)(i) of this section) —

* * *

(f) *Subsequent transfers.*—(1) *In general.*—Where there has been more than one transfer of a partnership interest, a transferee's basis adjustment is determined without regard to any prior transferee's basis adjustment. In the case of a gift of an interest in a partnership, the donor is treated as transferring, and the donee as receiving, that portion of the basis adjustment attributable to the gifted partnership interest. The following example illustrates the provisions of this paragraph (f)(1):

* * *

(2) *Special rules for substituted basis transactions.*—Where a partner had a basis adjustment under section 743(b) allocated pursuant to §1.755-1(b)(2) through (b)(4) that is attributable to an interest that is subsequently transferred in a substituted basis transaction (within the meaning of §1.755-1(b)(5)), the provisions of paragraph (f)(1) of this section do not apply. Instead, the transferee succeeds to that portion of the transferor's basis adjustment attributable to the transferred partnership interest. The basis adjustment to which the transferee succeeds is taken into account for purposes of determining the transferee's share of the adjusted basis to the partnership of the partnership's property for purposes of paragraph (b) of this section and §1.755-1(b)(5). To the extent a transferee would be required to decrease the adjusted basis of an item of partnership property pursuant to §§1.743-1(b)(2) and 1.755-1(b)(5), the decrease first reduces the positive section 743(b) adjustment, if any, that the transferee succeeds to. The following example illustrates the provisions of this paragraph (f)(2):

Example—(i) A and B are partners in LTP, a partnership. A owns a 60 percent interest, and B owns a 40 percent interest, in LTP. B owns the LTP interest with an adjusted basis of $50 and a fair market value of $70. LTP owns two assets: Capital Asset 1 with an adjusted basis of $25 and a fair market value of $100, and Capital Asset 2 with an adjusted basis of $100 and a fair market value of $75. B sells its interest in LTP to UTP. Both LTP and UTP have a section 754 election in effect. Pursuant to §1.755-1(b)(3), UTP's $20 section 743(b) adjustment is allocated $30 to Capital Asset 1 and ($10) to Capital Asset 2.

(ii) UTP distributes its LTP interest to C, a partner in UTP, when the adjusted bases and fair market values of the LTP interest and LTP's assets have not changed. C's adjusted basis in its UTP interest at the time of the distribution is $40. Pursuant to paragraph (f)(2) of this section, C succeeds to UTP's section 743(b) adjustment. Also pursuant to paragraph (f)(2) of this section, the section 743(b) adjustment is taken into account in determining C's share of the adjusted basis of LTP property. Thus, C also has a $30 negative section 743(b) adjustment that must be allocated pursuant to §1.755-1(b)(5). That is, C's interest in the partnership's previously taxed capital is $70 (C would be entitled to $70 cash on liquidation and there is no increase or decrease for tax gain or tax loss from the hypothetical transaction, taking into account UTP's section 743(b) adjustment to which C succeeds). Pursuant to §1.755-1(b)(5)(iii)(B), the $30 negative section 743(b) adjustment must be allocated within the capital class first to properties with unrealized depreciation in proportion to C's share of the respective amounts of unrealized depreciation before the decrease. Taking into account UTP's section 743(b) adjustment to which C succeeds, C has no share of LTP's unrealized depreciation. Pursuant to §1.755-1(b)(5)(iii)(B), any remaining decrease must be allocated among Capital Asset 1 and Capital Asset 2 in proportion to C's share of their adjusted bases. Taking into account UTP's section 743(b) adjustment to which C succeeds, C's share of the adjusted basis in Capital Asset 1 is $40 ($10 share of LTP's basis and $30 of UTP's section 743(b) adjustment to which C succeeded) and in Capital Asset 2 is $30 ($40 share of LTP's basis and ($10) of UTP's section 743(b) adjustment). Thus, 40/70 of the $30 adjustment, $17.14, is allocated to Capital Asset 1 and 30/70 of the $30 adjustment, $12.86, is allocated to Capital Asset 2. The decrease allocated to Capital Asset 1 first reduces UTP's section 743(b) adjustment to which C succeeds. Thus, C has a net section 743(b) adjustment in Capital Asset 1 of $12.86 ($30 minus $17.14) and in Capital Asset 2 of ($22.86) (($10) plus ($12.86)). If Capital Asset 1 is subject to the allowance for depreciation or amortization, C's net $12.86 positive basis adjustment is recovered pursuant to paragraph (j)(4)(i)(B).

(iii) If C later transfers its LTP interest to D in a transaction that is not a substituted basis transaction within the meaning of §1.755-1(b)(5), under paragraph (f)(1) of this section, D does not succeed to any of C's section 743(b) adjustment.

* * *

(j) * * *

(3) * * *

(ii) * * *

Example 1. A and B form equal partnership PRS. A and B each contribute $100 cash, and PRS purchases nondepreciable property for $200. Later, at a time when the property value has decreased to $100, C contributes $50 cash for a 1/3 interest in PRS. Under §1.704-1(b)(2)(iv)(f)(5), PRS revalues its property in connection with the admission of C, allocating the $100 unrealized loss in the property equally between A and B under the partnership agreement, which provides for the use of the traditional method under §1.704-3(b). A subsequently sells its interest in PRS to T for $50. PRS has an election in effect under section 754. T receives a negative $50 basis adjustment under section 743(b) that, under section 755, is allocated to the nondepreciable property. PRS later sells the property for $120. PRS recognizes a book gain of $20 (allocated equally between T, B, and C), and a tax loss of $80. T will receive an allocation of $40 of tax loss under the principles of section 704(c). However, because T has a negative $50 basis adjustment in the nondepreciable property, T recognizes a $10 gain from the partnership's sale of the property.

* * *

Example 3. A and B form equal partnership PRS. A and B each contribute $75 cash. PRS purchases nondepreciable property for $150. Later, at a time when the property value has decreased to $100, C contributes $50 cash for a 1/3 interest in PRS. Under §1.704-1(b)(2)(iv)(f)(5), PRS revalues its property in connection with the admission of C. The $50 unrealized loss in the property is allocated equally to A and B under the partnership agreement, which provides for the use of the remedial allocation method described in §1.704-3(d). A subsequently sells its interest in PRS to T for $50. PRS has an election in effect under section 754. T receives a negative $25 basis adjustment under section 743(b) that, under section 755, is allocated to the nondepreciable property. PRS later sells the property for $112. PRS recognizes a book gain of $12 (allocated equally between T, B, and C), and a tax loss of $38 (allocated equally between T and B). To match its share of book gain, C will be allocated $4 of remedial gain, and T and B will each be allocated an offsetting $2 remedial loss. T was allocated a total of $21 of tax loss with respect to the property. However, because T has a negative $25 basis adjustment in the nondepreciable property, T recognizes a $4 gain from the partnership's sale of the property.

* * *

(k) * * *

(1) * * *

(iii) *Rules for substantial built-in loss transactions.*—A partnership required to adjust the basis of partnership property following the transfer of an interest in a partnership by sale or exchange or on the death of a partner as the result of the partnership having a substantial built-in loss (as defined in paragraph (a)(2)(i) of this section) immediately after such transfer is subject to, and required to comply with, this paragraph (k)(1), and may rely on, and must comply with, paragraphs (k)(3), (k)(4), and (k)(5) of this section solely with respect to the transfer to which the substantial built-in loss relates as if an election under section 754 were in effect at the time of the transfer. *See* paragraph (k)(2) of this section for additional rules for transferees and paragraph (n) of this section for special reporting rules relating to electing investment partnerships.

(2) * * *

(iv) *Special rules for transferees subject to the substantial built-in loss provisions.*—The transferee of an interest in a partnership that is required to reduce the bases of partnership property in accordance with the rules in paragraph (a)(2) of this section must comply with this paragraph (k)(2) as if an election under section 754 were in effect at the time of the transfer.

(l) *Basis adjustments with respect to tiered partnerships.*—(1) *General rule.*—If an interest in an upper-tier partnership that holds an interest in a lower-tier partnership is transferred by sale or exchange or upon the death of a partner, and the upper-tier partnership and the lower-tier partnership both have elections in effect under section 754, then for purposes of section 743(b) and section 754, an interest in the lower-tier partnership will be deemed similarly transferred in an amount equal to the portion of the upper-tier partnership's interest in the lower-tier partnership that is attributable to the interest in the upper-tier partnership being transferred. Additionally, if an interest in an upper-tier partnership that holds (directly or indirectly through one or more partnerships) an interest in a lower-tier partnership is transferred by sale or exchange or on the death of a partner, and the upper-tier partnership has a substantial built-in loss (within the meaning of paragraph (a)(2)(i) of this section) with respect to the transfer, each lower-tier partnership is treated, solely with respect to the transfer, as if it had made a section 754 election for the taxable year of the transfer. For additional examples of the application of the principles of this paragraph (l), see Revenue Ruling 87-115, 1987-2 CB 163. *See* § 601.601(d)(2)(ii)(b).

(2) *Example.*—The following example illustrates the principles of this paragraph (l).

Example. A and B are equal partners in UTP, a partnership. UTP has no liabilities and owns a 25 percent interest in LTP, a partnership. UTP's interest in LTP has a fair market value of $100,000 and an adjusted basis of $500,000. LTP has no liabilities and owns Land, which has a fair market value of $400,000 and an adjusted basis of $2 million. In Year 3, when UTP and LTP do not have section 754 elections in effect, B sells 50 percent of its interest in UTP to C for its fair market value of $25,000. Because the adjusted basis of UTP's interest in LTP ($500,000) exceeds the fair market value of UTP's interest in LTP ($100,000) by more than $250,000 immediately after the transfer, UTP has a substantial built-in loss with respect to the transfer. Thus, pursuant to paragraph (l) of this section, UTP must adjust the basis of its interest in LTP, and LTP must adjust the basis of Land, as if it had made a section 754 election for Year 3.

(m) *Anti-abuse rule for substantial built-in loss transactions.*—Provisions relating to substantial built-in loss transactions in paragraph (a) and paragraphs (k), (l), (n), and (o) of this section must be applied in a manner consistent with the purposes of these paragraphs and the substance of the transaction. Accordingly, if a principal purpose of a transaction is to achieve a tax result that is inconsistent with the purpose of one or more of these paragraphs, the Commissioner may recast the transaction for Federal income tax purposes, as appropriate, to achieve tax results that are consistent with the purpose of these paragraphs. Whether a tax result is inconsistent with the purposes of the provisions is determined based on all the facts and circumstances. For example, under the provisions of this paragraph (m)—

(1) Property held by related partnerships may be aggregated if the properties were transferred to the related partnerships with a principal purpose of avoiding the application of the substantial built-in loss provisions in section 743 and the regulations; and

(2) A contribution of property to a partnership may be disregarded if the transfer of the property was made with a principal purpose of avoiding the application of the substantial built-in loss provisions in section 743 and the regulations thereunder.

(n) *Electing investment partnerships.*—(1) *No adjustment of partnership basis.*—For purposes of this section, an electing investment partnership (as defined in paragraph (n)(6) of this section) shall not be treated as having a substantial built-in loss (within the meaning of

paragraph (a)(2)(i) of this section) with respect to any transfer occurring while the election in paragraph (n)(6)(i) of this section is in effect.

(2) *Loss deferral for transferee partner.*—In the case of a transfer of an interest in an electing investment partnership, the transferee partner's distributive share of losses (without regard to gains) from the sale or exchange of partnership property shall not be allowed except to the extent that it is established that such losses exceed the loss (if any) recognized by the transferor partner (or by any prior transferor to the extent not fully offset by a prior disallowance under this paragraph (n)(2)) on the transfer of the partnership interest. If an electing investment partnership allocates losses with a different character from the sale or exchange of property to the transferee (such as ordinary or section 1231 losses and capital losses) and the losses allocated to that partner are limited by this paragraph (n)(2), then a proportionate amount of the losses disallowed under this paragraph (n)(2) shall consist of each loss of a separate character that is allocated to the transferee partner.

(3) *No reduction in partnership basis.*—Losses disallowed under paragraph (n)(2) of this section shall not decrease the transferee partner's basis in the partnership interest.

(4) *Effect of termination of partnership.*—This paragraph (n) shall be applied without regard to any termination of a partnership under section 708(b)(1)(B).

(5) *Certain basis reductions treated as losses.*—In the case of a transferee partner whose basis in property distributed by the partnership is reduced under section 732(a)(2), the amount of the loss recognized by the transferor on the transfer of the partnership interest that is taken into account under paragraph (n)(2) of this section shall be reduced by the amount of such basis reduction.

(6) *Electing investment partnership.*—For purposes of this section, the term *electing investment partnership* means any partnership if—

(i) The partnership makes an election under paragraph (n)(10) of this section to have this paragraph (n) apply;

(ii) The partnership would be an investment company under section 3(a)(1)(A) of the Investment Company Act of 1940 but for an exemption under paragraph (1) or (7) of section 3(c) of such Act;

(iii) The partnership has never been engaged in a trade or business (see paragraph (n)(7) of this section for additional rules regarding this paragraph (n)(6)(iii));

(iv) Substantially all of the assets of the partnership are held for investment;

(v) At least 95 percent of the assets contributed to the partnership consist of money;

(vi) No assets contributed to the partnership had an adjusted basis in excess of fair market value at the time of contribution;

(vii) All partnership interests of the partnership are issued by the partnership pursuant to a private offering before the date that is 24 months after the date of the first capital contribution to the partnership; (viii) The partnership agreement of the partnership has substantive restrictions on each partner's ability to cause a redemption of the partner's interest (see paragraphs (n)(8) and (n)(9) of this section for additional rules regarding this paragraph (n)(6)(viii)); and

(ix) The partnership agreement of the partnership provides for a term that is not in excess of 15 years (see paragraph (n)(9) of this section for additional rules regarding this paragraph (n)(6)(ix)).

(7) *Trade or business.*—For purposes of paragraph (n)(6)(iii) of this section, whether a partnership is engaged in a trade or business is based on the all the facts and circumstances. Notwithstanding the prior sentence—

(i) A partnership will not be treated as engaged in a trade or business if, based on all the facts and circumstances, the partnership is not engaged in a trade or business under the rules in § 1.731-2(e)(3).

(ii) In the case of a tiered partnership arrangement, a partnership (upper-tier partnership) will not be treated as engaged in a trade or business of a partnership in which it owns an interest (lower-tier partnership) if the upper-tier partnership can establish that, at all times during the period in which the upper-tier partnership owns an interest in the lower-tier partnership, the adjusted basis of its interest in the lower-tier partnership is less than 25 percent of the total capital that is required to be contributed to the upper-tier partnership by its partners during the entire term of the upper-tier partnership. Otherwise, the upper-tier partnership will be treated as engaged in the trade or business of the lower-tier partnership.

(8) *Substantive restrictions.*—For purposes of paragraph (n)(6)(viii) of this section, substantive restrictions include cases in which a redemption is permitted under a partnership agreement only if the redemption is necessary to avoid a violation of state, federal, or

local laws (such as ERISA or the Bank Holding Company Act) or the imposition of a federal excise tax on, or a change in the federal tax-exempt status of, a tax-exempt partner.

(9) *Special rules for partnerships in existence on June 4, 2004.*—In the case of a partnership in existence on June 4, 2004, paragraph (n)(6)(viii) of this section will not apply to the partnership and paragraph (n)(6)(ix) of this section is applied by substituting "20 years" for "15 years."

(10) *Election.*—(i) *Eligibility.*—A partnership is eligible to make the election described in paragraph (n)(6)(i) of this section if the partnership meets the definition of an electing investment partnership in paragraph (n)(6) of this section and does not have an election under section 754 in effect.

(ii) *Manner of making election.*—A partnership must make the election by attaching a written statement to an original return for the taxable year for which the election is effective. The original return must be filed not later than the time prescribed by § 1.6031(a)-1(e) of the Procedure and Administration Regulations (including extensions) for filing the return for the taxable year for which the election is effective. If the partnership is not otherwise required to file a partnership return, the election shall be made in accordance with the rules in § 1.6031(a)-1(b)(5) of the Procedure and Administration Regulations. The statement must—

(A) Set forth the name, address, and tax identification number of the partnership making the election;

(B) Contain a representation that the partnership is eligible to make the election; and

(C) Contain a declaration that the partnership elects to be treated as an electing investment partnership.

(iii) *Effect and duration of election.*—Once the election is made, the election is effective for all transfers during the partnership's taxable year for which the election is effective and all succeeding taxable years, except as provided in paragraphs (n)(10)(iv) and (n)(10)(v) of this section.

(iv) *Termination of election.*—(A) *In general.*—The election terminates if the partnership fails to meet the definition of an electing investment partnership. The electing investment partnership's election also terminates if the partnership files an election under section 754.

(B) *Effect of termination.*—If the election terminates, the partnership will be subject to the substantial built-in loss provisions in this section with respect to the first transfer of a partnership interest that occurs after the partnership ceases to meet the definition of an electing investment partnership (or the first transfer that occurs after the effective date of the section 754 election) and to each subsequent transfer. In addition, any losses that are subsequently allocated to a partner to whom a partnership interest was transferred while the election was in effect shall remain subject to the rules in paragraph (n)(2) of this section.

(v) *Revocation of election.*—(A) *In general.*—The election, once made, shall be irrevocable except with the consent of the Commissioner. The application for consent to revoke the election must be submitted to the Internal Revenue Service in the form of a letter ruling request.

(B) *Effect of revocation.*—If the election is properly revoked, the partnership will be subject to the substantial built-in loss provisions in this section with respect to the first transfer of a partnership interest that occurs after the effective date of the revocation and to each subsequent transfer. In addition, any losses that are subsequently allocated to a partner to whom a partnership interest was transferred while the election was in effect shall remain subject to the rules in paragraph (n)(2) of this section.

(11) *Transferor partner required to provide information to transferee partner and partnership.*—(i) *In general.*—Except as provided in paragraph (n)(11)(ii) of this section, if an electing investment partnership interest is transferred in a sale or exchange or upon the death of a partner, the transferor (or, in the case of a partner who dies, the partner's executor, personal representative, or other successor in interest) must notify the transferee and the partnership in writing. If the transferor is a nominee (within the meaning of § 1.6031(c)-1T), then the nominee, and not the beneficial owner of the transferred interest, must supply the information to the transferee and the partnership. The notice must be provided within 30 days after the date on which the transferor partner (or the executor, personal representative, or other successor in interest) receives a Schedule K-1 from the partnership for the partnership's taxable year in which the transfer occurred. The notice must be signed under penalties of perjury, must be retained by the transferee and the partnership as long as the contents thereof may be material in the administration of any internal revenue law, and must include—

(A) The name, address, and tax identification number of the transferor;

(B) The name, address, and tax identification number of the transferee (if ascertainable);

(C) The name of the electing investment partnership;

(D) The date of the transfer (and, in the case of the death of a partner, the date of the death of the partner);

(E) The amount of loss, if any, recognized by the transferor on the transfer of the interest, together with the computation of the loss;

(F) The amount of losses, if any, recognized by any prior transferors to the extent the losses were subject to disallowance under paragraph (n)(2) of this section in the hands of a prior transferee and have not been offset by prior loss disallowances under paragraph (n)(2) of this section; and

(G) Any other information necessary for the transferee to compute the amount of loss disallowed under paragraph (n)(2) of this section.

(ii) *Exception.*—The rules of paragraph (n)(11)(i) of this section do not apply if the transferor recognizes a gain on the transfer and no prior transferor recognized a loss on any transfer.

(iii) *Effect of failure to notify transferee partner.*—If the transferor partner, its legal representative in the case of a transfer by death, or the nominee (if the transferor is a nominee) fails to provide the transferee partner with the statement, the transferee partner must treat all losses allocated from the electing investment partnership as disallowed under paragraph (n)(2) of this section unless the transferee partner obtains, from the partnership or otherwise, the information necessary to determine the proper amount of losses disallowed under paragraph (n)(2) of this section. If the transferee does not have the information necessary to determine the proper amount of losses disallowed under paragraph (n)(2) of this section, but does have information sufficient to determine the maximum amount of losses that could be disallowed, then the transferee may treat the amount of losses disallowed under paragraph (n)(2) of this section as being equal to that maximum amount. For example, if the transferee is able to ascertain the adjusted basis that a prior transferor had in its partnership interest, but is not able to ascertain the amount realized by that transferor, the transferee may assume, for purposes of calculating the amount of losses disallowed under paragraph (n)(2) of this section, that the sales price when the prior transferor sold its interest was zero. If, following the filing of a return pursuant to the previous sentence, the transferor partner or the partnership provides the required information to the transferee partner, the transferee partner should make appropriate adjustments in an amended return for the year of the loss allocation from the partnership in accordance with section 6511 or other applicable rules.

(iv) *Additional rules.*.—See paragraph (n)(12)(i) of this section for additional reporting requirements when the electing investment partnership is not required to file a partnership return.

(12) *Electing investment partnership required to provide information to partners.*—(i) *Distributive shares of partnership items.*—An electing investment partnership is required to separately state on Schedule K and K-1 of the partnership's return (Form 1065) all allocations of losses to all of its partners under § 1.702-1(a)(8)(ii), including losses that, in the absence of section 743(e), could be netted against gains at the partnership level. If a partnership's election to be treated as an electing investment partnership is terminated or revoked under paragraphs (n)(10)(iv) or (n)(10)(v) of this section, the partnership must continue to state such gains and losses separately in future returns relating to any period during which the partnership has one or more transferee partners that are subject to section paragraph (n)(2) of this section. If an electing investment partnership is not required to file a partnership return, the transferee of a partnership interest may be required to provide the Commissioner similar information regarding the partner's distributive share of gross gains and losses of the partnership under § 1.6031(a)-1(b)(4).

(ii) *Annual statement.*—An electing investment partnership must provide an annual statement to all of its partners. The statement must be attached to every statement provided to a partner or nominee under section 6031(b) that is issued with respect to any taxable year for which an election to be treated as an electing investment partnership is in effect (whether or not the election is in effect for the entire taxable year). The statement must include the following—

(A) A statement that the partnership has elected to be treated as an electing investment partnership;

(B) A statement that, unless the transferor partner recognizes a gain on the transfer and no prior transferor recognized a loss on any transfer, if a partner transfers an interest in the partnership to another person, the transferor partner must, within 30 days after receiving a Schedule K-1 from the partnership for the taxable year that includes the date of the transfer, provide the transferee with

Reg. § 1.743-1(n)(12)(ii)(B)

certain information, including the amount, if any, of loss that the transferor recognized on the transfer of the partnership interest, and the amount of losses, if any, recognized by prior transferors with respect to the same interest; and

(C) A statement that if an interest in the partnership is transferred to a transferee partner, the transferee is required to reduce its distributive share of losses from the partnership, determined without regard to gains from the partnership, to the extent of any losses recognized by the transferor partner when that partner transferred the partnership interest to the transferee (and to the extent of other losses recognized on prior transfers of the same partnership interest that have not been offset by prior loss disallowances). The statement must also notify the transferee that it is required to reduce its share of losses as reported to the transferee by the partnership each year by the amount of any loss recognized by the transferor partner (or any prior transferor to the extent not already offset by prior loss disallowances) until the transferee has reduced its share of partnership losses by the total amount of losses required to be disallowed. Finally, the statement must state that if the transferor partner (or its nominee), or its legal representative in the case of a transfer by death, fails to provide the transferee with the required statement, the transferee must treat all losses allocated from the partnership as disallowed unless the transferee obtains, from the partnership or otherwise, the information necessary to determine the proper amount of losses disallowed.

(o) *Securitization partnerships.*—(1) *General rule.*—A securitization partnership (as defined in paragraph (o)(2) of this section) shall not be treated as having a substantial built-in loss with respect to any transfer.

(2) *Definition of securitization partnership.*—A *securitization partnership* means any partnership the sole business activity of which is to issue securities that provide for a fixed principal (or similar) amount and that are primarily serviced by the cash flows of a discrete pool (either fixed or revolving) of receivables or other financial assets that by their terms convert into cash in a finite period, but only if the sponsor of the pool reasonably believes that the receivables and other financial assets comprising the pool are not acquired for the purpose of being disposed of.

(p) *Effective/applicability date.*—* * * Paragraph (f)(2) of this section and the provisions relating to substantial built-in losses in paragraph (a) and paragraphs (k), (l), (m), (n), and (o) of this section are effective for transfers of partnership interests occurring on or after the date of publication of the Treasury decision adopting these rules as final regulations in the **Federal Register**.

Partners and Partnerships: Sales or Exchanges: Certain Distributions

Partners and Partnerships: Sales or Exchanges: Certain Distributions.—Amendments to Reg. §1.751-1, prescribing how a partner should measure its interest in a partnership's unrealized receivables and inventory items, and that provide guidance regarding the tax consequences of a distribution that causes a reduction in that interest, are proposed (published in the Federal Register on November 3, 2014) (corrected January 26, 2015) (REG-151416-06).

☐ Par. 7. Section 1.751-1 is amended by:

a. Revising paragraphs (a)(1) and (2).

b. Revising the first sentence of paragraph (b)(1)(i) and adding a new sentence at the end of paragraph (b)(1)(i).

c. Removing the last four sentences of paragraph (b)(1)(ii).

d. Revising paragraphs (b)(1)(iii) and (b)(2) and (3).

e. Redesignating paragraphs (b)(4) and (5) as paragraphs (b)(5) and (6).

f. Adding a new paragraph (b)(4).

g. Revising the paragraph heading of newly designated paragraph (b)(5).

h. Further redesignating newly redesignated paragraph (b)(5)(ii) as paragraph (b)(5)(vi) and adding paragraphs (b)(5)(ii), (iii), (iv), and (v).

i. Revising newly designated paragraph (b)(6).

j. Revising paragraph (c)(4)(vi).

k. Adding paragraph (c)(4)(x).

l. Removing paragraphs (c)(5) and (6).

m. Revising the first and second sentences of paragraph (d)(1).

n. Revising paragraphs (e), (f), and (g).

The additions and revisions read as follows:

§1.751-1. Unrealized receivables and inventory items.—(a) * * *

(1) *Character of amount realized.*—To the extent that money or property received by a partner in exchange for all or part of his partnership interest is attributable to his share of the value of partnership unrealized receivables or inventory items, the money or fair market value of the property received shall be considered as an amount realized from the sale or exchange of property other than a capital asset. The remainder of the total amount realized on the sale or exchange of the partnership interest is realized from the sale or exchange of a capital asset under section 741. For definition of "unrealized receivables" and "inventory items," see section 751(c) and (d). See paragraph (e) of this section for the definition of section 751 property.

(2) *Determination of gain or loss.*—The income or loss realized by a partner upon the sale or exchange of its interest in section 751 property is the amount of income or loss from section 751 property (taking into account allocations of tax items applying the principles of section 704(c), including any remedial allocations under §1.704-3(d), and any section 743 basis adjustment pursuant to §1.743-1(j)(3)) that would have been allocated to the partner (to the extent attributable to the partnership interest sold or exchanged) if the partnership had sold all of its property in a fully taxable transaction for cash in an amount equal to the fair market value of such property (taking into account section 7701(g)) immediately prior to the partner's transfer of the interest in the partnership. Any gain or loss recognized that is attributable to section 751 property will be ordinary gain or loss. The difference between the amount of capital gain or loss that the partner would realize in the absence of section 751 and the amount of ordinary income or loss determined under this paragraph (a)(2) is the transferor's capital gain or loss on the sale of its partnership interest. For purposes of section 751(a) and paragraph (a) of this section, the amount of money or the fair market value of property received by the partner in exchange for all or part of his partnership interest must take into account the partner's share of income or gain from section 751 property. See Example 1 in paragraph (g) of this section. See §1.460-4(k)(2)(iv)(E) for rules relating to the amount of ordinary income or loss attributable to a contract accounted for under a long-term contract method of accounting.

* * *

(b) *Certain distributions treated as sales or exchanges.*—(1) *In general.*—(i) Certain distributions to which section 751(b) applies are treated in whole or in part as sales or exchanges of property, and not as distributions to which sections 731 through 736 apply. * * * For purposes of section 751 and this section, a partner's interest in the partnership's section 751 property includes allocations of tax items applying the principles of section 704(c).

* * *

(iii) If a distribution is a section 751(b) distribution, as described in paragraph (b)(2)(i) of this section, the tax consequences of the section 751(b) distribution, as determined under paragraph (b)(3) of this section, shall first apply, and then the rules of sections 731 through 736 shall apply. See paragraph (b)(5)(vi) of this section for treatment of payments under section 736(a).

(2) *Distributions to which section 751(b) applies.*—(i) *Section 751(b) amount.*—A distribution is a section 751(b) distribution if it gives rise to a "section 751(b) amount" for any partner. A partner's section 751(b) amount (if any) associated with a distribution of partnership property (including money) equals the greatest of—

(A) The amount by which the partner's net section 751 unrealized gain immediately before the distribution exceeds the partner's net section 751 unrealized gain immediately after the distribution;

(B) The amount by which the partner's net section 751 unrealized loss immediately after the distribution exceeds the partner's net section 751 unrealized loss immediately before the distribution; and

(C) The amount of the partner's net section 751 unrealized gain immediately before the distribution, increased by the total amount of the partner's net section 751 unrealized loss immediately after the distribution (where neither of those numbers equals zero).

(ii) Net section 751 unrealized gain or loss before a distribution.—A partner's net section 751 unrealized gain or loss immediately before a distribution equals the amount of net income or loss, as the case may be, from section 751 property that would be allocated to the partner if the partnership disposed of all of the partnership's assets for cash in an amount equal to the fair market value of such property (taking into account section 7701(g)). For this purpose, a partner's net section 751 unrealized gain or loss includes any remedial allocations under §1.704-3(d), and takes into account any section 743(b) basis adjustment pursuant to §1.743-1(j)(3) and any carryover basis adjustment described in §§1.743-1(g)(2)(ii), 1.755-1(b)(5)(iii)(D), or 1.755-1(c)(4) as though the carryover basis adjustment was applied to the basis of new partnership section 751 property with fair market value of zero.

(iii) Net section 751 unrealized gain or loss after a distribution.—A partner's net section 751 unrealized gain or loss immediately after a distribution equals the sum of (to the extent applicable)—

(A) With respect to a partner remaining in the partnership immediately after the distribution (including a distributee partner remaining in the partnership), the amount of net income or loss, as the case may be (including any remedial allocations under §1.704-3(d) and taking into account any section 743(b) basis adjustment pursuant to §1.743-1(j)(3) and any carryover basis adjustment described in §§1.743-1(g)(2)(ii), 1.755-1(b)(5)(iii)(D), or 1.755-1(c)(4) as though the carryover basis adjustment was applied to the basis of new partnership section 751 property with fair market value of zero), from section 751 property that would be allocated to the partner if the partnership disposed of all of the partnership's assets for cash in an amount equal to the fair market value of such property (taking into account section 7701(g)); and

(B) With respect to a partner receiving a distribution, the amount of net income or loss, as the case may be, from section 751 property that would be recognized by the distributee if, immediately after the distribution, the distributee disposed of the distributed assets for cash in an amount equal to the fair market value of such property (taking into account section 7701(g)).

(iv) Revaluation of assets.—For a partnership that distributes money or property (other than a de minimis amount) to a partner as consideration for an interest in the partnership, and that owns section 751 property immediately after the distribution, if the partnership maintains capital accounts in accordance with §1.704-1(b)(2)(iv), the partnership must revalue its assets immediately prior to the distribution in accordance with §1.704-1(b)(2)(iv)(f). If a partnership does not maintain capital accounts in accordance with §1.704-1(b)(2)(iv), the partnership must comply with this section by computing its partners' shares of partnership gain or loss immediately before the distribution as if the partnership assets were sold for cash in a fully taxable transaction (taking into account section 7701(g)), and by taking those computed shares of gain or loss into account under the principles of section 704(c) (making subsequent adjustments for cost recovery and other events that affect the basis of the property). In addition, if the partnership (upper-tier partnership) owns another partnership directly or indirectly through one or more partnerships (lower-tier partnership), and the same persons own, directly or indirectly (through one or more entities), more than 50 percent of the capital and profits interests in both the upper-tier partnership and the lower-tier partnership, the lower-tier partnership must also revalue its assets immediately prior to the distribution in accordance with §1.704-1(b)(2)(iv)(f) if the lower-tier partnership owns section 751 property. If the same persons do not own, directly or indirectly, more than 50 percent of the capital and profits interests in both the upper-tier partnership and the lower-tier partnership, the upper-tier partnership must allocate its distributive share of the lower-tier partnership's items among its partners in a manner that reflects the allocations that would have been made had the lower-tier partnership revalued its property.

(3) Tax consequences of a section 751(b) distribution.—(i) *Reasonable approach.*—In the case of a section 751(b) distribution described in paragraph (b)(2) of this section, the partnership must choose a reasonable approach that is consistent with the purpose of section 751(b) under which each partner with a section 751(b) amount recognizes ordinary income (or takes it into account by eliminating a basis adjustment) equal to that section 751(b) amount immediately prior to the section 751(b) distribution. In certain circumstances described in paragraph (b)(3)(ii) of this section, a distributee partner may also be permitted or required to recognize capital gain. To be reasonable, an approach must conform to the general principles and anti-abuse rules described in paragraph (b)(4) of this section. An approach is not necessarily unreasonable merely because another approach would result in a higher aggregate tax liability. Once the partnership has adopted a reasonable approach, it must apply that approach consistently for all section 751(b) distributions, including for any distributions the partnership makes after a termination of the partnership under section 708(b)(1)(B). If the application

of the adopted approach to a later section 751(b) distribution produces results inconsistent with the purpose of section 751, the partnership must adopt another reasonable approach that achieves the purposes of section 751 for that distribution only. See *Example 3* through *Example 8* in paragraph (g) of this section.

(ii) Gain Recognition.—(A) *Mandatory recognition.*—A partner's net section 751 unrealized gain or net section 751 unrealized loss for purposes of paragraph (b)(3)(i) of this section is determined before taking into account any basis adjustments required by paragraph (b)(3)(iii) of this section. In certain instances, the application of paragraph (b)(3)(iii) of this section may cause a partner to receive distributed property with a basis that differs from the basis of the property in the hands of the distributing partnership. If an adjustment to the basis of the distributed section 751 property results in a section 734(b) basis adjustment, and that basis adjustment would have altered the amount of net section 751 unrealized gain or loss computed under paragraph (b)(2) of this section if the section 734(b) adjustment had been included immediately prior to the distribution, then the distributee partner must recognize capital gain immediately prior to the distribution in an amount sufficient to eliminate that section 734(b) basis adjustment. See *Examples 5* and *6* in paragraph (g) of this section. If, however, the partnership makes an election under §1.755-1(c)(2)(vi), then the partner must characterize all or a portion of the gain recognized under this paragraph as ordinary income or a dividend, as appropriate, to preserve the character of the gain in the adjusted asset. See *Example 9* in paragraph (g) of this section.

(B) *Elective recognition.*—A distributee partner may elect to recognize capital gain (in addition to amounts required to be recognized under this section) to eliminate section 732(a)(2) or (b) basis adjustments to the asset or assets received in distribution if, and to the extent that, the basis adjustments required by paragraph (b)(3)(iii) of this section would otherwise cause the distributee partner's net section 751 unrealized gain to be greater immediately after the distribution than it was immediately before the distribution or would cause the distributee partner's net section 751 unrealized loss to be less immediately after the distribution than it was immediately before the distribution. A distributee partner elects under this paragraph (b)(3)(ii)(B) by providing the partnership with written notification of its intent to make the election and reporting the capital gain on its return. An extension of time to make an election under this paragraph (b)(3)(ii)(B) will not be granted under §301.9100-3 of this chapter. The requirement in paragraph (b)(1)(i) of this section that a partnership apply a chosen reasonable method consistently across all partnership distributions does not apply for purposes of this paragraph. See *Example 7* in paragraph (g) of this section.

(iii) Adjustments to Basis.—The partnership and its partners must make appropriate adjustments to the adjusted basis of the partners' interests in the partnership, and of section 751 property and other property held by the partnership or partners, in a manner consistent with the adopted approach to reflect any ordinary income or capital gain recognized upon application of paragraph (b)(3) of this section, and section 704(c) amounts must be adjusted accordingly.

(4) General principles and anti-abuse rules.—(i) The purpose of section 751 is to prevent a partner from converting its rights to ordinary income into capital gain, including by relying on the rules of section 704(c) to defer ordinary income while monetizing most of the value of the partnership interest. The partnership and all partners of the partnership must apply the rules of section 751 and §1.751-1 in a manner consistent with the purpose of section 751. Accordingly, if a principal purpose of a transaction is to achieve a tax result that is inconsistent with the purpose of section 751, the Commissioner may recast the transaction for federal tax purposes as appropriate to achieve tax results that are consistent with the purpose of section 751. The Commissioner will determine whether a tax result is inconsistent with the purpose of section 751 based on all the facts and circumstances. The existence of one or more of the situations set forth below is presumed to establish that a transaction is inconsistent with the purpose of section 751 and disclosure to the Internal Revenue Service in accordance with §1.751-1(b)(4)(ii) is required.

(A) Circumstances in which a partner received a distribution that would otherwise be subject to section 751(b), but for the application of the principles of section 704(c), and one or more of the following conditions exist (whether at the time of the distribution or, in the case of paragraph (b)(4)(i)(A)(2), (3), (4), or (5) of this section, a later date):

(1) The partner's interest in net section 751 unrealized gain is at least four times greater than the partner's capital account immediately after the distribution, pursuant to §1.704-1(b)(2)(iv) (or comparable amount for partnerships not maintaining capital accounts under §1.704-1(b)(2)(iv));

(2) The partner is substantially protected from losses from the partnership's activities and has little or no participation in

the profits from the partnership's activities other than a preferred return that is in the nature of a payment for the use of capital;

    (3) The partner engages in a transaction that, at the time of the transaction, causes the net value of the partner (or its successor) to be less than the tax liability that the partner (or its successor) would incur with respect to its interest in the partnership's section 751 property upon a sale of its partnership interest for its fair market value at the time of the transaction. For this purpose, the net value of the partner (or its successor) equals—

    (i) The fair market value of all assets owned by the partner (or its successor) that may be subject to creditor's claims under local law (including the partner's enforceable right to contributions from its owner or owners), less

    (ii) All obligations of the partner (or its successor) other than the partner's obligation with respect to the tax liability for which the net value is being determined;

    (4) The partner transfers a portion of its partnership interest within five years after the distribution in a manner that does not trigger ordinary income recognition, and ordinary income or gain with respect to the partnership interest is subject to Federal income tax in the hands of the transferor partner immediately before the transfer, but any ordinary income or gain with respect to the partnership interest is exempt from, or otherwise not subject to, Federal income tax in the hands of the transferee partner immediately after the transfer;

    (5) The partnership transfers to a corporation in a nonrecognition transaction section 751 property other than pursuant to a transfer of all property used in a trade or business (excluding assets that are not material to a continuation of the trade or business); or

    (B) The partners agree to change (other than a de minimis change) the manner in which the partners share any item or class of items of income, gain, loss, deduction or credit of the partnership under the partnership agreement and that change reduces the partner's net section 751 unrealized gain.

    (ii) If a partner participates in a transaction described in paragraph (b)(4)(i)(A) or (B) of this section and does not recognize and report its share of ordinary income from section 751 property on its tax return for the taxable year of the transaction, the partner must file Form 8275-R, Regulation Disclosure Statement, or any appropriate successor form, disclosing its participation in the transaction for the taxable year in which the transaction occurred.

    (5) *Special rules.*—* * *

        * * *

    (ii) The transferee in a nonrecognition transaction of all or a portion of the partnership interest of a contributing partner is treated as the contributing partner for purposes of section 751(b)(2) in an amount attributable to the interest transferred.

    (iii) For purposes of section 751(b)(2), if a partnership disposes of contributed section 751 property in a nonrecognition transaction, the substituted basis property (within the meaning of section 7701(a)(42)) received in exchange for such substituted basis property is treated as the contributed section 751 property with regard to the contributing partner. If a partnership transfers contributed section 751 property together with other property in a nonrecognition transaction, the substituted basis property (within the meaning of section 7701(a)(42)) is treated as the contributed section 751 property with regard to the contributing partner in the same proportion as the fair market value of the contributed section 751 property, at the time of the transfer, bears to the fair market value of the other property transferred at the time of the transfer. If a transfer described in this paragraph (b)(5)(iii) was in exchange for an interest in an entity, the interest in the entity will not be treated as the contributed section 751 property with regard to the contributing partner to the extent the value of the interest is attributable to other property the partnership contributed to the entity.

    (iv) For purposes of section 751(b)(2), an interest in an entity previously contributed to the partnership is not treated as previously contributed property to the extent the value of the interest is attributable to property the partnership contributed to the entity after the interest was contributed to the partnership. The preceding sentence does not apply to the extent that the property contributed to the entity was contributed to the partnership by the partner that also contributed the interest in the entity to the partnership.

    (v) For purposes of section 751(b)(2), the distribution of an undivided interest in property is treated as the distribution of previously contributed property to the extent that the undivided interest does not exceed the undivided interest, if any, contributed by the distributee partner in the same property.

        * * *

    (6) *Statements required.*—(i) *Partnership.*—A partnership that makes a section 751(b) distribution must submit with its return for the year of the distribution a statement for each section 751(b) distribution made during the year that includes the following:

    (A) A caption identifying the statement as the disclosure of a section 751(b) distribution and the date of the distribution; and

    (B) A brief description of the reasonable approach adopted by the partnership pursuant to paragraph (b)(3)(i) of this section for recognizing the ordinary income; if applicable, the capital gain required to be recognized; and if relevant, whether the approach varies from an approach previously adopted within any of the three tax years preceding the current tax year.

    (ii) *Partner.*—A partnership that makes a section 751(b) distribution during the partnership's tax year must submit with its return for the year of the distribution a statement for each partner that has a section 751(b) amount greater than $0 in connection with that distribution. The statement must be attached to the statement for that partner required by section 6031(b) and §1.6031(b)-1T(a), and must include the following:

    (A) The date of the section 751(b) distribution;

    (B) The amount of ordinary income the partner recognized pursuant to paragraph (b)(3)(i) of this section; and

    (C) The amount of capital gain the partner recognized, if any, pursuant to paragraph (b)(3)(ii)(A) or (B) of this section.

    (c) * * *

    (4) * * *

    (vi) With respect to any taxable year of a partnership beginning after July 18, 1984, amounts treated as ordinary income under section 467 are treated as ordinary income under this section in the same manner as amounts treated as ordinary income under section 1245 (*see* paragraph (c)(4)(iii) of this section) or section 1250 (*see* paragraph (c)(4)(v) of this section).

        * * *

    (x) With respect to any taxable year of a partnership beginning after July 18, 1984, the term *unrealized receivables,* for purposes of this section and sections 731, 732, and 741 (but not for purposes of section 736), includes any market discount bond (as defined in section 1278) and any short-term obligation (as defined in section 1283) but only to the extent of the amount that would be treated as ordinary income if (at the time of the transaction described in this section or section 731, 732, or 741, as the case may be) such property had been sold by the partnership.

        * * *

    (d) *Inventory items which have substantially appreciated in value.*—(1) *Substantial appreciation.*—Partnership inventory items shall be considered to have appreciated substantially in value if, at the time of the distribution, the total fair market value of all the inventory items of the partnership exceeds 120 percent of the aggregate adjusted basis for such property in the hands of the partnership (without regard to any special basis adjustment to the partner). The terms "inventory items which have appreciated substantially in value" or "substantially appreciated inventory items" refer to the aggregate of all partnership inventory items but do not include any unrealized receivables. * * *

        * * *

    (e) *Section 751 property and other property.*—For purposes of paragraph (a) of this section, *section 751 property* means unrealized receivables or inventory items. For purposes of paragraph (b) of this section, *section 751 property* means unrealized receivables or substantially appreciated inventory items. For purposes of all paragraphs of this section, *other property* means all property (including money) that is not section 751 property.

    (f) *Applicability date.*—The rules contained in paragraph (a)(2) of this section apply to transfers of partnership interests that occur on or after November 3, 2014. The rules contained in paragraph (a)(3) of this section apply to transfers of partnership interests that occur on or after December 15, 1999. The rules contained in paragraphs (b)(2) and (3) of this section apply to distributions of partnership property that occur on or after the date of publication of a Treasury decision adopting these rules as final regulations in the **Federal Register**. However, a partnership and its partners may apply the rules contained in paragraph (b)(2) of this section for purposes of determining a partner's interest in the partnership's section 751 property on or after November 3, 2014, provided the partnership and its partners apply paragraphs (a)(2), (b)(2), and (b)(4) of this section, and proposed §1.704-1(b)(2)(iv)(f), consistently for all partnership sales, exchanges, and distributions occurring on or after November 3, 2014, including for any distributions the partnership makes after a termination of the partnership under section 708(b)(1)(B).

    (g) *Examples.*—Application of the provisions of section 751 may be illustrated by the following examples. In each of *Examples 2* through 9 of this paragraph (g), none of the section 751 property qualifies as property that the distributee previously contributed as described in section 751(b)(2)(A), and no distribution to a retiring partner is a payment described in section 736(a):

Example 1. (i)(A) A and B are equal partners in personal service partnership PRS. A contributed nondepreciable capital assets (the "Capital Assets") to PRS with a basis and fair market value of $14,000. B contributed unrealized receivables described in paragraph (c) of this section (the "Unrealized Receivables") to PRS with a basis

of zero and fair market value of $14,000. Later, when the fair market value of the Capital Assets had declined to $2,000, B transferred its interest in PRS to T for $9,000 when PRS's balance sheet (reflecting a cash receipts and disbursements method of accounting) was as follows:

Assets

	Adjusted Basis	Fair Market Value
Cash	$ 4,000	$ 4,000
Capital Assets	14,000	2,000
Unrealized Receivables	0	14,000
Total	18,000	20,000

Liabilities and Capital

	Adjusted Basis	Fair Market Value
Liabilities	$2,000	$2,000
Capital:		
A	15,000	9,000
B	1,000	9,000
Total	18,000	20,000

(B) The total amount realized by B is $10,000, consisting of the cash received, $9,000, plus $1,000, B's share of the partnership liabilities assumed by T. *See* section 752. B's interest in the partnership property includes an interest in the partnership's Unrealized Receivables. B's basis in its partnership interest is $2,000 ($1,000, plus $1,000, B's share of partnership liabilities). If section 751(a) did not apply to the sale, B would recognize $8,000 of capital gain from the sale of the interest in PRS. However, section 751(a) does apply to the sale.

(ii) For purposes of section 751(a), the amount of money or the fair market value of property received by the partner in exchange for all or part of his partnership interest must take into account the partner's share of income or gain from section 751 property. If PRS sold all of its section 751 property in a fully taxable transaction immediately prior to the transfer of B's partnership interest to T, B would have been allocated $14,000 of ordinary income from the sale of PRS's Unrealized Receivables under section 704(c). Therefore, B will recognize $14,000 of ordinary income with respect to the Unrealized Receivables. The difference between the amount of capital gain or loss that the partner would realize in the absence of section 751

($8,000) and the amount of ordinary income or loss determined under paragraph (a)(2) of this section ($14,000) is the transferor's capital gain or loss on the sale of its partnership interest. In this case, B will recognize a $6,000 capital loss.

Example 2. (i) A, B, and C each contribute $120 to partnership ABC in exchange for a 1/3 interest. A, B, and C each share in the profits and losses of ABC in accordance with their 1/3 interest. ABC purchases land for $100 in Year 1. At the end of Year 3, when ABC holds $260 in cash and land with a value of $100 and has generated $90 in zero-basis unrealized receivables, ABC distributes $50 cash to C in a current distribution, reducing C's interest in ABC from 1/3 to 1/4. ABC has a section 754 election in effect. To determine if the distribution is a distribution to which section 751(b) applies, ABC must apply the test set forth in paragraph (b)(2) of this section.

(ii)(A) Pursuant to paragraph (b)(2)(iv) of this section, ABC revalues its assets and its partners' capital accounts are increased under §1.704-1(b)(2)(iv)(f) to reflect each partner's share of the unrealized gain in the partnership's assets. Before the distribution, ABC's balance sheet is as follows:

	Tax	Book		Capital	Tax	Book
Cash	$260	$260		A	$120	$150
Unrealized Receivable	0	90		B	120	150
Real Property	100	100		C	120	150
Totals	360	450			360	450

(B) If ABC disposed of all of its assets for cash in an amount equal to the fair market value of such property immediately before the distribution, A, B, and C would each be allocated $30 of net income from ABC's section 751 property. Accordingly, A, B, and C's

net section 751 unrealized gain immediately before the distribution is $30 each under paragraph (b)(2)(ii) of this section.

(iii)(A) After the distribution (but before taking into account any consequences under this section), ABC's balance sheet would be as follows:

	Tax	Book		Capital	Tax	Book
Cash	$210	$210		A	$120	$150
Unrealized Receivable	0	90		B	120	150
Real Property	100	100		C	70	100
Totals	310	400			310	400

(B) If ABC disposed of all of its assets in exchange for cash in amounts equal to the fair market values of those assets immediately after the distribution, A, B, and C would each still be allocated $30 of net income from ABC's section 751 property pursuant to §1.704-3(a)(6). C did not receive any section 751 property in the distribution. Accordingly, A, B, and C's net section 751 unrealized gain immediately after the distribution is $30 each under paragraph (b)(2)(iii) of this section.

(iv) Because no partner's net section 751 unrealized gain is greater immediately before the distribution than immediately after the distribution, and because no partner's net section 751 unrealized loss is greater immediately after the distribution than immediately before the distribution, the distribution is not a section 751(b) distri-

bution under paragraph (b)(2)(i) of this section. Accordingly, section 751(b) does not apply to the distribution.

Example 3. (i) Assume the same facts as in *Example 2* of this paragraph (g), but assume ABC distributes $150 cash to C in complete liquidation of C's interest. To determine if the distribution is a distribution to which section 751(b) applies, ABC must apply the test set forth in paragraph (b)(2) of this section.

(ii)(A) Pursuant to paragraph (b)(2)(iv) of this section, ABC revalues its assets and its partners' capital accounts are increased under §1.704-1(b)(2)(iv)(f) to reflect each partner's share of the unrealized gain in the partnership's assets. Before the distribution, ABC's balance sheet is as follows:

	Tax	Book		Capital	Tax	Book
Cash	$260	$260		A	$120	$150
Unrealized Receivable	0	90		B	120	150
Real Property	100	100		C	120	150
Totals	360	450			360	450

(B) If ABC disposed of all of its assets in exchange for cash in amounts equal to the fair market values of these assets immediately before the distribution, A, B, and C would each be allocated $30 of net income from ABC's section 751 property. Accordingly, A, B, and

C's net section 751 unrealized gain immediately before the distribution is $30 each under paragraph (b)(2)(ii) of this section.

(iii)(A) Because ABC has elected under section 754, and because A recognizes $30 gain on the distribution of cash, the basis of the real property is increased to $130 under section 734(b). After the distribu-

	Tax	Book	Capital	Tax	Book
Cash	$110	$110	A	$120	$150
Unrealized Receivable	0	90	B	120	150
Real Property	130	100	C	0	0
Totals	240	300		240	300

(B) Because C is no longer a partner in ABC, C would not be allocated any net income from ABC's section 751 property immediately after the distribution. Also, C did not receive any section 751 property in the distribution. Accordingly, C's net section 751 unrealized gain immediately after the distribution is $0 under paragraph (b)(2)(iii) of this section.

(iv) Because C's net section 751 unrealized gain is greater immediately before the distribution than immediately after the distribution, section 751(b) applies to the distribution. Under paragraph (b)(2)(i) of this section, C has a section 751(b) amount equal to $30, the amount by which C's share of pre-distribution net section 751 unrealized gain ($30) exceeds C's share of post-distribution net section 751 unrealized gain ($0). Accordingly, paragraph (b)(3)(i) of this section requires C to recognize $30 of ordinary income using a reasonable approach consistent with the purpose of this section. ABC

	Tax	Book	Capital	Tax	Book
Cash	$260	$260	A	$120	$150
Unrealized Receivable	30	90	B	120	150
Real Property	100	100	C	150	150
Totals	390	450		390	450

(vi) After determining the tax consequences of the section 751(b) distribution, the rules of sections 731 through 736 apply. Accordingly, C recognizes no gain or loss under section 731(a) upon the

	Tax	Book	Capital	Tax	Book
Cash	$110	$110	A	$120	$150
Unrealized Receivable	30	90	B	120	150
Real Property	100	100	C	0	0
Totals	240	300		240	300

(vii) Assume alternatively that ABC adopts an approach under which, immediately before the section 751(b) distribution, C is deemed to—

(A) Receive a distribution of ABC's unrealized receivables with a fair market value of $30 and a tax basis of $0;

(B) Sell the unrealized receivable to ABC in exchange for $30, recognizing $30 of ordinary income; and

(C) Contribute the $30 to ABC. Provided the partnership applies the approach consistently for all section 751(b) distributions, ABC's adopted approach is reasonable. After taking into account the tax consequences of the section 751(b) distribution immediately prior to the cash distribution, ABC's modified balance sheet is the same as the balance sheet shown in paragraph (v) of this example.

(viii) After determining the tax consequences of the section 751(b) distribution, the rules of sections 731 through 736 apply. The

	Tax	Basis Adj.	Book	Capital	Tax	Special Basis	Book
Unrealized Receivable	0	25	50	A	25		75
Real Property	50		100	B	25	25	75
Totals	50	25	150		50	25	150

(B) If AB disposed of all of its assets in exchange for cash in amounts equal to the fair market values of these assets immediately before the distribution, A and B would each be allocated $25 of net income from AB's section 751 property. However, B's net income from Unrealized Receivable would be offset by its $25 section 743 adjustment. §1.743-1(j)(3). Accordingly, A and B's net section 751

	Tax	Basis Adj.	Book	Capital	Tax	Carryover Adjustment	Book
Carryover Adjustment		25	0	A	25		25
Real Property	50		100	B	25	25	75
Totals	50	25	100		50	25	100

(B) If AB disposed of all of its assets in exchange for cash in amounts equal to the fair market values of those assets immediately after the distribution, no partner would be allocated net income or loss from section 751 property. However, B has a carryover basis adjustment to ordinary income property of $25 under §§1.743-1(g)(2)(ii) and 1.755-1(c)(4), which B must treat as applied to section 751 property with fair market value of $0 pursuant to paragraph (b)(2)(ii) of this section. Accordingly, B's net section 751 unrealized loss immediately after the distribution is $25 under

tion (but before taking into account any consequences under this section), ABC's balance sheet would be as follows:

considers two approaches, the first of which is described in paragraphs (v) and (vi) of this example, and the second of which is described in paragraphs (vii) and (viii) of this example.

(v) Assume ABC adopts an approach under which, immediately before the section 751(b) distribution, C is deemed to recognize $30 of ordinary income. To reflect C's recognition of $30 of ordinary income, C increases its basis in its ABC partnership interest by $30, and the partnership increases its basis in the unrealized receivable by the $30 of income recognized by C, immediately before the distribution. Provided the partnership applies the approach consistently for all section 751(b) distributions, ABC's adopted approach is reasonable. After taking into account the tax consequences of the section 751(b) distribution immediately prior to the cash distribution, ABC's modified balance sheet is as follows:

distribution. Because C recognizes no gain on the distribution, the basis of the partnership real property is not adjusted. After the distribution, ABC's balance sheet is as follows:

tax consequences under the rules of sections 731 through 736 are the same tax consequences described in paragraph (vi) of this example.

Example 4. (i) A and B are equal partners in a partnership, AB, that owns Unrealized Receivable with a fair market value of $50 and nondepreciable real property with a basis of $50 and a fair market value of $100. A has an adjusted basis in its partnership interest of $25, and B has an adjusted basis in its partnership interest of $50. The partnership has a section 754 election in effect, and B has a basis adjustment under section 743(b) of $25 that is allocated to Unrealized Receivable. AB distributes Unrealized Receivable to A in a current distribution. To determine if the distribution is a distribution to which section 751(b) applies, AB must apply the test set forth in paragraph (b)(2) of this section.

(ii)(A) AB makes a non-mandatory revaluation of its assets and its partners' capital accounts are increased under §1.704-1(b)(2)(iv)(f) to reflect each partner's share of the unrealized gain in the partnership's assets. Before the distribution, AB's balance sheet is as follows:

unrealized gain immediately before the distribution is $25 and $0, respectively, under paragraph (b)(2)(ii) of this section.

(iii)(A) After the distribution (but before taking into account any consequences under this section), AB's balance sheet would be as follows:

paragraph (b)(2)(iii)(A) of this section. If, immediately after the distribution, A disposed of Unrealized Receivable in exchange for $50 cash, A would recognize $50 of net income from section 751 property. Accordingly, A's net section 751 unrealized gain immediately after the distribution is $50 under paragraph (b)(2)(iii)(B) of this section.

(iv) Because B's net section 751 unrealized loss immediately after the distribution ($25) exceeds B's net section 751 unrealized loss immediately before the distribution ($0), the distribution is a section 751(b) distribution. Under paragraph (b)(2)(i) of this section, B has a section 751(b) amount equal to $25, the difference of B's share of pre-distribution net section 751 unrealized gain ($0) and B's share of post-distribution net section 751 unrealized loss ($25). Accordingly, paragraph (b)(3)(i) of this section requires B to account for $25 of ordinary income using a reasonable approach consistent with the purpose of this section.

(v) Assume AB adopts an approach under which, immediately before the section 751(b) distribution, B is deemed to—

(A) Receive a distribution of Unrealized Receivable with a fair market value of $25 and a tax basis of $25 (which consists of B's section 743(b) basis adjustment and is determined solely for purposes

	Tax	Book	Capital	Tax	Book
			A	0	25
Real Property	50	100	B	50	75
Totals	50	100		50	100

(vi) After determining the tax consequences of the section 751(b) distribution, the rules of sections 731 through 736 apply. Accordingly, A recognizes no gain on the distribution of Unrealized Receivable, which A takes with a basis of $25.

Example 5. Capital Gain Recognition Required. (i) A, B, and C are each 1/3 partners in a partnership, ABC, that holds Unrealized Receivable 1 with a fair market value of $90, Unrealized Receivable 2 with a fair market value of $30, and nondepreciable real property with a fair market value of $180. The partnership has a section 754 election in effect. Each of the partners has an adjusted basis in its

	Tax	Book	Capital	Tax	Book
Unrealized Receivable 1	$0	$90	A	$0	$100
Unrealized Receivable 2	0	30	B	0	100
Real Property	0	180	C	0	100
Totals	0	300		0	300

(B) If ABC disposed of all of its assets for cash in an amount equal to the fair market value of such property immediately before the distribution, A, B, and C would each be allocated $40 of net income from ABC's section 751 property ($30 each from Unrealized Receivable 1 and $10 each from Unrealized Receivable 2). Accordingly, A, B, and C's net section 751 unrealized gain immediately

	Tax	Book	Capital	Tax	Book
Unrealized	$0	$30	A	$0	$10
Receivable 2			B	0	100
Real Property	0	180	C	0	100
Totals	0	210		0	210

(B) If ABC disposed of all of its assets in exchange for cash in amounts equal to the fair market values of those assets immediately after the distribution, A, B, and C would each be allocated $10 of net income from ABC's section 751 property ($10 each from Unrealized Receivable 2). If immediately after the distribution, A disposed of Unrealized Receivable 1 in exchange for $90 cash, A would recognize $90 of net income from section 751 property. Accordingly, B and C's net section 751 unrealized gain immediately after the distribution is $10 each under paragraph (b)(2)(iii)(A) of this section, and A's is $100 under paragraphs (b)(2)(iii)(A) and (B) of this section.

(iv) Because B and C's net section 751 unrealized gain is greater immediately before the distribution than immediately after the distribution, the distribution is a section 751(b) distribution. Under paragraph (b)(2)(i) of this section, each of B and C has a section 751(b) amount equal to $30, the amount by which each partner's share of pre-distribution net section 751 unrealized gain ($40) exceeds its share of post-distribution net section 751 unrealized gain ($10). Accordingly, paragraph (b)(3)(i) of this section requires each of B and C to recognize $30 of ordinary income using a reasonable approach consistent with the purpose of this section. ABC considers three approaches, the first of which is described in paragraphs (v) and (vi) of this example, the second of which is described in paragraphs (vii) and (viii) of this example, and the third of which is described in paragraph (ix) of this example.

	Tax	Book	Capital	Tax	Book
Unrealized Receivable 1	$60	$90	A	$60	$100
Unrealized Receivable 2	0	30	B	30	100
Real Property	60	180	C	30	100
Totals	120	300		120	300

(vi) After determining the tax consequences of the section 751(b) distribution, the rules of sections 731 through 736 apply. Thus, Unrealized Receivable 1 would take a $60 basis in A's hands under

of applying a reasonable method consistent with the purposes of section 751(b));

(B) Sell Unrealized Receivable to AB in exchange for $25, so that B recognizes $0 of ordinary income, and AB receives Unrealized Receivable with a basis of $25; and

(C) Contribute the $25 to AB. Provided the partnership applies the approach consistently for all section 751(b) distributions, AB's adopted approach is reasonable. After taking into account the tax consequences of the section 751(b) distribution, AB's modified balance sheet is as follows:

partnership interest of $0 with a fair market value of $100. None of the partners has a capital loss carryforward. ABC distributes to A Unrealized Receivable 1 in a current distribution. To determine if the distribution is a distribution to which section 751(b) applies, ABC must apply the test set forth in paragraph (b)(2) of this section.

(ii)(A) Pursuant to paragraph (b)(2)(iv) of this section, ABC revalues its assets and its partners' capital accounts are increased under §1.704-1(b)(2)(iv)(f) to reflect each partner's share of the unrealized gain in the partnership's assets. Before the distribution, ABC's balance sheet is as follows:

before the distribution is $40 each under paragraph (b)(2)(ii) of this section.

(iii)(A) After the distribution (but before taking into account any consequences under this section), ABC's balance sheet would be as follows:

(v) Assume ABC adopts an approach under which, immediately before the section 751(b) distribution, B and C are each deemed to recognize $30 of ordinary income. To reflect B and C's recognition of $30 of ordinary income, B and C increase their bases in their ABC partnership interests by $30 each, and the partnership increases its basis in Unrealized Receivable 1 by $60 immediately before the distribution to A. Following the distribution to A, A's basis in Unrealized Receivable 1 is $0 under section 732(a)(2). Because ABC has elected under section 754, the distribution of Unrealized Receivable 1 to A would result in a $60 section 734(b) adjustment to Unrealized Receivable 2. See §1.755-1(c)(1). Because that basis adjustment would have altered the amount of net section 751 unrealized gain or loss computed under paragraph (b)(2) of this section, A must recognize $60 of capital gain prior to the distribution of Unrealized Receivable 1 pursuant to paragraph (b)(3)(ii)(A) of this section. This gain recognition increases A's basis in its ABC partnership interest by $60 immediately before the distribution to A, eliminating the section 734(b) adjustment. See section 732(a)(2). In addition, the partnership increases its basis in Real Property by $60 pursuant to paragraph (b)(3)(iii) of this section, and treats A's gain recognized as reducing A's $60 reverse section 704(c) amount in the Real Property. Provided the partnership applies the approach consistently for all section 751(b) distributions, ABC's adopted approach is reasonable. After taking into account the tax consequences of the deemed gain approach described in this example, ABC's modified balance sheet immediately prior to the distribution is as follows:

section 732(a), and no section 734(b) adjustment would be made to Unrealized Receivable 2. After the distribution, ABC's balance sheet is as follows:

	Tax	Book	Capital	Tax	Book
Unrealized Receivable 2	$0	$30	A	$0	$10
			B	30	100
Real Property	60	180	C	30	100
Totals	60	210		60	210

(vii) Assume alternatively that ABC adopts an approach under which, immediately before the section 751(b) distribution, B and C are each deemed to:

(A) Receive a distribution of Unrealized Receivable 1 with a fair market value of $30 and tax basis of $0;

(B) Sell the unrealized receivable to ABC for $30, recognizing $30 of ordinary income; and

(C) Contribute the $30 to ABC. For the same reasons stated in paragraph (v) of this example, A recognizes capital gain of $60. To accomplish this, A, immediately before the section 751(b) distribution, is deemed to:

(1) Receive a distribution of Real Property with a fair market value of $60 and tax basis of $0;

(2) Sell the Real Property to ABC for $60, recognizing $60 of capital gain; and

(3) Contribute the $60 to ABC.

(viii) The partnership treats the $60 of gain recognized by A as reducing A's $60 reverse section 704(c) amount in the Real Property.

	Tax	Book	Capital	Tax	Book
Unrealized Receivable 1	$9	$90	A	$3	$100
Unrealized Receivable 2	0	30	B	3	100
Real Property	0	180	C	3	100
Totals	9	300		9	300

(B) If ABC disposed of all of its assets for cash in an amount equal to the fair market value of such property immediately before the distribution, A, B, and C would each be allocated $37 of net income from ABC's section 751 property ($27 each from Unrealized Receivable 1 and $10 each from Unrealized Receivable 2). Accordingly, A, B, and C's net section 751 unrealized gain immediately

	Tax	Book	Capital	Tax	Book
Unrealized Receivable 2	$6	$30	A	$0	$10
			B	3	100
Real Property	0	180	C	3	100
Totals	6	210		6	210

(B) If ABC disposed of all of its assets for cash in an amount equal to the fair market value of such property immediately after the distribution, taking into account the $6 section 734(b) adjustment allocated to Unrealized Receivable 2, A, B, and C would each be allocated $8 of net income from ABC's section 751 property ($8 each from Unrealized Receivable 2). If, immediately after the distribution, A disposed of Unrealized Receivable 1 for cash in an amount equal to its fair market value, A would recognize $87 of net income from section 751 property. Accordingly, B and C's net section 751 unrealized gain immediately after the distribution is $8 each under paragraph (b)(2)(iii)(A) of this section, and A's is $95 under paragraphs (b)(2)(iii)(A) and (B) of this section.

(iii) Because B and C's net section 751 unrealized gain is greater immediately before the distribution than immediately after the distribution, the distribution is a section 751(b) distribution. Under paragraph (b)(2)(i) of this section, each of B and C has a section 751(b) amount equal to $29, the amount by which each partner's share of pre-distribution net section 751 unrealized gain ($37) exceeds its share of post-distribution net section 751 unrealized gain ($8). Accordingly, paragraph (b)(3)(i) of this section requires each of B and C to recognize $29 of ordinary income using a reasonable approach consistent with the purpose of this section. ABC considers two approaches, the first of which is described in paragraphs (iv) and (v) of this example, and the second of which is described in paragraphs (vi) and (vii) of this example.

	Tax	Book	Capital	Tax	Book
Unrealized Receivable 1	$67	$90	A	$61	$100
Unrealized Receivable 2	0	30	B	32	100
Real Property	58	180	C	32	100
Totals	125	300		125	300

(v) After determining the tax consequences of the section 751(b) distribution, the rules of sections 731 through 736 apply. Thus, A would take a $61 tax basis in Unrealized Receivable 1 under section

Provided the partnership applies the approach consistently for all section 751(b) distributions, ABC's adopted approach is reasonable. Before taking into account the tax consequences of the section 751(b) distribution, ABC's balance sheet is the same as the balance sheet shown in paragraph (v) of this example. After determining the tax consequences of the section 751(b) distribution, the rules of sections 731 through 736 apply. The tax consequences under the rules of sections 731 through 736 are the same tax consequences described in paragraph (vi) of this example.

(ix) Assume alternatively that A does not recognize capital gain of $60. As a result, upon the distribution of Unrealized Receivable 1 to A, ABC makes a $60 section 734(b) adjustment to Unrealized Receivable 2. The adopted approach is not reasonable because it is contrary to paragraph (b)(3)(ii)(A) of this section.

Example 6. Capital Gain Recognition Required. (i)(A) Assume the same facts as *Example 5* of this paragraph (g), except that Unrealized Receivable 1 has a $9 tax basis, and each of the partners has an adjusted basis in its partnership interest of $3. Before the distribution, ABC's balance sheet is as follows:

before the distribution is $37 each under paragraph (b)(2)(ii) of this section.

(ii)(A) After the distribution (but before taking into account any consequences under this section), ABC's balance sheet would be as follows:

(iv) Assume ABC adopts an approach under which, immediately before the section 751(b) distribution, B and C are each deemed to recognize $29 of ordinary income. To reflect B and C's recognition of $29 of ordinary income, B and C increase their bases in their ABC partnership interests by $29 each, and the partnership increases its basis in Unrealized Receivable 1 by $58 to $67 immediately before the distribution to A. Following the distribution to A, A's basis in Unrealized Receivable 1 is $3 under section 732(a)(2). Because ABC has elected under section 754, the distribution of Unrealized Receivable 1 to A would result in a $64 section 734(b) adjustment to Unrealized Receivable 2 (rather than the $6 section 734(b) adjustment computed prior to the application of this section). See § 1.755-1(c)(1). Because that additional basis adjustment would have altered the amount of net section 751 unrealized gain or loss computed under paragraph (b)(2) of this section, A must recognize $58 of capital gain prior to the distribution of Unrealized Receivable 1 pursuant to paragraph (b)(3)(ii)(A) of this section. This gain recognition increases A's basis in its ABC partnership interest by $58 to $61 immediately before the distribution to A. In addition, the partnership increases its basis in Real Property by $58 pursuant to paragraph (b)(3)(iii) of this section, and treats A's gain recognized as reducing A's $60 reverse section 704(c) amount in the Real Property. Provided the partnership applies the approach consistently for all section 751(b) distributions, ABC's adopted approach is reasonable. After taking into account the tax consequences of the deemed gain approach described in this example, ABC's modified balance sheet immediately prior to the distribution is as follows:

732(a), and a $6 section 734(b) adjustment would be made to Unrealized Receivable 2. After the distribution, ABC's balance sheet is as follows:

	Tax	Book	Capital	Tax	Book
Unrealized Receivable 2	$6	$30	A	$0	$10
			B	32	100
Real Property	58	180	C	32	100
Totals	64	210		64	210

(vi) Assume alternatively that ABC adopts an approach under which, immediately before the section 751(b) distribution, B and C are each deemed to:

(A) Receive a distribution of Unrealized Receivable 1 with a fair market value of $29 and tax basis of $0;

(B) Sell the unrealized receivable to ABC for $29, recognizing $29 of ordinary income; and

(C) Contribute the $29 to ABC. For the same reasons stated in paragraph (iv) of this example, A recognizes capital gain of $58. To accomplish this, A, immediately before the section 751(b) distribution, is deemed to:

(1) Receive a distribution of Real Property with a fair market value of $58 and tax basis of $0;

(2) Sell the Real Property to ABC for $58, recognizing $58 of capital gain; and

(3) Contribute the $58 to ABC.

(vii) The partnership treats the $58 of gain recognized by A as reducing A's $60 reverse section 704(c) amount in the Real Property.

Provided the partnership applies the approach consistently for all section 751(b) distributions, ABC's adopted approach is reasonable. After taking into account the tax consequences of the section 751(b) distribution, ABC's balance sheet is the same as the balance sheet shown in paragraph (iv) of this example. After determining the tax consequences of the section 751(b) distribution, the rules of sections 731 through 736 apply. The tax consequences under the rules of sections 731 through 736 are the same tax consequences described in paragraph (v) of this example.

Example 7. Capital Gain Recognition Elective. (i)(A) Assume the same facts as described in Example 6 of this paragraph (g), including that ABC adopts the deemed gain approach described in paragraph (iv), except that ABC does not have a section 754 election in effect. As in *Example 6*, each of A, B, and C has net section 751 unrealized gain of $37 immediately before the distribution. After the distribution (but before taking into account any consequences under this section), ABC's balance sheet would be as follows:

	Tax	Book	Capital	Tax	Book
Unrealized Receivable 2	$0	$30	A	0	10
			B	3	100
Real Property	0	180	C	3	100
Totals	0	210		6	210

(B) If ABC disposed of all of its assets for cash in an amount equal to the fair market value of such property immediately after the distribution, because there is no section 734(b) adjustment allocated to Unrealized Receivable 2, A, B, and C would each be allocated $10 of net income from ABC's section 751 property ($10 each from Unrealized Receivable 2). If, immediately after the distribution, A disposed of Unrealized Receivable 1 for cash in an amount equal to its fair market value, A would recognize $87 of net income from section 751 property. Accordingly, B and C's net section 751 unrealized gain immediately after the distribution is $10 each under paragraph (b)(2)(iii)(A) of this section, and A's is $97 under paragraphs (b)(2)(iii)(A) and (B) of this section.

(ii) Because B and C's net section 751 unrealized gain is greater immediately before the distribution than immediately after the distribution, the distribution is a section 751(b) distribution. Under paragraph (b)(2)(i) of this section B and C each have a section 751(b) amount equal to $27, the amount by which those partners' shares of pre-distribution net section 751 unrealized gain ($37), exceeds their shares of post-distribution net section 751 unrealized gain ($10). Accordingly, paragraph (b)(3)(i) of this section requires each of B and C to recognize $27 of ordinary income using a reasonable approach consistent with the purpose of this section.

(iii) Assume ABC adopts an approach under which, immediately before the section 751(b) distribution, B and C are each deemed to recognize $27 of ordinary income. To reflect B and C's recognition of $27 of ordinary income, B and C increase their bases in their ABC

partnership interests by $27, and the partnership increases its basis in Unrealized Receivable 1 by $54 to $63 immediately before the distribution to A. The distribution to A results in an adjustment to the basis of the distributed Unrealized Receivable 1 under section 732(a)(2), reducing the basis of Unrealized Receivable 1 in the hands of A to $3. Because ABC has not elected under section 754 and does not have a substantial basis reduction under section 734(d), this $60 decrease to the basis of Unrealized Receivable 1 will not affect the basis of other assets held by ABC. Thus, the distribution does not alter the amount of net section 751 unrealized gain or loss computed under paragraph (b)(2) of this section. Accordingly, A is not obligated under paragraph (b)(3)(ii)(A) of this section to recognize gain or income upon the distribution of Unrealized Receivable 1. However, A may elect to recognize $60 of capital gain under paragraph (b)(3)(ii)(B) of this section to eliminate the section 732 basis adjustment to the distributed Unrealized Receivable 1 which would otherwise cause A's net section 751 unrealized gain to be greater immediately after the distribution than it was immediately before the distribution. This gain recognition increases A's basis in its ABC partnership interest by $60 immediately before the distribution to A. In addition, the partnership increases its basis in Real Property by $60 pursuant to paragraph (b)(3)(iii) of this section, and treats A's gain recognized as reducing A's $60 reverse section 704(c) amount in the Real Property. A receives the distributed Unrealized Receivable 1 with a basis of $63, so that the distribution does not increase A's net section 751 unrealized gain. After the distribution, ABC's balance sheet is as follows:

	Tax	Book	Capital	Tax	Book
Unrealized Receivable 2	$0	$30	A	0	10
			B	30	100
Real Property	60	180	C	30	100
Totals	60	210		60	210

Example 8. (i) A, B, and C, each domestic corporations, are 1/3 partners in a domestic partnership ABC. ABC purchased 100% of the stock in two foreign corporations, X and Y. X and Y each have one share of stock outstanding. ABC has a basis of $15 in its X share with a fair market value of $150, and a basis of $3 in its Y share with a fair market value of $30. The earnings and profits of X that are attributable to ABC's X stock under section 1248 are $135; the earnings and profits of Y that are attributable to ABC's Y stock are $27. ABC has a section 754 election in effect. Each of A, B, and C has a partnership interest with an adjusted basis of $6 and a fair market value of $60. On January 1, 2013, ABC distributes the Y share to A in a current

distribution. To determine if the distribution is a distribution to which section 751(b) applies, ABC must apply the test set forth in paragraph (b)(2) of this section.

(ii)(A) Pursuant to paragraph (b)(2)(iv) of this section, ABC revalues its assets. Its partners' capital accounts are increased under §1.704-1(b)(2)(iv)(f) to reflect each partner's share of the unrealized gain in the partnership's assets. Before the distribution, ABC's balance sheet is as follows (with the shares of X and Y each reflected as having both an unrealized receivable component and a capital gain component):

	Tax	Book	Capital	Tax	Book
X stock (total)	$15	$150	A	$6	$60
Unrealized receivable	0	135	B	6	60
Capital gain asset	15	15	C	6	60
Y stock (total)	3	30			

	Tax	Book	Capital	Tax	Book
Unrealized receivable	0	27			
Capital gain asset	3	3			
Totals	18	180		18	180

(B) If ABC disposed of all of its assets for cash in an amount equal to the assets' fair market value immediately before the distribution, A, B, and C would each be allocated $54 of net income from ABC's section 751 property ($45 each from X stock and $9 each from Y stock). Accordingly, A, B, and C's net section 751 unrealized gain immediately before the distribution is $54 each under paragraph (b)(2)(ii) of this section.

(iii)(A) After the distribution (but before taking into account any consequences under this section), ABC's balance sheet is as follows:

	Tax	Book	Capital	Tax	Book
X stock (total)	$15	$150	A	$3	$30
Unrealized receivable	0	135	B	6	60
Capital gain asset	15	15	C	6	60
Totals	15	150		15	150

(B) If ABC disposed of its asset for cash in an amount equal to the fair market value of that asset immediately after the distribution, A, B, and C would each be allocated $45 of net income from ABC's section 751 property pursuant to §1.704-3(a)(6). A, however, received Y stock, which continues to be section 751 property in A's hands under section 735(a), with a holding period that includes the partnership's holding period under section 735(b). If A disposed of its Y stock for cash in an amount equal to its fair market value, A would recognize $27 of gain under section 751(b) on the Y stock (a foreign corporation described in section 1248) that is included in A's income under section 1248 as a dividend to the extent of the attributable earnings. Accordingly, B and C's net section 751 unrealized gain immediately after the distribution is $45 each under paragraph (b)(2)(iii)(A) of this section, and A's is $72 under paragraphs (b)(2)(iii)(A) and (B) of this section.

(iv) Because B and C's net section 751 unrealized gain is greater immediately before the distribution than immediately after the distribution, the distribution is a section 751(b) distribution. Under paragraph (b)(2)(i) of this section, B and C each have a section 751(b) amount equal to $9, the amount by which those partners shares of pre-distribution net section 751 unrealized gain ($54) exceeds their shares of post-distribution net section 751 unrealized gain ($45). Accordingly, paragraph (b)(3)(i) of this section requires each of B and C to recognize $9 as a dividend under section 1248 using a reasonable approach consistent with the purpose of this section. ABC considers two approaches, the first of which is described in paragraphs (v) and (vi) of this example, and the second of which is described in paragraph (vii) of this example.

(v) Assume ABC adopts an approach under which, immediately before the section 751(b) distribution, B and C are each deemed to recognize $9 of gain includible as a dividend with respect to the distribution of the Y stock, which is treated as a sale or exchange for purposes of section 1248. To reflect B and C's recognition of $9 of dividend income, B and C increase the bases in their ABC partnership interests by $9 each, and the partnership increases its basis in the Y share unrealized receivable component by $18 immediately before the distribution. The portion of the unrealized receivable component of the Y share that is deemed to be sold or exchanged under section 1248 has a new holding period beginning on the day after the section 751(b) distribution ("the new holding period portion"). The earnings and profits of $18 attributable to the new holding period portion of the Y share are 2/3 of the total earnings and profits attributable to the Y share immediately before the distribution (B and C's $18 aggregate gain recognized under section 751(b) divided by $27, the aggregate of all the partners' net section 751 unrealized gain immediately before the distribution). The remaining earnings and profits are allocated to the remainder of the Y share. Provided the partnership applies the approach consistently for all section 751(b) distributions, ABC's adopted approach is reasonable. After taking into account the tax consequences of the deemed gain approach described in this example, ABC's modified balance sheet immediately before the distribution is as follows:

	Tax	Book	Capital	Tax	Book
X stock	$15	$150	A	$6	$60
Unrealized receivable	0	135	B	15	60
Capital gain asset	15	15	C	15	60
Y stock	21	30			
New holding period portion	18	18			
Unrealized receivable	0	9			
Capital gain asset	3	3			
Totals	36	180		36	180

(vi) After determining the tax consequences of the section 751(b) distribution, the rules of sections 731 through 736 apply. Accordingly, the basis of the distributed Y stock in A's hands is limited under section 732(a)(2) to A's $6 basis in its partnership interest. Pursuant to section 732(c)(3)(B), the $15 decrease in basis from $21 to $6 must be allocated to the distributed components of the Y stock in proportion to their respective adjusted bases. A must allocate the $15 decrease in basis in the Y stock between the new holding period portion (which has a basis of $18) and the remainder of the Y share (which has a basis of $3). Accordingly, A receives the new holding period portion of the Y share with an adjusted basis of $5.14 ($6 multiplied by ($18 divided by $21)), and the remainder of the Y share with an adjusted basis of $0.86 ($6 multiplied by ($3 divided by $21)). Because the basis of the distributed Y stock in A's hands was reduced from $21 (the basis of the Y stock in the hands of ABC) to $6 (the basis in A's hands), ABC must increase the basis of its remaining asset under section 734(b)(1)(B) by $15. ABC must allocate the $15 under §1.755-1(c)(1)(i) to the capital gain portion of the X stock. After the distribution, ABC's balance sheet is as follows:

	Tax	Book	Capital	Tax	Book
X stock	$30	$150	A	$0	$30
Unrealized receivable	0	135	B	15	60
Capital gain asset	30	15	C	15	60
Totals	30	150		30	150

(vii) Assume alternatively that ABC adopts an approach under which, immediately before the section 751(b) distribution, B and C are each deemed to:

(A) Receive a distribution of the portion of the partnership's Y stock with a fair market value of $9 and a tax basis of $0;

(B) Sell the Y stock back to ABC for $9, recognizing $9 of gain includible as a dividend; and

(C) Contribute the $9 to ABC. ABC will be deemed to have purchased for $18 a portion of the Y stock unrealized receivable component, which will have a new holding period. The deemed sale of Y stock by B and C to ABC will be treated as a sale or exchange for purposes of section 1248. Provided that the partnership applies the approach consistently for all section 751(b) distributions, Partnership

ABC's adopted approach is reasonable. After taking into account the tax consequences of the deemed transaction, ABC's balance sheet is the same as the balance sheet shown in paragraph (v) of this example. After taking into account the tax consequences of the section 751(b) distribution, ABC's balance sheet is the same as the balance sheet shown in paragraph (vi) of this example.

(viii) Assume that in a later unrelated transaction, A sells its Y stock at a time when its fair market value, earnings and profits, and adjusted basis have not changed. The sale of Y stock by A is a sale or exchange subject to section 1248. Pursuant to §1.732-1(c)(2)(v), in determining the dividend portion of its gain on the Y stock under section 1248, A does not take into account the $15 decrease in basis under section 732. Accordingly, upon the sale of the Y stock, A recognizes $9 of gain, the lesser of $9 ($0 gain on the new holding period portion ($18 fair market value minus $18 basis) plus $9 gain on the remainder ($12 fair market value minus $3 basis)) or $9 (earnings and profits attributable to the remainder of the Y share) as dividend income under section 1248. A recognizes $15 of capital gain in addition to the $9 of dividend income ($30 amount realized minus $15 ($6 aggregate basis in Y share plus $9 section 1248 dividend income)).

(ix) Assume that ABC also sells its X stock in a later unrelated transaction at a time when its fair market value has declined to $120 but earnings and profits have remained the same. ABC has not made an election under § 1.755-1(c)(2)(vi). In determining the dividend portion of its gain on the X stock under section 1248, ABC does not take into account the $15 increase in basis under section 734(b). Upon the sale of the stock, ABC recognizes $105, the lesser of $105 ($120 - $15) or $135 (earnings and profits attributable to the X stock for the partnership's holding period) as dividend income. In addition to the $105 of gain includible as a dividend, ABC recognizes $15 of capital loss ($120 amount realized minus $135 ($30 aggregate basis in X stock plus $105 section 1248 dividend income)).

Example 9. (i) Assume the same facts as in *Example 8* of this paragraph (g), except assume that Partnership ABC makes an election under § 1.755-1(c)(2)(vi). As in *Example 8*, paragraph (b)(3)(i) of this section requires each of B and C to recognize $9 as a dividend under section 1248 using a reasonable approach consistent with the purpose of this section for the reasons described in paragraphs (ii) through (iv) of *Example 8*. Further assume that ABC adopts the deemed gain approach described in paragraph (v) of *Example 8*. As in *Example 8*, B and C are each deemed to recognize $9 of dividend income with respect to the distribution of the Y stock, which is

treated as a sale or exchange for purposes of section 1248. To reflect B and C's recognition of $9 of dividend income, B and C increase the bases in their ABC partnership interests by $9 each. The partnership increases its basis in the Y share unrealized receivable component by $18 immediately before the distribution. The portion of the unrealized receivable component of the Y share that is deemed to be sold or exchanged under section 1248 has a new holding period beginning on the day after the section 751(b) distribution ("the new holding period portion").

(ii) Because ABC makes an election under § 1.755-1(c)(2)(vi), the distribution of the Y share to A results in a $15 section 734(b) adjustment to the unrealized receivable component of the X share. Because that basis adjustment would have altered the amount of net section 751 unrealized gain or loss computed under paragraph (b)(2) of this section, A must recognize $15 of gain with respect to the X share pursuant to paragraph (b)(3)(ii)(A) of this section. Also pursuant to paragraph (b)(3)(ii)(A) of this section, A's recognition of income with respect to the X stock is a sale or exchange for purposes of section 1248 and begins a new holding period for this portion of ABC's X stock, including for purposes of attributing earnings and profits. This income recognition increases A's basis in its ABC partnership interest by $15 immediately before the distribution to A. In addition, the partnership increases its basis in the X share by $15, immediately before the distribution to A. The partnership treats the $15 of dividend income recognized by A as reducing A's $15 reverse section 704(c) amount in the X stock. Provided the partnership applies the approach consistently for all section 751(b) distributions, ABC's adopted approach is reasonable. After taking into account the tax consequences of the deemed gain approach described above, ABC's balance sheet is as follows:

	Tax	Book	Capital	Tax	Book
X stock	$30	$150	A	$21	$60
Unrealized receivable	0	120	B	15	60
Capital gain asset	30	30	C	15	60
Y stock	21	30			
Unrealized receivable	0	9			
Capital gain asset	21	21			
Totals	51	180		51	180

(iii)(A) After determining the tax consequences of the section 751(b) distribution, the rules of sections 731 through 736 apply. Accordingly, the Y stock would take a $21 basis in A's hands under

section 732(a), and no section 734(b) adjustment would be made to the X stock. After the distribution, ABC's balance sheet is as follows:

	Tax	Book	Capital	Tax	Book
X stock	$30	$150	A	$0	$30
Unrealized receivable	0	120	B	15	60
Capital gain asset	30	30	C	15	60
Totals	30	150		30	150

(B) If the partnership sells the X stock, the gain recognized is $120 ($150 - $30), all of which is recharacterized as a dividend under section 1248. Because A's recognition of $15 of dividend income

reduced A's reverse section 704(c) amount in the X stock, this gain is allocated $45 to B, $45 to C, and $30 to A.

☐ Par. 18. For each section listed in the table, remove the language in the "Remove" column and add in its place the language in the "Add" column as set forth below:

Section	Remove	Add
§ 1.751-1, paragraph (c)(4)(i) first and last sentences	sections 731, 736, 741, and 751	sections 731, 732, and 741 (but not for purposes of section 736)
§ 1.751-1, paragraph (c)(4)(ii), first and last sentences	sections 731, 736, 741, and 751	sections 731, 732, and 741 (but not for purposes of section 736)
§ 1.751-1, paragraph (c)(4)(iii) first and last sentences	sections 731, 736, 741, and 751	sections 731, 732, and 741 (but not for purposes of section 736)
§ 1.751-1, paragraph (c)(4)(iv) first and last sentences	sections 731, 736, 741, and 751	sections 731, 732, and 741 (but not for purposes of section 736)
§ 1.751-1, paragraph (c)(4)(v) first and last sentences	sections 731, 736, 741, and 751	sections 731, 732, and 741 (but not for purposes of section 736)
§ 1.751-1, paragraph (c)(4)(vii) first and last sentences	sections 731, 736, 741, and 751	sections 731, 732, and 741 (but not for purposes of section 736)
§ 1.751-1, paragraph (c)(4)(viii) First and last sentences	sections 731, 736, 741, and 751	sections 731, 732, and 741 (but not for purposes of section 736)
§ 1.751-1, paragraph (c)(4)(ix) first and last sentences	sections 731, 736, 741, and 751	sections 731, 732, and 741 (but not for purposes of section 736)
§ 1.751-1, paragraph (d)(2)(i) last sentence	section 1221(1)	section 1221(a)(1)
§ 1.751-1, paragraph (d)(2)(ii) second sentence	section 1221(4)	section 1221(a)(4)

Section 752: Related Party Rules: Recourse Liabilities of a Partnership

Section 752: Related Party Rules: Recourse Liabilities of a Partnership.—Amendments to Reg. §§ 1.752-0 and 1.752-2, relating to recourse liabilities of a partnership and the special rules for related persons, are proposed (published in the Federal Register on December 16, 2013) (REG-136984-12).

☐ Par. 2. Section 1.752-0 is amended by:

1. Revising the entry for §1.752-2(a) and adding new entries for §1.752-2(a)(1) and (a)(2).

2. Revising the entry for §1.752-4(b)(2); removing the entries for §1.752-4(b)(2)(i), (b)(2)(ii), and (b)(2)(iii); redesignating the entries for §1.752-4(b)(2)(iv), (b)(2)(iv)(A) and (b)(2)(iv)(B) as §1.752-4(b)(4), (b)(4)(i), and (b)(4)(ii), respectively; and removing the entry for §1.752-4(b)(2)(iv)(C).

3. Adding new entries for §1.752-4(b)(3) and (b)(5).

The revisions and additions read as follows:

§1.752-0. Table of contents.

§1.752-2. Partner's share of recourse liabilities.

   (a) *Special rules.*—Partner's share of recourse liabilities.
     (1) In general.
     (2) Overlapping economic risk of loss.

         * * *

§1.752-4. Special rules.

         * * *

☐ Par. 3. Section 1.752-2 is amended by:

1. Redesignating paragraph (a) as paragraph (a)(1) and adding a heading to paragraph (a).

2. Adding paragraph (a)(2).

3. Adding *Example 9 to* paragraph (f).

4. Revising paragraphs (i)(1) and (2).

5. Adding a sentence to the end of paragraph (l).

The additions and revisions read as follows:

§1.752-2. Partner's share of recourse liabilities.—(a) *Partner's share of recourse liabilities.*—* * *

   (2) *Overlapping economic risk of loss.*—For purposes of determining a partner's share of a recourse partnership liability, the amount of the partnership liability is taken into account only once. If the aggregate amount of the economic risk of loss that all partners are determined to bear with respect to a partnership liability (or portion thereof) under paragraph (a)(1) of this section (without regard to this paragraph (a)(2)) exceeds the amount of such liability (or portion thereof), then the economic risk of loss borne by each partner with respect to such liability shall equal the amount determined by multiplying:

     (i) The amount of such liability (or portion thereof) by

     (ii) The fraction obtained by dividing the amount of the economic risk of loss that such partner is determined to bear with respect to that liability (or portion thereof) under paragraph (a)(1) of this section, by the sum of such amounts for all partners.

         * * *

   (f) * * *

Example 9. Overlapping economic risk of loss. (i) A and B are unrelated equal members of limited liability company, AB. AB is treated as a partnership for federal tax purposes. AB borrows $1,000 from Bank. A guarantees payment for the entire amount of AB's

$1,000 liability and B guarantees payment for $500 of the liability. Both A and B waive their rights of contribution against each other.

   (ii) Because the aggregate amount of A's and B's economic risk of loss under paragraph (a)(1) of this section ($1,500) exceeds the amount of AB's liability ($1,000), the economic risk of loss borne by A and B each is determined under paragraph (a)(2) of this section. Under paragraph (a)(2) of this section, A's economic risk of loss equals $1,000 multiplied by $1,000/$1,500 or $667, and B's economic risk of loss equals $1,000 multiplied by $500/$1,500 or $333.

         * * *

   (i) * * *

   (1) The amount of liabilities with respect to which the upper-tier partnership has the payment obligation or is the lender as provided in paragraph (c) of this section; and

   (2) The amount of any other liabilities with respect to which partners of the upper-tier partnership bear the economic risk of loss, provided the partner is not a partner in the lower-tier partnership.

         * * *

   (l) * * * Paragraphs (a)(2), (f) *Example 9,* and (i) of this section apply to liabilities incurred or assumed by a partnership on or after the date these proposed regulations are published as final regulations in the **Federal Register**, other than liabilities incurred or assumed by a partnership pursuant to a written binding contract in effect prior to that date.

Certain Interests in Partnerships: Treated as Stock or Indebtedness

Certain Interests in Partnerships: Treated as Stock or Indebtedness.—Amendments to Reg. §1.752-2, addressing the treatment of instruments issued by partnerships, consolidated groups, and certain transactions involving qualified cash-management arrangements, are proposed (published in the Federal Register on October 21, 2016) (REG-130314-16).

Par. 4. Section 1.752-2 is amended by:

1. Revising paragraph (c)(3).

2. Revising paragraph (l)(4).

The addition and revision read as follows

§1.752-2. Partner's share of recourse liabilities.

         * * *

   (c) * * *

   (3) [The text of the proposed amendment to §1.752-2(c)(3) is the same as the text of §1.752-2T(c)(3) as added by T.D. 9790.]

   (l) * * *

   (4) [The text of the proposed amendment to §1.752-2(l)(4) is the same as the text of §1.752-2T(l)(4) as added by T.D. 9790.]

Section 752: Related Party Rules: Recourse Liabilities of a Partnership

Section 752: Related Party Rules: Recourse Liabilities of a Partnership.—Amendments to Reg. §§1.752-4 and 1.752-5, relating to recourse liabilities of a partnership and the special rules for related persons, are proposed (published in the Federal Register on December 16, 2013) (REG-136984-12).

☐ Par. 4. Section 1.752-4 is amended by:

1. Removing the word "and" at the end of paragraph (b)(1)(ii).

2. Removing "267(f)(1)(A)." at the end of (b)(1)(iii) and adding in its place "267(f)(1)(A); and".

3. Adding paragraph (b)(1)(iv).

4. Revising paragraph (b)(2).

5. Adding paragraphs (b)(3), (4), and (5).

The additions and revisions read as follows:

§1.752-4. Special rules.

         * * *

   (b) * * *

   (1) * * *

§1.752-0. Table of contents. (continued)

§1.752-2. Partner's share of recourse liabilities.

   (b) * * *
     (2) Related partner exception.
     (3) Person related to more than one partner.
     (4) Special rule where entity structured to avoid related person status.
       (i) In general.
       (ii) Ownership interest.
     (5) Examples.

(iv) Disregard section 267(c)(1) in determining whether stock of a corporation owned, directly or indirectly, by or for a partnership is considered as being owned proportionately by or for its partners if the corporation is a lender as provided in § 1.752-2(c) or has a payment obligation with respect to a liability of the partnership.

(2) *Related partner exception.*—Notwithstanding paragraph (b)(1) of this section (which defines related person), if a person that owns (directly or indirectly through one or more partnerships) an interest in a partnership is a lender as provided in § 1.752-2(c) or has a payment obligation with respect to a partnership liability, or portion thereof, then other persons owning interests directly or indirectly (through one or more partnerships) in that partnership are not treated as related to that person for purposes of determining the economic risk of loss borne by each of them for such partnership liability, or portion thereof. This paragraph (b)(2) does not apply when determining a partner's interest under the de minimis rules in § 1.752-2(d) and (e).

(3) *Person related to more than one partner.*—If a person that is a lender as provided in § 1.752-2(c) or that has a payment obligation with respect to a partnership liability, or portion thereof, is related to more than one partner under paragraph (b)(1) of this section, the partnership liability, or a portion thereof, is shared equally among such partners.

(4) *Special rule where entity structured to avoid related person status.*—(i) *In general.*—If—

(A) A partnership liability is owed to or guaranteed by another entity that is a partnership, an S corporation, a C corporation, or a trust;

(B) A partner or related person owns (directly or indirectly) a 20 percent or more ownership interest in the other entity; and

(C) A principal purpose of having the other entity act as a lender or guarantor of the liability was to avoid the determination that the partner that owns the interest bears the economic risk of loss for federal income tax purposes for all or part of the liability; then the partner is treated as holding the other entity's interest as a creditor or guarantor to the extent of the partner's or related person's ownership interest in the entity.

(ii) *Ownership interest.*—For purposes of paragraph (b)(4)(i) of this section, a person's ownership interest in:

(A) A partnership equals the partner's highest percentage interest in any item of partnership loss or deduction for any taxable year;

(B) An S corporation equals the percentage of the outstanding stock in the S corporation owned by the shareholder;

(C) A C corporation equals the percentage of the fair market value of the issued and outstanding stock owned by the shareholder; and

(D) A trust equals the percentage of the actuarial interests owned by the beneficial owner of the trust.

(5) *Examples.*—The following examples illustrate the principles of paragraph (b) of this section.

Example 1. Person related to more than one partner. A owns 100 percent of X, a corporation. X owns 100 percent of Y, a corporation. A and X are equal members of P, a limited liability company treated as a partnership for federal tax purposes. Y guarantees payment of a liability of P of $1,000. A and X are not lenders as provided in § 1.752-2(c) and do not otherwise have a payment obligation with respect to the liability. Therefore, paragraph (b)(2) of this section does not apply for purposes of determining the economic risk of loss borne by A and X. Under paragraph (b)(1) of this section, Y is related to A and X. Therefore, under paragraph (b)(3) of this section, A and X each have a $500 share of the $1,000 liability.

Example 2. Related partner exception. A owns 100 percent of two corporations, X and Y. A and Y are members of P, a limited liability company treated as a partnership for federal tax purposes. P borrows $1,000 from Bank. A and X each guarantee payment of the $1,000 debt owed to Bank. A and Y are not treated as related to each other pursuant to paragraph (b)(2) of this section because A has the payment obligation with respect to the $1,000 debt pursuant to § 1.752-2(b). Y is therefore not treated as related to X. Because A is the only partner that bears the economic risk of loss for P's $1,000 liability, A's share of the liability is $1,000 under § 1.752-2(a)(1).

Example 3. Related partner exception. A owns 100 percent of two corporations, X and Y. X owns 79 percent of a corporation, Z, and Y owns the remaining 21 percent of Z. X and Y are members of P, a limited liability company treated as a partnership for federal tax purposes. P borrows $2,000 from Bank. Both X and Z guarantee payment of the $2,000 debt owed to Bank. X has a payment obligation with respect to P's $2,000 liability; therefore, paragraph (b)(2) of this section applies and X and Y are not treated as related for purposes of determining the economic risk of loss borne by each of them for P's $2,000 liability. Because X and Y are not treated as related, and neither owns an 80 percent or more interest in Z, neither X nor Y is treated as related to Z under paragraph (b)(1) of this section. Because X bears the economic risk of loss for P's $2,000 liability, X's share of the liability is $2,000 under § 1.752-2(a)(1).

Example 4. Related partner exception and person related to more than one partner. Same facts as in *Example 3*, but X guarantees payment of only $1,200 of the debt owed to Bank and Z guarantees payment of $2,000. Pursuant to paragraph (b)(2) of this section, X and Y are not treated as related to the extent of X's $1,200 guarantee. Because X bears the economic risk of loss for $1,200 of P's $2,000 liability, X's share of the liability is $1,200 under § 1.752-2(a)(1). In addition, because paragraph (b)(2) of this section does not apply with respect to the remaining portion of the liability that X did not guarantee, X and Y are treated as related for purposes of the remaining $800 of the liability pursuant to paragraph (b)(1) of this section. Therefore, Z is treated as related to X and Y under paragraph (b)(1) of this section. Pursuant to paragraph (b)(3) of this section, X and Y share the $800 equally. In sum, X's share of P's $2,000 liability is $1,600 ($1,200 under § 1.752-2(a)(1) and $400 under paragraph (b)(3) of this section) and Y's share of P's $2,000 liability is $400 under paragraph (b)(3) of this section.

Example 5. Entity structured to avoid related person status. A, B, and C form a general partnership, ΛBC. A, B, and C are equal partners, each contributing $1,000 to the partnership. A and B want to loan money to ABC and have the loan treated as nonrecourse for purposes of section 752. A and B form partnership AB to which each contributes $50,000. A and B share losses equally in partnership AB. Partnership AB loans partnership ABC $100,000 on a nonrecourse basis secured by the property ABC buys with the loan. Under these facts and circumstances, A and B bear the economic risk of loss with respect to the partnership liability equally based on their percentage interest in losses of partnership AB.

* * *

☐ Par. 5. Section 1.752-5 is amended by adding a second sentence in paragraph (a) and removing the word "However" at the beginning of the third sentence and adding in its place "In addition".

The addition reads as follows:

§ 1.752-5. Effective dates and transition rules.—(a) * * * However, § 1.752-4(b)(1)(iv), (b)(2), (b)(3), and (b)(5) *Examples 1, 2, 3,* and *4* apply to any liability incurred or assumed by a partnership on or after the date that these regulations are published as final regulations in the **Federal Register**, other than a liability incurred or assumed by a partnership pursuant to a written binding contract in effect prior to that date. * * *

* * *

Section 754 Election Statement: Steamlining

Section 754 Election Statement: Steamlining.—Amendments to Reg. § 1.754-1, relating to the requirements for making a valid election under section 754 of the Internal Revenue Code of 1986, are proposed (published in the Federal Register on October 12, 2017) (REG-116256-17).

Par 2. Section 1.754-1 is amended by revising the fourth sentence of paragraph (b)(1) and adding new paragraph (d) to read as follows:

§ 1.754-1. Time and manner of making election to adjust basis of partnership property.

* * *

(b) * * *

(1) * * * The statement required by this paragraph (b)(1) must set forth the name and address of the partnership making the election, and contain a declaration that the partnership elects under section 754 to apply the provisions of section 734(b) and section 743(b). * * *

* * *

(d) *Applicability date.*—The fourth sentence of paragraph (b)(1) of this section applies to taxable years ending on or after the date these regulations are published as final regulations in the Federal Register. Taxpayers may, however, rely on the fourth sentence of paragraph (b)(1) of this section for periods prior to the date these regulations are published as final regulations in the Federal Register.

Partners and Partnerships: American Jobs Creation Act of 2004 and Taxpayer Relief Act of 1997: Guidance

Partners and Partnerships: American Jobs Creation Act of 2004 and Taxpayer Relief Act of 1997: Guidance.—Amendments to Reg. §1.755-1, providing guidance on certain provisions of the American Jobs Creation Act of 2004, conforming the regulations to statutory changes in the Taxpayer Relief Act of 1997, modifying the basis allocation rules to prevent certain unintended consequences of the current basis allocation rules for substituted basis transactions and providing additional guidance on allocations resulting from revaluations of partnership property, are proposed (published in the Federal Register on January 16, 2014) (REG-144468-05) (corrected April 15, 2014).

☐ Par. 9. Section 1.755-1 is amended by:

1. Revising paragraph (b)(5).
2. Redesignating paragraph (e) as paragraph (f).
3. Adding a new paragraph (e).
4. Revising newly redesignated paragraph (f).

The revisions and addition read as follows:

§1.755-1. Rules for allocation of basis.

* * *

(b) * * *

* * *

(5) *Substituted basis transactions.*—(i) *In general.*—This paragraph (b)(5) applies to basis adjustments under section 743(b) that result from exchanges in which the transferee's basis in the partnership interest is determined in whole or in part by reference to the transferor's basis in that interest and from exchanges in which the transferee's basis in the partnership interest is determined by reference to other property held at any time by the transferee. For example, this paragraph (b)(5) applies if a partnership interest is contributed to a corporation in a transaction to which section 351 applies, if a partnership interest is contributed to a partnership in a transaction to which section 721(a) applies, or if a partnership interest is distributed by a partnership in a transaction to which section 731(a) applies.

(ii) *Allocations between classes of property.*—(A) *No adjustment.*—If the total amount of the basis adjustment under section 743(b) is zero, then no adjustment to the basis of partnership property will be made under this paragraph (b)(5).

(B) *Increases.*—If there is an increase in basis to be allocated to partnership assets, the increase must be allocated between capital gain property and ordinary income property in proportion to, and to the extent of, the gross gain or gross income (including any remedial allocations under §1.704-3(d)) that would be allocated to the transferee (to the extent attributable to the acquired partnership interest) from the hypothetical sale of all property in each class. Any remaining increase must be allocated between the classes in proportion to the fair market value of all property in each class.

(C) *Decreases.*—If there is a decrease in basis to be allocated to partnership assets, the decrease must be allocated between capital gain property and ordinary income property in proportion to, and to the extent of, the gross loss (including any remedial allocations under §1.704-3(d)) that would be allocated to the transferee (to the extent attributable to the acquired partnership interest) from the hypothetical sale of all property in each class. Any remaining decrease must be allocated between the classes in proportion to the transferee's shares of the adjusted bases of all property in each class (as adjusted under the preceding sentence).

Assets	Adjusted basis
Intangible 1	$30
Land	$200
50% interest in LTP	$190

LTP, a partnership, has a section 754 election in effect for the year of the distribution. LTP owns three assets with the following adjusted bases and fair market values:

Assets	Adjusted basis
Intangible 2	$340
Intangible 3	$20
Inventory	$20

UTP distributes its interest in LTP in redemption of A's interest in UTP. At the time of the distribution, A's adjusted basis in its UTP interest is $140. A recognizes no gain or loss on the distribution. Under section 732(b), A's basis in the distributed LTP interest is $140. Under sections 734(b) and 755, UTP increases its adjusted basis in Intangible 1 by $50, the amount of the basis adjustment to the LTP interest in the hands of A.

(ii) The amount of the basis adjustment with respect to LTP under section 743(b) is the difference between A's basis in LTP of

(iii) *Allocations within the classes.*—(A) *Increases.*—If, under paragraph (b)(5)(ii) of this section, there is an increase in basis to be allocated within a class, the increase must be allocated first to properties with unrealized appreciation in proportion to the transferee's share of the respective amounts of unrealized appreciation (to the extent attributable to the acquired partnership interest) before the increase (but only to the extent of the transferee's share of each property's unrealized appreciation). Any remaining increase must be allocated among the properties within the class in proportion to their fair market values.

(B) *Decreases.*—If, under paragraph (b)(5)(ii) of this section, there is a decrease in basis to be allocated within a class, the decrease must be allocated first to properties with unrealized depreciation in proportion to the transferee's shares of the respective amounts of unrealized depreciation (to the extent attributable to the acquired partnership interest) before the decrease (but only to the extent of the transferee's share of each property's unrealized depreciation). Any remaining decrease must be allocated among the properties within the class in proportion to the transferee's shares of their adjusted bases (as adjusted under the preceding sentence).

(C) *Limitation in decrease of basis.*—Where, as a result of a transaction to which this paragraph (b)(5) applies, a decrease in basis must be allocated to capital gain assets, ordinary income assets, or both, and the amount of the decrease otherwise allocable to a particular class exceeds the transferee's share of the adjusted basis to the partnership of all assets in that class, the basis of the property is reduced to zero (but not below zero).

(D) *Carryover adjustment.*—Where a transferee's negative basis adjustment under section 743(b) cannot be allocated to any asset, the adjustment is made when the partnership subsequently acquires property of a like character to which an adjustment can be made.

(iv) *Examples.*—The provisions of this paragraph (b)(5) are illustrated by the following examples—

Example 1. * * *

Example 2. * * *

Example 3—(i) A is a one-third partner in UTP, a partnership, which has a valid election in effect under section 754. The three partners in UTP have equal interests in the capital and profits of UTP. UTP has three assets with the following adjusted bases and fair market values:

	Fair market value
	$200
	$200
	$200

	Fair market value
	$100
	$280
	$20

$140 and A's share of the adjusted basis to LTP of partnership property. A's share of the adjusted basis to LTP of partnership property is equal to the sum of A's share of LTP's liabilities of $0 plus A's interest in the previously taxed capital of LTP of $190 ($200, A's cash on liquidation, increased by $120, the amount of tax loss allocated to A from the sale of Intangible 2 in the hypothetical transaction, decreased by $130, the amount of tax gain allocated to A from the sale of Intangible 3 in the hypothetical transaction). Therefore, the amount of the negative basis adjustment under section 743(b) to partnership property is $50.

(iii) Under this paragraph (b)(5), LTP must allocate $50 of A's negative basis adjustment between capital gain property and ordinary income property in proportion to, and to the extent of, the gross loss (including any remedial allocations under § 1.704-3(d)) that would be allocated to A from the hypothetical sale of all property in each class. If LTP disposed of its assets in a hypothetical sale, A would be allocated $120 of gross loss from Intangible 2 only. Accordingly, the $50 negative adjustment must be allocated to capital assets. Under paragraph (b)(5)(iii)(B) of this section, the $50 negative adjustment must be allocated to the assets in the capital class first to properties with unrealized depreciation in proportion to the transferee's shares of the respective amounts of unrealized depreciation. Thus, the $50 negative adjustment must be allocated entirely to Intangible 2.

Example 4—(i) A is a one-third partner in LTP. The three partners in LTP have equal interests in the capital and profits of LTP. LTP has two assets: accounts receivable with an adjusted basis of $300 and a fair market value of $240 and a nondepreciable capital asset with an adjusted basis of $60 and a fair market value of $240. A contributes its interest in LTP to UTP in a transaction described in section 721. At the time of the transfer, A's basis in its LTP interest is $90. Under section 723, UTP's basis in its interest in LTP is $90. LTP makes an election under section 754 in connection with the transfer.

(ii) The amount of the basis adjustment under section 743(b) is the difference between UTP's $90 basis in its LTP interest and UTP's share of the adjusted basis to LTP of LTP's property. UTP's share of the adjusted basis to LTP of LTP's property is equal to the sum of UTP's share of LTP's liabilities of $0 plus UTP's interest in the previously taxed capital of LTP of $120 ($160, the amount of cash on liquidation, increased by $20, the amount of tax loss allocated to UTP from the hypothetical transaction, and decreased by $60, the amount of tax gain allocated to UTP from the hypothetical transaction). Therefore, the amount of the negative basis adjustment under section 743(b) to partnership property is $30.

(iii) The total amount of gross loss that would be allocated to UTP from the hypothetical sale of LTP's ordinary income property is $20 (one third of the excess of the basis of the accounts receivable ($300) over their fair market value ($240)). The hypothetical sale of LTP's capital gain property would result in a net gain. Therefore, under this paragraph (b)(5), $20 of the $30 basis adjustment must be allocated to ordinary income property. Because LTP holds only one ordinary income property, the $20 decrease must be allocated entirely to the accounts receivable. Pursuant to paragraph (b)(5)(ii)(C) of this section, the remaining $10 basis adjustment must be allocated between ordinary income property and capital gain property according to UTP's share of the adjusted bases of such properties. Therefore, $8 ($10 multiplied by $80 divided by $100) would be allocated to the accounts receivable and $2 ($10 multiplied by $20 divided by $100) would be allocated to the nondepreciable capital asset. * * *

* * *

(e) *No allocation of basis decrease to stock of corporate partner.*—(1) *In general.*—In making an allocation under section 755(a) of any decrease in the adjusted basis of partnership property under section 734(b)—

(i) No allocation may be made to stock in a corporation (or any person related (within the meaning of sections 267(b) or 707(b)(1)) to such corporation) that is a partner in the partnership; and

(ii) Any amount not allocable to stock by reason of paragraph (c)(1) of this section shall be allocated under section 755(a) to other partnership property.

(2) *Recognition of gain.*—Gain shall be recognized to the partnership to the extent that the amount required to be allocated under paragraph (e)(1)(ii) of this section to other partnership property exceeds the aggregate adjusted basis of such other property immediately before the allocation required by paragraph (e)(1)(ii) of this section.

(3) *Example.*—A, B, and C are equal partners in PRS, a partnership. C is a corporation. The adjusted basis and fair market value for A's interests in PRS is $100. PRS owns Capital Asset 1 with an adjusted basis of $0 and a fair market value of $100, Capital Asset 2 with an adjusted basis of $150 and a fair market value of $50, and stock in Corp, a corporation that is related to C under section 267(b), with an adjusted basis of $250 and fair market value of $150. PRS has a section 754 election in effect. PRS distributes Capital Asset 1 to A in liquidation of A's interest in PRS. PRS will reduce the basis of its remaining assets under section 734(b) by $100, to be allocated under section 755. Pursuant to the general rule of paragraph (c) of this section, PRS would reduce the basis of Capital Asset 2 by $50 and the stock of Corp by $50. However, pursuant to paragraph (e)(1)(i) of this section, the basis of the Corp stock is not adjusted. Thus, the basis of Capital Asset 2 is reduced by $100 from $150 to $50.

(f) *Effective date.*—(1) *Generally.*—Except as provided in paragraph (f)(2) of this section, this section applies to transfers of partnership interests and distributions of property from a partnership that occur on or after December 15, 1999.

(2) *Special rules.*—Paragraphs (a) and (b)(3)(iii) of this section apply to transfers of partnership interests and distributions of property from a partnership that occur on or after June 9, 2003. Paragraph (b)(5) of this section applies to transfers of partnership interests occurring on or after January 16, 2014. Paragraph (e) of this section applies to transfers of partnership interests occurring on or after the date of publication of the Treasury decision adopting these rules as final regulations in the **Federal Register**.

* * *

Partners and Partnerships: Sales or Exchanges: Certain Distributions

Partners and Partnerships: Sales or Exchanges: Certain Distributions.—Amendments to Reg. § 1.755-1, prescribing how a partner should measure its interest in a partnership's unrealized receivables and inventory items, and that provide guidance regarding the tax consequences of a distribution that causes a reduction in that interest, are proposed (published in the Federal Register on November 3, 2014) (corrected January 26, 2015) (REG-151416-06).

☐ Par. 8. Section 1.755-1 is amended by:

a. Adding paragraphs (c)(2)(iii), (iv), (v), and (vi).

b. Revising the paragraph heading and the introductory text of paragraph (c)(6).

c. Removing the paragraph heading "*Example.*" in paragraph (c)(6) and adding "*Example 1.*" in its place.

d. Adding *Examples 2* and *3* to paragraph (c)(6).

e. Revising paragraph (e)(2).

The additions and revisions read as follows:

§1.755-1. Rules for allocation of basis.

* * *

(c) * * *

(2) * * *

(iii) *Coordination with section 1245 and similar provisions.*—Any increase in basis allocated to capital gain property pursuant to the second sentence in paragraph (c)(2)(i) of this section is not taken into account in determining the recomputed or adjusted basis in the property for purposes of section 1245(a)(1). Notwithstanding the prior sentence, any depreciation or amortization of the increase in basis that is allowed or allowable is taken into account in computing the property's recomputed basis. In the case of property that is subject to section 617(d)(1), 1250(a)(1), 1252(a)(1), or 1254(a)(1), rules similar to the rule in this paragraph (c)(2)(iii) shall apply.

(iv) *Coordination with section 1231.*—Any increase in basis allocated to capital gain property pursuant to the second sentence in paragraph (c)(2)(i) of this section is not taken into account in deter-

mining section 1231 gain and loss, as defined in section 1231(a)(3). Any basis adjustment to an asset not taken into account pursuant to this paragraph (c)(2)(iv) shall be treated as gain from the sale or exchange of a capital asset with the same holding period as the underlying asset.

(v) *Coordination with sections 1248 and 995.*—Any increase in basis allocated to stock in a foreign corporation pursuant to the second sentence in paragraph (c)(2)(i) of this section, or any decrease in basis allocated to stock in a foreign corporation pursuant to the second sentence in paragraph (c)(2)(ii) of this section, is not taken into account in determining the amount of gain recognized on the sale or exchange of such stock for purposes of section 1248(a). In the case of property that is subject to section 995(c), rules similar to the rule set forth in this paragraph (c)(2)(v) shall apply.

(vi) *Election not to apply the provisions of paragraphs (c)(2)(iii), (iv), and (v).*—A partnership may elect not to apply paragraphs (c)(2)(iii), (iv), and (v) of this section, and § 1.732-1(c)(2)(iii), (iv), and (v). An election made under this paragraph (c)(2)(vi) shall apply to all property distributions taking place in the partnership taxable year for which the election is made and in all subsequent partnership taxable years (including after a termination of the partnership under section 708(b)(1)(B)). An election under this paragraph (c)(2)(vi) must be made in a written statement filed with the partnership return for the first taxable year in which any of paragraph (c)(2)(iii), (iv), or (v) of this section, or §1.732-1(c)(2)(iii), (iv), or (v), would have applied if no election was made. An election under this paragraph (c)(2)(vi) is valid only if the required statement is included with a partnership return that is filed not later than the time prescribed by paragraph (e) of this section or §1.6031(a)-1 (including extensions thereof) for filing the return for such taxable year. This election is a method of accounting under section 446, and once the election is made, it can be revoked only with the consent of the Commissioner. The revocation of the election, or the making of a late election, under this paragraph (c)(2)(vi) is a change in method of accounting to which the provisions of section 446(e) and the regulations under section 446(e) apply. *See* paragraph (c)(6), *Example 3*, of this section for the treatment of a section 734(b) adjustment if an election under this paragraph (c)(2)(vi) is made, and certain consequences of the election under section 751(b). The statement required by this paragraph (c)(2)(vi) shall—

(A) Set forth the name and address of the partnership making the election;

(B) Be signed by any officer, manager, or member of the partnership who is authorized (under local law or the partnership's organizational documents) to make the election and who represents to having such authorization under penalties of perjury; and

(C) Contain a declaration that the partnership elects not to apply paragraphs (c)(2)(iii), (iv), and (v) of this section and §1.732-1(c)(2)(iii), (iv), and (v).

* * *

(6) *Examples.*—The following examples illustrate this paragraph (c):

* * *

Example 2. (i) A, B, and C are equal partners in ABC. Each partner has an outside basis in its partnership interest of $20. ABC owns depreciable equipment X with an adjusted basis of $30 and a fair market value of $150 and depreciable equipment Y with an adjusted basis of $30 and a fair market value of $30. ABC has made an election under section 754.

(ii) The depreciable equipment X has $120 of adjustments reflected in its adjusted basis within the meaning of §1.1245-2(a)(2). Accordingly, the entire $120 of the gain with respect to depreciable equipment X would be treated as gain to which section 1245(a)(1) would apply if the partnership sold the depreciable equipment X for its fair market value. ABC, therefore, has a $120 unrealized receivable within the meaning of §1.751-1(c)(4)(iii). Assume ABC makes a current distribution of the depreciable equipment Y to A. Because A's basis in his partnership interest is only $20, A's basis in the depreciable equipment Y will be limited to $20 under section 732(a). Under section 734(b), ABC will increase the basis in its capital gain property by $10 and will not adjust the basis of ordinary income property. Assume ABC has not made an election under §1.755-1(c)(2)(vi).

(iii) *Allocation between classes.* Pursuant to §1.755-1(a)(1), ABC's $120 unrealized receivable associated with the depreciable equipment X is treated as a separate asset that is ordinary income property. Thus, ABC is treated as having two assets (each actually a component of the single asset, equipment X) after the distribution, one that is capital gain property with a basis of $30 and a fair market value of $30, and one that is ordinary income property with a basis of $0 and a fair market value of $120.

(iv) *Allocation within class.* ABC must allocate the $10 basis increase entirely to the capital gain portion of the depreciable equipment X, as it holds no other capital gain property after it distributes the depreciable equipment Y to A. Therefore, ABC increases the basis of the capital gain property to $40.

(v) *Treatment of section 734(b) adjustment.* Pursuant to paragraph (c)(2)(iii) of this section, if ABC sold its depreciable equipment X for $150 immediately after the distribution to A, ABC would not take into account the $10 section 734(b) adjustment in determining ABC's recomputed or adjusted basis in the depreciable equipment X for purposes of section 1245(a)(1) and, accordingly, would recognize $120 of ordinary income. Also pursuant to paragraph (c)(2)(iv) of this section, the $10 section 734(b) adjustment is not taken into account for purposes of determining section 1231 gain or loss. Thus, pursuant

to paragraph (c)(2)(vi) of this section, ABC would recognize a $10 capital loss.

(vi) *Treatment of additional depreciation and appreciation.* (A) Assume, instead, that ABC continues to own the equipment and takes additional depreciation deductions of $16 ($15 with respect to the original remaining $30 basis and $1 with respect to the additional $10 basis resulting from the section 734(b) adjustment). At a time when the equipment has appreciated in value to $170, ABC sells the depreciable equipment X for $170 in a taxable transaction. In that same taxable year, ABC does not sell any other property used in its trade or business.

(B) Pursuant to section 1245(a)(1), ABC must recognize ordinary income in an amount by which the lesser of the following two amounts exceeds ABC's adjusted basis in the depreciable equipment X—

(1) ABC's recomputed basis in the depreciable equipment, or

(2) ABC's amount realized;

(C) Pursuant to section 1245(a)(2)(A), ABC's recomputed basis is an amount equal to the sum of—

(1) ABC's adjusted basis of the property, plus

(2) The amount of adjustments reflected in the adjusted basis on account of deductions allowed or allowable.

(D) Pursuant to (c)(2)(iii) of this section, the $9 remaining section 734(b) adjustment is not taken into account in determining ABC's recomputed or adjusted basis in the property for purposes of section 1245(a)(1). Thus, ABC's adjusted basis in the property is $15 (the remaining original basis). Also pursuant to (c)(2)(iii) of this section, however, any depreciation, or amortization of the section 734(b) adjustment that is allowed or allowable is taken into account in computing the property's recomputed basis. Thus, ABC's amount of adjustments reflected in the adjusted basis is $136 (the original $120 adjustment for depreciation deductions plus the additional $15 adjustment for depreciation deductions plus the additional $1 adjustment for depreciation deductions taken with respect to the section 734(b) adjustment). Accordingly, ABC's recomputed basis is $151 ($15 adjusted basis plus $136 of adjustments), which is lower than ABC's amount realized of $170. ABC, therefore, must recognize ordinary income in an amount by which ABC's recomputed basis of $151 exceeds ABC's adjusted basis in the depreciable equipment X. Pursuant to (c)(2)(iii) of this section, the $9 remaining section 734(b) adjustment is not taken into account in determining the adjusted basis in the property for purposes of section 1245(a)(1). Accordingly, ABC must recognize $136 of ordinary income (the excess of ABC's $151 recomputed basis in the depreciable equipment X over ABC's $15 adjusted basis in the depreciable equipment X).

(E) Pursuant to paragraph (c)(2)(iv) of this section, the section 734(b) adjustment is not taken into account in determining ABC's section 1231 gain or loss. Accordingly, pursuant to section 1231(a)(1), ABC recognizes $19 of capital gain (ABC's $170 amount realized on the disposition of the depreciable equipment X over ABC's adjusted basis of $15 in the depreciable equipment X, reduced by the $136 of ordinary income ABC recognized under section 1245(a)(1)). Pursuant to paragraph (c)(2)(vi) of this section, ABC also recognizes a capital loss equal to the remaining $9 section 734(b) adjustment.

Example 3. (i) Assume the same facts as *Example 2* of this paragraph (c), except ABC has made an election under paragraph (c)(2)(vi) of this section.

(ii) *Treatment of section 734(b) adjustment.* Because ABC has made an election under paragraph (c)(2)(vi) of this section, paragraph (c)(2)(iii) of this section does not apply. Thus, if ABC sold its depreciable equipment X immediately after the distribution to A, ABC would take into account the $10 section 734(b) adjustment in determining ABC's recomputed or adjusted basis in the depreciable equipment X for purposes of section 1245(a)(1) and, accordingly, would recognize $110 of ordinary income (including for purposes of applying section 751).

* * *

(e) * * *

(2) *Special rules.*—Paragraphs (a) and (b)(3)(iii) of this section apply to transfers of partnership interests and distributions of property from a partnership that occur on or after June 9, 2003, and paragraphs (c)(2)(iii), (iv), (v), (vi), and (c)(6) of this section and *Examples* 2 and 3 of paragraph (c) of this section apply to distributions of property from a partnership that occur on or after the date of publication of a Treasury decision adopting these rules as final regulations in the **Federal Register**.

Partnerships: Equity for Services

Partnerships: Equity for Services. Amendments to Reg. §1.761-1, providing that the transfer of a partnership interest in connection with the performance of services is subject to Code Sec. 83 and providing rules for coordinating Code Sec. 83 with partnership taxation principles, are proposed (published in the Federal Register on May 24, 2005) (REG-105346-03).

☐ Par. 8. Section 1.761-1(b) is amended by adding two sentences to the end of the paragraph to read as follows:

§1.761-1. Terms defined.

* * *

(b) * * * If a partnership interest is transferred in connection with the performance of services, and that partnership interest is substantially nonvested (within the meaning of §1.83-3(b)), then the holder of the partnership interest is not treated as a partner solely by reason of holding the interest, unless the holder makes an election with respect to the interest under section 83(b). The previous sentence applies to partnership interests that are transferred on or after the date final regulations are published in the Federal Register.

* * *

Partnership Interest: Treatment of Grantor of an Option

Partnership Interest: Treatment of Grantor of an Option.—Amendments to Reg. §1.761-3, relating to the tax treatment of noncompensatory options and convertible instruments issued by a partnership, are proposed (published in the Federal Register on February 5, 2013) (REG-106918-08).

☐ Par 2. Section 1.761-3 is amended by adding paragraph (c)(1)(iv) to read as follows:

§1.761-3. Certain option holders treated as partners.

* * *

(c) * * *

(1) * * *

(iv) An event described in paragraphs (c)(1)(iv)(A), (B), or (C) of this section, provided the event is pursuant to a plan in existence at the time of the issuance or modification of the noncompensatory option that has as a principal purpose the substantial reduction of the present value of the aggregate Federal tax liabilities of the partners and the noncompensatory option holder (under paragraph (a)(1)(ii) of this section):

(A) Issuance, transfer, or modification of an interest in, or liquidation of, the issuing partnership;

(B) Issuance, transfer, or modification of an interest in any look-through entity (as defined in paragraph (b)(1) of this section) that directly, or indirectly through one or more look-through entities, owns the noncompensatory option;

(C) Issuance, transfer, or modification of an interest in any look-through entity that directly, or indirectly through one or more look-through entities, owns an interest in the issuing partnership.

* * *

INSURANCE COMPANIES

Life Insurance Companies: Computation and Reporting of Reserves

Life Insurance Companies: Computation and Reporting of Reserves.—Amendments to Reg. §1.801-2, providing guidance on the computation of life insurance reserves and the change in basis of computing certain reserves of insurance companies, are proposed (published in the Federal Register on April 2, 2020) (REG-132529-17).

Par. 4. Section 1.801-2 is amended by removing the language "1.801-7" and adding the language "1.801-6" in its place.

§1.801-2. Taxable years affected.

Life Insurance Companies: Property and Casualty Insurance Companies: Life Insurance Reserves

Life Insurance Companies: Property and Casualty Insurance Companies: Life Insurance Reserves.—Amendments to Reg. §1.801-4, permitting the recomputation of certain life insurance reserves if such reserves were initially computed or estimated on other than an actuarial basis, are proposed (published in the Federal Register on January 2, 1997) (REG-246018-96).

Par. 2. Section 1.801-4 is amended by adding a new paragraph (g) to read as follows:

§1.801-4. Life insurance reserves.

* * *

(g) *Recomputation of life insurance reserves.*—(1) *General.*—If an insurance company does not compute or estimate its reserves for contracts involving, at the time with respect to which the reserves are computed, life, accident or health contingencies, on the basis of mortality or morbidity tables and assumed rates of interest, then the taxpayer or the Commissioner may recompute reserves for those contracts on the basis of mortality or morbidity tables and assumed rates of interest.

(2) *Effect of recomputation.*—If reserves are recomputed pursuant to paragraph (g)(1) of this section, the recomputed reserves satisfy the requirements of section 816(b)(1)(A).

(3) *Mean reserve.*—For purposes of section 816(b)(4) and §1.801-3(i), if reserves are recomputed pursuant to paragraph (g)(1) of this section for a taxable year, the reserves must be recomputed for both the beginning and the end of the taxable year.

(4) *Subsequently acquired information.*—No information acquired after the date as of which a reserve was initially computed or estimated may be taken into account in recomputing that reserve under paragraph (g)(1) of this section.

(5) *Effective date.*—This section is applicable with respect to returns filed for taxable years beginning after the date final regulations are filed with the Office of the Federal Register.

Life Insurance Companies: Computation and Reporting of Reserves

Life Insurance Companies: Computation and Reporting of Reserves.—Amendments to Reg. §§1.801-5, 1.801-7 and 1.801-8, providing guidance on the computation of life insurance reserves and the change in basis of computing certain reserves of insurance companies, are proposed (published in the Federal Register on April 2, 2020) (REG-132529-17).

Par. 5. Section 1.801-5 is amended by:

1. Removing paragraph (c) and redesignating paragraph (d) as paragraph (c).

2. In newly redesignated paragraph (c), designating the *Example* as paragraph (c)(1).

3. In newly designated paragraph (c)(1):

i. Designating the introductory text as paragraph (c)(1)(i).

ii. Adding a heading for the table in newly designated paragraph (c)(1)(i).

iii. Designating the undesignated paragraph following newly designated paragraph (c)(1)(i) as paragraph (c)(1)(ii).

4. Adding reserved paragraph (c)(2).

The addition reads as follows:

§1.801-5. Total reserves.

* * *

(c) * * *

(1) * * *

Par. 6. Section 1.801-7 is removed and reserved.

§1.801-7. Variable annuities.

(i) * * *

Table 1 to Paragraph (c)(1)(i)

* * *

Par. 7. In §1.801-8, paragraph (e) is removed and reserved.

§1.801-8. Contracts with reserves based on segregated asset accounts.

Life Insurance Companies: Computation and Reporting of Reserves

Life Insurance Companies: Computation and Reporting of Reserves.—Amendments to Reg. §1.806-4, providing guidance on the computation of life insurance reserves and the change in basis of computing certain reserves of insurance companies, are proposed (published in the Federal Register on April 2, 2020) (REG-132529-17).

Par. 8. Section 1.806-4 is removed.

§1.806-4. Change of basis in computing reserves.

Life Insurance Companies: Computation and Reporting of Reserves

Life Insurance Companies: Computation and Reporting of Reserves.—Reg. §§1.807-3 and 1.807-4 and amendments to Reg. §1.807-1, providing guidance on the computation of life insurance reserves and the change in basis of computing certain reserves of insurance companies, are proposed (published in the Federal Register on April 2, 2020) (REG-132529-17).

Par. 9. Section 1.807-1 is revised to read as follows:

§1.807-1. Computation of life insurance reserves.

(a) *No asset adequacy reserve.*—The life insurance reserve determined under section 807(d)(1) does not include any asset adequacy reserve. An asset adequacy reserve includes any reserve that is established as an additional reserve based upon an analysis of the adequacy of reserves that would otherwise be established or any reserve that is not held with respect to a particular contract. In determining whether a reserve is a life insurance reserve, the label placed on such reserve is not determinative, provided, however, any

reserve or portion of a reserve that would have been established pursuant to an asset adequacy analysis required by the National Association of Insurance Commissioner's Valuation Manual 30 as it existed on December 22, 2017, the date of enactment of Public Law 115-97, is an asset adequacy reserve.

(b) *Applicability date.*—The rules of this section apply to taxable years beginning on or after **[DATE FINAL REGULATIONS ARE PUBLISHED IN THE FEDERAL REGISTER]**.

Par. 10. Section 1.807-3 is added to read as follows:

§1.807-3. Reporting of reserves.

(a) *Reserve reporting.*—A life insurance company subject to tax under section 801 is required to make a return on Form 1120-L, *U.S. Life Insurance Company Income Tax Return*. The Internal Revenue Service may require reporting with respect to the opening balance and closing balance of items described in section 807(c) and with respect to the method of computing such items for purposes of determining

income. Such reporting may provide for the manner in which separate account items are reported. (See section 6011 and §301.6011-1 of this chapter.)

(b) *Applicability date.*—The rules of this section apply to taxable years beginning on or after **[DATE FINAL REGULATIONS ARE PUBLISHED IN THE FEDERAL REGISTER]**. [Reg. §1.807-3.]

Par. 11. Section 1.807-4 is added to read as follows:

§1.807-4. Adjustment for change in computing reserves.

(a) *Requirement to follow administrative procedures.*—Except as provided in §1.446-1(e), a change in basis of computing an item referred to in section 807(c) is a change in method of accounting for purposes of §1.446-1(e). Before computing such item under a new basis, a life insurance company must obtain the consent of the Commissioner of Internal Revenue or his delegate (Commissioner) pursuant to administrative procedures prescribed by the Commissioner. Similarly, an insurance company other than a life insurance company (a nonlife insurance company) that changes its basis of computing life insurance reserves must obtain the consent of the Commissioner pursuant to administrative procedures prescribed by the Commissioner.

(b) *Section 481 adjustment.*—(1) *In general.*—If the basis of computing any item referred to in section 807(c) as of the close of any taxable year (the year of change) differs from the basis of computing such item at the close of the preceding taxable year, then the difference between the amount of the item at the close of the taxable year computed on the new basis and the amount of the item at the close of the taxable year computed on the old basis that is attributable to contracts issued before the taxable year, is taken into account under section 481 and §§1.481-1 through 1.481-5 as an adjustment attributable to a change in method of accounting.

(2) *Loss of company status.*—If for any taxable year a taxpayer that was an insurance company for the year of change is no longer an insurance company, then the taxpayer must take into account in the preceding taxable year (that is, the last taxable year it was an insurance company) the balance of any section 481(a) adjustment determined under paragraph (b)(1) of this section. A taxpayer that was an insurance company for the year of change does not accelerate the balance of any section 481(a) adjustment determined under paragraph (b)(1) of this section merely because it changes from a life insurance company to a nonlife insurance company or because it changes from a nonlife insurance company to a life insurance company.

(c) *Effect on determining increase or decrease in reserves.*—(1) *Effect under section 807(a) and (b).*—If there is a change in basis of computing

any item described in section 807(c) for a taxable year, then, for purposes of section 807(a) and (b), the closing balance for such item for the year of change with respect to contracts issued before the year of change is determined on the old basis and the opening balance for such item for the next taxable year for such contracts is computed on the new basis.

(2) *Effect under section 832.*—The following rules apply for purposes of section 832(b)(4):

(i) For the year of change, life insurance reserves at the end of the year of change with respect to contracts issued before the year of change are determined on the old basis.

(ii) For the taxable year following the year of change, life insurance reserves at the end of the preceding taxable year (that is, the year of change) with respect to contracts issued before the year of change are determined on the new basis.

(d) *Examples.*—The principles of paragraphs (a) through (c) of this section are illustrated by the following examples. For purposes of these examples and except as otherwise provided, IC is a life insurance company within the meaning of section 816(a) that issues life insurance and annuity contracts. IC is required to determine the amount of life insurance reserves under section 807(d) and to take net increases or decreases in the reserves into account in computing life insurance company taxable income. IC's reserve for each insurance contract at issue exceeds the net surrender value for such contract and does not exceed the statutory reserve for such contract. IC uses a calendar year as its taxable year.

(1) *Example 1*—(i) *Facts.* In 2021, IC discovered that it had computed the amount of life insurance reserves for its 2019 and 2020 taxable years by using a mortality table that was not permitted by the tax reserve method (as defined in section 807(d)(3)).

(ii) *Analysis.* To comply with section 807(d), IC must use the appropriate mortality table to compute its life insurance reserves for the 2021 taxable year. This change is a change in basis of computing life insurance reserves and a change in method of accounting described in §1.446-1(e). IC is required to obtain the consent of the Commissioner to change its basis of computing its life insurance reserves by following the administrative procedures prescribed by the Commissioner.

(2) *Example 2*—(i) *Facts.* IC issues variable annuity contracts with guaranteed minimum benefits. In Year 1, the National Association of Insurance Commissioners makes a change to the Commissioners' Annuity Reserve Valuation Method that imposes a new computational requirement on issuers of variable annuities with guaranteed minimum benefits. The requirement applies to the determination of statutory reserves as of December 31, Year 1, for contracts issued on or prior to December 31, Year 1.

(ii) *Analysis.* To comply with section 807(d), IC must compute its life insurance reserves for variable annuities with guaranteed minimum benefits for the Year 1 taxable year using the new computational requirement. This change is a change in basis of computing life insurance reserves for such contracts issued prior to Year 1 and a change in method of accounting described in §1.446-1(e). IC is required to obtain the consent of the Commissioner to change its basis of computing its life insurance reserves by following the administrative procedures prescribed by the Commissioner.

(3) *Example 3*—(i) *Facts.* In 2021, IC changed the basis of computing the amount of life insurance reserves for a certain type of life insurance contract as described in section 807(f). Both the basis used for computing the reserves for the relevant contracts at the close of the 2020 taxable year (old basis) and the basis of computing the reserves for the relevant type of contract at the close of the 2021 taxable year (new basis) are consistent with the applicable Commissioners' Reserve Valuation Method. IC followed the administrative procedures prescribed by the Commissioner to obtain consent to change the basis of computing these reserves. IC determined that the life insurance reserves as of December 31, 2021, for the relevant contracts issued prior to 2021 were $110 if computed using the old method and $120 if computed using the new method. IC also determined that the life insurance reserves as of December 31, 2021, for the relevant contracts issued during 2021 were $15 using the new basis.

(ii) *Analysis.* IC must take into account under section 481 and the administrative procedures prescribed by the Commissioner the $10 difference between the reserves for the relevant contracts issued prior to 2021 computed under the old basis ($110) and the reserves for such contracts computed under the new basis ($120). For purposes of determining any net increase or net decrease in reserves in taxable year 2021 under section 807(a) or (b), IC's closing balance of life insurance reserves computed under section 807(d) with respect to the relevant contracts is $110 for contracts issued prior to 2021 (computed on the old basis) and $15 for contracts issued during 2021 (computed on the new basis). IC's opening balance in 2022 for life insurance reserves for the relevant contracts is $135 (computed on the new basis).

(4) *Example 4*—(i) *Facts.* The facts are the same as in paragraph (d)(3) of this section (the facts in *Example 3*), except that IC is an insurance company that is not a life insurance company. IC is required to compute taxable income under section 832.

(ii) *Analysis.* IC must take into account under section 481 and the administrative procedures prescribed by the Commissioner the $10 difference between the reserves for the relevant contracts issued prior to 2021 computed under the old basis ($110) and the reserves for such contracts computed under the new basis ($120). For purposes of determining the premiums earned on insurance contracts during the taxable year as described in section 832(b)(4) for the year of change, the life insurance reserves at the end of the taxable year are $110 for contracts issued prior to 2021 (computed on the old basis) and $15 for contracts issued during 2021 (computed on the new basis). For purposes of determining the premiums earned on insurance contracts during the taxable year as described in section 832(b)(4) for the taxable year following the year of change, the life insurance reserves at the end of the preceding taxable year (the year of change) with respect to relevant contracts are $135 (computed on the new basis).

(e) *Applicability date.*—The rules of this section apply to taxable years beginning on or after **[DATE FINAL REGULATIONS ARE PUBLISHED IN THE FEDERAL REGISTER]**. However, a taxpayer may choose to apply the rules of this section for taxable years beginning after December 31, 2017, the effective date of the revision of section 807 by Public Law 115-97, and ending before the first taxable year that begins on or after **[DATE FINAL REGULATIONS ARE PUBLISHED IN THE FEDERAL REGISTER]**. See section 7805(b)(7). [Reg. §1.807-4.]

Life Insurance Companies: Computation and Reporting of Reserves

Life Insurance Companies: Computation and Reporting of Reserves.—Amendments to Reg. §§1.809-2 and 1.809-5, providing guidance on the computation of life insurance reserves and the change in basis of computing certain reserves of insurance companies, are proposed (published in the Federal Register on April 2, 2020) (REG-132529-17).

Par. 12. Section 1.809-2 is removed.

§1.809-2. Exclusion of share of investment yield set aside for policyholders.

Par. 13. Section 1.809-5 is amended by removing the language "and §1.810-3" from the last sentence of paragraph (a)(5)(iii).

§1.809-5. Deductions.

Life Insurance Companies: Computation and Reporting of Reserves

Life Insurance Companies: Computation and Reporting of Reserves.—Amendments to Reg. §1.810-3, providing guidance on the computation of life insurance reserves and the change in basis of computing certain reserves of insurance companies, are proposed (published in the Federal Register on April 2, 2020) (REG-132529-17).

Par. 14. Section 1.810-3 is removed.

§1.810-3. Adjustment for change in computing reserves.

Life Insurance Companies: Computation and Reporting of Reserves

Life Insurance Companies: Computation and Reporting of Reserves.—Reg. §1.816-1, providing guidance on the computation of life insurance reserves and the change in basis of computing certain reserves of insurance companies, is proposed (published in the Federal Register on April 2, 2020) (REG-132529-17).

Par. 15. Section 1.816-1 is added before the undesignated center heading "Miscellaneous Provisions" to read as follows:

§1.816-1. Life insurance reserves.

(a) *Definition of life insurance reserves.*—Except as provided in section 816(h), a reserve that meets the requirements of section 816(b)(1) and (2) will not be disqualified as a life insurance reserve solely because the method used to compute the reserve takes into account other factors, provided that the method used to compute the reserve is a tax reserve method as defined in section 807(d)(3) and that such reserve is not an asset adequacy reserve as described in §1.807-1(a).

(b) *Applicability date.*—The section applies to taxable years beginning on or after **[DATE FINAL REGULATIONS ARE PUBLISHED IN THE FEDERAL REGISTER]**. However, a taxpayer may choose to apply the rules of this section for taxable years beginning after December 31, 2017, the effective date of the revision of section 807 by Public Law 115-97, and ending before the first taxable year that begins on or after **[DATE FINAL REGULATIONS ARE PUBLISHED IN THE FEDERAL REGISTER]**. See section 7805(b)(7). [Reg. §1.816-1.]

Life Insurance Companies: Computation and Reporting of Reserves

Life Insurance Companies: Computation and Reporting of Reserves.—Amendments to Reg. §§1.817A-0 and 1.817A-1, providing guidance on the computation of life insurance reserves and the change in basis of computing certain reserves of insurance companies, are proposed (published in the Federal Register on April 2, 2020) (REG-132529-17).

Par. 16. Section 1.817A-0 is removed.

§1.817A-0. Table of contents.

Par. 17. Section 1.817A-1 is amended by:

1. Revising the heading to paragraph (b) and paragraph (b)(1).

2. Removing paragraph (b)(2).

3. Redesignating paragraphs (b)(3) and (4) as paragraph (b)(2) and (3).

5. In newly redesignated paragraph (b)(3):

i. Revising the first sentence.

ii. Removing the word "None" in the second sentence and adding "Neither" in its place.

6. Removing paragraph (b)(5)

7. Revising paragraph (d).

The revisions read as follows:

§1.817A-1. Certain modified guaranteed contracts.

* * *

(b) *Applicable interest rates for certain non-equity-indexed modified guaranteed contracts.*—(1) *Tax reserves during temporary guarantee period under section 807(c)(3).*—An insurance company is required to determine the tax reserves for certain MGCs under section 807(c)(3). During the temporary guarantee period of such an MGC that is a non-equity-indexed MGC, the applicable interest rate to be used is the current market rate, as defined in paragraph (a)(5) of this section. For periods after the end of such a temporary guarantee period, section 807(c)(3) is not modified when applied to a non-equity indexed MGC. Section 807(c)(3) is not affected by the definition of current market rate contained in paragraph (a)(5) of this section once the temporary guarantee period has expired.

* * *

(3) *Periods after the end of the temporary guarantee period.*—For periods after the end of the temporary guarantee period, sections 807(c)(3) and 811(d) are not modified when applied to non-equity-indexed MGCs. * * *

* * *

(d) *Applicability dates.*—Paragraph (b) of this section applies to taxable years beginning on or after [DATE FINAL REGULATIONS ARE PUBLISHED IN THE FEDERAL REGISTER]. However, a taxpayer may choose to apply the rules of paragraph (b) of this section for taxable years beginning after December 31, 2017, the effective date of the revision of section 807 by Public Law 115-97, and ending before the first taxable year that begins on or after [DATE FINAL REGULATIONS ARE PUBLISHED IN THE FEDERAL REGISTER]. See section 7805(b)(7). For taxable years beginning before [DATE FINAL REGULATIONS ARE PUBLISHED IN THE FEDERAL REGISTER], see paragraph (b) of this section as contained in 26 CFR part 1 revised as of April 1, 2019.

Life Insurance Companies: Computation and Reporting of Reserves

Life Insurance Companies: Computation and Reporting of Reserves.—Amendments to Reg. §1.818-2, providing guidance on the computation of life insurance reserves and the change in basis of computing certain reserves of insurance companies, are proposed (published in the Federal Register on April 2, 2020) (REG-132529-17).

Par. 18. Section 1.818-2 is amended by removing paragraph (c).

§1.818-2. Accounting provisions.

Imputed Interest: Original Issue Discount: Safe Haven Rates

Imputed Interest: Original Issue Discount: Safe Haven Interest Rates.—Reproduced below is the text of a proposed amendment of Reg. §1.818-3, relating to (1) the tax treatment of debt instruments issued after July 1, 1982, that contain original issue discount, (2) the imputation of and the accounting for interest with respect to sales and exchanges of property occurring after December 31, 1984, and (3) safe haven interest rates for loans or advances between commonly controlled taxpayers and safe haven leases between such taxpayers (published in the Federal Register on April 8, 1986).

☐ Par. 16. In §1.818-3, paragraph (f) is amended by removing the phrase "section 1232(a) (relating to the taxation of bonds and other evidences of indebtedness)" and adding in its place the phrase "section 1271 (relating to the treatment of amounts received on retirement or sale or exchange of debt instruments)", and by removing the phrase "section 1232(a)(2)(C)" and adding in its place the phrase "section 1271(d)".

§1.818-3. Amortization of premium and accrual of discount.

Life Insurance Companies: Computation and Reporting of Reserves

Life Insurance Companies: Computation and Reporting of Reserves.—Amendments to Reg. §1.818-4, providing guidance on the computation of life insurance reserves and the change in basis of computing certain reserves of insurance companies, are proposed (published in the Federal Register on April 2, 2020) (REG-132529-17).

Par. 19. Section 1.818-4 is removed and reserved.

§1.818-4. Election with respect to life insurance reserves computed on preliminary term basis.

Life Insurance Companies: Computation and Reporting of Reserves

Life Insurance Companies: Computation and Reporting of Reserves.—Amendments to Reg. §1.848-1, providing guidance on the computation of life insurance reserves and the change in basis of computing certain reserves of insurance companies, are proposed (published in the Federal Register on April 2, 2020) (REG-132529-17).

Par. 20. Section 1.848-1 is amended by removing the language "section 807(e)(4)" in paragraph (b)(2)(i) and adding the language "section 807(e)(3)" in its place.

§1.848-1. Definitions and special provisions.

REGULATED INVESTMENT COMPANIES AND REAL ESTATE INVESTMENT TRUSTS

Transition of Tax Consequences: IBORs: Guidance

Transition of Tax Consequences: IBORs: Guidance.—Amendments to Reg. §1.860A-0, providing guidance on the tax consequences of the transition to the use of reference rates other than interbank offered rates in debt instruments and non-debt contracts, are proposed (published in the Federal Register on October 9, 2019) (REG-118784-18).

Par. 2. Section 1.860A-0 is amended by adding entries for §1.860G-1(e) to read as follows:

§1.860A-0. Outline of REMIC provisions.
* * *

§1.860G-1 *Definition of regular and residual interests.*
* * *

(e) Transition from interbank offered rates.
(1) In general.

(2) Change in reference rate for a regular interest after the startup day.
(3) Contingencies of rate on a regular interest.
(4) Reasonable expenses incurred to alter a regular interest.
(5) Applicability dates.
* * *

Deduction for Business Interest Expense: Limitation

Deduction for Business Interest Expense: Limitation.—Amendments to Reg. §1.860C-2, regarding the limitation on the deduction for business interest expense after the enactment of recent tax legislation, are proposed (published in the Federal Register on December 28, 2018) (REG-106089-18).

Par. 15. Section 1.860C-2 is amended by revising paragraph (b)(2) to read as follows:

§1.860C-2. Determination of REMIC taxable income or net loss.
* * *

(b) * * *

(2) *Deduction allowable under section 163.*—(i) A REMIC is allowed a deduction, determined without regard to section 163(d), for any interest expense accrued during the taxable year.

(ii) For taxable years beginning after December 31, 2017, a REMIC is allowed a deduction, determined without regard to section 163(j), for any interest expense accrued during the taxable year.
* * *

Definition of Registered Form: Guidance

Definition of Registered Form: Guidance.—Amendments to Reg. §1.860D-1, providing guidance on the definitions of registration-required obligation and registered form, including guidance on the issuance of pass-through certificates and participation interests in registered form, are proposed (published in the Federal Register on September 19, 2017) (REG-125374-16).

Par. 6. Section 1.860D-1(b)(5)(i)(A) is amended by removing the language "§ 5f.103-1(c)" and adding in its place the language "§ 1.163-5(b)."

§1.860D-1. Definition of a REMIC.

REMICs: Reporting Information: Extension of Time

REMICs: Reporting Information: Extension of Time.—An amendment to Reg. §1.860F-4, relating to real estate mortgage investment conduits, is proposed (published in the Federal Register on September 30, 1991).

☐ Par. 3. Section 1.860F-4 is amended by revising paragraph (e)(2)(i) to read as follows:

§1.860F-4. REMIC reporting requirements and other administrative rules.
* * *

(e) * * *
(2) * * *

(i) In general, Schedule Q must be mailed (or otherwise delivered) to each holder of a residual interest during a calendar quarter no later than the 41st day following the close of the calendar quarter.
* * *

Transition of Tax Consequences: IBORs: Guidance

Transition of Tax Consequences: IBORs: Guidance.—Amendments to Reg. §1.860G-1, providing guidance on the tax consequences of the transition to the use of reference rates other than interbank offered rates in debt instruments and non-debt contracts, are proposed (published in the Federal Register on October 9, 2019) (REG-118784-18).

Par. 3. Section 1.860G-1 is amended by adding paragraph (e) to read as follows:

§1.860G-1. Definition of regular and residual interests.
* * *

(e) *Transition from interbank offered rates.*—(1) *In general.*—This paragraph (e) applies to certain interests in a REMIC that provide for a rate referencing an interbank offered rate. See §1.1001-6 for additional rules that may apply to an interest in a REMIC that provides for a rate referencing an interbank offered rate.

(2) *Change in reference rate for a regular interest after the startup day.*—An alteration to a regular interest in a REMIC that occurs after the startup day and that is described in §1.1001-6(a)(1) or (3) is disregarded in determining whether the regular interest has fixed terms on the startup day under paragraph (a)(4) of this section.

(3) *Contingencies of rate on a regular interest.*—An interest in a REMIC does not fail to qualify as a regular interest solely because it is subject to a contingency whereby a rate that references an interbank offered rate and is a variable rate permitted under paragraph (a)(3) of this section may change to a fixed rate or a different variable rate permitted under paragraph (a)(3) of this section in anticipation of the interbank offered rate becoming unavailable or unreliable.

(4) *Reasonable expenses incurred to alter a regular interest.*—An interest in a REMIC does not fail to qualify as a regular interest solely

because it is subject to a contingency whereby the amount of payments of principal or interest (or other similar amounts) with respect to the interest in the REMIC is reduced by reasonable costs incurred to effect an alteration or modification described in § 1.1001-6(a)(1), (2), or (3). In addition, payment by a party other than the REMIC of reasonable costs incurred to effect an alteration or modification described in § 1.1001-6(a)(1), (2), or (3) is not a contribution to the REMIC for purposes of section 860G(d).

(5) *Applicability dates.*—(i) Paragraphs (e)(2) and (4) of this section apply with respect to an alteration or modification that occurs on or after the date of publication of a Treasury decision adopting these rules as final regulations in the **Federal Register**. However, taxpayers may apply paragraphs (e)(2) and (4) of this section with respect to an alteration or a modification that occurs before the date of publication of a Treasury decision adopting these rules as final regulations in the **Federal Register**. See section 7805(b)(7).

(ii) Paragraph (e)(3) of this section applies to a regular interest in a REMIC issued on or after the date of publication of a Treasury decision adopting these rules as final regulations in the **Federal Register**. However, a taxpayer may apply paragraph (e)(3) of this section to a regular interest in a REMIC issued before the date of publication of a Treasury decision adopting these rules as final regulations in the **Federal Register**. See section 7805(b)(7).

Stock and Rights to Acquire Stock: Deemed Distributions

Stock and Rights to Acquire Stock: Deemed Distributions.—Amendments to Reg. §1.860G-3, regarding deemed distributions of stock and rights to acquire stock and resolving ambiguities concerning the amount and timing of deemed distributions that are or result from adjustments to rights to acquire stock, are proposed (published in the Federal Register on April 13, 2016) (REG-133673-15).

Par. 5. Section 1.860G-3(b)(1) is amended by removing the language "1.1441-2(d)(4)" in the last sentence, and adding the language "1.1441-2(d)(1)(ii)(C)" in its place, and by removing the language "1.1441-5(b)(2)(i)(A), and" and adding the language "1.1441-5(b)(2)(i)(A), 1.1471-2(a)(4)(i)(B)(4), and" in its place.

§1.860G-3. Treatment of foreign persons.

SOURCES WITHIN OR WITHOUT THE U.S.

Imputed Interest: Original Issue Discount: Safe Haven Rates

Imputed Interest: Original Issue Discount: Safe Haven Interest Rates.—Reproduced below is the text of a proposed amendment of Reg. §1.861-2, relating to (1) the tax treatment of debt instruments issued after July 1, 1982, that contain original issue discount, (2) the imputation of and the accounting for interest with respect to sales and exchanges of property occurring after December 31, 1984, and (3) safe haven interest rates for loans or advances between commonly controlled taxpayers and safe haven leases between such taxpayers (published in the Federal Register on April 8, 1986).

§1.861-2. Interest.

☐ Par. 17. In §1.861-2, paragraph (a)(4) is amended by removing the phrase "section 1232(b)(1)" and adding in its place the phrase "section 1273(a)(1)".

Stock and Rights to Acquire Stock: Deemed Distributions

Stock and Rights to Acquire Stock: Deemed Distributions.—Amendments to Reg. §1.861-3, regarding deemed distributions of stock and rights to acquire stock and resolving ambiguities concerning the amount and timing of deemed distributions that are or result from adjustments to rights to acquire stock, are proposed (published in the Federal Register on April 13, 2016) (REG-133673-15).

Par. 6. Section 1.861-3 is amended by:

1. In paragraph (a)(6), removing "A substitute dividend payment is a payment" in the first sentence and adding "A substitute dividend payment is a payment or a deemed payment" in its place, and adding a new second sentence.

2. In paragraph (d), replacing the third sentence with a new sentence.

The additions read as follows:

§1.861-3. Dividends.—(a) * * *

(6) *Substitute dividend payments.*—* * * A deemed payment is a payment deemed to have been made in the amount (as determined under §1.305-7(c)(4)) of a deemed distribution (as defined in §1.305-1(d)(7)) that the owner of the transferred security is entitled to during the term of the transaction. * * *

* * *

(d) *Effective/applicability date.*—* * * Paragraph (a)(6) of this section applies to payments made on or after the date of publication of the Treasury decision adopting these rules as final regulations in the **Federal Register**; however, a taxpayer may rely on the rule in the second sentence of paragraph (a)(6) of this section for all deemed distributions (as defined in §1.305-1(d)(7)) occurring on or after January 1, 2016, until the date of publication of a Treasury decision adopting these rules as final regulations in the **Federal Register**. * * *

Compensation for Labor or Personal Services: Artists: Athletes

Compensation for Labor or Personal Services: Artists: Athletes.—Amendments to Reg. §1.861-4, clarifying the determination of source of compensation of a person, including an artist or athlete, who is compensated for labor or personal services performed at specific events, are proposed (filed in the Federal Register on October 17, 2007) (REG-114125-07).

☐ Par. 2. Section 1.861-4 is amended by:

1. Removing the heading for paragraph (b)(1)(i).

2. Redesignating paragraph (b)(1)(i) as paragraph (b)(1).

3. In the last sentence of newly designated paragraph (b)(1), adding the language "or on the event basis as defined in paragraph (b)(2)(ii)(G) of this section," after the language "paragraph (b)(2)(ii)(E) of this section,".

4. In the last sentence of paragraph (b)(2)(i), adding the language "or on the event basis as defined in paragraph (b)(2)(ii)(G) of this section," after the language "paragraph (b)(2)(ii)(E) of this section,".

5. In the first sentence of paragraph (b)(2)(ii)(C)(1)(i), adding the language ", including an event basis as defined in paragraph (b)(2)(ii)(G) of this section," after the language "alternative basis" wherever the language "alternative basis" appears in the sentence.

6. In the first sentence of paragraph (b)(2)(ii)(C)(1)(ii), adding the language "event basis as defined in paragraph (b)(2)(ii)(G) of this section or other" after the language "partly without the United States under an".

7. Removing paragraph (b)(2)(ii)(C)(3).

8. In the first sentence of paragraph (b)(2)(ii)(E), removing the language "individual's" and adding the language "person's" in its place, removing the language "individual" and adding the language "person" in its place, and removing the language "his or hers" and adding the language "such person's" in its place.

9. In the second sentence of paragraph (b)(2)(ii)(F), removing the language "an individual" and adding the language "a person" in its place.

10. Redesignating paragraphs (c) and (d) as new paragraphs (d) and (e), respectively.

11. Redesignating paragraph (b)(2)(ii)(G) as new paragraph (c).

12. Adding a new paragraph (b)(2)(ii)(G).

13. In the introductory language of newly-designated paragraph (c), removing the language "paragraph (b)(2)(ii)" and adding the language "section" in its place.

14. Adding new *Examples 7, 8, 9,* and *10* to newly-designated paragraph (c).

15. Redesignating paragraph (b)(1)(ii) *Example,* as new *Example 11* in newly-designated paragraph (c), revising the paragraph heading and removing paragraph (b)(1)(ii).

16. Adding a new sentence at the end of newly-designated paragraph (e) and revising the paragraph heading.

The additions read as follows:

§1.861-4. Compensation for labor or personal services.

* * *

(b) * * *

(2) * * *

(ii) * * *

(G) *Event basis.*—The amount of compensation for labor or personal services determined on an event basis is the amount of the person's compensation which, based on the facts and circumstances, is attributable to the labor or personal services performed at the location of a specific event. The source of compensation for labor or personal services determined on an event basis is the location of the specific event. A basis that purports to determine the source of compensation from the performance of labor or personal services at a specific event, whether on a time basis or otherwise, by taking into account the location of labor or personal services performed in preparation for the performance of labor or personal services at the specific event will generally not be the basis that most correctly determines the source of the compensation.

(c) *Examples.*—* * *

Example 7. P, a citizen and resident of Country A, is paid by Company Z to make a presentation in the United States in 2009. In 2010, Company Z pays P to make 10 presentations, four of which are in the United States and six of which are outside the United States. P is compensated separately by Company Z for each presentation. For some presentations P receives a flat fee from Company Z. For the remaining presentations P receives compensation that is based on a formula. Under the facts and circumstances of the particular case, the source of the compensation for each presentation is most correctly reflected on an event basis, as defined in paragraph (b)(2)(ii)(G) of this section. Because P is compensated separately for each presentation, the source of P's compensation from Company Z for the 2009 presentation within the United States and the four 2010 presentations in the United States will be from sources in the United States. The amounts will be determined based on the flat fee or the formula as contractually determined.

Example 8. (i) *Facts.* Group B, a Country N corporation, is a musical group. All of the members of Group B are citizens and residents of Country N. Group B has an employment arrangement with Corp Y, a Country N corporation, to perform as directed by Corp Y. Corp Y and a tour promoter enter into a contract to provide the services of Group B to perform in musical concerts in the United States and Country M during a 45-day period. Under the contract, Group B performs concerts in 15 cities, 10 of which are in the United States. Prior to entering the United States, Group B spends 60 days rehearsing and preparing in Country N. Under the contract with Corp Y, Group B receives a flat fee of $10,000,000 for performing in all 15 cities. The fee is based on expected revenues from the musical concerts. Each concert is expected to require a similar amount and type of labor or personal services by Group B. At the end of the tour, an analysis of the revenues from all of the concerts shows that 80% of the total revenues from the tour were from the performances within the United States.

(ii) *Analysis.* Under the facts and circumstances basis of paragraph (b)(1) of this section, the source of the compensation received under the contract is most correctly reflected on an event basis, as defined in paragraph (b)(2)(ii)(G) of this section, with amounts determined based on the relative gross receipts attributable to the performances within and without the United States. Thus, of the $10,000,000 of compensation included in Group B's gross income, $8,000,000 ($10,000,000 × .80) is attributable to labor or personal services performed by Group B within the United States and $2,000,000 ($10,000,000 × .20) is attributable to the labor or personal services performed by Group B without the United States.

Example 9. (i) *Facts.* A, a citizen and resident of Country M, is an employee of Corp X, a Country M corporation. During 2008, Corp X is contractually obligated to provide A's services to perform in a specific athletic event in the United States. Under A's employment contract with Corp X, A is required to perform at a professional level that requires training and other preparation prior to the event. A undertakes all of this preparation in Country M. Solely as a result of A's performance at the athletic event in the United States, A receives $2,000,000 from Corp. X.

(ii) *Analysis.* The entire $2,000,000 received by A for performing labor or personal services at the athletic event in the United States is income from sources within the United States on an event basis as defined in paragraph (b)(2)(ii)(G) of this section. A's compensation is attributable entirely to labor or personal services performed within the United States at the athletic event. It is inappropriate to conclude that the source of A's compensation for labor or personal services is performed partly within and partly without the United States simply because A's preparation for the athletic event involved activities in Country M.

Example 10. (i) *Facts.* X, a citizen and resident of Country M, is employed under a standard player's contract by a professional sports team (Team) that plays its games both within and without the United States during its season. The term of the contract is for twelve months beginning on October 1. Under the contract, X's salary could be paid in semi-monthly installments beginning with the first game of the regular season and ending with the final game played by the Team. Alternatively, because the regular playing season was shorter than the one-year period covered by the contract, X had the option to receive his salary over a twelve-month period. X elected this option. In addition, during the period of this employment contract, X, as an employee of Team, was required to practice at the direction of the Team as well as to participate in games. During 2008, X participated in all practices and games of Team and received a salary. Team qualified for postseason games in 2008. X also received in 2008 additional amounts for playing in preseason and postseason games for the Team.

(ii) *Analysis.* The salary paid to X by the Team is considered to be personal services compensation of X that X received as an employee of the Team. The source of this compensation within the United States is determined under the time basis method described in paragraph (b)(2)(ii)(A) of this section and accordingly is determined based upon the number of days X performed services for the Team within the United States during 2008 over the total number of days that X performed services for the Team during 2008. The source of the additional amounts X received for playing in preseason and postseason games is determined under the event basis method described in paragraph (b)(2)(ii)(G) of this section and accordingly is determined based on the location where each such preseason or postseason game was played.

Example 11. * * *

* * *

(e) *Effective/applicability date.*—* * * The revisions in paragraphs (b)(1), (b)(2)(i), and (b)(2)(ii)(C)(1)(i) and (ii) of this section which refer to the event basis; the revisions of paragraphs (b)(2)(ii)(C)(e), (b)(2)(ii)(E), (b)(2)(ii)(F), (b)(2)(ii)(G), and (c) of this section; and *Examples 7* through *11* of paragraph (c) of this section apply to taxable years beginning after the date final regulations are published in the Federal Register.

Cloud and Digital Content Transactions: Classification

Cloud and Digital Content Transactions: Classification.—Amendments to Reg. § 1.861-7, regarding the classification of cloud transactions for purposes of the international provisions of the Internal Revenue Code, are proposed (published in the Federal Register on August 14, 2019) (REG-130700-14).

Par. 2. Section 1.861-7 is amended by revising paragraph (c) to read as follows:

§1.861-7. Sale of personal property.

* * *

(c) *Country in which sold.*—For purposes of part I (section 861 and following), subchapter N, chapter 1 of the Code, and the regulations thereunder, a sale of personal property is consummated at the time when, and the place where, the rights, title, and interest of the seller in the property are transferred to the buyer. Where bare legal title is retained by the seller, the sale shall be deemed to have occurred at the time and place of passage to the buyer of beneficial ownership and the risk of loss. For determining the place of sale of copyrighted articles transferred in electronic medium, see § 1.861-18(f)(2)(ii). However, in any case in which the sales transaction is arranged in a particular manner for the primary purpose of tax avoidance, the foregoing rules will not be applied. In such cases, all factors of the transaction, such as negotiations, the execution of the agreement, the location of the property, and the place of payment, will be considered, and the sale will be treated as having been consummated at the place where the substance of the sale occurred.

* * *

Allocation and Apportionment of Deductions and Foreign Tax Credit: Guidance

Allocation and Apportionment of Deductions and Foreign Tax Credit: Guidance.—Amendments to Reg. §§1.861-8 and 1.861-9 and Temporary Reg. §§1.861-8T and 1.861-9T, relating to the allocation and apportionment of deductions and creditable foreign taxes, the definition of financial services income, foreign tax redeterminations, availability of foreign tax credits under the transition tax, and the application of the foreign tax credit limitation to consolidated groups, are proposed (published in the Federal Register on December 17, 2019) (REG-105495-19).

Par. 3. Section 1.861-8 is amended by:

1. Adding a sentence to the end of paragraph (a)(1).
2. Revising paragraph (d)(2)(ii)(B).
3. Adding paragraph (d)(2)(v).
4. Revising paragraph (e)(4)(ii).
5. Revising the heading of paragraph (e)(5) and adding five sentences to the end of paragraph (e)(5).
6. Revising the first sentence of paragraph (e)(6)(i).
7. Revising paragraphs (e)(7) and (8).
8. Adding paragraph (e)(16).
9. Adding paragraphs (g)(15) through (18) and paragraph (g)(24);
10. Revising paragraph (h).

The additions and revisions read as follows:

§1.861-8. Computation of taxable income from sources within the United States and from other sources and activities.—(a) * * *

(1) * * * The term "section 861 regulations" means this section, §§1.861-8T, 1.861-9, 1.861-9T, 1.861-10, 1.861-10T, 1.861-11, 1.861-11T, 1.861-12, 1.861-12T, 1.861-13, 1.861-14, 1.861-14T, 1.861-17, and §1.861-20.

* * *

(d) * * *

(2) * * *

(ii) * * *

(B) *Certain stock and dividends.*—The term "exempt income" includes the portion of the dividends that are deductible under section 243(a)(1) or (2) (relating to the dividends received deduction) or section 245(a) (relating to the dividends received deduction for dividends from certain foreign corporations). Thus, for purposes of apportioning deductions using a gross income method, gross income does not include a dividend to the extent that it gives rise to a dividend received deduction under either section 243(a)(1), section 243(a)(2), or section 245(a). In addition, for purposes of apportioning deductions using an asset method, assets do not include that portion of the value of the stock (determined in accordance with §1.861-9(g), and, as relevant, §§1.861-12 and 1.861-13) equal to the portion of dividends paid thereon that would be deductible under either section 243(a)(1), section 243(a)(2), or section 245(a). For example, in the case of stock for which all dividends would be allowed a deduction of 50 percent under section 243(a)(1), 50 percent of the value of the stock is treated as an exempt asset. In the case of stock which generates, has generated, or can reasonably be expected to generate qualifying dividends deductible under section 243(a)(3), such stock does not constitute an exempt asset. However, such stock and the qualifying dividends thereon are eliminated from consideration in the apportionment of interest expense under the consolidation rule set forth in §1.861-11T(c), and in the apportionment of other expenses under the consolidation rules set forth in §1.861-14T.

* * *

(v) *Dividends received deduction and tax-exempt interest of insurance companies.*—(A) *In general.*—For purposes of characterizing gross income or assets as exempt or not exempt under this section, the following rules apply on a company wide basis pursuant to the rules in paragraphs (d)(2)(v)(A)(1) and (2) of this section.

(1) In the case of an insurance company taxable under section 801, the term "exempt income" includes the portion of dividends received that satisfy the requirements of deductibility under sections 243(a)(1) and (2) and 245(a) but without regard to any disallowance under section 805(a)(4)(A)(ii) of the policyholder's share of the dividends or any similar disallowance under section 805(a)(4)(D), and also includes tax-exempt interest but without reduction for the policyholder's share of tax-exempt interest that reduces the closing balance of items described in section 807(c), as provided under section 807(a)(2)(B) and 807(b)(1)(B). The term "exempt assets" includes the corresponding portion of assets that give rise to exempt income described in the preceding sentence. See §1.861-8(e)(16) for a special rule concerning the allocation of reserve expenses to dividends received by a life insurance company.

(2) In the case of an insurance company taxable under section 831, the term "exempt income" includes the portion of interest and dividends deductible under sections 832(c)(7) and (12) or sections 834(c)(1) and (7). Exempt income also includes the amounts reducing the losses incurred under section 832(b)(5) to the extent such amounts are not already taken into account in the preceding sentence. The term "exempt assets" includes the corresponding portion of assets that give rise to exempt income described in the preceding two sentences.

(B) *Examples.*—The following examples illustrate the application of paragraph (d)(2)(v)(A) of this section.

(1) *Example 1*—(i) *Facts.* USC is a domestic life insurance company that has $300x of gross income, consisting of $100x of foreign source general category income and $200x of U.S. source passive category interest income, $100x of which is tax-exempt interest income from municipal bonds under section 103. USC's opening balance of its section 807(c) reserves is $50,000x and USP's closing balance of its section 807(c) reserves is $50,130x. Under section 807(b)(1)(B), USP's closing balance of its section 807(c) reserves, $50,130x, is reduced by the amount of the policyholder's share of tax-exempt interest. The policyholder's share of tax-exempt interest under section 812(b) is equal to 30 percent of the $100x of tax-exempt interest ($30x). Therefore, under sections 803(a)(2) and 807(b), USP's reserve deduction is $100x ($50,130x of reserve deduction minus $30x (30 percent of $100x of tax-exempt interest), minus $50,000x). USC has no other income or deductions.

(ii) *Analysis — allocation.* Under section 818(f)(1), USC's reserve deduction is treated as an item that cannot be definitely allocated to an item or class of gross income. Accordingly, under paragraph (b)(5) of this section, USC's reserve deduction is allocable to all of USC's gross income as a class.

(iii) *Analysis — apportionment.* Under paragraph (c)(3) of this section, the reserve deduction is ratably apportioned between the statutory grouping (foreign source general category income) and the residual grouping (U.S. source income) on the basis of the relative amounts of gross income in each grouping. For purposes of apportioning deductions under §1.861-8T(d)(2)(i)(B), exempt income is not taken into account. Under paragraph (d)(2)(v)(A)(1) of this section, in the case of an insurance company taxable under section 801, exempt income includes tax-exempt interest without regard to any reduction for the policyholder's share. USC has U.S. source income of $200x of which $100x is tax-exempt without regard to the reduction for the policyholder's share of tax-exempt interest that reduces the closing balance of items described in section 807(c). Thus, the gross income taken into account in apportioning USC's reserve deduction is $100x of foreign source general category gross income and $100x of U.S. source gross income. Of USC's $100x reserve deduction, $50x ($100x x $100x/$200x) is apportioned to foreign source general category gross income and $50x ($100x x $100x/$200x) is apportioned to U.S. source gross income.

(2) *Example 2*—(i) *Facts.* USC is a domestic life insurance company that has $300x of gross income consisting of $100x of foreign source general category income and $200x of U.S. source general category dividend income eligible for the 50% dividends received deduction (DRD) under section 243(a)(1). Under section 805(a)(4)(A)(ii), USC is allowed a 50% DRD on the company's share of the dividend received. Under section 812(a), the company's share is equal to 70% of the dividend income eligible for the DRD under section 243(a)(1), which results in a DRD of $70x (70% x 50% x $200x), and under section 812(b), the policyholder's share is equal to 30% of the dividend income eligible for the DRD under section 243(a)(1), or $30x. USC is entitled to a $130x deduction for an increase in its life insurance reserves under sections 803(a)(2) and 807(b). Unlike for tax-exempt interest income, there is no adjustment under section 807(b)(1)(B) to the reserve deduction for the policyholder's share of dividends eligible for the DRD under section 243(a)(1). USC has no other income or deductions.

(ii) *Analysis — allocation.* Under section 818(f)(1), USC's reserve is treated as an item that cannot be definitely allocated to an item or class of gross income except that, under §1.861-8(e)(16), an amount of reserve expenses of a life insurance company equal to the DRD that is disallowed because it is attributable to the policyholder's share of dividends is treated as definitely related to such dividends. Thus, USC has a life insurance reserve deduction of $130x, of which $30x (equal to the policyholder's share of the DRD that would have been allowed under section 243(a)(1)) is directly allocated and apportioned to U.S. source dividend income. Under paragraph (b)(5) of this section, the remaining portion of USC's reserve deduction ($100x) is allocable to all of USC's gross income as a class.

(iii) *Analysis — apportionment.* Under paragraph (c)(3) of this section, the deduction is ratably apportioned between the statutory grouping (foreign source general category income) and the residual grouping (U.S. source income) on the basis of the relative amounts of gross income in each grouping. For purposes of apportioning deductions under §1.861-8T(d)(2)(i)(B), exempt income is not taken into account. Under paragraph (d)(2)(v)(A)(1) of this section, in the case of an insurance company taxable under section 801, exempt income includes dividends deductible under section 805(a)(4) without regard to any reduction to the DRD for the policyholder's share in section 804(a)(4)(A)(ii). Thus, the gross income taken into account in apportioning $100x of USC's remaining reserve deduction is $100x of foreign source general category gross income and $100x of U.S. source gross income. Of USC's $100x remaining reserve deduction, $50x ($100x x $100x/$200x) is apportioned to foreign source general category gross income and $50x ($100x x $100x/$200x) is apportioned to U.S. source gross income.

* * *

(e) * * *

(4) * * *

(ii) *Stewardship expenses.*—(A) *In general.*—Stewardship expenses result from "overseeing" functions undertaken for a corporation's own benefit as an investor in a related corporation. For purposes of this section, stewardship expenses of a corporation are those expenses resulting from "duplicative activities" (as defined in §1.482-9(l)(3)(iii)) or "shareholder activities" (as defined in §1.482-9(l)(3)(iv)) of the corporation with respect to the related corporation. Thus, for example, stewardship expenses include expenses of an activity the sole effect of which is either to protect the corporation's capital investment in the related corporation or to facilitate compliance by the corporation with reporting, legal, or regulatory requirements applicable specifically to the corporation, or both. If a corporation has a foreign or international department which exercises overseeing functions with respect to related foreign corporations and, in addition, the department performs other functions that generate other foreign-source income (such as fees for services rendered outside of the United States for the benefit of foreign related corporations and foreign-source royalties), some part of the deductions with respect to that department are considered definitely related to the other foreign-source income. In some instances, the operations of a foreign or international department will also generate U.S. source income (such as fees for services performed in the United States).

(B) *Allocation.*—Stewardship expenses are considered definitely related and allocable to dividends and inclusions received or accrued, or to be received or accrued, under sections 78, 951 and 951A, as well as amounts included under sections 1291, 1293, and 1296, from the related corporation.

(C) *Apportionment.*—Stewardship expenses must be apportioned between the statutory grouping (or groupings) and residual grouping based on the relative values of the stock in each grouping held by a taxpayer, as determined and characterized under § 1.861-9T(g) (and, as relevant, § § 1.861-12 and 1.861-13) for purposes of allocating and apportioning the taxpayer's interest expense.

(D) *Partnerships.*—The principles of paragraph (e)(4)(ii)(A) of this section apply to determine if expenses incurred with respect to a partnership are stewardship expenses. Stewardship expenses incurred with respect to a partnership are considered definitely related and allocable to a partner's distributive share of partnership income. The principles of paragraph (e)(4)(ii)(C) of this section apply to apportion expenses incurred with respect to a partnership.

(5) *Legal and accounting fees and expenses; damages awards, prejudgment interest, and settlement payments.*—* * * Awards for litigation or arbitral damages, prejudgment interest, and payments in settlement of or in anticipation of claims for damages, including punitive damages, arising from product liability and similar or related claims are definitely related and allocable to the class of gross income produced by the specific sales of the products or services that gave rise to the claims for damage or injury. If the claims arise from an event incident to the production of products or provision of services rather than from damage or injury caused by the product or service, the payments are definitely related and allocable to the class of gross income ordinarily produced by the assets used to produce the products or services that are involved in the event. If necessary, the deductions arising from the event are apportioned among the statutory and residual groupings on the basis of the relative values (as determined under § 1.861-9T(g) and, as relevant, § § 1.861-12 and 1.861-13, for purposes of allocating and apportioning the taxpayer's interest expense) of the assets in each grouping. If the claims are made by investors in a corporation, arise from negligence, fraud, or other malfeasance of the corporation (or its representatives), and are not described in the preceding two sentences, then the damages, prejudgment interest, and settlement payments paid by the corporation are definitely related and allocable to all income of the corporation and are apportioned among the statutory and residual groupings based on the relative value of the corporation's assets in each grouping (as determined under § 1.861-9T(g) and, as relevant, § § 1.861-12 and 1.861-13, for purposes of allocating and apportioning the taxpayer's interest expense). The grouping (or groupings) of income to which damages, prejudgment interest, and settlement payments is allocated and apportioned is determined based on the groupings to which the related income would be assigned if the income were recognized in the taxable year in which the deduction is allowed.

(6) * * *

(i) * * * The deduction for foreign income, war profits and excess profits taxes allowed by section 164 is allocated and apportioned among the applicable statutory and residual groupings under § 1.861-20. * * *

* * *

(7) *Losses on the sale, exchange, or other disposition of property.*— See § § 1.865-1 and 1.865-2 for rules regarding the allocation of certain losses.

(8) *Net operating loss deduction.*—(i) *Components of net operating loss.*—A net operating loss is assigned to statutory or residual grouping components by reference to the losses in each such statutory or residual grouping that are not allocated to reduce income in other groupings in the taxable year of the loss. For example, for purposes of section 904, the source and separate category components of a net operating loss are determined by reference to the amounts of separate

rate limitation loss and U.S. source loss (determined without regard to adjustments required under section 904(b)) that are not allocated to reduce U.S. source income or income in other separate categories under the rules of sections 904(f) and 904(g) for the taxable year in which the net operating loss arose. *See* § 1.904(g)-3(d)(2). See § 1.1502-4 for rules applicable in computing the foreign tax credit limitation and determining the source and separate category of a net operating loss of a consolidated group.

(ii) *Components of section 172 deduction.*—A net operating loss deduction allowed under section 172 is allocated and apportioned to statutory and residual groupings by reference to the statutory and residual grouping components of the net operating loss that is deducted in the taxable year. Except as provided under the rules for an operative section, a partial net operating loss deduction is treated as ratably comprising the components of a net operating loss. See, for example, § 1.904(g)-3, which is an exception to the general rule described in the previous sentence and provides rules for determining the source and separate category of a partial net operating loss deduction for purposes of section 904 as the operative section.

* * *

(16) *Special rule for the allocation of reserve expenses of a life insurance company.*—An amount of reserve expenses of a life insurance company equal to the dividends received deduction that is disallowed because it is attributable to the policyholders' share of dividends received is treated as definitely related to such dividends. See paragraph (d)(2)(v)(B)(2) of this section (*Example 2*).

* * *

(g) * * *

(15) *Example 15: Payment in settlement of claim for damages allocated to specific class of gross income.*—(i) *Facts*—USP, a domestic corporation, designs, manufactures, and sells Product A in the United States. USP also operates a foreign branch, within the meaning of § 1.904-4(f)(3)(vii), in Country X through FDE, a disregarded entity organized in Country X, which manufactures and sells Product A in Country X. USP earns $300x of U.S. source income from sales of Product A to customers in the United States. The sales of Product A to customers in Country X result in aggregate gross income of $100x, of which $80x is U.S. source income attributable to USP's manufacturing activities and $20x is U.S. source income attributable to FDE's distribution activities. The $100x of income from sales of Product A to customers in Country X constitutes foreign branch category income. FDE is sued under Country X law for damages after Product A harms a customer in Country X. FDE makes a deductible payment to the Country X customer in settlement of the legal claims for damages.

(ii) *Analysis.* Because Product A caused the customer's injury, the claim for damages arose from the specific sales of Product A to the customer in Country X. Claims that might arise from damages caused by Product A to customers in the United States are irrelevant in allocating the deduction for the settlement payments made to the customer in Country X. Therefore, FDE's damages payment deduction is allocable to the class of gross income of sales of Product A in Country X. For purposes of section 904(d), because that class of gross income consists solely of U.S. source income, none of that income is included in the statutory grouping of foreign source foreign branch category income, and accordingly the damages payment deduction reduces USP's residual grouping of U.S. source income.

(16) *Example 16: Legal damages payment arising from event prior to sale.*—(i) *Facts*—The facts are the same as in paragraph (g)(15) of this section (the facts in *Example 15*) except that there is a disaster at FDE's warehouse in Country X arising from the negligence of an employee. The inventory of Product A in the warehouse is destroyed and FDE employees as well as residents in the vicinity of the warehouse are injured. USP's reputation in the United States suffers such that USP expects to subsequently lose market share in the United States. FDE makes damages payments totaling $80x to both its injured employees and the nearby residents.

(ii) *Analysis.* FDE's warehouse in Country X is used in connection with sales of Product A to customers in Country X. Thus, the $80x damages payment is allocable to the class of gross income ordinarily produced by the assets used to produce Product A. No apportionment of the $80x is necessary for purposes of applying section 904(d) because the class of gross income to which the deduction is allocated consists solely of U.S. source income

(17) *Example 17: Payment following a change in law.*—(i) *Facts.* The facts are the same as in paragraph (g)(15) (the facts in *Example 15*) except that FDE manufactures and sells Product A in Country X in 2015 (before the enactment of the section 904(d)(1)(B) separate category for foreign branch income) and is sued in 2016 under Country X law for damages after Product A harms a customer in Country X. FDE makes a deductible damages payment to the Country X customer pursuant to a court judgment in 2019.

(ii) *Analysis.* The specific sales of Product A in Country X in 2015 led to the customer's injury in Country X. The payment in 2019 of the deductible damages payment is definitely related and allocable to the class of gross income consisting of Product A sales in Country X. Although the income earned from the Product A sales in Country X in 2015 was foreign source general category income, in 2019 the assets used to produce such income is U.S. source foreign branch category income. Accordingly, the deductible damages payment is allocated to foreign branch category income. No apportionment of the payment is necessary because the class of gross income to which the deduction is allocated consists solely of U.S. source income.

(18) *Example 18: Stewardship and supportive expenses.*—(i) *Facts*—(A) USP, a domestic corporation, manufactures and sells Product A in the United States. USP owns 100% of the stock of USSub, a domestic corporation, and CFC1, CFC2, and CFC3, which are all controlled foreign corporations. USP and USSub file separate returns for U.S. Federal income tax purposes but are members of the same affiliated group under section 243(b)(2). USSub, CFC1, CFC2, and CFC3 perform similar functions in the United States and in the foreign countries T, U, and V, respectively. The tax book value of USP's stock in each of its four subsidiaries is $10,000x.

(B) USP's supervision department (the Department) incurs expenses of $1,500x. The Department is responsible for the supervision of its four subsidiaries and for rendering certain services to the subsidiaries, and the Department provides all the supportive functions necessary for USP's foreign activities. The Department performs three principal types of activities. First, the Department performs services outside the United States for the direct benefit of CFC2 for which a fee is paid by CFC2 to USP. The cost to the Department of the services for CFC2 is $900x, which results in a total charge (after a $100x markup) to CFC2 of $1,000x, all of which is foreign source income to USP. Second, the Department provides services related to license agreements that USP maintains with subsidiaries CFC1 and CFC2 and which give rise to foreign source income to USP. The cost of the services is $60x. Third, it performs activities described in §1.482-9(l)(3)(iii) that are in the nature of shareholder oversight, that duplicate functions performed by the subsidiaries' own employees, and that do not provide an additional benefit to the subsidiaries. For example, a team of auditors from USP's accounting department periodically audits the subsidiaries' books and prepares internal reports for use by USP's management. Similarly, USP's treasurer periodically reviews for the board of directors of USP the subsidiaries' financial policies. These activities do not provide an additional benefit to the related corporations. The cost of the duplicative services and related supportive expenses is $540x.

(C) USP also earns the following items of income. First, under section 951(a), USP includes $2,000x of subpart F income that is passive category income. Second, under section 951A and the section 951A regulations (as defined in §1.951A-1(a)(1)), USP has a GILTI inclusion amount of $2,000x. USP's deduction under section 250 is $1,000x ("section 250 deduction"), all of which is by reason of section 250(a)(1)(B)(i). No portion of USP's section 250 deduction is reduced by reason of section 250(a)(2)(B). Finally, USP also earns $1,000x of fees from CFC2 and receives royalties of $1,000x from CFC1 and CFC2.

(D) Under §1.861-9T(g)(3), USSub owns assets that generate income described in the residual grouping of gross income from U.S. sources. USP uses the asset method described in §1.861-12T(c)(3)(ii) to characterize the stock in its CFCs. After application of §1.861-13(a), USP determines that $5,000x of the stock of each of the three CFCs is assigned to the section 951A category ("section 951A category stock") in the non-section 245A subgroup; $2,000x of the stock of each of the three CFCs is assigned to the general category in the section 245A subgroup; and $3,000x of the stock of each of the three CFCs is assigned to the passive category in the non-section 245A subgroup. Additionally, under §1.861-8(d)(2)(ii)(C)(2), $2,500x of the stock of each of the three CFCs that is section 951A category stock is an exempt asset. Accordingly, with respect to the stock of its controlled foreign corporations in the aggregate, USP has $7,500x of section 951A category stock in a non-section 245A subgroup, $6,000x of general category stock in a section 245A subgroup, $9,000x of passive category stock in a non-section 245A subgroup, and $7,500x of stock that is an exempt asset.

(ii) *Analysis*—(A) *Character of USP Department services.* The first and second activities (the services rendered for the benefit of CFC2, and the provision of services related to license agreements with CFC1 and CFC2) are not properly characterized as stewardship expenses because they are not incurred solely to protect the corporation's capital investment in the related corporation or to facilitate compliance by the corporation with reporting, legal, or regulatory requirements applicable specifically to the corporation. The third activity described is in the nature of shareholder oversight and is characterized as stewardship as described in paragraph (e)(4)(ii)(A) of this section because the expense is related to duplicative activities.

(B) *Allocation.* First, the deduction of $900x for expenses related to services rendered for the benefit of CFC2 is definitely related (and therefore allocable) to the $1,000x in fees for services that USP receives from CFC2. Second, the $60x of deductions attributable to USP's license agreements with CFC1 and CFC2 are definitely related (and therefore allocable) solely to royalties received from CFC1 and CFC2. Third, the stewardship deduction of $540x is definitely related (and therefore allocable) to dividends and inclusions received from all the subsidiaries.

(C) *Apportionment*—(1) No apportionment of USP's deduction of $900x for expenses related to the services is necessary because the class of gross income to which the deduction is allocated consists entirely of a single statutory grouping, foreign source general category income.

(2) No apportionment of USP's deduction of $60x attributable to the ancillary services is necessary because the class of gross income to which the deduction is allocated consists entirely of a single statutory grouping, foreign source general category income.

(3) For purposes of apportioning USP's $540x stewardship expenses in determining the foreign tax credit limitation, the statutory groupings are foreign source general category income, foreign source passive category income, and foreign source section 951A category income. The residual grouping is U.S. source income.

(4) USP's deduction of $540x for the Department's stewardship expenses which are allocable to dividends and inclusions received from the subsidiaries are apportioned using the same value of USP's stock in USSub, CFC1, CFC2, and CFC3 that is used for purposes of allocating and apportioning USP's interest expense. However, the $10,000x value of USP's stock of USSub is eliminated because USSub generates qualifying dividends deductible under section 243(a)(3). *See* §1.861-8(d)(2)(ii)(B).

(5) Although USP may be allowed a section 245A deduction with respect to dividends from the CFCs, the value of the stock of the CFCs is not eliminated because the section 245A deduction does not create exempt income or result in the stock being treated as an exempt asset. *See* section 864(e)(3) and §1.861-8T(d)(2)(iii)(C). Therefore, the only asset value upon which stewardship expenses are apportioned is the stock in USP's CFCs.

(6) Taking into account the characterization of USP's stock in CFC1, CFC2, and CFC3, and excluding the exempt portion, the $540x of Department expenses is apportioned as follows: $180x ($540x x $7,500x/$22,500x) to section 951A category income, $144x ($540x x $6,000x/$22,500x) to general category income, and $216x ($540x x $9,000x/$22,500x) to passive category income. Section 904(b)(4)(B)(i) applies to $144x of the stewardship expense apportioned to the CFCs' stock that is characterized as being in the section 245A subgroup in the general category.

* * *

(24) For guidance, see §1.861-8T(g) *Example* 24.

* * *

(h) *Applicability date.*—(1) Except as provided in paragraph (h)(2) of this section, this section applies to taxable years that both begin after December 31, 2017, and end on or after December 4, 2018.

(2) Paragraphs (d)(2)(ii)(B), (d)(2)(v), (e)(4), (e)(5), (e)(6)(i), (e)(8), (e)(16), and (g)(15) through (g)(18) of this section apply to taxable years that end on or after December 16, 2019. For taxable years that both begin after December 31, 2017, and end on or after December 4, 2018, and also end before December 16, 2019, see §1.861-8(d)(2)(ii)(B), (e)(4), (e)(5), (e)(6)(i), and (e)(8) as in effect on December 17, 2019.

Par. 4. Section 1.861-8T is amended by revising paragraph (d)(2)(ii)(B) to read as follows:

§1.861-8T. Computation of taxable income from sources within the United States and from other sources and activities (temporary).

* * *

(d) ***

Par. 5. Section 1.861-9 is amended by:
1. Revising paragraphs (a) and (b).

(2) ***

(ii) ***

(B) For further guidance, see §1.861-8(d)(2)(ii)(B).

* * *

2. Revising paragraphs (c)(1) through (4).

3. Adding paragraph (e)(9).

4. Revising paragraph (k).

The revisions and additions read as follows:

§1.861-9. Allocation and apportionment of interest expense and rules for asset-based apportionment.—(a) For further guidance, see §1.861-9T(a).

(b) *Interest equivalent.*—(1) *Certain expenses and losses.*—(i) *General rule.*—Any expense or loss (to the extent deductible) incurred in a transaction or series of integrated or related transactions in which the taxpayer secures the use of funds for a period of time is subject to allocation and apportionment under the rules of this section and §1.861-9T(b) if such expense or loss is substantially incurred in consideration of the time value of money. However, the allocation and apportionment of a loss under this paragraph (b) and §1.861-9T(b) does not affect the characterization of such loss as capital or ordinary for any purpose other than for purposes of the section 861 regulations (as defined in §1.861-8(a)(1)).

(ii) *Examples.*—For further guidance, see §1.861-9T(b)(1)(ii).

(2) *Certain foreign currency borrowings.*—For further guidance, see §1.861-9T(b)(2) through (7).

(3) through (7) [Reserved]

(8) *Guaranteed payments.*—Any deductions for guaranteed payments for the use of capital under section 707(c) are allocated and apportioned in the same manner as interest expense.

(c)(1) *Disallowed deductions.*—For further guidance, see §1.861-9T(c)(1) through (4).

(2) through (4) [Reserved]

* * *

(e) * * *

(9) *Special rule for upstream partnership loans.*—(i) *In general.*—For purposes of apportioning interest expense that is not directly allocable under paragraph (e)(4) of this section or §1.861-10T, an upstream partnership loan debtor's (UPL debtor) pro rata share of the value of the upstream partnership loan (as determined under paragraph (h)(4)(i) of this section) is not considered an asset of the UPL debtor taken into account as described in paragraphs (e)(2) and (3) of this section.

(ii) *Treatment of interest expense and interest income attributable to an upstream partnership loan.*—If a UPL debtor (or any other person in the same affiliated group as the UPL debtor) takes into account a distributive share of upstream partnership loan interest income (UPL interest income), the UPL debtor assigns an amount of its distributive share of the UPL interest income equal to the matching expense amount for the taxable year that is attributable to the same loan to the same statutory and residual groupings using the same ratios as the statutory and residual groupings of gross income from which the upstream partnership loan interest expense (UPL interest expense) is deducted by the UPL debtor (or any other person in the same affiliated group as the UPL debtor). Therefore, the amount of the distributive share of UPL interest income that is assigned to each statutory and residual grouping is the amount that bears the same proportion to the matching expense amount as the UPL interest expense in that statutory or residual grouping bears to the total UPL interest expense of the UPL debtor (or any other person in the same affiliated group as the UPL debtor).

(iii) *Anti-avoidance rule for third party back-to-back loans.*—If, with a principal purpose of avoiding the rules in this paragraph (e)(9), a partnership makes a loan to a person that is not related (within the meaning of section 267(b) or 707) to the lender, the unrelated person makes a loan to a direct or indirect partner in the partnership (or any person in the same affiliated group as a direct or indirect partner), and the first loan would constitute an upstream partnership loan if made directly to the direct or indirect partner (or person in the same affiliated group as a direct or indirect partner), then the rules of this paragraph (e)(9) apply as if the first loan was made directly by the partnership to the partner (or affiliate of the partner), and the interest expense paid by the partner is treated as made with respect to the first loan. Such a series of loans will be subject to this recharacterization rule without regard to whether there was a principal purpose of avoiding the rules in this paragraph (e)(9) if the loan to the unrelated person would not have been made or maintained on substantially the same terms but for the loan of funds by the unrelated person to the direct or indirect partner (or affiliate of the partner). The principles of this paragraph (e)(9)(iii) also apply to similar transactions that involve more than two loans and regardless of the order in which the loans are made.

(iv) *Interest equivalents.*—The principles of this paragraph (e)(9) apply in the case of a partner, or any person in the same affiliated group as the partner, that takes into account a distributive share of income and has a matching expense amount (treating any interest equivalent described in §§1.861-9(b) and 1.861-9T(b) as interest income or expense for purposes of paragraph (e)(9)(v)(B) of this section) that is allocated and apportioned in the same manner as interest expense under §§1.861-9(b) and 1.861-9T(b).

(v) *Definitions.*—For purposes of this paragraph (e)(9), the following definitions apply.

(A) *Affiliated group.*—The term *affiliated group* has the meaning provided in §1.861-11(d)(1).

(B) *Matching expense amount.*—The term *matching expense amount* means the lesser of the total amount of the UPL interest expense taken into account directly or indirectly by the UPL debtor for the taxable year with respect to an upstream partnership loan or the total amount of the distributive shares of the UPL interest income of the UPL debtor (or any other person in the same affiliated group as the UPL debtor) with respect to the loan.

(C) *Upstream partnership loan debtor (UPL debtor).*—The term *upstream partnership loan debtor*, or *UPL debtor*, means the person that holds the payable with respect to a upstream partnership loan. If a partnership holds the payable, then any partner in the partnership (other than a partner described in paragraph (e)(4)(i) of this section) is also considered a UPL debtor.

(D) *Upstream partnership loan interest expense (UPL interest expense).*—The term *upstream partnership loan interest expense*, or *UPL interest expense*, means an item of interest expense paid or accrued with respect to a upstream partnership loan, without regard to whether the expense was currently deductible (for example, by reason of section 163(j)).

(E) *Upstream partnership loan interest income (UPL interest income).*—The term *upstream partnership loan interest income*, or *UPL interest income*, means an item of gross interest income received or accrued with respect to an upstream partnership loan.

(F) *Upstream partnership loan.*—The term *upstream partnership loan* means a loan by a partnership to a person that owns an interest, directly or indirectly through one or more other partnerships or other pass-through entities, in the partnership, or to any person in the same affiliated group as that person.

(vi) *Examples.*—The following examples illustrate the application of this paragraph (e)(9).

(A) *Example 1*—(1) *Facts.* US1, a domestic corporation, directly owns 60% of PRS, a foreign partnership that is not engaged in a U.S. trade or business. The remaining 40% of PRS is directly owned by US2, a domestic corporation that is unrelated to US1. US1, US2, and PRS all use the calendar year as their taxable year. In Year 1, PRS loans $1,000x to US1. For Year 1, US1 has $100x of interest expense with respect to the loan and PRS has $100x of interest income with respect to the loan. US1's distributive share of the interest income is $60x. Under paragraph (e)(2) of this section, $75x of US1's interest expense with respect to the loan is allocated to U.S. source income and $25x is allocated to foreign source foreign branch category income. Under paragraph (h)(4)(i) of this section, US1's share of the total value of the loan between US1 and PRS is $600x.

(2) *Analysis.* The loan by PRS to US1 is an upstream partnership loan and US1 is an UPL debtor. Under paragraph (e)(9)(iv)(B) of this section, the matching expense amount is $60x, the lesser of the UPL interest expense taken into account by US1 with respect to the loan for the taxable year ($100x) and US1's distributive share of the UPL interest income ($60x). Under paragraph (e)(9)(ii) of this section, US1 assigns $45x of the UPL interest income to U.S. source income ($60x x $75x/$100x) and $15x of the UPL interest income to foreign source foreign branch category income ($60x x $25x/$100x). Under paragraph (e)(9)(i) of this section, the disregarded portion of the upstream partnership loan is $600x.

(B) *Example 2*—(1) *Facts.* The facts are the same as in paragraph (e)(9)(vi)(A)(1) of this section (the facts in *Example 1*), except that US1 and US2 are part of the same affiliated group, US2's distributive share of the interest income is $40x, and under paragraph (h)(4)(i) of this section US2's share of the total value of the loan between US1 and PRS is $400x.

(2) *Analysis.* The loan by PRS to US1 is an upstream partnership loan and US1 is an UPL debtor. Under paragraph (e)(9)(iv)(B) of this section, the matching expense amount is $100x, the lesser of the

UPL interest expense taken into account by US1 with respect to the loan for the taxable year ($100x) and the total amount of US1 and US2's distributive shares of the UPL interest income ($100x). Under paragraph (e)(9)(ii) of this section, US1 assigns $75x of the UPL interest income to U.S. source income ($100x x $75x/$100x) and $25x of the UPL interest income to foreign source foreign branch category income ($100x x $25x/$100x). Under paragraph (e)(9)(i) of this section, the disregarded portion of the upstream partnership loan is $1,000x, the total amount of US1 and US2's share of the loan between US1 and PRS.

Par. 6. Section 1.861-9T is amended by revising paragraph (b)(1)(i) to read "For further guidance, see § 1.861-9(b)(1)(i)." and adding paragraph (b)(8) to read "For further guidance, see § 1.861-9(b)(8).".

§ 1.861-9T. Allocation and apportionment of interest expense (temporary).

* * *

(b) ***

  (1) ***

* * *

(k) *Applicability date.*—(1) Except as provided in paragraph (k)(2) of this section, this section applies to taxable years that both begin after December 31, 2017, and end on or after December 4, 2018.

(2) Paragraphs (b)(1)(i), (b)(8), and (e)(9) of this section apply to taxable years that end on or after December 16, 2019. For taxable years that both begin after December 31, 2017, and end on or after December 4, 2018, and also end before December 16, 2019, see § 1.861-9T(b)(1)(i) as contained in 26 CFR part 1 revised as of April 1, 2019.

  (i) General rule.—For further guidance, see § 1.861-9(b)(1)(i).

* * *

  (8) Guaranteed payments.—For further guidance, see § 1.861-9(b)(8).

* * *

Income from U.S. Sources: Allocation and Apportionment

Income from U.S. Sources: Allocation and Apportionment of Expenses.—Temporary Reg. §§ 1.861-8T—1.861-12T, relating to the allocation and apportionment of interest expense and certain other expenses for purposes of the foreign tax credit rules and certain other international tax provisions, are also proposed as final regulations and, when adopted, would become §§ 1.861-8—1.861-12 (published in the Federal Register on September 14, 1988).

§ 1.861-8. Computation of taxable income from sources within the United States and from other sources and activities.

§ 1.861-9. Allocation and apportionment of income expense.

§ 1.861-10. Special allocations of interest expense.

§ 1.861-11. Special rules for allocating and apportioning interest expense of an affiliated group of corporations.

§ 1.861-12. Characterization rules and adjustments for certain assets.

Income from U.S. Sources: Transition Rules

Income from Source: Interest Expense Allocation.—Amendments of Temporary Reg. § 1.861-9T, relating to transition rules for the allocation and apportionment of interest expense for the purposes of the foreign tax credit rules and certain other international tax provisions, are also proposed as final (published in the Federal Register on August 2, 1989).

§ 1.861-9. Allocation and apportionment of interest expense.

Allocation and Apportionment of Deductions and Foreign Tax Credit: Guidance

Allocation and Apportionment of Deductions and Foreign Tax Credit: Guidance.—Amendments to Reg. § 1.861-12 and Temporary Reg. § 1.861-12T, relating to the allocation and apportionment of deductions and creditable foreign taxes, the definition of financial services income, foreign tax redeterminations, availability of foreign tax credits under the transition tax, and the application of the foreign tax credit limitation to consolidated groups, are proposed (published in the Federal Register on December 17, 2019) (REG-105495-19).

Par. 7. Section 1.861-12 is amended by revising paragraphs (d) through (i) and adding paragraph (k) to read as follows:

§ 1.861-12. Characterization rules and adjustments for certain assets.

* * *

(d) Treatment of notes. For further guidance, see § 1.861-12T(d) through (e).

  (e) [Reserved]

(f) *Assets connected with capitalized, deferred, or disallowed interest.*—(1) In general.—In the case of any asset in connection with which interest expense accruing during a taxable year is capitalized, deferred, or disallowed under any provision of the Code, the value of the asset for allocation and apportionment purposes is reduced by the principal amount of indebtedness the interest on which is so capitalized, deferred, or disallowed. Assets are connected with debt (the interest on which is capitalized, deferred, or disallowed) only if using the debt proceeds to acquire or produce the asset causes the interest to be capitalized, deferred, or disallowed.

  (2) *Examples.*—The following examples illustrate the application of paragraph (f)(1) of this section.

(i) *Example 1: Capitalized interest under section 263A*—(A) Facts. X is a domestic corporation that uses the tax book value method of apportionment. X has $1,000x of indebtedness and incurs $100x of interest expense. Using $800x of the $1,000x debt proceeds to produce tangible property, X capitalizes $80x of interest expense under the

rules of section 263A. X deducts the remaining $20x of interest expense.

(B) *Analysis.* Because interest on $800x of debt is capitalized under section 263A by reason of the use of debt proceeds to produce the tangible property, $800x of the principal amount of X's debt is connected to the tangible property under paragraph (f)(1) of this section. Therefore, for purposes of apportioning the remaining $20x of X's interest expense, the adjusted basis of the tangible property is reduced by $800x.

(ii) *Example 2: Disallowed interest under section 163(l)*—(A) Facts. X, a domestic corporation, owns 100% of the stock of Y, a domestic corporation. X and Y file a consolidated return and use the tax book value method of apportionment. In Year 1, X makes a loan of $1,000x to Y (Loan A) and Y then uses the Loan A proceeds to acquire in a cash purchase all the stock of a foreign corporation, Z. Interest on Loan A is payable in U.S. dollars or, at the option of Y, in stock of Z.

(B) *Analysis.* Under section 163(l), Loan A is a disqualified debt instrument because interest on Loan A is payable at the option of Y in stock of a related party to Y. Because Loan A is a disqualified debt instrument, section 163(l)(1) disallows Y's interest deduction for interest payable on Loan A. In addition, the value of the Z stock is not reduced under paragraph (f)(1) of this section because the use of the Loan A proceeds to acquire the stock of Z is not the cause of Y's interest deduction being disallowed. Rather, the Loan A terms allowing interest to be paid in stock of Z is the cause of Y's interest deduction being disallowed under section 163(l). Therefore, no adjustment is made to Y's adjusted basis in the stock of Z for purposes of allocating the interest expense of X and Y.

(g) *Special rules for FSCs.*—For further guidance, see § 1.861-12T(g) through (j).

(h) [Reserved]

(i) [Reserved]

* * *

Par. 8. Section 1.861-12T is amended by revising paragraph (f) to read "For further guidance, see § 1.861-12(f)."

§1.861-12T. Characterization rules and adjustments for certain assets (Temporary regulations).

* * *

Income from U.S. Sources: Transition Rules

Income from Source: Interest Expense Allocation.—Temporary Reg. § 1.861-13T, relating to transition rules for the allocation and apportionment of interest expense for the purposes of the foreign tax credit rules and certain other international tax provisions, is also proposed as final (published in the Federal Register on August 2, 1989).

§1.861-13. Transition rules for interest expenses.

Allocation and Apportionment of Deductions and Foreign Tax Credit: Guidance

Allocation and Apportionment of Deductions and Foreign Tax Credit: Guidance.—Amendments to Reg. § 1.861-14 and Temporary Reg. § 1.861-14T, relating to the allocation and apportionment of deductions and creditable foreign taxes, the definition of financial services income, foreign tax redeterminations, availability of foreign tax credits under the transition tax, and the application of the foreign tax credit limitation to consolidated groups, are proposed (published in the Federal Register on December 17, 2019) (REG-105495-19).

Par. 9. Section 1.861-14 is amended by:

1. Removing the last sentence in paragraph (d)(1).

2. Revising paragraphs (d)(3) and (4).

3. Revising paragraphs (e)(1) through (5).

4. Redesignating paragraph (e)(6)(i) as paragraph (e)(6) and removing paragraph (e)(6)(ii).

5. Revising paragraphs (f) through (k).

The revisions read as follows:

§1.861-14. Special rules for allocating and apportioning certain expenses (other than interest expense) of an affiliated group of corporations.

* * *

(d) ***

(3) *Inclusion of financial corporations.*—For further guidance, see § 1.861-14T(d)(3) through (d)(4).

(4) [Reserved]

(e) *Expenses to be allocated and apportioned under this section.*— (1) *Expenses not directly allocable to specific income producing activities or property.*—(i) The expenses that are required to be allocated and apportioned under the rules of this section are expenses that are not directly allocable to specific income producing activities or property solely of the member of the affiliated group that incurred the expense, including (but not limited to) certain expenses related to supportive functions, research and experimental expenses, stewardship expenses, legal and accounting expenses, and litigation damages awards, prejudgment interest, and settlement payments. Interest expense of members of an affiliated group of corporations is allocated and apportioned under § 1.861-11T and not under the rules of this section. Expenses that are included in inventory costs or that are capitalized are not subject to allocation and apportionment under the rules of this section.

(ii) For further guidance, see § 1.861-14T(e)(1)(ii).

(2) *Research and experimental expenditures.*—R&E expenditures (as defined in § 1.861-17(a)) in the case of an affiliated group are allocated and apportioned under the rules of § 1.861-17 as if all members of the affiliated group were a single taxpayer. Thus, R&E expenditures are allocated to all gross intangible income of all members of the affiliated group reasonably connected with the relevant broad SIC code category. If fewer than all members of the affiliated group derive gross intangible income reasonably connected with that relevant broad SIC code category, then such expenditures are apportioned under the rules of this paragraph (e)(2) only among those members, as if those members were a single taxpayer.

(3) *Expenses related to supportive functions.*—For further guidance, see § 1.861-14T(e)(3).

(4) *Stewardship expenses.*—Stewardship expenses are allocated and apportioned in accordance with the rules of § 1.861-8(e)(4). In general, stewardship expenses are considered definitely related and allocable to dividends and inclusions received or accrued, or to be received or accrued, from a related corporation. If members of the affiliated group, other than the member that incurred the steward-

ship expense, receive or may receive dividends or accrue or may accrue inclusions from the related corporation, such expense must be allocated and apportioned in accordance with the rules of paragraph (c) of this section as if all such members of the affiliated group that receive or may receive dividends were a single corporation. Such expenses must be apportioned between statutory and residual groupings of income within the appropriate class of gross income by reference to the apportionment factors contributed by the members of the affiliated group treated as a single corporation.

(5) *Legal and accounting fees and expenses; damages awards, prejudgment interest, and settlement payments.*—Legal and accounting fees and expenses, as well as litigation or arbitral damages awards, prejudgment interest, and settlement payments, are allocated and apportioned under the rules of § 1.861-8(e)(5). To the extent that under § 1.861-14T(c)(2) and (e)(1)(ii) of this section such expenses are not directly allocable to specific income-producing activities or property of one or more members of the affiliated group, such expenses must be allocated and apportioned as if all members of the affiliated group were a single corporation. Specifically, such expenses must be allocated to a class of gross income that takes into account the gross income which is generated, has been generated, or is reasonably expected to be generated by the other members of the affiliated group. If the expenses relate to the gross income of fewer than all members of the affiliated group as determined under § 1.861-14T(c)(2), then those expenses must be apportioned under the rules of § 1.861-14T(c)(2), as if those fewer members were a single corporation. Such expenses must be apportioned taking into account the apportionment factors contributed by the members of the group that are treated as a single corporation.

* * *

(f) *Computation of FSC or DISC combined taxable income.*—For further guidance, see § 1.861-14T(f) through (g).

(g) [Reserved]

(h) *Allocation of section 818(f) expenses.*—Life insurance company expenses specified in section 818(f)(1) are allocated and apportioned on a separate entity basis, including with regard to members of a consolidated group. Those expenses are not allocated and apportioned on a life-nonlife group or a life subgroup basis. See also § 1.861-8(e)(16) for rules on the allocation of reserve expenses with respect to dividends received by a life insurance company.

(i) through (j) [Reserved]

(k) *Applicability date.*—This section applies to taxable years ending on or after December 16, 2019.

(k) *Applicability date.*—(1) Except as provided in paragraph (k)(2) of this section, this section applies to taxable years that both begin after December 31, 2017, and end on or after December 4, 2018.

(2) Paragraph (f) this section applies to taxable years that end on or after December 16, 2019. For taxable years that both begin after December 31, 2017, and end on or after December 4, 2018, and before December 16, 2019, see § 1.861-12T(f) as contained in 26 CFR part 1 revised as of April 1, 2019.

(f) *Assets connected with capitalized, deferred, or disallowed interest.*—For further guidance, see § 1.861-12(f).

* * *

Par. 10. Section 1.861-14T is amended by revising paragraphs (e)(1)(i), (e)(2)(i) and (ii), (e)(4) and (5), and (h) to read as follows:

§1.861-14T. Special rules for allocating and apportioning certain expenses (other than interest expense) of an affiliated group of corporations (Temporary).

* * *

(e)(1)(i) For further guidance, see §1.861-14(e)(1)(i).

* * *

(e)(2)(i) For further guidance, see §1.861-14(e)(2)(i) through §1.861-14(e)(2)(ii).

(ii) [Reserved]

* * *

(e)(4) *Stewardship expenses.*—For further guidance, see §1.861-14(e)(4) through §1.861-14(e)(5).

(5) [Reserved]

* * *

(h) *Allocation of section 818(f) expenses.*—For further guidance, see §1.861-14(h).

* * *

Income from U.S. Sources: Allocation and Apportionment

Income from U.S. Sources: Allocation and Apportionment of Expenses.—Temporary Reg. §1.861-14T, relating to the allocation and apportionment of interest expense and certain other expenses for purposes of the foreign tax credit rules and certain other international tax provisions, is also proposed as final regulations and, when adopted, would become §1.861-14 (published in the Federal Register on September 14, 1988).

§1.861-14. Special rules for allocating and apportioning certain expenses (other than interest expense) of an affiliated group of corporations.

Allocation and Apportionment of Deductions and Foreign Tax Credit: Guidance

Allocation and Apportionment of Deductions and Foreign Tax Credit: Guidance.—Amendments to Reg. §1.861-17, relating to the allocation and apportionment of deductions and creditable foreign taxes, the definition of financial services income, foreign tax redeterminations, availability of foreign tax credits under the transition tax, and the application of the foreign tax credit limitation to consolidated groups, are proposed (published in the Federal Register on December 17, 2019) (REG-105495-19).

Par. 11. Section 1.861-17 is revised to read as follows:

§1.861-17. Allocation and apportionment of research and experimental expenditures.—(a) *Scope.*—This section provides rules for the allocation and apportionment of research and experimental expenditures that a taxpayer deducts, or amortizes and deducts, in a taxable year under section 174 or section 59(e) (applicable to expenditures that are allowable as a deduction under section 174(a)) (*R&E expenditures*). R&E expenditures do not include any expenditures that are not deductible by reason of the second sentence under §1.482-7(j)(3)(i) (relating to CST Payments (as defined in §1.482-7(b)(1)) owed to a controlled participant in a cost sharing arrangement), because nondeductible amounts are not allocated and apportioned under §§1.861-8 through 1.861-17.

(b) *Allocation.*—(1) *In general.*—The method of allocation and apportionment of R&E expenditures set forth in this section recognizes that research and experimentation is an inherently speculative activity, that findings may contribute unexpected benefits, and that the gross income derived from successful research and experimentation must bear the cost of unsuccessful research and experimentation. In addition, the method set forth in this section recognizes that successful R&E expenditures ultimately result in the creation of intangible property that will be used to generate income. Therefore, R&E expenditures ordinarily are considered deductions that are definitely related to gross intangible income (as defined in paragraph (b)(2) of this section) reasonably connected with the relevant SIC code category (or categories) of the taxpayer and therefore allocable to gross intangible income as a class related to the SIC code category (or categories) and apportioned under the rules in this section. For purposes of this allocation, a taxpayer's SIC code category (or categories) are determined in accordance with the provisions of paragraph (b)(3) of this section. For purposes of this section, the term *intangible property* means intangible property, as defined in section 367(d)(4), that is derived from R&E expenditures.

(2) *Definition of gross intangible income.*—The term *gross intangible income* means all gross income earned by a taxpayer that is attributable (in whole or in part) to intangible property and includes gross income from sales or leases of products or services derived (in whole or in part) from intangible property, income from sales of intangible property, income from platform contribution transactions described in §1.482-7(b)(1)(ii), royalty income from the licensing of intangible property, and amounts taken into account under section 367(d) by reason of a transfer of intangible property. Gross intangible income also includes a distributive share of any amounts described in the previous sentence, but does not include dividends or any amounts included in income under sections 951, 951A, or 1293.

(3) *SIC code categories.*—(i) *Allocation based on SIC code categories.*—Ordinarily, a taxpayer's R&E expenditures are incurred to produce gross intangible income that is reasonably connected with one or more relevant SIC code categories. Where research and experimentation is conducted with respect to more than one SIC code category, the taxpayer may aggregate the categories for purposes of allocation and apportionment. However, the taxpayer may not subdivide any categories. Where research and experimentation is not clearly related

to any SIC code category (or categories), it will be considered conducted with respect to all of the taxpayer's SIC code categories.

(ii) *Use of three digit standard industrial classification codes.*—A taxpayer determines the relevant SIC code categories by reference to the three digit classification of the Standard Industrial Classification Manual (SIC code). The SIC Manual is available at https://www.osha.gov/pls/imis/sic_manual.html.

(iii) *Consistency.*—Once a taxpayer selects a SIC code category for the first taxable year for which this section applies to the taxpayer, it must continue to use that category in following years unless the taxpayer establishes to the satisfaction of the Commissioner that, due to changes in the relevant facts, a change in the category is appropriate.

(iv) *Wholesale trade and retail trade categories.*—A taxpayer must use a SIC code category within the divisions of "wholesale trade" or "retail trade" if it is engaged solely in sales-related activities with respect to a particular category of products. In the case of a taxpayer that conducts material non-sales-related activities with respect to a particular category of products, all R&E expenditures related to sales of the products must be allocated and apportioned as if the expenditures were reasonably connected to the most closely related three digit SIC code category other than those within the wholesale and retail trade divisions. For example, if a taxpayer engages in both the manufacturing and assembling of cars and trucks (SIC Code 371) and in a wholesaling activity related to motor vehicles and motor vehicle parts and supplies (SIC Code 501), the taxpayer must allocate and apportion all R&E expenditures related to both activities as if they relate solely to the manufacturing SIC Code 371. By contrast, if the taxpayer engages only in the wholesaling activity related to motor vehicles and motor vehicle parts and supplies, the taxpayer must allocate and apportion all R&E expenditures to the wholesaling SIC Code 501.

(c) *Exclusive apportionment.*—Solely for purposes of applying this section to section 904 as the operative section, an amount equal to fifty percent of a taxpayer's R&E expenditures in a SIC code category (or categories) is apportioned exclusively to the residual grouping of U.S. source gross intangible income if research and experimentation that accounts for at least fifty percent of such R&E expenditures was performed in the United States. Similarly, an amount equal to fifty percent of a taxpayer's R&E expenditures in a SIC code category (or categories) is apportioned exclusively to the statutory grouping (or groupings) of foreign source gross intangible income in that SIC code category if research and experimentation that accounts for more than fifty percent of such R&E expenditures was performed outside the United States. If there are multiple separate categories with foreign source gross intangible income in the SIC code category, the fifty percent of R&E expenditures apportioned under the previous sentence is apportioned ratably to foreign source gross intangible income based on the relative amounts of gross receipts from gross intangible income in the SIC code category in each separate category, as determined under paragraph (d) of this section.

(d) *Apportionment based on gross receipts from sales of products or services.*—(1) *In general.*—A taxpayer's R&E expenditures not apportioned under paragraph (c) of this section are apportioned between the statutory grouping (or among the statutory groupings) within the class of gross intangible income and the residual grouping within such class according to the rules in paragraph (d)(1)(i) through (iv) of this section. See paragraph (b) of this section for defining the class of gross intangible income in relation to SIC code categories.

(i) A taxpayer's R&E expenditures not apportioned under paragraph (c) of this section are apportioned in the same proportions that:

(A) The amounts of the taxpayer's gross receipts from sales and leases of products (as measured by gross receipts without regard to cost of goods sold) or services that are related to gross intangible income within the statutory grouping (or statutory groupings) and in the residual grouping bear, respectively, to

(B) The total amount of such gross receipts in the class.

(ii) For purposes of this paragraph (d), the amount of the gross receipts used to apportion R&E expenditures also includes gross receipts from sales and leases of products or services of any controlled or uncontrolled party to the extent described in paragraph (d)(3) and (4) of this section.

(iii) The statutory grouping (or groupings) or residual grouping to which the gross receipts are assigned is the grouping to which the gross intangible income related to the sale, lease, or service is assigned. In cases where the gross intangible income of the taxpayer is income not described in paragraph (d)(3) or (4) of this section, the grouping to which the taxpayer's gross receipts and the gross intangible income are assigned is the same. In cases where the taxpayer's gross intangible income is related to sales, leases, or services described in paragraphs (d)(3) or (4) of this section, the gross receipts that will be used for purposes of this paragraph (d) are the gross receipts of the controlled or uncontrolled parties that are exploiting the taxpayer's intangible property. The grouping to which the controlled or uncontrolled parties' gross receipts are assigned is determined based on the grouping of the taxpayer's gross intangible income attributable to the license, sale, or other transfer of intangible property to such controlled or uncontrolled party as described in paragraph (d)(3)(i) or (d)(4)(i) of this section, and not the grouping to which the gross receipts would be assigned if the assignment were based on the income earned by the controlled or uncontrolled party. See paragraph (g)(1) of this section (*Example 1*).

(iv) For purposes of applying this section to section 904 as the operative section, because a United States person's gross intangible income cannot include income assigned to the section 951A category, no R&E expenditures of a United States person are apportioned to foreign source income in the section 951A category.

(2) *Apportionment in excess of gross income.*—Amounts apportioned under this section may exceed the amount of gross income related to the SIC code category within the statutory or residual grouping. In such case, the excess is applied against other gross income within the statutory or residual grouping. See § 1.861-8(d)(1) for applicable rules where the apportionment results in an excess of deductions over gross income within the statutory or residual grouping.

(3) *Sales or services of uncontrolled parties.*—(i) *In general.*—For purposes of the apportionment within a class under paragraph (d)(1) of this section, the gross receipts of each uncontrolled party from particular products or services incorporating intangible property that was licensed, sold, or transferred by the taxpayer to such uncontrolled party (directly or indirectly) are taken into account for determining the taxpayer's apportionment if the taxpayer can reasonably be expected to license, sell, or transfer to that uncontrolled party, directly or indirectly, intangible property that would arise from the taxpayer's current R&E expenditures. If the taxpayer has previously licensed, sold, or transferred intangible property related to a SIC code category to an uncontrolled party, the taxpayer is presumed to expect to license, sell, or transfer to that uncontrolled party all future intangible property related to the same SIC code category.

(ii) *Definition of uncontrolled party.*—For purposes of this paragraph (d)(3), the term *uncontrolled party* means a party that is not a person with a relationship to the taxpayer specified in section 267(b), or is not a member of a controlled group of corporations to which the taxpayer belongs (within the meaning of section 993(a)(3)).

(iii) *Sales of components.*—In the case of a sale or lease of a product by an uncontrolled party that is derived from the taxpayer's intangible property but is incorporated as a component of a larger product (for example, where the product incorporating the intangible property is a component of a large machine), only the portion of the gross receipts from the larger product that are attributable to the component derived from the intangible property is included. For purposes of the preceding sentence, a reasonable estimate based on

the principles of section 482 must be made. See paragraph (g)(4)(ii)(B)(3) of this section (*Example 4*).

(iv) *Reasonable estimates of gross receipts.*—If the amount of gross receipts of an uncontrolled party is unknown, a reasonable estimate of gross receipts must be made annually. Appropriate economic analyses, based on the principles of section 482, must be used to estimate gross receipts. See paragraph (g)(5)(B)(3)(ii) of this section (*Example 5*).

(4) *Sales or services of controlled corporations.*—(i) *In general.*—For purposes of the apportionment within a class under paragraph (d)(1) of this section, the gross receipts from sales, leases, or services of a controlled corporation are taken into account if the taxpayer can reasonably be expected to license, sell, or transfer to that controlled corporation, directly or indirectly, intangible property that would arise from the taxpayer's current R&E expenditures. Except to the extent provided in paragraph (d)(4)(iv) of this section, if the taxpayer has previously licensed, sold, or transferred intangible property related to a SIC code category to a controlled corporation, the taxpayer is presumed to expect to license, sell, or transfer to that controlled corporation all future intangible property related to the same SIC code category.

(ii) *Definition of a corporation controlled by the taxpayer.*—For purposes of this paragraph (d)(4), the term *controlled corporation* means any corporation that has a relationship to the taxpayer specified in section 267(b) or is a member of a controlled group of corporations to which the taxpayer belongs (within the meaning of section 993(a)(3)). Because an affiliated group is treated as a single taxpayer, a member of an affiliated group is not a controlled corporation. See paragraph (e) of this section.

(iii) *Gross receipts not to be taken into account more than once.*—Sales, leases, or services between controlled corporations or between a controlled corporation and the taxpayer are not taken into account more than once; in such a situation, the amount of gross receipts of the selling corporation must be subtracted from the gross receipts of the buying corporation.

(iv) *Effect of cost sharing arrangements.*—If the controlled corporation has entered into a cost sharing arrangement, in accordance with the provisions of § 1.482-7, with the taxpayer for the purpose of developing intangible property, then the taxpayer is not reasonably expected to license, sell, or transfer to that controlled corporation, directly or indirectly, intangible property that would arise from the taxpayer's share of the R&E expenditures with respect to the cost shared intangibles as defined in § 1.482-7(j)(1)(i). Therefore, solely for purposes of apportioning a taxpayer's R&E expenditures (which does not include the amount of CST Payments received by the taxpayer; see paragraph (a) of this section) that are intangible development costs (as defined in § 1.482-7(d)) with respect to a cost sharing arrangement, the controlled corporation's gross receipts are not taken into account for purposes of paragraphs (d)(1) and (d)(4)(i) of this section.

(5) *Application of section 864(e)(3).*—Section 864(e)(3) and § 1.861-8(d)(2)(ii) do not apply for purposes of this section.

(e) *Affiliated groups.*—See § 1.861-14(e)(2) for rules on allocating and apportioning R&E expenditures of an affiliated group (as defined in § 1.861-14(d)).

(f) *Special rules for partnerships.*—(1) *R&E expenditures.*—For purposes of applying this section, if R&E expenditures are incurred by a partnership in which the taxpayer is a partner, the taxpayer's R&E expenditures include the taxpayer's distributive share of the partnership's R&E expenditures.

(2) *Purpose and location of expenditures.*—In applying exclusive apportionment under paragraph (c) of this section, a partner's distributive share of R&E expenditures incurred by a partnership is treated as incurred by the partner for the same purpose and in the same location as incurred by the partnership.

(3) *Apportionment based on gross receipts.*—In applying the remaining apportionment under paragraph (d) of this section, a taxpayer's gross receipts from a SIC code category include the full amount of any gross receipts from the SIC code category of any partnership not described in paragraph (d)(3)(ii) of this section in which the taxpayer is a direct or indirect partner if the gross receipts would have been included had the partnership been a corporation.

(g) *Examples.*—The following examples illustrate the application of the rules in this section.

(1) *Example 1*—(i) *Facts.* X, a domestic corporation, is a manufacturer and distributor of small gasoline engines for lawnmowers. Gasoline engines are a product within the category, Engines and Turbines (SIC Industry Group 351). Y, a wholly owned foreign subsidiary of X, also manufactures and sells these engines abroad. X

owns no other foreign subsidiaries. During Year 1, X incurred R&E expenditures of $60,000x, which it deducts under section 174 as a current expense, to invent and patent a new and improved gasoline engine. All of the research and experimentation was performed in the United States. Also in Year 1, the domestic gross receipts of X of gasoline engines total $500,000x and foreign gross receipts of Y total $300,000x. X provides technology for the manufacture of engines to Y through a license that requires the payment of an arm's length royalty. In Year 1, X's gross income is $200,000x, of which $140,000x is U.S. source income from domestic sales of gasoline engines, $40,000x is income included under section 951A all of which relates to Y's foreign source income from sales of gasoline engines, $10,000x is foreign source royalties from Y, and $10,000x is U.S. source interest income. None of the foreign source royalties are allocable to passive category income of Y, and therefore, under §§1.904-4(d) and 1.904-5(c)(3), the foreign source royalties are general category income to X.

(ii) *Analysis*—(A) *Allocation.* The R&E expenditures were incurred in connection with developing intangible property related to small gasoline engines and they are definitely related to the items of gross intangible income related to the SIC code category 351, namely gross income from the sale of small gasoline engines in the United States and royalties received from subsidiary Y, a foreign manufacturer of gasoline engines. Accordingly, under paragraph (b) of this section, the R&E expenditures are allocable to the class of gross intangible income related to SIC code category 351, all of which is general category income of X. X's U.S. source interest income and income included under section 951A are not within this class of gross intangible income and, therefore, no portion of the R&E expenditures are allocated to the U.S. source interest income or foreign source income in the section 951A category.

(B) *Apportionment*—(1) *In general.* For purposes of applying this section to section 904 as the operative section, the statutory grouping of gross intangible income is foreign source general category income and the residual grouping of gross intangible income is U.S. source income.

(2) *Exclusive apportionment.* Under paragraph (c) of this section, because at least 50% of X's research and experimental activity was performed in the United States, 50% of the R&E expenditures, or $30,000x ($60,000x x 50%), is apportioned exclusively to the residual grouping of U.S. source gross intangible income. The remaining 50% of the R&E expenditures is then apportioned between the statutory and residual groupings on the basis of the relative amounts of gross receipts from sales of small gasoline engines by X and Y that are related to the U.S. source sales income and foreign source royalty income, respectively.

(3) *Apportionment based on gross receipts.* After taking into account exclusive apportionment, X has $30,000x ($60,000x − $30,000x) of R&E expenditures that must be apportioned between the residual and statutory groupings. Because Y is a controlled corporation of X, its gross receipts within the SIC code are taken into account in apportioning X's R&E expenditures if X is reasonably expected to license, sell, or transfer intangible property that would arise from the R&E expenditures that result in the $60,000x deduction. Because Y has licensed the intangible property developed by X related to the SIC code, it is presumed it is reasonably expected to license the intangible property that would be developed from the current research and experimentation. Therefore, under paragraphs (d)(1) and (5) of this section, $11,250x ($30,000x x $300,000x/($500,000x + $300,000x)) is apportioned to the statutory grouping of X's gross intangible income attributable to its license of intangible property to Y, or foreign source general category income. No portion of the gross receipts by X or Y are disregarded under section 864(e)(3), regardless of whether the income related to those sales is eligible for a deduction under section 250(a)(1)(A). The remaining $18,750x ($30,000x x $500,000x/($500,000x + $300,000x)) is apportioned to the residual grouping of gross intangible income, or U.S. source income.

(4) *Summary.* Accordingly, for purposes of the foreign tax credit limitation, $11,250x of X's R&E expenditures are apportioned to foreign source general category income, and $48,750x ($30,000x + $18,750x) of X's R&E expenditures are apportioned to U.S. source income.

(2) *Example 2*—(i) *Facts.* The facts are the same as in paragraph (g)(1)(i) of this section (the facts in *Example 1*) except that X also spends $30,000x in Year 1 for research on steam turbines, all of which is performed in the United States, and X has steam turbine gross receipts in the United States of $400,000x. X's foreign subsidiary Y neither manufactures nor sells steam turbines. The steam turbine research is in addition to the $60,000x in R&E expenditures incurred by X on gasoline engines for lawnmowers. X thus has $90,000x of R&E expenditures. X's gross income is $250,000x, of which $140,000x is U.S. source income from domestic sales of gasoline engines, $50,000x is U.S. source income from domestic sales of steam turbines, $40,000x is income included under section 951A all of which relates to foreign source income derived from Y's sales of gasoline engines,

$10,000x is foreign source royalties from Y, and $10,000x is U.S. source interest income.

(ii) *Analysis*—(A) *Allocation.* X's R&E expenditures generate gross intangible income from sales of small gasoline engines and steam turbines. Both of these products are in the same three digit SIC code category, Engines and Turbines (SIC Industry Group 351). Therefore, under paragraph (a) of this section, X's R&E expenditures are definitely related to all items of gross intangible income attributable to SIC code category 351. These items of X's gross intangible income are gross income from the sale of small gasoline engines and steam turbines in the United States and royalties from foreign subsidiary Y, a foreign manufacturer and seller of small gasoline engines. X's U.S. source interest income and income included under section 951A is not within this class of gross intangible income and, therefore, no portion of X's R&E expenditures are allocated to the U.S. source interest income or income in the section 951A category.

(B) *Apportionment*—(1) *In general.* For purposes of applying this section to section 904 as the operative section, the statutory grouping of gross intangible income is foreign source general category income and the residual grouping of gross intangible income is U.S. source income.

(2) *Exclusive apportionment.* Under paragraph (c) of this section, because at least 50% of X's research and experimental activity was performed in the United States, 50% of the R&E expenditures, or $45,000x ($90,000x x 50%), are apportioned exclusively to the residual grouping of U.S. source gross intangible income. The remaining 50% of the R&E expenditures is then apportioned between the residual and statutory groupings on the basis of the relative amounts of gross receipts of small gasoline engines and steam turbines by X and Y with respect to which gross intangible income is foreign source general category income and U.S. source income.

(3) *Apportionment based on gross receipts.* After taking into account exclusive apportionment, X has $45,000x ($90,000x − $45,000x) of R&E expenditures that must be apportioned between the residual and statutory groupings. Even though a portion of the R&E expenditures that must be apportioned are attributable to research performed with respect to steam turbines, and Y does not sell steam turbines, because Y previously licensed intangible property related to SIC code category 351, it is presumed that X expects to license all intangible property related to SIC code category 351, including intangible property related to steam turbines. Therefore, under paragraph (d)(1) of this section, $11,250x ($45,000x x $300,000x/($500,000x + $400,000x + $300,000x)) is apportioned to the statutory grouping of gross intangible income of the royalty income to which the gross receipts by Y were related, or foreign source general category income. The remaining $33,750x ($45,000x x ($500,000x + $400,000x)/($500,000x + $400,000x + $300,000x)) is apportioned to the residual grouping of gross intangible income, or U.S. source gross income.

(4) *Summary.* Accordingly, for purposes of the foreign tax credit limitation, $11,250x of X's R&E expenditures are apportioned to foreign source general category income and $78,750x ($45,000x + $33,750x) of X's R&E expenditures are apportioned to U.S. source gross income.

(3) *Example 3*—(i) *Facts*—(A) *Acquisitions and transfers by X.* The facts are the same as in paragraph (g)(1)(i) of this section (the facts in *Example 1*) except that, in Year 2, X and Y terminate the license for the manufacture of engines that was in place in Year 1 and enter into an arm's length cost-sharing arrangement, in accordance with the provisions of §1.482-7, to share the funding of all of X's research activity. In Year 2, Y makes a PCT Payment (as defined in §1.482-7(b)(1)) of $50,000x that is sourced as a royalty and a CST Payment of $25,000x under the cost sharing arrangement.

(B) *Gross receipts and R&E expenditures.* In Year 2, X and Y continue to sell gasoline engines, with gross receipts of $600,000x in the United States and $400,000x abroad by Y. X incurs research costs of $85,000x in Year 2 for research activities conducted in the United States, but cannot deduct $25,000x of that amount by reason of the second sentence under §1.482-7(j)(3)(i) (relating to CST Payments).

(C) *Gross income of X.* In Year 2, X's gross income is $350,000x, of which $200,000x is U.S. source income from domestic sales of gasoline engines, $50,000x is foreign source income attributable to the PCT Payment, and $100,000x is income included under section 951A all of which relates to foreign source income derived from engine sales by Y.

(ii) *Analysis*—(A) *Allocation.* The $60,000x of R&E expenditures were incurred in connection with small gasoline engines and they are definitely related to the items of gross intangible income related to the SIC code category, namely gross income from the sale of small gasoline engines in the United States and PCT Payments from Y. Accordingly, under paragraph (a) of this section, the R&E expenditures are allocable to this class of gross intangible income. X's income included under section 951A is not within this class of gross intangible income and, therefore, no portion of X's R&E expenditures is allocated to X's section 951A category income.

(B) Apportionment—(1) In general. For purposes of applying this section to section 904 as the operative section, the statutory grouping of gross intangible income is foreign source general category income, and the residual grouping of gross intangible income is U.S. source income.

(2) Exclusive apportionment. Under paragraph (c) of this section, because at least 50% of X's research and experimentation was performed in the United States, 50% of the R&E expenditures, or $30,000x ($60,000x x 50%), is apportioned exclusively to the residual grouping of gross intangible income, U.S. source gross income.

(3) Apportionment based on gross receipts. Under paragraph (d)(5)(v) of this section, none of Y's gross receipts are taken into account because they are attributable to the cost shared intangible under the valid cost sharing arrangement. Because all of the gross receipts from sales that are taken into account under paragraph (d)(1) of this section relate to gross intangible income that is included in the residual grouping, $30,000x is apportioned to the residual grouping of gross intangible income, or U.S. source gross income.

(4) Summary. Accordingly, for purposes of the foreign tax credit limitation, $60,000x of X's R&E expenditures are apportioned to U.S. source income.

(4) Example 4—(i) Facts—(A) X's R&E expenditures. X, a domestic corporation, is engaged in continuous research and experimentation to improve the quality of the products that it manufactures and sells, which are floodlights, flashlights, fuse boxes, and solderless connectors. X incurs $100,000x of R&E expenditures in Year 1 that was performed exclusively in the United States. As a result of this research activity, X acquires patents that it uses in its own manufacturing activity.

(B) License to Y and Z. In Year 1, X licenses its floodlight patent to Y and Z, uncontrolled foreign corporations, for use in their own territories, Countries Y and Z, respectively. Corporation Y pays X a royalty of $3,000x plus $0.20x for each floodlight sold. Gross receipts from sales of floodlights by Y for the taxable year are $135,000x (at $4.50x per unit) or 30,000x units, and the royalty is $9,000x ($3,000x + $0.20x × 30,000x). Y has sales of other products of $500,000x. Z pays X a royalty of $3,000x plus $0.30x for each unit sold. Z manufactures 30,000x floodlights in the taxable year, and the royalty is $12,000x ($3,000x + $0.30x × 30,000x). The dollar value of Z's gross receipts from floodlight sales is not known because, in this case, the floodlights are not sold separately by Z but are instead used as a component in Z's manufacture of lighting equipment for theaters. However, a reasonable estimate of Z's gross receipts attributable to the floodlights, based on the principles of section 482, is $120,000x. The gross receipts from sales of all Z's products, including the lighting equipment for theaters, are $1,000,000x.

(C) X's gross receipts and gross income. X's gross receipts from sales of floodlights for the taxable year are $500,000x and its sales of its other products (flashlights, fuse boxes, and solderless connectors) are $400,000x. X has gross income of $500,000x, consisting of U.S. source gross income from domestic sales of floodlights, flashlights, fuse boxes, and solderless connectors of $479,000x, and foreign source royalty income of $9,000x and $12,000x from foreign corporations Y and Z respectively. The royalty income is general category income to X under section 904(d)(2)(A)(ii) and § 1.904-4(b)(2)(ii).

(ii) Analysis—(A) Allocation. X's R&E expenditures are definitely related to all of the gross intangible income from the products that it produces, which are floodlights, flashlights, fuse boxes, and solderless connectors. All of these products are in the same three digit SIC code category, Electric Lighting and Wiring Equipment (SIC Industry Group 364). Therefore, under paragraph (b) of this section, X's R&E expenditures are definitely related to the class of gross intangible income related to SIC code category 354 and to all items of gross intangible income attributable to the class. These items of X's gross intangible income are gross income from the sale of floodlights, flashlights, fuse boxes, and solderless connectors in the United States and royalties from Corporations Y and Z.

(B) Apportionment—(1) In general. For purposes of applying this section to section 904 as the operative section, the statutory grouping of gross intangible income is foreign source general category income, and the residual grouping of gross intangible income is U.S. source income.

(2) Exclusive apportionment. Under paragraph (c) of this section, because at least 50% of X's research and experimentation was performed in the United States, 50% of the R&E expenditures, or $50,000x ($100,000x x 50%), is apportioned exclusively to the residual grouping of U.S. source gross intangible income.

(3) Apportionment based on gross receipts. After taking into account exclusive apportionment, X has $50,000x ($100,000x − $50,000x) of R&E expenditures that must be apportioned between the residual and statutory groupings. Gross receipts from sales of Y and Z are taken into account in apportioning the R&E expenditures if X is reasonably expected to license, sell, or transfer the intangible property that would arise from the research and experimentation that results in the $100,000x deduction. Because X licensed intangible

property related to the SIC code in Year 1, it is presumed that it would continue to license the intangible property that would be developed from the current research and experimentation. Under paragraph (d)(3)(i) of this section, because Y and Z are uncontrolled parties with respect to X, only gross receipts from their sales of the licensed product, floodlights, are included for purposes of apportionment. In addition, under paragraph (d)(3)(iii) of this section, only the portion of Z's gross receipts that are attributable to the floodlights that incorporate the intangible property licensed from X, rather than Z's total gross receipts, are used for purposes of apportionment. All of X's gross receipts from sales in the entire SIC code category are included for purposes of apportionment on the basis of gross intangible income attributable to those sales. Under paragraph (d)(1) of this section, $11,039x ($50,000x × ($135,000x + $120,000x)/($900,000x + $135,000x + $120,000x)) is apportioned to the statutory grouping of gross intangible income, or foreign source general category income. The remaining $38,961x ($50,000x × $900,000x/($900,000x + $135,000x + $120,000x)) is apportioned to the residual grouping of gross intangible income, or U.S. source gross income.

(4) Summary. Accordingly, for purposes of the foreign tax credit limitation, $11,039x of X's R&E expenditures are apportioned to foreign source general category income and $88,961x ($50,000x + $38.961x) of X's R&E expenditures are apportioned to U.S. source gross income.

(5) Example 5—(i) Facts. X, a domestic corporation, is a cloud storage service provider. Cloud storage services are a service within the category, Computer Programming, Data Processing, and other Computer Related Services (SIC Industry Group 737). During Year 1, X incurred R&E expenditures of $50,000x to invent and copyright new storage monitoring and management software. All of the research and experimentation was performed in the United States. X uses this software in its own business to provide services to customers. X also licenses a version of the software that can be used by other businesses that provide cloud storage services. X licenses the software to uncontrolled party U, which sub-licenses the software to other businesses that provide cloud storage services to customers. U does not use the software except to sublicense it. As a part of the licensing agreement with U, U and its sub-licensees are only permitted to use the software in certain countries outside of the United States. Under the contract with U, U pays X a royalty of 50% on the amount it receives from its sub-licensees that use the software to provide services to customers. In Year 1, X earns $300,000x of gross receipts from providing cloud storage services within the U.S. Further, in Year 1 U receives $10,000x of royalty income from its sub-licensees and pays a royalty of $5,000x to X. Thus, X also earns $5,000x of foreign source royalty income from licensing its software to U for use outside of the United States.

(ii) Analysis—(A) Allocation. The R&E expenditures were incurred in connection with the development of cloud computing software and they are definitely related to the items of gross intangible income related to the SIC Code category, namely gross income from the storage monitoring and management software in the United States and royalties received from U. Accordingly, under paragraph (b) of this section, the R&E expenditures are allocable to this class of gross intangible income, all of which is general category income of X.

(B) Apportionment—(1) In general. For purposes of applying this section to section 904 as the operative section, the statutory grouping of gross intangible income is foreign source general category income, and the residual grouping of gross intangible income is U.S. source income.

(2) Exclusive apportionment. Under paragraph (c) of this section, because at least 50% of X's research and experimental activity was performed in the United States, 50% of the R&E expenditures, or $25,000x ($50,000x x 50%), is apportioned exclusively to the residual grouping of U.S. source gross intangible income.

(3) Apportionment based on gross receipts—(i) In general. After taking into account exclusive apportionment, X has $25,000x ($50,000x − $25,000x) of R&E expenditures that must be apportioned between the statutory and residual groupings. Because U's sub-licensees' gross receipts incorporate intangible property licensed by X, U's sub-licensees' gross receipts from services incorporating the licensed intangible property are taken into account in apportioning X's R&E expenditures if X is reasonably expected to license, sell, or transfer intangible property that would arise from the R&E expenditures incurred in Year 1. Because U has licensed and the sub-licensees have sublicensed the intangible property developed by X related to the SIC code, it is presumed that U would continue to license the intangible property that would be developed from the current research and experimentation.

(ii) Determination of U's sub-licensee's gross receipts. Under paragraph (d)(3)(iv) of this section, X can make a reasonable estimate of the gross receipts of U's sub-licensees from services incorporating the intangible property licensed by X by estimating, after an appropriate economic analysis, that U would charge a 5% royalty on the sub-licensee's sales. U received a royalty of $10,000x from the sub-licensees. X then determines U's sub-licensees' foreign sales by divid-

ing the total royalty payments received by U by the royalty estimated rate ($10,000x/.05x = $200,000x).

(*iii*) *Results of apportionment based on gross receipts.* Therefore, under paragraphs (d)(1) and (3) of this section, $10,000x ($25,000x x $200,000x/($300,000x + $200,000x)) is apportioned to the statutory grouping of gross intangible income, or foreign source general category income. The remaining $15,000x ($25,000x x $300,000x/($300,000x + $200,000x)) is apportioned to the residual grouping of gross intangible income, or U.S. source income.

(4) *Summary.* Accordingly, for purposes of the foreign tax credit limitation, $10,000x of X's R&E expenditures are apportioned to foreign source general category income and $40,000x ($25,000x + $15,000x) of X's R&E expenditures are apportioned to U.S. source income.

(h) *Applicability date.*—This section applies to taxable years beginning after December 31, 2019. [Reg. § 1.861-17.]

Cloud and Digital Content Transactions: Classification

Cloud and Digital Content Transactions: Classification.—Amendments to Reg. § 1.861-18, regarding the classification of cloud transactions for purposes of the international provisions of the Internal Revenue Code, are proposed (published in the Federal Register on August 14, 2019) (corrected October 2, 2019) (REG-130700-14).

Par. 3. Section 1.861-18 is amended as follows:

a. For each paragraph listed in the following table, removing the language in the "Remove" column and adding in its place the language in the "Add" column.

Paragraph	Remove	Add
(a)(1)	computer programs	digital content
(b)(1) introductory text	a computer program	digital content
(b)(1)(i)	computer program	digital content
(b)(1)(ii)	computer program	digital content
(b)(1)(iii)	computer program	digital content
(b)(1)(iv)	computer programming techniques	development of digital content
(b)(2), first sentence	Any transaction	Any arrangement
(b)(2), first sentence	computer programs	digital content
(b)(2), second sentence	overall transaction	overall arrangement
(c)(1)(i), first sentence	a computer program	digital content
(c)(1)(i), third sentence	a computer program	digital content
(c)(1)(i), third sentence	that program	that digital content
(c)(1)(ii)	a computer program	digital content
(c)(1)(ii)	the computer program	the digital content
(c)(2)(i)	computer program	digital content
(c)(2)(ii)	computer programs	digital content
(c)(2)(ii)	copyrighted computer program	digital content
(c)(3), first sentence	a computer program	digital content
(c)(3), second sentence	the magnetic medium of a floppy disk, or in the main memory or hard drive of a computer, or in any other medium	any medium
(d)	a newly developed or modified computer program	newly developed or modified digital content
(d)	computer program	digital content
(e) introductory text	a computer program	digital content
(e)(1)	computer programming techniques	the development of digital content
(f)(3), subject heading	computer programs	digital content
(f)(3), first sentence	computer programs	digital content
(f)(3), second sentence	a computer program on disk	digital content on a disk
(f)(3), third sentence	program	digital content
(g)(2)	a computer program	digital content
(g)(3)(i), first sentence	a computer program	digital content
(g)(3)(i), first sentence	the program	the digital content
(g)(3)(i), first sentence	software	digital content
(g)(3)(ii), first sentence	a computer program	digital content
(g)(3)(ii), first sentence	the program	the digital content
(g)(3)(ii), second sentence	a computer program	digital content
(g)(3)(ii), second sentence	the program	the digital content

b. Amend paragraph (a)(1) by:

i. Adding before "367" sections "59A, 245A, 250, 267A,";

ii. Removing "551,"; and

iii. Removing "chapter 3, chapter 5" and adding in its place "chapters 3 and 4,".

c. Revising paragraphs (a)(3), (c)(2)(iii) and (iv), and (f)(2).

d. Redesignating Examples 1 through 18 of paragraph (h) as paragraphs (h)(1) through (18), respectively.

e. Adding paragraphs (h)(19) through (21).

f. Revising paragraphs (i) and (j).

g. Removing paragraph (k).

The revisions and additions read as follows:

§1.861-18. Classification of transactions involving digital content.

* * *

(a) * * *

(3) *Digital content.*—For purposes of this section, digital content means a computer program or any other content in digital format that is either protected by copyright law or no longer protected by copyright law solely due to the passage of time. For example, digital content includes books in digital format, movies in digital format, and music in digital format. For purposes of this section, a computer program is a set of statements or instructions to be used directly or indirectly in a computer in order to bring about a certain result and includes any media, user manuals, documentation, data base, or similar item if the media, user manuals, documentation, data base, or other similar item is incidental to the operation of the computer program.

* * *

(c) * * *

(2) * * *

(iii) The right to make a public performance of digital content, other than a right to publicly perform digital content for the purpose of advertising the sale of the digital content performed; or

(iv) The right to publicly display digital content, other than a right to publicly display digital content for the purpose of advertising the sale of the digital content displayed.

* * *

(f) * * *

(2) *Transfers of copyrighted articles.*—(i) *Classification.*—The determination of whether a transfer of a copyrighted article is a sale or exchange is made on the basis of whether, taking into account all facts and circumstances, the benefits and burdens of ownership have been transferred. A transaction that does not constitute a sale or exchange because insufficient benefits and burdens of ownership of the copyrighted article have been transferred, such that a person other than the transferee is properly treated as the owner of the copyrighted article, will be classified as a lease generating rental income.

(ii) *Source.*—Income from transactions that are classified as sales or exchanges of copyrighted articles will be sourced under section 861(a)(6), 862(a)(6), 863, or 865(a), (b), (c), or (e), as appropriate. When a copyrighted article is sold and transferred through an electronic medium, the sale is deemed to have occurred at the location of download or installation onto the end-user's device used to access the digital content for purposes of §1.861-7(c), subject to the tax avoidance provisions in §1.861-7(c). However, in the absence of information about the location of download or installation onto the end-user's device used to access the digital content, the sale will be deemed to have occurred at the location of the customer, which is determined based on the taxpayer's recorded sales data for business or financial reporting purposes. Income derived from leasing a copyrighted article will be sourced under section 861(a)(4) or 862(a)(4), as appropriate.

* * *

(h) * * *

(19) *Example 19*—(i) *Facts.* Corp A operates a website that offers electronic books for download onto end-users' computers or other electronic devices. The books offered by Corp A are protected by copyright law. Under the agreements between content owners and Corp A, Corp A receives from the content owners a digital master copy of each book, which Corp A downloads onto its server, in addition to the nonexclusive right to distribute for sale to the public an unlimited number of copies in return for paying each content owner a specified amount for each copy sold. Corp A may not transfer any of the distribution rights it receives from the content owners. The term of each agreement Corp A has with a content owner is shorter than the remaining life of the copyright. Corp A charges each end-user a fixed fee for each book purchased. When purchasing a book on Corp A's website, the end-user must acknowledge the terms of a license agreement with the content owner that states that the end-user may view the electronic book but may not reproduce or distribute copies of it. In addition, the agreement provides that the end-user may download the book onto a limited number of its devices. Once the end-user downloads the book from Corp A's server onto a device, the end-user may access and view the book from that device, which does not need to be connected to the Internet in order for the end-user to view the book. The end-user owes no additional payment to Corp A for the ability to view the book in the future.

(ii) *Analysis.* (A) Notwithstanding the license agreement between each end-user and content owner granting the end-user rights to use the book, the relevant transactions are the transfer of a master copy of the book and rights to sell copies from the content owner to Corp A, and the transfers of copies of books by Corp A to end-users. Al-

though the content owner is identified as a party to the license agreement memorializing the end-user's rights with respect to the book, each end-user obtains those rights directly from Corp A, not from the content owner. Because the end-user receives only a copy of each book and does not receive any of the copyright rights described in paragraph (c)(2) of this section, the transaction between Corp A and the end-user is classified as the transfer of a copyrighted article under paragraph (c)(1)(ii) of this section. See paragraphs (h)(1) and (2) of this section (*Example 1* and *Example 2*). Under the benefits and burdens test of paragraph (f)(2) of this section, the transaction is classified as a sale and not a lease, because the end-user receives the right to view the book in perpetuity on its device.

(B) The transaction between each content owner and Corp A is a transfer of copyright rights. In obtaining a master copy of the book along with the right to sell an unlimited number of copies to customers, Corp A receives a copyright right described in paragraph (c)(2)(i) of this section. For purposes of paragraph (b)(2) of this section, the digital master copy is de minimis. Under paragraph (f)(1) of this section, there has not been a transfer of all substantial rights in the copyright rights to the content because each content owner retains the right to further license or sell the copyrights, subject to Corp A's interest; Corp A has acquired no right itself to transfer the copyright rights to any of the content; and the grant of distribution rights is for less than the remaining life of the copyright to each book. Therefore, the transaction between each content owner and Corp A is classified as a license, and not a sale, of copyright rights.

(20) *Example 20*—(i) *Facts.* Corp A offers end-users memberships that provide them with unlimited access to Corp A's catalog of copyrighted music in exchange for a monthly fee. In order to access the music, an end-user must download each song onto a computer or other electronic device. The end-user may download songs onto a limited number of its devices. Under the membership agreement terms, an end-user may listen to the songs but may not reproduce or distribute copies of them. Once the end-user stops paying Corp A the monthly membership fee, an electronic lock is activated so that the end-user can no longer access the music.

(ii) *Analysis.* The end-users receive none of the copyright rights described in paragraph (c)(2) of this section and instead receive only copies of the digital content. Therefore, under paragraph (c)(1)(ii) of this section, each download is classified as the transfer of a copyrighted article. Although an end-user will retain a copy of the content at the end of the payment term, the end-user cannot access the content after the electronic lock is activated. Taking into account the special characteristics of digital content as provided in paragraph (f)(3) of this section, the activation of the electronic lock is the equivalent of having to return the copy. Therefore, under paragraph (f)(2) of this section, each transaction is classified as a lease of a copyrighted article because the right to access the music is limited.

(21) *Example 21*—(i) *Facts.* Corp A offers a catalog of movies and TV shows, all of which are subject to copyright protection. Corp A gives end-users several options for viewing the content, each of which has a separate price. A "streaming" option allows an end-user to view the video, which is hosted on Corp A's servers, while connected to the Internet for as many times as the end-user wants during a limited period. A "rent" option allows an end-user to download the video to its computer or other electronic device (which does not need to be connected to the Internet for viewing) and watch the video as many times as the end-user wants for a limited period, after which an electronic lock is activated and the end-user may no longer view the content. A "purchase" option allows an end-user to download the video and view it as many times as the end-user chooses with no end date. Under all three options, the end-user may view the video but may not reproduce or distribute copies of it. Under the "rent" and "purchase" options, the end-user may download the video onto a limited number of its devices.

(ii) *Analysis.* (A) With respect to the "rent" and "purchase" options, the end-user receives none of the copyright rights described in paragraph (c)(2) of this section but, rather, receives only copies of the digital content. Therefore, transactions under those two options are transfers of copyrighted articles. Transactions for which the end-user chooses the "purchase" option are classified as sales of copyrighted articles under the benefits and burdens test of paragraph (f)(2) of this section because the end-user receives the right to view the videos in perpetuity. Transactions under the "rent" option are classified as leases of copyrighted articles under paragraph (f)(2) of this section because the end-user's right to view the videos is for a limited period.

(B) For transactions under the "streaming" option, there is no transfer of any copyright rights described in paragraph (c)(2) of this section. There is also no transfer of a copyrighted article, because the content is not downloaded by an end-user, but rather is accessed through an on-demand network. The transaction also does not constitute the provision of services for the development of digital content or the provision of know-how under paragraph (b)(1) of this section. Therefore, paragraph (h)(1) of this section does not apply to such transaction. Instead, the transaction is a cloud transaction that is classified under §1.861-19. See §1.861-19(d)(9).

(i) *Effective date.*—This section applies to transactions not subject to §1.861-19 involving the transfer of digital content, or the provision of services or of know-how in connection with digital content, pursuant to contracts entered into in taxable years beginning on or after the date of publication of a Treasury decision adopting these rules as final regulations in the **Federal Register**. For transactions involving computer programs occurring pursuant to contracts entered into in taxable years beginning before the date of publication of a Treasury decision adopting these rules as final regulations in the **Federal Register**, see §1.861-18(i) as contained in T.D. 8785 and T.D. 9870.

(j) *Change in method of accounting required by this section.*—In order to comply with this section, a taxpayer engaging in a transaction involving digital content pursuant to a contract entered into in taxable years beginning on or after the date described in paragraph (i) of this section may be required to change its method of accounting. If so required, the taxpayer must secure the consent of the Commissioner in accordance with the requirements of §1.446-1(e) and the applicable administrative procedures for obtaining the Commissioner's consent under section 446(e) for voluntary changes in methods of accounting.

Cloud and Digital Content Transactions: Classification

Cloud and Digital Content Transactions: Classification.—Reg. §1.861-19, regarding the classification of cloud transactions for purposes of the international provisions of the Internal Revenue Code, is proposed (published in the Federal Register on August 14, 2019) (REG-130700-14).

Par. 4. Section 1.861-19 is added to read as follows:

§1.861-19. Classification of cloud transactions.—(a) *In general.*—This section provides rules for classifying a cloud transaction (as defined in paragraph (b) of this section) either as a provision of services or as a lease of property. The rules of this section apply for purposes of Internal Revenue Code sections 59A, 245A, 250, 267A, 367, 404A, 482, 679, and 1059A; subchapter N of chapter 1; chapters 3 and 4; and sections 842 and 845 (to the extent involving a foreign person), and apply with respect to transfers to foreign trusts not covered by section 679.

(b) *Cloud transaction defined.*—A cloud transaction is a transaction through which a person obtains on-demand network access to computer hardware, digital content (as defined in §1.861-18(a)(3)), or other similar resources, other than on-demand network access that is de minimis taking into account the overall arrangement and the surrounding facts and circumstances. A cloud transaction does not include network access to download digital content for storage and use on a person's computer or other electronic device.

(c) *Classification of transactions.*—(1) *In general.*—A cloud transaction is classified solely as either a lease of computer hardware, digital content (as defined in §1.861-18(a)(3)), or other similar resources, or the provision of services, taking into account all relevant factors, including the factors set forth in paragraph (c)(2) of this section. The relevance of any factor varies depending on the factual situation, and one or more of the factors set forth in paragraph (c)(2) of this section may not be relevant in a given instance. For purposes of this paragraph (c), computer hardware, digital content, or other similar resources are referred to as "the property," and the party to the transaction making such property available to customers for use is referred to as "the provider."

(2) *Factors demonstrating classification as the provision of services.*—Factors demonstrating that a cloud transaction is classified as the provision of services rather than a lease of property include the following factors—

(i) The customer is not in physical possession of the property;

(ii) The customer does not control the property, beyond the customer's network access and use of the property;

(iii) The provider has the right to determine the specific property used in the cloud transaction and replace such property with comparable property;

(iv) The property is a component of an integrated operation in which the provider has other responsibilities, including ensuring the property is maintained and updated;

(v) The customer does not have a significant economic or possessory interest in the property;

(vi) The provider bears any risk of substantially diminished receipts or substantially increased expenditures if there is nonperformance under the contract;

(vii) The provider uses the property concurrently to provide significant services to entities unrelated to the customer;

(viii) The provider's fee is primarily based on a measure of work performed or the level of the customer's use rather than the mere passage of time; and

(ix) The total contract price substantially exceeds the rental value of the property for the contract period.

(3) *Application to arrangements comprised of multiple transactions.*—An arrangement comprised of multiple transactions generally requires separate classification for each transaction. If at least one of the transactions is a cloud transaction, but not all of the transactions are cloud transactions, this section applies only to classify the cloud transactions. However, any transaction that is de minimis, taking into account the overall arrangement and the surrounding facts and circumstances, will not be treated as a separate transaction, but as part of another transaction.

(d) *Examples.*—The provisions of this section may be illustrated by the examples in this paragraph (d). For purposes of this paragraph, unless otherwise indicated, Corp A is a domestic corporation; Corp B is a foreign corporation; end-users are individuals; and no rights described in §1.861-18(c)(2) (copyright rights) are transferred as part of the transactions described.

(1) *Example 1: Computing capacity*—(i) *Facts.* Corp A operates data centers on its premises in various locations. Corp A provides Corp B computing capacity on Corp A's servers in exchange for a monthly fee based on the amount of computing power made available to Corp B. Corp B provides its own software to run on Corp A's servers. Depending on utilization levels, the servers accessed by Corp B may also be used simultaneously by other customers. The computing capacity provided to Corp B can be sourced from a variety of servers in one or more of Corp A's data centers, and Corp A determines how its computing resources are allocated among customers. Corp A agrees to keep the servers operational, including by performing physical maintenance and repair, and may replace any server with another server of comparable functionality. Corp A agrees to provide Corp B with a payment credit for server downtime. Corp B has no ability to physically alter any server.

(ii) *Analysis.* (A) The computing capacity transaction between Corp A and Corp B is a cloud transaction described in paragraph (b) of this section because Corp B obtains a non-de minimis right to on-demand network access to computer hardware of Corp A.

(B) Corp B has neither physical possession of nor control of the servers, beyond Corp B's right to access and use the servers. Corp A may replace any server with a functionally comparable server. The servers are a component of an integrated operation in which Corp A has other responsibilities, including maintaining the servers. The transaction does not provide Corp B with a significant economic or possessory interest in the servers. The agreement provides that Corp A will provide Corp B with a payment credit for server downtime, such that Corp A bears risk of substantially diminished receipts in the event of contract nonperformance. The servers may, depending on utilization levels, be used by Corp A to provide significant computing capacity to entities unrelated to Corp B. Corp A is compensated according to the level of Corp B's use (that is, the amount of computing power made available) and not solely based on the passage of time. Taking into account all of the relevant factors, the transaction between Corp A and Corp B is classified as the provision of services under paragraph (c) of this section.

(2) *Example 2: Computing capacity on dedicated servers*—(i) *Facts.* The facts are the same as in paragraph (d)(1)(i) of this section (the facts in *Example 1*), except that, in order to offer more security to Corp B, Corp A provides Corp B computing capacity exclusively through designated servers, which are owned by Corp A and located at Corp A's facilities. Corp A agrees not to use a designated server for any other customer for the duration of its arrangement with Corp B. Corp A's compensation reflects a substantial return for maintaining the servers in addition to the rental value of the servers.

(ii) *Analysis.* (A) As in paragraph (d)(1) of this section, the transaction between Corp A and Corp B is a cloud transaction described in paragraph (b) of this section because Corp B obtains a non-de minimis right to on-demand network access to computer hardware resources of Corp A.

(B) The fact that Corp A provides computing capacity to Corp B through designated servers indicates that such servers are not used concurrently by other Corp A customers. However, Corp A retains physical possession of the servers. In addition, Corp A's sole responsibility for maintaining the servers, and its sole right to replace or physically alter the servers, indicate that Corp A controls the servers. Although Corp B obtains the exclusive right to use certain servers,

Corp B does not have a significant economic or possessory interest in the servers because, among other things, Corp A retains the right to replace the servers, Corp A bears the risk of damage to the servers, and Corp B does not share in cost savings associated with the servers because the fee paid by Corp B to Corp A does not vary based on Corp A's costs. The compensation to Corp A substantially exceeds the rental value of the servers. The other relevant factors are analyzed in the same manner as paragraph (d)(1) of this section. Taking into account all of these factors, the transaction between Corp A and Corp B is classified as a provision of services under paragraph (c) of this section.

(3) *Example 3: Access to software development platform and website hosting*—(i) *Facts.* Corp A provides Corp B a software platform that Corp B uses to develop and deploy websites with a range of features, including blogs, message boards, and other collaborative knowledge bases. The software development platform consists of an operating system, web server software, scripting languages, libraries, tools, and back-end relational database software and allows Corp B to use in its websites certain visual elements subject to copyrights held by Corp A. The software development platform is hosted on servers owned by Corp A and located at Corp A's facilities. Corp B's finished websites are also hosted on Corp A's servers. The software development platform and servers are also used concurrently to provide similar functionality to Corp A customers unrelated to Corp B. Corp B accesses the software development platform via a standard web browser. Corp B has no ability to alter the software code. A small amount of scripting code is downloaded onto Corp B's computers to facilitate secure logins and access to the software development platform. All other functions of the software development platform execute on Corp A's servers, and no portion of the core software code is ever downloaded by Corp B or Corp B's customers. Corp A is solely responsible for maintaining the servers and software development platform, including ensuring continued functionality and compatibility with Corp B's browser, providing updates and fixes to the software for the duration of the contract with Corp B, and replacing or upgrading the servers or software at any time with a functionally similar version. Corp B pays Corp A a monthly fee for the platform and website hosting that takes into account the storage requirements of Corp B's websites and the amount of website traffic supported, but there is no stand-alone fee for use of the software development platform. Corp B agrees to pay for Corp A's website hosting services for a minimum period, after which Corp B may continue to pay for Corp A's website hosting services or transfer its developed websites to a different hosting provider. Corp A agrees to provide Corp B with a payment credit for server downtime.

(ii) *Analysis.* (A) Corp A's provision to Corp B of access to the software platform is a cloud transaction described in paragraph (b) of this section because Corp B obtains a non-de minimis right to on-demand network access to computer hardware and software resources of Corp A. Corp A's hosting of Corp B's finished websites is part of the provision of access to the software platform and hardware.

(B) Corp B does not have physical possession of the software platform or servers. Although Corp B uses Corp A's platform to develop and deploy websites, Corp B does not maintain the software platform or the servers on which it is hosted, and Corp B cannot alter the software platform. Accordingly, Corp B does not control the software platform or the servers. Corp A maintains the right to replace or upgrade the software platform and servers with functionally similar versions. The servers and software platform are components of an integrated operation in which Corp A has various responsibilities, including maintaining the servers and updating the software. Corp B does not have a significant economic or possessory interest in Corp A's software platform or servers. Corp B may lose revenue with respect to the websites that it deploys on Corp A's servers when the servers are down; nonetheless, Corp A bears the risk of substantially diminished receipts in the event of contract nonperformance because Corp A will provide Corp B with a payment credit for server downtime. Corp A provides access to the servers and platform to Corp B and other customers concurrently. Corp A is compensated based on Corp B's level of use (that is, the amount of computing resources provided) and not solely by the passage of time. Taking into account all of the factors, the transaction between Corp A and Corp B is classified as a provision of services under paragraph (c) of this section.

(C) Although the download of a small amount of scripting code to facilitate logins and access to the software platform would otherwise constitute a transfer of a computer program, instead of a cloud transaction under paragraph (b) of this section, the download is de minimis in the context of the overall arrangement, and therefore, under paragraph (c)(3) of this section, there is no separate classification of the download. Similarly, the fact that Corp B receives rights to publicly display certain copyrighted visual elements resulting from Corp A's software development platform on Corp B's own websites, which would otherwise constitute a transfer of copyright rights under §1.861-18, instead of a cloud transaction under paragraph (b)

of this section, does not require separate classification because the right to use such elements is also de minimis. Thus, under paragraph (c) of this section, the entire arrangement is classified as a service.

(4) *Example 4: Access to software*—(i) *Facts.* The facts are the same as in paragraph (d)(3)(i) of this section (the facts in *Example 3*), except that, instead of providing website development software, Corp A provides Corp B access to customer relationship management software under several options such as "entry-level," "mid-level," and "advanced-level," via a standard web browser, which Corp A hosts on its servers for a monthly subscription fee. Corp B has no ability to alter the software code, and Corp A agrees to make available new versions of the software as they are developed for the duration of Corp B's contract, and to ensure servers' uptime in accordance with the service level agreement.

(ii) *Analysis.* (A) As in paragraph (d)(3) of this section, the transaction between Corp A and Corp B is a cloud transaction described in paragraph (b) of this section because Corp B obtains a non-de minimis right to on-demand network access to computer hardware and software resources of Corp A.

(B) The relevant factors are analyzed in the same manner as in paragraph (d)(3) of this section, except that compensation due to Corp A is determined based on the option chosen and the passage of time rather than a measure of computing resources utilized. Although as a general matter compensation based on the passage of time is more indicative of a lease than a service transaction, that factor is outweighed by the other factors, which support classification as a service transaction. Taking into account all of the factors, the transaction between Corp A and Corp B is classified as a provision of services under paragraph (c) of this section.

(5) *Example 5: Downloaded software subject to §1.861-18*—(i) *Facts.* Corp A provides software for download to Corp B that enables Corp B to create a scalable, shared pool of computing resources over Corp B's own network for use by Corp B's employees. Corp B downloads the software, which runs solely on Corp B's servers. Corp A provides Corp B with free updates for download as they become available. Corp B pays Corp A an annual fee, and, upon termination of the arrangement, an electronic lock is activated that prevents Corp B from further using the software.

(ii) *Analysis.* Under paragraph (b) of this section, the download of software for use with Corp B's computer hardware does not constitute on-demand network access by Corp B to Corp A's software. Accordingly, the transaction between Corp A and Corp B is not a cloud transaction described in paragraph (b) of this section. Because the transaction involves the transfer of digital content as defined in §1.861-18(a)(3), it is classified under §1.861-18.

(6) *Example 6: Access to online software via an application*—(i) *Facts.* Corp A provides Corp B word processing, spreadsheet, and presentation software and allows employees of Corp B to access the software over the Internet through a web browser or an application ("app"). In order to access the software from a mobile device, Corp B's employees usually download Corp A's app onto their devices. To access the full functionality of the app, the device must be connected to the Internet. Only a limited number of features on the app are available without an Internet connection. Corp B has no ability to alter the software code. The software is hosted on servers owned by Corp A and located at Corp A's facilities and is used concurrently by other Corp A customers. Corp A is solely responsible for maintaining and repairing the servers and software, and ensuring continued functionality and compatibility with Corp B's employees' devices and providing updates and fixes to the software (including the app) for the duration of the contract with Corp B. Corp B pays a monthly fee based on the number of employees with access to the software. Upon termination of the arrangement, Corp A activates an electronic lock preventing Corp B's employees from further utilizing the app, and Corp B's employees are no longer able to access the software via a web browser.

(ii) *Analysis.* (A) Corp A's provision to Corp B of a non-de minimis right to on-demand network access to Corp A's computer hardware and software resources for the purpose of fully utilizing Corp A's software is a cloud transaction described in paragraph (b) of this section.

(B) Corp B has neither physical possession of nor control over Corp A's word processing, spreadsheet, and presentation software or computer hardware. Additionally, the servers and software are part of an integrated operation in which Corp A maintains the servers and updates the software. Corp A makes available its word processing, spreadsheet, and presentation software and servers to Corp B and other customers concurrently. Corp A's compensation, though based in part on the passage of time, is also determined by reference to Corp B's level of use (that is, the number of Corp B employees with access to the software). Taking into account all of the factors, the transaction between Corp A and Corp B is classified as the provision of services under paragraph (c) of this section.

(C) The provision of the app to Corp B's employees by download onto their devices would be a transfer of a computer program rather than a cloud transaction subject to paragraph (b) of this section. However, under paragraph (c)(3) of this section, it is necessary to consider whether that transfer is de minimis in the context of the overall arrangement and in light of the surrounding facts and circumstances. Here, the significance of the download of the app by Corp B's employees is limited by the fact that the device running the app must be connected to Corp A's servers via the Internet to enable most of the app's core functions. The software that enables such functionality remains on Corp A's servers and is accessed through an on-demand network by Corp B's employees. Therefore, the download of the app is de minimis, and under paragraph (c)(3) of this section, the entire arrangement is classified as a service.

(7) *Example 7: Access to offline software with limited online functions*—(i) *Facts.* Corp A provides Corp B word processing, spreadsheet, and presentation software that is functionally similar to the software in paragraph (d)(6) of this section (*Example 6*). The software is made available for access over the Internet but only to download the software onto a computer or onto a mobile device in the form of an app. The downloaded software contains all the core functions of the software. Employees of Corp B can use the software on their computers or mobile devices regardless of whether their computer or mobile device is online. When online, the software provides a few ancillary functions that are not available offline, such as access to document templates and data collection for diagnosing problems with the software. Whether working online or offline, Corp B employees can store their files only on their own computer or mobile device, and not on Corp A's data storage servers. Because the software provides near full functionality without access to Corp A's servers, it requires more computing resources on employees' computers and devices than the app in paragraph (d)(6) of this section. Corp B's employees can also download updates to the software as part of the monthly fee arrangement. Upon termination of the arrangement, an electronic lock is activated so that the software can no longer be accessed.

(ii) *Analysis.* The provision of the software constitutes a lease of a copyrighted article under §1.861-18. See §1.861-18(h)(4). The access to the online ancillary functions otherwise would constitute a cloud transaction under paragraph (b) of this section, but the access to these functions is de minimis in the context of the overall arrangement, considering that the core functions are available offline through the downloaded software. Because there is no cloud transaction described in paragraph (b) of this section, this section does not apply.

(8) *Example 8: Data storage, separate from access to offline software*—(i) *Facts.* The facts are the same as in paragraph (d)(7)(i) of this section (the facts in *Example 7*), except that Corp A also provides data storage to Corp B on Corp A's server systems in exchange for a monthly fee based on the amount of data storage used by Corp B. Under the data storage terms, Corp B employees may store files created by Corp B employees using Corp A's software or other software. Although Corp A's word processing software is compatible with Corp A's data storage systems, the core functionality of Corp A's software is not dependent on Corp B's purchase of the storage plan. Depending on utilization levels, the server systems providing data storage to Corp B may also be used simultaneously for other customers. The data storage provided to Corp B can be sourced from a variety of server systems in one or more of Corp A's data centers, and Corp A determines how its computing resources are allocated among customers. Corp A agrees to keep the server systems operational, including by performing physical maintenance and repair, and may replace any server system with another one of comparable functionality. Corp A agrees to provide Corp B with a payment credit for server downtime. Corp B has no ability to physically alter the server systems.

(ii) *Analysis.* (A) Corp A's provision of software and data storage capacity constitute separate transactions, and neither is de minimis. Therefore, under paragraph (c)(3) of this section, the transactions are classified separately.

(B) As in paragraph (d)(7), Corp B's download of fully functional software, along with on-demand network access to certain limited online features, does not constitute a cloud transaction, but rather constitutes a lease of a copyrighted article under §1.861-18.

(C) Corp A's provision of data storage constitutes a cloud transaction because Corp B obtains a non-de minimis right to on-demand network access to computer hardware of Corp A.

(D) Corp B has neither physical possession of nor control of the server systems, beyond Corp B's right to access and use the servers. Corp A may replace any server with a functionally comparable server. The server systems are a component of an integrated operation in which Corp A has other responsibilities, including maintaining the server systems. The transaction does not provide Corp B with a significant economic or possessory interest in the servers. The servers may, depending on utilization levels, be used by Corp A to provide significant services to entities unrelated to Corp B. Corp A is compensated according to the level of Corp B's use (that is, the

amount of data storage used by Corp B) and not solely based on the passage of time. Because Corp A will provide Corp B with a payment credit for server downtime, Corp A bears risk of substantially diminished receipts in the event of contract nonperformance. Taking into account all of these factors, the transaction for data storage is classified as a provision of services under paragraph (c) of this section.

(9) *Example 9: Streaming digital content using third-party servers*—(i) *Facts.* Corp A streams digital content in the form of videos and music to end-users from servers located in data centers owned and operated by Data Center Operator. Data Center Operator's content delivery network facility services multiple customers. Each end-user uses a computer or other electronic device to access unlimited streaming video and music in exchange for payment of a flat monthly fee to Corp A. The end-user may select from among the available content the particular video or song to be streamed. Corp A continually updates its content catalog, replacing content with higher quality versions and adding new content at no additional charge to the end-user. Content that is streamed to the end-user is not stored locally on the end-user's computer or other electronic device and therefore can be played only while the end-user's computer or other electronic device is connected to the Internet. Corp A pays Data Center Operator a fee based on the amount of data storage used and computing power made available in connection with Corp A's content streaming. The storage and computing power provided to Corp A can be sourced from a variety of servers in one or more of Data Center Operator's facilities, and Data Center Operator determines how computing resources are allocated among its customers. Data Center Operator covenants to keep the servers operational, including performing physical maintenance and repair. Corp A has no right or ability to physically alter the servers.

(ii) *Analysis.* (A) The relevant factors for classifying the transaction between Corp A and Data Center Operator are analyzed in the same manner as the computing capacity and data storage transactions in paragraphs (d)(1) and (8) of this section (*Example 1* and *Example 8*), respectively, such that the transaction between Corp A and Data Center Operator is classified as a provision of services by Data Center Operator to Corp A under paragraph (c) of this section.

(B) A transaction between Corp A and an end-user is a cloud transaction described in paragraph (b) of this section because the end-user obtains a non-de minimis right to on-demand network access to digital content of Corp A.

(C) An end-user has neither physical possession of nor control of the digital content. Additionally, Corp A has the right to determine the digital content used in the cloud transaction and retains the right to modify its selection of digital content. Digital content accessed by end-users is a component of an integrated operation in which Corp A's other responsibilities include maintaining and updating its content catalog. Corp A's end-users do not obtain a significant economic or possessory interest in any of the digital content in Corp A's catalog. The digital content provided by Corp A may be accessed concurrently by multiple unrelated end-users. Although, as a general matter, compensation based on the passage of time is more indicative of a lease than a service transaction, that factor is outweighed by the other factors, which support a services classification. Taking into account all of the factors, a transaction between an end-user and Corp A is classified as a provision of services under paragraph (c) of this section.

(10) *Example 10: Downloaded digital content subject to §1.861-18*—(i) *Facts.* Corp A offers digital content in the form of videos and music solely for download onto end-users' computers or other electronic devices for a fee. Once downloaded, the end-user accesses the videos and songs from the end-user's computer or other electronic device, which does not need to be connected to the Internet in order to play the content. The end-user owes no additional payment to Corp A for the ability to play the content in the future.

(ii) *Analysis.* Under paragraph (b) of this section, the download of digital content onto an end-user's computer for storage and use on that computer does not constitute on-demand network access by the end-user to the digital content of Corp A. Accordingly, the transaction between the end-user and Corp A is not a cloud transaction described in paragraph (b) of this section, and this section does not apply to the transaction. Because the transaction involves the transfer of digital content as defined in §1.861-18(a)(3), it will be classified under §1.861-18. See §1.861-18(h)(21).

(11) *Example 11: Access to online database*—(i) *Facts.* Corp A offers an online database of industry-specific materials. End-users access the materials through Corp A's website, which aggregates and organizes information topically and hosts a proprietary search engine. Corp A hosts the website and database on its own servers and provides multiple end-users access to the website and database concurrently. Corp A is solely responsible for maintaining and replacing the servers, website, and database (including adding or updating materials in the database). End-users have no ability to alter the servers, website, or database. Most materials in Corp A's database are publicly available by other means, but Corp A's website offers an efficient way to locate and obtain the information on demand. Cer-

tain materials in Corp A's database constitute digital content within the meaning of §1.861-18(a)(3), and Corp A pays the copyright owners a license fee for using them. Each end-user may download any of the materials to its own computer and keep such materials without further payment. The end-user pays Corp A a fee based on the number of searches or the amount of time spent on the website, and such fee is not dependent on the amount of materials the end-user downloads. The fee that the end-user pays is substantially higher than the stand-alone charge for accessing the same digital content outside of Corp A's system.

(ii) *Analysis.* (A) Corp A's provision to an end-user of access to Corp A's website and online database is a cloud transaction described in paragraph (b) of this section because the end-user obtains a non-de minimis right to on-demand access to Corp A's computer hardware and software resources.

(B) An end-user's downloading of the digital content would be classified as a sale of copyrighted articles under §1.861-18. Nonetheless, taking into account the entire arrangement, including that the primary benefit to the end-user is access to Corp A's database and its proprietary search engine, and that the stand-alone charge for accessing the digital content would be substantially less than the fee Corp A charges, the downloads are de minimis. Accordingly, under paragraph (c)(3) of this section, there is no separate classification of the downloads.

(C) The end-user has neither physical possession of nor control of the database, software, or the servers that host the database or software. Corp A retains the right to replace its servers and update its software and database. The database, software, and servers are part of an integrated operation in which Corp A is responsible for curat-ing the database, updating the software, and maintaining the servers. Corp A provides each end-user on-demand network access to its software and online database concurrently with other end-users. Certain end-users pay Corp A a fee based on time spent on Corp A's website, which could be construed as compensation based on the passage of time and thus be more indicative of a lease than a service transaction. However, the fee that the end-user pays is substantially higher than the stand-alone charge for accessing the same digital content outside of Corp A's system. Accordingly, on balance, the fee arrangement supports the classification of the transaction as a service transaction. Taking into account all of these factors, the arrangement between end-users and Corp A is treated as the provision of services under paragraph (c) of this section.

(e) *Effective/applicability date.*—This section applies to cloud transactions occurring pursuant to contracts entered into in taxable years beginning on or after the date of publication of a Treasury decision adopting these rules as final regulations in the **Federal Register**.

(f) *Change in method of accounting required by this section.*—In order to comply with this section, a taxpayer engaging in a cloud transaction pursuant to a contract entered into on or after the date described in paragraph (e) of this section may be required to change its method of accounting. If so required, the taxpayer must secure the consent of the Commissioner in accordance with the requirements of §1.446-1(e) and the applicable administrative procedures for obtaining the Commissioner's consent under section 446(e) for voluntary changes in methods of accounting. [Reg. §1.861-19.]

Allocation and Apportionment of Deductions and Foreign Tax Credit: Guidance

Allocation and Apportionment of Deductions and Foreign Tax Credit: Guidance.—Reg. §1.861-20, relating to the allocation and apportionment of deductions and creditable foreign taxes, the definition of financial services income, foreign tax redeterminations, availability of foreign tax credits under the transition tax, and the application of the foreign tax credit limitation to consolidated groups, is proposed (published in the Federal Register on December 17, 2019) (REG-105495-19).

Par 12. Section 1.861-20 is added to read as follows:

§1.861-20. Allocation and apportionment of foreign income taxes.—(a) *Scope.*—This section provides rules for the allocation and apportionment of foreign income taxes, including allocating and apportioning foreign income taxes to separate categories for purposes of the foreign tax credit. The rules of this section apply except as modified under the rules for an operative section. See, for example, §§1.704-1(b)(4)(viii)(*d*)(*1*), 1.904-6, 1.960-1(d)(3)(ii), and 1.965-5(b)(2). Paragraph (b) of this section provides definitions for the purposes of this section. Paragraph (c) of this section provides the general rule for allocation and apportionment of foreign income taxes. Paragraph (d) of this section provides rules for assigning foreign gross income to statutory and residual groupings. Paragraph (e) of this section provides rules for allocating and apportioning foreign law deductions to foreign gross income in the statutory and residual groupings. Paragraph (f) of this section provides rules for apportioning foreign income taxes among statutory and residual groupings. Paragraph (g) of this section provides examples that illustrate the application of this section. Paragraph (h) of this section provides the applicability dates for this section.

(b) *Definitions.*—The following definitions apply for purposes of this section.

(1) *Corporation.*—The term *corporation* has the same meaning as set forth in §301.7701-2(b), except that it does not include a reverse hybrid.

(2) *Corresponding U.S. item.*—The term *corresponding U.S. item* means the item of U.S. gross income or U.S. loss, if any, that arises from the same transaction or other realization event from which an item of foreign gross income also arises. An item of U.S. gross income or U.S. loss is a corresponding U.S. item even if the item of foreign gross income that arises from the same transaction or realization event differs in amount from the item of U.S. gross income or U.S. loss. A corresponding U.S. item does not include an item of gross income that is exempt, excluded or eliminated from U.S. gross income, nor does it include an item of U.S. gross income or U.S. loss that is not realized, recognized or taken into account by the taxpayer in the U.S. taxable year in which the taxpayer paid or accrued the foreign income tax.

(3) *Foreign capital gain amount.*—The term *foreign capital gain amount* means the portion of a distribution that under foreign law gives rise to gross income of a type described in section 301(c)(3)(A).

(4) *Foreign dividend amount.*—The term *foreign dividend amount* means the portion of a distribution that is taxable as a dividend under foreign law.

(5) *Foreign gross income.*—The term *foreign gross income* means the items of gross income included in the base upon which a foreign income tax is imposed. This includes all items of foreign gross income included in the foreign tax base, even if the foreign taxable year begins in the U.S. taxable year that precedes the U.S. taxable year in which the taxpayer pays or accrues the foreign income tax.

(6) *Foreign income tax.*—The term *foreign income tax* means an income, war profits, or excess profits tax within the meaning of §1.901-2(a) that is a separate levy within the meaning of §1.901-2(d).

(7) *Foreign law CFC.*—The term *foreign law CFC* means a foreign corporation certain of the earnings of which are taxable to its shareholder under a foreign law subpart F regime.

(8) *Foreign law distribution.*—The term *foreign law distribution* has the meaning provided in paragraph (d)(3)(i)(C) of this section.

(9) *Foreign law subpart F income.*—The term foreign law subpart F income means the items of a foreign law CFC, computed under foreign law, that give rise to an inclusion in a taxpayer's foreign gross income by reason of a foreign law subpart F regime.

(10) *Foreign law subpart F regime.*—A foreign law subpart F regime is a foreign law tax regime similar to the subpart F regime described in sections 951 through 959 that imposes a tax on a shareholder of a corporation based on an inclusion in the shareholder's taxable income of certain of the corporation's current earnings that are of a type that is similar to subpart F income, whether or not the foreign law deems the corporation's earnings to be distributed.

(11) *Foreign taxable income.*—The term *foreign taxable income* means foreign gross income reduced by the deductions that are allowed under foreign law.

(12) *Foreign taxable year.*—The term *foreign taxable year* has the meaning set forth in section 7701(a)(23), applied by substituting "under foreign law" for the phrase "under subtitle A."

(13) *Reverse hybrid.*—The term *reverse hybrid* means an entity that is described in §301.7701-2(b) and that is a fiscally transparent entity (under the principles of §1.894-1(d)(3)) or a branch under the laws of a foreign country imposing tax on the income of the entity.

(14) *Taxpayer.*—The term *taxpayer* has the meaning described in §1.901-2(f)(1).

(15) *U.S. capital gain amount.*—The term *U.S. capital gain amount* means the portion of a distribution to which section 301(c)(3)(A) applies.

(16) *U.S. dividend amount.*—The term *U.S. dividend amount* means the portion of a distribution that is made out of earnings and profits under Federal income tax law or out of previously taxed earnings and profits described in section 959(a) or (b). It also includes amounts included in gross income as a dividend by reason of section 1248 or section 964(e).

(17) *U.S. gross income.*—The term *U.S. gross income* means the items of gross income that a taxpayer recognizes and includes in taxable income under Federal income tax law for its U.S. taxable year.

(18) *U.S. loss.*—The term *U.S. loss* means the item of loss that a taxpayer recognizes and includes in taxable income under Federal income tax law for its U.S. taxable year.

(19) *U.S. return of capital amount.*—The term *U.S. return of capital amount* means the portion of a distribution to which section 301(c)(2) applies.

(20) *U.S. taxable year.*—The term *U.S. taxable year* has the same meaning as that of the term *taxable year* set forth in section 7701(a)(23).

(c) *General rule.*—A foreign income tax is allocated or apportioned to the statutory and residual groupings that include the items of foreign gross income included in the base on which the tax is imposed. Each foreign income tax (that is, each separate levy) is allocated and apportioned separately under the rules in this section. A foreign income tax is allocated and apportioned to or among the statutory and residual groupings under the following steps:

(1) First, by assigning the items of foreign gross income to the groupings under the rules of paragraph (d) of this section;

(2) Second, by allocating and apportioning the deductions that are allowed under foreign law to the foreign gross income in the groupings under the rules of paragraph (e) of this section; and

(3) Third, by allocating and apportioning the foreign income tax by reference to the foreign taxable income in the groupings under the rules of paragraph (f) of this section.

(d) *Assigning items of foreign gross income to the statutory and residual groupings.*—(1) *In general.*—Each item of foreign gross income is assigned to a statutory or residual grouping. The amount of the item is determined under foreign law. However, Federal income tax law applies to characterize the item and the transaction or other realization event from which the item arose, and to assign it to a grouping. Except as provided in paragraph (d)(3) of this section, if a taxpayer pays or accrues a foreign income tax that is imposed on foreign taxable income that includes an item of foreign gross income in a U.S. taxable year in which the taxpayer also realizes, recognizes, or takes into account a corresponding U.S. item, then the item of foreign gross income is assigned to the grouping to which the corresponding U.S. item is assigned. If the corresponding U.S. item is a U.S. loss (or zero), the foreign gross income is assigned to the grouping to which a gain would be assigned had the transaction or other realization event given rise to a gain, rather than a U.S. loss (or zero), for Federal income tax purposes, and not (if different) to the grouping to which the U.S. loss is allocated and apportioned in computing U.S. taxable income. Paragraph (d)(3) of this section provides special rules regarding the assignment of the item of foreign gross income in particular circumstances.

(2) *Items of foreign gross income with no corresponding U.S. item.*—Except as provided in paragraph (d)(3) of this section, the rules in paragraphs (d)(2)(i) and (ii) of this section apply for purposes of characterizing an item of foreign gross income and assigning it to a grouping if the taxpayer does not realize, recognize, or take into account a corresponding U.S. item in the same U.S. taxable year in which the taxpayer pays or accrues foreign income tax that is imposed on foreign taxable income that includes the item of foreign gross income.

(i) *Foreign gross income from U.S. nonrecognition event, or U.S. recognition event that falls in a different U.S. taxable year.*—If a taxpayer recognizes an item of foreign gross income arising from a transaction or other foreign realization event that does not result in the recognition of gross income or loss under Federal income tax law in the same U.S. taxable year in which the foreign income tax is paid or accrued, then the item of foreign gross income is characterized and assigned to the grouping to which the corresponding U.S. item would be assigned if the event giving rise to the foreign gross income resulted in the recognition of gross income or loss under Federal income tax law in that U.S. taxable year. For example, if a foreign gross income item of gain arises from a distribution of property that is treated as a taxable disposition of the property under foreign law, and the realization event under foreign law does not cause the recognition of gain or loss under Federal income tax law, the foreign gross income item of gain is assigned to the grouping to which a

corresponding U.S. item of gain or loss on a taxable disposition of the property would be assigned. However, foreign gross income arising from the receipt of the distribution is assigned under the rules of paragraphs (d)(3)(i) and (ii) of this section. As another example, if a taxpayer pays or accrues a foreign income tax that is imposed on foreign taxable income that includes an item of foreign gross income by reason of a transaction or other realization event that also gave rise to an item of U.S. gross income or U.S. loss, but the U.S. and foreign taxable years end on different dates and the event occurred in the last U.S. taxable year that ends before the end of the foreign taxable year, then the item of foreign gross income is characterized and assigned to the grouping to which the corresponding U.S. item would be assigned if the item of U.S. gross income or U.S. loss were taken into account under Federal income tax law in the U.S. taxable year in which the foreign income tax is paid or accrued.

(ii) *Foreign gross income of a type that is recognized but excluded from U.S. gross income.*—(A) *In general.*—If a taxpayer recognizes an item of foreign gross income that is a type of recognized gross income that Federal income tax law excludes from U.S. gross income, then the item of foreign gross income is assigned to the grouping to which the item of gross income would be assigned if it were included in U.S. gross income. Notwithstanding the previous sentence, foreign gross income that is attributable to a base difference is assigned under paragraph (d)(2)(ii)(B) of this section.

(B) *Base differences.*—If a taxpayer recognizes an item of foreign gross income that is attributable to a base difference, then the item of foreign gross income is assigned to the residual grouping. *But see* § 1.904-6(b)(1) (assigning foreign gross income attributable to a base difference to foreign source income in the separate category described in section 904(d)(2)(H)(i)) for purposes of applying section 904 as the operative section). An item of foreign gross income is attributable to a base difference under this paragraph (d)(2)(ii)(B) only if it is one of the following items:

(1) Death benefits described in section 101;

(2) Gifts and inheritances described in section 102;

(3) Contributions to capital described in section 118;

(4) The receipt of money or other property in exchange for stock described in section 1032 (including by reason of a transfer described in section 351(a));

(5) The receipt of money or other property in exchange for a partnership interest described in section 721;

(6) The portion of a distribution of property by a corporation to its shareholder with respect to its stock that is described in section 301(c)(2); and

(7) A distribution to a partner described in section 733.

(3) *Special rules for assigning certain items of foreign gross income to a statutory or residual grouping.*—(i) *Items of foreign gross income included by a taxpayer in its capacity as a shareholder.*—(A) *Scope.*—The rules of this paragraph (d)(3)(i) apply to assign to a statutory or residual grouping an item of foreign gross income that a taxpayer includes in foreign taxable income in its capacity as a shareholder of a corporation as a result of a distribution, a foreign law distribution, an inclusion, or gain with respect to the stock of the corporation (as determined under foreign law).

(B) *Characterizing and assigning foreign gross income items that arise from a distribution.*—(1) *In general.*—If there is a distribution by a corporation that is recognized for both foreign law and Federal income tax purposes, a taxpayer first applies the rules of paragraph (d)(3)(i)(B)(2) of this section, and then (if necessary) applies the rules of paragraph (d)(3)(i)(B)(3) of this section to determine the amount and the character of the items of foreign gross income that arise from the distribution. Foreign gross income arising from any portion of a distribution that is not recognized as a distribution for Federal income tax purposes is characterized under the rules for foreign law distributions in paragraph (d)(3)(i)(C) of this section. *See* § 1.960-1(d)(3)(ii) for rules for assigning foreign gross income arising from a distribution described in this paragraph to income groups or PTEP groups for purposes of section 960 as the operative section.

(2) *Characterizing and assigning the foreign dividend amount.*—The foreign dividend amount is, to the extent of the U.S. dividend amount, assigned to the same statutory and residual groupings from which a distribution of the U.S. dividend amount is made under Federal income tax law. If the foreign dividend amount exceeds the U.S. dividend amount, the excess foreign dividend amount is an item of foreign gross income that is, to the extent of the U.S. return of capital amount, treated as attributable to a base difference described in paragraph (d)(2)(ii)(B)(6) of this section. Any additional excess of the foreign dividend amount over the sum of the U.S. dividend amount and the U.S. return of capital amount is an item of foreign gross income that is assigned to the statutory or residual grouping (or ratably to the groupings) to which the U.S. capital gain amount is assigned.

(3) *Characterizing and assigning the foreign capital gain amount.*—The foreign capital gain amount is, to the extent of the U.S. capital gain amount, assigned to the statutory and residual groupings to which the U.S. capital gain amount is assigned under Federal income tax law. If the foreign capital gain amount exceeds the U.S. capital gain amount, the excess is, to the extent of the U.S. return of capital amount, treated as attributable to a base difference described in paragraph (d)(2)(ii)(B)(6) of this section. Any additional excess of the foreign capital gain amount over the sum of the U.S. capital gain amount and the U.S. return of capital amount is assigned ratably to the statutory and residual groupings to which the U.S. dividend amount is assigned.

(C) *Foreign gross income items arising from a foreign law distribution.*—An item of foreign gross income that arises from an event that foreign law treats as a taxable distribution (other than by reason of a foreign law subpart F regime) but that Federal income tax law does not treat as a distribution of property (for example, a stock dividend described in section 305 or a foreign law consent dividend) (a *foreign law distribution*) is assigned under the rules of paragraph (d)(3)(i)(B) of this section to the same statutory or residual groupings to which the foreign gross income would be assigned if a distribution of property in the amount of the foreign law distribution were made for Federal income tax purposes in the U.S. taxable year in which the taxpayer paid or accrued the foreign income tax.

(D) *Foreign gross income from an inclusion under a foreign law subpart F regime.*—An item of foreign gross income that a taxpayer includes under foreign law in its capacity as a shareholder of a foreign law CFC under a foreign law subpart F regime is assigned to the same statutory and residual groupings as the item of foreign law subpart F income of the foreign law CFC that gives rise to the item of foreign gross income of the taxpayer. The assignment is made by treating the items of foreign gross income of the taxpayer attributable to the foreign law subpart F regime inclusion as the items of foreign gross income of the foreign law CFC and applying the rules in this paragraph (d) by treating the foreign law CFC as the taxpayer in its U.S. taxable year with or within which its foreign taxable year (under the law of the foreign jurisdiction imposing the shareholder-level tax) ends. See § 1.904-6(f) for special rules with respect to items of foreign gross income relating to items of the foreign law CFC that give rise to inclusions under section 951A for purposes of applying section 904 as the operative section.

(ii) *Tax imposed on disregarded payments.*—**(A)** *Disregarded payments made by a foreign branch.*—Except as provided in paragraph (d)(3)(ii)(C) of this section, an item of foreign gross income that a taxpayer includes by reason of the receipt of a disregarded payment made by a disregarded entity or other foreign branch is assigned to the statutory or residual grouping to which the income out of which the payment is made is assigned. For purposes of this paragraph (d)(3)(ii), a disregarded payment is considered to be made ratably out of all of the accumulated after-tax income of the foreign branch, as computed for Federal income tax purposes. The accumulated after-tax income of the foreign branch is deemed to have arisen in the statutory and residual groupings in the same ratio as the tax book value of the assets of the branch in the groupings, determined in accordance with § 1.987-6(b)(2), unless the payment was made with a principal purpose of avoiding the purposes of an operative section, or results in a material distortion in the association of foreign income tax with U.S. gross income in the same statutory or residual grouping as the foreign gross income from the payment. For purposes of applying § 1.987-6(b)(2) under this paragraph (d)(3)(ii), assets of the foreign branch include stock held by the foreign branch. *But see* § 1.904-6(b)(2)(i) (assigning certain items based on the separate category to which the U.S. gross income to which the disregarded payment is allocable is assigned under § 1.904-4(f)(2)(vi)(A) for purposes of applying section 904 as the operative section).

(B) *Disregarded payments made by an owner.*—Except as provided in paragraph (d)(3)(ii)(C) of this section, an item of foreign gross income that a taxpayer includes by reason of the receipt of a disregarded payment made to a foreign branch by a foreign branch owner is assigned to the residual grouping. *But see* § 1.904-6(b)(2)(ii) (assigning certain items to the foreign branch category for purposes of applying section 904 as the operative section).

(C) *Disregarded payments in connection with disregarded sales or exchanges of property.*—An item of foreign gross income attributable to gain recognized under foreign law by reason of a disregarded payment received in exchange for property is characterized and assigned under the rules of paragraph (d)(2)(i) of this section.

(D) *Definitions.*—For purposes of this paragraph (d)(3)(ii) and paragraph (g) of this section, the terms *disregarded entity, disregarded payment, foreign branch,* and *foreign branch owner* have the same meaning given to those terms in § 1.904-4(f)(3). A foreign branch owner can include a foreign corporation. *See* § 1.904-4(f)(3)(viii).

(iii) *Reverse hybrids.*—An item of foreign gross income that a taxpayer includes in foreign taxable income in its capacity as the owner of a reverse hybrid is assigned to a statutory or residual grouping by treating the taxpayer's items of foreign gross income included from the reverse hybrid as the foreign gross income of the reverse hybrid, and applying the rules in this paragraph (d) by treating the reverse hybrid as the taxpayer in the reverse hybrid's U.S. taxable year with or within which its foreign taxable year (under the law of the foreign jurisdiction imposing the owner-level tax) ends. See § 1.904-6(f) for special rules that apply for purposes of section 904 with respect to items of foreign gross income that under this paragraph (d)(3)(iii) would be assigned to a separate category that includes income that gives rise to inclusions under section 951A.

(iv) *Gain on sale of disregarded entity.*—An item of foreign gross income arising from gain recognized on the disposition of a disregarded entity that is characterized as a disposition of assets for Federal income tax purposes is assigned to statutory and residual groupings in the same proportion as the gain that would be treated as foreign gross income in each grouping if the transaction were treated as a disposition of assets for foreign tax law purposes.

(e) *Allocating and apportioning deductions (allowed under foreign law) to foreign gross income in a grouping.*—**(1)** *Application of foreign law expense allocation rules.*—In order to determine foreign taxable income in each statutory grouping, or the residual grouping, foreign gross income in each grouping is reduced by deducting any expenses, losses, or other amounts that are deductible under foreign law that are specifically allocable to the items of foreign gross income in the grouping under the laws of that foreign country. If expenses are not specifically allocated under foreign law, then the expenses are allocated and apportioned among the groupings under the principles of foreign law. Thus, for example, if foreign law provides that expenses will be apportioned on a gross income basis, the foreign law deductions are apportioned on the basis of the relative amounts of foreign gross income assigned to each grouping.

(2) *Application of U.S. expense allocation rules in the absence of foreign law rules.*—If foreign law does not provide rules for the allocation or apportionment of expenses, losses or other deductions to particular items of foreign gross income, then the principles of the section 861 regulations (as defined in § 1.861-8(a)(1)) apply in allocating and apportioning such expenses, losses, or other deductions to foreign gross income. For example, in the absence of foreign law expense allocation rules, the principles of the section 861 regulations apply to allocate definitely related expenses to particular categories of foreign gross income and provide the methods for apportioning foreign law expenses that are definitely related to more than one statutory grouping or that are not definitely related to any statutory grouping. For this purpose, the apportionment of expenses required to be made under the principles of the section 861 regulations need not be made on other than a separate company basis. If the taxpayer applies the principles of the section 861 regulations for purposes of allocating foreign law deductions under this paragraph (e), the taxpayer must apply the principles in the same manner as the taxpayer applies such principles in determining the income or earnings and profits for Federal income tax purposes of the taxpayer (or of the foreign branch, controlled foreign corporation, or other entity that paid or accrued the foreign taxes, as the case may be). For example, a taxpayer must use the modified gross income method under § 1.861-9T when applying the principles of that section for purposes of this paragraph (e) to determine the amount of foreign taxable income in each grouping if the taxpayer applies the modified gross income method in determining the income and earnings and profits of a controlled foreign corporation for Federal income tax purposes.

(f) *Apportionment of foreign income tax among groupings.*—If foreign taxable income is assigned to more than one grouping, then the foreign income tax is apportioned among the statutory and residual groupings by multiplying the foreign income tax by a fraction, the numerator of which is the foreign taxable income in a grouping and the denominator of which is all foreign taxable income on which the foreign income tax is imposed. If foreign law, including by reason of an income tax convention, exempts certain types of income from tax, or if foreign taxable income is reduced to or below zero by foreign law deductions, then no foreign income tax is allocated and apportioned to that income. A withholding tax (as defined in section 901(k)(1)(B)) is allocated and apportioned to the foreign gross income from which it is withheld. If foreign law, including by reason of an income tax convention, provides for a specific rate of tax with respect to certain types of income (for example, capital gains), or allows credits only against tax on particular items or types of income (for example, credit for foreign withholding taxes), then such provisions are taken into account in determining the amount of foreign tax imposed on such foreign taxable income.

(g) *Examples.*—The following examples illustrate the application of this section and § 1.904-6.

Reg. § 1.861-20(g)

(1) *Presumed facts.*—Except as otherwise provided, the following facts are assumed for purposes of the examples:

(i) USP and US2 are domestic corporations, which are unrelated;

(ii) USP elects to claim a foreign tax credit under section 901;

(iii) CFC, CFC1, and CFC2 are controlled foreign corporations organized in Country A, and are not reverse hybrids;

(iv) All parties have a U.S. dollar functional currency and a U.S. taxable year and foreign taxable year that corresponds to the calendar year;

(v) No party has expenses for Country A tax purposes or expenses for U.S. tax purposes (other than foreign income tax expense); and

(vi) Section 904 is the operative section, and terms have the meaning provided in this section or §§ 1.904-4 and 1.904-5.

(2) *Example 1: Corresponding U.S. item*—(i) *Facts.* USP conducts business in Country A that gives rise to a foreign branch. In Year 1, for Country A tax purposes, USP earns $600x of gross income from the sale of Asset X and incurs foreign income tax of $80x. Also in Year 1, for Federal income tax purposes, USP earns $800x of foreign branch category income from the sale of Asset X.

(ii) *Analysis.* For purposes of allocating and apportioning the $80x of Country A foreign income tax, the $600x of Country A gross income from the sale of Asset X is first assigned to separate categories. The $800x of foreign branch category income from the sale of Asset X is the corresponding U.S. item to the Country A item of gross income. Under paragraph (d)(1) of this section, because USP recognizes a corresponding U.S. item with respect to the Country A item of gross income in the same U.S. taxable year, the $600x of Country A gross income is assigned to the same separate category as the corresponding U.S. item. This is the case even though the amount of gross income recognized for Federal income tax purposes differs from the amount recognized for Country A tax purposes. Accordingly, the $600x of Country A gross income is assigned to the foreign branch category. Additionally, because all of the Country A taxable income is assigned to a single separate category, the $80x of Country A tax is also allocated to the foreign branch category. No apportionment of the $80x is necessary because the class of gross income to which the tax is allocated consists entirely of a single statutory grouping, foreign branch category income.

(3) *Example 2: Characterization of transactions*—(i) *Facts.* USP owns all of the outstanding stock of CFC, which conducts business in Country A. In Year 1, USP sells all of the stock of CFC to US2. For Country A tax purposes, USP recognizes $800x of gain on which Country A imposes $80x of foreign income tax based on its rules for taxing capital gains of nonresidents. For Federal income tax purposes, USP recognizes $800x of gain on the sale of the stock of CFC, all of which is included in the gross income of USP as a dividend under section 1248(a). Under §§ 1.904-4(d) and 1.904-5(c)(4), the $800x is general category income to USP.

(ii) *Analysis.* For purposes of allocating and apportioning the $80x of Country A foreign income tax, the $800x of Country A gross income from the sale of the stock of CFC is first assigned to separate categories. The $800x of general category income from the sale of the stock of CFC is the corresponding U.S. item to the Country A item of gross income. Under paragraph (d)(1) of this section, because USP recognizes a corresponding U.S. item with respect to the Country A gross income in the same U.S. taxable year, the $800x of Country A gross income is assigned to the same separate category as the corresponding U.S. item. Accordingly, the $800x of Country A gross income is assigned to the general category. This is the case even though for Country A tax purposes the $800x of Country A gross income is characterized as gain from the sale of stock, which would be passive category income under section 904(d)(2)(B)(i), because the income is assigned to a separate category based on the characterization of the gain as a dividend under Federal income tax law. Additionally, because all of the Country A taxable income is assigned to a single separate category, the $80x of Country A tax is also allocated to the general category. No apportionment of the $80x is necessary because the class of gross income to which the deduction is allocated consists entirely of a single statutory grouping, general category income.

(4) *Example 3: No corresponding U.S. item because of a timing difference*—(i) *Facts.* USP owns all of the outstanding stock of CFC, which conducts business in Country A. CFC sells Asset X. For Country A tax purposes, the sale of Asset X occurs in Year 1, and CFC recognizes $400x of foreign gross income and incurs $80x of foreign income tax. For Federal income tax purposes, the sale of Asset X occurs in Year 2 and CFC recognizes $500x of general category income.

(ii) *Analysis.* For purposes of allocating and apportioning the $80x of Country A foreign income tax in Year 1, the $400x of Country A gross income from the sale of Asset X is first assigned to separate categories. There is no corresponding U.S. item because the U.S.

gross income related to the sale is recognized in a different U.S. taxable year than the item of foreign gross income. Under paragraph (d)(2)(i) of this section, because there would be a corresponding U.S. item if the realization event occurred in the same U.S. taxable year for U.S. and foreign tax purposes, the item of foreign gross income (the $400x from the sale of Asset X) is characterized and assigned to the groupings to which the corresponding U.S. item would be assigned if it were recognized for Federal income tax purposes in the same U.S. taxable year in which the item of foreign gross income is recognized. This is the case even though the amount of gross income recognized for Federal income tax purposes differs from the amount recognized for Country A tax purposes. Accordingly, the $400x of Country A gross income is assigned to the general category. Additionally, because all of the Country A taxable income is assigned to a single separate category, the $80x of Country A tax is also allocated to the general category. No apportionment of the $80x is necessary because the class of gross income to which the deduction is allocated consists entirely of a single statutory grouping, general category income.

(5) *Example 4: No corresponding U.S. item because excluded from gross income*—(i) *Facts.* USP conducts business in Country A. In Year 1, USP earns $200x of interest income on a State or local bond. For Country A tax purposes, the $200x of income is included in gross income and incurs $10x of foreign income tax. For Federal income tax purposes, the $200x is excluded from gross income under section 103.

(ii) *Analysis.* For purposes of allocating and apportioning the $10x of Country A foreign income tax, the $200x of Country A gross income is first assigned to separate categories. There is no corresponding U.S. item because the interest income is excluded from U.S. gross income. Thus, the rules of paragraph (d)(2) of this section apply to characterize and assign the foreign gross income to the groupings to which a corresponding U.S. item would be assigned if it were recognized under Federal income tax law in that U.S. taxable year. The interest income is excluded from U.S. gross income, but is otherwise described or identified by section 103. Accordingly, under paragraph (d)(2)(ii)(A) of this section, the $200x of Country A gross income is assigned to the separate category to which the interest income would be assigned under Federal income tax law if the income were included in gross income. Under section 904(d)(2)(B)(i), the interest income would be passive category income. Accordingly, the $200x of Country A gross income is assigned to the passive category. Additionally, because all of the Country A taxable income is assigned to a single separate category, the $10x of Country A tax is also allocated to the passive category (subject to the rules in § 1.904-4(c)). No apportionment of the $10x is necessary because the class of gross income to which the deduction is allocated consists entirely of a single statutory grouping, passive category income.

(6) *Example 5: Actual distribution*—(1) *Facts.* USP owns all of the outstanding stock of CFC1, which in turn owns all of the outstanding stock of CFC2. CFC1 and CFC2 conduct business in Country A. In Year 1, CFC2 distributes $300x to CFC1. For Country A tax purposes, $100x of the distribution is the foreign dividend amount, $160x is treated as a nontaxable return of capital, and the remaining $40x is the foreign capital gain amount. CFC1 incurs $20x of foreign income tax with respect to the foreign dividend amount and $4x of foreign income tax with respect to the foreign capital gain amount. The $20x and $4x of foreign income tax are each a separate levy. For Federal income tax purposes, $150x of the distribution is the U.S. dividend amount, $100x is the U.S. return of capital amount, and the remaining $50x is the U.S. capital gain amount. Under section 904(d)(3)(D) and §§ 1.904-4(d) and 1.904-5(c)(4), the $150x of U.S. dividend amount consists solely of general category income in the hands of CFC1. Under section 904(d)(2)(B)(i) and § 1.904-4(b)(2)(i)(A), the $50x of U.S. capital gain amount is passive category income to CFC1.

(ii) *Analysis*—(A) *In general.* Because the $20x of Country A foreign income tax and the $4x of Country A foreign income tax are separate levies, the taxes are allocated and apportioned separately. For purposes of allocating and apportioning each foreign income tax, the relevant item of Country A gross income (the foreign dividend amount or foreign capital gain amount) is first assigned to separate categories. The U.S. dividend amount and U.S. capital gain amount are corresponding U.S. items. However, paragraph (d)(3)(i)(B) of this section (and not paragraph (d)(1) of this section) applies to assign the items of foreign gross income arising from the distribution.

(B) *Foreign dividend amount.* Under paragraph (d)(3)(i)(B)(2) of this section, the foreign dividend amount ($100x) is, to the extent of the U.S. dividend amount ($150x), assigned to the same separate category from which the distribution of the U.S. dividend amount is made under Federal income tax law. Thus, $100x of foreign gross income that is the foreign dividend amount is assigned to the general category. Additionally, because all of the Country A taxable income included in the base on which the $20x of foreign income tax is imposed is assigned to a single separate category, the $20x of Country A tax on the foreign dividend amount is also allocated to the general category. No apportionment of the $20x is necessary because the class of gross income to which the deduction is allocated consists entirely of a single statutory grouping, general category income.

(C) *Foreign capital gain amount.* Under paragraph (d)(3)(i)(B)(3) of this section, the foreign capital gain amount ($40x) is, to the extent of the U.S. capital gain amount ($50x), assigned to the same separate category to which the U.S. capital gain is assigned under Federal income tax law. Thus, the $40x of foreign gross income that is the foreign capital gain amount is assigned to the passive category. Additionally, because all of the Country A taxable income in the base on which the $4x of foreign income tax is imposed is assigned to a single separate category, the $4x of Country A tax on the foreign dividend amount is also allocated to the passive category. No apportionment of the $4x is necessary because the class of gross income to which the deduction is allocated consists entirely of a single statutory grouping, passive category income.

(7) *Example 6: Foreign law distribution*—(i) *Facts.* USP owns all of the outstanding stock of CFC. In Year 1, for Country A tax purposes, CFC distributes $1,000x of its stock that is treated as a dividend to USP, and Country A imposes a withholding tax on USP of $150x with respect to the $1,000x of foreign gross income. For Federal income tax purposes, the distribution is treated as a stock dividend described in section 305(a) and USP recognizes no U.S. gross income. At the time of the distribution, CFC has $800x of section 965(a) PTEP (as defined in §1.960-3(c)(2)(vi)) in a single annual PTEP account (as defined in §1.960-3(c)(1)), and $500x of earnings and profits described in section 959(c)(3). Section 965(g) is the operative section for purposes of applying this section. *See* §1.965-5(b)(2).

(ii) *Analysis.* For purposes of allocating and apportioning the $150x of Country A foreign income tax, the $1,000x of Country A gross income is first assigned to the relevant statutory and residual groupings for purposes of applying section 965(g) as the operative section. Under §1.965-5(b)(2), the statutory grouping is the portion of the distribution that is attributable to section 965(a) previously taxed earnings and profits and the residual grouping is the portion of the distribution attributable to other earnings and profits. There is no corresponding U.S. item because under section 305 USP recognizes no U.S. gross income with respect to the distribution. Under paragraph (d)(3)(i)(C) of this section, the item of foreign gross income (the $1,000x distribution) is assigned under the rules of paragraph (d)(3)(i)(B) of this section to the same statutory or residual groupings to which the foreign gross income would be assigned if a distribution of the same amount were made for Federal income tax purposes in Year 1. Under paragraph (d)(3)(i)(B)(2) of this section, the foreign dividend amount ($1,000x) is, to the extent of the U.S. dividend amount ($1,000x), assigned to the same statutory or residual groupings from which a distribution of the U.S. dividend amount would be made under Federal income tax law. Thus, $800x of foreign gross income related to the foreign dividend amount is assigned to the statutory grouping for the portion of the distribution attributable to section 965(a) previously taxed earnings and profits and $200x of foreign gross income is assigned to the residual grouping. Under paragraph (f) of this section, $120x ($150x x $800x/$1000x) of the Country A foreign income tax is apportioned to the statutory grouping and $30x ($150x x $200x/$1000x) of the Country A foreign income tax is apportioned to the residual grouping. See section 965(g) and §1.965-5(b) for application of the applicable percentage (as defined in §1.965-5(d)) to the foreign income tax allocated and apportioned to the statutory grouping.

(8) *Example 7: Foreign law subpart F regime, CFC shareholder*—(i) *Facts.* USP owns all of the outstanding stock of CFC1, which in turn owns all of the outstanding stock of CFC2. CFC2 is organized and conducts business in Country B. Country A has a foreign law subpart F regime that imposes a tax on CFC1 for certain earnings of CFC2, a foreign law CFC. In Year 1, CFC2 earns $400x of interest income and $200x of royalty income. CFC2 incurs no foreign income tax. For Country A tax purposes, the $400x of interest income and $200x of royalty income are each an item of foreign law subpart F income of CFC2 that are included in the gross income of CFC1. CFC1 incurs $150x of Country A foreign income tax with respect to the foreign law subpart F income. For Federal income tax purposes, with respect to CFC2, the $400x of interest income is passive category income under section 904(d)(2)(B)(i) and the $200x of royalty income is general category income under §1.904-4(b)(2)(iii).

(ii) *Analysis.* For purposes of allocating and apportioning CFC1's $150x of Country A foreign income tax, the $600x of Country A gross income is first assigned to separate categories. The $600x of foreign gross income is not included in the U.S. gross income of CFC1, and thus, there is no corresponding U.S. item. Under paragraph (d)(3)(i)(D) of this section, each item of foreign law subpart F income that is included in CFC1's foreign gross income is assigned to the same separate category as the item of foreign law subpart F income of CFC2. With respect to CFC2, the $400x of interest income and the $200x of royalty income would be corresponding U.S. items if CFC2 were the taxpayer. Accordingly, $400x of CFC1's foreign gross income is assigned to the passive category and $200x of CFC1's foreign gross income is assigned to the general category. Under paragraph (f) of this section, $100x ($150x x $400x/$600x) of the Country A foreign income tax is apportioned to the passive category and $50x ($150x x

$200x/$600x) of the Country A foreign income tax is apportioned to the general category.

(9) *Example 8: Foreign law subpart F regime, U.S. shareholder*—(i) *Facts.* The facts are the same as in paragraph (g)(8)(i) of this section (the facts in *Example 7*), except that both CFC1 and CFC2 are organized and conduct business in Country B, all of the outstanding stock of CFC1 is owned by Individual X, a U.S. citizen resident in Country A, and Country A imposes tax of $150x on foreign gross income of $600x under its foreign law subpart F regime on Individual X, rather than on CFC1. For Federal income tax purposes, in the hands of CFC2, the $400x of interest income is passive category subpart F income and the $200x of royalty income is general category tested income (as defined in §1.951A-2(b)(1)). CFC2's $400x of interest income gives rise to a passive category subpart F inclusion under section 951(a)(1)(A), and its $200x of tested income gives rise to a GILTI inclusion amount (as defined in §1.951A-1(c)(1)) of $200x, with respect to Individual X.

(ii) *Analysis.* The analysis is the same as in paragraph (g)(8)(ii) of this section (the analysis in *Example 7*) except that under §1.904-6(f), because $50x of the Country A foreign income tax is allocated and apportioned under paragraph (d)(3)(i)(D) of this section to CFC2's general category tested income group to which Individual X's inclusion under section 951A is attributable, the $50x of Country A foreign income tax is allocated and apportioned in the hands of Individual X to the section 951A category.

(10) *Example 9: Disregarded payment*—(i) *Facts.* USP owns all of the outstanding stock of CFC1. CFC1 owns all of the interests in FDE, a disregarded entity organized in Country A. FDE owns all of the outstanding stock of CFC2. In Year 1, FDE pays $400x of interest to CFC1. For Country A tax purposes, CFC1 includes the $400x of interest income in gross income and incurs foreign income tax of $80x. For Federal income tax purposes, the $400x payment is a disregarded payment and results in no income to CFC1. The tax book value of the assets of FDE, including the stock of CFC2, in each separate category (determined in accordance with §1.987-6(b)(2)) is as follows: $750x of general category assets and $250x of passive category assets. The payment of the $400x of interest is not made with the principal purpose of avoiding the purposes of section 904, and does not result in a material distortion of the association of foreign income tax with U.S. gross income in a separate category.

(ii) *Analysis.* For purposes of allocating and apportioning CFC1's $80x of foreign income tax, the $400x of Country A gross income is first assigned to separate categories. The $400x of foreign gross income is not included in the U.S. gross income of CFC1, and thus, there is no corresponding U.S. item. Under paragraph (d)(3)(ii)(A) of this section, the $400x payment is considered to be made ratably out of all of the accumulated after-tax income of FDE, which is deemed to have arisen in the separate categories in the same ratio of the tax book value of the assets in the separate categories (as determined under §1.987-6(b)(2)). Accordingly, $300x ($400x x $750x/$1,000x) of the Country A gross income is assigned to the general category and $100x ($400x x $250x/$1,000x) of the Country A gross income is assigned to the passive category. Under paragraph (f) of this section, $60x ($80x x $300x/$400x) of the Country A foreign income tax is apportioned to the general category and $20x ($80x x $100x/$400x) of the Country A foreign income tax is apportioned to the passive category.

(11) *Example 10: Disregarded transfer of built-in gain property*—(i) *Facts.* USP owns FDE, a foreign branch operating in Country A. FDE transfers Asset F, equipment used in FDE's trade or business in Country A, for no consideration to USP in a transaction that is disregarded for Federal income tax purposes but treated as a distribution of Asset F from a foreign corporation to its U.S. shareholder for Country A tax purposes. Asset F has a fair market value of $250x at the time of transfer and an adjusted basis of $100x for both Federal income tax and Country A tax purposes. Country A imposes $30x of tax on FDE with respect to the $150x of built-in gain on a deemed sale of Asset F, which is recognized for Country A tax purposes by reason of the transfer to USP. If FDE had sold Asset F for $250x in a transaction that was regarded for Federal income tax purposes, FDE would also have recognized gain of $150x for Federal income tax purposes, and that gain would have been characterized as foreign branch category income as defined in §1.904-4(f). Country A also imposes $25x of withholding tax on USP by reason of the distribution of Asset F, valued at $250x, to USP.

(ii) *Analysis*—(A) *Net basis tax on built-in gain.* For purposes of allocating and apportioning the $30x of Country A foreign income tax imposed on FDE by reason of the deemed sale of Asset F, the $150x of Country A gross income from the deemed sale of Asset F is first assigned to a separate category. Because the transaction is disregarded for Federal income tax purposes, there is no corresponding U.S. item. However, FDE would have recognized gain of $150x, which would have been a corresponding U.S. item, if the deemed sale had been recognized for Federal income tax purposes. Therefore, under paragraph (d)(2)(i) of this section the item of foreign gross income is characterized and assigned to the grouping to which such corresponding U.S. item would have been assigned if the deemed sale were recognized under Federal income tax law. Because the sale of Asset F in a regarded transaction would have resulted in foreign branch category income, the foreign gross income is characterized as foreign branch category income. Because all of the Country A foreign taxable income is assigned to a single separate category, the $30x of Country A tax is also allocated to the foreign branch category. No apportionment of the $30x is necessary because the class of gross income to which the tax is allocated consists entirely of a single statutory grouping, foreign branch category income.

(B) *Withholding tax on distribution.* For purposes of allocating and apportioning the $25x of Country A withholding tax imposed on USP by reason of the transfer of Asset F, the $250x of Country A gross income from the distribution of Asset F is first assigned to a separate category. The transfer is a remittance from FDE to USP that is disregarded for Federal income tax purposes (as described in § 1.904-4(f)(2)(vi)(C)(2) and § 1.904-4(f)(3)(ix)) and thus there is no corresponding U.S. item. Under paragraph (d)(3)(ii)(A) of this section the item of foreign gross income is assigned to the groupings to which the income out of which the payment is made is assigned, and the payment is considered to be made ratably out of all of the accumulated after-tax income of FDE, as computed for Federal income tax purposes. The accumulated after-tax income of FDE is deemed to have arisen in the statutory and residual groupings in the same ratio as the tax book value of the FDE's assets in the groupings, determined in accordance with § 1.987-6(b)(2). Because all of FDE's assets produce foreign branch category income, the foreign gross income is characterized as foreign branch category income. Because all of the Country A foreign taxable income from which the tax is withheld is assigned to a single separate category, under paragraph (f) of this section the $25x of Country A withholding tax is also allocated to the foreign branch category. No apportionment of the $25x is necessary because the class of gross income to which the tax is allocated consists entirely of a single statutory grouping, foreign branch category income.

(12) *Example 11: Sale of disregarded entity*—(i) *Facts.* USP sells FDE, a disregarded entity that is organized and operates in Country A, for $500x. FDE owns Asset X and Asset Y, each having a fair market value of $250x. For Country A tax purposes, FDE has a basis in Asset X of $100x and a basis in Asset Y of $200x; USP's basis in FDE is $100x; and the sale is treated as a sale of stock. Country A imposes foreign income tax of $40x on USP on the Country A gross income of $400x resulting from the sale of FDE, based on its rules for taxing capital gains of nonresidents. For Federal income tax purposes, USP has a basis of $150x in Asset X, which produces passive category income, and a basis of $150x in Asset Y, which produces general category income that would not be foreign personal holding company income if earned by a CFC. For Federal income tax purposes USP recognizes $100x of passive category income and $100x of general category income from the sale of FDE.

(ii) *Analysis.* For purposes of allocating and apportioning USP's $40x of Country A foreign income tax, the $400x of Country A gross income resulting from the sale of FDE is first assigned to separate categories. Under paragraph (d)(3)(iv) of this section, USP's $400x of Country A gross income is assigned among the statutory groupings in the same percentages as the foreign gross income in each category that would have resulted if the sale of FDE were treated as an asset sale for Country A tax purposes. Because for Country A tax purposes Asset X had a built-in gain of $150x and Asset Y had a built-in gain of $50x, $300x ($400x x $150x/$200x) of the Country A gross income is assigned to the passive category and $100x ($400x x $50x/$200x) is assigned to the general category. Under paragraph (f) of this section, $30x ($40x x $300x/$400x) of the Country A foreign income tax is apportioned to the passive category, and $10x ($40x x $100x/$400x) of the Country A foreign income tax is apportioned to the general category.

(h) *Applicability date.*—This section applies to taxable years beginning after December 31, 2019. [Reg. § 1.861-20.]

Sales of Inventory: Determining Source of Income

Sales of Inventory: Determining Source of Income.—Amendments to Reg. §§ 1.863-1—1.863-3, modifying the rules for determining the source of income from sales of inventory produced within the United States and sold without the United States or vice versa, are proposed (published in the Federal Register on December 30, 2019) (REG-100956-19).

Par. 2. Section 1.863-1 is amended as follows:

1. In paragraph (a):

i. Revising the third sentence.

ii. Removing "§ 1.863-3(g)" and adding in its place "§ 1.863-3(f)".

2. In paragraph (b)(1):

i. Removing ", must be allocated between sources within and without the United States based on the fair market value of the product at the export terminal (as defined in paragraph (b)(3)(iii) of this section)" from the first sentence and adding in its place "shall be treated as income from sources within the United States".

ii. Revising the second sentence.

iii. Removing the third, fourth, and fifth sentences.

3. Removing paragraphs (b)(1)(i) and (ii).

4. In paragraph (b)(2):

i. Removing "prior to export terminal" from the heading and adding in its place "activities".

ii. Removing "before the relevant product is shipped from the export terminal" from the first sentence.

5. Removing "§§ 1.1502-13 or 1.863-3(g)(2)" from paragraph (b)(3)(i) and adding in its place "§ 1.1502-13 or § 1.863-3(f)(2)".

6. Removing "to or from the export terminal" from the third sentence of paragraph (b)(3)(ii).

7. Removing paragraph (b)(3)(iii).

8. In paragraph (b)(6), removing "this paragraph (b)" from the first sentence and adding in its place "paragraph (b)(2) of this section".

9. Designating *Examples 1, 2, 3, 4,* and *5* of paragraph (b)(7) as paragraphs (b)(7)(i) through (v).

10. Revising newly designated paragraphs (b)(7)(i) through (iv).

11. In newly designated paragraph (b)(7)(v):

i. Removing "*Example 1*" from the first sentence and adding "paragraph (b)(7)(i) of this section (*Example 1*)".

ii. Removing "country" from the first sentence and adding in its place "Country".

iii. Removing "Mine's" from the seventh sentence and adding in its place "Mines'".

The revisions read as follows:

§ 1.863-1. Allocation of gross income under section 863(a).—(a) * * * See also section 865(b) for rules for sourcing income from the sale of inventory property, within the meaning of section 865(i)(1) (inventory), generally, and section 865(e)(2) and § 1.865-3 for sourcing income from the sale of personal property (including inventory) by a nonresident that is attributable to the nonresident's office or other fixed place of business in the United States. * * *

(b) * * *

(1) * * * Notwithstanding any other provision of this part, except to the extent provided in paragraph (b)(2) of this section or § 1.865-3, gross receipts from the sale within the United States of products derived from the ownership or operation of any farm, mine, oil or gas well, other natural deposit, or timber outside the United States shall be treated as attributable to production activities without the United States and therefore treated as income from sources without the United States.

* * *

(7) * * *

(i) *Example 1. No additional production.* U.S. Mines, a domestic corporation, operates a copper mine and mill in Country X. U.S. Mines extracts copper-bearing rocks from the ground and transports the rocks to the mill where the rocks are ground and processed to produce copper-bearing concentrate. The concentrate is transported to a port where it is dried in preparation for export, stored, and then shipped to purchasers in the United States. Because there is no additional production, paragraph (b)(3)(ii) of this section does not apply, and under paragraph (b)(1) of this section, gross receipts from the sale of the concentrate will be from sources without the United States.

(ii) *Example 2. No additional production.* U.S. Gas, a domestic corporation, extracts natural gas within the United States, and transports the natural gas to a Country X port where it is liquefied in preparation for shipment. The liquefied natural gas is then transported via freighter and sold without additional production activities in a foreign country. Liquefaction of natural gas is not an additional production activity because liquefaction prepares the natural gas for transportation. Therefore, under paragraph (b)(1) of this section, gross receipts from the sale of the liquefied natural gas will be from sources within the United States.

(iii) *Example 3. Production in United States.* U.S. Gold, a domestic corporation, mines gold in Country X, produces gold jewelry using production assets located in the United States, and sells the jewelry in Country Y. Assume that the fair market value of the gold before the additional production activities in the United States is $40x and that U.S. Gold ultimately sells the gold jewelry in Country Y for $100x. Under paragraph (b)(2) of this section, $40x of U.S. Gold's gross receipts will be allocated to sources without the United States,

and the remaining $60x of gross receipts will be U.S. source under §1.863-3.

(iv) *Example 4. Production in United States.* U.S. Oil, a domestic corporation, extracts oil in Country X, transports the oil via a pipeline to the United States, refines the oil using production assets located in the United States, and sells the refined product in the United States to unrelated persons. Assume that the fair market value of the oil before refinement in the United States is $80x and U.S. Oil ultimately sells the refined product for $100x. Under paragraph (b)(2) of this section, $80 of gross receipts will be allocated to sources without the United States, and the remaining $20 of gross receipts will be allocated to sources within the United States.

* * *

Par. 3. Section 1.863-2 is amended as follows:

1. Removing "(and that is treated as derived partly from sources within and partly from sources without the United States)" from the third sentence of paragraph (a) and adding a colon at the end of the paragraph.

2. Revising paragraph (b).

The revision reads as follows:

§1.863-2. Allocation and apportionment of taxable income.

* * *

(b) *Determination of source of taxable income.*—Income treated as derived from sources partly within and partly without the United States under paragraph (a) of this section may be allocated or apportioned to sources within and without the United States pursuant to §§1.863-1, 1.863-3, 1.863-4, 1.863-8, and 1.863-9. To determine the source of certain types of income described in paragraph (a)(1) of this section, see §1.863-4. To determine the source of gross income de-

scribed in paragraph (a)(2) of this section, see §1.863-1 for natural resources and §1.863-3 for all other sales of inventory property. Section 1.865-3 may apply instead of the provisions in this part to source gross income from sales of personal property (including inventory property) by nonresidents attributable to an office or other fixed place of business in the United States. To determine the source of income partly from sources within a possession of the United States, including income described in paragraph (a)(3) of this section, see §1.863-3(e).

* * *

Par. 4. Section 1.863-3 is amended as follows:

1. Revising paragraphs (a) and (b).

2. Removing "and sales activity" from the heading in paragraph (c).

3. In paragraph (c)(1)(i)(A):

i. Removing "(g)(2)(ii)" and adding in its place "(f)(2)(ii)";

ii. Removing "the income attributable to production activity" and adding in its place "gross income"; and

iii. Removing "(c)(1)(ii)" and adding in its place "(c)(2)".

4. Removing "(g)(2)(ii)" from paragraph (c)(1)(i)(B) and adding in its place "(f)(2)(ii)".

5. Removing "within the United States and within foreign countries" from the heading to paragraph (c)(1)(ii) and adding in its place "within and without the United States".

6. Removing "income attributable to the taxpayer's production activity" from paragraph (c)(1)(ii)(A) and adding in its place "gross income".

7. In paragraph (c)(1)(iii):

i. Removing "(c)(1)" from the first and second sentences and adding in its place "(c)";

ii. Removing "by manipulating the formula described in paragraph (c)(1)(ii)(A) of this section";

iii. Removing "production income" and adding in its place "gross income"; and

iv. Removing "income from production activity" and adding in its place "gross income".

8. Removing paragraph (c)(2) and the paragraph designation and heading for (c)(1);

9. In paragraphs (c)(i) through (iv), redesignating the paragraphs in the first column as the paragraphs in the second column:

Old paragraphs	New paragraphs
(c)(i)	(c)(1)
(c)(i)(A)	(c)(1)(i)
(c)(i)(B)	(c)(1)(ii)
(c)(i)(C)	(c)(1)(iii)
(c)(ii)	(c)(2)
(c)(ii)(A)	(c)(2)(i)
(c)(ii)(B)	(c)(2)(ii)
(c)(iii)	(c)(3)
(c)(iv)	(c)(4)

10. Revising newly redesignated paragraph (c)(2)(ii).

11. In newly redesignated paragraph (c)(4):

i. In the introductory text, removing "(c)(1)" and adding in its place "(c)"; and

ii. Designating *Examples 1, 2,* and *3* as paragraphs (c)(4)(i) through (iii).

12. In newly designated paragraph (c)(4)(i):

i. Removing "production" from the heading and adding in its place "gross"; and

ii. Redesignating paragraphs (c)(1)(i)(i) and (ii) as paragraphs (c)(4)(i)(A) and (B).

13. In newly redesignated paragraph (c)(4)(i)(A), removing the ninth sentence.

14. In newly redesignated paragraph (c)(4)(i)(B):

i. Removing "production", "one half of", and "or $6," from the first sentence;

ii. Removing "production" from the second sentence; and

iii. In the last sentence, removing "$2" and "$6" and adding in their places "$4" and "$12", respectively.

15. In newly designated paragraph (c)(4)(ii):

i. Removing "*Example 1*" from the first sentence and adding in its place "in paragraph (c)(4)(i)(A) of this section (*Example 1*)"; and

ii. Removing "from production activity" from the second sentence.

16. In newly designated paragraph (c)(4)(iii), redesignating paragraphs (c)(4)(iii)(i) and (ii) as paragraphs (c)(4)(iii)(A) and (B).

17. In newly redesignated paragraph (c)(4)(iii)(A):

i. Removing "*Example 1*" from the first sentence and adding in its place "in paragraph (c)(4)(i)(A) of this section (*Example 1*)"; and

ii. Removing "(c)(1)(ii)" and "production income" from the fourth sentence and adding in their places "(c)(2)" and "gross income", respectively.

18. In newly redesignated paragraph (c)(4)(iii)(B):

i. Removing "(c)(1)(ii)(A)" from the first sentence and adding in its place "(c)(2)(i)"; and

ii. Removing "production income" from the second sentence and adding in its place "gross income".

19. Revising paragraph (d).

20. Removing paragraph (e).

21. Redesignating paragraph (f) as paragraph (e).

22. Revising newly redesignated paragraphs (e)(1) and (2) and (e)(3)(i).

23. Removing "(f)(3)(ii)" from newly redesignated paragraph (e)(3)(ii)(B) introductory text and adding in its place "(e)(3)(ii)".

24. Revising newly redesignated paragraph (e)(3)(ii)(C)(*1*).

25. Removing newly redesignated paragraph (e)(4).

26. Further redesignating paragraph (e)(3)(iii) as paragraph (e)(4).

27. In newly redesignated paragraph (e)(4):

i. Removing "(f)(3)(ii)" from the introductory text and adding in its place "(e)(3)(ii)"; and

ii. Designating *Examples 1* and *2* as paragraphs (e)(4)(i) and (ii).

28. In newly designated paragraph (e)(4)(i), redesignating paragraphs (e)(4)(i)(i) and (ii) as paragraphs (e)(4)(i)(A) and (B).

29. In newly designated paragraph (e)(4)(ii), redesignating paragraphs (e)(4)(ii)(i) and (ii) as paragraphs (e)(4)(ii)(A) and (B).

30. In newly redesignated paragraph (e)(4)(ii)(A), removing "*Example 1*" and adding "paragraph (e)(4)(i)(A) of this section (*Example 1*)".

31. Removing "(f)" from newly redesignated paragraph (e)(5) and adding in its place "(e)" and removing "(g)" and adding in its place "(f)".

32. Removing newly redesignated paragraph (e)(6).

33. Redesignating paragraph (g) as paragraph (f).

34. In newly redesignated paragraph (f)(1), removing "(g)(2)" and adding in its place "(f)(2)".

35. In newly redesignated paragraph (f)(2)(ii), removing "(g)(2)(i)" and adding in its place "(f)(2)(i)" and removing "(c)(1)(ii)(B)" and adding in its place "(c)(2)(ii)".

36. Removing newly redesignated paragraph (f)(2)(iv).

37. In newly redesignated paragraph (f)(3):

i. Removing "(g)" from the introductory text and adding in its place "(f)"; and

ii. Designating *Examples 1* and *2* as paragraphs (f)(3)(i) and (ii).

38. In newly designated paragraph (f)(3)(ii):

i. Removing "*Example 1*" from the first sentence and adding in its place "paragraph (f)(3)(i) of this section (*Example 1*)";

ii. Removing "these regulations" in the fourth sentence and adding in its place "this section";

iii. Removing the fifth sentence; and

iii. Removing "(1)" from the last sentence.

39. Redesignating paragraph (h) as (g) and revising newly redesignated paragraph (g).

The revisions read as follows:

§1.863-3. Allocation and apportionment of income from certain sales of inventory.—(a) *In general.*—(1) *Scope.*—Subject to the rules of §1.865-3, paragraphs (a) through (d) of this section apply to determine the source of income derived from the sale of inventory property (inventory) that a taxpayer produces (in whole or in part) within the United States and sells without the United States, or that a taxpayer produces (in whole or in part) without the United States and sells within the United States (Section 863(b)(2) Sales). See section 865(i)(1) for the definition of inventory. Paragraph (b) of this section provides that the source of gross income from the sale or exchange of inventory in Section 863(b)(2) Sales is based solely on the production activities with respect to the inventory. Paragraph (c) of this section describes how to determine source based on production activity, including where inventory is produced partly within the United States and partly without the United States. Paragraph (d) of this section determines taxable income from Section 863(b)(2) Sales. Paragraph (e) of this section applies to determine the source of certain income derived from a possession of the United States. Paragraph (f) of this section provides special rules for partnerships for all sales subject to §§1.863-1 through 1.863-3. Paragraph (g) of this section provides applicability dates for the rules in this section.

(2) *Cross references.*—To determine the source of income derived from the sale of personal property (including inventory) by a nonresident that is attributable to the nonresident's office or other fixed place of business in the United States under section 865(e)(2), the rules of §1.865-3 apply, and the rules of this section do not apply. To determine the source of income from sales of property produced by the taxpayer, when the property is either produced in whole or in part in space or on or under water not within the jurisdiction (as recognized by the United States) of a foreign country, possession of the United States, or the United States (in international water), or is sold in space or international water, the rules of §1.863-8 apply, and the rules of this section do not apply except to the extent provided in §1.863-8.

(b) *Sourcing based solely on production activities.*—Subject to the rules of §1.865-3, all gain, profit, and income derived from Section 863(b)(2) Sales is allocated and apportioned solely on the basis of the production activities with respect to the inventory.

(c) * * *

(2) * * *

(ii) *Adjusted basis of production assets.*—(A) *In general.*—For purposes of paragraph (c)(2)(i) of this section, the adjusted basis of an asset is determined by using the alternative depreciation system under section 168(g)(2). The adjusted basis of all production assets

for purposes of paragraph (c)(2)(i) of this section is determined as though such production assets were subject to the alternative depreciation system set forth in section 168(g)(2) for the entire period that such property has been in service. The adjusted basis of the production assets is determined without regard to the election to expense certain depreciable assets under section 179 and without regard to any additional first-year depreciation provision (for example, sections 168(k), 168(l), and 168(m), and former sections 1400L(b) and 1400N(d)). The average adjusted basis is computed by averaging the adjusted basis of the asset at the beginning and end of the taxable year, unless by reason of material changes during the taxable year such average does not fairly represent the average for such year. In this event, the average adjusted basis is determined upon a more appropriate basis.

(B) *Production assets used to produce other property.*—If a production asset is used to produce inventory sold in Section 863(b)(2) Sales and also used to produce other property during the taxable year, the portion of its adjusted basis that is included in the fraction described in paragraph (c)(2)(i) of this section will be determined under any method that reasonably reflects the portion of the asset that produces inventory sold in Section 863(b)(2) Sales. For example, the portion of such an asset that is included in the formula may be determined by multiplying the asset's average adjusted basis by a fraction, the numerator of which is the gross receipts from sales of inventory from Section 863(b)(2) Sales produced by the asset, and the denominator of which is the gross receipts from all property produced by that asset.

* * *

(d) *Determination of source of taxable income.*—Once the source of gross income has been determined under paragraph (c) of this section, the taxpayer must properly allocate and apportion under §§1.861-8 through 1.861-14T and 1.861-17 its expenses, losses and other deductions to its respective amounts of gross income from sources within and without the United States from its Section 863(b)(2) Sales.

(e) *Income partly from sources within a possession of the United States.*—(1) *In general.*—This paragraph (e) relates to certain sales that give rise to gains, profits, and income that are treated as derived partly from sources within the United States and partly from sources within a possession of the United States (Section 863 Possession Sales). This paragraph (e) applies to determine the source of income derived from the sale of inventory produced (in whole or in part) by the taxpayer within the United States and sold within a possession, or produced (in whole or in part) by a taxpayer in a possession and sold within the United States (Possession Production Sales). It also applies to determine the source of income derived from the purchase of personal property within a possession of the United States and its sale within the United States (Possession Purchase Sales). A taxpayer subject to this paragraph (e) must apportion gross income from Section 863 Possession Sales under paragraph (e)(2) of this section (in the case of Possession Production Sales) or using the business activity method described in paragraph (e)(3)(i) of this section (in the case of Possession Purchase Sales). The source of gross income from each type of activity from Possession Purchase Sales must then be determined under paragraph (e)(3)(ii) of this section. The source of taxable income from Possession Production Sales is determined under paragraph (c) of this section. The source of taxable income from Section 863 Possession Sales is determined under paragraph (d) of this section.

(2) *Allocation or apportionment for Possession Production Sales.*—The source of gross income from Possession Production Sales is determined under the rules of paragraph (c) of this section, except that the term *possession* of the United States is substituted for *foreign country* wherever it appears.

(3) *Allocation or apportionment for Possession Purchase Sales.*—(i) *Determination of source of gross income for Possession Purchase Sales.*—Gross income from Possession Purchase Sales is allocated in its entirety to the taxpayer's business activity, and is then apportioned between sources within the United States and sources within a possession of the United States under paragraph (e)(3)(ii) of this section.

(ii) * * *

(C) * * *

(1) *Sales activity.*—The source of the taxpayer's income that is attributable to sales activity will be determined under the provisions of §1.861-7(c). Notwithstanding any other provision of this part, for rules regarding the source of income when a sale takes place in space or international water, the rules of §1.863-8 apply, and the rules of this section do not apply except to the extent provided in §1.863-8.

* * *

(g) *Applicability dates.*—This section applies to taxable years ending on or after December 23, 2019. However, taxpayers may apply this section in its entirety for taxable years beginning after December 31, 2017, and ending before December 23, 2019, provided that the taxpayer and persons that are related (within the meaning of section 267 or 707) to the taxpayer apply this section in its entirety.

Global Dealing Operations: Allocation and Sourcing of Income and Deductions

Global Dealing Operations: Allocation and Sourcing of Income and Deductions.—Amendments to Reg. §1.863-3, relating to the allocation and sourcing of income, deductions, gains and losses from a global dealing operation, are proposed (published in the Federal Register on March 6, 1998) (REG-208299-90).

☐ Par. 7. Section 1.863-3 is amended as follows:

1. Paragraph (h) is redesignated as paragraph (i).
2. A new paragraph (h) is added.

The addition reads as follows:

§1.863-3. Allocation and apportionment of income from certain sales of inventory.

* * *

(h) *Income from a global dealing operation.*—(1) *Purpose and scope.*—This paragraph (h) provides rules for sourcing income, gain and loss from a global dealing operation that, under the rules of §1.482-8, is earned by or allocated to a controlled taxpayer qualifying as a participant in a global dealing operation under §1.482-8(a)(2)(ii). This paragraph (h) does not apply to income earned by or allocated to a controlled taxpayer qualifying as a participant in a global dealing operation that is specifically sourced under sections 861, 862 or 865, or to substitute payments earned by a participant in a global dealing operation that are sourced under §1.861-2(a)(7) or §1.861-3(a)(6).

(2) *In general.*—The source of any income, gain or loss to which this section applies shall be determined by reference to the residence of the participant. For purposes of this paragraph (h), the residence of a participant shall be determined under section 988(a)(3)(B).

(3) *Qualified business units as participants in global dealing operations.*—(i) *In general.*—Except as otherwise provided in this paragraph (h), where a single controlled taxpayer conducts a global dealing operation through one or more qualified business units (QBUs), as defined in section 989(a) and §1.989(a)-1, the source of income, gain or loss generated by the global dealing operation and earned by or allocated to the controlled taxpayer shall be determined by applying the rules of §1.482-8 as if each QBU that performs activities of a regular dealer in securities as defined in §1.482-8(a)(2)(ii)(A) or the related activities described in §1.482-8(a)(2)(ii)(B) were a separate controlled taxpayer qualifying as a participant in the global dealing operation within the meaning of §1.482-8(a)(2)(ii). Accordingly, the amount of income sourced in the United States and outside of the United States shall be determined by treating the QBU as a participant in the global dealing operation, allocating income to each participant under §1.482-8, as modified by paragraph (h)(3)(ii) of this section, and sourcing the income to the United States or outside of the United States under §1.863-3(h)(2).

(ii) *Economic effects of a single legal entity.*—In applying the principles of §1.482-8, the taxpayer shall take into account the economic effects of conducting a global dealing operation through a single entity instead of multiple legal entities. For example, since the entire capital of a corporation supports all of the entity's transactions, regardless of where those transactions may be booked, the payment of a guarantee fee within the entity is inappropriate and will be disregarded.

(iii) *Treatment of interbranch and interdesk amounts.*—An agreement among QBUs of the same taxpayer to allocate income, gain or loss from transactions with third parties is not a transaction because a taxpayer cannot enter into a contract with itself. For purposes of this paragraph (h)(3), however, such an agreement, including a risk transfer agreement (as defined in §1.475(g)-2(b)) may be used to determine the source of global dealing income from transactions with third parties in the same manner and to the same extent that transactions between controlled taxpayers in a global dealing operation may be used to allocate income, gain or loss from the global dealing operation under the rules of §1.482-8.

(iv) *Deemed QBU.*—For purposes of this paragraph (h)(3), a QBU shall include a U.S. trade or business that is deemed to exist because of the activities of a dependent agent in the United States, without regard to the books and records requirement of §1.989(a)-1(b).

(v) *Examples.*—The following examples illustrate this paragraph (h)(3).

Example 1. Use of comparable uncontrolled financial transactions method to source global dealing income between branches. (i) F is a foreign bank that acts as a market maker in foreign currency through branch offices in London, New York, and Tokyo. In a typical business day, the foreign exchange desk in F's U.S. branch (USFX) enters into several hundred spot and forward contracts on the interbank market to purchase and sell Deutsche marks (DM) with unrelated third parties. Each of F's branches, including USFX, employs both marketers and traders for their foreign currency dealing. In addition, USFX occasionally transfers risk with respect to its third party DM contracts to F's London and Tokyo branches. These interbranch transfers are entered into in the same manner as trades with unrelated third parties. On a typical day, risk management responsibility for no more than 10% of USFX's DM trades are transferred interbranch. F records these transfers by making notations on the books of each branch that is a party to the transfers. The accounting procedures are nearly identical to those followed when a branch enters into an offsetting hedge with a third party. USFX maintains contemporaneous records of its interbranch transfers and third party transactions, separated according to type of trade and counterparty. Moreover, the volume of USFX's DM spot purchases and sales each day consistently provides USFX with third party transactions that are contemporaneous with the transfers between the branches.

(ii) As provided in paragraph (h)(3)(i) of this section, USFX and F's other branches that trade DM are participants in a global dealing operation. Accordingly, the principles of §1.482-8 apply in determining the source of income earned by F's qualified business units that are participants in a global dealing operation. Applying the comparability factors in §1.482-8(a)(3) shows that USFX's interbranch transfers and uncontrolled DM-denominated spot and forward contracts have no material differences. Because USFX sells DM in uncontrolled transactions and transfers risk management responsibility for DM-denominated contracts, and the uncontrolled transactions and interbranch transfers are consistently entered into contemporaneously, the interbranch transfers provide a reliable measure of an arm's length allocation of third party income from F's global dealing operation in DM-denominated contracts. This allocation of third party income is treated as U.S. source in accordance with §§1.863-3(h) and 1.988-4(h) and accordingly will be treated as income effectively connected with F's U.S. trade or business under §1.864-4.

Example 2. Residual profit split between branches. (i) F is a bank organized in country X that has a AAA credit rating and engages in a global dealing operation in foreign currency options through branch offices in London, New York, and Tokyo. F has dedicated marketers and traders in each branch who work closely together to design and sell foreign currency options that meet the particular needs of customers. Each branch also employs general salespeople who sell standardized foreign currency options, as well as other financial products and foreign currency offered by F. F's traders work from a common book of transactions that is risk managed at each branch during local business hours. Accordingly, all three branches share the responsibility for risk managing the book of products. Personnel in the home office of F process and confirm trades, reconcile trade tickets, and provide ongoing administrative support (back office services) for the other branches. The global dealing operation has generated $223 of operating profit for the period.

(ii) Under §1.863-3(h), F applies §1.482-8 to allocate global dealing income among its branches, because F's London, New York, and Tokyo branches are treated as participants in a global dealing operation that deals in foreign currency options under §1.482-8(a)(2). After analyzing the foreign currency options business, F has determined that the residual profit split method is the best method to determine an arm's length amount of compensation allocable to each participant in the global dealing operation.

(iii) Under the first step of the residual profit split method (§1.482-8(e)(6)(ii)), F identifies and compensates the routine contributions performed by each participant. F determines that an arm's length compensation for general salespeople is $3, $4, and $5 in New York, London, and Tokyo, respectively, and that the home office incurred $11 of expenses in providing the back office services. Since F's capital legally supports all of the obligations of the branches, no amount is allocated to the home office of F for the provision of capital.

(iv) The second step of the residual profit split method (§1.482-8(e)(6)(iii)) requires that the residual profit be allocated to participants according to their nonroutine contributions. F determines that a multi-factor formula best reflects these contributions. After a detailed functional analysis, and applying the comparability factors in §1.482-8(a)(3), 40% of the residual profit is allocated to the London branch, 35% to the New York branch, and the remaining 25% to the Tokyo branch. Thus, the residual profit of $200 ($223 operating profit minus $12 general salesperson commissions minus $11 back office allocation) is allocated $80 to London (40% allocation × $200), $70 to New York (35% × $200) and $50 to Tokyo (25% × $200).

Example 3. Residual profit split—deemed branches. (i) P, a U.K. corporation, conducts a global dealing operation in notional principal contracts, directly and through a U.S. subsidiary (USsub) and a Japanese subsidiary (Jsub). P is the counterparty to all transactions entered into with third parties. P, USsub, and Jsub each employ marketers and traders who work closely together to design and sell derivative products to meet the particular needs of customers. USsub also employs personnel who process and confirm trades, reconcile trade tickets and provide ongoing administrative support (back office services) for the global dealing operation. The global dealing operation maintains a single common book for each type of risk, and the

book is maintained where the head trader for that type of risk is located. However, P, USsub, and Jsub have authorized a trader located in each of the other affiliates to risk manage its books during periods when the primary trading location is closed. This grant of authority is necessary because marketers, regardless of their location, are expected to sell all of the group's products, and need to receive pricing information with respect to products during their clients' business hours, even if the booking location is closed. The global dealing operation has generated $180 of operating profit for the period.

(ii) Because employees of USsub have authority to enter into contracts in the name of P, P is treated as being engaged in a trade or business in the United States through a deemed QBU. §1.863-3(h)(3)(iv). Similarly, under U.S. principles, P would be treated as being engaged in business in Japan through a QBU. Under §1.482-8(a)(2), P, USsub, and Jsub are participants in the global dealing operation relating to notional principal contracts. Additionally, under §1.863-3(h)(3), the U.S. and Japanese QBUs are treated as participants in a global dealing operation for purposes of sourcing the income from that operation. Under §1.863-3(h), P applies the methods in §1.482-8 to determine the source of income allocated to the U.S. and non-U.S. QBUs of P.

(iii) After analyzing the notional principal contract business, P has concluded that the residual profit split method is the best method to allocate income under §1.482-8 and to source income under §1.863-3(h).

(iv) Under the first step of the residual profit split method (§1.482-8(e)(6)(ii)), P identifies and compensates the routine contributions performed by each participant. Although the back office function does not give rise to participant status, in the context of a residual profit split allocation, the back office function is relevant for purposes of receiving remuneration for a back contribution to a global dealing operation. P determines that an arm's length compensation for the back office is $20. Since the back office services constitute a routine contribution, $20 of income is allocated to USsub under step 1 of the residual profit split method. Similarly, as the arm's length compensation for the risk to which P is subject as counterparty is $40, $40 is allocated to P as compensation for acting as counterparty.

(v) The second step of the residual profit split method (§1.482-8(e)(6)(iii)) requires that the residual profit be allocated to participants according to the relative value of their nonroutine contributions. Under P's transfer pricing method, P allocates the residual profit of $120 ($180 gross income minus $20 for back office services minus $40 compensation for the routine contribution of acting as counterparty) using a multi-factor formula that reflects the relative value of the nonroutine contributions. Applying the comparability factors set out in §1.482-8(a)(3), P allocates 40% of the residual profit to P, 35% of the residual profit to USsub, and the remaining 25% of residual profit to Jsub. Accordingly, under step 2, $48 is allocated to P, $42 is allocated to USsub, and $30 is allocated to Jsub. Under §1.863-3(h), the amounts allocated under the residual profit split is sourced according to the residence of each participant to which it is allocated.

(vi) Because the $40 allocated to P consists of compensation for the use of capital, the allocation is sourced according to where the capital is employed. Accordingly, the $40 is sourced 35% to P's deemed QBU in the United States under §1.863-3(h)(3)(iv) and 65% to non-U.S. sources.

***

Income from U.S. Sources: Allocation and Apportionment

Income from U.S. Sources: Allocation and Apportionment of Expenses.—Temporary Reg. §1.863-3T (redesignated as Temporary Reg. §1.863-3AT by T.D. 8687), relating to the allocation and apportionment of interest expense and certain other expenses for purposes of the foreign tax credit rules and certain other international tax provisions, is also proposed as a final regulation and, when adopted, would become §1.863-3A (published in the Federal Register on September 14, 1988).

§1.863-3A. Income from the sale of personal property derived partly from within and partly from without the United States.

Global Dealing Operations: Allocation and Sourcing of Income and Deductions

Global Dealing Operations: Allocation and Sourcing of Income and Deductions.—Amendments to Reg. §1.863-7, relating to the allocation and sourcing of income, deductions, gains and losses from a global dealing operation, are proposed (published in the Federal Register on March 6, 1998) (REG-208299-90).

☐ Par. 8. Section 1.863-7(a)(1) is amended by revising the second sentence to read as follows:

§1.863-7. Allocation of income attributable to certain notional principal contracts under section 863(a).—(a) *Scope.*—(1) *Introduction.*—* * * This section does not apply to income from a section 988 transaction (as defined in section 988(c) and §1.988-1(a)), or to income from a global dealing operation (as defined in §1.482-8(a)(2)(i)(i)) that is sourced under the rules of §1.863-3(h). * * *

***

Section 1256 Contracts: Swap Exclusions

Section 1256 Contracts: Swap Exclusions.—Amendment to Reg. §1.863-7, providing guidance on the category of swaps and similar agreements that are within the scope of Code Sec. 1256(b)(2)(B), are proposed (published in the Federal Register on September 16, 2011) (REG-111283-11).

☐ Par. 4. Section 1.863-7 is amended by:

1. Revising the third sentence and removing the fourth sentence of paragraph (a)(1).

2. Adding two sentences to the end of paragraph (a)(2).

The revision and addition read as follows:

§1.863-7. **Allocation of income attributable to certain notional principal contracts under section 863(a).**—(a) *Scope.*—(1) *Introduction.*—* * * Notional principal contract income is income attributable to a notional principal contract as defined in §1.446-3(c). * * *

(2) * * * The rules of this section apply to notional principal contracts as defined in §1.446-3(c) that are entered into on or after the date of publication of a Treasury decision adopting these rules as

final regulations in the **Federal Register**. Section 1.863-7 as contained in 26 CFR part 1 revised April 1, 2011, continues to apply to notional principal contracts entered into before the date of publication of a Treasury decision adopting these rules as final regulations in the **Federal Register**.

* * *

Sales of Inventory: Determining Source of Income

Sales of Inventory: Determining Source of Income.—Amendments to Reg. §1.863-8, modifying the rules for determining the source of income from sales of inventory produced within the United States and sold without the United States or vice versa, are proposed (published in the Federal Register on December 30, 2019) (REG-100956-19).

Par. 5. Section 1.863-8 is amended as follows:

1. Revising paragraph (b)(3)(ii)(A).

2. In paragraph (b)(3)(ii)(B), removing "allocable to production activity" wherever it appears and by removing "§1.863-3(c)(1)" from the second sentence and adding in its place "§1.863-3(c)".

3. In paragraph (b)(3)(ii)(C), removing "allocable to production activity" wherever it appears and by removing "§1.863-3(c)(1)" from the fifth sentence and adding in its place "§1.863-3(c)".

4. Removing paragraph (b)(3)(ii)(D).

5. Designating *Examples 1* through *14* of paragraph (f) as paragraphs (f)(1) through (14).

6. In newly designated paragraphs (f)(1) through (14), removing the period between the second and third level paragraph headings and adding an em-dash in its place.

7. Removing "*Example 4*" from newly designated paragraph (f)(4)(i) and adding in its place "paragraph (f)(4)(i) (*Example 4*)".

8. Removing "*Example 4*" from newly designated paragraph (f)(5)(i) and adding in its place "paragraph (f)(4)(i) of this section (*Example 4*)".

9. Revising the first, second, and third sentences of newly designated paragraphs (f)(6)(ii).

10. Removing "*Example 8*" from newly designated paragraph (f)(9)(i) and adding in its place "in paragraph (f)(8)(i) of this section (*Example 8*)".

11. Removing "*Example 8*" from newly designated paragraph (f)(9)(ii) and adding in its place "paragraph (f)(8)(i) of this section (*Example 8*)".

12. Revising newly designated paragraph (f)(11)(ii).

13. In paragraph (g)(1), removing "(C)" from the first sentence.

14. In paragraph (g)(4) introductory text, removing "(C)" from the first sentence.

The revisions read as follows:

§1.863-8. **Source of income derived from space and ocean activity under section 863(d).**

* * *

(b) * * *

(3) * * *

(ii) *Sales of property produced by the taxpayer.*—(A) *General.*— If the taxpayer both produces property and sells such property, the taxpayer must allocate and apportion all gain, profit, and income derived from sales of such property solely on the basis of the production activities with respect to such property, and the source of that income will be determined under paragraph (b)(3)(ii)(B) or (C) of this section. To determine the source of income derived from the sale of personal property (including inventory) by a nonresident that is attributable to the nonresident's office or other fixed place of business in the United States under section 865(e)(2), the rules of §1.865-3 apply, and the rules of this section do not apply.

* * *

(f) * * *

(6) * * *

(ii) *Analysis.*—The collection of data and creation of images in space is characterized as the creation of property in space. Because S both produces and sells the data, the source of the gross income from the sale of the data is determined under paragraph (b)(3)(ii) of this section (by reference to §1.863-3(c)) solely on the basis of the production activities. The source of S's gross income is determined under §1.863-3(c)(2) because production activities occur both in space and on land. * * *

(11) * * *

(ii) *Analysis.*—Because S's rights, title, and interest in the satellite pass to the customer in space, the sale takes place in space under §1.861-7(c), and the sale transaction is space activity under paragraph (d)(1)(i) of this section. The source of income derived from the sale of the satellite in space is determined under paragraph (b)(3)(ii) of this section (by reference to §1.863-3(c)) solely on the basis of the production activities with respect to the satellite.

* * *

CFCs: U.S. Shareholders: Ownership Attribution

CFCs: U.S. Shareholders: Ownership Attribution.—Amendments to Reg. §§1.863-8 and 1.863-9, relating to the modification of section 958(b) of the Internal Revenue Code by the Tax Cuts and Jobs Act, which was enacted on December 22, 2017, are proposed (published in the Federal Register on October 2, 2019) (REG-104223-18).

Par. 7. Section 1.863-8 is amended by:

1. In paragraph (b)(2)(ii), revising the first sentence and adding a sentence at the end of the paragraph.

2. Revising paragraph (h).

The revisions and addition read as follows:

§1.863-8. **Source of income derived from space and ocean activity under section 863(d).**

* * *

(b) * * *

(2) * * *

(ii) * * * Space and ocean income derived by a controlled foreign corporation (CFC) is income from sources within the United States. * * * For purposes of this section, a controlled foreign corporation has the meaning provided in section 957, determined without applying subparagraphs (A), (B), and (C) of section 318(a)(3) so as to

consider a United States person as owning stock which is owned by a person who is not a United States person.

* * *

(h) *Applicability dates.*—Except as provided in this paragraph (h), this section applies to taxable years beginning on or after December 27, 2006. The provisions in paragraph (b)(2)(ii) of this section relating to the meaning of CFC apply to taxable years of foreign corporations ending on or after October 1, 2019. For taxable years of foreign corporations ending before October 1, 2019, a taxpayer may apply such provisions to the last taxable year of a foreign corporation beginning before January 1, 2018, and each subsequent taxable year of the foreign corporation, provided that the taxpayer and United States persons that are related (within the meaning of section 267 or 707) to the taxpayer consistently apply such provisions with respect to all foreign corporations.

Par. 8. Section 1.863-9 is amended by revising paragraphs (b)(2)(ii) and (l) to read as follows:

§1.863-9. Source of income derived from communications activity under section 863(a), (d), and (e).

* * *

(b) * * *

    (2) * * *

        (ii) *International communications income derived by a controlled foreign corporation.*—International communications income derived by a controlled foreign corporation (CFC) is one-half from sources within the United States and one-half from sources without the United States. For purposes of this section, a controlled foreign corporation has the meaning provided in section 957, determined without applying subparagraphs (A), (B), and (C) of section 318(a)(3) so as to consider a United States person as owning stock which is owned by a person who is not a United States person.

* * *

    (l) *Applicability dates.*—Except as otherwise provided in this paragraph (l), this section applies to taxable years beginning on or after December 27, 2006. The provisions in paragraph (b)(2)(ii) of this section relating to the meaning of CFC apply to taxable years of foreign corporations ending on or after October 1, 2019. For taxable years of foreign corporations ending before October 1, 2019, a taxpayer may apply such provisions to the last taxable year of a foreign corporation beginning before January 1, 2018, and each subsequent taxable year of the foreign corporation, provided that the taxpayer and United States persons that are related (within the meaning of section 267 or 707) to the taxpayer consistently apply such provisions with respect to all foreign corporations.

Global Dealing Operations: Allocation and Sourcing of Income and Deductions

Global Dealing Operations: Allocation and Sourcing of Income and Deductions.—Amendments to Reg. §§1.864-4 and 1.864-6, relating to the allocation and sourcing of income, deductions, gains and losses from a global dealing operation, are proposed (published in the Federal Register on March 6, 1998) (REG-208299-90).

☐ Par. 9. Section 1.864-4 is amended as follows:

1. Paragraphs (c)(2)(iv), (c)(2)(v), (c)(3)(ii), and (c)(5)(vi)(*a*) and (*b*) are redesignated as (c)(2)(v), (c)(2)(vi), (c)(3)(iii), and (c)(5)(vi)(*b*) and (*c*), respectively.

2. New paragraphs (c)(2)(iv), (c)(3)(ii), and (c)(5)(vi)(*a*) are added.

The additions read as follows:

§1.864-4. U.S. source income effectively connected with U.S. business.

* * *

(c) * * *

    (2) * * *

        (iv) *Special rule relating to a global dealing operation.*—An asset used in a global dealing operation, as defined in §1.482-8(a)(2)(i), will be treated as an asset used in a U.S. trade or business only if and to the extent that the U.S. trade or business is a participant in the global dealing operation under §1.863-3(h)(3), and income, gain or loss produced by the asset is U.S. source under §1.863-3(h) or would be treated as U.S. source if §1.863-3(h) were to apply to such amounts.

* * *

    (3) * * *

        (ii) *Special rule relating to a global dealing operation.*—A U.S. trade or business shall be treated as a material factor in the realization of income, gain or loss derived in a global dealing operation, as defined in §1.482-8(a)(2)(i), only if and to the extent that the U.S. trade or business is a participant in the global dealing operation under §1.863-3(h)(3), and income, gain or loss realized by the U.S. trade or business is U.S. source under §1.863-3(h) or would be treated as U.S. source if §1.863-3(h) were to apply to such amounts.

* * *

    (5) * * *

        (vi) * * *

        (a) *Certain income earned by a global dealing operation.*—Notwithstanding paragraph (c)(5)(ii) of this section, U.S. source interest, including substitute interest as defined in §1.861-2(a)(7), and dividend income, including substitute dividends as defined in §1.861-3(a)(6), derived by a participant in a global dealing operation, as defined in §1.482-8(a)(2)(i), shall be treated as attributable to the foreign corporation's U.S. trade or business, only if and to the extent that the income would be treated as U.S. source if §1.863-3(h) were to apply to such amounts.

☐ Par. 10. Section 1.864-6 is amended as follows: 1. Paragraph (b)(2)(ii)(*d*)(*3*) and (b)(3)(ii)(*c*) are added. 2. Paragraph (b)(3)(i) is revised by adding a new sentence after the last sentence. The additions and revision read as follows:

§1.864-6. Income, gain or loss attributable to an office or other fixed place of business in the United States.

* * *

(b) * * *

    (2) * * *

        (ii) * * *

        (d) * * *

        (3) *Certain income earned by a global dealing operation.*—Notwithstanding paragraphs (b)(2)(ii)(*a*) or (*b*) of this section, foreign source interest, including substitute interest as defined in §1.861-2(a)(7), or dividend income, including substitute dividends as defined in §1.861-3(a)(6), derived by a participant in a global dealing operation, as defined in §1.482-8(a)(2)(i) shall be treated as attributable to the foreign corporation's U.S. trade or business only if and to the extent that the income would be treated as U.S. source if §1.863-3(h) were to apply to such amounts. * * *

    (3) * * *

        (i) * * * Notwithstanding paragraphs (b)(3)(i)(*1*) and (*2*) of this section, an office or other fixed place of business of a nonresident alien individual or a foreign corporation which is located in the United States and which is a participant in a global dealing operation, as defined in §1.482-8(a)(2)(i), shall be considered to be a material factor in the realization of foreign source income, gain or loss, only if and to the extent that such income, gain or loss would be treated as U.S. source if §1.863-3(h) were to apply to such amounts.

        (ii) * * *

        (c) *Property sales in a global dealing operation.*—Notwithstanding paragraphs (b)(3)(ii)(*a*) or (*b*) of this section, personal property described in section 1221(1) and sold in the active conduct of a taxpayer's global dealing operation, as defined in §1.482-8(a)(2)(i), shall be presumed to have been sold for use, consumption, or disposition outside of the United States only if and to the extent that the income, gain or loss to which the sale gives rise would be sourced outside of the United States if §1.863-3(h) were to apply to such amounts.

Sales of Inventory: Determining Source of Income

Sales of Inventory: Determining Source of Income.—Amendments to Reg. §1.864-6, modifying the rules for determining the source of income from sales of inventory produced within the United States and sold without the United States or vice versa, are proposed (published in the Federal Register on December 30, 2019) (REG-100956-19).

Par. 6. Section 1.864-6 is amended by revising paragraphs (c)(2) and (3) and adding paragraph (c)(4) to read as follows:

§1.864-6. Income, gain, or loss attributable to an office or other fixed place of business in the United States.

* * *

(c) * * *

(2) *Special limitation in case of sales of goods or merchandise through U.S. office.*—Notwithstanding paragraph (c)(1) of this section, the special rules described in this paragraph (c)(2) apply with respect to a sale of goods or merchandise specified in § 1.864-5(b)(3), to which paragraph (b)(3)(i) of this section does not apply. In the case of a nonresident alien with a tax home within the United States, as defined in section 911(d)(3), the amount of income from the sale of goods or merchandise that is properly allocable to the individual's U.S. office is determined under § 1.865-3(d)

(3) *Examples.*—The application of this paragraph (c) may be illustrated by the following examples—

(i) *Example 1.* Nonresident alien individual A, who has a tax home in the United States, manufactures machinery in a foreign country and sells the machinery outside the United States through A's sales office in the United States for use in foreign countries. Title to the property sold is transferred to the foreign purchaser outside the United States, but no office or other fixed place of business of A in a foreign country participates materially in the sale made through its U.S. office. By reason of its sales activities in the United States, A is engaged in business in the United States during the taxable year. During the taxable year, A derives a total income of $250,000x from these sales. Under section 865(b)(2), all of A's income from these sales is foreign source as production occurs outside the United States. Under paragraph (c)(2) of this section, the amount of income that is allocable to A's U.S. office is determined under § 1.865-3(d)(2). The taxpayer does not allocate income from the sale under the books and records method described in § 1.865-3(d)(2)(ii). Thus, 50 percent of A's foreign source income, plus any additional income allocable

based on the location of production activities under § § 1.863-3(b) and 1.865-3(d)(2)(i) (in this case, $0x), is effectively connected for the taxable year with the conduct of A's U.S. trade or business, or $125,000x.

(ii) *Example 2.* Nonresident alien individual B, who has a tax home in the United States, has an office in a foreign country that purchases merchandise and sells it through B's sales office in the United States for use in various foreign countries, with title to the property passing outside the United States. No other office of B participates materially in these sales made through its U.S. office. By reason of its sales activities in the United States, B is engaged in business in the United States during the taxable year. During the taxable year, B derives income of $300,000x from these sales made through its U.S. sales office. Under section 865(b), all of B's income from these sales is foreign source as title to the merchandise passes outside the United States. The amount of income properly allocable to B's US office determined under § 1.865-3(d)(3) is $300,000x.

(iii) *Example 3.* The facts are the same as in paragraph (c)(3)(ii) of this section (*Example 2*), except that B has an office in a foreign country which participates materially in the sales which are made through its U.S. office. The income which is allocable to B's U.S. sales office is not effectively connected for the taxable year with the conduct of a trade or business in the United States by that corporation.

(4) *Applicability date.*—Paragraphs (c)(2) and (3) of this section, to the extent they apply to sales of inventory described in section 864(c)(4)(B)(iii), apply to sales occurring in taxable years ending on or after December 23, 2019. However, taxpayers may apply this section in its entirety for taxable years beginning after December 31, 2017, and ending before December 23, 2019, provided that the taxpayer and persons that are related (within the meaning of section 267 or 707) to the taxpayer apply this section in its entirety.

Income from U.S. Sources: Related Person

Controlled Foreign Corporations: Investment of Earnings in U.S. Property: Related Person Factoring Income.—Temporary Reg. § 1.864-8T, relating to the treatment of related person factoring income, is also proposed as a final regulation and, when adopted, would become Reg. § 1.864-8 (published in the Federal Register on June 14, 1988).

§1.864-8. Treatment of related persons.

Foreign Taxpayers: Derivative Financial Instruments: Safe Harbors

Foreign Taxpayers: Derivative Financial Instruments: Safe Harbors.—Reg. § 1.864(b)-1, providing that foreign taxpayers who effect transactions in derivative financial instruments for their own accounts are not thereby engaged in a trade or business in the United States if they are not dealers in stocks, securities, commodities or derivatives, is proposed (published in the Federal Register on June 12, 1998) (REG-106031-98) (corrected 7/15/98).

☐ Par. 2. Section 1.864(b)-1 is added to read as follows:

§1.864(b)-1. Trading in derivatives.—(a) *Trading for taxpayer's own account.*—As used in part I (section 861 and following) and part II (section 871 and following), subchapter N, chapter 1 of the Internal Revenue Code (Code), and chapter 3 (section 1441 and following) of the Code, and the regulations thereunder, if a taxpayer is an eligible nondealer, the term *engaged in trade or business within the United States* does not include effecting transactions in derivatives for the taxpayer's own account, including hedging transactions within the meaning of § 1.1221-2.

(b) *Definitions.*—(1) *Eligible nondealer.*—For purposes of this section, an *eligible nondealer* is a foreign corporation or a person that is not a resident of the United States, and either of which is not, at any place (domestic or foreign), nor at any time during that person's taxable year, any of the following—

(i) A dealer in stocks or securities as defined in § 1.864-2(c)(2)(iv)(*a*);

(ii) A dealer in commodities as that term is used in § 1.864-2(d); or

(iii) A person that regularly offers to enter into, assume, offset, assign or otherwise terminate positions in derivatives with customers in the ordinary course of a trade or business, including regularly holding oneself out, in the ordinary course of one's trade or business, as being willing and able to enter into either side of a derivative transaction.

(2) *Derivative.*—For purposes of this section, the term *derivative* includes—

(i) An interest rate, currency (as defined in paragraph (b)(3) of this section), equity, or commodity (as the term is used in section 864(b)(2)(B) and § 1.864-2(d)) notional principal contract (as the term is used in section 475(c)(2)); or

(ii) An evidence of an interest, or a derivative financial instrument (including any option, forward contract, short position and any similar financial instrument), in any—

(A) Commodity (as the term is used in section 864(b)(2)(B) and § 1.864-2(d));

(B) Currency (as defined in paragraph (b)(3) of this section);

(C) Share of stock (as the term is used in § 1.864-2(c)(2));

(D) Partnership or beneficial ownership interest in a widely held or publicly traded partnership or trust;

(E) Note, bond, debenture, or other evidence of indebtedness; or

(F) Notional principal contract described in paragraph (b)(2)(i) of this section.

(3) *Limitation.*—For purposes of this section, the term *currency* is limited to currencies of a kind customarily dealt in on an organized commodity exchange. [Reg. § 1.864(b)-1.]

Gain or Loss of Foreign Person: Sale or Exchange: Partnership Interest

Gain or Loss of Foreign Person: Sale or Exchange: Partnership Interest.—Reg. § 1.864(c)(8)-1, affecting certain foreign persons that recognize gain or loss from the sale or exchange of an interest in a partnership that is engaged in a trade or business within the United States, is proposed (published in the Federal Register on December 27, 2018) (REG-113604-18).

Par. 2. Section 1.864(c)(8)-1 is added to read as follows:

§1.864(c)(8)-1. Gain or loss by foreign persons on the disposition of certain partnership interests.—(a) *Overview.*—This section pro-

vides rules and definitions under section 864(c)(8). Paragraph (b) of this section provides the general rule treating gain or loss recognized by a nonresident alien individual or foreign corporation from the sale or exchange of a partnership interest as effectively connected gain or effectively connected loss. Paragraph (c) of this section provides rules for determining the limitation on the amount of effectively connected gain or effectively connected loss under section 864(c)(8) and paragraph (b) of this section. Paragraph (d) of this section provides rules regarding coordination with section 897. Paragraph (e) of this section provides rules regarding certain tiered partnerships. Paragraph (f) of this section provides rules regarding U.S. income tax treaties. Paragraph (g) of this section provides definitions. Paragraph (h) of this section provides a rule regarding certain contributions of property to a partnership. Paragraph (i) of this section contains examples illustrating the rules set forth in this section. Paragraph (j) of this section provides the applicability date.

(b) *Gain or loss treated as effectively connected gain or loss.*—(1) *In general.*—Notwithstanding any other provision of subtitle A of the Internal Revenue Code, if a foreign transferor owns, directly or indirectly, an interest in a partnership that is engaged in the conduct of a trade or business within the United States, outside capital gain, outside capital loss, outside ordinary gain, or outside ordinary loss (each as defined in paragraph (b)(2) of this section) recognized by the foreign transferor on the transfer of all (or any portion) of the interest is treated as effectively connected gain or effectively connected loss, subject to the limit described in paragraph (b)(3) of this section. Except as provided in paragraph (d) of this section, this section does not apply to prevent any portion of the gain or loss that is otherwise treated as effectively connected gain or effectively connected loss under provisions of the Internal Revenue Code other than section 864(c)(8) from being so treated.

(2) *Determination of outside gain and loss.*—(i) *In general.*—The amount of gain or loss recognized by the foreign transferor in connection with the transfer of its partnership interest is determined under all relevant provisions of the Internal Revenue Code and the regulations thereunder. See, e.g., § § 1.741-1(a) and 1.751-1(a)(2). For purposes of this section, the amount of gain or loss that is treated as capital gain or capital loss under sections 741 and 751 is referred to as *outside capital gain* or *outside capital loss*, respectively. The amount of gain or loss that is treated as ordinary gain or ordinary loss under sections 741 and 751 is referred to as *outside ordinary gain* or *outside ordinary loss*, respectively.

(ii) *Nonrecognition provisions.*—A foreign transferor's gain or loss recognized in connection with the transfer of its partnership interest does not include gain or loss to the extent that the gain or loss is not recognized by reason of one or more nonrecognition provisions of the Internal Revenue Code.

(3) *Limitations.*—This paragraph (b)(3) limits the amount of gain or loss recognized by a foreign transferor that may be treated as effectively connected gain or effectively connected loss.

(i) *Capital gain limitation.*—Outside capital gain recognized by a foreign transferor is treated as effectively connected gain to the extent it does not exceed aggregate deemed sale EC capital gain determined under paragraph (c)(3)(ii)(B) of this section.

(ii) *Capital loss limitation.*—Outside capital loss recognized by a foreign transferor is treated as effectively connected loss to the extent it does not exceed aggregate deemed sale EC capital loss determined under paragraph (c)(3)(ii)(B) of this section.

(iii) *Ordinary gain limitation.*—Outside ordinary gain recognized by a foreign transferor is treated as effectively connected gain to the extent it does not exceed aggregate deemed sale EC ordinary gain determined under paragraph (c)(3)(ii)(A) of this section.

(iv) *Ordinary loss limitation.*—Outside ordinary loss recognized by a foreign transferor is treated as effectively connected loss to the extent it does not exceed aggregate deemed sale EC ordinary loss determined under paragraph (c)(3)(ii)(A) of this section.

(c) *Amount treated as effectively connected with the conduct of a trade or business within the United States.*—This paragraph (c) describes the steps to be followed in computing the limitations described in paragraph (b)(3) of this section.

(1) *Step 1: Determine deemed sale gain and loss.*—Determine the amount of gain or loss that the partnership would recognize with respect to each of its assets (other than interests in partnerships described in paragraph (e) of this section) upon a deemed sale of all of the partnership's assets on the date of the transfer of the partnership interest described in paragraph (b)(1) of this section (deemed sale). For this purpose, a deemed sale is a hypothetical sale by the partnership to an unrelated person of each of its assets (tangible and intangible) in a fully taxable transaction for cash in an amount equal to the fair market value of each asset (taking into account section 7701(g)) immediately before the partner's transfer of the interest in

the partnership. For rules concerning the deemed sale of certain partnership interests, see paragraph (e) of this section.

(2) *Step 2: Determine deemed sale EC gain and loss.*—(i) *In general.*—With respect to each asset deemed sold in paragraph (c)(1) of this section, determine the amount of gain or loss from the deemed sale that would be treated as effectively connected gain or effectively connected loss (including by reason of section 897, taking into account any exceptions thereto, such as section 897(k) or section 897(l)). Gain described in this paragraph (c)(2) is referred to as *deemed sale EC gain*, and loss described in this paragraph (c)(2) is referred to as *deemed sale EC loss*. Section 864 and the regulations thereunder apply for purposes of determining whether gain or loss that would arise in a deemed asset sale would be treated as effectively connected gain or loss. For purposes of this paragraph (c)(2)(i), gain or loss from the deemed sale of an asset is treated as attributable to an office or other fixed place of business maintained by the partnership in the United States, and is not treated as sold for use, disposition, or consumption outside the United States in a sale in which an office or other fixed place of business maintained by the partnership in a foreign country materially participated in the sale.

(ii) *Exception.*—Gain or loss from the deemed sale of an asset described in paragraph (c)(2)(i) of this section (other than a United States real property interest) is not treated as deemed sale EC gain or deemed sale EC loss if—

(A) No income or gain produced by the asset was taxable as income that was effectively connected with the conduct of a trade or business within the United States by the partnership (or a predecessor of the partnership) during the ten-year period ending on the date of the transfer; and

(B) The asset has not been used, or held for use, in the conduct of a trade or business within the United States by the partnership (or a predecessor of the partnership) during the ten-year period ending on the date of the transfer.

(3) *Step 3: Determine the foreign transferor's distributive share of deemed sale EC gain or deemed sale EC loss.*—(i) *In general.*—Determine the foreign transferor's distributive share of deemed sale EC gain and deemed sale EC loss. A foreign transferor's distributive share of deemed sale EC gain or deemed sale EC loss with respect to each asset is the amount of the deemed sale EC gain and deemed sale EC loss determined under paragraph (c)(2) of this section that would have been allocated to the foreign transferor by the partnership under all applicable Code sections (including section 704) upon the deemed sale described in paragraph (c)(1) of this section, taking into account allocations of tax items applying the principles of section 704(c), including any remedial allocations under § 1.704-3(d), and any section 743 basis adjustment pursuant to § 1.743-1(j)(3)).

(ii) *Aggregate deemed sale EC items.*—(A) *Ordinary gain or loss.*—A foreign transferor's *aggregate deemed sale EC ordinary gain* (if the aggregate results in a gain) or *aggregate deemed sale EC ordinary loss* (if the aggregate results in a loss) is the sum of—

(1) The portion of the foreign transferor's distributive share of deemed sale EC gain and deemed sale EC loss that is attributable to the deemed sale of the partnership's assets that are section 751(a) property; and

(2) Deemed sale EC gain and deemed sale EC loss from the sale of assets that are section 751(a) property that would be allocated to the foreign transferor with respect to interests in partnerships that are engaged in the conduct of a trade or business within the United States under paragraph (e)(1)(ii) of this section upon the deemed asset sales described in paragraph (e)(1)(i) of this section.

(B) *Capital gain or loss.*—A foreign transferor's *aggregate deemed sale EC capital gain* (if the aggregate of the foreign transferor's distributive share of the deemed sale EC capital gain and loss results in a gain) or *aggregate deemed sale EC capital loss* (if the aggregate of the foreign transferor's distributive share of the deemed sale EC capital gain and loss results in a loss) is the sum of—

(1) The portion of the foreign transferor's distributive share of deemed sale EC gain and deemed sale EC loss that is attributable to the deemed sale of assets that are not section 751(a) property; and

(2) Deemed sale EC gain and deemed sale EC loss from the sale of assets that are not section 751(a) property and that would be allocated to the foreign transferor with respect to all interests in partnerships that are engaged in the conduct of a trade or business within the United States under paragraph (e)(1)(ii) of this section upon the deemed asset sales described in paragraph (e)(1)(i) of this section.

(iii) *Partial transfers.*—If a foreign transferor transfers less than all of its interest in a partnership, then for purposes of paragraph (c)(3)(i) of this section, the foreign transferor's distributive share of deemed sale EC gain and deemed sale EC loss is determined by reference to the amount of deemed sale EC gain or deemed sale

EC loss determined under paragraph (c)(3)(i) of this section that is attributable to the portion of the foreign transferor's partnership interest that was transferred.

(d) *Coordination with section 897.*—If a foreign transferor transfers an interest in a partnership in a transfer that is subject to section 864(c)(8), and the partnership owns one or more United States real property interests (as defined in section 897(c)), then the foreign transferor determines its effectively connected gain and effectively connected loss under this section, and not pursuant to section 897(g). Accordingly, with respect to a transfer described in the preceding sentence, section 864(c)(8)(C) does not reduce the amount of gain or loss treated as effectively connected gain or loss under this section. For rules regarding a transfer not subject to section 864(c)(8) of an interest in a partnership that owns one or more United States real property interests, see section 897(g) and the regulations thereunder.

(e) *Tiered partnerships.*—(1) *Transfers of upper-tier partnerships.*—Assets sold in a deemed sale described in paragraph (c)(1) of this section do not include interests in partnerships that are engaged in the conduct of a trade or business within the United States or interests in partnerships that hold, directly or indirectly, partnerships that are engaged in the conduct of a trade or business within the United States. Rather, if a foreign transferor transfers an interest in a partnership (upper-tier partnership) that owns, directly or indirectly, an interest in one or more partnerships that are engaged in the conduct of a trade or business within the United States, then—

(i) Beginning with the lowest-tier partnership that is engaged in the conduct of a trade or business within the United States in a chain of partnerships and going up the chain, each partnership that is engaged in the conduct of a trade or business within the United States is treated as selling its assets in a deemed sale in accordance with the principles of paragraph (c)(1) of this section; and

(ii) Each partnership must determine its deemed sale EC gain and deemed sale EC loss in accordance with the principles of paragraph (c)(2) of this section, and determine the distributive share of deemed sale EC gain and deemed sale EC loss for each partner that is either a partnership (in which the foreign transferor is a direct or indirect partner) or a foreign transferor, in accordance with the principles of paragraph (c)(3)(i) of this section.

(2) *Transfers by upper-tier partnerships.*—If a foreign transferor is a direct or indirect partner in an upper-tier partnership and the upper-tier partnership transfers an interest in a partnership that is engaged in the conduct of a trade or business within the United States (including a partnership held indirectly through one or more partnerships), then the principles of this section (including paragraph (e)(1) of this section) apply with respect to the gain or loss on the transfer that is allocated to the foreign transferor by the upper-tier partnership.

(3) *Coordination with section 897.*—For purposes of this paragraph (e), a lower-tier partnership that holds one or more United States real property interests is treated as engaged in the conduct of a trade or business within the United States.

(f) *Income tax treaties.*—(1) *In general.*—This paragraph (f) describes how the provisions of a U.S. income tax treaty apply to the transfer by a foreign transferor that is eligible for benefits under the treaty of an interest in a partnership that is engaged in the conduct of a trade or business within the United States.

(2) *Application of gains article.*—Treaty provisions applicable to gains from the alienation of property forming part of a permanent establishment, including gains from the alienation of a permanent establishment in the United States, apply to the transfer by a foreign transferor of an interest in a partnership with a permanent establishment in the United States.

(3) *Coordination rule.*—For purposes of applying paragraph (c) of this section to gains described in paragraph (f)(2) of this section, a foreign transferor's distributive share of deemed sale EC gain and deemed sale EC loss are determined with respect to the assets of the partnership that form part of the partnership's permanent establishment in the United States and that are not otherwise exempt from U.S. taxation under the treaty.

(g) *Definitions.*—The following definitions apply for purposes of this section.

(1) *Effectively connected gain.*—The term *effectively connected gain* means gain that is treated as effectively connected with the conduct of a trade or business within the United States.

(2) *Effectively connected loss.*—The term *effectively connected loss* means loss treated as effectively connected with the conduct of a trade or business within the United States.

(3) *Foreign transferor.*—The term *foreign transferor* means a nonresident alien individual or foreign corporation.

(4) *Section 751(a) property.*—The term *section 751(a) property* means unrealized receivables described in section 751(c) and inventory items described in section 751(d).

(5) *Transfer.*—The term *transfer* means a sale, exchange, or other disposition, and includes a distribution from a partnership to a partner to the extent that gain or loss is recognized on the distribution, as well as a transfer treated as a sale or exchange under section 707(a)(2)(B).

(h) *Anti-stuffing rule.*—If a foreign transferor (or a person that is related to a foreign transferor within the meaning of section 267(b) or 707(b)) transfers property (including another partnership interest) to a partnership in a transaction with a principal purpose of reducing the amount of gain treated as effectively connected gain, or increasing the amount of loss treated as effectively connected loss, under section 864(c)(8) or section 897, the transfer is disregarded for purposes of section 864(c)(8) or section 897, as appropriate, or otherwise recharacterized in accordance with its substance.

(i) *Examples.*—This paragraph provides examples that illustrate the rules of this section. For purposes of this paragraph, unless otherwise provided, the following facts are presumed. FP is a foreign corporation. USP is a domestic corporation. PRS is a partnership that was formed on January 1, 2018, when FP and USP each contributed $100x in cash. PRS has made no distributions and received no contributions other than those described in paragraph (i)(1)(iii) of this section. FP's adjusted basis in its interest in PRS is $100x. X is a foreign corporation that is unrelated to FP, USP, or PRS. Upon the formation of PRS, FP and USP entered into an agreement providing that all income, gain, loss, and deduction of PRS will be allocated equally between FP and USP. PRS is engaged in the conduct of a trade or business within the United States (the U.S. Business) and an unrelated business in Country A (the Country A Business). In a deemed sale described in paragraph (c)(1) of this section, gain or loss on assets of the U.S. Business would be treated as effectively connected gain or effectively connected loss, and gain or loss on assets of the Country A Business would not be so treated (including by reason of paragraph (c)(2)(ii) of this section). PRS has no liabilities. FP does not qualify for the benefits of an income tax treaty between the United States and another country.

(1) *Example 1. Deemed sale limitation*—(i) *Facts.* On January 1, 2019, FP sells its entire interest in PRS to X for $105x. Immediately before the sale, PRS's balance sheet appears as follows:

	Adjusted Basis	Fair Market Value
U.S. Business capital asset	$100x	$104x
Country A Business capital asset	100x	106x
Total	$200x	$210x

(ii) *Analysis*—(A) *Outside gain or loss.* FP is a foreign transferor (within the meaning of paragraph (g)(3) of this section) and transfers (within the meaning of paragraph (g)(5) of this section) its interest in PRS to X. FP recognizes a $5x capital gain under section 741, which is an outside capital gain within the meaning of paragraph (b)(2)(i) of this section. Under paragraph (b)(1) of this section, FP's $5x capital gain is treated as effectively connected gain to the extent that it does not exceed the limitation described in paragraph (b)(3)(i) of this section, which is FP's aggregate deemed sale EC capital gain.

(B) *Deemed sale.* FP's aggregate deemed sale EC capital gain is determined according to the three-step process set forth in paragraph (c) of this section. First, the amount of gain or loss that PRS would recognize with respect to each of its assets upon a deemed sale described in paragraph (c)(1) of this section is a $4x gain with respect

to the U.S. Business capital asset and a $6x gain with respect to the Country A Business capital asset. Second, under paragraph (c)(2) of this section, PRS's deemed sale EC gain is $4x. PRS recognizes no deemed sale EC gain or loss with respect to the Country A Business capital asset under section 864 and paragraph (c)(2)(ii) of this section. Third, under paragraph (c)(3)(ii)(B) of this section, FP's aggregate deemed sale EC capital gain is $2x (that is, the aggregate of its distributive share of deemed sale EC gain attributable to the deemed sale of assets that are not section 751(a) property, which is 50% of $4x).

(C) *Limitation.* Under paragraph (b)(3)(i) of this section, the $5x outside capital gain recognized by FP is treated as effectively connected gain to the extent that it does not exceed FP's $2x aggregate deemed sale EC capital gain. Accordingly, FP recognizes $2x of capital gain that is treated as effectively connected gain.

(ii) *Analysis*—(A) *Outside gain or loss.* FP is a foreign transferor (within the meaning of paragraph (g)(3) of this section) and transfers (within the meaning of paragraph (g)(5) of this section) its interest in PRS to X. FP recognizes a $10x capital gain under section 741, which is an outside capital gain within the meaning of paragraph (b)(2)(i) of this section. Under paragraph (b)(1) of this section, FP's $10x capital gain is treated as effectively connected gain to the extent that it does not exceed the limitation described in paragraph (b)(3)(i) of this section, which is FP's aggregate deemed sale EC capital gain.

(B) *Deemed sale.* FP's aggregate deemed sale EC capital gain is determined according to the three-step process set forth in paragraph (c) of this section. First, the amount of gain or loss that PRS would recognize with respect to each of its assets upon a deemed sale described in paragraph (c)(1) of this section is a $50x gain with respect to the U.S. Business capital asset and a $30x loss with respect to the Country A Business capital asset. Second, under paragraph (c)(2) of this section, PRS's deemed sale EC gain is $50x. PRS recog-

(2) *Example 2. Outside gain limitation*—(i) *Facts.* On January 1, 2019, FP sells its entire interest in PRS to X for $110x. Immediately before the sale, PRS's balance sheet appears as follows:

	Adjusted Basis	Fair Market Value
U.S. Business capital asset	$100x	$150x
Country A Business capital asset	100x	70x
Total	$200x	$220x

nizes no deemed sale EC gain or loss with respect to the Country A Business capital asset under section 864 and paragraph (c)(2)(ii) of this section. Third, under paragraph (c)(3) of this section, FP's aggregate deemed sale EC capital gain is $25x (that is, the aggregate of its distributive share of deemed sale EC gain attributable to the deemed sale of assets that are not section 751(a) property, which is 50% of $50x).

(C) *Limitation.* Under paragraph (b)(3)(i) of this section, the $10x outside capital gain recognized by FP is treated as effectively connected gain to the extent that it does not exceed FP's $25x aggregate deemed sale EC capital gain. Accordingly, FP recognizes $10x of capital gain that is treated as effectively connected gain.

(3) *Example 3. Interaction with section 751(a)*—(i) *Facts.* On January 1, 2019, FP sells its entire interest in PRS to X for $95x. Through both its U.S. Business and its Country A Business, PRS holds inventory items that are section 751 property (as defined in §1.751-1(a)). Immediately before the sale, PRS's balance sheet appears as follows:

	Adjusted Basis	Fair Market Value
U.S. Business capital asset	$20x	$50x
U.S. Business inventory	30x	50x
Country A Business capital asset	100x	80x
Country A Business inventory	50x	10x
Total	$200x	$190x

(ii) *Analysis*—(A) *Outside gain or loss.* FP is a foreign transferor (within the meaning of paragraph (g)(3) of this section) and transfers (within the meaning of paragraph (g)(5) of this section) its interest in PRS to X. Under sections 741 and 751, FP recognizes a $10x ordinary loss and a $5x capital gain. See §1.751-1(a). Under paragraph (b)(2)(i) of this section, FP has outside ordinary loss equal to $10x and outside capital gain equal to $5x. Under paragraph (b)(1) of this section, FP's outside ordinary loss and outside capital gain are treated as effectively connected loss and effectively connected gain to the extent that each does not exceed the applicable limitation described in para-

graph (b)(3) of this section. In the case of FP's outside ordinary loss, the applicable limitation is FP's aggregate deemed sale EC ordinary loss. In the case of FP's outside capital gain, the applicable limitation is FP's aggregate deemed sale EC capital gain.

(B) *Deemed sale.* FP's aggregate deemed sale EC ordinary loss and aggregate deemed sale EC capital gain are determined according to the three-step process set forth in paragraph (c) of this section.

(1) *Step 1.* The amount of gain or loss that PRS would recognize with respect to each of its assets upon a deemed sale described in paragraph (c)(1) of this section is as follows:

Asset	Gain/(Loss)
U.S. Business capital asset	$30x
U.S. Business inventory	20x
Country A Business capital asset	(20x)
Country A Business inventory	(40x)

(2) *Step 2.* Under paragraph (c)(2) of this section, PRS's deemed sale EC gain and deemed sale EC loss must be determined with

respect to each asset. The amounts determined under paragraph (c)(2) of this section are as follows:

Asset	Deemed Sale EC Gain/(Loss)
U.S. Business capital asset	$30x
U.S. Business inventory	20x
Country A Business capital asset	0
Country A Business inventory	0

(3) *Step 3.* Under paragraph (c)(3) of this section, FP's aggregate deemed sale EC capital gain is $15x (that is, the aggregate of its distributive share of deemed sale EC gain that is attributable to the deemed sale of assets that are not section 751(a) property, which is 50% of $30x) and FP's aggregate deemed sale EC ordinary loss is $0 (that is, the aggregate of its distributive share of deemed sale EC loss that is attributable to the deemed sale of assets that are section 751(a) property).

(C) *Limitation*—(i) *Capital gain.* Under paragraph (b)(3)(i) of this section, the $5x outside capital gain recognized by FP is treated as effectively connected gain to the extent that it does not exceed FP's

$15x aggregate deemed sale EC capital gain. Accordingly, the amount of FP's capital gain that is treated as effectively connected gain is $5x.

(ii) *Ordinary loss.* Under paragraph (b)(3)(iv) of this section, the $10x outside ordinary loss recognized by FP is treated as effectively connected loss to the extent that it does not exceed FP's $0 aggregate deemed sale EC ordinary loss. Accordingly, the amount of FP's ordinary loss that is treated as effectively connected loss is $0.

(j) *Applicability date.*—This section applies to transfers occurring on or after November 27, 2017. [Reg. §1.864(c)(8)-1.]

Interests in Partnerships: Withholding of Tax: Information Reporting

Interests in Partnerships: Withholding of Tax: Information Reporting.—Reg. §1.864(c)(8)-2, implementing certain sections of the Internal Revenue Code, including sections added to the Internal Revenue Code by the Tax Cuts and Jobs Act, that relate to the withholding of tax and information reporting with respect to certain dispositions of interests in partnerships engaged in the conduct of a trade or business within the United States, is proposed (published in the Federal Register on May 13, 2019) (REG-105476-18).

Par. 2. Section 1.864(c)(8)-2 is added to read as follows:

§1.864(c)(8)-2. Notification and reporting requirements.— (a) *Notification by foreign transferor.*—(1) *In general.*—Except as provided in paragraph (a)(2) of this section, a notifying transferor that transfers an interest in a specified partnership must notify the part-

nership of the transfer in writing within 30 days of the transfer. The notification must include—

(i) The names and addresses of the notifying transferor and the transferee or transferees;

(ii) The U.S. taxpayer identification number (TIN) of the notifying transferor and, if known, of the transferee or transferees; and

(iii) The date of the transfer.

(2) *Exceptions.*—(i) *Certain interests in publicly traded partnerships.*—Paragraph (a)(1) of this section does not apply to a notifying transferor that transfers an interest in a publicly traded partnership if the interest is publicly traded on an established securities market or is readily tradable on a secondary market (or the substantial equivalent thereof).

(ii) *Certain distributions.*—Paragraph (a)(1) of this section does not apply to a notifying transferor that is treated as transferring an interest in a specified partnership because it received a distribution from that specified partnership.

(3) *Section 6050K.*—The notification described in paragraph (a)(1) of this section may be combined with or provided at the same time as the notification described in §1.6050K-1(d), provided that it satisfies the requirements of both sections.

(4) *Other guidance.*—The notification described in paragraph (a)(1) of this section must also include any information required in forms, instructions, or other guidance.

(b) *Reporting by specified partnerships with notifying transferor.*— (1) *In general.*—(i) A specified partnership must provide to a notifying transferor the statement described in paragraph (b)(2) of this section if—

(A) The partnership receives the notice described in paragraph (a) of this section, or otherwise has actual knowledge that there has been a transfer of an interest in the partnership by a notifying transferor; and

(B) At the time of the transfer, the notifying transferor would have had a distributive share of deemed sale EC gain or deemed sale EC loss within the meaning of §1.864(c)(8)-1(c).

(ii) *Distributions.*—For purposes of paragraph (b)(1)(i)(B) of this section, a partnership that is a transferee because it makes a distribution is treated as having actual knowledge of that transfer.

(2) *Contents of statement.*—The statement required to be furnished by the specified partnership under paragraph (b)(1) of this section must include—

(i) The items described in §1.864(c)(8)-1(c)(3)(ii) (foreign transferor's aggregate deemed sale EC items, which includes items derived from lower-tier partnerships); and

(ii) Any other information as provided in forms, instructions, or other guidance.

(3) *Time for furnishing statement.*—The specified partnership must furnish the required information on or before the due date (with extensions) for issuing Schedule K-1 (Form 1065), *Partner's Share of Income, Deductions, Credits, etc.*, or its successor, to the transferor for the year of the transfer. *See* §1.6031(b)-1T(b).

(4) *Manner of furnishing statement.*—No specific format is required for the information except as provided in any forms, instructions, or other guidance.

(5) *Partnership notifying transferor.*—For purposes of this paragraph (b), a specified partnership must treat a notifying transferor that is a partnership as a nonresident alien individual.

(c) *Statement may be provided to agent.*—A partnership may provide a statement required under paragraph (b)(2) of this section to a person other than the notifying transferor if the person is described in §1.6031(b)-1T(c).

(d) *Definitions.*—The following definitions apply for purposes of this section.

(1) *Notifying transferor.*—The term *notifying transferor* means any foreign person, any domestic partnership that has a foreign person as a direct partner, and any domestic partnership that has actual knowledge that a foreign person indirectly holds, through one or more partnerships, an interest in the domestic partnership.

(2) *Specified partnership.*—The term *specified partnership* means a partnership that is engaged in the conduct of a trade or business within the United States or that owns (directly or indirectly) an interest in a partnership that is engaged in the conduct of a trade or business within the United States, and may include a publicly traded partnership as defined in section 7704 and §§1.7704-1 through 1.7704-4, but does not include a publicly traded partnership treated as a corporation under that section.

(3) *Transfer.*—The term *transfer* has the meaning provided in §1.864(c)(8)-1(g)(5).

(e) *Applicability dates.*—Paragraph (a) of this section applies to transfers that occur on or after the date that these regulations are published as final regulations in the **Federal Register**. Paragraphs (b) and (c) of this section apply to returns filed on or after the date that these regulations are published as final regulations in the **Federal Register**. Paragraph (d) of this section applies beginning on the date that these regulations are published as final regulations in the **Federal Register**. [Reg. 1.864(c)(8)-2.]

Sales of Inventory: Determining Source of Income

Sales of Inventory: Determining Source of Income.—Reg. §1.865-3, modifying the rules for determining the source of income from sales of inventory produced within the United States and sold without the United States or vice versa, is proposed (published in the Federal Register on December 30, 2019) (REG-100956-19).

Par. 7. Section 1.865-3 is added to read as follows:

§1.865-3. Source of income from sales of personal property (including inventory property) by a nonresident attributable to an office or other fixed place of business in the United States.—(a) *In general.*—Notwithstanding any other provisions of sections 861 through 865 or the regulations in this part except paragraph (b) of this section, if a nonresident, as defined in section 865(g)(1)(B), maintains an office or other fixed place of business in the United States, income from any sale of personal property (including inventory property) attributable to such office or other fixed place of business (as determined under paragraph (c) of this section) is sourced in the United States in an amount described in paragraph (d) of this section. See section 865(i)(1) for the definition of inventory property.

(b) *Exceptions for inventory property.*—Paragraph (a) of this section does not apply with respect to the income derived by a nonresident from any sale of inventory property that is sold for use, disposition, or consumption outside the United States if an office or other fixed place of business of the nonresident in a foreign country materially participated in the sale. See §1.864-6(b)(3) to determine whether a foreign office materially participated in the sale and whether the property was destined for foreign use.

(c) *Attribution of a sale to a United States office.*—In determining whether a sale of personal property by a nonresident is attributable to an office or other fixed place of business in the United States, the principles of section 864(c)(5)(B) as prescribed in §1.864-6(b) and (c) apply. The rule in this paragraph (c) applies without regard to whether the property is described in §1.864-5(b)(3)(iii). In determining whether a nonresident maintains an office or other fixed place of business in the United States, the principles of section 864(c)(5)(A) as prescribed in §1.864-7 apply, including the rules of paragraph (d) of

that section regarding the office or fixed place of business of a dependent agent of the nonresident.

(d) *Amount of income or loss on sale of personal property attributable to a U.S. office.*—(1) *In general.*—Subject to the special rules described in paragraphs (d)(2), (3), and (4) of this section, the amount of income, gain, or loss from the sale of personal property attributable to an office or other fixed place of business in the United States is determined under §1.864-6(c)(1).

(2) *Produced inventory property.*—(i) *In general.*—With respect to income from the sale of inventory property subject to paragraph (a) of this section that is produced by a nonresident, 50 percent of the gross income from such sale is properly allocable to the office or fixed place of business in the United States. The remaining 50 percent of the gross income is allocable to production activities and is sourced in accordance with §1.863-3 (the "50/50 method"). However, in lieu of the 50/50 method, a taxpayer may elect to allocate income from the sale of inventory property that is produced by a nonresident under the books and records method described in paragraph (d)(2)(ii) of this section, provided it satisfies all of the requirements described in that paragraph to the satisfaction of the Commissioner. For purposes of this paragraph (d)(2)(i), the term "produced" includes created, fabricated, manufactured, extracted, processed, cured, and aged. See section 864(a) and §1.864-1.

(ii) *Books and records method.*—(A) *Method.*—A taxpayer may elect to determine the amount of its gross income from the sale of inventory property subject to paragraph (a) of this section and produced by a nonresident that is allocable to production and sales activities for the taxable year based upon its books of account. The taxpayer must establish that the taxpayer, in good faith and unaffected by considerations of tax liability, regularly employs in its books of account a detailed allocation of receipts and expenditures that clearly reflects the amount of the taxpayer's gross income from its inventory sales that is attributable to its sales activities, and gross income from sales that is attributable to its production activities under the principles of section 482. For purposes of this paragraph (d)(2)(ii)(A), section 482 principles will apply as if the office or fixed place of business in the United States were a separate taxpayer from the nonresident (whether or not payments are made between the United States office or other fixed place of business and the nonresident taxpayer's other offices). The gross income allocable to sales activity under this method is treated as properly allocable to the office or other fixed place of business in the United States. The gross income allocable to production activities is sourced in accordance with § 1.863-3.

(B) *Election and reporting rules.*—(1) *In general.*—A taxpayer making an allocation of gross income under the books and records method in paragraph (d)(2)(ii)(A) of this section must satisfy the requirements of paragraphs (d)(2)(ii)(B)(2) and (3) of this section. Failure to satisfy the requirements in paragraphs (d)(2)(ii)(B)(2) and (3) in full and to the satisfaction of the Commissioner will result in application of the 50/50 method specified in paragraph (d)(2)(i) of this section.

(2) *Required records.*—A taxpayer electing the books and records method under paragraph (d)(2)(ii)(A) of this section must prepare and maintain records that are in existence when its return is filed regarding the allocation of gross income between sales and production activities in its books of account. The taxpayer must also prepare an explanation of how such allocation clearly reflects the taxpayer's income from production and sales activities under the principles of section 482. The taxpayer must make available such explanation and records for both the U.S. sales office and the entity or entities that perform the production activities upon request of the Commissioner, generally within 30 days or some other time period as agreed between the Commissioner and the taxpayer.

(3) *Disclosure on a tax return.*—A taxpayer who chooses to apply the books and records method under paragraph (d)(2)(ii)(A) of this section must indicate in a statement attached to a timely filed return (including extensions) that it elects to apply such method and has prepared the records described in paragraph (d)(2)(ii)(B)(2) of this section.

(3) *Purchased inventory property.*—With respect to income from the sale of inventory property subject to paragraph (a) of this section that is purchased by the nonresident, the entire income from such sale is properly allocable to the office or other fixed place of business in the United States.

(4) *Depreciable personal property.*—With respect to income from the sale of depreciable personal property subject to paragraph (a) of this section—

(i) The gain not in excess of the depreciation adjustments is allocable to an office or other fixed place of business in the United States to the same extent that the gain would be allocated to sources within the United States under the rules of section 865(c)(1). The remaining gain not in excess of the depreciation adjustments is allocated to sources without the United States in accordance with section 865(c)(1). However, notwithstanding the preceding sentences, if the property was predominantly used in the United States, within the meaning of section 865(c)(3)(B)(i), for a specific year, all of the gain not in excess of depreciation for that year is allocated to sources within the United States.

(ii) The gain in excess of the depreciation adjustments is treated as if such property were inventory and is sourced under paragraph (d)(2) or (3) of this section as applicable.

(e) *Determination of source of taxable income.*—For rules allocating and apportioning expenses to income effectively connected with the conduct of a trade or business in the United States, see §§ 1.882-4 and 1.882-5.

(f) *Export trade corporations.*—This section is not applicable for purposes of defining an export trade corporation under section 971.

(g) *Applicability date.*—This section applies to sales occurring in taxable years ending on or after December 23, 2019. However, taxpayers may apply this section in its entirety for taxable years beginning after December 31, 2017, and ending before December 23, 2019, provided that the taxpayer and persons that are related (within the meaning of section 267 or 707) to the taxpayer apply this section in its entirety. [Reg. § 1.865-3.]

Definition of Registered Form: Guidance

Definition of Registered Form: Guidance.—Amendments to Reg. § 1.871-14, providing guidance on the definitions of registration-required obligation and registered form, including guidance on the issuance of pass-through certificates and participation interests in registered form, are proposed (published in the Federal Register on September 19, 2017) (REG-125374-16).

Par. 7. Section 1.871-14 is amended by:

1. Revising the heading for paragraph (c).
2. Revising paragraph (c)(1)(i).
3. Revising the heading for paragraph (d).
4. Revising paragraphs (d)(1) and (2).
5. Adding paragraphs (j)(4) and (5).

The revisions and additions read as follows:

§ 1.871-14. Rules relating to repeal of tax on interest of nonresident alien individuals and foreign corporations received from certain portfolio debt investments.

* * *

(c) *Obligations in registered form.*—(1) *In general.*—(i) *Registered form.*—For purposes of this section, the rules of § 1.163-5(b) apply to determine when an obligation is in registered form.

* * *

(d) *Application of repeal of 30-percent withholding to pass-through certificates or participation interests.*—(1) *In general.*—(i) *Pass-through certificates.*—Interest received on a pass-through certificate (as defined in § 1.163-5(a)(3)(i)(B)) qualifies as portfolio interest under section 871(h)(2) or 881(c)(2) if the interest satisfies the conditions described in paragraph (c)(1)(ii) of this section or the conditions described in paragraph (e) of this section, without regard to whether any obligation held by the grantor trust, or similar fund, to which the pass-through certificate relates is described in paragraph (c)(1)(ii) or (e) of this section. For purposes of this paragraph (d)(1)(i), a similar fund includes an entity that, under §§ 301.7701-1 through 301.7701-3 of this chapter, is disregarded as an entity separate from its owner or classified as a partnership for federal tax purposes, without regard to the fund has the power to vary the assets in the fund or the sequence of payments made to holders. In addition, for purposes of this paragraph (d)(1)(i), a similar fund does not include a business entity that is classified as a corporation under § 301.7701-2 of this chapter.

(ii) *Participation interests.*—Interest received on a participation interest described in § 1.163-5(a)(3)(ii) qualifies as portfolio interest under section 871(h)(2) or 881(c)(2) if the interest satisfies the conditions described in paragraph (c)(1)(ii) of this section or the conditions described in paragraph (e) of this section, without regard to whether the obligation to which the participation interest relates is described in paragraph (c)(1)(ii) or (e) of this section.

(2) *Interest in REMICs.*—Interest received on a regular or residual interest in a REMIC, as defined in sections 860D and 860G and the regulations thereunder, qualifies as portfolio interest under section 871(h)(2) or 881(c)(2) if the interest satisfies the conditions described in paragraph (c)(1)(ii) of this section or the conditions described in paragraph (e) of this section. For purposes of paragraphs (c)(1)(ii) and (e) of this section, interest on a regular interest in a REMIC is not considered interest on any mortgage obligations held by the REMIC. The rule in the preceding sentence, however, applies only to payments made to the holder of the regular interest in the REMIC from the REMIC and does not apply to payments made to the REMIC. For purposes of paragraphs (c)(1)(ii) and (e) of this section, interest on a residual interest in a REMIC is considered to be interest on or with respect to the obligations held by the REMIC, and not on or with respect to the residual interest.

* * *

(j) * * *

(4) *Registered form.*—Paragraph (c)(1)(i) of this section applies to obligations issued after March 18, 2012. For the rules that apply to obligations issued on or before March 18, 2012, see § 1.871-14 as contained in 26 CFR part 1, revised as of the date of the most recent annual revision

(5) *Pass-through certificates, participation interests, and interests in REMICs.*—Paragraph (d) of this section applies to pass-through cer-

tificates, participation interests, or interests in REMICs issued after

Definition of Registered Form: Guidance

Definition of Registered Form: Guidance.—Amendments to Reg. §1.881-3, providing guidance on the definitions of registration-required obligation and registered form, including guidance on the issuance of pass-through certificates and participation interests in registered form, are proposed (published in the Federal Register on September 19, 2017) (REG-125374-16).

Par. 8. Section 1.881-3(e) is amended by:

1. Removing *Examples 10* and *19*.

2. Redesignating *Examples 11* through *18* as *Examples 10* through *17* and *Examples 20* through *26* as *Examples 18* through *24*.

§1.881-3. Conduit financing arrangements.

GILTI: Hybrid Arrangements: Allocation of Deductions

GILTI: Hybrid Arrangements: Allocation of Deductions.—Amendments to Reg. §1.881-3, adjusting hybrid deduction accounts to take into account earnings and profits of a controlled foreign corporation that are included in income by a United States shareholder, are proposed (published in the Federal Register on April 8, 2020) (REG-106013-19).

Par. 3. Section 1.881-3 is amended by:

1. Adding a sentence at the end of paragraph (a)(1).

2. Revising paragraph (a)(2)(i)(C).

3. In paragraph (a)(2)(ii)(B)(*1*) introductory text, removing "one of the following" and adding "one or more of the following" in its place.

4. In paragraph (a)(2)(ii)(B)(*1*)(*ii*), removing the word "or" at the end of the paragraph.

5. In paragraph (a)(2)(ii)(B)(*1*)(*iii*), removing the period at the end and adding a semicolon in its place.

6. Adding paragraphs (a)(2)(ii)(B)(*1*)(*iv*) and (*v*) and (d)(1)(iii).

7. Adding a sentence at the end of paragraph (e) introductory text.

8. In paragraph (e), designating Examples 1 through 26 as paragraphs (e)(1) through (26), respectively.

9. In newly designated paragraph (e)(3), removing "*Example 2*" and "§ 301.7701-3" and adding "paragraph (e)(2) of this section (the facts in *Example 2*)" and "§ 301.7701-3 of this chapter" in their places, respectively.

10. Redesignating newly designated paragraphs (e)(4) through (26) as paragraphs (e)(6) through (28), respectively.

11. Adding new paragraphs (e)(4) and (5);

12. In newly redesignated paragraph (e)(9)(ii), removing "(a)(4)(i)" and adding "(a)(4)(i) of this section" in its place.

13. In newly redesignated paragraph (e)(23)(i), removing "*Example 20*" and adding "paragraph (e)(22) of this section (the facts in *Example 22*)" in its place.

14. In newly redesignated paragraph (e)(23)(ii), removing "*Example 19*" and "paragraph (i) of this *Example 21*" and adding "paragraph (e)(21) of this section (*Example 21*)" and "paragraph (e)(23)(i) of this section (this *Example 23*)" in their places, respectively.

15. In newly redesignated paragraph (e)(25)(i), removing "Example 22" and adding "paragraph (e)(24) of this section (the facts in *Example 24*)" in its place.

16. In newly redesignated paragraph (e)(26)(i), removing "*Example 22*" and adding in its place "paragraph (e)(24) of this section (the facts in *Example 24*)".

17. Adding paragraph (e)(29).

18. In paragraph (f):

i. Revising the paragraph heading.

ii. Removing "Paragraph (a)(2)(i)(C) and *Example 3* of paragraph (e) of this section" and adding "Paragraphs (a)(2)(i)(C) and (e)(3) of this section" in its place.

iii. Adding a sentence at the end of the paragraph.

The additions and revision read as follows:

§1.881-3. Conduit financing arrangements.

(a) * * *

(1) * * * See § 1.1471-3(f)(5) for the application of a conduit transaction for purposes of sections 1471 and 1472. See also §§1.267A-1 and 1.267A-4 (disallowing a deduction for certain interest or royalty payments to the extent the income attributable to the payment is offset by a deduction with respect to equity).

(2) * * *

(i) * * *

(C) *Treatment of disregarded entities.*—For purposes of this section, the term person includes a business entity that is disregarded as an entity separate from its single member owner under §§301.7701-1 through 301.7701-3 of this chapter and therefore such entity may be treated as a party to a financing transaction with its owner.

(ii) * * *

(B) * * *

(*1*) * * *

(*iv*) The issuer is allowed a deduction or another tax benefit (such as an exemption, exclusion, credit, or a notional deduction determined with respect to the stock or similar interest) for amounts paid, accrued, or distributed (deemed or otherwise) with respect to the stock or similar interest, either under the laws of the issuer's country of residence or a country in which the issuer has a taxable presence, such as a permanent establishment, to which a payment on a financing transaction is attributable; or

(*v*) A person related to the issuer is, under the tax laws of the issuer's country of residence, allowed a refund (including through a credit), or similar tax benefit for taxes paid by the issuer to its country of residence on amounts paid, accrued, or distributed (deemed or otherwise) with respect to the stock or similar interest, without regard to any related person's tax liability under the laws of the issuer's country of residence.

(d) * * *

(1) * * *

(iii) *Limitation for certain types of stock.*—If a financing transaction linking one of the parties to the financing arrangement is stock (or a similar interest in a partnership, trust, or other person) described in paragraph (a)(2)(ii)(B)(*1*)(*iv*) of this section, and the issuer is allowed a notional interest deduction with respect to its stock or similar interest (under the laws of its country of residence or another country in which it has a place of business or permanent establishment), the portion of the payment made by the financed entity that is recharacterized under paragraph (d)(1)(i) of this section attributable to such financing transaction will not exceed the financing transaction's principal amount as determined under paragraph (d)(1)(ii) of this section multiplied by the rate used to compute the issuer's notional interest deduction for the taxable year in which the payment is made.

* * *

(e) *Examples.*—* * * For purposes of these examples, unless otherwise indicated, it is assumed that no stock is of the types described in paragraph (a)(2)(ii)(B)(*1*)(*iv*) or (*v*) of this section.

* * *

(4) *Example 4. Hybrid instrument as financing arrangement.*—The facts are the same as in paragraph (e)(2) of this section (the facts in *Example 2*), except that FP assigns the DS note to FS in exchange for stock issued by FS. The stock issued by FS is in form convertible debt with a 49-year term that is treated as debt under the tax laws of Country T. The FS stock is not subject to any of the redemption, acquisition, or payment rights or requirements specified in paragraphs (a)(2)(ii)(B)(*1*)(*i*) through (*iii*) of this section. Because the FS stock gives rise to a deduction under the tax laws of Country T, the FS stock is a financing transaction under paragraph

(a)(2)(ii)(B)(*1*)(*iv*) of this section. Therefore, the DS note held by FS and the FS stock held by FP are financing transactions within the meaning of paragraphs (a)(2)(ii)(A)(*1*) and (2) of this section, respectively, and together constitute a financing arrangement within the meaning of paragraph (a)(2)(i) of this section. See also § 1.267A-4 for rules applicable to disqualified imported mismatch amounts.

(5) *Example 5. Refundable tax credit treated as financing transaction.*—FS lends $1,000,000 to DS in exchange for a note issued by DS. Additionally, Country T has a regime whereby FP, as the sole shareholder of FS, is allowed a refund with respect to distributions of earnings by FS that is equal to 90% of the Country T taxes paid by FS associated with any such distributed earnings. FP is not itself subject to Country T tax on distributions from FS. The loan from FS to DS is a financing transaction within the meaning of paragraph (a)(2)(ii)(A)(*1*) of this section. FP's stock in FS constitutes a financing transaction within the meaning of paragraph (a)(2)(ii)(B)(*1*)(*v*) of this section because FP, a person related to FS, is allowed a refund of FS's Country T taxes even though FP is not subject to Country T tax on such payments. Together, the FS stock held by FP and the DS note held by FS constitute a financing arrangement within the meaning of paragraph (a)(2)(i) of this section.

* * *

(29) *Example 29. Amount of payment subject to recharacterization.*—(i) FP lends $10,000,000 to FS in exchange for a ten-year note with a stated interest rate of 6%. FP also contributes $5,000,000 to FS in exchange for FS stock. Pursuant to Country T tax law, FS is entitled to a notional interest deduction with respect to the stock equal to the prevailing Country T government bond rate multiplied by the taxpayer's net equity for the previous taxable year. FS, pursuant to a tax avoidance plan, lends $20,000,000 to DS in exchange for a note that pays 8% interest annually. DS makes its first $1,600,000 payment on this note in year X, when the prevailing Country T bond rate is 1%.

(ii) Both the note and the stock issued by FS to FP are financing transactions. The note is an advance of money under paragraph (a)(2)(i)(A) of this section. The stock is described in paragraph (a)(2)(ii)(A)(2) of this section, by reason of paragraph (a)(2)(ii)(B)(*1*)(*iv*) of this section, because Country T law entitles FS to a notional interest deduction with respect to its stock. The note issued by DS is also financing transaction by reason of paragraph (a)(2)(ii)(A)(*1*) of this section. Accordingly, FP is advancing money and DS receives money, effected through FS an intermediary entity, and the receipt and advance are effected through financing transactions (that is, the FS note, FS stock, and the DS note linking all three entities). As such, the arrangement may be treated as a financing arrangement. See paragraph (a)(2)(i)(A) of this section. FP is the financing entity, FS is the intermediate entity, and DS is the financed entity. The aggregate principal amount of financing transactions linking DS to the financing arrangement ($20,000,000) is greater than the aggregate principal amount of the financing transactions linking FP to the financing arrangement ($15,000,000). Therefore, under paragraph (d)(1)(i) of this section, the amount of DS's payment recharacterized as a payment directly between DS and FP would be $1,200,000 ($1,600,000 x $15,000,000 / $20,000,000) prior to the application of paragraph (d)(1)(iii) of this section. However, of the $1,200,000 subject to re-characterization, $400,000 ($1,200,000 x $5,000,000 / $15,000,000) is attributable to NID stock and thus subject to the limitation in paragraph (d)(1)(iii) of this section. Thus, only $50,000 ($5,000,000 x 1%) of the $400,000 may be recharacterized as a transaction between DS and FP. The remaining $800,000 is not subject to the limitation in paragraph (d)(1)(iii) of this section because it is not attributable to stock that entitles the issuer to a notional interest deduction. Accordingly, only $850,000 of DS's payment is recharacterized as going directly from DS to FP. See also § 1.267A-4 for rules applicable to disqualified imported mismatch amounts.

(f) *Applicability date.*—* * * Paragraphs (a)(2)(ii)(B)(*1*)(*iv*) and (*v*) and (d)(1)(iii) of this section apply to payments made on or after [date of publication of the final regulations in the **Federal Register**].

Foreign Corporations: Determination of Interest Expense Deduction: Branch Profits Tax

Foreign Corporations: Determination of Interest Expense Deduction: Branch Profits Tax.—Amendments to Reg. § 1.882-5, relating to the determination of the interest expense deduction of foreign corporations and the branch profits tax, are proposed (published in the Federal Register on March 8, 1996).

☐ Par. 2. Section 1.882-5 is amended as follows:

1. The text of paragraph (b)(2)(iv) is added.
2. The text of paragraph (c)(2)(v) is added.
3. In paragraph (c)(5), *Example 4, Example 6*, and *Example 7* are added.
4. The text of paragraph (d)(2)(vi) is added.
5. In paragraph (d)(6), *Example 4* is added.
6. The text of paragraph (e)(3) is added.
7. In paragraph (e)(5), *Example 2* is added.
8. The text of paragraph (f)(2) is added.

The added provisions read as follows:

§ 1.882-5. Determination of interest deduction
* * *

(b) * * *
(2) * * *

(iv) *Adjustment to basis of financial instruments.*—The basis of a security or contract that is marked to market pursuant to section 475 or section 1256 will be determined as if each determination date were the last business day of the taxpayer's taxable year. A financial instrument with a fair market value of less than zero is a liability, not an asset, for purposes of this section. [*NOTE*: Proposed Reg. § 1.882-5(b)(2)(iv) was adopted as Temporary Reg. § 1.882-5T(b)(3)(ii) by T.D. 9281 on August 15, 2006.]

* * *

(c) * * *
(2) * * *

(v) *Hedging transactions.*—A transaction (or transactions) that hedges an asset or liability, or a pool of assets or a pool of liabilities, will be taken into account in determining the value, amount and currency denomination of the asset or liability that it hedges. A transaction will be considered to hedge an asset or liability only if the transaction meets the requirements of § 1.1221-2.

* * *

(5) * * *

Example 4. Partnership liabilities. X and Y are each foreign corporations engaged in the active conduct of a trade or business within the United States through a partnership, P. Under the partnership agreement, X and Y each have a 50% interest in the capital and profits of P, and X is also entitled to a return of 6% per annum on its capital account that is a guaranteed payment under section 707(c). In addition, P has incurred a liability of $100x to an unrelated bank, B. Under paragraph (c)(2)(vi) of this section, X and Y each share equally in P's liability to B. In accordance with U.S. tax principles, P's obligation to make guaranteed payments to X does not constitute a liability of P, and therefore neither X nor Y take into account that obligation of the partnership in computing their actual ratio.

* * *

Example 6. Securities in ratio as assets. FC is a foreign corporation engaged in a trade or business in the United States through a U.S. branch. FC is a dealer in securities within the meaning of section 475(c)(1)(B) because it regularly offers to enter into positions in currency spot and forward contracts with customers in the ordinary course of its trade or business. FC has not elected to use the fixed ratio. On December 31, 1996, the end of FC's taxable year, the mark-to-market value of the spot and forward contracts entered into by FC worldwide is 1000x, which includes a mark-to-market gain of 500x with respect to the spot and forward contracts that are shown on the books of its U.S. branch and that produce effectively connected income. On its December 31, 1996, determination date, FC includes 500x in its U.S. assets, and 1000x in its worldwide assets.

Example 7. Securities in ratio as assets and liabilities. The facts are the same as in *Example 4*, except that on December 31, 1996, the mark-to-market value of the spot and forward contracts entered into by FC worldwide is 1000x, and FC has a mark-to-market loss of 500x with respect to the spot and forward contracts that are shown on the books of its U.S. branch and that would produce effectively connected income. On its December 31, 1996, determination date, FC includes the 1000x in its worldwide assets for purposes of determining its ratio of worldwide liabilities to worldwide assets. For purposes of Step 3, however, FC has U.S.-booked liabilities in the United States equal to the 500x U.S. loss position.

(d) * * *

(2) * * *

(vi) *Hedging transactions.*—A transaction (or transactions) that hedges a U.S. booked liability, or a pool of U.S. booked liabilities, will be taken into account in determining the currency denomination, amount of, and interest rate associated with, that liability. A transaction will be considered to hedge a U.S. booked liability only if the transaction meets the requirements of § 1.1221-2(a), (b), and (c), and is identified in accordance with the requirements of § 1.1221-2(e).

* * *

(6) * * *

Example 4. Liability hedge—(i) *Facts.* FC is a foreign corporation that meets the definition of a bank, as defined in section 585(a)(2)(B) (without regard to the second sentence thereof), and that is engaged in a banking business in the United States through its branch, B. FC's corporate policy is to match the currency denomination of its assets and liabilities, thereby minimizing potential gains and losses from currency fluctuations. Thus, at the close of each business day, FC enters into one or more hedging transactions as needed to maintain a balanced currency position, and instructs each branch to do the same. At the close of business on December 31, 1998, B has 100x of U.S. dollar assets, and U.S. booked liabilities of 90x U.S. dollars and 1000x Japanese yen (exchange rate: $1 = 100). To eliminate the currency mismatch in this situation, B enters into a forward contract with an unrelated third party that requires FC to pay 10x dollars in return for 1000x yen. Through this hedging transaction, FC has effectively converted its 1000x Japanese yen liability into a U.S. dollar liability. FC uses its actual ratio of 90% in 1998 for Step 2, the adjusted U.S. booked liabilities method for purposes of Step 3, and is a calendar year taxpayer.

(ii) *Analysis.* Under paragraph 1.882-5(d)(2)(vi), FC is required to take into account hedges of U.S. booked liabilities in determining the currency denomination, amount, and interest rate associated with those liabilities. Accordingly, FC must treat the Japanese yen liabilities booked in the United States on December 31, 1998, as U.S. dollar liabilities to determine both the amount of the liabilities and the interest paid or accrued on U.S. booked liabilities for purposes of this section. Moreover, in applying the scaling ratio prescribed in paragraph (d)(4)(i) of this section, FC must scale back both the U.S. booked liabilities and the hedge(s) of those liabilities. Assuming that FC's average U.S. booked liabilities for the year ending December 31, 1998, exceed its U.S.-connected liabilities determined under paragraphs (a)(1) through (c)(5) of this section by 10%, FC must scale back by 10% both its interest expense associated with U.S. booked liabilities, and any income or loss from the forward contract to purchase Japanese yen that hedges its U.S. booked liabilities.

(e) * * *

(3) *Hedging transactions.*—A transaction (or transactions) that hedges a liability, or a pool of liabilities, will be taken into account in determining the amount of, or interest rate associated with, that liability. A transaction will be considered to hedge a liability only if the transaction meets the requirements of § 1.1221-2(a),(b), and (c).

* * *

(5) * * *

Example 2. Asset hedge—(i) *Facts.* FC is a foreign corporation that meets the definition of a bank, as defined in section 585(a)(2)(B) (without regard to the second sentence thereof), and that is engaged in the banking business in the United States through its branch, B. FC's corporate policy is to match the currency denomination of its assets and liabilities, thereby minimizing potential gains and losses from currency fluctuations. Thus, at the close of each business day, FC enters into one or more hedging transactions as needed to maintain a balanced currency position, and instructs each branch to do the same. At the close of business on December 31, 1998, B has two U.S. assets, a loan of 90x U.S. dollars and a loan of 1000x Japanese yen (exchange rate: $1 = ¥100). B has U.S. booked liabilities, however, of 100x U.S. dollars. To eliminate the currency mismatch, B enters into a forward contract with an unrelated third party that requires FC to pay 1000x yen in return for 10x dollars. Through this hedging transaction, FC has effectively converted its 1000x Japanese yen asset into a U.S. dollar asset. FC uses its actual ratio of 90% in 1998 for Step 2, has elected the separate currency pools method in paragraph (e) of this section, and is a calendar year taxpayer.

(ii) *Analysis.* Under paragraph (e)(1)(i) of this section, FC must take into account any transaction that hedges a U.S. asset in determining the currency denomination and value of that asset. FC's Japanese yen asset will therefore be treated as a U.S. dollar asset in determining its U.S. assets in each currency. Accordingly, FC will be treated as having only U.S. dollar assets in making its separate currency pools computation.

(f) * * *

(2) *Special rules for financial products.*—Paragraphs (b)(2)(iv), (c)(2)(v), (d)(2)(vi), and (e)(3) of this section will be effective for taxable years beginning on or after the date these regulations are published as final regulations in the Federal Register.

Deduction for Business Interest Expense: Limitation

Deduction for Business Interest Expense: Limitation.—Amendments to Reg. § 1.882-5, regarding the limitation on the deduction for business interest expense after the enactment of recent tax legislation, are proposed (published in the Federal Register on December 28, 2018) (REG-106089-18).

Par. 16. Section 1.882-5 is amended by adding a sentence to the end of paragraph (a)(5) to read as follows:

§ 1.882-5. Determination of interest deduction.—(a) * * *

(5) * * * For rules regarding the coordination of this section and section 163(j), see § 1.163(j)-8(e).

* * *

Transition of Tax Consequences: IBORs: Guidance

Transition of Tax Consequences: IBORs: Guidance.—Amendments to Reg. § 1.882-5, providing guidance on the tax consequences of the transition to the use of reference rates other than interbank offered rates in debt instruments and non-debt contracts, are proposed (published in the Federal Register on October 9, 2019) (REG-118784-18).

Par. 4. Section 1.882-5 is amended by:

1. Revising the fourth sentence of paragraph (a)(7)(i).

2. Revising paragraph (d)(5)(ii)(B).

3. Removing the "(1)" from the "(f)(1)" paragraph designation and adding a subject heading to paragraph (f)(1).

4. Adding paragraph (f)(3).

The revisions and addition read as follows:

§ 1.882-5. Determination of interest deduction.—(a) * * *

(7) * * *

(i) * * * An elected method (other than the fair market value method under paragraph (b)(2)(ii) of this section, or the published rate election in paragraph (d)(5)(ii) of this section) must be used for a minimum period of five years before the taxpayer may elect a different method. * * *

* * *

(d) * * *

(5) * * *

(ii) * * *

(B) *Published rate election.*—For each taxable year in which a taxpayer is a bank within the meaning of section 585(a)(2)(B) (without regard to the second sentence thereof or whether any activities are effectively connected with a trade or business within the United States), the taxpayer may elect to compute the interest expense attributable to excess U.S.-connected liabilities by using the yearly average Secured Overnight Financing Rate (SOFR) published by the Federal Bank of New York for the taxable year rather than the interest rate provided in paragraph (d)(5)(ii)(A) of this section. A taxpayer may elect to apply the rate provided in paragraph (d)(5)(ii)(A) of this section or in this paragraph (d)(5)(ii)(B) on an annual basis and the taxpayer does not need the consent of the Commissioner to change this election in a subsequent taxable year. If a taxpayer that is eligible to make the published rate election either does not file a timely return or files a calculation with no excess U.S.-connected liabilities and it is later determined by the Director of Field Operations that the taxpayer has excess U.S.- connected liabilities, then the Director of Field Operations, and not the taxpayer, may choose whether to apply the interest rate provided under either paragraph (d)(5)(ii)(A) or (B) of this section to the taxpayer's excess U.S.-connected liabilities in determining interest expense.

* * *

(f) * * *—

  (1) *General rule.*—* * *

* * *

(3) *Applicability date for published rate election.*—Paragraph (d)(5)(ii)(B) of this section applies to taxable years ending after the date of publication of a Treasury decision adopting these rules as final regulations is published in the **Federal Register**.

Foreign Corporations: Determination of Interest Expense Deduction: Branch Profits Tax

Foreign Corporations: Determination of Interest Expense Deduction: Branch Profits Tax.—Amendments to Reg. §1.884-1, relating to the determination of the interest expense deduction of foreign corporations and the branch profits tax, are proposed (published in the Federal Register on March 8, 1996).

☐ Par. 3. Section 1.884-1 is amended as follows:

1. Paragraph (c)(2)(iii) is added.

2. Paragraph (d)(2) is amended as follows:

  a. Paragraph (d)(2)(vii) is revised.

  b. In paragraph (d)(2)(xi), *Example 6* through *Example 8* are added.

3. The text of paragraph (d)(6)(v) is added.

4. In paragraph (i)(4), a sentence is added at the end of the existing text.

The revised and added provisions read as follows:

§1.884-1. Branch profits tax.

* * *

(c) * * *

  (2) * * *

    (iii) *Hedging transactions.*—A transaction that hedges a U.S. asset, or a pool of U.S. assets, will be taken into account in determining the amount of that asset (or pool of assets) to the extent that income or loss from the hedging transaction produces ECI or reduces ECI. A transaction that hedges a U.S. asset, or pool of U.S. assets, is also taken into account in determining the currency denomination of the U.S. asset (or pool of U.S. assets). A transaction will be considered to hedge a U.S. asset only if the transaction meets the requirements of §1.1221-2(a), (b), and (c), and is identified in accordance with the requirements of §1.1221-2(e).

(d) * * *

  (2) * * *

    (vii) *Financial instruments.*—A financial instrument, including a security as defined in section 475 and a section 1256 contract, shall be treated as a U.S. asset of a foreign corporation in the same proportion that the income, gain, or loss from such security is ECI for the taxable year.

* * *

  (xi) * * *

  Example 6. Hedging transactions—(i) *Facts.* FC is a foreign corporation engaged in a trade or business in the United States through a U.S. branch. The functional currency of FC's U.S. branch is the U.S. dollar. On January 1, 1997, in the ordinary course of its business, the U.S. branch of FC enters into a forward contract with an unrelated party to purchase 100 German marks (DM) on March 31, 1997, for $50. To hedge the risk of currency fluctuation on this transaction, the U.S. branch also enters into a forward contract with another unrelated party to sell 100 DM on March 31, 1997, for $52, identifying this contract as a hedging transaction in accordance with the requirements of §1.1221-2(e). FC marks its foreign currency transactions to market for U.S. tax purposes.

  (ii) *Net assets.* At the end of FC's taxable year, the value of the forward contract to purchase 100 DM is marked to market, resulting in gain of $10 being realized and recognized as U.S. source effectively connected income by FC. Similarly, FC marks to market

the contract to sell 100 DM, resulting in $8 of realized and recognized loss by FC. Pursuant to paragraph (c)(2)(iii) of this section, FC must increase or decrease the amount of its U.S. assets to take into account any transaction that hedges the contract to purchase 100 DM. Consequently, FC has a U.S. asset of $2 ($10 (the adjusted basis of the contract to purchase 100 DM) - $8 (the loss on the contract to sell 100 DM)).

  Example 7. Split hedge. The facts are the same as in *Example 5*, except that the contract to sell 100 DM is entered into with an unrelated third party by the home office of FC. FC includes the contract to sell 100 DM in a pool of assets treated as producing income effectively connected with the U.S. trade or business of FC. Therefore, under paragraph (c)(2)(iii) of this section, at its next determination date FC will report a U.S. asset of $2, computed as in *Example 5*.

  Example 8. Securities. FC is a foreign corporation engaged in a U.S. trade or business through a branch in the United States. During the taxable year 1997, FC derives $100 of income from securities, of which $60 is treated as U.S. source effectively connected income under the terms of an Advance Pricing Agreement that uses a profit split methodology. Accordingly, pursuant to paragraph (d)(2)(vii) of this section, FC has a U.S. asset equal to 60% ($60 of ECI divided by $100 of gross income from securities) of the amount of the securities.

* * *

(6) * * *

    (v) *Computation of E&P basis of financial instruments.*—For purposes of this section, the E&P basis of a security that is marked to market under section 475 and a section 1256 contract shall be adjusted to take into account gains and losses recognized by reason of section 475 or section 1256. The E&P basis must be further adjusted to take into account a transaction that hedges a U.S. asset, as provided in paragraph (c)(2)(ii) of this section.

* * *

(i) * * *

  (4) * * * Paragraphs (c)(2)(iii), (d)(2)(vii), and (d)(6)(v) of this section will be effective for taxable years beginning on or after the date these regulations are published as final regulations in the Federal Register.

* * *

Foreign Corporations: Branch Profits Tax

Foreign Corporations: Branch Profits Tax.—Reg. §§1.884-2T and 1.884-3T, relating to the branch profits tax, are proposed (published in the Federal Register on September 2, 1988) (INTL-934-86). Reg. §§1.884-0, 1.884-1, 1.884-4 and 1.884-5 were adopted 9/10/92 by T.D. 8432.

§1.884-2. Special rules for termination or incorporation of a U.S. trade or business or liquidation or reorganization of a foreign corporation or its domestic subsidiary.

§1.884-3. Coordination of branch profits tax with second-tier withholding.

Foreign Governments and International Organizations

Income of Foreign Governments and International Organizations.—Temporary Reg. §§1.892-1T—1.892-7T, relating to current taxation of income of foreign governments from investment sources within the United States, are also proposed as final regulations and, when adopted, would become Reg. §§1.892-1—1.892-7 (published in the Federal Register on June 27, 1988).

§1.892-1. Purpose and scope of regulations.

§1.892-2. Foreign government defined.

§1.892-3. **Income of foreign governments**.

§1.892-4. **Commercial activities**.

§1.892-5. **Controlled commercial entity**.

§1.892-6. **Income of international organizations**.

§1.892-7. **Relationship to other Internal Revenue Code sections**.

Foreign Governments and International Organizations: Income from Sources within the United States

Foreign Governments and International Organizations: Income from Sources within the United States.—Reg. §1.892-4 and amendments to Reg. §1.892-5, relating to the taxation of the income of foreign governments from investments in the United States under section 892 of the Internal Revenue Code, are proposed (published in the Federal Register on November 3, 2011) (REG-146537-06) (corrected November 23, 2011).

☐ Par. 2. Section 1.892-4 is added to read as follows:

§1.892-4. **Commercial activities**.—(a) through (c) [Reserved]. For further guidance, see §1.892-4T(a) through (c).

(d) *In general*.—Except as provided in paragraph (e) of this section, all activities (whether conducted within or outside the United States) which are ordinarily conducted for the current or future production of income or gain are commercial activities. Only the nature of the activity, not the purpose or motivation for conducting the activity, is determinative of whether the activity is commercial in character. An activity may be considered a commercial activity even if such activity does not constitute a trade or business for purposes of section 162 or does not constitute (or would not constitute if undertaken in the United States) the conduct of a trade or business in the United States for purposes of section 864(b).

(e) *Activities that are not commercial*.—(1) *Investments*.—(i) *In general*.—Subject to the provisions of paragraphs (e)(1)(ii) and (iii) of this section, the following are not commercial activities: investments in stocks, bonds, and other securities (as defined in §1.892-3T(a)(3)); loans; investments in financial instruments (as defined in §1.892-3T(a)(4)); the holding of net leases on real property; the holding of real property which is not producing income (other than on its sale or from an investment in net leases on real property); and the holding of bank deposits in banks. Transferring securities under a loan agreement which meets the requirements of section 1058 is an investment for purposes of this paragraph (e)(1)(i). An activity will not cease to be an investment solely because of the volume of transactions of that activity or because of other unrelated activities.

(ii) *Trading*.—Effecting transactions in stocks, bonds, other securities (as defined in §1.892-3T(a)(3)), commodities, or financial instruments (as defined in §1.892-3T(a)(4)) for a foreign government's own account does not constitute a commercial activity regardless of whether such activity constitutes a trade or business for purposes of section 162 or constitutes (or would constitute if undertaken within the United States) the conduct of a trade or business in the United States for purposes of section 864(b). Such transactions are not commercial activities regardless of whether they are effected by the foreign government through its employees or through a broker, commission agent, custodian, or other independent agent and regardless of whether or not any such employee or agent has discretionary authority to make decisions in effecting the transactions. Such transactions undertaken as a dealer (as determined under the principles of §1.864-2(c)(2)(iv)(a)), however, constitute commercial activity. For purposes of this paragraph (e)(1)(ii), the term *commodities* means commodities of a kind customarily dealt in on an organized commodity exchange but only if the transaction is of a kind customarily consummated at such place.

(iii) *Banking, financing, etc.*—Investments (including loans) made by a banking, financing, or similar business constitute commercial activities, even if the income derived from such investments is not considered to be income effectively connected with the active conduct of a banking, financing, or similar business in the U.S. by reason of the application of §1.864-4(c)(5).

(iv) *Disposition of a U.S. real property interest*.—A disposition (including a deemed disposition under section 897(h)(1)) of a U.S. real property interest (as defined in section 897(c)), by itself, does not constitute the conduct of a commercial activity. As described in §1.892-3T(a), however, gain derived from a disposition of a U.S. real property interest defined in section 897(c)(1)(A)(i) will not qualify for exemption from tax under section 892.

(2) through (5) [Reserved]. For further guidance, see §1.892-4T(c)(2) through (c)(5).

(f) *Effective/applicability date*.—This section applies on the date the regulations are published as final regulations in the **FEDERAL REGISTER**. See §1.892-4T for the rules that apply before the date the regulations are published as final regulations in the **FEDERAL REGISTER**. [Reg. §1.892-4.]

☐ Par. 3. Section 1.892-5 is revised to read as follows:

§1.892-5. **Controlled commercial entity**.—(a) *In general*.—(1) *General rule and definition of the term "controlled commercial entity"*.—Under section 892(a)(2)(A)(ii) and (a)(2)(A)(iii), the exemption generally applicable to a foreign government (as defined in §1.892-2T) for income described in §1.892-3T does not apply to income received by a controlled commercial entity or received (directly or indirectly) from a controlled commercial entity, or to income derived from the disposition of any interest in a controlled commercial entity. For purposes of section 892 and the regulations thereunder, the term *entity* means and includes a corporation, a partnership, a trust (including a pension trust described in §1.892-2T(c)), and an estate, and the term *controlled commercial entity* means any entity (including a controlled entity as defined in §1.892-2T(a)(3)) engaged in commercial activities (as defined in §§1.892-4 and 1.892-4T) (whether conducted within or outside the United States) if the government—

(i) Holds (directly or indirectly) any interest in such entity which (by value or voting power) is 50 percent or more of the total of such interests in such entity, or

(ii) Holds (directly or indirectly) any other interest in such entity which provides the foreign government with effective practical control of such entity.

(2) *Inadvertent commercial activity*.—(i) *General rule*.—For purposes of determining whether an entity is a controlled commercial entity for purposes of section 892(a)(2)(B) and paragraph (a)(1) of this section, an entity that conducts only inadvertent commercial activity will not be considered to be engaged in commercial activities. How-ever, any income derived from such inadvertent commercial activity will not qualify for exemption from tax under section 892. Commercial activity of an entity will be treated as inadvertent commercial activity only if:

(A) Failure to avoid conducting the commercial activity is reasonable as described in paragraph (a)(2)(ii) of this section;

(B) The commercial activity is promptly cured as described in paragraph (a)(2)(iii) of this section; and

(C) The record maintenance requirements described in paragraph (a)(2)(iv) of this section are met.

(ii) *Reasonable failure to avoid commercial activity*.—(A) *In general*.—Subject to paragraphs (a)(2)(ii)(B) and (C) of this section, whether an entity's failure to prevent its worldwide activities from resulting in commercial activity is reasonable will be determined in light of all the facts and circumstances. Due regard will be given to the number of commercial activities conducted during the taxable year and in prior taxable years, as well as the amount of income earned from, and assets used in, the conduct of the commercial activities in relationship to the entity's total income and assets, respectively. For purposes of this paragraph (a)(2)(ii)(A) and paragraph (a)(2)(ii)(C) of this section, where a commercial activity conducted by a partnership is attributed under paragraph (d)(5)(i) of this section to an entity owning an interest in the partnership—

(1) Assets used in the conduct of the commercial activity by the partnership are treated as assets used in the conduct of commercial activity by the entity in proportion to the entity's interest in the partnership; and

(2) The entity's distributive share of the partnership's income from the conduct of the commercial activity shall be treated as income earned by the entity from the conduct of commercial activities.

(B) *Continuing due diligence requirement.*—A failure to avoid commercial activity will not be considered reasonable unless there is continuing due diligence to prevent the entity from engaging in commercial activities within or outside the United States as evidenced by having adequate written policies and operational procedures in place to monitor the entity's worldwide activities. A failure to avoid commercial activity will not be considered reasonable if the management-level employees of the entity have not undertaken reasonable efforts to establish, follow, and enforce such written policies and operational procedures.

(C) *Safe Harbor.*—Provided that adequate written policies and operational procedures are in place to monitor the entity's worldwide activities as required in paragraph (a)(2)(ii)(B) of this section, the entity's failure to avoid commercial activity during the taxable year will be considered reasonable if:

(1) The value of the assets used in, or held for use in, all commercial activity does not exceed five percent of the total value of the assets reflected on the entity's balance sheet for the taxable year as prepared for financial accounting purposes, and

(2) The income earned by the entity from commercial activity does not exceed five percent of the entity's gross income as reflected on its income statement for the taxable year as prepared for financial accounting purposes.

(iii) *Cure requirement.*—A timely cure shall be considered to have been made if the entity discontinues the conduct of the commercial activity within 120 days of discovering the commercial activity. For example, if an entity that holds an interest as a general partner in a partnership discovers that the partnership is conducting commercial activity, the entity will satisfy the cure requirement if, within 120 days of discovering the commercial activity, the entity discontinues the conduct of the activity by divesting itself of its interest in the partnership (including by transferring its interest in the partnership to a related entity), or the partnership discontinues its conduct of commercial activity.

(iv) *Record maintenance.*—Adequate records of each discovered commercial activity and the remedial action taken to cure that activity must be maintained. The records shall be retained so long as the contents thereof may become material in the administration of section 892.

(3) *Annual determination of controlled commercial entity status.*— If an entity described in paragraph (a)(1)(i) or (ii) of this section engages in commercial activities at any time during a taxable year, the entity will be considered a controlled commercial entity for the entire taxable year. An entity not otherwise engaged in commercial activities during a taxable year will not be considered a controlled commercial entity for a taxable year even if the entity engaged in commercial activities in a prior taxable year.

(b) through (d)(4) [Reserved]. For further guidance, see § 1.892-5T(b) through (d)(4).

(5) *Partnerships.*—(i) *General rule.*—Except as provided in paragraph (d)(5)(ii) or paragraph (d)(5)(iii) of this section, the commercial activities of an entity classified as a partnership for federal tax purposes will be attributable to its partners for purposes of section 892. For example, if an entity described in paragraph (a)(1)(i) or (ii) of this section holds an interest as a general partner in a partnership that is engaged in commercial activities, the partnership's commercial activities will be attributed to that entity for purposes of determining if the entity is a controlled commercial entity within the meaning of section 892(a)(2)(B) and paragraph (a) of this section.

(ii) *Trading activity exception.*—An entity not otherwise engaged in commercial activities will not be considered to be engaged in commercial activities solely because the entity is a member of a partnership (whether domestic or foreign) that effects transactions in stocks, bonds, other securities (as defined in § 1.892-3T(a)(3)), commodities (as defined in § 1.892-4(e)(1)(ii)), or financial instruments (as defined in § 1.892-3T(a)(4)) for the partnership's own account or solely because an employee of such partnership, or a broker, commission agent, custodian, or other agent, pursuant to discretionary authority granted by such partnership, effects such transactions for the account of the partnership. This exception shall not apply to any member in the case of a partnership that is a dealer in stocks, bonds, other securities, commodities, or financial instruments, as determined under the principles of § 1.864-2(c)(2)(iv)(a).

(iii) *Limited partner exception.*—(A) *General rule.*—An entity that is not otherwise engaged in commercial activities (including, for example, performing services for a partnership as described in sec-

tion 707(a) or section 707(c)) will not be deemed to be engaged in commercial activities solely because it holds an interest as a limited partner in a limited partnership. Nevertheless, pursuant to sections 875, 882, and 892(a)(2)(A)(i), a foreign government member's distributive share of partnership income will not be exempt from taxation under section 892 to the extent that the partnership derived such income from the conduct of a commercial activity. For example, where a controlled entity described in § 1.892-2T(a)(3) that is not otherwise engaged in commercial activities holds an interest as a limited partner in a limited partnership that is a dealer in stocks, bonds, other securities, commodities, or financial instruments in the United States, although the controlled entity partner will not be deemed to be engaged in commercial activities solely because of its interest in the limited partnership, its distributive share of partnership income derived from the partnership's activity as a dealer will not be exempt from tax under section 892 because it was derived from the conduct of a commercial activity.

(B) *Interest as a limited partner in a limited partnership.*— Solely for purposes of paragraph (d)(5)(iii) of this section, an interest in an entity classified as a partnership for federal tax purposes shall be treated as an interest as a limited partner in a limited partnership if the holder of such interest does not have rights to participate in the management and conduct of the partnership's business at any time during the partnership's taxable year under the law of the jurisdiction in which the partnership is organized or under the governing agreement. Rights to participate in the management and conduct of a partnership's business do not include consent rights in the case of extraordinary events such as admission or expulsion of a general or limited partner, amendment of the partnership agreement, dissolution of the partnership, disposition of all or substantially all of the partnership's property outside of the ordinary course of the partnership's activities, merger, or conversion.

(iv) *Illustration.*—The following example illustrates the application of this paragraph (d)(5):

Example 1. K, a controlled entity of a foreign sovereign, has investments in various stocks and bonds of United States corporations and in a 20% interest in Opco, a limited liability company that is classified as a partnership for federal tax purposes. Under the governing agreement of Opco, K has the authority to participate in the management and conduct of Opco's business. Opco has investments in various stocks and bonds of United States corporations and also owns and manages an office building in New York. Because K has authority to participate in the management and conduct of Opco's business, its interest in Opco is not a limited partner interest. Therefore, K will be deemed to be engaged in commercial activities because of attribution of Opco's commercial activity, even if K does not actually make management decisions with regard to Opco's commercial activity, the operation of the office building. Accordingly, K is a controlled commercial entity, and all of its income, including its distributive share of partnership income from its interest in Opco and its income from the stocks and bonds it owns directly, will not be exempt from tax under section 892.

Example 2. The facts are the same as in *Example 1*, except that Opco has hired a real estate management firm to lease offices and manage the office building. Notwithstanding the fact that an independent contractor is performing the activities, Opco will still be deemed to be engaged in commercial activities. Accordingly, K is a controlled commercial entity, and all of its income, including its distributive share of partnership income from its interest in Opco and its income from the stocks and bonds it owns directly, will not be exempt from tax under section 892.

Example 3. The facts are the same as in *Example 1*, except that K is a member that has no right to participate in the management and conduct of Opco's business. Assume further that K is not otherwise engaged in commercial activities. Under paragraph (d)(5)(iii) of this section, Opco's commercial activities will not be attributed to K. Accordingly, K will not be a controlled commercial entity, and its income derived from the stocks and bonds it owns directly and the portion of its distributive share of partnership income from its interest in Opco that is derived from stocks and bonds will be exempt from tax under section 892. The portion of K's distributive share of partnership income from its interest in Opco that is derived from the operation of the office building will not be exempt from tax under section 892 and § 1.892-3T(a)(1).

(e) *Effective/applicability date.*—This section applies on the date these regulations are published as final regulations in the **FEDERAL REGISTER**. See § 1.892-5(a) as issued under TD 9012 (August 1, 2002) for rules that apply on or after January 14, 2002, and before the date these regulations are published as final regulations in the **FEDERAL REGISTER**. See § 1.892-5T(a) for rules that apply before January 14, 2002, and § 1.892-5T(b) through (d) for rules that apply before the date these regulations are published as final regulations in the **FEDERAL REGISTER**. [Reg. § 1.892-5.]

Global Dealing Operations: Allocation and Sourcing of Income and Deductions

Global Dealing Operations: Allocation and Sourcing of Income and Deductions.—Amendments to Reg. §1.894-1, relating to the allocation and sourcing of income, deductions, gains and losses from a global dealing operation, are proposed (published in the Federal Register on March 6, 1998) (REG-208299-90).

☐ Par. 11. Section 1.894-1 is amended as follows:

1. Paragraph (d) is redesignated as paragraph (e).

2. New paragraph (d) is added.

The addition reads as follows:

§1.894-1. Income affected by treaty.

* * *

(d) *Income from a global dealing operation.*—If a taxpayer that is engaged in a global dealing operation, as defined in §1.482-8(a)(2)(i), has a permanent establishment in the United States under the princi-

ples of an applicable U.S. income tax treaty, the principles of §1.863-3(h), §1.864-4(c)(2)(iv), §1.864-4(c)(3)(ii), §1.864-4(c)(5)(vi)(a) or §1.864-6(b)(2)(ii)(*d*)(*3*) shall apply for purposes of determining the income attributable to that U.S. permanent establishment.

* * *

Dispositions of Investment in U.S. Real Property

Nonresident Aliens and Foreign Corporations: Disposition of Investment in U.S. Real Property.—Temporary Reg. §§1.897-4AT and 1.897-5T—1.897-9T, relating to dispositions of U.S. real property interests by nonresident aliens and foreign corporations, are also proposed as final regulations and, when adopted, would become Reg. §§1.897-4A and 1.897-5—1.897-9 (published in the Federal Register on May 5, 1988).

§1.897-4A. Table of contents.

§1.897-5. Corporate distributions.

§1.897-6. Nonrecognition exchanges applicable to corporations, their shareholders, and other taxpayers, and certain transfers of property in corporate reorganizations.

§1.897-7. Treatment of certain partnership interests as entirely U.S. real property interests under sections 897(g) and 1445(e).

§1.897-8. Status of a U.S. real property holding corporation as a condition for electing section 897(i) pursuant to §1.897-3.

§1.897-9. Treatment of certain interest in publicly traded corporations, definition of foreign person, and foreign governments and international organizations.

Gain or Loss of Foreign Person: Sale or Exchange: Partnership Interest

Gain or Loss of Foreign Person: Sale or Exchange: Partnership Interest.—Reg. §1.897-7, affecting certain foreign persons that recognize gain or loss from the sale or exchange of an interest in a partnership that is engaged in a trade or business within the United States, is proposed (published in the Federal Register on December 27, 2018) (REG-113604-18).

Par. 3. Section 1.897-7 is added to read as follows:

§1.897-7. Treatment of certain partnership interests, trusts and estates under section 897(g).—(a) through (b) [Reserved]. For further guidance, see §1.897-7T(a) through (b).

(c) *Coordination with section 864(c)(8).*—Except as provided in §1.864(c)(8)-1, the amount of any money, and the fair market value of any property, received by a nonresident alien individual or foreign

corporation in exchange for all or part of its interest in a partnership, trust, or estate shall, to the extent attributable to United States real property interests, be considered as an amount received from the sale or exchange in the United States of such property. See also §1.864(c)(8)-1(h) for an anti-stuffing rule that may apply to transactions subject to section 897. This paragraph applies to transfers occurring on or after November 27, 2017. [Reg. §1.897-7.]

Gain or Loss of Foreign Person: Sale or Exchange: Partnership Interest

Gain or Loss of Foreign Person: Sale or Exchange: Partnership Interest.—Amendments to Temporary Reg. §1.897-7T, affecting certain foreign persons that recognize gain or loss from the sale or exchange of an interest in a partnership that is engaged in a trade or business within the United States, are proposed (published in the Federal Register on December 27, 2018) (REG-113604-18).

Par. 4. Section 1.897-7T is amended by adding paragraph (c) to read as follows:

§1.897-7T. Treatment of certain partnership interests as entirely U.S. real property interests under sections 897(g) and 1445(e) (temporary).

* * *

(c) *Coordination with section 864(c)(8).* [Reserved]. For further guidance, see §1.897-7(c). [Reg. §1.897-7T.]

Foreign Pension Funds: Exception for Interests

Foreign Pension Funds: Exception for Interests.—Reg. §1.897(l)-1, regarding the exception from taxation with respect to gain or loss of a qualified foreign pension fund attributable to certain interests in United States real property, is proposed (published in the Federal Register on June 7, 2019) (REG-109826-17).

Par. 2. Section 1.897(l)-1 is added to read as follows:

§1.897(l)-1. Exception for interests held by foreign pension funds.—(a) *Overview.*—This section provides rules regarding the exception from section 897 for qualified holders. Paragraph (b) of this section provides the general rule excepting qualified holders from section 897. Paragraph (c) of this section provides the requirements that an eligible fund must satisfy to be treated as a qualified foreign pension fund. Paragraph (d) of this section provides definitions. Paragraph (e) of this section provides examples illustrating the application of the rules of this section. Paragraph (f) of this section provides applicability dates. For rules applicable to a qualified foreign pension fund or qualified controlled entity claiming an exemp-

tion from withholding under chapter 3, see generally §§1.1441-3, 1.1445-2, 1.1445-4, 1.1445-5, 1.1445-8, 1.1446-7.

(b) *Exception from section 897.*—(1) *In general.*—Gain or loss of a qualified holder from the disposition of a United States real property interest, including gain from a distribution described in section 897(h), is not subject to section 897(a).

(2) *Limitation.*—Paragraph (b)(1) of this section applies solely with respect to gain or loss that is attributable to one or more qualified segregated accounts maintained by a qualified holder.

Reg. §1.897(l)-1(b)(2)

(c) *Qualified foreign pension fund requirements.*—(1) *In general.*—This paragraph (c) provides rules regarding the application of the requirements of section 897(l)(2) to an eligible fund. Paragraph (c)(2) of this section provides requirements that an eligible fund must satisfy to be treated as a qualified foreign pension fund. Paragraph (c)(3) of this section provides rules on the application of the requirements in paragraph (c)(2) of this section, including rules regarding the application of the requirements in paragraph (c)(2) of this section to an eligible fund that is an organization or arrangement.

(2) *Requirements applicable to an eligible fund.*—(i) *Created or organized.*—An eligible fund must be created or organized under the law of a foreign country. For purposes of this paragraph (c)(2)(i), a governmental unit is treated as created or organized in the foreign country with respect to which it is, or is a part of, the foreign government.

(ii) *Purpose of eligible fund.*—(A) *In general.*—An eligible fund must be established by—

(1) The foreign country in which it is created or organized to provide retirement or pension benefits to participants or beneficiaries that are current or former employees or persons designated by such employees as a result of services rendered by such employees to their employers; or

(2) One or more employers to provide retirement or pension benefits to participants or beneficiaries that are current or former employees or persons designated by such employees in consideration for services rendered by such employees to such employers.

(B) *Established to provide retirement or pension benefits.*—An eligible fund is treated as satisfying the requirement of paragraph (c)(2)(ii)(A) of this section if and only if—

(1) All of the benefits that an eligible fund provides are qualified benefits provided to qualified recipients; and

(2) At least 85 percent of the present value of the qualified benefits that the eligible fund reasonably expects to provide are retirement or pension benefits.

(C) *Certain employers and employees.*—For purposes of this section, the following rules apply:

(1) A self-employed individual is treated as both an employer and an employee;

(2) Employees of an individual, trust, corporation, or partnership are treated as employees of each member of the employer group that includes the individual, trust, corporation, or partnership; and

(3) An eligible fund established by a trade union, professional association, or similar group is treated as established by any employer that funds, in whole or in part, the eligible fund.

(iii) *Single participant or beneficiary.*—(A) *In general.*—An eligible fund may not have a single qualified recipient that has a right to more than five percent of the assets or income of the eligible fund.

(B) *Constructive ownership.*—For purposes of paragraph (c)(2)(iii)(A) of this section, an individual is considered to have a right to the assets and income of an eligible fund to which any person who bears a relationship to the individual described in section 267(b) or 707(b) has a right.

(iv) *Regulation and information reporting.*—(A) *In general.*—An eligible fund must—

(1) Be subject to government regulation, and

(2) Provide annual information about its beneficiaries to the relevant tax authorities in the foreign country in which it is established or operates, or such information must otherwise be available to the relevant tax authorities in the foreign country in which it is established or operates.

(B) *Information to be provided.*—An eligible fund is treated as satisfying the requirement of paragraph (c)(2)(iv)(A)(2) of this section only if the eligible fund annually provides to the relevant tax authorities in the foreign country in which it is established or operates the amount of qualified benefits provided to each qualified recipient by the eligible fund (if any), or such information is otherwise available to such relevant tax authorities. An eligible fund is not treated as failing to satisfy the requirement of paragraph (c)(2)(iv)(A)(2) of this section as a result of the eligible fund not being required to provide information to the relevant tax authorities in a year in which no qualified benefits are provided to qualified recipients.

(C) *Relevant tax authorities.*—An eligible fund is treated as satisfying the requirement of paragraph (c)(2)(iv)(A)(2) of this section if the eligible fund is required, pursuant to the laws of the foreign country in which it is established or operates, to provide the information described in paragraph (c)(2)(iv)(B) of this section to one or more

governmental units of the foreign country in which the eligible fund is created or organized, or if such information is otherwise available to one or more governmental units of the foreign country in which the eligible fund is created or organized.

(D) *Treatment of certain governmental units.*—An eligible fund that is described in paragraph (c)(2)(ii)(A)(1) of this section, but is not also described in paragraph (c)(2)(ii)(A)(2) of this section, is deemed to satisfy the requirements of paragraph (c)(2)(iv)(A) of this section.

(v) *Tax treatment.*—(A) *In general.*—The laws of the foreign country in which the eligible fund is established or operates must provide that, due to the status of the eligible fund as a retirement or pension fund, either—

(1) Contributions to the eligible fund that would otherwise be subject to tax under such laws are deductible or excluded from the gross income of the eligible fund or taxed at a reduced rate; or

(2) Taxation of any investment income of the eligible fund is deferred or excluded from the gross income of the eligible fund or such income is taxed at a reduced rate.

(B) *Income subject to preferential tax treatment.*—An eligible fund is treated as satisfying the requirement of paragraph (c)(2)(v)(A) of this section in a taxable year if, under the income tax laws of the foreign country in which the eligible fund is established or operates—

(1) At least 85 percent of the contributions to the eligible fund are subject to the tax treatment described in paragraph (c)(2)(v)(A)(1) of this section, or

(2) At least 85 percent of the investment income of the eligible fund is subject to the tax treatment described in paragraph (c)(2)(v)(A)(2) of this section.

(C) *Income not subject to tax.*—An eligible fund is treated as satisfying the requirement of paragraph (c)(2)(v)(A) of this section if the eligible fund is exempt from the income tax of the foreign country in which it is established and operates or the foreign country in which it is established and operates has no income tax.

(D) *Other preferential tax regimes.*—An eligible fund that does not receive the tax treatment described in either paragraphs (c)(2)(v)(A)(1) or (2) of this section is nonetheless treated as satisfying the requirement of paragraph (c)(2)(v)(A) of this section if the eligible fund establishes that each of the conditions described in paragraphs (c)(2)(v)(D)(1) and (2) of this section is satisfied:

(1) Under the laws of the country in which the eligible fund is established and operates, the eligible fund is subject to a preferential tax regime due to its status as a retirement or pension fund; and

(2) The preferential tax regime described in paragraph (c)(2)(v)(D)(1) of this section has a substantially similar effect as the tax treatment described in paragraphs (c)(2)(v)(A)(1) or (2) of this section.

(E) *Subnational jurisdictions.*—Solely for purposes of this paragraph (c)(2)(v), a reference to a foreign country does not include a reference to a state, province, or political subdivision of a foreign country.

(3) *Rules on the application of the requirements in paragraph (c)(2) of this section.*—(i) *In general.*—Except as provided in paragraph (c)(3)(ii) of this section, an organization or arrangement is treated as a single entity for purposes of determining whether the requirements of paragraph (c)(2) of this section are satisfied.

(ii) *Foreign status determined independently.*—Each person or governmental unit that is part of an organization or arrangement must independently satisfy the requirement of paragraph (c)(2)(i) of this section.

(iii) *Relevant income, assets, and functions.*—The determination of whether an eligible fund satisfies the requirements of paragraphs (c)(2)(ii) through (v) of this section is made solely with respect to the income and assets held by the eligible fund in one or more qualified segregated accounts, the qualified benefits funded by the qualified segregated accounts, the information reporting and regulation related to the qualified segregated accounts, and the qualified recipients whose benefits are funded by the qualified segregated accounts. For this purpose, all qualified segregated accounts maintained by an eligible fund are treated as a single qualified segregated account.

(d) *Definitions.*—The following definitions apply for purposes of this section.

(1) *Ancillary benefits.*—The term *ancillary benefits* means benefits payable upon the diagnosis of a terminal illness, death benefits,

disability benefits, medical benefits, unemployment benefits, or similar benefits.

(2) *Eligible fund.*—The term *eligible fund* means a trust, corporation, or other organization or arrangement that maintains one or more qualified segregated accounts.

(3) *Employer group.*—The term *employer group* means all individuals, trusts, partnerships, and corporations with a relationship to each other specified in section 267(b) or section 707(b).

(4) *Foreign country.*—The term *foreign country* means a country other than the United States. Except for purposes of paragraph (c)(2)(v) of this section, references in this section to a foreign country include references to a state, province, or political subdivision of a foreign country. Solely for purposes of this section, the Commonwealth of Puerto Rico and any possession of the United States are treated as a foreign country.

(5) *Governmental unit.*—The term *governmental unit* means any foreign government or part thereof, including any person, body, group of persons, organization, agency, bureau, fund, or instrumentality, however designated, of a foreign government.

(6) *Organization or arrangement.*—The term *organization or arrangement* means one or more trusts, corporations, governmental units, or employers.

(7) *Qualification date.*—The term *qualification date* means, with respect to an entity or governmental unit, the earliest date during an uninterrupted period ending on the date of the disposition or the distribution, as the case may be, in which the trust, corporation, governmental unit, or employer is a qualified foreign pension fund or a qualified controlled entity.

(8) *Qualified benefits.*—The term *qualified benefits* means retirement, pension, or ancillary benefits.

(9) *Qualified controlled entity.*—The term *qualified controlled entity* means a trust or corporation organized under the laws of a foreign country all of the interests of which are held by one or more qualified foreign pension funds directly or indirectly through one or more qualified controlled entities or partnerships.

(10) *Qualified foreign pension fund.*—The term *qualified foreign pension fund* means an eligible fund that satisfies the requirements of paragraph (c) of this section.

(11) *Qualified holder.*—(i) *In general.*—The term *qualified holder* means a qualified foreign pension fund or a qualified controlled entity.

(ii) *Limitation.*—Notwithstanding paragraph (d)(11)(i) of this section, a qualified holder does not include any trust, corporation, governmental unit, or employer that, at any time during the testing period, determined without regard to this paragraph (d)(11)(ii), was not a qualified foreign pension fund, a part of a qualified foreign pension fund, or a qualified controlled entity. The preceding sentence does not apply to an entity that owned no United States real property interests as of the qualification date.

(12) *Qualified recipient.*—(i) *In general.*—The term *qualified recipient* means—

(A) With respect to an eligible fund described in paragraph (c)(2)(ii)(A)(*1*) of this section, any person eligible to be treated as a participant or beneficiary of such eligible fund and any person designated by such participant or beneficiary to receive qualified benefits, and

(B) With respect to an eligible fund described in paragraph (c)(2)(ii)(A)(*2*) of this section, a current or former employee or any person designated by such current or former employee to receive qualified benefits.

(ii) *Special rule regarding automatic designation.*—For purposes of paragraph (d)(12)(i) of this section, a person is treated as designating another person to receive benefits if the other person is, by reason of such person's relationship or other status with respect to the first person, entitled to receive benefits pursuant to the contractual terms applicable to the eligible fund or pursuant to the laws of the foreign country in which the eligible fund is created or organized, whether or not the first person expressly designated such person as a beneficiary.

(13) *Qualified segregated account.*—(i) *In general.*—The term *qualified segregated account* means an identifiable pool of assets maintained for the sole purpose of funding qualified benefits to qualified recipients.

(ii) *Assets held by eligible funds.*—For purposes of paragraph (d)(13)(i) of this section, an identifiable pool of assets of an eligible fund is treated as maintained for the sole purpose of funding qualified benefits to qualified recipients only if the contractual terms applicable to the eligible fund or the laws of the foreign country in which the eligible fund is established or operates require that all the assets in the pool, and all the income earned with respect to such assets, be used exclusively to fund the provision of qualified benefits to qualified recipients or to satisfy necessary reasonable expenses of the eligible fund, and that such assets or income may not inure to the benefit of a person other than a qualified recipient. For this purpose, the fact that assets or income may inure to the benefit of a governmental unit by operation of escheat or similar laws is ignored.

(iii) *Assets held by qualified controlled entities.*—For purposes of paragraph (d)(13)(i) of this section, the assets of a qualified controlled entity are treated as an identifiable pool of assets maintained for the sole purpose of funding qualified benefits to qualified recipients only if both of the following requirements are satisfied:

(A) All of the net earnings of the qualified controlled entity are credited to its own account or to the qualified segregated account of a qualified foreign pension fund or another qualified controlled entity, with no portion of its income inuring to the benefit of a person other than a qualified recipient; and

(B) All of the assets of the qualified controlled entity, after satisfaction of liabilities to persons having interests in the entity solely as creditors, vest in a qualified segregated account of a qualified foreign pension fund or another qualified controlled entity upon dissolution.

(14) *Testing period.*—The term *testing period* means, with respect to a trust, corporation, governmental unit, or employer and a disposition described in section 897(a) or a distribution described in section 897(h), as the case may be, the shortest of—

(i) The period beginning on December 18, 2015, and ending on the date of the disposition or the distribution;

(ii) The ten-year period ending on the date of the disposition or the distribution; and

(iii) The period during which the entity (or its predecessor) was in existence.

(e) *Examples.*—This paragraph (e) provides examples that illustrate the rules of this section. The following examples do not illustrate the application of the applicable withholding rules, including sections 1445 and 1446 and the regulations thereunder. For the purposes of the examples in this paragraph (e), unless otherwise stated, the following facts are presumed. No person is entitled to more than five percent of any eligible fund's assets or income, taking into account the constructive ownership rules in paragraph (d)(2)(iii)(B) of this section. The limitation described in paragraph (d)(11)(ii) of this section does not apply to any entity.

(1) *Example 1. No legal entity*—(i) *Facts.* Country A establishes Retirement Plan for the sole purpose of providing retirement benefits to all citizens of Country A aged 65 or older. Retirement Plan is comprised of Asset Pool and Agency. Asset Pool is a group of accounts maintained on the balance sheet of the government of Country A. Pursuant to the laws of Country A, income and gain earned by Asset Pool is used solely to support the provision of retirement benefits by Retirement Plan. Agency is a Country A agency that administers the provision of benefits by Retirement Plan and manages Asset Pool's investments. Under the laws of Country A, investment income earned by Retirement Plan is not subject to Country A's income tax. In Year 1, Agency sells Property, which is an interest in real property located in the United States owned by Asset Pool, recognizing $100x of gain with respect to Property that would be subject to tax under section 897(a) unless paragraph (b) of this section applies with respect to the gain.

(ii) *Analysis.* (A) Retirement Plan, which is comprised of Asset Pool and Agency, is comprised of one or more governmental units described in paragraph (d)(5) of this section. Accordingly, Retirement Plan is an organization or arrangement described in paragraph (d)(6) of this section. Furthermore, Retirement Plan maintains a qualified segregated account in the form of Asset Pool, an identifiable pool of assets maintained for the sole purpose of funding retirement benefits to beneficiaries of the Retirement Fund (qualified recipients as defined in paragraph (d)(12)(i)(A) of this section). Therefore, Retirement Plan is an eligible fund within the meaning of paragraph (d)(2) of this section.

(B) In determining whether or not Retirement Plan is an eligible fund that satisfies the requirements of paragraph (c)(2) of this section and is treated as a qualified foreign pension fund, the rules of paragraph (c)(3) of this section apply. Accordingly, the activities of Asset Pool and Agency are integrated and treated as undertaken by a single entity to determine whether the requirements of paragraphs (c)(2)(ii) through (v) of this section are met. However, Asset Pool and Agency must independently satisfy the requirement of paragraph (c)(2)(i) of this section.

(C) Retirement Plan is comprised of Asset Pool and Agency, each of which is a governmental unit and treated as created or organized under the law of Country A for purposes of paragraph (c)(2)(i) of this section. Accordingly, Retirement Plan satisfies the requirement of paragraph (c)(2)(i) of this section.

(D) Retirement Plan is established by Country A to provide retirement benefits, which are qualified benefits described in paragraph (d)(8) of this section, to all citizens of Country A, who are qualified recipients described in paragraph (d)(12)(i)(A) of this section because they are eligible to be participants or beneficiaries of Retirement Plan. In addition, all of the benefits that Retirement Plan provides are qualified benefits provided to qualified recipients, and at least 85 percent of the benefits that Retirement Plan reasonably expects to provide are retirement or pension benefits. Accordingly, Retirement Plan satisfies the requirement of paragraph (c)(2)(ii) of this section.

(E) Retirement Plan provides retirement benefits to all citizens of Country A aged 65 or older, with no citizen entitled to more than five percent of Retirement Fund's assets or to more than five percent of the income of the eligible fund. Accordingly, Retirement Plan satisfies the requirement of paragraph (c)(2)(iii) of this section.

(F) Retirement Plan is comprised solely of governmental units within the meaning of paragraph (d)(5) of this section. Accordingly, under paragraph (c)(2)(iv)(D) of this section, Retirement Plan is treated as satisfying the requirements of paragraph (c)(2)(iv)(A) of this section.

(G) Investment income earned by Retirement Plan is not subject to income tax in Country A. Accordingly, Retirement Plan satisfies the requirement of paragraph (c)(2)(v) of this section.

(H) Because Retirement Plan satisfies the requirements of paragraphs (c)(2)(i) through (v) of this section, Retirement Plan is a qualified foreign pension fund as defined in paragraph (d)(10) of this section. Because Retirement Plan is a qualified foreign pension fund and the limitation described in paragraph (d)(11)(ii) of this section does not apply, Retirement Plan is a qualified holder. Retirement Plan's gain with respect to Property is attributable solely to Asset Pool, a qualified segregated account maintained by Retirement Plan. Accordingly, under paragraph (b) of this section, the $100x gain recognized by Retirement Plan attributable to the disposition of Property is not subject to section 897(a).

(2) *Example 2. Fund established by an employer*—(i) *Facts.* Employer, a corporation organized in Country B, establishes Fund to provide retirement benefits to current and former employees of Employer and S1, a Country B corporation that is wholly owned by Employer. Fund is established as a trust under the law of Country B, and Employer retains discretion to invest assets and to administer benefits on Fund's behalf. Fund receives contributions from Employer and contributions from employees that are beneficiaries of Fund. All contributions to Fund and all of Fund's earnings are separately accounted for on Fund's books and records and are required by Fund's organizational documents to exclusively fund the provision of benefits to Fund's beneficiaries, except as necessary to satisfy reasonable expenses of the Fund. Fund currently has over 100 beneficiaries, a number that is reasonably expected to grow as Employer expands. Fund will pay benefits to employees upon retirement based on years of service and employee contributions, but, if a beneficiary dies before retirement, Fund will pay a death benefit to the beneficiary's designee (or deemed designee under local law if the beneficiary fails to identify a beneficiary). It is reasonably expected that such death benefits will account for less than fifteen percent of the present value of the qualified benefits that Fund expects to provide in the future. Fund annually provides to the tax authorities of Country B the amount of qualified benefits distributed to each participant (or designee). Country B's tax authorities prescribe rules and regulations governing Fund's operations. Under the laws of Country B, Fund is not taxed on its investment income.

(ii) *Analysis.* (A) Fund is a trust that maintains an identifiable pool of assets for the sole purpose of funding retirement and ancillary benefits to current and former employees of Employer (qualified recipients as defined in paragraph (d)(12)(i)(B) of this section). All assets held by Fund, and all income earned by Fund, are used to provide such benefits. Therefore, Fund is a trust that maintains a qualified segregated account within the meaning of paragraph (d)(13) of this section. Accordingly, Fund is an eligible fund within the meaning of paragraph (d)(2) of this section.

(B) Because Fund is created or organized under the law of Country B, Fund satisfies the requirement of paragraph (c)(2)(i) of this section.

(C) All of the benefits provided by Fund are qualified benefits because the only benefits that Fund provides are pension or retirement benefits or ancillary benefits described in paragraph (d)(1) of this section, which are qualified benefits described in paragraph (d)(8) of this section, to qualified recipients. Furthermore, Fund reasonably anticipates that more than 85 percent of the present value of benefits paid to qualified participants will be retirement or pension benefits. Accordingly, Fund is established by Employer to provide retirement or pension benefits to qualified recipients in consideration

for services rendered by such qualified recipients to such employers, and Fund satisfies the requirement of paragraph (c)(2)(ii) of this section.

(D) No single qualified recipient has a right to more than five percent of the assets or income of the eligible fund. Accordingly, Fund satisfies the requirement of paragraph (c)(2)(iii) of this section.

(E) Fund is regulated and annually provides to the relevant tax authorities in the foreign country in which it is established or operates the amount of qualified benefits provided to each qualified recipient by the eligible fund. Accordingly, Fund satisfies the requirements of paragraph (c)(2)(iv) of this section.

(F) Fund is not subject to income tax on its investment income. Accordingly, Fund satisfies the requirement of paragraph (c)(2)(v) of this section.

(G) Because Fund meets the requirements of paragraph (c)(2) of this section, Fund is treated as a qualified foreign pension fund described in paragraph (d)(10) of this section. As a qualified foreign pension fund with respect to which the limitation described in paragraph (d)(11)(ii) of this section does not apply, Fund is a qualified holder. All of Fund's assets are held in a qualified segregated account within the meaning of paragraph (d)(13) of this section. Consequently, under paragraph (b) of this section, any gain or loss of Fund from the disposition of a United States real property interest, including any distribution treated as gain from the disposition of a United States real property interest under section 897(h), is not subject to section 897(a).

(3) *Example 3. Employer controlled group*—(i) *Facts.* The facts are the same as in *Example 2*, except that S2, a Country B corporation that is wholly owned by Employer, performs all tax compliance functions for Employer, S1, and S2, including information reporting with respect to Fund participants.

(ii) *Analysis.* For purposes of testing the requirements of paragraph (c)(2) of this section, Fund and S2 are an organization or arrangement that is treated as a single entity under paragraph (c)(3)(i) of this section and an eligible fund under (d)(2) of this section with respect to the qualified segregated account held by Fund. Because the eligible fund comprised of Fund and S2 satisfies the requirements of paragraph (c)(2) of this section (including the requirement under paragraph (c)(3)(ii) of this section that each entity satisfy the foreign organization requirement of paragraph (c)(2)(i) of this section), the eligible fund that is comprised of Fund and S2 constitutes a qualified foreign pension fund described in paragraph (d)(10) of this section. Thus, under paragraph (b) of this section, gain or loss of Fund from the disposition of a United States real property interest, including any distribution treated as gain from the disposition of a United States real property interest under section 897(h), is not subject to section 897(a).

(4) *Example 4. Third-party assumption of pension liabilities*—(i) *Facts.* The facts are the same as in *Example 2*, except that Fund anticipates $100x of qualified benefits will be paid each year beginning in Year 5. Fund enters into an agreement with Guarantor, a privately held Country B corporation, which provides that Fund will, in Year 1, cede a portion of its assets to Guarantor in exchange for annual payments of $100x beginning in Year 5 and continuing until one or more previously identified participants (and their designees) ceases to be eligible to receive benefits. Guarantor has discretion to invest the ceded assets as it chooses, subject to certain agreed upon investment restrictions. Pursuant to its agreement with Fund, Guarantor must maintain Segregated Pool, a pool of assets securing its obligations under its agreement with Fund. The value of Segregated Pool must exceed a specified amount (determined based on an agreed upon formula) until Guarantor's payment obligations are completed, and any remaining assets in Segregated Pool (that is, assets exceeding the required payments to Fund) are retained by Guarantor. Guarantor bears all investment risk with respect to Segregated Pool. Accordingly, Guarantor is required to make annual payments of $100x to Fund regardless of the performance of Segregated Pool. In Year 2, Guarantor purchases stock in Company A, a United States real property holding company that is a United States real property interest, and holds the Company A stock in Segregated Pool. In Year 4, Guarantor sells the stock in Company A, realizing a gain of $100x.

(ii) *Analysis.* The Segregated Pool is not a qualified segregated account, because it is not maintained for the sole purpose of funding qualified benefits to qualified recipients, and because income attributable to assets in the Segregated Pool (including the Company A stock) may inure to Guarantor, which is not a qualified recipient. Accordingly, Fund and Guarantor do not qualify as an organization or arrangement that is an eligible fund with respect to the Company A stock. Therefore, Guarantor is not exempt under paragraph (b) of this section with respect to the $100x of gain realized in connection with the sale of its shares in Company A.

(5) *Example 5. Asset manager*—(i) *Facts.* The facts are the same as in *Example 4* except that instead of ceding legal ownership of the assets to Guarantor, Fund transfers assets to Guarantor to be held in Trust on behalf of Fund. Guarantor has exclusive management au-

thority over the assets, and is entitled to a reasonable fixed management fee which it withdraws annually from Trust's assets.

(ii) *Analysis*. Assets held by Fund, including its interest in Trust, are treated as held by Fund, a qualified holder within the meaning of paragraph (d)(11) of this section, in a qualified segregated account within the meaning of paragraph (d)(13) of this section. Paragraph (d)(13)(ii) of this section provides that the assets of the qualified segregated account may be used to satisfy reasonable expenses of the eligible fund, such that the reasonable fixed management fee paid to Guarantor does not cause the assets held in Trust to fail to be treated as held in a qualified segregated account. Consequently, the limitation of paragraph (b)(2) of this section does not apply and Fund Guarantor is exempt under paragraph (b) of this section with respect to the $100x of gain realized in connection with the sale of its shares in Company A.

(6) *Example 6. Partnership*—(i) *Facts*. The facts are the same as in *Example 4* except that instead of ceding legal ownership of the assets to Guarantor, Fund contributes the assets to a partnership (PRS) formed with Guarantor. Guarantor contributes nominal capital to the partnership, but receives a profits interest in the partnership that is reasonable in light of the Guarantor's management activity. Guarantor serves as the general partner of PRS and has discretionary authority to buy and sell PRS assets without approval from Fund.

(ii) *Analysis*. All of Fund's assets, including the partnership interest, are held in a qualified segregated account within the meaning of paragraph (d)(13) of this section. See *Example 2*, paragraph (ii)(A) of this section. Accordingly, Fund is exempt under paragraph (b) of this section with respect to gain or loss from the disposition of a United States real property interest, including any distribution treated as gain from the disposition of a United States real property interest under section 897(h), that is allocable to Fund from PRS. Guarantor is not exempt under paragraph (b) of this section with respect to gain or loss allocable to Guarantor from PRS.

(7) *Example 7. Wholly-owned entity*—(i) *Facts*. Fund is a qualified foreign pension fund organized in Country C that meets the requirements of paragraph (c)(2) of this section. Fund owns all the outstanding stock of OpCo, a manufacturing corporation organized in Country C, in a qualified segregated account maintained by Fund. Fund originally formed OpCo on January 1, 2016, for the purpose of conducting the manufacturing business and utilizing the business profits to fund pension liabilities. OpCo either retains or distributes to Fund all of its net earnings, and upon dissolution, must distribute all of its assets to stockholders after satisfaction of liabilities to its creditors. Fund has held all of the stock of OpCo since OpCo was formed. On June 1, 2017, OpCo realizes $100 of gain on the disposition of Property A, a United States real property interest.

(ii) *Analysis*. (A) A qualified holder described in paragraph (d)(11) of the section includes a qualified controlled entity described in paragraph (d)(9) of this section. A qualified controlled entity includes any corporation organized under the laws of a foreign country all the interests of which are owned by one or more qualified foreign pension funds directly or indirectly through one or more qualified controlled entities. Fund is a qualified foreign pension fund that wholly owns OpCo. Accordingly, OpCo is a qualified controlled entity.

(B) A qualified controlled entity is a qualified holder under paragraph (d)(11) of this section, but only if the qualified controlled entity was a qualified controlled entity throughout the entire testing period. The testing period under paragraph (d)(14) of this section is the shortest of the period beginning on December 18, 2015, and ending on the date of the disposition or the distribution; the ten-year period ending on the date of the disposition or the distribution; or the period during which the entity was in existence. Thus, the testing period is January 1, 2016 (the date of formation) to June 1, 2017 (the date of the disposition). Because OpCo was a qualified controlled entity as defined in paragraph (d)(9) of this section at all times during that period, the limitation in paragraph (d)(11)(ii) of this section does not apply to OpCo, and OpCo is a qualified holder under paragraph (d)(11) of this section.

(C) Under paragraph (b)(2) of this section, only gain or loss attributable to a qualified segregated account is exempt under section 897(l). All of OpCo's net earnings are credited to its own account or distributed to Fund and credited to Fund's qualified segregated account. Upon dissolution, all of OpCo's assets, after satisfaction of liabilities to persons having interests in the entity solely as creditors, would be distributed to OpCo's sole shareholder, Fund, and credited to Fund's qualified segregated account. Accordingly, all of OpCo's assets constitute a qualified segregated account. Therefore, the limitation in paragraph (b)(2) of this section does not apply, and the $100x gain realized by OpCo, a qualified holder, from the disposition of Property A on June 1, 2017, is not subject to tax under section 897(a).

(8) *Example 8. Not a qualified holder*—(i) *Facts*. The facts are the same as in *Example 7*, except that Opco was formed by a person other than Fund on January 1, 2016, and Fund acquired all the stock of OpCo on November 1, 2016. During the period from January 1, 2016, and October 31, 2016, Opco was not a qualified foreign pension fund, a part of a qualified foreign pension fund, or a qualified controlled entity. OpCo owned Property A before November 1, 2016.

(ii) *Analysis*. Under paragraph (d)(11)(ii) of this section, a qualified holder does not include any entity that was not a qualified foreign pension fund, a part of a qualified foreign pension fund, or a qualified controlled entity at any time during the testing period. The testing period with respect to OpCo is the period from January 1, 2016 (the date of formation of OpCo) to June 1, 2017 (the date of the disposition). Because OpCo was not a qualified foreign pension fund, a part of a qualified foreign pension fund, or a qualified controlled entity from January 1, 2016 to November 1, 2016, OpCo was not a qualified foreign pension fund, a part of a qualified foreign pension fund, or a qualified controlled entity at all times during the testing period. Accordingly, OpCo is not a qualified holder with respect to the disposition of Property A, and the $100x of gain recognized by OpCo is not exempt from tax under section 897(l), regardless of the amount of unrealized gain in Property A as of November 1, 2016.

(f) *Applicability date.*—(1) *In general.*—Except as otherwise provided in paragraph (f)(2) of this section, this section applies to a disposition of a United States real property interest, or a distribution described in section 897(h), occurring on or after the date of publication of the Treasury decision adopting these rules as final regulations in the **Federal Register**.

(2) *Certain Provisions.*—Paragraphs (b)(1), (d)(5), (7), (9), (11), and (14) of this section apply with respect to dispositions of United States real property interests and distributions described in section 897(h) occurring on or after June 6, 2019. [Reg. § 1.897(l)-1.]

Foreign Corporations: Tax Years

Foreign Corporations: Tax Years.—Reproduced below are the texts of proposed Reg. §§ 1.898-0—1.898-4, relating to the required taxable year of those foreign corporations beginning after July 10, 1989 (published in the Federal Register on January 5, 1993). See below for a proposed amendment to proposed Reg. § 1.898-4.

☐ Par. 6. Sections 1.898-0—1.898-4 are added as follows:

§ 1.898-0. Outline of regulations for section 898.—This section lists the major paragraphs contained in §§ 1.898-1 through 1.898-4.

§ 1.898-1. Taxable year of certain foreign corporations.
  (a) In general.
  (b) Effective dates.
  (c) Exceptions to section 898.
    (1) Specified foreign corporations with no section 951(a) or foreign personal holding company income.
    (2) Elections to be treated as domestic corporations.

§ 1.898-2. Definition of specified foreign corporation.
  (a) In general.
  (b) Ownership requirements.
    (1) In general.
    (2) Ownership by attribution.
    (3) Definition of United States shareholder.
      (i) In general.
      (ii) Certain captive insurance companies.
      (iii) Foreign personal holding companies

    (4) Illustrations.
  (c) Special rule for foreign personal holding companies that are not controlled foreign corporations.
    (1) In general.
    (2) Illustrations.

§ 1.898-3. Determining the required year.
  (a) Controlled foreign corporations.
    (1) In general.
    (2) One-month deferral election.
    (3) Majority U.S. shareholder year.
      (i) In general.
      (ii) Passthrough entities.
    (4) Inconsistent majority U.S. shareholder years.
      (i) In general.
      (ii) Formula for determining least aggregate deferral.
      (iii) Illustrations.
      (iv) Procedural requirements and effective date.
    (5) Testing days.

(i) In general.

(ii) Illustration.

(iii) Additional testing days.

(iv) Illustration.

(v) Anti-abuse rule.

(b) Foreign personal holding companies.

(1) In general.

(2) One-month deferral election not available.

(3) Testing days.

§ 1.898-4. Special rules.

(a) Changes in the required year of a specified foreign corporation for its first taxable year beginning after July 10, 1989.

(1) In general.

(2) Procedure for a specified foreign corporation to conform to the required year for the first taxable year beginning after July 10, 1989.

(i) No section 898(c)(1)(B) election.

(ii) With section 898(c)(1)(B) election.

(iii) Filing requirement.

(b) Changes in the required year of a specified foreign corporation during a taxable year of a specified foreign corporation subsequent to its first taxable year beginning after July 10, 1989.

(1) In general.

(2) Procedure for the change to a new required year of a specified foreign corporation for taxable years subsequent to its first taxable year beginning after July 10, 1989.

(i) Different majority shareholder year.

(ii) Election under section 898(c)(1)(B).

(iii) Procedure for prior years.

(iv) Making a second election under section 898(c)(1) (B).

(v) Procedure for obtaining the consent of the Commissioner to change the required year of specified foreign corporations.

(3) Short period.

(i) In general.

(ii) Illustrations.

(4) Conforming changes in the majority U.S. shareholder year.

(c) Nonconforming foreign and United States taxable years of a specified foreign corporation.

(1) In general.

(2) Computation of income and earnings and profits of a specified foreign corporation.

(i) Separate books of account.

(ii) Income and earnings and profits computation in lieu of separate books.

(iii) Illustration.

(3) 52-53-week taxable year.

(i) In general.

(ii) Majority United States shareholder with a 52-53 week taxable year.

(iii) Specified foreign corporation with a 52-53 week taxable year.

(iv) Illustrations.

(4) Certain captive insurance companies that elect to treat their related person insurance income as income effectively connected with the conduct of a United States trade or business.

(d) Four-year income spread.

[Reg. § 1.898-0.]

§1.898-1. Taxable year of certain foreign corporations.—(a) *In general.*—Pursuant to section 898(a), the taxable year of a specified foreign corporation is the required year. The required year is generally the majority U.S. shareholder year. These regulations define specified foreign corporation and United States shareholder, for purposes of these rules, at §1.898-2(a) and (b)(3), respectively. The ownership requirements of a specified foreign corporation, which are a part of the definition of specified foreign corporation, are set forth at §1.898-2 (b)(1) and (2). A special rule for determining whether a foreign corporation that meets the ownership requirements of a foreign personal holding company is a specified foreign corporation is located at §1.898-2(c). Section 1.898-3 sets forth the rules for the determination of the required year, including rules by which a specified foreign corporation that is a controlled foreign corporation may elect a taxable year beginning one month earlier than the majority U.S. shareholder year. Section 1.898-4 sets forth special rules including rules at paragraphs (a) and (b) of that section on changes in the required year, rules at paragraph (c) of that section covering situations where the required year under section 898 is different from the specified foreign corporation's foreign taxable year (the taxable year for purposes of computing income tax liabilities due a foreign country), and rules at paragraph (d) of that section regarding the four-year spread of certain income.

(b) *Effective dates.*—Sections 1.898-1 through 1.898-4 are effective for taxable years of specified foreign corporations beginning after July 10, 1989. However, §§1.898-3 (a)(4)(regarding situations in which inconsistent majority U.S. shareholder years exist) and 1.898-3 (a)(5)(iii)(regarding situations in which additional testing days are required) are effective for taxable years beginning after [INSERT DATE 120 DAYS AFTER DATE OF PUBLICATION OF FINAL REGULATIONS IN THE FEDERAL REGISTER], and section 1.898-4 (b) is effective for changes in the required year of a specified foreign corporation subsequent to its first taxable year beginning after July 10, 1989.

(c) *Exceptions to section 898.*—(1) *Specified foreign corporations with no section 951(a) or foreign personal holding company income.*—A specified foreign corporation is not required to conform its taxable year to the required year so long as its United States shareholders do not have any amount includible in gross income pursuant to section 951(a) and do not receive any actual or deemed distributions attributable to amounts described in section 553 with respect to that corporation. Once any United States shareholder of that specified foreign corporation has any amount includible in gross income pursuant to section 951(a) or receives any actual or deemed distributions attributable to amounts described in section 553 with respect to that corporation, then the specified foreign corporation must comply with section 898 and §§1.898-3 and 1.898-4 beginning with its first taxable year subsequent to the taxable year to which that shareholder's income is attributable. Once the specified foreign corporation is required to conform its taxable year to the required year, the fact that the shareholders of the corporation cease to have any such amount includible in gross income pursuant to section 951(a) or section 553 is not relevant. Section 898 continues to apply.

(2) *Elections to be treated as domestic corporations.*—A foreign corporation that is a foreign insurance company and that elects to be treated as a domestic corporation pursuant to section 953(d) is treated as a domestic corporation for all purposes of the Code and, thus, is not subject to section 898. Likewise, a foreign corporation organized under the laws of a contiguous foreign country and described in section 1504(d) is not subject to section 898 if the foreign corporation is treated as a domestic corporation in accordance with section 1504(d). [Reg. §1.898-1.]

§1.898-2. Definition of specified foreign corporation.—(a) *In general.*—For purposes of section 898 and §§1.898-1 through 1.898-4, a specified foreign corporation means any foreign corporation with respect to which the ownership requirements of section 898(b)(2) and paragraph (b) of this section are met and which either is treated as a controlled foreign corporation for any purpose under sections 951 through 964 of the Code (including sections 957(a), 957(b) and 953(c)), or is a foreign personal holding company, as defined in section 552.

(b) *Ownership requirements.*—(1) *In general.*—The ownership requirements of section 898(b)(2) and this paragraph (b)(1) are met with respect to any foreign corporation if a United States shareholder owns, or is considered to own by applying the attribution rules set forth in paragraph (b)(2) of this section, on each testing day, more than 50 percent of the total voting power of all classes of stock of the foreign corporation entitled to vote, or more than 50 percent of the total value of all classes of stock of the foreign corporation.

(2) *Ownership by attribution.*—For purposes of section 898(b)(2)(A) and paragraph (b)(1) of this section, the rules contained in the following sections of the Internal Revenue Code apply in determining ownership—

(i) Section 958(a) and (b) for determining direct, indirect, and constructive stock ownership of a controlled foreign corporation;

(ii) Section 551(f) pertaining to the stock of a foreign personal holding company held through a foreign entity; and,

(iii) Section 554 for determining stock ownership of a foreign personal holding company.

(3) *Definition of United States shareholder.*—(i) *In general.*—For purposes of §§1.898-1 through 1.898-4, United States shareholder has the meaning given to it by section 951(b), except that, in the case of a foreign corporation having related person insurance income, as defined in section 953(c)(2), a person will be treated as a United States shareholder for purposes of section 898 if that person is treated as a United States shareholder under section 953(c)(1). *See* section 898(b)(3)(A).

(ii) *Certain captive insurance companies.*—The determination of whether certain shareholders are United States shareholders under section 953(c)(1) and, consequently, whether the foreign corporation is a controlled foreign corporation for a particular taxable year, depends on the proportion of related person insurance income to total insurance income earned by the foreign corporation during the taxable year. If the related person insurance income of the foreign corporation is less than 20 percent of its total insurance income for the year, then the special rules of section 953(c) for captive insurance companies will not apply. The determination of whether the related person insurance income of a foreign corporation is less than 20 percent of its total insurance income for a particular taxable year cannot be made until the end of that year. Consequently, a foreign corporation that derives related person insurance income generally will not be required to consider non-10 percent United States shareholders (*i.e.*, persons who are United States shareholders only because of the special captive insurance rules) in determining whether it is a controlled foreign corporation on the first day of the foreign corporation's taxable year to determine further whether it is a specified foreign corporation and, therefore, subject to section 898, unless the foreign corporation was treated as a controlled foreign corporation because of the special captive insurance rules for the immediately preceding taxable year. When a foreign corporation is both a captive insurance company and a specified foreign corporation, it must consider all persons who are United States shareholders under both sections 951(b) and 953(c) in determining its required year.

(iii) *Foreign personal holding companies.*—In the case of any foreign personal holding company as defined in section 552, which is not also a specified foreign corporation by reason of being a controlled foreign corporation under section 898(b)(1)(A)(i), United States shareholder means any person who is treated as a United States shareholder under section 551(a).

(4) *Illustrations.*—The application of this paragraph (b) may be illustrated by the following examples:

Example 1. Z is a publicly traded United States corporation that owns all of the outstanding stock of FY, a foreign corporation. FY is not a foreign personal holding company. FY owns 51 percent (of both voting power and value) of all of the outstanding stock of FX, which is also a foreign corporation. The remainder of the stock is owned by an unrelated foreign corporation. FY is a controlled foreign corporation and a specified foreign corporation. In addition, pursuant to section 958(a)(2), Z is considered to own its proportionate share (*i.e.*, 51 percent) of the stock of FX which is owned by FY. Thus, FX is also both a controlled foreign corporation and [a] specified foreign corporation, as defined in section 898(b) and this section.

Example 2. Z is a United States citizen who owns 51 percent of the value, but none of the voting stock, of FY, a foreign corporation. The remaining 49 percent of the value of FY, as well as all of FY's voting stock, is owned by a nonresident alien individual who is not related to Z. FY owns 51 percent (of both voting power and value) of all of the outstanding stock of FX, which is also a foreign corporation. FY is not a controlled foreign corporation because it does not have a United States shareholder within the meaning of section 951(b)(although if FY had related person insurance income it may be a controlled foreign corporation under the rules of section 953(c)). FY was a foreign personal holding company for its prior year. FY is a foreign personal holding company and a specified foreign corporation for the current year for purposes of section 898 because Z is a United States shareholder within the meaning of section 551(a) who owns 51 percent of the total value of the stock of FY. *See* section 552(a)(2)(B). Under section 551(f), however, the stock of FX owned by FY is not treated as being owned proportionately by Z. Accordingly, FX is not subject to section 898.

Example 3. FX has 20 equal shareholders, all of whom are related United States persons. Thus, FX does not qualify as a controlled foreign corporation under the general subpart F rules applicable to insurance companies because none of the United States persons are United States shareholders. However, if FX earns related person insurance income in a particular taxable year, then it will be considered a controlled foreign corporation for that year, unless the amount of the related person insurance income was less than 20 percent of its total insurance income for that year. If, in its taxable year ending December 31, 1990, FX earns related person insurance income in an amount that is less than 20 percent of its total insurance income and, thus, is not considered a controlled foreign corporation, then FX would not be required to determine its required year on January 1, 1991. Alternatively, if FX earns related person insurance income in its taxable year ending December 31, 1990, in excess of the 20 percent *de minimis* amount and, thus, is considered a controlled foreign corporation, FX would be required to determine whether it is a specified foreign corporation on January 1, 1991, and in making that determination, would be required to treat all United States persons owning its stock as United States shareholders.

(c) *Special rule for foreign personal holding companies that are not controlled foreign corporations.*—(1) *In general.*—A foreign corporation that is not a controlled foreign corporation for 30 days or more during the current taxable year will be required to determine whether it is a specified foreign corporation on any testing day during the current year only if the foreign corporation—

(i) meets the ownership requirements of section 552(a)(2)(ownership requirements for a foreign personal holding company) for the current taxable year, and

(ii) was a foreign personal holding company for its taxable year immediately preceding the current taxable year.

(2) *Illustrations.*—The application of this paragraph (c) may be illustrated by the following examples:

Example 1. (i) FX is a foreign corporation that uses the calendar year as its taxable year. For calendar year 1989, its last taxable year beginning before the effective date of section 898, FX met the stock ownership requirements of section 552(a)(2) for a foreign personal holding company. More than 50 percent of the total value of all classes of stock of FX is owned by Y, a United States shareholder with a taxable year ending June 30. The remaining value of FX stock, and all of FX's voting stock, is owned by Z, a nonresident alien individual who is unrelated to Y. FX is not a controlled foreign corporation.

(ii) On January 1, 1990 (FX's first testing day after the effective date of section 898), FX examined its gross income for the taxable year ending December 31, 1989. FX met the gross income requirement of section 552(a)(1) for a foreign personal holding company for that year. Therefore, under the rules of this paragraph (c), FX was deemed to be a foreign personal holding company, for purposes of section 898, for the current taxable year beginning January 1, 1990. Accordingly, FX was required to determine whether it was a specified foreign corporation on January 1, 1990. FX was a specified foreign corporation on that date and, therefore, was required to change its taxable year to the required year ending on June 30.

Example 2. The facts are the same as in *Example 1*, with the additional fact that FX did not meet the gross income requirement for a foreign personal holding company for the short taxable year beginning January 1, 1990, and ending June 30, 1990. Nevertheless, FX will be required to maintain a taxable year beginning July 1, 1990, as its required year under section 898(c). [Reg. § 1.898-2.]

§1.898-3. Determining the required year.—(a) *Controlled foreign corporations.*—(1) *In general.*—The required year is the majority U.S. shareholder year prescribed in section 898(c)(1)(C) and paragraph (a)(3) of this section. If, however, there are inconsistent majority U.S. shareholder years, then the required year is the taxable year prescribed in section 898(c)(1)(A)(ii) and paragraph (a)(4) of this section.

(2) *One-month deferral election.*—A specified foreign corporation that is a controlled foreign corporation may elect under section 898(c)(1)(B) and § 1.898-4(a)(2)(ii) and (b)(2)(ii) of this section a taxable year beginning one month earlier than the majority U.S. shareholder year. The specified foreign corporation may revoke this election; see § 1.898-4(b). If the specified foreign corporation revokes the election, it may re-elect the one-month deferral only if it follows the procedures set forth in § 1.898-4(b)(2)(iv) and (v). A specified foreign corporation that is a foreign personal holding company, but is not a controlled foreign corporation, may not make this election. Also, this election may not be made by a specified foreign corporation that is a controlled foreign corporation, but whose required year is the taxable year prescribed by section 898(c)(1)(A)(ii) and paragraph (a)(4) of this section because there are inconsistent majority U.S. shareholder years.

(3) *Majority U.S. shareholder year.*—(i) *In general.*—For the purpose of determining the required year of a specified foreign corporation, the majority U.S. shareholder year under section 898(c)(1)(C)(i) means the taxable year (if any) which, on each testing day as defined in paragraph (a)(5) of this section, constitutes the taxable year of a United States shareholder described in either paragraph (a)(3)(i)(A) or (B) of this section.

(A) Each United States shareholder, as defined in section 898(b)(3)(A) and § 1.898-2(b)(3), that owns more than 50 percent of the voting power of all classes of stock of the specified foreign corporation entitled to vote, or more than 50 percent of the total value of all classes of stock of the specified foreign corporation, after application of the attribution rules of section 898(b)(2)(B). This shareholder is described in section 898(b)(2)(A) and is referred to in this section as a "more than 50 percent United States shareholder."

(B) Each United States shareholder, as defined in section 898(b)(3)(A) and § 1.898-2(b)(3), that is not a more than 50 percent United States shareholder and whose stock was treated as owned under section 898(b)(2)(B) (the attribution rules) by a more than 50 percent United States shareholder.

(ii) *Passthrough entities.*—For the purpose of determining the required year of a specified foreign corporation, if each United States shareholder described in paragraph (a)(3)(i)(A) or (B) of this section is a passthrough entity, such as an S corporation, partnership, trust, or estate, then the majority U.S. shareholder year is the taxable year which, on a testing day, constitutes the taxable year of the passthrough entity and not the taxable year or years of the passthrough entity's shareholders, partners, or beneficiaries.

(4) *Inconsistent majority U.S. shareholder years.*—(i) *In general.*— There may exist more than one majority U.S. shareholder year under section 898(c)(1)(C)(i) and paragraph (a)(3) of this section because the taxable years of shareholders described in paragraph (a)(3)(i)(A) or (B) of this section may be different taxable years. If the majority U.S. shareholder years are inconsistent, then the specified foreign corporation must adopt the taxable year that results in the least aggregate deferral of income to all United States shareholders of the specified foreign corporation, even if that taxable year is not a majority U.S. shareholder year. See paragraph (a)(4)(iii), *Example* 2, of this section. If the required year is the taxable year prescribed by this paragraph (a)(4) because there are inconsistent majority U.S. shareholder years, then the one-month deferral election under section 898(c)(1)(B) and paragraph (a)(2) of this section is not available.

(ii) *Formula for determining least aggregate deferral.*—The aggregate deferral of income for a particular year is equal to the sum of the products determined by multiplying, on each testing day as defined in paragraph (a)(5) of this section, the number of month(s) of deferral for each United States shareholder, that are shareholders on the testing day, that would be generated by that year end by that United States shareholder's percentage interest in deemed distributions from the specified foreign corporation. The United States shareholder's taxable year that produces the lowest sum when compared to the other United States shareholders' taxable years is the taxable year that results in the least aggregate deferral of income to the United States shareholders. For purposes of this section, the number of months of deferral for a United States shareholder of a specified foreign corporation is measured by the number of months from the end of the taxable year of the specified foreign corporation to the end of the taxable year of the United States shareholder. Part of a month is treated as a month. If the calculation results in more than one taxable year qualifying as the taxable year with the least aggregate deferral, the specified foreign corporation may select any one of such taxable years as its required year. However, if one of such qualifying taxable years is also the specified foreign corporation's existing taxable year, the specified foreign corporation must maintain its existing taxable year.

(iii) *Illustrations.*—The application of this paragraph (a)(4) may be illustrated by the following examples:

Example 1. (i) FX is a foreign corporation with two classes of stock, only one of which is voting stock. Each class of stock shares equally in distributions. FX has a June 30 taxable year. FX's shareholders, A, B and C are U.S. citizens. A owns 45 percent of each class of stock, B owns 35 percent of each class of stock, and C owns the remaining 20 percent of each class of stock. A is B's grandfather and C is unrelated to A and B. A and C are calendar year taxpayers. B's taxable year ends on June 30. Under sections 958(b)(1) and 318(a)(1)(A), A is considered to own the stock owned by B. Under section 898(c)(1)(C)(i) (I), A is a more than 50 percent United States shareholder and under section 898(c)(1)(C)(i)(II), B is a United States shareholder whose stock is considered to be owned by a more than 50 percent United States shareholder. Accordingly, FX has two majority U.S. shareholder years, the calendar year and the fiscal year ending June 30. These majority U.S. shareholder years are inconsistent.

(ii) Beginning July 1, 1990, the first day of FX's first taxable year beginning after July 10, 1989, FX must conform its taxable year to the required year by adopting the taxable year that results in the least aggregate deferral of income, taking into consideration the taxable year of each United States shareholder, including C. The taxable year ending December 31 produces .35 × 6 (B's percentage share of distributions from FX multiplied by the number of months of deferral if December 31 is the required year), or a product of 2.1. The taxable year ending June 30 produces [.45 × 6] plus [.20 × 6] (A and C's percentage shares of distributions from FX multiplied by the number of months of deferral if June 30 is the required year), or a product of 3.9. Accordingly, the taxable year ending December 31 is the required year. However, if C's year end were also June 30, or if only the nonvoting stock shared in distributions and B owned all of the nonvoting stock, then the taxable year ending June 30 would produce the least aggregate deferral of income, and would be the required year.

Example 2. (i) LX is a calendar year foreign corporation with one class of stock. LX's shareholders, A, B and C are U.S. citizens. A is B's grandfather and C is unrelated to A and B. A owns 10 percent of LX's stock and has a taxable year ending June 30. B owns 45 percent of LX's stock and has a taxable year ending March 31. C owns the remaining 45 percent of LX and has a September 30 taxable year. Under sections 958(b)(1) and 318(a)(1) (A), A is considered to own the stock owned by B. Under section 898(c)(1)(C)(i)(I), A is a more than 50 percent United States shareholder and under section 898(c)(1)(C) (i)(II), B is a United States shareholder whose stock is considered to be owned by a more than 50 percent United States shareholder. Accordingly, LX has two inconsistent majority U.S.

shareholder years, the fiscal year ending June 30 and the fiscal year ending March 31.

(ii) Beginning January 1, 1990, the first day of LX's first taxable year beginning after July 10, 1989, LX must conform its taxable year to the required year by adopting the taxable year that results in the least aggregate deferral of income, taking into consideration the taxable year of each United States shareholder. The taxable year ending June 30 produces [.45 × 3] plus [.45 × 9] (B and C's, respective percentage shares of distributions multiplied by the number of months of deferral), or a product of 5.4. The taxable year ending March 31 produces [.1 × 9] plus [.45 × 6] (A and C's percentage shares of distributions multiplied by the number of months of deferral), or a product of 3.6. The taxable year ending September 30 produces [.1 × 3] plus [.45 × 6] (A and B's percentage shares of distributions multiplied by the number of months of deferral), or a product of 3.0. Accordingly, September 30 is the required year.

(iv) *Procedural requirements and effective date.*—This paragraph (a)(4) is effective for taxable years beginning after [INSERT DATE 120 DAYS AFTER DATE OF PUBLICATION OF FINAL REGULATIONS IN THE FEDERAL REGISTER]. In order to show that the requirements of this paragraph (a)(4) are satisfied, a statement setting forth the computations required to establish the taxable year that results in the least aggregate deferral of income to the United States shareholders of the specified foreign corporation must be attached to Form 5471 and, if applicable, to Form 1120F, and must indicate the following at the top of page one of the statement: "FILED UNDER § 1.898-3(a)(4)."

(5) *Testing days.*—(i) *In general.*—A specified foreign corporation must identify its majority U.S. shareholder year(s), if any, for the purpose of determining its required year. The specified foreign corporation must determine its majority U.S. shareholder year on each testing day. In general, the testing day is the first day of the specified foreign corporation's taxable year for U.S. tax purposes, determined without regard to section 898. *See* section 898(c)(1)(C)(ii).

(ii) *Illustration.*—The application of paragraph (a)(5)(i) of this section may be illustrated by the following example:

Example. FX is a foreign corporation that, prior to the effective date of section 898, used the calendar year as its taxable year. Thus, on January 1, 1990, the first day of FX's first taxable year beginning after July 10, 1989, FX determined whether it was a specified foreign corporation and, thus, required to change its taxable year to the required year under section 898(c). Based on this test, FX changed to a taxable year ending on June 30 (because FX was a specified foreign corporation and its majority U.S. shareholder year ends on June 30). Accordingly, FX had a short period taxable year for the period beginning January 1, 1990, and ending June 30, 1990. On July 1, 1990, the first day of its new taxable year, FX again tested to determine whether it was using the required year.

(iii) *Additional testing days.*—For taxable years of specified foreign corporations beginning after [INSERT DATE THAT IS 120 DAYS AFTER FINAL REGULATIONS ARE PUBLISHED IN THE FEDERAL REGISTER], a specified foreign corporation must determine its majority U.S. shareholder year on each day, since the most recent testing day described in paragraph (a) (5)(i) of this section, on which a substantial change occurs in the United States ownership of the stock of the specified foreign corporation. A substantial change in the United States ownership of the stock of a specified foreign corporation is a change that results in a new more than 50 percent United States shareholder of the foreign corporation.

(iv) *Illustration.*—The application of paragraph (a) (5)(iii) of this section may be illustrated by the following example:

Example. FX is a controlled foreign corporation with one class of stock and a taxable year ending on June 30. Y, the majority United States shareholder of FX, owns 51 percent of the stock of FX. Y also has a taxable year ending June 30. Thus, FX is a specified foreign corporation subject to section 898. On May 1, 1994, Y sold 10 percent of the stock in FX to Z, an unrelated United States corporation that owned 41 percent of the stock of FX before the sale. Z obtained, therefore, a sufficient amount of FX stock to qualify as a "more than 50 percent United States shareholder" of FX. Z has a taxable year ending on April 30. Consequently, on May 1, 1994, FX determined that its new required year was a taxable year ending April 30. FX has a taxable year ending June 30, 1994, and a short taxable year beginning July 1, 1994, and ending April 30, 1995. *See* § 1.898-4(b)(3).

(v) *Anti-abuse rule.*—The district director may require the use of a testing day other than that identified in paragraph (a)(5)(i) or (iii) of this section that will reflect more accurately the ownership of the specified foreign corporation and thereby the aggregate deferral of income to the United States shareholders of the specified foreign corporation where the United States shareholders engage in a transaction (or transactions) that has as its principal purpose the avoidance of the principles of this section. Thus, the anti-abuse rule of the preceding sentence would apply, for example, when there is a transfer of an interest in a specified foreign corporation that results in a temporary transfer of that interest principally for the purpose of qualifying for a specific taxable year under the principles of this section.

(b) *Foreign personal holding companies.*—(1) *In general.*—The required year is the majority U.S. shareholder year prescribed by section 898(c)(1)(A) and paragraph (a) (3) of this section. If, however, there are inconsistent majority U.S. shareholder years, then the required year is the taxable year determined under the provisions of paragraph (a)(4) of this section.

(2) *One-month deferral election not available.*—A specified foreign corporation that is a foreign personal holding company, but is not a controlled foreign corporation, may not make the one-month deferral election of paragraph (a)(2) of this section.

(3) *Testing days. See.*—paragraph (a)(5) of this section. [Reg. § 1.898-3.]

§ 1.898-4. Special rules.—(a) *Changes in the required year of a specified foreign corporation for its first taxable year beginning after July 10, 1989.*—(1) *In general.*—A specified foreign corporation must conform its taxable year to the required year as defined in section 898(c) for taxable years beginning after July 10, 1989. In addition, section 898(c)(1)(B) permits a specified foreign corporation that is a controlled foreign corporation to elect a taxable year beginning one month earlier than the majority U.S. shareholder year.

(2) *Procedure for a specified foreign corporation to conform to the required year for the first taxable year beginning after July 10, 1989.*—(i) *No section 898(c)(1)(B) election.*—If no election under section 898(c)(1)(B) can be made because the specified foreign corporation is a foreign personal holding company, or no election is being made for a specified foreign corporation that is a controlled foreign corporation, but the specified foreign corporation is changing its first taxable year beginning after July 10, 1989, to conform to the required year, then unless the instructions to the forms provide otherwise, the words "Change in Taxable Year" must be placed in the upper left hand corner of the first page of Form 5471 and, if applicable, on Form 1120F, with respect to the specified foreign corporation for the taxable year for which the change is made. If a specified foreign corporation is not required to change its taxable year, then no notation concerning this fact need appear on Form 5471 and, if applicable, on Form 1120F.

(ii) *With section 898(c)(1)(B) election.*—The election under section 898(c)(1)(B) may be made for a specified foreign corporation that is a controlled foreign corporation for its first taxable year beginning after July 10, 1989, by indicating on Form 5471 and, if applicable, on Form 1120F, that the taxable year shown on the form with respect to the controlled foreign corporation was determined in accordance with section 898(c)(1)(B). The following words must be used unless the instructions to the forms provide otherwise:

(A) If the election involves a change in the taxable year of the controlled foreign corporation, the words "Section 898(c)(1)(B) Election – Change in Taxable Year" must be placed in the upper left hand corner of the first page of Form 5471 and, if applicable, on Form 1120F; and

(B) If the election does not involve a change in the taxable year of the controlled foreign corporation, the words, "Section 898(c)(1)(B) Election" must be placed in the upper left hand corner of the first page of Form 5471 and, if applicable, on Form 1120.

(iii) *Filing requirement.*—If a specified foreign corporation changed its required year for its first taxable year beginning after July 10, 1989, to conform to the requirements of section 898 and § 1.898-3 but did not follow the procedures set forth in Rev. Proc. 90-26 and this paragraph (a)(2), a statement must be attached to the first Form 5471 and, if applicable, Form 1120F, to be filed after [INSERT DATE THAT IS 120 DAYS AFTER DATE OF PUBLICATION OF FINAL REGULATIONS IN THE FEDERAL REGISTER]indicating that the corporation's taxable year was changed to conform to the requirements of section 898. If a specified foreign corporation has not conformed its first taxable year beginning after July 10, 1989, to the taxable year required by section 898 and § 1.898-3, an amended return with an amended Form 5471 (or Form 1120F) must be filed to satisfy the requirements of section 898, § 1.898-3 and this paragraph (a)(2).

(b) *Changes in the required year of a specified foreign corporation during a taxable year of a specified foreign corporation subsequent to its first taxable year beginning after July 10, 1989.*—(1) *In general.*—A specified foreign corporation must conform its taxable year to a different required year should circumstances arise in which the required year changes under the rules of § 1.898-3, such as when a substantial

change in ownership of a specified foreign corporation results in a new more than 50 percent United States shareholder with a different majority U.S. shareholder year. The change in taxable year of a specified foreign corporation made to conform to a different required year shall be treated as initiated by the taxpayer and as having been made with the consent of the Commissioner. The requirements set forth in this paragraph (b) are effective for taxable years subsequent to a specified foreign corporation's first taxable year beginning after July 10, 1989.

(2) *Procedure for the change to a new required year of a specified foreign corporation for taxable years subsequent to its first taxable year beginning after July 10, 1989.*—(i) *Different majority U.S. shareholder year.*—If the specified foreign corporation is changing its taxable year to conform to a different required year under paragraph (b)(1) of this section, unless the instructions to the forms provide otherwise, the words "Change in Taxable Year" must be placed in the upper left hand corner of the first page of Form 5471 and, if applicable, on Form 1120F, with respect to the specified foreign corporation for the taxable year for which the change is made. This paragraph covers terminations of prior elections under section 898(c)(1)(B) made in conjunction with that change.

(ii) *Election under section 898(c)(1)(B).*—If the specified foreign corporation that is a controlled foreign corporation is changing its taxable year to conform to a different required year under paragraph (b) of this section and an election under section 898(c)(1)(B) is made, the change in taxable year and the election under section 898(c)(1)(B) are to be noted on Form 5471 and, if applicable, on Form 1120F, with respect to that corporation for the taxable year for which the change and election are made. Unless the instructions to the forms provide otherwise, the words "Section 898(c)(1)(B) Election – Change in Taxable Year" must be placed in the upper left hand corner of the first page of each form. This paragraph covers terminations of prior elections under section 898(c)(1)(B) made in conjunction with that election.

(iii) *Procedure for prior years.*—If a specified foreign corporation conformed its taxable year to that required by section 898 and § 1.898-3 prior to [INSERT DATE THAT IS 120 DAYS AFTER DATE OF PUBLICATION OF FINAL REGULATIONS IN THE FEDERAL REGISTER] but did not follow the procedures set forth in this paragraph (b)(2), a statement must be attached to the first Form 5471 and, if applicable, Form 1120F, to be filed after [INSERT DATE THAT IS 120 DAYS AFTER DATE OF PUBLICATION OF FINAL REGULATIONS IN THE FEDERAL REGISTER] indicating that the corporation's taxable year was changed to conform to the requirements of section 898 and § 1.898-3. If a specified foreign corporation has not conformed a taxable year subsequent to its first taxable year beginning after July 10, 1989, to the taxable year required by section 898 and § 1.898-3, an amended return, with an amended Form 5471 (or Form 1120F) must be filed to satisfy the requirements of section 898, § 1.898-3 and this paragraph (b)(2).

(iv) *Making a second election under section 898(c)(1)(B).*—Except for an election under section 898(c)(1)(B) that is made in conjunction with a change in its taxable year to conform to a different required year under paragraph (b)(2)(ii) of this section, a specified foreign corporation that has elected the one-month deferral under section 898(c)(1)(B) and subsequently revoked that election shall not be eligible to make an election under section 898(c)(1)(B) for any taxable year before its fifth taxable year which begins after the first taxable year for which the revocation is effective, unless the consent of the Commissioner pursuant to the procedures set forth in paragraph (b)(2)(v) of this section is obtained.

(v) *Procedure for obtaining the consent of the Commissioner to change the required year of specified foreign corporations.*—In the circumstance described in paragraph (b)(2)(iv) of this section, a specified foreign corporation must request the approval of the Commissioner for a change in taxable year by completing and filing Form 1128 (Application for Change in Accounting Period) (or successor form) with the Commissioner. The application may be filed either by the majority United States shareholder on behalf of the specified foreign corporation or by the specified foreign corporation. The application must be filed on or before the 15th day of the second calendar month following the close of the short period for which a return is required to effect the change in taxable year. Reference to this regulation must be made part of the application by placing the following statement at the top of page one of the application: "FILED UNDER § 1.898-4." Approval of a change in taxable year described in paragraph (b)(2)(iv) of this section will not be granted unless the taxpayer agrees to the terms, conditions, and adjustments, as set forth by the Commissioner, under which the change will be effected. Unless the instructions to the forms indicate otherwise, re-election of section 898(c)(1)(B) must be noted on Form 5471 and, if applicable, on Form 1120F, for the taxable year for which the re-election is made. Unless the instructions to the forms indicate otherwise, the words "Re-elected Section 898(c)(1)(B) Election – Change in Taxable Year" must be placed in the upper left hand corner of the first page of each form.

(3) *Short period.*—(i) *In general.*—Any short period required for a specified foreign corporation to effect the change in taxable year described in paragraph (b)(1) of this section will begin on the first day of the specified foreign corporation's current taxable year and will end on the last day of the new required year within which the change in ownership of the specified foreign corporation (or other event that necessitates a change in taxable year) occurs. If, however, the last day of the specified foreign corporation's current taxable year occurs prior to the last day of the new required year within which the change in ownership of the specified foreign corporation (or other event resulting in a new required year) occurs, then the short period will begin the day following the last day of the specified foreign corporation's current taxable year and end on the last day of the new required year subsequent to the required year within which the change in ownership of the specified foreign corporation (or other event resulting in a new required year) occurred. In no case shall the taxable year of the specified foreign corporation be in excess of one year.

(ii) *Illustrations.*—The application of this paragraph (b)(3) may be illustrated by the following examples:

Example 1. FX is a foreign corporation that is a specified foreign corporation within the meaning of section 898(b). FX had been a calendar year taxpayer. On July 1, 1991, FX was purchased by a United States shareholder with a September 30 fiscal year. Accordingly, the short period required to change the taxable year of FX to the required year began on January 1, 1991, the first day of FX's current taxable year, and ended on September 30, 1991, the last day of the new required year within which the change in ownership of FX occurred.

Example 2. The facts are the same as in *Example 1* except that on July 1, 1991, FX was purchased by a United States shareholder with a June 30 fiscal year. Accordingly, the short period required to change the taxable year of FX to the required year did not begin until January 1, 1992, the day following the last day of FX's current taxable year because the last day of FX's current taxable year occurs prior to the last day of the new required year within which the change in ownership occurred. The short period will begin January 1, 1992, and will end June 30, 1992.

(4) *Conforming changes in the majority U.S. shareholder year.*—The requirements of section 898 and §§1.898-3 and 1.898-4 may be satisfied by a majority United States shareholder of a specified foreign corporation changing its taxable year to conform to the taxable year of the specified foreign corporation. However, any change to the United States shareholder's taxable year requires the approval of the Commissioner, and must be made in accordance with section 442 and the regulations under that section, relating to changes of annual accounting period.

(c) *Nonconforming foreign and United States taxable years of a specified foreign corporation.*—(1) *In general.*—If a specified foreign corporation's foreign taxable year (for purposes of computing income tax liabilities due a foreign country) does not conform to the required year pursuant to section 898(c) and §1.898-3, then the United States shareholders must compute any income inclusion relating to the specified foreign corporation including, but not limited to, subpart F income, increase in earnings invested in United States property, foreign personal holding company income, and section 864(d) income in accordance with the rules set forth in paragraphs (c)(2) and (3) of this section. However, see section 338 and the regulations under that section for rules applicable to certain domestic and foreign corporations, and the shareholders of those corporations where an election under that section is made.

(2) *Computation of income and earnings and profits of a specified foreign corporation.*—(i) *Separate books of account.*—A specified foreign corporation that has a foreign taxable year different from its required year, as determined under section 898(c) and §1.898-3, will have portions of two foreign annual accounting periods in each required year. In this case, either separate books of account for the specified foreign corporation based upon the required year may be maintained, or income (and earnings and profits) shall be computed as set forth in paragraph (c)(2)(ii) of this section. Books of account must be maintained on a consistent basis for each foreign annual accounting period.

(ii) *Income and earnings and profits computation in lieu of separate books.*—In lieu of maintaining separate books of account, income and earnings and profits shall be computed in two steps. First, for the foreign annual accounting period of the specified foreign corporation which ends within its required year, the income (and earnings and profits) of the specified foreign corporation is the entire income (or earnings and profits) of the foreign annual accounting period, less the income (or earnings and profits), if any, of that foreign annual

accounting period properly allocable to the preceding taxable year, determined under a consistent application of the principles of section 964 and the regulations under that section. Second, for the foreign annual accounting period of the specified foreign corporation which ends after its required year, the income (and earnings and profits) of the specified foreign corporation is the income (and earnings and profits) of each month (or quarter) which has ended within the required year determined on the basis of interim actual book closings and computed by a consistent application of the principles of section 964 and the regulations under that section. If the amount of income properly includable in the gross income of United States shareholders in the preceding taxable year is different from the amount of income actually included by United States shareholders in the preceding taxable year, then an adjustment must be made by each United States person affected by means of an amended return for that preceding taxable year.

(iii) *Illustration.*—The application of this paragraph (c)(2) may be illustrated by the following example:

Example. (i) FX is a specified foreign corporation organized in foreign country, FC. FX's annual accounting period and taxable year, for FC purposes, end March 31. FX's required year is the calendar year. FX did not conform its FC taxable year to the required year. Separate books for United States tax purposes are not maintained. Accordingly, FX's required year, Calendar Year 1, will include portions of two FC annual accounting periods and FC taxable years.

(ii) For the FC period ending March 31, during Calendar Year 1, FX's income (in U.S. dollars) was $1,000, all of which was foreign personal holding company income. This amount was determined on the basis of FX's annual March 31, FC financial reports, adjusted in accordance with section 964 and the regulations under that section. Of the $1,000, it was determined from the annual financial reports that $350 was earned during the months ending in Calendar Year 1. For the period April 1, during Calendar Year 1, to the end of Calendar Year 1, FX's income was $1,200, determined on the basis of FX's monthly interim FC books of account. Accordingly, the income of FX subject to inclusion in the gross income of United States shareholders for Calendar Year 1, is $1,550. However, based on FX's annual March 31, Year 2, financial reports (adjusted in accordance with section 964 and the regulations under that section), FX's income for the period April 1, during Calendar Year 1, to the end of Calendar Year 1 was $1,300, not $1,200. Accordingly, each United States shareholder of FX must file an amended return for Calendar Year 1 showing its portion of the additional $100 of income.

(3) *52-53-week taxable year.*—(i) *Majority United States shareholder with a 52-53-week taxable year.*—If a majority United States shareholder elects to follow a 52-53-week taxable year (determined under section 441(f) and the regulations under that section), and the specified foreign corporation does not intend to follow a 52-53-week taxable year, then the required year of the specified foreign corporation, as determined under section 898(c) and §1.898-3, shall be a 12-month taxable year, which must end on the last day of the same month used in determining the 52-53-week taxable year of its majority United States shareholder. If the election of the one-month deferral under section 898(c)(1)(B) and §1.898-3(a)(2) is made, the election will be valid, and the specified foreign corporation may retain a 12-month taxable year, subject to the condition that the 12-month taxable year must end on the last day of the month which immediately precedes the month used in determining the 52-53-week taxable year of its majority United States shareholder.

(ii) *Specified foreign corporation with a 52-53-week taxable year.*—If a specified foreign corporation elects to follow a 52-53-week taxable year, and the majority United States shareholder does not intend to follow a 52-53-week taxable year, then the required year, as determined under section 898(c) and §1.898-3, of the specified foreign corporation shall be a 52-53-week taxable year, which must end within a seven-day period from the last day of the 12-month taxable year of its majority United States shareholder. If the election of the one-month deferral under section 898(c)(1)(B) and §1.898-3(a)(2) is made, the election will be valid and the specified foreign corporation may retain a 52-53-week taxable year, subject to the condition that the 52-53-week taxable year must end within a seven-day period from the last day of the month which immediately precedes the 12-month taxable year of its majority United States shareholder.

(iii) *Illustrations.*—The application of this paragraph (c)(3) may be illustrated by the following examples:

Example 1. X is a United States corporation created on January 1, 1990, that elected to follow a 52-53-week taxable year which ends on the Friday nearest the end of December. Thus, X's first United States taxable year began on Monday, January 1, 1990, and ended on Friday, December 28, 1990; its next taxable year began on Saturday, December 29, 1990, and ended on Friday, January 3, 1992. X owns 100 percent of FY, a specified foreign corporation that is a controlled foreign corporation which follows a 12-month taxable year ending on November 30. In these circumstances, X's taxable year may end either earlier or later than one month after the end of FY's taxable year. Nonetheless, an election under section 898(c)(1)(B), which would permit FY to retain its current taxable year, will be effective because FY's taxable year ends on the last day of the month which immediately precedes the same month used in determining the 52-53-week taxable year of X, its majority United States shareholder.

> *Example 2.* Y is a United States person with a taxable year ending September 30. Y also is the majority United States shareholder of FX, a specified foreign corporation which is a controlled foreign corporation that wishes to make the one-month deferral election under section 898(c)(1)(B). FX follows a 52-53-week taxable year that ends on the Monday closest to the last day of August. In 1990, the last day of August fell on a Friday. Thus, FX's taxable year ended on Monday, September 3, 1990, a date within a seven-day period from the last day of the month which immediately precedes the 12-month taxable year of its majority United States shareholder, Y. In 1994, FX's taxable year will end on Monday, August 29, and its next taxable year will begin on August 30, 1994. Thus, in 1994, FX's taxable year will begin more than one month before the beginning of Y's United States taxable year. Nevertheless, the election made under section 898(c)(1)(B) will be effective because FX's taxable year will end within a seven-day period from the last day of the month which immediately precedes the 12-month taxable year of its majority United States shareholder.

> (4) *Certain captive insurance companies that elect to treat their related person insurance income as income effectively connected with the conduct of a United States trade or business.*—Section 953(c)(3)(C) permits a foreign corporation to elect to treat its related person insurance income as income effectively connected with the conduct of a trade or business in the United States. Under § 1.953-7(c)(3) of proposed regulations, such a foreign corporation must utilize the calendar year as its annual accounting period for United States tax purposes, as

required by section 843. Further, if an election is made for the first taxable year beginning after December 31, 1987, or any subsequent taxable year, the election is effective from the first day of the taxable year for which the election is made (and all subsequent taxable years). Therefore, a foreign corporation that has a fiscal taxable year prior to making the election must file a short-year return for the period from the first day the election becomes effective to the last day of the calendar year in which the election is made. The rules under section 953(c)(3)(C) and § 1.953-7 will prevail over the rules under section 898 and this section. Thus, if a captive insurance company that is a specified foreign corporation makes an election pursuant to section 953(c)(3)(C) and § 1.953-7(c), it must use the calendar year as its annual accounting period for United States tax purposes, regardless of the taxable year of its majority United States shareholder. However, if a captive insurance company that is a specified foreign corporation does not make the election pursuant to section 953(c)(3)(C) and the regulations thereunder, it must conform its United States taxable year to that of its majority United States shareholder.

(d) *Four-year income spread.*—For its first taxable year beginning after July 10, 1989, if, because of the change necessitated by section 898 in the taxable year of the specified foreign corporation, any United States person was required to include in gross income for one taxable year amounts attributable to two taxable years of the specified foreign corporation, the amount that the United States person would otherwise have included in gross income for the one taxable year by reason of the short taxable year of the specified foreign corporation resulting from the change shall be included in that person's gross income ratably over a four-taxable-year period beginning with that one taxable year. A United States person who is required by reason of section 898 to include in gross income amounts attributable to two taxable years of a specified foreign corporation may not waive the four-year ratable inclusion of such gross income. [Reg. § 1.898-4.]

Accounting Periods: Adoptions: Changes: Retentions

Accounting Periods: Adoptions: Changes: Retentions.—Amendments to proposed Reg. § 1.898-4 (see above), relating to certain adoptions, changes, and retentions of annual accounting periods, are proposed (published in the Federal Register on June 13, 2001) (REG-106917-99).

☐ Par. 9. Section 1.898-4, as proposed to be added at 58 FR 297, January 5, 1993, is amended by adding paragraph (c)(3)(iv) to read as follows:

§ 1.898-4. Special rules.

* * *

(c) * * *

(3) * * *

(iv) *Recognition of income and deductions.*—See § 1.441-2(e) for rules regarding the recognition of income and deductions (e.g.,

amounts includible in gross income pursuant to sections 951(a) or 553) if either the majority United States shareholder, or the specified foreign corporation, or both, elect to use a 52-53-week taxable year under this paragraph (c)(3).

* * *

Foreign Tax Credit: Determining the Amount of Taxes Paid

Foreign Tax Credit: Determining the Amount of Taxes Paid.—Amendments to Reg. § 1.901-2, providing guidance relating to the determination of the amount of taxes paid, are proposed (published in the Federal Register on March 30, 2007) (REG-156779-06). The amendments to Reg. § 1.901-2(e)(5)(iv) were adopted as Temporary Reg. § 1.901-2T(e)(5)(iv) by T.D. 9416 on July 15, 2008.

☐ Par. 2. Section 1.901-2 is amended by adding paragraphs (e)(5)(iii) and (iv) [see sentence, above, regarding (e)(5)(iv)], and revising paragraph (h) to read as follows:

⋙→ *Caution: Proposed Reg. § 1.901-2(e)(5)(iii) will be effective for tax years beginning after the final regulations are published in the Federal Register. Taxpayers can rely on Proposed Reg. § 1.901-2(e)(5)(iii) for tax years ending on or after March 29, 2007, and beginning on or before the date the final regulations are published. See Notice 2007-95.*

§ 1.901-2. Income, war profits, or excess profits tax paid or accrued.

* * *

(e)(5) * * *

(iii) *U.S.-owned foreign entities.*—(A) *In general.*—If a U.S. person described in section 901(b) directly or indirectly owns stock possessing 80 percent or more of the total voting power and total value of one or more foreign corporations (or, in the case of a non-corporate foreign entity, directly or indirectly owns an interest in 80 percent or more of the income of one or more such foreign entities), the group comprising such foreign corporations and entities (the "U.S.-owned group") shall be treated as a single taxpayer for purposes of paragraph (e)(5) of this section. Therefore, if one member of such a U.S.-owned group transfers or surrenders a net loss for the taxable year to a second member of the U.S.-owned group and the loss reduces the foreign tax due from the second member pursuant to a foreign law group relief or similar regime, foreign tax paid by the first member in a different year does not fail to be a compulsory payment solely because such tax would not have been due had the member that transferred or surrendered the net loss instead carried over the loss to reduce its own income and foreign tax liability in that year. Similarly, if one or more members of the U.S.-owned group enter into a combined settlement under foreign law of two or more issues involving different members of the group, such settlement will

be evaluated on an overall basis, not on an issue-by-issue or entity-by-entity basis, in determining whether an amount is a compulsory amount. The provisions of this paragraph (e)(5)(iii) apply solely for purposes of determining whether amounts paid are compulsory payments of foreign tax and do not, for example, modify the provisions of section 902 requiring separate pools of post-1986 undistributed earnings and post-1986 foreign income taxes for each member of a qualified group.

(B) *Special rules.*—All domestic corporations that are members of a consolidated group (as that term is defined in § 1.1502-1(h)) shall be treated as one domestic corporation for purposes of this paragraph (e)(5)(iii). For purposes of this paragraph (e)(5)(iii), indirect ownership of stock or another equity interest (such as an interest in a partnership) shall be determined in accordance with the principles of section 958(a)(2), whether the interest is owned by a U.S. or foreign person.

(C) *Examples.*—The following examples illustrate the rules of this paragraph (e)(5)(iii):

> *Example 1.* (i) *Facts.* A, a domestic corporation, wholly owns B, a country X corporation. B, in turn, wholly owns several country X corporations, including C and D. B, C, and D participate in group relief in country X. Under the country X group relief rules, a member with a net loss may choose to surrender the loss to another member of the group. In year 1, C has a net loss of (1,000x) and D has

⋙→ Caution: *Proposed Reg. §1.901-2(e)(5)(iii) will be effective for tax years beginning after the final regulations are published in the Federal Register. Taxpayers can rely on Proposed Reg. §1.901-2(e)(5)(iii) for tax years ending on or after March 29, 2007, and beginning on or before the date the final regulations are published. See Notice 2007-95.*

net income of 5,000x for country X tax purposes. Pursuant to the group relief rules in country X, C agrees to surrender its year 1 net loss to D and D agrees to claim the net loss. D uses the net loss to reduce its year 1 net income to 4,000x for country X tax purposes, which reduces the amount of country X tax D owes in year 1 by 300x. In year 2, C earns 3,000x with respect to which it pays 900x of country X tax. Country X permits a taxpayer to carry forward net losses for up to ten years.

    (ii) *Result.* Paragraph (e)(5)(i) of this section provides, in part, that an amount paid to a foreign country does not exceed the amount of liability under foreign law for tax if the taxpayer determines such amount in a manner that is consistent with a reasonable interpretation and application of the substantive and procedural provisions of foreign law (including applicable tax treaties) in such a way as to reduce, over time, the taxpayer's reasonably expected liability under foreign law for tax. Under paragraph (e)(5)(iii)(A) of this section, B, C, and D are treated as a single taxpayer for purposes of testing whether the reasonably expected foreign tax liability has been minimized over time, because A directly and indirectly owns 100 percent of each of B, C, and D. Accordingly, none of the 900x paid by C in year 2 fails to be a compulsory payment solely because C could have reduced its year 2 country X tax liability by 300x by choosing to carry forward its year 1 net loss to year 2 instead of surrendering it to D to reduce D's country X liability in year 1.

    Example 2. (i) *Facts.* L, M, and N are country Y corporations. L owns 100 percent of the common stock of M, which owns 100 percent of the stock of N. O, a domestic corporation, owns a security issued by M that is treated as debt for country Y tax purposes and as stock for U.S. tax purposes. As a result, L owns 100 percent of the stock of M for country Y purposes while O owns 99 percent of the stock of M for U.S. tax purposes. L, M, and N participate in group relief in country Y. Pursuant to the group relief rules in country Y, M may surrender its loss to any member of the group. In year 1, M has a net loss of $10 million, N has net income of $25 million, and L has net income of $15 million. M chooses to surrender its year 1 net loss to L. Country Y imposes tax of 30 percent on the net income of country Y corporations. Accordingly, in year 1, the loss surrender has the effect of reducing L's country Y tax by $3 million. In year 1, N makes a payment of $7.5 million to country Y with respect to its net income of $25 million. If M had surrendered its net loss to N instead of L, N would have had net income of $15 million, with respect to which it would have owed only $4.5 million of country Y tax.

    (ii) *Result.* M and N, but not L, are treated as a single taxpayer for purposes of paragraph (e)(5) of this section because O directly and indirectly owns 99 percent of each of M and N, but owns no direct or indirect interest in L. Accordingly, in testing whether M and N's reasonably expected foreign tax liability has been minimized over time, L is not considered the same taxpayer as M and N, collectively, and the $3 million reduction in L's year 1 country Y tax liability through the surrender to L of M's $10 million country Y net loss in year 1 is not considered to reduce M and N's collective country Y tax liability.

* * *

    (h) *Effective date.*—Paragraphs (a) through (e)(5)(ii) and paragraph (g) of this section, §1.901-2A, and §1.903-1 apply to taxable years beginning after November 14, 1983. Paragraphs (e)(5)(iii) and (iv) of this section are effective for foreign taxes paid or accrued during taxable years of the taxpayer ending on or after the date on which these regulations are published as final regulations in the Federal Register.

Section 301 Regulations: Statutory Changes Reflected

Section 301 Regulations: Statutory Changes Reflected.—Amendments to Reg. §1.902-1, updating existing regulations under section 301 to reflect statutory changes made by the Technical and Miscellaneous Revenue Act of 1988, which changes provide that the amount of a distribution of property made by a corporation to its shareholder is the fair market value of the distributed property, are proposed (published in the Federal Register on March 26, 2019) (REG-121694-16).

    Par. 5. In §1.902-1(a)(12), remove the reference "§1.301-1(b)" and add in its place "§1.301-1(c)".

§1.902-1. Credit for domestic corporate shareholder of a foreign corporation for foreign income taxes paid by the foreign corporation.

Section 301 Regulations: Statutory Changes Reflected

Section 301 Regulations: Statutory Changes Reflected.—Amendments to Reg. §1.902-3, updating existing regulations under section 301 to reflect statutory changes made by the Technical and Miscellaneous Revenue Act of 1988, which changes provide that the amount of a distribution of property made by a corporation to its shareholder is the fair market value of the distributed property, are proposed (published in the Federal Register on March 26, 2019) (REG-121694-16).

    Par. 6. In §1.902-3(a)(7), remove the reference "§1.301-1(b)" and add in its place "§1.301-1(c)".

§1.902-3. Credit for domestic corporate shareholder of a foreign corporation for foreign income taxes paid with respect to accumulated profits of taxable years of the foreign corporation beginning before January 1, 1987.

Allocation and Apportionment of Deductions and Foreign Tax Credit: Guidance

Allocation and Apportionment of Deductions and Foreign Tax Credit: Guidance.—Amendments to Reg. §1.904-4, relating to the allocation and apportionment of deductions and creditable foreign taxes, the definition of financial services income, foreign tax redeterminations, availability of foreign tax credits under the transition tax, and the application of the foreign tax credit limitation to consolidated groups, are proposed (published in the Federal Register on December 17, 2019) (REG-105495-19).

    Par. 13. Section 1.904-4 is amended by:

1. Revising paragraph (c)(7)(i).
2. Revising the third and fourth sentences of paragraph (c)(7)(ii).
3. Revising paragraph (c)(7)(iii).
4. Adding paragraphs (c)(8)(v) through (viii).
5. Revising paragraphs (e)(1)(ii) and (e)(2).
6. Removing paragraphs (e)(3) and (4).
7. Removing the language "§1.904-6(b)" in paragraph (o) and adding the language "1.904-6(e)" in its place.
8. Revising paragraph (q).

The revisions and additions read as follows:

§1.904-4. Separate application of section 904 with respect to certain categories of income.

* * *

    (c) * * *

    (7) * * *

    (i) *In general.*—If the effective rate of tax imposed by a foreign country on income of a foreign corporation that is included in a taxpayer's gross income is reduced under foreign law on distribu- tion of such income, the rules of this paragraph (c) apply at the time that the income is included in the taxpayer's gross income, without regard to the possibility of a subsequent reduction of foreign tax on the distribution. If the inclusion is considered to be high-taxed income, then the taxpayer must initially treat the inclusion as general category income, section 951A category income or income in a specified separate category as provided in paragraph (c)(1) of this section. When the foreign corporation distributes the earnings and profits to which the inclusion was attributable and the foreign tax on the inclusion is reduced, then if a redetermination of U.S. tax liability is required under §1.905-3(b)(2), the taxpayer must redetermine whether the revised inclusion (if any) should be considered to be high-taxed income. *See* §1.905-3(b)(2)(ii) (requiring a redetermination of the amount of the inclusion, the application of the high-tax exception under section 954(b)(4), and the amount of foreign taxes deemed paid). If, taking into account the reduction in foreign tax, the inclusion would not have been considered high-taxed income, then the taxpayer, in redetermining its U.S. tax liability for the year or years affected, must treat the inclusion and the associated taxes (as reduced on the distribution) as passive category income and taxes. For this purpose, the foreign tax on an inclusion under section 951(a)(1) or 951A(a) is considered reduced on distribution of the earnings and profits associated with the inclusion if the total taxes paid and deemed paid on the inclusion and the distribution (taking into account any reductions in tax and any withholding taxes) is less than the total taxes deemed paid in the year of inclusion. Therefore, any foreign currency gain associated with the earnings and profits that are distributed with respect to the inclusion is not taken into account in determining whether there is a reduction of tax requiring a redetermination of whether the inclusion is high-taxed income.

(ii) * * * If, however, foreign law does not attribute a reduction in taxes to a particular year or years, then the reduction in taxes shall be attributable, on an annual last in-first out (LIFO) basis, to foreign taxes potentially subject to reduction that are associated with previously taxed income, then on a LIFO basis to foreign taxes associated with income that under paragraph (c)(7)(iii) of this section remains as passive income but that was excluded from subpart F income or tested income under section 954(b)(4) or section 951A(c)(2)(A)(i)(III), and finally on a LIFO basis to foreign taxes associated with other earnings and profits. Furthermore, in applying the ordering rules of section 959(c), distributions shall be considered made on a LIFO basis first out of earnings described in section 959(c)(1) and (2), then on a LIFO basis out of earnings and profits associated with income that remains passive income under paragraph (c)(7)(iii) of this section but that was excluded from subpart F income or tested income under section 954(b)(4) or section 951A(c)(2)(A)(i)(III), and finally on a LIFO basis out of other earnings and profits. * * *

(iii) *Treatment of income excluded under section 954(b)(4) or section 951A(c)(2)(A)(i)(III).*—If the effective rate of tax imposed by a foreign country on income of a foreign corporation is reduced under foreign law on distribution of that income, the rules of section 954(b)(4) (including for purposes of determining tested income under section 951A(c)(2)(A)(i)(III)) are applied in the year of inclusion without regard to the possibility of a subsequent reduction of foreign tax. *See* §1.954-1(d)(3)(iii) and §1.951A-2(c)(6)(iv). If a taxpayer excludes passive income from a controlled foreign corporation's foreign personal holding company income or tested income under section 954(b)(4) or section 951A(c)(2)(A)(i)(III), then, notwithstanding the general rule of §1.904-5(d)(2), the income is considered to be passive category income until distribution of that income. At that time, if after the redetermination of U.S. tax liability required under §1.905-3(b)(2) the taxpayer still elects to exclude the passive income under section 954(b)(4) or section 951A(c)(2)(A)(i)(III), the rules of this paragraph (c)(7)(iii) apply to determine whether the income is high-taxed income upon distribution and, therefore, income in another separate category. For purposes of determining whether a reduction in tax is attributable to taxes on income excluded under section 954(b)(4) or section 951A(c)(2)(A)(i)(III), the rules of paragraph (c)(7)(ii) of this section apply. The rules of paragraph (c)(7)(ii) of this section also apply for purposes of ordering distributions to determine whether such distributions are out of earnings and profits associated with such excluded income. For an example illustrating the operation of this paragraph (c)(7)(iii), see paragraph (c)(8)(vi) of this section (*Example 6*).

(8) * * *

(v) *Example 5*— CFC, a controlled foreign corporation, is a wholly-owned subsidiary of USP, a domestic corporation. USP and CFC are calendar year taxpayers. In Year 1, CFC's only earnings consist of $200x of pre-tax passive income that is foreign personal holding company income that is earned in foreign Country X. Under Country X's tax system, the corporate tax on particular earnings is reduced on distribution of those earnings and no withholding tax is imposed. In Year 1, CFC pays $100x of foreign tax with respect to its passive income. USP does not elect to exclude this income from subpart F under section 954(b)(4) and includes $200x in gross income ($100x of net foreign personal holding company income and $100x of the amount under section 78 (the "section 78 dividend")). At the time of the inclusion, the income is considered to be high-taxed income under paragraphs (c)(1) and (c)(6)(i) of this section and is general category income to USP ($100x > $42x (21% x $200x)). CFC does not distribute any of its earnings in Year 1. In Year 2, CFC has no additional earnings. On December 31, Year 2, CFC distributes the $100x of earnings from Year 1. At that time, CFC receives a $60x

refund from Country X attributable to the reduction of the Country X corporate tax imposed on the Year 1 earnings. The refund is a foreign tax redetermination under §1.905-3(a) that under §1.905-3(b)(2) and §1.954-1(d)(3)(iii) requires a redetermination of CFC's Year 1 subpart F income and the application of section 954(b)(4), as well as a redetermination of USP's Year 1 inclusion under section 951(a)(1), its deemed paid taxes under section 960(a), and its Year 1 U.S. tax liability. As recomputed taking into account the $60x refund, CFC's Year 1 passive category net foreign personal holding company income is increased by $60x to $160x, CFC's foreign income taxes attributable to that income are reduced from $100x to $40x, and the income still qualifies to be excluded from CFC's subpart F income under section 954(b)(4) ($40x > $37.80x (90% x 21% x $200x)). Assuming USP does not change its Year 1 election, USP's Year 1 inclusion under section 951(a)(1) is increased by $60x to $160x, and the associated deemed paid tax and section 78 dividend are reduced by $60x to $40x. Under paragraph (c)(7)(i) of this section, in connection with the adjustments required under section 905(c), USP must redetermine whether the adjusted Year 1 inclusion is high-taxed income of USP. Taking into account the $60x refund, the inclusion is not considered high-taxed income of USP ($40x < $42x (21% x $200x)). Therefore, USP must treat the $200x of income ($160x inclusion plus $40x section 78 amount) and the $40x of taxes associated with the inclusion in Year 1 as passive category income and taxes. USP must also follow the appropriate procedures under §1.905-4.

(vi) *Example 6.* The facts are the same as in paragraph (c)(8)(v) of this section (the facts in *Example 5*), except that in Year 1, USP elects to apply section 954(b)(4) to exclude CFC's passive income from its subpart F income, both before and after the recomputation of CFC's Year 1 subpart F income and USP's Year 1 U.S. tax liability that is required by reason of the Year 2 $60x foreign tax redetermination. Although the income is not considered to be subpart F income, under paragraph (c)(7)(iii) of this section it remains passive category income until distribution. In Year 2, the $100x distribution is a dividend to USP, because CFC has $160x of accumulated earnings and profits described in section 959(c)(3) (the $100x of earnings in Year 1 increased by the $60x refund received in Year 2 that under §1.905-3(b)(2) is taken into account in Year 1). Under paragraph (c)(7)(iii) of this section, USP must determine whether the dividend income is high-taxed income to USP in Year 2. The treatment of the dividend as passive category income may be relevant in determining deductions allocable or apportioned to such dividend income or related stock that are excluded in the computation of USP's foreign tax credit limitation under section 904(a) in Year 2. *See* section 904(b)(4). Under paragraph (c)(1) of this section, the dividend income is passive category income to USP because the foreign taxes paid and deemed paid by USP ($0x) with respect to the dividend income do not exceed the highest U.S. tax rate on that income.

(vii) *Example 7.* The facts are the same as in paragraph (c)(8)(v) of this section (the facts in *Example 5*), except that the distribution in Year 2 is subject to a withholding tax of $25x. Under paragraph (c)(7)(i) of this section, USP must redetermine whether its Year 1 inclusion should be considered high-taxed income of USP because there is a net $35x reduction ($60x refund of foreign corporate tax − $25x withholding tax) of foreign tax. By taking into account both the reduction in foreign corporate tax and the additional withholding tax, the inclusion continues to be considered high-taxed income of USP in Year 1 ($65x > $42x (21% x $200). USP must follow the appropriate section 905(c) procedures. USP must redetermine its U.S. tax liability for Year 1, but the Year 1 inclusion and the $65x taxes ($40x of deemed paid tax in Year 1 and $25x withholding tax in Year 2) will continue to be treated as general category income and taxes.

(viii) *Example 8*—(A) CFC, a controlled foreign corporation operating in Country G, is a wholly-owned subsidiary of USP, a domestic corporation. USP and CFC are calendar year taxpayers. Country G imposes a tax of 50% on CFC's earnings. Under Country G's system, the foreign corporate tax on particular earnings is reduced on distribution of those earnings to 30% and no withholding tax is imposed. Under Country G's law, distributions are treated as made out of a pool of undistributed earnings subject to the 50% tax rate. For Year 1, CFC's only earnings consist of passive income that is foreign personal holding company income that is earned in foreign Country G. CFC has taxable income of $110x for Federal income tax purposes and $100x for Country G purposes. Country G, therefore, imposes a tax of $50x on the Year 1 earnings of CFC. USP does not elect to exclude this income from subpart F under section 954(b)(4) and includes $110x in gross income ($60x of net foreign personal holding company income under section 951(a) and $50x of the section 78 dividend). The highest rate of tax under section 11 in Year 1 is 34%. Therefore, at the time of the section 951(a) inclusion, the income is considered to be high-taxed income under paragraph (c) of this section and is general category income to USP. CFC does not distribute any of its earnings in Year 1.

(B) In Year 2, CFC earns general category income that is not subpart F income or tested income. CFC again has $110x in taxable income for Federal income tax purposes and $100x in taxable income for Country G purposes, and CFC pays $50x of tax to foreign Country G. In Year 3, CFC has no taxable income or earnings. On December 31, Year 3, CFC distributes $60x of its total $120x of earnings and receives a refund of foreign tax of $24x. The $24x refund is a foreign tax redetermination under §1.905-3(a) that under §1.905-3(b)(2) requires a redetermination of CFC's Year 1 subpart F income and USP's deemed paid taxes and Year 1 U.S. tax liability. Country G treats the distribution of earnings as out of the 50% tax rate pool of $200x of earnings accumulated in Year 1 and Year 2, as calculated for Country G tax purposes. However, under paragraph (c)(7)(ii) of this section, the distribution, and, therefore, the reduction of tax is treated as first attributable to the $60x of passive category earnings attributable to income previously taxed in Year 1, and none of the distribution is treated as made out of the $60x of earnings accumulated in Year 2 (which is not previously taxed). Because 40 percent (the reduction in tax rates from 50 percent to 30 percent is a 40 percent reduction in the tax) of the $50x of foreign taxes attributable to the $60x of Year 1 passive income as calculated for Federal income tax purposes is refunded, $20x of the $24x foreign tax refund reduces foreign taxes on CFC's Year 1 passive income from $50x to $30x. The other $4x of the tax refund reduces the taxes imposed in Year 2 on CFC's general category income from $50x to $46x.

(C) Under paragraph (c)(7) of this section, in connection with the section 905(c) adjustment USP must redetermine whether its Year 1 subpart F inclusion should be considered high-taxed income. By taking into account the reduction in foreign tax, the inclusion is increased by $20x to $80x, the deemed paid taxes are reduced by $20x to $30x, and the inclusion is not considered high-taxed income ($30x < 34% x $110x). Therefore, USP must treat the revised section 951(a) inclusion and the taxes associated with the section 951(a) inclusion as passive category income and taxes in Year 1. USP must follow the appropriate procedures under §1.905-4.

* * *

(e) * * *
(1) * * *

(ii) *Definition of financial services income.*—The term *financial services income* means income derived by a financial services entity, as defined in paragraph (e)(2) of this section, that is:

(A) Income derived in the active conduct of a banking, financing, or similar business under section 954(h)(3)(A)(i);

(B) Income that is of a kind that would be insurance income as defined in section 953(a)(1) (including related person insurance income as defined in section 953(c)(2) and without regard to the exception in section 953(a)(2) for income that is exempt insurance income under section 953(e));

(C) Income from the investment by an insurance company of its unearned premiums or reserves ordinary and necessary to the proper conduct of the insurance business; or

(D) Passive income as defined in section 904(d)(2)(B) and paragraph (b) of this section as determined before the application of the exception for high-taxed income but after the application of the exception for export financing interest.

* * *

(2) *Financial services entities.*—(i) *Definition of financial services entity.*—(A) *In general.*—The term *financial services entity* means an individual or corporation that is predominantly engaged in the active conduct of a banking, insurance, financing, or similar business (active financing business) within the meaning of paragraphs (e)(2)(i)(A)(1) through (4) of this section for any taxable year. Except as provided in paragraph (e)(2)(ii) of this section, a determination of whether an individual or corporation is a financial services entity is done on an individual or entity-by-entity basis. An individual or corporation is predominantly engaged in the active financing business for any year if for that year:

(1) It is predominantly engaged in the active conduct of a banking, financing, or similar business under section 954(h)(2)(B) (substituting the reference to "controlled foreign corporation" with "individual or corporation");

(2) It is an insurance company meeting the requirements of section 953(e)(3)(A) and (C) provided that the company's foreign personal holding company income does not exceed the amount that would be treated as derived in the active conduct of an insurance business under section 954(i) if all of the insurance and annuity contracts issued or reinsured by the company had qualified as exempt contracts under section 953(e)(2);

(3) It is a qualifying insurance corporation as defined in section 1297(f) that is engaged in the active conduct of an insurance business under section 1297(b)(2)(B) (but without regard to whether the corporation is a foreign corporation); or

(4) It is a domestic corporation, or a corporation that has elected to be treated as a domestic corporation under section 953(d), that is subject to Federal income tax under subchapter L on its net income and is subject to regulation as an insurance (or reinsurance) company in its jurisdiction of organization.

(B) *Certain gross income included and excluded.*—For purposes of applying the rules in paragraph (e)(2)(i)(A) of this section (including by reason of paragraph (e)(2)(ii) of this section), gross income includes interest on State and local bonds described in section 103(a), but does not include income from a distribution of previously taxed earnings and profits described in section 959(a) or (b).

(C) *Treatment of partnerships and other pass-through entities.*—For purposes of applying the rules in paragraph (e)(2)(i)(A) of this section (including by reason of paragraph (e)(2)(ii) of this section) with respect to an individual or corporation that is a direct or indirect partner in a partnership, the partner's distributive share of partnership income is characterized as if each partnership item of gross income were realized directly by the partner. For example, in applying section 954(h)(2)(B) under paragraph (e)(2)(i)(A) of this section, a customer with respect to a partnership is treated as a related person with respect to an individual or corporation that is a partner in the partnership if the customer is related to the individual or corporation under section 954(d)(3). Similar principles apply for an individual or corporation's share of income from any other pass-through entities.

(ii) *Financial services group.*—A corporation that is a member of a financial services group is deemed to be a financial services entity regardless of whether it is a financial services entity under paragraph (e)(2)(i) of this section. For purposes of this paragraph (e)(2)(ii), a financial services group means an affiliated group as defined in section 1504(a) (but determined without regard to paragraphs (2) or (3) of section 1504(b)) if the affiliated group as a whole meets the requirements of section 954(h)(2)(B)(i) (except that the reference to "controlled foreign corporation" is substituted with "affiliated group" in section 954(h)(2)(B)(i)). For purposes of determining whether an affiliated group is a financial services group under the previous sentence, only the income of group members that are domestic corporations or foreign corporations that are controlled foreign corporations in which U.S. members of the affiliated group own, directly or indirectly, at least 80 percent of the total voting power and value of the stock is included. In addition, indirect ownership is determined under section 318 and the regulations under that section, and the income of the group does not include any income from transactions with other members of the group.

(iii) *Examples.*—The following examples illustrate the application of paragraph (e)(2) of this section.

(A) *Example 1*—(1) *Facts.* USP is a domestic corporation that is the parent of a consolidated group which includes B (a domestic corporation that is primarily engaged in a manufacturing business), C (a domestic corporation whose primary function is to manage the treasury operations of the consolidated group), and D (a domestic corporation that is engaged in the active and regular conduct of financing purchases by unrelated customers of B's products). USP also owns a 20% partnership interest in PS, a domestic partnership that is engaged in the active and regular conduct of making loans to customers that are not related persons with respect to it or USP. The other 80% of PS is owned by USX, a domestic corporation unrelated to USP (or any other member of the USP consolidated group). B has gross income of $170x consisting of income from its manufacturing operations. C has gross income of $20x consisting of interest income from loans to B. D has gross income of $100x consisting of interest income from making loans to unrelated customers that purchase B's products. PS has gross income of $50x consisting of interest on loans that it makes to customers in the ordinary course of its business, $10x of which is attributable to loans to C, $30x of which is attributable to loans to Z (a wholly owned subsidiary of USX), and $10 of which is attributable to loans to customers unrelated to either the USP or USX affiliated groups. USP, B, C, and D have no other items of gross income and no other intercompany transactions.

(2) *Analysis*—(i) *Entity test.* Under paragraph (e)(2)(i)(A) of this section, B and C are not financial services entities because neither meets the requirements of being predominantly engaged in the active conduct of a banking, finance, insurance, or similar business. B does not meet the requirements because all of its income is derived from manufacturing. C does not meet the requirements because it lends solely to related persons. Under paragraph (e)(2)(i)(A)(1) of this section, D is a financial services entity because all of its gross income is derived from making loans to unrelated customers in the ordinary course of its lending business in a manner that meets the requirements of section 954(h)(2)(B)(i). Under paragraph (e)(2)(i)(C) of this section, USP's distributive share of partnership income from PS is characterized as if each item of PS's gross income were realized directly by USP. Thus, USP includes a $10x distributive share of income from PS, $2x of which is from related party loans to C and $8x of which is from loans to persons that are not related persons with respect to USP. Under paragraph (e)(2)(i)(A)(1) of this section, USP is a financial services entity because more than 70% of its gross income is derived from making loans to unrelated customers in the

ordinary course of a lending business ($8x/$10x > 70% x $10x) and meets the requirements of section 954(h)(2)(B)(i).

    (ii) Affiliated group test. Under paragraph (e)(2)(ii) of this section, a corporation that is a member of a financial services group is deemed to be a financial services entity regardless of whether it is a financial services entity under paragraph (e)(2)(i) of this section. This would apply if the USP, B, C, and D affiliated group as a whole meets the requirements of section 954(h)(2)(B)(i). The USP affiliated group derives $108x ($100x by D and $8x by USP) from loans to unrelated customers and derives $278x of total gross income after making the adjustments provided in paragraph (e)(2)(ii) of this section ($300x total gross income minus $20x interest on intercompany loan from C to B and $2x interest on loan from PS to C). Because the gross income USP's affiliated group derives directly from the active and regular conduct of a lending or finance business from transactions with customers which are not related persons is 39% ($108x divided by $278x), the USP affiliated group does not satisfy the more than 70% of gross income test of section 954(h)(2)(B)(i), and the USP affiliated group is not a financial services group. USP and D are financial services entities under paragraph (e)(2)(i)(A) of this section. B and C are not financial services entities under either of paragraphs (e)(2)(i) or (ii) of this section.

    (B) *Example 2*—(1) *Facts.* The facts are the same as in paragraph (e)(2)(iii)(A)(1) of this section (the facts in *Example 1*) except that USX is the parent of a consolidated group, which includes Y (a domestic corporation that is a U.S. licensed bank), and Z (a domestic corporation that is a non-bank lender that is engaged in the active and regular conduct of making loans to customers unrelated to USX or its affiliates). Y has gross income of $200x, consisting of $190x from making loans to unrelated customers in the ordinary course of its banking business and $10x of other income not described in section 954(h)(4). Z has gross income of $160x, consisting of interest income from making loans to unrelated customers. USX, Y, and Z have no other items of gross income and no other intercompany transactions.

    (2) *Analysis*—(i) *Entity test.* Under paragraph (e)(2)(i)(A) of this section, Y and Z are financial services entities. Y is a financial services entity because it satisfies the requirements of section 954(h)(2)(B)(ii). Z is a financial services entity because all of its gross income is derived from making loans to unrelated customers in the ordinary course of its lending business in a manner that meets the requirements of section 954(h)(2)(B)(i). Under paragraph (e)(2)(i)(C) of this section, USX's distributive share of partnership income from PS is characterized as if each item of PS's gross income were realized directly by USX. Thus, USX includes a $40x distributive share of

income from PS, $24x of which is from related party loans to Z and $16x of which is from loans to unrelated parties. Under paragraph (e)(2)(i)(A)(1) of this section, USX is not a financial services entity because only 60% ($24x divided by $40x) of its gross income is derived from making loans to unrelated customers in the ordinary course of a lending business and, therefore, USX does not meet the more than 70% of gross income test of section 954(h)(2)(B)(i).

    (ii) Affiliated group test. Under paragraph (e)(2)(ii) of this section, a corporation that is a member of a financial services group is deemed to be a financial services entity regardless of whether it is a financial services entity under paragraph (e)(2)(i) of this section. This would apply if the USX, Y, and Z affiliated group as a whole meets the requirements of section 954(h)(2)(B)(i). The USX affiliated group derives $366x ($190x by Y, $160x by Z, $16x by USP) from loans to unrelated customers and derives $376x of total gross income after making the adjustments provided in paragraph (e)(2)(ii) of this section ($400x total gross income minus $24x interest on loans from PS to Z). Because the gross income USX's affiliated group derives directly from the active and regular conduct of a lending or finance business from transactions with customers which are not related persons is 97% ($366x divided by $376x), the USX affiliated group satisfies the more than 70% of gross income test of section 954(h)(2)(B)(i), and the USX affiliated group is a financial services group. Y and Z are financial services entities under paragraph (e)(2)(i)(A). USX is a financial services entity under paragraph (e)(2)(ii) of this section.

* * *

    (q) *Applicability date.*—(1) Except as provided in paragraph (q)(2) and (3) of this section, this section applies for taxable years that both begin after December 31, 2017, and end on or after December 4, 2018.

    (2) Paragraphs (c)(7)(i), (c)(7)(iii), (c)(8)(v) through (viii) apply to taxable years ending on or after December 16, 2019. For taxable years that both begin after December 31, 2017, and end on or after December 4, 2018, and also end before December 16, 2019, see §1.904-4(c)(7)(i) and (c)(7)(iii) as in effect on December 17, 2019.

    (3) Paragraphs (e)(1)(ii) and (e)(2) of this section apply to taxable years ending on or after the date the final regulations are filed with the **Federal Register**. For taxable years that both begin after December 31, 2017, and end on or after December 4, 2018, and also end before the date the final regulations are filed with the **Federal Register**, see §1.904-4(e)(1)(i) and (e)(2) as in effect on December 17, 2019.

Controlled Foreign Corporations: Hybrid Branches: Subpart F Income

    Controlled Foreign Corporations: Hybrid Branches: Subpart F Income.—Amendments to Reg. §1.904-5, relating to the treatment under subpart F of certain transactions involving hybrid branches, are proposed (published in the Federal Register on July 13, 1999) (REG-113909-98).

    ☐ Par. 2. In §1.904-5, paragraph (k)(1) is revised to read as follows:

§1.904-5. Look-through rules as applied to controlled foreign corporations and other entities.

* * *

    (k) *Ordering rules.*—(1) *In general.*—Income received or accrued by a related person to which the look-through rules apply is characterized before amounts included from, or paid or distributed by, that person and received or accrued by a related person. For purposes of

determining the character of income received or accrued by a person from a related person if the payor or another related person also receives or accrues income from the recipient and the look-through rules apply to the income in all cases, the rules of paragraph (k)(2) of this section apply. Notwithstanding any other provision of this section, the principles of §1.954-1(c)(1)(i) will apply to any expense subject to §1.954-1(c)(1)(i).

* * *

CFCs: U.S. Shareholders: Ownership Attribution

    CFCs: U.S. Shareholders: Ownership Attribution.—Amendments to Reg. §1.904-5, relating to the modification of section 958(b) of the Internal Revenue Code by the Tax Cuts and Jobs Act, which was enacted on December 22, 2017, are proposed (published in the Federal Register on October 2, 2019) (REG-104223-18).

    Par. 9. Section 1.904-5, as proposed to be amended at 83 FR 63200 (December 7, 2018), is further amended by:

    1. Revising paragraph (a)(4)(i).

    2. Revising the first sentence of paragraph (a)(4)(vi).

    3. Revising paragraph (o).

    The revisions read as follows:

§1.904-5. Look-through rules as applied to controlled foreign corporations and other entities.—(a) * * *

    (4) * * *

    (i) The term *controlled foreign corporation* has the meaning given such term by section 957 (taking into account the special rule for certain captive insurance companies contained in section 953(c)), determined without applying subparagraphs (A), (B), and (C) of section 318(a)(3) so as to consider a United States person as owning stock which is owned by a person who is not a United States person.

* * *

    (vi) The term *United States shareholder* has the meaning given such term by section 951(b) (taking into account the special rule for certain captive insurance companies contained in section 953(c)), determined without applying subparagraphs (A), (B), and (C)

of section 318(a)(3) so as to consider a United States person as owning stock which is owned by a person who is not a United States person, except that for purposes of this section, a United States shareholder includes any member of the controlled group of the United States shareholder. * * *

* * *

    (o) *Applicability dates.*—Except as otherwise provided in this paragraph (o), this section applies to taxable years that both begin after December 31, 2017, and end on or after December 4, 2018. Paragraphs (a)(4)(i) and (vi) of this section apply to taxable years of foreign corporations ending on or after October 1, 2019, and taxable years of United States persons ending on or after October 1, 2019. For taxable years of foreign corporations ending before October 1, 2019, and taxable years of United States persons ending before October 1, 2019, a taxpayer may apply such provisions to the last taxable year of a foreign corporation beginning before January 1, 2018, and each subsequent taxable year of the foreign corporation, and to taxable years of United States shareholders in which or with which such taxable

years of the foreign corporation end, provided that the taxpayer and United States persons that are related (within the meaning of section 267 or 707) to the taxpayer consistently apply such provisions with respect to all foreign corporations.

Allocation and Apportionment of Deductions and Foreign Tax Credit: Guidance

Allocation and Apportionment of Deductions and Foreign Tax Credit: Guidance.—Amendments to Reg. § 1.904-6, relating to the allocation and apportionment of deductions and creditable foreign taxes, the definition of financial services income, foreign tax redeterminations, availability of foreign tax credits under the transition tax, and the application of the foreign tax credit limitation to consolidated groups, are proposed (published in the Federal Register on December 17, 2019) (REG-105495-19).

Par. 14. § 1.904-6 is amended by:

1. Revising the section heading.

2. Revising paragraph (a).

3. Redesignating paragraph (b) as paragraph (e) and adding a new paragraph (b).

4. Adding paragraph (c) and revising paragraph (d).

5. Removing the language "paragraph (b)(4)(ii)" in newly-redesignated paragraph (e)(4)(i) and adding the language "paragraph (e)(4)(ii)" in its place.

6. Removing the language "paragraph (b)(4)(ii)(B)" in newly-redesignated paragraph (e)(4)(ii)(C) and adding the language "paragraph (e)(4)(ii)(B)" in its place.

7. Adding paragraphs (f) through (h).

The revisions and additions read as follows:

§ 1.904-6. Allocation and apportionment of foreign income taxes.—(a) *In general.*—The amount of foreign income taxes paid or accrued with respect to a separate category (as defined in § 1.904-5(a)(4)(v)) of income (including U.S. source income assigned to the separate category) includes only those foreign income taxes that are allocated and apportioned to the separate category under the rules of § 1.861-20 (as modified by this section). In applying the foreign tax credit limitation under sections 904(a) and (d) to general category income described in section 904(d)(2)(A)(ii) and § 1.904-4(d), the general category is a statutory grouping. However, the general category income is the residual grouping of income for purposes of assigning foreign income taxes to separate categories. In addition, in determining the numerator of the foreign tax credit limitation under sections 904(a) and (d), where U.S. source income is the residual grouping, the amount of foreign income taxes paid or accrued for which a deduction is allowed, for example, under section 901(k)(7), with respect to foreign source income in a separate category includes only those foreign income taxes that are allocated and apportioned to foreign source income in the separate category under the rules of § 1.861-20 (as modified by this section). For purposes of this section, unless otherwise stated, terms have the same meaning as provided in § 1.861-20(b).

(b) *Assigning an item of foreign gross income to a separate category.*—For purposes of assigning an item of foreign gross income to a separate category or categories (or foreign source income in a separate category) under § 1.861-20, the rules of this paragraph (b) apply.

(1) *Base differences.*—Any item of foreign gross income that is attributable to a base difference described in § 1.861-20(d)(2)(ii)(B) is assigned to the separate category described in section 904(d)(2)(H)(i), and to foreign source income in that category.

(2) *Certain disregarded payments.*—(i) *Certain disregarded payments made by a foreign branch.*—Except in the case of disregarded payments in exchange for property described in § 1.861-20(d)(3)(ii)(C), if in connection with a disregarded payment made by a foreign branch to another foreign branch or to a foreign branch owner that is described in § 1.861-20(d)(3)(ii)(A), U.S. gross income that would otherwise be attributable to a foreign branch is attributed to another foreign branch or to the foreign branch owner under § 1.904-4(f)(2)(vi)(A) (including by reason of § 1.904-4(f)(2)(vi)(D)), the item of foreign gross income that arises by reason of the disregarded payment is assigned to the same separate category as the reattributed U.S. gross income.

(ii) *Certain disregarded payments made by a foreign branch owner.*—Except in the case of disregarded payments in exchange for property described in § 1.861-20(d)(3)(ii)(C), an item that a United States person includes in foreign gross income solely by reason of the receipt of a disregarded payment that is described in § 1.861-20(d)(3)(ii)(B) (payment to a foreign branch by a foreign branch owner) is assigned to the foreign branch category (or a specified separate category associated with the foreign branch category), or, in the case of a foreign branch owner that is a partnership, to the partnership's general category income that is attributable to the foreign branch. See § 1.960-1(d)(3)(ii)(A) and (e) for rules providing that foreign income tax on a disregarded payment by a foreign branch owner that is a controlled foreign corporation is assigned to the residual grouping and cannot be deemed paid under section 960.

(3) *Disposition of property resulting in reattribution of U.S. gross income to or from a foreign branch.*—If a disposition of property results

in the recognition of U.S. gross income that is reattributed under § 1.904-4(f)(2)(vi)(A) by reason of a disregarded payment described in § 1.904-4(f)(2)(vi)(B)(2) (or by reason of § 1.904-4(f)(2)(vi)(D)), any foreign gross income arising from that disposition of property under foreign law is assigned to a separate category under the rules in § 1.861-20(d)(1) applied without regard to the reattribution of U.S. gross income under § 1.904-4(f)(2)(vi)(A).

(c) *Allocating and apportioning deductions.*—For purposes of applying § 1.861-20(e) to allocate and apportion deductions allowed under foreign law to foreign gross income in the separate categories, before undertaking the steps outlined in § 1.861-20(e), foreign gross income in the passive category is first reduced by any related person interest expense that is allocated to the income under the principles of section 954(b)(5) and § 1.904-5(c)(2)(ii)(C). In allocating and apportioning expenses not specifically allocated under foreign law, the principles of foreign law are applied only after taking into account the reduction of passive income by the application of section 954(b)(5). In allocating and apportioning expenses when foreign law does not provide rules for the allocation or apportionment of expenses, losses or other deductions to particular items of foreign gross income, then the principles of section 954(b)(5), in addition to the principles of the section 861 regulations (as defined in § 1.861-8(a)(1)), apply to allocate and apportion expenses, losses or other foreign law deductions to foreign gross income after reduction of passive income by the amount of related person interest expense allocated to passive income under section 954(b)(5) and § 1.904-5(c)(2)(ii)(C).

(d) *Apportionment of taxes for purposes of applying the high-tax income tests.*—If taxes have been allocated and apportioned to passive income under the rules of paragraph (a) this section, the taxes must further be apportioned to the groups of income described in § 1.904-4(c)(3), (4) and (5) for purposes of determining if the group is high-taxed income that is recharacterized as income in another separate category under the rules of § 1.904-4(c). *See also* § 1.954-1(c)(1)(iii)(B) (defining a single item of passive category foreign personal holding company income by reference to the grouping rules under § 1.904-4(c)(3), (4) and (5)). Taxes are related to income in a particular group under the same rules as those in paragraph (a) of this section except that those rules are applied by apportioning foreign income taxes to the groups described in § 1.904-4(c)(3), (4) and (5) instead of separate categories.

* * *

(f) *Treatment of certain foreign income taxes paid or accrued by United States shareholders.*—Some or all of the foreign gross income of a United States shareholder of a controlled foreign corporation that is a foreign law CFC described in § 1.861-20(d)(3)(i)(D) or a reverse hybrid described in § 1.861-20(d)(3)(iii) is assigned to the section 951A category if, were the controlled foreign corporation the taxpayer that recognizes the foreign gross income, the foreign gross income would be assigned to the controlled foreign corporation's tested income group (as defined in § 1.960-1(b)(33)) within the general category to which an inclusion under section 951A is attributable. The amount of the United States shareholder's foreign gross income that is assigned to the section 951A category (or a specified separate category associated with the section 951A category) is based on the inclusion percentage (as defined in § 1.960-2(c)(2)) of the United States shareholder. For example, if a United States shareholder has an inclusion percentage of 60 percent, then 60 percent of the foreign gross income of a United States shareholder that would be assigned (under § 1.861-20(d)(3)(iii)) to the tested income group within the general category income of a reverse hybrid that is a controlled foreign corporation to which an inclusion under section 951A is attributable is assigned to the section 951A category or the specified separate category for income resourced under a tax treaty, and not to the general category.

(g) *Examples.*—For examples illustrating the application of this section, see § 1.861-20(g).

(h) *Applicability date.*—This section applies to taxable years beginning after December 31, 2019. For taxable years that both begin after December 31, 2017, and end on or after December 4, 2018, and also begin before January 1, 2020, see § 1.904-6 as in effect on December 17, 2019.

Allocation and Apportionment of Deductions and Foreign Tax Credit: Guidance

Allocation and Apportionment of Deductions and Foreign Tax Credit: Guidance.—Amendments to Reg. § 1.904(b)-3, relating to the allocation and apportionment of deductions and creditable foreign taxes, the definition of financial services income, foreign tax redeterminations, availability of foreign tax credits under the transition tax, and the application of the foreign tax credit limitation to consolidated groups, are proposed (published in the Federal Register on December 17, 2019) (REG-105495-19).

Par. 15. Section 1.904(b)-3 is amended by adding paragraph (d)(2) and revising paragraph (f) to read as follows:

§ 1.904(b)-3. Disregard of certain dividends and deductions under section 904(b)(4).

* * *

(d) * * *

(2) *Net operating losses.*—If the taxpayer has a net operating loss in the current taxable year, then solely for purposes of determining the source and separate category of the net operating loss, the overall foreign loss rules in section 904(f) and the overall domestic loss rules in section 904(g) are applied without taking into account the adjustments required under section 904(b) and this section.

* * *

(f) *Applicability dates.*—(1) Except as provided in paragraph (f)(2) of this section, this section applies to taxable years beginning after December 31, 2017.

(2) Paragraph (d)(2) of this section applies to taxable years ending on or after December 16, 2019.

Allocation and Apportionment of Deductions and Foreign Tax Credit: Guidance

Allocation and Apportionment of Deductions and Foreign Tax Credit: Guidance.—Amendments to Reg. § 1.904(g)-3, relating to the allocation and apportionment of deductions and creditable foreign taxes, the definition of financial services income, foreign tax redeterminations, availability of foreign tax credits under the transition tax, and the application of the foreign tax credit limitation to consolidated groups, are proposed (published in the Federal Register on December 17, 2019) (REG-105495-19).

Par. 16. Section 1.904(g)-3 is amended by:

1. Adding a sentence at the end of paragraph (b)(1).

2. Adding paragraph (j) and revising paragraph (l).

The addition and revisions read as follows:

§ 1.904(g)-3. Ordering rules for the allocation of net operating losses, net capital losses, U.S. source losses, and separate limitation losses, and for the recapture of separate limitation losses, overall foreign losses, and overall domestic losses.

* * *

(b) * * *

(1) * * * See §§ 1.861-8(e)(8), 1.904(b)-3(d)(2), and 1.1502-4(c)(1)(iii) for rules to determine the source and separate category components of a net operating loss.

* * *

(j) *Step Nine: Dispositions that result in additional income recognition under the branch loss recapture and dual consolidated loss recapture rules.*—(1) *In general.*—If, after any gain is required to be recognized under section 904(f)(3) on a transaction that is otherwise a nonrecognition transaction, an additional amount of income is recognized under section 91(d), section 367(a)(3)(C) (as applicable to losses incurred before January 1, 2018), or § 1.1503(d)-6, and that additional income amount is determined by taking into account an offset for the amount of gain recognized under section 904(f)(3) and so is not initially taken into account in applying paragraph (b) of this section, then paragraphs (b) through (h) of this section are applied to determine the allocation of any additional net operating loss deduction and other deductions or losses and the applicable increases in the taxpayer's overall foreign loss, separate limitation loss, and overall domestic loss accounts, as well as any additional recapture and reduction of the taxpayer's separate limitation loss, overall foreign loss, and overall domestic loss accounts.

(2) *Rules for additional recapture of loss accounts.*—For the purpose of recapturing and reducing loss accounts under paragraph (j)(1) of this section, the taxpayer also takes into account any creation of or addition to loss accounts that result from the application of paragraphs (b) through (i) of this section in the current tax year. If any of the additional income described in paragraph (j)(1) of this section is foreign source income in a separate category for which there is a remaining balance in an OFL account after applying paragraph (i) of this section, the section 904(f)(1) recapture amount under § 1.904(f)-2(c) for that additional income is determined by first computing a hypothetical recapture amount as it would have been determined prior to the application of paragraph (i) of this section but taking into account the additional foreign source income described in this paragraph (j)(2) and then subtracting the actual OFL recapture determined prior to the application of paragraph (i) of this section (that did not take into account the additional foreign source income). The remainder is the OFL recapture amount with respect to the additional foreign source income described in this paragraph (j)(2).

* * *

(l) *Applicability date.*—This section applies to taxable years ending on or after the date the final regulations are filed with the **Federal Register.**

Allocation and Apportionment of Deductions and Foreign Tax Credit: Guidance

Allocation and Apportionment of Deductions and Foreign Tax Credit: Guidance.—Amendments to Reg. §§ 1.905-3—1.905-5, relating to the allocation and apportionment of deductions and creditable foreign taxes, the definition of financial services income, foreign tax redeterminations, availability of foreign tax credits under the transition tax, and the application of the foreign tax credit limitation to consolidated groups, are proposed (published in the Federal Register on December 17, 2019) (REG-105495-19).

Par. 17. Section 1.905-3 is amended by:

1. Revising the section heading and the first sentence of paragraph (a).

2. Adding paragraphs (b)(2) and (3).

3. Revising paragraph (d).

The revisions and additions read as follows:

§ 1.905-3. Adjustments to U.S. tax liability and to current earnings and profits as a result of a foreign tax redetermination.—(a) * * * For purposes of this section and § 1.905-4, the term foreign tax redetermination means a change in the liability for foreign income taxes, as defined in § 1.960-1(b)(5), or certain other changes described in this paragraph (a) that may affect a taxpayer's U.S. tax liability, including by reason of a change in the amount of its foreign tax credit, the amount of its distributions or inclusions under sections 951, 951A, or 1293, the application of the high-tax exception described in section 954(b)(4) (including for purposes of determining tested income under section 951A(c)(2)(A)(i)(III)), or the amount of tax determined under sections 1291(c)(2) and 1291(g)(1)(C)(ii). * * *

(b) * * *

(2) *Foreign income taxes paid or accrued by foreign corporations.*—(i) *In general.*—A redetermination of U.S. tax liability is required to

account for the effect of a redetermination of foreign income taxes taken into account by a foreign corporation in the year accrued, or a refund of foreign income taxes taken into account by the foreign corporation in the year paid.

(ii) *Required adjustments.*—If a redetermination of U.S. tax liability is required for any taxable year under paragraph (b)(2)(i) of this section, the foreign corporation's taxable income, earnings and profits, and current year taxes (as defined in § 1.960-1(b)(4)) must be adjusted in the year to which the redetermined tax relates (or, in the case of a foreign corporation that receives a refund of foreign income tax and uses the cash basis of accounting, in the year the tax was paid). The redetermination of U.S. tax liability is made by treating the redetermined amount of foreign tax as the amount of tax paid or accrued by the foreign corporation in such year. For example, in the case of a refund of foreign income taxes taken into account in the year accrued, the foreign corporation's subpart F income, tested income, and earnings and profits are increased, as appropriate, in the year to which the foreign tax relates to reflect the functional currency amount of the foreign income tax refund. The required redetermination of U.S. tax liability must account for the effect of the foreign tax redetermination on the characterization and amount of distributions or inclusions under sections 951, 951A, or 1293 taken into account by each of the foreign corporation's United States shareholders, on the application of the high-tax exception described in section 954(b)(4) (including for purposes of determining tested income under section 951A(c)(2)(A)(i)(III)), and the amount of tax determined under sections 1291(c)(2) and 1291(g)(1)(C)(ii), as well as on the amount of foreign taxes deemed paid under section 960 in such year, regardless of whether any such shareholder chooses to deduct or credit its foreign income taxes in any taxable year. In addition, a redetermination of U.S. tax liability is required for any subsequent taxable year in which the characterization or amount of a United States share-holder's distribution or inclusion from the foreign corporation is affected by the foreign tax redetermination, up to and including the taxable year in which the foreign tax redetermination occurs, as well as any year to which unused foreign taxes from such year were carried under section 904(c).

(iii) *Reduction of corporate level tax on distribution of earnings and profits.*—If a United States shareholder of a controlled foreign corporation receives a distribution out of previously taxed earnings and profits described in section 959(c)(1) and (2) and a foreign country has imposed tax on the income of the controlled foreign corporation, which tax is reduced on distribution of the earnings and profits of the corporation (resulting in a foreign tax redetermination), then the United States shareholder must redetermine its U.S. tax liability for the year or years affected.

(iv) *Foreign tax redeterminations relating to taxable years beginning before January 1, 2018.*—In the case of a foreign tax redetermination of a foreign corporation that relates to a taxable year of the foreign corporation beginning before January 1, 2018, a redetermination of U.S. tax liability is required under the rules of § 1.905-5.

(v) *Examples.*—The following examples illustrate the application of this paragraph (b)(2).

(A) *Presumed Facts.*—Except as otherwise provided, the following facts are assumed for purposes of the examples:

(1) All parties are accrual basis taxpayers that use the calendar year as their taxable year both for Federal income tax purposes and for foreign tax purposes and use the average exchange rate to translate accrued foreign income taxes;

(2) CFC, CFC1, and CFC2 are controlled foreign corporations organized in Country X that use the "u" as their functional currency;

(3) No income adjustment is required to reflect exchange gain or loss (within the meaning of § 1.988-1(e)) with respect to the disposition of nonfunctional currency attributable to a refund of foreign income taxes received by any CFC, because all foreign income taxes are denominated and paid in the CFC's functional currency;

(4) The highest rate of U.S. tax in section 11 and the rate applicable to USP in all years is 21 percent; and

(5) USP's foreign tax credit limitation under section 904(a) exceeds the amount of foreign income taxes it is deemed to pay.

(B) *Example 1: Refund of tested foreign income taxes*—(1) *Facts.* CFC is a wholly-owned subsidiary of USP, a domestic corporation. In Year 1, CFC earns 3,660u of general category gross tested income and accrues and pays 300u of foreign income taxes with respect to that income. CFC has no allowable deductions other than the foreign income tax expense. Accordingly, CFC has tested income of 3,360u in Year 1. CFC has no qualified business asset investment (within the meaning of section 951A(d) and § 1.951A-3(b)). In Year 1, no portion of USP's deduction under section 250 ("section 250 deduction") is

reduced by reason of section 250(a)(2)(B)(ii). USP's inclusion percentage (as defined in § 1.960-2(c)(2)) is 100%. In Year 1, USP earns no other income and has no other expenses. The average exchange rate used to translate USP's inclusion under section 951A and CFC's foreign income taxes into dollars for Year 1 is $1x:1u. *See* section 989(b)(3) and §§ 1.951A-1(d)(1) and 1.986(a)-1(a)(1). Accordingly, for Year 1, USP's tested foreign income taxes (as defined in § 1.960-2(c)(3)) with respect to CFC are $300x. In Year 3, CFC carries back a loss for foreign tax purposes and receives a refund of foreign tax of 100u that relates to Year 1.

(2) *Analysis*—(i) *Result in Year 1.* In Year 1, CFC has tested income of 3,360u and tested foreign income taxes of $300x. Under section 951A(a) and § 1.951A-1(c)(1), USP has a GILTI inclusion amount of $3,360x (3,360u translated at $1x:1u). Under section 960(d) and § 1.960-2(c), USP is deemed to have paid $240x (80% x 100% x $300x) of foreign income taxes. Under section 78 and § 1.78-1(a), USP is treated as receiving a dividend of $300x (a "section 78 dividend"). USP's section 250 deduction is $1,830x (50% x ($3,360x + $300x)). Accordingly, for Year 1, USP has taxable income of $1,830x ($3,360x + $300x - $1,830x) and pre-credit U.S. tax liability of $384.3x (21% x $1,830x). Accordingly, USP pays U.S. tax of $144.3x ($384.3x - $240x).

(ii) *Result in Year 3.* The refund of 100u to CFC in Year 3 is a foreign tax redetermination under paragraph (a) of this section. Under paragraph (b)(2)(ii) of this section, USP must account for the effect of the foreign tax redetermination on its GILTI inclusion amount and foreign taxes deemed paid in Year 1. In redetermining USP's U.S. tax liability for Year 1, USP must increase CFC's tested income and its earnings and profits in Year 1 by the refunded tax amount of 100u, must determine the effect of that increase on its GILTI inclusion amount, and must adjust the amount of foreign taxes deemed paid and the section 78 dividend to account for CFC's refund of foreign tax. Under § 1.986(a)-1(c), the refund is translated into dollars at the exchange rate that was used to translate such amount when initially accrued. As a result of the foreign tax redetermination, for Year 1, CFC has tested income of 3,460u (3,360u + 100u) and tested foreign income taxes of $200x ($300x - $100x). Under section 951A(a) and § 1.951A-1(c)(1), USP has a redetermined GILTI inclusion amount of $3,460x (3,460u translated at $1x:1u). Under section 960(d) and § 1.960-2(c), USP is deemed to have paid $160x (80% x 100% x $200x) of foreign income taxes. Under section 78 and § 1.78-1(a), USP's section 78 dividend is $200x. USP's redetermined section 250 deduction is $1,830x (50% x ($3,460x + $200x)). Accordingly, USP's redetermined taxable income is $1,830x ($3,460x + $200x - $1,830x) and its pre-credit U.S. tax liability is $384.3x (21% x $1,830x). Therefore, USP's redetermined U.S. tax liability is $224.3x ($384.3x - $160x), an increase of $80x ($224.3x - $144.3x).

(C) *Example 2: High tax exception election following a foreign tax redetermination*—(1) *Facts.* CFC is a wholly-owned subsidiary of USP, a domestic corporation. In Year 1, CFC earns 1,000u of general category gross foreign base company sales income and accrues and pays 100u of foreign income taxes with respect to that income. CFC has no allowable deductions other than the foreign income tax expense. The average exchange rate used to translate USP's subpart F inclusion and CFC's foreign income taxes into dollars for Year 1 is $1x:1u. *See* section 989(b)(3) and § 1.986(a)-1(a)(1). In Year 1, USP earns no other income and has no other expenses. In Year 5, pursuant to a Country X audit CFC accrues and pays additional foreign income tax of 80u with respect to its 1,000u of general category foreign base company sales income earned in Year 1. The spot rate (as defined in § 1.988-1(d)) on the date of payment of the tax in Year 5 is $1x:0.8u. The foreign income taxes accrued and paid in Year 1 and Year 5 are properly attributable to CFC's foreign base company sales income that is included in income by USP under section 951(a)(1)(A) ("subpart F inclusion") in Year 1 with respect to CFC.

(2) *Analysis*—(i) *Result in Year 1.* In Year 1, CFC has subpart F income of 900u (1,000u - 100u). Accordingly, USP has a $900x (900u translated at $1x:1u) subpart F inclusion. Under section 960(a) and § 1.960-2(b), USP is deemed to have paid $100x (100u translated at $1x:1u) of foreign income taxes. Under section 78 and § 1.78-1(a), USP's section 78 dividend is $100x. Accordingly, for Year 1, USP has taxable income of $1,000x ($900x + $100x) and pre-credit U.S. tax liability of $210x (21% x $1,000x). Accordingly, USP's U.S. tax liability is $110x ($210x - $100x).

(ii) *Result in Year 5.* CFC's payment of 80u of additional foreign income tax in Year 5 with respect to Year 1 is a foreign tax redetermination as defined in paragraph (a) of this section. Under paragraph (b)(2)(ii) of this section, USP must reduce CFC's subpart F income and its earnings and profits in Year 1 by the additional tax amount of 80u. Further, USP must reduce its subpart F inclusion, adjust the amount of foreign taxes deemed paid, and adjust the amount of the section 78 dividend to account for CFC's additional payment of foreign tax. Under section 986(a)(1)(B)(i) and § 1.986(a)-1(a)(2)(i), because CFC's payment of additional tax occurs more than 24 months after the close of the taxable year to which it relates, the additional tax is translated into dollars at the spot rate on the date of payment ($1x:0.8u). Therefore, CFC has foreign income taxes of $200x (100u translated at $1x:1u plus 80u translated at $1x:0.8u) that are properly attributable to CFC's foreign base company sales income that gives rise to USP's subpart F inclusion in Year 1. As a result of the foreign tax redetermination, for Year 1, USP has a subpart F inclusion of $820x (1,000u - 180u = 820u translated at $1x:1u). Under section 960(a) and §1.960-2(b), USP is deemed to have paid $200x of foreign income taxes. Under section 78 and §1.78-1(a), USP's section 78 dividend is $200x. For purposes of section 954(b)(4), the effective tax rate on the general category foreign base company sales income is determined by dividing $200x, the U.S. dollar amount of the foreign taxes deemed paid, by the U.S. dollar amount of the net item of foreign base company sales income ($820x) plus the amount of the foreign income tax ($200x). Thus, the effective rate imposed on the general category foreign base company sales income in Year 1 is 19.6% ($200x/$1020x), which exceeds 18.9% (90% of 21%, the highest tax rate in section 11). Therefore, after the foreign tax redetermination, USP is eligible to elect to exclude the item of subpart F income under section 954(b)(4) and §1.954-1(d). If USP makes the election under §1.954-1(d), USP's taxable income, pre-credit U.S. tax liability, and allowable foreign tax credit is zero, resulting in a decrease in USP's U.S. tax liability of $110x. If USP does not make the election under §1.954-1(d), then USP's redetermined U.S. taxable income is $1020x ($820x + $200x) and its pre-credit U.S. tax liability is $214.2x (21% x $1020x). Therefore, USP's redetermined U.S. tax liability is $14.20x ($214.2x - $200x), a decrease of $95.80x ($110x - $14.20x). If USP makes a timely refund claim within the time period allowed by section 6511, USP will be entitled to a refund of any overpayment resulting from the redetermination of U.S. tax liability.

(D) *Example 3: Two-year rule*—(1) *Facts.* CFC is a wholly-owned subsidiary of USP, a domestic corporation. In Year 1, CFC earns 1,000u of general category gross foreign base company sales income and accrues 210u of foreign income taxes with respect to that income. In Year 1, USP earns no other income and has no other expenses. The average exchange rate used to translate USP's subpart F inclusion and CFC's foreign income taxes into dollars for Year 1 is $1x:1u. See sections 989(b)(3) and 986(a)(1)(A) and §1.986(a)-1(a)(1). USP does not elect to treat CFC's subpart F income as high taxed income under section 954(b)(4). CFC does not pay its foreign income taxes for Year 1 until September 1, Year 5, when the spot rate is $0.8x:1u. The foreign income taxes accrued and paid in Year 1 and Year 5, respectively, are properly attributable to CFC's foreign base company sales income that gives rise to USP's subpart F inclusion in Year 1 with respect to CFC.

(2) *Analysis*—(i) *Result in Year 1.* In Year 1, CFC has subpart F income of 790u (1,000u - 210u). Accordingly, USP has a $790x (790u translated at $1x:1u) subpart F inclusion. Under section 960(a) and §1.960-2(b), USP is deemed to have paid $210x (210u translated at $1x:1u) of foreign income taxes. Under section 78 and §1.78-1(a), USP's section 78 dividend is $210x. Accordingly, for Year 1, USP has taxable income of $1,000x ($790x + $210x) and pre-credit U.S. tax liability of $210x (21% x $1,000x). Accordingly, USP owes no U.S. tax ($210x - $210x = 0).

(ii) *Result in Year 3.* CFC's failure to pay the tax by the end of Year 3 results in a foreign tax redetermination under paragraph (a) of this section. Because the taxes are not paid on or before the date 24 months after the close of the taxable year to which the tax relates, under paragraph (a) of this section CFC must account for the redetermination as if the unpaid 210u of taxes were refunded on the last day of Year 3. Under paragraph (b)(2)(ii) of this section, USP must increase CFC's subpart F income and its earnings and profits in Year 1 by the unpaid tax amount of 210u. Further, USP must increase its subpart F inclusion, and decrease the amount of foreign taxes deemed paid and the amount of the section 78 dividend to account for the unpaid taxes. As a result of the foreign tax redetermination, for Year 1, USP has a subpart F inclusion of $1,000x (1,000u translated at $1x:1u). Under section 960(a) and §1.960-2(b), USP is deemed to have paid no foreign income taxes. Under section 78 and §1.78-1(a), USP has no section 78 dividend. Accordingly, USP's redetermined taxable income is $1,000x and its pre-credit U.S. tax liability is unchanged at $210x (21% x $1,000x). However, USP has no foreign tax credits. Therefore, USP's redetermined U.S. tax liability for Year 1 is $210x, an increase of $210x.

(iii) *Result in Year 5.* CFC's payment of the Year 1 tax liability of 210u on September 1, Year 5, results in a second foreign tax redetermination under paragraph (a) of this section. Under paragraph (b)(2)(ii) of this section, USP must decrease CFC's subpart F income and its earnings and profits in Year 1 by the tax paid amount of 210u. Further, USP must reduce its subpart F inclusion, and increase the amount of foreign taxes deemed paid and the amount of the section 78 dividend to account for CFC's payment of foreign tax. Under section 986(a)(1)(B)(i) and §1.986(a)-1(a)(2)(i), because the tax was paid more than 24 months after the close of the year to which the tax relates, CFC must translate the 210u of tax at the spot rate on the date of payment of the foreign taxes in Year 5. Therefore, CFC has foreign income taxes of $168x (210u translated at $0.8x:1u) that are properly attributable to CFC's foreign base company sales income

that gives rise to USP's subpart F inclusion in Year 1. As a result of the foreign tax redetermination, for Year 1, USP has a subpart F inclusion of $790x (1,000u - 210u = 790u translated at $1x:1u). Under section 960(a) and §1.960-2(b), USP is deemed to have paid $168x of foreign income taxes. Under section 78 and §1.78-1(a), USP's section 78 dividend is $168x. Accordingly, USP's redetermined taxable income is $958x ($790x + $168x) and its pre-credit U.S. tax liability is $201.18x (21% x $958x). Under section 904(a), USP's foreign tax credit limitation is $201.18x ($201.18x x $958x/$958x) and exceeds the $168x of foreign income tax that USP is deemed to have paid. Therefore USP's redetermined U.S. tax liability is $33.18 ($201.18x - $168x), a decrease of $176.82x ($210x - $33.18x).

(E) *Example 4: Contested tax*—(1) *Facts.* CFC is a wholly-owned subsidiary of USP, a domestic corporation. In Year 1, CFC earns 360u of general category gross tested income and accrues and pays 160u of current year taxes with respect to that income. CFC has no allowable deductions other than the foreign income tax expense. Accordingly, CFC has tested income of 200u in year 1. CFC has no qualified business asset investment (within the meaning of section 951A(d) and §1.951A-3(b)). In Year 1, no portion of USP's section 250 deduction is reduced by reason of section 250(a)(2)(B)(ii). USP's inclusion percentage (as defined in §1.960-2(c)(2)) is 100%. In Year 1, USP earns no other income and has no other expenses. The average exchange rate used to translate USP's section 951A inclusion and CFC's foreign income taxes into dollars for Year 1 is $1x:1u. See section 989(b)(3) and §§1.951A-1(d)(1) and 1.986(a)-1(a)(1). Accordingly, for Year 1, USP's tested foreign income taxes (as defined in §1.960-2(c)(3)) with respect to CFC are $160x. In Year 3, Country X assessed an additional 30u of tax with respect to CFC's Year 1 income. CFC did not pay the additional 30u of tax and contested the assessment. After exhausting all effective and practical remedies to reduce, over time, its liability for foreign tax, CFC settled the contest with Country X in Year 4 for 20u, which CFC did not pay until January 15, Year 5, when the spot rate was $1.1x:1u. CFC did not earn any other income or accrue any other foreign income taxes in Years 2 through 6 and made no distributions to USP. The additional taxes paid in Year 5 are also tested foreign income taxes of USP with respect to CFC.

(2) *Analysis*—(i) *Result in Year 1.* In Year 1, CFC has tested income of 200u and tested foreign income taxes of $160x. Under section 951A(a) and §1.951A-1(c)(1), USP has a GILTI inclusion amount of $200x (200u translated at $1x:1u). Under section 960(d) and §1.960-2(c), USP is deemed to have paid $128x (80% x 100% x $160x) of foreign income taxes. Under section 78 and §1.78-1(a), USP's section 78 dividend is $160x. USP's section 250 deduction is $180x (50% x ($200x + $160x)). Accordingly, for Year 1, USP has taxable income of $180x ($200x + $160x - $180x) and a pre-credit U.S. tax liability of $37.8x (21% x $180x). Under section 904(a), because all of USP's income is section 951A category income (see §1.904-4(g)), USP's foreign tax credit limitation is $37.8 ($37.8x x $180x/$180x), which is less than the $128x of foreign income tax that USP is deemed to have paid. Accordingly, USP owes no U.S. tax ($37.8x - $37.8x = 0).

(ii) *Result in Year 5.* CFC's accrual and payment of the additional 20u of foreign income tax with respect to Year 1 is a foreign tax redetermination under paragraph (a) of this section. Under §1.461-4(g)(6)(iii)(B), the additional taxes accrue when the tax contest is resolved, that is, in Year 4. However, because the taxes, which relate to Year 1, were not paid on or before the date 24 months after close of CFC's taxable year to which the tax relates, that is, Year 1, under section 905(c)(2) and paragraph (a) of this section CFC cannot take these taxes into account when they accrue in Year 4. Instead, the taxes are taken into account when they are paid in Year 5. Under paragraph (b)(2)(ii) of this section, USP must decrease CFC's tested income and its earnings and profits in Year 1 by the additional tax amount of 20u. Further, USP must adjust its GILTI inclusion amount, the amount of foreign taxes deemed paid, and the amount of the section 78 dividend to account for CFC's additional payment of tax. Under section 986(a)(1)(B)(i) and §1.986(a)-1(a)(2)(i), because CFC's payment of additional tax occurs more than 24 months after the close of the taxable year to which it relates, the additional tax is translated into dollars at the spot rate on the date of payment ($1.1x:1u). Therefore, CFC has tested foreign income taxes of $182x (160u translated at $1x:1u plus 20u translated at $1.1x:1u). As a result of the foreign tax redetermination, for Year 1, CFC has tested income of 180u (200u - 20u). Under section 951A(a) and §1.951A-1(c)(1), USP has a redetermined GILTI inclusion amount of $180x (180u, translated at $1x:1u). Under section 960(d) and §1.960-2(c), USP is deemed to have paid $145.6x (80% x 100% x $182x) of foreign income taxes. Under section 78 and §1.78-1(a), USP's section 78 dividend is $182x. USP's redetermined section 250 deduction is $181x (50% x ($180x + $182x)). Accordingly, USP's redetermined taxable income is $181x ($180x + $182x − $181x) and its pre-credit U.S. tax liability is $38.01x (21% x $181x). Under section 904(a), USP's foreign tax credit limitation is $38.01x ($38.01x x $181x/$181x), which is less than the $145.6x of foreign tax credits that USP is deemed to have paid. Therefore, USP's redetermined U.S. tax liability is zero ($38.01x - $38.01x).

(3) *Foreign tax redeterminations of successors or transferees.* If at the time of a foreign tax redetermination the person with legal liability for the tax (or in the case of a refund, the legal right to such refund) (the "successor") is a different person than the person that had legal liability for the tax in the year to which the redetermined tax relates (the "original taxpayer"), the required redetermination of U.S. tax liability is made as if the foreign tax redetermination occurred in the hands of the original taxpayer. Federal income tax principles apply to determine the tax consequences if the successor remits (or receives a refund of) a tax that in the year to which the

redetermined tax relates was the legal liability of, and thus under § 1.901-2(f) is considered paid by, the original taxpayer.

* * *

(d) *Applicability dates.*—This section applies to foreign tax redeterminations occurring in taxable years ending on or after December 16, 2019, and to foreign tax redeterminations of foreign corporations occurring in taxable years that end with or within a taxable year of a United States shareholder ending on or after December 16, 2019 and that relate to taxable years of foreign corporations beginning after December 31, 2017.

Par. 18. Section 1.905-4, as proposed to be added at 72 FR 62805 (November 7, 2007), is further revised to read as follows:

§1.905-4. Notification of foreign tax redetermination.— (a) *Application of this section.*—The rules of this section apply if, as a result of a foreign tax redetermination (as defined in § 1.905-3(a)), a redetermination of U.S. tax liability is required under section 905(c) and § 1.905-3(b).

(b) *Time and manner of notification.*—(1) *Redetermination of U.S. tax liability.*—(i) *In general.*—Except as provided in paragraphs (b)(1)(v) and (b)(2) through (b)(4) of this section, any taxpayer for which a redetermination of U.S. tax liability is required must notify the Internal Revenue Service (IRS) of the foreign tax redetermination by filing an amended return, Form 1118 (Foreign Tax Credit—Corporations) or Form 1116 (Foreign Tax Credit), and the statement described in paragraph (c) of this section for the taxable year with respect to which a redetermination of U.S. tax liability is required. Such notification must be filed within the time prescribed by this paragraph (b) and contain the information described in paragraph (c) of this section. If a foreign tax redetermination requires an individual to redetermine the individual's U.S. tax liability, and if, after taking into account such foreign tax redetermination, the amount of creditable foreign taxes (as defined in section 904(j)(3)(B)) that are paid or accrued by such individual during the taxable year does not exceed the applicable dollar limitation in section 904(j), the individual is not required to file Form 1116 with the amended return for such taxable year if the individual satisfies the requirements of section 904(j).

(ii) *Increase in amount of U.S. tax liability.*—Except as provided in paragraphs (b)(1)(iv) and (b)(2) through (b)(4) of this section, for each taxable year of the taxpayer with respect to which a redetermination of U.S. tax liability is required by reason of a foreign tax redetermination that increases the amount of U.S. tax liability, for example, by reason of a downward adjustment to the amount of foreign income taxes paid or accrued by the taxpayer or a foreign corporation with respect to which the taxpayer computes an amount of foreign taxes deemed paid, the taxpayer must file a separate notification by the due date (with extensions) of the original return for the taxpayer's taxable year in which the foreign tax redetermination occurs.

(iii) *Decrease in amount of U.S. tax liability.*—Except as provided in paragraphs (b)(1)(iv) and (b)(2) through (b)(4) of this section, for each taxable year of the taxpayer with respect to which a redetermination of U.S. tax liability is required by reason of a foreign tax redetermination that decreases the amount of U.S. tax liability and results in an overpayment, for example, by reason of an increase in the amount of foreign income taxes paid or accrued by the taxpayer or a foreign corporation with respect to which the taxpayer computes an amount of foreign taxes deemed paid, the taxpayer must file a claim for refund with the IRS within the period provided in section 6511. See section 6511(d)(3)(A) for the special refund period for refunds attributable to an increase in foreign tax credits.

(iv) *Multiple redeterminations of U.S. tax liability for same taxable year.*—The rules of this paragraph (b)(1)(iv) apply except as provided in paragraphs (b)(1)(v), (b)(2) through (b)(4) of this section. If more than one foreign tax redetermination requires a redetermination of U.S. tax liability for the same affected taxable year of the taxpayer and those foreign tax redeterminations occur within the same taxable year or within two consecutive taxable years of the taxpayer, the taxpayer may file for the affected taxable year one amended return, Form 1118 or Form 1116, and the statement described in paragraph (c) of this section that reflects all such foreign tax redeterminations. If the taxpayer chooses to file one notification for such redeterminations, one or more of such redeterminations would increase the U.S. tax liability, and the net effect of all such redeterminations is to increase the U.S. tax liability for the affected taxable year, the taxpayer must file such notification by the due date (with extensions) of the original return for the taxpayer's taxable year in which the first foreign tax redetermination that would result in an increased U.S. tax liability occurred. If the taxpayer chooses to file one notification for such redeterminations, one or more of such redeterminations would decrease the U.S. tax liability, and the net

effect of all such redeterminations is to decrease the total amount of U.S. tax liability for the affected taxable year, the taxpayer must file such notification as provided in paragraph (b)(1)(iii) of this section, within the period provided by section 6511. If a foreign tax redetermination with respect to the taxable year for which a redetermination of U.S. tax liability is required occurs after the date for providing such notification, more than one amended return may be required with respect to that taxable year.

(v) *Amended return required only if there is a change in amount of U.S. tax due.*—If a redetermination of U.S. tax liability is required by reason of a foreign tax redetermination, but does not change the amount of U.S. tax due for any taxable year, the taxpayer may, in lieu of applying the applicable rules of paragraphs (b)(1)(i) through (iv) of this section, notify the IRS of such redetermination by attaching a statement to the original return for the taxpayer's taxable year in which the foreign tax redetermination occurs. Such statement must be filed by the due date (with extensions) of the original return for the taxpayer's taxable year in which the foreign tax redetermination occurs and contain the information described in §1.904-2(f). If a redetermination of U.S. tax liability is required by reason of a foreign tax redetermination (either alone, or if the taxpayer chooses to apply paragraph (b)(1)(iv) of this section, in combination with other foreign tax redeterminations, as provided therein) and the redetermination of U.S. tax liability results in a change to the amount of U.S. tax due for a taxable year, but does not change the amount of U.S. tax due for other taxable years, for example, because of a carryback or carryover of an unused foreign tax under section 904(c), the notification requirements for such other taxable years are deemed to be satisfied if the taxpayer complies with the applicable rules of paragraphs (b)(1)(i) through (iv) of this section with respect to each taxable year for which the foreign tax redetermination changes the amount of U.S. tax due.

(2) *Notification with respect to a change in the amount of foreign tax reported to an owner by a pass-through entity.*—(i) *In general.*—If a partnership, trust, or other pass-through entity that reports to its beneficial owners (or to any intermediary on behalf its beneficial owners), including partners, shareholders, beneficiaries, or similar persons, an amount of creditable foreign income taxes, such pass-through entity must notify both the IRS and its owners of any foreign tax redetermination described in §1.905-3(a) with respect to the foreign tax so reported. For purposes of this paragraph (b)(2), whether or not a redetermination has occurred within the meaning of §1.905-3(a) is determined as if the pass-through entity were a domestic corporation which had elected to and claimed foreign tax credits in the amount reported for the year to which such foreign taxes relate. The notification required under this paragraph (b)(2) must include the statement described in paragraph (c) of this section along with any information necessary for the owners to redetermine their U.S. tax liability.

(ii) *Partnerships subject to subchapter C of chapter 63.*—Except as provided in paragraph (b)(4) of this section, if a redetermination of U.S. tax liability that is required under §1.905-3(b) by reason of a foreign tax redetermination described in §1.905-3(a) would require a partnership adjustment as defined in §301.6241-1(a)(6) of this chapter, the partnership must file an administrative adjustment request under section 6227 and make any adjustments required under section 6227. See §301.6227-2 and §301.6227-3 of this chapter for procedures for making adjustments with respect to an administrative adjustment request. An administrative adjustment request required under this paragraph (b)(2)(ii) must be filed by the due date (with extensions) of the original return for the partnership's taxable year in which the foreign tax redetermination occurs, and the restrictions in section 6227(c) do not apply to such filing. However, unless the administrative adjustment request may otherwise be filed after applying the limitations contained in section 6227(c), such a request is limited to adjustments that are required to be made under section 905(c). The requirements of paragraph (b)(2)(i) of this section are deemed to be satisfied with respect to any item taken into account in an administrative adjustment request filed under this paragraph (b)(2)(ii).

(3) *Alternative notification requirements.*—An amended return and Form 1118 (Foreign Tax Credit—Corporations) or Form 1116 (Foreign Tax Credit), is not required to notify the IRS of the foreign tax redetermination and redetermination of U.S. tax liability if the taxpayer satisfies alternative notification requirements that may be prescribed by the IRS through forms, instructions, publications, or other guidance.

(4) *Taxpayers under examination within the jurisdiction of the Large Business and International Division.*—(i) *In general.*—The alternative notification requirements of this paragraph (b)(4) apply if all of the following conditions are satisfied:

(A) A foreign tax redetermination occurs while the taxpayer is under examination within the jurisdiction of the Large Business and International Division (or a successor division);

(B) The foreign tax redetermination results in a downward adjustment to the amount of foreign income taxes paid or accrued by the taxpayer or a foreign corporation with respect to which the taxpayer computes an amount of foreign income taxes deemed paid;

(C) The foreign tax redetermination requires a redetermination of U.S. tax liability and accordingly, but for this paragraph (b)(4), the taxpayer would be required to notify the IRS of such foreign tax redetermination under paragraph (b)(1)(ii) of this section (determined without regard to paragraphs (b)(1)(iv) and (v) of this section) or (b)(2)(ii) of this section;

(D) The return for the taxable year for which a redetermination of U.S. tax liability is required is under examination; and

(E) The due date specified in paragraph (b)(1)(ii) or (b)(2) of this section for providing notice of such foreign tax redetermination is not before the later of the opening conference or the hand-delivery or postmark date of the opening letter concerning an examination of the return for the taxable year for which a redetermination of U.S. tax liability is required by reason of such foreign tax redetermination.

(ii) *Notification requirements.*—(A) *Foreign tax redetermination occurring before commencement of the examination.*—If a foreign tax redetermination described in paragraph (b)(4)(i)(B) and (C) of this section occurs before the later of the opening conference or the hand-delivery or postmark date of the opening letter and if the condition provided in paragraph (b)(4)(i)(E) of this section with respect to such foreign tax redetermination is met, the taxpayer, in lieu of applying the rules of paragraph (b)(1)(i) and (ii) of this section (requiring the filing of an amended return, Form 1118, and the statement described in paragraph (c) of this section) or (b)(2)(ii) of this section (requiring the filing of an administrative adjustment request), must notify the IRS of such redetermination by providing the statement described in paragraph (b)(4)(iii) of this section to the examiner no later than 120 days after the later of the date of the opening conference of the examination, or the hand-delivery or postmark date of the opening letter concerning the examination.

(B) *Foreign tax redetermination occurring within 180 days after commencement of the examination.*—If a foreign tax redetermination described in paragraph (b)(4)(i)(B) and (C) of this section occurs on or after the latest of the opening conference or the hand-delivery or postmark date of the opening letter and on or before the date that is 180 days after the later of the opening conference or the hand-delivery or postmark date of the opening letter, the taxpayer, in lieu of applying the rules of paragraph (b)(1)(i) and (ii) of this section or (b)(2) of this section, must notify the IRS of such redetermination by providing the statement described in paragraph (b)(4)(iii) of this section to the examiner no later than 120 days after the date the foreign tax redetermination occurs.

(C) *Foreign tax redetermination occurring more than 180 days after commencement of the examination.*—If a foreign tax redetermination described in paragraphs (b)(4)(i)(B) and (C) of this section occurs after the date that is 180 days after the later of the opening conference or the hand-delivery or postmark date of the opening letter, the taxpayer must either apply the rules of paragraphs (b)(1)(i) and (ii) of this section or (b)(2) of this section, or, in lieu of applying paragraphs (b)(1)(i) and (ii) of this section or (b)(2) of this section, provide the statement described in paragraph (b)(4)(iii) of this section to the examiner within 120 days after the date the foreign tax redetermination occurs. However, the IRS, in its discretion, may either accept such statement or require the taxpayer to comply with the rules of paragraphs (b)(1)(i) and (ii) of this section or (b)(2) of this section, as applicable.

(iii) *Statement.*—The statement required by paragraphs (b)(4)(ii)(A) and (B) of this section must provide the original amount of foreign income taxes paid or accrued, the revised amount of foreign income taxes paid or accrued, and documentation with respect to the revisions, including exchange rates and dates of accrual or payment, and, if applicable, the information described in para-

graph (c)(8) of this section. The statement must include the following declaration signed by a person authorized to sign the return of the taxpayer: "Under penalties of perjury, I declare that I have examined this written statement, and to the best of my knowledge and belief, this written statement is true, correct, and complete."

(iv) *Penalty for failure to file notice of a foreign tax redetermination.*—A taxpayer subject to the rules of this paragraph (b)(4) must satisfy the rules of paragraph (b)(4)(ii) of this section in order not to be subject to the penalty relating to the failure to file notice of a foreign tax redetermination under section 6689 and §301.6689-1 of this chapter.

(5) *Examples.*—The following examples illustrate the application of paragraph (b) of this section.

(i) *Example 1*—(A) X, a domestic corporation, is an accrual basis taxpayer and uses the calendar year as its U.S. taxable year. X conducts business through a branch in Country M, the currency of which is the m, and also conducts business through a branch in Country N, the currency of which is the n. X uses the average exchange rate to translate foreign income taxes. Assume that X is able to claim a credit under section 901 for all foreign income taxes paid or accrued.

(B) In Year 1, X accrued and paid 100m of Country M income taxes with respect to 400m of foreign source foreign branch category income. The average exchange rate for Year 1 was $1:1m. Also in Year 1, X accrued and paid 50n of Country N income taxes with respect to 150n of foreign source foreign branch category income. The average exchange rate for Year 1 was $1:1n. On its Year 1 Federal income tax return, X claimed a foreign tax credit under section 901 of $150 ($100 (100m translated at $1:1m) + $50 (50n translated at $1:1n)) with respect to its foreign source foreign branch category income. *See* §1.986(a)-1(a)(1).

(C) In Year 2, X accrued and paid 100n of Country N income taxes with respect to 300n of foreign source foreign branch category income. The average exchange rate for Year 2 was $1.50:1n. On its Year 2 Federal income tax return X claimed a foreign tax credit under section 901 of $150 (100n translated at $1.5:1n). *See* §1.986(a)-1(a)(1).

(D) On June 15, Year 5, when the spot rate was $1.40:1n, X received a refund of 10n from Country N, and, on March 15, Year 6, when the spot rate was $1.20:1m, X was assessed by and paid Country M an additional 20m of tax. Both payments were with respect to X's foreign source foreign branch category income in Year 1. On May 15, Year 6, when the spot rate was $1.45:1n, X received a refund of 5n from Country N with respect to its foreign source foreign branch category income in Year 2.

(E) Both the refunds and the assessment are foreign tax redeterminations under §1.905-3(a). Under §1.905-3(b)(1), X must redetermine its U.S. tax liability for both Year 1 and Year 2. With respect to Year 1, under paragraph (b)(1)(ii) of this section, X must notify the IRS of the June 15, Year 5, refund of 10n from Country N that increased X's U.S. tax liability by filing an amended return, Form 1118, and the statement required in paragraph (c) of this section for Year 1 by the due date of the original return (with extensions) for Year 5. The amended return and Form 1118 reduces the amount of foreign income taxes claimed as a credit under section 901 and increases X's U.S. tax liability by $10 (10n refund translated at the average exchange rate for Year 1, or $1:1n (see §1.986(a)-1(c)). With respect to the March 15, Year 6, additional assessment of 20m by Country M, under paragraph (b)(1)(iii) of this section, X must notify the IRS within the time period provided by section 6511, increasing the foreign income taxes available as a credit and reducing X's U.S. tax liability by $24 (20m translated at the spot rate on the date of payment, or $1.20:1m). *See* sections 986(a)(1)(B)(i) and 986(a)(2)(A) and §1.986(a)-1(a)(2)(i). X may so notify the IRS by filing a second amended return, Form 1118, and the statement described in paragraph (c) of this section for Year 1, within the time period provided by section 6511. Alternatively, under paragraph (b)(1)(iv) of this section, when X redetermines its U.S. tax liability for Year 1 to take into account the 10n refund from Country N that occurred in Year 5, X may also take into account the 20m additional assessment by Country M that occurred on March 15, Year 6. If X reflects both foreign tax redeterminations on the same amended return, Form 1118, and in the statement described in paragraph (c) of this section for Year 1, the amount of X's foreign income taxes available as a credit would be reduced by $10 (10n refund translated at $1:1n), and increased by $24 (20m additional assessment translated at the spot rate on the date of payment, March 15, Year 6, or $1.20:1m). The foreign income taxes available as a credit therefore would be increased by $14 ($24 (additional assessment) − $10 (refund)). Because the net effect of the foreign tax redeterminations is to increase the amount of foreign taxes paid or accrued and decrease X's U.S. tax liability, under paragraph (b)(1)(iv) of this section the Year 1 amended return, Form 1118, and the statement required in paragraph (c) of this section reflecting foreign tax redeterminations in both years must be filed within the time period provided by section 6511.

(F) With respect to Year 2, under paragraph (b)(1)(ii) of this section, X must notify the IRS by filing an amended return, Form 1118, and the statement required in paragraph (c) of this section for Year 2 that is separate from that filed for Year 1. The amended return, Form 1118, and the statement required in paragraph (c) of this section for Year 2 must be filed by the due date (with extensions) of X's original return for Year 6. The amended return and Form 1118 reduces the amount of foreign income taxes claimed as a credit under section 901 and increases X's U.S. tax liability by $7.50 (5n refund translated at the average exchange rate for Year 2, or $1.50:1n).

(ii) *Example 2.* X, a taxpayer within the jurisdiction of the Large Business and International Division, uses the calendar year as its U.S. taxable year. On November 15, Year 2, X receives a refund of foreign income taxes that constitutes a foreign tax redetermination and necessitates a redetermination of U.S. tax liability for X's Year 1 taxable year. Under paragraph (b)(1)(ii) of this section, X is required to notify the IRS of the foreign tax redetermination that increased its U.S. tax liability by filing an amended return, Form 1118, and the statement described in paragraph (c) of this section for its Year 1 taxable year by October 15, Year 3 (the due date (with extensions) of the original return for X's Year 2 taxable year). On December 15, Year 3, the IRS hand delivers an opening letter concerning the examination of the return for X's Year 1 taxable year, and the opening conference for such examination is scheduled for January 15, Year 4. Because the date for notifying the IRS of the foreign tax redetermination under paragraph (b)(1)(ii) of this section (October 15, Year 3) is before the date of the opening conference concerning the examination of the return for X's Year 1 taxable year (January 15, Year 4), the condition of paragraph (b)(4)(i)(E) of this section is not met, and so paragraph (b)(4)(i) of this section does not apply. Accordingly, X must notify the IRS of the foreign tax redetermination by filing an amended return, Form 1118, and the statement described in paragraph (c) of this section for the Year 1 taxable year by October 15, Year 3.

(c) *Notification contents.*—The statement required by paragraphs (b)(1)(i) through (iv) of this section and (b)(2) of this section must contain information sufficient for the IRS to redetermine U.S. tax liability if such a redetermination is required under section 905(c). The information must be in a form that enables the IRS to verify and compare the original computation of U.S. tax liability, the revised computation resulting from the foreign tax redetermination, and the net changes resulting therefrom. The statement must include the following:

(1) The taxpayer's name, address, identifying number, the taxable year or years of the taxpayer that are affected by the foreign tax redetermination, and, in the case of foreign taxes deemed paid, the name and identifying number, if any, of the foreign corporation;

(2) The date or dates the foreign income taxes were accrued, if applicable; the date or dates the foreign income taxes were paid; the amount of foreign income taxes paid or accrued on each date (in foreign currency) and the exchange rate used to translate each such amount, as provided in § 1.986(a)-1(a) or (b);

(3) Information sufficient to determine any change to the characterization of a distribution, the amount of any inclusion under section 951(a), 951A, or 1293, or the deferred tax amount under section 1291;

(4) Information sufficient to determine any interest due from or owing to the taxpayer, including the amount of any interest paid by the foreign government to the taxpayer and the dates received;

(5) In the case of any foreign income tax that is refunded in whole or in part, the taxpayer must provide the date of each such refund; the amount of such refund (in foreign currency); and the

exchange rate that was used to translate such amount when originally claimed as a credit (as provided in § 1.986(a)-1(c)) and the spot rate (as defined in § 1.988-1(d)) for the date the refund was received (for purposes of computing foreign currency gain or loss under section 988);

(6) In the case of any foreign income taxes that are not paid on or before the date that is 24 months after the close of the taxable year to which such taxes relate, the amount of such taxes in foreign currency, and the exchange rate that was used to translate such amount when originally claimed as a credit or added to PTEP group taxes (as defined in § 1.960-3(d)(1));

(7) If a redetermination of U.S. tax liability results in an amount of additional tax due, and the carryback or carryover of an unused foreign income tax under section 904(c) only partially eliminates such amount, the information required in § 1.904-2(f); and

(8) In the case of a pass-through entity, the name, address, and identifying number of each beneficial owner to which foreign taxes were reported for the taxable year or years to which the foreign tax redetermination relates, and the amount of foreign tax initially reported to each beneficial owner for each such year and the amount of foreign tax allocable to each beneficial owner for each such year after the foreign tax redetermination is taken into account.

(d) *Payment or refund of U.S. tax.*—The amount of tax, if any, due upon a redetermination of U.S. tax liability is paid by the taxpayer after notice and demand has been made by the IRS. Subchapter B of chapter 63 of the Internal Revenue Code (relating to deficiency procedures) does not apply with respect to the assessment of the amount due upon such redetermination. In accordance with sections 905(c) and 6501(c)(5), the amount of additional tax due is assessed and collected without regard to the provisions of section 6501(a) (relating to limitations on assessment and collection). The amount of tax, if any, shown by a redetermination of U.S. tax liability to have been overpaid is credited or refunded to the taxpayer in accordance with subchapter B of chapter 66 (section 6511 et seq.).

(e) *Interest and penalties.*—(1) *In general.*—If a redetermination of U.S. tax liability is required by reason of a foreign tax redetermination, interest is computed on the underpayment or overpayment in accordance with sections 6601 and 6611. No interest is assessed or collected on any underpayment resulting from a refund of foreign income taxes for any period before the receipt of the refund, except to the extent interest was paid by the foreign country or possession of the United States on the refund for the period before the receipt of the refund. *See* section 905(c)(5). In no case, however, will interest assessed and collected pursuant to the preceding sentence for any period before receipt of the refund exceed the amount that otherwise would have been assessed and collected under section 6601 for that period. Interest is assessed from the time the taxpayer (or the foreign corporation, partnership, trust, or other pass-through entity of which the taxpayer is a shareholder, partner, or beneficiary) receives a refund until the taxpayer pays the additional tax due the United States.

(2) *Imposition of penalty.*—Failure to comply with the provisions of this section subjects the taxpayer to the penalty provisions of section 6689 and § 301.6689-1 of this chapter.

(f) *Applicability date.*—This section applies to foreign tax redeterminations (as defined in § 1.905-3(a)) occurring in taxable years ending on or after December 16, 2019, and to foreign tax redeterminations of foreign corporations occurring in taxable years that end with or within a taxable year of a United States shareholder ending on or after December 16, 2019.

Par. 19. Section 1.905-5, as proposed to be added at 72 FR 62805 (November 7, 2007), is further revised to read as follows:

§1.905-5. Foreign tax redeterminations of foreign corporations that relate to taxable years of the foreign corporation beginning before January 1, 2018.—(a) *In general.*—(1) *Effect of foreign tax redetermination of a foreign corporation.*—A foreign tax redetermination (as defined in § 1.905-3(a)) of a foreign corporation that relates to a taxable year of the foreign corporation beginning before January 1, 2018, and that may affect a taxpayer's foreign tax credit in any taxable year, must be accounted for by adjusting the foreign corporation's taxable income and earnings and profits, post-1986 undistributed earnings as defined in § 1.902-1(a)(9), and post-1986 foreign income taxes as defined in § 1.902-1(a)(8) (or its pre-1987 accumulated profits as defined in § 1.902-1(a)(10)(i) and pre-1987 foreign income taxes as defined in § 1.902-1(a)(10)(iii), as applicable) in the taxable year of the foreign corporation to which the foreign taxes relate.

(2) *Requirement of U.S. tax redetermination.*—A redetermination of U.S. tax liability is required to account for the effect of the foreign tax redetermination on the earnings and profits and taxable income of the foreign corporation, the taxable income of a United States

shareholder, and the amount of foreign taxes deemed paid by the United States shareholder under section 902 or 960 (as in effect before December 22, 2017), in the year to which the redetermined foreign taxes relate. For example, in the case of a refund of foreign income taxes, the subpart F income, earnings and profits, and post-1986 undistributed earnings (or pre-1987 accumulated profits, as applicable) of the foreign corporation are increased in the year to which the foreign tax relates to reflect the functional currency amount of the foreign income tax refund. The required redetermination of U.S. tax liability must account for the effect of the foreign tax redetermination on the characterization and amount of distributions or inclusions under sections 951 or 1293 taken into account by each of the foreign corporation's United States shareholders and on the application of the high-tax exception described in section 954(b)(4), as well as on the amount of foreign income taxes deemed paid in such year. In addition, a redetermination of U.S. tax liability is required for any subsequent taxable year in which the United States shareholder received or accrued a distribution or inclusion from the foreign corporation, up to and including the taxable year in which the foreign tax redetermination occurs, as well as any year to which unused foreign taxes from such year were carried under section 904(c).

(b) *Notification requirements.*—(1) *In general.*—The notification requirements of §1.905-4, as modified by paragraphs (b)(2) and (3) of this section, apply if a redetermination of U.S. tax liability is required under paragraph (a) of this section.

(2) *Notification relating to post-1986 undistributed earnings and post-1986 foreign income taxes.*—In the case of foreign tax redeterminations with respect to taxes included in post-1986 foreign income taxes, in addition to the information required by §1.905-4(c), the taxpayer must provide the balances of the pools of post-1986 undistributed earnings and post-1986 foreign income taxes before and after adjusting the pools, the dates and amounts of any dividend distributions or other inclusions made out of earnings and profits for the affected year or years, and the amount of earnings and profits from which such dividends were paid or such inclusions were made for the affected year or years.

(3) *Notification relating to pre-1987 accumulated profits and pre-1987 foreign income taxes.*—In the case of foreign tax redeterminations with respect to pre-1987 accumulated profits, in addition to the information required by §1.905-4(c), the taxpayer must provide the following: the dates and amounts of any dividend distributions made out of earnings and profits for the affected year or years; the rate of exchange on the date of any such distribution; and the amount of earnings and profits from which such dividends were paid for the affected year or years.

(c) *Currency translation rules for adjustments to pre-1987 foreign income taxes.*—Foreign income taxes paid with respect to pre-1987 accumulated profits that are deemed paid under section 960 (or under section 902 in the case of an amount treated as a dividend under section 1248) are translated into dollars at the spot rate for the

date of the payment of the foreign income taxes, and refunds of such taxes are translated into dollars at the spot rate for the date of the refund. Foreign income taxes deemed paid by a taxpayer under section 902 with respect to an actual distribution of pre-1987 accumulated profits and refunds of such taxes are translated into dollars at the spot rate for the date of the distribution of the earnings to which the foreign income taxes relate. *See* section 902(c)(6) (as in effect before December 22, 2017) and §1.902-1(a)(10)(iii). For purposes of this section, the term *spot rate* has the meaning provided in §1.988-1(d).

(d) *Adjustments to pools of post-1986 foreign income taxes.*—The redetermination of U.S. tax liability required by paragraph (a) of this section is made in accordance with section 905(c) as in effect for those taxable years, without regard to rules that required prospective adjustments to a foreign corporation's pools of post-1986 undistributed earnings and post-1986 foreign income taxes in the year of the foreign tax redetermination in lieu of redeterminations of U.S. tax liability. No underpayment or overpayment of U.S. tax liability results from a foreign tax redetermination unless the required adjustments change the U.S. tax liability. Consequently, no interest is paid by or to a taxpayer as a result of adjustments, required by reason of a foreign tax redetermination, to a foreign corporation's pools of post-1986 undistributed earnings and post-1986 foreign income taxes in the year to which the redetermined foreign tax relates that did not result in a change to U.S. tax liability, for example, because no foreign taxes were deemed paid in that year.

(e) *Applicability date.*—This section applies to foreign tax redeterminations (as defined in §1.905-3(a)) of foreign corporations occurring in taxable years that end with or within taxable years of a United States shareholder ending on or after December 16, 2019 and that relate to taxable years of foreign corporations beginning before January 1, 2018.

Foreign Tax Credit

Foreign Tax Credits: Foreign Tax Redeterminations: Notification.—Temporary Reg. §§1.905-4T and 1.905-5T, relating to a taxpayer's obligation to file notification of a foreign tax redetermination, to make adjustments to a taxpayer's pools of foreign taxes and earnings and profits, and the imposition of the civil penalty for failure to file such notice or report such adjustments, are also proposed as final regulations and, when adopted, would become Reg. §§1.905-4 and 1.905-5 (published in the Federal Register on June 23, 1988).

§1.905-4. Notification and redetermination of United States tax liability.

§1.905-5. Foreign tax redeterminations and currency translation rules for foreign tax redeterminations occurring in taxable years beginning prior to January 1, 1987.

Foreign Tax Credit: Foreign Tax Redeterminations

Foreign Tax Credit: Foreign Tax Redeterminations.—Reg. §§1.905-4 and 1.905-5, relating to a taxpayer's obligation under Code Sec. 905(c) to notify the IRS of a foreign tax redetermination, are proposed (published in the Federal Register on November 7, 2007) (REG-209020-86).

☐ Par. 3. Section 1.905-4 is added to read as follows:

§1.905-4. Notification of foreign tax redetermination.
[The text of this section is the same as the text of §1.905-4T(a) through (f)(2) as added by T.D. 9362].

☐ Par. 3. Section 1.905-5 is added to read as follows:

§1.905-5. Foreign tax redeterminations and currency translation rules for foreign tax redeterminations occurring in taxable years beginning prior to January 1, 1987.
[The text of this section is the same as the text of §1.905-5T(a) through (f) as added by T.D. 9362].

Domestic International Sales Corporations

Domestic International Sales Corporations: Taxation of Income.—Reproduced below is the text of a proposed amendment of Temporary Reg. §1.921-1T, relating to the taxation to income allocable to a DISC for taxable years beginning after 1984 (published in the Federal Register on February 3, 1987).

☐ Par. 3. Paragraph (b)(6) of §1.921-1T is removed.

§1.921-1T. Temporary regulations providing transition rules for DISCs and FSCs.

FSCs: Export Property

Foreign Sales Corporations.—Temporary Reg. §§1.927(a)-1T and 1.927(d)-2T, relating to foreign sales corporations, are also proposed as final regulations and, when adopted, would become Reg. §§1.927(a)-1 and 1.927(d)-2, respectively (published in the Federal Register on March 3, 1987).

§1.927(a)-1. Definition of export property.

§1.927(d)-2. Definitions and special rules relating to foreign sales corporation.

Possessions Credit

Possessions Corporations Credit: Qualified Possession Source Investment Income.—Reproduced below are the texts of proposed Reg. §§1.936-2, 1.936-3 and 1.936-3A, defining the term "qualified possession source investment income" (published in the Federal Register on January 21, 1986).

* * *

☐ Par. 2. New §§1.936-2, 1.936-3 and 1.936-3A are added after §1.936-1 to read as follows:

§1.936-2. Source of income.—(a) *In general.*—Except as provided in §1.936-2(b) (relating to certain interest), for purposes of section 936(d)(2), the determination as to whether gross income is from sources within a particular possession shall be made in accordance with §1.863-6.

(b) *Certain interest.*—(1) Interest paid by a possessions corporation that meets the condition of section 936(a)(2)(A) with respect to a particular possession is from sources within that possession.

(2) Interest paid or credited on deposit accounts with a possession branch of a corporation or partnership is from sources within the possession if, at the time of payment or crediting, the branch is engaged within the possession in the commercial banking business or the business of a savings and loan or similar association. [Reg. §1.936-2.]

§1.936-3. Investment in a possession (for use therein).—For purposes of section 936(d)(2), interest and certain dividends derived after April 17, 1984 (less deductions allocable and apportionable thereto) by a domestic corporation engaged in the active conduct of a trade or business in Puerto Rico shall be treated as attributable to investment in Puerto Rico (for use therein) if the interest or certain dividends qualify for exemption from Puerto Rican Income Tax under regulations issued by the Secretary of the Treasury of Puerto Rico, as in effect on April 17, 1984 under the authority of the Acts No. 6 of December 15, 1953, 57 of June 13, 1963, and 25 of June 2, 1978, as amended, to determine the institutions which are eligible to receive funds from exempted businesses under those Acts.

In the case of any investment of funds made by the possessions corporation after [Date that is 30 days after the date of publication in the Federal Register of this regulation as a Treasury decision], the preceding sentence shall not apply unless the possessions corporation receives, at the time the funds are delivered for investment, the written agreement of the institution receiving the funds that the funds will be invested by the institution so as to qualify for exemption under the foregoing regulations of Puerto Rico. Interest derived after September 30, 1976 and before April 18, 1984 shall be treated as attributable to investment in Puerto Rico (for use therein) if the interest qualifies for exemption from Puerto Rican Income Tax under regulations issued by the Secretary of the Treasury of Puerto Rico as in effect on September 28, 1976 under the authority of section 2(j) of the Puerto Rico Industrial Incentive Act of 1963, as amended. [Reg. §1.936-3.]

§1.936-3A. Funds derived from a possession.—(a) *In general.*—Funds treated as derived from the active conduct of a trade or business in a possession or from investment of such funds in a possession ("qualified funds") include—

(1) Taxable income from sources without the United States derived from the active conduct of a trade or business in the possession, and

(2) Qualified possession source investment income,

reduced by any distributions paid with respect to such income and by any losses (not otherwise taken into account under subparagraph (1) or (2)) from such activity or investment. The amount of any capital contributions to a possessions corporation is not treated as qualified funds.

(b) *Limitation on investment.*—Notwithstanding paragraph (a), the amount of qualified funds which may be invested in a possession and give rise to income which is treated as qualified possession source investment income is limited to the total qualified funds for the taxable year and for all prior taxable years which are not already invested in a possession. For this purpose, qualified possession source investment income is not included in total qualified funds for the current taxable year, but is included with respect to prior taxable years.

(c) *Illustration:.*—The principles of paragraphs (a) and (b) of this section are illustrated by the following example:

Example: X has operated in Puerto Rico as a section 936 corporation since January 1, 1980. In 1980 X earned $30,000 from the active conduct of a business in Puerto Rico and paid a dividend of $20,000. On January 1, 1981 X invested $20,000 in a Puerto Rican financial institution. For the year 1981 X had a loss of $10,000 from the conduct of its business and received $1500 in interest. For the years 1982 and 1983 X earned $40,000 and $60,000 respectively from its business and $2000 each year from its investments which qualify under §1.936-3 and paid dividends of $20,000 and $30,000 respectively. On January 1, 1984 X deposited $80,000 in the same Puerto Rican financial institution for a total deposit of $100,000. For 1984 X had a $5000 loss from its business, but received $15,000 of interest from its investments.

For 1981, the interest received from the investment in the Puerto Rican financial institution was not qualified possession source investment income since there were no qualified funds for 1981. The $30,000 of income received by X from the active conduct of its business in 1980 was reduced to zero by a $20,000 dividend in 1980 and a $10,000 loss in 1981.

For 1982 and 1983 the $20,000 originally deposited in 1981 and not withdrawn are treated as qualified funds and all of the income derived therefrom as qualified possession source investment income assuming the requirements of §§1.936-2 and 1.936-3 are met. (The zero qualified funds at the end of 1981 were increased to $20,000 in 1982, representing $40,000 of active business income less $20,000 of dividends; in 1983, the qualified funds available for investment were further increased to $52,000, representing $60,000 of active business income in 1983 less dividend payment of $30,000 (or $30,000) plus $2000 of qualified possession source investment income accrued in 1982). The $1500 of interest earned in 1981 was not derived from qualified funds and, therefore, was not qualified possession source investment income. In addition, this amount and any amount of interest derived therefrom can never be qualified funds since the $1500 was neither derived initially from the active conduct of a trade or business in Puerto Rico nor was it qualified possession source investment income.

For 1984, $7350 of the $15,000 of interest received on the $100,000 investment constitutes qualified possession source investment income since only $49,000 of the $100,000 deposited was from qualified funds ($52,000 of qualified funds at the end of 1983 reduced by the $5000 of loss incurred in 1984 and increased by the $2000 of qualified possession source investment income accrued in 1983). [Reg. §1.936-3A.]

* * *

☐ Par. 4. Section 7.936-1 is removed.

§7.936-1. Qualified possession source investment income (temporary).

Qualified Caribbean Basin Countries: Investments: Requirements

Qualified Caribbean Basin Countries: Investments: Requirements.—Reproduced below is the text of a proposed amendment to Reg. §1.936-10, relating to the use of Code Sec. 936 funds to finance an investment that qualifies as a privatization (published in the Federal Register on May 13, 1991).

☐ Par. 2. Section 1.936-10 is amended as follows:

1. Paragraph (c)(5)(i)(A) is amended by adding a new sentence at the end of the paragraph to read as set forth below.

2. Paragraph (c)(5)(i)(B)(*1*) is amended by removing the word "or" at the end of the paragraph.

3. Paragraph (c)(5)(i)(B)(2) is amended by adding the word "or" at the end of the paragraph, and paragraph (c)(5)(i)(B)(*3*) is added to read as set forth below.

4. Paragraph (c)(5)(v) is added to read as set forth below.

5. Paragraphs (c)(9)(i) and (ii) are revised to read as set forth below.

§1.936-10.　Qualified investments.

* * *

(c) * * *

(5) * * *

(i) * * *

(A) * * * Solely for purposes of a qualified privatization described in paragraph (c)(5)(v) of this section, the amounts disbursed under the loan or bond issue may also be applied to an investment in a corporation, partnership, or trust.

(B) * * *

(3) A qualified privatization described in paragraph (c)(5)(v) of this section;

* * *

(v) *Qualified privatization.*—This paragraph (c)(5)(v) is effective for investments made by a possessions corporation in a financial institution for investments in accordance with a specific authorization granted by the Commissioner of Financial Institutions of Puerto Rico (or his delegate) on or after [INSERT DATE THAT IS 30 DAYS AFTER PUBLICATION OF THE FINAL REGULATIONS IN THE FEDERAL REGISTER]. For purposes of this section, a qualified privatization is a financing transaction that satisfies all of the requirements of this paragraph (c)(5)(v).

(A) The loan must be made to finance the acquisition, directly or through an investment in a corporation, partnership or trust, of any assets that are currently used in a trade or business or were used in a trade or business but are no longer so used at the time of acquisition and a plan exists to continue or resume using those assets in the conduct of an active trade or business. The loan can also be used to finance other costs associated with acquiring the trade or business or placing assets back in service, within the limits set forth in paragraph (c)(4)(iii) of this section.

(B) After the acquisition, the assets must be used in a trade or business conducted as a qualified business activity.

(C) The United States Agency for International Development (USAID) or the Overseas Private Investment Corporation (OPIC) must certify, prior to the acquisition, that, as a result of the transfer of the activity from the public to the private sector, the acquisition is expected to have a significant positive developmental impact in the qualified Caribbean Basin country where the trade or business is conducted. The determination of whether an acquisition has significant positive developmental impact depends upon an analysis measuring the extent to which incremental developmental benefits exceed incremental negative effects. Generally, developmental effects will be measured in relation to the impact of the acquisition on those economic factors generally used to measure the effect of an activity on the economy of a qualified Caribbean Basin country. Those factors include (but are not limited to) increased economic efficiency and innovation conducive to self-sustaining growth, decreased government expenditures or increased direct revenues to the government, an improved balance of payments of the qualified Caribbean Basin country (through expanded exports of goods or services), increased employment over time, reduced cost of capital, increased expenditures for maintenance and operations, increased capital expenditures, increased net output and improved market competitiveness. Negative factors include (but are not limited to) increased capital outflows (*e.g.,* expenditures abroad and repatriation to any foreign shareholders).

(D) During the 3-year period preceding the acquisition, the government of the qualified Caribbean Basin country must have owned an interest, directly or indirectly, in the acquired assets that, by value or voting interest, represented 50 percent or more of the total of such interests in the acquired assets, and such government must have exercised effective control over such assets.

(E) After the acquisition and during all the time that the loan is outstanding, no government or government-controlled entity may own, directly or indirectly, any interest in the acquired assets.

(F) No government or government-controlled entity may exercise any effective control, or managerial or operational responsibility or authority, over the acquired assets at any time during the time that the loan is outstanding. This restriction is not intended to restrict the normal exercise of regulatory authority by a government, provided such power is not exercised in a way that would defeat the intent of the provisions in this paragraph (c)(5)(v)(F).

* * *

(9) * * *

(i) In the case of an investment described in paragraph (c)(4) of this section (relating to investments in active business assets) or in paragraph (c)(5)(v) of this section (relating to qualified privatization), a qualified recipient is a person that carries on a qualified business activity in a qualified Caribbean Basin country, and complies with the agreement and certification requirements described in paragraph (c)(11)(i) of this section at all times during the period in which the investment remains outstanding.

(ii) In the case of an investment described in paragraph (c)(5) of this section (relating to investments in development projects), other than an investment described in paragraph (c)(5)(v) of this section, a qualified recipient is the borrower (including a person empowered by the borrower to authorize expenditures for the investment in the development project) that has authority to comply, and complies, with the agreement and certification requirements described in paragraph (c)(11)(i) of this section at all times during the period in which the investment remains outstanding.

U.S. Possessions: Residence Rules

U.S. Possessions: Residence Rules.—Amendments to Reg. §1.937-1, determining whether an individual is a bona fide resident of a U.S. territory and affecting individuals establishing bona fide residency in a U.S. territory by allowing additional days of constructive presence in a U.S. territory, are proposed (published in the Federal Register on August 27, 2015) (REG-109813-11).

Par. 2. Section 1.937-1 is amended as follows:

1. Revising paragraph (c)(3)(i)(B) and paragraph (c)(3)(i)(C)(2).
2. Adding paragraph (c)(3)(i)(D).
3. Revising *Example 1* of paragraph (g).
4. Redesignating *Examples 2* through *10* of paragraph (g) as *Examples 5* through *13* respectively.
5. Adding new *Examples 2, 3,* and *4* to paragraph (g).
6. Revising newly re-designated *Example 5* of paragraph (g).
7. Adding a new sentence to the end of paragraph (i).

The revisions and additions read as follows:

§1.937-1.　Bona fide residency in a possession.

* * *

(c) * * *

(3) * * *

(i) * * *

(B) Any day that an individual is outside of the relevant possession to receive, or to accompany on a full-time basis a parent, spouse, or child (as defined in section 152(f)(1)) who is receiving, qualifying medical treatment as defined in paragraph (c)(4) of this section;

(C) * * *

(1) * * *

(2) Period for which a mandatory evacuation order is in effect for the geographic area in the relevant possession in which the individual's place of abode is located; and

(D) Any day not described in paragraph (c)(3)(i)(B) or (C) of this section that an individual is outside of the United States and the relevant possession, except that an individual will not be considered present in the relevant possession under this paragraph (c)(3)(i)(D) for more than 30 days during the taxable year, and this paragraph (c)(3)(i)(D) does not apply for purposes of calculating the required minimum 60 days of presence in the relevant possession under paragraph (c)(1)(ii) of this section. Furthermore, this paragraph (c)(3)(i)(D) applies only if the number of days that the individual is considered to be present in the relevant possession during the taxable year, determined without regard to this paragraph (c)(3)(i)(D), exceeds the number of days that the individual is considered to be present in the United States during the taxable year.

* * *

(g) * * *

Example 1. Presence test. H, a U.S. citizen, is engaged in a profession that requires frequent travel. In each of the years 2016 and 2017, H spends 195 days in Possession N and the balance of the year in the United States. In 2018, H spends 160 days in Possession N and the balance of the year in the United States. Thus, H spends a total of 550 days in Possession N for the three-year period consisting of years 2016, 2017, and 2018. Under paragraph (c)(1)(ii) of this section, H satisfies the presence test of paragraph (c) of this section with respect to Possession N for taxable year 2018 because H is present in Possession N for more than the required 549 days during the three-year period of 2016 through 2018 and is present in Possession N for at least 60 days during each of those taxable years. Assuming that in 2018 H does not have a tax home outside of Possession N and does not have a closer connection to the United States or a foreign country under paragraphs (d) and (e) of this section respectively, then regardless of whether H was a bona fide resident of Possession N in 2016 and 2017, H is a bona fide resident of Possession N for taxable year 2018.

Example 2. Presence test. Same facts as *Example 1,* except that in 2018, H spends 130 days in Possession N, 110 days in foreign countries, and 125 days in the United States. Because H satisfies the requirements of paragraph (c)(3)(i)(D) of this section, 30 of the days spent in foreign countries during 2018 are treated as days of presence in Possession N. Thus, H will be treated as being present for 160 days in Possession N for 2018. Under paragraph (c)(1)(ii) of this section, H meets the presence test of paragraph (c) of this section with respect to Possession N for taxable year 2018 because H is present in Possession N for 550 days (more than the required 549 days) during the three-year period of 2016 through 2018 and is present in Possession N for at least 60 days in each of those taxable years. As in *Example 1,* assuming that in 2018 H does not have a tax home outside of Possession N and does not have a closer connection to the United States or a foreign country under paragraphs (d) and (e) of this section respectively, then regardless of whether H was a bona fide resident of Possession N in 2016 and 2017, H is a bona fide resident of Possession N in 2018.

Example 3. Presence test. Same facts as *Example 1,* except that in 2018, H spends 130 days in Possession N, 100 days in foreign countries, and 135 days in the United States. Under these facts, H does not satisfy paragraph (c)(1)(ii) of this section for taxable year 2018 because H is present in Possession N for only 520 days (less than the required 549 days) during the three-year period of 2016 through 2018. The rule of paragraph (c)(3)(i)(D) of this section (treating up to 30 days spent in foreign countries as days of presence in Possession N) is not available because H fails to satisfy the condition that H be present more days in Possession N than in the United States during 2018, determined without regard to the application of paragraph (c)(3)(i)(D) of this section.

Example 4. Presence test. Same facts as *Example 1,* except that in 2016, H spends 360 days in Possession N and six days in the United States; in 2017, H spends 45 days in Possession N, 290 days in foreign countries, and 30 days in the United States; and in 2018, H spends 180 days in Possession N and 185 days in the United States. Under these facts, H does not satisfy paragraph (c)(1)(ii) of this section for taxable year 2018. During the three-year period from 2016 through 2018, H is present in Possession N for 615 days, including 30 of the days spent in foreign countries in 2017, which are treated under paragraph (c)(3)(i)(D) of this section as days of presence in Possession N. Although H is present in Possession N for more than the required 549 days during the three-year period, H is only present for 45 days in Possession N during one of the taxable years (2017) of the period, less than the 60 days of minimum presence required under paragraph (c)(1)(ii) of this section. The rule of paragraph (c)(3)(i)(D) of this section does not apply for purposes of determining whether H is present in Possession N for the 60-day minimum required under paragraph (c)(1)(ii) of this section.

Example 5. Presence test. W, a U.S. citizen, owns a condominium in Possession P where she spends part of the taxable year. W also owns a house in State N near her grown children and grandchildren. W is retired and her income consists solely of pension payments, dividends, interest, and Social Security benefits. For 2016, W spends 145 days in Possession P, 101 days in Europe and Asia on vacation, and 120 days in State N. For taxable year 2016, W is not present in Possession P for at least 183 days, is present in the United States for more than 90 days, and has a significant connection to the United States by reason of her permanent home. However, under paragraph (c)(1)(iv) of this section, W still satisfies the presence test of paragraph (c) of this section with respect to Possession P for taxable year 2016 because she has no earned income in the United States and is present for more days in Possession P than in the United States.

* * *

(i) * * * Notwithstanding the foregoing, paragraph (c)(3)(i)(D) and *Examples 1, 2, 3, 4,* and *5* of paragraph (g) of this section apply for taxable years beginning after the date these regulations are published as final regulations in the **Federal Register**.

Sales of Inventory: Determining Source of Income

Sales of Inventory: Determining Source of Income.—Amendments to Reg. §§ 1.937-2 and 1.937-3, modifying the rules for determining the source of income from sales of inventory produced within the United States and sold without the United States or vice versa, are proposed (published in the Federal Register on December 30, 2019) (REG-100956-19).

Par. 8. Section 1.937-2 is amended by removing "§ 1.863-3(f)" from paragraph (d) and adding in its place "§ 1.863-3(e)".

§1.937-2. Income from sources within a possession.

Par. 9. Section 1.937-3 is amended by removing "§ 1.863-3(f)" from paragraph (d) and adding in its place "§ 1.863-3(e)".

§1.937-3. Income effectively connected with the conduct of a trade or business in a possession.

Cloud and Digital Content Transactions: Classification

Cloud and Digital Content Transactions: Classification.—Amendments to Reg. § 1.937-3, regarding the classification of cloud transactions for purposes of the international provisions of the Internal Revenue Code, are proposed (published in the Federal Register on August 14, 2019) (REG-130700-14).

Par. 5. Section 1.937-3 is amended by removing Examples 4 and 5 from paragraph (e).

§1.937-3. Income effectively connected with the conduct of a trade or business in a possession.

GILTI: Stock Ownership Determination: Guidance

GILTI: Stock Ownership Determination: Guidance.—Amendments to Reg. § 1.951-1, regarding the treatment of domestic partnerships for purposes of determining amounts included in the gross income of their partners with respect to foreign corporations and regarding gross income that is subject to a high rate of tax under the GILTI provisions, are proposed (published in the Federal Register on June 21, 2019) (REG-101828-19).

Par. 2. Section 1.951-1 is amended by adding paragraph (a)(4) and revising the last sentence of paragraph (i) to read as follows:

§1.951-1. Amounts included in gross income of United States shareholders.

* * *

(a) * * *

(4) See § 1.958-1(d)(1) for ownership of stock of a foreign corporation through a domestic partnership for purposes of sections 951 and 951A and for purposes of any other provision that applies by reference to section 951 or 951A.

* * *

(i) * * * Paragraph (h) of this section applies to taxable years of domestic partnerships ending on or after May 14, 2010, but does not apply to determine the stock of a controlled foreign corporation owned (within the meaning of section 958(a)) by a United States person for taxable years of the controlled foreign corporation beginning on or after the date of publication of the Treasury decision adopting these rules as final regulations in the Federal Register, and for taxable years of United States persons in which or with which such taxable years of the controlled foreign corporation end.

GILTI: Stock Ownership Determination: Guidance

GILTI: Stock Ownership Determination: Guidance.—Amendments to Reg. § 1.951A-0, regarding the treatment of domestic partnerships for purposes of determining amounts included in the gross income of their partners with respect to foreign corporations and regarding gross income that is subject to a high rate of tax under the GILTI provisions, are proposed (published in the Federal Register on June 21, 2019) (REG-101828-19).

Par. 3. Section 1.951A-0 is amended by adding entries for § 1.951A-7(a), § 1.951A-7(b), and § 1.951A-7(c) to read as follows:

§ 1.951A-0. Outline of section 951A regulations.

* * *

§ 1.951A-7 Applicability dates.

(a) In general.
(b) High tax exclusion.
(c) Domestic partnerships.

GILTI: Hybrid Arrangements: Allocation of Deductions

GILTI: Hybrid Arrangements: Allocation of Deductions.—Amendments to Reg. § 1.951A-0, adjusting hybrid deduction accounts to take into account earnings and profits of a controlled foreign corporation that are included in income by a United States shareholder, are proposed (published in the Federal Register on April 8, 2020) (REG-106013-19).

Par. 4. Section 1.951A-0, as proposed to be amended at 84 FR 29114 (June 21, 2019), is further amended by adding entries for § 1.951A-2(c)(6), (c)(6)(i) and (ii), (c)(6)(ii)(A) through (C), (c)(6)(iii), (c)(6)(iv), (c)(6)(iv)(A), (c)(6)(iv)(A)(1) and (2), (c)(6)(iv)(B), (c)(6)(iv)(B)(1) and (2), (c)(7), (c)(7)(i) and (ii), (c)(7)(ii)(A), (c)(7)(ii)(A)(1) and (2), (c)(7)(ii)(B), (c)(7)(iii) through (v), (c)(7)(v)(A) through (D), (c)(7)(v)(D)(1) and (2), (c)(7)(v)(D)(2)(i) and (ii), (c)(7)(v)(E), (c)(7)(v)(E)(1) and (2), (c)(7)(vi), (c)(7)(vi)(A), (c)(7)(vi)(A)(1) and (2), and (c)(7)(vi)(B) and § 1.951A-7(d) to read as follows:

§ 1.951A-0. Outline of section 951A regulations.

* * *

§ 1.951A-2 Tested income and tested loss.

* * *

(c) * * *

(6) Allocation of deductions attributable to certain disqualified payments.

(i) In general.
(ii) Definitions related to disqualified payment.
  (A) Disqualified payment.
  (B) Disqualified period.
  (C) Related recipient CFC.
(iii) Treatment of partnerships.
(iv) Examples.
  (A) Example 1: Deduction related directly to disqualified payment to related recipient CFC.
    (1) Facts.
    (2) Analysis.
  (B) Example 2: Deduction related indirectly to disqualified payment to partnership in which related recipient CFC is a partner.
    (1) Facts.
    (2) Analysis.

(7) Election for application of high tax exception of section 954(b)(4).

(i) In general.
(ii) Definitions.
  (A) Tentative gross tested income item.
    (1) In general.

    (2) Income attributable to a QBU.
  (B) Tentative net tested income item.
(iii) Effective rate at which taxes are imposed.
(iv) Taxes paid or accrued with respect to a tentative net tested income item.
(v) Rules regarding the election.
  (A) Manner of making election.
  (B) Scope of election.
  (C) Duration of election.
  (D) Revocation of election.
    (1) In general.
    (2) Limitations by reason of revocation.
     (i) In general.
     (ii) Exception for change of control.
  (E) Rules applicable to controlling domestic shareholder groups.
    (1) In general.
    (2) Definition of controlling domestic shareholder group.
(vi) Example.
  (A) Example: Effect of disregarded payments between QBUs.
    (1) Facts.
    (2) Analysis.
  (B) [Reserved]

§ 1.951A-7 Applicability dates.

* * *

(d) Deduction for certain disqualified payments.

GILTI: Stock Ownership Determination: Guidance

GILTI: Stock Ownership Determination: Guidance.—Amendments to Reg. § 1.951A-2, regarding the treatment of domestic partnerships for purposes of determining amounts included in the gross income of their partners with respect to foreign corporations and regarding gross income that is subject to a high rate of tax under the GILTI provisions, are proposed (published in the Federal Register on June 21, 2019) (corrected August 2, 2019) (REG-101828-19).

Par. 4. Section 1.951A-2 is amended by revising paragraph (c)(1)(iii) and adding paragraph (c)(6) to read as follows:

§ 1.951A-2. Tested income and tested loss.

* * *

(c) * * *

(1) * * *

(iii) Gross income excluded from the foreign base company income (as defined in section 954) or the insurance income (as defined in section 953) of the corporation by reason of the exception described in section 954(b)(4) pursuant to an election under § 1.954-1(d), or a tentative gross tested income item of the corporation that qualifies for the exception described in section 954(b)(4) pursuant to an election under paragraph (c)(6) of this section,

* * *

(6) *Election for application of high tax exception of section 954(b)(4).*—(i) *In general.*—For purposes of section 951A(c)(2)(A)(i)(III) and paragraph (c)(1)(iii) of this section, a tentative gross tested income item of a controlled foreign corporation for a CFC inclusion year qualifies for the exception described in section 954(b)(4) if—

(A) An election made under paragraph (c)(6)(v)(A) of this section is effective with respect to the controlled foreign corporation for the CFC inclusion year; and

(B) The tentative net tested income item with respect to the tentative gross tested income item was subject to foreign income taxes at an effective rate that is greater than 90 percent of the rate that would apply if the income were subject to the maximum rate of tax specified in section 11.

(ii) *Definitions.*—(A) *Tentative gross tested income item.*—(1) *In general.*—A single tentative gross tested income item with respect to a controlled foreign corporation for a CFC inclusion year is the aggregate of all items of gross income attributable to a single qualified business unit (QBU) of the controlled foreign corporation in such CFC inclusion year that would be gross tested income without regard to this paragraph (c)(6) and that would be in a single tested income group (as defined in § 1.960-1(d)(2)(ii)(C)). For this purpose, a QBU is defined in section 989(a) and the regulations under that section, and a controlled foreign corporation's QBUs includes QBUs owned by the controlled foreign corporation in addition to the QBU that is the controlled foreign corporation. Therefore, a controlled foreign corporation may have multiple tentative gross tested income items.

(2) *Income attributable to a QBU.*—Gross income is attributable to a QBU if the gross income is properly reflected on the books and records of the QBU. Such gross income must be deter

Reg. § 1.951A-2(c)(6)(ii)(A)(2)

mined under Federal income tax principles, except that the principles of §1.904-4(f)(2)(vi) (without regard to the exclusion described in §1.904-4(f)(2)(vi)(C)(*1*)) apply to adjust gross income of a QBU to reflect disregarded payments.

(B) *Tentative net tested income item.*—A tentative net tested income item with respect to a tentative gross tested income item is determined by allocating and apportioning deductions (not including any items described in §1.951A-2(c)(5)) to the tentative gross tested income item under the principles of §1.960-1(d)(3) by treating each single tentative gross tested income item as gross income in a separate tested income group.

(iii) *Effective rate at which taxes are imposed.*—For a CFC inclusion year of a controlled foreign corporation, the effective rate with respect to the controlled foreign corporation's tentative net tested income items is determined separately for each such item. The effective rate at which taxes are imposed on a tentative net tested income item is—

(A) The U.S. dollar amount of foreign income taxes paid or accrued with respect to the tentative net tested income item, determined by applying paragraph (c)(6)(iv) of this section; divided by

(B) The U.S. dollar amount of the tentative net tested income item, increased by the amount of foreign income taxes referred to in paragraph (c)(6)(iv) of this section.

(iv) *Taxes paid or accrued with respect to a tentative net tested income item.*—For a CFC inclusion year, the amount of foreign income taxes paid or accrued by a controlled foreign corporation with respect to a tentative net tested income item of the controlled foreign corporation for purposes of this paragraph (c)(6) is the U.S. dollar amount of the controlled foreign corporation's current year taxes (as defined in §1.960-1(b)(4)) that would be allocated and apportioned under the principles of §1.960-1(d)(3)(ii) to the tentative net tested income item by treating such tentative net tested income item as being in a separate tested income group. If the principles of §1.904-4(f)(2)(vi) apply to adjust the gross income of a QBU to account for disregarded payments as provided in paragraph (c)(6)(ii)(A)(2) of this section, the principles of §1.904-6(a)(2) apply to allocate and apportion foreign income taxes imposed by reason of the disregarded payments. Except to the extent provided in the next sentence, the amount of foreign income taxes paid or accrued with respect to a tentative net tested income item, determined in the manner provided in this paragraph (c)(6), will not be affected by a subsequent reduction in foreign income taxes attributable to a distribution to shareholders of all or part of such income. To the extent the foreign income taxes paid or accrued by the controlled foreign corporation are reasonably certain to be returned by the foreign jurisdiction imposing such taxes to a shareholder, directly or indirectly, through any means (including, but not limited to, a refund, credit, payment, discharge of an obligation, or any other method) on a subsequent distribution to such shareholder, the foreign income taxes are not treated as paid or accrued for purposes of this paragraph (c)(6)(iv).

(v) *Rules regarding the election.*—(A) *Manner of making election.*—An election is made under this paragraph (c)(6)(v)(A) with respect to a controlled foreign corporation for a CFC inclusion year—

(1) By the controlling domestic shareholders (as defined in §1.964-1(c)(5)), by attaching a statement to such effect with an original or amended income tax return for the U.S. shareholder inclusion year of each controlling domestic shareholder in which or with which such CFC inclusion year ends, and including any additional information required by applicable administrative pronouncements; or

(2) In accordance with the rules provided in forms or instructions.

(B) *Scope of election.*—An election made under paragraph (c)(6)(v)(A) of this section that is effective with respect to a controlled foreign corporation for a CFC inclusion year applies with respect to each tentative gross tested income item of the controlled foreign corporation for the CFC inclusion year and is binding on all United States shareholders of the controlled foreign corporation.

(C) *Duration of election.*—An election made under paragraph (c)(6)(v)(A) of this section is effective for a CFC inclusion year of a controlled foreign corporation for which the election is made and all subsequent CFC inclusion years of such corporation unless revoked by the controlling domestic shareholders of the controlled foreign corporation under paragraph (c)(6)(v)(D)(*1*) of this section.

(D) *Revocation of election.*—(*1*) *In general.*—Except as provided in paragraph (c)(6)(v)(D)(2) of this section, the election made under paragraph (c)(6)(v)(A) of this section with respect to a controlled foreign corporation for a CFC inclusion year is revoked by the controlling domestic shareholders of the controlled foreign corpora-

tion in the same manner as prescribed for an election in paragraph (c)(6)(v)(A) of this section.

(2) *Limitations by reason of revocation.*—(i) *In general.*—Except as provided in paragraph (c)(6)(v)(D)(2)(*ii*) of this section, if an election with respect to a controlled foreign corporation for a CFC inclusion year is revoked under paragraph (c)(6)(v)(D)(*1*) of this section, a new election cannot be made under paragraph (c)(6)(v)(A) of this section with respect to the controlled foreign corporation for any CFC inclusion year that begins within sixty months following the close of the CFC inclusion year for which the previous election was revoked, and such subsequent election cannot be revoked under paragraph (c)(6)(v)(D)(*1*) of this section with respect to the controlled foreign corporation for any CFC inclusion year that begins within sixty months following the close of the CFC inclusion year for which the subsequent election was made.

(ii) *Exception for change of control.*—The Commissioner may permit a controlled foreign corporation to make an election under paragraph (c)(6)(v)(A) of this section or revoke an election under paragraph (c)(6)(v)(D)(*1*) of this section with respect to any CFC inclusion year within the sixty-month period described in paragraph (c)(6)(v)(D)(2)(*i*) of this section if more than 50 percent of the total combined voting power of all classes of the stock of the controlled foreign corporation entitled to vote as of the beginning of such CFC inclusion year are owned (within the meaning of section 958(a)) by persons that did not own any interests in the controlled foreign corporation as of the close of the CFC inclusion year for which the prior election or revocation with respect to the controlled foreign corporation became effective. For purposes of the preceding sentence, a person includes any person bearing a relationship described in section 267(b) or 707(b)(1) with respect to the person.

(E) *Rules applicable to controlling domestic shareholder groups.*—(*1*) *In general.*—In the case of a controlled foreign corporation that is a member of a controlling domestic shareholder group, an election is made under paragraph (c)(6)(v)(A) of this section or revoked under paragraph (c)(6)(v)(D)(*1*) of this section with respect to each member of the controlling domestic shareholder group (including any member that joins the controlling domestic shareholder group after the election or revocation) and the rules in paragraphs (c)(6)(v)(A) through (D) of this section apply by reference to the controlling domestic shareholder group.

(2) *Definition of controlling domestic shareholder group.*—For purposes of paragraph (c)(6)(v)(E)(*1*) of this section, the term *controlling domestic shareholder group* means two or more controlled foreign corporations (each a *member*) if more than 50 percent of the total combined voting power of all classes of the stock of each corporation is owned (within the meaning of section 958(a)) by the same controlling domestic shareholder or, if no single controlling domestic shareholder owns (within the meaning of section 958(a)) more than 50 percent of the total combined voting power of all classes of the stock of each corporation, more than 50 percent of the total combined voting power of all classes of the stock of each corporation is owned (within the meaning of section 958(a)) by the same controlling domestic shareholders and each controlling domestic shareholder owns (within the meaning of section 958(a)) the same percentage of stock in each controlled foreign corporation. For purposes of the preceding sentence, a controlling domestic shareholder includes any person bearing a relationship described in section 267(b) or 707(b)(1) to the controlling domestic shareholder.

(vi) *Example.*—The following example illustrates the application of this paragraph (c)(6).

(A) *Example: Effect of disregarded payments between QBUs*—(1) *Facts*—(i) FP, a controlled foreign corporation organized in Country A, conducts a trade or business in Country A (the Country A Business) and reflects items of income, gain, loss, and expense attributable to the Country A Business on the books and records of FP's home office. Under §1.989(a)-1(b)(2)(i)(A), FP is a QBU. FP's functional currency is the U.S. dollar. FP has a calendar year taxable year in both the United States and Country A. An election is made under paragraph (c)(6)(v)(A) of this section that is effective for FP's CFC inclusion year.

(*ii*) FP owns FDE, a Country B disregarded entity (within the meaning of §1.904-4(f)(3)(i)). FDE conducts activities in Country B that constitute a trade or business within the meaning of §1.989(a)-1(c) (the Country B Business), and reflects items of income, gain, loss, and expense attributable to the Country B Business on the books and records of FDE. Under §1.989(a)-1(b)(2)(ii)(B), the Country B Business conducted through FDE is a QBU. The Country B Business's functional currency is the U.S. dollar. FDE has a calendar year taxable year in Country B.

(*iii*) On Date A in Year 1, FDE accrues $100x of interest income from X, an unrelated third party, and reflects the accrual on the books and records of the Country B business. FP excludes the $100x from foreign personal holding company income by reason of section 954(h). Subsequently, on Date B in Year 1, FDE accrues and pays $20x of interest to FP. FP reflects the interest income item on the books and records of the Country A Business. FDE reflects the $20x of interest expense on the books and records of the Country B Business.

(*iv*) Country A imposes no tax on income. Country B imposes a 25% tax on income. For Country B income tax purposes, FDE (which is not disregarded under Country B income tax principles) recognizes $80x of taxable income ($100x interest income, less a $20x deduction for the interest paid to FP). Accordingly, FDE incurs a Country B income tax liability with respect to Year 1, the U.S. dollar amount of which is $20x. For Federal income tax purposes, if FDE were not a disregarded entity (within the meaning of §1.904-4(f)(3)(i)), FP would recognize $20x of income in Year 1, and FDE would recognize $80x of taxable income in Year 1. Other than the $20x expense accrued with respect to the income tax imposed by Country B, FP incurs no deductions in Year 1 for Federal income tax purposes.

(*2*) *Analysis*—(*i*) Under paragraph (c)(6)(ii)(A)(*1*) of this section, a separate tentative gross tested income item must be determined with respect to FP's Country A Business and Country B Business (each of which is a QBU). To determine the separate tentative gross tested income items with respect to its Country A Business and Country B Business, FP must determine the gross income that is attributable to the Country A Business and the Country B Business under paragraph (c)(6)(ii)(A)(*2*) of this section. Without regard to the $20x interest payment from FDE to FP, gross income attributable to the Country A Business would be $0 (that is, $20x of interest income reflected on the books and records of the Country A Business, reduced by $20x attributable to a payment that is disregarded for Federal income tax purposes). Similarly, without regard to the $20x interest payment from FDE to FP, gross income attributable to the Country B Business would be $100x (that is, $100x of interest income reflected on the books and records of the Country B Business, unreduced by the $20x payment from FDE to FP). However, the $20x payment from FDE to FP is a disregarded payment within the meaning of §1.904-4(f)(3)(ii), and would, under the principles of §1.904-4(f)(2)(vi) (without regard to the exclusion described in §1.904-4(f)(2)(vi)(C)(*1*)), adjust the gross income of the Country A Business from $0 to $20x and the gross income of the Country B Business from $100x to $80x (in each case, by virtue of the $20x disregarded interest payment from FDE to FP). Accordingly, FP's

tentative gross tested income attributable to the Country A Business is $20x and its tentative gross tested income attributable to the Country B Business is $80x.

(*ii*) Under paragraph (c)(6)(ii)(B) of this section, because there are no deductions allocated or apportioned under §1.960-1(d)(3) to the tentative gross tested income items of the Country A Business, FP's tentative net tested income item attributable to the Country A Business is $20x. Taking into account the $20x deduction for Country B income taxes that are allocable to the Country B Business under §1.960-1(d)(3), FP's tentative net tested income item attributable to the Country B Business is $60x under paragraph (c)(6)(ii)(B) of this section (tentative gross tested income of $80x less the $20x deduction).

(*iii*) Under paragraphs (c)(6)(iii) and (iv) of this section, for Year 1 (a CFC inclusion year of FP), the effective rate with respect to FP's $60x tentative net tested income item attributable to its Country B Business is 25%: $20x (the U.S. dollar amount of the Country B taxes accrued with respect to FP's tentative tested net income item attributable to the Country B Business) divided by $80x (the U.S. dollar amount of FP's $60x tentative net tested income item, increased by the $20x amount of Country B income taxes accrued with respect to that tentative net tested income item), expressed as a percentage. Therefore, FP's tentative net tested income item attributable to the Country B Business was subject to foreign income taxes at an effective rate (25%) that is greater than 18.9% (which is 90% of the rate that would apply if the income were subject to the maximum rate of tax specified in section 11, which is 21%). Accordingly, the requirement of paragraph (c)(6)(i)(B) of this section is satisfied with respect to FP's tentative gross tested income item attributable to the Country B Business in Year 1. Further, the requirement of paragraph (c)(6)(i)(A) of this section is satisfied because an election described in paragraph (c)(6)(v)(A) of this section was made with respect to FP for Year 1. Accordingly, FP's $80x item of tentative gross tested income attributable to its Country B Business qualifies for the high tax exception of section 954(b)(4) under paragraph (c)(6)(i) of this section.

(*iv*) FP's $20x item of tentative net tested income attributable to its Country A Business is not subject to foreign income tax, and therefore does not satisfy the requirement of paragraph (c)(6)(i)(B) of this section. Accordingly, FP's $20x item of tentative gross tested income attributable to the Country A Business does not qualify for the high tax exception of section 954(b)(4) under paragraph (c)(6)(i) of this section.

GILTI: Hybrid Arrangements: Allocation of Deductions

GILTI: Hybrid Arrangements: Allocation of Deductions.—Amendments to Reg. §1.951A-2, adjusting hybrid deduction accounts to take into account earnings and profits of a controlled foreign corporation that are included in income by a United States shareholder, are proposed (published in the Federal Register on April 8, 2020) (REG-106013-19).

Par. 5. Section 1.951A-2, as proposed to be amended at 84 FR 29114 (June 21, 2019), is further amended by redesignating paragraph (c)(6) as paragraph (c)(7) and adding a new paragraph (c)(6) and a reserved paragraph (c)(7)(vi)(B) to read as follows:

§1.951A-2. Tested income and tested loss.

* * *

(c) * * *

(6) *Allocation of deductions attributable to certain disqualified payments.*—(i) *In general.*—A deduction related directly or indirectly to a disqualified payment is allocated or apportioned solely to residual CFC gross income, and any deduction related to a disqualified payment is not properly allocable to property produced or acquired for resale under section 263, section 263A, or section 471.

(ii) *Definitions related to disqualified payment.*—The following definitions apply for purposes of this paragraph (c)(6).

(A) *Disqualified payment.*—The term *disqualified payment* means a payment made by a person to a related recipient CFC during the disqualified period with respect to the related recipient CFC, to the extent the payment would constitute income described in section 951A(c)(2)(A)(i) and paragraph (c)(1) of this section without regard to whether section 951A applies.

(B) *Disqualified period.*—The term *disqualified period* has the meaning provided in §1.951A-3(h)(2)(ii)(C)(*1*), substituting "related recipient CFC" for "transferor CFC."

(C) *Related recipient CFC.*—The term *related recipient CFC* means, with respect to a payment by a person, a recipient of the payment that is a controlled foreign corporation that bears a relationship to the payor described in section 267(b) or 707(b) immediately before or after the payment.

(iii) *Treatment of partnerships.*—For purposes of determining whether a payment is made by a person to a related recipient CFC for purposes of paragraph (c)(6)(ii)(A) of this section, a payment by or to a partnership is treated as made proportionately by or to its partners, as applicable.

(iv) *Examples.*—The following examples illustrate the application of this paragraph (c)(6).

(A) *Example 1: Deduction related directly to disqualified payment to related recipient CFC.*—(1) *Facts.* USP, a domestic corporation, owns all of the stock in CFC1 and CFC2, each a controlled foreign corporation. Both USP and CFC2 use the calendar year as their taxable year. CFC1 uses a taxable year ending November 30. On October 15, 2018, before the start of its first CFC inclusion year, CFC1 receives and accrues a payment from CFC2 of $100x of prepaid royalties with respect to a license. The $100x payment is excluded from subpart F income pursuant to section 954(c)(6) and would constitute income described in section 951A(c)(2)(A)(i) and paragraph (c)(1) of this section without regard to whether section 951A applies.

(2) *Analysis.* CFC1 is a related recipient CFC (within the meaning of paragraph (c)(6)(ii)(C) of this section) with respect to the royalty prepayment by CFC2 because it is related to CFC2 within the meaning of section 267(b). The royalty prepayment is received by CFC1 during its disqualified period (within the meaning of paragraph (c)(6)(ii)(B) of this section) because it is received during the period beginning January 1, 2018, and ending November 30, 2018. Because it would constitute income described in section 951A(c)(2)(A)(i) and paragraph (c)(1) of this section without regard to whether section 951A applies, the payment is a disqualified payment. Accordingly, CFC2's deductions related to such payment accrued during taxable years ending on or after [*INSERT DATE OF FILING WITH THE FEDERAL REGISTER*] are allocated or apportioned solely to residual CFC gross income under paragraph (c)(6)(i) of this section.

(B) *Example 2: Deduction related indirectly to disqualified payment to partnership in which related recipient CFC is a partner.*—(1) *Facts.* The facts are the same as in paragraph (c)(6)(iv)(A)(*1*) of this section (the facts in *Example 1*), except that CFC1 and USP own 99%

and 1%, respectively of FPS, a foreign partnership, which has a taxable year ending November 30. USP receives a prepayment of $110x from CFC2 for the performance of future services. USP subcontracts the performance of these future services to FPS for which FPS receives and accrues a $100x prepayment from USP. The services will be performed in the same country under the laws of which CFC1 and FPS are created or organized, and the $100x prepayment is not foreign base company services income under section 954(e) and §1.954-4(a). The $100x prepayment would constitute income described in section 951A(c)(2)(A)(i) and paragraph (c)(1) of this section without regard to whether section 951A applies.

(2) *Analysis.* CFC1 is a related recipient CFC (within the meaning of paragraph (c)(6)(ii)(C) of this section) with respect to the services prepayment by USP because, under paragraph (c)(6)(iii) of this section, it is treated as receiving $99x (99% of $100x) of the services prepayment from USP, and it is related to USP within the meaning of section 267(b). The services prepayment is received by CFC1 during its disqualified period (within the meaning of paragraph (c)(6)(ii)(B) of this section) because it is received during the period beginning January 1, 2018, and ending November 30, 2018. Because it would constitute income described in section 951A(c)(2)(A)(i) and paragraph (c)(1) of this section without regard to whether section 951A applies, the prepayment is a disqualified payment. CFC2's deductions related to its prepayment to USP are indirectly related to the disqualified payment by USP. Accordingly, CFC2's deductions related to such payment accrued during taxable years ending on or after [*INSERT DATE OF FILING WITH THE FEDERAL REGISTER*] are allocated or apportioned solely to residual CFC gross income under paragraph (c)(6)(i) of this section.

* * *

GILTI: Stock Ownership Determination: Guidance

GILTI: Stock Ownership Determination: Guidance.—Amendments to Reg. §1.951A-7, regarding the treatment of domestic partnerships for purposes of determining amounts included in the gross income of their partners with respect to foreign corporations and regarding gross income that is subject to a high rate of tax under the GILTI provisions, are proposed (published in the Federal Register on June 21, 2019) (REG-101828-19).

Par. 5. Section 1.951A-7 is revised to read as follows:

§1.951A-7. Applicability dates.—(a) *In general.*—Except as otherwise provided in this section, sections 1.951A-1 through 1.951A-6 apply to taxable years of foreign corporations beginning after December 31, 2017, and to taxable years of United States shareholders in which or with which such taxable years of foreign corporations end.

(b) *High tax exclusion.*—Section 1.951A-2(c)(1)(iii) and (c)(6) applies to taxable years of foreign corporations beginning on or after the date of publication of the Treasury decision adopting these rules as final regulations in the **Federal Register**, and to taxable years of United States shareholders in which or with which such taxable years of foreign corporations end.

(c) *Domestic partnerships.*—Section 1.951A-1(e) applies to taxable years of foreign corporations beginning after December 31, 2017, and before the date of publication of the Treasury decision adopting these rules as final regulations in the **Federal Register**, and to taxable years of United States persons in which or with which such taxable years of foreign corporations end.

GILTI: Hybrid Arrangements: Allocation of Deductions

GILTI: Hybrid Arrangements: Allocation of Deductions.—Amendments to Reg. §1.951A-7, adjusting hybrid deduction accounts to take into account earnings and profits of a controlled foreign corporation that are included in income by a United States shareholder, are proposed (published in the Federal Register on April 8, 2020) (REG-106013-19).

Par. 6. Section 1.951A-7, as proposed to be amended at 84 FR 29114 (June 21, 2019), is further amended by adding paragraph (d) to read as follows:

§1.951A-7. Applicability dates.

* * *

(d) *Deduction for certain disqualified payments.*—Section §1.951A-2(c)(6) applies to taxable years of foreign corporations ending on or after [*INSERT DATE OF FILING WITH THE FEDERAL REGISTER*], and to taxable years of United States shareholders in which or with which such taxable years end.

CFCs: Insurance Income: After 1986

Controlled Foreign Corporations: Insurance Income: Tax Years After 1986.—Reproduced below are the texts of proposed Reg. §§1.953-0—1.953-7 and proposed amendments to Reg. §§1.953-1—1.953-6, relating to the election to expense certain depreciable business assets (published in the Federal Register on April 17, 1991).

☐ Par. 2. Sections 1.953-1—1.953-6 are redesignated as §§1.953-1A—1.953-6A, and a new center heading is added preceding newly designated §1.953-1A to read as follows:

REGULATIONS APPLICABLE TO TAXABLE YEARS BEGINNING BEFORE JANUARY 1, 1987

☐ Par. 5. A new center heading is added to follow newly designated §1.953-6A and to precede §1.960-1:

REGULATIONS APPLICABLE TO TAXABLE YEARS BEGINNING AFTER DECEMBER 31, 1986

☐ Par. 3. A new center heading and new §§1.953-0 through 1.953-7 are added to read as follows:

REGULATIONS APPLICABLE TO TAXABLE YEARS BEGINNING AFTER DECEMBER 31, 1986

§1.953-0. Introduction.—(a) This paragraph lists the topics covered in §§1.953-0 through 1.953-7.
§1.953-0. Introduction.
    (a) Outline.
    (b) Effective dates.
§1.953-1. Taxation of foreign insurance operations.
    (a) In general.
    (b) Determining subpart F inclusions of income from insurance operations.
        (1) Procedure.
        (2) Cross reference to additional provisions.
    (c) Effective date.
§1.953-2. Premiums attributable to the section 953 insurance income category and the SCI income category.
    (a) In general.
        (1) Section 953 insurance income premiums.
        (2) SCI income premiums.
    (b) Method of attributing premiums to the section 953 insurance income or SCI income categories.
        (1) In general.
        (2) Examples.
    (c) Definition of premiums.

    (d) Allocation and apportionment of premiums.
        (1) Risks both in and outside the home country.
        (2) Examples.
        (3) 80 percent rule.
            (i) In general.
            (ii) Example.
    (e) Location of risks in connection with property.
        (1) In general.
        (2) Specific rules for locating certain types of property.
            (i) Commercial transportation property.
            (ii) Examples.
            (iii) Noncommercial transportation property.
            (iv) Property exported by ship or aircraft.
            (v) Property imported by ship or aircraft.
            (vi) Shipments originating and terminating in the home country.
            (vii) Shipments originating and terminating in a country other than the home country.
        (3) Related assets and certain moveable property.
            (i) Related assets.
            (ii) Example.
            (iii) Moveable property.

(iv) Example.

(f) Location of risks in connection with liability arising out of activity.

(1) Definition of risks in connection with liability.

(2) Location of risk.

(i) In general.

(ii) Examples.

(3) Specific rules locating certain activities.

(i) Liability with respect to property manufactured, produced, constructed, or assembled.

(ii) Examples.

(iii) Location of activities in connection with transportation property.

(iv) Example.

(v) Selling activity.

(vi) Example.

(g) Location of risks in connection with life or health.

(1) In general.

(2) Example.

(h) Risks deemed to be located in a country other than the home country.

(1) Artificial arrangements.

(2) Evidence of arrangements.

(3) Examples.

§ 1.953-3. Allocation of premiums to the RPII or nonRPII categories of section 953 insurance income.

(a) In general.

(b) Related person insurance income.

(1) In general.

(2) Definitions.

(i) United States shareholder, related person, and controlled foreign corporation.

(ii) Examples.

(iii) United States shareholder: exception for indirect ownership; publicly traded stock.

(iv) Example.

(v) Controlled foreign corporation: shipowner's protection and indemnity association.

(3) Reinsurance.

(i) In general.

(ii) Examples.

(4) Indirectly insuring a related insured: fronting.

(i) In general.

(ii) Example.

(5) Cross-insurance arrangements.

(i) In general.

(ii) Example.

(6) Specific premium rules.

(i) Premiums received prior to January 1, 1987.

(ii) Apportionment of premiums if stock owned for less than entire taxable year.

(iii) Examples.

(iv) Anti-abuse rule.

(v) Example.

§ 1.953-4. Allocation and apportionment of items of investment income.

(a) In general.

(1) Investment income.

(2) Decreases in reserves.

(i) In general.

(ii) Examples.

(b) Allocation of investment income.

(1) In general.

(2) Examples.

(c) Apportionment of investment income.

(1) Life insurance companies.

(i) In general.

(ii) Section 807(c) items attributable to RPII, nonRPII, and SCI contracts.

(2) Property and casualty companies.

(i) In general.

(ii) Unpaid losses attributable to a particular category.

(3) Examples.

§ 1.953-5. Allocation and apportionment of expenses.

(a) Allocation of deductions to RPII, nonRPII, and SCI categories.

(b) Apportionment of expenses to RPII, nonRPII, and SCI categories.

(1) In general.

(2) Life insurance companies.

(i) Investment deductions.

(ii) Other deductions.

(3) Property and casualty companies.

(i) Investment deductions.

(ii) Other deductions.

(c) Allocation and apportionment of deductions between premium and investment income after the deductions have been allocated or apportioned to the SCI or RPII categories.

(1) In general.

(2) Examples.

(3) Apportionment of reserves, losses, policyholder dividends, and policy acquisition expenses and certain other deductions between investment and premium income.

(i) In general.

(ii) Deduction for reserves and losses defined.

(iii) Investment income required to be added to reserves and required to fund losses.

(iv) Investment income's proportionate share of policyholder dividends.

(v) Apportionment of policy acquisition expenses and certain other deductions.

(vi) Example.

(4) Alternative method for life insurance companies.

(i) In general.

(ii) Example.

(5) Losses in excess of premium or investment income.

(6) Losses within the RPII, nonRPII, and SCI categories.

§ 1.953-6. Application of subchapter L and certain sections of subchapter N of the Code.

(a) Applicability of subchapter L.

(1) In general.

(2) Applicability of section 7702. [Reserved]

(3) Applicability of section 817. [Reserved]

(b) Special rules regarding use of subchapter L to compute RPII, nonRPII, and SCI income.

(1) Certain provisions not to apply.

(2) Allocation and apportionment of certain items.

(c) Alternative tax for certain small companies.

(d) Computation of reserves to determine applicability of part I of subchapter L.

(1) Reserves required by law.

(i) Reserves with respect to United States business.

(ii) Reserves deemed to be required.

(iii) Reserves with respect to foreign business.

(2) SCI reserves to be taken into account.

(e) Computation of reserves for purposes of computing taxable income.

(1) Actual reserves required

(2) Life insurance reserves.

(3) Discounted unpaid losses of a property and casualty company.

(4) Interest rates used for determining reserves.

(i) Qualified foreign contracts and property and liability contracts.

(ii) Nonqualified foreign contracts.

(f) Corporations not qualifying as insurance companies.

(1) In general.

(2) Items of gross income attributable to insurance operations of a non-insurance company.

(i) Corporations computing taxable income under part I of subchapter L.

(ii) Example.

(iii) Corporations computing taxable income under part II of subchapter L.

(g) Relationship between sections 953 and 954.

(1) Priority of application.

(i) In general.

(ii) Examples.

(2) Decrease or increase in income not material.

(i) In general.

(ii) Examples.

(h) Inclusion of pro rata share of subpart F income derived from insurance operations.

(1) Inclusion of pro rata share of related person insurance income.

(2) Inclusion of subpart F income other than related person insurance income.

(3) Earnings and profits limitation.

(4) Examples.

(5) Controlled foreign corporation for less than entire year.

(i) In general.

(ii) Example.

(6) Distributions.
 (i) In general.
 (ii) Example.
(7) Mutual insurance companies.
(i) Application of sections 959, 961, and 1248.
(j) Application of section 367(b). [Reserved]
(k) Interaction with section 954(b)(3).
§ 1.953-7. Exceptions to inclusion of related person insurance income for certain shareholders.
 (a) Corporation not held by insureds.
  (1) In general.
  (2) Examples.
 (b) De minimis insurance exception.
  (1) In general.
  (2) Examples.
  (3) Anti-abuse rule.
   (i) In general.
   (ii) Examples.
 (c) Election to treat income as effectively connected.
  (1) In general.
  (2) Corporations which may make the election.
   (i) In general.
   (ii) Successor corporation.
   (iii) Examples.
  (3) Taxable year of corporation making election.
  (4) Period during which election is in effect.
   (i) Elections that become effective in taxable years beginning after December 31, 1987.
   (ii) Examples.
   (iii) Elections that become effective in first taxable year beginning after December 31, 1986.
   (iv) Examples.
  (5) Effect of election; taxation under section 882; alternative minimum tax; dividends received deduction; pre-1987 deficits in earnings and profits; and net operating losses.
  (6) Exemption from tax imposed by section 4371.
  (7) Procedure for making election under section 953(c)(3)(C).
   (i) In general.
   (ii) When election must be made.
   (iii) Election.
  (8) Closing agreement.
  (9) Letter of credit.
   (i) In general.
   (ii) Changes in the amount of the letter of credit.
  (10) Underpayment of tax due.
  (11) Termination or revocation of election.
   (i) Termination.
   (ii) Revocation with consent.
   (iii) Unilateral revocation by Commissioner.

(b) *Effective dates.*—(1) The provisions of §§ 1.953-1 through 1.953-7 apply to taxable years of a controlled foreign corporation beginning after December 31, 1986. However, the amendments to section 953(c)(2) and (c)(3) by section 1012(i)(3)(A) and (B)(i) and (ii) of the Technical and Miscellaneous Revenue Act of 1988 shall apply to taxable years beginning after December 31, 1987 to the extent such amendments add the phrase "(directly or indirectly)." Further, the risk location rules of § 1.953-2 shall apply only to periods of coverage that begin on or after June 17, 1991. Prior to the effective date of § 1.953-2, taxpayers may determine the location of risks by using the principles of § 1.953-2A of the regulations, but those principles shall be applied to determine whether risks are located in or outside the controlled foreign corporation's country of incorporation rather than in or outside the United States. Finally, the apportionment of reserves, losses, policyholder dividends, and policy acquisition expenses between premium and investment income within the SCI, and, in certain circumstances, within the RPII category as provided in § 1.953-5(c)(3) shall apply to taxable years beginning on or after April 17, 1991. For taxable years beginning prior to April 17, 1991, taxpayers may use a reasonable apportionment formula.

(2) The provisions of §§ 1.953-1A through 1.953-6A apply to taxable years of a controlled foreign corporation beginning before January 1, 1987. All references therein to sections of the Code are to the Internal Revenue Code of 1954 prior to the amendments made by the Tax Reform Act of 1986. [Reg. § 1.953-0.]

§ 1.953-1. Taxation of foreign insurance operations.—(a) *In general.*—The income from the insurance operations of a controlled foreign corporation may be subject to inclusion in the gross income of a United States shareholder under subpart F of the Code either as insurance income under section 953 or as foreign personal holding company income under sections 954(a)(1) and (c). Section 953 insurance income is income (including premium and investment income)

attributable to the issuing or reinsuring of any insurance or annuity contract in connection with risks located in a country other than the country (the "home country") under the laws of which the controlled foreign corporation is created or organized and which would be taxed under subchapter L of the Code if the income were the income of a domestic insurance company. The term "home country" includes any area within the jurisdiction (as recognized by the United States) of the country of incorporation of a controlled foreign corporation or within the jurisdiction of a possession of such country. A risk is located in a country other than the home country if it is located on the high seas outside the home country. Insurance income exists only with respect to bona fide contracts of insurance (or reinsurance) or annuity contracts. There are two categories of section 953 insurance income: income that constitutes related person insurance income under § 1.953-3(b)(1) (the "RPII category") and income that is subject to section 953 but is not related person insurance income (the "nonRPII category"). Income, whether premium or investment income, derived from issuing or reinsuring insurance or annuity contracts in connection with risks located in the country in which the controlled foreign corporation is created or organized is referred to as same country insurance ("SCI") income. Investment income attributable to premiums that constitute SCI income may be includable in the gross income of the United States shareholders of a controlled foreign corporation as foreign personal holding company income under sections 954(a)(1) and (c). However, the premiums attributable to issuing or reinsuring insurance or annuity contracts in connection with risks located in the controlled foreign corporation's home country are not generally treated as subpart F income.

(b) *Determining subpart F inclusions of income from insurance operations.*—(1) *Procedure.*—The following procedures are used to determine the amount of a controlled foreign corporation's section 953 insurance income and its foreign personal holding company income derived from insurance operations:

 (i) Determine whether premiums from insurance, reinsurance, and annuity contracts issued by the controlled foreign corporation constitute section 953 insurance income or SCI income by determining the location of the risks under the contracts (*see* § 1.953-2);

 (ii) Determine whether the premiums that constitute section 953 insurance income are attributable to the RPII or nonRPII categories (*see* § 1.953-3);

 (iii) Allocate and apportion investment income to the RPII, nonRPII, and SCI categories (*see* § 1.953-4); and

 (iv) Allocate and apportion deductions to the RPII, nonRPII, and SCI categories; within the SCI category and, under certain circumstances, within the RPII category, further allocate and apportion deductions between SCI premium income and SCI investment income (*see* § 1.953-5).

 (2) *Cross reference to additional provisions.*—Section 1.953-6 contains rules relating to the application of subchapter L of the Code (insurance companies), subpart F of part III of subchapter N (controlled foreign corporations), and certain additional Code provisions to income derived from the conduct of insurance operations. Section 1.953-7 contains rules regarding certain exceptions to the inclusion of related person insurance income in the gross income of certain United States shareholders.

(c) *Effective date.*—For regulations under section 953 that apply to the taxable years of a controlled foreign corporation beginning before January 1, 1987, *see* §§ 1.953-1A through 1.953-6A. The provisions of § 1.953-1 and §§ 1.953-3 through 1.953-7 apply to the taxable years of a controlled foreign corporation beginning after December 31, 1986. However, the amendments to section 953(c)(2) and (c)(3) by section 1012(i)(3)(A) and (B)(i) and (ii) of the Technical and Miscellaneous Revenue Act of 1988 shall apply to taxable years beginning after December 31, 1987 to the extent such amendments add the phrase "(directly or indirectly)." Also, the regulations under § 1.953-2 regarding the location of risks will apply only to periods of coverage, regardless of when the contract was issued, that begin on or after June 17, 1991. Prior to the effective date of § 1.953-2, taxpayers may determine the location of risks by using the principles of § 1.953-2A of the regulations, but those principles shall be applied to determine whether risks are located in or outside the controlled foreign corporation's country of incorporation rather than in or outside the United States. Finally, the apportionment of reserves, losses, policyholder dividends, and policy acquisition expenses between premium and investment income within the SCI, and, in certain circumstances, within the RPII category as provided in § 1.953-5(c)(3) shall apply to taxable years beginning on or after April 17, 1991. For taxable years beginning prior to April 17, 1991, taxpayers may use a reasonable apportionment formula. [Reg. § 1.953-1.]

§ 1.953-2. Premiums attributable to the section 953 insurance income category and the SCI income category.—(a) *In general.*—Premiums on any insurance, reinsurance, or any annuity contract (including an annuity certain, which is an annuity that guarantees payments for a fixed period without reference to life contingencies) must be classified as either section 953 insurance income or SCI income. To determine whether premiums paid for an annuity certain are section 953 insurance income or SCI income, the annuity certain shall be treated as a contract covering risks in connection with life or health. Premiums written (less return premiums and premiums paid for reinsurance) before the first taxable year of the controlled foreign corporation beginning after December 31, 1986 that become earned under section 832(b)(4) in such taxable year or succeeding taxable years must be classified as either section 953 insurance income or SCI income. (*See* §1.953-3, below, for rules allocating premiums that constitute section 953 insurance income to the RPII or nonRPII categories.)

(1) *Section 953 insurance income premiums.*—Premiums constitute section 953 insurance income if they relate to risks that are—

(i) In connection with property located in a country other than the home country, as described in paragraph (e) of this section;

(ii) In connection with a liability arising out of an activity conducted in a country other than the home country, as described in paragraph (f) of this section;

(iii) In connection with the life or health of a resident of a country other than the home country, as described in paragraph (g) of this section; or

(iv) In connection with risks not described in paragraph (a)(1)(i) through (iii) of this section as a result of any arrangement whereby another person receives a substantially equal amount of premiums or other consideration in respect of issuing (or reinsuring) a contract described in paragraph (a)(1)(i) through (iii) of this section. (*See* paragraph (h) of this section).

(2) *SCI income premiums.*—Premiums constitute SCI income if they relate to risks that are—

(i) In connection with property located in the home country, as described in paragraph (e) of this section;

(ii) In connection with a liability arising out of an activity conducted in the home country, as described in paragraph (f) of this section; or

(iii) In connection with the life or health of a resident of the home country, as described in paragraph (g) of this section.

(b) *Method of attributing premiums to the section 953 insurance income or SCI income categories.*—(1) *In general.*—Whether the premiums from an insurance, reinsurance, or annuity contract constitute section 953 insurance income or SCI income is determined by the location of the risks during the period or periods of coverage under the contract to which the premiums relate. A period of coverage is a period no longer than one year during which insurance coverage is provided or an annuity contract is in force and which begins or ends with or within the taxable year of the controlled foreign corporation. A period of coverage begins when coverage under the contract commences or on the anniversary of that date. A period of coverage ends on the last day preceding a new period of coverage, on the day the contract terminates or is canceled, or on the day the risk under the contract has been transferred in a reinsurance transaction in which the reinsurer assumes all rights and obligations under the reinsured policies. The determination of where a risk is located must be made separately for each period of coverage applicable to the taxable year.

(2) *Examples.*—The following examples illustrate the principles of paragraph (b)(1) of this section.

Example 1. Controlled foreign corporation X, incorporated in country M, issues to corporation Z an insurance contract which provides coverage for a 2 1/2 year period beginning on July 1, 1987. Under the insurance contract, premiums are paid monthly. Corporation X uses the calendar year as the taxable year. For premiums included in gross income for the 1987 taxable year, the period of coverage under the contract is July 1, 1987 to June 30, 1988. For premiums included in gross income for the 1988 taxable year, there are two applicable periods of coverage: July 1, 1987 to June 30, 1988 and July 1, 1988 to June 30, 1989. Whether the premiums attributable to each such period of coverage constitute section 953 insurance income or SCI insurance income must be made by considering only the facts pertinent to each period of coverage separately. For the 1989 taxable year, the periods of coverage are July 1, 1988 to June 30, 1989 and July 1, 1989 to December 31, 1989. Again, whether the premiums attributable to each such period of coverage constitute section 953 insurance income or SCI insurance income must be made by considering only the facts pertinent to each period of coverage separately.

Example 2. The facts are the same as in *Example 1* except that Z cancels the contract on August 31, 1987. For the 1987 taxable year, the period of coverage is July 1, 1987 to August 31, 1987.

Example 3. The facts are the same as in *Example 1* except that on January 15, 1989, X cedes risks under the insurance contract in a reinsurance transaction (other than a reinsurance transaction in

which the reinsurer assumes all rights and obligations under the reinsured contracts) to controlled foreign corporation W, which also uses the calendar year as the taxable year. For the 1988 taxable year, the periods of coverage for X are July 1, 1987 to June 30, 1988 and July 1, 1988 to June 30, 1989. For 1989, the periods of coverage for both X and W are July 1, 1988 to June 30, 1989 and July 1, 1989 to December 31, 1989.

Example 4. The facts are the same as in *Example 1* except that corporation X issues to corporation Z an insurance contract which covers the marine risks of shipping a machine to and from countries other than country M. The contract does not specify the dates during which the machine is covered, but provides coverage from the time the machine is delivered alongside a named vessel at the port of embarkation until the time the machine is delivered alongside the vessel at the port of debarkation. The deliveries are commenced and completed during the period beginning February 1, 1987 and ending February 28, 1987. For the 1987 taxable year, the period of coverage is February 1 to February 28, 1987.

(c) *Definition of premiums.*—For a controlled foreign corporation that would be taxed as a life insurance company under part I of subchapter L (relating to life insurance companies) of the Code if it were a domestic insurance company, the term "premiums," for purposes of this section and §1.953-3, means the items taken into account for the taxable year under section 803(a)(1). For a controlled foreign corporation that would be taxed under part II of subchapter L (relating to insurance companies other than life insurance companies), the term "premiums," for purposes of this section and §1.953-3, means premiums written, as defined in section 832(b)(4)(A). If a policy of insurance, such as a reporting form policy or other policy, does not require premiums to be paid until the policy term expires, then the deposits required during the term of the policy must be included in premiums. In the case of a mutual fire or flood insurance company described in section 832(b)(1)(D), the term "premiums," for purposes of this section and §1.953-3, means the entire amount of premiums deposited. In addition, for taxable years beginning after December 31, 1986 and before January 1, 1993, if the foreign corporation was a controlled foreign corporation (as defined in section 957 of the Code prior to its amendment by the Tax Reform Act of 1986) in the most recent taxable year beginning before January 1, 1987, the term "premiums" also includes an amount equal to $3\frac{1}{3}$ percent of the unearned premiums at the end of the most recent taxable year beginning before January 1, 1987 that are sourced within the United States under section 861(a)(7). *See* section 832(b)(4)(C). Premiums included in gross income by virtue of the preceding sentence are attributable to risks located outside the controlled foreign corporation's home country.

(d) *Allocation and apportionment of premiums.*—(1) *Risks both in and outside the home country.*—If the risks covered by a contract of insurance or reinsurance or annuity contract are located both in and outside the home country during any period of coverage, the premium for insuring the risks must be allocated to or apportioned between risks incurred in the home country and risks incurred outside the home country. Allocation of a premium means that there is a direct correlation between the premium charged and the location of the insured risks in or outside the home country. Apportionment means that there is a reasonable basis for dividing the premium between risks incurred in the home country and risks incurred outside the home country, but there is no direct correlation between the premium charged and the location of the risks. If a premium is apportioned between home country risks and risks incurred outside the home country, each premium payment shall be considered to be partly related to home country risks and partly related to risks incurred outside the home country. The allocation or apportionment of premiums to or between risks located in the home country and risks located outside the home country must be reasonable in relation to the location of the insured risks during the period of coverage. In considering whether a method of allocation or apportionment is reasonable, consideration shall be given to the types of risks covered and the terms of the insurance, reinsurance, or annuity contract including, but not limited to, provisions which separately describe each risk covered, the period of coverage of each risk, the special warranties for each risk, the premium for each risk, and the conditions for paying the premium for each risk. The allocation and apportionment of premiums must be consistent with the rules prescribed in paragraphs (e), (f), and (g) of this section. In addition, once a particular method has been adopted for allocating and apportioning premiums under a contract, that method must be used as long as the contract is in force.

(2) *Examples.*—The following examples illustrate the rules of paragraph (d)(1) of this section.

Example 1. X is a country F controlled foreign corporation with a calendar taxable year. X insures from July 1, 1987 through June 30, 1988 a particular piece of machinery that is located in country F. The machine is moved outside country F on January 1, 1988. The contract provides for $500 in premiums to be paid on June 30, 1987 and $1,000 on January 1, 1988. The larger premium payment on January 1, 1988 reflects the increased risks associated with locating the machine outside country F. For the 1987 and 1988 taxable years, the period of coverage is July 1, 1987 to June 30, 1988. Because there is a direct correlation between the premium payments and the location of the risks, the premiums must be allocated. The $500 premium payment included in X's gross income for the 1987 taxable year relates to risks incurred while the property is located in country F; therefore, all $500 in premiums constitute SCI income. The $1,000 included in X's gross income in the 1988 taxable year relates to coverage while the property is outside country F; therefore, all $1,000 constitutes section 953 insurance income.

Example 2. Z is a country F controlled foreign corporation with a calendar taxable year. Z issues a policy of insurance covering risks of damage to railroad rolling stock that only travels a particular route between country F and country M. The railroad rolling stock travels an equal number of miles in both countries. A $1,000 premium is required by Z to insure the railroad rolling stock from July 1, 1987 through June 30, 1988. The premium is paid in two installments: $500 on June 30, 1987 and $500 on January 1, 1988. Based on the types of risks covered by the contract of insurance and the terms of the contract, Z, in conformance with paragraph (e)(2)(i) of this section, chooses an apportionment method based on mileage. Because the premium is apportioned, $250 of the $500 premium included in the gross income of Z in the 1987 taxable year is attributable to home country risks and $250 is attributable to risks outside the home country. The result for the 1988 taxable year is the same.

(3) *80 percent rule.*—(i) *In general.*—If 80 percent or more of the premiums for a period of coverage of a particular contract are apportioned to risks located in the home country or to risks located outside the home country, then all of the premiums for the period of coverage are apportioned to risks incurred in or outside the home country, as the case may be.

(ii) *Example.*—The following example illustrates the operation of the 80 percent rule of paragraph (d)(3)(i) of this section.

Example. Controlled foreign corporation X, which is incorporated in country F and uses the calendar year as its taxable year, issues an insurance contract insuring a machine owned by Y against damage for a one year period commencing on May 1, 1987. When the contract was issued, the machine was located in country F; however, on April 1, 1988, Y moved the machine to a branch located outside country F. Y is required to pay premiums of $100 per month under the terms of the insurance contract. For the taxable years ending December 31, 1987 and December 31, 1988, the period of coverage is May 1, 1987 to April 30, 1988. For that period of coverage $1/12$ ($100/$1200) of the premiums are related to risks located outside country F. Because approximately 92% of the premiums are related to home country risks, all the premiums under the contract are attributable to home country risks. Therefore, the $800 of premiums received by X from Y in the taxable year ending December 31, 1987 and the $400 of premiums received in the taxable year ending December 31, 1988 are attributable entirely to home country risks and constitute SCI income.

(e) *Location of risks in connection with property.*—*(1) In general.*—Risks in connection with property covered by a contract of insurance or reinsurance are located where the property is located during the period or periods of coverage applicable to the taxable year. A risk is in connection with property if it is related to an interest of an insured in tangible (whether real or personal) or intangible property. An interest in real property includes, but is not limited to, the interest of an owner, landlord, tenant, licensee, licensor, mortgagor, mortgagee, trustee, beneficiary, or partner. Where property is located depends on all the facts and circumstances. (*See* paragraph (e)(2) of this section for specific rules locating certain types of property.) The determination of where property is located must be made separately under each contract of insurance or reinsurance and for each item of property covered by the contract for each period of coverage applicable to the taxable year. (However, *see* paragraph (e)(3)(i) of this section which permits property to be aggregated in certain circumstances for purposes of determining location of risks.)

(2) *Specific rules for locating certain types of property.*—(i) *Commercial transportation property.*—Premiums related to insuring or reinsuring risks in connection with any motor vehicle, ship or boat, aircraft, railroad rolling stock, or any container transported thereby ("commercial transportation property") that is used predominantly in the commercial transportation of persons or property are attributable to risks located in the home country if the property is located in the home country for the entire period of coverage, or outside the home country if the property is located outside the home country for the entire period of coverage. If the commercial transportation property is located both in and outside the home country, then the premiums shall be allocated or appor-

tioned between risks located in the home country and risks located outside the home country on any reasonable basis (such as time or mileage) that gives due regard to the risk being insured and that complies with the requirements of paragraphs (d)(1) and (d)(3) of this section. *See* paragraph (e)(3)(iii) of this section for rules relating to the location of moveable property, which includes commercial transportation property, if the location of such property cannot be determined by the end of the taxable year.

(ii) *Examples.*—The following examples illustrate the operation of paragraph (e)(2)(i) of this section.

Example 1. Controlled foreign corporation Y, which is incorporated in country F, issues a property and liability insurance contract covering a helicopter that is used in rescue operations in country F as well as other countries. More than 60 percent of the miles traversed by the helicopter are outside country F. However, the helicopter is located in a hangar in country F for more than 90 percent of the period of coverage. Y apportions the premiums based on the time the helicopter is located in and outside the country of incorporation. An apportionment based on the amount of time that the helicopter is located in and outside country F is not reasonable in light of the types of risks insured and the activities in which the helicopter is engaged. Therefore, Y's apportionment of the premium will not be respected.

Example 2. Corporation Y, a country F controlled foreign corporation, insures an airplane that is used exclusively for the commercial transportation of persons or property. Of the total miles travelled by the airplane, 60 percent are traversed outside country F, and 40 percent are traversed in country F. The airplane is grounded only for repairs, and the repairs are made at the location of the airplane at the time the repairs are needed. The premiums must be apportioned on a reasonable basis between risks incurred while the plane is in country F and risks incurred while it is outside country F. On the facts presented in this example, an apportionment based on total miles traversed in and outside country F would be reasonable. Thus, 60 percent of the premiums would constitute section 953 insurance income and 40 percent of the premiums would constitute SCI income.

Example 3. The facts are the same as in *Example 2* except that of the total miles travelled by the airplane, 85 percent are traversed outside the home country and 15 percent are traversed in the home country. Under the 80 percent rule of paragraph (d)(3) of this section, all of the premiums are apportioned to risks located outside country F.

(iii) *Noncommercial transportation property.*—Premiums related to risks incurred in connection with any motor vehicle, ship or boat, aircraft, or railroad rolling stock not used predominantly in the commercial transportation of persons or property are attributable to risks located outside the home country if the noncommercial transportation property is registered during the period of coverage with a country other than the home country (including any political subdivision or agency of such country) or if the owner of the property is a citizen of, resident of, or entity organized under the laws of a country other than the home country. In all other cases, noncommercial transportation property shall be deemed to be located in the home country.

(iv) *Property exported by ship or aircraft.*—Premiums related to risks in connection with property exported from the home country by ship or aircraft are attributable to risks incurred while the exported property is located in the home country if the insured risks terminate when the exported property is placed aboard the ship or aircraft for export. Premiums are attributable to risks incurred while the exported property is located outside the home country if the insured risks commence when the exported property is placed aboard the ship or aircraft for export. If the insured risks commence before the exported property is placed aboard the ship or aircraft for export and terminate after the departure of the ship or aircraft from the home country, the premiums must be allocated or apportioned between risks incurred while the exported property is located in the home country and risks incurred while the property is located outside the home country on any reasonable basis (such as time or mileage) that gives due regard to the risk being insured and that complies with the requirements of paragraphs (d)(1) and (d)(3) of this section.

(v) *Property imported by ship or aircraft.*—Premiums related to risks in connection with property imported into the home country by ship or aircraft are attributable to risks incurred outside the home country if the insured risks terminate when the imported property is unloaded at the home country port of entry. If the insured risks commence after the imported property is unloaded from the ship or aircraft at the home country port of entry, the premiums are attributable to risks incurred while the imported property is in the home country. If the insured risks commence before and terminate after the imported property is unloaded from the ship or aircraft at the home country port of entry, the premiums must be allocated or apportioned to or between risks incurred while the imported property is located in the home country and risks incurred while the imported property is located outside the home country on any reasonable basis (such as time or mileage) that gives due regard to the risk being insured and that complies with the requirements of paragraphs (d)(1) and (d)(3) of this section.

(vi) *Shipments originating and terminating in the home country.*—Premiums related to risks incurred in connection with property transported from one place in the home country to another place in the home country on or over another country, or on or over the high seas outside the territorial waters of the home country are attributable to risks in the home country unless the premiums are allocated, in a reasonable manner, under the terms of the insurance contract to risks incurred while the property is located in the home country and risks incurred while the property is located outside the home country.

(vii) *Shipments originating and terminating in a country other than the home country.*—Premiums related to risks in connection with property transported on or over the home country to and from points outside the home country are attributable to risks located outside the home country unless the premiums are allocated, in a reasonable manner, under the terms of the insurance contract to risks incurred while the property is located in the home country and risks incurred while the property is located outside the home country.

(3) *Related assets and certain moveable property.*—(i) *Related assets.*—If a contract of insurance or reinsurance covers a group of related assets, such as inventory, which are located in and outside the home country, premiums under the contract may be allocated or apportioned, on any reasonable basis, between risks located in the home country and risks located outside the home country by reference to such property taken in the aggregate.

(ii) *Example.*—The following example illustrates the related assets rule of paragraph (e)(3)(i) of this section.

Example. X is a controlled foreign corporation incorporated in country F. X issues a contract of insurance to M covering M's inventory. M maintains its inventory in warehouses in country F and other countries. The risks to which the inventory is exposed are similar in each country in which the inventory is stored. For the applicable period of coverage, 40 percent of M's inventory is located in country F and 60 percent is located outside country F. The location of the property is determined on the basis of the average value of inventory warehoused in and outside of country F during the period of coverage. X may apportion 40 percent of the premiums under the contract with M to the SCI income category and 60 percent to the section 953 insurance income category.

(iii) *Moveable property.*—In any case in which a contract of insurance or reinsurance covers moveable property (other than noncommercial transportation property) and the determination of the location of the property in or outside the home country during a period of coverage cannot practically be made by the close of the controlled foreign corporation's taxable year, the controlled foreign corporation may apportion the premiums in conformance with a reasonable expectation of where the property will be located during the period of coverage, provided that the apportionments made on all contracts to which this paragraph (e)(3)(iii) applies do not result in a material distortion. A material distortion results if the amount of premiums apportioned to the SCI or section 953 insurance income category determined by reference to the actual facts pertinent to the period of coverage, as ascertained within 90 days after the end of the period of coverage, would result in at least a 10 percentage point difference when compared to the amount of premiums apportioned to those categories under a reasonable expectation of where the property will be located during the period of coverage. In order to avail itself of this method, the controlled foreign corporation must maintain records that demonstrate the reasonableness of its apportionment, disclose the actual location of the property as ascertained within 90 days after the end of the period of coverage, and demonstrate that the apportionment did not result in a material distortion. If such records are not maintained, the apportionment method of this paragraph may not be used and the property shall be located under the rule of this paragraph (e) that would apply in absence of the method prescribed by this paragraph (e)(2)(iii). In the event of a material distortion, the United States shareholders or, if an election is made under § 1.953-7(c), the controlled foreign corporation, must file amended income tax returns and apportion premiums based on the actual location of the property and the rules of paragraphs (d) and (e) of this section.

(iv) *Example.*—The following example illustrates the moveable property rule of paragraph (e)(3)(iii) of this section.

Example. X is a controlled foreign corporation incorporated in country F. It uses the calendar year as its taxable year. X issues a

contract of insurance covering a ship from July 1, 1988 to June 30, 1989. The contract is the only one issued by X that covers moveable property. The owner of the ship leases the ship to third persons on a per voyage basis. Based on information provided by the shipowner, 30 percent of the total miles traversed during the 12 month period immediately preceding the issuance of the contract were in home country waters and 70 percent outside the home country. X may apportion 30 percent of the premiums received to the SCI income category and 70 percent to the section 953 insurance income category. Within 90 days after the end of the policy period, X obtains information demonstrating that the ship was used in the territorial waters of the home country 25 percent of the time and outside the territorial waters 75 percent of the time. The apportionment method used by X is reasonable and does not result in a material distortion because an apportionment based on the facts pertinent to the period of coverage would not have resulted in at least a 10 percentage point difference in the amount of premiums apportioned to the SCI or section 953 insurance income categories. Thus, X may use the apportionment method described in paragraph (e)(3)(iii) of this section provided it maintains the records required by that paragraph.

(f) *Location of risks in connection with liability arising out of activity.*—(1) *Definition of risks in connection with liability.*—A risk covered by a contract of insurance or reinsurance is in connection with liability arising out of an activity if the insured is covered against a liability resulting from the actions of a person or a juridical entity, including actions that result in a tort, violation of contract, violation of property rights, or any other cause of action pursuant to the operation of law. The term not only includes a direct liability, which, for example, may be incurred by a tortfeasor to the person harmed, but also an indirect liability, such as the liability of one person to another resulting from the actions of an independent contractor. Moreover, a risk in connection with liability includes any loss of an insured (except a loss in connection with property described in paragraph (e) of this section) which could arise from the occurrence of an event insured against. For example, in the case of a promoter of outdoor sporting events, a risk in connection with liability arising out of an activity includes the loss that could arise from the cancellation of a sporting event because of inclement weather.

(2) *Location of risk.*—(i) *In general.*—A risk in connection with an activity is located where the activity that could give rise to a liability or loss is performed. For purposes of allocating and apportioning premiums between risks located in and outside the home country, where an activity is performed depends on the facts and circumstances of each case. Among the factors to be considered in making the determination are the location of the assets associated with the activity, the place where services comprising the activity are performed, the place where activities intended to result in a sale occur, and the place where sales actually occur.

(ii) *Examples.*—The following examples illustrate the location of risk rules of paragraph (f)(2)(i) of this section.

Example 1. X is a controlled foreign corporation that issues liability insurance and is incorporated in country M. It uses a calendar year as its taxable year. X issues a contract of insurance to Z, which owns and operates department stores in country M and other countries. The contract covers all of Z's stores. It provides coverage against "liability for bodily injury or property damage arising out of the ownership, maintenance, or use of the insured premises and all operations necessary or incidental thereto." Assuming X cannot allocate the premiums between home country and other country risks, it must apportion the premiums between those risks on a reasonable basis taking into account where the stores are located and the level of covered activities in each of those stores.

Example 2. Y is a controlled foreign corporation incorporated in country F. Y writes worker's compensation coverage. Y issues a contract to Z, which has employees in country F and other countries, covering all of Z's employees. The premiums paid by Z are not allocable to risks located in the home country and risks located outside the home country. Z must apportion the premiums on a reasonable basis taking into account where Z's employees perform services.

(3) *Specific rules locating certain activities.*—(i) *Liability with respect to property manufactured, produced, constructed, or assembled.*—Premiums under a policy of insurance or reinsurance that insures a person that manufactures, produces, constructs, or assembles property against claims arising from the consumption or use of such property are attributable to risks from an activity performed where the consumption or use of the property takes place, or if the place of consumption or use cannot be known, where the property is manufactured, produced, constructed, or assembled. If the consumption or use of the property could arise in or outside the home country, the premiums must be allocated to or apportioned between risks located in the home country and risks located outside the home country on any reasonable basis that gives due regard to the risk being insured

and that complies with the requirements of paragraphs (d)(1) and (d)(3) of this section.

(ii) *Examples.*—The following examples illustrate the rule of paragraph (f)(3)(i) of this section.

Example 1. X is a contractor that constructs apartment buildings. X uses a system of pre-fabricated construction that entails constructing parts of the apartment buildings in country F and assembling them outside of country F. The only completed apartment buildings constructed by X are outside of country F. X is insured by Z, a country F controlled foreign corporation, against liability for the improper construction of, or the failure to construct, an apartment building. Z is insuring risks in connection with an activity that arises outside of country F because that is where the use of the property takes place.

Example 2. M manufactures automobiles in facilities located in country W. M is covered by a single policy of insurance issued by F, a controlled foreign corporation organized in country W. M sells its automobiles through independent dealers all over the world, including country F. F charges a single premium to insure M against any liability for harm to persons or damage to property arising from a manufacturing defect. F must apportion the premium between risks located in W and risks located outside W on a reasonable basis because the use of the automobiles occurs in and outside of country W. However, if it cannot be known where the automobiles are used, then F is deemed to be insuring risks in connection with an activity that arises in country W because that is where the automobiles are manufactured.

(iii) *Location of activities in connection with transportation property.*—Premiums under a contract of insurance or reinsurance covering risks in connection with the operation of a motor vehicle, ship or boat, aircraft, or railroad rolling stock are attributable to risks in connection with an activity performed where the transportation property is located under the principles of paragraph (e)(2)(i) and (iii) of this section relating to the location of transportation property.

(iv) *Example.*—The following example illustrates the rule of paragraph (f)(3)(iii) of this section.

Example. X is a controlled foreign corporation created under the laws of country F and uses the calendar year as its taxable year. X insures B, a pilot for a commercial airline, against any damage to persons or property arising from B's professional activities. X charges a $10,000 premium, payable $5,000 at the inception of the policy and $5,000 on January 1, 1988, for a one year policy providing coverage from July 1, 1987 to June 30, 1988. B always pilots the same round trip flight from country F to country R and back. For both the 1987 and 1988 taxable years, the period of coverage is July 1, 1987 to June 30, 1988. On each trip from F to R the aircraft traverses half of the total mileage in country F and half in country R. Because the aircraft B flies is located in the home country one-half of the time, a reasonable basis exists for apportioning one-half of the premiums paid by B to risks arising from his activities outside the home country and one-half to activities arising in the home country. Thus, for the 1987 taxable year, the $5,000 of premiums are apportioned so that $2,500 of the premiums are attributable to home country risks and $2,500 of the premiums are attributable to risks located outside the home country. For the 1988 taxable year, the results are the same.

(v) *Selling activity.*—The liability of a person arises from selling activity only if, and to the extent that, the liability does not relate to liability in connection with property manufactured, produced, constructed, or assembled, as described in paragraph (f)(3)(i) of this section, or liability for activities in connection with transportation property, as described in paragraph (f)(3)(iii) of this section. A person is engaged in selling activity if the person engages in any activity which is intended to result in the sale of property. Premiums received on a contract of insurance or reinsurance covering risks in connection with selling activity are attributable to risks incurred where the selling activity takes place regardless of whether the property passes through, or is delivered in, the country in which the selling activity is carried on. Selling activity takes place where the activities preparatory to the sale, such as advertising, negotiating, and distributing, take place.

(vi) *Example.*—The following example illustrates the rule of paragraph (f)(3)(v) of this section.

Example. Corporation M, a country W corporation, insures a wholesale distributor against liability arising out of a breach of warranty. The wholesale distributor negotiates and processes orders in country W, but sells its inventory exclusively in countries other than country W by advertising in trade publications and distributing sales catalogues in those countries. The premiums on the policy issued to M are attributable to risks arising from activities performed both in and outside country W and M must allocate and apportion, on a reasonable basis, the premiums received for insuring the whole-

sale distributor between risks located in country W and risks located outside country W.

(g) *Location of risks in connection with life or health.*—(1) *In general.*—Risks in connection with life or health include risks under contracts of insurance, reinsurance, annuity contracts, or noncancellable health and accident contracts defined in section 816(a) (relating to the definition of a life insurance company). Risks under cancelable health and accident contracts are also risks in connection with life or health. An annuity certain, under which annuity payments are not determined by reference to life contingencies, is treated, for purposes of section 953 as a contract covering risks in connection with life or health. The risk under any insurance, reinsurance, or annuity contract covered by this paragraph (g)(1) is located in the country where the person with respect to whom the risk is located (the "determining life") is resident. The determining life with respect to any life, accident, or health insurance or reinsurance contract is the person whose life or health is covered by the contract. The determining life with respect to a life annuity contract is the person by whose life the annuity payments are measured. The determining life with respect to an annuity certain is the life of the person who purchases the annuity contract and the life of the person for whose benefit the annuity was purchased. Thus, risks in connection with an annuity certain are deemed to be located in their entirety outside a controlled foreign corporation's home country if either the purchaser of the contract or the recipient of the annuity payments resides outside the home country, as determined in accordance with the rules of this paragraph. The person with the determining life is presumed to be resident at the last address given to the controlled foreign corporation as such person's residence, unless the controlled foreign corporation knows or has reason to know that such person is resident at a different address. Premiums received under a contract of group life or health insurance must be apportioned between risks located in the home country and risks outside the home country on the basis of the last known addresses of the residences of the persons insured under the contract or, in the case where the contract is issued to an employer, where the persons covered by the contract are employed.

(2) *Example.*—The following example illustrates the rules of paragraph (g)(1) of this section.

Example. Controlled foreign corporation X, a country F corporation and a calendar year taxpayer, is engaged in the life insurance business. On July 1, 1987, X issues a three year term life insurance contract on the life of B. Premiums under the contract are payable on July 1 and December 31 of each year the contract is in force. B gives to X an address in country F as the address of his primary residence. On November 1, 1987, B changes his primary residence from country F to country Z. B notifies X of the change of address on February 1, 1988. For X's 1987 taxable year the premiums received on July 1, 1987 and December 31, 1987 are allocable to the SCI income category. Because X did not have knowledge, and had no reason to know, of B's change of address until February 1, 1988, it may rely, for all premium payments received before February 1, 1988, on the address B initially provided at the time the contract was approved. However, all premiums received after February 1, 1988 constitute section 953 insurance income because X had knowledge at the time those premiums were received that B had his or her primary residence outside of country F.

(h) *Risks deemed to be located in a country other than the home country.*—(1) *Artificial arrangements.*—The section 953 insurance income of a controlled foreign corporation includes any insurance income from issuing or reinsuring insurance policies or annuity contracts covering risks located in the home country if the insurance, reinsurance, or annuity contracts are attributable to any direct or indirect cross-insurance arrangement whereby the controlled foreign corporation provides insurance, reinsurance, or annuity contracts relating to home country risks and, in exchange, another person provides insurance, reinsurance, or annuity contracts relating to risks located outside the home country. Arrangements to which this rule applies include those entered into by the controlled foreign corporation, persons related (within the meaning of section 954(d)(3)) to the controlled foreign corporation, the United States shareholders of the controlled foreign corporation, and persons related to such shareholders.

(2) *Evidence of arrangements.*—The determination of whether an arrangement referred to in paragraph (h)(1) of this section exists depends on all the facts and circumstances. Facts to be considered in determining the existence of such an arrangement include the premiums charged in relation to the risks insured, the profit margin expected from the contracts, and the loss experience of the risks which the other person insures or reinsures compared with the loss experience of the risks which the controlled foreign corporation insures or reinsures. Further, consideration will be given to the existence of common directors or owners between the parties executing the reciprocal insurance arrangement. The period in which the controlled

foreign corporation receives premiums and the period of coverage for which the premiums are received need not be the same as, or identical in length with, that of the other person or limited to a single taxable year of the controlled foreign corporation.

(3) *Examples.*—The following examples illustrate the principles of paragraph (h) of this section.

Example 1. Controlled foreign corporation X is incorporated in country F and is a wholly owned subsidiary of corporation M, a United States corporation. Foreign corporation Y is a wholly owned subsidiary of foreign corporation R. R is not a controlled foreign corporation. Corporations M and R, which are not related, agree that from July 1, 1987 through December 31, 1987, Y corporation will reinsure certain policies issued by M covering risks that are located outside country F, and that from January 1, 1988 through June 30, 1988, X will reinsure certain policies issued by R covering risks that are located in country F. The premiums received by X corporation from reinsuring the risks of R are attributable to risks located outside country F and constitute section 953 insurance income.

Example 2. The facts are the same as in *Example 1* except that one-third of the risks of M to be reinsured are reinsured with Y and two-thirds of the risks are reinsured with Z, another wholly owned foreign subsidiary of R. The premiums received by X from reinsuring the policies of R are attributable to risks located outside country F and constitute section 953 insurance income.

Example 3. The facts are the same as in *Example 1* except that X and V, another wholly owned foreign subsidiary of M, reinsure the risks of R. The premiums received by X and V from reinsuring the policies of R are attributable to risks located outside country F and constitute section 953 insurance income. [Reg. § 1.953-2.]

§1.953-3. Allocation of premiums to the RPII or nonRPII categories of section 953 insurance income.—(a) *In general.*—All premiums that constitute section 953 insurance income are included within one of two categories: premiums that constitute related person insurance income ("RPII premiums") under paragraph (b) of this section and premiums that do not constitute RPII premiums ("nonRPII premiums"). RPII premiums are not recharacterized as nonRPII premiums even though the exceptions of § 1.953-7 are applicable. However, if the exceptions of § 1.953-7(a) or (b) apply, persons that are United States shareholders solely by virtue of section 953(c)(1)(A) and paragraph (b)(2) of this section of a controlled foreign corporation, as defined in section 953(c)(1)(B) and paragraph (b)(2) of this section, do not include RPII income in their gross income. Persons that are United States shareholders within the meaning of section 951(b) of a controlled foreign corporation as defined in section 957 must always include RPII income in their gross income, regardless of whether the exceptions of § 1.953-7(a) or (b) apply. However, the special pro rata share rules of section 953(c)(5) and § 1.953-6(h)(1) shall not apply if the conditions of section 953(c)(3)(A) and (B) and § 1.953-7(a) and (b) are met.

(b) *Related person insurance income.*—(1) *In general.*—Related person insurance income is included within the meaning of the term "insurance income" as that term is used in section 953. Related person insurance income is premium and investment income attributable to a policy of insurance or reinsurance that provides insurance coverage to a related insured on risks located outside the controlled foreign corporation's country of incorporation, or premium and investment income attributable to an annuity contract that is purchased by or for the benefit of a related insured if the determining life is located outside the controlled foreign corporation's country of incorporation. For this purpose, a related insured is any insured, purchaser of an annuity contract, or recipient of annuity payments that is a United States shareholder of the controlled foreign corporation or a related person (within the meaning of section 954(d)(3)) to a United States shareholder.

(2) *Definitions.*—(i) *United States shareholder, related person, and controlled foreign corporation.*—For purposes of determining whether insurance income is related person insurance income, the terms "United States shareholder," "related person to a United States shareholder," and "controlled foreign corporation" are specifically defined. The term "controlled foreign corporation" means any foreign corporation if 25 percent or more of the total combined voting power of all classes of stock of the foreign corporation entitled to vote or 25 percent or more of the total value of the stock of the foreign corporation is owned (within the meaning of section 958(a)), or is considered as owned by applying the rules of ownership of section 958(b), by United States shareholders on any day during the taxable year of the foreign corporation. For purposes of applying this section to a foreign mutual insurance company, the term stock includes any certificate entitling the holder to voting power in the mutual company. *See* section 958(a)(3). A "United States shareholder" for these purposes is any United States person (as defined in section 957(c)) who owns (within the meaning of section 958(a)) any stock of the foreign corporation at any time during the foreign corporation's taxable year.

A person is a related person to a United States shareholder if the person is related within the meaning of section 954(d)(3) of the Code to the United States shareholder. Thus, a person is related to a United States shareholder if the person controls (within the meaning of section 954(d)(3)), or is controlled by, the United States shareholder, or the person is controlled by the same person (or persons) that controls the United States shareholder. In addition, in the case of any policy of insurance covering liability arising from services performed as a director, officer, or employee of a corporation, or as a partner or employee of a partnership, the person performing such services and the entity for which such services are performed shall be treated as related persons.

(ii) *Examples.*—The following examples illustrate the definitions of paragraph (b)(2)(i) of this section.

Example 1. X is a country F corporation that provides insurance coverage to its 100 shareholders. X has voting common stock and nonvoting preferred stock issued and outstanding. All of the voting common stock is owned by 75 foreign persons. None of the foreign shareholders are related persons within the meaning of section 954(d)(3). All of the nonvoting preferred stock is owned by 25 United States persons. The nonvoting preferred stock accounts for 25 percent of the total value of both classes of stock outstanding. Therefore, each United States person is a United States shareholder and X is a controlled foreign corporation under section 953(c)(2)(B). The premiums from policies of insurance issued to the twenty-five United States shareholders constitute RPII premiums to the extent those premiums relate to risks located outside country F. The premiums from the 75 foreign shareholders constitute nonRPII premiums to the extent those premiums relate to risks located outside country F.

Example 2. The facts are the same as in *Example 1* except that all of the nonvoting preferred stock is owned by a foreign corporation, all of the stock of which is owned by the 25 United States persons. Under section 958(a)(2), the United States persons are considered as owning the stock owned by the foreign corporation. Therefore, X is a controlled foreign corporation and the 25 United States persons are United States shareholders.

Example 3. The facts are the same as in *Example 1* except that 5 of the nonvoting preferred stock shareholders are insured by X and 20 are not. X is a controlled foreign corporation and all 25 United States persons are United States shareholders. A United States person need not be insured by the controlled foreign corporation to be a United States shareholder of that corporation.

Example 4. Y is a foreign corporation that issues polices of insurance and reinsurance. The one class of Y stock outstanding is owned equally by 25 shareholders who are United States persons. None of the shareholders of Y are insured by Y; however, five of the policies issued by Y are issued to wholly-owned foreign subsidiaries of five of Y's shareholders. The premiums attributable to the policies of insurance issued with respect to the foreign subsidiaries constitute RPII premiums. The insured foreign subsidiaries are related persons to United States shareholders because those subsidiaries are controlled, within the meaning of section 954(d)(3), by United States shareholders.

(iii) *United States shareholder: exception for indirect ownership; publicly traded stock.*—A United States person who is not insured or reinsured (directly or indirectly) by a foreign corporation (the "insuring foreign corporation") and is not related to a person insured (directly or indirectly) by the insuring foreign corporation shall not be treated as a United States shareholder of the insuring foreign corporation by virtue of section 958(a)(2) because of such person's ownership of stock in another foreign corporation which owns stock (directly or indirectly) in the insuring foreign corporation if:

(A) The stock of the other foreign corporation is publicly traded;

(B) The United States person owns less than five percent of the combined voting power of all classes of stock entitled to vote and less than five percent of the total value of the stock of the other foreign corporation; and

(C) The stock of the insuring foreign corporation constitutes less than five percent of the gross value of all the assets of the other foreign corporation.

(iv) *Example.*—The following example illustrates the indirect ownership exception of paragraph (b)(2)(iii) of this section.

Example. X is a foreign corporation which writes policies of insurance for its shareholders and unrelated persons. X has one class of stock outstanding. Five shareholders of X, who are United States persons, each own 4 percent of X's stock. These shareholders are also insured by X. The remaining 80 percent of the X stock is owned by corporation Y, a foreign corporation the stock of which is publicly traded. X insures certain risks of Y. All of the stock of Y is owned by United States persons, but no shareholder of Y owns more than 5 percent of the stock of Y by vote or value or is insured by X. None of the United States persons are related to Y or to each other. The X stock owned by Y constitutes less than five percent of the total value of all of Y's assets. The United States persons who own the stock of Y are not considered United States shareholders of X under section 958(a)(2) because the requirements of paragraph (b)(2)(iii) of this section are met. Therefore, only 20 percent of the X stock is owned by United States persons and X is not a controlled foreign corporation.

(v) *Controlled foreign corporation: shipowner's protection and indemnity association.*—A controlled foreign corporation meeting the definition of paragraph (b)(2)(i) of this section and also qualifying as a shipowner's protection and indemnity association under section 526 of the Code is a controlled foreign corporation subject to the provisions of §§ 1.953-1 through 1.953-7. Thus, a United States shareholder of such an association must include its pro rata share of the receipts of such an association that constitute section 953 insurance income, including premiums, dues, and assessments, less appropriately allocated and apportioned expenses, losses and other deductions, in such shareholder's gross income as required by § 1.953-6(h) notwithstanding section 526. See § 1.952-2(c)(1) which states that subchapter F does not apply in determining the gross income of a controlled foreign corporation.

(3) *Reinsurance.*—(i) *In general.*—Related person insurance income includes income attributable to contracts of reinsurance, including reinsurance arrangements in which the reinsurer accepts all the rights and obligations under the reinsured contracts, pursuant to which the controlled foreign corporation reinsures contracts issued by its United States shareholders, or related persons to such shareholders.

(ii) *Examples.*—The following examples illustrate the rule of paragraph (b)(3)(i) of this section.

Example 1. Twenty-five domestic corporations, which are engaged in the business of issuing property insurance policies to unrelated commercial entities, formed Z under the laws of country W to reinsure a portion of the risks insured by the domestic corporations. Each of the twenty-five domestic corporations owns an equal amount of the one class of stock of Z outstanding. Z has no business other than reinsuring the policies issued by its shareholders. The premiums received by Z constitute RPII premiums.

Example 2. The facts are the same as in *Example 1.* However, X, one of the shareholders of Z, enters a portfolio (assumption) reinsurance agreement with Z under which Z assumes all of the rights and obligations under certain policies issued by X. Z notifies the policyholders that it is assuming all the rights and obligations under the policies issued by X. The premiums from the reinsured policies constitute related person insurance income even though X no longer has any rights or obligations under the policies.

(4) *Indirectly insuring a related insured: fronting.*—(i) *In general.*—For taxable years beginning after December 31, 1987, premiums received on insurance contracts, or contracts reinsuring insurance contracts, that indirectly insure United States shareholders of a controlled foreign corporation or persons related to such shareholders are included within the definition of related person insurance income. A contract indirectly insures a United States shareholder or person related to such shareholder if the contract is issued by an unrelated person and the contract is ultimately reinsured with the controlled foreign corporation in which the United States shareholder owns stock. For taxable years beginning after December 31, 1987, premiums received on annuity contracts, or contracts reinsuring annuity contracts, that are indirectly purchased by, or indirectly provide annuity benefits to, a United States shareholder or persons related to such shareholders are included within the definition of related person insurance income.

(ii) *Example.*—The following example illustrates the rule of paragraph (b)(4)(i) of this section.

Example. Z is a domestic corporation that has issued a policy of insurance to Y. Y is a domestic corporation which owns stock in X, a controlled foreign corporation within the meaning of section § 1.953-3(b)(2)(i). Z does not own any of the stock of X. Z reinsures with X part of the risk it insures under the policy issued to Y. The premiums received by X for reinsuring the policy issued to Y are RPII premiums because one of its United States shareholders, Y, is indirectly an insured of X.

(5) *Cross-insurance arrangements.*—(i) *In general.*—Related person insurance income includes insurance income attributable to a direct or indirect cross-insurance arrangement whereby the controlled foreign corporation issues an insurance, reinsurance, or annuity contract to a person other than a related insured (as defined in paragraph (b)(1) of this section) in return for another person issuing an insurance, reinsurance, or annuity contract to a person that would be a related insured if the controlled foreign corporation were to issue an insurance, reinsurance, or annuity contract to such person. See § 1.953-2(h).

(ii) *Example.*—The following example illustrates the rule of paragraph (b)(5)(i) of this section.

Example. Controlled foreign corporation X is owned by 30 United States shareholders engaged in a similar line of business. Controlled foreign corporation Y is owned by 32 United States shareholders engaged in the same line of business as the 30 shareholders of X. Both X and Y provide insurance to businesses engaged in the line of business in which their shareholders are engaged as well as other types of business. X agrees to provide insurance protection to Y's shareholders and Y agrees to provide insurance to X's shareholders. The premiums of both X and Y that relate to insuring the shareholders of the other corporation constitute related person insurance income.

(6) *Specific premium rules.*—(i) *Premiums received prior to January 1, 1987.*—Related person insurance income includes premiums written (less return premiums and premiums paid for reinsurance) before the first taxable year of the controlled foreign corporation beginning after December 31, 1986 that become earned under section 832(b)(4) in a taxable year beginning after December 31, 1986, or succeeding taxable years, provided that the premiums otherwise qualify as related person insurance income.

(ii) *Apportionment of premiums if stock owned for less than entire taxable year.*—If, during a taxable year of a controlled foreign corporation, an insurance, reinsurance, or annuity contract that relates to a United States shareholder remains in force beyond the period during which the United States shareholder owns stock in the controlled foreign corporation, the amount of the premiums, as defined in § 1.953-2(c), attributable to the contract must be apportioned between the RPII category and the nonRPII category. The amount apportioned to the RPII category is equal to the amount of premiums on the contract included in the gross income of the controlled foreign corporation in the taxable year multiplied by a fraction, the numerator of which is the number of days in the period of coverage which fall within the taxable year during which the United States shareholder owned stock in the controlled foreign corporation, and the denominator of which is the total number of days in the period of coverage that fall within the taxable year. The remainder of the premiums on the contract are apportioned to the nonRPII category.

(iii) *Examples.*—The following examples illustrate the rule of paragraph (b)(6)(ii) of this section.

Example 1. Y is a country F controlled foreign corporation with a calendar taxable year. Y issues a policy of insurance to M, one of its United States shareholders, covering risks of property damage to a plant owned by M. The plant is located outside country F. The policy covers risks incurred from July 1, 1987 to June 30, 1988. M pays premiums of $1,000 on July 1, 1987 and $1,000 on January 1, 1988. On September 30, 1987, M sells all of its stock in Y. In Y's 1987 taxable year, there are 183 days during which M is insured. M is a stockholder in Y for 92 days during the 1987 taxable year. Therefore, of the $1,000 of premiums from M included in Y's gross income in its 1987 taxable year, $503 ($1,000 × $^{92}/_{183}$) is allocated to the RPII premium category and $497 is allocated to the nonRPII premium category. For the 1988 taxable year, all $1,000 of premiums from M are allocated to the nonRPII premium category because M owns no stock in Y on any day of the period of coverage falling within the 1988 taxable year.

Example 2. The facts are the same as in *Example 1* except that M sells only a part of its Y stock on September 30, 1987. Because M remains a shareholder in Y, all the premiums received from M in the 1987 and 1988 taxable years are allocated to the RPII premium category.

(iv) *Anti-abuse rule.*—If the facts and circumstances indicate that the premiums charged on an insurance, reinsurance, or annuity contract that gives rise to related person insurance income are below the premium rate charged on comparable contracts issued to unrelated persons, then the district director can recast capital contributions or other amounts paid or deposited by the United States shareholder as premiums on an insurance, reinsurance, or annuity contract. See also section 482 (allocation of income and deductions among taxpayers) and section 845 (certain reinsurance agreements).

(v) *Example.*—The following example illustrates the anti-abuse rule of paragraph (b)(6)(iv) of this section.

Example. X is a controlled foreign corporation incorporated in country F that insures the risks of its shareholders, all of whom are United States persons, as well as the risks of unrelated persons. In 1987, X issued fire insurance policies to some of its shareholders and to unrelated persons covering property located outside country F. The premium rates charged to the shareholders under the policies were less than those charged to similarly situated unrelated persons. The shareholders who are insured under the fire insurance policies also purchased preferred stock on which X has call rights which become effective on the same dates that the policies expire. The facts indicate that the amounts paid for the preferred stock are actually part of the cost of the insurance provided to the shareholders. All or part of the amounts paid for the preferred stock may be recharacterized as premiums paid on insurance policies. [Reg. § 1.953-3.]

§1.953-4. Allocation and apportionment of items of investment income.—(a) *In general.*—(1) *Investment income.*—This section prescribes the rules for determining the amount of investment income within the RPII, nonRPII, and SCI categories. Except as provided in paragraph (a)(2) of this section, investment income for this purpose is any type of income of a controlled foreign corporation for the taxable year other than premiums as defined in § 1.953-2(c). Thus, investment income includes, but is not limited to, gain from the sale or disposition of property under section 832(b)(1)(B), interest, dividends, and rents. Investment income also includes, to the extent prescribed in paragraph (a)(2) of this section, income resulting from the decrease in section 807(c) items under section 807(a), income resulting from the decrease in section 807(c)(1) items included in unearned premiums of a property and casualty insurance company under section 832(b)(4), and income resulting from a reduction of discounted unpaid losses under section 832(b)(5). An item of investment income is allocated to a particular category, whether the RPII, nonRPII, or SCI category, only if the income results from a decrease in reserves attributable under the principles of § 1.953-5(a) to a particular category or if the requirements of paragraph (b) of this section are met. If an item of investment income cannot be allocated to the RPII, nonRPII, or SCI categories, it is apportioned to the different categories in accordance with paragraph (c) of this section. If the investment income within each of the RPII, nonRPII, and SCI categories is determined under the apportionment method of paragraph (c) of this section, then the investment income within each category shall be deemed to consist of each type of investment income (*e.g.*, dividends, interest, tax-exempt interest, and capital gains) in the same proportion that the aggregate amount of a particular type of investment income earned during the taxable year bears to the total amount of all types of investment income earned during the taxable year.

(2) *Decreases in reserves.*—(i) *In general.*—In the case of each of the RPII, nonRPII, and SCI categories of income, if a decrease in section 807(c) items or a decrease in section 846 discounted unpaid losses occurs as the result of the payment of claims and benefits accrued and losses incurred, as described in section 805(a)(1), or as the result of losses paid, as described in section 832(b)(5)(A)(i), then the income resulting from the decrease in reserves shall be deemed to consist of premium and investment income in the same proportion that the claims, benefits, or losses that result in the decrease in the reserve are apportioned between premium and investment income under § 1.953-5(c)(3)(iii)(A). Section 807(c) items include section 807(c)(1) reserves included in the unearned premiums of a property and casualty insurance company under section 832(b)(4). If a decrease in section 807(c) items and section 846 unpaid losses attributable under the principles of § 1.953-5(a) to the SCI category and to the RPII category (if the elections under section 953(c)(3)(C) and section 831(b) are made) occurs as the result of any actuarial redetermination, the amount of income included in gross income in accordance with section 807(f), in the case of a foreign life insurance company, or in accordance with section 481, in the case of a foreign property and casualty insurance company, shall be considered investment income equal to the amount obtained by multiplying the decrease in section 807(c) items or section 846 discounted unpaid losses by a fraction. The numerator of the fraction shall be the amount of the increase in section 807(c) items or section 846 discounted unpaid losses that have been apportioned against investment income under § 1.953-5(c)(3)(iii)(B) and (C) during the five taxable years (or the period during which the controlled foreign corporation has been in existence, if less than five taxable years) preceding the current taxable year. The denominator of the fraction shall be the total amount of deductions attributable to the increases in section 807(c) items and section 846 discounted unpaid losses during the five taxable years (or shorter period, if applicable) preceding the current taxable year. The remainder of the decrease in section 807(c) items and section 846 discounted unpaid losses attributable to the SCI category and, if appropriate, the RPII category shall be treated as giving rise to premium income. In the case of section 807(c) items and section 846 discounted unpaid losses attributable to the nonRPII category and the RPII category, if the section 953(c)(3)(C) and section 831(b) elections have not been made, the entire decrease in section 807(c) items and section 846 discounted unpaid losses shall be treated as investment income.

(ii) *Examples.*—The following examples illustrate the principles of paragraph (a)(2)(i) of this section.

Example 1. Y is a life insurance company and is a controlled foreign corporation. In 1988 Y's section 807(c)(1) life insurance reserves decrease from $10,000 to $8,000, resulting in $2,000 of income under sections 803(a)(2) and 807(a). The decrease resulted from

the payment of a death benefit that, under § 1.953-5(c)(3)(iii)(A), is apportioned against investment income and premium income in the amount of $1,500 and $500, respectively. The $2,000 decrease results in $1,500 of investment income ($2,000 × $1,500/$2,000) and $500 of premium income ($2,000 × $500/$2,000).

Example 2. X is a property and casualty insurance company and is a controlled foreign corporation. Under section 832(b)(5), X had, for its 1987 taxable year, discounted unpaid losses of $100,000 attributable to contracts the premiums from which were allocable to the SCI category of income. For 1988, X had losses paid of $50,000 and discounted unpaid losses of $25,000 allocable to contracts giving rise to SCI premiums. Section 832(b)(5) requires X to reduce its 1988 losses paid by the excess of discounted unpaid losses for 1987 over the current year discounted unpaid losses. Thus, X has $25,000 of income resulting from the decrease in discounted unpaid losses computed as follows: 1988 losses paid of $50,000 minus the difference between 1987 discounted unpaid losses of $100,000 and 1988 discounted unpaid losses of $25,000 ($50,000 – [$100,000 – $25,000]) = $25,000. Assuming that section 481 applies, X will take the premium and investment income into account in accordance with that section. If over the past five years, the increase in discounted unpaid losses is $50,000, of which $10,000 was allocated to investment income and $40,000 to premium income under § 1.953-5(c)(3)(iii)(B) and (C), then 1/5th ($10,000/$50,000) of the amounts taken into income in each taxable year in accordance with section 481 will be treated as investment income and 4/5ths ($40,000/$50,000) will be treated as premium income.

(b) *Allocation of investment income.*—(1) *In general.*—An item of investment income is allocated to a particular category of income if the item directly relates to a contract (or that part of a contract) which gives rise to premiums allocable to the same category of income. An item of investment income is considered to be directly related to a contract (or that part of a contract) which gives rise to premiums allocable to a particular category if the income is derived from an asset which is identified on the controlled foreign corporation's books and records as an asset relating to RPII, nonRPII, or SCI contracts and the controlled foreign corporation separately accounts for the various income, exclusion, deduction, reserve, and other liability items properly attributable to such contracts.

(2) *Examples.*—The following examples illustrate the rules of paragraph (b)(1) of this section.

Example 1. The facts are the same as in *Example 2* of paragraph (a)(2)(ii) of this section. The amount of investment income included in gross income in each taxable year in accordance with section 481 is allocable to the SCI category.

Example 2. Z is a country F controlled foreign corporation which issues life insurance contracts. Among the contracts issued by Z are variable life insurance contracts issued to residents of country F. The life insurance contracts qualify as variable contracts under section 817(d) of the Code. The amounts received under the contracts are allocated pursuant to country F law to an account which is segregated from the general asset accounts of Z, and the amount of the death benefits under the contracts are adjusted on the basis of the investment return and the market value of the segregated asset account. Z's books of account identify the assets relating to the variable life insurance contracts issued to residents of country F, and Z separately accounts for the various income, exclusion, deduction, reserve, and other liability items properly attributable to such contracts. Therefore, all of the investment income attributable to the variable contracts is allocable to the SCI income category.

(c) *Apportionment of investment income.*—(1) *Life insurance companies.*—(i) *In general.*—A foreign corporation that would determine its insurance income under part I of subchapter L (relating to life insurance companies) if it were a domestic company shall apportion its investment income to each of the RPII, nonRPII, and SCI categories, in the same proportion that—

(A) The sum of the means of each of the items described in section 807(c) attributable to contracts which give rise to premiums within the particular income category bears to

(B) The sum of the means of the items described in section 807(c) for the taxable year attributable to all contracts.

(ii) *Section 807(c) items attributable to RPII, nonRPII, and SCI contracts.*—The amount of an item described in section 807(c) that is attributable to a particular income category is that amount which would result if the section 807(c) item were computed, using the assumptions required under section 807, as modified by § 1.953-6(e), only with respect to the contracts the premiums from which are apportioned to that particular income category.

(2) *Property and casualty companies.*—(i) *In general.*—A foreign corporation that would determine its insurance income under part II of subchapter L (relating to insurance companies other than life insurance companies) if it were a domestic company shall apportion

its investment income to each of the RPII, nonRPII, and SCI categories, in the same proportion that—

    (A) The sum of the premiums written, as defined in section 832(b)(4)(A), for the current taxable year, plus the amount of unearned premiums as of the close of the previous taxable year, plus the amount of the section 846 discounted unpaid losses as of the close of the previous taxable year attributable to the particular income category, bears to

    (B) The sum of the premiums written, as defined in section 832(b)(4)(A), for the current taxable year, plus the amount of unearned premiums as of the close of the previous taxable year, plus the amount of the section 846 discounted unpaid losses as of the close of the previous taxable year attributable to all categories of income.

    (ii) *Unpaid losses attributable to a particular category.*—The amount of the section 846 discounted unpaid losses that are attributable to a particular income category is that amount which would result if the unpaid losses were computed, using the assumptions required by section 846, as modified by § 1.953-6(e), only with respect to the contracts the premiums from which are apportioned to that particular income category.

    (3) *Examples.*—The following examples illustrate the principles of paragraph (c) of this section.

    Example 1. X is a property and casualty insurance company and a controlled foreign corporation that is not engaged in a trade or business in the United States. X is a calendar year taxpayer. In 1987, X had $600 of premiums written from contracts issued to related insureds and $300 of premiums written from contracts issued to unrelated persons. At the end of 1986, X had $400 in unearned premiums from contracts issued to related insureds and $200 of unearned premiums from contracts issued to unrelated persons. X

also had unpaid losses at the end of 1986 of $500 with respect to its related insured contracts and $250 with respect to its contracts issued to unrelated persons. In 1987, X had $1,000 of taxable interest income and $2,000 of tax exempt income. The total of X's premiums written for the current year, plus previous year unearned premiums, plus previous year unpaid loss reserves on RPII business is $1,500 ($600 + $400 + $500) and on nonRPII business is $750 ($300 + $200 + $250). Therefore, $2,000 of investment income ($1,500/$2,250 × $3,000) is apportioned to the RPII category and $1,000 ($750/$2,250 × $3,000) is apportioned to the nonRPII category. Pursuant to paragraph (a)(1) of this section, of the $2,000 apportioned to the RPII category, $666.67 ($2,000 × $1,000/$3,000) is taxable interest income and $1,333.33 ($2,000 × $2,000/$3,000) is tax-exempt interest. Of the $1,000 apportioned to the nonRPII category, $333.33 ($1,000 × $1,000/$3,000) is taxable interest income and $666.67 ($1,000 × $2,000/$3,000) is tax-exempt interest income.

    Example 2. Y is a controlled foreign corporation that issues life insurance policies and would, if it were a domestic corporation, be taxable under part I of subchapter L of the Code. Y is not engaged in a trade or business within the United States. In 1987, its first year in business, Y only issues insurance policies to its United States shareholders or persons related to its United States shareholders. Y received $3,000 in premiums for the year and at the end of the year had a reserve under section 807(c)(1) of $2,000. In 1988, Y only issues life insurance policies to persons other than its United States shareholders or persons related to those shareholders. Y receives $5,000 in premiums in 1988. In 1988, Y's year-end section 807(c)(1) reserves with respect to contracts issued to related persons is $1,000 and with respect to unrelated persons is $4,000. Investment income in 1988 is $1,000, all of which is taxable interest income. The mean of the 807(c) items for 1988 are computed in Table 1 below.

Table 1

Mean section 807(c) items attributable to RPII contracts in force in 1988:		
Mean of life insurance reserves attributable to RPII policies:		
1987 closing reserve	$2,000	
1988 closing reserve	$1,000	
Mean = ($2,000 + $1,000)/2		$1,500
Mean of life insurance reserves attributable to nonRPII policies:		
1987 closing reserve	$0	
1988 closing reserve	$4,000	
Mean = $4,000/2		$2,000

Based on the computations in Table 1, the investment income apportioned to the RPII category equals $1,000 × ($1,500/3,500) or $428.57, and investment income apportioned to the nonRPII category equals $1,000 × ($2,000/$3,500) or $571.42. [Reg. § 1.953-4.]

§ 1.953-5. Allocation and apportionment of expenses.—(a) *Allocation of deductions to RPII, nonRPII, and SCI categories.*—To compute the amount of section 953 insurance income or foreign personal holding company income that a controlled foreign corporation has derived from insurance operations, items of expenses, losses, and other deductions (collectively referred to as "deductions") must be allocated to and apportioned among the RPII, nonRPII, and SCI categories of income. Allocation of expenses shall be made in accordance with § § 1.861-8, 1.861-8T, 1.861-9T, 1.861-10T, and 1.861-12T, and this section. The deduction under section 832(b)(4)(B) for unearned premiums is allocable to the categories to which the unearned premiums relate as determined by § § 1.953-2 and 1.953-3. The deductions for death benefits, increases in reserves, policyholder dividends, consideration in respect of the assumption by another person of liabilities, and reimbursable dividends under section 805(a)(1), (2), (3), (6), and (7) are allocable to the particular category of income to which those deductions relate. The deductions for losses paid and discounted unpaid losses, under section 832(b)(5), and dividends and similar distributions paid or declared to policyholders in their capacity as such, under section 832(c)(11), are also allocable to the particular category of income to which those deductions relate. The amount of the deductions specified in the preceding two sentences of this paragraph shall be considered to relate to the RPII, nonRPII, and SCI categories to the extent the deduction is attributable to contracts that give rise to premiums allocated to a particular category. Deductions not specifically addressed in this paragraph (a) may be allocated to the RPII, nonRPII, or SCI category of income if the controlled foreign corporation identifies on its books and records the assets which relate to RPII, nonRPII, or SCI contracts, and the controlled foreign corporation separately accounts for the various income, exclusion, deduction, reserve, and other liability items properly attributable to such contracts.

    (b) *Apportionment of expenses to RPII, nonRPII, and SCI categories.*—(1) *In general.*—Those expenses which cannot be allocated must be apportioned among the RPII, nonRPII, and SCI categories.

    (2) *Life insurance companies.*—(i) *Investment deductions.*—A controlled foreign corporation that would be taxable under part I of

subchapter L (relating to life insurance companies) if it were a domestic insurance company shall apportion to the RPII, nonRPII, and SCI categories its deductions that are allocable or apportionable to investment income under § § 1.861-8, 1.861-8T, 1.861-9T, 1.861-10T, and 1.861-12T in the same proportion that investment income for the current taxable year is apportioned to those categories under § 1.953-4(c).

    (ii) *Other deductions.*—A controlled foreign corporation that would be taxable under part I of subchapter L (relating to life insurance companies) if it were a domestic insurance company shall apportion to the RPII, nonRPII, and SCI categories a deduction that is not allocable or apportionable to investment income under § § 1.861-8, 1.861-8T, 1.861-9T, 1.861-10T, and 1.861-12T in the same proportion as the numerator in paragraph (b)(2)(ii)(A) of this section bears to the denominator in paragraph (b)(2)(ii)(B) of this section.

    (A) *Numerator.*—For purposes of this paragraph (b)(2)(ii) the numerator equals:

    (1) The amount of premiums determined under section 803(a)(1) allocable to the income category, plus

    (2) The decrease in section 807(c) items allocable to the income category as determined under section 807(a), minus

    (3) The increase in section 807(c) items allocable to the income category as determined under section 807(b).

    (B) *Denominator.*—For purposes of this paragraph (b)(2)(ii) the denominator equals:

    (1) The amount of premiums determined under section 803(a)(1) for all categories of income, plus

    (2) The decrease in section 807(c) items for all categories of income as determined under section 807(a), minus

    (3) The increase in section 807(c) items for all categories of income as determined under section 807(b).

    (3) *Property and casualty companies.*—(i) *Investment deductions.*—A controlled foreign corporation that would be taxable under part II of subchapter L (relating to insurance companies other than life companies) if it were a domestic insurance company shall apportion to the RPII, nonRPII, and SCI categories its deductions that are allocable or apportionable to investment income under § § 1.861-8, 1.861-8T, 1.861-9T, 1.861-10T, and 1.861-12T in the same proportion that investment income for the current taxable year is apportioned to those categories under § 1.953-4(c).

(ii) *Other deductions.*—A controlled foreign corporation that would be taxable under part II of subchapter L (relating to insurance companies other than life insurance companies) if it were a domestic insurance company shall apportion to the RPII, nonRPII, and SCI categories a deduction that is not allocable or apportionable to investment income under §§ 1.861-8, 1.861-8T, 1.861-9T, 1.861-10T, and 1.861-12T in the same proportion that the premiums earned, as defined in section 832(b)(4), allocated to a particular income category bears to the total of the premiums earned in all of the income categories.

(c) *Allocation and apportionment of deductions between premium and investment income after the deductions have been allocated or apportioned to the SCI or RPII categories.*—(1) *In general.*—Deductions within the SCI category must be allocated to or apportioned between premium income and investment income. Deductions within the RPII category must be allocated to or apportioned between premium and investment income if an election is made under section 953(c)(3)(C) (relating to the treatment of RPII income as effectively connected with the conduct of a United States trade or business) and under section 831(b) (alternative tax for certain small companies). Allocation and apportionment of deductions to or between premium and investment income within the SCI category and, if applicable, the RPII category is made in accordance with §§ 1.861-8, 1.861-8T, 1.861-9T, 1.861-10T, and 1.861-12T and paragraph (c)(3) of this section.

(2) *Examples.*—The following examples illustrate the rule of paragraph (c)(1) of this section.

Example 1. X is a life insurance company that issues policies insuring the lives of persons residing in X's country of incorporation. X requires its insureds to undergo medical examinations by physicians approved and paid by X. Under the principles of §§ 1.861-8, 1.861-8T, 1.861-9T, 1.861-10T, and 1.861-12T and this section, the medical expenses paid by X are allocable to the class of gross income consisting of X's SCI premiums.

Example 2. Z is a life insurance company that issues policies only in its country of incorporation. Z has an investment department that is in charge of investing Z's funds. The amount expended by Z in compensating the employees of its investment department is allocable under the principles of § 1.861-8 and this section to the class of gross income consisting of Z's SCI investment income.

(3) *Apportionment of reserves, losses, policyholder dividends, and policy acquisition expenses and certain other deductions between investment and premium income.*—(i) *In general.*—For taxable years beginning on or after April 17, 1991, the amount of the deduction for reserves, the deduction for losses, the deduction for policyholder dividends, the deduction for policy acquisition expenses, and certain other deductions apportioned against investment income within the SCI category and, if applicable, within the RPII category, shall be—

(A) The amount of investment income required to be added to reserves and required to fund losses within the SCI and, if applicable, the RPII category as computed in paragraph (c)(3)(iii) of this section;

(B) Investment income's proportionate share of policyholder dividends within the SCI and, if applicable, the RPII category as determined under paragraph (c)(3)(iv) of this section; and

(C) The amount of policy acquisition expenses and certain other deductions determined under paragraph (c)(3)(v) of this section.

The remainder of the deductions for reserves, losses, policyholder dividends, policy acquisition expenses, and certain other deductions within the SCI and, if applicable, the RPII category shall be apportioned against and reduce premium income. For taxable years beginning prior to April 17 1991, taxpayers may use a reasonable apportionment formula.

(ii) *Deduction for reserves and losses defined.*—For purposes of paragraph (c)(3)(i) of this section, the phrase "deduction for losses" means current year deductions for claims, benefits, and losses under section 805(a)(1)(other than discounted unpaid losses under section 846), losses paid under section 832(b)(5)(A)(i), and unpaid losses on life insurance contracts. The phrase "deduction for reserves" means, for purposes of paragraph (c)(3)(i) of this section: the increase in section 807(c) reserves, as adjusted by section 807(b), of a foreign life insurance company; the increase in section 807(c)(1) reserves, as adjusted under section 807(b), included in unearned premiums of a foreign property and casualty company; and the increase in section 846 discounted unpaid losses as computed under section 832(b)(5)(ii).

(iii) *Investment income required to be added to reserves and required to fund losses.*—The total amount of investment income required to be added to reserves and to fund current year losses within the SCI and, if applicable, the RPII category is computed as the sum of the following:

(A) The investment income portion of current year losses within the SCI and, if applicable, the RPII category: This amount is the excess of—

(1) The amount of current year losses within the appropriate category, less

(2) The amount of current year losses within the appropriate category divided by one plus one-half of the annual interest rate specified in § 1.953-6(e)(4) for computing reserves.

(B) The investment income portion attributable to current-year premiums that have been added to reserves within the SCI and, if applicable, the RPII category: This amount shall be computed as—

(1) The amount of current-year premiums added to reserves within the appropriate category multiplied by one-half of the annual interest rate specified in § 1.953-6(e)(4) for computing reserves, or

(2) If the amount of current-year premiums added to the reserves is not known, the excess of—

(i) The year-end reserves within the appropriate category attributable to current-year premiums within the appropriate category, less

(ii) The year-end reserves within the appropriate category divided by one plus one-half of the annual interest rate specified in § 1.953-6(e)(4) for computing reserves.

(C) The investment income portion attributable to reserves within the SCI and, if applicable, the RPII category existing as of the end of the preceding taxable year and still in existence as of the end of the current taxable year: This amount shall be computed as the excess of—

(1) The amount of the reserves within the appropriate category at the end of the taxable year, less the sum of the amount of reserves within the appropriate category attributable to current-year premiums plus the investment income portion attributable to current-year premiums as computed under paragraph (c)(3)(iii)(B) of this section, over

(2) The amount obtained by dividing the amount computed under paragraph (c)(3)(iii)(C)(1) of this section by one plus the annual interest rate specified in § 1.953-6(e)(4) for computing reserves.

(D) If the amount of a reserve within the SCI and, if applicable, the RPII category is increased because of any actuarial redetermination, the investment income portion of the increase shall be treated as the amount of the adjustment multiplied by a fraction, the numerator of which is the amount of reserves within the appropriate category that have been deducted against gross investment income under paragraph (c)(3)(iii)(B) and (D) of this section during the five taxable years preceding the current taxable year (or for the life of the corporation preceding the current taxable year if the foreign corporation has been in existence for less than five taxable years), and the denominator of which is the total amount of deductions attributable to reserves within the appropriate category during the five taxable years preceding the current taxable year (or for the life of the corporation preceding the current taxable year, as may be applicable).

(iv) *Investment income's proportionate share of policyholder dividends.*—For purposes of this paragraph (c)(3), investment income's proportionate share of policyholder dividends, as defined in section 808(a) and (b) and section 832(c)(11), is an amount equal to the deduction for policyholder's dividends determined under sections 808, 809, and 832(c)(11) for the taxable year multiplied by a fraction, the numerator of which is gross investment income within the SCI and, if applicable, the RPII category, for the taxable year, reduced by the amounts determined under paragraph (c)(3)(i)(A) of this section, and the denominator of which is total gross income within the appropriate category reduced by the excess, if any, of the closing balance of items described in section 807(c) or discounted unpaid losses under section 846 within the appropriate category, over the opening balance of such items and losses within the appropriate category. For purposes of paragraph (c)(3)(iv) of this section, the denominator of the fraction shall be determined by including tax-exempt interest and by applying section 807(a)(2)(B) as if it did not contain section 807(a)(2)(B)(i) thereof.

(v) *Apportionment of policy acquisition expenses and certain other deductions.*—For purposes of this paragraph (c)(3), specified policy acquisition expenses, as defined in section 848(c)(1), and general deductions, as defined in section 848(c)(2), shall be apportioned to investment income within the SCI category and, if applicable, the RPII category, in the same proportion as the numerator in paragraph (c)(3)(v)(A) of this section bears to the denominator in paragraph (c)(3)(v)(B) of this section.

(A) *Numerator.*—For purposes of this paragraph (c)(3)(v), the numerator equals the amount of investment income allocated or apportioned to the SCI category and, if applicable, the RPII category, minus the amount of the deduction for reserves apportioned to investment income under this paragraph (c)(3), to the extent that such reserves qualify as life insurance reserves within the meaning of section 816(b).

(B) *Denominator.*—For purposes of this paragraph (c)(3)(v), the denominator equals the amount of premium income allocated or apportioned to the SCI category and, if applicable, the RPII category, plus the amount determined under paragraph (c)(3)(v)(A) of this section. For purposes of paragraph (c)(3)(v)(B) of this section, premium income is the amount of premiums within the meaning of section 803(a)(1) and (b), in the case of a controlled foreign corporation that would be taxable under part I of subchapter L (relating to life insurance companies) if it were a domestic insurance company. In the case of a controlled foreign corporation that would be taxable under part II of subchapter L (relating to insurance companies other than life companies) if it were a domestic insurance company, premium income is the amount of premiums within the meaning of section 832(b)(4). All computations entering into the determination of premium income for purposes of paragraph (c)(3)(v)(B) of this section shall be made in the manner required under section 811(a) for life insurance companies. The fraction set forth in this paragraph (c)(3)(v), determined for each taxable year, applies to the amount of specified policy acquisition expenses computed under section 848(c)(1) for that taxable year, which are capitalized and allowed as a deduction in such taxable year and in subsequent taxable years in accordance with section 848(a). The fraction set forth in this paragraph (c)(3)(v), determined for each taxable year, also applies to the amount, if any, by which general deductions (as defined in section 848(c)(2)) deductible in such taxable year exceed specified policy acquisition expenses for such year (as computed and capitalized under section 848). Such general deductions are subject to the apportionment formula set forth in this paragraph (c)(3)(v), even if the capitalization requirements of section 848 do not apply to the company or to certain contracts issued by it. For purposes of this paragraph (c)(3)(v), the terms "net premiums" and "general deductions," as defined in sections 848(d) and 848(c)(2), respectively, shall be computed by taking into account only amounts that have been allocated or apportioned to the SCI category and, if applicable, the RPII category.

(vi) *Example.*—The following example demonstrates the calculation of the amount of investment income required to be added to reserves and fund losses under paragraph (c)(3)(i) of this section.

Example. X is a country F controlled foreign corporation that has income from issuing life insurance contracts to persons who reside in country F. At the end of its 1988 taxable year, X has a reserve under section 807(c)(1) of $12,292 of which $7,000 is from the addition of current-year premiums plus $350 of investment income attributable to those premiums. At the end of the 1987 taxable year X's reserves were $7,350. Thus, X's reserves have increased a total of $4,942. X paid $3,000 in death benefits in 1988. The appropriate interest rate for computing X's life insurance reserves on all of X's policies is 10% per annum. The amount of reserves and losses apportioned to premium and investment income is computed as follows:

The investment income portion of X's current year losses paid:

Losses – [Losses/(1 + .5(10%)] $3,000 – ($3,000/1.05) = $142.86.

The investment income portion of X's current year premiums that have been added to reserves:

There are two methods for computing this amount:

(a) Current year premiums added to reserves × .5(annual interest rate for determining reserves).

$7,000 × .05 = $350

(b) Year-end reserves attributable to current-year premiums less [such year-end reserves divided by 1 + .5(annual interest rate)].

$7,350 – [$7,350/(1 + .5(10%)]=

$7,350 – $7,000 = $350.

The investment income portion attributable to section 807(c) reserves existing at the end of the preceding taxable year that were in existence at the end of the current taxable year.

[Year-end reserves less the sum of reserves attributable to current-year premiums plus the investment income portion attributable to current-year premiums minus the amount obtained in the previous term divided by (1 + 10%)]

[$12,292 – ($7,000 + $350)] – [($12,292 – ($7,000 + $350))/1.10] = $4,942 – $4,492.72 = $449.28

Thus, of $3,000 in losses, $142.86 is apportioned to gross investment income and $2,857.14 is allocated to premium income. Of the $4,942 increase in reserves, $350 is the amount of investment income required to be added to current-year premiums and $449.28 is the amount of investment income required to be added to reserves that were in existence throughout the year. Thus, $799.28 of the $4,942.28 increase in reserves is apportioned to investment income and $4,142.72 ($4,942 – $799.28) of the increase in reserves is apportioned to premium income.

(4) *Alternative method for life insurance companies.*—(i) *In general.*—As an alternative to the computations required by paragraph (c)(3)(i) of this section, a controlled foreign corporation that would be subject to part I of subchapter L if it were a domestic insurance company may apportion against investment income within the SCI and, if applicable, the RPII category, the deductions for reserves, losses, and policyholder dividends in an amount equal to the policy interest plus gross investment income's proportionate share of policyholder dividends as computed under section 812(b). The remaining amount, if any, of the deductions for reserves, losses, and policyholder dividends shall be apportioned to gross premium income.

(ii) *Example.*—The following example demonstrates the principles of paragraph (c)(4)(i) of this section.

Example. X is a controlled foreign corporation that would be taxable as a life insurance company under part I of subchapter L if it were a domestic insurance company. In 1988, X has a reserve of $1,000. In 1989, X has a reserve of $1,500. Under section 812(b)(2)(A), and using the interest rate prescribed in § 1.953-6(e)(4) for computing reserves, X has policy interest equal to $200. Rather than using the method set forth in paragraph (c)(3)(i) of this section, the increase in reserves may be apportioned between premium and investment income by apportioning the policy interest to investment income and by apportioning the increase in the reserves less the policy interest against premium income. Thus, $200 is apportioned to investment income and $300 ($500 – $200) is apportioned to premium income.

(5) *Losses in excess of premium or investment income.*—If the total amount of deductions allocated and apportioned to premium income within the RPII and nonRPII categories exceeds the amount of premium income within those categories, then the excess shall be allocated to investment income within the same category. If the total amount of deductions allocated and apportioned to premium income within the SCI category exceeds the amount of premium income within that category, then the excess shall not be allocated to investment income within the SCI category and shall not be allocated to any other category of subpart F income. However, if an election is made under section 952(c)(1)(B)(vii), the deductions allocated and apportioned to premium income within the SCI category shall be allocated to investment income within the SCI category. If the total amount of deductions allocated or apportioned to investment income within each of the RPII and nonRPII categories exceeds the amount of investment income within those categories, then the excess deductions shall be allocated to premium income within the same category. If the total amount of deductions allocated or apportioned to investment income within the SCI category exceeds the amount of investment income within that category, then the excess deductions shall be allocated to the RPII or nonRPII categories in accordance with paragraph (c)(6) of this section. However, if an election is made under section 952(c)(1)(B)(vii), deductions allocated or apportioned to investment income with the SCI category that exceed the income within that category shall first reduce premium income within the same category.

(6) *Losses within the RPII, nonRPII, and SCI categories.*—If, after allocating and apportioning deductions, there is a loss within the RPII or nonRPII categories, within the investment income portion of the SCI category, or, if an election is made under section 952(c)(1)(B)(vii), within the entire SCI category, then a loss in one category will be treated as reducing income in another category only for purposes of calculating the pro rata share of RPII, nonRPII, or SCI income to be included by United States shareholders as defined in section 951(b). Thus, persons that are United States shareholders solely by virtue of section 953(c)(1)(A) may not use a loss within the nonRPII or SCI categories to reduce income within the RPII category. [Reg. § 1.953-5.]

§ 1.953-6. Application of subchapter L and certain sections of subchapter N of the Code.—(a) *Applicability of subchapter L.*—(1) *In general.*—A controlled foreign corporation which has insurance income under section 953 or foreign personal holding company income that is SCI investment income shall compute its insurance income or SCI investment income either under part I of subchapter L of the Code (relating to life insurance companies) or under part II of subchapter L of the Code (relating to other insurance companies) as modified by this section and § 1.952-2. If a controlled foreign corporation does not file an annual statement with an insurance regulatory authority of any State, such corporation must complete those portions of the annual statement prescribed by the National Association of Insurance Commissioners which are necessary to make the determinations and computations required under subchapter L of the Code. If a controlled foreign corporation uses the reserves described in paragraph (d)(1)(ii) of this section (relating to reserves on United States business for which no NAIC statement is required) to qualify as a life insurance company subject to part I under subchapter L, then the foreign corporation shall compute its reserves, for purposes of the NAIC annual statement, by following the laws and regulations of

New York or the laws of the State of the United States where the insured risks are located, whichever is applicable under paragraph (d)(1)(ii) of this section. In all other circumstances, the controlled foreign corporation shall complete the necessary portion of the NAIC annual statement by following the rules prescribed in §§ 1.953-1 through 1.953-7 and, to the extent not inconsistent with those sections, the rules prescribed by the National Association of Insurance Commissioners.

(2) *Applicability of section 7702.*—[Reserved]

(3) *Applicability of section 817.*—[Reserved]

(b) *Special rules regarding use of subchapter L to compute RPII, nonRPII, and SCI income.*—(1) *Certain provisions not to apply.*—The following provisions of subchapter L do not apply in computing section 953 insurance income or foreign personal holding company income that is SCI investment income:

(i) Section 806, relating to the small life insurance company deduction;

(ii) Section 805(a)(5), relating to the operations loss deduction; and

(iii) Section 832(c)(5), relating to certain capital losses.

(2) *Allocation and apportionment of certain items.*—The items referred to in section 803(a)(1)(relating to gross amount of premiums and other considerations), section 803(a)(2)(relating to net decrease in reserves), section 805(a)(2)(relating to net increase in reserves), and section 832(b)(4)(relating to premiums earned on insurance contracts) shall be taken into account in computing income within a particular category, whether the RPII, nonRPII, and SCI, categories, only to the extent they relate to a contract issued or reinsured by the controlled foreign corporation that gives rise to premiums within that particular category. For rules relating to the allocation of premiums, *see* §§ 1.953-2 and 1.953-3. For rules relating to increases or decreases in reserves, *see* §§ 1.953-4 and 1.953-5.

(c) *Alternative tax for certain small companies.*—Any controlled foreign corporation that computes its taxable income under part II of subchapter L (relating to insurance companies other than life insurance companies) and makes the election under § 1.953-7(c) to have its related person insurance income treated as effectively connected with the conduct of a trade or business in the United States may elect to have its related person insurance income, as well as its income effectively connected with the conduct of a United States trade or business that is excluded from subpart F income under section 952(b), taxed under section 831(b)(alternative tax for certain small companies) if the requirements of that section are met. To determine whether a corporation meets the net written premium requirement of section 831(b), the premiums on all policies (including SCI policies) of insurance or reinsurance or annuity contracts issued by the corporation must be taken into account.

(d) *Computation of reserves to determine applicability of part I of subchapter L.*—(1) *Reserves required by law.*—The reserves set forth in this paragraph (d)(1) are the only reserves to be taken into account as reserves required by law under section 816(b)(2) to determine for any taxable year whether a controlled foreign corporation is subject to part I of subchapter L (relating to life insurance companies):

(i) *Reserves with respect to United States business.*—The reserves which are required by the law of the state or states of the United States, including the District of Columbia, to which the business of the controlled foreign corporation is subject, but only with respect to its United States business, if any, which is taxable under section 842(a).

(ii) *Reserves deemed to be required.*—To the extent the controlled foreign corporation is not subject to section 842(a) but issues a policy of insurance or an annuity contract to a resident of the United States—

(A) Except as provided in paragraph (d)(1)(ii)(B) of this section, the reserves that would be required by applying the minimum standards of the law of New York as if the controlled foreign corporation were an insurance company transacting all of its insurance business (other than its insurance business carried on within the United States that is subject to section 842(a)) for the taxable year in New York, and

(B) With respect to all United States risks covered by insurance ceded to the controlled foreign corporation by an insurance company subject to subchapter L of the Code, determined without regard to section 501, and in respect of which an election is made by or on behalf of the controlled foreign corporation to determine its reserves in accordance with paragraph (d)(1)(ii)(B) of this section, the amount of reserves against such risks which would result if the reserves were determined by applying the law of the state of the United States where the risks are located as if the controlled foreign

corporation were an insurance company in that state engaged in reinsuring the risks.

(iii) *Reserves with respect to foreign business.*—In the case of a reserve on a contract that is not described in paragraph (d)(1)(i) and (ii) of this section, the reserve determined under the laws, regulations, or administrative guidance of the insurance regulatory authority of the home country, or the reserve determined under the laws of the country of residence of the insured, if the controlled foreign corporation is subject to the insurance regulatory authority of the insured's country of residence. If the reserves of a controlled foreign corporation are subject to the laws of more than one foreign jurisdiction, the amount of reserves taken into account shall be the largest reserve required by any such foreign jurisdiction. If neither the home country nor the country of residence of the insured require reserves to be established, then the reserve shall be computed using the mortality tables prescribed by section 807(d) but using the interest rate prescribed in paragraph (e)(4) of this section applicable to qualified contracts.

(2) *SCI reserves to be taken into account.*—The total reserves of a controlled foreign corporation are taken into account to determine whether the corporation is to compute its taxable income under part I of subchapter L. Thus, reserves which relate to the lives or health of residents of the home country are taken into account.

(e) *Computation of reserves for purposes of computing taxable income.*—(1) *Actual reserves required.*—For all purposes of §§ 1.953-1 through 1.953-7, a controlled foreign corporation will be considered to have a reserve only to the extent the reserve has been actually held during the taxable year for which the reserve is claimed.

(2) *Life insurance reserves.*—For purposes of computing the taxable income from insurance operations, the section 807(c)(1) items of a controlled foreign corporation that would be taxable under part I or part II of subchapter L of the Code if it were a domestic insurance company that are related to a nonqualified contract, as defined in this paragraph, shall be determined under the rules of section 807(d). The amount of life insurance reserves under section 807(c)(1) relating to qualified foreign contracts shall be determined under the rules of section 807(e)(4) and paragraph (e)(4) of this section. For purposes of this paragraph, a qualified foreign contract means a contract insuring life or health issued by a controlled foreign corporation if the person with the determining life, as defined in § 1.953-2(g)(1), is a resident of the country in which the controlled foreign corporation is incorporated and such country is not contiguous to the United States. A nonqualified foreign contract is any contract that is not a qualified foreign contract.

(3) *Discounted unpaid losses of a property and casualty company.*— If a controlled foreign corporation would be taxable under part II of subchapter L of the Code if it were a domestic insurance company or if it would be subject to part I but has discounted unpaid losses as defined in section 846, the amount of its discounted unpaid losses shall be determined under the rules of section 846 except to the extent modified by paragraph (e)(4) of this section.

(4) *Interest rates used for determining reserves.*—(i) *Qualified foreign contracts and property and liability contracts.*—For purposes of applying section 807(d)(2)(B) and section 812(b)(2)(A) to qualified foreign contracts as defined in paragraph (e)(2) of this section, the term "prevailing State assumed interest rate" shall mean the highest assumed interest rate permitted to be used in computing life insurance reserves for insurance contracts or annuity contracts under the laws of each country in which the controlled foreign corporation conducts an insurance business. For purposes of applying sections 807 and 812 to qualified foreign contracts, as defined in paragraph (e)(2) of this section, and for purposes of applying section 846 to contracts covering risks located outside the United States, the applicable federal interest rate shall be a foreign currency rate of interest analogous to the applicable federal mid-term rates as defined in section 1274(d), but based on annual compounding. An analogous foreign currency rate of interest is a rate of interest based on yields (with an appropriate compounding period) of the highest grade of outstanding marketable obligations denominated in the currency of the country pursuant to the laws of which the controlled foreign corporation computes its reserves (excluding any obligations that benefit from special tax exemptions or preferential tax rates not available to debt instruments generally) with due consideration given to the maturities of the obligations. If a controlled foreign corporation that would be subject to part II of subchapter L if it were a domestic insurance company uses the loss payment patterns prescribed by the Secretary under section 846(d) for discounting unpaid losses (rather than the company's historical payment pattern as permitted under section 846(e)), the company must compute the year-end discounted fraction of unpaid losses and the reserve discount factors by using the applicable federal interest rate required by this paragraph and may not use the year end discounted fraction of

unpaid losses and the reserve discount factors prescribed by the Secretary for any accident year.

(ii) *Nonqualified foreign contracts.*—For purposes of applying sections 807 and 812 to nonqualified foreign contracts, as defined in paragraph (e)(2) of this section, the prevailing state assumed interest rate shall be the rate defined in section 807(d)(4)(B) and the applicable federal interest rate shall be the rate defined in section 807(d)(4)(A).

(f) *Corporations not qualifying as insurance companies.*—(1) *In general.*—The United States shareholders of a controlled foreign corporation must include their pro rata share of that corporation's section 953 insurance income even if the foreign corporation would not be taxed under subchapter L of the Code if it were a domestic corporation. Such a corporation shall compute its section 953 insurance income and its foreign personal holding company income that is SCI investment income under the rules of part I or part II of subchapter L as modified by section 953(b) and §§ 1.953-1 through 1.953-7, to the extent not inconsistent with the rules of this paragraph, as if it were a domestic insurance company. A controlled foreign corporation will compute its insurance income as if it were a domestic insurance company subject to part I of subchapter L (relating to life insurance companies) only if it can meet the requirements of section 816(a) of the Code taking into account only that portion of its business which involves the issuing or reinsuring of insurance or annuity contracts. If the requirements of section 816(a) cannot be met, then the controlled foreign corporation must compute its insurance income under part II of subchapter L.

(2) *Items of gross income attributable to insurance operations of a non-insurance company.*—(i) *Corporations computing taxable income under part I of subchapter L.*—The taxable income of a controlled foreign corporation described under paragraph (f)(1) of this section that computes its insurance income under part I of subchapter L, shall include in its insurance income, together with the items of gross income that directly relate to its life insurance business, the items of income described in section 803(a)(3) which are not directly related to its insurance business, and which are not directly related to any other trade or business, in the proportion that the numerator determined under paragraph (f)(2)(i)(A) of this section bears to the denominator determined under paragraph (f)(2)(i)(B) of this section.

(A) *Numerator.*—The numerator used for the apportionment under paragraph (f)(2)(i) of this section is the sum of the means of the items described in section 807(c) at the beginning and end of the taxable year.

(B) *Denominator.*—The denominator used for the apportionment under paragraph (f)(2)(ii) of this section is the mean of the value of the total assets held by the controlled foreign corporation at the beginning and the end of the taxable year, determined by taking bills, accounts, notes receivable, and open accounts at face value and all other assets at their adjusted basis under section 1011 of the Code, unless there is affirmative evidence that more accurately reflects the value of the assets.

(ii) *Example.*—The following example illustrates the principles of paragraph (f)(2)(i) of this section.

Example. X is a controlled foreign corporation incorporated in country M engaged in the business of selling product V. It uses the calendar year as its taxable year. All of X's sales are to persons who reside outside of country M. A division of X issues contracts of credit life insurance to ensure payment of the purchase price of X's products. X does not, however, do enough business as an insurer to qualify as an insurance company under subchapter L of the Code. In 1988, X receives $500 in premiums and $3,000 in sales from product V. X also has interest, dividends, and gains from the sale of investment properties in the amount of $10,000. The investment income is not specifically allocable to the insurance or non-insurance businesses. The mean of X's reserves under section 807(c) determined as of the beginning and end of 1988 is $1,000. The mean of the value of X's total assets held at the beginning and the end of the taxable year is $5,000. The $3,000 received as part of the sales price of product V are directly related to V's non-insurance business and do not constitute insurance income. The $500 in premiums are directly related to V's insurance business and do constitute insurance income under section 953. Of X's $10,000 in investment income $2,000 ($10,000 × $1,000/$5,000) is insurance income under section 953.

(iii) *Corporations computing taxable income under part II of subchapter L.*—The taxable income of a controlled foreign corporation described in paragraph (f)(1) of this section that computes its insurance income as if it were a domestic insurance company subject to part II of subchapter L shall include in its insurance income, together with the items of gross income that directly relate to its insurance business, the items of income described in section 832(b)(1) which are not directly related to its insurance business, and which are not

directly related to any other trade or business, in the proportion that the numerator determined under paragraph (f)(2)(iii)(A) of this section bears to the denominator determined under paragraph (f)(2)(iii)(B) of this section.

(A) *Numerator.*—The numerator used for the apportionment under paragraph (f)(2)(iii) of this section is the sum of—

(1) The mean of the controlled foreign corporation's unearned premiums at the beginning and end of the taxable year, determined under section 832(b)(4)(B);

(2) The mean of the controlled foreign corporation's discounted unpaid losses at the beginning and end of the taxable year, determined under section 846; plus

(3) The mean of the items described in section 807(c)(4) at the beginning and end of the taxable year, to the extent allowable under section 832(c)(11).

(B) *Denominator.*—The denominator used for the apportionment under paragraph (f)(2)(iii) of this section is the mean of the value of the total assets held by the controlled foreign corporation at the beginning and the end of the taxable year, determined by taking bills, accounts, notes receivable, and open accounts at face value and all other assets at their adjusted basis under section 1011 of the Code, unless there is affirmative evidence that more accurately reflects the value of the assets.

(g) *Relationship between sections 953 and 954.*—(1) *Priority of application.*—(i) *In general.*—For purposes of determining the subpart F income of a controlled foreign corporation, the provisions of section 953 and §§ 1.953-1 through 1.953-7 must be applied before the provisions of section 954 (relating to foreign base company income). Further, the provisions of section 954 apply only to income that is not insurance income under section 953. For example, the provisions of section 954 are applied to the investment income attributable to premiums received with respect to insured risks located in the controlled foreign corporation's country of incorporation only after §§ 1.953-1 through 1.953-7 have been applied to determine the amount of section 953 insurance income and SCI income and the deductions allocated and apportioned to those categories of income. Notwithstanding the foregoing, foreign base company oil related income as defined in section 954(a)(5) and (g) shall not be treated as insurance income subject to section 953 and shall not be subject to §§ 1.953-1 through 1.953-7.

(ii) *Examples.*—The following examples illustrate the principles of paragraph (g)(1)(i) of this section.

Example 1. X is a controlled foreign corporation incorporated in country F. X's only trade or business is the insurance business. All of X's premiums are received under contracts insuring risks located outside country F. X earns interest, dividends, and rents from the investment of the premiums it receives. The interest, dividends, and rents are insurance income under section 953 and not foreign personal holding company income under section 954.

Example 2. Y is a controlled foreign corporation incorporated in country W. Y owns all of the outstanding stock of Z, also a country W corporation. Y writes contracts that give rise to premiums allocable to the nonRPII and SCI categories. In its taxable year ending in 1988, Y receives a dividend from Z. Y must allocate or apportion that dividend income to the nonRPII and SCI categories under § 1.953-4 before applying the exception of section 954(c)(3)(relating to dividends from same-country related corporations) to the SCI investment income.

(2) *Decrease or increase in income not material.*—(i) *In general.*—For purposes of computing the subpart F income of a controlled foreign corporation deriving income from insurance, reinsurance, or annuity contracts, deductions are allowed if they are allowed under subchapter L of the Code as modified by section 953 regardless of whether they are allocated or apportioned to section 953 insurance income or SCI investment income which constitutes section 954(c) foreign personal holding company income. Further, the amount of section 953 insurance income and the amount of foreign personal holding company income attributable to SCI investment income shall be determined in accordance with subchapter L of the Code, as modified by section 953, even though those rules result in a greater amount of subpart F income compared to the amount determined under section 954. Thus, in applying section 953 to income of a controlled foreign corporation that would, but for section 953, be subject to the provisions of section 954, the exceptions under section 954(c) which would not require a United States shareholder to include in gross income dividends, interest, rents, royalties, gains from the sale or exchange of property described in section 954(c)(1)(B), net gains from commodities transactions described in section 954(c)(1)(C), and net gains from foreign currency transactions described in section 954(c)(1)(D), are irrelevant.

(ii) *Examples.*—The principles of this paragraph (g)(2) are illustrated in the following examples.

Example 1. Z is a controlled foreign corporation that only issues and reinsures property and casualty insurance policies covering home country risks. Z may allocate a part of its discounted unpaid losses under section 846 to its SCI investment income which is foreign personal holding company income under section 954(c).

Example 2. X, a controlled foreign corporation, receives dividends and interest from a subsidiary which is incorporated in the same country as X and has a substantial part of its trade or business assets located in that country. All of X's income is attributable to the RPII or nonRPII categories. The dividends, after the appropriate allocation and apportionment, are included in the gross income of X's United States shareholders without regard to section 954(c)(3)(relating to dividends and interest from same-country related corporations).

(h) *Inclusion of pro rata share of subpart F income derived from insurance operations.*—(1) *Inclusion of pro rata share of related person insurance income.*—Each section 953(c) shareholder, as defined in this paragraph (h)(1), must include in its gross income (subject to the section 952(c) earnings and profits limitation) the lesser of—

(i) The "pro rata amount," which is the amount that would be determined under section 951(a)(2) if only related person insurance income were taken into account; if the number of shares of stock owned (within the meaning of section 958(a)) by section 953(c) shareholders in the aggregate on the last day of the taxable year were the total number of shares in the foreign corporation; and if only distributions received by section 953(c) shareholders were taken into account under section 951(a)(2)(B); or

(ii) The "limitation amount," which is the amount that would be determined under section 951(a)(2) if all of the taxable income of the foreign corporation for the taxable year were subpart F income.

A section 953(c) shareholder is a United States shareholder as defined in section 953(c)(1)(A) and § 1.953-3(b)(2) and includes a United States shareholder as defined in section 951(b).

(2) *Inclusion of subpart F income other than related person insurance income.*—Each United States shareholder as defined in section

Computation of pro rata share of related person insurance income.

Lesser of:

Pro rata amount:

A:	$5/80 \times \$1,000$	
B:	$5/80 \times \$1,000$	
C:	$70/80 \times \$1,000$	

or

Limitation amount:

A:	$5/100 \times \$1,000$	
B:	$5/100 \times \$1,000$	
C:	$70/100 \times \$1,000$	

Example 2. The facts are the same as in *Example 1* except that there is $2,000 of related person insurance income and $1,500 of earnings and profits. The amount of related person insurance income

Computation of pro rata share of related person insurance income.

Lesser of:

Pro rata amount:

A:	$5/80 \times \$2,000$	
B:	$5/80 \times \$2,000$	
C:	$70/80 \times \$2,000$	

or

Limitation amount:

A:	$5/100 \times \$2,000$	
B:	$5/100 \times \$2,000$	
C:	$70/100 \times \$2,000$	

Computation of section 952(c)(1)(A) earnings and profits limitation.

A:	$5/100 \times \$1,500$	
B:	$5/100 \times \$1,500$	
C:	$70/100 \times \$1,500$	

The amount of related person insurance income included in the gross income of each shareholder is limited by their pro rata share of earnings and profits as computed under section 952(c) because that amount is less than both the pro rata amount and the limitation amount.

Computation of pro rata share of related person insurance income.

Lesser of:

Pro rata amount:

A:	$5/80 \times \$1,000$	
B:	$5/80 \times \$1,000$	
C:	$70/80 \times \$1,000$	

or

Limitation amount:

A:	$5/100 \times \$2,000$	
B:	$5/100 \times \$2,000$	
C:	$70/100 \times \$2,000$	

Computation of the pro rata share of subpart F income other than related person insurance income.

C is the only section 951(b) shareholder.

C:	$70/100 \times \$1,000$	

951(b)(a "section 951(b) shareholder") must include, in addition to its pro rata share of income within the RPII category computed under paragraph (h)(1) of this section, its pro rata share of subpart F income other than related person insurance income, as computed under section 951(a)(2) and paragraph (h)(3) of this section. A section 951(b) shareholder must include its pro rata share of income within the RPII category as computed under this paragraph (h)(2) regardless of whether the exceptions of section 953(c)(3)(A) and (B) and § 1.953-7(a) and (b) apply.

(3) *Earnings and profits limitation.*—Pursuant to section 952(c)(1)(A), the subpart F income of any controlled foreign corporation for any taxable year shall not exceed the earnings and profits of such corporation for such taxable year. Thus, a United States shareholder's inclusion of subpart F income shall not exceed such shareholder's pro rata share, computed under the principles of section 951(a)(2), of the earnings and profits of the controlled foreign corporation. If the sum of a United States shareholder's pro rata share of related person insurance income and subpart F income other than related person insurance income exceeds such shareholder's pro rata share of the controlled foreign corporation's earnings and profits, then the section 952(c)(1)(A) earnings and profits limitation shall be applied by first including the United States shareholder's pro rata share of related person insurance income.

(4) *Examples.*—The following examples illustrate the principles of paragraph (h) of this section.

Example 1. X is a country M corporation and is a controlled foreign corporation under section 957, section 953(c)(1)(B), and § 1.953-3(b)(2). It has 100 shares of one class of stock outstanding. A owns 5 shares, B owns 5 shares, C owns 70 shares, and F owns 20 shares. A, B, and C are unrelated United States persons; F is a foreign person. A, B and C are considered section 953(c) shareholders. Only C, however, is a section 951(b) shareholder. During the current taxable year, X has $1,000 of related person insurance income and $1,000 of earnings and profits. A and B will each include $50 and C will include $700 of related person insurance income in gross income, computed as set forth below.

=	$62.50	
=	$62.50	
=	$875.00	

=	$50.00	
=	$50.00	
=	$700.00	

included in gross income of A, B, and C is $75, $75, and $1,050, respectively, as computed below.

=	$125	
=	$125	
=	$1,750	

=	$100	
=	$100	
=	$1,400	

=	$75	
=	$75	
=	$1,050	

Example 3. The facts are the same as in *Example 1* except that X has $1,000 in related person insurance income, $1,000 in subpart F income other than related person insurance income, and $1,500 in earnings and profits.

=	$62.50	
=	$62.50	
=	$875.00	

=	$100	
=	$100	
=	$1,400	

=	$700	

Computation of pro rata share of earnings and profits.

A:	$5/100 \times \$1,500$	=	$75
B:	$5/100 \times \$1,500$	=	$75
C:	$70/100 \times \$1,500$	=	$1,050

With respect to A and B, the pro rata amount of related person insurance income is less than their pro rata share of X's earnings and profits. Thus, A and B will each include $62.50 in gross income as related person insurance income.

The sum of C's pro rata share of related person insurance income (the pro rata amount of $875) and subpart F income other than related person insurance income ($700) equals $1,575. That sum exceeds C's pro rata share of X's earnings and profits ($1,050). Thus, C must include $875 of related person insurance income and $175 ($1,050 – $875) of subpart F income other than related person insurance income.

(5) *Controlled foreign corporation for less than entire year.*—(i) *In general.*—If a foreign corporation with related person insurance income is a controlled foreign corporation for less than the entire taxable year, for purposes of computing the limitation amount, only the taxable income of the foreign corporation for that portion of the taxable year during which the foreign corporation was a controlled

Computation of pro rata share of related person insurance income.

Lesser of:

     Pro rata amount:

A:	$5/80 \times (182/365 \times \$1,000)$	=	$31.00
B:	$5/80 \times (182/365 \times \$1,000)$	=	$31.00
C:	$70/80 \times (182/365 \times \$1,000)$	=	$436.00

or

     Limitation amount:

A:	$5/100 \times (182/365 \times \$1,000)$	=	$25.00
B:	$5/100 \times (182/365 \times \$1,000)$	=	$25.00
C:	$70/100 \times (182/365 \times \$1,000)$	=	$349.00

Thus, the amount of related person insurance income to be included by A, B, and C is the limitation amount.

(6) *Distributions.*—(i) *In general.*—Only distributions to United States shareholders, as defined in section 951(b) or section 953(c)(1)(A), are to be taken into account for purposes of computing the pro rata amount, as defined in paragraph (h)(1)(i) of this section. However, for purposes of computing the limitation amount under paragraphs (h)(1)(ii) of this section, distributions to shareholders other than United States shareholders shall be taken into account.

(ii) *Example.*—The following example illustrates the rule of paragraph (h)(6)(i) of this section.

     Computation of pro rata share of related person insurance income.

       (i)   *Pro rata amount:*
               A: $60/60 \times 182/365 \times \$1,000$

       (ii)   *Limitation amount:*
               A: $60/100 \times 182/365 \times \$2,000$
                  minus lesser of:
                  $120 dividend on shares purchased
             or
                  $60\% \times 182/365 \times \$2,000$
                  ($598.00)

Thus, A must include $478 of related person insurance income in gross income.

(7) *Mutual insurance companies.*—For purposes of sections 951(a)(2) and 953(c)(5) and paragraph (h) of this section, a United States shareholder that is a policyholder in a mutual insurance company shall compute its pro rata share by reference to the amount that would be distributed with respect to the United States shareholder's policy or policies owned on the last day of the controlled foreign corporation's taxable year if all the related person insurance income and all the subpart F income other than related person insurance income were distributed to the policyholders. In making the determination of a mutual policyholder's pro rata share of subpart F income the rules set forth in paragraph (h)(7)(i) through (iii) of this section are applied in the order given and the first rule to result in the determination of a specific amount to be included in the policyholder's gross income is the rule that shall be applied. The mutual policyholder's pro rata share of subpart F income shall be determined as:

(i) The amount that would be distributed annually under the terms of the policy or the by-laws of the corporation;

(ii) The amount that would be distributed if the mutual company were liquidated; or

(iii) The amount that would be distributed to a policyholder if earnings and profits were distributed in the same proportion that premiums paid by the policyholder over a five-year period ending on the last day of the controlled foreign corporation's taxable year bears to the total amount of premiums paid by all policyholders who hold

foreign corporation, computed as if such income were earned ratably throughout the taxable year, shall be treated as subpart F income.

(ii) *Example.*—The rule of this paragraph (h)(5) is illustrated in the following example.

Example. X, a foreign corporation, was incorporated on January 1, 1987 by A, B and F. As of that date, A and B, who are United States persons, each own 5 shares and F, who is not a United States person, owns 90 shares of the 100 shares of the single class of stock issued and outstanding. On July 1, 1987, F sells 70 of his shares to C, a United States person. At the end of the calendar year, which is also X's taxable year, X has $1,000 of income from providing insurance to its United States shareholders and persons related to those shareholders. X also has $1,000 of earnings and profits for the year. A and B must each include $25.00 in gross income and C must include $349.00. The computations necessary to determine related person insurance income are set forth below.

Example. X is a controlled foreign corporation within the meaning of section 953(c)(1) and § 1.953-3(b)(2) and has 100 shares of one class of stock outstanding. F, who is not a United States person, owned all 100 shares of X's outstanding stock until July 1, 1987, when A, a United States person, acquired 60 shares of the stock from F. On June 30, 1987, before A had acquired X's stock from F, X made a distribution of $2 per share for a total of $200 to F. At the end of the calendar year, which is also X's taxable year, X had $2,000 of taxable income, of which $1,000 is related person insurance income. X also had earnings and profits for the taxable year of $2,000. The computation for determining A's pro rata share of related person insurance income is set forth below.

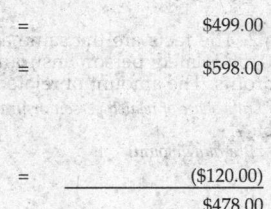

	=	$499.00
	=	$598.00
	=	($120.00)
		$478.00

ownership interests on the last day of the taxable year and have held their interest over the five-year period.

(i) *Application of sections 959, 961, and 1248.*—If a foreign corporation that is a controlled foreign corporation under section 953(c) makes a distribution with respect to its stock, section 959(a)(1) shall apply to any United States shareholder as defined in section 953(c)(1)(A) and § 1.953-3(b)(2). Earnings and profits attributable to related person insurance income included in the gross income of a United States shareholder with less than 10 percent of the combined voting power of the stock of the controlled foreign corporation shall be treated as earnings and profits which have been included in the gross income of a United States shareholder for purposes of sections 956 and 959(a)(2). In addition, the adjustments made to the basis of stock in a controlled foreign corporation required by section 961 shall apply to any United States shareholder as defined in section 953(c)(1)(A) and § 1.953-3(b)(2). Any United States person who is a United States shareholder, as defined in section 953(c)(1)(A) and § 1.953-3(b)(2), of a controlled foreign corporation, as defined in section 953(c)(1)(B) and § 1.953-3(b)(2), shall be treated as meeting the stock ownership requirements of section 1248(a)(2). In addition, any controlled foreign corporation, within the meaning of section 953(c)(1)(B) and § 1.953-3(b)(2), shall be treated as a controlled foreign corporation for purposes of section 1248.

(j) *Application of section 367(b).*—[Reserved]

(k) *Interaction with section 954(b)(3).*—Income that would not be considered subpart F income but for the operation of section

954(b)(3)(B) shall not be considered related person insurance income. Thus, if foreign base company income and insurance income exceed 70 percent of gross income, United States persons who are United States shareholders solely by operation of section 953(c)(1)(A) and §1.953-3(b)(2) must include in their gross income only their pro rata share of related person insurance income. Any person who is a United States shareholder as defined in section 951(b) shall, however, include his pro rata share, as determined under this section, of the entire amount of subpart F income of the controlled foreign corporation. [Reg. §1.953-6.]

§1.953-7. Exceptions to inclusion of related person insurance income for certain shareholders.—(a) *Corporation not held by insureds.*—(1) *In general.*—A person that is a United States shareholder solely by virtue of section 953(c)(1) shall not include in gross income such person's pro rata share of income that qualifies as related person insurance income if, at all times during the taxable year of the foreign corporation, less than 20 percent of the total combined voting power of all classes of stock of the corporation entitled to vote and less than 20 percent of the total value (both stock and policies) of the corporation is owned (directly or indirectly under the principles of section 883(c)(4)) by persons who are the insured under any insurance or reinsurance contract, who are the purchasers or beneficiaries of any annuity contract issued or reinsured by the foreign corporation, or who are related persons (within the meaning of section 954(d)(3)) to any such insured. For purposes of this paragraph, the term "insured" means only United States persons, as defined in section 957(c), or persons related to United States persons (within the meaning of section 954(d)(3)) who are insured or reinsured by the foreign corporation, persons who have purchased or are beneficiaries under any annuity contract issued or reinsured by the foreign corporation, or persons insured by the foreign corporation in a cross-insurance arrangement described in §1.953-3(b)(5).

(2) *Examples.*—The principles of this paragraph (a) are illustrated in the following examples.

Example 1. X is a country Y corporation which issues property and liability insurance policies for risks located outside country Y. X has one class of voting stock outstanding. Z, a domestic corporation, owns 60 percent of X's stock. Z has 100 shareholders each of which owns one percent of Z. Of the remaining shareholders of X, four are foreign corporations, each of which owns five percent of the X stock, and four are domestic corporations which also own five percent each. X has issued policies of insurance to 25 of Z's shareholders, the four foreign corporations which own stock in X, and to W, one of the domestic corporate shareholders of X. None of the other shareholders of X are insured by X. The 25 insureds who own stock in Z own, indirectly under the principles of section 883(c)(4), 15 percent of the stock of X (25% × 60%). The insurance income attributable to the policy of insurance issued to W is related person insurance income that is includable in the gross income of the four domestic corporate shareholders of X because 20 percent of the stock of X is owned directly or indirectly by insureds who are United States persons: 15 percent by 25 of the shareholders of Z plus 5 percent owned by W. In addition, because Z is a United States shareholder as defined in section 951(b), as well as in section 953(c)(1), it must include its pro rata share of the related person insurance of income of X, plus the section 953(a) insurance income that is not related person insurance income, regardless of whether 20 percent or more of the corporation is owned, directly or indirectly, by insureds who are United States persons.

Example 2. Y is a controlled foreign corporation. Its one class of stock outstanding is owned equally by 20 domestic corporations, none of which are insured by Y. Nine of the shareholder corporations are the parent corporations of nine unrelated, wholly owned foreign subsidiaries which are insured by Y. Because the insureds are related persons, within the meaning of section 954(d)(3), to United States shareholders (the domestic corporate shareholders), the income from insuring the foreign subsidiaries is related person insurance income. Moreover, because nine domestic corporate shareholders of Y control the subsidiaries, within the meaning of section 954(d)(3), they are related persons. Therefore, 45 percent (9 × 5%) of the stock of Y is owned by United States shareholders that are related to the insureds and the exception to inclusion in gross income of paragraph (a)(1) of this section is inapplicable. The 20 domestic shareholders must include Y's related person insurance income in their gross income.

(b) *De minimis insurance exception.*—(1) *In general.*—A person that is a United States shareholder solely by virtue of section 953(c)(1) shall not include in gross income such person's pro rata share of income that qualifies as related person insurance income if the related person insurance income, determined on a gross basis, of the foreign corporation is less than 20 percent of the foreign corporation's total insurance income for the taxable year, determined on a gross basis, without regard to those provisions of section 953(a)(1) and §1.953-2(a)(1) which limit section 953 insurance income to income from countries other than the country in which the corporation was

created or organized. Related person insurance income determined on a gross basis means life insurance gross income within the meaning of section 803 or gross income within the meaning of section 832(b)(1), whichever is applicable, except that the phrase "premiums earned (within the meaning of section 832(b)(4)" shall be substituted for the term "underwriting income," where that term appears in section 832(b)(1)(A).

(2) *Examples.*—The following examples illustrate the principles of paragraph (b)(1) of this section.

Example 1. X is a country Y corporation engaged in the business of issuing liability insurance. All of the stock of X is owned by United States shareholders. Each of the United States shareholders owns less than 10 percent of X's one class of stock outstanding. For its 1987 taxable year, X has $100,000 of gross income of which $10,000 constitutes section 953 insurance income within the RPII category and $50,000 constitutes section 953 insurance income within the nonRPII category. Of the remaining $40,000 of income, $10,000 would have been premium and investment income within the RPII category of section 953 insurance income and $30,000 would have been premium and investment income within the nonRPII category of insurance income except that those amounts relate to contracts insuring risks located in the home country. Thus, without regard to the same country exception, $20,000 of income ($10,000 from the RPII category and $10,000 from the SCI category) would have been within the RPII category of section 953 insurance income. X does not meet the de minimis insurance exception of paragraph (b)(1) of this section because 20 percent ($20,000/$100,000) of its insurance income, determined without regard to those provisions of section 953(a)(1) and §1.953-2(a)(3) which limit insurance income to income from insuring risks located outside the home country, is related person insurance income.

Example 2. The facts are the same as in *Example 1* except that $3,000 of premiums that constitute income within the RPII category is paid to another insurer pursuant to a reinsurance contract. X does meet the de minimis insurance exception because under section 832(b)(4)(A) premiums paid for reinsurance are deducted from premiums written in arriving at premiums earned. Thus, approximately 17.5 percent ($17,000/$97,000) of X's insurance income is related person insurance income.

(3) *Anti-abuse rule.*—(i) *In general.*—In determining insurance income on a gross basis, the District Director may exclude income attributable to an insurance or reinsurance contract covering the life, health, property, or liability of a person other than a United States shareholder, or person related to such shareholder, or attributable to an annuity contract, or a contract reinsuring annuity contracts, that are purchased by, or provide annuity payments to, a person other than a United States shareholder or person related to such shareholder, if the primary purpose for entering into the contract is to qualify for the de minimis insurance exception. *See also* section 845. In making this determination, the District Director will consider all the facts and circumstances. Among the factors to be considered are whether there is a true transfer of risk, whether the predominant purpose for the transaction is a bona fide business purpose, and whether the terms of the insurance or reinsurance contract reflect the terms that unrelated parties would agree to in a similar transaction.

(ii) *Examples.*—The following examples illustrate the principles of paragraph (b)(3) of this section.

Example 1. The facts are the same as in *Example 1* in paragraph (b)(2) of this section, except that near the end of its taxable year, X cedes to another insurance company, Z, under a contract of reinsurance some of the insurance policies that were issued by X to persons other than related insureds. X receives a ceding commission from Z of $30,000 and thereby increases its gross income other than RPII income by $30,000. Thus, approximately 15 percent ($20,000/$130,000) of X's income is RPII income without regard to the same country exception. At the beginning of the following taxable year, Z reinsures with S, a subsidiary controlled by X, a block of insurance which is similar to the policies X reinsured with Z. W pays Z a ceding commission of $30,000. Based on the facts and circumstances, X will be regarded as having engaged in the reinsurance transaction with Z in order to qualify for the de minimis exception. Therefore, the $30,000 of income from the reinsurance transaction will be ignored in determining whether X qualifies for the de minimis exception.

Example 2. The facts are the same as in *Example 1* in paragraph (b)(2) of this section except, that near the end of the taxable year, X enters a reinsurance agreement with M under which X receives $30,000 in nonRPII premiums. At the beginning of the following taxable year, X cedes to F all of the risks of M that X reinsured at the end of 1988, transferring the $30,000 in premiums to F. The $30,000 in nonRPII premiums received by X under the reinsurance agreement will be ignored for purposes of determining whether X qualifies for the de minimis related person insurance income exception.

(c) *Election to treat income as effectively connected.*—(1) *In general.*—A controlled foreign corporation, other than a disqualified corporation, may elect in accordance with the procedures set forth in this paragraph to treat its related person insurance income that is not actually effectively connected income under section 864(c) as if it were income effectively connected with the conduct of a trade or business in the United States. To make the election, the foreign corporation must waive all benefits (other than with respect to section 884) with respect to related person insurance income granted by the United States under any treaty, including any friendship, commerce and navigation treaty, between the United States and any foreign country.

(2) *Corporations which may make the election.*—(i) *In general.*— The election may be made by any corporation that is not a disqualified corporation. A corporation is a disqualified corporation if, for any taxable year beginning after December 31, 1986, it is a controlled foreign corporation as defined in section 957(a) or (b) (without regard to section 953(c)(1)(B) and §1.953-3(b)(2)) for an uninterrupted period of 30 days or more during the taxable year and a United States shareholder, as defined in section 951(b), owns, directly or indirectly, within the meaning of section 958(a) (without regard to the constructive ownership rules of section 958(b)), stock in the corporation at some time during the taxable year.

(ii) *Successor corporation.*—A corporation that is a successor to another corporation that, during any taxable year beginning after December 31, 1986, was a disqualified corporation may not make the election. The term "successor corporation" means any foreign corporation that acquires assets of another foreign corporation having a fair market value of 50 percent or more of the fair market value of all the assets held by the acquired foreign corporation immediately before the acquisition, if 50 percent or more of the combined voting power of all classes of stock entitled to vote or 50 percent or more of the value of all classes of stock in the acquiring corporation is owned, directly or indirectly, at the time of the acquisition by one or more persons who at any time during which the acquired foreign corporation was a disqualified corporation owned, directly or indirectly, 50 percent or more of the combined voting power of all classes of stock entitled to vote or 50 percent or more of the value of all classes of stock in the acquired foreign corporation.

(iii) *Examples.*—The following examples illustrate the principles of paragraph (c)(2) of this section.

Example 1. Subsequent to December 31, 1986, 50 domestic corporations, all engaged in business within the same industry, form M, a foreign corporation to insure the risks of the 50 corporations and their subsidiaries. Each of the corporations owns two percent of the one class of voting stock of M outstanding. M may make the election under section 953(c)(3)(C) to have its related person insurance income treated as if it were effectively connected with the conduct of a trade or business within the United States because it has never been a controlled foreign corporation within the meaning of section 957(a) or (b).

Example 2. The facts are the same as in *Example 1*, except that four of the 50 domestic corporate shareholders, W, X, Y, and Z, each own 7 percent of the stock of M and are wholly-owned subsidiaries of V, a domestic corporation. None of the other shareholders of M are 10 percent or greater shareholders. M is a controlled foreign corporation under section 957(b) because more than 25 percent of its stock is owned by United States shareholders as defined in section 951(b). Under the attribution rules of section 958(b), W, X, Y, and Z are each considered as owning 28 percent of the stock of M and therefore are United States shareholders under section 951(b) because each is considered as owning the stock of the others by attribution through V. Because each of W, X, Y, and Z own stock in M directly under section 958(a), M is a disqualified corporation.

Example 3. On January 1, 1987, X, a domestic corporation, formed Z under the laws of country F as a reinsurance company constituting a mutual insurance company under the laws of country F. X capitalized Z by contributing interest bearing reserve fund certificates which entitle X to 30 percent of the voting power in Z. Z reinsures policies issued by X, none of which relate to risks located in country F. Under the laws of country F, the policyholders under the policies issued by X and reinsured by Z are members of Z and have voting rights. None of these policyholders hold 10 percent or more of the voting power of Z. However, only those policyholders may receive policyholder dividends from Z. X is not entitled to any non-liquidating distributions from Z. Z is a controlled foreign corporation within the meaning of section 957(b). Even though neither X nor the United States policyholders have had inclusions of insurance income in their gross income by virtue of subpart F of the Code, because Z is a controlled foreign corporation under section 957(b) it cannot make the election under section 953(c)(3)(C) to have its related person insurance income treated as if it were effectively connected with the conduct of a trade or business within the United States.

(3) *Taxable year of corporation making election.*—A corporation making the election to treat related person insurance income as income effectively connected with the conduct of a trade or business in the United States must utilize the calendar year as its annual accounting period for United States tax purposes, as required by section 843.

(4) *Period during which election is in effect.*—(i) *Elections that become effective in taxable years beginning after December 31, 1987.*—If an election under paragraph (c)(3) of this section is made for the first taxable year beginning after December 31, 1987 or any subsequent taxable year, the election is effective from the first day of the taxable year for which the election is made (and all subsequent taxable years). Therefore, a foreign corporation that has a fiscal taxable year prior to making the election must file a short-year return for the period from the first day the election becomes effective to the last day of the calendar year in which the election is made.

(ii) *Examples.*—The following examples illustrate the rule of paragraph (c)(4)(i) of this section.

Example 1. X is a controlled foreign corporation that keeps its books and records on a calendar year basis. X makes an election under paragraph (c)(3) of this section for the 1988 taxable year. X's election is effective as of January 1, 1988.

Example 2. Y is a controlled foreign corporation that keeps its books and records on a July 1 to June 30 fiscal year basis. Y makes an election under paragraph (c)(3) of this section for the 1988 taxable year. Y's election is effective as of July 1, 1988. Y must file a short-year return covering the period from July 1, 1988 to December 31, 1988.

(iii) *Elections that become effective in first taxable year beginning after December 31, 1986.*—For any foreign corporation that makes an election under paragraph (c) of this section for the first taxable year beginning after December 31, 1986, the election is effective as of the date indicated by the corporation on its election statement and for all subsequent taxable years. A foreign corporation that had a fiscal taxable year prior to making the election must file a short-year return covering the period from the beginning of its 1987 fiscal year to the last day of its 1987 fiscal year. The foreign corporation must include in its gross income for the taxable year in which the election becomes effective the amount of related person insurance income that is attributable to the period from the date the election becomes effective through the last day of the calendar year. The amount of the related person insurance income attributable to such period is that amount determined by allocating to each day in the taxable year its ratable portion of related person insurance income. However, if the corporation keeps adequate books and records that, in the district director's discretion, accurately reflect the actual amount of the income earned in such period, the corporation may include such amount in gross income rather than the daily pro rata amount.

(iv) *Examples.*—The following examples illustrate the principles of paragraph (c)(4)(iii) of this section.

Example 1. X is a controlled foreign corporation that keeps its books and records on a calendar year basis. X makes an election under paragraph (c) of this section for the 1987 taxable year. In its election statement, X chose September 15, 1987 as the effective date of its election. X must include in gross income the related person insurance income attributable to the period from September 15, 1987 to December 31, 1987 in its calendar year 1987 tax return.

Example 2. Y is a controlled foreign corporation that keeps its books and records on a July 1 to June 30 fiscal year basis. Y makes an election under this paragraph (c) of this section for the 1987 taxable year and chooses to make the election effective as of September 1, 1987. Y must file a short-year return covering the period from July 1, 1987 to August 31, 1987. The related person insurance income of Y that, under Y's method of accounting, is attributable to the period from July 1, 1987 to August 31, 1987 must be included in the gross income of Y's United States shareholders. In addition, X must also file another short-year return covering the period from September 1, 1987 to December 31, 1987 and must include in its gross income for that period the related person insurance income attributable to that period.

(5) *Effect of election: taxation under section 882; alternative minimum tax; dividends received deduction; pre-1987 deficits in earnings and profits, and net operating losses.*—If a foreign corporation makes an election under paragraph (c) of this section, all income that is actually effectively connected with the conduct of a trade or business in the United States (as determined under sections 864(c) and 842) and all related person insurance income that is not effectively connected with the conduct of a trade or business within the United States but is treated as if it were effectively connected by virtue of the election under this paragraph (c) of this section will be taxable under section 882. The branch profits tax imposed by section 884 and the tax imposed on interest described in section 884(f) will apply to an

electing corporation to the same extent and in the same manner that those taxes would have applied if the corporation had not made the election. Thus, the exclusion from the branch profits tax contained in section 884(d)(2)(D) (relating to income treated as effectively connected under section 953(c)(3)(C)) does not apply to income which is actually effectively connected with the conduct of a trade or business within the United States under sections 864(c) and 842. Further, a controlled foreign corporation that makes the election under section 953(c)(3)(C) shall continue to be treated as a controlled foreign corporation for purposes of section 864(c)(4)(D)(ii). Thus, related person insurance income that is treated as income effectively connected with the conduct of a United States trade or business shall not be subject to the branch profits tax under section 884 solely by virtue of making the election under section 953(c)(3)(C). *But see* section 842(b) with respect to the minimum effectively connected net investment income of a foreign corporation conducting an insurance business within the United States. Related person insurance income that is treated as if it were effectively connected with the conduct of a United States trade or business is subject to the alternative minimum tax provisions of sections 55 and 56 of the Code. For purposes of section 245 (dividends from certain foreign corporations), related person insurance income that is treated as if it were effectively connected by virtue of an election under paragraph (c)(3) of this section shall be treated as effectively connected for purposes of determining post-1986 undistributed U.S. earnings under section 245(a)(5). Net operating loss deductions and deficits in earnings and profits of a corporation making the election under paragraph (c)(3) of this section that would be carried over from, or incurred in, taxable years beginning before January 1, 1986 cannot be carried over to, or used in, taxable years beginning after December 31, 1986.

(6) *Exemption from tax imposed by section 4371.*—The tax imposed by section 4371 (relating to policies issued or reinsured by foreign insurers) shall not apply to premiums that are subject to the election under paragraph (c) of this section to treat related person insurance income which is not otherwise effectively connected income under section 864(c) as if it were effectively connected with the conduct of a trade or business within the United States. The exemption from the tax imposed by section 4371 begins after the later of the

date of acceptance of the election or the first day of the first taxable year for which the election is made. An election is accepted on the date when the closing agreement has been executed by the taxpayer and the Commissioner. A copy of the election statement that has been stamped as accepted by the Commissioner will serve to place others on notice of the exemption. If an election has an effective date prior to the date on which the election is accepted, any excise taxes that have been paid on any related person insurance income received prior to the acceptance of the election may be refunded to the person who remitted the taxes. *See also* section 4373, which exempts from the excise tax under section 4371 income which is effectively connected with the conduct of a trade or business within the United States.

(7) *Procedure for making election under section 953(c)(3)(C).*—(i) *In general.*—In order to make a valid election to treat related person insurance income as income effectively connected with the conduct of a trade or business in the United States, a foreign corporation must provide the Internal Revenue Service with a signed election statement, a signed closing agreement, and a letter of credit.

(ii) *When election must be made.*—In order for the election to be effective for a taxable year, an election statement must be filed on or before the due date of the electing corporation's tax return reporting the related person insurance income earned during the taxable year.

(iii) *Election.*—An election is made by mailing an original and one copy of an election statement to the Internal Revenue Service, Assistant Commissioner (International), IN:C:C:51, 950 L'Enfant Plaza South, S.W., Washington, D.C. 20024. The statement must be signed under penalty of perjury by a responsible corporate officer, within the meaning of section 6062, stating that the statement and accompanying documents are true and complete to the best of the officer's knowledge and belief. A copy of the accepted election statement must be attached to the first tax return of the electing corporation that includes related person insurance income to which the election under paragraph (c) of this section applies. The election statement must be made in the following (or substantially similar) form:

FOREIGN CAPTIVE INSURANCE
COMPANY ELECTION UNDER
SECTION 953(c)(3)(C)

(1) _____

(Name, address, tax identification number [a number will automatically be assigned to those corporations not already having a number], and place of incorporation of the corporation) hereby elects under section 953(c)(3)(C) to treat its related person insurance income, as defined in section 953(c)(2), that is not actually effectively connected with the conduct of a trade or business in the United States under sections 864 or 842, as income effectively connected with the conduct of a trade or business within the United States.

(2) *(Name of corporation).*—waives all benefits (other than with respect to section 884) with respect to related person insurance income under any treaty, including any friendship, commerce and navigation treaty, between the United States and any foreign country.

(3) *(Name of corporation).*—agrees to timely file a United States income tax return and timely remit the income tax due on its related person insurance income, determined as if all such income were effectively connected with the conduct of a United States trade or business.

(4) Attached to this election statement is a complete list of all United States shareholders, as defined in section 953(c)(1)(A) and §1.953-3(b)(2), which own stock in *(Name of corporation)* as of a date no more than 90 days prior to the date this election statement is mailed. The list includes the name, address, tax identification number, and ownership percentage for each such United States shareholder. *(Name of corporation)* agrees to file an updated list containing the information prescribed in this paragraph determined as of the

last day of each taxable year. This updated list will be filed with the United States tax return reporting the related person insurance income earned by the corporation for each taxable year the election is in effect. [Attach listing].

(5) *(Name of corporation).*—agrees to file a complete list of all United States persons (whether or not listed as United States persons who own stock in *(Name of corporation)*) whose risks are insured or reinsured by *(Name of corporation)*, or who have purchased annuities or will receive annuity payments from *(Name of corporation)* as of the last day of each taxable year. The list will include the name, address, and tax identification number of each United States person so insured or reinsured. The list will be filed with the United States tax return reporting related person insurance income earned by *(Name of corporation)* for each taxable year the election is in effect.

(6) *(Name of corporation).*—agrees to provide security for the payment of tax due on its related person insurance income. The security will be in an amount and upon the terms as stated in a closing agreement to be executed between the Internal Revenue Service and *(Name of corporation)*.

(7) Attached is the power of attorney, Form 2848, of the person authorized to negotiate a closing agreement on behalf of *(Name of corporation)*.

The undersigned declares under penalty of perjury that the statements contained in this election and accompanying documents are true and complete to the best of his/her knowledge and belief.

_____	_____
Date	(Title) (Name of Corporation)

(8) *Closing agreement.*—After the receipt of the election statement, the controlled foreign corporation's designated representative will be provided with a model closing agreement and further instructions on completing the election process.

(9) *Letter of credit.*—(i) *In general.*—A foreign corporation that makes the election under paragraph (c)(3) of this section must provide a letter of credit issued in favor of the Internal Revenue Service. The letter of credit must generally be in an amount equal to 10 percent of the gross premium income from insuring or reinsuring the risks of United States shareholders and persons related to such

shareholders in the 12 month period preceding the filing of the election. In the case of a corporation that did not receive gross premiums from United States shareholders or related persons in the previous 12 month period, the amount of the letter of credit required will be based on an estimate of the projected gross premiums of the corporation for the first year of the election. For purposes of paragraph (c)(9)(i) and (ii) of this section, the term "gross premiums" means the amount of gross premiums written on insurance contracts during the taxable year without adjustment for return premiums, premiums for reinsurance, premiums and other consideration arising out of indemnity reinsurance, or increases in unearned premiums. In all cases, a minimum amount of $75,000 will be required and the maximum amount required will not exceed $10,000,000. The foreign corporation must provide, under penalty of perjury, evidence to support the computation of the amount of the letter of credit it proposes as security under paragraph (c) of this section.

(ii) *Changes in the amount of the letter of credit.*—Once the amount of the letter of credit has been determined for a taxable year, no change in the amount of the letter of credit is required unless in a subsequent taxable year there is an increase in gross premiums to more than 120 percent of the amount of the gross premiums used to compute the letter of credit (the "base year gross premiums"). If for any taxable year, the foreign corporation has gross premium income constituting more than 120 percent of the base year gross premiums, the amount of the letter of credit must be increased within 30 days of the filing of the tax return for that year. If a letter of credit in a greater amount must be provided, it must be in the amount of 10 percent of the gross premiums for the taxable year. No change in the letter of credit is required if gross premiums for a taxable year decline from the base year premium level; however, the taxpayer may submit a new letter of credit equal to 10 percent of the gross premiums for the taxable year in replacement of the outstanding letter of credit.

(10) *Underpayment of tax due.*—If it is determined that there is a deficiency or underpayment of any tax due pursuant to the election, the Commissioner will issue a notice of deficiency or notice and demand in the amount of the deficiency or underpayment determined, plus any applicable interest and penalties. Assessment and collection of any deficiency or underpayment of tax will be as provided by the Internal Revenue Code and payment of all additional amounts due will be in accordance with the terms specified in any statement of notice and demand sent to the foreign corporation. If the tax is not paid in accordance with the terms of the statement of notice and demand, collection of the deficiency will be made by resorting to the letter of credit before any levy or proceeding in court for collection is instituted against the controlled foreign corporation or its shareholders. However, nothing in paragraph (c)(3)(10) of this section shall be construed to preclude the Secretary's ability to use the jeopardy assessment procedures of sections 6861 through 6864 of the Code. If the letter of credit is drawn upon, it must be reinstated to the level as provided for under the closing agreement within 60 days after the date drawn upon.

(11) *Termination or revocation of election.*— (i) *Termination.*—If a controlled foreign corporation that made the election to treat its related person insurance income as effectively connected income for any taxable year becomes a disqualified corporation, as defined in paragraph (c)(2) of this section, in any subsequent taxable year, the election will not apply to any taxable year beginning after the taxable year in which the corporation becomes a disqualified corporation. If a foreign corporation's election is terminated by virtue of the corporation's becoming a disqualified corpora-

tion, the corporation will be barred from making another election under section 953(c)(3)(C).

(ii) *Revocation with consent.*—The election to treat related person insurance income as effectively connected with the conduct of a trade or business within the United States can be revoked only with the consent of the Commissioner. In order to obtain a revocation, the taxpayer must request a ruling from the Associate Chief Counsel (International). To determine whether a request for revocation should be granted, consideration will be given to all the facts and circumstances. Among the circumstances that will be considered as favorable to a determination to allow revocation of an election will be whether the foreign corporation would qualify for the de minimis ownership exception of paragraph (a)(1) of this section or the de minimis related person insurance exception of paragraph (b)(2) of this section. If after having made an election under paragraph (c) of this section the foreign corporation makes an election under section 953(d) (relating to the election of a foreign insurance company to be treated as a domestic corporation), the election under this paragraph shall be treated as revoked with the Commissioner's consent beginning with the period that the election under section 953(d) is in effect. The revocation of an election is effective for the taxable year indicated by the Commissioner in the consent. Any foreign corporation that receives the consent of the Commissioner to revoke an election may not make a subsequent election for a period of four years from the end of the first taxable year in which the election is not in effect.

(iii) *Unilateral revocation by Commissioner.*—If an electing corporation fails to timely file a return, fails to pay the tax due with respect to related person insurance income that it elects to have taxed as effectively connected income, fails to make the estimated tax payments required by section 6655, or fails to maintain or provide a letter of credit in the appropriate amount, the election may be revoked by the Commissioner for the taxable year in which the electing corporation fails to file a return, pay the tax due, pay the estimated tax, or fails to maintain or provide the appropriate letter of credit or in any subsequent taxable year. If the revocation is made in a taxable year subsequent to the taxable year in which the failure occurs, the Commissioner can make the revocation effective retroactively to the taxable year in which the failure occurred or any subsequent taxable year. Revocation of the election may cause the United States shareholders of the foreign corporation to be liable for subpart F inclusions and make the foreign corporation liable for the unpaid excise tax on premiums under section 4371 for insurance or reinsurance issued by the foreign corporation. Funds obtained under the letter of credit will be applied to the taxes due from the foreign corporation, its shareholders, or both, with respect to related person insurance income. Any foreign corporation (or successor corporation, as defined in paragraph (c)(2)(ii) of this section) the election of which is unilaterally revoked by the Commissioner shall be barred from making another election under section 953(c)(3)(C). [Reg. § 1.953-7.]

CFCs: Insurance Income: After 1986: Election to Expense

Controlled Foreign Corporations: Insurance Income: Tax Years After 1986.—Reproduced below is a proposed amendment to Temporary Reg. § 1.954-1T (Reg. § 1.954-1T was redesignated as Reg. § 4.954-1 by T.D. 8618 on 9/6/95), relating to the election to expense certain depreciable business assets (published in the Federal Register on April 17, 1991).

☐ Par. 4. Section 1.954-1T is amended by revising paragraph (c) to read as follows:

§ 1.954-1T. Foreign base company income; taxable years beginning after December 31, 1986 (Temporary).

* * *

(c) *Computation of net foreign base company income.*—(1) *General rule.*—The net foreign base company income of a controlled foreign corporation is computed by reducing (but not below zero) the amount of gross income in each of the categories of adjusted gross foreign base company income described in paragraph (b)(2) of this section, so as to take into account deductions allocable and apportionable to such income. For purposes of section 954 and this section, expenses must be allocated and apportioned consistent with the allocation and apportionment of expenses for purposes of section 904(d). For purposes of this § 1.954-1T, an item of net foreign base company income must be categorized according to the category of adjusted gross foreign base company income from which it is de-

rived. Thus, an item of net foreign base company income must be categorized as a net item of—

(i) Foreign personal holding company income,

(ii) Foreign base company sales income,

(iii) Foreign base company services income,

(iv) Foreign base company shipping income,

(v) Foreign base company oil related income, or

(vi) Full inclusion foreign base company income.

(2) *Computation of net foreign base company income derived from same country insurance income.*—Deductions relating to foreign base company income derived from insurance, reinsurance, or annuity contracts covering risks located in the country in which the controlled foreign corporation is created or organized shall be allocated and apportioned in accordance with the rules set forth in § 1.953-5.

Controlled Foreign Corporations: Hybrid Branches: Subpart F Income

Controlled Foreign Corporations: Hybrid Branches: Subpart F Income.—Amendments to Reg. §§ 1.954-0 and 1.954-1, relating to the treatment under subpart F of certain transactions involving hybrid branches, are proposed (published in the Federal Register on July 13, 1999) (REG-113909-98).

☐ Par. 3. Section 1.954-0(b) is amended as follows:

1. The entry for § 1.954-1(c)(1)(i) is revised.

2. Entries for § 1.954-1(c)(1)(i)(A) through (c)(1)(i)(E) are added.

3. An entry for § 1.954-2(a)(5) is added.

4. An entry for §1.954-2(a)(6) is added.
The revision and additions read as follows:

§1.954-0. Introduction.

* * *

(b) * * *

§ 1.954-1 Foreign base company income

* * *

(c) * * *

(1) * * *

(i) Deductions.

(A) Deductions against gross foreign base company income.

(B) Special rule for deductible payments to certain non-fiscally transparent entities.

(C) Limitations.

(D) Example.

(E) Effective date.

* * *

☐ Par. 4. Section 1.954-1 is amended as follows: **1.** Paragraphs (c)(1)(i) heading and introductory text and (c)(1)(i)(A) through (c)(1)(i)(D) are redesignated as paragraphs (c)(1)(i)(A) heading and introductory text and (c)(1)(i)(A)(1) through (c)(1)(i)(A)(4), respectively. **2.** A heading for paragraph (c)(1)(i) is added. **3.** Paragraphs (c)(1)(i)(B) through (c)(1))(i)(E) are added. The additions read as follows:

§1.954-1. Foreign base company income

* * *

(c) * * *

(1) * * *

(i) *Deductions.*—(A) *Deductions against gross foreign base company income.*—* * *

(B) *Special rule for deductible payments to certain non-fiscally transparent entities.*—Notwithstanding any other provision of this section, except as provided in paragraph (c)(1)(i)(C) of this section, an expense (including a distributive share of any expense) that would otherwise be allocable under section 954(b)(5) against the subpart F income of a controlled foreign corporation shall not be allocated against subpart F income of the controlled foreign corporation resulting from the payment giving rise to the expense if—

(1) Such expense arises from a payment between the controlled foreign corporation and a partnership in which the controlled foreign corporation is a partner and the partnership is not regarded as fiscally transparent, as defined in §1.954-9(a)(7), by any country in which the controlled foreign corporation does business or has substantial assets; and

(2) The payment from which the expense arises would have reduced foreign tax, under §1.954-9(a)(3), and would have fallen within the tax disparity rule of §1.954-9(a)(5)(iv), if those provisions had been applicable to the payment.

(C) *Limitations.*—Paragraph (c)(1)(i)(B) of this section shall not apply to the extent that the controlled foreign corporation partner has no income against which to allocate the expense, other than its distributive share of a payment described in paragraph (c)(1)(i)(B) of this section. Similarly, to the extent an expense described in paragraph (c)(1)(i)(B) of this section exceeds the controlled

foreign corporation partner's distributive share of the payment from which the expense arises, such excess amount of the expense may reduce subpart F income (other than such payment) to which it is properly allocable or apportionable under section 954(b)(5).

(D) *Example.*—The following example illustrates the application of paragraphs (c)(1)(i)(B) and (C) of this section:

Example. CFC, a controlled foreign corporation in Country A, is a 70 percent partner in partnership P, located in Country B. Country A's tax laws do not classify P as a fiscally transparent entity. The rate of tax in country B is 15 percent of the tax rate in country A. P loans $100 to CFC at a market rate of interest. In year 1, CFC pays P $10 of interest on the loan. The interest payment would have caused the recharacterization rules of §1.954-9 to apply if the payment were made between the entities described in §1.954-9(a)(2). CFC's distributive share of P's interest income is $7, which is foreign personal holding company income to CFC under section 954(c). Under paragraph (c)(1)(i)(B) of this section, $7 of the $10 interest expense may not be allocated against any of CFC's subpart F income. However, to the extent the remaining $3 of interest expense is properly allocable to subpart F income of CFC other than its distributive share of P's interest income, this expense may offset such other subpart F income.

(E) *Effective date.*—Paragraph (c)(1)(i)(B), (C) and (D) of this section shall be applicable for all payments made or accrued in taxable years commencing after [date that is 5 years after publication of the final regulations in the federal register], under hybrid arrangements, unless such payments are made pursuant to an arrangement that would qualify for permanent relief under §1.954-9(a)(2) if made between a controlled foreign corporation and its hybrid branch, in which case the relief afforded under that section shall also be afforded under this section.

* * *

§1.954-2 Foreign personal holding company income.

(a) * * *

(5) Special rules applicable to distributive share of partnership income.

(i) Application of related person exceptions where payment reduces foreign tax of payor.

(ii) Certain other exceptions applicable to foreign personal holding company income. [Reserved]

(iii) Effective date.

(6) Special rules applicable to exceptions from foreign personal holding company income treatment in circumstances involving hybrid branches.

(i) In general.

(ii) Exception where no tax reduction or tax disparity.

(iii) Effective date.

* * *

Foreign Personal Holding Company Income: Foreign Currency Gain or Loss: Exclusion

Foreign Personal Holding Company Income: Foreign Currency Gain or Loss: Exclusion.—Amendments to Reg. §1.954-0, providing guidance on the treatment of foreign currency gain or loss of a controlled foreign corporation under the business needs exclusion from foreign personal holding company income, are proposed (published in the Federal Register on December 19, 2017) (REG-119514-15).

Par. 3. Section 1.954-0(b) is amended by:

1. Redesignating the entry for §1.954-2(g)(2)(ii)(D) as the entry for §1.954-2(g)(2)(ii)(E).

2. Redesignating the entries for §1.954-2(g)(2)(ii)(C), (g)(2)(ii)(C)(1), (g)(2)(ii)(C)(2), (g)(2)(ii)(C)(2)(i), (g)(2)(ii)(C)(2)(ii), and (g)(2)(ii)(C)(2)t(iii) as the entries for §1.954-2(g)(2)(ii)(D), (g)(2)(ii)(D)(1), (g)(2)(ii)(D)(2), (g)(2)(ii)(D)(2)(i), (g)(2)(ii)(D)(2)(ii), and (g)(2)(ii)(D)(2)(iii), respectively.

3. Adding new entries for §1.954-2(g)(2)(ii)(C), (g)(2)(ii)(C)(1), and (g)(2)(ii)(C)(2).

4. Revising the entry for §1.954-2(g)(2)(iii).

The additions and revision read as follows:

§1.954-0. Introduction

* * *

(b) * * *

§ 1.954-2 Foreign personal holding company income.

* * *

(g) * * *

(2) * * *

(ii) * * *

(C) Foreign currency gains and losses arising from a transaction or property that gives rise to both non-subpart F income

and subpart F income or from a bona fide hedging transaction with respect to such a transaction or property.

(1) In general.

(2) Financial statement hedging transaction with respect to the net investment in a qualified business unit.

* * *

(iii) Special rule for foreign currency gain or loss from an interest-bearing liability and bona fide hedges of an interest-bearing liability.

* * *

GILTI: Stock Ownership Determination: Guidance

GILTI: Stock Ownership Determination: Guidance.—Amendments to Reg. §1.954-1, regarding the treatment of domestic partnerships for purposes of determining amounts included in the gross income of their partners with respect to foreign corporations and regarding gross income that is subject to a high rate of tax under the GILTI provisions, are proposed (published in the Federal Register on June 21, 2019) (REG-101828-19).

Par. 6. Section 1.954-1 is amended by:

1. Adding "or" to the end of paragraph (c)(1)(iii)(A)(2)(*ii*).

2. Removing and reserving paragraphs (c)(1)(iii)(A)(2)(*iii*) and (*iv*).

3. Adding paragraphs (c)(1)(iii)(A)(3) and (c)(1)(iv).

4. Removing the language "foreign base company oil related income, as defined in section 954(g), or" in the second sentence of paragraph (d)(1) introductory text.

5. Adding a new sentence after the fourth sentence in paragraph (d)(1) introductory text.

6. Removing the language "imposed by a foreign country or countries" in paragraph (d)(1)(ii).

7. Removing the language "in a chain of corporations through which a distribution is made" in the first sentence in paragraph (d)(2) introductory text.

8. Removing the language "(or deemed paid or accrued)" in paragraph (d)(2)(i).

9. Revising the heading and the first sentence of paragraph (d)(3)(i).

10. Removing the second sentence of paragraph (d)(3)(i).

11. Removing and reserving paragraphs (d)(4)(iii) and (d)(7).

The additions and revisions read as follows:

§1.954-1. Foreign base company income.

* * *

(c) * * *

  (1) * * *

    (iii) * * *

      (A) * * *

        (3) Amount of a single item.—For purposes of paragraph (c)(1)(iii)(A) of this section, the aggregate amount from all transactions that falls within a single separate category (as defined in §1.904-5(a)(4)(v)) and is described in paragraph (c)(1)(iii)(A)(*1*)(*i*) of this section is a single item of income. Similarly, the aggregate amount from all transactions that falls within a single separate category (as defined in §1.904-5(a)(4)(v)) and is described in each one of paragraphs (c)(1)(iii)(A)(*1*)(*ii*) through (c)(1)(iii)(A)(*1*)(*v*) of this section is in each case a separate single item of income. The same principles apply for transactions described in each one of paragraphs (c)(1)(iii)(A)(*2*)(*i*) through (*v*) of this section.

* * *

        (iv) *Treatment of deductions or loss attributable to disqualified basis.*—For purposes of paragraph (c)(1)(i) of this section (and in the case of insurance income, paragraph (a)(6) of this section), in determining the amount of a net item of foreign base company income or insurance income, deductions or loss described in §1.951A-2(c)(5) are not allocated and apportioned to gross foreign base company income or gross insurance income.

(d) * * *

  (1) * * * For rules concerning the application of the high tax exception of sections 954(b)(4) and 951A(c)(2)(A)(i)(III) to tentative gross tested income items, see §1.951A-2(c)(1)(iii) and (c)(6). * * *

* * *

  (3) * * *

    (i) *In general.*—The amount of foreign income taxes paid or accrued by a controlled foreign corporation with respect to a net item of income for purposes of section 954(b)(4) and this paragraph (d) is the U.S. dollar amount of the controlled foreign corporation's current year taxes (as defined in §1.960-1(b)(4)) that are allocated and apportioned under §1.960-1(d)(3)(ii) to the subpart F income group (as defined in §1.960-1(d)(2)(ii)(B)) that corresponds with the net item of income. * * *

* * *

GILTI: Stock Ownership Determination: Guidance

GILTI: Stock Ownership Determination: Guidance.—Amendments to Reg. §1.954-1, regarding the treatment of domestic partnerships for purposes of determining amounts included in the gross income of their partners with respect to foreign corporations and regarding gross income that is subject to a high rate of tax under the GILTI provisions, are proposed (published in the Federal Register on June 21, 2019) (REG-101828-19).

Par. 7. Section 1.954-1, as proposed to be amended at 83 FR 63200 (December 7, 2018), is further amended by:

1. Removing and reserving paragraph (d)(3)(ii).

2. Redesignating paragraphs (h)(1) and (h)(2) as paragraphs (h)(2) and (h)(3), respectively.

3. Adding a new paragraph (h)(1).

4. Removing the language "Paragraphs (d)(3)(i) and (ii)" in newly redesignated paragraph (h)(2) and adding "The last two sentences in paragraph (d)(3)(i)" in its place.

The addition reads as follows:

§1.954-1. Foreign base company income.

* * *

(h) * * *

  (1) *Paragraphs (c)(1)(iii)(A)(3) and (c)(1)(iv) of this section and portion of paragraph (d)(3)(i) of this section.*—Paragraphs (c)(1)(iii)(A)(3) and (c)(1)(iv) of this section and the first sentence of paragraph (d)(3)(i) of this section apply to taxable years of a controlled foreign corporation beginning on or after the date of publication of the Treasury decision adopting these rules as final regulations in the **Federal Register**.

* * *

Allocation and Apportionment of Deductions and Foreign Tax Credit: Guidance

Allocation and Apportionment of Deductions and Foreign Tax Credit: Guidance.—Amendments to Reg. §1.954-1, relating to the allocation and apportionment of deductions and creditable foreign taxes, the definition of financial services income, foreign tax redeterminations, availability of foreign tax credits under the transition tax, and the application of the foreign tax credit limitation to consolidated groups, are proposed (published in the Federal Register on December 17, 2019) (REG-105495-19).

Par. 20. Section 1.954-1 is amended by:

1. In paragraph (c)(1)(i)(C) removing the language "reduced by related person" and adding the language "reduced (but not below zero) by related person" in its place.

2. Adding two sentences to the end of paragraph (d)(3)(iii).

3. Revising paragraph (h)(1).

The revisions and additions read as follows:

§1.954-1. Foreign base company income.

* * *

(d) * * *

  (3) * * *

    (iii) * * * In addition, foreign income taxes that have not been paid or accrued because they are contingent on a future distribution of earnings are not taken into account for purposes of this paragraph (d)(3). If, pursuant to section 905(c) and §1.905-3(b)(2), a redetermination of U.S. tax liability is required to account for the effect of a foreign tax redetermination (as defined in §1.905-3(a)), this paragraph (d) is applied in the adjusted year taking into account the adjusted amount of the redetermined foreign tax.

* * *

(h) * * *

(1) *Paragraph (d)(3) of this section.*—Paragraph (d)(3) of this section applies to taxable years of a controlled foreign corporation ending on or after December 16, 2019. For taxable years of a controlled foreign corporation ending on or after December 4, 2018, but ending before December 16, 2019, see §1.954-1(d)(3) as contained in 26 CFR part 1 revised as of April 1, 2019.

* * *

Controlled Foreign Corporations: Hybrid Branches: Subpart F Income

Controlled Foreign Corporations: Hybrid Branches: Subpart F Income.—Amendments to Reg. §1.954-2, relating to the treatment under subpart F of certain transactions involving hybrid branches, are proposed (published in the Federal Register on July 13, 1999) (REG-113909-98).

☐ Par. 5. In §1-954-2, paragraphs (a)(5) and (a)(6) are added to read as follows:

§1.954-2. Foreign personal holding company income.—(a) * * *

(5) *Special rules applicable to distributive share of partnership income.*—(i) *Application of related person exceptions where payment reduces foreign tax of payor.*—If a partnership receives an item of income that reduced the foreign income tax of the payor (determined under the principles of §1.954-9(a)(3)), to determine the extent to which a controlled foreign corporation's distributive share of such item of income is foreign personal holding company income, the exceptions contained in section 954(c)(3) shall apply only if—

(A)(1) Any such exception would have applied to exclude the income from foreign personal holding company income if the controlled foreign corporation had earned the income directly (determined by testing, with reference to such controlled foreign corporation, whether an entity is a related person, within the meaning of section 954(d)(3), or is organized under the laws of, or uses property in, the foreign country in which the controlled foreign corporation is created or organized); and

(2) The distributive share of such income is not in respect of a payment made by the controlled foreign corporation to the partnership; and

(B)(1) The partnership is created or organized, and uses a substantial part of its assets in a trade or business in the country under the laws of which the controlled foreign corporation is created or organized (determined under the principles of paragraph (b)(4) of this section);

(2) The partnership is regarded as fiscally transparent, as defined in §1.954-9(a)(7), by all countries under the laws of which the controlled foreign corporation is created or organized or has substantial assets; or

(3) The income is taxed in the year when earned at an effective rate of tax (determined under the principles of §1.954-1(d)(2)) that is not less than 90 percent of, and not more than five percentage points less than, the effective rate of tax that would have applied to such income under the laws of the country in which the controlled foreign corporation is created or organized if such income were earned directly by the controlled foreign corporation partner from local sources.

(ii) *Certain other exceptions applicable to foreign personal holding company income.*—[Reserved].

(iii) *Effective date.*—Paragraph (a)(5)(i) of this section shall apply to all amounts paid or accrued in taxable years commencing after [date that is 5 years after publication of the final regulations in the federal register], under hybrid arrangements, unless such payments are made pursuant to an arrangement which would qualify for permanent relief under §1.954-9(c)(2) if made between a controlled foreign corporation and its hybrid branch, in which case the relief afforded under that section shall also be afforded under this section.

(6) *Special rules applicable to exceptions from foreign personal holding company income treatment in circumstances involving hybrid branches.*—(i) *In general.*—In the case of a payment between a controlled foreign corporation (or its hybrid branch, as defined in §1.954-9(a)(6)) and the hybrid branch of a related controlled foreign corporation, the exceptions contained in section 954(c)(3) shall apply only if the payment would have qualified for the exception if the payor were a separate controlled foreign corporation created or organized in the jurisdiction where foreign tax is reduced and the payee were a separate controlled foreign corporation created or organized under the laws of the jurisdiction in which the payment is subject to tax (other than a withholding tax).

(ii) *Exception where no tax reduction or tax disparity.*—Paragraph (a)(6)(i) of this section shall not apply unless the payment would have reduced foreign tax, under §1.954-9(a)(3), and fallen within the tax disparity rule of §1.954-9(a)(5)(iv) if those provisions had been applicable to the payment.

(iii) *Effective date.*—The rules of this section shall apply to all amounts paid or accrued in taxable years commencing after [date that is 5 years after publication of the final regulations in the federal register], under hybrid arrangements, unless such payments are made pursuant to an arrangement which would qualify for permanent relief under §1.954-9(c)(2) if made between a controlled foreign corporation and its hybrid branch, in which case the relief afforded under that section shall also be afforded under this section.

Section 1256 Contracts: Swap Exclusions

Section 1256 Contracts: Swap Exclusions.—Amendment to Reg. §1.954-2, providing guidance on the category of swaps and similar agreements that are within the scope of Code Sec. 1256(b)(2)(B), are proposed (published in the Federal Register on September 16, 2011) (REG-111283-11).

☐ Par. 5. Section 1.954-2 is amended by:

1. Revising paragraph (h)(3)(i).
2. Adding paragraph (h)(3)(iii).

The revision and addition read as follows:

§1.954-2. Foreign personal holding company income.

* * *

(3) *Notional principal contracts.*—(i) In general.—Income equivalent to interest includes income from notional principal contracts (as defined in §1.446-3(c)) denominated in the functional currency of the taxpayer (or a qualified business unit of the taxpayer, as defined in section 989(a)), the value of which is determined solely by reference to interest rates or interest rate indices, to the extent that the income from such transactions accrues on or after August 14, 1989.

* * *

(iii) *Effective/applicability date.*—The rules of paragraph (h)(3) of this section apply to notional principal contracts as defined in §1.446-3(c) that are entered into on or after the date of publication of a Treasury decision adopting these rules as final regulations in the **Federal Register**. Section 1.954-2(h)(3) as contained in 26 CFR part 1 revised April 1, 2011, continues to apply to notional principal contracts entered into before the date of publication of a Treasury decision adopting these rules as final regulations in the **Federal Register**.

* * *

Foreign Personal Holding Company Income: Foreign Currency Gain or Loss: Exclusion

Foreign Personal Holding Company Income: Foreign Currency Gain or Loss: Exclusion.—Amendments to Reg. §1.954-2, providing guidance on the treatment of foreign currency gain or loss of a controlled foreign corporation under the business needs exclusion from foreign personal holding company income, are proposed (published in the Federal Register on December 19, 2017) (REG-119514-15).

Par. 4. Section 1.954-2 is amended by:

1. Adding a sentence after the first sentence in paragraph (a)(4)(ii)(A).
2. Redesignating paragraph (g)(2)(ii)(D) as paragraph (g)(2)(ii)(E).
3. Redesignating paragraph (g)(2)(ii)(C) as paragraph (g)(2)(ii)(D).

4. In newly redesignated paragraph (g)(2)(ii)(D)(2)(*i*), removing "paragraph (g)(2)(ii)(C)" and adding "paragraph (g)(2)(ii)(D)" in its place and removing "paragraph (g)(2)(ii)(C)(*1*)" and adding "paragraph (g)(2)(ii)(D)(*1*)" in its place.

5. In newly redesignated paragraph (g)(2)(ii)(D)(2)(*ii*), removing "paragraph (g)(2)(ii)(C)(2)(*i*)" and adding "paragraph (g)(2)(ii)(D)(2)(*i*)" each place it appears.

6. In newly redesignated paragraph (g)(2)(ii)(D)(2)(*iii*), removing "paragraph (g)(2)(ii)(C)(2)" and adding "paragraph (g)(2)(ii)(D)(2)" in its place.

7. Adding new paragraph (g)(2)(ii)(C).

8. Revising paragraph (g)(2)(iii).

9. Revising paragraph (g)(3)(iii).

10. Revising paragraph (g)(4)(iii).

11. Adding two sentences after the third sentence in paragraph (i)(2).

The additions and revisions read as follows:

§1.954-2. Foreign personal holding company income.

(a) * * *

(4) * * *

(ii) * * *

(A) * * * Additionally, the acquisition of a debt instrument by a controlled foreign corporation may be treated as a bona fide hedging transaction with respect to an interest-bearing liability of the controlled foreign corporation, provided that the acquisition of the debt instrument has the effect of managing the controlled foreign corporation's exchange rate risk with respect to the liability within the meaning of §1.1221-2(c)(4) and (d), determined without regard to §1.1221-2(d)(5), and otherwise meets the requirements of paragraph (a)(4)(ii) of this section. * * *

* * *

(g) * * *

(2) * * *

(ii) * * *

(C) *Foreign currency gains and losses arising from a transaction or property that gives rise to both non-subpart F income and subpart F income or from a bona fide hedging transaction with respect to such a transaction or property.*—(*1*) *In general.*—If a foreign currency gain or loss would be directly related to the business needs of the controlled foreign corporation pursuant to paragraph (g)(2)(ii)(B)(*1*) or (2) of this section except that it arises from a transaction or property that gives rise, or is reasonably expected to give rise, to both non-subpart F income and subpart F income (other than foreign currency gain or loss), or from a bona fide hedging transaction with respect to such a transaction or property, the amount of foreign currency gain or loss that is allocable to non-subpart F income under this paragraph (g)(2)(ii)(C)(*1*) is directly related to the business needs of the controlled foreign corporation. The amount of foreign currency gain or loss arising from a transaction or property described in this paragraph (g)(2)(ii)(C)(*1*), or from a bona fide hedging transaction with respect to such a transaction or property, that is allocable to non-subpart F income equals the product of the total amount of foreign currency gain or loss arising from the transaction or property and the ratio of non-subpart F income (other than foreign currency gain or loss) that the transaction or property gives rise to, or is reasonably expected to give rise to, to the total income that the transaction or property gives rise to, or is reasonably expected to give rise to. However, none of the foreign currency gain or loss arising from property that does not give rise to income (as defined in paragraph (e)(3) of this section), or from a bona fide hedging transaction with respect to such property, is allocable to non-subpart F income.

(*2*) *Financial statement hedging transaction with respect to a qualified business unit.*—If foreign currency gain or loss arises from a financial statement hedging transaction (as defined in this paragraph (g)(2)(ii)(C)(*2*)) with respect to a qualified business unit (as defined in §1.989(a)-1) (QBU) of a controlled foreign corporation that is not treated as an entity separate from the controlled foreign corporation for federal income tax purposes, either because it is a branch or division of the controlled foreign corporation or because it is a business entity that is disregarded as separate from its owner under §301.7701-3 of this chapter, the amount of the qualifying portion (as determined under this paragraph (g)(2)(ii)(C)(*2*)) of foreign currency gain or loss that is allocable to non-subpart F income under this paragraph (g)(2)(ii)(C)(*2*) is directly related to the business needs of the controlled foreign corporation. Generally, the controlled foreign corporation must allocate the qualifying portion of foreign currency gain or loss arising from the financial statement hedging transaction between subpart F income and non-subpart F income in the same proportion as it would characterize gain or loss determined under section 987 as subpart F income and non-subpart F income under the principles of §1.987-6(b). A *financial statement hedging transaction* is a transaction that is entered into by a CFC for the purpose of managing exchange rate risk with respect to part or all of that CFC's net investment in a QBU that is included in the consolidated financial statements of a United States shareholder of the CFC (or a corporation that directly or indirectly owns such United States shareholder). The qualifying portion of foreign currency gain or loss is the amount

of foreign currency gain or loss arising from a financial statement hedging transaction that is properly accounted for under U.S. generally accepted accounting principles as a cumulative foreign currency translation adjustment to shareholders' equity.

* * *

(iii) *Special rule for foreign currency gain or loss from an interest-bearing liability and bona fide hedges of an interest-bearing liability.*—Except as provided in paragraph (g)(2)(ii)(D)(2) or (g)(5)(iv) of this section, foreign currency gain or loss arising from an interest-bearing liability is characterized as subpart F income and non-subpart F income in the same manner that interest expense associated with the liability would be allocated and apportioned between subpart F income and non-subpart F income under §§1.861-9T and 1.861-12T. Likewise, foreign currency gain or loss arising from a bona fide hedging transaction entered into by the controlled foreign corporation that has the effect of managing exchange rate risk with respect to an interest-bearing liability that is not subject to paragraph (g)(2)(ii)(D)(2) (certain interest-bearing liabilities treated as dealer property) or (g)(5)(iv) (gain or loss allocated under §1.861-9) of this section is characterized as subpart F income and non-subpart F income in the same manner that interest expense associated with the interest-bearing liability would be allocated and apportioned between subpart F income and non-subpart F income under §§1.861-9T and 1.861-12T. Paragraph (g)(2)(ii) of this section does not apply to any foreign currency gain or loss described in this paragraph (g)(2)(iii).

(3) * * *

(iii) *Revocation of election.*—This election is effective for the taxable year of the controlled foreign corporation for which it is made and all subsequent taxable years of such corporation unless revoked by the Commissioner or the controlling United States shareholders (as defined in §1.964-1(c)(5)) of the controlled foreign corporation. The controlling United States shareholders of a controlled foreign corporation may revoke such corporation's election at any time. If an election has been revoked under this paragraph (g)(3)(iii), a new election under paragraph (g)(3) of this section cannot be made until the sixth taxable year following the year in which the previous election was revoked, and such subsequent election cannot be revoked until the sixth taxable year following the year in which the subsequent election was made. The controlling United States shareholders revoke an election on behalf of a controlled foreign corporation by filing a statement that clearly indicates such election has been revoked with their original or amended income tax returns for the taxable year of such United States shareholders ending with or within the taxable year of the controlled foreign corporation for which the election is revoked.

* * *

(4) * * *

(iii) *Revocation of election.*—This election is effective for the taxable year of the controlled foreign corporation for which it is made and all subsequent taxable years of such corporation unless revoked by the Commissioner or the controlling United States shareholders (as defined in §1.964-1(c)(5)) of the controlled foreign corporation. The controlling United States shareholders of a controlled foreign corporation may revoke such corporation's election at any time. If an election has been revoked under this paragraph (g)(4)(iii), a new election under paragraph (g)(4) of this section cannot be made until the sixth taxable year following the year in which the previous election was revoked, and such subsequent election cannot be revoked until the sixth taxable year following the year in which the subsequent election was made. The controlling United States shareholders revoke an election on behalf of a controlled foreign corporation by filing a statement that clearly indicates such election has been revoked with their original or amended income tax returns for the taxable year of such United States shareholders ending with or within the taxable year of the controlled foreign corporation for which the election is revoked.

* * *

(i) * * *

(2) *Other paragraphs.*—* * * The second sentence of paragraph (a)(4)(ii)(A), paragraph (g)(2)(ii)(C)(1), and the second sentence of paragraph (g)(2)(iii) apply to a bona fide hedging transaction entered into on or after the date the proposed regulations are published as final regulations in the *Federal Register*. Paragraphs (g)(2)(ii)(C) (other

paragraph (g)(2)(ii)(C)(1), insofar as it applies to a bona fide hedging transaction), (g)(3)(iii), and (g)(4)(iii) of this section apply to taxable years of controlled foreign corporations ending on or after the date that these regulations are published as final regulations in the *Federal Register*.

Allocation and Apportionment of Deductions and Foreign Tax Credit: Guidance

Allocation and Apportionment of Deductions and Foreign Tax Credit: Guidance.—Amendments to Reg. §1.954-2, relating to the allocation and apportionment of deductions and creditable foreign taxes, the definition of financial services income, foreign tax redeterminations, availability of foreign tax credits under the transition tax, and the application of the foreign tax credit limitation to consolidated groups, are proposed (published in the Federal Register on December 17, 2019) (REG-105495-19).

Par. 21. Section 1.954-2 is amended by:

1. Removing the text "and" from paragraph (h)(2)(i)(H).

2. Redesignating paragraph (h)(2)(i)(I) as paragraph (h)(2)(i)(J).

3. Adding a new paragraph (h)(2)(i)(I).

4. Adding a sentence to the end of paragraph (i)(2).

The additions read as follows:

§1.954-2. Foreign personal holding company income.

* * *

(h) * * *

  (2) * * *

   (i) * * *

    (I) Any guaranteed payments for the use of capital under section 707(c); and

* * *

(i) * * *

  (2) * * * Paragraph (h)(2)(i)(I) of this section applies to taxable years of controlled foreign corporations ending on or after December 16, 2019, and to taxable years of United States shareholders in which or with which such taxable years end.

Controlled Foreign Corporations: Hybrid Branches: Subpart F Income

Controlled Foreign Corporations: Hybrid Branches: Subpart F Income.—Reg. §1.954-9, relating to the treatment under subpart F of certain transactions involving hybrid branches, is proposed (published in the Federal Register on July 13, 1999) (REG-113909-98).

☐ Par. 6. Section 1.954-9 is added to read as follows:

§1.954-9. Hybrid branches.—(a) *Subpart F income arising from certain payments involving hybrid branches.*—(1) *Payment causing foreign tax reduction gives rise to additional subpart F income.*—The non-subpart F income of a controlled foreign corporation will be recharacterized as subpart F income, to the extent provided in paragraph (a)(5) of this section, if—

(i) A hybrid branch payment, as defined in paragraph (a)(6) of this section, is made between the entities described in paragraph (a)(2) of this section;

(ii) The hybrid branch payment reduces foreign tax, as determined under paragraph (a)(3) of this section; and

(iii) The hybrid branch payment is treated as falling within a category of foreign personal holding company income under the rules of paragraph (a)(4) of this section.

(2) *Hybrid branch payment between certain entities.*—(i) *In general.*—Paragraph (a)(1) of this section shall apply to hybrid branch payments between—

(A) A controlled foreign corporation and its hybrid branch;

(B) Hybrid branches of a controlled foreign corporation;

(C) A partnership in which a controlled foreign corporation is a partner (either directly or through one or more branches or other partnerships) and a hybrid branch of the partnership; or

(D) Hybrid branches of a partnership in which a controlled foreign corporation is a partner (either directly or through one or more branches or other partnerships).

(ii) *Hybrid branch payment involving partnership.*—(A) *Fiscally transparent partnership.*—To the extent of the controlled foreign corporation's proportionate share of a hybrid branch payment, the rules of paragraphs (a)(3), (4) and (5) of this section shall be applied by treating the hybrid branch payment between the partnership and the hybrid branch as if it were made directly between the controlled foreign corporation and the hybrid branch, or as if the hybrid branches of the partnership were hybrid branches of the controlled foreign corporation, if the hybrid branch payment is made between—

(1) A fiscally transparent partnership in which a controlled foreign corporation is a partner (either directly or through one or more branches or other fiscally transparent partnerships) and the partnership's hybrid branch; or

(2) Hybrid branches of a fiscally transparent partnership in which a controlled foreign corporation is a partner (either directly or through one or more branches or other fiscally transparent partnerships).

(B) *Non-fiscally transparent partnership.*—To the extent of the controlled foreign corporation's proportionate share of a hybrid branch payment, the rules of paragraphs (a)(3) and (4) and (a)(5)(iv)

of this section shall be applied to the non-fiscally transparent partnership as if it were the controlled foreign corporation, if the hybrid branch payment is made between—

(1) A non-fiscally transparent partnership in which a controlled foreign corporation is a partner (either directly or through one or more branches or other partnerships) and the partnership's hybrid branch; or

(2) Hybrid branches of a non-fiscally transparent partnership in which a controlled foreign corporation is a partner (either directly or through one or more branches or other partnerships).

(C) *Examples.*—The following examples illustrate the application of this paragraph (a)(2)(ii):

Example 1. CFC, a controlled foreign corporation in Country A, is a 90 percent partner in partnership P, which is treated as fiscally transparent under the laws of Country A. P has a hybrid branch, BR, in Country B. P makes an interest payment of $100 to BR. Under Country A law, CFC's 90 percent share of the payment reduces CFC's Country A income tax. Under paragraph (a)(2)(ii)(A) of this section, the recharacterization rules of this section are applied by treating the payment as if made by CFC to BR. Ninety dollars of CFC's non-subpart F income, to the extent available, and subject to the earnings and profits and tax rate limitations of paragraph (a)(5) of this section, is recharacterized as subpart F income.

Example 2. CFC, a controlled foreign corporation in country A, is a 90 percent partner in partnership P, which is treated as fiscally transparent under the laws of Country A. P has two branches in Country B, BR1 and BR2. BR1 is treated as fiscally transparent under the laws of Country A. BR2 is a hybrid branch. BR1 makes an interest payment of $100 to BR2. Under paragraph (a)(2)(ii)(A) of this section, the payment by BR1, the fiscally transparent branch, is treated as a payment by P, and the deemed payment by P, a fiscally transparent partnership, is treated as made by CFC. Under Country A law, CFC's 90 percent share of BR1's payment reduces CFC's Country A income tax. Ninety dollars of CFC's non-subpart F income, to the extent available, and subject to the earnings and profits and tax rate limitations of paragraph (a)(5) of this section, is recharacterized as subpart F income.

(3) *Application when payment reduces foreign tax.*—For purposes of paragraph (a)(1) of this section, a hybrid branch payment reduces foreign tax when the foreign tax imposed on the income of the payor, or any person that is a related person with respect to the payor (as determined under the principles of section 954(d)(3)), is less than the foreign tax that would have been imposed on such income had the hybrid branch payment not been made, or the hybrid branch payment creates or increases a loss or deficit or other tax attribute which may be carried back or forward to reduce the foreign income tax of the payor or any owner in another year (determined by taking into account any refund of such tax made to the payor, payee or any other person).

(4) *Hybrid branch payment that is included within a category of foreign personal holding company income.*—(i) *In general.*—For purposes of paragraph (a)(1) of this section, whether the hybrid branch payment is treated as income included within a category of foreign personal holding company income is determined by treating a hybrid branch that is either the payor or recipient of the hybrid branch payment as a separate wholly-owned subsidiary corporation of the controlled foreign corporation that is incorporated in the jurisdiction under the laws of which such hybrid branch is created, organized for foreign law purposes, or has substantial assets. Thus, the hybrid branch payment will be treated as included within a category of foreign personal holding company income if, taking into account any specific exceptions for that category, the payment would be included within a category of foreign personal holding company income if the branch or branches were treated as separately incorporated for U.S. tax purposes.

(ii) *Extent to which controlled foreign corporation and hybrid branches treated as separate entities.*—For purposes of this section, other than the determination under paragraph (a)(4)(i) of this section, a controlled foreign corporation and its hybrid branch, a partnership and its hybrid branch, or hybrid branches shall not be treated as separate entities. Thus, for example, if a controlled foreign corporation, including all of its hybrid branches, has an overall deficit in earnings and profits to which section 952(c) applies, the limitation of such section on the amount includible in the subpart F income of such corporation will apply. Similarly, for purposes of applying the de minimis and full inclusion rules of section 954(b)(3), a controlled foreign corporation and its hybrid branch, or hybrid branches shall not be treated as separate corporations. Further, a hybrid branch payment that would reduce foreign personal holding company income under section 954(b)(5) if made between two separate entities will not create an expense if made between a controlled foreign corporation and its hybrid branch, a partnership and its hybrid branch, or hybrid branches.

(5) *Recharacterization of income attributable to current earnings and profits as subpart F income.*—(i) *General rule.*—Non-subpart F income of a controlled foreign corporation in an amount equal to the excess of earnings and profits of the controlled foreign corporation for the taxable year over subpart F income, as defined in section 952(a), will be recharacterized as subpart F income under paragraph (a)(1) of this section only to the extent provided under paragraphs (a)(5)(ii) through (vi) of this section.

(ii) *Subpart F income.*—For purposes of determining the excess of current earnings and profits over subpart F income under paragraph (a)(1) of this section, the amount of subpart F income is determined before the application of the rules of this section but after the application of the rules of sections 952(c) and 954(b). Further, such amount is determined by treating the controlled foreign corporation and all of its hybrid branches as a single corporation.

(iii) *Recharacterization limited to gross amount of hybrid branch payment.*—(A) *In general.*—The amount recharacterized as subpart F income under paragraph (a)(1) of this section is limited to the amount of the hybrid branch payment.

(B) *Exception for duplicative payments.*—[Reserved].

(iv) *Tax disparity rule.*—(A) *In general.*—Paragraph (a)(1) of this section will apply only if the hybrid branch payment falls within the tax disparity rule. The hybrid branch payment falls within the tax disparity rule if it is taxed in the year when earned at an effective rate of tax that is less than 90 percent of, and at least 5 percentage points less than, the hypothetical effective rate of tax imposed on the hybrid branch payment, as determined under paragraph (a)(5)(iv)(B) of this section.

(B) *Hypothetical effective rate of tax.*—(1) *In general.*—The hypothetical effective rate of tax imposed on the hybrid branch payment is—

(i) For the taxable year of the payor in which the hybrid branch payment is made, the amount of income taxes that would have been paid or accrued by the payor if the hybrid branch payment had not been made, less the amount of income taxes paid or accrued by the payor; divided by

(ii) The amount of the hybrid branch payment.

(2) *Hypothetical effective rate of tax when hybrid branch payment causes or increases loss or deficit.*—If the hybrid branch payment causes or increases a loss or deficit of the payor for foreign tax purposes, and such loss or deficit can be carried forward or back, the hypothetical effective rate of tax imposed on the hybrid branch payment is the effective rate of tax that would be imposed on the taxable income of the payor for the year in which the payment is made if the payor's taxable income were equal to the amount of the hybrid branch payment.

(C) *Examples.*—The application of this paragraph (a)(5)(iv) is illustrated by the following examples:

Example 1. In 2006, CFC organized in Country A had net income of $60 from manufacturing for Country A tax purposes. It also had a branch (BR) in Country B. BR is a hybrid entity under paragraph (a)(1) of this section. CFC made a payment of $40 to BR, which was a hybrid branch payment under paragraph (a)(6) of this section, and was treated by CFC as a deductible payment for Country A tax purposes. CFC paid $30 of Country A taxes in 2006. It would have paid $50 of Country A taxes without the deductible payment. Country A did not impose any withholding tax on the $40 payment to BR. Country B also did not impose a tax on the $40 received by BR. Therefore, the effective rate of tax on that payment is 0%. Furthermore, the hypothetical effective rate of tax on the $40 hybrid branch payment is 50% ($50 − $30/$40). The effective rate of tax (0%) is less than 90% of, and more than 5 percentage points less than, this hypothetical rate of tax of 50%. As a result, the $40 hybrid branch payment falls within the tax disparity rule of this paragraph (a)(5)(iv).

Example 2. Assume the same facts as in *Example 1*, except that CFC has a loss of $100 for the year for Country A tax purposes. Under Country A law, CFC can carry the loss forward for use in subsequent years. CFC paid no Country A taxes in 2006. The rate of tax in Country A is graduated from 20% to 50%. If the $40 hybrid branch payment were the only item of taxable income of CFC, Country A would have imposed tax at an effective rate of 30%. The effective rate of tax (0%) is less than 90% of, and more than 5 percentage points less than, the hypothetical effective rate of tax (30%) imposed on the hybrid branch payment. As a result, the $40 hybrid branch payment falls within the tax disparity rule of this paragraph (a)(5)(iv).

Example 3. Assume the same facts as in *Example 1*, except that Country B imposes tax on the $40 hybrid payment to BR at an effective rate of 50%. The effective rate of 50% is equal to the hypothetical effective rate of tax. As a result, the hybrid branch payment does not fall within the tax disparity rule of this paragraph (a)(5)(iv) and, thus, the recharacterization rules of paragraph (a)(1) of this section do not apply. See also the special high tax exception of paragraph (a)(5)(v) of this section.

(v) *Special high tax exception.*—(A) *In general.*—Paragraph (a)(1) of this section shall not apply if the non-subpart F income that would be recharacterized as subpart F income under this section was subject to foreign income taxes imposed by a foreign country or countries at an effective rate that is greater than 90 percent of the maximum rate of tax specified in section 11 for the taxable year of the controlled foreign corporation.

(B) *Effective rate of tax.*—The effective rate of tax imposed on the non-subpart F income that would be recharacterized as subpart F income under this section is determined under the principles of §1.954-1(d)(2) and (3). See paragraph (b) of this section for the application of section 960 to amounts recharacterized as subpart F income under this section.

(vi) *No carryback or carryforward of amounts in excess of current year earnings and profits limitation.*—To the extent that some or all of the amount required to be recharacterized under this section is not recharacterized as subpart F income because the hybrid branch payment exceeds the amount that can be recharacterized, as determined under paragraph (a)(5)(i) of this section, this excess shall not be carried back or forward to another year.

(6) *Definitions for this section.*—For purposes of this section:

(i) *Arrangement.*—shall mean any agreement to pay interest, rents, royalties or similar amounts. It shall also include the declaration and payment of a dividend (but not an agreement or undertaking to pay future, unspecified dividends). An arrangement shall not, however, include the mere formation or acquisition (or similar event) of a hybrid branch that is intended to become a party to an arrangement.

(ii) *Entity.*—means any person that is treated by the United States or any jurisdiction as other than an individual.

(iii) *Hybrid branch.*—means an entity that—

(A) Is disregarded as an entity separate from its owner for federal tax purposes and is owned (including ownership through branches) by either a controlled foreign corporation or a partnership in which a controlled foreign corporation is a partner (either directly or indirectly through one or more branches or partnerships);

(B) Is treated as fiscally transparent by the United States; and

(C) Is treated as non-fiscally transparent by the country in which the payor entity, any owner of a fiscally-transparent payor entity, the controlled foreign corporation, or any intermediary partnership is created, organized or has substantial assets.

(iv) Hybrid branch payment.—means the gross amount of any payment (including any accrual) which, under the tax laws of any foreign jurisdiction to which the payor is subject, is regarded as a payment between two separate entities but which, under U.S. income tax principles, is not income to the recipient because it is between two parts of a single entity.

(7) Fiscally transparent and non-fiscally transparent.—For purposes of this section an entity shall be treated as fiscally transparent with respect to an interest holder of the entity, if such interest holder is required, under the laws of any jurisdiction to which it is subject, to take into account separately, on a current basis, such interest holder's share of all items which, if separately taken into account by such interest holder, would result in an income tax liability for the interest holder in such jurisdiction different from that which would result if the interest holder did not take the share of such items into account separately. A non-fiscally transparent entity is an entity that is not fiscally transparent under this paragraph (a)(7).

(b) Application of section 960.—For purposes of determining the amount of taxes deemed paid under section 960, the amount of non-subpart F income recharacterized as subpart F income under this section shall be treated as attributable to income in separate categories, as defined in § 1.904-5(a)(1), in proportion to the ratio of non-subpart F income in each such category to the total amount of non-subpart F income of the controlled foreign corporation for the taxable year.

(c) Effective dates.—(1) *In general.*—This section shall be applicable for all amounts paid or accrued in taxable years commencing after [date that is 5 years after publication of the final regulations in the federal register], under hybrid arrangements, except as otherwise provided.

(2) Permanent relief.—(i) *In general.*—This section shall not apply to any payments made under hybrid arrangements entered into before June 19, 1998. This exception shall be permanent so long as the arrangement is not substantially modified, within the meaning of paragraph (c)(2)(ii) of this section, on or after June 19, 1998.

(ii) Substantial modification.—(A) *In general.*—Substantial modification of a hybrid arrangement includes—

(1) The expansion of the hybrid arrangement (other than de minimis expansion);

(2) A more than 50% change in the U.S. ownership (direct or indirect) of any entity that is a party to the hybrid arrangement, other than—

(i) A transfer of ownership of such party within a controlled group determined under section 1563(a), without regard to section 1563(a)(4); or

(ii) A change in ownership of the entire controlled group (determined under section 1563(a), without regard to section 1563(a)(4)) of which such party is a member;

(3) Any measure taken by a party to the arrangement (or any related party) that materially increases the tax benefit of the hybrid arrangement, regardless of whether such measure alters the legal relationship between the parties to the arrangement. For example, in the case of a hybrid branch payment determined with reference to a percentage of sales, a growth in the amount of the hybrid branch payment (and, thus, the tax benefit) caused by a growth of sales will not, in general, be a substantial modification. However, in the case of a significant sales growth resulting from a transfer of assets by a related party, that transfer would be a measure which materially increased the benefit of the arrangement, and that arrangement would be deemed to have been substantially modified.

(B) Transactions not treated as substantial modification.—Substantial modification of a hybrid arrangement does not include—

(1) The daily reissuance of a demand loan by operation of law;

(2) The renewal of a loan, license or rental agreement on the same terms and conditions if—

(i) The renewal occurs pursuant to the terms of the agreement and without more than a de minimis amount of action of any party thereto;

(ii) As contemplated by the original agreement, the same parties agree to renew the agreement without modification; or

(iii) The renewal occurs solely by reason of a subsequent drawdown under a grandfathered master credit facility agreement;

(3) The renewal of a loan, license, or rental agreement by the same parties on terms which do not increase the tax benefit of the arrangement (other than a de minimis increase);

(4) The making of payments under a license agreement in respect of copyrights or patents (or know-how associated with such copyrights or patents), not in existence at the time the agreement was entered into, but only where the development of such property was anticipated by the agreement, and such property is substantially derived from (or otherwise incorporates substantial features of) copyrights and patents (or know-how associated with such copyrights or patents) in existence at the time of, and covered under, the original agreement;

(5) A final transfer pricing adjustment made by the taxation authorities of the jurisdiction in which the tax reduction occurs, so long as such adjustment would not have been a substantial valuation misstatement (as defined in section 6662(e)(1)(B)) if the adjustment had been made by the Internal Revenue Service; or

(6) A de minimis periodic adjustment by the parties to the arrangement made annually (or more frequently) to conform the payments to the requirements of section 482. [Reg. § 1.954-9.]

Foreign Corporations: Limitation on Deduction for Dividends

Foreign Corporations: Limitation on Deduction for Dividends.—Reg. § 1.954(c)(6)-1, limiting the dividends received deduction available for certain dividends received from current or former controlled foreign corporations, is proposed (published in the Federal Register on June 18, 2019) (REG-106282-18).

Par. 3. Section 1.954(c)(6)-1 is added to read as follows:

§ 1.954(c)(6)-1. Certain cases in which section 954(c)(6) exception not available.—[The text of proposed § 1.954(c)(6)-1 is the same as the text of § 1.954(c)(6)-1T as added by T.D. 9865].

GILTI: Stock Ownership Determination: Guidance

GILTI: Stock Ownership Determination: Guidance.—Amendments to Reg. § 1.956-1, regarding the treatment of domestic partnerships for purposes of determining amounts included in the gross income of their partners with respect to foreign corporations and regarding gross income that is subject to a high rate of tax under the GILTI provisions, are proposed (published in the Federal Register on June 21, 2019) (REG-101828-19).

Par. 8. Section 1.956-1, as amended May 23, 2019, at 84 FR 23717, effective July 22, 2019, is further amended by revising the first sentence of paragraph (g)(4) to read as follows:

§ 1.956-1. Shareholder's pro rata share of the average of the amounts of United States property held by a controlled foreign corporation.

* * *

(g) * * *

(4) Paragraphs (a)(2) and (3) of this section apply to taxable years of controlled foreign corporations beginning on or after July 22, 2019, and to taxable years of a United States shareholder in which or with which such taxable years of the controlled foreign corporations end, but the last sentence of paragraph (a)(2)(i) and paragraphs (a)(2)(iii) and (a)(3)(iv) of this section do not apply to taxable years of controlled foreign corporations beginning on or after the date of publication of the Treasury decision adopting these rules as final regulations in the **Federal Register**, and to taxable years of a United States shareholder in which or with which such taxable years of the controlled foreign corporations end. * * *

* * *

CFCs: Earnings and Profits: Shareholder's Share

Controlled Foreign Corporations: Investment of Earnings in U.S. Property: Related Person Factoring Income.—Amendments to Temporary Reg. §§ 1.956-1T and 1.956-2T, relating to the treatment of related person factoring income, are proposed (published in the Federal Register on June 14, 1988). Amendments to Reg. §§ 1.956-1(b)(4), 1.956-2(d)(2) and 1.956-3(b)(2)(ii) withdrawn by REG-122387-16 on November 3, 2016; Temporary Reg. § 1.956-3T adopted by T.D. 9792 on November 2, 2016.

§1.956-1. **Shareholder's pro rata share of a controlled foreign corporation's increase in earnings invested in United States property**.

§1.956-2. **Definition of United States property**.

Notional Principal Contracts: Nonperiodic Payments: Swaps

Notional Principal Contracts: Nonperiodic Payments: Swaps.—Amendments to Reg. §1.956-2, providing that, subject to certain exceptions, a notional principal contract with a nonperiodic payment, regardless of whether it is significant, must be treated as two separate transactions consisting of one or more loans and an on-market, level payment swap, are proposed (published in the Federal Register on May 8, 2015) (REG-102656-15; REG-107548-11).

Par. 3. Section 1.956-2 is amended by revising paragraphs (b)(1)(xi) and (f) to read as follows:

§1.956-2. **Definition of United States property**.
* * *

(b)(1)(xi) [The text of this proposed amendment is the same as the text of §1.956-2T(b)(1)(xi) as added by T.D. 9719].

* * *

(f) [The text of this proposed amendment is the same as the text of §1.956-2T(f) as added by T.D. 9719].

United States Property: Controlled Foreign Corporations: Partnerships with Special Allocations

United States Property: Controlled Foreign Corporations: Partnerships with Special Allocations.—Amendments to Reg. §1.956-4, regarding the determination of the amount of United States property treated as held by a controlled foreign corporation (CFC) through a partnership, are proposed (published in the Federal Register on November 3, 2016) (corrected December 28, 2016) (REG-114734-16).

Par. 2. Section 1.956-4 is amended by:
1. Revising paragraph (b)(2)(ii).
2. Adding paragraph (b)(2)(iii).
3. Adding a sentence at the end of paragraph (i) of *Example 2* of paragraph (b)(3).
4. Revising paragraph (ii) of *Example 2* of paragraph (b)(3).
5. Revising *Example 3* of paragraph (b)(3).
6. Adding *Example 4* to paragraph (b)(3).
7. Revising paragraph (f)(1).
The revisions and additions read as follows:

§1.956-4. **Certain rules applicable to partnerships**.
* * *

(b) * * *
    (2) * * *

(ii) *Special allocations.*—Except as otherwise provided in paragraph (b)(2)(iii) of this section, for purposes of paragraph (b)(1) of this section, if a partnership agreement provides for the allocation of book income (or, where appropriate, book gain) from a subset of the property of the partnership to a partner other than in accordance with the partner's liquidation value percentage in a particular taxable year (a *special allocation)*, then the partner's attributable share of that property is determined solely by reference to the partner's special allocation with respect to the property, provided the special allocation will be respected for Federal income tax purposes under section 704(b) and the regulations thereunder and does not have a principal purpose of avoiding the purposes of section 956.

(iii) *Limitation on special allocations in the case of a controlled partnership.*—Paragraph (b)(2)(ii) of this section does not apply to determine a partner's attributable share of partnership property in the case of a partnership controlled by the partner. For purposes of this paragraph (b)(2)(iii), a partner controls a partnership when the partner and the partnership are related within the meaning of section 267(b) or section 707(b), determined by substituting "at least 80 percent" for "more than 50 percent" wherever it appears.

(3) * * *
Example 2. (i) *Facts.* * * * FS does not control FPRS within the meaning of paragraph (b)(2)(iii) of this section.

(ii) *Result.* Under paragraph (b)(1) of this section, for purposes of section 956, FS is treated as holding its attributable share of the property held by FPRS with an adjusted basis equal to its attributable share of FPRS's adjusted basis in such property. In general, FS's attributable share of property held by FPRS is determined in accordance with FS's liquidation value percentage. However, because FS does not control FPRS within the meaning of paragraph (b)(2)(iii) of this section and because the special allocation does not have a principal purpose of avoiding the purposes of section 956, under paragraph (b)(2)(ii) of this section, FS's attributable share of the FPRS property is determined by reference to its special allocation. FS's special allocation percentage for the FPRS property is 80%, and thus FS's attributable share of the FPRS property is 80% and its attributable share of FPRS's basis in the FPRS property is $80x. Accordingly, for purposes of determining the amount of United States property held by FS as of the close of quarter 1 of year 1, FS is treated as holding United States property with an adjusted basis of $80x.

Example 3. (i) *Facts.* USP, a domestic corporation, wholly owns FS, a controlled foreign corporation, which, in turn, owns a 25% capital and profits interest in FPRS, a foreign partnership. The remaining 75% capital and profits interest in FPRS is owned by an unrelated foreign person. Thus, FS does not control FPRS within the meaning of paragraph (b)(2)(iii) of this section. FPRS holds property (the "FPRS property") that would be United States property if held by FS directly. The FPRS property has an adjusted basis of $100x and is anticipated to appreciate in value but generate relatively little income. The FPRS partnership agreement, which satisfies the requirements of section 704(b), specially allocates 80% of the income with respect to the FPRS property to the unrelated foreign person and 80% of the gain with respect to the disposition of FPRS property to FS. The special allocation does not have a principal purpose of avoiding the purposes of section 956.

(ii) *Result.* Because FPRS is not controlled by FS within the meaning of paragraph (b)(2)(iii) of this section, and the special allocation does not have a principal purpose of avoiding the purposes of section 956, under paragraph (b)(2)(ii) of this section, FS's attributable share of the FPRS property is determined by reference to a special allocation with respect to the FPRS property. Given the income and gain anticipated with respect to the FPRS property, it is appropriate to determine FS's attributable share of the property in accordance with the special allocation of gain. Accordingly, for purposes of determining the amount of United States property held by FS in each year that FPRS holds the FPRS property, FS's attributable share of the FPRS property is 80% and its attributable share of FPRS's basis in the FPRS property is $80x. Thus, FS is treated as holding United States property with an adjusted basis of $80x.

Example 4. (i) *Facts.* The facts are the same as in *Example 3* of this paragraph (b)(3), except that USP owns the 75% capital and profits interest in FPRS rather than an unrelated foreign person. Thus, FS controls FPRS within the meaning of paragraph (b)(2)(iii) of this section. At the close of quarter 1 of year 1, the liquidation value percentage, as determined under paragraph (b)(2) of this section, for FS with respect to FPRS is 25%.

(ii) *Result.* Because FPRS is controlled by FS within the meaning of paragraph (b)(2)(iii) of this section, under paragraph (b)(2)(iii) of this section, FS's attributable share of the FPRS property is not determined by reference to the special allocation of gain with respect to the FPRS property. Accordingly, for purposes of determining the amount of United States property held by FS in each year that FPRS holds the FPRS property, FS's attributable share of the FPRS property is determined under paragraph (b)(2)(i) in accordance with FS's liquidation value percentage, which is 25%, and its attributable share of FPRS's basis in the FPRS property is $25x. Thus, FS is treated as holding United States property with an adjusted basis of $25x.

* * *

(f) * * *
(1) Except as otherwise provided in this paragraph (f)(1), paragraph (b) of this section applies to taxable years of controlled foreign corporations ending on or after November 3, 2016, and taxable years of United States shareholders in which or with which such taxable years end, with respect to property acquired on or after November 3, 2016. Paragraphs (b)(2)(ii) and (iii) of this section, as well as *Example 2*, *Example 3*, and *Example 4* of paragraph (b)(3) of this section, apply to taxable years of controlled foreign corporations ending on or after the date of publication in the **Federal Register** of the Treasury decision adopting this rule as a final regulation, and

taxable years of United States shareholders in which or with which such taxable years end, with respect to property acquired on or after the date of publication in the **Federal Register** of the Treasury decision adopting this rule as a final regulation. For purposes of this paragraph (f)(1), a deemed exchange of property pursuant to section 1001 on or after November 3, 2016 constitutes an acquisition of the property on or after that date, and a deemed exchange of property pursuant to section 1001 on or after the date of publication in the **Federal Register** of the Treasury decision adopting this rule as a final

regulation constitutes an acquisition of the property on or after that date.

See §1.956-2(a)(3), as contained in 26 CFR part 1 revised as of April 1, 2016, for the rules applicable to taxable years of a controlled foreign corporation beginning on or after July 23, 2002, and ending before November 3, 2016, and with respect to property acquired before November 3, 2016, to taxable years of a controlled foreign corporation beginning on or after July 23, 2002.

GILTI: Stock Ownership Determination: Guidance

GILTI: Stock Ownership Determination: Guidance.—Amendments to Reg. §1.958-1, regarding the treatment of domestic partnerships for purposes of determining amounts included in the gross income of their partners with respect to foreign corporations and regarding gross income that is subject to a high rate of tax under the GILTI provisions, are proposed (published in the Federal Register on June 21, 2019) (REG-101828-19).

Par. 9. Section 1.958-1 is amended by:

1. Redesignating paragraph (d) as paragraph (e).

2. Adding a new paragraph (d).

The addition reads as follows:

§1.958-1. Direct and indirect ownership of stock.

* * *

(d) *Stock owned through domestic partnerships.*—(1) *In general.*— Except as otherwise provided in paragraph (d)(2) of this section, for purposes of section 951 and section 951A, and for purposes of any other provision that applies by reference to section 951 or section 951A, a domestic partnership is not treated as owning stock of a foreign corporation within the meaning of section 958(a). When the preceding sentence applies, a domestic partnership is treated in the same manner as a foreign partnership under section 958(a)(2) and paragraph (b) of this section for purposes of determining the persons that own stock of the foreign corporation within the meaning of section 958(a).

(2) *Non-application for determination of status as United States shareholder or controlled foreign corporation.*—Paragraph (d)(1) of this section does not apply for purposes of determining whether any United States person is a United States shareholder (as defined in section 951(b)), whether any United States shareholder is a controlling domestic shareholder (as defined in §1.964-1(c)(5)), or whether any foreign corporation is a controlled foreign corporation (as defined in section 957(a)).

(3) *Examples.*—The following examples illustrate the application of this paragraph (d).

(i) *Example 1*—(A) *Facts.* USP, a domestic corporation, and Individual A, a United States citizen unrelated to USP, own 95% and 5%, respectively, of PRS, a domestic partnership. PRS owns 100% of the single class of stock of FC, a foreign corporation.

(B) *Analysis*—(1) *CFC and United States shareholder determinations.* Under paragraph (d)(2) of this section, the determination of whether PRS, USP, and Individual A (each a United States person) are United States shareholders of FC and whether FC is a controlled foreign corporation is made without regard to paragraph (d)(1) of this section. PRS, a United States person, owns 100% of the total combined voting power or value of the FC stock within the meaning of section 958(a). Accordingly, PRS is a United States shareholder under section 951(b), and FC is a controlled foreign corporation under section 957(a). USP is a United States shareholder of FC because it owns 95% of the total combined voting power or value of the FC stock under sections 958(b) and 318(a)(2)(A). Individual A, however, is not a United States shareholder of FC because Individual A owns only 5% of the total combined voting power or value of the FC stock under sections 958(b) and 318(a)(2)(A).

(2) *Application of sections 951 and 951A.* Under paragraph (d)(1) of this section, for purposes of sections 951 and 951A, PRS is not treated as owning (within the meaning of section 958(a)) the FC stock; instead, PRS is treated in the same manner as a foreign partnership for purposes of determining the FC stock owned by USP and Individual A under section 958(a)(2) and paragraph (b) of this section. Therefore, for purposes of sections 951 and 951A, USP is treated as owning 95% of the FC stock under section 958(a), and Individual A is treated as owning 5% of the FC stock under section 958(a). USP is a United States shareholder of FC, and therefore USP determines its income inclusions under section 951 and 951A based on its ownership of FC stock under section 958(a). However, because Individual A is not a United States shareholder of FC, Individual A does not have an income inclusion under section 951 with respect to

FC or a pro rata share of any amount of FC for purposes of section 951A.

(ii) *Example 2*—(A) *Facts.* USP, a domestic corporation, and Individual A, a United States citizen, own 90% and 10%, respectively, of PRS1, a domestic partnership. PRS1 and Individual B, a nonresident alien individual, own 90% and 10%, respectively, of PRS2, a domestic partnership. PRS2 owns 100% of the single class of stock of FC, a foreign corporation. USP, Individual A, and Individual B are unrelated to each other.

(B) *Analysis*—(1) *CFC and United States shareholder determination.* Under paragraph (d)(2) of this section, the determination of whether PRS1, PRS2, USP, and Individual A (each a United States person) are United States shareholders of FC and whether FC is a controlled foreign corporation is made without regard to paragraph (d)(1) of this section. PRS2 owns 100% of the total combined voting power or value of the FC stock within the meaning of section 958(a). Accordingly, PRS2 is a United States shareholder under section 951(b), and FC is a controlled foreign corporation under section 957(a). Under sections 958(b) and 318(a)(2)(A), PRS1 is treated as owning 90% of the FC stock owned by PRS2. Accordingly, PRS1 is a United States shareholder under section 951(b). Further, under section 958(b)(2), PRS1 is treated as owning 100% of the FC stock for purposes of determining the FC stock treated as owned by USP and Individual A under section 318(a)(2)(A). Therefore, USP is treated as owning 90% of the FC stock under section 958(b) (100% x 100% x 90%), and Individual A is treated as owning 10% of the FC stock under section 958(b) (100% x 100% x 10%). Accordingly, both USP and Individual A are United States shareholders of FC under section 951(b).

(2) *Application of sections 951 and 951A.* Under paragraph (d)(1) of this section, for purposes of sections 951 and 951A, PRS1 and PRS2 are not treated as owning (within the meaning of section 958(a)) the FC stock; instead, PRS1 and PRS2 are treated in the same manner as foreign partnerships for purposes of determining the FC stock owned by USP and Individual A under section 958(a)(2) and paragraph (b) of this section. Therefore, for purposes of determining the amount included in gross income under sections 951 and 951A, USP is treated as owning 81% (100% x 90% x 90%) of the FC stock under section 958(a), and Individual A is treated as owning 9% (100% x 90% x 10%) of the FC stock under section 958(a). Because USP and Individual A are both United States shareholders of FC, USP and Individual A determine their respective inclusions under sections 951 and 951A based on their ownership of FC stock under section 958(a).

(4) *Applicability date.*—Paragraphs (d)(1) through (3) of this section apply to taxable years of foreign corporations beginning on or after the date of publication of the Treasury decision adopting these rules as final regulations in the **Federal Register**, and to taxable years of United States persons in which or with which such taxable years of foreign corporations end. For taxable years that precede the taxable years described in the preceding sentence, a domestic partnership may apply those paragraphs to taxable years of a foreign corporation beginning after December 31, 2017, and to taxable years of the domestic partnership in which or with which such taxable years of the foreign corporation end, provided that the partnership, its partners that are United States shareholders of the foreign corporation, and other domestic partnerships that bear relationships described in section 267(b) or 707(b) to the partnership (and their United States shareholder partners) consistently apply paragraph (d) of this section

with respect to all foreign corporations whose stock the domestic partnerships own within the meaning of section 958(a) (determined without regard to paragraph (d)(1) of this section).

* * *

CFCs: U.S. Shareholders: Ownership Attribution

CFCs: U.S. Shareholders: Ownership Attribution.—Amendments to Reg. §1.958-2, relating to the modification of section 958(b) of the Internal Revenue Code by the Tax Cuts and Jobs Act, which was enacted on December 22, 2017, are proposed (published in the Federal Register on October 2, 2019) (REG-104223-18).

Par. 10. Section 1.958-2 is amended by:

1. Removing and reserving paragraph (d)(2).

2. In paragraph (g), designating *Examples 1* through *6* as paragraphs (g)(1) through (6), respectively.

3. In newly designated paragraphs (g)(1) and (2), removing the language "paragraph (c)(1)(iii) and (2) of this section" and adding "paragraphs (c)(1)(iii) and (c)(2) of this section" in its place.

4. Revising newly designated paragraph (g)(4).

5. Adding paragraph (h).

6. Removing the parenthetical authority citation at the end of the section.

The revisions and addition read as follows:

§1.958-2. Constructive ownership of stock.

* * *

(g) * * *

(4) *Example 4.*—Foreign corporation U owns 100 percent of the one class of stock in domestic corporation V and also 100 percent of the one class of stock in foreign corporation W. Because more than 50 percent in value of the stock of V Corporation is owned by its sole shareholder, U Corporation, V Corporation is considered under paragraph (d)(1)(iii) of this section as owning the stock owned by U Corporation in W Corporation, and accordingly is a United States shareholder of W Corporation.

* * *

(h) *Applicability date.*—Paragraphs (d)(2) and (g)(4) of this section apply to taxable years of foreign corporations ending on or after October 1, 2019, and taxable years of United States shareholders in which or with which such taxable years of foreign corporations end. For taxable years of foreign corporations ending before October 1, 2019, and taxable years of United States shareholders in which or with which such taxable years of foreign corporations end, a taxpayer may apply such provisions to the last taxable year of a foreign corporation beginning before January 1, 2018, and each subsequent taxable year of the foreign corporation, and to taxable years of United States shareholders in which or with which such taxable years of the foreign corporation end, provided that the taxpayer and United States persons that are related (within the meaning of section 267 or 707) to the taxpayer consistently apply such provisions with respect to all foreign corporations.

CFCs: Previously Taxed Earnings and Profits: Exclusion from Gross Income: Basis Adjustments

CFCs: Previously Taxed Earnings and Profits: Exclusion from Gross Income: Basis Adjustments.—Amendments to Reg. §§1.959-1—1.959-4, providing guidance relating to the exclusion from gross income of previously taxed earnings and profits under Code Sec. 959 and related basis adjustments under Code Sec. 961, are proposed (published in the Federal Register on August 29, 2006) (REG-121509-00) (corrected December 8, 2006).

☐ Par. 2. Section 1.959-1 is revised to read as follows:

§1.959-1. Exclusion from gross income of United States persons of previously taxed earnings and profits.—(a) *In general.*—Section 959(a) provides an exclusion whereby the earnings and profits of a foreign corporation attributable to amounts which are, or have been, included in a United States shareholder's gross income under section 951(a) are not taxed again when distributed (directly or indirectly through a chain of ownership described in section 958(a)) from such foreign corporation to such shareholder (or any other United States person who acquires from any person any portion of the interest of such United States shareholder in such foreign corporation, but only to the extent of such portion, and subject to such proof of the identity of such interest as the Secretary may by regulations prescribe). Section 959(a) also excludes from gross income of a United States shareholder earnings and profits attributable to amounts which are, or have been, included in the gross income of such shareholder under section 951(a) which would, but for section 959(a)(2), be again included in the gross income of such shareholder (or any other United States person who acquires from any person any portion of the interest of such United States shareholder in such foreign corporation, but only to the extent of such portion, and subject to such proof of the identity of such interest as the Secretary may by regulations prescribe) under section 951(a)(1)(B). Section 959(b) provides that for purposes of section 951(a), the earnings and profits of a CFC attributable to amounts that are, or have been, included in the gross income of a United States shareholder under section 951(a) shall not, when distributed through a chain of ownership described in section 958(a), be included in the gross income of a CFC in such chain for purposes of the application of section 951(a) to such CFC with respect to such United States shareholder (or any other United States person who acquires from any person any portion of the interest of such United States shareholder in such foreign corporation, but only to the extent of such portion, and subject to such proof of the identity of such interest as the Secretary may by regulations prescribe). Section 959(c) provides rules for the allocation of distributions to the various categories of previously taxed earnings and profits of a foreign corporation and the foreign corporation's non-previously taxed earnings and profits. Section 959(d) provides that, except as provided in section 960(a)(3), any distribution excluded from gross income under section 959(a) shall be treated as a distribution which is not a dividend; except that such distribution shall immediately reduce earnings and profits. Section 959(e) provides that, for purposes of sections 959 and 960(b), any amount included in the gross income of any person as a

dividend by reason of subsection (a) or (f) of section 1248 shall be treated as an amount included in the gross income of such person (or, in any case to which section 1248(e) applies, of the domestic corporation referred to in section 1248(e)(2)) under section 951(a)(1)(A). Section 959(f)(1) provides rules for the allocation of amounts which would, but for section 959(a)(2), be included in gross income under section 951(a)(1)(B) to certain previously taxed earnings and profits of a foreign corporation and non-previously taxed earnings and profits. Section 959(f)(2) provides an ordering rule pursuant to which the rules of section 959 are applied first to actual distributions and then to amounts which would, but for section 959, be included in gross income under section 951(a)(1)(B). Paragraph (b) of this section provides a list of definitions. Paragraph (c) of this section provides rules for the exclusion from gross income under section 959(a)(1) of distributions of earnings and profits by a foreign corporation and the exclusion from gross income under section 959(a)(2) of amounts which would, but for section 959, be included in gross income under section 951(a)(1)(B). Paragraph (d) of this section provides for the establishment and acquisition of previously taxed earnings and profits accounts by shareholders of foreign corporations. Section 1.959-2 provides rules for the exclusion from gross income of a CFC of distributions of previously taxed earnings and profits from another CFC in a chain of ownership described in section 958(a). Section 1.959-3 provides rules for the allocation of distributions and section 956 amounts to the earnings and profits of a CFC and for the maintenance and adjustment of previously taxed earnings and profits accounts by shareholders of foreign corporations. Section 1.959-4 provides for the treatment of actual distributions that are excluded from gross income under section 959(a).

(b) *Definitions.*—For purposes of this section through §1.959-4 and §1.961-1 through §1.961-4, the terms listed in this paragraph are defined as follows:

(1) *Previously taxed earnings and profits* means the earnings and profits of a foreign corporation, computed in accordance with sections 964 and 986(b) and the regulations thereunder, attributable to section 951(a) inclusions.

(2) *Previously taxed earnings and profits account* means an account reflecting the previously taxed earnings and profits of a foreign corporation (if any).

(3) *Dollar basis* means the United States dollar amounts included in a United States shareholder's income with respect to the

previously taxed earnings and profits included in a shareholder's previously taxed earnings and profits account.

(4) *Covered shareholder* means a person who is one of the following—

(i) A United States person who owns stock (within the meaning of section 958(a)) in a foreign corporation and who has had a section 951(a) inclusion with respect to its stock in such corporation;

(ii) A successor in interest, as defined in paragraph (b)(5) of this section; or

(iii) A corporation that is not described in paragraphs (b)(4)(i) or (ii) of this section and that owns stock (within the meaning of section 958(a)) in a foreign corporation in which another corporation is a covered shareholder described in paragraph (b)(4)(i) or (ii) of this section, if both the first mentioned corporation and the covered shareholder are members of the same consolidated group.

(5) *Successor in interest* means a United States person who acquires, from any person, ownership (within the meaning of section 958(a)) of stock in a foreign corporation, for which there is a previously taxed earnings and profits account and who establishes to the satisfaction of the Director of Field Operations the right to the exclusion from gross income provided by section 959(a) and this section. To establish the right to the exclusion, the shareholder must attach to its return for the taxable year a statement that provides that it is excluding amounts from gross income because it is a successor in interest succeeding to one or more previously taxed earnings and profits accounts with respect to shares it owns in a foreign corporation. Included in the statement shall be the name of the foreign corporation. In addition, that shareholder must be prepared to provide the following information within 30 days upon request by the Director of Field Operations—

(i) The name, address, and taxable year of the foreign corporation and of all the other corporations, partnerships, trusts, or estates in any applicable chain of ownership described in section 958(a);

(ii) The name, address, and taxpayer identification number, if any, of the person from whom the stock interest was acquired;

(iii) A description of the stock interest acquired and its relation, if any, to a chain of ownership described in section 958(a);

(iv) The amount for which an exclusion under section 959(a) and paragraph (c) of this section is claimed; and

(v) Evidence showing that the earnings and profits for which an exclusion is claimed are previously taxed earnings and profits, that such amounts were not previously excluded from the gross income of a United States person, and the identity of the United States shareholder who originally included such amounts in gross income under section 951(a). The acquiring person shall also furnish to the Director of Field Operations such other information as may be required by the Director of Field Operations in support of the exclusion.

(6) *Block of stock* shall have the meaning provided in § 1.1248-2(b) with the additional requirement that the previously taxed earnings and profits attributable to each share of stock in such block must be the same.

(7) *Consolidated group* shall have the meaning provided in § 1.1502-1(h).

(8) *Member* shall have the meaning provided in § 1.1502-1(b).

(9) *Section 951(a) inclusion* means a section 951(a)(1)(A) inclusion or an amount included in the gross income of a United States shareholder under section 951(a)(1)(B).

(10) *Section 951(a)(1)(A) inclusion* means—

(i) An amount included in a United States shareholder's gross income under section 951(a)(1)(A);

(ii) An amount included in the gross income of any person as a dividend by reason of subsection (a) or (f) of section 1248 (or, in any case to which section 1248(e) applies, an amount included in the gross income of the domestic corporation referred to in section 1248(e)(2)); or

(iii) An amount described in section 1293(c).

(11) *Section 956 amount* means an amount determined under section 956 for a United States shareholder with respect to a single share or, if a shareholder maintains a previously taxed earnings and profits account with respect to a block of stock, a block of such shareholder's stock in the CFC.

(12) *Section 959(c)(1) earnings and profits* means the previously taxed earnings and profits of a foreign corporation attributable to amounts that have been included in the gross income of a United States shareholder under section 951(a)(1)(B) (or which would have been included except for section 959(a)(2) and § 1.959-2) and amounts that have been included in gross income under section 951(a)(1)(C) as it existed prior to its repeal (or which would have been included except for section 959(a)(3) as it existed prior to its repeal).

(13) *Section 959(c)(2) earnings and profits* means the previously taxed earnings and profits of a foreign corporation attributable to section 951(a)(1)(A) inclusions.

(14) *Non-previously taxed earnings and profits* means the earnings and profits of a foreign corporation other than the corporation's previously taxed earnings and profits.

(15) *CFC* means a controlled foreign corporation within the meaning of either section 953(c)(1)(B) or section 957.

(16) *United States shareholder* means a United States person who qualifies as a United States shareholder under either section 951(b) or section 953(c)(1)(A).

(c) *Amount excluded from gross income.*—(1) *Distributions.*—In the case of a distribution of earnings and profits to a covered shareholder with respect to stock in a foreign corporation, an amount shall be excluded from such shareholder's gross income equal to the total amount by which such shareholder's previously taxed earnings and profits account with respect to such stock is decreased under § 1.959-3 because of the distribution.

(2) *Section 956 amounts.*—In a case where a covered shareholder has a section 956 amount for a CFC's taxable year, an amount shall be excluded from such shareholder's gross income equal to the amount of section 959(c)(2) earnings and profits in any shareholder's previously taxed earnings and profits account that are reclassified as section 959(c)(1) earnings and profits under § 1.959-3 because of that section 956 amount.

(d) *Shareholder accounts.*—(1) *In general.*—Any person who is subject to § 1.959-3 shall maintain a previously taxed earnings and profits account with respect to each share of stock it owns (within the meaning of section 958(a)) in a foreign corporation. Although the account is share specific, the account may be maintained with respect to each block of the stock in the foreign corporation. Such account shall be maintained in accordance with § 1.959-3.

(2) *Acquisition of account.*—(i) *In general.*—If any person acquires, from any other person, ownership of shares of stock in a foreign corporation (within the meaning of section 958(a)) the prior shareholder's previously taxed earnings and profits account with respect to such stock becomes the previously taxed earnings and profits account of the acquirer.

(ii) *Acquisition of account by a person other than a successor in interest.*—If such acquirer is not a successor in interest (a foreign person for example), the previously taxed earnings and profits account with respect to the stock acquired shall remain unchanged for the period that the stock is owned by such acquirer. See also § 1.959-3(e), providing account adjustment rules that apply only for acquired PTI accounts if the acquirer is a successors in interest.

(3) *Examples.*—The application of this paragraph (d) is illustrated by the following examples:

Example 1. Shareholder's previously taxed earnings and profits account. (i) *Facts.* DP, a United States shareholder owns all of the 100 shares of the only class of stock in FC, a CFC. The 100 shares are a block of stock. DP and FC use the calendar year as their taxable year and FC uses the U.S. dollar as its functional currency. In year 1, FC earns $100x of subpart F income and $100x of non-subpart F income. DP includes $100x in gross income under section 951(a).

(ii) *Analysis.* As a result of DP's inclusion of $100x of gross income under section 951(a), DP has a previously taxed earnings and profits account with respect to each of its 100 shares equal to $1x or should DP choose to maintain its previously taxed earnings and profits account on a block basis, an account of $100x with respect to its entire interest in FC.

Example 2. Acquisition of previously taxed earnings and profits account. (i) *Facts.* Assume the same facts as *Example 1*, but that in year 2, a nonresident alien, FP, contributes property to FC to acquire 1000 newly issued shares of FC of the same class held by DP. In year 10, DP sells all of its FC shares to FP. In year 15, FP sells all of its shares in FC to USP, a United States person. Any income earned by FC after year 1 is non-subpart F income. The only distributions by FC during this period are a $100x pre-sale distribution to FP in year 15 and another $100x distribution in year 16 to USP.

(ii) *Analysis.* In year 2, DP retains its previously taxed earnings and profits account of $100x as result of its section 951(a) inclusion in year 1 regardless of the fact that FC is no longer a CFC and DP no longer holds a sufficient interest in FC to be a United States shareholder with respect to FC. In year 10, pursuant to paragraph (d)(2)(i) of this section, FP acquires a $100x previously taxed earnings and profits account with respect to DP's block of stock in FC that FP acquired. In year 15, FP receives a distribution of $100x of earnings and profits from FC, but FP may not exclude any of this distribution from gross income because FP is a nonresident alien. Consequently, pursuant to paragraph (d)(2)(ii) of this section, even though it acquired a previously taxed earnings and profits account from DP of $100x the account remains unchanged during FP's ownership of the FC stock. However, if USP can make the showing required in paragraph (b)(5) of this section, USP may exclude the $100x distribution in year 16 under section 959(a)(1) and paragraph (c) of this section to the extent that the distribution results in a decrease of the $100x previously taxed earnings and profits account that USP acquired

☐ Par. 3. Section 1.959-2 is revised to read as follows:

§1.959-2. Exclusion from gross income of CFCs of previously taxed earnings and profits.—(a) *Exclusion from gross income.*—(1) *In general.*—The earnings and profits of a CFC (lower-tier CFC) attributable to amounts which are, or have been, included in the gross income of a United States shareholder under section 951(a) shall not, when distributed through a chain of ownership described in section 958(a), be also included in the gross income of the CFC receiving the distribution (upper-tier CFC) in such chain for purposes of the application of section 951(a) to such upper-tier CFC with respect to such United States shareholder. The amount of the exclusion provided under this paragraph is the entire amount distributed by the lower-tier CFC to the upper-tier CFC that gave rise (in whole or in part) to an adjustment of the United States shareholder's previously taxed earnings and profits accounts with respect to the stock it owns (within the meaning of section 958(a)) in the lower-and upper-tier CFC under §1.959-3(e)(3). This amount shall not exceed the earnings and profits of the lower-tier CFC attributable to amounts described in section 951(a)(1) (without regard to pro rata share). The exclusion from the income of such upper-tier CFC also applies with respect to any other United States shareholder who is a successor in interest.

(2) *Examples.*—The application of this paragraph (a) is illustrated by the following examples:

Example 1. Distribution attributable to subpart F income of lower-tier CFC. (i) *Facts.* FC, a CFC, is 70% owned by DP, a United States person, and 30% owned by FP, a nonresident alien. FC owns all the stock in FS, a CFC. DP, FP, FC and FS all use the calendar year as their taxable year and FC and FS use the U.S. dollar as their functional currency. In year 1, FS earns $100x of passive income described in section 954(c) and $50x of non-subpart F income. On the last day of year 1, FS distributes $100x to FC that would qualify as subpart F income of FC. On the last day of year 1, FC distributes $70x to DP and $30x to FP.

(ii) *Analysis.* DP is required to include $70x in its gross income under section 951(a) as a result of FS's earning $100x of subpart F income for the year. Consequently, the section 959(c)(2) earnings and profits in DP's previously taxed earnings and profits account with respect to its indirect ownership of stock in FS is increased to $70x. Under §1.959-3(e)(3), as a result of the $100x distribution paid by FS to FC, DP's previously taxed earnings and profits account is reduced by its pro rata share of the distribution ($70x). In addition, FS's non-previously taxed earnings and profits are reduced by the remaining $30x. Under paragraph (a) of this section, the amount of the exclusion under paragraph (a) is equal to the amount distributed, not to exceed the amount of earnings and profits that gave rise to the previously taxed income that is being distributed. Consequently, the entire $100x distribution (as opposed to only $70x) is excluded from FC's gross income for purposes of determining whether DP has an inclusion under section 951(a) as a result of FC's receiving the distribution from FS. The receipt of the distribution from FS increases FC's earnings and profits by $100x ($70x of which is previously taxed earnings and profits and $30x of which is non-previously taxed earnings and profits).

Example 2. Transferee shareholder. (i) *Facts.* The facts are the same as in *Example 1* except that neither FS nor FC makes any distributions in year 1. In year 2, FP sells its stock in FC to DT, a United States person. On the last day of year 2, FS distributes $100x to FC that would qualify as subpart F income of FC. FS has no earnings and profits for year 2, and FC has no earnings and profits for year 2 other than the distribution from FS.

(ii) *Analysis.* With respect to DP, the analysis is the same as that in *Example 1*. However, for purposes of DT's determination of the amount includible in its gross income under section 951(a) with respect to FC for year 2, none of the $100x distribution is excluded

from FP pursuant to the account adjustment rules of §1.959-3. [Reg. §1.959-1.]

from FC's gross income for purposes of applying section 951(a) with respect to DT's interest in FC because none of earnings and profits distributed by FS to FC are attributable to amounts which are, or have been, included in the gross income of DT or the person to whom DT is a successor in interest (FP). Consequently, DT must include $30x in gross income under section 951(a) for year 2 as its pro rata share of FC's subpart F income of $100x ($100x × 30%). Thereafter, DT has a previously taxed earnings and profits account consisting of $30x with respect to its stock in FC and FC has $100x of previously taxed earnings and profits.

Example 3. Mixed distribution. (i) *Facts.* The facts are the same as in *Example 1*, except that on the last day of year 1, FS distributes $150x to FC that would qualify as subpart F income of FC, which in turn distributes $105x to DP and $45x to FP.

(ii) *Analysis.* Under the analysis in *Example 1* and pursuant to paragraph (a) of this section, $100x of the distribution from FS to FC is excluded from FC's gross income for purposes of determining DP's inclusion under section 951(a) with respect to FC's receipt of the distribution from FS. However, DP's pro rata share of the remaining $50x, or $35x ($50x × 70%), is included in DP's gross income under section 951(a). Consequently, the previously taxed earnings and profits in DP's previously taxed earnings and profits account with respect to its stock in FC is increased from $70x to $105x pursuant to §1.959-3(e)(2)(i). That account is then reduced to $0, as a result of the distribution of $105x to DP pursuant to §1.959-3(e)(2)(ii) and DP excludes the distribution of $105x from FC from its gross income for year 1 under section 959(a)(1) and §1.959-1(c).

(b) *Section 304(a)(1) transactions.*—(1) *Deemed redemption treated as a distribution.*—In the case of a stock acquisition under section 304(a)(1) treated as a distribution to which section 301 applies, the selling CFC shall be deemed for purposes of section 959(b) and paragraph (a) of this section to receive such distributions through a chain of ownership described under section 958(a).

(2) *Example.*—The application of this paragraph (c) is illustrated by the following example:

Example. Cross-chain acquisition of CFC stock by a CFC from another CFC. (i) *Facts.* DP, a domestic corporation, owns all of the stock in two foreign corporations, FX and FY. FX owns all of the stock in foreign corporation FZ. DP, FX, FY, and FZ all use the calendar year as their taxable year and the U.S. dollar as their functional currency. During year 1, FY purchases all of the stock in FZ from FX for $80x in a transaction described in section 304(a)(1). At the end of year 1, before taking into account the purchase of FZ's stock, FY has section 959(c)(2) earnings and profits of $20x and non-previously taxed earnings and profits of $10x, and FZ has section 959(c)(2) earnings and profits of $50x and non-previously taxed earnings and profits of $0.

(ii) *Analysis.* Under section 304(a)(1), FX is deemed to have transferred the FZ stock to FY in exchange for FY stock in a transaction to which section 351 applies, and FY is treated as having redeemed, for $80x, the FY stock deemed issued to FX. The payment of $80x is treated as a distribution to which section 301 applies. Under section 304(b)(2), the determination of the amount which is a dividend (and the source) is made as if the distribution were made, first, by FY to the extent of its earnings and profits, $30x, and then by FX to the extent of its earnings and profits, $50x. Under paragraph (c)(1) of this section, FX is deemed to receive the distributions from FY and FZ through a chain of ownership described in section 958(a). Under paragraph (a) of this section, the amount of FY's previously taxed earnings and profits, $20x, and the amount of FZ's previously taxed earnings and profits, $50x, distributed to FX are excluded from the gross income of FX. Accordingly, only $10x is included in FX's gross income. [Reg. §1.959-2.]

☐ Par. 4. Section 1.959-3 is revised to read as follows:

§1.959-3. Maintenance and adjustment of previously taxed earnings and profits accounts.—(a) *In general.*—This section provides rules for the maintenance and adjustment of previously taxed earnings and profits accounts by shareholders and with respect to foreign corporations. Paragraph (b) of this section provides general rules governing the accounting of previously taxed earnings and profits at the shareholder level and corporate level. Paragraph (c) of this section provides rules regarding the treatment of foreign taxes when previously taxed earnings and profits are distributed by a foreign corporation through a chain of ownership described in section 958(a). Paragraph (d) of this section provides rules regarding the allocation of other expenses to previously taxed earnings and profits. Para-

graph (e)(1) of this section addresses the adjustment of shareholder-level previously taxed earnings and profits accounts as a result of certain transactions. Paragraph (e)(2) of this section provides rules establishing the order in which adjustments are to be made to a covered shareholder's previously taxed earnings and profits account. Paragraph (e)(3) of this section provides rules regarding distributions of previously taxed earnings and profits in a chain of ownership described in section 958(a). Paragraph (e)(4) of this section provides for the maintenance and adjustment of aggregate categories of previously taxed and non-previously taxed earnings and profits at the corporate level with adjustments to individual shareholder-level accounts. Paragraph (e)(5) of this section provides rules for the effect of a foreign corporation's deficit in earnings and profits on previously taxed earnings and profits. Paragraph (f) of this section provides rules regarding the treatment of previously taxed earnings and profits when a shareholder has multiple previously taxed earnings and profits accounts. Paragraph (g) of this section provides rules regarding the treatment of previously taxed earnings and profits when more than one shareholder in a foreign corporation is a member of the same consolidated group. Paragraph (h) of this section provides rules governing the adjustment of previously taxed earnings and profits accounts in the case of a redemption.

(b) *Corporate-level and shareholder-level accounting of previously taxed earnings and profits.*—(1) *Shareholder-level accounting.*—A shareholder's previously taxed earnings and profits account with respect to its stock in a foreign corporation shall identify the amount of section 959(c)(1) earnings and profits and the amount of section 959(c)(2) earnings and profits attributable to such stock for each taxable year of the foreign corporation and shall be maintained in the functional currency of such foreign corporation. A shareholder account must also reflect the annual dollar basis of each category of previously taxed earnings and profits in the account. See § 1.959-3(e) of this section for rules regarding the adjustment of shareholder previously taxed earnings and profits accounts.

(2) *Corporate-level accounting.*—Separate aggregate categories of section 959(c)(1), section 959(c)(2) and non-previously taxed earnings and profits (earnings and profits described in section 959(c)(3)) shall be maintained with respect to a foreign corporation. These categories of earnings and profits of the foreign corporation shall be maintained in the functional currency of the foreign corporation. For purposes of this section, distributions are allocated to a foreign corporation's earnings and profits under section 316(a) by applying first section 316(a)(2) and then section 316(a)(1) to each of these three categories of earnings and profits. Section 956 amounts shall be treated as attributable first to section 959(c)(2) earnings and profits and then to non-previously taxed earnings and profits. These allocations are made in conjunction with the rules for making corporate-level adjustments to previously taxed earnings and profits under § 1.959-3(e)(4).

(3) *Classification of earnings and profits.*— (i) *In general.*—For purposes of this section, earnings and profits are classified as to year and category of earnings and profits in the taxable year of the foreign corporation in which such amounts are included in gross income of a United States shareholder under section 951(a) and are reclassified as to category of earnings and profits in the taxable year of the foreign corporation in which such amounts would be so included in the gross income of a United States shareholder under section 951(a) but for the provisions of section 959(a)(2) and § 1.959-1(c)(2). Such classifications do not change by reason of a subsequent distribution of such amounts to an upper-tier corporation in a chain of ownership described in section 958(a). This paragraph shall apply to distributions by one foreign corporation to another foreign corporation and by a foreign corporation to a United States person.

(ii) *Dollar basis pooling election.*—For purposes of computing foreign currency gain or loss under section 986(c) and adjustments to stock basis under section 961(b) and (c) with respect to distributions of previously taxed earnings and profits of any foreign corporation, in lieu of maintaining annual dollar basis accounts with respect to previously taxed earnings and profits described in paragraph (b)(1) of this section, a taxpayer may maintain an aggregate dollar basis pool that reflects the dollar basis of all of the corporation's previously taxed earnings and profits described in sections 959(c)(1) and 959(c)(2) and treat a pro rata portion of the dollar basis pool as attributable to distributions of such previously taxed earnings and profits. A taxpayer makes this election by using a dollar basis pool to compute foreign currency gain or loss under section 986(c) with respect to distributions of previously taxed earnings and profits of the foreign corporation, or to compute gain or loss with respect to its stock in the foreign corporation, whichever occurs first. Any subsequent change in the taxpayer's method of assigning dollar basis may be made only with the consent of the Commissioner.

(4) *Examples.*—The application of this paragraph (b) is illustrated by the following examples:

Example 1. Distribution. (i) *Facts.* DP, a United States shareholder, owns 100% of the only class of stock in FC, a CFC, which, in turn, owns 100% of the only class of stock in FS, a CFC. DP, FC and FS all use the calendar year as their taxable year. FC and FS both use the u as their functional currency. During year 1, FC earns 100u of non-subpart F income and invests 100u in United States property. DP must include 100u in its gross income for year 1 under section 951(a)(1)(B) with respect to FC. For year 2, FS has no subpart F income or investment of earnings in United States property but FS has 100u of non-previously taxed earnings and profits which it distributes to FC. The distribution of 100u to FC is subpart F income of FC and DP must include the 100u in its gross income for year 2

under section 951(a)(1)(A). Also in year 2, FC has non-subpart F income of 100u. The exchange rates at all times in year 1 and year 2, respectively, are 1u = $1 and 1u = $1.20.

(ii) *Analysis.* With respect to FC, the earnings and profits are classified as follows: 100u of section 959(c)(1) earnings and profits from year 1, 100u of section 959(c)(2) earnings and profits from year 2, and 100u of non-previously taxed earnings and profits from year 2. The dollar basis with respect to the section 959(c)(1) earnings and profits is $100 and the dollar basis with respect to the section 959(c)(2) earnings and profits is $120.

Example 2. Subsequent distribution in a later year. (i) *Facts.* Assume the same facts as in *Example 1,* except that during year 3 neither FC nor FS has any earnings and profits or deficit in earnings and profits or section 956 amount, but FC distributes 100u to DP on December 31, year 3, at which time the spot exchange rate is 1u = $1.30.

(ii) *Analysis.* For purposes of section 959 and 961, the 100u distribution of FC shall be considered attributable to FC's section 959(c)(1) earnings and profits for year 1. The section 959(c)(1) earnings and profits are reduced by 100u and the dollar basis of the account is reduced by $100. Since the spot rate at the time of the 100u distribution to DP is 1u = $1.30, DP recognizes foreign currency gain of $30 ((100 × 1.3) – (100 × 1)).

Example 3. Dollar basis pooling election. (i) *Facts.* Assume the same facts as in *Example 2,* except that DP elected to maintain the dollar basis of its previously taxed earnings and profits account on a pooled basis for purposes of section 986(c) and section 961 as provided in paragraph (b)(3)(ii) of this section.

(ii) *Analysis.* The section 959(c)(1) earnings and profits are reduced by 100u, but the dollar basis of the account is reduced by $110 ((100u/200u) × $220). In addition, DP recognizes foreign currency gain under section 986(c) of $20 ($130 – ((100u/200u) × $220)).

(c) *Treatment of certain foreign taxes.*—(1) For purposes of this section, when previously taxed earnings and profits are distributed by a foreign corporation to another foreign corporation through a chain of ownership described in section 958(a) such earnings and profits shall be reduced by the functional currency amount of any income, war profits, or excess profits taxes imposed by any foreign country or a possession of the United States on or with respect to such earnings and profits. Any such taxes shall not be included in the distributee foreign corporation's pools of post-1986 foreign income taxes maintained for purposes of sections 902 and 960(a)(1). Such taxes shall be maintained in a separate account and allowed as a credit as provided under section 960(a)(3) when the associated previously taxed earnings and profits are distributed. The taxpayer's dollar basis in the previously taxed earnings and profits account shall be reduced by the dollar amount of such taxes, translated in accordance with section 986(a).

(2) *Example.*—The application of this paragraph (c) is illustrated by the following example:

Example. Imposition of foreign taxes on a CFC. (i) *Facts.* DP, a United States shareholder, owns 100% of the only class of stock in foreign corporation FC, a CFC, which, in turn, owns 100% of the only class of stock in FS, a CFC. DP, FC, and FS all use the calendar year as their taxable year. FC and FS both use the u as their functional currency. During year 1, FS earns 90u of subpart F income, after incurring 10u of foreign income tax allocable to such income under § 1.954-1(c), has earnings and profits in excess of 90u, and makes no distributions. DP must include 90u, translated at the average exchange rate for the year of 1u=$1 as provided in section 989(b)(3), in its gross income for year 1 under section 951(a)(1)(A)(i). As of the end of year 1, FS has section 959(c)(2) earnings and profits of 90u. During year 2, FS has neither earnings and profits nor a deficit in earnings and profits but distributes 90u to FC, and, by reason of section 959(b) and § 1.959-2, such amount is not includible in the gross income of DP for year 2 under section 951(a) with respect to FC. FC incurs a withholding tax of 9u on the 90u distribution from FS (10% of 90u) and an additional foreign income tax of 11u by reason of the inclusion of the distribution in its taxable income for foreign tax purposes in year 2. The average exchange rate for year 2 is 1u = $2.

(ii) *Analysis.* At the end of year 2, FS has section 959(c)(2) earnings and profits of 0 (90u - 90u); and FC has section 959(c)(2) earnings and profits of 70u (90u - 9u - 11u). DP's dollar basis in the 70u section 959(c)(2) earnings and profits account with respect to FC is $50 ($90 inclusion – $18 withholding tax – $22 income tax). The $40 of foreign taxes imposed on FC with respect to the previously taxed earnings and profits are not included in FC's post-1986 foreign income taxes pool. A foreign tax credit with respect to the $40 of foreign tax attributable to the 70u of previously taxed earnings and profits will be allowed under section 960(a)(3) upon distribution of such previously taxed earnings and profits.

(d) *Treatment of other expenses.*—Except as provided in paragraph (c) of this section, no expense paid or accrued by a foreign corporation shall be allocated or apportioned to the previously taxed earnings and profits of such corporation.

(e) *Adjustments to previously taxed earnings and profits account.*—(1) *In general.*—A covered shareholder's previously taxed earnings and profits account (including the dollar basis in such account) is adjusted in the manner provided in paragraphs (e)(2), (f) and (g) of this section, except as otherwise provided in paragraph (e)(3) of this section. For adjustments to a previously taxed earnings and profits account in the case of redemptions, see paragraph (h) of this section.

(2) *Order and amount of adjustments.*—As of the close of a foreign corporation's taxable year, and for the taxable year of the covered shareholder in which or with which such taxable year of the foreign corporation ends, the covered shareholder shall make any of the following adjustments that are applicable for that year to the previously taxed earnings and profits account for the stock owned for any portion of such year (within the meaning of section 958(a)) in the foreign corporation in the following order—

(i) *Step 1. Section 951(a)(1)(A) inclusion.*—Increase the amount of section 959(c)(2) earnings and profits and the associated dollar basis in the account by the amount of the section 951(a)(1)(A) inclusion with respect to such stock;

(ii) *Step 2. Distributions on such stock.*—(A) Decrease the amount of the section 959(c)(1) earnings and profits in the account (but not below zero), and then the amount of section 959(c)(2) earnings and profits in the account (but not below zero) by the amount of earnings and profits distributed to the covered shareholder during the year with respect to such stock, decrease the dollar basis in the account by the dollar amount attributable to the distributed earnings and profits; and

(B) Increase the amount of the earnings and profits and associated dollar basis, in the account first to the extent provided under paragraph (f)(1) of this section and then to the extent provided under paragraph (g)(1) of this section and then reduce the account to zero;

(iii) *Step 3. Reallocation from other accounts with respect to redemptions.*—Increase the amount of the earnings and profits and associated dollar basis in the account to the extent provided under paragraph (h)(3)(ii) of this section.

(iv) *Step 4. Section 956 amount.*—Reclassify the section 959(c)(2) earnings and profits and associated dollar basis in such shareholder's previously taxed earnings and profits account with respect to such stock as section 959(c)(1) earnings and profits in an amount equal to the lesser of—

(A) The covered shareholder's section 956 amount for the taxable year with respect to such stock; or

(B) The amount of the section 959(c)(2) earnings and profits attributable to such stock.

(v) *Step 5. Reallocation to other accounts with respect to distributions.*—Decrease the amount of section 959(c)(1) earnings and profits and associated dollar basis in the account, and thereafter the amount of section 959(c)(2) earnings and profits and associated dollar basis in the account to the extent provided under paragraph (f)(1) of this section and then under paragraph (g)(1) of this section;

(vi) *Step 6. Reclassification with respect to section 956 amounts.*—Reclassify the section 959(c)(2) earnings and profits and the associated dollar basis attributable to such stock as section 959(c)(1) earnings and profits to the extent provided under paragraph (f)(2) of this section and then to the extent provided in paragraph (g)(2) of this section.

(vii) *Step 7. Further adjustment for section 956 amounts.*—Increase the amount of section 959(c)(1) earnings and profits and the associated dollar basis in the account by any amount included in the covered shareholder's gross income for the year under section 951(a)(1)(B) with respect to such stock.

(3) *Intercorporate distributions.*—If a foreign corporation receives a distribution of earnings and profits from another foreign corporation that is in a chain of ownership described in section 958(a), a covered shareholder's previously taxed earnings and profits accounts with respect to the stock in each foreign corporation in such chain shall be adjusted at the end of the respective corporation's taxable year, and for the taxable year of the covered shareholder in which or with which such taxable year of the foreign corporation ends, as follows:

(i) The covered shareholder's previously taxed earnings and profits account with respect to stock in the distributor shall be decreased (but not below zero), at the same time that the covered shareholder would make adjustments under paragraph (e)(2)(ii) of this section, by the amount of the distribution and the associated dollar basis. Such decrease to the covered shareholder's previously

taxed earnings and profits account shall be made first to the section 959(c)(1) earnings and profits and thereafter to the section 959(c)(2) earnings and profits in such account.

(ii) Except as provided in paragraph (c) of this section, the section 959(c)(1) earnings and profits and section 959(c)(2) earnings and profits in the covered shareholder's previously taxed earnings and profits account with respect to the stock in the distributee shall be increased, at the same time that the covered shareholder would make adjustments under paragraph (e)(2)(i) of this section, by an amount equal to the decrease under paragraph (e)(3)(i) of this section and to the extent the distribution is out of non-previously taxed earnings and profits of the distributor, to the extent provided under paragraph (e)(2) of this section. If the receiving corporation uses a non-dollar functional currency that differs from the functional currency used by the distributing corporation, then—

(A) The amount of increase shall be the spot value of the distribution in the receiving corporation's functional currency at the time of the distribution; and

(B) The dollar basis of the amount distributed shall be carried over from the distributing corporation to the receiving corporation.

(4) *Effect on foreign corporation's earnings and profits.*—Adjustments to a shareholder's previously taxed earnings and profits account in accordance with this section shall result in corresponding adjustments to the appropriate aggregate category or categories of earnings and profits of the foreign corporation. If an adjustment to a foreign corporation's earnings and profits is required (other than as a result of the previous sentence) the adjustment shall be made only to the non-previously taxed earnings and profits of the corporation except to the extent provided in paragraph (h)(2)(i) of this section. Moreover, if a distribution to a taxpayer exceeds such taxpayer's previously taxed earnings and profits account with respect to stock it owns (within the meaning of section 958(a)) in the foreign corporation making the distribution, the distribution may only be treated as a dividend under section 316 by applying section 316(a)(1) and (2) to the non-previously taxed earnings and profits of the foreign corporation.

(5) *Deficits in earnings and profits.*—If a foreign corporation has a deficit in earnings and profits, as determined under section 964(a) and §1.964-1, for any taxable year, a covered shareholder's previously taxed earnings and profits account with respect to its stock in such foreign corporation shall not be adjusted to take into account the deficit and the deficit shall be applied only to the non-previously taxed earnings and profits of the foreign corporation.

(6) *Examples.*—The application of this paragraph (e) is illustrated by the following examples:

Example 1. Distribution to a United States shareholder. (i) *Facts.* DP, a United States shareholder, owns 100% of the only class of stock in FC, a CFC. Both DP and FC use the calendar year as their taxable year. FC uses the "u" as its functional currency. During year 1, FC derives 100u of subpart F income, and such amount is included in DP's gross income under section 951(a)(1)(A). The average exchange rate for year 1 is 1u = $1. At the end of year 1, FC's current and accumulated earnings and profits (before taking into account distributions made during year 1) are 500u. Also, on December 31, year 1, when the spot exchange rate is 1u = $1.10, FC distributes 50u of earnings and profits to DP.

(ii) *Analysis.* At the end of year 1, the section 959(c)(2) earnings and profits in DP's previously taxed earnings and profits account are first increased from 0 to 100u, pursuant to paragraph (e)(2)(i) of this section as a result of the subpart F inclusion of 100u and then reduced from 100u to 50u, pursuant to paragraph (e)(2)(ii) of this section as a result of the distribution. DP's dollar basis in the 100u of previously taxed earnings and profits is $100 (the dollar amount of the income inclusion under section 951(a)(1)(A)). See section 989(b)(3). The 50u distribution is excluded from DP's gross income pursuant to §1.959-1(c)(1). Pursuant to paragraph (e)(4) of this section, at the end of year 1, FC has section 959(c)(2) earnings and profits of 50u and non-previously taxed earnings and profits of 400u. DP's dollar basis in the previously taxed earnings and profits account is reduced by a pro rata share of the dollar amount included in income under section 951(a)(1)(A), or by $50 (50u distribution/100u previously taxed earnings and profits × $100 dollar basis). DP recognizes foreign currency gain under section 986(c) of $5 ($55 spot value of 50u distribution − $50 basis).

Example 2. Net deficit in earnings and profits. (i) *Facts.* Assume the same facts as in *Example 1*, except that FC has a net deficit in earnings and profits of 500u for year 2. At the end of Year 1, FC has 50u of section 959(c)(2) earnings and profits and 400u of non-previously taxed earnings and profits.

(ii) *Analysis.* At the end of year 2, DP's section 959(c)(2) earnings and profits for year 1 remains at 50u, pursuant to paragraph (e)(5) of this paragraph, because a shareholder's previously taxed earnings and profits account is not adjusted to take into account the

CFC's deficit in earnings and profits. Pursuant to paragraph (e)(4) of this section, at the end of year 2, FC's non-previously taxed earnings and profits are reduced to (100u), and no adjustment is made to FC's previously taxed earnings and profits, which remains at 50u.

Example 3. Distribution and section 956 inclusion in same year. Assume the same facts as in *Example 1*, except that DP also has a section 956 amount for year 1 with respect to its stock in FC of 200u.

(ii) *Analysis.* At the end of year 1, adjustments are made to DP's previously taxed earnings and profits account in its FC stock in the following order: First, the section 959(c)(2) earnings and profits in DP's previously taxed earnings and profits account are increased from 0 to 100u pursuant to paragraph (e)(2)(i) of this section as a result of the subpart F inclusion. Then, the section 959(c)(2) earnings and profits in DP's previously taxed earnings and profits account are reduced from 100u to 50u pursuant to paragraph (e)(2)(ii) of this section as a result of the distribution and the 50u distribution is excluded from DP's gross income pursuant to § 1.959-1(c)(1). Then, the remaining 50u of section 959(c)(2) earnings and profits in DP's previously taxed earnings and profits account are reclassified as section 959(c)(1) earnings and profits pursuant to paragraph (e)(2)(iv) of this section as a result of FC's investment in United States property and 50u of the 200u section 956 amount is excluded from DP's gross income pursuant to § 1.959-1(c)(2). Finally, the remaining 150u section 956 amount equal to $165 (150u × 1.1) is included in DP's gross income pursuant to section 951(a)(1)(B) and the section 959(c)(1) earnings and profits in DP's previously taxed earnings and profits account are increased from 50u to 200u pursuant to paragraph (e)(2)(vii) of this section. Pursuant to paragraph (e)(4) of this section, at the end of year 1, FC has section 959(c)(1) earnings and profits of 200u and non-previously taxed earnings and profits of 250u. DP's dollar basis in the previously taxed earnings and profits account at the end of year 1 is $215 (the $50 attributable to the reclassified 50u of earnings and $165 attributable to the 150u of section 956 inclusion). See section 989(b)(4).

Example 4. Section 956 amount in following year. (i) *Facts.* Assume the same facts as in *Example 3*, except that in year 2, DP has an additional section 956 amount of 200u with respect to its stock in FC and the spot exchange rate on December 31, year 2 is 1u = $1.20.

(ii) *Analysis.* As in *Example 3*, at the end of year 1, DP has a section 959(c)(1) earnings and profits account with respect to its stock in FC of 200u. Although DP has 200u of section 959(c)(1) earnings and profits in its previously taxed earnings and profits account with respect to its stock in FC, section 959(c)(1) earnings and profits are generated by the inclusion of a section 956 amount in a United States shareholder's gross income or the reclassification of section 959(c)(2) earnings and profits to exclude a section 956 amount from a United States shareholder's gross income and cannot be used to exclude any additional section 956 amounts from a United States shareholder's gross income. Consequently, at the end of year 2, the section 959(c)(1) earnings and profits in DP's previously taxed earnings and profits account are increased from 200u to 400u pursuant to paragraph (e)(2)(vii) of this section and the 200u section 956 amount is included in DP's gross income pursuant to section 959(a)(1)(B). Pursuant to paragraph (e)(4) of this section, at the end of year 2, FC has section 959(c)(1) earnings and profits of 400u and non-previously taxed earnings and profits of 50u. DP's dollar basis in its 200u of year 2 section 959(c)(1) earnings and profits is $240.

Example 5. Section 951(a)(1)(A) inclusion and distribution in following year. (i) *Facts.* Assume the same facts as in *Example 4*, except that in year 3, FC derives 250u of subpart F income, which is included in DP's income under section 951(a)(1)(A), makes a 250u distribution to DP, and has 700u of current and accumulated earnings and profits (before taking into account distributions made during year 3). The average exchange rate for year 3 is 1u = $1.10, so DP includes $275 in income (250u × $1.10/1u).

(ii) *Analysis.* As in *Example 4*, at the end of year 2, DP has a previously taxed earnings and profits account with respect to its stock in FC of 400u of section 959(c)(1) earnings and profits. At the end of year 3, adjustments are made in the following order. First, DP's section 959(c)(2) earnings and profits are increased from 0 to 250u pursuant to paragraph (e)(2)(i) of this section as a result of the subpart F inclusion. Then the section 959(c)(1) earnings and profits in DP's previously taxed earnings and profits account are reduced from 400u to 150u and the 250u distribution to DP is excluded from DP's gross income pursuant to § 1.959-1(c)(1). Pursuant to paragraph (e)(4) of this section, at the end of year 3, FC has 150u of section 959(c)(1) earnings and profits, 250u of section 959(c)(2) earnings and profits, and 50u of non-previously taxed earnings and profits. If DP has not made the dollar basis pooling election described in paragraph (b)(3)(ii) of this section, then the 250u distribution out of section 959(c)(1) earnings is assigned a dollar basis of $293.75 ($240 basis in 200u of year 2 earnings and $53.75 basis in 50u of year 1 earnings (50u/200u × $215)). DP's remaining dollar basis in the year 1 section 959(c)(1) earnings is $161.25 ($215 – $53.75). If DP elected to maintain the dollar basis of its previously taxed earnings and profits account on a pooled basis as provided in paragraph (b)(3)(ii) of this section,

then the 250u distribution out of section 959(c)(1) earnings is assigned a dollar basis of $280.77 (250u/650u × ($215 + $240 + $275)), and DP's dollar basis in its remaining 400u previously taxed earnings accounts is $449.23 ($730 – $280.77).

Example 6. Distribution to a United States shareholder and a foreign shareholder. (i) *Facts.* DP, a United States shareholder, owns 70% and FP, a nonresident alien, owns 30% of the only class of stock in FC, a CFC that uses the U.S. dollar as its functional currency. Both DP and FC use the calendar year as their taxable year. During year 1, FC derives $100x of subpart F income, $70x of which is included in DP's gross income under section 951(a)(1)(A). FC's current and accumulated earnings and profits (before taking into account distributions made during year 1) are $500x. Also, during year 1, FC distributes $50x of earnings and profits, $35x distribution to DP and $15x distribution to FP.

(ii) *Analysis.* At the end of year 1, the section 959(c)(2) earnings and profits in DP's previously taxed earnings and profits account are increased from $0 to $70x, pursuant to paragraph (e)(2)(i) of this section as a result of the subpart F inclusion. The section 959(c)(2) earnings and profits in DP's previously taxed earnings and profits account are then reduced from $70x to $35x, pursuant to paragraph (e)(2)(ii) of this section as a result of the distribution. Pursuant to paragraph (e)(4) of this section, at the end of year 1, FC has section 959(c)(2) earnings and profits of $35x and non-previously taxed earnings and profits of $415x.

Example 7. Intercorporate Distribution. (i) *Facts.* DP, a United States shareholder, owns 70% and FP, a nonresident alien, owns 30% of the only class of stock in FC, a CFC. FC owns 100% of the only class of stock in FS, a CFC. FC uses the "u" as its functional currency and FS uses the "y" as its functional currency. DP, FC, and FS all use the calendar year as their taxable year. During year 1, FS derives 100y of subpart F income. The average y:$ exchange rate for year 1 is 1y = $1. On December 31, year 2, FS distributes 100y to FC. The y:u exchange rate on December 31, year 2, is 1y = 0.5u.

(ii) *Analysis.* (A) *Year 1.* At the end of year 1, DP's pro rata share of 70y of subpart F income is included in DP's gross income pursuant to section 951(a)(1)(A)(i) and the section 959(c)(2) earnings and profits in DP's previously taxed earnings and profits account with respect to the stock it indirectly owns in FS are correspondingly increased from 0 to 70y pursuant to paragraph (e)(2)(i) of this section as a result of the subpart F income. The dollar basis of the previously taxed earnings and profits in DP's account with respect to its stock in FS is $70. At the end of year 2, FS has section 959(c)(2) earnings and profits of 70y and non-previously taxed earnings and profits of 30y.

(B) *Year 2.* Upon the distribution of 100y=50u from FS to FC on December 31, year 2, the section 959(c)(2) earnings and profits in DP's previously taxed earnings and profits account with respect to the stock it indirectly owns in FS are reduced from 70y to 0 and the section 959(c)(2) earnings and profits in DP's earnings and profits account with respect to its stock in FC are correspondingly increased from 0 to 35u pursuant to paragraph (e)(3) of this section. The entire 100y=50u distribution is excluded from FC's income for purposes of determining FC's subpart F income under section 951(a) for year 2 with respect to DP pursuant to § 1.959-2(a)(1). Pursuant to paragraph (e)(4) of this section, at the end of year 2, FS has 0 earnings and profits and FC has section 959(c)(2) earnings and profits of 35u and non-previously taxed earnings and profits of 15u. DP's dollar basis in its 35u of section 959(c)(2) earnings and profits in its earnings and profits account with respect to its stock in FC is $70, carried over from DP's original dollar basis in its 70y of section 959(c)(2) earnings and profits in its previously taxed earnings and profits account with respect to its stock in FS.

Example 8. Sale of CFC stock. (i) *Facts.* DP1, a United States shareholder, owns 100% of the only class of stock in FC, a CFC. At the beginning of year 1, DP1 has a zero basis in its stock in FC. Both DP1 and FC use the calendar year as their taxable year. FC uses the U.S. dollar as its functional currency. During year 1, FC derives $100x of subpart F income and $100x of other income. On December 31 of year 1, DP1 sells all of its stock in FC to DP2, a U.S. person for $200x. Year 1 is a year beginning on or after December 31, 1962.

(ii) *Analysis.* First, DP1 includes the $100x of subpart F income in gross income under section 951(a)(1)(A). The section 959(c)(2) earnings and profits in DP1's previously taxed earnings and profits account with respect to its stock in FC are increased from $0 to $100x pursuant to paragraph (e)(2)(i) of this section and DP1's basis in its FC stock is increased from $0 to $100x pursuant to § 1.961-1(b). FC's section 959(c)(2) earnings and profits are increased from $0 to $100x and its non-previously taxed earnings and profits are correspondingly increased from $0 to $100x pursuant to paragraph (e)(4) of this section. Then pursuant to section 1248(a), because FC has $100x of non-previously taxed earnings and profits attributable to DP1's stock that are attributable to a taxable year beginning on or after December 31, 1962 during which FC was a CFC and DP1 owned its stock in FC, the $100x of gain recognized by DP1 on the sale of its stock ($200x proceeds – $100x basis) is included in DP1's gross income as a dividend. Consequently, the section 959(c)(2) earnings and profits in

DP1's previously taxed earnings and profits account with respect to its stock in FC are increased from $100x to $200x pursuant to paragraph (e)(2)(i) of this section. Upon the sale, DP2 acquires from DP1 a previously taxed earnings and profits account with respect to the FC stock of $200x of section 959(c)(2) earnings and profits and takes a cost basis of $200x in the FC stock pursuant to section 1012.

(f) *Special rule for shareholders with more than one previously taxed earnings and profits account.*—(1) *Adjustments for distributions.*—If a covered shareholder owns (within the meaning of section 958(a)) more than one share of stock in a foreign corporation as of the last day of the foreign corporation's taxable year, to the extent that the total amount of any distributions of earnings and profits made with respect to any particular share for the foreign corporation's taxable year would exceed the previously taxed earnings and profits account with respect to such share (an excess distribution amount), the following adjustments shall be made:

(i) *Adjustment of other accounts.*—The covered shareholder's previously taxed earnings and profits accounts with respect to the shareholder's other shares of stock in the foreign corporation that are owned by the covered shareholder as of the last day of the CFC's taxable year shall be decreased, in the aggregate, by an amount equal to such excess distribution amount, but not below zero. Such decrease shall be made on a pro rata basis by reference to the amount of the previously taxed earnings and profits in those other accounts and shall be allocated to the section 959(c)(1) and (c)(2) earnings and profits in those accounts in the same manner as a distribution is allocated to such earnings and profits pursuant to the rules of section 959(c) and paragraph (e)(2)(ii)(A) of this section.

(ii) *Adjustment of deficient account.*—The covered shareholder's previously taxed earnings and profits account for the first-mentioned share of stock shall correspondingly be increased by the same amount, and then shall be adjusted to zero as provided under paragraph (e)(2)(ii)(B) of this section.

(2) *Adjustments for section 956 amounts.*—If a United States shareholder, who owns more than one share of stock in a CFC as of the last day of the CFC's taxable year, has a section 956 amount with respect to its stock in the CFC for a taxable year, to the extent that the section 956 amount with respect to any particular share of stock exceeds the section 959(c)(2) earnings and profits in such shareholder's previously taxed earnings and profits account with respect to such share (an excess section 956 amount), the covered shareholder's section 959(c)(2) earnings and profits in its previously taxed earnings and profits accounts with respect to its other shares of stock that are owned by the United States shareholder on the last day of the CFC's taxable year shall be reclassified as section 959(c)(1) earnings and profits, in the aggregate, by an amount equal to such excess section 956 amount. Such reclassification shall be made on a pro rata basis by reference to the amount of the section 959(c)(2) earnings and profits in each of the United States shareholder's other previously taxed earnings and profits accounts with respect to its stock in the CFC prior to reclassification under this paragraph (f)(2).

(3) *Examples.*—The application of this paragraph (f) is illustrated by the following examples:

Example 1. Two blocks of stock. (i) *Facts.* DP, a United States shareholder, owns two blocks, block 1 and block 2, of shares of class A stock in FC, a CFC that uses the U.S. dollar as its functional currency. Both DP and FC use the calendar year as their taxable year. Entering year 1, DP has a previously taxed earnings and profits account with respect to its block 1 shares consisting of $25x of section 959(c)(2) earnings and profits and a previously taxed earnings and profits account with respect to its block 2 shares consisting of $65x of section 959(c)(2) earnings and profits. Entering year 1, FC has section 959(c)(2) earnings and profits of $90x and non-previously taxed earnings and profits of $200x. During year 1, FC makes a distribution of earnings and profits on its Class A stock of $50x on each of block 1 and block 2.

(ii) *Analysis.* First, as a result of the distribution, the section 959(c)(2) earnings and profits in DP's previously taxed earnings and profits account with respect to block 1 are decreased from $25x to $0 and the section 959(c)(2) earnings and profits in DP's previously taxed earnings and profits account with respect to block 2 are decreased from $65x to $15x pursuant to paragraph (e)(2)(ii) of this section. Because there are insufficient previously taxed earnings and profits with respect to block 1, DP may access its excess previously taxed earnings and profits with respect to its block 2 stock, after taking into account any distributions or section 956 amounts with respect to block 2. Accordingly, the section 959(c)(2) earnings and profits in DP's previously taxed earnings and profits account with respect to block 2 are decreased from $15x to $0 pursuant to paragraphs (e)(2)(v) and (f)(1)(i) of this section and the section 959(c)(2) earnings and profits in DP's previously taxed earnings and profits account with respect to block 2 are increased from $0 to $15x and then decreased from $15x to $0 pursuant to paragraphs

(e)(2)(ii)(B) and (f)(1)(ii) of this section. The $40x ($25x + $15x) of the distribution with respect to block 1 and $50x of the distribution with respect to block 2 are excluded from DP's gross income pursuant to §1.959-1(c)(1). The remaining $10x of the distribution of earnings and profits with respect to block 1 is included in DP's gross income as a dividend. Pursuant to paragraph (e)(4) of this section, at the end of year 1, FC has section 959(c)(2) earnings and profits of $0 and non-previously taxed earnings and profits of $190x.

Example 2. Multiple classes of stock. (i) *Facts.* Assume the same facts as in *Example 1*, except that DP also owns a block, block 3, of class B stock in FC. Entering year 1, DP has a previously taxed earnings and profits account with respect to block 3 consisting of $60x of section 959(c)(2) earnings and profits. Entering year 1, FC has $150x of section 959(c)(2) earnings and profits and $200x of non-previously taxed earnings and profits.

(ii) *Analysis.* First, as in *Example 1*, the section 959(c)(2) earnings and profits in DP's previously taxed earnings and profits account with respect to block 1 are decreased from $25x to $0 and the section 959(c)(2) earnings and profits in DP's previously taxed earnings and profits account with respect to block 2 are decreased from $65x to $15x pursuant to paragraph (e)(2)(ii) of this section. Because there are insufficient previously taxed earnings and profits with respect to block 1, DP may access its excess previously taxed earnings and profits with respect to block 2 and block 3, after taking into account any distributions or section 956 amounts with respect to those blocks. In addition, the previously taxed earnings and profits from blocks 2 and 3 are decreased pro rata based on the relative previously taxed earnings and profits in the previously taxed earnings and profits accounts with respect to both blocks after taking into account any distributions or section 956 amounts with respect to those blocks. Thus, the section 959(c)(2) earnings and profits in DP's previously taxed earnings and profits account with respect to block 2 are decreased from $15x to $10x ($15x/$75x × $25x) and the section 959(c)(2) earnings and profits in DP's previously taxed earnings and profits account with respect to block 3 are decreased from $60x to $40x ($60x/$75x × $25x) pursuant to paragraphs (e)(2)(v) and (f)(1)(i) of this section. The section 959(c)(2) earnings and profits in DP's previously taxed earnings and profits account with respect to block 1 are increased from $0 to $25x and then decreased from $25x to $0 pursuant to paragraphs (e)(2)(ii)(B) and (f)(1)(ii) of this section. The entire $50x distribution with respect to block 1 and $50x distribution with respect to block 2 are excluded from DP's gross income pursuant to §1.959-1(c)(1). Pursuant to paragraph (e)(4) of this section, at the end of year 1, FC has section 959(c)(2) earnings and profits of $50x and non-previously taxed earnings and profits of $200x.

Example 3. Distribution in excess of aggregate previously taxed earnings and profits. (i) *Facts.* Assume the same facts as in *Example 2*, except that instead of a total distribution of $100x on Class A shares in year 1, FC makes a total distribution of $200x on its Class A shares in year 1, consisting of a $100x distribution to block 1 and a $100 distribution to block 2.

(ii) *Analysis.* First, as a result of the distribution, the section 959(c)(2) earnings and profits in DP's previously taxed earnings and profits account with respect to block 1 are decreased from $25x to $0 and the section 959(c)(2) earnings and profits in DP's previously taxed earnings and profits account with respect to block 2 are decreased from $65x to $0 pursuant to paragraph (e)(2)(ii) of this section. Because there are insufficient previously taxed earnings and profits in DP's previously taxed earning and profits accounts with respect to blocks 1 and 2, DP may access its excess previously taxed earnings and profits in its previously taxed earnings and profits account with respect to block3 after taking into account any distributions or section 956 amounts with respect to block 3. Consequently, the section 959(c)(2) earnings and profits in DP's previously taxed earnings and profits account with respect to block 3 are decreased from $60x to $0 pursuant to paragraphs (e)(2)(v) and (f)(1)(i) of this section. Of the total $200x distribution from FC to DP, $150x is excluded from DP's gross income pursuant to §1.959-1(c)(1). The remaining $50x of the distribution is included in DP's gross income pursuant to section 951(a)(1)(A). Pursuant to paragraph (e)(4) of this section, at the end of year 1, FC has section 959(c)(2) earnings and profits of $0 and non-previously taxed earnings and profits of $150x.

Example 4. Sale. (i) *Facts.* Assume the same facts as in *Example 2*, except that DP sells block 3 before the end of year 1.

(ii) *Analysis.* First, as in *Example 2*, the distribution results in a decrease of the section 959(c)(2) earnings and profits in DP's previously taxed earnings and profits account with respect to block 1 from $25x to $0 and the section 959(c)(2) earnings and profits in DP's previously taxed earnings and profits account with respect to block 2 from $65x to $15x pursuant to paragraph (e)(2)(ii) of this section. Because DP does not own block 3 on the last day of year 1, DP cannot use the previously taxed earnings and profits account with respect to block 3 to exclude a distribution in that year to block 1 or 2 from gross income. Therefore, the section 959(c)(2) earnings and profits in DP's previously taxed earnings and profits account with respect to block 2 are decreased from $15x to $0 pursuant to paragraphs (e)(2)(v) and (f)(1)(i) of this section and the section 959(c)(2) earnings and profits in DP's previously taxed earnings and profits account with respect to block 1 are increased from $0 to $15x and then decreased from $15x to $0 pursuant to paragraphs (e)(2)(ii)(B) and (f)(1)(ii) of this section. The $40x ($25x + $15x) of the distribution with respect to block 1 and $50x of the distribution with respect to block 2 are excluded from DP's gross income pursuant to § 1.959-1(c)(1). The remaining $10x of the distribution with respect to block 1 is included in DP's gross income as a dividend. Pursuant to paragraph (e)(4) of this section, at the end of year 1, FC has section 959(c)(2) earnings and profits of $60x and non-previously taxed earnings and profits of $190x.

Example 5. Section 956 amount. (i) *Facts.* Assume the same facts as in *Example 2,* except that, in addition, during year 1, FC has a section 956 amount of $30x, $5x of which is allocable to each of blocks 1 and 2, and $20x of which is allocable to block 3.

(ii) *Analysis.* Pursuant to paragraph (f)(2) of this section, account adjustments are made for the distribution from FC before any account adjustments are made for the section 956 amount. After account adjustments are made for the distribution from FC as illustrated in *Example 2,* DP has a previously taxed earnings and profits account with respect each block as follows: block 1: $0, block 2: $10x of section 959(c)(2) earnings and profits, block 3: $40x of section 959(c)(2) earnings and profits. As a result of the section 956 amount with respect to block 2, pursuant to paragraph (e)(2)(vi) of this section, $5x of DP's section 959(c)(2) earnings and profits in its previously taxed earnings and profits account with respect to block 2 is reclassified as section 959(c)(1) earnings and profits. Consequently, block 2 is left with a previously taxed earnings and profits account consisting of $5x of section 959(c)(1) earnings and profits and $5x of section 959(c)(2) earnings and profits. In addition, pursuant to paragraph (e)(2)(vi) of this section, $20x of DP's section 959(c)(2) earnings and profits in its previously taxed earnings and profits account with respect to block 3 are reclassified as section 959(c)(1) earnings and profits. Consequently, block 3 is left with a previously taxed earnings and profits account consisting of $20x of section 959(c)(1) earnings and profits and $20x of section 959(c)(2) earnings and profits. The total $25x section 956 amount with respect to blocks 2 and 3 is excluded from DP's gross income pursuant to § 1.959-1(c)(2). Because there are insufficient previously taxed earnings and profits in the previously taxed earnings and profits account with respect to block 1, DP may access its excess previously taxed earnings and profits in the previously taxed earnings and profits accounts with respect to blocks 2 and 3 after taking into account any distributions or section 956 amounts with respect to those blocks. In addition, the previously taxed earnings and profits in the previously taxed earnings and profits accounts with respect to blocks 2 and 3 are reclassified pro rata based on the relative previously taxed earnings and profits in those accounts after taking into account any distributions or section 956 amounts with respect to those blocks. Accordingly, pursuant to paragraphs (e)(2)(vi) and (f)(2) of this section, an additional $1x ($5x/$25x × $5x) of the section 959(c)(2) earnings and profits in DP's previously taxed earnings and profits account with respect to block 2 are reclassified as section 959(c)(1) earnings and profits and an additional $4x ($20x/$25x × $5x) of the section 959(c)(2) earnings and profits in DP's previously taxed earnings and profits account with respect to block 3 are reclassified as section 959(c)(1) earnings and profits. The $5x section 956 amount with respect to block 1 is also excluded from DP's gross income pursuant to § 1.959-1(c)(2). At the end of year 1, DP's previously taxed earnings and profits accounts with respect to its various blocks of stock are as follows: block 1 has no previously taxed earnings and profits, block 2 has $6x ($5x + $1x) of section 959(c)(1) earnings and profits and $4x ($5x – $1x) of section 959(c)(2) earnings and profits and block 3 has $24x ($20x + $4x) of section 959(c)(1) earnings and profits and $16x ($20x – $4x) of section 959(c)(2) earnings and profits. Pursuant to paragraph (e)(4) of this section, at the end of year 1, FC has $30x of section 959(c)(1) earnings and profits, $20x of section 959(c)(2) earnings and profits, and $200x of non-previously taxed earnings and profits.

(g) *Special rule for shareholder included in a consolidated group.*—(1) *Adjustments for distributions.*—(i) *In general.*—In the case of a covered shareholder who is a member of a consolidated group, to the extent that the total amount of any distributions of earnings and profits with respect to such covered shareholder's stock in a foreign corporation during such foreign corporation's taxable year would exceed the covered shareholder's previously taxed earnings and profits account with respect to all of the covered shareholder's stock of the foreign corporation (an excess distribution amount) the previously taxed earnings and profits accounts of the covered shareholder and of the other members of the covered shareholder's consolidated group that own stock in the same foreign corporation and are members of the covered shareholder's consolidated group on the last day of the foreign corporation's taxable year shall be adjusted as follows.

(A) *Adjustment of other members' accounts.*—The previously taxed earnings and profits accounts of the other members of the consolidated group that own (within the meaning of section 958(a)) stock in the same foreign corporation and are members of the covered shareholder's consolidated group on the last day of the foreign corporation's taxable year shall be decreased, in the aggregate, by the amount of such excess distribution amount, but not below zero. Such decrease shall be made on a pro rata basis by reference to the amount of such other members' previously taxed earnings and profits accounts and shall be allocated to the section 959(c)(1) and (c)(2) earnings and profits in such accounts in the same manner as a distribution is allocated to such earnings and profits pursuant to section 959(c) and paragraph (e)(2)(ii)(A) of this section.

(B) *Adjustment of the deficient account.*—The deficient previously taxed earnings and profits account of such covered shareholder shall correspondingly be increased by the same amount, and then adjusted to zero under paragraph (e)(2)(ii)(B) of this section.

(ii) *Insufficient previously taxed earnings and profits.*—If more than one member of the consolidated group is a covered shareholder that has an excess distribution amount with respect to all of its stock in the foreign corporation and there is insufficient previously taxed earnings and profits available in the previously taxed earnings and profits accounts of other consolidated group members to exclude the combined excess distribution amounts of the covered shareholders, the other consolidated group members' previously taxed earnings and profits shall be allocated between the covered shareholders' deficient previously taxed earnings and profits accounts in proportion to each covered shareholder's excess distribution amount.

(2) *Adjustments for section 956 amounts.*—(i) *In general.*—If a United States shareholder, who is a member of a consolidated group, has a section 956 amount with respect to its stock in a CFC for a taxable year, to the extent that the section 956 amount exceeds the section 959(c)(2) earnings and profits in such United States shareholder's previously taxed earnings and profits accounts with respect to all of its stock in the CFC (an excess section 956 amount), the section 959(c)(2) earnings and profits in the previously taxed earnings and profits accounts of consolidated group members, who are members of the United States shareholder's consolidated group on the last day of the CFC's taxable year, with respect to their stock in the CFC shall be reclassified as section 959(c)(1) earnings and profits, in the aggregate, by an amount equal to such excess section 956 amount. The amount that is reclassified with respect to each such account of such other members shall be proportionate to the amount of section 959(c)(2) earnings and profits in those accounts prior to reclassification under this paragraph (g).

(ii) *Insufficient section 959(c)(2) earnings and profits.*—If more than one member of the consolidated group is a United States shareholder that has an excess section 956 amount with respect to its stock in the CFC for the taxable year and there is insufficient aggregate section 959(c)(2) earnings and profits in other consolidated group members' previously taxed earnings and profits accounts to exclude the combined excess section 956 amounts of the Untied States shareholders, the amount of any consolidated group members' section 959(c)(2) earnings and profits that are reclassified on behalf of each United States shareholder shall be proportionate to the excess section 956 amount for each such United States shareholder.

(3) *Stock basis adjustments of members.*—See § 1.1502-32 for rules addressing investment adjustments resulting from the application of this paragraph.

(4) *Examples.*—The application of this paragraph (g) is illustrated by the following examples:

Example 1. Two consolidated group members. (i) *Facts.* DP1, a United States shareholder, owns one block, block 1, of shares of Class A stock in FC, a CFC that uses the U.S. dollar as its functional currency. DP2, a United States shareholder and a member of DP1's consolidated group, owns one block, block 2, of shares of Class A stock in FC. DP1, DP2 and FC all use the calendar year as their taxable year and FC uses the U.S. dollar as its functional currency. Entering year 1, DP1 has a previously taxed earnings and profits account with respect to block 1 consisting of $50x of section 959(c)(2) earnings and profits and DP2 has a previously taxed earnings and profits account with respect to block 2 consisting of $200x of section 959(c)(2) earnings and profits. Entering year 1, FC has section 959(c)(2) earnings and profits of $250x and non-previously taxed earnings and profits of $100x. In year 1, FC generates no earnings and profits and makes a distribution of earnings and profits on its Class A stock, a $100x distribution of earnings and profits to block 1 and a $100x distribution of earnings and profits to block 2.

(ii) *Analysis.* First, pursuant to paragraph (e)(2)(ii) of this section, the section 959(c)(2) earnings and profits in DP1's previously taxed earnings and profits account with respect to block 1 are decreased from $50x to $0 and the section 959(c)(2) earnings and profits in DP2's previously taxed earnings and profits account with respect to block 2 are decreased from $200x to $100x. Then, pursuant to paragraphs (e)(2)(v) and (g)(1)(i)(A) of this section, the section 959(c)(2) earnings and profits in DP2's previously taxed earnings and profits account with respect to block 2 are decreased from $100x to $50x and, pursuant to paragraphs (e)(2)(ii)(B) and (g)(1)(i)(B) of this section, the section 959(c)(2) earnings and profits in DP1's previously taxed earnings and profits account with respect to block 1 are increased from $0 to $50x and then decreased from $50x to $0. Pursuant to section 959(a) and §1.959-1(c), the entire $100x distribution to block 1 and $100x distribution to block 2 are excluded from DP1's and DP2's gross incomes respectively. Pursuant to paragraph (e)(4) of this section, at the end of year 1, FC has section 959(c)(2) earnings and profits of $50x and non-previously taxed earnings and profits of $100x.

Example 2. Two consolidated group members; multiple classes of stock. (i) *Facts.* Assume the same facts as in *Example 1,* except that DP1 also owns one block, block 3, of shares of class B stock in FC. DP1 has a previously taxed earnings and profits account with respect to block 3 consisting of $40x of section 959(c)(2) earnings and profits. Entering year 1, FC has section 959(c)(2) earnings and profits of $290x and non-previously taxed earnings and profits of $100x.

(ii) *Analysis.* First, pursuant to paragraph (e)(2)(ii) of this section, the section 959(c)(2) earnings and profits in DP1's previously taxed earnings and profits account with respect to block 1 are decreased from $50x to $0 and the section 959(c)(2) earnings and profits in DP2's previously taxed earnings and profits account with respect to block 2 are decreased from $200x to $100x. Then, pursuant to paragraphs (e)(2)(v) and (f)(1)(i) of this section, the section 959(c)(2) earnings and profits in DP1's previously taxed earnings and profits account with respect to block 3 are decreased from $40x to $0 and, pursuant to paragraphs (e)(2)(ii)(B) and (f)(1)(ii) of this section, the section 959(c)(2) earnings and profits in DP1's previously taxed earnings and profits account with respect to block 1 are increased from $0 to $40x and then decreased from $40x to $0. Finally, pursuant to paragraphs (e)(2)(v) and (g)(1)(i)(A) of this section, the section 959(c)(2) earnings and profits in DP2's previously taxed earnings and profits account with respect to block 2 are decreased from $100x to $90x and, pursuant to paragraphs (e)(2)(ii)(B) and (g)(1)(i)(B) of this section, the section 959(c)(2) earnings and profits in DP1's previously taxed earnings and profits account with respect to block 1 are increased from $0 to $10x and then decreased from $10x to $0. Pursuant to section 959(a) and §1.959-1(c), the entire $100x distribution to block 1 and $100x distribution to block 2 are excluded from DP1's and DP2's gross incomes respectively. Pursuant to paragraph (e)(4) of this section, at the end of year 1, FC has section 959(c)(2) earnings and profits of $90x and non-previously taxed earnings and profits of $100x.

Example 3. Three consolidated group members; multiple classes of stock. (i) *Facts.* Assume the same facts as in *Example 2,* except that DP3, a United States shareholder and a member of DP1's consolidated group, owns one block, block 4, of shares of class B stock in FC. DP3 has a previously taxed earnings and profits account with respect to block 4 consisting of $25x of section 959(c)(2) earnings and profits. Entering year 1, FC has section 959(c)(2) earnings and profits of $315x and non-previously taxed earnings and profits of $100x.

(ii) *Analysis.* First, pursuant to paragraph (e)(2)(ii) of this section, the section 959(c)(2) earnings and profits in DP1's previously taxed earnings and profits account with respect to block 1 are decreased from $50x to $0 and the section 959(c)(2) earnings and profits in DP2's previously taxed earnings and profits account with respect to block 2 are decreased from $200x to $100x. Then, pursuant to paragraphs (e)(2)(v) and (f)(1)(i) of this section, the section 959(c)(2) earnings and profits in DP1's previously taxed earnings and profits account with respect to block 3 are decreased from $40x to $0 and, pursuant to paragraphs (e)(2)(ii)(B) and (f)(1)(ii) of this section, the section 959(c)(2) earnings and profits in DP1's previously taxed earnings and profits account with respect to block 1 are increased from $0 to $40x and then decreased from $40x to $0. Finally, pursuant to paragraphs (e)(2)(v) and (g)(1)(i)(A) of this section, the section 959(c)(2) earnings and profits in DP2's and DP3's previously taxed earnings and profits accounts with respect to blocks 2 and 4 are decreased pro rata from $100x to $92x and from $25x to $23x respectively, and, pursuant to paragraphs (e)(2)(ii)(B) and (g)(1)(i)(B) of this section, the section 959(c)(2) earnings and profits in DP1's previously taxed earnings and profits account with respect to block 1 are increased from $0 to $10x and then decreased from $10x to $0. Pursuant to section 959(a) and §1.959-1(c), the entire amounts of the $100x distribution to block 1 and the $100x distribution to block 2 are excluded from DP1's and DP2's gross incomes respectively. Pursuant to paragraph (e)(4) of this section, at the end of year 1, FC has section 959(c)(2) earnings and profits of $115x and non-previously taxed earnings and profits of $100x.

Example 4. Section 956 Amount. (i) *Facts.* Assume the same facts as in *Example 3,* except that instead of a distribution of 200x on its class A stock, FC has a section 956 amount for year 1 of $180x, 45x of which is allocable to each of blocks 1 through 4.

(ii) *Analysis.* First, pursuant to paragraph (e)(2)(iv) of this section, the section 959(c)(2) earnings and profits in each shareholder's previously taxed earnings profits account are reclassified as section 959(c)(1) earnings and profits leaving each block of stock with the following account: block 1: $45x of section 959(c)(1) earnings and profits, $5x of section 959(c)(2) earnings and profits; block 2: $45x of section 959(c)(1) earnings and profits and $155x of section 959(c)(2) earnings and profits; block 3: $40x of section 959(c)(1) earnings and profits and $0 of section 959(c)(2) earnings and profits; block 4: $25x of section 959(c)(1) earnings and profits and $0 of section 959(c)(2) earnings and profits. After the above reclassifications, DP1 has an excess section 956 amount of $5x with respect to block 3. Therefore, pursuant to paragraphs (e)(2)(vi) and (f)(2) of this section, the remaining $5x of section 959(c)(2) earnings and profits in DP1's previously taxed earnings and profits account with respect to block 1 are reclassified as section 959(c)(1) earnings and profits, leaving DP1 with $50x of section 959(c)(1) earnings and profits and $0 of section 959(c)(2) earnings and profits in its previously taxed earnings and profits account with respect to block 1. The entire $45x section 956 amount with respect to blocks 1 and 3 are excluded from DP1's gross income pursuant to paragraph (c)(2) of this section. After the above reclassifications, DP3 has an excess section 956 amount of $20x with respect to block 4. Therefore, pursuant to paragraphs (e)(2)(vi) and (g)(2)(i) of this section, $20x of the section 959(c)(2) earnings and profits in DP2's previously taxed earnings and profits account with respect to block 2 are reclassified as section 959(c)(1) earnings and profits, leaving DP2 with $65x of section 959(c)(1) earnings and profits and $135x of section 959(c)(2) earnings and profits. The entire $45x section 956 amount with respect to blocks 2 and 4 are excluded from DP2's and DP3's gross incomes, respectively, pursuant to §1.959-1(c)(2). Pursuant to paragraph (e)(4) of this section, at the end of year 1, FC has section 959(c)(1) earnings and profits of $180x, section 959(c)(2) earnings and profits of $135x, and non-previously taxed earnings and profits of $100x.

Example 5. Ex-member. (i) *Facts.* DP1, a United States shareholder, owns one block, block 1, of shares of Class A stock in FC, a CFC that uses the U.S. dollar as its functional currency. DP2 and DP3, both United States shareholders and members of DP1's consolidated group, own one block each, blocks 2 and 3 respectively, of shares of Class A stock in FC. DP1, DP2, DP3 and FC all use the calendar year as their taxable year. Entering year 1, DP1 has a previously taxed earnings and profits account with respect to block 1 consisting of $50x of section 959(c)(2) earnings and profits, DP2 has a previously taxed earnings and profits account with respect to block 2 consisting of $100x of section 959(c)(2) earnings and profits, and DP3 has a previously taxed earnings and profits account with respect to block 3 consisting of $200x of section 959(c)(2) earnings and profits. Entering year 1, FC has section 959(c)(2) earnings and profits of $350x and non-previously taxed earnings and profits of $100x. On March 15 of year 1, FC makes a distribution of earnings and profits on its Class A stock consisting of a $100x distribution of earnings and profits to each of blocks 1, 2 and 3. On July 4 of year 1, DP3 is sold to DP4, a United States person who is not a member of the consolidated group, and DP3 ceases to be a member of the consolidated group.

(ii) *Analysis.* First, pursuant to paragraph (e)(2)(ii) of this section, the section 959(c)(2) earnings and profits in DP1's previously taxed earnings and profits account with respect to block 1 are decreased from $50x to $0, the section 959(c)(2) earnings and profits in DP2's previously taxed earnings and profits account with respect to block 2 are decreased from $100x to $0, and the section 959(c)(2) earnings and profits in DP3's previously taxed earnings and profits account with respect to block 3 are decreased from $200x to $100x. Because DP3 was not a member of DP1's consolidated group on the last day of year 1, the remaining $100x of section 959(c)(2) earnings and profits in DP3's previously taxed earnings and profits account with respect to its stock in FC cannot be used to exclude the remaining $50x distribution to DP1 from DP1's gross income. Consequently, pursuant to §1.959-1(c)(1), $50x of the distribution to block 1, the entire $100x of the distribution to block 2, and the entire $100x of the distribution to block 3 are excluded from DP1's, DP2's, and DP3's gross incomes respectively. The remaining $50x distribution to DP1 is included in DP1's gross income pursuant to section 951(a)(1)(a). Pursuant to paragraph (e)(4) of this section, at the end of year 1, FC has section 959(c)(2) earnings and profits of $150x and non-previously taxed earnings and profits of $50x.

Example 6. Insufficient excess previously taxed earnings and profits. (i) *Facts.* DP1, a United States shareholder, owns one block, block 1, of shares of Class A stock in FC, a CFC that uses the U.S. dollar as its functional currency. DP2 and DP3, both United States shareholders and members of DP1's consolidated group, own one block each, blocks 2 and 3 respectively, of shares of Class A stock in FC. DP1, DP2, DP3 and FC all use the calendar year as their taxable year. Entering year 1, DP1 has a previously taxed earnings and profits account with respect to block 1 consisting of $40x of section 959(c)(2) earnings and profits, DP2 has a previously taxed earnings and profits account with respect to block 2 consisting of $60x of section 959(c)(2) earnings and profits, and DP3 has a previously taxed earnings and profits account with respect to block 3 consisting of $150x of section 959(c)(2) earnings and profits. Entering year 1, FC has section 959(c)(2) earnings and profits of $250x and non-previously taxed earnings and profits of $100x. On March 15 of year 1, FC makes a distribution of earnings and profits on its Class A stock consisting of a $100x distribution of earnings and profits to each of blocks 1, 2 and 3.

(ii) *Analysis.* First, pursuant to paragraph (e)(2)(ii) of this section, the section 959(c)(2) earnings and profits in DP1's previously taxed earnings and profits account with respect to block 1 are decreased from $40x to $0, the section 959(c)(2) earnings and profits in DP2's previously taxed earnings and profits account with respect to block 2 are decreased from $60x to $0, and the section 959(c)(2) earnings and profits in DP3's previously taxed earnings and profits account with respect to block 3 are decreased from $150x to $50x. Then, pursuant to paragraph (g)(1)(i)(A) of this section, the section 959(c)(2) earnings and profits in DP3's previously taxed earnings and profits account with respect to its stock in FC are reduced from $50x to $0, and, pursuant to paragraphs (g)(1)(i)(B) and (g)(1)(ii) of this section, the section 959(c)(2) earnings and profits in DP1's and DP2's previously taxed earnings and profits accounts with respect to their stock in FC are increased from $0 to $30x ($60x /$100x x $50x) and $0 to $20x ($40x/$100x x $50x) respectively and then immediately reduce to $0. Pursuant to §1.959-1(c), $70x ($40x + $30x) of the distribution to DP1, $80x ($60x + $20x) of the distribution to DP2, and $100x of the distribution to DP3 are excluded from gross income. The remaining $30x distributed to DP1 and $20x distributed to DP2 are included in gross income pursuant to section 951(a)(1)(A). Pursuant to paragraph (e)(4) of this section, at the end of year 1, FC has non-previously taxed earnings and profits of $50x.

(h) *Adjustments in the case of redemptions.*—(1) *In general.*—In the case of a foreign corporation's redemption of stock (a redemption distribution), the effect on the covered shareholder's previously taxed earnings and profits account and on the earnings and profits of the redeeming corporation depends on whether the distribution is treated as a payment in exchange for stock or as a distribution of property to which section 301 applies. For the treatment of deemed redemption distributions in transactions described in section 304(a)(1), see paragraph (h)(4) of this section.

(2) *Exchange treatment.*—(i) *Effect on foreign corporation's earnings and profits.*—In the case of a redemption distribution that is treated as a payment in exchange for stock under section 302(a) or section 303, the amount of the distribution properly chargeable to the earnings and profits of the redeeming foreign corporation is the amount determined under section 312(a), subject to the limitation in section 312(n)(7) and this paragraph (h)(2)(i). For purposes of section 312(n)(7), the amount properly chargeable to the earnings and profits of the redeeming foreign corporation shall not exceed the sum of—

(A) The amount of the previously taxed earnings and profits account with respect to the redeemed shares of stock (without adjustment for any income inclusion under section 1248 resulting from the redemption); and

(B) A ratable portion of the redeeming corporation's non-previously taxed earnings and profits. Such chargeable amount of earnings and profits shall be allocated to earnings and profits in accordance with section 959(c) and this section.

(ii) *Cessation of previously taxed earnings and profits account.*—In the case of a redemption distribution that is treated as a payment in exchange for stock, the redeemed covered shareholder's previously taxed earnings and profits account with respect to the redeemed shares ceases to exist and is not transferred to any other previously taxed earnings and profits account. In such a case, any previously taxed earnings and profits in the redeemed covered shareholder's previously taxed earnings and profits account, after being reduced under paragraph (h)(2)(i) of this section, become non-previously taxed earnings and profits of the foreign corporation.

(iii) *Examples.*—The application of this paragraph (h)(2) is illustrated by the following examples:

Example 1. Complete redemption treated as exchange; previously taxed earnings and profits account is depleted. (i) *Facts.* DP, a United States shareholder, owns 70% and FP, a nonresident alien who is unrelated to DP under section 318, owns 30% of the only class of stock in FC, a CFC that uses the U.S. dollar as its functional currency. Both DP and FC use the calendar year as their taxable year and both DP and FC are wholly owned by the same domestic corporation, USP. DP has a previously taxed earnings and profits account consisting of $50x of section 959(c)(2) earnings and profits with respect to its stock in FC and DP has a $50 basis in its FC stock pursuant to section 961(a). FC has $50x of section 959(c)(2) earnings and profits and $50x of non-previously taxed earnings and profits attributable to taxable years of FC beginning on or after December 31, 1962 during which FC was a CFC and during which DP held its shares of stock in FC. FC

redeems all of DP's stock for $100x in a redemption that is treated as a payment in exchange for the stock under section 302(a).

(ii) *Analysis.* DP includes $35x ($50x × 70%) in gross income as a dividend pursuant to section 1248(a) as a result of the deemed exchange. FC adjusts its earnings and profits as a result of the exchange under paragraph (h)(2)(i) of this section in the following manner: first, FC's section 959(c)(2) earnings and profits are reduced from $50x to $0; then, FC's non-previously taxed earnings and profits are decreased from $50x to $15x to reflect DP's $35x ratable share of FC's non-previously taxed earnings and profits. DP's previously taxed earnings and profits account ceases to exist and is not transferred to any other previously taxed earnings and profits account.

Example 2. Complete redemption treated as exchange; previously taxed earnings and profits account is not depleted. (i) *Facts.* Assume the same facts as *Example 1,* except that the amount of the redemption distribution by FC to DP is $25x.

(ii) *Analysis.* DP recognizes a $25x loss as a result of the deemed exchange. FC's section 959(c)(2) earnings and profits are decreased from $50x to $25x, pursuant to paragraph (h)(2)(i) of this section. DP's previously taxed earnings and profits account ceases to exist, and the remaining $25x of section 959(c)(2) earnings and profits in such account is not transferred to any other previously taxed earnings and profits account. However, pursuant to paragraph (h)(2)(ii) of this section, the $25x of previously taxed earnings and profits is converted to non-previously taxed earnings and profits of DC.

(3) *Distribution treatment.*—(i) *Adjustment of shareholder previously taxed earnings and profits accounts and foreign corporation's earnings and profits.*—In the case of a redemption distribution by a foreign corporation that is treated as a distribution of property to which section 301 applies, §1.959-1 and this section shall apply in the same manner as they would apply to any distribution of property to which section 301 applies.

(ii) *Transfer to remaining shares.*—To the extent that the previously taxed earnings and profits account with respect to stock redeemed in a transaction described in paragraph (h)(3)(i) of this section exceeds the amount chargeable to the earnings and profits of the corporation under the rules of that paragraph, the excess previously taxed earnings and profits shall be reallocated to the previously taxed earnings and profits accounts with respect to the remaining stock in the foreign corporation in a manner consistent with, and in proportion to, the proper adjustments of the basis in the remaining shares pursuant to §1.302-2(c).

(iii) *Examples.*—The application of this paragraph (h)(3) is illustrated by the following examples:

Example 1. Redemption in exchange for cash that is treated as a distribution. (i) *Facts.* DP, a United States shareholder, owns 100% of the stock in FC, a CFC that uses the U.S. dollar as its functional currency. Both DP and FC use the calendar year as their taxable year. DP owns two blocks of stock in FC, block 1 and block 2. At the beginning of year 1, DP has a previously taxed earnings and profits account with respect to block 1 consisting of $50x of section 959(c)(2) earnings and profits and FC has section 959(c)(2) earnings and profits of $50x and non-previously taxed earnings and profits of $100x. In year 1, FC redeems block 1 for $100x in a redemption that is treated as a distribution of property to which section 301 applies under section 302(d).

(ii) *Analysis.* The section 959(c)(2) earnings and profits in DP's previously taxed earnings and profits account with respect to block 1 are reduced from $50x to $0 and FC's section 959(c)(2) earnings and profits are correspondingly reduced from $50x to $0. The remaining $50x is included in DP's gross income as a dividend under section 301(c)(1) and FC's non-previously taxed earnings and profits are reduced from $100x to $50x.

Example 2. Redemption in exchange for cash that is treated as a distribution. (i) *Facts.* Assume the same facts as *Example 1,* except that DP is redeemed for $25x.

(ii) *Analysis.* The section 959(c)(2) earnings and profits in DP's previously taxed earnings and profits account with respect to block 1 are reduced from $50x to $25x and FC's section 959(c)(2) earnings and profits are correspondingly reduced from $50x to $25x. FC's non-previously taxed earnings and profits remain at $100x. Pursuant to paragraph (h)(3)(ii) of this section the remaining $25x of section 959(c)(2) earnings and profits in DP's previously taxed earnings and profits account with respect to block 1 are reallocated with respect to the remaining stock in FC in a manner consistent with, and in proportion to, the proper adjustments of the basis of the remaining FC shares pursuant to §1.302-2(c).

(4) *Section 304 transactions.*—(i) *Deemed redemption treated as a distribution.*—In the case of a stock acquisition described in section 304(a)(1), that is treated as a distribution of property to which section 301 applies, a covered shareholder receiving an amount treated as a distribution of earnings and profits shall have a previously taxed

earnings and profits account with respect to stock in each foreign corporation treated as distributing its earnings and profits under section 304(b)(2), even if such person did not otherwise have a previously taxed earnings and profits account with respect to stock in such corporation or corporations. In such a case, §1.959-1 and this section shall apply in the same manner as these regulations would apply to any distribution to which section 301 applies.

(ii) *Example.*—The application of this paragraph (h)(4) is illustrated by the following example:

Example. Cross-chain acquisition of first-tier CFC. (i) *Facts.* DP, a domestic corporation, owns all of the stock in DS, a domestic corporation, and F1, a CFC. DP and DS are members of the same consolidated group. DS owns all of the stock in F2, a CFC. DP, DS, F1 and F2 all use the calendar year as their taxable year and F1 and F2 each use the U.S. dollar as its functional currency. During year 1, F1 purchases all the stock in F2 from DS for $80x in a transaction described in section 304(a)(1). At the end of year 1, before taking into account the purchase of F2's stock, DP has a previously taxed earnings and profits account consisting of $20x of section 959(c)(2) earnings and profits with respect to its stock in F1, and F1 has previously taxed earnings and profits consisting of $20x of section 959(c)(2) earnings and profits and non-previously taxed earnings and profits of $10x. At the end of year1, before taking into account the purchase of F2's stock, DS has a previously taxed earnings and profits account consisting of $50x of section 959(c)(2) earnings and profits with respect to its stock in F2, and F2 has section 959(c)(2) earnings and profits of $50x and non-previously taxed earnings and profits of $0.

(ii) *Analysis.* Under section 304(a)(1), DS is deemed to have transferred the F2 stock to F1 in exchange for F1 stock in a transaction to which section 351(a) applies, and F1 is treated as having re-

deemed, for $80x, the F1 stock deemed issued to DS. The payment of $80x is treated as a distribution of property to which section 301 applies. Under section 304(b)(2), the determination of the amount which is a dividend is made as if the distribution were made, first, by F1 to the extent of its earnings and profits ($30x), and then by F2 to the extent of its earnings and profits ($50x). Before taking into account the deemed distributions, DS had a previously taxed earnings and profits account consisting of $50x of section 959(c)(2) earnings and profits with respect to its stock in F2, and DP had a previously taxed earnings and profits account consisting of $20x of section 959(c)(2) earnings and profits with respect to its stock in F1. Under paragraph (h)(4)(i) of this section, DS has a previously taxed earnings and profits account with respect to the stock in F1. Under paragraph (g)(1)(i) of this section, the section 959(c)(2) earnings and profits in DP's previously taxed earnings and profits account with respect to the F1 stock are reduced from $20x to $0 and the section 959(c)(2) earnings and profits in DS's previously taxed earnings and profits account with respect to the F1 stock are increased from $0 to $20x. The distribution by F1 causes the section 959(c)(2) earnings and profits in DS's previously taxed earnings and profits account with respect to F1 stock to be reduced from $20x to $0, and causes F1's section 959(c)(2) earnings and profits to be reduced from $20x to $0 and its non-previously taxed earnings and profits to be reduced from $10x to $0. The deemed distribution by F2 causes the section 959(c)(2) earnings and profits in DS's previously taxed earnings and profits account with respect to F2 stock to be reduced from $50x to $0, and causes F2's section 959(c)(2) earnings and profits to be reduced from $50x to $0. Of the distribution of $80x, $70x is excluded from DS's gross income pursuant to §1.959-1(c)(1), and $10x is included in DS's gross income as a dividend.

[Reg. §1.959-3.]

□ Par. 5. Section 1.959-4 is revised to read as follows:

§1.959-4. Distributions of amounts excluded under section 959(a).—Except as provided in section 960(a)(3) and §1.960-1, any distribution excluded from gross income of a covered shareholder under section 959(a)(1) and §1.959-1(c)(1) shall be treated, for pur-

poses of chapter 1 (relating to normal taxes and surtaxes) of subtitle A (relating to income taxes) of the Internal Revenue Code as a distribution which is not a dividend, except such a distribution shall immediately reduce earnings and profits.

Allocation and Apportionment of Deductions and Foreign Tax Credit: Guidance

Allocation and Apportionment of Deductions and Foreign Tax Credit: Guidance.—Amendments to Reg. §1.960-1 and 1.960-2, relating to the allocation and apportionment of deductions and creditable foreign taxes, the definition of financial services income, foreign tax redeterminations, availability of foreign tax credits under the transition tax, and the application of the foreign tax credit limitation to consolidated groups, are proposed (published in the Federal Register on December 17, 2019) (REG-105495-19).

Par 22. Section 1.960-1 is amended by:

1. Adding a sentence at the end of paragraph (c)(2).

2. Revising the first three sentences, and adding two new sentences after the third sentence, in paragraph (d)(3)(ii)(A).

3. Removing and reserving paragraph (d)(3)(ii)(B).

4. Revising the second, third, and seventh sentences of paragraph (d)(3)(ii)(C).

The addition and revisions read as follows:

§1.960-1. Overview, definitions, and computational rules for determining foreign income taxes deemed paid under section 960(a), (b), and (d).

* * *

(c) * * *

(2) * * * An item of income with respect to a current taxable year does not include an amount included as subpart F income of a controlled foreign corporation by reason of the recharacterization of a recapture account established in a prior U.S. taxable year (and the corresponding earnings and profits) of the controlled foreign corporation under section 952(c)(2) and §1.952-1(f).

* * *

(d) * * *

(3) * * *

(ii) * * *

(A) *In general.*—* * * A current year tax is allocated and apportioned among the section 904 categories under the rules of §1.904-6. An amount of the current year tax that is allocated and apportioned to a section 904 category is then allocated and apportioned among the income groups within the section 904 category under §1.861-20 (as modified by §1.904-6(c)) by treating each income group as a statutory grouping and treating the residual income group as the residual grouping. Therefore, the portion of a current year tax that is attributable to foreign taxable income arising from a transaction that does not result in the recognition of gross income or loss for Federal income tax purposes in the current taxable year is assigned under §1.861-20(d)(2)(i) to the section 904 category and income

group within a section 904 category to which the corresponding U.S. item would be assigned if the event giving rise to the foreign taxable income resulted in the recognition of income or loss under Federal income tax law in that year. Foreign gross income arising from the receipt of a disregarded payment made by a disregarded entity or other foreign branch to its foreign branch owner that is a controlled foreign corporation is assigned to the income group or groups from which the payment is considered to be made under §1.861-20(d)(3)(ii)(A). Foreign gross income attributable to a base difference, or resulting from the receipt of a disregarded payment made to a foreign branch, is assigned to the residual income grouping under §§1.861-20(d)(2)(ii)(B) and 1.861-20(d)(3)(ii)(B). * * *

* * *

(C) * * * In such case, under §1.861-20, the portion of the foreign gross income (as defined in §1.861-20(b)(5)) that is characterized under Federal income tax principles as a distribution of previously taxed earnings and profits that results in the increase in the PTEP group in the current taxable year is assigned to that PTEP group. If a PTEP group is not treated as an income group under the first sentence of this paragraph (d)(3)(ii)(C), and the rules of §1.861-20 would otherwise apply to assign foreign gross income to a PTEP group, that foreign gross income is instead assigned to the subpart F income group or tested income group to which the income that gave rise to the previously taxed earnings and profits would be assigned if the income were recognized by the recipient controlled foreign corporation under Federal income tax principles in the current taxable year * * * That foreign gross income, however, may be assigned to a subpart F income group or tested income group.

Par 23. Section 1.960-2 is amended by adding a sentence at the end of paragraph (b)(3)(iii) to read as follows:

§1.960-2. Foreign income taxes deemed paid under sections 960(a) and (d).

* * *

(b) * * *

  (3) * * *

(iii) * * * *See* §1.960-1(c)(2) for rule regarding the treatment of an increase in the subpart F income of a controlled foreign corporation by reason of the recharacterization of a recapture account and the corresponding accumulated earnings and profits under section 952(c) and §1.952-1(f).

Allocation and Apportionment of Deductions and Foreign Tax Credit: Guidance

Allocation and Apportionment of Deductions and Foreign Tax Credit: Guidance.—Amendments to Reg. §1.960-7, relating to the allocation and apportionment of deductions and creditable foreign taxes, the definition of financial services income, foreign tax redeterminations, availability of foreign tax credits under the transition tax, and the application of the foreign tax credit limitation to consolidated groups, are proposed (published in the Federal Register on December 17, 2019) (REG-105495-19).

Par. 24. Section 1.960-7 is revised to read as follows:

§1.960-7. Applicability dates.—(a) Except as provided in paragraph (b) of this section, §§1.960-1 through 1.960-6 apply to each taxable year of a foreign corporation ending on or after December 4, 2018, and to each taxable year of a domestic corporation that is a United States shareholder of the foreign corporation in which or with which such taxable year of such foreign corporation ends.

(b) Section 1.960-1(d)(3)(ii) applies to taxable years of a foreign corporation beginning after December 31, 2019, and to each taxable year of a domestic corporation that is a United States shareholder of the foreign corporation in which or with which such taxable year of such foreign corporation ends. For taxable years of a foreign corporation that end on or after December 4, 2018, and also begin before January 1, 2020, see §1.960-1(d)(3)(ii) as in effect on December 17, 2019.

CFCs: Previously Taxed Earnings and Profits: Exclusion from Gross Income: Basis Adjustments

CFCs: Previously Taxed Earnings and Profits: Exclusion from Gross Income: Basis Adjustments.—Reg. §§1.961-3 and 1.961-4 and amendments to Reg. §§1.961-1 and 1.961-2, providing guidance relating to the exclusion from gross income of previously taxed earnings and profits under Code Sec. 959 and related basis adjustments under Code Sec. 961, are proposed (published in the Federal Register on August 29, 2006) (REG-121509-00) (corrected December 8, 2006).

☐ Par. 6. Section 1.961-1 is revised to read as follows:

§1.961-1. Increase in basis of stock in CFCs and of other property.—(a) *Definitions.*—See §1.959-1(b) for a list of defined terms applicable to §1.961-1 through §1.961-4.

(b) *Increase in basis.*—(1) *In general.*—Except as provided in paragraphs (b)(2) and (b)(3) of this section, the adjusted basis of a United States shareholder's stock in a CFC or property (as defined in paragraph (c)(1) of this section) by reason of the ownership of which such United States shareholder is considered under section 958(a) as owning stock in a CFC shall be increased under section 961(a) each time, and to the extent that, such United States shareholder's previously taxed earnings and profits account with respect to the stock in that CFC is increased pursuant to the steps outlined in §1.959-3(e)(2).

(2) *Limitation on amount of increase in case of election under section 962.*—[Reserved].

(3) *Deemed inclusions under sections 1293(c) and 959(e).*—Paragraph (b)(1) of this section shall not apply in the case of a deemed section 951(a) inclusion pursuant to section 1293(c) or 959(e).

(c) *Rules of application.*—(1) *Property defined.*—The property of a United States shareholder referred to in paragraph (b)(1) of this section shall consist of—

  (i) Stock in a foreign corporation;

  (ii) An interest in a foreign partnership; or

  (iii) A beneficial or ownership interest in a foreign estate or trust (as defined in section 7701(a)(31)).

(2) *Increase with respect to each share or ownership unit.*—Any increase under paragraph (b) of this section in the basis of a United States shareholder's stock in a foreign corporation or property (as defined in paragraph (c)(1) of this section) by reason of the ownership of which such United States shareholder is considered under section 958(a) as owning stock in a foreign corporation shall be made on a pro rata basis with respect to each share of such stock or each ownership unit of such property.

(3) *Translation rules.*—For purposes of determining an increase in basis under this section, in cases in which the previously taxed earnings and profits account is maintained in a non-United States dollar functional currency, section 951(a) inclusions shall be translated into United States dollars at the appropriate exchange rate as described in section 989(b). Any other increase in basis pursuant to paragraph (b) of this section (for example, a basis increase resulting from the application of §1.959-3(f) or (g)) shall be in the amount of the transferor's dollar basis attributable to the previously taxed earnings and profits transferred.

(c) [(d)] *Examples.*—The application of this section is illustrated by the following examples:

☐ Par. 7. Section 1.961-2 is revised to read as follows:

§1.961-2. Reduction in basis of stock in foreign corporations and of other property.—(a) *Reduction in basis.*—(1) *In general.*—Except as

Example 1. Basis adjustment for income inclusion. (i) *Facts.* DP, a United States shareholder, owns 800 of the 1,000 shares of the one class of stock in FC and has a basis of $50 in each of its shares. DP and FC use the calendar year as a taxable year and FC is a CFC. FC uses the u as its functional currency. The average exchange rate for year 1 is 1u = $1. In year 1, its first year of operation, FC has 100,000u of subpart F income after the payment of 11,250u of foreign income taxes. DP is required to include in gross income 80,000u (800/1,000 × 100,000u) equal to $80,000 under section 951(a), and 9,000u (80,000u/100,000u × 11,250u) equal to $9,000 under section 78.

(ii) *Analysis.* On December 31, of year 1, DP increases the section 959(c)(2) earnings and profits in its previously taxed earnings and profits account with respect to its stock in FC by 80,000u pursuant to §1.959-3(e)(2)(i) to reflect the inclusion of 80,000u, or $80,000, in DP's gross income pursuant to section 959(a), and correspondingly increases the basis of each share of its stock in FC by $100 ($80,000/800) from $50 to $150 pursuant to paragraphs (b)(1) and (c)(2) of this section.

Example 2. Sale of CFC stock. (i) *Facts.* Assume the same facts as in *Example 1*, except that in year 2, DP sells all of its stock in FC to DP2, a United States person that is DP's successor in interest (as defined in §1.959-1(b)(5)), for $200 per share. At the time of sale, the exchange rate is 1u = $1 and DP has a basis of $150 per share in its FC stock and a previously taxed earnings and profits account with respect to its FC stock consisting of 80,000u of section 959(c)(2) earnings and profits with a dollar basis of $80,000. Also, at the time of sale, FC has 50,000u of non-previously taxed earnings and profits, attributable to taxable years of FC beginning on or after December 31,1962 during which FC was a CFC and DP held its shares of stock in FC.

(ii) *Analysis.* Pursuant to section 1248(a), because FC has 40,000u of non-previously taxed earnings and profits attributable to DP's stock (50,000u × 800/1,000), the $40,000 of gain, equal to 40,000u, recognized by DP on the sale of it stock (($200 - $150) × 800) is included in DP's gross income as a dividend. Consequently, the section 959(c)(2) earnings and profits in DP's previously taxed earnings and profits account with respect to its stock in FC are increased from 80,000u to 120,000u pursuant to §1.959-3(e)(2)(i). DP's basis in each share of its stock in FC is not adjusted, pursuant to paragraph (b)(3) of this section, because the adjustment to DP's previously taxed earnings and profits account results from a deemed section 951(a) inclusion pursuant to section 959(e). Upon the sale, DP2 acquires a previously taxed earnings and profits account with respect to the FC stock of 120,000u pursuant to §1.959-1(d)(2)(i) and can utilize the account if it qualifies as a successor in interest under §1.959-1(b)(5). DP2 takes a cost basis of $200 per share in the FC stock pursuant to section 1012.

[Reg. §1.961-1.]

provided in paragraph (a)(2) of this section, the adjusted basis of a covered shareholder's stock in a foreign corporation or property (as defined in §1.961-1(c)) by reason of the ownership of which such covered shareholder is considered under section 958(a) as owning stock in a foreign corporation shall be reduced under section 961(b) each time, and to the extent, that such covered shareholder's dollar basis in a previously taxed earnings and profits account with respect to the stock in such foreign corporation is decreased pursuant to the steps outlined in §1.959-3(e)(2) and shall also be reduced by the dollar amount of any foreign income taxes allowed as a credit under section 960(a)(3) with respect to the earnings and profits accounted for by that decrease.

(2) *Limitation on amount of reduction in case of election under section 962.*—[Reserved].

(b) *Rules of application.*—(1) *Reduction with respect to each ownership unit.*—Any reduction under paragraph (a) of this section in the adjusted basis of a covered shareholder's stock in a foreign corporation or property (as defined in paragraph (b)(1) of this section) by reason of the ownership of which it is considered under section 958(a) as owning stock in a foreign corporation shall be made on a pro rata basis with respect to each share of such stock or each ownership unit of such property.

(2) *Translation rules.*—For purposes of determining a decrease in basis under this section, in cases in which the previously taxed earnings and profits account is maintained in a non-United States dollar functional currency, distributions of previously taxed earnings and profits shall be translated using the dollar basis of the earnings distributed. See §1.959-3(b)(1) and (b)(3)(ii) for rules regarding the dollar basis of previously taxed earnings and profits. If the covered shareholder elects to maintain dollar basis accounts of previously taxed earnings and profits as described in § 1.959-3(b)(3)(ii), the dollar basis of the earnings distributed shall be determined according to the following formula: (functional currency distributed/total functional currency previously taxed earnings and profits) × total dollar basis of previously taxed earnings and profits. See section 989(b)(1) for the appropriate exchange rate applicable to distributions for purposes of section 986(c).

(c) *Amount in excess of basis.*—To the extent that the amount of the reduction in the adjusted basis of property provided by paragraph (a) of this section exceeds such adjusted basis, the amount shall be treated as gain from the sale or exchange of property.

(d) *Examples.*—The application of this section is illustrated by the following examples:

Example 1. Successor in interest. (i) *Facts.* DP, a United States shareholder, owns all of the 1,000 shares of the one class of stock in FC, which owns all of the 500 shares of the one class of stock in FS. Each share of DP's stock in FC has a basis of $200. DP, FC, and FS use the calendar year as a taxable year and FC and FS are CFCs throughout the period here involved. FC and FS both use the u as their functional currency. In year 1, FS has 100,000u of subpart F income after the payment of 50,000u of foreign income taxes. The average exchange rate for year 1 and year 2 is 1u = $1. For year 1, DP includes 100,000u in gross income under section 951(a) with respect to FS. In accordance with the provisions of §1.961-1, DP increases the basis of each of its 1,000 shares of stock in FC to $300 ($200+$100,000/1,000)

☐ Par. 8. Section 1.961-3 is added to read as follows:

§1.961-3. Basis adjustments in stock held by foreign corporation.—(a) *Where the upper-tier entity is 100% owned by a single United States shareholder.*—(1) *In general.*—If a United States shareholder is treated under section 958(a) as owning stock in a CFC (lower-tier CFC) by reason of owning, either directly or pursuant to the application of section 958(a), stock in one or more other CFCs (each an "upper-tier CFC"), any increase to such United States shareholder's basis in stock or other property under §1.961-1 of this section resulting from an adjustment to such United States shareholder's previously taxed earnings and profits account with respect to its stock in the lower-tier CFC shall also be made to each upper-tier CFC's basis in either the stock in the lower-tier CFC or the property by reason of which it is considered to own stock in the lower-tier CFC under section 958(a), but only for purposes of determining the amount included under section 951 in the gross income of such United States shareholder or its successor in interest. In addition, any downward adjustment to such United States shareholder's (or its successor in interest's) previously taxed earnings and profits account with respect to its stock in a distributor under §1.959-3(e)(3) shall result in a corresponding reduction of the basis of the distributee's stock in the distributor for purposes of determining the amount included in such United States shareholder's gross income under section 951(a).

(2) *Examples.*—The application of this paragraph (a) is illustrated by the following examples:

as of December 31, of year 1. On July 31 of year 2, DP sells 250 of its shares of stock in FC to domestic corporation DT at a price of $350 per share. DT satisfies the requirements of paragraph (d) of §1.959-1 so as to qualify as DP's successor in interest. On September 30 of year 2, the earnings and profits attributable to the 100,000u included in DP's gross income under section 951(a) for year 1 are distributed to FC which incurs a withholding tax of 10,000u on such distribution (10% of 100,000u) and an additional foreign income tax of 33 1/3% or 30,000u by reason of the inclusion of the net distribution of 90,000u (100,000u minus 10,000u) in its taxable income for year 2. On June 30 of year 3, FC distributes the remaining 60,000u of such earnings and profits to DP and DT: DP receives 45,000u (750/1,000×60,000u) and excludes such amount from gross income under section 959(a) and §1.959-1(c); DT receives 15,000u (250/1,000×60,000u) and, as DP's successor in interest, excludes such amount from gross income under section 959(a) and §1.959-1(c).

(ii) *Analysis.* As of June 30 of year 3, DP must reduce the adjusted basis of each of its 750 shares of stock in FC to $200 ($300 minus ($45,000/750+$10,000/1,000+ $30,000/1,000)); and DT must reduce the basis of each of its 250 shares of stock in FC to $250 ($350 minus ($15,000/250+ $10,000/1,000+$30,000/1,000)).

Example 2. Sale of lower-tier CFC. (i) *Facts.* Assume the same facts as in *Example 1*, except that in addition, on July 31 of year 2, FC sells its 500 shares of stock in FS to domestic corporation DT2 at a price of $600 per share. DT2 satisfies the requirements of §1.959-1(b)(5) so as to qualify as DP's successor in interest. On September 30 of year 2, FS distributes 100,000u of earnings and profits to DT2, which earnings and profits are attributable to the 100,000u included in DP's gross income under section 951(a) for year 1. As DP's successor in interest, DT2 excludes the 100,000u it receives from gross income under section 959(a) and §1.959-1(c).

(ii) *Analysis.* As of September 30 of year 2, DT2 must reduce the basis of each of its 500 shares of stock in FS to $400 ($600 minus ($100,000/500)).

Example 3. Section 956 amount. (i) *Facts.* DP, a United States shareholder, owns all of the 1,000 shares of the one class of stock in FC, which owns all of the 500 shares of the one class of stock in FS. Each share of DP's stock in FC has a basis of $200. DP, FC, and FS use the calendar year as a taxable year and FC and FS are CFCs throughout the period here involved. FC and FS both use the u as their functional currency. In year 1, FS has 100,000u of subpart F income after the payment of 50,000u of foreign income taxes. The average exchange rate for year 1 and year 2 is 1u = $1. For year 1, DP includes 100,000u in gross income under section 951(a) with respect to FS. In accordance with the provisions of §1.959-3(e)(2)(i) and §1.961-1, DP increases the section 959(c)(2) earnings and profits in its earnings and profits account with respect to its FC stock by 100,000u and correspondingly adjusts the basis of each of its 1,000 shares of stock in FC to $300 ($200+$100,000/1,000) as of December 31 of year 1. In year 2, DP has a section 956 amount with respect to its stock in FC of 100,000u.

(ii) *Analysis.* On December 31 of year 2, DP reclassifies 100,000u of section 959(c)(2) earnings and profits as section 959(c)(1) earnings and profits pursuant to §1.959-3(e)(2)(iv). DP's basis in each of its 1,000 shares of stock in FC remains unchanged at $300 per share.

[Reg. §1.961-2.]

Example 1. Intercorporate dividend from lower-tier CFC to upper-tier CFC. (i) *Facts.* DP, a United States shareholder, owns all of the stock in FC, a CFC, and FC owns all of the stock in FS, a CFC. DP, FC and FS all use the calendar year as their taxable year and FC and FS both use the U.S. dollar as their functional currency. In year 1, FS has $100x of subpart F income that is included in DP's gross income under section 951(a)(1). In year 2, FS pays a dividend of $100x to FC.

(ii) *Analysis.* On December 31 of year 1, the section 959(c)(2) earnings and profits in DP's previously taxed earnings and profits account with respect to its stock in FS are increased by $100x pursuant to §1.959-3(e)(2)(i) to reflect the inclusion of $100x in DP's gross income under section 951(a)(1)(A). DP's basis in its stock in FC is correspondingly increased by $100x pursuant to §1.961-1(b). FC's basis in its stock in FS is also increased by $100x pursuant to paragraph (a) of this section, but only for purposes of determining the amount included in DP's gross income under section 951. At the end of year 2, the section 959(c)(2) earnings and profits in DP's previously taxed earnings and profits account with respect to its stock in FS are decreased by $100x and its previously taxed earnings and profits account with respect to its stock in FC are increased by $100x pursuant to §1.959-3(e)(3) to reflect the transfer of the previously taxed earnings and profits from FS to FC. The $100x distribution is excluded from FC's income for purposes of determining the amount included in DP's gross income pursuant to §1.959-2(a). FC's basis in its stock in FS, for purposes of determining the amount included in

DP's gross income under section 951, is decreased by $100x pursuant to paragraph (a) of this section.

Example 2. Sale of upper-tier CFC stock. (i) *Facts.* DP, a United States shareholder, owns all of the stock in FC, a CFC. FC owns all of the stock in FS1, a CFC, and FS1 owns all of the stock in FS2, a CFC. DP, FC, FS1, and FS2 all use the calendar year as their taxable year and FC, FS1 and FS2 all use the U.S. dollar as their functional currency. In year 1, FS2 has $100x of subpart F income which is included in DP's gross income under section 951(a)(1)(A). In year 2, FC sells FS1 to FT, a nonresident alien, and recognizes $100x of gain on the sale.

(ii) *Analysis.* On December 31 of year 1, the section 959(c)(2) earnings and profits in DP's previously taxed earnings and profits account with respect to its stock in FS2 are increased by $100x pursuant to §1.959-3(e)(2)(i) to reflect the inclusion of $100x in DP's gross income under section 951(a)(1). DP's basis in its stock in FC is correspondingly increased by $100x under §1.961-1(b). FC's basis in its stock in FS1 and FS1's basis in its stock in FS2 are also each increased by $100x under paragraph (a) of this section, but only for purposes of determining the amount included in the gross income of DP under section 951. In year 2, the $100x of gain on FC's sale of FS1 stock would be subpart F income that would be includible in DP gross income under section 951(a)(1)(A). However, since FC has an additional $100x of basis in its stock in FS1 for purposes of determining the amount included in DP's gross income under section 951, the sale of FS1 by FC does not generate any subpart F income to DP.

(b) *Exception where the upper-tier entity is less than 100 percent owned by a single United States shareholder.*—(1) *In general.*—If United States shareholders are treated, under section 958(a), as owning stock in a CFC (lower-tier CFC) by reason of owning, either directly or pursuant to the application of section 958(a), stock in one or more other CFCs (each an "upper-tier CFC"), and if, in the aggregate, the lower-tier CFC is less than wholly indirectly owned by a single United States shareholder, any increase to any United States shareholder's basis in stock or other property under §1.961-1(b) of this section resulting from an increase to such United States shareholder's previously taxed earnings and profits account with respect to its stock in such lower-tier CFC shall result in an increase to each upper-tier CFC's basis in either the stock in the lower-tier CFC or the property by reason of which such upper-tier CFC is considered to own stock in the lower-tier CFC under section 958(a), but only for purposes of determining the amount included under section 951 in the gross income of such United States shareholder or its successor in interest. The amount of the increase to each upper-tier CFC's basis in either the stock in the lower-tier CFC or the property by reason of which such upper-tier CFC is considered to own stock in the lower-tier CFC under section 958(a) shall be equal to the amount that would be excluded from the gross income of such upper-tier CFC

☐ Par. 9. Section 1.961-4 is added to read as follows:

§1.961-4. Section 304 transactions.—(a) *Deemed redemption treated as a distribution.*—(1) *In general.*—In the case of a stock acquisition described in section 304(a)(1) that is treated as a distribution of earnings and profits of a foreign acquiring corporation or a foreign issuing corporation or both, basis adjustments shall be made in accordance with the rules of §§1.961-1, 1.961-2, and 1.961-3.

(2) *Examples.*—The application of this section is illustrated by the following examples:

Example 1. Cross-chain acquisition of first-tier CFC. (i) *Facts.* DP, a domestic corporation, owns all of the stock in DS, a domestic corporation, and F1, a CFC. DS owns all of the stock in F2, a CFC. DP, DS, F1 and F2 all use the calendar year as their taxable year and F1 and F2 use the U.S. dollar as their functional currency. During year 1, F1 purchases all of the stock in F2 from DS for $80x in a transaction described in section 304(a)(1). At the end of year 1, before taking into account the purchase of F2's stock, DP has a previously taxed earnings and profits account consisting of $20x of section 959(c)(2) earnings and profits with respect to its stock in F1, and F1 has section 959(c)(2) earnings and profits of $20x and non-previously taxed earnings and profits of $10x. At the end of year 1, before taking into account the purchase of F2's stock, DS has a previously taxed earnings and profits account consisting of $50x of section 959(c)(2) earnings and profits with respect to its stock in F2 and F2 has section 959(c)(2) earnings and profits of $50x and non-previously taxed earnings and profits of $0. Before taking into account the purchase of F2's stock, DP's basis in F1's stock is $30x and DS's basis in F2's stock is $60x.

(ii) *Analysis.* Under section 304(a)(1), DS is deemed to have transferred the F2 stock to F1 in exchange for F1 stock in a transaction to which section 351(a) applies, and F1 is treated as having redeemed, for $80x, the F1 stock hypothetically issued to DS. The payment of $80x is treated as a distribution to which section 301 applies. Under section 304(b)(2), the determination of the amount

pursuant to section 959(b) and §1.959-2(a) if the amount that gave rise to the adjustment to the United States shareholder's previously taxed earnings and profits account with respect to its stock in the lower-tier CFC were actually distributed through a chain of ownership to such upper-tier CFC. In addition, any decrease to such United States shareholder's (or successor in interest's) previously taxed earnings and profits account with respect to its stock in a distributor under §1.959-3(e)(3) shall result in a corresponding reduction of the basis of the distributee's stock in the distributor. The reduction of the basis of the distributee's stock in the distributor shall be equal to the amount that would be excluded from the gross income of the distributee pursuant to section 959(b) and §1.959-2(a).

(2) *Example.*—The application of this paragraph (b) is illustrated by the following example:

Example. Less than wholly owned CFC. (i) *Facts.* DP, a United States shareholder, owns 70%, and FP, a nonresident alien, owns 30% of the stock in FC, a CFC. FC in turn owns 100% of the stock in FS, a CFC. Each of DP, FC, FN and FS use the calendar year as their taxable year and both FC and FS use the U.S. dollar as their functional currency. Entering year 1, DP has a basis of $50x in FC and FC has a basis of $50x in FS. In year 1, FS earns $100x of subpart F income. In year 2, FC sells FS for $150x.

(ii) *Analysis.* On December 31 of year 1, DP includes $70x of the $100x of subpart F income earned by FS in gross income under section 951(a)(1)(A). DP increases its section 959(c)(2) earnings and profits in its earnings and profits account with respect to its stock in FS by $70x pursuant to §1.959-3(e)(2)(i). DP increases its basis in FC from $50x to $120x pursuant to §1.961-1(b). FC increases its basis in FS from $50x to $150x pursuant to paragraph (b)(1) of this section (but only for purposes of determining FC's subpart F income with respect to DP) because if the $100x amount of subpart F income of FS that caused the $70x increase to DP's previously taxed earnings and profits account with respect to its stock in FS had been distributed to FC, the entire $100x would be excluded from FC's gross income pursuant to section 959(b) and §1.959-2(a) for purposes of determining DP's inclusion under section 951(a)(1)(A). In year 2, when FC sells FS, for purposes of determining DP's subpart F inclusion, FC is treated as recognizing $0 on the sale ($150x sale proceeds - $150x basis). Therefore, DP includes $0 in income under section 951(a)(1)(A) as a result of the sale. Although the sale does not generate gain for purposes of determining DP's subpart F inclusion, it does cause FC's non-previously taxed earnings and profits to be increased by $100x ($150x sale proceeds - $50x basis).

(c) *Translation rules.*—Rules similar to those provided in §1.961-1(c)(3) and §1.961-2(b)(3) shall apply for purposes of determining the exchange rates used to reflect any change to the basis of stock or other property under this section. [Reg. §1.961-3.]

which is a dividend is made as if the distribution were made, first, by F1 to the extent of its earnings and profits ($30x), and then by F2 to the extent of its earnings and profits ($50x). Before taking into account the deemed distributions, DS had a previously taxed earnings and profits account of $50x with respect to its stock in F2 and DP had a previously taxed earnings and profits account of $20x with respect to its stock in F1. Under §1.959-3(h)(4)(i), DS is deemed to have a previously taxed earnings and profits account with respect to stock in F1. Under §1.959-3(g)(1), the section 959(c)(2) earnings and profits in DP's previously taxed earnings and profits account with respect to F1 stock are reduced from $20x to $0. As a result, DP's basis in F1's stock is reduced from $30x to $10x under §1.961-2(a). The deemed distribution of earnings and profits by F2 causes the section 959(c)(2) earnings and profits in DS's previously taxed earnings and profits account with respect to F2 stock to be reduced from $50x to $0. Under §1.961-2(a) and §1.961-3(a), F1's basis in its newly acquired F2's stock is reduced from $60x to $10x. F1 has a transferred basis of $10x in F2's stock.

Example 2. Cross-chain acquisition of lower-tier CFC. (i) *Facts.* DP, a domestic corporation, owns all of the stock in two CFCs, FX and FY. FX owns all of the stock in FZ, a CFC. FX, FY and FZ use the U.S. dollar as their functional currency. During year 1, FY purchases all of the stock in FZ from FX for $80x in a transaction described in section 304(a)(1). On December 31 of year 1, before taking into account the purchase of FZ's stock, FY has section 959(c)(2) earnings and profits of $20x and non-previously taxed earnings and profits of $10x, and FZ has section 959(c)(2) earnings and profits of $50x and non-previously taxed earnings and profits of $0. Before taking into account FX's purchase of FZ's stock, DP's basis in FX's stock is $60x; DP's basis in FY's stock is $30x; and FX's basis in FZ's stock, for purposes of determining the amount includible in DP's gross income under section 951(a), is $60x.

(ii) *Analysis.* Under section 304(a)(1), FX is deemed to have transferred the FZ stock to FY in exchange for FY stock in a transaction to which section 351(a) applies, and FY is treated as having redeemed, for $80x, the FY stock hypothetically issued to FX. The payment of $80x is treated as a distribution of property to which section 301 applies. Under section 304(b)(2), the determination of the amount which is a dividend is made as if the distribution were made, first, by FY to the extent of its earnings and profits, $30x, and then by FX to the extent of its earnings and profits, $50x. Under §1.959-2(b), FX is deemed to receive the distributions from FY and FZ through a chain of ownership described in section 958(a), and $70x is excluded from FX's gross income under section 959(b) and §1.959-2(a). Under §1.959-3(e)(3), the section 959(c)(2) earnings and profits in DP's previously taxed earnings and profits account for the stock in FY are reduced from $20x to $0; the section 959(c)(2) earnings and profits in

DP's previously taxed earnings and profits account for the stock in FZ are reduced from $50x to $0; and the section 959(c)(2) earnings and profits in DP's previously taxed earnings and profits account for the stock in FX are increased from $0 to $70x (and such account is further increased to $80x due to the inclusion of $10x of subpart F income in DP's gross income under section 951(a)). Under §1.961-2(a), DP's basis in the stock in FY is reduced from $30x to $10x. DP's basis in the stock in FX is first reduced by $50x under §1.961-2(a), and then increased by $80x under §1.961-1(b), for a net increase of $30x, to $90x. Under §1.961-3(a), FY's basis in the stock in FZ, for purposes of determining the amount includible in DP's gross income under section 951(a), is reduced by $50x to $10x.

[Reg. §1.961-4.]

Foreign-Derived Intangible Income: Global Intangible Low-Taxed Income: Deduction

Foreign-Derived Intangible Income: Global Intangible Low-Taxed Income: Deduction.—Amendments to Reg. §1.962-1, providing guidance to determine the amount of the deduction for foreign-derived intangible income and global intangible low-taxed income, are proposed (published in the Federal Register on March 6, 2019) (REG-104464-18).

Par. 3. Section 1.962-1 is amended by adding paragraphs (b)(1)(i)(A)(2), (b)(1)(i)(B)(3), and revising paragraph (d) to read as follows:

§1.962-1. Limitation of tax for individuals on amounts included in gross income under section 951(a).

* * *

(b) * * *

(1) * * *

(i) * * *

(A) * * *

(2) His GILTI inclusion amount (as defined in §1.951A-1(c)(1)) for the taxable year; plus

* * *

(B) * * *

(3) The portion of the deduction under section 250 and §1.250(a)-1 that would be allowed to a domestic corporation equal to the percentage applicable to global intangible low-taxed income for the taxable year under section 250(a)(1)(B) (including as modified by

section 250(a)(3)(B)) multiplied by the sum of the amount described in paragraph (b)(1)(i)(A)(2) of this section and the amount described in paragraph (b)(1)(i)(A)(3) of this section that is attributable to the amount described in paragraph (b)(1)(i)(A)(2) of this section.

* * *

(d) *Applicability dates.*—Except as otherwise provided in this paragraph (d), paragraph (b)(1)(i) of this section applies beginning the last taxable year of a foreign corporation that begins before January 1, 2018, and with respect to a United States person, for the taxable year in which or with which such taxable year of the foreign corporation ends. Paragraph (b)(1)(i)(B)(3) applies to taxable years of a foreign corporation ending on or after March 4, 2019, and with respect to a United States person, for the taxable year in which or with which such taxable year of the foreign corporation ends.

CFCs: Insurance Income: After 1986: Tax Adjustments

Controlled Foreign Corporations: Insurance Income: Tax Years After 1986.—Reproduced below is a proposed amendment to Reg. §1.964-1, relating to the election to expense certain depreciable business assets (published in the Federal Register on April 17, 1991).

☐ Par. 6. Section 1.964-1 is amended by adding the following language to the end of paragraph (c)(5):

§1.964-1. Determination of the earnings and profits of a foreign corporation

* * *

(c) *Tax adjustments.*—* * *

(5) *Controlling United States shareholders.*—* * * In the event that a foreign corporation is a controlled foreign corporation solely by virtue of section 953(c)(1)(B), the controlling United States shareholders of the foreign corporation shall be those United States shareholders (as defined in section 953(c)(1)(A)) who, in the aggregate, own (within the meaning of section 958(a)) more than 25 percent of

the total combined voting power of all classes of the stock of such corporation entitled to vote. In the event that the foreign corporation is a controlled foreign corporation solely by virtue of section 953(c)(1)(B) but the United States shareholders (as defined in section 953(c)(1)(A)) do not, in the aggregate, own (within the meaning of section 958(a)) more than 25 percent of the total combined voting power of all classes of the stock of such corporation entitled to vote, the controlling shareholders of the foreign corporation shall be all those United States shareholders (within the meaning of section 953(c)(1)(A)) who own (within the meaning of section 958(a)) stock of such corporation.

Foreign Corporations: Tax Accounting Elections

Foreign Corporations: Tax Accounting Elections.—Amendments to Reg. §1.964-1, clarifying the rules for controlling domestic shareholders to adopt or change a method of accounting or taxable year on behalf of a foreign corporation, are proposed (published in the Federal Register on November 4, 2011) (REG-114749-09). Amendments to Reg. §§1.952-2 and 1.964-1, proposed on July 1, 1992, are withdrawn.

☐ Par. 2. Section 1.964-1 is amended as follows:

1. Adding a new paragraph (a)(4).

2. In paragraph (b)(3), revising the introductory text, redesignating *Example (1)* as *Example*, and removing *Example (2)*.

3. Revising the first sentence of paragraph (c)(1).

4. Revising paragraph (c)(1)(iii) and removing paragraphs (c)(1)(iii)(*a*), (c)(1)(iii)(*b*), and (c)(1)(iii)(*c*).

5. Revising paragraph (c)(1)(v).

6. Inserting a sentence after the fourth sentence of paragraph (c)(2), revising the fifth sentence of paragraph (c)(2), and adding a sentence at the end of paragraph (c)(2).

7. Revising paragraph (c)(8).

8. Adding a new paragraph (c)(9).

9. Revising paragraph (d).

The additions and revisions read as follows:

§1.964-1. Determination of the earnings and profits of a foreign corporation

* * *

(a)(4) *Example.*—The rules of this paragraph (a) are illustrated by the following example.

Example. (i) *Facts.* P, a domestic corporation, owns all of the outstanding stock of FX, a controlled foreign corporation. In preparing its books for purposes of accounting to its shareholders, FX uses an accounting method (Local Books Method) to determine the

amount of its depreciation expense that does not conform to accounting principles generally accepted in the United States (U.S. GAAP) or to U.S. income tax accounting standards as described in paragraph (c). The amount of the adjustment necessary to conform the depreciation expense determined under the Local Books Method with the amount that would be determined under U.S. GAAP for purposes of paragraph (a)(1)(ii) of this section if FX were a domestic corporation is not material. However, the adjustment necessary to conform the amount of the depreciation expense under the Local Books Method to U.S. income tax accounting standards for purposes of paragraph (a)(1)(iii) of this section is material.

(ii) *Result.* Although FX is not required to make the adjustment necessary to conform the amount of its tax expense reserve deduction determined under the Local Books Method to the amount that would be determined under U.S. GAAP, FX is required to make the adjustment necessary to conform the amount of the depreciation expense determined under the Local Books Method to the amount of depreciation expense for the current year that would be allowed under U.S. income tax accounting standards as described in paragraph (c).

(b) * * *

(3) *Example.*—The rules of this paragraph (b) are illustrated by the following example.

* * *

(c) * * *

(1) *In general.*—Except as otherwise provided in the Code and regulations (for example, section 952(c)(3) (earnings and profits determined without regard to section 312(n)(4)-(6) for purposes of section 952(c)), the tax accounting standards to be applied in making the adjustments required by paragraph (a)(1)(iii) of this section shall be those applied to domestic corporations, including but not limited to the following:

* * *

(iii) *Depreciation and amortization.*—Depreciation and amortization shall be computed in accordance with the provisions of section 312(k) and the regulations under that section. In the case of a foreign corporation described in section 312(k)(4) (one with less than 20 percent U.S.-source gross income), depreciation and amortization of items that are not described in section 312(k)(2) or (k)(3) shall be determined under the rules for determining taxable income. For example, amortization for amortizable section 197 intangibles (as defined in section 197(c)) is calculated in accordance with section 197, and depreciation for real property is calculated in accordance with section 168(g)(2)(C)(iii). For any taxable year beginning before July 1, 1972, depreciation shall be computed in accordance with section 167 and the regulations under that section.

* * *

(v) *Taxable years.*—The period for computation of taxable income and earnings and profits known as the taxable year shall reflect the provisions of sections 441 and 898 and the regulations under those sections.

* * *

(2) *Adoption or change of method or taxable year.*—* * * Once adopted, a method of accounting or taxable year may be changed by or on behalf of the foreign corporation only in accordance with the applicable provisions of the Code and regulations. Adjustments to the appropriate separate category (as defined in §1.904-5(a)(1)) of earnings and profits and income of the foreign corporation (including a category of subpart F income described in section 952(a) or, in the case of foreign base company income, described in §1.954-1(c)(1)(iii)) shall be required under section 481 to prevent any duplication or omission of amounts attributable to previous years that would otherwise result from any change in a method of accounting. * * * See paragraph (c)(9) of this section for rules if the change in method of accounting is required in connection with an audit of the foreign corporation's controlling domestic shareholders (as defined in paragraph (c)(5) of this section).

* * *

(8) *Examples.*—The following examples illustrate the application of paragraph (c) of this section:

Example 1. P, a domestic corporation, owns all of the outstanding stock of FX, a controlled foreign corporation organized in 2012. In maintaining its books for the purpose of accounting to its shareholders, FX deducts additions to a reserve for bad debts. Assume that if FX were a domestic corporation, it would be required to use the specific charge-off method under section 166 with respect to allowable bad debt losses. In accordance with paragraph (c)(1)(i) of this section, FX's reserve deductions must be adjusted (if the adjustments are material) in order to compute its earnings and profits in accordance with U.S. income tax accounting standards as described in paragraph (c). Accordingly, P must compute FX's earnings and profits using the specific charge-off method of accounting for bad debts in accordance with section 166.

Example 2. FX, a controlled foreign corporation, maintains its books for the purpose of accounting to its shareholders by capitalizing research and experimental expenses. A, B, and C, the United States shareholders (as defined in section 951(b)) of FX, own 45 percent, 30 percent, and 25 percent, respectively, of its only class of outstanding stock. For the first taxable year of FX, pursuant to paragraph (c)(3) of this section, B and C adopt on its behalf the section 174 method of currently deducting research and experimental

expenses. Regardless of whether A objects to this action or receives the notice required by paragraph (c)(3)(iii) of this section, adjustments must be made to reflect the use of the section 174 method in computing the earnings and profits of FX with respect to A as well as with respect to B and C.

Example 3. (i) P, a calendar year domestic corporation that uses the fair market value method of apportioning interest expense, owns all of the outstanding stock of FX, a controlled foreign corporation organized in 2002 that uses the calendar year as its taxable year for foreign tax purposes. On June 1, 2012, FX makes a distribution to P. Prior to that distribution, none of the significant events specified in paragraph (c)(6) of this section had occurred. In addition, neither P nor FX had ever made or adopted, or been required to make or adopt, an election or method of accounting or taxable year for United States tax purposes with respect to FX. FX does not act to make any election or adopt any method of accounting or a taxable year for United States tax purposes.

(ii) P must compute FX's earnings and profits for FX's 2002 through 2012 taxable years in order to determine if any portion of the 2012 distribution is taxable as a dividend and to determine P's deemed paid foreign tax credit on such portion under section 902. Under paragraph (c)(2) of this section, P may make an election or adopt a method or methods of accounting and a taxable year on behalf of FX by satisfying the requirements of paragraph (c)(3) of this section by the due date (with extensions) of P's Federal income tax return for 2012, its taxable year with which ends FX's 2012 taxable year. Under paragraph (c)(4) of this section, any such election or adoption will govern the computation of FX's earnings and profits for its taxable years beginning in 2002 and subsequent taxable years for purposes of determining the Federal income tax liability of P and any subsequent shareholders of FX in 2012 and subsequent taxable years, unless the Commissioner consents to a change.

(iii) If P fails to satisfy the requirements under paragraph (c)(3) of this section and such failure is not shown to the satisfaction of the Commissioner to be due to reasonable cause, the earnings and profits of FX will be computed on the basis of a calendar taxable year as if no elections were made and any permissible methods of accounting not requiring an election and reflected in FX's books were adopted. Any subsequent attempt by FX or P to change an accounting method or taxable year of FX shall be effective only if the Commissioner consents to the change.

Example 4. (i) The facts are the same as in *Example 3*, except that P owns 80 percent, rather than all, of the outstanding stock of FX. M, a calendar year domestic corporation, owns the remaining 20 percent of the stock of FX beginning in 2002. M uses the tax book value method to allocate its interest expense under section 864(e)(4).

(ii) M, but not P, must compute FX's earnings and profits beginning in 2002 in order to determine the adjustment under §1.861-12(c) and §1.861-12T(c) to M's basis in the stock of FX for M's 2002 through 2011 taxable years. Because P, the controlling domestic shareholder of FX, has not made or adopted, or been required to make or adopt, an election or a method of accounting or taxable year with respect to FX, the earnings and profits of FX for 2002 through 2011 will be computed on the basis of a calendar taxable year as if no elections were made and any permissible methods of accounting not requiring an election and reflected in FX's books were adopted. However, a properly filed, timely election or adoption of a method of accounting or taxable year by, or on behalf of, FX with respect to FX's taxable year ending in 2012, when FX's earnings and profits are first significant for United States tax purposes for P, FX's controlling domestic shareholder, shall not be treated as a change in accounting method or a change in taxable year for any pre-2012 taxable year of FX. M will not be required to recompute its basis adjustments for 2002 through 2011 by reason of P's adoption of a method or methods of accounting or taxable year with respect to FX for 2012. See paragraph (c)(4)(iii) of this section. However, any method of accounting or taxable year adopted on behalf of FX by P pursuant to this paragraph (c) with respect to FX is binding on P, FX, and M for purposes of computing FX's earnings and profits in 2002 and subsequent taxable years for purposes of determining the Federal income tax liability of P, M, and any subsequent shareholders of FX in 2012 and subsequent taxable years, unless the Commissioner consents to a change.

Example 5. (i) In 1987, P, a calendar year domestic corporation that uses the tax book value method to allocate its interest expense under section 864(e)(4), acquired 50 percent of the outstanding stock of 10/50 Corp, a noncontrolled section 902 corporation organized in 1980. For taxable years beginning on or before April 25, 2006, the provisions of this paragraph (c) did not provide a mechanism for shareholders of noncontrolled section 902 corporations to make elections or adopt methods of accounting or a taxable year on behalf of noncontrolled section 902 corporations. However, P had to compute 10/50 Corp's earnings and profits in order to determine the adjustment under §1.861-12(c) and §1.861-12T(c) to P's basis in the stock of 10/50 Corp beginning with P's 1987 taxable year.

(ii) For taxable years beginning on or before April 25, 2006, P was required to compute 10/50 Corp's earnings and profits as if any permissible method of accounting not requiring an election and reflected in 10/50 Corp's books had been adopted. See paragraph (c)(4)(ii) of this section. In taxable years beginning after April 25, 2006, in accordance with paragraph (c)(3) of this section P may request the consent of the Commissioner to change any method of accounting or the taxable year on behalf of 10/50 Corp.

(9) *Change of method on audit.*—If, in connection with an audit (or audits) of one or more shareholders of the foreign corporation who collectively would constitute the foreign corporation's controlling domestic shareholder(s) if they undertook to act on the corporation's behalf, the Commissioner determines that a method of accounting of the foreign corporation does not clearly reflect income, the computation of earnings and profits shall be made in a manner which, in the opinion of the Commissioner, does clearly reflect income. See section 446 and the related regulations. The Commissioner shall provide written notice of the change in method of accounting to each such shareholder and to all other persons known by the Commissioner to be domestic shareholders who own (within the meaning of section 958(a)) stock of the foreign corporation. However, the failure of the Commissioner to provide such notice to any such other person shall not invalidate the change of method, which shall bind both the foreign corporation and all of its domestic shareholders as to the computation of the foreign corporation's earnings and profits for the taxable year of the foreign corporation for which the method of accounting is changed and in subsequent taxable years unless the Commissioner consents to a change.

(d) *Effective/applicability date.*—This section applies in computing earnings and profits of foreign corporations in taxable years of foreign corporations beginning on or after the date of publication of these regulations as final regulations in the **Federal Register**, and taxable years of shareholders with or within which such taxable years of the foreign corporations end. See 26 CFR § 1.964-1 (revised as of April 1, 2011) for rules applicable to taxable years beginning before such date.

Allocation and Apportionment of Deductions and Foreign Tax Credit: Guidance

Allocation and Apportionment of Deductions and Foreign Tax Credit: Guidance.—Amendments to Reg. § 1.965-5, relating to the allocation and apportionment of deductions and creditable foreign taxes, the definition of financial services income, foreign tax redeterminations, availability of foreign tax credits under the transition tax, and the application of the foreign tax credit limitation to consolidated groups, are proposed (published in the Federal Register on December 17, 2019) (REG-105495-19).

Par. 25. Amend § 1.965-5 by:

1. Redesignating paragraph (b) as paragraph (b)(1).
2. Adding new introductory text for paragraph (b).
3. Revising the heading of newly redesignated paragraph (b)(1).
4. Adding paragraph (b)(2).

The revision and additions read as follows:

§ 1.965-5. Allowance of a credit or deduction for foreign income taxes.

* * *

(b) *Rules for foreign income taxes paid or accrued.*—(1) *In general.*— * * *

(2) *Attributing taxes to section 959(a) distributions of section 965 previously taxed earnings and profits.*—For purposes of paragraph (b)(1) of this section, foreign income taxes are attributable to a distribution of section 965(a) previously taxed earnings and profits or section 965(b) previously taxed earnings and profits if such taxes would be allocated and apportioned to a distribution of such previously taxed earnings and profits under the principles of § 1.904-6(a)(1)(iv), regardless of whether an actual distribution is made or recognized for Federal income tax purposes. Therefore, for example, a credit or deduction for the applicable percentage of foreign income taxes imposed on a United States shareholder that pays foreign tax on a distribution that is not recognized for Federal income tax purposes (for example, in the case of a consent dividend or stock dividend upon which a withholding tax is imposed) is not allowed under paragraph (b)(1) of this section to the extent it is attributable to a distribution of section 965(a) previously taxed earnings and profits or section 965(b) previously taxed earnings and profits under the principles of § 1.904-6(a)(1)(iv). For taxable years of foreign corporations beginning after December 31, 2019, in lieu of applying the principles of § 1.904-6 under this paragraph (b)(2), the rules in § 1.861-20 apply by treating the portion of a distribution attributable to section 965(a) previously taxed earnings and profits and the portion of a distribution attributable to section 965(b) previously taxed earnings and profits each as a statutory grouping, and the portion of the distribution that is attributable to other earnings and profits as the residual grouping. See § 1.861-20(g)(7) (*Example 6*).

* * *

Allocation and Apportionment of Deductions and Foreign Tax Credit: Guidance

Allocation and Apportionment of Deductions and Foreign Tax Credit: Guidance.—Amendments to Reg. § 1.965-9, relating to the allocation and apportionment of deductions and creditable foreign taxes, the definition of financial services income, foreign tax redeterminations, availability of foreign tax credits under the transition tax, and the application of the foreign tax credit limitation to consolidated groups, are proposed (published in the Federal Register on December 17, 2019) (REG-105495-19).

Par. 26. Section 1.965-9 is amended by adding a sentence to the end of paragraph (c) to read as follows:

§ 1.965-9. Applicability dates.

* * *

(c) * * * Section 1.965-5(b)(2) applies to taxable years of foreign corporations that end on or after December 16, 2019, and with respect to a United States person, to the taxable years in which or with which such taxable years of the foreign corporations end.

Foreign Currency Gain or Loss: Recognition and Deferral

Foreign Currency Gain or Loss: Recognition and Deferral.—Amendments to Reg. §§ 1.987-1, 1.987-3, 1.987-6 and 1.987-8, relating to the recognition and deferral of foreign currency gain or loss under section 987 with respect to a qualified business unit (QBU) in connection with certain QBU terminations and certain other transactions involving partnerships, are proposed (published in the Federal Register on December 8, 2016) (REG-128276-12). Amendments to Reg. §§ 1.987-2, 1.987-4 and 1.987-12 adopted and amendments to Reg. § 1.987-7 are withdrawn by T.D. 9857, May 10, 2019.

Par. 2. Section 1.987-1 is amended by adding paragraphs (b)(1)(iii), (b)(6), (c)(1)(ii)(B), (c)(3)(i)(E), (d)(3), (f), (g)(2)(i)(B) and (C), and (g)(3)(i)(E) through (H) to read as follows:

§ 1.987-1. Scope, definitions, and special rules.

* * *

(b) * * *

(1) * * *

(iii) [The text of the proposed amendment to § 1.987-1(b)(1)(iii) is the same as the text of § 1.987-1T(b)(1)(iii) as added by T.D. 9795].

* * *

(6) [The text of the proposed amendment to § 1.987-1(b)(6) is the same as the text of § 1.987-1T(b)(6) as added by T.D. 9795].

(c) * * *

(1) * * *

(ii) * * *

(B) [The text of the proposed amendment to § 1.987-1(c)(1)(ii)(B) is the same as the text of § 1.987-1T(c)(1)(ii)(B) as added by T.D. 9795]

* * *

(3) * * *

(i) * * *

(E) [The text of the proposed amendment to §1.987-1(c)(3)(i)(E) is the same as the text of §1.987-1T(c)(3)(i)(E) as added by T.D. 9795].

* * *

(d) * * *

(3) [The text of the proposed amendment to §1.987-1(d)(3) is the same as the text of §1.987-1T(d)(3) as added by T.D. 9795].

* * *

(f) [The text of the proposed amendment to §1.987-1(f) is the same as the text of §1.987-1T(f) as added by T.D. 9795].

* * *

(g) * * *

(2) * * *

(i) * * *

(B) [The text of the proposed amendment to §1.987-1(g)(2)(i)(B) is the same as the text of §1.987-1T(g)(2)(i)(B) as added by T.D. 9795].

Par. 4. Section 1.987-3 is amended by adding paragraphs (b)(2)(ii), (b)(4), (c)(2)(ii) and (v), (d), and *Example 9* through *Example 14* of paragraph (e) to read as follows:

§1.987-3. Determination of section 987 taxable income or loss of an owner of a section 987 QBU.

* * *

(b) * * *

(2) * * *

(ii) [The text of the proposed amendment to §1.987-3(b)(2)(ii) is the same as the text of §1.987-3T(b)(2)(ii) as added by T.D. 9795].

* * *

(4) [The text of the proposed amendment to §1.987-3(b)(4) is the same as the text of §1.987-3T(b)(4) as added by T.D. 9795].

* * *

(c) * * *

(2) * * *

(ii) [The text of the proposed amendment to §1.987-3(c)(2)(ii) is the same as the text of §1.987-3T(c)(2)(ii) as added by T.D. 9795].

* * *

(v) [The text of the proposed amendment to §1.987-3(c)(2)(v) is the same as the text of §1.987-3T(c)(2)(v) as added by T.D. 9795].

* * *

Par. 6. Section 1.987-6 is amended by adding paragraph (b)(4) to read as follows:

§1.987-6. Character and source of section 987 gain or loss.

* * *

(b) * * *

Par. 8. Section 1.987-8 is amended by adding paragraph (d) to read as follows:

§1.987-8. Termination of a section 987 QBU.

* * *

(C) [The text of the proposed amendment to §1.987-1(g)(2)(i)(C) is the same as the text of §1.987-1T(g)(2)(i)(C) as added by T.D. 9795].

* * *

(3) * * *

(i) * * *

(E) [The text of the proposed amendment to §1.987-1(g)(3)(i)(E) is the same as the text of §1.987-1T(g)(3)(i)(E) as added by T.D. 9795].

(F) [The text of the proposed amendment to §1.987-1(g)(3)(i)(F) is the same as the text of §1.987-1T(g)(3)(i)(F) as added by T.D. 9795].

(G) [The text of the proposed amendment to §1.987-1(g)(3)(i)(G) is the same as the text of §1.987-1T(g)(3)(i)(G) as added by T.D. 9795].

(H) [The text of the proposed amendment to §1.987-1(g)(3)(i)(H) is the same as the text of §1.987-1T(g)(3)(i)(H) as added by T.D. 9795].

* * *

(d) [The text of the proposed amendment to §1.987-3(d) is the same as the text of §1.987-3T(d) as added by T.D. 9795].

(e) *Examples.*—* * *

Example 9 [The text of the proposed amendment to §1.987-3(e) *Example 9* is the same as the text of §1.987-3T(e) *Example 9* as added by T.D. 9795].

Example 10 [The text of the proposed amendment to §1.987-3(e) *Example 10* is the same as the text of §1.987-3T(e) *Example 10* as added by T.D. 9795].

Example 11 [The text of the proposed amendment to §1.987-3(e) *Example 11* is the same as the text of §1.987-3T(e) *Example 11* as added by T.D. 9795].

Example 12 [The text of the proposed amendment to §1.987-3(e) *Example 12* is the same as the text of §1.987-3T(e) *Example 12* as added by T.D. 9795].

Example 13 [The text of the proposed amendment to §1.987-3(e) *Example 13* is the same as the text of §1.987-3T(e) *Example 13* as added by T.D. 9795].

Example 14 [The text of the proposed amendment to §1.987-3(e) *Example 14* is the same as the text of §1.987-3T(e) *Example 14* as added by T.D. 9795].

* * *

(4) [The text of the proposed amendment to §1.987-6(b)(4) is the same as the text of §1.987-6T(b)(4) as added by T.D. 9795].

* * *

(d) [The text of the proposed amendment to §1.987-8(d) is the same as the text of §1.987-8T(d) as added by T.D. 9795].

* * *

Gain or Loss: Nonfunctional Currency Transactions

Gain or Loss: Nonfunctional Currency Transactions.—Amendments to Reg. §§1.988-1 and 1.988-2, relating to the taxation of gain or loss from certain foreign currency transactions, are proposed (published in the Federal Register on March 17, 1992) (REG-208202-91) [originally issued as INTL-15-91]. Amendments to Reg. §1.988-2(b)(15), (d)(5), (e)(3)(iv) and (e)(7) were adopted 1/12/2000 by T.D. 8860. Amendments to Reg. §1.988-1(a)(3), (4) and (5) were withdrawn on 8/29/2003 by REG-106486-98; INTL-0015-91.

☐ Par. 2. Section 1.988-1 is amended by adding paragraphs (a)(3), (4), and (5), and adding *Example 12* to paragraph (a)(6) to read as follows [amendments to Reg. §1.988-1(a)(3), (4) and (5) were withdrawn on 8/29/2003 by REG-106486-98, leaving only the amendment to Reg. §1.988-1(a)(6), below]:

§1.988-1. Certain definitions and special rules.

(a) * * *

(6) * * *

Example 12. (i) On January 1, 1993, X issues a 3 year bond with the following terms. The bond is priced at par with a principal amount of $100. X agrees to make three payments on December 31 of each year of $5.28 and, upon maturity, will repay 200 Swiss francs (Sf) in satisfaction of the principal due. The spot rate on January 1, 1993 is Sf1 = $.50.

(ii) The debt instrument is a dual currency debt instrument within the meaning of paragraph (a)(4) of this section. The dual currency debt instrument is separated into two component hypothet-

ical debt instruments. The first is a hypothetical Swiss franc denominated zero coupon bond with a stated redemption price at maturity of Sf200 discounted at a rate consistent with the rules of §1.1273-2(d)(2)(iv) (assume 5% compounded annually) to determine an issue price of Sf172.77. The second is a 3 year hypothetical dollar self-amortizing installment obligation with annual payments of $5.28, a principal amount of $13.62 [$100 − (Sf172.77 × $.50)] and a yield to maturity of 8% compounded annually. Issuing a hypothetical dollar denominated installment obligation is not a section 988 transaction. Issuing the hypothetical Swiss franc zero coupon bond is a section 988 transaction subject to the computational rules of §1.988-2(b).

Reg. §1.988-1(a)(6)

☐ Par. 3. Section 1.988-2 is amended by adding paragraphs (b)(14) and (15), (d)(5), (e)(3)(iv) and (e)(7) as follows [amendments to Reg. § 1.988-2(b)(15), (d)(5), (e)(3)(iv) and (e)(7) were adopted 1/12/2000 by T.D. 8860, leaving only the amendments to Reg. § 1.988-2(b)(14), below]:

§ 1.988-2. Recognition and computation of exchange gain or loss.
* * *

(b) * * *

(14) *Nonfunctional currency debt replaced by other related person debt denominated in a different currency.*—(i) *In general.*—If a debt instrument denominated in a nonfunctional currency (or the payments of which are determined with reference to a nonfunctional currency) is entered into between related persons as defined in sections 267(b) and 707(b), and the instrument is disposed of or otherwise terminated prior to maturity in a transaction in which exchange gain or loss would be recognized, the District Director or the Assistant Commissioner (International) may defer such gain or loss if he determines that the debt has in effect been replaced with other debt denominated in a different currency (replacement debt) entered into with the same or another related person (regardless of whether the replacement debt is denominated in, or determined by reference to, the taxpayer's functional currency). Such deferral, however, shall not exceed the earlier of the date the replacement debt is terminated in a transaction in which gain or loss is recognized or the maturity date of the replacement debt (so long as such debt is not replaced with debt of a related person in a different currency).

(ii) *Debt for debt exchanges in the same nonfunctional currency.*—[RESERVED]

(iii) *Example.*—The following example illustrates the application of this paragraph (b)(14).

Example. X is a calendar year corporation with the dollar as its functional currency. On January 1, 1995, X issues a par bond with a principal amount of 3,500,000 British pounds (£) to Y, a related person under section 267(b). The bond pays interest at the rate of 10% compounded semi-annually and matures on December 31, 2009. The £3,500,000 have a spot value of $5,000,000 on January 1, 1995. On January 1, 1997, X and Y agree to convert X's pound obligation to a dollar obligation in the principal amount of $5,300,000, the spot value of the pound principal amount on that date. Assume that but for paragraph (b)(14) of this section, X would realize and recognize a $300,000 exchange loss on January 1, 1997. However, the District Director may defer X's $300,000 exchange loss until the $5,300,000 obligation matures or is otherwise terminated in a transaction in which gain or loss is recognized.

(iv) *Effective date.*—Paragraph (b)(14)(i) of this section shall be effective for transactions entered into after March 17, 1992.
* * *

Section 1256 Contracts: Swap Exclusions

Section 1256 Contracts: Swap Exclusions.—Amendment to Reg. § 1.988-1, providing guidance on the category of swaps and similar agreements that are within the scope of Code Sec. 1256(b)(2)(B), are proposed (published in the Federal Register on September 16, 2011) (REG-111283-11).

☐ Par. 6. Section 1.988-1 is amended by:

1. Revising paragraph (a)(2)(iii)(B)(*2*).

2. Adding two sentences to the end of paragraph (a)(2)(iii)(C) The revision and addition read as follows:

§ 1.988-1. Certain definitions and special rules.—(a) * * *

(2) * * *

(iii) * * *

(B) * * *

(*2*) Definition of notional principal contract. Generally, the term "notional principal contract" means a contract defined in § 1.446-3(c). However, a "notional principal contract" shall only be considered as described in paragraph (a)(2)(iii)(B)(*1*) of this section if the underlying property to which the instrument ultimately relates is money (for example, functional currency), nonfunctional currency, or property the value of which is determined by reference to an interest

rate. Thus, the term "notional principal contract" includes a currency swap as defined in § 1.988-2(e)(2)(ii), but does not include a swap referenced to a commodity or equity index.

(C) * * * The rules of this paragraph (a)(2)(iii) apply to notional principal contracts as defined in § 1.446-3(c) that are entered into on or after the date of publication of a Treasury decision adopting these rules as final regulations in the **Federal Register**. Section 1.988-1(a)(2)(iii) as contained in 26 CFR part 1 revised April 1, 2011, continues to apply to notional principal contracts entered into before the date of publication of a Treasury decision adopting these rules as final regulations in the **Federal Register**.
* * *

Foreign Currency Gain or Loss: Recognition and Deferral

Foreign Currency Gain or Loss: Recognition and Deferral.—Amendments to Reg. §§ 1.988-1 and 1.988-2, relating to the recognition and deferral of foreign currency gain or loss under section 987 with respect to a qualified business unit (QBU) in connection with certain QBU terminations and certain other transactions involving partnerships, are proposed (published in the Federal Register on December 8, 2016) (REG-128276-12).

Par. 10. Section 1.988-1 is amended by adding paragraph (a)(3) to read as follows:

§ 1.988-1. Certain definitions and special rules.
* * *

(a) * * *

(3) [The text of the proposed amendment to § 1.988-1(a)(3) is the same as the text of § 1.988-1T(a)(3) as added by T.D. 9795].
* * *

Par. 11. Section 1.988-2 is amended by revising paragraph (b)(16) and adding paragraph (i) to read as follows:

§ 1.988-2. Recognition and computation of exchange gain or loss.
* * *

(b) * * *

(16) [The text of the proposed amendment to § 1.988-2(b)(16) is the same as the text of § 1.988-2T(b)(16) as added by T.D. 9795].
* * *

(i) [The text of the proposed amendment to § 1.988-2(i) is the same as the text of § 1.988-2T(i) as added by T.D. 9795].

Global Dealing Operations: Allocation and Sourcing of Income and Deductions

Global Dealing Operations: Allocation and Sourcing of Income and Deductions.—Amendments to Reg. § 1.988-4, relating to the allocation and sourcing of income, deductions, gains and losses from a global dealing operation, are proposed (published in the Federal Register on March 6, 1998) (REG-208299-90).

☐ Par. 12. Section 1.988-4 is amended as follows:

1. Paragraph (h) is redesignated as paragraph (i).

2. A new paragraph (h) is added.

The addition and revision read as follows:

§ 1.988-4. Source of gain or loss realized on a section 988 transfer.
* * *

(h) *Exchange gain or loss from a global dealing operation.*—Notwithstanding the provisions of this section, exchange gain or loss derived

by a participant in a global dealing operation, as defined in § 1.482-8(a)(2)(i), shall be sourced under the rules set forth in § 1.863-3(h).
* * *

Gain or Loss: Nonfunctional Currency Transactions

Gain or Loss: Nonfunctional Currency Transactions.—Amendments to Reg. §1.988-5, relating to the taxation of gain or loss from certain foreign currency transactions, are proposed (published in the Federal Register on March 17, 1992) (REG-208202-91) [originally issued as INTL-15-91].

☐ Par. 4. Section 1.988-5 is amended by adding paragraphs (d) and (f) to read as follows:

§1.988-5. Section 988(d) hedging transactions.

* * *

(d) *Hedges of certain nonfunctional currency payments.*—(1) *In general.*—If a qualified payment, as defined in paragraph (d)(2)(ii) of this section, and a hedge, as defined [in] paragraph (d)(2)(iii) of this section, satisfy the requirements of paragraph (d)(2)(i) of this section, the qualified payment and the hedge shall be integrated as provided in paragraph (d)(3) of this section. A transaction integrated in accordance with the provisions of this section shall be referred to as a "hedged qualified payment." For purposes of this paragraph (d), the rules of paragraph (b)(3)(ii) of this section shall apply.

(2) *Requirements and definitions.*—(i) *Requirements of hedged qualified payment.*—A qualified payment as defined in paragraph (d)(2)(ii) of this section and a hedge as defined in paragraph (d)(2)(iii) of this section must satisfy the following requirements in order to be treated as a hedged qualified payment under paragraph (d)(1) of this section.

(A) The qualified payment and the hedge are identified as an integrated transaction under the rules of paragraph (b)(3) of this section.

(B) The hedge is entered into (or in the case of nonfunctional currency deposited in a separate account with a bank or other financial institution, such currency is acquired and deposited) on or after the date the qualified payment becomes fixed (or declared in the case of a dividend), and before the accrual date as defined in paragraph (d)(2)(iv) of this section.

(C) The qualified payment is hedged in whole or in part throughout the period beginning with the date the hedge is identified in accordance with paragraph (b)(3) of this section and ending on or after the accrual date (but not later than the payment date).

(D) None of the parties to the hedge are related. For this purpose, parties are related if they satisfy any of the relationships defined in sections 267(b) and 707(b).

(E) In the case of a qualified business unit with a residence, as defined in section 988(a)(3)(B), outside of the United States, both the qualified payment and the hedge are properly reflected on the books of that qualified business unit.

(F) Subject to the limitations of paragraph (d)(2)(i)(E) of this section, both the qualified payment and the hedge are entered into by the same individual, partnership, trust, estate, or corporation. With respect to a corporation, the same corporation must enter into both the qualified payment and the hedge whether or not such corporation is a member of an affiliated group of corporations that files a consolidated return.

(G) With respect to a foreign person engaged in a U.S. trade or business that enters into a qualified payment or hedge through such trade or business, all items of income and expense associated with the qualified payment and the hedge would have been effectively connected with such U.S. trade or business throughout the term of the hedged qualified payment had this paragraph (d) not applied.

(ii) *Qualified payment.*—A qualified payment is—

(A) A declared but unpaid dividend denominated in or determined by reference to a nonfunctional currency with respect to the recipient; or

(B) An unaccrued rent or royalty payment denominated in or determined by reference to a nonfunctional currency of the taxpayer (whether the taxpayer is the payor or recipient), the amount of which is fixed on the date the hedge is entered into.

(iii) *Hedge.*—(A) *In general.*—For purposes of this paragraph (d), the term hedge means a deposit of nonfunctional currency in a hedging account (as defined [in] paragraph (d)(3)(iii)(D) of this section), a contract described in §1.988-1(a)(1)(ii) and (2)(iii), or combination thereof, that reduces the risk of exchange rate fluctuations by reference to the taxpayer's functional currency with respect to nonfunctional currency payments made or received under a qualified payment (as defined in paragraph (d)(2)(ii) of this section). The term hedge includes an option contract described in §1.988-1(a)(1)(ii) and (2)(iii) only if the option contract expires on or before the accrual date and is exercised on or before such date. The premium paid for an option that lapses shall be integrated with the qualified payment.

(B) *Special rule for series of hedges.*—A series of hedges as defined in paragraph (d)(3)(iii)(A) of this section shall be considered a hedge if the qualified payment is hedged in whole or in part throughout the period beginning with the date the hedge is identi-

fied in accordance with paragraph (d)(2)(i)(A) of this section and ending on or after the accrual date. A taxpayer that enters into a series of hedges will be deemed to have satisfied the preceding sentence if the hedge that succeeds a hedge that has been terminated is entered into on the business day following such termination.

(C) *Special rules for historical rate rollovers.*—The principles of paragraph (b)(2)(iii)(C) of this section shall apply for purposes of this paragraph (d).

(D) *Special rules regarding deposits of nonfunctional currency in a hedging account.*—The principles of paragraph (b)(2)(iii)(D) of this section shall apply for purposes of this paragraph (d).

(E) *Interest income on deposit of nonfunctional currency in a hedging account.*—The principles of paragraph (b)(2)(iii)(E) of this section shall apply for purposes of this paragraph (d).

(iv) *Accrual date.*—The accrual date is the date when a dividend, rent or royalty that is a qualified payment is required to be accrued (or otherwise taken into account) under the taxpayer's method of accounting. A taxpayer may use any reasonable convention consistently applied to translate an accrued payment or receipt into the taxpayer's functional currency.

(v) *Payment date.*—The payment date is the date when payment is made or received with respect to a qualified payment or the subsequent account payable or receivable arising from such qualified payment.

(3) *Effect of hedged qualified payment.*—(i) *In general.*—A taxpayer that has entered into a transaction that is treated as a hedged qualified payment shall treat amounts paid or received under the hedge as paid or received under the qualified payment, or any subsequent account payable or receivable, or that portion to which the hedge relates. Thus, for example, any gain or loss on the hedge shall have the same source and character as the source and character of the qualified payment. The taxpayer shall recognize no exchange gain or loss on the hedge. The taxpayer shall recognize no exchange gain or loss with respect to an account payable or receivable that arises from a qualified payment during the period that the account payable or receivable is covered by the hedge.

(ii) *Partially hedged qualified payments.*—The effect of integrating a qualified payment and a hedge that partially hedges such qualified payment is to treat the amounts paid or received under the hedge as paid or received under the portion of the qualified payment being hedged, or any subsequent account payable or receivable. The income or expense resulting from qualified payment that is attributable to that portion of the qualified payment that is not hedged shall be translated into functional currency on the accrual date. The taxpayer shall realize exchange gain or loss shall with respect to any unhedged payable or receivable arising from the qualified payment.

(iii) *Disposition of a hedge or termination of the qualified payment prior to the accrual date.*—(A) *In general.*—If a taxpayer identifies a qualified payment as part of a hedged qualified payment as defined in paragraph (d)(2) of this section, and the qualified payment is disposed of or otherwise terminated prior to the accrual date (by transfer, cancellation, or otherwise), the taxpayer shall treat the hedge as sold for its fair market value on the date the qualified payment is terminated and shall realize and recognize any gain or loss with respect to that hedge on such date. Such gain or loss shall be an adjustment to the amount received or expended with respect to the disposition or termination, if any. The spot rate on the date the hedge is treated as sold shall be used to determine subsequent exchange gain or loss on the hedge. If a taxpayer identifies a hedge as part of a hedged qualified payment as defined in paragraph (d)(2) of this section, and disposes of the hedge prior to the accrual date, any gain or loss realized by the taxpayer on such disposition shall not be recognized and shall be an adjustment to the income or expense from the qualified payment.

(B) *Certain events in a series of hedges treated as a termination of the hedged qualified payment.*—If the rules of paragraph (d)(2)(iii)(B) of this section are not satisfied, the hedged qualified payment shall be terminated and the provisions of paragraph (d)(3)(iii)(A) of this section shall apply to any gain or loss actually realized with respect to such hedge. Any subsequent transactions entered into to reduce the risk of exchange rate movements with respect to such qualified payment shall not be considered a hedge as defined in paragraph (d)(2)(iii) of this section.

(C) *Qualified payments between related persons.*—(1) *In general.*—Notwithstanding any other provision of this paragraph (d), if the parties to a qualified payment are related within the meaning of sections 267(b) and 707(b), and the hedge or qualified payment is disposed of or otherwise terminated prior to the accrual date, the District Director or the Assistant Commissioner (International) may redetermine the timing, source, and character of gain or loss from the hedge or the qualified payment if he determines that a significant purpose for disposing of the hedge or terminating the qualified payment prior to the accrual date was to affect the timing, source, or character of income, gain, expense, or loss for Federal income tax purposes.

(2) *Special source rule for certain hedges of dividends between related persons.*—If a hedged qualified payment is entered into by a U.S. person and consists of a declared but unpaid dividend between related persons (as defined in section 267(b)) and a hedge, and the dividend is not paid, then any loss realized with respect to the hedge shall reduce foreign source income described in section 904 (d)(1)(I) and any gain shall be treated as from U.S. sources.

(iv) *Disposition of a hedge on or after the accrual date.*—If a taxpayer identifies a hedge as part of a hedged qualified payment as defined in paragraph (d)(2) of this section, and disposes of the hedge on or after the accrual date, the taxpayer shall recognize no gain or loss on the hedge and the booking date, as defined in § 1.988-2(c)(2), of the payable or receivable for purposes of computing exchange gain or loss shall be the date such hedge is disposed of.

(v) *Special rule for foreign persons that enter into hedged qualified payments giving rise to U.S. source income not effectively connected with a U.S. trade or business.*—If a foreign person enters into a hedged qualified payment that gives rise to U.S. source income not effectively connected with a U.S. trade or business of such foreign person, for purposes of sections 871(a), 881, 1441, 1442 and 6049, the provisions of this paragraph (d) shall not apply and such sections of the Internal Revenue Code shall be applied separately to the qualified payment and the hedge. To the extent relevant to any foreign person, if the requirements of this paragraph (d) are otherwise met, the provisions of this paragraph (d) shall apply for all other purposes of the Internal Revenue Code (*e.g.*, for purposes of calculating the earnings and profits of a controlled foreign corporation that enters into a hedged qualified payment through a qualified business unit resident outside the United States, income or expense with respect to such hedged qualified payment shall be calculated under the provisions of this paragraph (d)).

(vi) *Sections 263(g), 1092, and 1256 do not apply.*—Sections 263(g), 1092, and 1256 do not apply with respect to a qualified payment or hedge which comprises a hedged qualified payment as defined in paragraph (d)(2) of this section. However, sections 263(g), 1092 and 1256 may apply to the hedged qualified payment if such transaction is part of a straddle.

(vii) *Examples.*—The principles set forth in paragraph (d) of this section are illustrated in the following examples. The examples assume that K is an accrual method, calendar year U.S. corporation with the dollar as its functional currency.

Example 1. (i) K is a U.S. corporation that has a qualified business unit, Q. Q's principal place of business is in Canada, and it has the U.S. dollar (US$) as its functional currency. On January 1, 1993, Q enters into a 3 year lease to rent an office in Canada for annual payments of 50,000 Canadian dollars (C$). On February 1, 1993, 1994, and 1995, Q enters into a forward contract to buy C$50,00O for US$24,500, US$24,000, and US$23,500 respectively. Assume Q satisfies the identification requirements of paragraph (d)(2)(i)(A) of this section.

(ii) The obligation to pay rent denominated in nonfunctional currency as set forth above is a qualified payment as defined in paragraph (d)(2)(ii) of this section. Further, the forward contracts constitute a hedge as defined in paragraph (d)(2)(iii) of this section. Assuming the requirements of paragraph (d)(2)(i) of this section are satisfied, Q may integrate the forward contracts with the rental payments. Accordingly, Q is treated as having paid US$24,500 in rent in 1993, US$24,000 in rent in 1994, and US$23,500 in 1995.

Example 2. (i) B is a wholly owned Danish subsidiary of K, a U.S. corporation. B was organized on January 1, 1995, and its functional currency is the Danish Kroner. On September 1, 1995, the board of directors of B declares a dividend payable on December 31, 1995 in the amount of Kr100,000, which equals $10,000 at the spot rate on September 1, 1995. On the same day, K enters into a forward contract to sell Kr100,000 for $9,750 on September 1, 1995. Assume K satisfies the identification requirements of paragraph (d)(2)(i)(A) of this section. B pays a dividend of Kr100,000 on December 31, 1995. At the end of 1995, B's pool of post-1986 undistributed earnings is Kr300,000 of non-subpart F foreign source earnings and profits, and B's pool of post-1986 foreign income taxes is $3,000.

(ii) The declared dividend denominated in Kroner as set forth above is a qualified payment as defined in paragraph (d)(2)(ii) of this section. Further, the forward contract constitutes a hedge as defined in paragraph (d)(2)(iii) of this section. Assuming the requirements of paragraph (d)(2)(i) of this section are satisfied, K may integrate the forward contract with the dividend. Accordingly, K is treated as having received a $9,750 dividend in 1995.

(iii) The amount of foreign taxes deemed paid with respect to the dividend is $1,000 (Kr100,000/Kr300,000 × $3,000). If B had not hedged the dividend, the amount of the foreign taxes deemed paid would still be $1,000, computed in the same manner.

(iv) Assume that B does not pay the Kr100,000 dividend and K realizes a $250 loss on December 31, 1995, when the forward contract is terminated. Under paragraph (d)(3)(iii)(C)(2) of this section, the $250 loss shall reduce foreign source income described in section 904(d)(1)(I).

(4) *Effective date.*—This paragraph (d) shall be effective for transactions entered into on or after [DATE FINAL REGULATIONS ARE PUBLISHED IN THE FEDERAL REGISTER].

* * *

(f) *Mark to market method of accounting for taxpayers that are not acting in the capacity of a dealer.*—(1) *Scope.*—This paragraph (f) shall apply to any taxpayer that makes an election as provided in paragraph (f)(2) of this section. However, this election is not available to a qualified business unit that uses the United States dollar approximate separate transactions method of accounting described in § 1.985-3.

(2) *Operative rules.*—(i) *In general.*—A taxpayer described in paragraph (f)(1) of this section may elect to realize for the taxable year exchange gain or loss on section 988 transactions that results from changes in exchange rates between the date a financial accounting period begins and the date a financial accounting period closes (but no less frequently than quarterly), provided such treatment is consistent with the taxpayer's method of accounting for financial reporting purposes (and that method conforms to U.S. generally accepted accounting principles). Realizing the gain or loss resulting from changes in exchange rates between the date a financial accounting period begins and the date a financial accounting period closes shall hereafter be referred to as marking to market.

(ii) *Treatment of gain or loss.*—Proper adjustment for gain or loss realized under the preceding paragraph shall be made in the amount of any gain or loss subsequently realized. The character and source of gain or loss realized under the preceding paragraph shall be determined under § 1.988-3 and § 1.988-4.

(iii) *Exception.*—The method of accounting described in this paragraph (f) shall not apply to transactions entered into by a taxpayer in its capacity as a dealer or trader (as defined in § 1.446-4(b)) in nonfunctional currency or nonfunctional currency denominated instruments.

(3) *Treatment of hedging transactions.*—(i) *Hedging election by the taxpayer.*—Except as provided in this paragraph (f)(3), all section 988 transactions must be accounted for as if they were not hedging any transaction (*i.e.*, without regard to the taxpayer's treatment of hedging transaction for financial accounting purposes). A taxpayer that makes an election under this paragraph (f) shall account for section 988 hedging transactions as provided in paragraphs (a) through (e) of this section. Thus, if a taxpayer that has made an election under this paragraph (f) fully hedges all payments under a nonfunctional currency borrowing so as to create a synthetic functional currency borrowing that satisfies the requirements of paragraph (a) of this section, such nonfunctional currency borrowing and the related hedges shall not be marked to market under paragraph (f)(2) of this section. In contrast, if the taxpayer elects hedge accounting treatment for financial accounting purposes with respect to the transaction described in the preceding sentence, but does not comply with paragraph (a) of this section (*e.g.*, fails to satisfy the identification requirements of paragraph (a)(8) of this section), the nonfunctional currency borrowing and related hedges must be marked to market under paragraph (f)(2) of this section.

(ii) *Authority of the District Director.*—Nothing in this paragraph (f) shall prevent the District Director (or Assistant Commissioner (International)) from applying the rules of paragraphs (a) through (d) of this section.

(4) *Consistency rules.*—If a taxpayer elects the mark to market method of accounting of this paragraph (f) each person who is related to the taxpayer within the meaning of section 267(b) or 707(b) (whether or not such person is uses U.S. generally accepted accounting principles) shall be deemed to make the election described in paragraph (f)(2) of this section. The deemed election shall not apply to persons who otherwise would not be eligible to make the election described in paragraph (f)(2) of this section.

(5) *Time and manner of making election.*—(i) *Time for making the election.*—A taxpayer's election under this paragraph (f) is effective for any taxable year (and subsequent taxable years) only if it is made by the due date (including extensions) of the taxpayer's federal income tax return for the year.

(ii) *Manner of making the election.*—A taxpayer shall make the election provided in this paragraph (f) by attaching a statement entitled "Election of mark to market method of accounting with respect to section 988 transactions" to the taxpayer's return for the first taxable year for which the election is to be effective. The statement must contain the following information:

(A) A brief description of the taxpayer's method of accounting for financial purposes; and

(B) A statement that this method of accounting applies consistently to all related persons (except for the dealing or trading activities of such person) within the meaning of sections 267(b) and 707(b) except qualified business units that use the United States dollar approximate separate transactions method of accounting described in § 1.985-3.

(iii) *Election by a partnership, trust or controlled foreign corporation.*—In the case of a partnership, the election shall be made on behalf of all partners by the general partners; in the case of a trust (other than a grantor trust) the election shall be made by the trustees. In the case of a controlled foreign corporation, the election shall be made on behalf of all shareholders by its controlling United States shareholders under § 1.964-1(c)(3).

(iv) *Revocation.*—The election under this paragraph (f) cannot be revoked without the consent of the Commissioner.

(6) *Interaction with § 1.988-2(b)(14).*—Section 1.988-2(b)(14) (relating to nonfunctional currency related person debt replaced by other related person debt in a different currency) shall not apply to exchange gain or loss realized with respect to a debt instrument which is subject to the mark to market method of accounting elected under this paragraph (f).

(7) *Examples.*—The following examples illustrate the rules of this paragraph (f):

Example 1. (i) X is a calendar year U.S. corporation with the dollar as its functional currency. X is on the accrual method of accounting, and has properly elected the mark to market method of accounting of § 1.988-5(f) under which X's section 988 transactions are marked to market monthly. X also uses a spot rate convention to determine the spot rate as provided in § 1.988-1(d)(3). Pursuant to X's spot rate convention, the spot rate at which a transaction within a month is booked is determined by the spot rate at the end of the prior month. Under X's method of accounting, nonfunctional currency denominated transactions (other than inventory and property accounts) on the books at the end of the month are revalued at the spot rate on the last day of the month. Inventory and property accounts (which are not section 988 transactions and therefore are not eligible for mark to market treatment) on the balance sheet are recorded exclusively at historical cost translated on the day of purchase. On January 1, 1995, X's only financial asset is a £ 2,000 bank account, which pursuant to X's spot rate convention is equal to $4,000 (the December 31, 1994 spot rate is £1 = $2, multiplied by £ 2,000). X also has inventory of $500 (translated at the historical rate). Assume that all of X's inventory was purchased on the same day. X has no liabilities.

(ii) On January 15, 1995, X receives £100 from the issuance of a note payable on January 15, 2000, and deposits the £100 into the bank account. The December 31, 1994 spot rate of £1 = $2 is used to book the cash and the note, not the spot rate on January 15, 1995. X has no other transactions during the month of January. The spot rate at the

end of January is £1 = $2.50. Accordingly, X will realize $1,050 of exchange gain [(£2,100 × $2.50 = $5,250) – (£2,100 × $2.00 = $4,200)] with respect to X's pound cash account. Additionally, X will realize $50 of exchange loss [(£100 × $2.00 = $200) – (£100 × $2.50 = $250)] with respect to X's liability. Thus, X's total exchange gain for the [month of] January is $1,000. Because the acquisition of the inventory is not a section 988 transaction (and accordingly is recorded at historical cost and not revalued), no gain or loss is realized with respect to the inventory.

(iii) On February 21, 1995, X sells half of its inventory for £195, in exchange for an account receivable. The January 31, 1995 spot rate of £1 = $2.50 is used to book the receivable and to determine the amount realized on the inventory sale, not the spot rate on February 21, 1995. X has no other transactions during the month of February. The spot rate at the end of February is £ 1 = $2.75. X will realize $548.50 of exchange gain computed as follows:

(A) X will realize $573.50 of exchange gain on its assets subject to section 988 computed as follows. With respect to X's pound cash account, X will realize $525 of exchange gain [(£2,100 × $2.75 = $5,775) – (£2,100 × $2.50 = $5,250)]. With respect to the account receivable, X will realize $48.50 of exchange gain [(£195 × $2.75 = $536.25) – (£195 × $2.50 = $487.75)].

(B) X will realize $25 of exchange loss [(£100 × $2.50 = $250) – (£100 × $2.75 = $275)] with respect to X's £100 liability.

X will compute gain on the sale of its inventory by translating the £195 realized at the January 31, 1995 rate of £1 = $2.50 to equal $487.50 and subtracting the assumed basis of $250. Thus, X's gain on the sale of inventory is $237.50, none of which is exchange gain or loss under section 988.

(iv) On March 22, 1995, X is paid £195 in satisfaction of the account receivable, and deposits that amount in its bank account. The February 28, 1995 spot rate of £1 = $2.75 is used to book payment of the receivable and the amount deposited. X has no other transactions during the month of March. The spot rate at the end of March is £1 = $3.00. X will realize $550.75 of exchange gain computed as follows:

(A) X will realize $575.75 of exchange gain on its assets computed as follows. With respect to X's pound cash account, X will realize $575.75 of exchange gain [(£2,295 × $3.00 = $6,887) – (£2,295 × $2.75 = $6,311.25)]. With respect to the account receivable, X will not realize exchange gain or loss because it is terminated within the month of March.

(B) X will realize $25 of exchange loss [(£100 × $2.75 = $275) – (£100 × $3.00 = $300)] with respect to X's £100 liability.

(v) On April 15, 1995, (when the spot rate is £ 1 = $3.25) X withdraws £1000 from its bank account that it uses to purchase a machine. The basis of the machine is $3000 (the spot rate on March 31, 1995 of £1 = $3.00 times £1000).

Example 2. H is a calendar year U.S. corporation with the dollar as its functional currency that has properly elected the mark to market method of accounting of paragraph (f)(2) of this section. Under this method, H revalues its nonfunctional currency positions at the close of each month. H owns 100 percent of L, a foreign corporation. L has the local currency as its functional currency. On August 4, 1995, H enters into a forward contract which it designates for financial accounting purposes as a hedge of its net investment in L. Under H's method of financial accounting, gain or loss on the forward contract is not included in profit and loss but is treated as an adjustment to the equity account of H. Under paragraph (f)(2) of this section, the forward contract is not treated as hedging any transaction and therefore must be revalued on August 31, 1995 and gain or loss realized.

(8) *Effective date.*—This paragraph (f) shall be effective for taxable years ending on or after [DATE FINAL REGULATIONS ARE PUBLISHED IN THE FEDERAL REGISTER].

Foreign Personal Holding Company Income: Foreign Currency Gain or Loss: Exclusion

Foreign Personal Holding Company Income: Foreign Currency Gain or Loss: Exclusion.—Reg. § 1.988-7, providing guidance on the treatment of foreign currency gain or loss of a controlled foreign corporation under the business needs exclusion from foreign personal holding company income, is proposed (published in the Federal Register on December 19, 2017) (REG-119514-15).

Par. 5. Section 1.988-7 is added to read as follows:

§ 1.988-7. Election to mark-to-market foreign currency gain or loss on section 988 transactions.—(a) *In general.*—Except as provided in paragraph (b) of this section, a taxpayer may elect under this section to apply the foreign currency mark-to-market method of accounting described in this section with respect to all section 988 transactions (including the acquisition and holding of nonfunctional currency described in section 988(c)(1)(C)(ii)). Under the foreign currency mark-to-market method of accounting, the timing of section 988 gain or loss on section 988 transactions is determined under the principles of section 1256. Only section 988 gain or loss is taken into account under the foreign currency mark-to-market method of ac-

counting. Consistent with section 1256(a)(2), appropriate adjustments must be made to prevent the section 988 gain or loss from being taken into account again under section 988 or another provision of the Code or regulations. A section 988 transaction subject to this election is not subject to the "netting rule" of section 988(b) and § 1.988-2(b)(8), under which exchange gain or loss is limited to overall gain or loss realized in a transaction, in taxable years prior to the taxable year in which section 988 gain or loss would be recognized with respect to such section 988 transaction but for this election.

(b) *Exceptions.*—The election described in paragraph (a) of this section does not apply to:

(1) Any security, commodity, or section 1256 contract that is marked to market under any other provision, including section 475 or section 1256;

(2) Any security, commodity, or section 1256 contract that, pursuant to an election or an identification made by the taxpayer, is excepted from mark-to-market treatment under another provision, including section 475 or section 1256;

(3) Any transaction of a qualified business unit (as defined in section 1.989(a)-1(b)) that is subject to section 987; or

(4) Any section 988 transaction denominated in, or determined by reference to, a hyperinflationary currency. See §1.988-2(b)(15), (d)(5), and (e)(7) for rules relating to such transactions.

(c) *Time and manner of election.*—A taxpayer makes the election under paragraph (a) of this section by filing a statement that clearly indicates that such election has been made with the taxpayer's timely-filed original federal income tax return for the taxable year for which the election is made. In the case of a controlled foreign corporation, the controlling United States shareholders (as defined in §1.964-1(c)(5)) make the election under paragraph (a) of this section on behalf of the controlled foreign corporation by filing a statement that clearly indicates that such election has been made with their timely-filed, original federal income tax returns for the taxable year of such United States shareholders ending with or within the taxable year of the controlled foreign corporation for which the election is made.

(d) *Revocation and subsequent election.*—A taxpayer may revoke its election under paragraph (a) of this section at any time. If an election has been revoked under this paragraph (d), a new election under paragraph (a) of this section cannot be made until the sixth taxable year following the year in which the previous election was revoked, and such subsequent election cannot be revoked until the sixth taxable year following the year in which the subsequent election was made. A taxpayer revokes the election by filing a statement that clearly indicates that such election has been revoked with its original or amended federal income tax return for the taxable year for which the election is revoked. In the case of a controlled foreign corporation, the controlling United States shareholders revoke the election on behalf of the controlled foreign corporation by filing a statement that clearly indicates that such election has been revoked with their original or amended federal income tax returns for the taxable year of such United States shareholders ending with or within the taxable year of the controlled foreign corporation for which the election is revoked.

(e) *Applicability dates.*—This section applies to taxable years of taxpayers (including controlled foreign corporations) ending on or after the date these regulations are published as final regulations in the *Federal Register*. [Reg. §1.988-7.]

DISCs: Taxation of Income

Domestic International Sales Corporations: Taxation of Income.—Reproduced below are the texts of proposed amendments of Reg. §1.991-1, relating to the taxation of income allocable to a DISC for taxable years beginning after 1984 (published in the Federal Register on February 3, 1987).

* * *

☐ Par. 4. Section 1.991-1 is amended as follows:

1. In the third sentence of paragraph (a), the phrase "and the interest equalization tax" is removed, and three new sentences are added at the end of paragraph (a).

2. a. In paragraph (b)(1) the third sentence is revised;

b. In paragraph (b)(2) a new sentence is added immediately after the fourth sentence;

c. Paragraph (b)(3) is revised; and

d. Paragraphs (b)(4) and (5) are removed.

3. New paragraphs (e) and (f) are added immediately after paragraph (d).

§1.991-1. Taxation of a domestic international sales corporation (DISC).—(a) *In general.*—* * * For taxable years of a DISC beginning after 1984, the shareholders of the DISC are required to pay an annual interest charge on the shareholder's DISC-related deferred tax liability. The interest charge is imposed on the DISC shareholder, not the DISC. See section 995(f) and §1.995(f)-1.

* * *

(b) *Determination of taxable income.*—(1) *In general.*—* * * For example, a DISC may choose its accounting methods and inventory method, or elect, under section 168(b)(3), different recovery percentages for its recovery property than those prescribed under section 168(b)(1), as if the DISC were a domestic corporation which had not elected to be treated as a DISC. * * *

(2) *Choice of accounting methods.*—* * * See also, section 267 for rules that may apply to transactions between a DISC and a related taxpayer requiring the matching of certain items of income and deduction and the deferral of certain losses. * * *

(3) *Annual accounting period.*—For taxable years beginning after March 21, 1984, a DISC cannot choose or change its taxable year without regard to the taxable year of its principal shareholder. In general, a DISC and its principal shareholder must use the same taxable year. See section 441(h) and §1.441-1.

* * *

(e) *Close of taxable year and termination of DISC election for all DISCs on December 31, 1984; Reelection required; Exemption of pre-1985 accumulated DISC income from tax.*—Under section 805(b)(1)(A) of the Tax Reform Act of 1984, Pub. L. 98-369, the last taxable year of a DISC beginning before 1985 ended on December 31, 1984. The corporation's DISC election is also deemed revoked as of the close of business on December 31, 1984. A new DISC election must be made on Form 4876A in order for the corporation to be treated as a DISC for any taxable year beginning after December 31, 1984. See §1.921-1T(b). See section 805(b)(2) of the Act and §1.921-1T(a) for the tax treatment after 1984 of the accumulated DISC income derived before 1985 by certain DISCs.

(f) *Interest charge imposed on DISC shareholders after 1984.*—Section 995(f) requires that for each taxable year beginning after 1984, each shareholder of a DISC shall pay an interest charge on the shareholder's DISC-related deferred tax liability. The shareholder's DISC-related deferred tax liability is computed only with reference to the DISC's accumulated DISC income (earned in periods after 1984) and deferred by the DISC for more than one taxable year. Thus, in general, a DISC shareholder will not have a DISC-related deferred tax liability (and thus, no interest charge) until the close of the shareholder's taxable year following the taxable year with which or within which the first taxable year of the DISC (ending after 1984) ends. See §1.995(f)-1.

DISCs: Taxation of Income: Elections

Domestic International Sales Corporations: Taxation of Income.—Reproduced below are the texts of proposed amendments of Reg. §§1.992-1 and 1.992-2, relating to the taxation of income allocable to a DISC for taxable years beginning after 1984 (published in the Federal Register on February 3, 1987).

☐ Par. 5. Section 1.992-1 is amended as follows:

1. At the end of paragraph (a)(7), "and" is removed; at the end of paragraph (a)(8), the period is removed and ", and" is added in its place; immediately following paragraph (a)(8) the following new paragraph is added: "(9) Is not a member of any controlled group (as defined in section 993(a)(3) and §1.993-1(k)) of which a FSC or a small FSC (as defined in section 992) is a member. See paragraph (j) of this section."; and in the sentence immediately following paragraph (a)(9), the language "subparagraphs (1) through (8) of this paragraph" is removed and the language "paragraphs (a)(1), through (a)(9) of this section" is added in its place.

2. The text of paragraph (e) is redesignated as paragraph (e)(1) and new paragraph (e)(2) is added to read as set forth below.

3. A new paragraph (j) is added to read as set forth below

§1.992-1. Requirements of a DISC.—

* * *

(e) *Election in effect.*—(1) * * *

(2) Section 805(b)(1)(A) of the Tax Reform Act of 1984 provides that the last taxable year of any DISC beginning in 1984, shall end on December 31, 1984, and under §1.921-1T(a)(1) the corporation's DISC election is also deemed revoked as of the close of business on that date. A new DISC election must be filed on Form 4876A in order for the corporation to be treated as a DISC for any taxable year beginning after December 31, 1984. See §1.992-2(a) and (b).

* * *

(j) *Effect on a DISC of a FSC election.*—(1) *General rule.*—(i) Under section 992(a)(1)(E) and paragraph (a)(9) of this section, a corporation shall not be treated as a DISC for a taxable year if at any time during such taxable year such corporation is a member of a controlled group (as defined in section 993(a)(3) and §1.993-1(k)) of which a FSC or a small FSC (as defined in section 922) is a member. For purposes of this paragraph (j), a FSC also includes a small FSC. A FSC election within a group will prevail over any DISC election within such group. Thus, no corporation can make an election to be treated as a DISC for any taxable year if on any day of such taxable year such corporation is a member of a controlled group of which a FSC is a member. Further, the election of a corporation to be treated as a DISC is terminated on the first day for which the election of another corporation to be treated as a FSC becomes effective, if at any time during the DISC's taxable year such corporations are members of the same controlled group. Except as provided in paragraph (j)(2) of this section (relating to certain corporate acquisitions and reorganizations), the termination of the DISC election on such date means that such corporation shall not be treated as a DISC for its entire taxable year which includes such date, and the corporation shall be subject to tax on its taxable income for such entire taxable year. A revocation of the corporation's DISC election under section 992(b)(3) is not required.

(ii) The following example illustrates the provisions of this paragraph (j)(1):

Example. D, a calendar year corporation, has made a proper DISC election for 1985 and succeeding years. F, a corporation having a fiscal year beginning on July 1, is a member of the same controlled group of which D is a member. On May 1, 1986, F files an election to be treated as a FSC effective for F's taxable year beginning July 1, 1986. D's DISC election is treated as terminated on July 1, 1986, and D is not a DISC for its taxable year which begins January 1, 1986, and ends on December 31, 1986. F's election to be treated as a FSC for its taxable year beginning July 1, 1986, is not affected by the termination of D's DISC election.

(2) *Exception for certain acquisitions and reorganizations.*—(i) In the case of a DISC and a FSC described in paragraph (j)(2)(ii) of this section for a taxable year, paragraph (j)(1) of this section shall not apply, and the domestic corporation may be treated as a DISC or the foreign corporation may be treated as a FSC for a short taxable year ending on the day preceding the day the DISC and the FSC became members of the same controlled group. If the DISC election is terminated, the DISC is required to satisfy all requirements to be treated as a DISC (including the 95 percent qualified export receipts and assets requirement of section 992(a)(1)) for the short taxable year, and may satisfy those requirements by making the distributions to meet such requirements provided in section 992(c). The $10 million limitation on qualified export receipts under section 995(b)(1)(E) for the short taxable year must be pro rated on a daily basis as provided in §1.995-8(a). If the FSC election is terminated, the FSC is required to

satisfy all requirements to be treated as a FSC for the short taxable year, and if the FSC is a small FSC, the $5 million foreign trading gross receipts limitation under section 924(b)(2) for the short taxable year must be pro rated on a daily basis. The controlled group of corporations shall make its choice to terminate the election of either the DISC or the FSC by filing the short period return required for the corporation whose election as a DISC or FSC (as the case may be) is to be terminated within the due date (including extensions) prescribed by section 6072(b). If the group fails to terminate the election of either the DISC or the FSC within such period, the DISC election of the domestic corporation shall be terminated as provided by paragraph (j)(1) of this section.

(ii) A DISC and a FSC are described in this paragraph (j)(2)(ii) for a taxable year if—

(A) Both the DISC and the FSC had an immediately preceding taxable year and each was treated as a DISC and as a FSC, respectively, for such immediately preceding taxable year,

(B) The DISC and the FSC were not members of the same controlled group on the first day of the taxable year, and

(C) The DISC and the FSC became members of the same controlled group of corporations during the taxable year by reason of the acquisition, directly or indirectly, of a member of the controlled group which includes such DISC (or FSC, as the case may be) by either—

(1) A member of the controlled group which includes such FSC (or DISC, as the case may be) (thereby making the DISC and the FSC members of the same parent-subsidiary controlled group), or

(2) The 5 or fewer persons who are individuals, estates or trusts who control the corporation which controls such FSC (or DISC, as the case may be) (thereby making the DISC and the FSC members of the same brother-sister controlled group).

(iii) The provisions of this paragraph (j)(2) may be illustrated by the following example:

Example—(i) *Facts.* Z corporation owns all the stock of D, a corporation which has elected to be treated as a DISC. X corporation owns all the stock of F, a corporation which has elected to be treated as a small FSC. Z, X, D and F use the calendar year as the taxable year. D was treated as a DISC, and F was treated as a small FSC, for their taxable years ending December 31, 1986. On January 1, 1987, Z and X are not members of the same controlled group. On August 1, 1987, Z purchases all of the stock of X, thereby making D and F members of the same controlled group.

(ii) *Result.* (A) If the group chose to retain the small FSC and terminate the DISC, under paragraph (j)(2)(i) of this section, D is permitted to end its taxable year on July 31, 1987, and may be treated as a DISC for such short year if it satisfies the requirements of section 992(a)(1) with respect to such short taxable year. The $10 million amount under section 995(b)(1)(E) for the short taxable year is limited to $5,808,219 ($10 million × 212/365). D's DISC election is terminated on August 1, 1987. F's small FSC election and $5 million amount under section 924(b)(2) are not affected by the acquisition.

(B) Alternatively, the group could choose to retain the DISC and terminate the small FSC with the same short taxable year ending July 31, 1987. F's $5 million amount for such short year would be limited to $2,904,110 ($5 million × 212/365), and D's DISC election and $10 million amount under section 995(b)(1)(E) would not be affected by the acquisition.

☐ Par. 6. Section 1.992-2 is amended by removing "Form 4876" each place it appears and adding in their place the words "Form 4876A", and by revising paragraphs (a) and (b)(2) to read as follows:

§1.992-2. Election to be treated as a DISC.—(a) *Manner and Time of election.*—(1) *Manner.*—The election to be treated as a DISC is made by the corporation by filing Form 4876A (Form 4876 for taxable years beginning before January 1, 1985) with the service center with which it would file its income tax return if the corporation were subject for such taxable year to all the taxes imposed by subtitle A of the Internal Revenue Code. The Form 4876A shall be signed by any person authorized to sign the corporation's return under section 6062, and shall contain the information required by such Form. Except as provided in paragraphs (b)(3) and (c) of this section, such election to be treated as a DISC shall be valid only if the statement of consent of every person who is a shareholder of the corporation as of the beginning of the first taxable year for which such election is to be effective is made on or is attached to such Form 4876A when filed with the service center.

(2) *Time for making election.*—In the case of a corporation making an election to be treated as a DISC for the corporation's first taxable year, the election shall be made within 90 days after the beginning of such taxable year. In the case of a corporation making an election to be treated as a DISC for a taxable year which is not the corporation's first taxable year, the election shall be made during the

90 day period immediately preceding the first day of such taxable year.

(3) *Special rule for re-electing DISC status in 1985.*—Under section 805(b) of the Tax Reform Act of 1985, the last taxable year of any DISC beginning in 1984 ended on December 31, 1984, and under §1.921-1T(a)(1), the corporation's election to be treated as a DISC is deemed revoked after the close of business on such date. A corporation which was a DISC on December 31, 1984, and which wishes to be treated as a DISC for its first taxable year beginning after December 31, 1984, must make a new DISC election by filing Form 4876A in accordance with the instructions thereon and in accordance with paragraph (a)(1) of this section on or before June 3, 1987. The Form 4876A is to be filed within such period with the service center with which the corporation files its DISC return.

(b) *Consent by shareholders.*—* * *

(2) *Transitional rule for certain corporations re-electing DISC status in 1985.*—Notwithstanding paragraph (b)(1) of this section, if the corporation was a DISC on December 31, 1984, and the corporation files its election to be treated as a DISC for the corporation's first taxable year beginning after December 31, 1984, within the time

prescribed in paragraph (a)(3) of this section, the election shall be valid if the consent of each person who was a shareholder of the corporation on January 1, 1985, is filed with the service center with which the election was filed on or before December 31, 1987. The

form of such consent shall be the same as that prescribed in paragraph (b)(1) of this section. A copy of the corporation's statement of election, Form 4876A, shall be attached to the consent.

* * *

Imputed Interest: OID: Safe Haven Interest Rates

Imputed Interest: Original Issue Discount: Safe Haven Interest Rates.—Reproduced below is the text of a proposed amendment of Reg. §1.993-1, relating to (1) the tax treatment of debt instruments issued after July 1, 1982, that contain original issue discount, (2) the imputation of and the accounting for interest with respect to sales and exchanges of property occurring after December 31, 1984, and (3) safe haven interest rates for loans or advances between commonly controlled taxpayers and safe haven leases between such taxpayers (published in the Federal Register on April 8, 1986).

* * *

☐ Par. 18. In §1.993-1, paragraph (g) is amended by removing the phrase "section 1232" and adding in its place the phrase "section 1272".

* * *

DISCs: Deemed Distributions

Domestic International Sales Corporations: Taxation of Income.—Reproduced below are the texts of proposed Reg. §1.995-2A and proposed amendments to Reg. §1.995-2, relating to the taxation of income allocable to a DISC for taxable years beginning after 1984 (published in the Federal Register on February 3, 1987).

* * *

☐ Par. 7. Section 1.995-2 is amended by revising the title of the section and by adding two new sentences immediately before the first sentence in paragraph (a) to read as follows:

§1.995-2. Deemed distributions in qualified years ending before 1985.—(a) *General rule.*—This section applies to taxable years of a DISC ending before January 1, 1985. See §1.995-2A for taxable years of a DISC beginning after December 31, 1984. * * *

☐ Par. 8. New section 1.995-2A is added immediately after §1.995-2 to read as follows:

§1.995-2A. Deemed distributions in qualified years beginning after 1984.—(a) *General rule.*—This section applies to taxable years of a DISC beginning after December 31, 1984. See §1.995-2 for taxable years beginning before January 1, 1985. Under section 995(b)(1), each shareholder of a DISC shall be treated as having received a distribution taxable as a dividend with respect to the shareholder's stock on the last day of each taxable year of the DISC beginning after December 31, 1984, in an amount equal to the shareholder's pro rata share of the sum (as limited by paragraph (b) of this section) of the following items:

(1) The gross interest derived by the DISC during such year from producer's loans (as defined in §1.993-4).

(2) The lower of—

(i) Any gain recognized by the DISC during such year on the sale or exchange of property (other than property which in the hands of the DISC is a qualified export asset) which was previously transferred to it in a transaction in which the transferor realized gain which was not recognized in whole or in part, or

(ii) The amount of the transferor's gain which was not recognized on the previous transfer of the property to the DISC. For purposes of this paragraph (a)(2), each item of property shall be considered separately. See paragraph (d) of this section for special rules with respect to certain tax-free acquisitions of property by the DISC.

(3) The lower of—

(i) Any gain recognized by the DISC during such year on the sale or exchange of property which in the hands of the DISC is a qualified export asset (other than stock in trade or property described in section 1221(1)) and which was previously transferred to the DISC in a transaction in which the transferor realized gain which was not recognized in whole or in part, or

(ii) The amount of the transferor's gain which was not recognized on the previous transfer of the property to the DISC and which would have been includible in the transferor's gross income as ordinary income if its entire realized gain had been recognized upon the transfer. For purposes of this paragraph (a)(3), each item of property shall be considered separately. See paragraph (d) of this section for special rules with respect to certain tax-free acquisitions of property by the DISC.

(4) Fifty (50) percent of the taxable income of the DISC for the taxable year attributable to military property (as defined in §1.995-6).

(5) The taxable income of the DISC for the taxable year attributable to qualified export receipts of the DISC for such year which exceed $10,000,000 (as determined under §1.995-8).

(6) The sum of—

(i) In the case of a shareholder which is a C corporation, an amount equal to one-seventeenth ($1/17$) of the excess, if any, of the taxable income of the DISC for the taxable year, before reduction for any distributions during such year, over the sum of the amounts deemed distributed for the taxable year in accordance with paragraphs (a)(1) through (5) of this section,

(ii)(A) In the case of a shareholder which is a C corporation—

(1) An amount equal to $16/17$ of the excess described in paragraph (a)(6)(i), multiplied by the international boycott factor as determined under section 999(c)(1), or

(2) In lieu of the amount determined under subparagraph (ii)(A)(1), $16/17$ of such excess as is described in section 999(c)(2), or

(B) In the case of a shareholder which is not a C corporation—

(1) An amount equal to all of the excess described in paragraph (a)(6)(i), multiplied by the international boycott factor as determined under section 999(c)(1), or

(2) In lieu of the amount determined under subparagraph (ii)(B)(1), the amount of such excess as is described in section 999(c)(2), and

(iii) An amount equal to the sum of any illegal bribes, kickbacks, or other payments paid by or on behalf of the DISC directly or indirectly to an official, employee, or agent in fact of a government. An amount is paid by a DISC where it *is* paid directly or indirectly by any officer, director, employee, shareholder, or agent of the DISC for the benefit of such DISC. For purposes of this section, the principles of section 162(c) and the regulations thereunder shall apply. The amount of an illegal payment made in the form of property or services shall be considered to be equal to the fair market value of such property or services at the time such property is transferred or such services are performed.

(7) The amount of foreign investment attributable to producer's loans of the DISC, as of the close of the "group taxable year" ending with such taxable year of the DISC, determined in accordance with §1.995-5. The amount of such foreign investment attributable to producer's loans so determined for any taxable year of a former DISC shall be deemed distributed as a dividend to the shareholders of such former DISC on the last day of such taxable year. See §1.995-3(e) for the effect that such deemed distribution has on scheduled installments of deemed distributions or accumulated DISC income under §1.995-3(a) upon disqualification.

(b) *Limitation on amount of deemed distributions under section 995(b)(1).*—(1) *General rule.*—The sum of the amounts described in paragraphs (a)(1) through (a)(6) of this section which is deemed distributed pro rata to the DISC's shareholders as a dividend for any taxable year of the DISC shall not exceed the DISC's earnings and profits for such year.

(2) *Foreign investment attributable to producer's loans.*—The amount of foreign investment attributable to producer's loans of the DISC (as described in paragraph (a)(7) of this section) which is deemed to be distributed pro rata to the DISC's shareholders as a dividend for any taxable year of the DISC shall not exceed the lesser of the DISC's accumulated DISC income at the beginning of such year or the corporation's accumulated earnings and profits at the beginning of such year (but not less than zero)—

(i) Increased by any DISC income of the corporation for such year as defined in §1.996-3(b)(2) (that is, any excess of the DISC's earnings and profits for such year over the sum of the amounts described in paragraphs (a)(1) through (a)(6) of this section), or

(ii) Decreased by any deficit in the DISC's earnings and profits for such year.

For example, if a DISC has a deficit in accumulated earnings and profits at the beginning of a taxable year of $10,000, current earnings and profits of $12,000, no amounts described in paragraphs (a)(1) through (a)(6) of this section for the year, and foreign investment attributable to producer's loans for the taxable year of $5,000, the DISC would have a deemed distribution described in paragraph (a)(7) of this section of $5,000 for the taxable year. As a further example, assume that the DISC had accumulated earnings and profits of $13,000 at the beginning of the taxable year, accumulated DISC income of $10,000 at the beginning of the taxable year, a deficit in earnings and profits for the taxable year of $12,000, no amounts described in paragraphs (a)(1) through (a)(6) of this section for the taxable year, and foreign investment attributable to producer's loans for the taxable year of $5,000. Under these facts the DISC would have no deemed distribution described in paragraph (a)(7) of this section for the taxable year because the DISC had no DISC income for the taxable year and the current year's deficit in earnings and profits subtracted from the DISC's accumulated DISC income at the beginning of the year produces a negative amount. For rules relating to the carryover to a subsequent year of the $5,000 of foreign investment attributable to producer's loans, see § 1.995-5(a)(6).

(3) *Ordering rule when limitation applies.*—If, by reason of the limitation described in paragraph (b)(1) of this section, less than the sum of the amounts described in paragraphs (a)(1) through (a)(6) of this section is deemed distributed, then the portion of such sum which is deemed distributed shall be attributed first to the amount described in paragraph (a)(1), to the extent thereof; second to the amount described in paragraph (a)(2), to the extent thereof; third to the amount described in paragraph (a)(3), to the extent thereof; and so forth, and finally to the amount described in paragraph (a)(6).

(c) *Examples.*—Paragraphs (a) and (b) of this section may be illustrated by the following examples:

Example (1). Y is a corporation which uses the calendar year as its taxable year and elects to be treated as a DISC beginning with its taxable year beginning January 1, 1985. X, a corporation, is Y's sole shareholder. In 1985, X transfers certain property to Y in exchange for Y's stock in a transaction in which X does not recognize gain or loss by reason of the application of section 351(a). Included in the property transferred to Y is depreciable property described in paragraph (a)(3) of this section on which X realizes, and does not recognize by reason of the application of section 1245(b)(3), a gain of $20,000. If X had sold such property for cash, the $20,000 gain would have been recognized as ordinary income under section 1245. Also included in the transfer to Y are 100 shares of stock in a third corporation (which is not a related foreign export corporation) on which X realizes, but does not recognize, a gain of $5,000. In 1986, Y sells such property and recognizes a gain of $25,000 on the depreciable property and $8,000 on the 100 shares of stock. Y has accumulated earnings and profits at the beginning of 1986 of $5,000, earnings and profits for 1986 of $72,000, and taxable income for 1986 of $100,000. At the beginning of 1986, Y has $6,000 of accumulated DISC income, no previously taxed income, and a deficit of $1,000 of other earnings and profits. The total qualified export receipts of Y for 1986 are less than $10 million and there were no transactions in military property. Under these facts and the additional facts assumed in the table below, X is treated as having received a deemed distribution taxable as a dividend of $46,000 on December 31, 1986, determined as follows:

(1)	Gross interest derived by Y in 1986 from producer's loans		$7,000
(2)	Amount of gain on depreciable property (lesser of Y's recognized gain ($25,000) or X's gain not recognized on section 1245 property ($20,000))		20,000
(3)	Amount of gain on stock (lesser of Y's recognized gain ($8,000) or X's gain not recognized ($5,000))		5,000
(4)	One-seventeenth of the excess of the DISC's taxable income for 1986 over the sum of lines (1), (2) and (3) ($^1\!/_{17}$ of $100,000 minus $32,000))		$4,000
(5)	Limitation on lines (1) through (4):		
	(a)	Sum of lines (1) through (4)	$36,000
	(b)	Earnings and profits for 1986	72,000
	(c)	Lesser of lines (5)(a) or (b)	$36,000
(6)	Amount determined under paragraph (a)(7) of this section:		
	(a)	Foreign investment attributable to producer's loans under § 1.995-5	$10,000
	(b)	Sum of the lesser of accumulated earnings and profits at beginning of 1986 ($5,000) or accumulated DISC income at beginning of 1986 ($6,000), plus excess of earnings and profits for 1986 over line (5)(c) ($72,000 minus $36,000)	$41,000
	(c)	Lesser of lines (6)(a) or (b)	$10,000
(7)	Total deemed distribution for 1986 (sum of lines (5)(c) and (6)(c))		$46,000

Example (2). Assume the facts are the same as in example (1), except that the earnings and profits for 1986 are only $30,000. Under these facts, X is treated as receiving a deemed distribution taxable as a dividend of $35,000 on December 31, 1986, determined as follows:

(5)	Limitation on lines (1) through (4) of example (1):		
	(a)	Line (5)(a) of example (1)	$36,000
	(b)	Earnings and profits for 1986	$30,000
	(c)	Lesser of lines (5)(a) or (b)	$30,000
(6)	Amount determined under paragraph (a)(7) of this section:		
	(a)	Line (6)(a) of example (1)	$10,000
	(b)	Sum of the lesser of accumulated earnings and profits at beginning of 1986 ($5,000) or accumulated DISC income at beginning of 1986 ($6,000), plus excess of earnings and profits for 1986 over line (5)(c) ($30,000 minus $30,000)	$5,000
	(c)	Lesser of lines (6)(a) or (b)	$5,000
(7)	Total deemed distribution for 1986 (sum of lines (5)(c) and (6)(c))		$35,000

Example (3). Assume the facts are the same as in example (1), except that Y has a deficit in accumulated earnings and profits at the beginning 1986 of $4,000. This deficit is comprised of accumulated DISC income of $1,000, no previously taxed income and a deficit in other earnings and profits of $5,000. Assume also that Y has earnings and profits for 1986 of $45,000. Under these facts, X is treated as receiving a deemed distribution taxable as a dividend in the amount of $45,000 on December 31, 1986, determined as follows:

(5)	Limitation on lines (1) through (4) of example (1):		
	(a)	Line (5)(a) of example (1)	$36,000
	(b)	Earnings and profits for 1986	$45,000
	(c)	Lesser of lines (5)(a) or (b)	$36,000
(6)	Amount determined under paragraph (a)(7) of this section:		
	(a)	Line (6)(a) of example (1)	$10,000
	(b)	Sum of the lesser of accumulated earnings and profits at beginning of 1986 ($4,000 deficit—but not less than zero) or accumulated DISC income at beginning of 1986 ($1,000), plus excess of earnings and profits for 1986 over amount on line (5)(c) ($45,000 minus $36,000)	$9,000

(c)	Lesser of lines (6)(a) or (b)	$9,000
(7)	Total deemed distribution for 1986 (sum of lines (5)(c) and (6)(c))	$45,000

(d) *Special rules for certain tax-free acquisitions of property by the DISC.*—(1) *Exchanges by DISC.*—For purposes of paragraph (a)(2)(i) and (3)(i) of this section, if—

(i) A DISC acquires property in a first transaction and in a second transaction it disposes of such property in exchange for other property, and

(ii) By reason of the application of section 1031 (relating to like-kind exchanges) or section 1033 (relating to involuntary conversions), the basis in the DISC's hands of the other property acquired in such second transaction is determined in whole or in part with reference to the basis of the property acquired in the first transaction,

then upon a disposition of such other property in a third transaction by the DISC such other property shall be treated as though it had been transferred to the DISC in the first transaction. Thus, if the first transaction is a purchase of the property for cash, then paragraph (a)(2) and (3) of this section will not apply to a sale by the DISC of the other property acquired in the second transaction.

(2) *Transfer to another DISC.*—For purposes of paragraph (a)(2)(i) and (3)(i) of this section, if a DISC acquires property in a first transaction and it transfers such property to a transferee DISC in a second transaction in which the transferor DISC's gain is not recognized in whole or in part, then such property shall be treated as though it had been transferred to the transferee DISC in the same manner in which it was acquired in the first transaction by the transferor DISC. For example, if X and Y are both DISCs, and if X transfers property to Y in a second transaction in which gain or loss is not recognized, paragraph (a)(2) or (3) of this section does not apply to a sale of such property by Y in a third transaction if X had acquired the property in a first transaction by a cash purchase. If, however, X acquired the property from a transferor other than a DISC in the first transaction in which the transferor's realized gain was not recognized, then paragraph (a)(2) or (3) of this section may apply to a sale by Y if the other conditions of paragraph (a)(2) or (3) are met.

(3) *Limitation on amount recognized by DISC.*—If a DISC acquires property in a second transaction described in paragraph (d)(1) or (2) of this section in which it (or, in the case of a second transaction described in paragraph (d)(2), the transferor DISC) recognizes a portion (but not all) of the realized gain, then the amount described in paragraph (a)(2)(ii) or (a)(3)(ii) of this section with respect to a disposition by the DISC of such acquired property in a third transaction shall not exceed the amount of the transferor's gain which was not recognized on the first transaction minus the amount of gain recognized by the DISC (or transferor DISC) on the second transaction.

(4) *Examples.*—The provisions of this paragraph (d) are illustrated by the following examples:

Example (1). X and Y are corporations each of which qualifies as a DISC and uses the calendar year as its taxable year. In 1985, X acquires section 1245 property in a first transaction in which the transferor's entire realized gain of $17 is not recognized. In 1986, X transfers such property to Y in a second transaction in which X realizes a gain of $20 of which only $4 is recognized. (On December 31, 1986, X's shareholders are treated as having received a distribution taxable as a dividend which includes such $4 under paragraph (a)(3) of this section, provided the limitation in paragraph (b) of this section is met.) Assume further that in a third transaction in 1987, Y sells such property and recognizes a gain of $25. Under section 995(b)(1)(C) and paragraph (a)(3)(ii) of this section, Y's shareholders are treated as having received a distribution taxable as a dividend on December 31, 1987, of $13, which is the amount of the gain not recognized on the first transaction ($17) reduced by the amount recognized by X on the second transaction ($4).

Example (2). Z is a DISC which uses the calendar year as its taxable year. In a first transaction in 1985, Z acquires section 1245 property in exchange for its stock from A, an individual who is Z's sole shareholder, in a transaction in which A's realized gain of $30 is not recognized by reason of section 351(a). In a second transaction in 1986, Z exchanges such property for other property in a like-kind exchange to which section 1031(b) applies and recognizes $10 of a realized gain of $35. (On December 31, 1986, A is treated as having received a distribution taxable as a dividend which includes such $10 under paragraph (a)(3) of this section, provided the limitation in paragraph (b) of this section is met.) In a third transaction in 1987, Z sells the property acquired in the like-kind exchange and recognizes a gain of $25. Under section 995(b)(1)(C) and paragraph (a)(3)(ii) of this section, A is treated as having received a distribution taxable as a dividend on December 31, 1987, of $20, which is the amount of gain not recognized by A on the first transaction ($30) reduced by the amount of gain recognized by Z on the second transaction ($10).

(e) *Carryback of net operating loss and capital loss to prior DISC taxable year.*—For purposes of sections 991, 995 and 996, the amount of the deduction for the taxable year under section 172 for a net operating loss carryback or carryover or under section 1212 for a capital loss carryback or carryover shall be determined in the same manner as if the DISC were a domestic corporation which had not elected to be treated as a DISC. Thus, the amount of the deduction will be the same whether or not the corporation was a DISC in the year the loss is incurred or in the year to which the loss is carried. For provisions setting forth adjustments to the DISCs, or former DISCs, deemed distributions, adjustments to its divisions of earnings and profits, and other tax consequences arising from such carrybacks, see §1.996-8. See §1.996-9 for the reduction of the amount of any net operating loss or capital loss carryforward of a DISC to the extent of the DISC's accumulated DISC income as of December 31, 1984. [Reg. §1.995-2A.]

* * *

Partners and Partnerships: Sales or Exchanges: Certain Distributions

Partners and Partnerships: Sales or Exchanges: Certain Distributions.—Amendments to Reg. §1.995-4, prescribing how a partner should measure its interest in a partnership's unrealized receivables and inventory items, and that provide guidance regarding the tax consequences of a distribution that causes a reduction in that interest, are proposed (published in the Federal Register on November 3, 2014) (REG-151416-06).

☐ Par. 9. Section 1.995-4 is amended by revising the section heading and adding a new sentence at the end of paragraph (a)(1) to read as follows:

§1.995-4. Gain on certain dispositions of stock in a DISC.—(a) * * *

(1) * * * *But see* §§1.732-1(c)(2)(v) and 1.755-1(c)(2)(v) for rules governing the application of section 995(c) to partnership property in

situations in which the basis of the property is increased or decreased under section 732 or 734(b).

* * *

DISCs: Deemed Distributions

Domestic International Sales Corporations: Taxation of Income.—Reproduced below are the texts of proposed Reg. §§1.995-8 and 1.995-(f)-1, relating to the taxation of income allocable to a DISC for taxable years beginning after 1984 (published in the Federal Register on February 3, 1987).

* * *

☐ Par. 10. A new section 1.995-8 is added immediately after §1.995-7, to read as follows:

§1.995-8. Taxable income attributable to qualified export receipts which exceed $10 million for a taxable year ending after 1984.—(a) *In general.*—This section provides rules for the computation of the taxable income of the DISC attributable to qualified export receipts (as defined in section 993(a) and the regulations thereunder) of the DISC which exceed $10 million for a taxable year beginning after December 31, 1984. Section 995(b)(1)(E) treats the amount of such taxable income as a deemed distribution pro rata to the shareholders of the DISC for taxable years of the DISC beginning after

December 31, 1984. If the DISC's qualified export receipts for the taxable year exceed the $10 million amount, the corporation does not lose its status as a DISC, but there will be a deemed distribution of all of the DISC's taxable income attributable to the qualified export receipts for the taxable year which exceed the $10 million amount. Under section 995(b)(4) and paragraph (f) of this section, only one $10 million amount is allowed among all DISCs which are members of the same controlled group (as defined in section 993(a)(3)). If the DISC's taxable year is a short period as defined in section 443, and for such year the DISC is not a member of a controlled group which includes any other DISC, the $10 million amount for such year shall be reduced to the amount which bears the same ratio to $10 million as the number of days in such short period bears to 365, and for purposes of this section, all references to the $10 million amount shall refer to such reduced amount. If the qualified export receipts of the DISC for the taxable year do not exceed the $10 million amount, section 995(b)(1)(E) and this section do not apply. The $10 million amount is an annual amount; thus, if $10 million exceeds the DISC's qualified export receipts for the taxable year, such excess may not be carried or applied to any other taxable year. For purposes of this section, the term "excess receipts" means the qualified export receipts of the DISC for the taxable year which exceed the $10 million amount. See paragraph (d) of this section for coordination of the deemed distribution under section 995(b)(1)(E) and the other deemed distributions under section 995(b)(1).

(b) *Determination of qualified export receipts which exceed $10 million.*—(1) *General rule.*—If the qualified export receipts of the DISC for the taxable year exceed the $10 million amount, the DISC shall segregate the qualified export receipts for the taxable year into two amounts, those which shall be considered not to exceed the $10 million amount, and those which shall be considered to exceed the $10 million amount. Except as provided in paragraphs (b)(2) and (3) of this section, the selection of the excess receipts may be made by the DISC in any manner. In general, the selection of the excess receipts permits the DISC to allocate the $10 million amount to the qualified export receipts of those transactions during the taxable year which permit the greatest amount of taxable income to be allocated to the DISC under the inter-company pricing rules of section 994. Except as provided in paragraphs (b)(2) and (3) of this section, the allocation may be made on a transaction-by-transaction basis among all the transactions occurring during the taxable year, or on the basis of groupings consistent with the groupings used by the DISC for purposes of applying the inter-company pricing rules under §1.994-1(c)(7). Specifically, the $10 million amount is not required to be allocated to transactions in the order in which they occur during the taxable year, nor is the amount required to be allocated ratably to all transactions occurring during the taxable year. The allocation of the $10 million amount shall be made by the DISC on or before the due date of the DISC's return for the taxable year. The allocation of the $10 million amount may thereafter be amended only if (i) the DISC and all of the DISC's shareholders file amended returns consistent with any change in the allocation of the $10 million amount, and (ii) at the time such amended returns are filed, at least 12 full months remain in the statutory period (including extensions) for the assessment of a deficiency against any shareholder of the DISC. If less than 12 full months of such period remain with respect to any such shareholder, the director of the service center with which such shareholder files its income tax return will, upon request, enter into an agreement extending such statutory period for the limited purpose of assessing any deficiency against such shareholder attributable to the change in the allocation of the $10 million amount.

(2) *Exception for related and subsidiary services.*—Notwithstanding paragraph (b)(1) of this section, if qualified export receipts for the taxable year arise from a transaction in which services are or are to be provided which are related and subsidiary to any qualified sale, exchange, lease, rental, or other disposition of export property (within meaning of section 993(a)(1)(C) and §1.993-1(d)), the total amount of the qualified export receipts derived from such transaction must either be allocated in total, or not allocated at all to the $10 million amount. For example, if the qualified export receipts derived from a transaction are $50, of which $4 are attributable to related and subsidiary services and $46 are attributable to the sale of export property, the DISC must allocate either $50 or $0 of the qualified export receipts from such transaction to the $10 million amount; the DISC may not chose to allocate to the $10 million amount only the $4 attributable to the services or only the $46 attributable to the export property.

(3) *Ratable allocation where last transaction selected exceeds $10 million amount.*—If, in selecting among the qualified export receipts of

the taxable year, the qualified export receipts of the last transaction so selected by the DISC (when added to the receipts selected from other transactions) result in the DISC exceeding the $10 million amount for such year, the amount of qualified export receipts and taxable income attributable to such transaction which, for purposes of section 995(b)(1)(E) and this section shall be considered not to exceed the $10 million amount, shall be apportioned in proportion to (i) the amount of the qualified export receipts of the transaction that do not (when added to the receipts selected from other transactions) cause the DISC to exceed the $10 million amount, to (ii) the total amount of qualified export receipts from such transaction. The remainder shall be considered attributable to excess receipts for the taxable year. The deductions and the taxable income attributable to such transaction shall also be apportioned in the same manner. For example, assume that for the taxable year the DISC has selected nine transactions having total qualified export receipts of $9,975,000 as transactions to which the $10 million amount is to be applied, and that the tenth transaction the DISC would select has qualified export receipts of $40,000. In this instance, $25,000 ($10,000,000 – $9,975,000) of the qualified export receipts from such tenth transaction shall be considered not to exceed the $10 million amount, and $15,000 ($40,000 – $25,000) of such receipts shall be considered to be excess receipts. Accordingly, 37.5 percent (15/40) of the taxable income attributable to such transaction shall be deemed to be attributable to excess receipts.

(c) *Deductions taken into account.*—After identifying the transactions of the taxable year which are considered to exceed the $10 million amount, the DISC shall reduce such excess receipts by, where applicable, the cost of goods sold attributable to such excess receipts, and the deductions of the DISC properly allocated and apportioned to such excess receipts in accordance with §1.861-8. Such deductions include all applicable deductions from gross income for the taxable year provided under part VI of subchapter B of chapter 1 of the Code. The difference between the amount of the excess receipts and the deductions attributable to such excess receipts is the taxable income of the DISC attributable to qualified export receipts of the DISC for the taxable year which exceed the $10 million amount. Except as provided in paragraph (d) of this section, this amount of taxable income is treated as the deemed distribution under section 995(b)(1)(E) for the taxable year.

(d) *Coordination with other deemed distributions under section 995(b)(1).*—If (but for this paragraph (d)) an amount of taxable income would be treated as distributed for the taxable year under section 995(b)(1)(E) and also under subparagraph (A), (B), (C) or (D) of section 995(b)(1), such amount of taxable income shall be treated as distributed for such taxable year under that other subparagraph and not under section 995(b)(1)(E) and shall be subtracted from the amount determined under paragraph (c) of this section. In the case of military property, as defined in section 995(b)(3)(B) and §1.995-6(c), 50 percent of the taxable income of the DISC for the taxable year attributable to such property is deemed distributed under section 995(b)(1)(D) and §1.995-6. The remainder of the taxable income attributable to military property is deemed distributed under section 995(b)(1)(E) unless all of the gross receipts attributable to such property is allocated to the $10 million amount.

(e) *Illustration.*—The principles of this section may be illustrated by the following example:

Example—(i) *Facts.* P is a C corporation that uses the fiscal year ending September 30 as the taxable year. P owns all of the stock in Corporation D. D elects to be treated as a DISC for its taxable year beginning January 1, 1985. Under section 441(h), D must use the same taxable year as P. Accordingly, D's taxable year beginning January 1, 1985, will end on September 30, 1985. Assume that in D's taxable year ending September 30, 1985, D sold four aircraft in separate transactions (S1, S2, M1, M2). Two of the sales (M1 and M2) were of military property. D also derived $12,000 of interest from producer's loans during the taxable year. D's qualified export receipts for the taxable year are $9,762,000, and assume that the deductions properly allocated and apportioned thereto are $8,550,000, as follows:

	Receipts	Deductions	Taxable income
Producer's loan interest	$12,000	–0–	$12,000
Sales: S1	3,750,000	3,330,000	420,000
S2	3,000,000	2,670,000	330,000
M1	1,500,000	1,200,000	300,000
M2	1,500,000	1,350,000	150,000
	$9,762,000	$8,550,000	$1,212,000

(ii) *Limitation on $10 million amount.* D's taxable year ending September 30, 1985, is a short period consisting of 273 days. Accordingly, the $10 million amount specified in section 995(b)(1)(E) is limited to $7,479,452 (273/365 × $10 million) for the taxable year.

(iii) *Amount distributed under section 995(b)(1)(E).* D allocates all of the qualified export receipts from S1 and S2, and $729,452 of the

receipts from M1 against the $7,479,452 amount ($3,750,000 + $3,000,000 + $729,452 = $7,479,452), leaving the following amounts, reduced by the deductions properly apportioned and allocated thereto, as the amount distributed for the taxable year under section 995(b)(1)(E):

	Excess Receipts	Deductions	Taxable income
M1	$1,500,000	$1,200,000	$300,000
Less: Amount of M1 not in excess of limitation	(729,452)	(583,562)[1]	(145,890)
M1 Excess receipts	$770,548	$616,438	$154,110
M2	1,500,000	1,350,000	150,000
Producer's loan interest	12,000	–0–	12,000
Taxable income attributable to excess receipts, see §1.995-8(c)			$316,110
Less: Amounts otherwise distributed under section 995(b)(1), see §1.995-8(d):			
Section 995(b)(1)(A)—Producer's loan interest			$(12,000)
Section 995(b)(1)(D)—50% of taxable income attributable to sales of military property:			
M1 $154,110 × 50%			(77,055)
M2 $150,000 × 50%			(75,000)
Deemed distribution under section 995(b)(1)(E) for taxable year			$152,055

[1] $729,452/$1,500,000 × $1,200,000 = $583,562. See paragraph (b)(3) of this section.

(iv) *Deemed distribution for 1985.* The amount of D's deemed distribution under section 995(b)(1) for D's taxable year ending September 30, 1985, is $437,464 determined as follows:

Section 995(b)(1):	Amount
(A) Producer's loan interest	$12,000
(D) One-half of taxable income attributable to military property (50% of $450,000)	225,000
(E) Taxable income attributable to excess receipts	152,055
(F) One-seventeenth of the excess of taxable income less amounts in (A), (D) and (E) $^{17}/_1 × ($1,212,000 – $12,000 – $225,000 – $152,055)$	48,409
	$437,464

(f) *Members of a controlled group limited to one $10 million amount.*—(1) *General rule.*—For purposes of section 995(b)(1)(E) and this section, in the case of a controlled group of corporations (as defined in section 993(a)(3) and §1.993-1(k)), all DISCs which are members of such controlled group on a December 31, shall, for their taxable years which include such December 31, be limited to one $10 million amount. The $10 million amount shall be allocated equally among the member DISCs of such controlled group for their taxable years including such December 31, unless all of the member DISCs consent to an apportionment plan providing for an unequal allocation of the $10 million amount. Such a plan shall provide for the apportionment of a fixed dollar amount to one or more of the corporations, and the sum of the amounts so apportioned shall not exceed the $10 million amount. If the taxable year including such December 31 of any member DISC is a short period (as defined in section 443), the portion of the $10 million amount allocated to such member DISC for such short period under the preceding sentence shall be reduced to the amount which bears the same ratio to the amount so allocated as the number of days in such short period bears to 365. The consent of each member DISC to the apportionment plan for the taxable year shall be signified by a statement which satisfies the requirements of and is filed in the manner specified in §1.1561-3(b). An apportionment plan may be amended in the manner prescribed in §1.1561-3(c), except that an original or an amended plan may not be adopted with respect to a particular December 31 if at the time such original or amended plan is sought to be adopted, less than 12 full months remain in the statutory period (including extensions) for the assessment of a deficiency against any shareholder of a member DISC the tax liability of which would change by

the adoption of such original or amended plan. If less than 12 full months of such period remain with respect to any such shareholder, the director of the service center with which such shareholder files its income tax return will, upon request, enter into an agreement extending such statutory period for the limited purpose of assessing any deficiency against such shareholder attributable to the adoption of such original or amended apportionment plan.

(2) *Membership determined under section 1563(b).*—For purposes of paragraph (f) of this section, the determination of whether a DISC is a member of a controlled group of corporations with respect to any taxable year shall be made in the manner prescribed in section 1563(b) and the regulations thereunder.

(3) *Certain short taxable years.*—(i) *General rule.*—If a DISC has a short period (as defined in section 443) which does not include a December 31, and such DISC is a member of a controlled group of corporations which includes one or more other DISCs with respect to such short period, then the amount described in section 995(b)(1)(E) with respect to the short period of such DISC shall be determined by (A) dividing $10 million by the number of DISCs which are members of such group on the last day of such short period, and (B) multiplying the result by a fraction, the numerator of which is the number of days in such short period and the denominator of which is 365. For purposes of the preceding sentence, section 1563(b) shall be applied as if the last day of such short period were substituted for December 31. Except as provided in paragraph (f)(3)(ii) of this section, a DISC having a short period not including a December 31 may not enter into an apportionment plan with respect to such short period.

(ii) *Exception.*—If the short period not including a December 31 of two or more DISCs begins on the same date and ends on the same date and such DISCs are members of the same controlled group, such DISCs may enter into an apportionment plan for such short period in the manner provided in paragraph (f)(1) of this section with respect to the combined amount allowed to each of such DISCs under paragraph (f)(3)(i).

(4) *Effect on DISC shareholders.*—The computation of the deemed distribution under section 995(b)(1)(E) and this section for a taxable year, as affected by the controlled group rules of this paragraph (f), applies to a shareholder of a DISC whether or not such shareholder is a member of the controlled group which includes such DISC. [Reg. §1.995-8.]

☐ Par. 11. New §1.995(f)-1 is added immediately after §1.995-8 to read as follows:

§1.995(f)-1. Interest charge on DISC-related deferred tax liability for periods after 1984.—(a) *Interest charge.*—(1) *In general.*—Effective for taxable years ending after December 31, 1984, section 995(f) requires that each shareholder of a DISC shall pay for each taxable year interest on the shareholder's DISC-related deferred tax liability (as defined in paragraph (d) of this section) for such year at a rate of interest equal to the base period T-bill rate (as defined in paragraph (b)(2) of this section). See paragraph (b) of this section for the computation of the amount of the interest charge. The interest charge is computed on Form 8404. For purposes of this section, the term "DISC" includes a former DISC as defined in section 992(a)(3). Accordingly, a shareholder of a former DISC is required to pay the annual interest charge on such shareholder's DISC-related deferred tax liability.

(2) *Related rules.*—(i) The interest charge is an annual charge and is imposed on the shareholder of the DISC. The interest charge is not imposed on the DISC. Under section 995(f)(6), the amount of a shareholder's interest charge for any taxable year is treated for all purposes of the Code as interest paid or accrued on an underpay-

ment of tax. Accordingly, subject to all otherwise applicable limitations on the deduction for interest, the amount of the annual interest charge imposed on the shareholder is deductible by the shareholder for the taxable year in which the amount of the interest charge is paid, in the case of a shareholder which uses the cash receipts and disbursements method of accounting, or accrued, in the case of a shareholder which uses the accrual method of accounting. See paragraph (j)(2) of this section. Because the interest charge imposed on the shareholder is treated as interest, the payment or accrual of the interest charge does not increase or decrease the shareholder's basis in the stock of the DISC, and does not increase or decrease the taxable income or earnings and profits of the DISC.

(ii) Under section 995(f)(2), the shareholder's DISC-related deferred tax liability for a taxable year, that is, the amount considered to be the "principal" amount of the "loan" on which the interest charge is computed, is determined only with reference to the accumulated DISC income (A) derived by the DISC in periods after 1984, and (B) derived by the DISC in taxable years of the DISC that ended before the taxable year of the shareholder for which the interest charge is being determined.

(iii) No payments of estimated tax under section 6654 (in the case of individuals) or 6154 (in the case of corporations) are required with respect to the interest charge imposed by section 995(f)(1).

(iv) Paragraph (g) of this section contains rules for determining the interest charge for a taxable year in which shares in the DISC are transferred or redeemed. Paragraph (h) of this section proivdes rules for the computation and allocation of the interest charge where the DISC's shares are held by S corporations, trusts, estates or partnerships.

(b) *Computation of the interest charge.*—(1) *General rule.*—Under section 995(f)(1), the amount of the interest charge imposed on a DISC shareholder for a taxable year is equal to the product of—

(i) The shareholder's DISC-related deferred tax liability for such year, multiplied by,

(ii) A factor which is equal to the base period T-bill rate compounded daily for the number of days in the shareholder's taxable year for which the interest charge is being computed. See section 6622 for the requirement that all interest required to be paid under the Code be compounded daily. See paragraph (c) of this section for obtaining the table of base period T-bill rate factors reflecting daily compounding of the base period T-bill rate. See paragraph (g) of this section for special rules for computing the amount of the interest charge for a taxable year in which the shareholder transfers or acquires stock in the DISC.

(2) *Base period T-bill rate.*—Under section 995(f)(4), the "base period T-bill rate" is the annual rate of interest determined by the Secretary to be equivalent to the average investment yield of United States Treasury bills with maturities of 52 weeks which were auctioned during the one-year period ending on September 30 of the calendar year ending with (or, if the shareholder's taxable year is not the calendar year, of the most recent calendar year ending before) the close of the taxable year of the DISC shareholder for which the shareholder's interest charge is being determined. For example, if a DISC shareholder's taxable year is a fiscal year ending on June 30, the base period T-bill rate applicable to the shareholder's taxable year ending June 30, 1987, would be the rate determined for the one-year period ending September 30, 1986. If the shareholder's taxable year is the calendar year, the base period T-bill rate applicable to the shareholder's taxable year ending December 31, 1987, would be the rate determined for the one-year period ending September 30, 1987.

(c) *Publication of base period T-bill rate and use of the table of factors for daily compounding.*—The base period T-bill rate for each one-year period ending on September 30, as determined by the Secretary, shall be certified to the Commissioner and shall be published in a revenue ruling in the Internal Revenue Bulletin. Such revenue ruling shall also contain a table of factors reflecting daily compounding of the base period T-bill rate. To compute the amount of the interest charge for the taxable year under paragraph (b) of this section the shareholder shall use the base period T-bill rate factor corresponding to the number of days in the shareholder's taxable year for which the interest charge is being computed. Generally, the factor to be used will be the factor for 365 days. The factor to be used will be other than the factor for 365 days if the shareholder's taxable year for which the interest charge is being determined is a short taxable year, if the shareholder uses the 52-53 week taxable year, or if the shareholder's taxable year is a leap year. For example, if a DISC shareholder which had been using the calendar year as the taxable year changes its taxable year to the fiscal year ending January 31, then in computing the interest charge for the short taxable year January 1 to January 31 required to effect such change, the shareholder will use the factor for a taxable year of 31 days.

(d) *DISC-related deferred tax liability.*—(1) *Purpose.*—For taxable years of a DISC shareholder ending after December 31, 1984, the shareholder's DISC-related deferred tax liability represents, in general terms, the cumulative amount of income tax that is considered to have been deferred from taxation in prior taxable years (ending after 1984) of the shareholder by use of the DISC. A separate interest charge is imposed on the shareholder for each taxable year of the shareholder until the deferred DISC income is distributed or deemed distributed by the DISC. The amount of the shareholder's DISC-related deferred tax liability is determined for each taxable year by taking the difference between the shareholder's income tax liability for the taxable year computed first with, and then without, the accumulated DISC income that has been deferred from taxation in prior taxable years of the shareholder. See paragraph (f) of this section for the definition of "deferred DISC income." This paragraph (d) provides certain special rules to be used solely for the purpose of determining the amount of the shareholder's DISC-related deferred tax liability. For any taxable year, these rules may result in the amount of the shareholder's DISC-related deferred tax liability being different than the amount of additional income tax that the shareholder would owe for such year if the deferred DISC income were

received by the shareholder in an actual distribution to which section 996(a) applies.

(2) *In general.*—(i) Under section 995(f)(2), the "shareholder's DISC-related deferred tax liability", with respect to any taxable year of a DISC shareholder ending after 1984, is the excess of—

(A) The amount which would be the tax liability (as defined in paragraph (e) of this section) of the shareholder for the taxable year if the amount of the deferred DISC income (as described in paragraph (f) of this section) of such shareholder for such taxable year were included in the shareholder's gross income as ordinary income, over

(B) The actual amount of the shareholder's tax liability for such taxable year.

(ii) If in the taxable year the shareholder owns stock in more than one DISC, the deferred DISC income of such shareholder for the taxable year is the sum of the amounts of deferred DISC income of such shareholder with respect to each of such DISCs.

(iii) Where the DISC shareholder is a member of an affiliated group of corporations that files a consolidated return, the affiliated group's DISC-related deferred tax liability for the taxable year is the excess of (A) the amount which would be the group's tax liability (as defined in paragraph (e) of this section) including in gross income the deferred DISC income for the taxable year of each DISC shareholder which is a member of the group, over (B) the amount of the group's actual tax liability for such taxable year.

(iv) Except as provided in paragraphs (d) and (e) of this section, the computations necessary to determine the shareholder's DISC-related deferred tax liability shall be made under the law and the rates of tax applicable to the shareholder's taxable year for which the computations are made.

(v) The shareholder's DISC-related deferred tax liability for a taxable year is computed on Form 8404. See paragraph (j) of this section for the manner and time for filing or amending Form 8404 and paying the interest charge.

(3) *Carrybacks not taken into account.*—Under section 995(f)(2)(A), the shareholder's DISC-related deferred tax liability for any taxable year is determined without regard to any net operating loss or capital loss carryback or any credit carryback to such taxable year from any succeeding taxable year. For example, if for 1987 a calendar year shareholder of a DISC has a DISC-related deferred tax liability for the taxable year and thereby incurs an interest charge for such taxable year, and if the shareholder thereafter has a net operating loss (as defined in section 172(c)) for calendar year 1988, all or a portion of which is a net operating loss carryback to the 1987 taxable year, the shareholder's DISC-related deferred tax liability and interest charge for the 1987 taxable year are not affected by such net operating loss carryback, even if the shareholder recovers the total amount of the tax it paid for taxable year 1987, and has a net operating loss carryover to future taxable years.

(4) *Carryovers not taken into account.*—(i) *General rule.*—Under section 995(f)(2)(A)(i), the determination of the shareholder's tax liability for the taxable year including the deferred DISC income shall be made by not taking into account any loss, deduction or credit to the extent that such loss, deduction or credit may be carried by the shareholder to any other taxable year. If, however, the taxable year is the last taxable year to which the amount of a carryforward (of either a deduction or a credit) may be carried, the shareholder's tax liability including the deferred DISC income shall be computed with regard to the full amount of such carryforward, because the amount of the carryforward cannot be carried to another taxable year of the shareholder.

(ii) *Examples.*—The provisions of this paragraph (d)(4) may be illustrated by the following examples:

Example (1). Assume that in 1986, a calendar year DISC shareholder recognizes only ordinary business income of $10,000, and has deferred DISC income for the taxable year of $5000. If the shareholder also had a net operating loss carryforward to 1986 of $12,000, the shareholder would be allowed a $10,000 net operating loss deduction for 1986 and would have a net operating loss carryforward to 1987 of $2000. For purposes of determining the shareholder's DISC-related deferred tax liability for 1986, the shareholder's computation of its tax liability including the deferred DISC income under section 995(f)(2)(A)(i) may take into account a net operating loss deduction of only $10,000, because $2000 of the total loss carryforward may be carried to the shareholder's following taxable year. Accordingly, the shareholder's taxable income for 1986 including the deferred DISC income is $5000 ($10,000 of ordinary income, plus $5000 of deferred DISC income, less the net operating loss deduction of $10,000). However, if 1986 were the last taxable year to which the $12,000 net operating loss carryforward could be carried, then the shareholder's tax liability including the deferred DISC income under section 995(f)(2)(A)(i) may be computed by taking the full amount of the loss carryforward into account.

Reg. § 1.995(f)-1(d)(4)(ii)

Example (2). Assume that in 1986, a calendar year DISC shareholder places in service an amount of property such that the amount of the investment credit determined for the taxable year under section 46 is $25,000, and that the shareholder has no credit carryforwards to the taxable year from any earlier taxable year. Assume that for the shareholder's 1986 taxable year the amount of the credit allowed is limited to $20,000, because of the limitation on the amount of the credit allowed under section 38(c), and that the remaining $5000 of the credit determined for the taxable year may be carried back 3 years or forward 15 years. In determining the shareholder's DISC-related deferred tax liability for the 1986 taxable year, the amount of the credit that may be allowed to reduce the shareholder's tax liability including the deferred DISC income under section 995(f)(2)(A)(i) is limited to $20,000, because the remaining $5000 of the credit may be carried to another taxable year.

Example (3). The facts are the same as in example (2). Assume that $2000 of the $5000 excess credit for 1986 was applied to reduce 1985 taxes, and that none of the remaining $3000 could be carried back to any other taxable year. If in 1987, all of the $3000 credit carried over from 1986 is applied to reduce the shareholder's 1987 actual tax liability, that $3000 credit is also to be used to reduce the shareholder's 1987 tax liability including the deferred DISC income under section 995(f)(2)(A)(i).

(5) *Adjustments not involving carryovers or carrybacks.*—In computing the amount of the DISC shareholder's taxable income and tax liability including the deferred DISC income under section 995(f)(2)(A)(i), there shall be taken into account adjustments in amounts allowable as deductions and in amounts excluded from or included in gross income to the extent that such adjustments do not result in amounts which may be carried back or forward by the shareholder to any other taxable year. For example, in the case of a DISC shareholder who is an individual, the amount of medical expenses allowable as a deduction under section 213 must be redetermined when computing the individual's taxable income and tax liability including the deferred DISC income under section 995(f)(2)(A)(i). The amount of medical expenses allowable as a deduction decreases because the taxpayer's adjusted gross income, increased by the amount of the deferred DISC income, would increase the limitation on the deductible amount of medical expenses, and the medical expenses not allowed may not be carried to any other taxable year. As a further example, in the case of an individual or a corporation which is a DISC shareholder, the amount allowable as a charitable deduction under section 170 is not redetermined when computing the taxpayer's taxable income and tax liability including the deferred DISC income under section 995(f)(2)(A)(i), because the amount of charitable contributions made for the taxable year which are not allowable as a deduction for such year by reason of the percentage of income limitations under section 170(b) may be carried over to subsequent taxable years under section 170(d).

(6) *Deferred tax liability determined without regard to any consequential deduction or credit.*—Except as provided in paragraph (d)(8) of this section, in computing the amount of the DISC shareholder's tax liability including the deferred DISC income under section 995(f)(2)(A)(i), there shall not be taken into account any additional deduction or credit that would be allowable for any item that would be paid or accrued if the deferred DISC income were actually distributed to the shareholder. For example, when computing the shareholder's tax liability including the deferred DISC income, no deduction shall be taken into account for the additional state or local income or franchise taxes that would be due if such deferred DISC income were actually distributed to the shareholder. In addition, to simplify the calculations, in the case of a DISC shareholder who uses the accrual method of accounting, no deduction for the current year's interest charge shall be taken into account in computing the shareholder's DISC-related deferred tax liability for the current taxable year. However, after the amount of the interest charge for the current taxable year has been determined, such amount may be taken into account as a deduction for the current taxable year in determining the amount of the shareholder's income tax liability under chapter 1 of the Code for the taxable year in the circumstances described in paragraph (j)(2)(ii) of this section.

(7) *Source of deferred DISC income.*—The source of the deferred DISC income which is considered included in the shareholder's gross income for purposes of section 995(f)(2)(A)(i) shall be determined under section 861(a)(2)(D) and § 1.861-3(a)(5) in the same manner as if such amount were actually distributed to the DISC shareholder as a dividend.

(8) *Deemed paid foreign tax credit; separate limitation.*—In the case of a DISC shareholder that is a corporation, if the shareholder elects the foreign tax credit for the taxable year, such shareholder shall, in computing its tax liability including the deferred DISC income, take into account any increase in the amount of the deemed

paid foreign tax credit under section 902(a) for foreign income taxes paid by the DISC to the extent that the deferred DISC income is treated as income from sources without the United States. In such case, in accordance with section 78, the shareholder shall also include the amount of such foreign income tax in computing its gross income including the deferred DISC income. Any increase in the amount of the foreign tax credit that would be allowable against the tax liability determined under section 995(f)(2)(A)(i) with respect to the amount of the deferred DISC income shall be subject to the separate limitation required by section 904(d)(1)(F) in the same manner as if such amount were actually distributed to the DISC shareholder as a dividend.

(e) *Tax liability.*—(1) *General rule.*—Except as provided in paragraphs (e)(2) and (e)(3) of this section, for purposes of the two tax computations ("with and without" the deferred DISC income) required by section 995(f)(2) and paragraph (d) of this section, the term "tax liability" means the amount of the tax imposed on the DISC shareholder for the taxable year by chapter 1 of the Code, reduced by the credits (but not the credit carrybacks or carryovers described in paragraphs (d)(3) and (d)(4) of this section) allowable against such tax.

(2) *Certain taxes not to be taken into account.*—For purposes of section 995 (f)(2) and paragraph (e)(1) of this section, any tax imposed by any of the following provisions shall not be treated as tax imposed by chapter 1 of the Code:

(i) Section 55 (relating to the alternative minimum tax) and

(ii) Any other provisions described in section 26(b)(2) (relating to certain other taxes treated as not imposed by chapter 1 of the Code).

(3) *Certain credits not taken into account.*—For purposes of section 995(f)(2) and paragraph (e)(1) of this section, the credits allowed for the taxable year by the following sections shall not be taken into account in determining the DISC shareholder's tax liability:

(i) Section 31 (relating to taxes withheld on wages),

(ii) Section 32 (relating to the earned income credit), and

(iii) Section 34 (relating to the fuels credit).

(f) *Deferred DISC income.*—(1) *In general.*—Under section 995(f)(3)(A), for any taxable year of a DISC shareholder, the term "deferred DISC income" means the excess of—

(i) The shareholder's pro rata share of the DISC's accumulated DISC income (earned by the DISC in taxable years ending after December 31, 1984) as of the close of the computation year (as defined in paragraph (f)(2) of this section), over

(ii) The amount (if any) of distributions-in-excess-of-income (as defined in paragraph (f)(3) of this section) made by the DISC during the taxable year of the DISC immediately following the computation year.

Thus, in the simple case where the DISC has only one shareholder and the DISC and the shareholder have the same taxable year, the shareholder's deferred DISC income for the taxable year is the excess of the DISC's accumulated DISC income (derived from periods after 1984) at the beginning of the taxable year over the amount (if any) by which actual distributions for the taxable year which are considered to be made out of accumulated DISC income exceed the amount of DISC income for such year. Where shareholders of the DISC have a taxable year different from that of the DISC, the deferred DISC income is measured from the computation year, as described in paragraph (f)(2) of this section.

(2) *Computation year.*—(i) *General rule.*—Under section 995(f)(3)(B), with respect to any taxable year of a DISC shareholder, the "computation year" is the taxable year of the DISC ending with (or within, if the DISC and the shareholder do not have the same taxable year) the taxable year of the shareholder which precedes the taxable year of the shareholder for which the amount of deferred DISC income is being determined.

(ii) *Example.*—The following example illustrates the relationship between the shareholder's taxable year and the DISC's computation year:

Example. Assume that a DISC, D, has two shareholders, A, the principal shareholder, and B, a minority shareholder. Shareholder A uses the calendar year as the taxable year, and shareholder B's taxable year is the fiscal year ending June 30. Under section 441(h), D must use the calendar year as the taxable year. In determining the amount of shareholder A's deferred DISC income for A's taxable year ending December 31, 1987, the computation year is D's taxable year ending December 31, 1986, that is, D's taxable year ending with shareholder A's taxable year preceding the taxable year of A for which A's deferred DISC income is being determined. In determining the amount of shareholder B's deferred DISC income for B's taxable year ending June 30, 1987, the computation year is D's taxable year ending December 31, 1985, that is, D's taxable year ending within B's taxable year preceding the taxable year of B for which B's deferred DISC income is being determined.

(3) *Distributions-in-excess-of-income.*—Under section 995(f)(3)(C), with respect to any taxable year of a DISC, the term "distributions-in-excess-of-income", means the excess (if any) of—

(i) The amount of actual distributions made to the shareholder during such taxable year out of accumulated DISC income (as determined under section 996), over

(ii) The shareholder's pro rata share of the DISC income (as defined in section 996(f)) for such taxable year.

	1985	1986	1987
Taxable income and earnings and profits for the year	$45,000	$60,000	$40,000
Deemed distribution under section 995(b)(1)	5,000	10,000	15,000
DISC income for year	$40,000	$50,000	$25,000
Actual distributions during year	$–0–	$20,000	$60,000
Accumulated DISC income—end of year	$40,000	$85,000	$65,000
Previously taxed income—end of year	5,000	–0–	–0–
Accumulated earnings and profits—end of year	$45,000	$85,000	$65,000

(ii) *Result—1985.* Under section 995(f)(3), P will have no deferred DISC income for P's taxable year ending December 31, 1985, because D does not have accumulated DISC income derived from periods after 1984 as of the close of the computation year. With respect to P's taxable year ending December 31, 1985, the computation year under section 995(f)(3)(B) would be D's taxable year ending with or within P's taxable year ending December 31, 1984, which is prior to D's current election to be treated as a DISC. Accordingly, because P has no deferred DISC income for its taxable year ending December 31, 1985, P will have no DISC-related deferred tax liability and therefore no interest charge for the taxable year.

(iii) *Result—1986.* Under section 995(f)(3), P will have deferred DISC income for P's taxable year ending December 31, 1986, of $40,000 determined as follows. With respect to P's taxable year ending December 31, 1986, the computation year is D's taxable year ending December 31, 1985. D's accumulated DISC income as of the close of the computation year is $40,000, and D made no distributions-in-excess-of-income in D's taxable year following the computation year (that is, in D's taxable year ending December 31, 1986, of the actual distributions of $20,000, only $5000 of this amount is treated as made out of accumulated DISC income, and because the DISC income for the year is $50,000, none of the actual distributions for the year reduce the accumulated DISC income as of the beginning of the taxable year.)

Accordingly, because P's deferred DISC income for the taxable year ending December 31, 1986, is $40,000, P must compute its tax liability for the year with and then without the $40,000 amount under section 995(f)(2) to determine its DISC-related deferred tax liability. P's interest charge for the taxable year ending December 31, 1986, under section 995(f)(1) will be the amount of the DISC-related deferred tax liability (the tax on $40,000) multiplied by the base period T-bill rate factor for the 365 day taxable year. See paragraph (b) of this section.

(iv) *Result-1987.* Under section 995 (f)(3), P will have deferred DISC income for P's taxable year ending December 31, 1987, of $65,000 computed as follows:

	D's accumulated DISC income derived from periods after 1984 as of the close of the computation year (D's taxable year ending December 31, 1986)	$85,000
Less:	Amount of D's distributions-in-excess-of-income made in D's taxable year ending December 31, 1987	20,000
	P's deferred DISC income for taxable year ending December 31, 1987	$65,000

The $20,000 amount of distributions-in-excess-of-income for D's taxable year ending December 31, 1987, may be determined as follows:

	Amount of D's actual distributions for D's taxable year ending December 31, 1987		$60,000
Less:	D's previously taxed income at close of previous taxable year	$–0–	
	Deemed distribution for current year . .	15,000	
	Total amount of previously taxed income available for distributions during D's taxable year ending December 31, 1987	$15,000	15,000
	Difference-Amount of actual distributions for current year out of accumulated DISC income		$45,000
Less:	DISC income for current year		25,000
	Distributions-in-excess-of-income for D's taxable year ending December 31, 1987		$20,000

Accordingly, because P's deferred DISC income for its taxable year ending December 31, 1987 is $65,000, P must compute its tax

(4) *Illustrations.*—The provisions of paragraph (f) of this section may be illustrated by the following example:

Example—(i) *Facts.* P corporation, which uses the calendar year as the taxable year, owns all of the stock of D, a domestic corporation which elects to be treated as a DISC for its taxable year beginning January 1, 1985. Under section 441(h), D must adopt the same taxable year as P; accordingly, D's taxable year beginning January 1, 1985, will end on December 31, 1985.

Assume that D has the following amounts for its three taxable years ending December 31, 1985, 1986 and 1987:

liability for the taxable year with and then without the $65,000 amount to determine its DISC-related deferred tax liability under section 995(f)(2). P's interest charge for the taxable year ending December 31, 1987, under section 995(f)(1) will be the amount of the DISC-related deferred tax liability (the tax on the $65,000) multiplied by the base period T-bill rate factor for the 365 day taxable year.

(g) *Special rules for computation of the interest charge where DISC stock is transferred during taxable year.*—(1) *General rule.*—If the same number of shares of stock in the DISC are not held by the shareholder for the shareholder's entire taxable year, the amount of the interest charge for the taxable year with respect to the shares transferred or acquired by the shareholder shall be equal to the amount of the DISC-related deferred tax liability with respect to such transferred or acquired shares computed as if the shareholder held such shares for the shareholder's entire taxable year, multiplied by the base period T-bill rate factor corresponding to the number of days in the shareholder's taxable year that the shareholder held such transferred or acquired shares. In determining the number of days in the shareholder's taxable year that the shareholder held such transferred or acquired shares, the transferor shareholder shall include the day of the transfer and the transferee shareholder shall exclude the day of the transfer.

(2) *Adjustment for gain recognized on disposition.*—(i) *Transferor.*—For purposes of determining the deferred DISC income for the taxable year of a shareholder who disposes of stock in the DISC during the taxable year, the amount of gain recognized with respect to such stock which is treated under section 995(c) and §1.995-4 as a dividend shall be treated as an actual distribution made by the DISC to such shareholder out of accumulated DISC income for the taxable year of the DISC which includes the date of such disposition. Accordingly, the amount of such gain which exceeds the shareholder's pro rata share of the DISC income for such taxable year shall be treated under section 995(f)(3)(C) and paragraph (f) of this section as a distribution-in-excess-of-income which reduces the amount of such shareholder's deferred DISC income for the taxable year of the shareholder in which the disposition of the shares occurs.

(ii) *Transferee.*—For purposes of determining the amount of any transferee shareholder's deferred DISC income for a taxable year, if under section 996(d)(1) and §1.996-4(a) such shareholder would be permitted to treat an amount of an actual distribution by the DISC made out of accumulated DISC income as made out of previously taxed income, such transferee shareholder's deferred DISC income for such taxable year shall be reduced by such amount.

(3) *Examples.*—The provisions of this paragraph (g) may be illustrated by the following examples:

Example (1). X, an individual, uses the calendar year as the taxable year and owns all of the stock of D, a calendar year corporation which elects to be treated as a DISC for 1985. On May 1, 1987, X makes a gift to Y, a calendar year individual, of all the stock in D. On December 31, 1986, D had accumulated DISC income of $1000, and during its taxable year ending December 31, 1987, D made no distributions-in-excess-of-income. X recognizes no gain on the transfer of stock to Y. Accordingly, for the taxable year ending December 31, 1987, X and Y each have deferred DISC income of $1000, and each must compute a DISC-related deferred tax liability for 1987 with respect to this $1000 of deferred DISC income as if each of them owned the stock for the entire year. X will multiply X's DISC-related deferred tax liability by the base period T-bill rate factor for 121 days, and Y will multiply Y's DISC-related deferred tax liability by the base period T-bill rate factor for 244 days, to reflect the number of days during their taxable year that each held the stock in the DISC. If during the taxable year Y received a distribution in excess of income of $200, Y's deferred DISC income for the taxable year would be $800, and X's deferred DISC income for the year would also be $800, even though the actual distribution was received by Y.

Example (2). (i) Corporations A and D use the calendar year as the taxable year. A owns all of the stock of D, which elects to be treated as a DISC for 1985. On December 31, 1987, A sells all of its stock in D to B corporation, and recognizes a gain on the sale of $400. B corporation uses the fiscal year ending June 30 as the taxable year. Assume that D had accumulated DISC income at the close of 1986 of $600, and that D realized $250 of DISC income for 1987. Assume also that D made no actual distributions out of accumulated DISC income during 1987. Accordingly, D has accumulated DISC income at December 31, 1987, of $850 ($600 plus $250), all of which was accumulated during the period A held the stock in the DISC. Under section 995(c) and §1.995-4, all of A's recognized gain of $400 on the disposition of the stock in the DISC is treated as a dividend, because A's recognized gain ($400) does not exceed the accumulated DISC income of D attributable to the stock disposed of by A ($850).

(ii) Under paragraph (g)(2) of this section, for purposes of section 995(f)(3), the $400 amount that A must treat as a dividend is treated as an actual distribution to A for 1987 out of accumulated DISC income. Accordingly, A's deferred DISC income for its taxable year ending December 31, 1987, is $450, determined as follows:

Accumulated DISC income of D at close of computation year (1986)		$600
Amount of gain realized by A in 1987 treated as an actual distribution out of accumulated DISC income	$400	
Less: DISC income for 1978	250	
Difference: Amount treated as a distribution-in-excess-of- income	$150	150
Deferred DISC income		$450

A will use this $450 amount of deferred DISC income to compute its DISC-related deferred tax liability and interest charge for A's 365 day taxable year ending December 31, 1987.

(iii) Because B purchased the stock in D on December 31, 1987, B will have a part-year interest charge for B's taxable year ending June 30, 1988. D's computation year with respect to B's taxable year ending June 30, 1988, is D's taxable year ending December 31, 1986. B's deferred DISC income for its taxable year ending June 30, 1988, is $450, the same amount that A had with respect to A's taxable year ended December 31, 1987, because B is permitted, under section 996(d), to take into account as a reduction in accumulated DISC income, the amount of gain recognized on the disposition which was treated as an actual distribution to A out of accumulated DISC income. Accordingly, B must compute its DISC-related deferred tax liability and interest charge for the taxable year ending June 30, 1988, with respect to the $450 of deferred DISC income. The interest charge for B's taxable year ending June 30, 1988, is determined by multiplying B's DISC-related deferred tax liability (the tax on the $450 of deferred DISC income) by the base period T-bill rate factor for 182 days (January 1 to June 30, 1988), because B held the stock for only 182 days in B's taxable year ended June 30, 1988.

(iv) Note that under section 441(h), D must change its taxable year from the calendar year to the fiscal year ending June 30, because there has been a change in the taxable year of D's "principal shareholder" by reason of B's acquisition of D. See §1.441-1(h)(3).

(h) *Special rules for computation of the interest charge where DISC stock is held by certain pass-through entities.*—(1) *Partnerships.*—For purposes of section 995(f) and this section, if stock in a DISC is held by a partnership, the deferred DISC income of such partnership for the taxable year shall be attributed to each partner in proportion to the partner's interest in partnership income for the taxable year. Thus, each partner shall take into account its share of the partnership's deferred DISC income for the partnership taxable year ending with or within the taxable year of the partner, and each partner shall determine its DISC-related deferred tax liability and the interest charge thereon for the partner's taxable year as if the partner directly owned stock in the DISC.

(2) *S corporations.*—For purposes of section 995(f) and this section, if stock in a DISC is held by an S corporation, the deferred DISC income of such S corporation for the taxable year shall be attributed to each shareholder in proportion to the shareholder's pro rata share of the S corporation's nonseparately computed income or loss (determined under section 1366(a)(1)(B)) for the taxable year. Thus, each shareholder shall take into account its share of the S corporation's deferred DISC income for the taxable year of the S corporation ending with or within the taxable year of the shareholder, and shall determine its DISC-related deferred tax liability and the interest charge thereon for the taxable year as if the shareholder directly owned stock in the DISC.

(3) *Estates or trusts.*—For purposes of section 995(f) and this section, if stock in a DISC is held by an estate or trust, the deferred DISC income allocable to the stock in the DISC held by the estate or trust shall not be attributed to the beneficiaries of such estate or trust. The interest charge is imposed on the estate or trust. The estate or trust is required to determine its DISC-related deferred tax liability and interest charge for the taxable year in the same manner as other taxpayers. For this purpose, the tax rates applicable to estates and trusts for the taxable year under section 1(e) shall apply. In computing the taxable income of the estate or trust for the taxable year including the deferred DISC income under section 995(f)(2)(A)(i), the estate or trust shall not take into account a deduction under section 651 or 661 (relating to deductions for distributions) greater than the deduction for distributions allowed in computing the estate or trust's actual tax liability for such year under section 995(f)(2)(A)(ii).

(i) [There is no paragraph (i).]

(j) *Character, payment, assessment and collection of the interest charge.*—(1) *Character.*—Under section 995(f)(6), the interest charge imposed on a DISC shareholder for any taxable year is treated for all purposes of the Code in the same manner as interest on an underpayment of tax under section 6601. Thus, the interest charge may be deducted from the shareholder's gross income only to the extent the shareholder may deduct interest on an underpayment of tax, and subject to all applicable limitations on the deduction for interest.

(2) *Taxable year for which interest charge is deductible.*—(i) *Cash method shareholder.*—If the DISC shareholder uses the cash receipts and disbursements method of accounting, to the extent that the interest charge for a taxable year is deductible, it is deductible in the taxable year in which the shareholder pays the interest charge. For example, assume that on March 15, 1987, a cash method, calendar year DISC shareholder that is a C corporation pays $100, representing the full amount of the shareholder's interest charge for its taxable year ending December 31, 1986. The $100 amount is a proper interest deduction for the shareholder's taxable year ending December 31, 1987, the taxable year in which the cash method shareholder paid the interest charge.

(ii) *Accrual method shareholder.*—If the DISC shareholder uses the accrual method of accounting, under the all events test the fact of the shareholder's liability for the interest charge for a taxable year is not fixed, and the amount of the interest charge cannot be determined, until the close of the period in which the shareholder can receive a distribution-in-excess-of-income with respect to such year. Prior to that time, all or any amount of the interest charge for the taxable year may be eliminated by such a distribution. Generally, however, if the DISC shareholder uses the accrual method and if the DISC and the shareholder have the same taxable year, then to the extent that the interest charge for a taxable year is deductible, the amount of the shareholder's interest charge is a proper deduction for such taxable year, because the period in which the DISC can make a distribution-in-excess-of-income to the shareholder with respect to such taxable year ends on the last day of such shareholder's taxable year. For example, assume that on March 10, 1987, an accrual method, calendar year DISC shareholder that is a C corporation pays $150, representing the full amount of the shareholder's interest charge for its taxable year ending December 31, 1986. Assume also that the DISC uses the calendar year as the taxable year. When the DISC's 1986 taxable year closed, the shareholder could no longer receive a distribution-in-excess-of-income under section 995(f)(3)(A)(ii) with respect to the shareholder's 1986 taxable year. Accordingly, the $150 interest charge is a proper interest deduction for the shareholder's taxable year ending December 31, 1986, the taxable year in which the interest charge accrued under section 461.

(3) *Payment, assessment and collection of the interest charge.*—(i) Under section 995(f)(6), the interest charge imposed on the DISC shareholder for any taxable year is required to be paid on the same date the shareholder's income tax return for such taxable year is required to be filed, without regard to extensions.

If the interest charge is not paid by that date, interest, compounded daily, at the rate specified under section 6621 shall be imposed on the amount of the unpaid interest charge from that date until the date the interest charge is paid. The interest charge for the taxable year shall be computed on a current Form 8404, which must be completed in accordance with the instructions thereon, and filed by the DISC shareholder together with a separate payment of the interest charge. The payment of the interest charge shall be made, and the Form 8404 shall be filed with the service center with which the shareholder's income tax return for the taxable year is required to be filed. In order to assure proper handling of the Form 8404 and crediting of payment of the interest charge to the shareholder's account, the Form 8404 and the payment of the interest charge should not be attached to or mailed together with the shareholder's income tax return for the taxable year. Payment of the interest charge may not be made by designating any portion of an overpayment of tax as an amount to be applied in payment of the interest charge.

(ii) Payments of estimated tax under section 6654 (in the case of an individual), or 6154 (in the case of a corporation) are not required with respect to the interest charge.

(iii) The interest charge is to be assessed, and may be collected in the same manner as interest on an underpayment of tax under section 6601.

(4) *Subsequent change in interest charge amount; amended Form 8404.*—If the shareholder's actual tax liability for a taxable year changes, either by reason of an audit adjustment or by the filing of an amended return, the shareholder is required to file an amended Form 8404 only if the amount of the shareholder's DISC-related deferred

tax liability (as defined in §1.995(f)-1(d)) for such taxable year also changes. If so required, the shareholder shall file the amended Form 8404 by (i) clearly labeling across the top of a Form 8404 "Amended Form 8404 for Shareholder's Taxable Year Ending 19XX", (ii) by attaching to the amended Form 8404 a computation and an explanation of the change in the shareholder's DISC-related deferred tax liability and interest charge for such taxable year, and (iii) by enclosing payment for the amount of any additional interest charge or a statement of the amount of the interest charge required to be refunded to the shareholder. The amended Form 8404 should be attached to the copy of the shareholder's amended income tax return for the taxable year involved, or mailed separately to the service center with which the shareholder would file an amended income tax return for the taxable year involved. [Reg. §1.995(f)-1.]

DISCs: Deemed Distributions

Domestic International Sales Corporations: Taxation of Income.—Reproduced below are the texts of proposed Reg. §1.996-9 and proposed amendments to Reg. §1.996-1, relating to the taxation of income allocable to a DISC for taxable years beginning after 1984 (published in the Federal Register on February 3, 1987).

* * *

☐ Par. 12. Paragraph (b)(2) of §1.996-1 is revised to read as follows:

§1.996-1. Rules for actual distributions and certain deemed distributions.—* * *

(b) *Rules for qualifying distributions and deemed distributions under section 995(b)(1)(G).*—* * *

(2) *Special rules.*—(i) *1976-1984.*—For taxable years beginning after December 31, 1975, and before January 1, 1985, paragraph (b)(1) of this section shall apply to one-half of the amount of an actual distribution made pursuant to §1.992-3 to satisfy the condition of

§1.992-1(b) (the gross receipts test) and paragraph (a) of this section shall apply to the remaining one-half of such amount.

(ii) *After 1984.*—For taxable years beginning after December 31, 1984, in the case of a DISC shareholder which is a C corporation, paragraph (b)(1) of this section shall apply to $^{16}/_{17}$ of the amount of an actual distribution made pursuant to §1.992-3 to satisfy the condition of §1.992-1(b) (the gross receipts test) and paragraph (a) of this section shall apply to one-seventeenth ($^{1}/_{17}$) of such amount.

* * *

☐ Par. 12. A new section 1.996-9 is added immediately after §1.996-8 to read as follows:

§1.996-9. Adjustments attributable to the Tax Reform Act of 1984.—(a) *Exemption of pre-1985 accumulated DISC income from tax.*—(1) *In general.*—Under section 805(b)(2) of the Tax Reform Act of 1984, Pub. L. 98-369, 98 Stat. 494, 1001, in the case of actual distributions made after December 31, 1984, by a DISC or former DISC which was a DISC on such date, any accumulated DISC income of such DISC or former DISC which was derived before January 1, 1985, shall be treated as previously taxed income with respect to which there had previously been a deemed distribution to which section 996(e)(1) applied. For purposes of this section such accumulated DISC income shall be referred to as "exempt accumulated DISC income". For purposes of this section, a distribution includes any distribution in liquidation of a corporation.

(2) *Exception for previously disqualified DISCs.*—Paragraph (a)(1) of this section does not apply to the amount of any actual or deemed distribution of any accumulated DISC income of a DISC or former DISC derived before January 1, 1985, which is scheduled to be received as a deemed distribution under section 995(b)(2) and §1.995-3 by reason of the disqualification, termination or revocation of the DISC election of such corporation (a "disqualified DISC"). Thus, in the case of a corporation which was a disqualified DISC with respect to one or more prior taxable years ending before 1985, but which has re-elected to be treated as a DISC for one or more succeeding taxable years including the taxable year ending December 31, 1984, this paragraph (a)(2) applies to any accumulated DISC income scheduled to be received as a deemed distribution under section 995(b)(2), and paragraph (a)(1) of this section applies to any accumulated DISC income derived before 1985 which is not required to be distributed under section 995(b)(2).

(3) *Exception for amounts distributed to meet qualification requirements.*—Paragraph (a)(1) of this section does not apply to the amount of any accumulated DISC income derived before January 1, 1985, which is distributed (or is required to be distributed) under section 992(c) after December 31, 1984, in order to satisfy the requirements of section 992(a)(1)(A) (relating to the 95 percent qualified export receipts test) or section 992(a)(1)(B) (relating to the 95 percent qualified export assets test), with respect to any taxable year ending before January 1, 1985.

(b) *Effect of distributions by DISC to shareholders.*—(1) *Scope.*—This paragraph (b) applies only to distributions made after December 31, 1984, by a DISC (including a corporation which has elected to be treated as an interest charge DISC for any period after 1984) or a former DISC which has any amount of exempt accumulated DISC income (as defined in paragraph (a)(1) of this section), and it shall not apply after such corporation has distributed, under the ordering rules of this paragraph (b), all of its exempt accumulated DISC

income. This paragraph (b) shall apply notwithstanding section 996(a)(1).

(2) *Ordering rule for distributions made before July 1, 1985.*—Any actual distribution to a shareholder after December 31, 1984, and before July 1, 1985, by a DISC or former DISC described in paragraph (b)(1) of this section, which is made out of earnings and profits shall be treated as made—

(i) First, out of previously taxed income, to the extent thereof,

(ii) Second, out of accumulated DISC income derived after 1984, to the extent thereof, and

(iii) Third, out of other earnings and profits (including current earnings and profits in the case of a former DISC).

Any distribution which is treated as made out of previously taxed income under paragraph (b)(2)(i) shall be treated as made first out of exempt accumulated DISC income, to the extent thereof, and second, out of other previously taxed income.

(3) *Ordering rule for distributions made after June 30, 1985.*—Any actual distribution to a shareholder after June 30, 1985, by a DISC or former DISC described in paragraph (b)(1) of this section, which is made out of earnings and profits shall be treated as made—

(i) First, out of other earnings and profits (including current earnings and profits in the case of a former DISC), to the extent thereof,

(ii) Second, out of previously taxed income, to the extent thereof, and

(iii) Third, out of accumulated DISC income derived after 1984.

Any distribution which is treated as made out of previously taxed income under paragraph (b)(3)(ii) shall be treated as made first out exempt accumulated DISC income, to the extent thereof, and second, out of other previously taxed income.

(4) *Exception for qualifying distributions and foreign investments attributable to producer's loans.*—This paragraph (b) shall not apply to any actual distribution made pursuant to section 992(c) (relating to distributions to meet qualification requirements), or to any deemed distribution pursuant to section 995(b)(1)(G) (relating to foreign investment attributable to producer's loans). Such distributions shall be treated as described in section 996(a)(2).

(c) *Earnings and profits attributable to exempt income.*—The earnings and profits of a corporation which receives a distribution directly or indirectly from a DISC or former DISC shall be increased by the amount of money and the adjusted basis of any property received in a distribution which is treated as made out of previously taxed income attributable to exempt accumulated DISC income.

(d) *No adjustment to basis in stock of DISC for exempt income.*—Notwithstanding section 996(e), a shareholder's basis in the stock of a DISC or former DISC shall not be increased by the amount of exempt accumulated DISC income which is treated as previously taxed income, and such basis shall not be reduced by the receipt of such amount as previously taxed income in a distribution to which paragraph (b) of this section applies.

(e) *Carryover basis in property received in a distribution of exempt income.*—If property other than money is received in a distribution of exempt accumulated DISC income as previously taxed income, and if such property was a qualified export asset (as defined in section 993(b)) on December 31, 1984, then for purposes of section 311, no gain or loss shall be recognized on the distribution of such property, and the shareholder who receives such property shall have a basis in such property equal to the basis of such property in the hands of the DISC or former DISC.

(f) *Reduction of net operating loss and capital loss carryovers.*—In the case of a DISC (including a corporation which has elected to be treated as an interest charge DISC for any period after 1984) or a former DISC which was a DISC on December 31, 1984, the amount of any net operating loss or capital loss of such corporation that was incurred in a taxable year in which such corporation was a DISC and which is a net operating loss or capital loss carryover to any taxable year ending after December 31, 1984, shall be reduced by the amount of exempt accumulated DISC income (as defined in paragraph (a)(1) of this section) of such corporation as of December 31, 1984. If the sum of such carryovers exceeds the amount of such exempt accumulated DISC income, the exempt accumulated DISC income shall first be applied to reduce the amount of such net operating loss carryover, and the amount of such exempt accumulated DISC income (if any) which exceeds such net operating loss carryover shall be applied to reduce the amount of such capital loss carryover to the extent of such excess.

(g) *No credit allowed for foreign taxes attributable to exempt accumulated DISC income.*—Notwithstanding sections 901(d) and 902, no credit shall be allowed for the amount of any income, war profits, or excess profits taxes paid or deemed paid to any foreign country or possession of the United States to the extent that such taxes are attributable to any exempt accumulated DISC income of a DISC or former DISC. [Reg. §1.996-9.]

* * *

International Boycotts

International Boycotts: Loss of Tax Benefits: Computation of International Boycott Factor.—Reproduced below is the text of proposed Reg. §1.999-1, relating to the computation of the international boycott factor (published in the Federal Register on February 24, 1977).

§1.999-1. Computation of the International Boycott Factor.—(a) *In general.*—Sections 908(a), 952(a)(3), and 995(b)(1)(F) provide that certain benefits of the foreign tax credit, deferral of earnings of foreign corporations, and DISC are denied if a person or a member of a controlled group (within the meaning of section 993(a)(3)) that includes that person participates in or cooperates with an international boycott (within the meaning of section 999(b)(3)). The loss of tax benefits may be determined by multiplying the otherwise allowable tax benefits by the "international boycott factor." Section 999(c)(1) provides that the international boycott factor is to be determined under regulations prescribed by the Secretary. The method of computing the international boycott factor is set forth in paragraph (c) of this section. A special rule for computing the international boycott factor of a person that is a member of two or more controlled groups is set forth in paragraph (d). Transitional rules for making adjustments to the international boycott factor for years affected by the effective dates are set forth in paragraph (e). The definitions of the terms used in this section are set forth in paragraph (b).

(b) *Definitions.*—For purposes of this section:

(1) *Boycotting country.*—In respect of a particular international boycott, the term "boycotting country" means any country described in section 999(a)(1)(A) or (B) that requires participation in or cooperation with that particular international boycott.

(2) *Participation in or cooperation with an international boycott.*—For the definition of the term "participation in or cooperation with an international boycott", see section 999(b)(3) and Parts H through M of the Treasury Department's International Boycott Guidelines.

(3) *Operations in or related to a boycotting country.*—For the definitions of the terms "operations", "operations in a boycotting country", "operations related to a boycotting country", and "operations with the government, a company, or a national of a boycotting country", see Part B of the Treasury Department's International Boycott Guidelines.

(4) *Clearly demonstrating clearly separate and identifiable operations.*—For the rules for "clearly demonstrating clearly separate and identifiable operations", see Part D of the Treasury Department's International Boycott Guidelines.

(5) *Purchase made from a country.*—The terms "purchase made from a boycotting country" and "purchases made from any country other than the United States" mean, in respect of any particular country, the gross amount paid in connection with the purchase of, the use of, or the right to use:

(i) Tangible personal property (including money) from a stock of goods located in that country,

(ii) Intangible property (other than securities) in that country,

(iii) Securities by a dealer to a beneficial owner that is a resident of that country (but only if the dealer knows or has reason to know the country of residence of the beneficial owner),

(iv) Real property located in that country, or

(v) Services performed in, and the end product of services performed in, that country (other than payroll paid to a person that is an officer or employee of the payor).

(6) *Sales made to a country.*—The terms "sales made to a boycotting country" and "sales made to any country other than the United States" mean, in respect of any particular country, the gross receipts from the sale, exchange, other disposition, or use of:

(i) Tangible personal property (including money) for direct use, consumption, or disposition in that country,

(ii) Services performed in that country,

(iii) The end product of services (wherever performed) for direct use, consumption, or disposition in that country,

(iv) Intangible property (other than securities) in that country,

(v) Securities by a dealer to a beneficial owner that is a resident of that country (but only if the dealer knows or has reason to know the country of residence of the beneficial owner), or

(vi) Real property located in that country.

To determine the country of direct use, consumption, or disposition of tangible personal property and the end product of services, see paragraph (b)(10) of this section.

(7) *Sales made from a country.*—The terms "sales made from a boycotting country" and "sales made from any country other than the United States" mean, in respect of a particular country, the gross receipts from the sale, exchange, other disposition, or use of:

(i) Tangible personal property (including money) from a stock of goods located in that country,

(ii) Intangible property (other than securities) in that country, or

(iii) Services performed in, and the end product of services performed in, that country.

However, gross receipts from any such sale, exchange, other disposition, or use by a person that are included in the numerator of that person's international boycott factor by reason of paragraph (b)(6) of this section shall not again be included in the numerator by reason of this subparagraph.

(8) *Payroll paid or accrued for services performed in a country.*—The terms "payroll paid or accrued for services performed in a boycotting country" and "payroll paid or accrued for services performed in any country other than the United States" mean, in respect of a particular country, the total amount paid or accrued as compensation to officers and employees, including wages, salaries, commissions, and bonuses, for services performed in that country.

(9) *Services performed partly within and partly without a country.*—(i) *In general.*—Except as provided in paragraph (b)(9)(ii) of this section, for purposes of allocating to a particular country—

(A) The gross amount paid in connection with the purchase or use of,

(B) The gross receipts from the sale, exchange, other disposition or use of, and

(C) the payroll paid or accrued for

services performed, or the end product of services performed, partly within and partly without that country, the amount paid, received, or accrued to be allocated to that country, unless the facts and circumstances of a particular case warrant a different amount, will be that amount that bears the same relation to the total amount paid, received, or accrued as the number of days of performance of the services within that country bears to the total number of days of performance of services for which the total amount is paid, received, or accrued.

(ii) *Transportation, telegraph, and cable services.*—Transportation, telegraph, and cable services performed partly within one country and partly within another country are allocated between the two countries as follows:

(A) In the case of a purchase of such services performed from Country A to Country B, fifty percent of the gross amount paid is deemed to be a purchase made from Country A and the remaining fifty percent is deemed to be a purchase made from Country B.

(B) In the case of a sale of such services performed from Country A to Country B, fifty percent of the gross receipts is deemed to be a sale made from Country A and the remaining fifty percent is deemed to be a sale made to Country B.

(10) *Country of use, consumption, or disposition.*—As a general rule, the country of use, consumption, or disposition of a tangible personal property (including money) and the end product of services (wherever performed) is deemed to be the country of destination of the tangible personal property or the end product of the services. (Thus, if legal services are performed in one country and an opinion is given for use by a client in a second country, the end product of the legal services is used, consumed, or disposed of in the second country.) The occurrence in a country of a temporary interruption in the shipment of the tangible personal property or the delivery of the end product of services shall not constitute such country the country of destination. However, if at the time of the transaction the person providing the tangible personal property or the end product of services knew, or should have known from the facts and circumstances surrounding the transaction, that the tangible personal property or the end product of services probably would not be used, consumed, or disposed of in the country of destination, that person must determine the country of ultimate use, consumption or disposition of the tangible personal property or the end product of services. Notwithstanding the preceding provisions of this subparagraph, a person that sells, exchanges, otherwise disposes of, or makes available for use, tangible personal property to any person all of whose business except for an insubstantial part consists of selling from inventory to retail customers at retail outlets all within one country may assume at the time of such sale to such person that the tangible personal property will be used, consumed, or disposed of within such country.

(11) *Controlled group taxable year.*—The term "controlled group taxable year" means the taxable year of the controlled group's common parent corporation. In the event that no common parent corporation exists, the members of the group shall elect the taxable year of one of the members of the controlled group to serve as the controlled group taxable year. The taxable year election is a binding election to be changed only with the approval of the Secretary or his delegate. The election is to be made in accordance with the procedures set forth in the instructions to Form 5713, the International Boycott Report.

(c) *Computation of international boycott factor.*—(1) *In general.*—The method of computing the international boycott factor of a person that is not a member of a controlled group is set forth in paragraph (c)(2) of this section. The method of computing the international boycott factor of a person that is a member of a controlled group is set forth in paragraph (c)(3) of this section. For purposes of paragraphs (c)(2) and (3), purchases and sales made by, and payroll paid or accrued by, a partnership are deemed to be made or paid or accrued by a partner in that production that the partner's distributive share bears to the purchases and sales made by, and the payroll paid or accrued by, the partnership. Also for purposes of paragraphs (c)(2) and (3), purchases and sales made by, and payroll paid or accrued by, a trust referred to in section 671 are deemed to be made both by the trust (for purposes of determining the trust's international boycott factor), and by a person treated under section 671 as the owner of the trust (but only in that proportion that the portion of the trust that such person is considered as owning under section 671 through 679 bears to the purchases and sales made by, and the payroll paid and accrued by, the trust).

(2) *International boycott factor of a person that is not a member of a controlled group.*—The international boycott factor to be applied by a person that is not a member of a controlled group (within the meaning of section 993(a)(3)) is a fraction.

(i) The numerator of the fraction is the sum of the—

(A) Purchases made from all boycotting countries associated in carrying out a particular international boycott,

(B) Sales made to or from all boycotting countries associated in carrying out a particular international boycott, and

(C) Payroll paid or accrued for services performed in all boycotting countries associated in carrying out a particular international boycott

by that person during that person's taxable year, minus the amount of such purchases, sales, and payroll that is clearly demonstrated to be attributable to clearly separate and identifiable operations in connection with which there was no participation in or cooperation with that international boycott.

(ii) The denominator of the fraction is the sum of the—

(A) Purchases made from any country other than the United States,

(B) Sales made to or from any country other than the United States, and

(C) Payroll paid or accrued for services performed in any country other than the United States

by that person during that person's taxable year.

(3) *International boycott factor of a person that is a member of a controlled group.*—The international boycott factor to be applied by a person that is a member of a controlled group (within the meaning of section 993(a)(3)) shall be computed in the manner described in paragraph (c)(2) of this section, except that there shall be taken into account the purchases and sales made by, and the payroll paid or accrued by, each member of the controlled group during each member's own taxable year that ends with or within the controlled group taxable year that ends with or within that person's taxable year.

(d) *Computation of the international boycott factor of a person that is a member of two or more controlled groups.*—The international boycott factor to be applied under sections 908(a), 952(a)(3), and 995(b)(1)(F) by a person that is a member of two or more controlled groups shall be determined in the manner described in paragraph (c)(3), except that the purchases, sales, and payroll included in the numerator and denominator shall include the purchases, sales, and payroll of that person and of all other members of the two or more controlled groups of which that person is a member.

(e) *Transitional rules.*—(1) *Pre-November 3, 1976 boycotting operations.*—The international boycott factor to be applied under sections 908(a), 952(a)(3), and 995(b)(1)(F) by a person that is not a member of a controlled group, for that person's taxable year that includes November 3, 1976, or a person that is a member of a controlled group, for the controlled group taxable year that includes November 3, 1976, shall be computed in the manner described in paragraphs (c)(2) and (c)(3), respectively, of this section. However, the following adjustments shall be made—

(i) There shall be excluded from the numerators described in paragraphs (c)(2)(i) and (c)(3)(i) of this section purchases, sales, and payroll clearly demonstrated to be attributable to clearly separate and identifiable operations—

(A) that were completed on or before November 3, 1976, or

(B) in respect of which it is demonstrated that the agreements constituting participation in or cooperation with the international boycott were renounced, the renunciations were communicated on or before November 3, 1976, to the governments or persons with which the agreements were made, and the agreements have not been reaffirmed after November 3, 1976, and

(ii) The international boycott factor resulting after the numerator has been modified in accordance with paragraph (e)(1)(i) of this section shall be further modified by multiplying it by a fraction. The numerator of that fraction shall be the number of days in that person's taxable year (or, if applicable, in that person's controlled group taxable year) remaining after November 3, 1976, and the denominator shall be 366.

The principles of this subparagraph are illustrated in the following example:

Example. Corporation A, a calendar year taxpayer, is not a member of a controlled group. During the 1976 calendar year, Corporation A had three operations in a boycotting country under three separate contracts, each of which contained agreements constituting participation in or cooperation with an international boycott. Each contract was entered into on or after September 2, 1976. Operation (1) was completed on November 1, 1976. The sales made to a boycotting country in connection with Operation (1) amounted to $10. Operation (2) was not completed during the taxable year, but on November 1, 1976, Corporation A communicated a renunciation of the boycott agreement covering that operation to the government of the boycott country. The sales made to a boycotting country in connection with Operation (2) amounted to $40. Operation (3) was not completed during the taxable year, nor was any renunciation of the boycott agreement made. The sales made to a boycotting country in connection with Operation (3) amounted to $25. Corporation A had no purchases made from, sales made from, or payroll paid or accrued for services performed in, a boycotting country. Corporation A had $500 of purchases made from, sales made from, sales made to, or payroll paid or accrued for services performed in, countries other than the United States. Company A's boycott factor for 1976, con-puted under paragraph (c)(2) of this section (before the application of this subparagraph) would be:

$$\frac{\$10 + \$40 + \$25}{\$500} = \frac{\$75}{\$500}$$

However, the $10 is eliminated from the numerator by reason of paragraph (e)(1)(i)(A) of this section, and the $40 is eliminated from the numerator by reason of paragraph (e)(1)(i)(B) of this section. Thus, before the application of paragraph (e)(1)(ii) of this section, Corporation A's international boycott factor is $25/$500. After the application of paragraph (e)(1)(ii), Corporation A's international boycott factor is:

$$\frac{\$25}{\$500} \times \frac{58}{366}$$

(2) *Pre-December 31, 1977 boycotting operations.*—The international boycott factor to be applied under sections 908(a), 952(a)(3), and 995(b)(1)(F) by a person that is not a member of a controlled group, for that person's taxable year that includes December 31, 1977, or by a person that is a member of a controlled group, for the controlled group taxable year that includes December 31, 1977, shall be computed in the manner described in paragraphs (c)(2) and (c)(3), respectively, of this section. However, the following adjustments shall be made—

(i) There shall be excluded from the numerators described in paragraphs (c)(2)(i) and (c)(3)(i) of this section purchases, sales, and payroll clearly demonstrated to be attributable to clearly separate and identifiable operations that were carried out in accordance with the terms of binding contracts entered into before September 2, 1976, and—

(A) That were completed on or before December 31, 1977, or

(B) In respect of which it is demonstrated that the agreements constituting participation in or cooperation with the international boycott were renounced, the renunciations were communicated on or before December 31, 1977, to the governments or persons with which the agreements were made, and the agreements were not reaffirmed after December 31, 1977, and

(ii) In the case of clearly separate and identifiable operations that are carried out in accordance with the terms of binding contracts entered into before September 2, 1976, but that do not meet the requirements of paragraph (e)(2)(i) of this section, the numerators described in paragraphs (c)(2)(i) and (c)(3)(i) of this section shall be adjusted by multiplying the purchases, sales, and payroll clearly demonstrated to be attributable to those operations by a fraction, the numerator of which is the number of days in such person's taxable year (or, if applicable, in such person's controlled group taxable year) remaining after December 31, 1977, and the denominator of which is 365.

The principles of this subparagraph are illustrated in the following example:

Example. Corporation A is not a member of a controlled group and reports on the basis of a July 1—June 30 fiscal year. During the 1977-1978 fiscal year, Corporation A had 2 operations carried out pursuant to the terms of separate contracts, each of which had a clause that constituted participation in or cooperation with an international boycott. Neither operation was completed during the fiscal year, nor were either of the boycotting clauses renounced. Operation (1) was carried out in accordance with the terms of a contract entered into on November 15, 1976. Operation (2) was carried out in accordance with the terms of a binding contract entered into before September 2, 1976. Corporation A had sales made to a boycotting country in connection with Operation (1) in the amount of $50, and in connection with Operation (2) in the amount of $100. Corporation A had sales made to countries other than the United States in the amount of $500. Corporation A had no purchases made from, sales made from, or payroll paid or accrued for services performed in, any country other than the United States. In the absence of this subparagraph, Corporation A's international boycott factor would be

$$\frac{\$50 + \$100}{\$500}$$

However, by reason of the application of this subparagraph, Corporation A's international boycott factor is reduced to

$$\frac{\$50 + \$100 \quad (\frac{181}{365})}{\$500}$$

(3) *Incomplete controlled group taxable year.*—If, at the end of the taxable year of a person that is a member of a controlled group, the controlled group taxable year that includes November 3, 1976 has not ended, or the taxable year of one or more members of the controlled group that includes November 3, 1976 has not ended, then the international boycott factor to be applied under sections 908(a), 952(a)(3) and 995(b)(1)(F) by such person for the taxable year shall be computed in the manner described in paragraph (c)(3) of this section. However, the numerator and the denominator in that paragraph shall include only the purchases, sales, and payroll of those members of the controlled group whose taxable years ending after November 3, 1976 have ended as the end of the taxable year of such person.

(f) *Effective date.*—This section applies to participation in or cooperation with an international boycott after November 3, 1976. In the case of operations which constitute participation in or cooperation with an international boycott and which are carried out in accordance with the terms of a binding contract entered into before September 2, 1976, this section applies to such participation or cooperation after December 31, 1977. [Reg. § 1.999-1].

GAIN OR LOSS ON DISPOSITION OF PROPERTY

Annuity Contracts: Exchanges of Property

Annuity Contracts: Exchanges of Property.—Amendments to Reg. § 1.1001-1, providing guidance on the taxation of the exchange of property for an annuity contract, are proposed (published in the Federal Register on October 18, 2006) (REG-141901-05).

☐ Par. 3. In § 1.1001-1, paragraphs (h), (i) and (j) are added to read as follows:

§ 1.1001-1. Computation of gain or loss.

* * *

(h) [Reserved.]

(i) [Reserved.]

(j) *Certain annuity contracts received in exchange for property.*— (1) *In general.*—If an annuity contract (other than an annuity contract that either is a debt instrument subject to sections 1271 through 1275, or is received from a charitable organization in a bargain sale governed by § 1.1011-2) is received in exchange for property, receipt of the contract shall be treated as a receipt of property in an amount equal to the fair market value of the contract, whether or not the contract is the equivalent of cash. The amount realized attributable to the annuity contract is the fair market value of the annuity contract at the time of the exchange, determined under section 7520. For the timing of the recognition of gain or loss, if any, see § 1.451-1(a). In the case of a transfer in part a sale and in part a gift, see paragraph (e) of this section. In the case of an annuity contract that is a debt instrument subject to sections 1271 through 1275, see paragraph (g) of this section. In the case of a bargain sale to a charitable organization, see § 1.1011-2.

(2) *Effective date.*—(i) *In general.*—Except as provided in paragraph (j)(2)(ii), this paragraph (j) is effective for exchanges of property for an annuity contract (other than an annuity contract that either is a debt instrument subject to sections 1271 through 1275, or is received from a charitable organization in a bargain sale governed by § 1.1011-2) after October 18, 2006.

(ii) This paragraph (j) is effective for exchanges of property for an annuity contract (other than an annuity contract that either is a debt instrument subject to sections 1271 through 1275, or is received from a charitable organization in a bargain sale governed by § 1.1011-2) after April 18, 2007, if the following conditions are met —

(A) The issuer of the annuity contract is an individual;

(B) The obligations under the annuity contract are not secured, either directly or indirectly; and

(C) The property transferred in exchange for the annuity contract is not subsequently sold or otherwise disposed of by the transferee during the two-year period beginning on the date of the exchange. For purposes of this provision, a disposition includes without limitation a transfer to a trust (whether a grantor trust, a revocable trust, or any other trust) or to any other entity even if solely owned by the transferor.

State and Local Governments: Tax-Exempt Bonds

State and Local Governments: Tax-Exempt Bonds.—Amendments to Reg. §1.1001-3, addressing when tax-exempt bonds are treated as retired for purposes of section 103 and sections 141 through 150 of the Internal Revenue Code, are proposed (published in the Federal Register on December 31, 2018) (REG-141739-08).

Par. 3. Section 1.1001-3 is amended by:

1. Revising paragraph (a)(2).
2. Revising the paragraph (h) subject heading.
3. Revising the first sentence of paragraph (h)(1).
4. Revising the paragraph (h)(2) subject heading.
5. Adding paragraph (h)(3).

The revisions and addition read as follows:

§1.1001-3. Modifications of debt instruments.—(a) * * *

(2) *Qualified tender bonds.*—For special rules governing whether tax-exempt bonds that are qualified tender bonds are retired for purposes of sections 103 and 141 through 150, see §1.150-3.

* * *

(h) *Applicability date.*—* * *

(1) * * * Except as otherwise provided in paragraphs (h)(2) and (3) of this section, this section applies to alterations of the terms of a debt instrument on or after September 24, 1996. * * *

(2) *Alteration or modification results in an instrument or property right that is not debt.* * * *

(3) *Qualified tender bonds.*—Paragraph (a)(2) of this section applies to events and actions taken with respect to qualified tender bonds that occur on or after the date that is 90 days after the date of publication of the Treasury decision adopting these rules as final regulations in the **Federal Register**.

Transition of Tax Consequences: IBORs: Guidance

Transition of Tax Consequences: IBORs: Guidance.—Reg. §1.1001-6, providing guidance on the tax consequences of the transition to the use of reference rates other than interbank offered rates in debt instruments and non-debt contracts, is proposed (published in the Federal Register on October 9, 2019) (REG-118784-18).

Par. 5. Section 1.1001-6 is added to read as follows:

§1.1001-6. Transition from interbank offered rates.—

(a) *Treatment under section 1001.*—(1) *Debt instruments.*—An alteration of the terms of a debt instrument to replace a rate referencing an interbank offered rate (IBOR) with a qualified rate as defined in paragraph (b) of this section (qualified rate) and any associated alteration as defined in paragraph (a)(5) of this section (associated alteration) are not treated as modifications and therefore do not result in an exchange of the debt instrument for purposes of §1.1001-3. For example, if the terms of a debt instrument that pays interest at a rate referencing the U.S.-dollar London Interbank Offered Rate (USD LIBOR) are altered to provide that the instrument pays interest at a qualified rate referencing the Secured Overnight Financing Rate published by the Federal Reserve Bank of New York, that alteration of terms is not treated as a modification and therefore does not result in an exchange for purposes of §1.1001-3.

(2) *Non-debt contracts.*—A modification of the terms of a contract other than a debt instrument (a non-debt contract) to replace a rate referencing an IBOR with a qualified rate and any associated modification as defined in paragraph (a)(5) of this section (associated modification) are not treated as the exchange of property for other property differing materially in kind or extent for purposes of §1.1001-1(a). A non-debt contract includes but is not limited to a derivative, stock, an insurance contract, and a lease agreement.

(3) *Fallback rate.*—An alteration of the terms of a debt instrument to include a qualified rate as a fallback to a rate referencing an IBOR and any associated alteration are not treated as modifications and therefore do not result in an exchange of the debt instrument for purposes of §1.1001-3. In addition, an alteration of the terms of a debt instrument to substitute a qualified rate in place of a rate referencing an IBOR as a fallback to another rate and any associated alteration are not treated as modifications and therefore do not result in an exchange of the debt instrument for purposes of §1.1001-3. A modification of the terms of a non-debt contract to include a qualified rate as a fallback to a rate referencing an IBOR and any associated modification are not treated as the exchange of property for other property differing materially in kind or extent for purposes of §1.1001-1(a). In addition, a modification of the terms of a non-debt contract to substitute a qualified rate in place of a rate referencing an IBOR as a fallback to another rate and any associated modification are not treated as the exchange of property for other property differing materially in kind or extent for purposes of §1.1001-1(a).

(4) *Other contemporaneous alterations and modifications.*—Whether an alteration of the terms of a debt instrument that is not described in paragraph (a)(1) or (3) of this section and that is made contemporaneously with an alteration described in paragraph (a)(1) or (3) of this section results in an exchange of the debt instrument is determined under §1.1001-3. Similarly, whether a modification of the terms of a non-debt contract that is not described in paragraph (a)(2) or (3) of this section and that is made contemporaneously with a modification described in paragraph (a)(2) or (3) of this section results in an exchange of property for other property differing materially in kind or extent is determined under §1.1001-1(a). In applying

§1.1001-3 or §1.1001-1(a) for this purpose, the altered or modified terms described in paragraph (a)(1), (2), or (3) of this section are treated as part of the terms of the debt instrument or non-debt contract prior to any alteration or modification that is not so described. For example, if the parties to a debt instrument change the interest rate from a rate referencing USD LIBOR to a qualified rate and at the same time increase the interest rate to account for deterioration of the issuer's credit since the issue date, the qualified rate is treated as a term of the instrument prior to the alteration and only the addition of the risk premium is analyzed under §1.1001-3.

(5) *Associated alteration or modification.*—For purposes of this section, *associated alteration* or *associated modification* means any alteration of a debt instrument or modification of a non-debt contract that is associated with the alteration or modification by which a qualified rate replaces, or is included as a fallback to, the IBOR-referencing rate and that is reasonably necessary to adopt or to implement that replacement or inclusion. An associated alteration or associated modification may be a technical, administrative, or operational alteration or modification, such as a change to the definition of interest period or a change to the timing and frequency of determining rates and making payments of interest (for example, delaying payment dates on a debt instrument by two days to allow sufficient time to compute and pay interest at a qualified rate computed in arrears). An associated alteration or associated modification may also be the addition of an obligation for one party to make a one-time payment in connection with the replacement of the IBOR-referencing rate with a qualified rate to offset the change in value of the debt instrument or non-debt contract that results from that replacement (a one-time payment).

(b) *Qualified rate.*—(1) *In general.*—For purposes of this section, a *qualified rate* is any one of the following rates, provided that the rate satisfies the fair market value requirement of paragraph (b)(2) of this section and the currency requirement of paragraph (b)(3) of this section:

(i) The Secured Overnight Financing Rate published by the Federal Reserve Bank of New York (SOFR);

(ii) The Sterling Overnight Index Average (SONIA);

(iii) The Tokyo Overnight Average Rate (TONAR or TONA);

(iv) The Swiss Average Rate Overnight (SARON);

(v) The Canadian Overnight Repo Rate Average (CORRA);

(vi) The Hong Kong Dollar Overnight Index (HONIA);

(vii) The interbank overnight cash rate administered by the Reserve Bank of Australia (RBA Cash Rate);

(viii) The euro short-term rate administered by the European Central Bank (€STR);

(ix) Any alternative, substitute or successor rate selected, endorsed or recommended by the central bank, reserve bank, monetary authority or similar institution (including any committee or working group thereof) as a replacement for an IBOR or its local currency equivalent in that jurisdiction;

Reg. §1.1001-6(b)(1)(ix)

(x) Any qualified floating rate, as defined in §1.1275-5(b) (but without regard to the limitations on multiples set forth in §1.1275-5(b)), that is not described in paragraphs (b)(1)(i) through (ix) of this section;

(xi) Any rate that is determined by reference to a rate described in paragraphs (b)(1)(i) through (x) of this section, including a rate determined by adding or subtracting a specified number of basis points to or from the rate or by multiplying the rate by a specified number; or

(xii) Any rate identified as a qualified rate in guidance published in the Internal Revenue Bulletin (see §601.601(d)(2)(ii)(a) of this chapter) for purposes of this section.

(2) *Substantial equivalence of fair market value.*—(i) *In general.*—Notwithstanding paragraph (b)(1) of this section, a rate is a qualified rate only if the fair market value of the debt instrument or non-debt contract after the alteration or modification described in paragraph (a)(1), (2), or (3) of this section is substantially equivalent to the fair market value of the debt instrument or non-debt contract before the alteration or modification. In determining fair market value for this purpose, the parties may use any reasonable, consistently applied valuation method and must take into account the value of any onetime payment that is made in connection with the alteration or modification. A reasonable valuation method may (but need not) be based in whole or in part on past or projected values of the relevant rate. The requirements of this paragraph (b)(2)(i) are deemed to be satisfied if the rate meets the safe harbor set forth in paragraph (b)(2)(ii)(A) of this section or if the parties satisfy the safe harbor set forth in paragraph (b)(2)(ii)(B) of this section.

(ii) *Safe harbors.*—(A) *Historic average of rates.*—Paragraph (b)(2)(i) of this section is satisfied if, on the date of the alteration or modification described in paragraph (a)(1), (2), or (3) of this section, the historic average of the relevant IBOR-referencing rate does not differ by more than 25 basis points from the historic average of the replacement rate, taking into account any spread or other adjustment to the rate, and adjusted to take into account the value of any onetime payment that is made in connection with the alteration or modification. For this purpose, an historic average may be determined by using an industry-wide standard, such as a method of determining an historic average recommended by the International Swaps and Derivatives Association for the purpose of computing the spread adjustment on a rate included as a fallback to an IBOR-referencing rate on a derivative or a method of determining an historic average recommended by the Alternative Reference Rates Committee (or a comparable non-U.S. organization or non-U.S. regulator) for the purpose of computing the spread adjustment for a rate that replaces an IBOR-referencing rate on a debt instrument. An historic average may also be determined by any reasonable method that takes into account every instance of the relevant rate published during a continuous period beginning no earlier than 10 years before the alteration or modification and ending no earlier than three months before the alteration or modification. For purposes of this safe harbor, the historic average must be determined for both rates using the same method and historical data from the same timeframes and must be determined in good faith by the parties with the goal of making the fair market value of the debt instrument or non-debt contract after the alteration or modification substantially equivalent to the fair market value of the debt instrument or non-debt contract before the alteration or modification.

(B) *Arm's length negotiations.*—Paragraph (b)(2)(i) of this section is satisfied if the parties to the debt instrument or non-debt contract are not related (within the meaning of section 267(b) or section 707(b)(1)) and the parties determine, based on bona fide, arm's length negotiations between the parties, that the fair market value of the debt instrument or non-debt contract before the alteration or modification described in paragraph (a)(1), (2), or (3) of this section is substantially equivalent to the fair market value after the alteration or modification. For this purpose, the fair market value of the debt instrument or non-debt contract after the alteration or modification must take into account the value of any one-time payment that is made in connection with the alteration or modification.

(C) *Published in the Internal Revenue Bulletin.*—In guidance published in the Internal Revenue Bulletin, the Commissioner may set forth additional circumstances in which a rate is treated as satisfying the requirement of paragraph (b)(2)(i) of this section (see §601.601(d)(2)(ii)(a) of this chapter).

(3) *Currency of the interest rate benchmark.*—Notwithstanding paragraph (b)(1) of this section, a rate is a qualified rate only if the interest rate benchmark to which the rate refers after the alteration or modification described in paragraph (a)(1), (2), or (3) of this section and the IBOR to which the debt instrument or non-debt contract referred before that alteration or modification are based on transactions conducted in the same currency or are otherwise reasonably expected to measure contemporaneous variations in the cost of newly borrowed funds in the same currency.

(c) *Effect of an alteration of the terms of a debt instrument or a modification of the terms of a derivative on integrated transactions and hedges.*—An alteration of the terms of a debt instrument or a modification of the terms of a derivative to replace a rate referencing an IBOR with a qualified rate on one or more legs of a transaction that is integrated under §1.988-5 or §1.1275-6 is not treated as legging-out of the transaction, provided that the §1.1275-6 hedge (as defined in §1.1275-6(b)(2)) or the §1.988-5(a) hedge (as defined in §1.988-5(a)(4)) as modified continues to meet the requirements for a §1.1275-6 hedge or §1.988-5(a) hedge, whichever is applicable. Similarly, an alteration of the terms of a debt instrument or a modification of the terms of a derivative to replace an interest rate referencing an IBOR with a qualified rate on one or more legs of a transaction that is subject to the hedge accounting rules described in §1.446-4 will not be treated as a disposition or termination (within the meaning of §1.446-4(e)(6)) of either leg of the transaction. In addition, a modification to replace an interest rate referencing an IBOR with a qualified rate on a hedging transaction for bonds that is integrated as a qualified hedge under §1.148-4(h) for purposes of the arbitrage investment restrictions applicable to State and local tax-exempt bonds and other tax-advantaged bonds (as defined in §1.150-1(b)) is not treated as a termination of that qualified hedge under §1.148-4(h)(3)(iv)(B), provided that the hedge as modified continues to meet the requirements for a qualified hedge under §1.148-4(h), as determined by applying the special rules for certain modifications of qualified hedges under §1.148-4(h)(3)(iv)(C).

(d) *Source and character of a one-time payment.*—For all purposes of the Internal Revenue Code, the source and character of a one-time payment that is made by a payor in connection with the alteration or modification described in paragraph (a)(1), (2), or (3) of this section is the same as the source and character that would otherwise apply to a payment made by the payor with respect to the debt instrument or non-debt contract that is altered or modified.

(e) *Coordination with provision for grandfathered obligations under chapter 4.*—A non-debt contract that is modified only as described in paragraph (a)(2) or (3) of this section is not materially modified for purposes of §1.1471-2(b)(2)(iv).

(f) *Coordination with the OID and REMIC rules.*—For rules regarding original issue discount on certain debt instruments that provide for a rate referencing an IBOR, see §1.1275-2(m). For rules regarding certain interests in a REMIC that provide for a rate referencing an IBOR, see §1.860G-1(e).

(g) *Applicability date.*—This section applies to an alteration of the terms of a debt instrument or a modification of the terms of a non-debt contract that occurs on or after the date of publication of a Treasury decision adopting these rules as final regulations in the **Federal Register**. Taxpayers and their related parties, within the meaning of sections 267(b) and 707(b)(1), may apply this section to an alteration of the terms of a debt instrument or a modification of the terms of a non-debt contract that occurs before the date of publication of a Treasury decision adopting these rules as final regulations in the **Federal Register**, provided that the taxpayers and their related parties consistently apply the rules of this section before that date. See section 7805(b)(7). [Reg. §1.1001-6.]

Imputed Interest: OID: Safe Haven Rates: Related Party Sales

Imputed Interest: Original Issue Discount: Safe Haven Interest Rates.—Reproduced below is the text of a proposed amendment to Reg. §1.1012-2, relating to (1) the tax treatment of debt instruments issued after July 1, 1982, that contain original issue discount, (2) the imputation of and the accounting for interest with respect to sales and exchanges of property occurring after December 31, 1984, and (3) safe haven interest rates for loans or advances between commonly controlled taxpayers and safe haven leases between such taxpayers (published in the Federal Register on April 8, 1986).

☐ Par. 21. Section 1.1012-2 is revised to read as follows:

§1.1012-2. Certain sales or exchanges between related parties.— (a) *In general.*—In the case of a sale or exchange of property in which the relationship between the seller and the buyer is such that the sale or exchange is not necessarily an arm's-length transaction, the trans-

action shall be examined to determine whether the value of the consideration provided by the buyer is greater than or less than the value of the property. If the value of the consideration exceeds the value of the property, this excess shall not be treated as relating to the sale or exchange and will be recharacterized according to the relationship between the parties. If the value of the property exceeds the value of the consideration, this excess generally shall be treated as transferred from the seller to the buyer based on the relationship between the parties and not as transferred in exchange for the debt instrument. The preceding sentence shall not apply to any transaction that would be characterized as in part a gift and in part a sale under § 1.170A-4(c)(2) and § 1.1011-2(b) or under § 1.1015-4.

(b) *Value.*—In applying this section to any sale or exchange where all or a part of the consideration furnished by the buyer consists of one or more debt instruments issued by the buyer to the seller, then, for purposes of this section—

(1) The value of any such debt instrument to which section 1274 applies or which has adequate stated interest within the meaning of section 1274(c)(2) or § 1.483-2 shall be its issue price;

(2) The value of any such debt instrument issued under a contract to which section 483 applies shall be the amount described in § 1.483-3(a)(2)(i); and

(3) In determining whether the value of the consideration furnished by the buyer exceeds the value of the property, the value of the property shall be determined by reference to the price that an unrelated buyer (having the same creditworthiness as the actual buyer) would be willing to pay for the property in an arm's-length transaction if seller financing (taken into account at its issue price) were offered on the same terms as those offered to the actual buyer.

(c) *Examples.*—The provisions of this section may be illustrated by the following examples:

Example (1). (i) On January 1, 1986, Corporation X sells nonpublicly traded property to A, the sole shareholder of X. In consideration for the sale, A makes a down payment of $200,000 and issues a debt instrument calling for a single payment of $1,000,000 due in five years. No interest is provided for in the debt instrument. Because A is the sole shareholder of X, the transaction must be examined to determine whether the value of the property exceeds the value of the consideration furnished by A. For this purpose, the value of the property is its fair market value (determined without regard to any seller financing).

(ii) Assume that the fair market value of the property is $900,000 and that the issue price of the debt instrument under § 1.1274-4 is $643,928. Thus, the value of the consideration furnished by A is $843,928 (the sum of $200,000 (the portion of the consideration attributable to the down payment) and $643,928 (the portion of the consideration attributable to the debt instrument)). Since the value of the property ($900,000) exceeds the value of the consideration ($843,928),

X Corporation is treated as having made a distribution to shareholder A to which section 301 applies. The amount of the distribution is $56,072 (the difference between $900,000 and $843,928). The basis of the property in the hands of A is $900,000 ($843,928 (consideration actually furnished by A) increased by $56,072 (the amount of the section 301 distribution)).

Example (2). The facts are the same as in Example (1) except that the fair market value of the property is $800,000. X is not treated as having made a section 301 distribution to A and A's basis in the property is $800,000. The transaction need not be examined for excessive consideration since a sale from a corporation to a shareholder ordinarily would not be used to disguise a contribution to capital from the shareholder to the corporation.

Example (3). (i) C sells nonpublicly traded property to his employer D for $300,000 in cash and D's debt instrument having a face amount of $1,000,000, payable in 5 years with interest payable semiannually at a rate of 9 percent. Because D is C's employer, the transaction must be examined to determine if a portion of the amount designated as consideration for the property is in fact disguised compensation.

(ii) Assume that the fair market value of the property (assuming no seller financing), is $1,000,000 and that the issue price of D's debt instrument is $1,000,000. Assume further that a buyer unrelated to D and having the same creditworthiness as C would be willing to pay $1,200,000 for the property if allowed to pay $300,000 in cash and $900,000 in the form of a 5-year debt instrument calling for semiannual payments of interest at a rate of 9 percent. The value of the consideration furnished by D is $1,300,000 (cash of $300,000 plus a debt instrument having an issue price of $1,000,000). Since this amount exceeds the value of the property by $100,000, only $200,000 of the $300,000 transferred from D to C is treated as consideration furnished for the property. The remaining $100,000 is treated as compensation. D's basis in the property is $1,200,000 (cash consideration of $200,000 plus a debt instrument with an issue price of $1,000,000).

Example (4). The facts are the same as in Example (3) except that the property could be sold to the unrelated buyer for $1,400,000 (assuming a down payment of $300,000 and 5-year seller financing at 9 percent for the balance of the purchase price). Because the value of the consideration furnished by D ($1,300,000) does not exceed the value of the property ($1,400,000), D is not treated as having paid compensation to C. D's basis in the property is $1,300,000. The transaction need not be examined for insufficient consideration since employees ordinarily do not make bargain sales to their employers. [Reg. § 1.1012-2.]

Estate and Person Acquiring Property from Decedent: Consistent Basis Reporting

Estate and Person Acquiring Property from Decedent: Consistent Basis Reporting.—Reg. § 1.1014-10, providing guidance regarding the requirement that a recipient's basis in certain property acquired from a decedent be consistent with the value of the property as finally determined for Federal estate tax purposes, is proposed (published in the Federal Register on March 4, 2016) (REG-127923-15).

Par. 2. Section 1.1014-10 is added to read as follows:

§ 1.1014-10. Basis of property acquired from a decedent must be consistent with Federal estate tax return.—(a) *Consistent basis requirement.*—(1) *In general.*—The taxpayer's initial basis in property described in paragraph (b) of this section may not exceed the property's final value within the meaning of paragraph (c) of this section. This requirement applies whenever the taxpayer reports a taxable event with respect to the property to the Internal Revenue Service (IRS) (for example depreciation or amortization) and continues to apply until the property is sold, exchanged, or otherwise disposed of in one or more transactions that result in the recognition of gain or loss for Federal income tax purposes, regardless of whether the owner on the date of the sale, exchange, or disposition is the same taxpayer who acquired the property from the decedent or as a result of the decedent's death.

(2) *Subsequent basis adjustments.*—The final value within the meaning of paragraph (c) of this section is the taxpayer's initial basis in the property. In computing at any time after the decedent's date of death the taxpayer's basis in property acquired from the decedent or as a result of the decedent's death, the taxpayer's initial basis in that property may be adjusted due to the operation of other provisions of the Internal Revenue Code (Code) governing basis without violating paragraph (a)(1) of this section. Such adjustments may include, for example, gain recognized by the decedent's estate or trust upon distribution of the property, post-death capital improvements and depreciation, and post-death adjustments to the basis of an interest in a partnership or S corporation. The existence of recourse or nonrecourse debt secured by property at the time of the decedent's death does not affect the property's basis, whether the gross value of the property and the outstanding debt are reported separately on the estate tax return or the net value of the property is reported. There-

fore, post-death payments on such debt do not result in an adjustment to the property's basis.

(b) *Property subject to consistency requirement.*—(1) *In general.*—Property subject to the consistency requirement in paragraph (a)(1) of this section is any property that is includable in the decedent's gross estate under section 2031, any property subject to tax under section 2106, and any other property the basis of which is determined in whole or in part by reference to the basis of such property (for example as the result of a like-kind exchange or involuntary conversion) that generates a tax liability under chapter 11 of subtitle B of the Code (chapter 11) on the decedent's estate in excess of allowable credits, except the credit for prepayment of tax under chapter 11.

(2) *Exclusions.*—For purposes of paragraph (b)(1) of this section, property that qualifies for an estate tax charitable or marital deduction under section 2055, 2056, or 2056A, respectively, does not generate a tax liability under chapter 11 and therefore is excluded from the property subject to the consistency requirement in paragraph (a)(1) of this section. For purposes of paragraph (b)(1) of this section, tangible personal property for which an appraisal is not required under § 20.2031-6(b) is deemed not to generate a tax liability under chapter 11 and therefore also is excluded from the property subject to the consistency requirement in paragraph (a)(1) of this section.

(3) *Application.*—For purposes of paragraph (b)(1) of this section, if a liability under chapter 11 is payable after the application of all available credits (other than a credit for a prepayment of estate tax), the consistency requirement in paragraph (a)(1) of this section applies to the entire gross estate (other than property excluded under paragraph (b)(2) of this section) because all such property contributes to the liability under chapter 11 and therefore is treated as generating

a tax liability under chapter 11. If, however, after the application of all such available credits, no tax under chapter 11 is payable, the entire gross estate is excluded from the application of the consistency requirement.

(c) *Final value.*—(1) *Finality of estate tax value.*—The *final value* of property reported on a return filed pursuant to section 6018 is its value as finally determined for purposes of the tax imposed by chapter 11. That value is —

(i) The value reported on a return filed with the Internal Revenue Service (IRS) pursuant to section 6018 once the period of limitations for assessment of the tax under chapter 11 has expired without that value having been timely adjusted or contested by the IRS,

(ii) If paragraph (c)(1)(i) of this section does not apply, the value determined or specified by the IRS once the periods of limitations for assessment and for claim for refund or credit of the tax under chapter 11 have expired without that value having been timely contested;

(iii) If paragraphs (c)(1)(i) and (ii) of this section do not apply, the value determined in an agreement, once that agreement is final and binding on all parties; or

(iv) If paragraphs (c)(1)(i), (ii), and (iii) of this section do not apply, the value determined by a court, once the court's determination is final.

(2) *No finality of estate tax value.*—Prior to the determination, in accordance with paragraph (c)(1) of this section, of the final value of property described in paragraph (b) of this section, the recipient of that property may not claim an initial basis in that property in excess of the value reported on the statement required to be furnished under section 6035(a). If the final value of the property subsequently is determined under paragraph (c)(1) of this section and that value differs from the value reported on the statement required to be furnished under section 6035(a), then the taxpayer may not rely on the statement initially furnished under section 6035(a) for the value of the property and the taxpayer may have a deficiency and underpayment resulting from this difference.

(3) *After-discovered or omitted property.*—(i) *Return under section 6018 filed.*—In the event property described in paragraph (b)(1) of this section is discovered after the estate tax return under section 6018 has been filed or otherwise is omitted from that return (after-discovered or omitted property), the final value of that property is determined under section (c)(3)(i)(A) or (B) of this section.

(A) *Reporting prior to expiration of period of limitation on assessment.*—The final value of the after-discovered or omitted property is determined in accordance with paragraph (c)(1) or (2) of this section if the executor, prior to the expiration of the period of limitation on assessment of the tax imposed on the estate by chapter 11, files with the IRS an initial or supplemental estate tax return under section 6018 reporting the property.

(B) *No reporting prior to expiration of period of limitation on assessment.*—If the executor does not report the after-discovered or omitted property on an initial or supplemental Federal estate tax return filed prior to the expiration of the period of limitation on assessment of the tax imposed on the estate by chapter 11, the final value of that unreported property is zero. See *Example 3* of paragraph (e) of this section.

(ii) *No return under section 6018 filed.*—If no return described in section 6018 has been filed, and if the inclusion in the decedent's gross estate of the after-discovered or omitted property would have generated or increased the estate's tax liability under chapter 11, the final value, for purposes of section 1014(f), of all property described in paragraph (b) of this section is zero until the final value is determined under paragraph (c)(1) or (2) of this section. Specifically, if the executor files a return pursuant to section 6018(a) or (b) that includes this property or the IRS determines a value for the property, the final value of all property described in paragraph (b) of this section includible in the gross estate then is determined under paragraph (c)(1) or (2) of this section.

(d) *Executor.*—For purposes of this section, *executor* has the same meaning as in section 2203 and includes any other person required under section 6018(b) to file a return.

(e) *Examples.*—The following examples illustrate the application of this section.

Example 1. (i) At D's death, D owned 50% of Partnership P, which owned a rental building with a fair market value of $10 million subject to nonrecourse debt of $2 million. D's sole beneficiary is C, D's child. P is valued at $8 million. D's interest in P is reported

on the return required by section 6018(a) at $4 million. The IRS accepts the return as filed and the time for assessing the tax under chapter 11 expires. C sells the interest for $6 million in cash shortly thereafter.

(ii) Under these facts, the final value of D's interest is $4 million under paragraph (c)(1)(i) of this section. Under section 742 and §1.742-1, C's basis in the interest in P at the time of its sale is $5 million (the final value of D's interest ($4 million) plus 50% of the $2 million nonrecourse debt). Following the sale of the interest, C reports taxable gain of $1 million. C has complied with the consistency requirement of paragraph (a)(1) of this section.

(iii) Assume instead that the IRS adjusts the value of the interest in P to $4.5 million, and that value is not contested before the expiration of the time for assessing the tax under chapter 11. The final value of D's interest in P is $4.5 million under paragraph (c)(1)(ii) of this section. Under section 742 and § 1.742-1, C claims a basis of $5.5 million at the time of sale and reports gain on the sale of $500,000. C has complied with the consistency requirement of paragraph (a)(1) of this section.

Example 2. (i) At D's death, D owned (among other assets) a private residence that was not encumbered. D's sole beneficiary is C. D's executor reports the value of the residence on the return required by section 6018(a) as $600,000 and pays the tax liability under chapter 11. The IRS timely contests the reported value and determines that the value of the residence is $725,000. The parties enter into a settlement agreement that provides that the value of the residence for purposes of the tax imposed by chapter 11 is $650,000. Pursuant to paragraph (c)(1)(iii) of this section, the final value of the residence is $650,000.

(ii) Several years later, C adds a master suite to the residence at a cost of $45,000. Pursuant to section 1016(a), C's basis in the residence is increased by $45,000 to $695,000. Subsequently, C sells the residence to an unrelated third party for $900,000. C claims a basis in the residence of $695,000 and reports a gain of $205,000 ($900,000 – $695,000). C has complied with the consistency requirement of paragraph (a)(1) of this section.

Example 3. (i) The facts are the same as in *Example 2* but, after the expiration of the period for assessing the tax imposed by chapter 11, the executor discovers property that had not been reported on the return required by section 6018(a) but which, if reported, would have generated additional chapter 11 tax on the entire value of the newly discovered property. Pursuant to paragraph (c)(3)(i)(B) of this section, C's basis in the residence of $695,000 does not change, but the final value of the additional unreported property is zero.

(ii) Alternatively, assume that no return was required to be filed under section 6018 before discovering the additional property (and none in fact was filed) but, after the application of the applicable credit amount, D's taxable estate including the unreported property would have been $200,000. Pursuant to paragraph (c)(3)(ii) of this section, the final value of all property included in D's gross estate that is described in paragraph (b) of this section is zero until the executor files an estate tax return with the IRS pursuant to section 6018 or the IRS determines a value for the property. In either of those events, the final value of property described in paragraph (b) of this section reported on the return is determined in accordance with paragraph (c)(1) or (c)(2) of this section.

Example 4. (i) At D's death, D's gross estate includes a residence valued at $300,000 encumbered by nonrecourse debt in the amount of $100,000. Title to the residence is held jointly by D and C (D's daughter) with rights of survivorship. D provided all the consideration for the residence and the entire value of the residence was included in D's gross estate. The executor reports the value of the residence as $200,000 on the return required by section 6018 filed with the IRS for D's estate and claims no other deduction for the debt. The statement required by section 6035 reports the value of the residence as $300,000. C sells the residence before the final value is determined under paragraph (c)(1) of this section for $375,000 and claims a gain of $75,000 on C's Federal income tax return.

(ii) A court subsequently determines that the value of the residence was $290,000 and the time for contesting this value in any court expires before the expiration of the period for assessing C's income tax for the year of C's sale of the property. The final value of the residence is $290,000 pursuant to paragraphs (c)(1)(iv) and (c)(2) of this section. Because C claimed a basis in the residence that exceeds the final value, C may have a deficiency and underpayment.

(f) *Effective/applicability date.*—Upon the publication of the Treasury Decision adopting these rules as final in the **Federal Register**, this section will apply to property acquired from a decedent or by reason of the death of a decedent whose return required by section 6018 is filed after July 31, 2015. Persons may rely upon these rules before the date of publication of the Treasury Decision adopting these rules as final in the **Federal Register**. [Reg. §1.1014-10.]

Accelerated Cost Recovery System

Accelerated Cost Recovery System.—Reproduced below are the texts of proposed amendments of Reg. §§1.1016-3 and 1.1016-4, relating to the Accelerated Cost Recovery System for recovering capital costs of eligible property (published in the Federal Register on February 16, 1984).

☐ Par. 4. Paragraph (a)(3) of §1.1016-3 is redesignated as (a)(4), and a new paragraph (a)(3) is added to read as follows:

§1.1016-3. Exhaustion, wear and tear, obsolescence, amortization, and depletion for periods since February 28, 1913.—(a) *In general.*—* * *

(3) *Adjustment for amount allowable where no cost recovery deduction claimed under section 168.*—(i) Except as provided in subdivision (iii) of this subparagraph (3), if the taxpayer has not taken a deduction under section 168 (hereinafter referred to as ACRS deduction) either in the taxable year or for any prior taxable year, the adjustments to basis of the property for the ACRS deduction allowable shall be determined by using the recovery method described in section 168(b)(1) or (2) or, where applicable, section 168(f)(2)(A) or (B).

(ii) If the taxpayer with respect to any recovery property has properly taken an ACRS deduction under one of the methods provided in section 168 for one or more years but has omitted the deduction in other years, the adjustment to basis for the ACRS deduction allowable in such a case will be the deduction under the method which was used by the taxpayer with respect to that property. Thus, for example, A acquired property in 1981 for which he properly elected to compute his ACRS deduction by use of one of the optional straight line percentages described in section 168(b)(3) for the first recovery year but did not take a deduction in the second and third years of the asset's recovery period. The adjustment to basis for the ACRS deduction allowable for the second and third recovery years will be computed using the optional straight line percentages which were elected.

(iii) If the taxpayer has made an election under §1.168-5(e)(5) (relating to special election rules for foreign taxpayers)

to use an optional straight line percentage with respect to recovery property, the adjustments to basis of the property for the ACRS deduction allowable shall be determined pursuant to that election.

(iv) The provisions of subdivision (iii) of this subparagraph (3) may be illustrated by the following example:

Example. In 1981, Corporation F (a calendar year taxpayer) purchases for $100,000 and places in service in a foreign country 5-year recovery property which has a present class life of 7.5 years. F is not subject to United States income tax, other than under section 881, and is not required to compute earnings and profits under section 964. On January 1, 1983, F begins engaging in a trade or business in the United States (making it subject to tax under section 882), and uses the property in the United States in connection with that trade or business. Under §1.168-5(e)(5)(ii), F may elect to use the optional recovery percentages with respect to the property placed in service in 1981 by submitting the requisite information on its income tax return for the taxable year beginning in 1983. That election will apply with respect to such property from the taxable year in which it is placed in service. Thus, if F elects the optional recovery percentages based on a 12-year recovery period under §1.168-2(g)(3), the allowable ACRS deductions for 1981 and 1982 would be $4,000 (*i.e.*, .04 × $100,000) and $9,000 (*i.e.*, .09 × $100,000), respectively, and F's adjusted basis in the property on January 1, 1983, would be $87,000 (*i.e.*, $100,000 − $13,000). For the deduction allowable to F with respect to the property in 1983, see §1.168-2(j)(4)(i) and (j)(6) (relating to change in status).

* * *

☐ Par. 5. Section 1.1016-4 is amended by adding a new sentence at the end of paragraph (b) thereof, to read as follows:

§1.1016-4. Exhaustion, wear and tear, obsolescence, amortization, and depletion; periods during which income was not subject to tax.—

* * *

(b) * * *

For purposes of this section, the amount that would have been allowable as a deduction shall be determined without reference to section 168.

Imputed Interest: OID: Safe Haven Rates: Basis Adjustments

Imputed Interest: Original Issue Discount: Safe Haven Interest Rates.—Reproduced below is the text of a proposed amendment of Reg. §1.1016-5, relating to (1) the tax treatment of debt instruments issued after July 1, 1982, that contain original issue discount, (2) the imputation of and the accounting for interest with respect to sales and exchanges of property occurring after December 31, 1984, and (3) safe haven interest rates for loans or advances between commonly controlled taxpayers and safe haven leases between such taxpayers (published in the Federal Register on April 8, 1986).

☐ Par. 22. In §1.1016-5, paragraph(s) is revised to read as follows:

§1.1016-5. Miscellaneous adjustments to basis.

* * *

(s) *Original issue discount.*—In the case of certain debt instruments issued at a discount after May 27, 1969, the basis shall be

increased under section 1272(b)(2) by the amount of original issue discount included in the holder's gross income pursuant to section 1272.

Allocation Rules: Code Sec. 1060 Coordination

Gains and Losses: Asset Acquisitions: Allocation Rules.—Temporary Reg. §1.1031(d)-1T, relating to allocation rules for certain asset acquisitions under Code Sec. 1060, is also proposed as a final regulation and, when adopted, would become Reg. §1.1031(d)-1 (published in the Federal Register on July 18, 1988).

§1.1031(d)-1. Coordination of section 1060 with section 1031 (temporary).

Imputed Interest: OID: Safe Haven Rates: Certain Exchanges

Imputed Interest: Original Issue Discount: Safe Haven Interest Rates.—Reproduced below is the text of a proposed amendment of Reg. §1.1037-1, relating to (1) the tax treatment of debt instruments issued after July 1, 1982, that contain original issue discount, (2) the imputation of and the accounting for interest with respect to sales and exchanges of property occurring after December 31, 1984, and (3) safe haven interest rates for loans or advances between commonly controlled taxpayers and safe haven leases between such taxpayers (published in the Federal Register on April 8, 1986).

☐ Par. 23. Section 1.1037-1 is amended as follows:

1. In paragraph (a) by removing the phrase "the first sentence of section 1232(a)(2)(B)," and adding in its place "section 1271(c)(2)(A)", by removing the phrase "section 1232(b)(2)" each place that is appears in *Example* (6) and *Example* (7) and adding in its place the phrase "section 1273(b)(1)", by removing the phrase "section 1232(a)(2)(B)" each place it appears in *Example* (7) and adding in its place the phrase "section 1271(c)(2)(A)", and by removing the phrase "section 1232(a)(2)(B)(ii)" each place it appears in *Example* (6) and *Example* (7) and adding in its place the phrase "section 1271(c)(2)(A)(ii)".

2. In paragraph (b) by removing the phrase "section 1232" from the heading and adding in its place the phrase "section 1271", by removing the phrase "section 1232(a)(2)(B)" each place that it appears and adding in its place the phrase "section 1271(c)(2)(A)", and by removing the phrase "section 1232" from the heading of paragraph (b)(6) and adding in its place the phrase "section 1271".

§1.1037-1. Certain exchanges of United States obligations.

Transfers Between Spouses

Transfers: Alimony, Separate Maintenance, and Dependency Exemption.—Temporary Reg. §1.1041-1T, relating to the treatment of transfers of property between spouses and former spouses, the tax treatments of alimony and separate maintenance payments, and the dependency exemption in the case of a child of divorced parents, is also proposed as a final regulation and, when adopted, would become Reg. §1.1041-1 (published in the Federal Register on August 31, 1984).

§1.1041-1. Treatment of transfers of property between spouses or incident to divorce.

Employee Trusts: Effective Dates

Employee Trusts: Tax Reform Act of 1984: Effective Dates.—Temporary Reg. §1.1042-1T is also proposed as a final regulation and, when adopted, would become Reg. §1.1042-1 (published in the Federal Register on February 4, 1986).

§1.1042-1. Questions and answers relating to the sales of stock to employee stock ownership plans or certain cooperatives.

Employee Stock Ownership Plans: Sale of Stock: Notarized Statements of Purchase

Employee Stock Ownership Plans: Sale of Stock: Notarized Statements of Purchase.— Amendments to Temporary Reg. §1.1042-1T, relating to notarized statements of purchase under Code Sec. 1042 and affecting taxpayers making an election to defer the recognition of gain under Code Sec. 1042 on the sale of stock to an employee stock ownership plan, are proposed (published in the Federal Register on July 10, 2003) (REG-121122-03).

□ Par. 2. In §1.1042-1T, A-3, in the undesignated paragraph following paragraph (b)(6), the penultimate sentence is removed and three sentences added in its place to read as follows:

§1.1042-1T. Questions and answers relating to the sales of stock to employee stock ownership plans or certain cooperatives (temporary).

* * *

Q-3. * * *

A-3. * * *

(b) * * *

(6) * * *

* * * Such statement of purchase must be notarized not later than the time the taxpayer files the income tax return for the taxable year in which the sale of qualified securities occurred in any case in which any qualified replacement property was purchased by such time and during the qualified replacement period. If qualified replacement property is purchased after such filing date but during the qualified replacement period, the statement of purchase must be notarized not later than the time the taxpayer's income tax return is filed for the taxable year following the year for which the election under section 1042(a) was made. The previous two sentences apply to taxable years of sellers ending on or after the date final regulations are published in the Federal Register. * * *

* * *

Transfers of Securities Under Agreements

Transfers of Securities Under Agreements.—Reproduced below are the texts of proposed Reg. §§1.1058-1 and 1.1058-2, relating to transfers of securities under certain agreements (published in the Federal Register on July 26, 1983).

□ Paragraph 1. The following sections are inserted in the appropriate place.

§1.1058-1. Transfers of securities under certain agreements.— (a) *In general.*—Section 1058 provides rules for the nonrecognition of gain or loss with respect to certain transfers of securities occurring after December 31, 1976. In order to qualify for treatment under this section, the transfer must be pursuant to an agreement which contains the provisions required by paragraph (b) of this section and those provisions must be complied with. If this section does apply, the lender will not recognize gain or loss on the exchange of the securities for the obligation of the borrower under the agreement nor will the lender recognize gain or loss on the exchange of the rights under such agreement in return for securities identical to the securities transferred by the lender.

(b) *Agreement requirements.*—The agreement between the borrower and lender described in paragraph (a) of this section must be in writing and must—

(1) Require the borrower to return to the lender securities identical to those which were lent to the borrower. For the purposes of this section securities are defined in section 1236(c). Identical securities are securities of the same class and issue as the securities lent to the borrower. If, however, the agreement permits the borrower to return equivalent securities in the event of reorganization, recapitalization or merger of the issuer of the securities during the term of the loan, this requirement will be deemed to be satisfied.

(2) Require the borrower to make payments to the lender of amounts equivalent to all interest, dividends, and other distributions which the owner of the securities is entitled to for the period during which the securities are borrowed.

(3) Not reduce the lender's risk of loss or opportunity for gain. Accordingly, the agreement must provide that the lender may terminate the loan upon notice of not more than 5 business days. See section 512(a)(5) and the regulations thereunder for additional requirements with respect to loans of securities made by exempt organizations.

(c) *Basis.*—(1) *Lender's basis in securities.*—If this section applies, the lender's basis in the identical securities returned by the borrower shall be the same as the lender's basis in the securities lent to the borrower.

(2) *Lender's basis in contractual obligation.*—If this section applies, the lender's basis in the contractual obligation received from the borrower in exchange for the lender's securities is equal to the lender's basis in the securities exchanged.

(d) *Treatment of payments to lender.*—Except as otherwise provided in section 512(a)(5), a payment of amounts required to be paid by the borrower that are equivalent to all interest, dividends, and other distributions as provided in paragraph (b)(2) of this section, shall be treated by the lender as a fee for the temporary use of property. Thus, for example, an amount received by the lender that is equivalent to a dividend paid during the term of the loan shall not constitute a dividend to the lender for purposes of the Internal Revenue Code, but shall be taken into account as ordinary income.

(e) *Noncompliance with section 1058.*—(1) If a transfer of securities is intended to comply with section 1058 and fails to do so because the contractual obligation does not meet the requirements of section 1058(b) and §1.1058-1(b), gain or loss is recognized in accordance with section 1001 and §1.1001-1(a) upon the initial transfer of the securities. However, see section 1091 of the Code for disallowance of loss from wash sales of stock or securities.

(2) If securities are transferred pursuant to an agreement which meets the requirements of section 1058(b) and §1.1058-1(b) and the borrower fails to return to the lender securities identical to the securities transferred as required by the agreement, or otherwise defaults under the agreement, gain or loss is recognized on the day the borrower fails to return identical securities as required by the agreement, or otherwise defaults under the agreement. However, see section 1091 of the Code for disallowance of loss from wash sales of stock or securities.

(f) *Special rule.*—For purposes of determining the tax consequences to the lender of securities when a merger, recapitalization or reorganization (including, but not limited to, a reorganization described in section 368(a)(1) of the Internal Revenue Code) of the issuer occurs during the term of a loan to which section 1058 applies, the section 1058 loan transaction is deemed terminated immediately prior to the merger, recapitalization or reorganization and a second section 1058 transaction is deemed entered into immediately following the merger, recapitalization or reorganization. Therefore, the borrower of the securities is deemed to have returned the securities to the lender immediately prior to the merger, recapitalization or reorganization and immediately following the merger, recapitalization or reorganization the lender and borrower are deemed to have entered into a second section 1058 loan transaction, on terms identical to the original section 1058 loan transaction. The special rule in this paragraph (f) shall not apply in the case where the lender ultimately is repaid with securities identical to the securities originally transferred.

(g) *Cross reference.*—For rules relating to the lender's holding period, see §1.1223-2. [Reg. §1.1058-1.]

§1.1058-2. Examples.—The provisions of §1.1058-1 may be illustrated by the following examples:

Example (1). A owns 1,000 shares of XYZ common stock. A instructs A's broker, B, to sell the XYZ stock. B sells to C. After the sale, B learns that A will not be able to deliver to B certificates representing the 1,000 shares in time for B to deliver them to C on the settlement date. B decides to effect the delivery by borrowing stock from a third party. To this end, B enters into a written agreement with D, a non-exempt corporation having a large stock portfolio of XYZ common stock. The agreement includes the following terms:

(1) D will transfer to B certificates representing 1,000 shares of XYZ common stock.

(2) B will pay D an amount equivalent to any dividends or other distributions paid on the XYZ stock during the period of the loan.

(3) Regardless of any increases or decreases in the market value of XYZ common stock, B will transfer to D 1,000 shares of the XYZ common stock of the same issue as that of the XYZ common stock transferred from D to B.

(4) B agrees that upon notice of 5 business days, B will return identical securities to D.

The agreement between B and D satisfies the requirements of paragraph (b) of §1.1058-1. The agreement is in writing. It requires the borrower, B, to return to the lender, D, identical securities and to pay to the lender, D, amounts equivalent to any dividends or other distributions paid on the stock during the period of the loan. It does not reduce D's risk of loss or opportunity for gain because, regardless of fluctuations in the market value of XYZ common stock, B is obligated to return 1,000 shares of XYZ common stock.

Example (2). Assume the same facts as in Example (1) except that the agreement between B and D includes the following additional terms:

(1) Upon D's transfer to B of the certificates representing the 1,000 shares of XYZ common stock, B will transfer to D, cash equal to the market value of the XYZ common stock on the business day preceding the transfer, as collateral for the stock. The collateral will be increased or decreased daily to reflect increases or decreases in the market value of the XYZ stock during the period of the loan.

(2) B agrees that upon notice of 5 business days, B will return to D 1,000 shares of XYZ common stock, or the equivalent thereof in the event of reorganization, recapitalization, or merger of XYZ during the term of the loan. Upon delivery of the stock to D, D will return the cash collateral to B.

The agreement between B and D satisfies the requirements of paragraph (b) of this section. If XYZ is merged into another corporation and B returns to D an equivalent amount of stock in the resulting corporation, paragraph (f) of this section provides that the section 1058 transaction is deemed terminated immediately before the merger. Thus, D is deemed to be the owner of the XYZ common stock at the time of the merger. Furthermore, paragraph (a) of this section provides that D does not recognize gain or loss upon the transfer of the XYZ common stock to B or upon the return of the stock of the resulting corporation to D. Nonetheless, gain or loss may be recognized with respect to the merger. If the merger is described in section 368(a)(1), gain will be recognized to the extent section 354(a)(2) or 356 applies to the merger. If the merger is not described in section 368(a)(1), D generally will recognize the entire gain or loss with respect to such stock as a result of the merger.

Example (3). Assume the same facts as in example (2) and in addition that on March 1, D transfers certificates representing 1,000 shares of XYZ common stock to B. D's basis in the stock is $60,000. On the business day preceding the transfer, the stock has a market value of $75 a share. Consequently, B transfers to D $75,000 as collateral for the stock. B then uses the certificates to complete a timely delivery to C. On March 20, when the market value of XYZ common stock is $69 a share, D gives B notice of termination. On March 24, B delivers to D 1,000 shares of XYZ common stock of the same issue as that of the XYZ common stock transferred to B on March 1. D returns the $69,000 cash collateral to B. (Because the market value of the stock had declined during the period of the loan, the collateral was adjusted to reflect the new market value and the $6,000 had previously been returned to B.) Because the agreement between B and D contains the provisions required by paragraph (b) of §1.1058-1 and such provisions were complied with, D does not recognize gain on the transfer of the XYZ common stock to B. Nor does D recognize gain upon the return of XYZ common stock. D's basis in the XYZ common stock returned to it by B is $60,000. As to the holding period of the XYZ common stock returned to D, see §1.1223-2(a).

Example (4). Assume the same facts as in example (3) and in addition that on March 3, XYZ pays a dividend on its common stock. B pays to D an amount equivalent to the dividend. The amount paid by B does not constitute a dividend to D, but rather constitutes a fee for the temporary use of property as provided in §1.1058-1(d).

Example (5). (i) Assume the same facts as in example (3) except that on March 24 B notifies D that delivery of the 1,000 shares of XYZ common stock, of the same issue as that of the XYZ common stock transferred to B on March 1, cannot be completed on March 24. Assume further that B informs D that delivery would be completed on March 27.

(ii) If B and D agree to extend the time period in which B is to return the identical securities to D till March 27, then the section 1058 agreement will not be treated as breached when B delivers the securities on March 27, pursuant to the modified section 1058 agreement. As a result, D does not recognize gain on the transfer of XYZ common stock to B. Nor does D recognize gain upon the return of XYZ common stock.

(iii) If B and D do not agree to extend the time period, in which B is to return the identical securities to D, then as of March 25 B's failure to transfer the identical securities as required by the agreement will be treated as a breach of the agreement. As a result D will be treated as selling the XYZ common stock on March 25. D must then recognize gain or (subject to section 1091) loss, whichever is appropriate, on the sale of the securities. [Reg. §1.1058-2.]

Tax Straddles: Loss Deferral: Wash Sales

Tax Straddles: Loss Deferral: Wash Sales.—Temporary Reg. §§1.1092(b)-1T, 1.1092(b)-2T and 1.1092(b)-5T, relating to the application of the loss deferral and wash sale rules and treatment of holding periods and losses with respect to straddle positions, are also proposed as final regulations and, when adopted, would become Reg. §§1.1092(b)-1, 1.1092(b)-2 and 1.1092(b)-5, respectively (published in the Federal Register on January 24, 1985).

§1.1092(b)-1. Coordination of loss deferral rules and wash sale rules.

§1.1092(b)-2. Treatment of holding periods and losses with respect to straddle positions.

§1.1092(b)-5. Definitions.

Tax Straddles: Mixed Straddles

Tax Straddles: Mixed Straddles: Identification.—Temporary Reg. §§1.1092(b)-3T and 1.1092(b)-4T, relating to mixed straddles, are also proposed as final regulations and, when adopted, would become Reg. §§1.1092(b)-3 and 1.1092(b)-4 (published in the Federal Register on January 24, 1985).

§1.1092(b)-3. Mixed straddles; straddle-by-straddle identification under section 1092(b)(2)(A)(i)(I).

§1.1092(b)-4. Mixed straddles; mixed straddle account.

Straddles: Personal Property Defined

Straddles: Personal Property Defined.—An amendment to Reg. §1.1092(d)-2, relating to the definition of personal property for purposes of the straddle rules, is proposed (published in the Federal Register on May 2, 1995).

☐ Par. 2. Section 1.1092(d)-2 is revised to read as follows:

§1.1092(d)-2. Personal property.—(a) *Special rules for stock.*—As defined by section 1092(d)(1), *personal property* includes—

(1) Any stock if the stock is of a type that is actively traded and the stock is part of a straddle at least one of the offsetting positions of which is—

(i) An option with respect to that stock or substantially identical stock or securities; or

(ii) Under paragraphs (b) and (c) of this section, a position with respect to substantially similar or related property (other than stock); and

(2) Any stock, whether or not of a type that is actively traded, of a corporation formed or availed of to take positions in personal property as defined by section 1092(d)(1) that offset positions taken, directly or indirectly, by any shareholder.

(b) *Substantially similar or related property.*—For purposes of section 1092(d)(3)(B)(i)(II) and this section, the term *substantially similar or related property* is defined in §1.246-5 (other than §1.246-5(b)(3)). The rule in §1.246-5(c)(6) does not narrow the related party rule in section 1092(d)(4).

(c) *Position with respect to substantially similar or related property (other than stock).*—For purposes of section 1092(d)(3)(B)(i)(II) and this section, a *position with respect to substantially similar or related property (other than stock)* does not include direct ownership of stock or a short sale of stock but includes any other position with respect to substantially similar or related property.

(d) *Example.*—The following example illustrates the application of this section.

(1) *Facts*—(i) *The stock.* A acquired 10,000 shares of actively traded X stock during 1990. On September 29, 1995, those shares had a fair market value of $1,000,000.

(ii) *The swap.* On September 29, 1995, A entered into an *equity swap* contract with unrelated counterparty C, for a term of three years. Under the terms of that contract, on the last business day of each calendar quarter, A must pay to C an amount equal to the appreciation, if any, during the quarter on 10,000 shares of X stock. A also must pay to C an amount equal to the dividends, if any, that were paid during the quarter on 10,000 shares of X stock. On the last business day of each calendar quarter, A is to receive from C an amount equal to the depreciation, if any, during the quarter on 10,000 shares of X stock. A also is to receive from C an amount equal to the 3-month London Interbank Offered Rate (LIBOR), as determined at the close of the prior quarter, multiplied by the value of the X stock on that date.

(2) *Holdings*—(i) *The two legs as offsetting positions.* Because holding the equity swap substantially diminishes A's risk of loss from holding the X stock, the X stock and the equity swap are offsetting positions within the meaning of section 1092(c). The remaining question is whether these are positions with respect to personal property.

(ii) *The swap leg as a position with respect to personal property.* The equity swap contract is a position with respect to personal property as defined by section 1092(d)(1). Although section 1092(d)(3)(A) generally excludes stock from the definition of personal property, this exclusion does not apply to interests in stock. Therefore, stock can be personal property when testing whether an interest in the stock, other than a direct interest in, or a short sale of, the stock, is a position with respect to personal property. Because the equity swap contract is an interest in actively traded stock, the equity swap contract is a position with respect to personal property.

(iii) *The stock leg as personal property.* As described below, ownership of the X stock is also a position with respect to personal property.

(A) *The rule of section 1092(d)(3)(B)(i)(II).* Under section 1092(d)(3)(B)(i)(II) and paragraph (a)(1)(ii) of this section, stock is not excluded from the definition of personal property if it is part of a straddle at least one of the offsetting positions of which is a position with respect to substantially similar or related property (other than stock).

(B) *The swap as a position with respect to substantially similar or related property (other than stock) for purposes of section 1092(d)(3)(B)(i)(II).* Under paragraph (b) of this section, the equity swap contract is a position with respect to property that is substantially similar or related to the X stock because A is entitled to payments under the equity swap contract that are attributable to the decline in the value of the X stock. See §1.246-5(c)(7). Under section 1092(d)(3)(B)(i)(II) and paragraph (c) of this section, the equity swap contract is a position with respect to substantially similar or related property (other than stock) because it is not direct ownership of stock or a short sale of stock.

(C) *The stock as part of a straddle for purposes of the test of section 1092(d)(3)(B)(i)(II).* In determining whether the X stock is part of a straddle for purposes of the test of section 1092(d)(3)(B)(i) and paragraph (a)(1) of this section, section 1092(d)(3)(C) treats the X stock as personal property. Because the stock is treated as personal property for this purpose, because the equity swap contract is a position with respect to personal property (see paragraph (d)(2)(ii) of this section), and because the X stock and the equity swap contract are offsetting positions (see paragraph (d)(2)(i) of this section), the straddle test in section 1092(d)(3)(B)(i) and paragraph (a)(1) of this section is satisfied. Accordingly, under section 1092(d)(3)(B), the stock is personal property for all purposes of section 1092.

(iv) *The two legs as a straddle.* Because ownership of the X stock and the equity swap contract are offsetting positions with respect to personal property, the X stock and the equity swap contract are a straddle to A within the meaning of section 1092(c)(1).

(e) *Effective dates.*—(1) *In general.*—Except as provided in paragraph (e)(2) of this section, this section applies to positions established on or after May 1, 1995.

(2) *Special rules for substantially similar or related property.*—(i) *In general.*—Paragraph (b) of this section applies to positions established on or after March 17, 1995.

(ii) *Special rule for certain straddles.*—Paragraph (b) of this section applies to positions established after March 1, 1984, if the taxpayer substantially diminished its risk of loss by holding substantially similar or related property involving the following types of transactions—

(A) Holding offsetting positions consisting of stock and a convertible debenture of the same corporation where the price movements of the two positions are related; or

(B) Holding a short position in a stock index regulated futures contract (or alternatively an option on such a regulated futures contract or an option on the stock index) and stock in an investment company whose principal holdings mimic the performance of the stocks included in the stock index (or alternatively a portfolio of stocks whose performance mimics the performance of the stocks included in the stock index).

CAPITAL GAINS AND LOSSES

Transfers of Securities Under Agreements

Transfers of Securities Under Agreements.—Reproduced below is the text of proposed Reg. §1.1223-2, relating to transfers of securities under certain agreements (published in the Federal Register on July 26, 1983).

☐ Par. 2. The following is inserted immediately after §1.1223-1.

§1.1223-2. Rules relating to securities lending transactions.—(a) *General rule.*—In the case of a transfer of securities pursuant to an agreement which meets the requirements of section 1058 (relating to transfers of securities under certain agreements), the holding period in the hands of the lender of the securities received by the lender from the borrower shall include—

(1) The period for which the lender held the securities which were transferred to the borrower; and

(2) The period between the transfer of the securities from the lender to the borrower and the return of the securities to the lender.

(b) *Failure to comply with section 1058.*—(1) If a transfer of securities is intended to comply with section 1058 and fails to do so because the contractual obligation does not meet the requirements of section 1058(b) and §1.1058-1(b), the holding period in the hands of the lender of the securities transferred to the borrower shall terminate on the day the securities are transferred to the borrower, and the holding period in the hands of the borrower of the property transferred to it shall begin on the date that the securities are delivered pursuant to the transfer loan agreement.

(2) If securities are transferred pursuant to an agreement which meets the requirements of section 1058(b) and §1.1058-1(b) and the borrower fails to return identical securities as required by the agreement or otherwise defaults under the agreement, the holding period in the hands of the lender of the securities transferred to the borrower shall terminate on the day the borrower fails to return identical securities as required by the agreement or otherwise defaults under the agreement, and the holding period in the hands of the borrower of the securities transferred to it shall begin on the day the borrower fails to return identical securities as required by the agreement or otherwise defaults under the agreement. [Reg. §1.1223-2.]

Partners and Partnerships: Sales or Exchanges: Certain Distributions

Partners and Partnerships: Sales or Exchanges: Certain Distributions.—Amendments to Reg. §1.1231-1, prescribing how a partner should measure its interest in a partnership's unrealized receivables and inventory items, and that provide guidance regarding the tax consequences of a distribution that causes a reduction in that interest, are proposed (published in the Federal Register on November 3, 2014) (REG-151416-06).

☐ Par. 10. Section 1.1231-1 is amended by adding a new sentence after the third sentence in the introductory text of paragraph (d) to read as follows:

§1.1231-1. Gains and losses from the sale or exchange of certain property used in the trade or business.

(d) * * * *See also* §§1.732-1(c)(2)(iv) and 1.755-1(c)(2)(iv) for rules governing the application of section 1231 to partnership property in situations in which the basis of the property is increased under section 732 or 734(b). * * *

* * *

Imputed Interest: OID: Safe Haven Rates

Imputed Interest: Original Issue Discount: Safe Haven Interest Rates.—Reproduced below are the texts of proposed amendments of Reg. §§1.1232-1—1.1232-3 and 1.1232-3A, relating to (1) the tax treatment of debt instruments issued after July 1, 1982, that contain original issue discount, (2) the imputation of and the accounting for interest with respect to sales and exchanges of property occurring after December 31, 1984, and (3) safe haven interest rates for loans or advances between commonly controlled taxpayers and safe haven leases between such taxpayers (published in the Federal Register on April 8, 1986).

☐ Par. 24. Section 1.1232-1 is amended as follows:

1. In paragraph (a) by revising the heading to read "Bonds and other evidences of indebtedness issued before July 2, 1982; scope of section"; by removing the first sentence and adding the following new sentence as the first sentence of the paragraph, and by removing the phrase "after May 27, 1969," from the fourth sentence and adding in its place the phrase "after May 27, 1969, and before July 2, 1982,". The added sentence reads as follows: "Section 1232 as in effect before its repeal by section 42(a) of the Tax Reform Act of 1984 applies to any bond, debenture, note, or certificate of indebtedness (referred to in this section and §§1.1232-2 through 1.1232-4 as an obligation) (1) which is a capital asset in the hand of the taxpayer, and (2) which is issued by any corporation, or by any government or political subdivision thereof."

2. In paragraph (c)(3) by removing the phrase "December 31, 1975," from the heading and adding in its place the phrase "December 31, 1975, and before July 2, 1982"; and by adding the phrase "and before July 2, 1982" immediately after the first parenthetical in the first sentence thereof.

§1.1232-1. Bonds and other evidences of indebtedness; scope of section.

☐ Par. 25. The heading of §1.1232-2 is revised to read "Retirement of an obligation issued before July 2, 1982."

§1.1232-2. Retirement.

☐ Par. 26. Section 1.1232-3 is amended as follows: **1.** The heading is amended by adding the phrase "and before July 2, 1982," immediately following the phrase "December 31, 1954." **2.** Paragraph (a) is amended by removing the phrase "after May 27, 1969" from the heading and from each place that it appears and adding in its place the phrase "after May 27, 1969, and before July 2, 1982". **3.** Paragraph (f), the first sentence, is amended by removing the phrase "after December 31, 1954," and inserting the phrase "after December 31, 1954, and before August 17, 1984," in its place.

§1.1232-3. Gain upon sale or exchange of obligations issued at a discount.

☐ Par. 27. Section 1.1232-3A is amended as follows: **1.** The heading and paragraph (a) are amended by removing the phrase "after May 27, 1969," and adding in its place the phrase "after May 27, 1969, and before July 2, 1982." **2.** Paragraph (f) is amended by removing the phrase "after December 31, 1975" and by adding in its place the phrase "after December 31, 1975, and before July 2, 1982."

§1.1232-3A. Inclusion as interest of original issue discount on certain obligations issued after May 27, 1969.

Partnership Interest: Treatment of Grantor of an Option

Partnership Interest: Treatment of Grantor of an Option.—Amendments to Reg. §1.1234-3, relating to the tax treatment of noncompensatory options and convertible instruments issued by a partnership, are proposed (published in the Federal Register on February 5, 2013) (REG-106918-08).

☐ Par 3. Section 1.1234-3 is amended by adding a sentence at the end of paragraph (b)(2) to read as follows:

§1.1234-3. Special rules for the treatment of grantors of certain options granted after September 1, 1976.

* * *

(b) * * *

(2) * * * For purposes of the preceding sentence, for options granted on or after February 5, 2013, the term *securities* includes partnership interests.

* * *

Notional Principal Contracts: Contingent Nonperiodic Payments

Notional Principal Contracts: Contingent Nonperiodic Payments.—Reg. §1.1234A-1, relating to the inclusion into income or deduction of a contingent nonperiodic payment provided for under a notional principal contract, is proposed (published in the Federal Register on February 26, 2004) (REG-166012-02).

☐ Par. 5. Section 1.1234A-1 is added to read as follows:

§1.1234A-1. Notional principal contracts, bullet swaps, and forward contracts.—(a) *General rule.*—If a taxpayer has a position in a notional principal contract governed by the rules of §1.446-3, any gain or loss arising from a termination payment as defined in §1.446-3(h)(1) is treated as gain or loss from a termination of the notional principal contract.

(b) *Nonapplicability to payments other than termination payments.*— For purposes of section 1234A, none of the following payments terminate or cancel a right or obligation: a periodic payment described in §1.446-3(e), a nonperiodic payment described in §1.446-3(f), a contingent nonperiodic payment described in §1.446-3(g)(6) to which §1.446-3(g)(6)(ii) applies, or mark-to-market income inclusions and deductions described in §1.446-3(i)(1). Accordingly, section 1234A does not apply to any of these items, including any final scheduled payment. If a payment made or received pursuant to a notional principal contract is not a termination payment as defined in §1.446-3(h)(1), the payment constitutes ordinary income or expense. See sections 162 and 212 and the regulations thereunder.

(c) *Bullets swaps and forward contracts.*—(1) Any gain or loss arising from the settlement of obligations under a bullet swap or forward contract (including a payment pursuant to the terms of the obligations) is treated as gain or loss from a termination of the bullet swap or forward contract.

(2) *Definition of bullet swap.*—A bullet swap is a financial instrument that is not an excluded contract as defined in §1.446-3(c)(1)(ii), that provides for the computation of an amount or amounts due from one party to another by reference to a specified index upon a notional principal amount, and that provides for settlement of all the parties' obligations at or close to maturity of the contract.

(d) *Effective date.*—Paragraphs (b)(1) and (c) of this section are applicable to notional principal contracts, bullet swaps, and forward contracts entered into on or after 30 days after the date a Treasury decision based on these proposed regulations is published in the Federal Register. [Reg. §1.1234A-1.]

Partners and Partnerships: Sales or Exchanges: Certain Distributions

Partners and Partnerships: Sales or Exchanges: Certain Distributions.—Amendments to Reg. §1.1245-1, prescribing how a partner should measure its interest in a partnership's unrealized receivables and inventory items, and that provide guidance regarding the tax consequences of a distribution that causes a reduction in that interest, are proposed (published in the Federal Register on November 3, 2014) (REG-151416-06).

□ Par. 18. For each section listed in the table, remove the language in the "Remove" column and add in its place the language in the "Add" column as set forth below:

§1.1245-1. General rule for treatment of gain from dispositions of certain depreciable property.

Section	Remove	Add
§1.1245-1, paragraph (a) last sentence	see section 1245(b) and §1.1245-4.	*see* section 1245(b), and §§1.732-1(c)(2)(iii), 1.755-1(c)(2)(iii), and 1.1245-4.

Partners and Partnerships: Sales or Exchanges: Certain Distributions

Partners and Partnerships: Sales or Exchanges: Certain Distributions.—Amendments to Reg. §§1.1245-2 and 1.1245-4, prescribing how a partner should measure its interest in a partnership's unrealized receivables and inventory items, and that provide guidance regarding the tax consequences of a distribution that causes a reduction in that interest, are proposed (published in the Federal Register on November 3, 2014) (REG-151416-06).

□ Par. 11. Section 1.1245-2 is amended by removing paragraph (c)(6)(ii) and redesignating paragraph (c)(6)(iii) as paragraph (c)(6)(ii).

□ Par. 18. For each section listed in the table, remove the language in the "Remove" column and add in its place the language in the "Add" column as set forth below:

§1.1245-2. Definition of recomputed basis.

Section	Remove	Add
§1.1245-2, paragraph (c)(6)(i)	1245(b)(6)(B)	1245(b)(5)(B)

□ Par. 12. Section 1.1245-4 is amended by revising paragraphs (f)(2)(ii) and (f)(3) and *Example 2* to read as follows:

§1.1245-4. Exceptions and limitations.

* * *

(f) * * *

(2) * * *

(ii) The portion of such potential section 1245 income which is recognized as ordinary income under paragraphs (b)(3)(i) and (b)(4)(i) of §1.751-1.

(3) * * *

Example 2. Assume the same facts as in *Example 1* of this paragraph (f) except that the machine had been purchased by the partnership. Assume further that upon the distribution, $4,000 of gain is recognized as ordinary income under section 751(b). Under section 1245(b)(3), gain to be taken into account under section 1245(a)(1) by the partnership is limited to $4,000. Immediately after the distribution, the amount of adjustments reflected in the adjusted basis of the property is $2,000 (that is, potential section 1245 income of the partnership, $6,000, minus gain recognized under section 751(b), $4,000). Thus, if the adjusted basis of the machine in the hands of C were $10,000, the recomputed basis of the machine would be $12,000 ($10,000 plus $2,000).

* * *

Controlled Foreign Corporations: Insurance Income: Tax Years After 1986

Controlled Foreign Corporations: Insurance Income: Tax Years After 1986.—Reproduced below is a proposed amendment to Reg. §1.1248-1, relating to the election to expense certain depreciable business assets (published in the Federal Register on April 17, 1991).

□ Par. 7. Section 1.1248-1 is amended by revising paragraph (a)(2) to read as follows:

§1.1248-1. Treatment of gain from certain sales or exchanges of stock in certain foreign corporations.—(a) *In general.*—* * *

(2) In respect of a United States person who sells or exchanges stock in a foreign corporation, the conditions referred to in paragraph (a)(1) of this section are satisfied only if—

(i) Such person owned, within the meaning of section 958(a), or was considered as owning by applying the rules of ownership of section 958(b), 10 percent or more of the total combined voting power of all classes of stock entitled to vote of the foreign corporation at any time during the 5-year period ending on the date of the sale or exchange and during that time the foreign corporation was a controlled foreign corporation as defined in section 957, or

(ii) Such person owned, within the meaning of section 958(a), any stock in the foreign corporation at any time during the 5-year period ending on the date of the sale or exchange and during that time the foreign corporation was a controlled foreign corporation as defined in section 953(c)(1)(B).

Partners and Partnerships: Sales or Exchanges: Certain Distributions

Partners and Partnerships: Sales or Exchanges: Certain Distributions.—Amendments to Reg. §1.1248-1, prescribing how a partner should measure its interest in a partnership's unrealized receivables and inventory items, and that provide guidance regarding the tax consequences of a distribution that causes a reduction in that interest, are proposed (published in the Federal Register on November 3, 2014) (REG-151416-06).

□ Par. 13. Section 1.1248-1 is amended by adding a new sentence at the end of paragraph (a)(1) to read as follows:

§1.1248-1. Treatment of gain from certain sales or exchanges of stock in certain foreign corporations.—(a) * * *

(1) * * * *See also* §§1.732-1(c)(2)(v) and 1.755-1(c)(2)(v) for rules governing the application of section 1248 to partnership property in situations in which the basis of the property is increased or decreased under section 732 or 734(b).

* * *

Partners and Partnerships: Sales or Exchanges: Certain Distributions

Partners and Partnerships: Sales or Exchanges: Certain Distributions.—Amendments to Reg. §1.1250-1, prescribing how a partner should measure its interest in a partnership's unrealized receivables and inventory items, and that provide guidance regarding the tax consequences of a distribution that causes a reduction in that interest, are proposed (published in the Federal Register on November 3, 2014) (REG-151416-06).

□ Par. 14. Section 1.1250-1 is amended by revising the section heading and adding a new sentence at the end of paragraph (f) to read as follows:

§1.1250-1. Gain from disposition of certain depreciable property.

(f) * * * *See also* §§1.732-1(c)(2)(iii) and 1.755-1(c)(2)(iii) for rules governing the application of section 1250 to partnership property in situations in which the basis of the property is increased under section 732 or 734(b).

* * *

Partners and Partnerships: Sales or Exchanges: Certain Distributions

Partners and Partnerships: Sales or Exchanges: Certain Distributions.—Amendments to Reg. §1.1252-2, prescribing how a partner should measure its interest in a partnership's unrealized receivables and inventory items, and that provide guidance regarding the tax consequences of a distribution that causes a reduction in that interest, are proposed (published in the Federal Register on November 3, 2014) (REG-151416-06).

□ Par. 15. Section 1.1252-2 is amended by adding a new sentence at the end of paragraph (c)(2)(vii) to read as follows:

§1.1252-2. Special rules.

* * *

(c) * * *

(2) * * *

(vii) * * * *See also* §§1.732-1(c)(2)(iii) and 1.755-1(c)(2)(iii) for rules governing the application of section 1252 to partnership property in situations in which the basis of the property is increased under section 732 or 734(b).

* * *

Partners and Partnerships: Sales or Exchanges: Certain Distributions

Partners and Partnerships: Sales or Exchanges: Certain Distributions.—Amendments to Reg. §1.1254-5, prescribing how a partner should measure its interest in a partnership's unrealized receivables and inventory items, and that provide guidance regarding the tax consequences of a distribution that causes a reduction in that interest, are proposed (published in the Federal Register on November 3, 2014) (REG-151416-06).

□ Par. 16. Section 1.1254-5 is amended by revising the introductory text of paragraph (b)(1) to read as follows:

§1.1254-5. Special rules for partnerships and their partners.

* * *

(b) *Determination of gain treated as ordinary income under section 1254 upon the disposition of natural resource recapture property by a partnership.*—(1) *General rule.*—Upon a disposition of natural resource recapture property by a partnership, the amount treated as ordinary income under section 1254 is determined at the partner level. *See also* §§1.732-1(c)(2)(iii) and 1.755-1(c)(2)(iii) for rules governing the application of section 1254 to partnership property in certain situations. Each partner must recognize as ordinary income under section 1254 the lesser of—

* * *

Cost-Sharing Payments: Conservation Payments

Cost-Sharing Payments: Conservation Payments: Exclusions: Recapture.—Temporary Reg. §§16A.1255-1 and 16A.1255-2, relating to cost-sharing payments, are also proposed as final regulations (published in the Federal Register on May 21, 1981).

§16A.1255-1. General rule for treatment of gain from disposition of section 126 property.

§16A.1255-2. Special rules.

Section 1256 Contracts: Swap Exclusions

Section 1256 Contracts: Swap Exclusions.—Reg. §§1.1256(b)-1 and 1.1256(g)-1, providing guidance on the category of swaps and similar agreements that are within the scope of Code Sec. 1256(b)(2)(B), are proposed (published in the Federal Register on September 16, 2011) (REG-111283-11).

□ Par. 7. Section 1.1256(b)-1 is added to read as follows:

§1.1256(b)-1. Section 1256 contract defined.—(a) *General rule.*—A section 1256 contract does not include any contract, or option on such contract, that is a notional principal contract as defined in §1.446-3(c). A contract that is defined as both a notional principal contract in §1.446-3(c) and as a section 1256 contract in section 1256(b)(1) is treated as a notional principal contract and not as a section 1256 contract.

(b) *Regulated futures contract.*—A regulated futures contract is a section 1256 contract only if the contract is a futures contract—

(1) With respect to which the amount required to be deposited and the amount which may be withdrawn depends on a system of marking to market;

(2) That is traded on or subject to the rules of a qualified board or exchange; and

(3) That is not required to be reported as a swap under the Commodity Exchange Act.

(c) *Effective/applicability date.*—The rules of this section apply to contracts entered into on or after the date the final regulations are published in the **Federal Register**. [Reg. §1.1256(b)-1.]

□ Par. 8. Section 1.1256(g)-1 is added to read as follows:

§1.1256(g)-1. Qualified board or exchange defined.—(a) *General rule.*—A qualified board or exchange means a national securities exchange registered with the Securities Exchange Commission, a domestic board of trade designated as a contract market by the Commodity Futures Trading Commission, or any other exchange, board of trade, or other market for which the Secretary determines in published guidance in the **Federal Register** or in the Internal Revenue Bulletin (see §601.601(d)(2)(ii) of this chapter) that such market has rules adequate to carry out the purposes of section 1256.

(b) *Effective/applicability date.*—The rule of this section applies to taxable years ending on or after the date the final regulations are published in the **Federal Register**. [Reg. §1.1256(g)-1.]

Transition of Tax Consequences: IBORs: Guidance

Transition of Tax Consequences: IBORs: Guidance.—Amendments to Reg. §1.1271-0, providing guidance on the tax consequences of the transition to the use of reference rates other than interbank offered rates in debt instruments and non-debt contracts, are proposed (published in the Federal Register on October 9, 2019) (REG-118784-18).

Par. 6. Section 1.1271-0 is amended by adding a reserved entry for §1.1275-2(l) and by adding entries for §1.1275-2(m) to read as follows:

§1.1271-0. Original issue discount; effective date; table of contents.

* * *

§1.1275-2 Special rules relating to debt instruments.

* * *

(l) [Reserved]

(m) Transition from interbank offered rates.

(1) In general.

(2) Single qualified floating rate.

(3) Remote contingency.

(4) Change in circumstances.

(5) Applicability date.

* * *

REMICs: Regular Interests: Accrual of OID

REMICs: Regular Interests: Accrual of OID.—Amendments to Reg. §§1.1271-0 and 1.1275-2, relating to the accrual of original issue discount (OID) on certain real estate mortgage investment conduit (REMIC) regular interests and providing guidance to REMICs, REMIC regular interest holders and information reporters regarding the accrual of OID, are proposed (published in the Federal Register on August 25, 2004) (REG-108637-03).

☐ Par. 2. Section 1.1271-0 is amended by adding entries for §1.1275-2(l) and (m) to read as follows:

§1.1271-0. Original issue discount; effective date; table of contents.

* * *

§1.1275-2 Special rules relating to debt instruments.

* * *

(l) [Reserved]

(m) Special rule for certain REMIC regular interests.

(1) Scope.

(2) General rules.

(3) Special rule for calculation of OID in final accrual period.

(4) Definition of record date.

(5) Accrual of qualified stated interest.

(6) Example.

(7) Treatment of REMIC regular interests if the record dates and the payment dates are separated by more than thirty-one days.

(8) Effective date.

* * *

☐ Par. 3. Section 1.1275-2 is amended by adding new paragraphs (l) and (m) to read as follows:

§1.1275-2. Special rules relating to debt instruments.

* * *

(l) [Reserved].

(m) *Special rules for certain REMIC regular interests.*—(1) *Scope.*—If the terms of a REMIC regular interest (as defined in section 860G(a)(1)) provide for a delay between its record dates and the associated payment dates, the initial accrual period and final accrual period for that regular interest are determined under this paragraph (m). Except as provided in paragraph (m)(7) of this section, this paragraph (m) does not apply to a REMIC regular interest if the record dates and the payment dates are separated by more than thirty-one days.

(2) *General rules.*—(i) *Initial accrual period.*—The initial accrual period for a REMIC regular interest subject to this paragraph (m) begins on issuance of the REMIC regular interest.

(ii) *Final accrual period.*—The final accrual period for a REMIC regular interest subject to this paragraph (m) ends on the final record date of the REMIC regular interest.

(3) *Special rule for calculation of OID in final accrual period.*—In applying section 1272(a)(6)(A) to calculate OID in the final accrual period for a REMIC regular interest subject to this paragraph (m), payments after the end of the final accrual period of amounts included in the stated redemption price at maturity are treated as payments during the final accrual period.

(4) *Definition of record date.*—For purposes of this paragraph (m), a *record date* of a REMIC regular interest is a date, provided by the terms of the REMIC regular interest, on which the holder becomes entitled to a payment (of interest or principal) that is to be made on a subsequent payment date.

(5) *Accrual of qualified stated interest.*—See §1.446-2 for the accrual of qualified stated interest.

(6) *Example.*—The following example illustrates the application of this paragraph (m).

Example. REMIC X issues regular interests on January 1, 2009. The terms of the regular interests provide for payments of interest and principal to the persons who hold the regular interests on the last day of the calendar month (the record date). Each such payment is to be made on the fifteenth day of the succeeding calendar month (the payment date). The last payment with respect to the regular interests issued by REMIC X is to be made on January 15, 2014, to persons who hold the regular interests on December 31, 2013. Under this paragraph (m), the initial accrual period begins on the date of issuance, January 1, 2009, and the last accrual period ends on the last record date, December 31, 2013.

(7) *Treatment of REMIC regular interests if the record dates and the payment dates are separated by more than thirty-one days.*—[Reserved]

(8) *Effective date.*—(i) *In general.*—This paragraph (m) applies to REMIC regular interests issued after the date the final regulations are published in the Federal Register.

(ii) *Automatic consent to change method of accounting.*—Taxpayers are hereby granted the Commissioner's consent under section 446(e) to change their method of accounting for REMIC regular interests to which this paragraph (m) applies if—

(A) The change involves changing accrual periods to accrual periods allowed by this paragraph (m);

(B) The change is made for the first taxable year of the taxpayer during which the taxpayer holds a REMIC regular interest to which the rules of this paragraph (m) apply; and

(C) The change in method of accounting is effected on a cut-off basis.

Accrual Method of Accounting: Income Inclusion

Accrual Method of Accounting: Income Inclusion.—Amendments to Reg. §1.1275-2, regarding the timing of income inclusion under section 451 of the Internal Revenue Code (Code), are proposed (published in the Federal Register on September 9, 2019) (REG-104870-18).

Par. 6. Section 1.1275-2 is amended by adding paragraph (l) to read as follows:

§1.1275-2. Special rules relating to debt instruments.

* * *

(l) *OID rule for income item subject to section 451(b).*—(1) *In general.*—Notwithstanding any other rule in sections 1271 through 1275 and §§1.1271-1 through 1.1275-7, if, and to the extent, a taxpayer's item of income with respect to a debt instrument is subject to the timing rules in §1.451-3(i) (including credit card late fees, credit card cash advance fees, or interchange fees), then the taxpayer does not take the item into account to determine whether the debt instrument has any OID. As a result, the taxpayer does not treat the item as creating or increasing any OID on the debt instrument.

(2) *Applicability dates.*—(i) *In general.*—Except as provided in paragraphs (l)(2)(ii) and (iii) of this section, paragraph (l)(1) of this section applies for taxable years beginning after the date the Treasury decision adopting these regulations as final is published in the **Federal Register**.

(ii) *Early adoption.*—Until the date the Treasury decision adopting these regulations as final regulations is published in the

Federal Register, a taxpayer may rely on these proposed regulations for taxable years beginning after December 31, 2018, for a specified credit card fee as defined in §1.451-3(i)(2), if applied consistently to all specified credit card fees subject to §1.451-3(i).

(iii) *Applicability date for purposes of accounting method changes.*—Paragraph (l)(1) of this section will not apply for purposes of applying section 13221(e) of the Tax Cuts and Jobs Act, Public Law No. 115-97 (131 Stat. 2054) to determine the section 481(a) adjustment period for any adjustment under section 481(a) for a qualified change in method of accounting required under section 451(b) and §1.451-3(i) for the items subject to §1.451-3(i).

Transition of Tax Consequences: IBORs: Guidance

Transition of Tax Consequences: IBORs: Guidance.—Amendments to Reg. §1.1275-2, providing guidance on the tax consequences of the transition to the use of reference rates other than interbank offered rates in debt instruments and non-debt contracts, are proposed (published in the Federal Register on October 9, 2019) (REG-118784-18).

Par. 7. Section 1.1275-2, as proposed to be amended at 84 FR 47210, September 9, 2019, is further amended by adding paragraph (m) to read as follows:

§1.1275-2. Special rules relating to debt instruments.

* * *

(m) *Transition from interbank offered rates.*—(1) *In general.*—This paragraph (m) applies to a variable rate debt instrument (as defined in §1.1275-5(a)) that provides both for a qualified floating rate that references an interbank offered rate (IBOR) and for a methodology to change the IBOR-referencing rate to a different rate in anticipation of the IBOR becoming unavailable or unreliable. See §1.1001-6 for additional rules that may apply to a debt instrument that provides for a rate referencing an IBOR.

(2) *Single qualified floating rate.*—If a debt instrument is described in paragraph (m)(1) of this section, the IBOR-referencing rate and the different rate are treated as a single qualified floating rate for purposes of §1.1275-5.

(3) *Remote contingency.*—If a debt instrument is described in paragraph (m)(1) of this section, the possibility that the IBOR will become unavailable or unreliable is treated as a remote contingency for purposes of paragraph (h) of this section.

(4) *Change in circumstances.*—If a debt instrument is described in paragraph (m)(1) of this section, the fact that the IBOR has become unavailable or unreliable is not treated as a change in circumstances for purposes of paragraph (h)(6) of this section.

(5) *Applicability date.*—Paragraph (m) of this section applies to debt instruments issued on or after the date of publication of a Treasury decision adopting these rules as final regulations in the **Federal Register**. However, a taxpayer may apply paragraph (m) of this section to debt instruments issued before the date of publication of a Treasury decision adopting these rules as final regulations in the **Federal Register**. See section 7805(b)(7).

Definition of Registered Form: Guidance

Definition of Registered Form: Guidance.—Amendments to Reg. §1.1287-1, providing guidance on the definitions of registration-required obligation and registered form, including guidance on the issuance of pass-through certificates and participation interests in registered form, are proposed (published in the Federal Register on September 19, 2017) (REG-125374-16).

Par. 9. Section 1.1287-1 is amended by:
1. Revising paragraph (a).
2. Redesignating paragraphs (b)(1) and (2) as (b)(2) and (3), respectively.
3. Adding a new paragraph (b)(1).
4. Revising the paragraph heading and first sentence of newly redesignated paragraph (b)(2).
5. Redesignating paragraph (d) as paragraph (d)(1).
6. Revising the paragraph heading and the first sentence of newly redesignated paragraph (d)(1).
7. Adding a new paragraph heading for paragraph (d).
8. Adding paragraph (d)(2).
The revisions and additions read as follows:

§1.1287-1. Denial of capital gains treatment for gains on registration-required obligations not in registered form.—(a) *In general.*— Except as provided in paragraph (c) of this section, any gain on the sale or other disposition of a registration-required obligation held after December 31, 1982, that is not in registered form shall be treated as ordinary income unless the issuance of the obligation was subject to tax under section 4701. The term *registration-required obligation* has the meaning given to that term in section 163(f)(2) and §1.163-5(a)(2)(i). The term *holder* means the person that would be denied a loss deduction under section 165(j)(1) or denied capital gain treatment under section 1287(a).

(b) *Registered form.*—(1) *Obligations issued after March 18, 2012.*— With respect to obligations issued after March 18, 2012, the term *registered form* has the meaning given that term in §1.163-5(b).

(2) *Obligations issued after September 21, 1984 and on or before March 18, 2012.*—With respect to any obligation originally issued after September 21, 1984, and on or before March 18, 2012, the term *registered form* has the meaning given that term in §5f.103-1 of this chapter. * * *

* * *

(d) *Applicability date.*—(1) *In general.*—Except as provided in paragraph (d)(2) of this section, these regulations apply generally to obligations issued after January 20, 1987. * * *

(2) *Obligations issued after March 18, 2012.*—Paragraph (a) of this section applies to obligations issued after March 18, 2012.

Passive Foreign Investment Companies: Passive Income Characterization: Certain Foreign Banks and Securities Dealers: Exceptions To

Passive Foreign Investment Companies: Passive Income Characterization: Certain Foreign Banks and Securities Dealers: Exception To.— Amendments to Reg. §1.1291-0, relating to the application of the exceptions to passive income contained in section 1296(b) for foreign banks, securities dealers and brokers, are proposed (published in the Federal Register on April 28, 1995).

☐ Par. 2. Section 1.1291-0T is redesignated as §1.1291-0.

☐ Par. 3. Newly designated §1.1291-0 is amended as follows:

1. The section heading for newly designated §1.1291-0 is revised.

2. The introductory language for newly designated §1.1291-0 is revised.

3. Entries for §§1.1296-4 and 1.1296-6 are added in numerical order.

The revisions and additions read as follows:

§1.1291-0. Passive foreign investment companies—table of contents.—This section lists headings under sections 1291, 1294, 1296 and 1297 of the Internal Revenue Code.

* * *

§1.1296-4. Characterization of certain banking income of foreign banks as nonpassive.
  (a) General rule.
  (b) Active bank.
    (1) U.S. licensed banks.
    (2) Other foreign banks.
  (c) Licensing requirements.
  (d) Deposit-taking requirements.
    (1) General rule.
    (2) Deposit.
    (3) Substantiality of deposits.
  (e) Lending activities test.
  (f) Banking income.
    (1) General rule.
    (2) Banking activities.
  (g) Certain restricted reserves.
  (h) Customer relationship.
  (i) Income earned by qualified bank affiliates.
    (1) General rule.
    (2) Affiliate income requirement.
    (3) Group income requirements.
    (4) Related group.
  (j) Income from nonbank activities.

  (k) Effective date.

§1.1296-6. Characterization of certain securities income.
  (a) General rule.
  (b) Active dealer or broker.
    (1) General rule.
    (2) U.S. licensed dealers and brokers.
    (3) Other dealers and brokers.
     (i) General rule.
     (ii) Licensing requirements.
  (c) Securities dealer.
  (d) Securities broker.
  (e) Securities income.
    (1) General rule.
    (2) Securities activities.
  (f) Certain deposits of capital.
  (g) Dealer-customer relationship.
  (h) Investment income.
  (i) Calculation of gross income from a matched book.
  (j) Income earned by qualified securities affiliates.
    (1) General rule.
    (2) Affiliate income requirement.
    (3) Group income requirements.
    (4) Related group.
    (5) Example.
  (k) Income from nonsecurities activities.
  (l) Effective date.

* * *

Passive Foreign Investment Companies: Guidance

Passive Foreign Investment Companies: Guidance.—Amendments to Reg. §§1.1291-0 and 1.1291-1, regarding the determination of ownership in a passive foreign investment company within the meaning of section 1297(a) and the treatment of certain income received or accrued by a foreign corporation and assets held by a foreign corporation for purposes of section 1297, are proposed (published in the Federal Register on July 11, 2019) (REG-105474-18).

Par. 2. Section 1.1291-0 is amended by revising the heading for §1.1291-1 and adding entries for §1.1291-1(b)(8)(iv)(A) and (B), (b)(8)(iv)(B)(*1*) and (*2*), (b)(8)(iv)(C), and (b)(8)(iv)(C)(*1*) and (*2*) to read as follows:

§1.1291-0. Treatment of shareholders of certain passive foreign investment companies; table of contents.

* * *

§1.1291-1 Taxation of United States persons that indirectly own PFIC stock.

* * *

  (b) ***
    (8) ***
      (iv) ***

  (A) Example 1.
  (B) Example 2.
    (*1*) Facts.
    (*2*) Results.
  (C) Example 3.
    (*1*) Facts.
    (*2*) Results.

* * *

Par. 3. Section 1.1291-1 is amended by:
1. Revising the section heading.
2. Revising the second sentence of paragraph (b)(8)(ii)(B).
3. Revising paragraphs (b)(8)(iii)(A), (B), and (C).
4. Designating *Example 1* in paragraph (b)(8)(iv) as paragraph (b)(8)(iv)(A).
5. Adding paragraphs (b)(8)(iv)(B) and (C).
6. Revising paragraph (j)(3).
7. Adding paragraph (j)(4).
The revision and additions read as follows:

§1.1291-1. Taxation of United States persons that indirectly own PFIC stock.

* * *

  (b) ***
    (8) ***
      (ii) ***

    (B) * * * Sections 1297(d) and 1298(b)(7) and §1.1297-4(b)(2) and (f)(2) do not apply in determining whether a foreign corporation is a PFIC for purposes of this paragraph (b)(8)(ii)(B).

* * *

    (iii) *Ownership through pass-through entities.*—(A) *Partnerships.*—Except as otherwise provided in this paragraph (b)(8)(iii)(A), if a foreign or domestic partnership directly or indirectly owns stock, the partners of the partnership are considered to own such stock proportionally in accordance with their ownership interests in the partnership. Solely for purposes of determining whether a person satisfies the ownership threshold described in paragraph (b)(8)(ii)(A) of this section with respect to a foreign corporation that is not a PFIC (determined without applying sections 1297(d) and 1298(b)(7)), the first sentence of this paragraph (b)(8)(iii)(A) applies only in the case of a partner that owns 50 percent

or more of the ownership interests in the partnership that directly or indirectly owns the stock of the foreign corporation.

    (B) *S Corporations.*—Except as otherwise provided in this paragraph (b)(8)(iii)(B), if an S corporation directly or indirectly owns stock, each S corporation shareholder is considered to own such stock proportionately in accordance with the shareholder's ownership interest in the S corporation. Solely for purposes of determining whether a person satisfies the ownership threshold described in paragraph (b)(8)(ii)(A) of this section with respect to a foreign corporation that is not a PFIC (determined without applying sections 1297(d) and 1298(b)(7)), the first sentence of this paragraph (b)(8)(iii)(B) applies only in the case of a S corporation shareholder that owns 50 percent or more of the ownership interests in the S corporation that directly or indirectly owns the stock of the foreign corporation.

    (C) *Estates and nongrantor trusts.*—Except as otherwise provided in this paragraph (b)(8)(iii)(C), if a foreign or domestic estate or nongrantor trust (other than an employees' trust described in section 401(a) that is exempt from tax under section 501(a)) directly or indirectly owns stock, each beneficiary of the estate or trust is considered to own a proportionate amount of such stock. For purposes of this paragraph (b)(8)(iii)(C), a nongrantor trust is any trust or portion of a trust that is not treated as owned by one or more persons under sections 671 through 679. Solely for purposes of determining whether a person satisfies the ownership threshold described in paragraph (b)(8)(ii)(A) of this section with respect to a foreign corporation that is not a PFIC (determined without applying sections 1297(d) and 1298(b)(7)), the first sentence of this paragraph (b)(8)(iii)(C) applies only in the case of a beneficiary whose proportionate share of the estate or trust that directly or indirectly owns the stock of the foreign corporation is 50 percent or more.

* * *

(iv) * * *

(B) *Example 2.*—(1) *Facts.* A, a United States citizen, owns 50% of the interests in Foreign Partnership, a foreign partnership, the remaining interests in which are owned by an unrelated foreign person. Foreign Partnership owns 100% of the stock of FC1 and 50% of the stock of FC2, the remainder of which is owned by an unrelated foreign person. Both FC1 and FC2 are foreign corporations that are not PFICs (determined without applying sections 1297(d) and 1298(b)(7)). FC1 and FC2 each own 50% of the stock of FC3, a foreign corporation that is a PFIC.

(2) *Results.* Under paragraph (b)(8)(iii)(A) of this section, for purposes of determining whether A is a shareholder of FC3, A is considered to own 50% (50%x100%), or 50% or more, of FC1, because A owns 50% or more of Foreign Partnership, but 25% (50%x50%) of FC2. Thus, under paragraph (b)(8) of this section, A is considered to own 25% of the stock of FC3 (50%x100%x50%) indirectly through FC1, and thus is a shareholder of FC3 for purposes of the PFIC provisions, but is not considered to own any stock of FC3 indirectly through FC2.

(C) *Example 3.*—(1) *Facts.* The facts are the same as in paragraph (b)(8)(iv)(B)(1) of this section (the facts in *Example 2*), except that A owns 40% of the interests in Foreign Partnership.

(2) *Results.* Under paragraph (b)(8)(iii)(A) of this section, for purposes of determining whether A is a shareholder of FC3, A is not considered to own 50% or more of FC1 or FC2 because it does not own 50% or more of the interests in Foreign Partnership. Thus, under paragraph (b)(8) of this section, A is not considered to own any stock of FC3 indirectly through FC1 or FC2.

* * *

(j) * * *

(3) Except as otherwise provided in paragraph (j)(4) of this section, paragraphs (b)(2)(ii) and (v), (b)(7) and (8), and (e)(2) of this section apply to taxable years of shareholders ending on or after December 31, 2013.

(4) Paragraphs (b)(8)(ii)(B), (b)(8)(iii)(A), (B), and (C), and (b)(8)(iv)(B) and (C) of this section apply to taxable years of shareholders beginning on or after the date of publication of a Treasury decision adopting these rules as final regulations in the **Federal Register**.

Passive Foreign Investment Companies: Qualified Electing Funds: Shareholders

Passive Foreign Investment Companies: Qualified Electing Funds: Shareholders.—Reproduced below is the text of proposed Reg. §1.1291-1, relating to the taxation of shareholders of certain passive foreign investment companies (PFICs) upon payment of distributions by such companies or upon the disposition of stock of such companies (published in the Federal Register on April 1, 1992) (INTL-941-86; INTL-656-87; INTL-704-87). Proposed Reg. §1.1291-1(b)(2)(ii), (b)(2)(v), (b)(7), (b)(8) and (i) withdrawn by REG-113350-13 on December 31, 2013.

☐ Par. 5. Section 1.1291-1 is added to read as follows:

§1.1291-1. Taxation of U.S. persons that are shareholders of section 1291 funds.—(a) *In general.*—A U.S. person that is a shareholder (within the meaning of paragraph (b)(7) of this section) of a section 1291 fund (as defined in paragraph (b)(2)(v) of this section) is subject to the special rules under section 1291 and these regulations with respect to gain recognized on direct and indirect dispositions of stock of the section 1291 fund and upon certain direct and indirect distributions by the section 1291 fund. This section provides definitions and rules applicable to all PFICs and their shareholders. For rules governing the taxation of distributions and dispositions, see §§1.1291-2 and 1.1291-3, respectively. For rules governing the determination of the deferred tax amount, see §1.1291-4. For rules governing the determination of the foreign tax credit that a shareholder of a section 1291 fund may claim on distributions and certain dispositions, see §1.1291-5. For rules governing the recognition of gain on a direct or indirect disposition of stock of a section 1291 fund notwithstanding an otherwise applicable nonrecognition provision, see §1.1291-6. For guidance for regulated investment companies making a mark-to-market election, see §1.1291-8. For the time and manner of making the deemed sale and dividend elections under section 1291(d)(2), see §§1.1291-9 and 1.1291-10, respectively.

(b) *Definitions.*—(1) *PFIC.*—(i) *In general.*—A passive foreign investment company (PFIC) is a foreign corporation that satisfies either the income test of section 1296(a)(1) or the asset test of section 1296(a)(2). A corporation will not be treated as a PFIC with respect to a shareholder for those days included in the shareholder's holding period before the shareholder became a United States person within the meaning of section 7701(a)(30).

(ii) *PFIC characterization continued.*—A corporation will be treated as a PFIC with respect to a shareholder even if the corporation satisfies neither the income test nor the asset test of section 1296(a), if the corporation (or its predecessor in a reorganization described in section 368(a)(1)(F)) was a section 1291 fund with respect to the shareholder at any time during the shareholder's holding period of the corporation's stock.

(2) *Types of PFICs.*—(i) *QEF.*—A PFIC is a qualified electing fund (QEF) with respect to a shareholder that has elected under section 1295 to be taxed currently on its share of the PFIC's earnings and profits pursuant to section 1293.

(ii) [Withdrawn by REG-113350-13 on December 31, 2013.]

(iii) *Unpedigreed QEF.*—A PFIC is an unpedigreed QEF for a taxable year if—

(A) An election under section 1295 is in effect for that year;

(B) The PFIC has been a QEF with respect to the shareholder for at least one, but not all, of the taxable years that are included wholly or partly in the shareholder's holding period of the PFIC stock and during which the corporation was a PFIC; and

(C) The shareholder has not made an election under section 1291(d)(2) and §1.1291-9 or 1.1291-10 with respect to the PFIC to purge the prior PFIC years from the shareholder's holding period. For the effect on a shareholder's holding period of an election under section 1291(d)(2), see §§1.1291-9(f) and 1.1291-10(f).

(iv) *Nonqualified fund.*—A PFIC is a nonqualified fund with respect to a shareholder if the shareholder has not elected under section 1295 to treat the PFIC as a QEF.

(v) [Withdrawn by REG-113350-13 on December 31, 2013.]

(3) *PrePFIC year and day.*—A prePFIC year is a taxable year (or portion thereof) of the shareholder, included in its holding period of the stock of a corporation, during which the corporation was not a PFIC within the meaning of paragraph (b)(1) of this section. A prePFIC day is a day in a prePFIC year of the shareholder. Thus, the days in a taxable year of a shareholder beginning after 1986 that are included in a taxable year of the corporation that began before 1987 are prePFIC days.

(4) *Prior PFIC year and day.*—A prior PFIC year is a taxable year (or portion thereof) of a shareholder, other than the current shareholder year, included in its holding period of stock of a corporation during which the corporation was a section 1291 fund. A prior PFIC day is a day in a prior PFIC year of a shareholder.

(5) *Current shareholder year.*—The current shareholder year is the taxable year of the shareholder in which occurs a distribution by, or disposition of stock of, a section 1291 fund.

(6) *Stock.*—The term stock includes any equity interest in a corporation, without regard to whether there is a certificate or other representation of the equity interest in the corporation. For a rule that treats an option holder as a shareholder of a section 1291 fund, see §1.1291-1(d).

(7) [Withdrawn by REG-113350-13 on December 31, 2013.]

(8) [Withdrawn by REG-113350-13 on December 31, 2013.]

(c) *Coordination with QEF rules.*—(1) *Pedigreed QEFs.*—Section 1291 and these regulations do not apply to direct and indirect distributions by, and direct and indirect dispositions of stock of, a PFIC that, with respect to the shareholder, is a pedigreed QEF as defined in paragraph (b)(2)(ii) of this section.

(2) *Unpedigreed QEFs.*—Section 1291 and these regulations apply to direct and indirect distributions by, and direct and indirect dispositions of stock of, a PFIC that, with respect to the shareholder, is an unpedigreed QEF, as defined in paragraph (b)(2)(iii) of this section. For the treatment under section 1291 and these regulations of inclusions in income under section 1293(a) and distributions of amounts not includible in income by reason of section 1293(c), see §1.1291-2(b)(2).

(d) *Option holder as shareholder.*—If a U.S. person has an option to acquire stock of a PFIC (other than stock with respect to which the PFIC is a pedigreed QEF), such option is considered to be stock of a section 1291 fund for purposes of applying section 1291 and these regulations to a disposition of the option. For purposes of this paragraph (d), the exercise of an option is not a disposition to which section 1291 applies. For purposes of this paragraph (d), an option to acquire an option, and each one of a series of such options, are considered an option to acquire stock. For the holding period of stock acquired upon the exercise of an option, *see* § 1.1291-1(h)(3).

(e) *Exempt organization as shareholder.*—If the shareholder of a section 1291 fund is an organization exempt from tax under this chapter, section 1291 and these regulations apply to such shareholder only if a dividend from the section 1291 fund would be taxable to the organization under subchapter F.

(f) *Excess distribution from sources within Puerto Rico.*—A deferred tax amount, as defined in § 1.1291-4, will be determined under section 1291 and these regulations on amounts derived from sources within Puerto Rico (within the meaning of section 933(1)) by an individual shareholder who is a bona fide resident of Puerto Rico, but only to the extent such amounts are allocated under § 1.1291-2(e)(2) to a taxable year in the shareholder's holding period during which the shareholder was not entitled to the benefits of section 933.

(g) *Regulated investment companies and real estate investment trusts.*—A regulated investment company, as defined in section 851, and a real estate investment trust, as defined in section 856, that are shareholders of a section 1291 fund are taxable under section 1291 and these regulations on direct or indirect distributions from a section 1291 fund and on direct or indirect dispositions of the stock of a section 1291 fund, and are therefore liable for the deferred tax amount, as defined in section 1291(c) and § 1.1291-4. For a mark-to-market election that may be made by a regulated investment company that is a shareholder of a section 1291 fund, *see* § 1.1291-8.

(h) *Holding period.*—(1) *In general.*—Except as otherwise provided in this paragraph (h), § 1.1291-6(b)(5), 1.1291-9(f), or 1.1291-10(f), a shareholder's holding period of stock of a PFIC is determined under the general rules of the Code and regulations concerning the holding period of stock. The following example illustrates the rule of this paragraph (h)(1).

Example. T purchased the stock of FC, a foreign corporation, on December 31, 1985. FC has qualified as a PFIC since its taxable year beginning January 1, 1987. For purposes of sections 1291 through 1297 and the regulations under those sections, as well as other provisions of the Code and regulations, T's holding period of the FC stock began on January 1, 1986.

(2) *Stock acquired from U.S. decedent or domestic estate.*—For purposes of section 1291 and these regulations, a shareholder's holding period of a share of stock of a PFIC includes the period the share was held by another U.S. person if the shareholder acquired the share by reason of the death of that other U.S. person (the decedent), the PFIC was a section 1291 fund with respect to the decedent, and the decedent did not recognize gain pursuant to § 1.1291-6(c)(2)(iii) (or would not have recognized gain had there been any) on the transfer to the shareholder.

(3) *Stock acquired upon exercise of option.*—The holding period of a share of stock of a PFIC acquired upon the exercise of an option includes the period the option was held. The following example illustrates the rule of this paragraph (h)(3).

Example. X is a domestic corporation that owns all of the stock of Y, a PFIC. On January 1, 1993, X issues a debt instrument to G, a U.S. person. Under the terms of the instrument, G may convert the debt instrument into 20 shares of the stock of Y on any date prior to the maturity date of December 31, 2002. On August 14, 1997, G exercises the conversion right and receives 20 shares of Y stock. Pursuant to § 1.1291-1(h)(3), G's holding period of the Y stock begins at the time of the acquisition of the debt instrument, not at the time of acquisition of the Y stock.

(4) *Stock owned directly and indirectly.*—(i) *In general.*—Except as provided in paragraph (h)(2), (3), (4)(ii), (5), or (6) of this section, 1.1291-6(b)(5), 1.1291-9(f), or 1.1291-10(f), a shareholder's holding period of stock of a PFIC owned indirectly begins on the first day that a shareholder is considered to own stock of the PFIC (or of another PFIC that was a predecessor of that PFIC) under § 1.1291-1(b)(8). If a shareholder has owned a share of stock of a PFIC both directly and indirectly, the shareholder's holding period of that share begins on the earlier of—

(A) The first day that the shareholder owned the stock of the PFIC directly; or

(B) The first day that the shareholder was an indirect shareholder with respect to the share of stock of the PFIC (or of another PFIC that was a predecessor of that PFIC).

(ii) *Examples.*—The following examples illustrate the operation of the rule of paragraph (h)(4)(i) of this section.

Example 1. A's holding period of stock of X began on August 14, 1990. X is a corporation that always has been an S corporation. At the time A acquired the X stock, X held stock of FC, a PFIC. For purposes of sections 1291 through 1297, A's holding period of the FC stock began on August 14, 1990, even though X's holding period of that stock began on an earlier day.

Example 2. B, a U.S. person, owns all the stock of FP, a foreign corporation that is not a PFIC; under section 1223, B's holding period of the FP stock began on August 1, 1987. FP owns 50 percent of the stock of FS, a foreign corporation that is not a PFIC; FP's holding period of the FS stock began on December 13, 1987. FS owns 10 percent of FC, a PFIC; under section 1223, FS's holding period of the FC stock began on November 20, 1986. For purposes of section 1291, B's holding period of the FC stock began on December 13, 1987, the first day that ownership of the FC stock is attributed to B under § 1.1291-1(b)(8).

(iii) *Section 1291 fund stock held by former C corporation.*—For purposes of § 1.1291-2(e)(2)(i), if an S corporation's holding period of stock of a section 1291 fund includes any period during which the S corporation was a C corporation, the S corporation shareholder's holding period is the S corporation's holding period of such stock.

(5) *New holding period.*—If a shareholder recognizes all of the gain realized on a direct or indirect disposition of stock of a section 1291 fund, within the meaning of § 1.1291-3(c), (d), or (e), but continues to be a shareholder with respect to such stock immediately after such disposition, the shareholder's holding period for such stock will be treated as beginning on the day after the disposition. For an illustration of this rule as applied to a disposition pursuant to § 1.1291-3(d) (regarding pledged stock), *see* § 1.1291-3(d)(7), *Example 1.*

(6) *Stock transferred to a member of a consolidated return group.*—For the holding period of stock of a section 1291 fund transferred from one member of a consolidated return group to another member of the group for purposes of § 1.1291-2(e)(2)(i), *see* § 1.1291-3(f).

(7) *PFIC character of holding period.*—(i) *In general.*—If a shareholder's holding period of stock of a PFIC includes a period described in section 1223(1), the character of the days in such latter period as prePFIC or prior PFIC days is determined by reference to the character of those days in the shareholder's holding period immediately prior to the exchange. If a shareholder's holding period of stock of a PFIC includes a period described in section 1223(2), the character of the days in such latter period as prePFIC or prior PFIC days is determined by reference to the character, immediately prior to the transfer, of those days in the holding period of the person from whom the stock was acquired.

(ii) *Anti-avoidance rule.*—If a shareholder's holding period of stock of a PFIC includes a period described in section 1223(1), the character of the days in such latter period will be deemed to be prior PFIC days if a purpose for the exchange described in section 1223(1) was avoidance of the interest charge rules under section 1291.

(i) [Withdrawn by REG-113350-13 on December 31, 2013.]

(j) *Effective date.*—(1) *In general.*—Except as otherwise provided in this paragraph (j), §§ 1.1291-1 through 1.1291-9 and the new parts of § 1.1291-10 are effective on April 11, 1992. However, sections 1291 through 1297, inclusive, are effective for taxable years of foreign corporations beginning after December 31, 1986. Accordingly, shareholders of PFICs are subject to sections 1291 through 1297 with respect to transactions occurring within those taxable years. Shareholders of section 1291 funds, in determining their liability under sections 1291 through 1297 during those years, must apply reasonable interpretations of the statute and legislative history and employ reasonable methods to preserve the interest charge.

(2) *Section 1.1291-3(d)(6).*—For purposes of applying section 1297(b)(6), concerning a disposition resulting from the use of PFIC stock as security for a loan, the transition rule provided in § 1.1291-3(d)(6) is effective for taxable years of foreign corporations beginning after 1986.

(3) *Section 1.1291-8.*—Section 1.1291-8 is effective for taxable years of RICs ending after [*INSERT DATE OF PUBLICATION OF THIS DOCUMENT AS A FINAL REGULATION*]. [Reg. § 1.1291-1.]

Passive Foreign Investment Companies: Qualified Electing Funds: Shareholders

Passive Foreign Investment Companies: Qualified Electing Funds: Shareholders.—Reproduced below are the texts of proposed Reg. §§1.1291-2—1.1291-7, relating to the taxation of shareholders of certain passive foreign investment companies (PFICs) upon payment of distributions by such companies or upon the disposition of stock of such companies (published in the Federal Register on April 1, 1992) (INTL-941-86; INTL-656-87; INTL-704-87). Reg. §§1.1291-0, 1.1291-9 and 1.1291-10 were adopted by T.D. 8701 on December 26, 1996. Proposed Reg. §1.1291-8 was withdrawn on February 2, 1999.

☐ Par. 5. Sections 1.1291-2 through 1.1291-8 [1.1291-7]are added to read as follows:

§1.1291-2. Taxation of distributions by section 1291 funds.— (a) *In general.*—Notwithstanding section 301 and the regulations under that section, a shareholder is subject to the rules of section 1291, this section, and §1.1291-4 with respect to a distribution (including an indirect distribution as defined in paragraph (f) of this section) by a section 1291 fund, if any portion of such distribution is an excess distribution. An excess distribution is defined in paragraph (c)(1) of this section. Under paragraph (e)(2)(i) of this section, the excess distribution is allocated ratably over the shareholder's holding period of the stock of the section 1291 fund. The portions of the excess distribution allocated to the current shareholder year and to prePFIC years are included in the shareholder's gross income as ordinary income in the current shareholder year under paragraph (e)(2)(ii) of this section. The portions of the excess distribution allocated to prior PFIC years are not included in the shareholder's gross income pursuant to paragraph (e)(2)(iii) of this section. Instead, the shareholder incurs tax plus interest (the deferred tax amount) on those portions of the excess distribution, as provided in §1.1291-4.

(b) *Distribution.*—(1) *In general.*—For purposes of section 1291 and these regulations, unless otherwise provided in this paragraph (b), a distribution is any actual or constructive transfer of money or property by a section 1291 fund with respect to its stock. For example, a distribution includes a transfer of stock taxable pursuant to section 305(b) and (c), a transfer in redemption of stock taxable under section 301 pursuant to section 302(d), and an amount treated as a dividend under section 78. A distribution, however, does not include a transfer that qualifies under section 305(a) or 355(a). Transfers with respect to stock that are treated as dispositions of the stock under §1.1291-3 are not treated as distributions under this section. For transfers with respect to stock (including transfers that qualify under section 355(a)) that are treated as dispositions, *see* §1.1291-3.

(2) *Coordination with current inclusion rules.*—(i) *Deemed dividend or income inclusions; distributions of previously taxed amounts.*—Amounts included in gross income under section 551(a), 951(a), or 1293(a), and transfers of amounts not included in gross income by reason of section 551(d), 959, or 1293(c), are not treated as distributions for purposes of this section. The following example illustrates the rule of this paragraph (b)(2)(i).

Example. USP, a domestic corporation, purchased in 1989 10 percent of the stock of FC, a section 1291 fund that also is a CFC. Both USP and FC use the calendar year as their taxable year. In 1989, USP, pursuant to section 951(a)(1), included in income $100 of subpart F income of FC, none of which was distributed in 1989. The $100 of subpart F income is not treated as a distribution taxable under section 1291. In 1990, FC did not have any subpart F income. In that year, FC distributed $200 to USP. Of the $200 distribution, $100 had been previously taxed to USP. Because $100 of the $200 distribution is not included in gross income by reason of section 959, pursuant to §1.1291-2(b)(2) that amount is not treated as a distribution for purposes of §1.1291-2(c)(2)(i). Therefore, the total distribution, for purposes of calculating the excess distribution for 1990, is $100.

(ii) *Other rules.*—For treatment of amounts that would be taxable in the same taxable year under section 951(a) or 1293(a) and section 1291, *see* §§1.1291-2(f)(3) and 1.1291-3(e)(4)(ii).

(3) *Section 304 transactions.*—(i) *In general.*—If, in a transaction described in section 304(a), the issuing corporation is a section 1291 fund, any amount treated as paid out of the earnings and profits of such section 1291 fund by virtue of section 304(b)(2) is treated as an excess distribution by such fund for purposes of section 1291 and this section. In addition, the transfer of the stock of such fund will be treated as a disposition to which §§1.1291-3 and 1.1291-6 apply. If, in a transaction described in section 304(a), the acquiring corporation is a section 1291 fund, any amount paid by such corporation to the transferor is treated as a distribution by such fund (notwithstanding the provisions of section 304(b)(2)), and the transferor is treated for purposes of section 1291 and this section as the owner of any stock of the fund that it owns directly or constructively under section 304(c). The following example illustrates the rule of this paragraph (b)(3)(i).

Example. USP, a domestic corporation, owns all the stock of FS1 and FS2. FS1 and FS2 each have accumulated earnings and profits of $100 that were not previously taxed under any other section of the Code. FS1, but not FS2, is a PFIC. USP has not elected under section 1295 to treat FS1 as a QEF. However, USP plans to make a section 1295 election to treat FS1 as a QEF, as well as the

deemed dividend election under section 1291(d)(2)(B) to purge USP's holding period of the FS1 stock of its prior PFIC years. Before it makes those elections, USP plans to sell the stock of FS1 to FS2 for its fair market value of $200. The transfer of the FS1 stock to FS2 is a transaction to which section 304 applies. Section 304(b)(2) provides that $100 of the $200 payment to USP is treated as paid directly by FS1 out of its earnings and profits. Pursuant to §1.1291-2(b)(3)(i), the $100 distribution to USP is taxable as an excess distribution. The transfer will not be a taxable disposition under §1.1291-3 because USP's interest in FS1 is not reduced as a result of the transfer. *See* section 304(a)(1) and §1.1291-6(c)(1)(i).

(ii) *Limitation.*—[Reserved]

(c) *Excess distribution and nonexcess distribution.*—(1) *Excess distribution.*—An excess distribution is that portion of any direct or indirect distribution with respect to a share of stock of a section 1291 fund during the current shareholder year that is the ratable portion (as defined in paragraph (c)(4) of this section) of the total excess distribution (as defined in paragraph (c)(3) of this section), if any. Except as provided in §1.1291-5, an excess distribution and the taxation thereof are determined without regard to the amount or character of the earnings and profits of the section 1291 fund. Except as provided in paragraph (d)(2) of this section (concerning shares of stock having the same holding period), the excess distribution is calculated separately for each share of stock held.

(2) *Nonexcess distribution.*—(i) *In general.*—A nonexcess distribution with respect to a share of section 1291 stock is the portion of the total amount of all distributions during the current shareholder year with respect to the share that does not exceed 125 percent of the average amount of the distributions with respect to the share during the three taxable years of the shareholder's holding period (or during the lesser number of taxable years in the shareholder's holding period) that immediately precede the current shareholder year. Distributions in any of the preceding three (or fewer) taxable years of the shareholder included in the shareholder's holding period that began before 1987 are included in determining the nonexcess distribution.

(ii) *Amount not included in income.*—The portion of an excess distribution in a prior taxable year that was not included in income pursuant to §1.1291-2 (e)(2)(iii) is not treated as a distribution in that prior year for purposes of paragraph (c)(2)(i) or (iii) of this section. For an illustration of the rule of this paragraph (c)(2)(ii), *see* paragraph (e)(4), *Example 1*, of this section.

(iii) *Distributions received by predecessors.*—If a shareholder's holding period of the stock of a section 1291 fund includes the period the stock was held by another person, distributions made during the holding period of such other person with respect to the stock will be treated as if they had been received by the shareholder for purposes of paragraph (c)(2)(i) of this section.

(3) *Total excess distribution.*—(i) *In general.*—The total excess distribution with respect to a share of stock of a section 1291 fund is the excess, if any, of—

(A) The total amount of all distributions during the current shareholder year with respect to the share, over

(B) The nonexcess distribution with respect to that stock.

(ii) *Exception.*—Notwithstanding paragraph (c)(3)(i) of this section, the total excess distribution is zero for the taxable year of the shareholder in which the shareholder's holding period of the stock begins. The following example illustrates the rule of this paragraph (c)(3)(ii).

Example. On January 1, 1989, X, a U.S. person, gave his son Y, also a U.S. person, one share of stock of FC, a section 1291 fund, that X had purchased in 1986. Y purchased another share of FC stock on January 3, 1989. Y did not make the section 1295 election with respect to FC. In 1989, FC distributed $100 for each outstanding share of its stock. Pursuant to §1.1291-2(c)(3)(ii), no portion of the distribution in respect of the share Y purchased in 1989 is treated as an excess distribution. However, the distribution paid to Y with respect to the stock given to him by his father may be wholly or partly an excess distribution. Although Y first held that share of FC stock in 1989, Y's holding period includes the period X held that share of stock, as provided in section 1223(2), and therefore does not begin in 1989.

(4) *Ratable portion.*—The total excess distribution is allocated ratably to each distribution received with respect to a share of stock

during the current shareholder year. A distribution's ratable portion of the total excess distribution is the product of the total excess distribution and the ratio of the distribution to the total distribution with respect to the share of stock during the current shareholder year. Each ratable portion of the total excess distribution is an excess distribution.

(d) *Special rules.*—The following rules apply for purposes of calculating the nonexcess distribution and the total excess distribution—

(1) *Stock acquired during the year.*—In general, a distribution in a prior taxable year with respect to a share of stock may only be taken into account in determining a nonexcess distribution under paragraph (c)(2)(i) of this section if the shareholder was a shareholder at the time of such distribution, or the distribution was received by a person whose holding period of the stock is included in the shareholder's holding period. However, with respect to a prior taxable year during which a person became a shareholder, the shareholder may instead take into account the total amount (or portion thereof) that the shareholder determines was actually paid by the section 1291 fund with respect to that share of stock during that taxable year. No other annualization rule will apply under section 1291(b)(3)(C). The following example illustrates the rule of this paragraph (d)(1).

Example. R, a U.S. person, became an indirect shareholder of one share of FC stock on August 1, 1991. R did not elect under section 1295 to treat FC, a PFIC, as a QEF. R and FC both use the calendar year as their taxable years. R determines, based on dividend information provided in FC's 1991 annual report, that FC distributed $100 with respect to each outstanding share of its stock at the end of each quarter during that year. For purposes of calculating nonexcess distributions in 1992, 1993, and 1994, R may treat $400 as the amount received in 1991. If R had been unable to determine the amount distributed in 1991 before August 1, the 1991 distribution would have been limited to the $200 actually distributed after August 1 with respect to the one share of FC stock attributed to R.

(2) *Calculations for shares with same holding period.*—The calculation of the nonexcess distribution and the total excess distribution may be made on an aggregate basis for shares of stock having the same holding period (block of stock). The following example illustrates the rule of this paragraph (d)(2).

Example. (i) *Facts.* X, a U.S. person that is a calendar year taxpayer, owns 12 shares of stock of FC, a PFIC. X has not elected under section 1295 to treat FC as a QEF. X acquired two of the 12 shares on December 31, 1986 (Block #1), four shares on December 31, 1987 (Block #2), and six shares on December 31, 1988 (Block #3). On June 30 of 1987 and 1988, FC distributed $10 in respect of each outstanding share of its stock; no portion of either distribution was an excess distribution. On June 30, 1989, FC distributed $30 in respect of each outstanding share of its stock. For purposes of determining the taxation of the 1989 distribution, the excess distribution may be calculated for each of the three blocks of stock held by X instead of on a share-by-share basis.

(ii) *Block #1 excess distribution.* The nonexcess distribution for Block #1 is $25 (125% times $20 [($20 + $20)/2]). The total excess distribution for Block #1 is $35 ($60 – $25).

(iii) *Block #2 excess distribution.* The nonexcess distribution for Block #2 is $50 (125% × $40, the distribution made in the only preceding taxable year in the holding period of the Block #2 shares). The total excess distribution for Block #2 is $70 ($120 – $50).

(iv) *Block #3.* There is no excess distribution with respect to the Block #3 stock because the first taxable year of the holding period of that block of stock is 1989, the taxable year of the distribution.

(3) *Effect of nontaxable distribution or exchange.*—(i) *Tax-free distributions of stock.*—A distribution with respect to a share of stock, made during the shareholder's holding period for the share but before a distribution of stock under section 305(a) with respect to that share, will be treated ratably as a distribution with respect to the shares in the block of stock composed of the original share and the shares distributed with respect to that share pursuant to the stock distribution.

(ii) *Nontaxable exchange of stock.*—Distributions with respect to stock include distributions with respect to stock exchanged therefor in a nonrecognition transfer in which gain was not recognized pursuant to § 1.1291-6(c).

(iii) *Example.*—The following example illustrates the rule of paragraph (d)(3) of this section.

Example. On December 31, 1985, X, a U.S. person, purchased one share of stock of FC, a corporation. FC has been a section 1291 fund with respect to X since FC's taxable year that began January 1, 1987. In both 1986 and 1987, FC distributed $6 with respect to each share of its stock. FC transferred all its assets and liabilities to F, a PFIC, in a transaction that qualified as a reorganization defined in

section 368(a)(1)(C) and that was effective on January 1, 1988. X exchanged his share of FC stock for one share of stock of F in an exchange to which section 354 applied and no gain was recognized pursuant to § 1.1291-6(c)(1). On December 31, 1988, F distributed $3 with respect to each share of its stock. No part of the 1986, 1987, and 1988 distributions was an excess distribution. On December 31, 1989, F distributed $10 with respect to each share of its stock. In calculating the total excess distribution for 1989, the $6 distributions paid in 1986 and 1987 by FC with respect to the FC stock held by X, as well as the $3 distribution paid by F in 1988 on the F stock received in exchange for the FC stock, are taken into account. Accordingly, the total excess distribution for 1989 is $3.75 ($10 – [125% × $5 (the average distribution for the three preceding taxable years)]).

(4) *Distributions in a foreign currency.*—(i) *In general.*—Except as provided in paragraph (d)(4)(ii) of this section, the nonexcess distribution and the total excess distribution are determined in U.S. dollars. Each distribution that must be taken into account for purposes of the calculation is translated into the U.S. dollar at the spot rate (within the meaning of § 1.988-1T (d)) on the date on which such distribution was made. The following example illustrates the rule of this paragraph (d)(4)(i).

Example. USP, a domestic corporation, purchased on December 31, 1986, five percent of the stock of FC, a country X corporation that is a section 1291 fund with respect to USP. The functional currency of FC is the "LC", the currency of country X. FC made no distributions during 1987. FC distributed $100 to USP on August 1, 1988; LC20 on November 20, 1989; and 100 units of country Y currency on December 13, 1990. In order to calculate the 1989 and 1990 excess distributions, USP must convert the 1989 distribution of LC20 into U.S. dollars at the spot rate on November 20, 1989, and the 1990 distribution of 100 units of country Y currency into U.S. dollars at the spot rate on December 13, 1990.

(ii) *Exception.*—If all distributions that must be taken into account for purposes of calculating the nonexcess distribution and the total excess distribution for the current shareholder year were made in a single currency (other than the U.S. dollar), the nonexcess distribution and total excess distribution will be determined in the currency in which the distributions were made. Each ratable portion of a total excess distribution determined in a foreign currency is translated into U.S. dollars at the spot rate on the date of the distribution to which the ratable portion is allocated.

(5) *Adjustments for section 642(c) charitable deduction.*—(i) *In general.*—A trust that is permitted to deduct the amount of its fixed annual charitable obligation from gross income pursuant to section 642(c)(1) (the section 642(c) deduction) generally may adjust an excess distribution from a section 1291 fund as provided in this paragraph (d)(5) by the amount of the section 642(c) deduction. Except as otherwise provided in this paragraph (d)(5), the trust may adjust an excess distribution if, in satisfaction of its fixed annual obligation, it distributes—

(A) amounts received from the section 1291 fund;

(B) the stock of a section 1291 fund; or

(C) the proceeds from the sale thereof, to an organization described in section 170(c), as required under the terms of the governing instrument of the trust.

The adjustment provided in this paragraph (d)(5) is limited to the amount of the trust's fixed annual charitable obligation.

(ii) *Exception.*—This paragraph (d)(5) does not apply to a grantor of a trust if the grantor deducted from income, as provided in section 170(f)(2)(B), the value of an interest in any share of stock of the section 1291 fund upon its transfer to the trust.

(iii) *Adjustments.*—(A) *Corpus consisting only of section 1291 fund stock.*—Where the assets of the trust consist only of stock of one or more section 1291 funds, the section 642(c) deduction first reduces the nonexcess distributions, if any, determined under paragraph (c)(2)(i) of this section. The amount of the section 642(c) deduction remaining after reduction of the nonexcess distributions reduces the portions of the excess distributions allocated to the prePFIC and current shareholder years. Finally, the amount of the section 642(c) deduction remaining after the prior two reductions reduces pro rata the portions of the excess distributions allocated to the prior PFIC years. The deferred tax amount, as defined in § 1.1291-4, is determined with respect to the adjusted allocations of the excess distributions.

(B) *Corpus consisting of section 1291 fund stock and other property.*—(1) *Income from both section 1291 fund stock and other property.*—A distribution of income in satisfaction of a fixed annual charitable obligation is treated as distributed out of income, if any, derived from the trust property other than the stock of a section 1291 fund to the extent thereof, before being treated as distributed out of amounts received from a section 1291 fund. An adjustment will be permitted in the manner provided in paragraph (d)(5)(iii)(A) of this section only after the deduction permitted under section 642(c) has reduced income from other property to zero.

(2) Use of corpus to satisfy obligation.—The trust will not be entitled to the adjustment permitted under this paragraph (d)(5) if the trust uses stock of a section 1291 fund instead of its other property to satisfy its fixed annual charitable obligation.

(6) PFIC for part of current shareholder year.—This paragraph (d)(6) applies if the section 1291 fund first qualified as a PFIC for its taxable year beginning after the first day of the current shareholder year and therefore is a section 1291 fund for only a portion of the current shareholder year. Distributions during the portion of the current shareholder year before the corporation qualified as a PFIC are taken into account for purposes of calculating the nonexcess distribution and the total excess distribution. However, those distributions are taxable under the general rules applicable to distributions by a corporation to its shareholder with respect to its stock, notwithstanding that a ratable portion thereof may be an excess distribution within the meaning of paragraph (c)(1) of this section. The following example illustrates the rule of this paragraph (d)(6).

Example. X, a U.S. person, purchased one share of stock of FC, a corporation, on December 31, 1986. X uses the calendar year as its taxable year; FC's taxable year ends November 30. FC first qualified as a PFIC for its taxable year that began December 1, 1990. X did not elect under section 1295 to treat FC as a QEF. X received a distribution of $100 in 1987, but did not receive another distribution from FC until August 1, 1990, when FC distributed $100 per share. On December 13, 1990, FC made another $100 per share distribution. The August distribution is taken into account for purposes of calculating the nonexcess distribution and total excess distribution for 1990 and the ratable portion of the December 13 distribution that is an excess distribution. However, pursuant to §1.1291-2(d)(6), the August distribution is not subject to section 1291 notwithstanding that a ratable portion of that distribution is an excess distribution within the meaning of §1.1291-2(c)(1). The August distribution is included in X's 1990 gross income to the extent provided in section 301(c).

(e) Taxation of a distribution and effect on earnings and profits.— (1) *Nonexcess distribution.*—A nonexcess distribution, as defined in paragraph (c)(2)(i) of this section, is taxable to a shareholder according to the general rules of taxation applicable to distributions made by a corporation to a shareholder with respect to its stock. *See, e.g.,* section 301 and the regulations under that section.

(2) Excess distribution.—(i) *In general.*—To determine the taxation of an excess distribution, the excess distribution is first allocated pro rata to each day in the shareholder's holding period (as determined under §1.1291-1(h)) of the share of stock with respect to which the distribution was made. The holding period of a share of stock of a section 1291 fund is treated as ending on (and including) the date of each excess distribution solely for purposes of allocating the excess distribution.

(ii) Allocations included in income.—The portions of an excess distribution allocated to prePFIC years and the current shareholder year are included in the shareholder's gross income for the current shareholder year as ordinary income.

(iii) Allocations not included in income.—The portions of an excess distribution allocated to prior PFIC years are not included in the shareholder's gross income for purposes of this title. These amounts are subject to the deferred tax amount. The deferred tax amount is an additional liability of the shareholder for tax and interest for the current shareholder year. For the calculation of the deferred tax amount and the foreign tax credit that may be taken to reduce the deferred tax amount, *see* §§1.1291-4 and 1.1291-5.

(3) Allocation of earnings and profits.—For purposes of determining the taxation of a nonexcess distribution and calculating the

TAXABLE YEAR	
1986	
1987	
1988	
1989	

Excess distribution:

The allocation to 1986, the prePFIC year, and the allocation to 1989, the current shareholder year, are included in X's gross income for 1989 as ordinary income. The allocations to 1987 and 1988, the prior PFIC years, are not included in X's gross income in 1989, but are subject to the deferred tax amount.

(iii) July 31 distribution. The excess distribution allocated to the July 31 distribution, which is the ratable portion of the total excess distribution allocated to the distribution made on that date, is

foreign tax credit under §1.1291-5, the earnings and profits of a section 1291 fund are allocated proportionately between the nonexcess distribution (as defined in paragraph (c)(2)(i) of this section) and the total excess distribution (as defined in paragraph (c)(3) of this section) and reduced (but not below zero) by the amounts thereof.

(4) Examples.—The following examples illustrate the operation of paragraphs (c), (d), and (e) of this section.

Example 1. (i) *Facts.* X, a U.S. person, purchased a share of stock of FC, a corporation, on December 31, 1985. FC has been a section 1291 fund since its taxable year that began January 1, 1987. X received distributions from FC of $50 on December 31, 1987, $80 on December 31, 1988, and $150 on December 31, 1989. FC made no distributions in 1986.

(ii) *1987 excess distribution.* Because X did not receive a distribution from FC during 1986, the only preceding taxable year in its holding period, the total distribution of $50 is the total excess distribution for 1987. That amount is allocated pro rata over X's two-year holding period, as provided in §1.1291-2(e)(2)(i): $25 is allocated to 1986, a prePFIC year, and $25 to 1987, the current shareholder year. The entire $50 therefore is included in X's gross income for 1987 as ordinary income.

(iii) *1988 excess distribution.* In 1988, of the $80 total distribution, $31.25 (125% × $25 [(0 + $50) / 2]) is the nonexcess distribution, and is taxable as a corporate distribution as provided in section 301(c). The total excess distribution for 1988, $48.75 ($80 − $31.25), is allocated over X's three-year holding period; $16.25 is allocated to each year. The portions of the excess distribution allocated to the prePFIC year (1986) and the current shareholder year (1988) total $32.50; that amount is included in X's gross income as ordinary income. The $16.25 portion of the excess distribution allocated to 1987, the prior PFIC year, is not included in X's gross income, but is subject to the deferred tax amount. Of the $80 distribution, $63.75 ($31.25 + $32.50) is included in X's gross income in 1988.

(iv) *1989 excess distribution.* In 1989, of the $150 total distribution, $47.40 (125% × $37.90 [(0 + $50 + $63.75) / 3]) is the nonexcess distribution, and is taxable as a corporate distribution as provided in section 301(c). The total excess distribution for 1989, $102.60 ($150 −$47.40), is allocated over X's four-year holding period; $25.65 is allocated to each year. The portions of the excess distribution allocated to the prePFIC year (1986) and the current shareholder year (1989) total $51.30; that amount is included in X's gross income as ordinary income. The portions of the excess distribution allocated to the prior PFIC years (1987 and 1988) total $51.30; that amount is not included in X's gross income but is subject to the deferred tax amount. Of the total $150 distribution, $98.70 ($47.40 + $51.30) is included in X's gross income in 1989.

Example 2. (i) *Facts.* X, a U.S. person with a calendar taxable year, purchased 1,000 shares of stock of FC, a corporation, on December 31, 1985. FC has been a section 1291 fund since its taxable year that began January 1, 1987. FC distributed $100,000 to X on January 31, 1989, and $200,000 to X on July 31, 1989. X determined the total excess distribution for 1989 to be $150,000.

(ii) *January 31 distribution.* The excess distribution allocated to the January 31 distribution, which is the ratable portion of the total excess distribution allocated to the $100,000 distribution made on that date, is $50,000 [$150,000 × ($100,000 / $300,000)]. For purposes of allocating the $50,000 excess distribution over X's holding period, X's holding period is treated as ending on (and including) January 31, 1989. X thus held the stock for 1,127 days (365 days in both 1986 and 1987, 366 days in 1988, and 31 days in 1989) at the time of the January 31 distribution. The $50,000 excess distribution allocated to the January 31 distribution is allocated pro rata to the 1,127 days; approximately $44.37 is allocated to each day in the holding period. The total allocations to each of the taxable years in X's holding period are as follows:

	TOTAL ALLOCATION PER YEAR
	$16,193.70
	$16,193.70
	$16,237.70
	$1,374.90
	$50,000.00

$100,000 [$150,000 × ($200,000 / $300,000)]. For purposes of the allocation of this excess distribution, X's holding period is treated as ending on July 31, 1989. X thus held the stock for 1,308 days (365 days in both 1986 and 1987, 366 days in 1988, and 212 days in 1989) at the time of the July 31 distribution. The $100,000 excess distribution allocated to the July 31 excess distribution is allocated pro rata to the 1,308 days; approximately $76.45 is allocated to each day in the holding period. The total allocations of the July 31 excess distribution to each of the taxable years in X's holding period are as follows:

TAXABLE YEAR	TOTAL ALLOCATION PER YEAR
1986	$27,905.20
1987	$27,905.20
1988	$27,981.65
1989	$16,207.95
	$100,000.00

Excess distribution:

The portions of the excess distribution allocated to 1986, the prePFIC year, and to 1989, the current shareholder year, are included as ordinary income in X's gross income for 1989. The portions of the excess distribution allocated to 1987 and 1988, the prior PFIC years, are not included in X's gross income in 1989, but are subject to the deferred tax amount.

Example 3. (i) *Facts.* X, a U.S. person, holds six shares of the stock of FC, a section 1291 fund. Two shares were purchased on December 31, 1986 (Block #1), and four shares were purchased on December 31, 1987 (Block #2). On June 30 of 1987 and 1988, FC distributed $10,000 in respect of each outstanding share of its stock. No portion of the distributions in either year was an excess distribution. On June 30, 1989, FC distributed $30,000 in respect of each outstanding share of its stock.

(ii) *Calculation of the 1989 excess distributions.* The excess distribution is determined separately for each block of stock.

TAXABLE YEAR
1987
1988
1989

Excess distribution:

The portion of the excess distribution allocated to 1989, the current shareholder year, of $6,946.20, is included as ordinary income in X's gross income for 1989. The portions of the excess distribution allocated to the prior PFIC years, 1987 and 1988, an aggregate of $28,053.80, are not included in X's gross income in 1989, but are subject to the deferred tax amount.

TAXABLE YEAR
1988
1989

Excess distribution:

The portion of the excess distribution allocated to 1989, the current shareholder year, of $23,162.60, is included as ordinary income in X's gross income for 1989. The portion of the excess distribution allocated to 1988, $46,837.40, is not included in X's gross income in 1989, but is subject to the deferred tax amount.

Example 4. X is a U.S. person that owns all the stock of FC, a section 1291 fund. At the end of its 1991 taxable year, FC has accumulated earnings and profits, before reduction for distributions made during the year, of $100, none of which was previously taxed to X under section 951 or 1293. FC distributes $200 to X on the last day of FC's taxable year. X determines that, of the $200 distribution, $50 is a nonexcess distribution, and $150 is the total excess distribution. FC's earnings and profits of $100 are allocated proportionately between the nonexcess distribution of $50 and the excess distribution of $150, and reduced to zero. Accordingly, $25 of FC's earnings and profits are allocated to the nonexcess distribution and $75 of FC's earnings and profits are allocated to the excess distribution. Therefore, $25 of the $50 nonexcess distribution is taxable as a dividend under section 301(c)(1), and the remaining $25 is taxable to the extent provided in section 301(c)(2) and (3). The excess distribution of $150 is taxable as provided in §1.1291-2(e)(2).

(f) *Indirect distributions.*—(1) *In general.*—A distribution (as defined in §1.1291-2(b)) by a section 1291 fund to the actual owner of stock of the section 1291 fund is an indirect distribution if such stock is considered owned by a U.S. person pursuant to §1.1291-1(b)(8). Except as otherwise provided in this paragraph (f), an indirect shareholder is taxable on the total distribution paid by the section 1291 fund with respect to the stock attributed to the indirect shareholder, as if the indirect shareholder had actually received that amount. The following example illustrates the rule of this paragraph (f)(1).

Example. (i) X, an S corporation under section 1361, purchased 100 shares of stock of FC, a corporation, on December 31, 1985. FC has been a section 1291 fund since its taxable year that began January 1, 1987. A purchased 10 percent of the stock of X on December 31, 1986, and thus became an indirect shareholder of 10 shares of FC stock. Pursuant to §1.1291-1(h)(4)(i), A's holding period of the FC stock began on January 1, 1987.

(ii) FC distributed $5 per share of stock to its shareholders in 1986, and $8 per share in 1987. In 1987 A is treated as receiving a distribution of $80 from FC. A did not have a total excess distribution in 1987, the taxable year in which A's holding period of the FC stock began

(A) *Block #1 excess distribution.* The nonexcess distribution for Block #1 is $25,000 [125% times ($20,000 + $20,000) / 2]. The total excess distribution for Block #1 is $35,000 ($60,000 – $25,000).

(B) *Block #2 excess distribution.* The nonexcess distribution for Block #2 is $50,000 [125% times $40,000 (the distribution received in the only preceding taxable year included in X's holding period]. The total excess distribution for Block #2 is $70,000 ($120,000 – $50,000).

(iii) *Block #1 allocation.* The holding period of the Block #1 stock began on January 1, 1987, and ended, for purposes of section 1291, on June 30, 1989, for a total of 912 days (365 days in 1987, 366 days in 1988 and 181 days in 1989). The $35,000 excess distribution for Block #1 is allocated pro rata to each of the 912 days. Accordingly, approximately $38.38 is allocated to each day. The total allocations to each of the taxable years in X's holding period are as follows:

TOTAL ALLOCATION PER YEAR
$14,007.70
$14,046.10
$6,946.20
$35,000.00

(iv) *Block #2 allocation.* The holding period of the Block #2 stock began on January 1, 1988, and ended, for purposes of section 1291, on June 30, 1989, for a total of 547 days (366 days in 1988 and 181 days in 1989). The excess distribution of $70,000 in respect of the Block #2 stock is allocated pro rata to each of the 547 days. Accordingly, approximately $127.97 is allocated to each day. The total allocations to each of the taxable years in X's holding period are as follows:

TOTAL ALLOCATION PER YEAR
$46,837.40
$23,162.60
$70,000.00

(iii) FC distributed $12 per share in 1988, all of which was paid on June 30, 1988. A therefore is treated as receiving a distribution of $120 from FC. The nonexcess distribution is $100 [125% times $80]. Accordingly, the excess distribution is $20 ($120 – $100). That amount is allocated under §1.1291-2(e)(2)(i) to each day in A's holding period of the FC stock, which began on January 1, 1987, and ended, for purposes of the allocation of the excess distribution, on June 30, 1988.

(2) *Pass-through entities.*—(i) *Taxation of trusts, estates, and their beneficiaries.*—[Reserved]

(ii) *Information reporting.*—(A) *In general.*—A domestic partnership that is a direct or indirect shareholder of a section 1291 fund must separately state the total distribution as a distribution from a section 1291 fund on its federal income tax return (if any) and on any Schedule K-1 filed by the partnership or provided to a partner to which a distributive share of the distribution from the section 1291 fund is allocated pursuant to section 704. In addition, the partnership must state on the Schedule K-1 the information needed by the partner to compute its excess distribution with respect to such total distribution, and provide the name, address and stock basis, where appropriate, of the actual owner of the section 1291 fund that paid the distribution (or whose stock was transferred in an indirect disposition). Any partner receiving such a Schedule K-1 that is itself a domestic partnership is in turn obligated to separately state such information according to the same rules. Similar rules apply to S corporations.

(B) *Trusts and estates.*—[Reserved]

(3) *Coordination with subpart F.*—If, but for this paragraph (f)(3), an indirect distribution would be taxable to an indirect shareholder under this section and also included in the gross income of the indirect shareholder under section 551(a), 951(a)(1), or 1293(a), the indirect distribution is taxable only under this section.

(4) *Exceptions.*—(i) *Distribution to sole shareholder.*—A distribution by a section 1291 fund (distributing fund) to another section 1291 fund (distributee fund) will not be taxable to the direct shareholder of the distributee fund if—

(A) The distributee fund owns all the stock of the distributing fund; and

(B) The distributing fund distributed all its earnings and profits in the current shareholder year and annually distributed all its earnings and profits for each year that is included in the shareholder's holding period of the distributing fund.

(ii) *Other exceptions.*—[Reserved]

(5) *Adjustment to basis.*—The shareholder's adjusted basis of the stock or other property that is owned directly by the shareholder and through which ownership of the section 1291 fund is attributed to the shareholder is increased by the amount of the indirect distribution taxed to the shareholder pursuant to paragraph (f)(1) of this section.

(6) *Treatment of previously taxed amounts.*—The principles of sections 959 and 961 apply with respect to amounts previously taxed under this paragraph (f). The following example illustrates the rule of this paragraph (f)(6).

Example. USP owns 50% of CFC1. CFC1 and its wholly owned subsidiary, CFC2, are both controlled foreign corporations within the meaning of section 957(a), but are not PFICs. CFC2 owns 10% of the stock of NQF, a PFIC. USP is an indirect shareholder of NQF pursuant to §1.1291-1(b)(8)(ii). USP has not elected to treated NQF as a QEF. In 1992, NQF distributes $100 to CFC2, and CFC1 distributes $100 to USP, but CFC2 makes no distributions to CFC1. At the end of 1992, CFC1 has accumulated earnings and profits of $200, none of which was previously taxed to USP under section 951(a)(1). USP is taxable pursuant to §1.1291-2(f) on its pro rata share of the indirect distribution paid to CFC2, and also is taxable on CFC1's distribution pursuant to section 301(c). No part of the distribution by CFC1 to USP is attributable to the amount taxed to USP under §1.1291-2(f) because no part of the distribution can be attributed to NQF's distribution to CFC2. [Reg. §1.1291-2.]

§1.1291-3. Dispositions.—(a) *Purpose and scope.*—Any direct or indirect disposition of stock of a section 1291 fund within the meaning of paragraphs (b), (c), (d), and (e) of this section is taxable to the extent provided in section 1291, this section, and §1.1291-6. For dispositions of stock of a section 1291 fund that qualify for nonrecognition treatment, *see* §1.1291-6. Gain is determined on a share-by-share basis and is taxed as an excess distribution as provided in §1.1291-2(e)(2). Unless otherwise provided under another provision of the Code, a loss realized on a disposition of stock of a section 1291 fund is not recognized.

(b) *Disposition.*—(1) *In general.*—For purposes of this section, a disposition is any transaction or event that constitutes an actual or deemed transfer of property for any purpose of the Code and the regulations thereunder, including (but not limited to) a sale, exchange, gift, or transfer at death, an exchange pursuant to a liquidation or section 302(a) redemption, or a distribution described in section 311, 336, 337, 355(c) or 361(c). For purposes of this paragraph (b), any person receiving a distribution that qualifies under section 355 will be treated as disposing of all of its stock in the distributing corporation (whether or not there is an actual disposition of such stock) in exchange for stock of the distributing corporation, the controlled corporation, or both, as the case may be.

(2) *Change of U.S. residence or citizenship.*—If a shareholder of a section 1291 fund becomes a nonresident alien for U.S. tax purposes, the shareholder will be treated as having disposed of the shareholder's stock in the section 1291 fund for purposes of section 1291 on the last day that the shareholder is a U.S. person. Termination of an election under section 6013(g) is treated as a change of residence (within the meaning of this paragraph (b)(2)) of the spouse who was a resident solely by reason of the section 6013(g) election.

(c) *Direct disposition of stock of a section 1291 fund.*—Except to the extent provided in §1.1291-6, a direct shareholder of a section 1291 fund recognizes all gain that it realizes on a disposition of the stock of such fund.

(d) *Stock of a section 1291 fund used as security for an obligation.*—(1) *In general.*—Except to the extent provided in paragraphs (d)(3) and (6) of this section, the use of stock of a section 1291 fund as security for the performance of an obligation of a direct or indirect shareholder (or of a person related within the meaning of section 267(b) to that shareholder), in connection with a loan, guarantee, margin account, or otherwise (a pledge of stock), is a transaction that results in a disposition of the stock of the section 1291 fund within the meaning of paragraph (b) of this section. Such pledged stock will be treated as having been disposed of on the later of the date when such stock is first used as security with respect to such obligation, or the first day of the first taxable year of the foreign corporation as a PFIC. Such pledged stock will be treated as having been disposed of for consideration equal to the lesser of—

(i) The unpaid principal of the obligation secured by the stock on the date of disposition; or

(ii) The fair market value of the stock immediately before such disposition.

(2) *Indirect pledge.*—A pledge of stock of a section 1291 fund, as described in paragraph (d)(1) of this section, will be deemed to occur if such stock serves indirectly as security for the performance

of an obligation described in that paragraph, and a principal purpose for the structure of the security arrangement was to avoid the rule of that paragraph.

(3) *Requirement of gain realized.*—This paragraph (d) does not apply if the shareholder would realize a loss on an actual disposition of the stock of the section 1291 fund at the time the obligation was secured by the stock.

(4) *Increase in value of pledged stock.*—An increase in the value of stock being used to secure the performance of an obligation will not be treated as a disposition of the stock unless the pledged stock is used to secure additional principal or new indebtedness.

(5) *Adjustment to basis; holding period.*—If stock of a section 1291 fund is treated as disposed of under this paragraph (d), adjustments to basis will be made in accordance with rules similar to those in §1.1291-6(b)(4). For the holding period of pledged stock, *see* §1.1291-1(h)(5).

(6) *Transition rule.*—Stock of a section 1291 fund that secured an obligation within the meaning of paragraph (d)(1) of this section as of the effective date of section 1297(b)(6) is not treated as disposed of as of the first day of the first taxable year of the foreign corporation as a PFIC, unless such stock continued to secure such obligation 180 days after the effective date. For a special effective date pertaining to this rule, *see* §1.1291-1(j)(2).

(7) *Examples.*—The following examples illustrate the operation of this paragraph (d).

Example 1. On November 20, 1995, X, a U.S. person that was a shareholder of FC, a section 1291 fund, used its stock in FC, valued immediately before the loan at $120,000, as security for a $100,000 loan. X's basis in the stock is $70,000. The pledge is treated as a disposition of the stock for $100,000, which is the lesser of the loan principal secured by the stock and the fair market value of the stock. S recognizes $30,000 on the disposition, which gain is taxed as an excess distribution under section 1291 and §1.1291-2(e)(2). X's basis in the FC stock is increased by $30,000, the amount of gain recognized on the deemed disposition. The holding period of the pledged stock is not adjusted to reflect the disposition because the full amount of the gain inherent in the stock was not recognized (*see* §1.1291-1(h)(5)).

Example 2. The facts are the same as in *Example 1.* In addition, on August 12, 1996, X borrows an additional $30,000 (for a total outstanding loan balance on that day of $130,000). The value of the FC stock immediately before the additional loan is $130,000. Pursuant to §1.1291-3(d)(4), there is a disposition within the meaning of §1.1291-3(d)(1) to the extent the value of the FC stock secures additional indebtedness. The FC stock first secured a loan of $100,000, which was less than its full value. The second loan results in a disposition to the extent that the previously unrecognized appreciation and any additional appreciation secure additional indebtedness. Accordingly, there is an excess distribution of $30,000. X's basis in its FC stock is increased by $30,000, the amount of gain recognized. X's holding period in the FC stock for section 1291 purposes is treated as beginning on the day after the effective date of the second borrowing (*see* §1.1291-1(h)(5)).

(e) *Indirect dispositions.*—(1) *In general.*—Except as otherwise provided in this paragraph (e) and §1.1291-6, an indirect shareholder of a section 1291 fund is taxable under section 1291 and this section on an indirect disposition of stock of the section 1291 fund.

(2) *Indirect disposition defined.*—An indirect disposition is—

(i) Any disposition of stock of a section 1291 fund by its actual owner if such stock is attributed to an indirect shareholder under §1.1291-1(b)(8);

(ii) Any disposition, by an indirect shareholder or any other person, of any interest in a person, if by virtue of such interest the indirect shareholder was treated as owning stock of a section 1291 fund under §1.1291-1(b)(8); or

(iii) Any other transaction as a result of which an indirect shareholder's ownership of a section 1291 fund is reduced or terminated.

Paragraph (e)(2)(i) of this section applies without regard to whether the indirect shareholder's ownership of a section 1291 fund is changed by the disposition. However, paragraph (e)(2)(ii) of this section does not apply if the disposition does not result in a reduction in the indirect shareholder's ownership of the fund or an increase in the basis of the stock of the fund in the hands of the actual owner.

(3) *Examples.*—The following examples illustrate paragraph (e)(2) of this section.

Example 1. T, a U.S. person, and M, a foreign person, are equal partners of FP, a foreign partnership that owns 10 shares of stock of FC, a PFIC. Pursuant to §1.1291-1(b)(8)(iii), T is an indirect shareholder of one half of the shares of FC stock held by FP. T did not elect under section 1295 to treat FC as a QEF. On August 14, 1994, H, a U.S. person, joins the partnership as an equal partner. As a result of H's acquisition of one-third of FP, H is an indirect shareholder of one-third of the FC stock held by FP. H's acquisition of the FP interest is a disposition pursuant to §1.1291-3(e)(2)(iii), taxable to T, of one-third of T's interest in the FC stock.

Example 2. E, a U.S. person, and R, a foreign person, each own 50% of the outstanding stock of Distributing, a foreign corporation that is not a PFIC or a controlled foreign corporation within the meaning of section 957(a). Distributing owns all the stock of Controlled, a PFIC. Pursuant to §1.1291-1(b)(8)(ii)(A), E is an indirect shareholder of Controlled. E did not elect under section 1295 to treat Controlled as a QEF. In a transaction that qualifies under section 355(a), Distributing distributes all the Controlled stock to R. As a result of the distribution, E's interest in Controlled is terminated. The distribution is an indirect disposition of E's ownership of Controlled, within the meaning of §1.1291-3(e)(2)(i), taxable to E under §1.1291-3(e).

Example 3. C, a U.S. person, owns 51% of the stock of CFC, a foreign corporation that is not a PFIC. Several foreign persons own the remaining 49% of CFC. CFC owns 100 shares of FYZ, a PFIC. Pursuant to §1.1291-1(b)(8)(ii)(A), C is an indirect shareholder of 51 shares of the FYZ stock held by CFC. C did not elect under section 1295 to treat FYZ as a QEF. To raise capital, CFC makes a public offering of its stock. After the offering, C owns only 35% of the CFC stock. The reduction of C's ownership of CFC terminated C's indirect ownership of the FYZ stock, and therefore is an indirect disposition of the FYZ stock, pursuant to §1.1291-3(e)(2)(iii), taxable to C under §1.1291-3(e).

(4) *General rules.*—(i) *Amount and treatment of gain.*—If a shareholder with respect to a share of stock of a section 1291 fund is taxable on an indirect disposition of that share, the shareholder is treated as recognizing an amount of gain with respect to that share equal to the shareholder's pro rata share of the gain realized by the actual owner of that share (in the case of a disposition described in paragraph (e)(2)(i) of this section), or the gain the actual owner would have realized on an actual disposition of such stock (in the case of other dispositions). The gain taxable to the shareholder is an excess distribution, taxable in the manner provided in §1.1291-2(e)(2). The gain is allocated over the shareholder's holding period of the stock of the section 1291 fund as determined in §1.1291-1(h)(4).

(ii) *Coordination with current inclusion rules.*—If gain from an indirect disposition would be taxable to a shareholder under this section, and would, but for this paragraph (e)(4)(ii), also be included in the gross income of the shareholder under section 551(a), 951(a)(1), or 1293(a), the indirect disposition is taxable only under this section.

(iii) *Adjustment to basis; holding period.*—The shareholder's adjusted basis of the stock or other property that is owned directly by the shareholder and through which ownership of the section 1291 fund is attributed to the shareholder is increased by the amount of gain recognized by the shareholder pursuant to paragraph (e)(4)(i) of this section. In addition, solely for purposes of determining the subsequent treatment under the Code of a direct or indirect shareholder of the stock of the section 1291 fund treated as transferred in an indirect disposition, the adjusted basis of the actual owner of the stock of the section 1291 fund is increased by the amount of gain recognized by the shareholder. For the holding period rule for stock that is treated as disposed of under paragraph (e)(2) of this section, see §1.1291-1(h)(5).

(iv) *Treatment of previously taxed amounts.*—The principles of sections 959 and 961 apply with respect to distributions by a foreign corporation through which a shareholder was considered to own stock of a section 1291 fund, to the extent that such distributions are attributable to amounts previously taxed under this paragraph (e) on a disposition of the stock of such fund.

(5) *Pass-through entities.*—(i) *Section 1291 fund stock held by former C corporation.*—Solely for purposes of calculating the aggregate amount of interest under §1.1291-4(d)(1), the S corporation shareholder's gain is determined without regard to section 1366(f)(2). Accordingly, the excess distribution for this purpose includes the amount of the S corporation's liability for tax attributable to the built-in gain in the stock of the section 1291 fund pursuant to section 1374. For an illustration of the rule of this paragraph (e)(5)(i), see §1.1291-4(e), *Example 2.* For the taxation of the S corporation on the disposition of the stock of a section 1291 fund, see section 1374.

(ii) *Taxation of trusts, estates, and their beneficiaries.*—[Reserved]

(iii) *Information reporting.*—The information reporting obligations to which pass-through entities are subject with respect to

indirect distributions also apply with respect to indirect dispositions. See §1.1291-2(f)(2)(ii).

(6) *Exceptions.*—(i) *Disposition of PFIC's wholly-owned PFIC.*—A direct shareholder of a section 1291 fund (first-tier fund) will not be taxable on an indirect disposition of a section 1291 fund (second-tier fund) that is a wholly owned subsidiary of the first-tier fund if the second-tier fund annually distributed all its earnings and profits for each year that is included in the shareholder's holding period of the second-tier fund.

(ii) *Other exceptions.*—[Reserved]

(f) *Transfers within a consolidated group.*—For purposes of applying sections 1291 through 1297 to the stock of a PFIC, transfers by one member of a consolidated group to another member are ignored. Thus, the basis of the transferred stock in the hands of the transferee is the adjusted basis of such stock in the hands of the transferor, and the holding period of such stock held by a member of the consolidated group includes the holding period of all members of the group that have transferred the stock.

(g) *Installment sales.*—If the gain from a disposition of a share of stock of a section 1291 fund is reported on the installment basis, there is an excess distribution on the receipt of each installment or portion thereof in the amount of the gain to be reported in accordance with section 453 with respect to such share. For purposes of allocating each excess distribution under §1.1291-2(e)(2)(i), the holding period of the transferred stock, which begins on the date determined under §1.1291-1(h), is treated as ending on the date of each installment.

(h) *Series of liquidation distributions.*—For purposes of allocating the gain recognized on a distribution of property that is one of a series of distributions in liquidation of a section 1291 fund, the holding period of the stock of the liquidating corporation, which begins on the date determined under §1.1291-1(h), is treated as ending on the date of each liquidation distribution with respect to which gain is recognized.

(i) *Sections 1246 and 1248 inapplicable.*—Sections 1246 and 1248 do not apply to the disposition of stock of a section 1291 fund that is taxable under section 1291. See sections 1246(g) and 1248(g)(2).

(j) *Estate tax deduction.*—If a shareholder acquired the stock of a section 1291 fund from a decedent (other than a decedent who was a nonresident alien at all times during the holding period of the stock), and the decedent did not recognize any gain on the transfer of his or her stock at death pursuant to §1.1291-6(c)(2)(iii)(A), the shareholder may deduct from gross income, for the taxable year of the disposition of the stock of the section 1291 fund that is taxable to the shareholder, an amount equal to that portion of the decedent's estate tax deemed paid which is attributable to the excess of (A) the value at which such stock was taken into account for purposes of determining the value of the decedent's gross estate, over (B) the value at which it would have been so taken into account if such value had been the basis of the stock in the hands of the shareholder determined under §1.1291-6(b)(4)(iii). [Reg. §1.1291-3.]

§1.1291-4. The deferred tax amount.—(a) *In general.*—The deferred tax amount is the sum of the aggregate increases in taxes (defined in paragraph (c)(5) of this section) and the aggregate amount of interest (defined in paragraph (d) of this section) determined with respect to the aggregate increases in taxes. The deferred tax amount is computed for the portions of each excess distribution allocated to different prior PFIC years, as defined in §1.1291-1(b)(4).

(b) *Character of deferred tax amount.*—The aggregate increases in taxes are an additional amount of tax imposed on the shareholder for the current shareholder year. The aggregate increases in taxes are treated as an income tax for purposes of subtitle F (Procedure and Administration), and therefore will be assessed, collected, paid, and subject to penalties and interest in the same manner as other taxes on income. The aggregate amount of interest is treated as interest under section 6601. To determine the extent to which such interest may be deducted for federal income tax purposes, see section 163 and the regulations under that section.

(c) *Increase in tax.*—(1) *In general.*—An increase in tax is determined for each portion of an excess distribution allocated to a prior PFIC year. Each increase in tax is determined by multiplying the amount of the excess distribution allocated to the prior PFIC year by the highest statutory rate of tax in effect under either section 1 or section 11, as applicable, for that prior PFIC year.

(2) *Rate of tax in effect.*—The highest statutory rate of tax is determined without regard to the actual rate of tax to which the shareholder was subject in that prior PFIC year. The rate of tax in effect in the case of a distribution or disposition taxable to an indirect shareholder is the rate in effect for the indirect shareholder. For taxable years of the shareholder beginning after 1987 and before

January 1, 1991, the highest statutory rate of tax in effect under section 1 is 28 percent. If there was a change of tax rates during a taxable year, the highest rate of tax is determined in the manner described in section 15(e) using the highest statutory rates of tax in effect before and after the change of rates.

(3) *Reduction for foreign taxes.*—To the extent provided in section 1291(g) and §1.1291-5, each increase in tax is reduced by the foreign tax credit calculated with respect to the increase in tax.

(4) *Net increase in tax.*—The net increase in tax is the amount of the increase in tax after reduction for creditable foreign taxes. *See* paragraph (d) of this section.

(5) *Aggregate increases in taxes.*—The term aggregate increases in taxes means the sum of all net increases in tax calculated for an excess distribution.

(d) *Aggregate amount of interest.*—(1) *In general.*—The aggregate amount of interest is the sum of the interest charges computed on all net increases in tax calculated for an excess distribution. An interest charge is computed separately for the interest period of each net increase in tax by using the applicable rates and method under section 6621. The interest period for a net increase in tax is the period beginning on the due date of the income tax return for the prior PFIC year for which the net increase in tax was computed and ending on the due date for the income tax return for the current shareholder year. For purposes of this paragraph, the term due date means the date prescribed by law, determined without regard to extensions, for filing the income tax return for the taxable year of the shareholder.

46% rate: 181/365 × 46% =
34% rate: 184/365 × 34% =

The increase in tax for 1987 is $49.94 ($125 × 39.95%).

(iii) *Calculation of the other increases in tax.* The highest statutory rate of tax applicable to X that was in effect for both 1988 and 1989 was 34 percent. The increase in tax for each of 1988 and 1989 is $42.50 ($125 × 34%).

Year of Allocation	Increase in Tax
1987	$49.94
1988	42.50
1989	42.50

Example 2. (i) *Facts.* The facts are the same as in *Example 1* except that X was a C corporation until it elected to be treated as an S corporation effective for its taxable year beginning January 1, 1988. A is a U.S. person who has been a shareholder of X since January 1, 1988. A's holding period of the FC stock began on January 1, 1988, pursuant to §1.1291-1(h)(4)(i). As of January 1, 1988, the FC stock had appreciated in value to $800; X therefore had $300 of built-in gain within the meaning of section 1374. Assume X pays a built-in gain tax of $102 because of the sale of the FC stock in 1990.

(ii) *Calculation of the aggregate increases in taxes owed by A.* The $500 gain recognized, reduced as provided in section 1366(f)(2) by the amount of built-in gain tax of $102 paid by X pursuant to section 1374 to $398, is taxable to A as an excess distribution as provided in §1.1291-2(e)(2). The $398 excess distribution is allocated pro rata over X's four-year holding period (not A's three-year holding period) as provided in §1.1291-3(e)(5). The allocation of $99.50 to 1990, the current shareholder year, is included in A's ordinary income. The allocations of $99.50 to 1987, 1988, and 1989 are not included in income, but are subject to the deferred tax amount. The aggregate increases in taxes are determined based on those $99.50 allocations.

(A) *Calculation of the 1987 increase in tax.* The highest statutory rate of tax applicable to A that was in effect in 1987 was 38.5 percent. The increase in tax for the portion of the excess distribution allocated to 1987 is $38.31 ($99.50 × 38.5%).

Year of Allocation	Increase in Tax
1987	$48.12
1988	35.00
1989	35.00

(iv) *The deferred tax amount.* The deferred tax amount is the sum of the aggregate increases in taxes determined in (ii) and the aggregate amount of interest determined in (iii). [Reg. §1.1291-4.]

§1.1291-5. Coordination with the foreign tax credit rules.—

(a) *Scope.*—This section provides rules for determining the amount of foreign tax credit that a shareholder may claim on a distribution from a section 1291 fund, and in certain cases, on a disposition of stock of a section 1291 fund. This section applies to a shareholder that has chosen under section 901 for the current shareholder year to claim a credit for foreign taxes paid. The rules of this section apply separately with respect to each section 1291 fund in which the share-

(2) *Reduction for interest paid under section 453A(c).*—A disposition may be subject to both sections 1291 and 453A(c). The aggregate amount of interest determined in paragraph (d)(1) of this section is reduced by the amount of interest paid under section 453A(c) that is attributable to an excess distribution arising from the disposition. The shareholder may use any reasonable method of determining the amount of the reduction.

(e) *Examples.*—The following examples illustrate the rules of this section.

Example 1. (i) *Facts.* X is a domestic corporation that is a calendar year taxpayer. The due date (without regard to extensions) for its federal income tax return is March 15. X acquired a share of stock of FC, a corporation, on December 31, 1986, for $500. FC has been a section 1291 fund with respect to X since FC's taxable year that began January 1, 1987. On December 31, 1990, X sold the FC stock for $1000. X did not incur any foreign tax on the disposition of the FC stock. X's gain on the sale, $500, is taxed as an excess distribution. The excess distribution is allocated pro rata over X's four-year holding period. Accordingly, $125 is allocated to each year in X's holding period. The $125 allocated to 1990, the current shareholder year, is included in X's ordinary income for that year. The allocations to 1987, 1988 and 1989, the prior PFIC years, are subject to the deferred tax amount under §1.1291-4.

(ii) *Calculation of the 1987 increase in tax.* The increase in tax for the $125 allocated to 1987 is determined in the manner described in section 15(e) by using a weighted average rate. The weighted average rate is 40 percent:

$$\begin{array}{r} 22.81\% \\ 17.14\% \\ \hline 39.95\% \end{array}$$

(iv) *Aggregate increases in taxes.* The aggregate increases in taxes are $134.94 ($49.94 + $42.50 + $42.50).

(v) *Interest charge.* Interest on each of the three increases in tax ($49.94, $42.50, and $42.50) is computed using the rates and method provided in section 6621 for the respective interest period. The following are the interest periods:

	Interest Period	
Beginning on		Ending on
March 15, 1988		March 15, 1991
March 15, 1989		March 15, 1991
March 15, 1990		March 15, 1991

(B) *Calculation of the other increases in tax.* The highest statutory rate of tax applicable to A that was in effect for both 1988 and 1989 is 28 percent. The increase in tax for each of 1988 and 1989 is $27.86 ($99.50 × 28%).

(C) *Calculation of the aggregate increases in taxes.* The aggregate increases in taxes are $94.03 ($38.31 + 27.86 + 27.86).

(iii) *Calculation of the aggregate amount of interest.* For purposes of calculating the aggregate amount of interest, the reduction provided under section 1366(f)(2) is disregarded and the excess distribution is $500. Accordingly, for purposes of calculating the aggregate amount of interest, $125 is allocated to 1987, 1988, and 1989.

(A) *Calculation of the 1987 hypothetical increase in tax.* The highest statutory rate of tax applicable to A that was in effect in 1987 was 38.5 percent. The hypothetical increase in tax for the portion of the excess distribution allocated to 1987 is $48.12 ($125 × 38.5%).

(B) *Calculation of the other hypothetical increases in tax.* The highest statutory rate of tax applicable to A that was in effect for both 1988 and 1989 is 28 percent. The hypothetical increase in tax for each of 1988 and 1989 is $35.00 ($125 × 28%).

(C) *Interest charge.* Interest on each of the three hypothetical increases in tax ($48.12, $35, and $35) is computed using the rates and method provided in section 6621 for the respective interest period. The following are the interest periods:

	Interest Period	
Beginning on		Ending on
April 15, 1988		April 15, 1991
April 15, 1989		April 15, 1991
April 15, 1990		April 15, 1991.

holder directly or indirectly owns stock. For purposes of this section, an S corporation is treated as a partnership, and its shareholders as partners of the partnership. *See* section 1373.

(b) *Distributions from section 1291 funds to shareholders that are not entitled to a foreign tax credit for foreign taxes deemed paid.*—(1) *Rule.*—If a section 1291 fund makes a distribution with respect to which a shareholder (other than a shareholder described in paragraph (c) of this section) is subject to tax under §1.1291-2, and the shareholder would be entitled to a foreign tax credit for foreign taxes paid (including withholding taxes) with respect to such distribution, but not for foreign taxes deemed paid with respect to such distribution (determined in both cases without regard to section 1291 and this section), the foreign tax credit with respect to that distribution is determined under the steps provided in this paragraph (b). The excess distribution is treated as foreign source income described in section 904(d)(1)(A).

Foreign taxes paid with respect to the total distribution   × $\dfrac{\text{Total excess distribution}}{\text{Total distribution}}$

The remainder of the creditable foreign taxes are allocated to the nonexcess distribution.

(ii) *Step 2.*—The shareholder allocates the total excess distribution and the excess distribution taxes ratably to each distribution received during the shareholder's taxable year in the manner provided in § 1.1291-2 (c)(4). The shareholder then allocates each excess distribution and the excess distribution taxes allocated to that distribution to each taxable year included in the shareholder's holding period based on the number of days in each such taxable year.

(iii) *Step 3.*—The shareholder determines the tentative increase in tax for each prior PFIC year. The term tentative increase in tax means the increase in tax determined in the manner provided in § 1.1291-4(c) for each prior PFIC year. The tentative increase in tax for a prior PFIC year is the foreign tax credit limitation for the excess distribution taxes allocated to that prior PFIC year.

(iv) *Step 4.*—The shareholder claims as a foreign tax credit with respect to an increase in tax for a prior PFIC year the lesser of the tentative increase in tax for that year determined in *Step 3* or the excess distribution taxes allocated to that prior PFIC year in *Step 2*.

(v) *Step 5.*—The shareholder determines the net increase in tax for each prior PFIC year by reducing the tentative increase in tax for a prior PFIC year determined in *Step 3* by the foreign tax credit determined for that year in *Step 4*. For the calculation of the interest charge for each net increase in tax, see § 1.1291-4(d).

(vi) *Step 6.*—The portions of the excess distribution and excess distribution taxes allocated to the current shareholder year and pre-PFIC years, if any, as well as the creditable foreign taxes allocated to the nonexcess distribution, are taken into account in the current shareholder year under the general foreign tax credit rules.

(2) *Carryovers disallowed.*—The amount by which the excess distribution taxes allocated to a prior PFIC year exceed the tentative increase in tax for that year may not be claimed as a foreign tax credit against any federal income tax.

(c) *Distributions from section 1291 funds that are CFCs.*—(1) *Rule.*—If a controlled foreign corporation (CFC) (as defined in

$\dfrac{\text{Distribution allocable to a separate category (including gross-up) (Step 1(A))}}{\text{Total distribution (including gross-up)}}$

(iii) *Step 3.*—The shareholder determines the U.S. source portion of each separate category excess distribution as follows:

$\dfrac{\text{U.S. source portion of distribution allocable to a separate category (Step 1(C))}}{\text{Total distribution allocable to that category (Step 1 (A))}}$

(iv) *Step 4.*—The shareholder determines the excess distribution taxes with respect to each separate category (separate category excess distribution taxes) as follows:

$\dfrac{\text{Creditable foreign taxes with respect to the distribution and allocable to the separate category (Step 1 (B))}}{}$

(v) *Step 5.*—(A) The shareholder allocates—
    (1) The separate category excess distribution;
    (2) The separate category excess distribution taxes; and
    (3) The U.S. source portion of the separate category excess distribution ratably to each distribution received during the shareholder's taxable year in the manner provided in § 1.1291-2(c)(4).
    (B) The shareholder then allocates—
    (1) The amount determined in *Step 5* (A)(1) for each distribution to each taxable year included in the shareholder's holding period based on the number of days in each such taxable year;
    (2) The amount determined in *Step 5* (A)(2) for each distribution to each taxable year included in the shareholder's holding period based on the number of days in each such taxable year; and
    (3) The amount determined in *Step 5* (A)(3) for each distribution to each taxable year included in the shareholder's holding period based on the number of days in each such taxable year.

(i) *Step 1.*—The shareholder determines the total excess distribution under § 1.1291-2 (c)(3), and the excess distribution taxes. The excess distribution taxes are the creditable foreign taxes (within the meaning of section 1291(g)(2)(A)), paid or accrued with respect to the total distribution for the current shareholder year, allocated to the total excess distribution as follows:

section 904(d)(4)) that is a section 1291 fund makes a distribution with respect to which a United States shareholder (also as defined in section 904(d)(4)) is subject to tax under § 1.1291-2, the foreign tax credit with respect to that excess distribution is determined by applying the rules of section 1291(g) on a separate category basis within the meaning of section 904. *See* section 904(d)(3)(A) and the regulations under that section. A distribution described in this paragraph (c) from a section 1291 fund is foreign source income except to the extent the distribution is determined to be derived from U.S. sources pursuant to section 904(g). The foreign tax credit of a United States shareholder with respect to a distribution by a CFC that is taxable as an excess distribution to the shareholder under § 1.1291-2(e)(2) is determined according to the following steps.

(i) *Step 1.*—The shareholder determines—
    (A) The separate category or categories (as defined in § 1.904-5(a)(1)) to which the total distribution (including the amount of the gross-up determined under section 78) for the taxable year is allocable under the rules of section 904(d)(3) and the regulations under that section (see § 1.904-5(c)(4));
    (B) The creditable foreign taxes, which are the foreign taxes paid or deemed paid on the distribution (determined without regard to section 1291 and this section) with respect to each separate category under the rules of sections 901, 902, 904, and 960 and the regulations under those sections (see § 1.904-6(b)(3)); and
    (C) The portion of the total distribution (including the gross-up) in each separate category that is from U.S. sources pursuant to section 904(g) (see § 1.904-5(m)(4) and (6)).
Solely for purposes of section 1291, any portion of the total excess distribution that would not be allocated to a separate category under normally applicable rules because it exceeds the fund's earnings and profits is deemed to be foreign source income allocated to the separate category defined in section 904(d)(1)(A).

(ii) *Step 2.*—The shareholder determines—
    (A) The total excess distribution under § 1.1291-2(c)(3) with respect to the total distribution (including the gross-up); and
    (B) The portion of the total excess distribution allocable to each separate category (the separate category excess distribution). Each separate category excess distribution is calculated as follows:

×   Total excess distribution(*Step 2 (A)*)

×   Separate category excess distribution (*Step 2 (B)*)

× $\dfrac{\text{Separate category excess distribution (Step 2 (B))}}{\text{Total distribution allocable to that category (Step 1 (A))}}$

Solely for purposes of determining the foreign tax credit limitation for the current shareholder year, the portion of an excess distribution that is allocated to the current shareholder year and prePFIC years, and included in income, is treated as a dividend from a CFC that is not a PFIC. The excess distribution taxes allocated to that portion of the excess distribution are treated as foreign taxes paid with respect to a dividend from a CFC that is not a PFIC and taken into account in the current shareholder year under general foreign tax credit rules.

(vi) *Step 6.*—The shareholder determines a tentative increase in tax for each prior PFIC year for each allocation of a separate category excess distribution determined under *Step 5* (B)(1) (separate category tentative increase in tax).

(vii) *Step 7.*—The shareholder determines a foreign tax credit limitation for each prior PFIC year to which the separate category excess distribution is allocated. The limitation is determined as follows:

Separate category tentative increase in tax for prior PFIC year
(*Step 6*)

×

$$\frac{\text{Foreign source separate category excess distribution allocated to that prior PFIC year }(Step\ 5\ (B)(1) - Step\ 5\ (B)(3))}{\text{Separate category excess distribution allocated to that prior PFIC year }(Step\ 5\ (B)(1))}$$

(viii) *Step 8.*—The shareholder may claim a foreign tax credit for each separate category tentative increase in tax. The foreign tax credit for a prior PFIC year is the lesser of the foreign tax credit limitation determined in *Step 7* for the prior PFIC year or the amount of the separate category excess distribution taxes allocated to that prior PFIC year under *Step 5* (B)(2).

(ix) *Step 9.*—The shareholder determines the separate category net increase in tax for each prior PFIC year by reducing the separate category tentative increase in tax determined for that year in *Step 6* by the amount of the foreign tax credit determined for that year in *Step 8*. For the calculation of the interest charge on each net increase in tax, *see* § 1.1291-4(d).

(2) *Carryovers disallowed.*—The amount by which the excess distribution taxes allocated to a prior PFIC year exceed the separate category tentative increase in tax for that year may not be claimed as a foreign tax credit against any federal income tax.

(3) *Example.*—The following example illustrates the rules of paragraph (c) of this section.

Example. (i) *Facts.* USP, a domestic corporation, has been a United States shareholder of FC, a CFC that is a section 1291 fund, since December 31, 1986. USP and FC both use the calendar year as their taxable year. USP has not included any amount in income under section 951 with respect to FC. On March 31, 1989, FC distributed $1000 to USP. As of that date, USP had held the FC stock for 821 days (365 days in 1987, 366 days in 1988, and 90 days in 1989). USP elects to credit foreign taxes for 1989, and determines the total creditable taxes with respect to the distribution from FC to be $485, $425 of which are deemed paid taxes and $60 of which are withholding taxes. The total distribution for 1989, including the section 78 gross-up, is $1425.

(ii) *Step 1: Determination of separate category income, U.S. source portions, and foreign taxes.* Applying the look through rules of section 904(d)(3), USP determines that $1125 of the total distribution of $1425 is allocable to distributions from a noncontrolled section 902 corporation, and that the remaining $300 is allocable to general limitation income. USP determines that $390 of creditable foreign taxes were paid and deemed paid with respect to the distributions from the noncontrolled section 902 corporation, and $95 were paid and deemed paid with respect to the general limitation income. USP determines that the distributions from the noncontrolled section 902 corporation and the general limitation income are from foreign sources. Accordingly, *Steps 3* and *5* (A)(3) will not be performed.

(iii) *Step 2: Calculation of total excess distribution and separate category excess distributions.* USP determines, based on FC distributions during the preceding three taxable years, that the total excess distribution for the current taxable year is $800. Of that amount, $631.58 [[$1125 (distribution allocable to distributions from a noncontrolled section 902 corporation)/$1425 (total distribution)] × $800 (total excess distribution)] is allocable to distributions from a noncontrolled section 902 corporation, and $168.42 [[$300 (distribution allocable to general limitation income)/$1425 (total distribution)] × $800 (total excess distribution)] is allocable to general limitation income.

(iv) *Step 4: Calculation of separate category excess distribution taxes.* USP calculates the excess distribution taxes (EDT) allocable to the separate category excess distributions. The noncontrolled section 902 corporation excess distribution taxes are $218.95 [$390 (creditable foreign taxes paid and deemed paid with respect to distributions from a noncontrolled section 902 corporation) × [$631.58 (noncontrolled section 902 corporation excess distribution)/$1125 (distribution from noncontrolled section 902 corporation)]], and the general limitation income excess distribution taxes are $53.33 [$95 (creditable foreign taxes paid and deemed paid with respect to general limitation income) × [$168.42 (general limitation income excess distribution)/$300 (distribution allocable to general limitation income)]].

(v) *Step 5: Allocations of separate category excess distributions and excess distribution taxes over holding period.* The separate category excess distributions and the separate category EDT are allocated to each taxable year in USP's holding period based on the number of days in each such taxable year. (Discrepancies may be observed in the following presentation. These discrepancies reflect rounding to the nearest penny of the different calculations performed.)

(A) *Noncontrolled section 902 corporation excess distribution:* $.77 of the noncontrolled section 902 corporation excess distribution ($631.58/821 days) and $.27 of EDT ($218.95/821 days) are allocated to each day. The allocations to each taxable year are as follows:

Taxable year in holding period	Allocations to taxable year	
	Excess distribution	EDT
1987 (365 days)	$281.05	$98 55
1988 (366 days)	281.82	98.82
1989 (90 days)	69.30	24.30

(B) General limitation excess distribution: $.21 of the general limitation excess distribution ($168.42/821 days) and $.065 of EDT ($53.33/821 days) are allocated to each day. The allocations to each taxable year are as follows:

Taxable year in holding period	Allocations to taxable year	
	Excess distribution	EDT
1987 (365 days)	$76.65	$23.73
1988 (366 days)	76.86	23.79
1989 (90 days)	18.90	5.85

(vi) *Step 6: Calculation of separate category tentative increases in taxes.* USP determines the tentative increases in tax (TIIT) for the allocations of each separate category excess distribution to 1987 and 1988, the prior PFIC years in USP's holding period. The noncontrolled section 902 corporation excess distribution TIIT for 1987 is $112.28 [$281.05 (allocation of noncontrolled section 902 corporation excess distribution to 1987) × 39.95% (the highest corporate tax rate in effect in 1987], and for 1988, $95.82 [$281.82 (allocation of noncontrolled section 902 corporation excess distribution to 1988) × 34% (highest corporate tax rate in effect in 1988)]. The general limitation excess distribution TIIT for 1987 is $30.62 [$76.65 (allocation of general limitation income excess distribution to 1987) × 39.95% (highest corporate tax rate in effect in 1987], and for 1988, $26.13 [$76.86 (allocation of general limitation income excess distribution to 1988) × 34% (highest corporate tax rate in effect in 1988)].

(vii) *Step 7: Calculation of the foreign tax credit limitations.* USP determines the foreign tax credit (FTC) limitations for each prior PFIC year on a separate category basis. The FTC limitations are the same as the tentative increases in tax because none of the separate category distributions are from U.S. sources. Therefore, the FTC limitation for the noncontrolled section 902 corporation excess distribution for 1987 is $112.28, and for 1988, $95.82. The FTC limitation for the general limitation excess distribution for 1987 is $30.62, and for 1988, $26.13.

(viii) *Step 8: Calculation of the foreign tax credit.* The FTC for the noncontrolled section 902 corporation excess distribution for 1987 is $98.55 [lower of $112.28 (1987 noncontrolled section 902 corporation FTC limitation) and $98.55 (1987 noncontrolled section 902 corporation EDT)], and for 1988, $95.82 [lower of $95.82 (1988 noncontrolled section 902 corporation FTC limitation) and $98.82 (1988 noncontrolled section 902 corporation EDT)]. The FTC for the general limitation excess distribution for 1987 is $23.73 [lower of $30.62 (1987 general limitation FTC limitation) and $23.73 (1987 general limitation income EDT)], and for 1988 is $23.79 [lower of $26.13 (1988 general limitation income FTC limitation) and $23.79 (1988 general limitation EDT)].

(ix) *Step 9: Calculation of the separate category net increases in taxes.* As provided in § 1.1291-4(c)(3), USP determines the net increase in tax (NIIT) for each separate category excess distribution allocated to a prior PFIC year. The noncontrolled section 902 corporation NIIT for 1987 is $13.73 [$112.28 (1987 noncontrolled section 902 corporation TIIT) less $98.55 (1987 noncontrolled section 902 corporation FTC)], and the noncontrolled section 902 corporation NIIT for 1988 is 0 [$95.82 (1988 noncontrolled section 902 corporation TIIT) less $95.82 (1988 noncontrolled section 902 corporation FTC)]. The general limitation income NIIT for 1987 is $6.89 [$30.62 (1987 general limitation income TIIT) less $23.73 (1987 general limitation income FTC)], and the general limitation NIIT for 1988 is $2.34 [$26.13 (1988 general limitation income TIIT) less $23.79 (1988 general limitation income FTC)]. An interest charge is calculated for each NIIT as provided in § 1.1291-4(d). The $3 excess of noncontrolled section 902 EDT allocated to 1988 ($98.82) over the FTC limitation calculated for the 1988 allocation of the noncontrolled section 902 excess distribution ($95.82) may not be used to reduce any federal income tax. The calculations of *Steps 5* through *9* are summarized as follows:

(A) *Noncontrolled section 902 corporation excess distribution—*

Taxable year (days) in holding period	Excess distribution	EDT	Step 6 TIIT	Step 8 FTC	Step 9 NIIT
	Allocations to taxable year—Step 5				
1987 (365)	$281.05	$98.55	$112.28	$98.55	$13.73
1988 (366)	281.82	98.82	95.82	95.82	0
1989 (90)	69.30	24.30			

(B) *General limitation income excess distribution—*

Taxable year (days) in holding period	Excess distribution	EDT	Step 6 TIIT	Step 8 FTC	Step 9 NIIT
	Allocations to taxable year—Step 5				
1987 (365)	$76.65	$23.73	$30.62	$23.73	$6.89
1988 (366)	76.86	23.79	26.13	23.79	2.34
1989 (90)	69.30	24.30			

(x) *Current shareholder year foreign tax credit*. The allocations of the separate category excess distributions to 1989, the current shareholder year, are included in USP's ordinary income. Such income is treated as a dividend from a CFC that is not a PFIC, and the EDT allocated to that income are treated as foreign taxes paid with respect to a dividend from a CFC that is not a PFIC.

(d) *Distributions from section 1291 funds that are noncontrolled section 902 corporations.*—If a noncontrolled section 902 corporation (as defined in section 904(d)(2)(E) and the regulations under that section) that is a section 1291 fund makes a distribution with respect to which a domestic shareholder (as defined in section 902 and the regulations under that section) is subject to tax under §1.1291-2, the rules of paragraph (c) of this section apply for purposes of determining the amount of the foreign tax credit with respect to that distribution; however, the only separate category is described in section 904(d)(1)(E). This paragraph (d) does not apply to a United States shareholder of a CFC to whom paragraph (c) of this section applies.

(e) *Section 1248 gain.*—For purposes of determining the foreign tax credit under this section, a shareholder treats gain from a disposition of stock of a section 1291 fund as a distribution only to the extent that the gain would be, but for section 1291, includible in gross income as a dividend under section 1248. [Reg. §1.1291-5.]

§1.1291-6. **Nonrecognition transfers of stock of section 1291 funds.**—(a) *In general.*—(1) *Scope.*—This section provides rules concerning the recognition of gain by a shareholder on a direct or indirect disposition of stock of a section 1291 fund that results from a transaction in which, but for section 1291 and these regulations, there would not be full recognition of gain under the Code and regulations (the transaction hereinafter referred to as a nonrecognition transfer). This section also provides coordination between section 1291 and other provisions of the Code and regulations under which gain must be recognized in transactions that would otherwise be entitled to nonrecognition.

(2) *Nonrecognition transfers.*—A nonrecognition transfer includes, but is not limited to, a gift, a transfer by reason of death, a distribution to a beneficiary by a trust or estate (other than a distribution to which section 643(e)(3) applies), and a transfer in which gain or loss is not fully recognized pursuant to any of the following provisions: Sections 311(a), 332, 336(e), 337, 351, 354, 355, 361, 721, 731, 852(b)(6), 1036, and 1041.

(3) *Application of section to transfer of stock of a pedigreed QEF.*—This section does not apply to a nonrecognition transfer of stock of a pedigreed QEF. The following example illustrates the rule of this paragraph (a)(3).

Example. X is a U.S. person that is a shareholder of FC, a corporation. FC owns all the stock of FS. Both FC and FS are pedigreed QEFs with respect to X. Pursuant to a plan of complete liquidation, satisfying the requirements of section 332, FS distributes all its assets and liabilities to FC. No gain or loss will be recognized to FC, FS, or X under section 1291(f) or 1297(b)(5).

(b) *Recognition of gain or loss.*—(1) *In general.*—Unless otherwise provided in paragraph (c) of this section, a shareholder recognizes gain on any direct or indirect disposition of stock of a section 1291 fund in accordance with the rules of §1.1291-3, without regard to whether the disposition is a result of a nonrecognition transfer as defined in paragraph (a)(2) of this section.

(2) *Coordination with other recognition provisions.*—A direct or indirect disposition of stock to which an exception to the gain recognition rule of paragraph (b)(1) of this section applies will nevertheless be a disposition taxable under §1.1291-3 if the gain must be recognized pursuant to another provision of the Code or regulations. For coordination with section 367, *see* paragraph (d)(1) of this section.

(3) *No recognition of loss.*—This section does not permit or require the recognition of loss on a direct or indirect disposition of stock of a section 1291 fund if such loss would not otherwise be recognized under another section of the Code or regulations. For the effect on the holding period of a disposition resulting from a nonrec-

ognition transfer that would be subject to the gain recognition rule but for the fact that a loss is realized, *see* paragraph (b)(5) of this section.

(4) *Special basis rules.*—(i) *Direct shareholders.*—If the gain recognition rule of paragraph (b)(1) of this section applies to a nonrecognition transfer in which a direct shareholder transfers stock of a section 1291 fund, proper adjustment is made to the basis of such stock in the hands of the transferee, as well as to the basis of the property, if any, received by the shareholder in the transaction.

(ii) *Indirect shareholders.*—If the gain recognition rule of paragraph (b)(1) of this section applies to a disposition by an indirect shareholder that results from a nonrecognition transfer, the shareholder's adjusted basis of the stock or other property owned directly by the shareholder through which ownership of the section 1291 fund is attributed to the shareholder is increased by the amount of gain recognized by the shareholder. In addition, solely for purposes of determining the subsequent treatment under the Code and regulations of a direct or indirect shareholder of the stock of the section 1291 fund treated as disposed of, the adjusted basis of the actual owner of the stock of the section 1291 fund is increased by the amount of gain recognized by the shareholder.

(iii) *Stock acquired by reason of death.*—Unless all of the gain is recognized to a shareholder (the decedent) pursuant to paragraph (c)(2)(iii)(B) of this section, the basis of stock received on the death of the decedent by the decedent's estate (other than a foreign estate within the meaning of section 7701(a)(31)), or directly by another U.S. person, is the lower of the fair market value or adjusted basis of the transferred stock in the hands of the shareholder immediately before death. If gain is recognized by the decedent, the decedent's adjusted basis of the stock of the section 1291 fund is increased by the gain recognized with respect thereto.

(iv) *Assets distributed in certain subsidiary liquidations.*—The bases of the assets of a section 1291 fund distributed to an 80 percent corporate distributee (within the meaning of section 337(c)), in complete liquidation of the section 1291 fund pursuant to section 332, is increased by the amount by which the gain recognized by the shareholder exceeds the amount that would have been taxed as a dividend under section 367(b). Except as otherwise provided in this paragraph (b)(4)(iv), the adjusted basis of each distributed asset is increased (but not in excess of its fair market value) by a pro rata portion of the excess described in the preceding sentence, based on the realized but unrecognized gain with respect to such asset relative to the realized but unrecognized gain with respect to all distributed assets. For purposes of the preceding sentence, money is not treated as an asset. The adjusted basis of a receivable may not be increased pursuant to this paragraph (b)(4)(iv) to an amount that exceeds the receivable's face amount.

(5) *Special holding period rule for transfers subject to gain recognition rule.*—If a loss is realized on a direct or indirect disposition of stock of a section 1291 fund in a transaction in which any gain, if realized, would have been recognized under this section, the shareholder's holding period for stock received in the transaction, if any, as well as the transferee's holding period of the transferred stock, begins on the day after the disposition, but only for purposes of applying sections 1291 through 1297 to the shareholder or the transferee with respect to such stock, as appropriate.

(c) *Exceptions to general rule.*—(1) *Transfer of section 1291 fund stock for PFIC stock.*—Gain is not recognized on a direct or indirect disposition of stock of a section 1291 fund that results from a nonrecognition transfer if in the transfer, stock of the section 1291 fund, or an interest in another person that causes the shareholder to be an indirect shareholder, is exchanged solely for either—

(i) Stock of the same or another corporation that either qualifies under section 1296(a) as a PFIC for its taxable year that includes the day after the nonrecognition transfer or is the acquiring foreign corporation in a section 368(a)(1)(F) reorganization; or

(ii) An interest in another person that owns directly or indirectly stock of the transferred section 1291 fund or of another

PFIC, but only to the extent (by value) that the shareholder is treated under § 1.1291-1(b)(8) as owning after the transfer at least as great an interest in the section 1291 fund or other PFIC that the indirect shareholder owned before the transfer. Stock in another PFIC owned before the transfer is not taken into account for purposes of the preceding sentence. For the definition of an indirect disposition, *see* generally § 1.1291-3(e)(2).

(2) *Transfer to U.S. person.*—(i) *In general.*—Unless otherwise provided, a shareholder does not recognize gain on a direct or indirect disposition of stock of a section 1291 fund that results from a nonrecognition transfer if immediately after the transfer such stock is owned or considered owned by a U.S. person (U.S. transferee), provided that—

(A) The basis of the stock that is the subject of the disposition, in the hands of its actual owner immediately after the transfer, is no greater than the basis of such stock in the hands of its actual owner immediately before the transfer;

(B) The U.S. transferee's holding period for the transferred stock is at least as long as the holding period of the shareholder immediately before the transfer; and

(C) The aggregate ownership (determined under § 1.1291-1(b)(8)) of the shareholder and the U.S. transferee immediately after the transfer (determined without regard to stock held by the U.S. transferee prior to the transfer) is the same as or greater than the shareholder's proportionate ownership immediately before the transfer.

This paragraph (c)(2)(i) does not apply to a transfer to a partnership, S corporation, trust or estate. For those rules, *see* paragraph (c)(3) of this section.

(ii) *Transitory ownership.*—Gain is not recognized to a domestic corporation that is a party to a reorganization within the meaning of section 368(b) if, pursuant to a plan of reorganization, the corporation acquires stock of a PFIC that is a party to the reorganization in exchange for the domestic corporation's assets, and transfers the PFIC stock under section 361(c) to a shareholder that is a U.S. person in exchange for the shareholder's stock of the domestic corporation.

(iii) *Transfer by reason of death.*—(A) *In general.*—Except as provided in paragraph (c)(2)(iii)(B) of this section, gain is not recognized to a shareholder upon a disposition of stock of a section 1291 fund that results from a nonrecognition transfer to the shareholder's domestic estate or directly to another U.S. person upon the death of the shareholder.

(B) *Exception.*—Gain is recognized to a shareholder on the transfer of stock of a section 1291 fund to the shareholder's domestic estate if, pursuant to the terms of the will, the section 1291 fund stock may be transferred to either a foreign beneficiary or a trust established in the will.

(iv) *Section 355 distribution of stock of section 1291 fund.*—Gain is not recognized to a shareholder that is the distributing corporation upon a direct or indirect disposition of stock of a section 1291 fund that results from the distribution of stock of a controlled corporation to another U.S. person (the distributee) in a transaction qualifying under section 355(a) if the distributee is a shareholder with respect to such stock immediately after the distribution. The distributee in such a transaction takes a holding period in the stock of the controlled corporation equal to the longer of the holding period determined under section 1223(1) or the distributing corporation's holding period of the stock of the controlled corporation. If the controlled corporation is itself the section 1291 fund, the distributee in such a transaction takes a basis in the stock of the controlled corporation equal to the lesser of the adjusted basis determined under section 358 or the distributing corporation's adjusted basis of the stock of the controlled corporation immediately prior to the distribution.

(v) *Gifts incurring gift tax.*—If a shareholder makes a gift of stock of a section 1291 fund to a U.S. person and thereby incurs gift tax, the shareholder will not recognize gain, but will be liable for the deferred tax amount as if the shareholder recognized gain in the amount of the gift tax that is added to the basis of the transferred stock under section 1015(d). The adjusted basis of the transferred stock may only be increased, to the extent provided in section 1015(d), by the amount of gift tax paid. The following example illustrates the rule of this paragraph (c)(2)(v).

Example. M, a U.S. person, purchased 1,000 shares of NQF, a PFIC, on December 31, 1989. M did not elect to treat NQF as a QEF. M gave the NQF stock to her daughter, H, also a U.S. person, on December 31, 1993. M paid $100x of gift tax. As provided in section 1015(a) and (d)(6), H's adjusted basis in the NQF stock is M's adjusted basis, increased by $60x of gift tax paid. As a result, pursuant to § 1.1291-6(c)(2)(v), M is liable for the deferred tax amount that

M would have owed if M recognized $60x of gain on a taxable transfer of the NQF stock. For purposes of calculating the deferred tax amount, the $60x is allocated over M's four-year holding period, with the deferred tax amount calculated with respect to the $45x allocated to 1991, 1992, and 1993. Other than for the $60x of gift tax paid, there are no further adjustments to H's basis in the NQF.

(vi) *Exception inapplicable.*—Paragraph (c)(2) of this section does not apply to a disposition of stock of a section 1291 fund that results from a nonrecognition transfer of stock of a section 1291 fund if the U.S. transferee is—

(A) An organization that will not be subject to section 1291 and these regulations pursuant to § 1.1291-1(e) with respect to that section 1291 fund; or

(B) A trust, including a testamentary trust or other irrevocable trust, that is not a grantor trust or beneficiary-owned section 678 trust to which paragraph (c)(3)(iv) of this section applies.

(3) *Transfers involving pass-through entities.*—(i) *Section 721 transfer to partnership.*—Gain is not recognized to a shareholder on a disposition of stock of a section 1291 fund that results from a transfer to a partnership under section 721, but only to the extent that the shareholder is treated as owning such stock immediately after the transfer pursuant to § 1.1291-1(b)(8)(iii)(A).

(ii) *Section 731 distribution by partnership.*—Gain is not recognized to a partner on a disposition of stock of a section 1291 fund that results from a distribution under section 731, but only to the extent that the partner is treated as owning such stock immediately after the distribution pursuant to § 1.1291-1(b)(8).

(iii) *Transfer to S corporation.*—Gain is not recognized to a shareholder on a disposition of stock of a section 1291 fund that results from a transfer to an S corporation under section 351, but only to the extent that the shareholder is treated as owning such stock immediately after the transfer pursuant to § 1.1291-1(b)(8)(iii)(B).

(iv) *Transfer to grantor trust.*—Gain is not recognized on a disposition of stock of a section 1291 fund that results from a nonrecognition transfer to a trust by the grantor of the trust if the grantor is treated as owning the portion of the trust that includes both the income and corpus portions of the stock that is disposed of. If a person other than the grantor is treated as the owner of the portion of a beneficiary-owned section 678 trust that includes the income and corpus portions of the stock transferred to the trust, that person is treated as acquiring the stock by gift from the grantor, which is a transfer subject to the general rules of this section. Stock owned directly or indirectly by a grantor of a grantor trust or by a beneficiary of a beneficiary-owned section 678 trust will be treated as transferred by the grantor or other person considered the owner thereof for purposes of this section at the time the grantor or beneficiary is no longer considered the owner of both the income and corpus portions of the stock of the section 1291 fund. For special rules applicable to a grantor or beneficiary-owned section 678 trust, *see* sections 671 through 679 and the regulations under those sections.

(4) *Transfer to nonresident alien spouse who files joint return.*—Gain is not recognized on a disposition of stock of a section 1291 fund that results from a nonrecognition transfer to the shareholder's nonresident alien spouse who has made the election under section 6013(g) and is treated as a resident for purposes of chapter 1 of the Code. A termination of the election pursuant to section 6013(g)(4) will be treated as a disposition of the stock by the transferee spouse as provided in § 1.1291-3(b)(2).

(d) *Special rules.*—(1) *Section 367 or 1492 transfer.*—(i) *Gain recognition transfer.*—If the gain recognition rule of paragraph (b)(1) of this section applies to a disposition of stock of a section 1291 fund that results from a transfer with respect to which section 367 or 1492 requires the shareholder to recognize gain or include an amount in income as a distribution under section 301, the gain realized on the transfer is taxable as an excess distribution as provided in § 1.1291-2(e)(2). The excess, if any, of the amount to be included in income pursuant to section 367(b) over the gain realized is taxable as provided in the regulations under section 367(b).

(ii) *Disposition to which exception applies.*—If an exception to the gain recognition rule of paragraph (b)(1) of this section applies to a disposition to which section 367(b) applies, and section 367(b) requires the shareholder to include an amount in income as a distribution taxable under section 301, that amount is an excess distribution taxable as provided in § 1.1291-2(e)(2).

(2) *Taxable year of disposition by reason of death.*—A disposition of stock of a section 1291 fund by reason of a shareholder's death, to which the gain recognition rule of paragraph (b)(1) or (c)(2)(iii)(B) of this section applies, will be treated as a disposition by the shareholder effected immediately before death and taxable to the shareholder in the shareholder's last taxable year.

(3) *Section 643(e)(3) election.*—An election by a foreign estate or trust under section 643(e)(3) will not apply to stock of a section 1291 fund distributed to a U.S. person if the gain recognized by reason of the election is not taxable in the United States.

(e) *Receipt of nonqualifying property.*—If a nonrecognition transfer results in a disposition of stock of a section 1291 fund to which an exception to the gain recognition rule of paragraph (b)(1) of this section would apply but for the fact that the property received in the transfer includes money or property (nonqualifying property) in addition to property permitted to be received pursuant to paragraph (c) of this section, gain is recognized only to the extent of the nonqualifying property. If such nonqualifying property is treated as a distribution by the section 1291 fund under otherwise applicable provisions of the Code, the distribution will be taxable on an excess distribution as provided in §1.1291-2(e)(2).

(f) *Examples.*—The following examples illustrate the operation of this section.

Example 1. A is a shareholder of PFIC, a corporation organized under the laws of Country X. PFIC is a section 1291 fund with respect to A. To avoid expropriation of the assets of PFIC by the government of Country X, PFIC's management has decided to relocate to Country Y. To effect the relocation, PFIC adopted a plan of reorganization pursuant to which PFIC will transfer all of its assets to Newco, a newly organized Country Y corporation, in exchange for Newco stock and the assumption of PFIC's liabilities in a transaction that will qualify as a reorganization described in section 368(a)(1)(F). PFIC will distribute the Newco stock to its shareholders in exchange for its stock. A will transfer all of its PFIC stock in exchange for Newco stock of equal value. A will not recognize gain on the transfer of PFIC stock in exchange for Newco stock pursuant to section 354 and §1.1291-6(c)(1)(i), and the days in A's holding period of the Newco stock will retain the prePFIC and prior PFIC character of the days in A's holding period of the PFIC stock pursuant to §1.1291-1(h)(7). *See* §1.1291-1(b)(1)(ii).

Example 2. X is a domestic corporation that owns 75 percent of F, a foreign corporation that is not a PFIC. F owns 100 percent of the stock of FS, a PFIC. X is treated under §1.1291-1(b)(8)(ii)(A) as owning 75 percent of the stock of FS. X has not elected under section 1295 to treat FS as a QEF. FC, a foreign corporation, will acquire substantially all the assets of F in exchange for FC stock and the assumption of the liabilities of F in a transaction that will qualify as a reorganization described in section 368(a)(1)(C). FC never qualified as a PFIC and will not qualify as a PFIC at the beginning of the day after the transaction. F will distribute the FC stock to its shareholders in exchange for their F stock. X will transfer all its F stock to F in exchange for FC stock of equal value. After the reorganization, X will hold 49 percent of the outstanding FC stock, and therefore will no longer be treated under §1.1291-1(b)(8)(ii)(A) as owning stock of FS. Pursuant to §§1.1291-6(b)(1) and 1.1291-3(e)(1), X will be taxed on the indirect disposition of the FS stock.

Example 3. X, a domestic corporation, owns stock of PFIC, a corporation that is a section 1291 fund with respect to X. Pursuant to a plan of reorganization, X will transfer to FC, a foreign corporation, substantially all of its assets in exchange for FC voting stock and FC's assumption of the liabilities of X in a transaction that will qualify as a reorganization described in section 368(a)(1)(C). It is assumed that the transaction is not taxable under section 367(a) (including section 367(a)(5)). X will distribute the FC stock to its shareholders in exchange for their X stock. FC is not a PFIC and will not qualify as a PFIC for the taxable year that includes the day after the transfer. In addition, after the reorganization, no U.S. person will own 50 percent or more of FC. Pursuant to §1.1291-6(b)(1), section 361(a) will not apply to X's transfer of the PFIC stock to FC. X therefore will recognize the gain realized on the transfer of the stock of PFIC. The gain will be taxed to X as an excess distribution pursuant to §1.1291-3.

Example 4. X, a domestic corporation, satisfies the stock ownership requirements specified in section 332(b) with respect to PFIC, a corporation that is a section 1291 fund with respect to X. Pursuant to a plan of complete liquidation, PFIC will distribute all its assets and liabilities to X in exchange for its stock and liquidate. Pursuant to §1.1291-6(b)(1) and (d)(1)(i), section 332(a) will not apply to the complete liquidation of PFIC. X therefore will recognize gain on the disposition of the stock of PFIC, which gain will be taxed as an excess distribution pursuant to §1.1291-3. The adjusted basis of the assets of X will be increased as provided in §1.1291-6(b)(4)(iv).

Example 5. USP, a domestic corporation, owns all the stock of USS, also a domestic corporation. USS owns stock of FS, a corporation that is a section 1291 fund with respect to USS. Pursuant to a plan of reorganization that will qualify under section 368(a)(1)(C), USS will transfer substantially all its assets to FC, a PFIC, in exchange for FC stock and the assumption by FC of the liabilities of USS. USS will transfer the FC stock to USP in exchange for its stock. Pursuant to §1.1291-6(c)(1), section 361 applies to USS's transfer to FC of the FS stock. As provided in §1.1291-6(c)(2)(ii), USS will not recognize any gain on the transfer of the FC stock to USP in exchange for its stock.

Example 6. A, a U.S. person, owns all the stock of FC, a corporation that is both a controlled foreign corporation and a section 1291 fund with respect to A. Pursuant to a reorganization plan, FC will transfer all its assets to F, a foreign corporation that is a PFIC but not a controlled foreign corporation after the transfer, in exchange for F stock and the assumption of FC's liabilities in a transaction that will qualify as a reorganization described in section 368(a)(1)(C). FC will distribute the F stock to A in exchange for A's FC stock. A will not recognize gain on the transfer of FC stock in exchange for F stock pursuant to section 354 and §1.1291-6(c)(1). However, the regulations under section 367(b) require A to include a certain amount in gross income as a distribution taxable under section 301. As provided in §1.1291-6(d)(1)(ii), A will treat that amount as an excess distribution taxable as provided in §1.1291-2(e)(2).

Example 7. M, a U.S. person, purchased 100 shares of the stock of NQF on December 31, 1989, for $100. NQF is a corporation that is a section 1291 fund with respect to M. On January 1, 1992, when the 100 shares of NQF stock had a fair market value of $200, M transferred its NQF stock to P, a domestic partnership, of which M and N, also a U.S. person, are equal partners. After the transfer to P, M will be considered to own only 50 shares of the NQF stock pursuant to §1.1291-1(b)(8)(iii)(A), notwithstanding that gain recognized with respect to all 100 shares would be allocated to M pursuant to section 704(c). M therefore is taxable on the disposition of 50 shares of NQF stock in accordance with §1.1291-6(c)(3)(i).

(g) *Reporting requirements for transfers entitled to nonrecognition treatment under this section.*—If an exception to the gain recognition rule of paragraph (b)(1) of this section applies wholly or partly to a disposition of stock of a section 1291 fund that results from a nonrecognition transfer, the shareholder must provide the following information in an attachment to Form 8621, which must be filed with the shareholder's federal income tax return for the taxable year in which the transfer occurs:

(1) A complete description of the transfer, including a complete description of the stock, securities or other property received directly or indirectly in the transfer.

(2) The name, address, and taxpayer identification number (if available) of the transferor and transferee of the transferred property.

(3) A statement citing the applicable exception to the gain recognition rule and stating why the exception is applicable.

(h) *Transfers involving QEF stock.*—For rules concerning the effect of a transfer of stock of a QEF on the section 1295 election, *see* §1.1295-1. [Reg. §1.1291-6.]

§1.1291-7. Section 1291(e) rules similar to section 1246.—[Reserved]

Passive Foreign Investment Companies: Qualified Electing Funds: Shareholders

Passive Foreign Investment Companies: Qualified Electing Funds: Shareholders.—Reproduced below is the text of proposed Reg. §1.1293-1, relating to the taxation of shareholders of certain passive foreign investment companies (PFICs) upon payment of distributions by such companies or upon the disposition of stock of such companies (published in the Federal Register on April 1, 1992) (INTL-941-86; INTL-656-87; INTL-704-87). Reg. §§1.1291-0, 1.1291-9 and 1.1291-10 were adopted by T.D. 8701 on December 26, 1996. Proposed Reg. §1.1291-8 was withdrawn on February 2, 1999.

☐ Par. 6. Section 1.1293-1 is added to read as follows:

§1.1293-1. Current taxation of income from qualified electing funds. (a) *In general.*—Pursuant to section 1293(a)(1), every U.S. person that is a direct or indirect shareholder of a PFIC during a taxable year of the PFIC for which the shareholder has in effect a section 1295 election (within the meaning of §1.1295-1(a)) includes in gross income the shareholder's pro rata share of the ordinary earnings and net capital gain of such fund for that taxable year. Such amounts are included in income in the taxable year of the shareholder in which or with which the taxable year of the PFIC ends. Section 1293 applies to a shareholder of a pedigreed QEF (as defined in § 1.1291-1(b)(2)(ii)) only for those taxable years during which the corporation qualifies as a PFIC under section 1296(a). Section 1293 applies to a shareholder of an unpedigreed QEF (as defined in § 1.1291-1(b)(2)(iii)) for those taxable years during which the corporation is a PFIC (as defined in § 1.1291-1(b)(1)).

(b) *Other rules.*—[Reserved][Reg. § 1.1293-1.]

PFICs: Shareholders: Qualified Electing Fund Elections

PFICs: Shareholders: Qualified Electing Fund Elections.—**Reg. § 1.1293-2, relating to permitting certain shareholders to make a special election under Code Sec. 1295, in lieu of the election currently provided for under that section, with respect to certain preferred shares of a passive foreign investment company (PFIC), is proposed (published in the Federal Register on December 24, 1996) (REG-209040-88).**

☐ Par. 2. Section 1.1293-2 is added to read as follows:

§ 1.1293-2. Special inclusion rules for special preferred QEF election.—(a) *In general.*—A shareholder (including a shareholder that is a pass-through entity, as described in § 1.1295-2(c)(1)) that makes a special preferred QEF election under § 1.1295-2 must, regardless of the shareholder's method of accounting, include in income in respect of each share subject to the election, an annual amount (preferred QEF amount) determined according to the rules of paragraph (b) of this section. A shareholder that makes a special preferred QEF election must include the preferred QEF amount in income under this section for each year in which the taxpayer continues to hold a share that is subject to the election. The rules of this section apply in lieu of the general rules of section 1293 and § 1.1293-1.[1]

(b) *Preferred QEF amount.*—(1) *In general.*—The preferred QEF amount for any share subject to a special preferred QEF election is the sum of the ratable daily portion of each periodic dividend amount (as described in paragraph (b)(2) of this section) on the share for the taxable year of the shareholder to which that portion relates, plus the preferred discount amount (as defined below), if any, for the taxable year. For purposes of this section, the preferred discount amount for a taxable year is the amount that bears the same ratio to the total amount of preferred discount (as described in § 1.1295-2(b)(2)(i)) on the share as the number of days that the taxpayer held the share in the taxable year bears to the number of days after the date the taxpayer acquired the share and up to (and including) the share's redemption date as established under the principles of § 1.305-5(b). Notwithstanding the preceding sentence, the preferred discount amount for a taxable year is zero if the preferred discount on the share at the time of its acquisition by the shareholder was less than an amount equal to 1/4 of 1 percent of the redemption price of the stock, multiplied by the number of complete years from the date of acquisition of the stock to the redemption date of the stock.

(2) *Periodic dividend amount.*—A periodic dividend amount is the amount payable with respect to a share, whether on a cumulative or noncumulative basis, for a period (wholly or partly within the shareholder's taxable year) for which dividends on the share are calculated based upon the redemption or liquidation price of the share multiplied by a fixed percentage rate.

(c) *Special rules of application.*—(1) *Earnings and profits disregarded.*—The amounts to be included in income pursuant to this section are determined without regard to the earnings and profits of the foreign corporation with respect to which the special preferred QEF election applies.

(2) *Year of inclusion.*—The shareholder includes the preferred QEF amount in its taxable year without regard to the taxable year of the foreign corporation with respect to which the special preferred QEF election applies.

(3) *Character of inclusions.*—The shareholder includes all preferred QEF amounts in income as ordinary earnings.

(4) *Treatment of distributions.*—Distributions received by a shareholder on shares subject to a special preferred QEF election that are paid out of earnings and profits of the foreign corporation are not included in gross income of the shareholder to the extent the distributions do not exceed the preferred QEF amounts (other than any portion of preferred QEF amounts consisting of preferred discount amounts) previously includible in income pursuant to this section. These distributions will, however, be treated as dividends for all other purposes of the Code and regulations. Amounts distributed to a shareholder with respect to shares subject to a special preferred QEF election that exceed amounts previously included in income under this section with respect to such shares are treated for all purposes of the Code and regulations as a distribution of property subject to the rules of section 301.

(5) *Basis adjustment rules.*—The adjusted basis of a shareholder in shares that are subject to a special preferred QEF election shall be—

(i) Increased by any amount that is included in the gross income of the shareholder under paragraph (a) of this section; and

(ii) Decreased by any dividends (not to exceed the amount included in gross income under paragraph (a) of this section) actually paid to the shareholder in respect of such shares.

(6) *Effect limited to electing shareholder.*—This section does not apply to the foreign corporation with respect to which a special preferred QEF election applies. Accordingly, the provisions of this section will not affect the foreign corporation's calculation of its earnings and profits for any purpose of the Code or regulations. In addition, the rules of this section apply only for purposes of determining the tax consequences for holders of shares subject to the election. Thus, the election shall have no effect on the application of the Code or regulations with respect to the tax consequences of the ownership of shares that are not subject to the election, including for purposes of determining whether any distributions from the foreign corporation with respect to such shares should be treated as having been included in the income of any United States person pursuant to section 1293(c) or section 959.

(d) *Examples.*—The following examples illustrate the rules of paragraphs (a), (b) and (c) of this section. Although these examples assume a 30-day month, 360-day year, any reasonable counting method may be used to compute the length of accrual periods. For purposes of simplicity, the relevant amounts as stated are rounded to two decimal places. However, the computations do not reflect any such rounding convention. The examples are as follows:

Example 1. Preferred QEF amount—(i) *Facts.* (A) On May 1, 1998, A, an individual who files his returns on a calendar year basis, purchased for $10,000 in a single secondary market transaction 100 shares of nonconvertible Class A $100 par value preferred stock (the Class A Stock) of FC, a foreign corporation with a taxable year ending on March 31.

(B) The terms of the Class A Stock provide for a mandatory redemption of the Class A Stock by the issuer at par on June 1, 2012. The Class A Stock is not redeemable pursuant to an issuer call or holder put on any other date. Each share of Class A Stock provides for a semi-annual cumulative distribution payable in dollars on June 1 and December 1 equal to one-half the product of the par value of the Class A Stock and the applicable annual dollar LIBOR in effect on the distribution date immediately prior to the relevant distribution date. The shares of the Class A stock are qualified preferred shares in the hands of A. A purchases no other qualified preferred shares of FC during its 1998 or 1999 taxable years.

(C) A made a special preferred QEF election for A's taxable year ended December 31, 1998, which applies to the Class A Stock acquired by A on May 1, 1998. FC is a PFIC under section 1296 for its taxable year ending March 31, 1999, but FC is not a PFIC for its taxable year ending March 31, 2000. FC paid no current dividends on June 1, 1998, and December 1, 1998, paid the June 1, 1999, dividend currently on June 1, 1999, together with accumulated distributions from June 1, 1998, and December 1, 1998, and paid the December 1, 1999, dividend currently on December 1, 1999. The applicable annual LIBOR is 8 percent on December 1, 1997, 7 percent on June 1, 1998, 9 percent on December 1, 1998, 10 percent on June 1, 1999, and 9 percent on December 1, 1999. FC had sufficient earnings and profits, within the meaning of section 312, for its taxable year ending on March 31, 2000, so that actual distributions to all shareholders of Class A Stock in that year were treated as paid out of earnings and profits of FC.

(ii) *Tax consequences to A for A's taxable year ending December 31, 1998.* As required under paragraph (a) of this section, A must include in gross income for its 1998 taxable year the 1998 preferred QEF amount. The preferred QEF amount, as determined under paragraph (b) of this section, for A's 1998 taxable year is the ratable portion of each periodic dividend amount for that year. For 1998, there are three periodic dividend amounts: The periodic dividend amount for the period from December 1, 1997, to June 1, 1998 (periodic dividend amount 1), the periodic dividend amount for the period from June 1, 1998, to December 1, 1998 (periodic dividend amount 2), and the periodic dividend amount for the period from December 1, 1998, to

---

[1] This proposed regulation was published on April 1, 1992, at 57 Fed. Reg. 11024.

June 1, 1999 (periodic dividend amount 3). Periodic dividend amount 1 in respect of each share owned by A is $4 (1/2 multiplied by the applicable annual LIBOR of 8 percent set on December 1, 1997, multiplied by the $100 amount payable on redemption). Because A acquired the shares on May 1, 1998, A's ratable portion of periodic dividend amount 1 for 1998 is approximately $.67 (30/180 multiplied by $4) per share. Periodic dividend amount 2 in respect of each share owned by A is $3.50 (1/2 multiplied by the applicable annual LIBOR of 7 percent set on June 1, 1998, multiplied by $100). Because A owned the shares for the entire period associated with periodic dividend amount 2, A's ratable portion of periodic dividend amount 2 for 1998 is the full $3.50 per share. Periodic dividend amount 3 in respect of each share owned by A is $4.50 (1/2 multiplied by the applicable annual LIBOR of 9 percent set on December 1, 1998, multiplied by $100). Because the portion of 1998 associated with periodic dividend amount 3 is only the month of December, 1998, A's ratable portion of periodic dividend amount 3 for 1998 is approximately $.75 (30/180 multiplied by $4.50). Accordingly, A's preferred QEF amount for 1998 is approximately $4.92 ($.67 + $3.5 + $.75) per share. A must include approximately $492 (approximately $4.92 per share, multiplied by 100 shares) in income as ordinary earnings for its 1998 tax year even though FC paid no actual dividend to shareholders of Class A Stock for the period in 1998 during which A held the Class A Stock.

(iii) *Tax consequences to A for A's taxable year ending December 31, 1999*. As required under paragraph (a) of this section, A includes in gross income for its 1999 taxable year its preferred QEF amount for 1999. The preferred QEF amount, as determined under paragraph (b) of this section, for A's 1999 taxable year is the ratable portion of each periodic dividend amount for that year. For 1999, there are three periodic dividend amounts: The periodic dividend amount for the period from December 1, 1998, to June 1, 1999 (periodic dividend amount 1), the periodic dividend amount for the period from June 1, 1999, to December 1, 1999 (periodic dividend amount 2), and the periodic dividend amount for the period from December 1, 1999, to June 1, 2000 (periodic dividend amount 3). Periodic dividend amount 1 in respect of each share owned by A is $4.50 (1/2 multiplied by the applicable annual LIBOR of 9 percent set on December 1, 1998, multiplied by $100). Because A held each share of Class A Stock for five months in 1999 for the period associated with periodic dividend amount 1, A's ratable portion of periodic dividend amount 1 for 1999 is approximately $3.75 (150/180 multiplied by $4.50). Periodic dividend amount 2 in respect of each share owned by A is $5 (1/2 multiplied by the applicable annual LIBOR of 10 percent set on June 1, 1999, multiplied by $100). Because A owned the share for the entire period associated with periodic dividend amount 2, A's ratable portion of periodic dividend amount 2 for 1999 is the full $5. Periodic dividend amount 3 in respect of each share owned by A is $4.50 (1/2

multiplied by the applicable annual LIBOR of 9 percent set on December 1, 1999, multiplied by $100). Because A held each share of Class A Stock for one month in 1999 for the period associated with periodic dividend amount 3, A's ratable portion of periodic dividend amount 3 for 1999 is approximately $.75 (30/180 multiplied by $4.50). Accordingly, A's preferred QEF amount for 1998 is approximately $9.50 ($3.75 + $5 + $.75). A must include approximately $950 ($9.50 per share, multiplied by 100 shares) in income as ordinary income for its 1999 taxable year even though FC was not a PFIC for FC's taxable year ending in 2000. The current distributions and arrearages actually paid to A with respect to the Class A Stock are not includible in income by A under paragraph (c)(4) of this section because they constitute amounts previously included in income.

Example 2. Preferred Discount—(i) *Facts*. The facts are the same as in *Example 1* except that A acquired the 100 shares of Class A Stock for $9000.

(ii) *Tax Consequences to A for A's taxable year ending December 31, 1998*. (A) Because the Class A Stock is fixed term preferred stock (as described in §1.1295-2(b)(1)(vii)) and A acquired each share of the Class A stock with $10 of preferred discount, as described in §1.1295-2(b)(2), A's preferred QEF amount to be included by A for the taxable year consists of the sum of the ratable daily portion of each periodic dividend amount, as calculated in paragraph (d)(ii) of *Example 1* of this section, plus the preferred discount amount described in paragraph (b)(1) of this section.

(B) The preferred discount amount with respect to each share is approximately $.47 ($10 multiplied by 240 days/5070 days to maturity). A must include approximately $47 ($.47 per share, multiplied by 100 shares), together with the amount calculated in paragraph (d)(ii) of *Example 1* of this section, in income as ordinary earnings for its 1998 tax year even though FC paid no actual dividend to shareholders of Class A Shares for the period in 1998 during which A held the Class A Stock.

(iii) *Tax consequences to A for A's taxable year ending December 31, 1999*. The portion of the preferred discount on each share includible under paragraph (a) of this section is approximately $.71 ($10 multiplied by 360 days/5070 days to maturity). A must include this amount, together with the amount calculated in paragraph (d)(iii) of *Example 1* of this section, in income as ordinary earnings for its 1999 tax year even though FC was not a PFIC for FC's taxable year ending in 2000. The current distributions and arrearages actually paid to A in 1999 with respect to the Class A Stock are not includible in income by A under paragraph (c)(4) of this section, because they constitute amounts previously included in income.

(e) *Effective date*.—The rules under this section apply with respect to qualified preferred stock subject to a special preferred QEF election made after the date that is 30 days after the date of publication of this document as a final regulation. [Reg. §1.1293-2.]

Passive Foreign Investment Companies

Passive Foreign Investment Companies: Elections.—Temporary Reg. §1.1294-1T, relating to requirements for making certain elections by passive foreign investment companies and their shareholders that are United States persons, is also proposed as a final regulation and, when adopted, would become Reg. §1.1294-1 (published in the Federal Register on March 2, 1988). Temporary Reg. §1.1295-1T was removed by T.D. 8404, March 31, 1992. Temporary Reg. §1.1291-0T was reserved by T.D. 8750, December 31, 1997. Temporary Reg. §1.1297-3T was adopted by T.D. 9231, December 7, 2005.

§1.1294-1. Extension to extend the time for payment of tax on undistributed earnings of a qualified electing fund.

Passive Foreign Investment Companies: Qualified Electing Funds: Shareholders

Passive Foreign Investment Companies: Qualified Electing Funds: Shareholders.—Reproduced below is the text of proposed Reg. §1.1295-1, relating to the taxation of shareholders of certain passive foreign investment companies (PFICs) upon payment of distributions by such companies or upon the disposition of stock of such companies (published in the Federal Register on April 1, 1992) (INTL-941-86; INTL-656-87; INTL-704-87). Reg. §§1.1291-0, 1.1291-9 and 1.1291-10 were adopted by T.D. 8701 on December 26, 1996. Proposed Reg. §1.1291-8 was withdrawn on February 2, 1999.

☐ Par. 7. Section 1.1295-1 is added to read as follows:

§1.1295-1. Qualified electing funds.—(a) *In general*.—This section provides certain rules under section 1295 applicable to a U.S. person that has elected to treat a PFIC (as defined in §1.1291-1(b)(1)) as a QEF (as defined in §1.1291-1(b)(2)(i)). A U.S. person that has elected to treat a PFIC as a QEF is taxable annually, pursuant to section 1293, on its pro rata share of the ordinary earnings and net capital gain of the QEF.

(b) *Application of section 1295 election*.—(1) *Election personal to shareholder*.—An election under section 1295 and this section (section 1295 election) applies only to the shareholder that makes the election. Accordingly, a shareholder's section 1295 election will not apply to a U.S. transferee (as defined in §1.1291-6(c)(2)(i)) of stock of a PFIC with respect to which the shareholder made a section 1295 election. A section 1295 election made by a common parent of a consolidated group as agent for members of the group is considered made by each

member of the group that owns stock of the PFIC at the time of the election and at any time thereafter.

(2) *Election applicable to specific corporation only*.—(i) *In general*.—Only a corporation with respect to which a shareholder makes a section 1295 election is a QEF. The shareholder's section 1295 election applies to all of the stock of the QEF that the shareholder owns at the time of the election or acquires thereafter. Except as provided in paragraph (b)(2)(ii) of this section, if a shareholder transfers stock of a QEF in exchange for stock of another PFIC, the latter PFIC is not a QEF unless the shareholder makes a section 1295 election to treat it as a QEF. If a shareholder disposes of stock of a QEF in exchange for stock of another PFIC in a nonrecognition transfer (as defined in §1.1291-6(a)(2)) effected prior to April 1, 1992, and the shareholder has consistently treated the other PFIC as a QEF, the shareholder may make a section 1295 election with respect to the other PFIC

whose stock was received for the taxable year of the PFIC that includes the day the transfer was effected. Such election must be made by the later of—

(A) The due date provided in section 1295(b); or

(B) The due date for the return for the taxable year of the shareholder that includes April 1, 1992.

For the deadline for making the section 1295 election in the case of nonrecognition transfers effected after April 1, 1992, *see* section 1295(b).

(ii) *Stock of QEF received in a nonrecognition transfer.*—If a U.S. person is a U.S. transferee (as defined in §1.1291-6(c)(2)(i)) of stock of a PFIC in a nonrecognition transfer in which the shareholder disposing of such stock does not fully recognize the gain with respect to such stock, and the U.S. transferee, at the time of the transaction, has in effect a section 1295 election with respect to that PFIC, the section 1295 election will apply to the newly acquired stock on the day after the transaction. The newly acquired stock will be treated as stock of an unpedigreed QEF for which an election under section 1291(d)(2) and §1.1291-9 or 1.1291-10 may be made. For purposes of making a section 1291(d)(2) election pursuant to this paragraph (b)(2)(ii), the qualification date is the day after the nonrecognition transaction. The following example illustrates the rule of this paragraph (b)(2)(ii).

Example. (i) X, a domestic corporation, owns stock of NQF, a section 1291 fund with respect to X, and stock of FC, a pedigreed QEF with respect to X. Pursuant to a plan of reorganization, X and the other shareholders of NQF exchange their NQF stock for voting stock of FC in a transaction that qualifies as a reorganization described in section 368(a)(1)(C). Pursuant to §1.1291-6(c)(1), the gain recognition rule of §1.1291-6(b)(1) does not apply to X's disposition of NQF stock. X therefore does not recognize gain on the exchange of NQF stock for FC stock. X's adjusted basis in the FC stock received in the reorganization is equal to X's adjusted basis in the NQF stock immediately prior to the transfer. The holding period of the FC stock received includes the period during which X held the NQF stock, and, as provided in §1.1291-1(h)(7), the character of the days during that period as prePFIC and prior PFIC carry over to the FC stock.

(ii) As provided in §1.1295-1(b)(2)(ii), the section 1295 election that X made with respect to FC applies to the FC stock received in the reorganization. However, because the holding period of the FC stock received in exchange for the NQF stock includes days that are treated as prior PFIC days, the FC stock received in the reorganization is treated as stock of an unpedigreed QEF. X may make an election under section 1291(d)(2) to purge the holding period of the FC stock received of the prior PFIC days carried over with the NQF holding period. [Reg. §1.1295-1.]

PFICs: Shareholders: Qualified Electing Fund Elections

PFICs: Shareholders: Qualified Electing Fund Elections.—Reg. §1.1295-2, relating to permitting certain shareholders to make a special election under Code Sec. 1295, in lieu of the election currently provided for under that section, with respect to certain preferred shares of a passive foreign investment company (PFIC), is proposed (published in the Federal Register on December 24, 1996) (REG-209040-88).

☐ Par. 3. Section 1.1295-2 is added to read as follows:

§1.1295-2. Special preferred QEF election.—(a) *In general.*—This section provides rules permitting certain shareholders to make a special election under section 1295 (special preferred QEF election) in lieu of the election described in §1.1295-1[1] and Notice 88-125, 1988-2 C.B. 535 (see §601.601(d)(2)(ii)(*b*) of this chapter), with respect to certain preferred shares (qualified preferred shares) of a foreign corporation that certifies either that it is a PFIC (as defined in §1.1291-1(b)(1)(i))[1] or that it reasonably believes that it is a PFIC. In order to make a special preferred QEF election, a shareholder must satisfy the stock ownership requirement of paragraph (c)(2) of this section. A special preferred QEF election of a shareholder applies only to those qualified preferred shares acquired and held directly by the shareholder in the taxable year of the shareholder for which the election is made. A shareholder making a special preferred QEF election must account for dividend income on shares subject to the election under the special income inclusion rules described in §1.1293-2, rather than under the general income inclusion rules of section 1293 and §1.1293-1. In addition, for purposes of determining the tax consequences of owning shares subject to the special preferred QEF election, an electing shareholder must treat the foreign corporation as a PFIC for the entire period during which the shareholder continues to hold any of such shares. Paragraph (b) of this section defines qualified preferred shares. Paragraph (c) of this section provides rules for determining who may make the special preferred QEF election. Paragraph (d) of this section provides rules concerning the effect of the election. Paragraph (e) of this section provides rules for the time and manner of making the election. Paragraph (f) of this section sets forth the annual reporting requirement for the election. Paragraph (g) of this section provides rules concerning the possible termination or invalidation of the election. For the applicability date of this section, see paragraph (h) of this section.

(b) *Qualified preferred share defined.*—(1) *In general.*—For purposes of this section, a share of a foreign corporation is a qualified preferred share only if—

(i) The share was originally issued for cash or in exchange for qualified preferred shares of the foreign corporation in a transaction to which section 354(a)(1) applied;

(ii) If the share were to constitute a debt obligation, the share would be in registered form within the meaning of §5f.103-1(c) of this chapter;

(iii) All amounts payable with respect to the share are denominated in U.S. dollars and are not determined by reference to the value of a currency other than the U.S. dollar;

(iv) The share is limited and preferred as to dividends and does not participate in corporate growth to any significant extent within the meaning of section 1504(a)(4)(B);

(v) The share has a fixed redemption or liquidation price;

(vi) The share provides for cumulative or noncumulative dividend rights that are limited to an annual (or shorter period) amount computed by multiplying either the redemption or liquidation price of the share by a specified index described in §1.446-3(c)(2)(i), (iii), or (iv) (specified index), or by a specified index periodically re-established pursuant to an auction reset mechanism, set in advance of the period with respect to which the specified index applies;

(vii) If the share may be redeemed under circumstances described in §1.305-5(b) such that redemption premium (as described in §1.305-5(b)) could be treated under section 305(c) as a constructive distribution (fixed term preferred stock), the share was not issued with redemption premium exceeding the de minimis amount described in section 305(c)(1) and §1.305-5(b)(1);

(viii) If the share may not be redeemed under circumstances described in §1.305-5(b) such that redemption premium would not be treated under section 305 as a constructive distribution (perpetual preferred stock), the share does not provide shareholders with the right to receive an amount upon liquidation or redemption that exceeds the issue price of the share (as determined under the principles of section 1273(b)) by an amount in excess of 5 percent of such liquidation or redemption amount;

(ix) If redeemable, the share is redeemable only in whole and not in part and is not subject to mandatory redemption within five years of the issue date of the share. Further, the share is not subject to a holder put or issuer call that, based on all the facts and circumstances as of the issue date of the share, is more likely than not to be exercised at a time within five years of the issue date;

(x) If convertible, the share is not convertible into a share other than a share meeting all the conditions set forth in paragraphs (b)(1)(i) through (b)(1)(ix) of this section; and

(xi) The issuer of the share has indicated in an offering document relating to the original issuance of the share or in a written statement available to U.S. holders that the issuer has no current intention or belief that it will not pay dividends on the share on a current basis and that the share meets the conditions set forth in paragraphs (b)(1)(i) through (b)(1)(x) of this section and this paragraph (b)(1)(xi).

(2) *Special rules for shares acquired in secondary market transactions.*—(i) *Fixed term preferred stock.*—A share of fixed term preferred stock (as described in paragraph (b)(1)(vii) of this section) that satisfies the conditions set forth in paragraph (b)(1) of this section and that is acquired in a transaction other than in connection with the initial issuance of the share (a secondary market transaction), shall constitute a qualified preferred share with respect to a shareholder, but only if the shareholder acquires the share for cash and the share has preferred discount (as defined below) that is less than or equal to an amount equal to 1 percent of the redemption price, multiplied by the number of complete years from the date of acquisition of the share to the redemption date as established under the principles of §1.305-5(b). Sales of shares to bond houses, brokers, or similar persons or organizations acting in the capacity as underwriters, placement agents, or wholesalers are ignored for purposes of determining

[1] This proposed regulation was published on April 1, 1992, at 57 Fed. Reg. 11024.

whether a share is acquired in connection with the initial issuance of the share. For purposes of this section, the preferred discount for a share is the excess of the redemption price of the share payable on the redemption date over the shareholder's acquisition cost for the share.

(ii) *Perpetual preferred stock.*—A share of perpetual preferred stock, within the meaning of paragraph (b)(1)(viii) of this section, that satisfies the conditions set forth in paragraph (b)(1) of this section and that is acquired in a secondary market transaction, shall constitute a qualified preferred share with respect to the shareholder, but only if the shareholder acquires the share for cash and the amount payable upon liquidation of the share exceeds the shareholder's acquisition cost for the share by an amount less than or equal to 10 percent of such liquidation amount.

(iii) *Examples.*—The following examples illustrate the rules of this paragraph (b)(2).

Example 1—(i) *Facts.* On May 1, 1998, A, an individual who files her return on a calendar year basis, purchases for $9000 cash in a single secondary market transaction (as defined in paragraph (b)(2)(i) of this section) 100 shares of nonconvertible Class A $100 par value preferred stock (Class A Stock) of FC, a foreign corporation with a taxable year ending March 31. The terms of the Class A Stock satisfy all the conditions described in paragraph (b)(1) of this section and provide for a mandatory redemption of the Class A Stock by the issuer in U.S. dollars at par on June 1, 2012. The Class A Stock is not redeemable pursuant to an issuer call or holder put on any other date.

(ii) *Analysis.* In order for A to make a special preferred QEF election with respect to the Class A Stock acquired by A, the Class A Stock acquired must constitute qualified preferred shares. Although the Class A Stock meets the requirements for qualified preferred shares set forth in paragraph (b)(1) of this section, the stock also must satisfy the requirements described in paragraph (b)(2) because A acquired the stock in a secondary market transaction. Because the terms of the Class A Stock provide that the stock will be redeemed by the issuer on June 1, 2012, the stock constitutes fixed term preferred stock within the meaning of paragraph (b)(1)(vii) of this section. A purchased the Class A Stock for $90 per share, representing a $10 discount ($100 June 1, 2012, per share redemption price less $90 acquisition cost). Because this $10 discount, which constitutes preferred discount within the meaning of paragraph (b)(2)(i) of this section, is less than $14 (1 percent of the redemption price multiplied by 14 (the number of complete years until the mandatory redemption date)), the Class A Stock acquired by A satisfies the conditions of paragraph (b)(2)(i) of this section and therefore constitutes qualified preferred shares.

Example 2—(i) *Facts.* The facts are the same as in *Example 1*, except that A acquires the 100 shares of Class A Stock for $8000.

(ii) *Analysis.* In this case, A purchased the Class A Stock for $80 per share, representing a $20 discount ($100 June 1, 2012, redemption price less $80 acquisition cost). Because this $20 of preferred discount is greater than $14 (1 percent of the redemption price multiplied by 14 (the number of complete years until the mandatory redemption date)), the Class A Stock fails to satisfy the conditions of paragraph (b)(2)(i) of this section and therefore fails to qualify as qualified preferred shares.

(c) *Who may make the election.*—(1) *In general.*—A U.S. person that acquires qualified preferred shares for cash or in a nonrecognition transaction described in §1.1291-6(a)[2] (nonrecognition transaction) and that holds such shares directly may make a special preferred QEF election, provided that, in the case of shares acquired in a nonrecognition transaction, either the qualified preferred shares are treated as stock of a pedigreed QEF, as defined in §1.1291-1(b)(2)(ii), immediately prior to the nonrecognition transaction, or the gain, if any, realized on the transaction would be recognized under §1.1291-6(b) with respect to the nonrecognition transaction. A special preferred QEF election will not apply to any shares with respect to which the electing shareholder is an indirect shareholder, within the meaning of §1.1291-1(b)(8). Solely for purposes of this section, partnerships, S corporations, trusts and estates (pass-through entities) that directly own qualified preferred shares are treated as shareholders that may make a special preferred QEF election. A shareholder may not make a special preferred QEF election if at any time the shareholder made a section 1295 election (other than a special preferred QEF election) with respect to the foreign corporation. A shareholder may not make a special preferred QEF election unless the shareholder satisfies the stock ownership requirements set forth in paragraph (c)(2) of this section, and the shareholder receives from the foreign corporation the statement described in paragraph (c)(3) of this section.

(2) *Ownership requirement.*—A holder of qualified preferred shares of a foreign corporation may make a special preferred QEF election only if, at all times during the taxable year of the shareholder, the shareholder does not own, directly, indirectly, or constructively, within the meaning of section 958, five percent or more of the vote or value of any class of stock of the foreign corporation. The five percent vote or value limitation must be satisfied for each taxable year of the shareholder during which the shareholder continues to hold shares subject to the special preferred QEF election.

(3) *Statement from corporation.*—A shareholder may make the special preferred QEF election only if the foreign corporation has provided a written statement relating to the taxable year of the corporation that ends with or within the taxable year of the shareholder for which the election is made certifying either that the foreign corporation is, or that it reasonably believes that it is, a PFIC, and that it is not a controlled foreign corporation within the meaning of section 957(a) for such taxable year of the corporation. The statement must be provided directly to the electing shareholder or in a disclosure or other document generally available to all U.S. holders. Electing shareholders must retain a copy of the statement for their records.

(d) *Effect of election.*—(1) *In general.*—Unless terminated or invalidated pursuant to paragraph (g) of this section, shares subject to a special preferred QEF election will be treated as shares of a pedigreed QEF (as defined in §1.1291-1(b)(2)(ii)) for all taxable years of the foreign corporation that are included wholly or partly in the shareholder's holding period of the shares. A special preferred QEF election applies to all qualified preferred shares owned directly by the shareholder that are acquired in the taxable year of the election. Separate special preferred QEF elections may be made for qualified preferred shares acquired in other taxable years of the taxpayer. A special preferred QEF election is personal to the shareholder that made the election and does not apply to a transferee of the shares. A shareholder that has made a special preferred QEF election may not make, with respect to the foreign corporation, any other election permitted under sections 1291 through 1297 and the regulations under those sections, including a section 1295 election as described in §1.1295-1 and Notice 88-125, 1988-2 C.B. 535 (see §601.601(d)(2)(ii)(*b*) of this chapter), for any period during which the special preferred QEF election remains in effect with respect to any shares of the shareholder.

(2) *Continued PFIC Characterization.*—By making the special preferred QEF election, the shareholder agrees to treat the foreign corporation as a PFIC with respect to qualified preferred shares subject to the election at all times during its holding period for such shares, without regard to whether the foreign corporation is a PFIC for any taxable year of the foreign corporation during which the preferred QEF election remains in effect.

(3) *Section 1293 inclusions.*—For each taxable year of the shareholder to which an election under this section applies, the shareholder must include in income the preferred QEF amount, as defined in §1.1293-2, in the manner and under the rules provided in that section.

(e) *Time for and manner of making the special preferred QEF election.*—(1) *Time for making the election.*—A special preferred QEF election must be made on or before the due date, as extended, for filing the shareholder's return for the taxable year during which the shareholder acquired the qualified preferred shares for which the election is being made. A special preferred QEF election may not be made for those shares at any other time pursuant to any other provision of the Code or regulations.

(2) *Manner of making the election.*—(i) *In general.*—A shareholder makes the special preferred QEF election under this section for all qualified preferred shares of a foreign corporation acquired during the shareholder's taxable year by checking the appropriate box in Form 8621 (Return by a Shareholder of a Passive Foreign Investment Company or Qualified Electing Fund), Part I, for making the section 1295 election, and indicating in the margin of Part I that the shareholder is making a special preferred QEF election with respect to certain specified shares. The shareholder also must report the preferred QEF amount for the taxable year of the election on Line 6a of Part II of Form 8621. In addition, the shareholder must attach to Form 8621 the statement (preferred QEF statement) described in paragraph (e)(2)(ii) of this section, signed by the shareholder under penalties of perjury, stating that the information and representations provided in the preferred QEF statement are true, correct, and complete to the best of the shareholder's knowledge and belief.

---

[2] This proposed regulation was published on April 1, 1992, at 57 Fed. Reg. 11024.

(ii) *Preferred QEF statement contents.*—The preferred QEF statement must include the following information and representations:

(A) The first taxable year of the shareholder for which the special preferred QEF election is made;

(B) The number of shares subject to the election, their acquisition date(s) and acquisition price(s), and the class designation(s) of the shares;

(C) A representation by the shareholder that it did not at any time during its taxable year own directly, indirectly, or constructively, within the meaning of section 958, five percent or more of the vote or value of any class of stock of the foreign corporation with respect to which the election applies;

(D) A representation by the shareholder that it has obtained the written statement described in paragraph (c)(3) of this section; and

(E) A representation by the shareholder that it has never made a section 1295 election other than a special preferred QEF election with respect to the foreign corporation.

(f) *Annual reporting requirement.*—For each taxable year of a shareholder during which the shareholder holds shares of a foreign corporation subject to one or more special preferred QEF elections, the shareholder must file Form 8621 with respect to the foreign corporation regardless of whether the foreign corporation is or is not a PFIC under section 1296 during any portion of the taxable year. The shareholder must indicate in the margin of Part I of Form 8621 the number of special preferred QEF elections of the shareholder that remain in effect with respect to the foreign corporation. In addition, the shareholder must report, on Line 6a of Part II of Form 8621, the aggregate of the preferred QEF amounts for all relevant special preferred QEF elections in effect for the taxable year.

(g) *Termination or invalidation of election.*—(1) *In general.*—A sale, exchange or other disposition of a share that is subject to a special preferred QEF election will terminate the special preferred QEF election with respect to that share. In addition, the Commissioner may, in the Commissioner's discretion, terminate or invalidate a special preferred QEF election if a shareholder that made the election fails to satisfy the initial or ongoing requirements of the election. Once made, a special preferred QEF election may not be terminated or invalidated by the shareholder.

(2) *Effect of termination or invalidation.*—Termination of a special preferred QEF election by the Commissioner will be effective on the first day of the shareholder's first taxable year following the last taxable year of the shareholder for which the requirements of the election are satisfied. For purposes of sections 1291 through 1297 and the regulations thereunder, the holding period of qualified preferred shares subject to an election that has been terminated will be treated as beginning on the effective date of the termination. A shareholder that has made an election that is invalidated by the Commissioner will be treated for purposes of sections 1291 through 1297 and the regulations thereunder as if the shareholder never made the election.

(h) *Effective date.*—An election under this section may only be made with respect to qualified preferred shares that are issued after the date that is 30 days after the date of publication of this document as a final regulation. [Reg. § 1.1295-2.]

Passive Foreign Investment Companies: Passive Income Characterization: Certain Foreign Banks and Securities Dealers: Exceptions To

Passive Foreign Investment Companies: Passive Income Characterization: Certain Foreign Banks and Securities Dealers: Exceptions To.—Reg. §§1.1296-4 and 1.1296-6, relating to the application of the exceptions to passive income contained in section 1296(b) for foreign banks, securities dealers and brokers, are proposed (published in the Federal Register on April 28, 1995) (INTL-65-93). See below (REG-115795-97) for a proposed amendment to proposed Reg. §1.1296-4.

☐ Par. 4. Sections 1.1296-4 and 1.1296-6 are added to read as follows:

§1.1296-4. Characterization of certain banking income of foreign banks as nonpassive.—(a) *General rule.*—For purposes of section 1296, banking income earned by an active bank, as defined in either paragraph (b)(1) or (2) of this section, or by a qualified bank affiliate, as defined in paragraph (i) of this section, is nonpassive income.

(b) *Active bank.*—(1) *U.S. licensed banks.*—A corporation (whether domestic or foreign) is an active bank if it is licensed by federal or state bank regulatory authorities to do business as a bank in the United States. A foreign corporation will not satisfy the requirements of this paragraph (b)(1) if, under its federal or state license or licenses, the foreign corporation is permitted to maintain only an office, such as a representative office, that is prohibited by federal or state law from taking deposits or making loans.

(2) *Other foreign banks.*—A foreign corporation is an active bank if it meets the licensing requirement of paragraph (c) of this section and it actively conducts, within the meaning of §1.367(a)-2T(b)(3), a banking business that is a trade or business within the meaning of §1.367(a)-2T(b)(2). In order for the business conducted by a foreign corporation to be considered a banking business, the foreign corporation must also meet the deposit-taking requirements of paragraph (d) of this section and the lending requirements of paragraph (e) of this section.

(c) *Licensing requirements.*—To be an active bank under paragraph (b)(2) of this section, a foreign corporation must be licensed or authorized to accept deposits from residents of the country in which it is chartered or incorporated and to conduct, in that country, one or more of the banking activities described in paragraph (f)(2) of this section. However, in no case will a foreign corporation satisfy the requirements of this paragraph (c) if one of the principal purposes for its obtaining a license or authorization was to satisfy the requirements of this section.

(d) *Deposit-taking requirements.*—(1) *General rule.*—To be an active bank under paragraph (b)(2) of this section—

(i) A foreign corporation must, in the ordinary course of the corporation's trade or business, regularly accept deposits from customers who are residents of the country in which it is licensed or authorized; and

(ii) The amount of deposits shown on the corporation's balance sheet must be substantial.

(2) *Deposit.*—Whether a liability constitutes a deposit for purposes of this paragraph (d) is determined by reference to the characteristics of the relevant instrument and does not depend solely on whether the instrument is designated as a deposit.

(3) *Substantiality of deposits.*—Whether the amount of deposits (including interbank deposits) shown on a corporation's balance sheet is substantial depends on all the facts and circumstances, including whether the corporation's capital structure and funding sources as a whole are similar to that of banking institutions engaged in the same types of activities and subject to the jurisdiction of the same bank regulatory authorities.

(e) *Lending activities test.*—To be an active bank under paragraph (b)(2) of this section, a corporation must regularly make loans to customers in the ordinary course of its trade or business. A note, bond, debenture or other evidence of indebtedness will be treated as a loan for purposes of this section only if the debt instrument is received by the corporation on an extension of credit made pursuant to a loan agreement entered into in the ordinary course of the corporation's banking business. Such debt instruments generally will not be considered loans for purposes of this section if the instruments are not treated as loans (but are classified as securities or other investment assets, for example) for purposes of the foreign corporation's financial statements.

(f) *Banking income.*—(1) *General rule.*—Banking income is the gross income derived from the active conduct (within the meaning of §1.367(a)-2T(b)(3)) of any banking activity described in paragraph (f)(2) of this section.

(2) *Banking activities.*—For purposes of this section, the following are banking activities—

(i) Lending activities described in paragraph (e) of this section;

(ii) Factoring evidences of indebtedness for customers;

(iii) Purchasing, selling, discounting, or negotiating for customers notes, drafts, checks, bills of exchange, acceptances, or other evidences of indebtedness;

(iv) Issuing letters of credit and negotiating drafts drawn thereunder for customers;

(v) Performing trust services, including activities as a fiduciary, agent or custodian, for customers, provided such trust activities are not performed in connection with services provided by a dealer in stock, securities or similar financial instruments;

(vi) Arranging foreign exchange transactions (including any section 988 transaction within the meaning of section 988(c)(1)) for, or engaging in foreign exchange transactions with, customers;

(vii) Arranging interest rate or currency futures, forwards, options or notional principal contracts for, or entering into such transactions with, customers;

(viii) Underwriting issues of stock, debt instruments or other securities under best efforts or firm commitment agreements for customers;

(ix) Engaging in finance leases, as defined in §1.904-4(e)(2)(i)(V);

(x) Providing charge and credit card services for customers or factoring receivables obtained in the course of providing such services;

(xi) Providing traveler's check and money order services for customers;

(xii) Providing correspondent bank services for customers;

(xiii) Providing paying agency and collection agency services for customers;

(xiv) Maintaining restricted reserves (including money or securities) as described in paragraph (g) of this section; and

(xv) Any other activity that the Commissioner determines, through a revenue ruling or other formal published guidance (see §601.601(d)(2) of this chapter), to be a banking activity generally conducted by active banks in the ordinary course of their banking business.

(g) *Certain restricted reserves.*—A deposit of assets in a reserve is, for purposes of this section, a banking activity if the deposit is maintained in a segregated account in order to satisfy a capital or reserve requirement under the laws of a jurisdiction in which the corporation actively conducts (within the meaning of §1.367(a)-2T(b)(3)) a banking business that is a trade or business (within the meaning of §1.367(a)-2T(b)(2)). A deposit of assets into a reserve qualifies under this paragraph (g) if and only to the extent that the assets are not available for use in connection with the corporation's banking business because of significant regulatory restrictions on the investment of such assets. This paragraph (g) does not apply to ordinary working capital, which is available for unrestricted use.

(h) *Customer relationship.*—Whether a customer relationship exists is determined by reference to all the facts and circumstances. Such a relationship does not exist with respect to transactions between members of a related group, as defined in paragraph (i)(4) of this section, or transactions with any shareholders, officers, directors or other employees of any person that would otherwise be treated as an active bank or qualified bank affiliate if one of the principal purposes for such transactions was to satisfy the requirements of this section.

(i) *Income earned by qualified bank affiliates.*—(1) *General rule.*—A foreign corporation that is not an active bank but which derives banking income, as defined in paragraph (f)(1) of this section, is a qualified bank affiliate for purposes of this section if such corporation meets the requirements of paragraph (i)(2) of this section and the related group of which it is a member meets the requirements of paragraph (i)(3) of this section. Banking income earned by a qualified bank affiliate is nonpassive only for purposes of determining whether any member of the related group is a passive foreign investment company or holds stock in a passive foreign investment company or for purposes of applying section 956A(c)(2)(A). However, banking income of a qualified bank affiliate remains passive with respect to persons who own stock in that affiliate but who are not members of the related group of which the affiliate is a member.

(2) *Affiliate income requirement.*—To be a qualified bank affiliate, at least 60 percent of the foreign corporation's total gross income for the taxable year must be banking income, securities income, as defined in §1.1296-6(e)(1), or gross income described in section 1296(b)(2)(B) (relating to insurance activities). For purposes of applying this paragraph (i)(2), the look-through rules of sections 1296(b)(2)(C) and 1296(c) do not apply.

(3) *Group income requirements.*—The related group qualifies under this paragraph (i) if—

(i) At least 30 percent of the aggregate gross financial services income, as defined in §1.904-4(e)(1), earned during the taxable year by members of the related group is banking income earned by active banks who are members of the related group during the current taxable year; and

(ii) At least 70 percent of the aggregate gross financial services income earned during the taxable year by members of the related group is banking income, securities income, or gross income described in section 1296(b)(2)(B) (relating to insurance activities).

(4) *Related group.*—The related group is the group of persons consisting of the entity being tested under this paragraph (i) and all entities that are related within the meaning of section 954(d)(3) to such entity, substituting "person" for "controlled foreign corporation" each time the latter term appears.

(j) *Income from nonbank activities.*—Income derived from the conduct of activities other than banking activities described in paragraph (f)(2) of this section and income from assets held for the conduct of such other activities are nonpassive only to the extent otherwise provided in section 1296.

(k) *Effective date.*—This section is effective for taxable years beginning after December 31, 1994. However, taxpayers may apply this section to a taxable year beginning after December 31, 1986, but must consistently apply this section to such taxable year and all subsequent years. [Reg. §1.1296-4.]

§1.1296-6. Characterization of certain securities income.—(a) *General rule.*—For purposes of section 1296, securities income earned by an active dealer or active broker, as defined in paragraph (b) of this section, or a qualified securities affiliate, as defined in paragraph (j) of this section, is nonpassive income. This section applies only for purposes of determining whether a controlled foreign corporation, as defined in section 957(a), is a passive foreign investment company with respect to its United States shareholders as defined in section 951(b), or for the purpose of determining whether an asset is passive under section 956A(c)(2)(A).

(b) *Active dealer or broker.*—(1) *General rule.*—A securities dealer, as defined in paragraph (c) of this section, or a securities broker, as defined in paragraph (d) of this section, is an active dealer or an active broker for purposes of this section if it meets the requirements of either paragraph (b)(2) or (3) of this section.

(2) *U.S. licensed dealers and brokers.*—A securities dealer or securities broker (whether foreign or domestic) is an active dealer or an active broker if it is registered as a securities dealer or broker under section 15(a) of the Securities Exchange Act of 1934 or is registered as a Government securities dealer or broker under section 15C(a) of such Act.

(3) *Other dealers and brokers.*—(i) *General rule.*—A securities dealer or a securities broker is an active dealer or an active broker if it meets the licensing requirements of paragraph (b)(3)(ii) of this section and actively conducts, within the meaning of §1.367(a)-2T(b)(3), one or more securities activities, as defined in paragraph (e)(2) of this section, as a trade or business within the meaning of §1.367(a)-2T(b)(2).

(ii) *Licensing requirements.*—To be an active dealer or an active broker under paragraph (b)(3) of this section, a securities dealer or securities broker must be licensed or authorized in the country in which it is chartered, incorporated or organized to conduct one or more of the securities activities described in paragraph (e)(2) of this section with residents of that country. The conduct of such activities must be subject to *bona fide* regulation, including appropriate reporting, monitoring and prudential (including capital adequacy) requirements, by a securities regulatory authority in that country that regularly enforces compliance with such requirements and prudential standards.

(c) *Securities dealer.*—For purposes of this section, a securities dealer is a dealer (whether foreign or domestic) in securities within the meaning of section 475(c)(1).

(d) *Securities broker.*—For purposes of this section, a securities broker is a corporation (whether domestic or foreign) that, during its taxable year, stands ready, in the ordinary course of its trade or business, to effect transactions in securities and other financial instruments for the account of customers, including the arrangement of loans of securities owned by customers.

(e) *Securities income.*—(1) *General rule.*—Securities income means the gross income (except as provided in paragraph (i) of this section) derived from the active conduct (within the meaning of §1.367(a)-2T(b)(3)) of any securities activity described in paragraph (e)(2) of this section.

(2) *Securities activities.*—For purposes of this section, the following are securities activities—

(i) Purchasing or selling stock, debt instruments, interest rate or currency futures or other securities or derivative financial products (including notional principal contracts) from or to customers and holding stock, debt instruments and other securities as inventory for sale to customers, unless the relevant securities or derivative financial products (including notional principal contracts) are not held in a dealer capacity;

(ii) Effecting transactions in securities for customers as a securities broker;

(iii) Arranging futures, forwards, options, or notional principal contracts for, or entering into such transactions with, customers;

(iv) Arranging foreign exchange transactions (including any section 988 transaction within the meaning of section 988(c)(1)) for, or engaging in foreign exchange transactions with, customers;

(v) Underwriting issues of stocks, debt instruments, or other securities under best efforts or firm commitment agreements with customers;

(vi) Purchasing, selling, discounting, or negotiating for customers on a regular basis notes, drafts, checks, bills of exchange, acceptances or other evidences of indebtedness;

(vii) Borrowing or lending stocks or securities for customers;

(viii) Engaging in securities repurchase or reverse repurchase transactions with customers;

(ix) Engaging in hedging activities directly related to another securities activity described in this paragraph (e)(2);

(x) Repackaging mortgages and other financial assets into securities and servicing activities with respect to such financial assets (including the accrual of interest incidental to such activities);

(xi) Engaging in financing activities typically provided by an investment bank, such as—

(A) Project financing provided in connection with, for example, construction projects;

(B) Structured finance, including the extension of a loan and the sale of participations or interests in the loan to other financial institutions or investors; and

(C) Leasing activities to the extent incidental to financing activities described in this paragraph (e)(2)(xi) or to advisory services described in paragraph (e)(2)(xii) of this section;

(xii) Providing financial or investment advisory services, investment management services, fiduciary services, trust services or custodial services;

(xiii) Providing margin or any other financing for a customer secured by securities or money market instruments, including repurchase agreements, or providing financing in connection with any of the activities listed in paragraphs (e)(2)(i) through (e)(2)(xii) of this section;

(xiv) Maintaining deposits of capital (including money or securities) described in paragraph (f) of this section; and

(xv) Any other activity that the Commissioner determines, through a revenue ruling or other formal published guidance, to be a securities activity generally conducted by active dealers or active brokers in the ordinary course of their securities business.

(f) *Certain deposits of capital.*—A deposit of capital is, for purposes of this section, a securities activity if the deposit is maintained in a segregated account in order to satisfy a capital requirement for registration as a securities broker or dealer under the laws of a jurisdiction in which the broker or dealer actively conducts (within the meaning of § 1.367(a)-2T(b)(3)) a trade or business (within the meaning of § 1.367(a)-2T(b)(2)) as a securities broker or dealer. A deposit of capital qualifies under this paragraph (f) if and only to the extent that the assets are not available for use in connection with the controlled foreign corporation's activities as a securities broker or dealer because of significant regulatory restrictions on the investment of such assets. This paragraph (f) does not apply to ordinary working capital, which is available for unrestricted use.

(g) *Dealer-customer relationship.*—Whether a dealer-customer relationship exists is determined by reference to all the facts and circumstances. Such a relationship does not exist with respect to transactions between members of a related group, as defined in paragraph (j)(4) of this section, or transactions with any shareholders, officers, directors or other employees of any person that would otherwise be treated as an active dealer, active broker or qualified securities affiliate if one of the principal purposes for such transactions was to satisfy the requirements of this section.

(h) *Investment income.*—Income earned on any securities held for investment within the meaning of section 475(b)(1)(A) or not held for sale within the meaning of section 475(b)(1)(B), is passive for purposes of sections 1296(a)(1), 1296(a)(2) and 956A(c)(2)(A).

(i) *Calculation of gross income from a matched book.*—Securities income includes only the net (not gross) income from matched transactions. For purposes of this section, a matched transaction is a sale and repurchase agreement with respect to the same security properly treated as offsetting agreements in a matched book.

(j) *Income earned by qualified securities affiliates.*—(1) *General rule.*—A foreign corporation that is not an active dealer or an active broker but which derives securities income described in paragraph (e)(1) of this section is a qualified securities affiliate for purposes of this section if such corporation meets the requirements of paragraph (j)(2) of this section and is a member of a related group that meets the requirements of paragraph (j)(3) of this section. Securities income earned by a qualified securities affiliate is nonpassive only for purposes of determining whether any member of the related group is a passive foreign investment company or holds stock in a passive foreign investment company or for purposes of applying section 956A(c)(2)(A). However, securities income of a qualified securities affiliate remains passive with respect to persons who own stock in

that affiliate but who are not members of the related group of which the affiliate is a member.

(2) *Affiliate income requirement.*—To be a qualified securities affiliate, at least 60 percent of the foreign corporation's total gross income for the taxable year must be banking income, as defined in § 1.1296-4(f)(1), securities income, as defined in paragraph (e)(1) of this section, or gross income described in section 1296(b)(2)(B) (relating to insurance activities). For purposes of this paragraph (j)(2), the look-through rules of sections 1296(b)(2)(C) and 1296(c) do not apply.

(3) *Group income requirements.*—The related group qualifies under this paragraph (j) if—

(i) At least 30 percent of the aggregate gross financial services income, as defined in § 1.904-4(e)(1), earned during the taxable year by members of the related group is securities income earned by active dealers or active brokers who are members of the related group during the current taxable year; and

(ii) At least 70 percent of the aggregate gross financial services income earned during the taxable year by members of the related group is banking income, securities income, or gross income described in section 1296(b)(2)(B) (relating to insurance activities).

(4) *Related group.*—The related group is the group of persons consisting of the entity being tested under this paragraph (j) and all entities that are related within the meaning of section 954(d)(3) to such entity, substituting "person" for "controlled foreign corporation" each time the latter term appears.

(5) *Example.*—The following example illustrates the rules of this paragraph (j).

Example. (i) *Facts.* SD is a country Y corporation that owns 85 percent of the stock of M, a country Z corporation. A, a U.S. person, owns the remaining 15 percent of the stock of M. B, C, and D, all unrelated U.S. persons, own 5, 15, and 36 percent, respectively, of the stock of SD. The rest of SD's stock is publicly held. SD is a securities dealer within the meaning of section 475(c)(1) and satisfies the licensing requirements of paragraph (b)(3)(ii) of this section. Because M's sole activity is conducting a matched book repo business, M is not a securities dealer within the meaning of section 475. For its taxable year ending December 31, 1994, SD earns $100 of gross income from trading profits and interest and dividends on inventory. For its taxable year ending December 31, 1994, M earns $50 of net interest income from its matched book repo business. SD and M earn no other income. All of SD and M's assets are held in connection with their securities businesses and none has been identified as having been held for investment.

(ii) *Securities income earned by SD.* SD is an active dealer under paragraph (b) of this section because it is a securities dealer under section 475 and satisfies the licensing requirements of paragraph (b)(3)(ii) of this section. Therefore, because SD is a controlled foreign corporation, SD's securities income is nonpassive under paragraph (a) of this section.

(iii) *Securities income earned by M.* (A) SD and M are financial services entities that are the only members of a related group as defined in paragraph (j)(4) of this section. The percentage of the SD-M related group's financial services income that is securities income earned by active dealers (SD), is 66.66 percent (($100/$150) × 100). The percentage of the SD-M related group's financial services income that is securities income, banking income (as defined in § 1.1296-4(f)), or insurance income (as defined in section 1296(b)(2)(B)) is 100 percent (($150/$150) × 100). In addition, the percentage of M's income that is securities income is 100 percent (($50/$50) × 100).

(B) M is a qualified securities affiliate because the gross income tests of paragraphs (j)(2) and (3) of this section are satisfied. Accordingly, because M is a controlled foreign corporation, M's securities income is nonpassive for purposes of determining whether C or D own an interest in a PFIC (whether SD or M). M is thus not a PFIC with respect to C or D because it does not meet the income or asset tests of section 1296(a). SD also is not a PFIC with respect to C or D because it does not meet the income or assets tests of section 1296(a), after applying the look-through rule of section 1296(c).

(C) However, because B owns less than 10 percent of the stock of SD, and is therefore not a United States shareholder with respect to SD under section 951(b), M's interest income is passive (even though it is securities income) for purposes of determining whether B's indirect interest in M is an interest in a PFIC. Moreover, M's interest income is passive for purposes of determining whether A owns an interest in a PFIC. As a result, M meets the income and asset tests of section 1296(a) and is therefore a PFIC with respect to A and B.

(k) *Income from nonsecurities activities.*—Income derived from the conduct of activities other than securities activities described in paragraph (e)(2) of this section and income from assets held for the conduct of such other activities are nonpassive only to the extent otherwise provided in section 1296.

(l) *Effective date.*—This section is effective for taxable years beginning after September 30, 1993. [Reg. § 1.1296-6.]

PFICs: Shareholders: Qualified Electing Fund Election: Rules

PFICs: Shareholders: Qualified Electing Fund Elections: Rules.—Amendments to proposed Reg. §1.1296-4 (see above (INTL-65-93)), relating to rules for a passive foreign investment company shareholder that makes the election under Code Sec. 1295 to treat the passive foreign investment company as a qualified electing fund, are proposed (published in the Federal Register on January 2, 1998) (REG-115795-97).

☐ Par. 7. Section 1.1296-4(e) as proposed at 60 FR 20922 (April 28, 1995) is amended by adding a sentence at the end of the paragraph to read as follows:

§1.1296-4. Characterization of certain banking income of foreign banks as passive.

* * *

(e) *Lending activities test.*—* * * An interbank deposit made in the ordinary course of a corporation's banking business will be treated as a loan for purposes of this section. For the effective date of this paragraph (e), see paragraph (k) of this section.

Passive Foreign Investment Companies: Guidance

Passive Foreign Investment Companies: Guidance.—Amendments to Reg. §1.1297-0, regarding the determination of ownership in a passive foreign investment company within the meaning of section 1297(a) and the treatment of certain income received or accrued by a foreign corporation and assets held by a foreign corporation for purposes of section 1297, are proposed (published in the Federal Register on July 11, 2019) (REG-105474-18).

Par. 4. Section 1.1297-0 is amended by revising the introductory text and adding entries for §§1.1297-1, 1.1297-2, and 1.1297-4 in numerical order to read as follows:

§1.1297-0. Table of contents.—This section contains a listing of the headings for §§1.1297-1, 1.1297-2, 1.1297-3, 1.1297-4, and 1.1297-5.

§1.1297-1 Definition of passive foreign investment company.

(a) Overview.

(b) Dividends included in gross income.

(1) General rule.

(2) Example.

(i) Facts.

(ii) Results.

(c) Passive income.

(1) Foreign personal holding company income.

(i) General rule.

(ii) Determination of gross income or gain on a net basis for certain items of foreign personal holding company income.

(iii) Dividends.

(2) Treatment of share of partnership income.

(i) Look-through partnership.

(ii) Less-than-25-percent-owned partnership.

(3) Exception for certain interest, dividends, rents, and royalties received from a related person.

(i) Allocation of interest.

(ii) Allocation of dividends.

(iii) Allocation of rents and royalties.

(iv) Determination of whether amounts are received or accrued from a related person.

(d) Asset test.

(1) Calculation of average annual value (or adjusted bases).

(i) General rule.

(ii) Measuring period.

(A) General rule.

(B) Election to use alternative measuring period.

(C) Short taxable year.

(iii) Adjusted basis.

(A) [Reserved]

(B) Election.

(iv) Time and manner of elections and revocations.

(A) Elections.

(B) Revocations and subsequent elections.

(v) Change in method of measuring assets.

(A) General rule.

(B) Example.

(1) Facts.

(2) Results.

(2) Dual-character assets.

(i) General rule.

(ii) Special rule when only part of an asset produces income.

(iii) Special rule for stock that produced income that was excluded from passive income under section 1297(b)(2)(C).

(iv) Example.

(A) Facts.

(B) Results.

(3) Partnership interest.

(i) Look-through partnership.

(ii) Less-than-25-percent-owned partnership.

(4) Dealer property.

(e) Stapled stock.

(f) Definitions.

(1) Look-through partnership.

(2) Measuring date.

(3) Measuring period.

(4) Non-passive asset.

(5) Non-passive income.

(6) Passive asset.

(7) Passive income.

(8) Tested foreign corporation.

(g) Applicability date.

(1) [Reserved]

(2) In general.

§1.1297-2 Special rules regarding look-through subsidiaries.

(a) Overview.

(b) General rules.

(1) Tested foreign corporation's ownership of a corporation.

(2) Tested foreign corporation's proportionate share of the assets and income of a look-through subsidiary.

(i) Proportionate share of assets.

(ii) Proportionate share of income.

(A) General rule.

(B) Special rule.

(iii) Coordination of section 1297(c) with section 1298(b)(7).

(3) Examples.

(i) Example 1.

(A) Facts.

(B) Results.

(ii) Example 2.

(A) Facts.

(B) Results.

(iii) Example 3.

(A) Facts.

(B) Results.

(c) Elimination of certain intercompany assets and income.

(1) General rule for asset test.

(2) General rule for income test.

(3) Partnerships.

(4) Examples.

(i) Example 1.

(A) Facts.

(B) Results.

(ii) Example 2.

(A) Facts.

(B) Results.

(iii) Example 3.

(A) Facts.

(B) Results.

(d) Related person determination for purposes of section 1297(b)(2)(C).

(1) General rule.

(2) Example.

(i) Facts.

(ii) Results.

(e) Treatment of activities of certain look-through subsidiaries and look-through partnerships for purposes of section 954(c)(2)(A) active rents and royalties exception.

(1) General rule.
(2) Examples.
(i) Example 1.
(A) Facts.
(B) Results.
(ii) Example 2.
(A) Facts.
(B) Results.
(f) Gain on disposition of stock in a look-through subsidiary.
(1) Amount of gain taken into account.
(2) Characterization of residual gain as passive income.
(3) Examples.
(i) Example 1.
(A) Facts.
(B) Results.
(ii) Example 2.
(A) Facts.
(B) Results.
(iii) Example 3.
(A) Facts.
(B) Results.
(g) Definitions.
(1) Look-through subsidiary.
(2) LTS debt.
(3) LTS stock.
(4) Residual gain.
(5) Unremitted earnings.
(h) Applicability date.

* * *

§1.1297-4 *Qualifying insurance corporation.*
(a) Scope.
(b) Qualifying insurance corporation.
(c) 25 percent test.
(d) Election to apply the alternative facts and circumstances test.
(1) In general.
(2) Predominantly engaged in an insurance business.
(i) In general.
(ii) Facts and circumstances.
(iii) Examples of facts indicating a foreign corporation is not predominantly engaged in an insurance business.
(3) Runoff-related circumstances.
(4) Rating-related circumstances.
(5) Election.
(i) In general.
(ii) Information provided by foreign corporation.
(iii) Time and manner for making the election.
(e) Rules limiting the amount of applicable insurance liabilities.
(1) In general.
(2) General limitation on applicable insurance liabilities.

(3) Additional limitation on amount of applicable insurance liabilities for a foreign corporation that does not prepare a financial statement based on a financial reporting standard.
(i) In general.
(ii) Choice of accounting method.
(4) Changes to financial statements prepared.
(f) Definitions.
(1) Applicable financial statement.
(2) Applicable insurance liabilities.
(3) Applicable insurance regulatory body.
(4) Financial reporting standard.
(5) Generally accepted accounting principles or GAAP.
(6) Insurance business.
(7) Total assets.
(g) Applicability date.
§1.1297-5 *Exception from the definition of passive income for active insurance income.*
(a) Scope.
(b) Exclusion from passive income of active insurance income.
(c) Income derived by a QIC in the active conduct of an insurance business.
(1) In general.
(2) Insurance business.
(3) Active conduct of an insurance business.
(i) In general.
(ii) Control test.
(A) Ownership.
(1) Ownership by or of a corporation.
(2) Ownership of a partnership.
(B) Control and supervision.
(C) Compensation.
(4) Active conduct percentage.
(i) In general.
(ii) Related expense determination.
(iii) Ceding commission.
(d) Income of qualifying domestic insurance corporation.
(e) Exclusion of assets for purposes of the passive asset test under section 1297(a)(2).
(f) Treatment of income and assets of certain look-through subsidiaries and look-through partnerships for purposes of the section 1297(b)(2)(B) exception.
(1) General rule.
(2) Applicable statement for tested foreign corporations applying paragraph (g)(1) of this section.
(g) No double counting.
(h) Definitions.
(1) Insurance services.
(2) Investment activity.
(3) Qualifying insurance corporation or QIC.
(i) Applicability date.

CFCs: U.S. Shareholders: Ownership Attribution

CFCs: U.S. Shareholders: Ownership Attribution.—Amendments to Reg. §1.1297-1, relating to the modification of section 958(b) of the Internal Revenue Code by the Tax Cuts and Jobs Act, which was enacted on December 22, 2017, are proposed (published in the Federal Register on October 2, 2019) (REG-104223-18).

Par. 11. Section 1.1297-1, as proposed to be added at 84 FR 33120 (July 11, 2019), is amended by revising paragraphs (d)(1)(iii)(A) and (g)(1) to read as follows:

§1.1297-1. Definition of passive foreign investment company.

* * *

(d) * * *
(1) * * *

(A) *Controlled foreign corporation.*—For purposes of section 1297(e)(2)(A), the term *controlled foreign corporation* has the meaning provided in section 957, determined without applying subparagraphs (A), (B), and (C) of section 318(a)(3) so as to consider a United States person as owning stock which is owned by a person who is not a United States person.

* * *

(g) * * *

(1) *Paragraph (d)(1)(iii)(A) of this section.*—Paragraph (d)(1)(iii)(A) of this section applies to taxable years of shareholders ending on or after October 1, 2019. For taxable years of shareholders ending before October 1, 2019, a shareholder may apply paragraph (d)(1)(iii)(A) of this section to the last taxable year of a foreign corporation beginning before January 1, 2018, and each subsequent taxable year of the foreign corporation, provided that the shareholder and United States persons that are related (within the meaning of section 267 or 707) to the taxpayer consistently apply such paragraph with respect to all foreign corporations.

* * *

Passive Foreign Investment Companies: Guidance

Passive Foreign Investment Companies: Guidance.—Reg. §§1.1297-1 and 1.1297-2, regarding the determination of ownership in a passive foreign investment company within the meaning of section 1297(a) and the treatment of certain income received or accrued by a foreign corporation and assets held by a foreign corporation for purposes of section 1297, are proposed (published in the Federal Register on July 11, 2019) (REG-105474-18).

Par. 5. Sections 1.1297-1 and 1.1297-2 are added to read as follows:

§1.1297-1. Definition of passive foreign investment company.—
(a) *Overview.*—This section provides rules concerning the income

test set forth in section 1297(a)(1) and the asset test set forth in section 1297(a)(2). Paragraph (b) of this section provides a rule relating to the definition of gross income for purposes of section 1297. Paragraph (c) of this section sets forth rules relating to the definition of passive income for purposes of section 1297. Paragraph (d) of this section provides rules relating to the asset test of section 1297. See §§ 1.1297-2 and 1.1298-4 for additional rules concerning the treatment of the income and assets of a corporation subject to look-through treatment under section 1297(c). Paragraph (e) of this section sets forth rules relating to the determination of passive foreign investment company (PFIC) status for stapled entities. Paragraph (f) of this section sets forth definitions applicable for this section, and paragraph (g) of this section sets forth the applicability date of this section.

(b) *Dividends included in gross income.*—(1) *General rule.*—For purposes of section 1297, gross income includes dividends that are excluded from gross income under section 1502 and § 1.1502-13.

(2) *Example.*—(i) *Facts.* USP is a domestic corporation that owns 30% of TFC, a foreign corporation. The remaining 70% of TFC is owned by FP, a foreign corporation that is unrelated to USP. TFC owns 25% of the value of USS1, a domestic corporation. USS1 owns 80% of the value of USS2, a domestic corporation. USS1 and USS2 are members of an affiliated group (as defined in section 1504(a)) filing a consolidated return. USS2 distributes a dividend to USS1 that is excluded from USS1's income pursuant to § 1.1502-13 for purposes of determining the U.S. Federal income tax liability of the affiliated group of which USS1 and USS2 are members.

(ii) *Results.* Although the dividend received by USS1 from USS2 is excluded from USS1's income for purposes of determining the U.S. Federal income tax liability of the affiliated group of which USS1 and USS2 are members, pursuant to paragraph (b)(1) of this section, for purposes of section 1297, USS1's gross income includes the USS2 dividend. Accordingly, for purposes of section 1297, TFC's gross income includes 25% of the dividend received by USS1 from USS2 pursuant to section 1297(c) and § 1.1297-2(b)(2)(ii). See section 1298(b)(7) and § 1.1298-4 for rules concerning the characterization of the USS2 dividend.

(c) *Passive income.*—(1) *Foreign personal holding company income.*—(i) *General rule.*—For purposes of section 1297, except as otherwise provided in section 1297(b)(2), this section, and § 1.1297-4, the term passive income means income of a kind that would be foreign personal holding company income as defined under section 954(c)(1). For the purpose of this paragraph (c)(1)—

(A) The exceptions to foreign personal holding company income in section 954(c)(1), 954(c)(2)(A) (relating to active rents and royalties), 954(c)(2)(B) (relating to export financing income), 954(c)(2)(C) (relating to dealers), and 954(h) (relating to entities engaged in the active conduct of a banking, financing, or similar business) are taken into account;

(B) The exceptions in section 954(c)(3) (relating to certain income received from related persons), 954(c)(6) (relating to certain amounts received from related controlled foreign corporations), and 954(i) (relating to entities engaged in the active conduct of an insurance business) are not taken into account;

(C) The rules in section 954(c)(4) (relating to sales of certain partnership interests) and 954(c)(5) (relating to certain commodity hedging transactions) are taken into account; and

(D) An entity is treated as a controlled foreign corporation within the meaning of section 957(a) for purposes of applying an exception to foreign personal holding company income in section 954(c) and (h) and for purposes of identifying whether a person is a related person with respect to such entity within the meaning of section 954(d)(3).

(ii) *Determination of gross income on a net basis for certain items of foreign personal holding company income.*—For purposes of section 1297, the excess of gains over losses from property transactions described in section 954(c)(1)(B), the excess of gains over losses from transactions in commodities described in section 954(c)(1)(C), the excess of foreign currency gains over foreign currency losses described in section 954(c)(1)(D), and positive net income from notional principal contracts described in section 954(c)(1)(F) are taken into account as gross income. The excess of gains over losses and positive net income is calculated separately with respect to the tested foreign corporation and each look-through subsidiary (as defined in § 1.1297-2(g)(1)).

(iii) *Dividends.*—For purposes of section 1297, the term dividend includes all amounts treated as dividends for purposes of this chapter, including amounts treated as dividends pursuant to sections 302, 304, 356(a)(2), 964(e), and 1248.

(2) *Treatment of share of partnership income.*—(i) *Look-through partnership.*—A tested foreign corporation is treated as if it received directly its share of any item of income of a look-through partnership, and the exceptions to passive income in section 1297(b)(2) and

the relevant exceptions to foreign personal holding company income in section 954(c) and (h) that are based on whether income is derived in the active conduct of a business or whether a corporation is engaged in the active conduct of a business apply to such income only if the exception would have applied to exclude the income from passive income or foreign personal holding company in the hands of the partnership, determined by taking into account only the activities of the partnership. See § 1.1297-2(e) for rules that allow the activities of certain other entities to be taken into account for purposes of determining the characterization of a tested foreign corporation's share of partnership income. See also § 1.1297-2(d) for rules determining whether a person is a related person for purposes of applying section 1297(b)(2)(C) in the case of income received or accrued by a partnership that is treated as received directly by a tested foreign corporation pursuant to this paragraph (c)(2).

(ii) *Less-than-25-percent-owned partnership.*—For purposes of section 1297, a tested foreign corporation's share of any item of income of a partnership in which the corporation owns, directly or indirectly, less than 25 percent of the value is treated as passive income.

(3) *Exception for certain interest, dividends, rents, and royalties received from a related person.*—(i) *Allocation of interest.*—For purposes of section 1297(b)(2)(C), interest that is received or accrued, as applicable based on the recipient's method of accounting, from a related person (as defined in section 1297(b)) is allocated to income of the related person that is not passive income in proportion to the ratio of the portion of the related person's non-passive income for its taxable year to the total amount of the related person's income for the taxable year that ends with or within the taxable year of the recipient.

(ii) *Allocation of dividends.*—For purposes of section 1297(b)(2)(C), dividends that are received or accrued, as applicable based on the recipient's method of accounting, from a related person are allocated to income of the related person that is not passive income based on the relative portion of the related person's current earnings and profits for its taxable year that ends with or within the taxable year of the recipient that are attributable to non-passive income.

(iii) *Allocation of rents and royalties.*—For purposes of section 1297(b)(2)(C), rents and royalties that are received or accrued, as applicable based on the recipient's method of accounting, from a related person are allocated to income of the related person that is not passive income to the extent the related person's deduction for the rent or royalty is allocated to non-passive income of the related person under the principles of §§ 1.861-8 through 1.861-14T.

(iv) *Determination of whether amounts are received or accrued from a related person.*—For purposes of section 1297(b)(2)(C), the determination of whether interest, dividends, rents, and royalties are received or accrued from a related person is made on the date of the receipt or accrual, as applicable based on the recipient's method of accounting, of the interest, dividend, rent, or royalty.

(d) *Asset test.*—(1) *Calculation of average annual value (or adjusted bases).*—(i) *General rule.*—For purposes of section 1297, the calculation of the average percentage of assets held by a tested foreign corporation during its taxable year that produce passive income or that are held for the production of passive income is determined based on the average of the fair market values (or the average of the adjusted bases) of the passive assets and total assets held by the foreign corporation on the last day of each measuring period (*measuring date*) of the foreign corporation's taxable year. The average of the fair market values (or the average of the adjusted bases) of the foreign corporation's passive assets or total assets for the taxable year is equal to the sum of the values (or adjusted bases) of the passive assets or total assets, as applicable, on each measuring date of the foreign corporation's taxable year, divided by the number of measuring dates in the taxable year.

(ii) *Measuring period.*—(A) *General rule.*—Except as otherwise provided in paragraph (d)(1)(ii)(B) of this section, the measuring periods for a tested foreign corporation are the four quarters that make up the foreign corporation's taxable year.

(B) *Election to use alternative measuring period.*—The average percentage of assets held by a tested foreign corporation during its taxable year that produce passive income or that are held for the production of passive income may be calculated using a period that is shorter than a quarter (such as a week or month). The same period must be used to measure the assets of the foreign corporation for the first year (including a short taxable year) that this alternative measuring period is used, and for any and all subsequent years, unless a revocation is made. An election to use an alternative measuring period or a revocation of such an election must be made in accordance with the rules of paragraph (d)(1)(iv) of this section.

(C) *Short taxable year.*—For purposes of applying section 1297 to a tested foreign corporation that has a taxable year of less than twelve months (short taxable year), the average values (or adjusted bases) are determined based on the measuring dates of the foreign corporation's taxable year (determined as if the taxable year were not a short taxable year), and by treating the last day of the short taxable year as a measuring date.

(iii) *Adjusted basis.*—(A) [Reserved]

(B) *Election.*—An election under section 1297(e)(2)(B) with respect to an eligible tested foreign corporation or a revocation of such an election must be made in accordance with the rules of paragraph (d)(1)(iv) of this section.

(iv) *Time and manner of elections and revocations.*—(A) *Elections.*—An owner (as defined in this paragraph (d)(1)(iv)) of a foreign corporation makes an election described in paragraph (d)(1)(ii)(B) or (d)(1)(iii)(B) of this section for a taxable year in the manner provided in the Instructions to Form 8621 (or successor form), if the owner is required to file a Form 8621 (or successor form) with respect to the foreign corporation for the taxable year of the owner in which or with which the taxable year of the foreign corporation for which the election is made ends. If the owner is not required to file Form 8621 (or successor form) with respect to the foreign corporation for the taxable year, the owner makes such an election by filing a written statement providing for the election and attaching the statement to an original or amended Federal income tax return for the taxable year of the owner in which or with which the taxable year of the foreign corporation for which the election is made ends clearly indicating that such election has been made. An election can be made by an owner only if the owner's taxable year for which the election is made, and all taxable years that are affected by the election, are not closed by the period of limitations on assessments under section 6501. Elections described in in paragraphs (d)(1)(ii)(B) and (d)(1)(iii)(B) of this section are not eligible for relief under § 301.9100-3 of this chapter. For purposes of this paragraph (d)(1)(iv), an owner of a foreign corporation is a United States person that is eligible under § 1.1295-1(d) to make a section 1295 election with respect to the foreign corporation, or would be eligible under § 1.1295-1(d) to make a section 1295 election if the foreign corporation were a PFIC.

(B) *Revocations and subsequent elections.*—An election described in paragraph (d)(1)(ii)(B) or (d)(1)(iii)(B) of this section made pursuant to paragraph (d)(1)(iv)(A) of this section is effective for the taxable year of the foreign corporation for which it is made and all subsequent taxable years of such corporation unless revoked by the Commissioner or the owner (as defined in paragraph (d)(1)(iv)(A) of this section) of the foreign corporation. The owner of a foreign corporation may revoke such an election at any time. If an election described in paragraph (d)(1)(ii)(B) or (d)(1)(iii)(B) of this section has been revoked under this paragraph (d)(1)(iv)(B), a new election described in paragraph (d)(1)(ii)(B) or (d)(1)(iii)(B) of this section, as applicable, cannot be made until the sixth taxable year following the year for which the previous such election was revoked, and such subsequent election cannot be revoked until the sixth taxable year following the year for which the subsequent election was made. The owner revokes the election for a taxable year in the manner provided in the Instructions to Form 8621 (or successor form), if the owner is required to file a Form 8621 (or successor form) with respect to the foreign corporation for the taxable year of the owner in which or with which the taxable year of the foreign corporation for which the election is revoked ends, or by filing a written statement providing for the revocation and attaching the statement to an original or amended Federal income tax return for the taxable year of the owner in which or with which the taxable year of the foreign corporation for which the election is revoked ends clearly indicating that such election has been revoked, if the owner is not required to file Form 8621 (or successor form) with respect to the foreign corporation for the taxable year.

(v) *Change in method of measuring assets.*—(A) *General rule.*—For purposes of section 1297, when stock of a foreign corporation is not publicly traded for an entire taxable year, the assets of the foreign corporation must be measured for all measuring periods of the taxable year on the basis of value if the corporation was publicly traded on the majority of days during the year or section 1297(e)(2) did not otherwise apply to the corporation on the majority of days of the year, and on the basis of adjusted basis otherwise.

(B) *Example.*—The following example illustrates the application of this paragraph (d)(1)(v).

(1) *Facts.* TFC is a controlled foreign corporation, 90% of the stock of which is wholly owned by USP at the beginning of its taxable year ending December 31 and throughout the year. The remaining 10% of its stock has historically been regularly traded on a national securities exchange that is registered with the Securities and Exchange Commission and continues to be until September 1 of the taxable year, when USP acquires all of it pursuant to a tender offer.

(2) *Results.* Because TFC was publicly traded on the majority of days during the year, the assets of the foreign corporation must be measured for all measuring periods of the taxable year on the basis of value.

(2) *Dual-character assets.*—(i) *General rule.*—Except as otherwise provided in paragraph (d)(2)(ii) of this section, for purposes of section 1297, an asset (or portion of an asset) that produces both passive income and non-passive income during a taxable year (dual-character asset) is treated as two assets for each measuring period in the taxable year, one of which is a passive asset and one of which is a non-passive asset. The value (or adjusted basis) of the dual-character asset is allocated between the passive asset and the non-passive asset in proportion to the relative amounts of passive income and non-passive income produced by the asset (or portion of an asset) during the taxable year. See paragraph (d)(2)(iii) of this section for a special rule concerning stock that has previously produced dividends subject to the exception provided in section 1297(b)(2)(C).

(ii) *Special rule when only part of an asset produces income.*—For purposes of section 1297, when only a portion of an asset produces income during a taxable year, the asset is treated as two assets, one of which is characterized as a passive asset or a non-passive asset based on the income that it produces, and one of which is characterized based on the income that it is held to produce. The value (or adjusted basis) of the asset is allocated between the two assets pursuant to the method that most reasonably reflects the uses of the property. In the case of real property, an allocation based on the physical use of the property generally is the most reasonable method.

(iii) *Special rule for stock that produced income that was excluded from passive income under section 1297(b)(2)(C).*—Stock with respect to which no dividends are accrued or received, as applicable based on the recipient's method of accounting, during a taxable year but with respect to which dividends accrued or received, as applicable based on the recipient's method of accounting, during a prior taxable year were in whole or in part excluded from passive income under section 1297(b)(2)(C) and paragraph (c)(3)(ii) of this section is treated as two assets, one of which is a passive asset and one of which is a non-passive asset. The value (or adjusted basis) of the asset is allocated between the two assets in proportion to the average percentage of dividends that were characterized as passive income, and the average percentage of dividends characterized as non-passive income, for the previous two taxable years pursuant to section 1297(b)(2)(C) and paragraph (c)(3)(ii) of this section.

(iv) *Example.*—The following example illustrates the application of this paragraph (d)(2).

(A) *Facts.* (1) USP is a domestic corporation that owns 30% of TFC, a foreign corporation. The remaining 70% of TFC is owned by FP, a foreign corporation that is unrelated to USP. TFC owns 20% of the value of FS1, a foreign corporation, and FP owns the remaining 80% of the value of FS1. FP, TFC, and FS1 are not controlled foreign corporations within the meaning of section 957(a), and each has a calendar year taxable year. For purposes of section 1297(b)(2)(C), FP is a "related person" with respect to TFC because FP owns more than 50% of the vote or value of TFC, and FS1 is a "related person" with respect to TFC because FP owns more than 50% of the vote or value of both TFC and of FS1.

(2) During Year 3, FP has only passive income, and FS1 has passive income of $200x and non-passive income of $800x. FS1 does not pay dividends during Year 3, but did pay $100x of dividends in Year 2 and $300x of dividends in Year 1. In Year 2, FS1 had current earnings and profits of $1000x, attributable to passive income of $100x and non-passive income of $900x; and, in Year 1, FS1 had current earnings and profits of $1000x, attributable to passive income of $500x and non-passive income of $500x. Throughout Year 3, TFC holds an obligation of FS1 with respect to which FS1 pays $100x of interest.

(3) In addition to the stock in FS1 and the FS1 obligation, TFC holds an office building, 40% of which is rented to FP throughout Year 3 for $100x per quarter. For the first two quarters of Year 3, 60% of the office building is used by TFC in a trade or business generating non-passive income. For the last two quarters of Year 3, 60% of the office building is rented to an unrelated person for $300x per quarter, and TFC's own officers or staff of employees regularly perform active and substantial management and operational functions while the property is leased.

(B) *Results.* (1) Under paragraph (c)(3)(ii) of this section, the dividends paid by FS1 in Year 2 were characterized as 10% passive income and 90% non-passive income. Under paragraph (c)(3)(ii) of this section, the dividends paid by FS1 in Year 1 were characterized as 50% passive income and 50% non-passive income. Accordingly, the average percentage of dividends for the previous two taxable years that were characterized as passive income is 40% (((10% x

$100x) + (50\% \times \$300x))/(\$100x + \$300x))$, and the average percentage of dividends characterized as non-passive income is 60% ((($90\% \times \$100x) + (50\% \times \$300x))/(\$100x + \$300x))$. Thus, under paragraph (d)(2)(iii) of this section, 60% of each share of stock of FS1 is characterized as a non-passive asset and 40% is characterized as a passive asset for each quarter of Year 3 for purposes of applying section 1297(a)(2) to determine whether TFC is a PFIC.

(2) Under paragraph (c)(3)(i) of this section, the interest received by TFC from FS1 is characterized as 20% ($200x/($200x+$800x))$ passive income and thus 80% non-passive income for purposes of applying section 1297(a)(1) to determine whether TFC is a PFIC. Accordingly, under paragraph (d)(2)(i) of this section, 20% of the obligation of FS1 is characterized as a passive asset and 80% as a non-passive asset for each quarter of Year 3 for purposes of applying section 1297(a)(2) to determine whether TFC is a PFIC.

(3) Under paragraph (c)(3)(iii) of this section, the rent received from FP throughout Year 3 is characterized as 100% passive income. Under paragraph (c)(1)(i)(A) of this section and section 954(c)(2)(A), the rent received from the unrelated person during the last two quarters is characterized as 100% non-passive income. Accordingly, under paragraph (d)(2)(i) of this section, 40% (($100x \times 4)/(($100x \times 4)+($300x \times 2)))$ of the office building is a passive asset, and 60% (($300x \times 2)/(($100x \times 4)+($300x \times 2)))$ is a non-passive asset for purposes of applying section 1297(a)(2) to determine whether TFC is a PFIC. Paragraph (d)(2)(ii) of this section does not apply because both portions of the office building generate income during Year 3.

(3) *Partnership interest.*—(i) *Look-through partnership.*—A tested foreign corporation is treated as holding directly its proportionate share of the assets held by a look-through partnership. The rules and principles of sections 701 through 761 apply to determine the corporate partner's proportionate share of the value of the partnership assets, as well as the proportionate share of the partnership's adjusted basis in the partnership's assets (taking into account any adjustments to such basis with respect to such partner under section 743). A tested foreign corporation's proportionate share of a partnership asset is treated as producing passive income, or being held to produce passive income, to the extent the asset produced, or was held to produce, passive income in the hands of the partnership under the rules in paragraph (c)(2) of this section.

(ii) *Less-than-25-percent-owned partnership.*—For purposes of section 1297, a tested foreign corporation's interest in a partnership in which the corporation owns, directly or indirectly, less than 25 percent of the value is treated as a passive asset.

(4) *Dealer property.*—For purposes of section 1297(a)(2), an asset that produces, or would produce upon disposition, income or gain that is, or would be, excluded from passive income pursuant to section 954(c)(2)(C) is treated as a non-passive asset.

(e) *Stapled stock.*—For purposes of determining whether stapled entities (as defined in section 269B(c)(2)) are a PFIC, all entities that are stapled entities with respect to each other are treated as a single entity that holds all of the assets of the stapled entities, conducts all of the activities of the stapled entities, and derives all of the income of the stapled entities.

(f) *Definitions.*—The following definitions apply for purposes of this section:

(1) *Look-through partnership.*—The term *look-through partnership* means, with respect to a tested foreign corporation—

(i) For purposes of section 1297(a)(2), a partnership at least 25 percent of the value of which is owned (as determined under § 1.1297-2(b)(1) as if the partnership were a corporation) by the tested foreign corporation on the measuring date; and

(ii) For purposes of section 1297(a)(1), a partnership for which the value owned (as determined under § 1.1297-2(b)(1) as if the partnership were a corporation) by the tested foreign corporation on the date on which income is received or accrued by the partnership is at least 25 percent of the value of the partnership.

(2) *Measuring date.*—The term *measuring date* has the meaning provided in paragraph (d)(1)(i) of this section.

(3) *Measuring period.*—The term *measuring period* means a quarter or an alternative measuring period, as determined in accordance with paragraph (d)(1)(ii) of this section.

(4) *Non-passive asset.*—The term *non-passive asset* means an asset other than a passive asset.

(5) *Non-passive income.*—The term *non-passive income* means income other than passive income.

(6) *Passive asset.*—The term *passive asset* means an asset that produces passive income, or which is held for the production of

passive income, taking into account the rules in paragraphs (c) and (d) of this section.

(7) *Passive income.*—The term *passive income* has the meaning provided in paragraph (c)(1) of this section.

(8) *Tested foreign corporation.*—The term *tested foreign corporation* means a foreign corporation the PFIC status of which is being tested under section 1297(a).

(g) *Applicability date.*—(1) [Reserved]

(2) *In general.*—The rules of this section apply to taxable years of shareholders beginning on or after the date of publication of the Treasury decision adopting these rules as final regulations in the **Federal Register**. [Reg. § 1.1297-1.]

§ 1.1297-2. Special rules regarding look-through subsidiaries.—(a) *Overview.*—This section provides rules concerning the treatment of income and assets of a look-through subsidiary for purposes of determining whether a tested foreign corporation (as defined in § 1.1297-1(f)(8)) is a passive foreign investment company (PFIC) under section 1297(a). Paragraph (b) of this section provides guidance for purposes of section 1297(c) on how to determine a tested foreign corporation's ownership in a corporation and how to determine a tested foreign corporation's proportionate share of a look-through subsidiary's assets and income. Paragraph (c) of this section provides rules that eliminate certain income and assets related to look-through subsidiaries and look-through partnerships (as defined in § 1.1297-1(f)(1)) for purposes of determining a tested foreign corporation's PFIC status. Paragraph (d) of this section sets forth a rule to determine whether certain income received or accrued by look-through subsidiaries and look-through partnerships is received or accrued from a related person for purposes of section 1297(b)(2)(C). Paragraph (e) of this section sets forth rules concerning the attribution of activities from a look-through subsidiary or look-through partnership. Paragraph (f) of this section provides rules for determining the amount of gain from the sale or exchange of stock of a look-through subsidiary that is taken into account under section 1297(a) and for determining the passive or non-passive character of the gain. Paragraph (g) of this section sets forth definitions applicable for this section, and paragraph (h) of this section sets forth the applicability date of this section.

(b) *General rules.*—(1) *Tested foreign corporation's ownership of a corporation.*—For purposes of section 1297(c) and the regulations in this section, the principles of section 958(a) and the regulations in this chapter under that section applicable to determining direct or indirect ownership by value apply to determine a tested foreign corporation's percentage ownership (by value) in the stock of another corporation. These principles apply whether an intermediate entity is domestic or foreign.

(2) *Tested foreign corporation's proportionate share of the assets and income of a look-through subsidiary.*—(i) *Proportionate share of assets.*—For each measuring period (as defined in § 1.1297-1(f)(3)), a tested foreign corporation is treated as if it held its proportionate share of each asset of a look-through subsidiary, determined based on the tested foreign corporation's percentage ownership (by value) (as determined under paragraph (b)(1) of this section)) of the look-through subsidiary on the measuring date (as defined in § 1.1297-1(f)(2)).

(ii) *Proportionate share of income.*—(A) *General rule.*—A tested foreign corporation is treated as if it received directly its proportionate share of each item of gross income of a corporation for a taxable year if the corporation is a look-through subsidiary with respect to the tested foreign corporation for the taxable year of the tested foreign corporation. In such case, a tested foreign corporation's proportionate share of a look-through subsidiary's gross income is determined based on the corporation's average percentage ownership (by value) of the look-through subsidiary.

(B) *Special rule.*—When a corporation is not a look-through subsidiary with respect to a tested foreign corporation for a taxable year of the tested foreign corporation, the tested foreign corporation may be treated as if it received directly its proportionate share of the gross income of the first corporation for each measuring period in the year for which the first corporation is a look-through subsidiary, provided that the gross income of the first corporation for each such measuring period can be established. In such case, a tested foreign corporation's proportionate share of a look-through subsidiary's gross income is determined based on the tested foreign corporation's percentage ownership (by value) (as determined under paragraph (b)(1) of this section) of the look-through subsidiary on the relevant measuring date.

(iii) *Coordination of section 1297(c) with section 1298(b)(7).*—A tested foreign corporation is not treated under section 1297(c) and this paragraph (b) as holding its proportionate share of the assets of a domestic corporation, or receiving directly its proportionate share of the gross income of such corporation, if the stock of the corporation is treated as an asset that is not a passive asset (as defined in §1.1297-1(f)(6)) that produces income that is not passive income (as defined in §1.1297-1(f)(7)) under section 1298(b)(7) (concerning the treatment of certain foreign corporations owning stock in certain 25 percent owned domestic corporations). See §1.1298-4 for rules governing the application of section 1298(b)(7).

(3) *Examples.*—The following examples illustrate the rules of this paragraph (b). For purposes of the examples in this paragraph (b)(3), for TFC's and LTS's entire taxable years, USP is a domestic corporation; USP owns 30% of TFC; TFC owns the amount of stock of LTS provided in each example; LTS owns 25% of the only class of FS stock; and TFC, LTS, and FS are foreign corporations that are not controlled foreign corporations within the meaning of section 957(a).

(i) *Example 1*—(A) *Facts.* TFC directly owns 80% of the only class of LTS stock for TFC's and LTS's entire taxable year. Pursuant to the principles of section 958(a), TFC owns 80% of the value of LTS, LTS owns 25% of the value of FS, and TFC owns 20% of the value of FS.

(B) *Results.* Under paragraph (b) of this section, in determining whether LTS is a PFIC under section 1297(a), LTS is treated as if it held 25% of each of FS's assets on each of the measuring dates in its taxable year, and received directly 25% of the gross income of FS for the taxable year. In determining whether TFC is a PFIC under section 1297(a), TFC is treated as if it held an 80% interest in each of LTS's assets on each of the measuring dates in its taxable year, and received directly 80% of the income of LTS for the taxable year. However, TFC is treated as if it held a 20% interest in the stock of FS (and not the assets of FS), and received 80% of any dividends paid from FS to LTS (and not any income of FS).

(ii) *Example 2*—(A) *Facts.* TFC directly owns 25% of the only class of LTS stock on the last day of each of the first three quarters of its taxable year, but disposes of its entire interest in LTS during the fourth quarter of its taxable year. Pursuant to the principles of section 958(a), on each of its first three measuring dates, TFC owns 25% of the value of LTS and 6.25% of the value of FS.

(B) *Results.* Under paragraph (b) of this section, in determining whether TFC is a PFIC under section 1297(a), TFC is treated as if it held 25% of LTS's assets on each of the first three measuring dates in its taxable year. However, because it held an average of 18.75% of the value of LTS on the measuring dates in the taxable year, it is not treated as receiving directly the gross income of LTS for the taxable year. If information about the gross income for LTS for each of the first three quarters of its taxable year is available, TFC may be treated as receiving directly 25% of the income of LTS for each of those quarters, because it owned 25% of the value of LTS on the measuring dates with respect to those measuring periods. For each of its first three quarters, TFC is treated as if it held a 6.25% interest in the stock of FS (and not the assets of FS) and may, if information about the income for LTS for each of the first three quarters of its taxable year is available, be treated as receiving 25% of any dividends paid from FS to LTS (and not any income of FS).

(iii) *Example 3*—(A) *Facts.* TFC directly owns 100% of the only class of LTS stock for TFC's and LTS's entire taxable year. Pursuant to the principles of section 958(a), TFC owns 100% of the value of LTS, and TFC owns 25% of the value of FS. TFC earns $5x of rents from renting a building to LTS, a related person with respect to TFC within the meaning of section 954(d)(3). TFC also sells one item of property described in section 954(c)(1)(B)(i) for a gain of $25x and another for a loss of $10x, and no exception from passive income applies to either amount. LTS has $100x of revenues from selling property described in section 1221(a)(1) to unrelated persons, but $150x of cost of goods sold with respect to such property. None of LTS's deduction for the rent paid to TFC is allocated to non-passive income under the principles of §§1.861-8 through 1.861-14T. During the taxable year, FS sells one item of property described in section 954(c)(1)(B)(i) for a gain of $50x and another for a loss of $100x, and no exception from passive income applies to either amount.

(B) *Results.* Under paragraph (b) of this section, in determining whether TFC is a PFIC under section 1297(a), TFC is treated as if it held 100% of LTS's assets on each of the measuring dates in its taxable year, and received directly 100% of the gross income of LTS for the taxable year. Accordingly, TFC is treated as receiving directly $0x of gross income from the sale of property by LTS given that LTS revenues are fully offset by costs of goods sold. Furthermore, TFC is treated as if it held a 25% interest in FS's assets, and received directly 25% of the gross income of FS. Pursuant to §1.1297-1(c)(1)(ii), only the excess of gains over losses from property transactions described in section 954(c)(1)(B) is taken into account as gross income for purposes of section 1297. Accordingly, TFC is treated as receiving directly $0x of gross income from the sales of property by FS. TFC's rental income constitutes passive income pursuant to §1.1297-1(c) and section 954(c)(1)(A), the exception in section 954(c)(2)(A) does

not apply, and, taking into account §1.1297-1(c)(3)(iii), section 1297(b)(2)(c) does not apply to characterize any of the rental income as non-passive income. TFC's income from its sales of property constitutes passive income pursuant to §1.1297-1(c) and section 954(c)(1)(B), although, pursuant to §1.1297-1(c)(1)(ii), only the excess of gains over losses is taken into account as gross income for purposes of section 1297. As a result, TFC's income, all of which is passive income, equals $20x ($5x + ($25x-$10x)) of gross income.

(c) *Elimination of certain intercompany assets and income.*—(1) *General rule for asset test.*—For purposes of section 1297, a tested foreign corporation does not take into account the value (or adjusted basis) of stock of a look-through subsidiary (*LTS stock*) or its proportionate share of an obligation of a look-through subsidiary (*LTS debt*) that it owns on a measuring date, including LTS stock and LTS debt that it is treated as owning pursuant to section 1297(c) and paragraph (b)(2) of this section or §1.1297-1(c)(2). The tested foreign corporation's proportionate share of a LTS debt is the value (or adjusted basis) of the debt multiplied by the tested foreign corporation's percentage ownership (by value) in the debtor look-through subsidiary. Furthermore, for purposes of section 1297, a tested foreign corporation does not take into account the value (or adjusted basis) of stock or obligations of the tested foreign corporation that it is treated as owning pursuant to section 1297(c) and paragraph (b)(2) of this section or §1.1297-1(c)(2).

(2) *General rule for income test.*—For purposes of section 1297, a tested foreign corporation does not take into account dividends derived with respect to LTS stock or its proportionate share of interest derived with respect to LTS debt, including amounts that it is treated as receiving pursuant to section 1297(c) and paragraph (b)(2) of this section or §1.1297-1(c)(2), other than dividends that are attributable to income that was not treated as received directly by the tested foreign corporation pursuant to paragraph (b)(2) of this section. The tested foreign corporation's proportionate share of interest is the amount of interest multiplied by the tested foreign corporation's percentage ownership (by value) in the debtor look-through subsidiary. Furthermore, for purposes of section 1297, a tested foreign corporation does not take into account dividends or interest with respect to stock or obligations of the tested foreign corporation that it is treated as receiving pursuant to section 1297(c) and paragraph (b)(2) of this section or §1.1297-1(c)(2).

(3) *Partnerships.*—For purposes of section 1297, the principles of paragraphs (c)(1) and (2) of this section apply with respect to ownership interests in and debt of a look-through partnership and with respect to distributions by a look-through partnership, other than distributions that are attributable to income that was not treated as received directly by the tested foreign corporation pursuant to §1.1297-1(c)(2), and interest derived with respect to the debt of a look-through partnership.

(4) *Examples.*—The following examples illustrate the rules of this paragraph (c). For purposes of the examples in this paragraph (c)(4), USP is a domestic corporation; USP owns 30% of TFC; TFC, LTS1, and LTS2 are foreign corporations that are not controlled foreign corporations within the meaning of section 957(a); FPS is a foreign partnership; and TFC, LTS1, and LTS2 measure assets for purposes of section 1297(a)(2) based on value.

(i) *Example 1*—(A) *Facts.* TFC directly owns 40% of the value of LTS1 stock on each of the measuring dates, and thus is treated under paragraph (b)(1) of this section as owning 40% of LTS1 on each of the measuring dates. TFC's assets include a loan to LTS1 with a balance of $1,000x on each of the measuring dates. During the first quarter of the taxable year, TFC received $20x of dividends from LTS1, which were attributable to income of LTS1 treated as received directly by TFC pursuant to paragraph (b)(2) of this section, and $30x of interest on the loan, both of which were paid in cash.

(B) *Results.* Under paragraph (c) of this section, for purposes of applying section 1297(a), TFC's assets do not include the stock of LTS1, and TFC's income does not include the $20x of dividends received from LTS1. Similarly, TFC's assets include only $600x ($1,000x loan - (40% x $1,000x)) of the loan to LTS1, and TFC's income includes only $18x ($30x interest - (40% x $30x)) of the interest from LTS1. However, TFC's assets include the entire $50x of cash ($20x of dividends and $30x of interest) received from LTS1.

(ii) *Example 2*—(A) *Facts.* The facts are the same as in paragraph (c)(4)(i)(A) of this section (the facts in *Example 1*), except that TFC also directly owns 30% of the value of LTS2 stock on each of the measuring dates, and thus is treated under paragraph (b)(1) of this section as owning 30% of LTS2, and LTS1's assets also include a loan to LTS2 with a balance of $200x on each of the measuring dates. During the first quarter of the taxable year, LTS1 received $5x of interest on the loan, which was paid in cash.

(B) *Results.* The results are the same as in paragraph (c)(4)(i)(B) of this section (the results in *Example 1*), except that TFC's assets also do not include the stock of LTS2. Similarly, although TFC would be treated under paragraph (b)(2) of this section as owning $80x (40% x $200x) of the LTS1 loan to LTS2, under paragraph (c) of this section, TFC does not take into account $60x (30% x $200x) of the loan to LTS2, and accordingly, its assets include only $20x ($80x-$60x) of the loan to LTS1. Furthermore, although TFC would be treated under paragraph (b)(2) of this section as receiving $2x (40% x $5x) of the interest received by LTS1 from LTS2, under paragraph (c) of this section, TFC does not take into account $1.5x (30% x $5x) of the interest received by LTS1, and accordingly, its income includes only $0.5x ($2x-$1.5x) of the interest from LTS2. Furthermore, TFC's assets include $2x (40% x $5x) of LTS1's cash received from LTS2.

(iii) *Example 3*—(A) *Facts.* TFC directly owns 80% of the value of LTS1 stock on each of the measuring dates, and thus is treated under paragraph (b)(1) of this section as owning 80% of LTS1 on each of the measuring dates. TFC also directly owns 50% of the value in FPS on each of the measuring dates. LTS1's assets include the remaining 50% of the value in FPS and a loan to FPS with a balance of $500x on each of the measuring dates. FPS's assets include a loan to TFC with a balance of $1000x on each of the measuring dates. During the first measuring period of the taxable year, FPS received $30x of interest from TFC, and LTS1 received $15x of interest from FPS, both of which were paid in cash. During the last measuring period of the taxable year, FPS received $80x of income from an unrelated person in cash and distributed $60x of such income in cash to TFC and LTS1 in proportion to their interests in FPS.

(B) *Results.* Under paragraph (c) of this section, for purposes of applying section 1297(a), TFC's assets do not include the stock of LTS1, the interests in FPS owned by TFC directly and through LTS1, any of the loan by FPS to TFC, or any of the loan by LTS1 to FPS. Similarly, TFC's income does not include any of the $30x of interest received by FPS from TFC, any of the $15x of interest received by LTS1 from FPS, or any of the $60x of distributions received by TFC and LTS1 from FPS. However, on each of the measuring dates, TFC's assets include $27x ((50% x $30x) + (80% x 50% x $30x)) of the $30 of cash received by FPS from TFC and $12x (80% x $15x) of the $15 of cash received by LTS1 from FPS. Moreover, on the last measuring date of the taxable year, TFC's assets include $18x ((50% x $20x) + (80% x 50% x $20x)) of the $20x ($80x - $60x) of cash received by FPS from the unrelated person and retained and $54 ((50% x $60x) + (80% x 50% x $60x)) of the $60x cash received by FPS from the unrelated person and distributed. Furthermore, TFC's income includes $72x ((50% x $80x) + (80% x 50% x $80x)) of the $80x of income received by FPS from an unrelated person.

(d) *Related person determination for purposes of section 1297(b)(2)(C).*—(1) *General rule.*—For purposes of section 1297(b)(2)(C), interest, dividends, rents, or royalties received or accrued by a look-through subsidiary (and treated as received directly by a tested foreign corporation pursuant to section 1297(c) and paragraph (b)(2) of this section) are considered received or accrued from a related person only if the payor of the interest, dividend, rent or royalty is a related person (within the meaning of section 954(d)(3)) with respect to the look-through subsidiary, taking into account § 1.1297-1(c)(1)(i)(D). Similarly, for purposes of 1297(b)(2)(C), interest, dividends, rents, or royalties received or accrued by a look-through partnership (and treated as received directly by a tested foreign corporation pursuant to § 1.1297-1(c)(2)) are considered received or accrued from a related person only if the payor of the interest, dividend, rent or royalty is a related person (within the meaning of section 954(d)(3)) with respect to the look-through partnership, taking into account § 1.1297-1(c)(1)(i)(D).

(2) *Example.*—The following example illustrates the rule of this paragraph (d).

(i) *Facts.* USP is a domestic corporation that owns 30% of TFC. TFC directly owns 30% of the value of FS1 stock, and thus under paragraph (b) of this section is treated as owning 30% of FS1. FS1 directly owns 60% of the vote of FS2 stock and 20% of the value of FS2 stock. The remaining vote and value of FS2 stock are owned by an unrelated foreign person. TFC, FS1, and FS2 are foreign corporations that are not controlled foreign corporations within the meaning of section 957(a). FS1 receives a $100x dividend from FS2.

(ii) *Results.* Pursuant to section 1297(c) and paragraph (b)(2) of this section, TFC is treated as receiving directly $30x of the dividend income received by FS1. FS2 is a "related person" with respect to FS1 for purposes of section 1297(b)(2)(C) because FS1 owns more than 50% of the vote of FS2. FS2 is not a "related person" with respect to TFC for purposes of section 1297(b)(2)(C). Under paragraph (d) of this section, for purposes of determining whether the dividend income received by FS1 is subject to the exception in section 1297(b)(2)(C) for purposes of testing the PFIC status of TFC, the dividend is treated as received from a related person because FS1 and FS2 are related persons within the meaning of section 1297(b)(2)(C). Therefore, to the extent the dividend income received by FS1 would be properly allocable to income of FS2 that is not passive income, the dividend income that TFC is treated as receiving under section

1297(c) is treated as non-passive income (as defined in § 1.1297-1(f)(5)).

(e) *Treatment of activities of certain look-through subsidiaries and look-through partnerships for purposes of section 954(c)(2)(A) active rents and royalties exception.*—(1) *General rule.*—An item of rent or royalty income received by a tested foreign corporation (including an amount treated as received or accrued pursuant to section 1297(c) and paragraph (b)(2) of this section or pursuant to § 1.1297-1(c)(2)) that would be passive income in the hands of the entity that actually received or accrued it is not passive income pursuant to § 1.1297-1(c)(1)(i)(A) and section 954(c)(2)(A) if the item would be excluded from foreign personal holding company income under section 954(c)(2)(A) and § 1.954-2(b)(6), (c), and (d), determined by taking into account the activities performed by the officers and staff of employees of the tested foreign corporation as well as activities performed by the officers and staff of employees of any look-through subsidiary in which the tested foreign corporation owns more than 50 percent by value (as determined under paragraph (b)(1) of this section) and any look-through partnership in which the tested foreign corporation owns, directly or indirectly, more than 50 percent.

(2) *Examples.*—The following examples illustrate the rule of this paragraph (e).

(i) *Example 1*—(A) *Facts.* USP is a domestic corporation that directly owns 20% of the outstanding stock of FS1. The remaining 80% of the outstanding stock of FS1 is directly owned by a foreign person that is not related to USP. FS1 directly owns 100% of the value of the outstanding stock of FS2 and directly owns 80% of the value of the outstanding stock of FS3. The remaining 20% of the outstanding stock of the value of the FS3 is directly owned by a foreign person that is not related to USP. FS2 directly owns 80% of the value of the outstanding stock of FS4. The remaining 20% of the value of the outstanding stock of FS4 is directly owned by a foreign person that is not related to USP. FS1, FS2, FS3 and FS4 are all organized in Country A and are not controlled foreign corporations within the meaning of section 957(a). FS4 owns real property that is leased to a person that is not a related person, but does not perform any activities. FS1 and FS2 also do not perform any activities. Officers and employees of FS3 in Country A perform activities with respect to the real property of FS4 that, if performed by officers or employees of FS4, would allow the rental income in the hands of FS4 to qualify for the exception from foreign personal holding company income in section 954(c)(2)(A) and § 1.954-2(b)(6) and (c)(1)(ii).

(B) *Results.* Under this paragraph (e), for purposes of determining whether the rental income treated under section 1297(c) and paragraph (b)(2) of this section as received directly by FS1 with respect to the real property owned and rented by FS4 is passive income for purposes of section 1297, the activities of FS3 are taken into account as a result of FS1's ownership of 80% by value (as determined under paragraph (b)(1) of this section) of FS3. Thus, the exception in section 954(c)(2)(A) would apply, and the rental income treated as received by FS1 would be treated as non-passive income for purposes of determining whether FS1 is a PFIC. Because FS2 and FS4 do not own more than 50 percent by value (as determined under paragraph (b)(1) of this section) of FS3, the activities of FS3 are not taken into account for purposes of determining whether the rental income treated as received by FS2 and actually received by FS4 with respect to the real property owned and rented by FS4 is passive income for purposes of section 1297. Thus, the exception in section 954(c)(2)(A) would not apply, and the rental income treated as received by FS2 and actually received by FS4 would be treated as passive income for purposes of determining whether FS2 and FS4 are PFICs.

(ii) *Example 2*—(A) *Facts.* The facts are the same as in paragraph (e)(2)(i)(A) of this section (the facts in *Example 1*), except that FS2 also owns real property that is leased to a person that is not a related person, and the officers and employees of FS2 in Country A engage in activities that would allow rental income received by FS2 with respect to its real property to qualify for the exception in section 954(c)(2)(A) and § 1.954-2(b)(6) and (c)(1)(iv), relying on the rule in § 1.954-2(c)(2)(ii) that provides that an organization is substantial in relation to rents if active leasing expenses equal or exceed 25 percent of adjusted leasing profit. However, the active leasing expenses of FS1 are less than 25 percent of its adjusted leasing profit, which includes the rental income of FS4 treated as received directly by FS1 as well as the rental income of FS2 treated as received directly by FS1.

(B) *Results.* Because FS2's rental income constitutes non-passive income as a result of the application of § 1.1297-1(c)(1)(i)(A) and section 954(c)(2)(A), it is treated as non-passive income treated as received by FS1 for purposes of determining whether FS1 is a PFIC, and accordingly, it is not necessary to rely on paragraph (e) of this section.

(f) *Gain on disposition of stock in a look-through subsidiary.*—(1) *Amount of gain taken into account.*—The amount of gain derived from a tested foreign corporation's direct disposition of stock of a look-through subsidiary, or an indirect disposition resulting from the disposition of stock of a look-through subsidiary by other look-through subsidiaries or by look-through partnerships, that is taken into account by the tested foreign corporation for purposes of section 1297(a)(1), section 1298(b)(3), and §1.1298-2 is the residual gain. The residual gain equals the total gain recognized by the tested foreign corporation (including gain treated as recognized by the tested foreign corporation pursuant to section 1297(c) and paragraph (b)(2) of this section or §1.1297-1(c)(2)) from the disposition of the stock of the look-through subsidiary reduced (but not below zero) by unremitted earnings. *Unremitted earnings* are the excess (if any) of the aggregate income (if any) taken into account by the tested foreign corporation pursuant to section 1297(c) and paragraph (b)(2) of this section or §1.1297-1(c)(2) with respect to the stock of the disposed-of look-through subsidiary (including with respect to any other look-through subsidiary, to the extent it is owned by the tested foreign corporation indirectly through the disposed-of look-through subsidiary) over the aggregate dividends (if any) received by the tested foreign corporation from the disposed-of look-through subsidiary with respect to the stock. For purposes of this paragraph (f)(1), the amount of gain derived from the disposition of stock of a look-through subsidiary and income of and dividends received from the look-through subsidiary is determined on a share-by-share basis.

(2) *Characterization of residual gain as passive income.*—For purposes of section 1297(a)(1), section 1298(b)(3), and §1.1298-2, the residual gain is characterized as passive income or non-passive income based on the relative amounts of passive assets and non-passive assets (as defined in §1.1297-1(f)(6) and (4), respectively) of the disposed-of look-through subsidiary (and any other look-through subsidiary to the extent owned indirectly through the look-through subsidiary) treated as held by the tested foreign corporation on the date of the disposition of the look-through subsidiary. For the purpose of this paragraph (f)(2), the relative amounts of passive assets and non-passive assets held by the look-through subsidiary are measured under the same method (value or adjusted bases) used to measure the assets of the tested foreign corporation for purposes of section 1297(a)(2).

(3) *Examples.*—The following examples illustrate the rules of this paragraph (f). For purposes of the examples in this paragraph (f)(3), USP is a domestic corporation, TFC and FS are foreign corporations that are not controlled foreign corporations within the meaning of section 957(a), and USP, TFC, and FS each has outstanding a single class of stock with 100 shares outstanding and a calendar taxable year.

(i) *Example 1*—(A) *Facts.* USP owned 30% of the outstanding stock of TFC throughout Years 1, 2, 3, and 4. In Year 1, TFC purchased 5 shares of FS stock, representing 5% of the stock of FS, from an unrelated person. On the first day of Year 3, TFC purchased 20 shares of FS stock, representing 20% of the stock of FS, from an unrelated person. TFC owned 25% of the outstanding stock of FS throughout Years 3 and 4. Prior to Year 3, TFC did not include any amount in income with respect to FS under section 1297(c)(2). During Years 3 and 4, for purposes of section 1297(a)(1), TFC included in income, in the aggregate, $40x of income with respect to FS under section 1297(c) and paragraph (b)(2) of this section. TFC did not receive dividends from FS during Year 1, 2, 3, or 4. For purposes of section 1297(a)(2), TFC measures its assets based on their fair market value as provided under section 1297(e). On the last day of Year 4, TFC recognizes a loss with respect to the sale of 5 shares of FS stock, and a $110x gain with respect to the sale of 20 shares of FS stock. On the date of the sale, FS owns non-passive assets with an aggregate fair market value of $150x, and passive assets with an aggregate fair market value of $50x.

(B) *Results.* For purposes of applying section 1297(a)(1) to TFC for Year 4, TFC must take into account $78x of residual gain, as provided by paragraph (f)(1) of this section, which equals the amount by which the $110x gain recognized on the sale of 20 shares exceeds the aggregate pro rata share of $32x income ($40x x 20/25) taken into account by TFC with respect to the 20 shares in FS under section 1297(c) and paragraph (b)(2) of this section during Years 3 and 4. There is zero residual gain on the sale of 5 shares of FS stock because they were sold at a loss. Under paragraph (f)(2) of this section, $58.50x of the residual gain is non-passive income ($78x x ($150x/$200x)) and $19.50x is passive income ($78x x ($50x/$200x)).

(ii) *Example 2*—(A) *Facts.* The facts are the same as in paragraph (f)(3)(i)(A) of this section (the facts in *Example 1*), except that in Year 1, TFC purchased 15 shares of FS stock, representing 15% of the stock of FS, from an unrelated person, and on the first day of Year 3, TFC purchased an additional 15 shares of FS stock, representing 15%

of the stock of FS, from an unrelated person, and on the last day of Year 4, TFC recognizes gain of $10x of the sale of 15 shares of FS stock purchased in Year 1, and gain of $60x on the sale of the other 15 shares of FS stock purchased in Year 3.

(B) *Results.* For purposes of applying section 1297(a)(1) to TFC for Year 4, TFC must take into account $40x of residual gain, as provided by paragraph (f)(1) of this section, which equals the amount by which the $60x gain recognized on the sale of the 15 shares acquired in Year 3 exceeds the pro rata aggregate share of $20x income ($40x x 15/30) taken into account by TFC with respect to the 15 shares in FS under section 1297(c)(2) during Years 3 and 4. There is zero residual gain on the sale of the other 15 shares of FS stock because the $10x of gain does not exceed the aggregate pro rata share of $20x income taken into account by TFC with respect to the other 15 shares of FS under section 1297(c) and paragraph (b)(2) of this section. Under paragraph (f)(2) of this section, $30x of the residual gain is non-passive income ($40x x ($150x/$200x)) and $10x is passive income ($40x x ($50x/$200x)).

(iii) *Example 3*—(i) *Facts.* The facts are the same as in paragraph (f)(3)(ii)(A) of this section (the facts in *Example 2*), except that TFC received, in the aggregate, $20x of dividends from FS during Year 2.

(B) *Results.* The results are the same as in paragraph (f)(3)(ii)(B) of this section (the results in *Example 2*), except that the residual gain is $50x, which equals the $40x of residual gain attributable to the 15 shares acquired in Year 3, as computed in paragraph (f)(3)(ii)(B) of this section (the results in *Example 2*), plus the $10x of gain recognized on the 15 shares acquired in Year 1 reduced by $0x, the amount by which the pro rata share of aggregate income ($20x) taken into account by TFC with respect to those 15 shares of FS stock under section 1297(c) and paragraph (b)(2) of this section exceeds the aggregate pro rata amount of dividends with respect to those 15 shares of FS stock ($20x) received by TFC from FS. Under paragraph (f)(2) of this section, $35x of the residual gain is non-passive income ($50x x ($150x/$200x)) and $15x is passive income ($50x x ($50x/$200x)).

(g) *Definitions.*—The following definitions apply for purposes of this section:

(1) *Look-through subsidiary.*—The term *look-through subsidiary* means, with respect to a tested foreign corporation—

(i) For purposes of section 1297(a)(2) and paragraph (b)(2)(i) of this section, a corporation at least 25 percent of the value of the stock of which is owned (as determined under paragraph (b)(1) of this section) by the tested foreign corporation on the measuring date;

(ii) For purposes of section 1297(a)(1)—

(A) For the taxable year, a corporation with respect to which the average percentage ownership (which is equal to the percentage ownership (by value) (as determined under paragraph (b)(1) of this section) on each measuring date during the taxable year, divided by the number of measuring dates in the year) by the tested foreign corporation during the tested foreign corporation's taxable year is at least 25 percent; or

(B) For a measuring period, a corporation at least 25 percent of the value of the stock of which is owned (as determined under paragraph (b)(1) of this section) by the tested foreign corporation on the measuring date, provided all items of gross income of the corporation for each of the measuring periods in the taxable year for which the tested foreign corporation owns at least 25 percent of the value (as determined under paragraph (b)(1) of this section) on the relevant measuring dates can be established; and

(iii) For purposes of paragraph (f) of this section and §1.1298-2, a corporation at least 25 percent of the value of the stock of which is owned (as determined under paragraph (b)(1) of this section) by the tested foreign corporation immediately before the disposition of stock of the corporation.

(2) *LTS debt.*—The term *LTS debt* has the meaning provided in paragraph (c)(1) of this section.

(3) *LTS stock.*—The term *LTS stock* has the meaning provided in paragraph (c)(1) of this section.

(4) *Residual gain.*—The term *residual gain* has the meaning provided in paragraph (f)(1) of this section.

(5) *Unremitted earnings.*—The term *unremitted earnings* has the meaning provided in paragraph (f)(1) of this section.

(h) *Applicability date.*—The rules of this section apply to taxable years of shareholders beginning on or after the date of publication of the Treasury decision adopting these rules as final regulations in the **Federal Register**. [Reg. §1.1297-2.]

Application of the Grantor Trust Rules to Nonexempt Employees' Trusts

Application of the Grantor Trust Rules to Nonexempt Employees' Trusts.—Reg. §1.1297-4, relating to the application of the grantor trust rules to nonexempt employees' trusts, is proposed (published in the Federal Register on September 27, 1996) (REG-209826-96).

☐ Par. 4. Section 1.1297-4 is added to read as follows:

§1.1297-4. Application of subpart E of subchapter J with respect to foreign employees' trusts.—(a) *General rules.*—For purposes of part VI of subchapter P, chapter 1 of the Code, a foreign employer that is not a controlled foreign corporation is not treated as the owner of any portion of a foreign employees' trust (as defined in §1.671-1(h)(2)) except as provided in this paragraph (a), regardless of whether the employer has a power or interest described in sections 673 through 677 over any portion of the trust.

(1) *Principal purpose to avoid classification as a passive foreign investment company.*—If a principal purpose for a transfer of property by any person to a foreign employees' trust (as defined in §1.671-1(h)(2)) is to avoid classification of a foreign corporation as a passive foreign investment company, then the following rule applies. If the foreign employer has a power or interest described in sections 673 through 677 over the trust, then the grantor trust rules of subpart E of part I of subchapter J, chapter 1 of the Code will apply, for purposes of part VI of subchapter P, to a fixed dollar amount in the trust that is equal to the fair market value of the property that is transferred for the purpose of avoiding classification as a passive foreign investment company. Whether a principal purpose for a transfer is the avoidance of classification as a passive foreign investment company will be determined on the basis of all of the facts and circumstances, including whether the amount of assets held by the foreign employees' trust is reasonably related to the plan's anticipated liabilities, taking into account any local law and practice relating to proper funding levels.

(2) *Principal purpose to reduce or eliminate taxation under section 1291 or 1293.*—If a principal purpose for a transfer of property by any person to a foreign employees' trust (as defined in §1.671-1(h)(2)) is to reduce or eliminate taxation under section 1291 or 1293, then the following rule applies. If the foreign employer has a power or interest described in sections 673 through 677 over the trust, then the provisions of subpart E will apply, for purposes of part VI of subchapter P, to a fixed dollar amount in the trust that is equal to the fair market value of the property transferred for the purpose of reducing or eliminating taxation under section 1291 or 1293. Whether a principal purpose for a transfer is to reduce or eliminate taxation under section 1291 or 1293 will be determined on the basis of all the facts and circumstances, including whether the amount of assets held by the foreign employees' trust is reasonably related to the plan's anticipated liabilities, taking into account any local law and practice relating to proper funding levels.

(3) *Application to employer entity.*—The rules of this section apply to the employer whose employees benefit under the deferred compensation plan funded through the foreign employees' trust, or, in the case of a deferred compensation plan covering independent contractors, the recipient of services performed by those independent contractors, regardless of whether the plan is maintained through another entity. Thus, for example, where a deferred compensation plan benefitting employees of a foreign employer that is not a controlled foreign corporation is funded through a foreign employees' trust, the foreign employer is considered to be the grantor of the foreign employees' trust for purposes of this paragraph (a).

(b) *Effective date.*—This section applies to taxable years of a foreign corporation ending after September 27, 1996. [Reg. §1.1297-4.]

Passive Foreign Investment Companies: Guidance

Passive Foreign Investment Companies: Guidance.—Reg. §§1.1297-4 and 1.1297-5, regarding the determination of ownership in a passive foreign investment company within the meaning of section 1297(a) and the treatment of certain income received or accrued by a foreign corporation and assets held by a foreign corporation for purposes of section 1297, are proposed (published in the Federal Register on July 11, 2019) (REG-105474-18).

Par. 6. Sections 1.1297-4 and 1.1297-5 are added to read as follows:

§1.1297-4. Qualifying insurance corporation.—(a) *Scope.*—This section provides rules for determining whether a foreign corporation is a qualifying insurance corporation for purposes of section 1297(f). Paragraph (b) of this section provides the general rule for determining whether a foreign corporation is a qualifying insurance corporation. Paragraph (c) of this section describes the 25 percent test in section 1297(f)(1)(B). Paragraph (d) of this section contains rules for applying the alternative facts and circumstances test in section 1297(f)(2). Paragraph (e) of this section contains rules limiting the amount of applicable insurance liabilities for purposes of the 25 percent test described in paragraph (c) of this section and the alternative facts and circumstances test described in paragraph (d) of this section. Paragraph (f) of this section provides definitions that apply for purposes of this section. Paragraph (g) of this section provides the applicability date of this section.

(b) *Qualifying insurance corporation.*—For purposes of section 1297(b)(2)(B), this section and §1.1297-5, a qualifying insurance corporation (QIC) is a foreign corporation that—

(1) Is an insurance company as defined in section 816(a) that would be subject to tax under subchapter L if the corporation were a domestic corporation; and

(2) Satisfies—

(i) The 25 percent test described in paragraph (c) of this section; or

(ii) The requirements for an election to apply the alternative facts and circumstances test as described in paragraph (d) of this section and a United States person has made an election as described in paragraph (d)(5) of this section.

(c) *25 percent test.*—A foreign corporation satisfies the 25 percent test if the amount of its applicable insurance liabilities exceeds 25 percent of its total assets. This determination is made on the basis of the liabilities and assets reported on the corporation's applicable financial statement for the last year ending with or within the taxable year.

(d) *Election to apply the alternative facts and circumstances test.*—(1) *In general.*—A United States person that owns stock in a foreign corporation that fails to qualify as a QIC solely because of the 25 percent test may elect to treat the stock of the corporation as stock of a QIC if the foreign corporation—

(i) Is predominantly engaged in an insurance business as described in paragraph (d)(2) of this section;

(ii) Failed to satisfy the 25 percent test solely due to runoff-related circumstances, as described in paragraph (d)(3) of this section, or rating-related circumstances, as described in paragraph (d)(4) of this section; and

(iii) Reports an amount of applicable insurance liabilities that is at least 10 percent of the amount of the total assets on its applicable financial statement for the last annual reporting period ending with or within the corporation's taxable year (the *10 percent test*).

(2) *Predominantly engaged in an insurance business.*—(i) *In general.*—A foreign corporation is predominantly engaged in an insurance business in any taxable year during which more than half of the business of the foreign corporation is the issuing of insurance or annuity contracts or the reinsuring of risks underwritten by insurance companies. This determination is made based on whether the particular facts and circumstances of the foreign corporation are comparable to commercial insurance arrangements providing similar lines of coverage to unrelated parties in arm's length transactions. The fact that a foreign corporation has been holding itself out as an insurer for a long period is not determinative of whether the foreign corporation is predominantly engaged in an insurance business.

(ii) *Facts and circumstances.*—Facts and circumstances to consider in determining whether a foreign corporation is predominantly engaged in an insurance business include—

(A) Claims payment patterns for the current year and prior years;

(B) The foreign corporation's loss exposure as calculated for a regulator or for a credit rating agency, or, if those are not calculated, for internal pricing purposes;

(C) The percentage of gross receipts constituting premiums for the current and prior years; and

(D) The number and size of insurance contracts issued or taken on through reinsurance by the foreign corporation.

(iii) *Examples of facts indicating a foreign corporation is not predominantly engaged in an insurance business.*—Examples of facts that may indicate a foreign corporation is not predominantly engaged in an insurance business include—

(A) A small overall number of insured risks with low likelihood but large potential costs;

(B) Employees and agents of the foreign corporation focused to a greater degree on investment activities than underwriting activities; and

(C) Low loss exposure.

(3) *Runoff-related circumstances.*—During the annual reporting period covered by the applicable financial statement, a foreign corporation fails to satisfy the 25 percent test solely due to runoff-related circumstances only if the corporation—

(i) Was actively engaged in the process of terminating its pre-existing, active insurance or reinsurance underwriting operations pursuant to an adopted plan of liquidation or a termination of operations under the supervision of its applicable insurance regulatory body;

(ii) Did not issue or enter into any insurance, annuity, or reinsurance contract, other than a contractually obligated renewal of an existing insurance contract or a reinsurance contract pursuant to and consistent with the plan of liquidation or a termination of operations; and

(iii) Made payments during the annual reporting period covered by the applicable financial statement to satisfy the claims under insurance, annuity, or reinsurance contracts, and the payments cause the corporation to fail to satisfy the 25 percent test.

(4) *Rating-related circumstances.*—A foreign corporation fails to satisfy the 25 percent test solely due to rating-related circumstances only if—

(i) The 25 percent test is not met as a result of the specific requirements with respect to capital and surplus that a generally recognized credit rating agency imposes; and

(ii) The foreign corporation complies with the requirements of the credit rating agency in order to maintain the minimum credit rating required for the foreign corporation to be classified as secure to write new insurance business for the current year.

(5) *Election.*—(i) *In general.*—A United States person may make the election under section 1297(f)(2) if the foreign corporation directly provides the United States person a statement, signed by a responsible officer of the foreign corporation or an authorized representative of the foreign corporation, or the foreign corporation makes a publicly available statement (such as in a public filing, disclosure statement, or other notice provided to United States persons that are shareholders of the foreign corporation) that it satisfied the requirements of section 1297(f)(2) and paragraph (d)(1) of this section during the foreign corporation's the taxable year. However, a United States person may not rely upon any statement by the foreign corporation to make the election under section 1297(f)(2) if the shareholder knows or has reason to know that the statement made by the foreign corporation was incorrect.

(ii) *Information provided by foreign corporation.*—In addition to a statement that the foreign corporation satisfied the requirements of section 1297(f)(2) and paragraph (d)(1) of this section, the statement described in paragraph (d)(5)(i) of this section also must include:

(A) The ratio of applicable insurance liabilities to total assets for the taxable year; and

(B) A statement indicating whether the failure to satisfy the 25 percent test described in paragraph (c) of this section was the result of runoff-related or rating-related circumstances, along with a brief description of those circumstances.

(iii) *Time and manner for making the election.*—The election described in paragraph (d)(1) of this section must be made by a United States person who owns stock in the foreign corporation (directly or indirectly) by completing the appropriate part of Form 8621 (or successor form) for each year in which the election applies. A United States person must attach the Form 8621 (or successor form) to its Federal income tax return for the taxable year to which the election relates on or before the due date (including extensions) for the filing of the return. The United States person must attach to the Form 8621 the statement provided by the foreign corporation described in paragraph (d)(1) of this section. If the foreign corporation makes a publicly available statement instead of providing a statement to the United States person, the United States person must attach a statement to the Form 8621 incorporating the information provided in the publicly available statement.

(e) *Rules limiting the amount of applicable insurance liabilities.*—(1) *In general.*—For purposes of determining whether a foreign corporation satisfies the 25 percent test described in paragraph (c) of this section or the 10 percent test described in paragraph (d)(1)(iii) of this section, the rules of this paragraph (e) apply to limit the amount of applicable insurance liabilities of the foreign corporation.

(2) *General limitation on applicable insurance liabilities.*—The amount of applicable insurance liabilities may not exceed the lesser of:

(i) The amount of applicable insurance liabilities shown on the most recent applicable financial statement;

(ii) The minimum amount of applicable insurance liabilities required by the applicable law or regulation of the jurisdiction of the applicable regulatory body; or

(iii) For a foreign corporation that prepares a financial statement on the basis of a financial reporting standard for a purpose other than financial reporting, the amount of the applicable insurance liabilities on that financial statement.

(3) *Additional limitation on amount of applicable insurance liabilities for a foreign corporation that does not prepare a financial statement based on a financial reporting standard.*—(i) *In general.*—If a foreign corporation has an applicable financial statement described in paragraph (f)(1)(iii) of this section and the applicable financial statement does not discount incurred but unpaid losses and loss reserves on an economically reasonable basis, the amount of applicable insurance liabilities may not exceed the amount of applicable insurance liabilities on the applicable financial statement reduced in accordance with the discounting principles that would have applied under a financial reporting standard, if the foreign corporation had prepared a financial statement under a financial reporting standard for the last year ending with or within the taxable year.

(ii) *Choice of accounting method.*—The foreign corporation may choose whether to apply generally accepted accounting principles or international financial reporting principles to calculate the discounted amount of its applicable insurance liabilities for purposes of paragraph (e)(3)(i)(B) of this section. If the foreign corporation does not choose between these financial reporting standards, generally accepted accounting principles will apply.

(4) *Changes to financial statements prepared.*—Any foreign corporation that has prepared a financial statement on the basis of a financial reporting standard for an annual reporting period that included December 22, 2017, or any subsequent annual reporting period, must continue to prepare its applicable financial statement using a financial reporting standard unless the foreign corporation has a non-Federal tax business purpose for using the annual statement described in paragraph (f)(1)(iii) of this section. If a foreign corporation has no non-Federal tax business purpose for using the annual statement described in paragraph (f)(1)(iii) of this section and does not continue to prepare an applicable financial statement using a financial reporting standard, its applicable insurance liabilities are treated as $0 for purposes of this section.

(f) *Definitions.*—For purposes of this section, the following terms have the meanings described in this paragraph (f).

(1) *Applicable financial statement.*—The term *applicable financial statement* means the financial statement that is used by the foreign corporation for financial reporting purposes and that is—

(i) Made on the basis of generally accepted accounting principles;

(ii) Made on the basis of international financial reporting standards, if there is no statement that is made on the basis of generally accepted accounting principles; or

(iii) The annual statement required to be filed with the applicable insurance regulatory body, as defined in paragraph (f)(3) of this section, if there is no statement made on the basis of either general accounting principles or international financial reporting standards. The annual statement required to be filed with the applicable insurance regulatory body must provide complete information regarding the foreign corporation's operations and financial condition for the annual reporting period ending with or within the taxable year.

(2) *Applicable insurance liabilities.*—With respect to any life or property and casualty insurance business of a foreign corporation, the term *applicable insurance liabilities* means—

(i) Occurred losses for which the foreign corporation has become liable but has not paid before the end of the last annual reporting period ending with or within the taxable year, including unpaid claims for death benefits, annuity contracts, and health insurance benefits;

(ii) Unpaid expenses (including reasonable estimates of anticipated expenses) of investigating and adjusted unpaid losses described in paragraph (f)(2)(i) of this section; and

(iii) The aggregate amount of reserves (excluding deficiency, contingency, or unearned premium reserves) held for future, unaccrued health insurance claims and claims with respect to contracts providing coverage for mortality or morbidity risks, including annuity benefits dependent upon the life expectancy of one or more individuals.

(3) *Applicable insurance regulatory body.*—The term *applicable insurance regulatory body* means the entity that has been established by law to license or authorize a corporation to engage in an insurance business, to regulate insurance company solvency and to which the applicable financial statement is provided.

(4) *Financial reporting standard.*—The term *financial reporting standard* means either GAAP or international financial reporting standards.

(5) *Generally accepted accounting principles or GAAP.*—The term *generally accepted accounting principles* or *GAAP* means United States generally accepted accounting principles.

(6) *Insurance business.*—Solely for purposes of this section, *insurance business* has the meaning described in § 1.1297-5(c)(2).

(7) *Total assets.*—For purposes of section 1297(f) and this section, a foreign corporation's *total assets* are the aggregate end-of-period value of the real property and personal property that the foreign corporation reports on its applicable financial statement for the last annual accounting period ending with or within the taxable year.

(g) *Applicability date.*—This section applies to taxable years of United States persons that are shareholders in certain foreign corporations beginning on or after the date of publication of the Treasury decision adopting these rules as final regulations in the **Federal Register**. [Reg. § 1.1297-4.]

§ 1.1297-5. Exception from the definition of passive income for active insurance income.—(a) *Scope.*—This section provides rules pertaining to the exception from passive income under section 1297(b)(2)(B) for income derived in the active conduct of an insurance business and rules related to certain income of a qualifying domestic insurance corporation. Paragraph (b) of this section provides a general rule that excludes from passive income certain income of a qualifying insurance corporation (QIC) and certain income of a qualifying domestic insurance corporation. Paragraph (c) of this section provides rules for determining the amount of income derived by a QIC in the active conduct of an insurance business. Paragraph (d) of this section defines income of a qualifying domestic insurance corporation that is not treated as passive for purposes of section 1297. Paragraph (e) of this section provides rules excluding certain assets for purposes of the passive asset test under section 1297(a)(2). Paragraph (f) of this section provides rules concerning the treatment of income and assets of certain look-through subsidiaries and look-through partnerships of a QIC. Paragraph (g) of this section provides a rule prohibiting the double counting of any item for purposes of this section. Paragraph (h) of this section provides definitions applicable to the rules of this section. Paragraph (i) of this section provides the applicability date of this section.

(b) *Exclusion from passive income of active insurance income.*—For purposes of section 1297 and § 1.1297-1, passive income does not include—

(1) Income that a QIC derives in the active conduct of an insurance business as determined under paragraph (c) of this section; and

(2) Income from a qualifying domestic insurance corporation as determined under paragraph (d) of this section, except that this exclusion does not apply to determine whether a tested foreign corporation (as defined in § 1.1297-1(f)(8)) is a PFIC for purposes of section 1298(a)(2) and § 1.1291-1b(8)(ii).

(c) *Income derived by a QIC in the active conduct of an insurance business.*—(1) *In general.*—Income that a QIC derives in the active conduct of an insurance business is an amount equal to the QIC's passive income (as defined in § 1.1297-1(c) and taking into account the exceptions in section 1297(b)(2) other than the exception provided in section 1297(b)(2)(B) and this section) earned with respect to assets of a QIC that are available to satisfy liabilities of the QIC related to its insurance business (as described in paragraph (c)(2) of this section), multiplied by—

(i) 100 percent if the active conduct percentage determined under paragraph (c)(4) of this section equals or exceeds 50 percent; or

(ii) Zero if the active conduct percentage determined under paragraph (c)(4) of this section is less than 50 percent.

(2) *Insurance business.*—Solely for purposes of § 1.1297-4 and this section, an insurance business is the business of issuing insurance and annuity contracts and the reinsuring of risks underwritten by insurance companies, together with those investment activities and administrative services that are required to support (or that are substantially related to) those insurance, annuity, or reinsurance contracts issued or entered into by the QIC.

(3) *Active conduct of an insurance business.*—(i) *In general.*—For purposes of determining whether a QIC engages in the active conduct of an insurance business, active conduct is determined based on all the facts and circumstances. In general, a QIC actively conducts an insurance business only if the officers and employees of the QIC carry out substantial managerial and operational activities. A QIC's officers and employees are considered to include the officers and employees of another entity only if the QIC satisfies the control test

described in paragraph (c)(3)(ii) with respect to the officers and employees of the other entity. In determining whether the officers and employees of the QIC carry out substantial managerial and operational activities, however, the activities of independent contractors are disregarded.

(ii) *Control test.*—A QIC's officers and employees are considered to include the officers and employees of another entity when the requirements of paragraphs (c)(3)(ii)(A) through (C) of this section are satisfied.

(A) *Ownership.*—(1) *Ownership by or of a corporation.*—If the other entity is a corporation—

(i) The QIC owns, or is considered to own within the meaning of section 958(a), determined without regard to whether an intermediate entity is domestic or foreign, more than 50 percent of the total combined voting power of all classes of stock of the other corporation entitled to vote, and more than 50 percent of the total value of the stock of the other corporation; or

(ii) A common parent owns, or is considered to own within the meaning of section 958(a), determined without regard to whether an intermediate entity is domestic or foreign, more than 80 percent of the total combined voting power of all classes of stock entitled to vote and more than 80 percent of the total value of the stock of each of the QIC and the other corporation.

(2) *Ownership of a partnership.*—If the other entity is a partnership—

(i) The QIC owns, directly or indirectly, more than 50 percent of the interests in the capital and profits in the entity; or

(ii) A common parent owns, directly or indirectly, more than 80 percent of the interests in the capital and profits in the entity and owns, or is considered to own within the meaning of section 958(a), determined without regard to whether an intermediate entity is domestic or foreign, more than 80 percent of the total combined voting power of all classes of stock entitled to vote and more than 80 percent of the total value of the stock of the QIC.

(B) *Control and supervision.*—The QIC exercises regular oversight and supervision over the services performed by the other entity's officers and employees for the QIC.

(C) *Compensation.*—The QIC either—

(1) Pays directly all the compensation of the other entity's officers and employees attributable to services performed for the production or acquisition of premiums and investment income on assets held to meet its obligations under the insurance, annuity, or reinsurance contracts issued or entered into by the QIC (*insurance services*);

(2) Reimburses the other entity for the portion of its expenses, including compensation and related expenses (determined in accordance with section 482 and taking into account all expenses that would be included in the total services costs under § 1.482-9(j) and (k)(2)) for the insurance services performed for the QIC or by the other entity's officers and employees; or

(3) Otherwise pays arm's length compensation in accordance with section 482 on a fee-related basis to the other entity for the insurance services provided.

(4) *Active conduct percentage.*—(i) *In general.*—A QIC's active conduct percentage for a taxable year is the percentage calculated (to the nearest percent) by dividing—

(A) The aggregate amount of expenses, including compensation (or reimbursement of compensation) and related expenses, for services of the officers and employees of the QIC (or another entity under an arrangement that satisfies the requirements of paragraph (c)(3)(ii) of this section) incurred by the QIC for the taxable year that are related to the production or acquisition of premiums and investment income on assets held to meet its obligations under the insurance, annuity, or reinsurance contracts issued or entered into by the QIC, by;

(B) The aggregate of—

(1) The amount described in paragraph (c)(4)(i)(A) of this section; and

(2) The amount of all expenses paid for the taxable year by the QIC to a person other than a person whose services for the QIC are covered by the expenses included in paragraph (c)(4)(i)(A) of this section for the production or acquisition of premiums and investment income on assets held to meet obligations under the insurance, annuity, or reinsurance contracts issued or entered into by the QIC.

(ii) *Related expense determination.*—For purposes of determining the amount included in the numerator under paragraph (c)(4)(i)(A) of this section, the cost of compensation and related expenses include all costs in cash or in kind (including stock-based compensation) that, based on analysis of the facts and circumstances, are directly identified with, or reasonably allocated in accordance with the principles of § 1.482-9(k)(2) to, the services of the officers and employees of the insurance company (or related party, as appropriate). In general, costs for the purpose of this paragraph (c)(4)(ii) include all resources expended, used, or made available to achieve the specific objective for which the service of the officer or employee is rendered. For the purpose of this paragraph (c)(4)(ii), reference to generally accepted accounting principles or Federal income tax accounting rules may provide a useful starting point but will not necessarily be conclusive regarding inclusion of costs, and such costs do not include interest expense, foreign income taxes (as defined in §1.901-2(a)), or Federal income taxes.

(iii) *Ceding commission.*—For purposes of paragraph (c)(4)(i) of this section, ceding commissions are not taken into account in either the numerator or denominator of the active conduct percentage.

(d) *Income of qualifying domestic insurance corporation.*—The income of a domestic corporation is income of a qualifying domestic insurance corporation if the domestic corporation is subject to—

(1) Tax as an insurance company under subchapter L of chapter 1 of subtitle A of the Internal Revenue Code; and

(2) Federal income tax on its net income.

(e) *Exclusion of assets for purposes of the passive asset test under section 1297(a)(2).*—For purposes of section 1297 and §1.1297-1, passive assets (as defined in §1.1297-1(f)(6)), do not include—

(1) Assets of a QIC available to satisfy liabilities of the QIC related to its insurance business (as described in paragraph (c)(2) of this section), if the active conduct percentage of the QIC equals or exceeds 50 percent; and

(2) Assets of a qualifying domestic insurance corporation that meets the requirements described in paragraph (d) of this section, except that this exclusion does not apply to determine whether a tested foreign corporation (as defined in §1.1297-1(f)(8)) is a PFIC for purposes of section 1298(a)(2) and §1.1291-1(b)(8)(ii).

(f) *Treatment of income and assets of certain look-through subsidiaries and look-through partnerships for purposes of the section 1297(b)(2)(B) exception.*—(1) *General rule.*—An item of income treated as received or accrued or an asset treated as held by a QIC pursuant to section 1297(c) and §1.1297-2(b)(2) or pursuant to §1.1297-1(c)(2) or (d)(3)

that would be passive income or a passive asset is treated as an item of income or an asset of the QIC for purposes of paragraphs (c) and (e) of this section.

(2) *Applicable statements for tested foreign corporations applying paragraph (f)(1) of this section.*—For purposes of paragraph (f)(1) of this section, an item of passive income or passive asset in the hands of an entity other than a QIC (subsidiary entity) may only be treated as an item of income or an asset used in the active conduct of an insurance business by a foreign corporation treated as a QIC for purposes of paragraphs (c) and (e) of this section if the applicable financial statement used to test the QIC status of the foreign corporation includes the assets and liabilities of the subsidiary entity.

(g) *No double counting.*—Nothing in this section or §1.1297-4 permits any item to be counted more than once.

(h) *Definitions.*—For purposes of this section, the following terms have the meanings described in this paragraph (h).

(1) *Insurance services.*—The term *insurance services* has the meaning provided in paragraph (c)(3)(ii)(C)(1) of this section.

(2) *Investment activity.*—The term *investment activity* means any activity engaged in by a QIC to produce income of a kind that would be passive income (as defined in §1.1297-1(c)). Investment activities include those activities that are required to support or are substantially related to insurance and annuity contracts issued or reinsured by a QIC only to the extent that income produced by the activities is generated by assets available to satisfy liabilities of the QIC related to the insurance business, as described in paragraph (c)(2) of this section.

(3) *Qualifying insurance corporation* or *QIC.*—The term *qualifying insurance corporation* or *QIC* has the meaning described in §1.1297-4.

(i) *Applicability date.*—This section applies to taxable years of United States persons that are shareholders in certain foreign corporations beginning on or after the date of publication of the Treasury decision adopting these rules as final regulations in the **Federal Register**. [Reg. §1.1297-5.]

Passive Foreign Investment Companies: Guidance

Passive Foreign Investment Companies: Guidance.—Amendments to Reg. §1.1298-0, regarding the determination of ownership in a passive foreign investment company within the meaning of section 1297(a) and the treatment of certain income received or accrued by a foreign corporation and assets held by a foreign corporation for purposes of section 1297, are proposed (published in the Federal Register on July 11, 2019) (REG-105474-18).

Par. 7. Section 1.1298-0 is amended by:
1. Revising the introductory text.
2. Adding entries for §§1.1298-2 and 1.1298-4 in numerical order.
The revision and additions read as follows:

§1.1298-0. Passive foreign investment company—table of contents.—This section contains a listing of the paragraph headings for §§1.1298-1, 1.1298-2, 1.1298-3, and 1.1298-4.

* * *

§1.1298-2 Rules for certain corporations changing businesses.
(a) Overview.
(b) Change of business exception.
(c) Special rules.
(d) Disposition of stock in a look-through subsidiary.
(e) Application of change of business exception.
(f) Examples.
(1) Example 1.
(i) Facts
(ii) Results.
(2) Example 2.
(i) Facts
(ii) Results.
(g) Applicability date.

* * *

§1.1298-4 Rules for certain foreign corporations owning stock in 25-percent owned domestic corporations.
(a) Overview.
(b) Treatment of certain foreign corporations owning stock in a 25-percent-owned domestic corporation.
(1) General rule.
(2) Qualified stock.
(c) Indirect ownership of stock through a partnership.
(d) Section 531 tax.
(1) Subject to section 531 tax.
(2) Waiver of treaty benefits.
(i) Tested foreign corporation that files, or is required to file, a Federal income tax return.
(ii) Tested foreign corporation that is not required to file a Federal income tax return.
(e) Interaction of section 1298(b)(7) and section 1298(a)(2).
(f) Anti-abuse rules.
(1) Classification as PFIC excluding qualified stock.
(2) Avoidance principal purposes.
(g) Applicability date.

Passive Foreign Investment Companies: Guidance

Passive Foreign Investment Companies: Guidance.—Reg. §1.1298-2, regarding the determination of ownership in a passive foreign investment company within the meaning of section 1297(a) and the treatment of certain income received or accrued by a foreign corporation and assets held by a foreign corporation for purposes of section 1297, is proposed (published in the Federal Register on July 11, 2019) (REG-105474-18).

Par. 8. Section 1.1298-2 is added to read as follows:

§1.1298-2. Rules for certain corporations changing businesses.—(a) *Overview.*—This section provides rules under section 1298(b)(3) and 1298(g) that apply to certain foreign corporations that dispose of

one or more active trades or businesses for purposes of determining whether a foreign corporation is treated as a passive foreign investment company (PFIC). Paragraph (b) of this section sets forth a rule that applies to certain foreign corporations that dispose of one or more active trades or businesses. Paragraph (c) of this section provides special rules. Paragraph (d) of this section sets forth a rule for the treatment of the disposition of the stock of a look-through subsidiary (as defined in §1.1297-2(g)(1)). Paragraph (e) of this section provides guidance on the application of the rules in this section. Paragraph (f) provides examples illustrating the application of the rules in this section. Paragraph (g) sets forth the applicability date for this section.

(b) *Change of business exception.*—A corporation is not treated as a PFIC for a taxable year if—

(1) Neither the corporation (nor any predecessor) was a PFIC for any prior taxable year;

(2) Either—

(i) Substantially all of the passive income of the corporation for the taxable year is attributable to proceeds from the disposition of one or more active trades or businesses; or

(ii) Following the disposition of one or more active trades or businesses, substantially all of the passive assets of the corporation on each of the measuring dates that occur during the taxable year and after the disposition are attributable to proceeds from the disposition; and

(3) The corporation is not a PFIC for either of the first two taxable years following the taxable year.

(c) *Special rules.*—The rules in this paragraph (c) apply for purposes of section 1298(b)(3) and this section.

(1) Income is attributable to proceeds from the disposition of one or more active trades or businesses to the extent the income is derived from the investment of the proceeds from the disposition of assets used in the active trade or businesses.

(2) Assets are attributable to proceeds from the disposition of one or more active trades or businesses only to the extent the assets are the proceeds of the disposition of assets used in the active trade or businesses, or are derived from the investment of the proceeds.

(3) The determination of the existence of an active trade or business and whether assets are used in an active trade or business is made under §1.367(a)-2(d)(2), (3), and (5), except that officers and employees do not include the officers and employees of related entities as provided in §1.367(a)-2(d)(3). However, if activities performed by the officers and staff of employees of a look-through subsidiary of a corporation (including a look-through subsidiary with respect to which paragraph (d) of this section applies) or of a look-through partnership would be taken into account by the corporation pursuant to §1.1297-2(e) if it applied, or if activities performed by a related person would be taken into account by the corporation pursuant to section 954(h)(3)(E), such activities are taken into account for purposes of the determination of the existence of an active trade or business and the determination of whether assets are used in an active trade or business.

(4) In the case of a corporation that satisfies the condition in paragraph (b)(2)(ii) of this section, the condition in paragraph (b)(3) of this section is deemed to be satisfied if the corporation completely liquidates by the end of the taxable year following the year with respect to which the shareholder applies the exception in paragraph (b) of this section.

(d) *Disposition of stock of a look-through subsidiary.*—For purposes of paragraph (b) of this section, the proceeds from a tested foreign corporation's disposition of the stock of a look-through subsidiary are treated as proceeds from the disposition of a proportionate share of the assets held by the look-through subsidiary on the date of the disposition, based on the method (value or adjusted bases) used to measure the assets of the tested foreign corporation for purposes of section 1297(a)(2). The proceeds attributable to assets used by the look-through subsidiary in an active trade or business are treated as proceeds attributable to the disposition of an active trade or business.

(e) *Application of change of business exception.*—A shareholder can apply the exception in paragraph (b) of this section with respect to a taxable year of a disposition of an active trade or business or an immediately succeeding taxable year, but cannot apply the exception with respect to more than one taxable year for a disposition.

(f) *Examples.*—The following examples illustrate the rules of this section. For purposes of the examples in this paragraph (f): USP is a domestic corporation; TFC and FS are foreign corporations that are not controlled foreign corporations (within the meaning of section 957(a)); each corporation has outstanding a single class of stock; USP has owned its interest in TFC since the formation of TFC; each of USP, TFC, and FS have a calendar taxable year; and for purposes of section 1297(a)(2), TFC measures the amount of its assets based on value.

(1) *Example 1*—(i) *Facts.* (A) USP owns 15% of the outstanding stock of TFC. TFC owns 30% of the outstanding stock of FS. FS

operates an active trade or business and 100% of its assets are used in the active trade or business. The value of FS's non-passive assets (as defined in §1.1297-1(f)) is $900x; the value of FS's passive assets (which include cash and accounts receivable) is $100x. TFC has not been treated as a PFIC for any taxable year prior to Year 1 and has no predecessor corporations. In addition to holding the FS stock, TFC directly conducts its own active trade or business. The value of TFC's non-passive assets (other than FS stock) is $50x; the value of TFC's passive assets (other than FS stock and assets received during Year 1) is $30x. TFC earns $1x of non-passive income (as defined in §1.1297-1(f)) from its directly conducted active trade or business.

(B) On January 1, Year 1, TFC sells all of its FS stock for $300x. The residual gain computed under §1.1297-2(f)(1) on the sale of the FS stock is $10x. Under §1.1297-2(f)(2), $9x of residual gain is characterized as non-passive income and $1x of residual gain is characterized as passive income. During the first quarter of Year 1 and apart from the sale of the FS stock, TFC earned $20x of passive income from the investment of the proceeds from the disposition of the FS stock, and TFC maintained such earnings as well as the disposition proceeds in cash for the remainder of the year. TFC reinvests the proceeds of the FS stock sale in an active trade or business during Year 2, and, thus, TFC is not a PFIC in Year 2 and Year 3. Less than 75% of TFC's gross income in Year 1 is passive income (($20x + $1x)/ ($10x + $20x + $1x) = 68%). However, subject to the application of section 1298(b)(3) and this section, TFC would be a PFIC in Year 1 under section 1297(a)(2) because the proceeds from the sale of the FS stock ($300x) together with TFC's other passive assets ($30x + $20x) exceed 50% of TFC's total assets ($300x + $30x + $20x + $50x).

(ii) *Results.* (A) Under paragraph (d) of this section, for purposes of applying section 1298(b)(3)(B)(i) in Year 1, TFC's proceeds from the disposition of the stock of FS that are attributable to assets used by FS in an active trade or business are considered as from the disposition of an active trade or business. Because 100% of FS's assets are used in its active trade or business, all of TFC's proceeds are considered as from the disposition of an active trade or business. Therefore, under paragraph (c)(1) of this section, the passive income considered attributable to proceeds from a disposition of one or more active trades or businesses is $20x (from investment of disposition proceeds). Because TFC reasonably does not expect to be a PFIC in Year 2 and Year 3, and TFC is not, in fact, a PFIC for those years, TFC will not be treated as a PFIC in Year 1 by reason of section 1298(b)(3) and paragraph (b) of this section, based on the satisfaction of the condition in paragraph (b)(2)(i) of this section, assuming that the 95% (($20x/($20x + $1x)) of TFC's passive income for Year 1 that is attributable to proceeds of the disposition of FS's active trade or business constitutes substantially all of its passive income.

(B) TFC would also not be treated as a PFIC in Year 1 by reason of section 1298(b)(3) and paragraph (b) of this section, based on the satisfaction of the condition in paragraph (b)(2)(ii) of this section, assuming that the 91% (($320x x 4)/(($320x + $30x) x 4)) of TFC's passive assets on the quarterly measuring dates during Year 1 following the disposition of the stock of FS that is attributable to proceeds of the disposition of FS's active trade or business constitutes substantially all of its passive assets.

(C) Under paragraph (e) of this section, TFC cannot claim the section 1298(b)(3) exception in relation to the income attributable to the proceeds of the FS stock sale in Year 2.

(2) *Example 2*—(i) *Facts.* The facts are the same as in paragraph (f)(1)(i) of this section (the facts in *Example 1*), except that during the first quarter of Year 1, TFC earned only $10x of passive income from the investment of the proceeds from the disposition of the FS stock and $10x of passive income from its other passive assets and maintained such earnings in cash for the remainder of the year.

(ii) *Results.* The results are the same as in paragraph (f)(1)(ii) of this section (the facts in *Example 1*), except that under paragraph (c)(1) of this section, the passive income considered attributable to proceeds from a disposition of one or more active trades or businesses is $10x. Because 48% ($10x/($10x + $10x + $1x)), and not substantially all, of TFC's passive income for Year 1 is attributable to proceeds of the disposition of FS's active trade or business, TFC does not qualify for the exception from treatment as a PFIC in section 1298(b)(3) for Year 1. However, under paragraphs (b)(2) and (d) of this section, $310x ($300x disposition proceeds + $10x from investment of disposition proceeds) of TFC's passive assets held on each quarterly measuring date after the disposition is considered attributable to the disposition of an active trade or business. Because TFC reasonably does not expect to be a PFIC in Year 2 and Year 3, and TFC is not, in fact, a PFIC for those years, TFC will not be treated as a PFIC in Year 1 by reason of paragraph (b) of this section, based on the satisfaction of the condition in paragraph (b)(2)(ii) of this section, assuming that the 89% (($310x x 4)/(($310x + $10x + $30x) x 4)) of TFC's passive assets on the quarterly measuring dates during Year 1 following the disposition of the stock of FS that is attributable to proceeds of the disposition of FS's active trade or business constitutes substantially all of its passive assets.

(g) *Applicability date.*—The rules of this section apply to taxable years of shareholders beginning on or after the date of publication of the Treasury decision adopting these rules as final regulations in the **Federal Register**. [Reg. § 1.1298-2.]

Passive Foreign Investment Companies: Guidance

Passive Foreign Investment Companies: Guidance.—Reg. § 1.1298-4, regarding the determination of ownership in a passive foreign investment company within the meaning of section 1297(a) and the treatment of certain income received or accrued by a foreign corporation and assets held by a foreign corporation for purposes of section 1297, is proposed (published in the Federal Register on July 11, 2019) (REG-105474-18).

Par. 9. Section 1.1298-4 is added to read as follows:

§ 1.1298-4. Rules for certain foreign corporations owning stock in 25-percent-owned domestic corporations.—(a) *Overview.*—This section provides rules under section 1298(b)(7) that apply to certain foreign corporations that own stock in 25-percent-owned domestic corporations (as defined in paragraph (b) of this section) for purposes of determining whether a foreign corporation is a passive foreign investment company (PFIC). Paragraph (b) of this section provides the general rule. Paragraph (c) of this section sets forth rules concerning ownership of 25-percent-owned domestic corporations or qualified stock (as defined in paragraph (b)(2) of this section) through partnerships. Paragraph (d) of this section sets forth rules for determining whether a foreign corporation is subject to the tax imposed by section 531 (the section 531 tax) and for waiving treaty benefits that would prevent the imposition of such tax. Paragraph (e) of this section sets forth a rule governing the interaction of section 1298(b)(7) and section 1298(a)(2). Paragraph (f) of this section sets forth anti-abuse rules for the application of section 1298(b)(7). Paragraph (g) sets forth the applicability date for this section.

(b) *Treatment of certain foreign corporations owning stock in a 25-percent-owned domestic corporation.*—(1) *General rule.*—Except as otherwise provided in paragraphs (e) and (f) of this section, when a tested foreign corporation (as defined in § 1.1297-1(f)) is subject to the section 531 tax (or waives any benefit under any treaty that would otherwise prevent the imposition of the tax), and owns (directly or indirectly under the rules in paragraph (c) of this section) at least 25 percent (by value) of the stock of a domestic corporation (a *25-percent-owned domestic corporation*), for purposes of determining whether the foreign corporation is a PFIC, any qualified stock held directly or indirectly under the rules in paragraph (c) of this section by the 25-percent-owned domestic corporation is treated as an asset that does not produce passive income (and is not held for the production of passive income), and any amount included in gross income with respect to the qualified stock is not treated as passive income.

(2) *Qualified stock.*—For purposes of paragraph (b)(1) of this section, the term *qualified stock* means any stock in a C corporation that is a domestic corporation and that is not a regulated investment company or real estate investment trust.

(c) *Indirect ownership of stock through a partnership.*—For purposes of paragraph (b)(1) of this section, a tested foreign corporation that is a partner in a partnership is considered to own its proportionate share of any stock of a domestic corporation held by the partnership, and a domestic corporation that is a partner in a partnership is considered to own its proportionate share of any qualified stock held by the partnership. The rules and principles of sections 701 through 761 apply to determine the corporation's proportionate share of the stock of the domestic corporation or of the qualified stock. An upper-tier partnership's attributable share of the stock of a domestic corporation or of qualified stock held by a lower-tier partnership is treated as held by the upper-tier partnership for purposes of applying the rule in this paragraph (c).

(d) *Section 531 tax.*—(1) *Subject to section 531 tax.*—For purposes of paragraph (b) of this section, a tested foreign corporation is considered subject to the section 531 tax regardless of whether the tax is imposed on the corporation and of whether the requirements of § 1.532-1(c) are met.

(2) *Waiver of treaty benefits.*—(i) *Tested foreign corporation that files, or is required to file, a Federal income tax return.*—For purposes of paragraph (b) of this section, a tested foreign corporation that files, or is required to file, a Federal income tax return waives the benefit under a treaty that would otherwise prevent the imposition of the section 531 tax by attaching to its original or amended return for the taxable year for which section 1298(b)(7) and paragraph (b)(1) of this section are applied or any prior taxable year a statement that it irrevocably waives treaty protection against the imposition of the section 531 tax, effective for all prior, current, and future taxable years, provided the taxable year for which the return is filed and all subsequent taxable years are not closed by the period of limitations on assessments under section 6501.

(ii) *Tested foreign corporation that is not required to file a Federal income tax return.*—For purposes of paragraph (b) of this section, a tested foreign corporation that is not required to file a Federal income tax return waives the benefit under a treaty that would otherwise prevent the imposition of the section 531 tax by a date no later than nine months following the close of the taxable year for which section 1298(b)(7) and paragraph (b)(1) of this section are applied by—

(A) Adopting a resolution or similar governance document that confirms that it has irrevocably waived any treaty protection against the imposition of the section 531 tax, effective for all prior, current, and future taxable years, and maintaining a copy of the resolution (or other governance document) in its records; or

(B) In the case of a tested foreign corporation described in section 1297(e)(3), including in its public filings a statement that it irrevocably waives treaty protection against the imposition of the section 531 tax, effective for all prior, current, and future taxable years.

(e) *Interaction of section 1298(b)(7) and section 1298(a)(2).*—Section 1298(b)(7) does not apply to determine whether a tested foreign corporation is a PFIC for purposes of section 1298(a)(2) and § 1.1291-1(b)(8)(ii).

(f) *Anti-abuse rules.*—(1) *Classification as PFIC excluding qualified stock.*—Paragraph (b) of this section does not apply when—

(i) 75 percent or more of the gross income of the tested foreign corporation for the taxable year (taking into account § 1.1297-2 and excluding any amount included in gross income with respect to qualified stock) is passive income (as defined in § 1.1297-1(c)(1)); or

(ii) The average percentage of assets held by the tested foreign corporation (taking into account § 1.1297-2 and excluding qualified stock) that are passive assets (as defined in § 1.1297-1(f)) is at least 50 percent.

(2) *Avoidance principal purpose.*—Paragraph (b) of this section does not apply when a principal purpose for the tested foreign corporation's formation or acquisition of the stock of the 25-percent-owned domestic corporation that holds the qualified stock is to avoid classification of the tested foreign corporation as a PFIC. A principal purpose to avoid classification of the tested foreign corporation as a PFIC is deemed to exist when the 25-percent-owned domestic corporation is not engaged in an active trade or business in the United States. The existence of an active trade or business is determined under § 1.367(a)-2(d)(2) and (3), except that officers and employees of the 25-percent-owned domestic corporation do not include the officers and employees of related entities as provided in § 1.367(a)-2(d)(3). However, activities performed by the officers and staff of employees of a look-through subsidiary of the 25-percent-owned domestic corporation or a partnership that would be taken into account by the corporation pursuant to § 1.1297-2(e) if it applied are taken into account for purposes of the determination of the existence of an active trade or business.

(g) *Applicability date.*—The rules of this section apply to taxable years of shareholders beginning on or after the date of publication of the Treasury decision adopting these rules as final regulations in the **Federal Register**. [Reg. § 1.1298-4.]

TAX TREATMENT OF S CORPORATIONS AND THEIR SHAREHOLDERS

Subchapter S Corporations: Elections

Subchapter S Corporations: Elections, Consents and Refusals.—Temporary Reg. § 18.0, relating to the time and manner of making certain elections, consents, and refusals under the Subchapter S Revision Act of 1982, is also proposed as a final regulation (published in the Federal Register on January 26, 1983).

§ 18.0. Effective date of temporary regulations under the Subchapter S Revision Act of 1982.

Reporting Income and Deductions: Consolidated Group

Reporting Income and Deductions: Consolidated Group.—Amendments to Reg. §§1.1361-5 and 1.1362-3, revising the rules for reporting certain items of income and deduction that are reportable on the day a corporation joins or leaves a consolidated group, are proposed (published in the Federal Register on March 6, 2015) (REG-100400-14).

Par. 2. Section 1.1361-5 is amended:

1. In paragraph (a)(3), by removing "§1.1502-76(b)(1)(ii)(A)(2) (relating to a special rule" and adding "§1.1502-76(b)(1)(ii)(B) (relating to special rules" in its place.

2. In paragraph (a)(4), *Example 4*, by removing "§1.1502-76(b)(1)(ii)(A)(2)" and adding "§1.1502-76(b)(1)(ii)(B)(*1*)" in its place..

§1.1361-5. Termination of QSub election.

Par. 3. Section 1.1362-3 is amended in paragraph (a) by removing "§1.1502-76(b)(1)(ii)(A)(2)" and adding "§1.1502-76(b)(1)(ii)(B)" in its place.

§1.1362-3. Effect of election on corporation.

Eligible Terminated S Corporations: Definition: Distributions of Money

Eligible Terminated S Corporations: Definition: Distributions of Money.—Reg. §§1.1371-1 and 1.1371-2, regarding the definition of an eligible terminated S corporation (ETSC) and providing rules relating to distributions of money by an ETSC after the post-termination transition period, are proposed (published in the Federal Register on November 7, 2019) (REG-131071-18).

Par. 6. Sections 1.1371-1 and 1.1371-2 are added to read as follows:

§1.1371-1. Distributions of money by an eligible terminated S corporation.—(a) *Scope and definitions.*—(1) *Scope.*—This section provides rules relating to qualified distributions (as defined in paragraph (a)(2)(xii) of this section) and distributions to which section 301 applies during each taxable year of the ETSC period (as defined in paragraph (a)(2)(vii) of this section), including the taxable year in which the ETSC period ends. If the ETSC (as defined in paragraph (a)(2)(vi) of this section) does not make any qualified distributions during a taxable year, then no distribution by the ETSC is governed by section 1371(f) or this section. Paragraph (a)(2) of this section contains definitions that apply for purposes of this section. Paragraph (b) of this section contains rules regarding the characterization of a qualified distribution. Paragraph (c) of this section contains rules regarding the characterization of any excess qualified distribution (as defined in paragraph (a)(2)(viii) of this section) and non-qualified distribution (as defined in paragraph (a)(2)(xi) of this section) during each taxable year of the ETSC period, including the taxable year in which the ETSC period ends. Paragraph (d) of this section contains examples illustrating the rules of this section. Paragraph (e) of this section contains the applicability date of this section.

(2) *Definitions.*—The following definitions apply for purposes of this section—

(i) *AAA.*—The term *AAA* means the accumulated adjustments account, within the meaning of section 1368(e)(1)(A) and §1.1368-2(a)(1).

(ii) *AAA ratio.*—Except as provided in this paragraph (a)(2)(ii) or paragraph (b)(3)(iv) of this section, the term *AAA ratio* means the fraction of which the numerator is historical AAA and the denominator is the sum of historical AAA and historical AE&P. Notwithstanding the preceding sentence, if the AE&P of the ETSC is less than or equal to zero as of the beginning of a taxable year, then the AAA ratio is one for such year and all subsequent taxable years of the ETSC period.

(iii) *AE&P.*—The term *AE&P* means earnings and profits described in section 316(a)(1).

(iv) *AE&P ratio.*—Except as provided in this paragraph (a)(2)(iv) or paragraph (b)(3)(iv) of this section, the term *AE&P ratio* means the fraction of which the numerator is historical AE&P, and the denominator is the sum of historical AAA and historical AE&P. Notwithstanding the preceding sentence, if the AE&P of the ETSC is less than or equal to zero as of the beginning of a taxable year, then the AE&P ratio is zero for such year and all subsequent taxable years of the ETSC period.

(v) *CE&P.*—The term *CE&P* means earnings and profits that are described in section 316(a)(2).

(vi) *ETSC.*—The term *ETSC* means an eligible terminated S corporation, within the meaning of section 481(d) and §1.481-5.

(vii) *ETSC period.*—In general, the term *ETSC period* means any taxable year, or portion thereof, of an ETSC beginning on the first day after the post-termination period within the meaning of section 1377(b)(1)(A) and ending on the date on which the ETSC's AAA balance is zero. Additionally, an ETSC does not have an ETSC period if the ETSC's AAA balance is not greater than zero at the end of its post-termination transition period. See §1.1371-2 for rules

governing the impact of a post-termination period, within the meaning of section 1377(b)(1)(B), on the ETSC period.

(viii) *Excess qualified distribution.*—The term *excess qualified distribution* means the portion of a qualified distribution that is not characterized pursuant to paragraph (b)(2) or (3) of this section.

(ix) *Historical AAA.*—The term *historical AAA* means the AAA of the ETSC as of the beginning of the day on which the revocation of an election under section 1362(a) is effective pursuant to section 1362(d)(1).

(x) *Historical AE&P.*—The term *historical AE&P* means the AE&P of the ETSC as of the beginning of the day on which the revocation of an election under section 1362(a) is effective pursuant to section 1362(d)(1). For purposes of the preceding sentence, if the ETSC's historical AE&P is less than zero, then the historical AE&P is treated as zero.

(xi) *Non-qualified distribution.*—The term *non-qualified distribution* means a distribution to which section 301 applies, which is not a qualified distribution.

(xii) *Qualified distribution.*—The term *qualified distribution* means a distribution of money by an ETSC during the ETSC period to which, absent application of section 1371(f) and this section, section 301 would apply.

(b) *Characterization of qualified distribution.*—(1) *In general.*—Paragraph (b)(2) of this section provides rules regarding the determination of the amount of a qualified distribution that is sourced from AAA and the corollary effects of such a characterization. Paragraph (b)(3) of this section provides rules regarding the determination of the amount of a qualified distribution that is sourced from AE&P and the corollary effects of such a characterization. Paragraph (b)(4) of this section provides rules regarding the characterization of an excess qualified distribution as a separate qualified distribution. The rules in paragraphs (b)(2) through (4) of this section are applied before the application of paragraph (c) of this section.

(2) *Distribution of AAA.*—(i) *Amount.*—The portion of a qualified distribution that is sourced from the ETSC's AAA is equal to the lesser of:

(A) The product of the qualified distribution and the AAA ratio; and

(B) The ETSC's AAA immediately before the qualified distribution.

(ii) *Reduction or elimination of ETSC's AAA.*—The ETSC's AAA is reduced by the amount of the distribution described in paragraph (b)(2)(i) of this section. If, with respect to a qualified distribution, the amount described in paragraph (b)(2)(i)(A) of this section equals or exceeds the amount described in paragraph (b)(2)(i)(B) of this section, then the rules in this paragraph (b) do not apply to any subsequent distributions by the ETSC. Instead, the subsequent distributions are treated in the manner provided in paragraph (c) of this section.

(iii) *Effect on the shareholder.*—The amount described in paragraph (b)(2)(i) of this section is applied against and reduces the shareholder's adjusted basis of the shares of stock with respect to which the distribution is made under the principles of section

301(c)(2). If the application of the amount described in paragraph (b)(2)(i) of this section would result in a reduction of basis that exceeds the shareholder's adjusted basis of any share of stock with respect to which the distribution is made, such excess is treated as gain from the sale or exchange of property. The reduction of the shareholder's basis described in this paragraph (b)(2)(iii) with respect to a qualified distribution occurs prior to the application of paragraph (c) of this section to the excess qualified distribution, if any, with respect to such qualified distribution.

(3) *Distribution of AE&P.*—(i) *Amount.*—This paragraph (b)(3) applies if the ETSC's AE&P ratio is greater than zero. If this paragraph (b)(3) applies, the portion of a qualified distribution that is sourced from the ETSC's AE&P is equal to the lesser of:

(A) The product of the qualified distribution and the AE&P ratio; and

(B) The ETSC's AE&P immediately before the qualified distribution. For purposes of the preceding sentence, if the ETSC's AE&P immediately before the qualified distribution is less than zero, then the ETSC's AE&P is treated as zero.

(ii) *Effect on ETSC's AE&P.*—The ETSC's AE&P is reduced, as described in section 312(a)(1), by the amount of the distribution described in paragraph (b)(3)(i) of this section. The AE&P reduction described in this paragraph occurs prior to the application of paragraph (c) of this section, even if a distribution to which paragraph (c) of this section applies (regarding excess qualified distributions and non-qualified distributions) occurs earlier in time than the qualified distribution to which this paragraph (b)(3)(ii) applies.

(iii) *Effect on the shareholder.*—The amount of the qualified distribution that is sourced from the ETSC's AE&P described in paragraph (b)(3)(i) of this section is included in the gross income of the shareholder as a dividend under section 301(c)(1).

(iv) *Adjustment to the AAA ratio and the AE&P ratio.*—After the application of paragraph (b)(3)(ii) of this section, if the ETSC's AE&P is zero and the ETSC's AAA is greater than zero, then the ETSC's AAA ratio is one and the ETSC's AE&P ratio is zero for all subsequent qualified distributions during:

(A) That taxable year; and

(B) All subsequent taxable years of the ETSC period.

(4) *Excess qualified distribution treated as a separate qualified distribution.*—(i) *In general.*—After the application of paragraph (b)(2)(ii) of this section with respect to a qualified distribution, if the ETSC has any remaining AAA, then any amount of excess qualified distribution, with respect to such qualified distribution, is treated as a separate qualified distribution and is analyzed pursuant to paragraph (b) of this section.

(ii) *No change in characterization of previously characterized portion of qualified distribution.*—Paragraph (b)(4)(i) will not change the characterization of any portion of a qualified distribution that was previously characterized pursuant to paragraphs (b)(2) and (3) of this section and will reflect the application of paragraphs (b)(2) and (3) of this section to the portion of the qualified distribution previously characterized.

(c) *Characterization of excess qualified distribution and non-qualified distributions.*—After application of paragraph (b) of this section, the excess qualified distributions, if any, and non-qualified distributions, if any, are treated in the manner provided in sections 301(c) and 316.

(d) *Examples.*—The following examples illustrate the rules of this section. For purposes of the examples in this paragraph (d), X is a calendar year S corporation with a single share of stock outstanding. A, an individual, purchased its share of X stock prior to December 22, 2017 and, except as otherwise indicated, never contributed any amounts to X's capital. A remained the sole shareholder of X when X made a valid revocation on March 15, 2018, pursuant to section 1362(d)(1) and §1.1362-2 and 1.1362-6, of its S election and when that election became effective on January 1, 2018. X qualified as an ETSC pursuant to §1.481-5(b) and its ETSC period began on January 1, 2019. Additionally, X did not make any distributions during its post-termination transition period, within the meaning of section 1377(b)(1)(A). Furthermore, A remains the sole shareholder of X at the time of the distribution(s) described.

(1) *Example 1: Historical AE&P is zero*—(i) *Facts.* At the beginning of January 1, 2018, X had AAA of $100 and AE&P of $0. During 2018, X had $300 of CE&P and made no distributions. At the beginning of January 1, 2019, X has AAA of $100 and AE&P of $300, and A's adjusted basis in its share of X stock is $460. During 2019, the only distribution that X makes is a $60 distribution of money to A on December 27. X's CE&P during 2019 is $150, without diminution by reason of any distributions made during the taxable year.

(ii) *Analysis*—(A) *Calculation of AAA ratio and AE&P ratio.* Pursuant to paragraphs (a)(2)(ix) and (x) of this section, respectively, X's

historical AAA and X's historical AE&P are determined as of the beginning of January 1, 2018, the beginning of the day on which the revocation of X's election under section 1362(a) is effective pursuant to section 1362(d)(1). Accordingly, X's historical AAA is $100 and X's historical AE&P is $0. Therefore, X's AAA ratio is 1 ($100/($100 + $0)), and X's AE&P ratio is zero ($0/($100 + $0)).

(B) *Characterization of distribution.* Pursuant to paragraph (a)(2)(xii) of this section, the $60 distribution on December 27, 2019, is a qualified distribution because it is a distribution of money by an ETSC during the ETSC period to which section 301 would apply absent the application of section 1371(f) and this section.

(C) *Analysis of qualified distribution*—(1) *Distribution of AAA.* Pursuant to paragraph (b)(2)(i) of this section, the portion of the qualified distribution that is sourced from AAA is equal to the lesser of: the product of the qualified distribution and the AAA ratio ($60 x 1, or $60), and X's AAA immediately before the qualified distribution ($100). Therefore, $60 is sourced from AAA. Pursuant to paragraph (b)(2)(ii) of this section, after the distribution, X's AAA is reduced by $60 to $40. Pursuant to paragraph (b)(2)(iii) of this section, A's basis in its X stock is reduced by $60 to $400.

(2) *Distribution of AE&P.* Pursuant to paragraph (b)(3)(i) of this section, the portion of the distribution that is sourced from AE&P is equal to the lesser of: the product of the qualified distribution and the AE&P ratio ($60 x 0, or $0), and X's AE&P immediately before the qualified distribution ($300). Therefore, $0 is sourced from AE&P.

(2) *Example 2: Qualified distributions with both historical AAA and historical AE&P*—(i) *Facts.* At the beginning of January 1, 2018, X had AAA of $200 and AE&P of $100. During 2018, X had $0 of CE&P and made no distributions. At the beginning of January 1, 2019, X has AAA of $200 and AE&P of $100, and A's adjusted basis in its share of X stock is $500. During 2019, X makes a $90 distribution of money on February 9 and a $150 distribution of money on June 5. X's CE&P during 2019 is $500, without diminution by reason of any distributions made during the taxable year.

(ii) *Analysis*—(A) *Calculation of AAA ratio and AE&P ratio.* Pursuant to paragraphs (a)(2)(ix) and (x) of this section, respectively, X's historical AAA and X's historical AE&P are determined as of the beginning of January 1, 2018, the beginning of the day on which the revocation of X's election under section 1362(a) is effective pursuant to section 1362(d)(1). Accordingly, X's historical AAA is $200 and X's historical AE&P is $100. Therefore, X's AAA ratio is 0.67 ($200/($200 + $100)), and X's AE&P ratio is 0.33 ($100/($200 + $100)).

(B) *Characterization of distributions.* Pursuant to paragraph (a)(2)(xii) of this section, the $90 distribution on February 9, 2019, and the $150 distribution on June 5, 2019, are both qualified distributions because they are distributions of money by an ETSC during the FTSC period to which section 301 would apply absent the application of section 1371(f) and this section.

(C) *Analysis of qualified distributions*—(1) *February 9, 2019 distribution*—(i) *Distribution of AAA.* Pursuant to paragraph (b)(2)(i) of this section, the portion of the qualified distribution that is sourced from AAA is equal to the lesser of: the product of the qualified distribution and the AAA ratio ($90 x 0.67, or $60), and X's AAA immediately before the qualified distribution ($200). Therefore, $60 is sourced from AAA. Pursuant to paragraph (b)(2)(ii) of this section, after the distribution, X's AAA is reduced by $60 to $140. Pursuant to paragraph (b)(2)(iii) of this section, A's basis in its X stock is reduced by $60 to $440.

(ii) *Distribution of AE&P.* Pursuant to paragraph (b)(3)(i) of this section, the portion of the distribution that is sourced from AE&P is equal to the lesser of: the product of the qualified distribution and the AE&P ratio ($90 x 0.33, or $30), and X's AE&P immediately before the qualified distribution ($100). Therefore, $30 is sourced from AE&P. Pursuant to paragraph (b)(3)(ii) of this section, after the distribution, X's AE&P is reduced by $30 to $70. Pursuant to paragraph (b)(3)(iii) of this section, the $30 distribution is characterized as a dividend.

(2) *June 5, 2019 distribution*—(i) *Distribution of AAA.* Pursuant to paragraph (b)(2)(i) of this section, the portion of the qualified distribution that is sourced from AAA is equal to the lesser of: the product of the qualified distribution and the AAA ratio ($150 x 0.67, or $100), and X's AAA immediately before the qualified distribution ($140). Therefore, $100 is sourced from AAA. Pursuant to paragraph (b)(2)(ii) of this section, after the distribution, X's AAA is reduced by $100 to $40. Pursuant to paragraph (b)(2)(iii) of this section, A's basis in its X stock is reduced by $100 to $340.

(ii) *Distribution of AE&P.* Pursuant to paragraph (b)(3)(i) of this section, the portion of the distribution that is sourced from AE&P is equal to the lesser of: the product of the qualified distribution and the AE&P ratio ($150 x 0.33, or $50), and X's AE&P immediately before the qualified distribution ($70). Therefore, $50 is sourced from AE&P. Pursuant to paragraph (b)(3)(ii) of this section, after the distribution, X's AE&P is reduced by $50 to $20. Pursuant to paragraph (b)(3)(iii) of this section, the $50 distribution is characterized as a dividend.

(3) *Example 3: Limitation on amount characterized as AAA*—(i) *Facts.* At the beginning of January 1, 2018, X had AAA of $100 and AE&P of $300. During 2018, X had $280 of CE&P and made no distributions. At the beginning of January 1, 2019, X has AAA of $100 and AE&P of $580, and A's adjusted basis in its share of X stock is $450. During 2019, the only distribution that X makes is a $500 distribution of money to A on October 5. X's CE&P during 2019 is $150, without diminution by reason of any distributions made during the taxable year.

(ii) *Analysis*—(A) *Calculation of AAA ratio and AE&P ratio.* Pursuant to paragraphs (a)(2)(ix) and (x) of this section, respectively, X's historical AAA and X's historical AE&P are determined as of the beginning of January 1, 2018, the beginning of the day on which the revocation of X's election under section 1362(a) is effective pursuant to section 1362(d)(1). Accordingly, X's historical AAA is $100 and X's historical AE&P is $300. Therefore, X's AAA ratio is 0.25 ($100/($100 + $300)), and X's AE&P ratio is 0.75 ($300/($100 + $300)).

(B) *Characterization of distribution.* Pursuant to paragraph (a)(2)(xii) of this section, the $500 distribution on October 5, 2019, is a qualified distribution because it is a distribution of money by an ETSC during the ETSC period to which section 301 would apply absent the application of section 1371(f) and this section.

(C) *Analysis of qualified distribution*—(1) *Distribution of AAA.* Pursuant to paragraph (b)(2)(i) of this section, the portion of the qualified distribution that is sourced from AAA is equal to the lesser of: the product of the qualified distribution and the AAA ratio ($500 x 0.25, or $125), and X's AAA immediately before the qualified distribution ($100). Therefore, $100 is sourced from AAA. Pursuant to paragraph (b)(2)(ii) of this section, after the distribution, X's AAA is reduced by $100 to $0. Pursuant to paragraph (b)(2)(iii) of this section, A's basis in its X stock is reduced by $100 to $350.

(2) *Distribution of AE&P.* Pursuant to paragraph (b)(3)(i) of this section, the portion of the distribution that is sourced from AE&P is equal to the lesser of: the product of the qualified distribution and the AE&P ratio ($500 x 0.75, or $375), and X's AE&P immediately before the qualified distribution ($580). Therefore, $375 is sourced from AE&P. Pursuant to paragraph (b)(3)(ii) of this section, after the distribution, X's AE&P is reduced by $375 to $205. Pursuant to paragraph (b)(3)(iii) of this section, the $375 distribution is characterized as a dividend.

(D) *Effect of qualified distribution on ETSC period.* Pursuant to paragraph (a)(2)(vii) of this section, X's ETSC period ends because X's AAA balance is zero following the October 5, 2019 distribution.

(E) *Analysis of excess qualified distribution*—(1) *Amount of excess qualified distribution.* Pursuant to paragraph (a)(2)(viii) of this section, the amount of the excess qualified distribution is $25, the portion of the qualified distribution ($500) not characterized pursuant to paragraph (b)(2) or (3) of this section ($100 AAA distribution + $375 AE&P distribution).

(2) *Characterization of excess qualified distribution.* Paragraph (b)(4) of this section does not apply to the excess qualified distribution because X's AAA balance is zero after the application of paragraph (b)(2)(ii) of this section (see paragraph (d)(3)(ii)(C)(1) of this section). Pursuant to paragraph (c) of this section, section 301(c) applies to the excess qualified distribution. Pursuant to sections 301(c)(1) and 316, the $25 excess qualified distribution is sourced from CE&P.

(iii) *Subsequent contribution.* The facts are the same as paragraph (d)(3)(i) of this section, except that at the time of the October 5, 2019 distribution, A's adjusted basis in its X stock is $90. Further, on December 27, 2019, A contributes $100 to X in a transaction described in section 351(a). The analysis in paragraph (d)(3)(ii) of this section remains the same, except that, unlike the second to last sentence of paragraph (d)(3)(ii)(C)(1) of this section, A's basis in its X stock is reduced by $90 to $0 and pursuant to paragraph (b)(2)(iii) of this section, $10 is treated as gain from the sale or exchange of property. Additionally, as a result of the December 27, 2019 contribution of $100, A's basis in its X stock is increased by $100, so that at the end of 2019, A's basis in its X stock is $100.

(4) *Example 4: Limitation on the amount characterized as AE&P*—(i) *Facts.* At the beginning of January 1, 2018, X had AAA of $100 and AE&P of $100. During 2018, X had CE&P of $(75) and made no distributions. At the beginning of January 1, 2019, X has AAA of $100 and AE&P of $25, and A's adjusted basis in its share of X stock is $500. During 2019, the only distributions that X makes are a $100 distribution of money to A on July 9 and a $40 distribution of money to A on September 27. X's CE&P during 2019 is $20, without diminution by reason of any distributions made during the taxable year.

(ii) *Analysis*—(A) *Calculation of AAA ratio and AE&P ratio.* Pursuant to paragraphs (a)(2)(ix) and (x) of this section, respectively, X's historical AAA and X's historical AE&P are determined as of the beginning of January 1, 2018, the beginning of the day on which the revocation of X's election under section 1362(a) is effective pursuant to section 1362(d)(1). Accordingly, X's historical AAA is $100 and X's historical AE&P is $100. Therefore, X's AAA ratio is 0.5 ($100/($100 + $100)), and X's AE&P ratio is 0.5 ($100/($100 + $100)).

(B) *Analysis of July 9, 2019 distribution*—(1) *Characterization of distribution.* Pursuant to paragraph (a)(2)(xii) of this section, the $100 distribution on July 9, 2019, is a qualified distribution because it is a distribution of money by an ETSC during the ETSC period to which section 301 would apply absent the application of section 1371(f) and this section.

(2) *Analysis of qualified distribution*—(i) *Distribution of AAA.* Pursuant to paragraph (b)(2)(i) of this section, the portion of the distribution that is sourced from AAA is equal to the lesser of: the product of the qualified distribution and the AAA ratio ($100 x 0.5, or $50), and X's AAA immediately before the qualified distribution ($100). Therefore, $50 is sourced from AAA. Pursuant to paragraph (b)(2)(ii) of this section, after the distribution, X's AAA is reduced by $50 to $50. Pursuant to paragraph (b)(2)(iii) of this section, A's basis in its X stock is reduced by $50 to $450.

(ii) *Distribution of AE&P.* Pursuant to paragraph (b)(3)(i) of this section, the portion of the distribution that is sourced from AE&P is equal to the lesser of: the product of the qualified distribution and the AE&P ratio ($100 x 0.5, or $50), and X's AE&P immediately before the qualified distribution ($25). Therefore, $25 is sourced from AE&P. Pursuant to paragraph (b)(3)(ii) of this section, after the distribution, X's AE&P is reduced by $25 to $0. Pursuant to paragraph (b)(3)(iii) of this section, the $25 distribution is characterized as a dividend.

(3) *Recalculation of AAA and AE&P ratios.* Pursuant to paragraph (b)(3)(iv) of this section, because the July 9, 2019 distribution caused X's AE&P to be reduced to zero, the AAA ratio is one and the AE&P ratio is zero for all subsequent qualified distributions during the 2019 taxable year and subsequent taxable years of the ETSC period.

(4) *Excess qualified distribution*—(i) *Amount of excess qualified distribution.* Pursuant to paragraph (a)(2)(viii) of this section, the amount of the excess qualified distribution is $25, the amount of the qualified distribution ($100) not characterized pursuant to paragraph (b)(2) or (3) of this section ($50 AAA distribution + $25 AE&P distribution).

(ii) *Characterization of excess qualified distribution as a separate qualified distribution.* Pursuant to paragraph (b)(4) of this section, because X has AAA remaining after characterizing the qualified distribution (see paragraph (d)(4)(ii)(B)(2)(i) of this section), the $25 excess qualified distribution is treated as a separate qualified distribution and is analyzed pursuant to paragraph (b) of this section.

(iii) *Analysis of excess qualified distribution that is treated as a separate qualified distribution.* Pursuant to paragraph (b)(2)(i) of this section, the portion of the distribution that is sourced from AAA is equal to the lesser of: the product of the excess qualified distribution and the AAA ratio ($25 x 1, or $25), and X's AAA immediately before the excess qualified distribution ($50). Therefore, $25 is sourced from AAA. Pursuant to paragraph (b)(2)(ii) of this section, after the distribution, X's AAA is reduced by $25 to $25. Pursuant to paragraph (b)(2)(iii) of this section, A's basis in its X stock is reduced by $25 to $425. Pursuant to paragraph (b)(3)(i) of this section, because X's AE&P ratio is zero, paragraph (b)(3) of this section does not apply.

(C) *Analysis of September 27, 2020 distribution*—(1) *Characterization of the distribution.* Pursuant to paragraph (a)(2)(xii) of this section, the $40 distribution on September 27, 2020, is a qualified distribution because it is a distribution of money by an ETSC during the ETSC period to which section 301 would apply absent the application of section 1371(f) and this section.

(2) *Analysis of qualified distribution*—(i) *Distribution of AAA.* Pursuant to paragraph (b)(2)(i) of this section, the portion of the distribution that is sourced from AAA is equal to the lesser of: the product of the qualified distribution and the AAA ratio ($40 x 1, or $40), and X's AAA immediately before the qualified distribution ($25) (see paragraph (d)(4)(ii)(B)(4)(iii) of this section). Therefore, $25 is sourced from AAA. Pursuant to paragraph (b)(2)(ii) of this section, after the distribution, X's AAA is reduced by $25 to $0. Pursuant to paragraph (b)(2)(iii) of this section, A's basis in its X stock is reduced by $25 to $400.

(ii) *Distribution of AE&P.* Pursuant to paragraph (b)(3)(i) of this section, because X's AE&P ratio is zero, paragraph (b)(3) of this section does not apply.

(3) *Excess qualified distribution*—(i) *Amount of excess qualified distribution.* Pursuant to paragraph (a)(2)(viii) of this section, the amount of the excess qualified distribution is $15, the portion of the qualified distribution ($40) not characterized pursuant to paragraph (b)(2) or (3) of this section ($25 AAA distribution + $0 AE&P distribution).

(ii) *Excess qualified distribution not characterized as a separate qualified distribution.* Pursuant to paragraph (b)(4) of this section, because X has AAA of $0 after characterizing the qualified distribution (see paragraph (d)(4)(ii)(C)(2)(i) of this section), the $15 excess qualified distribution is not treated as a separate qualified distribution.

(iii) *Analysis of excess qualified distribution that is not treated as a separate qualified distribution.* Pursuant to paragraph (c) of this section, section 301(c) applies to the excess qualified distribution. Pursuant to sections 301(c)(1) and 316, the $15 excess qualified distribution is sourced from CE&P.

(5) *Example 5: Distributions include non-qualified distributions* —(i) *Facts.* At the beginning of January 1, 2018, X had AAA of $100 and AE&P of $100. During 2018, X had $0 of CE&P and made no distributions. At the beginning of January 1, 2019, X has AAA of $100 and AE&P of $100, and A's adjusted basis in its X stock is $200. During 2019, X makes a $100 distribution of money on June 14; a $300 distribution of property on November 9; and a $200 distribution of money on December 18. X's CE&P during 2019 is $160, without diminution by reason of any distributions made during the taxable year.

(ii) *Analysis*—(A) *Calculation of AAA ratio and AE&P ratio.* Pursuant to paragraphs (a)(2)(ix) and (x) of this section, respectively, X's historical AAA is $100 and X's historical AE&P is $100. Therefore, X's AAA ratio is 0.5 ($100/($100 + $100)), and X's AE&P ratio is 0.5 ($100/($100 + $100)).

(B) *Characterization of distributions.* Pursuant to paragraph (a)(2)(xii) of this section, the $100 distribution on June 14, 2019, and the $200 distribution on December 18, 2019, are both qualified distributions because they are distributions of money by an ETSC during the ETSC period to which section 301 would apply absent the application of section 1371(f) and this section. Pursuant to paragraph (a)(2)(xi) of this section, the $300 distribution of property on November 9, 2019, is non-qualified distribution. Pursuant to paragraph (b)(1) of this section, the rules of paragraphs (b)(2) through (4) of this section apply to the qualified distributions before the rules of paragraph (c) of this section apply to the non-qualified distribution and any excess qualified distributions.

(C) *Analysis of qualified distributions*—(1) *June 14, 2019 distribution*—(i) *Distribution of AAA.* Pursuant to paragraph (b)(2)(i) of this section, the portion of the distribution that is sourced from AAA is equal to the lesser of: the product of the qualified distribution and the AAA ratio ($100 x 0.5, or $50), and X's AAA immediately before the qualified distribution ($100). Therefore, $50 is sourced from AAA. Pursuant to paragraph (b)(2)(ii) of this section, after the distribution, X's AAA is reduced by $50 to $50. Pursuant to paragraph (b)(2)(iii) of this section, on June 14, 2019, A's basis in its X stock is reduced by $50 to $150.

(ii) *Distribution of AE&P.* Pursuant to paragraph (b)(3)(i) of this section, the portion of the distribution that is sourced from AE&P is equal to the lesser of: the product of the qualified distribution and the AE&P ratio ($100 x 0.5, or $50), and X's AE&P immediately before the qualified distribution ($100). Therefore, $50 is sourced from AE&P. Pursuant to paragraph (b)(3)(ii) of this section, after the distribution, X's AE&P is reduced by $50 to $50. Pursuant to paragraph (b)(3)(iii) of this section, the $50 distribution is characterized as a dividend.

(iii) *Amount of excess qualified distribution* The amount of the excess qualified distribution is $0, the amount of the qualified distribution ($100) not characterized pursuant to paragraph (b)(2) or (3) of this section ($50 AAA distribution + $50 AE&P distribution).

(2) *December 18, 2019 distribution*—(i) *Distribution of AAA.* Pursuant to paragraph (b)(2)(i) of this section, the portion of the distribution that is sourced from AAA is equal to the lesser of: the product of the qualified distribution and the AAA ratio ($200 x 0.5, or $100), and X's AAA immediately before the qualified distribution ($50). Therefore, $50 is sourced from AAA. Pursuant to paragraph (b)(2)(ii) of this section, after the distribution, X's AAA is reduced by $50 to $0. Pursuant to paragraph (b)(2)(iii) of this section, A must determine its basis as of December 18, 2019, in order to determine the consequences of receiving the $50 AAA distribution. Because the non-qualified distribution on November 9, 2019, which precedes the December 18, 2019 qualified distribution, could have the effect of reducing A's basis, any effect on A's basis from that non-qualified distribution must be analyzed prior to determining the effect of the December 18, 2019 distribution of AAA on A's basis. See paragraphs (d)(5)(ii)(D)(3) and (4) of this section. Pursuant to paragraph (a)(2)(vii) of this section, X's ETSC period ends because X's AAA balance is zero following the December 18, 2019 distribution.

(ii) *Distribution of AE&P.* Pursuant to paragraph (b)(3)(i) of this section, the portion of the distribution that is sourced from AE&P is equal to the lesser of: the product of the qualified distribution and the AE&P ratio ($200 x 0.5, or $100), and X's AE&P immediately before the qualified distribution ($50). Therefore, $50 is sourced from AE&P. Pursuant to paragraph (b)(3)(ii) of this section, after the distribution, X's AE&P is reduced by $50 to $0. Pursuant to paragraph (b)(3)(iii) of this section, the $50 distribution is characterized as a dividend.

(iii) *Amount of excess qualified distribution.* The amount of the excess qualified distribution is $100, the amount of the qualified distribution ($200) not characterized pursuant to paragraph (b)(2) or (3) of this section ($50 AAA distribution + $50 AE&P distribution).

(D) *Analysis of non-qualified and excess qualified distributions*—(1) *In general.* The $300 non-qualified distribution on November 9, 2019, and the $100 excess qualified distribution on December 18, 2019, are treated in the manner provided in section 301(c).

(2) *Allocation of CE&P.* Pursuant to section 316 and §1.316-2, X's CE&P is allocated proportionately among the excess qualified and the non-qualified distributions. Therefore, the portion of X's CE&P that is allocated to the November 9, 2019 distribution and the December 18, 2019 distribution is $120 ($160 X's CE&P x ($300 distribution / $400 total excess qualified and non-qualified distributions during 2019) and $40 ($160 X's CE&P x ($100 distribution / $400 total excess qualified and non-qualified distributions during 2019), respectively.

(3) *November 9, 2019 distribution.* Pursuant to paragraph (d)(5)(ii)(D)(2) of this section, $120 of the $300 distribution is characterized as a distribution of CE&P. Pursuant to paragraph (d)(5)(ii)(C)(2)(ii) of this section, the amount of X's AE&P available to allocate the November 9, 2019 distribution is $0. Therefore the remaining $180 is characterized pursuant to section 301(c)(2) and (3). Pursuant to paragraph (d)(5)(ii)(C)(1)(i) of this section, A's basis in its X stock prior to the November 9, 2019 distribution is $150. Therefore, $150 is applied against basis pursuant to section 301(c)(2) (reducing A's basis to $0) and $30 is treated as gain from the sale or exchange of property pursuant to section 301(c)(3).

(4) *December 18, 2019 distribution*—(i) *Consequences of AAA distribution.* As of December 18, 2019, A's basis in its X stock is $0. See paragraph (d)(5)(ii)(D)(3) of this *section.* Pursuant to paragraph (d)(5)(ii)(C)(2)(i) of this section, $50 of the distribution is characterized as a distribution of AAA. Because the amount of the distribution of AAA ($50) exceeds A's basis in its X stock ($0), pursuant to paragraph (b)(2)(iii) of this section, on December 18, 2019, $50 is treated as gain from the sale or exchange of property.

(ii) *Characterization of excess qualified distribution.* Pursuant to paragraph (d)(5)(ii)(C)(2)(iii) of this section, $100 of the December 18, 2019 distribution is an excess qualified distribution. Paragraph (b)(4) of this section does not apply to the excess qualified distribution because X's AAA balance is zero after the application of paragraph (b)(2)(ii) of this section (see paragraph (d)(5)(ii)(C)(2)(i) of this section). Pursuant to paragraph (c) of this section, section 301(c) applies to the excess qualified distribution. Pursuant to paragraph (d)(5)(ii)(D)(2) of this section, $40 of the $100 excess qualified distribution is characterized as a distribution of CE&P. Pursuant to paragraph (d)(5)(ii)(D)(3) of this section, X's AE&P as the time of the December 18, 2019 distribution is $0. Therefore the remaining $60 is characterized pursuant to section 301(c)(2) and (3). Pursuant to paragraph (d)(5)(ii)(D)(4)(i) of this section, A's basis in its X stock prior to characterization of the excess qualified distribution is $0. Therefore, $60 is treated as gain from the sale or exchange of property pursuant to section 301(c)(3).

(e) *Applicability date.*—This section generally applies to taxable years beginning after [DATE OF PUBLICATION OF THE FINAL RULES IN THE **FEDERAL REGISTER**]. However, corporations may choose to apply the rules in §§1.316-2, 1.481-5, 1.1371-1, 1.1371-2, and 1.1377-2 in their entirety, to the extent applicable, to taxable years that began on or before [DATE OF PUBLICATION OF THE FINAL RULES IN THE **FEDERAL REGISTER**] and with respect to which the period described in section 6511(a) has not expired. If the corporation makes the choice described in the previous sentence, all shareholders of the corporation must report consistently. [Reg. §1.1371-1.]

§1.1371-2. Impact of Audit PTTP on ETSC Period.— (a) *Definitions.*—For purposes of this section, the definitions used in §1.1371-1(a)(2) are applicable. Additionally, the following definitions apply for purposes of this section—

(1) *Audit PTTP.*—The term *audit PTTP* means a post-termination transition period described in section 1377(b)(1)(B).

(2) *Initial PTTP.*—The term *initial PTTP* means a post-termination transition period described in section 1377(b)(1)(A).

(3) *Intervening audit PTTP.*—The term *intervening audit PTTP* means an audit PTTP arising during the ETSC period.

(b) *In general.*—If an intervening audit PTTP arises, the ETSC period shall immediately stop. Immediately following the end of the intervening audit PTTP, the ETSC period will resume if the ETSC's AAA balance is greater than zero. Otherwise, any subsequent distributions by the ETSC are treated in the manner provided in section 301(c).

(c) *Examples.*—The following examples illustrate the rules of this section. For purposes of the examples in this paragraph (c), X is a calendar year S corporation. A, an individual, purchased all of the outstanding shares of X in a single transaction at the same price per share prior to December 22, 2017, and was the sole shareholder of X at all times. Pursuant to section 1362(d)(1) and §§1.1362-2 and 1.1362-6, X made a valid revocation of its S election on March 15, 2019, that became effective on January 1, 2019. No amount distributed by X is an extraordinary dividend within the meaning of section 1059.

(1) *Example 1: No ETSC period following initial PTTP* —(i) *Facts*. At the beginning of January 1, 2019, X had AAA of $49,000 and AE&P of $2,000, and A's adjusted basis in its shares of X stock was $50,000. During 2019, the only distribution that X made was a $49,000 distribution of money to A on March 13, 2019. X's CE&P during 2019 was $0, without regard to any diminution by reason of any distributions made during the taxable year.

(ii) *Analysis* —(A) *Distribution during initial PTTP.* Pursuant to sections 1371(e) and 1377(b)(1)(A), the $49,000 distribution of money on March 13, 2019, is characterized as a distribution of AAA because it was made during the initial PTTP.

(B) *Effect on corporation* Pursuant to §1.1368-2(a)(3)(iii), X's AAA is reduced by $49,000 to $0. Following the initial PTTP, even if X satisfies the requirements of section 481(d)(2) and §1.481-5(b) to be an ETSC, X does not have an ETSC period because its AAA balance is zero at the end of its initial PTTP. Therefore, section 1371(f) and §1.1371-1 will not apply to any subsequent distributions by X.

(C) *Effect on shareholder* Pursuant to section 1371(e)(1), A reduces its basis in its X stock by $49,000 to $1,000.

(2) *Example 2: Intervening audit PTTP*—(i) *Facts.* The facts are the same as the facts in paragraph (c)(1) of this section. On May 20, 2020, which is after X's initial PTTP, the IRS begins an audit of X's 2018 return. During the audit it is agreed that X overstated its advertising expense deduction by $10,000. On July 6, 2020, A signs a closing agreement whereby X's overstatement results in an additional tax on A's 2018 individual return. As a result, at the beginning of January 1, 2019, X had AAA of $59,000 ($49,000 + $10,000) and AE&P of $2,000. Additionally, at the beginning of January 1, 2019, A's adjusted basis in its shares of X stock was $60,000 ($50,000 + $10,000). During 2020, the only distribution X makes is a $6,000 distribution of money to A on September 1, 2020. X's CE&P during 2020 was $0, without regard to any diminution by reason of any distributions made during the taxable year.

(ii) *Analysis*—(A) *Analysis of March 15, 2019 distribution.* The treatment of the March 15, 2019, distribution is the same as described in paragraph (c)(1)(ii)(A) of this section, because the amount of the distribution ($49,000) does not exceed X's AAA balance at the beginning of January 1, 2019 ($59,000), and so the entirety of the $49,000 distribution is properly characterized as a distribution of AAA.

(1) *Effect on corporation.* As described in paragraph (c)(1)(ii)(B) of this section, X's AAA ($59,000 at the beginning of January 1, 2019) is reduced by $49,000 to $10,000. At the conclusion of X's initial PTTP (ending on December 31, 2019), X's AAA balance is $10,000. Pursuant

to §1.1371-1(a)(2)(vii), X has an ETSC period. Therefore, section 1371(f) and §1.1371-1 will apply to any subsequent qualified distributions by X.

(2) *Effect on shareholder.* As described in paragraph (c)(1)(ii)(C) of this section, A reduces its basis in its X stock ($60,000 at the beginning of January 1, 2019) by $49,000 to $11,000.

(B) *Intervening audit PTTP* Pursuant to section 1377(b)(1)(B), X enters an intervening audit PTTP that begins on July 6, 2020, and ends on November 2, 2020. The application of section 1371(f) and the regulatory provisions in this part under section 1371 of the Code to distributions during the intervening audit PTTP is stopped. Instead, sections 1371(e) and 1377(b)(1)(B), and the regulatory provisions in this part under sections 1371 and 1377 of the Code, apply for the duration of the intervening audit PTTP. During the intervening audit PTTP, the only distribution X made is a $6,000 distribution of money to A on September 1, 2020. Pursuant to sections 1371(e) and 1377(b)(1)(B), the $6,000 distribution is characterized as a distribution of AAA because it was made during the intervening audit PTTP.

(1) *Effect on corporation.* Pursuant to §1.1368-2(a)(3)(iii), X's AAA is reduced by $6,000 to $4,000. Beginning on November 3, 2020, pursuant to §1.1371-1(a)(2)(vii), X's ETSC period resumes (after the intervening audit PTTP's conclusion) because its AAA balance is greater than zero.

(2) *Effect on shareholder.* Pursuant to section 1371(e)(1), A reduces its basis in its X stock by $6,000 to $5,000.

(C) *ETSC period.* Beginning on November 3, 2020, X's ETSC period resumes, and distributions of money are subject to section 1371(f) and the regulatory provisions in this part under section 1371 of the Code until X's AAA balance is zero. For purposes of calculating each of X's AAA and AE&P ratios, X's historical AAA is $59,000 (at the beginning of January 1, 2019, which includes the $10,000 increase as a result of the July 6, 2020, closing agreement).

(d) *Applicability date.*—This section generally applies to taxable years beginning after [DATE OF PUBLICATION OF THE FINAL RULES IN THE **FEDERAL REGISTER**]. However, corporations may choose to apply the rules in §§1.316-2, 1.481-5, 1.1371-1, 1.1371-2, and 1.1377-2 in their entirety, to the extent applicable, to taxable years that began on or before [DATE OF PUBLICATION OF THE FINAL RULES IN THE **FEDERAL REGISTER**] and with respect to which the period described in section 6511(a) has not expired. If the corporation makes the choice described in the previous sentence, all shareholders of the corporation must report consistently. [Reg. §1.1371-2.]

Eligible Terminated S Corporations: Definition: Distributions of Money

Eligible Terminated S Corporations: Definition: Distributions of Money.—Amendments to Reg. §§1.1377-2 and 1.1377-3, regarding the definition of an eligible terminated S corporation (ETSC) and providing rules relating to distributions of money by an ETSC after the post-termination transition period, are proposed (published in the Federal Register on November 7, 2019) (REG-131071-18).

Par. 7. Section 1.1377-2 is amended by removing the last sentence of paragraph (b).

§1.1377-2. Post-termination transition period.

Par. 8. Section 1.1377-3 is amended by:
a. Removing "and 1.1377-2 apply" and adding "applies" in its place; and
b. Adding three sentences at the end of the paragraph.
The addition reads as follows:

§1.1377-3. Effective dates.—* * * Section 1.1377-2 generally applies to taxable years beginning after [DATE OF PUBLICATION OF THE FINAL RULES IN THE **FEDERAL REGISTER**], however, corporations may choose to apply the rules in §§1.316-2, 1.481-5, 1.1371-1, 1.1371-2, and 1.1377-2 in their entirety, to the extent applicable, to taxable years that began on or before [DATE OF PUBLICATION OF THE FINAL RULES IN THE **FEDERAL REGISTER**] and with re-

spect to which the period described in section 6511(a) has not expired. If the corporation makes the choice described in the previous sentence, all shareholders of the corporation must report consistently. For taxable years beginning on or before [DATE OF PUBLICATION OF THE FINAL RULES IN THE **FEDERAL REGISTER**], see §1.1377-2(b) as contained in 26 CFR part 1, revised April 1, 2019.

Subchapter S Corporations: Elections

Subchapter S Corporations: Elections, Consents and Refusals.—Temporary Reg. §§ 18.1379-1 and 18.1379-2, relating to the time and manner of making certain elections, consents, and refusals under the Subchapter S Revision Act of 1982, are also proposed as final regulations (published in the Federal Register on January 26, 1983). Reg. §18.1377-1 removed by T.D. 8696 on December 20, 1996, and Reg. §18.1378-1 removed by T.D. 8996, May 16, 2002.

§18.1379-1. Transitional rules on enactment.

§18.1379-2. Special rules for all elections, consents, and refusals.

COOPRATIVES AND THEIR PATRONS

Section 199A Rules: Cooperatives and Patrons

Section 199A Rules: Cooperatives and Patrons.—Amendments to Reg. §1.1388-1, providing guidance to cooperatives to which sections 1381 through 1388 of the Code apply (Cooperatives) and their patrons regarding the deduction for qualified business income under section 199A(a) of the Code as well as guidance to specified agricultural or horticultural cooperatives (Specified Cooperatives) and their patrons regarding the deduction for domestic production activities under section 199A(g) of the Code, are proposed (published in the Federal Register on June 19, 2019) (REG-118425-18).

Par. 3. Section 1.1388-1 is amended by adding paragraphs (f) and (g).

The additions read as follows:

§1.1388-1. Definitions and special rules.

* * *

(f) *Patronage and nonpatronage.*—Whether an item of income or deduction is patronage or nonpatronage sourced is determined by applying the directly related use test. The directly related use test provides that if the income or deduction is produced by a transaction that actually facilitates the accomplishment of the cooperative's marketing, purchasing, or services activities, the income or deduction is from patronage sources. However, if the transaction producing the income or deduction does not actually facilitate the accomplishment of these activities but merely enhances the overall profitability of the cooperative, being merely incidental to the association's cooperative operation, the income or deduction is from nonpatronage sources. Patronage and nonpatronage income or deductions cannot be netted unless otherwise permitted by the Internal Revenue Code or regulations issued under the relevant section of the Internal Revenue Code, or guidance published in the Internal Revenue Bulletin (*see* § 601.601(d)(2) of this chapter).

(g) *Effective/applicability date.*—The provisions of paragraph (f) of this section apply to taxable years ending after the date the Treasury decision adopting these regulations as final regulations is published in the *Federal Register*. However, taxpayers may rely on the provisions of paragraph (f) of this section until the date the Treasury decision adopting these regulations as final regulations is published in the *Federal Register*.

TAX ON SELF-EMPLOYMENT INCOME

Qualified Opportunity Funds: Deferred Gains

Qualified Opportunity Funds: Deferred Gains.—Reg. §1.1400Z-2(a)-1, relating to gains that may be deferred as a result of a taxpayer's investment in a qualified opportunity fund (QOF), was adopted by T.D. 9889 on December 31, 2019 (published in the Federal Register on October 29, 2018) (REG-115420-18).

≫→ *Caution: Proposed Reg. §1.1400Z-2(a)-1, below, was adopted by T.D. 9889; however, for an exception regarding when this proposed regulation may be relied upon, see final Reg. §1.1400Z2(a)-1(g).*

Par. 2. Section 1.1400Z-2(a)-1 is added to read as follows:

§1.1400Z-2(a)-1. Deferring tax on capital gains by investing in opportunity zones.—(a) *In general.*—Under section 1400Z-2(a) of the Internal Revenue Code (Code) and this section, an eligible taxpayer may elect to defer recognition of some or all of its eligible gains to the extent that the taxpayer timely invests (as provided for by section 1400Z-2(a)(1)(A)) in eligible interests of a qualified opportunity fund (QOF), as defined in section 1400Z-2(d)(1). Paragraph (b) of this section defines eligible taxpayers, eligible gains, and eligible interests and contains related operational rules. Paragraph (c) of this section provides rules for applying section 1400Z-2 to a partnership, S corporation, trust, or estate that recognizes an eligible gain or would recognize such a gain if it did not elect to defer the gain under section 1400Z-2(a).

(b) *Definitions and related operating rules.*—The following definitions and rules apply for purposes of section 1400Z-2 and the regulations thereunder:

(1) *Eligible taxpayer.*—An *eligible taxpayer* is a person that may recognize gains for purposes of Federal income tax accounting. Thus, eligible taxpayers include individuals; C corporations, including regulated investment companies (RICs) and real estate investment trusts (REITs); partnerships; S corporations; trusts and estates. An eligible taxpayer may elect to defer recognition of one or more eligible gains in accordance with the requirements of section 1400Z-2.

(2) *Eligible gain.*—(i) *In general.*—An amount of gain is an *eligible gain*, and thus is eligible for deferral under section 1400Z-2(a), if the gain—

(A) Is treated as a capital gain for Federal income tax purposes;

(B) Would be recognized for Federal income tax purposes before January 1, 2027, if section 1400Z-2(a)(1) did not apply to defer recognition of the gain; and

(C) Does not arise from a sale or exchange with a person that, within the meaning of section 1400Z-2(e)(2), is related to the taxpayer that recognizes the gain or that would recognize the gain if section 1400Z-2(a)(1) did not apply to defer recognition of the gain.

(ii) *Gain not already subject to an election.*—In the case of a taxpayer who has made an election under section 1400Z-2(a) with respect to some but not all of an eligible gain, the term "eligible gain" includes the portion of that eligible gain with respect to which no election has yet been made.

(iii) *Gains under section 1256 contracts.*—(A) *General rule.*—The only gain arising from section 1256 contracts that is eligible for deferral under section 1400Z-2(a)(1) is capital gain net income for a taxable year. This net amount is determined by taking into account the capital gains and losses for a taxable year on all of a taxpayer's section 1256 contracts, including all amounts determined under section 1256(a), both those determined on the last business day of a taxable year and those that section 1256(c) requires to be determined under section 1256(a) because of the termination or transfer during the taxable year of the taxpayer's position with respect to a contract. The 180-day period with respect to any capital gain net income from section 1256 contracts for a taxable year begins on the last day of the taxable year, and the character of that gain when it is later included under section 1400Z-2(a)(1)(B) and (b) is determined under the general rule in paragraph (b)(5) of this section. See paragraph (b)(2)(iii)(B) of this section for limitations on the capital gains eligible for deferral under this paragraph (b)(2)(iii)(A).

(B) *Limitation on deferral for gain from 1256 contracts.*—If, at any time during the taxable year, any of the taxpayer's section 1256 contracts was part of an offsetting positions transaction (as defined in paragraph (b)(2)(iv) of this section) and any other position in that transaction was not a section 1256 contract, then no gain from any section 1256 contract is an eligible gain with respect to that taxpayer in that taxable year.

(iv) *No deferral for gain from a position that is or has been part of an offsetting-positions transaction.*—If a capital gain is from a position that is or has been part of an offsetting-positions transaction, the gain is not eligible for deferral under section 1400Z-2(a)(1). For purposes of this paragraph (b)(2)(iv), an offsetting-positions transaction is a transaction in which a taxpayer has substantially diminished the taxpayer's risk of loss from holding one position with respect to personal property by holding one or more other positions with respect to personal property (whether or not of the same kind). It does not matter whether either of the positions is with respect to actively traded personal property. An offsetting-positions transaction includes a straddle as defined in section 1092 and the regulations thereunder, including section 1092(d)(4), which provides rules for positions held by related persons and certain flow-through entities (for example, a partnership). An offsetting-positions transaction also includes a transaction that would be a straddle (taking into account the principles referred to in the preceding sentence) if the straddle definition did not contain the active trading requirement in section 1092(d)(1). For example, an offsetting-positions transaction includes positions in closely held stock or other non-traded personal property and substantially offsetting derivatives.

(3) *Eligible interest.*—(i) *In general.*—For purposes of section 1400Z-2, an *eligible interest* in a QOF is an equity interest issued by the QOF, including preferred stock or a partnership interest with special allocations. Thus, the term eligible interest excludes any debt instrument within the meaning of section 1275(a)(1) and § 1.1275-1(d).

(ii) *Use as collateral permitted.*—Provided that the eligible taxpayer is the owner of the equity interest for Federal income tax purposes, status as an eligible interest is not impaired by using the interest as collateral for a loan, whether as part of a purchase-money borrowing or otherwise.

(iii) *Deemed contributions not constituting investment.*—See § 1.1400Z-2(e)-1(a)(2) for rules regarding deemed contributions of money to a partnership pursuant to section 752(a).

(4) *180-day period.*—(i) *In general.*—Except as otherwise provided elsewhere in this section, the 180-day period referred to in section 1400Z-2(a)(1)(A) with respect to any eligible gain (180-day

period) begins on the day on which the gain would be recognized for Federal income tax purposes if the taxpayer did not elect under section 1400Z-2 to defer recognition of that gain.

(ii) *Examples.*—The following examples illustrate the principles of paragraph (b)(4)(i) of this section.

Example 1. Regular-way trades of stock. If stock is sold at a gain in a regular-way trade on an exchange, the 180-day period with respect to the gain on the stock begins on the trade date.

Example 2. Capital gain dividends received by RIC and REIT shareholders. If an individual RIC or REIT shareholder receives a capital gain dividend (as described in section 852(b)(3) or section 857(b)(3)), the shareholder's 180-day period with respect to that gain begins on the day on which the dividend is paid.

Example 3. Undistributed capital gains received by RIC and REIT shareholders. If section 852(b)(3)(D) or section 857(b)(3)(D) (concerning undistributed capital gains) requires the holder of shares in a RIC or REIT to include an amount in the shareholder's long-term capital gains, the shareholder's 180-day period with respect to that gain begins on the last day of the RIC or REIT's taxable year.

Example 4. Additional deferral of previously deferred gains—(i) *Facts.* Taxpayer A invested in a QOF and properly elected to defer realized gain. During 2025, taxpayer A disposes of its entire investment in the QOF in a transaction that, under section 1400Z-2(a)(1)(B) and (b), triggers an inclusion of gain in A's gross income. Section 1400Z-2(b) determines the date and amount of the gain included in A's income. That date is the date on which A disposed of its entire interest in the QOF. A wants to elect under section 1400Z-2 to defer the amount that is required to be included in income.

(ii) *Analysis.*—Under paragraph (b)(4)(i) of this section, the 180-day period for making another investment in a QOF begins on the day on which section 1400Z-2(b) requires the prior gain to be included. As prescribed by section 1400Z-2(b)(1)(A), that is the date of the inclusion-triggering disposition. Thus, in order to make a deferral election under section 1400Z-2, A must invest the amount of the inclusion in the original QOF or in another QOF during the 180-day period beginning on the date when A disposed of its entire investment in the QOF.

(5) *Attributes of gains that section 1400Z-2(a)(1)(B) includes in income.*—If section 1400Z-2(a)(1)(B) and (b) require a taxpayer to include in income some or all of a previously deferred gain, the gain so included has the same attributes in the taxable year of inclusion that it would have had if tax on the gain had not been deferred. These attributes include those taken into account by sections 1(h), 1222, 1256, and any other applicable provisions of the Code.

(6) *First-In, First-Out (FIFO) method to identify which interest in a QOF has been disposed of.*—(i) *FIFO requirement.*—If a taxpayer holds investment interests with identical rights (fungible interests) in a QOF that were acquired on different days and if, on a single day, the taxpayer disposes of less than all of these interests, then the first-in-first-out (FIFO) method must be used to identify which interests were disposed of. Fungible interests may be equivalent shares of stock in a corporation or partnership interests with identical rights.

(ii) *Consequences of identification.*—The FIFO method determines—

(A) Whether an investment is described in section 1400Z-2(e)(1)(A)(i)(an investment to which a gain deferral election under section 1400Z-2(a) applies) or section 1400Z-2(e)(1)(A)(ii) (an investment which was not part of a gain deferral election under section 1400Z-2(a));

(B) In the case of investments described in section 1400Z-2(e)(1)(A)(i), the attributes of the gain subject to a deferral election under section 1400Z-2(a), at the time the gain is included in income (the attributes addressed in paragraph (b)(5) of this section); and

(C) The extent, if any, of an increase under section 1400Z-2(b)(2)(B) in the basis of an investment interest that is disposed of.

(7) *Pro-rata method.*—If, after application of the FIFO method, a taxpayer is treated as having disposed of less than all of the investment interests that the taxpayer acquired on one day and if the interests acquired on that day vary with respect to the characteristics described in paragraph (b)(6)(ii) of this section, then a proportionate allocation must be made to determine which interests were disposed of (pro-rata method).

(8) *Examples.*—The following examples illustrate the rules of paragraph (b)(5) through (7) of this section.

Example 1. Short-term gain. For 2018, taxpayer B properly made an election under section 1400Z-2 to defer $100 of gain that, if not deferred, would have been recognized as short-term capital gain, as defined in section 1222(1). In 2022, section 1400Z-2(a)(1)(B) and (b)

requires taxpayer B to include the gain in gross income. Under paragraph (b)(5) of this section, the gain included is short-term capital gain.

Example 2. Collectibles gain. For 2018, taxpayer C properly made an election under section 1400Z-2 to defer a gain that, if not deferred, would have been collectibles gain as defined in IRC section 1(h)(5). In a later taxable year, section 1400Z-2(a)(1)(B) and (b) requires some or all of that deferred gain to be included in gross income. The gain included is collectibles gain.

Example 3. Net gains from section 1256 contracts. For 2019, taxpayer D had $100 of capital gain net income from section 1256 contracts. D timely invested $100 in a QOF and properly made an election under section 1400Z-2 to defer that $100 of gain. In 2023, section 1400Z-2(a)(1)(B) and (b) requires taxpayer D to include that deferred gain in gross income. Under paragraph (b)(5) of this section, the character of the inclusion is governed by section 1256(a)(3) (which requires a 40:60 split between short-term and long-term capital gain). Accordingly, $40 of the inclusion is short-term capital gain and $60 of the inclusion is long-term capital gain.

Example 4. FIFO method. For 2018, taxpayer E properly made an election under section 1400Z-2 to defer $300 of short-term capital gain. For 2020, E properly made a second election under section 1400Z-2 to defer $200 of long-term capital gain. In both cases, E properly invested in QOF Q the amount of the gain to be deferred. The two investments are fungible interests and the price of the interests was the same at the time of the two investments. E did not purchase any additional interest in QOF Q or sell any of its interest in QOF Q until 2024, when E sold for a gain 60 percent of its interest in QOF Q. Under paragraph (b)(6)(i) of this section, E must apply the FIFO method to identify which investments in QOF Q that E disposed of. As determined by this identification, E sold the entire 2018 initial investment in QOF Q. Under section 1400Z-2(a)(1)(B) and (b), the sale triggered an inclusion of deferred gain. Because the inclusion has the same character as the gain that had been deferred, the inclusion is short-term capital gain.

Example 5. FIFO method. In 2018, before Corporation R became a QOF, Taxpayer F invested $100 cash to R in exchange for 100 R common shares. Later in 2018, after R was a QOF, F invested $500 cash to R in exchange for 400 R common shares and properly elected under section 1400Z-2 to defer $500 of independently realized short-term capital gain. Even later in 2018, on different days, F realized $300 of short-term capital gain and $700 of long-term capital gain. On a single day that fell during the 180-day period for both of those gains, F invested $1,000 cash in R in exchange for 800 R common shares and properly elected under section 1400Z-2 to defer the two gains. In 2020, F sold 100 R common shares. Under paragraph (b)(6)(i) of this section, F must apply the FIFO method to identify which investments in R F disposed of. As determined by that identification, F sold the initially acquired 100 R common shares, which were not part of a deferral election under section 1400Z-2. R must recognize gain or loss on the sale of its R shares under the generally applicable Federal income tax rules, but the sale does not trigger an inclusion of any deferred gain.

Example 6. FIFO method. The facts are the same as example 5, except that, in addition, during 2021 F sold an additional 400 R common shares. Under paragraph (b)(6)(i) of this section, F must apply the FIFO method to identify which investments in R were disposed of. As determined by this identification, F sold the 400 common shares which were associated with the deferral of $500 of short-term capital gain. Thus, the deferred gain that must be included upon sale of the 400 R common shares is short-term capital gain.

Example 7. Pro-rata method. The facts are the same as in examples 5 and 6, except that, in addition, during 2022 F sold an additional 400 R common shares. Under paragraph (b)(6)(i) of this section, F must apply the FIFO method to identify which investments in R were disposed of. In 2022, F is treated as holding only the 800 R common shares purchased on a single day, and the section 1400Z-2 deferral election associated with these shares applies to gain with different characteristics (described in paragraph (b)(6)(ii) of this section). Under paragraph (b)(7) of this section, therefore, R must use the pro-rata method to determine which of the characteristics pertain to the deferred gain required to be included as a result of the sale of the 400 R common shares. Under the pro-rata method, $150 of the inclusion is short-term capital gain ($300 ×400/800) and $350 is long-term capital gain ($700 × 400/800).

(c) *Special rules for pass-through entities.*—(1) *Eligible gains that a partnership elects to defer.*—A partnership is an eligible taxpayer under paragraph (b)(1) of this section and may elect to defer recognition of some or all of its eligible gains under section 1400Z-2(a)(2).

(i) *Partnership election.*—If a partnership properly makes an election under section 1400Z-2(a)(2), then—

(A) The partnership defers recognition of the gain under the rules of section 1400Z-2 (that is, the partnership does not recognize gain at the time it otherwise would have in the absence of the election to defer gain recognition);

(B) The deferred gain is not included in the distributive shares of the partners under section 702 and is not subject to section 705(a)(1); and

(ii) *Subsequent recognition.*—Absent any additional deferral under section 1400Z-2(a)(1)(A), any amount of deferred gain that an electing partnership subsequently must include in income under sections 1400Z-2(a)(1)(B) and (b) is recognized by the electing partnership at the time of inclusion and is subject to sections 702 and 705(a)(1) in a manner consistent with recognition at that time.

(2) *Eligible gains that the partnership does not defer.*—(i) *Tax treatment of the partnership.*—If a partnership does not elect to defer some, or all, of the gains for which it could make a deferral election under section 1400Z-2, the partnership's treatment of any such amounts is unaffected by the fact that the eligible gain could have been deferred under section 1400Z-2.

(ii) *Tax treatment by the partners.*—If a partnership does not elect to defer some, or all, of the gains for which it could make a deferral election under section 1400Z-2—

(A) The gains for which a deferral election are not made are included in the partners' distributive shares under section 702 and are subject to section 705(a)(1);

(B) If a partner's distributive share includes one or more gains that are eligible gains with respect to the partner, the partner may elect under section 1400Z-2(a)(1)(A) to defer some or all of its eligible gains; and

(C) A gain in a partner's distributive share is an eligible gain with respect to the partner only if it is an eligible gain with respect to the partnership and it did not arise from a sale or exchange with a person that, within the meaning of section 1400Z-2(e)(2), is related to the partner.

(iii) *180-day period for a partner electing deferral.*—(A) *General rule.*—If a partner's distributive share includes a gain that is described in paragraph (c)(2)(ii)(C) of this section (gains that are eligible gains with respect to the partner), the 180-day period with respect to the partner's eligible gains in the partner's distributive share generally begins on the last day of the partnership taxable year in which the partner's allocable share of the partnership's eligible gain is taken into account under section 706(a).

(B) *Elective rule.*—Notwithstanding the general rule in paragraph (c)(2)(iii)(A) of this section, if a partnership does not elect to defer all of its eligible gain, the partner may elect to treat the partner's own 180-day period with respect to the partner's distributive share of that gain as being the same as the partnership's 180-day period.

(C) The following example illustrates the principles of this paragraph (c)(2)(iii).

Example. Five individuals have identical interests in partnership P, there are no other partners, and P's taxable year is the calendar year. On January 17, 2019, P realizes a capital gain of $1000*x* that it decides not to elect to defer. Two of the partners, however, want to defer their allocable portions of that gain. One of these two partners invests $200*x* in a QOF during February 2020. Under the general rule in paragraph (c)(2)(iii)(A) of this section, this investment is within the 180-day period for that partner (which begins on December 31, 2019). The fifth partner, on the other hand, decides to make the election provided in paragraph (c)(2)(iii)(B) of this section and invests $200*x* in a QOF during February 2019. Under that elective rule, this investment is within the 180-day period for that partner (which begins on January 17, 2019).

(3) *Pass-through entities other than partnerships.*—If an S corporation; a trust; or a decedent's estate recognizes an eligible gain, or would recognize an eligible gain if it did not elect to defer recognition of the gain under section 1400Z-2(a), then rules analogous to the rules of paragraph (c)(1) and (2) of this section apply to that entity and to its shareholders or beneficiaries, as the case may be.

(d) *Elections.*—The Commissioner may prescribe in guidance published in the Internal Revenue Bulletin or in forms and instructions (*see* §§ 601.601(d)(2) and 601.602 of this chapter), both the time, form, and manner in which an eligible taxpayer may elect to defer eligible gains under section 1400Z-2(a) and also the time, form, and manner in which a partner may elect to apply the elective 180-day period provided in paragraph (c)(2)(iii)(B) of this section.

(e) *Applicability date.*—This section applies to eligible gains that would be recognized in the absence of deferral on or after the date of publication in the **Federal Register** of a Treasury decision adopting these proposed rules as final regulations. An eligible taxpayer, however, may rely on the proposed rules in this section with respect to eligible gains that would be recognized before that date, but only if the taxpayer applies the rules in their entirety and in a consistent manner. [Reg. § 1.1400Z-2(a)-1.]

Qualified Opportunity Funds: Investment

Qualified Opportunity Funds: Investment.—Amendments to Reg. § 1.1400Z2(a)-1, relating to gains that may be deferred as a result of a taxpayer's investment in a qualified opportunity fund, as well as special rules for an investment in a QOF held by a taxpayer for at least 10 years, were adopted by T.D. 9889 on December 31, 2019 (published in the Federal Register on May 1, 2019) (REG-120186-18).

⫸→ *Caution: Proposed Reg. § 1.1400Z2(a)-1, below, was adopted by T.D. 9889; however, for an exception regarding when this proposed regulation may be relied upon, see final Reg. § 1.1400Z2(a)-1(g).*

Par. 2. Section 1.1400Z2(a)-1, as proposed to be added by 83 FR 54279, October 29, 2018 is amended by:

1. Redesignating (b)(2)(iii) and (iv) as paragraphs (b)(2)(v) and (vi), respectively.
2. Adding new paragraphs (b)(2)(iii) and (iv) and paragraphs (b)(9) and (10).

The revisions and additions read as follows:

§ 1.1400Z2(a)-1. Deferring tax on capital gains by investing in opportunity zones.

* * *

(b) * * *
(2) * * *

(iii) *Gains from section 1231 property.*—The only gain arising from section 1231 property that is eligible for deferral under section 1400Z-2(a)(1) is capital gain net income for a taxable year. This net amount is determined by taking into account the capital gains and losses for a taxable year on all of the taxpayer's section 1231 property. The 180-day period described in paragraph (b)(4) of this section with respect to any capital gain net income from section 1231 property for a taxable year begins on the last day of the taxable year.

(iv) *No deferral for gain realized upon the acquisition of an eligible interest.*—Gain is not eligible for deferral under section 1400Z-2(a)(1) if such gain is realized upon the sale or other transfer of property to a QOF in exchange for an eligible interest (*see* paragraph (b)(10)(i)(C) of this section) or the transfer of property to an eligible taxpayer in exchange for an eligible interest (*see* paragraph (b)(10)(iii) of this section).

* * *

(9) *Making an investment for purposes of an election under section 1400Z-2(a).*—(i) *Transfer of cash or other property to a QOF.*—A taxpayer makes an investment for purposes of an election under section 1400Z-2(a)(1)(A) (section 1400Z-2(a)(1)(A) investment) by transferring cash or other property to a QOF in exchange for eligible interests

in the QOF, regardless of whether the transfer is one in which the transferor would recognize gain or loss on the property transferred.

(ii) *Furnishing services.*—Services rendered to a QOF are not considered the making of a section 1400Z-2(a)(1)(A) investment. Thus, if a taxpayer receives an eligible interest in a QOF for services rendered to the QOF or to a person in which the QOF holds any direct or indirect equity interest, then the interest in the QOF that the taxpayer receives is not a section 1400Z-2(a)(1)(A) investment but is an investment to which section 1400Z-2(e)(1)(A)(ii) applies.

(iii) *Acquisition of eligible interest from person other than QOF.*—A taxpayer may make a section 1400Z-2(a)(1)(A) investment by acquiring an eligible interest in a QOF from a person other than the QOF.

(10) *Amount invested for purposes of section 1400Z-2(a)(1)(A).*—In the case of any investments described in this paragraph (b)(10), the amount of a taxpayer's section 1400Z-2(a)(1)(A) investment cannot exceed the amount of gain to be deferred under the election. If the amount of the taxpayer's investment as determined under this paragraph (b)(10) exceeds the amount of gain to be deferred under the section 1400Z-2(a) election, the amount of the excess is treated as an investment to which section 1400Z-2(e)(1)(A)(ii) applies. See paragraph (b)(10)(ii) of this section for special rules applicable to transfers to QOF partnerships.

(i) *Transfers to a QOF.*—(A) *Cash.*—If a taxpayer makes a section 1400Z-2(a)(1)(A) investment by transferring cash to a QOF, the amount of the taxpayer's section 1400Z-2(a)(1)(A) investment is that amount of cash.

(B) *Property other than cash—Nonrecognition transactions.*—This paragraph (b)(10)(i)(B) applies if a taxpayer makes a section 1400Z-2(a)(1)(A) investment by transferring property other than cash to a QOF and if, but for the application of section 1400Z-2(b)(2)(B), the taxpayer's basis in the resulting investment in the QOF would be determined, in whole or in part, by reference to the taxpayer's basis in the transferred property.

(1) *Amount of section 1400Z-2(a)(1)(A) investment.*—If paragraph (b)(10)(i)(B) of this section applies, the amount of the taxpayer's section 1400Z-2(a)(1)(A) investment is the lesser of the taxpayer's adjusted basis in the eligible interest received in the transaction, without regard to section 1400Z-2(b)(2)(B), or the fair market value of the eligible interest received in the transaction, both as determined immediately after the contribution. Paragraph (b)(10)(i)(B) of this section applies separately to each item of property contributed to a QOF.

(2) *Fair market value of the eligible interest received exceeds its adjusted basis.*—If paragraph (b)(10)(i)(B) of this section applies, and if the fair market value of the eligible interest received is in excess of the taxpayer's adjusted basis in the eligible interest received, without regard to section 1400Z-2(b)(2)(B), then the taxpayer's investment is an investment with mixed funds to which section 1400Z-2(e)(1) applies. Paragraph (b)(10)(i)(B)(1) of this section determines the amount of the taxpayer's investment to which section 1400Z-2(e)(1)(A)(i) applies. Section 1400Z-2(e)(1)(A)(ii) applies to the excess of the fair market value of the investment to which section 1400Z-2(e)(1)(A)(i) applies over the taxpayer's adjusted basis therein, determined without regard to section 1400Z-2(b)(2)(B).

(3) *Transfer of built-in loss property and section 362(e)(2).*—If paragraph (b)(10)(i)(B) of this section and section 362(e)(2) both apply to a transaction, the taxpayer is deemed to have made an election under section 362(e)(2)(C).

(C) *Property other than cash—Taxable transactions.*—This paragraph (b)(10)(i)(C) applies if a taxpayer makes a section 1400Z-2(a)(1)(A) investment by transferring property other than cash to a QOF and if, without regard to section 1400Z-2(b)(2)(B), the taxpayer's basis in the eligible interest received would not be determined, in whole or in part, by reference to the taxpayer's basis in the transferred property. If this paragraph (b)(10)(i)(C) applies, the amount of the taxpayer's section 1400Z-2(a)(1)(A) investment is the fair market value of the transferred property, as determined immediately before the transfer. This paragraph (b)(10)(i)(C) applies separately to each item of property transferred to a QOF.

(D) *Basis in an investment with mixed funds.*—If a taxpayer's investment in a QOF is an investment with mixed funds to which section 1400Z-2(e)(1) applies, the taxpayer's basis in the investment to which section 1400Z-2(e)(1)(A)(ii) applies is equal to the taxpayer's basis in all of the QOF interests received, determined without regard to section 1400Z-2(b)(2)(B), and reduced by the basis of the taxpayer's investment to which section 1400Z-2(e)(1)(A)(i) applies, determined without regard to section 1400Z-2(b)(2)(B).

(ii) *Special rules for transfers to QOF partnerships.*—In the case of an investment in a QOF partnership, the following rules apply:

(A) *Amounts not treated as an investment.*—(1) *Non-contributions in general.*—To the extent the transfer of property to a QOF partnership is characterized other than as a contribution (for example, as a sale for purposes of section 707), the transfer is not a section 1400Z-2(a)(1)(A) investment.

(2) *Reductions in investments otherwise treated as contributions.*—To the extent any transfer of cash or other property to a partnership is not disregarded under paragraph (b)(10)(ii)(A)(1) of this section (for example, it is not treated as a disguised sale of the property transferred to the partnership under section 707), the transfer to the partnership will not be treated as a section 1400Z-2(a)(1)(A) investment to the extent the partnership makes a distribution to the partner and the transfer to the partnership and the distribution would be recharacterized as a disguised sale under section 707 if:

(i) Any cash contributed were non-cash property; and

(ii) In the case of a distribution by the partnership to which § 1.707-5(b) (relating to debt-financed distributions) applies, the partner's share of liabilities is zero.

(B) *Amount invested in a QOF partnership.*—(1) *Calculation of amount of qualifying and non-qualifying investments.*—To the extent paragraph (b)(10)(ii)(A) of this section does not apply, the amount of the taxpayer's qualifying investment in a QOF partnership is the lesser of the taxpayer's net basis in the property contributed to the

QOF partnership, or the net value of the property contributed by the taxpayer to the QOF partnership. The amount of the taxpayer's non-qualifying investment in the partnership is the excess, if any, of the net value of the contribution over the amount treated as a qualifying investment.

(2) *Net basis.*—For purposes of paragraph (b)(10)(ii)(B) of this section, net basis is the excess, if any, of—

(i) The adjusted basis of the property contributed to the partnership; over

(ii) The amount of any debt to which the property is subject or that is assumed by the partnership in the transaction.

(3) *Net value.*—For purposes of paragraph (b)(10)(ii)(B) of this section, net value is the excess of—

(i) The gross fair market value of the property contributed; over

(ii) The amount of the debt described in paragraph (b)(10)(ii)(B)(2)(ii) of this section.

(4) *Basis of qualifying and non-qualifying investments.*—The basis of a qualifying investment is the net basis of the property contributed, determined without regard to section 1400Z-2(b)(2)(B) or any share of debt under section 752(a). The basis of a non-qualifying investment (before any section 752 debt allocation) is the remaining net basis. The bases of qualifying and non-qualifying investments are increased by any debt allocated to such investments under the rules of § 1.1400Z2(b)-1(c)(6)(iv)(B).

(5) *Rules applicable to mixed-funds investments.*—If one portion of an investment in a QOF partnership is a qualifying investment and another portion is a non-qualifying investment, see § 1.1400Z2(b)-1(c)(6)(iv) for the rules that apply.

(iii) *Acquisitions from another person.*—If a taxpayer makes a section 1400Z-2(a)(1)(A) investment by acquiring an eligible interest in a QOF from a person other than the QOF, then the amount of the taxpayer's section 1400Z-2(a)(1)(A) investment is the amount of the cash, or the fair market value of the other property, as determined immediately before the exchange, that the taxpayer exchanged for the eligible interest in the QOF.

(iv) *Examples.*—The following examples illustrate the rules of paragraph (b)(10) of this section. For purposes of the following examples, B is an individual and Q is a QOF corporation.

(A) *Example 1: Transfer of built-in gain property with basis less than gain to be deferred.* B realizes $100 of eligible gain within the meaning of paragraph (b)(2) of this section. B transfers unencumbered property with a fair market value of $100 and an adjusted basis of $60 to Q in a transaction that is described in section 351(a). Paragraph (b)(10)(i)(B) of this section applies because B transferred property other than cash to Q and, but for the application of section 1400Z-2(b)(2)(B), B's basis in the eligible interests in Q would be determined, in whole or in part, by reference to B's basis in the transferred property. The fair market value of the eligible interest B received is $100, and, without regard to section 1400Z-2(b)(2)(B), B's basis in the eligible interest received would be $60. Thus, pursuant to paragraph (b)(10)(i)(B)(2) of this section, B's investment is an investment with mixed funds to which section 1400Z-2(e)(1) applies. Pursuant to paragraphs (b)(10)(i)(B)(1) and (2) of this section, B's section 1400Z-2(a)(1)(A) investment is $60 (the lesser of the taxpayer's adjusted basis in the eligible interest, without regard to section 1400Z-2(b)(2)(B), of $60 and the $100 fair market value of the eligible interest received). Pursuant to section 1400Z-2(b)(2)(B)(i), B's basis in the section 1400Z-2(a)(1)(A) investment is $0. Additionally, B's other investment is $40 (the excess of the fair market value of the eligible interest received ($100) over the taxpayer's adjusted basis in the eligible interest, without regard to section 1400Z-2(b)(2)(B) ($60)). B's basis in the other investment is $0 (B's $60 basis in its investment determined without regard to section 1400Z-2(b)(2)(B), reduced by the $60 of adjusted basis allocated to the investment to which section 1400Z-2(e)(1)(A)(i) applies, determined without regard to section 1400Z-2(b)(2)(B)). *See* paragraph (b)(10)(i)(D) of this section. Pursuant to section 362, Q's basis in the transferred property is $60.

(B) *Example 2: Transfer of built-in gain property with basis in excess of eligible gain to be deferred.* The facts are the same as *Example 1* in paragraph (b)(10)(iv)(A) of this section, except that B realizes $50 of eligible gain within the meaning of paragraph (b)(2) of this section. Pursuant to paragraph (b)(10) of this section, B's section 1400Z-2(a)(1)(A) investment cannot exceed the amount of eligible gain to be deferred (that is, the $50 of eligible gain) under the section 1400Z-2(a) election. Therefore, pursuant to paragraph (b)(10)(i)(B)(1) of this section, B's section 1400Z-2(a)(1)(A) investment is $50 (the lesser of the taxpayer's adjusted basis in the eligible interest received, without regard to section 1400Z-2(b)(2)(B), of $60 and the $100 fair market value of the eligible interest, limited by the amount of eligible gain to be deferred under the section 1400Z-2(a) election). B's section 1400Z-2(a)(1)(A) investment has an adjusted basis of $0, as provided in section 1400Z-2(b)(2)(B)(i). Additionally, B's other investment is $50 (the excess of the fair market value of the eligible interest received ($100) over the amount ($50) of B's section 1400Z-2(a)(1)(A) investment). B's basis in the other investment is $10 (B's $60 basis in its investment determined without regard to section 1400Z-2(b)(2)(B)), reduced by the $50 of adjusted basis allocated to B's section 1400Z-2(a)(1)(A) investment, determined without regard to section 1400Z-2(b)(2)(B)).

(C) *Example 3: Transfers to QOF partnerships—(1) Facts.* A and B each realized $100 of eligible gain and each transfers $100 of cash to a QOF partnership. At a later date, the partnership borrows $120 from an unrelated lender and distributes the cash of $120 equally to A and B.

(2) *Analysis.* If the contributions had been of property other than cash, the contributions and distributions would have been tested under the disguised sale rules of §1.707-5(b) by, among other things, determining the timing of the distribution and amount of the debt allocated to each partner. Under paragraph (b)(10)(ii)(A)(2) of this section, the cash of $200 ($100 from A and $100 from B) is treated as property that could be sold in a disguised sale transaction and each partner's share of the debt is zero for purposes of determining the amount of the investment. To the extent there would have been a disguised sale applying the rule of paragraph (b)(10)(ii)(A)(2) of this section, the amount of the investment would be reduced by the amount of the contribution so recharacterized.

(3) *Property contributed has built-in gain.* The facts are the same as in this *Example 3* in paragraph (b)(10)(iv)(C)(1) of this section, except that the property contributed by A had a value of $100 and basis of $20 and the partnership did not borrow money or make a distribution. Under paragraph (b)(10)(ii)(B)(1) of this section, the amount of A's qualifying investment is $20 (the lesser of the net value or the net basis of the property that A contributed), and the

excess of the $100 contribution over the $20 qualifying investment constitutes a non-qualifying investment. Under paragraph (b)(10)(ii)(B)(2) of this section, A's basis in the qualifying investment (determined without regard to section 1400Z-2(b)(2)(B) or section 752(a)) is $20. After the application of section 1400Z-2(b)(2)(B) but before the application of section 752(a), A's basis in the qualifying investment is zero. A's basis in the non-qualifying investment is zero without regard to the application of section 752(a).

(4) *Property contributed has built-in gain and is subject to debt.* The facts are the same as in this *Example 3* in paragraph (b)(10)(iv)(C)(3) of this section, except that the property contributed by A has a gross value of $130 and is subject to debt of $30. Under paragraph (b)(10)(ii)(B)(1) of this section, the amount of A's qualifying investment is zero, the lesser of the property's $100 net value ($130 minus $30) or zero net basis ($20 minus $30, but limited to zero). The entire contribution constitutes a non-qualifying investment.

(5) *Property contributed has built-in loss and is subject to debt.* The facts are the same as in this *Example 3* in paragraph (b)(10)(iv)(C)(4) of this section, except that the property contributed by A has a basis of $150. Under paragraph (b)(10)(ii)(B)(1) of this section, the amount of A's qualifying investment is $100, the lesser of the property's $100 net value ($130 minus $30) or $120 net basis ($150 minus $30). The non-qualifying investment is $0, the excess of the qualifying investment ($100) over the net value ($100). A's basis in the qualifying investment (determined without regard to section 1400Z-2(b)(2)(B) and section 752(a)) is $120, the net basis. After the application of section 1400Z-2(b)(2)(B), A's basis in the qualifying investment is zero, plus its share of partnership debt under section 752(a).

* * *

Qualified Opportunity Funds: Investment

Qualified Opportunity Funds: Investment.—Reg. §1.1400Z2(b)-1, relating to gains that may be deferred as a result of a taxpayer's investment in a qualified opportunity fund, as well as special rules for an investment in a QOF held by a taxpayer for at least 10 years, was adopted by T.D. 9889 on December 31, 2019 (published in the Federal Register on May 1, 2019) (REG-120186-18).

⋙→ *Caution: Proposed Reg. §1.1400Z2(b)-1, below, was adopted by T.D. 9889; however, for an exception regarding when this proposed regulation may be relied upon, see final Reg. §1.1400Z2(b)-1(j).*

Par. 3. Section 1.1400Z2(b)-1 is added to read as follows:

§1.1400Z2(b)-1. Inclusion of gains that have been deferred under section 1400Z-2(a).—(a) *Scope and definitions.—*(1) *Scope.—*This section provides rules under section 1400Z-2(b) of the Internal Revenue Code regarding the inclusion in income of gain deferred under section 1400Z-2(a)(1)(A). This section applies to a QOF owner only until all of such owner's gain deferred pursuant to section 1400Z-2(a)(1)(A) has been included in income, subject to the limitations described in paragraph (e)(5) of this section. Paragraph (a)(2) of this section provides additional definitions used in this section and §§1.1400Z2(c)-1 through 1.1400Z2(g)-1. Paragraph (b) of this section provides general rules under section 1400Z-2(b)(1) regarding the timing of the inclusion in income of the deferred gain. Paragraph (c) of this section provides rules regarding the determination of the extent to which an event triggers the inclusion in income of all, or a portion, of the deferred gain. Paragraph (d) of this section provides rules regarding holding periods for qualifying investments. Paragraph (e) of this section provides rules regarding the amount of deferred gain included in gross income under section 1400Z-2(a)(1)(B) and (b), including special rules for QOF partnerships and QOF S corporations. Paragraph (f) of this section provides examples illustrating the rules of paragraphs (c), (d), and (e) of this section. Paragraph (g) of this section provides rules regarding basis adjustments under section 1400Z-2(b)(2)(B). Paragraph (h) of this section provides special reporting rules applicable to partners, partnerships, and direct or indirect owners of QOF partnerships. Paragraph (i) of this section provides dates of applicability.

(2) *Definitions.—*The following definitions apply for purposes of this section and §§1.1400Z2(c)-1 and 1.1400Z2(g)-1:

(i) *Boot.—*The term *boot* means money or other property that section 354 or 355 does not permit to be received without the recognition of gain.

(ii) *Consolidated group.—*The term *consolidated group* has the meaning provided in §1.1502-1(h).

(iii) *Deferral election.—*The term *deferral election* means an election under section 1400Z-2(a) made before January 1, 2027, with respect to an eligible interest.

(iv) *Inclusion event.—*The term *inclusion event* means an event described in paragraph (c) of this section.

(v) *Mixed-funds investment.—*The term *mixed-funds investment* means an investment a portion of which is a qualifying investment and a portion of which is a non-qualifying investment.

(vi) *Non-qualifying investment.—*The term *non-qualifying investment* means an investment in a QOF described in section 1400Z-2(e)(1)(A)(ii).

(vii) *Property.—*(A) *In general.—*The term *property* means money, securities, or any other property.

(B) *Inclusion events regarding QOF corporation distributions.—*For purposes of paragraph (c) of this section, in the context in which a QOF corporation makes a distribution, the term property does not include stock (or rights to acquire stock) in the QOF corporation that makes the distribution.

(viii) *QOF.—*The term *QOF* means a qualified opportunity fund, as defined in section 1400Z-2(d)(1) and associated regulations.

(ix) *QOF C corporation.—*The term *QOF C corporation* means a QOF corporation other than a QOF S corporation.

(x) *QOF corporation.—*The term *QOF corporation* means a QOF that is classified as a corporation for Federal income tax purposes.

(xi) *QOF owner.—*The term *QOF owner* means a QOF shareholder or a QOF partner.

(xii) *QOF partner.—*The term *QOF partner* means a person that directly owns a qualifying investment in a QOF partnership or a person that owns such a qualifying investment through equity interests solely in one or more partnerships.

(xiii) *QOF partnership.—*The term *QOF partnership* means a QOF that is classified as a partnership for Federal income tax purposes.

(xiv) *QOF S corporation.—*The term *QOF S corporation* means a QOF corporation that has elected under section 1362 to be an S corporation.

(xv) *QOF shareholder.—*The term *QOF shareholder* means a person that directly owns a qualifying investment in a QOF corporation.

(xvi) *Qualifying investment.*—The term *qualifying investment* means an eligible interest (as defined in §1.1400Z2(a)-1(b)(3)), or portion thereof, in a QOF to the extent that a deferral election applies with respect to such eligible interest or portion thereof.

(xvii) *Qualifying QOF partnership interest.*—The term *qualifying QOF partnership interest* means a direct or indirect interest in a QOF partnership that is a qualifying investment.

(xviii) *Qualifying QOF stock.*—The term *qualifying QOF stock* means stock in a QOF corporation that is a qualifying investment.

(xix) *Qualifying section 355 transaction.*—The term *qualifying section 355 transaction* means a distribution described in paragraph (c)(11)(i)(B) of this section.

(xx) *Qualifying section 381 transaction.*—The term *qualifying section 381 transaction* means a transaction described in section 381(a)(2), except the following transactions:

(A) An acquisition of assets of a QOF by a QOF shareholder that holds a qualifying investment in the QOF;

(B) An acquisition of assets of a QOF by a tax-exempt entity as defined in §1.337(d)-4(c)(2);

(C) An acquisition of assets of a QOF by an entity operating on a cooperative basis within the meaning of section 1381;

(D) An acquisition by a QOF of assets of a QOF shareholder that holds a qualifying investment in the QOF;

(E) A reorganization of a QOF in a transaction that qualifies under section 368(a)(1)(G);

(F) A transaction, immediately after which one QOF owns an investment in another QOF; and

(G) A triangular reorganization of a QOF within the meaning of §1.358-6(b)(2)(i), (ii), or (iii).

(xxi) *Remaining deferred gain.*—The term *remaining deferred gain* means the full amount of gain that was deferred under section 1400Z-2(a)(1)(A), reduced by the amount of gain previously included under paragraph (b) of this section.

(b) *General inclusion rule.*—The gain to which a deferral election applies is included in gross income, to the extent provided in paragraph (e) of this section, in the taxable year that includes the earlier of:

(1) The date of an inclusion event; or

(2) December 31, 2026.

(c) *Inclusion events.*—(1) *General rule.*—Except as otherwise provided in this paragraph (c), the following events are inclusion events (which result in the inclusion of gain under paragraph (b) of this section) if, and to the extent that—

(i) *Reduction of interest in QOF.*—A taxpayer's transfer of a qualifying investment reduces the taxpayer's equity interest in the qualifying investment;

(ii) *Distribution of property regardless of whether the taxpayer's direct interest in the QOF is reduced.*—A taxpayer receives property in a transaction that is treated as a distribution for Federal income tax purposes, whether or not the receipt reduces the taxpayer's ownership of the QOF; or

(iii) *Claim of worthlessness.*—A taxpayer claims a loss for worthless stock under section 165(g) or otherwise claims a worthlessness deduction with respect to its qualifying investment.

(2) *Termination or liquidation of QOF or QOF owner.*—(i) *Termination or liquidation of QOF.*—Except as otherwise provided in this paragraph (c), a taxpayer has an inclusion event with respect to all of its qualifying investment if the QOF ceases to exist for Federal income tax purposes.

(ii) *Liquidation of QOF owner.*—(A) *Portion of distribution treated as sale.*—A distribution of a qualifying investment in a complete liquidation of a QOF owner is an inclusion event to the extent that section 336(a) treats the distribution as if the qualifying investment were sold to the distributee at its fair market value, without regard to section 336(d).

(B) *Distribution to 80-percent distributee.*—A distribution of a qualifying investment in a complete liquidation of a QOF owner is not an inclusion event to the extent section 337(a) applies to the distribution.

(3) *Transfer of an investment in a QOF by gift.*—A taxpayer's transfer of a qualifying investment by gift, whether outright or in trust, is an inclusion event, regardless of whether that transfer is a completed gift for Federal gift tax purposes, and regardless of the taxable or tax-exempt status of the donee of the gift.

(4) *Transfer of an investment in a QOF by reason of the taxpayer's death.*—(i) *In general.*—Except as provided in paragraph (c)(4)(ii) of this section, a transfer of a qualifying investment by reason of the taxpayer's death is not an inclusion event. Transfers by reason of death include, for example:

(A) A transfer by reason of death to the deceased owner's estate;

(B) A distribution of a qualifying investment by the deceased owner's estate;

(C) A distribution of a qualifying investment by the deceased owner's trust that is made by reason of the deceased owner's death;

(D) The passing of a jointly owned qualifying investment to the surviving co-owner by operation of law; and

(E) Any other transfer of a qualifying investment at death by operation of law.

(ii) *Exceptions.*—The following transfers are not included as a transfer by reason of the taxpayer's death, and thus are inclusion events, and the amount recognized is includible in the gross income of the transferor as provided in section 691:

(A) A sale, exchange, or other disposition by the deceased taxpayer's estate or trust, other than a distribution described in paragraph (c)(4)(i) of this section;

(B) Any disposition by the legatee, heir, or beneficiary who received the qualifying investment by reason of the taxpayer's death; and

(C) Any disposition by the surviving joint owner or other recipient who received the qualifying investment by operation of law on the taxpayer's death.

(5) *Grantor trusts.*—(i) *Contributions to grantor trusts.*—If the owner of a qualifying investment contributes it to a trust and, under the grantor trust rules, the owner of the investment is the deemed owner of the trust, the contribution is not an inclusion event.

(ii) *Changes in grantor trust status.*—In general, a change in the status of a grantor trust, whether the termination of grantor trust status or the creation of grantor trust status, is an inclusion event. Notwithstanding the previous sentence, the termination of grantor trust status as the result of the death of the owner of a qualifying investment is not an inclusion event, but the provisions of paragraph (c)(4) of this section apply to distributions or dispositions by the trust.

(6) *Special rules for partners and partnerships.*—(i) *Scope.*—Except as otherwise provided in this paragraph (c)(6), in the case of a partnership that is a QOF or, directly or indirectly solely through one or more partnerships, owns an interest in a QOF, the inclusion rules of this paragraph (c) apply to transactions involving any direct or indirect partner of the QOF to the extent of such partner's share of any eligible gain of the QOF.

(ii) *Transactions that are not inclusion events.*—(A) *In general.*—Notwithstanding paragraphs (c)(1) and (2) and (c)(6)(iii) of this section, and except as otherwise provided in paragraph (c)(6) of this section, no transaction described in paragraph (c)(6)(ii) of this section is an inclusion event.

(B) *Section 721 contributions.*—Subject to paragraph (c)(6)(v) of this section, a contribution by a QOF owner, including any contribution by a partner of a partnership that, solely through one or more upper-tier partnerships, owns an interest in a QOF (contributing partner), of its direct or indirect partnership interest in a qualifying investment to a partnership (transferee partnership) in a transaction governed all or in part by section 721(a) is not an inclusion event, provided the interest transfer does not cause a partnership termination of a QOF partnership, or the direct or indirect owner of a QOF, under section 708(b)(1). *See* paragraph (c)(6)(ii)(C) of this section for transactions governed by section 708(b)(2)(A). Notwithstanding the rules in this paragraph (c)(6)(ii)(B), the inclusion rules in paragraph (c) of this section apply to any part of the transaction to which section 721(a) does not apply. The transferee partnership becomes subject to section 1400Z-2 and all section 1400Z-2 regulations in this chapter with respect to the eligible gain associated with the contributed qualifying investment. The transferee partnership must allocate and report the gain that is associated with the contributed qualifying investment to the contributing partner to the same extent that the gain would have been allocated and reported to the contributing partner in the absence of the contribution.

(C) *Section 708(b)(2)(A) mergers or consolidations.*—Subject to paragraph (c)(6)(v) of this section, a merger or consolidation of a partnership holding a qualifying investment, or of a partnership that holds an interest in such partnership solely through one or more partnerships, with another partnership in a transaction to which section 708(b)(2)(A) applies is not an inclusion event. The resulting partnership or new partnership, as determined under §1.708-1(c)(1), becomes subject to section 1400Z-2, and all section 1400Z-2 regulations in this chapter, to the same extent that the original partnership was so subject prior to the transaction, and must allocate and report any eligible gain to the same extent and to the same partners that the original partnership allocated and reported such items prior to the transaction. Notwithstanding the rules in this paragraph (c)(6)(ii)(C), the general inclusion rules of paragraph (c) of this section apply to the portion of the transaction that is otherwise treated as a sale or exchange under paragraph (c) of this section.

(iii) *Partnership distributions.*—Notwithstanding paragraph (c)(6)(i) of this section, and subject to paragraph (c)(6)(v) of this section, and except as provided in paragraph (c)(6)(ii)(C) of this section, an actual or deemed distribution of property (including cash) by a QOF partnership to a partner with respect to its qualifying investment is an inclusion event only to the extent that the distributed property has a fair market value in excess of the partner's basis in its qualifying investment. Similar rules apply to distributions involving tiered partnerships. *See* paragraph (c)(6)(iv) of this section for special rules relating to mixed-funds investments.

(iv) *Special rules for mixed-funds investments.*—(A) *General rule.*—The rules of paragraph (c)(6)(iv) of this section apply solely for purposes of section 1400Z-2. A partner that holds a mixed-funds investment in a QOF partnership (a mixed-funds partner) shall be treated as holding two separate interests in the QOF partnership, one a qualifying investment and the other a non-qualifying investment (the separate interests). The basis of each separate interest is determined under the rules described in paragraphs (c)(6)(iv)(B) and (g) of this section as if each interest were held by different taxpayers.

(B) *Allocations and distributions.*—All section 704(b) allocations of income, gain, loss, and deduction, all section 752 allocations of debt, and all distributions made to a mixed-funds partner shall be treated as made to the separate interests based on the allocation percentages of such interests as defined in paragraph (c)(6)(iv)(D) of this section. For purposes of this paragraph (c)(6)(iv)(B), in allocating income, gain, loss, or deduction between these separate interests, section 704(c) principles shall apply to account for any value-basis disparities attributable to the qualifying investment or non-qualifying investment. Any distribution (whether actual or deemed) to the holder of a qualifying investment is subject to the rules of paragraphs (c)(6)(iii) and (v) of this section, without regard to the presence or absence of gain under other provisions of subchapter K of chapter 1 of subtitle A of the Code.

(C) *Subsequent contributions.*—In the event of an increase in a partner's qualifying or non-qualifying investment (for example, as in the case of an additional contribution for a qualifying investment or for an interest that is a non-qualifying investment or a change in allocations for services rendered), the partner's interest in the separate interests shall be valued immediately prior to such event and the allocation percentages shall be adjusted to reflect the relative values of these separate interests and the additional contribution, if any.

(D) *Allocation percentages.*—The allocation percentages of the separate interests shall be determined based on the relative capital contributions attributable to the qualifying investment and the non-qualifying investment. In the event a partner receives a profits interest in the partnership for services rendered to or for the benefit of the partnership, the allocation percentages with respect to such partner shall be calculated based on:

(1) With respect to the profits interest received, the highest share of residual profits the mixed-funds partner would receive with respect to that interest; and

(2) With respect to the remaining interest, the percentage interests for the capital interests described in the immediately preceding sentence.

(v) *Remaining deferred gain reduction rule.*—An inclusion event occurs when and to the extent that a transaction has the effect of reducing—

(A) The amount of remaining deferred gain of one or more direct or indirect partners; or

(B) The amount of gain that would be recognized by such partner or partners under paragraph (e)(4)(ii) of this section to the extent that such amount would reduce such gain to an amount that is less than the remaining deferred gain.

(7) *Special rule for S corporations.*—(i) *In general.*—Except as provided in paragraphs (c)(7)(ii), (iii), and (iv) of this section, none of the following is an inclusion event:

(A) An election, revocation, or termination of a corporation's status as an S corporation under section 1362;

(B) A conversion of a qualified subchapter S trust (as defined in section 1361(d)(3)) to an electing small business trust (as defined in section 1361(e)(1));

(C) A conversion of an electing small business trust to a qualified subchapter S trust;

(D) A valid modification of a trust agreement of an S-corporation shareholder whether by an amendment, a decanting, a judicial reformation, or a material modification;

(E) A 25 percent or less aggregate change in ownership pursuant to paragraph (c)(7)(iii) of this section in the equity investment in an S corporation that directly holds a qualifying investment; and

(F) A disposition of assets by a QOF S corporation.

(ii) *Distributions by QOF S corporation.*—(A) *General rule.*—An actual or constructive distribution of property by a QOF S corporation to a shareholder with respect to its qualifying investment is an inclusion event to the extent that the distribution is treated as gain from the sale or exchange of property under section 1368(b)(2) and (c).

(B) *Spill-over rule.*—For purposes of applying paragraph (c)(7)(ii) of this section to the adjusted basis of a qualifying investment, or non-qualifying investment, as appropriate, in a QOF S corporation, the second sentence of §1.1367-1(c)(3) applies—

(1) With regard to multiple qualifying investments, solely to the respective bases of such qualifying investments, and does not take into account the basis of any non-qualifying investment; and

(2) With regard to multiple non-qualifying investments, solely to the respective bases of such non-qualifying investments, and does not take into account the basis of any qualifying investment.

(iii) *Aggregate change in ownership of an S corporation that is a QOF owner.*—(A) *General rule.*—Solely for purposes of section 1400Z-2, an inclusion event occurs when there is an aggregate change in ownership, within the meaning of paragraph (c)(7)(iii)(B) of this section, of an S corporation that directly holds a qualifying investment in a QOF. The S corporation is treated as having disposed of its entire qualifying investment in the QOF, and neither section 1400Z-2(b)(2)(B)(iii) or (iv) nor section 1400Z-2(c) applies to the S corporation's qualifying investment after that date. The disposition under this paragraph (c)(7)(iii)(A) is treated as occurring on the date the requirements of paragraph (c)(7)(iii)(B) of this section are satisfied.

(B) *Aggregate ownership change threshold.*—For purposes of paragraph (c)(7)(iii)(A) of this section, there is an *aggregate change in ownership* of an S corporation if, immediately after any change in ownership of the S corporation, the percentage of the stock of the S corporation owned directly by the shareholders who owned the S corporation at the time of its deferral election has decreased by more than 25 percent. The ownership percentage of each shareholder referred to in this paragraph (c)(7)(iii)(B) is measured separately from the ownership percentage of all other shareholders. Any decrease in ownership is determined with regard to the percentage held by the relevant shareholder at the time of the election under section 1400Z-2(a), and all decreases are then aggregated. Decreases in ownership may result from, for example, the sale of shares, the redemption of shares, the issuance of new shares, or the occurrence of section 381(a) transactions. The aggregate change in ownership is measured separately for each qualifying investment of the S corporation.

(iv) *Conversion from S corporation to partnership or disregarded entity.*—(A) *General rule.*—Notwithstanding paragraph (c)(7)(i) of this section, and except as provided in paragraph (c)(7)(iv)(B) of this section, a conversion of an S corporation to a partnership or an entity disregarded as separate from its owner under §301.7701-3(b)(1)(ii) of this chapter is an inclusion event.

(B) *Exception for qualifying section 381 transaction.*—A conversion described in paragraph (c)(7)(iv)(A) of this section is not an inclusion event if the conversion comprises a step in a series of related transactions that together qualify as a qualifying section 381 transaction.

(v) *Treatment of separate blocks of stock in mixed-funds investments.*—With regard to a mixed-funds investment in a QOF S corporation, if different blocks of stock are created for otherwise qualifying investments to track basis in such qualifying investments, the separate blocks are not treated as different classes of stock for purposes of S corporation eligibility under section 1361(b)(1).

(vi) *Applicability.*—Paragraph (c)(7) of this section applies regardless of whether the S corporation is a QOF or a QOF shareholder.

(8) *Distributions by a QOF C corporation.*—A distribution of property by a QOF C corporation with respect to a qualifying investment is not an inclusion event except to the extent section 301(c)(3) applies to the distribution. For purposes of this paragraph (c)(8), a

distribution of property also includes a distribution of stock by a QOF C corporation that is treated as a distribution of property to which section 301 applies pursuant to section 305(b).

(9) *Dividend-equivalent redemptions.*—(i) *General rule.*—Except as provided in paragraph (c)(9)(ii) or (iii) of this section, a transaction described in section 302(d) is an inclusion event with respect to the full amount of the distribution.

(ii) *Redemption of stock of wholly owned QOF.*—If all stock in a QOF is held directly by a single shareholder, or directly by members of the same consolidated group, and if shares are redeemed in a transaction to which section 302(d) applies, *see* paragraph (c)(8) of this section (applicable to distributions by QOF corporations).

(iii) *S corporations.*—S corporation section 302(d) transactions are an inclusion event to the extent the distribution exceeds basis in the QOF as adjusted under paragraph (c)(7)(ii) of this section.

(10) *Qualifying section 381 transactions.*—(i) *Assets of a QOF are acquired.*—(A) *In general.*—Except to the extent provided in paragraph (c)(10)(i)(C) of this section, if the assets of a QOF corporation are acquired in a qualifying section 381 transaction, and if the acquiring corporation is a QOF immediately after the acquisition, then the transaction is not an inclusion event.

(B) *Determination of acquiring corporation's status as a QOF.*—For purposes of paragraph (c)(10)(i)(A) of this section, the acquiring corporation is treated as a QOF immediately after the qualifying section 381 transaction if the acquiring corporation satisfies the certification requirements in §1.1400Z2(d)-1 immediately after the transaction and holds at least 90 percent of its assets in qualified opportunity zone property on the first testing date after the transaction (*see* section 1400Z-2(d)(1) and §1.1400Z2(d)-1).

(C) *Receipt of boot by QOF shareholder in qualifying section 381 transaction.*—(1) *General rule.*—Except as provided in paragraph (c)(10)(i)(C)(2) of this section, if assets of a QOF corporation are acquired in a qualifying section 381 transaction and a taxpayer that is a QOF shareholder receives boot with respect to its qualifying investment, the taxpayer has an inclusion event. If the taxpayer realizes a gain on the transaction, the amount that gives rise to the inclusion event is the amount of gain under section 356 that is not treated as a dividend under section 356(a)(2). If the taxpayer realizes a loss on the transaction, the amount that gives rise to the inclusion event is an amount equal to the fair market value of the boot received.

(2) *Receipt of boot from wholly owned QOF.*—If all stock in both a QOF and the corporation that acquires the QOF's assets in a qualifying section 381 transaction are held directly by a single shareholder, or directly by members of the same consolidated group, and if the shareholder receives (or group members receive) boot with respect to the qualifying investment in the qualifying section 381 transaction, paragraph (c)(8) of this section (applicable to distributions by QOF corporations) applies to the boot as if it were distributed from the QOF to the shareholder(s) in a separate transaction to which section 301 applied.

(ii) *Assets of a QOF shareholder are acquired.*—(A) *In general.*—Except to the extent provided in paragraph (c)(10)(ii)(B) of this section, a qualifying section 381 transaction in which the assets of a QOF shareholder are acquired is not an inclusion event with respect to the qualifying investment. However, if the qualifying section 381 transaction causes a QOF shareholder that is an S corporation to have an aggregate change in ownership within the meaning of paragraph (c)(7)(iii)(B) of this section, *see* paragraph (c)(7)(iii)(A) of this section.

(B) *Qualifying section 381 transaction in which QOF shareholder's qualifying investment is not completely acquired.*—If the assets of a QOF shareholder are acquired in a qualifying section 381 transaction in which the acquiring corporation does not acquire all of the QOF shareholder's qualifying investment, there is an inclusion event to the extent that the QOF shareholder's qualifying investment is not transferred to the acquiring corporation.

(11) *Section 355 transactions.*—(i) *Distribution by a QOF.*—(A) *In general.*—Except as provided in paragraph (c)(11)(i)(B) of this section, if a QOF corporation distributes stock or securities of a controlled corporation to a taxpayer in a transaction to which section 355, or so much of section 356 as relates to section 355, applies, the taxpayer has an inclusion event with respect to its qualifying investment. The amount that gives rise to such inclusion event is equal to the fair market value of the shares of the controlled corporation and the boot received by the taxpayer in the distribution with respect to its qualifying investment.

(B) *Controlled corporation becomes a QOF.*—(1) *In general.*—Except as provided in paragraph (c)(11)(i)(B)(3) of this section, if a QOF corporation distributes stock or securities of a controlled corpo-

ration in a transaction to which section 355, or so much of section 356 as relates to section 355, applies, and if both the distributing corporation and the controlled corporation are QOFs immediately after the final distribution (qualifying section 355 transaction), then the distribution is not an inclusion event with respect to the taxpayer's qualifying investment in the distributing QOF corporation or the controlled QOF corporation. This paragraph (c)(11)(i)(B) does not apply unless the distributing corporation distributes all of the stock and securities in the controlled corporation held by it immediately before the distribution within a 30-day period. For purposes of this paragraph (c)(11)(i)(B), the term *final distribution* means the last distribution that satisfies the preceding sentence.

(2) *Determination of distributing corporation's and controlled corporation's status as QOFs.*—For purposes of paragraph (c)(11)(i)(B)(1) of this section, each of the distributing corporation and the controlled corporation is treated as a QOF immediately after the final distribution if the corporation satisfies the certification requirements in §1.1400Z2(d)-1 immediately after the final distribution and holds at least 90 percent of its assets in qualified opportunity zone property on the first testing date after the final distribution (*see* section 1400Z-2(d)(1) and §1.1400Z2(d)-1).

(3) *Receipt of boot.*—If a taxpayer receives boot in a qualifying section 355 transaction with respect to its qualifying investment, and if section 356(a) applies to the transaction, the taxpayer has an inclusion event, and the amount that gives rise to the inclusion event is the amount of gain under section 356 that is not treated as a dividend under section 356(a)(2). If a taxpayer receives boot in a qualifying section 355 transaction with respect to its qualifying investment, and if section 356(b) applies to the transaction, *see* paragraph (c)(8) of this section (applicable to distributions by QOF corporations).

(4) *Treatment of controlled corporation stock as qualified opportunity zone stock.*—If stock or securities of a controlled corporation are distributed in a qualifying section 355 transaction, and if the distributing corporation retains a portion of the controlled corporation stock after the initial distribution, the retained stock will not cease to qualify as qualified opportunity zone stock in the hands of the distributing corporation solely as a result of the qualifying section 355 transaction. This paragraph (c)(11)(i)(B)(4) does not apply unless the distributing corporation distributes all of the stock and securities in the controlled corporation held by it immediately before the distribution within a 30-day period.

(ii) *Distribution by a QOF shareholder.*—If a QOF shareholder distributes stock or securities of a controlled QOF corporation in a transaction to which section 355 applies, then for purposes of section 1400Z-2(b)(1) and paragraph (b) of this section, the taxpayer has an inclusion event to the extent the distribution reduces the taxpayer's direct tax ownership of its qualifying QOF stock. For distributions by a QOF shareholder that is an S corporation, *see also* paragraph (c)(7)(iii) of this section.

(12) *Recapitalizations and section 1036 transactions.*—(i) *No reduction in proportionate interest in qualifying QOF stock.*—(A) *In general.*—Except as otherwise provided in paragraph (c)(8) of this section (relating to distributions subject to section 305(b)) or paragraph (c)(12)(i)(B) of this section, if a QOF corporation engages in a transaction that qualifies as a reorganization described in section 368(a)(1)(E), or if a QOF shareholder engages in a transaction that is described in section 1036, and if the transaction does not have the result of decreasing the taxpayer's proportionate interest in the QOF corporation, the transaction is not an inclusion event.

(B) *Receipt of property or boot by QOF shareholder.*—If the taxpayer receives property or boot in a transaction described in paragraph (c)(12)(i)(A) of this section and section 368(a)(1)(E), then the property or boot is treated as property or boot to which section 301 or section 356 applies, as determined under general tax principles. If the taxpayer receives property that is not permitted to be received without the recognition of gain in a transaction described in paragraph (c)(12)(i)(A) of this section and section 1036, then, for purposes of this section, the property is treated in a similar manner as boot in a transaction described in section 368(a)(1)(E). For the treatment of property to which section 301 applies, *see* paragraph (c)(8) of this section. For the treatment of boot to which section 356 applies (including in situations in which the QOF is wholly and directly owned by a single shareholder or by members of the same consolidated group), *see* paragraph (c)(10) of this section.

(ii) *Reduction in proportionate interest in the QOF corporation.*—If a QOF engages in a transaction that qualifies as a reorganization described in section 368(a)(1)(E), or if a QOF shareholder engages in a transaction that is described in section 1036, and if the transaction has the result of decreasing the taxpayer's proportionate qualifying interest in the QOF corporation, then the taxpayer has an inclusion event in an amount equal to the amount of the reduction in the fair market value of the taxpayer's qualifying QOF stock.

(13) *Section 304 transactions.*—A transfer of a qualifying investment in a transaction described in section 304(a) is an inclusion event with respect to the full amount of the consideration.

(14) *Deduction for worthlessness.*—If a taxpayer claims a loss for worthless stock under section 165(g) or otherwise claims a worthlessness deduction with respect to all or a portion of its qualifying investment, then for purposes of section 1400Z-2 and all section 1400Z-2 regulations in this chapter, the taxpayer is treated as having disposed of that portion of its qualifying investment on the date it became worthless. Thus, the taxpayer has an inclusion event with respect to that portion of its qualifying investment, and neither section 1400Z-2(b)(2)(B)(iii) or (iv) nor section 1400Z-2(c) applies to that portion of the taxpayer's qualifying investment after the date it became worthless.

(15) *Other inclusion and non-inclusion events.*—Notwithstanding any other provision of this paragraph (c), the Commissioner may determine by published guidance that a type of transaction is or is not an inclusion event.

(d) *Holding periods.*—(1) *Holding period for QOF investment.*—(i) *General rule.*—Solely for purposes of sections 1400Z-2(b)(2)(B) and 1400Z-2(c), and except as otherwise provided in this paragraph (d)(1), the length of time a qualifying investment has been held is determined without regard to the period for which the taxpayer had held property exchanged for such investment.

(ii) *Holding period for QOF investment received in a qualifying section 381 transaction, a reorganization described in section 368(a)(1)(E), or a section 1036 exchange.*—For purposes of section 1400Z-2(b)(2)(B) and 1400Z-2(c), the holding period for QOF stock received by a taxpayer in a qualifying section 381 transaction in which the target corporation was a QOF immediately before the acquisition and the acquiring corporation is a QOF immediately after the acquisition, in a reorganization described in section 368(a)(1)(E), or in a section 1036 exchange, is determined by applying the principles of section 1223(1).

(iii) *Holding period for controlled corporation stock.*—For purposes of section 1400Z-2(b)(2)(B) and 1400Z-2(c), the holding period of a qualifying investment in a controlled corporation received by a taxpayer on its qualifying investment in the distributing corporation in a qualifying section 355 transaction is determined by applying the principles of section 1223(1).

(iv) *Tacking with donor or deceased owner.*—For purposes of section 1400Z-2(b)(2)(B) and 1400Z-2(c), the holding period of a qualifying investment held by a taxpayer who received that qualifying investment as a gift that was not an inclusion event, or by reason of the prior owner's death, includes the time during which that qualifying investment was held by the donor or the deceased owner, respectively.

(2) *Determination of original use of QOF assets.*—(i) *Assets acquired in a section 381 transaction.*—For purposes of section 1400Z-2(d), including for purposes of determining whether the original use of qualified opportunity zone business property commences with the acquiring corporation, any qualified opportunity zone property transferred by the transferor QOF to the acquiring corporation in connection with a qualifying section 381 transaction does not lose its status as qualified opportunity zone property solely as a result of its transfer to the acquiring corporation.

(ii) *Assets contributed to a controlled corporation.*—For purposes of section 1400Z-2(d), including for purposes of determining whether the original use of qualified opportunity zone business property commences with the controlled corporation, any qualified opportunity zone property contributed by the distributing corporation to the controlled corporation in connection with a qualifying section 355 transaction does not lose its status as qualified opportunity zone property solely as a result of its contribution to the controlled corporation.

(3) *Application to partnerships.*—The principles of paragraphs (d)(1) and (2) of this section apply to qualifying QOF partnership interests with regard to non-inclusion transactions described in paragraph (c)(6)(ii) of this section.

(e) *Amount includible.*—Except as provided in §1.1400Z2(a)-1(b)(4), the amount of gain included in gross income under section 1400Z-2(a)(1)(B) on a date described in paragraph (b) of this section is determined under this paragraph (e).

(1) *In general.*—Except as provided in paragraphs (e)(2) and (4) of this section, and subject to paragraph (e)(5) of this section, in the case of an inclusion event, the amount of gain included in gross income is equal to the excess of the amount described in paragraph

(e)(1)(i) of this section over the amount described in paragraph (e)(1)(ii) of this section.

(i) The amount described in this paragraph (e)(1)(i) is equal to the lesser of:

(A) An amount which bears the same proportion to the remaining deferred gain, as:

(1) The fair market value of the portion of the qualifying investment that is disposed of in the inclusion event, as determined as of the date of the inclusion event, bears to;

(2) The fair market value of the total qualifying investment immediately before the inclusion event; or

(B) The amount described in paragraph (e)(1)(i)(A)(*1*) of this section.

(ii) The amount described in this paragraph (e)(1)(ii) is the taxpayer's basis in the portion of the qualifying investment that is disposed of in the inclusion event.

(iii) For purposes of paragraph (e)(1)(i)(A)(*1*) of this section, the fair market value of that portion is determined by multiplying the fair market value of the taxpayer's entire qualifying investment in the QOF, valued as of the date of the inclusion event, by the percentage of the taxpayer's qualifying investment that is represented by the portion disposed of in the inclusion event.

(2) *Property received from a QOF in certain transactions.*—In the case of an inclusion event described in paragraph (c)(6)(iii) or (v) or (c)(8), (9), (10), (11), or (12) of this section, the amount of gain included in gross income is equal to the lesser of:

(i) The remaining deferred gain; or

(ii) The amount that gave rise to the inclusion event. *See* paragraph (c) of this section for rules regarding the amount that gave rise to the inclusion event, and *see* paragraph (g) of this section for applicable ordering rules.

(3) *Gain recognized on December 31, 2026.*—The amount of gain included in gross income on December 31, 2026 is equal to the excess of—

(i) The lesser of—

(A) The remaining deferred gain; and

(B) The fair market value of the qualifying investment held on December 31, 2026; over

(ii) The taxpayer's basis in the qualifying investment as of December 31, 2026, taking into account only section 1400Z-2(b)(2)(B).

(4) *Special amount includible rule for partnerships and S corporations.*—For purposes of paragraphs (e)(1) and (3) of this section, in the case of an inclusion event involving a qualifying investment in a QOF partnership or S corporation, or in the case of a qualifying investment in a QOF partnership or S corporation held on December 31, 2026, the amount of gain included in gross income is equal to the lesser of:

(i) The product of:

(A) The percentage of the qualifying investment that gave rise to the inclusion event; and

(B) The remaining deferred gain, less any basis adjustments pursuant to section 1400Z-2(b)(2)(B)(iii) and (iv); or

(ii) The gain that would be recognized on a fully taxable disposition of the qualifying investment that gave rise to the inclusion event.

(5) *Limitation on amount of gain included after statutory five- and seven-year basis increases.*—The total amount of gain included in gross income under this paragraph (e) is limited to the amount deferred under section 1400Z-2(a)(1), reduced by any increase in the basis of the qualifying investment made pursuant to section 1400Z-2(b)(2)(B)(iii) or (iv). *See* paragraph (g)(2) of this section for limitations on the amount of basis adjustments under section 1400Z-2(b)(2)(B)(iii) and (iv).

(f) *Examples.*—The following examples illustrate the rules of paragraphs (c), (d) and (e) of this section. For purposes of the following examples: A, B, C, W, X, Y, and Z are C corporations that do not file a consolidated Federal income tax return; Q is a QOF corporation or a QOF partnership, as specified in each example; and each divisive corporate transaction satisfies the requirements of section 355.

(1) *Example 1: Determination of basis, holding period, and qualifying investment*—(i) *Facts.* A wholly and directly owns Q, a QOF corporation. On May 31, 2019, A sells a capital asset to an unrelated party and realizes $500 of capital gain. On October 31, 2019, A transfers unencumbered asset N to Q in exchange for a qualifying investment. Asset N, which A has held for 10 years, has a basis of $500 and a fair market value of $500. A elects to defer the inclusion of $500 in gross income under section 1400Z-2(a) and §1.1400Z2(a)-1.

(ii) *Analysis.* Under §1.1400Z2(a)-1(b)(10)(i)(B)(*1*), A made a qualifying investment of $500. Under section 1400Z-2(b)(2)(B)(i), A's basis in its qualifying investment in Q is $0. For purposes of sections

1400Z-2(b)(2)(B) and 1400Z-2(c), A's holding period in its new investment in Q begins on October 31, 2019. *See* paragraph (d)(1)(i) of this section. Other than for purposes of applying section 1400Z-2, A has a 10-year holding period in its new Q investment as of October 31, 2019.

(iii) *Transfer of built-in gain property.* The facts are the same as in this *Example* 1 in paragraph (f)(1)(i) of this section, but A's basis in transferred asset N is $200. Under § 1.1400Z2(a)-1(b)(10)(i)(B)(*1*), A made a qualifying investment of $200 and a non-qualifying investment of $300.

(2) *Example 2: Transfer of qualifying investment*—(i) *Facts.* On May 31, 2019, A sells a capital asset to an unrelated party and realizes $500 of capital gain. On October 31, 2019, A transfers $500 to newly formed Q, a QOF corporation, in exchange for a qualifying investment. On February 29, 2020, A transfers 25 percent of its qualifying investment in Q to newly formed Y in exchange for 100 percent of Y's stock in a transfer to which section 351 applies (the Transfer), at a time when the fair market value of A's qualifying investment in Q is $800.

(ii) *Analysis.* Under § 1.1400Z2(a)-1(b)(10)(i)(A), A made a qualifying investment of $500 on October 31, 2019. In the Transfer, A exchanged 25 percent of its qualifying investment for Federal income tax purposes, which reduced A's direct qualifying investment. Under paragraph (c)(1)(i) of this section, the Transfer is an inclusion event to the extent of the reduction in A's direct qualifying investment. Under paragraph (e)(1) of this section, A therefore includes in income an amount equal to the excess of the amount described in paragraph (e)(1)(i) of this section over A's basis in the portion of the qualifying investment that was disposed of, which in this case is $0. The amount described in paragraph (e)(1)(i) is the lesser of:

(A) $125 ($500 x ($200 / $800)); or

(B) $200. As a result, A must include $125 of its deferred capital gain in income in 2020. After the Transfer, the Q stock is not qualifying Q stock in Y's hands.

(iii) *Disregarded transfer.* The facts are the same as in this *Example* 2 in paragraph (f)(2)(i) of this section, except that Y elects to be treated as an entity that is disregarded as an entity separate from its owner for Federal income tax purposes effective prior to the Contribution. Since the Transfer would be disregarded for Federal income tax purposes, A's transfer of its qualifying investment in Q would not be treated as a reduction in direct tax ownership for Federal income tax purposes, and the Transfer would not be an inclusion event with respect to A's qualifying investment in Q for purposes of section 1400Z-2(b)(1) and paragraph (b) of this section. Thus, A would not be required to include in income any portion of its deferred capital gain.

(iv) *Election to be treated as a corporation.* The facts are the same as in this *Example* 2 in paragraph (f)(2)(iii) of this section, except that Y (a disregarded entity) subsequently elects to be treated as a corporation for Federal income tax purposes. A's deemed transfer of its qualifying investment in Q to Y under § 301.7701-3(g)(1)(iv) of this chapter is an inclusion event for purposes of section 1400Z-2(b)(1) and paragraph (b) of this section.

(3) *Example 3: Part sale of qualifying QOF partnership interest in Year 6 when value of the QOF interest has increased*—(i) *Facts.* In October 2018, A and B each realize $200 of eligible gain, and C realizes $600 of eligible gain. On January 1, 2019, A, B, and C form Q, a QOF partnership. A contributes $200 of cash, B contributes $200 of cash, and C contributes $600 of cash to Q in exchange for qualifying QOF partnership interests in Q. A, B, and C hold 20 percent, 20 percent, and 60 percent interests in Q, respectively. On January 30, 2019, Q obtains a nonrecourse loan from a bank for $1,000. Under section 752, the loan is allocated $200 to A, $200 to B, and $600 to C. On February 1, 2019, Q purchases qualified opportunity zone business property for $2,000. On July 31, 2024, A sells 50 percent of its qualifying QOF partnership interest in Q to B for $400 cash. Prior to the sale, there were no inclusion events, distributions, partner changes, income or loss allocations, or changes in the amount or allocation of debt outstanding. At the time of the sale, the fair market value of Q's qualified opportunity zone business property is $5,000.

(ii) *Analysis.* Because A held its qualifying QOF partnership interest for at least five years, A's basis in its partnership interest at the time of the sale is $220 (the original zero basis with respect to the contribution, plus the $200 debt allocation, plus the 10% increase for interests held for five years). The sale of 50 percent of A's qualifying QOF partnership interest to B requires A to recognize $90 of eligible gain, the lesser of 50 percent of the remaining $180 deferred gain ($90) or the gain that would be recognized on a taxable sale of 50 percent of the interest ($390). A also recognizes $300 of gain relating to the appreciation of its interest in Q.

(4) *Example 4: Sale of qualifying QOF partnership interest when value of the QOF interest has decreased*—(i) *Facts.* The facts are the same as in *Example* 3 in paragraph (f)(3) of this section, except that A sells 50 percent of its qualifying QOF partnership interest in Q to B for cash of $50, and at the time of the sale, the fair market value of Q's qualified opportunity zone business property is $1,500.

(ii) *Analysis.* Because A held its qualifying QOF partnership interest for at least five years, A's basis at the time of the sale is $220. Under section 1400Z-2(b)(2)(A), the sale of 50 percent of A's qualifying QOF partnership interest to B requires A to recognize $40 of eligible gain, the lesser of $90 (50 percent of A's remaining deferred gain of $180) or $40 (the gain that would be recognized by A on a sale of 50 percent of its QOF interest). A's remaining basis in its qualifying QOF partnership interest is $110.

(5) *Example 5: Amount includible on December 31, 2026*—(i) *Facts.* The facts are the same as in *Example 3* in paragraph (f)(3) of this section, except that no sale of QOF interests takes place in 2024. Prior to December 31, 2026, there were no inclusion events, distributions, partner changes, income or loss allocations, or changes in the amount or allocation of debt outstanding.

(ii) *Analysis.* For purposes of calculating the amount includible on December 31, 2026, each of A's basis and B's basis is increased by $30 to $230, and C's basis is increased by $90 to $690 because they held their qualifying QOF partnership interests for at least seven years. Each of A and B is required to recognize $170 of eligible gain, and C is required to recognize $510 of eligible gain.

(iii) *Sale of qualifying QOF partnership interests.* The facts are the same as in this *Example 5* in paragraph (f)(5)(i) of this section, except that, on March 2, 2030, C sells its entire qualifying QOF partnership interest in Q to an unrelated buyer for cash of $4,200. Assuming an election under section 1400Z-2(c) is made, the basis of C's Q interest is increased to its fair market value immediately before the sale by C. C is treated as purchasing the interest immediately before the sale and the bases of the partnership's assets are increased in the manner they would be if the partnership had an election under section 754 in effect.

(6) *Example 6: Mixed-funds investment*—(i) *Facts.* On January 1, 2019, A and B form Q, a QOF partnership. A contributes $200 to Q, $100 of which is a qualifying investment, and B contributes $200 to Q in exchange for a qualifying investment. All the cash is used to purchase qualified opportunity zone property. Q has no liabilities. On March 30, 2023, when the values and bases of the qualifying investments remain unchanged, Q distributes $50 to A.

(ii) *Analysis.* Under paragraph (c)(6)(iv) of this section, A is a mixed-funds partner holding two separate interests, a qualifying investment and a non-qualifying investment. One half of the $50 distribution is treated under that provision as being made with respect to A's qualifying investment. For the $25 distribution made with respect to the qualifying investment, A is required to recognize $25 of eligible gain.

(iii) *Basis adjustments.* Under paragraph (g)(1)(ii)(B) of this section, prior to determining the tax consequences of the distribution, A increases its basis in its qualifying QOF partnership interest by $25 under section 1400Z-2(b)(2)(B)(ii). The distribution of $25 results in no gain under section 731. After the distribution, A's basis in its qualifying QOF partnership interest is $0 ($25-$25).

(7) *Example 7: Qualifying section 381 transaction of a QOF corporation*—(i) *Facts.* X wholly and directly owns Q, a QOF corporation. On May 31, 2019, X sells a capital asset to an unrelated party and realizes $500 of capital gain. On October 31, 2019, X contributes $500 to Q in exchange for a qualifying investment. In 2020, Q merges with and into unrelated Y (with Y surviving) in a transaction that qualifies as a reorganization under section 368(a)(1)(A) (the Merger). X does not receive any boot in the Merger with respect to its qualifying investment in Q. Immediately after the Merger, Y satisfies the requirements for QOF status under section 1400Z-2(d)(1) (*see* paragraph (c)(10)(i)(B) of this section).

(ii) *Analysis.* The Merger is not an inclusion event for purposes of section 1400Z-2(b)(1) and paragraph (b) of this section. *See* paragraph (c)(10)(i)(A) of this section. Accordingly, X is not required to include in income in 2020 its $500 of deferred capital gain as a result of the Merger. For purposes of section 1400Z-2(b)(2)(B) and 1400Z-2(c), X's holding period for its investment in Y is treated as beginning on October 31, 2019. For purposes of section 1400Z-2(d), Y's holding period in its assets includes Q's holding period in its assets, and Q's qualified opportunity zone business property continues to qualify as such. *See* paragraph (d)(2)(i) of this section.

(iii) *Merger of QOF shareholder.* The facts are the same as in this *Example 7* in paragraph (f)(7)(i) of this section, except that, in 2020, X (rather than Q) merges with and into Y in a section 381 transaction in which Y acquires all of X's qualifying interest in Q, and Y does not qualify as a QOF immediately after the merger. The merger transaction is not an inclusion event for purposes of section 1400Z-2(b)(1) and paragraph (b) of this section. *See* paragraph (c)(10)(ii) of this section.

(iv) *Receipt of boot.* The facts are the same as in this *Example 7* in paragraph (f)(7)(i) of this section, except that the value of X's qualifying investment immediately before the Merger is $1,000, X receives $100 of cash in addition to Y stock in the Merger in exchange for its qualifying investment, and neither Q nor Y has any earnings and profits. X realizes $1,000 of gain in the Merger. Under paragraphs (c)(10)(i)(C)(*1*) and (e)(2) of this section, X is required to include $100 of its deferred capital gain in income in 2020.

(v) *Realization of loss.* The facts are the same as in this *Example 7* in paragraph (f)(7)(iv) of this section, except that the Merger occurs in 2025, the value of X's qualifying investment immediately before the Merger is $25, and X receives $10 of boot in the Merger. X realizes $25 of loss in the Merger. Under paragraphs (c)(10)(i)(C)(*1*) and (e)(2) of this section, X is required to include $10 of its deferred capital gain in income in 2020.

(8) *Example 8: Section 355 distribution by a QOF*—(i) *Facts.* A wholly and directly owns Q, a QOF corporation, which wholly and directly owns Y, a corporation that is a qualified opportunity zone business. On May 31, 2019, A sells a capital asset to an unrelated party and realizes $500 of capital gain. On October 31, 2019, A contributes $500 to Q in exchange for a qualifying investment. On June 26, 2025, Q distributes all of the stock of Y to A in a transaction in which no gain or loss is recognized under section 355 (the Distribution). Immediately after the Distribution, each of Q and Y satisfies the requirements for QOF status (*see* paragraph (c)(11)(i)(B)(*2*) of this section).

(ii) *Analysis.* Because each of Q (the distributing corporation) and Y (the controlled corporation) is a QOF immediately after the Distribution, the Distribution is a qualifying section 355 transaction. Thus, the Distribution is not an inclusion event for purposes of section 1400Z-2(b)(1) and paragraph (b) of this section.. *See* paragraph (c)(11)(i)(B) of this section. Accordingly, A is not required to include in income in 2025 any of its $500 of deferred capital gain as a result of the Distribution. For purposes of section 1400Z-2(b)(2)(B) and 1400Z-2(c), A's holding period for its qualifying investment in Y is treated as beginning on October 31, 2019. See paragraph (d)(2)(i) of this section.

(iii) *Section 355 distribution by a QOF shareholder.* The facts are the same as in this *Example 8* in paragraph (f)(8)(i) of this section, except that A distributes 80 percent of the stock of Q (all of which is a qualifying investment in the hands of A) to A's shareholders in a transaction in which no gain or loss is recognized under section 355. The distribution is an inclusion event for purposes of section 1400Z-2(b)(1) and paragraph (b) of this section, and A is required to include in income $400 (80 percent of its $500 of deferred capital gain) as a result of the distribution. *See* paragraphs (c)(1) and (c)(11)(ii) of this section.

(iv) *Distribution of boot.* The facts are the same as in this *Example 8* in paragraph (f)(8)(i) of this section, except that A receives boot in the Distribution. Under paragraphs (c)(8) and (c)(11)(i)(B)(*3*) of this section, the receipt of boot in the Distribution is an inclusion event for purposes of section 1400Z-2(b)(1) and paragraph (b) of this section to the extent of gain recognized pursuant to section 301(c)(3).

(v) *Section 355 split-off.* The facts are the same as in this *Example 8* in paragraph (f)(8)(i) of this section, except that Q stock is directly owned by both A and B (each of which has made a qualifying investment in Q), and Q distributes all of the Y stock to B in exchange for B's Q stock in a transaction in which no gain or loss is recognized under section 355. The distribution is a qualifying section 355 transaction and is not an inclusion event for purposes of section 1400Z-2(b)(1) and paragraph (b) of this section. Neither A nor B is required to include its deferred capital gain in income in 2025 as a result of the distribution.

(vi) *Section 355 split-up.* The facts are the same as in this *Example 8* in paragraph (f)(8)(v) of this section, except that Q wholly and directly owns both Y and Z; Q distributes all of the Y stock to A in exchange for A's Q stock and distributes all of the Z stock to B in exchange for B's Q stock in a transaction in which no gain or loss is recognized under section 355; Q then liquidates; and immediately after the Distribution, each of Y and Z satisfies the requirements for QOF status. The distribution is a qualifying section 355 transaction and is not an inclusion event for purposes of section 1400Z-2(b)(1) and paragraph (b) of this section. Neither A nor B is required to include its deferred capital gain in income in 2025 as a result of the transaction.

(vii) *Section 355 split-off with boot.* The facts are the same as in this *Example 8* in paragraph (f)(8)(v) of this section, except that B also receives boot. Under paragraph (c)(11)(i)(B)(*3*) of this section, B has an inclusion event, and the amount that gives rise to the inclusion event is the amount of gain under section 356 that is not treated as a dividend under section 356(a)(2).

(9) *Example 9: Recapitalization*—(i) *Facts.* On May 31, 2019, each of A and B sells a capital asset to an unrelated party and realizes $500 of capital gain. On October 31, 2019, A contributes $500 to newly formed Q in exchange for 50 shares of Q nonvoting stock (A's qualifying investment) and B contributes $500 to Q in exchange for 50 shares of Q voting stock (B's qualifying investment). A and B are the sole shareholders of Q. In 2020, when A's qualifying investment is worth $600, A exchanges all of its Q non-voting stock for $120 and 40 shares of Q voting stock in a transaction that qualifies as a reorganization under section 368(a)(1)(E).

(ii) *Analysis.* Because A's proportionate interest in Q has decreased in this transaction, the recapitalization is an inclusion event under paragraph (c)(12)(ii) of this section. Thus, A is treated as having reduced its direct tax ownership of its investment in Q to the extent of the reduction in the fair market value of its qualifying QOF stock. The $120 that A received in the reorganization represents the difference in fair market value between its qualifying investment before and after the reorganization. Under paragraphs (c)(12)(i)(B) and (e)(2) of this section, A is required to include $120 of its deferred capital gain in income in 2020. Because B's proportionate interest in Q has not decreased, and because B did not receive any property in the recapitalization, B does not have an inclusion event with respect to its qualifying investment in Q. *See* paragraph (c)(12)(i) of this section. Therefore, B is not required to include any of its deferred gain in income as a result of this transaction.

(10) *Example 10: Debt financed distribution*—(i) *Facts.* On January 1, 2019, A and B form Q, a QOF partnership, each contributing $200 that is deferred under the section 1400Z-2(a) election to Q in exchange for a qualifying investment. On November 18, 2022, Q obtains a nonrecourse loan from a bank for $300. Under section 752, the loan is allocated $150 to A and $150 to B. On November 30, 2022, when the values and bases of the investments remain unchanged, Q distributes $50 to A.

(ii) *Analysis.* A is not required to recognize gain under §1.1400Z2(b)-1(c) because A's basis in its qualifying investment is $150 (the original zero basis with respect to the contribution, plus the $150 debt allocation). The distribution reduces A's basis to $100.

(11) *Example 11: Debt financed distribution in excess of basis*—(i) *Facts.* The facts are the same as in *Example 10* in paragraph (f)(10) of this section, except that the loan is entirely allocated to B under section 752. On November 30, 2024, when the values of the investments remain unchanged, Q distributes $50 to A.

(ii) *Analysis.* Under §1.1400Z2(b)-1(c)(6)(iii), A is required to recognize $30 of eligible gain under section §1.1400Z2(b)-1(c) because the $50 distributed to A exceeds A's $20 basis in its qualifying investment (the original zero basis with respect to its contribution, plus $20 with regard to section 1400Z-2(b)(2)(B)(iii)).

(12) *Example 12: Aggregate ownership change threshold*—(i) *Facts.* On May 31, 2019, B, an S corporation, sells a capital asset to an unrelated party for cash and realizes $500 of capital gain. On July 15, 2019, B makes a deferral election and transfers the $500 to Q, a QOF partnership in exchange for a qualifying investment. On that date, B has outstanding 100 shares, of which each of individuals D, E, F, and G owns 25 shares. On September 30, 2019, D sells 10 shares of its B stock. On September 30, 2020, E sells 16 shares of its B stock.

(ii) *Analysis.* Under paragraph (c)(7)(iii)(A) of this section, the sales of stock by D and E caused an aggregate change in ownership of B because, the percentage of the stock of B owned directly by D, E, F, and G at the time of B's deferral election decreased by more than 25 percent. Solely for purposes of section 1400Z-2, B's qualifying investment in Q would be treated as disposed of. Consequently, B would have an inclusion event with respect to all of B's remaining deferred gain of $500, and neither section 1400Z-2(b)(2)(B)(iii) or (iv), nor section 1400Z-2(c), would apply to B's qualifying investment after that date.

(g) *Basis adjustments.*—(1) *Timing of section 1400Z-2(b)(2)(B)(ii) adjustments.*—(i) *In general.*—Except as provided in paragraph (g)(1)(ii) of this section, basis adjustments under section 1400Z-2(b)(2)(B)(ii) are made immediately after the amount of gain determined under section 1400Z-2(b)(2)(A) is included in income under section 1400Z-2(b)(1). If the basis adjustment under section 1400Z-2(b)(2)(B)(ii) is being made as a result of an inclusion event, then the basis adjustment is made before determining the other tax consequences of the inclusion event.

(ii) *Specific application to section 301(c)(3) gain, S corporation shareholder gain, or partner gain.*—(A) *General rule.*—This paragraph (g)(1)(ii) applies if a QOF makes a distribution to its owner, and if, without regard to any basis adjustment under section 1400Z-2(b)(2)(B)(ii), at least a portion of the distribution would be characterized as gain under section 301(c)(3) or paragraphs (c)(6)(iii) and (c)(7)(ii) of this section with respect to its qualifying investment.

(B) *Ordering rule.*—If paragraph (g)(1)(ii) of this section applies, the taxpayer is treated as having an inclusion event to the extent provided in paragraph (c)(6)(iii) or (c)(7), (8), (9), (10), (11), or (12) of this section, as applicable. Then, the taxpayer increases its basis under section 1400Z-2(b)(2)(B)(ii), before determining the tax consequences of the distribution.

(C) *Example.*—The following example illustrates the rules of this paragraph (g)(1)(ii).

(*1*) *Example 1*—(i) *Facts.* On May 31, 2019, A sells a capital asset to an unrelated party and realizes $500 of capital gain. On October 31, 2019, A contributes $500 to Q, a newly formed QOF corporation, in exchange for all of the outstanding Q common stock and elects to defer the recognition of $500 of capital gain under section 1400Z-2(a) and §1.1400Z2(a)-1. In 2020, when Q has $40 of earnings and profits, Q distributes $100 to A (the Distribution).

(ii) *Recognition of gain.* Under paragraph (g)(1)(ii)(A) of this section, the Distribution is first evaluated without regard to any basis adjustment under section 1400Z-2(b)(2)(B)(ii). Of the $100 distribution, $40 is treated as a dividend and $60 is treated as gain from the sale or exchange of property under section 301(c)(3), because A's basis in its Q stock is $0 under section 1400Z-2(b)(2)(B)(i). Under paragraphs (c)(8) and (e)(2) of this section, $60 of A's gain that was deferred under section 1400Z-2(a) and §1.1400Z2(a)-1 is recognized in 2020.

(iii) *Basis adjustments.* Under paragraph (g)(1)(ii)(B) of this section, prior to determining the further tax consequences of the Distribution, A increases its basis in its Q stock by $60 in accordance with section 1400Z-2(b)(2)(B)(ii). As a result, the Distribution is characterized as a dividend of $40 under section 301(c)(1) and a return of basis of $60 under section 301(c)(2). Therefore, after the section 301 distribution, A's basis in Q is $0 ($60 - $60).

(2) [Reserved]

(2) *Amount of basis adjustment.*—The increases in basis under section 1400Z-2(b)(2)(B)(iii) and (iv) only apply to that portion of the qualifying investment that has not been subject to previous gain inclusion under section 1400Z-2(b)(2)(A).

(3) *Special partnership rules.*—(i) *General rule.*—The initial basis under section 1400Z-2(b)(2)(B)(i) of a qualifying investment in a QOF partnership is zero, as adjusted to take into account the contributing partner's share of partnership debt under section 752.

(ii) *Tiered arrangements.*—Any basis adjustment described in section 1400Z-2(b)(2)(B)(iii) and (iv) and section 1400Z-2(c) (the basis adjustment rules) shall be treated as an item of income described in section 705(a)(1) and shall be reported in accordance with the applicable forms and instructions. Any amount to which the basis adjustment rules or to which section 1400Z-2(b)(1) applies shall be allocated to the owners of the QOF, and to the owners of any partnership that directly or indirectly (solely through one or more partnerships) owns such QOF interest, and shall track to such owners' interests, based on their shares of the remaining deferred gain to which such amounts relate.

(4) *Basis adjustments in S corporation stock.*—(i) *S corporation investor in QOF.*—(A) *S corporation.*—If an S corporation is an investor in a QOF, the S corporation must adjust the basis of its qualifying investment as set forth in this paragraph (g). The rule in this paragraph (g)(4)(i)(A) does not affect adjustments to the basis of any other asset of the S corporation.

(B) *S corporation shareholder.*—(1) *In general.*—The S corporation shareholder's pro-rata share of any recognized capital gain that has been deferred at the S corporation level will be separately stated under section 1366 and will adjust the shareholders' stock basis under section 1367.

(2) *Basis adjustments to qualifying investments.*—Any adjustment made to the basis of an S corporation's qualifying invest-

ment under section 1400Z-2(b)(2)(B)(iii) or (iv), or section 1400Z-2(c), will not:

(i) Be separately stated under section 1366; or

(ii) Until the date on which an inclusion event with respect to the S corporation's qualifying investment occurs, adjust the shareholders' stock basis under section 1367.

(3) *Basis adjustments resulting from inclusion events.*—If the basis adjustment under section 1400Z-2(b)(2)(B)(ii) is being made as a result of an inclusion event, then the basis adjustment is made before determining the other tax consequences of the inclusion event.

(ii) *QOF S corporation.*—(A) *Transferred basis of assets received.*—If a QOF S corporation receives an asset in exchange for a qualifying investment, the basis of the asset shall be the same as it would be in the hands of the transferor, increased by the amount of the gain recognized by the transferor on such transfer.

(B) *Basis adjustments resulting from inclusion events.*—If the basis adjustment under section 1400Z-2(b)(2)(B)(ii) for the shareholder of the QOF S corporation is being made as a result of an inclusion event, then the basis adjustment is made before determining the other tax consequences of the inclusion event.

(h) *Notifications by partners and partnerships, and shareholders and S corporations.*—(1) *Notification of deferral election.*—A partnership that makes a deferral election must notify all of its partners of the deferral election and state each partner's distributive share of the eligible gain in accordance with applicable forms and instructions. A partner that makes a deferral election must notify the partnership in writing of its deferral election, including the amount of the eligible gain deferred.

(2) *Notification of deferred gain recognition by indirect QOF owner.*—If an indirect owner of a QOF partnership or QOF S corporation sells a portion of its partnership interest or S corporation shares in a transaction to which §1.1400Z2(b)-1(c)(6)(iv) applies, or which is subject to §1.1400Z2(b)-1(c)(7)(iii), such indirect owner must provide to the QOF owner notification and information sufficient to enable the QOF owner, in a timely manner, to recognize an appropriate amount of deferred gain.

(3) *Notification of section 1400Z-2(c) election by QOF partner or QOF partnership.*—A QOF partner must notify the QOF partnership of an election under section 1400Z-2(c) to adjust the basis of the qualifying QOF partnership interest that is disposed of in a taxable transaction. Notification of the section 1400Z-2(c) election, and the adjustments to the basis of the qualifying QOF partnership interest(s) disposed of or to the QOF partnership asset(s) disposed of, is to be made in accordance with applicable forms and instructions.

(4) *S corporations.*—Similar rules to those in paragraphs (h)(1) and (3) of this section apply to S corporations as appropriate.

(i) *Applicability dates.*—This section applies for taxable years that begin on or after the date of publication in the **Federal Register** of a Treasury decision adopting these proposed rules as final regulations. However, a taxpayer may rely on the proposed rules in this section with respect to taxable years that begin before that date, but only if the taxpayer applies the rules in their entirety and in a consistent manner. [Reg. §1.1400Z2(b)-1.]

Qualified Opportunity Funds: Deferred Gains

Qualified Opportunity Funds: Deferred Gains.—Reg. §1.1400Z-2(d)-1, relating to gains that may be deferred as a result of a taxpayer's investment in a qualified opportunity fund (QOF), was adopted by T.D. 9889 on December 31, 2019 (published in the **Federal Register** on October 29, 2018) (REG-115420-18). Proposed amendments to Reg. §1.1400Z2(d)-1(c)(4)(i), (c)(5), (c)(6), (c)(7), (d)(2)(i)(A), (d)(2)(ii), (d)(2)(iii), (d)(5)(i), and (d)(5)(ii)(B) withdrawn by REG-120186-18 on May 1, 2019.

⟫⟫→ *Caution: Proposed Reg. §1.1400Z-2(d)-1, below, was adopted by T.D. 9889; however, for an exception regarding when this proposed regulation may be relied upon, see final Reg. §1.1400Z2(d)-1(e).*

Par. 4. Section 1.1400Z-2(d)-1 is added to read as follows:

§1.1400Z-2(d)-1. Qualified Opportunity Funds.—(a) *Becoming a QOF.*—(1) *Self-certification.*—Except as provided in paragraph (e)(1) of this section, if a taxpayer that is classified as a corporation or partnership for Federal tax purposes is eligible to be a QOF, the taxpayer may self-certify that it is QOF. This section refers to such a taxpayer as an *eligible entity*. The following rules apply to the self-certification:

(i) *Time, form, and manner.*—The self-certification must be effected at such time and in such form and manner as may be prescribed by the Commissioner in IRS forms or instructions or in publications or guidance published in the Internal Revenue Bulletin (*see* §§601.601(d)(2) and 601.602 of this chapter).

(ii) *First taxable year.*—The self-certification must identify the first taxable year that the eligible entity wants to be a QOF.

(iii) *First month.*—The self-certification may identify the first month (in that initial taxable year) in which the eligible entity wants to be a QOF.

(A) *Failure to specify first month.*—If the self-certification fails to specify the month in the initial taxable year that the eligible entity first wants to be a QOF, then the first month of the eligible entity's initial taxable year as a QOF is the first month that the eligible entity is a QOF.

(B) *Investments before first month not eligible for deferral.*—If an investment in eligible interests of an eligible entity occurs prior to the eligible entity's first month as a QOF, any election under section 1400Z-2(a)(1) made for that investment is invalid.

(2) *Becoming a QOF in a month that is not the first month of the taxable year.*—If an eligible entity's self-certification as a QOF is first

effective for a month that is not the first month of that entity's taxable year—

(i) For purposes of section 1400Z-2(d)(1)(A) and (B) in the first year of the QOF's existence, the phrase *first 6-month period of the taxable year of the fund* means the first 6 months each of which is in the taxable year and in each of which the entity is a QOF. Thus, if an eligible entity becomes a QOF in the seventh or later month of a 12-month taxable year, the 90-percent test in section 1400Z-2(d)(1) takes into account only the QOF's assets on the last day of the taxable year.

(ii) The computation of any penalty under section 1400Z-2(f)(1) does not take into account any months before the first month in which an eligible entity is a QOF.

(3) *Pre-existing entities.*—There is no legal barrier to a pre-existing eligible entity becoming a QOF, but the eligible entity must satisfy all of the requirements of section 1400Z-2 and the regulations thereunder, including the requirements regarding qualified opportunity zone property, as defined in section 1400Z-2(d)(2). In particular, that property must be acquired after December 31, 2017.

(b) *Valuation of assets for purposes of the 90-percent asset test.*— (1) *In general.*—For a taxable year, if a QOF has an applicable financial statement within the meaning of § 1.475(a)-4(h), then the value of each asset of the QOF for purposes of the 90-percent asset test in section 1400Z-2(d)(1) is the value of that asset as reported on the QOF's applicable financial statement for the relevant reporting period.

(2) *QOF without an applicable financial statement.*—If paragraph (b)(1) of this section does not apply to a QOF, then the value of each asset of the QOF for purposes of the 90-percent asset test in section 1400Z-2(d)(1) is the QOF's cost of the asset.

(c) *Qualified opportunity zone property.*—(1) *In general.*—Pursuant to section 1400Z-2(d)(2)(A), the following property is *qualified opportunity zone property*:

(i) Qualified opportunity zone stock as defined in paragraph (c)(2) of this section,

(ii) Qualified opportunity zone partnership interest as defined in paragraph (c)(3) of this section, and

(iii) Qualified opportunity zone business property as defined in paragraph (c)(4) of this section.

(2) *Qualified opportunity zone stock.*—(i) *In general.*—Except as provided in paragraphs (c)(2)(ii) and (e)(2) of this section, if an entity is classified as a corporation for Federal tax purposes (corporation), then an equity interest (stock) in the entity is *qualified opportunity zone stock* if—

(A) The stock is acquired by a QOF after December 31, 2017, at its original issue (directly or through an underwriter) from the corporation solely in exchange for cash,

(B) As of the time the stock was issued, the corporation was a qualified opportunity zone business as defined in section 1400Z-2(d)(3) and paragraph (d) of this section (or, in the case of a new corporation, the corporation was being organized for purposes of being such a qualified opportunity zone business), and

(C) During substantially all of the QOF's holding period for the stock, the corporation qualified as a qualified opportunity zone business as defined in section 1400Z-2(d)(3) and paragraph (d) of this section.

(ii) *Redemptions of stock.*—Pursuant to section 1400Z-2(d)(2)(B)(ii), rules similar to the rules of section 1202(c)(3) apply for purposes of determining whether stock in a corporation qualifies as qualified opportunity zone stock.

(A) *Redemptions from taxpayer or related person.*—Stock acquired by a QOF is not treated as qualified opportunity zone stock if, at any time during the 4-year period beginning on the date 2 years before the issuance of the stock, the corporation issuing the stock purchased (directly or indirectly) any of its stock from the QOF or from a person related (within the meaning of section 267(b) or 707(b)) to the QOF. Even if the purchase occurs after the issuance, the stock was never qualified opportunity zone stock.

(B) *Significant redemptions.*—Stock issued by a corporation is not treated as qualified opportunity zone stock if, at any time during the 2-year period beginning on the date 1 year before the issuance of the stock, the corporation made 1 or more purchases of its stock with an aggregate value (as of the time of the respective purchases) exceeding 5 percent of the aggregate value of all of its stock as of the beginning of the 2-year period. Even if one or more of the disqualifying purchases occurs after the issuance, the stock was never qualified opportunity zone stock.

(C) *Treatment of certain transactions.*—If any transaction is treated under section 304(a) as a distribution in redemption of the stock of any corporation, for purposes of paragraphs (c)(2)(ii)(A) and

(B) of this section, that corporation is treated as purchasing an amount of its stock equal to the amount that is treated as such a distribution under section 304(a).

(3) *Qualified opportunity zone partnership interest.*—Except as provided in paragraph (e)(2) of this section, if an entity is classified as a partnership for Federal tax purposes (partnership), any capital or profits interest (partnership interest) in the entity is a *qualified opportunity zone partnership interest* if—

(i) The partnership interest is acquired by a QOF after December 31, 2017, from the partnership solely in exchange for cash,

(ii) As of the time the partnership interest was acquired, the partnership was a qualified opportunity zone business as defined in section 1400Z-2(d)(3) and paragraph (d) of this section (or, in the case of a new partnership, the partnership was being organized for purposes of being a qualified opportunity zone business), and

(iii) During substantially all of the QOF's holding period for the partnership interest, the partnership qualified as a qualified opportunity zone business as defined in section 1400Z-2(d)(3) and paragraph (d) of this section.

(4) *Qualified opportunity zone business property of a QOF.*—Tangible property used in a trade or business of a QOF is qualified opportunity zone business property for purposes of paragraph (c)(1)(iii) of this section if—

(i) [Withdrawn by REG-120186-18 on May 1, 2019.]

(ii) The original use of the tangible property in the qualified opportunity zone, within the meaning of paragraph (c)(7) of this section, commences with the QOF, or the QOF substantially improves the tangible property within the meaning of paragraph (c)(8) of this section (which defines substantial improvement in this context); and

(iii) During substantially all of the QOF's holding period for the tangible property, substantially all of the use of the tangible property was in a qualified opportunity zone.

(5) [Withdrawn by REG-120186-18 on May 1, 2019.]

(6) [Withdrawn by REG-120186-18 on May 1, 2019.]

(7) [Withdrawn by REG-120186-18 on May 1, 2019.]

(8) *Substantial improvement of tangible property.*—(i) *In general.*—Except as provided in paragraph (c)(8)(ii) of this section, for purposes of paragraph (c)(4)(ii) of this section, tangible property is treated as substantially improved by a QOF only if, during any 30-month period beginning after the date of acquisition of the property, additions to the basis of the property in the hands of the QOF exceed an amount equal to the adjusted basis of the property at the beginning of the 30-month period in the hands of the QOF.

(ii) *Special rules for land and improvements on land.*— (A) *Buildings located in the zone.*—If a QOF purchases a building located on land wholly within a QOZ, under section 1400Z-2(d)(2)(D)(ii) a substantial improvement to the purchased tangible property is measured by the QOF's additions to the adjusted basis of the building. Under section 1400Z-2(d), measuring a substantial improvement to the building by additions to the QOF's adjusted basis of the building does not require the QOF to separately substantially improve the land upon which the building is located.

(B) [*Reserved*].

(d) *Qualified opportunity zone business.*—(1) *In general.*—A trade or business is a *qualified opportunity zone business* if—

(i) Substantially all of the tangible property owned or leased by the trade or business is qualified opportunity zone business property as defined in paragraph (d)(2) of this section,

(ii) Pursuant to section 1400Z-2(d)(3)(A)(iii), the trade or business satisfies the requirements of section 1397C(b)(2), (4), and (8) as defined in paragraph (d)(5) of this section, and

(iii) Pursuant to section 1400Z-2(d)(3)(A)(iii), the trade or business is not described in section 144(c)(6)(B) as defined in paragraph (d)(6) of this section.

(2) *Qualified opportunity zone business property of the qualified opportunity zone business for purposes of paragraph (d)(1)(i) of this section.*—(i) *In general.*—The tangible property used in a trade or business of an entity is qualified opportunity zone business property for purposes of paragraph (d)(1)(i) of this section if—

(A) [Withdrawn by REG-120186-18 on May 1, 2019.]

(B) The original use of the tangible property in the qualified opportunity zone commences with the entity or the entity substantially improves the tangible property within the meaning of paragraph (d)(4) of this section (which defines substantial improvement in this context); and

(C) During substantially all of the entity's holding period for the tangible property, substantially all of the use of the tangible property was in a qualified opportunity zone.

(ii) [Withdrawn by REG-120186-18 on May 1, 2019.]

(iii) [Withdrawn by REG-120186-18 on May 1, 2019.]

(3) *Substantially all requirement of paragraph (d)(1)(i) of this section.*—(i) *In general.*—A trade or business of an entity is treated as satisfying the *substantially all* requirement of paragraph (d)(1)(i) of this section if at least 70 percent of the tangible property owned or leased by the trade or business is qualified opportunity zone business property as defined in paragraph (d)(2) of this section.

(ii) *Calculating percent of tangible property owned or leased in a trade or business.*—(A) *In general.*—If an entity has an applicable financial statement within the meaning of § 1.475(a)-4(h), then the value of each asset of the entity as reported on the entity's applicable financial statement for the relevant reporting period is used for determining whether a trade or business of the entity satisfies the first sentence of paragraph (d)(3)(i) of this section (concerning whether the trade or business is a qualified opportunity zone business).

(B) *Entity without an applicable financial statement.*—If paragraph (d)(3)(ii)(A) of this section does not apply to an entity and a taxpayer both holds an equity interest in the entity and has self-certified as a QOF, then that taxpayer may value the entity's assets using the same methodology under paragraph (b) of this section that the taxpayer uses for determining its own compliance with the 90-percent asset requirement of section 1400Z-2(d)(1) (Compliance Methodology), provided that no other equity holder in the entity is a Five-Percent Zone Taxpayer. If paragraph (d)(3)(ii)(A) of this section does not apply to an entity and if two or more taxpayers that have self-certified as QOFs hold equity interests in the entity and at least one of them is a Five-Percent Zone Taxpayer, then the values of the entity's assets may be calculated using the Compliance Methodology that both is used by a Five-Percent Zone Taxpayer and that produces the highest percentage of qualified opportunity zone business property for the entity.

(C) *Five Percent Zone Taxpayer.*—A *Five-Percent Zone Taxpayer* is a taxpayer that has self-certified as a QOF and that holds stock in the entity (if it is a corporation) representing at least 5 percent in voting rights and value or holds an interest of at least 5 percent in the profits and capital of the entity (if it is a partnership).

(iii) *Example.*—The following example illustrates the principles of paragraph (d)(3)(ii) of this section.

Example. Entity ZS is a corporation that has issued only one class of stock and that conducts a trade or business. Taxpayer X holds 94% of the ZS stock, and Taxpayer Y holds the remaining 6% of that stock. (Thus, both X and Y are Five Percent Zone Taxpayers within the meaning of paragraph (d)(3)(ii)(C) of this section.) ZS does not have an applicable financial statement, and, for that reason, a determination of whether ZS is conducting a qualified opportunity zone business may employ the Compliance Methodology of X or Y. X and Y use different Compliance Methodologies permitted under paragraph (d)(3)(ii) (B) of this section for purposes of satisfying the 90-percent asset test of section 1400Z-2(d)(1). Under X's Compliance Methodology (which is based on X's applicable financial statement), 65% of the tangible property owned or leased by ZS's trade or business is qualified opportunity zone business property. Under Y's Compliance Methodology (which is based on Y's cost), 73% of the tangible property owned or leased by ZS's trade or business is qualified opportunity zone business property. Because Y's Compliance Methodology would produce the higher percentage of qualified opportunity zone business property for ZS (73%), both X and Y may use Y's Compliance Methodology to value ZS's owned or leased tangible property. If ZS's trade or business satisfies all additional requirements in section 1400Z-2(d)(3), the trade or business is a qualified opportunity zone business. Thus, if all of the additional requirements in section 1400Z-2(d)(2)(B) are satisfied, stock in ZS is qualified opportunity zone stock in the hands of a taxpayer that has self-certified as a QOF.

(4) *Substantial improvement of tangible property for purposes of paragraph (d)(2)(i)(B) of this section.*—(i) *In general.*—Except as provided in paragraph (d)(4)(ii) of this section, for purposes of paragraph (d)(2)(i)(B) of this section, tangible property is treated as substantially improved by a qualified opportunity zone business only if, during any 30-month period beginning after the date of acquisition of such tangible property, additions to the basis of such tangible property in the hands of the qualified opportunity zone business exceed an amount equal to the adjusted basis of such tangible property at the beginning of such 30-month period in the hands of the qualified opportunity zone business.

(ii) *Special rules for land and improvements on land.*—(A) *Buildings located in the zone.*—If a QOF purchases a building located on land wholly within a QOZ, under section 1400Z-2(d)(2)(D)(ii) a substantial improvement to the purchased tangible property is measured by the QOF's additions to the adjusted basis of the building. Under section 1400Z-2(d), measuring a substantial improvement to the building by additions to the QOF's adjusted

basis of the building does not require the QOF to separately substantially improve the land upon which the building is located.

(B) [*Reserved*].

(5) *Operation of section 1397C requirements incorporated by reference.*—(i) [Withdrawn by REG-120186-18 on May 1, 2019.]

(ii) *Use of intangible property requirement.*—(A) *In general.*—Section 1400Z-2(d)(3) incorporates section 1397C(b)(4), requiring that, with respect to any taxable year, a substantial portion of the intangible property of an opportunity zone business is used in the active conduct of a trade or business in the qualified opportunity zone.

(B) [Withdrawn by REG-120186-18 on May 1, 2019.]

(iii) *Nonqualified financial property limitation.*—Section 1400Z-2(d)(3) incorporates section 1397C(b)(8), limiting in each taxable year the average of the aggregate unadjusted bases of the property of a qualified opportunity zone business that may be attributable to nonqualified financial property. Section 1397C(e)(1), which defines the term *nonqualified financial property* for purposes of section 1397C(b)(8), excludes from that term reasonable amounts of working capital held in cash, cash equivalents, or debt instruments with a term of 18 months or less (working capital assets).

(iv) *Safe harbor for reasonable amount of working capital.*—Solely for purposes of applying section 1397C(e)(1) to the definition of a qualified opportunity zone business under section 1400Z-2(d)(3), working capital assets are treated as reasonable in amount for purposes of sections 1397C(b)(2) and 1400Z-2(d)(3)(A)(ii), if all of the following three requirements are satisfied:

(A) *Designated in writing.*—These amounts are designated in writing for the acquisition, construction, and/or substantial improvement of tangible property in a qualified opportunity zone, as defined in section 1400Z-1(a).

(B) *Reasonable written schedule.*—There is a written schedule consistent with the ordinary start-up of a trade or business for the expenditure of the working capital assets. Under the schedule, the working capital assets must be spent within 31 months of the receipt by the business of the assets.

(C) *Property consumption consistent.*—The working capital assets are actually used in a manner that is substantially consistent with paragraph (d)(5)(iv)(A) and (B) of this section.

(v) *Safe harbor for gross income derived from the active conduct of business.*—Solely for purposes of applying the 50-percent test in section 1397C(b)(2) to the definition of a qualified opportunity zone business in section 1400Z-2(d)(3), if any gross income is derived from property that paragraph (d)(5)(iv) of this section treats as a reasonable amount of working capital, then that gross income is counted toward satisfaction of the 50-percent test.

(vi) *Safe harbor for use of intangible property.*—Solely for purposes of applying the use requirement in section 1397C(b)(4) to the definition of a qualified opportunity zone business under section 1400Z-2(d)(3), the use requirement is treated as being satisfied during any period in which the business is proceeding in a manner that is substantially consistent with paragraphs (d)(5)(iv)(A) through (C) of this section.

(vii) *Safe harbor for property on which working capital is being expended.*—If paragraph (d)(5)(iv) of this section treats some financial property as being a reasonable amount of working capital because of compliance with the three requirements of paragraph (d)(5)(iv)(A)-(C) and if the tangible property referred to in paragraph (d)(5)(iv)(A) is expected to satisfy the requirements of section 1400Z-2(d)(2)(D)(1) as a result of the planned expenditure of those working capital assets, then that tangible property is not treated as failing to satisfy those requirements solely because the scheduled consumption of the working capital is not yet complete.

(viii) *Example.*—The following example illustrates the rules of this paragraph (d)(5):

(i) *Facts.* In 2019, Taxpayer H realized $w million of capital gains and within the 180-day period invested $w million in QOF T, a qualified opportunity fund. QOF T immediately acquired from partnership P a partnership interest in P, solely in exchange for $w million of cash. P immediately placed the $w million in working capital assets, which remained in working capital assets until used. P had written plans to acquire land in a qualified opportunity zone on which it planned to construct a commercial building. Of the $w million, $x million was dedicated to the land purchase, $y million to the construction of the building, and $z million to ancillary but necessary expenditures for the project. The written plans provided for purchase of the land within a month of receipt of the cash from QOF T and for the remaining $y and $z million to be spent within the next 30 months on construction of the building and on the ancillary expenditures. All expenditures were made on schedule, consuming the $w million. During the taxable years that overlap with the first 31-month period, P had no gross income other than that derived from the amounts held in those working capital assets. Prior to completion of the building, P's only assets were the land it purchased, the unspent amounts in the working capital assets, and P's work in process as the building was constructed.

(ii) *Analysis of construction*—(A) P met the three requirements of the safe harbor provided in paragraph (d)(5)(iv) of this section. P had a written plan to spend the $w received from QOF T for the acquisition, construction, and/or substantial improvement of tangible property in a qualified opportunity zone, as defined in section 1400Z-1(a). P had a written schedule consistent with the ordinary start-up for a business for the expenditure of the working capital assets. And, finally, P's working capital assets were actually used in a manner that was substantially consistent with its written plan and the ordinary start-up of a business. Therefore, the $x million, the $y million, and the $z million are treated as reasonable in amount for purposes of sections 1397C(b)(2) and 1400Z-2(d)(3)(A)(ii).

(B) Because P had no other gross income during the 31 months at issue, 100 percent of P's gross income during that time is treated as derived from an active trade or business in the qualified opportunity zone for purposes of satisfying the 50-percent test of section 1397C(b)(2).

(C) For purposes of satisfying the requirement of section 1397C(b)(4), during the period of land acquisition and building construction a substantial portion of P's intangible property is treated as being used in the active conduct of a trade or business in the qualified opportunity zone.

(D) All of the facts described are consistent with QOF T's interest in P being a qualified opportunity zone partnership interest for purposes of satisfying the 90-percent test in section 1400Z-2(d)(1).

(iii) *Analysis of substantial improvement.* The above conclusions would also apply if P's plans had been to buy and substantially improve a pre-existing commercial building. In addition, the fact that P's basis in the building has not yet doubled does not cause the building to fail to satisfy section 1400Z-2(d)(2)(D)1)(III).

(6) *Trade or businesses described in section 144(c)(6)(B) not eligible.*—Pursuant to section 1400Z-2(d)(3)(A)(iii), the following trades or businesses described in section 144(c)(6)(B) cannot qualify as a qualified opportunity zone business:

(i) Any private or commercial golf course,

(ii) Country club,

(iii) Massage parlor,

(iv) Hot tub facility,

(v) Suntan facility,

(vi) Racetrack or other facility used for gambling, or

(vii) Any store the principal business of which is the sale of alcoholic beverages for consumption off premises.

(e) *Exceptions based on where an entity is created, formed, or organized.*—(1) *QOFs.*—If a partnership or corporation (an entity) is not organized in one of the 50 states, the District of Columbia, or the U.S. possessions, it is ineligible to be a QOF. If an entity is organized in a U.S. possession but not in one of the 50 States or the District of Columbia, it may be a QOF only if it is organized for the purpose of investing in qualified opportunity zone property that relates to a trade or business operated in the U.S. possession in which the entity is organized.

(2) *Entities that can issue qualified opportunity zone stock or qualified opportunity zone partnership interests.*—If an entity is not organized in one of the 50 states, the District of Columbia, or the U.S. possessions, an equity interest in the entity is neither qualified opportunity zone stock nor a qualified opportunity zone partnership interest. If an entity is organized in a U.S. possession but not in one of the 50 States or the District of Columbia, an equity interest in the entity may be qualified opportunity zone stock or a qualified opportunity zone partnership interest, as the case may be, only if the entity conducts a qualified opportunity zone business in the U.S. possession in which the entity is organized. An entity described in the preceding sentence is treated as satisfying the "domestic" requirement in section 1400Z-2(d)(2)(B)(i) or section 1400Z-2(C)(i).

(3) *U.S. possession defined.*—For purposes of this paragraph (e), a U.S. possession means any jurisdiction other than the 50 States and the District of Columbia where a designated qualified opportunity zone exists under section 1400Z-1.

(f) *Applicability date.*—This section applies for QOF taxable years that begin on or after the date of publication in the **Federal Register** of a Treasury decision adopting these proposed rules as final regulations. A QOF, however, may rely on the proposed rules in this section with respect to taxable years that begin before the date of applicability of this section, but only if the QOF applies the rules in their entirety and in a consistent manner. [Reg. 1.1400Z-2(d)-1.]

Qualified Opportunity Funds: Investment

Qualified Opportunity Funds: Investment.—Amendments to Reg. §1.1400Z2(d)-1, relating to gains that may be deferred as a result of a taxpayer's investment in a qualified opportunity fund, as well as special rules for an investment in a QOF held by a taxpayer for at least 10 years, were adopted by T.D. 9889 on December 31, 2019 (published in the Federal Register on May 1, 2019) (REG-120186-18).

⟫➔ *Caution: Proposed Reg. §1.1400Z2(d)-1, below, was adopted by T.D. 9889; however, for an exception regarding when this proposed regulation may be relied upon, see final Reg. §1.1400Z2(d)-1(e).*

Par. 5. Section 1.1400Z2(d)-1, as proposed to be added by 83 FR 54279, October 29, 2018, is amended by:

1. Revising paragraphs (b) and (c)(4) through (7).

2. Revising the heading of paragraph (c)(8).

3. In paragraph (c)(8)(i), removing "paragraph (c)(4)(ii) of this section" and adding in its place "this paragraph (c)(8)(i)".

4. Adding paragraphs (c)(8)(ii)(B) and (c)(9).

5. Revising paragraph (d)(2)(i)(A) through (C) and adding paragraphs (d)(2)(i)(D) and (E).

6. Redesignating paragraph (d)(2)(iii) as (d)(2)(iv) and revising newly redesignated paragraph (d)(2)(iv).

7. Redesignating paragraphs (d)(2)(ii) as (d)(2)(iii) and revising newly redesignated paragraph (d)(2)(iii).

8. Adding new paragraph (d)(2)(ii).

9. Revising paragraphs (d)(3)(ii)(A) through (C) and (d)(4)(ii) and the heading of paragraph (d)(5).

10. Adding a sentence at the end of paragraph (d)(5)(i) and adding paragraphs (d)(5)(i)(A) through (E).

11. Adding a sentence at the end of paragraph (d)(5)(ii)(A).

12. Revising paragraphs (d)(5)(ii)(B), (d)(5)(iv) introductory text, and (d)(5)(iv)(A) and (C) and adding paragraphs (d)(5)(iv)(D) and (E).

13. Redesignating paragraph (d)(5)(viii) as (d)(5)(ix) and adding a new paragraph (d)(5)(viii).

14. Adding a sentence at the end of paragraph (f).

The revisions and additions read as follows:

§1.1400Z2(d)-1. Qualified Opportunity Funds.

* * *

(b) *Valuation of assets for purposes of the 90-percent asset test.*—(1) *In general.*—For purposes of the 90-percent asset test in section 1400Z-2(d)(1), on an annual basis, a QOF may value its assets using the applicable financial statement valuation method set forth in paragraph (b)(2) of this section, if the QOF has an applicable financial statement within the meaning of §1.475(a)-4(h), or the alternative valuation method set forth in paragraph (b)(3) of this section. During each taxable year, a QOF must apply consistently the valuation method that it selects under this paragraph (b)(1) to all assets valued with respect to the taxable year.

(2) *Applicable financial statement valuation method.*—(i) *In general.*—Under the applicable financial statement valuation method set forth in this paragraph (b)(2), the value of each asset that is owned or leased by the QOF is the value of that asset as reported on the QOF's applicable financial statement for the relevant reporting period.

(ii) *Requirement for selection of method.*—A QOF may select the applicable financial statement valuation method set forth in this paragraph (b)(2) to value an asset leased by the QOF only if the applicable financial statement of the QOF is prepared according to U.S. generally accepted accounting principles (GAAP) and requires an assignment of value to the lease of the asset.

(3) *Alternative valuation method.*—(i) *In general.*—Under the alternative valuation method set forth in this paragraph (b)(3), the value of the assets owned by a QOF is calculated under paragraph (b)(3)(ii) of this section, and the value of the assets leased by a QOF is calculated under paragraph (b)(3)(iii) of this section.

Reg. §1.1400Z2(d)-1(b)(3)(i)

(ii) *Assets that are owned by a QOF.*—The value of each asset that is owned by a QOF is the QOF's unadjusted cost basis of the asset under section 1012.

(iii) *Assets that are leased by a QOF.*—(A) *In general.*—The value of each asset that is leased by a QOF is equal to the present value of the leased asset as defined in paragraph (b)(3)(iii)(C) of this section.

(B) *Discount rate.*—For purposes of calculating present value under paragraph (b)(3)(iii) of this section, the discount rate is the applicable Federal rate under section 1274(d)(1), determined by substituting the term "lease" for "debt instrument."

(C) *Present value.*—For purposes of paragraph (b)(3)(iii) of this section, present value of a leased asset—

(1) Is equal to the sum of the present values of each payment under the lease for the asset;

(2) Is calculated at the time the QOF enters into the lease for the asset; and

(3) Once calculated, is used as the value for the asset by the QOF for all testing dates for purposes of the 90-percent asset test.

(D) *Term of a lease.*—For purposes of paragraph (b)(3)(iii) of this section, the term of a lease includes periods during which the lessee may extend the lease at a predefined rent.

(4) *Option to disregard recently contributed property.*—A QOF may choose to determine compliance with the 90-percent asset test by excluding from both the numerator and denominator of the test any property that satisfies all the criteria in paragraphs (b)(4)(i) through (iii) of this section. A QOF need not be consistent from one semi-annual test to another in whether it avails itself of this option.

(i) As the case may be, the amount of the property was received by the QOF partnership as a contribution or by the QOF corporation solely in exchange for stock of the corporation;

(ii) This contribution or exchange occurred not more than 6 months before the test from which it is being excluded; and

(iii) Between the date of that contribution or exchange and the date of the asset test, the amount was held continuously in cash, cash equivalents, or debt instruments with a term of 18 months or less.

(c) * * *

(4) *Qualified opportunity zone business property of a QOF.*—(i) *In general.*—Tangible property used in a trade or business of a QOF is qualified opportunity zone business property for purposes of paragraph (c)(1)(iii) of this section if the requirements of paragraphs (c)(4)(i)(A) through (E) of this section, as applicable, are satisfied.

(A) In the case of property that the QOF owns, the property was acquired by the QOF after December 31, 2017, by purchase as defined by section 179(d)(2) from a person that is not a related person within the meaning of section 1400Z-2(e)(2).

(B) In the case of property that the QOF leases—

(1) *Qualifying acquisition of possession.*—The property was acquired by the QOF under a lease entered into after December 31, 2017;

(2) *Arms-length terms.*—The terms of the lease were market rate (that is, the terms of the lease reflect common, arms-length market practice in the locale that includes the qualified opportunity zone as determined under section 482 and all section 482 regulations in this chapter) at the time that the lease was entered into; and

(3) *Additional requirements for leases from a related person.*—If the lessee and the lessor are related parties, paragraph (c)(4)(i)(B)(4) and (5) of this section must be satisfied.

(4) *Prepayments of not more than one year.*—The lessee at no time makes any prepayment in connection with the lease relating to a period of use of the property that exceeds 12 months.

(5) *Purchase of other QOZBP.*—If the original use of leased tangible personal property in a qualified opportunity zone (within the meaning of in paragraph (c)(4)(i)(B)(6) of this section) does not commence with the lessee, the property is not qualified opportunity zone business property unless, during the relevant testing period (as defined in paragraph (c)(4)(i)(B)(7) of this section), the lessee becomes the owner of tangible property that is qualified opportunity zone business property having a value not less than the value of that leased tangible personal property. There must be substantial overlap of the zone(s) in which the owner of the property so acquired uses it and the zone(s) in which that person uses the leased property.

(6) *Original use of leased tangible property.*—For purposes of paragraph (c)(4)(i)(B)(5) of this section, the original use of leased

tangible property in a qualified opportunity zone commences on the date any person first places the property in service in the qualified opportunity zone for purposes of depreciation (or first uses it in a manner that would allow depreciation or amortization if that person were the property's owner). For purposes of this paragraph (c)(4)(i)(B)(6), if property has been unused or vacant for an uninterrupted period of at least 5 years, original use in the zone commences on the date after that period when any person first uses or places the property in service in the qualified opportunity zone within the meaning of the preceding sentence. Used tangible property satisfies the original use requirement if the property has not been previously so used or placed in service in the qualified opportunity zone.

(7) *Relevant testing period.*—For purposes of paragraph (c)(4)(i)(B)(5) of this section, the *relevant testing period* is the period that begins on the date that the lessee receives possession under the lease of the leased tangible personal property and ends on the earlier of—the date 30-months after the date the lessee receives possession of the property under the lease; or the last day of the term of the lease (within the meaning of paragraph (b)(3)(iii)(D) of this section).

(8) *Valuation of owned or leased property.*—For purposes of paragraph (c)(4)(i)(B)(5) of this section, the value of owned or leased property is required to be determined in accordance with the valuation methodologies provided in paragraph (b) of this section, and such value in the case of leased tangible personal property is to be determined on the date the lessee receives possession of the property under the lease.

(C) In the case of tangible property owned by the QOF, the original use of the owned tangible property in the qualified opportunity zone, within the meaning of paragraph (c)(7) of this section, commences with the QOF, or the QOF substantially improves the owned tangible property within the meaning of paragraph (c)(8) of this section (which defines substantial improvement in this context).

(D) In the case of tangible property that is owned or leased by the QOF, during substantially all of the QOF's holding period for the tangible property, substantially all of the use of the tangible property was in a qualified opportunity zone.

(E) In the case of real property (other than unimproved land) that is leased by a QOF, if, at the time the lease is entered into, there was a plan, intent, or expectation for the real property to be purchased by the QOF for an amount of consideration other than the fair market value of the real property determined at the time of the purchase without regard to any prior lease payments, the leased real property is not qualified opportunity zone business property at any time.

(ii) *Trade or business of a QOF.*—The term *trade or business* means a trade or business within the meaning of section 162.

(iii) *Safe harbor for inventory in transit.*—In determining whether tangible property is used in a qualified opportunity zone for purposes of section 1400Z-2(d)(2)(D)(i)(III), and of paragraphs (c)(4)(i)(D), (c)(6), (d)(2)(i)(D), and (d)(2)(iv) of this section, inventory (including raw materials) of a trade or business does not fail to be used in a qualified opportunity zone solely because the inventory is in transit—

(A) From a vendor to a facility of the trade or business that is in a qualified opportunity zone; or

(B) From a facility of the trade or business that is in a qualified opportunity zone to customers of the trade or business that are not located in a qualified opportunity zone.

(5) *Substantially all of a QOF's holding period for property described in paragraphs (c)(2) and (3) and (c)(4)(i)(D) of this section.*—For purposes of determining whether the holding period requirements in paragraphs (c)(2) and (3) and (c)(4)(i)(D) of this section are satisfied, the term *substantially all* means at least 90 percent.

(6) *Substantially all of the usage of tangible property by a QOF in a qualified opportunity zone.*—A trade or business of an entity is treated as satisfying the *substantially all* requirement of paragraph (c)(4)(i)(D) of this section if at least 70 percent of the use of the tangible property is in a qualified opportunity zone.

(7) *Original use of tangible property acquired by purchase.*—(i) *In general.*—For purposes of paragraph (c)(4)(i)(C) of this section, the original use of tangible property in a qualified opportunity zone commences on the date any person first places the property in service in the qualified opportunity zone for purposes of depreciation or amortization (or first uses it in a manner that would allow depreciation or amortization if that person were the property's owner). For purposes of this paragraph (c)(7), if property has been unused or vacant for an uninterrupted period of at least 5 years, original use in the qualified opportunity zone commences on the date after that period when any person first so uses or places the property in service in the qualified opportunity zone. Used tangible property satisfies

the original use requirement if the property has not been previously so used or placed in service in the qualified opportunity zone. If the tangible property had been so used or placed in service in the qualified opportunity zone before it is acquired by purchase, it must be substantially improved in order to satisfy the requirements of section 1400Z-2(d)(2)(D)(i)(II).

(ii) *Lessee improvements to leased property.*—Improvements made by a lessee to leased property satisfy the original use requirement in section 1400Z-2(d)(2)(D)(i)(II) as purchased property for the amount of the unadjusted cost basis under section 1012 of such improvements.

(8) *Substantial improvement of tangible property acquired by purchase—* * * *

(ii) * * *

(B) *Unimproved land.*—Unimproved land that is within a qualified opportunity zone and acquired by purchase in accordance with section 1400Z-2(d)(2)(D)(i)(I) is not required to be substantially improved within the meaning of section 1400Z-2(d)(2)(D)(i)(II) and (d)(2)(D)(ii).

(9) *Substantially all of tangible property owned or leased by a QOF.*—(i) *Tangible property owned by a QOF.*—Whether a QOF has satisfied the "substantially all" threshold set forth in paragraph (c)(6) of this section is to be determined by a fraction—

(A) The numerator of which is the total value of all qualified opportunity zone business property owned or leased by the QOF that meets the requirements in paragraph (c)(4)(i) of this section; and

(B) The denominator of which is the total value of all tangible property owned or leased by the QOF, whether located inside or outside of a qualified opportunity zone.

(d) * * *

(2) * * *

(i) * * *

(A) In the case of tangible property that the entity owns, the tangible property was acquired by the entity after December 31, 2017, by purchase as defined by section 179(d)(2) from a person who is not a related person within the meaning of section 1400Z-2(e)(2).

(B) In the case of tangible property that the entity leases—

(1) *Qualifying acquisition of possession.*—The property was acquired by the entity under a lease entered into after December 31, 2017;

(2) *Arms-length terms.*—The terms of the lease are market rate (that is, the terms of the lease reflect common, arms-length market practice in the locale that includes the qualified opportunity zone as determined under section 482 and all section 482 regulations in this chapter) at the time that the lease was entered into; and

(3) *Additional requirements for leases from a related person.*—If the lessee and the lessor are related parties, paragraphs (d)(2)(i)(B)(4) and (5) of this section must be satisfied.

(4) *Prepayments of not more than one year.*—The lessee at no time makes any prepayment in connection with the lease relating to a period of use of the property that exceeds 12 months.

(5) *Purchase of other QOZBP.*—If the original use of leased tangible personal property in a qualified opportunity zone (within the meaning of in paragraph (d)(2)(i)(B)(6) of this section) does not commence with the lessee, the property is not qualified opportunity zone business property unless, during the relevant testing period (as defined in paragraph (d)(2)(i)(B)(7) of this section), the lessee becomes the owner of tangible property that is qualified opportunity zone business property having a value not less than the value of that leased tangible personal property. There must be substantial overlap of the zone(s) in which the owner of the property so acquired uses it and the zone(s) in which that person uses the leased property.

(6) *Original use of leased tangible property.*—For purposes of paragraph (d)(2)(i)(B)(5) of this section, the original use of leased tangible property in a qualified opportunity zone commences on the date any person first places the property in service in the qualified opportunity zone for purposes of depreciation (or first uses it in a manner that would allow depreciation or amortization if that person were the property's owner). For purposes of this paragraph (d)(2)(i)(B)(6), if property has been unused or vacant for an uninterrupted period of at least 5 years, original use in the qualified opportunity zone commences on the date after that period when any person first uses or places the property in service in the qualified opportunity zone within the meaning of the preceding sentence. Used tangible property satisfies the original use requirement if the

property has not been previously so used or placed in service in the qualified opportunity zone.

(7) *Relevant testing period.*—For purposes of paragraph (d)(2)(i)(B)(5) of this section, the *relevant testing period* is the period that begins on the date that the lessee receives possession under the lease of the leased tangible personal property and ends on the earlier of—the date 30-months after the date the lessee receives possession of the property under the lease; or the last day of the term of the lease (within the meaning of paragraph (b)(3)(iii)(D) of this section).

(8) *Valuation of owned or leased property.*—For purposes of paragraph (d)(2)(i)(B)(5) of this section, the value of owned or leased property is required to be determined in accordance with the valuation methodologies provided in paragraph (b) of this section, and such value in the case of leased tangible personal property is to be determined on the date the lessee receives possession of the property under the lease.

(C) In the case of tangible property owned by the entity, the original use of the owned tangible property in the qualified opportunity zone, within the meaning of paragraph (c)(7) of this section, commences with the entity, or the entity substantially improves the owned tangible property within the meaning of paragraph (d)(4) of this section (which defines substantial improvement in this context).

(D) In the case of tangible property that is owned or leased by the entity, during substantially all of the entity's holding period for the tangible property, substantially all of the use of the tangible property was in a qualified opportunity zone.

(E) In the case of real property (other than unimproved land) that is leased by the entity, if, at the time the lease is entered into, there was a plan, intent, or expectation for the real property to be purchased by the entity for an amount of consideration other than the fair market value of the real property determined at the time of the purchase without regard to any prior lease payments, the leased real property is not qualified opportunity zone business property at any time.

(ii) *Trade or business of an entity.*—The term *trade or business* means a trade or business within the meaning of section 162.

(iii) *Substantially all of a qualified opportunity zone business's holding period for property described in paragraph (d)(2)(i)(D) of this section.*—For purposes of the holding period requirement in paragraph (d)(2)(i)(D) of this section, the term *substantially all* means at least 90 percent.

(iv) *Substantially all of the use of tangible property by a qualified opportunity zone business in a qualified opportunity zone.*—The substantially all of the use requirement of paragraph (d)(2)(i)(D) of this section is satisfied if at least 70 percent of the use of the tangible property is in a qualified opportunity zone.

(3) * * *

(ii) * * *

(A) *In general.*—Whether a trade or business of the entity satisfies the 70-percent "substantially all" threshold set forth in paragraph (d)(3)(i) of this section is to be determined by a fraction—

(1) The numerator of which is the total value of all qualified opportunity zone business property owned or leased by the qualified opportunity zone business that meets the requirements in paragraph (d)(2)(i) of this section; and

(2) The denominator of which is the total value of all tangible property owned or leased by the qualified opportunity zone business, whether located inside or outside of a qualified opportunity zone.

(B) *Value of tangible property owned or leased by a qualified opportunity zone business.*—(1) *In general.*—For purposes of the fraction set forth in paragraph (d)(3)(ii)(A) of this section, on an annual basis, the owned or leased tangible property of a qualified opportunity zone business may be valued using the applicable financial statement valuation method set forth in paragraph (d)(3)(ii)(B)(2) of this section, if the qualified opportunity zone business has an applicable financial statement within the meaning of § 1.475(a)-4(h), or the alternative valuation method set forth in paragraph (d)(3)(ii)(B)(3) of this section. During each taxable year, the valuation method selected under this paragraph (d)(3)(ii)(B)(1) must be applied consistently to all tangible property valued with respect to the taxable year.

(2) *Applicable financial statement valuation method.*—(i) *In general.*—Under the applicable financial statement valuation method set forth in this paragraph (d)(3)(ii)(B)(2), the value of tangible property of the qualified opportunity zone business, whether owned or leased, is the value of that property as reported, or as otherwise would be reported, on the qualified opportunity zone business's applicable financial statement for the relevant reporting period.

(ii) Requirement for selection of method.—A qualified opportunity zone business may select the applicable financial statement valuation method set forth in this paragraph (d)(3)(ii)(B)(2) to value tangible property leased by the qualified opportunity zone business only if the applicable financial statement of the qualified opportunity zone business requires, or would otherwise require, an assignment of value to the lease of the tangible property.

(3) Alternative valuation method.—*(i) In general.*—Under the alternative valuation method set forth in this paragraph (d)(3)(ii)(B)(3), the value of tangible property that is owned by the qualified opportunity zone business is calculated under paragraph (d)(3)(ii)(B)(3)(ii) of this section, and the value of tangible property that is leased by the qualified opportunity zone business is calculated under paragraph (d)(3)(ii)(B)(4) of this section.

(ii) Tangible property owned by a qualified opportunity zone business.—The value of tangible property that is owned by the qualified opportunity zone business is the unadjusted cost basis of the property under section 1012 in the hands of the qualified opportunity zone business for each testing date of a QOF during the year.

(4) Tangible property leased by a qualified opportunity zone business.—*(i) In general.*—For purposes of paragraph (d)(3)(ii)(B)(3) of this section, the value of tangible property that is leased by the qualified opportunity zone business is equal to the present value of the leased tangible property as defined in paragraph (d)(3)(ii)(B)(5) of this section.

(ii) Discount rate.—For purposes of calculating present value under paragraph (d)(3)(ii)(B)(4) of this section, the discount rate is the applicable Federal rate under section 1274(d)(1), determined by substituting the term "lease" for "debt instrument."

(5) Present value.—For purposes of paragraph (d)(3)(ii)(B)(4), present value of leased tangible property

(i) Is equal to the sum of the present values of each payment under the lease for such tangible property;

(ii) Is calculated at the time the qualified opportunity zone business enters into the lease for such leased tangible property; and

(iii) Once calculated, is used as the value for such asset by the qualified opportunity zone business for all testing dates for purposes of the 90-percent asset test.

(6) Term of a lease.—For purposes of paragraph (d)(3)(ii)(B)(4) of this section, the term of a lease includes periods during which the lessee may extend the lease at a predefined rent.

(C) *Five-Percent Zone Taxpayer.*—If a taxpayer both holds an equity interest in the entity and has self-certified as a QOF, then that taxpayer may value the entity's assets using the same methodology under paragraph (b) of this section that the taxpayer uses for determining its own compliance with the 90-percent asset requirement of section 1400Z-2(d)(1) (Compliance Methodology), provided that no other equity holder in the entity is a Five-Percent Zone Taxpayer. If two or more taxpayers that have self-certified as QOFs hold equity interests in the entity and at least one of them is a Five-Percent Zone Taxpayer, then the values of the entity's assets may be calculated using the Compliance Methodology that both is used by a Five-Percent Zone Taxpayer and that produces the highest percentage of qualified opportunity zone business property for the entity. A *Five-Percent Zone Taxpayer* is a taxpayer that has self-certified as a QOF and that holds stock in the entity (if it is a corporation) representing at least 5 percent in voting rights and value or holds an interest of at least 5 percent in the profits and capital of the entity (if it is a partnership).

* * *

(4) * * *

(ii) Special rules for land and improvements on land.—(A) *Buildings located in the qualified opportunity zone.*—If a qualified opportunity zone business purchases a building located on land wholly within a QOZ, under section 1400Z-2(d)(2)(D)(ii) a substantial improvement to the purchased tangible property is measured in relation to the qualified opportunity zone business's additions to the adjusted basis of the building. Under section 1400Z-2(d), measuring a substantial improvement to the building by additions to the qualified opportunity zone business's adjusted basis of the building does not require the qualified opportunity zone business to separately substantially improve the land upon which the building is located.

(B) *Unimproved land.*—Unimproved land that is within a qualified opportunity zone and acquired by purchase in accordance with section 1400Z-2(d)(2)(D)(i)(I) is not required to be substantially improved within the meaning of section 1400Z-2(d)(2)(D)(i)(II) and (d)(2)(D)(ii).

(5) Operation of section 1397C requirements adopted by reference.—(i) * * * A trade or business meets the 50-percent gross income requirement in the preceding sentence if the trade or business satisfies any one of the four criteria described in paragraph (d)(5)(i)(A), (B), (C), or (D) of this section, or any criteria identified in published guidance issued by the IRS under § 601.601(d)(2) of this chapter.

(A) *Services performed in qualified opportunity zone based on hours.*—At least 50 percent of the services performed for the trade or business are performed in the qualified opportunity zone, determined by a fraction—

(1) The numerator of which is the total number of hours performed by employees and independent contractors, and employees of independent contractors, for services performed in a qualified opportunity zone during the taxable year; and

(2) The denominator of which is the total number of hours performed by employees and independent contractors, and employees of independent contractors, for services performed during the taxable year.

(B) *Services performed in qualified opportunity zone based on amounts paid for services.*—At least 50 percent of the services performed for the trade or business are performed in the qualified opportunity zone, determined by a fraction—

(1) The numerator of which is the total amount paid by the entity for services performed in a qualified opportunity zone during the taxable year, whether by employees, independent contractors, or employees of independent contractors; and

(2) The denominator of which is the total amount paid by the entity for services performed during the taxable year, whether by employees, independent contractors, or employees of independent contractors.

(C) *Necessary tangible property and business functions.*—The tangible property of the trade or business located in a qualified opportunity zone and the management or operational functions performed in the qualified opportunity zone are each necessary for the generation of at least 50 percent of the gross income of the trade or business.

(D) *Facts and circumstances.*—Based on all the facts and circumstances, at least 50 percent of the gross income of a qualified opportunity zone business is derived from the active conduct of a trade or business in the qualified opportunity zone.

(E) *Examples.*—The following examples illustrate the principles of paragraphs (d)(5)(i)(C) and (D) of this section.

(1) Example 1. A landscaping business has its headquarters in a qualified opportunity zone, its officers and employees manage the daily operations of the business (within and without the qualified opportunity zone) from its headquarters, and all its equipment and supplies are stored in the headquarters facilities. The activities occurring and the storage of equipment and supplies in the qualified opportunity zone are, taken together, a material factor in the generation of the income of the business.

(2) Example 2. A trade or business is formed or organized under the laws of the jurisdiction within which a qualified opportunity zone is located, and the business has a PO Box located in the qualified opportunity zone. The mail received at that PO Box is fundamental to the income of the trade or business, but there is no other basis for concluding that the income of the trade or business is derived from activities in the qualified opportunity zone. The mere location of the PO Box is not a material factor in the generation of gross income by the trade or business.

(3) Example 3. In 2019, Taxpayer X realized $w million of capital gains and within the 180-day period invested $w million in QOF Y, a qualified opportunity fund. QOF Y immediately acquired from partnership P a partnership interest in P, solely in exchange for $w million of cash. P is a real estate developer that has written plans to acquire land in a qualified opportunity zone on which it plans to construct a commercial building for lease to other trades or businesses. In 2023, P's commercial building is placed in service and is fully leased up to other trades or businesses. For the 2023 taxable year, because at least 50 percent of P's gross income is derived from P's rental of its tangible property in the qualified opportunity zone. Thus, under P's facts and circumstances, P satisfies the gross income test under section 1397C(b)(2).

(ii) Use of intangible property requirement.—(A) * * * For purposes of section 1400Z-2(d)(3)(ii) and the preceding sentence, the term *substantial portion* means at least 40 percent.

(B) *Active conduct of a trade or business.*—(1) [Reserved]

(2) Operating real property.—Solely for the purposes of section 1400Z-2(d)(3)(A), the ownership and operation (including leasing) of real property is the active conduct of a trade or business. However, merely entering into a triple-net-lease with respect to real

property owned by a taxpayer is not the active conduct of a trade or business by such taxpayer.

(3) *Trade or business defined.*—The term *trade or business* means a trade or business within the meaning of section 162.

* * *

(iv) *Safe harbor for reasonable amount of working capital.*—Solely for purposes of applying section 1397C(e)(1) to the definition of a qualified opportunity zone business under section 1400Z-2(d)(3), working capital assets are treated as reasonable in amount for purposes of sections 1397C(b)(2) and 1400Z-2(d)(3)(A)(ii), if all of the requirements in paragraphs (d)(5)(iv)(A) through (C) of this section are satisfied.

(A) *Designated in writing.*—These amounts are designated in writing for the development of a trade or business in a qualified opportunity zone (as defined in section 1400Z-1(a)), including when appropriate the acquisition, construction, and/or substantial improvement of tangible property in such a zone.

* * *

(C) *Property consumption consistent.*—The working capital assets are actually used in a manner that is substantially consistent with paragraphs (d)(5)(iv)(A) and (B) of this section. If consumption of the working capital assets is delayed by waiting for governmental action the application for which is complete, that delay does not cause a failure of this paragraph (d)(5)(iv)(C).

(D) *Ability of a single business to benefit from more than a single application of the safe harbor.*—A business may benefit from multiple overlapping or sequential applications of the working capital safe harbor, provided that each application independently satisfies all of the requirements in paragraphs (d)(5)(iv)(A) through (C) of this section.

(E) *Examples.*—The following examples illustrate the rules of paragraph (d)(5)(iv) of this section.

(1) *Example 1: General application of working capital safe harbor*—(i) *Facts.* QOF F creates a business entity E to open a fast-food restaurant and acquires almost all of the equity of E in exchange for cash. E has a written plan and a 20-month schedule for the use of this cash to establish the restaurant. Among the planned uses for the cash are identification of favorable locations in the qualified opportunity zone, leasing a building suitable for such a restaurant, outfitting the building with appropriate equipment and furniture (both owned and leased), necessary security deposits, obtaining a franchise and local permits, and the hiring and training of kitchen and wait staff. Not-yet-disbursed amounts were held in assets described in section 1397C(e)(1), and these assets were eventually expended in a manner consistent with the plan and schedule.

(ii) *Analysis.* E's use of the cash qualifies for the working capital safe harbor described in paragraph (d)(5)(iv) of this section.

(2) *Example 2: Multiple applications of working capital safe harbor*—(i) *Facts.* QOF G creates a business entity H to start a new technology company and acquires equity of H in exchange for cash on Date 1. In addition to H's rapid deployment of capital received from other equity investors, H writes a plan with a 30-month schedule for the use of the Date 1 cash. The plan describes use of the cash to research and develop a new technology (Technology), including paying salaries for engineers and other scientists to conduct the research, purchasing, and leasing equipment to be used in research and furnishing office and laboratory space. Approximately a year-and-a-half after Date 1, on Date 2, G acquires additional equity in H for cash, and H writes a second plan. This new plan has a 25-month schedule for the development of a new application of existing software (Application), to be marketed to government agencies. Among the planned uses for the cash received on Date 2 are paying development costs, including salaries for software engineers, other employees, and third-party consultants to assist in developing and marketing the new application to the anticipated customers. Not-yet-disbursed amounts that were scheduled for development of the Technology and the Application were held in assets described in section 1397C(e)(1), and these assets were eventually expended in a manner substantially consistent with the plans and schedules for both the Technology and the Application.

(ii) *Analysis.* H's use of both the cash received on Date 1 and the cash received on Date 2 qualifies for the working capital safe harbor described in paragraph (d)(5)(iv) of this section.

* * *

(viii) *Real property straddling a qualified opportunity zone.*—For purposes of satisfying the requirements in this paragraph (d)(5), when it is necessary to determine whether a qualified opportunity zone is the location of services, tangible property, or business functions, section 1397C(f) applies (substituting "qualified opportunity zone" for "empowerment zone"). If the amount of real property based on square footage located within the qualified opportunity zone is substantial as compared to the amount of real property based on square footage outside of the qualified opportunity zone, and the real property outside of the qualified opportunity zone is contiguous to part or all of the real property located inside the qualified opportunity zone, then all of the property is deemed to be located within a qualified opportunity zone.

* * *

(f) * * * Notwithstanding the preceding sentence, a QOF may not rely on the proposed rules in paragraphs (c)(8)(ii)(B) and (d)(4)(ii)(B) of this section (which concern the qualification of land as QOZBP) if the land is unimproved or minimally improved and the QOF or the QOZB purchases the land with an expectation, an intention, or a view not to improve the land by more than an insubstantial amount within 30 months after the date of purchase.

Qualified Opportunity Funds: Investment

Qualified Opportunity Funds: Investment.—Reg. §1.1400Z2(f)-1, relating to gains that may be deferred as a result of a taxpayer's investment in a qualified opportunity fund, as well as special rules for an investment in a QOF held by a taxpayer for at least 10 years, was adopted by T.D. 9889 on December 31, 2019 (published in the Federal Register on May 1, 2019) (REG-120186-18).

⟫⟫→ *Caution: Proposed Reg. §1.1400Z2(f)-1, below, was adopted by T.D. 9889; however, for an exception regarding when this proposed regulation may be relied upon, see final Reg. §1.1400Z2(f)-1(d).*

Par. 6. Section 1.1400Z2(f)-1 is added to read as follows:

§1.1400Z2(f)-1. Failure of qualified opportunity fund to maintain investment standard.—(a) *In general.*—Except as provided by §1.1400Z2(d)-1a(2)(ii) with respect to a taxpayer's first taxable year as a QOF, if a QOF fails to satisfy the 90-percent asset test in section 1400Z-2(d)(1), then the fund must pay the statutory penalty set forth in section 1400Z-2(f) for each month it fails meet the 90-percent asset test.

(b) *Time period for a QOF to reinvest certain proceeds.*—If a QOF receives proceeds from the return of capital or the sale or disposition of some or all of its qualified opportunity zone property within the meaning of section 1400Z-2(d)(2)(A), and if the QOF reinvests some or all of the proceeds in qualified opportunity zone property by the last day of the 12-month period beginning on the date of the distribution, sale, or disposition, then the proceeds, to the extent that they are so reinvested, are treated as qualified opportunity zone property for purposes of the 90-percent asset test in section 1400Z-2(d)(1), but only to the extent that prior to the reinvestment in qualified opportunity zone property the proceeds are continuously held in cash, cash equivalents, or debt instruments with a term of 18 months or less. If reinvestment of the proceeds is delayed by waiting for governmental action the application for which is complete, that delay does not cause a failure of the 12-month requirement in this paragraph (b).

(c) *Anti-abuse rule.*—(1) *In general.*—Pursuant to section 1400Z-2(e)(4)(C), the rules of section 1400Z-2 and §§1.1400Z2(a)-1 through 1.1400Z2(g)-1 must be applied in a manner consistent with the purposes of section 1400Z-2. Accordingly, if a significant purpose of a transaction is to achieve a tax result that is inconsistent with the purposes of section 1400Z-2, the Commissioner can recast a transaction (or series of transactions) for Federal tax purposes as appropriate to achieve tax results that are consistent with the purposes of section 1400Z-2. Whether a tax result is inconsistent with the purposes of section 1400Z-2 must be determined based on all the facts and circumstances.

(2) [Reserved]

(d) *Applicability date.*—This section applies to taxable years of a QOF that end on or after the date of publication in the **Federal Register** of a Treasury decision adopting these proposed rules as final regulations. However, an eligible taxpayer may rely on the proposed rules in this section (other than paragraph (c) of this section) with respect to taxable years before the date of applicability of this section, but only if the eligible taxpayer applies the rules in their entirety and in a consistent manner. An eligible taxpayer may rely on the proposed rules in paragraph (c) of this section with respect to taxable years before the date of applicability of this section, but only if the eligible taxpayer applies the rules of section 1400Z-2 and §§1.1400Z2(a)-1 through 1.1400Z2(g)-1, as applicable, in their entirety and in a consistent manner. [Reg. §1.1400Z2(f)-1.]

Qualified Opportunity Funds: Investment

Qualified Opportunity Funds: Investment.—Reg. §1.1400Z2(g)-1, relating to gains that may be deferred as a result of a taxpayer's investment in a qualified opportunity fund, as well as special rules for an investment in a QOF held by a taxpayer for at least 10 years, was adopted by T.D. 9889 on December 31, 2019 (published in the Federal Register on May 1, 2019) (REG-120186-18).

>>>→ *Caution: Proposed Reg. §1.1400Z2(g)-1, below, was adopted by T.D. 9889 as Reg. §§1.1502-14Z and 1.1504-3; however, for an exception regarding when this proposed regulation may be relied upon, see final Reg. §§1.1502-14Z(k) and 1.1504-3(e).*

Par. 7. Section 1.1400Z2(g)-1 is added to read as follows:

§1.1400Z2(g)-1. Application of opportunity zone rules to members of a consolidated group.—(a) *Scope and definitions.*—(1) *Scope.*—This section provides rules regarding the Federal income tax treatment of QOFs owned by members of consolidated groups.

(2) *Definitions.*—The definitions provided in §1.1400Z2(b)-1(a)(2) apply for purposes of this section.

(b) *QOF stock not stock for purposes of affiliation.*—(1) *In general.*—Stock in a QOF corporation (whether qualifying QOF stock or otherwise) is not treated as stock for purposes of determining whether the issuer is a member of an affiliated group within the meaning of section 1504. Therefore, a QOF corporation can be the common parent of a consolidated group, but a QOF corporation cannot be a subsidiary member of a consolidated group.

(2) *Example.*—The following example illustrates the rules of this paragraph (b).

(i) *Facts.* Corporation P wholly owns corporation S, which wholly owns corporation Q. P, S, and Q are members of a U.S. consolidated group (P group). In 2018, S sells an asset to an unrelated party and realizes $500 of capital gain. S contributes $500 to Q and properly elects to defer recognition of the gain under section 1400Z-2. At such time, Q qualifies and elects to be treated as a QOF.

(ii) *Analysis.* Under paragraph (b) of this section, stock of a QOF (qualifying or otherwise) is not treated as stock for purposes of affiliation under section 1504. Thus, once Q becomes a QOF, Q ceases to be affiliated with the P group members under section 1504(a), and it deconsolidates from the P group.

(c) *Qualifying investments by members of a consolidated group.*—Except as otherwise provided in this section or in §1.1400Z2(b)-1, section 1400Z-2 applies separately to each member of a consolidated group. Therefore, for example, the same member of the group must both engage in the sale of a capital asset giving rise to gain and timely invest an amount equal to some or all of such gain in a QOF (as provided in section 1400Z-2(a)(1)) in order to qualify for deferral of such gain under section 1400Z-2.

(d) *Tiering up of investment adjustments provided by section 1400Z-2.*—Basis increases in a qualifying investment in a QOF under sections 1400Z-2(b)(2)(B)(iii), 1400Z-2(b)(2)(B)(iv), and 1400Z-2(c) are treated as satisfying the requirements of §1.1502-32(b)(3)(ii)(A), and thus qualify as tax-exempt income to the QOF owner. Therefore, if the QOF owner is a member of a consolidated group and is owned by other members of the same group (upper-tier members), the group members increase their bases in the shares of the QOF owner under §1.1502-32(b)(2)(ii). However, there is no basis increase under §1.1502-32(b)(2)(ii) in shares of upper-tier members with regard to basis increases under section 1400Z-2(c) and the regulations at §1.1400Z2(c)-1 unless and until the basis of the qualifying investment is increased to its fair market value, as provided in section 1400Z-2(c) and the regulations at §1.1400Z2(c)-1.

(e) *Application of §1.1502-36(d).*—This paragraph (e) clarifies how §1.1502-36(d) applies if a member (M) transfers a loss share of another member (S) and S is a QOF owner that owns a qualifying investment in a QOF. To determine S's attribute reduction amount under §1.1502-36(d)(3), S's basis in its qualifying investment is included in S's net inside attribute amount to compute S's aggregate inside loss under §1.1502-36(d)(3)(iii)(A). However, S's basis in the qualifying investment is not included in S's category D attributes available for attribute reduction under §1.1502-36(d)(4). Thus, S's basis in the qualifying investment cannot be reduced under §1.1502-36(d). If S's attribute reduction amount exceeds S's attributes available for reduction, then to the extent of S's basis in the qualifying investment (limited by the remaining attribute reduction amount), the common parent is treated as making the election under §1.1502-36(d)(6) to reduce M's basis in the transferred loss S shares.

(f) *Examples.*—The following examples illustrate the rules of this section.

(1) *Example 1: Basis adjustment when member owns qualifying QOF stock*—(i) *Facts.* Corporation P is the common parent of a consolidated group (P group), and P wholly owns Corporation S, a member of the P group. In 2018, S sells an asset to an unrelated party and realizes $500 of capital gain. S contributes $500 to Q (a QOF corporation) and properly elects to defer the gain under section 1400Z-2(a) and §1.1400Z2(a)-1. S does not otherwise own stock in Q. In 2029, when S still owns its qualifying investment in Q, P sells all of the stock of S to an unrelated party.

(ii) *Analysis*—(A) *5-year and 7-year basis increase and §1.1502-32 tier-up.* In 2023, when S has held the stock of Q for five years, under section 1400Z-2(b)(2)(B)(iii), S increases its basis in its Q stock by $50 (10 percent of $500, the amount of gain deferred by reason of section 1400Z-2(a)(1)(A)). The 10-percent basis increase qualifies as tax-exempt income to S under paragraph (d) of this section. Thus, P (an upper-tier member) increases its basis in S's stock by $50 under §1.1502-32(b)(2)(ii). Similarly, in 2025, when S has held the stock of Q for seven years, under section 1400Z-2(b)(2)(B)(iv), S increases its basis in its Q stock by an additional $25 (5 percent of $500). The 5 percent basis increase also qualifies as tax-exempt income to S under paragraph (d) of this section, and P increases its basis in S's stock by an additional $25 under §1.1502-32(b)(2)(ii).

(B) *S's recognition of deferred capital gain in 2026.* S did not dispose of its Q stock prior to December 31, 2026. Therefore, under section 1400Z-2(b)(1)(B) and §1.1400Z2(b)-1(b)(2), S's deferred capital gain is included in S's income on December 31, 2026. The amount of gain included under section 1400Z-2(b)(2)(A) is $425 ($500 of deferred gain less S's $75 basis in Q). S's basis in Q is increased by $425 to $500, and P's basis in S also is increased by $425.

(C) *P's disposition of S.* P's sale of S stock in 2029 results in the deconsolidation of S. Q remains a non-consolidated subsidiary of S, and S is not treated as selling or exchanging its Q stock for purposes of section 1400Z-2(c). Therefore, no basis adjustments under section 1400Z-2 are made as a result of P's sale of S stock.

(iii) *S sells the stock of Q after 10 years.* The facts are the same as in this *Example 1* in paragraph (f)(1)(i) of this section, except that in 2029, instead of P selling all of the stock of S, S sells all of the stock of Q to an unrelated party for its fair market value of $800. At the time of the sale, S has owned the Q stock for over 10 years, and S elects under section 1400Z-2(c) to increase its stock basis in Q from $500 (*see* the analysis in this *Example 1* in paragraph (f)(1)(ii)(B) of this section) to the fair market value of Q on the date of the sale, $800. As a result of the election, S's basis in Q is $800 and S has no gain on the sale of Q stock. Additionally, the $300 basis increase in Q is treated as tax-exempt income to S pursuant to paragraph (d) of this section. Thus, P increases its basis in P's stock by $300 under §1.1502-32(b)(2)(ii).

(2) *Example 2: Computation and application of the attribute reduction amount under §1.1502-36(d) when S owns a QOF*—(i) *Facts.* Corporation P (the common parent of a consolidated group) wholly owns corporation M, which wholly owns corporation S, which wholly owns Q (a QOF corporation). In 2018, S sells an asset to an unrelated party and realizes $5,000 of capital gain. S contributes $5,000 to Q and properly elects to defer the gain under section 1400Z-2. In 2024, M sells all of its S stock to an unrelated party for fair market value of $100, and M's basis in the stock of S is $300. At the time of sale, S owns the stock of Q with a basis of $500 (S's basis in Q was increased under section 1400Z-2(b)(2)(B)(iii) to $500 in 2023), and S has a net operating loss carryover of $50. M's transfer of the S shares is a transfer of loss shares under §1.1502-36. Assume that no basis redetermination is required under §1.1502-36(b) and no basis reduction is required under §1.1502-36(c).

(ii) *Attribute reduction under §1.1502-36(d).* Under §1.1502-36(d), S's attributes are reduced by S's attribute reduction amount. Section 1.1502-36(d)(3) provides that S's attribute reduction amount is the lesser of the net stock loss and S's aggregate inside loss. The net stock loss is the excess of the $300 aggregate basis of the transferred S shares over the $100 aggregate value of those shares, or $200. S's aggregate inside loss, which includes the basis of the stock of Q as provided by paragraph (e) of this section, is the excess of S's net inside attribute amount over the value of the S share. S's net inside attribute amount is $550, computed as the sum of S's $50 loss carryover and its $500 basis in Q. S's aggregate inside loss is therefore $450 ($550 net inside attribute amount over the $100 value of the S share). Accordingly, S's attribute reduction amount is the lesser of the $200 net stock loss and the $450 aggregate inside loss, or $200. Under §1.1502-36(d)(4), S's $200 attribute reduction is first allocated and applied to reduce S's $50 loss carryover to $0. Under §

§1.1502-36(d)(4)(i)(D), S generally would be able to reduce the basis of its category D assets (including stock in other corporations) by the remaining attribute reduction amount ($150). However, paragraph (e) of this section provides that S's basis in the QOF (Q) shares is not included in S's category D attributes that are available for reduction under §1.1502-36(d)(4), and the remaining $150 of attribute reduction amount cannot be used to reduce the basis of Q shares under §1.1502-36(d). Rather, under paragraph (e) of this section, P is treated as making the election under §1.1502-36(d)(6) to reduce M's basis in the transferred loss S shares by $150. As a result, P's basis in its M stock will also be reduced by $150.

(g) *Applicability date.*—Except as otherwise provided in this paragraph (g), this section applies for taxable years that begin on or after the date of publication in the **Federal Register** of a Treasury decision adopting these proposed rules as final regulations. However, a QOF may rely on the proposed rules in this section with respect to taxable years that begin before the applicability date of this section, but only if the QOF applies the rules in their entirety and in a consistent manner. [Reg. §1.1400Z2(g)-1.]

Self-Employment Tax: Limited Partner: Definition

Self-Employment Tax: Limited Partner: Definition.—Amendments to Reg. §1.1402(a)-2, relating to the self-employment tax imposed under Code Sec. 1402, are proposed (published in the Federal Register on January 13, 1997) (REG-209824-96).

☐ Par. 2. Section 1.1402(a)-2 is amended by:

1. Revising the first sentence of paragraph (d).
2. Removing the reference "section 702(a)(9)" in the first sentence of paragraph (e) and adding "section 702(a)(8)" in its place.
3. Revising the last sentence of paragraph (f).
4. Revising paragraphs (g) and (h).
5. Adding new paragraphs (i) and (j).

The revisions and additions read as follows:

§1.1402(a)-2. Computation of net earnings from self-employment.

* * *

(d) * * * Except as otherwise provided in section 1402(a) and paragraph (g) of this section, an individual's net earnings from self-employment include the individual's distributive share (whether or not distributed) of income or loss described in section 702(a)(8) from any trade or business carried on by each partnership of which the individual is a partner. * * *

* * *

(f) * * * For rules governing the classification of an organization as a partnership or otherwise, see §§301.7701-1, 301.7701-2, and 301.7701-3 of this chapter.

(g) *Distributive share of limited partner.*—An individual's net earnings from self-employment do not include the individual's distributive share of income or loss as a limited partner described in paragraph (h) of this section. However, guaranteed payments described in section 707(c) made to the individual for services actually rendered to or on behalf of the partnership engaged in a trade or business are included in the individual's net earnings from self-employment.

(h) *Definition of limited partner.*—(1) *In general.*—Solely for purposes of section 1402(a)(13) and paragraph (g) of this section, an individual is considered to be a limited partner to the extent provided in paragraphs (h)(2), (h)(3), (h)(4), and (h)(5) of this section.

(2) *Limited partner.*—An individual is treated as a limited partner under this paragraph (h)(2) unless the individual—

(i) Has personal liability (as defined in §301.7701-3(b)(2)(ii) of this chapter for the debts of or claims against the partnership by reason of being a partner;

(ii) Has authority (under the law of the jurisdiction in which the partnership is formed) to contract on behalf of the partnership; or

(iii) Participates in the partnership's trade or business for more than 500 hours during the partnership's taxable year.

(3) *Exception for holders of more than one class of interest.*—An individual holding more than one class of interest in the partnership who is not treated as a limited partner under paragraph (h)(2) of this section is treated as a limited partner under this paragraph (h)(3) with respect to a specific class of partnership interest held by such individual if, immediately after the individual acquires that class of interest—

(i) Limited partners within the meaning of paragraph (h)(2) of this section own a substantial, continuing interest in that specific class of partnership interest; and,

(ii) The individual's rights and obligations with respect to that specific class of interest are identical to the rights and obligations of that specific class of partnership interest held by the limited partners described in paragraph (h)(3)(i) of this section.

(4) *Exception for holders of only one class of interest.*—An individual who is not treated as a limited partner under paragraph (h)(2) of this section solely because that individual participates in the partnership's trade or business for more than 500 hours during the partnership's taxable year is treated as a limited partner under this paragraph (h)(4) with respect to the individual's partnership interest if, immediately after the individual acquires that interest—

(i) Limited partners within the meaning of paragraph (h)(2) of this section own a substantial, continuing interest in that specific class of partnership interest; and

(ii) The individual's rights and obligations with respect to the specific class of interest are identical to the rights and obligations of the specific class of partnership interest held by the limited partners described in paragraph (h)(4)(i) of this section.

(5) *Exception for service partners in service partnerships.*—An individual who is a service partner in a service partnership may not be a limited partner under paragraphs (h)(2), (h)(3), or (h)(4) of this section.

(6) *Additional definitions.*—Solely for purposes of this paragraph (h)—

(i) A *class of interest* is an interest that grants the holder specific rights and obligations. If a holder's rights and obligations from an interest are different from another holder's rights and obligations, each holder's interest belongs to a separate class of interest. An individual may hold more than one class of interest in the same partnership provided that each class grants the individual different rights or obligations. The existence of a guaranteed payment described in section 707(c) made to an individual for services rendered to or on behalf of a partnership, however, is not a factor in determining the rights and obligations of a class of interest.

(ii) A *service partner* is a partner who provides services to or on behalf of the service partnership's trade or business. A partner is not considered to be a service partner if that partner only provides a de minimis amount of services to or on behalf of the partnership.

(iii) A *service partnership* is a partnership substantially all the activities of which involve the performance of services in the fields of health, law, engineering, architecture, accounting, actuarial science, or consulting.

(iv) A *substantial interest in a class of interest* is determined based on all of the relevant facts and circumstances. In all cases, however, ownership of 20 percent or more of a specific class of interest is considered substantial.

(i) *Example.*—The following example illustrates the principles of paragraphs (g) and (h) of this section:

Example. (i) A, B, and C form LLC, a limited liability company, under the laws of State to engage in a business that is not a service partnership described in paragraph (h)(6)(iii) of this section. LLC, classified as a partnership for federal tax purposes, allocates all items of income, deduction, and credit of LLC to A, B, and C in proportion to their ownership of LLC. A and C each contribute $1x for one LLC unit. B contributes $2x for two LLC units. Each LLC unit entitles its holder to receive 25 percent of LLC's tax items, including profits. A does not perform services for LLC; however, each year B receives a guaranteed payment of $6x for 600 hours of services rendered to LLC and C receives a guaranteed payment of $10x for 1000 hours of services rendered to LLC. C also is elected LLC's manager. Under State's law, C has the authority to contract on behalf of LLC.

(ii) *Application of general rule of paragraph (h)(2) of this section.* A is treated as a limited partner in LLC under paragraph (h)(2) of this section because A is not liable personally for debts of or claims against LLC, A does not have authority to contract for LLC under State's law, and A does not participate in LLC's trade or business for more than 500 hours during the taxable year. Therefore, A's distributive share attributable to A's LLC unit is excluded from A's net earnings from self-employment under section 1402(a)(13).

(iii) *Distributive share not included in net earnings from self-employment under paragraph (h)(4) of this section.* B's guaranteed payment of $6x is included in B's net earnings from self-employment under section 1402(a)(13). B is not treated as a limited partner under paragraph (h)(2) of this section because, although B is not liable for debts of or claims against LLC and B does not have authority to contract for LLC under State's law, B does participates in LLC's trade or business for more than 500 hours during the taxable year. Further, B is not treated as a limited partner under paragraph (h)(3) of this section because B does not hold more than one class of interest in LLC. However, B is treated as a limited partner under paragraph (h)(4) of this section because B is not treated as a limited partner under paragraph (h)(2) of this section solely because B participated in LLC's business for more than 500 hours and because A is a limited partner under paragraph (h)(2) of this section who owns a substantial interest with rights and obligations that are identical to B's rights and obligations. In this example, B's distributive share is deemed to be a return on B's investment in LLC and not remuneration for B's service to LLC. Thus, B's distributive share attributable to B's two LLC units is not net earnings from self-employment under section 1402(a)(13).

(iv) *Distributive share included in net earnings from self-employment.* C's guaranteed payment of $10x is included in C's net earnings from self-employment under section 1402(a). In addition, C's distributive share attributable to C's LLC unit also is net earnings from self-employment under section 1402(a) because C is not a limited partner under paragraphs (h)(2), (h)(3), or (h)(4) of this section. C is not treated as a limited partner under paragraph (h)(2) of this section because C has the authority under State's law to enter into a binding contract on behalf of LLC and because C participates in LLC's trade or business for more than 500 hours during the taxable year. Further, C is not treated as a limited partner under paragraph (h)(3) of this section because C does not hold more than one class of interest in LLC. Finally, C is not treated as a limited partner under paragraph (h)(4) of this section because C has the power to bind LLC. Thus, C's guaranteed payment and distributive share both are included in C's net earnings from self-employment under section 1402(a).

(j) *Effective date.*—Paragraphs (d), (e), (f), (g), (h), and (i) are applicable beginning with the individual's first taxable year beginning on or after the date this section is published as a final regulation in the Federal Register.

UNEARNED INCOME MEDICARE CONTRIBUTION

Net Investment Income Tax: Guidance Under Section 1411

Net Investment Income Tax: Guidance Under Section 1411.—Amendments to Reg. §1.1411-0, providing guidance on the computation of net investment income, are proposed (published in the Federal Register on December 2, 2013) (REG-130843-13).

☐ Par. 2. Section 1.1411-0 is amended by:

1. Revising the entries under §1.1411-3 for paragraphs (d)(2)(ii), (d)(3) and adding entries (d)(3)(i) through (iii).

2. Revising the entries under §1.1411-4 for paragraphs (d)(4)(iii), (e)(3), and (g)(10) through (13).

3. Adding entries to §1.1411-7.

The revisions and additions to read as follows:

§1.1411-0. Table of contents.

* * *

§1.1411-3 Application to estates and trusts.

* * *

(d) * * *

  (2) * * *

    (ii) Special rules for CRTs with income from certain CFCs or PFICs.

  (3) Elective simplified method.

    (i) Treatment of annuity or unitrust distributions.

    (ii) Properly allocable deductions in excess of gross income.

    (iii) Procedural requirements for making election.

* * *

§1.1411-4 Definition of net investment income.

* * *

(d) * * *

  (4) * * *

    (iii) Adjustment for capital loss carryforwards for previously excluded income

* * *

(e) * * *

  (3) Treatment of income from common trust funds.

* * *

(g) * * *

  (10) Treatment of section 707(c) guaranteed payments.

  (11) Treatment of section 736 payments.

    (i) In general.

    (ii) Treatment of section 736(a)(1) payments.

      (A) General rule.

      (B) Examples.

    (iii) Treatment of section 736(a)(2) payments.

      (A) Payments for unrealized receivables and goodwill.

      (B) Payments not for unrealized receivables or goodwill.

    (iv) Treatment of section 736(b) payments.

    (v) Application of section 1411(c)(4) to section 736 payments.

  (12) Income and deductions from certain notional principal contracts.

    (i) In general.

    (ii) Notional principal contracts.

  (13) Treatment of income or loss from REMIC residual interests.

* * *

§1.1411-7 Exception for dispositions of certain active interests in partnerships and S corporations

  (a) In general.

    (1) General application.

    (2) Definitions.

    (3) Section 1411(c)(4) dispositions.

      (i) Transfers by individuals, estates, and trusts.

      (ii) Transfers by passthrough entities.

    (4) Special rules.

      (i) Certain liquidations.

      (ii) Excluded gain or loss.

      (iii) Rules applicable to S corporation shareholders.

        (A) Certain S corporation dispositions.

        (B) S corporations subject to section 1374.

        (C) Treatment of Qualified Subchapter S Trusts (QSSTs).

  (b) Calculation.

    (1) In general.

      (i) Gain on disposition of interest.

      (ii) Loss on disposition of interest.

    (2) Examples.

  (c) Optional simplified reporting.

    (1) In general.

    (2) Qualifications.

      (i) Minimal section 1411 property.

      (ii) Minimal gain or loss.

    (3) Nonapplicability.

    (4) Optional simplified reporting calculation.

    (5) Examples.

  (d) Deferred recognition transactions.

  (e) Tiered passthrough disposition. [Reserved]

  (f) Adjustment to net gain or loss.

  (g) Information reporting.

    (1) Information to be provided by passthrough entity to transferor.

    (2) Information reporting by transferors.

  (h) Effective/applicability date.

Net Investment Income Tax: Guidance Under Section 1411

Net Investment Income Tax: Guidance Under Section 1411.—Amendments to Reg. §§1.1411-3 and 1.1411-4, providing guidance on the computation of net investment income, are proposed (published in the Federal Register on December 2, 2013) (REG-130843-13) (corrected February 24, 2014).

☐ Par 3. Section 1.1411-3 is amended by:

1. Revising paragraph (d)(2)(ii).
2. Revising paragraph (d)(2)(iii) by adding *Example 2* through *Example 5*.
3. Revising paragraph (d)(3).
4. Revising paragraph (f).
The revisions and additions read as follows:

§1.1411-3. Application to estates and trusts.

* * *

(d) * * *

(2) * * *

(ii) *Special rules for CRTs with income from certain CFCs or PFICs.*—If a CRT is a trust described in §1.1411-10(a), and the CRT includes an amount in gross income under section 951(a) or section 1293(a) from a CFC or QEF that is not also income derived from a trade or business described in section 1411(c)(2) and §1.1411-5 (except as provided in §1.1411-10(b)(2)) and an election under §1.1411-10(g) is not in effect with respect to the CFC or QEF, or the CRT is treated as receiving an excess distribution within the meaning of section 1291(b) or recognizing gain treated as an excess distribution under section 1291(a)(2), then the following rules apply for purposes of section 1411 with regard to income derived from the CFC, QEF, or PFIC—

(A) Amounts included in gross income for chapter 1 purposes under section 951(a) or section 1293(a) in a calendar year with respect to the CFC or QEF, and in one or more categories described in §1.664-1(d)(1) are considered excluded income in that calendar year;

(B) For the year in which the CRT is treated as receiving any of the items of net investment income described in paragraphs (c)(1)(i), (c)(1)(ii), (c)(2)(i), and (c)(4) of §1.1411-10 that otherwise are not included in gross income for purposes of chapter 1 for that year ("*NII Inclusion Amount*") with respect to the CFC, QEF, or PFIC, the rules of this paragraph (d)(2)(ii)(B) apply; and

(1) For purposes of determining the character under section 664 of a distribution to the unitrust or annuity recipient of a CRT, the NII Inclusion Amount treated as received by the CRT shall be allocated among the categories described in section 664(b)(1) through (b)(3), and among the classes within each category as described in §1.664-1(d)(1), in the manner described in this paragraph (d)(2)(ii)(B). Specifically, to the extent the CRT has amounts of excluded income in the categories described in section 664(b)(1) (the Ordinary Income Category) or section 664(b)(2) (the Capital Gain Category), the NII Inclusion Amount shall be allocated to the CRT's classes of excluded income in the Ordinary Income Category, and then to the classes of excluded income in the Capital Gain Category, in turn, until exhaustion of each such class, beginning with the class of excluded income within a category with the highest Federal income tax rate.

(2) Any remaining NII Inclusion Amount not so allocated to classes within the Ordinary Income and Capital Gain Categories shall be placed in the category described in section 664(b)(3) (the Other Income Category). To the extent the CRT distributes amounts from this Other Income Category, that distribution shall constitute a distribution described in §1.1411-10(c)(4).

(3) A distribution by the CRT of excluded income first is deemed to carry out net investment income to the extent of the NII Inclusion Amount that has been allocated to excluded income in that class.

(4) As a result, a distribution of excluded income will carry out to the unitrust or annuity recipient net investment income attributable to the items described in this paragraph (d)(2)(ii)(B).

. (C) In the case of a difference between the amount calculated with respect to a disposition under paragraph (c)(2)(iii) or (c)(2)(iv) of §1.1411-10 and the amount attributable to the relevant disposition for purposes of chapter 1, the following rules apply—

(1) If the amount of the gain from the disposition for purposes of section 1411 is higher (or the loss smaller) than the amount of the gain (or loss) calculated for purposes of chapter 1, such difference shall be considered an NII Inclusion Amount and shall be allocated as described in paragraph (d)(2)(ii)(B) of this section. However, in applying paragraph (d)(2)(ii)(B) of this section to this increase, the order of the classes and categories to which the allocation is made shall be changed as follows: the increase shall be allocated first to the class in the Capital Gain Category that reflects the nature of the increase (short-term or long-term), then to other classes in that category, in turn until exhausted, then to the classes in the Ordinary Income Category, and finally to the Other Income Category.

(2) If the amount of the gain from the disposition for purposes of section 1411 is smaller (or the loss higher) than the amount of the gain (or loss) calculated for purposes of chapter 1, such difference shall reduce accumulated net investment income in the CRT's categories and their respective classes as follows—

(i) To the extent that the CRT has amounts in the Other Income Category by reason of the application of paragraph (d)(2)(ii)(B) or (d)(2)(ii)(C)(1) of this section for the current or prior years, to the Other Income Category; and

(ii) Any excess difference in the same order as specified in paragraph (d)(2)(ii)(C)(1) of this section.

(iii) * * *

Example 2. (i) In 2010, A creates a net income with makeup CRT (NIMCRUT). A is the sole income beneficiary of the NIMCRUT for 15 years. As of December 31, 2012, the NIMCRUT had $2,000 of dividend income and $180,000 of long-term capital gain within the Ordinary Income and Capital Gain Categories, respectively. Because both of these amounts were received by the NIMCRUT during a taxable year beginning before 2013, both constitute excluded income within the meaning of §1.1411-1(d). In Year 1, the NIMCRUT acquires an interest in a CFC. The NIMCRUT does not make the §1.1411-10(g) election with respect to the CFC. In Year 1, the NIMCRUT receives a section 951(a) inclusion of $5,000 and makes no distributions to A. For all years, income derived with respect to the CFC is not income derived in a trade or business described in section 1411(c)(2) and §1.1411-5.

(ii) In Year 1, §1.1411-3(d)(2)(ii)(A) treats the section 951 inclusion as excluded income and allocates it to the class of non-NII with a 39.6% tax rate in the Ordinary Income Category under §1.664-1(d)(1).

Year 1 ending Category and Class Balances

Category	Class	Excluded / NII	Tax Rate	Amount
Ordinary Income				
	Interest and Other Income (including section 951 Inclusions)	Excluded	39.6%	$5,000
	Qualified Dividends	Excluded	20.0%	$2,000
Capital Gain				
	Long-Term	NII	23.8%	$ 0
	Long-Term	Excluded	20.0%	$180,000
Other Income				None

(iii) The NIMCRUT makes no distributions to its sole income beneficiary in Year 2. In Year 3, the CFC distributes $4,000 to the NIMCRUT (which constitutes net investment income under §1.1411-10(c)(1)(i)), the NIMCRUT has a total of $800 of post-2012 interest, and the NIMCRUT distributes $4,000 to the beneficiary.

Category and Class Balances immediately before both the CFC distribution and the NIMCRUT's Year 3 distribution to A

Category	Class	Excluded / NII	Tax Rate	Amount
Ordinary Income				
	Interest (post-2012)	NII	43.4%	$800
	Interest and Other Income (including section 951 Inclusions)	Excluded	39.6%	$5,000
	Qualified Dividends	Excluded	20.0%	$2,000
Capital Gain				
	Long-Term	NII	23.8%	$ 0
	Long-Term	Excluded	20.0%	$180,000
Other Income				None

Section 1.1411-3(d)(2)(ii)(B) will cause the $4,000 distribution from the CFC to be allocated first to the class of excluded income within the Ordinary Income Category with the highest Federal tax rate (the Interest and Other Income class). The distribution to A consists of $800 of post-2012 interest (subject to section 1411) and $3,200 from the Interest and Other Income class, of which all $3,200 constitutes NII by reason of the allocation under

§ 1.1411-3(d)(2)(ii)(B). Of the $1,800 remaining in that category after the distribution to A, $800 will carry out NII to A, and will be includable in A's net investment income, when it is distributed to A in the future. Because the $3,200 distributed to A from this class is subject to both income tax and tax under section 1411 for Year 3, the timing differential attributable to the rules in § 1.1411-10 has been corrected within the NIMCRUT before the income is distributed to A.

Year 3 ending Category and Class Balances (immediately following the distribution to A)

Category	Class	Excluded / NII	Tax Rate	Amount
Ordinary Income				
	Interest (post-2012)	NII	43.4%	$0
	Interest & Other Income (including section 951 Inclusions)	Excluded	39.6%	$1,800*
	Qualified Dividends	Excluded	20.0%	$2,000
Capital Gain				
	Long-Term	NII	23.8%	$0
	Long-Term	Excluded	20.0%	$180,000
Other Income				None

* Of which $800 will carry out NII to A when distributed

Example 3. (i) Assume the same facts as in *Example 2*, except that, in Year 2, the NIMCRUT has a section 951 inclusion in the amount of $4,000, taxable interest income of $800, tax exempt interest of $4,000. Assume the CRT has $1,100 undistributed capital gain from a taxable year ending before December 31, 2012.

Category and Class Balances immediately before the Year 2 distribution to A

Category	Class	Excluded / NII	Tax Rate	Amount
Ordinary Income				
	Interest (post-2012)	NII	43.4%	$800
	Interest and Other Income (including section 951 Inclusions)	Excluded	39.6%	$9,000
	Qualified Dividends	Excluded	20.0%	$2,000
Capital Gain				
	Long-Term	NII	23.8%	$ 0
	Long-Term	Excluded	20.0%	$1,100
Other Income		Excluded		$4,000

(ii) In Year 2, the NIMCRUT made a $4,800 distribution to A in that same year (leaving a net balance in the Interest and Other Income class of $5,000 at the end of Year 2).

Category and Class Balances as of December 31, Year 2 (immediately following the distribution to A)

Category	Class	Excluded / NII	Tax Rate	Amount
Ordinary Income				
	Interest (post-2012)	NII	43.4%	$0
	Interest and Other Income (including section 951 Inclusions)	Excluded	39.6%	$5,000
	Qualified Dividends	Excluded	20.0%	$2,000
Capital Gain				
	Long-Term	NII	23.8%	$0
	Long-Term	Excluded	20.0%	$1,100
Other Income		Excluded		$4,000

A's net investment income in Year 2 will include $800 of taxable interest income, but will not include the $4,000 of other ordinary income.

(iii) In Year 3, the NIMCRUT received a distribution from the CFC of $9,000, and assume, for purposes of this example, that the NIMCRUT distributes $6,000 to A. Section 1.1411-3(d)(2)(ii)(B) will cause the $9,000 distribution from the CFC to be allocated first to the class of excluded income within the Ordinary Income Category with the highest Federal tax rate (thus, $5,000 to the Other Income class and $2,000 to Qualified Dividends). The $2,000 balance of the Year 3

distribution from the CFC is allocated under § 1.1411-3(d)(2)(ii)(B) as follows: $1,100 to the Long-Term Capital Gain class of non-NII (so the distribution to A from this class in the future will carry out $1,100 of NII to A), and the remaining $900 to the Other Income Category (so the distribution to A from this class in the future will carry out $900 of NII to A).

The distribution to A consists of $5,000 of Interest and Other Income class and $1,000 of Qualified Dividends, all of which constitutes NII by reason of the allocation under § 1.1411-3(d)(2)(ii)(B).

Category and Class Balances as of December 31, Year 3 (immediately following the distribution to A)

Category	Class	Excluded / NII	Tax Rate	Amount
Ordinary Income				
	Interest (post-2012)	NII	43.4%	$0
	Interest & Other Income (section 951 inclusion)	Excluded	39.6%	$0
	Qualified Dividends	Excluded	20.0%	$1,000*
Capital Gain				
	Long-Term	NII	23.8%	$0
	Long-Term	Excluded	20.0%	$1,100*
Other Income		NII	3.8%	$900
Other Income		Excluded	0.0%	$3,100

* All of which will carry out NII to A when distributed in the future

A's net investment income in Year 3 will include $5,000 of other ordinary income and $1,000 of qualified dividend income.

Example 4. (i) Same facts as in *Example 2*, except that the NIMCRUT distributes $7,000 to A in Year 2. This distribution consists of the section 951 inclusion and the accumulated qualified dividends.

(ii) In Year 2, the NIMCRUT will report $5,000 of ordinary income and $2,000 of qualified dividends to A. Both amounts will constitute excluded income to A. In this case, A does not have to adjust MAGI because the section 951 inclusion is treated in the same way as any other type of excluded income within the Ordinary Income Category.

Year 2 ending Category and Class Balances (immediately following the distribution to A)

Category	Class	Excluded / NII	Tax Rate	Amount
Ordinary Income				
	Interest and Other Income (including section 951 Inclusions)	Excluded	39.6%	$0
	Qualified Dividends	Excluded	20.0%	$0
Capital Gain				
	Long-Term	NII	23.8%	$0
	Long-Term	Excluded	20.0%	$180,000
Other Income				None

(iii) When the CFC distributes $4,000 to the NIMCRUT in Year 3, §1.1411-3(d)(2)(ii)(B)(*1*) requires the NIMCRUT to allocate that $4,000 to the NIMCRUT's accumulated balance of long-term

capital gains recognized by the NIMCRUT prior to December 31, 2012, so that the first $4,000 of the NIMCRUT's long-term capital gains distributed to A in the future will carry out NII to A.

Category and Class Balances immediately before the Year 3 distribution to A

Category	Class	Excluded / NII	Tax Rate	Amount
Ordinary Income				
	Interest and Other Income (including section 951 Inclusions)	Excluded	39.6%	$0
	Qualified Dividends	Excluded	20.0%	$0
Capital Gain				
	Long-Term	Excluded	20.0%	$180,000*
Other Income				None

* Of which $4,000 will carry out NII to A when distributed in the future

When the NIMCRUT distributes the $4,000 to A in the future, the NIMCRUT will report $4,000 of long-term capital gain to

A that also constitutes net investment income. No MAGI adjustments associated with that distribution will be required by A.

Year 3 ending Category and Class Balances (immediately following the distribution to A)

Category	Class	Excluded / NII	Tax Rate	Amount
Ordinary Income				
	Interest and Other Income (including section 951 Inclusions)	Excluded	39.6%	$0
	Qualified Dividends	Excluded	20.0%	$0
Capital Gain				
	Long-Term	Excluded	20.0%	$176,000
Other Income				None

Example 5. (i) Same facts as in *Example 4*, except that the NIMCRUT's entire balance of accumulated long-term capital gain was received after 2012 and thus is ANII.

(ii) When the CFC distributes $4,000 to the NIMCRUT in Year 3, §1.1411-3(d)(2)(ii)(B)(*1*) requires the NIMCRUT to allocate that $4,000 to excluded income within the Ordinary Income or Capi-

tal Gain Categories. In this case, the NIMCRUT does not have any excluded income remaining within those categories. As a result, §1.1411-3(d)(2)(ii)(B)(*2*) requires the excess portion of the CFC distribution not allocable to excluded income in the Ordinary Income or Capital Gain Categories ($4,000 in this case) to be allocated to the Other Income Category.

Category and Class Balances immediately before the Year 3 distribution to A

Category	Class	Excluded / NII	Tax Rate	Amount
Ordinary Income				
	Interest and Other Income (including section 951 Inclusions)	Excluded	39.6%	$0
	Qualified Dividends	Excluded	20.0%	$0
Capital Gain				
	Long-Term	NII	23.8%	$180,000
	Long-Term	Excluded	20.0%	$0
Other Income		NII	3.8%	$4,000

When the NIMCRUT distributes the $4,000 to A, the NIM-CRUT will report $4,000 of long-term capital gains to A that also

constitute net investment income. No MAGI adjustments associated with the distribution are required by A.

Year 3 ending Category and Class Balances (immediately following the distribution to A)

Category	Class	Excluded / NII	Tax Rate	Amount
Ordinary Income				
	Interest and Other Income (including section 951 Inclusions)	Excluded	39.6%	$0
	Qualified Dividends	Excluded	20.0%	$0
Capital Gain				
	Long-Term	NII	23.8%	$176,000
	Long-Term	Excluded	20.0%	$0
Other Income		NII	3.8%	$4,000

After the NIMCRUT distributes all income within the Ordinary and Capital Gain categories, the NIMCRUT will distribute the $4,000 of Other Income to A. Such income will have a zero percent tax rate for chapter 1 purposes but will constitute net investment income. In this case, §1.1411-3(d)(2)(ii)(B)(*2*) provides that the future distribution will be considered a distribution of net investment income from a trust within the meaning of §1.1411-10(c)(4). As a result, §1.1411-10(e) requires A to increase MAGI for the year of that distribution.

(3) *Elective simplified method.*—(i) *Treatment of annuity or unitrust distributions.*—If a CRT makes a valid election under this paragraph (d)(3), the rules of paragraph (d)(2) of this section shall not apply, and the net investment income of the beneficiary attributable

to the beneficiary's annuity or unitrust distribution from the CRT shall include an amount equal to the lesser of—

(A) The beneficiary's share of the total amount of the distributions for that year; or

(B) The beneficiary's same share of the accumulated net investment income (as defined in paragraph (d)(1)(iii) of this section) of the CRT.

(ii) *Properly allocable deductions in excess of gross income.*—In computing the amount described in paragraph (d)(3)(i)(B) of this section, notwithstanding §1.1411-4(f)(1)(ii) (limitations on deductions in excess of income), if in a taxable year a CRT's properly allocable deductions described in section 1411(c)(1)(B) and the regulations thereunder exceed the gross investment income and net gain de-

Reg. §1.1411-3(d)(3)(ii)

scribed in section 1411(c)(1)(A) and the regulations thereunder, then such excess deductions shall reduce the amount described in paragraph (d)(3)(i)(B) of this section for that taxable year and, to the extent of any remaining excess deductions, for subsequent taxable years of the CRT.

(iii) *Procedural requirements for making election.*—In the case of a CRT established after December 31, 2012, a CRT wanting to make the election under paragraph (d)(3) of this section must do so on its income tax return for the taxable year in which the CRT is established. In the case of a CRT established before January 1, 2013, the CRT wanting to make the election under paragraph (d)(3) of this section must do so on the return for its first taxable year beginning on or after January 1, 2013. Once made, the election is irrevocable. In lieu of the relief provisions under §301.9100-3, the CRT may make the election on an amended return for that year only if the taxable year for which the election is made, and all taxable years that are affected by the election, for both the CRT and its beneficiaries, are not closed by the period of limitations on assessments under section 6501.

* * *

(f) *Effective/applicability date.*—This section applies to taxable years beginning after December 31, 2013, except that paragraphs (d)(1), (d)(2)(i), *Example 1* of (d)(2)(iii), and (d)(3) of this section applies to taxable years of CRTs that begin after December 31, 2012. However, taxpayers may apply this section to taxable years beginning after December 31, 2012, in accordance with §1.1411-1(f).

* * *

☐ Par 4. Section 1.1411-4 is amended by revising paragraphs (d)(4)(iii), (e)(3), and (g)(10) through (13) to read as follows:

§1.1411-4. Definition of net investment income.

* * *

(d) * * *

(4) * * *

(iii) *Adjustment for capital loss carryforwards for previously excluded income.*—(A) *General rule.*—For purposes of calculating net gain in paragraph (d) of this section (and any allowable loss described in paragraph (f)(4) of this section, if applicable), capital losses are reduced by the lesser of—

(1) The amount of capital loss taken into account in the current year by reason of section 1212(b)(1); or

(2) The amount of net capital loss excluded from net investment income in the preceding year by reason of paragraph (d)(4) of this section.

(B) *Example.*—The following example illustrates the provisions of this paragraph (d)(4)(iii). For purposes of this example, assume the taxpayer is a United States citizen, uses a calendar taxable year, and Year 1 and all subsequent years are taxable years in which section 1411 is in effect:

Example. (i)(A) In Year 1, A, an unmarried individual, disposes of 100 shares of publicly traded stock for a short-term capital gain of $4,000. In addition, A disposes of a partnership interest and recognizes a long-term capital loss of $19,000. Assume that the entire amount of $19,000 loss is not allowed against net investment income pursuant to section 1411(c)(4)(B), §1.1411-7, and paragraph (d)(4)(ii) of this section. A has no capital loss carryovers from the year preceding Year 1.

(B) For purposes of chapter 1, A reports net capital loss of $15,000, of which $3,000 is allowed as a deduction in computing taxable income under section 1211(b)(1), and the remaining $12,000 is carried forward into Year 2 as a long-term capital loss pursuant to section 1212(b)(1).

(C) For purposes of calculating net investment income, A reports $4,000 of net gain. The $19,000 loss taken into account in computing A's taxable income in Year 1 is not taken into account in computing net gain. Therefore, there are no losses in excess of gains in Year 1 for which a deduction is allowed under paragraph (f)(4) of this section.

(ii)(A) In Year 2, A has no capital gain or loss transactions.

(B) For purposes of chapter 1, A reports net capital loss of $12,000, of which $3,000 is allowed as a deduction in computing taxable income under section 1211(b)(1), and the remaining $9,000 is carried forward into Year 3 as a long-term capital loss pursuant to section 1212(b)(1).

(C) For purposes of calculating net investment income, A must adjust the $12,000 capital loss carryover from Year 1 pursuant to paragraph (d)(4)(iii) of this section. The amount of the adjustment is the lesser of—

(1) The amount of capital loss taken into account in the current year by reason of section 1212(b)(1) ($12,000), or

(2) The amount of net capital loss excluded from net investment income in Year 1 by reason of paragraph (d)(4) of this section ($19,000). The $19,000 loss was the amount disallowed by reason of paragraph (d)(4)(ii) of this section, and there were no other adjustments under paragraphs (d)(4)(i) or (d)(4)(iii) of this section in Year 1.

(D) The amount of capital loss carryover that is taken into account by A in computing net investment income in Year 2 is $0 ($12,000 carryover amount less the adjustment of $12,000). Accordingly, when calculating net investment income, A has no losses in excess of gains, and no deduction is available to A under paragraph (f)(4) of this section.

(iii)(A) In Year 3, A recognizes a $5,000 short-term capital gain from the disposition of property described in paragraph (d)(4)(i) of this section, and a $1,000 short-term capital loss from the disposition of publicly traded stock.

(B) For purposes of chapter 1, A reports net capital loss carryover from Year 2 of $9,000. In addition, the short-term capital gain of $5,000 and $1,000 short-term capital loss net to produce $4,000 of short-term capital gain. A reports a net capital loss of $5,000 ($5,000 - $1,000 - $9,000), of which $3,000 is allowed as a deduction in computing taxable income under section 1211(b)(1), and the remaining $2,000 is carried forward into Year 4 as a long-term capital loss pursuant to section 1212(b)(1).

(C) For purposes of calculating net investment income, A may exclude the $5,000 capital gain from the calculation of net gain pursuant to paragraph (d)(4)(i) of this section. In addition, A must adjust the $9,000 capital loss carryover from Year 2 pursuant to paragraph (d)(4)(iii) of this section. The amount of the adjustment is the lesser of—

(1) The amount of capital loss taken into account in the current year by reason of section 1212(b)(1) ($9,000); or

(2) The amount of net capital loss excluded from net investment income in Year 2 by reason of paragraph (d)(4) of this section ($12,000). The $12,000 loss was the amount disallowed by reason of paragraph (d)(4)(iii) of this section, and there were no other adjustments under paragraphs (d)(4)(i) or (d)(4)(ii) of this section in Year 2.

(D) The amount of capital loss carryover that is taken into account by A in computing net investment income in Year 3 is $0 ($9,000 carryover amount less the adjustment of $9,000). Accordingly, when calculating net investment income, A excludes $5,000 of gain under paragraph (d)(4)(i) of this section and the $9,000 capital loss carryover under paragraph (d)(4)(iii) of this section. The amount of losses taken into account for purposes of computing net gain is $1,000 (attributable to the $1,000 short-term capital loss from the disposition of publicly traded stock). Pursuant to paragraph (f)(4) of this section, A is entitled to a deduction of $1,000 because the $1,000 capital loss exceeds the gains, and the loss is less than the amount of allowable loss for chapter 1 purposes ($3,000).

(iv)(A) In Year 4, A recognizes a $8,000 long-term capital loss on the disposition of raw land to which paragraph (d)(4)(i) of this section does not apply.

(B) For purposes of chapter 1, A reports net capital loss carryover from Year 3 of $2,000. The $8,000 long-term capital loss is added to the $2,000 capital loss carryforward to produce a $10,000 long-term capital loss, of which $3,000 is allowed as a deduction in computing taxable income under section 1211(b)(1), and the remaining $7,000 is carried forward into Year 5 as a long-term capital loss pursuant to section 1212(b)(1).

(C) For purposes of calculating net investment income, A takes into account the $8,000 capital loss from the sale of the land. In addition, A must adjust the $2,000 capital loss carryover from Year 3 pursuant to paragraph (d)(4)(iii) of this section. The amount of the adjustment is the lesser of—

(1) The amount of capital loss taken into account in the current year by reason of section 1212(b)(1) ($2,000); or

(2) The amount of net capital loss excluded from net investment income in Year 3 by reason of paragraph (d)(4) of this section ($4,000). The $4,000 loss is the sum of the $5,000 gain disallowed by reason of paragraph (d)(4)(i) of this section and the $9,000 loss disallowed by reason of paragraph (d)(4)(iii) of this section, and there were no other adjustments under paragraph (d)(4)(ii) of this section in Year 3.

(D) The amount of capital loss carryover that is taken into account by A in computing net investment income in Year 3 is $0 ($2,000 carryover amount less the adjustment of $2,000). The amount of losses taken into account for purposes of computing net gain is $8,000 (attributable to the $8,000 capital loss from the disposition of raw land). Pursuant to paragraph (f)(4) of this section, A is entitled to a deduction of $3,000 because the $8,000 capital loss exceeds the gains, and only $3,000 of the loss is allowable for chapter 1 purposes under section 1211(b)(1).

(v)(A) In Year 5, A has no capital gain or loss transactions.

(B) For purposes of chapter 1, A reports net capital loss carryover from Year 4 of $7,000: $3,000 is allowed as a deduction in computing taxable income under section 1211(b)(1), and the remaining $4,000 is carried forward into Year 6 as a long-term capital loss pursuant to section 1212(b)(1).

(C) For purposes of calculating net investment income, A must adjust the $7,000 capital loss carryover from Year 4 pursuant to paragraph (d)(4)(iii) of this section. The amount of the adjustment is the lesser of—

(1) The amount of capital loss taken into account in the current year by reason of section 1212(b)(1) ($7,000); or

(2) The amount of net capital loss excluded from net investment income in Year 4 by reason of paragraph (d)(4) of this section ($2,000). The $2,000 loss was the amount disallowed by reason of paragraph (d)(4)(iii) of this section, and there were no other adjustments under paragraphs (d)(4)(i) or (d)(4)(ii) of this section in Year 4.

(D) The amount of capital loss carryover that is taken into account by A in computing net investment income in Year 5 is $5,000 ($7,000 carryover amount less the adjustment of $2,000). The amount of losses taken into account for purposes of computing net gain is $5,000 carried over from Year 4. Pursuant to paragraph (f)(4) of this section, A is entitled to a deduction of $3,000 because the $5,000 capital loss exceeds the gains, and only $3,000 of the loss is allowable for chapter 1 purposes under section 1211(b)(1).

(vi)(A) In Year 6, A has no capital gain or loss transactions.

(B) For purposes of chapter 1, A reports net capital loss carryover from Year 5 of $4,000: $3,000 is allowed as a deduction in computing taxable income under section 1211(b)(1), and the remaining $1,000 is carried forward into Year 7 as a long-term capital loss pursuant to section 1212(b)(1).

(C) For purposes of calculating net investment income, A must adjust the $4,000 capital loss carryover from Year 5 pursuant to paragraph (d)(4)(iii) of this section. The amount of the adjustment is the lesser of—

(1) The amount of capital loss taken into account in the current year by reason of section 1212(b)(1) ($4,000); or

(2) The amount of net capital loss excluded from net investment income in Year 5 by reason of paragraph (d)(4) of this section ($2,000). The $2,000 loss was the amount disallowed by reason of paragraph (d)(4)(iii) of this section, and there were no other adjustments under paragraphs (d)(4)(i) or (d)(4)(ii) of this section in Year 5.

(D) The amount of capital loss carryover that is taken into account by A in computing net investment income in Year 6 is $2,000 ($4,000 carryover amount less the adjustment of $2,000). The amount of losses taken into account for purposes of computing net gain is $2,000 carried over from Year 5. Pursuant to paragraph (f)(4) of this section, A is entitled to a deduction of $2,000 because the $2,000 capital loss exceeds the gains, and the loss is less than the amount of allowable loss for chapter 1 purposes ($3,000). As a result, the entire $8,000 loss from the raw land has been taken into account in computing A's net investment income ($3,000 in Years 4 and 5, and $2,000 in Year 6).

(vii)(A) In Year 7, A has no capital gain or loss transactions.

(B) For purposes of chapter 1, A reports net capital loss carryover from Year 6 of $1,000. The entire $1,000 is allowed as a deduction in computing taxable income under section 1211(b)(1). A has no capital losses to carry over to Year 8.

(C) For purposes of calculating net investment income, A must adjust the $1,000 capital loss carryover from Year 6 pursuant to paragraph (d)(4)(iii) of this section. The amount of the adjustment is the lesser of—

(1) The amount of capital loss taken into account in the current year by reason of section 1212(b)(1) ($1,000); or

(2) The amount of net capital loss excluded from net investment income in Year 6 by reason of paragraph (d)(4) of this section ($2,000). The $2,000 loss was the amount disallowed by reason of paragraph (d)(4)(iii) of this section, and there were no other adjustments under paragraphs (d)(4)(i) or (d)(4)(ii) of this section in Year 6.

(D) The amount of capital loss carryover that is taken into account by A in computing net investment income in Year 6 is $0 ($1,000 carryover amount less the adjustment of $1,000). Therefore, when calculating net investment income, A has no losses in excess of gains, and no deduction is available to A under paragraph (f)(4) of this section.

(e) * * *

(3) *Treatment of income from common trust funds.*—If a taxpayer is a participant in a common trust fund and the taxpayer includes under section 584 any item of income, deduction, gain, or loss, then section 1411 and the regulations thereunder apply to that item to the same extent as if the participant had made directly the investments of the common trust fund to which the items are attributable.

* * *

(g) * * *

(10) *Treatment of section 707(c) guaranteed payments.*—Net investment income does not include section 707(c) payments received for services. Except to the extent provided in paragraph (g)(11)(iii)(A) of this section, section 707(c) payments received for the use of capital are net investment income within the meaning of section 1411(c)(1)(A)(i) and paragraph (a)(1)(i) of this section.

(11) *Treatment of section 736 payments.*—(i) *In general.*—The treatment of payments received by a retiring partner or a deceased partner's successor in interest described in section 736 is determined under the rules of this paragraph (g)(11). Section 736 payments are not distributions from a plan or arrangement described in section 1411(c)(5) and § 1.1411-8. To the extent that any portion of a section 736 payment is taken into account in computing a taxpayer's net earnings from self-employment (within the meaning of § 1.1411-9), then such amount is not taken into account in computing net investment income by reason of section 1411(c)(6) and § 1.1411-9.

(ii) *Treatment of section 736(a)(1) payments.*—(A) *General rule.*—In the case of a payment described in section 736(a)(1) as a distributive share of partnership income, the items of income, gain, loss, and deduction attributable to such distributive share are taken into account in computing net investment income in section 1411(c) in a manner consistent with the item's character and treatment for chapter 1 purposes. See § 1.469-2(e)(2)(iii) for rules concerning the item's character and treatment for chapter 1.

(B) *Examples.*—The following examples illustrate the provisions of this paragraph (g)(11)(ii). For purposes of these examples, assume the taxpayer is a United States citizen, uses a calendar taxable year, and Year 1 and all subsequent years are taxable years in which section 1411 is in effect:

Example 1. Distributive share for unrealized receivables. (i) A retires from PRS, a business entity classified as a partnership for Federal Income tax purposes for which capital is not a material income producing factor. A is entitled, pursuant to the partnership agreement, to receive 10% of PRS's net income for 60 months commencing immediately following A's retirement in exchange for A's fair market value share of PRS's unrealized receivables. A will provide no services to PRS for the 60-month period following A's retirement. Prior to A's retirement, A materially participated in PRS's trade or business within the meaning of § 1.469-5T. Prior to A's retirement, A materially participated as a general partner in PRS's trade or business within the meaning of § 1.469-5T. For purposes of section 1411, PRS was not a trade or business described in section 1411(c)(2)(A) prior to A's retirement.

(ii) In Year 3, pursuant to the partnership agreement, A received a cash payment of $20,000. A's distributive share of PRS income in Year 3 included $70,000 of gross income from operations and $50,000 of deductions from operations. PRS's status as a passive or nonpassive activity is determined under § 1.469-2(e)(2)(iii) at the time the liquidation of A's partnership interest commenced, and remains fixed for the duration of A's liquidation payments. Therefore, PRS is a nonpassive activity with respect to A in Year 3 pursuant to § 1.469-2(e)(2)(iii). As a result, the gross income is not attributable to a trade or business described in section 1411(c)(2)(A) or § 1.1411-5(a)(1). Accordingly, A's distributive share of $70,000 of gross income and $50,000 of associated deductions are not includable in A's net investment income in Year 3.

(iii) If PRS's distributive share of operational income and deductions was attributable to a trade or business described in section 1411(c)(2)(B) or § 1.1411-5(a)(2), the $70,000 of gross income amounts would be included in A's net investment income under section 1411(c)(1)(A)(ii) and paragraph (c) of this section and the $50,000 of associated deductions would be properly allocable to such income under section 1411(c)(1)(B) and § 1.1411-4(f)(2)(ii).

Example 2. Excess distributive share payments. Assume the same facts as in *Example 1* except that PRS provides A an additional 2% of PRS's net income for 48 months commencing immediately following A's retirement as an incentive for A to retire earlier than planned. In the case of the additional 2% distributive share, the section 736(a) income characterization rule in § 1.469-2(e)(2)(iii) does not apply because the payment exceeds the value of PRS's unrealized receivables (which was established to equal 10% of PRS's income for 60 months in *Example 1*). As a result, A must determine whether PRS is a trade or business described in section 1411(c)(2)(A) and § 1.1411-5(a)(1) in Year 3 in order to determine whether the distributive share of operating income and deductions is includable in net investment income. If PRS is engaged in a trade or business described in section 1411(c)(2)(A) and §1.1411-5(a)(1) with respect to A in Year 3, then the distributive share will be taken into account in computing A's net investment income.

(iii) *Treatment of section 736(a)(2) payments.*—(A) *Payments for unrealized receivables and goodwill.*—In the case of a payment described in section 736(a)(2), the portion (if any) of the payment that is allocable to the unrealized receivables (within the meaning of section 751(c)) and goodwill of the partnership (as described and calculated in §1.469-2(e)(2)(iii)(B)) is included in net investment income under section 1411(c)(1)(A)(iii) and paragraphs (a)(1)(iii) and (d) of this section as gain from the disposition of a partnership interest.

(B) *Payments not for unrealized receivables or goodwill.*—In the case of a section 736(a)(2) payment not described in paragraph (g)(11)(iii)(A) of this section, the payment is characterized as a payment for services or as the payment of interest in a manner consistent with the payment's characterization under §1.469-2(e)(2)(ii). See paragraph (g)(9) of this section.

(iv) *Treatment of section 736(b) payments.*—Gain or loss attributable to section 736(b) payments is included in net investment income under section 1411(c)(1)(A)(iii) and paragraphs (a)(1)(iii) and (d) of this section as gain or loss from the disposition of a partnership interest. A taxpayer who elects under §1.736-1(b)(6) must apply the principles that are applied to installment sales in §1.1411-7(d).

(v) *Application of section 1411(c)(4) to section 736 payments.*—Section 1411(c)(4) and §1.1411-7 apply to gain or loss attributable to section 736 payments described in paragraphs (g)(11)(iii)(A) and (g)(11)(iv) of this section. In the case of section 736 payments that are received in more than one taxable year, the rules for calculating gain or loss under section 1411(c)(4) and §1.1411-7 are applied at the time the liquidation of the partner's interest commenced. The principles that are applied to installment sales in §1.1411-7(d) also apply for purposes of this section.

(12) *Income and deductions from certain notional principal contracts.*—(i) *In general.*—Net income for a taxable year taken into account by a taxpayer under §1.446-3(d) that is attributable to a notional principal contract described in paragraph (g)(12)(ii) of this section is net investment income described in section 1411(c)(1)(A) and paragraph (a)(1) of this section. A net deduction for a taxable year taken into account by a taxpayer under §1.446-3(d) that is attributable to a notional principal contract described in paragraph (g)(12)(ii) of this section is a properly allocable deduction described in section 1411(c)(1)(B) and paragraph (f) of this section.

(ii) *Notional principal contracts.*—For purposes of paragraph (g)(12)(i) of this section, a notional principal contract is any notional principal contract described in §1.446-3(c)(1) that is referenced to property (including an index) that produces (or would produce if the property were to produce income) interest, dividends, royalties, or rents if the property were held directly by the taxpayer. For purposes of the preceding sentence, an interest rate swap, cap, or floor is treated as a notional principal contract that is referenced to a debt instrument.

(13) *Treatment of income or loss from REMIC residual interests.*—The daily portion of taxable income determined under section 860C(a)(2) taken into account in determining tax under chapter 1 by the holder of a residual interest in a REMIC and any inducement fee included in income under §1.446-6(a) are treated as net investment income under section 1411(c)(1)(A) and paragraph (a)(1) of this section. The daily portion of net loss determined under section 860C(a)(2) taken into account in determining tax under Chapter 1 by the holder of a residual interest in a REMIC is a properly allocable deduction described in section 1411(c)(1)(B) and paragraph (f) of this section.

* * *

Net Investment Income Tax: Guidance Under Section 1411

Net Investment Income Tax: Guidance Under Section 1411.—Reg. §1.1411-7, providing guidance on the computation of net investment income, is proposed (published in the Federal Register on December 2, 2013) (REG-130843-13) (corrected February 24,2014).

☐ Par. 5. Section 1.1411-7 is added to read as follows:

§1.1411-7. Exception for dispositions of certain active interests in partnerships and S corporations.—(a) *In general.*—(1) *General application.*—In the case of a transferor that disposes of an interest in a partnership or S corporation described in paragraph (a)(3) of this section (transferor), the gain or loss from the disposition recognized under chapter 1 that is taken into account under §1.1411-4(a)(1)(iii) shall be calculated in accordance with this section. The calculation in paragraph (b) of this section reflects the net gain or net loss that the transferor would take into account if the partnership or S corporation sold all of its Section 1411 Property (as defined in paragraph (a)(2)(iv) of this section) for fair market value immediately before the disposition of such interest. In certain instances, transferors may qualify to use an alternative calculation described in paragraph (c) of this section in lieu of the calculation described in paragraph (b) of this section. Paragraph (d) of this section contains additional rules for Section 1411(c)(4) Dispositions (as defined in paragraph (a)(2)(ii) of this section) in deferred recognition transactions. Paragraph (f) of this section provides rules for adjusting the amount of gain or loss computed under this paragraph (a)(1) for transferors subject to basis adjustments required by §1.1411-10(d). Paragraph (g) of this section provides rules for information disclosures by a partnership or S corporation to transferors and for information reporting by individuals, trusts, and estates. If a transferor disposes of an interest in a partnership or S corporation not described in paragraph (a)(3) of this section, then this section does not apply and the full amount of the gain or loss, as computed under chapter 1 and adjusted by §1.1411-10(d) (if applicable), is taken into account in computing the transferor's net investment income.

(2) *Definitions.*—For purposes of this section—

(i) The term *Passthrough Entity* means an entity taxed as a partnership or an S corporation. For purposes of this section, a reference to an interest in any S corporation shall mean a reference to stock in such S corporation.

(ii) The term *Section 1411(c)(4) Disposition* means a disposition of an interest in a Passthrough Entity described in paragraph (a)(3) of this section.

(iii) The term *Section 1411 Holding Period* means the year of disposition and the transferor's two taxable years preceding the disposition or the time period the transferor held the interest, whichever is less; provided, however, that for purposes of applying this paragraph (a)(2)(iii), the transferor will—

(A) Include the period that a previous owner or owners held the interest transferred if the transferor acquired its interest from another Passthrough Entity in a nonrecognition transaction during the year of disposition or the prior two taxable years;

(B) Include the period that the transferor held an interest in a Subsidiary Passthrough Entity if the transferor transferred that interest to a Passthrough Entity in a nonrecognition transaction during the year of disposition or the prior two taxable years; and

(C) Include the period that a previous owner or owners held the interest transferred if the transferor acquired its interest by gift.

(iv) The term *Section 1411 Property* means property owned by or held through the Passthrough Entity that, if disposed of by the entity, would result in net gain or loss allocable to the transferor of a type that is includable in determining net investment income of the transferor under §1.1411-4(a)(1)(iii).

(v) The term *Subsidiary Passthrough Entity* means an interest in a Passthrough Entity owned, directly or indirectly, by another Passthrough Entity.

(3) *Section 1411(c)(4) Dispositions.*—(i) *Transfers by individuals, estates, and trusts.*—The disposition by a transferor of an interest in a Passthrough Entity is a Section 1411(c)(4) Disposition only if—

(A) The Passthrough Entity is engaged in one or more trades or businesses (within the meaning of section 162), or owns an interest (directly or indirectly) in a Subsidiary Passthrough Entity that is engaged in one or more trades or businesses (within the meaning of section 162), that is not described in §1.1411-5(a)(2) (trading in financial instruments or commodities); and

(B) One or more of the trades or businesses of the Passthrough Entity described in paragraph (a)(3)(i)(A) of this section is not a §1.1411-5(a)(1) (passive activity) trade or business of the transferor.

(ii) *Transfers by Passthrough Entities.*—Where a Passthrough Entity (the "holder") disposes of an interest in a Subsidiary Passthrough Entity, that disposition qualifies as a Section 1411(c)(4) Disposition with respect to a partner or shareholder of the Passthrough Entity if the partner or shareholder would satisfy the requirements of paragraph (a)(3)(i) of this section if it held the interest in the Subsidiary Passthrough Entity directly. For this purpose, the partner or shareholder shall be treated as owning a proportionate share of any Subsidiary Passthrough Entity in which the partner or shareholder owns an indirect interest through one or more tiers of Passthrough Entities.

(4) *Special rules.*—(i) *Certain liquidations.*—If a fully taxable disposition of all of the Passthrough Entity's assets is followed by the complete liquidation of the Passthrough Entity as part of a single plan, then the disposition will be treated as an asset sale for purposes of section 1411, and no additional gain or loss will be included in net investment income under §1.1411-4(a)(1)(iii) on the subsequent liquidation of the Passthrough Entity by any transferor who would have satisfied paragraph (a)(3) of this section prior to the sale. A sale of stock in an S corporation with respect to which an election under section 336(e) or section 338(h)(10) is made shall be treated as a fully taxable disposition of the Passthrough Entity's assets followed by the liquidation of the Passthrough Entity for purposes of this paragraph (a)(4)(i).

(ii) *Excluded gain or loss.*—The difference between the amount of gain or loss taken into account in computing taxable income for purposes of chapter 1 and the amount of gain or loss taken into account after the application of this section shall constitute excluded income or excluded loss, as applicable, for purposes of §1.1411-4(d)(4)(ii).

(iii) *Rules applicable to S corporation shareholders.*—(A) *Certain S corporation dispositions.*—If the transfer of an interest in an S corporation causes the S election to terminate on the day of the transfer, then the corporation shall continue to be treated as an S corporation for purposes of applying the rules of this section to the transferor notwithstanding that §1.1362-3(a) treats the day of the transfer as the first day of the corporation's C corporation short year (as defined therein).

(B) *S corporations subject to section 1374.*—For purposes of the calculation under paragraph (b) of this section, the amount of gain or loss allocated to the transferor is determined under section 1366(a), and the allocation does not take into account any reduction in the transferor's pro rata share of gains under section 1366(f)(2) resulting from the hypothetical imposition of tax under section 1374 as a result of the deemed sale.

(C) *Treatment of Qualified Subchapter S Trusts (QSSTs).*—In the case of a disposition of S corporation stock by a QSST, the rules of this section are applied by treating the QSST as the owner of the S corporation stock.

(b) *Calculation.*—(1) *In general.*—A transfer of an interest in a Passthrough Entity who disposes of that interest in a Section 1411(c)(4) Disposition may use the simplified calculation in paragraph (c) of this section if it meets the eligibility requirements set forth in paragraph (c)(2) of this section. Any other transferor who disposes of an interest in a Passthrough Entity in a Section 1411(c)(4) Disposition must include gain or loss under §1.1411-4(a)(1)(iii) determined in accordance with this paragraph (b).

(i) *Gain on disposition of interest.*—If the transferor recognized a gain from the disposition, the amount of the net gain included in §1.1411-4(a)(1)(iii) is the lesser of—

(A) the transferor's gain on the disposition of the interest in the Passthrough Entity as determined in accordance with chapter 1; or

(B) the transferor's allocable share of the chapter 1 net gain from a deemed sale of the Passthrough Entity's Section 1411 Property as determined using the principles of §1.469-2T(e)(3) (allocation of gain or loss to activities of the Passthrough Entity) where the net gain is the sum of the amounts of net gain and net loss allocable to the transferor as determined under §§1.469-2T(e)(3)(ii)(B)(1)(i) and 1.469-2T(e)(3)(ii)(B)(2)(i) that would constitute income to the transferor for purposes of section 1411 if sold by the Passthrough Entity. The general rules of §1.469-2T(e)(3) apply in calculating the transferor's allocable share of the net gain under this section; however, the gain recharacterization rule of §1.469-2T(e)(3)(iii) shall not apply in any case. The calculation of net gain in this paragraph (b)(1)(i) shall not be less than zero.

(ii) *Loss on disposition of interest.*—If the transferor recognizes a loss from the disposition, the amount of the net loss included in §1.1411-4(a)(1)(iii) is the lesser of—

(A) The transferor's loss (expressed as a positive number) on the disposition of the interest in the Passthrough Entity as determined in accordance with chapter 1; or

(B) The transferor's allocable share of the chapter 1 net loss (expressed as a positive number) from the deemed sale of the entity's Section 1411 Property as determined in accordance with §1.469-2T(e)(3) (allocation of gain or loss to activities of the Passthrough Entity) where the net loss is the sum of the amounts of net gain and net loss allocable to the transferor as determined under §§1.469-2T(e)(3)(ii)(B)(1)(i) and 1.469-2T(e)(3)(ii)(B)(2)(i) that would constitute income or loss to the transferor for purposes of section 1411 if sold by the Passthrough Entity. The general rules of §1.469-2T(e)(3) apply in calculating the transferor's allocable share of the net gain under this section; however, the gain recharacterization rule of §1.469-2T(e)(3)(iii) shall not apply in any case. The calculation of net gain in this paragraph (b)(1)(ii) shall not be less than zero. For purposes of this paragraph (b)(1)(ii), the loss limitation provisions imposed by sections 704(d) and 1366(d) shall not apply.

(2) *Examples.*—The following examples illustrate the principles of paragraph (b)(1) of this section. For purposes of these examples, assume that the taxpayer is a United States citizen, uses a calendar taxable year, and Year 1 and all subsequent years are taxable years in which section 1411 is in effect:

Example 1. (i) *Facts.* A owns a one-half interest in P, a calendar year partnership. In Year 1, A sells its interest for $200,000. A's adjusted basis for the interest sold is $120,000. Thus, A recognizes $80,000 of gain from the sale (chapter 1 gain). P is engaged in three trade or business activities, X, Y, and Z, none of which are §1.1411-5(a)(2) (trading in financial instruments or commodities) trades or businesses. P also owns marketable securities. For Year 1, A materially participates in activity Z, thus it is not a §1.1411-5(a)(1) (passive activity) trade or business of A. A, however, does not materially participate in activities X and Y, so these activities are §1.1411-5(a)(1) trades or businesses of A. Because P is engaged in at least one trade or business and at least one of those trades or businesses is not passive to the transferor A, A determines its amount of §1.1411-4(a)(1)(iii) gain or loss from net investment income under §1.1411-7. Assume for purposes of this example, A is not eligible to compute its §1.1411-4(a)(1)(iii) gain or loss under the optional simplified reporting method discussed in paragraph (c) of this section. The fair market value and adjusted basis of the gross assets used in P's activities are as follows:

	Adjusted basis	Fair market value	Gain/Loss	A's Share Gain/Loss
X (Passive as to A)	$136,000	$96,000	($40,000)	($20,000)
Y (Passive as to A)	60,000	124,000	64,000	32,000
Z (Non-passive as to A)	40,000	160,000	120,000	60,000
Marketable securities	4,000	20,000	16,000	8,000
Total	240,000	400,000	160,000	80,000

(ii) *Analysis.* Under paragraph (b)(1) of this section, A must determine the portion of gain or loss from the sale of P's Section 1411 Property allocable to A. Under paragraph (b)(1)(ii) of this section, A's allocable share of gain from P's Section 1411 Property is $20,000 (($20,000) from X + $32,000 from Y + $8,000 from the marketable securities). Because the $20,000 allocable to A from a deemed sale of P's Section 1411 Property is less than A's $80,000 chapter 1 gain, A will include $20,000 under §1.1411-4(a)(1)(iii).

Example 2. Assume the same facts as *Example 1*, but A materially participates in activities Y and Z and does not materially participate in activity X. Under paragraph (b)(1)(i) of this section, A's allocable share of P's Section 1411 Property is ($12,000) (($20,000) from X + $8,000 from the marketable securities). Because A sold its interest for a chapter 1 gain, the amount allocable to A from a deemed sale of P's Section 1411 Property cannot be less than zero. Accordingly, A includes no gain or loss under §1.1411-4(a)(1)(iii).

(c) *Optional simplified reporting.*—(1) *In general.*—A transferor of an interest in a Passthrough Entity in a Section 1411(c)(4) Disposition may use the simplified reporting rules of paragraph (c)(4) of this section if it satisfies the eligibility requirements set forth in paragraph (c)(2) of this section and is not described in paragraph (c)(3) of this section. All other transferors of interests in Passthrough Entities in Section 1411(c)(4) Dispositions must use the calculation set forth in paragraph (b) of this section. Paragraph (d) of this section contains additional rules for Section 1411(c)(4) Dispositions in deferred recognition transactions.

(2) *Qualifications.*—Unless described in paragraph (c)(3) of this section, a transferor of an interest in a Passthrough Entity in a Section 1411(c)(4) Disposition may determine the amount of net gain or net loss that is taken into account under §1.1411-4(a)(1)(iii) in accordance with paragraph (c)(4) of this section if either or both of the requirements in paragraph (c)(2)(i) or (c)(2)(ii) of this section are satisfied:

(i) *Five percent threshold.*—The sum of separately stated income, gain, loss, and deduction items (with any separately stated loss and deduction items included as positive numbers) of a type the transferor would take into account in calculating net investment income (as defined in §1.1411-1(d)) that are allocated to the transferor in respect of the transferred interest is five percent or less of the sum of all separately stated items of income, gain, loss, and deduction (with any separately stated loss and deduction items included as positive numbers) allocated to the transferor in respect of the transferred interest during the Section 1411 Holding Period, and the total amount of chapter 1 gain or loss recognized by the transferor from the disposition of interests in the Passthrough Entity does not exceed $5 million (including gains or losses from multiple dispositions as part of a plan). All dispositions of interests in the Passthrough Entity that occur during the taxable year will be presumed to be part of a plan. In calculating the percentage described in the first sentence of this paragraph (c)(2)(i), if the transferor acquired the transferred interest in a transaction described in paragraph (a)(2)(iii)(A) or (a)(2)(iii)(C) of this section, then items of income, gain, loss, or deduction allocated to the transferor include any such items allocated to the transferor's predecessor (or predecessors) in interest during the Section 1411 Holding Period. If the transferor transferred an interest in a Subsidiary Passthrough Entity to the Passthrough Entity in a transaction described in paragraph (a)(2)(iii)(B) of this section, then items of income, gain, loss or deduction allocated to the transferor include any items allocated to the transferor during the Section 1411 Holding Period in respect of the interest in the Subsidiary Passthrough Entity.

(ii) *$250,000 gain or loss threshold.*—The total amount of chapter 1 gain or loss recognized by the transferor from the disposition of interests in the Passthrough Entity does not exceed $250,000 (including gains or losses from multiple dispositions as part of a plan). All dispositions of interests in the Passthrough Entity that occur during the taxable year will be presumed to be part of a plan.

(3) *Nonapplicability.*—A transferor is not eligible to use the simplified reporting method of paragraph (c)(4) of this section if any of the following conditions are met:

(i) The transferor has held directly the interest in the Passthrough Entity (or held the interest indirectly in the case of a Subsidiary Passthrough Entity) for less than twelve months preceding the Section 1411(c)(4) Disposition.

(ii) The transferor transferred, directly or indirectly, Section 1411 Property (other than cash or cash equivalents) to the Passthrough Entity (or a Subsidiary Passthrough Entity described in paragraph (a)(2)(v) of this section), or received a distribution of property (other than Section 1411 property) from the Passthrough Entity (or a Subsidiary Passthrough Entity described in paragraph (a)(2)(v) of this section), during the Section 1411 Holding Period as part of a plan that includes the transfer of the transferor's interest in the Passthrough Entity. A transferor who contributed, directly or indirectly, Section 1411 Property (other than cash or cash equivalents) within 120 days of the disposition of the interest in the Passthrough Entity is presumed to have made the contribution as part of a plan that includes the transfer of the interest in the Passthrough Entity.

(iii) The Passthrough Entity is a partnership, and the transferor transfers a partial interest that represents other than a proportionate share of all of the transferring partner's economic rights in the partnership.

(iv) The transferor knows or has reason to know that the percentage of the Passthrough Entity's gross assets that consist of Section 1411 Property has increased or decreased by 25 percentage points or more during the transferor's Section 1411 Holding Period due to contributions, distributions, or asset acquisitions or dispositions in taxable or nonrecognition transactions.

(v) The Passthrough Entity, which is the subject of the Section 1411(c)(4) Disposition, was taxable as a C corporation during the Section 1411 Holding Period, but during that period elects under section 1362 to be taxable as an S corporation under section 1361.

(4) *Optional simplified reporting calculation.*—The amount of net gain or loss from the transferor's Section 1411(c)(4) Disposition that is includable in § 1.1411-4(a)(1)(iii) is determined by multiplying the transferor's chapter 1 gain or loss on the disposition by a fraction, the numerator of which is the sum of income, gain, loss, and deduction items (with any separately stated loss and deduction items netted as negative numbers) of a type that are taken into account in the calculation of net investment income (as defined in § 1.1411-1(d)) that are allocated to the transferor during the Section 1411 Holding Period and the denominator of which is the sum of all items of income, gain, loss, and deduction allocated to the transferor during the Section 1411 Holding Period (with any separately stated loss and deduction items netted as negative numbers). If the quotient of the fraction is either greater than one or less than zero, then the fraction shall be one; provided, however, that if the numerator is a negative amount in connection with a computation of overall chapter 1 gain on the sale or a positive amount in connection with a computation of overall chapter 1 loss on the sale, then the fraction shall be zero. In calculating the fraction described in the first sentence of this paragraph (c)(4), if the transferor acquired the transferred interest in a transaction described in paragraph (a)(2)(iii)(A) or (C) of this section, then items

of income, gain, loss, or deduction allocated to the transferor include any such items allocated to the transferor's predecessor (or predecessors) in interest during the Section 1411 Holding Period. If the transferor transferred an interest in a Subsidiary Passthrough Entity to the Passthrough Entity in a transaction described in paragraph (a)(2)(iii)(B) of this section, then items of income, gain, loss or deduction allocated to the transferor include any items allocated to the transferor during the Section 1411 Holding Period in respect of the interest in the Subsidiary Passthrough Entity.

(5) *Examples.*—The following examples illustrate the principles of paragraph (c)(4) of this section. For purposes of these examples, assume that the taxpayer is a United States citizen, uses a calendar taxable year, and Year 1 and all subsequent years are taxable years in which section 1411 is in effect:

Example 1. Facts. A owns a one-half interest in P, a partnership. In Year 1, A sells the interest for $2,000,000. A's adjusted basis for the interest sold is $1,100,000. Because P is engaged in at least one trade or business and at least one of those trades or businesses is not passive to the transferor A, A determines its amount of § 1.1411-4(a)(1)(iii) gain or loss from net investment income under § 1.1411-7. None of the nonapplicability conditions set forth in section 1.1411-7(c)(3) apply. The aggregate net income from P's activities allocable to A for the year of disposition and the two preceding tax years are as follows:

	Aggregate Income/ (loss)
X (Non-Passive as to A)	$1,800,000
Y (Passive as to A)	(10,000)
Marketable securities	20,000

(ii) *Analysis.* During A's Section 1411 Holding Period, A was allocated $30,000 of gross items of a type taken into account in the calculation of net investment income ($10,000 of loss from activity Y and $20,000 of income from marketable securities). The total amount of A's allocated net items during the Section 1411 Holding Period equals $1,830,000 ($1,800,000 income from activity X, $10,000 loss from activity Y, and $20,000 income from marketable securities). Thus, less than 5% ($30,000/1,830,000) of A's allocations during the Section 1411 Holding Period are of a type that are taken into account in the computation of net investment income, and because A's chapter 1 gain recognized of $900,000 is less than $5,000,000, A qualifies under § 1.1411-7(c)(2)(ii) to use the optional simplified method.

(iii) Under paragraph (c)(4) of this section, A's percentage of Section 1411 Property is determined by dividing A's allocable shares of income and loss of a type that are taken into account in the calculation of net investment income (as defined in § 1.1411-1(d)) that are allocated to the transferor by the Passthrough Entity during the Section 1411 Holding Period is $10,000 ($10,000 loss from Y + $20,000 income from marketable securities) by $1,810,000, which is the sum of A's share of income and loss from all of P's activities ($1,800,000 + ($10,000) + 20,000). Thus, A's gain for purposes of § 1.1411-4(a)(1)(iii) is $4,972.32 ($900,000 chapter 1 gain multiplied by the fraction 10,000/1,810,000).

Example 2. Assume the same facts as *Example 1*, but A sells the interest in P for $900,000. Under paragraph (c)(4) of this section, A's percentage of Section 1411 Property is determined by dividing A's allocable share of income and loss of a type that are taken into account in the calculation of a net investment income (as defined in § 1.1411-1(d)) that are allocated to the transferor by the Passthrough Entity during the Section 1411 Holding Period is $10,000 ($10,000 loss from Y + $20,000 income from marketable securities) by $1,810,000, which is the sum of A's share of income and loss from all of P's activates ($1,800,000 + ($10,000) + 20,000). Because A's allocable share during the Section 1411 Holding Period of income and loss of a type that is taken into account in calculating net investment income was a positive amount, and A sells its interest for an overall chapter 1 loss, A uses a fraction of 0 to compute its net investment income under paragraph (c)(4) of this section. Thus, A has no gain or loss for purposes of § 1.1411-4(a)(1)(iii) ($200,000 chapter 1 loss multiplied by a fraction of 0).

(d) *Deferred recognition transactions.*—In the case of a disposition of a Passthrough Entity in an installment sale under section 453 (or in exchange for an annuity contract), the calculations described in paragraphs (b) and (c) of this section shall be applied in the year of the disposition as if the entire amount of gain recognized for chapter 1 is taken into account by the transferor in the year of the disposition. For this purpose, it is assumed that any contingencies potentially affecting consideration to the transferor that are reasonably expected to occur will occur, and in the case of annuities based on the life expectancy of one or more individuals, the present value of the annuity (using existing Federal tax valuation methods) is used to determine the estimated gain. If the calculations in this section result in a transferor excluding only a portion of the chapter 1 gain from net investment income, the amount of excluded gain will constitute an addition to basis for purposes of applying section 453 to determine the amount of gain is includable in net investment income under §1.1411-4(a)(1)(iii) as payments are received.

(e) *Disposition of tiered Passthrough Entities.*—[Reserved]

(f) *Adjustment to net gain or loss.*—In the case of a disposition of an interest in a Passthrough Entity where the transferor's basis in the interest for section 1411 purposes does not equal the transferor's basis for chapter 1 purposes due to basis adjustments required by §1.1411-10(d), then the following rules apply:

(i) If the transferor's basis for section 1411 purposes is higher than the transferor's basis for chapter 1 purposes, then the difference reduces the amount of gain or increases the amount of loss, as applicable, that is includable in net investment income under this section.

(ii) If the transferor's basis for section 1411 purposes is lower than the transferor's basis for chapter 1 purposes, then the difference increases the amount of gain or reduces the amount of loss, as applicable, that is includable in net investment income under this section.

(iii) The adjustments to gain or loss includable in net investment income under this paragraph (f) are taken into account by the transferor immediately following the calculation of gain or loss under paragraphs (a)(4)(i), (b)(1) or (c)(4) of this section, as applicable.

(g) *Information reporting.*—(1) *Information to be provided by passthrough entity to transferor.*—Where the Passthrough Entity knows, or has reason to know, that the transferor satisfies paragraph (a)(3)(i) of this section but does not satisfy paragraph (c) of this section, then the Passthrough Entity shall provide the transferor with information as to the transferor's allocable share of the net gain or loss from the deemed sale of the Passthrough Entity's Section 1411 Property as described in paragraph (b)(1) of this section and such other information as may be required by forms, instructions, or in other guidance to allow the transferor to compute gain or loss under this section.

(2) *Information reporting by transferors.*—Any transferor making a calculation under this section must attach a statement to the transferor's return for the year of disposition containing certain information as required by this paragraph (g)(2) and any other information required by guidance and applicable forms and instructions issued by the Commissioner to allow the transferor to compute gain or loss under this section. In the case of a disposition in a transaction described in paragraph (d) of this section, the information required by this paragraph (g)(2) shall apply in the year of the disposition, or in the first year the taxpayer is subject to section 1411 (determined without regard to the effect of this section), whichever is later. The statement must include—

(i) The name and taxpayer identification number of the Passthrough Entity of which the interest was transferred;

(ii) The amount of the transferor's gain or loss on the disposition of the interest for purposes of chapter 1;

(iii) The information provided by the Passthrough Entity to the transferor by reason of paragraph (g)(1) of this section; and

(iv) The amount of adjustment to gain or loss by reason of paragraph (f) of this section, if any.

(h) *Effective/applicability date.*—This section applies to taxable years beginning after December 31, 2013. However, taxpayers may apply this section to taxable years beginning after December 31, 2012 in accordance with §1.1411-1(f). [Reg. §1.1411-7.]

WITHHOLDING OF TAX ON NONRESIDENT ALIENS AND FOREIGN CORPORATIONS

Withholding: Nonresident Aliens: Form W-8: Electronic Transmission

Withholding: Nonresident Aliens: Form W-8: Electronic Transmission.—Amendments to Reg. §1.1441-1, relating to the establishment by withholding agents and payors of an electronic system for use by beneficial owners or payees in furnishing Form W-8 (Certificate of Foreign Status), are proposed (published in the Federal Register on October 14, 1997) (REG-107872-97).

☐ Par. 2. In §1.1441-1, paragraph (e)(4)(iv) is revised to read as follows:

§1.1441-1. Requirement for the deduction and withholding of tax on payments to foreign persons.

* * *

(e) * * *

(4) * * *

(iv) *Electronic transmission of information.*—(A) *In general.*—A withholding agent may establish a system for beneficial owners or payees to furnish electronically Forms W-8 (or such other form as the Internal Revenue Service may prescribe). The system also may enable the withholding agent to electronically transmit Forms W-8 to another person. The system must meet the requirements described in paragraph (e)(4)(iv)(B) of this section.

(B) *Requirements.*—(1) *In general.*—The electronic system must ensure that the information received is the information sent, and must document all occasions of user access that result in the submission, renewal, or modification of a Form W-8. In addition, the design and operation of the electronic system, including access procedures, must make it reasonably certain that the person accessing the system and furnishing Form W-8 is the person named in the form.

(2) *Same information as paper Form W-8.*—The electronic transmission must provide the withholding agent or payor with exactly the same information as the paper Form W-8.

(3) *Perjury statement and signature requirements.*—The electronic transmission must be signed by way of an electronic signature by the person whose name is on the Form W-8 and the signature must be under penalties of perjury in the manner described in this paragraph (e)(4)(iv)(B)(3).

(i) *Perjury statement.*—The perjury statement must contain the language that appears on the paper Form W-8. The electronic system must inform the person whose name is on the Form W-8 that the person must make the declaration contained in the perjury statement and that the declaration is made by signing the Form W-8. The instructions and the language of the perjury statement must immediately follow the person's certifying statements and immediately precede the person's electronic signature.

(ii) *Electronic signature.*—The act of the electronic signature must be effected by the person whose name is on the electronic Form W-8. The signature must also authenticate and verify the submission. For this purpose, the terms *authenticate* and *verify* have the same meanings as they do when applied to a written signature on a paper Form W-8. An electronic signature can be in any form that satisfies the foregoing requirements. The electronic signature must be the final entry in the person's Form W-8 submission.

(4) *Requests for electronic Forms W-8 data.*—Upon request by the Internal Revenue Service during an examination, the withholding agent must supply a hard copy of the electronic Form W-8 and a statement that, to the best of the withholding agent's knowledge, the electronic Form W-8 was filed by the person whose name is on the form. The hard copy of the electronic Form W-8 must provide exactly the same information as, but need not be a facsimile of, the paper Form W-8.

(C) *Special requirements for transmission of Forms W-8 by an intermediary.*—[Reserved].

* * *

Stock and Rights to Acquire Stock: Deemed Distributions

Stock and Rights to Acquire Stock: Deemed Distributions.—Amendments to Reg. §§1.1441-2 and 1.1441-3, regarding deemed distributions of stock and rights to acquire stock and resolving ambiguities concerning the amount and timing of deemed distributions that are or result from adjustments to rights to acquire stock, are proposed (published in the Federal Register on April 13, 2016) (REG-133673-15).

Par. 7. Section 1.1441-2 is amended by:

1. Revising paragraphs (d)(1) and (4).

2. Amending paragraph (f) by removing the language "(d)(4)" in the second sentence and adding in its place "(d)(1)(ii)(C)," and adding a fourth and fifth sentence.

The revisions and addition read as follows:

§1.1441-2. Amounts subject to withholding.

* * *

(d) * * *

(1) *General rule.*—(i) *Control or custody and knowledge.*—Except as provided in paragraph (d)(1)(ii) of this section, a withholding agent has an obligation to withhold under section 1441 only to the extent that, at any time between the date that the obligation to withhold would arise (but for the provisions of this paragraph (d)) and the due date (including extensions) for filing Form 1042 with respect to the calendar year in which the payment occurs, it has—

(A) Control over, or custody of, money or property owned by the recipient or beneficial owner from which to withhold an amount; and

(B) Knowledge of the facts that give rise to the payment.

(ii) *Exception not available.*—The exception from the obligation to withhold under paragraph (d)(1)(i) of this section does not apply if—

(A) The withholding agent is related (within the meaning of section 482) to the recipient or the beneficial owner of the payment;

(B) The payment is a distribution with respect to stock (including a deemed distribution (as defined in §1.305-1(d)(7)) of stock or a right to acquire stock); *see*, however, paragraph (d)(4) of this section, which provides a limited exception from the obligation to withhold on a deemed distribution;

(C) The amounts are described in §1.860G-3(b)(1) (regarding certain partnership allocations of REMIC net income with respect to a REMIC residual interest);

(D) The lack of control over or custody of money or property from which to withhold is part of a pre-arranged plan known to the withholding agent to avoid withholding under section 1441, 1442, or 1443; or

(E) The payment is a deemed payment (as defined in §1.861-3(a)(6)); *see*, however, paragraph (d)(4) of this section, which provides a limited exception from the obligation to withhold on a deemed payment.

(iii) *Documentation.*—Any exception from withholding pursuant to paragraph (d)(1)(i) of this section applies without a requirement that documentation be furnished to the withholding agent. However, documentation may have to be furnished for purposes of the information reporting provisions under chapter 61 of the Code and backup withholding under section 3406.

(iv) *Scope of exception.*—The exception from withholding under this paragraph (d) is not a determination that the amounts are not fixed or determinable annual or periodical income, nor is it an exception from reporting the amount under §1.1461-1(b) and (c).

(v) *Lack of money or property or lack of knowledge.*—A withholding agent does not lack control over money or property for purposes of this paragraph (d)(1) if the withholding agent directs another party to make the payment. Thus, for example, a principal does not cease to have control over a payment when it contracts with a paying agent to make the payments to its account holders in lieu of paying the account holders directly. Further, a withholding agent does not lack knowledge of the facts that give rise to a payment merely because the withholding agent does not know the character or source of the payment for U.S. tax purposes. *See* §1.1441-3(d)(1) for rules addressing a withholding agent's obligations when the withholding agent has knowledge of the facts that give rise to the payment, but the character or source of the payment is not known.

(vi) *Example.*—A, an individual, owns stock in DC, a domestic corporation, through a custodian, Bank 1. A also has a money market account at Bank 2. DC pays a dividend of $1,000 that is deposited in A's custodial account at Bank 1. A then directs Bank 1 to transfer $1,000 to A's money market account at Bank 2. With respect to the payment of the dividend into A's custodial account with Bank 1, both DC and Bank 1 are withholding agents making a payment of an amount subject to withholding for which they have custody, control, and knowledge. *See* §§1.1441-2(b)(1) and 1.1441-7(a)(1). Therefore, both DC and Bank 1 have an obligation to withhold on the payment unless they can reliably associate the payment with documentation sufficient to treat the respective payees as not subject to withholding under chapter 3. With respect to the wire transfer of $1,000 from A's account at Bank 1 to A's account at Bank 2, neither Bank 1 nor Bank 2 is required to withhold on the transfer because neither bank has knowledge of the facts that gave rise to the payment. Even though Bank 1 is a custodian for A's stock in DC and has knowledge regarding the $1,000 dividend paid to A, once Bank 1 credits the $1,000 dividend to A's account, the $1,000 becomes A's property. When A transfers the $1,000 to its account at Bank 2, this is a separate transfer about which Bank 1 has no knowledge regarding the type of payment made. Further, Bank 2 only has knowledge that

it receives $1,000 to be credited to A's account but has no knowledge regarding the type of payment made. Accordingly, Bank 1 and Bank 2 have no withholding obligation with respect to the transfer from A's custodial account at Bank 1 to A's money market account at Bank 2.

* * *

(4) *Deemed distributions under section 305(c) and deemed payments.*—(i) *General rule.*—Subject to the rules in this paragraph (d)(4)(i) and paragraph (d)(4)(iii) of this section, and any other exception to withholding (for example, under §1.1441-4), a withholding agent has an obligation to withhold on a deemed distribution (as defined in §1.305-1(d)(7)) or a deemed payment (as defined in §1.861-3(a)(6)) on a security. However, a withholding agent other than the issuer of a specified security (as defined in §1.6045-1(a)(14)) has an obligation to withhold on a deemed distribution (as defined in §1.305-1(d)(7)) on a specified security or a deemed payment (as defined in §1.861-3(a)(6)) that is determined with respect to a deemed distribution on a specified security only if:

(A) The issuer of the specified security reports the information required under §1.6045B-1 regarding the deemed distribution before the due date (not including extensions) for the withholding agent to file Form 1042 for the calendar year in which the deemed distribution or the deemed payment occurred; or

(B) The withholding agent has actual knowledge of the deemed distribution before the due date (not including extensions) for it to file Form 1042 for the calendar year in which the deemed distribution or the deemed payment occurred, but in such case the requirements of this paragraph (d)(4)(i) will not be considered to be met until January 15 of the year following the calendar year in which the deemed distribution or the deemed payment occurred.

(ii) *Time to withhold on a deemed distribution or deemed payment.*—After the requirements of paragraph (d)(4)(i) of this section have been met, except as provided in §1.1441-5 regarding the time to withhold for partnerships and trusts, a withholding agent must withhold on a deemed distribution (as defined in §1.305-1(d)(7)) or a deemed payment (as defined in §1.861-3(a)(6)) on the earliest of:

(A) The date on which a payment of cash is made with respect to the security or the securities lending or sales-repurchase transaction;

(B) The date on which the security is sold, exchanged, or otherwise disposed of (including a transfer of the security to a separate account not maintained by the withholding agent or a termination of the account relationship); or

(C) The due date (not including extensions) for the withholding agent to file Form 1042 for the calendar year in which the deemed distribution or the deemed payment occurred.

(iii) *Treatment of foreign entities assuming withholding responsibilities.*—Notwithstanding §1.1441-1(b)(1), a withholding agent may not treat a foreign entity as having assumed primary withholding responsibility under §1.1441-1(e)(5), §1.1441-1(b)(2)(iv), §1.1441-5(c)(2)(i), or §1.1441-5(e)(5)(v) for a deemed distribution (as defined in §1.305-1(d)(7)) on a specified security (as defined in §1.6045-1(a)(14)) or a deemed payment (as defined in §1.861-3(a)(6)) that is determined with respect to a deemed distribution on a specified security unless the withholding agent has provided the foreign entity a copy of the issuer statement described in §1.6045B-1(b)(1) within 10 days of the issuer furnishing the statement to the holder of record (or its nominee), or the issuer has met the public reporting requirements described in §1.6045B-1(a)(3). A foreign entity described in the preceding sentence has an obligation to withhold on the deemed distribution or the deemed payment (unless an exception to withholding under section 1441 applies) if it receives a copy of the statement described in §1.6045B-1(b)(1) or the issuer has met the public reporting requirements described in §1.6045B-1(a)(3) by the due date (not including extensions) for filing Form 1042 with respect to the calendar year in which the deemed distribution or the deemed payment occurred. *See* §1.1441-3(c)(5)(i) for when the foreign entity may rely on the copy of the issuer statement that it receives to determine the amount to withhold.

(iv) *Examples.*—The following examples illustrate when a withholding agent must satisfy its obligation to withhold under paragraph (d)(4) of this section on a deemed distribution.

Example 1 (i) *Facts.* WA is a U.S. custodian that holds a convertible debt instrument (CDI) of Corporation X that is a specified security (as defined in §1.6045-1(a)(14)) on behalf of A, a foreign person. On March 1 of Year 1, there is a change in the conversion ratio of the CDI that is treated as a deemed distribution under §1.305-7(b) and (c). On March 15 of Year 1, Corporation X makes an interest payment on the CDI to WA as custodian for A. On April 1 of Year 1, Corporation X reports the information required under §1.6045B-1 regarding the deemed distribution on its public website. On April 15 of Year 1, Corporation X makes another interest payment on the CDI to WA as custodian for A.

(ii) *Analysis.* Under paragraph (d)(4)(i) of this section, WA does not have an obligation to withhold on the deemed distribution on the CDI that it holds on behalf of A until April 1 of Year 1, the date on which Corporation X satisfied its reporting requirements under §1.6045B-1 regarding the deemed distribution. WA must withhold on the April 15 cash payment, which is the earliest of the dates specified in paragraph (d)(4)(ii) of this section for withholding on the deemed distribution.

Example 2 (i) *Facts.* The facts are the same as in Example 1, except that an interest payment is not made on the Corporation X CDI on April 15 of Year 1, and the CDI is transferred to a separate account of A that is not maintained by WA on April 15 of Year 1.

(ii) *Analysis.* Because WA is a withholding agent under §1.1441-7(a)(4) with respect to the deemed distribution on March 1 of Year 1 and Corporation X reports the information required under §1.6045B-1, WA is required to satisfy the withholding obligation even though the CDI was transferred before a cash payment is made with respect to the CDI. WA does not have an obligation to withhold on the deemed distribution until April 1 of Year 1, the date on which Corporation X reported the conversion ratio adjustment as required by §1.6045B-1 regarding the deemed distribution. WA must withhold upon the transfer of the CDI to an account not maintained by WA on April 15 of Year 1, which is the earliest of the dates specified in paragraph (d)(4)(ii) of this section for withholding.

Example 3 (i) *Facts.* The facts are the same as in Example 2, except that the CDI is transferred to a separate account of A that is not maintained by WA on March 30 of Year 1.

Par. 8. Section 1.1441-3 is amended by:

1. Adding paragraph (c)(5).

2. Amending paragraph (i) by removing the language "paragraphs (g) and (h)" and adding in its place "paragraphs (c)(5), (g), and (h)".

The addition reads as follows:

§1.1441-3. Determination of amounts to be withheld.

* * *

(c) * * *

(5) *Reliance rule for applicable adjustments.*—(i) *In general.*—For purposes of determining the amount of a deemed distribution (as defined in §1.305-1(d)(7)) on a specified security (as defined in §1.6045-1(a)(14)) or a deemed payment (as defined in §1.861-3(a)(6)) that is determined with respect to a deemed distribution on a specified security, a withholding agent other than the issuer of the specified security (as defined in §1.6045-1(a)(14)) may rely on the information provided by the issuer under §1.6045B-1 (or a copy of the issuer statement in the circumstances described in

(ii) *Analysis.* Because WA is a withholding agent under §1.1441-7(a)(4) with respect to the deemed distribution on March 1 of Year 1 and Corporation X has satisfied its reporting requirements with respect to the deemed distribution, WA is required to satisfy the withholding obligation even though the CDI was transferred before WA received the issuer reporting from Corporation X under §1.6045B-1 regarding the deemed distribution. WA does not have an obligation to withhold on the deemed distribution until April 1 of Year 1, the date on which Corporation X satisfied its reporting requirements under §1.6045B-1 regarding the deemed distribution. Because neither of the events specified in paragraphs (d)(4)(ii)(A) and (B) of this section occurred after April 1 of Year 1, WA must satisfy its withholding obligation by the due date (not including extensions) for filing Form 1042 (that is, by March 15 of Year 2), as provided in paragraph (d)(4)(ii)(C) of this section. WA may apply §1.1461-2(b) in order to collect the underwithheld amount.

* * *

(f) *Effective/applicability date.*—* * * Paragraphs (d)(1) and (d)(4) of this section apply to payments made on or after the date of publication of the Treasury decision adopting these rules as final regulations in the **Federal Register**. A withholding agent may, however, rely on the rules in paragraphs (d)(1) and (d)(4) of this section for all deemed distributions (as defined in §1.305-1(d)(7)) or deemed payments (as defined in §1.861-3(a)(6)) occurring on or after January 1, 2016, until the date of publication of a Treasury decision adopting these rules as final regulations in the **Federal Register**.

§1.1441-2(d)(4)(iii)) unless it knows that such information is incorrect or unreliable. *See* §1.1441-2(d)(4) for a withholding agent's obligation to withhold on a deemed distribution or a deemed payment.

(ii) *Effective/applicability date.*—Paragraph (c)(5)(i) of this section applies to payments made on or after the date of publication of the Treasury decision adopting these rules as final regulations in the **Federal Register**. A withholding agent may, however, rely on the rules in paragraph (c)(5)(i) of this section for all deemed distributions (as defined in §1.305-1(d)(7)) or deemed payments (as defined in §1.861-3(a)(6)) occurring on or after January 1, 2016, until the date of publication of a Treasury decision adopting these rules as final regulations in the **Federal Register**.

* * *

Withholding: Nonresident Aliens: Sale of Obligations: Between Interest Payment Dates

Withholding: Nonresident Aliens: Sale of Obligations: Between Interest Payment Dates.—Amendments to Reg. §1.1441-3, relating to the obligation to withhold on interest paid with respect to obligations in the case of sales of obligations between interest payment dates, are proposed (published in the Federal Register on October 14, 1997) (REG-114000-97).

☐ Par. 2. In §1.1441-3, paragraph (b) is revised to read as follows:

§1.1441-3. Determination of amount to be withheld.

* * *

(b) *Withholding on payments on certain obligations.*—(1) *Withholding at time of payment of interest.*—When making a payment on an interest-bearing obligation, a withholding agent must withhold under §1.1441-1 upon the gross amount of stated interest payable on the interest payment date, regardless of whether the payment constitutes a return of capital or the payment of income within the meaning of section 61, unless the withholding agent has knowledge of the actual amount of interest paid. For this purpose, the withholding agent may rely on information provided by the issuer (or its paying agent), on a representation from the beneficial owner, or on information that the withholding agent has in its records. To the extent an amount was withheld on an amount of capital rather than interest, see rules for adjustments, refunds, or credits under §1.1441-1(b)(8).

(2) *No withholding between interest payment dates.*—(i) *General rule.*—A withholding agent is not required to withhold under §1.1441-1 upon interest accrued on the date of a sale of debt obligations when that sale occurs between two interest payment dates (even though the amount is treated as interest under §1.61-7(c) or (d) and is subject to tax under section 871(a) or 881(a)), unless the withholding agent has knowledge of the amount paid as interest. For purposes of this paragraph (b)(2)(i), a withholding agent is treated as having knowledge in the same manner as a withholding agent has

knowledge for purposes of §1.1441-2(b)(3)(ii), dealing with withholding on original issue discount. In addition, notwithstanding lack of knowledge (within the meaning of §1.1441-2(b)(3)(ii)), withholding is required on the entire amount of stated interest paid with respect to the obligation as determined as of the date of original issue if the withholding agent, pursuant to the provisions in §1.1441-1(b)(3), treats the payment as made to a foreign payee because it cannot associate the payment with required documentation and the amount would qualify as portfolio interest. See §1.1441-1(b)(8) for adjustments to any amount that has been overwithheld as a result of this provision.

(ii) *Applicable rules.*—Any exemption from withholding pursuant to paragraph (b)(2)(i) of this section applies without a requirement that documentation be furnished to the withholding agent. However, documentation may have to be furnished for purposes of the information reporting provisions under section 6049 and backup withholding under section 3406. See §1.6045-1(c) for reporting requirements by brokers with respect to sale proceeds. Any exemption from withholding under paragraph (b)(2)(i) of this section is not a determination that the accrued interest is not fixed or determinable annual or periodical income. See §1.61-7(c) regarding the character of payments received by the acquirer of an obligation subsequent to such acquisition (that is, as a return of capital or interest accrued after the acquisition).

* * *

Withholding: Distributions in Redemption of Stock

Withholding: Distributions in Redemption of Stock.—Amendments to Reg. §1.1441-3, providing an escrow procedure that a withholding agent must apply while making the determination under Code Sec. 302 as to whether the distribution in redemption of the stock held by a foreign shareholder is treated as a dividend subject to withholding or a distribution in part or full payment in exchange for stock, are proposed (published in the Federal Register on October 17, 2007) (REG-140206-06).

□ Par. 2. Section 1.1441-3 is amended as follows:

1. A sentence is added at the end of paragraph (c)(2)(i)(B).
2. Paragraph (c)(5) is added.
3. A sentence is added at the end of paragraph (d)(1).

The additions read as follows:

§1.1441-3. Determination of amounts to be withheld.

* * *

(c) * * *

(2) * * *

(i) * * *

(B) * * * The preceding sentence shall not apply to a public section 302 distribution to which paragraph (c)(5) applies.

* * *

(5) *Special rules for certain distributions to which section 302 applies.*—(i) *Withholding responsibility.*—(A) *General rule.*—A corporation that makes a public section 302 distribution, or any intermediary (described in §1.1441-1(c)(13)) making a payment of such a distribution, is required to withhold under section 1441, 1442 or 1443 on the entire amount of the distribution unless the provisions of paragraph (c)(5)(iii) of this section have been applied. The provisions of paragraph (c)(2)(i)(B) or (d)(1) of this section do not apply to a public section 302 distribution.

(B) *Effective/applicability date.*—The rules of this paragraph (c)(5) apply to public section 302 distributions made after December 31, 2008.

(ii) *Definitions.*—Solely for purposes of this paragraph (c)(5), the following definitions shall apply:

(A) *Public section 302 distribution* means a distribution by a corporation in redemption of its stock for which there is an established financial market within the meaning of §1.1092(d)-1.

(B) *Section 302 payment* means payment of a public section 302 distribution.

(C) *Distributing corporation* means a corporation making or treated as making a public section 302 distribution.

(iii) *Escrow procedure.*—(A) *Application.*—(1) *In general.*— The escrow procedure in this paragraph (c)(5)(iii) may be applied only by an intermediary (described in §1.1441-1(c)(13)) that is a U.S. financial institution. A U.S. financial institution making a section 302 payment to a foreign account holder, and applying this escrow procedure, is not required to withhold on the entire amount of a section 302 payment under the general rule of paragraph (c)(5)(i).

(B) *Escrow account.*—(1) *In general.*—A U.S. financial institution shall set aside in an escrow account on the date it receives a section 302 payment from a distributing corporation with respect to stock of a foreign account holder 30 percent (or the applicable dividend rate provided by a tax treaty for a qualifying foreign account holder) of the amount and shall credit the foreign account holder's account with the balance of the section 302 payment.

(2) *Qualified intermediaries.*—The amount set aside, under paragraph (c)(5)(iii)(B)(1) of this section shall include 30 percent (or the applicable dividend rate provided by a treaty) of the amount paid to any qualified intermediary (QI) (whether or not the QI has assumed primary withholding responsibility) and to any withholding foreign partnership or withholding foreign trust (WP/WT).

(C) *Request for section 302 payment certification.*—On or before the date it receives the section 302 payment, the U.S. financial institution shall provide the following information and instructions, in writing, to the foreign beneficial owner—

(1) The total number of distributing corporation's shares outstanding before and after the public section 302 distribution;

(2) An explanation of the conditions under which the section 302 payment will be treated as a dividend or a payment in exchange for stock for Federal income tax purposes (including an explanation of any applicable constructive ownership rules); and

(3) A request that the beneficial owner of the account provide a certification (section 302 payment certification), within 60 days of the section 302 payment, stating whether the section 302 payment is either a dividend or a payment in exchange for stock under the Internal Revenue Code.

(D) *Content of section 302 payment certification.*—The section 302 payment certification must include the following information:

(1) The beneficial owner's name and account number.

(2) The distributing corporation's name.

(3) The total shares of the distributing corporation outstanding immediately before and immediately after the public section 302 distribution.

(4) A certification from the beneficial owner that either—

(i) The section 302 payment is a payment in exchange for stock because the beneficial owner's proportionate interest has been reduced but not completely terminated;

(ii) The section 302 payment is a payment in exchange for stock because the beneficial owner's interest in the distributing corporation is completely terminated; or

(iii) The section 302 payment is a dividend.

(5) With respect to the certifications in paragraph (c)(5)(iii)(D)(4)(i) and (ii) of this section, the number of shares actually and constructively owned by the beneficial owner before and after the distribution and the beneficial owner's percentage ownership before and after the distribution.

(6) A penalties of perjury statement.

(7) The signature of the beneficial owner and date of signature.

(E) *Receipt of section 302 payment certification.*—(1) *Payment in exchange for stock.*—If, within the 60-day period described in paragraph (c)(5)(iii)(C)(3), the U.S. financial institution receives from the foreign beneficial owner a section 302 payment certification stating that the section 302 payment is a payment in exchange for stock, and if the U.S. financial institution does not know or have reason to know that the information in the section 302 payment certification is unreliable or incorrect, the U.S. financial institution shall credit the account with the amount set aside with respect to the beneficial owner who provides the certification. The entire amount paid (including the amount initially set aside) shall be reported as capital gains on Form 1042-S Foreign Person's U.S. Source Income Subject to Withholding.

(2) *Unreliable or incorrect exchange certification.*—If the U.S. financial institution knows or has reason to know that the information in the section 302 payment certification is unreliable or incorrect, the U.S. financial institution shall treat the payment as a payment for which no section 302 payment certification has been received and shall follow the withholding and reporting procedures in paragraph (c)(5)(iii)(E)(4) of this section.

(3) *Dividend.*—If, within the 60-day period, the U.S. financial institution receives a section 302 payment certification from the foreign beneficial owner stating that the section 302 payment is a dividend, the U.S. financial institution shall treat the amount set aside as tax withheld as of the time it receives the section 302 payment certification, and shall deposit that amount pursuant to the applicable regulations. The entire amount paid shall be reported on Form 1042-S as dividends.

(4) *No timely certification received.*—If, within the 60-day period, the U.S. financial institution does not receive a section 302 payment certification, or is treated under paragraph (c)(5)(iii)(E)(2) of this section as not receiving a section 302 payment certification, the U.S. financial institution shall treat the amount set aside as tax withheld as of the 61st day, and shall deposit that amount pursuant to the applicable regulations. The entire amount paid shall be reported on Form 1042-S as dividends.

(5) *Late certification.*—If, after the 60-day period has expired, the U.S. financial institution receives a section 302 payment certification from a foreign beneficial owner that the section 302 payment is a payment in exchange for stock and the conditions stated in §1.1461-2(a) are satisfied, the U.S. financial institution may apply the refund or offset procedures of that paragraph.

(6) *Determination of incorrect treatment.*—If, after the 60-day period has expired, the U.S. financial institution determines

that the section 302 payment was incorrectly treated as a distribution in exchange for stock, the procedures set forth regarding underwithholding in §1.1461-2(b) are applicable.

(7) Undocumented beneficial owners.—The U.S. financial institution shall withhold at 30 percent on the entire amount paid to a beneficial owner that is not properly documented under §§1.1441-1, 1.1441-5, etc. and that is presumed to be a foreign person, whether or not the U.S. financial institution has received a section 302 payment certification from such beneficial owner. The U.S. financial institution shall report the entire amount paid on Form 1042-S as dividends.

(F) Amounts in excess of section 302 payment.—If the amount the U.S. financial institution credits to the account of the foreign beneficial owner from the escrow account includes an amount in excess of the section 302 payment, such as interest accrued on the escrowed funds, the U.S. financial institution shall report and withhold on such excess amount in accordance with the rules under Chapter 3 of the Internal Revenue Code.

(G) U.S. non-exempt recipients.—The U.S. financial institution shall treat beneficial owners that are U.S. non-exempt recipients, and that hold stock in the distributing corporation through QIs, WPs/WTs, NQIs and flow-throughs, in accordance with the section 302 payment certifications obtained from those U.S. non-exempt recipients and shall instruct foreign intermediaries and foreign flow-through entities to do the same.

(H) Notice to distributing corporation.—The U.S. financial institution shall notify the distributing corporation, in writing, by the filing date of Form 1042-S, of the aggregate amount of the section 302 payment that the U.S. financial institution has reported on Forms 1042-S as capital gains, and the aggregate amount of the section 302 payment that it has reported on Forms 1042-S as dividends.

(I) Application of Escrow Procedure to Qualified Intermediaries.—As provided in paragraph (c)(5)(iii)(A) of this section, only the U.S. financial institution may establish an escrow account and the amounts set aside in the escrow account shall include 30 percent (or the applicable treaty rate applicable to dividends) on payments made to a direct account holder that is a QI (including a QI that has assumed primary withholding responsibility). Under the procedure described in paragraph (c)(5)(iii)(I)(3), a QI shall provide the U.S. financial institution with a withholding statement as required in the QI Agreement. If there is a chain of QIs, each QI in the chain shall apply the procedure. The procedures described in this paragraph (I) shall be applied to withholding foreign partnerships and withholding foreign trusts within the meaning of §§1.1441-5(c)(2) and (e)(5)(v), respectively, in the same manner as the procedures apply to a QI.

(1) Request for section 302 payment certification.—The U.S. financial institution shall provide the information and instructions described in paragraph (c)(5)(iii)(C) of this section to the QI, and the QI shall provide the same information and instructions to its account holders including account holders that are U.S. non-exempt recipients.

(2) Content of section 302 payment certification.—The content of the section 302 payment certification shall include the information described in paragraph (c)(5)(iii)(D) of this section.

(3) Receipt of section 302 payment certification.—*(i) Payment in exchange for stock.*—If, within the 60-day period described in paragraph (c)(5)(iii)(C), the QI receives from the beneficial owner a section 302 payment certification stating that the section 302 payment is a payment in exchange for stock and if the QI does not know or have reason to know that the information in the section 302 payment certification is unreliable or incorrect, the QI shall reflect such treatment in its withholding statement provided to the U.S. financial institution, and, based upon the withholding statement, the U.S. financial institution shall release payment from its escrow and the QI shall credit the beneficial owner's account with the amount set aside by the U.S. financial institution with respect to the beneficial owner who provided the certification. The entire amount paid (including the amount initially set aside) shall be reported on the QI's pooled basis Form 1042-S as capital gains.

(ii) Unreliable or incorrect exchange certification.—If the QI knows or has reason to know that the information in the section

302 payment certification is unreliable or incorrect, the QI shall treat the payment as a payment for which no section 302 payment certification has been received and shall follow the withholding and reporting procedures in paragraph (c)(5)(iii)(I)(3)(iv) of this section.

(iii) Dividend.—If, within the 60-day period, QI receives a section 302 payment certification stating that the section 302 payment is a dividend, the QI shall reflect such treatment in its withholding statement and shall treat the payment as a dividend for purposes of its reporting and withholding responsibilities under the QI agreement. The entire amount paid shall be reported on its pooled basis Form 1042-S as dividends.

(iv) No timely certification received.—If, within the 60-day period, the QI does not receive a section 302 payment certification, or is treated under paragraph (c)(5)(iii)(I)(3)(ii) of this section as not receiving a section 302 payment certification, the QI shall reflect such treatment in its withholding statement provided to the U.S. financial institution and shall treat the payment as a dividend for purposes of its reporting and withholding responsibilities under the QI agreement. The entire amount paid shall be reported on its pooled basis Form 1042-S as dividends.

(v) Late certification.—If, after the 60-day period has expired, the QI receives a section 302 payment certification from a beneficial owner that the section 302 payment is a payment in exchange for stock and the conditions stated in the QI agreement regarding the refund and offset procedures are satisfied, the QI may apply such refund or offset procedures.

(vi) Determination of incorrect treatment.—If, after the 60-day period has expired, the QI determines that the section 302 payment was incorrectly treated as a distribution in exchange for stock, the procedures set forth regarding adjustments for underwithholding in the QI agreement are applicable.

(vii) Undocumented beneficial owners.—The QI shall withhold at 30 percent on the entire amount paid to a beneficial owner that is not properly documented and that is presumed to be a foreign person, whether or not the QI has received a section 302 payment certification from such beneficial owner. The QI shall report the entire amount paid on its pooled basis Form 1042-S as dividends.

(4) U.S. non-exempt recipients.—The QI shall treat direct account holders that are U.S. non-exempt recipients, and that hold stock in the distributing corporation, in accordance with the section 302 payment certifications obtained from those U.S. non-exempt recipients and shall instruct foreign intermediaries and foreign flow-through entities to do the same.

(J) Intermediaries that are not qualified intermediaries.—If the U.S. financial institution has an account holder that is an intermediary that is not a QI ("NQI"), the U.S. financial institution shall apply the rules of paragraph (c)(5)(iii)(J)(1) through (4) of this section. Where the provisions of this paragraph (J) refer only to the U.S. financial institution, they shall apply in the same manner to a QI or WP/WT and where they refer to an NQI, they shall apply in the same manner to a flow-through that is not a WP or WT.

(1) The U.S. financial institution shall provide the information and instructions described in paragraph (c)(5)(iii)(C) of this section to the NQI and the NQI shall provide the same information and instructions to its account holders.

(2) The content of the section 302 payment certification shall include the information described in paragraph (c)(5)(iii)(D) of this section.

(3) The NQI shall provide the section 302 payment certification to the U.S. financial institution together with the otherwise required documentation and a withholding statement made in accordance with the section 302 payment certification.

(4) The U.S. financial institution shall treat the section 302 payment as a dividend or a payment in exchange for stock based on the information and documentation provided to it under paragraph (c)(5)(iii)(J)(3) of this section. The U.S. financial institution shall withhold and report on a specific payee basis in accordance with this information.

(d) * * *

(1) * * * This paragraph does not apply to a public section 302 distribution to which paragraph (c)(5) applies.

* * *

Foreign Pension Funds: Exception for Interests

Foreign Pension Funds: Exception for Interests.—Amendments to Reg. §1.1441-3, regarding the exception from taxation with respect to gain or loss of a qualified foreign pension fund attributable to certain interests in United States real property, are proposed (published in the Federal Register on June 7, 2019) (REG-109826-17).

Par. 3. Section 1.1441-3 is amended by adding paragraph (c)(4)(iii) to read as follows:

§1.1441-3. Determination of amounts to be withheld.

* * *

(c) * * *

(4) * * *

(iii) *Special rule for qualified holders*.—(A) *In general*.—Any corporate distribution made by a USRPHC or a QIE to a payee that is a qualified holder (as defined in §1.897(l)-1(d)(11)) shall not be subject to the rules of this paragraph (c)(4) but shall be subject to the requirements of paragraphs (c)(1) through (3) of this section.

(B) *Applicability date*.—Paragraph (c)(4)(iii)(A) of this section applies to distributions made by a USRPHC or a QIE occurring on or after the date of publication of the Treasury decision adopting these rules as final regulations in the **Federal Register**.

* * *

Stock and Rights to Acquire Stock: Deemed Distributions

Stock and Rights to Acquire Stock: Deemed Distributions.—Amendments to Reg. §1.1441-7, regarding deemed distributions of stock and rights to acquire stock and resolving ambiguities concerning the amount and timing of deemed distributions that are or result from adjustments to rights to acquire stock, are proposed (published in the Federal Register on April 13, 2016) (REG-133673-15).

Par. 9. Section 1.1441-7 is amended by:

1. Redesignating paragraph (a)(4) as (a)(5) and adding a second and third sentence to newly redesignated (a)(5).

2. Adding a new paragraph (a)(4).

3. Amending paragraph (g) by removing the language "paragraphs (a)(4)" and adding in its place "paragraphs (a)(5)."

The addition reads as follows:

§1.1441-7. General provisions relating to withholding agents.— (a) * * *

(4) *Withholding agent with respect to deemed distributions under section 305(c)*.—Any person that issues or holds directly or indirectly (for example, through an account maintained for another intermediary) on behalf of a beneficial owner, or a flow through entity that owns directly or indirectly (through another flow-through entity), a security upon which a deemed distribution (as defined in §1.305-1(d)(7)) is made has custody of or control over the deemed distribution. *See* §1.1441-2(d)(4) for a withholding agent's obligation to withhold on the deemed distribution and §1.1441-3(c)(5)(i) for when a withholding agent may rely on the information reported by the issuer under §1.6045B-1 to determine the amount to withhold.

(5) * * * Paragraph (a)(4) of this section applies to payments made on or after the date of publication of the Treasury decision adopting these rules as final regulations in the **Federal Register**. A withholding agent may, however, rely on the rules in paragraph (a)(4) of this section for all deemed distributions (as defined in §1.305-1(d)(7)) occurring on or after January 1, 2016, until the date of publication of a Treasury decision adopting these rules as final regulations in the **Federal Register**.

Interests in Partnerships: Withholding of Tax: Information Reporting

Interests in Partnerships: Withholding of Tax: Information Reporting.—Amendments to Reg. §1.1445-2, implementing certain sections of the Internal Revenue Code, including sections added to the Internal Revenue Code by the Tax Cuts and Jobs Act, that relate to the withholding of tax and information reporting with respect to certain dispositions of interests in partnerships engaged in the conduct of a trade or business within the United States, are proposed (published in the Federal Register on May 13, 2019) (REG-105476-18).

Par. 3. Section 1.1445-2 is amended by adding paragraph (b)(2)(v) and a sentence to the end of paragraph (e) to read as follows:

§1.1445-2. Situations in which withholding is not required under section 1445(a).

* * *

(b) * * *

(2) * * *

(v) *Form W-9*.—For purposes of paragraph (b)(2)(i) of this section, a certification of non-foreign status includes a valid Form W-9, *Request for Taxpayer Identification Number and Certification*, or its successor, submitted to the transferee by the transferor.

* * *

(e) *Applicability dates*.—* * * Paragraph (b)(2)(v) of this section applies to certifications provided on or after May 7, 2019, except that a taxpayer may apply it with respect to certifications provided before that date.

Foreign Pension Funds: Exception for Interests

Foreign Pension Funds: Exception for Interests.—Amendments to Reg. §1.1445-2, regarding the exception from taxation with respect to gain or loss of a qualified foreign pension fund attributable to certain interests in United States real property, are proposed (published in the Federal Register on June 7, 2019) (REG-109826-17).

Par. 4. Section 1.1445-2 is amended by revising paragraphs (b)(1) and (b)(2)(i)(C) and adding paragraph (b)(2)(v) and a new sentence at the end of paragraph (e) to read as follows:

§1.1445-2. Situations in which withholding is not required under section 1445(a).

* * *

(b) * * *

(1) *In general*.—No withholding is required under section 1445 if the transferor of a U.S. real property interest is not a foreign person. Therefore, paragraph (b)(2) of this section provides rules pursuant to which the transferor can provide a certification of non-foreign status to inform the transferee that withholding is not required. A transferee that obtains such a certification must retain that document for five years, as provided in paragraph (b)(3) of this section. Except to the extent provided in paragraph (b)(4) of this section, obtaining this certification excuses the transferee from any liability otherwise imposed by section 1445 and §1.1445-1(e). However, section 1445 and the rules of this section do not impose any obligation upon a transferee to obtain a certification from the transferor; thus, a transferee may instead rely upon other means to ascertain the non-foreign status of the transferor. If, however, the transferee relies upon other means and the transferor was, in fact, a foreign person, then the transferee is subject to the liability imposed by section 1445 and §1.1445-1(e).

(i) A transferee is in no event required to rely upon other means to ascertain the non-foreign status of the transferor and may demand a certification of non-foreign status or Form W-8EXP in the case of a qualified holder (as defined in §1.897(l)-1(d)(11)). If the certification or form is not provided, the transferee may withhold tax under section 1445 and will be considered, for purposes of sections 1461 through 1463, to have been required to withhold such tax.

(ii) [Reserved]

(2) * * *

(i) * * *

(C)*(1)* Is signed under penalties of perjury.

(2) In general, a foreign person is a nonresident alien individual, foreign corporation, foreign partnership, foreign trust, or foreign estate, except that a qualified holder (as defined in §1.897(l)-1(d)(11)) is not a foreign person. Additionally, a foreign corporation that has made a valid election under section 897(i) is generally not treated as a foreign person for purposes of section 1445. In this regard, see §1.1445-7. Pursuant to §1.897-1(p), an individual's identifying number is the individual's Social Security number and any other person's identifying number is its U.S. employer identification number (EIN). A certification pursuant to this paragraph (b) must be verified as true and signed under penalties of perjury by a responsible officer in the case of a corporation, by a general partner in the case of a partnership, and by a trustee, executor, or equivalent fiduciary in the case of a trust or estate. No particular form is needed for a certification pursuant to this paragraph (b), nor is any particular language required, so long as the document meets the requirements of this paragraph (b)(2)(i). Samples of acceptable certifications are provided in paragraph (b)(2)(iv) of this section.

* * *

(v) *Qualified holders*.—As an alternative to a certification of non-foreign status described in paragraph (b)(2)(i) of this section, a qualified holder (as defined in §1.897(l)-1(d)(11)) may provide a Form W-8EXP to certify that it is treated as not foreign for purposes of section 1445. A Form W-8EXP provided for this purpose is subject to the general requirements of a certification of non-foreign status. For example, a Form W-8EXP provided for this purpose must be retained for the five-year period described in paragraph (b)(3) of this section regardless of whether it is required to be retained for purposes of section 1441 and the regulations thereunder.

* * *

(e) * * * Paragraphs (b)(1), (b)(2)(i) and (v) of this section, as revised by the Treasury decision adopting these rules as final regulations, apply with respect to dispositions of U.S. real property interests and distributions described in section 897(h) occurring on or after the date of publication of the Treasury decision adopting these rules as final regulations in the **Federal Register**.

Foreign Pension Funds: Exception for Interests

Foreign Pension Funds: Exception for Interests.—Amendments to Reg. §§1.1445-4 and 1.1445-5, regarding the exception from taxation with respect to gain or loss of a qualified foreign pension fund attributable to certain interests in United States real property, are proposed (published in the Federal Register on June 7, 2019) (REG-109826-17).

Par. 5. Section 1.1445-4 is amended by revising paragraphs (a)(2) and (b)(2) and adding paragraph (g) to read as follows:

§1.1445-4. Liability of agents.—(a) * * *

(2) The transferee is furnished with a non-foreign certification pursuant to §1.1445-2(b)(2) or a certification regarding qualified holder status provided on Form W-8EXP and either:

(i) The agent knows that the certification is false; or

(ii) The agent represents a transferor that is a foreign corporation that is not a qualified holder. An agent that represents a transferor that is a foreign corporation is not required to provide notice to the transferee if the foreign corporation provided a non-foreign certification or certification regarding qualified holder status provided on Form W-8EXP, as applicable, to the transferee prior to such agent's employment and the agent does not know that the corporation did so.

(b) * * *

Par. 6. Section 1.1445-5 is amended by revising paragraph (b)(3)(ii)(A) and adding a new sentence at the end of paragraph (h) to read as follows:

§1.1445-5. Special rules concerning distributions and other transactions by corporations, partnerships, trusts, and estates.

* * *

(b) * * *

(3) * * *

(ii) * * *

(A) *In general.*—For purposes of this section, an entity or fiduciary may treat any holder of an interest in the entity as a U.S. person if that interest-holder furnishes to the entity or fiduciary a certification stating that the interest-holder is not a foreign person, in accordance with the provisions of paragraph (b)(3)(ii)(B) of this sec-

(2) The entity or fiduciary is furnished with a non-foreign certification pursuant to §1.1445-5(b)(3)(ii) or a certification regarding qualified holder status provided on Form W-8EXP and either:

(i) The agent knows that such certification is false; or

(ii) The agent represents a foreign corporation (other than a qualified holder) that made such a certification.

* * *

(g) *Certain applicability dates.*—Paragraphs (a)(2) and (b)(2) of this section, as revised by the Treasury decision adopting these rules as final regulations, apply with respect to dispositions of U.S. real property interests and distributions described in section 897(h) occurring on or after the date of publication of the Treasury decision adopting these rules as final regulations in the **Federal Register**.

tion. In general, a foreign person is a nonresident alien individual, foreign corporation, foreign partnership, foreign trust, or foreign estate, except that a qualified holder (as defined in §1.897(l)-1(d)(11)) is not a foreign person.

* * *

(h) * * * Paragraph (b)(3)(ii)(A) of this section, as revised by the Treasury decision adopting these rules as final regulations, applies with respect to dispositions of U.S. real property interests and distributions described in section 897(h) occurring on or after the date of publication of the Treasury decision adopting these rules as final regulations in the **Federal Register**.

Interests in Partnerships: Withholding of Tax: Information Reporting

Interests in Partnerships: Withholding of Tax: Information Reporting.—Amendments to Reg. §1.1445-5, implementing certain sections of the Internal Revenue Code, including sections added to the Internal Revenue Code by the Tax Cuts and Jobs Act, that relate to the withholding of tax and information reporting with respect to certain dispositions of interests in partnerships engaged in the conduct of a trade or business within the United States, are proposed (published in the Federal Register on May 13, 2019) (REG-105476-18).

Par. 4. Section 1.1445-5 is amended by adding paragraph (b)(3)(iv) and a sentence to the end of paragraph (h) to read as follows:

§1.1445-5. Special rules concerning distributions and other transactions by corporations, partnerships, trusts, and estates.

* * *

(b) * * *

(3) * * *

(iv) *Form W-9.*—For purposes of paragraph (b)(3)(i) of this section, a certification of non-foreign status includes a valid Form

W-9, *Request for Taxpayer Identification Number and Certification,* or its successor, submitted to the transferee by the transferor.

* * *

(h) *Applicability dates.*—* * * Paragraph (b)(3)(iv) of this section applies to certifications provided on or after May 7, 2019, except that a taxpayer may apply it with respect to certifications provided before that date.

Interests in Partnerships: Withholding of Tax: Information Reporting

Interests in Partnerships: Withholding of Tax: Information Reporting.—Amendments to Reg. §1.1445-8, implementing certain sections of the Internal Revenue Code, including sections added to the Internal Revenue Code by the Tax Cuts and Jobs Act, that relate to the withholding of tax and information reporting with respect to certain dispositions of interests in partnerships engaged in the conduct of a trade or business within the United States, are proposed (published in the Federal Register on May 13, 2019) (REG-105476-18).

Par. 5. Section 1.1445-8 is amended by revising paragraph (f) to read as follows:

§1.1445-8. Special rules regarding publicly traded partnerships, publicly traded trusts and real estate investment trusts (REITs).

* * *

(f) *Qualified notice.*—(1) *In general.*—A qualified notice for purposes of paragraph (b)(3)(iv) of this section is a notice provided in the manner described in §1.1446-4(b)(4) by a partnership, trust, or REIT regarding a distribution that is attributable to the disposition of a United States real property interest. In the case of a REIT, a qualified notice is only a notice of a distribution, all or any portion of which the REIT actually designates, or characterizes in accordance with paragraph (c)(2)(ii)(C) of this section, as a capital gain dividend in the

manner described in §1.1446-4(b)(4), with respect to each share or certificate of beneficial interest. A deemed designation under paragraph (c)(2)(ii)(A) of this section may not be the subject of a qualified notice under this paragraph (f). A person described in paragraph (b)(3) of this section is treated as receiving a qualified notice when the notice is provided in accordance with §1.1446-4(b)(4).

(2) *Applicability dates.*—Paragraph (f)(1) of this section applies to distributions made on or after the date that is 60 days after the date that these regulations are published as final regulations in the **Federal Register**.

* * *

Foreign Pension Funds: Exception for Interests

Foreign Pension Funds: Exception for Interests.—Amendments to Reg. §1.1445-8, regarding the exception from taxation with respect to gain or loss of a qualified foreign pension fund attributable to certain interests in United States real property, are proposed (published in the Federal Register on June 7, 2019) (REG-109826-17).

Par. 7. Section 1.1445-8 is amended by revising paragraph (e) and adding paragraph (j) to read as follows:

§1.1445-8. Special rules regarding publicly traded partnerships, publicly traded trusts and real estate investment trusts (REITs).

* * *

(e) *Determination of non-foreign status by withholding agent.*—A withholding agent may rely on a certificate of non-foreign status pursuant to §1.1445-2(b), a Form W-9, a Form W-8EXP (in the case of a qualified holder (as defined in §1.897(l)-1(d)(11)), or a form that is substantially similar to such forms, to determine whether an interest holder is not a foreign person. Reliance on these documents will excuse the withholding agent from liability imposed under section 1445(e)(1) in the absence of actual knowledge that the interest holder is a foreign person. A withholding agent may also employ other means to determine the status of an interest holder, but, if the agent relies on such other means and the interest holder proves, in fact, to be a foreign person, then the withholding agent is subject to any liability imposed pursuant to section 1445 and the regulations thereunder for failure to withhold.

* * *

(j) *Certain applicability dates.*—Paragraph (e) of this section, as revised by the Treasury decision adopting these rules as final regulations, applies with respect to dispositions of U.S. real property interests and distributions described in section 897(h) occurring on or after the date of publication of the Treasury decision adopting these rules as final regulations in the **Federal Register**.

Disposition of Investment in U.S. Real Property

Nonresident Aliens and Foreign Corporations: Disposition of Investment in U.S. Real Property.—Temporary Reg. §§1.1445-10T and 1.1445-11T, relating to dispositions of U.S. real property interests by nonresident aliens and foreign corporations, are also proposed as final regulations and, when adopted, would become Reg. §§1.1445-10 and 1.1445-11 (published in the Federal Register on May 5, 1988). Temporary Reg. §1.1445-9T was removed by T.D. 9082 on August 4, 2003.

§1.1445-10. Special rule for foreign governments.

§1.1445-11. Special rules requiring withholding under §1.1445-5.

Foreign Pension Funds: Exception for Interests

Foreign Pension Funds: Exception for Interests.—Amendments to Reg. §§1.1446-1 and 1.1446-2, regarding the exception from taxation with respect to gain or loss of a qualified foreign pension fund attributable to certain interests in United States real property, are proposed (published in the Federal Register on June 7, 2019) (REG-109826-17).

Par. 8. Section 1.1446-1 is amended by revising the second sentence of paragraph (c)(2)(ii)(G) and revising paragraph (c)(2)(ii)(H) to read as follows:

§1.1446-1. Withholding tax on foreign partners' share of effectively connected taxable income.

* * *

(c) * * *

(2) * * *

(ii) * * *

(G) * * * However, except as set forth in §1.1446-2(b)(2)(iii)(B) (regarding certain qualified holders described in §1.897(l)-1(d)(11)) and §1.1446-3(c)(3) (regarding certain tax-exempt organizations described in section 501(c)), the submission of Form W-8EXP will have no effect on whether there is a 1446 tax due with respect to such partner's allocable share of partnership ECTI. * * *

(H) *Foreign corporations, certain foreign trusts, and foreign estates.*—Consistent with the rules of this paragraph (c)(2) and (3) of this section, a foreign corporation, a foreign trust (other than a foreign grantor trust described in paragraph (c)(2)(ii)(E) of this section), or a foreign estate may generally submit any appropriate Form W-8 (e.g., Form W-8BEN-E or Form W-8IMY) to the partnership to establish its foreign status for purposes of section 1446. In addition to Form W-8BEN-E, a foreign entity may also submit Form W-8EXP or a certification of non-foreign status described in §1.1445-5(b)(3) for purposes of documenting itself as a qualified holder (as defined in §1.897(l)-1(d)(11)).

* * *

Par. 9. Section 1.1446-2 is amended by adding paragraph (b)(4)(iii) to read as follows:

§1.1446-2. Determining a partnership's effectively connected taxable income allocable to foreign partners under section 704.

* * *

(b) * * *

(4) * * *

(iii) *Special rule for qualified holders.*—With respect to a foreign partner that is a qualified holder (as defined in §1.897(l)-1(d)(11)), the foreign partner's allocable share of partnership ECTI does not include gain or loss that is not taken into account by the qualified holder under §1.897(l)-1(b) and that is not otherwise treated as effectively connected with a trade or business in the United States. The partnership must have received from the partner a valid certificate of non-foreign status or Form W-8EXP. See §1.1446-1(c)(2)(ii)(G) and (H) regarding documentation of qualified holders.

* * *

Interests in Partnerships: Withholding of Tax: Information Reporting

Interests in Partnerships: Withholding of Tax: Information Reporting.—Amendments to Reg. §§1.1446-3 and 1.1446-4, implementing certain sections of the Internal Revenue Code, including sections added to the Internal Revenue Code by the Tax Cuts and Jobs Act, that relate to the withholding of tax and information reporting with respect to certain dispositions of interests in partnerships engaged in the conduct of a trade or business within the United States, are proposed (published in the Federal Register on May 13, 2019) (REG-105476-18).

Par. 6. Section 1.1446-3 is amended:

1. In the first sentence of paragraph (a)(2)(i), by removing "section 11(b)(1)" and adding in its place "section 11(b)".

2. By adding paragraph (c)(4).

The addition reads as follows:

§1.1446-3. Time and manner of calculating and paying the 1446 tax.

* * *

(c) * * *

(4) *Coordination with section 1446(f).*—A partnership that is directly or indirectly subject to withholding under section 1446(f)(1) during its taxable year may credit the amount withheld under section 1446(f)(1) against its section 1446 tax liability for that taxable year only to the extent the amount is allocable to foreign partners.

* * *

Par. 7. Section 1.1446-4 is amended by:
1. By revising paragraphs (b)(3) and (4).
2. By removing the second sentence of paragraph (c).
3. By revising paragraphs (d) and (f)(3).
The revisions and additions read as follows:

§1.1446-4.　Publicly traded partnerships.

* * *

(b) * * *

(3) *Nominee.*—For purposes of this section, the term nominee means a person that holds an interest in a publicly traded partnership on behalf of a foreign person and that is either a U.S. person, a qualified intermediary (as defined in § 1.1441-1(e)(5)(ii)) that assumes primary withholding responsibility for a payment, or a U.S. branch of a foreign person that agrees to be treated as a U.S. person (as described in § 1.1441-1(b)(2)(iv)) with respect to a payment.

(4) *Qualified notice.*—For purposes of this section, a qualified notice is a notice posted by a publicly traded partnership that states the amount of a distribution that is attributable to each type of income described in paragraphs (f)(3)(i) through (v) of this section. A qualified notice may also include the information described in § 1.1446(f)-4(b)(3), relating to an exception from withholding under section 1446(f)(1) for transfers of certain partnership interests. The notice must be posted in a readily accessible format in an area of the primary public Web site of the publicly traded partnership that is dedicated to this purpose. A qualified notice must be posted by the date required for providing notice with respect to dividends described in 17 CFR 240.10b-17(b)(1) or (3) (or any successor regulation) issued pursuant to the Securities Exchange Act of 1934 (15 U.S.C. 78a) and contain the information described therein as it would relate to the distribution. The publicly traded partnership must keep the notice accessible to the public for ten years on its primary public Web site or the primary public Web site of any successor organization. No specific format is required unless provided in forms, instructions, or other guidance. See paragraph (d) of this section regarding when a nominee is considered to have received a qualified notice.

* * *

(d) *Rules for designation of nominees to withhold tax under section 1446.*—A nominee that receives a distribution from a publicly traded partnership subject to withholding under this section, and which is to be paid to (or for the account of) any foreign person, may be treated as a withholding agent under this section. A nominee is treated as receiving a qualified notice on the date that the notice is posted in accordance with paragraph (b)(4) of this section. When a nominee is treated as a withholding agent with respect to a foreign partner of the partnership, the obligation to withhold on distributions to the foreign partner in accordance with the rules of this section is imposed solely on the nominee. A nominee responsible for withholding under the rules of this section is subject to liability under sections 1461 and 6655, as well as all applicable penalties and interest, as if the nominee were a partnership responsible for withholding under this section. A nominee may rely on a qualified notice that meets the requirements in paragraph (b)(4) of this section to determine the amounts on which it must withhold. If a notice a publicly traded partnership issues relating to its distribution does not meet the requirements in paragraph (b)(4) of this section, the nominee must withhold on the distribution with respect to—

(1) Foreign partners that are corporations, at the greater of the highest rate of tax specified in section 11(b) or section 881; and

(2) Foreign partners that are not corporations, at the greater of the highest rate of tax specified in section 1 or section 871.

* * *

(f) * * *

(3) *Ordering rule relating to distributions.*—Distributions from publicly traded partnerships are deemed to be paid out of the following types of income in the order indicated—

(i) Amounts attributable to income described in section 1441 or 1442 that are not effectively connected with the conduct of a trade or business in the United States but are subject to withholding, before taking into account any treaty exemptions;

(ii) Amounts attributable to income described in section 1441 or 1442 that are not effectively connected with the conduct of a trade or business in the United States and are not subject to withholding because of an exemption under a provision of the Code;

(iii) Amounts attributable to income effectively connected with the conduct of a trade or business in the United States that are not subject to withholding under §§ 1.1446-1 through 1.1446-6 (for example, amounts exempt by treaty);

(iv) Amounts subject to withholding under §§ 1.1446-1 through 1.1446-6; and

(v) Amounts not listed in paragraphs (f)(3)(i) through (iv) of this section.

* * *

Interests in Partnerships: Withholding of Tax: Information Reporting

Interests in Partnerships: Withholding of Tax: Information Reporting.—Amendments to Reg. § 1.1446-7, implementing certain sections of the Internal Revenue Code, including sections added to the Internal Revenue Code by the Tax Cuts and Jobs Act, that relate to the withholding of tax and information reporting with respect to certain dispositions of interests in partnerships engaged in the conduct of a trade or business within the United States, are proposed (published in the Federal Register on May 13, 2019) (REG-105476-18).

Par. 8. Section 1.1446-7 is amended by revising the section heading and adding two sentences at the end of the section to read as follows:

§1.1446-7.　Applicability dates.—* * * The addition of § 1.1446-3(c)(4) applies to partnership taxable years that include transfers that occur on or after the date that is 60 days after the date that these regulations are published as final regulations in the **Federal Register**. The revisions to § 1.1446-4(b)(3) and (4), the removal of the second sentence of § 1.1446-4(c), and the revisions to § 1.1446-4(d) and (f)(3) apply to distributions made on or after the date that is 60 days after the date that these regulations are published as final regulations in the **Federal Register**.

Foreign Pension Funds: Exception for Interests

Foreign Pension Funds: Exception for Interests.—Amendments to Reg. § 1.1446-7, regarding the exception from taxation with respect to gain or loss of a qualified foreign pension fund attributable to certain interests in United States real property, are proposed (published in the Federal Register on June 7, 2019) (REG-109826-17).

Par. 10. Section 1.1446-7 is amended by revising the section heading and adding a new sentence at the end of the paragraph to read as follows:

§1.1446-7.　Effective/Applicability date.—* * * Sections 1.1446-1(c)(2)(ii)(G) and (H) and 1.1446-2(b)(2)(iii)(A) and (B), as revised by the Treasury decision adopting these rules as final regulations, apply with respect to dispositions of U.S. real property interests and distributions described in section 897(h) occurring on or after the date of publication of the Treasury decision adopting these rules as final regulations in the **Federal Register**.

Interests in Partnerships: Withholding of Tax: Information Reporting

Interests in Partnerships: Withholding of Tax: Information Reporting.—Reg. §§ 1.1446(f)-1—1.1446(f)-5, implementing certain sections of the Internal Revenue Code, including sections added to the Internal Revenue Code by the Tax Cuts and Jobs Act, that relate to the withholding of tax and information reporting with respect to certain dispositions of interests in partnerships engaged in the conduct of a trade or business within the United States, are proposed (published in the Federal Register on May 13, 2019) (REG-105476-18).

Par. 9. Sections 1.1446(f)-1 through 1.1446(f)-5 are added to read as follows:

§1.1446(f)-1.　General rules.—(a) *Overview.*—These regulations provide rules for withholding, reporting, and paying tax under section 1446(f) upon the sale, exchange, or other disposition of certain interests in partnerships. This section provides definitions and general rules of applicability that apply for purposes of section 1446(f). Section 1.1446(f)-2 provides withholding rules for the transfer of a

non-publicly traded partnership interest under section 1446(f)(1). Section 1.1446(f)-3 provides rules that apply when a partnership is required to withhold under section 1446(f)(4) on distributions made to the transferee in an amount equal to the amount that the transferee failed to withhold plus interest. Section 1.1446(f)-4 provides special rules for the sale, exchange, or disposition of publicly traded partnership interests, for which the withholding obligation under section 1446(f)(1) is generally imposed on certain brokers that act on behalf of the transferor. Section 1.1446(f)-5 provides rules that address the liability for failure to withhold under section 1446(f) and rules regarding the liability of a transferor's or transferee's agent.

(b) *Definitions.*—This paragraph (b) provides definitions that apply for purposes of § § 1.1446(f)-1 through 1.1446(f)-5.

(1) The term *broker* means any person, foreign or domestic, that, in the ordinary course of a trade or business during the calendar year, stands ready to effect sales made by others, and that, in connection with a transfer of a PTP interest, receives all or a portion of the amount realized on behalf of the transferor. The term broker also includes any clearing organization (as defined in § 1.1471-1(b)(21)) that effects the transfer of a PTP interest on behalf of the transferor. The term broker does not include an escrow agent that effects no sales other than such transactions that are incidental to the purpose of escrow (such as sales to collect on collateral).

(2) The term *controlling partner* means a partner that, together with any person that bears a relationship described in sections 267(b) or 707(b)(1) to the partner, owns directly or indirectly a 50 percent or greater interest in the capital, profits, deductions, or losses of the partnership in the 12 months before the determination date.

(3) The term *effect* has the meaning provided in § 1.6045-1(a)(10).

(4) The term *foreign person* means a person that is not a United States person.

(5) The term *PTP interest* means an interest in a publicly traded partnership if the interest is publicly traded on an established securities market or is readily tradable on a secondary market (or the substantial equivalent thereof).

(6) The term *publicly traded partnership* has the same meaning as in section 7704 and § § 1.7704-1 through 1.7704-4 but does not include a publicly traded partnership treated as a corporation under that section.

(8) The term *TIN* means the tax identifying number assigned to a person under section 6109.

(9) The term *transfer* means a sale, exchange, or other disposition, and includes a distribution from a partnership to a partner.

(10) The term *transferee* means any person, foreign or domestic, that acquires a partnership interest through a transfer, and includes a partnership that makes a distribution.

(11) Except as otherwise provided in this paragraph, the term *transferor* means any person, foreign or domestic, that transfers a partnership interest. In the case of a trust, to the extent all or a portion of the income of the trust is treated as owned by the grantor or another person under sections 671 through 679 (such trust, a grantor trust), the term transferor means the grantor or other person.

(12) The term *transferor's agent* or *transferee's agent* means any person who represents the transferor or transferee (respectively) in any negotiation with another person relating to the transaction or in settling the transaction. A person will not be treated as a transferor's agent or a transferee's agent solely because it performs one or more of the activities described in § 1.1445-4(f)(3) (relating to activities of settlement officers and clerical personnel).

(13) The term *United States person* or *U.S. person* means a person described in section 7701(a)(30).

(c) *General rules of applicability.*—(1) *In general.*—This paragraph (c) provides general rules that apply for purposes of § § 1.1446(f)-1 through 1.1446(f)-5.

(2) *Certifications.*—(i) *In general.*—This paragraph (c)(2) provides rules that are applicable to certifications described in § § 1.1446(f)-1 through 1.1446(f)-5, except as otherwise provided therein, or in forms, instructions, or other guidance. A certification must provide the name and address of the person providing it. A certification must also be signed under penalties of perjury and, if the certification is provided by the transferor, must include a TIN if the transferor has, or is required to have, a TIN. A transferee (or other person required to withhold) may not rely on a certification if it knows that a transferor has, or is required to have, a TIN, and that TIN has not been provided with the certification. A certification includes any documents associated with the certification, such as statements from the partnership, IRS forms, withholding certificates, withholding statements, certifications, or other documentation. Documents associated with the certification form an integral part of the certification, and the penalties of perjury statement provided on the certification also applies to the documents. A certification (other than the certification described in § 1.1446(f)-2(d)(2)) may not be relied upon if it is obtained earlier than 30 days before the transfer or any time after the transfer.

(ii) *Penalties of perjury.*—A certification signed under penalties of perjury must provide the following: "Under penalties of perjury, I declare that I have examined the information on this document, and to the best of my knowledge and belief, it is true, correct, and complete."

(iii) *Authority to sign certifications on behalf of a business entity.*—A certification provided by a business entity must be signed by an individual who is an officer, director, general partner, or managing member of the entity, or, if the general partner or managing member is itself a business entity, an individual who is an officer, director, or managing member of the entity that is the general partner or managing member.

(iv) *Electronic submission.*—A certification may be sent electronically, including as text in an email, an image embedded in an email, or a Portable Document Format (.pdf) attached to an email. An electronic certification, however, may not be relied upon if the person receiving the submission knows that the certification was transmitted by a person not authorized to do so by the person required to execute the certification.

(v) *Retention period.*—Any person that relies on a certification pursuant to § § 1.1446(f)-1 through 1.1446(f)-5 must retain the certification (including any documentation) for the longer of five calendar years following the close of the last calendar year in which it relied on the certification or for as long as it may be relevant to the determination of its withholding obligation under section 1446(f) or its withholding tax liability under section 1461.

(vi) *Submission to IRS.*—Except as provided in § 1.1446(f)-2(b)(7) and 1.1446(f)-2(c)(4)(vi) (involving certifications relating to an income tax treaty), or in any forms, instructions, or other guidance, the recipient of a certification is not required to mail a copy to the IRS.

(vii) *Grantor trusts.*—A certification provided by a transferor that is a grantor or other owner of a grantor trust must identify the portion of the amount realized that is attributable to the grantor or other owner.

(3) *Books and records.*—A partnership that relies on its books and records pursuant to § § 1.1446(f)-1 through 1.1446(f)-5 (including for purposes of providing a certification or other statement) must identify in its books and records the date on which the transfer occurred, the information on which the partnership relied, and the provisions of § § 1.1446(f)-1 through 1.1446(f)-5 supporting an exception from, or adjustment to, the partnership's obligation to withhold. The identification required by this paragraph (c)(3) must be made no later than 30 days after the date of the transfer. The partnership must retain the identified information in its books and records for the longer of five calendar years following the close of the last calendar year in which it relied on the information or for as long as it may be relevant to the determination of its withholding obligation under section 1446(f) or its withholding tax liability under section 1461.

(4) *Determination date.*—(i) *In general.*—This paragraph (c)(4) provides rules for the determination date. The same determination date must be used for all purposes with respect to a transfer. Any statement, certification, or books and records with regard to a transfer must state the determination date. The determination date of a transfer must be one of the following—

(A) The date of the transfer;

(B) Any date that is no more than 60 days before the date of the transfer; or

(C) The date that is the later of—

(1) The first day of the partnership's taxable year in which the transfer occurs, as determined under section 706; or

(2) The date, before the date of the transfer, of the most recent event described in § 1.704-1(b)(2)(iv)(f)(5) or § 1.704-1(b)(2)(iv)(s)(1) (revaluation event), irrespective of whether the capital accounts of the partners are adjusted in accordance with § 1.704-1(b)(2)(iv)(f).

(ii) *Controlling partner.*—The determination date for a transferor that is a controlling partner is determined without regard to paragraph (c)(4)(i)(C) of this section.

(5) *IRS forms and instructions.*—Any reference to an IRS form includes its successor form. Any form must be filed in the manner provided in the instructions to the forms or in other guidance.

(d) *Coordination with section 1445.*—A transferee that is otherwise required to withhold under section 1445(e)(5) or § 1.1445-11T(d)(1) with respect to the amount realized, as well as under section 1446(f)(1), will be subject to the payment and reporting requirements of section 1445 only, and not section 1446(f)(1), with respect to that amount. However, if the transferor has applied for a withholding certificate under the last sentence of §1.1445-11T(d)(1), the transferee must withhold the greater of the amounts required under section 1445(e)(5) or section 1446(f)(1). A transferee that has complied with the withholding requirements under either section 1445(e)(5) or section 1446(f)(1), as applicable under this paragraph (d), will be deemed to satisfy the other withholding requirement.

(e) *Applicability date.*—This section applies to transfers that occur on or after the date that is 60 days after the date that these regulations are published as final regulations in the **Federal Register**. [Reg. 1.1446(f)-1.]

§1.1446(f)-2. Withholding on the transfer of a non-publicly traded partnership interest.—(a) *Transferee's obligation to withhold.*— Except as otherwise provided in this section, a transferee is required to withhold under section 1446(f)(1) a tax equal to 10 percent of the amount realized on any transfer of a partnership interest. This section does not apply to a transfer of a PTP interest that is effected through one or more brokers, including a distribution made with respect to a PTP interest held in an account with a broker. For rules regarding those transfers, see §1.1446(f)-4.

(b) *Exceptions to withholding.*—(1) *In general.*—A transferee is not required to withhold under this section if it properly relies on a certification or its books and records as described in this paragraph (b). A transferee may not rely on a certification if it has actual knowledge that the certification is incorrect or unreliable. A partnership that is a transferee because it makes a distribution may not rely on its books and records if it knows, or has reason to know, that the information is incorrect or unreliable.

(2) *Certification of non-foreign status by transferor.*—A transferee may rely on a certification of non-foreign status from the transferor that states that the transferor is not a foreign person, states the transferor's name, TIN, and address, and is signed under penalties of perjury. For this purpose, a certification of non-foreign status includes a valid Form W-9, *Request for Taxpayer Identification Number and Certification.* For purposes of this paragraph (b)(2), a transferee may rely on a valid Form W-9 from the transferor that it already possesses if the form meets these requirements.

(3) *No realized gain by transferor.*—(i) *In general.*—A transferee (other than a partnership that is a transferee because it makes a distribution) may rely on a certification from the transferor that states that the transfer of the partnership interest would not result in any realized gain (including ordinary income arising from application of section 751 §1.751-1) to the transferor as of the determination date. See paragraph (b)(6) of this section for rules that apply when the transferor realizes gain but is not required to recognize the gain under a provision of the Internal Revenue Code.

(ii) *Partnership distributions.*—A partnership that is a transferee because it makes a distribution may rely on its books and records, or on a certification from the transferor, to determine that the distribution would not result in any realized gain to the transferor as of the determination date.

(4) *Less than 10 percent effectively connected gain.*—(i) *In general.*—A transferee (other than a partnership that is a transferee because it makes a distribution) may rely on a certification from the partnership that states that if the partnership sold all of its assets at fair market value as of the determination date in the manner described in §1.864(c)(8)-1(c), either—

(A) The amount of net gain that would have been effectively connected with the conduct of a trade or business within the United States would be less than 10 percent of the total net gain; or

(B) No gain would have been effectively connected with the conduct of a trade or business within the United States.

(ii) *Partnership distributions.*—A partnership that is a transferee because it makes a distribution may rely on its books and records to determine that as of the determination date either paragraph (b)(4)(i)(A) or (B) of this section is satisfied.

(5) *Less than 10 percent effectively connected taxable income.*— (i) *In general.*—A transferee (other than a partnership making a distribution) may rely on a certification from the transferor that states that—

(A) For the transferor's immediately prior taxable year and the two preceding taxable years, the transferor was at all times a partner in the partnership;

(B) The transferor's allocable share of effectively connected taxable income determined under §1.1446-2 (as provided on Form 8805, *Foreign Partner's Information Statement of Section 1446 Withholding Tax*) (ECTI), including any ECTI allocable to a partner that bears a relationship to the transferor described in sections 267(b)

or 707(b)(1), was less than $1 million in each of the taxable years described in paragraph (b)(5)(i)(A) of this section;

(C) The transferor's allocable share of ECTI in each of the taxable years described in paragraph (b)(5)(i)(A) of this section was less than 10 percent of the transferor's total distributive share of net income from the partnership for that year as determined under subchapter K of the Internal Revenue Code (as provided on Schedule K-1 (Form 1065), *Partner's Share of Income, Deductions, Credits, etc.*); and

(D) The transferor's distributive share of income or gain that is effectively connected with the conduct of a trade or business within the United States or deductions or losses properly allocated and apportioned to that income in each of the taxable years described in paragraph (b)(5)(i)(A) of this section has been reported on a Federal income tax return (either filed by the transferor or, in the case of transferor that is a partnership, filed by its direct or indirect nonresident alien individual or foreign corporate partners) on or before the due date (including extensions), and all amounts due with respect to the reported amounts has been timely paid to the IRS, provided that the return was required to be filed when the transferor furnishes the certification (taking into account any extensions of time to file).

(ii) *Immediately prior taxable year.*—(A) *In general.*—The transferor's immediately prior taxable year is the transferor's most recent taxable year—

(1) With or within which a taxable year of the partnership ended; and

(2) For which a Schedule K-1 (Form 1065) was due (including extensions) or furnished (if earlier) before the transfer.

(B) *Limitation.*—A transferee may not rely on a certification that is provided before the transferor's receipt of the Schedule K-1 (Form 1065) described in paragraph (b)(5)(ii)(A) of this section.

(iii) *No Form 8805.*—(A) *In general.*—Except as provided in paragraph (b)(5)(iii)(B) of this section, a transferor that does not receive Form 8805 because it had no ECTI for which the partnership paid section 1446 tax (within the meaning in §1.1446-2(a)) in any of the years described in paragraph (b)(5)(i)(A) of this section may not make the certification provided in this paragraph (b)(5).

(B) *Exception.*—If, in any of the years described in paragraph (b)(5)(i)(A) of this section, a transferor has an allocable share of loss that is effectively connected with the conduct of a trade or business within the United States, or has deductions properly allocated and apportioned to income that is effectively connected with the conduct of a trade or business within the United States from the partnership, paragraph (b)(5)(iii)(A) of this section does not apply by reason of a lack of Form 8805 with respect to that year, and the transferor is treated as having an allocable share of ECTI of zero in that year for purposes of paragraph (b)(5)(i)(C) of this section.

(iv) *No net distributive share of income.*—A transferor that did not have a net distributive share of income in any year described in paragraph (b)(5)(i)(A) of this section cannot provide the certification described in this paragraph (b)(5).

(v) *Partnership distributions.*—A partnership that is a transferee by reason of making a distribution may rely on its books and records to determine that the requirements in paragraphs (b)(5)(i)(A) through (C) of this section have been satisfied (subject to the rules in paragraphs (b)(5)(ii) through (iv) of this section). The partnership must also obtain a representation from the transferor stating that the requirement in paragraph (b)(5)(i)(D) of this section has been satisfied.

(vi) *No certification when reporting is incorrect.*—A transferor may not make the certification described in this paragraph (b)(5) if it has actual knowledge that the information relevant to the certification that is reported by the partnership on any Form 8805 or Schedule K-1 (Form 1065) is incorrect.

(6) *Certification of nonrecognition by transferor.*—(i) *In general.*— A transferee may rely on a certification from the transferor that states that by reason of the operation of a nonrecognition provision of the Internal Revenue Code the transferor is not required to recognize any gain or loss with respect to the transfer. The certification must briefly describe the transfer and provide the relevant law and facts relating to the certification.

(ii) *Partial nonrecognition.*—Paragraph (b)(6)(i) of this section does not apply if only a portion of the gain realized on the transfer is subject to a nonrecognition provision. However, see paragraph (c)(4)(v) of this section for rules applicable to a transferor's claim for partial nonrecognition.

(7) *Income tax treaties.*—(i) *In general.*—A transferee may rely on a certification from the transferor that states that the transferor is

not subject to tax on any gain from the transfer pursuant to an income tax treaty in effect between the United States and a foreign country if the requirements of this paragraph (b)(7) are met. The transferor must include with the certification a withholding certificate (on a Form W-8BEN, *Certificate of Foreign Status of Beneficial Owner for United States Tax Withholding and Reporting (Individuals)*, or Form W-8BEN-E, *Certificate of Status of Beneficial Owner for United States Tax Withholding and Reporting (Entities)*) that meets the requirements for validity under § 1.1446-1(c)(2)(iv) (or an applicable substitute form that meets the requirements under § 1.1446-1(c)(5)) and that contains the information necessary to support the claim for treaty benefits. A transferee may rely on a certification of treaty benefits only if, within 30 days after the date of the transfer, the transferee mails a copy of the certification to the Internal Revenue Service, at the address provided in § 1.1445-1(g)(10), together with a cover letter providing the name, TIN, and address of the transferee and the partnership in which an interest was transferred.

(ii) *Treaty claim for less than all of the gain.*—Paragraph (b)(7)(i) of this section does not apply if treaty benefits apply to only a portion of the gain from the transfer. However, see paragraph (c)(4)(vi) of this section for rules applicable to situations in which treaty benefits apply to only a portion of the gain.

(iii) *Exclusive means to claim an exception from withholding based on treaty benefits.*—A transferor claiming treaty benefits with respect to all of the gain from the transfer must use the exception in this paragraph (b)(6) and not any other exception or determination procedure in paragraphs (b) and (c) of this section to claim an exception to withholding by reason of a claim of treaty benefits.

(c) *Determining the amount to withhold.*—(1) *In general.*—A transferee that is required to withhold under this section must withhold 10 percent of the amount realized on the transfer of the partnership interest, except as otherwise provided in this paragraph (c). Any procedures in this paragraph (c) apply solely for purposes of determining the amount to withhold under section 1446(f)(1) and this section. A transferee may not rely on a certification if it has actual knowledge that the certification is incorrect or unreliable. A partnership that is a transferee because it makes a distribution may not rely on its books and records if it knows, or has reason to know, that the information is incorrect or unreliable.

(2) *Amount realized.*—(i) *In general.*—The amount realized on the transfer of the partnership interest is determined under section 1001 (including §§ 1.1001-1 through 1.1001-5) and section 752 (including § 1.752-1 through 1.752-7). Thus, the amount realized includes the amount of cash paid (or to be paid), the fair market value of other property transferred (or to be transferred), the amount of any liabilities assumed by the transferee or to which the partnership interest is subject, and the reduction in the transferor's share of partnership liabilities. In the case of a distribution, the amount realized is the sum of the amount of cash distributed (or to be distributed), the fair market value of property distributed (or to be distributed), and the reduction in the transferor's share of partnership liabilities.

(ii) *Alternative procedures for transferee to determine share of partnership liabilities.*—(A) *In general.*—A transferee (other than a partnership that is a transferee because it makes a distribution), as an alternative to determining the share of partnership liabilities under paragraph (c)(2)(i) of this section, may use the procedures of this paragraph (c)(2)(ii) to determine the extent to which a reduction in partnership liabilities is included in the amount realized.

(B) *Certification of liabilities by transferor.*—Except as otherwise provided in this section, a transferee may rely on a certification from a transferor, other than a controlling partner, that provides the amount of the transferor's share of partnership liabilities reported on the most recent Schedule K-1 (Form 1065) issued by the partnership. If the transferor's actual share of liabilities at the time of the transfer differs from the amount reported on that Schedule K-1 (Form 1065), the certification will not be treated as incorrect or unreliable if the transferor also certifies that it does not have actual knowledge of any events occurring after receiving the Schedule K-1 (Form 1065) that would cause the amount of the transferor's share of partnership liabilities at the time of the transfer to differ by more than 25 percent from the amount shown on the Schedule K-1 (Form 1065). A transferee may not rely on a certification if the last day of the partnership taxable year for which the Schedule K-1 (Form 1065) was provided was more than 22 months before the date of the transfer.

(C) *Certification of liabilities by partnership.*—A transferee may rely on a certification from a partnership that provides the amount of the transferor's share of partnership liabilities on the determination date. If the transferor's actual share of liabilities at the time of the transfer differs from the amount on the certification, the certification will not be treated as incorrect or unreliable if the part-

nership also certifies that it does not have actual knowledge of any events occurring after the determination date that would cause the amount of the transferor's share of partnership liabilities at the time of the transfer to differ by more than 25 percent from the amount shown on the certification by the partnership for the determination date.

(iii) *Partnership's determination of partnership liabilities for distributions.*—A partnership that is a transferee because it makes a distribution may rely on its books and records to determine the extent to which the transferor's share of partnership liabilities on the determination date are included in the amount realized. The information in the books and records will not be treated as incorrect or unreliable unless the partnership has actual knowledge, on or before the date of the distribution, of any events occurring after the determination date that would cause the amount of the transferor's share of partnership liabilities at the time of the transfer to differ by more than 25 percent from the amount determined by the partnership as of the determination date.

(iv) *Certification by a foreign partnership of non-foreign status of its partners.*—(A) *In general.*—When a transferor is a foreign partnership, a transferee may use the procedures of this paragraph (c)(2)(iv) to determine the amount realized. For this purpose, the transferee may rely on a certification from the transferor providing the modified amount realized, and may treat the modified amount realized as the amount realized.

(B) *Determining modified amount realized.*—The modified amount realized is determined by multiplying the amount realized (as determined under this paragraph (c)(2), without regard to this paragraph (c)(2)(iv)) by the aggregate percentage computed as of the determination date. The aggregate percentage is the percentage of the gain (if any) arising from the transfer that would be allocated to presumed foreign persons. For this purpose, a presumed foreign person is any direct or indirect partner of the transferor that has not provided a certification of non-foreign status that meets the requirements of paragraph (b)(2) of this section. For purposes of this paragraph (c)(2)(iv), an indirect partner is a person that owns an interest in the transferor indirectly through one or more foreign partnerships.

(C) *Certification.*—The certification is made by providing a withholding certificate (on Form W-8IMY, *Certificate of Foreign Intermediary, Foreign Flow-Through Entity, or Certain U.S. Branches for United States Tax Withholding and Reporting*) and a withholding statement that provides the percentage of gain allocable to each direct or indirect partner and that provides whether each such person is a United States person or presumed foreign person. The certification must also include a certification of non-foreign status that meets the requirements of paragraph (b)(2) of this section from each of the United States persons that are direct or indirect partners of the transferor that are identified as a United States person on the withholding statement.

(3) *Lack of money or property or lack of knowledge regarding liabilities.*—The amount to withhold equals the amount realized determined without regard to any decrease in the transferor's share of partnership liabilities if—

(i) The amount otherwise required to be withheld under this paragraph (c) would exceed the amount realized determined without regard to the decrease in the transferor's share of partnership liabilities; or

(ii) The transferee is unable to determine the amount realized because it does not have actual knowledge of the transferor's share of partnership liabilities (and has not received or cannot rely on a certification described in paragraph (c)(2)(ii)(B) or (C) of this section).

(4) *Certification of maximum tax liability.*—(i) *In general.*—A transferee may use the procedures of this paragraph (c)(4) for determining the amount to withhold for purposes of section 1446(f)(1) and paragraph (a) of this section. A transferee (other than a partnership that is a transferee because it makes a distribution) may rely on a certification from a transferor that is a foreign corporation, a nonresident alien individual or a foreign partnership regarding the transferor's maximum tax liability as described in paragraph (c)(4)(ii) of this section. A partnership that is a transferee because it makes a distribution may instead rely on its books and records to determine the transferor's maximum tax liability if the books and records includes the information required by paragraphs (c)(4)(iii) and (c)(4)(iv) of this section. A transferor that is a foreign partnership is treated as a nonresident alien individual for purposes of determining the transferor's maximum tax liability.

(ii) *Maximum tax liability.*—For purposes of this paragraph (c)(4), the term *maximum tax liability* means the amount of the transferor's effectively connected gain (as determined under paragraph (c)(4)(iii)(E) of this section) multiplied by the applicable percentage, as defined in § 1.1446-3(a)(2).

(iii) *Required information.*—The certification must include—

(A) A statement that the transferor is either a nonresident alien individual, a foreign corporation, or a foreign partnership;

(B) The transferor's adjusted basis in the transferred interest on the determination date;

(C) The transferor's amount realized (determined in accordance with paragraph (c)(2) of this section) on the determination date;

(D) Whether the transferor remains a partner immediately after the transfer;

(E) The amount of outside ordinary gain and outside capital gain that would be recognized and treated as effectively connected gain under § 1.864(c)(8)-1(b) on the determination date (effectively connected gain);

(F) The transferor's maximum tax liability on the determination date;

(G) A representation from the transferor that the transferor determined the amounts described in paragraph (c)(4)(iii)(E) of this section based on the statement described in paragraph (c)(4)(iv) of this section; and

(H) A representation from the transferor that it has provided the transferee with a copy of the statement described in paragraph (c)(4)(iv) of this section.

(iv) *Partnership statement.*—A transferor may make the representation in paragraph (c)(4)(iii)(G) of this section only if the partnership provides to the transferor a statement (that meets the requirements for a certification under the general rules for applicability in § 1.1446(f)-1(c)) that includes—

(A) The partnership's name, address, and TIN; and

(B) The transferor's aggregate deemed sale EC ordinary gain, within the meaning of § 1.864(c)(8)-1(c)(3)(ii)(A) (if any) and the transferor's aggregate deemed sale EC capital gain, within the meaning of § 1.864(c)(8)-1(c)(3)(ii)(B) (if any), in each case, on the determination date.

(v) *Partial nonrecognition.*—If a nonrecognition provision applies to only a portion of the gain realized on the transfer, a certification described in this paragraph (c)(4) may be relied upon only if the certification also includes the information required in paragraph (b)(6) of this section.

(vi) *Income tax treaties.*—If only a portion of the gain on the transfer is not subject to tax pursuant to an income tax treaty in effect between the United States and a foreign country, a certification described in paragraph (c)(4)(i) of this section may be relied upon only if the certification also complies with the requirements of paragraph (b)(7) of this section, including the requirement that the determination that gain from the transfer is not subject to tax pursuant to an income tax treaty be made with respect to the transferor, and that the transferee mail a copy of the relevant certification described in this paragraph (c)(4) to the IRS.

(d) *Reporting and paying withheld amounts.*—(1) *In general.*—A transferee required to withhold under this section must report and pay any tax withheld by the 20th day after the date of the transfer using Forms 8288, *U.S. Withholding Tax Return for Dispositions by Foreign Persons of U.S. Real Property Interests*, and 8288-A, *Statement of Withholding on Dispositions by Foreign Persons of U.S. Real Property Interests*, in accordance with the instructions to those forms. The IRS will stamp Form 8288-A to show receipt and mail a stamped copy to the transferor (at the address reported on the form). *See* paragraph (e)(2) of this section for the procedures for the transferor to claim a credit for amounts withheld. Forms 8288 and 8288-A must include the TINs of both the transferor and the transferee. If any required TIN is not provided, the transferee must still report and pay any tax withheld on Form 8288.

(2) *Certification of withholding to partnership for purposes of section 1446(f)(4).*—A transferee (other than a partnership that is a transferee because it makes a distribution) must certify to the partnership the extent to which it has satisfied its obligation to withhold under this section no later than 10 days after the transfer. The certification must either include a copy of Form 8288-A that the transferee files with respect to the transfer, or state the amount realized and the amount withheld on the transfer of the partnership interest. The certification must also include any certifications that the transferee relied on to apply an exception to withholding under paragraph (b) of this section or to determine the amount to withhold under paragraph (c) of this section. See § 1.1446(f)-3 for rules regarding a partnership's obligation to withhold on distributions to a transferee when this certification establishes only partial satisfaction of the required amount, is not provided, or cannot be relied upon.

(e) *Effect of withholding on transferor.*—(1) *In general.*—The withholding of tax by a transferee under this section does not relieve a foreign person from filing a U.S. tax return with respect to the transfer. See §§ 1.6012-1(b)(1), 1.6012-2(g)(1), and 1.6031(a)-1. Further, the withholding of tax by a transferee does not relieve a nonresident alien individual or foreign corporation subject to tax under section 864(c)(8) from paying any tax due with the return that has not been fully satisfied through withholding.

(2) *Manner of obtaining credit.*—(i) *Individuals and corporations.*—Except as provided in paragraph (e)(3) of this section, an individual or corporation may claim a credit under section 33 for the amount withheld under this section by attaching to its applicable return the stamped copy of Form 8288-A provided to it under paragraph (d)(1) of this section. *See also* § 1.1462-1.

(ii) *Partnerships.*—For a rule allowing a foreign partnership that is a transferor to claim a credit for the amount withheld under this section against its tax liability under section 1446(a), see § 1.1446-3(c)(4).

(3) *Failure to receive Form 8288-A.*—If a stamped copy of Form 8288-A has not been provided to the transferor by the IRS, the transferor may establish the amount of tax withheld by the transferee by attaching to its return substantial evidence of the amount. The transferor must attach to its return a statement that includes all of the information otherwise required to be provided on Form 8288-A.

(f) *Applicability date.*—This section applies to transfers that occur on or after the date that is 60 days after the date that these regulations are published as final regulations in the **Federal Register**. [Reg. 1.1446(f)-2.]

§ 1.1446(f)-3. Partnership's requirement to withhold under section 1446(f)(4) on distributions to transferee.—(a) *Partnership's obligation to withhold amounts not withheld by the transferee.*—(1) *In general.*—If a transferee fails to withhold any amount required to be withheld under § 1.1446(f)-2, the partnership in which the interest was transferred must withhold from any distributions made to the transferee pursuant to this section. To determine its withholding obligation under this paragraph (a)(1), a partnership may rely on a certification received from the transferee described in § 1.1446(f)-2(d)(2) unless it knows, or has reason to know, that the certification is incorrect or unreliable.

(2) *Notification by IRS.*—A partnership that receives notification from the IRS that a transferee has provided incorrect information regarding the amount realized or amount withheld on the certification described in § 1.1446(f)-2(d)(2), or has failed to pay the IRS the amount reported as withheld on the certification, must withhold the amount prescribed in the notification on distributions to the transferee made on or after the date that is 15 days after it receives the notification. For this purpose, the amount realized is not treated as incorrect if the transferee properly relied on a certification to compute the amount realized pursuant to § 1.1446(f)-2(c)(2).

(b) *Exceptions to withholding.*—(1) *Withholding has been satisfied by transferee.*—A partnership is not required to withhold under paragraph (a)(1) of this section if it relies on a certification described in § 1.1446(f)-2(d)(2) received from the transferee (within the time prescribed in that section) that states that an exception to withholding described in § 1.1446(f)-2(b) applies or that the transferee withheld the full amount required to be withheld (taking into account any adjustments under § 1.1446(f)-2(c)) under § 1.1446(f)-2.

(2) *PTP interests.*—(i) *In general.*—Except as provided in paragraph (b)(2)(ii) of this section, a partnership is not required to withhold under this section on distributions made with respect to a PTP interest.

(ii) *Exception for a false qualified notice.*—If a publicly traded partnership determines (including by reason of notification from the IRS) that it has published a qualified notice that falsely states that either the exception described in § 1.1446(f)-4(b)(3) (the 10-percent exception) or the exception described in § 1.1446(f)-4(b)(4) (the qualified current income exception) applies, the publicly traded partnership must withhold under this section on distributions to the transferee in an amount equal to the amount that a broker failed to withhold under § 1.1446(f)-4 due to reliance on the qualified notice, plus interest.

(3) *Distributing partnerships.*—A partnership that is a transferee because it makes a distribution is not required to withhold under this section.

(c) *Withholding rules.*—(1) *Timing of withholding.*—(i) *In general.*—A partnership required to withhold under paragraph (a)(1) of this section must withhold on distributions made to the transferee beginning on the later of—

(A) The date that is 30 days after the date of transfer; or

(B) The date that is 15 days after the date on which the partnership acquires actual knowledge that the transfer has occurred.

(ii) *Satisfaction of withholding obligation.*—A partnership is treated as satisfying its withholding obligation under paragraph (a)(1) of this section and may stop withholding on distributions to the transferee on the earlier of—

(A) The date on which the partnership completes withholding and paying the amount required to be withheld under paragraph (c)(2) of this section;

(B) The date on which the partnership receives and may rely on a certification from the transferee described in §1.1446(f)-2(d)(2) (without regard to whether the certification is received by the time prescribed in that section) that claims an exception to withholding under §1.1446(f)-2(b); or

(C) If a partnership interest is not a PTP interest, the date on which the transferee no longer owns an interest in the partnership, unless the partnership has actual knowledge that any successor to the transferee is a person that bears a relationship described in section 267(b) or 707(b)(1) with respect to the transferee or the transferor from which the transferee acquired the interest.

(2) *Amount to withhold.*—(i) *In general.*—A partnership required to withhold under paragraph (a)(1) of this section must withhold the full amount of each distribution made to the transferee until it has withheld—

(A) A tax of 10 percent of the amount realized (determined solely under §1.1446(f)-2(c)(2)(i) or, in the case of a publicly traded partnership, solely under §1.1446(f)-4(c)(2)(i)) on the transfer, reduced by any amount withheld by the transferee, plus

(B) Any interest computed under paragraph (c)(2)(ii) of this section.

(ii) *Computation of interest.*—The amount of interest required to be withheld under paragraph (a)(1) of this section is the amount of interest that would be required to be paid under section 6601 and §301.6601-1 if the amount that should have been withheld by the transferee was considered an underpayment of tax. For this purpose, interest is payable between the date that is 20 days after the date of the transfer and the date on which the tax due under paragraph (a)(1) of this section is paid to the IRS.

(iii) *Certifications required.*—For purposes of paragraph (c)(2)(i)(A) of this section, a partnership must determine the amount realized on the transfer and any amount withheld by the transferee based on a certification from the transferee described in §1.1446(f)-2(d)(2), without regard to whether the certification is received by the time prescribed in that section. A partnership that does not receive or cannot rely on a certification from the transferee described in §1.1446(f)-2(d)(2) must withhold tax equal to the full amount of each distribution made to the transferee until it receives a certification that it can rely on.

(3) *Coordination with other withholding provisions.*—Any amount required to be withheld on a distribution under any other provision of the Internal Revenue Code is not also required to be withheld under section 1446(f)(4) or this section.

(d) *Reporting and paying withheld amounts.*—The partnership must report and pay the tax withheld using Forms 8288, *U.S. Withholding Tax Return for Dispositions by Foreign Persons of U.S. Real Property Interests*, and 8288-C, *Statement of Withholding Under Section 1446(f)(4) for Withholding on Dispositions by Foreign Persons of Partnership Interests*, as provided in forms, instructions, or other guidance.

(e) *Effect of withholding on transferor and transferee.*—(1) *Transferor.*—The withholding of tax by a partnership under this section does not relieve a foreign person from filing a U.S. income tax return with respect to the transfer. See §§1.6012-1(b)(1), 1.6012-2(g)(1), and 1.6031(a)-1. Further, the withholding of tax by a partnership does not relieve a nonresident alien individual or foreign corporation subject to tax under section 864(c)(8) from paying any tax due with the return that has not been fully satisfied through withholding. An individual or corporation is not allowed a credit under section 33 for amounts withheld on distributions to the transferee under this section. See, however, §§1.1446(f)-5(a) and 1.1463-1(a), which generally provide that tax will not be recollected if paid by another person.

(2) *Transferee.*—A transferee is treated as satisfying its withholding tax liability under §1.1446(f)-2 to the extent that a partnership withholds tax (which does not include interest) from the transferee under this section. Interest computed under paragraph (c)(2)(ii) of this section that is withheld by the partnership from the transferee is treated as interest paid by the transferee with respect to its withholding tax liability under §1.1446(f)-2. A transferee may not obtain a refund when the amount of tax withheld under this section exceeds the transferee's withholding tax liability under §1.1446(f)-2.

Instead, only the partnership may claim a refund on behalf of the transferee for the excess amount under this section.

(f) *Applicability date.*—This section applies to transfers that occur on or after the date that is 60 days after the date that these regulations are published as final regulations in the **Federal Register**. [Reg. 1.1446(f)-3.]

§1.1446(f)-4. Withholding on the transfer of a publicly traded partnership interest.—(a) *Broker's obligation to withhold on a transfer of a PTP interest.*—(1) *In general.*—If a transfer of a PTP interest is effected through one or more brokers, the transferee is not required to withhold under section 1446(f)(1) and §1.1446(f)-2. Rather, any broker required to withhold under paragraph (a)(2) of this section must withhold a tax equal to 10 percent of the amount realized (as defined in paragraph (c)(2) of this section) on the transfer of a PTP interest, except as otherwise provided in this section. For rules regarding the application of section 1446(f)(4) and §1.1446(f)-3 to a publicly traded partnership, see §1.1446(f)-3(b)(2).

(2) *Broker's requirement to withhold.*—(i) *Payments to foreign brokers.*—A broker that pays the amount realized from the transfer of a PTP interest to another broker that is a foreign person must withhold under this section unless the foreign person is—

(A) A qualified intermediary (as defined in §1.1441-1(e)(5)(ii)) that provides a valid qualified intermediary withholding certificate (as described in §1.1441-1(e)(3)(ii)) that states that it assumes primary withholding responsibility under chapter 3; or

(B) A U.S. branch of a foreign person (as described in §1.1441-1(b)(2)(iv)) that provides a valid U.S. branch withholding certificate (as described in §1.1441-1(e)(3)(v)) that states that it agrees to be treated as a U.S. person with respect to any payment associated with the certificate.

(ii) *Brokers with customer relationship with transferor.*—A broker that effects the transfer for the transferor as its customer (as defined in §1.6045-1(a)(2)) is required to withhold under this section.

(iii) *Exception.*—A broker is not required to withhold under this section if it knows that the withholding obligation has already been satisfied.

(iv) *Determination of foreign broker's status.*—For purposes of paragraph (a)(2)(i) of this section, a broker must treat another broker as a foreign person unless it obtains documentation (including a certification of non-foreign status) establishing that the other broker is a U.S. person.

(b) *Exceptions to withholding.*—(1) *In general.*—A broker is not required to withhold under this section if it properly relies on a certification described in paragraph (b)(2) or (b)(6) of this section, a qualified notice described in paragraph (b)(3) or (b)(4) of this section, or if the exception described in paragraph (b)(5) of this section applies. A broker may not rely on a certification described in this paragraph (b) if it has actual knowledge that the certification is incorrect or unreliable.

(2) *Certification of non-foreign status.*—A broker may rely on a certification of non-foreign status that it obtains from the transferor. A certification of non-foreign status under this section means a Form W-9, *Request for Taxpayer Identification Number and Certification*, or valid substitute form, that meets the requirements of §1.1441-1(d)(2). For this purpose, a broker may rely on a valid form that it already possesses from the transferor. A broker may instead rely on certification from a second broker (as defined in §1.6045-1(a)(1)) that acts as an agent for the transferor when the second broker does not receive the amount realized from the transfer of the PTP interest. This certification must state that the second broker has collected a valid certification of non-foreign status (within the meaning of this paragraph (b)(2)) from the transferor, and it must include the transferor's TIN and status as a foreign or U.S. person.

(3) *Less than 10 percent effectively connected gain by partnership.*—(i) *In general.*—A broker may rely on a qualified notice described in paragraph (b)(3)(iii) of this section that states that the 10-percent exception applies, as determined under paragraph (b)(3)(ii) of this section.

(ii) *10-percent exception.*—(A) *In general.*—The 10-percent exception applies to a transfer if, on the PTP designated date described in paragraph (b)(3)(ii)(B) of this section, had the publicly traded partnership sold all of its assets at fair market value in the manner described in §1.864(c)(8)-1(c), either—

(1) The amount of gain that would have been effectively connected with the conduct of a trade or business within the United States would be less than 10 percent of the total gain; or

(2) No gain would have been effectively connected with the conduct of a trade or business within the United States.

(B) *PTP designated date.*—The PTP designated date for a transfer is any date for a deemed sale determination that is designated by the publicly traded partnership in a qualified notice described in paragraph (b)(3)(iii) of this section, provided that the PTP designated date occurs on or after the date that is 92 days before the date on which the publicly traded partnership posted the qualified notice naming the PTP designated date.

(iii) *Qualified notice.*—(A) *In general.*—Except as provided in paragraph (b)(3)(iii)(B) and (C) of this section, a qualified notice described in this paragraph (b)(3)(iii) is the most recent qualified notice (within the meaning of §1.1446-4(b)(4)) posted by the publicly traded partnership.

(B) *Qualified notice posting date requirement.*—A qualified notice is described in this paragraph (b)(3)(iii) only if the publicly traded partnership has posted it within the 92-day period ending on the date of the transfer.

(C) *Recent posting of qualified notice.*—If the most recent qualified notice posted by the publicly traded partnership was posted during the 10-day period ending on the date of the transfer, a broker may instead rely on the immediately preceding qualified notice (within the meaning of §1.1446-4(b)(4)) posted by the publicly traded partnership, provided that it satisfies the condition described in paragraph (b)(3)(iii)(B) of this section.

(4) *Distribution made from current income.*—(i) *In general.*—A broker is not required to withhold under this section on a distribution by a publicly traded partnership if the entire amount of a distribution is designated, on a qualified notice (within the meaning of §1.1446-4(b)(4)) posted with respect to that distribution, as a qualified current income distribution (within the meaning of paragraph (b)(4)(ii) of this section).

(ii) *Qualified current income distribution.*—A qualified current income distribution is a distribution that does not exceed the net income of the publicly traded partnership since the record date (within the meaning of 17 CFR 240.14a-1(h) or its successor provision) of the immediately preceding distribution made by the publicly traded partnership.

(5) *Amount subject to withholding under section 3406.*—A broker is not required to withhold under this section if the amount realized from the transfer of the PTP interest is subject to withholding under §31.3406(b)(3)-2 of this chapter.

(6) *Income tax treaties.*—A broker may rely on a certification from the transferor that states that the transferor is not subject to tax on any gain from the transfer pursuant to an income tax treaty in effect between the United States and a foreign country if the requirements of this paragraph (b)(6) are met. The transferor must include with the certification a withholding certificate (on a Form W-8BEN, *Certificate of Foreign Status of Beneficial Owner for United States Tax Withholding and Reporting (Individuals)*, or Form W-8BEN-E, *Certificate of Status of Beneficial Owner for United States Tax Withholding and Reporting (Entities)*) that meets the requirements for validity under §1.1446-1(c)(2)(iv) (or an applicable substitute form that meets the requirements under §1.1446-1(c)(5)) and that contains the information necessary to support the claim for treaty benefits. For purposes of this paragraph (b)(6), a broker may rely on a withholding certificate that it already possesses from the transferor unless it has actual knowledge that the information is incorrect or unreliable. This exception does not apply if treaty benefits apply to only a portion of the gain from the transfer.

(c) *Determining the amount to withhold.*—(1) *In general.*—A broker that is required to withhold under this section must withhold 10 percent of the amount realized on the transfer of the PTP interest, except as provided in this paragraph (c). Any procedures in this paragraph (c) apply solely for purposes of determining the amount to withhold under section 1446(f)(1) and this section. A broker may not rely on a certification described in this paragraph (c) if it has actual knowledge that the certification is incorrect or unreliable.

(2) *Amount realized.*—(i) *In general.*—Solely for purposes of this section, the amount realized is the amount of gross proceeds (as defined in §1.6045-1(d)(5)) paid or credited upon the transfer to the customer or other broker (as applicable), or, in the case of a distribution, the amount of cash distributed (or to be distributed) and the fair market value of property distributed (or to be distributed).

(ii) *Certification by a foreign partnership of non-foreign status of its partners.*—(A) *In general.*—When a transferor is a foreign partnership, a broker may use the procedures of this paragraph (c)(2)(ii) to determine the amount realized. For this purpose, the broker may rely on a certification from the transferor providing the modified amount realized, and may treat the modified amount realized as the amount realized.

(B) *Determining modified amount realized.*—The modified amount realized is determined by multiplying the amount realized (as determined under this paragraph (c)(2), without regard to this paragraph (c)(2)(ii)) by the aggregate percentage computed as of the determination date. The aggregate percentage is the percentage of the gain (if any) arising from the transfer that would be allocated to presumed foreign persons. For this purpose, a presumed foreign person is any direct or indirect partner of the transferor that has not provided a certification of non-foreign status that meets the requirements of paragraph (b)(2) of this section. For purposes of this paragraph (c)(2)(ii), an indirect partner is a person that owns an interest in the transferor indirectly through one or more foreign partnerships.

(C) *Certification.*—The certification is made by providing a withholding certificate (on Form W-8IMY, *Certificate of Foreign Intermediary, Foreign Flow-Through Entity, or Certain U.S. Branches for United States Tax Withholding and Reporting*) and a withholding statement that provides the percentage of gain allocable to each direct or indirect partner and that provides whether each such person is a United States person or presumed foreign person. The certification must also include a certification of non-foreign status that meets the requirements of paragraph (b)(2) of this section from each of the United States persons that are direct or indirect partners of the transferor that are identified as a United States person on the withholding statement. For purposes of this paragraph (c)(2)(ii), a broker may rely on a withholding certificate and withholding statement that it already possesses from the partnership unless it has actual knowledge that the information is incorrect or unreliable.

(d) *Reporting and paying withheld amounts.*—A broker that is required to withhold under this section must pay the withheld tax pursuant to the deposit rules in §1.6302-2. For rules regarding reporting on Forms 1042, *Annual Withholding Tax Return for U.S. Source Income of Foreign Persons*, and 1042-S, *Foreign Person's U.S. Source Income Subject to Withholding*, that apply to a broker that withholds under this section, see §1.1461-1(b) and (c). For rules regarding when an amount realized on the transfer of a PTP interest is an amount subject to reporting, see §1.1461-1(c)(2)(i)(Q). A broker that pays the amount realized to a foreign partnership must issue a Form 1042-S directly to the partnership rather than issuing a form to each of the partners of the partnership. *See* §1.1461-1(c)(1)(ii)(A)(8) (treating the foreign partnership as a recipient for reporting purposes). A broker making a payment to a U.S. branch treated as a U.S. person must not treat the branch as a U.S. person for purposes of reporting the payment made to the branch. Therefore, a payment to that U.S. branch must be reported on Form 1042-S. *See* §1.1461-1(c). A Form 1042-S issued directly to the transferor must include the TIN of the transferor unless the broker does not know the TIN at the time of issuance.

(e) *Effect of withholding on transferor.*—(1) *In general.*—The withholding of tax under this section does not relieve a foreign person from filing a U.S. tax return with respect to the transfer. *See* §§1.6012-1(b)(1), 1.6012-2(g)(1), and 1.6031(a)-1. Further, the withholding of tax by a broker does not relieve a nonresident alien individual or foreign corporation subject to tax under section 864(c)(8) from paying any tax due with the return that has not been fully satisfied through withholding.

(2) *Manner of obtaining credit.*—(i) *Individuals and corporations.*—An individual or corporation may claim a credit under section 33 for the amount withheld under this section by attaching to its applicable return a copy of a Form 1042-S that includes its TIN.

(ii) *Partnerships.*—For a rule allowing a foreign partnership that is a transferor to claim a credit for the amount withheld under this section against its obligation to withhold under section 1446(a), see §1.1446-3(c)(4).

(f) *Applicability date.*—This section applies to transfers that occur on or after the date that is 60 days after the date that these regulations are published as final regulations in the **Federal Register**. [Reg. 1.1446(f)-4.]

§1.1446(f)-5. Liability for failure to withhold.—(a) *Liability for failure to withhold.*—Every person required to withhold and pay tax under section 1446(f), but that fails to do so, is liable for the tax under section 1461. Under section 1463, if the tax required to be withheld is paid by another person required to withhold under section 1446(f) or by the nonresident alien individual or foreign corporation subject to tax under section 864(c)(8), the tax will not be recollected. However, any person that failed to withhold under section 1446(f) is in no case relieved from liability for any interest, penalties, or additions to tax that would otherwise apply. A partnership that failed to withhold and pay tax under §1.1446(f)-3 is only liable for the amount of tax that it failed to collect (but not any interest computed on that amount under §1.1446(f)-3(c)(2)(ii)), plus any interest, penalties, or additions to tax with regard to the partnership's failure to withhold.

(b) *Liability of agents.*—(1) *Duty to provide notice of false certification.*—A transferee's or transferor's agent (other than a broker required to withhold under §1.1446(f)-4) must provide notice to a transferee (or other person required to withhold) if that person is furnished with a certification described in §§1.1446(f)-1 through 1.1446(f)-4 and the agent knows that the certification is false. A person required to withhold may not rely on a certification if it receives the notice described in this paragraph (b)(1).

(2) *Procedural requirements.*—Any agent who is required to provide notice under paragraph (b)(1) of this section must do so in writing (including by electronic submission) as soon as possible after learning of the false certification. If the agent first learns of the false certification before the date of transfer, notice must be given by the third day following that discovery but no later than the date of transfer (before the transferee's payment of consideration). If an agent first learns of a false certification after the date of transfer, notice must be given by the third day following that discovery. The notice must also explain the possible consequences to the recipient of a failure to withhold. The notice need not disclose the information on which the agent's statement is based. The agent must also furnish a copy of the notice to the IRS by the date on which the notice is required to be given to the recipient. The copy of the notice must be delivered to the address provided in §1.1445-1(g)(10) and must be accompanied by a cover letter stating that the copy is being filed pursuant to the requirements of §1.1446(f)-5(b)(2).

(3) *Failure to provide notice.*—Any agent who is required to provide notice under paragraph (b)(1) of this section, but fails to do so in the manner required in paragraph (b)(2) of this section, is liable for the tax that the person who should have been provided notice in accordance with paragraph (b)(2) of this section was required to withhold under section 1446(f) if the notice had been given.

(4) *Limitation on liability.*—An agent's liability under paragraph (b)(3) of this section is limited to the amount of compensation that the agent derives from the transaction. In addition, an agent that assists in the preparation of, or fails to disclose knowledge of, a false certification may be liable for civil and criminal penalties.

(c) *Applicability date.*—This section applies to transfers that occur on or after the date that is 60 days after the date that these regulations are published as final regulations in the **Federal Register**. [Reg. 1.1446(f)-5.]

Withholding: Reducing Burden under FATCA

Withholding: Reducing Burden under FATCA.—Amendments to Reg. §§1.1461-1 and 1.1461-2, eliminating withholding on payments of gross proceeds, deferring withholding on foreign passthru payments, eliminating withholding on certain insurance premiums, and clarifying the definition of investment entity, are proposed (published in the Federal Register on December 18, 2018) (REG-132881-17).

Par. 4. Section 1.1461-1 is amended by:

1. Adding two sentences after the first sentence in paragraph (a)(1).
2. Redesignating paragraph (c)(1)(i) as paragraph (c)(1)(i)(A) and adding paragraphs (c)(1)(i) introductory text and (c)(1)(i)(B).
3. Adding a sentence at the end of paragraph (c)(4)(iv).

The additions read as follows:

§1.1461-1. Payment and returns of tax withheld.—(a) * * *

(1) * * * In a case in which a withholding agent is permitted to withhold on an amount subject to reporting (as defined in paragraph (c)(2) of this section) in a calendar year (subsequent year) following the calendar year (preceding year) in which the withholding agent paid such amount (or, for a partnership or trust withholding with respect to a foreign partner, beneficiary, or owner, the year the partnership or trust received such amount), the withholding agent shall designate the deposit of the withholding as made for the preceding year and report the tax liability on Form 1042 for the preceding year. In the case of a partnership that withholds as described in the preceding sentence and does not file its federal income tax return on a calendar-year basis, however, such partnership may instead designate the deposit as made for the subsequent year and report the tax liability on Form 1042 for the subsequent year. * * *

* * *

(c) * * *

(1) * * *

(i) *Withholding agent information reporting.*—This paragraph (c)(1)(i) describes the general requirements for a withholding agent to file an information return on Form 1042-S and describes a special rule for a withholding agent that withholds in a subsequent year as described in paragraph (a)(1) of this section.

* * *

(B) *Special reporting by withholding agents that withhold in a subsequent year.*—Notwithstanding the first sentence of paragraph (c)(1)(i)(A) of this section, if a withholding agent designates the deposit of such withholding as made for the preceding calendar year as described in paragraph (a)(1) of this section, the withholding agent is required to report the amount on Form 1042-S for the preceding year. With respect to a withholding agent described in the previous sentence that is a partnership and that withholds after March 15 of the subsequent year, such partnership may file and furnish the Form 1042-S on or before September 15 of that year. In the case of a partnership that designates the deposit of such withholding as made for the subsequent year as permitted in paragraph (a)(1) of this section, however, the partnership shall report the amount on Form 1042-S for the subsequent year.

* * *

(4) * * *

(iv) * * * If a nonqualified intermediary that is a participating FFI or a registered deemed-compliant FFI receives a payment that has been withheld upon at a 30-percent rate under chapter 4 by another withholding agent and that is reported as made to an unknown recipient on Form 1042-S provided to the nonqualified intermediary, the nonqualified intermediary may report the payment (or portion of the payment) on Form 1042-S as made to a recipient that has been withheld upon under chapter 3 when the payment is not an amount for which withholding is required under chapter 4 based on the payee's chapter 4 status and the nonqualified intermediary reports the correct withholding rate for the recipient.

* * *

Par. 5. Section 1.1461-2 is amended by:

1. Revising the second sentence of paragraph (a)(2)(i) introductory text.
2. Revising paragraphs (a)(2)(i)(A) and (B).
3. Adding paragraph (a)(2)(i)(C).
4. Revising paragraph (a)(3).

The revisions and addition read as follows:

§1.1461-2. Adjustments for overwithholding or underwithholding of tax.—(a) * * *

(2) * * *

(i) * * * In such a case, the withholding agent may reimburse itself by reducing, by the amount of tax actually repaid to the beneficial owner or payee, the amount of any deposit of withholding tax otherwise required to be made by the withholding agent under §1.6302-2(a)(1)(iii) for any subsequent payment period occurring before the end of the calendar year following the calendar year of overwithholding. * * *

(A) The repayment to the beneficial owner or payee occurs before the earliest of the due date (including extensions) for filing the Form 1042-S for the calendar year of overwithholding, the date the Form 1042-S is actually filed with the IRS, or the date the Form 1042-S is furnished to the beneficial owner or payee;

(B) The withholding agent states on a timely filed (including extensions) Form 1042-S for the calendar year of overwithholding the amount of tax withheld and the amount of any actual repayment; and

(C) The withholding agent states on a timely filed (including extensions) Form 1042 for the calendar year of overwithholding the amount of adjustments made to overwithholding under paragraph (a)(1) of this section and the amount of any credit claimed under §1.6414-1.

* * *

(3) *Set-off.*—Under the set-off procedure, the withholding agent may repay the beneficial owner or payee by applying the amount overwithheld against any amount of tax which otherwise would be required under chapter 3 or 4 of the Internal Revenue Code

or the regulations under part 1 of this chapter to be withheld from income paid by the withholding agent to such person. Any such set-off that occurs for a payment period in the calendar year following the calendar year of overwithholding shall be allowed only if—

(i) The repayment to the beneficial owner or payee occurs before the earliest of the due date (including extensions) for filing the Form 1042-S for the calendar year of overwithholding, the date the Form 1042-S is actually filed with the IRS, or the date the Form 1042-S is furnished to the beneficial owner or payee;

(ii) The withholding agent states on a timely filed (including extensions) Form 1042-S for the calendar year of overwithholding the amount of tax withheld and the amount of any repayment made through set-off; and

(iii) The withholding agent states on a timely filed (including extensions) Form 1042 for the calendar year of overwithholding the amount of adjustments made to overwithholding under paragraph (a)(1) of this section and the amount of any credit claimed under § 1.6414-1.

* * *

Interests in Partnerships: Withholding of Tax: Information Reporting

Interests in Partnerships: Withholding of Tax: Information Reporting.—Amendments to Reg. §§ 1.1461-1—1.1461-3, implementing certain sections of the Internal Revenue Code, including sections added to the Internal Revenue Code by the Tax Cuts and Jobs Act, that relate to the withholding of tax and information reporting with respect to certain dispositions of interests in partnerships engaged in the conduct of a trade or business within the United States, are proposed (published in the Federal Register on May 13, 2019) (REG-105476-18).

Par. 10. Section 1.1461-1 is amended:

1. As proposed to be amended December 18, 2018, at 83 FR 64757:

i. Paragraph (a)(1) is further amended by revising the sixth, seventh, and eighth sentences.

ii. Paragraph (c)(1)(i)(A) is further amended by revising the second and third sentences.

2. By revising paragraph (c)(1)(ii)(A)(8).

3. By adding paragraph (c)(1)(ii)(B)(5).

4. In paragraph (c)(2)(i) introductory text, by revising the first and second sentences.

5. In paragraph (c)(2)(i)(N), by removing the word "and" that follows the semi-colon.

6. In paragraph (c)(2)(i)(O), by removing the period at the end of the paragraph and adding "; and" in its place.

7. By adding paragraphs (c)(2)(i)(P) and (Q).

8. By adding a sentence at the end of paragraph (c)(4)(ii)(A).

9. Revising paragraph (i).

The revisions and additions read as follows:

§ 1.1461-1. Payment and returns of tax withheld.—(a) * * *

(1) *Deposits of tax.*—* * * With respect to withholding under section 1446, this section shall apply only to publicly traded partnerships and nominees that withhold under § 1.1446-4 and brokers that withhold under § 1.1446(f)-4 on transfers of publicly traded partnership interests. See § 1.1461-3 for penalties that apply for failure to withhold under section 1446(a) on effectively connected taxable income allocable to foreign partners or under section 1446(f) on transfers of partnership interests by foreign partners. The references in the previous two sentences to § 1.1446(f)-4 and section 1446(f) shall apply to transfers of partnership interests that occur on or after 60 days after the date that these regulations are published as final regulations in the **Federal Register**.

* * *

(c) * * *

(1) * * *

(i) * * *

(A) *In general.*—* * * Notwithstanding the preceding sentence, any person that withholds or is required to withhold an amount under sections 1441, 1442, 1443, § 1.1446-4(a) (applicable to publicly traded partnerships required to pay tax under section 1446(a) on distributions), or § 1.1446(f)-4(a) (applicable to brokers required to withhold on transfers of publicly traded partnership interests) must file a Form 1042-S for the payment withheld upon whether or not that person is engaged in the conduct of a trade or business and whether or not the payment is an amount subject to reporting. The reference in the previous sentence to § 1.1446(f)-4(a) shall apply with respect to returns for transfers that occur on or after 60 days after the date that these regulations are published as final regulations in the **Federal Register**. * * *

* * *

(ii) * * *

(A) * * *

(8) A partner (including a foreign partnership) receiving a distribution from a publicly traded partnership subject to withholding under section 1446(a) and § 1.1446-4 on distributions of effectively connected income, and a partner (including a foreign partnership) receiving an amount realized from a transfer of a publicly traded partnership interest subject to withholding under section 1446(f)(1) and § 1.1446(f)-4. The references in this paragraph (c)(1)(ii)(A)(8) to section 1446(f)(1) and § 1.1446(f)-4 shall apply with respect to returns for transfers that occur on or after 60 days after the date that these regulations are published as final regulations in the **Federal Register**.

* * *

(B) * * *

(5) A foreign broker withheld upon under § 1.1446(f)-4(a)(2)(i) by another broker paying an amount realized from the transfer of a PTP interest.

(2) * * *

(i) *In general.*—Subject to the exceptions described in paragraph (c)(2)(ii) of this section, amounts subject to reporting on Form 1042-S are amounts paid to a foreign payee or partner (including persons presumed to be foreign) that are amounts subject to withholding as defined in § 1.1441-2(a), § 1.1446-4(a) (addressing publicly traded partnerships required to pay withholding tax under section 1446(a) on distributions of effectively connected income), or § 1.1446(f)-4(a) (addressing brokers required to withhold and pay tax on the amount realized on the transfer of an interest in a publicly traded partnership). The reference in the previous sentence to withholding under § 1.1446-4(f) shall apply with respect to returns for transfers that occur on or after 60 days after the date that these regulations are published as final regulations in the **Federal Register**. * * *

* * *

(P) The amount of any distribution made by a publicly traded partnership that is an amount subject to withholding under § 1.1446-4, or that is paid to a qualified intermediary that assumes primary withholding responsibility for the payment or a U.S. branch of a foreign person that agrees to be treated as a U.S. person described in § 1.1446-4(b)(2); and

(Q) An amount realized on the transfer of a publicly traded partnership interest subject to § 1.1446(f)-4 (unless an exception to withholding applies under § 1.1446(f)-4(b)(2) through (5)).

* * *

(4) * * *

(ii) * * *

(A) *Amounts paid to a nonqualified intermediary, a flow-through entity, and certain U.S. branches.*—* * * For a payment to a foreign partnership on the transfer of a publicly traded partnership interest subject to § 1.1446(f)-4(a), see paragraph (c)(1)(ii)(A)(8) of this section (treating the foreign partnership as a recipient).

* * *

(i) *Applicability date.*—(1) *In general.*—Except as provided in paragraph (i)(2) of this section, this section applies to returns required for payments made on or after January 6, 2017. For payments made after June 30, 2014, and before January 6, 2017, see this section as in effect and contained in 26 CFR part 1, as revised April 1, 2016. For payments made after December 31, 2000, and before July 1, 2014, see this section as in effect and contained in 26 CFR part 1, as revised April 1, 2013.

(2) *Exceptions.*—Paragraphs (a)(1), (c)(1)(i)(A), (c)(1)(ii)(A)(8), (c)(2)(i), and (c)(2)(iii) of this section apply as provided in those paragraphs. Paragraphs (c)(1)(ii)(A)(11), (c)(1)(ii)(B)(5), (c)(2)(i)(P) and (Q), and (c)(4)(ii)(A) apply with respect to returns for transfers that occur on or after 60 days after the date that these regulations are published as final regulations in the **Federal Register**.

Par. 11. Section 1.1461-2 is amended:

1. By revising paragraph (a)(1).

2. As proposed to be amended April 13, 2016, at 81 FR 21795, by revising the first and last sentences of paragraph (b).

The revisions and addition read as follows:

§1.1461-2. Adjustments for overwithholding or underwithholding of tax.—(a) * * *

(1) *In general.*—Except as otherwise provided in this paragraph (a)(1), a withholding agent that has overwithheld under chapter 3 of the Internal Revenue Code, and made a deposit of the tax as provided in §1.6302-2(a), may adjust the overwithheld amount either pursuant to the reimbursement procedure described in paragraph (a)(2) of this section or pursuant to the set-off procedure described in paragraph (a)(3) of this section. These rules do not apply to partnerships or nominees required to withhold under section 1446(a), other than on a distribution by a publicly traded partnership subject to withholding under §1.1446-4(a) and a payment of an amount realized on the transfer of an interest in a publicly traded partnership subject to §1.1446(f)-4. The reference in the previous sentence to

withholding under §1.1446-4(f) shall apply with respect to returns for transfers that occur on or after 60 days after the date that these regulations are published as final regulations in the **Federal Register**.

* * *

(b) * * * A withholding agent may withhold from future payments (including distributions of effectively connected income subject to withholding under §1.1446-4 and the amount realized from the transfer of a partnership interest subject to §1.1446(f)-4) made to a beneficial owner the tax that should have been withheld from previous payments to that beneficial owner under chapter 3 of the Code. * * * The reference in this paragraph (b) to withholding under §1.1446-4(f)-4 shall apply with respect to returns for transfers that occur on or after 60 days after the date that these regulations are published as final regulations in the **Federal Register**.

* * *

Par. 12. Section 1.1461-3 is amended by revising the first sentence and last sentences to read as follows:

§1.1461-3. Withholding under section 1446.—For rules relating to the withholding tax liability of a partnership, nominee, or transferee under section 1446, see §§1.1446-1 through 1.1446-7 and 1.1446(f)-1 through 1.1446(f)-5. * * * The references in this section to §§1.1446-1 through 1.1446-7 apply to partnership taxable years beginning after May 18, 2005, or such earlier time as the regulations under

§§1.1446-1 through 1.1446-5 apply by reason of an election under §1.1446-7, and the references in this section to §1.1446(f)-1 through 1.1446(f)-5 shall apply with respect to returns for transfers that occur on or after 60 days after the date that these regulations are published as final regulations in the **Federal Register**.

Stock and Rights to Acquire Stock: Deemed Distributions

Stock and Rights to Acquire Stock: Deemed Distributions.—Amendments to Reg. §1.1461-2, regarding deemed distributions of stock and rights to acquire stock and resolving ambiguities concerning the amount and timing of deemed distributions that are or result from adjustments to rights to acquire stock, are proposed (published in the Federal Register on April 13, 2016) (REG-133673-15).

Par. 10. Section 1.1461-2 is amended by revising the second sentence to paragraph (b), adding a fourth sentence to paragraph (b), and adding a second and third sentence to paragraph (d) to read as follows:

§1.1461-2. Adjustments for overwithholding or underwithholding of tax.

* * *

(b) *Withholding of additional tax when underwithholding occurs.*—* * * In the alternative, the withholding agent may satisfy the tax from property that it holds in custody for the beneficial owner, property over which it has control, or additional contributions of property obtained directly or indirectly from the beneficial owner. * * * A withholding agent that adjusts its underwithholding under the procedure described in this paragraph (b) will not be subject to any penalties or additions to tax described in §1.1461-1(a)(2) if it timely

deposits the amounts that it withholds from future payments, proceeds from the liquidation of property, or additional contributions of property obtained directly or indirectly from the beneficial owner. * * *

(d) * * * Paragraph (b) of this section applies to payments made on or after the date of publication of the Treasury decision adopting these rules as final regulations in the **Federal Register**. A withholding agent may, however, rely on the rules in paragraph (b) of this section for payments occurring on or after January 1, 2016, until the date of publication of a Treasury decision adopting these rules as final regulations in the **Federal Register**.

Interests in Partnerships: Withholding of Tax: Information Reporting

Interests in Partnerships: Withholding of Tax: Information Reporting.—Amendments to Reg. §1.1463-1, implementing certain sections of the Internal Revenue Code, including sections added to the Internal Revenue Code by the Tax Cuts and Jobs Act, that relate to the withholding of tax and information reporting with respect to certain dispositions of interests in partnerships engaged in the conduct of a trade or business within the United States, are proposed (published in the Federal Register on May 13, 2019) (REG-105476-18).

Par. 13. Section 1.1463-1 is amended by revising the fourth and fifth sentences of paragraph (a) to read as follows:

§1.1463-1. Tax paid by recipient of income.—(a) * * * See §§1.1446-3(e), 1.1446-3(f) and 1.1446(f)-5(a) for application of the rule of this paragraph (a), and for additional rules, in which the withholding tax was required to be paid under section 1446. The references in the previous sentence to §1.1446-3(e) and 1.1446-3(f) apply to partnership taxable years beginning after May 18, 2005, or such earlier time as the regulations under §§1.1446-1 through 1.1446-5 apply by

reason of an election under §1.1446-7, and the reference in the previous sentence to §1.1446(f)-5(a) shall apply to the tax required to be withheld under section 1446(f) for transfers that occur on or after 60 days after the date that these regulations are published as final regulations in the **Federal Register**.

* * *

Interests in Partnerships: Withholding of Tax: Information Reporting

Interests in Partnerships: Withholding of Tax: Information Reporting.—Amendments to Reg. §1.1464-1, implementing certain sections of the Internal Revenue Code, including sections added to the Internal Revenue Code by the Tax Cuts and Jobs Act, that relate to the withholding of tax and information reporting with respect to certain dispositions of interests in partnerships engaged in the conduct of a trade or business within the United States, are proposed (published in the Federal Register on May 13, 2019) (REG-105476-18).

Par. 14. Section 1.1464-1 is amended by revising the last sentence of paragraph (a) and by revising paragraph (c) to read as follows:

§1.1464-1. Refunds or credits.—(a) *In general.*—* * * With respect to section 1446 (other than section 1446(f)), this section applies only to a publicly traded partnership described in §1.1446-4.

* * *

(c) *Applicability date.*—The last sentence of paragraph (a) applies to publicly traded partnerships described in §1.1446-4 for partnership taxable years beginning after April 29, 2008, and to brokers required to withhold under §1.1446(f)-4 on transfers that occur on or after the date that is 60 days after the date that these regulations are published as final regulations in the **Federal Register**.

Stock and Rights to Acquire Stock: Deemed Distributions

Stock and Rights to Acquire Stock: Deemed Distributions.—Amendments to Reg. §1.1471-2, regarding deemed distributions of stock and rights to acquire stock and resolving ambiguities concerning the amount and timing of deemed distributions that are or result from adjustments to rights to acquire stock, are proposed (published in the Federal Register on April 13, 2016) (REG-133673-15).

Par. 11. Section 1.1471-2 is amended by:

1. Revising paragraph (a)(4)(i)(A), redesignating paragraph (B) as new paragraph (E), and adding new paragraphs (B) through (D).

2. Amending paragraph (c) by adding a third and fourth sentence.

The revisions and addition read as follows:

§1.1471-2. Requirement to deduct and withhold tax on withholdable payments to certain FFIs.

* * *

(a) * * *

(4) * * *

(i) * * *

(A) *In general.*—Except as provided in paragraph (a)(4)(i)(B) of this section, a withholding agent has an obligation to withhold under chapter 4 only to the extent that, at any time between the date that the obligation to withhold would arise (but for the provisions of this paragraph (a)(4)(i)(A)) and the due date (including extensions) for filing Form 1042 (including extensions) with respect to the calendar year in which the payment occurs, it has—

(1) Control over, or custody of, money or property owned by the recipient or beneficial owner from which to withhold an amount, and

(2) Knowledge of the facts that give rise to the payment.

(B) *Exception not available.*—The exception from the obligation to withhold under paragraph (a)(4)(i)(A) of this section does not apply if—

(1) The withholding agent is related (within the meaning of section 482) to the recipient or the beneficial owner of the payment;

(2) The payment is with respect to stock (including a deemed distribution (as defined in §1.305-1(d)(7)) of stock or a right to acquire stock) or other securities; however, the limited exception from the obligation to withhold on a deemed distribution provided in §1.1441-2(d)(4) also applies to a deemed distribution that is a withholdable payment under chapter 4;

(3) The lack of control over or custody of money or property from which to withhold is part of a pre-arranged plan known to the withholding agent to avoid withholding under section 1471 or 1472;

(4) The amounts are described in §1.860G-3(b)(1) (regarding certain partnership allocations of REMIC net income with respect to a REMIC residual interest);

(5) Any of the special rules described in §1.1441-2(d)(2) or (3), regarding the obligation of a withholding agent with respect to cancellation of debt or the satisfaction of tax liability following underwithholding by a withholding agent, apply with respect to the payment (by applying such rules to payments that are withholdable payments under chapter 4); or

(6) The payment is a deemed payment (as defined in §1.861-3(a)(6)); however, the limited exception from the obligation to withhold on a deemed payment provided in §1.1441-2(d)(4) also applies to a deemed payment that is determined with respect to a deemed distribution on a specified security and that is a withholdable payment under chapter 4.

(C) *Documentation.*—Any exception from withholding pursuant to paragraph (a)(4)(i)(A) of this section applies without a requirement that documentation be furnished to the withholding agent. However, documentation may have to be furnished for purposes of the information reporting provisions under chapter 61 of the Code and backup withholding under section 3406.

(D) *Lack of money or property or lack of knowledge.*—A withholding agent does not lack control over money or property for purposes of this paragraph (a)(4)(i)(A) if the withholding agent directs another party to make the payment. Thus, for example, a principal does not cease to have control over a payment when it contracts with a paying agent to make the payments to its account holders in lieu of paying the account holders directly. Further, a withholding agent does not lack knowledge of the facts that give rise to a payment merely because the withholding agent does not know the character or source of the payment for U.S. tax purposes. *See* paragraph (a)(5) of this section for rules addressing a withholding agent's obligations when the withholding agent has knowledge of the facts that give rise to the payment, but the character or source of the payment is not known.

* * *

(c) * * * Paragraph (a)(4)(i) of this section applies to payments made on or after the date of publication of the Treasury decision adopting these rules as final regulations in the **Federal Register**. A withholding agent may, however, rely on the rules in paragraph (a)(4)(i) of this section (together with the rules in §1.1441-2(d)(4)), for all deemed distributions (as defined in §1.305-1(d)(7)) or deemed payments (as defined in §1.861-3(a)(6)) that are withholdable payments occurring on or after January 1, 2016, until the date of publication of a Treasury decision adopting these rules as final regulations in the **Federal Register**.

Withholding: Reducing Burden under FATCA

Withholding: Reducing Burden under FATCA.—Amendments to Reg. §§1.1471-2—1.1471-5, eliminating withholding on payments of gross proceeds, deferring withholding on foreign passthru payments, eliminating withholding on certain insurance premiums, and clarifying the definition of investment entity, are proposed (published in the Federal Register on December 18, 2018) (REG-132881-17). Proposed amendments to Reg. §1.1471-1 were adopted by T.D. 9890 on December 31, 2019.

Par. 7. Section 1.1471-2 is amended by:

1. Removing the language "or constitutes gross proceeds from the disposition of such an obligation" from the first sentence of paragraph (a)(1).

2. Removing and reserving paragraph (a)(2)(iii)(B).

3. Removing paragraph (a)(2)(vi).

4. Removing the language ", or any gross proceeds from the disposition of such an obligation" from the first and second sentences of paragraph (b)(1).

5. Removing the language "and the gross proceeds allocated to a partner from the disposition of such obligation as determined under §1.1473-1(a)(5)(vii)" from paragraph (b)(3)(i).

6. Removing the language "and further includes a beneficiary's share of the gross proceeds from a disposition of such obligation as determined under §1.1473-1(a)(5)(vii)" from paragraph (b)(3)(ii).

7. Removing the language "and the gross proceeds from the disposition of such obligation to the extent such owner is treated as owning the portion of the trust that consists of the obligation" from paragraph (b)(3)(iii).

The revision reads as follows:

§1.1471-2. Requirement to deduct and withhold tax on withholdable payments to certain FFIs.—(a) * * *

(2) * * *

(iii) * * *

(B) [Reserved]

* * *

Par. 8. Section 1.1471-3 is amended by:

1. Removing the language that reads "and that is excluded from the definition of a withholdable payment under §1.1473-1(a)(4)" from paragraph (a)(3)(ii)(A)(4).

2. Removing paragraph (c)(8)(iv) and redesignating paragraph (c)(8)(v) as new paragraph (c)(8)(iv).

§1.1471-3. Identification of payee.

Par. 9. Section 1.1471-4 is amended by:

1. Removing the language "or the gross proceeds from the disposition of such an obligation" from the seventh sentence of paragraph (b)(1).

2. Revising paragraph (b)(4).

The revision reads as follows:

§1.1471-4. FFI agreement.

* * *

(b) * * *

(4) *Foreign passthru payments.*—A participating FFI is not required to deduct and withhold tax on a foreign passthru payment made by such participating FFI to an account held by a recalcitrant account holder or to a nonparticipating FFI before the date that is two years after the date of publication in the **Federal Register** of final regulations defining the term *foreign passthru payment.*

* * *

Par. 10. Section 1.1471-5 is amended by adding a sentence at the end of paragraph (e)(4)(i)(B) to read as follows:

§1.1471-5. Definitions applicable to section 1471.

* * *

(e) * * *

(4) * * *

(i) * * *

(B) * * * Notwithstanding the preceding sentence, an entity is not managed by another entity for purposes of this paragraph (e)(4)(i)(B) solely because the first-mentioned entity invests all or a portion of its assets in such other entity, if such other entity is a mutual fund, exchange traded fund, or a collective investment entity that is widely-held and is subject to investor protection regulation.

* * *

Stock and Rights to Acquire Stock: Deemed Distributions

Stock and Rights to Acquire Stock: Deemed Distributions.—Amendments to Reg. §1.1473-1, regarding deemed distributions of stock and rights to acquire stock and resolving ambiguities concerning the amount and timing of deemed distributions that are or result from adjustments to rights to acquire stock, are proposed (published in the Federal Register on April 13, 2016) (corrected July 5, 2016) (REG-133673-15).

Par. 12. Section 1.1473-1 is amended by:

1. Amending paragraph (a)(2)(vii)(A) by adding a sentence to the end of the paragraph.

2. Adding paragraph (d)(7).

3. Amending paragraph (f) by adding a third and fourth sentence.

The additions read as follows:

§1.1473-1. Section 1473 definitions.—(a) * * *

(2) * * *

(vii) * * *

(A) * * * For purposes of determining the amount of a deemed distribution (as defined in §1.305-1(d)(7)) on a specified security (as defined in §1.6045-1(a)(14)) or a deemed payment (as defined in §1.861-3(a)(6)) that is determined with respect to a deemed distribution on a specified security, a withholding agent other than the issuer of the specified security may rely on issuer reporting by applying the rule under §1.1441-3(c)(5)(i) to deemed distributions or deemed payments that are withholdable payments under chapter 4.

* * *

(d) * * *

(7) *Withholding agent with respect to deemed distributions under section 305(c).*—Any person that issues or holds directly or indirectly (for example, through an account maintained for another intermediary) on behalf of a beneficial owner, or a flow through entity that owns directly or indirectly (through another flow-through entity), a security upon which a deemed distribution (as defined in §1.305-1(d)(7)) is made has custody of or control over the deemed distribution.

* * *

(f) * * * Paragraphs (a)(2)(vii) and (d)(7) of this section apply to payments made on or after the date of publication of the Treasury decision adopting these rules as final regulations in the **Federal Register**. A withholding agent may, however, rely on the rules in paragraphs (a)(2)(vii) and (d)(7) of this section for all deemed distributions (as defined in §1.305-1(d)(7)) or deemed payments (as defined in §1.861-3(a)(6)) that are withholdable payments occurring on or after January 1, 2016, until the date of publication of a Treasury decision adopting these rules as final regulations in the **Federal Register**.

Withholding: Reducing Burden under FATCA

Withholding: Reducing Burden under FATCA.—Amendments to Reg. §1.1473-1, eliminating withholding on payments of gross proceeds, deferring withholding on foreign passthru payments, eliminating withholding on certain insurance premiums, and clarifying the definition of investment entity, are proposed (published in the Federal Register on December 18, 2018) (REG-132881-17).

Par. 11. Section 1.1473-1 is amended by:

1. Revising paragraph (a)(1).

2. Removing the fourth sentence of paragraph (a)(2)(vii)(A).

3. Removing and reserving paragraph (a)(3).

4. Revising paragraph (a)(4)(iii).

5. Removing paragraph (a)(4)(iv) and redesignating paragraphs (a)(4)(v) through (viii) as new paragraphs (a)(4)(iv) through (vii).

6. Removing paragraph (a)(5)(vii).

The revisions read as follows:

§1.1473-1. Section 1473 definitions.—(a) *Definition of withholdable payment.*—(1) *In general.*—Except as otherwise provided in this paragraph (a) and §1.1471-2(b) (regarding grandfathered obligations), the term *withholdable payment* means any payment of U.S. source FDAP income (as defined in paragraph (a)(2) of this section).

* * *

(3) [Reserved]

(4) * * *

(iii) *Excluded nonfinancial payments.*—Payments for the following: services (including wages and other forms of employee compensation (such as stock options)), the use of property, office and equipment leases, software licenses, transportation, freight, gambling winnings, awards, prizes, scholarships, interest on outstanding accounts payable arising from the acquisition of goods or services, and premiums for insurance contracts that do not have cash value (as defined in §1.1471-5(b)(3)(vii)(B)). Notwithstanding the preceding sentence, excluded nonfinancial payments do not include the following: payments in connection with a lending transaction (including loans of securities), a forward, futures, option, or notional principal contract, or a similar financial instrument; premiums for cash value insurance contracts or annuity contracts; amounts paid under cash value insurance or annuity contracts; dividends; interest (including substitute interest described in §1.861-2(a)(7)) other than interest described in the preceding sentence; investment advisory fees; custodial fees; and bank or brokerage fees.

* * *

Withholding: Reducing Burden under FATCA

Withholding: Reducing Burden under FATCA.—Amendments to Reg. §§1.1474-1 and 1.1474-2, eliminating withholding on payments of gross proceeds, deferring withholding on foreign passthru payments, eliminating withholding on certain insurance premiums, and clarifying the definition of investment entity, are proposed (published in the Federal Register on December 18, 2018) (REG-132881-17).

Par. 12. Section 1.1474-1 is amended by:

1. Adding two sentences after the first sentence in paragraph (b)(1).

2. Revising paragraph (b)(2).

3. Redesignating paragraph (d)(1)(i) as paragraph (d)(1)(i)(A) and adding paragraphs (d)(1)(i) introductory text and (d)(1)(i)(B).

4. Adding a sentence after the first sentence in paragraph (d)(2)(ii).

The revisions and additions read as follows:

§1.1474-1. Liability for withheld tax and withholding agent reporting.

* * *

(b) * * *

(1) * * * In a case in which a withholding agent is permitted to withhold on a chapter 4 reportable amount (as defined in paragraph (d)(2) of this section) in a calendar year (subsequent year) following the calendar year (preceding year) in which the withholding agent paid such amount (or, for a partnership or trust withholding with respect to a foreign partner, beneficiary, or owner, the year the partnership or trust received such amount), the withholding agent shall designate the deposit of the withholding as made for the preceding year and shall report the tax liability on Form 1042 for the preceding year. In the case of a partnership that withholds as described in the preceding sentence and does not file its federal income tax return on a calendar-year basis, however, such partnership may instead designate the deposit as made for the subsequent year and report the tax liability on Form 1042 for the subsequent year.* * *

(2) *Special rule for foreign passthru payments that include an undetermined amount of income subject to tax.*—[Reserved]

* * *

(d) * * *

(1) * * *

(i) *Withholding agent information reporting.*—This paragraph (d)(1)(i) describes the general requirements for a withholding agent to file an information return on Form 1042-S and describes a special rule for a withholding agent that withholds in a subsequent year as described in paragraph (b)(1) of this section.

* * *

(B) *Special reporting by withholding agents that withhold in a subsequent year.*—Notwithstanding the first sentence of paragraph (d)(1)(i)(A) of this section, if a withholding agent designates the deposit of such withholding as made for the preceding calendar year as described in paragraph (b)(1) of this section, the withholding agent is required to report the amount on Form 1042-S for the preceding year. With respect to a withholding agent described in the previous sentence that is a partnership and that withholds after March 15 of the subsequent year, such partnership may file and furnish the Form 1042-S on or before September 15 of that year. In the case of a partnership that designates the deposit of such withholding as made for the subsequent year as permitted in paragraph (b)(1) of this section, however, the partnership shall report the chapter 4 reportable amount on Form 1042-S for the subsequent year.

* * *

(2) * * *

(ii) * * * A chapter 4 reportable amount also does not include an amount received by a nonqualified intermediary that is a participating FFI or a registered deemed-compliant FFI if the nonqualified intermediary reports such amount as having been withheld upon under chapter 3 to the extent permitted under §1.1461-1(c)(4)(iv). * * *

* * *

Par. 13. Section 1.1474-2 is amended by revising the second sentence of paragraph (a)(3)(i) introductory text, paragraphs (a)(3)(i)(A) through (C), and paragraph (a)(4) to read as follows:

§1.1474-2. Adjustments for overwithholding or underwithholding of tax.—(a) * * *

(3) * * *

(i) * * * In such a case, the withholding agent may reimburse itself by reducing, by the amount of tax actually repaid to the beneficial owner or payee, the amount of any deposit of withholding tax otherwise required to be made by the withholding agent under §1.6302-2(a)(1)(iii) for any subsequent payment period occurring before the end of the calendar year following the calendar year of overwithholding. * * *

(A) The repayment to the beneficial owner or payee occurs before the earliest of the due date (including extensions) for filing the Form 1042-S for the calendar year of overwithholding, the date the Form 1042-S is actually filed with the IRS, or the date the Form 1042-S is furnished to the beneficial owner or payee;

(B) The withholding agent states on a timely filed (including extensions) Form 1042-S for the calendar year of overwithholding the amount of tax withheld and the amount of any actual repayment; and

(C) The withholding agent states on a timely filed (including extensions) Form 1042 for the calendar year of overwithholding the amount of adjustments made to overwithholding under paragraph (a)(1) of this section and the amount of any credit claimed under §1.6414-1.

* * *

(4) *Set-off.*—Under the set-off procedure, the withholding agent may repay the beneficial owner or payee by applying the amount overwithheld against any amount of tax which otherwise would be required under chapter 3 or 4 of the Internal Revenue Code or the regulations under part 1 of this chapter to be withheld from income paid by the withholding agent to such person. Any such set-off that occurs for a payment period in the calendar year following the calendar year of overwithholding shall be allowed only if—

(i) The repayment to the beneficial owner or payee occurs before the earliest of the due date (including extensions) for filing the Form 1042-S for the calendar year of overwithholding, the date the Form 1042-S is actually filed with the IRS, or the date the Form 1042-S is furnished to the beneficial owner or payee;

(ii) The withholding agent states on a timely filed (including extensions) Form 1042-S for the calendar year of overwithholding the amount of tax withheld and the amount of any repayment made through set-off; and

(iii) The withholding agent states on a timely filed (including extensions) Form 1042 for the calendar year of overwithholding the amount of adjustments made to overwithholding under paragraph (a)(1) of this section and the amount of any credit claimed under §1.6414-1.

* * *

CONSOLIDATED RETURNS

Consolidated Returns: AMT: Definitions

Consolidated Returns: Alternative Minimum Tax.—Reproduced below is the text of a proposed amendment to Reg. §1.1502-1, relating to the computation of the alternative minimum tax by consolidated groups (published in the Federal Register on December 30, 1992).

☐ Par. 3. Section 1.1502-1 is amended by reserving paragraph (i) and adding paragraph (j) to read as follows:

§1.1502-1. Definitions.

* * *

(i) [Reserved]

(j) *Tax liability.*—Except as provided otherwise, references relating to the "tax liability" of a consolidated group are to the consolidated tax liability determined in accordance with §1.1502-2.

However, references in §1.1552-1 (a) through (f) (relating to the computation of earnings and profits) to the tax liability of a consolidated group are to the regular tax liability of the group, determined in accordance with section 26 (b), reduced by the credits allowable under part IV of subchapter A of the Internal Revenue Code (other than the consolidated minimum tax credit under §1.1502-55(h)). Similarly, references to a member's tax liability determined as if it had filed separate returns under §1.1502-33(d), or the separate return tax liability of a member under §1.1552-1(a)(3)(ii)(*b*), are to the regular tax liability of the member under section 26(b), reduced by the above-referenced credits.

Allocation and Apportionment of Deductions and Foreign Tax Credit: Guidance

Allocation and Apportionment of Deductions and Foreign Tax Credit: Guidance.—Amendments to Reg. §1.1502-4, relating to the allocation and apportionment of deductions and creditable foreign taxes, the definition of financial services income, foreign tax redeterminations, availability of foreign tax credits under the transition tax, and the application of the foreign tax credit limitation to consolidated groups, are proposed (published in the Federal Register on December 17, 2019) (REG-105495-19).

Par. 27. Section 1.1502-4 is revised to read as follows:

§1.1502-4. Consolidated foreign tax credit.—(a) *In general.*—The credit under section 901 for taxes paid or accrued to any foreign country or possession of the United States is allowed to the group only if the agent for the group (as defined in §1.1502-77(a)) chooses to use the credit in the computation of the consolidated tax liability of the group for the consolidated return year. If that choice is made, section 275(a)(4) provides that no deduction against taxable income may be taken on the consolidated return for foreign taxes paid or accrued by any member. However, if section 275(a)(4) does not apply, a deduction against consolidated taxable income may be allowed for certain taxes for which a credit is not allowed, even though the choice is made to claim a credit for other taxes. See, for example, sections 901(j)(3), 901(k)(7), 901(l)(4), 901(m)(6), and 908(b).

(b) *Computation of foreign tax credit.*—The foreign tax credit for the consolidated return year is determined on a consolidated basis under the principles of sections 901 through 909 and 960. Taxes paid or accrued to all foreign countries and possessions by members of the group for the year (including those deemed paid under section 960 and paragraph (d) of this section) must be aggregated.

(c) *Computation of limitation on credit.*—For purposes of computing the group's limiting fraction under section 904, the following rules apply:

(1) *Computation of taxable income from foreign sources.*—(i) *Separate categories.*—The group must compute a separate foreign tax credit limitation for income in each separate category (as defined in §1.904-5(a)(4)(v) for purposes of this section). The numerator of the limiting fraction in any separate category is the consolidated taxable income of the group determined in accordance with §1.1502-11, taking into account adjustments required under section 904(b), if any, from sources without the United States in that category, determined in accordance with the rules of §1.904-4, 1.904-5, and the section 861 regulations (as defined in §1.861-8(a)(1)).

(ii) *Adjustments under sections 904(f) and (g).*—The rules for allocation and recapture of separate limitation losses and overall foreign losses under section 904(f) and §1.1502-9 apply to determine the foreign source and U.S. source taxable income in each separate category of the consolidated group. Similarly, the rules for allocation and recapture of overall domestic losses under section 904(g) and §1.1502-9 apply to determine the foreign source and U.S. source taxable income in each separate category of the consolidated group. See §1.904(g)-3 for allocation rules under sections 904(f) and 904(g). The rules of sections 904(f) and 904(g) do not operate to recharacterize foreign income tax attributable to any separate category.

(iii) *Computation of consolidated net operating loss.*—The source and separate category of the group's consolidated net operating loss ("CNOL"), as that term is defined in §1.1502-21(e), for the taxable year, if any, is determined based on the amounts of any separate limitation losses and U.S. source loss that are not allocated to reduce U.S. source income or income in other separate categories under the rules of sections 904(f) and 904(g) in computing the group's consolidated foreign tax credit limitations for the taxable year under paragraphs (c)(1)(i) and (ii) of this section.

(iv) *Characterization of CNOL carried to a separate return year.*—(A) *In general.*—The total amount of CNOL attributable to a member that is carried to a separate return year is determined under the rules of §1.1502-21(b)(2). The source and separate category of the portion of the CNOL that is attributable to a member is determined under this paragraph (c)(1)(iv).

(B) *Tentative apportionment.*—For the portion of the CNOL that is attributable to the member described in paragraph (c)(1)(iv) of this section, the consolidated group determines a tentative allocation and apportionment to each statutory and residual grouping (as described in §1.861-8(a)(4) with respect to section 904 as the operative section) under the principles of §1.1502-9(c)(2)(i), (ii), (iv) and (v) by treating the portion of the group's CNOL in each statutory and residual grouping as if it were a CSLL account, as that term is described in §1.1502 9(b)(4). This determination is made as of the end of the taxable year of the consolidated group in which the CNOL arose or, if earlier and applicable, when the member leaves the consolidated group.

(C) *Adjustments.*—(1) If the total tentative apportionment for all statutory and residual groupings exceeds the portion of the CNOL attributable to the member described in paragraph (c)(1)(iv)(A) of this section (the "excess amount"), then the tentative apportionment in each grouping is reduced by an amount equal to the excess amount multiplied by a fraction, the numerator of which is the tentative apportionment in that grouping, and the denominator of which is the total tentative apportionments in all groupings.

(2) If the total tentative apportionment for all statutory and residual groupings is less than the total CNOL attributable to the member described in paragraph (c)(1)(iv)(A) (the "deficiency"), then the tentative apportionment in each grouping is increased by an amount equal to the deficiency multiplied by a fraction, the numerator of which is the CNOL in that grouping that was not tentatively apportioned, and the denominator of which is the total CNOL in all groupings that was not tentatively apportioned.

(v) *Consolidated net capital losses.*—The principles of the rules in paragraphs (c)(1)(i) through (iv) of this section apply for purposes of determining the source and separate category of consolidated net capital losses described in §1.1502-22(e).

(2) *Computation of consolidated taxable income.*—The denominator of the limiting fraction in any separate category is the consolidated taxable income of the group determined in accordance with §1.1502-11, taking into account adjustments required under section 904(b), if any.

(3) *Computation of tax against which credit is taken.*—The tax against which the limiting fraction under section 904(a) is applied will be the consolidated tax liability of the group determined under §1.1502-2, but without regard to §1.1502-2(a)(2), (3), (4), (8), and (9), and without regard to any credit against such liability. See sections 26(b) and 901(a).

(d) *Carryover and carryback of unused foreign tax.*—(1) *Allowance of unused foreign tax as consolidated carryover or carryback.*—The consolidated group's carryovers and carrybacks of unused foreign tax (as defined in §1.904-2(c)(1)) to the taxable year is determined on a consolidated basis under the principles of section 904(c) and §1.904-2 and is deemed to be paid or accrued to a foreign country or possession for that year. The consolidated group's unused foreign tax carryovers and carrybacks to the taxable year consist of any unused foreign tax of the consolidated group, plus any unused foreign tax of members for separate return years, which may be carried over or back to the taxable year under the principles of section 904(c) and §1.904-2. The consolidated group's unused foreign tax carryovers and carrybacks do not include any unused foreign taxes apportioned to a corporation for a separate return year pursuant to §1.1502-79(d). A consolidated group's unused foreign tax in each separate category is the excess of the foreign taxes paid, accrued or deemed paid under section 960 by the consolidated group over the limitation in the applicable separate category for the consolidated return year. See paragraph (c) of this section.

(2) *Absorption rules.*—For purposes of determining the amount, if any, of an unused foreign tax which can be carried to a taxable year (whether a consolidated or separate return year), the amount of the unused foreign tax that is absorbed in a prior consolidated return year under section 904(c) shall be determined by—

(i) Applying all unused foreign taxes which can be carried to a prior year in the order of the taxable years in which those unused foreign taxes arose, beginning with the taxable year that ends earliest, and

(ii) All the unused foreign taxes which can be carried to such prior year from taxable years ending on the same date on a pro rata basis.

(e) *Example.*—The following example illustrates the application of this section:

(1) *Facts*—(i) Domestic corporation P is incorporated on January 1, Year 1. On that same day, P incorporates domestic corporations S and T as wholly owned subsidiaries. P, S, and T file consolidated returns for Years 1 and 2 on the basis of a calendar year. T engages in business solely through a qualified business unit in Country A. S engages in business solely through qualified business units in countries A and B. P does business solely in the United States. During

Year 1, T sold an item of inventory to P at a gain of $2,000. Under §1.1502-13 the intercompany gain has not been taken into account as of the close of Year 1. The taxable income of each member for Year 1

from foreign and U.S. sources, and the foreign taxes paid on such foreign income, are as follows:

Table 1 to paragraph (e)(1)(i)

Corporation	U.S. Source taxable income	Foreign branch category foreign source taxable income	Foreign branch category foreign tax paid	Total taxable income
P	$40,000			$40,000
T		$20,000	$12,000	20,000
S		20,000	9,000	20,000
Group				$80,000

(ii) The separate taxable income of each member was computed by taking into account the rules under §1.1502-12. Accordingly, T's intercompany gain of $2,000 is not included in T's taxable income for Year 1. The group's consolidated taxable income (computed in accordance with §1.1502-11) is $80,000. The consolidated tax liability against which the credit may be taken (computed in accordance with paragraph (c)(3) of this section) is $16,800.

(2) *Analysis.* The aggregate taxes paid to all foreign countries with respect to the foreign branch category income of $21,000 ($12,000 + $9,000) is limited to $8,400 ($16,800 x $40,000/$80,000). Assuming P, as the agent for the group, chooses to use the foreign taxes paid as a credit, the group may claim a $8,400 foreign tax credit.

(f) *Applicability date.*—This section applies to taxable years for which the original consolidated Federal income tax return is due (without extensions) after December 17, 2019.

Consolidated Returns: AMT: Estimated Tax

Consolidated Returns: Alternative Minimum Tax.—Reproduced below is the text of a proposed amendment to Reg. §1.1502-5, relating to the computation of the alternative minimum tax by consolidated groups (published in the Federal Register on December 30, 1992).

☐ Par. 5. Section 1.1502-5 is revised to read as follows:

§1.1502-5. Estimated tax.—(a) *General rule.*—(1) *Consolidated estimated tax.*—If a group files a consolidated return for two consecutive taxable years, it must make payments of estimated tax on a consolidated basis for each subsequent taxable year, until separate returns are filed. When filing on a consolidated basis, the group is generally treated as a single corporation for purposes of section 6655 (relating to payment of estimated tax by corporations). If separate returns are filed by the members for a taxable year, the amount of any estimated tax payments made with respect to a consolidated estimated tax for the year is credited against the separate tax liabilities of the members in any reasonable manner designated by the common parent. Consolidated payments of estimated tax must be deposited with the authorized commercial depositary or Federal Reserve Bank with which the common parent deposits its estimated tax payments. A statement must be attached to the payment setting forth the name, address, employer identification number, and Internal Revenue Service Center of each member.

(2) *First two consolidated return years.*—For its first two consolidated return years, a group may make payments of estimated tax on either a consolidated or a separate member basis, and the amount of any separate estimated tax payments is credited against the consolidated tax liability of the group.

(b) *Addition to tax for failure to pay estimated tax under section 6655.*—(1) *Consolidated return filed.*—For its first two consolidated return years, a group may compute the amount of the penalty (if any) under section 6655 on a consolidated basis or a separate member basis, regardless of the method of payment. Thereafter, the group must compute the penalty for any consolidated return year on a consolidated basis.

(2) *Computation of penalty on consolidated basis.*—(i) This paragraph (b)(2) provides rules for computing the penalty under section 6655 on a consolidated basis.

(ii) The tax shown on the return for the preceding taxable year referred to in section 6655(d)(1)(B)(ii) is, if a consolidated return was filed for that preceding year, the tax shown on the consolidated return for that preceding year or, if a consolidated return was not filed for that preceding year, the aggregate of the taxes shown on the separate returns of the common parent and any other corporation that was a member of the same affiliated group as the common parent for that preceding year.

(iii) If estimated tax was not paid on a consolidated basis, the amount of the group's payments of estimated tax for the taxable year is the aggregate of the payments made by all members for the year.

(iv) If the common parent is otherwise eligible to use the section 6655(d)(1)(B)(ii) required annual payment rule, that rule applies only if the group's consolidated return, or each member's separate return if the group did not file a consolidated return, for the preceding taxable year was a taxable year of 12 months.

(3) *Computation of penalty on separate member basis.*—To compute any penalty under section 6655 on a separate member basis, for purposes of section 6655(d)(1)(B)(i), the "tax shown on the return" for the taxable year is the portion of the tax shown on the consolidated

return allocable to the member under paragraph (b)(6) of this section. If the member was included in the consolidated return filed by the group for the preceding taxable year, for purposes of section 6655(d)(1)(B)(ii), the "tax shown on the return" for the preceding taxable year for any member is the portion of the tax shown on the consolidated return for the preceding year allocable to the member under paragraph (b)(6) of this section.

(4) *Consolidated payments if separate returns filed.*—If the group does not file a consolidated return for the taxable year but makes payments of estimated tax on a consolidated basis, for purposes of section 6655(b)(1)(B), the "amount (if any) of the installment paid" by any member is an amount apportioned to the member in any reasonable manner designated by the common parent. If a member was included in the consolidated return filed by the group for the preceding taxable year, the amount of the member's penalty under section 6655 is computed on the separate member basis described in paragraph (b)(3) of this section.

(5) *Tax defined.*—For purposes of this section, "tax" means the excess of—

(i) The sum of—

(A) The consolidated tax imposed by section 11, section 1201(a), or subchapter L of chapter 1, whichever applies;

(B) The consolidated AMT determined under §1.1502-55; and

(C) The consolidated environmental tax defined under §1.1552-1(h)(2); over

(ii) The credits allowable under part IV of subchapter A of chapter 1 of the Internal Revenue Code against the consolidated taxes in paragraphs (b)(5)(i)(A), (B), and (C) of this section.

(6) *Rules for allocation of consolidated tax liability.*—For purposes of this section, the tax shown on a consolidated return shall be allocated to the members of the group by allocating—

(i) Any tax described in paragraph (b)(5)(i)(A) of this section, net of allowable credits under paragraph (b)(5)(ii) (other than the allowable consolidated MTC defined in §1.1502-55(h)), under the method that the group has elected pursuant to section 1552 and §1.1502-33(d);

(ii) Any allowable consolidated MTC (as defined in §1.1502-55(h)) in accordance with the requirements of §1.1552-1(g);

(iii) Any consolidated AMT described in paragraph (b)(5)(i)(B) of this section in accordance with the requirements of §1.1552-1(g); and

(iv) Any consolidated environmental tax described in paragraph (b)(5)(i)(C) of this section in accordance with the requirements of §1.1552-1(h).

(c) *Examples.* The provisions of this section are illustrated by the following examples.

Example 1. Corporations P and S1 file a consolidated return for the first time for calendar year 1992. P and S1 also file consolidated returns for 1993 and 1994. Under paragraph (a)(2) of this section, for 1992 and 1993 P and S1 may pay estimated tax on either a separate or consolidated basis. Under paragraph (a)(1) of this section, for 1994 the group must pay its estimated tax on a consolidated basis. In determining whether P and S1 come within the exception provided in section 6655(d)(1)(B)(ii) for 1994, the "tax shown on the return" is the tax shown on the consolidated return for 1993.

Example 2. Corporations P, S1, and S2 file a consolidated return for the first time for calendar year 1992 and file their second consolidated return in 1993. S2 ceases to be a member of the group on September 15, 1994. Under paragraph (b)(2) of this section, in determining whether the group (which no longer includes S2) comes within the exception provided in section 6655(d)(1)(B)(ii) for 1994, the "tax shown on the return" is the tax shown on the consolidated return for 1993.

Example 3. Corporations P and S1 file a consolidated return for the first time for calendar year 1992 and file their second consolidated return in 1993. Corporation S2 becomes a member of the group on July 1, 1994, and joins in the filing of the consolidated return for 1994. Under paragraph (b)(2) of this section, in determining whether the group (which now includes S2) comes within the exception provided in section 6655(d)(1)(B)(ii) for 1994, the "tax shown on the return" is the tax shown on the consolidated return for 1993. Any tax of S2 for any separate return year is not included as a part of the "tax

shown on the return" for purposes of applying section 6655(d)(1)(B)(ii).

Example 4. Corporations X and Y file consolidated returns for the calendar years 1992 and 1993 and separate returns for 1994. Under paragraph (b)(3) of this section, in determining whether X or Y comes within the exception provided in section 6655(d)(1)(B)(ii) for 1994, the "tax shown on the return" is the amount of tax shown on the consolidated return for 1993 allocable to X and to Y in accordance with paragraph (b)(6) of this section.

(d) *Cross reference.*—For provisions relating to quick refunds of corporate estimated tax payments, *see* § 1.1502-78 and § § 1.6425-1 through 1.6425-3.

(e) *Effective date.*—This section applies to any taxable year for which the due date of the income tax return (without regard to extensions) is on or after [the date that is sixty days after final regulations are filed with the Federal Register]. For prior years, *see* § 1.1502-5 (as contained in the 26 CFR edition revised as of April 1, 1992).

Elimination of Circular Adjustments to Basis: Absorption of Losses

Elimination of Circular Adjustments to Basis: Absorption of Losses.—Amendments to Reg. § § 1.1502-11 and 1.1502-12, revising the rules concerning the use of a consolidated group's losses in a consolidated return year in which stock of a subsidiary is disposed of, are proposed (published in the Federal Register on June 11, 2015) (REG-101652-10).

Par. 2. Section 1.1502-11 is amended by:

1. Revising paragraphs (a) introductory text, (a)(2), (a)(3), and (a)(4).

2. Removing and reserving paragraph (a)(6).

3. Revising paragraphs (b), (c)(2)(i), and (c)(2)(ii).

4. Removing in paragraph (c)(2)(vi) the phrase "unlimited deductions and losses that are absorbed" and adding "S's absorbed amount of losses" in its place.

5. Revising paragraph (c)(4).

6. Revising the heading of paragraph (c)(7) and adding a sentence at the end of the paragraph.

7. Adding paragraph (e).

The revisions and additions read as follows:

§ 1.1502-11. Consolidated taxable income.—(a) *In general.*—The consolidated taxable income (CTI) for a consolidated return year shall be determined by taking into account—

* * *

(2) Any consolidated net operating loss (CNOL) deduction (see § 1.1502-21 for the computation of the CNOL deduction);

(3) Any consolidated capital gain net income (see § 1.1502-22 for the computation of the consolidated capital gain net income);

(4) Any consolidated section 1231 net loss (see § 1.1502-23 for the computation of the consolidated section 1231 net loss);

* * *

(6) [Reserved]

* * *

(b) *Elimination of circular basis adjustments if there is no excluded COD income.*—(1) *In general.*—If a member (P) disposes of a share of stock of one or more subsidiaries (S), this paragraph (b) applies to determine the amount of S's losses that will be used in the consolidated return year of disposition and in a carryback year. The purpose of these rules is to prevent P's income, gain, deduction, or loss from the disposition of a share of S's stock from affecting the amount of S's deductions and losses that are absorbed. A change to the amount of S's absorbed losses would affect P's basis in S's stock under § 1.1502-32, which in turn affects P's gain or loss on the disposition of S's stock. For purposes of this section, P is treated as disposing of a share of a subsidiary's stock if any event described in § 1.1502-19(c) occurs or, if for any reason, a member recognizes gain or loss (including an excess loss account included in income) with respect to the share. However, to the extent income, gain, deduction, or loss from a disposition of a share of S's stock is deferred under any rule of law (for example, § 1.1502-13 and section 267(f)), the taxable year in which the deferred amount is taken into account is treated as the taxable year of disposition. This paragraph (b) does not apply if any member realizes discharge of indebtedness income that is excluded from gross income under section 108(a) during the consolidated return year of the disposition. If a member realizes such income, see paragraph (c) of this section. For purposes of this section, S's ordinary loss means its separate net operating loss (as defined in § 1.1502-21(b)(2)(iv)(B)). Solely for purposes of this section, any reference to a member's capital gain includes amounts treated as capital gain. Furthermore, for those purposes, a member's capital loss means a consolidated net capital loss determined by reference to only that member's capital gain and capital loss items.

(2) *Deductions and losses of disposed subsidiaries.* (i) *Determination of absorbed amounts.*—If P disposes of a share of S's stock in a transaction to which this paragraph (b) applies, the extent

to which S's ordinary loss and capital loss (including losses carried over from a prior year) that are absorbed in the consolidated return year of the disposition or in a prior year as a carryback (the absorbed amount) is determined under this paragraph (b)(2). S's absorbed amount is the amount that would be absorbed in a computation of the group's consolidated taxable income (CTI) for the consolidated return year of the disposition (and any taxable year to which losses may be carried back) without taking into account any member's income, gain, deduction, or loss from the disposition of any share of any subsidiary's stock in that year. S's absorbed amount is determined after first applying other applicable limitations and ordering rules (for example, limitations imposed by section 382(a) and § 1.1502-21 and the ordering rules of section 382(l)(2)) to S's deductions and losses. Any election that the group makes on its actual return for the consolidated return year (for example, an election to relinquish a carryback under § 1.1502-21(b)(3)) must be used in this computation. Once S's absorbed amount is determined, that amount is not redetermined. Except as provided in paragraph (b)(2)(iii)(B)(*1*) of this section, the amount determined under this paragraph (b)(2)(i) fixes only the amount of S's losses that will be absorbed. Thus, under paragraph (b)(2)(iii)(A) of this section, the character of the losses that are absorbed in the actual computation of the group's CTI for the year (or as a carryback to a prior year) may not be the same as the character of the losses that are absorbed in determining the absorbed amount. However, if the alternative computation of paragraph (b)(2)(iii)(B)(*1*) of this section is required, the character of the absorbed amount as determined under this paragraph (b)(2)(i) is retained.

(ii) *Stock basis reduction and gain or loss on disposition.*—After the determination of S's absorbed amount, P reduces its basis in S's stock under the investment adjustment rules of § 1.1502-32(b)(2) by the absorbed amount. If any share is a loss share, P then adjusts its basis in S's stock by applying paragraphs (b) and (c) of § 1.1502-36, and, if an election is actually made under § 1.1502-36(d)(6), by applying § 1.1502-36(d) to the extent necessary to give effect to the election. P then computes its gain or loss on the disposed of shares after taking into account those adjustments.

(iii) *Actual computation of CTI.*—(A) *In general.*—The group's CTI and any carryback of a portion of a CNOL are determined under applicable provisions of the Internal Revenue Code (Code) and regulations, taking into account gain or loss on any subsidiary's stock, and taking into account losses of disposed of subsidiaries equal to each such subsidiary's absorbed amount.

(B) *Alternative computation.*—If the computation of the group's CTI under paragraph (b)(2)(iii)(A) of this section would result in an absorption of less than all of any disposed of subsidiary's absorbed amount, then the group's CTI is computed by applying the following steps, rather than the computation under that paragraph:

(1) First, losses of each disposed of subsidiary equal in both amount and character and from the same taxable years as losses used in the computation of its absorbed amount under paragraph (b)(2)(i) of this section offset income and gain of other members without taking into account any gain or loss on any share of subsidiary stock and without regard to net losses of other members.

(2) Second, a disposing member offsets its gain on subsidiary stock with its losses on subsidiary stock of the same character. For this purpose, a loss on subsidiary stock is determined after applying §1.1502-36(b) and (c), and so much of §1.1502-36(d) as is necessary to give effect to an election actually made under §1.1502-36(d)(6). If the disposing member has net income or gain on subsidiary stock, and if the member also has a loss of the same character (determined without regard to the net income, gain, deduction or loss on subsidiary stock), the loss offsets that net income or gain and any remaining income or gain is added to the amount determined after the application of paragraph (b)(2)(ii)(B)(1) of this section. For example, if P has a net capital loss on portfolio stock, that net loss is not taken into account in applying paragraph (b)(2)(iii)(B)(1). However, under this paragraph (b)(2)(iii)(B)(2), that net capital loss is absorbed to the extent of that member's net capital gain on subsidiary stock.

(3) Third, if, after the application of paragraph (b)(2)(iii)(B)(2) of this section, the group has remaining income or gain and a disposing member has a net loss on subsidiary stock (determined after applying §1.1502-36(b) and (c), and so much of §1.1502-36(d) as is necessary to give effect to an election actually made under §1.1502-36(d)(6), that remaining income or gain is then offset by a loss on the disposition of subsidiary stock, subject to the applicable rules of the Code and regulations. The amount of the offset, however, is limited to the lesser of the total remaining ordinary income or capital gain of the group (determined after the application of paragraph (b)(2)(iii)(B)(2) of this section), or the amount of the disposing member's ordinary income or capital gain of the same character (determined without regard to the stock loss). If the preceding sentence applies to more than one disposing member, and the sum of the amounts determined under that sentence exceeds the group's remaining ordinary or capital gain, the amounts offset capital gain or ordinary income on a pro rata basis under the principles of paragraph (e) of this section.

(4) Fourth, if, after application of paragraph (b)(2)(iii)(B)(3) of this section, the group has remaining ordinary income or capital gain, those amounts are offset by the unused losses of all members on a pro rata basis under paragraph (e) of this section.

(C) *Priority of rules.*—The computation of CTI under this paragraph (b)(2)(iii) applies notwithstanding other rules for the absorption of a portion of a member's current year loss, such as paragraphs (a) and (e) of this section, §§1.1502-12 and 1.1502-22(a), and the absorption of a member's portion of a CNOL or consolidated net capital loss carryover from a prior year under §§1.1502-21(b) and 1.1502-22(b), respectively. For example, in some circumstances, an ordinary loss of a disposed of subsidiary may offset capital gain of another member notwithstanding that under general rules a capital loss of another member would be allowed to the extent of capital gains before an ordinary loss is taken into account. Similarly, an ordinary loss with respect to a subsidiary's stock, which would generally offset ordinary income of the owning member and be included in determining that member's separate taxable income, may become a loss carryover if use of that loss would cause less than all of a disposed of subsidiary's absorbed amount to be used.

(D) *Deductions determined by reference to CTI.*—In the case of any deduction of any member that is determined by reference to or limited by the amount of CTI (for example, a charitable contribution deduction under §1.1502-24(c) and a percentage depletion deduction under §1.1502-44(b)), the amount of the deduction is determined without regard to any gain or loss on subsidiary stock.

(iv) *Losses not absorbed.*—To the extent S's losses in the consolidated return year of the disposition of its stock do not offset income or gain by reason of the rules of this paragraph (b), S ceases to be a member, and S's losses are not reattributed under §1.1502-36(d)(6), the losses are carried over to its separate return years (if any) under the applicable principles of the Code and regulations thereunder. Those losses are not taken into account in determining the percentage of CNOL or consolidated net capital loss attributable to members under §1.1502-21(b)(2)(iv) or §1.1502-22(b)(3), respectively. If S remains a member, its unused losses are included in the CNOL or consolidated net capital loss carryovers and are subject to the allocation rules of those sections.

(v) *Disposition of stock of a higher-tier subsidiary.*—If a subsidiary (T) is a lower-tier subsidiary (as described in §1.1502-36(f)(4)) of a higher-tier subsidiary (S), and S's stock is disposed of during a

consolidated return year, T's losses are subject to this paragraph (b) as if T's stock had been disposed of. Thus, T's absorbed amount is determined by disregarding any gain or loss (for example, an excess loss account taken into account under §1.1502-19(b)) on a deemed disposition of T's stock as provided under this paragraph (b), as well as any gain or loss on the disposition of a share of any other subsidiary's stock.

(vi) *Examples.*—For purposes of the examples in this paragraph (b)(2)(vi), unless otherwise stated, P is the common parent of a calendar-year consolidated group and owns all of the only class of stock of subsidiaries S, S1, S2, M, M1, and M2 for the entire year; S, S1, S2, M, M1, M2, and T own no stock of lower-tier subsidiaries; all persons use the accrual method of accounting; the facts set forth the only corporate activity; all transactions are between unrelated persons; tax liabilities are disregarded; and §1.1502-36 will not cause P to adjust its basis in S's stock immediately before a disposition. The rules of this paragraph (b)(2) are illustrated by the following examples:

Example 1. Absorption of disposed of subsidiary's losses. (i) *Facts.* P has a $500 basis in S's stock. P sells S's stock for $520 at the close of Year 1. For Year 1, P has ordinary income of $30 (determined without taking into account P's gain or loss from the disposition of S's stock) and S an $80 ordinary loss.

(ii) *Determination of absorbed amount.* To determine S's absorbed amount and the effect of the absorption of its losses under §1.1502-32(b)(2) on P's basis in S's stock, the group's taxable income is computed without taking into account P's gain or loss from the disposition of S's stock. The P group is treated as having a CNOL of $50 (P's $30 of income minus S's $80 separate net operating loss). Accordingly, S's absorbed amount determined under paragraph (b)(2)(i) of this section is $30.

(iii) *Loss absorption and basis reduction.* Under paragraph (b)(2)(ii) of this section, P's basis in S's stock is reduced by S's $30 absorbed amount from $500 to $470 immediately before the disposition. Consequently, P recognizes a $50 gain from the sale of S's stock, and the P group has CTI of $50 for Year 1 (P's $30 of ordinary income plus its $50 of gain from the sale of S's stock, minus $30 of S's ordinary loss equal to its absorbed amount). In addition, S's $50 of unabsorbed loss is carried to S's first separate return year.

Example 2, Carrybacks and carryovers. (i) *Facts.* For Year 1, the P group has CTI of $30 (all of which is attributable to P) and a consolidated net capital loss of $100 ($50 attributable to P and $50 to S), which cannot be carried back. At the beginning of Year 2, P has a $300 basis in S's stock. P sells S's stock for $280 at the close of Year 2. For Year 2, P has ordinary income of $30, and a $20 capital gain (determined without taking into account the consolidated net capital loss carryover from Year 1 or P's gain or loss from the disposition of S's stock), and S has a $100 ordinary loss.

(ii) *Determination of absorbed amount.* To determine S's absorbed amount and the effect of the absorption of its losses under §1.1502-32(b)(2) on P's basis in S's stock, the group's taxable income for Year 2 is computed without taking into account P's gain or loss from the disposition of S's stock. Under section 1212(a)(1)(B), P's $20 capital gain for Year 2 would be offset by $20 of the group's consolidated capital loss carryover from Year 1 ($10 attributable to P and $10 attributable to S). P's $30 of ordinary income in Year 2 would be offset by $30 of S's $100 ordinary loss in that year. P's $30 of ordinary income in Year 1 would be offset by a $30 CNOL carryback from Year 2, all of which is attributable to S. Accordingly, S's absorbed amount under paragraph (b)(2)(i) of this section is $70 ($10 of S's portion of the consolidated capital loss carryover from Year 1 plus $60 of S's loss from Year 2).

(iii) *Loss absorption and basis reduction.* Under paragraph (b)(2)(ii) of this section, P's basis in S's stock is reduced by S's $70 absorbed amount from $300 to $230, immediately before the disposition, resulting in $50 of capital gain to P from the sale of S's stock for $280 in Year 2. Thus, for Year 2 P will have $70 of capital gain ($50 from the stock sale plus $20 from its other capital gain for that year), which will be offset by $70 of the consolidated capital loss carryover from Year 1, $35 of which is attributable to P and $35 of which is attributable to S. Another $30 of S's ordinary loss offsets P's $30 of ordinary income in Year 2. An amount of S's ordinary loss equal to its remaining $5 absorbed amount may be carried back to Year 1 to offset $5 of the group's CTI in that year. P will have a $15 ($50 - $35) capital loss carryover from Year 1, and S will carry over a $15 ($50 - $35) capital loss from Year 1 and a $65 ($100 - $35) NOL to its first separate return year.

Example 3. Chain of subsidiaries. (i) *Facts.* P has a $500 basis in the stock of S and S has a $500 basis in the stock of T, its wholly owned subsidiary. P sells all of its S stock for $520 at the close of Year 1. For Year 1, P has ordinary income of $30, S has no income or loss, and T has an $80 ordinary loss.

(ii) *Determination of absorbed amount, basis reduction, and loss absorption.* Under §1.1502-19(c)(1)(ii), T's stock is treated as disposed of when it becomes a nonmember, and its losses are subject to paragraph (b) of this section. Thus, T's absorbed amount is determined by taking into account P's $30 of ordinary income but without taking into account any gain or loss on P's disposition of S's stock. Accordingly, T's absorbed amount determined under paragraph (b)(2)(i) of this section is $30. Under paragraph (b)(2)(ii) of this section, S's basis in T's stock is reduced by $30, from $500 to $470. Furthermore, under §1.1502-32(a)(3)(iii), P's basis in S's stock is reduced by $30, from $500 to $470, immediately before the sale. Consequently, P recognizes a $50 gain from the sale of S's stock ($520 - $470), and T will have a $50 ($80 - $30) NOL carryover to its first separate return year.

(iii) *Excess loss account in lower-tier stock.* The facts are the same as in paragraph (i) of this *Example 3*, except that S has a $10 excess loss account (ELA) in T's stock (rather than a $500 basis). Under paragraph (b)(1) of this section, T's stock is treated as disposed of and its absorbed amount is determined under paragraph (b)(2)(i) of this section. Thus, T's absorbed amount is determined by taking into account P's $30 of ordinary income but without taking into account P's gain or loss on the disposition of S's stock and S's inclusion of its ELA with respect to T's stock under §1.1502-19(b)(1). Accordingly, T's absorbed amount determined under paragraph (b)(2)(i) of this section is $30. Under paragraph (b)(2)(ii) of this section, S's ELA in its T stock is increased by $30, from $10 to $40, immediately before the disposition of T's stock. Under §1.1502-19(b), the ELA is included in S's income. Moreover, under §1.1502-32(b)(2), P's basis in S's stock is increased immediately before the sale by a net $10 (S's $40 inclusion of T's ELA under §1.1502-19(b) minus T's $30 absorbed loss that tiers up under §1.1502-32(a)(3)(iii)) from $500 to $510. Thus, P recognizes $10 of gain on the sale of S's stock ($520 - $510), and S takes into account $40 of gain from the inclusion of its ELA in T's stock. T will have a $50 ($80 - $30) NOL carryover to its first separate return year.

Example 4. Sale of S's stock and S remains in the group. (i) *Facts.* For Year 1, the P group has CTI of $100 (all of which is attributable to P). At the beginning of Year 2, P has a $40 basis in each of the 10 shares of S's stock. P sells 2 shares of S's stock for $85 each at the close of Year 2. For Year 2, P has an $80 ordinary loss (determined without taking into account P's gain or loss from the sale of S's stock), and S has an $80 ordinary loss.

(ii) *Determination of absorbed amount.* To determine S's absorbed amount and the effect of the absorption of its losses under §1.1502-32(b)(2) on P's basis in S's stock, the group's CTI for Year 2 is computed without taking into account P's gain or loss from the sale of S's stock. Thus, the group would have a $160 CNOL for Year 2, $100 of which is carried back to Year 1 ($50 attributable to S and $50 attributable to P) and offsets $100 of CTI in that year. Accordingly, S's absorbed amount determined under paragraph (b)(2)(i) of this section is $50.

(iii) *Loss absorption and basis reduction.* Under paragraph (b)(2)(ii) of this section, P's basis in all of S's stock is reduced by $50. Each of P's 10 shares of S stock is reduced by $5 from $40 to $35. Consequently, on the sale of each of the 2 shares of S's stock, P recognizes a $50 gain ($85 - $35). The losses available to offset the $100 gain on the sale of S's 2 shares consist of P's $80 ordinary loss and $50 of S's ordinary loss equal its absorbed amount. Under paragraph (e) of this section, P's and S's losses are absorbed on a pro rata basis. Therefore, the group absorbs approximately $62 ($100 x 80/80 + 50) of P's ordinary loss from Year 2, and approximately $38 ($100 x 50/80 + 50) of S's ordinary loss in that year. P's remaining $18 ($80 - $62) of ordinary loss in Year 2 and S's remaining $12 ($50 - $38) of ordinary loss equal to its remaining absorbed amount may be carried back to Year 1 to offset $30 of the $100 of CTI in that year. For Year 2, the P group has $30 remaining of its CNOL (all of which is attributable to S) which is carried to the P group's Year 3 consolidated return year.

(iv) *Lower-tier subsidiary.* The facts are the same as in paragraph (i) of this *Example 4*, except that S has no income or loss for Year 2, but S's wholly owned subsidiary, T, has an $80 ordinary loss. Under paragraph (b)(2)(v) of this section, T's loss is subject to paragraph (b) of this section as if T's stock had disposed of. To determine T's absorbed amount, and the effect of the absorption of its losses under §1.1502-32 on S's basis in its T stock and P's basis in its S stock, the group's taxable income is computed without taking into account P's gain or loss from the sale of S's stock. Of the group's $160 CNOL for Year 2, $100 is carried back to Year 1 ($50 attributable to P and $50 attributable to T) and offsets $100 of CTI in that year. Accordingly, T's absorbed amount determined under paragraph (b)(2)(i) of this section is $50. Under paragraph (b)(2)(ii) of this section, S's basis in T's stock is reduced by $50. Under §1.1502-32(a)(3)(iii), the $50 reduction to S's basis in T's stock tiers up and reduces P's basis in its 10 shares of S stock by $50. Consequently, P's basis in each of the 10 shares of S stock will be decreased by $5 from $40 to $35. On the sale of each of the 2 shares of S's stock, P recognizes a $50 gain ($85 - $35). Under the actual computation, the group has P's $80 ordinary loss and $50 of T's $80 ordinary loss (limited by its absorbed amount) available to offset P's $100 gain on

the sale of S's stock. Under paragraph (e) of this section, P's gain is offset on a pro rata basis by approximately $62 ($100 x 80/($80 + $50)) of P's ordinary loss in Year 2, and approximately $38 ($100 x ($50/($80 + $50)) of T's ordinary loss in that year. P's remaining $18 of ordinary loss in Year 2 and $12 of T's ordinary loss equal to its remaining absorbed amount may be carried back to Year 1 to offset $30 of the $100 of CTI in that year. For Year 2, the P group has $30 remaining of its CNOL (all of which is attributable to T) which is carried to the P group's Year 3 consolidated return year.

Example 5. Alternative Computation. (i) *Facts.* At the beginning of Year 1, P has a $200 basis in S's stock. P sells all of its S stock for $100 at the close of Year 1. For Year 1, P has $10 capital gain on portfolio stock. In addition to S, P has two other subsidiaries, M1 and M2. M1 has capital gain of $50; M2 has a capital loss of $30, and S has a capital loss of $60.

(ii) *Determination of absorbed amount.* To determine S's absorbed amounts and the effect of the absorption of its loss under §1.1502-32(b)(2) on P's basis in S's stock, the group's taxable income is computed without taking into account P's gain or loss from the disposition of S's stock. Under that computation, S's capital loss would offset $40 ($60 x $60/$90) of the group's $60 of capital gain. Accordingly, S's absorbed amount is $40.

(iii) *Basis reduction.* Under paragraph (b)(2)(ii) of this section, S's $40 absorbed amount reduces P's basis in S's stock by $40 from $200 to $160. On the sale of S's stock, P recognizes a capital loss of $60 ($100 - $160).

(iv) *Computation of CTI under generally applicable rules.* In the actual computation under paragraph (b)(2)(iii)(A) of this section, P is treated as having a $50 capital loss ($60 capital loss on the sale of S's stock plus $10 capital gain). Therefore, the only capital gain in the actual computation is M1's $50. There is a total of $120 of capital loss in the computation: S's $40 of capital loss (equal to its absorbed amount), as well as P's $50 and M2's $30 capital losses. M1's $50 of capital gain would be offset on a pro rata basis by approximately $16.50 of S's loss ($50 x $40/$120), approximately $21.00 ($50 x $50/$120) of P's $50 capital loss, and $12.50 ($50 x $30/$120) of M2's capital loss. Because less than all of S's absorbed amount of $40 would be used, the group's CTI is determined under the alternative computation of paragraph (b)(2)(iii)(B) of this section.

(v) *Alternative computation of CTI.* Under paragraph (b)(2)(iii)(B)(1) of this section, S's $40 capital loss (the amount and character of S's absorbed amount) first offsets $40 of the $60 of capital gain (determined without taking into account any gain or loss on P's sale of S stock and without regard to M2's capital loss of $30) generated by other members. Accordingly, $20 of capital gain (P's $10 capital gain determined without regard to its loss on S's stock plus M1's $50 capital gain minus S's $40 absorbed amount) remains. Because P has no net stock gain, paragraph (b)(2)(iii)(B)(2) of this section is inapplicable. Under paragraph (b)(2)(iii)(B)(3) of this section, $10 (the amount of P's capital loss on S's stock limited by the amount of its income included in the computation under paragraph (b)(2)(i) of this section) of P's capital loss offsets the group's $20 remaining capital gain. Under paragraph (b)(2)(iii)(B)(4) of this section, capital losses of members other than S offset the group's remaining $10 of capital gain on a pro rata basis. Therefore, the group will use $3.75 of M2's $30 capital loss ($10 x $30/$80) and $6.25 of P's $50 remaining capital loss ($10 x $50/$80). The group will have a $70 consolidated net capital loss carryover to Year 2 ($43.75 attributable to P and $26.25 attributable to M2). Paragraphs (b), (c), and (d)(6) of §1.1502-36 will not cause P to adjust its basis in S's stock immediately before P's sale of the S stock. However, S's $20 unabsorbed capital loss that may be carried to its first separate return year may be reduced under the attribute reduction rule of §1.1502-36(d)(2).

Example 6. Loss disposition. (i) *Facts.* For Year 1, the P group has a consolidated net capital loss of $100, all of which is attributable to S, and P and M have no income or loss. At the beginning of Year 2, P has a $300 basis in S's stock. P sells all of S's stock for $100 at the close of Year 2. For Year 2, P and S have no income or loss (determined without taking into account P's gain or loss from the disposition of S's stock) and the group has consolidated capital gain net income of $100 attributable solely to M.

(ii) *Determination of absorbed amount.* To determine S's absorbed amount and the effect of the absorption of its losses under §1.1502-32(b)(2) on P's basis in S's stock, the group's taxable income for Year 2 is computed without taking into account P's gain or loss from the disposition of S's stock. The $100 consolidated net capital loss carryover from Year 1 attributable to S offsets the group's $100 of consolidated capital gain net income in Year 2. Accordingly, S's absorbed amount determined under paragraph (b)(2)(i) of this section is $100.

(iii) *Loss absorption and basis reduction.* Under paragraph (b)(2)(ii) of this section, P's basis in S's stock is reduced from $300 to $200 immediately before the disposition. Consequently, P recognizes a $100 capital loss on the sale of S's stock. In an actual computation of CTI, P's $100 capital loss on S's stock in Year 2 would offset M's $100 capital gain in Year 2 before the consolidated capital loss carryover from Year 1 and, as a result, S's $100 absorbed amount would not be used. Because less than all of S's absorbed amount of $100 would be used, the group's CTI is determined under the alternative computation of paragraph (b)(2)(iii)(B) of this section.

(iv) *Alternative Computation of CTI.* Under paragraph (b)(2)(iii)(B)(*1*) of section, S's $100 consolidated net capital loss carryover from Year 1 first offsets M's $100 of capital gain in Year 2. Because P has no net stock gain to be added to the computation, the amount under paragraph (b)(2)(iii)(B)(2) of this section is zero. Because there is no remaining income to offset, paragraphs (b)(2)(iii)(B)(3) and (b)(2)(iii)(B)(4) of this section are inapplicable. Therefore, P's $100 loss on S's stock becomes a consolidated net capital loss carryover to the group's Year 3 consolidated return year.

Example 7: Netting of Disposing Member's Gains and Losses. (i) *Facts.* At the beginning of Year 1, P has a $120 basis in S's stock. P sells all of S's stock for $80 at the close of Year 1. In addition, P has $60 capital loss on the sale of portfolio stock. S has a capital loss of $180. M1 has a capital gain of $100 and M2 has a capital loss of $120.

(ii) *Determination of absorbed amount.* To determine S's absorbed amount and the effect of the absorption of its loss under § 1.1502-32(b)(2) on P's basis in S's stock, the group's taxable income is computed without taking into account P's gain or loss from the disposition of S's stock. Under that computation, S's capital loss would offset $50 ($100 x $180/($180 + $120 + $60)) of M1's $100 capital gain. Accordingly, S's absorbed amount is $50.

(iii) *Basis reduction and computation of CTI under generally applicable rules.* Under paragraph (b)(2)(ii) of this section, P's basis in S's stock is reduced by $50 from $120 to $70 immediately before the sale. Consequently, P recognizes a $10 capital gain on the sale of S's stock. In an actual computation of CTI, P's $10 capital gain on the sale of S's stock would be offset by $10 of P's $60 capital loss. M1's $100 capital gain would be offset by $22.73 ($100 x $50/($50 + $120 + $50)) of P's $50 of net capital loss, $ 54.54 ($100 x $120/$220) of M2's $120 capital loss and $22.73 ($100 x $50/$220) of S's $50 capital loss. Because less than all of S's absorbed amount of $50 would be used, the group's CTI is determined under the alternative computation of paragraph (b)(2)(iii)(B) of this section.

(iv) *Alternative computation of CTI.* Under paragraph (b)(2)(iii)(B)(*1*) of this section, $50 of S's capital loss (the amount and character of S's absorbed amount) first offsets $50 of the $100 capital gain (determined without taking into account any gain or loss on P's sale of S stock and without regard to P's and M2's capital losses). Therefore, after the absorption of S's loss equal to its absorbed amount, there is $50 of remaining capital gain. P will have a $10 capital gain on the sale of S's stock, a $60 capital loss on portfolio stock, and M2 will have a $120 capital loss. Under paragraph (b)(2)(iii)(B)(2) of this section, $10 of P's $60 loss on portfolio stock offsets its $10 gain on S's stock before M2's $120 capital loss is taken into account. No member has a net loss on subsidiary stock, and therefore paragraph (b)(2)(iii)(B)(3) of this section does not apply. Under paragraph (b)(2)(iii)(B)(4) of this section, the remaining capital gain of $50 after the application of paragraph (b)(2)(iii)(B)(3) is offset pro rata by $14.70 ($50 x $50/($50 + $120)) of P's capital loss and $35.30 ($50 x $120/$170) of M2's capital loss. P's unused capital loss of $35.30 and M2's unused capital loss of $84.70 become a $120 consolidated net capital loss carryover to the group's Year 2 consolidated return year.

Example 8. Character of Absorbed Amount. (i) *Facts.* At the beginning of Year 1, P has a $550 basis in S's stock. P sells all of S's stock for $50 at the close of Year 1. In addition, P has a capital gain of $200 (without regard to gain or loss on the sale of S's stock). S has an ordinary loss of $50 and M has an ordinary loss of $25.

(ii) *Determination of absorbed amount.* To determine S's absorbed amount and the effect of the absorption of its losses under § 1.1502-32(b)(2) on P's basis in S's stock, the group's taxable income is computed without taking into account P's gain or loss from the disposition of S's stock. Under that computation, S's $50 ordinary loss and M's $25 ordinary loss offset $75 of P's $200 capital gain. Accordingly, S's absorbed amount determined under paragraph (b)(2)(i) of this section is $50.

(iii) *Basis reduction and computation of CTI under generally applicable rules.* Under paragraph (b)(2)(ii) of this section, P's basis in S's stock is reduced by $50 from $550 to $500 immediately before the sale. Consequently, P recognizes a $450 capital loss on the sale of S's stock. In an actual computation of CTI, $200 of P's $450 capital loss on its sale of S's stock would offset its $200 capital gain and none of S's absorbed amount would be used. Because less than all of S's absorbed amount of $50 would be used, the group's CTI is determined under the alternative computation of paragraph (b)(2)(iii)(B) of this section.

(iv) *Alternative computation of CTI.* Under paragraph (b)(2)(iii)(B)(*1*) of this section, S's $50 ordinary loss first offsets $50 of P's $200 capital gain. Therefore, after the absorption of S's loss equal to its absorbed amount, the group will have $150 ($200 - $50) of remaining capital gain. Because P has no net stock gain to be added

to the computation, paragraph (b)(2)(iii)(B)(2) of this section is inapplicable. Under paragraph (b)(2)(iii)(B)(3) of this section, $150 of P's $450 loss on S's stock (the lesser of P's $200 capital gain or the group's $150 remaining capital gain) offsets the group's remaining $150 of capital gain. Because there is no more income in the group for M's loss to offset, the amount under paragraph (b)(2)(iii)(B)(4) of this section is zero. Therefore, P's remaining unused capital loss on S's stock of $300 and M's $25 ordinary loss become carryovers to the group's Year 2 consolidated return year.

Example 9. Worthless Stock Loss. (i) *Facts.* At the beginning of Year 1, P has a $120 basis in S's stock. For Year 1, P has $100 of ordinary income (determined without taking into account P's gain or loss on the disposition of S's stock) and S generates an $80 ordinary loss. At the close of Year 1, S issues stock to its creditors in a bankruptcy proceeding, and P's stock in S is canceled. The aggregate of S's historic gross receipts meets the requirements of section 165(g)(3)(B), which allows P to claim an ordinary loss with respect to S's stock.

(ii) *Determination of absorbed amount.* To determine S's absorbed amount and the effect of the absorption under § 1.1502-32(b)(2) on P's basis in S's stock, the group's CTI is computed without taking into account P's gain or loss from the disposition of S's stock. Under that computation, S's $80 ordinary loss would offset $80 of P's $100 of ordinary income. Accordingly, S's absorbed amount under paragraph (b)(2)(i) of this section is $80.

(iii) *Basis reduction and computation of CTI under generally applicable rules.* Under paragraph (b)(2)(ii) of this section, S's $80 absorbed amount reduces P's basis in S's stock from $120 to $40. Therefore, P's worthless stock deduction with respect to S's stock is $40. In an actual computation of CTI, P's separate taxable income under § 1.1502-12 would be determined by offsetting P's $100 of ordinary income with its $40 worthless stock deduction with respect to S's stock, leaving $60 of ordinary income that would be offset by S's ordinary loss. However, that computation would result in the absorption of only $60 of S's losses. Because less than all of S's absorbed amount of $80 would be used, the group's CTI is determined under the alternative computation of paragraph (b)(2)(iii)(B) of this section.

(iv) *Alternative computation of CTI.* Under paragraph (b)(2)(iii)(B)(*1*) of this section, S's $80 ordinary loss first offsets $80 of P's $100 of ordinary income. Therefore, after the absorption of S's loss equal to its absorbed amount, the group will have $20 of remaining ordinary income. Because P has no net stock gain to be added to the computation, the amount under paragraph (b)(2)(iii)(B)(2) of this section is zero. Under paragraph (b)(2)(iii)(B)(3) of this section, the group uses $20 of P's $40 ordinary loss on S's stock to offset the remaining $20 income of the group. Because there remains no more income in the group, the amount under paragraph (b)(2)(iii)(B)(4) of this section is zero. P's remaining $20 ordinary loss becomes a CNOL carryover to the group's Year 2 consolidated return year.

Example 10. Charitable Contributions. (i) *Facts.* At the beginning of Year 1, P has a $1,000 basis in S's stock. P sells all of its S stock for $900 at the close of Year 1. For Year 1, P has $1,000 of ordinary income (determined without taking into account P's gain or loss on the disposition of S's stock). For Year 1, S makes a $100 charitable contribution and incurs $200 of ordinary and necessary business expenses that are deductible under section 162(a). In addition, P has a subsidiary M, which also makes a $100 charitable contribution.

(ii) *Determination of S's portion of consolidated charitable contributions deduction.* Under § 1.1502-24(a), a group's consolidated charitable contributions deduction is limited to ten percent of its adjusted consolidated taxable income as defined in § 1.1502-24(c). Under paragraph (b)(2)(iii)(D) of this section, S's portion of the group's consolidated charitable contributions deduction is determined by computing the group's taxable income without regard to P's gain or loss on S's stock. Thus, for purposes of determining the consolidated charitable contributions deduction for Year 1, the group's CTI would be $800 (P's $1,000 of income minus S's $200 of section 162 expenses). Accordingly, the consolidated charitable contributions deduction for Year 1 is limited to $80 ($800 x 10%), $40 attributable to S and $40 attributable to M. Accordingly, S's ordinary loss for Year 1 is $240 ($200 + $40).

(iii) *Determination of absorbed amount.* To determine S's absorbed amount and the effect of the absorption of its losses under § 1.1502-32(b)(2) on P's basis in S's stock, the group's CTI is computed without taking into account P's gain or loss from the disposition of S's stock. S's $240 ordinary loss offsets $240 of P's $1,000 of ordinary income. Accordingly, S's absorbed amount is $240.

(iv) *Loss absorption and basis reduction.* Under paragraph (b)(2)(ii) of this section, S's $240 absorbed amount reduces P's basis in S's stock from $1,000 to $760. On the sale of S's stock, P recognizes capital gain of $140 ($900 - $760). P's ordinary income is offset by $240 of S's ordinary loss and $40 of M's portion of the group's consolidated charitable contributions deduction, resulting in CTI of $860 ($1,000 + $140 - $280). Of the group's excess charitable contributions of $120, $60 will be apportioned to S and carried to its first separate return year. The remaining $60 of excess consolidated charitable contributions is the group's consolidated charitable contribution carryover under § 1.1502-24(b).

    Example 11. Application of Unified Loss Rule. (i) *Facts.* In Year 1, P purchases the sole share of S's stock for $500. At the time of the purchase, S owns Land with a basis of $420. During Year 1, P incurs a $100 ordinary loss and S earns $100 in rental income, which increases P's basis in S's stock to $600. For Year 2, P has ordinary income of $30 (determined without taking into account P's gain or loss from the disposition of S's stock) and S incurs an ordinary loss of $80. At the close of Year 2, S has $20 of cash in addition to Land. In addition to S, P has another subsidiary M, which has an ordinary loss of $40 for Year 2. At the close of Year 2, when the value of Land has declined, P sells the sole share of S's stock for $480. No election is made under § 1.1502-36(d)(6) to reduce P's basis in S's stock or reattribute S's attributes to P.

    (ii) *Determination of absorbed amount.* To determine S's absorbed amount and the effect of the absorption of its losses under § 1.1502-32(b)(2) on P's basis in S's stock, the group's CTI is computed without taking into account P's gain or loss from the disposition of S's stock. Under paragraph (e)(1) of this section, P's $30 of ordinary income would be offset by $10 ($30 x $40/$120) of M's ordinary loss for Year 2 and $20 ($30 x $80/$120) of S's ordinary loss for Year 2. Accordingly, S's absorbed amount determined under paragraph (b)(2)(i) of this section is $20.

    (iii) *Loss absorption and basis reduction.* Under paragraph (b)(2)(ii) of this section, S's $20 absorbed amount reduces P's basis in S's stock from $600 (P's $500 purchase price plus the $100 positive adjustment in Year 1) to $580. After taking into account the effects of all applicable rules of law, including paragraph (b)(2)(ii) of this section, P would recognize a $100 ($480 - $580) loss on the sale of S's stock. Thus, P's sale of the S share is a transfer of a loss share and therefore subject to § 1.1502-36. Under § 1.1502-36(b)(1)(ii), P's basis in its sole share of S's stock is not subject to redetermination. Under § 1.1502-36(c), P's basis in the S share ($580) is reduced, but not below value, by the lesser of the share's net positive adjustment and disconformity amount. The share's net positive adjustment is the greater of zero and the sum of all investment adjustments (as defined in § 1.1502-36(b)(1)(iii)) applied to the basis of the share. The net positive adjustment applied to the basis of the share is $80, S's $100 income for Year 1 and its $20 absorbed amount for Year 2. The share's disconformity amount is the excess, if any, of its basis ($580) over its allocable portion of S's net inside attribute amount. S's net inside attribute amount of $500 is the sum of S's $20 cash, S's basis in Land of $420, and S's $60 loss carryover ($80 - $20). Thus, the share's disconformity amount is $80 ($580 - $500). The lesser of the net positive adjustment ($80) and the share's disconformity amount ($80) is $80. Accordingly, under § 1.1502-36(c), P's basis in S's share is reduced by $80 from $580 to $500, and after taking into account the adjustments under paragraphs (b) and (c) of § 1.1502-36, the transferred S share is still a loss share ($480 sale price minus $500 basis).

    (iv) *Computation of CTI.* In an actual computation of CTI, P's $30 of ordinary income would be offset on a pro rata basis by $20 ($30 x $40/$60) of M's ordinary loss and $10 ($30 x $20/$60) of S's ordinary loss. Because less than all of S's absorbed amount of $20 would be used, the group's CTI is determined under the alternative computation of paragraph (b)(2)(iii)(B) of this section. Under paragraph (b)(2)(iii)(B)(1) of this section, the computation of CTI is made by first computing the group's taxable income without taking into account P's loss on the disposition of S's stock and using only S's loss equal to its $20 absorbed amount. Accordingly, the group's $30 of ordinary income is reduced by $20 of S's ordinary loss, leaving $10 of remaining ordinary income. Because P has no net stock gain to be added to the computation, paragraph (b)(2)(iii)(B)(2) of this section is inapplicable. Under paragraph (b)(2)(iii)(B)(3) of this section, the group's remaining $10 of ordinary income is offset by a loss on the disposition of subsidiary stock, subject to applicable principles of the Code and regulations. The group's remaining $10 of income may not be offset by P's capital loss on the sale of S's stock, because P has no income of the same character on its loss on S's stock. Under paragraph (b)(2)(iii)(B)(4) of this section, the group's remaining $10 of ordinary income is offset by $10 of M's ordinary loss. M's $30 unabsorbed loss is carried over as a CNOL and P's remaining $20 capital loss from the sale of S's stock is carried over as a consolidated net capital loss to the group's Year 3 consolidated return year. S's $60 unused loss would be carried over to its separate return year subject to § 1.1502-36(d). Under § 1.1502-36(d)(2), S's attributes are reduced by S's attribute reduction amount. Under § 1.1502-36(d)(3), S's attri-

bute reduction amount is the lesser of the net stock loss and S's aggregate inside loss. The net stock loss is $20, the excess of the $500 basis of the transferred share over the $480 value of the transferred share. S's aggregate inside loss is $20, the excess of its $500 net inside attribute amount over the $480 value of the S share. Therefore, the attribute reduction amount is $20, the lesser of the $20 net stock loss and the $20 aggregate inside loss. Accordingly, S's $20 attribute reduction amount is applied to reduce from $60 to $40 the amount of S's NOL carryover to its separate return year.

    (v) *Election to reduce stock basis.* The facts are the same as in paragraph (i) of this *Example 11* except that P elects under § 1.1502-36(d)(6)(i)(B) to reattribute S's losses to the full extent of the attribute reduction amount ($20). Accordingly, P is treated as succeeding to $20 of S's losses as if acquired in a transaction described in section 381(a) (see § 1.1502-36(d)(6)(i)(B) and (iv)(A)) and, as a result, P's basis in the S share is reduced from $500 to $480. After giving effect to the election, P will have no loss on S's stock, the group will have a $50 CNOL carryover to Year 3 ($30 attributable to M and $20 attributable to P), and S will have a $40 NOL carryover to its separate return year.

    (3) *Effective/applicability date.*—This paragraph (b) applies to dispositions of subsidiary stock occurring in consolidated return years beginning on or after the date these regulations are published as final regulations in the **Federal Register**.

    (c) * * *

      (2) * * *

        (i) *Limitation on deductions and losses to offset income or gain.*—First, the determination of the extent to which S's deductions and losses for the consolidated return year of the disposition (and its deductions and losses carried over from prior years) may offset income and gain is made pursuant to paragraph (b)(2) of this section.

        (ii) *Tentative adjustment of stock basis.*—Second, § 1.1502-32 is tentatively applied to adjust the basis of the S stock to reflect the amount of S's income and gain included, and S's absorbed amount of losses, in the computation of consolidated taxable income or loss for the year of disposition (and any prior years) that is made pursuant to paragraph (b)(2) of this section, but not to reflect the realization of excluded COD income and the reduction of attributes in respect thereof.

                  * * *

    (4) *Definition of lower-tier corporation.*—For purposes of this paragraph (c), lower-tier corporation means a lower-tier subsidiary described in § 1.1502-36(f)(4).

                  * * *

    (7) *Effective/applicability date.*—* * * However, paragraphs (c)(2) and (4) of this section apply to consolidated return years beginning on or after the date these regulations are published as final regulations in the **Federal Register**.

                  * * *

    (e) *Absorption rule.*—(1) *Pro rata absorption of ordinary losses.*—If the group has a CNOL for a consolidated return year, the amount of each member's separate net operating loss, as defined in § 1.1502-21(b)(2)(iv)(B)(1), for the year that offsets the income or gain of other members is determined on a pro rata basis under the principles of § 1.1502-21(b)(2)(iv). For example, if, for the consolidated return year, P and S1 have a separate net operating loss of $60 and $30, respectively, and S2 (the only other member of the P group) has $21 of income, $14 of P's net operating loss and $7 of S1's net operating loss offset S2's $21 of income and are absorbed in the year.

    (2) *Pro-rata absorption of capital losses.*—If the group has a consolidated net capital loss for a consolidated return year and any member has capital gain net income for the year (taking into account only its capital gains and losses), the amount of each member's capital loss (as defined in paragraph (b)(1) of this section) that offsets the sum of the capital gain net income of other members (computed separately for each member) is determined on a pro rata basis under the principles of § 1.1502-21(b)(2)(iv). For purposes of this paragraph (e)(2), the character of each member's gains and losses is first determined on a consolidated basis. See §§ 1.1502-22 and 1.1502-23.

    (3) *Effective/applicability date.*—This paragraph (e) applies to consolidated return years beginning on or after the date these regulations are published as final regulations in the **Federal Register**.

    Par. 3. Section 1.1502-12 is amended by:

    1. Revising paragraphs (b) and (e).

    2. Removing and reserving paragraph (m).

    The revisions read as follows:

§1.1502-12. Separate taxable income.

* * *

(b) Any deduction that is disallowed under §1.1502-15 shall be taken into account as provided in that section;

* * *

(e) If a member disposes of a share of a subsidiary's stock, the member's deduction or loss (if any) on the stock that will be used in the consolidated return year of the disposition and as a carryback to prior years is computed in accordance with §1.1502-11(b) or (c), as appropriate.

* * *

(m) [Reserved]

* * *

CFCs: Previously Taxed Earnings and Profits: Exclusion from Gross Income: Basis Adjustments

CFCs: Previously Taxed Earnings and Profits: Exclusion from Gross Income: Basis Adjustments.—Amendments to Reg. §1.1502-12, providing guidance relating to the exclusion from gross income of previously taxed earnings and profits under Code Sec. 959 and related basis adjustments under Code Sec. 961, are proposed (published in the Federal Register on August 29, 2006) (REG-121509-00).

☐ Par. 10. Section 1.1502-12 as amended by adding paragraph (s) to read as follows:

§1.1502-12. Separate taxable income.

* * *

(s) The exclusion from gross income of previously taxed earnings and profits shall be determined by the rules of §1.959-3(g).

Foreign-Derived Intangible Income: Global Intangible Low-Taxed Income: Deduction

Foreign-Derived Intangible Income: Global Intangible Low-Taxed Income: Deduction.—Amendments to Reg. §§1.1502-12 and 1.1502-13, providing guidance to determine the amount of the deduction for foreign-derived intangible income and global intangible low-taxed income, are proposed (published in the Federal Register on March 6, 2019) (REG-104464-18).

Par. 4. Section 1.1502-12, as proposed to be amended in 83 FR 51072 (Oct. 10, 2018), is further amended by adding paragraph (t) to read as follows:

§1.1502-12. Separate taxable income.

* * *

(t) See §1.1502-50 for rules relating to the computation of a member's deduction under section 250.

Par. 5. Section 1.1502-13, as proposed to be amended in 83 FR 67490 (Dec. 28, 2018), is further amended:

1. In paragraph (a)(6)(ii), under the heading "Matching rule. (§1.1502-13(c)(7)(ii))", by adding entry (T); and

2. Adding paragraph (c)(7)(ii)(T).

The additions read as follows:

§1.1502-13. Intercompany transactions.—(a) * * *

(6) * * *

(ii) * * *

Matching rule. (§1.1502-13(c)(7)(ii))

* * *

(T) Example 20. Redetermination of attributes for section 250 purposes.

* * *

(c) * * *

(7) * * *

(ii) * * *

(T) *Example 20: Redetermination of attributes for section 250 purposes*—(1) *Facts.* S manufactures equipment in the United States and recognizes $75 of gross income included in gross DEI (as defined in §1.250(b)-1(c)(14)) on the sale of Asset, which is not depreciable property, to B in Year 1 for $100. In Year 2, B sells Asset to X for $125 and recognizes $25 of gross income. The sale is a FDDEI sale (as defined in §1.250(b)-1(c)(8)), and thus the $25 of income is included in B's gross FDDEI (as defined in §1.250(b)-1(c)(15)) for Year 2.

(2) *Timing and attributes.* S's $75 of intercompany income is taken into account in Year 2 under the matching rule to reflect the $75 difference between B's $25 corresponding item taken into account (based on B's $100 cost basis in Asset) and the recomputed corresponding item (based on the $25 basis that B would have if S and B were divisions of a single corporation and B's basis were determined by reference to S's basis). In determining whether S's gross income included in gross DEI from the sale of Asset is included in gross FDDEI, S and B are treated as divisions of a single corporation. See paragraph (a)(6) of this section. In determining the amount of income included in gross DEI that is included in gross FDDEI, the attributes of S's intercompany item and B's corresponding item may be redetermined to the extent necessary to produce the same effect on consoli-

dated taxable income (and consolidated tax liability) as if S and B were divisions of a single corporation. See paragraph (c)(1)(i) of this section. Applying section 250 and §1.1502-50 on a single entity basis, all $100 of income included in gross DEI would be gross FDDEI. On a separate entity basis, S would have $75 of gross income included in gross DEI that is included in gross non-FDDEI (as defined in §1.250(b)-1(c)(16)) and B would have $25 of gross income included in gross DEI that is included in gross FDDEI. Thus, on a separate entity basis, S and B would have, in the aggregate, $100 of gross income included in gross DEI, of which only $25 is included gross FDDEI. Accordingly, under single entity treatment, $75 that would be treated as gross income included in gross DEI that is included in gross non-FDDEI on a separate entity basis is redetermined to be included in gross FDDEI.

(3) *Intercompany sale for loss.* The facts are the same as in paragraph (c)(7)(ii)(T)(1) (the facts in *Example 20*), except that S recognizes $25 of loss on the sale of Asset. S's $25 of intercompany loss is taken into account under the matching rule to reflect the $25 difference between B's $25 corresponding item taken into account (based on B's $100 cost basis in Asset) and the recomputed corresponding item (based on the $125 basis that B would have if S and B were divisions of a single corporation and B's basis were determined by reference to S's $125 of costs). Applying section 250 and §1.1502-50 on a single entity basis, $0 of income would be included in gross DEI. In order to reflect this result, under the matching rule, S's $25 loss is allocated and apportioned solely to B's $25 of gross income from the sale of Asset for purposes of determining B's DEI and FDDEI. Furthermore, B's $25 of gross income is not taken into account for purposes of apportioning any other deductions under section 861 and the regulations under that section for purposes of determining any member's DEI or FDDEI.

* * *

Consolidated Returns: Intercompany Obligations: Disallowance of Interest Expense Deductions

Consolidated Returns: Intercompany Obligations: Disallowance of Interest Expense Deductions.—Amendments to Reg. §1.1502-13, affecting corporations filing consolidated returns by providing special rules for the treatment of certain intercompany transactions involving interest on intercompany obligations, are proposed (published in the Federal Register on May 7, 2004) (REG-128590-03).

☐ Par. 3. Section 1.1502-13 is amended by:

1. Adding a sentence after the second sentence of paragraph (c)(6)(ii)(A).

2. Adding paragraph (c)(6)(iii).

3. Revising the first sentence of *Example 1*(d) of paragraph (g)(5).

The revisions and additions read as follows:

§1.1502-13. Intercompany transactions.

* * *

(c) * * *

(6) * * *

(ii) * * *

(A) * * * However, see §1.265-2(c) for special rules related to the application of paragraph (c)(6)(i) of this section to interest income with respect to certain intercompany obligations the interest deduction on which is disallowed under section 265(a)(2). * * *

* * *

(iii) *Effective date.*—The third sentence of paragraph (c)(6)(ii)(A) of this section shall apply to taxable years beginning on or after the date these regulations are published as final regulations in the Federal Register.

* * *

(g) * * *

(5) * * *

Example 1 * * *

(d) *Tax-exempt income.* The facts are the same as in paragraph (a) of this *Example 1*, except that B's borrowing from S is allocable under section 265 to B's purchase of state and local bonds to which section 103 applies and § 1.265-2(c) does not apply. * * *

* * *

Partners and Partnerships: American Jobs Creation Act of 2004 and Taxpayer Relief Act of 1997: Guidance

Partners and Partnerships: American Jobs Creation Act of 2004 and Taxpayer Relief Act of 1997: Guidance.—Amendments to Reg. § 1.1502-13, providing guidance on certain provisions of the American Jobs Creation Act of 2004, conforming the regulations to statutory changes in the Taxpayer Relief Act of 1997, modifying the basis allocation rules to prevent certain unintended consequences of the current basis allocation rules for substituted basis transactions and providing additional guidance on allocations resulting from revaluations of partnership property, are proposed (published in the Federal Register on January 16, 2014) (REG-144468-05).

☐ Par. 10. Section 1.1502-13 is amended by:

1. Amending paragraph (h)(2), *Example 4*, by removing "Five years" and adding in its place "Seven years".

§ 1.1502-13. Intercompany transactions.

Reporting Income and Deductions: Consolidated Group

Reporting Income and Deductions: Consolidated Group.—An amendment to Reg. § 1.1502-13, revising the rules for reporting certain items of income and deduction that are reportable on the day a corporation joins or leaves a consolidated group, is proposed (published in the Federal Register on March 6, 2015) (REG-100400-14).

Par. 4. Section 1.1502-13 is amended by adding *Example 3(e)* to paragraph (c)(7)(ii) to read as follows:

§ 1.1502-13. Intercompany transactions.—

* * *

(c) * * *

(7) * * *

(ii) * * *

Example 3. * * *

(e) *Liability in excess of basis.* The facts are the same as in paragraph (a) of this *Example 3*, except that S and B are not members of the same consolidated group immediately before S's transfer of the land to B, and the land is encumbered with an $80 liability. Immediately after the transfer, S and B are members of the same consolidated group. Thus, the transfer is an intercompany transaction to which section 357(c) does not apply pursuant to § 1.1502-80(d).

* * *

Deduction for Business Interest Expense: Limitation

Deduction for Business Interest Expense: Limitation.—Amendments to Reg. § 1.1502-13, regarding the limitation on the deduction for business interest expense after the enactment of recent tax legislation, are proposed (published in the Federal Register on December 28, 2018) (REG-106089-18).

Par. 17. Section 1.1502-13 is amended by—

1. In paragraph (a)(6)(ii)—

a. Under the heading "Matching rule. (§ 1.1502-13(c)(7)(ii))":

i. Designating *Examples* 1 through *17* as entries (A) through (Q).

ii. Adding entries (R) and (S).

b. Under the heading "Anti-avoidance rules. (§ 1.1502-13(h)(2))":

i. Designating *Examples* 1 through 5 as entries (i) through (v).

ii. Adding an entry (vi).

2. In paragraph (c)(7)(ii):

a. Designating *Examples 1* through 17 as paragraphs (c)(7)(ii)(A) through (Q), respectively.

b. In newly designated paragraphs (c)(7)(ii)(A) through (Q):

i. Redesignating paragraphs (c)(7)(ii)(A)(a) through (i) as paragraphs (c)(7)(ii)(A)(1) through (9).

ii. Redesignating paragraphs (c)(7)(ii)(B)(a) and (b) as paragraphs (c)(7)(ii)(B)(1) and (2).

iii. Redesignating paragraphs (c)(7)(ii)(C)(a) through (d) as paragraphs (c)(7)(ii)(C)(1) through (4).

iv. Redesignating paragraphs (c)(7)(ii)(D)(a) through (e) as paragraphs (c)(7)(ii)(D)(1) through (5).

v. Redesignating paragraphs (c)(7)(ii)(E)(a) through (f) as paragraphs (c)(7)(ii)(E)(1) through (6).

vi. Redesignating paragraphs (c)(7)(ii)(F)(a) through (d) as paragraphs (c)(7)(ii)(F)(1) through (4).

v. Redesignating paragraphs (c)(7)(ii)(G)(a) through (d) as paragraphs (c)(7)(ii)(G)(1) through (4).

vi. Redesignating paragraphs (c)(7)(ii)(I)(a) through (e) as paragraphs (c)(7)(ii)(I)(1) through (5).

vii. Redesignating paragraphs (c)(7)(ii)(J)(a) through (d) as paragraphs (c)(7)(ii)(J)(1) through (4).

viii. Redesignating paragraphs (c)(7)(ii)(K)(a) through (d) as paragraphs (c)(7)(ii)(K)(1) through (4).

ix. Redesignating paragraphs (c)(7)(ii)(L)(a) and (b) as paragraphs (c)(7)(ii)(L)(1) and (2).

x. Redesignating paragraphs (c)(7)(ii)(N)(a) through (c) as paragraphs (c)(7)(ii)(N)(1) through (3).

xi. Redesignating paragraphs (c)(7)(ii)(O)(a) through (d) as paragraphs (c)(7)(ii)(O)(1) through (4).

xii. Redesignating paragraphs (c)(7)(ii)(P)(a) and (b) as paragraphs (c)(7)(ii)(P)(1) and (2).

xiii. Redesignating paragraphs (c)(7)(ii)(Q)(a) through (c) as paragraphs (c)(7)(Q)(1) through (3).

c. In the table below, for each newly redesignated paragraph listed in the "Paragraph" column, remove the text indicated in the "Remove" column and add in its place the text indicated in the "Add" column:

Paragraph	Remove	Add
(c)(7)(ii)(A)(5)	paragraph (a) of this *Example 1*	*Example 1* in paragraph (c)(7)(ii)(A)(1) of this section
(c)(7)(ii)(A)(5)	paragraphs (c) and (d) of this *Example 1*	*Example 1* in paragraphs (c)(7)(ii)(A)(3) and (4) of this section
(c)(7)(ii)(A)(6)	paragraph (a) of this *Example 1*	*Example 1* in paragraph (c)(7)(ii)(A)(1) of this section

Paragraph	Remove	Add
(c)(7)(ii)(A)(7)	paragraph (a) of this *Example 1*	*Example 1* in paragraph (c)(7)(ii)(A)(*1*) of this section
(c)(7)(ii)(A)(8)	paragraph (a) of this *Example 1*	*Example 1* in paragraph (c)(7)(ii)(A)(*1*) of this section
(c)(7)(ii)(A)(9)	paragraph (a) of this *Example 1*	*Example 1* in paragraph (c)(7)(ii)(A)(*1*) of this section
(c)(7)(ii)(C)(3)	paragraph (a) of this *Example 3*	*Example 3* in paragraph (c)(7)(ii)(C)(*1*) of this section
(c)(7)(ii)(C)(4)	paragraph (c) of this *Example 3*	*Example 3* in paragraph (c)(7)(ii)(C)(*3*) of this section
(c)(7)(ii)(C)(4)	paragraph (b) of this *Example 3*	*Example 3* in paragraph (c)(7)(ii)(C)(*2*) of this section
(c)(7)(ii)(D)(5)	paragraph (a) of this *Example 4*	*Example 4* in paragraph (c)(7)(ii)(D)(*1*) of this section
(c)(7)(ii)(D)(5)	paragraphs (c) and (d) of this *Example 4*	*Example 4* in paragraphs (c)(7)(ii)(D)(*3*) and (*4*) of this section
(c)(7)(ii)(E)(3)	paragraph (a) of this *Example 5*	*Example 5* in paragraph (c)(7)(ii)(E)(*1*) of this section
(c)(7)(ii)(E)(4)	paragraph (a) of this *Example 5*	*Example 5* in paragraph (c)(7)(ii)(E)(*1*) of this section
(c)(7)(ii)(E)(5)	paragraph (a) of this *Example 5*	*Example 5* in paragraph (c)(7)(ii)(E)(*1*) of this section
(c)(7)(ii)(E)(6)	paragraph (a) of this *Example 5*	*Example 5* in paragraph (c)(7)(ii)(E)(*1*) of this section
(c)(7)(ii)(F)(3)	paragraph (a) of this *Example 6*	*Example 6* in paragraph (c)(7)(ii)(F)(*1*) of this section
(c)(7)(ii)(F)(4)	paragraph (a) of this *Example 6*	*Example 6* in paragraph (c)(7)(ii)(F)(*1*) of this section
(c)(7)(ii)(G)(4)	paragraph (a) of this *Example 7*	*Example 7* in paragraph (c)(7)(ii)(G)(*1*) of this section
(c)(7)(ii)(G)(4)	paragraph (c) of this *Example 7*	*Example 7* in paragraph (c)(7)(ii)(G)(*3*) of this section
(c)(7)(ii)(I)(3)	paragraph (a) of this *Example 9*	*Example 9* in paragraph (c)(7)(ii)(I)(*1*) of this section
(c)(7)(ii)(I)(4)	paragraph (a) of this *Example 9*	*Example 9* in paragraph (c)(7)(ii)(I)(*1*) of this section
(c)(7)(ii)(I)(5)	paragraph (d) of this *Example 9*	*Example 9* in paragraph (c)(7)(ii)(I)(*4*) of this section
(c)(7)(ii)(J)(3)	paragraph (a) of this *Example 10*	*Example 10* in paragraph (c)(7)(ii)(J)(*1*) of this section
(c)(7)(ii)(J)(4)	paragraph (a) of this *Example 10*	*Example 10* in paragraph (c)(7)(ii)(J)(*1*) of this section
(c)(7)(ii)(K)(4)	paragraph (a) of this *Example 11*	*Example 11* in paragraph (c)(7)(ii)(K)(*1*) of this section
(c)(7)(ii)(N)(2)	paragraph (a) of this *Example 14*	*Example 14* in paragraph (c)(7)(ii)(N)(*1*) of this section
(c)(7)(ii)(O)(4)	paragraph (a) of this *Example 15*	*Example 15* in paragraph (c)(7)(ii)(O)(*1*) of this section
(c)(7)(ii)(Q)(*1*)	*Example 16*	*Example 16* in paragraph (c)(7)(ii)(P) of this section
(c)(7)(ii)(Q)(*2*)	paragraph (f)(7), *Example 2* of this section	*Example 2* in paragraph (f)(7) of this section
(c)(7)(iii)(A)	Paragraphs (c)(6)(ii)(C), (c)(6)(ii)(D), and (c)(7)(ii), Examples 16 and 17 of this section	Paragraphs (c)(6)(ii)(C) and (D) of this section, *Example 16* in paragraph (c)(7)(ii)(P) of this section, and *Example 17* in paragraph (c)(7)(ii)(Q) of this section

d. Adding paragraphs (c)(7)(ii)(R) and (S).

3. In paragraph (h)(2):

a. Designating *Examples 1* through 5 as paragraphs (h)(2)(i) through (v), respectively.

b. In newly designated paragraphs (h)(2)(i) through (v):

i. Redesignating paragraphs (h)(2)(i)(a) and (b) as paragraphs (h)(2)(i)(A) and (B).

ii. Redesignating paragraphs (h)(2)(ii)(a) and (b) as paragraphs (h)(2)(ii)(A) and (B).

iii. Redesignating paragraphs (h)(2)(iii)(a) and (b) as paragraphs (h)(2)(iii)(A) and (B).

iv. Redesignating paragraphs (h)(2)(iv)(a) and (b) as paragraphs (h)(2)(iv)(A) and (B).

v. Redesiganting paragraphs (h)(2)(v)(a) and (b) as paragraphs (h)(2)(iv)(A) and (B).

c. Adding paragraph (h)(2)(vi).

The additions read as follows:

§1.1502-13. Intercompany transactions.—(a) * * *

  (6) * * *

    (ii) * * *

    Matching rule. (§1.1502-13(c)(7)(ii))

         * * *

(R) Example 18. Transfer of partnership interests in an intercompany sale.

(S) Example 19. Intercompany transfer of partnership interests in a non-recognition transaction.

         * * *

Anti-avoidance rules. (§1.1502-13(h)(2))

* * *

(vi) Example 6. Section 163 interest limitation.

* * *

(c) * * *

(7) * * *

(ii) * * *

(R) *Example 18: Transfer of partnership interests in an intercompany sale—(1) Facts.* P wholly owns S and B, both of which are members of the consolidated group of which P is the common parent. S and A (an unrelated third party) are equal partners in PS1, which was formed in Year 1. At the end of Year 1, the fair market value of PS1 is $200x, and S's adjusted basis in its partnership interest is $100x. During Year 2, PS1 borrows money, pays $100x of business interest expense, and repays the debt. PS1's section 163(j) limitation is $0; thus, the $100x of Year 2 business interest expense is disallowed as a deduction to PS1, is characterized as excess business interest expense, and is allocated proportionally to PS1's partners. S reduces its basis in its PS1 interest under §1.163(j)-6(h) to reflect the $50x of excess business interest expense allocated to S, but the reduction is not treated as a noncapital, nondeductible expense (see §1.163(j)-4(d)(4)(ii). On the last day of Year 2, S sells its PS1 partnership interest to B for $50x. S has not used any of the excess business interest expense allocated from PS1; thus, immediately before the sale, S's basis in its PS1 interest is increased by $50x (to $100x) under §1.163(j)-6(h). This basis increase is not treated as tax-exempt income (see §1.163(j)-4(d)(4)(ii). During Year 3, PS1 earns $50x of income, all of which is reported to the partners as excess taxable income, and $25x of which is allocated to B. B's basis in its PS1 interest is increased accordingly. Additionally, during Year 3, B earns $25x of business interest income and has no business interest expense other than its allocation of business interest expense from PS1. At the close of business on the last day of Year 4, B sells its PS1 partnership interest to Z (an unrelated third party) for $85x. At the time of the sale, B's basis in its PS1 interest is $75x.

(2) *Definitions.* Under paragraph (b)(1) of this section, S's sale of its PS1 interest to B in Year 2 is an intercompany transaction, with S as the selling member and B as the buying member. S's $50x capital loss on the sale is an intercompany item within the meaning of paragraph (b)(2)(i) of this section. B's $25 of ordinary income in Year 3 and its $10x gain on the sale of the PS1 interest to Z in Year 4 are both corresponding items within the meaning of paragraph (b)(3)(i) of this section.

(3) *Timing and attributes.* S takes its $50x loss into account to reflect the difference in each consolidated return year between B's corresponding items taken into account for the year and the recomputed corresponding item for the year. If S and B were divisions of a single corporation and the intercompany sale were a transfer between divisions, the single entity would have had zero income inclusion in Year 3, as the $25x of excess taxable income attributable to the single entity's interest in PS1 would have allowed the single entity to use $25x of the excess business interest expense allocation from PS1 in Year 2. However, on a separate entity basis, B's corresponding item for Year 3 is $25x of ordinary income (the excess taxable income from PS1). As a result, under §1.1502-13(c)(ii), S takes into account $25x of its loss in Year 3, the difference between the recomputed corresponding item and B's corresponding item in Year 3 ($0 - $25x = - $25x). Under paragraphs (c)(1)(i) and (c)(4)(i)(A) of this section, the $25x is redetermined to be ordinary. The remaining $25x of S's loss continues to be deferred. The recomputed corresponding item in Year 4 is a $15x capital loss ($85x of sales proceeds minus

$100x basis (the original $100x basis, minus a $50 reduction in basis under §1.163(j)-6(h), plus a $25x increase for its allocable share of PS1's income, plus a $25x increase under §1.163(j)-6(h)). B's corresponding item is a $10x capital gain ($85x sales proceeds minus $75x basis). Accordingly, the remaining $25x of S's $50x Year 2 capital loss is taken into account in Year 4.

(S) *Example 19: Intercompany transfer of partnership interests in a nonrecognition transaction—(1) Facts.* P wholly owns B, which is a member of the consolidated group of which P is the common parent. P and A (an unrelated third party) are equal partners in PS1, which was formed in Year 1. At the end of Year 1, the fair market value of PS1 is $200x, and P's adjusted basis in its partnership interest is $100x. At the beginning of Year 2, PS1 borrows money and purchases inventory. During Year 2, PS1 pays $100x of business interest expense, sells inventory for $100x (net of cost of goods sold), and repays the debt in full. PS1's section 163(j) limitation for Year 2 is $30x (30 percent x $100x). Thus, $70x of PS1's Year 2 business interest expense is disallowed as a deduction to PS1, is characterized as excess business interest, and is allocated proportionally to PS1's partners. P reduces its basis in its PS1 interest under §1.163(j)-6(h) to reflect the $35x of excess business interest allocated to P. P's basis in its PS1 interest also is increased to reflect the $35x of income allocated to P, leaving P with a basis in its PS1 interest of $100x at the end of Year 2. On the first day of Year 3, P contributes its PS1 partnership interest to B in exchange for B stock in a non-recognition exchange under section 351. At the time, P had not used any of the excess business interest expense allocated from PS1. During Year 4, B sells its PS1 partnership interest to Z (an unrelated third party) for $200x.

(2) *Analysis.* P's transfer of its interest in PS1 to B is an intercompany transaction. The transfer also is a disposition for purposes of §1.163(j)-6(h). Therefore, immediately before the transfer, P increases its $100x basis in its PS1 interest by $35x (the amount of P's unused excess business interest expense). Under section 362, B receives a carryover basis of $135x in the PS1 interest. P has no intercompany item, but B's $65x of capital gain from its sale of the PS1 interest to Z is a corresponding item because the PS1 interest was acquired in an intercompany transaction. B takes the $65x of capital gain into account in Year 4.

* * *

(h) * * *

(2) * * *

(vi) *Example 6: Section163(j) interest limitation—(A) Facts.* S1 and S2 are members of a consolidated group of which P is the common parent. S1 is engaged in an excepted trade or business, and S2 is engaged in a non-excepted trade or business. If S1 were to lend funds directly to S2 in an intercompany transaction, under §1.163(j)-10(a)(4)(i), the intercompany obligation of S2 would not be considered an asset of S1 for purposes of §1.163(j)-10 (concerning allocations of interest and other taxable items between excepted and non-excepted trades or businesses for purposes of section 163(j)). With a principal purpose of avoiding treatment of a lending transaction between S1 and S2 as an intercompany transaction (and increasing the P group's basis in its assets allocable to excepted trades or businesses), S1 lends funds to X (an unrelated third party). X then on-lends funds to S2 on substantially similar terms.

(B) *Analysis.* A principal purpose of the steps undertaken was to avoid treatment of a lending transaction between S1 and S2 as an intercompany transaction. Therefore, under paragraph (h)(1) of this section, appropriate adjustments are made, and the X obligation in the hands of S1 is not treated as an asset of S1 for purposes of §1.163(j)-10, to the extent of the loan from X to S2.

* * *

Sales of Inventory: Determining Source of Income

Sales of Inventory: Determining Source of Income.—Amendments to Reg. §1.1502-13, modifying the rules for determining the source of income from sales of inventory produced within the United States and sold without the United States or vice versa, are proposed (published in the Federal Register on December 30, 2019) (REG-100956-19).

Par. 10. Section 1.1502-13, as proposed to be amended at 83 FR 67490 (December 28, 2018), is further amended by revising paragraph (c)(7)(ii)(N) to read as follows:

§1.1502-13. Intercompany transactions.

* * *

(c) * * *

(7) * * *

(ii) * * *

(N) *Example (14): Source of income under section 863—(1) Intercompany sale—(i) Facts.* S manufactures inventory property solely in the United States, and recognizes $75x of income on sales to B in Year 1. B conducts further production activity on the inventory property solely in Country Y and then sells the inventory property to X in Country Y and recognizes $25x of income on the sale to X, also in Year 1. Title passes from S to B, and from B to X, in Country Y. Assume that applying §1.863-3 on a single entity basis, including the formula for apportionment of multi-country production activities by

reference to the basis of production assets, $10x is treated as foreign source income and $90x is treated as U.S. source income (that is, 10 percent of the production occurred outside the United States and 90 percent occurred within the United States, as measured by the basis of assets used in production activities with respect to the property). Assume further that, on a separate entity basis, S would have $0 of foreign source income and $75x of U.S. source income and all of B's $25x of income would be foreign source income.

(ii) *Analysis.* Under the matching rule, both S's $75x intercompany income and B's $25x corresponding income are taken into account in Year 1. In determining the source of S and B's income from the inventory property sales, the attributes of S's intercompany item and B's corresponding item are redetermined to the extent necessary to produce the same effect on consolidated taxable income (and consolidated tax liability) as if S and B were divisions of a single corporation. See paragraph (c)(1)(i) of this section. On a separate entity basis, S would have $75x of U.S. source income because the product would be treated as produced wholly in the United States and sold outside the United States, and B would have $25x of foreign source income because the product would be treated as produced wholly outside the United States and sold outside the United States. On a single entity basis, S and B are treated as divisions of a single corporation, and section 863 applies as if $100x of income were recognized from producing partly in the United States and partly in Country Y and selling in Country Y. This results in $10x of foreign source income and $90x of U.S. source income. Accordingly, under single entity treatment, $15x of B's sales income that would be treated as foreign source income on a separate entity basis is redetermined to be U.S. source income. Under paragraph (c)(1)(i) of this section, attributes are redetermined only to the extent of the $15x necessary to achieve the same effect as if S and B were divisions of a single corporation. Under paragraph (c)(4)(ii) of this section, the redetermined attribute must be allocated between S and B using a reasonable method. In this case, only B would have foreign source income on a separate entity basis, and thus $15x of B's foreign source income must be recharacterized as U.S. source income.

(2) *Sale of property reflecting intercompany services or intangibles—(i) Facts.* S earns $10x of income performing services in the United States for B. B capitalizes S's fees into the basis of inventory property that it manufactures in the United States and sells to an unrelated person in Year 1 at a $90x profit, with title passing in Country Y. Assume that on a single entity basis, $100x is treated as U.S. source income and $0 is treated as foreign source income. Further assume that on a separate entity basis, S would have $10x of U.S. source income, and B would have $90x of U.S. source income, with neither having any foreign source income.

(ii) *Analysis.* Under the matching rule, S's $10x income and B's $90x income are taken into account in Year 1. In determining the source of S and B's income, the attributes of S's intercompany item and B's corresponding item are redetermined to the extent necessary to produce the same effect on consolidated taxable income (and consolidated tax liability) as if S and B were divisions of a single corporation, such that section 863 applies as if $100x were earned from manufacturing in the United States and selling in Country Y. Because the results are the same on a single entity basis and a separate entity basis ($100x of U.S. source income and $0x of foreign source income), the attributes are not redetermined under paragraph (c)(1)(i) of this section.

* * *

Consolidated Groups: Carryback of Consolidated NOLs: Separate Return Years

Consolidated Groups: Carryback of Consolidated NOLs: Separate Return Years.—Amendments to Reg. §1.1502-21, permitting certain acquiring consolidated groups to elect to waive all or a portion of the pre-acquisition portion of the 5-year carryback period under Code Sec. 172(b)(1)(H) for certain losses attributable to certain acquired members, are proposed (published in the Federal Register on May 31, 2002) (REG-122564-02).

☐ Par. 2. Section 1.1502-21 is amended by adding paragraph (b)(3)(ii)(C) to read as follows:

§1.1502-21. Net operating losses.
[The text of proposed §1.1502-21(b)(3)(ii)(C) is the same as the text of §1.1502-21T(b)(3)(ii)(C) as added by T.D. 8997].

Consolidated Group: Extended Carryback of Losses

Consolidated Group: Extended Carryback of Losses.—Amendments to Reg. §1.1502-21, providing guidance to consolidated groups that implements the revision to section 172(b)(1)(H), are proposed (published in the Federal Register on June 23, 2010) (REG-151605-09).

Par. 2. Section 1.1502-21 is revised to read as follows:

§1.1502-21. Net operating losses.—[The text of proposed §1.1502-21 is the same as the text for §1.1502-21T(a) through (h)(9)(i) as added by T.D. 9490].

Application of Section 172(h): Regulations: Consolidated Groups

Application of Section 172(h): Regulations: Consolidated Groups.—Amendments to Reg. §1.1502-21, providing guidance regarding the treatment of corporate equity reduction transactions (CERTs), including the treatment of multiple step plans for the acquisition of stock and CERTs involving members of a consolidated group, are proposed (published in the Federal Register on September 17, 2012) (REG-140668-07).

☐ Par. 3. Section 1.1502-21 is amended by adding paragraphs (b)(2)(iv)(C) and (h)(1)(iv) and revising paragraphs (b)(3)(ii)(B) and (h)(5) to read as follows:

§1.1502-21. Net operating losses.
* * *
(b) * * *
  (2) * * *
    (iv) * * *

     (C) *Apportionment of special status losses.—(1) In general.*— The amount of the group's CNOL that is determined to constitute a corporate equity reduction interest loss (CERIL) (as defined in section 172(h)(1) and §1.172(h)-2(a)(2)), specified liability loss (as defined in section 172(f)(1)), or any other net operating loss (NOL) that is subject to special carryback or carryover rules (special status loss), is apportioned to each member separately from the remainder of the CNOL, based on the percentage of CNOL attributable to the member as determined under paragraph (b)(2)(iv)(B) of this section. This apportionment is made without regard to whether a particular member actually incurred specific expenses or engaged in specific activities required by the special status loss provisions. If a consolidated group must apply §1.172(h)-3(d)(4) to allocate its CERIL for a loss limitation year between multiple corporate equity reduction transactions (CERTs), then the portion of the CERIL allocable to each CERT is treated as a separate CERIL for purposes of applying this paragraph (b)(2)(iv)(C) to apportion special status losses among members of the group.

     (2) *Example.*—The following example illustrates the rules of this paragraph (b)(2)(iv)(C):
     Example. (i) *Facts.* P is the parent of a group that includes S and that maintains a calendar taxable year. S has been a member of the group for all relevant years. In Year 3, the P group engages in a CERT. T is included in the P group beginning on January 1, Year 4, as a result of a transaction that does not constitute a CERT. In Year 4, the P group has a CNOL of $1,200. Under the CERT rules (in section 172(b)(1)(E) and (h), §§1.172(h)-1 through 1.172(h)-5, and §1.1502-72), $300 of the CNOL (25%) constitutes a CERIL. Assume that, absent application of this paragraph (b)(2)(iv)(C), under paragraph (b)(2)(iv)(B) of this section, 2/3 of the CNOL ($800) is attributable to T and the remaining 1/3 of the CNOL ($400) is attributable to S.

     (ii) *Analysis.* Under this paragraph (b)(2)(iv)(C), the CNOL is divided into its special status (CERIL) component, and its non-special status component. Because T has separate return year carryback years, each component of the CNOL (the non-special status CNOL and the CERIL) is apportioned under paragraph (b)(2)(iv)(B) of this section. Under that apportionment rule, 2/3 of each amount is apportioned to T, and the remainder of the CNOL is attributable to S and can be carried back to prior P group years, subject to any applicable limitations. Therefore, $200 of the $300 CERIL is apportioned to T, and $600 of the $900 non-special status CNOL is also apportioned to T. The $200 CERIL cannot be carried back to certain taxable years of T under the CERT rules. Likewise, $100 of the $300 CERIL is apportioned to S, and $300 of the $900 non-special status CNOL is also apportioned to S. Under the CERT rules, the $100 CERIL cannot be carried back to certain taxable years.

* * *

  (3) * * *
    (ii) * * *

    (B) *Election on acquisition to waive carryback to separate return years.—(1) In general.*—A corporation may make one of three mutually exclusive, irrevocable elections to waive carryback of CNOLs to separate return years of acquired members. Any election that is made with regard to an acquired corporation that was a member of a consolidated group (the former group) immediately before becoming a member of an acquiring group must include all other corporations that were members of the former group and that joined the acquiring group during the same consolidated return year of the acquiring group.

(2) *Annual election.*—If a corporation becomes a member of an acquiring group, the acquiring group may make an irrevocable election to relinquish, with respect to the part of any CNOL attributable to the member, the portion of the carryback period for which the member filed a separate return. This is an annual election, applicable to the CNOL of a single year. The election is made in a separate statement entitled, "THIS IS AN ELECTION UNDER §1.1502-21(b)(3)(ii)(B)(2) TO WAIVE THE PRE- [insert the first taxable year in which the member(s) joined the group] CARRYBACK PERIOD FOR THE PORTION OF THE [insert taxable year] CNOL ATTRIBUTABLE TO [insert the name(s) and EIN(s) of the corporation(s)]." The statement must be filed with the acquiring group's timely filed original return for the consolidated return year of the particular CNOL.

(3) *Single election.*—If a corporation becomes a member of an acquiring group, the acquiring group may make an irrevocable election to relinquish, with respect to all CNOLs attributable to the member, the portion of the carryback period for which the member filed a separate return. The election is not an annual election and applies to all losses that would otherwise be subject to a carryback to separate return years under section 172 or paragraph (b) of this section. The election is made in a separate statement entitled, "THIS IS AN ELECTION UNDER §1.1502-21(b)(3)(ii)(B)(3) TO WAIVE THE PRE- [insert the first taxable year in which the member(s) joined the group] CARRYBACK PERIOD FOR THE PORTION FOR ALL NOLs (and ALL CNOLs) ATTRIBUTABLE TO [insert the name(s) and EIN of the corporation(s)]." The statement must be filed with the acquiring group's timely filed original income tax return for the consolidated return year the corporation (or corporations) became a member.

(4) *Special one-time election for deconsolidating member.*— Section 1.1502-72(e)(1) makes available an election by a deconsolidating member (or its new common parent immediately following deconsolidation) to relinquish in whole the carryback of all NOLs to taxable years of the former group and any preceding taxable year. An election under §1.1502-72(e)(1) will control whether the deconsolidating corporation is treated as an applicable corporation under section 172(b)(1)(E)(iii) and §1.172(h)-1(b)(1) following the deconsolidation with regard to a CERT of the former group. See §1.1502-72(b). Further, an election under §1.1502-72(e)(1) may affect the computation of the CERIL under section 172(h)(1) and §1.172(h)-2(a)(2) with regard to any CERT for which the deconsolidating corporation (or any group of which the deconsolidating corporation is a member) is an applicable corporation under section 172(b)(1)(E)(iii) and §1.172(h)-1(b)(1) following the deconsolidation. See §1.1502-72(c)(4) and (d)(3)(ii).

* * *

(h) * * *

(1) * * *

(iv) Paragraph (b)(2)(iv)(C) of this section applies to taxable years for which the due date of the original return (without extensions) is on or after the date of publication of the Treasury decision adopting these rules as final regulations in the **Federal Register**.

* * *

(5) *Waiver of carrybacks.*—Paragraph (b)(3)(ii)(B) of this section (relating to the waiver of carrybacks to separate return years) applies to acquisitions occurring on or after the date of publication of the Treasury decision adopting these rules as final regulations in the **Federal Register**, except that it does not apply to any acquisition occurring pursuant to a written agreement that is binding before the date of publication of the Treasury decision adopting these rules as final regulations in the **Federal Register**. For original consolidated Federal income tax returns due (without extensions) before the date of the publication of the Treasury decision adopting these rules as final regulations in the **Federal Register**, see paragraph (b)(3)(ii)(B) of this section as contained in 26 CFR part 1 in effect on April 1, 1999.

* * *

Deduction for Business Interest Expense: Limitation

Deduction for Business Interest Expense: Limitation.—Amendments to Reg. §1.1502-21, regarding the limitation on the deduction for business interest expense after the enactment of recent tax legislation, are proposed (published in the Federal Register on December 28, 2018) (REG-106089-18).

Par. 18. Section 1.1502-21 is amended by revising paragraph (d) to read as follows:

§1.1502-21. Net operating losses.

* * *

(d) *Cross-reference.*—For rules governing the application of a SRLY limitation to business interest expense for which a deduction is disallowed under section 163(j), see §1.163(j)-5(d) and (f).

* * *

Allocation and Apportionment of Deductions and Foreign Tax Credit: Guidance

Allocation and Apportionment of Deductions and Foreign Tax Credit: Guidance.—Amendments to Reg. §1.1502-21, relating to the allocation and apportionment of deductions and creditable foreign taxes, the definition of financial services income, foreign tax redeterminations, availability of foreign tax credits under the transition tax, and the application of the foreign tax credit limitation to consolidated groups, are proposed (published in the Federal Register on December 17, 2019) (REG-105495-19).

Par. 28. Section 1.1502-21 is amended by adding a sentence to the end of paragraph (b)(2)(iv)(B) to read as follows:

§1.1502-21. Net operating losses.

* * *

(b) * * *

(2) * * *

(iv) * * *

(B) * * * The source and section 904(d) separate category of the CNOL attributable to a member is determined under §1.1502-4(c)(1)(iii).

* * *

Reporting Income and Deductions: Consolidated Group

Reporting Income and Deductions: Consolidated Group.—Amendments to Reg. §§1.1502-21, 1.1502-22 and 1.1502-28, revising the rules for reporting certain items of income and deduction that are reportable on the day a corporation joins or leaves a consolidated group, are proposed (published in the Federal Register on March 6, 2015) (REG-100400-14).

Par. 5. Section 1.1502-21 is amended by revising paragraph (b)(3)(iii) and adding paragraph (h)(1)(iv) to read as follows:

§1.1502-21. Net operating losses.

* * *

(b) * * *

(3) * * *

(iii) *Short years in connection with intercompany transactions to which section 381(a) applies.* If a member distributes or transfers assets in an intercompany transaction to which section 381(a) applies, see §1.1502-76(b)(2)(i).

* * *

(h) * * *

(1) * * *

(iv) Paragraph (b)(3)(iii) of this section applies to consolidated return years beginning on or after the date these regulations are published as final regulations in the **Federal Register**. For transactions occurring before the date these regulations are published as final regulations in the **Federal Register**, see §1.1502-21(b) as contained in 26 CFR part 1, revised as of April 1 preceding the date these regulations are published as final regulations in the **Federal Register**.

* * *

Par. 6. Section 1.1502-22 is amended by:

1. Revising paragraph (b)(4)(i).
2. Revising the heading of paragraph (h).
3. Adding paragraph (h)(1)(iii).
The revisions and addition read as follows:

§1.1502-22. Consolidated capital gain and loss.

* * *

(b) * * *

(4) *Special rules.*—(i) *Short years in connection with intercompany transactions to which section 381(a) applies.*—If a member distributes or transfers assets in an intercompany transaction to which section 381(a) applies, see §1.1502-76(b)(2)(i).

* * *

Par. 7. Section 1.1502-28 is amended in paragraph (b)(11) by removing "§1.1502-76(b)(1)(ii)(B)" and adding "§1.1502-76(b)(1)(ii)(A)(2)" in its place.

§1.1502-28. Consolidated section 108.

Elimination of Circular Adjustments to Basis: Absorption of Losses

Elimination of Circular Adjustments to Basis: Absorption of Losses.—Amendments to Reg. §§1.1502-21, 1.1502-21A, 1.1502-22, 1.1502-22A, 1.1502-23A and 1.1502-24, revising the rules concerning the use of a consolidated group's losses in a consolidated return year in which stock of a subsidiary is disposed of, are proposed (published in the Federal Register on June 11, 2015) (REG-101652-10).

Par. 4. Section 1.1502-21 is amended by:
1. Revising paragraph (b)(2)(iv)(B).
2. Adding paragraphs (b)(3)(vi) and (h)(1)(iv).
The revision and additions read as follows:

§1.1502-21. Net operating losses.

* * *

(b) ***

(2) ***

(iv) ***

(B) *Percentage of CNOL attributable to a member.*—(1) *In general.*—Except as provided in paragraph (b)(2)(iv)(B)(2) of this section, the percentage of the CNOL attributable to a member shall equal the separate net operating loss of the member for the consolidated return year divided by the sum of the separate net operating losses of all members having such losses for that year. For this purpose, the separate net operating loss of a member is determined by computing the CNOL by reference to only the member's items of income, gain, deduction, and loss (excluding capital gains and amounts treated as capital gains), including the member's losses and deductions actually absorbed by the group in the consolidated return year (whether or not absorbed by the member).

(2) *Recomputed percentage.*—If, for any reason, a member's portion of a CNOL is absorbed or reduced on a non pro rata basis (for example, under §§1.1502-11(b) or (c), 1.1502-28, 1.1502-36(d), or as the result of a carryback to a separate return year), the percentage of the CNOL attributable to each member is recom-

puted. In addition, if a member with a separate net operating loss ceases to be a member, the percentage of the CNOL attributable to each remaining member is recomputed under paragraph (b)(2)(iv)(B)(1) of this section. The recomputed percentage of the CNOL attributable to each member shall equal the remaining CNOL attributable to the member at the time of the recomputation divided by the sum of the remaining CNOL attributable to all of the remaining members at the time of the recomputation.

* * *

(3) * * *

(vi) *Amount of subsidiary's absorbed deductions and losses if subsidiary's stock is disposed of.*—For special rules regarding the amount of a subsidiary's deductions and losses that is absorbed if a member disposes of a share of the subsidiary's stock, see §1.1502-11(b) and (c).

* * *

(h) * * *

(1) * * *

(iv) Paragraphs (b)(2)(iv)(B) and (b)(3)(vi) of this section apply to consolidated return years beginning on or after the date these regulations are published as final regulations in the **Federal Register**.

* * *

Par. 5. Section 1.1502-21A is removed.

§1.1502-21A. Consolidated net operating loss deduction generally applicable for consolidated return years beginning before January 1, 1997.

Par. 6. Section 1.1502-22 is amended by:
1. Revising paragraphs (a)(2) and (3).
2. Adding paragraph (a)(4).
The revisions and addition read as follows:

§1.1502-22. Payment and returns of tax withheld by the acquiring agency.

* * *

(a) * * *

(2) The consolidated net section 1231 gain for the year (determined under §1.1502-23);

Par. 7. Section 1.1502-22A is removed.

§1.1502-22A. Consolidated net capital gain or loss generally applicable for consolidated return years beginning before January 1, 1997.

Par. 8. Section 1.1502-23A is removed.

(3) The net capital loss carryovers or carrybacks to the year; and

(4) Applying the ordering rules of §1.1502-11(b) if stock of a subsidiary is disposed of.

* * *

§1.1502-23A. Consolidated net section 1231 gain or loss generally applicable for consolidated return years beginning before January 1, 1997.

Par. 9. Section 1.1502-24 is amended by:

1. Removing the words "Five percent" in paragraph (a)(2) and adding "The percentage limitation on the total charitable contribution deduction provided in section 170(b)(2)(A)" in its place.

2. Removing "section 242," and §1.1502-25," in paragraph (c).

§1.1502-24. Consolidated charitable contributions deductions.

CFCs: Previously Taxed Earnings and Profits: Exclusion from Gross Income: Basis Adjustments

CFCs: Previously Taxed Earnings and Profits: Exclusion from Gross Income: Basis Adjustments.—Amendments to Reg. §1.1502-32, providing guidance relating to the exclusion from gross income of previously taxed earnings and profits under Code Sec. 959 and related basis adjustments under Code Sec. 961, are proposed (published in the Federal Register on August 29, 2006) (REG-121509-00).

☐ Par. 11. In section 1.1502-32, add a sentence after the second sentence in paragraph (b)(3)(ii)(D), add a sentence after the fourth sentence in paragraph (b)(3)(iii)(B) and add *Example 11* in paragraph (b)(5)(ii) to read as follows:

§1.1502-32. Investment adjustments.

* * *

(b) * * *

(3) * * *

(ii) * * *

(D) * * * Further, an increase to a member's previously taxed earnings and profits account under §1.959-3(g)(1)(i)(B) that pursuant to section 961(a) and §1.961-1(b) results in an increase to a member's basis in the stock in a CFC shall be treated as the receipt of tax exempt income. * * *

(iii) * * *

(B) * * * Also included as a noncapital, nondeductible expense is a decrease to a member's previously taxed earnings and profits account under §1.959-3(g)(1)(i)(A) that results in a decrease to a member's basis in the stock in a CFC pursuant to section 961(b) and §1.961-2(a). * * *

* * *

(5) * * *

(ii) * * *

Example 11. (a) *Facts.* P owns all of the stock of S and S1. S, a United States shareholder, owns 50 percent of the stock in FC, a CFC that uses the U.S. dollar as its functional currency. S1, a United States shareholder owns the remaining 50 percent of the stock in FC. Entering year 1, S has a previously taxed earnings and profits account with respect to its stock in FC consisting of $50x of section 959(c)(2) earnings and profits and S1 has a previously taxed earnings and profits account with respect to its stock in FC consisting of $200x of section 959(c)(2) earnings and profits. Entering year 1, FC has section 959(c)(2) earnings and profits of $250x and non-previously taxed earnings and profits of $100x. In year 1, FC generates no earnings and profits and makes a $100x distribution of earnings and profits on FC stock held by S and a $100x distribution of earnings and profits on the FC stock held by S1.

(b) *Analysis.* First, pursuant to §1.959-3(e)(2)(ii), the section 959(c)(2) earnings and profits in S's previously taxed earnings and profits account with respect to its FC stock are decreased from $50x to $0 and the section 959(c)(2) earnings and profits in S1's previously taxed earnings and profits account with respect to its FC stock are decreased from $200x to $100x. Then, pursuant to §1.959-2(e)(2)(v) and (g)(1)(i)(A), the section 959(c)(2) earnings and profits in S1's previously taxed earnings and profits account with respect to its FC stock are decreased from $100x to $50x and, pursuant to §1.959-3(e)(2)(ii)(B) and (g)(1)(i)(B), the section 959(c)(2) earnings and profits in S's previously taxed earnings and profits account with respect to its FC stock are increased from $0 to $50x and then decreased from $50x to $0. Pursuant to §1.959-1(c) of this section, the entire $100x distribution to S and $100x distribution to S1 are excluded from S's and S1's gross incomes. Pursuant to paragraph (b)(3)(ii)(D) of this section, the $50x increase to the section 959(c)(2) earnings and profits in S's previously taxed earnings and profits account with respect to its FC stock pursuant to §1.959-3(g)(1)(i)(B) is treated as the receipt of $50x of tax-exempt income by S. Pursuant to paragraph (b)(2)(ii) of this section, P's basis in S's stock is increased by $50x. Pursuant to paragraph (b)(3)(iii)(B) of this section, the $50x decrease to the section 959(c)(2) earnings and profits in S1's previously taxed earnings and profits account with respect to its FC stock pursuant to §1.959-3(g)(1)(i)(A) is treated as a noncapital nondeductible expense to S1. Pursuant to paragraph (b)(2)(iii) of this section, P's basis in S1's stock is decreased by $50x.

* * *

Consolidated Returns: AMT: General Computations

Consolidated Returns: Alternative Minimum Tax.—Amendments to Reg. §1.1502-33, relating to the computation of the alternative minimum tax by consolidated groups, are proposed (published in the Federal Register on December 30, 1992).

☐ Par. 6. Proposed §1.1502-33, published in the Federal Register on November 12, 1992 (57 FR 53634), is amended by adding the following sentence at the end of paragraph (d)(1)(i) to read as follows:

§1.1502-33. Earnings and profits.

* * *

(d) * * *

(1) * * *

(i) * * * *See* paragraphs (g), (h), and (j) of §1.1552-1 for rules relating to the allocation of the consolidated AMT (as computed under §1.1502-55), the consolidated environmental tax (defined in §1.1552-1(h)), and the consolidated additional taxes (defined in §1.1502-2(b)) among members of the group.

* * *

Deduction for Business Interest Expense: Limitation

Deduction for Business Interest Expense: Limitation.—Amendments to Reg. §1.1502-36, regarding the limitation on the deduction for business interest expense after the enactment of recent tax legislation, are proposed (published in the Federal Register on December 28, 2018) (REG-106089-18).

Par. 19. Section 1.1502-36 is amended by:

1. Revising the second sentence of paragraph (f)(2);

2. Revising the paragraph (h) heading;

3. Designating the text of paragraph (h) as paragraph (h)(1) and adding a heading to newly designated paragraph (h)(1); and

4. Adding paragraph (h)(2).

The revisions and addition read as follows:

§1.1502-36. Unified loss rule.

* * *

(f) * * *

(2) * * * Such provisions include, for example, sections 163(j), 267(f), and 469, and §1.1502-13. * * *

* * *

(h) *Applicability date.*—(1) *In general.*—* * *

(2) *Definition in paragraph (f)(2) of this section.*—Paragraph (f)(2) of this section applies to taxable years ending after the date of the Treasury decision adopting these regulations as final regulations is published in the **Federal Register**. For taxable years ending before the date of the Treasury decision adopting these regulations as final

regulations is published in the **Federal Register**, see § 1.1502-36 as contained in 26 CFR part 1, revised April 1, 2018. However, taxpayers and their related parties, within the meaning of sections 267(b) and 707(b)(1), may apply the rules of this section to a taxable year beginning after December 31, 2017, so long as the taxpayers and their related parties consistently apply the rules of this section, the section 163(j) regulations (within the meaning of § 1.163(j)-1(b)(32)), and if applicable, § § 1.263A-9, 1.381(c)(20)-1, 1.469-9, 1.882-5, 1.1502-13, 1.1502-21, 1.1502-79, 1.1502-91 through 1.1502-99 (to the extent they effectuate the rules of § § 1.382-6 and 1.383-1), and 1.1504-4 to those taxable years.

Foreign-Derived Intangible Income: Global Intangible Low-Taxed Income: Deduction

Foreign-Derived Intangible Income: Global Intangible Low-Taxed Income: Deduction.—Reg. § 1.1502-50, providing guidance to determine the amount of the deduction for foreign-derived intangible income and global intangible low-taxed income, is proposed (published in the Federal Register on March 6, 2019) (REG-104464-18).

Par. 6. Section 1.1502-50 is added to read as follows:

§ 1.1502-50. Consolidated section 250.—(a) *In general.*— (1) *Scope.*—This section provides rules for applying section 250 and the regulations thereunder (the *section 250 regulations*, see § § 1.250(a)-1 through 1.250(b)-6) to a member of a consolidated group (*member*). Paragraph (b) of this section provides rules for the determination of the amount of the deduction allowed to a member under section 250(a)(1). Paragraph (c) of this section provides rules governing the impact of intercompany transactions on the determination of a member's qualified business asset investment and the effect of intercompany transactions on the determination of a member's foreign-derived deduction eligible income. Paragraph (d) of this section provides rules governing basis adjustments to member stock resulting from the application of paragraph (b)(1) of this section. Paragraph (e) of this section provides definitions. Paragraph (f) of this section provides examples illustrating the rules of this section. Paragraph (g) of this section provides an applicability date.

(2) *Overview.*—The rules of this section ensure that the aggregate amount of deductions allowed under section 250 to members appropriately reflects the income, expenses, gains, losses, and property of all members. Paragraph (b) of this section allocates the consolidated group's overall deduction amount under section 250 to each member on the basis of its contribution to the consolidated foreign-derived deduction eligible income and consolidated global intangible low-taxed income. The definitions in paragraph (e) of this section provide for the aggregation of the deduction eligible income, foreign-derived deduction eligible income, deemed tangible income return, and global intangible low-taxed income of all members in order to calculate the consolidated group's overall deduction amount under section 250.

(b) *Allowance of deduction.*—(1) *In general.*—A member is allowed a deduction for a consolidated return year under section 250. See § 1.250(a)-1(b). The amount of the deduction is equal to the sum of—

(i) The product of the consolidated FDII deduction amount and the member's FDII deduction allocation ratio; and

(ii) The product of the consolidated GILTI deduction amount and the member's GILTI deduction allocation ratio.

(2) *Consolidated taxable income limitation.*—For purposes of applying the limitation described in § 1.250(a)-1(b)(2) to the determination of the consolidated FDII deduction amount and the consolidated GILTI deduction amount of a consolidated group for a consolidated return year—

(i) The consolidated foreign-derived intangible income (if any) is reduced (but not below zero) by an amount which bears the same ratio to the consolidated section 250(a)(2) amount that such consolidated foreign-derived intangible income bears to the sum of the consolidated foreign-derived intangible income and the consolidated global intangible low-taxed income; and

(ii) The consolidated global intangible low-taxed income (if any) is reduced (but not below zero) by the excess of the consolidated section 250(a)(2) amount over the reduction described in paragraph (b)(2)(i) of this section.

(c) *Impact of intercompany transactions.*—(1) *Impact on qualified business asset investment determination.*—For purposes of determining a member's qualified business asset investment, the basis of specified tangible property does not include an amount equal to any gain or loss realized with respect to such property by another member in an intercompany transaction (as defined in § 1.1502-13(b)(1)), whether or not such gain or loss is deferred. Thus, for example, if a selling member owns specified tangible property with an adjusted basis (within the meaning of section 1011) of $60x and an adjusted basis (for purposes of calculating qualified business asset investment) of $80x, and sells it for $50x to the purchasing member, the basis of such property for purposes of computing the purchasing member's qualified business asset investment is $80x.

(2) *Impact on foreign-derived deduction eligible income characterization.*—For purposes of redetermining attributes of members from an intercompany transaction as foreign-derived deduction eligible income, see § 1.1502-13(c)(1)(i) and (c)(7)(ii)(T), *Example 20.*

(d) *Adjustments to the basis of a member.*—For adjustments to the basis of a member related to paragraph (b)(1) of this section, see § 1.1502-32(b)(3)(ii)(B).

(e) *Definitions.*—The following definitions apply for purposes of this section.

(1) *Consolidated deduction eligible income.*—With respect to a consolidated group for a consolidated return year, the term *consolidated deduction eligible income* means the greater of the sum of the deduction eligible income (whether positive or negative) of all members or zero.

(2) *Consolidated deemed intangible income.*—With respect to a consolidated group for a consolidated return year, the term *consolidated deemed intangible income* means the excess (if any) of the consolidated deduction eligible income, over the consolidated deemed tangible income return.

(3) *Consolidated deemed tangible income return.*—With respect to a consolidated group for a consolidated return year, the term *consolidated deemed tangible income return* means the sum of the deemed tangible income return of all members.

(4) *Consolidated FDII deduction amount.*—With respect to a consolidated group for a consolidated return year, the term *consolidated FDII deduction amount* means the product of the FDII deduction rate and the consolidated foreign-derived intangible income, as adjusted by paragraph (b)(2) of this section.

(5) *Consolidated foreign-derived deduction eligible income.*—With respect to a consolidated group for a consolidated return year, the term *consolidated foreign-derived deduction eligible income* means the greater of the sum of the foreign-derived deduction eligible income (whether positive or negative) of all members or zero.

(6) *Consolidated foreign-derived intangible income.*—With respect to a consolidated group for a consolidated return year, the term *consolidated foreign-derived intangible income* means, except as provided in paragraph (e) of this section, the product of the consolidated deemed intangible income and the consolidated foreign-derived ratio.

(7) *Consolidated foreign-derived ratio.*—With respect to a consolidated group for a consolidated return year, the term *consolidated foreign-derived ratio* means the ratio (not to exceed one) of—

(i) The consolidated foreign-derived deduction eligible income; to

(ii) The consolidated deduction eligible income.

(8) *Consolidated GILTI deduction amount.*—With respect to a consolidated group for a consolidated return year, the term *consolidated GILTI deduction amount* means the product of the GILTI deduction rate and the sum of the consolidated global intangible low-taxed income, as adjusted by paragraph (b)(2) of this section, and the amounts treated as dividends received by the members under section 78 which are attributable to their global intangible low-taxed income for the consolidated return year.

(9) *Consolidated global intangible low-taxed income.*—With respect to a consolidated group for a consolidated return year, the term *consolidated global intangible low-taxed income* means the sum of the global intangible low-taxed income of all members.

(10) *Consolidated section 250(a)(2) amount.*—With respect to a consolidated group for a consolidated return year, the term *consolidated section 250(a)(2) amount* means the excess (if any) of the sum of the consolidated foreign-derived intangible income and the consolidated global intangible low-taxed income (determined without regard to section 250(a)(2) and paragraph (b)(2) of this section), over the consolidated taxable income of the consolidated group (within the meaning of § 1.1502-11) determined with regard to all items of income, deductions, or loss, except for the deduction allowed under

section 250 and this section. Therefore, for example, consolidated taxable income under this paragraph (f)(10) is determined taking into account the application of sections 163(j) and 172(a).

(11) *Deduction eligible income.*—With respect to a member for a consolidated return year, the term *deduction eligible income* means the member's gross DEI for the year (within the meaning of § 1.250(b)-1(c)(14)) reduced (including below zero) by the deductions properly allocable to gross DEI for the year (as determined under § 1.250(b)-1(d)(2)).

(12) *Deemed tangible income return.*—With respect to a member for a consolidated return year, the term *deemed tangible income return* means an amount equal to 10 percent of the member's qualified business asset investment, as adjusted by paragraph (c)(1) of this section.

(13) *FDII deduction allocation ratio.*—With respect to a member for a consolidated return year, the term *FDII deduction allocation ratio* means the ratio of—

(i) The member's positive foreign-derived deduction eligible income (if any); to

(ii) The sum of the positive foreign-derived deduction eligible income of all members.

(14) *FDII deduction rate.*—The term *FDII deduction rate* means 37.5 percent for consolidated return years beginning before January 1, 2026, and 21.875 percent for consolidated return years beginning after December 31, 2025.

(15) *Foreign-derived deduction eligible income.*—With respect to a member for a consolidated return year, the term *foreign-derived deduction eligible income* means the member's gross FDDEI for the year (within the meaning of § 1.250(b)-1(c)(15)) reduced (including below zero) by the deductions properly allocable to gross FDDEI for the year (as determined under § 1.250(b)-1(d)(2)).

(16) *GILTI deduction allocation ratio.*—With respect to a member for a consolidated return year, the term *GILTI deduction allocation ratio* means the ratio of—

(i) The sum of the member's global intangible low-taxed income and the amount treated as a dividend received by the member under section 78 which is attributable to its global intangible low-taxed income for the consolidated return year; to

(ii) The sum of consolidated global intangible low-taxed income and the amounts treated as dividends received by the members under section 78 which are attributable to their global intangible low-taxed income for the consolidated return year.

(17) *GILTI deduction rate.*—The term *GILTI deduction rate* means 50 percent for consolidated return years beginning before January 1, 2026, and 37.5 percent for consolidated return years beginning after December 31, 2025.

(18) *Global intangible low-taxed income.*—With respect to a member for a consolidated return year, the term *global intangible low-taxed income* means the sum of the member's GILTI inclusion amount under § 1.1502-51(b) and the member's distributive share of any domestic partnership's GILTI inclusion amount under § 1.951A-5(b)(2).

(19) *Qualified business asset investment.*—The term *qualified business asset investment* has the meaning provided in § 1.250(b)-2(b).

(20) *Specified tangible property.*—The term *specified tangible property* has the meaning provided in § 1.250(b)-2(c)(1).

(f) *Examples.*—The following examples illustrate the rules of this section.

(1) *Example 1: Calculation of deduction attributable to foreign-derived intangible income*—(i) *Facts.* P is the common parent of the P group and owns all of the only class of stock of subsidiaries USS1 and USS2. The consolidated return year of all persons is the calendar year. In 2018, P has deduction eligible income of $400x, foreign-derived deduction eligible income of $0, and qualified business asset investment of $0; USS1 has deduction eligible income of $200x, foreign-derived deduction eligible income of $200x, and qualified business asset investment of $600x; and USS2 has deduction eligible income of -$100x, foreign-derived deduction eligible income of $100x, and qualified business asset investment of $400x. The P group has consolidated taxable income that is sufficient to make inapplicable the limitation in paragraph (b)(2) of this section. No member of the P group has global intangible low-taxed income.

(ii) *Analysis.* (A) *Consolidated deduction eligible income.* Under paragraph (e)(1) of this section, the P group's consolidated deduction eligible income is $500x, the greater of the sum of the deduction eligible income (whether positive or negative) of all members ($400x + $200x - $100x) or zero.

(B) *Consolidated foreign-derived deduction eligible income.* Under paragraph (e)(5) of this section, the P group's consolidated foreign-derived deduction eligible income is $300x, the greater of the sum of the foreign-derived deduction eligible income (whether positive or negative) of all members ($0 + $200x + $100x) or zero.

(C) *Consolidated deemed tangible income return.* Under paragraph (e)(12) of this section, a member's deemed tangible income return is 10% of its qualified business asset investment. Therefore, P's deemed tangible income return is $0 (0.10 x $0), USS1's deemed tangible income return is $60x (0.10 x $600x), and USS2's deemed tangible income return is $40x (0.10 x $400x). Under paragraph (e)(3) of this section, the P group's consolidated deemed tangible income return is $100x, the sum of the deemed tangible income return of all members ($0 + $60x + $40x).

(D) *Consolidated deemed intangible income.* Under paragraph (e)(2) of this section, the P group's consolidated deemed intangible income is $400x, the excess of its consolidated deduction eligible income over its consolidated deemed tangible income return ($500x - $100x).

(E) *Consolidated foreign-derived intangible income.* Under paragraph (e)(7) of this section, the P group's consolidated foreign-derived ratio is 0.60, the ratio of its consolidated deduction eligible income to its consolidated deduction eligible income ($300x / $500x). Under paragraph (e)(6) of this section, the P group's consolidated foreign-derived intangible income is $240x, the product of its consolidated deemed intangible income and its consolidated foreign-derived ratio ($400x x 0.60).

(F) *Consolidated FDII deduction amount.* Under paragraph (e)(4) of this section, the P group's consolidated FDII deduction amount is $90x, the product of the FDII deduction rate and the consolidated foreign-derived intangible income (0.375 x $240x).

(G) *Member's deduction attributable to consolidated FDII deduction amount.* Under paragraph (b)(1) of this section, a member is allowed a deduction equal, in part, to the product of the consolidated FDII deduction amount of the consolidated group to which the member belongs and the member's FDII deduction allocation ratio. Under paragraph (e)(13) of this section, a member's FDII deduction allocation ratio is the ratio of its positive foreign-derived deduction eligible income to the sum of each member's positive foreign-derived deduction eligible income for such consolidated return year. As a result, the FDII deduction allocation ratios of P, USS1, and USS2 are 0 ($0 / $300x), 2/3 ($200x / $300x), and 1/3 ($100x / $300x), respectively. Therefore, P, USS1, and USS2 are permitted deductions under paragraph (b)(1) of this section in the amount of $0 (0 x $90x), $60x (2/3 x $90x), and $30x (1/3 x $90x), respectively.

(2) *Example 2: Limitation on consolidated foreign-derived deduction eligible income*—(i) *Facts.* The facts are the same as in paragraph (f)(1)(i) of this section (the facts in *Example 1*), except that P's foreign-derived deduction eligible income is $300x.

(ii) *Analysis.* (A) *Consolidated deduction eligible income and consolidated deemed tangible income return.* As in paragraphs (f)(1)(ii)(A) and (C) of this section (the analysis in *Example 1*), the P group's consolidated deduction eligible income is $500x and the P group's consolidated deemed tangible income return is $100x.

(B) *Consolidated foreign-derived deduction eligible income.* Under paragraph (e)(5) of this section, the P group's consolidated foreign-derived deduction eligible income is $600x, the greater of the sum of the foreign-derived deduction eligible income (whether positive or negative) of all members ($300x + $200x + $100x) or zero.

(C) *Consolidated deemed intangible income and consolidated foreign-derived intangible income.* Under paragraph (e)(2) of this section, the P group's consolidated deemed intangible income is $400x ($500x - $100x). Under paragraph (e)(7) of this section, the P group's consolidated foreign-derived ratio is 1.00 ($600x / $500x, but not in excess of one). Under paragraph (e)(6) of this section, the P group's consolidated foreign-derived intangible income is $400x ($400x x 1.00).

(D) *Consolidated FDII deduction amount and member's deduction attributable to consolidated FDII deduction amount.* Under paragraph (e)(4) of this section, the P group's consolidated FDII deduction amount is $150x (0.375 x $400x). Under paragraph (e)(13) of this section, the FDII deduction allocation ratios of P, USS1, and USS2 are 1/2 ($300 / $600x), 1/3 ($200x / $600x), and 1/6 ($100x / $600x), respectively. Therefore, P, USS1, and USS2 are permitted deductions under paragraph (b)(1) of this section in the amounts of $75x (1/2 x $150x), $50x (1/3 x $150x), and $25x (1/6 x $150x), respectively.

(3) *Example 3: Member with negative foreign-derived deduction eligible income*—(i) *Facts.* The facts are the same as in paragraph (f)(1)(i) of this section (the facts in *Example 1*), except that P's foreign-derived deduction eligible income is -$100x.

(ii) *Analysis.* (A) *Consolidated deduction eligible income and consolidated deemed tangible income return.* As in paragraphs (f)(1)(ii)(A) and (C) of this section (the facts in *Example 1*), the P group's consolidated deduction eligible income is $500x and the P group's consolidated deemed tangible income return is $100x.

(B) *Consolidated foreign-derived deduction eligible income.* Under paragraph (e)(5) of this section, the P group's consolidated foreign-derived deduction eligible income is $200x, the greater of the sum of the foreign-derived deduction eligible income (whether positive or negative) of all members (-$100x + $200x + $100x) or zero.

(C) *Consolidated deemed intangible income and consolidated foreign-derived intangible income.* Under paragraphs (e)(2) and (6) of this section, the P group's consolidated deemed intangible income is $400x ($500x - $100x), and the P group's consolidated foreign-derived intangible income is $160x ($400x x ($200x / $500x)).

(D) *Consolidated FDII deduction amount and member's deduction attributable to consolidated FDII deduction amount.* Under paragraph (e)(4) of this section, the P group's consolidated FDII deduction amount is $60x (0.375 x $160x). Under paragraph (e)(13) of this section, the FDII deduction allocation ratios of P, USS1, and USS2 are 0 ($0 / $300x), 2/3 ($200x / $300x), and 1/3 ($100x / $300x), respectively. Therefore, P, USS1, and USS2 are permitted deductions under paragraph (b)(1) of this section in the amounts of $0 (0 x $60x), $40x (2/3 x $60x), and $20x (1/3 x $60x), respectively.

(4) *Example 4: Calculation of deduction attributable to global intangible low-taxed income*—(i) *Facts.* The facts are the same as in paragraph (f)(1)(i) of this section (the facts in *Example 1*), except that USS1 owns CFC1 and USS2 owns CFC2. USS1 and USS2 have global intangible low-taxed income of $65x and $20x, respectively, and amounts treated as dividends received under section 78 attributable to their global intangible low-taxed income of $10x and $5x, respectively.

(ii) *Analysis.* (A) *Consolidated global intangible low-taxed income.* Under paragraph (e)(9) of this section, the P group's consolidated global intangible low-taxed income is $85x, the sum of the global intangible low-taxed income of all members ($0 + $65x + $20x).

(B) *Consolidated GILTI deduction amount.* Under paragraph (e)(8) of this section, the P group's consolidated GILTI deduction amount is $50x, the product of the GILTI deduction rate and the sum of its consolidated global intangible low-taxed income and the amounts treated as dividends received by the members under section 78 which are attributable to their global intangible low-taxed income for the consolidated return year (0.50 x ($85x + $10x + $5x)).

(C) *Member's deduction attributable to consolidated GILTI deduction amount.* Under paragraph (b)(1) of this section, a member is allowed a deduction equal, in part, to the product of the consolidated GILTI deduction amount of the consolidated group to which the member belongs and the member's GILTI deduction allocation ratio. Under paragraph (e)(16) of this section, a member's GILTI deduction allocation ratio is the ratio of the sum of its global intangible low-taxed income and the amount treated as a dividend received by the member under section 78 which is attributable to its global intangible low-taxed income for the consolidated return year to the sum of the consolidated global intangible low-taxed income and the amounts treated as dividends received by the members under section 78 which are attributable to their global intangible low-taxed income for the consolidated return year. As a result, the GILTI deduction allocation ratios of P, USS1, and USS2 are 0 ($0 / ($85x + $10x + $5x)), 3/4 (($65x + $10x) / ($85x + $10x + $5x)), and 1/4 (($20x + $5x) / ($85x + $10x + $5x)), respectively. Therefore, P, USS1, and USS2 are permitted deductions of $0 (0 x $50x), $37.50x (3/4 x $50x), and $12.50x (1/4 x $50x), respectively.

(D) *Member's deduction under section 250.* Under paragraph (b)(1) of this section, a member is allowed a deduction equal to the sum of the member's deduction attributable to the consolidated FDII deduction amount and the member's deduction attributable to the consolidated GILTI deduction amount. As a result P, USS1, and USS2 are entitled to deductions under paragraph (b)(1) of this section of $0 ($0 + $0), $97.50x ($60x + $37.50x), and $42.50x ($30x + $12.50x), respectively.

(5) *Example 5: Taxable income limitation*—(i) *Facts.* The facts are the same as in paragraph (f)(4)(i) of this section (the facts in *Example 4*), except that the P group's consolidated taxable income (within the meaning of paragraph (e)(10) of this section) is $300x.

(ii) *Analysis.* (A) *Determination of whether the limitation described in paragraph (b)(2) of this section applies.* Under paragraph (b)(2) of this section, in the case of a consolidated group with a consolidated section 250(a)(2) amount for a consolidated year, the amount of the consolidated foreign-derived intangible income and the consolidated global intangible low-taxed income otherwise taken into account in the determination of the consolidated FDII deduction amount and the consolidated GILTI deduction amount are subject to reduction. As in paragraph (f)(1)(ii)(E) of this section (the facts in *Example 1*), the P group's consolidated foreign-derived intangible income is $240x. As in paragraph (f)(4)(ii)(A) of this section (the analysis in *Example 4*), the P group's consolidated global intangible low-taxed income is $85x. The P group's consolidated taxable income is $300x. Under paragraph (e)(10) of this section, the P group's consolidated section 250(a)(2) amount is $25x (($240x + $85x) - $300x), the excess of the sum of the consolidated foreign-derived intangible income and the consolidated global intangible low-taxed income, over the P group's consolidated taxable income. Therefore, the limitation described in paragraph (b)(2) of this section applies.

(B) *Allocation of reduction.* Under paragraph (b)(2)(i) of this section, the P group's consolidated foreign-derived intangible income is reduced by an amount which bears the same ratio to the consolidated section 250(a)(2) amount as the consolidated foreign-derived intangible income bears to the sum of the consolidated foreign-derived intangible income and consolidated global intangible low-taxed income, and the P group's consolidated global intangible low-taxed income is reduced by the excess of the consolidated section 250(a)(2) amount over the reduction described in paragraph (b)(2)(i) of this section. Therefore, for purposes of determining the P group's consolidated FDII deduction amount and consolidated GILTI deduction amount, its consolidated foreign-derived intangible income is reduced to $221.54x ($240x - ($25x x ($240x / $325x))) and its consolidated global intangible low-taxed income is reduced to $78.46x ($85x - ($25x - ($25x x ($240x / $325x)))).

(C) *Calculation of consolidated FDII deduction amount and consolidated GILTI deduction amount.* Under paragraph (e)(4) of this section, the P group's consolidated FDII deduction amount is $83.08x ($221.54x x 0.375). Under paragraph (e)(8) of this section, the P group's consolidated GILTI deduction amount is $39.23x ($78.46x x 0.50).

(D) *Member's deduction attributable to the consolidated FDII deduction amount.* As in paragraph (f)(1)(ii)(G) of this section (the analysis in *Example 1*), the FDII deduction allocation ratios of P, USS1, and USS2 are 0, 2/3, and 1/3, respectively. Therefore, P, USS1, and USS2 are permitted deductions attributable to the consolidated FDII deduction amount of $0 (0 x $83.08x), $55.39x (2/3 x $83.08x), and $27.69x (1/3 x $83.08x), respectively.

(E) *Member's deduction attributable to the consolidated GILTI deduction amount.* As in paragraph (f)(4)(ii)(C) of this section (the analysis in *Example 4*), the GILTI deduction allocation ratios of P, USS1, and USS2 are 0, 3/4, and 1/4, respectively. Therefore, P, USS1, and USS2 are permitted deductions attributable to the consolidated GILTI deduction amount of $0 (0 x $39.23x), $29.42x (3/4 x $39.23x), and $9.81x (1/4 x $39.23x), respectively.

(F) *Member's deduction pursuant section 250.* Under paragraph (b)(1) of this section, a member is allowed a deduction equal to the sum of the member's deduction attributable to consolidated FDII deduction amount and the member's deduction attributable to consolidated GILTI deduction amount. As a result P, USS1, and USS2 are entitled to deductions under paragraph (b)(1) of this section of $0 ($0 + $0), $84.81x ($55.39x + $29.42x), and $37.50x ($27.69x + $9.81x), respectively.

(g) *Applicability date.*—This section applies to consolidated return years ending on or after the date of publication of the Treasury decision adopting these rules as final regulations in the **Federal Register**. [Reg. § 1.1502-50.]

GILTI: Stock Ownership Determination: Guidance

GILTI: Stock Ownership Determination: Guidance.—Amendments to Reg. § 1.1502-51, regarding the treatment of domestic partnerships for purposes of determining amounts included in the gross income of their partners with respect to foreign corporations and regarding gross income that is subject to a high rate of tax under the GILTI provisions, are proposed (published in the Federal Register on June 21, 2019) (REG-101828-19).

Par. 10. Section 1.1502-51 is amended by revising the last sentence in paragraph (b) and adding paragraph (g)(2) to read as follows:

§ 1.1502-51. Consolidated section 951A.

* * *

(b) * * * In addition, see § 1.958-1(d).

* * *

(g) * * *

(2) *The last sentence of paragraph (b) of this section.*—The last sentence of paragraph (b) of this section applies to taxable years of United States shareholders described in § 1.958-1(d)(4).

Consolidated Returns: AMT: General Computations

Consolidated Returns: Alternative Minimum Tax.—Reproduced below is the text of proposed Reg. § 1.1502-55, relating to the computation of the alternative minimum tax by consolidated groups (published in the Federal Register on December 30, 1992).

☐ Par. 7. Section 1.1502-55 is added to read as follows:

§1.1502-55. Computation of alternative minimum tax of consolidated groups.—(a) *In general.*—(1) *Overview.*—This section provides rules for determining a consolidated group's alternative minimum tax liability (its consolidated AMT) and for allocating various consolidated AMT attributes to members of the group. *See also* section 1561.

(2) *Principles.*—The consolidated AMT is determined under an approach that generally parallels the determination of the group's consolidated regular tax liability. The statutory scheme and definitions in sections 55 through 59 apply in determining consolidated AMT. For example, section 55(b)(1) defines tentative minimum tax (TMT), and that term is modified under this section and referred to as "consolidated TMT." Generally, this section provides further refinements to the "consolidated" AMT terms only where necessary to illustrate the adjustments required to compute the consolidated AMT or to allocate consolidated AMT attributes among members.

(b) *Consolidated AMTI.*—(1) *In general.*—Consolidated alternative minimum taxable income (AMTI), computed in accordance with the principles of §§1.1502-11 and 1.1502-12 (relating to the computation of consolidated taxable income), equals consolidated pre-adjustment AMTI—

(i) Increased or decreased by the consolidated adjustment for adjusted current earnings (consolidated ACE adjustment), computed under paragraph (b)(3) of this section; and

(ii) Decreased by the consolidated alternative tax net operating loss deduction (consolidated ATNOL deduction), computed under paragraph (b)(4) of this section.

(2) *Consolidated pre-adjustment AMTI.*—(i) *In general.*—Consolidated pre-adjustment AMTI is determined in accordance with the principles of §1.1502-11, taking into account the adjustments and preferences provided in sections 56 (excluding the section 56(g) adjustment), 57, and 58. The consolidated NOL deduction, however, is not taken into account in computing consolidated pre-adjustment AMTI. In determining consolidated pre-adjustment AMTI, a consolidated appreciated property charitable deduction preference must be computed. The consolidated appreciated property charitable deduction preference is the amount by which the consolidated charitable contribution deduction determined under the principles of §1.1502-24, computed by taking into account the adjustments pro-

vided in sections 56 (excluding the section 56(g) adjustment) and 58, would be reduced if all capital gain property of the group were taken into account at its adjusted basis.

(ii) *Separate pre-adjustment AMTI.*—(A) *In general.*—In computing consolidated pre-adjustment AMTI, each member must compute its separate pre-adjustment AMTI. The separate preadjustment AMTI of a member is determined in accordance with the principles of §1.1502-12, taking into account the adjustments and preferences provided in sections 56 (excluding the section 56(g) adjustment), 57, and 58.

(B) *Computation of member's section 57(a)(2) preference for excess IDCs.*—(1) *In general.*—In computing separate pre-adjustment AMTI, a member's preference under section 57(a)(2) is the member's allocable share of the consolidated IDC preference. A member's allocable share of the consolidated IDC preference is determined by multiplying the consolidated IDC preference by a fraction, the numerator of which is the separate IDC preference of the member, and the denominator of which is the sum of the separate IDC preferences of all members that have a separate IDC preference.

(2) *Consolidated IDC preference.*—The consolidated IDC preference is the excess of—

(i) The aggregate of each member's excess IDCs (as defined in section 57(a)(2)(B)) arising in the consolidated return year; over

(ii) 65 percent of the consolidated net income arising during the consolidated return year from all oil, gas, and geothermal properties (as defined in section 57(a)(2)(C)) of the group's members.

(3) *Separate IDC preference.*—A member's separate IDC preference is the amount, if any, by which the member's excess IDCs arising in the taxable year from all properties of the member is greater than 65 percent of the net income from oil, gas and geothermal properties of the member for the taxable year.

(iii) *Example.*—The following example illustrates the computation of consolidated pre-adjustment AMTI under this paragraph (b)(2).

Example. (i) P, S1, and S2 file a consolidated return, and have the following items of income and deduction for AMT purposes.

	P	S1	S2	Consolidated
Income	$1,000	$1,000	$1,000	
Depreciation	(300)	(100)	(200)	
Section 57(a)(2) IDC preference	240	—0—	160	
Section 57(a)(5) tax-exempt interest preference	100	50	—0—	
Separate pre-adjustment AMTI	$1,040	$950	$960	$2,950
AMT capital gains	300	150	100	550
Consolidated pre-adjustment AMTI				$3,500

(ii) Under paragraph (b)(2)(ii)(B) of this section, the section 57(a)(2) IDC preference for each of the members is computed as follows:

	P	S1	S2	Consolidated
IDCs	$460	$100	$395	$955
65% of net income from oil, gas, and geothermal properties	(160)	(200)	(195)	(555)
IDC preference	$300	$-0-	$200	$400

(iii) The $400 consolidated IDC preference is allocated among the members that have a separate IDC preference (P and S2). Each member's allocable share of the consolidated IDC preference,

P

$$\$400 \text{ consolidated IDC preference} \times \frac{\$300, \text{ separate IDC preference}}{\$500, \text{ sum of separate IDC preferences of all members}} = \$240$$

S2

$$\$400 \text{ consolidated IDC preference} \times \frac{\$200, \text{ separate IDC preference}}{\$500, \text{ sum of separate IDC preferences of all members}} = \$160$$

which is included in its separate pre-adjustment AMTI, is computed as follows:

(3) *Consolidated ACE adjustment.*—(i) *In general.*—In computing consolidated AMTI, subject to the limitation of paragraph (b)(3)(iii) of this section, consolidated pre-adjustment AMTI is increased (or decreased) by 75 percent of the excess (or deficit) for the consolidated return year of—

(A) The consolidated ACE (as defined in paragraph (b)(3)(ii) of this section) for the year; over

(B) The consolidated pre-adjustment AMTI (as defined in paragraph (b)(2) of this section) for the year.

(ii) *Consolidated ACE.*—(A) *In general.*—Consolidated ACE is determined in accordance with the principles of §1.1502-11, taking

into account the adjustments and preferences provided in sections 56, 57, and 58. The consolidated NOL deduction and the consolidated section 247 deduction, however, are not taken into account in computing consolidated ACE.

(B) *Separate ACE.*—In computing consolidated ACE, each member must compute its separate ACE. The separate ACE of a member is the separate pre-adjustment AMTI of the member, as defined in paragraph (b)(2)(ii) of this section, adjusted as provided in section 56(g) and §1.56(g)-1.

(iii) *Limitation on consolidated negative ACE adjustments.*—(A) *In general.*—Under the principles of section 56(g)(2)(B), the amount of the consolidated negative ACE adjustment for any consolidated return year is limited to the sum of—

    (1) The consolidated return year cumulative ACE adjustment (as defined in paragraph (b)(3)(iii)(B)(*1*) of this section); and

    (2) The separate return year cumulative ACE adjustment (as defined in paragraph (b)(3)(iii)(B)(*2*) of this section).

    (B) Definitions.—(1) Consolidated return year cumulative ACE adjustment.—The consolidated return year cumulative ACE adjustment equals the excess, if any, of the consolidated positive ACE adjustments for prior consolidated return years, over the sum of—

    (i) Consolidated negative ACE adjustments for prior consolidated return years (other than any portion of those consolidated negative ACE adjustments attributable to separate return year positive ACE adjustments, as determined under paragraph (b)(3)(iii)(C) of this section); and

    (ii) Consolidated positive ACE adjustments for prior consolidated return years apportioned to a corporation that ceases to be a member and carried to its separate return years in accordance with paragraph (e)(2) of this section (or, for consolidated return years for which the due date of the income tax return (without regard to extensions) is before [the date that is sixty days after final regulations are filed with the Federal Register], in accordance with any reasonable method used by the group).

    (2) Separate return year cumulative ACE adjustment.—The separate return year cumulative ACE adjustment equals the excess, if any, of the separate return year positive ACE adjustments of the members for prior taxable years (as defined in paragraph (b)(3)(iii)(B)(*3*) of this section), over the sum of—

    (i) The separate return year negative ACE adjustments of the members for prior taxable years (as defined in paragraph (b)(3)(iii)(B)(*4*) of this section); and

    (ii) The portion of the consolidated negative ACE adjustments of the group for prior consolidated return years attributable to prior year separate return year positive ACE adjustments of the members (as determined under paragraph (b)(3)(iii)(C) of this section).

    (3) Separate return year positive ACE adjustments.—Separate return year positive ACE adjustments are—

    (i) For each member, the increases in AMTI for prior separate return years (other than years for which the member joined in the filing of a consolidated return) due to the ACE adjustment under section 56(g); and

    (ii) For any prior separate return years for which a member joined in the filing of a consolidated return with another group, the member's allocable share of that group's consolidated

positive ACE adjustments determined under paragraph (e)(2) of this section (or, for taxable years for which the due date of the income tax return (without regard to extensions) is before [the date that is sixty days after final regulations are filed with the Federal Register], determined in accordance with any reasonable method used by that other group).

    (4) Separate return year negative ACE adjustments.—Separate return year negative ACE adjustments include the aggregate decreases in AMTI for prior separate return years (other than years for which the member joined in the filing of a consolidated return) due to the ACE adjustment under section 56(g).

    (C) Consolidated negative ACE adjustments attributable to separate return year positive ACE adjustments.—The portion of a consolidated negative ACE adjustment attributable to separate return year positive ACE adjustments is equal to the consolidated negative ACE adjustment multiplied by a fraction, the numerator of which is the separate return year cumulative ACE adjustment (as of the beginning of the consolidated return year) and the denominator of which is the aggregate of the separate return year cumulative ACE adjustment and the consolidated return year cumulative ACE adjustment (both determined as of the beginning of the consolidated return year).

    (4) Consolidated ATNOL deduction.—After taking into account the group's consolidated ACE adjustment for the year, the group takes the consolidated ATNOL deduction into account in computing consolidated AMTI. Subject to applicable limitations (*e.g.,* section 382) and the provisions of section 56(d), the consolidated ATNOL deduction is the aggregate of the consolidated ATNOL carryovers and carrybacks determined under the principles of §1.1502-21. The consolidated ATNOL for a consolidated return year is the consolidated net operating loss determined under the principles of §1.1502-21(e) for the year, taking into account the adjustments and preferences provided in sections 56, 57, and 58 for that year.

    (5) Example.—The following example illustrates certain general principles of this paragraph (b).

    Example. (i) *Separate returns.* P and S file separate returns. P's and S's items of income and deduction for regular tax (RT), AMT, and ACE purposes, and P's and S's tax liability are provided below. The effects of the lower section 11 brackets and the section 55(d) AMT exemption amount are ignored.

    (A) P has pre-adjustment AMTI of $700 and ACE of $900, resulting in a $150 positive ACE adjustment (75 percent of the difference between P's ACE and P's pre-adjustment AMTI). P's ATNOL deduction ($100) reduces its AMTI to $750. P's TMT is therefore $150 (20 percent of AMTI). Thus, P has an AMT liability of $48, the difference between P's TMT ($150) and P's regular tax ($102).

P	RT	AMT	ACE
Gross income	$1,000	$1,000	$1,000
Depreciation	(500)	(300)	(100)
Pre-adjustment AMTI		$700	
ACE			900
ACE adjustment		150	
NOL deduction	(200)		
ATNOL deduction		(100)	
Taxable income	$300		
AMTI		$750	
TMT (20%)		$150	
RT liability (34%)	$102		
AMT		$48	

    (B) S has pre-adjustment AMTI of $900 and ACE of $800, resulting in a $75 negative ACE adjustment (75 percent of the difference between S's pre-adjustment AMTI and S's ACE. (Assume that S may use the negative adjustment because of prior year positive ACE

adjustments). S's ATNOL deduction ($200) reduces its AMTI to $625. Thus, S has no AMT liability because S's regular tax ($306) exceeds its TMT ($125).

S	RT	AMT	ACE
Gross income	$1,000	$1,000	$1,000
Depreciation	0	(100)	(200)
Pre-adjustment AMTI		$900	
ACE			$800
ACE adjustment		(75)	
NOL deduction	(100)		
ATNOL deduction		(200)	
Taxable income	$900		
AMTI		$625	
TMT (20%)		$125	
RT liability (34%)	$306		
AMT		0	

    (ii) *Consolidated return filed.* (A) If P and S instead elect to file a consolidated return, the group would have the following results:

P group

RT

	P	S	Consolidated
Gross income	$1,000	$1,000	$2,000
Depreciation	(500)	0	(500)
Aggregate separate taxable income	$500	$1,000	$1,500
Consolidated NOL deduction			(300)
Consolidated taxable income			$1,200
Consolidated RT (34%)			$408

AMT

	P	S	Consolidated
Gross income	$1,000	$1,000	$2,000
Depreciation	(300)	(100)	(400)
Consolidated pre-adjustment AMTI	$700	$900	$1,600
ACE depreciation adjustment	200	(100)	100
Consolidated ACE	$900	$800	$1,700
Consolidated ACE adjustment			75
Consolidated ATNOL deduction			(300)
Consolidated AMTI			$1,375
Consolidated TMT (20%)			$275
Consolidated AMT			$0

(B) The P group has consolidated pre-adjustment AMTI of $1,600. In addition, the group has consolidated ACE of $1,700, resulting in a $75 positive consolidated ACE adjustment (75 percent of the difference between the group's ACE and the group's pre-adjustment AMTI). The consolidated ATNOL deduction reduces consolidated AMTI to $1,375. The consolidated TMT is $275. Thus, the P group has no consolidated AMT liability because its consolidated regular tax ($408) exceeds its consolidated TMT ($275).

(c) *Consolidated alternative minimum tax foreign tax credit.*—[Reserved]

(d) *Separate return limitation years.*—[Reserved]

(e) *Separate return years.*—(1) *Carryovers and carrybacks of consolidated AMT attributes to separate return years.*—(i) *In general.*—This paragraph (e)(1) provides principles under which various consolidated AMT attributes are allocated among members of a consolidated group, generally for purposes of apportioning the attribute to a corporation that ceases to be a member. The apportionment of consolidated AMT attributes that have regular tax counterparts is based on the principles applicable to the regular tax counterparts. *See, e.g.,* § 1.1502-21(b) (principles applicable to consolidated net operating losses).

(ii) *Examples.*—The following examples illustrate the application of this paragraph (e)(1).

Example 1. Allocation of consolidated ATNOL. (i) P, S1, and S2 are members of a consolidated group. In 1993, the group has a consolidated ATNOL of $100. P has a separate ATNOL of $150, S1 has a separate ATNOL of $50, and S2 has separate AMTI of $100. The separate ATNOLs for P and S1 are determined by computing the consolidated ATNOL, taking into account only the member's income, gain, deduction, and loss, including the member's losses and deductions actually absorbed by the group in the taxable year (whether or not absorbed by the member). *See* § 1.1502-21(b)(2)(iv).

(ii) Under this paragraph (e)(1), the portion of the consolidated ATNOL allocable to each member is determined in accordance with the principles of the regulations relating to the carryover and carryback of the consolidated NOL to separate return years. *See* § 1.1502-21(b). Thus, the portion of the consolidated ATNOL allocable to P and S1 is determined by multiplying the consolidated ATNOL by a fraction, the numerator of which is the member's separate ATNOL and the denominator of which is the sum of all members' separate ATNOLs. The portion of the consolidated ATNOL allocable to P is $75 ($100 multiplied by $150/$200). The portion of the consolidated ATNOL allocable to S1 is $25 ($100 multiplied by $50/$200). S2 is not allocated a portion of the consolidated ATNOL because S2 had no separate ATNOL.

Example 2. Allocation of consolidated ACE net capital loss. (i) P, S1, and S2 are members of a consolidated group. In 1993, the group has a consolidated ACE net capital loss of $210. P has a separate ACE net capital loss of $90, S1 has a separate ACE net capital gain of $60, and S2 has a separate ACE net capital loss of $180. The separate ACE net capital losses for P and S2 are determined by computing the consolidated ACE net capital loss by taking into account only the

member's gains and losses, including the member's losses actually absorbed by the group in the taxable year (whether or not absorbed by the member). *See* §§ 1.1502-22(b)(3) and 1.1502-21(b)(2)(iv).

(ii) Under this paragraph (e)(1), the portion of the consolidated ACE net capital loss allocable to each member is determined in accordance with the principles of the regulations relating to the carryover and carryback of the consolidated net capital loss to separate return years. *See* § 1.1502-22(b). Thus, the portion of the consolidated ACE net capital loss allocable to P and S2 is determined by multiplying the consolidated ACE net capital loss by a fraction, the numerator of which is the member's separate ACE net capital loss and the denominator of which is the sum of all members' separate ACE net capital losses. The portion of the consolidated ACE net capital loss allocable to P is $70 ($210 multiplied by $90/$270). The portion of the consolidated ACE net capital loss allocable to S2 is $140 ($210 multiplied by $180/$270). S1 is not allocated a portion of the consolidated ACE net capital loss because S1 had no separate ACE net capital loss.

(2) *Carryover of consolidated positive ACE adjustments to separate return years.*—(i) *In general.*—If a corporation ceases to be a member, the portion of the consolidated positive ACE adjustments allocated to the corporation is taken into account in its separate return years in accordance with the principles of §§ 1.56(g)-1(a)(2) and 1.1502-21(b). Any separate return year cumulative ACE adjustment attributable to a corporation as of the close of the taxable year in which the corporation ceases to be a member is also taken into account in its separate return year.

(ii) *Portion of consolidated positive ACE adjustments allocable to a member.*—(A) *In general.*—The portion of the consolidated positive ACE adjustments allocated to a member is the consolidated return year cumulative ACE adjustment as of the close of the consolidated return year in which the corporation ceases to be a member, multiplied by a fraction. The numerator of the fraction is the separate cumulative ACE adjustment of the member as of the close of the consolidated return year in which the corporation ceases to be a member, and the denominator of the fraction is the sum of the separate cumulative ACE adjustments of all members having separate cumulative ACE adjustments as of the close of the consolidated return year in which the corporation ceases to be a member.

(B) *Separate cumulative ACE adjustment.*—The separate cumulative ACE adjustment of a member is the consolidated return year cumulative ACE adjustment, if any, taking into account only the member's items of income, gain, deduction, and loss, including the member's losses and deductions actually absorbed by the group (whether or not absorbed by the member).

(f) *Deferral and restoration of gain or loss.*—The principles of the Internal Revenue Code and regulations that affect the timing of inclusion of items in consolidated taxable income generally apply for purposes of computing consolidated pre-adjustment AMTI and consolidated ACE. *See, e.g.,* § 1.1502-13. Applicable adjustments and preferences provided in sections 56, 57, and 58 must be taken into account.

(g) *Stock basis adjustments in computing consolidated AMT.*—(1) *Parallel approach.*—The principles set forth in §§1.1502-19 and 1.1502-32 for determining the regular tax basis in (or the regular tax excess loss account with respect to) a member's stock generally apply in determining both the corresponding AMT stock basis (or AMT excess loss account) and ACE stock basis (or ACE excess loss account).

(2) *Modifications to regular tax stock basis principles in computing consolidated pre-adjustment AMTI and consolidated ACE.*—The following modifications to the stock basis adjustment principles of §§1.1502-19 and 1.1502-32 apply for purposes of computing AMT stock basis (or AMT excess loss account) used in determining consolidated pre-adjustment AMTI and ACE stock basis (or ACE excess loss account) used in determining consolidated ACE—

(i) Adjustments may be determined annually but are required only if a difference between the regular tax and AMT or ACE basis in (or excess loss with respect to) a member's stock will affect the tax liability of any person (*e.g.*, on a sale of the stock);

(ii) The annual reporting requirements of §1.1502-32(g) do not apply under the AMT or ACE systems;

(iii) In determining the adjustments under §1.1502-32(b)(3)(i), any section 57 preference items includible in AMTI are not taken into account (while tax-exempt interest described in section 57(a)(5) is not taken into account in determining the adjustments for AMTI under §1.1502-32(b)(3)(i), it does result in a positive stock basis adjustment under §1.1502-32(b)(3)(ii));

(iv) A member's portion of any disallowed consolidated negative ACE adjustment for a consolidated return year is treated as a non-capital, non-deductible expense under §1.1502-32(b)(3)(iii) for purposes of determining the adjustments to another member's AMT basis in (or excess loss account with respect to) the stock of the member; and

(v) Solely for purposes of computing adjustments to the ACE basis in (or ACE excess loss account with respect to) the stock of a member, the member's excess of ACE deductions over ACE income for a consolidated return year is treated as a tax loss under §1.1502-32(b)(3)(i) that is absorbed in the same year that it arises.

(3) *Tax payments and refunds.*—The amount of any section 275 tax liability or refund of federal income tax taken into account under §§1.1502-19 and 1.1502-32 for regular tax purposes is also taken into account in computing AMT and ACE stock basis (or excess loss account).

(4) *Example.*—The following example illustrates the principles of this paragraph (g).

Example. (i) *Background.* (A) Corporations P and S file a consolidated return. On January 1, 1994, P has a $0 basis in S's stock. S has gross income for regular tax, AMT, and ACE purposes of $10,000 in 1994 and a loss from operations (before taking into account its depreciation deduction) for regular tax, AMT, and ACE purposes of $5,000 in 1995. The P group's tax liability (whether attributable to the regular tax or the AMT) is solely attributable to S, and the consolidated regular tax liability and consolidated AMT liability allocations under §1.1552-1 are the same as the separate liabilities of S. Finally, the effects of the lower section 11 tax rate brackets and the section 55(d) AMT exemption amount are ignored.

(B) On December 31, 1995, P sells a portion of the S stock. Under paragraph (g)(2)(i) of this section, no adjustments to P's basis in S's stock are required for purposes of computing consolidated pre-adjustment AMTI and consolidated ACE in 1994. However, because there was a stock sale in 1995, P's basis in S's stock must be adjusted for AMT and ACE purposes in 1995 as follows:

(ii) *Stock basis adjustments for 1994*—(A) *Adjustments*—

	RT	AMT	ACE
Gross income	$10,000	$10,000	$10,000
Depreciation	(5,000)	(4,000)	(3,000)
Taxable income	$5,000		
Pre-adjustment AMTI		$6,000	
ACE			$7,000
ACE adjustment		750	
AMTI		$6,750	
TMT (20%)		$1,350	
RT liability (34%)	$1,700		
AMT		$-0-	

(B) *Stock basis adjustments*—

P's basis in S's stock on 1/1/94	$-0-	$-0-	$-0-
§1.1502-32(b)(3)(i)	5,000	6,750	7,000
§1.1502-32(b)(3)(iii)	(1,700)	(1,700)	(1,700)
P's Basis in S stock on 12/31/94	$3,300	$5,050	$5,300

(iii)(A) *Stock basis adjustments for 1995.*

	RT	AMT	ACE
Gross income	$(5,000)	$(5,000)	$(5,000)
Depreciation	(5,000)	(4,000)	(3,000)
Taxable income	$(10,000)		
Pre-adjustment AMTI		$(9,000)	
ACE			$(8,000)
ACE adjustment		750	
AMTI		$(8,250)	
TMT (20%)		$-0-	
RT liability (34%)	$-0-		
AMT		$-0-	

Because of the section 56(d) 90-percent limitation on the amount of AMTI that may be offset by an ATNOL deduction, only $6,075 of the $8,250 ATNOL for 1995 is carried back to 1994 under the principles of §1.1502-21(b). Thus, since all $5,000 of the 1994 regular taxable income was offset by the 1995 NOL, but only $6,075 of the 1994

AMTI was offset by the 1995 ATNOL, an AMT liability for 1994 of $135 results. Accordingly, only $1,565 of the $1,700 Federal income taxes paid in 1994 is refunded in 1995.

(B) *Stock basis adjustments*—

P's basis in S stock on 12/31/94	$3,300	$5,050	$5,300
§1.1502-32(b)(3)(i)	(5,000)	(6,075)	(8,000)
§1.1502-32(b)(3)(ii)	1,565	1,565	1,565
§1.1502-32(b)(3)(iii)	(-0-)	(-0-)	(-0-)
P's basis (ELA) in S stock when sold on 12/31/95	$(135)	$540	$(1,135)

(h) *Consolidated MTC.*—(1) *Overview.*—A group's consolidated minimum tax credit (MTC) is generally based on the consolidated adjusted net minimum tax for prior years. Adjustments are made to take into account a member's adjusted net minimum tax from prior separate return years. *See* paragraphs (h)(2) through (4) of this sec-

tion. Adjustments are also made for the portion of the consolidated adjusted net minimum tax that is allocable to a corporation that ceases to be a member (and thus may be carried to the member's separate return years). *See* paragraph (h)(6) of this section.

(2) *Computation of the consolidated MTC.*—The consolidated MTC available as of the beginning of any consolidated return year is the sum of—

(i) The consolidated return year MTC (as defined in paragraph (h)(3) of this section); and

(ii) The separate return year MTC (as defined in paragraph (h)(4) of this section).

(3) *Consolidated return year MTC.*—(i) *General rule.*—The consolidated return year MTC is the excess (if any) of—

(A) The consolidated adjusted net minimum tax (as defined in paragraph (h)(3)(ii) of this section) for all prior consolidated return years beginning after 1986; over

(B) The sum of—

(1) The amount of the consolidated adjusted net minimum tax for prior consolidated return years that is allowable as a consolidated MTC in prior years; and

(2) The amount of the consolidated adjusted minimum tax for prior consolidated return years that is allowed to be carried to a separate return year of a member in accordance with paragraph (h)(6) of this section (or, for consolidated return years for which the due date of the income tax return (without regard to extensions) is before [the date that is sixty days after the final regulations are filed with the Federal Register], in accordance with any reasonable method used by the group).

(ii) *Consolidated adjusted net minimum tax.*—(A) *In general.*—Except as provided in paragraphs (h)(3)(ii)(B) and (C) of this section, consolidated adjusted net minimum tax is the amount of the consolidated AMT.

(B) *Exception for taxable years beginning after 1986 and before 1990.*—For taxable years beginning after December 31, 1986, and before January 1, 1990, consolidated adjusted net minimum tax is the amount of the consolidated AMT, reduced by the amount that would be the consolidated AMT for the taxable year if the only adjustments and tax preference items were those in section 56(c)(3), section 57(a)(1), section 57(a)(5), and section 57(a)(6).

(C) *Special rule for groups with consolidated disallowed section 29 or section 28 credits.*—The amounts determined under paragraphs (h)(3)(ii)(A) and (B) of this section for a taxable year are increased by the amount, if any, of a group's consolidated disallowed section 29 credit or consolidated disallowed section 28 credit for the year. For this purpose, the consolidated disallowed section 29 credit is the sum of the section 29 credits of all the members that are not allowable under section 29 solely by reason of the application of section 29(b)(6)(B). The consolidated disallowed section 28 credit is the sum of the section 28 credits of all the members that are not allowable under section 28 solely by reason of the application of section 28(d)(2)(B).

(4) *Separate return year MTC.*—(i) *In general.*—The separate return year MTC is, subject to applicable limitations (*e.g*, section 383), the excess (if any) of—

(A) The adjusted net minimum tax (as defined in section 53 (d)) for all prior separate return years of the group members beginning after 1986; over

(B) The sum of—

(1) The amount allowable as an MTC for such prior separate return years; and

(2) The amount described in paragraph (h)(4)(i)(A) of this section that is allowable as a consolidated MTC in prior years.

(ii) *Adjusted net minimum tax arising in another consolidated group.*—In the case of a member that filed a consolidated return in a prior year with another group, the amount described in paragraph (h)(4)(i)(A) of this section includes any consolidated MTC of another group that is attributable to that member and that is apportioned to it and available in the consolidated return year in accordance with paragraph (h)(6) of this section (or, for taxable years for which the due date of the income tax return (without regard to extensions) is before [the date that is sixty days after final regulations are filed with the Federal Register], in accordance with any reasonable method used by that other group).

(iii) *Limitation on portion of separate return year MTC arising in separate return limitation years.*—[Reserved]

(5) *Limitation on allowable consolidated MTC.*—(i) *In general.*—The available consolidated MTC allowable under this paragraph (h) for any consolidated return year is limited to the excess (if any) of—

(A) The modified consolidated regular tax liability (as defined in paragraph (h)(5)(ii) of this section) for the year; over

(B) The consolidated TMT for the year.

(ii) *Modified consolidated regular tax liability.*—Modified consolidated regular tax liability is the consolidated regular tax liability, computed in accordance with section 26(b), reduced by the sum of the consolidated credits allowable under subparts A, B, D, E, and F of part III of subchapter A of chapter 1 of the Internal Revenue Code.

(6) *Carryover of the consolidated MTC to separate return years.*—(i) *In general.*—When a corporation ceases to be a member of a group, the group is required to allocate to that corporation a portion of the group's consolidated MTC. The allocation is generally based on the corporation's contributions to the group's consolidated adjusted net minimum tax during the consolidated return years for which the corporation was a member of the group. The amount of the consolidated MTC properly allocable to a departing member is taken into account by the member in its succeeding separate return years.

(ii) *Consolidated MTC allocable to a member.*—(A) *In general.*—The amount of the consolidated MTC allocable to a corporation equals the corporation's allocable share of the consolidated MTC available as of the beginning of the consolidated return year in which the corporation ceases to be a member of a group—

(1) Increased by the corporation's allocable share of the consolidated adjusted net minimum tax, if any, for the consolidated return year in which the corporation ceases to be a member (as determined under paragraph (h)(6)(iii) of this section); and

(2) Decreased by the corporation's allocable share of any allowable consolidated MTC for the consolidated return year in which the corporation ceases to be a member (as determined under paragraphs (h)(6)(vi) and (7) of this section).

(B) *Reference to rules for determining a member's allocable share.*—For purposes of determining a corporation's allocable share of the consolidated MTC available as of the beginning of the consolidated return year in which the corporation ceases to be a member of a group (as described in paragraph (h)(6)(ii)(A) of this section), the rules of paragraph (h)(6)(iii) of this section apply to determine the corporation's allocable share of consolidated adjusted net minimum tax in each prior consolidated return year, and the rules of paragraphs (h)(6)(vi) and (7) of this section apply to determine the corporation's allocable share of any allowable consolidated MTC in prior consolidated return years. The rules of paragraph (h)(7) of this section are also applicable in determining the remaining amount of the departing member's separate return year MTC (from years prior to joining the consolidated group) that is taken into account in succeeding separate return years.

(iii) *Member's allocable share of consolidated adjusted net minimum tax.*—(A) *In general.*—A member's allocable share of the consolidated adjusted net minimum tax for a consolidated return year is determined by multiplying the consolidated AMT for the year by a fraction, the numerator of which is the separate adjusted AMT of the member (as defined in paragraph (h)(6)(iv) of this section) for the year, and the denominator of which is the sum of the separate adjusted AMTs of each member for the year.

(B) *Special allocation rule for groups with consolidated disallowed section 29 or section 28 credits.*—(1) *General rule.*—In a consolidated return year in which the group has a consolidated disallowed section 29 or 28 credit, in addition to the amount determined under paragraph (h)(6)(iii)(A) of this section, a member's allocable share of consolidated adjusted net minimum tax for the year includes its allocable share of the consolidated disallowed section 29 or 28 credit.

(2) *Allocable share of disallowed credit.*—A member's allocable share of the consolidated disallowed section 29 credit or consolidated disallowed section 28 credit for a consolidated return year is determined by multiplying the consolidated disallowed section 29 credit amount (or the consolidated disallowed section 28 credit amount) for the year by a fraction. The numerator of the fraction is the total section 29 credits (or section 28 credits) of the member for the taxable year, and the denominator is the total section 29 credits (or section 28 credits) of all members for the year.

(iv) *Separate adjusted AMT.*—(A) *In general.*—Subject to paragraph (h)(6)(iv)(B) of this section, the separate adjusted AMT of a member for a consolidated return year is the excess (if any) of—

(1) The consolidated AMT for the year; over

(2) The consolidated AMT for the year, computed by excluding the member's items of income, gain, deduction, and loss, and the member's credits.

(B) *Special rule in computing separate adjusted AMT.*—If, in computing a member's separate adjusted AMT, there is no consolidated AMT computed without that member's items (*i.e.*, the amount in paragraph (h)(6)(iv)(A)(2) of this section is zero), the amount determined under paragraph (h)(6)(iv)(A) of this section must be increased by the excess (if any) of the consolidated regular tax computed without the member's items, over consolidated TMT computed without the member's items.

(v) *Examples.*—The provisions of paragraphs (h)(1) through (6)(iv) of this section are illustrated by the following examples. In the examples, corporations P, S1, and S2 file a consolidated return. In each example, the group has no consolidated disallowed section 28 or section 29 credits for the year. The effects of the lower section 11 brackets and the section 55(d) exemption amount are ignored.

Example 1. (i) *1993 regular tax and AMT computation.*

	P	S1	S2	Consolidated
Taxable income	$1,200	$(200)	$3,000	$4,000
Adjustments and preferences	1,800	100	2,000	3,900
AMTI	$3,000	$(100)	$5,000	$7,900
TMT (20%)				$1,580
RT liability (34%)				1,360
AMT				$220

(ii) *Computation of separate adjusted AMT.*

(A) *Computation of consolidated AMT excluding P's items:*

Taxable income	$2,800
Adjustments and preferences	2,100
AMTI	$4,900
TMT (20%)	$980
RT liability (34%)	952
AMT	$28

Consolidated AMT computed without P's items is $28. Accordingly, P's separate adjusted AMT is $192 ($220 – $28).

(B) *Computation of consolidated AMT excluding S1's items:*

Taxable income	$4,200
Adjustments and preferences	3,800
AMTI	$8,000
TMT (20%)	$1,600
RT liability (34%)	1,428
AMT	$172

Consolidated AMT computed without S1's items is $172. Accordingly, S1's separate adjusted AMT is $48 ($220 – $172).

(C) *Computation of consolidated AMT excluding S2's items:*

Taxable income	$1,000
Adjustments and preferences	1,900
AMTI	$2,900
TMT (20%)	$580
RT liability (34%)	340
AMT	$240

Consolidated AMT computed without S2's items is $240. Because consolidated AMT computed without S2's items more than that amount computed with S2's items, S2 has no separate adjusted AMT.

(iii) *Allocation of 1993 consolidated adjusted net minimum tax to members of group.* Under paragraph (h)(6)(iii)(A) of this section, the amount of the 1993 consolidated adjusted net minimum tax allocable to P and S1 is determined as follows (S2 is allocated no portion of the 1993 consolidated adjusted net minimum tax because S2 has no separate adjusted AMT):

P

$$\$220 \text{ consolidated AMT} \times \frac{\$192, \text{ P's separate adjusted AMT}}{\$240, \text{ the sum of all members' separate adjusted AMTs}} = \$176$$

S1

$$\$220 \text{ consolidated AMT} \times \frac{\$48, \text{ S1's separate adjusted AMT}}{\$240, \text{ the sum of all members' separate adjusted AMTs}} = \$44$$

Example 2. (i) *1994 regular tax and AMT computation.*

	P	S1	S2	Consolidated
Taxable income	$5,000	$-0-	$2,000	$7,000
Adjustments and preferences	(5,000)	8,000	3,400	6,400
AMTI	$-0-	$8,000	$5,400	$13,400
TMT (20%)				$2,680
RT liability (34%)				2,380
AMT				$300

(ii) *Computation of separate adjusted AMT.*

(A) *Computation of consolidated AMT excluding P's items:*

Taxable income	$2,000
Adjustments and preferences	11,400
AMTI	$13,400
TMT (20%)	$2,680
RT liability (34%)	680
AMT	$2,000

Consolidated AMT computed without P's items is $2,000. Because the consolidated AMT with P is only $300, P has no separate adjusted AMT.

(B) *Computation of consolidated AMT excluding S1's items:*

Taxable income	$7,000
Adjustments and preferences	(1,600)
AMTI	$5,400
TMT (20%)	$1,080
RT liability (34%)	2,380
AMT	$-0-

The group has no consolidated AMT if S2's items are excluded. Accordingly, under paragraph (h)(6)(iv)(B) of this section, S2's separate adjusted AMT is $400, the sum of $300 (consolidated AMT computed with S2's items minus consolidated AMT computed without S2's items), and $100 (the excess of the consolidated regular tax computed without S2's items ($1,700) over the consolidated TMT computed without S2's items ($1,600)).

The group has no consolidated AMT if S1's items are excluded. Accordingly, under paragraph (h)(6)(iv)(B) of this section, S1's separate adjusted AMT is $1,600, the sum of $300 (consolidated AMT computed with S1's items minus consolidated AMT computed without S1's items), and $1,300 (the excess of the consolidated regular tax computed without S1's items ($2,380) over the consolidated TMT computed without S1's items ($1,080)).

(C) *Computation of consolidated AMT excluding S2's items:*

Taxable income	$5,000
Adjustments and preferences	3,000
AMTI	$8,000
TMT (20%)	1,600
RT liability (34%)	1,700
AMT	$-0-

(iii) *Allocation of 1994 consolidated MTC to members of the group.* Under paragraph (h)(6)(iii)(A) of this section, the amount of the 1994 consolidated adjusted net minimum tax allocable to S1 and S2 is determined as follows (P is allocated no portion of the consolidated MTC because P has no separate adjusted AMT):

S1

$$\$300 \text{ consolidated AMT} \times \frac{\$1,600, \text{ S1's separate adjusted AMT}}{\$2,000, \text{ the sum of all members' separate adjusted AMTs}} = \$225$$

S2

$$\$300 \text{ consolidated AMT} \times \frac{\$400, \text{ S2's separate adjusted AMT}}{\$2,000, \text{ the sum of all members' separate adjusted AMTs}} = \$75$$

(vi) *Member's allocable share of allowable consolidated MTC in a consolidated return year*— (A) *In general.* For purposes of determining the amount of the consolidated MTC allocable to a member under this paragraph (h)(6), a member's allocable share of the consolidated adjusted net minimum tax for a consolidated return year must, as described in paragraph (h)(6)(ii) of this section, be reduced by the member's allocable share of that amount allowable in a subsequent consolidated return year as a consolidated MTC. The member's allocable share of consolidated adjusted net minimum tax for a year that is allowable as a consolidated MTC in a subsequent taxable year is determined by multiplying the consolidated adjusted net minimum tax for the year allowable as a consolidated MTC (taking into account the ordering rules of paragraph (h)(7) of this section) by a fraction, the numerator of which is the member's allocable share of that consolidated adjusted net minimum tax and the denominator of which is the total amount of that consolidated adjusted net minimum tax.

(B) *Example.* The provisions of this paragraph (h)(6)(vi) are illustrated by the following example.

Example. (i) P, S1, and S2 file a consolidated return. In 1994, the group has consolidated adjusted net minimum tax of $100. Pursuant to the allocation method provided in paragraph (h)(6)(iii) of this section, P's, S1's, and S2's allocable shares of the 1994 consolidated adjusted net minimum tax are $60, $30, and $10, respectively. The group has no separate return year MTC as defined in paragraph (h)(4) of this section.

(ii) In 1995, the group has an $80 excess of modified consolidated regular tax over consolidated tentative minimum tax. Accordingly, $80 of the 1994 consolidated adjusted net minimum tax is allowable as a consolidated MTC in 1995 to offset consolidated regular tax.

(iii) As described in paragraph (h)(6)(ii) of this section, each member's allocable share of the 1994 consolidated adjusted net minimum tax is reduced by its allocable share of that $80 amount allowable as a consolidated MTC in 1995. The reduction amount is, under paragraph (h)(6)(vi) of this section, determined by multiplying the consolidated adjusted net minimum tax allowable as a consolidated MTC by a fraction, the numerator of which is the member's allocable share of that consolidated adjusted net minimum tax and the denominator of which is the total amount of that consolidated adjusted net minimum tax. As provided above, P's allocable share of the consoli-

dated adjusted net minimum tax is 60 percent (60/100), S1's allocable share is 30 percent (30/100), and S2's allocable share is 10 percent (10/100). Accordingly, P's allocable share of the consolidated adjusted net minimum tax is reduced by $48 ($80 multiplied by .60). S1's allocable share of the consolidated adjusted net minimum tax is reduced by $24 ($80 multiplied by .30). S2's allocable share of the consolidated adjusted net minimum tax is reduced by $8 ($80 multiplied by .10).

(7) *Amount of adjusted net minimum tax allowable as a consolidated MTC.*—Under the rules provided in paragraphs (h)(3)(i)(B)(1), (h)(4)(i)(B)(2), (h)(6)(ii), and (h)(6)(vi) of this section, adjusted net minimum tax, whether consolidated adjusted net minimum tax or adjusted net minimum tax from separate return years, must be reduced by the amount of that adjusted net minimum tax allowable in a subsequent consolidated return year as a consolidated MTC. For purposes of those rules, consolidated adjusted net minimum tax and adjusted net minimum tax from separate return years are allowable as a consolidated MTC in the order of the taxable year in which the adjusted net minimum tax is imposed, with the adjusted net minimum tax imposed in the taxable year with the earliest year end allowable first. Consolidated adjusted net minimum tax and adjusted net minimum tax from separate return years imposed in taxable years ending on the same date are considered to be allowable as a consolidated MTC in proportion to the total consolidated adjusted net minimum tax and adjusted net minimum tax from separate return years incurred in that same taxable year. If, however, there is a limitation on the use of a consolidated MTC (*e.g.,* under section 383), the adjusted net minimum tax unable to be used as a credit because of the limitation is disregarded for purposes of the computation provided in this paragraph (h)(7).

(i) [Reserved].

(j) *Successor and predecessor.*—For purposes of this section any reference to a corporation or member includes, as the context may require, a reference to a successor or predecessor.

(k) *Effective date.*—This section applies to any consolidated return year for which the due date of the income tax return (without regard to extensions) is on or after [the date that is sixty days after final regulations are filed with the Federal Register]. [Reg. § 1.1502-55.]

Application of Section 172(h): Regulations: Consolidated Groups

Application of Section 172(h): Regulations: Consolidated Groups.—Reg. § 1.1502-72, providing guidance regarding the treatment of corporate equity reduction transactions (CERTs), including the treatment of multiple step plans for the acquisition of stock and CERTs involving members of a consolidated group, are proposed (published in the Federal Register on September 17, 2012) (REG-140668-07) (corrected October 23, 2012).

☐ Par. 4. Section 1.1502-72 is added to read as follows:

§ 1.1502-72. Corporate equity reduction transactions.—(a) *In general.*—(1) *Scope.*—Section 172(b)(1)(E) and (h), §§ 1.172(h)-1 through 1.172(h)-5, and the rules of this section (the CERT rules) apply to determine whether a corporate equity reduction transaction (CERT) has occurred and to determine the consequences of the CERT, including rules governing the carryback of losses following a CERT, with respect to corporations that become, are, or cease to be members of a consolidated group.

(2) *Single entity treatment.*—(i) *In general.*—All members of a group are treated as a single taxpayer for purposes of the CERT rules. For example, if multiple members of a group acquire in total 50 percent or more (by vote or value) of the stock of another corporation, the group has engaged in a major stock acquisition (MSA) as defined in section 172(h)(3)(B) and § 1.172(h)-1(c)(2). The transactions and expenditures undertaken by a particular group member are generally not separately tracked; instead, the entire group is treated as a single applicable corporation.

(ii) *Debt and interest of group members.*—(A) *In general.*—The computation of a group's corporate equity reduction interest loss (CERIL) under section 172(h)(1) and § 1.172(h)-2(a)(2) for any loss limitation year (as defined in paragraph (a)(3) of this section) that is a consolidated return year includes the debt of all members and all interest deductions that are allowed on the group's consolidated return for that year. This rule applies regardless of whether any particular debt or interest expense is directly related to the CERT, whether any particular member was included in the group on the date of the CERT, or whether any particular debt would not exist in the group if the group had not engaged in the CERT. But see paragraph (a)(2)(iii) of this section (providing that intercompany transactions are generally disregarded).

(B) *Debt of acquired corporation.*—With respect to a corporation that joins a consolidated group (acquired corporation), in applying the CERT rules to consolidated return years that are loss limitation years, any debt of the acquired corporation is treated as debt of the acquiring group for purposes of applying the avoided cost rules of section 263A(f)(2)(A) on any measurement date after the inclusion of the corporation in the group. See section 172(h)(2) and § 1.172(h)-2(b) (applying the principles of section 263A(f)(2)(A)(ii)); see also § 1.263A-9(f)(2) (defining measurement dates).

(iii) *Intercompany transactions.*—In applying the CERT rules, intercompany transactions as defined in § 1.1502-13 are generally disregarded. For example, interest expense attributable to an intercompany obligation is not taken into account in computing the CERIL or three-year average of a group. However, a transaction between group members is not disregarded if a party to the transaction becomes a non-member pursuant to the same plan or arrangement. In such case, any transaction between group members, including a potential excess distribution (ED) as defined in section 172(h)(3)(C), § 1.172(h)-1(c)(3), and paragraph (f)(1) of this section, is tested on a separate entity basis under the CERT rules. It may also be tested as part of a larger, multi-step MSA. See § 1.172(h)-1(d)(2).

(iv) *Applicable corporation status following inclusion of member with preexisting CERT.*—(A) *Acquiring group treated as applicable corporation.*—If a corporation that is an applicable corporation (including by application of paragraph (b) of this section) with regard to a CERT occurring in a separate return year (pre-existing CERT member) joins a consolidated group, the group is treated as a single applicable corporation with regard to that CERT in the consolidated return year of the acquisition and any succeeding year. A corporation is a pre-existing CERT member regardless of whether the transaction at issue is an MSA that constitutes a CERT with respect to both a consolidated return year of the acquiring group and a separate return year of the acquired corporation.

(B) *End of separate tracking of target.*—Beginning on the first day on which a pre-existing CERT member is included in a consolidated group, the member ceases to be separately tracked as an applicable corporation. See paragraph (a)(2)(i) of this section. The CERT rules thereafter apply to the group, rather than to the member, with regard to any CERT for which the member had been an applicable corporation, including an MSA in which the member was acquired by the group. Therefore, beginning on the day on which the pre-existing CERT member is included in the group, no CERIL is computed with regard to the member, independent of the CERIL computed for the group. But see §1.1502-21(b)(2)(iv)(C) (providing for allocation and apportionment of a group's CERIL to specific group members) and §1.172(h)-5(b)(1) (relating to prohibition on carryback of a CERIL).

(3) *Loss limitation years.*—(i) *In general.*—This paragraph applies to identify loss limitation years of a consolidated group and corporations that have been members of a consolidated group. The taxable year in which a CERT actually occurs is a loss limitation year. Any other taxable year (potential loss limitation year) of any applicable corporation (including a consolidated group) constitutes a loss limitation year with regard to the CERT only if, under the carryforward rules of sections 172(b)(1)(A)(ii) and 381(c)(1), the potential loss limitation year would constitute the first or second taxable year following the taxable year of the corporation or consolidated group that actually engaged in the CERT that includes the date on which the CERT occurred. Except as otherwise provided in paragraph (a)(3)(ii) of this section, for purposes of this paragraph (a)(3), sections 172 and 381 are applied as if the inclusion of any corporation in a consolidated group or the deconsolidation of any member from a group were a transaction listed in section 381(a).

(ii) *Corporation joins group in an MSA.*—If a corporation joins a group in an MSA, no separate return year of the acquired corporation ending on or before it joined the acquiring group is treated as a loss limitation year for the purpose of determining the loss limitation years of the acquiring group or any corporation that deconsolidates from that group that relate to the MSA.

(iii) *Deconsolidating members.*—Under this paragraph (a)(3)(iii), a corporation that deconsolidates (deconsolidating member) from a group (former group) that is an applicable corporation may have loss limitation years with regard to a CERT of its former group. See paragraphs (b) (relating to postdeconsolidation status as applicable corporation) and (e)(1) of this section (providing for an irrevocable waiver of carrybacks such that a deconsolidating member is not treated as an applicable corporation). If the consolidated return year during which the deconsolidation occurs (year of deconsolidation) is a first or second loss limitation year with regard to the CERT, then certain separate return years of a deconsolidating member that is treated as an applicable corporation will constitute loss limitation years. If the year of deconsolidation is a first loss limitation year with regard to the CERT, the following two separate return years will constitute loss limitation years. If the year of deconsolidation is a second loss limitation year with regard to the CERT, the separate return year that immediately follows the year of deconsolidation will constitute a loss limitation year. If the deconsolidating member joins another consolidated group, the consolidated return years of that group may also constitute loss limitation years with regard to the CERT of the former group. See paragraph (a)(2)(iv) of this section (relating to inclusion of member with pre-existing CERT).

(4) *Application of rules to reverse acquisitions.*—In the case of any acquisition to which §1.1502-75(d)(3) applies (a reverse acquisition), for purposes of applying the CERT rules, the first corporation (as defined in §1.1502-75(d)(3)(i)) is treated as the corporation the stock of which is acquired, and the second corporation (as defined in §1.1502-75(d)(3)(i)) is treated as the corporation that acquires stock. In addition, for purposes of §1.172(h)-2(b)(3)(i) (identifying CERT costs of an MSA) in the case of a reverse acquisition, the fair market value of the stock acquired equals the fair market value of the stock of the first corporation that the stockholders (immediately before the acquisition) of the first corporation own immediately after the acquisition, rather than the fair market value of the stock of the second corporation.

(b) *Applicable corporation status following deconsolidation.*—(1) *In general.*—If a corporation deconsolidates in a loss limitation year from a group that is treated as an applicable corporation with regard to a CERT, the deconsolidating corporation and the former group are both treated as applicable corporations following the deconsolidation. If the corporation joins another consolidated group (acquiring group) following the deconsolidation, the rules of this section apply to the acquiring group, and this paragraph (b) applies with regard to the deconsolidation of any member from the acquiring group during

a loss limitation year associated with the CERT. See paragraph (a)(2)(iv) of this section regarding treatment of a group as a single applicable corporation following an acquisition; see also paragraph (a)(3)(ii) of this section for identification of loss limitation years following a deconsolidation. This paragraph (b) applies without regard to whether any particular corporation would on a separate entity basis have constituted an applicable corporation with regard to the CERT under section 172(b)(1)(E)(iii) and §1.172(h)-1(b), with or without the application of section 172(h)(4)(C) and paragraph (a)(2) of this section, or whether the CERT occurred in a consolidated return year. However, under this paragraph (b), the deconsolidating corporation may be treated as an applicable corporation with regard to a CERT of a former group only if the group engages in the CERT on or before the date of the deconsolidation, or if a pre-existing CERT member, as described in paragraph (a)(2)(iv)(A) of this section, joins the group on or before the date of the deconsolidation.

(2) *Exception if waiver filed.*—In general, a corporation that deconsolidates from a group (or the parent of a group acquiring the deconsolidating member), may, pursuant to paragraph (e)(1) of this section, make an irrevocable election to relinquish the carryback of all net operating losses (NOLs) (and attributable portions of consolidated net operating losses (CNOLs)) to taxable years of the former group and any preceding years. If such an election is made, the deconsolidating member is not treated as an applicable corporation with regard to any CERT of the former group after the deconsolidation. Any group that acquires the deconsolidating member is not treated as an applicable corporation with regard to any CERT of the former group solely as a result of the acquisition of that member. The former group will continue to be treated as an applicable corporation with regard to the CERT.

(3) *Examples.*—The following examples illustrate the rules of paragraph (a) of this section and this paragraph (b). For purposes of these examples, assume that all entities are domestic C corporations unless otherwise stated. Assume that all applicable corporations have substantial NOLs in their loss limitation years:

Example 1. Single entity treatment of acquisition indebtedness. (i) *Facts.* Corporation T is a calendar-year taxpayer that has significant debt outstanding, which was incurred to fund operations. Unrelated P is the common parent of a calendar-year consolidated group. The following steps occur pursuant to an integrated plan. On May 1, Year 5, P acquires 10 percent of the T stock for $100. On June 30, Year 5, T borrows $700 and immediately thereafter uses the money to redeem some of its shares from its shareholders. On the same day, the P group acquires all of the remaining T stock in exchange for $200. Assume that the $700 cash payment from T to the T shareholders is treated as a redemption. T is first included in the P group on July 1, Year 5. Under §1.172(h)-1(d)(2), the steps of the integrated plan (including the redemption of the former T shareholders) constitute a single MSA.

(ii) *Analysis.* T's short taxable year ending June 30, Year 5 is T's year of the CERT. The P group's consolidated return Year 5 is the taxable year of the CERT for the group. For purposes of allocating to the single MSA interest paid or accrued during the P group's loss limitation years (Years 5, 6, and 7) under §1.172(h)-2(b), the P group takes into account the debt of all members, including the $700 loan and all of T's other debt. See paragraph (a)(2)(ii)(B) of this section. The allocation of interest also takes into account all deductions for interest paid or accrued that are included in the consolidated return for the relevant loss limitation year. See paragraph (a)(2)(ii)(A) of this section.

Example 2. Loss limitation years if a corporation joins group in an MSA. Corporation T maintains a taxable year ending June 30. Unrelated X is the common parent of a calendar-year consolidated group. On March 31, Year 5, the X group acquires all of the T stock in a CERT, and T is first included in the X group on April 1, Year 5. On the date of the acquisition, both the X group and T constitute applicable corporations with regard to the Year 5 CERT. See §1.172(h)-1(b) and paragraph (a)(2) of this section. T's short taxable year ending on March 31, Year 5, was T's taxable year in which the CERT occurred. T's only loss limitation year with respect to the Year 5 CERT is its short taxable year ending on March 31, Year 5. See §1.172(h)-1(e) and paragraph (a)(3) of this section. Beginning on April 1, Year 5, T ceases to be separately tracked as an applicable corporation. See paragraph (a)(2)(i) and (iv)(B) of this section. The X group's year in which the CERT occurred is its consolidated return Year 5. The X group's loss limitation years with respect to the Year 5 CERT are its full taxable calendar Years 5, 6, and 7. See paragraph (a)(3)(i) and (ii) of this section.

Example 3. Loss limitation years of a group and deconsolidating member. (i) *Facts.* P is the common parent of a calendar-year consolidated group that includes S. On June 30, Year 6, a member of the P group engages in an acquisition that constitutes a CERT. S is not a party to the acquisition. On September 30, Year 6, S deconsolidates from the P group. No election under paragraph (e)(1) of this section is made with respect to the deconsolidation of S. Following its deconsolidation, S does not join in the filing of a consolidated return with another group, and it maintains a calendar taxable year.

(ii) *Analysis*. Because no election is made under paragraph (e)(1) of this section, following the deconsolidation, both the P group and S are treated as applicable corporations with regard to the Year 6 CERT. See paragraph (b)(1) of this section. The P group's loss limitation years with regard to the CERT are its consolidated return Years 6, 7, and 8. See section 172(b)(1)(E)(ii) and paragraph (a)(3)(i) of this section. S deconsolidates from the P group during consolidated return Year 6, which is the first loss limitation year with regard to the CERT. See paragraph (a)(3)(i) of this section. For purposes of applying paragraph (a)(3) of this section to identify loss limitation years, S is treated as deconsolidating from the P group in a transaction to which section 381(a) applies. Therefore, S's two taxable years that follow the deconsolidation, the short year ending December 31, Year 6, and the full taxable calendar Year 7, are its additional loss limitation years with regard to the Year 6 CERT. See paragraph (a)(3)(iii) of this section. See section 172(b)(1)(E)(i) and § 1.172(h)-5(b)(1) for rules regarding the prohibition on carryback of a CERIL.

Example 4. Loss limitation years if a pre-existing CERT member joins the group. (i) *Acquiring group has loss limitation years.* Corporation T maintains a calendar taxable year and does not join in the filing of a consolidated return. On July 1, Year 5, T engages in a CERT (Year 5 CERT). Unrelated X is the common parent of a calendar-year consolidated group that includes S. On December 31, Year 5, the X group acquires all of the outstanding T stock. T is first included in the X group on January 1, Year 6. The first loss limitation year with respect to the Year 5 CERT is T's calendar Year 5. See § 1.172(h)-1(e). As a result of the X group's acquisition of T, the X group is treated as a single applicable corporation with respect to the Year 5 CERT. See paragraph (a)(2)(iv) of this section. For purposes of applying paragraph (a)(3) of this section to identify loss limitation years, T is treated as joining the X group in a transaction to which section 381(a) applies. Because T has one loss limitation year with regard to the CERT before it joins the X group, the X group has two loss limitation years with respect to the Year 5 CERT: its calendar Years 6 and 7. See paragraph (a)(3)(i) of this section. However, the X group must test its acquisition of T under the CERT rules.

(ii) *Acquiring group has no loss limitation years.* The facts are the same as in paragraph (i) of this *Example 4*, except that the X group acquires T on January 31, Year 7. Because T has three loss limitation years before it is included in the X group (calendar Years 5 and 6, and a short taxable year ending on January 31, Year 7), none of the X group's consolidated return years are loss limitation years with regard to the Year 5 CERT. See section 172(b)(1)(E)(ii) and paragraph (a)(3)(i) of this section.

(iii) *Member deconsolidates from acquiring group.* The facts are the same as in paragraph (i) of this *Example 4*, except that S deconsolidates from the X group on June 30, Year 6. No election under paragraph (e)(1) of this section is made on the deconsolidation of S. Following its deconsolidation from the X group, S does not join in the filing of a consolidated return. T and the X group's loss limitation years remain the same as in paragraph (i) of this *Example 4*. Because no election is made under paragraph (e)(1) of this section with respect to S's deconsolidation, following the deconsolidation, S and the X group are both treated as applicable corporations with regard to T's Year 5 CERT. See paragraph (b)(1) of this section. S deconsolidates from the P group during consolidated return Year 6, which is the second loss limitation year with regard to the CERT. See paragraph (a)(3)(i) of this section. Therefore, following its deconsolidation, S's only loss limitation year with respect to the Year 5 CERT is its short taxable year July 1, Year 6 through December 31, Year 6. See paragraph (a)(3)(iii) of this section.

Example 5. Deconsolidation before group engages in CERT. Corporation T is a member of the P group, which maintains a calendar taxable year. On February 28, Year 4, T deconsolidates from the P group due to T's acquisition by the X group, which also maintains a calendar taxable year. T is included in the X group as of March 1, Year 4. No election under paragraph (e)(1) of this section is made on the deconsolidation of T from the P group. On March 31, Year 4, the P group engages in a CERT. Because the P group engages in the CERT after the date of the deconsolidation, T is not treated as an applicable corporation following the deconsolidation. See paragraph (b)(1) of this section. However, the X group must apply the CERT rules to the X group's acquisition of T.

Example 6. Member that engages in CERT deconsolidates with a waiver election. (i) *Facts.* P is the common parent of a calendar-year consolidated group. On March 31, Year 4, the P group engages in an MSA, when member T acquires all of the stock of T1. On June 30, Year 4, T and its subsidiaries (including T1) deconsolidate from the P group due to the acquisition of T by the X group. T and its subsidiaries are first included in the X group as of July 1, Year 4. The X group makes an election under paragraph (e)(1) of this section on the deconsolidation.

(ii) *Analysis.* Because an election under paragraph (e)(1) of this section is made on the deconsolidation of T and its subsidiaries from the P group, following the deconsolidation, only the P group is treated as an applicable corporation with regard to the March 31, Year 4 CERT. Neither T, T1, nor the X group is treated as an applicable corporation with regard to the March 31, Year 4 CERT, even though T directly engaged in the MSA, and T1 was the acquired corporation in that MSA. See paragraph (b)(2) of this section. However, the X group must apply the CERT rules to the X group's acquisition of T.

(c) *Identification and allocation of CERT costs.*—(1) *In general.*— The portion of an NOL that is treated as a CERIL is subject to limitation on carryback. See section 172(b)(1)(E)(i) and § 1.172(h)-5(b)(1). A CERIL is computed in part by identifying the deductions allowed for interest allocable to the CERT. The computation of interest allocable to a CERT under section 172(h)(2) and § 1.172(h)-2(b) takes into account all CERT costs as defined in § 1.172(h)-2(b)(3). This paragraph (c) contains rules applicable to the identification and allocation of CERT costs of a consolidated group.

(2) *Single entity treatment of CERT costs.*—The computation of interest allocable to a CERT in any particular loss limitation year of a consolidated group includes CERT costs incurred (including costs deemed incurred under this paragraph (c)) with regard to the CERT by all corporations that are members of a group during the loss limitation year.

(3) *CERT costs of acquired corporation.*—With respect to a corporation that joins a consolidated group (acquired corporation), for purposes of applying the CERT rules, any CERT costs incurred (or treated as incurred under this paragraph (c)) by the acquired corporation during separate return years prior to the acquired corporation's inclusion in the group are attributed to the acquiring group. Such costs are treated as having been incurred by the acquiring group for purposes of applying the avoided cost rules of section 263A(f)(2)(A) to any measurement date after the acquisition of the corporation. Those CERT costs are no longer separately identified as CERT costs incurred by the acquired corporation.

(4) *Allocation of CERT costs on deconsolidation.*—(i) *In general.*— This paragraph (c)(4) applies to determine the CERT costs allocable to a corporation that deconsolidates in a loss limitation year from a group that is treated as an applicable corporation with regard to a CERT. Under this paragraph (c)(4), CERT costs may be allocated to a deconsolidating corporation only if the group engages in the relevant CERT on or before the date of the deconsolidation, or if a pre-existing CERT member, as described in paragraph (a)(2)(iv)(A) of this section, joins the group on or before the date of the deconsolidation. This paragraph (c)(4) applies regardless of whether any particular corporation would have constituted an applicable corporation under section 172(b)(1)(E)(iii) and § 1.172(h)-1(b) without the application of section 172(h)(4)(C) and paragraph (a)(2) of this section, whether the CERT occurred in a consolidated return year, or whether any particular corporation actually incurred CERT costs.

(ii) *No waiver election made.*—If no election under paragraph (e)(1) of this section is made with regard to the deconsolidation, CERT costs incurred by the group (including costs treated as incurred by the group under this paragraph (c)) are allocated between the deconsolidating corporation and the former group, solely for purposes of computing allocable interest deductions of the deconsolidating corporation and the continuing group with regard to the CERT under section 172(h)(2) and § 1.172(h)-2(b). For purposes of computing interest allocable to the CERT under section 172(h)(2) and § 1.172(h)-2(b) during the loss limitation year of the former group that is the year of the deconsolidation, the CERT costs allocated to the deconsolidating member are included in the group's accumulated CERT costs on those measurement dates on which the deconsolidating corporation was included in the group. The portion of the group's total CERT costs that is allocated to a deconsolidating member equals the group's total CERT costs multiplied by a fraction, the numerator of which equals the value of the deconsolidating corporation immediately after its deconsolidation, and the denominator of which equals the value of the entire group immediately prior to the deconsolidation.

(iii) *Waiver election made.*—If an election under paragraph (e)(1) of this section is made with regard to a deconsolidation, no CERT costs are allocated to the deconsolidating corporation. All CERT costs remain with the former group for purposes of identifying its allocable interest deductions under section 172(h)(2) and § 1.172(h)-2(b) with regard to the CERT.

(5) *Examples.*—The following examples illustrate the rules of this paragraph (c). For purposes of the examples in this paragraph (c)(5), assume that all entities are domestic C corporations unless

otherwise stated. Assume that all applicable corporations have substantial NOLs in their loss limitation years:

Example 1. Aggregation of CERT costs of consolidated group and target. (i) *Facts.* P is the common parent of a calendar-year consolidated group that includes S1 and S2. On June 30, Year 5, S1 acquires all of the stock of T for $10 million. P incurs CERT costs of $100,000 and $250,000 for work performed by its outside counsel and an investment banker, respectively, that facilitates the acquisition. In addition, T incurs CERT costs of $175,000 for work performed by its outside counsel that facilitates the acquisition. All of these costs are incurred on or before the date of the acquisition. In all relevant years preceding its acquisition, T does not join in the filing of a consolidated return.

(ii) *Analysis.* For purposes of computing the P group's allocable interest deductions under section 172(h)(2) and § 1.172(h)-2(b), the P group's CERT costs include CERT costs incurred by all members of the P group. See paragraph (c)(2) of this section. In addition, when T joins the P group, the CERT costs incurred by T prior to its inclusion in the P group are attributed to the P group and are treated as having been incurred by the P group for purposes of applying the avoided cost rules of section 263A(f)(2)(A) to any measurement date after the acquisition of T. See paragraph (c)(3) of this section. As a result, the P group's accumulated CERT costs on July 1, Year 5, are $10,525,000 [$10,000,000 + $100,000 + $250,000 + $175,000]. See § 1.172(h)-2(b)(3) for rules defining CERT costs.

Example 2. Acquiring group treated as incurring CERT costs associated with unrelated CERT of target. T is a calendar-year taxpayer that does not join in the filing of a consolidated return. P is the common parent of a calendar-year consolidated group. P also owns 70 percent of the only class of T stock. During Year 4, T engages in a CERT. On June 30, Year 5, P acquires the remainder of the stock of T, and T is first included in the P group on July 1, Year 5. Following the acquisition, the P group is treated as an applicable corporation with regard to T's Year 4 CERT. See paragraph (a)(2)(iv) of this section. The P group's consolidated return Year 5 is the third and final loss limitation year with regard to the Year 4 CERT. See paragraph (a)(3)(i) of this section. The P group is treated as having incurred all of T's expenses allocable to the CERT for purposes of computing any CERIL for consolidated return Year 5. Because T was a member of the P group for less than the entire calendar taxable Year 5, T's CERT costs are included in the P group's accumulated CERT costs only on those measurement dates on which T is included in the group (that is, measurement dates on or after July 1, Year 5). See paragraph (c)(3) of this section and § 1.172(h)-2(b)(4). See also paragraph (d)(3)(iii) for rules relating to the interest history of a partial-year member.

Example 3. Allocation of CERT costs to deconsolidating member. (i) *Facts.* P is the common parent of a calendar-year consolidated group. P owns 60 percent of the sole class of stock of T, a calendar-year taxpayer. On January 31, Year 5, the P group engages in a CERT. On March 31, Year 5, P acquires the remainder of the stock of T, and T is first included in the P group on April 1, Year 5. On June 30, Year 6, T deconsolidates from the P group, with no election made under paragraph (e)(1) of this section.

(ii) *Analysis.* T is not a member of the P group at the time of the CERT. However, following its deconsolidation, T is treated as an applicable corporation with regard to the Year 5 CERT because the P group engages in the CERT before T deconsolidates, and no election is made under paragraph (e)(1) of this section on the deconsolidation. See paragraph (b)(1) of this section. Further, a portion of the P group's CERT costs is allocated to T for purposes of computing any CERIL of T (or of any group of which T becomes a member following its deconsolidation from the P group) with regard to the Year 5 CERT. See paragraphs (b)(1) and (c)(4)(ii) of this section. However, the CERT costs of the group otherwise allocated to T are included in the P group's accumulated CERT costs on those measurement dates during which T is included in the group (that is, measurement dates before July 1, Year 6). See paragraph (c)(4)(ii) of this section and § 1.172(h)-2(b)(4).

(d) *Determining the three-year average of a group.*—(1) *In general.*—Section 172(h)(2)(C) and § 1.172(h)-3(a) limit the amount of allocable interest deductions to the excess (if any) of the amount allowable as a deduction for interest paid or accrued by the taxpayer during the loss limitation year, over the average of interest paid or accrued by the taxpayer (the three-year average) for the three taxable years preceding the taxable year in which the CERT occurred (the lookback period). The computation under section 172(h)(2)(C)(ii) and § 1.172(h)-3(b) of a group's three-year average for the lookback period that is relevant to any loss limitation year includes interest paid or accrued (or treated as paid or accrued under this paragraph (d)) during the lookback period by all corporations that are members of the consolidated group during the loss limitation year.

(2) *Varying group membership.*—If group membership varies from one loss limitation year to another, a different three-year average is computed with regard to each loss limitation year of the group.

(3) *Interest history.*—(i) *Combination of interest history of acquired member with group history.*—With respect to a corporation that joins a consolidated group (acquired corporation), for purposes of applying the CERT rules, the interest paid or accrued (or treated as paid or accrued under this paragraph (d)) by the acquired corporation during each separate return year prior to its inclusion in the group is apportioned equally to each day within each of its separate return years. The interest apportioned to dates within the lookback period is then combined with the interest paid or accrued by the acquiring group and is treated as interest paid or accrued by the acquiring group during the lookback period for purposes of computing the three-year average that is relevant to any loss limitation year beginning with the consolidated return year during which the acquired corporation is first included in the group. For purposes of the CERT rules, the interest from the separate return years is no longer separately traced as interest paid or accrued by the acquired corporation. But see paragraph (d)(3)(iii) of this section for rules requiring proration of interest history attributable to corporations that are members of a group for less than an entire loss limitation year. The interest paid or accrued by a predecessor (as defined in § 1.172(h)-(1)(b)(2)) of a member of the group is similarly combined with the interest paid or accrued by the group. See § 1.172(h)-4(c)(2)(ii)(A).

(ii) *Interest treated as paid or accrued by a corporation that deconsolidates.*—(A) *In general.*—This paragraph (d)(3)(ii) provides rules that apply for purposes of determining any three-year average of a corporation that deconsolidates from a group (or a three-year average of any other group of which it becomes a member) and any three-year average of the group from which the corporation deconsolidates (former group). These rules apply to the computation of any three-year average with regard to a CERT of the former group or any other CERT.

(B) *Waiver election made.*—If an election under paragraph (e)(1) of this section is made with respect to the deconsolidation of a corporation from a group, then, following the deconsolidation, the deconsolidating member is treated as having paid or accrued zero interest during the period of its inclusion in the former group and preceding years. The group retains the interest history that would otherwise be allocated and apportioned to the deconsolidating member under this paragraph (d)(3)(ii).

(C) *No waiver election made.*—If no election under paragraph (e)(1) of this section is made with respect to the deconsolidation of a corporation, a portion of the group's amount of interest treated as paid or accrued during the period of the corporation's consolidation and any preceding years is allocated and apportioned to the deconsolidating corporation. The allocated and apportioned interest is subtracted from the group's interest history and is unavailable to the group (or any other group member) for purposes of computing a three-year average with regard to any loss limitation year of the group (or any other group member) after the year of deconsolidation. But see paragraph (d)(3)(iii) of this section for rules requiring proration of interest history attributable to corporations that are members of a group for less than an entire loss limitation year.

(D) *Method of allocation.*—If no election under paragraph (e)(1) of this section is made when a corporation deconsolidates, solely for purposes of the CERT rules, the corporation is treated as having paid or accrued interest equal to the amount of interest paid or accrued by the group in each consolidated return year through the date of the deconsolidation (including any combination of interest history pursuant to paragraph (d)(3)(i) of this section), multiplied by a fraction, the numerator of which equals the value of the deconsolidating corporation immediately after its deconsolidation, and the denominator of which equals the value of the entire group immediately prior to the deconsolidation.

(iii) *Proration of lookback period interest for members that are part of a group for less than the entire loss limitation year.*—If any member is included in the group for less than an entire consolidated return year that is a loss limitation year (partial-year member), then the group takes into account a pro rata portion of the partial-year member's amount of interest paid or accrued during the lookback period for purposes of determining a group's three-year average relevant to that loss limitation year. The amount of interest treated as paid or accrued that is subject to proration under this paragraph (d)(3)(iii) is the interest of the partial-year member that would otherwise be fully combined with the interest history of the acquiring group under paragraph (d)(3)(i) of this section (with regard to corporations acquired during the loss limitation year) or the interest that is otherwise allocated to a deconsolidating member under paragraph (d)(3)(ii) of this section. The pro rata amount equals the partial-year member's interest treated as paid or accrued for the dates of the lookback period, multiplied by a fraction, the numerator of which equals the number of days of the loss limitation year during which the partial-year member was a member of the group, and the denominator of which equals the number of days in the loss limitation year. This proration applies to interest paid or accrued during the entire lookback period, including portions of the lookback period during which the partial-year member was a member of the group.

(4) *Lookback period.*—(i) *In general.*—The lookback period with regard to a CERT is the three taxable years preceding the taxable year in which the CERT occurs. See section 172(h)(2)(C)(ii) and §1.172(h)-3(a). The lookback period that is relevant to any CERIL of a consolidated group is the three taxable years preceding the taxable year of the group that includes the date on which the CERT occurred. See §1.172(h)-5(a) (defining the date on which a CERT occurs if the CERT consists of multiple steps). This rule applies whether the group actually engaged in the CERT or is treated as an applicable corporation with regard to a CERT solely by application of paragraph (a)(2)(iv) of this section.

(ii) *Group not in existence for entire lookback period.*—If a group was not in existence for three taxable years prior to the consolidated return year that includes the date of the CERT, the lookback period includes the group's taxable years preceding the year of the CERT plus the preceding taxable years of the corporation that was the common parent of the group on the first day of the group's first consolidated return year (original common parent). If the group and the original common parent together have fewer than three taxable years that precede the consolidated return year that includes the date of the CERT, the lookback period will be deemed to include full 12-month periods that end on the calendar date that is one day prior to the date of organization of the original common parent.

(iii) *Group not in existence on date of CERT.*—If a group was not in existence on the date on which the CERT occurred, for purposes of determining the lookback period, the group's taxable years will be deemed to include the taxable years of the group's original common parent. If the original common parent was not in existence on the date of the CERT, or it does not have three taxable years that precede its taxable year that includes the date of the CERT, the group will be deemed to have additional 12-month taxable periods that end on the calendar date that is one day prior to the date of the original common parent's organization. From these deemed taxable periods, the group will identify the deemed period that includes the date on which the CERT occurred and the three immediately preceding deemed periods that constitute the lookback period. See §1.172(h)-5(a) regarding date on which CERT occurred in multi-step transaction.

(iv) *Interest history of corporations not in existence.*—If any member of a group is not in existence for the entire lookback period, for purposes of the CERT rules, that member is treated as having paid or accrued zero interest before its organization. But see §1.172(h)-4(c)(2)(ii) (regarding interest history of successors).

(5) *Examples.*—The following examples illustrate the rules of this paragraph (d). Unless otherwise stated, assume that all entities are domestic C corporations that have full, 12-month taxable years. Assume that all applicable corporations have substantial NOLs in their loss limitation years:

Example 1. Acquired member's interest history combined with interest history of group. (i) *Facts.* P is the common parent of a calendar-year consolidated group that includes S on all relevant dates. On December 31, Year 5, S acquires the stock of T in a CERT, and T is first included in the P group on January 1, Year 6. Membership in the P group is otherwise stable for all relevant years. Prior to joining the P group, T does not join in the filing of a consolidated return and maintains a calendar taxable year. T's amounts of interest paid or accrued in Years 2, 3, and 4, respectively, are $600, $200, and $400. The P group's amounts of interest paid or accrued in Years 2, 3, and 4, respectively, are $1,400, $1,000, and $1,200.

(ii) *Analysis.* The P group's loss limitation years are calendar Years 5, 6, and 7. See paragraph (a)(3)(i) of this section. Year 5 is also a loss limitation year for T. The P group's lookback period with regard to the CERT is calendar Years 2, 3, and 4. See paragraph (d)(4)(i) of this section. For purposes of computing any three-year average of the P group for its lookback period, on the acquisition of T, the interest history of T is generally combined with the interest history of the P group. See paragraph (d)(3)(i) of this section. However, because T is not a member of the P group on any date during consolidated return Year 5, the computation of the P group's three-year average relevant to Year 5 will not include any of T's interest paid or accrued during the lookback period. See paragraph (d)(3)(iii) of this section. Thus, the P group's three-year average for loss limitation Year 5 is $1,200 ([$1,400 + $1,000 + $1,200]/3). Because T is a member of the P group during each day of loss limitation Years 6 and 7, T's history of interest paid or accrued during the lookback period is fully included in the P group's computation of its three-year average relevant to loss limitation Years 6 and 7. See paragraph (d)(3)(i) and (iii) of this section. Thus, the P group's three-year average for loss limitation

Years 6 and 7 is $1,600 ([$1,400 + $1,000 + $1,200 + $600 + $200 + $400]/3).

(iii) *Interest combination if acquired member included in group for part of loss limitation year.* The facts are the same as in paragraph (i) of this *Example 1,* except that S acquires the stock of T on March 31, Year 5, and T is included in the P group for 275 days. Because T is a partial-year member of the P group during loss limitation Year 5, the computation of the three-year average relevant to loss limitation Year 5 includes the interest of T for the lookback period, prorated as required under paragraph (d)(3)(iii) of this section. Because T is in the P group for 275 days during Year 5, the computation of the P group's three-year average relevant to Year 5 takes into account an amount of T's interest history equal to T's actual amount of interest paid or accrued for each year of the lookback period, multiplied by a fraction equal to 275/365 (number of days of the loss limitation year during which T is a member of the P group divided by the number of days in the loss limitation year), or $452 ($600 x [275/365]), $151 ($200 x [275/365]), and $301 ($400 x [275/365]) for Years 2, 3, and 4, respectively.

Example 2. Lookback period if corporation with CERT history joins group. (i) *Facts.* P is the common parent of a calendar-year consolidated group. P also owns 55 percent of the sole class of stock of Corporation T, which maintains a taxable year ending June 30. On September 30, Year 4, T engages in a CERT. On December 31, Year 5, P acquires the remainder of the stock of T, and T is first included in the P group on January 1, Year 6.

(ii) *Analysis.* T's full taxable year ending June 30, Year 5, and its short year ending December 31, Year 5 are loss limitation years with regard to the September Year 4 CERT. The lookback period for the CERT relevant to these two loss limitation years is T's three taxable years ending on June 30, Years 2, 3, and 4. See section 172(h)(2)(C)(ii) and §1.172(h)-3(a). The P group's calendar Year 6 is its sole loss limitation year with regard to T's September Year 4 CERT. See paragraph (a)(3)(i) of this section. In determining any CERIL with regard to the P group's calendar Year 6, the lookback period is the three taxable years prior to the taxable year of the group that includes the date on which the CERT occurred. See paragraph (d)(4)(i) of this section. Therefore, the lookback period with regard to the P group's loss limitation Year 6 is calendar consolidated return Years 1, 2, and 3.

Example 3. Interest history if no waiver election made on member deconsolidation. (i) *Facts.* P is the common parent of a calendar-year consolidated group that includes S. The P group engaged in a CERT on December 27, Year 5. S deconsolidates from the P group on December 31, Year 5. No election under paragraph (e)(1) of this section is made on the deconsolidation of S. S's value immediately after its deconsolidation is $4,000. The P group's value immediately before S's deconsolidation is $10,000. The P group and its members engaged in no prior CERTs.

(ii) *Analysis.* Because the CERT occurs during the P group's calendar consolidated return Year 5, Years 5, 6, and 7 are the P group's loss limitation years. Because no election is made under paragraph (e)(1) of this section with regard to the deconsolidation of S, S is treated as an applicable corporation with regard to the Year 5 CERT under paragraph (b)(1) of this section and the interest history of the P group during the period of S's consolidation and any preceding years is allocated to S and the remaining members of the P group. See paragraph (d)(3)(ii)(C) of this section. The amount of the P group's interest for each year that is allocated to S is the amount of interest paid or accrued by the P group in the relevant consolidated return year multiplied by a fraction equal to 4,000 divided by 10,000 (the value of the deconsolidating corporation immediately after its deconsolidation divided by the value of the entire group immediately prior to the deconsolidation), or 2/5. See paragraph (d)(3)(ii)(D) of this section. The interest allocated to S is subtracted from the interest history of the group and is unavailable to the P group for purposes of computing a three-year average with regard to any loss limitation year of the P group after the year of the deconsolidation, including Years 6 and 7. The interest history allocated to S will be maintained by S to be used in the computation of any CERIL of S, or any CERIL of any group of which S is later a member. See paragraph (d)(3)(ii)(C) of this section.

(iii) *Waiver election filed.* The facts are the same as in paragraph (i) of this *Example 3,* except that an election under paragraph (e)(1) of this section is filed on the deconsolidation of S. As a result of that election, S is not treated as an applicable corporation with regard to the Year 5 CERT under paragraph (b)(2) of this section and none of the interest history of the P group is allocated to S under paragraph (d)(3)(ii)(B) of this section. Therefore, in any post-deconsolidation year, for purposes of computing a CERIL in connection with any CERT with regard to which S (or of any group of which S is later a member) is an applicable corporation, S is treated as having paid or accrued zero interest for the period of its inclusion in the P group and preceding years. The P group will retain the interest history that would otherwise be allocated to S. See paragraph (d)(3)(ii)(B) of this section.

Example 4. Interest history if no waiver election made for member that deconsolidates prior to CERT. (i) *Facts.* P is the parent of a calendar-year consolidated group that includes S. On December 31, Year 4, S deconsolidates from the P group. No election is made under paragraph (e)(1) of this section with regard to the deconsolidation. On July 1, Year 5, the P group engages in a CERT. The P group and its members engaged in no prior CERTs.

(ii) *Analysis.* Because no election is made under paragraph (e)(1) of this section with regard to the deconsolidation of S, the interest history of the P group is allocated between S and the remaining members of the P group. See paragraph (d)(3)(ii)(C) of this section. This allocation occurs despite the fact that, at the time of the deconsolidation, the P group has not engaged in a CERT. Therefore, for purposes of computing any three-year average for the P group relevant to the Year 5 CERT, the portion of the interest history allocated to S is unavailable to the P group for purposes of computing a three-year average with regard to any loss limitation year of the P group after the year of the deconsolidation. See paragraph (d)(3)(ii)(C) of this section.

Example 5. Interest history if waiver election made for member that deconsolidates and then engages in a CERT. (i) *Facts.* P is the parent of a calendar-year consolidated group that includes X. On December 31, Year 5, X deconsolidates from the P group and makes an election under paragraph (e)(1) of this section. After its deconsolidation, X maintains a calendar taxable year. During Year 7, X engages in a CERT.

(ii) *Analysis.* X's loss limitation years with regard to the Year 7 CERT are Years 7, 8, and 9. X's lookback period with regard to the CERT is comprised of its Years 4 and 5 in the P consolidated group, and X's separate return Year 6. See section 172(h)(2)(C)(ii) and paragraph (d)(4)(i) of this section. As a result of the filing of the election under paragraph (e)(1) of this section, none of the interest history of the P group is allocated to X. Therefore, for purposes of computing X's three-year average for loss limitation Years 7, 8, and 9, X is treated as having paid or accrued zero interest during Years 4 and 5 of the lookback period. See paragraph (d)(3)(ii)(B) of this section.

Example 6. Interest history if member deconsolidates mid-year. (i) *Facts.* P is the common parent of a calendar-year consolidated group that includes S. S deconsolidates from the P group on June 30, Year 5. No election under paragraph (e)(1) of this section is made on the deconsolidation of S. During Year 5, but prior to the deconsolidation, the P group engages in a CERT. S is not a party to the CERT, and, throughout its history in the group, S paid or accrued only nominal interest.

(ii) *Analysis.* The P group's lookback period is calendar Years 2, 3, and 4. Consolidated return Years 5, 6, and 7 are the P group's loss limitation years. Because no election is made under paragraph (e)(1) of this section with regard to the deconsolidation of S, the interest history of the P group is allocated between S and the remaining members of the P group. See paragraph (d)(3)(ii)(C) of this section. This is true although S played no part in the CERT, and it actually paid or accrued only nominal interest. In the consolidated return year of the deconsolidation (here, the P group's Year 5), S was a member for 181 days. Therefore, the P group includes in the computation of its three-year average relevant to Year 5 a pro rata portion of the interest history allocated to S. See paragraph (d)(3)(ii)(C) and (iii) of this section. The pro rata portion equals the group's interest history allocated to S under paragraph (d)(3)(ii)(C) and (D) of this section, multiplied by a fraction equal to 181/365 (number of days of the loss limitation year during which S is a member divided by the number of days in the loss limitation year). See paragraph (d)(3)(iii) of this section. The portion of the interest history allocated to S is excluded in its entirety from the computation of the group's three-year average relevant to Years 6 and 7. The interest history allocated to S will be used in the computation of any CERIL of S, and any CERIL of any group of which S is later a member. See paragraph (d)(3)(ii)(C) of this section.

Example 7. Group not in existence for the entire lookback period. (i) *Facts.* Corporation P is formed on October 1, Year 3, and maintains a calendar taxable year. On January 1, Year 4, P forms S in a transaction meeting the requirements of section 351. Beginning in Year 4, P files consolidated returns with S, its only subsidiary. The P group maintains a calendar taxable year. During Year 5, the P group engages in an ED.

(ii) *Analysis.* For purposes of limiting any CERIL related to the Year 5 CERT, the P group must measure its interest deductions for the three years preceding the taxable year in which the CERT occurs (three-year average). See section 172(h)(2)(C)(ii) and §1.172(h)-3(a). However, the P group was not in existence for three taxable years before the year that includes the date of the CERT (calendar Year 5). Rather, the P group was in existence for one full calendar taxable year (Year 4). Because the group does not have a three-year history, the lookback period includes the common parent's (P's) short taxable year (October 1 through December 31, Year 3), and is also deemed to include an additional taxable period (October 1, Year 2 through September 30, Year 3). See paragraph (d)(4)(ii) of this section. Further,

in computing the three-year average, the P group members are treated as having paid or accrued zero interest for dates on which they did not exist. However, the P group is treated as having paid any interest paid by P during its short taxable year (October 1 through December 31, Year 3). See paragraph (d)(4)(iv) of this section.

Example 8. Group not in existence prior to year of the CERT but target in existence. (i) *Facts.* Corporation P is formed on January 1, Year 4. On the same day, P organizes wholly-owned, special-purpose corporation S. T is an unrelated, calendar-year corporation with a significant tax history. On February 1, Year 4, S merges into T, with T surviving. In the merger, all of T's historic shareholders receive cash in exchange for their shares. Following the merger, P owns all of the outstanding stock of T, and P is treated as acquiring all the stock of T in an MSA. The P group files consolidated returns beginning in Year 4 and maintains a calendar taxable year. T is first included in the P group on February 2, Year 4.

(ii) *Analysis.* Neither P (the original common parent) nor the P group is in existence before the year that includes the date of the CERT (calendar Year 4). Therefore, for purposes of applying the interest allocation limitation of section 172(h)(2)(C) and §1.172(h)-3(a), the P group's lookback period is deemed to include three additional taxable periods (January 1 through December 31 for Years 1, 2, and 3). See paragraph (d)(4)(ii) of this section. Further in computing the three-year average, P is treated as having paid or accrued zero interest during the deemed years (January 1, Year 1 through December 30, Year 3). See paragraph (d)(4)(iv) of this section. However, with respect to the group's acquisition of T, the interest history of T is combined with the interest history of the P group. Because T is not a member of the P group for each day of loss limitation Year 4, the computation of the three-year average applicable to loss limitation Year 4 will include only a pro rata portion of the interest of T for the lookback period. See paragraph (d)(3)(i), (d)(3)(iii), and paragraph (iii) of Example 1 of paragraph (d)(5) of this section.

(e) *Election to waive carryback from all separate return years.*—(1) *In general.*—In addition to any other elections available under section 172(b)(3) and §1.1502-21(b)(3), if a member becomes a non-member of a group (former group), the former member may make an irrevocable election to relinquish the carryback of all NOLs (and attributable portions of CNOLs) to taxable years of the former group and any preceding years. If the former member becomes a member of another group (acquiring group) immediately after its deconsolidation from the former group, the election described in this paragraph (e)(1) is available only to the common parent of the acquiring group. The election is not an annual election and applies to all losses that would otherwise be subject to carryback to years of the former group (or preceding years) under section 172 or §1.1502-21(b). The election is binding on the deconsolidating corporation and any group of which it may become a member. Further, the election is available without regard to whether the former group is treated as an applicable corporation with regard to any CERT at the time of the deconsolidation. Any election under this paragraph (e)(1) by the common parent of an acquiring group must include all deconsolidating corporations that were members of the former group and that joined the acquiring group during the same consolidated return year of the acquiring group. The election is made in a separate statement entitled, "THIS IS AN ELECTION UNDER §1.1502-72(e)(1) TO WAIVE THE PRE- [insert the first taxable year following the deconsolidation of the former member(s) from the former group] CARRYBACK PERIOD FOR ALL NOLs AND ALL CNOLs ATTRIBUTABLE TO [insert the name(s) and EIN(s) of the corporation(s)]." The statement must be filed with the timely filed original return of the former member or the acquiring group for the first taxable year following the deconsolidation of the former member from the former group. See paragraphs (b)(2), (c)(4)(iii), and (d)(3)(ii)(B) of this section relating to treatment of a deconsolidating member making an election under this paragraph (e)(1).

(2) *Example.*—The following example illustrates the rules of this paragraph (e):

Example. P, a publicly-held corporation, is the common parent of a calendar-year consolidated group that includes T. On July 30, Year 5, the P group engages in a CERT. On December 31, Year 5, T deconsolidates from the P group, and it continues to maintain a calendar taxable year. With respect to its deconsolidation, T makes an election under paragraph (e)(1) of this section. As a result of such election, T is not treated as an applicable corporation with regard to the P group's Year 5 CERT and none of the CERT costs or interest history of the P group are allocated to T. See paragraphs (b)(2), (c)(4)(iii), and (d)(3)(ii)(B) of this section. On March 30, Year 6, the X group acquires all of the stock of T. The X group maintains a calendar taxable year. A portion of the X group's Year 6 CNOL is attributable to T under §1.1502-21(b)(2)(iv)(B). Because T filed an election under paragraph (e)(1) of this section with respect to its deconsolidation from the P group, no portion of the X group's Year 6 CNOL attributable to T can be carried back to any taxable years of T, of the P group, or any preceding years.

(f) *Excess distribution.*—(1) *Defined.*—Section 172(h)(3)(C) and § 1.172(h)-1(c)(3) provide that an ED means the excess (if any) of the aggregate distributions (including redemptions) made during a taxable year by a corporation with respect to its stock, over the greater of 150 percent of the average of such distributions (three-year distribution average) for the three taxable years immediately preceding such taxable year (distribution lookback period), or 10 percent of the fair market value of the stock of such corporation as of the beginning of such taxable year.

(2) *Determination of an ED by a group.*—(i) *Aggregation of distributions to non-members.*—For purposes of determining whether a group has made an ED during any consolidated return year (potential ED year), distributions by all members of the group to non-members during the potential ED year are aggregated and tested under section 172(h)(3)(C), § 1.172(h)-1(c)(3), and paragraph (f)(1) of this section.

(ii) *Distributions between members of the same group.*—Distributions between members of the same group are generally disregarded for purposes of applying the CERT rules. However, the preceding sentence does not apply if a party to the transaction is deconsolidated pursuant to the same plan or arrangement. See paragraph (a)(2)(iii) of this section.

(3) *Computation of three-year distribution average.*—(i) *In general.*—The computation under section 172(h)(3)(C)(ii)(I) and § 1.172(h)-1(f) of the group's three-year distribution average includes distributions made during the distribution lookback period to non-members by each corporation that is a member of the consolidated group during the potential ED year. Distributions made during the distribution lookback period by predecessors of those members are also included. See § 1.172(h)-4(d). The computation includes distributions made by corporations during separate return years, subject to additional rules of this paragraph (f) and paragraph (a)(2)(iii) of this section. If a corporation was a member of a prior group during a portion of a distribution lookback period, the distribution history of that corporation during taxable years of the prior group includes only distributions made by that corporation to non-members of the prior group.

(ii) *Corporation deconsolidated from a group.*—If a corporation deconsolidates from a group (former group), the corporation's actual distribution history is subtracted from the group's distribution history and is available to the deconsolidating corporation (or any group of which it becomes a member) for purposes of computing any three-year distribution average following the deconsolidation. The deconsolidating member's distribution history will be unavailable to the former group for purposes of computing its three-year distribution average with regard to any potential ED year of the former group after the year of deconsolidation. See § 1.172(h)-1(f)(1) (excluding from three-year distribution average those distributions treated as part of an MSA).

(iii) *Members included in group for less than entire loss limitation year.*—If any member is included in the group for less than an entire potential ED year (partial-year member), then a pro rata portion of the partial-year member's distribution history is computed under the principles of paragraph (d)(3)(iii) of this section and is included for purposes of determining the group's three-year distribution average relevant to that potential ED year.

(4) *Stock value and stock issuances of a group.*—(i) *Stock issuances taken into account in computing distributions.*—Stock issued by a member of a group is taken into account in applying section 172(h)(3)(E)(ii) and § 1.172(h)-5(c)(1) only if the stock is issued to a non-member. Intercompany stock issuances are disregarded. This rule is applicable whether the stock issuance occurred in the current group or a previous group.

(ii) *Value of stock of group.*—For purposes of applying section 172(h)(3)(C)(ii)(II), § 1.172(h)-1(c)(3), and paragraph (f)(1) of this section (relating to the fair market value of the stock of a distributing corporation), the value of the stock of the group is the value of the stock of all members, other than stock that is owned directly or indirectly by another member. But see section 172(h)(3)(E)(i) for rules regarding the exclusion of certain preferred stock for purposes of applying sections 172(h)(3)(C), § 1.172(h)-1(c)(3), and (f), and this paragraph (f). See also paragraphs (a)(2)(iii) and (f)(2)(ii) of this section, requiring separate entity analysis of certain transactions between members of a consolidated group.

(5) *Examples.*—The following examples illustrate the rules of this paragraph (f). For purposes of these examples, assume that all entities are domestic C corporations:

Example 1. Corporation deconsolidates from group. (i) *Facts.* P is the common parent of a calendar-year consolidated group that includes T. P owns 90 percent of the outstanding stock of T, and A (an unrelated party) owns the remaining 10 percent of the outstanding stock of T. T regularly makes distributions to its shareholders, P and A. On December 31, Year 4, X, the common parent of another calendar-year consolidated group, acquires all of the outstanding stock of T, and T deconsolidates from the P group. T is first included in the X group on January 1, Year 5. On March 31, Year 5, X makes a large distribution to its non-member shareholders. X makes no further distributions during its taxable year.

(ii) *Analysis.* The X group's distribution to its non-member shareholders on March 31, Year 5, is tested as a potential ED under section 172(h)(3)(C), § 1.172(h)-1(c)(3) and (f), and paragraph (f) of this section. The X group's distribution lookback period with regard to the potential ED is January 1 through December 31, for each of Years 2, 3, and 4. For purposes of computing the X group's three-year distribution average, the computation includes any distributions made by T to A, its former non-member shareholder, during the distribution lookback period, because T is a member of the X group during the year of the potential ED. See paragraph (f)(3) of this section. Distributions between members of the X group and between members of the P group are disregarded. See paragraph (f)(2)(ii) of this section.

Example 2. Integrated plan to deconsolidate. T is a wholly-owned subsidiary of P, and is a member of the P group. As part of a plan that includes the deconsolidation of T from the P group, T makes a distribution to P. Because T's distribution to P is part of an integrated plan that results in the deconsolidation of T, T's distribution to P is tested on a separate entity basis as a potential ED under section 172(h)(3)(C), § 1.172(h)-1(c)(3) and (f), and paragraph (f) of this section. See paragraphs (a)(2)(iii) and (f)(2)(ii) of this section. Therefore, the rules of section 172(h)(3)(C), § 1.172(h)-1(c)(3) and (f), and paragraph (f) of this section are applied based on the separate entity value and distribution history of T. See § 1.172(h)-1(d)(2) regarding testing of the distribution as part of a plan of major stock acquisition.

(g) *Life-nonlife groups.*—(1) *Scope.*—This paragraph (g) provides rules for applying the CERT rules to a group that elects under section 1504(c)(2) to file a consolidated return (life-nonlife group). See § 1.1502-47 (rules regarding lifenonlife groups).

(2) *Single entity treatment.*—(i) *In general.*—All members of a life-nonlife group are generally treated as a single taxpayer for purposes of the CERT rules. Accordingly, the rules of paragraphs (a) through (f) and (h) of this section and the rules of § § 1.172(h)-1 through 1.172(h)-5 are applied by treating the life-nonlife group as a single taxpayer, and are not applied on a subgroup basis. For example, all members of a life-nonlife group are treated as a single entity for purposes of determining whether a CERT has occurred under sections 172(h)(3)(B) and (C) and § 1.172(h)-1. See paragraph (a)(2)(i) of this section. Furthermore, all intercompany transactions between and within subgroups are generally disregarded. In addition, if a pre-existing CERT member becomes a member of a life-nonlife group, the life-nonlife group is treated as a single applicable corporation with regard to that CERT in the consolidated return year of the acquisition and any succeeding year. See paragraph (a)(2)(iv) of this section. If it is determined that a CERT exists, the amount of the CERIL is determined for the entire life-nonlife consolidated group as described in paragraph (g)(2)(ii)(A) of this section, and the CERIL is allocated to each subgroup as described in paragraph (g)(3) of this section.

(ii) *CERIL.*—(A) *Single CERIL computation.*—For any loss limitation year, a single CERIL is computed under section 172(h)(1) and § 1.172(h)-2(a)(2) for the life-nonlife group. The computation of the life-nonlife group's CERIL for any loss limitation year includes all life-nonlife group members' CERT costs, debt, and interest paid or accrued for that year.

(B) *Net operating loss.*—For purposes of determining CERIL of a lifenonlife group under section 172(h)(1) and § 1.172(h)-2(a)(2), the *net operating loss* of the group in any loss limitation year is the sum of the nonlife consolidated net operating loss (nonlife CNOL) (if any) and the consolidated loss from operations (consolidated LO) (if any) for that year. For this purpose, nonlife consolidated taxable income does not offset any LO, and consolidated partial life insurance company taxable income (as used in § 1.1502-47(g)) does not offset any nonlife CNOL.

(iii) *Carryover to separate return years.*—If any nonlife CNOL or consolidated LO that is attributable to a member of a subgroup may be carried to a separate return year (as defined in § 1.1502-47(d)(10)), the CERIL that is associated with the nonlife CNOL or consolidated LO is apportioned to each member, as relevant, under the method provided by § 1.1502-21(b)(2)(iv)(C)(1).

(iv) *Deconsolidation.*—If a member deconsolidates from a life-nonlife group without an election under paragraph (e)(1) of this section, then paragraphs (b)(1), (c)(4)(i) and (ii), and (d)(3)(ii)(A) and (C) of this section (relating to treatment of a deconsolidating member) apply to allocate CERT status, CERT costs, and interest history from the entire life-nonlife group to the deconsolidating member, and not from a specific subgroup.

(3) *Allocation of a CERIL.*—If a CERIL exists under paragraph (g)(2)(ii)(A) of this section, that CERIL is allocated to each subgroup that has a nonlife CNOL or consolidated LO. The amount of the nonlife CNOL and consolidated LO in a loss limitation year that constitutes a CERIL is equal to the total amount of the CERIL for the loss limitation year multiplied by a fraction, the numerator of which equals the nonlife CNOL or consolidated LO (as relevant), and the denominator of which equals the nonlife CNOL plus the consolidated LO.

(h) *Effective/applicability date.*—(1) *In general.*—Other than paragraph (e) of this section, the rules of this section apply to CERTs occurring on or after the date of publication of the Treasury decision adopting these rules as final regulations in the **Federal Register**. The rules of this section also apply to the deconsolidation of a member from, or the acquisition of a corporation by, a consolidated group that occurs on or after the date of publication of the Treasury decision adopting these rules as final regulations in the **Federal Register**. However, in each case, this section does not apply to any CERT, deconsolidation, or acquisition occurring pursuant to a written agreement that is binding before the date of publication of the Treasury decision adopting these rules as final regulations in the **Federal Register**.

(2) *Waiver election.*—Paragraph (e) of this section applies to the deconsolidation of a member from a consolidated group that occurs on or after the date of publication of Treasury decision adopting these rules as final regulations in the **Federal Register**, except that it does not apply to any deconsolidation occurring pursuant to a written agreement that is binding before the date of publication of the Treasury decision adopting these rules as final regulations in the **Federal Register**. [Reg. § 1.1502-72.]

Reporting Income and Deductions: Consolidated Group

Reporting Income and Deductions: Consolidated Group.—Amendments to Reg. §1.1502-76, revising the rules for reporting certain items of income and deduction that are reportable on the day a corporation joins or leaves a consolidated group, are proposed (published in the Federal Register on March 6, 2015) (REG-100400-14).

Par. 8. Section 1.1502-76 is amended:

1. By adding a sentence at the end of paragraph (b)(1)(i).
2. By revising paragraphs (b)(1)(ii)(A) and (B).
3. By adding paragraph (b)(1)(ii)(D).
4. By adding a sentence at the end of paragraph (b)(2)(i).
5. By revising paragraph (b)(2)(ii)(C)(9).
6. By removing the last sentence of paragraph (b)(2)(iii).
7. By removing the last sentence of paragraph (b)(2)(v).
8. In paragraph (b)(2)(vi)(C) by removing "paragraph (b)(2)(v)" and adding "paragraph (b)(2)(vi)" in its place.
9. By revising paragraph (b)(3).
10. By adding a sentence at the end of paragraph (b)(4).
11. By adding *Examples 8, 9*, and *10* to paragraph (b)(5).
12. By revising paragraph (b)(6).

The revisions and additions read as follows:

§1.1502-76. Taxable year of members of group.

* * *

(b) * * *

(1) * * *

(i) * * * If a corporation (S) becomes or ceases to be a member in a stock disposition or purchase for which an election under section 336(e) or section 338 is made, paragraphs (b)(1)(ii), (b)(2)(ii), and (b)(2)(iii) of this section do not apply to the transaction.

(ii) * * *

(A) *In general.*—(1) *End of the day rule.*—If S becomes or ceases to be a member during a consolidated return year, S's tax year ends, and (except as provided in paragraph (b)(1)(ii)(A)(2) or paragraph (b)(1)(ii)(B) of this section) for purposes of determining the period in which S must report an item of income, gain, deduction, loss, or credit, S is treated as becoming or ceasing to be a member at the end of the day on which its status as a member changes (end of the day rule).

(2) *Next day rule.*—If an extraordinary item (as defined in paragraph (b)(2)(ii)(C) of this section) results from a transaction that occurs on the day of S's change in status as a member, but after the event resulting in the change, and the item would be taken into account by S on that day, the transaction resulting in the extraordinary item is treated as occurring at the beginning of the following day for purposes of determining the period in which S must report the item (next day rule). The next day rule does not apply to any extraordinary item that becomes includible or deductible simultaneously with the event that causes the change in S's status.

(B) *Special rules for former S corporations.*—(1) *Beginning of the day rule.*—If an election under section 1362(a) is in effect for S immediately before S becomes a member, S is treated as becoming a member at the beginning of the day the termination of its election under section 1362(a) is effective (termination date), and S's taxable year ends at the end of the day preceding the termination date. See §1.1361-5(a)(3) for the treatment of certain qualified S corporation subsidiaries.

(2) *Previous day rule.*—If an extraordinary item (as defined in paragraph (b)(2)(ii)(C) of this section) results from a transaction that occurs on the termination date, but before or simultaneously with the event resulting in the termination of S's election under section 1362(a), and the item would be taken into account by S on that day, the transaction resulting in the extraordinary item is treated as occurring at the end of the previous day for purposes of determining the period in which S must report the item (previous day rule). See §1.1361-5(a)(3) for the treatment of certain qualified S corporation subsidiaries.

* * *

(D) *Coordination with sections 382 and 1374.*—If the day of S's change in status is also the date of an ownership change for purposes of section 382, the rules and principles of this section apply in determining the treatment of any item or asset for purposes of section 382(h). Accordingly, if the day of S's change in status is also a change date, the determination of net unrealized built-in gain or loss will reflect the application of both the end of the day rule and the next day rule, to the extent each applies. Moreover, items includible in the taxable year that ends as a result of S's change in status are not treated as occurring in the recognition period described in section 382(h)(7)(A), and items includible in the taxable year that begins as a result of S's change in status are treated as occurring in the recognition period. If S ceases to be a corporation subject to the tax imposed by section 1374 upon becoming a member of a consolidated group, or if S elects to be a corporation that is subject to such tax for its first separate return year after ceasing to be a member, S's items of recognized built-in gain or loss for purposes of section 1374 will include only the amounts reported on S's separate return (including items reported on that return under the previous day rule or the next day rule).

* * *

(2) * * *

(i) * * * If a member distributes or transfers assets in an intercompany transaction to which section 381(a) applies, a short taxable year of the distributor or transferor corporation is not taken into account either for purposes of determining the taxable years to which any tax attribute of the distributor or transferor corporation may be carried or for purposes of determining the taxable years in which an adjustment under section 481(a) is taken into account.

(ii) * * *

(C) * * *

(9) Any compensation-related deduction in connection with S's change in status (including, for example, a deduction for fees for services rendered in connection with S's change in status and for bonus, severance, and option cancellation payments made in connection with S's change in status);

* * *

(3) *Anti-avoidance rule.*—If any person acts with a principal purpose contrary to the purposes of this paragraph (b) to substan-

tially reduce the federal income tax liability of any person (including by modifying an existing contract or other agreement in anticipation of a change in S's status to shift an item between the taxable years that end and begin as a result of S's change in status), adjustments must be made as necessary to carry out the purposes of this section.

(4) * * * In addition, if S ceases to exist in the same consolidated return year in which S becomes a member, the due date for filing S's separate return shall be determined without regard to S's ceasing to exist in that year.

(5) * * *

Example 8. Allocation of certain amounts that become deductible on the day of S's change in status—(a) *Facts.* P purchases all of the stock of S, an accrual-basis, stand-alone C corporation, on June 30 pursuant to a stock purchase agreement. At the time of the stock purchase, S has outstanding nonqualified stock options issued to certain employees. The options did not have a readily ascertainable fair market value when granted, and the options do not provide for a deferral of compensation (as defined in §1.409A-1(b)). Under the option agreements, S is obligated to pay its employees certain amounts in cancellation of their stock options upon a change in control of S. P's purchase of S's stock causes a change in control of S, and S's obligation to make option cancellation payments to its employees becomes fixed and determinable upon the closing of the stock purchase. Several days after the closing of the stock purchase, S pays its employees the amounts required under the option agreements.

(b) *Analysis.* P's purchase of S's stock causes S to become a member of the P group at the end of the day on June 30. Under paragraph (b)(2)(ii)(C)(9) of this section, a deduction arising from S's liability to pay its employees in cancellation of their stock options in connection with S's change in status is an extraordinary item that cannot be prorated and must be allocated to June 30. The next day rule is inapplicable to this deduction because S's liability to pay its employees becomes deductible on the day of S's change in status simultaneously with the event that causes S's change in status. Consequently, a deduction for the option cancellation payments must be reported under the end of the day rule on S's tax return for the period ending June 30.

(c) *Success-based fees.* The facts are the same as in paragraph (a) of this *Example 8,* except that S also engages a consulting firm to provide services in connection with P's purchase of S's stock. Under the terms of the engagement letter, S's obligation to pay for these services is contingent upon the successful closing of the stock purchase. The stock purchase closes successfully, and S's obligation to pay its consultants becomes fixed and determinable at closing. To the extent S's payment of a success-based fee to its consultants is otherwise deductible, this item is an extraordinary item that cannot be prorated and must be reported under the end of the day rule on S's return for the period ending June 30. (See paragraph (b)(2)(ii)(C)(9) of this section.) The next day rule is inapplicable to the deduction because S's liability to pay its consultants becomes deductible on the day of S's change in status simultaneously with the event that causes S's change in status.

(d) *Unwanted assets.* The facts are the same as in paragraph (a) of this *Example 8,* except that, after closing on June 30, S sells to an unrelated party certain assets used in S's trade or business that are not wanted by the P group. Gain or loss on the sale of these assets is an extraordinary item that results from a transaction that occurs on the day of S's change in status, but after the event resulting in the change. Consequently, under the next day rule, the gain or loss must be reported on S's tax return for the period beginning July 1.

Example 9. Redemption that causes a change in status—(a) *Facts.* P owns 80 shares of S's only class of outstanding stock, and a person whose ownership of S stock is not attributed to P under section 302(c) owns the remaining 20 shares. On June 30, S distributes land with a basis of $100 and a fair market value of $140 to P in redemption of all of P's stock in S.

(b) *Analysis.* As a result of the redemption, S ceases to be a member of P's consolidated group on June 30. S will recognize $40 of gain under section 311(b) on the distribution of the land to P. The next day rule is inapplicable because S's gain becomes includible on the day of S's change in status simultaneously with the event that causes S's change in status. Consequently, S's gain must be reported under the end of the day rule in its taxable year ending June 30, during which S was a member of the P group. Under §1.1502-32(b)(2)(i), P's basis in its S stock is increased to reflect S's $40 gain immediately before the redemption of S's stock.

(c) *Partial redemption.* The facts are the same as in paragraph (a) of this *Example 9,* except that S distributes the land to P in redemption of 20 shares of P's stock in S. Thus, immediately after the redemption, P owns 75% (60 shares / 80 shares) of S's outstanding stock, and S's minority shareholder owns 25% (20 shares / 80 shares). The redemption does not satisfy the requirements of section 302(b) and is treated under section 302(d) as a distribution to which section 301 applies. The end of the day rule does not apply for purposes of determining whether P and S are members of the same consolidated group immediately after the redemption. Because P owns only 75% of S's stock immediately after the redemption, the distribution is not an intercompany distribution described in §1.1502-13(f)(2)(i). Thus, P may not exclude any amount of the distribution that is a dividend, and P's basis in S's stock is not reduced under §1.1502-32(b)(2)(iv). P may be entitled to a dividends received deduction under section 243(c) (but see section 1059(e)). For the reasons discussed in paragraph (b) of this *Example 9,* S's gain under section 311(b) must be reported under the end of the day rule in S's taxable year ending June 30, during which S was a member of the P group.

(d) *Distribution of loss property.* The facts are the same as in paragraph (a) of this *Example 9,* except that the land distributed by S to P has a fair market value of $60 rather than $140. The end of the day rule applies for purposes of determining the taxable year in which S must take into account its realized loss on the distribution of the land. Thus, under the end of the day rule, S's loss on the distribution of the land, which occurs simultaneously with S's ceasing to be a member, is taken into account in S's taxable year that ends as a result of the redemption. However, the end of the day rule does not apply for other purposes; for example, the rule does not apply in determining whether the transaction is an intercompany distribution or in determining the attributes (as defined in §1.1502-13(b)(6)) of the loss. Therefore, because S is not a member immediately after the distribution, S's loss on the distribution is not recognized under section 311(a). Under the end of the day rule, the loss is taken into account as a noncapital, nondeductible expense on the P group's consolidated return, and under §1.1502-32(b)(1)(i), P's basis in its S stock is decreased by $40 immediately before S leaves the group.

Example 10. Extraordinary item of S corporation—(a) *Facts.* On July 1, P purchases all the stock of S, an accrual-basis corporation with an election in effect under section 1362(a). Prior to the sale, S had engaged a consulting firm to find a buyer for S's stock, and the consulting firm's fee was contingent upon the successful closing of the sale of S's stock.

(b) *Analysis.* To the extent S's payment of the success-based fee to its consultants is otherwise deductible, this item is an extraordinary item (see paragraph (b)(2)(ii)(C)(9) of this section) that becomes deductible on July 1 simultaneously with the event that terminates S's election as an S corporation. Under paragraph (b)(1)(ii)(B)(2) of this section, S's obligation to pay the fee is treated as becoming deductible on June 30 under the previous day rule.

(6) *Effective/applicability date.*—Paragraphs (b)(2)(i) and (b)(4) of this section apply to consolidated return years beginning on or after the date these regulations are published as final regulations in the **Federal Register**. Otherwise, this paragraph (b) applies to corporations becoming or ceasing to be members of consolidated groups on or after the date these regulations are published as final regulations in the **Federal Register**.

* * *

Deduction for Business Interest Expense: Limitation

Deduction for Business Interest Expense: Limitation.—Amendments to Reg. §1.1502-79, regarding the limitation on the deduction for business interest expense after the enactment of recent tax legislation, are proposed (published in the Federal Register on December 28, 2018) (REG-106089-18).

Par. 20. Section 1.1502-79 is amended by adding paragraph (f) to read as follows:

§1.1502-79. Separate return years.

* * *

(f) *Disallowed business interest expense carryforwards.*—For the treatment of disallowed business interest expense carryforwards (within the meaning of §1.163(j)-1) of a member arising in a separate return limitation year, see §1.163(j)-5(d) and (f).

Consolidated Returns: Nonapplicability of Code Sec. 357(c)

Consolidated Returns: Nonapplicability of Code Sec. 357(c).—Amendments to Reg. §1.1502-80, clarifying that, in certain transfers described in Code Sec. 351 between members of a consolidated group, a transferee's assumption of certain liabilities described in section 357(c)(3) will not reduce the transferor's basis in the transferee's stock received in the transfer, are proposed (published in the Federal Register on November 14, 2001) (REG-137519-01).

☐ Par. 2. In §1.1502-80, paragraph (d) is revised to read as follows:

§1.1502-80. Applicability of other provisions of law.

* * *

(d) *Non-applicability of section 357(c).*—(1) *In general.*—Section 357(c) does not apply to cause the transferor to recognize gain in any transaction to which §1.1502-13 applies, if such transaction occurs in a consolidated return year beginning on or after the date these regulations are published as final regulations in the Federal Register. Notwithstanding the foregoing, for purposes of determining the transferor's basis in property under section 358(a) received in a transfer described in section 351, section 358(d)(2) shall operate to exclude liabilities described in section 357(c)(3)(A), other than those also described in section 357(c)(3)(B), from the computation of the amount of liabilities assumed that is treated as money received under section 358(d)(1), if such transfer occurs in a consolidated return year beginning on or after the date these regulations are published as final regulations in the Federal Register. This paragraph (d)(1) does not apply to a transaction if the transferor or transferee becomes a nonmember as part of the same plan or arrangement. The transferor (or transferee) is treated as becoming a nonmember once it is no longer a member of a consolidated group that includes the transferee (or transferor). For purposes of this paragraph (d)(1), any reference to a transferor or transferee includes, as the context may require, a reference to a successor or predecessor. For rules regarding the application of section 357(c) to transactions occurring in consolidated return years beginning on or after January 1, 1995, but before the date these regulations are published as final regulations in the Federal Register, see §1.1502-80(d) in effect prior to the date these regulations are published as final regulations in the Federal Register (see 26 CFR part 1 revised April 1, 2001).

(2) *Examples.*—The principles of paragraph (d)(1) of this section are illustrated by the following examples:

Example 1. P, S, and T are members of a consolidated group. P owns all of the stock of S and T with bases of $30 and $20, respectively. S has assets with a total fair market value equal to $100 and an aggregate basis of $30 and liabilities of $40. S merges into T in a transaction described in section 368(a)(1)(A) (and in section 368(a)(1)(D)). Section 357(c) does not apply to cause S to recognize gain in the merger. P's basis in T's stock increases to $50 ($30 plus $20), and T succeeds to S's $30 basis in the assets transferred and the $40 of liabilities.

Example 2. P owns all the stock of S1. S1 has assets with a total fair market value equal to $100 and an aggregate basis of $30. S1 has $40 of liabilities, $5 of which are described in section 357(c)(3)(A), but not section 357(c)(3)(B), and $35 of which are not described in section 357(c)(3)(A). S1 transfers its assets to a newly formed subsidiary, S2, in exchange for stock of S2 and S2's assumption of the liabilities of $40 in a transaction to which section 351 applies. Section 357(c) does not apply to cause S1 to recognize gain in connection with the transfer. For purposes of determining S1's basis in the S2 stock it received in the exchange, section 358(d)(2) operates to exclude $5 of the liabilities from the computation of the amount of liabilities assumed that are treated as money received under section 358(d)(1). S1's basis in the S2 stock received in the exchange is a $5 excess loss account (reflecting its $30 basis in the assets transferred reduced by $35, the amount of liabilities assumed that are not described in section 357(c)(3)(A)).

* * *

Consolidated Groups: Loss Limitation Rules

Consolidated Groups: Loss Limitation Rules.—Amendments to Reg. §1.1502-80, relating to the deductibility of losses recognized on dispositions of subsidiary stock by members of a consolidated group, the consequences of treating subsidiary stock as worthless, and when stock of a member of a consolidated group may be treated as worthless, are proposed (published in the Federal Register on March 18, 2004) (REG-153172-03).

☐ Par. 4. In §1.1502-80, paragraph (c) is revised to read as follows:

§1.1502-80. Applicability of other provisions of law.

[The text of this proposed §1.1502-80(c) is the same as the text of §1.1502-80T(c) as added by T.D. 9118.]

Consolidated Returns: Alaska Native Corporations

Consolidated Returns: Alaska Native Corporations.—Temporary Reg. §1.1502-81T, relating to corporations included in a consolidated return with a Native Corporation established under the Alaska Native Claims Settlement Act, is also proposed as a final regulation and, when adopted, would become Reg. §1.1502-81 (published in the Federal Register on March 18, 1987).

§1.1502-81. Alaska Native Corporations.

Deduction for Business Interest Expense: Limitation

Deduction for Business Interest Expense: Limitation.—Amendments to Reg. §§1.1502-90 and 1.1502-91, regarding the limitation on the deduction for business interest expense after the enactment of recent tax legislation, are proposed (published in the Federal Register on December 28, 2018) (REG-106089-18).

Par. 21. Section 1.1502-90 is amended by revising the entry for §1.1502-98 and adding an entry for §1.1502-99(d) to read as follows:

§1.1502-90. Table of contents.

* * *

§1.1502-98 Coordination with sections 383 and 163(j).

§1.1502-99 Effective dates.

* * *

(d) Application to section 163(j).

Par. 22. Section 1.1502-91 is amended by revising paragraph (e)(2) to read as follows:

§1.1502-91. Application of section 382 with respect to a consolidated group.

* * *

(e) * * *

(2) *Example*—(i) *Facts.* The L group has a consolidated net operating loss arising in Year 1 that is carried over to Year 2. The L loss group has an ownership change at the beginning of Year 2.

(ii) *Analysis.* The net operating loss carryover of the L loss group from Year 1 is a pre-change consolidated attribute because the L group was entitled to use the loss in Year 2 and therefore the loss was described in paragraph (c)(1)(i) of this section. Under paragraph (a)(2)(i) of this section, the amount of consolidated taxable income of the L group for Year 2 that may be offset by this loss carryover may not exceed the consolidated section 382 limitation of the L group for that year. See §1.1502-93 for rules relating to the computation of the consolidated section 382 limitation.

(iii) *Business interest expense.* The facts are the same as in the *Example* in paragraph (e)(2)(i) of this section, except that, rather than a consolidated net operating loss, a member of the L group pays or accrues a business interest expense in Year 1 for which a deduction is disallowed in that year under section 163(j) and §1.163(j)-2(b). The disallowed business interest expense is carried over to Year 2 under section 163(j)(2) and §1.163(j)-2(c). Thus, the disallowed business interest expense carryforward is a pre-change loss. Under section 163(j), the L loss group is entitled to deduct the carryforward in Year 2; however, the amount of consolidated taxable income of the L group for Year 2 that may be offset by this carryforward may not exceed the consolidated section 382 limitation of the L group for that year. See §1.1502-98(b) (providing that §§1.1502-91 through 1.1502-96 apply section 382 to business interest expense, with appropriate adjustments).

* * *

Consolidated Returns: Redetermination of Unrealized Built-In Gain and Loss

Consolidated Returns: Redetermination of Unrealized Built-In Gain and Loss.—Amendments to Reg. § 1.1502-91, requiring a loss group or loss subgroup to redetermine its consolidated net unrealized built-in gain and loss in certain circumstances, are proposed (published in the Federal Register on October 24, 2011) (REG-133002-10).

☐ Par. 2. Section 1.1502-91 is amended by:

1. Revising paragraph (g)(1).
2. Adding paragraphs (g)(7) and (g)(8).
3. Revising paragraph (h)(2) and the heading of paragraph (h)(4).
4. Adding paragraph (k).

The revisions and additions read as follows:

§ 1.1502-91. Application of section 382 with respect to a consolidated group.

* * *

(g) *Net unrealized built-in gain and loss.*—(1) *In general.*—The determination of whether a loss group or loss subgroup has a net unrealized built-in gain (NUBIG) or loss (NUBIL) under section 382(h)(3) is based on the aggregate amount of the separately determined NUBIGs or NUBILs (including items of built-in income and deduction described in section 382(h)(6)) of each member that is included in the loss group or loss subgroup, as the case may be, under paragraph (g)(2) of this section. The threshold requirement under section 382(h)(3)(B) applies on an aggregate basis.

(i) *Members included in group.*—If a member is not included in the determination of whether a loss group or loss subgroup has a NUBIL under paragraph (g)(2)(ii) or (g)(2)(iv) of this section, that member is not included in the loss group or loss subgroup. See § 1.1502-94(c) (relating to built-in gain or loss of a new loss member) and § 1.1502-96(a) (relating to the end of separate tracking of certain losses).

(ii) *Determination of separate NUBIG or NUBIL.*—For purposes of determining a member's separate NUBIG or NUBIL—

(A) Stock of a subsidiary that is a member of the loss group or loss subgroup (an included subsidiary) is disregarded, except as provided for in paragraph (g)(7) of this section. For this purpose, the term stock includes stock described in section 1504(a)(4) and § 1.382-2T(f)(18)(ii) and (f)(18)(iii);

(B) Intercompany obligations are disregarded; and

(C) Deferred amounts, such as amounts deferred under section 267 or § 1.1502-13, are built-in items unless they are deferred with respect to—

(1) An intercompany obligation; or

(2) A share of stock of an included subsidiary; however, if an amount deferred with respect to a share of such stock is taken into account at any time during the recognition period (whether or not any such loss amount is absorbed), NUBIG or NUBIL must be redetermined in accordance with paragraph (g)(7) of this section.

* * *

(7) *Redetermination of NUBIG or NUBIL of a loss group or loss subgroup to reflect unduplicated built-in gain or loss with respect to stock of an included subsidiary.*—(i) *In general.*—This paragraph (g)(7) applies if, during the recognition period, any member of the consolidated group directly or indirectly takes into account any gain or loss with respect to a share of stock of an included subsidiary (S) that was held by another member of the loss group or loss subgroup immediately before the change date, regardless of whether any such loss is absorbed. If this paragraph (g)(7) applies, the loss group or loss subgroup must redetermine its NUBIG or NUBIL to include any unduplicated built-in gain or loss with respect to the S share in accordance with the provisions of paragraphs (g)(7)(ii) and (g)(7)(iii) of this section. The redetermination is given effect immediately before the time the gain or loss on stock of an included subsidiary is taken into account. The redetermined NUBIG or NUBIL does not affect the tax treatment of transactions taken into account prior to the event that causes a redetermination of NUBIG or NUBIL under this paragraph (g)(7). However, the redetermined NUBIG or NUBIL is effective for all purposes immediately before the gain or loss on stock of an included subsidiary is taken into account. Thus, for example, the redetermined NUBIG or NUBIL is used to determine whether the loss group or subgroup is a NUBIG or NUBIL group, as well as whether the group meets the threshold requirement of section 382(h)(3)(B), at the time of the redetermination.

(ii) *Computation of unduplicated built-in gain or loss with respect to shares of S stock that are subject to this paragraph (g)(7).*—The loss group or loss subgroup computes its unduplicated built-in gain or loss with respect to each share of S stock that is subject to this paragraph (g)(7) by first treating the basis in the share as tentatively adjusted immediately before the change date or, in the case of an amount with respect to S stock that was deferred on the change date,

as of the date of the transaction that gave rise to the amount, as though the following occurred immediately before the ownership change or the transaction that gave rise to the deferred amount—

(A) *Deemed recognition of built-in gain or loss of lower-tier included subsidiaries.*—The separate NUBIG and NUBIL of S and all included subsidiaries that are lower-tier to S are treated as recognized, taken into account, and absorbed.

(B) *Tiering up of recognized amounts.*—All amounts deemed recognized, taken into account, and absorbed under paragraph (g)(7)(ii)(A) of this section are then deemed to tier up under the principles of § 1.1502-32 to tentatively adjust the basis in all of the S shares that are subject to this paragraph (g)(7).

(C) *Unduplicated gain or loss with respect to S stock.*—If the aggregate tentatively adjusted basis in the S shares subject to this paragraph (g)(7) exceeds the aggregate fair market value of those shares immediately before the change date or, in the case of a deferred amount, on the date of the transaction that gave rise to the item, the excess is the unduplicated loss with respect to those shares. Alternatively, if the aggregate fair market value of the S shares subject to this paragraph (g)(7) exceeds the aggregate tentatively adjusted basis in those shares on such date, the excess is the unduplicated gain with respect to those shares.

(iii) *Redetermination of the group's NUBIG or NUBIL.*—The loss group or loss subgroup's redetermined NUBIG or NUBIL is the sum of—

(A) The loss group or loss subgroup's NUBIG or NUBIL as originally determined without regard to the stock of any included subsidiary;

(B) Any unduplicated gain or loss with respect to a share of stock of an included subsidiary that was previously included in the loss group or loss subgroup's NUBIG or NUBIL under this paragraph (g)(7); and

(C) The unduplicated gain or loss on shares of S stock computed under paragraph (g)(7)(ii) of this section.

(iv) *Anti-avoidance rule.*—If any person acts with a principal purpose contrary to the purposes of this paragraph (g), to avoid the effect of the rules of this paragraph (g), or to apply the rules of this paragraph (g) to avoid the effect of any other provision of the consolidated return regulations, adjustments must be made as necessary to carry out the purposes of this paragraph (g).

(8) *Examples.*—The following examples illustrate the application of the provisions of paragraph (g) of this section. Unless otherwise stated, P is the common parent of a consolidated group that is a loss group and all members of the P group are included subsidiaries with respect to the loss group. P can establish that its gains are recognized built-in gains; P cannot establish that its losses are not recognized built-in losses. In addition, the threshold requirement of section 382(h)(3)(B) is satisfied. All other relevant facts are set forth in the examples.

Example 1. Basic application of provision. (i) *Facts.* On January 1, Year 1, P owns the sole outstanding share of S stock (basis $210, value $160) and the sole outstanding share of M stock. S owns the sole outstanding share of S1 stock (basis $100, value $80) and Truck (basis $70, value $80). S1 owns three of the five outstanding shares of S2 common stock (basis $40, value $20 for each share; thus, basis $120, value $60 in the aggregate). S2 owns Truck 2 (basis $70, value $40) and Truck 3 (basis $30, value $40). M owns the fourth of the five outstanding shares of S2 stock. X, a nonmember of the P group, owns the fifth outstanding share of S2 stock. January 1, Year 1, is a change date for the P group.

(ii) *Determination of the separate NUBIG or NUBIL of each member of the P loss group.* (A) *S2's separate NUBIG or NUBIL.* S2's assets are Truck 2 (with a built-in loss of $30) and Truck 3 (with a built-in gain of $10); therefore, S2 has a NUBIL of $20.

(B) *S1's separate NUBIG or NUBIL.* S1's only assets are the shares of S2 stock, which are disregarded under paragraph (g)(1)(ii)(A) of this section; therefore, S1 has a NUBIG or NUBIL of zero.

(C) *S's separate NUBIG or NUBIL.* S's assets are Truck (with a built-in gain of $10) and the share of S1 stock (which is disregarded); therefore, S has a NUBIG of $10.

(D) *M's separate NUBIG or NUBIL.* M's only asset is the share of S2 stock, which is disregarded under paragraph (g)(1)(ii)(A) of this section; therefore, M has a NUBIG or NUBIL of zero.

(E) *P's separate NUBIG or NUBIL.* P's only assets are the shares of M and S stock, which are disregarded; therefore, P has a NUBIG or NUBIL of zero.

(iii) *Determination of the P group's NUBIG or NUBIL.* The P group has a NUBIL of $10, reflecting the sum of S2's $20 NUBIL and S's $10 NUBIG.

Example 2. Transfer of shares of stock of an included subsidiary during recognition period. (i) *Sale to nonmember.* (A) *Facts.* The facts are the same as in *Example 1.* In addition, in Year 4, S sells its share of S1 stock for $65 to an unrelated party. At the time of the sale, S's basis in the share had been reduced to $90 due to adjustments for depreciation on S2's assets that tiered up under § 1.1502-32. (No adjustments are made to S's basis in the S1 share under § 1.1502-36, including by reason of an election to waive stock loss or reattribute losses.) As a result of the sale of the S1 share during the recognition period, the P group must redetermine its NUBIL under paragraph (g)(7) of this section.

(B) *Redetermination of the P group's NUBIG or NUBIL.* (1) *Unduplicated built-in gain or loss with respect to S1 share.* Under paragraph (g)(7)(ii)(A) of this section, the unduplicated built-in gain or loss with respect to the S1 share sold in Year 4 is computed by first treating the separate NUBIG or NUBIL of S1 and S2 (the only included subsidiary that is lower-tier to S1) as having been recognized, taken into account, and absorbed immediately before the change date. Under paragraph (g)(7)(ii)(B) of this section, those amounts are then treated as tiering up under the principles of § 1.1502-32 and tentatively adjusting S's basis in its S1 share, in order to identify the unduplicated gain or loss in the basis of the share under paragraph (g)(7)(ii)(C) of this section. S1 has no separate NUBIG or NUBIL to be treated as recognized, taken into account, and absorbed. S2 has a $20 separate NUBIL that is treated as recognized, taken into account, and absorbed and that is then treated as tiering up to adjust S's basis in the S1 share under the principles of § 1.1502-32. As a result, $12 of S2's $20 NUBIL would be treated as tiering up to S1 through the three S2 shares (of the total five outstanding) held by S1, and that $12 would then be treated as tiering up through S1 to tentatively adjust S's basis in the S1 share. S's tentatively reduced basis in the S1 share is therefore $100 - $12, or $88. Because the tentatively reduced basis of the share exceeds the value of the share by $8 ($88 - $80), S has an $8 unduplicated loss in its basis in its S1 stock.

(2) *Redetermined NUBIG or NUBIL of the P group.* Immediately before S takes into account the $25 loss on the sale of its share of S1 stock, the P group's NUBIL is redetermined to be $18, the sum of S2's NUBIL of $20, S1's NUBIL of $0, S's NUBIG of $10, P's NUBIG or NUBIL of $0, M's NUBIG or NUBIL of $0, and the $8 unduplicated loss in the S1 stock.

(C) *Effect of redetermination.* Of the $25 loss on the sale of the S1 share, $20 is recognized built-in loss, but the group only has an $18 NUBIL and so only $18 of the recognized built-in loss is subject to limitation under section 382.

(ii) *Nonrecognition transfer to member followed by sale to nonmember.* The facts are the same as in paragraph (i)(A) of this *Example 2,* except that, in Year 3, M1 joined the P group and S transferred its share of S1 stock to M1 in a transaction qualifying under section 351; as a result, it is M1, not S, that sells the S1 share to X in Year 4. The analysis and results are the same as in paragraphs (i)(B) and (i)(C) of this *Example 2* because this section applies when any member of the group recognizes gain or loss with respect to stock of an included subsidiary that was held by a member of the loss group immediately before the change date.

Example 3. Recognition of built-in loss prior to stock sale. (i) *Facts.* The facts are the same as in paragraph (i)(A) of *Example 2* except that, in addition, in Year 2, S2 sold Truck 2 and recognized the $30 built-in loss on Truck 2, and the P group absorbed the $30 loss. The loss is a recognized built-in loss under section 382(h)(2)(B) and thus subject to limitation to the extent of the originally determined $10 NUBIL.

(ii) *Redetermination of the P group's NUBIG or NUBIL.* (A) *Unduplicated built-in gain or loss with respect to the S1 share.* Because unduplicated stock gain or loss is computed immediately before the change date, the unduplicated stock loss is $8 for the reasons set forth in paragraph (i)(B)(1) of *Example 2.*

(B) *Redetermined NUBIG or NUBIL of the P group.* The computation of the P group's redetermined NUBIG or NUBIL is the same as in paragraph (i)(B)(2) of *Example 2,* except that the $30 of recognized built-in loss in Year 2 reduces the P group's $10 NUBIL (before NUBIL is redetermined under paragraph (g)(7) of this section) to zero. As a result, immediately before the sale of the S1 share, the P group's NUBIL is redetermined to be $8, which is the sum of zero and the $8 unduplicated loss in the S1 stock.

(iii) *Effect of redetermination.* Of the $25 loss on the sale of the S1 share, $20 is recognized built-in loss, but the group only has an $8 NUBIL and so only $8 of the recognized built-in loss is subject to limitation under section 382. The treatment of the loss recognized on the Year 2 sale of Truck 2 is not affected by the Year 4 redetermination.

Example 4. Sale of less than all shares of stock of an included subsidiary. (i) *Facts.* The facts are the same as in paragraph (i)(A) of *Example 2,* except that S1 has ten shares of stock outstanding, designated Share 1 through Share 10, all of which are owned by S. S's basis in Share 1 is $15.50, and S's basis in Share 2 is $4.50. In addition, instead of selling its one share of S1 stock, on January 1, Year 4, S sells Share 1 and Share 2 to an unrelated party for $16 (their aggregate fair market value).

(ii) *Redetermination of the P group's NUBIG or NUBIL.* (A) *Unduplicated built-in gain or loss with respect to S1 Share 1 and S1 Share 2.* The analysis is the same as in paragraph (i)(B)(1) of *Example 2* except that the unduplicated loss is $1.60, computed as the excess of $17.60 ($20 aggregate basis in the shares that are sold, tentatively reduced by $2.40, the shares' portion (2/10) of the $12 tentative adjustment that tiered-up from S2) over $16 (the shares' aggregate value).

(B) *Redetermined NUBIG or NUBIL of the P group.* The P group's redetermined NUBIL is $11.60, which is the sum of S2's NUBIL of $20, S1's NUBIL of $0, S's NUBIG of $10, P's NUBIG or NUBIL of $0, M's NUBIG or NUBIL of $0, and the unduplicated stock loss of $1.60.

(C) *Effect of redetermination.* Of the $4 loss recognized on the Year 4 sale of Share 1 and Share 2, all $4 is recognized built-in loss. The group's redetermined NUBIL is $11.60, and thus all $4 of the $4 recognized built-in loss is subject to limitation under section 382.

Example 5. NUBIL redetermined to be NUBIG. (i) *Disposition of stock of included member.* (A) *Facts.* On January 1, Year 1, P owns the sole outstanding share of S stock (basis $10, value $100). S owns Truck 1 (basis $65, value $50) and Truck 2 (basis $45, value $50). January 1, Year 1, is a change date for the P group. In Year 3, P sells its S share for $100.

(B) *Determination of the P group's NUBIG or NUBIL on change date.* S's assets are Truck 1 (with a built-in loss of $15) and Truck 2 (with a built-in gain of $5); therefore S has a separate NUBIL of $10. P's sole asset is the share of S stock, which is disregarded; therefore, P has a separate NUBIG or NUBIL of zero. Accordingly, on the change date, the P group has a NUBIL of $10, reflecting the sum of S's $10 NUBIL and P's $0 NUBIG/NUBIL.

(C) *Redetermination of the P group's NUBIG or NUBIL on disposition of stock of included subsidiary.* (1) *Unduplicated built-in gain or loss with respect to the S share.* Under paragraph (g)(7)(ii)(A) of this section, the unduplicated built-in gain or loss with respect to the S share sold in Year 3 is computed by first treating S's $10 NUBIL as having been recognized, taken into account, and absorbed immediately before the ownership change. Then, under paragraph (g)(7)(ii)(B) of this section, S's $10 NUBIL is treated as tentatively adjusting P's basis in the S share under the principles of § 1.1502-32. Accordingly, P's tentatively reduced basis in the S share is $10 - $10, or $0. Further, the value of the S share was $100 immediately before the change date. The share's $100 value exceeds the $0 tentatively reduced basis in the share by $100, and thus P has a $100 unduplicated gain in its S stock.

(2) *Redetermined NUBIG or NUBIL of the P group.* Immediately before P takes into account the $90 gain on the sale of its share of S stock, the P group's $10 NUBIL is redetermined to be a $90 NUBIG, the sum of S's NUBIL of $10 and the unduplicated gain in the S stock of $100.

(D) *Effect of redetermination.* Of the $90 gain P recognized on the sale of the S share, all $90 is recognized built-in gain and therefore, under section 382(h)(2)(A), the group's section 382 limitation is increased by $90.

(ii) *Disposition of loss asset prior to disposition of stock of included subsidiary.* (A) *Facts.* The facts are the same as in paragraph (i)(A) of this *Example 5,* except that, in addition, in Year 2, S sells Truck 1 for $50, recognizing a $15 loss that is taken into account and absorbed. As a result of the $15 loss absorption, P's basis in the S share is reduced to an excess loss account of $5 in Year 2 and, thus, when P sells the S share in Year 3, P recognizes $105 gain on the sale ($100 sale proceeds + $5 excess loss account recapture).

(B) *Determination of the P group's NUBIG or NUBIL on change date.* For the reasons set forth in paragraph (i)(B) of this *Example 5,* the P group has a NUBIL of $10 on the change date. Accordingly, S's $15 loss on Truck 1 is a recognized built-in loss under section 382(h)(2)(B), and therefore subject to limitation to the extent of the $10 NUBIL.

(C) *Redetermination of the P group's NUBIG or NUBIL on disposition of stock of included subsidiary.* (1) *Unduplicated built-in gain or loss with respect to the S share.* For the reasons set forth in paragraph (i)(C)(1) of this *Example 5,* the unduplicated built-in gain with respect to the S share is $100.

(2) *Redetermined NUBIG or NUBIL of the P group.* For the reasons set forth in paragraph (i)(C)(2) of this *Example 5*, the P group's NUBIG is redetermined to be $90. Immediately before P takes into account the $100 gain on the sale of its share of S stock, the P group's $10 NUBIL is redetermined to be a $90 NUBIG, the sum of S's NUBIL of $10 and P's NUBIG of $100.

(D) *Effect of redetermination.* Of the $105 gain P recognized on the sale of the S share, $90 is recognized built-in gain and therefore, under section 382(h)(2)(A), the group's section 382 limitation is increased by $90. The redetermination of P's original $10 NUBIL to a $100 NUBIG in Year 4 has no effect on the treatment of the Year 2 recognized built-in loss from the sale of Truck 1.

(h) * * *

(2) *Disposition of stock or an intercompany obligation of a member.*—Built-in gain or loss recognized by a member on the disposition of stock (including stock described in section 1504(a)(4) and §1.382-2T(f)(18)(ii) and (f)(18)(iii)) of another member is treated as a recognized gain or loss for purposes of section 382(h)(2) (unless disallowed) without regard to the extent to which such gain or loss was included in the determination of a net unrealized built-in gain or loss under paragraph (g) of this section. Built-in gain or loss recognized by a member with respect to an intercompany obligation is treated as recognized gain or loss only to the extent (if any) that the transaction gives rise to aggregate income or loss within the consolidated group.

* * *

(4) Successor assets. * * *

* * *

(k) *Effective/Applicability date.*—Paragraphs (g)(1), (g)(7), (g)(8), (h)(2) and (h)(4) of this section apply to amounts taken into account with respect to a share of stock of an included subsidiary on or after the date that final regulations are published in the **FEDERAL REGISTER**, but only with respect to ownership changes occurring on or after October 24, 2011. For amounts taken into account with respect to a share of stock of an included subsidiary not described in the preceding sentence, see §§1.1502-91(g) and 1.1502-91(h) as contained in 26 CFR part 1 in effect on April 1, 2011.

Deduction for Business Interest Expense: Limitation

Deduction for Business Interest Expense: Limitation.—Amendments to Reg. §1.1502-95, regarding the limitation on the deduction for business interest expense after the enactment of recent tax legislation, are proposed (published in the Federal Register on December 28, 2018) (REG-106089-18).

Par. 23. Section 1.1502-95 is amended in paragraph (b)(4) by:

1. Designating *Examples 1* and 2 as paragraphs (b)(4)(i) and (ii), respectively;

2. In newly designated paragraph (b)(4)(i), redesignating paragraphs (b)(4)(i)(i) and (ii) as paragraphs (b)(4)(i)(A) and (B), respectively;

3. In newly designated paragraph (b)(4)(ii), redesignating paragraphs (b)(4)(ii)(i) and (ii) as paragraphs (b)(4)(ii)(A) and (B), respectively; and

4. Adding two sentences at the end of newly redesignated paragraph (b)(4)(ii)(B).

The additions read follows:

§1.1502-95. Rules on ceasing to be a member of a consolidated group (or loss subgroup).

* * *

(b) * * *

(4) * * *

(ii) * * *

(B) * * * The analysis would be similar if the L loss group had an ownership change under §1.1502-92 in Year 2 with respect to disallowed business interest expense paid or accrued by L2 in Year 1 and carried forward under section 163(j)(2) to Year 2 and Year 3. See §1.1502-98(b) (providing that §§1.1502-91 through 1.1502-96 apply section 382 to business interest expense, with appropriate adjustments).

* * *

Deduction for Business Interest Expense: Limitation

Deduction for Business Interest Expense: Limitation.—Amendments to Reg. §§1.1502-98 and 1.1502-99, regarding the limitation on the deduction for business interest expense after the enactment of recent tax legislation, are proposed (published in the Federal Register on December 28, 2018) (REG-106089-18).

Par. 24. Section 1.1502-98 is amended by:

1. Revising the section heading;

2. Designating the undesignated text as paragraph (a) and adding a heading for newly designated paragraph (a); and

3. Adding paragraph (b).

The revision and additions read as follows:

§1.1502-98. Coordination with sections 383 and 163(j).— (a) *Coordination with section 383.*—* * *

(b) *Application to section 163(j).*—(1) *In general.*—The regulations under sections 163(j), 382, and 383 contain rules governing the application of section 382 to interest expense governed by section 163(j) and the regulations thereunder. See, for example, §§1.163(j)-11(b), 1.382-2, 1.382-6, and 1.383-1. The rules contained in §§1.1502-91 through 1.1502-96 apply these rules to members of a consolidated group, or corporations that join or leave a consolidated group, with appropriate adjustments. For example, for purposes of §§1.1502-91 through 1.1502-96, the term *loss group* includes a consolidated group in which any member is entitled to use a disallowed business interest expense carryforward, within the meaning of §1.163(j)-1(b)(9), that did not arise, and is not treated as arising, in a SRLY with regard to that group. Additionally, a reference to net operating loss carryovers in §§1.1502-91 through 1.1502-96 generally includes a reference to disallowed business interest expense carryforwards. References to a loss or losses in §§1.1502-91 through 1.1502-96 include references to disallowed business interest expense carryforwards or section 382 disallowed business interest carryforwards, within the meaning of §1.382-2(a)(7), as appropriate.

(2) *Appropriate adjustments.*—For purposes of applying the rules in §§1.1502-91 through 1.1502-96 to current-year business interest expense (within the meaning of §1.163(j)-5(a)(2)(i)), disallowed business interest expense carryforwards, and section 382 disallowed business interest carryforwards, appropriate adjustments are required.

Par. 25. Section 1.1502-99 is amended by adding paragraph (d) to read as follows:

§1.1502-99. Effective/applicability dates.

* * *

(d) *Application to section 163(j).*—(1) *Sections 1.382-2 and 1.382-5.*—To the extent the rules of §§1.1502-91 through 1.1502-99 effectuate the rules of §§1.382-2 and 1.382-5, the provisions apply with respect to ownership changes occurring on or after the date the Treasury decision adopting these regulations as final regulations is published in the **Federal Register**. For loss corporations that have ownership changes occurring before the date the Treasury decision adopting these regulations as final regulations is published in the **Federal Register**, see §§1.1502-91 through 1.1502-99 as contained in 26 CFR part 1, revised April 1, 2018. However, taxpayers and their related parties, within the meaning of sections 267(b) and 707(b)(1), may apply the rules of §§1.1502-91 through 1.1502-99 to the extent they apply the rules of §§1.382-2 and 1.382-5, to ownership changes occurring during a taxable year beginning after December 31, 2017, as well as consistently applying the rules of the §§1.1502-91 through 1.1502-99 to the extent they effectuate the rules of §§1.382-2, 1.382-5, 1.382-6, and 1.383-1, the section 163(j) regulations (within the meaning of §1.163(j)-1(b)(32)), and if applicable, §§1.263A-9, 1.381(c)(20)-1, 1.469-9, 1.882-5, 1.1502-13, 1.1502-21, 1.1502-36, 1.1502-79, and 1.1504-4 to taxable years beginning after December 31, 2017.

(2) *Sections 1.382-6 and 1.383-1.*—To the extent the rules of §§1.1502-91 through 1.1502-98 effectuate the rules of §§1.382-6 and 1.383-1, the provisions apply with respect to ownership changes

occurring during a taxable year ending after the date the Treasury decision adopting these regulations as final regulations is published in the **Federal Register**. For the application of these rules to an ownership change with respect to an ownership change occurring during a taxable year ending before the date the Treasury decision adopting these regulations as final regulations is published in the **Federal Register**, see §§1.1502-91 through 1.1502-99 as contained in 26 CFR part 1, revised April 1, 2018. However, taxpayers and their related parties, within the meaning of sections 267(b) and 707(b)(1),

may apply the rules of §§1.1502-91 through 1.1502-99 (to the extent that those rules effectuate the rules of §§1.382-6 and 1.383-1), to ownership changes occurring during a taxable year beginning after December 31, 2017, so long as the taxpayers and their related parties consistently apply the rules of the section 163(j) regulations (within the meaning of §1.163(j)-1(b)(32)), and if applicable, §§1.263A-9, 1.381(c)(20)-1, 1.469-9, 1.882-5, 1.1502-13, 1.1502-21, 1.1502-36, 1.1502-79, and 1.1504-4 to taxable years beginning after December 31, 2017.

Deduction for Business Interest Expense: Limitation

Deduction for Business Interest Expense: Limitation.—Amendments to Reg. §1.1504-4, regarding the limitation on the deduction for business interest expense after the enactment of recent tax legislation, are proposed (published in the Federal Register on December 28, 2018) (REG-106089-18).

Par. 26. Section 1.1504-4 is amended by:

1. Removing "163(j), 864(e)," from paragraph the first sentence of paragraph (a)(2) and adding "864(e)" in its place; and

2. Adding two sentences at the end of paragraph (i).

The addition reads as follows:

§1.1504-4. Treatment of warrants, options, convertible obligations, and other similar interests.

* * *

(i) * * * Paragraph (a)(2) of this section applies with respect to taxable years ending after the date the Treasury decision adopting these regulations as final regulations is published in the **Federal Register**. However, taxpayers and their related parties, within the

meaning of sections 267(b) and 707(b)(1), may apply the rules of this section to a taxable year beginning after December 31, 2017, so long as the taxpayers and their related parties consistently apply the rules of this section, the section 163(j) regulations (within the meaning of §1.163(j)-1(b)(32)), and if applicable, §§1.263A-9, 1.381(c)(20)-1, 1.382-6, 1.383-1, 1.469-9, 1.882-5, 1.1502-13, 1.1502-21, 1.1502-36, 1.1502-79, and 1.1502-91 through 1.1502-99 (to the extent they effectuate the rules of §§1.382-6, and 1.383-1), to those taxable years.

Consolidated Returns: AMT

Consolidated Returns: Alternative Minimum Tax.—Reproduced below is the text of a proposed amendment to Reg. §1.1552-1, relating to the computation of the alternative minimum tax by consolidated groups (published in the Federal Register on December 30, 1992).

☐ Par. 8. Section 1.1552-1 is amended by adding paragraphs (g) through (j) to read as follows:

§1.1552-1. Earnings and profits.

* * *

(g) *Allocation of consolidated AMT and allowable consolidated MTC to members*.—(1) *In general*.—For purposes of determining the earnings and profits of each member of a consolidated group, the consolidated AMT and allowable consolidated MTC (computed under §1.1502-55) must be allocated among the members in accordance with this paragraph (g).

(2) *Amount of consolidated AMT allocated to a member*.—The amount of consolidated AMT allocated to a member is determined by multiplying the consolidated AMT by a fraction, the numerator of which is the separate adjusted AMT (as defined in §1.1502-55(h)(6)(iv)) of the member for the year, and the denominator of which is the sum of each member's separate adjusted AMT for the year.

(3) *Amount of allowable consolidated MTC allocated to a member*.—The amount of allowable consolidated MTC in a taxable year must be allocated among the consolidated group members in accordance with the principles of §1.1502-55(h)(6)(vi) and (7).

(4) *Effective date*.—Paragraph (g) of this section applies to any consolidated return year for which the due date of the income tax return (without regard to extensions) is on or after [the date that is sixty days after final regulations are filed with the Federal Register].

(h) *Allocation of consolidated environmental tax*.—(1) *In general*.—For purposes of determining the earnings and profits of each member of a consolidated group, the consolidated environmental tax (as defined in paragraph (h)(2) of this section) must be allocated among the members in accordance with paragraph (h)(3) of this section.

(2) *Consolidated environmental tax*.—(i) *In general*.—The consolidated environmental tax is equal to 0.12 percent of the excess of—

(A) Consolidated modified AMTI; over

(B) $2,000,000.

(ii) *Consolidated modified AMTI*.—For purposes of determining the consolidated environmental tax, consolidated modified AMTI

is equal to the consolidated AMTI (as defined in §1.1502-55(b)), but determined without taking into account—

(A) The consolidated ATNOL deduction (as defined in §1.1502-55(b)(4)); and

(B) The deduction for the payment of an environmental tax under section 164(a)(5).

(3) *Amount of consolidated environmental tax to be allocated to a member*.—(i) *In general*.—The amount of consolidated environmental tax to be allocated to a member is determined by multiplying the consolidated environmental tax by a fraction, the numerator of which is the separate modified AMTI of the member, and denominator of which is the sum of each member's separate modified AMTI.

(ii) *Separate modified AMTI*.—For purposes of the allocation of consolidated environmental tax, separate modified AMTI of a member is the consolidated modified AMTI determined by taking into account only the member's items of income, gain, deduction, and loss, including the member's losses and deductions actually absorbed by the group in the taxable year (whether or not absorbed by the member). For purposes of this allocation, a member is considered to have separate modified AMTI only if the computation in this paragraph (h)(3)(ii) produces a number that is greater than zero.

(4) *Effective date*.—Paragraph (h) of this section applies to any consolidated return year for which the due date of the income tax return (without regard to extensions) is on or after [the date that is sixty days after final regulations are filed with the Federal Register].

(i) [Reserved]

(j) *Allocation of consolidated additional taxes to members*.—For purposes of determining the earnings and profits of each member of a consolidated group, the consolidated additional taxes (as defined in §1.1502-2(b)) are allocated to the members in accordance with any reasonable method used by the group. This paragraph (j) applies to any consolidated return year for which the due date of the income tax return (without regard to extensions) is on or after [the date that is sixty days after final regulations are filed with the Federal Register].

ESTATE TAX

Below-Market Loans

Below-Market Interest Rate Loans: Tax Reform Act of 1984.—Reproduced below is the text of a proposed amendment of Reg. §20.2031-4, detailing the estate tax treatment of lenders and borrowers with respect to below-market term loans made after June 6, 1984, and below-market demand loans outstanding after such date (published in the Federal Register on August 20, 1985).

☐ Par. 7. Section 20.2031-4 is amended by adding a new sentence at the end to read as follows:

§ 20.2031-4. Valuation of notes.
* * * See § 20.7872-1 for special rules in the case of gift loans (within the meaning of § 1.7872-4(b)) made after June 6, 1984.

* * *

Annuities: Interests: Valuation: Actuarial Tables

Annuities: Interests: Valuation: Actuarial Tables.—Amendments to Reg. § 20.2032-1, relating to the use of actuarial tables in valuing annuities, interests for life or terms of years, and remainder or reversionary interests, are proposed (published in the Federal Register on May 7, 2009) (REG-107845-08).

Par. 8. Section 20.2032-1 is amended by revising paragraphs (f)(1) and (h) to read as follows:

§ 20.2032-1. Alternate valuation.

* * *

(f) * * *

(1) [The text of this proposed paragraph (f)(1) is the same as the text of § 20.2032-1T(f)(1) as added by T.D. 9448].

* * *

(h) [The text of this proposed paragraph (h) is the same as the text of § 20.2032-1T(h) as added by T.D. 9448].

Estate Tax: Gross Estate: Alternate Valuation Date: Election

Estate Tax: Gross Estate: Alternate Valuation Date: Election.—Amendments to Reg. § 20.2032-1, providing guidance respecting the election to use the alternate valuation method under Code Sec. 2032, are proposed (published in the Federal Register on November 18, 2011) (REG-112196-07).

☐ Par. 2. For each entry in the table, each paragraph in the "Old Paragraph" column is redesignated as indicated in the "New Paragraph" column:

Old Paragraph	New Paragraph
20.2032-1(c)(1)	20.2032-1(c)(1)(i)
20.2032-1(c)(3)	20.2032-1(c)(3)(i)
20.2032-1(c)(3)(i)	20.2032-1(c)(3)(i)(A)
20.2032-1(c)(3)(ii)	20.2032-1(c)(3)(i)(B)
20.2032-1(c)(3)(iii)	20.2032-1(c)(3)(i)(C)
20.2032-1(c)(3)(iv)	20.2032-1(c)(3)(i)(D)
20.2032-1(c)(3)(v)	20.2032-1(c)(3)(i)(E)
20.2032-1(f)	20.2032-1(f)(2)
20.2032-1(f)(1)	20.2032-1(f)(2)(i)
20.2032-1(f)(2)	20.2032-1(f)(2)(ii)

☐ Par. 3. Section 20.2032-1 is amended by:

1. Revising paragraph (a) introductory text.

2. Revising paragraphs (a)(1) and (a)(2).

3. Revising newly-designated paragraph (c)(1)(i), newly-designated paragraph (c)(3)(i)(C), paragraph (e) introductory text, the introductory text of paragraph (e) *Example 1* preceding the table, the last sentence in newly-designated paragraph (f)(2) introductory text, newly-designated paragraph (f)(2)(i), and the second sentence in newly-designated paragraph (f)(2)(ii).

4. Adding new paragraphs (c)(1)(ii), (c)(1)(iii), (c)(1)(iv), (c)(4), (c)(5), (f)(1), and (f)(3).

5. Adding a paragraph heading and a new second sentence in paragraph (c)(2) introductory text.

6. Adding a paragraph heading to paragraph (c)(3).

7. Designating the undesignated language following newly-designated paragraph (c)(3)(i)(E) as paragraph (c)(3)(ii) and adding a paragraph heading to this paragraph.

8. Designating the table in paragraph (e) as *Example 1* and adding paragraph (e) *Example 2* following the table.

9. Revising the paragraph heading and adding two sentences at the end of paragraph (h).

The additions and revisions read as follows.

§ 20.2032-1. Alternate valuation.—(a) *In general.*—In general, section 2032 provides for the valuation of a decedent's gross estate at a date (alternate valuation date) other than the date of the decedent's death. More specifically, if an executor elects the alternate valuation method under section 2032, the property includible in the decedent's gross estate on the date of death (decedent's interest) is valued as of whichever of the following dates is applicable:

(1) Any property distributed, sold, exchanged, or otherwise disposed of within 6 months (1 year, if the decedent died on or before December 31, 1970) after the decedent's death (alternate valuation period) is valued as of the date on which it is first distributed, sold, exchanged, or otherwise disposed of (transaction date).

(2) Any property not distributed, sold, exchanged, or otherwise disposed of during the alternate valuation period is valued as of the date 6 months (1 year, if the decedent died on or before December 31, 1970) after the date of the decedent's death (6-month date).

* * *

(c) *Meaning of "distributed, sold, exchanged, or otherwise disposed of".*—(1) *In general.*

(i) *Transactions included.*—The phrase "distributed, sold, exchanged, or otherwise disposed of" comprehends all possible ways by which property ceases to form a part of the gross estate. This phrase includes, but is not limited to:

(A) The use of money on hand at the date of the decedent's death to pay funeral or other expenses of the decedent's estate;

(B) The use of money on hand at the date of the decedent's death to invest in other property;

(C) The exercise of employee stock options;

(D) The surrender of stock for corporate assets in partial or complete liquidation of a corporation, and similar transactions involving partnerships or other entities;

(E) The distribution by the estate (or other holder) of included property as defined in paragraph (d) of this section;

(F) The transfer or exchange of property for other property, whether or not gain or loss is currently recognized for income tax purposes;

(G) The contribution of cash or other property to a corporation, partnership, or other entity, whether or not gain or loss is currently recognized for income tax purposes;

(H) The exchange of interests in a corporation, partnership, or other entity (entity) for one or more different interests (for example, a different class of stock) in the same entity or in an acquiring or resulting entity or entities (see, however, paragraph (c)(1)(ii) of this section); and

(I) Any other change in the ownership structure or interests in, or in the assets of, a corporation, partnership, or other entity, an interest in which is includible in the gross estate, such that the included property after the change does not reasonably represent the included property at the decedent's date of death (see, however, paragraph (c)(1)(iii)(A) of this section). Such a change in the ownership structure or interests in or in the assets of an entity includes, without limitation—

(1) The dilution of the decedent's ownership interest in the entity due to the issuance of additional ownership interests in that entity;

(2) An increase in the decedent's ownership interest in the entity due to the entity's redemption of the interest of a different owner;

(3) A reinvestment of the entity's assets; and

(4) A distribution or disbursement of property (other than excluded property as defined in paragraph (d) of this section) by the entity (other than expenses, such as rents and salaries, paid in the ordinary course of the entity's business), with the effect that the fair market value of the entity before the occurrence does not equal the fair market value of the entity immediately thereafter.

(ii) *Exchange of an interest in an existing corporation, partnership, or other entity includible in the gross estate.*—If an interest in a corporation, partnership, or other entity (entity is includible in the gross estate at death and that interest is exchanged as described in paragraph (c)(1)(i)(H) of this section for one or more different interests in the same entity or in an acquiring or resulting entity or entities, the transaction does not result in an exchange or disposition under section 2032(a)(1) and paragraph (c)(1)(i)(H) of this section if, on the date of the exchange, the fair market value of the interest in the entity equals the fair market value of the interest(s) in the same entity or the acquiring or resulting entity or entities. Such transactions may include, without limitation, reorganizations, recapitalizations, mergers, or similar transactions. In determining whether the exchanged properties have the same fair market value, a difference in value equal to or less than 5 percent of the fair market value, as of the transaction date, of the property interest includible in the gross estate on the decedent's date of death is ignored. If the transaction satisfies the requirements of this paragraph, the property to be valued on the 6-month date (or on the transaction date, if any, subsequent to this transaction) is the property received in the exchange, rather than the property includible in the decedent's gross estate at the date of death. This paragraph has no effect on any other provision of the Internal Revenue Code that is applicable to the transaction. For example, even if the transaction does not result in a deemed exchange as a result of satisfying the requirements of this paragraph, the provisions of chapter 14 may be applicable to determine fair market value for Federal estate tax purposes.

(iii) *Distributions from an account or entity in which the decedent held an interest at death.*

(A) *In general.*—If during the alternate valuation period, an estate (or other holder of the decedent's interest) receives a distribution or disbursement (to the extent the distribution or disbursement consists of included property, as defined in paragraph (d) of this section) (payment) from a partnership, corporation, trust (including an IRA, Roth IRA, 403(b), 401(k), Thrift Savings Plan, etc.), bank account or similar asset, or other entity (entity), and an interest in that entity is includible in the gross estate, the payment does not result in a distribution under paragraph (c)(1)(i)(I) of this section. However, this rule applies only if, on the date of the payment, the fair market value of the decedent's interest in the entity before the payment equals the sum of the fair market value of the payment made to the estate (or other holder of the decedent's interest in the entity) and the fair market value of the decedent's interest in the entity, not including any excluded property, after the payment. In this case, the alternate valuation date of the payment is the date of the payment, and the alternate valuation date of the decedent's remaining interest in the entity, if any, is the 6-month date (or the transaction date, if any, subsequent to this payment). If this requirement is not met, the payment is a distribution under paragraph (c)(1)(i) of this section, and the alternate valuation date of the decedent's entire interest in the entity is the date of the payment. For purposes of this section, a distribution or disbursement is deemed to consist first of excluded property, if any, and then of included property, as those terms are defined in paragraph (d) of this section.

(B) *Special rule.*—If the decedent's interest in an entity that is includible in the gross estate consists of the amount needed to produce an annuity, unitrust, remainder, or other such payment valued under section 2036, then assuming the distribution satisfies the general rule set forth in paragraph (c)(1)(iii)(A) of this section, the value of each distribution (to the extent it is deemed to consist of included property) payable (whether or not actually paid) during the alternate valuation period shall be added to the value of the entity on the alternate valuation date. The sum of the fair market value of these distributions when made and the fair market value of the entity on the alternate valuation date shall be used as the fair market value of the entity in computing the amount, valued as of the alternate valuation date, to be included in the decedent's gross estate under section 2036. See *Example 2* of paragraph (e) of this section.

(iv) *Aggregation.*—For purposes of this section, a special aggregation rule applies in two situations to determine the value to be included in the gross estate pursuant to an alternate valuation election. Those two situations arise when, during the alternate valuation period, less than all of the interest includible in the decedent's gross estate in a particular property is the subject of a transaction described in paragraphs (c)(1)(i), (c)(1)(ii), (c)(1)(iii), or (c)(2) of this section. In one situation, one or more portions of the includible

interest are subject to such a transaction and a portion is still held on the 6-month date. In the other situation, the entire interest includible in the gross estate is disposed of in two or more such transactions during the alternate valuation period, so that no part of that interest remains on the 6-month date. In both of these situations, the fair market value of each portion of the interest includible in the gross estate is to be determined as follows. The fair market value of each portion subject to such a transaction, and the portion remaining, if any, on the 6-month date, is the fair market value, as of the transaction date, or the 6-month date for any remaining portion, of the entire interest includible in the gross estate on the decedent's date of death, multiplied by a fraction. The numerator of that fraction is the portion of the interest subject to that transaction, or the portion remaining on the 6-month date, and the denominator is the entire interest includible in the gross estate at the decedent's date of death.

(2) *Property distributed.*—* * * Property is not considered "distributed" merely because property passes directly at death as a result of a beneficiary designation or other contractual arrangement or by operation of law. * * *

(3) *Person able to sell, exchange, or otherwise dispose of property includible in the gross estate.*—(i) * * *

(A) * * *

(B) * * *

(C) An heir, devisee, or other person to whom title to property passes directly on death by reason of a beneficiary designation or other contractual arrangement or by operation of law;

(D) * * *

(E) * * *

(ii) *Binding contracts.*—* * *

(4) *Certain post-death events.*—If the effect of any other provision of the Internal Revenue Code is that a post-death event is deemed to have occurred on the date of death, the post-death event will not be considered a transaction described in paragraph (c)(1)(i) of this section. For example, the grant, during the alternate valuation period, of a qualified conservation easement in accordance with section 2031(c) is not a transaction described in paragraph (c)(1)(i) of this section. Pursuant to section 2031(c), the post-death grant of the easement is effective for Federal estate tax purposes as of the date of the decedent's death. As a result, for purposes of determining both the estate's eligibility to make an election under this section and the value of the property on the alternate valuation date, the fair market value of the property as of the date of death must be compared to the fair market value of that property as of the alternate valuation date, in each case as that value is adjusted by reason of the existence of the section 2031(c) qualified easement.

(5) *Examples.*—The application of paragraph (c) of this section is illustrated in the following examples. In each example, decedent's (D's) estate elects to value D's gross estate under the alternate valuation method, so that the alternate valuation date of the property includible in the gross estate on D's date of death is either the transaction date or the 6-month date. In each example, assume that the only factors affecting value during the alternate valuation period, and the only occurrences described in paragraphs (c)(1)(i) and (c)(2) of this section, are those described in the example.

Example 1. At D's death, D owned property with a fair market value of $100X. Two months after D's death (Date 1), D's executor and D's family members formed a limited partnership. D's executor contributed all of the property to the partnership and received an interest in the partnership in exchange. The investment of the property in the partnership is a transaction described in paragraph (c)(1)(i)(F) and/or (G) of this section. As a result, the alternate valuation date of the property is the date of its contribution and the value to be included in D's gross estate is the fair market value of the property immediately prior to its contribution to the partnership. The result would be the same if D's estate instead had contributed property to a limited partnership formed prior to D's death by D and/or other parties, related or unrelated to D. Further, the result would be the same if D's estate had contributed the property to a corporation, publicly traded or otherwise, or other entity after D's death and prior to the 6-month date.

Example 2. At D's death, D held incentive stock options that were qualified under section 422. D's executor exercised all of the stock options prior to the 6-month date. The exercise of the stock options is a transaction described in paragraph (c)(1)(i)(C) of this section. Thus, the alternate valuation date of the stock options is the date of their exercise and the value to be included in D's gross estate is the fair market value of the stock options immediately prior to their exercise. The result would be the same if the stock options were not qualified under section 422 and were taxable under section 83 upon exercise.

Example 3. D's gross estate includes a controlling interest in Y, a corporation. During the alternate valuation period, Y issued additional shares of stock and awarded them to certain key employees. D's interest in Y was diluted to a non-controlling interest by Y's issuance of the additional stock. Y's issuance of the stock is a transaction described in paragraph (c)(1)(i)(I) of this section. The value to be included in D's gross estate is the fair market value of D's stock immediately prior to Y's issuance of the additional stock. The result would be the same if D's estate included a minority interest in Y on the date of death and that interest became a controlling interest during the alternate valuation period as the result of Y's redemption of the shares of another shareholder.

Example 4. At D's death, D owned stock in Y, a corporation. During the alternate valuation period, the Board of Directors of Y contributed all of Y's assets to a partnership in exchange for interests therein. The contribution is a transaction described in paragraph (c)(1)(i)(I)(3) of this section. Therefore, the alternate valuation date of D's stock in Y is the date of the reinvestment of Y's assets and the value to be included in D's gross estate is the fair market value of D's stock in Y immediately prior to the reinvestment. The result would be the same even if the Board of Directors had contributed only a portion of Y's assets to the partnership during the alternate valuation period.

Example 5. (i) At D's death, D owned common stock in Y, a corporation. Two months after D's death (Date 1), there was a reorganization of Y. In the reorganization, D's estate exchanged all of its stock for a new class of stock in X. On the date of the reorganization, the difference between the fair market value of the stock D's estate received and the fair market value on that date of the stock includible in D's gross estate at death was greater than 5% of the fair market value, as of the date of the reorganization, of the stock D held at death. The reorganization is a transaction described in paragraph (c)(1)(i)(H) of this section and does not satisfy the exception described in paragraph (c)(1)(ii) of this section. Thus, the alternate valuation date is the date of the reorganization and the value to be included in D's gross estate is the fair market value of the stock immediately prior to the reorganization. This result is not affected by whether or not the reorganization is a tax-free reorganization for Federal income tax purposes. The result would be the same if the stock had been held, for example, in an IRA with designated beneficiaries. See paragraph (c)(3)(i)(C) of this section.

(ii) If, instead, the difference between the two fair market values as of the date of the reorganization was equal to or less than 5% of the fair market value, as of the date of the reorganization, of the stock D held at death, the reorganization would satisfy the exception provided in paragraph (c)(1)(ii) of this section. Thus, the alternate valuation date would be the 6-month date. The value to be included in D's gross estate would be the fair market value, determined as of the 6-month date, of the new class of stock in Y that D's estate received in the reorganization.

Example 6. (i) At D's death, D owned an interest in Partnership X that is includible in D's gross estate. During the alternate valuation period, X made a cash distribution to each of the partners. The distribution consists entirely of included property as defined in paragraph (d) of this section. The distribution is a transaction described in paragraph (c)(1)(i)(I)(4) of this section. On the date of the distribution, the fair market value of D's interest in X before the distribution equaled the sum of the distribution paid to D's estate and the fair market value of D's interest in X immediately after the distribution. Thus, pursuant to paragraph (c)(1)(iii)(A) of this section, the alternate valuation date of the property distributed is the date of the distribution, and the alternate valuation date of D's interest in X is the 6-month date.

(ii) If, instead, the fair market value of D's interest in X before the distribution did not equal the sum of the distribution paid to D's estate and the fair market value of D's interest in X (not including any excluded property) immediately after the distribution, then pursuant to paragraph (c)(1)(i)(I)(4) of this section, the alternate valuation date of D's entire interest in X would be the date of the distribution.

Example 7. D died owning 100% of Blackacre. D's will directs that an undivided 70% interest in Blackacre is to pass to Trust A for the benefit of D's surviving spouse, and an undivided 30% interest is to pass to Trust B for the benefit of D's surviving child. Three months after D's death (Date 1), the executor of D's estate distributed a 70% interest in Blackacre to Trust A. Four months after D's death (Date 2), the executor of D's estate distributed a 30% interest in Blackacre to Trust B. The following values are includible in D's gross estate pursuant to paragraphs (c)(1)(i)(E) and (c)(1)(iv): the fair market value of the 70% interest in Blackacre, determined by calculating 70% of the fair market value of all (100%) of Blackacre as of Date 1; and the fair market value of the 30% interest in Blackacre, determined by calculating 30% of the fair market value of all (100%) of Blackacre as of Date 2.

Example 8. At D's death, D owned 100% of the units of a limited liability company (LLC). Two months after D's death (Date 1), D's executor sold 20% of the LLC units to an unrelated third party. Three months after D's death (Date 2), D's executor sold 40% of the

LLC units to D's child. On the 6-month date, the estate held the remaining 40% of the units in the LLC. The alternate valuation date of the units sold is their sale date (Date 1 and Date 2, respectively) pursuant to paragraph (a) of this section. The alternate valuation date of the units remaining in the estate is the 6-month date, as these units have not been distributed, sold, exchanged, or otherwise disposed of in a transaction described in paragraphs (c)(1)(i) or (c)(2) of this section prior to this date. Pursuant to paragraph (c)(1)(iv) of this section, the value of the units disposed of on Date 1 and Date 2 is the fair market value of the 20% and 40% interests, determined by calculating 20% and 40% of the fair market value as of Date 1 and Date 2, respectively, of all the units (100%) includible in the gross estate at D's death. Similarly, the value of the units held on the 6-month date to be included in D's gross estate is the fair market value of those units, determined by taking 40% of the fair market value on the 6-month date of all of the units (100%) includible in the gross estate at D's death. As a result, the fact that the partial sales resulted in the creation of three minority interests is not taken into account in valuing under section 2032 any portion of the LLC interests held by D at D's death.

Example 9. Husband died owning an interest in a brokerage account titled in the names of Husband and Wife with rights of survivorship. On Husband's death, the account held marketable securities, corporate bonds, municipal bonds, certificates of deposit, and cash. During the alternate valuation period, Wife's stockbroker advised her that the account could not be held under the social security number of a deceased individual. Accordingly, approximately one month after Husband's death, Wife directed the stockbroker to transfer the account into an account titled in Wife's sole name. Because title to the joint account passes to Wife at the moment of Husband's death by operation of law, the transfer of the joint account into an account in Wife's sole name is not a transaction described in paragraph (c)(1)(i) of this section. Accordingly, the value of the assets held in Wife's solely owned account will be includible in Husband's gross estate at their fair market value on the 6-month date. The result would be the same if the brokerage firm automatically transferred title to the account into Wife's name, or if Wife changed the beneficiary designation for the account. Finally, the result would be the same if, instead of an account with a brokerage firm, the assets were held in Husband's retirement account (IRA or similar trust such as a Roth IRA, 403(b) plan, or 401(k) plan) or Wife's ownership of the account was the result of a contract (a beneficiary designation form) rather than operation of law.

Example 10. Assume the same facts as in *Example 9* except that, during the alternate valuation period, Wife directed the stockbroker to sell a bond in the account. The sale is a transaction described in paragraph (c)(1)(i)(I)(4) of this section. Wife is an individual described in paragraph (c)(3)(i)(D) of this section. Thus, the alternate valuation date of the bond is the date of its sale. The values to be included in D's gross estate are the fair market value of the bond on date of its sale, and the fair market value of the balance of the account on the 6-month date. The result would be the same if the bond had matured and was retired during the alternate valuation period. The result also would be the same if the bond was held within a retirement account (IRA or similar trust such as a Roth IRA, 403(b) plan, or 401(k) plan).

Example 11. Assume the same facts as in *Example 9* except that, during the alternate valuation period, Wife withdrew cash from the account or otherwise received income or other disbursements from the account. Each such withdrawal or disbursement from the account (to the extent it consists of included property as defined in paragraph (d) of this section) is a distribution described in paragraph (c)(1)(i)(I)(4) of this section. Provided that, on the date of each distribution, the fair market value of the account before the distribution (not including excluded property) equals the sum of the included property distributed and the fair market value of the included property in the account immediately after the distribution in accordance with paragraph (c)(1)(iii)(A) of this section, the alternate valuation date for each distribution is the date of the distribution and the alternate valuation date for the account is the 6-month date. The value to be included in the gross estate is the fair market value of each distribution of included property (determined as of the date of distribution) and the fair market value of the account on the 6-month date. The result would be the same if the assets were held in an IRA or similar trust, such as a Roth IRA, 403(b) plan, or 401(k) plan.

Example 12. Husband died with a retirement account, having named his three children, in specified shares totaling 100%, as the designated beneficiaries of that account. During the alternate valuation period, the account was divided into three separate retirement accounts, each in the name of a different child and funded with that child's designated share. The division of the retirement account is not a transaction described in paragraph (c)(1)(i) of this section by reason of paragraph (c)(2) of this section, so the alternate valuation date for each of the new accounts is the 6-month date.

Example 13. (i) D's gross estate includes real property. During the alternate valuation period, D's executor grants a conservation easement that restricts the property's use under local law but does not satisfy the requirements of section 2031(c). The easement reduces the fair market value of the property. The executor's grant of the conservation easement is a transaction described in paragraph (c)(1)(i)(E) of this section and does not satisfy the exception described in paragraph (c)(4) of this section. Therefore, the alternate valuation date for the property is the date the easement was granted, and the value to be included in D's gross estate is the fair market value of the property immediately prior to the grant.

(ii) Assume, instead, that the easement satisfied the requirements of section 2031(c) and, thus, satisfied the exception described in paragraph (c)(4) of this section. Pursuant to paragraph (c)(4), for purposes of determining both the estate's eligibility to make an election under section 2032 and the value of the property on the 6-month date, the section 2031(c) qualified easement is taken into account in determining both the fair market value of the property on D's date of death and the fair market value of the property on the 6-month date.

* * *

(e) *Examples.*—The application of paragraph (d) of this section regarding "included property" and "excluded property" is illustrated by the following examples.

Example 1. Assume that the decedent (D) died on January 1, 1955:* * *

Example 2. (i) At death, D held a qualified interest described in section 2702(b) in the form of an annuity in a grantor retained annuity trust (GRAT) D had created and funded with $150,000. The trust agreement provides for an annual annuity payment of $12,000 per year to D or D's estate for a term of 10 years. At the expiration of the 10-year term, the remainder is to be distributed to D's child. D dies prior to the expiration of the 10-year term. On D's date of death, the fair market value of the property in the GRAT is $325,000.

(ii) The only assets in the GRAT are an apartment building and a bank account. Three months after D's date of death, an annuity payment of $12,000 is paid in cash to D's estate. The monthly rents from the apartment building total $500. After the date of death and prior to the payment date, the GRAT received $1,500 in excluded property in the form of rent. Pursuant to paragraph (c)(1)(iii)(A) of this section, $1,500 of the $12,000 distributed is deemed to be excluded property for purposes of section 2032. The distribution is a transaction described in paragraph (c)(1)(i)(I)(4) of this section. On the date of the distribution, the fair market value of D's interest in the GRAT before the distribution equals the sum of the distribution paid to D's estate and the fair market value of D's interest in the GRAT immediately after the distribution. Thus, pursuant to paragraph (c)(1)(iii)(A) of this section, the alternate valuation date for the $10,500 cash distribution, which is included property, is the date of its distribution, and the alternate valuation date of the GRAT is the 6-month date.

(iii) The calculation of the value of D's interest in the GRAT includible in D's gross estate at D's death pursuant to section 2036 must be computed under the special rule of paragraph (c)(1)(iii)(B) of this section as a result of the estate's election to use the alternate valuation method under section 2032. On the 6-month date, the section 7520 interest rate is 6% and the fair market value of the property in the GRAT is $289,500. Pursuant to paragraph (c)(1)(iii)(B) of this section, the fair market value of the GRAT property deemed to be included property is $300,000 ($289,500 plus $10,500). Accordingly, for purposes of determining the fair market value of the corpus includible in D's gross estate under section 2036(a)(1) as of the 6-month date, see § 20.2036-1(c)(2), using a GRAT corpus of $300,000 and, pursuant to paragraph (f)(2)(i) of this section, a section 7520 rate of 6%.

(f) *Post-death factors and occurrences.*—(1) *In general.*—The election to use the alternate valuation method under section 2032 permits property includible in the gross estate on the decedent's date of death to be valued on the 6-month date, rather than on the date of death. Thus, the election permits a valuation for Federal estate tax purposes that reflects the impact of factors such as economic or market conditions, occurrences described in section 2054 (to the extent not compensated by insurance or otherwise, and not deducted under that section), and other factors or occurrences during the alternate valuation period, as set forth in guidance issued by the Secretary. Those factors and occurrences do not include the mere lapse of time described in paragraph (f)(2) of this section, or transactions described in paragraph (c)(1)(i) or (c)(2) of this section that are not excluded under paragraphs (c)(1)(ii), (c)(1)(iii)(A), and (c)(4) of this section. Generally, management decisions made in the ordinary course of operating a business, such as a corporation, a partnership, or other business entity, are taken into account under this section as occurrences related to economic or market conditions. To the extent, however, that these decisions change the ownership or control structure of the business entity, or otherwise are included in paragraph (c)(1)(i) or (c)(2) of this section and are not excluded by paragraphs (c)(1)(ii),

(c)(1)(iii)(A), or (c)(4) of this section, they will be treated as described in paragraph (c)(1)(i) of this section.

(2) *Mere lapse of time.*—* * * The application of this paragraph is illustrated in paragraphs (f)(2)(i) and (f)(2)(ii) of this section:

(i) *Life estates, remainders, and similar interests.*—(A) The fair market value of a life estate, remainder, term interest or similar interest as of the alternate valuation date is determined by applying the methodology prescribed in § 20.2031-7, subject to the following two sentences. The age of each person whose life expectancy may affect the fair market value of the interest shall be determined as of the date of the decedent's death. The fair market value of the property and the applicable interest rate under section 7520 shall be determined using values applicable on the alternate valuation date.

(B) *Examples.*—The application of paragraph (f)(2)(i)(A) of this section is illustrated in the following examples.

Example 1. Assume that the decedent (D) or D's estate was entitled to receive certain property upon the death of A, who was entitled to the income from the property for life. At the time of D's death after April 30, 2009, the fair market value of the property was $50,000, and A was 47 years and 5 months old. In the month in which D died, the section 7520 rate was 6.2%, but rose to 7.4% on the 6-month date. The fair market value of D's remainder interest as of D's date of death was $9,336.00 ($50,000 × 0.18672, the single life remainder factor from Table S for a 47 year old at a 6.2% interest rate), as illustrated in *Example 1* of § 20.2031-7T(d)(5). If, because of economic conditions, the property declined in value during the alternate valuation period and was worth only $40,000 on the 6-month date, the fair market value of the remainder interest would be $5,827 ($40,000 × 0.14568, the Table S value for a 47 year old at a 7.4% interest rate), even though A would have been 48 years old on the 6-month date.

Example 2. D created an intervivos charitable remainder annuity trust (CRAT) described in section 664(d)(1). The trust instrument directs the trustee to hold, invest, and reinvest the corpus of the trust and to pay to D for D's life, and then to D's child (C) for C's life, an amount each year equal to 6% of the initial fair market value of the trust. At the termination of the trust, the corpus, together with the accumulated income, is to be distributed to N, a charitable organization described in sections 170(c), 2055(a), and 2522(a). D died, survived by C. D's estate is entitled to a charitable deduction under section 2055 for the present value of N's remainder interest in the CRAT. Pursuant to § 1.664-2(c) and § 20.7520-2, in determining the fair market value of the remainder interest as of the alternate valuation date, D's executor may elect to use the section 7520 rate in effect for either of the two months immediately preceding the month in which the alternate valuation date occurs. Regardless of the section 7520 rate selected, however, the factor to be used to value the remainder interest is the appropriate factor for C's age on the date of D's death.

(2)(ii) *Patents.*—* * * Six months after the date of the decedent's death, the patent was sold for its then fair market value that had decreased to $60,000 because of the lapse of time. * * *

(3) *Examples.* The following examples illustrate the application of this paragraph (f). In each example, decedent's (D's) estate elects to value D's gross estate under the alternate valuation method, so that the alternate valuation date of the property includible in the gross estate on D's date of death is either the transaction date or the 6-month date. In each example, assume that the only factors affecting value, and the only occurrences described in paragraph (c)(1)(i) or (c)(2) of this section, taking place during the alternate valuation period are those described in the example.

Example 1. At D's death, D's gross estate includes a residence. During the alternate valuation period, the fair market value of the residence (as well as the residential market in the area generally) declines due to a reduction in the availability of credit throughout the United States and, consequently, a decline in the availability of mortgages. The decline in the availability of mortgages is an economic or market condition. Therefore, in valuing the residence on the 6-month date, the effect of this decline on the fair market value of the residence is to be taken into account.

Example 2. (i) At D's death, D is the sole shareholder of corporation Y, a manufacturing company. Four months after D's death, Y's physical plant is destroyed as a result of a natural disaster. The disaster affects a large geographic area and, as a result, the economy of that area is negatively affected. Five months after D's death, Y's Board of Directors votes to liquidate and dissolve Y. The liquidation and dissolution proceeding is not completed as of the 6-month date. The natural disaster is a factor that affects economic and market conditions. Therefore, the disaster, to the extent not compensated by insurance or otherwise, is taken into account in valuing the Y stock on the 6-month date.

(ii) Assume instead that Y's plant is severely damaged due to flooding from the failure of pipes in the facility. The damage is an occurrence described in section 2054. Therefore, the damage, to the extent not compensated by insurance or otherwise, is taken into account in valuing the property on the 6-month date.

    Example 3. At D's death, D has an interest in an S corporation, W. During the alternate valuation period, it is discovered that an employee of W has embezzled significant assets from W. W does not reasonably expect to recover the funds or any damages from the employee, and insurance proceeds are not sufficient to cover the loss. The theft is an occurrence described in section 2054. Therefore, the theft, to the extent not compensated by insurance or otherwise, is taken into account in valuing D's interest in W on the 6-month date.

    (h) *Effective/applicability date.*—* * * All of paragraph (c)(2) of this section except the second sentence of the introductory text, all of

paragraph (c)(3) of this section except paragraph (c)(3)(i)(C) of this section, the chart in *Example 1* of paragraph (e) of this section, all of paragraph (f)(2) of this section except the last sentence, and the first and third sentences in paragraph (f)(2)(ii) of this section are applicable to decedents dying after August 16, 1954. All of paragraphs (a) introductory text, (a)(1), (a)(2), (c)(1)(i), (c)(1)(ii), (c)(1)(iii), (c)(1)(iv), (c)(3)(i)(C), (c)(4), (c)(5), (f)(1), (f)(2)(i), and (f)(3) of this section, the second sentence of the introductory text in paragraph (c)(2) of this section, all of paragraph (e) of this section except the chart in *Example 1*, the last sentence in the introductory text of paragraph (f)(2) of this section, and the second sentence in paragraph (f)(2)(ii) of this section are applicable to estates of decedents dying on or after the date of publication of the Treasury decision adopting these rules as final in the **Federal Register**.

Retention of Stock Voting Rights

    Gross Estate: Property in Which Decedent Had Interest: Shares of Stock.—Reproduced below is the text of proposed Reg. §20.2036-2, relating to the estate tax consequences of a decedent's retention of voting rights in a lifetime transfer of stock (published in the Federal Register on August 3, 1983).

    ☐ Par. There is added immediately after §20.2036-1 the following new section:

    §20.2036-2. Special treatment of retained voting rights.—(a) *In general.*—For purposes of section 2036(a)(1) and §20.2036-1(a), the retention of the right to vote (directly or indirectly) shares of stock of a controlled corporation is a retention of the enjoyment of the transferred property if:

    (1) The transfer was made after June 22, 1976;

    (2) The corporation was a controlled corporation at any time after transfer of that stock; and

    (3) The corporation was a controlled corporation at any time during the three-year period ending on the decedent's death

The rule of this section does not require inclusion of stock in the gross estate if the transferred stock has no voting rights or if the donor has not retained voting rights in the stock transferred. Thus, for example, if a person owning 100 percent of the voting and nonvoting stock of a corporation transfers the nonvoting stock, that person shall not be treated as having retained the enjoyment of the property transferred merely because of voting rights in the stock retained. Stock carrying voting rights that will vest only when conditions occur, such as preferred stock which gains voting rights only if no dividends are paid, is subject to this section. However, if the decedent's right to vote such stock is only in a fiduciary capacity (*e.g.*, because the decedent is trustee of a trust to which the stock has been transferred), such stock is subject to this section only if, after the transfer by the decedent, the conditions occur that give the decedent the right to vote the stock. Stock that possesses voting rights in only extraordinary matters, such as mergers or liquidations shall be subject to this section unless the decedent's retention of voting rights is only in a fiduciary capacity.

    (b) *Relinquishment or cessation of voting rights within three years of death.*—In general, the relinquishment or cessation of retained voting rights shall be treated as a "transfer of property" for purposes of section 2035 (transfer within three years of death) if:

    (1) The voting rights were retained in a transfer made after June 22, 1976; and

    (2) The corporation was a controlled corporation at some point in time occurring after the transfer, before the relinquishment or cessation of voting rights, and within three years of death. However, to the extent that a relinquishment of voting rights is in exchange for voting rights in another controlled corporation, the relinquishment shall not be treated as a "transfer of property" for purposes of section 2035. See paragraph (e)(3) of this section for the treatment of voting rights in such other corporation.

    (c) *Meaning of right to vote.*—For purposes of this section, the term "right to vote" means the power to vote, whether exercisable alone or in conjunction with other persons. The capacity in which the decedent can exercise voting power is immaterial. Accordingly, a fiduciary power exercisable as trustee, co-trustee, or as officer of a corporation is a right to vote stock within the meaning of this section. For purposes of section 2036(b)(1) and §20.2036-2(a), the constructive ownership rules of section 318 shall not be used to attribute the retention of voting rights to the decedent. Therefore, the fact that a relative of the decedent is trustee of a trust to which the decedent has transferred stock shall not in itself require a finding that the decedent indirectly retained the right to vote that stock. However, any arrangement to shift formal voting power away from the decedent will not be treated for this purpose as a relinquishment of all voting rights if, in substance, the decedent has retained voting power. Moreover, voting power shall be deemed retained in cases where there is any agreement with the decedent, express or implied, that the shareholder, or other holder of the power to vote stock, either will vote the stock in a specified manner or will not vote the stock. If the decedent has the power to obtain the right to vote, such as where he may

appoint himself as a trustee of a trust holding the stock, the decedent has retained the right to vote for purposes of section 2036.

    (d) *Meaning of controlled corporation.*—(1) *In general.*—For purposes of this section, the term "controlled corporation" means a corporation in which the decedent, with application of the constructive ownership rules of section 318, is deemed to own or have a right to vote stock possessing at least 20 percent of the total combined voting power of all classes of stock.

    (2) *Computations.*—(i) *Total combined voting power of all classes of stock.*—For purposes of this paragraph, the total combined voting power of all classes of stock shall include only stock that currently has voting power. Stock that may vote only on extraordinary matters, such as mergers or liquidations, shall be disregarded. Similarly, treasury stock and stock that is authorized but unissued shall be disregarded.

    (ii) *Decedent's percentage of total combined voting power.*—For purposes of this paragraph, in determining whether the voting power possessed by the decedent is at least 20 percent of the total combined voting power of all classes of stock, consideration will be given to all the facts and circumstances. Generally, the percentage of voting power possessed by a person in a corporation may be determined by reference to the power of stock to vote for the election of directors. Instruments that do not have voting rights shall be disregarded. Instruments having no voting rights but which may be converted into voting stock shall be disregarded until such conversion occurs. Instruments carrying voting rights that will vest only when conditions, the occurrence of which is indeterminate, have been met will be disregarded until the conditions have occurred which cause the voting rights to vest. An example of such an instrument is preferred stock which gains voting rights only if no dividends are paid.

    (iii) *Example.*—The following example illustrates the application of paragraphs (d)(1) through (d)(2)(ii) of this section.

    Example. A corporation has three classes of stock outstanding, consisting of 40 shares of class A voting stock, 50 shares of class B voting stock, and 60 shares of class C preferred stock which is nonvoting except for extraordinary matters or unless the arrearages in dividends exceed a specified amount. Assume for purposes of this example that except for extraordinary business matters, the voting stock's only voting power is the right to vote in the election of directors. The class A stockholders are entitled to elect 7 of the 10 corporate directors, and the class B stockholders are entitled to elect the other 3 of the 10 directors. Thus, the class A stock (as a class) possesses 70 percent of the total combined voting power of all classes of stock, and the class B stock (as a class) possesses 30 percent of such voting power. At the time of D's death, D has voting rights in 9 shares of class A stock directly; and with the constructive ownership rules of section 318, D is deemed to have voting rights in 3 additional shares of class A stock. D has no interest in the class B stock and owns all 60 shares of the class C stock. Thus, D is deemed to possess 21 percent ((9 + 3) shares/40 shares × 70 percent) of the total combined voting power of all classes of stock. By reason of such voting power, the corporation is a controlled corporation within the meaning of this section.

    (e) *Direct versus indirect retention of voting rights.*—(1) *Direct transfers.*—Subject to the limitations contained in paragraph (a) of this section, if the decedent transfers stock of a controlled corporation (except in case of a bona fide sale for adequate and full consideration in money or money's worth), the retention of voting rights in the stock transferred shall require a portion of the fair market value of the stock to be included in the gross estate. For purposes of this paragraph (e)(1), transfers of stock in exchange for, in whole or in part, either property donated by the decedent or property for which the decedent supplied the purchase consideration, will not be considered a bona fide sale for adequate and full consideration. The amount included in the gross estate under this paragraph (e)(1) shall be an amount, not less than zero, equal to the fair market value at death of the stock transferred less the value of any consideration the decedent received in exchange.

(2) *Indirect transfer.*—Section 2036 applies to indirect as well as direct transfers. The acquisition of voting rights in stock acquired through the exercise of other instruments transferred by the decedent (such as through the exercise of warrants or options, or the conversion rights on convertible nonvoting stock or indebtedness) shall cause the stock to be treated as acquired with consideration furnished by the decedent and an indirect transfer by the decedent. If a third party makes a transfer to the trust and the consideration for the transfer was furnished by the decedent, the transfer by the third party to the trust will be treated as a transfer by the decedent to the trust. In addition, if the decedent makes a transfer by gift to a trust, and the trust subsequently acquires stock in which the decedent has voting rights, then for purposes of section 2036(a), the transaction will be treated as an indirect transfer of stock by the decedent (irrespective of whether the acquisition of the stock can be traced to the gift). The amount included in the gross estate in such a case is equal to the fair market value at death of the portion of the stock acquired with funds provided by the decedent. In the case of a purchase of stock from a third party by a trust, the stock shall be treated as purchased with funds provided by the decedent to the extent there are funds in the trust treated as provided by the decedent. For this purpose, the portion of the funds in the trust treated as provided by the decedent shall be determined after each addition to the trust and is equal to a fraction. The numerator of the fraction is the sum of—

(i) The total value of the trust immediately prior to the latest addition multiplied by the fraction of such value treated as provided by the decedent because of prior additions, and

Fair market value of instruments at death	$150,000
Less consideration received by D	50,000
Amount included in D's gross estate	$100,000

Example (2). The facts are the same as in *example (1)* except that the 1979 transfer to the trust (1000 shares of ABC Corporation) was in exchange for $100,000 cash. As a result of the stock transfer, the

Fair market value of instruments at death	$150,000
Less consideration received by D	100,000
Amount included in D's gross estate	$50,000

The 1979 transfer is not considered a *bona fide* sale for adequate and full consideration in money or money's worth since D provided the consideration by virtue of his 1977 transfer to the trust.

Example (3). During 1979, D transferred by gift 1000 shares of ABC Corporation voting stock worth $100,000 to his wife W. During 1980, W made a gift of the same stock to a trust. Assume that D becomes trustee of the trust and hence acquires the right to vote the stock in that capacity. Assume further that, at some time after D's transfer, ABC Corporation is a controlled corporation within the meaning of this section. D dies during 1981, at which time the stock is worth $150,000. The full $150,000 is included in D's gross estate under section 2036.

Example (4). During 1979, D transferred by gift $90,000 to a trust that already had $90,000 of funds, all of which is attributable to

(ii) The amount of the latest addition to the extent provided by the decedent.

The denominator of the fraction is the total value of the trust immediately after the latest addition.

(3) *Exchange of voting rights.*—For purposes of this section, if a decedent is deemed to have retained the right to vote shares of stock of a controlled corporation in a transfer occurring after June 22, 1976, the subsequent relinquishment of those voting rights, in exchange for voting rights in other stock of a controlled corporation, shall be treated as a retention of voting rights in such other stock. Furthermore, for purposes of section 2036(a), such other stock shall be treated as property transferred by the decedent. For example, if a person transfers stock in ABC Corporation (a controlled corporation) after June 22, 1976, to a trust for which that person is a trustee—thus retaining voting rights in a fiduciary capacity—and the trust later sells the ABC Corporation stock, using the proceeds to purchase stock in XYZ Corporation (a controlled corporation), that person will be treated as having retained the right to vote the shares of XYZ Corporation. In such a transaction, the shares of XYZ Corporation shall be treated as transferred by that person. If the stock in XYZ Corporation is acquired directly from the decedent, the amount included in the gross estate shall be determined under paragraph (e)(1) of this section. If the stock in XYZ Corporation is acquired from someone other than the decedent, the amount included in the decedent's gross estate shall be determined under paragraph (e)(2) of this section.

(4) *Examples.*—The following examples illustrate the application of section 2043 and paragraph (e)(1) and (e)(2) of this section.

Example (1). During 1977, D transferred by gift $100,000 cash to a trust. During 1979, D transferred to the trust 1000 shares of ABC Corporation voting stock worth $100,000. The 1979 transfer was in exchange for $50,000 cash and D retained voting rights in all the stock transferred. Assume that at some time after the stock transfer, ABC Corporation is a controlled corporation within the meaning of this section. D dies during 1981, at which time the stock is worth $150,000. As a result of the stock transfer, the amount included in D's gross estate under section 2036 is $100,000, computed as follows:

amount included in D's gross estate under section 2036 is $50,000, computed as follows:

contributions by persons other than D. During 1980, the trust purchased at full fair market value 1000 shares of ABC Corporation voting stock worth $100,000, at which time, because of appreciation, the value of the trust was $210,000. Assume that D acquires the right to vote the stock as trustee of the trust and that at some time after the stock purchase, ABC Corporation is a controlled corporation within the meaning of this section. D dies during 1981, at which time the stock is worth $150,000. Pursuant to paragraph (e)(2) of this section, at the time of the stock purchase, $105,000 (50 percent of $210,000) of funds in the trust were funds supplied by D, $100,000 of which are treated as used to purchase the stock. Accordingly, the amount included in D's gross estate under section 2036, $150,000, is the value at death of the portion of the stock acquired with funds provided by D.

Qualified Plan Benefits

Gross Estate: Annuities: Exclusion for Qualified Plan and IRA Benefits.—Temporary Reg. §20.2039-1T, providing guidance with respect to qualified employee benefit plans, welfare benefit funds and employees receiving benefits through such plans, is proposed (published in the Federal Register on January 29, 1986).

§20.2039-1T. Limitations and repeal of estate tax exclusion for qualified plans and individual retirement plans (IRAs) (temporary).

Individual Retirement Plans: Simplified Employee Pensions: Qualified Voluntary Employee Contributions

Individual Retirement Plans: Simplified Employee Pensions: Qualified Voluntary Employee Contributions.—Reproduced below are the texts of proposed amendments of Reg. §§20.2039-2 and 20.2039-4, relating to individual retirement plans, simplified employee pensions and qualified voluntary employee contributions (published in the Federal Register on January 23, 1984).

☐ Par. 10. Section 20.2039-2 is revised by adding a new subdivision (ix) to paragraph (c)(1) to read as follows:

§20.2039-2. Annuities under "qualified plans" and section 403(b) annuity contracts.

* * *

(c) *Amounts excludable from the gross estate.*

(1) * * *

☐ Par. 11. Section 20.2039-4 is revised by adding a new paragraph (h) to read as follows:

§20.2039-4. Lump sum distributions from "qualified plans;" decedents dying after December 31, 1978.

* * *

(h) *Accumulated deductible employee contributions.*—For purposes of this section, a lump sum distribution includes an amount attributable to accumulated deductible employee contributions (as defined in section 72(o)(5)(B)) in any qualified plan taken into account for purposes of determining whether any distribution from that quali-

(ix) Any deductible employee contributions (within the meaning of section 72(o)(5)) are considered amounts contributed by the employer.

* * *

fied plan is a lump sum distribution as determined under paragraph (b) of this section. Thus, amounts attributable to accumulated deductible employee contributions in a qualified plan under which amounts are payable in a lump sum distribution are not excludible from the decedent's gross estate under §20.2039-2, unless the recipient makes the section 402(a)/403(c) taxation election with respect to a lump sum distribution payable from that qualified plan.

* * *

Charitable Remainder Trusts

Charitable Remainder Trusts: Election: Extended Date.—Reproduced below is the text of a proposed amendment of Reg. §20.2055-2, relating to the granting of an extension to permit the reformation of charitable remainder trusts (published in the Federal Register on December 19, 1975).

☐ Par. 3. §20.2055-2 is amended by adding a sentence at the end of paragraph (a) and by adding a new paragraph (g) immediately following §20.2055-2(f). These added and amended provisions read as follows:

§20.2055-2. Transfers not exclusively for charitable purposes.—
(a) *Remainders and similar interests.*—* * * See paragraph (g) of this section for special rules relating to certain wills and trusts in existence on September 21, 1974.

* * *

(g) *Special rules applicable in the case of certain wills and trusts in existence on September 21, 1974.*—(1) In general, in the case of a will executed before September 21, 1974, or a trust created (within the meaning of applicable local law) after July 31, 1969, and before September 21, 1974, if—

(i) At the time of the decedent's death a deduction is not allowable solely because of the failure of an interest in property which passes or has passed from the decedent to a person, or for a use, described in section 2055(a) to meet the requirements of section 2055(e)(2)(A), and

(ii) The governing instrument is amended or conformed in accordance with this paragraph so that the interest is in a trust which is a charitable remainder annuity trust or a charitable remainder unitrust (described in section 664) or a pooled income fund (described in section 642(c)(5)), or the governing instrument is treated under paragraph (g)(8) of this section as if it were amended, a deduction shall nevertheless be allowed.

(2) An amendment or conformation pursuant to this paragraph must be made before January 1, 1976, or, if later, on or before the 30th day after the date on which judicial proceedings begun before January 1, 1976 (which are required to amend or conform the governing instrument) become final.

(3) A governing instrument may be amended or conformed under this paragraph only where:

(i) The transfer is not in trust but passes under a will executed before September 21, 1974;

(ii) The transfer is in the form of a testamentary trust created under a will executed before September 21, 1974;

(iii) The transfer was in trust, which was created (within the meaning of applicable local law) after July 31, 1969, and before September 21, 1974, but only if, at the time of the creation of the trust, the governing instrument provides that an organization described in section 170(c) receives an irrevocable remainder interest in such trust;

(iv) Property was transferred inter vivos after July 31, 1969, and before October 18, 1971, to a trust created (within the meaning of applicable local law) before August 1, 1969, which trust provides that an organization described in section 170(c) receives an irrevocable remainder interest in such trust, and the transferred property and any undistributed income therefrom is severed and placed in a separate trust before the applicable date specified in paragraph (g)(2) of this section. An instrument governing a transfer under this subdivision (iv), which is amended pursuant to this paragraph, shall be treated as having made such transfer to a trust deemed created on the date of such transfer;

(v) In the case of a transfer to a pooled income fund made before September 21, 1974 (or a transfer made under a will which was executed before September 21, 1974), the instrument governing the transfer fails to satisfy the requirements of §1.642(c)-5(b). However, a governing instrument may not be amended pursuant to this paragraph unless, at the time of the decedent's death, the interest is an irrevocable remainder interest for which a deduction, but for section 2055(e)(2)(A), would be allowable under section 2055(a) and

the regulations thereunder. The provisions of section 508(d)(2)(A) (relating to disallowance of certain charitable, etc., deductions) shall not apply to such interest if the governing instrument is amended so as to comply with the requirements of section 508(e) (relating to governing instruments) by the applicable date described in paragraph (g)(2) of this section.

(4) The decree resulting from any judicial proceedings begun to amend a governing instrument pursuant to paragraph (g)(1) of this section must be binding, under local law, on all parties having an interest in the bequest or transfer as well as the fiduciary of the decedent's estate and trustee of the trust to be amended. In the event local law does not require judicial proceedings to amend or conform a governing instrument, a deduction may nevertheless be allowed if the governing instrument is amended or conformed by nonjudicial agreement between all parties having an interest in the bequest or transfer as well as the fiduciary of the decedent's estate and trustee of the trust to be amended, provided that the agreement is binding, under local law, on all such parties. The judicial proceedings or nonjudicial agreement must also account for any distributions made from the deemed date of creation to the date of the amendment in the following manner:

(i) Where the amount of the distributions which would have been made by the trust to a recipient had the amendment pursuant to paragraph (g)(1) of this section been in effect since the creation of the trust exceeds the amount of the distributions made by the trust prior to the amendment, the trust must pay an amount equal to such excess to the recipient;

(ii) Where the amount of the distributions made to the recipient prior to the amendment pursuant to paragraph (g)(1) of this section exceeds the amount of the distributions which would have been made by such trust if the amended provisions of such trust had been in effect from the time of creation of such trust, the recipient must pay an amount equal to such excess to the trust.

See §1.664-1(d)(4) for rules relating to the year of inclusion in the case of an underpayment to a recipient and the allowance of a deduction in the case of an overpayment to a recipient.

(5) Where a charitable remainder trust (as described in §1.664-1(a)(1)(iii)(a)) results from an amendment pursuant to this paragraph, the trust will be treated as a charitable remainder trust for all purposes from the date it would be deemed created under §1.664-1(a)(4) and (5), whether or not such date is after September 20, 1974. Subject to the limitations imposed by section 6511, the estate tax charitable deduction is allowable and the charitable remainder trust is exempt from Federal income taxation. For the application of certain excise taxes pursuant to section 4947(a)(2) see §53.4947-1(c)(1)(iii) and (c)(6). In amending a governing instrument pursuant to paragraph (g)(1) of this section, the exchange of a noncharitable beneficiary's interest in an unqualified transfer in trust for an interest in a qualified transfer in trust will not be treated as an act of self-dealing (described in section 4941) or a taxable expenditure (described in section 4945).

(6) If, on the due date for filing the estate tax return (including any extensions thereof), proceedings to amend or conform a governing instrument pursuant to paragraph (g)(1) of this section have not become final, such return shall be filed with the tax computed as if no deduction were allowable under this paragraph. When the proceedings to amend or conform such instrument have become final (within the applicable date described in paragraph (g)(2) of this

section), a deduction shall be allowed upon the filing of a claim for credit or refund (within the limitations of section 6511). In the case of a credit or refund as a result of an amendment or conformation made pursuant to this paragraph, no interest shall be allowed for the period prior to the expiration of the 180th day after the date on which the claim for credit or refund is filed.

(7) If a governing instrument is amended under this paragraph, then, except as provided in paragraph (g)(8)(ii) of this section, the amount of the deduction allowable under this section shall be the amount that equals the value of the interest which, under the rules of section 2055 (including the rules governing disclaimers) passes to, or for the use of, an organization described in section 2055(a).

(8)(i) In the case of a will executed before September 21, 1974, or a trust created (within the meaning of applicable local law) before such date and after July 31, 1969, that creates an interest for which a deduction would be allowable under section 2055(a) but for section 2055(e)(2)(A), if the date of death of the decedent is prior to January 1, 1976, and if on or before the filing date of the estate tax return (including any extension thereof)—

(A) The interest is in a charitable trust which, if a deduction under section 2055(a) had been allowed, would be in a trust described in section 4947(a)(1), or

(B) Such interest passes directly to a person or for a use described in section 2055(a) (as, for example, by reason of the termination of an intervening interest),

the governing instrument shall be treated as if it were amended or conformed pursuant to paragraph (g)(1) of this section and a deduction shall be allowed. See section 508(d)(2) and §1.508-2(b) for the disallowance of such a deduction in the case of an interest in a trust

described in section 4947(a)(1) if the governing instrument fails to meet the requirements of section 508(e) by the end of the taxable year of the trust in which the filing date of the estate tax return occurs. A governing instrument treated as amended under this subdivision (i) may not thereafter be amended. The provisions of this subparagraph shall not apply if the requirements of subdivision (A) or (B) of this subdivision (ii) are satisfied as a result of an amendment of a dispositive provision of the governing instrument occurring since the date of death of the decedent.

(ii) The amount of the deduction for a transfer which is treated under this paragraph as if it were amended will be determined as if the transfer were a charitable remainder annuity trust which provides an annuity of 6 percent of the initial fair market value payable from the date of death—

(A) In the case of a transfer providing a life estate, for the expected lives of the noncharitable beneficiaries as determined on the date of death of the decedent, or

(B) In the case of a transfer providing a term of years, for the term of years as expressed in the governing instrument, but not to exceed 20 years.

Any distributions made to a recipient from the date of death of the decedent to the date on which the transfer is deemed to be amended (i.e., the date the transfer satisfies the requirements of paragraph (g)(8)(i) of this section) must be taken into account under this subdivision (ii) in determining the amount of the deduction, to the extent that the adjustments in such distributions required by paragraph (g)(4) of this section, determined as if the charitable remainder annuity trust were deemed created at the date of death of the decedent, have not been made on or before the filing date of the estate tax return. [Reg. §20.2055-2.]

GIFT TAX

Guidance under Section 529A: Qualified ABLE Programs

Guidance under Section 529A: Qualified ABLE Programs.—Amendments to Reg. §§25.2501-1 and 25.2503-3, regarding programs under The Stephen Beck, Jr., Achieving a Better Life Experience Act of 2014 and rules under which States or State agencies or instrumentalities may establish and maintain a new type of tax-favored savings program through which contributions may be made to the account of an eligible disabled individual to meet qualified disability expenses, are proposed (published in the Federal Register on June 22, 2015) (REG-102837-15).

Par. 6. Section 25.2501-1 is amended by adding a sentence at the end of paragraph (a)(1) to read as follows:

§25.2501-1. Imposition of Tax.—(a) * * *   * * *

(1) * * * For gift tax rules related to an ABLE account established under section 529A, *see* regulations promulgated thereunder.

Par. 7. Section 25.2503-3 is amended by adding a sentence at the end of paragraph (a) to read as follows:

§25.2503-3. Future interests in property.—(a) * * * A contribution   * * *
to an ABLE account established under section 529A is not a future interest.

Annual Exclusion for Spousal IRA Transfers

Annual Exclusion: Contributions to Spousal Individual Retirement Accounts.—Reproduced below is the text of proposed Reg. §25.2503-5, providing that contributions by a working spouse to an individual retirement account for the benefit of a nonworking spouse qualify for the annual gift tax exclusion to the extent that they are deductible for income tax purposes (published in the Federal Register on July 14, 1981).

* * *

☐ Par. 13. There is added after §25.2503-4 the following new section:

§25.2503-5. Individual retirement plan for spouse.—(a) *In general.*—For purposes of section 2503(b), any payment made by an individual for the benefit of his or her spouse—

(1) To an individual retirement account described in section 408(a),

(2) To an individual retirement subaccount described in §1.220-1(b)(3),

(3) For an individual retirement annuity described in section 408(b), or

(4) For a retirement bond described in section 409,

shall not be considered a gift of a future interest in property to the extent that such payment is allowable as a deduction under section 220 for the taxable year for which the contribution is made. Thus, for example, if individual A paid $900 to an individual retirement account for 1980 on behalf of A's spouse, B, of which $875 was deductible, $875 would not be a gift of a future interest.

(b) *Effective date.*—Paragraph (a) of this section is effective for transfers made after December 31, 1976.

Guidance under Section 529A: Qualified ABLE Programs

Guidance under Section 529A: Qualified ABLE Programs.—Amendments to Reg. §25.2503-6 regarding programs under The Stephen Beck, Jr., Achieving a Better Life Experience Act of 2014 and rules under which States or State agencies or instrumentalities may establish and maintain a new type of tax-favored savings program through which contributions may be made to the account of an eligible disabled individual to meet qualified disability expenses, are proposed (published in the Federal Register on June 22, 2015) (REG-102837-15).

Par. 8. Section 25.2503-6 is amended by adding a sentence at the end of paragraph (a) to read as follows:

§25.2503-6. Exclusion for certain qualified transfers to tuition or medical expenses.—(a) * * * A contribution to an ABLE account established under section 529A is not a qualified transfer.   * * *

Guidance under Section 529A: Qualified ABLE Programs

Guidance under Section 529A: Qualified ABLE Programs.—Amendments to Reg. §25.2511-2 regarding programs under The Stephen Beck, Jr., Achieving a Better Life Experience Act of 2014 and rules under which States or State agencies or instrumentalities may establish and maintain a new type of tax-favored savings program through which contributions may be made to the account of an eligible disabled individual to meet qualified disability expenses, are proposed (published in the Federal Register on June 22, 2015) (REG-102837-15).

Par. 9. Section 25.2511-2 is amended by adding a sentence at the end of paragraph (a) to read as follows:

§25.2511-2. Cessation of donor's dominion and control.—(a) * * * For gift tax rules related to an ABLE account established under section 529A, *see* regulations promulgated thereunder.

* * *

Imputed Interest: OID: Safe Haven Rates

Imputed Interest: Original Issue Discount: Safe Haven Interest Rates.—Amendments to Reg. §25.2512-4 and 25.2512-8, relating to (1) the tax treatment of debt instruments issued after July 1, 1982, that contain original issue discount, (2) the imputation of and the accounting for interest with respect to sales and exchanges of property occurring after December 31, 1984, and (3) safe haven interest rates for loans or advances between commonly controlled taxpayers and safe haven leases between such taxpayers, are proposed (published in the Federal Register on August 20, 1985; Reg. §25.2512-4 was reproposed in the Federal Register on April 8, 1986).

☐ Par. 43. Section 25.2512-4 is revised to read as follows:

§25.2512-4. Valuation of notes.—The fair market value of notes, secured or unsecured, is presumed to be the amount of unpaid principal, plus accrued interest to the date of the gift, unless the donor establishes a lower value. The fair market value of a debt instrument (as defined in §1.1275-1(b)) whose issue price is determined under section 1273(b)(1), (2), or (3), or section 1274 is presumed to be its revised issue price (as defined in §1.1275-1(h)). Unless returned at this value, it must be shown by satisfactory evidence that the note is worth less than the unpaid amount (because

of the interest rate, or date of maturity, or other cause), or that the note is uncollectible in part (by reason of the insolvency of the party or parties liable, or for other cause), and that the property, if any, pledged or mortgaged as security is insufficient to satisfy it. See §25.2512-8 and §1.1012-2 for special rules relating to certain sales or exchanges of property. See §25.7872-1 for special rules in the case of gift loans (within the meaning of §1.7872-4(b)) made after June 6, 1984. [Reg. §25.2512-4.]

☐ Par. 44. Section 25.2512-8 is revised to read as follows:

§25.2512-8. Transfers for insufficient or excessive consideration.—Transfers reached by the gift tax are not confined to those only which, being without a valuable consideration, accord with the common law concept of gifts, but embrace as well sales, exchanges, and other dispositions of property for a consideration to the extent that the value of the property transferred by the donor differs from the value in money or money's worth of the consideration given therefor. However, a sale, exchange, or other transfer of property made in the ordinary course of business (a transaction which is bona fide, at arm's length, and free from any donative intent), will be considered as made for consideration in money or money's worth equal to the value of the property transferred. If the buyer issues one or more debt instruments as all or a part of the consideration for the property,

then the property and the debt instruments shall be valued in accordance with the rules set forth in §1.1012-2. A consideration not reducible to a value in money or money's worth, as love and affection, promise of marriage, etc., is to be wholly disregarded, and the entire value of the property transferred contitutes the amount of the gift. Similarly, a relinquishment or promised relinquishment of dower or curtesy, or of a statutory estate created in lieu of dower or curtesy, or of other marital rights in the spouse's property or estate, shall not be considered to any extent a consideration "in money or money's worth." See, however, section 2516 and the regulations thereunder with respect to certain transfers incident to a divorce. [Reg. §25.2512-8.]

TAX ON GENERATION-SKIPPING TRANSFERS

Guidance under Section 529A: Qualified ABLE Programs

Guidance under Section 529A: Qualified ABLE Programs.—Amendments to Reg. §26.2642-1, regarding programs under The Stephen Beck, Jr., Achieving a Better Life Experience Act of 2014 and rules under which States or State agencies or instrumentalities may establish and maintain a new type of tax-favored savings program through which contributions may be made to the account of an eligible disabled individual to meet qualified disability expenses, are proposed (published in the Federal Register on June 22, 2015) (REG-102837-15).

Par. 11. Section 26.2642-1 is amended by adding a sentence at the end of paragraph (a) to read as follows:

§26.2642-1. Inclusion ratio
(a) * * * For generation-skipping transfer tax rules related to an ABLE account established under section 529A, *see* regulations promulgated thereunder.

* * *

GST Exemption: Extension of Time

GST Exemption: Extension of Time.—Reg. §26.2642-7, describing the circumstances and procedures under which an extension of time will be granted under Code Sec. 2642(g)(1), is proposed (published in the Federal Register on April 17, 2008) (REG-147775-06).

☐ Par. 2. Section 26.2642-7 is added to read as follows:

§26.2642-7. Relief under section 2642(g)(1).—(a) *In general.*— Under section 2642(g)(1)(A), the Secretary has the authority to issue regulations describing the circumstances in which a transferor, as defined in section 2652(a), or the executor of a transferor's estate, as defined in section 2203, will be granted an extension of time to allocate generation-skipping transfer (GST) exemption as described in sections 2642(b)(1) and (2). The Secretary also has the authority to issue regulations describing the circumstances under which a transferor or the executor of a transferor's estate will be granted an extension of time to make the elections described in section 2632(b)(3) and (c)(5). Section 2632(b)(3) provides that an election may be made by or on behalf of a transferor not to have the transferor's GST exemption automatically allocated under section 2632(b)(1) to a direct skip, as defined in section 2612(c), made by the transferor during life. Section 2632(c)(5)(A)(i) provides that an election may be made by or on behalf of a transferor not to have the transferor's GST

exemption automatically allocated under section 2632(c)(1) to an indirect skip, as defined in section 2632(c)(3)(A), or to any or all transfers made by such transferor to a particular trust. Section 2632(c)(5)(A)(ii) provides that an election may be made by or on behalf of a transferor to treat any trust as a GST trust, as defined in section 2632(c)(3)(B), for purposes of section 2632(c) with respect to any or all transfers made by that transferor to the trust. This section generally describes the factors that the Internal Revenue Service (IRS) will consider when an extension of time is sought by or on behalf of a transferor to timely allocate GST exemption and/or to make an election under section 2632(b)(3) or (c)(5). Relief provided under this section will be granted through the IRS letter ruling program. See paragraph (h) of this section.

(b) *Effect of Relief.*—If an extension of time to allocate GST exemption is granted under this section, the allocation of GST exemption will be considered effective as of the date of the transfer, and the value of the property transferred for purposes of chapter 11 or chapter 12 will determine the amount of GST exemption to be allocated. If an extension of time to elect out of the automatic allocation of GST exemption under section 2632(b)(3) or (c)(5) is granted under this section, the election will be considered effective as of the date of the transfer. If an extension of time to elect to treat any trust as a GST trust under section 2632(c)(5)(A)(ii) is granted under this section, the election will be considered effective as of the date of the first (or each) transfer covered by that election.

(c) *Limitation on relief.*—The amount of GST exemption that may be allocated to a transfer as the result of relief granted under this section is limited to the amount of the transferor's unused GST exemption under section 2631(c) as of the date of the transfer. Thus, if, by the time of the making of the allocation or election pursuant to relief granted under this section, the GST exemption amount under section 2631(c) has increased to an amount in excess of the amount in effect for the date of the transfer, no portion of the increased amount may be applied to that earlier transfer by reason of the relief granted under this section.

(d) *Basis for determination.*—(1) *In general.*—Requests for relief under this section will be granted when the transferor or the executor of the transferor's estate provides evidence (including the affidavits described in paragraph (h) of this section) to establish to the satisfaction of the IRS that the transferor or the executor of the transferor's estate acted reasonably and in good faith, and that the grant of relief will not prejudice the interests of the Government. Paragraphs (d)(2) and (d)(3) of this section set forth nonexclusive lists of factors the IRS will consider in determining whether this standard of reasonableness, good faith, and lack of prejudice to the interests of the Government has been met so that such relief will be granted. In making this determination, IRS will consider these factors, as well as all other relevant facts and circumstances. Paragraph (e) of this section sets forth situations in which this standard has not been met and, as a result, in which relief under this section will not be granted.

(2) *Reasonableness and good faith.*—The following is a nonexclusive list of factors that will be considered to determine whether the transferor or the executor of the transferor's estate acted reasonably and in good faith for purposes of this section:

(i) The intent of the transferor to timely allocate GST exemption to a transfer or to timely make an election under section 2632(b)(3) or (c)(5), as evidenced in the trust instrument, the instrument of transfer, or other relevant documents contemporaneous with the transfer, such as Federal gift and estate tax returns and correspondence. This may include evidence of the intended GST tax status of the transfer or the trust (for example, exempt, non-exempt, or partially exempt), or more explicit evidence of intent with regard to the allocation of GST exemption or the election under section 2632(b)(3) or (c)(5).

(ii) Intervening events beyond the control of the transferor or of the executor of the transferor's estate as the cause of the failure to allocate GST exemption to a transfer or the failure to make an election under section 2632(b)(3) or (c)(5).

(iii) Lack of awareness by the transferor or the executor of the transferor's estate of the need to allocate GST exemption to the transfer, despite the exercise of reasonable diligence, taking into account the experience of the transferor or the executor of the transferor's estate and the complexity of the GST issue, as the cause of the failure to allocate GST exemption to a transfer or to make an election under section 2632(b)(3) or (c)(5).

(iv) Consistency by the transferor with regard to the allocation of the transferor's GST exemption (for example, the transferor's consistent allocation of GST exemption to transfers to skip persons or to a particular trust, or the transferor's consistent election not to have the automatic allocation of GST exemption apply to transfers to one or more trusts or skip persons pursuant to section 2632(b)(3) or (c)(5)). Evidence of consistency may be less relevant if there has been a change of circumstances or change of trust beneficiaries that would otherwise explain a deviation from prior GST exemption allocation decisions.

(v) Reasonable reliance by the transferor or the executor of the transferor's estate on the advice of a qualified tax professional retained or employed by one or both of them and, in reliance on or consistent with that advice, the failure of the transferor or the executor to allocate GST exemption to the transfer or to make an election described in section 2632(b)(3) or (c)(5). Reliance on a qualified tax professional will not be considered to have been reasonable if the transferor or the executor of the transferor's estate knew or should have known that the professional either—

(A) Was not competent to render advice on the GST exemption; or

(B) Was not aware of all relevant facts.

(3) *Prejudice to the interests of the Government.*—The following is a nonexclusive list of factors that will be considered to determine whether the interests of the Government would be prejudiced for purposes of this section:

(i) The interests of the Government would be prejudiced to the extent to which the request for relief is an effort to benefit from hindsight. The interests of the Government would be prejudiced if the IRS determines that the requested relief is an attempt to benefit from hindsight rather than to achieve the result the transferor or the executor of the transferor's estate intended at the time when the transfer was made. A factor relevant to this determination is whether the grant of the requested relief would permit an economic advantage or other benefit that would not have been available if the allocation or election had been timely made. Similarly, there would be prejudice if a grant of the requested relief would permit an economic advantage or other benefit that results from the selection of one out of a number of alternatives (other than whether or not to make an allocation or election) that were available at the time the allocation or election could have been timely made, if hindsight makes the selected alternative more beneficial than the other alternatives. Finally, in a situation where the only choices were whether or not to make a timely allocation or election, prejudice would exist if the transferor failed to make the allocation or election in order to wait to see (thus, with the benefit of hindsight) whether or not the making of the allocation of exemption or election would be more beneficial.

(ii) The timing of the request for relief will be considered in determining whether the interests of the Government would be prejudiced by granting relief under this section. The interests of the Government would be prejudiced if the transferor or the executor of the transferor's estate delayed the filing of the request for relief with the intent to deprive the IRS of sufficient time to challenge the claimed identity of the transferor of the transferred property that is the subject of the request for relief, the value of that transferred property for Federal gift or estate tax purposes, or any other aspect of the transfer that is relevant for Federal gift or estate tax purposes. The fact that any period of limitations on the assessment or collection of transfer taxes has expired prior to the filing of a request for relief under this section, however, will not by itself prohibit a grant of relief under this section. Similarly, the combination of the expiration of any such period of limitations with the fact that the asset or interest was valued for transfer tax purposes with the use of a valuation discount will not by itself prohibit a grant of relief under this section.

(iii) The occurrence and effect of an intervening taxable termination or taxable distribution will be considered in determining whether the interests of the Government would be prejudiced by granting relief under this section. The interests of the Government may be prejudiced if a taxable termination or taxable distribution occurred between the time for making a timely allocation of GST exemption or a timely election described in section 2632(b)(3) or (c)(5) and the time at which the request for relief under this section was filed. The impact of a grant of relief on (and the difficulty of adjusting) the GST tax consequences of that intervening termination or distribution will be considered in determining whether the occurrence of a taxable termination or taxable distribution constitutes prejudice.

(e) *Situations in which the standard of reasonableness, good faith, and lack of prejudice to the interests of the Government has not been met.*—Relief under this section will not be granted if the IRS determines that the transferor or the executor of the transferor's estate has not acted reasonably and in good faith, and/or that the grant of relief would prejudice the interests of the Government. The following situations provide illustrations of some circumstances under which the standard of reasonableness, good faith, and lack of prejudice to the interests of the Government has not been met, and, as a result, in which relief under this section will not be granted:

(1) *Timely allocations and elections.*—Relief will not be granted under this section to decrease or revoke a timely allocation of GST exemption as described in § 26.2632-1(b)(4)(ii)(A)(*1*), or to revoke an election under section 2632(b)(3) or (c)(5) made on a timely filed Federal gift or estate tax return.

(2) *Timing.*—Relief will not be granted if the transferor or executor delayed the filing of the request for relief with the intent to deprive the IRS of sufficient time to challenge the claimed identity of the transferor or the valuation of the transferred property for Federal gift or estate tax purposes. (However, see paragraph (d)(3)(ii) of this section for examples of facts which alone do not constitute prejudice.)

(3) *Failure after being accurately informed.*—Relief will not be granted under this section if the decision made by the transferor or the executor of the transferor's estate (who had been accurately informed in all material respects by a qualified tax professional retained or employed by either (or both) of them with regard to the allocation of GST exemption or an election described in section 2632(b)(3) or (c)(5)) was reflected or implemented by the action or inaction that is the subject of the request for relief.

(4) *Hindsight.*—Relief under this section will not be granted if the IRS determines that the requested relief is an attempt to benefit from hindsight rather than an attempt to achieve the result the transferor or the executor of the transferor's estate intended when the transfer was made. One factor that will be relevant to this determination is whether the grant of relief will give the transferor the benefit of hindsight by providing an economic advantage that may not have been available if the allocation or election had been timely made. Thus, relief will not be granted if that relief will shift GST exemption from one trust to another trust unless the beneficiaries of the two trusts, and their respective interests in those trusts, are the same. Similarly, relief will not be granted if there is evidence that the transferor or executor had not made a timely allocation of the exemption in order to determine which of the various trusts achieved the greatest asset appreciation before selecting the trust that should have a zero inclusion ratio.

(f) *Period of limitations under section 6501.*—A request for relief under this section does not reopen, suspend, or extend the period of limitations on assessment or collection of any estate, gift, or GST tax under section 6501. Thus, the IRS may request that the transferor or the transferor's executor consent, under section 6501(c)(4), to an extension of the period of limitation on assessment or collection of any or all gift and GST taxes for the transfer(s) that are the subject of the requested relief. The transferor or the transferor's executor has the right to refuse to extend the period of limitations, or to limit such extension to particular issues or to a particular period of time. See section 6501(c)(4)(B).

(g) *Refunds.*—The filing of a request for relief under section 2642(g)(1) with the IRS does not constitute a claim for refund or credit of an overpayment and no implied right to refund will arise from the filing of such a request for relief. Similarly, the filing of such a request for relief does not extend the period of limitations under section 6511 for filing a claim for refund or credit of an overpayment. In the event the grant of relief under section 2642(g)(1) results in a potential claim for refund or credit of an overpayment, no such refund or credit will be allowed to the taxpayer or to the taxpayer's estate if the period of limitations under section 6511 for filing a claim for a refund or credit of the Federal gift, estate, or GST tax that was reduced by the granted relief has expired. The period of limitations under section 6511 is generally the later of three years from the time the original return is filed or two years from the time the tax was paid. If the IRS and the taxpayer agree to extend the period for assessment of tax, the period for filing a claim for refund or credit will be extended. Section 6511(c). The taxpayer or the taxpayer's estate is responsible for preserving any potential claim for refund or credit. A taxpayer who seeks and is granted relief under section 2642(g)(1) will not be regarded as having filed a claim for refund or credit by requesting such relief. In order to preserve a right of refund or credit, the taxpayer or the executor of the taxpayer's estate also must file before the expiration of the period of limitations under section 6511 for filing such a claim any required forms for requesting a refund or credit in accordance with the instructions to such forms and applicable regulations.

(h) *Procedural requirements.*—(1) *Letter ruling program.*—The relief described in this section is provided through the IRS's private letter ruling program. See Revenue Procedure 2008-1 (2008-1 IRB 1), or its successor, (which are available at *www.irs.gov*). Requests for relief under this section that do not meet the requirements of §301.9100-2 of this chapter must be made under the rules of this section.

(2) *Affidavit and declaration of transferor or the executor of the transferor's estate.*—(i) The transferor or the executor of the transferor's estate must submit a detailed affidavit describing the events that led to the failure to timely allocate GST exemption to a transfer or the failure to timely elect under section 2632(b)(3) or (c)(5), and the events that led to the discovery of the failure. If the transferor or the executor of the transferor's estate relied on a tax professional for advice with respect to the allocation or election, the affidavit must describe—

(A) The scope of the engagement;

(B) The responsibilities the transferor or the executor of the transferor's estate believed the professional had assumed, if any; and

(C) The extent to which the transferor or the executor of the transferor's estate relied on the professional.

(ii) Attached to each affidavit must be copies of any writing (including, without limitation, notes and e-mails) and other contemporaneous documents within the possession of the affiant relevant to the transferor's intent with regard to the application of GST tax to the transaction for which relief under this section is being requested.

(iii) The affidavit must be accompanied by a dated declaration, signed by the transferor or the executor of the transferor's estate that states: "Under penalties of perjury, I declare that I have examined this affidavit, including any attachments thereto, and to the best of my knowledge and belief, this affidavit, including any attachments thereto, is true, correct, and complete. In addition, under penalties of perjury, I declare that I have examined all the documents included as part of this request for relief, and, to the best of my knowledge and belief, these documents collectively contain all the relevant facts relating to the request for relief, and such facts are true, correct, and complete."

(3) *Affidavits and declarations from other parties.*—(i) The transferor or the executor of the transferor's estate must submit detailed affidavits from individuals who have knowledge or information about the events that led to the failure to allocate GST exemption or to elect under section 2632(b)(3) or (c)(5), and/or to the discovery of the failure. These individuals may include individuals whose knowledge or information is not within the personal knowledge of the transferor or the executor of the transferor's estate. The individuals described in paragraph (h)(3)(i) of this section must include—

(A) Each agent or legal representative of the transferor who participated in the transaction and/or the preparation of the return for which relief is being requested;

(B) The preparer of the relevant Federal estate and/or gift tax return(s);

(C) Each individual (including an employee of the transferor or the executor of the transferor's estate) who made a substantial contribution to the preparation of the relevant Federal estate and/or gift tax return(s); and

(D) Each tax professional who advised or was consulted by the transferor or the executor of the transferor's estate with regard to any aspect of the transfer, the trust, the allocation of GST exemption, and/or the election under section 2632(b)(3) or (c)(5).

(ii) Each affidavit must describe the scope of the engagement and the responsibilities of the individual as well as the advice or service(s) the individual provided to the transferor or the executor of the transferor's estate.

(iii) Attached to each affidavit must be copies of any writing (including, without limitation, notes and e-mails) and other contemporaneous documents within the possession of the affiant relevant to the transferor's intent with regard to the application of GST tax to the transaction for which relief under this section is being requested.

(iv) Each affidavit also must include the name, and current address of the individual, and be accompanied by a dated declaration, signed by the individual that states: "Under penalties of perjury, I declare that I have personal knowledge of the information set forth in this affidavit, including any attachments thereto. In addition, under penalties of perjury, I declare that I have examined this affidavit, including any attachments thereto, and, to the best of my knowledge and belief, the affidavit contains all the relevant facts of which I am aware relating to the request for relief filed by or on behalf of [transferor or the executor of the transferor's estate], and such facts are true, correct, and complete."

(v) If an individual who would be required to provide an affidavit under paragraph (h)(3)(i) of this section has died or is not competent, the affidavit required under paragraph (h)(2) of this section must include a statement to that effect, as well as a statement describing the relationship between that individual and the transferor or the executor of the transferor's estate and the information or knowledge the transferor or the executor of the transferor's estate believes that individual had about the transfer, the trust, the allocation of exemption, or the election. If an individual who would be required to provide an affidavit under paragraph (h)(3)(i) of this section refuses to provide the transferor or the executor of the transferor's estate with such an affidavit, the affidavit required under paragraph (h)(2) of this section must include a statement that the individual has refused to provide the affidavit, a description of the efforts made to obtain the affidavit from the individual, the information or knowledge the transferor or the executor of the transferor's estate believes the individual had about the transfer, and the relationship between the individual and the transferor or the executor of the transferor's estate.

(i) *Effective/applicability date.*—Section 26.2642-7 applies to requests for relief filed on or after the date of publication of the Treasury decision adopting these proposed rules as final regulations in the **Federal Register**. [Reg. §26.2642-7.]

Guidance under Section 529A: Qualified ABLE Programs

Guidance under Section 529A: Qualified ABLE Programs.—An amendment to Reg. §26.2652-1, regarding programs under The Stephen Beck, Jr., Achieving a Better Life Experience Act of 2014 and rules under which States or State agencies or instrumentalities may establish and maintain a new type of tax-favored savings program through which contributions may be made to the account of an eligible disabled individual to meet qualified disability expenses, is proposed (published in the Federal Register on June 22, 2015) (REG-102837-15).

Par. 12. Section 26.2652-1 is amended by adding a sentence at the end of paragraph (a)(1) to read as follows:

§ 26.2652-1. Transferor defined; other definitions.—(a) * * *   * * *

(1) * * * For generation-skipping transfer tax rules related to an ABLE account established under section 529A, *see* regulations promulgated thereunder.

GIFTS AND BEQUESTS FROM EXPATRIATES

Gifts and Bequests from Covered Expatriates: Imposition of Tax

Gifts and Bequests from Covered Expatriates: Imposition of Tax.—Reg. §§ 28.2801-0—28.2801-7, relating to a tax on United States citizens and residents who receive gifts or bequests from certain individuals who relinquished United States citizenship or ceased to be lawful permanent residents of the United States on or after June 17, 2008, are proposed (published in the Federal Register on September 10, 2015) (REG-112997-10).

Sections 28.2801-0 to 28.2801-7 are added to read as follows:

[Reg. § 28.2801-0.]

§ 28.2801-1. Tax on certain gifts and bequests from covered expatriates.—(a) *In general.*—Section 2801 of the Internal Revenue Code (Code) imposes a tax (section 2801 tax) on covered gifts and covered bequests, including distributions from foreign trusts attributable to covered gifts or covered bequests, received by a United States citizen or resident (U.S. citizen or resident) from a covered expatriate during a calendar year. Domestic trusts, as well as foreign trusts electing to be treated as domestic trusts for purposes of section 2801, are subject to tax under section 2801 in the same manner as if the trusts were U.S. citizens. See section 2801(e)(4)(A)(i) and (e)(4)(B)(iii). Accordingly, the section 2801 tax is paid by the U.S. citizen or resident, domestic trust, or foreign trust electing to be treated as a domestic trust for purposes of section 2801 that receives the covered gift or covered bequest. For purposes of this part 28, references to a U.S. citizen or U.S. citizens are considered to include a domestic trust and a foreign trust electing to be treated as a domestic trust for purposes of section 2801.

(b) *Effective/applicability date.*—This section applies on and after the date of publication of a Treasury decision adopting these rules as final regulations in the **Federal Register**. Once these regulations have been published as final regulations in the **Federal Register**, taxpayers may rely upon the final rules of this part for the period beginning June 17, 2008, and ending on the date preceding the date these regulations are published as final regulations in the **Federal Register**. [Reg. § 28.2801-1.]

§ 28.2801-2. Definitions.—(a) *Overview.*—This section provides definitions of terms applicable solely for purposes of section 2801 and the corresponding regulations.

(b) *Citizen or resident of the United States.*—A citizen or resident of the United States (U.S. citizen or resident) is an individual who is a citizen or resident of the United States under the rules applicable for purposes of chapter 11 or 12 of the Code, as the case may be, at the time of receipt of the covered gift or covered bequest. Furthermore, for purposes of this part 28, references to U.S. citizens also include domestic trusts, as well as foreign trusts electing to be treated as a domestic trust under § 28.2801-5(d). See § 28.2801-1(a)(1).

(c) *Domestic trust.*—The term *domestic trust* means a trust defined in section 7701(a)(30)(E). For purposes of this part 28, references to a domestic trust include a foreign trust that elects under § 28.2801-5(d) to be treated as a domestic trust solely for purposes of section 2801.

(d) *Foreign trust.*—(1) *In general.*—The term *foreign trust* means a trust defined in section 7701(a)(31).

(2) *Electing foreign trust.*—The term *electing foreign trust* is a foreign trust that has in effect a valid election to be treated as a domestic trust solely for purposes of section 2801. See § 28.2801-5(d).

(e) *U.S. recipient.*—The term *U.S. recipient* means a citizen or resident of the United States, a domestic trust, and an electing foreign trust that receives a covered gift or covered bequest, whether directly or indirectly, during the calendar year. The term U.S. recipient includes U.S. citizens or residents receiving a distribution from a foreign trust not electing to be treated as a domestic trust for purposes of section 2801 if the distributions are attributable (in whole or in part) to one or more covered gifts or covered bequests received by the foreign trust. This term also includes the U.S. citizen or resident shareholders, partners, members, or other interest-holders, as the case may be (if any), of a domestic entity that receives a covered gift or covered bequest.

(f) *Covered bequest.*—The term *covered bequest* means any property acquired directly or indirectly by reason of the death of a covered expatriate, regardless of its situs and of whether such property was acquired by the covered expatriate before or after expatriation from the United States. The term also includes distributions made by reason of the death of a covered expatriate from a foreign trust that has not elected under § 28.2801-5(d) to be treated as a domestic trust for purposes of section 2801 to the extent the distributions are attributable to covered gifts or covered bequests made to the foreign trust. See § 28.2801-3 for additional rules and exceptions applicable to the term *covered bequest*.

(g) *Covered gift.*—The term *covered gift* means any property acquired by gift directly or indirectly from an individual who is a covered expatriate at the time the property is received by a U.S. citizen or resident, regardless of its situs and of whether such property was acquired by the covered expatriate before or after expatriation from the United States. The term also includes distributions made, other than by reason of the death of a covered expatriate, from a foreign trust that has not elected under § 28.2801-5(d) to be treated as a domestic trust for purposes of section 2801 to the extent the distributions are attributable to covered gifts or covered bequests

made to the foreign trust. See § 28.2801-3 for additional rules and exceptions applicable to the term *covered gift*.

(h) *Expatriate and covered expatriate.*—The term *expatriate* has the same meaning for purposes of section 2801 as that term has in section 877A(g)(2). The term *covered expatriate* has the same meaning for purposes of section 2801 as that term has in section 877A(g)(1). The determination of whether an individual is a covered expatriate is made as of the expatriation date as defined in section 877A(g)(3), and if an expatriate meets the definition of a covered expatriate, the expatriate is considered a covered expatriate for purposes of section 2801 at all times after the expatriation date. However, an expatriate (as defined in section 877A(g)(2)) is not treated as a covered expatriate for purposes of section 2801 during any period beginning after the expatriation date during which such individual is subject to United States estate or gift tax (chapter 11 or chapter 12 of subtitle B) as a U.S. citizen or resident. See section 877A(g)(1)(C). An individual's status as a covered expatriate will be determined as of the date of the most recent expatriation, if there has been more than one.

(i) *Indirect acquisition of property.*—An indirect acquisition of property, as referred to in the definitions of a covered gift and covered bequest, includes—

(1) Property acquired as a result of a transfer that is a covered gift or covered bequest to a corporation or other entity other than a trust or estate, to the extent of the respective ownership interest of the recipient U.S. citizen or resident in the corporation or other entity;

(2) Property acquired by or on behalf of a U.S. citizen or resident, either from a covered expatriate or from a foreign trust that received a covered gift or covered bequest, through one or more other foreign trusts, other entities, or a person not subject to the section 2801 tax;

(3) Property paid by a covered expatriate, or distributed from a foreign trust that received a covered gift or covered bequest, in satisfaction of a debt or liability of a U.S. citizen or resident, regardless of the payee of that payment or distribution;

(4) Property acquired by or on behalf of a U.S. citizen or resident pursuant to a non-covered expatriate's power of appointment granted by a covered expatriate over property not in trust, unless the property previously was subjected to section 2801 tax upon the grant of the power or the covered expatriate had no more than a non-general power of appointment over that property; and

(5) Property acquired by or on behalf of a U.S. citizen or resident in other transfers not made directly by the covered expatriate to the U.S. citizen or resident.

(j) *Power of appointment.*—The term *power of appointment* refers to both a general and non-general power of appointment. A general power of appointment is as defined in sections 2041(b) and 2514(c) of the Code and a non-general power of appointment is any power of appointment that is not a general power of appointment.

(k) *Effective/applicability date.*—This section applies on and after the date of publication of a Treasury decision adopting these rules as final regulations in the **Federal Register**. Once these regulations have been published as final regulations in the **Federal Register**, taxpayers may rely upon the final rules of this part for the period beginning June 17, 2008, and ending on the date preceding the date these regulations are published as final regulations in the **Federal Register**. [Reg. § 28.2801-2.]

§ 28.2801-3. Rules and exceptions applicable to covered gifts and covered bequests.—(a) *Covered gift.*—Subject to the provisions of paragraphs (c), (d), and (e) of this section, the term *gift* as used in the definition of covered gift in § 28.2801-2(g) has the same meaning as in chapter 12 of subtitle B, but without regard to the exceptions in section 2501(a)(2), (a)(4), and (a)(5), the per-donee exclusion under section 2503(b) for certain transfers of a present interest, the exclusion under section 2503(e) for certain educational or medical expenses, and the waiver of certain pension rights under section 2503(f).

(b) *Covered bequest.*—Subject to the provisions of paragraphs (c), (d), and (e) of this section, property acquired "by reason of the death of a covered expatriate" as described in the definition of covered bequest in § 28.2801-2(f) includes any property that would have been includible in the gross estate of the covered expatriate under chapter 11 of subtitle B if the covered expatriate had been a U.S. citizen at the time of death. Therefore, in addition to the items described in § 28.2801-2(f), the term *covered bequest* includes, without limitation, property or an interest in property acquired by reason of a covered expatriate's death—

(1) By bequest, devise, trust provision, beneficiary designation or other contractual arrangement, or by operation of law;

(2) That was transferred by the covered expatriate during life, either before or after expatriation, and which would have been includible in the covered expatriate's gross estate under section 2036, section 2037, or section 2038 had the covered expatriate been a U.S. citizen at the time of death;

(3) That was received for the benefit of a covered expatriate from such covered expatriate's spouse, or predeceased spouse, for which a valid qualified terminable interest property (QTIP) election was made on such spouse's, or predeceased spouse's, Form 709, "U.S. Gift (and Generation-Skipping Transfer) Tax Return," Form 706, "United States Estate (and Generation-Skipping Transfer) Tax Return," or Form 706-NA, "United States Estate (and Generation-Skipping Transfer) Tax Return, Estate of nonresident not a citizen of the United States," which would have been included in the covered expatriate's gross estate under section 2044 if the covered expatriate was a U.S. citizen at the time of death; or

(4) That otherwise passed from the covered expatriate by reason of death, such as—

(i) Property held by the covered expatriate and another person as joint tenants with right of survivorship or as tenants by the entirety, but only to the extent such property would have been included in the covered expatriate's gross estate under section 2040 if the covered expatriate had been a U.S. citizen at the time of death;

(ii) Any annuity or other payment that would have been includible in the covered expatriate's gross estate if the covered expatriate had been a U.S. citizen at the time of death;

(iii) Property subject to a general power of appointment held by the covered expatriate at death; or

(iv) Life insurance proceeds payable upon the covered expatriate's death that would have been includible in the covered expatriate's gross estate under section 2042 if the covered expatriate had been a U.S. citizen at the time of death.

(c) *Exceptions to covered gift and covered bequest.*—The following transfers from a covered expatriate are exceptions to the definition of covered gift and covered bequest.

(1) *Reported taxable gifts.*—A transfer of property that is a taxable gift under section 2503(a) and is reported on the donor's timely filed Form 709 is not a covered gift, provided that the donor also timely pays the gift tax, if any, shown as due on that return. A transfer excluded from the definition of a taxable gift, such as a transfer of a present interest not in excess of the annual exclusion amount under section 2503(b), is not excluded from the definition of a covered gift under this paragraph (c)(1) even if reported on the donor's Form 709.

(2) *Property reported as subject to estate tax.*—Property that is included in the gross estate of the covered expatriate and is reported on a timely filed Form 706 or Form 706-NA is not a covered bequest, provided that the estate also timely pays the estate tax, if any, shown as due on that return. For this purpose, estate tax imposed on distributions from or on the remainder of a qualified domestic trust (QDOT) are deemed to be reported on a timely filed Form 706, if the tax due thereon was timely paid. Thus, if the covered expatriate's gross estate is not of sufficient value to require the filing of a Form 706-NA, for example, and no Form 706-NA is timely filed, the property passing from that covered expatriate is not excluded from the definition of a covered bequest under the rule of this paragraph (c)(2). Further, this exclusion does not apply to the property not on such a form, whether or not subject to United States estate tax (that is, non U.S.-situs property that passes to U.S. citizens or residents).

(3) *Transfers to charity.*—A gift to a donee described in section 2522(b) or a bequest to a beneficiary described in section 2055(a) is not a covered gift or covered bequest to the extent a charitable deduction under section 2522 or section 2055 would have been allowed if the covered expatriate had been a U.S. citizen or resident at the time of the transfer.

(4) *Transfers to spouse.*—A transfer from a covered expatriate to the covered expatriate's spouse is not a covered gift or covered bequest to the extent a marital deduction under section 2523 or section 2056 would have been allowed if the covered expatriate had been a U.S. citizen or resident at the time of the transfer. To the extent that a gift or bequest to a trust (or to a separate share of the trust) would qualify for the marital deduction, the gift or bequest is not a covered gift or covered bequest. For purposes of this paragraph (c)(4), a marital deduction is deemed not to be allowed for qualified terminable interest property (QTIP) or for property in a qualified domestic trust (QDOT) unless a valid QTIP and/or QDOT election is made. The term *covered bequest* also does not include assets in a QDOT funded for the benefit of a covered expatriate by the covered expatriate's predeceased spouse, but only if a valid election was made on the predeceased spouse's Form 706 or Form 706-NA to treat the trust as a QDOT.

(5) *Qualified disclaimers.*—A transfer pursuant to a covered expatriate's qualified disclaimer, as defined in section 2518(b), is not a covered gift or covered bequest from that covered expatriate.

(d) *Covered gifts and covered bequests made in trust.*—For purposes of section 2801, when a covered expatriate transfers property to a trust in a transfer that is a covered gift or covered bequest as determined under this section, the transfer of property is treated as a covered gift or covered bequest to the trust, without regard to the beneficial interests in the trust or whether any person has a general power of appointment or a power of withdrawal over trust property. Accordingly, the rules in section 2801(e)(4) and §28.2801-4(a) apply to determine liability for payment of the section 2801 tax. The U.S. recipient of a covered gift or a covered bequest to a domestic trust or an electing foreign trust is the domestic or electing foreign trust, and the U.S. recipient of a covered gift or a covered bequest to a non-electing foreign trust is any U.S. citizen or resident receiving a distribution from the non-electing foreign trust. See §28.2801-2(e) for the definition of a U.S. recipient.

(e) *Powers of appointment.*—(1) *Covered expatriate as holder of power.*—The exercise or release of a general power of appointment held by a covered expatriate over property, whether or not in trust (even if that covered expatriate was a U.S. citizen or resident when the general power of appointment was granted), for the benefit of a U.S. citizen or resident is a covered gift or covered bequest. The lapse of a general power of appointment is treated as a release to the extent provided in sections 2041(b)(2) and 2514(e). Furthermore, the exercise of a power of appointment by a covered expatriate that creates another power of appointment as described in section 2041(a)(3) or section 2514(d) for the benefit of a U.S. citizen or resident is a covered gift or a covered bequest.

(2) *Covered expatriate as grantor of power.*—The grant by a covered expatriate to an individual who is a U.S. citizen or resident of a general power of appointment over property not transferred in trust by the covered expatriate is a covered gift or covered bequest to the powerholder. For the rule applying to the grant by a covered expatriate of a general power of appointment over property in trust, see paragraph (d) of this section.

(f) *Examples.*—The provisions of this section are illustrated by the following examples:

Example 1. Transfer to spouse. In Year 1, CE, a covered expatriate domiciled in Country F, a foreign country with which the United States does not have a gift tax treaty, gives $300,000 cash to his wife, W, a U.S. resident and citizen of Country F. Under paragraph (c)(4) of this section, the $100,000 exemption for a noncitizen spouse, as indexed for inflation in Year 1, is excluded from the definition of a covered gift under section 2801 because only that amount of the transfer would have qualified for the gift tax marital deduction if CE had been a U.S. citizen at the time of the gift. See sections 2801(e)(3) and 2523(i). The remaining amount ($300,000 less the $100,000 exemption for a noncitizen spouse as indexed for inflation), however, is a covered gift from CE to W. W must timely file Form 708, "U.S. Return of Gifts or Bequests from Covered Expatriates," and timely pay the tax. See §§28.6011-1(a), 28.6071-1(a), and 28.6151-1(a). W also must report the transfer on Form 3520, "Annual Return to Report Transactions with Foreign Trusts and Receipt of Certain Foreign Gifts," and any other required form. See §28.2801-6(c)(1).

Example 2. Reporting property as subject to estate tax. (i) CE, a covered expatriate domiciled in Country F, a foreign country with which the United States does not have an estate tax treaty, owns a condominium in the United States with son, S, a U.S. citizen. CE and S each contributed their actuarial share of the purchase price when purchasing the condominium and own it as joint tenants with rights of survivorship. On December 14, Year 1, CE dies. At the time of CE's death, the fair market value of CE's share of the condominium, $250,000, is included in CE's gross estate under sections 2040 and 2103.

(ii) On September 14 of the following calendar year, Year 2, the executor of CE's estate timely files a Form 4768, "Application for Extension of Time to File a Return and/or Pay U.S. Estate (and Generation-Skipping Transfer) Taxes," requesting a 6-month extension of time to file Form 706-NA, and a 1-year extension of time to pay the estate tax. The IRS grants both extensions but CE's executor fails to file the Form 706-NA until after March 14 of the calendar year immediately following Year 2.

(iii) S learns that the executor of CE's estate did not timely file Form 706-NA. Because CE is a covered expatriate, S received a covered bequest as defined under §28.2801-2(f) and paragraph (b) of this section. S must timely file Form 708 and pay the section 2801 tax. See §§28.6011-1(a), 28.6071-1(a), and 28.6151-1(a). S also must file Form 3520 to report a large gift or bequest from a foreign person, and any other required form. See §28.2801-6(c)(1).

Example 3. Covered gift in trust with grant of general power of appointment over trust property. (i) On October 20, Year 1, CE, a covered expatriate domiciled in Country F, a foreign country with which the United States does not have a gift tax treaty, transfers $500,000 in cash from an account in Country F to an irrevocable foreign trust created on that same date. Under section 2511(a), no gift tax is imposed on the transfer and thus, CE is not required to file a U.S. gift tax return. Under the terms of the foreign trust, A, CE's child and a U.S. resident, and Q, A's child and a U.S. citizen, may receive discretionary distributions of income and principal during life. At A's death, the assets remaining in the foreign trust will be distributed to B, CE's other U.S. resident child, or if B is not living at the time of A's death, then to CE's then-living issue, *per stirpes.* The terms of the foreign trust also allow A to appoint trust principal and/or income to A, A's estate, A's creditors, the creditors of A's estate, or A's issue at any time. On March 5, Year 2, A exercises this power to appoint and causes the trustee to distribute $100,000 to Q.

(ii) On October 20, Year 1, the irrevocable foreign trust receives a covered gift for purposes of section 2801, but no section 2801 tax is imposed at that time. On March 5, Year 2, when Q receives $100,000 from the irrevocable foreign trust pursuant to the exercise of A's power of appointment, Q has received a distribution attributable to a covered gift and section 2801 tax is imposed on Q as of the date of the distribution. *See* §28.2801-4(d). Q must timely file Form 708 to report the covered gift from a foreign person (specifically, from CE). See section 6039F(a) and §§28.6011-1(a), 28.6071-1(a), and 28.6151-1(a). Under section 2501, A makes a taxable gift to Q of $100,000 when A exercises the general power of appointment for Q's benefit. See section 2514(b). Accordingly, A must report A's $100,000 gift to Q on a timely filed Form 709. See section 6019. Because A is considered the transferor of the $100,000 for gift and GST tax purposes, the distribution to Q is not a generation-skipping transfer under chapter 13. See §26.2652-1(a)(1). Furthermore, because the $100,000 is being distributed from a foreign trust, Q must report the gift on a Form 3520 as a distribution from a foreign trust. See §28.2801-6(c)(2).

Example 4. Lapse of power of appointment held by covered expatriate. (i) A, a U.S. citizen, creates an irrevocable domestic trust for the benefit of A's issue, CE, and CE's children. CE is a covered expatriate, but CE's children are U.S. citizens. CE has the right to withdraw $5,000 in each year in which A makes a contribution to the trust, but the withdrawal right lapses 30 days after the date of the contribution. In Year 1, A funds the trust, but CE fails to exercise CE's right to withdraw $5,000 within 30 days of the contribution. The $5,000 lapse is not considered to be a release of the power, so it is neither a gift for U.S. gift tax purposes, nor a covered gift for purposes of section 2801 under paragraph (e)(1) of this section.

(g) *Effective/applicability date.*—This section applies on and after the date of publication of a Treasury decision adopting these rules as final regulations in the **Federal Register**. Once these regulations have been published as final regulations in the **Federal Register**, taxpayers may rely upon the final rules of this part for the period beginning June 17, 2008, and ending on the date preceding the date these regulations are published as final regulations in the **Federal Register**. [Reg. §28.2801-3.]

§28.2801-4. Liability for and payment of tax on covered gifts and covered bequests; computation of tax.—(a) *Liability for tax.*— (1) *U.S. citizen or resident.*—A U.S. citizen or resident who receives a covered gift or covered bequest is liable for payment of the section 2801 tax.

(2) *Domestic trust.*—(i) *In general.*—A domestic trust that receives a covered gift or covered bequest is treated as a U.S. citizen and is liable for payment of the section 2801 tax. See section 2801(e)(4)(A)(i) and §28.2801-2(b).

(ii) *Generation-skipping transfer tax.*—A trust's payment of the section 2801 tax does not result in a taxable distribution under section 2621 to any trust beneficiary for purposes of the generation-skipping transfer tax to the extent that the trust, rather than the beneficiary, is liable for the section 2801 tax.

(iii) *Charitable remainder trust.*—A domestic trust qualifying as a charitable remainder trust (as that term is defined in §1.664-1(a)(1)(iii)(*a*)) is subject to section 2801 when it receives a covered gift or covered bequest. Section 2801(e)(3) excepts from the definition of covered gift and covered bequest property with respect to which a deduction under section 2522 or section 2055, respectively, would have been allowed if the covered expatriate had been a U.S. citizen or resident at the time of the transfer. See §28.2801-3(c)(3). As a result, the charitable remainder interest's share of each transfer to the charitable remainder trust is not a covered gift or covered bequest. To compute the amount of covered gifts and covered bequests taxable to the charitable remainder trust for a calendar year, the charitable remainder trust will (A) calculate, in accordance with the regulations under section 664 and as of the date of the trust's receipt of the contribution, the value of the remainder interest in each contribution received in such calendar year that would have been a covered gift or covered bequest without regard to section 2801(e)(3), (B) subtract the remainder interest in each such contribution from the amount of that contribution to compute the annuity or unitrust (income) interest in that contribution, and (C) add the total of such income interests, each of which is the portion of the contribution that constitutes a covered gift or covered bequest to the trust. The charita-

ble remainder trust then computes its section 2801 tax in accordance with paragraph (b) of this section.

(iv) *Migrated foreign trust.*—A foreign trust (other than one electing to be treated as a domestic trust under §28.2801-5(d)) that has previously received a covered gift or covered bequest and that subsequently becomes a domestic trust as defined under section 7701(a)(30)(E) (migrated foreign trust), must file a timely Form 708, "U.S. Return of Gifts or Bequests from Covered Expatriates," for the taxable year in which the trust becomes a domestic trust. The section 2801 tax, if any, must be paid by the due date of that Form 708. On that Form 708, the section 2801 tax is calculated in the same manner as if such trust was making an election under §28.2801-5(d) to be treated as a domestic trust solely for purposes of the section 2801 tax. Accordingly, the trustee must report and pay the section 2801 tax on all covered gifts and covered bequests received by the trust during the year in which the trust becomes a domestic trust, as well as on the portion of the trust's value at the end of the year preceding the year in which the trust becomes a domestic trust that is attributable to all prior covered gifts and covered bequests. Because the migrated foreign trust will be treated solely for purposes of section 2801 as a domestic trust for the entire year during which it became a domestic trust, distributions made to U.S. citizens or residents during that year but before the date on which the trust became a domestic trust will not be subject to section 2801.

(3) *Foreign trust.*—(i) *In general.*—A foreign trust that receives a covered gift or covered bequest is not liable for payment of the section 2801 tax unless the trust makes an election to be treated as a domestic trust solely for purposes of section 2801 as provided in §28.2801-5(d). Absent such an election, each U.S. recipient is liable for payment of the section 2801 tax on that person's receipt, either directly or indirectly, of a distribution from the foreign trust to the extent that the distribution is attributable to a covered gift or covered bequest made to the foreign trust. See §28.2801-5(b) and (c) regarding distributions from foreign trusts.

(ii) *Income tax deduction.*—The U.S. recipient of a distribution from a foreign trust is allowed a deduction against income tax under section 164 in the calendar year in which the section 2801 tax is paid or accrued. The amount of the deduction is equal to the portion of the section 2801 tax attributable to such distribution, but only to the extent that portion of the distribution is included in the U.S. recipient's gross income. The amount of the deduction allowed under section 164 is calculated as follows:

(A) First, the U.S. recipient must determine the total amount of distribution(s) from the foreign trust treated as covered gifts and covered bequests received by that U.S. recipient during the calendar year to which the section 2801 tax payment relates.

(B) Second, of the amount determined in paragraph (a)(3)(ii)(A) of this section, the U.S. recipient must determine the amount that also is includable in the U.S. recipient's gross income for that calendar year. For purposes of this paragraph (a)(3)(ii)(B), distributions from foreign trusts includable in the U.S. recipient's gross income are deemed first to consist of the portion of those distributions, if any, that are attributable to covered gifts and covered bequests.

(C) Finally, the U.S. recipient must determine the portion of the section 2801 tax paid for that calendar year that is attributable to the amount determined in paragraph (a)(3)(ii)(B) of this section, the covered gifts and covered bequests received from the foreign trust that are also included in the U.S. recipient's gross income. This amount is the allowable deduction. Thus, for a calendar year taxpayer, the deduction is determined by multiplying the section 2801 tax paid during the calendar year by the ratio of the amount determined in paragraph (a)(3)(ii)(B) of this section to the total covered gifts and covered bequests received by the U.S. recipient during the calendar year to which that tax payment relates (that is, 2801 tax liability x [foreign trust distributions attributable to covered gifts and covered bequests that are also included in gross income / total covered gifts or covered bequests received]).

(b) *Computation of tax.*—(1) *In general.*—The section 2801 tax is computed by multiplying the net covered gifts and covered bequests (as defined in paragraph (b)(2) of this section) received by a U.S. recipient during the calendar year by the greater of—

(i) The highest rate of estate tax under section 2001(c) in effect for that calendar year; or

(ii) The highest rate of gift tax under section 2502(a) in effect for that calendar year. See paragraph (f) of this section, *Example 1.*

(2) *Net covered gifts and covered bequests.*—The net covered gifts and covered bequests received by a U.S. recipient during the calendar year is the total value of all covered gifts and covered bequests received by that U.S. recipient during the calendar year, less the

section 2801(c) amount, which is the dollar amount of the per-donee exclusion in effect under section 2503(b) for that calendar year.

(c) *Value of covered gift or covered bequest.*—The value of a covered gift or covered bequest is the fair market value of the property as of the date of its receipt by the U.S. recipient. See paragraph (d) of this section regarding the determination of the date of receipt. As in the case of chapters 11 and 12, the fair market value of a covered gift or covered bequest is the price at which such property would change hands between a willing buyer and a willing seller, neither being under any compulsion to buy or to sell and both having reasonable knowledge of relevant facts. The fair market value of a covered gift is determined in accordance with the federal gift tax valuation principles of section 2512 and chapter 14 and the corresponding regulations. The fair market value of a covered bequest is determined by applying the federal estate tax valuation principles of section 2031 and chapter 14 and the corresponding regulations, but without regard to sections 2032 and 2032A.

(d) *Date of receipt.*—(1) *In general.*—The section 2801 tax is imposed upon the receipt of a covered gift or covered bequest by a U.S. recipient.

(2) *Covered gift.*—The date of receipt of a covered gift is the same as the date of the gift for purposes of chapter 12 as if the covered expatriate had been a U.S. citizen at the time of the transfer. Thus, for a gift of stock, if the covered expatriate delivers a properly endorsed stock certificate to the U.S. recipient, the date of delivery is the date of receipt for purposes of this section. Alternatively, if the covered expatriate delivers the stock certificate to the issuing corporation or its transfer agent in order to transfer title to the U.S. recipient, the date of receipt is the date the stock is transferred on the books of the corporation. For a transfer of assets by a covered expatriate to a domestic revocable trust, the trust receives the transfer on the date the covered expatriate relinquishes the right to revoke the trust. If, before the donor's relinquishment of the right to revoke the trust, the revocable trust distributes property to a U.S. citizen or resident not in discharge of a support or other obligation of the donor, then the U.S. recipient receives a covered gift on the date of that distribution. For an asset subject to a claim of right of another involving a bona fide dispute, the date of receipt is the date on which such claim is extinguished.

(3) *Covered bequest.*—The date of receipt of a covered bequest is the date of distribution from the estate or the decedent's revocable trust rather than the date of death of the covered expatriate. However, the date of receipt is the date of death for property passing on the death of the covered expatriate by operation of law, or by beneficiary designation or other contractual agreement. Notwithstanding the previous sentences, for an asset subject to a claim of right of another involving a bona fide dispute, the date of receipt is the date on which such claim is extinguished.

(4) *Foreign trusts.*—The date of receipt by a U.S. citizen or resident of property from a foreign trust that has not elected to be treated as a domestic trust under § 28.2801-5(d) is the date of its distribution from the foreign trust.

(5) *Powers of appointment.*—(i) *Covered expatriate as holder of power.*—In the case of the exercise, release, or lapse of a power of appointment held by a covered expatriate that is a covered gift pursuant to § 28.2801-3(e)(1), the date of receipt is the date of the exercise, release, or lapse of the power. In the case of the exercise, release, or lapse of a power of appointment held by a covered expatriate that is a covered bequest pursuant to § 28.2801-3(e)(1), the date of receipt is (A) the date the property subject to the power is distributed from the decedent's estate or revocable trust when the power of appointment is over property in such estate or trust, or (B) the date of the covered expatriate's death when the power of appointment is over property passing on the covered expatriate's death by operation of law, by beneficiary designation, or by other contractual agreement.

(ii) *Covered expatriate as grantor of power.*—The date of receipt of property subject to a general power of appointment granted by a covered expatriate to a U.S. citizen or resident over property not transferred in trust that constitutes a covered gift or covered bequest pursuant to § 28.2801-3(e)(2) is the first date on which both the power is exercisable by the U.S. citizen or resident and the property subject to the general power has been irrevocably transferred by the covered expatriate. The date of receipt of property subject to a general power of appointment over property in a domestic trust or an electing foreign trust is determined in accordance with paragraphs (d)(2) and (d)(3) of this section, and over property in a non-electing foreign trust is determined in accordance with paragraph (d)(4) of this section. See § 28.2801-3(d) for the rule applying to covered gifts and covered bequests made in trust.

(6) *Indirect receipts.*—The date of receipt by a U.S. citizen or resident of a covered gift or covered bequest received indirectly from a covered expatriate is the date of its receipt, as determined under paragraph (d)(2) or (d)(3) of this section, by the U.S. citizen or resident who is the first recipient of that property from the covered expatriate to be subject to section 2801 with regard to that property. For example, the date of receipt of property (i) subject to a non-general power of appointment over property not held in trust given by a covered expatriate to a foreign person (other than another covered expatriate) is the date that property is received by the U.S. citizen or resident in whose favor the power was exercised, and (ii) received through one or more entities not subject to section 2801 is the date of its receipt by the U.S. citizen or resident from a conduit entity.

(e) *Reduction of tax for foreign estate or gift tax paid.*—The section 2801 tax is reduced by the amount of any gift or estate tax paid to a foreign country with respect to the covered gift or covered bequest. For this purpose, the term *foreign country* includes possessions and political subdivisions of foreign states. However, no reduction is allowable for interest and penalties paid in connection with those foreign taxes. To claim the reduction of section 2801 tax, the U.S. recipient must attach to the Form 708 a copy of the foreign estate or gift tax return and a copy of the receipt or cancelled check for payment of the foreign estate or gift tax. The U.S. recipient also must report, on an attachment to the Form 708:

(1) The amount of foreign estate or gift tax paid with respect to each covered gift or covered bequest and the amount and date of each payment thereof;

(2) A description and the value of the property with respect to which such taxes were imposed;

(3) Whether any refund of part or all of the foreign estate or gift tax has been or will be claimed or allowed, and the amount; and

(4) All other information necessary for the verification and computation of the amount of the reduction of section 2801 tax.

(f) *Examples.*—The provisions of this section are illustrated by the following examples.

Example 1. Computation of tax. In Year 1, A, a U.S. citizen, receives a $50,000 covered gift from B and an $80,000 covered bequest from C. Both B and C are covered expatriates. In Year 1, the highest estate and gift tax rate is 40 percent and the section 2801(c) amount is $14,000. A's section 2801 tax for Year 1 is computed by multiplying A's net covered gifts and covered bequests by 40 percent. A's net covered gifts and covered bequests for Year 1 are $116,000, which is determined by reducing A's total covered gifts and covered bequests received during Year 1, $130,000 ($50,000 + $80,000), by the section 2801(c) amount of $14,000. A's section 2801 tax liability is then reduced by any foreign estate or gift tax paid under paragraph (e) of this section. Assuming A, B, and C paid no foreign estate or gift tax on the transfers, A's section 2801 tax liability for Year 1 is $46,400 ($116,000 x 0.4).

Example 2. Deduction of section 2801 tax for income tax purposes. In Year 1, B receives a covered bequest of $25,000. Also in Year 1, B receives an aggregate $500,000 of distributions from a non-electing foreign trust of which $100,000 was attributable to a covered gift. In Year 1, the highest estate and gift tax rate is 40 percent and the section 2801(c) amount is $14,000. Based on information provided by the trustee of the foreign trust, B includes $50,000 of the aggregate distributions from the foreign trust in B's gross income for Year 1. Under paragraph (a)(3)(ii) of this section, B (a cash basis taxpayer) is entitled to an income tax deduction under section 164 for the calendar year in which the section 2801 tax is paid. In Year 2, B timely reports the distributions from the foreign trust and pays $44,400 in section 2801 tax (($125,000 - $14,000) x 0.4). In Year 2, B is entitled to an income tax deduction because B paid the section 2801 tax in Year 2 on the Year 1 covered gift and covered bequest. B's Year 2 income tax deduction is computed as follows:

(i) $100,000 of B's total covered gifts and covered bequests of $125,000 received in Year 1 consisted of the portion of the distributions from the foreign trust attributable to covered gifts and covered bequests received by the trust. See paragraph (a)(3)(ii)(A) of this section.

(ii) $50,000 of the $500,000 of trust distributions were includable in B's gross income for Year 1. This amount is deemed to consist first of distributions subject to the section 2801 tax ($100,000). Thus, the entire amount included in B's gross income ($50,000) also is subject to the section 2801 tax, and is used in the numerator to determine the income tax deduction available to B. See paragraph (a)(3)(ii)(B) of this section.

(iii) The portion of B's section 2801 tax liability attributable to distributions from a foreign trust is $17,760 ($44,400 x ($50,000/$125,000)). Therefore, B's deduction under section 164 is $17,760. See paragraph (a)(3)(ii)(C) of this section.

Example 3. Date of receipt; bona fide claim. On October 10, Year 1, CE, a covered expatriate, died testate as a resident of Country F, a foreign country with which the United States does not have an estate tax treaty. CE designated his son, S, as the beneficiary of CE's retirement account. S is a U.S. citizen. CE's wife, W, who is a citizen and resident of Country F, elects to take her elective share of CE's estate under local law. S contests whether the retirement account is property subject to the elective share. S and W agree to settle their respective claims by dividing CE's assets equally between them. On December 15 of Year 2, Country F's court enters an order accepting the terms of the settlement agreement and dismissing the case. Under paragraph (d)(3) of this section, S received a covered bequest of one-half of CE's retirement account on December 15, Year 2, when W's claim of right was extinguished.

(g) *Effective/applicability date.*—This section applies on and after the date of publication of a Treasury decision adopting these rules as final regulations in the **Federal Register**. Once these regulations have been published as final regulations in the **Federal Register**, taxpayers may rely upon the final rules of this part for the period beginning June 17, 2008, and ending on the date preceding the date these regulations are published as final regulations in the **Federal Register**. [Reg. § 28.2801-4.]

§ 28.2801-5. Foreign trusts.—(a) *In general.*—The section 2801 tax is imposed on a U.S. recipient who receives distributions, whether of income or principal, from a foreign trust to the extent the distributions are attributable to one or more covered gifts or covered bequests made to that foreign trust. See paragraph (d) of this section regarding a foreign trust's election to be treated as a domestic trust for purposes of section 2801.

(b) *Distribution defined.*—For purposes of determining whether a U.S. recipient has received a distribution from a foreign trust, the term *distribution* means any direct, indirect, or constructive transfer from a foreign trust. This determination is made without regard to whether any portion of the trust is treated as owned by the U.S. recipient or any other person under subpart E of part I, subchapter J, chapter 1 of the Code (pertaining to grantors and others treated as substantial owners) and without regard to whether the U.S. recipient of the transfer is designated as a beneficiary by the terms of the trust. For purposes of section 2801, the term distribution also includes each disbursement from a foreign trust pursuant to the exercise, release, or lapse of a power of appointment, whether or not a general power. In addition to the reporting requirements under this section, see section 6048(c) regarding the information reporting requirement for U.S. persons receiving a distribution or deemed distribution from a foreign trust during the year.

(c) *Amount of distribution attributable to covered gift or covered bequest.*—(1) *Section 2801 ratio.*—(i) *In general.*—A foreign trust may have received covered gifts and covered bequests as well as contributions that were not covered gifts or covered bequests. Under such circumstances, the fair market value of the foreign trust at any time consists in part of a portion of the trust attributable to the covered gifts and covered bequests it has received (covered portion) and in part of a portion of the trust attributable to other contributions (non-covered portion). The covered portion of the trust includes the ratable portion of appreciation and income that has accrued on the foreign trust's assets from the date of the contribution of the covered gifts and covered bequests to the foreign trust. For purposes of section 2801, the amount of each distribution from the foreign trust, whether made from the income or principal of the trust, that is considered attributable to the foreign trust's covered gifts and covered bequests is determined on a proportional basis, by reference to the section 2801 ratio (as described in paragraph (c)(1)(ii) of this section), and not by the identification or tracing of particular trust assets. Specifically, this portion of each distribution is determined by multiplying the distributed amount by the percentage of the trust that consists of its covered portion immediately prior to that distribution (section 2801 ratio). Thus, for example, the section 2801 ratio of a foreign trust whose assets are comprised exclusively of covered gifts or covered bequests and the income and appreciation thereon, would be 1 and the full amount of each distribution from that foreign trust to a U.S. citizen or resident would be subject to section 2801.

(ii) *Computation.*—The section 2801 ratio, which must be redetermined after each contribution to the foreign trust, is computed by using the following fraction:

$$\text{Section 2801 ratio} = \frac{(X + Y)}{Z}$$

where,

X = The value of the trust attributable to covered gifts and covered bequests, if any, immediately before the contribution (pre-contribution value); this value is determined by multiplying the fair market value of the trust assets immediately prior to the contribution by the section 2801 ratio in effect immediately prior to the current contribution. This amount will be zero for all years prior to the year in which the foreign trust receives its first covered gift or covered bequest;

Y = The portion, if any, of the fair market value of the current contribution that constitutes a covered gift or covered bequest; and

Z = The fair market value of the trust immediately after the current contribution. See paragraph (e) of this section, *Example 1*, for an illustration of this computation.

(2) *Effect of reported transfer and tax payment.*—Once a section 2801 tax has been timely paid on property that thereafter remains in a foreign trust, that property is no longer considered to be, or to be attributable to, a covered gift or covered bequest to the foreign trust for purposes of the computation described in paragraph (c)(1)(ii) of this section. For purposes of the prior sentence, a section 2801 tax is deemed to have been timely paid on amounts for which no section 2801 tax was due as long as those amounts were reported as a covered gift or covered bequest on a timely filed Form 708, "U.S. Return of Gifts or Bequests from Covered Expatriates."

(3) *Inadequate information to calculate section 2801 ratio.*—If the trustee of the foreign trust does not have sufficient books and records to calculate the section 2801 ratio, or if the U.S. recipient is unable to obtain the necessary information with regard to the foreign trust, the U.S. recipient must proceed upon the assumption that the entire distribution for purposes of section 2801 is attributable to a covered gift or covered bequest.

(d) *Foreign trust treated as domestic trust.*—(1) *Election required.*—To be considered an electing foreign trust, so that the foreign trust is treated as a domestic trust solely for purposes of the section 2801 tax, a valid election is required.

(2) *Effect of election.*—(i) A valid election subjects the electing foreign trust to the section 2801 tax on (A) all covered gifts and covered bequests received by the foreign trust during that calendar year, (B) the portion of the trust attributable to covered gifts and covered bequests received by the trust in prior years, as determined in paragraph (d)(3)(iii) of this section, and (C) all covered gifts and covered bequests received by the foreign trust during calendar years subsequent to the first year in which the election is effective, unless and until the election is terminated. To the extent that covered gifts and covered bequests are subject to the section 2801 tax under the prior sentence, those trust receipts are no longer treated as a covered gift or covered bequest for purposes of determining the portion of the trust attributable to covered gifts and covered bequests. Therefore, upon making a valid election, the foreign trust's section 2801 ratio described in paragraph (c)(1)(ii) of this section will be zero until the effective date of any termination of the election and the subsequent receipt of any covered gift or covered bequest, and a distribution made from the foreign trust while this election is in effect is not taxable under section 2801 to the recipient trust beneficiary.

(ii) This election has no effect on any distribution from the foreign trust that was made to a U.S. recipient in a calendar year prior to the calendar year for which the election is made. Thus, even after a valid election is made, a distribution to a U.S. recipient in a calendar year prior to the calendar year for which the election is made that was attributable to one or more covered gifts or covered bequests continues to be a distribution attributable to one or more covered gifts or covered bequests and the section 2801 ratio in place at the time of the distribution continues to apply to that distribution. Furthermore, an election under this section does not relieve the U.S. recipient from the information reporting requirements of section 6048(c).

(3) *Time and manner of making the election.*—(i) *When to make the election.*—The election is made on a timely filed Form 708 for the calendar year for which the foreign trust seeks to subject itself to the section 2801 tax as described in paragraph (d)(2)(i) of this section. The election may be made for a calendar year whether or not the foreign trust received a covered gift or covered bequest during that calendar year. See § 28.6071-1.

(ii) *Requirements for a valid election.*—To make a valid election to be treated as a domestic trust for purposes of section 2801, the electing foreign trust must timely file a Form 708 and must, on such form—

(A) Make the election, timely pay the section 2801 tax, if any, as determined under paragraph (d)(3)(iii) of this section, and include a computation illustrating how the trustee of the electing foreign trust calculated both the section 2801 ratio described in paragraph (c)(1)(ii) of this section and the section 2801 tax;

(B) Designate and authorize a U.S. agent as provided in paragraph (d)(3)(iv) of this section;

(C) Agree to file Form 708 annually;

(D) List the amount and year of all prior distributions attributable to covered gifts and covered bequests made to a U.S.

recipient and provide the name, address, and taxpayer identification number of each U.S. recipient; and

(E) Notify each permissible distributee that the trustee is making the election under this paragraph (d) and provide to the IRS a list of the name, address, and taxpayer identification number of each permissible distributee. For this purpose, a permissible distributee is any U.S. citizen or resident who:

(1) Currently may or must receive distributions from the trust, whether of income or principal;

(2) May withdraw income or principal from the trust, regardless of whether the right arises or lapses upon the occurrence of a future event; or

(3) Would have been described in paragraph (d)(3)(ii)(E)(1) of this section if either the interests of all persons described in (d)(3)(ii)(E)(1) or (E)(2) had just terminated or the trust had just terminated.

(iii) *Section 2801 tax payable with the election.*—To make a valid election to be treated as a domestic trust for purposes of section 2801, the electing foreign trust must timely pay the section 2801 tax on all covered gifts and covered bequests received by the electing foreign trust in the calendar year for which the Form 708 is being filed. In some cases, an electing foreign trust may have received covered gifts or covered bequests in prior calendar years during which no such election was in effect. In those cases, the trustee must also, at the same time, report and pay the tax on the fair market value, determined as of the last day of the calendar year immediately preceding the year for which the Form 708 is being filed, of the portion of the trust attributable to covered gifts and covered bequests received by such trust in prior calendar years (except as provided in paragraph (d)(6)(iii) of this section with regard to an imperfect election). That portion is determined by multiplying the fair market value of the trust, as of the December 31 immediately preceding the year for which the election is made, by the section 2801 ratio in effect on that date, as calculated under paragraph (c)(1)(ii) of this section. If the trustee does not have sufficient books and records to determine what amount of the corpus and undistributed income is attributable to undistributed prior covered gifts and covered bequests, then that amount is deemed to be the entire fair market value of the trust as of that December 31. See paragraph (c)(3) of this section.

(iv) *Designation of U.S. agent.*—(A) *In general.*—The trustee of an electing foreign trust must designate and authorize a U.S. person, as defined in section 7701(a)(30), to act as an agent for the trust solely for purposes of section 2801. By designating a U.S. agent, the trustee of the foreign trust agrees to provide the agent with all information necessary to comply with any information request or summons issued by the Secretary. Such information may include, without limitation, copies of the books and records of the trust, financial statements, and appraisals of trust property.

(B) *Role of designated agent.*—Acting as an agent for the trust for purposes of section 2801 includes serving as the electing foreign trust's agent for purposes of section 7602 ("Examination of books and witnesses"), section 7603 ("Service of summons"), and section 7604 ("Enforcement of summons") with respect to—

(1) Any request by the Secretary to examine records or produce testimony related to the proper identification or treatment of covered gifts or covered bequests contributed to the electing foreign trust and distributions attributable to such contributions; and

(2) Any summons by the Secretary for records or testimony related to the proper identification or treatment of covered gifts or covered bequests contributed to the electing foreign trust and distributions attributable to such contributions.

(C) *Effect of appointment of U.S. agent.*—An electing foreign trust that appoints such an agent is not considered to have an office or a permanent establishment in the United States, or to be engaged in a trade or business in the United States, solely because of the agent's activities as an agent pursuant to this section.

(4) *Annual certification or filing requirement.*—The trustee of an electing foreign trust must file a timely Form 708 annually either to report and pay the section 2801 tax on all covered gifts and covered bequests received by the trust during the calendar year, or to certify that the electing foreign trust did not receive any covered gifts or covered bequests during the calendar year.

(5) *Duration of status as electing foreign trust.*—(i) *In general.*—A valid election (one that meets all of the requirements of paragraph (d)(3) of this section) is effective as of January 1 of the calendar year for which the Form 708 on which the election is made is filed. The election, once made, applies for all calendar years until the election is terminated as described in paragraph (d)(5)(ii) of this section.

(ii) *Termination.*—An election to be treated as a domestic trust for purposes of section 2801 is terminated either by the failure of the foreign trust to make the annual filing, together with any

payment of the section 2801 tax, as required by paragraph (d)(4) of this section, or by the failure of the foreign trust to timely pay any additional amount of section 2801 tax (in accordance with the requirements of paragraph (d)(6)(ii) of this section) with respect to recalculations described in paragraph (d)(6) of this section (a failure that results in an imperfect election). A termination, if any, is effective as of the beginning of the calendar year for which the trustee fails to make the annual filing required by paragraph (d)(4) of this section or for which the trustee fails to pay any of the amounts described in this paragraph (d)(5)(ii). In the case of a terminated election, the trustee should notify promptly each permissible distributee, as defined in paragraph (d)(3)(ii)(E) of this section, that the foreign trust's election was terminated as of January 1 of the applicable year (with the actual year of the termination being set forth in the notice), and that each U.S. recipient of a distribution made from the foreign trust on and after that date is subject to the section 2801 tax on the portion of each such distribution that is attributable to covered gifts and covered bequests. See paragraph (d)(6)(iii)(B) of this section for an additional notification requirement in the case of an imperfect election.

(iii) *Subsequent elections.*—If a foreign trust's election is terminated under paragraph (d)(5)(ii) of this section, the foreign trust is not prohibited from making another election in a future year, subject to the requirements of paragraph (d)(3) of this section.

(6) *Dispute as to amount of section 2801 tax owed by electing foreign trust.*—(i) *Procedure.*—If the Commissioner disputes the value of a covered gift or covered bequest, or otherwise challenges the computation of the section 2801 tax, that is reported on the electing foreign trust's timely filed Form 708 for any calendar year, the Commissioner will issue a letter (but not a notice of deficiency as defined in section 6212) to the trustee of the electing foreign trust and the appointed U.S. agent that details the disputed information and the proper amount of section 2801 tax as recalculated. The foreign trust must pay the additional amount of section 2801 tax including interest and penalties, if any, in accordance with the requirements of paragraph (d)(6)(ii) of this section, on or before the due date specified in the letter to maintain its election.

(ii) *Effect of timely paying the additional section 2801 tax amount.*—If the trustee of the foreign trust timely pays the additional amount(s) specified in the Commissioner's letter, or such other amount as agreed to by the Commissioner, and enters into a closing agreement with the IRS as described in section 7121, then the foreign trust's election to be treated as a domestic trust under paragraph (d) of this section remains in effect. In addition, in the absence of fraud, malfeasance, or misrepresentation of a material fact, that payment, in conjunction with the closing agreement, will be deemed to render any determination of value to which the closing agreement applies as final and binding on both the IRS and the foreign trust. Thus, subsequently, the IRS will not be able to challenge the section 2801 tax due from either the foreign trust or any of its beneficiaries who are U.S. citizens or residents for the year for which that Form 708 was filed by the foreign trust, except with respect to any covered gifts or covered bequests not reported on that return, and neither the foreign trust nor any of its beneficiaries will be able to file a claim for refund with respect to section 2801 tax paid by the foreign trust on the covered gifts and covered bequests reported on that Form 708.

(iii) *Effect of failing to timely pay the additional section 2801 tax amount (imperfect election).*—(A) *In general.*—If the foreign trust fails to timely pay the additional amount of section 2801 tax with interest and penalties, if any, claimed to be due by the IRS in accordance with the requirements of paragraph (d)(6)(ii) of this section, then the foreign trust's valid election is terminated and becomes an imperfect election. The foreign trust's election is terminated, and is converted into an imperfect election, retroactively as of the first day of the calendar year for which was filed the Form 708 with respect to which the additional amount of section 2801 tax is claimed to be due by the IRS. Thus, the value the foreign trust has reported on the Form 708 and on which the trust has paid the section 2801 tax is no longer considered to be attributable to covered gifts or covered bequests when computing the section 2801 ratio described in paragraph (c)(1)(ii) of this section applicable to distributions made by the foreign trust to U.S. recipients during the calendar year for which the Form 708 was filed and thereafter. The U.S. recipients of distributions from the foreign trust, however, should take into consideration the additional value determined by the IRS, on which the foreign trust did not timely pay the section 2801 tax, when computing the section 2801 ratio to be applied to a distribution from the trust. See paragraph (c) of this section. Any disagreement with regard to that additional value will be an issue to be resolved as part of the review of that U.S. recipient's own Form 708 reporting a distribution.

(B) *Notice to permissible beneficiaries.*—If the trustee of the foreign trust fails to remit the additional payment of the section 2801 tax including all interest and penalties, if any, in accordance with the requirements of paragraph (d)(6)(ii) of this section, by the due date stated in the IRS letter, the trustee should notify promptly each permissible distributee, as defined in paragraph (d)(3)(ii)(E) of this section, of the amount of additional value on which the foreign trust did not timely pay the section 2801 tax as determined by the IRS and that:

(1) The foreign trust's election was terminated as of January 1 of the applicable year (with the actual year of the termination being set forth in the notice); and

(2) Each U.S. recipient of a distribution made from the foreign trust on and after that termination date is subject to the section 2801 tax on the portion of each such distribution attributable to covered gifts and covered bequests.

(C) *Reasonable cause.*—If a U.S. recipient received a distribution from such trust on or after January 1 of the year for which the election was terminated and the election became an imperfect election, provided the U.S. recipient files a Form 708 and pays the section 2801 tax within a reasonable period of time after being notified by the trustee of the foreign trust or otherwise becoming aware that a valid election was not in effect when the distribution was made, the U.S. recipient's failure to timely file and pay are due to reasonable cause and not willful neglect for purposes of section 6651. For this purpose, a reasonable period of time is not more than six months after the U.S. recipient is notified by the trustee or the U.S. recipient otherwise becomes aware that a valid election is not in effect.

(D) *Interim period.*—If a foreign trust's valid election is terminated and becomes an imperfect election, there is a period of time (interim period) after the effective date of the termination of the election during which both the foreign trust and its U.S. beneficiaries are likely to continue to comply with section 2801 as it applies to an electing foreign trust with a valid election in place. The interim period begins on the effective date of the termination of the foreign trust's election that resulted in an imperfect election as described in paragraph (d)(6)(iii)(A) of this section, and ends on December 31 of the calendar year immediately preceding the calendar year in which the additional section 2801 tax claimed by the IRS is due. As under the rule in paragraph (d)(6)(iii)(A) of this section regarding imperfect elections, the covered gifts and covered bequests received by the foreign trust during this interim period, which the foreign trust has reported on its timely filed Form 708 and on which the foreign trust has timely paid the section 2801 tax, are no longer considered to be covered gifts and covered bequests for purposes of computing the section 2801 ratio described in paragraph (c)(1)(ii) of this section as it applies to distributions made by non-electing foreign trusts to their U.S. beneficiaries. In addition, each distribution made by the foreign trust to a U.S. citizen or resident during this interim period must be reported on that U.S. recipient's Form 708 by applying the section 2801 ratio to that distribution. Once the interim period has ended, the foreign trust has no election in place and the rules of section 2801(e)(4)(B)(i) will apply until the foreign trust subsequently (if ever) makes another valid election to be treated as a domestic trust for purposes of section 2801.

(7) *No overpayment caused solely by virtue of defect in election.*— Any remittance of section 2801 tax made by a foreign trust electing to be treated as a domestic trust does not become an overpayment solely by virtue of a defect in the election. Instead, if at some subsequent time the IRS determines that the election was not in fact a valid election, then the election shall be considered valid only with respect to the covered gifts or covered bequests on which the section 2801 tax was timely paid by the foreign trust and each covered gift and covered bequest on which the section 2801 tax has been timely paid is no longer treated as a covered gift or covered bequest for purposes of determining the portion of the foreign trust attributable to covered gifts and covered bequests. See paragraphs (d)(2)(i) and (d)(6)(iii) of this section.

(e) *Examples.*—The provisions of this section are illustrated by the following examples.

Example 1. Computation of section 2801 ratio. A and B each contribute $100,000 to a foreign trust. A (but not B) is a covered expatriate and A's contribution is a covered gift. The section 2801 ratio immediately after these two contributions is 0.50, computed as follows: the pre-contribution value of the trust ($0) times the pre-contribution section 2801 ratio (-0-), plus the current covered gift ($100,000), divided by the post-contribution fair market value of the trust ($200,000). See § 28.2801-5(c). Therefore, 50 percent of each distribution from the trust is subject to the section 2801 tax until the next contribution is made to the trust. If the trustee distributes $40,000 to C, a U.S. citizen, before the trust receives any other contributions, then $20,000 ($40,000 x 0.5) is a covered gift to C.

Example 2. Computation of section 2801 ratio when multiple contributions are made to foreign trust. (i) In 2005, A, a U.S. citizen, established and funded an irrevocable foreign trust with $200,000 and reported the transfer as a completed gift. On January 1 of each of the following

three years (2006 through 2008), A contributed an additional $100,000 to the foreign trust. A reported A's contributions to the foreign trust as completed gifts on timely filed Forms 709, for calendar years 2005 through 2008. On August 8, 2008, a date after the effective date of section 2801 (June 17, 2008), A expatriated and became a covered expatriate. On January 1 of a year after 2008 (Year X), A makes an additional $100,000 contribution to the trust. The aggregate $600,000 contributed to the trust by A, both before and after expatriation, are the only contributions to the trust. Each year, the trustee of the foreign trust provides beneficiary B, a U.S. citizen, with an accounting of the trust showing each receipt and disbursement of the trust during that year, including the date and amount of each contribution by A.

(ii) The fair market value of the trust was $610,000 immediately prior to A's contribution to the trust on January 1, Year X. Therefore, upon the Year X contribution of A's first and only covered gift, the portion of the trust attributable to covered gifts and covered bequests (covered portion) changed from zero to 0.14 ([(section 2801 ratio of 0 x $610,000 fair market value pre-contribution) plus the $100,000 covered gift]/ $710,000 fair market value post-contribution). See paragraph (c) of this section.

(iii) In February of Year X, B received a distribution of $225,000 from the foreign trust. Although A contributed a total of $600,000 to the foreign trust, A contributed only $100,000 while A was a covered expatriate. Under paragraph (c) of this section, the portion of the $225,000 distribution from the foreign trust attributable to a covered gift is $31,500 ($225,000 x 0.14 (section 2801 ratio)) because the distribution is made proportionally from the covered and non-covered portions of the trust. See paragraph (c)(1) of this section. Accordingly, B received a covered gift of $31,500.

(iv) Pursuant to the terms of the foreign trust, the trust made a terminating distribution on August 5, Year X, when B turned 35, and B received the balance of the appreciated trust, $505,000. The portion of this distribution attributable to covered gifts and covered bequests is $70,700 ($505,000 x 0.14). Therefore, B has received covered gifts from the foreign trust during Year X in the total amount of $102,200 ($31,500 + $70,700).

Example 3. Termination of foreign trust election. The trustee of a foreign trust that received a covered gift makes a valid election to be treated as a domestic trust under § 28.2801-5(d) for Year 1. However, the trustee fails to file timely the Form 708 for the next year, Year 2. The foreign trust election is terminated as of January 1, Year 2, under paragraph (d)(5)(ii) of this section. Thus, any distributions made to U.S. recipients during Year 1 have a section 2801 ratio of zero and are not subject to the section 2801 tax. However, any such distributions made during Year 2 are subject to the section 2801 tax to the extent the distributions are attributable to a covered gift or covered bequest received by the trust during Year 2. Unless the trustee makes a new election as described in paragraph (d)(5)(iii) of this section, beginning in Year 2, the foreign trust's section 2801 ratio must be recomputed each time the foreign trust receives a contribution.

Example 4. Imperfect election by foreign trust. (i) In Year 1, CE, a covered expatriate, gives a 20 percent limited partnership interest in a closely held business to a foreign trust created for the benefit of CE's child, A, who is a U.S. citizen. The limited partnership interest is a covered gift. The trustee of the foreign trust makes a valid election to have the trust treated as a domestic trust for purposes of section 2801, trustee timely files a Form 708, and timely pays the section 2801 tax on the reported fair market value of the covered gift ($500,000). Later in Year 1, the trust makes a $100,000 distribution to A.

(ii) In Year 2, CE contributes $200,000 in cash to the foreign trust. The cash is a covered gift. The trustee of the foreign trust timely files a Form 708 reporting the transfer and pays the section 2801 tax. The trust does not make a distribution to any beneficiary during Year 2. Late in Year 3, the IRS disputes the reported value of the partnership interest transferred in Year 1 and determines that the proper valuation on the date of the gift was $800,000. In Year 3, the IRS issues a letter to the trustee of the foreign trust detailing its finding of the increased valuation and of the resulting additional section 2801 tax including accrued interest, if any, due on or before a later date in Year 3 specified in the letter. The foreign trust fails to pay the additional section 2801 tax liability on or before that due date.

(iii) Under paragraph (d)(6)(iii) of this section, the foreign trust's election for Year 1 is an imperfect election; although it timely filed its return reporting the transfer and paid the tax, it failed to timely pay the additional section 2801 tax when the IRS notified the trust of an additional amount of section 2801 tax claimed to be due. Accordingly, the foreign trust's election is deemed to have terminated as of January 1 of Year 1. In computing the foreign trust's section 2801 ratio upon the receipt of the covered gift in Year 1, the $500,000 of value on which the section 2801 tax was timely paid is no longer deemed to be a covered gift. See paragraph (d)(6)(iii) of this section. When the trustee advises A of the letter from the IRS, A must file a late Form 708 reporting the portion of the Year 1 distribution attributable to covered gifts and covered bequests. Although A may owe section 2801 tax and interest, A will not owe any penalties under section 6651 as long as A files the Form 708 and pays the tax within a reasonable period of time after A receives notice of the termination of the election from the trustee of the foreign trust or otherwise becomes aware of the termination of the election. See paragraph (d)(6)(iii)(C) of this section.

(iv) When A files the Form 708, the IRS will verify whether A treated the $300,000 undervaluation claimed by the IRS as a covered gift in computing the section 2801 ratio. As with any other item reported on that return, A has the burden to prove the value of the covered gift to the foreign trust, and the IRS may challenge that value. If A treats the $300,000 as a covered gift to the trust, under paragraph (c)(1)(ii) of this section, the section 2801 ratio after the Year 1 contribution is 0.375 ($0 + ($300,000)/$800,000)). Thus, 37.5 percent of all distributions made to A from the foreign trust during Year 1 are subject to the section 2801 tax.

(v) The foreign trust's timely filing of the Form 708 for Year 2 and the timely payment of the section 2801 tax shown on that return is not a valid election under paragraph (d)(5)(iii) of this section because the trust did not timely pay the section 2801 tax on all covered gifts and covered bequests in prior years as required in paragraph (d)(3) of this section; that is, the tax on the additional $300,000 of value of the Year 1 transfer. However, under paragraph (d)(6)(iii)(D) of this section, because the foreign trust timely filed and paid the section 2801 tax on the Year 2 covered gift of $200,000, and the additional unpaid tax was not due until Year 3, the $200,000 amount is no longer considered a covered gift for purposes of computing the section 2801 ratio.

Example 5. Subsequent election after termination of foreign trust election. The facts are the same as in *Example 4.* In Year 3, the foreign trust does not receive a covered gift or covered bequest. However, the trustee decides that making another election to be treated as a domestic trust would be in the best interests of the trust's beneficiaries. Accordingly, by the due date for the Form 708 for Year 3, the trustee timely files the return and pays the section 2801 tax on the portion of the trust attributable to covered gifts and covered bequests. See paragraph (d)(5)(iii) of this section. The trustee calculates the portion of the trust attributable to covered gifts and covered bequests received by the trust in prior calendar years by multiplying the fair market value of the trust on December 31, Year 2, by the section 2801 ratio in effect on that date. See paragraph (d)(3)(iii) of this section. The foreign trust is an electing foreign trust in Year 3.

(f) *Effective/applicability date.*—This section applies on and after the date of publication of a Treasury decision adopting these rules as final regulations in the **Federal Register**. Once these regulations have been published as final regulations in the **Federal Register**, taxpayers may rely upon the final rules of this part for the period beginning June 17, 2008, and ending on the date preceding the date these regulations are published as final regulations in the **Federal Register**. [Reg. § 28.2801-5.]

§ 28.2801-6. Special rules and cross-references.—(a) *Determination of basis.*—For purposes of determining the U.S. recipient's basis in property received as a covered gift or covered bequest, see sections 1015 and 1014, respectively. However, section 1015(d) does not apply to increase the basis in a covered gift to reflect the tax paid under this section. For purposes of determining a U.S. recipient's basis in property received as a covered bequest from a decedent who died during 2010 and whose executor elected under section 301(c) of the Tax Relief, Unemployment Insurance Reauthorization, and Job Creation Act of 2010 not to have the estate tax provisions apply, see section 1022.

(b) *Generation-skipping transfer tax.*—Transfers made by a nonresident not a citizen of the United States (NRA transferor) are subject to generation-skipping transfer (GST) tax only to the extent those transfers are subject to federal estate or gift tax as defined in § 26.2652-1(a)(2). In applying this rule, taxable distributions from a trust and taxable terminations are subject to the GST tax only to the extent the NRA transferor's contributions to the trust were subject to federal estate or gift tax as defined in § 26.2652-1(a)(2). See § 26.2663-2. A transfer is subject to federal estate or gift tax, regardless of whether a federal estate or gift tax return reporting the transfer is timely filed and regardless of whether chapter 15 applies because of a covered expatriate's failure to timely file and pay the section 2801 tax, if applicable.

(c) *Information returns.*—(1) *Gifts and bequests.*—Pursuant to section 6039F and the corresponding regulations, and to the extent provided in Notice 97-34, 1997-1 CB 422, and Form 3520, Part IV, each U.S. person (other than an organization described in section 501(c) and exempt from tax under section 501(a)) who treats an amount received from a foreign person (other than through a foreign trust) as a gift or bequest (including a covered gift or covered bequest) must report such gift or bequest on Part IV of Form 3520 if the value of the total of such gifts and bequests exceeds a certain threshold. A U.S. citizen or resident, as defined in § 28.2801-2(b) but

not including a foreign trust that elects to be treated as a domestic trust, is included within the definition of a U.S. person for purposes of section 6039F.

(2) *Foreign trust distributions.*—Pursuant to section 6048(c) and the corresponding regulations, and to the extent provided in Notice 97-34 and Part III of Form 3520, U.S. persons must report each distribution received during the taxable year from a foreign trust on Part III of Form 3520. Under section 6677(a), a penalty of the greater of $10,000 or 35 percent of the gross value of the distribution may be imposed on a U.S. person who fails to timely report the distribution. A U.S. citizen or resident as defined in § 28.2801-2(b), but not including a foreign trust that elects to be treated as a domestic trust, generally is required to report such a distribution under section 6048(c).

(3) *Penalties and use of information.*—The filing of Form 706, Form 706-NA, or Form 709 does not relieve a U.S. citizen or resident who is required to file Form 3520 from any penalties imposed under section 6677(a) for failure to comply with section 6048(c), or from any penalties imposed under section 6039F(c) for failure to comply with section 6039F(a). Pursuant to section 6039F(c)(1)(A), the Secretary may determine the tax consequences of the receipt of a purported foreign gift or bequest.

(d) *Application of penalties.*—(1) *Accuracy-related penalties on underpayments.*—The section 6662 accuracy-related penalty may be imposed upon any underpayment of tax attributable to—

(i) A substantial valuation understatement under section 6662(g) of a covered gift or covered bequest; or

(ii) A gross valuation misstatement under section 6662(h) of a covered gift or covered bequest.

(2) *Penalty for substantial and gross valuation misstatements attributable to incorrect appraisals.*—The section 6695A penalty for substantial and gross valuation misstatements attributable to incorrect appraisals may be imposed upon any person who prepares an appraisal of the value of a covered gift or covered bequest.

(3) *Penalty for failure to file a return and to pay tax.*—See section 6651 for the application of a penalty for the failure to file Form 708, or the failure to pay the section 2801 tax.

(e) *Effective/applicability date.*—This section applies on and after the date of publication of a Treasury decision adopting these rules as final regulations in the **Federal Register**. Once these regulations have been published as final regulations in the **Federal Register**, taxpayers may rely upon the final rules of this part for the period beginning June 17, 2008, and ending on the date preceding the date these regulations are published as final regulations in the **Federal Register**. [Reg. § 28.2801-6.]

§ 28.2801-7. Determining responsibility under section 2801.—(a) *Responsibility of recipients of gifts and bequests from expatriates.*—It is the responsibility of the taxpayer (in this case, the U.S. citizen or resident receiving a gift or bequest from an expatriate or a distribution from a foreign trust funded at least in part by an expatriate) to ascertain the taxpayer's obligations under section 2801, which includes making the determination of whether the transferor is a covered expatriate and whether the transfer is a covered gift or covered bequest.

(b) *Disclosure of return and return information.*—(1) *In general.*—In certain circumstances, the Internal Revenue Service (IRS) may be permitted, upon request of a U.S. citizen or resident in receipt of a gift or bequest from an expatriate, to disclose to the U.S. citizen or resident return or return information of the donor or decedent expatriate that may assist the U.S. citizen or resident in determining whether the donor or decedent was a covered expatriate and whether the transfer was a covered gift or covered bequest. The U.S. citizen or resident may not rely upon this information, however, if the U.S. citizen or resident knows, or has reason to know, that the information received from the IRS is incorrect. The circumstances under which such information may be disclosed to a U.S. citizen or resident, and the procedures for requesting such information from the IRS, will be as provided by publication in the Internal Revenue Bulletin (see § 601.601(d)(2)(ii)(b)).

(2) *Rebuttable presumption.*—Unless a living donor expatriate authorizes the disclosure of his or her relevant return or return information to the U.S. citizen or resident receiving the gift, there is a rebuttable presumption that the donor is a covered expatriate and that the gift is a covered gift. A taxpayer who reasonably concludes that a gift or bequest is not subject to section 2801 may file a protective Form 708 in accordance with § 28.6011-1(b) to start the period for the assessment of any section 2801 tax.

(c) *Effective/applicability date.*—This section applies on and after the date of publication of a Treasury decision adopting these rules as final regulations in the **Federal Register**. Once these regulations have been published as final regulations in the **Federal Register**, taxpayers may rely upon the final rules of this part for the period beginning June 17, 2008, and ending on the date preceding the date these regulations are published as final regulations in the **Federal Register**. [Reg. § 28.2801-7.]

WITHHOLDING FROM WAGES

Fringe Benefits: Taxability

Fringe Benefits: Taxability.—Reg. §31.3401(a)-1T, relating to the treatment of taxable and nontaxable fringe benefits, is proposed (published in the Federal Register on January 7, 1985) (LR-216-84).

§31.3401(a)-1T. Question and answer relating to the definition of wages in section 3401(a).

Income Tax: Withholding from Wages

Income Tax: Withholding from Wages.—Amendments to Reg. §§ 31.3401(e)-1, 31.3402(a)-1, 31.3402(b)-1, 31.3402(c)-1, 31.3402(f)(1)-1, 31.3402(f)(2)-1, 31.3402(f)(3)-1, 31.3402(f)(4)-1, 31.3402(f)(4)-2, 31.3402(f)(5)-1, 31.3402(f)(6)-1, 31.3402(g)-1, 31.3402(h)(4)-1, 31.3402(i)-1, 31.3402(i)-2, 31.3402(l)-1, 31.3402(m)-1 and 31.3402(n)-1, providing guidance for employers concerning the amount of Federal income tax to withhold from employee's wages, implementing recent changes in the Internal Revenue Code made by the Tax Cuts and Jobs Act, and reflecting the redesigned 2020 Form W-4 and related IRS publications (published in the Federal Register on February 13, 2020) (REG-132741-17).

Par. 2. Section 31.3401(e)-1 is removed.

§31.3401(e)-1. Number of withholding exemptions claimed.

Par. 3. Section 31.3402(a)-1 is amended by adding paragraphs (g) and (h) to read as follows:

§31.3402(a)-1. Requirement of withholding.

* * *

(g) *Definitions and Interchangeable Terms.*—For purposes of Chapter 24 and this Subpart E of Part 31 of the Employment Tax Regulations:

(1) References to "withholding exemption certificate" include "withholding allowance certificate" unless otherwise stated in Subpart E of Part 31 of the Employment Tax Regulations.

(2) [Reserved]

(h) *Applicability date.*—The provisions of paragraph (g) of this section apply on and after **[DATE OF PUBLICATION OF FINAL REGULATIONS IN THE FEDERAL REGISTER]**. Under section 7805(b)(7) a taxpayer may choose to apply paragraph (g) of this section on and after January 1, 2020.

Par. 4. Section 31.3402(b)-1 is revised to read as follows:

§31.3402(b)-1. **Percentage method of withholding.**— (a) *Percentage method of withholding.*—The amount of tax to be deducted and withheld from an employee's wages under the percentage method of withholding is determined based on the entry for the employee's anticipated filing status or marital status and other entries on the employee's withholding allowance certificate using the applicable percentage method tables and computational procedures set forth in the applicable forms, instructions, publications, and other guidance prescribed by the Commissioner issued with respect to the period in which wages are paid.

(b) *Applicability date.*—The provisions of this section apply on and after **[DATE OF PUBLICATION OF FINAL REGULATIONS IN THE FEDERAL REGISTER]**. For rules that apply before **[DATE OF PUBLICATION OF FINAL REGULATIONS IN THE FEDERAL REGISTER]**, see 26 CFR part 31, revised as of March 14, 2019. Under section 7805(b)(7) a taxpayer may choose to apply this section on and after January 1, 2020.

Par. 5. Section 31.3402(c)-1 is amended by:
1. Revising paragraph (a)(1).
2. Redesignating paragraph (a)(2) as paragraph (a)(3).
3. Adding a new paragraph (a)(2).
4. Revising paragraph (b).
5. In paragraph (c)(1), revising the first sentence
6. Adding paragraph (f).
The revisions and additions read as follows:

§31.3402(c)-1. **Wage bracket withholding.**—(a) * * *
(1) The employer may elect to use the wage bracket method provided in section 3402(c) instead of the percentage method with respect to any employee. The tax computed under the wage bracket method shall be in lieu of the tax required to be deducted and withheld under section 3402(a).

(2) The amount of tax to be deducted and withheld from an employee's wages under the wage bracket method of withholding is determined based on the entry for the employee's anticipated filing status or marital status and other entries on the employee's withholding allowance certificate using the applicable wage bracket method tables and computational procedures set forth in the applicable forms, instructions, publications, and other guidance prescribed by the Commissioner issued with respect to the period in which wages are paid.

* * *

(b) *Established payroll periods, other than daily or miscellaneous, covered by wage bracket withholding tables.*—The wage bracket withholding tables applicable to the employee's filing status set forth in forms, instructions, publications, and other guidance prescribed by the Commissioner for established periods other than daily or miscellaneous should be used in determining the tax to be deducted and withheld for any such period without reference to the time the employee is actually engaged in the performance of services during such payroll period.

(c) * * *
(1) * * * The tables applicable to a daily or miscellaneous payroll period show the tentative amount of tax to be deducted and withheld from an employee's wages for the employee's filing status for one day.* * *

* * *

(f) *Applicability date.*—The provisions of this section apply on and after **[DATE OF PUBLICATION OF FINAL REGULATIONS IN THE FEDERAL REGISTER]**. For rules that apply before **[DATE OF PUBLICATION OF FINAL REGULATIONS IN THE FEDERAL REGISTER]**, see 26 CFR part 31, revised as of March 14, 2019. Under section 7805(b)(7) a taxpayer may choose to apply this section on and after January 1, 2020.

Par. 6. Section 31.3402(f)(1)-1 is revised to read as follows:

§31.3402(f)(1)-1. Withholding allowance.—(a) *In general.*— (1) Except as otherwise provided in section 3402(f)(6) (see §31.3402(f)(6)-1), an employee receiving wages will, on any day, be entitled to a withholding allowance as provided in section 3402(f)(1) and paragraph (b) of this section. In order to receive the benefit of the withholding allowance, the employee must furnish to the employer a valid withholding allowance certificate in effect for the calendar year as provided in section 3402(f)(2) and §31.3402(f)(2)-1.

(2) The employer is not required to ascertain whether the withholding allowance claimed is greater than the withholding allowance to which the employee is entitled. For rules relating to invalid withholding allowance certificates, see §31.3402(f)(2)-1(f)(3), for rules relating to required submission of copies of certain withholding allowance certificates to the Internal Revenue Service, see §31.3402(f)(2)-1(g)(1), and for rules relating to the notice of the maximum withholding allowance permitted, see §31.3402(f)(2)-1(g)(2).

(b) *Withholding allowance defined.*—(1) Generally, the withholding allowance to which an employee is entitled is determined under the computational procedures prescribed by the Commissioner in forms, instructions, publications, and other guidance for the calendar year for which the withholding allowance certificate is in effect.

(2) The withholding allowance is determined based on the following—

(i) Whether the employee is an individual for whom a deduction is allowable with respect to another taxpayer under section 151;

(ii) If the employee is married, whether the employee's spouse is an individual for whom a deduction is allowable with respect to another taxpayer under section 151 but only if such spouse does not have in effect a withholding allowance certificate claiming such deduction;

(iii) If the employee is married, whether the employee's spouse is entitled to additional deductions, credits, or other items the employee elects to take into account under §31.3402(m)-1 or would be so entitled if the employee's spouse were an employee receiving

Par. 7. Section 31.3402(f)(2)-1 is revised to read as follows:

§31.3402(f)(2)-1. Furnishing of withholding allowance certificates.—(a) *On commencement of employment.*—(1) On or before the date on which an individual commences employment with an employer, the individual must furnish the employer with a signed withholding allowance certificate (see §31.3402(f)(5)-1) relating to the filing status the employee reasonably expects to claim under §31.3402(l)-1(b) for the calendar year for which the withholding allowance certificate is in effect and the withholding allowance under §31.3402(f)(1)-1(b) that the employee claims.

(2) In no event may the withholding allowance exceed the withholding allowance that the employee is entitled to as determined based on the employee's reasonable expectations and the instructions set forth in forms, instructions, publications, and other guidance prescribed by the Commissioner.

(3) The employee may claim exemption from withholding if the certifications described in section 3402(n) and §31.3402(n)-1(a)(1) and (2) are true with respect to the employee.

(4) If an employee has no valid withholding allowance certificate in effect with the employer at the time of the payment of the wages, and fails to furnish a valid withholding allowance certificate to the employer, the employee will be treated as single but having the withholding allowance provided in forms, instructions, publications, and other guidance prescribed by the Commissioner.

(b) *Change of status that affects calendar year.*—(1) *General rule.*— If, on any day during the calendar year, the employee experiences a change of status that reduces the employee's withholding allowances, or withholding allowance in the manner described in paragraph (b)(2) of this section, the employee must, within 10 days after the change occurs, furnish the employer with a new withholding allowance certificate claiming the withholding allowance to which the employee is entitled under §31.3402(f)(1)-1(b), unless paragraph (b)(3) of this section applies to the employee.

(2) *Changes of status.*—A change of status occurs if any of the following changes occur on any day during the calendar year:

(i) The employee's filing status changes in the manner described in §31.3402(l)-1(c).

(ii) The employee no longer has only one withholding allowance certificate in effect for the employee, the employee's spouse, or both, and the employee or the employee's spouse selects higher withholding rate tables on the additional withholding allowance certificate, but higher withholding rate tables are not selected on any previously furnished withholding allowance certificate.

(iii) The employee has multiple withholding allowance certificates in effect on which higher withholding rate tables are not

wages, but only if such spouse does not have in effect a withholding allowance certificate claiming such allowance;

(iv) Any credit under section 24(a) that the employee reasonably expects to be able to claim on the employee's income tax return for the calendar year for which the withholding allowance certificate is in effect, except that the employee may not take into account any credit under section 24(a) if this credit is claimed on another valid withholding allowance certificate in effect with respect to another employer of the employee or the employee's spouse. In addition, an employee whose employer must withhold for that employee pursuant to a notice under §31.3402(f)(2)-1(g)(2) must offset any tax benefit resulting from a credit under section 24(a) with any anticipated income tax attributable to items other than wages includible in the employee's gross income in the manner prescribed by the Commissioner;

(v) Any additional deductions, credits, or other items the employee elects to take into account under §31.3402(m)-1 for the calendar year for which the withholding allowance certificate is in effect;

(vi) The basic standard deduction (as defined in section 63(c)(2)) relating to the filing status the employee reasonably expects to claim on the employee's income tax return for the calendar year for which the withholding allowance certificate is in effect; and

(vii) Any adjustment resulting from multiple withholding allowance certificates the employee, the employee's spouse, or both have or reasonably expect to have in effect with respect to one or more employers, determined based on the instructions to the withholding allowance certificate and other guidance for the calendar year for which the withholding allowance certificate is in effect.

(c) *Applicability date.*—The provisions of this section apply on and after **[DATE OF PUBLICATION OF FINAL REGULATIONS IN THE FEDERAL REGISTER]**. For rules that apply before **[DATE OF PUBLICATION OF FINAL REGULATIONS IN THE FEDERAL REGISTER]**, see 26 CFR part 31, revised as of March 14, 2019. Under section 7805(b)(7) a taxpayer may choose to apply this section on and after January 1, 2020.

selected, and the employee or the employee's spouse reasonably expects an increase in regular wages for the calendar year (as defined in §31.3402(g)-1(a)(1)(ii)) in excess of $10,000.

(iv) The employee has included on a valid withholding allowance certificate the child tax credit allowed under section 24(a) but reasonably expects the number of individuals who satisfy the definition of "qualifying child" as defined in section 24(c) who will be reported on the employee's income tax return for the year for which tax is being withheld to be less than the number taken into account in completing the withholding allowance certificate.

(v) The employee has included on a valid withholding allowance certificate a tax credit allowed under section 24(a) or other tax credits allowed under §31.3402(m)-1 but reasonably expects the employee's tax credits that will be reported on the employee's income tax return for the year for which tax is being withheld to decrease by more than $500 from the amount taken into account in completing the withholding allowance certificate.

(vi) The employee has included on a valid withholding allowance certificate deductions allowed under §31.3402(m)-1 but reasonably expects the employee's included income tax deductions that will be reported on the employee's income tax return for the year for which tax is being withheld to decrease by more than $2,300 from the amount taken into account in completing the withholding allowance certificate.

(vii) It is no longer reasonable for an employee who has furnished the employer with a withholding allowance certificate which relies upon the certifications described in §31.3402(n)-1(a) to anticipate that the employee will incur no liability for income tax imposed under subtitle A of the Code for the current or previous taxable year.

(3) *Exception.*—If one or more of the changes described in paragraph (b)(2) of this section occurs, but the total effect of the changes together with any other changes affecting the employee's anticipated tax liability under Subtitle A is not anticipated to result in an amount of tax to be deducted and withheld from the employee's wages under section 3402 for the year that is less than the employee's anticipated tax liability under Subtitle A, the employee is not required to furnish a new withholding allowance certificate.

(c) *Increase in withholding allowance.*—If, on any day during the calendar year, the employee experiences a change of status that increases the employee's withholding allowance, the employee may furnish the employer with a new withholding allowance certificate claiming the withholding allowance the employee is entitled to under §31.3402(f)(1)-1(b).

(d) *Exemption from withholding.*—If, on any day during the calendar year, the certifications described in section 3402(n) and §31.3402(n)-1(a)(1) and (2) are true with respect to an employee, the employee may furnish his employer with a withholding allowance certificate claiming exemption from withholding in the manner described in forms, instructions, publications, and other guidance prescribed by the Commissioner.

(e) *Change of status which affects next calendar year.*—(1) *General rule.*—If, on any day during the calendar year, the withholding allowance to which the employee will be, or may reasonably be expected to be, entitled under §31.3402(f)(1)-1(b) for the next calendar year, but not for the current calendar year, decreases in the manner prescribed in paragraph (b)(2) of this section, the employee must furnish a new withholding allowance certificate claiming the withholding allowance the employee is entitled to under §31.3402(f)(1)-1(b) to take effect in the next calendar year by the later of December 1 of the calendar year of the year in which the change occurs or within 10 days after the change occurs, unless paragraph (e)(2) of this section applies to the employee.

(2) *Exception.*—If one or more of the changes in paragraph (b)(2) of this section occurs, but the total effect of the changes together with any other changes affecting the employee's anticipated tax liability under subtitle A is not anticipated to result in an amount of tax to be deducted and withheld from the employee's wages under section 3402 for the employee's next year that is less than the employee's anticipated tax liability under Subtitle A, the employee is not required to furnish a new withholding allowance certificate.

(f) *Special rules.*—(1) *Employer requests.*—Before December 1 of each year, every employer should request each employee to furnish a new withholding allowance certificate for the next calendar year, in the event of a change to the employee's withholding allowance.

(2) *Social security account numbers.*—Every individual to whom a social security number has been assigned must include such number on any withholding allowance certificate furnished to an employer. An employee may not use a truncated social security number (see §301.6109-4) in completing the withholding allowance certificate. For provisions relating to the obtaining of an account number from the Social Security Administration, see §31.6011(b)-2.

(3) *Invalid withholding allowance certificates.*—(i) *General rule.*—Any alteration of or unauthorized addition to a withholding allowance certificate causes such certificate to be invalid; see §31.3402(f)(5)-1(b) for the definitions of alteration and unauthorized addition. Any withholding allowance certificate which the employee clearly indicates to be false by an oral statement or by a written statement (other than one made on the withholding allowance certificate itself) made by the employee to the employer on or before the date on which the employee furnishes such certificate is also invalid. For purposes of the preceding sentence, the term "employer" includes any individual authorized by the employer either to receive withholding allowance certificates, to make withholding computations, or to make payroll distributions.

(ii) *Employer disregard of invalid withholding allowance certificate.*—If an employer receives an invalid withholding allowance certificate, the employer must disregard it for purposes of computing withholding. The employer must inform the employee who furnished the certificate that it is invalid, and must request another withholding allowance certificate from the employee. If the employee who furnished the invalid certificate fails to comply with the employer's request, the employer must treat the employee as single but having the withholding allowance provided by the forms, instructions, publications, and other guidance prescribed by the Commissioner. If, however, a prior certificate is in effect with respect to the employee, the employer must continue to withhold in accordance with the prior certificate.

(g) *Submission of certain withholding allowance certificates and notice of maximum withholding allowance permitted.*—(1) *Submission of certain withholding allowance certificates.*—(i) *In general.*—An employer must submit to the Internal Revenue Service (IRS) a copy of any currently effective withholding allowance certificate as directed in a written notice to the employer from the IRS or as directed in published guidance.

(A) *Notice to submit withholding allowance certificates.*—A notice to the employer to submit withholding allowance certificates may relate either to one or more named employees, to one or more reasonably segregable units of the employer, or to withholding allowance certificates under certain specified criteria. The notice will designate the IRS office to which the copies of the withholding allowance certificates must be submitted. Alternatively, upon notice from the IRS, the employer must make available for inspection by an IRS employee withholding allowance certificates received from one or more named employees, from one or more reasonably segregable

units of the employer, or from employees who have furnished withholding allowance certificates under certain specified criteria.

(B) *Published guidance.*—Employers may also be required to submit copies of withholding allowance certificates under certain specified criteria when directed to do so by the IRS in published guidance in the Internal Revenue Bulletin (see §601.601(d)(2) of this chapter).

(ii) *Withholding after submission of withholding allowance certificate.*—After a copy of a withholding allowance certificate has been submitted to the IRS under this paragraph (g)(1), the employer must withhold tax on the basis of the withholding allowance certificate, if the withholding allowance certificate meets the requirements of §31.3402(f)(5)-1. However, the employer may not withhold on the basis of the withholding allowance certificate if the certificate must be disregarded based on a notice of the maximum withholding allowance permitted under the provisions of paragraph (g)(2) of this section.

(2) *Notice of the maximum withholding allowance permitted.*—(i) *Notice to employer.*—The IRS may notify the employer in writing that the employee is not entitled to claim a complete exemption from withholding or more than the maximum withholding allowance specified by the IRS in the written notice. The notice will also specify the applicable filing status for purposes of calculating the required amount of withholding. The notice will specify the IRS office to be contacted for further information. The notice of maximum withholding allowance permitted may be issued if—

(A) The IRS determines that a copy of a withholding allowance certificate submitted under paragraph (g)(1) of this section or otherwise provided to the IRS includes a materially incorrect statement or determines, after a request to the employee for verification of the statements on the certificate, that the IRS lacks sufficient information to determine if the certificate is correct; or

(B) The IRS otherwise determines that the employee is not entitled to claim a complete exemption from withholding and is not entitled to claim more than a specified number of withholding exemptions, withholding allowances, or a specified withholding allowance.

(ii) *Notice to employee.*—If the IRS provides a notice to the employer under this paragraph (g)(2), the IRS will also provide the employer with a similar notice for the employee (employee notice) that identifies the maximum withholding allowance permitted and specifies the filing status to be used for calculating the required amount of withholding for the employee. The employee notice will also indicate the process by which the employee can provide additional information to the IRS for purposes of determining the appropriate withholding allowance and/or modifying the specified filing status. The IRS will also mail a similar notice to the employee's last known address. For further guidance regarding the definition of last known address, see §301.6212-2 of this chapter. If the IRS is unable to determine a last known address for the employee, the IRS will use other available information as appropriate to mail the notice to the employee.

(iii) *Requirement to furnish.*—If the employee is employed by the employer as of the date of the notice, the employer must furnish the employee notice to the employee within 10 business days of receipt. The employer may follow any reasonable business practice to furnish the copy of the notice to the employee. For purposes of this paragraph (g)(2)(iii), the determination of whether an employee is employed as of the date of the notice is based on all the facts and circumstances, including whether the employer has treated the employment relationship as terminated for other purposes. An employee who is not performing services for the employer as of the date of the notice is employed by the employer as of the date of the notice for purposes of this paragraph (g)(2)(iii) if—

(A) The employer pays wages with respect to prior employment to the employee subject to income tax withholding on or after the date specified in the notice;

(B) The employer reasonably expects the employee to resume the performance of services for the employer within twelve months of the date of the notice; or

(C) The employee is on a bona fide leave of absence and either the period of such leave does not exceed twelve months or the employee retains a right to reemployment with the employer under an applicable statute or by contract.

(iv) *Requirement to withhold based on the notice.*—If the employer is required to furnish the employee notice to the employee under paragraph (g)(2)(iii) of this section, then the employer must withhold tax on the basis of the maximum withholding allowance and the filing status specified in the notice for any wages paid after the date specified in the notice, except as provided in paragraphs (g)(2)(v) through (ix) of this section. The employer must withhold tax in accordance with the notice as of the date specified in the notice, which shall be no earlier than 45 calendar days after the date of the notice.

(v) *Employment resumes after twelve months.*—If the employer is required to furnish the employee notice to the employee only pursuant to paragraph (g)(2)(iii)(B) of this section and the employee resumes the performance of services for the employer more than 12 months after the date of the notice, then the employer is not required to withhold based on the notice.

(vi) *Requirement to withhold based on an existing Form W-4.*—If a withholding allowance certificate is in effect with respect to the employee before the employer receives a notice of the maximum withholding allowance permitted under this paragraph (g)(2), the employer must continue to withhold tax in accordance with the existing withholding allowance certificate, rather than on the basis of the notice, if the existing withholding allowance certificate does not claim complete exemption from withholding and claims a filing status, a withholding allowance, and any additional amount under §31.3402(i)-1(a)(1) and (2) that results in more withholding than would result from applying the filing status and withholding allowance specified in the notice.

(vii) *Modification notice.*—After issuing the notice specifying the maximum withholding allowance permitted and the filing status, the IRS may issue a subsequent notice to the employer and the employee that modifies the original notice (modification notice). The modification notice may change the filing status and/or the withholding allowance permitted. The employer must withhold based on the modification notice as of the date specified in the modification notice.

(viii) *Requirement to withhold after termination of employment.*—If the employee is employed as of the date of the notice under paragraph (g)(2)(iii) of this section but the employer or employee terminates the employment relationship after the date of the notice, the employer must continue to withhold based on the maximum withholding allowance and the filing status specified in the notice or a modification notice if any wages subject to income tax withholding are paid with respect to the prior employment after such date. Furthermore, the employer must withhold based on the notice or modification notice if the employee resumes an employment relationship with the employer within 12 months after the termination of the employment relationship. Whether the employment relationship is terminated is based on all the facts and circumstances.

(ix) *Requirement to withhold based on new Form W-4.*—The employee may furnish a new withholding allowance certificate after the employer receives a notice or modification notice from the IRS of the maximum withholding allowance permitted under this paragraph (g)(2).

(A) *Employee requests more withholding.*—If the employee furnishes a new withholding allowance certificate after the employer receives the notice or modification notice, the employer must withhold tax on the basis of that new certificate only if the new certificate does not claim complete exemption from withholding and claims a filing status, a withholding allowance, and any additional amount under §31.3402(i)-1(a)(1) and (2) that results in more withholding than would result under the notice or modification notice.

(B) *Employee requests less withholding.*—If the employee furnishes a new withholding allowance certificate after the employer receives the notice or modification notice, the employer must disregard the new certificate and withhold on the basis of the notice or modification notice if the employee claims complete exemption from withholding or claims a filing status, a withholding allowance, and any additional amount under §31.3402(i)-1(a)(1) and (2) that results in less withholding than would result under the notice or modification notice. If the employee wants to put a new certificate into effect that results in less withholding than that required under the notice or modification notice, the employee must contact the IRS. The employer must withhold on the basis of the notice or modification notice unless the IRS subsequently notifies the employer to withhold based on the new certificate.

(3) *Definition of employer.*—For purposes of this paragraph (g), the term employer includes any person authorized by the employer to receive withholding allowance certificates, to make withholding computations, or to make payroll distributions.

(4) *Examples.*—The following examples illustrate the rules of this section.

(i) *Example 1.* Employer U receives a notice from the IRS that identifies the maximum withholding allowance permitted and specifies the filing status for Employee A. Employee A is not currently performing any services for Employer U. However, Employer U is continuing to make certain wage payments to Employee A. Employer U must furnish the employee notice to Employee A within 10 business days of receipt and must withhold based on the notice on any wages paid to Employee A on or after the date specified in the notice.

(ii) *Example 2.* Employer V receives a notice in October of Year 1 from the IRS that identifies the maximum withholding allowance permitted and specifies the filing status for Employee B. Employee B has not performed services for Employer V since August of Year 1. However, since Employee B has performed services for Employer V for several years on a seasonal basis, Employer V reasonably expects Employee B to resume the performance of services for Employer V in June of Year 2, a date that is within 12 months of the date of the notice. Employer V is required to furnish the notice to Employee B within 10 business days of receipt. Employee B does not resume the performance of services with Employer V until June of Year 3. Employer V is not required to withhold based on the notice.

(iii) *Example 3.* Employer W receives a notice from the IRS that identifies the maximum withholding allowance permitted and specifies the filing status for Employee C. Employee C began a 4-month unpaid maternity leave of absence three weeks before Employer W received the notice. Employer W must furnish the employee notice to Employee C within 10 business days of receipt. When her maternity leave ends and Employee C resumes performing services for Employer W, Employer W must withhold based on the notice.

(iv) *Example 4.* Employer X receives a notice from the IRS in Year 1 that identifies the maximum withholding allowance permitted and specifies the filing status for Employee D. Employer X must furnish the employee notice to Employee D within 10 business days of receipt and withhold based on the notice. In Year 2, Employee D terminates the employment relationship. Employee D applies for a different position with Employer X and resumes employment 10 months after having left her previous position with Employer X. Since Employer X rehired Employee D within 12 months after the termination of employment, Employer X must withhold based on the notice.

(v) *Example 5.* Employer Y receives a notice from the IRS that identifies the maximum withholding allowance permitted and specifies the filing status for Employee E. Employer Y must furnish the employee notice to Employee E within 10 business days of receipt. After receipt of this notice, Employee E contacts the IRS and establishes that the employee is entitled to claim a modified filing status and withholding allowance. Employer Y receives a modification notice from the IRS that changes the maximum withholding allowance permitted for Employee E. Employer Y must withhold tax based on the modification notice as of the date specified in such notice.

(vi) *Example 6.* Employer Z pays remuneration to Employee F, a United States citizen, for services performed in Country M. Employer Z receives a notice from the IRS in Year 1 that identifies the maximum withholding allowance permitted and specifies the filing status for Employee F. Employer Z must furnish the employee notice to Employee F within 10 business days of receipt. Employer Z reasonably believes all the remuneration paid to Employee F in Year 1 is excluded from Employee F's gross income under section 911. Since section 3401(a)(8)(B) excludes such remuneration from wages for income tax withholding purposes, Employer X does not have to withhold on such remuneration, notwithstanding the maximum withholding allowance permitted and filing status specified in the notice. In Year 2, Employee F returns to the United States to perform services. Employer Z does not reasonably believe any part of Employee F's remuneration paid in Year 2 is excluded from Employee F's gross income under section 911. Rather, Employer Z reasonably believes that remuneration paid to Employee F in Year 2 is subject to income tax withholding. Employer Z must withhold on the remuneration paid to Employee F in Year 2 based on the notice.

(h) *Applicability date.*—The provisions of paragraph (g) of this section apply on February 13, 2020. For rules that apply under paragraph (g) before February 13, 2020, see 26 CFR part 31, revised as of March 14, 2019. The provisions of paragraphs (a) through (f) of this section apply on and after **[DATE OF PUBLICATION OF FINAL REGULATIONS IN THE FEDERAL REGISTER]**. For rules that apply before **[DATE OF PUBLICATION OF FINAL REGULATIONS IN THE FEDERAL REGISTER]**, see 26 CFR part 31, revised as of March 14, 2019. Under section 7805(b)(7) a taxpayer may choose to apply paragraphs (a) through (g) of this section on and after January 1, 2020.

Par. 8. Section 31.3402(f)(3)-1 is revised to read as follows:

§31.3402(f)(3)-1. When withholding allowance certificate takes effect.—(a) *No withholding allowance certificate on file.*—A withholding

allowance certificate furnished to the employer in any case in which no previous withholding allowance certificate is in effect with such employer, takes effect as of the beginning of the first payroll period ending, or the first payment of wages made without regard to a payroll period, on or after the date on which such certificate is so furnished.

(b) *Withholding allowance certificate on file.*—Except as provided in paragraph (c) of this section, a withholding allowance certificate furnished to the employer in any case in which a previous withholding allowance certificate is in effect with such employer takes effect as of the beginning of the 1st payroll period ending (or the 1st payment of wages made without regard to a payroll period) on or after the 30th day after the day on which such certificate is so furnished. However, the employer may elect to put a withholding allowance certificate into effect earlier, beginning with any payment of wages on or after the day on which the certificate is so furnished.

Par. 9. Section 31.3402(f)(4)-1 is removed.

§31.3402(f)(4)-1. Period during which withholding exemption certificate remains in effect.

Par. 10 and 11. Redesignate §31.3402(f)(4)-2 as 31.3402(f)(4)-1 and revise newly-redesignated §31.3402(f)(4)-1 to read as follows:

§31.3402(f)(4)-1. Effective period of a withholding allowance certificate.—(a) *In general.*—Except as provided in paragraph (b) of this section and §31.3402(f)(2)-1(g)(2), a withholding allowance certificate that takes effect under section 3402(f) of the Internal Revenue Code of 1986 continues in effect with respect to the employee until another withholding allowance certificate takes effect under section 3402(f).

(b) *Certifications under section 3402(n) eliminating requirement of withholding.*—The certifications described in §31.3402(n)-1(a) made by an employee with respect to the employee's preceding taxable year and current taxable year are effective until either a new withholding allowance certificate furnished by the employee takes effect or the existing certificate that relies upon such certifications expires. If an employee's certificate expires and the employee fails to furnish a valid withholding allowance certificate, the employee will be treated as single but having the withholding allowance provided in forms, instructions, publications, and other guidance prescribed by the IRS. In no case shall a withholding allowance certificate that relies upon such certifications be effective with respect to any payment of wages made to an employee:

(1) In the case of an employee whose liability for tax under subtitle A is determined on a calendar year basis, after February 15 of the calendar year following the estimation year, or

(2) In the case of an employee to whom paragraph (b)(1) of this section does not apply, after the 15th day of the 2nd calendar month following the last day of the estimation year.

Par. 12. Section 31.3402(f)(5)-1 is revised to read as follows:

§31.3402(f)(5)-1. Form and contents of withholding allowance certificates.—(a) *In general.*—(1) *Form W-4.*—Form W-4, "Employee's Withholding Certificate," previously called "Employee's Withholding Allowance Certificate," is the form prescribed for the withholding allowance certificate required to be furnished under section 3402(f)(2). A withholding allowance certificate must be prepared in accordance with the instructions applicable thereto, and must set forth fully and clearly the information that is called for therein. In lieu of the prescribed form, an employer may prepare and provide to employees a form the provisions of which are identical to those of the prescribed form, but only if the employer also provides employees with all the tables, instructions, and worksheets set forth in the Form W-4 in effect at that time, and only if the employer complies with all revenue procedures relating to substitute forms in effect at that time.

(2) *Employee substitute forms.*—Employers are prohibited from accepting a substitute form developed by an employee, and an employee furnishing such form will be treated as failing to furnish a withholding allowance certificate. For further guidance regarding the employer's obligations when an employee is treated as failing to furnish a withholding allowance certificate, see §31.3402(f)(2)-1.

(3) *Current year revision.*—Only the Form W-4 revision in effect for a calendar year may be furnished by an employee in that calendar year and given legal effect by the employer, unless provided otherwise in forms, instructions, publications, or other guidance, except that an employee may furnish the Form W-4 revision for the following calendar year in the current calendar year to take effect for the following calendar year.

(4) *Examples.*—The following examples illustrate the rule in paragraph (a)(3) of this section.

(c) *Withholding allowance certificate furnished to take effect in next calendar year.*—A withholding allowance certificate furnished to the employer pursuant to section 3402(f)(2)(C) (see §31.3402(f)(2)-1(e) or §31.3402(l)-1(c)) which effects a change for the next calendar year, does not take effect, and may not be made effective, with respect to the calendar year in which the certificate is furnished.

(d) *Applicability date.*—The provisions of this section apply on [DATE OF PUBLICATION OF FINAL REGULATIONS IN THE FEDERAL REGISTER]. For rules that apply before [DATE OF PUBLICATION OF FINAL REGULATIONS IN THE FEDERAL REGISTER], see 26 CFR part 31, revised as of March 14, 2019. Under section 7805(b)(7) a taxpayer may choose to apply this section on and after January 1, 2020.

(c) *Estimation year.*—The estimation year is the taxable year including the day on which the employee furnishes the withholding allowance certificate to the employer, except that if the employee furnishes the withholding allowance certificate to the employer and specifies on the certificate that the certificate is not to take effect until a specified future date, the estimation year will be the taxable year including that specified future date.

(d) *Applicability to notice of maximum withholding allowance.*—If a withholding allowance certificate is no longer in effect because of the application of §31.3402(f)(2)-1(g)(2), the employer is no longer required to withhold pursuant to any notice under §31.3402(f)(2)-1(g)(2), and the employee fails to furnish the employer a valid withholding allowance certificate, then the employee will be treated as single but having the withholding allowance provided in forms, instructions, publications, and other guidance prescribed by the Commissioner, in accordance with §31.3402(f)(2)-1(a)(4).

(e) *Applicability date.*—The provisions of this section apply on and after [DATE OF PUBLICATION OF FINAL REGULATIONS IN THE FEDERAL REGISTER]. For rules that apply before [DATE OF PUBLICATION OF FINAL REGULATIONS IN THE FEDERAL REGISTER], see 26 CFR part 31, revised as of March 14, 2019. Under section 7805(b)(7) a taxpayer may choose to apply this section on and after January 1, 2020.

(i) *Example 1.* Employee A furnishes a 2019 Form W-4 to Employer X in calendar year 2020. The 2019 Form W-4 furnished by Employee A in 2020 has no legal effect. Employer X must disregard this 2019 Form W-4 furnished in 2020 and continue to withhold based on a previously furnished Form W-4 that has been in effect for Employee A, if any. If Employee A has no Form W-4 in effect, she is treated as having no valid withholding allowance certificate in effect.

(ii) *Example 2.* Employee A furnishes a 2021 Form W-4 to Employer X in calendar year 2020 to take effect in calendar year 2021. The 2021 Form W-4 is valid, and the employer must put this form in effect in 2021 in accordance with the timing rules in §31.3402(f)(3)-1.

(b) *Invalid Form W-4.*—A Form W-4 does not meet the requirements of section 3402(f)(5) or this section and is invalid if it includes an alteration or unauthorized addition. For purposes of §31.3402(f)(2)-1(f)(3) and this paragraph (b)—

(1) An alteration of a withholding allowance certificate is any deletion of the language of the jurat or other similar provision of such certificate by which the employee certifies or affirms the correctness of the completed certificate, or any material defacing of such certificate;

(2) An unauthorized addition to a withholding allowance certificate is any writing on such certificate other than the entries requested on the Form W-4 (*e.g.*, name, address, and filing status) or permitted by instructions or other guidance. For purposes of this rule, an entry claiming exemption from withholding that is accompanied by other entries on the Form W-4 (other than the employee's filing status) that could potentially affect the amount of income tax deducted and withheld from the employee's pay is an unauthorized addition; consequently, the employer must treat the Form W-4 as an invalid Form W-4.

(c) *Electronic Form W-4.*—(1) *In general.*—An employer may establish a system for its employees to furnish withholding allowance certificates electronically.

(2) *Requirements.*—(i) *In general.*—The electronic system must ensure that the information received is the information sent, and must document all occasions of employee access that result in the furnishing of a Form W-4. In addition, the design and operation of the electronic system, including access procedures, must make it reasonably certain that the person accessing the system and furnishing the Form W-4 is the employee identified in the form.

(ii) *Information to employer.*—The electronic furnishing must provide the employer with exactly the same information as the current version of the official Internal Revenue Service (IRS) Form W-4 available on irs.gov.

(iii) *Information to employee.*—The electronic Form W-4 system must provide the employee with the same information as the current version of the official IRS Form W-4 available on irs.gov and must satisfy any requirements specified by the IRS in forms, publications, and other guidance. The electronic Form W-4 system must provide employees the ability to claim exemption from withholding under section 3402(n) and must include the two certifications described in § 31.3402(n)-1(a).

(iv) *Jurat and signature requirements.*—The electronic furnishing must be signed by the employee under penalties of perjury.

(A) *Jurat.*—The jurat (perjury statement) must contain the language that appears on the paper Form W-4. The electronic program must inform the employee that he or she must make the

declaration set forth in the jurat and that the declaration is made by signing the Form W-4. The instructions and the language of the jurat must immediately follow the employee's income tax withholding selections and immediately precede the employee's electronic signature.

(B) *Electronic signature.*—The electronic signature must identify the employee furnishing the electronic Form W-4 and authenticate and verify the furnishing. For this purpose, the terms "authenticate" and "verify" have the same meanings as they do when applied to a written signature on a paper Form W-4. An electronic signature can be in any form that satisfies the foregoing requirements. The electronic signature must be the final entry in the employee's Form W-4 furnishing.

(v) *Copies of electronic Forms W-4.*—Upon request by the Internal Revenue Service, the employer must supply a hard copy of the electronic Form W-4 and a statement that, to the best of the employer's knowledge, the electronic Form W-4 was furnished by the named employee. The hardcopy of the electronic Form W-4 must provide exactly the same information as, but need not be a facsimile of, the paper Form W-4.

(d) *Applicability date.*—The provisions of this section apply on and after **[DATE OF PUBLICATION OF FINAL REGULATIONS IN THE FEDERAL REGISTER]**, except that paragraph (a)(3) of this section applies on and after March 16, 2020. For rules that apply before **[DATE OF PUBLICATION OF FINAL REGULATIONS IN THE FEDERAL REGISTER]**, see 26 CFR part 31, revised as of March 14, 2019. Under section 7805(b)(7) a taxpayer may choose to apply this section on and after January 1, 2020.

Par. 13. Section 31.3402(f)(6)-1 is revised to read as follows:

§ 31.3402(f)(6)-1. Withholding exemptions for nonresident alien individuals.—(a) *In general.*—(1) A nonresident alien individual (other than a nonresident alien individual treated as a resident under section 6013(g) or (h)) subject to withholding under section 3402 is on any one day entitled to the number of withholding exemptions corresponding to the number of personal exemptions to which the nonresident alien is entitled on such day by reason of the application of section 873(b)(3) or section 876, whichever applies. Thus, a nonresident alien individual who is not a resident of Canada or Mexico and who is not a resident of Puerto Rico during the entire taxable year, is allowed only one withholding exemption.

(2) The withholding exemption in paragraph (a) of this section and section 3402(f)(6) is the deduction allowed to the nonresident alien individual under section 151.

Par. 14. Section 31.3402(g)-1 is amended by
1. In paragraph (a)(2), revising the second sentence.
2. In paragraph (a)(7)(ii), revising the first sentence.
3. Adding paragraph (d).
The revisions and addition read as follows:

§ 31.3402(g)-1. Supplemental wage payments.—(a) * * *

(2) * * * This flat rate shall be applied without regard to whether income tax has been withheld from the employee's regular wages, and without regard to any entries on Form W-4, including whether the employee has claimed exempt status on Form W-4 or whether the employee has requested additional withholding on Form W-4, and without regard to the withholding method used by the employer. * * *

* * *

(7) * * *

(b) *Additional guidance.*—A nonresident alien individual (other than a nonresident alien individual treated as a resident under section 6013(g) or (h)) subject to withholding must follow administrative guidance such as forms, instructions, publications, or other guidance prescribed by the IRS to determine the nonresident alien's withholding allowance.

(c) *Applicability date.*—The provisions of this section apply on and after **[DATE OF PUBLICATION OF FINAL REGULATIONS IN THE FEDERAL REGISTER]**. For rules that apply before **[DATE OF PUBLICATION OF FINAL REGULATIONS IN THE FEDERAL REGISTER]**, see 26 CFR part 31, revised as of March 14, 2019. Under section 7805(b)(7) a taxpayer may choose to apply this section on and after January 1, 2020.

(ii) * * * The determination of the tax to be withheld under paragraph (a)(7)(iii) of this section is made without reference to any payment of regular wages and without regard to any entries on the Form W-4 other than the entry claiming exempt status on Form W-4 (see § 31.3402(n)-1(b)). * * *

* * *

(d) *Applicability date.*—The provisions of paragraph (a)(2) and (a)(7)(ii) of this section apply on and after **[DATE OF PUBLICATION OF FINAL REGULATIONS IN THE FEDERAL REGISTER]**. Under section 7805(b)(7) a taxpayer may choose to apply paragraph (a)(2) and (a)(7)(ii) of this section on and after January 1, 2020.

Par. 15. Section 31.3402(h)(4)-1 is amended by removing paragraph (b) and redesignating paragraph (c) as paragraph (b).

§ 31.3402(h)(4)-1. Other methods.

Par. 16. Section 31.3402(i)-1 is removed.

§ 31.3402(i)-1. Additional withholding.

Par. 17 and 18. Redesignate § 31.3402(i)-2 as 31.3402(i)-1 and revise newly-redesignated § 31.3402(i)-1 is amended by:
1. Revising the section heading.
2. Revising paragraph (a)(2).
3. Adding paragraph (a)(3).
4. Revising paragraph (b).
The revisions and addition read as follows:

§31.3402(i)-1. **Increases in withholding.**—(a) * * *

(2) *Increases in withholding based on additional income.*—(i) The employee may request that the employer add an additional amount to the employee's wages and that the employer deduct and withhold an additional amount of income tax resulting from this addition under the computational procedures prescribed by the IRS in forms, instructions, publications, and other guidance for the calendar year for which the withholding allowance certificate claiming an additional amount to add to the employee's wages is furnished;

(ii) The employee may request that the employer deduct and withhold additional amounts of income tax resulting from the employee selecting higher withholding rate tables on the withholding allowance certificate;

(iii) The employer must comply with the employee's request under paragraph (a)(1)(i) or (ii) of this section, except that the employer shall comply with the employee's request only to the extent that the amount that the employee requests to be deducted and withheld under this section does not exceed the amount that remains after the employer has deducted and withheld all amounts

Par. 19. Section 31.3402(l)-1 is revised to read as follows:

§31.3402(l)-1. **Determination and disclosure of marital or filing status.**—(a) *In general.*—An employer shall apply the applicable percentage method or wage bracket method withholding tables corresponding to the marital status or filing status that the employee selects on a valid withholding allowance certificate as set forth in forms, instructions, publications, and other guidance prescribed by the Commissioner.

(b) *Employee's filing status.*—An employee will be treated as single unless the employee selects head of household or married filing jointly filing status on a valid withholding allowance certificate. Employees may select a filing status other than single, subject to the following conditions:

(1) The employee may select head of household filing status on the employee's withholding allowance certificate only if the employee reasonably expects to be eligible to claim head of household filing status under section 2(b) and §1.2-2(b) of this chapter on the employee's income tax return.

(2) The employee may select married filing jointly filing status on the employee's withholding allowance certificate only if paragraph (d) of this section applies to the employee and the employee reasonably expects to file jointly a single return of income under Subtitle A with the employee's spouse. If an employee is married and expects to file a separate return from the employee's spouse, the employee must select single or married filing separately filing status on the employee's withholding allowance certificate.

(c) *Change in filing status.*—(1) *In general.*—Unless paragraph (c)(2) of this section applies, the employee must within 10 days furnish the employer with a new withholding allowance certificate if the employee's filing status changes—

(i) From married filing jointly (or qualifying widow(er)) to head of household, married filing separately, or single, or

(ii) From head of household to married filing separately or single.

(2) *Exception.*—If the employee's filing status changes in the manner described in paragraph (c)(1)(i) or (ii) of this section, but the total effect of the changes together with other changes affecting the employee's anticipated tax liability under Subtitle A does not result in an amount of tax to be deducted and withheld from the employee's wages for the taxable year that is less than the employee's

Par. 20. Section 31.3402(m)-1 is revised to read as follows:

§31.3402(m)-1. **Additional withholding allowance.**—(a) *In general.*—In determining the withholding allowance or additional reductions in withholding under section 3402(m) on employee withholding allowance certificates furnished to the employer to be effective on or after January 1, 2020, employees may take into account the estimated tax deductions described in paragraph (b) of this section, the estimated tax credits described in paragraph (c) of this section, and estimated tax payments described in paragraph (d) of this section. Employees may only claim items in paragraphs (b), (c), and (d) of this section to the extent provided in paragraph (e) of this section.

(b) *Estimated tax deductions.*—Employees may take into account the following income tax deductions in chapter 1:

(1) Estimated itemized deductions (as defined in section 63(d)) allowable under chapter 1;

otherwise required to be deducted and withheld by Federal law (other than by section 3402(i) and this section), State law, and local law (other than by State or local law that provides for voluntary withholding); and

(iv) The employer must comply with the employee's request in accordance with the time limitations in §31.3402(f)(3)-1. The employee must make the request on Form W-4 as provided in §31.3402(f)(5)-1 (relating to form and contents of withholding allowance certificates), and this Form W-4 shall take effect and remain effective in accordance with section 3402(f) and §31.3402(f)(4)-1.

(3) *Amount deducted treated as tax.*—The amount deducted and withheld pursuant to paragraphs (a)(1) and (2) of this section shall be treated as tax required to be deducted and withheld under section 3402.

(b) *Applicability date.*—The provisions of paragraph (a)(2) and (3) of this section apply on and after **[DATE OF PUBLICATION OF FINAL REGULATIONS IN THE FEDERAL REGISTER]**. Under section 7805(b)(7) a taxpayer may choose to apply paragraphs (a)(2) and (3) of this section on and after January 1, 2020.

anticipated tax liability under Subtitle A, the employee is not required to furnish a new withholding allowance certificate within 10 days. However, the employee must furnish a new withholding allowance certificate to take effect the following calendar year by the later of December 1 of the calendar year in which the employee's filing status changes, or within 10 days of such change.

(d) *Determination of marital status.*—For the purposes of section 3402(l)(2) and paragraph (b) of this section, paragraphs (d)(1) and (2) of this section shall be applied in determining whether an employee is a single person or a married person:

(1) An employee shall on any day be considered as a single person and not married if—

(i) The employee is legally separated from the employee's spouse under a decree of divorce or separate maintenance, or

(ii) Either the employee or the employee's spouse is, or on any preceding day within the same calendar year was, a nonresident alien unless the employee has made or reasonably expects to make an election under section 6013(g) in the time and manner prescribed in §1.6013-6(a)(4) of this chapter.

(2) An employee shall on any day be considered as a married person if paragraph (d)(1) of this section does not apply and—

(i) The employee is married within the meaning of §301.7701-18(b) of this chapter on the day the withholding allowance certificate is furnished;

(ii) The employee's spouse died during the employee's taxable year; or

(iii) The employee's spouse died during one of the two taxable years immediately preceding the current taxable year and, on the basis of facts existing at the beginning of such day, the employee reasonably expects, at the close of the taxable year, to be a surviving spouse as defined in section 2 and §1.2-2(a) of this chapter. The employee must reasonably expect to file an income tax return claiming qualifying widow(er) status.

(e) *Applicability date.*—The provisions of this section apply on and after **[DATE OF PUBLICATION OF FINAL REGULATIONS IN THE FEDERAL REGISTER]**. For rules that apply before **[DATE OF PUBLICATION OF FINAL REGULATIONS IN THE FEDERAL REGISTER]**, see 26 CFR part 31, revised as of March 14, 2019. Under section 7805(b)(7) a taxpayer may choose to apply this section on and after January 1, 2020.

(2) Estimated deductions described in section 62(a), except for—

(i) Any deduction described in section 62(a)(1);

(ii) Any deduction described in section 62(a)(2) if the reimbursement or payment for the amount allowable as such deduction is excludable from wages subject to income tax withholding;

(iii) Any deduction described in section 62(a)(3);

(iv) Any deduction described in section 62(a)(4); and

(v) Any deduction described in section 62(a)(5).

(3) Estimated deductions for net operating loss carryovers under section 172;

(4) The estimated aggregate net losses from schedules C (Profit or Loss from Business), D (Capital Gains and Losses), E (Supplemental Income and Loss), and F (Profit or Loss from Farming) of Form 1040 and from the last line of Part II of Form 4797 (Sale of Business Property);

(5) Estimated additional standard deduction for the aged and blind provided under section 63(c)(3) and section 63(f);

(6) Estimated deduction allowed under section 199A; and

(7) Estimated deduction or deductions allowed under section 151.

(c) *Estimated tax credits.*—Employees may take into account the estimated income tax credits allowable under chapter 1, except for—

(1) The credit under section 31(a) for taxes withheld under chapter 24 (which includes taxes withheld on wages and amounts treated as wages for chapter 24 purposes, such as pension withholding under section 3405 and backup withholding under section 3406) unless, on the day the employee estimates this amount, the amount has been actually withheld from the employee's wages (or another payment treated as wages for this purpose), the employee enters this amount of tax withheld pursuant to the instructions in the Tax Withholding Estimator (or successor) or Publication 505 (or successor), and the employee is not an employee whose employer must withhold for that employee pursuant to a notice under § 31.3402(f)(2)-1(g)(2);

(2) The credit for tax withheld at source for nonresident aliens and foreign corporations under section 33; and

(3) Any credit to the extent that the employee has filed or expects to file any IRS form claiming such credit other than the employee's United States Individual Income Tax Return (Form 1040).

(d) *Estimated tax payments.*—Employees may take into account estimated tax payments paid to date only if—

(1) The employee's employer is not obligated to withhold on the employee's wages pursuant to a notice under § 31.3402(f)(2)-1(g)(2);

(2) The amount claimed has been paid with the payment voucher from Form 1040-ES (or was otherwise designated by the taxpayer as a payment of estimated tax);

(3) The employee uses the Tax Withholding Estimator (or successor) and enters the amount claimed pursuant to the instructions in the Tax Withholding Estimator (or successor); and

(4) In using the Tax Withholding Estimator (or successor product), the employee includes all items of nonwage income the Tax Withholding Estimator (or successor product) prompts the employee to enter.

(e) *Definitions and special rules.*—(1) *Estimated.*—The term "estimated" as used in this section to modify the terms "deduction," "deductions," "credits," "losses," and "amount of decrease" means with respect to an employee the aggregate dollar amount of a particular item that the employee reasonably expects will be allowable to the employee on the employee's income tax return for the estimation year under the section of the Code specified for each item. In no event shall that amount exceed the sum of:

(i) The amount shown for that particular item on the income tax return that the employee has filed for the taxable year preceding the estimation year (or, if such return has not yet been filed, then the income tax return that the employee filed for the taxable year preceding such year), which amount the employee also reasonably expects to show on the income tax return for the estimation year, plus

(ii) The determinable additional amounts (as defined in paragraph (e)(1)(iii) of this section) for each item for the estimation year.

(iii) The determinable additional amounts are amounts that are not included in paragraph (e)(1)(i) of this section and that are demonstrably attributable to identifiable events during the estimation year or the preceding year. Amounts are demonstrably attributable to identifiable events if they relate to payments already made during the estimation year, to binding obligations to make payments (including the payment of taxes) during the year, and to other transactions or occurrences, the implementation of which has begun and is verifiable at the time the employee furnishes a withholding allowance certificate. The estimation year is the taxable year including the day on which the employee furnishes the withholding allowance certificate to the employer, except that if the employee furnishes

the withholding allowance certificate to the employer and specifies on the certificate that the certificate is not to take effect until a specified future date, the estimation year shall be the taxable year including that specified future date. It is not reasonable for an employee to include in his or her withholding computation for the estimation year any amount that is shown for a particular item on the income tax return that the employee has filed for the taxable year preceding the estimation year (or, if such return has not yet been filed, then the income tax return that the employee filed for the taxable year preceding such year) and that has been disallowed by the Service as part of an adjustment described in § 601.103(b) of this chapter (relating to examination and determination of tax liability) and § 601.105(b) through (d) of this chapter (relating to examination of returns), without regard to any pending request for reconsideration, protest, request for consideration by an Appeals office, or civil action in which such proposed adjustment is at issue.

(2) *Restriction for employees with non-wage income.*—The employee must offset any deduction described in paragraph (b) of this section with items includible in the employee's gross income for which no Federal income tax is withheld in accordance with forms, instructions, publications, and other guidance prescribed by the Commissioner. In addition, an employee whose employer must withhold for that employee pursuant to a notice under § 31.3402(f)(2)-1(g)(2) must offset any tax benefit resulting from any deduction or credit described in paragraph (b) or (c) of this section with the anticipated income tax attributable to items other than wages includible in the employee's gross income in the manner determined by the Commissioner.

(3) *Multiple withholding allowance certificates.*—(i) *In general.*—The employee may not take into account deductions, credits, or estimated tax payments described in paragraph (b), (c), or (d) of this section if these deductions, credits, or estimated tax payments are claimed on another valid withholding allowance certificate in effect with respect to another employer of the employee or any employer of the employee's spouse.

(ii) *Married taxpayers filing jointly.*—Married taxpayers who reasonably expect to file as married filing jointly on their federal income tax return for the estimation year determine the withholding allowance to which they are entitled under section 3402(m) on the basis of their combined wages, allowable credits or deductions, and estimated tax payments permitted to be taken into account. The deductions, credits, or estimated tax payments described in paragraphs (b), (c), and (d) of this section to which either spouse is entitled may be claimed by either spouse or may be allocated between both spouses. However, one spouse may not claim deductions, credits, or estimated tax payments described in paragraphs (b), (c), and (d) of this section claimed on the other spouse's withholding allowance certificate.

(iii) *Married taxpayers filing separately.*—A married taxpayer who reasonably expects to file a separate income tax return from the employee's spouse for the estimation year determines the withholding allowance deductions, credits, or estimated tax payments described in paragraphs (b), (c), and (d) of this section on the basis of the employee's individual wages, deductions, credits, and estimated tax payments.

(4) *IRS instructions.*—An employee must follow the instructions to the Form W-4, and other IRS forms, instructions, publications, and related guidance in determining the employee's withholding allowance or other reductions in withholding permitted under section 3402(m) for deductions, credits, or estimated tax payments described in paragraphs (b), (c), and (d) of this section.

(f) *Applicability date.*—The provisions of this section apply on or after **[DATE OF PUBLICATION OF FINAL REGULATIONS IN THE FEDERAL REGISTER]**. For rules that apply before **[DATE OF PUBLICATION OF FINAL REGULATIONS IN THE FEDERAL REGISTER]**, see 26 CFR part 31, revised as of March 14, 2019. Under section 7805(b)(7) a taxpayer may choose to apply this section on and after January 1, 2020.

Par. 21. Section 31.3402(n)-1 is revised to read as follows:

§ 31.3402(n)-1. Employees incurring no income tax liability.—(a) *In general.*—Notwithstanding any other provision of this subpart (except to the extent a payment of wages is subject to withholding under § 31.3402(g)-1(a)(2)), an employer shall not deduct and withhold any tax under chapter 24 upon a payment of wages made to an employee, if there is in effect with respect to the payment a withholding allowance certificate furnished to the employer by the employee which certifies that—

(1) The employee incurred no liability for income tax imposed under subtitle A of the Internal Revenue Code for the employee's preceding taxable year; and

(2) The employee anticipates that the employee will incur no liability for income tax imposed under subtitle A for the employee's current taxable year.

(b) *Mandatory flat rate withholding.*—To the extent wages are subject to income tax withholding under § 31.3402(g)-1(a)(2), such wages are subject to such income tax withholding regardless of whether a withholding allowance certificate under section 3402(n) and this section has been furnished to the employer.

(c) *Liability for income tax.*—For purposes of section 3402(n) and this section, an employee is not considered to incur liability for income tax imposed under subtitle A if the amount of such tax imposed is equal to or less than the total amount of credits against such tax which are allowable under chapter 1 of the Internal Revenue Code, other than those credits allowable under section 31 or 34. For purposes of this section, an employee who files a joint return under section 6013 is considered to incur liability for any tax shown on such return. An employee who is entitled to file a joint return under section 6013 shall not certify that the employee anticipates that he or she will incur no liability for income tax imposed by subtitle A for the employee's current taxable year if such statement would not be true in the event that the employee files a joint return for such year, unless the employee filed a separate return for the preceding taxable year and anticipates that the employee will file a separate return for the current taxable year.

(d) *Rules about withholding allowance certificates.*—For rules relating to invalid withholding allowance certificates, see §31.3402(f)(2)-1(h), and for rules relating to disregarding certain withholding allowance certificates on which an employee claims a complete exemption from withholding, see §31.3402(f)(2)-1(i).

(e) *Examples.*—The following examples illustrate this section:

(1) *Example 1.* A, an unmarried, calendar-year basis taxpayer, files an income tax return for 2020 on April 10, 2021, showing that A had adjusted gross income of $5,000 and is not liable for any income tax for 2020. A had $180 of income tax withheld during 2020. A anticipates that A's gross income for 2021 will be approximately the same amount, and that A will not incur income tax liability for that year. On April 20, 2021, A commences employment and furnishes the employer a withholding allowance certificate certifying that A incurred no liability for income tax imposed under subtitle A for 2020, and that A anticipates that A will incur no liability for income tax imposed under subtitle A for 2021. A's employer shall not deduct and withhold on payments of wages made to A on or after April 20,

2021. Under §31.3402(f)(4)-1(b), unless A furnishes a new withholding allowance certificate including the certifications described in paragraph (a) of this section to the employer, the employer is required to deduct and withhold upon payments of wages to A made after February 15, 2022.

(2) *Example 2.* Assume the facts are the same as in Example 1 in paragraph (e)(1) of this section except that A had been employed by the employer prior to April 20, 2021, and had furnished the employer a withholding allowance certificate prior to furnishing the withholding allowance certificate including the certifications described in paragraph (a) of this section on April 20, 2021. Under §31.3402(f)(3)-1(b), the employer would be required to give effect to the new withholding allowance certificate no later than the beginning of the first payroll period ending (or the first payment of wages made without regard to a payroll period) on or after May 20, 2021. However, under §31.3402(f)(3)-1(b), the employer could, if it chose, make the new withholding allowance certificate effective with respect to any payment of wages made on or after April 20, 2021, and before the effective date mandated by section 3402(f)(3)(B)(i) and §31.3402(f)(3)-1(b). Under §31.3402(f)(4)-1(b), unless A furnishes a new withholding allowance certificate including the certifications described in §31.3402(n)-1(a) to A's employer, the employer is required to deduct and withhold upon payments of wages to A made after February 15, 2022.

(3) *Example 3.* Assume the facts are the same as in Example 1 in paragraph (e)(1) of this section except that for 2020 A has taxable income of $8,000, income tax liability of $839, and income tax withheld of $1,195. Although A received a refund of $356 due to income tax withholding of $1,195, A may not certify on A's withholding allowance certificate that A incurred no liability for income tax imposed by subtitle A for 2020.

(f) *Applicability date.*—The provisions of this section apply on and after **[DATE OF PUBLICATION OF FINAL REGULATIONS IN THE FEDERAL REGISTER]**. For rules that apply before **[DATE OF PUBLICATION OF FINAL REGULATIONS IN THE FEDERAL REGISTER]**, see 26 CFR part 31, revised as of March 14, 2019. Under section 7805(b)(7) a taxpayer may choose to apply this section on and after January 1, 2020.

Periodic and Nonperiodic Distributions: Withholding

Periodic and Nonperiodic Distributions: Withholding.—Reg. §31.3405(e)-1, regarding withholding on certain periodic and nonperiodic distributions under section 3405, other than eligible rollover distributions, is proposed (published in the Federal Register on May 31, 2019) (REG-132240-15).

Par. 2. Section 31.3405(e)-1 is added to read as follows:

§31.3405(e)-1. Questions and answers relating to withholding on pensions, annuities, and certain other deferred income.—(a) The following questions and answers apply for purposes of determining whether a payor of a distribution described in section 3405(a) or (b) must withhold income tax under this section. For purposes of this section, references to the United States include possessions of the United States.

(b)(1) Q-1: Is an Army Post Office (APO), Fleet Post Office (FPO), or Diplomatic Post Office (DPO) address an address located within the United States for purposes of section 3405(e)(13)(A)?

(2) A-1: For purposes of section 3405(e)(13)(A), an APO, FPO, or DPO address is an address located within the United States.

(c)(1) Q-2: Is the payor required to withhold income tax from any distribution described in section 3405(a) or (b) if the payee's residence address that is provided to the payor is located within the United States?

(2) A-2: If the payee's residence address that is provided to the payor is located within the United States, the payor is required to withhold income tax from any distribution described in section 3405(a) or (b) unless the payee has made a valid election of no withholding in accordance with section 3405(a)(2) or (b)(2). Any election of no withholding with respect to a distribution under section 3405(a)(2) or (b)(2) is not valid if the payee instructs the payor to do one or more of the following in connection with the distribution:

(i) Send the distribution to a financial institution or other person located outside of the United States;

(ii) Send the distribution to a financial institution or other person located within the United States with further instructions (such as "for further credit to" instructions) directing that the funds be forwarded to a financial institution or other person located outside of the United States; or

(iii) Send the distribution to a financial institution or other person pursuant to payment instructions (including addenda information) that reference an International Automated Clearing House Transaction (IAT), International Bank Account Number (IBAN), or Society for Worldwide Interbank Financial Telecommunication (SWIFT) Business Identifier Code (BIC) linked to a financial institution or other person located outside of the United States.

(d)(1) Q-3: Is the payor required to withhold income tax from a distribution described in section 3405(a) or (b) if the payee's residence address that is provided to the payor is located outside of the United States?

(2) A-3: Unless section 3405(e)(13)(B) (which provides an exception for certain nonresident aliens) applies, if the payee's residence address that is provided to the payor is located outside of the United States, the payor is required to withhold income tax from a distribution described in section 3405(a) or (b), without regard to the delivery instructions and without regard to any request by the payee to elect no withholding. Withholding would be required, in this case, even if the payee has requested that the distribution be delivered to a financial institution or other person located within the United States.

(e)(1) Q-4: Is the payor required to withhold income tax from a distribution described in section 3405(a) or (b) if the payee has not provided the payor with the payee's residence address?

(2) A-4: If a payee has not provided the payor with the payee's residence address, the payor is required to withhold income tax from a distribution described in section 3405(a) or (b). A payee may not elect no withholding under section 3405(a)(2) or (b)(2) and any purported election of no withholding by such payee is not valid. For purposes of this section, a payee who has provided the payor with an address for the payee's nominee, trustee, or agent without also providing the payee's residence address has not provided a residence address.

(f)(1) Q-5: Do the withholding rules under section 3405(a) and (b) apply to a payee who is to receive a distribution that is subject to withholding under subchapter A of chapter 3 (or that would be so subject but for a tax treaty)?

(2) A-5: In accordance with section 3405(e)(1)(B)(iii), a designated distribution does not include a distribution of a United States-source payment that is subject to withholding under the rules of section 1441 and §1.1441-1(b)(1) of this chapter (or that would be so subject but for a tax treaty), such as a pension or other deferred compensation plan distribution to be made to a payee who is a nonresident alien (or other individual payee who is presumed to be a foreign person under the presumption rules of §1.1441-1(b)(3) of this chapter). Withholding under the rules of section 1441 and

§ 1.1441-1(b)(1) of this chapter, rather than under the rules of section 3405(a) or (b), would apply to such a distribution.

(g)(1) Q-6: What is the effective date and applicability date of this section?

(2) A-6: This section is effective on the date of publication of the Treasury decision adopting these rules as a final regulation in the Federal Register. The regulation in this section applies with respect to distributions on or after the applicability date of the final regulation. [Reg. § 31.3405(e)-1.]

Securities: Basis Reporting: Basis Determination

Securities: Basis Reporting: Basis Determination.—Amendments to Reg. § 31.3406(b)(3)-2, relating to reporting sales of securities by brokers and determining the basis of securities, are proposed (published in the Federal Register on December 17, 2009) (REG-101896-09).

Par. 16. Section 31.3406(b)(3)-2 is amended by revising paragraph (b)(4) to read as follows:

§ 31.3406(b)(3)-2. Reportable barter exchanges and gross proceeds of sales of securities or commodities by brokers.

* * *

(b) * * *

(4) *Security short sales.*—(i) *Short sales closed before January 1, 2011.*—(A) *Amount subject to backup withholding.*—The amount subject to withholding under section 3406 with respect to a short sale of securities closed before January 1, 2011, is the gross proceeds (as defined in § 1.6045-1(d)(5) of this chapter) of the short sale. At the option of the broker, however, the amount subject to withholding may be the gain upon the closing of the short sale (if any); consequently, the obligation to withhold under section 3406 is deferred until the closing transaction. A broker may use this alternative method of determining the amount subject to withholding under section 3406 for a short sale only if at the time the short sale is initiated, the broker expects that the amount of gain realized upon the closing of the short sale will be determinable from the broker's records. If, due to events unforeseen at the time the short sale was initiated, the broker is unable to determine the basis of the property used to close the short sale, the property is assumed for this purpose to have a basis of zero.

(B) *Time of backup withholding.*—For short sales closed before January 1, 2011, the determination of whether a short seller is subject to withholding under section 3406 must be made on the date of the initiation or closing, as the case may be, or on the date that the initiation or closing, as the case may be, is entered on the broker's books and records.

(ii) *Short sales closed on or after January 1, 2011.*—For short sales closed on or after January 1, 2011, the obligation to withhold under section 3406 is deferred until the short sale is considered closed under section 1233. The determination of whether a short seller is subject to withholding under section 3406 may be made as of either this date or the date that the closing transaction is entered on the broker's books and records. The amount subject to withholding under section 3406 is the gross proceeds (as defined in § 1.6045-1(d)(5) of this chapter) of the short sale. At the option of the broker, however, the amount subject to withholding may be the gain upon the closing of the short sale (if any) if the broker reports both the gross proceeds and basis of the securities on the return of information required by section 6045.

* * *

GENERAL PROVISIONS RELATING TO EMPLOYMENT TAXES

Fringe Benefits: Taxability

Fringe Benefits: Taxability.—Reg. § 31.3501(a)-1T, relating to the treatment of taxable and nontaxable fringe benefits, is proposed and, when adopted, would become Reg. § 31.3501(a)-1 (published in the Federal Register on January 7, 1985) (LR-216-84).

§ 31.3501(a)-1. Question and answer relting to the time employers must collect and pay the taxes on noncash fringe benefits.

Employment Taxes

Employment Taxes: Real Estate Agents and Direct Sellers: Employer's Liability.—Reproduced below are the texts of proposed Reg. §§ 31.3508-1 and 31.3509-1, relating to the treatment of qualified real estate agents and direct sellers as nonemployees, to the determination of employer liability for income tax withholding and employee social security taxes where the employer treated an employee as a nonemployee for purposes of such taxes, and to information reporting of direct sales and payments of remuneration for services (published in the Federal Register on January 7, 1986).

☐ Par. 2. There are inserted immediately after § 31.3507-2 the following two new sections.

§ 31.3508-1. Treatment of qualified real estate agents and direct sellers as nonemployees.—(a) *In general.*—For Federal income and employment tax purposes,

(1) An individual who performs services after December 31, 1982, as a qualified real estate agent or as a direct seller shall not be treated as an employee with respect to such services, and

(2) The service-recipient shall not be treated as an employer with respect to such services.

(b) *Qualified real estate agent defined.*—(1) *In general.*—For purposes of section 3508 and this section, the term "qualified real estate agent" means any individual who is a sales person (including an individual who does not personally make sales but who recruits, trains, or supervises other individuals who make sales) if—

(i) Such individual is a licensed real estate agent,

(ii) Substantially all of the remuneration (whether or not paid in cash) for the services performed by such individual as a real estate agent is directly related to sales or other output (including the performance of services) rather than to the number of hours worked, and

(iii) The services performed by such individual as a real estate agent are performed pursuant to a written contract between such individual and the service-recipient and the contract provides that such individual will not be treated as an employee with respect to such services for Federal tax purposes.

(2) *Services performed as a real estate agent.*—For purposes of this section, the services performed by an individual as a real estate agent include any activities that customarily are performed in con-

nection with the sale of an interest in real property. Such services include the advertising or showing of real property, the acquisition of a lease to real property, and the recruitment, training, or supervision of other real estate sales persons. Such services also include the appraisal activities of a licensed real estate agent in connection with the sale of real property. Services performed as a real estate agent do not include the management of property.

(c) *Direct seller defined.*—(1) *In general.*—For purposes of section 3508 and this section, the term "direct seller" means any person if—

(i) Such person—

(A) Is engaged in the trade or business of selling (or soliciting the sale of) consumer products to any buyer on a buy-sell or deposit-commission basis for resale by the buyer or any other person in the home or in some other place that does not constitute a permanent retail establishment, or

(B) Is engaged in the trade or business of selling (or soliciting the sale of) consumer products in the home or in some other place that does not constitute a permanent retail establishment,

(ii) Substantially all the remuneration (whether or not paid in cash) for the performance of the services described in paragraph (c)(2) of this section is directly related to sales or other output (including the performance of services) rather than to the number of hours worked, and

(iii) Such person performs the services described in paragraph (c)(2) of this section pursuant to a written contract between such person and the service-recipient, and the contract provides that such person will not be treated as an employee with respect to such services for Federal tax purposes.

(2) *Services performed as a direct seller.*—(i) *In general.*—The services described in this paragraph (c)(2) are any services that customarily are directly related to the trade or business of selling (or soliciting the sale of) consumer products in the home or in any other location that does not constitute a permanent retail establishment. Such services include any activity to increase the productivity of other individuals engaged in such sales, such as recruiting, training, motivating, and counseling such individuals. Except as provided in paragraph (c)(2)(ii) of this section, such services do not include the installation or construction on the customer's property of a consumer product. See paragraphs (f) and (g)(3) of this section for the inapplicability of section 3508 where the sale or use of consumer products is only incidental to the rendering of services.

(ii) *Installation of consumer product in conjunction with the sale of such product.*—If an individual engaged in the trade or business of selling consumer products performs installation services in conjunction with the sale of a consumer product such services shall be included as services performed as a direct seller only if the value of such installation services is 10 percent or less of the purchase price of such consumer product (including installation). If the value of such installation services exceeds 10 percent of the purchase price of the consumer product (including installation) the installation services shall not be included as services performed as a direct seller. See paragraph (j) of this section for treatment of dual services under section 3508.

(d) *Substantially all remuneration directly related to sales or other output.*—(1) *Substantially all remuneration.*—(i) *In general.*—The requirement of paragraph (b)(1)(ii) or (c)(1)(ii) of this section is satisfied for any calendar year with respect to the services described in such paragraph if at least 90 percent of the total remuneration, including advances and draws (except as provided in paragraph (d)(1)(ii) of this section), received by the individual from the service-recipient for performing such services during that calendar year is directly related to sales or other output rather than to the number of hours worked.

(ii) *Repayment of advances or draws.*—For purposes of paragraph (d)(1)(i) of this section, total remuneration received by an individual does not include any portion of an advance or draw that is repaid directly or indirectly (including repayment by a debit against the individual's account with the service-recipient) pursuant to a binding written agreement which on the date the advance or draw is received requires repayment of the amount by which such advance or draw exceeds the amount which is directly related to sales or other output (as defined in paragraph (d)(2) of this section). The determination of whether any amounts not excluded under this paragraph (d)(1)(ii) from the total remuneration received by an individual is directly related to sales or other output for purposes of paragraph (d)(1)(i) of this section is made on the basis of all the facts and circumstances (see paragraph (d)(2)(i) of this section).

(2) *Directly relating to sales or other output.*—(i) *In general.*—An item of remuneration is directly related to sales or other output if that item is paid, awarded, or credited to the individual on the basis of the individual's services with respect to one or more specific sales transactions or the accomplishment of one or more specific tasks rather than on the basis of the number of hours worked. Whether an item of remuneration is directly related to sales or other output shall be determined on the basis of all the facts and circumstances. For purposes of this section an item of remuneration that is in the nature of salary, that is, a fixed periodical compensation paid for services rendered without regard to the amount of services rendered, shall be treated as an item or remuneration that is paid, awarded, or credited on the basis of the number of hours worked.

(ii) *Directly related to sales or output of some other person.*—For purposes of this section, remuneration received by an individual based on the sale or productivity of some other individual shall be treated as directly related to sales or other output if it was paid, awarded, or credited on the basis of such other individual's services with respect to one or more particular sales transactions or the accomplishment of one or more specific tasks.

(iii) *Remuneration received from a pool.*—Remuneration received by an individual under an arrangement whereby a service-recipient pools the remuneration of several individuals and a portion of the aggregate pooled remuneration is periodically distributed to each pool participant shall be treated as directly related to sales or other output only to the extent that the amount of remuneration received by that individual from the pool does not exceed the amount of remuneration that, in the absence of the pool arrangement, such individual would have received on the basis of the individual's services with respect to one or more specific sale transactions or the accomplishment of one or more specific tasks. Amounts received from the pool in excess of the amount that person would have ordinarily received for performing services in connection with such

specific sales transactions or specific tasks are not directly related to sales or other output.

(e) *Written contract requirement.*—(1) *In general.*—Except as otherwise provided in paragraph (e)(2) of this section, a written contract that states that the individual will not be treated as an employee without specifically stating "for Federal tax purposes" does not meet the written contract requirements set forth in paragraph (b)(1)(iii) and (c)(1)(iii).

(2) *Existing contracts.*—(i) *In general.*—A contract which—

(A) Is in effect on or before February 28, 1983, and

(B) States that the individual performing the services will not be treated as an employee but does not specifically include the phrase "for Federal tax purposes," will be deemed to satisfy the written contract requirement if the service-recipient furnishes to the individual performing the services a written notice that specifically states that the individual will not be treated as an employee "for Federal tax purposes."

(ii) *Date contract requirement deemed satisfied.*—If the notice described in paragraph (e)(2)(i) of this section is mailed or otherwise furnished on or before February 28, 1983, the written contract requirement shall be deemed satisfied as of the date of the original contract. If the notice is furnished after that date, the written contract requirement is deemed satisfied as of the date the notice is furnished.

(f) *Trade or business of selling consumer products.*—For purposes of section 3508 and this section, a person is not engaged in the trade or business of selling (or soliciting the sale of) consumer products if the sale or use of such products is in an incidental part of a trade or business in which such person primarily renders services to clients. Whether the sale or use of a product is an incidental part of a trade or business that primarily consists of rendering services shall be determined on the basis of all the facts and circumstances, taking into account such factors as the cost of the product in relation to the cost of the service. Generally, the sale or use of a product is an incidental part of a trade or business that primarily consists of rendering services if the use of the product is necessary to the performance of the particular service (*e.g.,* insecticide in a pest control business). See paragraph (c)(2) of this section for the applicability of this section to individuals who install consumer products in conjunction with the sale of such products.

(g) *Definitions.*—(1) *Buy-sell basis.*—A transaction is on a buy-sell basis if the buyer performing the services is entitled to retain part or all of the difference between the price at which the buyer purchases the product and the price at which the buyer sells the product as part or all of the buyer's remuneration for the services.

(2) *Deposit-commission basis.*—A transaction is on a deposit-commission basis if the buyer performing the service is entitled to retain part or all of a purchase deposit paid by the consumer in connection with the transaction as part or all of the buyer's remuneration for the services.

(3) *Consumer product.*—The term "consumer product" means any tangible personal property which is distributed in commerce and which is normally used for personal, family, or household purposes (including any such property intended to be attached to or installed in any real property without regard to whether it is so attached or installed). The term "consumer product" does not include any product used in the manufacture of another product to be distributed in commerce or any product used only incidentally in providing a service (*e.g.,* insecticide used in a pest control service, materials used in an appliance repair business).

(4) *Permanent retail establishment.*—A permanent retail establishment is any retail business operating in a structure or facility that remains stationary for a substantial period of time to which consumers go to purchase consumer goods. Examples of these establishments are: grocery stores, hardware stores, clothing stores, hotels, restaurants, drug stores, and newsstands.

In addition, amusement areas, such as amusement parks and sports arenas, at which consumer products are sold are permanent retail establishments. Portable or mobile structures, facilities, or equipment, such as street vendor stands and mobile carts or vehicles, generally do not constitute permanent retail establishments. However, sales of consumer products may occur in a permanent retail establishment for purposes of this section even though portable or mobile structures, facilities, or equipment is used. For example, a vendor who sells consumer products, such as souvenirs or food, in the stands of a sports arena or on the grounds of an amusement park sells consumer products in a permanent retail establishment. Also, a vendor who sells consumer products in a parking lot or other property which is near to and serving a sports arena or other amusement area pursuant to an agreement which grants to the vendor or to the service-recipient the right to sell consumer products on such property sells consumer products in a permanent retail establishment, regardless of whether the sale is made within a permanent structure.

(5) *Service-recipient.*—The term "service-recipient" means the person (other than a client or customer) for whom the services as a qualified real estate agent or direct seller are performed (*e.g.,* a real estate firm or a company whose consumer products are sold door-to-door).

(h) *No inference.*—The fact that an individual does not qualify under section 3508 and this section as a qualified real estate agent or as a direct seller with respect to any services does not create an inference that such individual is an employee or the service-recipient is an employer with respect to such services.

(i) *Application to statutory employees.*—A statutory employee (that is, an individual in one of the categories of workers defined in section 3121(d)(3) or 3306(i) to be employees) who meets the requirements of prargraph (b) or (c) of this section for classification as a qualified real estate agent or as a direct seller shall be treated as a nonemployee for Federal income tax, Federal Insurance Contribution Act (FICA), and Federal Unemployment Tax Act (FUTA) purposes with respect to services performed as a qualified real estate agent or as a direct seller (as described in paragraphs (b)(2) and (c)(2) of this section, respectively).

(j) *Dual services.*—(1) *In general.*—Section 3508 shall apply only with respect to services performed as a qualified real estate agent or a direct seller. Whether an individual is treated as an employee or as a self-employed individual with respect to services other than those performed as a qualified real estate agent or a direct seller shall be determined under common-law principles.

(2) *Examples.*—The following examples illustrate the principles set forth in this paragraph (j).

Example (1). A is a licensed real estate agent who performs services as a real estate agent pursuant to a written contract described in paragraph (b)(1)(iii) of this section. In addition to performing services as a real estate agent A performs general bookkeeping duties for the same service-recipient. All of the remuneration for the services performed as a real estate agent is directly related to sales. A will be treated as a nonemployee under section 3508 only with respect to A's services as a real estate agent. Whether A is treated as an employee or as a self-employed individual with respect to the bookkeeping duties will be determined under common-law principles.

Example (2). B is engaged in the trade or business of selling aluminum siding. B performs services as a direct seller pursuant to a written contract described in paragraph (c)(1)(iii) of this section. All sales are made in the customer's home and the purchase price includes installation. B installs all aluminum siding which he sells and receives a commission based upon the purchase price as compensation for his services with respect to both the sale and the installation. The value of such installation services exceeds 10 percent of the purchase price of the siding. B will be treated as a nonemployee under section 3508 only with respect to his services as a direct seller. Whether B is treated as an employee or as a self-employed individual with respect to services performed in installing the siding will be determined under common-law principles.

Example (3). The facts are the same as in example (2) excepts that B sells and installs personal computers and that the value of the installation services performed by B is less than 10 percent of the purchase price of the computers including installation. B is treated as a nonemployee under section 3508 with respect to both his services in selling the computers and in installing them. See paragraph (c)(2)(ii) of this section.

Example (4). Assume all the requirements of section 3508(b)(1) and paragraph (b) of this section are satisfied with respect to A, a real estate agent, except that A did not obtain a real estate license until March 29. The license was valid for the remainder of the year. A is treated as self-employed under section 3508 for that portion of the year beginning on March 29. Whether for Federal tax purposes A is to be treated as self-employed for the other portion of the year shall be determined under common law.

(k) *Coordination with retirement plans for self-employed.*—This section shall not prevent an individual who is treated as a self-employed under section 3508 from being covered under a qualified retirement plan for self-employed individuals pursuant to section 401(c)(1) of the Code. [Reg. §31.3508-1.]

§31.3509-1. Determination of employer's liability for certain employment taxes.—(a) *In general.*—Except as otherwise provided in this section, if during any calendar year any employer fails to deduct and withhold any tax under chapter 24 (relating to withholding of income tax) or subchapter A of chapter 21 (relating to the social security tax on employees) of the Internal Revenue Code of 1954 with respect to any employee by reason of treating such employee as not

being an employee for purposes of such chapter or subchapter, the amount of the employer's liability for such tax with respect to such year shall be determined under this paragraph (a).

(1) *Income tax withholding.*—The employer's liability for tax under chapter 24 for such year with respect to such employee shall be determined as if the amount required to be deducted and withheld were equal to 1.5 percent of the wages (defined in section 3401(a)) paid to such employee for such year.

(2) *Employee social security taxes.*—The employer's liability for employee social security taxes under subchapter A of chapter 21 for such year with respect to such employee shall be determined as if the taxes imposed under such subchapter were 20 percent of the amount imposed under such subchapter for such year without regard to this paragraph (a)(2).

Section 3509 and this section do not affect an employer's liability for taxes under subchapter B of chapter 21 (relating to employer social security taxes) of the Internal Revenue Code of 1954. See paragraph (c) of this section for increased employer liability where an employer fails to meet certain reporting requirements.

(b) *Definitions.*—(1) *Fails to deduct and withhold any tax.*—(i) *In general.*—For purposes of section 3509 and this section, an employer fails to deduct and withhold any tax under chapter 24 or under subchapter A of chapter 21 with respect to an employee for a calendar year if such employer fails to pay over the full amount of such tax required to be deducted and withheld during calendar year (determined without regard to section 3509 and this section) on or before the due date for the return relating to such tax for the final quarter of such calendar year.

(ii) *Example.*—The provisions of this paragraph (b)(1) may be illustrated by the following example:

Example. M, an employer, does not deduct and withhold income and social security taxes with respect to A, an employee, for the first quarter of 1985 because of M's erroneous belief that A is not an employee. On April 1, 1985, M ascertains the error and begins to withhold and deduct the full amount of income and social security taxes with respect to A for the remaining three quarters of 1985. M also makes timely adjustments under section 6205 with respect to the first quarter's taxes not deducted and withheld, and pays over the full amount of income and social security taxes which were required to be deducted and withheld during 1985 on or before the due date for the return for the fourth quarter of 1985. M has not failed to deduct and withhold income and social security taxes with respect to A during 1985 for purposes of section 3509 and this section.

(2) *Treatment of employee as not being an employee.*—For purposes of section 3509 and this section, an employer has treated an employee as not being an employee for purposes of the withholding requirements of chapter 24 or subchapter A of chapter 21 if, because of his belief that the employee was not an employee, the employer (i) has failed to deduct and withhold such tax as defined in paragraph (b)(1) of this section for the calendar year and (ii) has also failed to file one or more employment tax returns (including, where applicable, Forms 940 (Employer's Annual Federal Unemployment (FUTA) Tax Return), 941 (Employer's Quarterly Federal Tax Return), 942 (Employer's Quarterly Tax Return for Household Employees), 943 (Employer's Annual Tax Return for Agricultural Employees), and W-2 (Wage and Tax Statement)) for any period during the calendar year with respect to such employee. For purposes of this paragraph (b)(2) an employer who has filed a delinquent or amended employment tax return as a result of Internal Revenue Service compliance procedures (*i.e.,* examination or collection activities) has failed to file an employment tax return.

(c) *Employer's liability increased where employer fails to meet reporting requirements.*—(1) *In general.*—In the case of an employer who fails to meet the applicable requirements of section 6041(a), 6041A, or 6051 with respect to any employee, unless such failure is due to reasonable cause, paragraph (a) of this section shall be applied with respect to such employee:

(i) By substituting "3 percent" for "1.5 percent" in paragraph (a)(1) of this section; and

(ii) By substituting "40 percent" for "20 percent" in paragraph (a)(2) of this section.

(2) *Applicable requirement.*—For purposes of paragraph (c)(1) of this section, an employer has failed to meet the applicable requirements of section 6041(a), 6041A, or 6051 with respect to an employee if—

(i) The employer has treated such employee as not being an employee for purposes of the withholding requirements of chapter 24 or subchapter A of chapter 21, and

(ii) The employer has failed to satisfy any of the requirements described in sections 6041(a), 6041A, and 6051 and the regulations thereunder (relating to information returns and statements) which would be applicable consistent with the treatment described in paragraph (c)(2)(i) of this section.

An employer who has failed to timely file any return or statement required under section 6041(a), 6041A, or 6051 has failed to meet the applicable requirements of that section.

(d) *Special rules.*—For purposes of section 3509 and this section:

(1) *Determination of liability.*—If the amount of any employer's liability for tax with respect to an employee is determined under section 3509 and this section:

(i) Such employee's liability for income tax or employee social security taxes shall not be affected by the assessment or collection of any tax so determined and any amount assessed or collected as a result of the application of this section shall not be credited against the employee's tax liability;

(ii) Such employer shall not be entitled to recover from such employee any tax determined under this section;

(iii) Sections 3402(d) and 6521 shall not apply with respect to such employer's liability determined under this section, although section 6521 may apply with respect to an employee's liability regardless of whether the employer's liability is determined under section 3509; and

(iv) Tax imposed by section 3101 or 3402 (including amounts determined under section 3509) for any calendar year that the employer has reported and paid over with respect to such employee shall be allowed as a credit against tax determined under section 3509 with respect to such employee for such calendar year. If the amount of such reported and paid over tax exceeds the employer's liability for tax as determined under section 3509, however, such excess does not constitute an overpayment of tax and does not entitle the employer to a refund or credit for the amount of such excess.

(2) *Section not to apply where employer deducts and withholds income tax but not social security taxes.*—Section 3509 and this section shall not apply to any employer with respect to any wages if:

(i) The employer deducted and withheld any amount of the tax imposed by chapter 24 with respect to such wages, but

(ii) Failed to deduct and withhold the amount of the taxes imposed by subchapter A of chapter 21 with respect to such wages.

(3) *Section not to apply to social security tax with respect to certain statutory employees.*—Section 3509 and this section shall not apply to any tax under subchapter A of chapter 21 with respect to an individual described in section 3121(d)(3). For purposes of the preceding sentence, if an individual would be an employee under section 3121(d)(3) but for the fact that such individual is an employee under section 3121(d)(1) or (2), such individual shall be treated as an individual described in section 3121(d)(3).

(4) *Section not to apply in cases of intentional disregard.*—Section 3509 and this section shall not apply to the determination of any employer's liability for tax under chapter 24 or subchapter A of chapter 21 for any calendar year if any part of such liability is due to the employer's intentional disregard of the requirement to deduct and withhold such tax. For purposes of the preceding sentence, an employer has intentionally disregarded the requirement to deduct and withhold a tax if the employer intentionally failed to deduct and withhold the full amount of such tax with respect to any wages paid on or after the date on which the employer ascertained the employee status of a worker.

(5) *Section not to apply to assessments made before January 1, 1983.*—Section 3509 and this section shall not apply to any tax assessed before January 1, 1983.

(6) *Penalties.*—Section 3509 and this section do not relieve an employer from liability for any penalties, additions to tax, or additional amounts otherwise applicable with respect to a failure to deduct and withhold any taxes. However, for purposes of applying any penalty, addition to tax, or additional amount with respect to any tax for which an employer's liability is determined under section 3509, the employer's tax liability as determined under that section shall be treated as the tax the employer should have withheld, deducted, and paid over. [Reg. § 31.3509-1.]

EXCISE TAXES

Retail Excise Taxes on Certain Luxury Items

Luxury Items Tax.—Reproduced below are the texts of proposed Reg. § 48.4001-1 and a proposed amendment to Reg. § 48.0-2, relating to the retailers' excise taxes on certain passenger vehicles (published in the Federal Register on January 2, 1991). The Revenue Reconciliation Act 0f 1993 (P.L. 103-66) repealed the luxury tax on boats, aircraft, jewelry and furs; thus, the text of the proposed regulations under former Code Secs. 4002, 4003, 4004, 4006, 4007, 4011 and 4012 (Reg. §§ 48.4002-1—48.4012-1) are no longer reproduced.

☐ Par. 3. Section 48.0-2 is amended as follows: 1. Sections 48.0-2(a)(6) and (7) are revised as set forth below; and 2. In paragraph (b)(1), the words "For the purposes of this part, the" are removed and the word "The" is added in their place, and new introductory text is added to paragraph (b) to read as set forth below.

§ 48.0-2. General definitions and attachment of tax.

(a) *Meaning of terms.*—* * *

(6) The term "taxable article" means any article taxable under chapter 31 or 32 of the Code.

☐ Par. 4. A new subpart B (only Reg. § 48.4001-1 currently reproduced) is added immediately following § 48.0-3 to read as follows:

§ 48.4001-1. Luxury tax imposed on passenger vehicles.—(a) *In general.*—(1) *Imposition of tax.*—Section 4001 imposes a tax (the luxury automobile tax) on the first retail sale of a passenger vehicle if the sales price of the vehicle exceeds $30,000.

(2) *Amount of tax.*—The luxury automobile tax is equal to 10 percent of the amount by which the sales price of the vehicle exceeds $30,000.

(3) *Liability for tax.*—The luxury automobile tax shall be paid by the person who makes the first retail sale.

(b) *Passenger vehicle defined.*—(1) *In general.*—For purposes of this section, the term "passenger vehicle" means a 4-wheeled vehicle that is manufactured or sold primarily for use on public streets, roads, and highways, and that is—

(i) Rated (except in the case of a truck, van, or limousine) at 6,000 pounds unloaded gross vehicle weight or less;

(ii) A truck or van rated at 6,000 pounds gross vehicle weight or less; or

(iii) A limousine.

(2) *Meaning of terms.*—The following definitions set forth the meanings of certain terms for purposes of this paragraph (b)—

(7) The term "vendor" or "seller" includes a lessor except that, with respect to the manufacturer's excise taxes, this rule applies only where the lessor is also the manufacturer of the article.

* * *

(b) *Attachment of tax.*—For purposes of this part, unless otherwise expressly indicated:

(i) *Unloaded gross vehicle weight.*—The term "unloaded gross vehicle weight" means the curb weight of a vehicle fully equipped for service, but without passengers or cargo.

(ii) *Gross vehicle weight.*—The term "gross vehicle weight" has the meaning given such term by § 145.4051-1(e)(3).

(iii) *Truck or van.*—(A) *Van.*—The term "van" means a vehicle (whether configured to transport cargo or passengers behind the driver's position) that—

(1) Is built on a truck chassis; and
(2) Has an enclosed body.

(B) *Multi-purpose and sport utility vehicles included.*—The term "truck or van" includes vehicles that are commonly known as minivans or sport utility vehicles.

(iv) *Limousines.*—The term "limousine" means any sedan seating four or more passengers behind the driver.

(c) *Exemption from luxury automobile tax for taxicabs. etc.*—The luxury automobile tax is not imposed on the sale of a passenger vehicle for use by the purchaser exclusively (except for incidental and *de minimis* uses) in the active conduct of a trade or business of transporting persons or property for compensation or hire. A person who is otherwise responsible for the payment of the luxury automobile tax must establish the applicability of this exemption by evidence satisfactory to the Commissioner and may, for that purpose, rely upon an exemption certificate received from the purchaser.

(d) *Cross-references.*—(1) *Exemption certificates.*—See § 48.4011-7 for rules relating to exemption certificates.

(2) *Additional exemptions.*—See §§ 48.4004-2 and 48.4011-2 for additional exemptions from the luxury automobile tax.

(3) *First retail sale and sales price.*—See § 48.4011-3 for the definition of the term "first retail sale." See § 48.4011-4 for the definition of the term "sales price."

(4) *Tax imposed on use.*—See § 48.4011-5 for rules relating to the tax imposed on passenger vehicles that are used before there has been a first retail sale.

(5) *Special rules for payment of tax in case of qualified lease or installment sale.*—See § 48.4011-6 for rules relating to the payment of tax on qualified leases and installment sales.

(6) *Procedural rules.*—For rules relating to the requirements for filing returns and for paying and depositing luxury automobile tax, see 26 CFR Part 40.

(7) *Effective date and termination.*—See § 48.4011-8 for the effective date of this section, and § 48.4012-1 for the termination of the luxury automobile tax. [Reg. § 48.4001-1.]

Excise Taxes: Taxable Fuel: Returns: Definitions

Excise Taxes: Taxable Fuel: Returns: Definitions.—Reg. § 48.0-4 and amendments to Reg. § 48.0-1, relating to credits and payments for alcohol mixtures, biodiesel mixtures, renewable diesel mixtures, alternative fuel mixtures, and alternative fuel sold for use or used as a fuel and relating to the definition of gasoline and diesel fuel, are proposed (published in the Federal Register on July 29, 2008) (REG-155087-05).

Par. 8. Section 48.0-1 is amended as follows:

1. In the second sentence, "and related credits, refunds, and payments" is added after "Code".
2. In the third sentence, "certain luxury items," is removed.
3. In the fourth sentence, "aviation fuel," is removed.

§ 48.0-1. Introduction.

Par. 9. Section 48.0-4 is added to read as follows:

§ 48.0-4. Forms.—Any reference to a form in this part is also a reference to any other form designated for the same use by the Commissioner after the date these regulations are published in the **Federal Register** as final regulations. All such forms must be completed in accordance with the instructions for the forms and contain any additional information required by this part.

Excise Tax: Tractors, Trailers, Trucks, and Tires: Highway Vehicle: Definition

Excise Tax: Tractors, Trailers, Trucks, and Tires: Highway Vehicle: Definition.—Reg. § 48.0-4 and amendments to Reg. §§ 48.0-1 and 48.0-2, relating to the excise taxes imposed on the sale of highway tractors, trailers, trucks, and tires, the use of heavy vehicles on the highway, and the definition of highway vehicle related to these and other taxes, are proposed (published in the Federal Register on March 31, 2016) (REG-103380-05).

Par. 4. Section 48.0-1, fourth sentence, is amended by removing the language "highway-type tires" and adding "taxable tires" in its place.

§ 48.0-1. Introduction.

Par. 5. In § 48.0-2, paragraph (b)(5), first sentence, is amended by removing the language "In the case of a lease," and adding "Except as provided in § 48.4052-1(e), in the case of a lease," in its place.

§ 48.0-2. Introduction.

Par. 6. Section 48.0-4 is added to subpart A to read as follows:

§ 48.0-4. Introduction.—(a) *Overview.*—(1) The definitions of *highway vehicle* and *mobile machinery* in this section apply for purposes of this part and part 41 of this chapter. See § 41.4482(a)-1(a)(2) of this chapter.

(2) The taxes imposed by sections 4051 and 4481 do not apply to mobile machinery (as defined in paragraph (b)(3)(iii) of this section), and the tax imposed by section 4071 does not apply to tires of a type used exclusively on such mobile machinery. In addition, for purposes of determining whether use of a vehicle qualifies as *off-highway business use* under section 6421(e)(2)(C) (relating to uses in mobile machinery), mobile machinery (as defined in this section) satisfies the design-based test of section 6421(e)(2)(C)(iii). To qualify as off-highway business use, however, the use of the vehicle must also satisfy the use-based test of section 6421(e)(2)(C)(iv).

(b) *Highway vehicle.*—(1) *In general.*—Except as otherwise provided in paragraph (b)(3) of this section, *highway vehicle* means any self-propelled vehicle, or any truck trailer or semitrailer, designed to perform a function of transporting a load over public highways.

(2) *Explanation.*—(i) A vehicle consists of a chassis, or a chassis and a body if the vehicle has a body, but does not include the vehicle's load.

(ii) Except as otherwise provided in paragraph (b)(3) of this section, in determining whether a vehicle is a highway vehicle, it is immaterial whether—
(A) The vehicle can perform functions other than transporting a load over the public highways;
(B) The vehicle is designed to perform a highway transportation function for only a particular kind of load, such as passengers, furnishings and personal effects (as in a house, office, or utility trailer), a special type of cargo, goods, supplies, or materials, or machinery or equipment specially designed to perform some off-highway task unrelated to highway transportation; and

(C) In the case of a vehicle specially designed to transport machinery or equipment, such machinery or equipment is permanently mounted on the vehicle.

(iii) Examples of vehicles that are designed to perform a function of transporting a load over the public highways are passenger automobiles, motorcycles, buses, motor homes, and highway-type trucks, truck tractors, trailers, and semitrailers.

(iv) Examples of vehicles that are not designed to perform a function of transporting a load over the public highways are farm tractors, bulldozers, road graders, and forklifts.

(v) The term *public highway* includes any road (whether a federal highway, state highway, city street, or otherwise) in the United States that is not a private roadway.

(vi) The term *transport* includes tow.

(3) *Exceptions.*—(i) *Certain vehicles specially designed for off-highway transportation.*—(A) *In general.*—The term *highway vehicle* does not include a vehicle if the vehicle is specially designed for the primary function of transporting a particular type of load other than over a public highway and because of this special design such vehicle's capability to transport a load over a public highway is substantially limited or impaired.

(B) *Determination of vehicle's design.*—For purposes of paragraph (c)(3)(i)(A) of this section, a vehicle's design is determined solely on the basis of its physical characteristics.

(C) *Determination of substantial limitation or impairment.*—For purposes of paragraph (c)(3)(i)(A) of this section, in determining whether substantial limitation or impairment exists, account may be taken of factors such as the size of the vehicle, whether the vehicle is subject to the licensing, safety, and other requirements applicable to highway vehicles, and whether the vehicle can transport a load at a sustained speed of at least 25 miles per hour. It is immaterial that a vehicle can transport a greater load off the public highway than the vehicle is permitted to transport over the public highway.

(ii) *Nontransportation truck trailers and semitrailers.*—The term *highway vehicle* does not include a truck trailer or semitrailer if it is specially designed to function only as an enclosed stationary shelter for the carrying on of an off-highway function at an off-highway site.

(iii) *Mobile machinery.*—The term highway vehicle does not include any vehicle that consists of a chassis—

(A) To which there has been permanently mounted (by welding, bolting, riveting, or other means) machinery or equipment to perform a construction, manufacturing, processing, farming, mining, drilling, timbering, or similar operation if the operation of the machinery or equipment is unrelated to transportation on or off the public highways;

(B) That has been specially designed to serve only as a mobile carriage and mount (and a power source, where applicable) for the particular machinery or equipment involved, whether or not such machinery or equipment is in operation; and

(C) That, by reason of such special design, could not, without substantial structural modification, be used as a component of a vehicle designed to perform a function of transporting any load other than that particular machinery or equipment or similar machinery or equipment requiring such a specially designed chassis.

(c) *Examples.*—The following examples illustrate the rules of this section:

Example 1; Off-highway transportation. (1) *Facts.* (i) A tri-axle semitrailer that is used in highway construction, maintenance, and repair work also hauls highway construction and repair materials to job sites. The semitrailer's floor is equipped with a continuous rubber belt attached to a steel slatted roller chain that carries payload to the rear tailgate at a controllable discharge rate. The semitrailer has insulated double sidewalls and a baffled hopper. This equipment enables the semitrailer to transport and unload hot-mix asphalt, asphalt-related materials, and low-slump concrete for highway construction and repair. When used as an asphalt transporter, the semitrailer unloads the asphalt at the job site through the rear tailgate into a trailing asphalt paving machine. The semitrailer is designed to perform a function of transporting a load over public highways.

(ii) A highway tractor tows the semitrailer at normal highway speeds. The semitrailer complies with all federal and state regulations governing highway use, may be legally operated on the public highways when loaded within legal weight limits (80,000 pounds), and does not exceed state maximum highway length, width, or height limitations. Loaded to its capacity with asphalt, the combined weight of the semitrailer, the asphalt, and the tractor exceeds 100,000 pounds. Special state permits may be purchased to operate the tractor/semitrailer combination above the legal weight limit on public highways.

(2) *Analysis.* For purposes of the exception provided by paragraph (b)(3)(i) of this section for vehicles specially designed for off-highway transportation, paragraph (b)(3)(i)(B) of this section provides that a vehicle's design is determined solely on the basis of its physical characteristics. The physical characteristics of this semitrailer include insulated double sidewalls, a baffled hopper, and an unloading mechanism on the floor of the trailer that moves hot road building materials to the back of the trailer and delivers these materials into a paving machine at controlled rates. Examples of the type of machinery or equipment that contribute to the highway transportation function are unloading equipment and machinery that contribute to the preservation of the cargo. The semitrailer's conveyor discharge system and insulated walls are designed to contribute to the highway transportation functions of unloading (discharge conveyor system) and preserving (insulated sidewalls) the load. This equipment is not designed for the job-site function of applying asphalt or low-slump concrete.

(3) *Conclusion.* The semitrailer is not a vehicle described in paragraph (b)(3)(i)(A) of this section. The semitrailer's physical characteristics, such as sidewalls, a hopper, and the unloading mechanism, demonstrate that this semitrailer is capable of transporting asphalt or low-slump concrete over a public highway without substantial limitation or impairment.

Example 2; Mobile machinery. (1) *Facts.* A chassis manufacturer built a truck chassis with a reinforced chassis frame, a heavy-duty engine, and a structure to accommodate the manufacturer's mounting of drilling equipment on the chassis and the use of that drilling equipment off the highways. The manufacturer also bolted a pintle-type trailer hitch to a beam that is welded to, and operates as a rear cross member of, the chassis frame rails. The truck is designed to perform a function of transporting a load over public highways.

(2) *Analysis.* This chassis can perform two functions. First, the chassis serves as a mobile carriage and mount for the drilling equipment installed on its bed. Second, the chassis can tow a trailer because it has a pintle-type trailer hitch. These dual capabilities demonstrate that the chassis was not specially designed to serve only as a mobile carriage and mount for its machinery.

(3) *Conclusion.* The chassis fails to meet the test in paragraph (c)(3)(iii) of this section for treatment as mobile machinery because the chassis is not specially designed to serve only as a mobile carriage and mount for the drilling equipment. A similar conclusion would apply if the manufacturer reinforced the chassis to make the chassis capable of towing a trailer, but the manufacturer did not install the pintle hook.

(d) *Effective/applicability date.*—This section applies on and after the date of publication of these regulations in the **Federal Register** as final regulations. [Reg. § 48.0-4.]

Excise Tax: Tractors, Trailers, Trucks, and Tires: Highway Vehicle: Definition

Excise Tax: Tractors, Trailers, Trucks, and Tires: Highway Vehicle: Definition.—Amendments to Reg. § 48.4041-8, relating to the excise taxes imposed on the sale of highway tractors, trailers, trucks, and tires, the use of heavy vehicles on the highway, and the definition of highway vehicle related to these and other taxes, are proposed (published in the Federal Register on March 31, 2016) (REG-103380-05).

Par. 7. Section 48.4041-8 is amended as follows:

1. Paragraph (b)(2)(ii), first sentence, is amended by removing the language "A self-propelled" and adding "Before January 1, 2005, a self-propelled" in its place.

2. Paragraph (b)(2)(iv) is added.

The addition reads as follows:

§ 48.4041-8. Definitions.

* * *

(b) * * *

(2) * * *

(iv) *Off-highway transportation vehicles after December 31, 2004.*—For a description of certain vehicles that are not treated as highway vehicles after December 31, 2004, see § 48.0-5(b)(3).

* * *

Excise Taxes: Taxable Fuel: Returns: Definitions

Excise Taxes: Taxable Fuel: Returns: Definitions.—Amendments to Reg. §§ 48.4041-0, 48.4041-18, 48.4041-19 and 48.4041-20, relating to credits and payments for alcohol mixtures, biodiesel mixtures, renewable diesel mixtures, alternative fuel mixtures, and alternative fuel sold for use or used as a fuel and relating to the definition of gasoline and diesel fuel, are proposed (published in the Federal Register on July 29, 2008) (REG-155087-05).

Par. 10. Section 48.4041-0 is amended as follows:

1. In the first sentence, the language "sales or uses of diesel fuel" is removed and "any liquid (other than biodiesel) that is sold for use or used as a fuel in a diesel-powered highway vehicle or diesel-powered train" is added in its place.

2. In the second sentence, the language "diesel fuel tax" is removed and "tax with respect to these liquids" is added in its place.

§ 48.4041-0. Applicability of regulations relating to diesel fuel after December 31, 1993.

Par. 11. Section 48.4041-18 is removed and reserved.

§ 48.4041-18. Fuels containing alcohol.

Par. 12. Section 48.4041-19 is revised to read as follows:

§ 48.4041-19. Reduction in tax for qualified methanol or ethanol fuel and partially exempt methanol or ethanol fuel.—(a) *In general.*—Section 4041(b)(2) provides a reduced rate of tax under sections 4041(a)(2) and (d) for qualified methanol or ethanol fuel. Section 4041(m) provides a reduced rate of tax under section 4041(a)(2) for partially exempt methanol or ethanol fuel.

(b) *Qualified methanol or ethanol fuel and partially exempt methanol or ethanol fuel defined.*—For purposes of section 4041(b)(2) and this section, qualified methanol or ethanol fuel is liquid motor fuel, at least 85 percent of which (by volume) consists of alcohol produced from coal (including peat). For purposes of section 4041(m) and this section, partially exempt methanol or ethanol fuel is a liquid motor fuel, at least 85 percent of which (by volume) consists of alcohol produced from natural gas (including ethanol produced through the process of thermally cracking ethane that is a constituent of natural gas). The actual gallonage of each component of the mixture (without adjustment for temperature) shall be used in determining whether, at the time of the taxable sale or use, the applicable 85 percent alcohol requirement has been met. A mixture containing less than 85 percent alcohol produced from coal (or less than 85 percent alcohol produced from natural gas) may be treated as satisfying the applicable percentage requirement. In determining whether a particular mixture should be so treated, the Commissioner shall take into account the existence of any facts and circumstances establishing that, but for the commercial and operational realities of the blending process, it may reasonably be concluded that the mixture would have contained at least 85 percent alcohol from the appropriate source. The necessary facts and circumstances will not be found to exist if over a period of time the mixtures blended by a blender show a consistent pattern of failing to contain at least 85 percent alcohol from the appropriate source.

(c) *Effective/applicablity date.*—This section is applicable on and after the date of publication of these regulations in the **Federal Register** as final regulations. For provisions applicable to prior periods, see 26 CFR 48.4041-19 (revised as of April 1, 2008). [Reg. § 48.4081-19.]

Par. 13. Section 48.4041-20 is removed and reserved.

§ 48.4041-20. Partially exempt methanol and ethanol fuel.

Excise Tax: Tractors, Trailers, Trucks, and Tires: Highway Vehicle: Definition

Excise Tax: Tractors, Trailers, Trucks, and Tires: Highway Vehicle: Definition.—Reg. §§ 48.4051-0—48.4051-2 and amendments to Reg. § 145.4051-1, relating to the excise taxes imposed on the sale of highway tractors, trailers, trucks, and tires, the use of heavy vehicles on the highway, and the definition of highway vehicle related to these and other taxes, are proposed (published in the Federal Register on March 31, 2016) (REG-103380-05).

Par. 9. New §§ 48.4051-0, 48.4051-1, and 48.4051-2 are added to subpart H to read as follows:

§ 48.4051-0. Overview; Heavy trucks, tractors, and trailers sold at retail.—Sections 48.4051-1, 48.4051-2, and 48.4052-1 provide guidance under sections 4051 and 4052 relating to the tax on the first retail sale of certain truck and trailer chassis and bodies and certain tractors. This guidance includes rules relating to the imposition of tax, liability for tax, exclusions, and definitions. For rules under sections 4051 and 4052 on the treatment of leases, uses treated as sales, and the determination of price for which an article is sold, see § 145.4052-1 of this chapter. [Reg. § 48.4051-0.]

§ 48.4051-1. Imposition of tax; Heavy trucks, tractors, and trailers sold at retail.—(a) *Imposition of tax.*—Section 4051 imposes a tax on the first retail sale of the following articles (including in each case parts or accessories sold on or in connection with the article or with the sale of the article):

(1) Automobile truck chassis and bodies.

(2) Truck trailer and semitrailer chassis and bodies.

(3) Tractors of the kind chiefly used for highway transportation in combination with a truck trailer or semitrailer.

(b) *Tax base and rate of tax.*—The tax is the applicable percentage of the price for which the article is sold. The applicable percentage is prescribed in section 4051(a)(1). For rules for the determination of price, see paragraph (d)(4) of this section and § 145.4052-1(d) of this chapter.

(c) *Liability for tax.*—(1) *In general.*—Except as provided in paragraph (c)(2) of this section, the person that makes the first retail sale (as defined in § 48.4052-1(a)) of a taxable article listed in paragraph (a) of this section is liable for the tax imposed by section 4051. This person is referred to as the *retailer* in this section and § 48.4051-2.

(2) *Exceptions; cross references.*—For cases in which a person other than the retailer is liable for the tax imposed under paragraph (a) of this section, see §§ 48.4051-1(d)(2)(ii) and (iii) (relating to chassis and bodies sold for use as a component part of a highway vehicle) and § 48.4051-1(e)(6)(ii) (relating to certain chassis completed as tractors).

(d) *Special rules.*—(1) *Separate taxation of chassis and body.*—If a chassis is a component part of a highway vehicle, the taxability of the chassis is determined independently of, and without regard to, the body that is installed on the chassis. If a body is a component part of a highway vehicle, the taxability of the body is determined independently of, and without regard to, the chassis on which the body is installed.

(2) *Chassis and bodies sold for use as a component part of a highway vehicle.*—(i) *In general.*—A chassis or body listed in paragraph (a) of this section is taxable under section 4051 only if such chassis or body is sold for use as a component part of a highway vehicle that is an automobile truck, truck trailer or semitrailer, or a tractor of the kind chiefly used for highway transportation in combination with a trailer or semitrailer. A chassis or body that is not listed in paragraph (a) of this section (for example, a chassis or body of a passenger automobile) is not taxable under section 4051 even though such chassis or body is used as a component part of a highway vehicle.

(ii) *Retailer; conditions for avoidance of liability.*—The retailer is not liable for tax on a chassis or body if, at the time of the first retail sale, the retailer—

(A) Has obtained from the buyer a certificate described in paragraph (d)(2)(iv) of this section stating, among other things, that the buyer will use the chassis or body as a component part of a vehicle that is not a highway vehicle;

(B) Has no reason to believe that any information in the certificate is false; and

(C) Has not received a notification from the IRS under paragraph (d)(2)(iv) of this section with respect to the buyer or the type of chassis or body.

(iii) *Liability of buyer.*—If a buyer that provides a certificate described in paragraph (d)(2)(iv) of this section uses the chassis or body to which the certificate relates as a component part of a highway vehicle, the buyer is liable for the tax imposed on the first retail sale of such chassis or body.

(iv) *Form of certificate.*—The certificate described in this paragraph (d)(2)(iv) consists of a statement that is signed under penalties of perjury by a person with authority to bind the buyer, is in substantially the same form as the model certificate in paragraph (d)(2)(v) of this section, and includes all the information necessary to complete the model certificate. The IRS may withdraw the right of a buyer to provide a certificate under this section if the buyer uses the chassis or body to which a certificate relates other than as stated in the certificate. The IRS may notify any retailer that the buyer's right to provide a certificate has been withdrawn. The IRS may also notify a retailer that sales of a specified type or types of chassis or bodies may not be made tax-free under this paragraph (d)(2) until further notification. The certificate may be included as part of any business records used to document a sale.

(v) *Model Certificate.*

Certificate
(To support the tax-free sale of a chassis or body that is to be used as a component part of a non-highway vehicle)
The undersigned buyer of a chassis or body listed in section 4051 ("Buyer") hereby certifies the following under penalties of perjury:

1. _____

Seller's name, address, and employer identification number
2. _____
_____
_____

Buyer's name, address, and employer identification number
3. _____
Date and location of sale to Buyer
4. The article(s) listed below will not be used as a component part of a highway vehicle. If the article is a chassis, Buyer has listed the chassis Vehicle Identification Number. If the article is a body, Buyer has listed the body's identification number.

5. Buyer understands that it must be prepared to establish, by evidence satisfactory to an examining agent, how Buyer used the article.

6. Buyer has not been notified by the Internal Revenue Service that its right to provide a certificate has been withdrawn.

7. Buyer understands that if it uses a chassis or body listed in this certificate as a component part of a highway vehicle, Buyer is liable for the tax imposed by section 4051 of the Internal Revenue Code.

8. Buyer understands that Buyer may be liable for the section 6701 penalty (relating to aiding and abetting an understatement of tax liability) if this is an erroneous certification.

9. Buyer understands that the fraudulent use of this certificate may subject Buyer and all parties making any fraudulent use of this statement to a fine or imprisonment, or both, together with the costs of prosecution.

Printed or typed name of person signing this certificate
_____

Title of person signing
_____

Signature and date signed

(3) *Sale of a completed unit.*—A sale of an automobile truck, truck trailer, or semitrailer is considered a sale of a chassis and of a body listed in paragraph (a) of this section.

(4) *Equipment installed on chassis or bodies.*—For purposes of section 4051, the sale price of a chassis or body includes any amount paid for equipment or machinery that is installed on and is an integral part of the chassis or body. Equipment or machinery is an integral part of a chassis or body if the equipment or machinery contributes to the highway transportation function of the chassis or body. Examples of machinery or equipment that contributes to the highway transportation function of a chassis or body are loading and unloading equipment; towing winches; and all other machinery or equipment that contributes to the maintenance or safety of the vehicle, the preservation of cargo (other than refrigeration units), or the comfort or convenience of the driver or passengers.

(5) *Vehicle use.*—In determining whether a tractor, a truck body or chassis, or a truck trailer or semitrailer chassis or body is subject to the tax imposed by section 4051, the use (whether commercial, personal, recreational, or otherwise) of an article is immaterial.

(e) *Explanation of terms and exclusions; tractors, trucks, trailers.*—(1) *Tractor.*—The term *tractor* means a highway vehicle primarily designed to tow a vehicle, such as a truck trailer or semitrailer. A vehicle equipped with air brakes and/or a towing package will be presumed to be a tractor unless it is established, based on all the vehicle's characteristics, that the vehicle is not primarily designed to tow a vehicle. However, a vehicle that is not equipped with air brakes and/or a towing package is a tractor if the vehicle is primarily designed to tow a vehicle.

(2) *Truck.*—The term *truck* means a highway vehicle primarily designed to transport its load on the same chassis as the engine even if it is also equipped to tow a vehicle, such as a trailer or semitrailer.

(3) *Primarily designed.*—The term *primarily* means principally or of first importance. *Primarily* does not mean exclusively. The function for which a vehicle is primarily designed is evidenced by physical characteristics such as the vehicle's capacity to tow a vehicle, carry cargo, and operate (including brake) safely when towing or carrying cargo. Towing capacity depends on the vehicle's gross vehicle weight (GVW) rating and gross combination weight (GCW) rating and whether the vehicle is configured to tow a trailer or semitrailer. Cargo carrying capacity depends on the vehicle's GVW rating and the configuration of the vehicle's bed or platform. If a vehicle is capable of more than one function, such as towing a vehicle and carrying cargo on the same chassis as the engine, the physical characteristics of the vehicle determine the purpose for which the vehicle is primarily designed. A vehicle that can both carry cargo on its chassis and tow a trailer is either a truck or tractor depending on which function is of greater importance.

(4) *Trailer.*—(i) *In general.*—The term *trailer* means a non-self-propelled vehicle hauled, towed, or drawn by a separate truck or tractor. A trailer consists of a chassis and a body. A chassis is the frame that supports the trailer's suspension, axles, wheels, tires, and brakes. A body is the structure usually installed on the trailer chassis to accommodate the intended load of the trailer. In some instances, the body may itself constitute all or part of the intended load.

(ii) *Truck trailer.*—The term *truck trailer* means a trailer that carries all of its weight and the weight of its load on its own chassis.

(iii) *Semitrailer.*—The term *semitrailer* means a trailer, the front end of which is designed to be attached to, and rest upon, the vehicle that tows it. A portion of the semitrailer's weight and load also rests upon the towing vehicle.

(5) *Incomplete chassis cab; classification as a truck.*—An incomplete chassis cab is classified as a truck at the time of its sale if, at such time—

(i) The incomplete chassis cab is not equipped with any of the features listed in paragraph (e)(7) of this section; and

(ii) The seller—

(A) Has obtained from the buyer a certificate described in paragraph (e)(8) of this section stating, among other things, that the buyer will equip the incomplete chassis cab as a truck;

(B) Has no reason to believe that any information in the certificate is false; and

(C) Has not received a notification under paragraph (e)(8) of this section with respect to the buyer.

(6) *Incomplete chassis cab; classification as a tractor.*—(i) *In general.*—An incomplete chassis cab is classified as a tractor at the time of its sale if, at such time—

(A) The incomplete chassis cab is equipped with any of the features listed in paragraph (e)(7) of this section; or

(B) The seller fails to satisfy one or more of the conditions set forth in paragraph (e)(5)(ii) of this section.

(ii) *Completion as a tractor.*—If no tax is imposed under section 4051(a)(1) on the sale of an incomplete chassis cab classified as a truck under paragraph (e)(5) of this section and the purchaser completes the incomplete chassis cab as a taxable tractor, the purchaser is liable for tax under section 4051(a)(1) on the purchaser's sale or use of the taxable tractor.

(7) *Incomplete chassis cab; features.*—The features referred to in paragraphs (e)(5)(i) and (e)(6)(i)(A) of this section are the following:

(i) A device for supplying air or hydraulic pressure or electric or other power from the incomplete chassis cab to the brake system of a towed vehicle.

(ii) A mechanism for protecting the incomplete chassis cab brake system from the effects of a loss of pressure in the brake system of a towed vehicle.

(iii) A control linking the brake system of the incomplete chassis cab to the brake system of a towed vehicle.

(iv) A control in the incomplete chassis cab for operating a towed vehicle's brakes independently of the incomplete chassis cab's brakes.

(v) Any other equipment designed to establish or enhance the incomplete chassis cab's use as a tractor.

(8) *Incomplete chassis cab; certificate.*—(i) *In general.*—The certificate described in this paragraph (e)(8) consists of a statement that is signed under penalties of perjury by a person with authority to bind the buyer, is in substantially the same form as the model certificate in paragraph (e)(8)(ii) of this section, and includes all the information necessary to complete the model certificate. The IRS may withdraw

the right of a buyer of vehicles to provide a certificate under this section if the buyer uses the vehicles to which a certificate relates other than as stated in the certificate. The IRS may notify any seller that the buyer's right to provide a certificate has been withdrawn. The certificate may be included as part of any business records normally used to document a sale.

(ii) *Model Certificate.*

Certificate
(To support the completion of an incomplete chassis cab as a truck)
The undersigned buyer of articles listed in section 4051 ("Buyer") hereby certifies the following under penalties of perjury:
1. _____

_____

Seller's name, address, and employer identification number
2. _____

_____

Buyer's name, address, and employer identification number
3. _____
Date and location of sale to Buyer
4. Buyer certifies that Buyer will complete these incomplete chassis cabs listed below as trucks:

VIN:	VIN:
VIN:	VIN:
VIN:	VIN:
VIN:	VIN:

5. Buyer has not been notified by the Internal Revenue Service that its right to provide a certificate has been withdrawn.
6. Buyer understands that if Buyer completes an incomplete chassis cab listed in this certificate as a taxable tractor described in section 4051(a)(1)(E) and then uses it or sells it, Buyer may be liable for the tax imposed by section 4051 on this sale or use. See 26 CFR 48.4051-1(e)(6)(ii) and 145.4052-1(c).
7. Buyer understands that Buyer may be liable for the section 6701 penalty (relating to aiding and abetting an understatement of tax liability) if this is an erroneous certification.
8. Buyer understands that the fraudulent use of this certificate may subject Buyer and all parties making any fraudulent use of this statement to a fine or imprisonment, or both, together with the costs of prosecution.

_____

Printed or typed name of person signing this certificate

_____

Title of person signing

_____

Signature and date signed

(f) *Exclusions.*—(1) *In general.*—Tax is not imposed by section 4051 on the first retail sale of the following articles:

(i) Automobile truck chassis or bodies that have practical and commercial fitness for use with a vehicle that has a GVW of 33,000 pounds or less.

(ii) Truck trailer and semitrailer chassis or bodies that have practical and commercial fitness for use with a truck trailer or semitrailer that has a GVW of 26,000 pounds or less.

(iii) Tractors that have—

(A) A GVW of 19,500 pounds or less; and

(B) A GCW of 33,000 pounds or less.

(2) *Practical and commercial fitness.*—A chassis or body possesses practical fitness for use with a vehicle if it performs its intended function up to a generally acceptable standard of efficiency with the vehicle, and a chassis or body possesses commercial fitness for use with a vehicle if it is generally available for use with the vehicle at a price that is reasonably competitive with other articles that may be used for the same purpose. A truck chassis that has practical and commercial fitness for use with a vehicle having a GVW of 33,000 pounds or less is not subject to the tax imposed by section 4051 regardless of the body actually mounted on the chassis. A truck trailer or semitrailer chassis that has practical and commercial fitness for use with a vehicle having a GVW of 26,000 pounds or less is not subject to tax regardless of the body actually mounted on the chassis. A taxable chassis or body, as the case may be, remains subject to tax—

(i) Even if an exempt body is mounted on a taxable chassis or a taxable body is mounted on an exempt chassis; and

(ii) The resulting vehicle is a highway vehicle.

(3) *Gross vehicle weight.*—(i) The term *gross vehicle weight* means the maximum total weight of a loaded vehicle. Except as otherwise provided in this paragraph (f)(3), the maximum total weight is the GVW rating of the article as specified by the manufacturer on the Manufacturer's Statement of Origin (or comparable document) or by the retailer of the completed article on a comparable document. In determining the GVW, the following rules apply:

(A) The GVW rating must take into account, among other things, the strength of the chassis frame, the axle capacity and

placement, and, if an article is specially equipped to the buyer's specifications, those specifications.

(B) The manufacturer or retailer of an article listed in paragraph (a) of this section must specify the article's GVW rating at the time the article requires no additional manufacture other than—

(1) The addition of readily attachable articles, such as tire or rim assemblies or minor accessories;

(2) The performance of minor finishing operations, such as painting; or

(3) In the case of a chassis, the addition of a body.

(C) If the IRS finds that a GVW rating by the manufacturer or a later seller is unreasonable in light of the facts and circumstances in a particular case, that GVW rating will not be used for purposes of section 4051.

(D) The IRS may exclude from a GVW rating any readily attachable parts to the extent the IRS finds that the use of such parts in computing the GVW rating results in an inaccurate GVW rating.

(E) If the following or similar ratings are inconsistent, the highest of these ratings is the GVW rating:

(1) The rating indicated in a label or identifying device affixed to an article.

(2) The rating set forth in sales invoice or warranty agreement.

(3) The advertised rating for that article (or identical articles).

(ii) The retailer must keep a record of the GVW rating for each chassis, body, or vehicle it sells. For this purpose, a record of the serial number of each such article is treated as a record of the GVW rating of the article if such rating is indicated by the serial number. The GVW rating must be retained as part of the retailer's records for each of its chassis, bodies, or vehicles.

(4) *Gross combination weight.*—(i) The term *gross combination weight* means the GVW of the tractor plus the GVW of any trailer or semitrailer that the tractor may safely tow. Unless a particular rating is unreasonable in light of the facts and circumstances in a particular case, the IRS will consider the GCW of a tractor to be the highest GCW rating specified on any of the following documents:

(A) The Manufacturer's Statement of Origin (or comparable document) or a comparable document of a seller of the completed tractor.

(B) A label or identifying device affixed to the completed tractor by the manufacturer or the seller.

(C) A sales invoice or warranty agreement.

(D) An advertisement for the tractor (or identical tractors).

(ii) The retailer must keep a record of the GCW rating for each tractor it sells. The GCW rating must be retained as part of the retailer's records for each of its tractors.

(g) *Example.*—The following example illustrates the application of paragraphs (e)(1), (2), (3), and (4) of this section:

Example. (1) Facts. (i) A vehicle has the capacity to tow truck trailers and semitrailers (trailers) that have a GVW of 20,000 pounds. The vehicle has a standard chassis cab (4-door with crew cab), accommodating five passengers, and is outfitted with certain luxury features. The cab has an electric trailer brake control that connects to the brakes of a towed trailer and to a hook up for trailer lights. The vehicle has two storage boxes behind the cab that can accommodate incidental items such as small tools and vehicle repair equipment.

(ii) The vehicle has a GVW rating of 23,000 pounds and a GCW rating of 43,000 pounds. The vehicle is equipped with hydraulic disc brakes with a four wheel automatic braking system, a 300 horsepower engine, and a six-speed automatic transmission. The front axle of the vehicle has an 8,000 pound rating and the rear axle has a 15,000 pound rating.

(iii) The vehicle has three types of hitching devices: a removable ball gooseneck hitch, a fifth wheel hitch, and a heavy duty trailer receiver hitch. The vehicle's platform, which is approximately 139 inches long, is designed with a rectangular well to accommodate the gooseneck and fifth wheel hitches (bed hitches). This platform slopes at the rear of the rectangular well and has tie down hooks. Optional removable steel stake rails can be placed around the platform.

(2) *Analysis.* (i) Some characteristics of the vehicle such as its chassis cab with a GVW rating of 23,000 pounds, a 300 horsepower engine, a front axle with an 8,000 pound rating, and a rear axle with a 15,000 pound rating are consistent with either a cargo carrying or a towing function. In this case, however, the vehicle also has a GCW rating of 43,000 pounds and its engine, brakes, transmission, axle ratings, electric trailer brake control, trailer hook up lights, and hitches enable it to tow a trailer that has a GVW rating of 20,000 pounds.

(ii) When the vehicle's bed hitches are used to tow, the cargo carrying capacity of the vehicle is limited to the storage boxes behind the cab and is minimal in comparison to the GVW rating of the towed truck trailer or semitrailer. Neither the steel stake bed rails nor the tie down hooks significantly increase cargo carrying capacity when either of the bed hitches is used. Even if neither of the vehicle's two bed hitches is used, the design of the vehicle significantly reduces its cargo carrying capacity when compared to the cargo carrying capacity of a pickup truck body or a flatbed truck body installed on a comparable chassis. The significant reduction in cargo carrying capacity resulting from the vehicle's platform with its rectangular well and sloping platform at the rear of the rectangular well is evidence that the vehicle is not primarily designed to carry cargo. By accommodating the bed hitches, however, this platform configuration increases the vehicle's towing capacity and, in conjunction with the other features described above, makes it possible to safely tow a trailer with a GVW rating of 20,000 pounds.

(3) *Conclusion.* The vehicle's physical characteristics, which maximize towing capacity at the expense of carrying capacity, establish that the vehicle is primarily designed to tow a vehicle, such as a truck trailer or semitrailer, rather than to carry cargo on its chassis. Thus, the vehicle is a tractor.

(h) *Effective/applicability date.*—This section applies on and after the date of publication of these regulations in the **Federal Register** as final regulations. [Reg. § 48.4051-1.]

§ 48.4051-2. Imposition of tax; parts and accessories.—(a) *Parts or accessories sold on or in connection with the sale of chassis, bodies, and tractors.*—(1) *In general.*—(i) The tax imposed by section 4051 applies to parts or accessories sold on or in connection with, or with the sale of, any article specified in § 48.4051-1(a). The tax applies whether or not the parts or accessories are separately billed by the retailer.

Par. 28. Section 145.4051-1 is revised to read as follows:

§ 145.4051-1. Imposition of tax on heavy trucks, tractors, and trailers sold at retail.—(a) For rules relating to the imposition of the tax imposed by section 4051 and related rules on the tax base,

(ii) If a taxable chassis or body is sold by the retailer without parts or accessories that are considered equipment essential for the operation or appearance of the taxable article, the sale of these parts or accessories by the retailer to the buyer of the taxable article will be considered, in the absence of evidence to the contrary, to have been made in connection with the sale of the taxable article even though they are shipped separately, whether at the same time or on a different date.

(iii) Parts and accessories that are spares or replacements are not subject to the tax described in paragraph (a)(1)(i) of this section.

(2) *Example.*—The following example illustrates the application of this paragraph (a):

Example. X buys from Retailer a chassis in a sale subject to the tax imposed by section 4051. At the time of the sale, bumpers were not attached to the chassis; rather, they had been ordered from Retailer and delivered to X at a later date. For purposes of the tax imposed by section 4051, the price of the chassis includes the price of the bumpers, regardless of when the Retailer delivered the bumpers or billed X for the bumpers.

(b) *Parts or accessories not sold on or in connection with the sale of chassis, bodies, and tractors.*—(1) *In general.*—Section 4051(b)(1) imposes a tax on the installation of a part or accessory on a taxable article specified in § 48.4051-1(a) within six months after the article was first placed in service. However, the tax imposed by section 4051(b)(1) does not apply if—

(i) The part or accessory is a replacement part or accessory; or

(ii) The aggregate price of non-replacement parts and accessories (and their installation) for any vehicle does not exceed $1,000.

(2) *Application and rate of tax.*—The tax is the applicable percentage of the price of the part or accessory and its installation. The applicable percentage is prescribed in section 4051(b)(1).

(3) *Liability for tax.*—The owner, lessee, or operator of the vehicle on which the parts or accessories are installed is liable for this tax. The owner(s) of the trade or business that installs the parts or accessories is secondarily liable for this tax.

(4) *Definitions.*—(i) *First placed in service.*—For purposes of this section, a vehicle is *first placed in service* on the date on which the owner of the vehicle took actual possession of the vehicle. This date can be established by the delivery ticket signed by the owner or other comparable document indicating delivery to, and acceptance by, the owner.

(ii) *Replacement part.*—The term *replacement part* means an item that is substantially similar to and intended to take the place of a vehicle part that has worn out or broken down, regardless of when it is ordered.

(5) *Example.*—The following example illustrates the application of this paragraph (b). Assume that during the periods described, the rate of tax is 12 percent of the price of the part or accessory and its installation.

Example. X bought a vehicle in a sale that was subject to the tax imposed by section 4051 and first placed it in service on September 1, 2013. On October 1, 2013, X purchases and has installed non-replacement parts at a cost of $750. On November 1, 2013, X purchases and has installed additional non-replacement parts at a cost of $450. On December 1, 2013, X purchases and has installed additional non-replacement parts and accessories at a cost of $900. Although the price of each separate purchase and installation is less than $1,000, the aggregate price exceeds the $1,000 limit on November 1, 2013. Accordingly, on November 1, 2013, X is liable for tax of $144 (12 percent x ($750 + $450)) on account of the installations on October 1, and November 1, 2013. On December 1, 2013, X is liable for a tax of $108 (12 percent x $900) on account of the installation on that date. To report its liability X must file Form 720, Quarterly Federal Excise Tax Return, for the fourth calendar quarter of 2013 by January 31, 2014.

(c) *Effective/applicability date.*—This section applies on and after the date of publication of these regulations in the **Federal Register** as final regulations. [Reg. § 48.4051-2.]

liability for tax, explanation of terms, and exclusions, see § 48.4051-1 through § 48.4052-2 of this chapter.

(b) This section applies on and after the date on which these regulations are published as final regulations in the **Federal Register**.

Excise Tax: Tractors, Trailers, Trucks, and Tires: Highway Vehicle: Definition

Excise Tax: Tractors, Trailers, Trucks, and Tires: Highway Vehicle: Definition.—Amendments to Reg. §§48.4052-1 and 145.4052-1, relating to the excise taxes imposed on the sale of highway tractors, trailers, trucks, and tires, the use of heavy vehicles on the highway, and the definition of highway vehicle related to these and other taxes, are proposed (published in the Federal Register on March 31, 2016) (REG-103380-05).

Par. 10. Section 48.4052-1 is revised to read as follows:

§48.4052-1. Definition; first retail sale.—(a) *In general.*—For purposes of the tax imposed by section 4051, *first retail sale* means a taxable sale defined in paragraph (b) of this section.

(b) *Taxable sale; in general.*—A sale of an article described in §48.4051-1(a) is a taxable sale except in the following cases:

(1) The sale is an exempt sale. A sale is an exempt sale if—

(i) The sale is a tax-free sale under section 4221;

(ii) The sale is of a used article that had previously been sold tax-free under section 4221; or

(iii) The article is sold for resale or leasing in a long-term lease and, at the time of sale, the seller—

(A) Has obtained from the buyer a certificate described in paragraph (d) of this section stating, among other things, that the buyer will either resell the vehicle or lease it in a long-term lease;

(B) Has no reason to believe that any information in the certificate is false; and

(C) Has not received a notification from the IRS under paragraph (d)(1) of this section with respect to the buyer.

(2) There has been a prior sale of the article that is not an exempt sale. The previous sentence does not apply if the prior sale is described in paragraph (c)(1) of this section.

(c) *Special rule for trailers and semitrailers.*—(1) *In general.*—A sale is described in this paragraph (c)(1) if the sale—

(i) Is a sale of a chassis or body of a truck trailer or semi-trailer ("trailer or semitrailer");

(ii) Is not an exempt sale; and

(iii) Occurs less than six months after the first sale of the trailer or semitrailer that is not an exempt sale.

(2) *Credit.*—In the case of a sale described in paragraph (c)(1) of this section, any tax paid by the prior seller on account of its sale (and not at any time refunded to or credited against any other liability of the prior seller) is treated as a payment on behalf of the person (the subsequent seller) liable for the tax on the sale described in paragraph (c)(1) of this section. The subsequent seller may claim such payment as a credit against its liability for tax on the sale described in paragraph (c)(1) of this section if the following conditions are met:

(i) The claim is made on Form 720, "Quarterly Federal Excise Tax Return" (or such other form as the IRS may designate) in accordance with the instructions for that form.

(ii) The subsequent seller has not been repaid any portion of the tax by the prior seller and has not provided the prior seller with a written consent to the allowance of a credit or refund.

(iii) The subsequent seller has records substantiating the amount of tax paid by the prior seller on its sale of the truck trailer or semitrailer.

(d) *Certificate.*—(1) *In general.*—The certificate referred to in paragraph (b)(1)(iii) of this section is a statement that is signed under penalties of perjury by a person with authority to bind the buyer, is in substantially the same form as the model certificate provided in paragraph (d)(3) of this section, and contains all information necessary to complete the model certificate. The IRS may withdraw the right of a buyer of vehicles to provide a certificate under this section if the buyer uses the vehicles to which a certificate relates other than as stated in the certificate. The IRS may notify any seller that the buyer's right to provide a certificate has been withdrawn. The certificate may be included as part of any business records normally used to document a sale.

(2) *Effect of use other than as stated in certificate.*—If a buyer that provides a certificate described in paragraph (b)(1)(iii)(A) of this section uses or leases (in a short term lease) an article listed in the certificate, the sale of such article to the buyer is treated as the first retail sale of the article and the buyer is liable for the tax imposed on such sale. If the conditions of paragraph (b)(1)(iii)(A), (B), and (C) of this section are satisfied, the seller will not be liable for the tax imposed on such sale.

(3) *Model certificate.*

Certificate

(To support nontaxable sale of articles listed in section 4051 for resale or long term lease under section 4052 of the Internal Revenue Code)
The undersigned buyer of articles listed in section 4051 ("Buyer") hereby certifies the following under penalties of perjury:

1. _____

_____

Seller's name, address, and employer identification number

2. _____

_____

Buyer's name, address, and employer identification number

3. _____

Date and location of sale to Buyer

4. The articles listed below will be either resold by Buyer or leased on a long term basis by Buyer. If the article is a chassis, Buyer has listed the chassis Vehicle Identification Number. If the article is a body, Buyer has listed the body's identification number.

5. Buyer understands that it must be prepared to establish, by evidence satisfactory to an examining agent, how each article bought under this certificate was used.

6. Buyer has not been notified by the Internal Revenue Service that its right to provide a certificate has been withdrawn.

7. Buyer understands that if it uses or leases (in a short term lease) an article listed in this certificate, Buyer will be liable for the tax imposed by section 4051(a)(1) on the article. See 26 CFR 48.4051-1 and 145.4052-1(c).

8. Buyer understands that Buyer may be liable for the section 6701 penalty (relating to aiding and abetting an understatement of tax liability) if this is an erroneous certification.

9. Buyer understands that the fraudulent use of this certificate may subject Buyer and all parties making any fraudulent use of this statement to a fine or imprisonment, or both, together with the costs of prosecution.

_____

Printed or typed name of person signing this certificate

_____

Title of person signing

_____

Signature and date signed

(e) *No installment payment of tax.*—If a lease is a taxable sale under §145.4052-1(b) of this chapter or an installment sale (or another form of sale under which the sales price is paid in installments), then the liability for the entire tax arises at the time of the lease or installment sale. No portion of the tax is deferred by reason of the fact that the sales price is paid in installments.

Reg. §48.4052-1(e)

(f) *Effective/applicability date.*—This section applies on and after the date of publication of these regulations in the **Federal Register** as final regulations.

Par. 29. Section 145.4052-1 is amended by:
1. Revising paragraph (a).
2. Adding two sentences after the first sentence in paragraph (d)(1).
3. Removing the last sentence in paragraph (d)(8)(iii).
4. Revising paragraph (g).
The revisions read as follows:

§145.4052-1. Special rules and definitions.—(a) *First retail sale.*— For the definition of first retail sale, see § 48.4052-1 of this chapter.

* * *

(d) * * *
(1) * * *. Total consideration paid for a chassis or body includes charges for equipment installed on the chassis or body. See §48.4051-1(d)(4).* * *

(g) *Effective/applicability date.*—This section applies on and after the date of publication of these regulations in the **Federal Register** as final regulations.

Par. 31. For each section listed in the tables, remove the language in the "Remove" column and add in its place the language in the "Add" column as set forth below:

Section	Remove	Add
§ 145.4052-1(b)(1) First sentence	§ 145.4051-1	§ 48.4051-1 of this chapter
Second sentence	paragraph (a)(2) of this section	§ 48.4052-1(b) of this chapter
§ 145.4052-1(b)(2)	§ 145.4051-1	§ 48.4051-1 of this chapter
	paragraph (a)(2) of this section	§ 48.4052-1(b) of this chapter
§ 145.4052-1(c)(1)	§ 145.4051-1	§ 48.4051-1 of this chapter
§ 145.4052-1(c)(5)(ii)	4216(a), 4216(f)	4052(b)(1)(A) and (B), 4216(a)
§ 145.4052-1(d)(1) Fourth sentence	Installatioin	installation

Excise Tax: Tractors, Trailers, Trucks, and Tires: Highway Vehicle: Definition

Excise Tax: Tractors, Trailers, Trucks, and Tires: Highway Vehicle: Definition.—Amendments to Reg. §§145.4061-1 and 48.4061(a)-1, relating to the excise taxes imposed on the sale of highway tractors, trailers, trucks, and tires, the use of heavy vehicles on the highway, and the definition of highway vehicle related to these and other taxes, are proposed (published in the Federal Register on March 31, 2016) (REG-103380-05).

Par. 11. Section 48.4061(a)-1 is amended as follows:
1. Paragraph (d)(2)(ii), first sentence, is amended by removing the language "A self-propelled" and adding "Before January 1, 2005, a self-propelled" in its place.
2. Paragraph (d)(2)(iv) is added.
The addition reads as follows:

§48.4061(a)-1. Imposition of tax; exclusion for light-duty trucks, etc.

* * *

(d) * * *
(2) * * *

Par. 30. Section 145.4061-1 is removed.

§145.4061-1. Application to manufacturers tax.

(iv) *Off-highway transportation vehicles after October 21, 2004.*—For a description of certain vehicles that are not treated as highway vehicles after October 21, 2004, see § 48.0-5(b)(3).

* * *

Excise Tax: Tractors, Trailers, Trucks, and Tires: Highway Vehicle: Definition

Excise Tax: Tractors, Trailers, Trucks, and Tires: Highway Vehicle: Definition.—Amendments to Reg. § 48.4071-1—48.4071-4, relating to the excise taxes imposed on the sale of highway tractors, trailers, trucks, and tires, the use of heavy vehicles on the highway, and the definition of highway vehicle related to these and other taxes, are proposed (published in the Federal Register on March 31, 2016) (REG-103380-05).

Par. 13. Section 48.4071-1 is revised to read as follows:

§48.4071-1. Tires; imposition of tax.—(a) *In general.*—(1) Tax is imposed by section 4071 on the sale by the manufacturer of a taxable tire with a maximum rated load capacity greater than 3,500 pounds.

(2) See § 48.4072-1(b) for the definition of the term *taxable tire.*

(b) *Tax base and computation of tax.*—The tax base is equal to the number of 10-pound increments, rounded down to the nearest ten pounds, by which the maximum rated load capacity exceeds 3,500 pounds. The tax is determined by multiplying this tax base by the rate of tax specified in section 4071(a). Thus, for example, a taxable tire with a maximum rated load capacity of 4,005 pounds is treated as having a maximum rated load capacity of 4,000 pounds and a tax base of 50 ((4000 - 3,500) ÷ 10). The tax imposed on the tire is the rate of tax under section 4071(a) times 50.

(c) *Liability for tax.*—The manufacturer of a taxable tire is liable for the tax imposed by section 4071.

(d) *Effective/applicability date.*—This section applies on and after the date of publication of these regulations in the **Federal Register** as final regulations.

Par. 14. Section 48.4071-2 is revised to read as follows:

§48.4071-2. Determination of maximum rated load capacity.— (a) *In general.*—For purposes of the tax imposed by section 4071, the maximum rated load capacity is the maximum rated load rating inscribed on a taxable tire's sidewall provided the inscription meets the standards prescribed by the National Highway Traffic Safety Administration in its regulations. If a taxable tire has multiple maxi-

mum load ratings, the taxable tire's highest maximum load rating is the taxable tire's maximum rated load capacity for purposes of the tax.

(b) *Tampering.*—In the event of any tampering with, or the appearance of tampering with, the inscription of a taxable tire's maximum rated load capacity as described in paragraph (a) of this section, the tire's maximum rated load capacity is the maximum rated load capacity of a comparable tire.

Par. 15. Section 48.4071-3 is amended by:
1. Revising the section heading and paragraph (a).
2. Revising paragraph (c)(1).
3. Adding paragraph (e).
4. Removing the undesignated authority citation at the end of the section.
The revisions and addition read as follows:

§ 48.4071-3. Imposition of tax on tires delivered to manufacturer's retail outlet.—(a) *General rule.*—If a tire manufacturer delivers a taxable tire it manufactured to one of its retail outlets, the manufacturer is liable for the tax imposed by section 4071 on this tire in the same manner as if the tire had been sold upon delivery to the retail outlet. The amount of tax is computed under § 48.4071-1.

* * *

(c) * * *

(1) *Delivery.*—(i) *Delivery options.*—A manufacturer of taxable tires may, at its option, treat either of the following events as constituting delivery to a retail outlet:

(A) Delivery of taxable tires to a common carrier (or, where the taxable tires are transported by the manufacturer, the placing of the taxable tires into the manufacturer's highway vehicle) for shipment from the plant in which the taxable tires are manufactured, or from a regional distribution center of taxable tires, to a retail outlet or to a location in the immediate vicinity of a retail outlet primarily for future delivery to the retail outlet.

(B) Arrival of the taxable tires at the retail outlet, or, where shipment is to a location in the immediate vicinity of a retail outlet primarily for future delivery to the retail outlet, the arrival of the taxable tires at such location.

(ii) *Delivery election.*—A manufacturer that has elected to treat one of the events listed in paragraph (c)(1)(i)(A) or (B) of this section as constituting delivery to a retail outlet may not use a different criterion for a later return period unless the manufacturer obtains permission from the IRS in advance.

* * *

(e) *Effective/applicability date.*—This section applies on and after the date of publication of these regulations in the **Federal Register** as final regulations.

(c) *Effective/applicability date.*—This section applies on and after the date of publication of these regulations in the **Federal Register** as final regulations.

Par. 26. For each section listed in the tables, remove the language in the "Remove" column from wherever it appears in the paragraph and add in its place the language in the "Add" column as set forth below:

Section	Remove	Add
§ 48.4071-3(b) Second sentence	tires or tubes	taxable tires
Fourth sentence	tires or inner tubes	taxable tires
Fifth sentence	tires	taxable tires
Sixth sentence	taxable tires and inner tubes	taxable tires
§ 48.4071-3(c)(1) Introductory text	tires or inner tubes	taxable tires
§ 48.4071-3(c)(1)(i)	tires or inner tubes	taxable tires
	tires or tubes	taxable tires
	tires and inner tubes	taxable tires
§ 48.4071-3(c)(2)(i) Second sentence	tires and inner tubes	taxable tires
Third sentence	tires or inner tubes	taxable tires
Fourth sentence	Tires and inner tubes	Taxable tires
	tires and tubes	taxable tires
Seventh sentence	tires and inner tubes tires and tubes tires or tubes	taxable tires
Eighth sentence	tires and inner tubes tire or inner tube	taxable tires
§ 48.4071-3(c)(2)(ii) First sentence (Example)	tires and tubes	taxable tires
Third sentence (Example)	tires and inner tubes	taxable tires
Fourth sentence (Example)	tires or inner tubes tires and tubes	taxable tires
§ 48.4071-3(c)(3)(i)	tire or inner tube	taxable tire
§ 48.4071-3(c)(3)(ii)	tire or inner tube	taxable tire
§ 48.4071-3(d)(1) First sentence	tires and inner tubes	taxable tires
Second sentence	tires or inner tubes	taxable tires
§ 48.4071-3(d)(2)	tires and inner tubes	taxable tires
§ 48.4071-3(d)(3)(i) First sentence	tire or inner tube	taxable tire
Second sentence	tire or inner tube	taxable tire
§ 48.4071-3(d)(3)(ii) Third sentence (Example)	tires and tubes (each of the two times it appears)	taxable tires
Fourth sentence (Example)	tires or inner tubes	taxable tires

Par. 16. Section 48.4071-4 is removed.

§48.4071-4. Original equipment tires on imported articles.

Excise Tax: Tractors, Trailers, Trucks, and Tires: Highway Vehicle: Definition

Excise Tax: Tractors, Trailers, Trucks, and Tires: Highway Vehicle: Definition.—Amendments to Reg. §48.4072-1, relating to the excise taxes imposed on the sale of highway tractors, trailers, trucks, and tires, the use of heavy vehicles on the highway, and the definition of highway vehicle related to these and other taxes, are proposed (published in the Federal Register on March 31, 2016) (REG-103380-05).

Par. 17. Section 48.4072-1 is amended by:

1. Revising paragraphs (b), (c), and (d).
2. Amending paragraph (e) by removing the second, third, and fourth sentences.
3. Revising paragraphs (f), (g), and (h).
4. Removing the undesignated authority citation at the end of the section. The revisions and addition read as follows:

§48.4072-1. Definitions.

* * *

(b) *Taxable tire.*—(1) *In general.*—The term *taxable tire* means a tire—

(i) Of the type used on highway vehicles;

(ii) That is wholly or in part made of rubber; and

(iii) That is marked pursuant to federal regulations for for highway use.

(2) *Recapped and retreaded tires.*—The term *taxable tire* includes a used tire that is recapped or retreaded (whether from shoulder-to-shoulder or bead-to-bead) only if—

(i) The used tire had not previously been sold in the United States;

(ii) The used tire is recapped or retreaded outside the United States; and

(iii) When imported into the United States, the recapped or retreaded tire meets the requirements of section (b)(1) of this section.

(c) *Tires of the type used on highway vehicles.*—The term *tires of the type used on highway vehicles* means tires (other than tires of a type used exclusively on mobile machinery (within the meaning of §48.0-5(c))) of the type used on—

(1) Highway vehicles; or

(2) Vehicles of the type used in connection with highway vehicles.

(d) *Rated load capacity.*—The term *rated load capacity* means the maximum load a tire is rated to carry at a specified inflation pressure.

* * *

(f) *Super single tire.*—The term *super single tire* means a single tire greater than 13 inches in cross section width designed to replace two tires in a dual fitment. The term does not include any tire designed for steering or an all position tire.

(g) Examples. The following examples illustrate the application of this section.

Example 1. (1) *Facts.* (i) A foreign tire manufacturer manufactures a tire that meets the Federal Motor Vehicle Safety Standard for truck tires prescribed by the DOT. The tire is not of a type used exclusively on mobile machinery (within the meaning of §48.0-5(c)). This tire is partially made of rubber. The foreign manufacturer marks this tire for highway use pursuant to DOT regulations. The foreign manufacturer sells the tire for use in the foreign country.

(ii) After use in the foreign country, a tire importer buys the tire and imports it into the United States. At the time of importation, the tread on this tire's casing meets the criteria for minimal tread on trucks used in interstate commerce as prescribed by the DOT.

(2) *Analysis.* The imported tire is a taxable tire because the tire is of the type used on a highway vehicle and is not of a type used exclusively on mobile machinery, the tire is wholly or in part made of rubber, and the tire is marked pursuant to federal regulations for highway use.

Example 2. (1) *Facts.* A tire manufacturer pays the tax imposed by section 4071(a) when it sells a tire that is (1) of the type used on highway vehicles; (2) wholly or in part made of rubber; and (3) marked pursuant to federal regulations for highway use. The tire does not have any design features to indicate that it is a tire of a type used exclusively on mobile machinery (within the meaning of §48.0-5(b)(3)(iii)). The purchaser of this tire puts the tire on mobile machinery described in §48.0-5(b)(3)(iii).

(2) *Analysis.* A tire that is "of the type used on highway vehicles" and "not of a type used exclusively on mobile machinery" retains those characteristics regardless of how the tire is actually used. Therefore, the characterization of a tire as a taxable tire is not changed because the tire is actually used on a vehicle that is mobile machinery.

(h) *Effective/applicability date.*—This section applies on and after the date of publication of these regulations in the **Federal Register** as final regulations.

Excise Tax: Tractors, Trailers, Trucks, and Tires: Highway Vehicle: Definition

Excise Tax: Tractors, Trailers, Trucks, and Tires: Highway Vehicle: Definition.—Amendments to Reg. §§48.4073-1—48.4073-4, relating to the excise taxes imposed on the sale of highway tractors, trailers, trucks, and tires, the use of heavy vehicles on the highway, and the definition of highway vehicle related to these and other taxes, are proposed (published in the Federal Register on March 31, 2016) (REG-103380-05).

Par. 19. Section 48.4073-1 is revised to read as follows:

§48.4073-1. Exemption for tires sold for the exclusive use of the Department of Defense or the Coast Guard.—(a) *In general.*—Tax is not imposed by section 4071 on the sale of a taxable tire if—

(1) The manufacturer of the taxable tire meets the registration requirements of section 4222; and

(2) The sale of the taxable tire is to the Department of Defense or the Coast Guard for the exclusive use of the Department of Defense or the Coast Guard,

(b) *Sales for resale.*—A manufacturer may sell a taxable tire tax-free under section 4073 and this section only if the sale is directly made to either the Department of Defense or the Coast Guard for such agency's exclusive use. Accordingly, a sale may not be made taxfree to a dealer for resale to the Department of Defense or the Coast Guard for its exclusive use, even though it is known at the time of sale by the manufacturer that the article will be so resold.

(c) *Certificate.*—(1) *Effect of certificate.*—A manufacturer will not be liable for tax on the sale of a taxable tire if, at the time of the sale, the manufacturer has obtained from the buyer an unexpired certificate described in paragraph (c)(2) of this section and has no reason to believe any information in the certificate is false. A buyer that provides an erroneous certificate described in paragraph (c)(2) of this section is liable for any tax imposed on the sale to which the certificate relates.

(2) *Form of certificate.*—The certificate described in this paragraph (c)(2) is a statement by the Department of Defense or the Coast Guard that is signed under penalties of perjury by a person with authority to bind the Department of Defense or the Coast Guard, is in substantially the same form as the model certificate provided in paragraph (c)(3) of this section, and contains all information necessary to complete the model certificate. A new certificate or notice that the current certificate is invalid must be given if any information in the current certificate changes. The certificate may be included as part of any business records normally used to document a sale.

(3) *Model Certificate.*

Certificate

(To support the tax-free sales of tires to the Department of Defense or the Coast Guard under section 4073 of the Internal Revenue Code)
The undersigned buyer of taxable tires ("Buyer") hereby certifies the following under penalties of perjury:

1. _____

_____

_____

Manufacturer's name, address, and employer identification number

2. _____

Buyer's name, address, and employer identification number
3.

Date and location of sale to Buyer
4. The tire(s) to which this certificate applies will be for the exclusive use of Buyer (that is, the Department of Defense or the Coast Guard).
5. This certificate applies to Buyer's purchases from Manufacturer as follows (complete as applicable):
   a. A single purchase on invoice or delivery ticket number _____
   b. All purchases between __(effective date) and __(expiration date), a period not exceeding 12 calendar quarters after the effective date, under account or order number(s) ____. If this certificate applies only to Buyer's purchases for certain locations, check here ____ and list the locations.

6. Buyer will provide a new certificate to the Manufacturer if any information in this certificate changes.
7. Buyer understands that Buyer may be liable for the section 6701 penalty (relating to aiding and abetting an understatement of tax liability) if this is an erroneous certification.
8. Buyer understands that the fraudulent use of this certificate may subject Buyer and all parties making any fraudulent use of this statement to a fine or imprisonment, or both, together with the costs of prosecution.

Printed or typed name of person signing this certificate

Title of person signing

Signature and date signed

(d) *Effective/applicability date.*—This section applies on and after the date of publication of these regulations in the **Federal Register** as final regulations.

Par. 20. Section 48.4073-2 is revised to read as follows:

§48.4073-2. American National Red Cross.—(a) For the exemption allowed to the American National Red Cross from the tax imposed by section 4071, see the Secretary's Authorization, 1979-1 C.B. 478 (See §601.601(d)(2)(ii)(*b*) of this chapter.)

Par. 21. Sections 48.4073-3 and 48.4073-4 are removed.

§48.4073-3. Exemption of tread rubber used for recapping non-highway tires.

Par. 21. Sections 48.4073-3 and 48.4073-4 are removed.

§48.4073-4. Other tax-free sales.

(b) *Effective/applicability date.*—This section applies on and after the date of publication of these regulations in the **Federal Register** as final regulations.

Excise Taxes: Taxable Fuel: Returns: Definitions

Excise Taxes: Taxable Fuel: Returns: Definitions.—Amendments to Reg. §§48.4081-1, 48.4081-2, 48.4081-3 and 48.4081-6, relating to credits and payments for alcohol mixtures, biodiesel mixtures, renewable diesel mixtures, alternative fuel mixtures, and alternative fuel sold for use or used as a fuel and relating to the definition of gasoline and diesel fuel, are proposed (published in the Federal Register on July 29, 2008) (REG-155087-05) (corrected August 25, 2008).

Par. 14. Section 48.4081-1 is amended as follows:
1. Paragraph (b) is amended by:
a. Revising the definition of Blender.
b. Adding the definition of Diesel-water fuel emulsion in alphabetical order.
c. Adding the language "(other than a mixture as defined in §48.6426-1(b))" after "any liquid" in the introductory text of the definition of Excluded liquid.
d. Revising the definition of Finished gasoline.
e. Revising the definition of Gasoline.
f. Adding the definition of Gasoline blend in alphabetical order.
g. Revising the definition of Refinery.
h. Removing the language "effective January 2, 1998," from the last sentence in the definition of Terminal.
2. Paragraph (c) is amended by:
a. In paragraph (c)(1)(i), removing the language "paragraphs (c)(1)(ii) and (c)(1)(iii)" in the introductory phrase and adding "paragraph (c)(1)(ii)" in its place.
b. In paragraph (c)(1)(ii), removing the language "A mixture" and adding "In calendar quarters beginning before the date of publication of these regulations in the **Federal Register** as final regulations, a mixture" in its place.
c. Removing paragraph (c)(1)(iii).
d. In paragraph (c)(2)(i), first sentence, adding the language "any of the following: a mixture (as defined in §48.6426-1(b)) that contains diesel fuel; renewable diesel as defined in section 40A(f)(3); transmix (as defined in section 4083(a)(3)(B)); and" after "*diesel fuel* means".
e. In paragraph (c)(2)(ii), first sentence, adding the language "biodiesel, alternative fuel (as defined in section 6426(d)(2)), qualified methanol or ethanol fuel (as defined in section 4041(b)(2)(B)), partially exempt methanol or ethanol fuel (as defined in section 4041(m)(2))," after "kerosene,".
f. In paragraph (c)(3)(i)(V) removing the language "gasoline;" and adding "gasoline; and" in its place.
g. In paragraph (c)(3)(i)(W), removing the language "Toluene; and" and adding "Toluene." in its place.
h. Removing paragraph (c)(3)(i)(X).
3. Paragraph (e) is amended by removing the language "48.4081-6(b)," and by adding the language "48.6426-1(b)" after "48.4101-1(b),".
4. Revising paragraph (f).
The revisions and additions read as follows:

§ 48.4081-1. Taxable fuel; definitions

* * *

(b) * * *

Blender means the person that has title to blended taxable fuel immediately after it is created.

* * *

Diesel-water fuel emulsion means diesel fuel at least 14 percent of which is water and with respect to which the emulsion additive is registered by a United States manufacturer with the Environmental Protection Agency pursuant to section 211 of the Clean Air Act (as in effect on March 31, 2003).

* * *

Finished gasoline means all products that are commonly or commercially known or sold as gasoline and are suitable for use as a motor fuel, other than—

(1) Products that have an ASTM octane number of less than 75 as determined by the motor method; and

(2) Alternative fuel as defined in section 6426(d)(2).

Par. 15. Section 48.4081-2 is amended by removing the last sentence of paragraph (d).

§ 48.4081-2. Taxable fuel; tax on removal at a terminal rack.

Par. 16. Section 48.4081-3 is amended as follows:
1. Paragraph (b)(1)(iii) is removed.
2. Removing the last sentence in paragraphs (g)(1) and (h).

§ 48.4081-3. Taxable fuel; taxable events other than removal at the terminal rack.

Par. 17. Section 48.4081-6 is removed and reserved.

§ 48.4081-6. Gasoline; gasohol.

Gasoline means aviation gasoline, finished gasoline, gasoline blends, gasoline blendstocks, and leaded gasoline.

Gasoline blend includes any liquid (other than finished gasoline) that contains at least 0.1 percent (by volume) of finished gasoline and that is suitable for use as a fuel in a motor vehicle or motorboat. However, the term does not include qualified methanol or ethanol fuel (as defined in section 4041(b)(2)(B)), partially exempt methanol or ethanol fuel (as defined in section 4041(m)(2)), or alcohol that is denatured under a formula approved by the Secretary.

* * *

Refinery means a facility used to produce taxable fuel and from which taxable fuel may be removed by pipeline, by vessel, or at a rack. However, the term does not include a facility where only blended taxable fuel, and no other type of taxable fuel, is produced.

* * *

(f) *Effective/applicability date.*—This section is applicable on and after the date of publication of these regulations in the **Federal Register** as final regulations. For provisions applicable to prior periods, see 26 CFR 48.4081-1 (revised as of April 1, 2008).

Excise Tax: Tractors, Trailers, Trucks, and Tires: Highway Vehicle: Definition

Excise Tax: Tractors, Trailers, Trucks, and Tires: Highway Vehicle: Definition.—Amendments to Reg. § 48.4081-1, relating to the excise taxes imposed on the sale of highway tractors, trailers, trucks, and tires, the use of heavy vehicles on the highway, and the definition of highway vehicle related to these and other taxes, are proposed (published in the Federal Register on March 31, 2016) (REG-103380-05).

Par. 22. Section 48.4081-1(b) is amended by removing the language "§ 48.4061(a)-1(d)" in the definition of *Diesel-powered highway vehicle* and adding "§ 48.0-5" in its place.

§ 48.4081-1. Taxable fuel; definitions.

Par. 26. For each section listed in the tables, remove the language in the "Remove" column from wherever it appears in the paragraph and add in its place the language in the "Add" column as set forth below:

Section	Remove	Add
§ 48.4081-1(b)	48.4061(a)-1(d)	48.0-5 of this chapter

Excise Taxes: Diesel Fuel and Kerosene: Dye Injections

Excise Taxes: Diesel Fuel and Kerosene: Dye Injections.—Amendments to Reg. §§ 48.4082-1 and 48.4101-1, relating to the mechanical dye injection of diesel fuel and kerosene, are proposed (published in the Federal Register on April 26, 2005) (REG-154000-04).

☐ Par. 2. In § 48.4082-1, paragraphs (d) and (e)(2) are revised to read as follows:

§ 48.4082-1. Diesel fuel and kerosene; exemption for dyed fuel.

* * *

(d) [The text of this proposed paragraph (d) is the same as the text of § 48.4082-1T(d) as added by T.D. 9199].

(e) * * *

(e)(2) [The text of this proposed paragraph (e)(2) is the same as the text of § 48.4082-1T(e)(2) as added by T.D. 9199].

☐ Par. 3. Section 48.4101-1 is amended by revising paragraph (h)(3)(iv) to read as follows:

§ 48.4101-1. Taxable fuel; registration.

* * *

(h) * * *

(3) * * *

(iv) [The text of this proposed paragraph (h)(3)(iv) is the same as the text of § 48.4101-1T(h)(3)(iv) as added by T.D. 9199].

Excise Taxes: Taxable Fuel: Returns: Definitions

Excise Taxes: Taxable Fuel: Returns: Definitions.—Amendments to Reg. §§ 48.4082-4 and 48.4101-1, relating to credits and payments for alcohol mixtures, biodiesel mixtures, renewable diesel mixtures, alternative fuel mixtures, and alternative fuel sold for use or used as a fuel and relating to the definition of gasoline and diesel fuel, are proposed (published in the Federal Register on July 29, 2008) (REG-155087-05).

Par. 18. Section 48.4082-4, is amended by adding the language "or biodiesel" after "taxable fuel" in paragraphs (a)(1)(iii) and (b)(1)(iii).

§ 48.4082-4. Diesel fuel and kerosene; back-up tax.

Par. 19. Section 48.4101-1 is amended as follows:
1. Paragraph (a)(1) is amended by removing the language "4081 and" and adding "4081, for certain producers and importers of alcohol, biodiesel, and renewable diesel, and alternative fuelers under sections 6426 and 6427, and for purposes of" in its place.

2. Revising paragraphs (a)(2), (c)(1)(vi), (c)(1)(vii), and adding paragraph (c)(1)(viii).

3. Paragraphs (a)(3) and (b)(3) are removed and reserved.

4. Paragraph (b)(9) is amended by removing the language "48.4081-6(b), 48.4082-5(b), 48.4082-6(b), 48.4082-7(b)" and adding "48.4082-5(b), 48.4082-7(b), 48.6426-1(b)," in its place.

5. Revising paragraph (d)(2) and adding paragraph (d)(7).

6. Paragraph (d)(5) is amended by, removing the language "vendor; or" and adding "vendor;" in its place.

7. Paragraph (d)(6) is amended by removing the language "pump)." and adding "pump); or" in its place.

8. Paragraph (f)(1)(i) is amended by removing from the heading the language "and vessel operators." and adding "vessel operators, alternative fuelers, producers or importers of alcohol, biodiesel, or renewable diesel, and diesel-water fuel emulsion producers." in its place.

9. Paragraph (f)(1)(ii) is amended by removing the language in the heading "and vessel operators" and adding "vessel operators, alternative fuelers, producers or importers of alcohol, biodiesel, or renewable diesel, and dieselwater fuel emulsion producers" in its place.

10. Paragraph (f)(1)(ii) is amended by removing the language in the introductory text "or vessel operator" and adding "vessel operator, alternative fueler, producer or importer of alcohol, biodiesel, or renewable diesel, or dieselwater fuel emulsion producer" in its place.

11. Paragraph (f)(1)(ii)(B) is amended by adding the language "reporting," after "payment,".

12. Paragraph (f)(4)(ii)(A) is amended by removing the language in the introductory text "district director" and adding "Commissioner" in its place.

13. Paragraph (f)(4)(ii)(A)(1) is amended by removing the language "district director);" and adding "Commissioner); and" in its place.

14. Paragraph (f)(4)(ii)(A)(2) is amended by removing the language "district director); and" and adding "Commissioner." in its place.

15. Removing paragraph (f)(4)(i)(A)(3).

16. Paragraph (f)(4)(iii) is amended by removing the language "deposit, and payment" and adding "deposit, payment, reporting, and claim" in its place.

17. Revising paragraph (h)(2)(iii).

18. Paragraph (j)(2) is amended by removing the language in the introductory text "district director" and adding "Commissioner" in its place.

19. Paragraph (j)(2)(i), is amended by removing the language "district director);" and adding "Commissioner); and" in its place.

20. Paragraph (j)(2)(ii) is amended by removing the language "district director); and" and adding "Commissioner)." in its place.

21. Removing paragraph (j)(2)(iii).

22. Paragraph (k) is amended by adding a new sentence between the existing second and third sentences.

23. Paragraph (l)(5) is added.

The revisions and additions read as follows:

§48.4101-1. Taxable fuel; registration.—(a) * * *

(2) A person is registered under section 4101 only if the Commissioner has issued a registration letter to the person and the registration has not been revoked or suspended or the person is treated under this paragraph (a)(2) as registered under section 4101. The following persons are treated as registered under section 4101:

(i) The United States is treated as registered under section 4101 for all purposes.

(ii) A partner in a partnership is treated as registered under section 4101 for purposes of claims filed under section 34 if the partnership is registered under section 4101 for purposes of filing claims under section 6426 or 6427.

(iii) A taxable fuel registrant is treated as registered under section 4101 as a diesel-water fuel emulsion producer.

(iv) A foreign person is treated as registered under section 4101 as a producer of alcohol, biodiesel, or renewable diesel if—

(A) The person produces alcohol, biodiesel, or renewable diesel outside the United States and does not produce alcohol, biodiesel, or renewable diesel within the United States; and

(B) The alcohol, biodiesel, or renewable diesel is imported into the United States by a person registered under section 4101 as a producer or importer of alcohol, biodiesel, or renewable diesel.

* * *

(c) * * *

(1) * * *

(vi) A terminal operator;

(vii) A vessel operator; or

(viii) A producer or importer of alcohol, biodiesel, or renewable diesel.

* * *

(d) * * *

(2) An alternative fueler;

* * *

(7) A diesel-water fuel emulsion producer.

* * *

(h) * * *

(2) * * *

(iii) Make any false statement on, or violate the terms of, any certificate given to another person to support—

(A) Any claim for credit, refund, or payment; or

(B) An exemption from, or reduced rate of, tax imposed by section 4081; or

* * *

(k) * * * For rules relating to claims with respect to alcohol, biodiesel, renewable diesel and alternative fuel, see §§48.6426-1 through 48.6426-7. * * *

(l) * * *

(5) References in this section to biodiesel and alcohol are applicable after December 31, 2004. References in this section to renewable diesel and diesel-water fuel emulsion are applicable after December 31, 2005. References in this section to alternative fuel are applicable after September 30, 2006.

Excise Tax: Tractors, Trailers, Trucks, and Tires: Highway Vehicle: Definition

Excise Tax: Tractors, Trailers, Trucks, and Tires: Highway Vehicle: Definition.—Amendments to Reg. §§48.4221-7 and 48.4221-8, relating to the excise taxes imposed on the sale of highway tractors, trailers, trucks, and tires, the use of heavy vehicles on the highway, and the definition of highway vehicle related to these and other taxes, are proposed (published in the Federal Register on March 31, 2016) (REG-103380-05).

Par. 23. Section 48.4221-7 is amended by:

1. Revising the section heading and paragraph (a).

2. Removing paragraph (b) and redesignating paragraph (c) as paragraph (b).

3. Revising redesignated paragraph (b)(2).

4. Adding new paragraph (c).

The revisions and addition read as follows:

§48.4221-7. Tax-free sale of tires for use on other articles.—(a) *In general.*—Under section 4221(e)(2), tax is not imposed by section 4071 on the sale of a taxable tire if—

(1) The taxable tire is sold for use by the purchaser for sale on or in connection with the sale of another article manufactured or produced by the purchaser;

(2) The other article is to be sold by the purchaser—

(i) In a tax-free sale for export, for use as supplies for vessels or aircraft, to a state or local government for its exclusive use, or to a nonprofit educational organization for its exclusive use; or

(ii) For any of such purposes in a sale that would be tax-free but for the fact that the other article is not subject to tax under section 4051 or 4064;

(3) The registration requirements of section 4222 and the regulations thereunder are met; and

(4) The proof, described in paragraph (b) of this section, of the disposition of the other article, is timely received by the manufacturer.

(b) * * *

(2) *Required information.*—(i) *In general.*—The information referred to in paragraph (b)(1) of this section is a statement that is signed under penalties of perjury by a person with authority to bind

the purchaser, is in substantially the same form as the model certificate provided in paragraph (b)(2)(ii) of this section, and contains all information necessary to complete the model certificate. For purchasers that are not required to be registered under section 4222, the IRS may withdraw the right of a purchaser of a taxable tire to provide a certificate under this section if the purchaser uses the tire to which a certificate relates other than as stated in the certificate. The IRS may notify any manufacturer to whom such purchaser has provided a certificate that the purchaser's right to provide a certificate has been withdrawn. The certificate may be included as part of any business records normally used to document a sale.

(ii) *Model certificate.*

Certificate

(To support the nontaxable sale of taxable tires by the manufacturer when sold for use on or in connection with the sale of another article manufactured or produced by the buyer and sold by the buyer in a sale that meets the requirements of section 4221(e)(2))

The undersigned buyer of taxable tires ("Buyer") hereby certifies the following under penalties of perjury:

1. _____

_____

Manufacturer's name, address, employer identification number, and registration number

2. _____

_____

Buyer's name, address, employer identification number, and registration number (if required)

3. _____

Date and location of sale to Buyer

4. The taxable tire(s) listed below, by its (their) United States Department of Transportation identification number(s), are covered by this certificate

5. The taxable tire(s) listed in this certificate that were purchased or shipped on the date specified in entry 3 have been used on or in connection with the sale of _____ (describe product sold by Buyer) by Buyer and such sale was—*(complete line (i), (ii), (iii), or (iv), whichever is applicable)*

(i) for export by _____ (Name of carrier) to _____ (Name of foreign country or possession) and was so exported on _____, _____ (Date). (A copy of the bill of lading or other proof of exportation is attached.)

(ii) for use as supplies on _____ (Name of vessel or aircraft) that is registered in _____ (Name of country in which vessel or aircraft is registered).

(iii) to _____ (Name of state or local government).

(iv) to _____ (Name and address of the nonprofit educational organization).

6. Buyer understands that it must be prepared to establish, by evidence satisfactory to an examining agent, how each tire bought under this certificate was used.

7. Check here ____ if Buyer is not required to be registered with the Internal Revenue Service because Buyer is a state or local government, a foreign person buying for export, or the United States.

8. Buyer understands that Buyer may be liable for the section 6701 penalty (relating to aiding and abetting an understatement of tax liability) if this is an erroneous certification.

9. Buyer understands that the fraudulent use of this certificate may subject Buyer and all parties making any fraudulent use of this statement to a fine or imprisonment, or both, together with the costs of prosecution.

_____

Printed or typed name of person signing this certificate

_____

Title of person signing

_____

Signature and date signed

(c) *Effective/applicability date.*—This section applies on and after the date of publication of these regulations in the **Federal Register** as final regulations.

Par. 26. For each section listed in the tables, remove the language in the "Remove" column from wherever it appears in the paragraph and add in its place the language in the "Add" column as set forth below:

Section	Remove	Add
Redesignated § 48.4221-7 (b)(1)	tire or inner tube	taxable tire
Second sentence	tire or inner tube	taxable tire
Third sentence	tire or inner tube	taxable tire

Par. 24. Section 48.4221-8 is amended by:

1. Revising the section heading and paragraph (a).

2. Removing the second paragraph (b), *Registration requirements for tires, tubes, and tread rubber; vendees purchasing tax-free.*

3. Revising paragraphs (c) and (d).

4. Removing paragraphs (e) and (f).

The revisions read as follows:

§48.4221-8. Tax-free sales of tires used on intercity, local, and school buses.—(a) *In general.*—Under section 4221(e)(3), tax is not imposed by section 4071 on the sale of a taxable tire for use by the buyer on or in connection with a qualified bus, as defined in paragraph (b) of this section, if—

(1) The registration requirements of section 4222 and the regulations thereunder are met;

(2) At the time of sale, the manufacturer of the taxable tire—

(i) Possesses a certificate (in the form described in paragraph (c)(2) of this section) from the buyer of a taxable tire, in which, among other things, the buyer certifies that the buyer will use the taxable tire on or in connection with a qualified bus;

(ii) Has no reason to believe that any information in the certificate described in paragraph (c) of this section is false; and

(iii) Has not received a notification from the IRS under paragraph (c)(2) of this section with respect to the buyer.

* * *

(c) *Certificate.*—(1) *Effect of certificate.*—A manufacturer will not be liable for tax on the sale of a taxable tire if the conditions of paragraph (a)(2) of this section are satisfied. In such a case, a buyer that provides an erroneous certificate described in paragraph (c)(2) of this section is liable for any tax imposed on the sale to which the certificate relates.

(2) *In general.*—The certificate referred to in paragraph (a)(2) of this section is a statement that is signed under penalties of perjury by a person with authority to bind the buyer, is in substantially the same form as the model certificate provided in paragraph (c)(3) of this section, and contains all information necessary to complete the model certificate. For purchasers that are not required to be registered under section 4222, the IRS may withdraw the right of a buyer of a taxable tire to provide a certificate under this section if the buyer uses the tires to which a certificate relates other than as stated in the certificate. The IRS may notify any manufacturer to whom the buyer has provided a certificate that the buyer's right to provide a certificate has been withdrawn. The certificate may be included as part of any business records normally used to document a sale.

(3) *Model certificate.*

Certificate
(To support the nontaxable sale of taxable tires used on intercity, local, and school buses)

The undersigned buyer of taxable tires ("Buyer") hereby certifies the following under penalties of perjury:

1. _____

_____

Manufacturer's name, address, employer identification number, and registration number

2. _____

_____

Buyer's name, address, employer identification number, and registration number

3. _____

Date and location of sale to Buyer

4. The taxable tire(s) listed below, by its (their) United States Department of Transportation identification number(s), will be used on intercity, local, and school buses.

5. Buyer understands that it must be prepared to establish, by evidence satisfactory to an examining agent, how each tire bought under this certificate was used.

6. Check here _____ if Buyer is not required to be registered with the Internal Revenue Service because Purchaser is a state or local government or the United States.

7. Buyer understands that Buyer may be liable for the section 6701 penalty (relating to aiding and abetting an understatement of tax liability) if this is an erroneous certification.

8. Buyer understands that the fraudulent use of this certificate may subject Buyer and all parties making any fraudulent use of this statement to a fine or imprisonment, or both, together with the costs of prosecution.

_____

Printed or typed name of person signing this certificate

_____

Title of person signing

_____

Signature and date signed

(d) *Effective/applicability date.*—This section applies on and after the date of publication of these regulations in the **Federal Register** as final regulations.

Communication Excise Tax: Toll Telephone Service: Distance

Communication Excise Tax: Toll Telephone Service: Distance Sensitivity.—Reg. §49.4252-0, relating to the definition of toll telephone service for purposes of the communications excise tax, is proposed (published in the Federal Register on April 1, 2003) (REG-141097-02).

☐ Par. 2. Section 49.4252-0 is added to read as follows:

§49.4252-0. Section 4252(b)(1); distance sensitivity.—(a) *In general.*—For a communications service to constitute toll telephone service described in section 4252(b)(1), the charge for the service need not vary with the distance of each individual communication.

(b) *Effective date.*—This section applies to amounts paid on and after the date of publication of these regulations in the Federal Register as final regulations. [Reg. §49.4252-0.]

Expatriate Health Plans: Issuers: Excepted Benefits

Expatriate Health Plans: Issuers: Excepted Benefits.—Amendments to Reg. §46.4377-1, relating to the rules for expatriate health plans, expatriate health plan issuers, and qualified expatriates under the Expatriate Health Coverage Clarification Act of 2014 (EHCCA), are proposed (published in the Federal Register on June 10, 2016) (REG-135702-15).

6. Section 46.4377-1 is amended by redesignating paragraph (c) as paragraph (d) and adding new paragraph (c) to read as follows:

§46.4377-1. Definitions and special rules.

* * *

(c) *Treatment of expatriate health plans.*—For policy years and plan years that end after January 1, 2017, the fees imposed by sections 4375 and 4376 do not apply to an expatriate health plan within the meaning of §54.9831-1(f)(3).

* * *

Excise Tax: Tractors, Trailers, Trucks, and Tires: Highway Vehicle: Definition

Excise Tax: Tractors, Trailers, Trucks, and Tires: Highway Vehicle: Definition.—Amendments to Reg. §41.4482(a)-1, relating to the excise taxes imposed on the sale of highway tractors, trailers, trucks, and tires, the use of heavy vehicles on the highway, and the definition of highway vehicle related to these and other taxes, are proposed (published in the Federal Register on March 31, 2016) (REG-103380-05).

Par. 2. Section 41.4482(a)-1(a)(2) is amended by removing the language "§48.4061(a)-1(d)" and adding "§48.0-5" in its place.

§41.4482(a)-1. Definition of highway motor vehicle.

REGISTRATION-REQUIRED OBLIGATIONS

Definition of Registered Form: Guidance

Definition of Registered Form: Guidance.—Amendments to Reg. §46.4701-1, providing guidance on the definitions of registration-required obligation and registered form, including guidance on the issuance of pass-through certificates and participation interests in registered form, are proposed (published in the Federal Register on September 19, 2017) (REG-125374-16).

Par. 16. Section 46.4701-1 is amended by:

1. Revising paragraphs (b)(3), (4), and (5).

2. Redesignating paragraph (e) as paragraph (e)(1).

3. Revising the paragraph heading of newly redesignated paragraph (e)(1).

4. Adding a new paragraph heading for paragraph (e).

5. Adding paragraph (e)(2).

The revisions and additions read as follows:

§46.4701-1. Tax on issuer of registration-required obligation not in registered form.

* * *

(b) * * *

(3) *Registration-required obligation.*—The term *registration-required obligation* has the same meaning as in section 163(f) and §1.163-5(a)(2)(i) of this chapter, except that the term does not include an obligation described in section 4701(b)(1)(B) or any obligation that is required to be registered under section 149(a), such as bonds that are tax-exempt under section 103. For purposes of determining whether an obligation is described in section 4701(b)(1)(B), the rules of §1.163-5(c) of this chapter apply.

(4) *Registered form.*—The term *registered form* has the same meaning as in §1.163-5(b) of this chapter.

(5) *Issuer.*—(i) *In general.*—Except as provided in paragraph (b)(5)(ii) of this section, the term *issuer* is the person whose interest deduction would be disallowed solely by reason of section 163(f)(1).

(ii) *Sponsor treated as issuer.*—A pass-through certificate (as defined in §1.163-5(a)(3)(i)(B) of this chapter), a participation interest described in §1.163-5(a)(3)(ii) of this chapter, or a regular interest in a REMIC, as defined in sections 860D and 860G and the regulations thereunder, is considered to be issued solely by the recipient of the proceeds from the issuance of the certificate or interest (the *sponsor*). The sponsor is therefore liable for any excise tax under section 4701 that may be imposed with reference to the principal amount of the pass-through certificate, participation interest, or regular interest.

* * *

(e) *Applicability date.*—(1) *In general.*—* * *

(2) *Exception.*—Notwithstanding paragraph (e)(1) of this section, paragraphs (b)(3), (4), and (5) of this section apply to obligations issued after March 18, 2012. For the rules that apply to obligations issued on or before March 18, 2012, see §46.4701-1 as contained in 26 CFR part 46, revised as of the date of the most recent annual revision.

PRIVATE FOUNDATIONS

Below-Market Loans

Below-Market Loans: Interest.—Reproduced below is the text of a proposed amendment of Reg. §53.4941(d)-2, relating to the tax treatment of both lender and borrower in certain below-market interest rate loan transactions (published in the Federal Register on August 20, 1985).

* * *

☐ Par. 10. Section 53.4941(d)-2 is amended by revising paragraph (c)(2) to read as follows:

§53.4941(d)-2. Specific acts of self-dealing.—

* * *

(c) Loans. * * *

(2) *Loans without interest.*—Subparagraph (1) of this paragraph shall not apply to the lending of money or other extension of credit by a disqualified person to a private foundation if the loan or other extension of credit is without interest (determined without regard to foregone interest described in section 7872) or other charge.

EXCISE TAX BASED ON INVESTMENT INCOME OF PRIVATE COLLEGES AND UNIVERSITIES

Private Colleges and Universities: Investment Income: Excise Tax

Private Colleges and Universities: Investment Income: Excise Tax.—Reg. §53.4968-1, determining the excise tax applicable to the net investment income of certain private colleges and universities, as provided by the Tax Cuts and Jobs Act, is proposed (published in the Federal Register on July 3, 2019) (REG-106877-18).

Par. 2. Section 53.4968-1 is added to read as follows:

§53.4968-1. Excise tax based on investment income of certain private colleges and universities.—(a) *Excise tax on the investment income of certain private colleges and universities.*—(1) *In general.*—For taxable years beginning after December 31, 2017, section 4968 imposes a tax equal to 1.4 percent of the net investment income (as defined in section 4968(c) and paragraph (b) of this section) of an applicable educational institution (as defined in section 4968(b)(1) and paragraph (a)(2) of this section).

(2) *Applicable educational institution.*—Under section 4968(b)(1) and for purposes of this section, the term *applicable educational institution* means any eligible educational institution as defined in section 25A(f)(2) and §1.25A-2(b) of this chapter—

(i) Which had at least 500 tuition-paying students attending the institution during the preceding taxable year;

(ii) More than 50 percent of the tuition-paying students attending the institution are located in the United States;

(iii) Which is not described in the first sentence of section 511(a)(2)(B) (relating to state colleges and universities); and

(iv) The aggregate fair market value of the assets of which at the end of such preceding taxable year (other than those assets that are used directly in carrying out the institution's exempt purpose) is at least $500,000 per student attending the institution.

(3) *Student.*—(i) *In general.*—For purposes of section 4968 and paragraph (a) of this section, the term *student* means a person enrolled in a degree, certification, or other program (including a program of study abroad approved for credit by the eligible institution at which such student is enrolled) leading to a recognized educational credential at an institution, and who is not enrolled in an elementary or secondary school.

(ii) *Tuition-paying.*—(A) *In general.*—For purposes of section 4968 and paragraph (a) of this section, the term *tuition-paying* means the payment of any tuition or fees required for the enrollment or attendance of a student for a course of instruction at an educational institution. The term *tuition-paying* does not include payment for supplies or equipment required during a specific course once a student is enrolled in and attending the course or the payment of room and board or other personal living expenses.

(B) *Treatment of a comprehensive or bundled fee.*—If a student is required to pay a fee (such as a comprehensive fee or a bundled fee) to an educational institution that combines charges for tuition with charges for personal expenses such as room and board, the student is a tuition-paying student.

(C) *Scholarships and work study programs operated directly by the applicable educational institution.*—Whether a student is tuition-paying is determined after taking into account any scholarships provided directly by the educational institution and any work study programs operated directly by the institution. Scholarship payments provided by third parties, even if administered by the institution, are considered payments of tuition on behalf of the student. Accordingly, a student will be considered a tuition-paying student if payment of tuition or a fee is required for the enrollment or attendance of the student for courses of instruction after the application of any scholarships offered directly by the institution or work study program operated directly by the institution.

(iii) *Located in the United States.*—For purposes of section 4968 and paragraph (a) of this section, the term *located in the United States* refers to the location of a student. A student is considered to have been located in the United States if the student resided in the United States for at least a portion of the time the student attended the institution during the applicable educational institution's preceding taxable year.

(iv) *Full-time/part-time students.*—For purposes of section 4968 and paragraph (a) of this section, the number of students of an educational institution (including for purposes of determining the number of students at a particular location) is based on the daily average number of full-time students attending such institution (with part-time students taken into account on a full-time student equivalent basis). The standards for determining part-time students, full-time students, full-time equivalents, and daily average are determined by each educational institution. However, the standards may not be lower than the applicable standards established by the Department of Education under the Higher Education Act of 1965 (20 U.S.C. 1088).

(4) *Assets used directly in carrying out an institution's exempt purpose.*—(i) *In general.*—For purposes of section 4968 and this paragraph (a)(4), an asset is used directly in carrying out an educational institution's exempt purpose only if the asset is actually used by the institution in carrying out its exempt purpose. Whether an asset is used directly by the institution to carry out its exempt purpose must be determined based on all the facts and circumstances. If property is used for an exempt purpose and for other purposes, and the exempt use represents 95 percent or more of the total use, the property is considered to be used exclusively for an exempt purpose. If the exempt use of such property represents less than 95 percent of the total use, the institution must make a reasonable allocation between such exempt and nonexempt uses.

(ii) *Illustrations.*—Examples of assets that are used directly in carrying out an institution's exempt purpose include, but are not limited to, the following—

(A) Administrative assets, such as office equipment and supplies used by the institution directly in the administration of its exempt activities;

(B) Real estate or the portion of any building used by the institution directly in its exempt activities;

(C) Physical property such as paintings or other works of art owned by the institution which are on public display, fixtures and equipment in classrooms, research facilities and related equipment which under the facts and circumstances serve a useful purpose in the conduct of the institution's exempt activities;

(D) The reasonable cash balances necessary to cover current administrative expenses and other normal and current disbursements directly connected with the educational institution's exempt activities. For purposes of this paragraph (a)(4)(ii)(D), the portion of an educational institution's actual cash balances at the end of a year that does not exceed 1.5 percent of the fair market value of the institution's non-charitable use assets, determined without regard to any reduction for reasonable cash balances, will be deemed to be a reasonable cash balance; and

(E) Any property the educational institution leases to other persons at no cost (or at a nominal rent) to the lessee in furtherance of the institution's exempt purposes.

(iii) *Exceptions.*—The following assets are examples of assets not used directly in carrying out an institution's exempt purpose—

(A) Assets that are held for the production of income or for investment (for example, stocks, bonds, interest-bearing notes, endowment funds, or leased real estate), even if the income from such assets is used to carry out such exempt purpose; and

(B) Property (such as offices) used for the purpose of managing the institution's endowment funds.

(iv) *Valuation of assets not used directly in carrying out an institution's exempt purpose.*—(A) *In general.*—The valuation of assets not used directly in carrying out an institution's exempt purpose is determined under the rules of section 4942(e) and §53.4942(a)-2(c)(4), as modified by paragraph (a)(4)(iv)(B) of this section.

(B) *Special rules.*—In applying the rules of §53.4942(a)-2(c)(4), an educational institution must—

(1) Substitute "educational institution" for "private foundation" or "foundation" every place they appear; and

(2) Make such adjustments as are reasonable and necessary to obtain the fair market value of any and all assets as of the last day of the preceding taxable year, rather than any other times permitted or required by §53.4942(a)-2(c)(4).

(b) *Net investment income.*—(1) *In general.*—An applicable educational institution described in paragraph (a)(2) of this section is subject to the 1.4 percent tax on its net investment income, and, as described in paragraph (c) of this section, also on certain amounts of net investment income of certain related organizations, for the taxable year.

(2) *Calculation of net investment income.*—For purposes of paragraph (b)(1) of this section, net investment income will be determined under the rules of section 4940(c) and §53.4940-1(c) through (f), as modified by paragraph (b)(3) of this section.

(3) *Special rules.*—In applying §53.4940-1(c) through (f):

(i) Substitute "Applicable educational institution" for "private foundation" and "foundation" each place they appear.

(ii) Section 53.4940-1(d)(3), relating to certain distributions in redemption of stock, does not apply.

(iii) Substitute "December 31, 2017" for "December 31, 1969" each place it appears.

(iv) If an applicable educational institution held an interest in a partnership (including through one or more tiers of partnerships) on December 31, 2017, and continuously thereafter, and the partnership held assets on December 31, 2017 and continuously thereafter to the date of disposition, the partnership's basis in its assets with respect to the applicable educational institution for purposes of determining the applicable educational institution's share of gain upon sale or disposition of the assets is not less than the fair market value of such asset on December 31, 2017, plus or minus all adjustments as provided under §53.4940-1(f)(2)(i) after December 31, 2017, and before the date of disposition. To avail itself of this special partnership basis rule, an institution must obtain documentation from the partnership to substantiate the basis used.

(v) For purposes of §53.4940-1(f), overall net losses from sales or other dispositions of property by one related organization (or by the applicable educational institution) reduce (but not below zero) overall net gains from such sales or other dispositions by other related organizations (or by the applicable educational institution).

(c) *Related organizations.*—(1) *Definition of related organization.*—(i) *In general.*—The term "related organization" means, with respect to an applicable educational institution, any organization which—

(A) Controls, or is controlled by, such institution;

(B) Is controlled by one or more persons which also control such institution; or

(C) Is a supported organization (as defined in section 509(f)(3)) or a supporting organization (as described in section 509(a)(3)) during the taxable year with respect to such institution.

(ii) *Control.*—The term control generally means—

(A) *Stock corporation.*—In the case of a corporation, ownership (by vote or value) of more than 50 percent of the stock of the corporation;

(B) *Partnership.*—In the case of a partnership, ownership of more than 50 percent of the profits interests or capital interests in such partnership; or

(C) *Trust.*—In the case of a trust with beneficial interests, ownership of more than 50 percent of the beneficial interests in the trust.

(D) *Nonstock organization.*—In the case of a nonprofit organization or other organization without owners or persons having beneficial interests (nonstock organization), including a governmental entity, control means that—

(1) More than 50 percent of the directors or trustees of the applicable educational institution or nonstock organization are either representatives of, or are directly or indirectly controlled by, the other entity; or

(2) More than 50 percent of the directors or trustees of the nonstock organization are either representatives of, or are directly or indirectly controlled by, one or more persons that control the applicable educational institution. For purposes of this paragraph (c)(1)(ii)(D)(2), a "representative" means a trustee, director, agent, or employee, and control includes the power to remove a trustee or director and designate a new trustee or director.

(iii) *Constructive ownership.*—The principles of section 318 apply for purposes of determining ownership of stock in a corporation, and similar principles apply for purposes of determining ownership of interest in any other entity.

Reg. §53.4968-1(c)(1)(iii)

(2) *Assets and net investment income of related organizations.*—(i) *In general.*—For purposes of determining the aggregate fair market value of the assets and net investment income of an educational institution, the assets and net investment income of any related organization are treated as the assets and net investment income, respectively, of the institution unless an exception provided in paragraph (c)(2)(ii) of this section applies.

(ii) *Exceptions.*—For purposes of section 4968 and this paragraph (c)(2)—

(A) *No amount taken into account with respect to more than one educational institution.*—In determining the aggregate fair market value of the assets and net investment income of an educational institution, assets and net investment income of a related organization are not taken into account with respect to more than one educational institution. Thus, in any case in which an organization is a related organization with respect to more than one educational institution, the assets and net investment income of the related organization must be allocated between the educational institutions being supported by the related organization. Such allocation must be made in a reasonable manner, taking into account all facts and circumstances, and must be used consistently across all related organizations.

(B) *Not intended or available for the use or benefit of the educational institution.*—(1) *In general.*—Except as provided by paragraph (c)(2)(ii)(B)(3) of this section, for purposes of determining the aggregate fair market value of the assets and net investment income of an educational institution, the assets and net investment income of a related organization are taken into account as assets and net investment income of the educational institution unless the assets and net investment are not intended or available for the use and benefit of the educational institution.

(2) *Determining whether assets and net investment income of a related organization are intended or available for the use and benefit of an educational institution.*—Assets and net investment income of a related organization are intended or available for the use and benefit of an educational institution if such assets and net investment income are specifically earmarked or restricted for the benefit of, or are otherwise fairly attributable to, the educational institution. Conversely, assets and net investment income of a related organization are not intended or available for the use and benefit of an educational institution if such assets and net investment income are specifically earmarked or restricted for another entity or for unrelated purposes or are otherwise not fairly attributable to the educational institution. The assets and net investment income of a related organization must be allocated between those intended or available for the use and benefit of an educational institution and those not intended or not available for the use and benefit of an educational institution. Such allocation must be made in a reasonable manner, taking into account all facts and circumstances, and must be used consistently across all related organizations.

(3) *Organizations controlled by the institution or described in section 509(a)(3) with respect to the institution for the taxable year.*—(i) *In general.*—If a related organization is controlled, as defined in paragraph (c)(1) of this section, by an educational institution, or is a supporting organization described in section 509(a)(3) with respect to the educational institution, the assets and net investment income of the related organization are taken into account as assets and net investment income of the educational institution regardless of whether the assets and net investment income are earmarked or restricted for the benefit of, or otherwise fairly attributable to, the educational institution and even if they are specifically earmarked or restricted for another entity or for unrelated purposes or are otherwise not fairly attributable to the educational institution, subject to paragraph (c)(2)(ii)(A) of this section.

(ii) *Special rule for Type III supporting organizations with respect to such institution as of December 31, 2017.*—An educational institution with a related organization that was a Type III supporting organization with respect to the educational institution on December 31, 2017, takes into account only the assets and net investment income of such Type III supporting organization that are intended or available for the use and benefit of, or otherwise fairly attributable to, the educational institution, as described in paragraph (c)(2)(ii)(B)(2) of this section. An educational institution may determine whether the assets and net investment income of such Type III supporting organization are intended or available for the use and benefit of, or otherwise fairly attributable to, the educational institution using any reasonable method. A method treating all the distributions received from such Type III supporting organization as net investment income of the school each year is deemed to be reasonable. Similarly, a method using the distributions received from the Type III supporting organization to calculate the percentage of the Type III supporting organization's total net income that was distributed to the educational institution, and then using the same percentage to calculate the value of the underlying assets of the Type III supporting organization that are intended or available for the use and benefit of the educational institution each year, will be deemed to be reasonable.

(d) *Applicability date.*—The rules of this section apply to taxable years beginning after the date of publication of the Treasury decision adopting these rules as final regulations in the **Federal Register**. A taxpayer may rely on these regulations for taxable years beginning before publication of final regulations. [Reg. § 53.4968-1.]

QUALIFIED PENSION, ETC., PLANS

Employees' Trusts: Minimum Funding Requirements

Employees' Trusts: Minimum Funding Requirements: Minimum Funding Excise Taxes.—Reproduced below are the texts of proposed Reg. §§ 54.4971-1—54.4971-3, relating to the minimum funding requirements for employee pension benefit plans, and to excise taxes for failure to meet the minimum funding standards (published in the Federal Register on December 1, 1982).

☐ Par. 8. The Pension Excise Tax Regulations, 26 CFR Part 54, are amended by adding in the appropriate place the following new sections:

§ 54.4971-1. General rules relating to excise tax on failure to meet minimum funding standards.—(a) [Reserved]

(b) [Reserved]

(c) *Additional tax.*—Section 4971(b) imposes an excise tax in any case in which an initial tax is imposed under section 4971(a) on an accumulated funding deficiency and the accumulated funding deficiency is not corrected within the taxable period (as defined in section 4971(c)(3)). The additional tax is 100 percent of the accumulated funding deficiency to the extent not corrected.

(d) [Reserved]

(e) *Definition of taxable period.*—(1) *In general.*—For purposes of any accumulated funding deficiency, the term "taxable period" means the period beginning with the end of the plan year in which there is an accumulated funding deficiency and ending on the earlier of:

(i) The date of mailing of a notice of deficiency under section 6212 with respect to the tax imposed by section 4971(a), or

(ii) The date on which the tax imposed by section 4971(a) is assessed.

(2) *Special rule.*—Where a notice of deficiency referred to in paragraph (e)(1)(i) of this section is not mailed because a waiver of the restrictions on assessment and collection of a deficiency has been accepted or because the deficiency is paid, the date of filing of the waiver or the date of such payment, respectively, shall be treated as the end of the taxable period. [Reg. § 54.4971-1.]

§ 54.4971-2. Operational rules and special definitions relating to excise tax on failure to meet minimum funding standards.—(a) *Correction.*—(1) *General rule.*—To correct an accumulated funding deficiency for a plan year, a contribution must be made to the plan that reduces the deficiency, as of the end of that plan year, to zero. To reduce the deficiency to zero, the contribution must include interest at the plan's actuarial valuation rate for the period between the end of that plan year and the date of the contribution.

(2) *Corrective effect of certain retroactive amendments.*—Certain retroactive plan amendments that meet the requirements of section 412(c)(8) may reduce an accumulated funding deficiency for a plan year to zero.

(3) *Optional corrective actions when employers withdraw from certain plans.*—See § 54.4971-3(e)(2) for correcting deficiencies attributable to certain withdrawing employers.

(b) *No deduction.*—Under section 275(a)(6), no deduction is allowed for a tax imposed under section 4971(a) or (b).

(c) *Waiver of imposition of tax.*—Under section 3002(b) of the Employee Retirement Income Security Act of 1974 (ERISA), the Commissioner may waive the imposition of the additional tax under section 4971(b) in appropriate cases. This authority does not extend to the imposition of the initial tax under section 4971(a).

(d) *Notification of the Secretary of Labor.*—(1) *In general.*—Except as provided in paragraph (d)(2) of this section, before issuing a notice of deficiency with respect to the tax imposed under section 4971(a) or (b), the Commissioner must notify the Secretary of Labor that the Internal Revenue Service proposes to assess the tax. The purpose of this notice is to give the Secretary of Labor a reasonable opportunity to obtain a correction of the accumulated funding deficiency or to comment on the imposition of the tax. (See section 4971(d) and section 3002(b) of ERISA.) The Commissioner may issue a notice of deficiency with respect to the tax imposed under section 4971(a) or (b) 60 days after the mailing of the notice of proposed deficiency to the Secretary of Labor. Any action taken by the Secretary of Labor will not affect the imposition of the 5-percent initial tax imposed by section 4971(a). See paragraph (c) of this section, however, concerning the Commissioner's authority to waive the 100-percent additional tax imposed by section 4971(b).

(2) *Jeopardy assessments.*—The Commissioner may determine that the assessment or collection of the tax imposed under section 4971(a) or (b) will be jeopardized by delay. If the Commissioner makes this determination, the Internal Revenue Service may immediately assess a deficiency under section 6861 without prior notice to the Secretary of Labor. Abatement of the assessment may be granted upon correction of the deficiency. See section 6861 and §301.6861-1 concerning abatement of assessments.

(e) *Request for investigation with respect to tax imposed under section 4971.*—Under section 3002(b) of ERISA, upon receiving a written request from the Secretary of Labor or from the Pension Benefit Guaranty Corporation, the Commissioner will investigate whether the taxes under section 4971(a) and (b) should be imposed on any employer referred to in the request. [Reg. §54.4971-2.]

§54.4971-3. Rules relating to liability for excise tax on failure to meet minimum funding standards.—(a) *General rule.*—(1) *One employer.*—An excise tax imposed under section 4971(a) or (b) with respect to a plan to or under which only one employer is responsible for contributing must be paid by that employer.

(2) *More than one employer.*—An excise tax imposed under section 4971(a) or (b) with respect to a plan to or under which more than one employer is responsible for contributing must be allocated between these employers under paragraph (b) of this section.

(3) *Related employers.*—Related corporations, trades, and businesses described in section 414(b) and (c) are "related employers" for purposes of this section. All related employers are treated as one employer for purposes of paragraph (b) of this section. The tax liability of each such related employer is determined separately by allocations under paragraph (c) of this section.

(b) *Allocation of tax liability.*—(1) *In general.*—Section 413(b)(6) and (c)(5) and section 414(b) and (c) discuss liability for tax under section 4971(a) or (b) with respect to collectively bargained plans and plans of more than one employer. Each employer's tax liability relates to an accumulated funding deficiency under a plan. However, the funding deficiency is determined with respect to a plan as a whole, not with respect to individual employers adopting the plan. Therefore, the deficiency must be allocated among employers adopting or maintaining the plan to determine their individual liability for a tax. Except as otherwise provided in paragraphs (c) and (d) of this section, this liability must be determined in a reasonable manner that is not inconsistent with the requirements of this paragraph (b).

(2) *Failure of individual employer to meet obligation under plan or contract.*—(i) *Single delinquency.*—An accumulated funding deficiency may be attributable, in whole or in part, to a delinquent contribution, that is, the failure of an individual employer to contribute to the plan as required by its terms or by the terms of a collectively bargained agreement pursuant to which the plan is maintained. To the extent that an accumulated funding deficiency is attributable to a delinquent contribution, the delinquent employer is solely liable for the resulting tax imposed under section 4971(a) or (b).

(ii) *Multiple delinquency.*—If an accumulated funding deficiency is attributable to more than one delinquent employer, liability for tax is allocated in proportion to each employer's share of the delinquency.

(iii) *Further liability.*—A delinquent employer may also be liable for the portion of tax determined by an allocation under paragraph (b)(3) of this section.

(3) *Failure of employers in the aggregate to avoid accumulated funding deficiency.*—(i) *Aggregate failure.*—An accumulated funding deficiency may be attributable, in whole or in part, to the failure of employers in the aggregate to contribute to the plan a sufficient amount to avoid an accumulated funding deficiency. To the extent that a deficiency for a plan year is not attributable to a delinquent contribution for that year, the deficiency is attributable to an aggre-

gate failure described in this subparagraph (3). Thus, for example, if 10 percent of the deficiency results from a delinquent contribution described in paragraph (b)(2) of this section, 90 percent results from failures described in this subparagraph (3). The allocation of tax liability to an individual employer for such an aggregate failure to avoid an accumulated funding deficiency is made under paragraph (b)(3)(ii) of this section.

(ii) *Allocation rule for aggregate failure.*—An individual employer's liability for tax attributable to an aggregate failure described in this subparagraph (3) is the product of the tax attributable to the aggregate failure times a fraction. The numerator of this fraction is the contribution the employer is required to make for the plan year under the plan or under the collectively bargained agreement pursuant to which the plan is maintained. The denominator of this fraction is the total contribution all employers are required to make for the plan year under the plan or under the collectively bargained agreement pursuant to which the plan is maintained. Thus, for example, if an employer is responsible for one-half of a plan's required contribution and 90 percent of an accumulated funding deficiency arises under this subparagraph (3), that employer is liable under this subparagraph (3) for 45 percent of the tax under section 4971(a) or (b), as the case may be, with respect to that deficiency.

(c) *Allocation rules for related employers.*—(1) *In general.*—To the extent that an accumulated funding deficiency is attributable to related employers, those employers are jointly and severally liable for an excise tax imposed under section 4971(a) or (b) with respect to that deficiency.

(2) *Plans not solely maintained by related employers.*—A plan that is not solely maintained by related employers first allocates tax liability under paragraph (b) of this section by treating the related employers as a single employer. The related employers are jointly and severally liable for the tax liability so allocated to any of the related employers.

(d) *Effect of plan termination on employer's tax liability.*—No tax is imposed under section 4971(a) for years after the plan year in which a plan terminates. An employer is liable only for unpaid 5-percent initial taxes under section 4971(a) and any additional tax which has been imposed under section 4971(b).

(e) *Effect of employer withdrawal from plan.*—(1) *General rule.*—An employer that withdraws from a plan remains liable for tax imposed with respect to the portion of an accumulated funding deficiency attributable to that employer for plan years before withdrawal.

(2) *Years subsequent to withdrawal.*—For any plan year with an accumulated funding deficiency, the tax is allocated between the employers responsible for contributing to the plan for that plan year in accordance with paragraphs (b) or (c) even if the deficiency in that year is attributable to an uncorrected deficiency from a prior year.

(f) *Examples.*—The provisions of paragraphs (a)-(c) of this section may be illustrated by the following examples:

Example (1). Employers W, X, Y and Z maintain a collectively bargained plan. Y and Z are related employers under paragraph (a)(3). W and X are each unrelated to any other employer. For plan year 1982, the employers are obligated, under the collectively bargained agreement, to contribute the following amount: W —$10x; X —$20x; Y —$30x; Z —$40x. As of the last date for making plan contributions, there is a delinquency of $10x attributable to W and $30x attributable to Y. Under paragraph (b)(2)(ii), W is liable for 10/40 of the tax imposed for 1982. Under paragraphs (b)(2)(ii) and (c)(2), Y and Z are jointly and severally liable for 30/40 of the tax.

Example (2). Assume the same facts as in Example (1). For plan year 1983, the minimum funding requirement is $145x. Contributions totaling $110x are made for 1983 in the amounts provided by the agreement: W —$15x; X —$20x; Y —$30x; Z —$45x. Under paragraph (b)(3)(i) of this section, there is an aggregate failure to avoid an accumulated funding deficiency, as the minimum funding requirement exceeds plan contributions by $35x. The tax attributable to the aggregate failure is allocated under paragraphs (b)(3)(ii) and (c)(2) as follows: W is liable for 15/110, or 13.6 percent of the tax; X is liable for 20/110, or 18.2 percent. Y and Z are jointly and severally liable for 75/110, or 68.2 percent.

Example (3). Assume the same facts as in Example (1). For 1984, the minimum funding requirement is $210x and employers are obligated under the agreement to contribute $130x: W —$15x; X —$25x; Y —$30x; Z —$60x. There is a funding deficiency due in part to a delinquency attributable to Y. Under paragraph (b)(3)(i), the remaining deficiency is an aggregate failure. Under paragraphs (b)(2)(i) and (c), Y and Z are jointly and severally liable for the 23 percent (30/130) of the excise tax attributable to the delinquency. The remaining 76.9 percent of the tax is allocated as follows: W —15/130 (11.5 percent) of the 76.9 percent; X —25/130 (19.2 percent) of the aggregate failure tax; Y and Z, combined under paragraph (c)(2)—90/130 (69.2 percent) of the aggregate failure tax. Y and Z are jointly and severally liable for approximately 76.3 percent of the total tax under section 4971 for the year: 23.1 percent attributable to Y 's delinquency and

53.2 percent (69.2 × 76.9 attributable to the aggregate failure under paragraph (b)(3)). [Reg. § 54.4971-3.]

Individual Retirement Plans: Simplified Employee Pensions

Individual Retirement Plans: Simplified Employee Pensions.—Reproduced below are the texts of proposed Reg. § 54.4973-1 and a proposed amendment of Reg. § 54.4974-1, relating to individual retirement plans and simplified employee pensions (published in the Federal Register on July 14, 1981).

* * *

☐ Par. 16. There is inserted in the appropriate place the following new section:

§ 54.4973-1. Excess contributions to certain accounts, contract and bonds.—(a) *In general.*—Under section 4973, in the case of an individual retirement account (described in section 408(a)), an individual retirement annuity (described in section 408(b)), a custodial account treated as an annuity contract under section 403(b)(7)(A), or an individual retirement bond described in section 409, a tax equal to 6 percent of the amount of excess contributions (as defined in paragraph (c) or (d) of this section) to such account, annuity or bond is imposed.

(b) *Individual liable for tax.*—(1) *Individual retirement plans.*—In the case of an individual retirement account, individual retirement annuity for individual retirement bond the tax imposed by section 4973 shall be paid by the individual to whom a deduction is or would be allowed with respect to contributions for the taxable year under section 219 (determined without regard to subsection (b)(1) thereof) or section 220 (determined without regard to subsection (b)(1) thereof), whichever is appropriate.

(2) *Custodial accounts under section 403(b)(7)(A).*—In the case of a custodial account treated as an annuity contract under section 403(b)(7)(A), the tax imposed by section 4973 shall be paid by the individual for whose benefit the account is maintained.

(c) *Excess contributions defined for individual retirement plans.*—For purposes of section 4973, in the case of individual retirement accounts, individual retirement annuities, or individual retirement bonds, the term "excess contributions" means the sum of—

(1) The excess (if any) of—

(i) The amount contributed for the taxable year to the accounts or for the annuities or bonds (other than a valid rollover contribution described in section 402(a)(5), 402(a)(7), 403(a)(4), 403(b)(8), 408(d)(3) or 409(b)(3)(C)), over

(ii) The amount allowable as a deduction under section 219 or 220 for such contributions, and

(2) The amount determined under this subsection for the preceding taxable year, reduced by the sum of—

(i) The distributions out of the account for the taxable year which were included in the gross income of the payee under section 408(d)(1),

(ii) The distributions out of the account for the taxable year to which section 408(d)(5) applies, and

(iii) The excess (if any) of the maximum amount allowable as a deduction under section 219 or 220 for the taxable year over the amount contributed (determined without regard to sections 219(c)(5) and 220(c)(6)) to the accounts or for the annuities or bonds for the taxable year. For purposes of this paragraph, any contribution which is distributed from the individual retirement account, individual retirement annuity, or bond in a distribution to which section 408(d)(4) applies shall be treated as an amount not contributed.

(d) *Excess contributions defined for custodial accounts under section 403(b)(7)(A).*—For purposes of section 4973, in the case of a custodial account referred to in paragraph (b)(2) of this section, the term "excess contributions" means the sum of—

(1) The excess (if any) of the amount contributed for the taxable year to such account (other than a valid rollover contribution described in section 403(b)(8), 408(d)(3)(A)(iii), or 409(b)(3)(C)), over the lesser of the amount excludable from gross income under section 403(b) or the amount permitted to be contributed under the limitations contained in section 415 (or under whichever such section is applicable, if only one is applicable), and

(2) The amount determined under this subsection for the preceding taxable year, reduced by—

(i) The excess (if any) of the lesser of (A) the amount excludable from gross income under section 403(b) or (B) the amount permitted to be contributed under the limitations contained in section 415 over the amount contributed to the account for the taxable year (or under whichever such section is applicable, if only one is applicable), and

(ii) The sum of the distributions out of the account (for the taxable year) which are included in gross income under section 72(e).

(e) *Special rules.*—(1) The tax imposed by section 4973 cannot exceed 6 percent of the value (determined as of the close of the individual's taxable year) of the account, annuity or bond.

(2) In the case of an endowment contract described in section 408(b), the tax imposed by section 4973 is not applicable to any amount allocable under § 1.219-1(b)(3) to the cost of life insurance under the contract.

(f) *Examples.*—The provisions of this section may be illustrated by the following examples:

Example (1). On April 20, 1979, A, a single individual, establishes an individual retirement account (IRA) and contributes $1,500. On January 11, 1980, A determines he has compensation for 1979 within the meaning of section 219(c) and the regulations thereafter of $8,000. Under section 219, the maximum amount allowable as a deduction for retirement savings available to A is $1,200. On April 15, 1980, A files his income tax return for 1979 taking a deduction of $1,200 for his contribution to his IRA, and as of such date there had been no distribution from the IRA. Under section 4973, A would have $300 of excess contribution in his account for 1979 [($1,500 – $1,200) + 0] and A would be liable for an excise tax of $18 on such excess contribution.

Example (2). Assume the same facts as in Example (1). Assume further that on July 1, 1980, A contributes $1,500 to his account. On January 9, 1981, A determines that he has compensation for 1980 of $12,000. Under section 219, the maximum amount allowable to A as a deduction for retirement savings is $1,500 for 1980. On April 15, 1981, A files his income tax return for 1980 taking a deduction of $1,500 for his contribution to his IRA. As of such date, there had been no distribution from the account. Under section 4973, A would have $300 of excess contributions in his IRA for 1980 [($1,500 – $1,500) + ($300 – $0)] and would be liable for an excise tax of $18 on such excess contribution.

Example (3). Assume the same facts as in Examples (1) and (2). Assume further that on July 1, 1981, A contributes $1,000 to his account. On January 9, 1982, A determines that he has compensation for 1981 of $15,000. Under section 219, the maximum amount allowable as a deduction to A as a deduction for retirement savings is $1,500 for 1981. On April 15, 1982, A files his income tax return for 1981 taking a deduction of $1,000 for his 1981 contribution to his IRA and an additional deduction of $300 under section 219(c)(5). A will have no excess contributions in his IRA for 1981 because he made no excess contributions for 1981 and the previous year's excess contribution has been eliminated by the underutilization (section 4973(b)(2)(C)) of 1981's allowable contribution.

Example (4). Assume the same facts as in Examples (1) and (2). Assume further that on July 1, 1981, A contributes $1,500 to his account. On December 1, 1981, A withdraws $300 from his IRA. On January 9, 1982, A determines that he has compensation for 1981 of $15,000. Under section 219, the maximum amount allowable as a deduction to A as a deduction for retirement savings is $1,500 for 1981. On April 15, 1982, A files his income tax return for 1981 taking a deduction of $1,500 for his 1981 contribution to his IRA. A will have no excess contributions in his IRA for 1981 because he made no excess contributions for 1981 and the previous year's excess contribution has been eliminated in a distribution described in section 408(d)(5).

Example (5). On February 1, 1979, H, an individual, establishes an IRA for himself and one for his nonworking spouse W. He contributes $875 to his account and $775 to his wife's account. On January 31, 1980, H determines that he has compensation for 1979 within the meaning of section 220(c) and the regulations thereunder of $20,000. Under section 220(b)(1), the maximum amount allowable as a deduction for retirement savings to A is $1,550. On April 15, 1980, H files a joint income tax return for 1979 and takes a deduction of $1,550 for his contribution to the IRA of himself and his spouse. As of such date, there had been no distribution from either IRA. Under section 4973, H would have $100 of excess contributions in his account for 1979 [($1,650 – $1,550) + 0] and H would be liable for an excise tax of $6 on such excess contribution.

Example (6). Assume the same facts as in Example (5). Assume further that on June 1, 1980, H contributes $875 to his account and $875 to his wife's account. On January 31, 1981, H determines that he has compensation for 1980 within the meaning of section 220(c) and the regulations thereunder of $20,000. Under section 220(b)(1), the maximum amount allowable as a deduction for retirement savings is $1,750. On April 15, 1981, H files his income tax return for 1980 taking a deduction of $1,750 for his contribution to the individual retirement account of himself and his wife. As of such date, there had been no distribution from either account. Under section 4973, H would have $100 of excess contributions in his account for 1980 and would be liable for an excise tax of $6 for such excess contribution.

Example (7). Assume the same facts as in Example (5). Assume further that on June 1, 1980, A contributes $1,000 to his account and nothing to his wife's account. On January 31, 1981, A determines that he has compensation for 1980 within the meaning of section 219(c) of $22,000. On April 15, 1981, H files his income tax return for 1980 and takes a $1,000 deduction under section 219(a) for the 1980 contribution to his IRA and a $100 deduction under section 219(c)(5) for the

1979 excess contribution. Under section 4973, H would have $0 excess contributions for 1980 because the previous year's excess contribution has been eliminated under section 4973(b)(2)(C).

Example (8). On March 1, 1979, a custodial account under section 403(b)(7)(A) is established for the benefit of T who is otherwise eligible to have such an account established and a contribution of $7,000 is made to such account by A's employer which is a tax-exempt organization described in section 501(c)(3). The amount excludable from T's gross income in 1979 under section 403(b) is $4,000 and the amount permitted to be contributed for 1979 under section 415 is $5,000. Under section 4973, T would have an excess contribution of $3,000 [($7,000 − $4,000) + 0] in his account for 1979 and would be liable for an excise tax of $180. [Reg. § 54.4973-1.]

☐ Par. 17. A new paragraph (d) is added to § 54.4974-1 to read as follows.

§ 54.4974-1. Excise tax on accumulations in individual retirement accounts or annuities.—

* * *

(d) *Waiver of tax in certain cases.—*(1) *In general.—*If the payee described in section 4974(a) establishes to the satisfaction of the Commissioner that—

(i) The shortfall described in section 4974(a) in the amount distributed during any taxable year was due to reasonable error, and

(ii) Reasonable steps are being taken to remedy the shortfall, the tax imposed by section 4974(a) may be waived.

(2) *Reasonable error.—*Examples of reasonable error leading to an underdistribution include: erroneous advice from the sponsoring organization or other pension advisors or organizations which misled the payee, attempts by the payee to apply the required formula which led to a miscalculation, or misunderstanding of the formula.

* * *

Employee Trusts: Effective Dates

Employee Trusts: Tax Reform Act of 1984: Effective Dates.—Temporary Reg. §§ 54.4976-1T and 54.4978-1T are also proposed as final regulations and, when adopted, would become Reg. §§ 54.4976-1 and 54.4978-1 (published in the Federal Register on February 4, 1986).

§ 54.4976-1. Questions and answers relating to taxes with respect to welfare benefit funds.

§ 54.4978-1. Questions and answers relating to the tax on certain dispositions by employee stock ownership plans and certain cooperatives.

Fringe Benefits: Taxability

Fringe Benefits: Taxability.—Reg. § 54.4977-1T, relating to the treatment of taxable and nontaxable fringe benefits, is proposed (published in the Federal Register on January 7, 1985) (LR-216-84).

§ 54.4977-1. Questions and answers relating to the election concerning lines of business in existence on January 1, 1984.

Qualified Plans: Automatic Contribution Arrangements

Qualified Plans: Automatic Contribution Arrangements.—Amendments to Reg. § 54.4979-1, relating to automatic contribution arrangements allowed by certain qualified plans, are proposed (published in the Federal Register on November 8, 2007) (REG-133300-07).

☐ Par. 15. Section 54.4979-1(c)(1) is amended by:
Revising the first and second sentences of paragraph (c)(1) to read as follows:

§ 54.4979-1. Excise tax on certain excess contributions and excess aggregate contributions.

* * *

(c) *No tax when excess distributed within 2 1/2 months of close of year or additional employer contributions made.—*(1) *General rule.—*No tax is imposed under this section on any excess contribution or excess aggregate contribution, as the case may be, to the extent the contribution (together with any income allocable thereto) is corrected before the close of the first 2 1/2 months of the following plan year (6 months in the case of a plan that includes an eligible automatic

contribution arrangement within the meaning of section 414(w)). Qualified nonelective contributions and qualified matching contributions taken into account under § 1.401(k)-2(a)(6) of this Chapter or qualified nonelective contributions or elective contributions taken into account under § 1.401(m)-2(a)(6) of this Chapter for a plan year may permit a plan to avoid excess contributions or excess aggregate contributions, respectively, even if made after the close of the 2 1/2 month period (6 months in the case of a plan that includes an eligible automatic contribution arrangement within the meaning of section 414(w)). * * *

* * *

HRAs: Group Health Plans: Employer Shared Responsibility: Nondiscrimination Rules

HRAs: Group Health Plans: Employer Shared Responsibility: Nondiscrimination Rules.—Amendments to Reg. §§ 54.4980H-4 and 54.4980H-5, clarifying the application of the employer shared responsibility provisions and certain nondiscrimination rules under the Internal Revenue Code to health reimbursement arrangements and other account-based group health plans integrated with individual health insurance coverage or Medicare (individual coverage HRAs), and to provide certain safe harbors with respect to the application of those provisions to individual coverage HRAs, are proposed (published in the Federal Register on September 30, 2019) (REG-136401-18).

Par. 4. Section 54.4980H-4 is amended by removing "9.5 percent of" and adding in its place "the product of the required contribution percentage (as defined in § 1.36B-2(c)(3)(v)(C) of this chapter) and" in the first sentence of paragraph (b)(1).

§ 54.4980H-4. Assessable payments under section 4980H(a).

Par. 5. Section 54.4980H-5 is amended by:
a. Revising paragraph (e)(2) introductory text;
b. In paragraph (e)(2)(i):
i Removing "an" and adding in its place "a general" in the heading; and
ii. Removing "affordability" and adding in its place "general affordability" in the first sentence;

c. Removing "9.5 percent of" and adding in its place "the product of the required contribution percentage (as defined in §1.36B-2(c)(3)(v)(C)) and" in the first sentence of paragraphs (e)(2)(ii)(A) and (B), the first and second sentences of paragraph (e)(2)(iii), and the first sentence of paragraph (e)(2)(iv);

d. In paragraph (e)(2)(v):

i. Adding a sentence to the end of the introductory text; and

ii. Designating *Examples 1* through *6* as paragraphs (e)(2)(v)(A) through (F), respectively;

e. In newly designated paragraphs (e)(2)(v)(A) through (F), redesignating the paragraphs in the first column as the paragraphs in the second column:

Old Paragraphs	New Paragraphs
(e)(2)(v)(A)(i) and (ii)	(e)(2)(v)(A)(*1*) and (*2*)
(e)(2)(v)(B)(i) and (ii)	(e)(2)(v)(B)(*1*) and (*2*)
(e)(2)(v)(C)(i) and (ii)	(e)(2)(v)(C)(*1*) and (*2*)
(e)(2)(v)(D)(i) and (ii)	(e)(2)(v)(D)(*1*) and (*2*)
(e)(2)(v)(E)(i) and (ii)	(e)(2)(v)(E)(*1*) and (*2*)
(e)(2)(v)(F)(i) and (ii)	(e)(2)(v)(F)(*1*) and (*2*)

f. Redesignating paragraphs (f) and (g) as paragraphs (g) and (h), respectively;

g. Adding a new paragraph (f); and

h. Revising newly redesignated paragraph (h).

The revisions and additions read as follows:

§54.4980H-5. Assessable payments under section 4980H(b).

* * *

(e) * * *

(2) *Affordability safe harbors for section 4980H(b) purposes.*—The affordability safe harbors set forth in paragraphs (e)(2)(ii) through (iv) of this section (general affordability safe harbors) apply solely for purposes of section 4980H(b), so that an applicable large employer member that offers minimum essential coverage providing minimum value will not be subject to an assessable payment under section 4980H(b) with respect to any employee receiving the applicable premium tax credit or cost-sharing reduction for a period for which the coverage is determined to be affordable under the requirements of a general affordability safe harbor. The preceding sentence applies even if the applicable large employer member's offer of coverage that meets the requirements of a general affordability safe harbor is not affordable for a particular employee under section 36B(c)(2)(C)(i) and §1.36B-2(c)(3)(v) of this chapter, and an applicable premium tax credit or cost-sharing reduction is allowed or paid with respect to that employee. The general affordability safe harbors apply with respect to offers of minimum essential coverage other than the offer of an individual coverage HRA, as defined in paragraph (f)(7) of this section. Paragraph (f) of this section sets forth affordability and minimum value safe harbors that apply to the offer of an individual coverage HRA (individual coverage HRA safe harbors).

* * *

(v) * * * For purposes of simplicity, the examples in this paragraph (e)(2)(v) assume 9.5 percent is the required contribution percentage for 2015 and 2016, although the required contribution percentage in 2015 and 2016 was adjusted for those years pursuant to §1.36B-2(c)(3)(v)(C) of this chapter.

* * *

(f) *Affordability and minimum value safe harbors for individual coverage HRAs.*—(1) *In general.*—Whether an offer of an individual coverage HRA is treated as affordable and providing minimum value, in general, is determined under §1.36B-2(c)(3)(i)(B), (c)(3)(vi), and (c)(5) of this chapter. This paragraph (f) sets forth safe harbors that an applicable large employer member may use in determining whether an offer of an individual coverage HRA is affordable or provides minimum value for purposes of section 4980H(b), even if the offer of the individual coverage HRA is not affordable or does not provide minimum value under §1.36B-2(c)(3)(i)(B), (c)(3)(vi), and (c)(5) of this chapter. An applicable large employer member that offers an individual coverage HRA is not subject to an assessable payment under section 4980H(b) with respect to any full-time employee receiving the applicable premium tax credit or cost-sharing reduction for a period for which the individual coverage HRA is determined to be affordable and to provide minimum value applying the safe harbors provided in this paragraph (f). The preceding sentence applies even if the applicable large employer member's offer of an individual coverage HRA that is affordable and provides minimum value applying the safe harbors under this paragraph (f) is not affordable or does not provide minimum value for a particular employee under §1.36B-2(c)(3)(i)(B), (c)(3)(vi), and (c)(5) of this chapter, and an applicable premium tax credit or cost-sharing reduction is allowed or paid with respect to that employee. To the extent not addressed in this paragraph (f), the rules under §1.36B-2(c)(3)(i)(B), (c)(3)(vi), and (c)(5) of this chapter apply in determining whether an offer of an individual coverage HRA is affordable and provides minimum value for purposes of section 4980H(b). Further, an applicable large employer member may rely on information provided by an Exchange in determining whether the offer of an individual coverage HRA is affordable and provides minimum value. See paragraph (f)(7) of this section for definitions that apply to this paragraph (f), which are in addition to the definitions set forth in §54.4980H-1(a).

(2) *Conditions of using an individual coverage HRA safe harbor.*—An applicable large employer member may use one or more of the safe harbors described in this paragraph (f) only with respect to the full-time employees and their dependents to whom the applicable large employer member offered the opportunity to enroll in an individual coverage HRA. The safe harbors in this paragraph (f) apply only to the offer of an individual coverage HRA, but to the extent an applicable large employer member offers some full-time employees and their dependents an individual coverage HRA and other full-time employees and their dependents other coverage under an eligible employer-sponsored plan that provides minimum value with respect to the self-only coverage offered to the employee, the applicable large employer member may use the safe harbors under this paragraph (f) for the offers of the individual coverage HRA and the general affordability safe harbors under paragraph (e)(2) of this section for the offers of other coverage. Use of any of the safe harbors in this paragraph (f) is optional for an applicable large employer member, and an applicable large employer member may choose to apply the safe harbors for any class of employees (as defined in paragraph (f)(7) of this section), provided it does so on a uniform and consistent basis for all employees in the class of employees. Each of the safe harbors set forth in this paragraph (f) may be used in combination with the other safe harbors provided in this paragraph (f), subject to the conditions of the safe harbors.

(3) *Minimum value.*—An individual coverage HRA that is affordable for a calendar month under §1.36B-2(c)(5) of this chapter, taking into account any applicable safe harbors under this paragraph (f), is treated as providing minimum value for the calendar month, for purposes of section 4980H(b).

(4) *Look-back month safe harbor.*—(i) *In general.*—In determining an employee's required HRA contribution for a calendar month, for purposes of section 4980H(b), an applicable large employer member may use the monthly premium for the applicable lowest cost silver plan for the month specified in either paragraph (f)(4)(i)(A) or (B) of this section, as applicable (the look-back month):

(A) *Calendar year plan.*—For an individual coverage HRA with a plan year that is the calendar year, an applicable large employer member may use the monthly premium for the applicable lowest cost silver plan for January of the prior calendar year.

(B) *Plan year that is not the calendar year.*—For an individual coverage HRA with a plan year that is not the calendar year, an applicable large employer member may use the monthly premium for the applicable lowest cost silver plan for January of the current calendar year.

(ii) *Application of look-back month safe harbor to employee's current circumstances.*—In determining the monthly premium for the applicable lowest cost silver plan based on the applicable look-back month, the applicable large employer member must use the employee's applicable age for the current plan year and the employee's applicable location for the current calendar month. In general, the applicable large employer member may use the monthly premium of the applicable lowest cost silver plan for the applicable look-back month for all calendar months of the plan year. However, to the extent the employee's applicable location changes during the plan year, although the applicable large employer member may continue to determine the monthly premium based on the applicable look-back month, the applicable large employer member must use the employee's new applicable location, in accordance with the rules set forth under paragraph (f)(6) of this section if applicable, to determine the applicable lowest cost silver plan used to determine the monthly premium.

(5) *Application of the general affordability safe harbors to individual coverage HRAs.*—The general affordability safe harbors set forth in paragraphs (e)(2)(ii), (iii), and (iv) of this section may apply to an offer of an individual coverage HRA by an applicable large employer member to a full-time employee for purposes of section 4980H(b), subject to the modifications set forth in this paragraph (f)(5).

(i) *Form W-2 safe harbor applied to individual coverage HRAs.*—An applicable large employer member satisfies the Form W-2 safe harbor of paragraph (e)(2)(ii) of this section with respect to an offer of an individual coverage HRA to an employee for a calendar year, or if applicable, part of a calendar year, if the individual coverage HRA is affordable under the Form W-2 safe harbor under paragraph (e)(2)(ii) of this section but substituting "the employee's required HRA contribution, as determined taking into account any other safe harbors in paragraph (f) of this section, if applicable" for each of the following phrases — "that employee's required contribution for the calendar year for the employer's lowest cost self-only coverage that provides minimum value", "the required employee contribution", "the employee's required contribution", and "the employee's required contribution for the employer's lowest cost self-only coverage that provides minimum value."

(ii) *Rate of pay safe harbor applied to individual coverage HRAs.*—An applicable large employer member satisfies the rate of pay safe harbor of paragraph (e)(2)(iii) of this section with respect to an offer of an individual coverage HRA to an employee for a calendar month if the individual coverage HRA is affordable under the rate of pay safe harbor of paragraph (e)(2)(iii) of this section but substituting "the employee's required HRA contribution, as determined taking into account any other safe harbors in paragraph (f) of this section, if applicable," for "the employee's required contribution for the calendar month for the applicable large employer member's lowest cost self-only coverage that provides minimum value."

(iii) *Federal poverty line safe harbor applied to individual coverage HRAs.*—An applicable large employer member satisfies the Federal poverty line safe harbor of paragraph (e)(2)(iv) of this section with respect to an offer of an individual coverage HRA to an employee for a calendar month if the individual coverage HRA is affordable under the federal poverty line safe harbor of paragraph (e)(2)(iv) of this section but substituting "the employee's required HRA contribution, as determined taking into account any other safe harbors in paragraph (f) of this section, if applicable," for "the employee's required contribution for the calendar month for the applicable large employer member's lowest cost self-only coverage that provides minimum value."

(6) *Location safe harbor.*—(i) *In general.*—For purposes of section 4980H(b), an applicable large employer member may determine an employee's required HRA contribution for a calendar month based on the cost of the applicable lowest cost silver plan for the location of the employee's primary site of employment.

(ii) *Primary site of employment.*—(A) *In general.*—An employee's primary site of employment generally is the location at which the applicable large employer member reasonably expects the employee to perform services on the first day of the plan year (or on the first day the individual coverage HRA may take effect, for an employee who is not eligible for the individual coverage HRA on the first day of the plan year). However, the employee's primary site of employment is treated as changing if the location at which the employee performs services changes and the employer expects the change to be permanent or indefinite; in that case, in general, the employee's primary site of employment is treated as changing no later than the first day of the second calendar month after the employee has begun performing services at the new location. Nonetheless, if an applicable large employer member is first offering an individual coverage HRA to a class of employees, and the change in location occurs prior to the individual coverage HRA's initial plan year, the employee's primary site of employment is treated as changing no later than the later of the first day of the plan year or the first day of the second calendar month after the employee has begun performing services at the new location.

(B) *Remote workers.*—In the case of an employee who regularly performs services from home or another location that is not on the applicable large employer member's premises, but who may be required by his or her employer to work at, or report to, a particular location, such as a teleworker with an assigned office space or available workspace at a particular location to which he or she may be required to report, the location to which the employee would report to provide services if requested is the primary site of employment. In the case of an employee who works remotely from home or at another location that is not on the premises of the applicable large employer member and who otherwise does not have an assigned office space or a particular location to which to report, the employee's residence is the primary site of employment.

(7) *Definitions.*—The definitions in this paragraph (f)(7) apply for purposes of this paragraph (f).

(i) *Applicable age.*—For an employee who is or will be eligible for an individual coverage HRA on the first day of the plan year, the employee's applicable age for the plan year is the employee's age on the first day of the plan year. For an employee who becomes eligible for an individual coverage HRA during the plan year, the employee's applicable age for the remainder of the plan year is the employee's age on the date the individual coverage HRA can first become effective with respect to the employee.

(ii) *Applicable location.*—An employee's applicable location is where the employee resides for the calendar month, or, if the applicable large employer member is applying the location safe harbor under paragraph (f)(6) of this section, the employee's primary site of employment for the calendar month.

(iii) *Applicable lowest cost silver plan.*—(A) *In general.*—The applicable lowest cost silver plan for an employee for a calendar month generally is the lowest cost silver plan for self-only coverage of the employee offered through the Exchange for the employee's applicable location for the month.

(B) *Different lowest cost silver plans in different parts of the same rating area.*—If there are different lowest cost silver plans in different parts of a rating area, an employee's applicable lowest cost silver plan is the lowest cost silver plan in the part of the rating area in which the employee's applicable location is located.

(C) *Lowest cost silver plan identified for use for employees of all ages.*—The applicable lowest cost silver plan for an employee is the lowest cost silver plan for the lowest age band in the individual market for the employee's applicable location.

(iv) *Class of employees.*—A class of employees means a class of employees as set forth in §54.9802-4(d)(2).

(v) *Individual coverage HRA.*—An individual coverage HRA means an individual coverage HRA as set forth in §54.9802-4.

(vi) *Required contribution percentage.*—Required contribution percentage means the required contribution percentage as defined in §1.36B-2(c)(3)(v)(C) of this chapter.

(vii) *Required HRA contribution.*—In general, the required HRA contribution means the required HRA contribution as defined in §1.36B-2(c)(5)(ii) of this chapter. However, for purposes of the safe harbors set forth in this paragraph (f), the required HRA contribution is determined based on the applicable lowest cost silver plan as defined in paragraph (f)(7)(iii) of this section and the monthly premium for the applicable lowest cost silver plan is determined based on the employee's applicable age, as defined in paragraph (f)(7)(i) of this section, and the employee's applicable location, as defined in paragraph (f)(7)(ii) of this section.

(8) *Examples.*—The following examples illustrate the application of the safe harbors under this paragraph (f) to applicable large employer members that offer an individual coverage HRA to at least some of their full-time employees.

(i) *Example 1 (Location safe harbor and look-back month safe harbor applied to calendar-year individual coverage HRA)*—(A) *Facts.* For 2020, Employer Y offers all full-time employees and their dependents an individual coverage HRA with a calendar-year plan year and makes $6,000 available in the HRA for the 2020 calendar-year plan year to each full-time employee without regard to family size, which means the monthly HRA amount for each full-time employee is $500. All of Employer Y's employees have a primary site of employment in City A. Employer Y chooses to use the location safe harbor and the look-back month safe harbor. Employer Y also chooses to use the rate of pay safe harbor for its full-time employees. Employee M is 40 years old on January 1, 2020, the first day of the plan year. The monthly premium for the applicable lowest cost silver plan for a 40 year old offered through the Exchange in City A for January 2019 is $600. Employee M's required HRA contribution for each month of 2020 is $100 (cost of the applicable lowest cost silver plan determined under the location safe harbor and the look-back month safe harbor ($600) minus the monthly HRA amount ($500)). The monthly amount determined under the rate of pay safe harbor for Employee M is $2,000 for each month in 2020.

(B) *Conclusion.* Employer Y has made an offer of affordable, minimum value coverage to Employee M for purposes of section 4980H(b) for each month of 2020 because Employee M's required HRA contribution ($100) is less than the amount equal to the required contribution percentage for 2020 multiplied by the monthly amount determined under the rate of pay safe harbor for Employee M (9.78 percent of $2,000 = $196). Employer Y will not be liable for an assessable payment under section 4980H(b) with respect to Employee M for any calendar month in 2020. (Also, Employer Y will not be liable for an assessable payment under section 4980H(a) for any calendar month in 2020 because it offered an individual coverage HRA, an eligible employer-sponsored plan that is minimum essential coverage, to all full-time employees and their dependents for each calendar month in 2020.)

(ii) *Example 2 (Location safe harbor and look-back month safe harbor applied to non-calendar year individual coverage HRA)*—(A) *Facts.* Employer Z offers all full-time employees and their dependents an individual coverage HRA with a non-calendar year plan year of July 1, 2020 through June 30, 2021, and makes $6,000 available in the HRA for the plan year to each full-time employee without regard to family size, which means the monthly HRA amount for each full-time employee is $500. All of Employer Z's employees have a primary site of employment in City B. Employer Z chooses to use the location safe harbor and the look-back month safe harbor. Employer Z also chooses to use the rate of pay safe harbor for its full-time employees. Employee N is 40 years old on July 1, 2020, the first day of the plan year. The monthly premium for the applicable lowest cost silver plan for a 40 year old offered through the Exchange in City B for January

2020 is $600. Employee N's required HRA contribution for each month of the plan year beginning July 1, 2020, is $100 (cost of the applicable lowest cost silver plan determined under the location safe harbor and the look-back month safe harbor ($600) minus the monthly HRA amount ($500)). The monthly amount determined under the rate of pay safe harbor for Employee N is $2,000 for each month of the plan year beginning July 1, 2020.

(B) *Conclusion.* Employer Z has made an offer of affordable, minimum value coverage to Employee N for purposes of section 4980H(b) for each month of the plan year beginning July 1, 2020, because Employee N's required HRA contribution ($100) is less than the amount equal to the required contribution percentage for plan years beginning in 2020 multiplied by the monthly amount determined under the rate of pay safe harbor for Employee N (9.78 percent of $2,000 = $196). Employer Z will not be liable for an assessable payment under section 4980H(b) with respect to Employee N for any calendar month in the plan year beginning July 1, 2020. (Also, Employer Z will not be liable for an assessable payment under section 4980H(a) for any calendar month in the plan year beginning July 1, 2020, because it offered an individual coverage HRA, an eligible employer-sponsored plan that is minimum essential coverage, to all full-time employees and their dependents for each calendar month in that plan year.)

* * *

(h) *Applicability date.*—Paragraphs (a) through (e) and (g) of this section are applicable for periods after December 31, 2014. Paragraph (f) of this section is applicable for periods after December 31, 2019.

HEALTH INSURANCE PROVIDERS FEE

Expatriate Health Plans: Issuers: Excepted Benefits

Expatriate Health Plans: Issuers: Excepted Benefits.—Amendments to Reg. §§57.2, 57.4 and 57.10, relating to the rules for expatriate health plans, expatriate health plan issuers, and qualified expatriates under the Expatriate Health Coverage Clarification Act of 2014 (EHCCA), are proposed (published in the Federal Register on June 10, 2016) (REG-135702-15).

14. Section 57.2 is amended by revising paragraph (n) to read as follows:

§57.2. Explanation of terms.

* * *

(n) *United States health risk.*—(1) *In general.*—The term *United States health risk* means the health risk of any individual who is—

(i) A United States citizen;

(ii) A resident of the United States (within the meaning of section 7701(b)(1)(A)); or

(iii) Located in the United States (within the meaning of paragraph (i) of this section) during the period such individual is so located.

(2) *Qualified expatriates, spouses, and dependents.*—The term *United States health risk* does not include the health risk of any individual who is a qualified expatriate (within the meaning of §54.9831-1(f)(6)) enrolled in an expatriate health plan (within the meaning of §54.9831-1(f)(3)). For purposes of this paragraph, a qualified expatriate includes any spouse, dependent, or any other individual enrolled in the expatriate health plan.

* * *

15. Section 57.4 is amended by adding a sentence to the end of paragraph (b)(2) and adding paragraph (b)(3) to read as follows:

§57.4. Fee calculation.

* * *

(b) * * *

(2) * * * This presumption does not apply to excluded premiums for qualified expatriates in expatriate health plans as described in §57.2(n)(2).

(3) *Manner of determining excluded premiums for qualified expatriates in expatriate health plans.*—The IRS may specify in other guidance published in the Internal Revenue Bulletin the manner of determining excluded premiums for qualified expatriates in expatriate health plans as described in §57.2(n)(2).

* * *

16. Section 57.10 is amended by revising paragraph (a) and adding paragraph (c) to read as follows:

§57.10. Effective/applicability dates.—(a) *In general.*—Except as provided in paragraphs (b) and (c) of this section, §§57.1 through 57.9 apply to any fee that is due on or after September 30, 2014.

(c) *Qualified expatriates in expatriate health plans.*—Section 57.2(n)(2), the last sentence of §57.4(b)(2), and §57.4(b)(3) apply to any fee that is due on or after the date the final regulations are published in the Federal Register. Until the date the final regulations are published in the Federal Register, taxpayers may rely on these rules for any fee that is due on or after September 30, 2018.

* * *

Health Insurance Providers Fee: Net Premiums Written

Health Insurance Providers Fee: Net Premiums Written.—Amendments to Reg. §57.2, modifying the current definition of "net premiums written" for purposes of the fee imposed by section 9010 of the Patient Protection and Affordable Care Act, as amended, are proposed (published in the Federal Register on December 9, 2016) (REG-134438-15).

2. Section 57.2 is amended by revising paragraph (k) to read as follows:

§57.2. Explanation of terms.

* * *

(k) *Net premiums written.*—(1) *In general.*—The term *net premiums written* means premiums written, adjusted as provided in paragraph (k)(2) of this section.

(2) *Adjustments.*—Net premiums written include adjustments to account for:

(i) *Assumption reinsurance, but not indemnity reinsurance.*—Net premiums written include reinsurance premiums written, reduced by reinsurance ceded, and reduced by ceding commissions with respect to the data *year. Net* premiums written do not include premiums written for indemnity reinsurance and are not reduced by indemnity reinsurance ceded because indemnity reinsurance within the meaning of paragraph (h)(5)(i) of this section is not health insurance under paragraph (h)(1) of this section. However, in the case of assumption reinsurance within the meaning of paragraph (h)(5)(ii) of this section, net premiums written include premiums written for assumption reinsurance, reduced by assumption reinsurance premiums ceded.

(ii) *Medical loss ratio (MLR) rebates.*—Net premiums written are reduced by MLR rebates with respect to the data year. For this purpose, MLR rebates are computed on an accrual basis.

(iii) *Premium adjustments related to retrospectively rated contracts.*—Net premiums written include retrospectively rated contract receipts and are reduced by retrospectively rated contract payments with respect to the data year. For this purpose, net premium adjustments related to retrospectively rated contracts are computed on an accrual basis.

(iv) *Amounts related to the risk adjustment program under section 1343 of the ACA.*—Net premiums written include risk adjustment payments (within the meaning of 42 U.S.C. 18063(b)) received with respect to the data year and are reduced by risk adjustment charges (within the meaning of 42 U.S.C. 18063(a)) paid with respect to the data year. For this purpose, risk adjustment payments and risk adjustment charges are computed on an accrual basis.

(v) *Additional adjustments published in the Internal Revenue Bulletin.*—The IRS may provide rules in guidance published in the Internal Revenue Bulletin (see § 601.601(d)(2) of this chapter) for additional adjustments against premiums written in determining net premiums written.

Health Insurance Providers Fee: Net Premiums Written

Health Insurance Providers Fee: Net Premiums Written.—Amendments to Reg. § 57.10, modifying the current definition of "net premiums written" for purposes of the fee imposed by section 9010 of the Patient Protection and Affordable Care Act, as amended, are proposed (published in the Federal Register on December 9, 2016) (REG-134438-15).

3. Section 57.10 is amended by revising paragraph (a) and adding paragraph (c) to read as follows:

§ 57.10. Effective/applicability date.—(a) *In general.*—Except as provided in paragraphs (b) and (c) of this section, §§ 57.1 through 57.9 apply to any fee that is due on or after September 30, 2014.

* * *

(c) *Paragraph (k) of § 57.2.*—Paragraph (k) of § 57.2 applies to any fee that is due on or after September 30, 2018.

MAINTENANCE OF MINIMUM ESSENTIAL COVERAGE

Expatriate Health Plans: Issuers: Excepted Benefits

Expatriate Health Plans: Issuers: Excepted Benefits.—Amendments to Reg. § 1.5000A-2, relating to the rules for expatriate health plans, expatriate health plan issuers, and qualified expatriates under the Expatriate Health Coverage Clarification Act of 2014 (EHCCA), are proposed (published in the Federal Register on June 10, 2016) (REG-135702-15).

3. Section 1.5000A-2 is amended by adding paragraphs (c)(1)(i)(D) and (d)(3) to read as follows:

§ 1.5000A-2. Minimum essential coverage.

* * *

(c) * * *

(1) * * *

(i) * * *

(D) A group health plan that is an expatriate health plan within the meaning of § 54.9831-1(f)(3) of this chapter if the requirements of § 54.9831-1(f)(3)(i) of this chapter are met by providing

coverage for qualified expatriates described in § 54.9831-1(f)(6)(i) or (ii) of this chapter.

* * *

(d) * * *

(3) *Certain expatriate health plans.*—An expatriate health plan within the meaning of § 54.9831-1(f)(3) of this chapter that is not an eligible employer-sponsored plan under paragraph (c)(1)(i)(D) of this section is a plan in the individual market.

* * *

Premium Tax Credit: Individual Shared Responsibility

Premium Tax Credit: Individual Shared Responsibility.—Amendments to Reg. § 1.5000A-3, relating to the health insurance premium tax credit (premium tax credit) and the individual shared responsibility provision, are proposed (published in the Federal Register on July 8, 2016) (REG-109086-15).

Par. 7: Section 1.5000A-3 is amended by adding a new paragraph (e)(3)(ii)(G) to read as follows:

§ 1.5000A-3. Exempt individuals.

* * *

(e) * * *

(3) * * *

(ii) * * *

(G) *Opt-out arrangements.*—*(1) In general.*—Except as otherwise provided in this paragraph (e)(3)(ii)(G), the amount of an opt-out payment made available to an employee under an opt-out arrangement increases the employee's (or related individual's) required contribution for purposes of determining the affordability of the eligible employer-sponsored plan to which the opt-out arrangement relates, regardless of whether the employee (or related individual) enrolls in the eligible employer-sponsored plan or declines to enroll in that coverage and is paid the opt-out payment.

(2) *Eligible opt-out arrangements.*—The amount of an opt-out payment made available to an employee under an eligible opt-out arrangement does not increase the employee's (or related individual's) required contribution for purposes of determining the affordability of the eligible employer-sponsored plan to which the eligible opt-out arrangement relates, regardless of whether the employee (or related individual) enrolls in the eligible employer-sponsored plan or is paid the opt-out payment.

(3) *Definitions.*—The following definitions apply for purposes of this paragraph (e)(3)(ii)(G):

(A) *Opt-out payment.*—The term *opt-out payment* means a payment that is available only if an employee declines coverage, including waiving coverage in which the employee would otherwise be enrolled, under an eligible employer-sponsored plan and that is not permitted to be used to pay for coverage under the

eligible employer-sponsored plan. An amount provided as an employer contribution to a cafeteria plan that is permitted to be used by the employee to purchase minimum essential coverage is not an opt-out payment, whether or not the employee may receive the amount as a taxable benefit. See paragraph (e)(3)(ii)(E) of this section for the treatment of employer contributions to a cafeteria plan.

(B) *Opt-out arrangement.*—The term *opt-out arrangement* means the arrangement under which an opt-out payment is made available.

(C) *Eligible opt-out arrangement.*—The term *eligible opt-out arrangement* means an arrangement under which an employee's right to receive an opt-out payment is conditioned on the employee providing reasonable evidence that the employee and all other individuals for whom the employee reasonably expects to claim a personal exemption deduction for the taxable year or years that begin or end in or with the employer's plan year to which the opt-out arrangement applies (employee's expected tax family) have, or will have, minimum essential coverage (other than coverage in the individual market, whether or not obtained through the Marketplace) during the period of coverage to which the opt-out arrangement applies. For this purpose, reasonable evidence of alternative coverage may include the employee's attestation that the employee and all other members of the employee's expected tax family have, or will have, minimum essential coverage (other than coverage in the individual market, whether or not obtained through the Marketplace) for the relevant period. Regardless of the evidence of alternative coverage required under the arrangement, to be an eligible opt-out arrangement, the arrangement must provide that the opt-out payment will not be made, and the employer in fact must not make the payment, if the employer knows or has reason to know that the employee or any other member of the employee's expected tax

Reg. § 1.5000A-3(e)(3)(ii)(G)(3)(C)

family does not have, or will not have, the alternative coverage. The arrangement must also require that the evidence of the alternative coverage be provided no less frequently than every plan year to which the eligible opt-out arrangement applies, and that it must be provided no earlier than a reasonable period of time before the commencement of the period of coverage to which the eligible opt-out arrangement applies. If the reasonable evidence (such as an attestation) is obtained as part of the regular annual open enrollment period that occurs within a few months before the commencement of the next plan year of employer-sponsored coverage, it will qualify as being provided no earlier than a reasonable period of time before commencement of the applicable period of coverage. An eligible opt-out arrangement is also permitted to require evidence of alternative coverage to be provided at a later date, such as after the plan year starts, which would enable the employer to require evidence that the employee and all other members of the employee's expected tax

family have already obtained the alternative coverage. Nothing in this rule prohibits an employer from requiring reasonable evidence of alternative coverage other than an attestation in order for an employee to qualify for an opt-out payment under an eligible opt-out arrangement. Further, provided that the reasonable evidence requirement is met, the amount of an opt-out payment made available under an eligible opt-out arrangement continues to be excluded from the employee's required contribution for the remainder of the period of coverage to which the opt-out payment originally applied even if the alternative coverage subsequently terminates for the employee or for any other member of the employee's expected tax family, regardless of whether the opt-out payment is required to be adjusted or terminated due to the loss of alternative coverage, and regardless of whether the employee is required to provide notice of the loss of alternative coverage to the employer.

* * *

INFORMATION AND RETURNS

Gifts and Bequests from Covered Expatriates: Imposition of Tax

Gifts and Bequests from Covered Expatriates: Imposition of Tax.—Reg. §28.6001-1, relating to a tax on United States citizens and residents who receive gifts or bequests from certain individuals who relinquished United States citizenship or ceased to be lawful permanent residents of the United States on or after June 17, 2008, is proposed (published in the Federal Register on September 10, 2015) (REG-112997-10).

Section 28.6001-1 is added to read as follows:

§28.6001-1. **Records required to be kept.**—(a) *In general.*—Every U.S. recipient as defined in §28.2801-2(e) subject to taxation under chapter 15 of the Internal Revenue Code must keep, for the purpose of determining the total amount of covered gifts and covered bequests, such permanent books of account or records as are necessary to establish the amount of that person's aggregate covered gifts and covered bequests, and the other information required to be shown on Form 708, "United States Return of Tax for Gifts and Bequests from Covered Expatriates." All documents and vouchers used in preparing the Form 708 must be retained by the person required to file the return so as to be available for inspection whenever required.

(b) *Supplemental information.*—In order that the Internal Revenue Service (IRS) may determine the correct tax, the U.S. recipient as defined in §28.2801-2(e) must furnish such supplemental information

as may be deemed necessary by the IRS. Therefore, the U.S. recipient must furnish, upon request, copies of all documents relating to the covered gift or covered bequest, appraisals of any items included in the aggregate amount of covered gifts and covered bequests, copies of balance sheets and other financial statements obtainable by that person relating to the value of stock or other property constituting the covered gift or covered bequest, and any other information obtainable by that person that may be necessary in the determination of the tax. See section 2801 and the corresponding regulations. For every policy of life insurance listed on the return, the U.S. recipient must procure a statement from the insurance company on Form 712 and file it with the IRS office where the return is filed. If specifically requested by the Commissioner, the insurance company must file this statement directly with the Commissioner. [Reg. §28.6001-1.]

Gifts and Bequests from Covered Expatriates: Imposition of Tax

Gifts and Bequests from Covered Expatriates: Imposition of Tax.—Reg. §28.6011-1, relating to a tax on United States citizens and residents who receive gifts or bequests from certain individuals who relinquished United States citizenship or ceased to be lawful permanent residents of the United States on or after June 17, 2008, is proposed (published in the Federal Register on September 10, 2015) (REG-112997-10).

Section 28.6011-1 is added to read as follows:

§28.6011-1. **Returns.**—(a) *Return required.*—The return of any tax to which this part 28 applies must be made on Form 708, "United States Return of Tax for Gifts and Bequests from Covered Expatriates," according to the instructions applicable to the form. With respect to each covered gift and covered bequest received during the calendar year, the U.S. recipient as defined in §28.2801-2(e) must include on Form 708 the information set forth in §25.6019-4. The U.S. recipient must file Form 708 for each calendar year in which a covered gift or covered bequest is received. The U.S. recipient who receives the covered gift or covered bequest during the calendar year is the person required to file the return. A U.S. recipient is not required to file such form, however, for a calendar year in which the total fair market value of all covered gifts and covered bequests received by that person during that calendar year is less than or equal to the section 2801(c) amount, which is the dollar amount of the per-donee exclusion in effect under section 2503(b) for that calendar year.

(b) *Protective return.*—(i) A U.S. citizen or resident (as defined in §28.2801-2(b)) that receives a gift or bequest from an expatriate and reasonably concludes that the gift or bequest is not a covered gift or a covered bequest from a covered expatriate may file a protective Form 708 in order to start the period for assessment of tax. To be a protective Form 708, it must provide all of the information otherwise required on Form 708, along with an affidavit, signed under penalties of perjury, setting forth the information on which that U.S. citizen or resident has relied in concluding that the donor or decedent, as the case may be, was not a covered expatriate, or that the transfer was not a covered gift or a covered bequest, as well as that person's efforts to obtain other information that might be relevant to these

determinations. If that U.S. citizen or resident has obtained information from the Internal Revenue Service (IRS) (as described in §28.2801-7(b)(1)), it must attach a copy of such information. The U.S. citizen or resident also must attach a copy of a completed Form 3520, Part III, for all trust distributions, or Part IV for all gifts and bequests, if applicable. If the return meets the requirements of this paragraph (b)(i), and if the IRS does not assess a section 2801 tax liability for that tax year within the limitations period for assessment stated in section 6501, the IRS may not later assess a section 2801 tax with regard to any transfer reported on that Form 708.

(ii) A U.S. citizen or resident who receives a gift or bequest from an expatriate and who files a protective Form 708 meeting the requirements of paragraph (b)(i) of this section showing no tax due, absent fraud or other special factors, will not be subject to any additions to tax for late filing under section 6651(a)(1) or for late payment under section 6651(a)(2), even if the gift or bequest is determined to be a covered gift or covered bequest from a covered expatriate within the limitations period for assessment stated in section 6501. Notwithstanding the foregoing, however, if a U.S. citizen or resident knows, or has reason to know, that the information provided by the IRS or any other source is incorrect or incomplete, that U.S. citizen or resident may not rely on that information, and except as provided in the preceding paragraph (b)(i) of this section, may be subject to all of the generally applicable provisions governing assessment of tax, collection of tax, and penalties. See sections 6501, 6502, 6651 and 6662.

(c) *Effective/applicability dates.*—This section applies on and after the date of publication of a Treasury decision adopting these rules as final regulations in the **Federal Register**. [Reg. §28.6011-1.]

Qualified Plans: Excise Taxes

Qualified Plans: Excise Taxes.—Temporary Reg. §54.6011-1T, relating to the payment of excise tax by employers receiving reversions of qualified plan assets required by the Tax Reform Act of 1986, is also proposed as a final regulation and, when adopted, would become Reg. §54.6011-1 (published in the Federal Register on April 3, 1987).

§ 54.6011-1. **General requirement of return, statement, or list.**

Domestic International Sales Corporations

Domestic International Sales Corporations: Taxation of Income.—Reproduced below is the text of a proposed amendment of Reg. § 1.6011-2, relating to the taxation of income allocable to a DISC for taxable years beginning after 1984 (published in the Federal Register on February 3, 1987).

* * *

☐ Par. 13. In § 1.6011-2, a new sentence is added immediately after the third sentence in paragraph (a) to read as follows:

§ 1.6011-2. **Returns, etc. of DISCs and former DISCs.**—
(a) *Records and information.*—* * * For taxable years beginning after 1984, every DISC or former DISC shall also disclose on the Schedule K (Form 1120-DISC) the amount of the shareholder's deferred DISC income for the shareholder's taxable year (as defined in section 995(f)(3)). * * *

* * *

Guidance under Section 529A: Qualified ABLE Programs

Guidance under Section 529A: Qualified ABLE Programs.—Amendments to Reg. § 301.6011-2, regarding programs under The Stephen Beck, Jr., Achieving a Better Life Experience Act of 2014 and rules under which States or State agencies or instrumentalities may establish and maintain a new type of tax-favored savings program through which contributions may be made to the account of an eligible disabled individual to meet qualified disability expenses, are proposed (published in the Federal Register on June 22, 2015) (REG-102837-15).

Par. 14. Section 301.6011-2 is amended by adding the word "series" after "5498" in the first sentence of paragraph (b)(1).

§ 301.6011-2. **Required use of magnetic media.**

Information Returns: Using Magnetic Media

Information Returns: Using Magnetic Media.—Amendments to Reg. § 301.6011-2, amending the rules for determining whether information returns must be filed using magnetic media (electronically), are proposed (published in the Federal Register on May 31, 2018) (REG-102951-16).

Par. 2. Section 301.6011-2 is amended as follows:
a. Paragraphs (b)(4) through (6) are added.
b. Paragraphs (c)(1)(iii) and (iv) are removed.
c. Paragraph (g)(2) is revised.
The additions and revisions read as follows:

§ 301.6011-2. **Required use of magnetic media.**

* * *

(b) * * *

(4) *Aggregation of returns.*—For purposes of determining whether the number of returns a person is required to file meets the 250-return threshold under paragraph (c)(1)(i) of this section, all types of returns covered by paragraphs (b)(1) and (2) of this section required to be filed during the calendar year are aggregated. Corrected returns are not taken into account in determining whether the 250-return threshold is met.

(5) *Corrected returns.*—Any person required to file returns covered by paragraphs (b)(1) and (2) of this section on magnetic media for a calendar year must file corrected returns covered by paragraphs (b)(1) and (2) of this section for such calendar year on magnetic media.

(6) *Examples.*—The provisions of paragraphs (b)(4) and (5) of this section are illustrated by the following examples:

Example 1. For the 2018 calendar year, Company W is required to file 200 Forms 1099-INT, "Interest Income," and 200 Forms 1099-DIV, "Dividends and Distributions," for a total of 400 returns. Because Company W is required to file 250 or more returns covered by paragraphs (b)(1) and (2) of this section for the calendar year, Company W must file all Forms 1099-INT and Forms 1099-DIV electronically.

Example 2. During the 2018 calendar year, Company X has 200 employees in Puerto Rico and 75 employees in American Samoa, for a total of 275 returns. Because Company X is required to file 250 or more returns covered by paragraphs (b)(1) and (2) of this section for the calendar year, Company X must file Forms 499R-2/W-2PR, "Commonwealth of Puerto Rico Withholding Statement," and Forms W-2AS, "American Samoa Wage and Tax Statement," electronically.

Example 3. For the 2018 calendar year, Company Y files 300 original Forms 1099-MISC, "Miscellaneous Income." Later, Company Y files 70 corrected Forms 1099-MISC for the 2018 calendar year. Because Company Y is required to file 250 or more returns covered by paragraphs (b)(1) and (2) of this section for the calendar year, Company Y must file its original 300 Forms 1099-MISC, as well as its 70 corrected Forms 1099-MISC for the 2018 calendar year, electronically.

* * *

(g) * * *

(2) Paragraphs (a)(1), (b)(1) and (2), (c)(1)(i), (c)(2), (d), (e), and (f) of this section are effective for information returns required to be filed after December 31, 1996. For information returns required to be filed after December 31, 1989, and before January 1, 1997, see section 6011(e) [26 USC 6011(e)]. Paragraph (b)(4) of this section is effective for information returns required to be filed after December 31, 2018. Paragraph (b)(5) of this section is effective for corrected information returns filed after December 31, 2018.

* * *

Reportable Transactions: Disclosure: Patented Transactions

Reportable Transactions: Disclosure: Patented Transactions.—Amendments to Reg. § 1.6011-4, providing rules to the disclosure of reportable transactions, including patented transactions, under Code Secs. 6011 and 6111, are proposed (published in the Federal Register on September 26, 2007) (REG-129916-07).

☐ Par. 2. Section 1.6011-4 is amended by:
1. Revising paragraphs (b)(7) and (c)(3)(i)(F).
2. Adding to paragraph (c)(3)(ii) *Examples 4, 5, 6,* and 7.
3. Revising paragraph (h)(2).
The revisions and additions read as follows:

§ 1.6011-4. **Requirement of statement disclosing participation in certain transactions by taxpayers.**

* * *

(b) * * *

(7) *Patented transactions.*—(i) *In general.*—A patented transaction is a transaction for which a taxpayer pays (directly or indirectly) a fee in any amount to a patent holder or the patent holder's agent for the legal right to use a tax planning method that the taxpayer knows or has reason to know is the subject of the patent. A patented transaction also is a transaction for which a taxpayer (the patent holder or the patent holder's agent) has the right to payment for another person's use of a tax planning method that is the subject of the patent.

(ii) *Definitions.*—For purposes of this paragraph (b)(7), the following definitions apply:

(A) *Fee.*—The term *fee* means consideration in whatever form paid, whether in cash or in kind, for the right to use a tax

Reg. § 1.6011-4(b)(7)(ii)(A)

planning method that is the subject of a patent. The term *fee* includes any consideration the taxpayer knows or has reason to know will be paid indirectly to the patent holder or patent holder's agent, such as through a referral fee, fee-sharing arrangement, or license. The term *fee* does not include amounts paid in settlement of, or as the award of damages in, a suit for damages for infringement of the patent.

(B) *Patent.*—The term *patent* means a patent granted under the provisions of title 35 of the United States Code, or any foreign patent granting rights generally similar to those under a United States patent. See §1.1235-2(a). The term *patent* includes patents that have been applied for but not yet granted.

(C) *Patent holder.*—A person is a patent holder if—

(1) The person is a holder as defined in §1.1235-2(d) and (e);

(2) The person would be a holder as defined in §1.1235-2(d)(2) if the phrase *S corporation or trust* was substituted for the word *partnership* and the phrase *shareholder or beneficiary* was substituted for the words *member* and *partner*;

(3) The person is an employer of a holder as defined in §1.1235-2(d) and the holder transferred to the employer all substantial rights to the patent as defined in §1.1235-2(b); or

(4) The person receives all substantial rights to the patent as defined in §1.1235-2(b) in exchange (directly or indirectly) for consideration in any form.

(D) *Patent holder's agent.*—The term *patent holder's agent* means any person who has the permission of the patent holder to offer for sale or exchange, to sell or exchange, or to market a tax planning method that is the subject of a patent. The term *patent holder's agent* also means any person who receives (directly or indirectly) for or on behalf of a patent holder a fee in any amount for a tax planning method that is the subject of a patent.

(E) *Payment.*—The term *payment* includes consideration in whatever form paid, whether in cash or in kind, for the right to use a tax planning method that is the subject of a patent. For example, if a patent holder or patent holder's agent receives payment for a patented transaction and a separate payment for another transaction, part or all of the payment for the other transaction may be treated as payment for the patented transaction if the facts and circumstances indicate that the payment for the other transaction is in consideration for the patented transaction. The term *payment* also includes amounts paid in settlement of, or as the award of damages in, a suit for damages for infringement of the patent.

(F) *Tax planning method.*—The term *tax planning method* means any plan, strategy, technique, or structure designed to affect Federal income, estate, gift, generation skipping transfer, employment, or excise taxes. A patent issued solely for tax preparation software or other tools used to perform or model mathematical calculations or to provide mechanical assistance in the preparation of tax or information returns is not a tax planning method.

(iii) *Related parties.*—For purposes of this paragraph (b)(7), persons who bear a relationship to each other as described in section 267(b) or 707(b) will be treated as the same person.

* * *

(c) * * *

(3) * * *

(i) * * *

(F) *Patented transactions.*—A taxpayer has participated in a patented transaction, as defined in paragraph (b)(7) of this section, if the taxpayer's tax return reflects a tax benefit from the transaction (including a deduction for fees paid in any amount to the patent holder or patent holder's agent). A taxpayer also has participated in a patented transaction, as defined in paragraph (b)(7) of this section, if the taxpayer is the patent holder or patent holder's agent and the taxpayer's tax return reflects a tax benefit in relation to obtaining a patent for a tax planning method (including any deduction for amounts paid to the United States Patent and Trademark Office as required by title 35 of the United States Code and attorney's fees) or reflects income from a payment received from another person for the use of the tax planning method that is the subject of the patent.

* * *

(ii) * * *

Example 4. (i) A, an individual, creates a tax planning method and applies for a U.S. patent. A pays attorney fees in relation to obtaining the patent and A pays the fee required under title 35 of the United States Code for the patent application. Subsequently, C pays a fee to A for the legal right to use the tax planning method that C knows or has reason to know is the subject of A's patent. A's tax return reflects both a deduction for an amount paid in relation to obtaining a patent and income from C's payment to A for the legal right to use the tax planning method that is the subject of the patent.

C's tax return reflects a deduction for an amount paid to A for the right to use the tax planning method that is the subject of the patent.

(ii) A is a patent holder under paragraph (b)(7)(ii)(C)(1) of this section. The transaction is a reportable transaction for A under paragraph (b)(7) of this section because A has the right to payment for another person's use of the tax planning method that is the subject of the patent. The transaction is a reportable transaction for C under paragraph (b)(7) of this section, because C paid a fee to A for the legal right to use a tax planning method that C knew or had reason to know was the subject of a patent. A has participated in the transaction in the year in which A's tax return reflects a tax benefit in relation to obtaining the patent or reflects income from C's payment to A for the legal right to use the tax planning method that is the subject of the patent. C has participated in the transaction in the year in which C's tax return reflects the deduction for any amount paid to A for the legal right to use the tax planning method that is the subject of the patent. C also participates in the transaction for any years for which any other tax benefit from the transaction is reflected on C's tax return.

Example 5. (i) A, an individual, is the employee of B, a corporation. A creates a tax planning method and applies for a U.S. patent but B pays the fee required under title 35 of the United States Code for A's patent application. Pursuant to A's employment contract with B, B holds all substantial rights to the patent. B's tax return reflects a deduction for the amount paid in relation to obtaining the patent.

(ii) A and B are patent holders under paragraph (b)(7)(ii)(C)(1) and (3) of this section, respectively. The transaction is not a reportable transaction for A under paragraph (b)(7) of this section because A does not have the right to payment for another person's use of the tax planning method that is the subject of the patent. The transaction is a reportable transaction for B under paragraph (b)(7) of this section because B holds all substantial rights to the patent and has the right to payment for another person's use of the tax planning method that is the subject of the patent. B has participated in the transaction in the year in which B's tax return reflects a tax benefit in relation to obtaining the patent. B also participates in the transaction for any years for which B's tax return reflects income from a payment received from another person for the use of the tax planning method that is the subject of the patent.

Example 6. (i) Assume the facts as in *Example 4*, except that A agrees to license the patent to F, a financial institution. The license agreement between A and F provides that F may offer the tax planning method to its clients and if a client decides to use the tax planning method, F must pay A for each client's use of the tax planning method. F offers the tax planning method to G who uses the tax planning method and knows or has reason to know it is the subject of a patent. F charges G for financial planning services and pays A for G's use of the tax planning method. A's tax return reflects income from the payment received from F. F's tax return reflects income from the payment received from G, and G's tax return reflects a deduction for the fees paid to F.

(ii) F is a patent holder's agent under paragraph (b)(7)(ii)(D) of this section because F has the permission of the patent holder to offer for sale or exchange, to sell or exchange, or to market a tax planning method that is the subject of a patent. F also is a patent holder's agent under paragraph (b)(7)(ii)(D) of this section because F receives (directly or indirectly) a fee in any amount for a tax planning method that is the subject of a patent for or on behalf of a patent holder. The transaction is a reportable transaction for both A and F under paragraph (b)(7) of this section because A and F each have the right to payment for another person's use of the tax planning method that is the subject of the patent. The transaction is a reportable transaction for G under paragraph (b)(7) of this section because G paid a fee (directly or indirectly) to a patent holder or a patent holder's agent for the legal right to use a tax planning method that G knew or had reason to know was the subject of the patent. A has participated in the transaction in the years in which A's tax return reflects income from the payment received from F for G's use of the tax planning method that is the subject of the patent. F has participated in the transaction in the years in which F's tax return reflects income from the payment received from G for use of the tax planning method that is the subject of the patent. G has participated in the transaction in the years in which G's tax return reflects a deduction for the fees paid to F. G also participates in the transaction for any years for which any other tax benefit from the transaction is reflected on G's tax return.

Example 7. Assume the same facts as in *Example 4*. J uses a tax planning method that is the same as the tax planning method that is the subject of A's patent. J does not pay any fees to any patent holder or patent holder's agent with respect to the tax planning method that is the subject of the patent. A sues J for infringement of the patent and J pays A an amount for damages. A's tax return reflects as income the amounts for damages received from J. The transaction is not a reportable transaction for J under paragraph (b)(7) of this section because J did not pay any fees (as defined in paragraph (b)(7)(ii)(A) of this section) (directly or indirectly) to a patent holder or patent holder's agent for the legal right to use a tax planning method that J knew or had reason to know was the subject of the patent. A has participated in a reportable transaction under paragraph (b)(7) of this section in the year in which A's tax return reflects income from a payment (the amount received as an award for damages in a suit for damages for infringement of the patent) received from another person for the use of the tax planning method that is the subject of a patent.

***

(h) ***

(2) *Patented transactions.*—Upon the publication of the Treasury decision adopting these rules as final regulations in the **Federal Register**, paragraphs (b)(7), (c)(3)(i)(F), and (c)(3)(ii) *Examples 4* through 7 of this section will apply to transactions entered into on or after September 26, 2007.

Classification: Cell Companies: Series LLCs

Classification: Cell Companies: Series LLCs.—Reg. §301.6011-6, regarding the classification for Federal tax purposes of a series of a domestic series limited liability company (LLC), a cell of a domestic cell company, or a foreign series or cell that conducts an insurance business, is proposed (published in the Federal Register on September 14, 2010) (REG-119921-09).

Par. 2. Section 301.6011-6 is added to read as follows:

§301.6011-6. Statements of series and series organizations.— (a) *Statement required.*—Each series and series organization (as defined in paragraph (b) of this section) shall file a statement for each taxable year containing the identifying information with respect to the series or series organization as prescribed by the Internal Revenue Service for this purpose and shall include the information required by the statement and its instructions.

(b) *Definitions.*—(1) *Series.*—The term *series* has the same meaning as in §301.7701-1(a)(5)(viii)(C).

(2) *Series organization.*—The term *series organization* has the same meaning as in §301.7701-1(a)(5)(viii)(A).

(c) *Effective/applicability date.*—This section applies to taxable years beginning after the date of publication of the Treasury decision adopting these rules as final regulations in the **Federal Register**.

Information Reporting: Minimum Essential Coverage

Information Reporting: Minimum Essential Coverage.—Reg. §301.6011-8, affecting health insurance issuers, employers, governments, and other persons that provide minimum essential coverage to individuals, are proposed (published in the Federal Register on September 9, 2013) (REG-132455-11).

☐ Par. 5. Section 301.6011-8 is added to read as follows:

§301.6011-8. Required use of magnetic media to report minimum essential coverage.—(a) *Returns reporting minimum essential coverage must be filed on magnetic media.*—A person required to file an information return reporting minimum essential coverage under §1.6055-1 of this chapter must file the return on magnetic media if the person is required to file to least 250 returns during the calendar year. Returns filed on magnetic media must be made in accordance with applicable publications, forms, instructions, or published guidance, see §§601.601(d) and 601.602 of this chapter.

(b) *Magnetic media.*—For purposes of this section, the term *magnetic media* has the same meaning as in §301.6011-2(a)(1).

(c) *Determination of 250 returns.*—For purposes of this section, a person is required to file at least 250 returns if, during the calendar year, the person is required to file at least 250 returns of any type, including information returns (for example, Forms W-2, Forms 1099), income tax returns, employment tax returns, and excise tax returns.

(d) *Waiver.*—The Commissioner may waive the requirements of this section in cases of hardship in accordance with §301.6011-2(c)(2)(i).

(e) *Failure to file.*—If a person fails to file an information return on magnetic media when required by this section, the person is deemed to have failed to file the return. See section 6721 for penalties for failure to file returns and see section 6724 and the regulations under section 6721 for failure to file on magnetic media.

(f) *Effective/applicability date.*—This section applies to returns on Form 1095-B or another form the IRS designates required to be filed after December 31, 2015. Reporting entities will not be subject to penalties under section 6721 with respect to the reporting requirements for 2014 (for information returns that would have been required to be filed in 2015 with respect to 2014). [Reg. §301.6011-8.]

Information Reporting: Health Insurance Coverage: Applicable Large Employers

Information Reporting: Health Insurance Coverage: Applicable Large Employers.—Reg. §301.6011-9, providing guidance to employers that are subject to the information reporting requirements under section 6056 of the Internal Revenue Code (Code), enacted by the Affordable Care Act, is proposed (published in the Federal Register on September 9, 2013) (REG-136630-12).

☐ Par. 2. Section 301.6011-9 is added to read as follows:

§301.6011-9. Electronic filing of section 6056 returns.— (a) *Returns required under section 6056.*—An applicable large employer member, as defined in §301.6056-1(b)(2), is required to file electronically an information return under section 6056 and §301.6056-1, except as otherwise provided in paragraph (b) of this section.

(b) *Exceptions.*—(1) *Low-volume filers/250-return threshold.*—(i) *In general.*—An applicable large employer member will not be required to file electronically the section 6056 information return described in paragraph (a) of this section unless it is required to file 250 or more returns during the calendar year. Each section 6056 information return for a full-time employee is a separate return. For purposes of this section, an applicable large employer member is required to file at least 250 returns if, during the calendar year, the applicable large employer member is required to file at least 250 returns of any type, including information returns (for example, Forms W-2, Forms 1099), income tax returns, employment tax returns, and excise tax returns. An applicable large employer member filing fewer than 250 returns during the calendar year may make the returns on the prescribed paper form.

(ii) *Examples.*—The following examples illustrate the provisions of paragraph (b)(1) of this section:

Example 1. Company X is an applicable large employer member. For the calendar year ending December 31, 2015, Company X is required to file 275 section 6056 returns. Company X is required to file section 6056 returns electronically for that calendar year because 275 section 6056 information returns exceed the 250-return threshold.

Example 2. Company Y is an applicable large employer member. For the calendar year ending December 31, 2015, Company Y is required to file 200 returns on Form W-2 and 150 section 6056 returns. Company Y is required to file the section 6056 returns electronically for that calendar year because it is required to file more than 250 returns (that is, the 200 Forms W-2 plus the 150 section 6056 returns).

(2) *Waiver.*—(i) *In general.*—The Commissioner may waive the requirements of this section if hardship is shown in a request for waiver filed in accordance with this paragraph (b)(2)(i). The principal factor in determining hardship will be the amount, if any, by which the cost of filing the section 6056 returns in accordance with this section exceeds the costs of filing the returns on other media. A request for waiver must be made in accordance with applicable revenue procedures or publications (see §601.601(d)(2)(ii)(*b*) of this chapter). Pursuant to these procedures, a request for waiver should be filed at least 45 days before the due date of the section 6056 return in order for the IRS to have adequate time to respond to the request for waiver. The waiver will specify the type of information return (that is, section 6056 information return) and the period to which it applies and will be subject to such terms and conditions regarding the method of reporting as may be prescribed by the Commissioner.

Reg. §301.6011-9(b)(2)(i)

(ii) *Supplemental rules.*—The Commissioner may prescribe rules that supplement the provisions of paragraph (b)(2)(i) of this section.

(c) *Effective/applicability date.*—The rules of this section are effective as of the date of publication of the Treasury decision adopting these rules as final regulations in the **Federal Register**. This section applies to returns on "Form 1095-C" or another form the IRS designates required to be filed after December 31, 2014. However, reporting entities will not be subject to penalties under sections 6721 or 6722 with respect to the reporting requirements for 2014 (for information returns filed and for statements furnished to employees in 2015). [Reg. §301.6011-9.]

Excise Taxes: Taxable Fuel: Returns: Definitions

Excise Taxes: Taxable Fuel: Returns: Definitions.—Amendments to Reg. §40.0-1, relating to credits and payments for alcohol mixtures, biodiesel mixtures, renewable diesel mixtures, alternative fuel mixtures, and alternative fuel sold for use or used as a fuel and relating to the definition of gasoline and diesel fuel, are proposed (published in the Federal Register on July 29, 2008) (REG-155087-05).

Par. 5. Section 40.0-1 is amended by revising paragraph (d) and adding paragraph (e) to read as follows:

§40.0-1. Introduction.

* * *

(d) *Person.*—For purposes of this part, each business unit that has, or is required to have, a separate employer identification number is treated as a separate person. Thus, business units (for example, a parent corporation and a subsidiary corporation, a proprietorship and a related partnership, or the various members of a consolidated group), each of which has a different employer identification number, are separate persons.

(e) *Effective/applicability date.*—This part is effective for returns and deposits that relate to calendar quarters beginning after September 30, 2008. For rules applicable to returns and deposits that relate to prior periods, see 26 CFR part 40 (revised as of April 1, 2008).

Life Insurance Companies: Computation and Reporting of Reserves

Life Insurance Companies: Computation and Reporting of Reserves.—Amendments to Reg. §1.6012-2, providing guidance on the computation of life insurance reserves and the change in basis of computing certain reserves of insurance companies, are proposed (published in the Federal Register on April 2, 2020) (REG-132529-17).

Par. 21. Section 1.6012-2 is amended by:

1. In the second sentence of paragraph (c)(1)(i), removing "Except as provided in paragraph (c)(4) of this section, such" and adding "Such" in its place.

2. In the third sentence of paragraph (c)(2), removing "Except as provided in paragraph (c)(4) of this section, such" and adding "Such" in its place.

3. Removing paragraph (c)(4).

4. Redesignating paragraph (c)(5) as paragraph (c)(4).

5. Revising paragraph (l).

The revision reads as follows.

§1.6012-2. Corporations required to make returns of income.

* * *

(l) *Applicability date.*—Except as provided in this paragraph (l), paragraph (c) of this section applies to any taxable year beginning on or after **[DATE FINAL REGULATIONS ARE PUBLISHED IN THE FEDERAL REGISTER]**. However, a taxpayer may choose to apply paragraph (c) of this section to any original Federal income tax return (including any amended return filed on or before the due date (including extensions) of such original return) timely filed on or after **[DATE FINAL REGULATIONS ARE PUBLISHED IN THE FEDERAL REGISTER]**. For taxable years beginning before **[DATE FINAL REGULATIONS ARE PUBLISHED IN THE FEDERAL REGISTER]** see paragraph (c) of this section as contained in 26 CFR part 1 in effect on April 1, 2019.

Dependency Exemption: Authorized Placement Agency: Definition

Dependency Exemption: Authorized Placement Agency: Definition.—Amendments to Reg. §1.6013-1, relating to the definition of an authorized placement agency for purposes of a dependency exemption for a child placed for adoption that were issued prior to the changes made to the law by the Working Families Tax Relief Act of 2004, are proposed (published in the Federal Register on January 19, 2017) (REG-137604-07).

Par. 18. Section 1.6013-1 is amended by removing paragraph (e).

§1.6013-1. Joint returns.

Tax Liability: Relief from Joint and Several Liability

Tax Liability: Relief from Joint and Several Liability.—Amendments to Reg. §1.6015-0, providing guidance to taxpayers on when and how to request relief under sections 66 and 6015, are proposed (published in the Federal Register on August 13, 2013) (REG-132251-11).

☐ Par. 4. Section 1.6015-0 is amended as follows:

1. In §1.6015-5, revising the entry for paragraph (a) as new entry for paragraph (a)(1) and adding a new entry for paragraph (a)(2); entries for paragraphs (b)(1) through (b)(5) are revised; entries for paragraphs (b)(2)(i) and (b)(2)(ii) are removed; and new entries are added for paragraphs (b)(3)(i), (b)(3)(ii), (b)(6), (c)(1), (c)(2), and (c)(3).

2. Section 1.6015-9 heading is revised.

The additions and revisions read as follows:

§1.6015-0. Table of contents.

* * *

§1.6015-5 Time and manner for requesting relief.
  (a) Requesting relief.
    (1) In general.
    (2) Requesting relief as part of a collection due process hearing.
  (b) * * *
    (1) Relief other than equitable relief.
    (2) Equitable relief.
    (3) Definitions.
      (i) Collection activity.
      (ii) Section 6330 notice.
    (4) Requests for relief made before commencement of collection activity.
    (5) Examples.
    (6) Premature requests for relief.
  (c) * * *
    (1) In general.
    (2) Reconsideration process.
    (3) Examples.

* * *

§1.6015-9 Effective/applicability date.

Tax Liability: Relief from Joint and Several Liability

Tax Liability: Relief from Joint and Several Liability.—Amendments to Reg. §1.6015-5, providing guidance to taxpayers on when and how to request relief under sections 66 and 6015, are proposed (published in the Federal Register on August 13, 2013) (REG-132251-11).

☐ Par. 5. Section 1.6015-5 is amended to read as follows:

1. Paragraph (a) is amended by designating the introductory text as (a)(1), adding a new heading for paragraph (a)(1) introductory text, and adding new paragraph (a)(2).

2. Paragraph (b)(1) is revised.

3. Paragraphs (b)(2), (b)(3), (b)(4), and (b)(5) are redesignated as paragraphs (b)(3), (b)(4), (b)(5), and (b)(6).

4. New paragraph (b)(2) is added.

5. Newly-designated paragraphs (b)(3)(ii), (b)(4), (b)(5), and (b)(6) are revised.

6. Paragraph (c)(1) is amended by adding a new sentence at the end of the paragraph.

7. Paragraph (c)(2) is redesignated as paragraph (c)(3) and revised and new paragraph (c)(2) is added.

The revisions and additions read as follows:

§1.6015-5. Time and manner for requesting relief.—
(a) *Requesting relief.*—(1) *In general.*—* * *

(2) *Requesting relief as part of a collection due process hearing.*—A requesting spouse may also elect the application of §1.6015-2 or 1.6015-3, or request equitable relief under §1.6015-4, pursuant to the collection due process (CDP) hearing procedures under sections 6320 and 6330, by attaching Form 8857, "Request for Innocent Spouse Relief," or an equivalent written statement to Form 12153, "Request for a Collection Due Process or Equivalent Hearing" (or other specified form).

(b) * * *.—(1) *Relief other than equitable relief.*—To elect the application of §1.6015-2 or 1.6015-3, a requesting spouse must file Form 8857 or other similar statement with the IRS no later than two years from the date of the first collection activity against the requesting spouse after July 22, 1998, with respect to the joint tax liability.

(2) *Equitable relief.*—To request equitable relief under §1.6015-4, a requesting spouse must file Form 8857 or other similar statement with the IRS within the period of limitation on collection of tax in section 6502 or within the period of limitation on credit or refund of tax in section 6511, as applicable to the joint tax liability. If a requesting spouse files a request for equitable relief under §1.6015-4 within the period of limitation on collection of tax, the IRS will consider the request for equitable relief, but the requesting spouse will be eligible for a credit or refund of tax only if the limitation period for credit or refund of tax is open when the request is filed (assuming all other requirements are met, including the limit on amount of credit or refund prescribed in section 6511(b)(2)). Alternatively, if a requesting spouse files a request for equitable relief after the period of limitation on collection of tax has expired but while the limitation period on credit or refund of tax remains open, the IRS will consider the request for equitable relief insofar as tax was paid by or collected from the requesting spouse, and the requesting spouse will be eligible for a potential credit or refund of tax. If neither the section 6502 nor section 6511 limitation period is open when a requesting spouse files a request for equitable relief, the IRS will not consider the request for equitable relief. See §1.6015-1(g).

(3) * * *.—(ii) *Section 6330 notice.*—A section 6330 notice refers to the notice sent, pursuant to section 6330, providing taxpayers notice of the IRS's intent to levy and of their right to a CDP hearing. The mailing of a section 6330 notice by certified mail to the requesting spouse's last known address is sufficient to start the two-year period, described in paragraph (b)(1), regardless of whether the requesting spouse actually receives the notice.

(4) *Requests for relief made before commencement of collection activity.*—Except as provided in paragraph (b)(6) of this section, an election under §1.6015-2 or 1.6015-3 or a request for equitable relief under §1.6015-4 may be made before any collection activity has commenced. For example, an election or request for equitable relief may be made in connection with an examination of a joint Federal income tax return or a demand for payment, or pursuant to the CDP hearing procedures of section 6320 with respect to the filing of a Notice of Federal Tax Lien. A request for equitable relief under §1.6015-4 for a liability that is properly reported on a joint Federal income tax return but not paid with the return or by the due date for payment is properly submitted at any time after the return is filed.

(5) *Examples.*—The following examples illustrate the rules of this paragraph (b):

Example 1. On January 12, 2009, the IRS mailed a section 6330 notice to H and W, by certified mail to their last known address, regarding their 2007 joint Federal income tax liability, which was the result of an understatement. The section 6330 notice was the first collection activity the IRS initiated against H and W to collect the 2007 joint liability. H and W did not request a CDP hearing in response to the section 6330 notice. On June 5, 2009, the IRS issued a levy on W's wages to W's employer. On July 10, 2009, the IRS issued a levy on H's wages to H's employer. To be considered for relief under §1.6015-2 or 1.6015-3, a Form 8857 or other request for relief must be filed on or before January 12, 2011, which is two years after the IRS sent the section 6330 notice. The two-year period for purposes of §§1.6015-2 and 1.6015-3 (not applicable to §1.6015-4) runs from the date the section 6330 notice was mailed and not from the date of the actual levy.

Example 2. On May 5, 2011, the IRS offset W's overpayment from W's 2010 separate Federal income tax return in the amount of $2,000 to H and W's joint tax liability for 2009 of $5,000, for which H and W filed a joint return on April 15, 2010. The offset is the first collection activity the IRS initiated against W to collect the 2009 joint liability. On October 3, 2013, W requests relief under section 6015. W's request is not timely under §§1.6015-2 and 1.6015-3 because the request was made more than two years after the IRS's first collection activity against W - the offset of W's overpayment from 2010. As to equitable relief under §1.6015-4, the period of limitation on collection is open when W files her request, and the request can be considered for equitable relief of the unpaid tax of $3,000. W is not, however, eligible for any credit or refund of the $2,000 amount that the IRS applied against H and W's 2009 joint liability, because the period of limitation on credit or refund of tax for 2009 is no longer open when W files her request for relief. Under section 6511(a), a credit or refund of tax must generally be claimed within three years after the filing date of a tax return for the tax year or two years after payment of the tax, whichever is later. Thus, the last day for W to claim a credit or refund of the $2,000 amount was May 5, 2013, but her request for relief was not filed until October 3, 2013.

Example 3. On June 14, 2011, the IRS offset W's overpayment from her separate Federal income tax return for 2010 against H and W's joint liability for 2009, which was the result of an understatement. On July 5, 2012, the IRS offset H's overpayment from his separate Federal income tax return for 2011 against H and W's joint liability for 2009. The offset is the first collection activity the IRS initiated against H to collect the 2009 joint liability. On November 25, 2013, H requests relief under section 6015 by filing Form 8857. H's request is timely. For purposes of §§1.6015-2 and 1.6015-3, the request was filed within two years of the IRS's first collection activity against H. The IRS's collection activity against W does not start the two-year period for H to request relief. Additionally, for purposes of §1.6015-4, the period of limitation on collection was open when H filed Form 8857, making him eligible for equitable relief from any unpaid liability for 2009, and the period of limitation on a credit or refund of tax for 2009 that was paid through the offset of H's overpayment for 2011 was likewise open when H filed his Form 8857.

Example 4. On April 15, 2008, H and W filed a joint Federal income tax return for tax year 2007. On October 1, 2009, additional liability was assessed against H and W as a result of income attributable to H being omitted from the return. H and W divorced soon after and, in late December 2009, W moved out of the family home without notifying the United States Postal Service or the IRS of her change of address until the end of January 2010. On January 15, 2010, the IRS mailed a section 6330 notice regarding H and W's 2007 joint Federal income tax liability to H and W's last known address (the address on H and W's joint Federal income tax return for tax year 2008, filed on April 15, 2009). H and W did not request a CDP hearing in response to the section 6330 notice. The IRS issued a levy on W's wages to W's employer on June 2, 2010. W filed Form 8857 requesting relief under section 6015 on May 15, 2012. Actual receipt of a section 6330 notice is not required to start the two-year period for purposes of §1.6015-2 or 1.6015-3, as long as the notice is sent to the taxpayer at the taxpayer's last known address by certified or registered mail. The two-year period, therefore, expired on January 15, 2012. Accordingly, W's request for relief is too late to be considered for any relief under §1.6015-2 or 1.6015-3, as the request was filed more than two years after the IRS sent the section 6330 notice. But because the period of limitation on collection was open (generally until October 1, 2019) when W filed the Form 8857, the IRS will consider whether W is entitled to equitable relief under §1.6015- 4. Further, to the extent W's request for equitable relief under §1.6015-4 seeks a refund of tax W paid through the levy, W's Form 8857 is a timely claim for refund because it was filed within the applicable period of limitation for credit or refund of tax (in this case, two years from payment of the tax).

Example 5. H and W timely filed a joint Federal income tax return for tax year 1999. The IRS selected the 1999 return for examination and determined a deficiency in tax of $10,000. The IRS assessed the tax on December 1, 2001. The taxpayers were divorced in 2005. On her separate Federal income tax return for tax year 2005, W reported an overpayment of $2,500, which the IRS applied on May 3, 2006, to the joint liability for 1999. On her separate Federal income tax return for tax year 2009, W reported an overpayment of $1,750, which the IRS applied on May 15, 2010, to the joint liability for 1999. On May 1, 2012, W filed with the IRS a Form 8857 requesting relief under section 6015. The IRS will not consider whether W is entitled to any relief under §1.6015-2 or 1.6015-3 because W's election is untimely as W's Form 8857 was filed after the end of the two-year period running from the offset of W's overpayment from her tax year 2005 return. Although the collection period expired on December 1, 2011, the IRS will consider whether W is entitled to equitable relief under §1.6015-4 for tax year 1999 because W filed Form 8857 within the two-year period for claiming a credit or refund of tax under section 6511(a). Under section 6511(b)(2), the amount of any refund to which W might be entitled is limited to $1,750 (the amount paid within the two years preceding the filing of W's Form 8857), and the $2,500 collected in May 2006 is not available for refund.

Example 6. Assume the same facts as in Example 5, except that W's separate Federal income tax return for tax year 2009 did not report an overpayment, and there was no offset against the joint liability for 1999. The IRS will not consider whether W is entitled to any relief under §1.6015-2 or 1.6015-3 because W's election is untimely as W's Form 8857 was filed after the end of the two-year period running from the offset of W's overpayment from her tax year 2005 return. Further, as the collection period expired on December 1, 2011, and the period for claiming a credit or refund of tax under section 6511(a) expired on May 3, 2008, IRS will not consider whether W is entitled to equitable relief under §1.6015-4 for tax year 1999.

(6) *Premature requests for relief.*—The IRS will not consider for relief under §§1.6015-2, 1.6015-3, or 1.6015-4 any election or request for relief from joint and several liability that is premature. A premature election or request for relief is an election or request, other than a request for relief for a liability that is properly reported on a joint Federal income tax return but not paid, that is filed for a tax year prior to the receipt of a notification of an examination or a letter or notice from the IRS indicating that there may be an outstanding liability with regard to that year. These notices or letters do not include notices issued pursuant to section 6223 relating to Tax Equity and Fiscal Responsibility Act of 1982 (TEFRA) partnership proceedings. A premature request for relief is not considered an election or request under §1.6015-1(h)(5).

(c) * * *.—(1) * * * A requesting spouse who receives a final administrative determination of relief under §1.6015-1 may not later elect the application of §1.6015-2 or 1.6015-3, or request equitable relief under §1.6015-4, including through the CDP hearing procedures under sections 6320 and 6330.

(2) *Reconsideration process.*—Pursuant to §§1.6015-1(h)(5) and 1.6015-5(c)(1), a requesting spouse is generally entitled to submit only one request for relief and receive only one final administrative determination. Nevertheless, if a requesting spouse submits new information (including new facts, evidence, and arguments not previously considered) to the IRS after the IRS issues a final administrative determination to the requesting spouse, the IRS may reconsider the requesting spouse's request for relief under its established reconsideration process. A request for a reconsideration is not a qualifying election under §1.6015-2 or 1.6015-3, or a request under §1.6015-4, for purposes of §1.6015-1(h)(5). Any reconsideration of a final administrative determination by the IRS, and any notice or letter issued to the requesting spouse as a result of the reconsideration (such as Letter 4277C, Letter 5186C, Letter 5187C, or Letter 5188C), is not the IRS's final determination for purposes of section 6015(e) and is not subject to review by the Tax Court under section 6015(e) or §1.6015-7.

(3) *Examples.*—The following examples illustrate the rules of this paragraph (c):

Example 1. In January 2008, W became a limited partner in partnership P, and in February 2009, she started her own business from which she earned $100,000 of gross income for the taxable year 2009. H and W filed a joint Federal income tax return for 2009, on which they claimed $20,000 in losses from the investment in P, and they omitted W's self-employment tax. In March 2011, the IRS commenced an examination under the provisions of the Code for TEFRA partnership proceedings and sent H and W a notice of the proceeding under section 6223(a)(1). In September 2011, the IRS opened an examination of H and W's 2009 joint return regarding the omitted self-employment tax. In 2012, H decides to pursue relief under section 6015. H may file a request for relief as to liability for self-employment tax because he has received a notification of an examination informing him of potential liability. A request for relief regarding the TEFRA partnership proceeding, however, is premature under paragraph (b)(6) of this section. H must wait until the IRS sends him a notice of computational adjustment or assesses any liability resulting from the TEFRA partnership proceeding before he may file a request for relief from that liability. An assessment of tax in the TEFRA partnership proceeding would be separate from an assessment for the self-employment tax. Therefore, a subsequent request from H for relief from any liability resulting from the TEFRA partnership proceeding will not be precluded under this paragraph (c) by a previous request that H filed for relief from self-employment tax liability.

Example 2. On October 21, 2009, H filed a Form 8857 requesting relief under §§1.6015-2, 1.6015-3, and 1.6015-4 for an assessed deficiency relating to his joint income tax return for tax year 2004. On August 11, 2010, the IRS issued a final administrative determination denying H relief from the liability for tax year 2004. Under section 6015(e), H had until November 9, 2010, to file a petition to the Tax Court to challenge the denial of relief. H did not timely file a petition. On October 3, 2011, H submitted information with respect to his claim for relief for tax year 2004 that he did not previously provide. The IRS considered the new information pursuant to its established reconsideration process in IRM 25.15.17 (Rev. 03/08/2013) and informed H on January 25, 2012, via Letter 4277C that he was still not entitled to relief under any subsection of section 6015. Letter 4277C is not a final administrative determination and did not confer any new rights for H to file a petition to the Tax Court to challenge the final administrative determination issued on August 11, 2010, or the denial of relief from the IRS's reconsideration.

Tax Liability: Relief from Joint and Several Liability

Tax Liability: Relief from Joint and Several Liability.—Amendments to Reg. §1.6015-9, providing guidance to taxpayers on when and how to request relief under sections 66 and 6015, are proposed (published in the Federal Register on August 13, 2013) (REG-132251-11).

☐ Par 6. Section 1.6015-9 is revised to read as follows:

§1.6015-9. Effective/applicability date.—(a) *In general.*—Except as provided in paragraph (b) of this section, §§1.6015-0 through 1.6015-9 are applicable for all elections under §1.6015-2 or 1.6015-3 or any requests for relief under §1.6015-4 filed on or after July 18, 2002.

(b) Except for the rules for determining the timeliness of an election under §1.6015-2 or 1.6015-3, or a request for equitable relief under §1.6015-4 in paragraphs (b)(1) and (b)(2) of §1.6015-5, §1.6015-5 is applicable to any election under §1.6015-2 or 1.6015-3, or to any request for equitable relief under §1.6015-4, filed on or after the date of publication of the Treasury decision adopting these rules as final regulations in the **Federal Register**. The rules for determining the timeliness of an election under §1.6015-2 or 1.6015-3, or a request for equitable relief under §1.6015-4 in paragraphs (b)(1) and (b)(2) of §1.6015-5 are applicable to any election under §1.6015-2 or 1.6015-3, or to any request for equitable relief under §1.6015-4, filed on or after July 25, 2011 (the date that Notice 2011-70, 2011-32 IRB 135, was issued to the public). [Reg. §1.6015-9.]

Taxable Income: Relief from Joint and Several Liability

Taxable Income: Relief from Joint and Several Liability.—Amendments to Reg. §§1.6015-0—1.6015-9, relating to relief from joint and several liability under section 6015 of the Internal Revenue Code and reflecting changes in the law made by the Tax Relief and Health Care Act of 2006 as well as changes in the law arising from litigation, are proposed (published in the Federal Register on November 20, 2015) (REG-134219-08).

Par. 7. Section 1.6015-0 is amended by:

1. In §1.6015-1, entries for paragraphs (e)(1), (e)(2), (e)(3), (e)(4), (e)(5), (h)(6), (h)(7), (h)(8), (k), (l), (m), (n), (o), and (p) are added and the entry for paragraph (h)(5) is revised.

2. In §1.6015-2, entries for paragraphs (b), (c), (d), and (e) are revised and the entries for paragraphs (e)(1) and (e)(2) are removed.

3. In § 1.6015-3, entries for paragraphs (a) and (c)(2)(v) are revised and entries for paragraphs (c)(2)(vi), (d)(2)(i)(A), (d)(2)(i)(B), and (e) are added.

4. In § 1.6015-4, an entry for paragraph (d) is added.

5. In § 1.6015-5, an entry for paragraph (d) is added.

6. In § 1.6015-6, an entry for paragraph (d) is added.

7. In § 1.6015-7, entries for paragraphs (c)(1) and (c)(4)(iii) are revised and entries for paragraphs (c)(1)(i), (c)(1)(ii), (c)(1)(iii), and (d) are added.

8. In § 1.6015-8, an entry for paragraph (d) is added.

9. Section 1.6015-9 entry is removed.

The revisions and additions read as follows:

Par. 8. Section 1.6015-1 is amended by:

1. Paragraphs (a)(2), (e), (h)(1), and (h)(5) are revised.

2. The last three sentences of paragraph (h)(4) are removed.

3. Paragraphs (h)(6), (7), and (8) and (k) are added.

4. Paragraph (l) is added and reserved.

5. Paragraphs (m), (n), (o), and (p) are added.

The revisions and additions read as follows:

§ 1.6015-1. Relief from joint and several liability on a joint return.—(a) * * *

(2) A requesting spouse may submit a single request for relief under § § 1.6015-2, 1.6015-3, and 1.6015-4. Upon submitting a request for relief, the IRS will consider whether relief is appropriate under § § 1.6015-2 and 1.6015-3 and, to the extent relief is unavailable under both of those provisions, under § 1.6015-4. Equitable relief under § 1.6015-4 is available only to a requesting spouse who fails to qualify for relief under § § 1.6015-2 and 1.6015-3.

* * *

(e) *Res judicata and collateral estoppel.*—(1) *In general.*—A requesting spouse is barred from relief from joint and several liability under section 6015 by res judicata for any tax year for which a court of competent jurisdiction has rendered a final decision on the requesting spouse's tax liability if relief under section 6015 was at issue in the prior proceeding, or if the requesting spouse meaningfully participated in that proceeding and could have raised the issue of relief under section 6015.

(2) *Situations in which relief under § 1.6015-3 will not be considered to have been at issue in the prior proceeding.*—Relief under § 1.6015-3

will not be considered to have been at issue in a prior proceeding if the requesting spouse only raised the issue of relief under section 6015 in general and did not specify under which subsection relief was being requested, and the requesting spouse was not eligible for relief under § 1.6015-3 during the prior proceeding because the requesting spouse was not divorced, widowed, or legally separated, or had been a member of the same household as the nonrequesting spouse during the prior 12 months.

(3) *Meaningful participation.*—A requesting spouse meaningfully participated in the prior proceeding if the requesting spouse was involved in the proceeding so that the requesting spouse could have raised the issue of relief under section 6015 in that proceeding. Meaningful participation is a facts and circumstances determination. Absent abuse as set forth in paragraph (i) of this section, the following is a nonexclusive list of acts to be considered in making the facts and circumstances determination: whether the requesting spouse participated in the IRS Appeals process while the prior proceeding was docketed; whether the requesting spouse participated in pretrial meetings; whether the requesting spouse participated in discovery; whether the requesting spouse participated in settlement negotiations; whether the requesting spouse signed court documents, such

as a petition, a stipulation of facts, motions, briefs, or any other documents; whether the requesting spouse participated at trial (for example, the requesting spouse was present or testified at the prior proceeding); and whether the requesting spouse was represented by counsel in the prior proceeding. No one act necessarily determines the outcome. The degree of importance of each act varies depending on the requesting spouse's facts and circumstances.

(i) Notwithstanding the fact that a requesting spouse performed any of the acts listed in paragraph (e)(3) of this section in the prior proceeding, the requesting spouse will not be considered to have meaningfully participated in the prior proceeding if the requesting spouse establishes that the requesting spouse performed the acts because the nonrequesting spouse abused (as described in paragraph (o) of this section) or maintained control over the requesting spouse, and the requesting spouse did not challenge the nonrequesting spouse for fear of the nonrequesting spouse's retaliation.

(ii) A requesting spouse did not meaningfully participate in a prior proceeding if, due to the effective date of section 6015, relief under section 6015 was not available in that proceeding.

(iii) In a case petitioned from a statutory notice of deficiency under section 6213, the fact that the requesting spouse did not have the ability to effectively contest the underlying deficiency is irrelevant for purposes of determining whether the requesting spouse meaningfully participated in the court proceeding for purposes of paragraph (e)(1) of this section.

(4) *Examples.*—The following examples illustrate the rules of this paragraph (e):

Example 1. In a prior court proceeding involving a petition from a notice of deficiency related to a joint income tax return, H and W were still married and filed a timely joint petition to the United States Tax Court. The petition stated that W was entitled to relief under section 6015 without specifying under which subsection she was requesting relief. Before trial, H negotiates with the IRS Chief Counsel attorney and settles the case. W did not meaningfully participate. A stipulated decision was entered that did not mention relief under section 6015. One year later W files a request for relief under section 6015. While W did not meaningfully participate in the prior court proceeding, because relief under section 6015 was at issue in that case, res judicata applies except with respect to relief under § 1.6015-3. Because W did not specify that she was requesting relief under § 1.6015-3, and W was not eligible to request relief under that section because she was still married to the nonrequesting spouse throughout the court proceeding, relief under § 1.6015-3 is not considered to have been at issue in that case. Thus, W is not barred by res judicata from raising relief under § 1.6015-3 in a later case. However, any later claim from W requesting relief under § 1.6015-2 or § 1.6015-4 would be barred by res judicata.

Example 2. Same facts as in *Example 1* of this paragraph (e)(4) except that H and W are divorced at the time the petition was filed. Because W was eligible to request relief under § 1.6015-3 as she was divorced from H, relief under § 1.6015-3 is considered to be at issue in the prior court proceeding and W is barred by res judicata from raising relief under § 1.6015-3 in a later case. Thus, any later claim from W requesting relief under any subsection of section 6015 would be barred by res judicata.

Example 3. The IRS issued a notice of deficiency to H and W determining a deficiency on H and W's joint income tax return based on H's Schedule C business. H and W timely filed a petition in the United States Tax Court. W signed the petition and numerous other documents, participated in discussions regarding the case with the IRS Chief Counsel attorney, and ultimately agreed to a settlement of the case. W could have raised any issue, but W did not have any access to H's records regarding his Schedule C business, over which H maintained exclusive control. Relief under section 6015 was never raised in the court proceeding. If W were to later file a request for relief under section 6015, W's claim would be barred by res judicata. Considering these facts and circumstances, W meaningfully participated in the prior court proceeding regarding the deficiency. The fact that W could not have effectively contested the underlying deficiency because she had no access to H's Schedule C records is not relevant to the determination of whether W meaningfully participated. Instead the meaningful participation exception looks to W's involvement in the prior court proceeding and her ability to raise relief under section 6015 as a defense.

Example 4. Same facts as *Example 3* of this paragraph (e)(4), except that W's participation in discussions with the IRS Chief Counsel attorney were clearly controlled by H, and W was fearful of H when she agreed to settle the case. In this situation, her involvement in the prior proceeding would not be considered meaningful participation because W was able to establish that H maintained control over her and that she did not challenge H for fear of the H's retaliation. If W were to later file a request for relief under section 6015, her claim would not be barred by res judicata.

Example 5. In March 2014, the IRS issued a notice of deficiency to H and W determining a deficiency on H and W's joint income tax

return for tax year 2011. H and W timely filed a pro se petition in the United States Tax Court for redetermination of the deficiency. W signed the petition, but otherwise, H handled the entire litigation, from discussing the case with the IRS Chief Counsel attorney to agreeing to a settlement of the case. Relief under section 6015 was never raised. W signed the decision document that H had agreed to with the IRS Chief Counsel attorney. If W were to later file a claim requesting relief under section 6015, W's claim would not be barred by res judicata. Considering these facts and circumstances, W's involvement in the prior court proceeding regarding the deficiency did not rise to the level of meaningful participation.

Example 6. Same facts as in *Example 5* of this paragraph (e)(4) except that W also participated in settlement negotiations with the IRS Chief Counsel attorney that resulted in the decision document entered in the case. Considering these facts and circumstances—signing the petition and the decision document, along with participating in the negotiations that led to the settlement reflected in the decision document—W meaningfully participated in the prior court proceeding regarding the deficiency because W could have raised relief under section 6015. Any later claim from W requesting relief under section 6015 would be barred by res judicata.

Example 7. In a prior court proceeding involving a petition from a notice of deficiency, H and W hired counsel, C, to represent them in the United States Tax Court. W agreed to C's representation, but otherwise, only H met and communicated with C about the case. C signed and filed the petition, discussed the case with the IRS Chief Counsel attorney, and agreed to a settlement of the case after discussing it with H. Relief under section 6015 was never raised. C signed the decision document on behalf of H and W. If W were to later file a claim requesting relief under section 6015, W's claim would not be barred by res judicata. Even though W was represented by counsel in the prior court proceeding regarding the deficiency, considering all the facts and circumstances, W's involvement in the prior court proceeding did not rise to the level of meaningful participation.

Example 8. In a prior court proceeding involving a petition from a notice of deficiency, H did not sign the petition or other court documents, participate in the Appeals or Counsel settlement negotiations, attend pretrial meetings, or hire separate counsel. H did, however, attend the trial and testify. Considering these facts and circumstances, H's participation in the trial is sufficient to establish that H meaningfully participated in the prior court proceeding regarding the deficiency because H's participation provided H with a definite opportunity to raise relief under section 6015 in that proceeding. Any later claim from H requesting relief under section 6015 would be barred by res judicata.

Example 9. The IRS issued a joint notice of deficiency to H and W determining a deficiency on H and W's joint income tax return based on H's Schedule C business. Only W timely filed a petition in the United States Tax Court. W conceded the deficiency shortly before trial and signed a decision document. W did not raise relief under section 6015. If W were to later file a claim requesting relief under section 6015, W's claim would be barred by res judicata. Because W was the only petitioner in the prior court proceeding, W's participation in that proceeding was meaningful participation.

(5) *Collateral estoppel.*—Any final decisions rendered by a court of competent jurisdiction regarding issues relevant to section 6015 are conclusive, and the requesting spouse may be collaterally estopped from relitigating those issues.

* * *

(h) *Definitions.*—(1) *Requesting spouse.*—A requesting spouse is an individual who filed a joint income tax return and requests relief from Federal income tax liability arising from that return under § 1.6015-2, § 1.6015-3, or § 1.6015-4.

* * *

(5) *Request for relief.*—A qualifying request under § 1.6015-2, § 1.6015-3, or § 1.6015-4 is the first timely request for relief from joint and several liability for the tax year for which relief is sought. A qualifying request also includes a requesting spouse's second request for relief from joint and several liability for the same tax year under § 1.6015-3 when the additional qualifications of paragraphs (h)(5)(i) and (ii) of this section are met—

(i) The requesting spouse did not qualify for relief under § 1.6015-3 at the time of the first request solely because the qualifications of § 1.6015-3(a) were not satisfied; and

(ii) At the time of the second request, the qualifications for relief under § 1.6015-3(a) were satisfied.

(6) *Unpaid tax and underpayment.*—Unpaid tax and underpayment for purposes of § 1.6015-4 means the balance due shown on the joint return, reduced by the tax paid with the joint return. The balance due shown on the joint return is determined after application of the credits for tax withheld under section 31, any amounts paid as estimated income tax, any amounts paid with an extension of time to file, or any other credits applied against the total tax reported on the

return. Tax paid with the joint return includes a check or money order remitted with the return or Form 1040-V, "Payment Voucher," or payment by direct debit, credit card, or other commercially acceptable means under section 6311. If the joint return is filed on or before the last day prescribed for filing under section 6072 (determined without regard to any extension of time to file under section 6081), the tax paid with the joint return includes any tax paid on or before the last day prescribed for payment under section 6151. If the joint return is filed after the last day prescribed for filing, the tax paid with the joint return includes any tax paid on or before the date the joint return is filed. A requesting spouse is not entitled to be considered for relief under §1.6015-4 for any tax paid with the joint return. If the tax paid with the joint return completely satisfies the balance due shown on the return, then there is no unpaid tax for purposes of §1.6015-4.

(7) *Understatement.*—The term understatement means the excess of the amount of tax required to be shown on the return for the taxable year over the amount of the tax imposed which is shown on the return, reduced by any rebate (within the meaning of section 6211(b)(2)).

(8) *Deficiency.*—The term deficiency has the same meaning given to that term in section 6211 and §301.6211-1 of this chapter.

* * *

(k) *Credit or refund.*—(1) *In general.*—Except as provided in paragraphs (k)(2) through (5) of this section, a requesting spouse who is eligible for relief can receive a credit or refund of payments made to satisfy the joint income tax liability, whether the liability resulted from an understatement or an underpayment.

(2) *No credit or refund allowed under §1.6015-3.*—A requesting spouse is not entitled to a credit or refund of any payments made on the joint income tax liability as a result of allocating the deficiency under §1.6015-3. See section 6015(g)(3) and §1.6015-3(c)(1).

(3) *No circumvention of §§1.6015-1(k)(2) and 1.6015-3(c)(1).*— Section 1.6015-4 may not be used to circumvent the limitation of §1.6015-3(c)(1) (such as, no refunds under §1.6015-3). Therefore, relief is not available under this section to obtain a credit or refund of liabilities already paid, for which the requesting spouse would otherwise qualify for relief under §1.6015-3. For purposes of determining whether the requesting spouse qualifies for relief under §1.6015-3, the fact that a refund was barred by section 6015(g)(2) and paragraph (k)(2) of this section does not mean that the requesting spouse did not receive full relief. A requesting spouse is entitled to full relief under §1.6015-3 if the requesting spouse was eligible to allocate the deficiency in full to the nonrequesting spouse.

(4) *Limitations on credit or refund.*—The availability of credit or refund is subject to the limitations provided by sections 6511 and 6512(b). Generally the filing of Form 8857, "Request for Innocent Spouse Relief," will be treated as the filing of a claim for credit or refund even if the requesting spouse does not specifically request a credit or refund. The amount allowable as a credit or refund, assuming the requesting spouse is eligible for relief, includes payments made after the filing of the Form 8857, as well as payments made within the applicable look-back period provided by section 6511(b).

(5) *Requesting spouse limited to credit or refund of payments made by the requesting spouse.*—A requesting spouse is only eligible for a credit or refund of payments to the extent the requesting spouse establishes that he or she provided the funds used to make the payment for which he or she seeks a credit or refund. Thus, a requesting spouse is not eligible for a credit or refund of payments made by the nonrequesting spouse. A requesting spouse is also generally not eligible for a credit or refund of joint payments made with the nonrequesting spouse. A requesting spouse, however, may be eligible for a credit or refund of the requesting spouse's portion of an overpayment from a joint return filed with the nonrequesting spouse that was offset under section 6402 to the spouses' joint income tax liability, to the extent that the requesting spouse can establish his or her contribution to the overpayment.

(l) [Reserved]

(m) *Penalties and interest.*—Generally, a spouse who is entitled to relief under §1.6015-2, §1.6015-3, or §1.6015-4 is also entitled to relief from related penalties, additions to tax, additional amounts, and interest (collectively, penalties and interest). Penalties and interest, however, are not separate erroneous items (as defined in paragraph (h)(4) of this section) from which a requesting spouse can be relieved separate from the tax. Rather relief from penalties and interest related to an understatement or deficiency will generally be determined based on the proportion of the total erroneous items from which the requesting spouse is relieved. For penalties that relate to a particular erroneous item, see §1.6015-3(d)(4)(iv)(B). Penalties and interest on an underpayment are also not separate items from which a requesting spouse may obtain relief under §1.6015-4. Relief from penalties

and interest on the underpayment will be determined based on the amount of relief from the underpayment to which the requesting spouse is entitled. If the underlying tax liability (whether an assessed deficiency or an underpayment) was paid in full after the joint return was filed but penalties and interest remain unpaid, the requesting spouse may be relieved from the penalties and interest if the requesting spouse is entitled to relief from the underlying tax. The fact that the requesting spouse is entitled to relief from the underlying tax but is not entitled to a refund because of §1.6015-1(k) does not prevent the requesting spouse from being relieved from liability for the penalties and interest.

(n) *Attribution of understatement or deficiency resulting from an increase to adjusted gross income.*—(1) *In general.*—Any portion of an understatement or deficiency relating to the disallowance of an item (or increase to an amount of tax) separately listed on an individual income tax return solely due to the increase of adjusted gross income (or modified adjusted gross income or other similar phase-out thresholds) as a result of an erroneous item solely attributable to the nonrequesting spouse will also be attributable to the nonrequesting spouse unless the evidence shows that a different result is appropriate. If the increase to adjusted gross income is the result of an erroneous item(s) of both the requesting and nonrequesting spouses, the item disallowed (or increased tax) due to the increase to adjusted gross income will be attributable to the requesting spouse in the same ratio as the amount of the item or items attributable to the requesting spouse over the total amount of the items that resulted in the increase to adjusted gross income.

(2) *Examples.*—The following examples illustrate the rules of this paragraph (n):

Example 1. H and W file a joint Federal income tax return. After applying withholding credits there is a tax liability of $500. Based on the earned income reported on the return and the number of qualifying children, H and W are entitled to an Earned Income Tax Credit (EITC) in the amount of $1,500. The EITC satisfies the $500 in tax due and H and W receive a refund in the amount of $1,000. Later the IRS concludes that H had additional unreported income, which increased the tax liability on the return to $1,000 and resulted in H and W's EITC being reduced to zero due to their adjusted gross income exceeding the maximum amount. The IRS determines a deficiency in the amount of $2,000 – $1,500 of which relates to the EITC and $500 of which relates to H's erroneous item – the omitted income. If W requests relief under section 6015, the entire $2,000 deficiency is attributable to H because the EITC was disallowed solely due to the increase of adjusted gross income as a result of H's omitted income. W satisfies the attribution factor of §1.6015-2(a)(2) and the threshold condition in section 4.01(7) of Rev. Proc. 2013-34 with respect to the entire deficiency. Under §1.6015-3(d)(4)(ii), the portion of the deficiency related to the disallowance of the EITC is initially allocated to H.

Example 2. H and W file a joint Federal income tax return reporting a total tax liability of $22,000. Later the IRS concludes that H had additional unreported income in the amount of $20,000, which increased H and W's adjusted gross income and their alternative minimum taxable income. As a result, H and W now owe the Alternative Minimum Tax (AMT). The IRS determines a deficiency in the amount of $5,250 – $250 of which relates to H and W's AMT liability as determined under section 55 and $5,000 of which relates to the increase in H and W's section 1 income tax liability. If W requests relief under section 6015, the entire $5,250 deficiency is attributable to H because H and W owe the AMT solely due to H's erroneous item – the omitted income. W satisfies the attribution factor of §1.6015-2(a)(2) and the threshold condition in section 4.01(7) of Rev. Proc. 2013-34 with respect to the entire deficiency. Under §1.6015-3(d)(4)(ii), the portion of the deficiency related to the AMT is initially allocated to H.

Example 3. H and W file a joint Federal income tax return reporting itemized deductions on Schedule A, "Itemized Deductions," in the amount of $50,000. Later the IRS concludes that $10,000 of W's expenses reported on her Schedule C, "Profit or Loss From Business," were not allowable, which increased H and W's adjusted gross income. As a result, H and W's itemized expenses are reduced to $45,000 as their adjusted gross income exceeded the phase-out amount. The IRS determines a deficiency in the amount of $5,000. If H requests relief under section 6015, the entire $5,000 deficiency is attributable to W because the itemized deductions were reduced solely due to the increase of adjusted gross income as a result of W's erroneous item – the Schedule C expenses. H satisfies the attribution factor of §1.6015-2(a)(2) and the threshold condition in section 4.01(7) of Rev. Proc. 2013-34 with respect to the entire deficiency. Under §1.6015-3(d)(2)(iv), the portion of the deficiency related to the disallowance of the Schedule A deductions is initially allocated to W.

Example 4. H and W file a joint Federal income tax return reporting itemized deductions on Schedule A in the amount of $50,000. Later the IRS concludes that H had additional unreported income in the amount of $4,000 and W had additional unreported income in the amount of $6,000, which increased H and W's adjusted gross income. As a result, H and W's itemized expenses are reduced to $45,000 as their adjusted gross income exceeded the phase-out amount. The IRS determines a deficiency in the amount of $6,000 – $1,500 of which relates to H's erroneous item, $2,500 of which relates to W's erroneous item, and $2,000 of which relates to the reduced itemized deductions. Assuming the conditions for relief under section 6015 are otherwise satisfied, the $2,500 deficiency from W's omitted income is attributable to W and the $1,500 deficiency from H's omitted income is attributable to H. Because the increase to adjusted gross income as a result of both H and W's erroneous items reduced the itemized deductions, the portion of the deficiency related to the disallowed itemized deductions is partially attributable to both H and W. Of the $2,000 deficiency from the disallowed itemized deductions, $800 is attributable to H because 40 percent ($4,000/$10,000) of the items that resulted in the increase to adjusted gross income are attributable to H, and $1,200 is attributable to W because 60 percent ($6,000/$10,000) of the items that resulted in the increase to adjusted gross income are attributable to W. If both H and

W requested relief the most H could be relieved from is $3700, the amount attributable to W ($2500 + $1200), and the most W could be relieved from is $2300, the amount attributable to H ($1500 + $800).

(o) *Abuse by the nonrequesting spouse.*—Abuse comes in many forms and can include physical, psychological, sexual, or emotional abuse, including efforts to control, isolate, humiliate, and intimidate the requesting spouse, or to undermine the requesting spouse's ability to reason independently and be able to do what is required under the tax laws. All the facts and circumstances are considered in determining whether a requesting spouse was abused. The impact of a nonrequesting spouse's alcohol or drug abuse is also considered in determining whether a requesting spouse was abused. Depending on the facts and circumstances, abuse of the requesting spouse's child or other family member living in the household may constitute abuse of the requesting spouse.

(p) *Effective/applicability date.*—This section will be applicable on the date of publication of a Treasury decision adopting these rules as final regulations in the **Federal Register**.

Par. 9. Section 1.6015-2 is amended by:

1. Paragraph (a) introductory text is revised.

2. Paragraph (b) is removed.

3. Paragraphs (c), (d), and (e) are redesignated as paragraphs (b), (c), and (d).

4. Newly designated paragraph (b) is revised.

5. The last sentence of newly designated paragraph (c) is revised.

6. Newly designated paragraph (d) is revised.

7. Paragraph (e) is added.

The revisions and addition read as follows:

§1.6015-2. Relief from liability applicable to all qualifying joint filers.—(a) *In general.*—A requesting spouse may be relieved from joint and several liability for tax (including related additions to tax, additional amounts, penalties, and interest) from an understatement for a taxable year under this section if the requesting spouse requests relief in accordance with §§1.6015-1(h)(5) and 1.6015-5, and—

* * *

(b) *Knowledge or reason to know.*—A requesting spouse has knowledge or reason to know of an understatement if he or she actually knew of the understatement, or if a reasonable person in similar circumstances would have known of the understatement. For rules relating to a requesting spouse's actual knowledge, see §1.6015-3(c)(2). All of the facts and circumstances are considered in determining whether a requesting spouse had reason to know of an understatement. The facts and circumstances that are considered include, but are not limited to, the nature of the erroneous item and the amount of the erroneous item relative to other items; any deceit or evasiveness of the nonrequesting spouse; the couple's financial situation; the requesting spouse's educational background and business experience; the extent of the requesting spouse's participation in the activity that resulted in the erroneous item; the requesting spouse's involvement in business or household financial matters; whether the requesting spouse failed to inquire, at or before the time the return was signed, about items on the return or omitted from the return that a reasonable person would question; any lavish or unusual expenditures compared with past spending levels; and whether the erroneous item represented a departure from a recurring pattern reflected in prior years' returns (for example, omitted income from an investment regularly reported on prior years' returns). A requesting spouse has knowledge or reason to know of the portion of an understatement related to an item attributable to the nonrequesting spouse under §1.6015-1(n) if the requesting spouse knows or has reason to know of the nonrequesting spouse's erroneous item or items that resulted in the increase to adjusted gross income. Depending on the facts and circumstances, if the requesting spouse was abused by the nonrequesting spouse (as described in §1.6015-1(o)), or the nonrequesting spouse maintained control of the household finances by restricting the requesting spouse's access to financial information, and because of the abuse or financial control, the requesting spouse was not able to challenge the treatment of any items on the joint return for fear of the nonrequesting spouse's retaliation,

the requesting spouse will be treated as not having knowledge or reason to know of the items giving rise to the understatement. If, however, the requesting spouse involuntarily executed the return, the requesting spouse may choose to establish that the return was signed under duress. In such a case, §1.6013-4(d) applies.

(c) * * * For guidance concerning the criteria to be used in determining whether it is inequitable to hold a requesting spouse jointly and severally liable under this section, see Rev. Proc. 2013-34 (2013-2 CB 397), or other guidance published by the Treasury and IRS (see §601.601(d)(2) of this chapter).

(d) *Partial relief.*—(1) *In general.*—If a requesting spouse had no knowledge or reason to know of a portion of an erroneous item, the requesting spouse may be relieved of the liability attributable to that portion of that item, if all other requirements are met with respect to that portion.

(2) *Example.*—The following example illustrates the rules of this paragraph (d):

Example. H and W are married and file their 2014 joint income tax return in March 2015. In April 2016, H is convicted of embezzling $2 million from his employer during 2014. H kept all of his embezzlement income in an individual bank account, and he used most of the funds to support his gambling habit. H and W had a joint bank account into which H and W deposited all of their reported income. Each month during 2014, H transferred an additional $10,000 from the individual account to H and W's joint bank account. Although H paid the household expenses using this joint account, W regularly received the bank statements relating to the account. W did not know or have reason to know of H's embezzling activities. W did, however, know or have reason to know of $120,000 of the $2 million of H's embezzlement income at the time she signed the joint return because that amount passed through the couple's joint bank account and she regularly received bank statements showing the monthly deposits from H's individual account. Therefore, W may be relieved of the liability arising from $1,880,000 of the unreported embezzlement income, but she may not be relieved of the liability for the deficiency arising from $120,000 of the unreported embezzlement income of which she knew and had reason to know.

(e) *Effective/applicability date.*—This section will be applicable on the date of publication of a Treasury decision adopting these rules as final regulations in the **Federal Register**.

Par. 10. Section 1.6015-3 is amended by:

1. The paragraph heading and first sentence of paragraph (a) are revised.

2. Paragraphs (c)(1) and (c)(2)(iv) are revised.

3. A sentence is added at the end of paragraph (c)(2)(i).

4. Paragraph (c)(2)(v) is redesignated as paragraph (c)(2)(vi) and paragraph (c)(2)(v) is added.

5. Newly redesignated paragraph (c)(2)(vi) is revised.

6. Paragraphs (d)(2)(i) and (d)(5) introductory text are revised.

7. In paragraph (d)(5), *Examples 7, 8, 9, 10,* and *11* are added.

8. Paragraph (e) is added.

The revisions and additions read as follows:

§1.6015-3. Allocation of deficiency for individuals who are no longer married, are legally separated, or are not members of the same household.—(a) *Allocation of deficiency.*—A requesting spouse may allocate a deficiency (as defined in §1.6015-1(h)(8)) if, as defined in paragraph (b) of this section, the requesting spouse is divorced, widowed, or legally separated, or has not been a member of the same household as the nonrequesting spouse at any time during the 12-month period ending on the date the request for relief is filed. * * *

(c) * * * (1) *No refunds.* Although a requesting spouse may be eligible to allocate the deficiency to the nonrequesting spouse, refunds are not authorized under this section. Refunds of paid liabilities for which a requesting spouse was entitled to allocate the deficiency under this section may be considered under §1.6015-2 but not under §1.6015-4. See §1.6015-1(k)(3).

(2) * * * (i) * * * A requesting spouse has actual knowledge of the portion of an understatement related to an item attributable to the nonrequesting spouse under §1.6015-1(n) and allocable to the nonrequesting spouse under paragraph (d) of this section if the requesting spouse has actual knowledge of the nonrequesting spouse's erroneous item or items that resulted in the increase to adjusted gross income.

* * *

(iv) *Factors supporting actual knowledge.*—To demonstrate that a requesting spouse had actual knowledge of an erroneous item at the time the return was signed, the Internal Revenue Service (IRS) will consider all the facts and circumstances, including but not limited to, whether the requesting spouse made a deliberate effort to avoid learning about the item to be shielded from liability; whether the erroneous item would have been allocable to the requesting spouse but for the tax benefit rule in paragraph (d)(2)(i) of this section; and whether the requesting spouse and the nonrequesting spouse jointly owned the property that resulted in the erroneous item. These factors, together with all other facts and circumstances, may demonstrate that the requesting spouse had actual knowledge of the item. If the requesting spouse had actual knowledge of an erroneous item, the portion of the deficiency with respect to that item will not be allocated to the nonrequesting spouse.

(v) *Actual knowledge and community property.*—A requesting spouse will not be considered to have had an ownership interest in an item based solely on the operation of community property law. Rather, a requesting spouse who resided in a community property state at the time the return was signed will be considered to have had an ownership interest in an item only if the requesting spouse's name appeared on the ownership documents, or there otherwise is an indication that the requesting spouse asserted dominion and control over the item. For example, assume H and W live in State A, a community property state. After their marriage, H opens a bank account in his name. Under the operation of the community property laws of State A, W owns one-half of the bank account. Assuming there is no other indication that she asserted dominion and control over the item, W does not have an ownership interest in the account for purposes of this paragraph (c)(2)(v) because she does not hold the account in her name.

(vi) *Abuse exception.*—Depending on the facts and circumstances, if the requesting spouse was abused by the nonrequesting spouse (as described in §1.6015-1(o)), or the nonrequesting spouse maintained control of the household finances by restricting the requesting spouse's access to financial information, and because of the abuse or financial control, the requesting spouse was not able to challenge the treatment of any items on the joint return for fear of the nonrequesting spouse's retaliation, the limitation on the requesting spouse's ability to allocate the deficiency because of actual knowledge will not apply. The requesting spouse will be treated as not having knowledge of the items giving rise to the deficiency. If, however, the requesting spouse involuntarily executed the return, the requesting spouse may choose to establish that the return was signed under duress. In such a case, §1.6013-4(d) applies.

* * *

(d) * * *

(2) * * *

(i) *Benefit on the return.*—(A) *In general.*—An erroneous item that would otherwise be allocated to one spouse is allocated to the second spouse to the extent that the second spouse received a tax benefit on the joint return and the first spouse did not receive a tax benefit. An erroneous item under this paragraph can be allocated to a requesting spouse or a nonrequesting spouse, but only a spouse who requests relief under this section may allocate the deficiency. A spouse who does not request relief under section 6015 remains fully liable for the deficiency. An allocation from a requesting spouse to a nonrequesting spouse reduces the amount for which a requesting spouse remains liable while an allocation from a nonrequesting spouse to a requesting spouse increases the amount for which a requesting spouse remains liable.

(B) *Calculating separate taxable income and tax due.*—Under section 6015(d)(3)(A), the items giving rise to the deficiency must be allocated to each spouse in the same manner as the items would have been allocated if the spouses had filed separate returns. In determining whether a spouse received a tax benefit from the item, it may be necessary to calculate each spouse's hypothetical separate return taxable income, determined without regard to the erroneous items, and taking into consideration adjusted gross income, allowable deductions and losses, and allowable credits against tax.

* * *

(5) *Examples.*—The following examples illustrate the rules of this paragraph (d). In each example, assume that the requesting spouse or spouses qualify to allocate the deficiency, that a request under section 6015 was timely made, and that the deficiency remains unpaid. In addition, unless otherwise stated, assume that neither spouse actually knew of the erroneous items allocable to the other spouse. The examples are as follows:

* * *

Example 7. Calculation of tax benefit based on taxable income. (i) On their joint Federal income tax return for tax year 2009, H reports $60,000 of wage income; W reports $25,000 of wage income; and H and W report joint interest income of $2,000 and joint ordinary income from investments in the amount of $6,000. In addition, H and W properly deduct $30,000 for their two personal exemptions and itemized deductions, and W erroneously reports a loss from her separate investment in a partnership in the amount of $20,000. On May 3, 2012, a $5,000 deficiency is assessed with respect to their 2009 joint return. W dies in November 2012. H requests innocent spouse relief. The deficiency on the joint return results from a disallowance of all of W's $20,000 loss (which is initially allocable to W).

(ii) After taking all sources of income and all allowable deductions into consideration, H's separate taxable income is $49,000 and W's separate taxable income is $14,000, calculated as follows:

	H	W
Wages	$60,000	$25,000
Interest Income	$1,000	$1,000
Investment Income	$3,000	$3,000
Adj. Gross Income	$64,000	$29,000
Exemptions and Deductions	($15,000)	($15,000)
Taxable Income	$49,000	$14,000
W's Disallowed Loss		($20,000)
Tax Benefit Not Used by W		($6,000)
Tax Benefit to W		($14,000)
Tax Benefit to H	($6,000)	

(iii) As W only used $14,000 of her $20,000 loss from her separate investment in a partnership to offset her separate taxable income, H benefited from the other $6,000 of the disallowed loss used to offset his separate taxable income. Therefore, $14,000 of the disallowed $20,000 loss is allocable to W (7/10) and $6,000 of the disallowed loss is allocable to H (3/10). H's liability is limited to $1,500 (3/10 of the $5,000 deficiency).

Example 8. Nonrequesting spouse receives a benefit on the joint return from the requesting spouse's erroneous item. (i) On their joint Federal income tax return for tax year 2008, W reports $40,000 of wage income and H reports $12,000 of wage income. In addition, H and W properly deduct $20,000 for their two personal exemptions and itemized deductions, H erroneously deducts a casualty loss in the amount of $5,000 related to a loss on his separately held property, and W erroneously takes a loss in the amount of $7,000 from an investment in a tax shelter. H and W legally separate in 2010, and on October 21, 2011, a $2,400 deficiency is assessed with respect to their 2008 joint return. H requests innocent spouse relief. The deficiency on the joint return results from a disallowance of all of H's $5,000 loss and all of W's $7,000 loss (which is allocable to W and for which H did not have actual knowledge).

(ii) The $5,000 casualty loss is initially allocated to H. As H's separate taxable income is only $2,000 ($12,000 wage income less $10,000 - 50 percent of the exemptions and itemized deductions), H only used $2,000 of his $5,000 casualty loss to offset his separate taxable income, and W benefited from the other $3,000 of the disallowed loss, which offset a portion of her separate taxable income. Therefore, $3,000 of the disallowed loss is allocable to W even though the loss is H's item, and $2,000 of the loss is allocable to H. The $7,000 tax shelter loss is also allocable to W as H did not have knowledge of the facts that made the tax shelter item unallowable as a loss. H's allocation percentage is 1/6 ($2,000/$12,000) and H's liability is limited to $400 (1/6 of $2,400 deficiency). The IRS may collect up to $400 from H and up to $2,400 from W (although the total amount collected may not exceed $2,400).

(iii) If the IRS could establish that H had knowledge of the facts that made the deduction for his casualty loss unallowable, the entire $5,000 casualty loss would be allocable to H. H's allocation percentage would be 5/12 ($5,000/$12,000) and H's liability would be limited to $1,000 (5/12 of $2,400 deficiency).

(iv) If W also requested innocent spouse relief (and H did not have knowledge of the facts that made his loss unallowable), there would be no remaining joint and several liability, and the IRS would be permitted to collect $400 from H (1/6 ($2,000/$12,000) of the $2,400 deficiency) and $2,000 (5/6 ($10,000/$12,000) of $2,400 deficiency) from W. If the IRS could establish that W had knowledge of the facts that made the deduction for the casualty loss unallowable, W would then be liable for the entire $2,400 deficiency, while H would remain liable for up to $400.

Example 9. Allocation of liability based on joint erroneous loss item. (i) On their joint Federal income tax return for tax year 2009, H reports $100,000 of wage income and W reports $50,000 of wage income. In addition, H and W properly deduct $40,000 for their two personal exemptions and itemized deductions, and erroneously report a loss in the amount of $50,000 from a jointly-held investment in a tax shelter. H and W divorce in 2011, and on August 14, 2012, a $12,000 deficiency is assessed with respect to their 2009 joint return. W requests innocent spouse relief. The deficiency on the joint return results from a disallowance of all of the $50,000 loss.

(ii) Under paragraph (d)(2)(iv) of this section, in the absence of clear and convincing evidence supporting a different allocation, an erroneous deduction item related to a jointly-owned investment is generally allocated 50 percent to each spouse. Thus, $25,000 of the loss is allocated to each spouse. In determining the effect, if any, of the tax benefit rule of § 1.6015-1(d)(2)(i), H's separate taxable income is $80,000: $100,000 wage income minus $20,000, or 50 percent of the exemptions and itemized deductions; and W's separate taxable income is $30,000: $50,000 minus $20,000. As both H's and W's separate

taxable income exceeds their allocated share of the disallowed loss, no additional amount is allocated between the spouses. W's allocation percentage is 1/2 ($25,000/$50,000) and W's liability is limited to $6,000 (1/2 of $12,000 deficiency). The IRS may collect up to $6,000 from W and up to $12,000 from H (although the total amount collected may not exceed $12,000).

(iii) If the IRS could establish that W had knowledge of the facts that made the loss unallowable, both H and W would then remain jointly and severally liable for the $12,000 deficiency.

Example 10. Calculation of tax benefit based on joint erroneous item. Assume the same facts as in *Example 9* of this paragraph (d)(5), except that W's wage income is only $40,000. W's separate taxable income would then be only $20,000 ($40,000 wage income minus $20,000 - 50 percent of the exemptions and itemized deductions). W would only be able to use $20,000 of the $25,000 loss from the tax shelter to offset her separate taxable income. Accordingly, H benefited from the other $5,000 of the disallowed loss, which was used to offset a portion of his separate taxable income. Therefore, $20,000 of the disallowed loss is allocable to W, and $30,000 is allocable to H: $25,000 (H's 50 percent of the disallowed loss) plus $5,000 (the portion of W's 50 percent that is allocable to H because H received a tax benefit). W's allocation percentage is 2/5 ($20,000/$50,000) and W's liability is limited to $4,800 (2/5 of $12,000 deficiency). The IRS may collect up to $4,800 from W and up to $12,000 from H (although the total amount collected may not exceed $12,000).

Example 11. Allocation of erroneous item based on fraud of the nonrequesting spouse. During 2009, W fraudulently accesses H's brokerage account to sell stock that H had separately received from an inheritance. W deposits the funds from the sale in a separate bank account to which H did not have access. H and W file a joint Federal income tax return for tax year 2009. The return did not include the income from the sale of the stock. H and W divorce in November 2010. The divorce decree states that W committed forgery and defrauded H with respect to his brokerage account. The IRS commences an audit in March 2011 and determines a deficiency based on the omission of the income from the sale of the stock. H requests innocent spouse relief. Under paragraph (d)(2)(iii) of this section, items of investment income are generally allocated to the spouse who owned the investment, which in this case would be H. Under paragraph (d)(2)(ii) of this section, however, the IRS may allocate any item between the spouses if the IRS determines that the allocation is appropriate due to fraud by one or both spouses. The IRS determines that W committed fraud with respect to H and as a result it is appropriate to allocate the deficiency to W under paragraph (d)(2)(ii).

(e) *Effective/applicability date.*—This section will be applicable on the date of publication of a Treasury decision adopting these rules as final regulations in the **Federal Register**.

Par. 17. For each entry for Section 1.6015-3 in the "Section" column remove the language in the "Remove" column and add the language in the "Add" column in its place.

Section	Remove	Add
1.6015-3(c)(4) *Example 4* (ii), (iii), (iv), and (v), first sentence	*Example 5*	*Example 4*
1.6015-3(c)(4) *Example 5* (ii), (iii), and (iv), first sentence	*Example 6*	*Example 5*

Par. 11. Section 1.6015-4 is revised to read as follows:

§1.6015-4. Equitable relief.—(a) A requesting spouse who files a joint return for which an understatement or deficiency (as defined by § 1.6015-1(h)(7) and (8)) was determined or for which there was unpaid tax (as defined by § 1.6015-1(h)(6)), and who does not qualify for full relief under § 1.6015-2 or § 1.6015-3, may be entitled to equitable relief under this section. The Internal Revenue Service (IRS) has the discretion to grant equitable relief from joint and several liability to a requesting spouse when, considering all of the facts and circumstances, it would be inequitable to hold the requesting spouse jointly and severally liable.

(b) This section may not be used to circumvent the limitation of § 1.6015-3(c)(1). Therefore, relief is not available under this section to obtain a refund of liabilities already paid, for which the requesting spouse would otherwise qualify for relief under § 1.6015-3. See

§ 1.6015-1(k)(3). If the requesting spouse is only eligible for partial relief under § 1.6015-3 (i.e., some portion of the deficiency is allocable to the requesting spouse), then the requesting spouse may be considered for relief under this section with respect to the portion of the deficiency for which the requesting spouse was not entitled to relief.

(c) For guidance concerning the criteria to be used in determining whether it is inequitable to hold a requesting spouse jointly and severally liable under this section, see Rev. Proc. 2013-34 (2013-1 IRB 397), or other guidance published by the Treasury and IRS (see § 601.601(d)(2) of this chapter).

(d) *Effective/applicability date.*—This section will be applicable on the date of publication of a Treasury decision adopting these rules as final regulations in the **Federal Register**.

Par. 12. Section 1.6015-5 is amended by adding paragraph (d) to read as follows:

§1.6015-5. Time and manner for requesting relief.

* * *

(d) *Effective/applicability date.*—This section will be applicable on the date of publication of a Treasury decision adopting these rules as final regulations in the **Federal Register**.

Par. 13. Section 1.6015-6 is amended by revising the first sentence of paragraph (a)(1), adding a sentence at the end of paragraph (a)(2), and adding paragraph (d) to read as follows:

§1.6015-6. Nonrequesting spouse's notice and opportunity to participate in administrative proceedings.—(a) * * * (1) When the Internal Revenue Service (IRS) receives a request for relief under §1.6015-2, §1.6015-3, or §1.6015-4, the IRS must send a notice to the nonrequesting spouse's last known address that informs the nonrequesting spouse of the requesting spouse's request for relief. * * *

(2) * * * For guidance concerning the nonrequesting spouse's right to appeal the preliminary determination to IRS Appeals, see

Par. 14. In §1.6015-7, paragraphs (b), (c)(1), (c)(3), and (c)(4)(iii) are revised and paragraph (d) is added to read as follows:

§1.6015-7. Tax Court review.

* * *

(b) *Time period for petitioning the Tax Court.*—Pursuant to section 6015(e), the requesting spouse may petition the Tax Court to review the denial of relief under §1.6015-1 within 90 days after the date the Internal Revenue Service's (IRS) final determination is mailed by certified or registered mail (the 90-day period). If the IRS does not mail the requesting spouse a final determination letter within 6 months of the date the requesting spouse files a request for relief under section 6015, the requesting spouse may petition the Tax Court to review the request at any time after the expiration of the 6-month period and before the expiration of the 90-day period. The Tax Court also may review a request for relief if the Tax Court has jurisdiction under another section of the Internal Revenue Code, such as section 6213(a) or section 6330(d). This paragraph (b) applies to liabilities arising on or after December 20, 2006, or arising prior to December 20, 2006, and remaining unpaid as of that date. For liabilities arising prior to December 20, 2006, which were fully paid prior to that date, the requesting spouse may petition the Tax Court to review the denial of relief as discussed above, but only with respect to denials of relief involving understatements under §1.6015-2, §1.6015-3, or §1.6015-4.

(c) *Restrictions on collection and suspension of the running of the period of limitations.*—(1) *Restrictions on collection.*—(i) *Restrictions on collection for requests for relief made on or after December 20, 2006.*—Unless the IRS determines that collection will be jeopardized by delay, no levy or proceeding in court shall be made, begun, or prosecuted against a spouse requesting relief under §1.6015-2, §1.6015-3, or §1.6015-4 (except for certain requests for relief made solely under §1.6015-4) for the collection of any assessment to which the request relates until the expiration of the 90-day period described in paragraph (b) of this section, or, if a petition is filed with the Tax Court, until the decision of the Tax Court becomes final under section 7481. For requests for relief made solely under §1.6015-4, the restrictions on collection only apply if the liability arose on or after December 20, 2006, or arose prior to December 20, 2006, and remained unpaid as of that date. The restrictions on collection begin on the date the request is filed.

(ii) *Restriction on collection for requests for relief made before December 20, 2006.*—Unless the IRS determines that collection will be jeopardized by delay, no levy or proceeding in court shall be made, begun, or prosecuted against a requesting spouse requesting relief

Rev. Proc. 2003-19 (2003-1 CB 371), or other guidance published by the Treasury Department and the IRS (see §601.601(d)(2) of this chapter).

* * *

(d) *Effective/applicability date.*—This section will be applicable on the date of publication of a Treasury decision adopting these rules as final regulations in the **Federal Register**.

under §1.6015-2 or §1.6015-3 for the collection of any assessment to which the request relates until the expiration of the 90-day period described in paragraph (b) of this section, or if a petition is filed with the Tax Court, until the decision of the Tax Court becomes final under section 7481. The restrictions on collection begin on the date the request is filed with the IRS. For requests for relief made solely under §1.6015-4, the restrictions on collection do not begin until December 20, 2006, and only apply with respect to liabilities remaining unpaid on or after that date.

(iii) *Rules for determining the period of the restrictions on collection.*—For more information regarding the date on which a decision of the Tax Court becomes final, see section 7481 and the regulations thereunder. Notwithstanding paragraphs (c)(1)(i) and (ii) of this section, if the requesting spouse appeals the Tax Court's decision, the IRS may resume collection of the liability from the requesting spouse on the date the requesting spouse files the notice of appeal, unless the requesting spouse files an appeal bond pursuant to the rules of section 7485. Jeopardy under paragraphs (c)(1)(i) and (ii) of this section means conditions exist that would require an assessment under section 6851 or 6861 and the regulations thereunder.

* * *

(3) *Suspension of the running of the period of limitations.*—The running of the period of limitations in section 6502 on collection against the requesting spouse of the assessment to which the request under §1.6015-2, §1.6015-3, or §1.6015-4 relates is suspended for the period during which the IRS is prohibited by paragraph (c)(1) of this section from collecting by levy or a proceeding in court and for 60 days thereafter. If the requesting spouse, however, signs a waiver of the restrictions on collection in accordance with paragraph (c)(2) of this section, the suspension of the period of limitations in section 6502 on collection against the requesting spouse will terminate on the date that is 60 days after the date the waiver is filed with the IRS.

(4) * * *

(iii) *Assessment to which the request relates.*—For purposes of this paragraph (c), the assessment to which the request relates is the entire assessment of the understatement or the balance due shown on the return to which the request relates, even if the request for relief is made with respect to only part of that understatement or balance due.

(d) *Effective/applicability date.*—This section will be applicable on the date of publication of a Treasury decision adopting these rules as final regulations in the **Federal Register**.

Par. 15. Section 1.6015-8 is amended by adding paragraph (d) to read as follows:

§1.6015-8. Applicable liabilities.

* * *

(d) *Effective/applicability date.*—This section will be applicable on the date of publication of a Treasury decision adopting these rules as final regulations in the **Federal Register**.

Par. 17. For each entry for Section 1.6015-8 in the "Section" column remove the language in the "Remove" column and add the language in the "Add" column in its place.

Section	Remove	Add
1.6015-8(c) *Example 1*, fifth sentence	6015(b)	6015

Par. 16. Section 1.6015-9 is removed.

§1.6015-9. Effective/applicability date.

Base Erosion and Anti-Abuse Tax: Additional Rules

Base Erosion and Anti-Abuse Tax: Additional Rules.—Amendments to Reg. §1.6031(a)-1, regarding the base erosion and anti-abuse tax imposed on certain large corporate taxpayers with respect to certain payments made to foreign related parties, are proposed (published in the Federal Register on December 6, 2019) (REG-112607-19).

Par. 7. Section 1.6031(a)-1 is amended by adding paragraphs (b)(7) and (f)(3) to read as follows:

§1.6031(a)-1. Return of partnership income.

* * *

(b) * * *

(7) *Filing obligation for certain partners of certain foreign partnerships with respect to base erosion payments.*—If a foreign partnership is not required to file a partnership return and the foreign partnership has made a payment or accrual that is treated as a base erosion payment of a partner as provided in §1.59A-7(b)(2), a person re-

quired to file a Form 8991 (or successor) who is a partner in the partnership must provide the information necessary to report any base erosion payments on Form 8991 (or successor) or the related instructions. This paragraph does not apply to any partner described in § 1.59A-7(b)(4).

* * *

(f) * * *

(3) Paragraph (b)(7) of this section applies to taxable years ending on or after the date that final regulations are filed with the **Federal Register**.

Returns: Partnerships: Partnership Information

Returns: Partnerships: Partnership Information.—Temporary Reg. §§1.6031(b)-1T and 1.6031(c)-1T, relating to partnership statements and nominee reporting of partnership information, are also proposed as final regulations and, when adopted, would become Reg. §§1.6031(b)-1 and 1.6031(c)-1, respectively (published in the Federal Register on September 7, 1988).

§1.6031(b)-1. Statements to partners.

§1.6031(c)-1. Nominee reporting of partnership infomation.

Expenditures Incurred in Attempts to Influence Legislation

Business Expenses: Private Foundations, Excise Taxes: Expenditures Incurred in Attempts to Influence Legislation.—Reproduced below is the text of a proposed amendment to Reg. §1.6033-2, relating to the treatment, for federal income tax purposes, of expenditures incurred in attempts to influence legislation (published in the Federal Register on November 25, 1980).

* * *

☐ Par. 3. Section 1.6033-2 is amended by revising paragraph (k), by redesignating revised paragraph (k) as paragraph (l), and by adding a new paragraph (k). These revised, redesignated, and added provisions read as follows:

§1.6033-2. Returns by exempt organizations; taxable years beginning after December 31, 1969.

* * *

(k) *Statements about certain expenditures.*—For years after 1980, every organization which is described in section 501(c)(5) or (6) and any other organization exempt under section 501(a) whose members or contributors may deduct dues or contributions as business expenses under section 162 shall furnish to its members and contributors a statement showing what percentage of its total expenditures during the calendar year were lobbying or political expenditures of a type for which §1.162-20 denies deductions to taxpayers. The statement required by the preceding sentence shall be furnished on or before January 31 of the following calendar year. This paragraph shall not apply to an organization for any year during which the

organization makes no lobbying or political expenditures of a type for which §1.162-20 denies deductions to taxpayers. Furthermore, an organization is not required under this paragraph to furnish any statement to a member or contributor for any year if the portion of that person's payments to the organization for that year which is allocable to the type of expenditures for which §1.162-20 denies deductions is

(1) Less than $25, or

(2) Less than $50 and less than 5 percent of the total payments made by that person to the organization for the year.

(l) *Effective date.*—The provisions of this section, other than paragraph (k), shall apply with respect to returns filed for taxable years beginning after December 31, 1969.

Exempt Organizations: Reporting Requirements: Guidance

Exempt Organizations: Reporting Requirements: Guidance.—Amendments to Reg. §1.6033-2, reporting regulations under section 6033 that are generally applicable to organizations exempt from tax under section 501(a) to reflect statutory amendments and certain grants of reporting relief announced through subregulatory guidance that have been made since the current regulations were adopted, particularly with respect to tax-exempt organizations required to file an annual Form 990 or 990-EZ information return, are proposed (published in the Federal Register on September 10, 2019) (REG-102508-16).

Par. 2. Section 1.6033-2 is amended by:
1. Revising the section heading;
2. In paragraph (a)(2)(ii) introductory text, removing "The" and adding "Subject to paragraph (a)(1) of this section, the" in its place;
3. In paragraph (a)(2)(ii)(*f*), revising the first sentence and removing "subdivision (iii) of this subparagraph" and adding "paragraph (a)(2)(iii) of this section" in its place;
4. Redesignating paragraphs (a)(2)(ii)(*k*) and (*l*) as paragraphs (a)(2)(ii)(*m*) and (*n*);
5. Adding new paragraphs (a)(2)(ii)(*k*) and (*l*);
6. Revising the first sentence of paragraph (a)(2)(iii)(*d*)(*1*);
7. Adding paragraphs (a)(5), (6), (7), and (8);
8. Revising paragraph (g)(1)(iii);
9. Removing the "or" at the end of paragraph (g)(1)(vi);
10. Removing the period at the end of paragraph (g)(1)(vii) and adding "; or" in its place;
11. Adding paragraph (g)(1)(viii);
12. Revising paragraph (g)(3);
13. Adding paragraph (g)(5) and a sentence at the end of paragraph (g)(6);
14. Redesignating paragraph (k) as paragraph (l);
15. Adding a new paragraph (k); and
16. Adding paragraph (l)(5).
The revisions and additions read as follows:

§1.6033-2. Returns by exempt organizations and returns by certain nonexempt organizations.—(a) * * *

(2) * * *

(ii) * * *

(*f*) The total of the contributions, gifts, grants and similar amounts received by it during the taxable year, and, in the case of an organization described in section 501(c)(3), the names and addresses of all persons that contributed, bequeathed, or devised $5,000 or more (in money or other property) during the taxable year. * * *

* * *

(*k*) In the case of organizations described in section 501(c)(3), the respective amounts (if any) of the taxes imposed on the organization, or any organization manager of the organization, during the taxable year under any of the following provisions (and the respective amounts (if any) of reimbursements paid by the organiza-

tion during the taxable year with respect to taxes imposed on any such organization manager under any of such provisions):

(*1*) Section 4911 (relating to tax on excess expenditures to influence legislation);

(*2*) Section 4912 (relating to tax on disqualifying lobbying expenditures of certain organizations); and

(*3*) Section 4955 (relating to taxes on political expenditures of section 501(c)(3) organizations), except to the extent that, by reason of section 4962, the taxes imposed under such section are not required to be paid or are credited or refunded.

(*l*) In the case of organizations described in section 501(c)(3), (4), or (29), the respective amounts (if any) of—

(*1*) The taxes imposed with respect to the organization on any organization manager, or any disqualified person, during the taxable year under section 4958 (relating to taxes on excess benefit transactions); and

(2) Reimbursements paid by the organization during the taxable year with respect to taxes imposed under such section, except to the extent that, by reason of section 4962, the taxes imposed under such section are not required to be paid or are credited or refunded.

* * *

(iii) * * *

(d)(1) Organizations described in section 501(c)(7), (8), or (10) that receive contributions or bequests to be used exclusively for purposes described in section 170(c)(4), 2055(a)(3), or 2522(a)(3), must attach a schedule with respect to all gifts that aggregate more than $1,000 from any one person showing the total amount of the contributions or bequests from each such person, the specific purpose or purposes for which such amount was received, and the specific use or uses to which such amount was put. * * *

* * *

(5) Political organizations, as defined by section 527(e)(1), that have gross receipts of $25,000 or more for the taxable year (or in the case of a qualified State or local political organization, as defined in section 527(e)(5), that has gross receipts of $100,000 or more for the taxable year) generally must comply with the requirements of section 6033 and this section in the same manner as organizations exempt from tax under section 501(a), except to the extent that the Commissioner may modify such requirements through forms, instructions to forms, or guidance published in the Internal Revenue Bulletin as appropriate for carrying out the purposes of section 527. For the purposes of this section, all references to organizations exempt from tax under section 501(a) shall include political organizations referred to in section 6033(g), other than those referred to in section 6033(g)(3) and except to the extent the Commissioner exercises discretion under section 6033(g)(4). This discretion may be exercised through forms, instructions to forms, or guidance published in the Internal Revenue Bulletin. In addition to the reporting requirements applicable to organizations exempt under section 501(a), such political organizations generally must report the names and addresses of all persons that contributed, bequeathed, or devised $5,000 or more (in money or other property) during the taxable year.

(6) Each controlling organization (within the meaning of section 512(b)(13)) that is subject to the requirements of section 6033(a) shall include on its annual return such information required by that return regarding –

(i) Any interest, annuities, royalties, or rents received from each controlled entity (within the meaning of section 512(b)(13));

(ii) Any loans made to each such controlled entity; and

(iii) Any transfers of funds between such controlling organization and each such controlled entity.

(7) Every organization described in section 4966(d)(1) shall, on its annual return for the taxable year—

(i) List the total number of donor advised funds (as defined in section 4966(d)(2)) it owns at the end of such taxable year;

(ii) Report the aggregate value of assets held in such funds at the end of such taxable year; and

(iii) Report the aggregate contributions to and grants made from such funds during such taxable year.

(8) Every organization described in section 509(a)(3) shall, on its annual return—

(i) List the supported organizations (as defined in section 509(f)(3)) with respect to which such organization provides support;

(ii) Specify whether the organization meets the requirements of clause (i), (ii), or (iii) of section 509(a)(3)(B); and

(iii) Certify that the organization meets the requirements of section 509(a)(3)(C).

* * *

(g) * * *

(1) * * *

(iii) Except as provided in paragraph (g)(1)(viii) of this section, an organization described in section 501(c) (other than a private foundation or a supporting organization described in section

509(a)(3)) the gross receipts of which in each taxable year are normally not more than $50,000 (as described in paragraph (g)(3) of this section);

* * *

(viii) A foreign organization (described in paragraph (k)(1) of this section) or a United States possession organization (described in paragraph (k)(2) of this section) (other than a private foundation or a supporting organization described in section 509(a)(3)) –

(A) The gross receipts of which in each taxable year from sources within the United States (as determined under paragraph (k)(3) of this section) are normally not more than $50,000 (as described in paragraph (g)(3) of this section); and

(B) That has no significant activity (including lobbying and political activity and the operation of a trade or business, but excluding investment activity) in the United States.

* * *

(3) For purposes of paragraphs (g)(1)(iii) and (viii) of this section, the gross receipts (as defined in paragraph (g)(4) of this section) of an organization are normally not more than $50,000 if:

(i) In the case of an organization that has been in existence for 1 year or less, the organization has received, or donors have pledged to give, gross receipts of $75,000 or less during the first taxable year of the organization;

(ii) In the case of an organization which has been in existence for more than one but less than 3 years, the average of the gross receipts received by the organization in its first 2 taxable years is $60,000 or less; and

(iii) In the case of an organization which has been in existence for 3 years or more, the average of the gross receipts received by the organization in the immediately preceding 3 taxable years, including the year for which the return would be required to be filed, is $50,000 or less.

* * *

(5) An organization that is not required to file an annual return by virtue of paragraphs (g)(1)(iii) and (viii) of this section must submit an annual electronic notification as described in section 6033(i). See § 1.6033-6.

(6) * * * This discretion may be exercised through forms, instructions to forms, or guidance published in the Internal Revenue Bulletin.

* * *

(k) *Foreign organizations and United States possession organizations.*—(1) *Foreign organization.*—For purposes of this section, a "foreign organization" is any organization not described in section 170(c)(2)(A).

(2) *United States possession organization.*—For purposes of this section, a "United States possession organization" is any organization created or organized in a possession of the United States.

(3) *Source of funds.*—For purposes of paragraph (g)(1)(viii) of this section, the source of an organization's gross receipts from gifts, grants, contributions or membership fees is determined by applying the rules found in § 53.4948-1(b) of this chapter. For purposes of paragraph (g)(1)(viii) of this section, the source of an organization's gross receipts other than gifts, grants, contributions, and membership fees is determined by applying the rules in sections 861 through 865 and the regulations in this part issued under section 861 through 865. For purposes of applying this paragraph (k)(3) regarding United States possession organizations, a United States person does not include individuals who are *bona fide* residents of a United States possession.

(l) * * *

(5) Paragraphs (a)(2)(ii)(*f*), (a)(2)(iii)(*d*)(1), (g)(1)(iii) and (viii), and (g)(3) of this section apply to annual information returns filed after [DATE OF PUBLICATION OF FINAL REGULATIONS IN THE **FEDERAL REGISTER**]. Under section 7805(b)(7) an organization may choose to apply the paragraphs listed in this paragraph (l)(5) to returns filed after September 6, 2019.

Estate and Person Acquiring Property from Decedent: Consistent Basis Reporting

Estate and Person Acquiring Property from Decedent: Consistent Basis Reporting.—Amendments to Reg. § 1.6035-1, providing guidance regarding the requirement that a recipient's basis in certain property acquired from a decedent be consistent with the value of the property as finally determined for Federal estate tax purposes, are proposed (published in the Federal Register on March 4, 2016) (REG-127923-15). Proposed Reg. § 1.6035-2 has been adopted by T.D. 9797 on December 1, 2016. Proposed Reg. § 1.6035-3 was removed by T.D. 9849 on March 11, 2019.

Par. 3. Section 1.6035-1 is revised to read as follows:

§ 1.6035-1. Basis information to persons acquiring property from decedent.—(a) *Required Information Return and Statement(s).*—(1) *In general.*—An executor (defined in paragraph (g)(1) of this section) required to file a return under section 6018 for an estate must file an Information Return (defined in paragraph (g)(2) of this section) with

the Internal Revenue Service (IRS) to report the value of certain property (described in paragraph (b)(1) of this section) included in the decedent's gross estate for purposes of the tax imposed by chapter 11 of subtitle B of the Internal Revenue Code (chapter 11) and other information prescribed by the Information Return and the instructions thereto. The value to be reported is the final value of the property as described in § 1.1014-10(c). This executor also must furnish a Statement (defined in paragraph (g)(3) of this section) to each beneficiary who has (or will) acquire, whether from the decedent or by reason of the death of the decedent, property reported on the Information Return to identify the property the beneficiary is to receive and to report the value of that property and other information prescribed by the Statement and instructions thereto. The Information Return and each Statement are required to be filed and furnished by the date provided in paragraph (d) of this section. If, after the Information Return and Statement are filed and furnished, there are certain changes in the final value and/or the recipient of property as described in paragraph (e) or (f) of this section, the executor must file a supplemental Information Return with the IRS and furnish a supplemental Statement to the beneficiary. Subsequent transfers of all or a portion of property previously reported (or required to be reported) on the Information Return required by paragraph (a) of this section, in transactions in which the transferee acquires the property with the transferor's basis, require additional reporting as described in paragraph (f) of this section.

(2) *Exception.*—Paragraph (a)(1) of this section applies only to the executor of an estate required by section 6018 to file an estate tax return. Accordingly, notwithstanding § 20.2010-2(a)(1), the executor does not have to file or furnish the Information Return or Statement(s) referred to in paragraph (a)(1) of this section if the executor is not required by section 6018 to file an estate tax return for the estate, even if the executor does file such a return for other purposes, e.g., to make a generation-skipping transfer tax exemption allocation or election, to make the portability election under section 2010(c)(5), or to make a protective filing to avoid any penalty if an asset value is later determined to cause a return to be required or otherwise.

(b) *Property for which reporting is required.*—(1) *In general.*—The property to which the reporting requirement under paragraph (a)(1) of this section applies is all property reported or required to be reported on a return under section 6018. This includes, for example, any other property whose basis is determined in whole or in part by reference to that property (for example as the result of a like-kind exchange or involuntary conversion). Of the property of a deceased nonresident non-citizen, this includes only the property that is subject to U.S. estate tax; similarly, this includes only the decedent's one-half of community property. Nevertheless, the following property is excepted from the reporting requirements—

(i) Cash (other than a coin collection or other coins or bills with numismatic value);

(ii) Income in respect of a decedent (as defined in section 691);

(iii) Tangible personal property for which an appraisal is not required under § 20.2031-6(b); and

(iv) Property sold, exchanged, or otherwise disposed of (and therefore not distributed to a beneficiary) by the estate in a transaction in which capital gain or loss is recognized.

(2) *Examples.*—The following examples illustrate the provisions of paragraph (b)(1) of this section.

Example 1. Included in D's gross estate are the contents of his residence. Pursuant to § 20.2031-6(a), the executor attaches to the return required by section 6018 filed for D's estate a room by room itemization of household and personal effects. All articles are named specifically. In each room a number of articles, none of which has a value in excess of $100, are grouped. A value is provided for each named article. Included in the household and personal effects are a painting, a rug, and a clock, each of which has a value in excess of $3,000. Pursuant to § 20.2031-6(b), the executor obtains an appraisal from a disinterested, competent appraiser(s) of recognized standing and ability, or a disinterested dealer(s) in the class of personalty involved for the painting, rug, and clock. The executor attaches these appraisals to the estate tax return for D's estate. Pursuant to paragraph (b)(1)(iii) of this section, the reporting requirements of paragraph (a)(1) of this section apply only to the painting, rug, and clock.

Example 2. Included in D's estate are shares in C, a publicly traded company. Shortly after D's death but prior to the filing of the estate tax return for D's estate, C is acquired by T, also a publicly traded company. For the shares in C includible in D's estate, the estate receives new shares in T and cash in a fully taxable transaction. Pursuant to paragraph (b)(1)(iv) of this section, the reporting requirements of paragraph (a)(1) of this section do not apply to the new shares in T or the cash.

(c) *Beneficiaries.*—(1) *In general.*—As provided in paragraph (a)(1) of this section, the executor must furnish to each beneficiary (including a beneficiary who is also an executor) receiving property that must be reported on the Information Return filed with the IRS, the Statement containing the required information regarding that beneficiary's property. For purposes of this provision, the beneficiary of a life estate is the life tenant, the beneficiary of a remainder interest

is the remainderman(men) identified as if the life tenant were to die immediately after the decedent, and the beneficiary of a contingent interest is a beneficiary, unless the contingency has occurred prior to the filing of the Form 8971. If the contingency subsequently negates the inheritance of the beneficiary, the executor must do supplemental reporting in accordance with paragraph (e) of this section to report the change of beneficiary.

(2) *Beneficiary not an individual.*—If the beneficiary is a trust or another estate, the executor must furnish the beneficiary's Statement to the trustee or executor of the trust or estate, rather than to the beneficiaries of that trust or estate. If the beneficiary is a business entity, the executor must furnish the Statement to the entity. However, see paragraph (f) of this section for additional reporting requirements in the event the trust, estate, or entity transfers all or a portion of the property in a transaction in which the transferee acquires the basis of the trust, estate, or entity.

(3) *Beneficiary not determined.*—If, by the due date provided in paragraph (d) of this section, the executor has not determined what property will be used to satisfy the interest of each beneficiary, the executor must report on the Statement for each such beneficiary all of the property that the executor could use to satisfy that beneficiary's interest. Once the exact distribution has been determined, the executor may, but is not required to, file and furnish a supplemental Information Return and Statement as provided in paragraph (e)(3) of this section.

(4) *Beneficiary not located.*—An executor must use reasonable due diligence to identify and locate all beneficiaries. If the executor is unable to locate a beneficiary by the due date of the Information Return provided in paragraph (d) of this section, the executor must so report on that Information Return and explain the efforts the executor has taken to locate the beneficiary and to satisfy the obligation of reasonable due diligence. If the executor subsequently locates the beneficiary, the executor must furnish the beneficiary with that beneficiary's Statement and file a supplemental Information Return with the IRS within 30 days of locating the beneficiary. A copy of the beneficiary's Statement must be attached to the supplemental Information Return. If the executor is unable to locate a beneficiary and distributes the property to a different beneficiary who was not identified in the Information Return as the recipient of that property, the executor must file a supplemental Information Return with the IRS and furnish the substitute beneficiary with that beneficiary's Statement within 30 days after the property is distributed. See paragraph (e)(1) of this section. A copy of the substitute beneficiary's Statement must be attached to the supplemental Information Return.

(d) *Due dates.*—(1) *In general.*—Except as provided in § 1.6035-2T, the executor must file the Information Return with the IRS, and must furnish to each beneficiary the Statement with regard to the property to be received by that beneficiary, on or before the earlier of—

(i) The date that is 30 days after the due date of the estate tax return required by section 6018 (including extensions, if any), or

(ii) The date that is 30 days after the date on which that return is filed with the IRS.

(2) *Transition rule.*—If the due date of an estate tax return required to be filed by section 6018 is on or before July 31, 2015, but the executor does not file the return with the IRS until after July 31, 2015, then the Information Return and Statement(s) are due on or before the date that is 30 days after the date on which the estate tax return is filed, except as provided in § 1.6035-2T.

(e) *Duty to supplement.*—(1) *In general.*—In the event of any adjustment to the information required to be reported on the Information Return or any Statement as described in paragraph (e)(2) of this section, the executor must file a supplemental Information Return with the IRS including all supplemental Statements and furnish a corresponding supplemental Statement to each affected beneficiary by the due date described in paragraph (e)(4) of this section.

(2) *Adjustments requiring supplement.*—Except as provided in paragraph (e)(3) of this section, an adjustment to which the duty to supplement applies is any change to the information required to be reported on the Information Return or Statement that causes the information as reported to be incorrect or incomplete. Such changes include, for example, the discovery of property that should have been (but was not) reported on an estate tax return described in section 6018, a change in the value of property pursuant to an examination or litigation, or a change in the identity of the beneficiary to whom the property is to be distributed (pursuant to a death, disclaimer, bankruptcy, or otherwise). Such changes also include the executor's disposition of property acquired from the decedent or as a result of the death of the decedent in a transaction in which the basis of new property received by the estate is determined in whole or in part by reference to the property acquired from the decedent or as a

result of the death of the decedent (for example as the result of a like-kind exchange or involuntary conversion). Changes requiring supplement pursuant to this paragraph (e)(2) are not inconsequential errors or omissions within the meaning of §301.6722-1(b) of this chapter.

(3) *Adjustments not requiring supplement.*—(i) *In general.*—A supplemental Information Return and Statement may but they are not required to be filed or furnished-

(A) To correct an inconsequential error or omission within the meaning of §301.6722-1(b) of this chapter, or

(B) To specify the actual distribution of property previously reported as being available to satisfy the interests of multiple beneficiaries in the situation described in paragraph (c)(3) of this section.

(ii) *Example.*—Paragraph (e)(3)(i)(B) of this section is illustrated by the following example.

Example 1. D's Will provided for D's residuary estate to be distributed to D's three children (E, F, and G). D's residuary estate included stock in a publicly traded company (X), a personal residence, and three paintings. On the due date of the Information Return and Statement required by paragraph (a)(1) of this section, D's executor had not yet determined which property each child would receive from D's residuary estate in satisfaction of that child's bequest. In accordance with paragraph (c)(3) of this section, D's executor reported on the Information Return filed with the IRS and on each child's own Statement that E, F, and G each might receive an interest in the stock in X, the personal residence, and the three paintings. Several months later, the executor determined that E would receive the stock in X, F would receive the residence, and G would receive the paintings. Paragraph (e)(3)(i)(B) of this section provides that the executor may but is not required to file a supplemental Information Return with the IRS and furnish supplemental Statements to E, F, and G to accurately report which beneficiary received what property.

Example 2. D's Will provided that D's jewelry and household effects (personalty) are to be distributed among D's three children (E, F, and G) as determined by E, F, and G. In accordance with paragraph (c)(3) of this section, D's executor reports on the Information Return filed with the IRS and on each child's own Statement each item of personalty other than items described in paragraph (b)(1)(iii) of this section. Several months later, E, F, and G determine who is to receive each item of personalty. Paragraph (e)(3)(i)(B) of this section provides that the executor may but is not required to file a supplemental Information Return with the IRS and furnish supplemental Statements to E, F, and G to accurately report which beneficiary received which item(s) of personalty.

(4) *Due date of supplemental reporting.*—(i) *In general.*—Except as provided in paragraph (e)(4)(ii) of this section, the supplemental Information Return must be filed and each supplemental Statement must be furnished on or before 30 days after—

(A) The final value within the meaning of §1.1014-10(c)(1) is determined;

(B) The executor discovers that the information reported on the Information Return or Statement is otherwise incorrect or incomplete, except to the extent described in paragraph (e)(3)(i) of this section; or

(C) A supplemental estate tax return under section 6018 is filed reporting property not reported on a previously filed estate tax return pursuant to §1.1014-10(c)(3)(i). In this case, a copy of the supplemental Statement provided to each beneficiary of an interest in this property must be attached to the supplemental Information Return.

(ii) *Probate property or property from decedent's revocable trust.*—With respect to property in the probate estate or held by a revocable trust at the decedent's death, if an event described in paragraph (e)(4)(i)(A), (B), or (C) of this section occurs after the decedent's date of death but before or on the date the property is distributed to the beneficiary, the due date for the supplemental Information Return and corresponding supplemental Statement is the date that is 30 days after the date the property is distributed to the beneficiary. If the executor chooses to furnish to the beneficiary on the Statement information regarding any changes to the basis of the reported property as described in §1.1014-10(a)(2) that occurred after the date of death but before or on the date of distribution, that basis adjustment information (which is not part of the requirement under section 6035) must be shown separately from the final value required to be reported on that Statement.

(f) *Subsequent transfers.*—If all or any portion of property that previously was reported or is required to be reported on an Information Return (and thus on the recipient's Statement or supplemental Statement) is distributed or transferred (by gift or otherwise) by the recipient in a transaction in which a related transferee determines its basis, in whole or in part, by reference to the recipient/transferor's basis, the recipient/transferor must, no later than 30 days after the date of the distribution or other transfer, file with the IRS a supplemental Statement and furnish a copy of the same supplemental Statement to the transferee. The requirement to file a supplemental Statement and furnish a copy to the transferee similarly applies to the distribution or transfer of any other property the basis of which is determined in whole or in part by reference to that property (for example as the result of a like-kind exchange or involuntary conversion). In the case of a supplemental Statement filed by the recipient/transferor before the recipient/transferor's receipt of the Statement described in paragraph (a) of this section, the supplemental Statement will report the change in the ownership of the property and need not provide the value information that would otherwise be required on the supplemental Statement. In the event the transfer occurs before the final value is determined within the meaning of proposed §1.1014-10(c), the transferor must provide the executor with a copy of the supplemental Statement filed with the IRS and furnished to the transferee in order to notify the executor of the change in ownership of the property. When the executor subsequently files any Return and issues any Statement required by paragraphs (a) or (e) of this section, the executor must provide the Statement (or supplemental Statement) to the new transferee instead of to the transferor. For purposes of this provision, a related transferee means any member of the transferor's family as defined in section 2704(c)(2), any controlled entity (a corporation or any other entity in which the transferor and members of the transferor's family (as defined in section 2704(c)(2)), whether directly or indirectly, have control within the meaning of section 2701(b)(2)(A) or (B)), and any trust of which the transferor is a deemed owner for income tax purposes. If the transferor chooses to include on the supplemental Statement provided to the transferee information regarding any changes to the basis of the reported property as described in §1.1014-10(a)(2) that occurred during the transferor's ownership of the property, that basis adjustment information (which is not part of the requirement under section 6035) must be shown separately from the final value required to be reported on that Statement.

(g) *Definitions.*—For purposes of this section, the following terms are defined as follows—

(1) *Executor* has the same meaning as in section 2203 and includes any other person required under section 6018(b) to file a return.

(2) *Information Return* means the Form 8971, including each beneficiary's Statement as defined in paragraph (g)(3) of this section required to be furnished, or any successor form issued by the IRS for this purpose.

(3) *Statement* means the payee statement described as Schedule A of the Information Return furnished to a beneficiary or any successor form or schedule issued by the IRS for this purpose.

(h) *Penalties.*—(1) *Failure to timely file complete and correct Information Return.*—For provisions relating to the penalty provided for failure to file an Information Return required by section 6035(a)(1) on or before the required filing date, failure to include all of the required information on an Information Return, or the filing of an Information Return that includes incorrect information, see section 6721 and the regulations thereunder. See section 6724 and the regulations thereunder for rules relating to waivers of penalties for certain failures due to reasonable cause.

(2) *Failure to timely furnish correct Statements.*—For provisions relating to the penalty provided for failure to furnish a Statement required by section 6035(a)(2) on or before the prescribed date, failure to include all of the required information on a Statement, or the filing of a Statement that includes incorrect information, see section 6722 and the regulations thereunder. See section 6724 and the regulations thereunder for rules relating to waivers of penalties for certain failures due to reasonable cause.

(i) *Effective/applicability date.*—Upon the publication of the Treasury Decision adopting these rules as final in the **Federal Register**, this section will apply to property acquired from a decedent or by reason of the death of a decedent whose return required by section 6018 is filed after July 31, 2015. Persons may rely upon these rules before the date of publication of the Treasury Decision adopting these rules as final in the **Federal Register**.

Foreign Corporations: Limitation on Deduction for Dividends

Foreign Corporations: Limitation on Deduction for Dividends.—Amendments to Reg. §1.6038-2, limiting the dividends received deduction available for certain dividends received from current or former controlled foreign corporations, are proposed (published in the Federal Register on June 18, 2019) (REG-106282-18).

Par. 4. Section 1.6038-2 is amended by:
1. Adding reserved paragraphs (f)(13) through (15).
2. Adding paragraph (f)(16).
3. Revising paragraph (m).
The additions and revision read as follows:

§1.6038-2. Information returns required of United States persons with respect to annual accounting periods of certain foreign corporations beginning after December 31, 1962.

* * *

(f) * * *

(13) through (15) [Reserved].

(16) [The text of proposed §1.6038-2(f)(16) is the same as the text of §1.6038-2T(f)(16) as added by T.D. 9865].

* * *

(m) [The text of proposed §1.6038-2(m) is the same as the text of §1.6038-2T(m) as added by T.D. 9865].

Foreign-Derived Intangible Income: Global Intangible Low-Taxed Income: Deduction

Foreign-Derived Intangible Income: Global Intangible Low-Taxed Income: Deduction.—Amendments to Reg. §§1.6038-2 and 1.6038-3, providing guidance to determine the amount of the deduction for foreign-derived intangible income and global intangible low-taxed income, are proposed (published in the Federal Register on March 6, 2019) (REG-104464-18).

Par. 7. Section 1.6038-2, as proposed to be amended at 83 FR 67612 (Dec. 28, 2018), is further amended by adding paragraph (f)(15) and a sentence at the end of paragraph (m) to read as follows:

§1.6038-2. Information returns required of United States persons with respect to annual accounting periods of certain foreign corporations beginning after December 31, 1962.

* * *

(f) * * *

(15) *Information reporting under section 250.*—If the person required to file Form 5471 (or any successor form) claims a deduction under section 250(a) that is determined, in whole or part, by reference to its foreign-derived intangible income, and any amount re-

quired to be reported under paragraph (f)(11) of this section is included in its computation of foreign-derived deduction eligible income, such person will provide on Form 5471 (or any successor form) such information that is prescribed by the form, instructions, publication, or other guidance.

* * *

(m) * * * Paragraph (f)(15) of this section applies with respect to information for annual accounting periods beginning on or after March 4, 2019.

Par. 8. Section 1.6038-3, as proposed to be amended at 83 FR 67612 (Dec. 28, 2018), is further amended by adding paragraph (g)(4) and a sentence to the end of paragraph (l) to read as follows:

§1.6038-3. Information returns required of certain United States persons with respect to controlled foreign partnerships (CFPs).

* * *

(g) * * *

(4) *Additional information required to be submitted by a controlling ten-percent or a controlling fifty-percent partner that has a deduction under section 250 by reason of FDII.*—In addition to the information required pursuant to paragraphs (g)(1), (2), and (3) of this section, if, with respect to the partnership's tax year for which the Form 8865 is being filed, a controlling ten-percent partner or a controlling fifty-percent partner has a deduction under section 250 (by reason of having foreign-derived intangible income), determined, in whole or in part,

by reference to the income, assets, or activities of the partnership, or transactions between the controlling-ten percent partner or controlling fifty-percent partner and the partnership, the controlling ten-percent partner or controlling fifty-percent partner must provide its share of the partnership's gross DEI, gross FDDEI, deductions that are definitely related to the partnership's gross DEI and gross FDDEI, and partnership QBAI (as those terms are defined in the section 250 regulations) in the form and manner and to the extent prescribed by Form 8865 (or any successor form), instruction, publication, or other guidance.

* * *

(l) * * * Paragraph (g)(4) of this section applies for tax years of a foreign partnership beginning on or after March 4, 2019.

Foreign-Derived Intangible Income: Global Intangible Low-Taxed Income: Deduction

Foreign-Derived Intangible Income: Global Intangible Low-Taxed Income: Deduction.—Amendments to Reg. §1.6038A-2, providing guidance to determine the amount of the deduction for foreign-derived intangible income and global intangible low-taxed income, are proposed (published in the Federal Register on March 6, 2019) (REG-104464-18).

Par. 9. Section 1.6038A-2, as proposed to be amended at 83 FR 67612 (Dec. 28, 2018), is further amended by adding paragraph (b)(5)(iv) and a sentence at the end of paragraph (g) to read as follows:

§1.6038A-2. Requirements of return.

* * *

(b) * * *

(5) * * *

(iv) *Information reporting under section 250.*—If, for the taxable year, the reporting corporation has a deduction under section 250 (by reason of having foreign-derived intangible income) with respect to any amount required to be reported under paragraph (b)(3) or (4)

of this section, the reporting corporation will provide on Form 5472 (or any successor form) such information about the deduction in the form and manner and to the extent prescribed by Form 5472 (or any successor form), instruction, publication, or other guidance.

* * *

(g) * * * Paragraph (b)(5)(iv) of this section applies with respect to information for annual accounting periods beginning on or after March 4, 2019.

Foreign Corporations: Transfer of Property

Reorganizations: Foreign Corporations: Transfer of Property.—Temporary Reg. §1.6038B-1T, relating to transfers of property to foreign corporations, is proposed (published in the Federal Register on May 16, 1986) (LR-3-86).

§1.6038B-1T. Reporting of certain transfers to foreign corporations (temporary).

Foreign-Owned Corporations: Information Returns

Foreign-Owned Corporations: Information Returns: Records.—Reproduced below is the text of proposed Reg. §1.6038C-1, relating to foreign-owned corporations (published in the Federal Register on December 10, 1990).

☐ Par. 5. New §1.6038C-1 is added to read as follows:

§1.6038C-1. General rule.—The rules of §§1.6038A-1 through 1.6038A-7 generally will apply for purposes of section 6038C.

Employment Taxes

Employment Taxes: Real Estate Agents and Direct Sellers: Employer's Liability.—Reproduced below is the text of proposed Reg. §1.6041A-1, relating to the treatment of qualified real estate agents and direct sellers as nonemployees, to the determination of employer liability for income tax withholding and employee social security taxes where the employer treated an employee as a nonemployee for purposes of such taxes, and to information reporting of direct sales and payments of remuneration for services (published in the Federal Register on January 7, 1986) (INTL-214-82).

☐ Par. 4. A new §1.6041A-1 is added immediately after §1.6041-7 to read as set forth below:

§1.6041A-1. Returns regarding payments of remuneration for services and certain direct sales.—(a) *Returns regarding remuneration for services*—

(1) *In general.*—If—

(i) Any service-recipient engaged in a trade or business pays in the course of that trade or business during any calendar year after 1982 remuneration to any person for services performed by that person, and

(ii) The aggregate amount of remuneration paid to such person during such calendar year is $600 or more,

then the service-recipient shall make a return in accordance with paragraph (e) of this section. For purposes of the preceding sentence, the term "service-recipient" means the person for whom the service is performed (*e.g.*, in the case of a real estate agent, the real estate firm for which such agent performs services). For purposes of this paragraph (a)(1) only, the term remuneration does not include amounts paid to any person for services performed by such person if the service-recipient knows that such amounts are excludable from the gross income of the person performing such services. For example, a return is not required with respect to amounts paid to a foster parent which are known by the service-recipient to constitute foster care payments that are excludable from gross income under section 131. For purposes of this paragraph (a)(1), a service-recipient shall be considered to know facts set forth in a written statement provided to the service-recipient, made under the penalties of perjury and signed by the person performing such services, in the absence of knowledge by the service-recipient that such statement is untrue. See section 6041A (d) for rules relating to the application of section 6041A and this section to governmental units (and agencies or instrumentalities thereof).

(2) *Payment attributable to parts and materials.*—For purposes of section 6041A and this section, the aggregate amount of remuneration paid to any person for services rendered includes any payments for parts or materials used by such person in rendering the services unless the trade or business of such person is primarily that of selling parts or materials. Whether a person is engaged primarily in the trade or business of selling parts and materials rather than providing services shall be determined on the basis of all facts and circumstances, taking into account such factors as whether such person holds himself or herself out as a dealer in parts and whether, with respect to the type of services rendered, a service-recipient ordinarily would specify the type or brand of parts or materials to be used.

Example. X Company makes a payment to an unincorporated repair shop for repairs to one of the company's automobiles. The automobile sustained body damage in an accident. The repair contract requires payment of $300 for labor and $400 for new parts that were installed. The repair shop does not hold itself out as a dealer in parts. Generally, customers of the repair shop do not specify the type or brand of replacement parts to be installed. Therefore, the aggregate amount of remuneration that is required to be reported pursuant to section 6041A(a) includes the payment for parts.

(b) *Returns regarding direct sales of $5,000 or more.*—(1) *In general.*—If—

(i) Any person engaged in a trade or business in the course of such trade or business during any calendar year sells consumer products to any buyer on a buy-sell, deposit-commission, or other commission basis for resale (by the buyer or any other person) in the home or otherwise than in a permanent retail establishment, and

(ii) The aggregate amount of such sales made by such person to such buyer during such calendar year is $5,000 or more,

then such person shall make a return with respect to such buyer in accordance with paragraph (e) of this section. This requirement shall apply to sales made in any calendar year after 1982.

(2) *Sale defined.*—For purposes of this paragraph (b), a person will be considered to sell a product to a buyer for resale even though such buyer does not acquire title to the product prior to selling it to the consumer. For example, a company sales person, paid on a commission basis, who does not acquire title to a product before selling it to the consumer is considered to have bought the product for resale for purposes of section 6041A(b) and this paragraph.

(3) *Acquisition for resale in a permanent retail establishment.*—Section 6041A(b) and this paragraph do not apply to sales of a product to a buyer who sells the product only in a permanent retail establishment, as defined in §31.3508-1(g)(4) of this chapter (Employment Tax Regulations). If a buyer acquires consumer products from a person for resale both in the home (or otherwise than in a permanent retail establishment) as well as in a permanent retail establishment, then such person shall, for purposes of determining the aggregate amount of sales made to such buyer under paragraph (b)(1)(i) of this section, take into account all sales of such products made to such buyer during the calendar year.

(4) *Products purchased for personal use or consumption.*—All sales to a buyer of consumer products on a buy-sell, deposit-commission, or other commission basis that are suitable for resale to another person shall be taken into account in determining the aggregate amount of sales made to such buyer under paragraph (b)(1)(i) of this section even if such buyer purchases some of the products for the buyer's personal use or consumption or disposes of some of the products other than by resale (for example, gifts to relatives). Sales of products that cannot be resold, such as samples and catalogues, are not taken into account in determining the aggregate amount of sales to a buyer during the calendar year.

(5) *Consumer product defined.*—For purposes of section 6041A(b) and this paragraph, the term "consumer product" means any tangible personal property which is distributed in commerce and which is normally used for personal, family, or household purposes (including any such property intended to be attached to or installed in any real property without regard to whether it is so attached or installed). The term "consumer product" does not include any product used to manufacture another product to be distributed in commerce or any product used only incidentally in providing a service (*e.g.*, insecticide used in a pest control service, material used in an appliance repair business).

(c) *Engaged in trade or business.*—For purposes of section 6041A(a)(1) or (b)(1) and this section, whether a service-recipient or other person is engaged in a trade or business shall be determined under the rules set forth in §1.6041-1(b).

(d) *Exceptions to return requirement.*—(1) *Return required under another section.*—No return shall be required under paragraph (a) of this section if a statement with respect to the services is required to be furnished under section 6051, 6052, or 6053.

(2) *Transactions exempt from reporting under section 6041.*—No return shall be required under paragraph (a) of this section with respect to a payment which is exempted under §1.6041-3 from the reporting requirement of section 6041, and no return shall be required under paragraph (b) of this section with respect to sales made to a corporation.

(e) *Time and manner of filing.*—(1) *Form.*—The return required to be filed under section 6041A(a) or (b) and paragraph (a) or (b) of this section shall be filed on Forms 1096 and 1099 in accordance with the instructions accompanying those forms.

(2) *Time for filing.*—The return shall be filed on or before February 28 of the year following the calendar year for which the return is filed.

(3) *Place of filing.*—The return shall be filed with the appropriate Internal Revenue Center, at the address listed in the instructions for Forms 1096 and 1099.

(4) *Contents.*—(i) *In general.*—Unless otherwise provided in the instructions to Form 1099, the return required under section 6041A(a) or (b) and paragraph (a) or (b) of this section shall set forth the information contained in paragraph (e)(4)(ii) or (iii) of this section.

(ii) *Return required under section 6041A(a).*—The return required to be filed under section 6041A(a) and paragraph (a)(1) of this section shall set forth the aggregate amount of remuneration paid to the person with respect to whom the return is made during the calendar year for services rendered, the name, address, and taxpayer identification number of the person making the payment, and the name, address, and taxpayer identification number of the recipient of the remuneration.

(iii) *Return required under section 6041A(b).*—A return required to be filed under section 6041A(b) and paragraph (b)(1) of this section shall set forth the name, address, and taxpayer identification number of the person making the sales, and the name, address, and taxpayer identification number of the buyer.

(f) *Statements to be furnished to persons with respect to whom information is required to be furnished.*—(1) *In general.*—Every person required to file a return pursuant to section 6041A(a) or (b) and paragraph (a) or (b) of this section shall furnish a written statement to each person whose name is required to be set forth in that return.

(2) *Time for furnishing statement.*—The written statement required under paragraph (f)(1) of this section shall be furnished to the person on or before January 31 of the year following the calendar year for which the return under section 6041A(a) or (b) was made.

(3) *Contents of statement.*—The statement shall contain—

(i) The name, address, and taxpayer identification number of the person required to make the return, and

(ii) In the case of a return required to be filed under section 6041A(a) and paragraph (a)(1) of this section, the aggregate amount of payments to the person required to be shown on the return.

(g) *Recipient to furnish name, address, and identification number.*—Any person with respect to whom a return or statement is required to be made pursuant to section 6041A and this section by another person shall furnish to that other person his name, address, and identification number upon demand by the person required to make the return.

(h) *Penalties.*—For provisions relating to the penalties for failure to file a return or to furnish a statement under section 6041A and this section, see sections 6652 and 6678 of the Code. For provisions relating to the penalty for failure to supply identification numbers under this section, see section 6676. [Reg. § 1.6041A-1.]

Consolidated Returns: Dual Consolidated Losses

Consolidated Returns: Dual Consolidated Losses.—Amendments to Reg. § 1.6043-4T, relating to various dual consolidated loss issues, including exceptions to the general prohibition against using a dual consolidated loss to reduce the taxable income of any other member of the affiliated group, are proposed (published in the Federal Register on May 24, 2005) (REG-102144-04).

☐ Par. 4. In § 1.6043-4T, paragraph (a)(1)(iii) is amended by removing the language "§ 1.1503-2(c)(2)" and adding "§ 1.1503(d)-1(b)(2)" in its place.

§ 1.6043-4T. Information returns relating to certain acquisitions of control and changes in capital structure (temporary).

Imputed Interest: Original Issue Discount: Safe Haven Interest Rates

Imputed Interest: Original Issue Discount: Safe Haven Interest Rates.—Reproduced below is the text of a proposed amendment of Reg. § 1.6045-1, relating to (1) the tax treatment of debt instruments issued after July 1, 1982, that contain original issue discount, (2) the imputation of and the accounting for interest with respect to sales and exchanges of property occurring after December 31, 1984, and (3) safe haven interest rates for loans or advances between commonly controlled taxpayers and safe haven leases between such taxpayers (published in the Federal Register on April 8, 1986).

☐ Par. 29. Paragraph (c) of § 1.6045-1 is amended by removing the phrase "section 1232(b)(1)" every place it appears and adding in its place the phrase "section 1273(a)(1)".

§ 1.6045-1. Returns of information of brokers and barter exchanges.

Definition of Registered Form: Guidance

Definition of Registered Form: Guidance.—Amendments to Reg. § 1.6045-1, providing guidance on the definitions of registration-required obligation and registered form, including guidance on the issuance of pass-through certificates and participation interests in registered form, are proposed (published in the Federal Register on September 19, 2017) (REG-125374-16).

Par. 10. Section 1.6045-1(n)(2)(ii)(J) is amended by removing the language "§ 1.1471-1(b)(18)" and adding in its place the language "§ 1.1471-1(b)(21)".

§ 1.6045-1. Returns of information of brokers and barter exchanges.

Correct Payee Statements: Failure to File Correct Information: Penalties

Correct Payee Statements: Failure to File Correct Information: Penalties.—Amendments to Reg. § 1.6045-1, relating to penalties for failure to file correct information returns or furnish correct payee statements, are proposed (published in the Federal Register on October 17, 2018) (REG-118826-16).

Par. 2. Section 1.6045-1 is amended by redesignating paragraph (d)(6)(vii) as paragraph (d)(6)(viii), adding paragraphs (d)(6)(vii) and (ix), and revising paragraphs (k)(4), (l), and (q) to read as follows:

§ 1.6045-1. Returns of information of brokers and barter exchanges.

* * *

(d) * * *

(6) * * *

(vii) *Treatment of de minimis errors.*—For purposes of this section, a customer's adjusted basis shall generally be determined by treating any incorrect dollar amount which is not required to be corrected by reason of section 6721(c)(3) or section 6722(c)(3) as the correct amount. However if a broker, upon identifying a dollar amount as incorrect, voluntarily both files a corrected information return and issues a corrected payee statement showing the correct dollar amount, then regardless of any requirement under section 6721 or section 6722, the adjusted basis shall be the correct dollar amount as reported on the corrected information return and corrected payee statement.

* * *

(ix) *Applicability date.*—Paragraph (d)(6)(vii) of this section applies with respect to information returns required to be filed and payee statements required to be furnished on or after January 1 of the calendar year immediately following the date of publication of a Treasury decision adopting these rules as final regulations in the **Federal Register**.

* * *

(k) * * *

(4) *Cross-reference to penalty.*—For provisions for failure to furnish timely a correct payee statement, see § 301.6722-1 of this chapter (Procedure and Administration Regulations). See § 301.6724-1 of this chapter for the waiver of a penalty if the failure is due to reasonable cause and is not due to willful neglect.

(l) *Use of magnetic media.*—See § 301.6011-2 of this chapter for rules relating to filing information returns on magnetic media and for rules relating to waivers granted for undue hardship. A broker or barter exchange that fails to file a Form 1099 on magnetic media, when required, may be subject to a penalty under section 6721 for each such failure. See paragraph (j) of this section.

* * *

(q) *Applicability date*.—Except as otherwise provided in paragraphs (d)(6)(ix), (m)(2)(ii), and (n)(12)(ii) of this section, and in this paragraph (q), this section applies on or after January 6, 2017.

Paragraphs (k)(4) and (l) of this section apply with respect to information returns required to be filed and payee statements required to be furnished on or after January 1 of the calendar year immediately following the date of publication of a Treasury decision adopting these rules as final regulations in the **Federal Register**. (For rules that apply after June 30, 2014, and before January 6, 2017, see this section as in effect and contained in 26 CFR part 1, as revised April 1, 2016.)

Stock and Rights to Acquire Stock: Deemed Distributions

Stock and Rights to Acquire Stock: Deemed Distributions.—Amendments to Reg. §1.6045B-1, regarding deemed distributions of stock and rights to acquire stock and resolving ambiguities concerning the amount and timing of deemed distributions that are or result from adjustments to rights to acquire stock, are proposed (published in the Federal Register on April 13, 2016) (REG-133673-15).

Par. 13. Section 1.6045B-1 is amended by adding paragraph (i) to read as follows:

§1.6045B-1. Returns relating to actions affecting basis of securities.

* * *

(i) *Deemed distribution under section 305(c)*.—(1) *In general.*—This paragraph (i) provides special rules for an organizational action resulting in a deemed distribution under section 305(c) that affects the basis of a specified security, including a deemed distribution resulting from an applicable adjustment (for example, a conversion ratio adjustment). *See* paragraph (j) of this section to determine when this section applies to an organizational action that affects the basis of a specified security. For example, under paragraph (j)(4) of this section, this section applies to a deemed distribution under section 305(c) resulting from an applicable adjustment to a convertible debt instrument if the deemed distribution occurs on or after January 1, 2016, and the deemed distribution could affect the basis of the convertible debt instrument.

(2) *Mandatory reporting.*—Notwithstanding any other provision in this section (including the reporting exceptions for exempt recipients in paragraphs (a)(4) and (b)(5) of this section), for an organizational action described in paragraph (i)(1) of this section the issuer must file an issuer return in accordance with paragraphs (a)(1) and (2) of this section and issuer statements in accordance with paragraphs (b)(1), (2), and (3) of this section. However, the requirement to file an issuer return and issuer statement in accordance with the preceding sentence does not apply if the issuer satisfies the public reporting requirements of paragraph (a)(3) of this section.

(3) *Information required to be reported.*—For purposes of paragraph (i)(2) of this section, an issuer must provide the information required under paragraph (a)(1) of this section, including—

(i) The date of the deemed distribution under section 305(c) as determined in accordance with §1.305-7(c)(5) (pursuant to paragraph (a)(1)(iv) of this section); and

(ii) The amount of the deemed distribution under section 305(c) as determined in accordance with §1.305-7(c)(4) (pursuant to paragraph (a)(1)(v) of this section).

(4) *Effective/applicability date.*—Paragraph (i)(2) of this section applies to a deemed distribution under section 305(c) occurring on or after the date of publication of the Treasury decision adopting these rules as final regulations in the **Federal Register**. For purposes of paragraphs (a)(1)(v) and (i)(3)(ii) of this section, an issuer must determine the amount of a deemed distribution under section 305(c) in accordance with §1.305-7(c)(4) for a deemed distribution occurring on or after the date of publication. For purposes of reporting the amount of a deemed distribution occurring prior to the date of publication, an issuer may determine the amount of the deemed distribution by treating such distribution either as a distribution of a right to acquire stock in accordance with §1.305-7(c)(4), or as a distribution of the shares of stock that would be received upon exercise of the right. For purposes of paragraphs (a)(1)(iv) and (i)(3)(i) of this section, an issuer must determine the date of a deemed distribution under section 305(c) occurring on or after the date of publication in accordance with §1.305-7(c)(5). An issuer, however, may rely on §1.305-7(c)(5) to determine the date of a deemed distribution that occurs prior to the date of publication.

* * *

CFCs: Insurance Income: Tax Years After 1986

Controlled Foreign Corporations: Insurance Income: Tax Years After 1986.—Reproduced below is a proposed amendment to Reg. §1.6046-1, relating to the election to expense certain depreciable business assets (published in the Federal Register on April 17, 1991).

☐ Par. 8. Section 1.6046-1 is amended as follows:

1. Paragraph (a)(2)(i) is revised.

2. Paragraph (c)(1)(i) and (c)(1)(ii)(*c*) is revised.

3. New paragraph (c)(1)(iii) is added preceding the concluding text of paragraph (c)(1).

4. The added and revised provisions read as follows:

§1.6046-1. Returns as to organization or reorganization of foreign corporations and as to acquisitions of their stock, on or after January 1, 1963.—(a) *Officers or directors.*—* * *

(2) *When liability arises after January 1, 1963.*—(i) *Requirement of return.*—Each United States citizen or resident who is at any time after January 1, 1963, an officer or director of a foreign corporation shall make a return on Form 5471 setting forth the information described in paragraph (a)(2)(ii) of this section with respect to each United States person who, during the time such citizen or resident is such an officer or director—

(*a*) Acquires (whether in one or more transactions) outstanding stock of such corporation which has, or which when added to any such stock then owned by him (excluding any stock owned by him on January 1, 1963, if on that date he owned 5 percent or more in value of such stock) has, a value equal to 5 percent or more in value of the outstanding stock of such foreign corporation,

(*b*) Acquires (whether in one or more transactions) an additional 5 percent or more in value of the outstanding stock of such foreign corporation, or

(*c*) Is not described in paragraph (a)(2)(i)(*a*) or (*b*) of this section, and who, at any time after January 1, 1987, is treated as a

United States shareholder under section 953(c) and §1.953-3(b)(2)(i) with respect to a foreign corporation.

* * *

(c) *Returns required of United States persons when liability to file arises after January 1, 1963.*—(1) *United States persons required to file.*—* * *

(i) Such person acquires (whether in one or more transactions) outstanding stock of such foreign corporation which has, or which when added to any such stock then owned by him (excluding any stock owned by him on January 1, 1963, if on that date he owned 5 percent or more in value of such stock) has, a value equal to 5 percent or more in value of the outstanding stock of such foreign corporation,

(ii) * * *

(*c*) Disposes of sufficient stock in such foreign corporation to reduce his interest to less than 5 percent in value of the outstanding stock of such foreign corporation, or

(iii) Such person is, at any time after January 1, 1987, treated as a United States shareholder under section 953(c) with respect to a foreign corporation.

* * *

Imputed Interest: OID: Safe Haven Rates

Imputed Interest: Original Issue Discount: Safe Haven Interest Rates.—Reproduced below is the text of a proposed amendment of Reg. §1.6049-4, relating to (1) the tax treatment of debt instruments issued after July 1, 1982, that contain original issue discount, (2) the imputation of and the accounting for interest with respect to sales and exchanges of property occurring after December 31, 1984, and (3) safe haven interest rates for loans or advances between commonly controlled taxpayers and safe haven leases between such taxpayers (published in the Federal Register on April 8, 1986).

☐ Par. 30. Paragraph (e)(2) of §1.6049-4 is amended by removing the phrase "section 1232(a)(3)" and adding in its place the phrase "section 1271(a)(3)(A)".

§1.6049-4. Return of information as to interest paid and original issue discount includible in gross income after December 31, 1982.

Imputed Interest: OID: Safe Haven Interest Rates

Imputed Interest: Original Issue Discount: Safe Haven Interest Rates.—Reproduced below is the text of a proposed amendment of Reg. §1.6049-5, relating (1) the tax treatment of debt instruments issued after July 1, 1982, that contain original issue discount, (2) the imputation of and the accounting for interest with respect to sales and exchanges of property occurring after December 31, 1984, and (3) safe haven interest rates for loans or advances between commonly controlled taxpayers and safe haven leases between such taxpayers (published in the Federal Register on April 8, 1986).

☐ Par. 31. Section 1.6049-5 is amended as follows:

1. In paragraph (b)(1)(vi)(B)(4) by removing the phrase "section 1232(b)(1)" and adding in its place the phrase "section 1273(a)(1)".

2. In paragraph (c) by removing the ninth sentence thereof and by revising the second, fourth and seventh sentences to read as follows:

§1.6049-5. Interest and original issue discount subject to reporting after December 31, 1982.

* * *

(c) *Original issue discount treated as payment of interest.*—* * * In the case of an obligation as to which there is during any calendar year an amount of original issue discount includible in the gross income of any holder (as determined under section 1272 and the regulations thereunder), the issuer of the obligation or a middleman (as defined in §1.6049-4(f)(4)) shall be treated as having paid to such holder during such calendar year an amount of interest equal to the amount of original issue discount so includible without regard to any reduction by reason of an acquisition premium under section 1272(a)(6) and (b)(4) or a purchase at a premium under section 1272(c)()1) and §1.1275-1(f). * * *

In the case of (1) an obligation to which section 1272 does not apply (for example, a short-term government obligation as defined in section 1271(a)(3)(A)) and (2) an obligation issued on or before December 31, 1982, in bearer form, the amount of original issue discount includible in gross income shall be treated as if paid in the calendar year in which the date of maturity occurs or in which the date of redemption occurs if redemption occurs before maturity. * * *

Discount on short term government obligations as defined in section 1271(a)(3)(B), such as Treasury bills, and discount on other obligations with a maturity at the date of issue of not more than 1 year (a short term obligation), including commercial paper, when paid at maturity or redemption if redemption occurs before maturity, shall constitute a payment of interest for purposes of section 6049. * * *

* * *

CFCs: U.S. Shareholders: Ownership Attribution

CFCs: U.S. Shareholders: Ownership Attribution.—Amendments to Reg. §1.6049-5, relating to the modification of section 958(b) of the Internal Revenue Code by the Tax Cuts and Jobs Act, which was enacted on December 22, 2017, are proposed (published in the Federal Register on October 2, 2019) (REG-104223-18).

Par. 12. Section 1.6049-5 is amended by revising paragraphs (c)(5)(i)(C) and (g) to read as follows:

§1.6049-5. Interest and original issue discount subject to reporting after December 31, 1982.

* * *

(c) * * *

(5) * * *

(i) * * *

(C) A controlled foreign corporation within the meaning of section 957, determined without applying subparagraphs (A), (B), and (C) of section 318(a)(3) so as to consider a United States person as owning stock which is owned by a person who is not a United States person.

* * *

(g) *Applicability dates.*—Except as otherwise provided in this paragraph (g), this section applies to payments made on or after January 6, 2017. (For payments made after June 30, 2014, and before January 6, 2017, see this section as in effect and contained in 26 CFR part 1, as revised April 1, 2016. For payments made after December 31, 2000, and before July 1, 2014, see this section as in effect and contained in 26 CFR part 1, as revised April 1, 2013.) Paragraph (c)(5)(i)(C) of this section applies to payments made on or after October 1, 2019. For payments made before October 1, 2019, a taxpayer may apply paragraph (c)(5)(i)(C) of this section for payments during the last taxable year of a foreign corporation beginning before January 1, 2018, and each subsequent taxable year of the foreign corporation, provided that the taxpayer and United States persons that are related (within the meaning of section 267 or 707) to the taxpayer consistently apply such paragraph with respect to all foreign corporations.

Information Returns: OID

Information Returns: Original Issue Discount; Brokers.—Temporary Reg. §1.6049-5T, relating to reporting requirements for original issue discount debt instruments, is also proposed as a final regulation and, when adopted, would become Reg. §1.6049-5 (published in the Federal Register on December 17, 1986).

§1.6049-5. Reporting by brokers of interest and original issue discount on and after January 1, 1986.

Definition of Registered Form: Guidance

Definition of Registered Form: Guidance.—Amendments to Reg. §1.6049-5, providing guidance on the definitions of registration-required obligation and registered form, including guidance on the issuance of pass-through certificates and participation interests in registered form, are proposed (published in the Federal Register on September 19, 2017) (REG-125374-16).

Par. 11. Section 1.6049-5 is amended by:

2. Removing "§5f.103-1(c))," and adding in its place "§1.163-5(b));" in paragraph (a)(1)(i).

3. Removing the language "§5f.163-1" and adding in its place the language "§1.163-5(a)(2)" in paragraph (a)(1)(ii).

§1.6049-5. Interest and original issue discount subject to reporting after December 31, 1982.

Imputed Interest: OID: Safe Haven Interest Rates

Imputed Interest: Original Issue Discount: Safe Haven Interest Rates.—Reproduced below is the text of a proposed amendment of Reg. §1.6049-6, relating to (1) the tax treatment of debt instruments issued after July 1, 1982, that contain original issue discount, (2) the imputation of and the accounting for interest with respect to sales and exchanges of property occurring after December 31, 1984, and (3) safe haven interest rates for loans or advances between commonly controlled taxpayers and safe haven leases between such taxpayers (published in the Federal Register on April 8, 1986).

§1.6049-6. Statements to recipients of interest payments and holders of obligations for attributed original issue discount..

☐ Par. 32. Paragraph (d) of §1.6049-6 is amended by removing the phrase "section 1232A" and adding in its place the phrase "section 1272(a)".

REMICs: Reporting Information: Extension of Time

REMICs: Reporting Information: Extension of Time.—Reproduced below is the text of a proposed amendment to Reg. §1.6049-7, relating to real estate mortgage investment conduits (published in the Federal Register on September 30, 1991).

☐ Par 4. Section 1.6049-7 is amended by revising paragraphs (e)(3)(ii)(A) and (f)(7)(ii) to read as follows:

§1.6049-7. Returns of information with respect to REMIC regular interests and collateralized debt obligations.

* * *

(e) * * *

  (3) * * *

    (ii) * * *

      (A) The 41st day after the close of the calendar quarter for which the information was requested, or

* * *

(f) * * *

  (7) * * *

    (ii) *Time for furnishing information.*—The statement required in paragraph (f)(7)(i) of this section must be furnished on or before the later of—

      (A) The 45th day after receipt of the request,

      (B) The 55th day after the close of the calendar quarter for which the information was requested, or

      (C) If the information is requested for the last calendar quarter in a calendar year, March 15 of the year following the calendar quarter for which the information was requested.

* * *

Returns: Foreclosures: Abandonment of Security

Information Returns: Loan Security: Abandonments, Foreclosure and Other Acquisitions.—Temporary Reg. §1.6050J-1T, relating to the requirement of reporting abandonments, foreclosures, and other acquisitions of property securing indebtedness, is also proposed as a final regulation and, when adopted, would become Reg. §1.6050J-1 (published in the Federal Register on August 31, 1984).

§1.6050J-1. Questions and answers concerning information returns relating to foreclosures and abandonments of security.

Partners and Partnerships: Sales or Exchanges: Certain Distributions

Partners and Partnerships: Sales or Exchanges: Certain Distributions.—Amendments to Reg. §1.6050K-1, prescribing how a partner should measure its interest in a partnership's unrealized receivables and inventory items, and that provide guidance regarding the tax consequences of a distribution that causes a reduction in that interest, are proposed (published in the Federal Register on November 3, 2014) (REG-151416-06).

☐ Par. 17. Section 1.6050K-1 is amended by revising paragraph (a)(4)(ii) and adding a new sentence after the third sentence of paragraph (c) introductory text to read as follows:

§1.6050K-1. Returns relating to sales or exchanges of certain partnership interests.—(a) * * *

(4) * * *

  (ii) *Section 751 property.*—For purposes of this section, the term "section 751 property" means unrealized receivables, as defined in section 751(c) and the regulations, and inventory items, as defined in section 751(d) and the regulations.

* * *

(c) * * * With respect to any statement required to be furnished to a transferor, the statement shall, in addition to the other information required, include the amount of any gain or loss attributable to section 751 property that is required to be recognized pursuant to paragraph (a)(2) of §1.751-1. * * *

* * *

Interests in Partnerships: Withholding of Tax: Information Reporting

Interests in Partnerships: Withholding of Tax: Information Reporting.—Amendments to Reg. §1.6050K-1, implementing certain sections of the Internal Revenue Code, including sections added to the Internal Revenue Code by the Tax Cuts and Jobs Act, that relate to the withholding of tax and information reporting with respect to certain dispositions of interests in partnerships engaged in the conduct of a trade or business within the United States, are proposed (published in the Federal Register on May 13, 2019) (REG-105476-18).

Par. 15. Section 1.6050K-1 is amended by:

1. Redesignating the introductory text of paragraph (c) and paragraphs (c)(1) through (3) as the introductory text of paragraph (c)(1) and paragraphs (c)(1)(i) through (iii), respectively.

2. Adding a subject heading to newly-redesignated paragraph (c)(1).

3. Adding paragraphs (c)(2) and (3), (d)(3), and (h).

The revision and additions read as follows:

§1.6050K-1. Returns relating to sales or exchanges of certain partnership interests.

* * *

(c) *Statements to be furnished to transferor and transferee.*—(1) *In general.*—* * *

(2) *Information to be provided to transferors.*—The statement a partnership must provide to a transferor partner pursuant to paragraph (c)(1) of this section must also include the information necessary for the transferor to make the transferor's required statement under §1.751-1(a)(3).

(3) *Transfers of partnership interests by foreign persons.*—For additional information required to be provided by the partnership if

section 864(c)(8) applies to the transfer of a partnership interest by a foreign person, see §1.864(c)(8)-2(b).

(d) * * *

(3) *Transfers of partnership interests by foreign persons.*—For notifications required by foreign transferors of partnership interests, see §1.864(c)(8)-2(a).

* * *

(h) *Applicability date.*—Paragraphs (c)(2) and (3) of this section apply to returns filed on or after the date that these regulations are published as final regulations in the **Federal Register**. Paragraph (d)(3) of this section applies to transfers that occur on or after the date that these regulations are published as final regulations in the **Federal Register**.

Qualified Tuition: Related Expenses: Reporting

Qualified Tuition: Related Expenses: Reporting.—Amendments to Reg. §§1.6050S-0 and 1.6050S-1, revising the rules for reporting qualified tuition and related expenses under section 6050S on a Form 1098-T, "Tuition Statement," and conforming the regulations to changes made to section 6050S by the Protecting Americans from Tax Hikes Act of 2015, are proposed (published in the Federal Register on August 2, 2016) (corrected September 26, 2016) (REG-131418-14).

Par. 6. Section 1.6050S-0 is amended by:

1. Revising the entry for §1.6050S-1(a)(2)(i).

2. Removing the entries for §1.6050S-1(a)(2)(iii) and (iv).

3. Revising the entries for §1.6050S-1(b)(2) introductory text and (b)(2)(ii).

4. Revising the entry for §1.6050S-1(b)(3) introductory text.

5. Removing the entries for §1.6050S-1(b)(3)(iii), (iv) and (v).

6. Revising the entry for §1.6050S-1(b)(4).

7. Removing the entry for §1.6050S-1(b)(5).

8. Redesignating the entry for §1.6050S-1(b)(6) as §1.6050S-1(b)(5).

9. Adding entries for §1.6050S-1(c)(1)(i), (ii) and (iii).

10. Removing the entry for §1.6050S-1(c)(2)(ii).

11. Redesignating the entry for §1.6050S-1(c)(2)(iii) as §1.6050S-1(c)(2)(ii).

12. Redesignating the entries for §1.6050S-1(e) and §1.6050S-1(f) as §1.6050S-1(f) and §1.6050S-1(g), respectively.

13. Adding a new entry for §1.6050S-1(e).

14. Revising the newly redesignated entry for §1.6050S-1(f)(4).

15. Adding a new entry for §1.6050S-1(f)(5).

The revisions and additions to read as follows:

§1.6050S-0. Table of Contents.

* * *

§1.6050S-1. Information reporting for qualified tuition and related expenses.

(a) * * *

(2) * * *

(i) No reporting of amounts for books, supplies and equipment unless the amount is a fee required to be paid to the institution.

(A) In general.

(B) Examples.

* * *

(b) * * *

(2) Information reporting requirements for educational institutions for qualified tuition and related expenses.

* * *

(ii) Information included on return.

(A) Name, address and TIN of institution

(B) Name address and TIN of individual enrolled at institution

(C) Amount of payments of qualified tuition and related expenses

(D) Indication of whether payments pertain to academic period commencing in first three months of following calendar year

(E) Amount of scholarships or grants

(F) Amount of reimbursements or refunds pertaining to expenses reported in prior year

(G) Amount of reductions of scholarships or grants

(H) Statement of whether individual enrolled for at least half of normal full-time work load

(I) Number of months during which individual enrolled for normal full-time workload

(J) Statement of individual's enrollment in graduate-level program

(K) Any additional information required by Form 1098-T or instructions

* * *

(3) Requirements for insurers.

* * *

(4) Time and place for filing return.

(i) In general.

(ii) Extensions of time.

* * *

(c) * * *

(1) * * *

(i) Required information.

(ii) Legend identifying statement as important tax information.

(iii) Instructions.

(A) Statement of payments made or reimbursements or refunds made.

(B) Statement regarding extent of individual's eligibility for credit under section 25A.

(C) Statement regarding reduction in tax credit due to grant or scholarship.

(D) Statement notifying individual of ability to allocate scholarship or grant.

(E) Statement notifying individual of consequences of refunds, reimbursements, reductions in tuition charges or grants or scholarships for prior taxable year.

(F) Statement informing individual of consequences of reimbursement or refund by institution or insurer.

(G) Statement notifying individual to consult forms and publications of IRS.

(H) Name, address and phone number of educational institution or insurer.

* * *

(e) Definitions.

(1) Administered and processed.

(i) In general.

(ii) Examples.

(2) Cost of attendance.

(f) * * *

(4) No penalty imposed on eligible educational institutions that certify compliance with paragraph (f)(3) of this section at the time of filing the return.

(5) Failure to furnish TIN.

Par. 7. Section 1.6050S-1 is amended by:

1. Revising paragraph (a)(2)(i) and removing paragraphs (a)(2)(iii) and (iv).

2. Revising paragraphs (b)(1), (b)(2)(i), and (b)(2)(ii)(D), (E), (G) and (H).

3. Redesignating paragraphs (b)(2)(ii)(I) and (J) as paragraphs (b)(2)(ii)(J) and (K), respectively, and adding a new paragraph (b)(2)(ii)(I).

4. Revising newly redesignated paragraph (b)(2)(ii)(J).

5. Revising paragraphs (b)(2)(iv), (v), (vi) and *Example 1, 2, 3,* and *4* in paragraph (b)(2)(vii).

6. In paragraph (b)(2)(vii), adding *Example 5* and *6*.

7. Removing paragraph (b)(3) and redesignating paragraphs (b)(4), (5) and (6) as paragraphs (b)(3), (4) and (5), respectively.

8. Revising newly redesignated paragraph (b)(4)(i).

9. Removing newly redesignated paragraph (b)(4)(ii) and further redesignating paragraph (b)(4)(iii) as paragraph (b)(4)(ii).

10. Revising paragraphs (c)(1)(iii)(A), (B) and (C).

11. Redesignating paragraphs (c)(1)(iii)(D), (E), (F), and (G) as paragraphs (c)(1)(iii)(E), (F), (G), and (H), respectively.

12. Revising newly re-designated paragraphs (c)(1)(iii)(E), (F), (G), and (H).

13. Adding a new paragraph (c)(1)(iii)(D).

14. Revising paragraph (c)(2)(i).

15. Removing paragraph (c)(2)(ii) and redesignating paragraph (c)(2)(iii) as paragraph (c)(2)(ii).

16. Redesignating paragraphs (e) and (f) as paragraphs (f) and (g), respectively.

17. Adding a new paragraph (e).

18. In newly redesignated paragraph (f):

i. Revising paragraph (f)(3)(ii).

ii. In paragraph (f)(3)(iii), removing the language "(e)(3)(iii)" and adding "(f)(3)(iii)" in its place.

iii. Further redesignating paragraph (f)(4) as paragraph (f)(5).

iv. Adding new paragraph (f)(4).

19. Revising newly redesignated paragraph (g).

The revisions and additions read as follows:

§1.6050S-1. Information reporting for qualified tuition and related expenses.—(a) * * *

(2) * * *

(i) *No reporting of amounts for books, supplies and equipment unless the amount is a fee required to be paid to the institution.*—(A) *In general.*—The information reporting requirements of this section do not apply to amounts paid for books, supplies, and equipment unless the amount is a fee that must be paid to the eligible educational institution as a condition of enrollment or attendance under §1.25A-2(d)(2)(ii).

(B) *Examples.*—The following examples illustrates the rules of this paragraph (a)(2):

Example 1. First-year students at College W are required to obtain books and other materials used in its mandatory first-year curriculum. The books and other materials are not required to be purchased from College W and may be borrowed from other students or purchased from off-campus bookstores, as well as from College W's bookstore. College W bills students for any books and materials purchased from College W's bookstore. Because the first-year books and materials may be purchased from any vendor, the amount is not a fee that must be paid to the eligible educational institution as a condition of enrollment or attendance and, therefore, is not subject to reporting under paragraph (a)(2)(i) of this section. No amount is reportable even if a first-year student pays College W for the required books and other materials purchased from College W's bookstore.

Example 2. Assume the same facts as *Example 1* of this paragraph (a)(2), except College W furnishes the books and other materials to each first-year student and the books may not be borrowed or purchased from other sources. College W charges a separate fee for books and materials to all first-year students for these items as part of the bill required to be paid to attend the institution. Under paragraph (a)(2)(i) of this section, because the amount is a fee that must be paid to the eligible educational institution as a condition of enrollment or attendance, the fee, if paid by or on behalf of the student, must be reported on the Form 1098-T as part of the qualified tuition and related expenses.

* * *

(b) *Requirement to file return.*—(1) *In general.*—Eligible educational institutions must report the information described in paragraph (b)(2) of this section, which requires institutions to report, among other information, the amount of payments received during the calendar year for qualified tuition and related expenses. Institutions must report separately adjustments made during the calendar year that relate to payments received for qualified tuition and related expenses that were reported for a prior calendar year. For purposes of paragraph (b)(2) of this section, an adjustment made to payments received means a reimbursement or refund. Insurers must report the information described in paragraph (b)(3) of this section.

(2) *Information reporting requirements.*—(i) *In general.*—Except as provided in paragraph (a)(2) of this section (regarding exceptions where no information reporting is required), an eligible educational institution must file an information return with the IRS on Form 1098-T, "Tuition Statement," with respect to each individual enrolled (as determined in paragraph (d)(1) of this section) for an academic period beginning during the calendar year (including an academic period beginning during the first three months of the next calendar year) or during a prior calendar year and for whom a transaction described in paragraph (b)(2)(ii)(C), (E), (F), or (G) of this section is made during the calendar year. An eligible educational institution may use a substitute Form 1098-T if the substitute form complies with applicable revenue procedures relating to substitute forms (see §601.601(d)(2) of this chapter).

(ii) * * *

(D) An indication by the institution whether any payments received for qualified tuition and related expenses reported for the calendar year relate to an academic period that begins during the first three months of the next calendar year and the amount of such payments;

(E) The amount of any scholarships or grants for the payment of the individual's cost of attendance (as defined in paragraph (e)(2) of this section) that the institution administered and processed (as defined in paragraph (e)(1) of this section) during the calendar year;

* * *

(G) The amount of any reductions to the amount of scholarships or grants for the payment of the individual's cost of attendance (as defined in paragraph (e)(2) of this section) that were reported by the eligible educational institution with respect to the individual for a prior calendar year;

(H) A statement or other indication showing whether the individual was enrolled for at least half of the normal full-time work load for the course of study the individual is pursuing for at least one academic period that begins during the calendar year (see section 25A and the regulations thereunder for more information regarding workload requirements);

(I) A statement or other indication showing the number of months (for this purpose, one day in a month is treated as an entire month) during the calendar year that the individual was enrolled for the normal full-time workload for the course of study the individual is pursuing at the institution;

(J) A statement or other indication showing whether the individual was enrolled in a program leading to a graduate-level degree, graduate-level certificate, or other recognized graduate-level educational credential, unless the student is enrolled in both a graduate-level program and an undergraduate level program during the same calendar year at the same institution in which case no statement or indication is required; and

* * *

(iv) *Separate reporting of reimbursements or refunds of payments of qualified tuition and related expenses that were reported for a prior calendar year.*—An institution must separately report on Form 1098-T any reimbursements or refunds (as defined in paragraph (b)(2)(vi) of this section) made during the current calendar year that relate to payments of qualified tuition and related expenses that were reported by the institution for a prior calendar year. Such reimbursements or refunds are not netted against the payments received for qualified tuition and related expenses during the current calendar year.

(v) *Payments received for qualified tuition and related expenses determined.*—For purposes of determining the amount of payments received for qualified tuition and related expenses during a calendar year, payments received with respect to an individual during the calendar year from any source (except for any scholarship or grant that, by its terms, must be applied to expenses other than qualified tuition and related expenses, such as room and board) are treated first as payments of qualified tuition and related expenses up to the total amount billed by the institution for qualified tuition and related expenses for enrollment during the calendar year, and then as payments of expenses other than qualified tuition and related expenses for enrollment during the calendar year. Payments received with respect to an amount billed for enrollment during an academic period beginning in the first 3 months of the following calendar year in which the payment is made are treated as payment of qualified tuition and related expenses in the calendar year during which the payment is received by the institution. For purposes of this section, a payment includes any positive account balance (such as any reimbursement or refund credited to an individual's account) that an institution applies toward current charges.

(vi) *Reimbursements or refunds of payments for qualified tuition and related expenses determined.*—For purposes of determining the amount of reimbursements or refunds made of payments received for qualified tuition and related expenses, any reimbursement or refund made with respect to an individual during a calendar year (except for any refund of a scholarship or grant that, by its terms, was required to be applied to expenses other than qualified tuition and related expenses, such as room and board) is treated as a reimbursement or refund of payments for qualified tuition and related expenses up to the amount of any reduction in charges for qualified tuition and related expenses. For purposes of this section, a reimbursement or refund includes amounts that an institution credits to an individual's account, as well as amounts disbursed to, or on behalf of, the individual.

(vii) * * *

Example 1. (i) Student A enrolls in University X as a full-time student for the 2016 fall semester. In early August 2016, University X sends a bill to Student A for $16,000 for the 2016 fall semester breaking out the current charges as follows: $10,000 for qualified tuition and related expenses and $6,000 for room and board. In late

August 2016, Student A pays $11,000 to University X, leaving a remaining balance to be paid of $5,000. In early September 2016, Student A drops to half-time enrollment for the 2016 fall semester but remains in on-campus housing. In late September 2016, University X credits $5,000 to Student A's account, reflecting a $5,000 reduction in the $10,000 charge for qualified tuition and related expenses as a result of dropping from full-time to half-time status. No other transactions occur with respect to Student A's account with University X. In late September 2016, University X applies the $5,000 credit toward Student A's current charges, eliminating any outstanding balance on Student A's account with University X.

(ii) Under paragraph (b)(2)(v) of this section, the $11,000 payment is treated as a payment of qualified tuition and related expenses up to the $10,000 billed for qualified tuition and related expenses. Under paragraph (b)(2)(vi) of this section, the $5,000 credited to the student's account is treated as a reimbursement or refund of payments for qualified tuition and related expenses because there is a reduction in charges for qualified tuition and related expenses equal to the $5,000 credit due to Student A dropping to half-time for the 2016 fall semester. Under paragraph (b)(2)(iii) of this section, the $10,000 payment received for qualified tuition and related expenses during 2016 is reduced by the $5,000 reimbursement or refund of payments received for qualified tuition and related expenses during 2016. Therefore, University X is required to report $5,000 of payments received for qualified tuition and related expenses during 2016 on a 2016 Form 1098-T.

Example 2. (i) The facts are the same as in *Example 1* of this paragraph (b)(2)(vii), except that Student A pays the full $16,000 in late August 2016. In late September 2016, University X reduces the tuition charges by $5,000 and issues a $5,000 refund to Student A.

(ii) Under paragraph (b)(2)(v) of this section, the $16,000 payment is treated as a payment of qualified tuition and related expenses up to the $10,000 billed for qualified tuition and related expenses. Under paragraph (b)(2)(vi) of this section, the $5,000 refund is treated as reimbursement or refund of payments for qualified tuition and related expenses because University X reduced the charges for qualified tuition and related expenses equal to the $5,000 refund disbursed to the student due to dropping to half-time for the 2016 fall semester. Under paragraph (b)(2)(iii) of this section, the $10,000 payment received for qualified tuition and related expenses during 2016 is reduced by the $5,000 reimbursement or refund of payments received for qualified tuition and related expenses during 2016. Therefore, University X is required to report $5,000 of payments received for qualified tuition and related expenses during 2016 on a 2016 Form 1098-T.

Example 3. (i) The facts are the same as in *Example 1* of this paragraph (b)(2)(vii), except that Student A is enrolled full-time, and, in early September 2016, Student A decides to live at home with her parents. In late September 2016, University X adjusts Student A's account to eliminate room and board charges and issues a $1,000 refund to Student A.

(ii) Under paragraph (b)(2)(v) of this section, the $11,000 payment is treated as a payment of qualified tuition and related expenses up to the $10,000 billed for qualified tuition and related expenses. Under paragraph (b)(2)(vi) of this section, the $1,000 refund is not treated as reimbursement or refund of payments for qualified tuition and related expenses because University X has reduced room and board charges for the 2016 fall semester, rather than reducing charges for qualified tuition and related expenses for the 2016 fall semester. Therefore, under paragraph (b)(2)(iii) of this section, University X is required to report $10,000 of payments received for qualified tuition and related expenses during 2016 on a 2016 Form 1098-T.

Example 4. (i) Student B enrolls in College Y as a full-time student for the 2017 spring semester. In early December 2016, College Y sends a bill to Student B for $16,000 for the 2017 spring semester breaking out current charges as follows: $10,000 for qualified tuition and related expenses and $6,000 for room and board. In late December 2016, College Y receives a payment of $16,000 from Student B. In mid-January 2017, after the 2017 spring semester classes begin, Student B drops to half-time enrollment. In mid-January 2017, College Y credits Student B's account with $5,000, reflecting a $5,000 reduction in charges for qualified tuition and related expenses, but does not issue a refund to Student B. Thereafter, Student B's account reflects a positive balance of $5,000 due to the credit and there is no other activity on Student B's account until early August when College Y sends a bill for $16,000 for the 2017 fall semester breaking out the current charges as follows: $10,000 for qualified tuition and related expenses and $6,000 for room and board. In early September 2017, College Y applies the $5,000 positive account balance (credit) toward Student B's $16,000 bill for the 2017 fall semester. In late September 2017, Student B pays $6,000 towards the charges for the 2017 fall semester.

(ii) For calendar year 2016, under paragraph (b)(2)(v) of this section, $10,000 of the $16,000 payment received by College Y in December 2016 is treated as a payment of qualified tuition and

related expenses. Therefore, College Y is required to report $10,000 of payments received for qualified tuition and related expenses during 2016 on a 2016 Form 1098-T. In addition, College Y is required to indicate that $10,000 of the payments reported on the 2016 Form 1098-T relate to an academic period that begins during the first three months of the next calendar year.

(iii) Under paragraph (b)(2)(vi) of this section, the $5,000 credited to Student B's account in January 2017 is treated as a reimbursement or refund of qualified tuition and related expenses because there is a reduction in charges for qualified tuition and related expenses of $5,000 for the 2017 spring semester. Under paragraph (b)(2)(iv) of this section, however, this reduction is a reimbursement or refund of qualified tuition and related expenses made during 2017 and, therefore, must be separately reported on the 2017 Form 1098-T. The 2016 Form 1098-T reporting $10,000 of qualified tuition and related expenses for 2016 is unchanged.

(iv) Under paragraph (b)(2)(v) of this section, the $5,000 positive account balance that is applied toward charges for the 2017 fall semester is treated as a payment made in 2017. Therefore, College Y received total payments of $11,000 during 2017 (the $5,000 credit plus the $6,000 payment). Under paragraph (b)(2)(v) of this section, the $11,000 of total payments made during 2017 are treated as a payment of qualified tuition and related expenses up to the $10,000 billed for qualified tuition and related expenses for the 2017 fall semester. Therefore, for 2017, College Y is required to report $10,000 of payments received for qualified tuition and related expenses during 2017 and a $5,000 refund of payments of qualified tuition and related expenses reported for 2016 on the 2017 Form 1098-T.

Example 5. (i) Student C enrolls in College Z as a full-time student for the 2016 fall semester and the 2017 spring semester. Student C was not enrolled in, and did not attend, any institution of higher education prior to the 2016 fall semester. In August 2016, College Z sends a bill to Student C for $11,000 for the 2016 fall semester. In December 2016, College Z sends a bill to Student C for $11,000 for the 2017 spring semester. Qualified tuition and related expenses billed for each semester is $6,000 and room and board billed for each semester is $5,000. In September 2016, College Z receives a payment of $11,000 which is applied toward the amount billed for Student C's attendance during the 2016 fall semester. In December 2016, College Z receives a payment of $4,500 which is applied toward the amount billed for Student C's attendance during the 2017 spring semester. In February 2017, College Z receives a payment of $6,500, the remainder of the amount billed for enrollment during the 2017 spring semester.

(ii) On the 2016 Form 1098-T, College Z reports the payment of $10,500 of qualified tuition and related expenses determined as follows: $6,000 for the payment received in September 2016 with respect to the amount billed for qualified tuition and related expenses for the 2016 fall semester and $4,500 for the payment received in December 2016 with respect to the amount billed for qualified tuition and related expenses for the 2017 spring semester. On the 2017 Form 1098-T, College Z reports the payment of $1,500 of qualified tuition and related expenses received in February 2017 with respect to the amount billed for qualified tuition and related expenses for the 2017 spring semester.

Example 6. The facts are the same as *Example 5* of this paragraph (b)(2)(vii) except in January 2017 College Z receives payment of $11,000 for the entire amount billed for the 2017 spring semester. On the 2016 Form 1098-T, College Z reports the payment of $6,000 for the payment received in September 2016 with respect to the amount billed for qualified tuition and related expenses for the 2016 fall semester. On the 2017 Form 1098-T, College Z reports the payment of $6,000 of qualified tuition and related expenses received in January 2017 with respect to the amount billed for qualified tuition and related expenses for the 2017 spring semester.

* * *

(4) *Time and place for filing return.*—(i) *In general.*—Except as provided in paragraph (b)(4)(ii) of this section, Form 1098-T must be filed on or before February 28 (March 31 if filed electronically) of the year following the calendar year in which payments were received for qualified tuition or related expenses, or reimbursements, refunds, or reductions of such amounts were made. An institution or insurer must file Form 1098-T with the IRS according to the instructions for Form 1098-T.

* * *

(c) * * *

(1) * * *

(iii) * * *

(A) State that the statement reports total payments received by the institution for qualified tuition and related expenses during the calendar year, or the total reimbursements or refunds made by the insurer;

(B) State that, under section 25A and the regulations thereunder, the taxpayer may claim an education tax credit only with

Reg. §1.6050S-1(b)(4)(i)

respect to qualified tuition and related expenses actually paid during the calendar year; and that the taxpayer may not be able to claim an education tax credit with respect to the entire amount of payments received for qualified tuition and related expenses reported on the Form 1098-T for the calendar year;

(C) State that the amount of any scholarships or grants reported on the Form 1098-T for the calendar year and other similar amounts not reported on the Form 1098-T (because they are not administered and processed by the eligible educational institution as defined in paragraph (e)(1) of this section) that are allocated by the student to pay qualified tuition and related expenses may reduce the amount of any allowable education tax credit for the taxable year;

(D) State that even if the eligible educational institution applies scholarships or grants reported on the Form 1098-T for the calendar year to qualified tuition and related expenses, the student may, for tax purposes, be able to allocate all or a portion of the scholarships or grants to expenses other than qualified tuition and related expenses (and, therefore, forego having to reduce the amount of the education tax credit the student may claim) if the terms of the scholarship or grant permit it to be used for expenses other than qualified tuition and related expenses and the student includes the amount in income on his federal income tax return.

* * *

(E) State that the amount of any reimbursements or refunds of payments received, or reductions in charges, for qualified tuition and related expenses, or any reductions to the amount of scholarships or grants, reported by the eligible educational institution with respect to the individual for a prior calendar year on Form 1098-T may affect the amount of any allowable education tax credit for the prior calendar year (and may result in an increase in tax liability for the year of the refund);

(F) State that the amount of any reimbursements or refunds of qualified tuition and related expenses reported on a Form 1098-T by an eligible educational institution or insurer may reduce the amount of an allowable education tax credit for a taxable year (and may result in an increase in tax liability for the year of the refund);

(G) State that the taxpayer should refer to relevant IRS forms and publications, such as Publication 970, "Tax Benefits for Education," and should not refer to the institution or the insurer, for explanations relating to the eligibility requirements for, and calculation of, any allowable education tax credit; and

(H) Include the name, address, and phone number of the information contact of the eligible educational institution or insurer that filed the Form 1098-T.

(2) *Time and manner for furnishing statement.*—(i) *In general.*— Except as provided in paragraph (c)(2)(ii) of this section, an institution or insurer must furnish the statement described in paragraph (c)(1) of this section to each individual for whom it is required to file a return, on or before January 31 of the year following the calendar year in which payments were received for qualified tuition and related expenses, or reimbursements, refunds or reductions of such amounts were made. If mailed, the statement must be sent to the individual's permanent address or the individual's temporary address if the institution or insurer does not know the individual's permanent address. If furnished electronically, the statement must be furnished in accordance with applicable regulations.

* * *

(e) *Definitions.*—The following definitions apply with respect to this section:

(1) *Administered and processed.*—(i) *In general.*—A scholarship or grant is "administered and processed" by an eligible educational institution if the institution receives payment of an amount (whether by cash, check, or other means of payment) that the institution knows or reasonably should know, is a scholarship or grant, regardless of whether the institution is named payee or co-payee of such amount and regardless of whether, in the case of a payment other than in cash, the student endorses the check or other means of payment for the benefit of the institution. For instance, Pell Grants, described in the Higher Education Act of 1965 (20 U.S.C. 1070), as amended, are administered and processed by an institution in all cases.

(ii) *Examples.*—The following examples illustrate the definition in this paragraph (e)(1):

Example 1. University M received a Pell Grant on behalf of Student B, a student enrolled in a degree program at University M.

University M provides all required notifications to and obtains all the necessary paperwork from Student B and applies the Pell Grant to Student B's account. Because University M received the Pell Grant and University M knows or should know that the Pell Grant is a scholarship or grant, under paragraph (e)(1)(i) of this section, the Pell Grant is administered and processed by University M.

Example 2. University N receives a check from Organization Y made out to Student C. University N is not named as a payee on the check. The cover letter accompanying the check provides University N with sufficient information to reasonably know that the check represents payment of a scholarship that may be used to pay Student C's qualified tuition and related expenses. Under paragraph (e)(1)(i) of this section, the scholarship from Organization Y is administered and processed by University N. This is the case even though University N is not named on the check as a payee and regardless of whether Student C endorses the check over to University N.

(2) *Cost of attendance.*—The term "cost of attendance" has the same meaning as section 472 of the Higher Education Act of 1965, 20 U.S.C. 1087ll.

(f) * * *

(3) * * *

(ii) *Acting in a responsible manner.*—An institution or insurer must request the TIN of each individual for whom it is required to file a return if it does not already have a record of the individual's correct TIN. If the institution or insurer does not have a record of the individual's correct TIN, then it must solicit the TIN in the manner described in paragraph (f)(3)(iii) of this section on or before December 31 of each year during which it receives payments of qualified tuition and related expenses or makes reimbursements, refunds, or reductions of such amounts with respect to the individual. If an individual refuses to provide his or her TIN upon request, the institution or insurer must file the return and furnish the statement required by this section without the individual's TIN, but with all other required information. The specific solicitation requirements of paragraph (f)(3)(iii) of this section apply in lieu of the solicitation requirements of § 301.6724-1(e) and (f) of this chapter for the purpose of determining whether an institution or insurer acted in a responsible manner in attempting to obtain a correct TIN. An institution or insurer that complies with the requirements of this paragraph (f)(3) will be considered to have acted in a responsible manner within the meaning of § 301.6724-1(d) of this chapter with respect to any failure to include the correct TIN of an individual on a return or statement required by section 6050S and this section.

* * *

(4) *No penalty imposed on eligible educational institutions that certify compliance with paragraph (f)(3) of this section at the time of filing the return.*—In the case of returns required to be filed and statements required to be furnished after December 31, 2015, the IRS will not impose a penalty against an eligible educational institution under section 6721 or 6722 for failure to include the individual's correct TIN on the return or statement if the institution makes a true and accurate certification to the IRS under penalties of perjury (in the form and manner prescribed by the Secretary in publications, forms and instructions, or other published guidance) at the time of filing of the return that the institution complied with the requirements in paragraphs (f)(3)(ii) and (iii) of this section. Nothing in this paragraph (f)(4) prevents the IRS from imposing a penalty under section 6721 or 6722 if after the IRS receives the certification described in this paragraph (f)(4) the IRS determines that the requirements of paragraph (f)(3) of this section are not satisfied or the failure is unrelated to an incorrect or missing TIN for the individual for whom the institution is required to file a return or statement.

* * *

(g) *Applicability date.*—The rules in this section apply to information returns required to be filed, and statements required to be furnished, after December 31, 2003, except that paragraphs (a)(2), (b)(1), (b)(2)(i), (b)(2)(ii)(D), (E), and (G) through (K), (b)(2)(iv) through (vii), (b)(4)(i) and (ii), (c)(1)(iii)(B) through (H), (e), and (f)(4) apply to information returns required to be filed, and statements required to be furnished, after the date of publication of the Treasury decision adopting these rules as final regulations in the **Federal Register**. For information returns required to be filed, and statements required to be furnished, on or before the date of publication of the Treasury decision adopting these rules as final regulations in the **Federal Register**, § 1.6050S-1 (as contained in 26 CFR part 1, revised April 2014) applies.

Catastrophic Health Coverage: Information Reporting

Catastrophic Health Coverage: Information Reporting.—Amendments to Reg. § 1.6055-1, relating to information reporting of minimum essential coverage under section 6055 of the Internal Revenue Code, are proposed (published in the Federal Register on August 2, 2016) (REG-103058-16).

Par. 2. Section 1.6055-1 is amended by:

1. Adding paragraphs (b)(13) and (14).
2. Redesignating paragraph (c)(1)(iv) as (c)(1)(v) and adding a new paragraph (c)(1)(iv).
3. Revising paragraphs (d)(1) and (2).
4. Redesignating paragraph (d)(3) as (d)(5) and adding a new paragraph (d)(3).
5. Adding paragraphs (d)(4) and (6).
6. Revising paragraph (g)(3).
7. Revising paragraph (h)(1).
8. Adding paragraph (h)(3).
9. Revising paragraph (j).

The revisions and additions read as follows:

§1.6055-1. Information reporting for minimum essential coverage.

* * *

(b) * * *

(13) *Catastrophic plan.*—The term catastrophic plan has the same meaning as in section 1302(e) of the Affordable Care Act (42 U.S.C. 18022(e)).

(14) *Basic health program.*—The term basic health program means a basic health program established under section 1331 of the Affordable Care Act (42 U.S.C. 18051).

(c) * * *

(1) * * *

(iv) The state agency that administers a Basic Health Program;

* * *

(d) *Reporting not required.*—(1) *Qualified health plans.*—Except for coverage under a catastrophic plan, a health insurance issuer is not required to file a return or furnish a report under this section for coverage in a qualified health plan in the individual market enrolled in through an Exchange.

(2) *Duplicative coverage.*—If an individual is covered for a month by more than one minimum essential coverage plan or program provided by the same reporting entity, reporting is required for only one of the plans or programs for that month.

(3) *Supplemental coverage.*—Reporting is not required for minimum essential coverage of an individual for a month if that individual is eligible for that coverage only if enrolled in other minimum essential coverage for which section 6055 reporting is required and is not waived under this paragraph (d)(3). This paragraph (d)(3) applies with respect to eligible employer-sponsored coverage only if the supplemental coverage is offered by the same employer that offered the eligible employer-sponsored coverage for which reporting is required. For this purpose, an employer is treated as offering minimum essential coverage offered by any other person that is a member of a controlled group of entities under section 414(b) or (c), an affiliated service group under section 414(m), or an entity in an arrangement described under section 414(o) of which the employer is also a member.

(4) *Certain coverage provided by Territories and Possessions.*—The agencies that administer Medicaid and the Children's Health Insurance Program in American Samoa, the Commonwealth of the Northern Mariana Islands, Guam, Puerto Rico, and the United States Virgin Islands are not required to report that coverage under section 6055.

* * *

(6) *Examples.*—The following examples illustrate the rules of this paragraph (d).

Example 1. Upon being hired, Taxpayer A enrolls in a self-insured major medical group health plan and a health reimbursement arrangement (HRA), both offered by A's employer, V. Both the group health plan and the HRA are minimum essential coverage, and V is the reporting entity for both. Because V is the reporting entity for both the self-insured major medical group health plan and the HRA, under paragraph (d)(2) of this section V must report under paragraph (a) of this section for either its self-insured major medical group health plan or its HRA for A for the months in which A is enrolled in both plans.

Example 2. Taxpayer B is enrolled in an insured employer-sponsored group health plan offered by B's employer, W. B is also covered by an HRA offered by W. Under the terms of the HRA, B is eligible for the HRA because B is enrolled in W's insured employer-sponsored group health plan. W's insured employer-sponsored group health plan is minimum essential coverage and, under paragraphs (a) and (c)(1)(i) of this section, the issuer of the insured employer-sponsored group health plan must report coverage under the plan. Therefore, for the months in which B is enrolled in both plans, under paragraph (d)(3) of this section, W does not need to report the HRA for B because the issuer is required to report on coverage for B in the insured employer-sponsored group health plan offered by W for those months.

Example 3. Taxpayer C enrolls in a Medicare Savings Program administered by X, a state Medicaid agency, which provides financial assistance with Medicare Part A premiums. Only individuals enrolled in Medicare Part A are offered coverage in this Medicare Savings Program. Medicare Part A is government-sponsored minimum essential coverage and, under paragraphs (a) and (c)(1)(iii) of this section, Medicare must report coverage under the program. Therefore, under paragraph (d)(3) of this section, X does not need to report under paragraph (a) of this section for C's coverage under the Medicare Savings Program.

Example 4. Taxpayer E obtains a Medicare supplemental insurance (Medigap) policy that provides financial assistance with costs not covered by Medicare Part A from Z, a health insurance issuer. Only individuals enrolled in Medicare Part A are offered coverage under this Medigap policy. Medicare Part A is minimum essential coverage and, under paragraphs (a) and (c)(1)(iii) of this section, Medicare is required to report E's coverage under Medicare Part A. Therefore, under paragraph (d)(3) of this section, Z does not need to report E's coverage under the Medigap policy.

Example 5. Taxpayer F is covered by an HRA offered by F's employer, P. F is also enrolled in a non-HRA group health plan that is self-insured and sponsored by F's spouse's employer, Q. P and Q are not treated as one employer under section 414(b), (c), (m), or (o). Under the terms of the HRA, F is eligible for the HRA only because F is enrolled in a non-HRA group health plan, which in this case is the group health plan offered by Q. However, because the HRA and the non-HRA group health plan are offered by different employers, paragraph (d)(3) of this section does not apply. Accordingly, under paragraphs (a) and (c)(2)(i)(A) of this section, P must report F's enrollment in the HRA, and Q must report F's (and F's spouse's) enrollment in the non-HRA group health plan.

* * *

(g) * * *

(3) *Form of the statement.*—A statement required under this paragraph (g) may be made either by furnishing to the responsible individual a copy of the return filed with the Internal Revenue Service or on a substitute statement. A substitute statement must include the information required to be shown on the return filed with the Internal Revenue Service and must comply with requirements in published guidance (see §601.601(d)(2) of this chapter) relating to substitute statements. An individual's identifying number may be truncated to appear in the form of an IRS truncated taxpayer identification number (TTIN) on the statement furnished to the responsible individual. The identifying number of the employer may also be truncated to appear in the form of a TTIN on the statement furnished to the responsible individual. For provisions relating to the use of TTINs, see §301.6109-4 of this chapter (Procedure and Administration Regulations).

* * *

(h) * * *

(1) *In general.*—For provisions relating to the penalty for failure to file timely a correct information return required under section 6055, see section 6721 and the regulations under that section. For provisions relating to the penalty for failure to furnish timely a correct statement to responsible individuals required under section 6055, see section 6722 and the regulations under that section. See section 6724, and the regulations thereunder, and paragraph (h)(3) of this section for provisions relating to the waiver of penalties if a failure to file or furnish timely or accurately is due to reasonable cause and not due to willful neglect.

* * *

(3) *Application of section 6724 waiver of penalties to section 6055 reporting.*—(i) *In general.*—Paragraphs (e) and (f) of §301.6724-1 of this chapter, as modified by this paragraph (h)(3), apply to reasonable cause waivers of penalties under sections 6721 and 6722 for failure to file timely or accurate information returns or to furnish individual statements required to be filed or furnished under section 6055.

(ii) *Account opened.*—For purposes of section 6055 reporting and the solicitation rules contained in paragraphs (i), (ii), (iii), and (v) of §301.6724-1(e)(1) of this chapter and paragraph (i) of

§ 301.6724-1(f)(1) of this chapter, an account is considered opened at the time the reporting entity receives a substantially complete application for coverage (including an application to add an individual to existing coverage) from or on behalf of an individual for whom the reporting entity does not already provide coverage.

(iii) *First annual solicitation deadline for missing TINs.*—In lieu of the deadline for the first annual solicitation contained in paragraph (ii) of § 301.6724-1(e)(1) of this chapter, the first annual solicitation must be made on or before the seventy-fifth day after the date on which an account is opened (or, in the case of retroactive coverage, the seventy-fifth day after the determination of retroactive coverage is made). The period from the date on which the reporting entity receives an application for coverage to the last day on which the first annual solicitation may be made is the first annual solicitation period.

(iv) *Failures to which a solicitation relates.*—(A) *Missing TIN.*—For purposes of reporting under section 6055 and the solicitation rules contained in paragraph (1) of § 301.6724-1(e) of this chapter, the initial and first annual solicitations relate to failures on returns required to be filed for the year which includes the first effective date of coverage for a covered individual. The second annual solicitation relates to failures on returns filed for the year immediately following the year to which the first annual solicitation relates and for succeeding calendar years.

(B) *Incorrect TIN.*—For purposes of reporting under section 6055 and the solicitation rules contained in paragraph (i) of § 301.6724-1(f)(1) of this chapter, the initial solicitation relates to failures on returns required to be filed for the year which includes the first effective date of coverage for a covered individual.

(v) *Solicitations made to responsible individual.*—For purposes of reporting under section 6055 and the solicitation rules contained in § 301.6724-1(e) and (f) of this chapter, an initial or annual solicitation made to the responsible individual is treated as a solicitation made to a covered individual.

* * *

(j) *Applicability date.*—(1) Except as provided in paragraphs (j)(2) and (3) of this section, this section applies for calendar years ending after December 31, 2014.

(2) Paragraphs (b)(14), (c)(1)(v), (d)(2) through (6), and (g)(3) of this section apply to calendar years ending after December 31, 2015. Paragraphs (d)(2), (d)(3), and (g)(3) of § 1.6055-1 as contained in 26 CFR part 1 edition revision as of April 1, 2016, apply to calendar years ending after December 31, 2014 and beginning before January 1, 2016.

(3) Paragraphs (b)(13) and (d)(1) of this section apply to calendar years beginning after December 31, 2016. Paragraph (d)(1) of § 1.6055-1 as contained in 26 CFR part 1 edition revised as of April 1, 2016, applies to calendar years ending after December 31, 2015 and beginning before January 1, 2017.

Expatriate Health Plans: Issuers: Excepted Benefits

Expatriate Health Plans: Issuers: Excepted Benefits.—Amendments to Reg. § 1.6055-2, relating to the rules for expatriate health plans, expatriate health plan issuers, and qualified expatriates under the Expatriate Health Coverage Clarification Act of 2014 (EHCCA), are proposed (published in the Federal Register on June 10, 2016) (REG-135702-15).

4. Section 1.6055-2 is amended by adding paragraph (a)(8) to read as follows:

§ 1.6055-2. Electronic furnishing of statements.—(a) * * *

(8) *Special rule for expatriate health plan coverage.*—(i) *In general.*—In the case of an individual covered under an expatriate health plan (within the meaning of § 54.9831-1(f)(3) of this chapter), the recipient is treated as having consented under paragraph (a)(2) of this section unless the recipient has explicitly refused to consent to receive the statement in an electronic format. The refusal to consent may be made electronically or in a paper document. A recipient's request for a paper statement is treated as an explicit refusal to receive the statement in electronic format. A furnisher relying on this paragraph (a)(8) must satisfy the requirements of paragraphs (a)(3) through (7) of this section, except that the statement required under paragraph (a)(3) must be provided at least 30 days prior to the time for furnishing under § 1.6055-1(g)(4)(i)(A) of this chapter of the first statement that the furnisher intends to furnish electronically to the

recipient, and the other requirements of paragraph (a)(3) are modified to reflect that the statement will be furnished electronically unless the recipient explicitly refuses to consent to receive the statement in an electronic format.

(ii) *Manner and time of notifying recipient.*—The IRS may specify in other guidance published in the Internal Revenue Bulletin the manner and timing for the initial notification of recipients that the statement required under paragraph (a)(3) of this section will be furnished electronically unless the recipient explicitly refuses to consent to receive the statement in an electronic format. See § 601.601(d)(2)(ii)(B) of this chapter.

(iii) *Effective/applicability date.*—The provisions of this paragraph (a)(8) apply as of January 1, 2017.

* * *

Expatriate Health Plans: Issuers: Excepted Benefits

Expatriate Health Plans: Issuers: Excepted Benefits.—Amendments to Reg. § 301.6056-2, relating to the rules for expatriate health plans, expatriate health plan issuers, and qualified expatriates under the Expatriate Health Coverage Clarification Act of 2014 (EHCCA), are proposed (published in the Federal Register on June 10, 2016) (REG-135702-15).

18. Section 301.6056-2 is amended by adding paragraph (a)(8) to read as follows:

§ 301.6056-2. Electronic furnishing of statements.—(a) * * *

(8) *Special rule for expatriate health plan coverage.*—(i) *In general.*—In the case of an individual covered under an expatriate health plan (within the meaning of § 54.9831-1(f)(3) of this chapter), the recipient is treated as having consented under paragraph (a)(2) of this section unless the recipient has explicitly refused to consent to receive the statement in an electronic format. The refusal to consent may be made electronically or in a paper document. A recipient's request for a paper statement is treated as an explicit refusal to receive the statement in electronic format. A furnisher relying on this paragraph (a)(8) must satisfy the requirements of paragraphs (a)(3) through (7) of this section, except that the statement required under paragraph (a)(3) must be provided at least 30 days prior to the time for furnishing under § 301.6056-1(g)(4)(i)(A) of this chapter of the first statement that the furnisher intends to furnish electronically to the

recipient, and the other requirements of paragraph (a)(3) are modified to reflect that the statement will be furnished electronically unless the recipient explicitly refuses consent to receive the statement in an electronic format.

(ii) *Manner and time of notifying recipient.*—The IRS may specify in other guidance published in the Internal Revenue Bulletin the manner and timing for the initial notification of recipients that the statement required under paragraph (a)(3) of this section will be furnished electronically unless the recipient explicitly refuses to consent to receive the statement in an electronic format. See § 601.601(d)(2)(ii)(B) of this chapter.

(iii) *Effective/applicability date.*—The provisions of this paragraph (a)(8) apply as of January 1, 2017.

* * *

Deferred Vested Benefits: Reporting and Notice Requirements

Deferred Vested Benefits: Reporting and Notice Requirements.—Amendments to Reg. §§ 301.6057-1 and 301.6057-2, relating to automatic extensions of time for filing certain employee plan returns by adding the Form 8955-SSA, "Annual Registration Statement Identifying Separated Participants With Deferred Vested Benefits," to the list of forms that are covered by the Income Tax Regulations on automatic extensions, are proposed (published in the Federal Register on June 21, 2012) (REG-153627-08).

☐ Par. 4. Section 301.6057-1 is amended by:

1. Revising paragraphs (a)(4) and (a)(5)(ii).

2. Removing paragraph (b)(2)(iii) and redesignating paragraph (b)(2)(iv) as (b)(2)(iii).

3. Revising newly designated paragraph (b)(2)(iii).

4. Revising paragraphs (b)(3)(ii), (b)(3)(iii), (c), (d), (f), and (g).

☐ Par. 5. Section 301.6057–1 is amended by removing the language "schedule SSA" and adding "Form 8955-SSA" in its place.

The revisions read as follows:

§301.6057-1. Employee retirement benefit plans; identification of participant with deferred vested retirement benefit.—

(a) * * *

(4) *Filing requirements.*—(i) *In general.*—Information relating to the deferred vested retirement benefit of a plan participant must be filed on Form 8955-SSA, "Annual Registration Statement Identifying Separated Participants With Deferred Vested Benefits." Form 8955-SSA shall be filed on behalf of an employee retirement benefit plan for each plan year for which information relating to the deferred vested retirement benefit of a plan participant is filed under paragraph (a)(5) or (b)(2) of this section. There shall be reported on Form 8955-SSA the name and Social Security number of the participant, a description of the nature, form and amount of the deferred vested retirement benefit to which the participant is entitled, and such other information as is required by section 6057(a) or Form 8955-SSA and the accompanying instructions. The form of the benefit reported on Form 8955-SSA shall be the normal form of benefit under the plan, or, if the plan administrator (within the meaning of section 414(g)) considers it more appropriate, any other form of benefit.

(ii) *General due date for filing.*—The forms prescribed by section 6057(a), including Form 8955-SSA, shall be filed in the manner and at the time as required by the forms and related instructions applicable to the annual period.

(iii) *Delegation of authority to Commissioner.*—The Commissioner may provide special rules under section 6057 (including designating the form used to comply with section 6057) in revenue rulings, notices, or other guidance published in the Internal Revenue Bulletin (see §601.601(d)(2)(ii)(b) of this chapter) that the Commissioner determines to be necessary or appropriate with respect to the filing requirements under section 6057.

(5) * * *

(ii) *Exception.*—Notwithstanding paragraph (a)(5)(i) of this section, no information relating to the deferred vested retirement benefit of a separated participant is required to be filed on Form 8955-SSA if, before the date such Form 8955-SSA is required to be filed (including any extension of time for filing granted pursuant to section 6081), the participant—

(A) Is paid some or all of the deferred vested retirement benefit under the plan;

(B) Returns to service covered under the plan; or

(C) Forfeits all of the deferred vested retirement benefit under the plan.

(b) * * *

(2) * * *

(iii) *Exception.*—Notwithstanding paragraph (b)(2)(i) of this section, no information relating to a participant's deferred vested retirement benefit is required to be filed on Form 8955-SSA if, before the date such Form 8955-SSA is required to be filed (including any extension of time for filing granted pursuant to section 6081), the participant—

(A) Is paid some or all of the deferred vested retirement benefit under the plan;

(B) Accrues additional retirement benefits under the plan; or

(C) Forfeits all of the deferred vested retirement benefit under the plan.

(3) * * *

(ii) *Inability to determine correct amount of participant's deferred vested retirement benefit.*—The plan administrator must indicate on Form 8955-SSA that the amount of a participant's deferred vested retirement benefit showed therein may be other than that to which the participant is actually entitled if such amount is computed on the basis of plan records that the plan administrator maintains and such records—

(A) Are incomplete with respect to the participant's service covered by the plan (as described in paragraph (b)(3)(i) of this section); or

(B) Fail to account for the participant's service not covered by the plan which is relevant to a determination of the participant's deferred vested retirement benefit under the plan (as described in paragraph (b)(3)(i) of this section).

(iii) *Inability to determine whether participant vested in deferred retirement benefit.*—Where, as described in paragraph (b)(3)(i) of this section, information to be reported on Form 8955-SSA is to be based upon records which are incomplete with respect to a participant's service covered by the plan or which fail to take into account relevant service not covered by the plan, the plan administrator may be unable to determine whether or not the participant is vested in any deferred retirement benefit. If, in view of information provided either by the incomplete records or the plan participant, there is a significant likelihood that the plan participant is vested in a deferred retirement benefit under the plan, information relating to the participant must be filed on Form 8955-SSA with the notation that the participant may be entitled to a deferred vested benefit under the plan, but information relating to the amount of the benefit may be omitted. This paragraph (b)(3)(iii) does not apply in a case in which it can be determined from plan records maintained by the plan administrator that the participant is vested in a deferred retirement benefit. Paragraph (b)(3)(ii) of this section, however, may apply in such a case.

(c) *Voluntary filing.*—(1) *In general.*—The plan administrator of an employee retirement benefit plan described in paragraph (a)(3) of this section, or any other employee retirement benefit plan (including a governmental plan within the meaning of section 414(d) or a church plan within the meaning of section 414(e)), may, at its option, file on Form 8955-SSA information relating to the deferred vested retirement benefit of any plan participant who separates at any time from service covered by the plan.

(2) *Deleting previously filed information.*—If, after information relating to the deferred vested retirement benefit of a plan participant is filed on Form 8955-SSA (or a predecessor to Form 8955-SSA), the plan participant is paid some or all of the deferred vested retirement benefit under the plan or forfeits all of the deferred vested retirement benefit under the plan, the plan administrator may, at its option, file on Form 8955-SSA (or such other form as may be provided for this purpose) the name and Social Security number of the plan participant with the notation that information previously filed relating to the participant's deferred vested retirement benefit should be deleted.

(d) *Filing incident to cessation of payment of benefits.*—(1) *In general.*

No information relating to the deferred vested retirement benefit of a plan participant is required to be filed on Form 8955-SSA if before the date such Form 8955-SSA is required to be filed, some of the deferred vested retirement benefit is paid to the participant, and information relating to a participant's deferred vested retirement benefit which was previously filed on Form 8955-SSA (or a predecessor to Form 8955-SSA) may be deleted if the participant is paid some of the deferred vested retirement benefit. If payment of the deferred vested retirement benefit ceases before all of the benefit to which the participant is entitled is paid to the participant, information relating to the deferred vested retirement benefit to which the participant remains entitled shall be filed on the Form 8955-SSA filed for the plan year following the last plan year within which a portion of the benefit is paid to the participant.

(2) *Exception.*—Notwithstanding paragraph (d)(1) of this section, no information relating to the deferred vested retirement benefit to which the participant remains entitled is required to be filed on Form 8955-SSA if, before the date such Form 8955-SSA is required to be filed (including any extension of time for filing granted pursuant to section 6081), the participant—

(i) Returns to service covered by the plan;

(ii) Accrues additional retirement benefits under the plan; or

(iii) Forfeits the benefit under the plan.

* * *

(f) *Penalties.*—For amounts imposed in the case of failure to file the report of deferred vested retirement benefits required by section 6057(a) and paragraph (a) or (b) of this section, see section 6652(d)(1).

(g) *Effective/applicability date.*—(1) *In general.*—Except as otherwise provided in this paragraph (g), this section is applicable for filings on or after June 21, 2012.

(2) *Special effective date rules for periods before the general effective date.*—Section 301.6057-1 of this chapter, as it appeared in the April 1, 2008 edition of 26 CFR part 301, applies for periods before the general effective date.

☐ Par. 6. Section 301.6057-2 is amended by revising paragraph (c) as follows:

§301.6057-2. Employee retirement benefit plans; notification of change in plan status.

* * *

(c) *Penalty.*—For amounts imposed in the case of failure to file a notification of a change in plan status required by section 6057(b) and this section, see section 6652(d)(2).

* * *

Gifts and Bequests from Covered Expatriates: Imposition of Tax

Gifts and Bequests from Covered Expatriates: Imposition of Tax.—Reg. §28.6060-1, relating to a tax on United States citizens and residents who receive gifts or bequests from certain individuals who relinquished United States citizenship or ceased to be lawful permanent residents of the United States on or after June 17, 2008, is proposed (published in the Federal Register on September 10, 2015) (REG-112997-10).

Section 28.6060-1 is added to read as follows:

§28.6060-1. Reporting requirements for tax return preparers.— (a) *In general.*—A person that employs one or more signing tax return preparers to prepare a return or claim for refund of any tax to which this part 28 applies, other than for the person, at any time during a return period, must satisfy the recordkeeping and inspection requirements in the manner stated in §1.6060-1 of this chapter.

(b) *Effective/applicability date.*—This section applies to returns and claims for refund filed on or after the date of publication of a Treasury decision adopting these rules as final regulations in the **Federal Register**. [Reg. §28.6060-1.]

Gifts and Bequests from Covered Expatriates: Imposition of Tax

Gifts and Bequests from Covered Expatriates: Imposition of Tax.—Reg. §28.6071-1, relating to a tax on United States citizens and residents who receive gifts or bequests from certain individuals who relinquished United States citizenship or ceased to be lawful permanent residents of the United States on or after June 17, 2008, is proposed (published in the Federal Register on September 10, 2015) (REG-112997-10).

Section 28.6071-1 is added to read as follows:

§28.6071-1. Time for filing returns.—(a) *In general.*—(1) A U.S. recipient as defined in §28.2801-2(e) must file Form 708, "U.S. Return of Gifts or Bequests from Covered Expatriates," on or before the fifteenth day of the eighteenth calendar month following the close of the calendar year in which the covered gift or covered bequest was received. Notwithstanding the preceding sentence, the due date for a Form 708 reporting a covered bequest that is not received on the decedent's date of death under §28.2801-4(d)(3) is the later of—

(i) The fifteenth day of the eighteenth calendar month following the close of the calendar year in which the covered expatriate died; or

(ii) The fifteenth day of the sixth month of the calendar year following the close of the calendar year in which the covered bequest was received.

(2) If a U.S. recipient receives multiple covered gifts and covered bequests during the same calendar year, the rule in paragraph (a)(1) of this section may result in different due dates and the filing of multiple returns reporting the different transfers received during the same calendar year.

(b) *Migrated foreign trust.*—The due date for a Form 708 for the year in which a foreign trust becomes a domestic trust is the fifteenth day of the sixth month of the calendar year following the close of calendar year in which the foreign trust becomes a domestic trust.

(c) *Certain returns by foreign trusts.*—(1) *Election under §28.2801-5(d) for calendar year in which no covered gift or covered bequest*

received.—A foreign trust making an election to be treated as a domestic trust for purposes of section 2801 under §28.2801-5(d) for a calendar year in which the foreign trust received no covered gifts or covered bequests must file a Form 708 on or before the fifteenth day of the sixth month of the calendar year following the close of the calendar year for which the election is made.

(2) *Certification to maintain election under §28.2801-5(d) for calendar year in which no covered gift or covered bequest received.*—An electing foreign trust filing a Form 708 to certify that the electing foreign trust did not receive any covered gifts or covered bequests during the calendar year must file the Form 708 on or before the fifteenth day of the sixth month of the calendar year following the close of that calendar year. See §28.2801-5(d)(4).

(d) *Transition period.*—The Form 708 reporting covered gifts or covered bequests received on or after June 17, 2008, and before the date of publication of a Treasury decision adopting these rules as final regulations in the **Federal Register**, will be due within a reasonable period of time after the date of that publication as specified in the final regulations, but in no event before the due date of the first return required under the final regulations for covered gifts or covered bequests received after the final regulations are published.

(e) *Effective/applicability dates.*—This section applies to each Form 708 filed on or after the date on which a Treasury decision is published adopting these rules as final regulations in the **Federal Register**. [Reg. §28.6071-1.]

Classification: Cell Companies: Series LLCs

Classification: Cell Companies: Series LLCs.—Reg. §301.6071-2, regarding the classification for Federal tax purposes of a series of a domestic series limited liability company (LLC), a cell of a domestic cell company, or a foreign series or cell that conducts an insurance business, is proposed (published in the Federal Register on September 14, 2010) (REG-119921-09).

Par. 3. Section 301.6071-2 is added to read as follows:

§301.6071-2. Time for filing statements of series and series organizations.—(a) *In general.*—Statements required by §301.6011-6 must be filed on or before March 15 of the year following the period for which the return is made.

(b) *Effective/applicability date.*—This section applies to taxable years beginning after the date of publication of the Treasury decision adopting these rules as final regulations in the **Federal Register**.

Gifts and Bequests from Covered Expatriates: Imposition of Tax

Gifts and Bequests from Covered Expatriates: Imposition of Tax.—Reg. §28.6081-1, relating to a tax on United States citizens and residents who receive gifts or bequests from certain individuals who relinquished United States citizenship or ceased to be lawful permanent residents of the United States on or after June 17, 2008, is proposed (published in the Federal Register on September 10, 2015) (REG-112997-10).

Section 28.6081-1 is added to read as follows:

§28.6081-1. Automatic extension of time for filing returns reporting gifts and bequests from covered expatriates.—(a) *In general.*—A U.S. recipient as defined in §28.2801-2(e) may request an extension of time to file a Form 708, "U.S. Return of Gifts or Bequests from Covered Expatriates," by filing Form 7004, "Application for Automatic Extension of Time to file Certain Business Income Tax, Information, and Other Returns." A U.S. recipient must include on Form 7004 an estimate of the amount of section 2801 tax liability and must file Form 7004 with the Internal Revenue Service office designated in the Form's instructions (except as provided in §301.6091-1(b) of this chapter for hand-carried documents).

(b) *Automatic extension.*—A U.S. recipient as defined in §28.2801-2(e) will be allowed an automatic six-month extension of time beyond the date prescribed in §28.6071-1 to file Form 708 if Form 7004 is filed on or before the due date for filing Form 708 in accordance with the procedures under paragraph (a) of this section.

(c) *No extension of time for the payment of tax.*—An automatic extension of time for filing a return granted under paragraph (b) of this section will not extend the time for payment of any tax due with such return.

Reg. §28.6081-1(c)

(d) *Penalties.*—See section 6651 regarding penalties for failure to file the required tax return or failure to pay the amount shown as tax on the return.

(e) *Effective/applicability dates.*—This section applies to applications for an extension of time to file Form 708 filed on or after the date of publication of a Treasury decision adopting these rules as final regulations in the **Federal Register**. [Reg. § 28.6081-1.]

Deferred Vested Benefits: Reporting and Notice Requirements

Deferred Vested Benefits: Reporting and Notice Requirements.—Amendments to Reg. § 1.6081-11, relating to automatic extensions of time for filing certain employee plan returns by adding the Form 8955-SSA, "Annual Registration Statement Identifying Separated Participants With Deferred Vested Benefits," to the list of forms that are covered by the Income Tax Regulations on automatic extensions, are proposed (published in the Federal Register on June 21, 2012) (REG-153627-08).

☐ Par. 2. Section 1.6081-11 is amended by:

1. Revising paragraph (a).
2. Adding paragraph (b)(3).
3. Revising the paragraph heading of paragraph (d) and adding paragraph (d)(2).
4. Revising the paragraph heading of paragraph (e) and adding paragraph (e)(2).

The revisions and additions read as follows:

§ 1.6081-11. Automatic extension of time for filing certain employee plan returns.—(a) *In general.*—An administrator or sponsor of an employee benefit plan required to file a return under the provisions of subpart E of part III of chapter 61 or the regulations under that chapter on Form 5500 (series), "Annual Return/Report of Employee Benefit Plan" or Form 8955-SSA, "Annual Registration Statement Identifying Separated Participants with Deferred Vested Benefits," will be allowed an automatic extension of time to file the return until the 15th day of the third month following the date prescribed for filing the return if the administrator or sponsor files an application under this section in accordance with paragraph (b) of this section.

(b) * * *

(3) A signature is not required for an automatic extension of time to file Form 5500 (series) and Form 8955-SSA.

* * *

(d) *Penalties.*—(1) *Form 5500.*—* * *

(2) *Form 8955-SSA.*—See section 6652 for penalties for failure to file a timely and complete Form 8955-SSA.

(e) *Effective/Applicability dates.*—(1) *Form 5500.*—* * *

(2) *Form 8955-SSA.*—This section is applicable for applications for an automatic extension of time to file Form 8955-SSA filed after June 21, 2012.

Gifts and Bequests from Covered Expatriates: Imposition of Tax

Gifts and Bequests from Covered Expatriates: Imposition of Tax.—Reg. § 28.6091-1, relating to a tax on United States citizens and residents who receive gifts or bequests from certain individuals who relinquished United States citizenship or ceased to be lawful permanent residents of the United States on or after June 17, 2008, is proposed (published in the Federal Register on September 10, 2015) (REG-112997-10).

Section 28.6091-1 is added to read as follows:

§ 28.6091-1. Place for filing returns.—A U.S. recipient as defined in § 28.2801-2(e) must file Form 708, "U.S. Return of Gifts and Bequests from Covered Expatriates," with the Internal Revenue Service office designated in the instructions applicable to the Form. [Reg. § 28.6091-1.]

Gifts and Bequests from Covered Expatriates: Imposition of Tax

Gifts and Bequests from Covered Expatriates: Imposition of Tax.—Reg. § 28.6101-1, relating to a tax on United States citizens and residents who receive gifts or bequests from certain individuals who relinquished United States citizenship or ceased to be lawful permanent residents of the United States on or after June 17, 2008, is proposed (published in the Federal Register on September 10, 2015) (REG-112997-10).

Section 28.6101-1 is added to read as follows:

§ 28.6101-1. Period covered by returns.—See § 28.6011-1 for the rules relating to the period covered by the return. [Reg. § 28.6101-1.]

Disclosure of Returns and Return Information: Contractors

Disclosure of Returns and Return Information: Contractors.—Amendments to Reg. § 301.6103(n)-1, authorizing the Department of State to disclose returns and return information to its contractors who assist the Department of State in carrying out its responsibilities under section 32101 of the Fixing America's Surface Transportation Act, are proposed (published in the Federal Register on March 13, 2018) (REG-129260-16).

Par. 2. Sections [301.]6103(n)-1(a)(1) and (e)(4)(i) are amended by removing the language "or the Department of Justice" and adding the language "the Department of Justice, or the Department of State" in its place.

Par. 3. Section 301.6103(n)-1(g) is amended to read as follows:

§ 301.6103(n)-1. Disclosure of returns and return information in connection with written contracts or agreements for the acquisition of property or services for tax administration purposes.

* * *

(g) *Applicability date.*—This section is applicable on June 5, 2007, except that paragraphs (a) and (e)(4)(i) of this section apply to the Department of State on or after March 12, 2018.

Disclosure of Information: Tax-Exempt Organizations

Disclosure of Information: Tax-Exempt Organizations.—Amendments to Reg. § 301.6104(c)-1, providing guidance to states regarding the process by which they may obtain or inspect certain returns and return information (including information about final and proposed denials and revocations of tax-exempt status) for the purpose of administering state laws governing certain tax-exempt organizations and their activities, are proposed (published in the Federal Register on March 15, 2011) (REG-140108-08).

☐ Par. 2. Section 301.6104(c)-1 is revised to read as follows:

§ 301.6104(c)-1. Disclosure of certain information to state officials.—(a) *In general.*—(1) Subject to the disclosure, recordkeeping, and safeguard provisions of section 6103, and upon written request by an appropriate state officer (ASO, as defined in paragraph (i)(1) of this section), the IRS may disclose or make available to the ASO the returns and return information described in paragraph (c) of this section with respect to—

(i) any organization described or formerly described in section 501(c)(3) and exempt or formerly exempt from taxation under section 501(a) (a charitable organization); or

(ii) any organization that has applied for recognition as an organization described in section 501(c)(3) (an applicant). Such information shall be disclosed or made available only as necessary to administer state laws regulating charitable organizations.

(2) Subject to the disclosure, recordkeeping, and safeguard provisions of section 6103, and upon written request by an ASO, the

IRS may disclose or make available to the ASO returns and return information regarding any organization described or formerly described in section 501(c) other than section 501(c)(1) or (c)(3). Such information shall be disclosed or made available only as necessary to administer state laws regulating the solicitation or administration of the charitable funds or charitable assets of these organizations.

(b) *Disclosure agreement.*—The IRS may require an ASO to execute a disclosure agreement or similar document specifying the procedures, terms, and conditions for the disclosure or inspection of information under section 6104(c), including compliance with the safeguards prescribed by section 6103(p)(4), as well as specifying the information to be disclosed. Such an agreement or similar document shall constitute the request for disclosure required by section 6104(c)(1)(C), as well as the written request required by section 6104(c)(2)(C)(i) and (c)(3). For security guidelines and other safeguards for protecting returns and return information, see guidance published by the IRS. See, for example, IRS Publication 1075, "Tax Information Security Guidelines for Federal, State and Local Agencies and Entities."

(c) *Disclosures regarding charitable organizations and applicants.*— (1) With respect to any organization described in paragraph (d) of this section, the IRS may disclose or make available for inspection under section 6104(c)(1) and (c)(2) to an ASO the following returns and return information with respect to a charitable organization or applicant:

(i) A refusal or proposed refusal to recognize an organization's exemption as a charitable organization (a final or proposed denial letter).

(ii) Information regarding a grant of exemption following a proposed denial.

(iii) A revocation of exemption as a charitable organization (a final revocation letter), including a notice of termination or dissolution.

(iv) A proposed revocation of recognition of exemption as a charitable organization (a proposed revocation letter).

(v) Information regarding the final disposition of a proposed revocation of recognition other than by final revocation.

(vi) A notice of deficiency or proposed notice of deficiency of tax imposed under section 507 or chapter 41 or 42 on the organization or a taxable person (as described in paragraph (i)(4) of this section).

(vii) Information regarding the final disposition of a proposed notice of deficiency of tax imposed under section 507 or chapter 41 or 42 on the organization other than by issuance of a final notice of deficiency.

(viii) The names, addresses, and taxpayer identification numbers of applicants for charitable status, provided on an applicant-by-applicant basis or by periodic lists of applicants. Under this provision the IRS may respond to inquiries from an ASO as to whether a particular organization has applied for recognition of exemption as a charitable organization.

(ix) Information regarding the final disposition of an application for recognition of exemption where no proposed denial letter is issued, including whether the application was withdrawn or whether the applicant failed to establish its exemption.

(x) Returns and other return information relating to the return information described in this paragraph (c)(1), except for returns and return information relating to proposed notices of deficiency described in paragraph (c)(1)(vi) of this section with respect to taxable persons.

(2) The IRS may disclose or make available for inspection returns and return information of a charitable organization or applicant, if the IRS determines that such information might constitute evidence of noncompliance with the laws under the jurisdiction of the ASO regulating charitable organizations and applicants. Such information may be disclosed on the IRS' own initiative. Disclosures under this paragraph (c)(2) may be made before the IRS issues a proposed determination (denial of recognition, revocation, or notice of deficiency) or any other action by the IRS described in this section.

(d) *Organizations to which disclosure applies.*—Regarding the information described in paragraphs (a)(2) and (c) of this section, the IRS will disclose or make available for inspection to an ASO such information only with respect to—

(1) an organization formed under the laws of the ASO's state;

(2) an organization, the principal office of which is located in the ASO's state;

(3) an organization that, as determined by the IRS, is or might be subject to the laws of the ASO's state regulating charitable organizations or the solicitation or administration of charitable funds or charitable assets; or

(4) a private foundation required by § 1.6033-2(a)(iv) to list the ASO's state on any of the foundation's returns filed for its last five years.

(e) *Disclosure limitations.*—Notwithstanding any other provision of this section, the IRS will not disclose or make available for inspection under section 6104(c) any information, the disclosure of which it determines would seriously impair federal tax administration, including, but not limited to—

(1) identification of a confidential informant or interference with a civil or criminal tax investigation; and

(2) information obtained pursuant to a tax convention between the United States and a foreign government (see section 6105(c)(2) for the definition of *tax convention*).

(f) *Disclosure recipients.*—(1) *In general.*—The IRS may disclose returns and return information under section 6104(c) to, or make it available for inspection by—

(i) an ASO, as defined in paragraph (i)(1) of this section, or

(ii) a person other than an ASO, but only if that person is a state officer or employee designated by the ASO to receive information under section 6104(c) on behalf of the ASO, as specified in paragraph (f)(2) of this section.

(2) *Designation by ASO.*—An ASO may designate state officers or employees to receive information under section 6104(c) on the ASO's behalf by specifying in writing each person's name and job title, and the name and address of the person's office. The ASO must promptly notify the IRS in writing of any additions, deletions, or other changes to the list of designated persons.

(g) *Redisclosure.*—An ASO to whom a return or return information has been disclosed may thereafter disclose such information—

(1) to another state officer or employee only as necessary to administer state laws governing charitable organizations or state laws regulating the solicitation or administration of charitable funds or charitable assets of noncharitable exempt organizations; or

(2) except as provided in paragraph (h)(1) of this section, to another state officer or employee who is personally and directly preparing for a civil proceeding before a state administrative body or court in a matter involving the enforcement of state laws regulating organizations with respect to which information can be disclosed under this section, solely for use in such a proceeding, but only if—

(i) the organization or a taxable person is a party to the proceeding, or the proceeding arose out of, or in connection with, determining the civil liability of the organization or a taxable person, or collecting such civil liability, under state laws governing organizations with respect to which information can be disclosed under this section;

(ii) the treatment of an item reflected on such a return is directly related to the resolution of an issue in the proceeding; or

(iii) the return or return information directly relates to a transactional relationship between the organization or a taxable person and a person who is a party to the proceeding that directly affects the resolution of an issue in the proceeding.

(h) *Redisclosure limitations.*—(1) Before disclosing in a state administrative or judicial proceeding, or to any party as provided by paragraph (g)(2) of this section, any return or return information received under section 6104(c), the ASO shall notify the IRS of the intention to make such a disclosure. No state officer or employee shall make such a disclosure except in accordance with any conditions the IRS might impose in response to the ASO's notice of intent. No such disclosure shall be made if the IRS determines that the disclosure would seriously impair federal tax administration.

(2) An ASO to whom a return or return information has been disclosed shall not disclose that information to an agent or contractor.

(i) *Definitions.*—(1) *Appropriate state officer* means—

(i) the state attorney general;

(ii) the state tax officer;

(iii) with respect to a charitable organization or applicant, any state officer other than the attorney general or tax officer charged with overseeing charitable organizations; and

(iv) with respect to a section 501(c) organization that is not described in section 501(c)(1) or (c)(3), the head of the agency designated by the state attorney general as having primary responsibility for overseeing the solicitation of funds for charitable purposes. A state officer described in paragraph (i)(1)(iii) or (i)(1)(iv) of this section must show that the officer is an ASO by presenting a letter from the state attorney general describing the functions and authority of the officer under state law, with sufficient facts for the IRS to determine that the officer is an ASO.

(2) *Return* has the same meaning as in section 6103(b)(1).

(3) *Return information* has the same meaning as in section 6103(b)(2).

(4) *Taxable person* means any person who is liable or potentially liable for excise taxes under chapter 41 or 42. Such a person includes—

Reg. § 301.6104(c)-1(h)(2)(i)(4)

(i) a disqualified person described in section 4946(a)(1), 4951(e)(4), or 4958(f);

(ii) a foundation manager described in section 4946(b);

(iii) an organization manager described in section 4955(f)(2) or 4958(f)(2);

(iv) a person described in section 4958(c)(3)(B);

(v) an entity manager described in section 4965(d); and

(vi) a fund manager described in section 4966(d)(3).

(j) *Failure to comply.*—Upon a determination that an ASO has failed to comply with the requirements of section 6103(p)(4), the IRS may take the actions it deems necessary to ensure compliance, including the refusal to disclose any further returns or return information to the ASO until the IRS determines that the requirements have been met. For procedures for the administrative review of a determination that an authorized recipient has failed to safeguard returns or return information, see § 301.6103(p)(7)-1.

(k) *Effective/applicability date.*—The rules of this section apply to taxable years beginning on or after the date of publication in the **Federal Register** of the Treasury decision adopting these rules as final regulations. [Reg. § 301.6104(c)-1.]

Gifts and Bequests from Covered Expatriates: Imposition of Tax

Gifts and Bequests from Covered Expatriates: Imposition of Tax.—Reg. § 28.6107-1, relating to a tax on United States citizens and residents who receive gifts or bequests from certain individuals who relinquished United States citizenship or ceased to be lawful permanent residents of the United States on or after June 17, 2008, is proposed (published in the Federal Register on September 10, 2015) (REG-112997-10).

Section 28.6107-1 is added to read as follows:

§ 28.6107-1. Tax return preparer must furnish copy of return or claim for refund to taxpayer and must retain a copy or record.— (a) *In general.*—A person who is a signing tax return preparer of any return or claim for refund of any tax to which this part 28 applies must furnish a completed copy of the return or claim for refund to the taxpayer and retain a completed copy or record in the manner stated in § 1.6107-1 of this chapter.

(b) *Effective/applicability dates.*—This section applies to returns and claims for refund filed on or after the date of publication of a Treasury decision adopting these rules as final regulations in the **Federal Register**. [Reg. § 28.6107-1.]

Gifts and Bequests from Covered Expatriates: Imposition of Tax

Gifts and Bequests from Covered Expatriates: Imposition of Tax.—Reg. § 28.6109-1, relating to a tax on United States citizens and residents who receive gifts or bequests from certain individuals who relinquished United States citizenship or ceased to be lawful permanent residents of the United States on or after June 17, 2008, is proposed (published in the Federal Register on September 10, 2015) (REG-112997-10).

Section 28.6109-1 is added to read as follows:

§ 28.6109-1. Tax return preparers furnishing identifying numbers for returns or claims for refund.— (a) *In general.*—Each tax return or claim for refund of the tax under chapter 15 of subtitle B of the Internal Revenue Code prepared by one or more signing tax return preparers must include the identifying number of the preparer required by § 1.6695-1(b) of this chapter to sign the return or claim for refund in the manner stated in § 1.6109-2 of this chapter.

(b) *Effective/applicability date.*—This section applies on and after the date of publication of a Treasury decision adopting these rules as final regulations in the **Federal Register**. [Reg. § 28.6109-1.]

Tax Return Preparer: Furnishing Identifying Number

Tax Return Preparer: Furnishing Identifying Number.—Amendments to Reg. § 1.6109-2, providing guidance on the eligibility of tax return preparers to obtain a preparer tax identification number (PTIN), are proposed (published in the Federal Register on February 15, 2012) (REG-124791-11).

☐ Par. 2. Section 1.6109-2 is amended by adding a new sentence to the end of paragraph (a)(1) and revising paragraphs (d), (f), (h) and (i) to read as follows:

§ 1.6109-2. Tax return preparers furnishing identifying numbers for returns or claims for refund and related requirements.

(a) * * *

(1) * * * For purposes of this section only, the terms *tax return* and *claim for refund of tax* include all tax forms submitted to the Internal Revenue Service unless specifically excluded by the Internal Revenue Service in other appropriate guidance.

* * *

(d)(1) Beginning after December 31, 2010, all tax return preparers must have a preparer tax identification number or other prescribed identifying number that was applied for and received at the time and in the manner, including the payment of a user fee, as may be prescribed by the Internal Revenue Service in forms, instructions, or other appropriate guidance.

(2) Except as provided in paragraph (h) of this section, to obtain a preparer tax identification number or other prescribed identifying number, a tax return preparer must be one of the following:

(i) An attorney;

(ii) A certified public accountant;

(iii) An enrolled agent;

(iv) A registered tax return preparer authorized to practice before the Internal Revenue Service under 31 U.S.C. 330 and the regulations thereunder;

(v) An individual 18 years of age or older who is supervised, in the manner the Internal Revenue Service prescribes in forms, instructions, or other appropriate guidance, as a tax return preparer by an attorney, certified public accountant, enrolled agent, enrolled retirement plan agent, or enrolled actuary authorized to practice before the Internal Revenue Service under 31 U.S.C. 330 and the regulations thereunder; or

(vi) An individual 18 years of age or older who certifies that the individual is a tax return preparer exclusively with respect to returns and claims for refund of tax that are not covered, at the time the tax return preparer applies for or renews the number, by a minimum competency examination prescribed by the Internal Revenue Service in forms, instructions, or other appropriate guidance. An individual must comply with any requirements at the time and in the manner that the Internal Revenue Service may prescribe in forms, instructions, or other appropriate guidance.

* * *

(f) As may be prescribed in forms, instructions, or other appropriate guidance, the Internal Revenue Service may conduct a Federal tax compliance check and a suitability check on a tax return preparer who applies for or renews a preparer tax identification number or other prescribed identifying number.

* * *

(h) The Internal Revenue Service, through forms, instructions, or other appropriate guidance, may prescribe exceptions to the requirements of this section, including the requirement that an individual be authorized to practice before the Internal Revenue Service before receiving a preparer tax identification number or other prescribed identifying number, as necessary in the interest of effective tax administration.

(i) *Effective/applicability date.*—Paragraph (a)(1) of this section applies to tax returns and claims for refund filed after December 31, 2008, except the last sentence of paragraph (a)(1), which applies to tax returns and claims for refund filed on or after the date that final regulations are published in the **Federal Register**. Paragraph (a)(2)(i) of this section applies to tax returns and claims for refund filed on or before December 31, 2010. Paragraph (a)(2)(ii) of this section applies to tax returns and claims for refund filed after December 31, 2010. Paragraph (d)(1) of this section applies to tax return preparers after December 31, 2010. Paragraph (d)(2) of this section applies to tax return preparers on or after the date that final regulations are published in the **Federal Register**. Paragraph (e) of this section applies after September 30, 2010. Paragraph (f) of this section applies on or after the date that final regulations are published in the **Federal Register**. Paragraphs (g) and (h) of this section apply after September 30, 2010.

Dependency Exemption: Authorized Placement Agency: Definition

Dependency Exemption: Authorized Placement Agency: Definition.—Amendments to Reg. §301.6109-3, relating to the definition of an authorized placement agency for purposes of a dependency exemption for a child placed for adoption that were issued prior to the changes made to the law by the Working Families Tax Relief Act of 2004, are proposed (published in the Federal Register on January 19, 2017) (REG-137604-07).

Par. 20. Section 301.6109-3 is amended by:

1. Revising the first sentence and adding a sentence to the end of the paragraph in paragraph (a)(1).

2. Revising paragraphs (b), (c)(1)(ii), the fourth and fifth sentences of (c)(2) introductory text, and paragraph (d).

The revisions and addition read as follows:

§301.6109-3. IRS adoption taxpayer identification numbers.—
(a) *In general.*—(1) *Definition.*—An IRS adoption taxpayer identification number (ATIN) is a temporary taxpayer identifying number assigned by the Internal Revenue Service (IRS) to a child (other than an alien individual as defined in §301.6109-1(d)(3)(i)) who has been placed lawfully with a prospective adoptive parent for legal adoption by that person. * * * A child lawfully placed with a prospective adoptive parent for legal adoption includes a child placed for legal adoption by the child's parent or parents by blood, an authorized placement agency, or any other person authorized by State law to place a child for legal adoption.

* * *

(b) *Definitions.*—(1) Authorized placement agency has the same meaning as in §1.152-1(b)(1)(iv).

(2) *Child* means a child who has not been adopted but has been placed lawfully with a prospective adoptive parent for legal adoption by that person.

(3) *Prospective adoptive parent* means a person in whose household a child has been placed lawfully for legal adoption by that person.

(c) * * *

(1) * * *

(ii) The child has been placed lawfully with the prospective adoptive parent for legal adoption by that person;

* * *

(2) * * * In addition, the application must include documentary evidence the IRS prescribes to establish that a child has been placed lawfully with the prospective adoptive parent for legal adoption by that person. Examples of acceptable documentary evidence establishing lawful placement for a legal adoption may include—

* * *

(d) *Applicability date.*—(1) *In general.*—Except as otherwise provided in paragraph (d)(2) of this section, the provisions of this section apply to income tax returns due (without regard to extension) on or after April 15, 1998.

(2) *Exception.*—Paragraphs (a)(1), (b), (c)(1)(ii), and (c)(2) of this section apply to income tax returns due (without regard to extension) on or after the date these regulations are published as final regulations in the **Federal Register**.

Tax Shelter Registration: Questions and Answers

Tax Shelter Registration: Questions and Answers.—Temporary Reg. §301.6111-1T, relating to tax shelter registration, is also proposed as a final regulation and, when adopted, would become Reg. §301.6111-1 (published in the Federal Register on August 15, 1984).

§301.6111-1. Questions and answers relating to tax shelter registration.

Tax Shelter Registration: Abusers: Lists

Tax Shelter Registration: List of Potential Abusers.—An amendment to Temporary Reg. §301.6111-1T, relating to tax shelter registration and the requirement to maintain lists of investors in potentially abusive tax shelters, is also proposed as final (published in the Federal Register on October 31, 1984).

§301.6111-1. Questions and answers relating to tax shelter registration.

Tax Shelter Registration: Amended Application

Registration of Tax Shelters: Amended Application.—An amendment to Temporary Reg. §301.6111-1T, relating to the registration of tax shelters, is also proposed as final (published in the Federal Register on March 4, 1986).

§301.6111-1. Questions and answers relating to tax shelter registration.

Reportable Transactions: Disclosure: Patented Transactions

Reportable Transactions: Disclosure: Patented Transactions.—Amendments to Reg. §301.6111-3, providing rules to the disclosure of reportable transactions, including patented transactions, under Code Secs. 6011 and 6111, are proposed (published in the Federal Register on September 26, 2007) (REG-129916-07).

☐ Par. 4. Section 301.6111-3 is amended by revising paragraphs (b)(2)(ii)(E), (b)(3)(i)(C), and (i)(2) to read as follows:

§301.6111-3. Disclosures of reportable transactions.

* * *

(b) * * *

(2) * * *

(ii) * * *

(E) *Patented transactions.*—A statement relates to a tax aspect of a transaction that causes it to be a patented transaction if the statement is made or provided by the patent holder or by the patent holder's agent, as defined in §1.6011-4(b)(7)(ii)(C) or (D) of this chapter, and concerns the tax planning method that is the subject of the patent.

* * *

(3) * * *

(i) * * *

(C) *Patented transactions.*—For patented transactions described in §1.6011-4(b)(7) of this chapter, the threshold amounts in §301.6111-3(b)(3)(i)(A) are reduced from $50,000 to $250 and from $250,000 to $500.

* * *

(i) * * *

(2) *Patented transactions.*—Upon the publication of the Treasury decision adopting these rules as final regulations in the Federal Register, paragraphs (b)(2)(ii)(E) and (b)(3)(i)(C) of this section will apply to transactions with respect to which a material advisor makes a tax statement on or after September 26, 2007.

Reg. §301.6111-3(i)(2)

TIME AND PLACE FOR PAYING TAX

Gifts and Bequests from Covered Expatriates: Imposition of Tax

Gifts and Bequests from Covered Expatriates: Imposition of Tax.—Reg. §28.6151-1, relating to a tax on United States citizens and residents who receive gifts or bequests from certain individuals who relinquished United States citizenship or ceased to be lawful permanent residents of the United States on or after June 17, 2008, is proposed (published in the Federal Register on September 10, 2015) (REG-112997-10).

Section 28.6151-1 is added to read as follows:

§28.6151-1. Time and place for paying tax shown on returns.— The tax due under this part 28 must be paid at the time prescribed in §28.6071-1 for filing the return, and at the place prescribed in §28.6091-1 for filing the return. [Reg. §28.6151-1.]

Preparer Tax Identification Number: User Fee

Preparer Tax Identification Number: User Fee.—Amendments to Reg. §300.12, relating to the imposition of certain user fees on tax return preparers, are proposed (published in the Federal Register on April 16, 2020) (REG-117138-17).

Par. 2. Section 300.12 is amended by revising paragraphs (b) and (d) to read as follows:

§300.12. Fee for obtaining a preparer tax identification number.
* * *

(b) *Fee.*—The fee to apply for or renew a preparer tax identification number is $21 per year and is in addition to the fee charged by the contractor.

* * *

(d) *Applicability date.*—This section applies to applications for or renewal of a preparer tax identification number filed on or after [date that is 30 days after these regulations are published as final regulations in the **Federal Register**].

Estimated Tax: Corporations

Estimated Tax: Corporations.—Reproduced below are the texts of proposed amendments to Reg. §§1.6164-4 and 1.6164-8, relating to estimated tax requirements for corporations (published in the Federal Register on March 26, 1984).

☐ Par. 2. Paragraph (a) of §1.6164-4 is revised to read as follows:

§1.6164-4. Payment of remainder of tax where extension relates only to part of the tax.—(a) *Time for payment.*—If an extension of time relates only to part of the tax, the time for payment of the remainder of the tax shall be considered to be the date on which payment would have been required if such remainder had been the tax:

* * *

☐ Par. 3. Paragraph (a) of §1.6164-8 is revised to read as follows:

§1.6164-8. Payments on termination.—(a) *In general.*—If an extension of time under section 6164 is terminated with respect to any amount either (1) by the filing of a new statement by the taxpayer under section 6164(e) extending the time for payment of a lesser amount than was extended in a prior statement, or (2) by action of the district director under section 6164(f) after making an examination of the statement filed by the corporation, no further extension of time may be made under section 6164 with respect to such amount. The time for payment of such amount shall be the date on which payment would have been required if there had been no extension with respect to such amount.

* * *

ASSESSMENT

Partnerships: Centralized Partnership Audit Regime

Partnerships: Centralized Partnership Audit Regime.—Reg. 301.6225-4, implementing the centralized partnership audit regime that have not been finalized to reflect the changes made by the Technical Corrections Act of 2018, contained in Title II of the Consolidated Appropriations Act of 2018 (TTCA), is proposed (published in the Federal Register on August 17, 2018) (REG-136118-15; REG-119337-17; REG-118067-17; REG-120232-17 and REG-120233-17).

Par. 11. Section 301.6225-4 is added to read as follows:

§301.6225-4. Effect of a partnership adjustment on specified tax attributes of partnerships and their partners.—(a) *Adjustments to specified tax attributes.*—(1) *In general.*—When there is a partnership adjustment (as defined in §301.6241-1(a)(6)), the partnership and its adjustment year partners (as defined in §301.6241-1(a)(2)) generally must adjust their specified tax attributes (as defined in paragraph (a)(2) of this section) in accordance with the rules in this section. For a partnership adjustment that results in an imputed underpayment (as defined in §301.6241-1(a)(3)), specified tax attributes are generally adjusted by making appropriate adjustments to the book value and basis of partnership property under paragraph (b)(2) of this section, creating notional items based on the partnership adjustment under paragraph (b)(3) of this section, allocating those notional items as described in paragraph (b)(5) of this section, and determining the effect of those notional items for the partnership and its reviewed year partners (as defined in §301.6241-1(a)(9)) or their successors (as defined in §1.704-1(b)(1)(viii)(*b*) of this chapter) under paragraph (b)(6) of this section. Paragraph (c) of this section describes how to treat an expenditure for any payment required to be made by a partnership under subchapter C of chapter 63 of the Internal Revenue Code (subchapter C of chapter 63) including any imputed underpayment. Paragraph (d) of this section describes adjustments to tax attributes of a partnership and its partners in the case of a partnership adjustment that does not result in an imputed underpayment (as described in §301.6225-1(f)).

(2) *Specified tax attributes.*—Specified tax attributes are the tax basis and book value of a partnership's property, amounts determined under section 704(c), adjustment year partners' bases in their partnership interests, adjustment year partners' capital accounts determined and maintained in accordance with §1.704-1(b)(2) of this chapter, and earnings and profits under section 312.

(3) *Timing.*—Adjustments to specified tax attributes under this section are made in the adjustment year (as defined in §301.6241-1(a)(1)). Thus, to the extent that an adjustment to a specified tax attribute under this section is reflected on a federal tax return, the partnership adjustment is generally first reflected on any return filed with respect to the adjustment year.

(4) *Effect of other sections.*—The determination of specified tax attributes under this section is not conclusive as to tax attributes of a partnership or its partners determined under other sections of the Internal Revenue Code (Code), including the subchapter C of chapter 63. For example, a partnership that files an administrative adjustment request (AAR) under section 6227 adjusts partnership tax attributes as appropriate. Further, to the extent a partner or partnership appropriately adjusted its tax attributes prior to a final determination under subchapter C of chapter 63 with respect to a partnership adjustment (for example, in the context of an amended return modification described in §301.6225-2(d)(2), the alternative procedure to filing amended returns as described in §301.6225-2(d)(2)(x), or a closing agreement described in §301.6225-2(d)(8)), those tax attributes are not adjusted under this section. Similarly, to the extent a partner filed a return inconsistent with the treatment of items on a partnership return, a reviewed year partner (or its successor) does not adjust its tax attributes to the extent the partner's prior return was consistent with the partnership adjustment. For the rules regarding consistent treatment by partners, see §301.6222-1.

(5) *Election under section 6226.*—(i) *In general.*—Except as otherwise provided in paragraph (a)(5)(ii) of this section, tax attributes of a partnership and its partners are adjusted for a partnership adjustment that results in an imputed underpayment with respect to which an election is made under § 301.6226-1 in accordance with § 301.6226-4, and not the rules of this section.

(ii) *Pass-through partners and indirect partners.*—A pass-through partner (as defined in § 301.6241-1(a)(5)) that is a partnership and pays an imputed underpayment under § 301.6226-3(e)(4) treats its share of each partnership adjustment reflected on the relevant statement as a partnership adjustment described in paragraph (a)(1) of this section, treats the imputed underpayment under § 301.6226-3(e)(4)(iii) as an imputed underpayment determined under § 301.6225-1 for purposes of § 1.704-1(b)(2)(iii)(*a*) and (*f*) of this chapter, treats items arising from an adjustment that does not result in an imputed underpayment as an item under paragraph (d) of this section, and finally treats amounts with respect to any penalties, additions to tax, and additional amounts and interest computed as an amount described in § 1.704-1(b)(2)(iii)(*f*)(3) of this chapter.

(6) *Reflection of economic arrangement.*—This section and the rules in § 1.704-1(b)(1)(viii), (b)(2)(iii)(*a*) and (*f*), (b)(2)(iv)(*i*)(4), and (b)(4)(xi), (xii), (xiii), (xiv), and (xv) of this chapter must be interpreted in a manner that reflects the economic arrangement of the parties and the principles of subchapter K of the Code, taking into account the rules of the centralized partnership audit regime.

(b) *Adjusting specified tax attributes in the case of a partnership adjustment that results in an imputed underpayment.*—(1) *In general.*— This paragraph (b) applies with respect to each partnership adjustment that was taken into account in the determination of the imputed underpayment under § 301.6225-1, except to the extent partner or partnership tax attributes were already adjusted as part of the partnership adjustment.

(2) *Book value and basis of partnership property.*—Partnership-level specified tax attributes must be adjusted under this paragraph (b)(2). Specifically, the partnership must make appropriate adjustments to the book value and basis of property to take into account any partnership adjustment. No adjustments are made with respect to property that was held by the partnership in the reviewed year but is no longer held by the partnership in the adjustment year. Amounts determined under section 704(c) must also be adjusted to take into account the partnership adjustment.

(3) *Creation of notional items based on partnership adjustment.*— (i) *In general.*—In order to give appropriate effect to each partnership adjustment for partner-level specified tax attributes, notional items are created with respect to each partnership adjustment, except as provided in paragraph (b)(4) of this section.

(ii) *Increase in income or gain.*—In the case of a partnership adjustment that is an increase to income or gain, a notional item of income or gain is created in an amount equal to the partnership adjustment.

(iii) *Increase in expense or loss.*—In the case of a partnership adjustment that is an increase to an expense or a loss, a notional item of an expense or loss is created in an amount equal to the partnership adjustment.

(iv) *Decrease in income or gain.*—In the case of a partnership adjustment that is a decrease to income or gain, a notional item of expense or loss is created in an amount equal to the partnership adjustment.

(v) *Decrease in expense or loss.*—In the case of a partnership adjustment that is a decrease to an expense or to a loss, a notional item of income or gain is created in an amount equal to the partnership adjustment.

(vi) *Credits.*—If a partnership adjustment reflects a net increase or net decrease in credits as determined in accordance with § 301.6225-1, the partnership may have one or more notional items of income, gain, loss, or deduction that reflects the change in the item that gives rise to the credit, and those items are treated as items in paragraph (b)(3)(ii), (iii), (iv), or (v) of this section. For example, if a partnership adjustment is to a credit, a notional item of deduction may be created when appropriate. See section 280C.

(4) *Situations in which notional items are not created.*—(i) *In general.*—In the case of a partnership adjustment described in this paragraph (b)(4), or when the creation of a notional item would duplicate a specified tax attribute or an actual item already taken into account, notional items are not created. Nevertheless, in these situations specified tax attributes are adjusted for the partnership and its reviewed year partners or their successors (as defined in § 1.704-1(b)(i)(viii)(*b*) of this chapter) in a manner that is consistent with how the partnership adjustment would have been taken into account under the

partnership agreement in effect for the reviewed year taking into account all facts and circumstances. See § 1.704-1(b)(2)(iii)(*f*)(4) of this chapter for rules for allocating the expenditure for an imputed underpayment in these circumstances.

(ii) *Adjustments for non-section 704(b) items.*—Notional items are not created for a partnership adjustment that does not derive from items that would have been allocated in the reviewed year under section 704(b). See paragraph (e) of this section, *Example 5*.

(iii) *Section 705(a)(2)(B) expenditures.*—Notional items are not created for a partnership adjustment that is a change of an item of deduction to a section 705(a)(2)(B) expenditure.

(iv) *Tax-exempt income.*—Notional items are not created for a partnership adjustment to an item of income of a partnership exempt from tax under subtitle A of the Code.

(5) *Allocation of the notional items.*—Notional items are allocated to the reviewed year partners or their successors under § 1.704-1(b)(4)(xi) of this chapter.

(6) *Effect of notional items.*—(i) *In general.*—The partnership creates notional items of income, gain, loss, deduction, or credit in order to make appropriate adjustments to specified tax attributes. See paragraph (e), *Example 1* of this section.

(ii) *Partner capital accounts.*—For purposes of capital accounts determined and maintained in accordance with § 1.704-1(b)(2) of this chapter, a notional item of income, gain, loss, deduction or credit is treated as an item of income, gain, loss, deduction or credit (including for purposes of determining book value). Similar adjustments may be appropriate for partnerships that do not determine and maintain capital accounts in accordance with § 1.704-1(b)(2) of this chapter.

(iii) *Partner's basis in its interest.*—(A) *In general.*—Except as otherwise provided, the basis of a partner's interest in a partnership is adjusted (but not below zero) to reflect any notional item allocated to the partner by treating the notional item as an item described in section 705(a).

(B) *Special basis rules.*—The basis of a partner's interest in a partnership is not adjusted for any notional items allocated to the partner —

(1) When a partner that is not a tax-exempt entity (as defined in § 301.6225-2(d)(3)(ii)) is a successor under § 1.704-1(b)(1)(viii)(*b*) of this chapter to a reviewed year tax-exempt partner, to the extent that the IRS approved a modification under § 301.6225-2 because the tax-exempt partner was not subject to tax; or

(2) When the notional item would be allocated to a successor that is related (within the meaning of sections 267(b) or 707(b)) to the reviewed year partner, the successor acquired its interest from the reviewed year partner in a transaction (or series of transactions) in which not all gain or loss is recognized during an administrative adjustment proceeding with respect to the partnership's reviewed year under subchapter C of chapter 63, and a principal purpose of the interest transfer (or transfers) was to shift the economic burden of the imputed underpayment among the related parties.

(c) *Determining a partner's share of an expenditure for any payment required to be made by a partnership under subchapter C of chapter 63.*— Payment by a partnership of any amount required to be paid under subchapter C of chapter 63 as described in § 301.6241-4(a) is treated as an expenditure described in section 705(a)(2)(B). Rules for determining whether the economic effect of an allocation of these expenses is substantial are provided in § 1.704-1(b)(2)(iii)(*f*) of this chapter and rules for determining whether an allocation of these expenses is deemed to be in accordance with the partners' interests in the partnership are provided in § 1.704-1(b)(4)(xii) of this chapter.

(d) *Adjusting tax attributes for a partnership adjustment that does not result in an imputed underpayment.*—The rules under subchapter K of the Code apply in the case of a partnership adjustment that does not result in an imputed underpayment. See § 301.6225-3(c). Accordingly, tax attributes (as defined in § 301.6241-1(a)(10)) of a partnership and its partners are adjusted under those rules. An item arising from a partnership adjustment that does not result in an imputed underpayment (as defined in § 301.6225-1(f)) is allocated under § 1.704-1(b)(4)(xiii) of this chapter.

(e) *Examples.*—The following examples illustrate the rules of this section. For purposes of these examples, unless otherwise stated, Partnership is subject to the provisions of subchapter C of chapter 63, Partnership and its partners are calendar year taxpayers, all partners are U.S. persons, and the highest rate of income tax in effect for all taxpayers is 20 percent for all relevant periods.

Example 1. (i) In 2019, A, B, and C are individuals that form Partnership. A contributes Whiteacre, which is unimproved land with an adjusted basis of $400 and a fair market value of $1000, and B and C each contribute $1000 in cash. The partnership agreement provides that all income, gain, loss, and deduction will be allocated in equal 1/3 shares among the partners. The partnership agreement also provides that the partners' capital accounts will be determined and maintained in accordance with §1.704-1(b)(2)(iv) of this chapter, distributions in liquidation of the partnership (or any partner's inter-

	Partnership Basis	Book	Value
Cash	$2000	$2000	$2000
Whiteacre	400	1000	1000
Totals	2400	3000	3000

(iii) In 2019, Partnership makes a $120 payment for Asset that it treats as a deductible expense on its partnership return.

	Partnership Basis	Book	Value
Cash	$1880	$1880	$1880
Whiteacre	400	1000	1000
Asset	0	0	120
Totals	2280	2880	3000

(iv) Partnership does not file an AAR for 2020. In 2021 (the adjustment year) it is finally determined that Partnership's $120 expenditure was not allowed as a deduction in 2019 (the reviewed year), but rather was the acquisition of an asset for which cost recovery deductions are unavailable. Accordingly, the IRS makes a partnership adjustment that disallows the entire $120 deduction, which results in an imputed underpayment of $48 ($120 x 40 percent). Partnership did not request modification under §301.6225-2. Partnership pays the $48 imputed underpayment.

(v) Partnership first determines its tax attribute adjustments resulting from the partnership adjustment by applying paragraph (b) of this section. Pursuant to paragraph (b)(2) of this section, Partnership must re-state the basis and book value of Asset to $120. Further, pursuant to paragraph (b)(3)(v) of this section, a $120 notional item of income is created. The $120 item of notional income is allocated in equal shares ($40) to A, B, and C in 2021 under §1.704-1(b)(4)(xi) of this chapter. Accordingly, in 2021 Partnership increases the capital accounts of A, B, and C by $40 each, and increases A, B, and C's outside bases by $40 each under paragraph (b)(6)(ii) and (iii) of this section, respectively.

	Partnership Basis	Book	Value
Cash	$1832	$1832	$1832
Whiteacre	400	1000	1000
Asset	120	120	120
Totals	2352	2952	2952

Example 2. (i) The facts are the same as in *Example 1* of this paragraph (e), except the IRS approves modification under §301.6225-2(d)(3) with respect to A, which is a tax-exempt entity, and under §301.6225-2(d)(4) with respect to C, which is a corporation subject to a tax rate of 20 percent. These modifications reduce Partnership's overall imputed underpayment from $48 to $30.

(ii) As in *Example 1* of this paragraph (e), Partnership determines its tax attribute adjustments resulting from the partnership adjustment by applying paragraph (b) of this section. Pursuant to paragraph (b)(3)(v) of this section, a $120 notional item of income is created. The $120 item of notional income is allocated in equal shares ($40) to A, B, and C in 2021 under §1.704-1(b)(4)(xi) of this chapter. Accordingly, in 2021 Partnership increases the capital accounts of A, B, and C by $40 each, and increases A, B, and C's outside bases by $40 each under paragraph (b)(6)(ii) and (iii) of this section, respectively.

(iii) However, the modifications affect how Partnership must allocate the imputed underpayment expenditure among A, B, and C

	Partnership Basis	Book	Value
Cash	$1856	$1856	$1856
Whiteacre	400	1000	1000
Asset	120	120	120
Totals	2376	2976	2976

Example 3. The facts are the same as in *Example 1* of this paragraph (e). However, in 2020, C transfers its entire interest in Partnership to D (an individual) for cash. Under §1.704-1(b)(2)(iv)(l) of this chapter, C's capital account carries over to D. In 2021, the year the IRS determines that Partnership's $120 expense is not allowed as a deduction, D is C's successor under §1.704-1(b)(1)(viii)(b)(2) of this chapter with respect to specified tax attributes and the payment of the imputed underpayment treated as an expenditure under section 705(a)(2)(B).

Example 4. The facts are the same as in *Example 1* of this paragraph (e), except that the partnership agreement provides that the

est) will be made in accordance with the partners' positive capital account balances, and any partner with a deficit balance in his capital account following the liquidation of his interest must restore that deficit to the partnership (as provided in §1.704-1(b)(2)(ii)(b)(2) and (3) of this chapter).

(ii) Upon formation, Partnership has the following assets and capital accounts:

	Outside Basis	Book	Value
A	$400	$1000	$1000
B	1000	1000	1000
C	1000	1000	1000
	2400	3000	3000

	Outside Basis	Book	Value
A	$360	$960	$1000
B	960	960	1000
C	960	960	1000
	2280	2880	3000

(vi) As described in paragraph (c) of this section, Partnership's payment of the $48 imputed underpayment is treated as an expenditure described in section 705(a)(2)(B) under §301.6241-4. Under §1.704-1(b)(4)(xii) of this chapter, Partnership determines each partner's properly allocable share of this expenditure in 2021 by allocating the expenditure in proportion to the allocations of the notional item to which the expenditure relates. Accordingly, each of A, B, and C have a properly allocable share of $16 each, which is the same proportion (1/3 each) in which A, B, and C share the $120 item of notional income. Thus, A, B and C's capital accounts are each decreased by $16 in 2021 and A, B and C's outside bases are each decreased by $16 in 2021. The allocation of the expenditure under the partnership agreement has economic effect under §1.704-1(b)(2)(ii) of this chapter and, because the allocation of the expenditure is determined in accordance with §1.704-1(b)(2)(iii)(f) of this chapter, the economic effect of these allocations is deemed to be substantial.

(vii) The payment is also reflected by a $48 decrease in partnership cash for book purposes under §1.704-1(b)(4)(ii) of this chapter. Therefore, in 2021, A's basis in Partnership is $384 and his capital account is $984. B and C each have a basis and capital account of $984.

	Outside Basis	Book	Value
A	$384	$984	$984
B	984	984	984
C	984	984	984
	2352	2952	2952

in 2021 (the adjustment year) pursuant to §1.704-1(b)(2)(iii)(f) of this chapter. Specifically, Partnership allocates the $24 expenditure in 2021 in proportion to the allocation of the notional item to which it relates (which is 1/3 each as in *Example 1* of this paragraph (e)), but it must also take into account modifications attributable to each partner. Accordingly, B's allocation is $16 (its share of the imputed underpayment, for which no modification occurred), and A and C have properly allocable shares of $0 and $8, respectively (their shares, taking into account modification). Thus, A's capital account is decreased by $0, B's capital account is decreased by $16, and C's capital account is decreased by $8 in 2021 and their respective outside bases are decreased by the same amounts in 2021.

(iv) The payment is also reflected by a $24 decrease in partnership cash for book purposes. Therefore, in 2021, A's basis in Partnership is $400 and his capital account is $1000, B's basis and capital account are both $984, and C's basis and capital account are both $992.

	Outside Basis	Book	Value
A	$400	$1000	$1000
B	984	984	984
C	992	992	992
Totals	2376	2976	2976

section 705(a)(2)(B) expenditure for imputed underpayments made by the partnership are specially allocated to A (all other items continue to be allocated in equal shares). Accordingly, in 2021, the section 705(a)(2)(B) expenditure is allocated entirely to A, which reduces its capital account by $48, which has economic effect under §1.704-1(b)(2)(ii) of this chapter. However, the economic effect of this allocation is not substantial under §1.704-1(b)(2)(iii)(a) of this chapter because it is not allocated in the manner described in §1.704-1(b)(2)(iii)(f) of this chapter. The allocation will also not be deemed to be in accordance with the partners' interests in the partnership under §1.704-1(b)(3)(ix) of this chapter because it is not allocated pursuant to the rules under §1.704-1(b)(4)(xii) of this chapter.

Example 5. (i) In 2019, Partnership has two partners, A and B. Both A and B have a $0 basis in their interests in Partnership. Further, Partnership has a $200 liability as defined in §1.752-1(a)(4) of this chapter. The liability is treated as a nonrecourse liability as defined in §1.752-1(a)(2) of this chapter so that A and B both are treated as having a $100 share of the liability under §1.752-3 of this chapter. In 2021 (the adjustment year), the IRS determines that the liability was inappropriately classified as a nonrecourse liability, should have been classified as a recourse liability as defined in §1.752-1(a)(1) of this chapter, and that A should have no share of the recourse liability under §1.752-2 of this chapter. The recharacterization of the liability from nonrecourse to recourse and the decrease in A's share of partnership liabilities are adjustments that are not allocated under section 704(b) under §301.6225-1(c)(5)(ii). As a result of the adjustments, the IRS includes in the residual grouping $100 of increased income to account for the cumulative effects of these adjustments to reflect the $100 decrease in A's share of partnership liabilities under §§1.752-1(c) and 1.731-1(a)(1)(i) of this chapter and determines an imputed underpayment of $40 ($100 x 40 percent). Partnership does not request modification under §301.6225-2. Partnership pays the $40 imputed underpayment.

(ii) Pursuant to paragraph (b)(4)(ii) of this of this section, notional items are not created with respect to this partnership adjustment. Instead, under paragraph (b)(4)(i) of this section, specified tax attributes are adjusted in a manner that is consistent with how the partnership adjustment would have been taken into account under the partnership agreement in effect for the reviewed year taking into account all facts and circumstances. In this case, no specified tax attributes are adjusted.

(iii) However, because A would have borne the economic burden of the partnership adjustment if the partnership and its partners had originally reported in a manner consistent with the partnership adjustment, the $40 imputed underpayment section 705(a)(2)(B) expenditure is allocated to A under §1.704-1(b)(2)(iii)(*f*)(4) of this chapter.

(f) *Applicability date.*—(1) *In general.*—Except as provided in paragraph (f)(2) of this section, this section applies to partnership taxable years beginning after December 31, 2017.

(2) *Election under §301.9100-22 in effect.*—This section applies to any partnership taxable year beginning after November 2, 2015 and before January 1, 2018 for which a valid election under §301.9100-22 is in effect. [Reg. §301.6225-4.]

Partnerships: Centralized Partnership Audit Regime

Partnerships: Centralized Partnership Audit Regime.—Reg. §301.6226-4, implementing the centralized partnership audit regime that have not been finalized to reflect the changes made by the Technical Corrections Act of 2018, contained in Title II of the Consolidated Appropriations Act of 2018 (TTCA), is proposed (published in the Federal Register on August 17, 2018) (REG-136118-15; REG-119337-17; REG-118067-17; REG-120232-17 and REG-120233-17).

Par. 15. Section 301.6226-4 is added to read as follows:

§301.6226-4. Effect of a partnership adjustment on tax attributes of partnerships and their partners.—(a) *Adjustments to tax attributes.*—(1) *In general.*—When a partnership adjustment (as defined in §301.6241-1(a)(6)) is taken into account by the reviewed year partners (as defined in §301.6241-1(a)(9)) or affected partners (as described in §301.6226-3(e)(3)(i)) pursuant to an election made by a partnership under §301.6226-1, the partnership and its reviewed year partners or affected partners must adjust their tax attributes (as defined in §301.6241-1(a)(10)) in accordance with the rules in this section.

(2) *Application to pass-through partners and indirect partners.*—To the extent a pass-through partner (as defined in §301.6241-1(a)(5)) pays an imputed underpayment under §301.6226-3(e)(4)(iii), such pass-through partner and its affected partners or their successors must make adjustments to their tax attributes in accordance with the rules in §301.6225-4.

(3) *Allocation of partnership adjustments.*—Partnership adjustments are allocated to the reviewed year partners or affected partners under §1.704-1(b)(4)(xiv) of this chapter.

(b) *Adjusting tax attributes of a partnership and its partners when an election under section 6226 is made.*—For partnership adjustments that are taken into account by the reviewed year partners or affected partners because an election is made under §301.6226-1, the partnership adjustments to be taken into account by each partner are determined under §301.6226-2(f). Accordingly, the reviewed year partners or affected partners must take into account the partnership adjustments as reflected on the statements described in §301.6226-2 or §301.6226-3(e)(3) in accordance with §301.6226-3. The reviewed year partners or affected partners and the partnership adjust partnership tax attributes affected by reason of an adjustment reflected on the statements described in §301.6226-2 or §301.6226-3(e)(3) with respect to the reviewed year (as defined in §301.6241-1(a)(8)), except to the extent partner or partnership tax attributes were already adjusted as part of the partnership adjustment. Additionally, reviewed year partners or affected partners adjust their partner tax attributes that are affected by the adjustments reflected on the statements described in §301.6226-2 or §301.6226-3(e)(3), but these adjustments to partner tax attributes are calculated with respect to each year beginning with the first affected year (as defined in §301.6226-3(b)(2)(i)), followed by any intervening years (as defined in §301.6226-3(b)(3)(i)), concluding with the reporting year (as defined in §301.6226-3(a)).

(c) *Example.*—The following example illustrates the rules of this section. For purposes of this example, Partnership is subject to the provisions of subchapter C of chapter 63 of the Internal Revenue Code, Partnership and its partners are calendar year taxpayers, all partners are U.S. persons, and the highest rate of income tax in effect for all taxpayers is 40 percent for all relevant periods.

Example. (i) In 2021, J, K and L form Partnership by each contributing $500 in exchange for partnership interests that share all items of income, gain, loss and deduction in identical shares. Partnership immediately purchases Asset on January 1, 2021 for $1,500, which it depreciates using the straight-line method with a 10-year recovery period beginning in 2021 ($150) so that each partner has a $50 distributive share of the depreciation, resulting in an outside basis of $450 for each partner. Accordingly, at the end of 2022, J, K and L have an outside basis and capital account of $400 each ($500 less $50 of their respective allocable shares of depreciation in 2021 and $50 in 2022).

	Partnership Basis	Book	Value
Asset	$1200	$1200	$1500
Totals	1200	1200	1500

		Outside Basis	Book	Value
	J	$400	$400	$500
	K	400	400	500
	L	400	400	500
		1200	1200	1500

(ii) The IRS initiates an administrative proceeding with respect to Partnership's 2021 taxable year (reviewed year) and in 2023 (adjustment year) finally determines that Asset should have been depreciated with a 20-year recovery period beginning in 2021, resulting in a $75 partnership adjustment that results in an imputed underpayment. The IRS does not initiate an administrative proceeding with respect to Partnership's 2022 taxable year, and Partnership does not file an administrative adjustment request for that taxable year. Partnership makes an election under §301.6226-1 with respect to the imputed underpayment. Therefore, J, K and L each are furnished a statement described in §301.6226-2 by Partnership reflecting the $25 income adjustment for 2021.

(iii) Tax attributes of the partners must be adjusted to reflect the $75 partnership adjustment reflected on the statements described in §301.6226-2 that is taken into account in equal shares ($25) by J, K, and L with respect to 2021. Specifically, J, K and L's outside bases and capital accounts must be increased $25 each with respect to the 2021 tax year. As a result, J, K and L each have an outside basis and capital account of $425 ($400 plus $25 of income realized with respect to 2021). Asset's basis and book value must also be changed in 2023. Thus, after adjusting tax attributes of the partners to take into account the election under §301.6226-1 and taking into account other activities of Partnership in 2023, accounts are stated as follows:

	Partnership Basis	Book	Value
Asset	$1275	$1275	$1500
Totals	1275	1275	1500

		Outside Basis	Book	Value
	J	$425	$425	$500
	K	425	425	500
	L	425	425	500
		1275	1275	1500

(d) *Applicability date.*—(1) *In general.*—Except as provided in paragraph (d)(2) of this section, this section applies to partnership taxable years beginning after December 31, 2017.

(2) *Election under § 301.9100-22 in effect.*—This section applies to any partnership taxable year beginning after November 2, 2015 and before January 1, 2018 for which a valid election under § 301.9100-22 is in effect. [Reg. § 301.6226-4.]

Allocation and Apportionment of Deductions and Foreign Tax Credit: Guidance

Allocation and Apportionment of Deductions and Foreign Tax Credit: Guidance.—Amendments to Reg. § 301.6227-1, relating to the allocation and apportionment of deductions and creditable foreign taxes, the definition of financial services income, foreign tax redeterminations, availability of foreign tax credits under the transition tax, and the application of the foreign tax credit limitation to consolidated groups, are proposed (published in the Federal Register on December 17, 2019) (REG-105495-19).

Par. 30. Section 301.6227-1 is amended by adding paragraph (g) to read as follows:

§ 301.6227-1. Administrative adjustment request by partnership.

* * *

(g) *Notice requirement and partnership adjustments required as a result of a foreign tax redetermination.*—For special rules applicable when an adjustment to a partnership related item (as defined in

section 6241(2)) is required as part of a redetermination of U.S. tax liability under section 905(c) and § 1.905-3(b) of this chapter as a result of a foreign tax redetermination (as defined in § 1.905-3(a) of this chapter), see § 1.905-4(b)(2)(ii) of this chapter.

* * *

COLLECTION

Excise Taxes: Taxable Fuel: Returns: Definitions

Excise Taxes: Taxable Fuel: Returns: Definitions.—Amendments to Reg. § 40.6302(c)-1, relating to credits and payments for alcohol mixtures, biodiesel mixtures, renewable diesel mixtures, alternative fuel mixtures, and alternative fuel sold for use or used as a fuel and relating to the definition of gasoline and diesel fuel, are proposed (published in the Federal Register on July 29, 2008) (REG-155087-05).

Par. 6. Section 40.6302(c)-1 is amended as follows:

1. Paragraph (e)(1)(ii) is amended by removing the language "components);" and adding "components); and" in its place.

2. Paragraph (e)(1)(iii) is amended by removing the language "chemicals); and" and adding "chemicals)." in its place.

3. Paragraph (e)(1)(iv) is removed.

§ 40.6302(c)-1. Use of Government depositaries.

ABATEMENTS, CREDITS, AND REFUNDS

Misdirected Direct Deposit Refunds: Identification and Recovery

Misdirected Direct Deposit Refunds: Identification and Recovery.—Amendments to Reg. § 301.6402-2, concerning the procedures for identification and recovery of a misdirected direct deposit refund, are proposed (published in the Federal Register on December 23, 2019) (REG-116163-19).

Par. 2. Section 6402-2 is amended by:

1. Redesignating paragraph (g) as paragraph (h) and adding new paragraph (g).

2. Revising the paragraph heading of newly redesignated paragraph (h) and adding a sentence at the end of the paragraph.

The additions and revisions read as follows:

§ 301.6402-2. Claims for credit or refund.

* * *

(g) *Misdirected direct deposit refund.*—(1) *Definition.*—The term *misdirected direct deposit refund* includes any refund of an overpayment of tax that is disbursed as a direct deposit but is not deposited into the account designated on the claim for refund to receive the direct deposit refund. A misdirected direct deposit refund does not include any amount that is credited or offset pursuant to the law in effect immediately prior to the direct deposit being disbursed.

(2) *Procedures for reporting a misdirected direct deposit refund.*—(i) *In general.*—A taxpayer or a taxpayer's authorized representative may report to the IRS that the taxpayer never received a direct deposit refund and request a replacement refund. The report must include the name of the taxpayer who requested the refund, the taxpayer identification number of the taxpayer, the taxpayer's mailing address, the type of return to which the refund is related, the account number and routing number that the taxpayer requested the refund be directly deposited into, and any other information necessary to locate the misdirected direct deposit refund.

(ii) *How to report a misdirected direct deposit refund.*—A reporting described in paragraph (g)(2)(i) of this section may be made in the following ways:

(A) By calling the IRS;

(B) On the form prescribed by the IRS and in accordance with the applicable publications, instructions, or other appropriate guidance;

(C) By contacting the Office of the Taxpayer Advocate by telephone, by mail, facsimile, or in person; or

(D) By submitting the appropriate form in person at a Taxpayer Assistance Center.

(3) *Procedures for coordination with financial institutions.*—(i) *Identification of the account that received the misdirected direct deposit*

refund.—If the IRS receives a report described in paragraph (g)(2)(ii) of this section and confirms that the refund described in the report was issued as a direct deposit, the IRS will initiate a refund trace to request the assistance of the Department of the Treasury's Bureau of the Fiscal Service. In accordance with its own procedures, the Bureau of the Fiscal Service coordinates with the financial institution that holds directly or indirectly the deposit account into which the refund was made, requesting from the financial institution such information as is necessary to identify whether the financial institution received the refund; whether the financial institution returned, or will return, the refund to the IRS, or if no funds are available for return; whether a deposit was made into the account designated on the claim for refund; and the identity of the deposit account owner to whom the deposit was disbursed.

(ii) *Coordination to recover the amounts transferred.*—Recovery of the misdirected direct deposit refund from a financial institution shall follow the procedures established by the Bureau of the Fiscal Service. The Bureau of the Fiscal Service shall request the return of the misdirected direct deposit refund from the financial institution that received it. The IRS may contact the financial institution directly to recover the misdirected direct deposit refund.

(4) *Issuance of replacement refund.*—When the IRS has determined that a misdirected direct deposit refund has occurred, the IRS will issue a replacement refund in the full amount of the refund that was misdirected. The replacement refund may be issued as a direct deposit or as a paper check sent to the taxpayer's last known address.

(5) *Applicability of this paragraph (g) to missing refunds.*—The provisions of paragraphs (g)(2) through (3)(i) of this section should be used for any refund that was disbursed as a direct deposit and that the taxpayer reports as missing. For example, although a refund that was deposited into an incorrect bank account because the taxpayer transposed two digits in their bank account number is not considered to be a misdirected direct deposit refund, the provisions

of paragraphs (g)(2) through (3)(i) of this section should be used. If the application of these procedures results in an amount recovered by the IRS, the recovered amount will be refunded or credited as allowed by law.

* * *

(h) *Applicability dates.*—* * * Paragraph (g) of this section applies to claims for refund filed after [**DATE THE FINAL REGULATIONS ARE PUBLISHED IN THE Federal Register**].

Elimination of Circular Adjustments to Basis: Absorption of Losses

Elimination of Circular Adjustments to Basis: Absorption of Losses.—Amendments to Reg. §301.6402-7, revising the rules concerning the use of a consolidated group's losses in a consolidated return year in which stock of a subsidiary is disposed of, are proposed (published in the Federal Register on June 11, 2015) (REG-101652-10).

Par. 11. Section 301.6402-7 is amended by revising the last sentence of paragraph (g)(2)(ii) and paragraph (l) to read as follows:

§301.6402-7. Claims for refund and applications for tentative carryback adjustments involving consolidated groups that include insolvent financial institutions.

* * *

(g) * * *
  (2) * * *
    (ii) * * * For this purpose, the separate net operating loss of a member is determined by computing the consolidated net operating loss by reference to only the member's items of income, gain, deduction, and loss (excluding capital gains and amounts treated as capital gains), including the member's losses and deductions actually absorbed by the group in the consolidated return year (whether or not absorbed by the member).

* * *

(l) *Effective/applicability dates.*—This section applies to refunds and tentative carryback adjustments paid after December 30, 1991. However, the last sentence of paragraph (g)(2)(ii) of this section applies to separate net operating losses of members incurred in consolidated return years beginning on or after the date these regulations are published as final regulations in the **Federal Register**.

Excise Tax: Tractors, Trailers, Trucks, and Tires: Highway Vehicle: Definition

Excise Tax: Tractors, Trailers, Trucks, and Tires: Highway Vehicle: Definition.—Amendments to Reg. §48.6416(c)-1, relating to the excise taxes imposed on the sale of highway tractors, trailers, trucks, and tires, the use of heavy vehicles on the highway, and the definition of highway vehicle related to these and other taxes, are proposed (published in the Federal Register on March 31, 2016) (REG-103380-05).

Par. 25. Section 48.6416(c)-1 is removed.

§48.6416(c)-1. Credit for tax paid on tires or, prior to January 1, 1984, inner tubes.

Excise Tax: Tractors, Trailers, Trucks, and Tires: Highway Vehicle: Definition

Excise Tax: Tractors, Trailers, Trucks, and Tires: Highway Vehicle: Definition.—Amendments to Reg. §48.6421-4,relating to the excise taxes imposed on the sale of highway tractors, trailers, trucks, and tires, the use of heavy vehicles on the highway, and the definition of highway vehicle related to these and other taxes, are proposed (published in the Federal Register on March 31, 2016) (REG-103380-05).

Par. 26. For each section listed in the tables, remove the language in the "Remove" column from wherever it appears in the paragraph and add in its place the language in the "Add" column as set forth below:

§48.6421-4. Meaning of terms.

Section	Remove	Add
§48.6421-4(c)	48.4061(a)-1(d)	48.0-5

Excise Taxes: Taxable Fuel: Returns: Definitions

Excise Taxes: Taxable Fuel: Returns: Definitions.—Reg. §§48.6426-1—48.6426-7, relating to credits and payments for alcohol mixtures, biodiesel mixtures, renewable diesel mixtures, alternative fuel mixtures, and alternative fuel sold for use or used as a fuel and relating to the definition of gasoline and diesel fuel, are proposed (published in the Federal Register on July 29, 2008) (REG-155087-05).

Par. 20. Sections 48.6426-1 through 48.6426-7 are added to read as follows:

§48.6426-1. Renewable and alternative fuels; explanation of terms.—(a) *Overview.*—This section provides an explanation of terms for purposes of the credits allowed by sections 34 and 6426 and the payments allowed by section 6427(e). The definition of *alcohol* in paragraph (c) of this section is also applicable for purposes of the credits allowed by section 40. The definitions of *biodiesel* and *renewable diesel* in paragraph (b) of this section are also applicable for purposes of the credits allowed by section 40A.

(b) *Explanation of terms.*

Agri-biodiesel means biodiesel derived solely from virgin oils. Virgin oils include virgin vegetable oils from the sources listed in section 40A(d)(2), as well as virgin oils not listed, such as palm oil and fish oil. Biodiesel produced from a feedstock that includes any recycled oils (such as recycled cooking oils) is not agri-biodiesel because it is not derived solely from virgin oils.

Alcohol is defined in paragraph (c) of this section.

Alcohol fuel mixture means a mixture of alcohol and taxable fuel that contains at least 0.1 percent (by volume) of taxable fuel.

Alternative fuel means, except as otherwise provided in the following sentence, liquefied petroleum gas, P Series Fuels (as defined by the Secretary of Energy under 42 U.S.C. 13211(2)), compressed or liquefied natural gas, liquefied hydrogen, any liquid fuel derived from coal (including peat) through the Fischer-Tropsch process, and liquid fuel derived from biomass (as defined in section 0.45K(c)(3)). The term does not include ethanol, methanol, biodiesel, or renewable diesel.

Alternative fuel mixture means a mixture of alternative fuel and taxable fuel that contains at least 0.1 percent (by volume) of taxable fuel.

Alternative fueler means a person that—
(1) Is an alternative fueler (unmixed fuel); or
(2) Produces alternative fuel mixtures for sale or use in its trade or business.

Alternative fueler (unmixed fuel) with respect to any alternative fuel that is sold for use or used as a fuel in a motor vehicle or motorboat is—

(1) In the case of alternative fuel on which tax is imposed by section 4041(a)(2) or (3), the person liable for such tax (determined in the case of compressed natural gas after the application of §48.4041-21 and in the case of any other alternative fuel after the application of rules similar to the rules of §§48.4041-3 and 48.4041-5);

(2) In the case of alternative fuel that is not described in paragraph (1) or (3) of this definition, the person that would be so liable for such tax but for the application of an exemption provided by section 4041(a)(3)(B), (b), (f), (g), or (h); and

(3) In the case of liquefied natural gas (LNG) that is sold in bulk for the exclusive use of a State that provides the written waiver described in §48.6426-6(c)(4) and is delivered into a bulk supply tank that can only fuel motor vehicles and motorboats of the State, the person that sells the alternative fuel to the State.

Biodiesel means biodiesel as defined in section 40A(d)(1). Biodiesel may be produced either within or outside the United States. Fuel meets the Environmental Protection Agency (EPA) registration requirements described in section 40A(d)(1)(A) if the EPA does not require the fuel to be registered.

Reg. §48.6426-1(b)

Biodiesel mixture means a mixture of biodiesel and diesel fuel that contains at least 0.1 percent (by volume) of diesel fuel. The kerosene in a biodiesel mixture is not included in either the overall volume of the mixture or the volume of diesel fuel in the mixture for purposes of determining whether the biodiesel mixture satisfies the 0.1 percent requirement. The diesel fuel in a biodiesel mixture may be dyed or undyed. See, however, section 6715 for the penalty for willful alteration of the strength or composition of any dye in dyed fuel and § 48.6715-1 for related rules.

Commingled biodiesel means biodiesel that is held by—

(1) Its producer in a storage tank at a time when the tank is used only for the storage of biodiesel and is used to store both biodiesel (other than agribiodiesel) and agri-biodiesel; or

(2) A person other than its producer in a storage tank at a time when the tank is used only for the storage of biodiesel and is used to store biodiesel to which more than a single Certificate for Biodiesel applies.

Commingled renewable diesel means renewable diesel held by a person other than its producer in a storage tank at a time when the tank is used only for the storage of renewable diesel and is used to store renewable diesel to which more than a single Certificate for Renewable Diesel applies.

Mixture means an alcohol fuel mixture, a biodiesel mixture, a renewable diesel mixture, or an alternative fuel mixture.

Mixture producer is the person that has title to the mixture immediately after it is created.

Motor vehicle has the meaning given to the term by § 48.4041-8(c). Thus, for example, the term includes forklift trucks used to carry loads at industrial plants and warehouses.

Producer means the person that produces alcohol, biodiesel, or renewable diesel.

Registered biodiesel producer means a biodiesel producer that is registered under section 4101 as a producer of biodiesel.

Registered renewable diesel producer means a renewable diesel producer that is registered under section 4101 as a producer of renewable diesel.

Renewable diesel means renewable diesel as defined in section 40A(f)(3). For this purpose, a fuel meets the Environmental Protection Agency's (EPA) registration requirements described in section 40A(f)(3)(A) if the EPA does not require the fuel to be registered or if diesel fuel coproduced from renewable diesel and petroleum feedstocks is registered. Renewable diesel may be produced either within or outside the United States.

Renewable diesel mixture is defined in paragraph (d) of this section.

Reseller means, with respect to any biodiesel or renewable diesel, a person that buys and subsequently sells such fuel without using the fuel to produce a biodiesel or renewable diesel mixture.

Thermal depolymerization process means, for purposes of the definition of *renewable diesel* in section 40A(f)(3), a process for the reduction of complex organic materials through the use of pressure and heat to decompose long chain polymers of hydrogen, oxygen, and carbon into short-chain petroleum hydrocarbons with a maximum length of around 18 carbons. A process may qualify as thermal depolymerization even if catalysts are used in the process.

Use as a fuel is defined in paragraph (e) of this section.

(c) *Alcohol; definition.*—(1) *In general.*—Except as otherwise provided in this paragraph (c), *alcohol* means any alcohol, including methanol and ethanol, that is not a derivative product of petroleum, natural gas, or coal (including peat). Thus, for example, the term does not include an ethanol by-product produced from a derivative of petroleum or natural gas. However, the term does include alcohol made from renewable resources, such as agricultural or forestry products. The term also includes alcohol made from urban wastes, such as methanol made from methane gas formed at waste disposal sites.

(2) *Source of the alcohol.*—Alcohol may be produced either within or outside the United States.

(3) *Proof and denaturants.*—Except for purposes of section 40, alcohol does not include alcohol with a proof of less than 190 degrees (determined without regard to added denaturants). For purposes of section 40, alcohol does not include alcohol with a proof of less than 150 degrees (determined without regard to added denaturants). If alcohol includes impurities or denaturants, the volume of alcohol is determined under the following rules:

(i) Except for purposes of section 40, the volume of alcohol includes the volume of any impurities (other than added denaturants and any fuel with which the alcohol is mixed) that reduce the purity of the alcohol to not less than 190 proof (determined without regard to added denaturants and any fuel with which the alcohol is mixed).

(ii) For purposes of section 40, the volume of alcohol includes the volume of any impurities (other than added denaturants

and any fuel with which the alcohol is mixed) that reduce the purity of the alcohol to not less than 150 proof (determined without regard to added denaturants and any fuel with which the alcohol is mixed).

(iii) The volume of alcohol includes the volume of any approved denaturants that reduce the purity of the alcohol, but only to the extent that the volume of the approved denaturants does not exceed five percent of the unadjusted volume of the alcohol. The unadjusted volume of the alcohol is determined for this purpose by including in unadjusted volume the approved denaturants and the impurities included in volume under paragraph (c)(3)(i) or (ii) of this section. If the volume of the approved denaturants exceeds five percent of the unadjusted volume of the alcohol, the excess over five percent is not considered alcohol.

(iv) For purposes of this paragraph (c)(3), approved denaturants are any denaturants (including gasoline and other nonalcohol fuel denaturants) that reduce the purity of the alcohol and are added to such alcohol under a formula approved by the Secretary.

(4) *ETBE.*—Ethyl tertiary butyl ether (ETBE) and other ethers produced from alcohol are treated as alcohol. The ether is treated as alcohol of the same type as the alcohol used to produce the ether and the volume of alcohol resulting from such treatment is the volume of alcohol of such type with an energy content equal to the energy content of the ether.

(d) *Renewable diesel mixture; definition.*—(1) *In general.*—Renewable diesel mixture means—

(i) A mixture of renewable diesel and diesel fuel (other than renewable diesel) that contains at least 0.1 percent (by volume) of diesel fuel (other than renewable diesel); and

(ii) Fuel produced from biomass (as defined in section 45K(c)(3)) and petroleum feedstocks using a thermal depolymerization process if such fuel has been registered by the Environmental Protection Agency (EPA) under section 211 of the Clean Air Act (42 U.S.C. 7545) and meets the requirements of ASTM D975 or D396.

(2) *Special rules.*—The kerosene in a renewable diesel mixture is not included in either the overall volume of the mixture or the volume of diesel fuel in the mixture for purposes of determining whether the renewable diesel mixture satisfies the 0.1 percent requirement. The diesel fuel in the renewable diesel mixture may be dyed or undyed. See, however, section 6715 for the penalty for willful alteration of the strength or composition of any dye in dyed fuel and § 48.6715-1 for related rules. For availability for ASTM specifications, see § 48.4081-1(d).

(e) *Use as a fuel; definitions.*—(1) A mixture is *used as a fuel* when it is consumed in the production of energy. Thus, for example, a mixture is used as a fuel when it is consumed in an internal combustion engine to power a vehicle or in a furnace to produce heat. However, a mixture that is destroyed in a fire or other casualty loss is not used as a fuel.

(2) A mixture is *sold for use as a fuel* if the producer sells the fuel and has reason to believe that the fuel will be used as a fuel by either the producer's buyer or any later buyer of the mixture.

(3) Alternative fuel (not in a mixture) is sold for use or used as a fuel in a motor vehicle or motorboat when the alternative fueler (unmixed fuel) with respect to the fuel delivers it into the fuel supply tank of a motor vehicle or motor boat or sells it in bulk for use by the buyer as a fuel in a motor vehicle or motorboat.

(f) *Other definitions.*—For the definitions of taxable fuel and diesel fuel, see § 48.4081-1.

(g) *Effective/applicability date.*—This section is applicable on and after the date these regulations are published as final regulations in the **Federal Register**. [Reg. § 48.6426-1.]

§ 48.6426-2. Alcohol fuel mixtures.—(a) *Overview.*—This section provides rules under which an alcohol fuel mixture producer may claim an excise tax credit under section 6426, a payment under section 6427, or an income tax credit under section 34. These claims relate to the mixture producer's sale or use of an alcohol fuel mixture and are based on the amount of alcohol used to produce the alcohol fuel mixture. For the applicable claim rate, see section 6426.

(b) *Conditions to allowance.*—(1) *Excise tax credit.*—A claim for the alcohol fuel mixture credit with respect to an alcohol fuel mixture is allowed under section 6426 only if each of the following conditions is satisfied:

(i) The claimant produced the alcohol fuel mixture for sale or use in the trade or business of the claimant.

(ii) The claimant sold the alcohol fuel mixture for use as a fuel or used the alcohol fuel mixture as a fuel.

(iii) The claimant has made no other claim with respect to the alcohol in the mixture or, if another claim has been made, such other claim is disregarded under this paragraph (b)(1)(iii). A claim is disregarded under this paragraph (b)(1)(iii) if it is—

(A) A claim for the small ethanol producer credit under section 40; or

(B) An erroneous claim under section 6427 and either the claim has been disallowed or the claimant has repaid the government the amount received under section 6427 with interest.

(iv) The claimant has filed a timely claim on Form 720, "Quarterly Federal Excise Tax Return," that contains all the information required in paragraph (c) of this section.

(2) *Payment or income tax credit.*—A claim for an alcohol fuel mixture payment under section 6427 or an income tax credit under section 34 is allowed only if—

(i) The conditions of paragraphs (b)(1)(i) and (ii) of this section are met; and

(ii) The claimant has filed a timely claim for payment on Form 720 or Form 8849, "Claim for Refund of Excise Taxes," or for a credit on Form 4136, "Credit for Federal Tax Paid on Fuels," that contains all the information required by paragraph (c) of this section.

(3) *ETBE; sold for use or used as a fuel.*—An alcohol fuel mixture that is produced at a refinery and that includes ethyl tertiary butyl ether or other ethers produced from alcohol is treated as meeting the requirement of paragraph (b)(1)(ii) of this section when the mixture is removed from the refinery and any subsequent sale or use of the mixture is disregarded for purposes of this section.

(4) *Overall limitations on credits and payments.*—See § 48.6426-7(a) for overall limitations on credits and payments allowed with respect to mixtures under sections 34, 6426, and 6427.

(c) *Content of claim.*—Each claim for an alcohol fuel mixture credit or payment must contain the following information with respect to the mixture covered by the claim:

(1) The amount of alcohol in the alcohol fuel mixture.

(2) A statement that the conditions to allowance described in paragraph (b) of this section have been met.

(3) A statement that the claimant either—

(i) Produced the alcohol it used in the mixture; or

(ii) Has in its possession a record of the name, address, and employer identification number of the person(s) that sold the alcohol to the claimant and the date of purchase.

(d) *Effective/applicability date.*—This section is applicable on and after the date these regulations are published as final regulations in the **Federal Register**. [Reg. § 48.6426-2.]

§ 48.6426-3. Biodiesel mixtures.—(a) *Overview.*—This section provides rules under which a biodiesel mixture producer may claim an excise tax credit under section 6426, a payment under section 6427, or an income tax credit under section 34. These claims relate to the mixture producer's sale or use of a biodiesel mixture and are based on the amount of biodiesel used to produce the biodiesel mixture. For the applicable claim rate, see section 6426.

(b) *Conditions to allowance.*—(1) *Excise tax credit.*—A claim for the biodiesel mixture credit with respect to a biodiesel mixture is allowed under section 6426 only if each of the following conditions is satisfied:

(i) The claimant produced the biodiesel mixture for sale or use in the trade or business of the claimant.

(ii) The claimant sold the biodiesel mixture for use as a fuel or used the biodiesel mixture as a fuel.

(iii) The claimant—

(A) Produced the biodiesel in the mixture; or

(B) Has obtained a certificate from the registered biodiesel producer as described in paragraph (e) of this section and, if applicable, a statement described in paragraph (f) of this section, for such biodiesel and has no reason to believe any information in the certificate and statement is false.

(iv) The claimant has made no other claim with respect to the biodiesel in the mixture or, if another claim has been made, such other claim is disregarded under this paragraph (b)(1)(iv). A claim is disregarded under this paragraph (b)(1)(iv) if it is—

(A) A claim for the small agri-biodiesel producer credit under section 40A; or

(B) An erroneous claim under section 6427 and either the claim has been disallowed or the claimant has repaid the government the amount received under section 6427 with interest.

(v) The claimant has filed a timely claim on Form 720, "Quarterly Federal Excise Tax Return," that contains all the information required in paragraph (c) of this section.

(2) *Payment or income tax credit.*—A claim for a biodiesel mixture payment under section 6427 or an income tax credit under section 34 is allowed only if—

(i) The conditions of paragraphs (b)(1)(i), (ii), and (iii) of this section are met; and

(ii) The claimant has filed a timely claim for payment on Form 720 or Form 8849, "Claim for Refund of Excise Tax," or for a credit on Form 4136, "Credit for Federal Tax Paid on Fuels," that contains all the information required by paragraph (c) of this section.

(3) *Overall limitations on credits and payments.*—See § 48.6426-7(a) for overall limitations on credits and payments allowed with respect to mixtures under sections 34, 6426, and 6427.

(c) *Content of claim.*—Each claim for a biodiesel mixture credit or payment must contain the following information with respect to the mixture covered by the claim:

(1) The amount of agri-biodiesel and biodiesel other than agri-biodiesel in the biodiesel mixture.

(2) Unless the claimant is the producer of the biodiesel in the biodiesel mixture, a copy of the applicable Certificate for Biodiesel described in paragraph (e) of this section and Statement(s) of Biodiesel Reseller described in paragraph (f) of this section. In the case of a certificate and statement that support a claim made on more than one claim form, the certificate and statement are to be included with the first claim and the claimant is to provide information related to the certificate and statement on any subsequent claim in accordance with the instructions applicable to the claim form.

(3) A statement that the conditions to allowance described in paragraph (b) of this section have been met.

(4) A statement that the claimant either—

(i) Is a registered biodiesel producer and produced the biodiesel it used in the mixture; or

(ii) Has in its possession a record of the name, address, and employer identification number of the person(s) that sold the biodiesel to the claimant and the date of purchase.

(d) *Commingled biodiesel; accounting method.*—For purposes of determining the certificate applicable to commingled biodiesel, a person that holds commingled biodiesel may identify the biodiesel it sells or uses by any reasonable method, including the first-in, first-out method applied either on a tank-by-tank basis or on an aggregate basis to all commingled biodiesel the person holds.

(e) *Certificate for Biodiesel.*—(1) *In general.*—The certificate to be obtained by the claimant is a statement that is signed under penalties of perjury by a person with authority to bind the registered biodiesel producer, is in substantially the same form as the model certificate in paragraph (e)(4) of this section, and contains all the information necessary to complete such model certificate.

(2) *Certificate identification number.*—The certificate identification number is determined by the producer and must be unique to each certificate.

(3) *Multiple certificates for single sale.*—A registered biodiesel producer may, with respect to a particular sale of biodiesel, provide multiple separate certificates, each applicable to a portion of the total volume of biodiesel sold. Thus, for example, a biodiesel producer that sells 5,000 gallons of biodiesel may provide its buyer with five certificates for 1,000 gallons each. The multiple certificates may be provided either to the buyer at or after the time of sale or to a reseller in the circumstances described in paragraph (f)(2) of this section.

(4) *Model certificate.*

CERTIFICATE FOR BIODIESEL

Certificate Identification Number: _____

(To support a claim related to biodiesel or a biodiesel mixture under the Internal Revenue Code)

The undersigned biodiesel producer ("Producer") hereby certifies the following under penalties of perjury:

1. _____
_____
_____

Producer's name, address, and employer identification number

2. _____
_____
_____

Name, address, and employer identification number of person buying the biodiesel from Producer

Reg. § 48.6426-3(e)(4)

3. _____

Date and location of sale to buyer

4. This certificate applies to _____gallons of biodiesel.

5. Producer certifies that the biodiesel to which this certificate relates is:

_____% Agri-biodiesel (derived solely from virgin oils)

_____% Biodiesel other than agri-biodiesel

6. This certificate applies to the following sale:

_____Invoice or delivery ticket number

_____Total number of gallons of biodiesel sold under that invoice or delivery ticket number (including biodiesel not covered by this certificate)

7. _____Total number of certificates issued for that invoice or delivery ticket number

8. _____
_____
_____

Name, address, and employer identification number of reseller to whom certificate is issued (only in the case of certificates reissued to a reseller after the return of the original certificate)

9. _____Original Certificate Identification Number (only in the case of certificates reissued to a reseller after return of the original certificate)

10. Producer is registered as a biodiesel producer with registration number _____. Producer's registration has not been suspended or revoked by the Internal Revenue Service.

Producer certifies that the biodiesel to which this certificate relates is monoalkyl esters of long chain fatty acids derived from plant or animal matter and that it meets the requirements of the American Society of Testing and Materials D6751 and the registration requirements for fuels and fuel additives established by EPA under section 211 of the Clean Air Act (42 U.S.C. 7545).

Producer understands that the fraudulent use of this certificate may subject Producer and all parties making any fraudulent use of this certificate to a fine or imprisonment, or both, together with the costs of prosecution.

_____

Printed or typed name of person signing this certificate

_____

Title of person signing

_____

Signature and date signed

(f) *Statement of Biodiesel Reseller.*—(1) *In general.*—A person that receives a Certificate for Biodiesel, and subsequently sells the biodiesel without producing a biodiesel mixture, is to give the certificate and a statement that satisfies the requirements of this paragraph (f) to its buyer. The statement must contain all of the information necessary to complete the model statement in paragraph (f)(4) of this section and be attached to the Certificate for Biodiesel. A reseller cannot make multiple copies of a Certificate for Biodiesel to divide the certificate between multiple buyers.

(2) *Multiple resales.*—If a single Certificate for Biodiesel applies to biodiesel that a reseller expects to sell to multiple buyers, the reseller should return the certificate (together with any statements provided by intervening resellers) to the producer who may reissue to the reseller multiple Certificates for Biodiesel in the appropriate volumes. The reissued certificates must include the Certificate Identification Number from the certificate that has been returned.

(3) *Withdrawal of the right to provide a certificate.*—The Internal Revenue Service may withdraw the right of a reseller of biodiesel to provide the certificate and a statement under this section if the Internal Revenue Service cannot verify the accuracy of the reseller's statements. The Internal Revenue Service may notify any person to whom the buyer has provided a statement that the reseller's right to provide the certificate and a statement has been withdrawn.

(4) *Model statement of biodiesel reseller.*

STATEMENT OF BIODIESEL RESELLER

(To support a claim related to biodiesel or a biodiesel mixture under the Internal Revenue Code)

The undersigned biodiesel reseller ("Reseller") hereby certifies the following under penalties of perjury:

1. _____
_____

Reseller's name, address, and employer identification number

2. _____
_____

Name, address, and employer identification number of Reseller's buyer

3. _____

Date and location of sale to buyer

4. _____

Volume of biodiesel sold

5. _____

Certificate Identification Number on the Certificate for Biodiesel

Reseller has bought the biodiesel described in the accompanying Certificate for Biodiesel and Reseller has no reason to believe that any information in the certificate is false.

Reseller has not been notified by the Internal Revenue Service that its right to provide a certificate and a statement has been withdrawn.

Reseller understands that the fraudulent use of this statement may subject Reseller and all parties making any fraudulent use of this statement to a fine or imprisonment, or both, together with the costs of prosecution.

_____

Printed or typed name of person signing this certificate

_____

Title of person signing

_____

Signature and date signed

(g) *Erroneous certificates; reasonable cause.*—If a claim for credit or payment described in this section is based on erroneous information in a certificate or statement described in paragraph (e)(4) or (f)(4) of this section, the claim is not allowed. Thus, for example, if a producer identifies a product as agribiodiesel on a Certificate for Biodiesel and the product does not meet the registration requirements established by EPA, a claim for a biodiesel mixture credit based on the certificate is not allowed. However, if the claimant has met the conditions of paragraph (b)(1)(iii)(B) of this section with respect to the certificate or statement, reliance on the certificate or statement will be treated as reasonable cause for purposes of the penalties imposed by sections 6651 (relating to failure to pay) and 6675 (relating to excessive claims).

(h) *Effective/applicability date.*—This section is applicable on and after the date of publication of these regulations as final regulations in the **Federal Register**. [Reg. § 48.6426-3.]

§48.6426-4. Renewable diesel mixtures.—(a) *Overview.*—This section provides rules under which a renewable diesel mixture producer may claim an excise tax credit under section 6426, a payment under section 6427, or an income tax credit under section 34. These claims relate to the mixture producer's sale or use of a renewable diesel mixture and are based on the amount of renewable diesel used to produce the renewable diesel mixture. For the applicable claim rate, see section 40A(f)(2).

(b) *Conditions to allowance.*—(1) *Excise tax credit.*—A claim for the renewable diesel mixture credit with respect to a renewable diesel mixture is allowed under section 6426 only if each of the following conditions is satisfied:

(i) The claimant produced the renewable diesel mixture for sale or use in the trade or business of the claimant.

(ii) The claimant sold the renewable diesel mixture for use as a fuel or used the renewable diesel mixture as a fuel.

(iii) The claimant—

(A) Produced the renewable diesel in the mixture; or

(B) Has obtained a certificate from the registered renewable diesel producer as described in paragraph (e) of this section and, if applicable, a statement described in paragraph (f) of this section, for such renewable diesel and has no reason to believe any information in the certificate and statement is false.

(iv) The claimant has made no other claim with respect to the renewable diesel in the mixture or, if another claim has been made, such other claim is disregarded under this paragraph (b)(1)(iv). A claim is disregarded under this paragraph (b)(1)(iv) if it is an erroneous claim under section 6427 and either the claim has been disallowed or the claimant has repaid the government the amount received under section 6427 with interest.

(v) The claimant has filed a timely claim on Form 720, "Quarterly Federal Excise Tax Return," that contains all the information required in paragraph (c) of this section.

(2) *Payment or income tax credit.*—A claim for a renewable diesel mixture payment under section 6427 or an income tax credit under section 34 is allowed only if—

(i) The conditions of paragraphs (b)(1)(i), (ii), and (iii) of this section are met; and

(ii) The claimant has filed a timely claim for payment on Form 720 or Form 8849, "Claim for Refund of Excise Taxes," or for a credit on Form 4136, "Credit for Federal Tax Paid on Fuels," that contains all the information required by paragraph (c) of this section.

(3) *Overall limitations on credits and payments.*—See § 48.6426-7(a) for overall limitations on credits and payments allowed with respect to mixtures under sections 34, 6426, and 6427.

(c) *Content of claim.*—Each claim for a renewable diesel mixture credit or payment must contain the following information with respect to the mixture covered by the claim:

(1) The amount of renewable diesel in the renewable diesel mixture.

(2) Unless the claimant is the producer of the renewable diesel in the renewable diesel mixture, a copy of the applicable Certificate for Renewable Diesel described in paragraph (e) of this section and Statement(s) of Renewable Diesel Reseller described in paragraph (f) of this section. In the case of a certificate and statement that support a claim made on more than one claim form, the certificate and statement are to be included with the first claim and the claimant is to provide information related to the certificate and statement on any subsequent claim in accordance with the instructions applicable to the claim form.

(3) A statement that the conditions to allowance described in paragraph (b) of this section have been met.

(4) A statement that the claimant either—

(i) Is a registered renewable diesel producer and produced the renewable diesel it used in the mixture; or

(ii) Has in its possession a record of the name, address, and employer identification number of the person(s) that sold the renewable diesel to the claimant and the date of purchase.

(d) *Commingled renewable diesel; accounting method.*—For purposes of determining the certificate applicable to commingled renewable diesel, a person that holds commingled renewable diesel may identify the renewable diesel it sells or uses by any reasonable method, including the first-in, first-out method applied either on a tank-by-tank basis or on an aggregate basis to all commingled renewable diesel the person holds.

(e) *Certificate for Renewable Diesel.*—(1) *In general.*—The certificate to be obtained by the claimant is a statement that is signed under penalties of perjury by a person with authority to bind the registered renewable diesel producer, is substantially in the same form as the model certificate in paragraph (e)(4) of this section, and contains all the information necessary to complete such model certificate.

(2) *Certificate identification number.*—The certificate identification number is determined by the producer and must be unique to each certificate.

(3) *Multiple certificates for single sale.*—A registered renewable diesel producer may, with respect to a particular sale of renewable diesel, provide multiple separate certificates, each applicable to a portion of the total volume of renewable diesel sold. Thus, for example, a renewable diesel producer that sells 5,000 gallons of renewable diesel may provide its buyer with five certificates for 1,000 gallons each. The multiple certificates may be provided either to the buyer at or after the time of sale or to a reseller in the circumstances described in paragraph (f)(2) of this section.

(4) *Model certificate.*

CERTIFICATE FOR RENEWABLE DIESEL

Certificate Identification Number: _____

(To support a claim related to renewable diesel or a renewable diesel mixture under the Internal Revenue Code)

The undersigned renewable diesel producer ("Producer") hereby certifies the following under penalties of perjury:

1. _____

_____

Producer's name, address, and employer identification number

2. _____

_____

Name, address, and employer identification number of person buying the renewable diesel from Producer

3. _____

Date and location of sale to buyer

4. This certificate applies to ____gallons of renewable diesel.

5. This certificate applies to the following sale:

____Invoice or delivery ticket number

____Total number of gallons of renewable diesel sold under that invoice or delivery ticket number (including renewable diesel not covered by this certificate)

6. ____Total number of certificates issued for that invoice or delivery ticket number

7. _____

_____

Name, address, and employer identification number of reseller to whom certificate is issued (only in the case of certificates reissued to a reseller after the return of the original certificate)

8. ____Original Certificate Identification Number (only in the case of certificates reissued to a reseller after return of the original certificate)

9. Producer is registered as a renewable diesel producer with registration number ____. Producer's registration has not been suspended or revoked by the Internal Revenue Service.

Reg. §48.6426-4(e)(4)

Producer certifies that the renewable diesel to which this certificate relates is diesel fuel derived from biomass (as defined in section 45K(c)(3) of the Internal Revenue Code) using a thermal depolymerization process and that it meets the requirements of the American Society of Testing and Materials D975 or D396 and the registration requirements for fuels and fuel additives established by EPA under section 211 of the Clean Air Act (42 U.S.C. 7545).

Producer understands that the fraudulent use of this certificate may subject Producer and all parties making any fraudulent use of this certificate to a fine or imprisonment, or both, together with the costs of prosecution.

_____
Printed or typed name of person signing this certificate

_____
Title of person signing

_____
Signature and date signed

(f) *Statement of Renewable Diesel Reseller.*—(1) *In general.*—A person that receives a Certificate for Renewable Diesel, and subsequently sells the renewable diesel without producing a renewable diesel mixture, is to give the certificate and a statement that satisfies the requirements of this paragraph (f) to its buyer. The statement must contain all of the information necessary to complete the model statement in paragraph (f)(4) of this section and be attached to the Certificate for Renewable Diesel. A reseller cannot make multiple copies of a Certificate for Renewable Diesel to divide the certificate between multiple buyers.

(2) *Multiple resales.*—If a single Certificate for Renewable Diesel applies to renewable diesel that a reseller expects to sell to multiple buyers, the reseller should return the certificate (together with any statements provided by intervening resellers) to the pro-ducer who may reissue to the reseller multiple Certificates for Renewable Diesel in the appropriate volumes. The reissued certificates must include the Certificate Identification Number from the certificate that has been returned.

(3) *Withdrawal of the right to provide a certificate.*—The Internal Revenue Service may withdraw the right of a reseller of renewable diesel to provide the certificate and a statement under this section if the Internal Revenue Service cannot verify the accuracy of the reseller's statements. The Internal Revenue Service may notify any person to whom the buyer has provided a statement that the reseller's right to provide the certificate and a statement has been withdrawn.

(4) *Model statement of renewable diesel reseller.*

STATEMENT OF RENEWABLE DIESEL RESELLER

(To support a claim related to renewable diesel or a renewable diesel mixture under the Internal Revenue Code)

The undersigned renewable diesel reseller ("Reseller") hereby certifies the following under penalties of perjury:
1. _____
_____
_____
Reseller's name, address, and employer identification number
2. _____
_____
Name, address, and employer identification number of Reseller's buyer
3. _____
Date and location of sale to buyer
4. _____
Volume of renewable diesel sold
5. _____
Certificate Identification Number on the Certificate for Renewable Diesel

Reseller has bought the renewable diesel described in the accompanying Certificate for Renewable Diesel and Reseller has no reason to believe that any information in the certificate is false.

Reseller has not been notified by the Internal Revenue Service that its right to provide a certificate and a statement has been withdrawn.

Reseller understands that the fraudulent use of this statement may subject Reseller and all parties making any fraudulent use of this statement to a fine or imprisonment, or both, together with the costs of prosecution.

_____
Printed or typed name of person signing this certificate

_____
Title of person signing

_____
Signature and date signed

(g) *Erroneous certificates; reasonable cause.*—If a claim for credit or payment described in this section is based on erroneous information in a certificate or statement described in paragraph (e)(4) or (f)(4) of this section, the claim is not allowed. Thus, for example, if a producer identifies a product as renewable diesel on a Certificate for Renewable Diesel and the product does not meet the registration requirements established by EPA, a claim for a renewable diesel mixture credit based on the certificate is not allowed. However, if the claimant has met the conditions of paragraph (b)(1)(iii)(B) of this section with respect to the certificate or statement, reliance on the certificate or statement will be treated as reasonable cause for purposes of the penalties imposed by sections 6651 (relating to failure to pay) and 6675 (relating to excessive claims).

(h) *Effective/applicability date.*—This section is applicable on and after the date these regulations are published as final regulations in the **Federal Register**. [Reg. § 48.6426-4.]

§ 48.6426-5. Alternative fuel mixtures.—(a) *Overview.*—This section provides rules under which an alternative fueler that produces an alternative fuel mixture may claim an excise tax credit under section 6426, a payment under section 6427, or an income tax credit under section 34. These claims relate to the mixture producer's sale or use of an alternative fuel mixture and are based on the amount of alternative fuel used to produce the alternative fuel mixture. For the applicable claim rate, see section 6426.

(b) *Conditions to allowance.*—(1) *Excise tax credit.*—A claim for the alternative fuel mixture credit with respect to an alternative fuel mixture is allowed under section 6426 only if each of the following conditions is satisfied:

(i) The claimant produced the alternative fuel mixture for sale or use in the trade or business of the claimant.

(ii) The claimant sold the alternative fuel mixture for use as a fuel or used the alternative fuel mixture as a fuel.

(iii) The claimant is registered under section 4101 as an alternative fueler.

(iv) The claimant has made no other claim with respect to the alternative fuel in the mixture or, if another claim has been made, such other claim is disregarded under this paragraph (b)(1)(iv). A claim is disregarded under this paragraph (b)(1)(iv) if it is an erroneous claim under section 6427 and either the claim has been disallowed or the claimant has repaid the government the amount received under section 6427 with interest.

(v) The claimant has filed a timely claim on Form 720, "Quarterly Federal Excise Tax Return," that contains all the information required by the claim form described in paragraph (c) of this section.

(2) *Payment or income tax credit.* A claim for an alternative fuel mixture payment under section 6427 or an alternative fuel mixture credit under sections 34 and 6427 is allowed only if—

(i) The conditions of paragraphs (b)(1)(i), (ii), and (iii) of this section are met; and

(ii) The claimant has filed a timely claim for payment on Form 720 or Form 8849, "Claim for Refund of Excise Taxes," or for a credit on Form 4136, "Credit for Fuel Tax Paid on Fuels," that contains all the information required by the claim form described in paragraph (c) of this section.

(3) *Overall limitations on credits and payments.*—See §48.6426-7(a) for overall limitations on credits and payments allowed with respect to mixtures under sections 34, 6426, and 6427.

(c) *Content of claim.*—Each claim for an alternative fuel mixture credit or payment must contain the following information with respect to the mixture covered by the claim:

(1) The amount of alternative fuel in the alternative fuel mixture.

(2) A statement that the conditions to allowance described in paragraph (b) of this section have been met.

(3) A statement that the claimant either—

(i) Produced the alternative fuel it used in the mixture; or

(ii) Has in its possession—

(A) A record of the name, address, and employer identification number of the person(s) that sold the alternative fuel to the claimant and the date of purchase; and

(B) An invoice or other purchase documentation identifying the alternative fuel.

(d) *Effective/applicability date.*—This section is applicable on and after the date these regulations are published as final regulations in the **Federal Register**. [Reg. §48.6426-5.]

§48.6426-6. Alternative fuel.—(a) *Overview.*—This section provides rules under which an alternative fueler (unmixed fuel) may claim an excise tax credit under section 6426, a payment under section 6427, or an income tax credit under section 34. These claims are based on the amount of alternative fuel sold or used. For the applicable claim rate, see section 6426.

(b) *Conditions to allowance.*—(1) *Excise tax credit.*—A claim for the alternative fuel excise tax credit with respect to alternative fuel sold for use or used as a fuel in a motor vehicle or motorboat is allowed under section 6426 only if each of the following conditions is satisfied:

(i) The claimant is the alternative fueler (unmixed fuel) with respect to the fuel.

(ii) The claimant is registered under section 4101 as an alternative fueler (unmixed fuel).

(iii) The claimant has made no other claim with respect to the alternative fuel or, if another claim has been made, such other claim is disregarded under this paragraph (b)(1)(iii). A claim is disregarded under this paragraph (b)(1)(iii) if it is an erroneous claim under section 6427 and either the claim has been disallowed or the claimant has repaid the government the amount received under section 6427 with interest.

(iv) The claimant has filed a timely claim on Form 720, "Quarterly Federal Excise Tax Return," that contains all the information required by the claim form described in paragraph (c) of this section.

(2) *Payment or income tax credit.*—A claim for an alternative fuel payment under section 6427 or an income tax credit under section 34 is allowed only if—

(i) The conditions of paragraphs (b)(1)(i) and (ii) of this section are met;

(ii) The sale or use is in the claimant's trade or business; and

(iii) The claimant has filed a timely claim for payment on Form 8849, "Claim for Refund of Excise Taxes," or for a credit on Form 4136, "Credit for Fuel Tax Paid on Fuels," that contains all the information required by paragraph (c) of this section.

(3) *Overall limitations on credits and payments.*—See §48.6426-7(b) for overall limitations on credits and payments allowed with respect to alternative fuel under sections 34, 6426, and 6427.

(c) *Content of claim.*—Each claim for an alternative fuel credit or payment must contain the following information with respect to the alternative fuel covered by the claim:

(1) The amount of alternative fuel sold or used.

(2) A statement that the conditions to allowance described in paragraph (b) of this section have been met.

(3) A statement that the claimant either—

(i) Produced the alternative fuel it sold or used; or

(ii) Has in its possession—

(A) A record of the name, address, and employer identification number of the person(s) that sold the alternative fuel to the claimant and the date of purchase; and

(B) An invoice or other purchase documentation identifying the alternative fuel.

(4) In the case of liquefied natural gas (LNG) that the claimant sold in bulk for the exclusive use of the State and delivered into a bulk supply tank that can only fuel motor vehicles or motorboats of the State, a statement that the claimant has in its possession a written waiver, signed under penalties of perjury by a person with authority to bind the State, stating that the LNG is delivered in bulk for the exclusive use of the State in a motor vehicle or motorboat and that the State gives up its right to claim any alternative fuel credit for such LNG.

(d) *Effective/applicability date.*—This section is applicable on and after the date these regulations are published as final regulations in the **Federal Register**. [Reg. §48.6426-6.]

§48.6426-7. Overall limitations on credits and payments.—(a) *Limitations applicable to mixtures.*—In the case of mixtures, the following limitations apply:

(1) The aggregate amount that, but for the coordination rules in sections 6426(g) and 6427(e)(3), would be allowable to a claimant either as a credit under section 6426 or a payment under section 6427 with respect to sales and uses of mixtures during a calendar quarter is allowed only as a credit under section 6426 to the extent such amount does not exceed the claimant's tax liability under section 4081 for the calendar quarter.

(2) The aggregate amount allowed to a claimant as a payment under section 6427 or an income tax credit under section 34 with respect to sales and uses of mixtures during a calendar quarter shall not exceed the amount that, but for the coordination rules in sections 6426(g) and 6427(e)(3), would be allowable to the claimant with respect to such sales and uses reduced by the claimant's tax liability under section 4081 for the calendar quarter.

(b) *Limitations applicable to alternative fuel.*—In the case of alternative fuel, the following limitations apply:

(1) The aggregate amount that, but for the coordination rules in sections 6426(g) and 6427(e)(3), would be allowable to a claimant either as a credit under section 6426 or a payment under section 6427 with respect to sales and uses of alternative fuel during a calendar quarter is allowed only as a credit under section 6426 to the extent such amount does not exceed the claimant's tax liability under section 4041 for the calendar quarter.

(2) The aggregate amount allowed to a claimant as a payment under section 6427 or an income tax credit under section 34 with respect to sales and uses of alternative fuel during a calendar quarter shall not exceed the amount that, but for the coordination rules in sections 6426(g) and 6427(e)(3), would be allowable to the claimant with respect to such sales and uses reduced by the claimant's tax liability under section 4041 for the calendar quarter.

(c) *Effective/applicability dates.*—This section is applicable on and after the date of publication of these regulations as final regulations in the **Federal Register**. [Reg. §48.6426-7.]

Excise Taxes: Taxable Fuel: Returns: Definitions

Excise Taxes: Taxable Fuel: Returns: Definitions.—Amendments to Reg. §48.6427-8, relating to credits and payments for alcohol mixtures, biodiesel mixtures, renewable diesel mixtures, alternative fuel mixtures, and alternative fuel sold for use or used as a fuel and relating to the definition of gasoline and diesel fuel, are proposed (published in the Federal Register on July 29, 2008) (REG-155087-05).

Par. 21. Section 48.6427-8 is amended as follows:

1. Revising paragraph (b)(1)(v) and adding (b)(1)(vii)(E).

2. Paragraph (b)(1)(vii)(C) is amended by removing the language "vehicle; or" and adding "vehicle;" in its place.

3. Paragraph (b)(1)(vii)(D) is amended by removing the language "6427(b)(3))." and adding "6427(b)(3)); or" in its place.

4. Paragraph (f) is amended by removing the language from the first sentence "1994." and adding "1994, and paragraph (b)(1)(vii)(E), which is applicable after the date these regulations are published as final regulations in the **Federal Register**." in its place."

The revision and addition read as follows:

§ 48.6427-8. Diesel fuel and kerosene; claims by ultimate purchasers.

* * *

(b) * * *

(1) * * *

(v) The diesel fuel or kerosene was not used on a farm for farming purposes (as defined in § 48.6420-4) or, except in the case of fuel described in paragraph (b)(1)(vii)(E) of the section, by a State;

* * *

(vii) * * *

(E) For the exclusive use, in the case of blended taxable fuel that is produced by a State and is both diesel fuel and a mixture (as defined in § 48.6426-1(b)), of the State that produced the blended taxable fuel.

* * *

Gasoline and Diesel Fuel Excise Tax: Rules Relating to Gasohol: Tax on Compressed Natural Gas

Gasoline and Diesel Fuel Excise Tax: Rules Relating to Gasohol: Tax on Compressed Natural Gas.—Reg. § 48.6427-10, relating to gasohol blending and the taxes on diesel fuel and compressed natural gas, is proposed (published in the Federal Register on October 19, 1994).

☐ Par. 29. Section 48.6427-10 is added to read as follows:

§ 48.6427-10. Credit or payment with respect to gasoline used to produce gasohol.—(a) *Conditions to allowance of credit or payment.*—A claim for credit or payment with respect to gasoline is allowed under section 6427(f) only if—

(1) The gasoline to which the claim relates was taxed at the aggregate rate of tax imposed by section 4081 without regard to section 4081(c);

(2) The claimant used the gasoline to produce gasohol (as defined in § 48.4081-6(b)(2)) that was sold or used in the claimant's trade or business; and

(3) The claimant has filed a timely claim for a credit or payment that contains the information required under paragraph (c) of this section.

(b) *Form of claim.*—Each claim for a payment under section 6427(f) must be made on Form 8849 (or such other form as the Commissioner may designate) in accordance with the instructions for that form. Each claim for a credit under section 6427(f) must be made on Form 4136 (or such other form as the Commissioner may designate) in accordance with the instructions for that form.

(c) *Content of claim.*—Each claim for credit or payment under section 6427(f) must contain the following information with respect to each batch of gasohol that contains the gasoline covered by the claim:

(1) The claimant's registration number, if the claimant is a registered gasohol blender (as defined in § 48.4081-6(b)(4)).

(2) The name, address, and employer identification number of the person that sold the claimant the gasoline.

(3) The date and location of the sale of the gasoline.

(4) The volume of the gasoline.

(5) The name, address, and employer identification number of the person that sold the claimant the alcohol.

(6) The date and location of the sale of the alcohol.

(7) The volume and type of the alcohol.

(8) In the case of a claim for a payment, a copy of the invoice or other record of sale relating to each purchase of alcohol.

(9) The written or typed name of the individual signing the claim and the telephone number of that individual.

(10) The amount of credit or payment claimed.

(d) *Time for filing claim.*—For rules relating to the time for filing a claim under section 6427(f), see section 6427(i). A claim under section 6427(f) is not considered to be filed unless it contains all the information required by paragraph (c) of this section and received at the place required by the form.

(e) *Effective date.*—This section is effective with respect to claims relating to gasohol produced after December 31, 1994. [Reg. § 48.6427-10.]

Excise Taxes: Taxable Fuel: Returns: Definitions

Excise Taxes: Taxable Fuel: Returns: Definitions.—Reg. § 48.6427-12, relating to credits and payments for alcohol mixtures, biodiesel mixtures, renewable diesel mixtures, alternative fuel mixtures, and alternative fuel sold for use or used as a fuel and relating to the definition of gasoline and diesel fuel, is proposed (published in the Federal Register on July 29, 2008) (REG-155087-05).

Par. 22. Section 48.6427-12 is added to read as follows:

§ 48.6427-12. Alcohol, alternative fuel, biodiesel, and renewable diesel.—(a) *In general.*—This section contains special rules for payments related to fuels containing alcohol, alternative fuel, biodiesel, and renewable diesel. Other rules for these payments are in §§ 48.6426-1 through 48.6426-7.

(b) *Coordination with excise tax credit.*—If the aggregate amount a person receives as a payment under section 6427(e) with respect to sales and uses of mixtures during a calendar quarter exceeds the amount allowed under § 48.6426-7(a), the excess constitutes an excessive amount for purposes of section 6206 and such amount, as well as the civil penalty under section 6675, may be assessed as if it were a tax imposed by section 4081. If the excessive amount is repaid to the government, with interest from the date of the payment (section 6602), on or before the due date of the Form 720, "Quarterly Federal Excise Tax Return," for the calendar quarter, the claim for the excessive amount will be treated as due to reasonable cause and the penalty under section 6675 will not be imposed with respect to the claim. If a person claims an income tax credit under section 34 in lieu of a payment under section 6427(e) with respect to sales and uses of mixtures during a calendar quarter and the aggregate amount claimed as an income tax credit with respect to such sales and uses exceeds the amount allowed under § 48.6426-7(a)(2), the income tax rules related to assessing an underpayment of income tax liability apply. The section 6675 penalty for excessive claims with respect to fuels does not apply in the case of section 34 income tax credits. Similar rules apply to excessive claims under sections 34 or 6427 with respect to sales and uses of alternative fuel.

(c) *Payment computation for certain blenders.*—(1) *In general.*—This paragraph (c) applies to a blender for any calendar quarter in which the blender's entire tax liability under section 4081 is based solely on the volume of alcohol in alcohol fuel mixtures, biodiesel in biodiesel mixtures, renewable diesel in renewable diesel mixtures, or alternative fuel in alternative fuel mixtures. If this paragraph (c) applies for a calendar quarter, the blender may use the following procedure to determine the amount it may claim as an income tax credit under

section 34 or a payment under section 6427(e) with respect to each mixture that it sells or uses during the quarter:

(i) First, determine the amount allowed under section 6426 as a credit on Form 720 by multiplying the volume of untaxed liquid used to produce the mixture by the tax imposed per gallon on the untaxed liquid.

(ii) Then, determine the total credit and payment allowable by multiplying the volume of untaxed liquid used to produce the mixture by the tax credit rate per gallon.

(iii) Then, subtract the amount determined in paragraph (c)(1)(i) of this section (the section 6426 credit amount) from the amount determined in paragraph (c)(1)(ii) of this section. This difference is the amount of the payment or income tax credit that may be claimed with respect to that mixture.

(2) *Example.*—The following example illustrates the provisions of this paragraph (c):

(i) P is a biodiesel mixture producer. P produces blended taxable fuel outside of the bulk transfer/terminal system by adding biodiesel that is agribiodiesel to taxed diesel fuel. See §§ 48.4081-1(c)(1) and 48.4081-3(g). P has no § 4081 liability other than its liability as a blender on its sale of the biodiesel mixture. During the period August 1 through August 10 (at which time the tax rate on diesel fuel is $0.244 per gallon and the claim amount on agri-biodiesel is $1.00 per gallon), P uses 5,000 gallons of agri-biodiesel to produce a biodiesel mixture. P determines that it may claim $3,780 as a payment under section 6427(e) with respect to this mixture. P computes this amount by—

(A) Multiplying 5,000 (gallons of agri-biodiesel) × $0.244 (tax imposed per gallon) = $1,220;

(B) Multiplying 5,000 (gallons of agri-biodiesel) × $1.00 (tax credit rate per gallon) = $5,000; and

(C) Subtracting $1,220 from $5,000 = $3,780.

(ii) On August 11, P files Form 8849 for the period August 1 - August 10. To avoid an excessive claim, P limits the claim on Form 8849 to $3,780 reporting 3,780 gallons of agri-biodiesel.

(iii) On Form 720 P reports liability for IRS No. 60(c) of $1,220 (5,000 gallons × $.244) and claims a credit on Schedule C for $1,220 for period August 1 -August 10, reporting on Schedule C 1,220 gallons of agri-biodiesel.

(d) *Effective/applicability date.*—This section is applicable on and after the date these regulations are published as final regulations in the **Federal Register**. [Reg. § 48.6427-12.]

INTEREST

Modification of Interest Payments for Certain Periods

Modification of Interest Payments for Certain Periods.—Reproduced below is the text of proposed amendments to Reg. § 301.6601-1, relating to the accrual of interest on overpayments and underpayments of tax (published in the Federal Register on October 9, 1984).

☐ Paragraph 1. Section 301.6601-1 is amended as follows:

1. Paragraph (d) is revised to read as set forth below.

2. Paragraphs (e)(1) and (e)(3) are revised to read as set forth below.

3. New paragraphs (e)(4) and (e)(5) are added as set forth below.

§ 301.6601-1. Interest on underpayments.
* * *

(d) *Suspension of interest; waiver of restrictions on assessment.*—In the case of a deficiency determined by a district director (or an assistant regional commissioner, appellate) with respect to any income, estate, gift tax, or excise tax imposed by chapters 41, 42, 43, 44, and 45, if the taxpayer files with such internal revenue officer an agreement waiving the restrictions on assessment of such deficiency, and if notice and demand for payment of such deficiency is not made within 30 days after the filing of such waiver, no interest shall be imposed on the deficiency for the period beginning immediately after such 30th day and ending on the date notice and demand is made. In the case of an agreement with respect to a portion of the deficiency, the rules as set forth in this paragraph are applicable only to that portion of the deficiency to which the agreement relates.

(e) *Income tax reduced by carryback.*—(1)(i) The carryback of a net operating loss, net capital loss, or a credit carryback as defined by § 301.6611-1(f)(1) shall not affect the computation of interest on any income tax for the period commencing with the last day prescribed for the payment of such tax and ending with the filing date, as defined in paragraph (e)(4) of this section, for the taxable year in which the loss or credit arises. For example, if the carryback of a net operating loss, a net capital loss, or a credit carryback to a prior taxable period eliminates or reduces a deficiency in income tax for that period, the full amount of the deficiency will bear interest at the annual rate established under section 6621 from the last date prescribed for payment of such tax until the filing date for the taxable year in which the loss or credit arose. Interest will continue to run beyond such filing date on any portion of the deficiency which is not eliminated by the carryback. With respect to any portion of a credit carryback from a taxable year attributable to a net operating loss carryback, a capital loss carryback or other credit carryback from a subsequent taxable year, such credit carryback shall not affect the computation of interest on any income tax for the period commencing with the last day prescribed for the payment of such tax and ending with the filing date for such subsequent taxable year.

(ii) The provisions of paragraph (e)(1)(i) of this section are illustrated by the following examples.

Example (1). Corporation L is a calendar year taxpayer. For taxable years 1980 and 1981, L reported no income tax liability. For 1982, L has an underpayment of income tax of $500. In 1983, L has a net operating loss which L carries back to 1982, reducing the underpayment to $200. For purposes of computing the interest on the underpayment of income tax for 1982, interest will accrue on the $500 beginning on March 15, 1983. Beginning on March 16, 1984, interest on the 1982 income tax underpayment will accrue on only $200.

Example (2). Corporation R is a calendar year taxpayer. For taxable years 1980, 1981 and 1982, R reported no income tax liability. In 1983, R had a net operating loss which could not be carried forward to 1984 because R had reported no income tax liability for 1984. As a result of an audit conducted on R in 1985, a $500 deficiency is assessed on R for taxable year 1982. R applied the 1983 net operating loss to the $500 assessed deficiency, thus reducing the deficiency to $200. Interest begins accruing on the $500 deficiency on March 15, 1983. Beginning on March 16, 1984, interest on the 1982 deficiency will accrue on only $200.

* * *

(3) Where there has been an allowance of an overpayment attributable to a net operating loss carryback, a capital loss carryback or a credit carryback as defined by § 301.6611-1(f)(1) and all or part of such allowance is later determined to be excessive, interest shall be computed on the excessive amount from the filing date for the year in which the net operating loss, net capital loss, or credit arose until the date on which the repayment of such excessive amount is received. Where there has been an allowance of an overpayment with respect to any portion of a credit carryback from a taxable year attributable to a net operating loss carryback or a capital loss carryback from a subsequent taxable year and all or part of such allowance is later determined to be excessive, interest shall be computed on the excessive amount from the filing date for such subsequent taxable year until the date on which the repayment of such excessive amount is received.

(4) For purposes of paragraph (e) of this section, the term "filing date" means the last day fixed by law or regulation for filing the return of income tax for the taxable year (determined without regard to any extension of time).

(5) Section 301.6601-1(e)(1), (3) and (4) apply to interest accruing after October 3, 1982. See 26 CFR 301.6601-1(e) (revised as of April 1, 1982) for rules applicable to interest accruing before October 4, 1982.

Modification of Interest Payments for Certain Periods

Modification of Interest Payments for Certain Periods.—Reproduced below is the text of proposed amendments to Reg. § 301.6611-1, relating to the accrual of interest on overpayments and underpayments of tax (published in the Federal Register on October 9, 1984).

☐ Par. 2. Section 301.6611-1 is revised to read as follows:

§ 301.6611-1. Interest on overpayments.—(a) *General rule.*—Except as otherwise provided, interest shall be allowed on any overpayment of any tax at the annual rate established under section 6621 from the date of overpayment of the tax.

(b) *Date of overpayment.*—(1) *In general.*—Except as provided in section 6401(a), relating to assessment and collection after the expiration of the applicable period of limitation, there can be no overpayment of tax until the entire tax liability has been satisfied. Therefore, the dates of overpayment of any tax are the date of payment of the first amount which (when added to previous payments) is in excess of the tax liability (including any interest, addition to the tax, or additional amount) and the dates of payment of all amounts subsequently paid with respect to such tax liability. For rules relating to the determination of the date of payment in the case of an advance payment of tax, a payment of estimated tax, and a credit for income tax withholding, see paragraph (d) of this section.

(2) *Period for which interest is allowable in the case of credits of overpayment.*—(i) *General rule.*—If an overpayment of tax is credited,

interest shall be allowed from the date of overpayment to the due date (as determined under paragraph (b)(2)(ii) of this section) of the amount against which such overpayment is credited. See paragraph (b)(4) of this section for late returns.

(ii) *Determination of due date.*—(A) *In general.*—The term "due date", as used in this section, means the last day fixed by law or regulations for the payment of the tax (determined without regard to any extension of time), and not the date on which the district director or the director of the regional service center makes demand for the payment of the tax. Therefore, the due date of a tax is the date fixed for the payment of the tax or the several installments thereof.

(B) *Tax payable in installments.*—(1) *In general.*—In the case of a credit against a tax, where the taxpayer had properly elected to pay the tax in installments, the due date is the date prescribed for the payment of the installment against which the credit is applied.

(2) *Delinquent installment.*—If the taxpayer is delinquent in payment of an installment of tax and a notice and demand has been issued for the payment of the delinquent installment and

the remaining installments, the due date of each remaining installment shall then be the date of such notice and demand.

(C) *Tax or installment not yet due.*—If a taxpayer agrees to the crediting of an overpayment against tax or an installment of tax and the schedule of allowance is signed prior to the date on which such tax or installment would otherwise become due, then the due date of such tax or installment shall be the date on which such schedule is signed.

(D) *Assessed interest.*—In the case of a credit against assessed interest, the due date is the date of the assessment of such interest.

(E) *Additional amount, addition to the tax, or assessable penalty.*—In the case of a credit against an amount assessed as an additional amount, addition to the tax, or assessable penalty, the due date is the date of the assessment.

(F) *Estimated income tax for succeeding year.*—If the taxpayer elects to have all or part of the overpayment shown by his return applied to his estimated tax for his succeeding taxable year, no interest shall be allowed on such portion of the overpayment credited and such amount shall be applied as a payment on account of the estimated tax for such year or the installments thereof.

(3) *Period for which interest is allowable in the case of refunds of overpayment.*—If an overpayment of tax is refunded, interest shall be

Tax liability

Assessed	$1,000
Correct liability	900
Overassessment	100

Record of payments

Mar. 15, 1955	500
June 15, 1955	500

Since the correct liability in this case is $900, the payment of $500 made on March 15, 1955, and $400 of the payment made on June 15, 1955, are applied in satisfaction of the tax liability. The balance of the payment made on June 15, 1955 ($100) constitutes the amount of the overpayment, and the date on which such payment was made would be the date of the overpayment from which interest would be computed.

Tax liability

Original assessment	$50,000
Deficiency assessment	10,000
Total assessed	60,000
Correct liability	35,000
Overassessment	25,000

Record of payments

Mar. 15, 1955	25,000
June 15, 1955	25,000
Nov. 15, 1956	5,000
Nov. 26, 1956	5,000

Since the correct liability in this case is $35,000, the entire payment of $25,000 made on March 15, 1955, and $10,000 of the payment made on June 15, 1955, are applied in satisfaction of the tax liability. The balance of the payment made on June 15, 1955 ($15,000), plus the

Date	Amount of overpayment
June 15, 1955	$15,000
Nov. 15, 1956	5,000
Nov. 26, 1956	5,000

The amount of any interest paid with respect to the deficiency of $10,000 is also an overpayment.

Example (3). Corporation Z failed to file a timely income tax return for the calendar year 1982. Z filed the 1982 return on Novem-

TAX LIABILITY

Original assessment	$50,000
Deficiency assessment	10,000
Total assessed	$60,000
Correct liability	35,000
Overassessment	$25,000

RECORD OF PAYMENTS

March 15, 1983	$50,000
Nov. 15, 1984	10,000

Since the correct liability in this case is $35,000, only $35,000 of the $50,000 payment made on March 15, 1983 is applied in satisfaction of the tax liability. The balance of the payment made on March 15, 1983

Date	Amount of overpayment
Nov. 20, 1983	$15,000
Nov. 15, 1984	10,000

The amount of any interest paid with respect to the deficiency of $10,000 is also an overpayment.

allowed from the date of the overpayment to a date determined by the district director or the director of the regional service center, which shall be not more than 30 days prior to the date of the refund check. The acceptance of a refund check shall not deprive the taxpayer of the right to make a claim for any additional overpayment and interest thereon, provided the claim is made within the applicable period of limitation. However, if a taxpayer does not accept a refund check, no additional interest on the amount of the overpayment included in such check shall be allowed. See paragraph (b)(4) of this section for late returns.

(4) *Late returns.*—For the purpose of paragraphs (b)(2), (b)(3) and (f) of this section, if, after October 3, 1982, a return is filed after the last date prescribed for filing such return (including any extension of time for filing the return), no interest shall be allowed or paid for any day before the date on which the return is filed. A return will not be treated as filed until it is filed in processible form. For rules relating to the processible form requirement, see paragraph (h)(1) of this section.

(c) *Examples.*—The provisions of paragraph (b) of this section may be illustrated by the following examples:

Example (1). Corporation X files an income tax return on March 15, 1955, for the calendar year 1954 disclosing a tax liability of $1,000 and elects to pay the tax in installments. Subsequent to payment of the final installment, the correct tax liability is determined to be $900.

Example (2). Corporation Y files an income tax return for the calendar year 1954 on March 15, 1955, disclosing a tax liability of $50,000, and elects to pay the tax in installments. On October 15, 1956, a deficiency in the amount of $10,000 is assessed and is paid in equal amounts on November 15 and November 26, 1956. On April 15, 1957, it is determined that the correct tax liability of the taxpayer for 1954 is only $35,000.

amounts paid on November 15 ($5,000), and November 26, 1956 ($5,000), constitute the amount of the overpayment. The dates of the overpayments from which interest would be computed are as follows:

ber 20, 1983, disclosing a tax liability of $50,000 which was paid in full on March 15, 1983. On October 15, 1984, a deficiency in the amount of $10,000 is assessed and is paid on November 15, 1984. On April 15, 1985, it is determined that the correct tax liability of the taxpayer for 1982 is only $35,000.

($15,000), plus the amount paid on November 15, 1984 ($10,000), constitute the amount of the overpayment. The dates of the overpayment from which interest would be computed are as follows:

(d) *Advance payment of tax, payment of estimated tax, and credit for income tax withholding.*—In the case of an advance payment of tax, a payment of estimated income tax, or a credit for income tax withholding, the provisions of section 6513 (except the provisions of subsection (c) thereof), applicable in determining the date of payment of tax for purposes of the period of limitations on credit or refund, shall apply in determining the date of overpayment for purposes of computing interest thereon.

(e) *Refund of overpayment within 45 days after return is filed.*—No interest shall be allowed on any overpayment of tax imposed by subtitle A of the Code if such overpayment is refunded—

(1) In the case of a return filed on or before the last date prescribed for filing the return of such tax (determined without regard to any extension of time for filing such return), within 45 days after such last date, or

(2) After December 17, 1966, in the case of a return filed after the last day prescribed for filing the return, within 45 days after the date on which the return is filed.

For the purpose of this paragraph (e), a return filed after October 3, 1982, will not be considered filed until it is filed in processible form, (as determined under paragraph (h)(1) of this section).

(f) *Refund of income tax caused by carrybacks.*—(1) *In general.*—If any overpayment of tax imposed by subtitle A of the Code results from the carryback of net operating loss, a net capital loss, or a credit carryback, such overpayment, for purposes of this section, shall be deemed not to have been made prior to the filing date for the taxable year in which the loss or credit arises, or, with respect to any portion of a credit carryback from a taxable year attributable to a net operating loss carryback, a capital loss carryback, or other credit carryback from a subsequent taxable year, such overpayment shall be deemed not to have been made prior to the close of the filing date for such subsequent taxable year. The term "credit carryback" means any investment credit carryback, work incentive program credit carryback, new employee credit carryback, research credit carryback, or employee stock ownership credit carryback. The term "filing date" means the last day fixed by law or regulation for filing the return of tax imposed by subtitle A for the taxable year (determined without regard to any extension of time).

(2) *Special rules for carrybacks.*—(i) *In general.*—An overpayment of tax described in paragraph (f)(1) of this section is treated as an overpayment for the loss year (as defined in paragraph (f)(2)(ii) of this section). In applying sections 6611(e) and 6611(f)(3)(B), and solely for purposes of those sections, the following rules apply:

(A) No interest is payable if the overpayment for the loss year is refunded within 45 days after the later of the filing of the claim for refund of the overpayment or the filing date of the return of tax imposed by subtitle A for that year. For this purpose, if an application for tentative carryback adjustment (an application under section 6411(a)) with respect to a particular overpayment is filed after the filing of a claim for refund for the overpayment, the claim for refund is treated as filed on the date the application for tentative carryback adjustment is filed;

(B) A claim for refund of the overpayment will not be treated as filed unless it is filed in processible form (as described in paragraph (h)(1) of this section);

(C) The term "claim" includes claim for credit or refund (*e.g.*, an amended tax return (the Form 1040X or Form 1120X for individuals or corporations, respectively)) and an application for a tentative carryback adjustment; and

(D) The filing date of the return of tax imposed by subtitle A may not be earlier than the last date prescribed for filing such return (determined without extensions).

(ii) *Loss year.*—The term "loss year" means—

(A) In the case of a carryback of a net operating loss or net capital loss, the taxable year in which such loss arises;

(B) In the case of a credit carryback (as defined by paragraph (f)(1) of this section), the taxable year in which such credit carryback arises; and

(C) In the case of any portion of a credit carryback from a taxable year to which a net operating loss, a net capital loss, or any other credit carryback was carried from a subsequent taxable year, the subsequent taxable year.

(iii) *Cross references.*—See section 6611(i) which treats the return of tax imposed by subtitle A for the loss year as not filed for purposes of section 6611(e) unless it is filed in processible form. Also see section 6611(b)(3) and paragraph (b)(4) of this section for rules that apply to late returns.

(iv) *Effective date.*—Section 301.6611-1(f) applies to interest accruing after October 3, 1982. See 26 CFR 301.6611-1(f) (revised as of April 1, 1982) for rules applicable to interest accruing before October 4, 1982.

(v) *Examples.*—The provisions of this section may be illustrated by the following examples:

Example (1). Corporation Q is a calendar year taxpayer. For taxable years 1978, 1979, and 1980, net capital gains were reported. However, for 1981 Q had a net capital loss which Q could carry back to 1978, resulting in an overpayment for that year. Q properly filed the 1981 tax return on March 15, 1982. Q properly filed the claim for refund of the overpayment resulting from the carryback on November 15, 1982.

(a) If the refund is made within 45 days after filing the claim then interest will accrue between January 1, 1982 and October 3, 1982.

(b) If the refund is made more than 45 days after filing the claim then interest will accrue from January 1, 1982.

Example (2). Corporation R reports income on a fiscal year ending August 31. For taxable years ending August 31, 1979, 1980, and 1981, net capital gains were reported. However, for the taxable year ending August 31, 1982, R had a net capital loss which R could carry back to 1979, resulting in an overpayment for that year. R properly filed the 1982 tax return on October 15, 1982. R properly filed the claim for refund of the overpayment on November 10, 1982.

(a) If the refund is made within 45 days after November 15, 1982, then interest will accrue from September 1, 1982 until October 3, 1982.

(b) If the refund is made more than 45 days after November 15, 1982, then interest will accrue from September 1, 1982 until October 3, 1982 and from November 15, 1982.

Example (3). Corporation S is a calendar year taxpayer. For taxable years 1979, 1980, and 1981, net capital gains were reported. However, for 1982, S had a net capital loss which S could carry back to 1979, resulting in an overpayment for that year. S properly filed the 1982 tax return on February 4, 1983. S properly filed the claim for refund of the overpayment on February 15, 1983.

(a) If the refund is made within 45 days after March 15, 1983, then no interest will accrue on the overpayment.

(b) If the refund is made after 45 days of March 15, 1983, then interest will accrue from March 15, 1983.

Example (4). Corporation Y is a calendar year taxpayer. For taxable years 1979, 1980, and 1981 net capital gains were reported. However, for 1982, Y had a net capital loss which Y could carry back to 1979, resulting in an overpayment for that year. Y properly filed the 1982 tax return on March 1, 1983. Y properly filed the claim for refund of the overpayment on May 15, 1983.

(a) If the refund is made within 45 days after May 15, 1983, then no interest will accrue on the overpayment.

(b) If the refund is made more than 45 days after May 15, 1983, then interest will accrue from March 15, 1983.

Example (5). Corporation Z is a calendar year taxpayer. For taxable years 1979, 1980, and 1981, net capital gains were reported. However, for 1982, Z had a net capital loss which Z could carry back to 1979, resulting in an overpayment for that year. Z filed the 1982 tax return late, on November 1, 1983. Z properly filed the claim for refund for overpayment on November 15, 1983.

(a) If the refund is made within 45 days after November 15, 1983, then no interest will accrue on the overpayment.

(b) If the refund is made more than 45 days after November 15, 1983, then interest will accrue from November 1, 1983.

(g) *Refund of income tax caused by carryback of foreign taxes.*—(1) *In general.*—For purposes of paragraph (a) of this section, any overpayment of tax resulting from a carryback of tax paid or accrued to foreign countries or possessions of the United States shall be deemed not to have been paid or accrued before the filing date (as defined in section 6611(f)(3)) for the taxable year under subtitle F of the Code in which such taxes were in fact paid or accrued.

(2) *Effective date.*—Section 301.6611-1(g) applies to interest accruing after October 3, 1982. See 26 CFR 301.6611-1(g) (revised as of April 1, 1982) for rules applicable to interest accruing before October 4, 1982.

(h) *Processible form.*—(1) *In general.*—A return is in processible form if—

(i) The return is filed on a form permitted under the Code or regulations (see paragraph (h)(2) of this section), and

(ii) The return contains the required information described in paragraph (h)(3) of this section.

(2) *Return on permitted form; components of return.*—In applying paragraph (h)(1)(i) of this section, the term "return" includes all components of the return. A component of the return is a required attachment, supporting document, or schedule required by the return, whether or not the information from the document or schedule appears on the return itself. Supporting documents and schedules include, for example, Form W-2, relating to wages; Schedule D, relating to capital gain or loss; Form 3903, relating to moving expenses; Schedule G, relating to income averaging; Form 3468, relating to investment credit; and Form 4625, relating to minimum tax. The term "form permitted under the Code or regulations" includes a

substitute form, schedule, or chart containing the same general provisions as the proper form, so long as the taxpayer complies with all revenue procedures relating to substitute forms in effect at that time.

(3) *Information required.*—The return must contain—

(i) The taxpayer's name, address, identifying number, and authorized signature, and

(ii) Sufficient required information on the return and its components (as defined in paragraph (h)(2) of this section) to permit the mathematical verification of the tax liability as shown on the return.

However, the information required by subdivisions (i) and (ii) is required in the case of a component of the return (within the meaning of paragraph (h)(2) of this section) only to the extent required by that component.

(4) *Examples.*—The provisions of paragraph (h) of this section may be illustrated by the following examples:

Example (1). A, an individual calendar year taxpayer, filed A's 1982 tax return on the due date, April 15, 1983. The return was properly completed except for A's failure to include schedule D, relating to capital gains or losses, with the filed return. On June 17, 1983, A's schedule D was filed. Because A did not file schedule D until June 17, 1983, there was insufficient information to mathematically verify the tax liability. Therefore, A's return is treated as filed on June 17, 1983 for purposes of section 6611(b)(3) and (e).

Example (2). B, an individual calendar year taxpayer, filed B's 1982 tax return on the due date, April 15, 1983. The return was completed properly except for B's mathematical error in totaling B's sources of income resulting in an incorrect computation of liability.

The error was discovered, and on July 24, 1983, B paid the additional tax. There was sufficient information filed with the return to compute the proper tax liability. Therefore, the return is treated as filed on April 15, 1983.

Example (3). Corporation X, a calendar year taxpayer, filed its 1982 tax return on the due date, March 15, 1983. The return was properly completed except that X did not use schedule A for cost of goods sold. However, X did include with the filed return its own schedule of cost of goods sold drafted on a substitute form and containing provisions identical with schedule A as required by the revenue procedures relating to substitute forms in effect at the time. Therefore, the return will be treated as filed on March 15, 1983.

Example (4). C, an individual calendar year taxpayer, filed C's 1982 tax return on the due date, April 15, 1983. The return was properly completed except for C's failure to include Schedule A, relating to itemized deductions, with the filed return. Because C's 1040 return reflects C's choice to utilize Schedule A, and C failed to file Schedule A, there was insufficient information for mathematically verifying the tax liability. Therefore, for purposes of sections 611(b)(3) and (e), C's return is not treated as filed. The return will be treated as filed when either Schedule A is filed or an amended return, reflecting C's election not to itemize, is filed.

(5) *Application.*—The requirements of section 6611(i) and this paragraph (h), relating to the processible form requirement, apply to sections 6611(b)(3), relating to late returns, 6611(e), relating to income tax refund within 45 days of a return, and 6611(h), relating to the windfall profit tax. See also, paragraph (f)(2)(i)(B) of this section (relating to interest on overpayments relating to certain carrybacks).

Interest Rate: Overpayments and Underpayments

Interest Rate: Overpayments and Underpayments: Determination.—Temporary Reg. §301.6621-2T, relating to the increased rate of interest on substantial underpayments attributable to tax motivated transactions, is also proposed as a final regulation and, when adopted, will become Reg. §301.6621-2 (published in the Federal Register on December 28, 1984).

§301.6621-2. Questions and answers relating to the increased rate of interest on substantial underpayments attributable to certain tax motivated transactions.

ADDITIONS TO TAX, ADDITIONAL AMOUNTS, ASSESSABLE PENALTIES

Individual Retirement Plans: Simplified Employee Pensions: Qualified Voluntary Employee Contributions

Individual Retirement Plans: Simplified Employee Pensions: Qualified Voluntary Employee Contributions.—Reproduced below is the text of proposed Reg. §301.6652-4, relating to individual retirement plans, simplified employee pensions and qualified voluntary employee contributions (published in the Federal Register on January 23, 1984).

* * *

☐ Par. 13. There is added after §301.6652-3 the following new section:

§301.6652-4. Failure to file information with respect to qualified voluntary employee contributions.—(a) *Failure to make annual reports to employees.*—In the case of a failure to make an annual report required by §1.219(a)-5(g) which contains the information required by such section on the date prescribed therefor, there shall be paid (on notice and demand by the Secretary and in the same manner as tax) by the person failing to make such annual report an amount

equal to $25 for each participant with respect to when there was a failure to make such report, multiplied by the number of years during which such failure continues.

(b) *Limitation.*—The total amount imposed under this section on any person shall not exceed $10,000 with respect to any calendar year.

Estate and Person Acquiring Property from Decedent: Consistent Basis Reporting

Estate and Person Acquiring Property from Decedent: Consistent Basis Reporting—Reg. §1.6662-8, providing guidance regarding the requirement that a recipient's basis in certain property acquired from a decedent be consistent with the value of the property as finally determined for Federal estate tax purposes, is proposed (published in the Federal Register on March 4, 2016) (REG-127923-15).

Par. 6. Section 1.6662-8 is added to read as follows:

§1.6662-8. Inconsistent estate basis reporting.—(a) *In general.*—Section 6662(a) and (b)(8) impose an accuracy-related penalty on the portion of any underpayment of tax required to be shown on a return that is attributable to an inconsistent estate basis.

(b) *Inconsistent estate basis.*—In accordance with section 6662(k), there is an *inconsistent estate basis* to the extent that a taxpayer claims a basis, without regard to the adjustments described in §1.1014-10(a)(2), in property described in paragraph (c) of this section that exceeds that property's final value as determined under §1.1014-10(c).

(c) *Applicable property.*—The property to which this section applies is property described in §1.1014-10(b) that is reported or required to be reported on a return required by section 6018 filed after July 31, 2015.

(d) *Effective/applicability date.*—Upon the publication of the Treasury Decision adopting these rules as final in the **Federal Register**, this section will apply to property described in §1.1014-10(b) acquired from a decedent or by reason of the death of a decedent whose return required by section 6018 is filed after July 31, 2015. Persons may rely upon these rules before the date of publication of the Treasury Decision adopting these rules as final in the **Federal Register**. [Reg. §1.6662-8.]

Allocation and Apportionment of Deductions and Foreign Tax Credit: Guidance

Allocation and Apportionment of Deductions and Foreign Tax Credit: Guidance.—Amendments to Reg. §301.6689-1, relating to the allocation and apportionment of deductions and creditable foreign taxes, the definition of financial services income, foreign tax redeterminations, availability of foreign tax credits under the transition tax, and the application of the foreign tax credit limitation to consolidated groups, are proposed (published in the Federal Register on December 17, 2019) (REG-105495-19).

Par. 31. Section 301.6689-1, as proposed to be added at 72 FR 62807 (November 7, 2007), is further revised to read as follows:

§ 301.6689-1. Failure to file notice of redetermination of foreign income taxes.—(a) *Application of civil penalty.*—If a foreign tax redetermination occurs, and the taxpayer failed to notify the Internal Revenue Service (IRS) on or before the date and in the manner prescribed in § 1.905-4 of this chapter, or as required under section 404A(g)(2), for giving notice of a foreign tax redetermination, then, unless paragraph (d) of this section applies, there is added to the deficiency (or the imputed underpayment as determined under section 6225) attributable to such redetermination an amount determined under paragraph (b) of this section. Subchapter B of chapter 63 of the Internal Revenue Code (relating to deficiency proceedings) does not apply with respect to the assessment of the amount of the penalty.

(b) *Amount of the penalty.*—The amount of the penalty shall be equal to—

(1) Five percent of the deficiency (or imputed underpayment) if the failure is for not more than one month, plus

(2) An additional five percent of the deficiency (or imputed underpayment) for each month (or fraction thereof) during which the failure continues, but not to exceed in the aggregate twenty-five percent of the deficiency (or imputed underpayment).

(c) *Foreign tax redetermination defined.*—For purposes of this section, a foreign tax redetermination is any redetermination for which a notice is required under sections 905(c) or 404A(g)(2). See §§ 1.905-3 through 1.905-5 of this chapter for rules relating to the notice requirement under section 905(c).

(d) *Reasonable cause.*—The penalty set forth in this section shall not apply if it is established to the satisfaction of the IRS that the failure to file the notification within the prescribed time was due to reasonable cause and not due to willful neglect. An affirmative showing of reasonable cause must be made in the form of a written statement that sets forth all the facts alleged as reasonable cause for the failure to file the notification on time and that contains a declaration by the taxpayer that the statement is made under the penalties of perjury. This statement must be filed with the Internal Revenue Service Center in which the notification was required to be filed. The taxpayer must file this statement with the notice required under section 905(c) or section 404A(g)(2). If the taxpayer exercised ordinary business care and prudence and was nevertheless unable to file the notification within the prescribed time, then the delay will be considered to be due to reasonable cause and not willful neglect.

(e) *Applicability date.*—This section applies to foreign tax redeterminations occurring in taxable years ending on or after December 16, 2019, and to foreign tax redeterminations of foreign corporations occurring in taxable years that end with or within a taxable year of a United States shareholder ending on or after December 16, 2019.

Foreign Tax Credits

Foreign Tax Credits: Foreign Tax Redeterminations: Notifications.—Temporary Reg. § 301.6689-1T, relating to a taxpayer's obligation to file notification of a foreign tax redetermination, to make adjustments to a taxpayer's pools of foreign taxes and earnings and profits, and the imposition of the civil penalty for failure to file such notice or report such adjustments, is also proposed as a final regulation and, when adopted, would become Reg. § 301.6689-1 (published in the Federal Register on June 23, 1988).

§ 301.6689-1. Failure to file notice of redetermination of foreign tax.

Foreign Tax Credit: Foreign Tax Redeterminations

Foreign Tax Credit: Foreign Tax Redeterminations.—Reg. § 301.6689-1, relating to a taxpayer's obligation under Code Sec. 905(c) to notify the IRS of a foreign tax redetermination, is proposed (published in the Federal Register on November 7, 2007) (REG-209020-86).

☐ Par. 5. Section 301.6689-1 is added to read as follows:

§ 301.6689-1. Failure to file notice of redetermination of foreign tax.—(a) [The text of the proposed amendments to § 301.6689-1(a) is the same as the text of § 301.6689-1T(a) as added by T.D. 9362].

(b) through (d) [Reserved]. For further guidance, see § 301.6689-1T(b) through (d).

(e) [The text of the proposed amendments to § 301.6689-1(e)(1) is the same as the text of § 301.6689-1T(e)(1) as added by T.D. 9362].

Individual Retirement Plans: Simplified Employee Pensions

Individual Retirement Plans: Simplified Employee Pensions.—Reproduced below is the text of a proposed amendment to Reg. § 301.6693-1, relating to individual retirement plans and simplified employee pensions (published in the Federal Register on July 14, 1981).

☐ Par. 18. Section 301.6693-1 is revised by changing its title, adding after paragraph (a)(2) a new paragraph (a)(3), and amending paragraph (e). Section 301.6693-1, as revised, reads as follows:

§ 301.6693-1. Penalty for failure to provide reports and documents concerning individual retirement accounts, individual retirement annuities and simplified employee pensions.—(a) *In general.*—* * *

(3) *Simplified employee pensions.*—An employer who makes a contribution on behalf of an employee to a simplified employee pension who fails to furnish or file a report or any other document required under section 408(1) or § 1.408-9 within the time and in the manner prescribed for furnishing or filing such item shall pay a penalty of $10 for each failure unless it is shown that such failure is due to reasonable cause.

* * *

(e) *Effective date.*—This section shall take effect on January 1, 1975, except for paragraph (a)(3) which is effective for years beginning after December 31, 1978.

Gifts and Bequests from Covered Expatriates: Imposition of Tax

Gifts and Bequests from Covered Expatriates: Imposition of Tax.—Reg. §§ 28.6694-1—28.6694-4, relating to a tax on United States citizens and residents who receive gifts or bequests from certain individuals who relinquished United States citizenship or ceased to be lawful permanent residents of the United States on or after June 17, 2008, is proposed (published in the Federal Register on September 10, 2015) (REG-112997-10).

Sections 28.6694-1 to 28.6694-4 are added to read as follows:

§ 28.6694-1. Section 6694 penalties applicable to return preparer.—(a) *In general.*—For general rules regarding section 6694 penalties applicable to preparers of returns or claims for refund of the tax under chapter 15 of subtitle B of the Internal Revenue Code (Code), see § 1.6694-1 of this chapter.

(b) *Effective/applicability date.*—This section applies to returns and claims for refund filed, and advice provided, on or after the date of publication of a Treasury decision adopting these rules as final regulations in the **Federal Register**. [Reg. § 28.6694-1.]

§ 28.6694-2. Penalties for understatement due to an unreasonable position.—(a) *In general.*—A person who is a tax return preparer of any return or claim for refund of any tax under chapter 15 of subtitle B of the Code is subject to penalties under section 6694(a) in the manner stated in § 1.6694-2 of this chapter.

(b) *Effective/applicability date.*—This section applies to returns and claims for refund filed, and advice provided, on or after the date of publication of a Treasury decision adopting these rules as final regulations in the **Federal Register**. [Reg. § 28.6694-2.]

§ 28.6694-3. **Penalties for understatement due to an unreasonable position.**—(a) *In general.*—A person who is a tax return preparer of any return or claim for refund of any tax under chapter 15 of subtitle B of the Code is subject to penalties under section 6694(b) in the manner stated in § 1.6694-3 of this chapter.

(b) *Effective/applicability date.*—This section applies to returns and claims for refund filed, and advice provided, on or after the date of publication of a Treasury decision adopting these rules as final regulations in the **Federal Register**. [Reg. § 28.6694-3.]

§ 28.6694-4. **Extension of period of collection when tax return preparer pays 15 percent of a penalty for understatement of tax-** payer's liability and certain other procedural matters.—(a) *In general.*—For rules relating to the extension of the period of collection when a tax return preparer who prepared a return or claim for refund of tax under chapter 15 of subtitle B of the Code pays 15 percent of a penalty for understatement of taxpayer's liability, and for procedural matters relating to the investigation, assessment, and collection of the penalties under section 6694(a) and (b), the rules under § 1.6694-4 of this chapter apply.

(b) *Effective/applicability date.*—This section applies to returns and claims for refund filed, and advice provided, on or after the date of publication of a Treasury decision adopting these rules as final regulations in the **Federal Register**. [Reg. § 28.6694-4.]

Gifts and Bequests from Covered Expatriates: Imposition of Tax

Gifts and Bequests from Covered Expatriates: Imposition of Tax.—Reg. §§ 28.6695-1 and 28.6696-1, relating to a tax on United States citizens and residents who receive gifts or bequests from certain individuals who relinquished United States citizenship or ceased to be lawful permanent residents of the United States on or after June 17, 2008, is proposed (published in the Federal Register on September 10, 2015) (REG-112997-10).

Section 28.6695-1 is added to read as follows:

§ 28.6695-1. **Other assessable penalties with respect to the preparation of tax returns for other persons.**—(a) *In general.*—A person who is a tax return preparer of any return or claim for refund of any tax under chapter 15 of subtitle B of the Internal Revenue Code (Code) is subject to penalties for failure to furnish a copy to the taxpayer under section 6695(a) of the Code, failure to sign the return under section 6695(b) of the Code, failure to furnish an identification number under section 6695(c) of the Code, failure to retain a copy or list under section 6695(d) of the Code, failure to file a correct information return under section 6695(e) of the Code, and negotiation of a check under section 6695(f) of the Code, in the manner stated in § 1.6695-1 of this chapter.

(b) *Effective/applicability date.*—This section applies to returns and claims for refund filed on or after the date of publication of a Treasury decision adopting these rules as final regulations in the **Federal Register**.[Reg. § 28.6695-1.]

Section 28.6696-1 is added to read as follows:

§ 28.6696-1. **Claims for credit or refund by tax return preparers and appraisers.**—(a) *In general.*—For rules regarding claims for credit or refund by a tax return preparer who prepared a return or claim for refund for any tax under chapter 15 of subtitle B of the Internal Revenue Code (Code), or by an appraiser that prepared an appraisal in connection with such a return or claim for refund under section 6695A of the Code, the rules under § 1.6696-1 of this chapter will apply.

(b) *Effective/applicability date.*—This section applies to returns and claims for refund filed, appraisals, and advice provided, on or after the date of publication of a Treasury decision adopting these rules as final regulations in the **Federal Register**. [Reg. § 28.6696-1.]

Tax Shelters: List of Investors

Tax Shelters: List of Investors.—Temporary Reg. § 301.6708-1T, relating to the requirement to maintain a list of investors in potentially abusive tax shelters, is also proposed as a final regulation and, when adopted, would become Reg. § 301.6708-1 (published in the Federal Register on August 29, 1984).

§ 301.6708-1. **Failure to maintain list of investors in potentially abusive tax shelters**.

Mortgage Credit Certificates

Mortgage Credit Certificates: Issuance Penalties.—Temporary Reg. § 1.6709-1T, relating to the issuance of mortgage credit certificates, is also proposed as final and, when adopted, would become Reg. § 1.6709-1 (published in the Federal Register on May 8, 1985).

§ 301.6709-1. **Penalties with respect to mortgage credit certificates**.

Correct Payee Statements: Failure to File Correct Information: Penalties

Correct Payee Statements: Failure to File Correct Information: Penalties.—Amendments to Reg. §§ 301.6721-0 and 301.6721-1, relating to penalties for failure to file correct information returns or furnish correct payee statements, are proposed (published in the Federal Register on October 17, 2018) (REG-118826-16).

Par. 4. Section 301.6721-0 is revised to read as follows:

§ 301.6721-0. **Table of Contents**.—In order to facilitate the use of §§ 301.6721-1 through 6724-1, this section lists the paragraph headings contained in these sections.

§ 301.6721-1 Failure to file correct information returns.
  (a) Imposition of penalty.
    (1) General rule.
    (2) Failures subject to the penalty.
  (b) Reduction in the penalty when a correction is made within specified periods.
    (1) Correction within 30 days.
    (2) Correction after 30 days but on or before August 1.
    (3) Required filing date defined.
    (4) Penalty amount for return with multiple failures.
    (5) Examples.
    (6) Applications to returns not due on January 31, February 28, or March 15.
  (c) Exception for inconsequential errors or omissions.
    (1) In general.
    (2) Errors or omissions that are never inconsequential.

    (3) Examples.
  (d) Exception for a de minimis number of failures.
    (1) Requirements.
    (2) Calculation of the de minimis exception.
    (3) Examples.
    (4) Nonapplication to returns not due on January 31, February 28, or March 15.
  (e) Safe harbor exception for certain de minimis errors.
    (1) In general.
    (2) Definition of de minimis error.
    (3) Election to override the safe harbor exception.
  (f) Lower limitations on the $3,000,000 maximum penalty amount with respect to persons with gross receipts of not more than $5,000,000.
    (1) In general.
    (2) Gross receipts test.
  (g) Higher penalty for intentional disregard of requirement to file timely correct information returns.
    (1) Application of section 6721(e).

(2) Meaning of "intentional disregard."

(3) Facts and circumstances considered.

(4) Amount of the penalty.

(5) Computation of the penalty; aggregate dollar amount of the items required to be reported correctly.

(6) Examples.

(h) Definitions.

(1) Information return.

(2) Statements.

(3) Returns.

(4) Other items.

(5) Payee.

(6) Filer.

(i) Adjustment for inflation.

(j) Applicability date.

§ 301.6722-1 *Failure to furnish correct payee statements.*

(a) Imposition of penalty.

(1) General rule.

(2) Failures subject to the penalty.

(b) Exception for inconsequential errors or omissions.

(1) In general.

(2) Errors or omissions that are never inconsequential.

(3) Examples.

(c) Higher penalty for intentional disregard of requirement to furnish timely correct payee statements.

(1) Application of section 6722(e).

(2) Amount of the penalty.

(3) Computation of the penalty; aggregate dollar amount of items required to be shown correctly.

(d) Safe harbor exception for certain de minimis errors.

(1) In general.

(2) Definition of de minimis error.

(3) Election to override the safe harbor exception.

(4) Record retention.

(6) Examples.

(e) Definitions.

(1) Payee.

(2) Payee statement.

(3) Other items.

(4) Filer.

(f) Adjustment for inflation.

(g) Applicability date.

§ 301.6723-1 *Failure to comply with other information reporting requirements.*

(a) Imposition of penalty.

(1) General rule.

(2) Failures subject to the penalty.

(3) Exception for inconsequential errors or omissions.

(4) Specified information reporting requirement defined.

(b) Examples.

§ 301.6724-1 *Reasonable cause.*

(a) Waiver of the penalty.

(1) General rule.

(2) Reasonable cause defined.

(b) Significant mitigating factors.

(c) Events beyond the filer's control.

(1) In general.

(2) Unavailability of the relevant business records.

(3) Undue economic hardship relating to filing on magnetic media.

(4) Actions of the Internal Revenue Service.

(5) Actions of agent—imputed reasonable cause.

(6) Actions of the payee or any other person.

(d) Responsible manner.

(1) In general.

(2) Special rule for filers seeking a waiver pursuant to paragraph (c)(6) of this section.

(e) Acting in a responsible manner—special rules for missing TINs.

(1) In general.

(i) Initial solicitation.

(ii) First annual solicitation.

(iii) Second annual solicitation.

(iv) Additional requirements.

(v) Failures to which a solicitation relates.

(vi) Exceptions and limitations.

(2) Manner of making annual solicitations—by mail or telephone.

(i) By mail.

(ii) By telephone.

(f) Acting in a responsible manner—special rules for incorrect TINs.

(1) In general.

(i) Initial solicitation.

(ii) First annual solicitation.

(iii) Second annual solicitation.

(iv) Additional requirements.

(2) Manner of making annual solicitation if notified pursuant to section 3406(a)(1)(B) and the regulations thereunder.

(3) Manner of making annual solicitation if notified pursuant to section 6721.

(4) Failures to which a solicitation relates.

(5) Exceptions and limitations.

(g) Due diligence safe harbor.

(1) In general.

(2) Special rules relating to TINs.

(3) Effective dates.

(h) Reasonable cause safe harbor after election under section 6722(c)(3)(B).

(1) [Reserved]

(j) Failures to which this section relates.

(k) Examples.

(l) [Reserved]

(m) Procedure for seeking a waiver.

(n) Manner of payment.

(o) Applicability date.

Par. 5. Section 301.6721-1 is amended by:

1. Revising paragraph (a)(1).

2. Revising the ninth sentence of paragraph (a)(2)(ii).

3. Revising paragraphs (b)(1), (2), (5), and (6), (c)(1), (c)(2)(iii), (c)(3), and (d).

4. Redesignating paragraphs (e), (f), and (g) as paragraphs (f), (g), and (h).

5. Adding a new paragraph (e).

6. Revising newly redesignated paragraphs (f)(1), (g)(1) and (4) through (6), (h)(1), and (h)(2)(x) and (xi) and adding paragraph (h)(2)(xii).

7. Revising newly redesignated paragraphs (h)(3)(xvii), (xviii), (xxiv), and (xxv) and adding paragraph (h)(3)(xxvi).

8. Revising newly redesignated paragraphs (h)(4) and (6).

9. Adding paragraphs (i) and (j).

The revisions and additions read as follows:

§301.6721-1. Failure to file correct information returns.—(a) *Imposition of penalty.*—(1) *General rule.*—A penalty of $250 is imposed for each information return (as defined in section 6724(d)(1) and paragraph (h) of this section) with respect to which a failure (as defined in section 6721(a)(2) and paragraph (a)(2) of this section) occurs. No more than one penalty will be imposed under this paragraph (a)(1) with respect to a single information return even though there may be more than one failure with respect to such return. The total amount imposed on any person for all failures during any calendar year with respect to all information returns shall not exceed $3,000,000. See paragraph (b) of this section for a reduction in the penalty when the failures are corrected within specified periods. See paragraph (c) of this section for an exception to the penalty for inconsequential errors or omissions. See paragraph (d) of this section for an exception to the penalty for a de minimis number of failures.

See paragraph (e) of this section for a safe harbor exception for certain de minimis errors. See paragraph (f) of this section for lower limitations to the $3,000,000 maximum penalty. See paragraph (g) of this section for higher penalties when a failure is due to intentional disregard of the requirement to file timely correct information returns. See paragraph (i) of this section for inflation adjustments to penalty amounts. See § 301.6724–1(a)(1) for waiver of the penalty for a failure that is due to reasonable cause.

(2) * * *

(ii) * * * Except as provided in paragraph (c)(1) or (e)(1) of this section, a failure to include correct information encompasses a failure to include the information required by applicable information reporting statutes or by any administrative pronouncements issued thereunder (such as regulations, revenue rulings, revenue procedures, or information reporting forms and form instructions). * * *

(b) *Reduction in the penalty when a correction is made within specified periods.*—(1) *Correction within 30 days.*—The penalty imposed under section 6721(a) for a failure to file timely or for a failure to include correct information shall be $50 in lieu of $250 if the failure is corrected on or before the 30th day after the required filing date ("within 30 days"). The total amount imposed on a person for all failures during any calendar year that are corrected within 30 days shall not exceed $500,000.

(2) *Correction after 30 days but on or before August 1.*—The penalty imposed under section 6721(a) for a failure to file timely or for a failure to include correct information shall be $100 in lieu of $250 if the failure is corrected after the 30–day period described in paragraph (b)(1) of this section but on or before August 1 of the year in which the required filing date occurs ("after 30 days but on or before August 1"). See paragraph (b)(6) of this section for an exception to the provisions of this paragraph (b)(2) for returns that are not due on January 31, February 28, or March 15. The total amount imposed on a person for all failures during any calendar year corrected after 30 days but on or before August 1 shall not exceed $1,500,000.

* * *

(5) *Examples.*—The provisions of paragraphs (a) and (b)(1) through (4) of this section may be illustrated by the following examples. These examples do not take into account any possible application of the de minimis exception under paragraph (d) of this section, the safe harbor exception for certain de minimis errors under paragraph (e) of this section, the lower small business limitations under paragraph (f) of this section, the penalty for intentional disregard under paragraph (g) of this section, any adjustments for inflation under paragraph (i) of this section, or the reasonable cause waiver under § 301.6724-1(a):

(i) *Example 1.*—Corporation R fails to file timely 23,000 Forms 1099–MISC (relating to miscellaneous income) for the 2018 calendar year. Five thousand of these returns are filed with correct information within 30 days, and 18,000 after 30 days but on or before August 1, 2019. For the same year R fails to file timely 400 Forms 1099–INT (relating to payments of interest) which R eventually files on September 28, 2019, after the period for reduction of the penalty has elapsed. R is subject to a penalty of $100,000 for the 400 forms which were not filed by August 1 ($250 x 400 = $100,000), $1,500,000 for the 18,000 forms filed after 30 days ($100 x 18,000 = $1,800,000, limited to $1,500,000 under paragraph (b)(2) of this section), and $250,000 for the 5,000 forms filed within 30 days ($50 x 5,000 = $250,000), for a total penalty of $1,850,000.

(ii) *Example 2.*—Corporation T fails to file timely 14,000 Forms 1099–MISC for the 2018 calendar year. T files the 14,000 Forms 1099–MISC on September 1, 2019. Because T does not correct the failure by August 1, 2019, T is subject to a penalty of $3,000,000, the maximum penalty under paragraph (a) of this section. Without the limitation of paragraph (a), T would be subject to a $3,500,000 penalty ($250 x 14,000 = $3,500,000).

(iii) *Example 3.*—Corporation U files timely 300 Forms 1099–MISC on paper for the 2018 calendar year with correct information. Under section 6011(e)(2) a person required to file at least 250 returns during a calendar year must file those returns on magnetic media. U does not correct its failures to file these returns on magnetic media by August 1, 2019. It is therefore subject to a penalty for a failure to file timely under paragraph (a)(2) of this section. However, pursuant to section 6724(c) and paragraph (a)(2) of this section, the penalty for a failure to file timely on magnetic media applies only to the extent the number of returns exceeds 250. As U was required to file 300 returns on magnetic media, U is subject to a penalty of $12,500 for 50 returns ($250 x 50 = $12,500).

(iv) *Example 4.*—Corporation V files 300 Forms 1099–B (relating to proceeds from broker and barter exchange transactions) on paper for the 2018 calendar year. The forms were filed on March 15, 2019, rather than on the required filing date of February 28, 2019. Under section 6011(e)(2), a person required to file at least 250 returns during a calendar year must file those returns on magnetic media. V does not correctly file these returns on magnetic media by August 1, 2019. V is subject to a penalty of $12,500 for filing 250 of the returns late ($50 x 250) and $12,500 for failing to file 50 returns on magnetic media ($250 x 50) for a total penalty of $25,000.

(6) *Application to returns not due on January 31, February 28, or March 15.*—For returns that are not due on January 31, February 28, or March 15 (for example, Forms 8300 reporting certain cash payments of $10,000 or more), the penalty is $50 if the failure is corrected within 30 days. If the failure is corrected after 30 days, the penalty is $250 rather than $100. There is no period during which the penalty is reduced to $100 under paragraph (b)(2) of this section.

(c) *Exception for inconsequential errors or omissions.*—(1) *In general.*—An inconsequential error or omission is not considered a failure to include correct information. For purposes of this paragraph (c)(1), the term "inconsequential error or omission" means any failure that does not prevent or hinder the Internal Revenue Service from processing the return, from correlating the information required to be shown on the return with the information shown on the payee's tax return, or from otherwise putting the return to its intended use. See paragraph (h)(5) of this section for the definition of "payee."

(2) * * *

(iii) Any monetary amounts, except as provided in paragraph (e) of this section. The Internal Revenue Service may, by administrative pronouncement, specify other types of errors or omissions that are never inconsequential.

(3) *Examples.*—The provisions of this paragraph (c) may be illustrated by the following examples, which do not take into account any possible application of the penalty for intentional disregard under paragraph (g) of this section or the reasonable cause waiver under § 301.6724-1(a):

(i) *Example 1.*—A filer files a Form 1099–MISC (relating to miscellaneous income) with the Internal Revenue Service. The Form 1099–MISC is complete and correct except that the word "street" is misspelled in the payee's address. The error does not prevent or hinder the Internal Revenue Service from processing the return, from correlating the information required to be shown on the return with the information shown on the payee's tax return, or from otherwise putting the return to its intended use. Therefore, no penalty is imposed under paragraph (a) of this section.

(ii) *Example 2.*—A filer files a Form 1099–MISC with the Internal Revenue Service. The Form 1099–MISC is complete and correct except that the payee's first name, William, is misspelled as "Willaim." The error does not prevent or hinder the Internal Revenue Service from processing the return, from correlating the information required to be shown on the return with the information shown on the payee's tax return, or from otherwise putting the return to its intended use. See paragraph (c)(2) of this section. Therefore, no penalty is imposed under paragraph (a) of this section.

(iii) *Example 3.*—A filer files a Form 1099–MISC with the Internal Revenue Service. The Form 1099–MISC is complete and correct except that the payee's name, "John Doe," is misspelled as "John Ode." Under paragraph (c)(2) of this section, supplying an incorrect surname for a payee is never considered an inconsequential error. Therefore, a penalty is imposed under paragraph (a) of this section.

(d) *Exception for a de minimis number of failures.*—(1) *Requirements.*—The penalty under paragraph (a) of this section is not imposed for a de minimis number of failures to include correct information if the filer corrects such failures on or before August 1 of the year in which the required filing date occurs. See paragraph (d)(4) of this section for special rules relating to returns that are not due on January 31, February 28, or March 15.

(2) *Calculation of the de minimis exception.*—The number of returns to which the de minimis exception applies for any calendar year shall not exceed the greater of 10 or one-half of one percent of the total number of all information returns the filer is required to file during the year. If the number of returns on which the filer fails to include correct information exceeds the number of returns to which the de minimis exception applies, the de minimis exception applies to those returns that will afford the filer the greatest reduction in penalty. The de minimis exception applies to failures to include correct information that exist after the application (if any) of the safe harbor exception for certain de minimis errors under paragraph (e) of this section and after the application (if any) of the waiver for reasonable cause under section 6724(a) and § 301.6724-1. Returns to which the de minimis exception applies are treated as having been originally filed with correct information.

(3) *Examples.*—The provisions of this paragraph (d) may be illustrated by the following examples. In each of the examples, the failures to file and to include correct information are subject to penalty under paragraph (a) of this section. The examples do not take into account any possible application of the safe harbor exception for certain de minimis errors under paragraph (e) of this section, the lower small business limitations under paragraph (f) of this section, the penalty for intentional disregard under paragraph (g) of this section, any adjustment for inflation under paragraph (i) of this section, or the reasonable cause waiver under § 301.6724-1(a).

(i) *Example 1.*—Corporation T files timely 10,000 Forms 1099–INT (relating to payments of interest) for 2018 by February 28, 2019. The 10,000 returns are all the information returns that T is required to file during the 2019 calendar year. Of the returns filed, 70 contained incorrect information. T corrects the failures on July 12,

2019. No penalty is imposed for 50 of the failures (that is, the greater of 10 or .005 x 10,000 = 50) even though the total failures, 70, exceed the number to which the de minimis exception may apply. The $100 penalty under paragraph (b)(2) of this section is imposed, in lieu of $250, for the remaining 20 failures, which were corrected after 30 days but on or before August 1, resulting in a total penalty of $2000 ($100 x 20 = $2000).

(ii) *Example 2.*—Corporation U files timely 9,500 Forms 1099–INT for 2018 by February 28, 2019. Fifty of these returns contain incorrect information with respect to which U files correct information on August 1, 2019. U also files 500 Forms 1099–INT for 2018 on August 30, 2019, after the required filing date. The 10,000 returns are all the information returns that U is required to file during the 2019 calendar year. The calculation of the de minimis exception is based on the 10,000 returns required to be filed during the 2019 calendar year even though 500 of the returns filed during the year were not filed timely. Therefore, the number of failures for which the de minimis exception applies is 50, and accordingly no penalty is imposed for the 50 Forms 1099–INT that were corrected on August 1, 2019. However, the $250 penalty under paragraph (a)(1) of this section is imposed for each failure to file timely, resulting in a total penalty of $125,000 ($250 x 500 = $125,000).

(iii) *Example 3.*—Corporation V files timely 9,950 Forms 1099–INT for 2018 by February 28, 2019. However, V fails to file timely 50 of its Forms 1099–INT. The 10,000 returns are all the information returns that V is required to file during the 2019 calendar year. Upon discovering the error, V files the 50 returns within 30 days of February 28, 2019. The 50 returns are complete and correct except that V fails to include the taxpayer identification numbers of the payees on the returns. V files corrected returns on August 1, 2019. Absent application of the de minimis exception, the penalty imposed for the failure to include correct information would be $5,000 ($100 x 50 = $5,000). Because the incorrect returns are corrected on August 1, the 50 forms are treated under the de minimis exception as originally filed with correct information, and therefore no penalty is imposed under paragraph (a) of this section for the failure to include correct information. Nevertheless, the penalty under paragraph (a) of this section is imposed for the failure to file timely the 50 returns because the de minimis exception does not apply to the penalty for the failure to file timely. Hence, a penalty of $2,500 ($50 x 50 = $2500) is imposed.

(iv) *Example 4.*—Corporation W files timely 100 Forms 1099–DIV and files an additional 50 Forms 1099–DIV late, but within 30 days of February 28, 2019. These are all the information returns that W was required to file during the 2019 calendar year. W discovers errors on 10 of the returns that were filed timely, and on 5 of the returns that were filed late. W corrects all the errors on August 1. The de minimis exception applies to 10 of the corrected returns. The exception will be allocated to the 10 returns that were filed timely with incorrect information, because that allocation is most favorable to W (that is, applying the exception to a return filed late with incorrect information would save W $50, by reducing the penalty on that return from $100 to $50, but applying the exception to a return filed timely would save W $100, by reducing the penalty on that return from $100 to $0). (See paragraph (b)(4) of this section.)

(4) *Nonapplication to returns not due on January 31, February 28, or March 15.*—The exception for a de minimis number of failures provided in paragraph (d)(1) of this section does not apply to failures with respect to returns that are not due on January 31, February 28, or March 15 (for example, Forms 8300 reporting certain cash payments of $10,000 or more). Nevertheless, the returns that are not due on January 31, February 28, or March 15 are included in the total number of all information returns that the filer is required to file during a year for purposes of calculating the number of the returns subject to the de minimis exception under paragraph (d)(2) of this section.

(e) *Safe harbor exception for certain de minimis errors.*—(1) *In general.*—Except as provided in paragraph (e)(3) or (g)(4) of this section, the penalty under section 6721(a) and paragraph (a) of this section is not imposed for a failure described in section 6721(a)(2)(B) and paragraph (a)(2)(ii) of this section (failure to include correct information on information return) when the failure relates to an incorrect dollar amount and is a de minimis error. When this safe harbor applies to an information return and the information return was otherwise correct and timely filed, no correction is required and, for purposes of this section, the information return is treated as having been filed with all of the correct required information.

(2) *Definition of de minimis error.*—For the definition of de minimis error, see § 301.6722–1(d)(2).

(3) *Election to override the safe harbor exception.*—The safe harbor exception provided for by paragraph (e)(1) of this section does not apply to any information return if the incorrect dollar amount that would qualify as a de minimis error for purposes of this paragraph (e) relates to an amount with respect to which an election has been made (and has not been revoked) under section 6722(c)(3)(B) and § 301.6722–1(d)(3). See § 301.6722–1(d)(3) for additional rules relating to the election under section 6722(c)(3)(B) and § 301.6722–1(d)(3), including rules relating to the revocation of the election and the inapplicability of the election to certain information. See § 301.6724–1(h) for rules relating to waiver of the section 6721 penalty in cases where the safe harbor exception provided for by paragraph (e)(1) of this section does not apply because of an election under § 301.6722–1(d)(3).

(f) *Lower limitations on the $3,000,000 maximum penalty amount with respect to persons with gross receipts of not more than $5,000,000.*—(1) *In general.*—If a person meets the gross receipts test (as defined in paragraph (f)(2) of this section) for any calendar year, the total amount of the penalty imposed on such person for all failures described in section 6721(a)(2) and paragraph (a)(2) of this section during such calendar year shall not exceed $1,000,000. The total amount of the penalty imposed under paragraph (b)(1) of this section for failures corrected within 30 days shall not exceed $175,000 for such calendar year. The total amount of the penalty imposed under paragraph (b)(2) of this section for failures corrected after 30 days but on or before August 1 shall not exceed $500,000 for such calendar year.

* * *

(g) *Higher penalty for intentional disregard of requirement to file timely correct information returns.*—(1) *Application of section 6721(e).*—If a failure is due to intentional disregard of the requirement to file timely or to include correct information on a return as described in paragraph (h) of this section, the amount of the penalty imposed under paragraph (a) of this section shall be determined under paragraph (g)(4) of this section.

* * *

(4) *Amount of the penalty.*—If one or more failures to file timely or to include correct information are due to intentional disregard of the requirement to file timely or to include correct information, then, with respect to each such failure determined under this paragraph (g)—

(i) Paragraphs (b), (d), (e), and (f) of this section shall not apply;

(ii) The $3,000,000 limitation under paragraph (a) of this section shall not apply, and the penalty under this paragraph (g) shall not be taken into account in applying the $3,000,000 limitation (or any similar limitation under paragraph (b) or (f) of this section) to penalties not determined under this paragraph (g);

(iii) The penalty imposed under paragraph (a) of this section shall be $500 or, if greater, the statutory percentage; and

(iv) The term "statutory percentage" means—

(A) In the case of a return other than a return required under section 6045(a), 6041A(b), 6050H, 6050I, 6050J, 6050K, 6050L, or 6050V, 10 percent of the aggregate dollar amount of the items required to be reported correctly;

(B) In the case of a return required to be filed by section 6045(a), 6050K, or 6050L, 5 percent of the aggregate dollar amount of the items required to be reported correctly;

(C) In the case of a return required to be filed under section 6050I(a), for any transaction (or related transactions), the greater of $25,000 or the amount of cash (within the meaning of section 6050I(d)) received in such transaction to the extent the amount of such cash does not exceed $100,000; or

(D) In the case of a return required to be filed under section 6050V, 10 percent of the value of the benefit of any contract with respect to which information is required to be included on the return.

(5) *Computation of the penalty; aggregate dollar amount of the items required to be reported correctly.*—The aggregate dollar amount used in computing the penalty under this paragraph (g) is the amount that is not reported or is reported incorrectly. If the intentional disregard relates to a dollar amount, the statutory percentage is applied to the difference between the dollar amount reported and the amount required to be reported correctly. If the intentional disregard relates to any other item on the return, the statutory percentage is applied to the aggregate amount of items required to be reported correctly. In determining the aggregate amount of items required to be reported correctly, no item shall be taken into account more than once. For example, if a filer willfully fails to file a Form 1099–INT on which $800 of interest and $160 of Federal income tax withheld (that is, backup withholding) is required to be reported, only the $800 amount is taken into account in computing the penalty.

(6) *Examples.*—The provisions of this paragraph (g) may be illustrated by the following examples, which do not take into account any adjustments for inflation under paragraph (i) of this section:

(i) *Example 1.*—On December 1, 2018, Automobile dealer P receives $55,000 from an individual for the purchase of an automobile in a transaction subject to reporting under section 6050I. The individual presents documents to P that identify him as "John Doe." However, P completes the Form 8300 (relating to cash received in a trade or business) and reflects the name of a cartoon character as the filer. Because P knew at the time of filing the Form 8300 that the filer's name was not the name of the cartoon character, he willfully failed to include correct information as described under paragraph (g)(2) of this section. Therefore, the penalty under paragraph (g)(4) of this section is imposed for the intentional disregard of the requirement to include correct information. The amount used in computing the penalty under paragraph (g)(5) of this section is $55,000 (that is, the amount required to be reported on the return with respect to which the payee is not correctly identified). The amount of the penalty determined under paragraph (g)(4)(iv)(C) of this section is $55,000 (that is, the greater of $25,000 or the amount of cash received in the transaction up to $100,000).

(ii) *Example 2.*—On December 1, 2018, Individual B contacts his agent, F, to act as his intermediary in the purchase of an automobile. B gives F $20,000 and requests F to purchase the automobile in F's name, which F does. F prepares the Form 8300 as required under section 6050I, but in the area designated for the name of the filer, F writes "confidential." Because F knew at the time the return was filed that it contained incomplete information, the penalty under paragraph (g)(4) of this section is imposed for the intentional disregard of the requirement to include correct information. The amount used in computing the penalty under paragraph (g)(5) of this section is $20,000 (that is, the amount required to be reported on the return with respect to which the payee is not correctly identified). The amount of the penalty determined under paragraph (g)(4)(iv)(C) of this section is $25,000 (that is, the greater of $25,000 or the amount of cash received in the transaction up to $100,000).

(iii) *Example 3.*—Corporation M deliberately does not include $5,000 of dividends on a Form 1099–DIV (relating to payments of dividends) on which a total of $200,000 (including the $5,000 dividends) is required to be reported under section 6042(a). Because the failure was deliberate, Corporation M's failure is due to intentional disregard of the requirement to include correct information. Accordingly, the amount of the penalty imposed under paragraph (a) is determined under paragraph (g)(4) of this section. Because the Form 1099–DIV is required to be filed under section 6042(a), under paragraph (g)(4)(iv)(A) the amount of the penalty with respect to such failure is 10 percent of the aggregate dollar amount of the items that were required to be but that were not reported correctly. Under paragraph (g)(5) of this section, $5,000 is the difference between the dollar amount reported and the amount required to be reported correctly. Therefore, the amount of the penalty is $500 ($5,000 x .10 = $500).

(iv) *Example 4.*—Form 8027 requires certain large food and beverage establishments to report certain information with respect to tips. The form requires (among other things) that the establishment report its gross receipts from food and beverage operations. Establishment A, in intentional disregard of the information reporting requirement, reported gross receipts of $1,000,000, when the correct amount was $1,500,000. The significance of the gross receipts reporting requirement is that section 6053(c)(3)(A) requires an establishment to allocate as tips among its employees the excess of 8 percent of its gross receipts over the aggregate amount reported by employees to the establishment as tips under section 6053(a). A's misstatement of its gross receipts caused A to show $80,000 on the Form 8027 as 8 percent of its gross receipts, rather than the correct amount of $120,000. A correctly reported the amount of tips reported to it by employees under section 6053(a) as $80,000. Thus A reported the excess of 8 percent of its gross receipts over tips reported to it as zero, rather than as the correct amount of $40,000. The requirement of reporting gross receipts is considered merely a step in the computa-

tion of the excess of 8 percent of gross receipts over tips reported to A under section 6053(a), so that the penalty for intentional disregard will be $4,000 (that is, 10 percent of the difference between the $40,000 required to be reported as the excess of 8 percent of gross receipts over tips reported under section 6053(a), and the zero amount actually reported).

(h) *Definitions.*—(1) *Information return.*—For purposes of this section, the term "information return" has the same meaning as "information return" as defined in section 6724(d)(1), including any statement described in paragraph (h)(2) of this section, any return described in paragraph (h)(3) of this section, and any other items described in paragraph (h)(4) of this section.

(2) * * *

(x) Section 408(i) (relating to reports with respect to individual retirement accounts or annuities on Form 1099–R, "Distributions From Pensions, Annuities, Retirement or Profit-Sharing Plans, IRAs, Insurance Contracts, etc.");

(xi) Section 6047(d) (relating to reports by employers, plan administrators, etc., on Form 1099–R); or

(xii) Section 6035 (relating to basis information with respect to property acquired from decedents, generally Form 8971, "Information Regarding Beneficiaries Acquiring Property From a Decedent" and the Schedule(s) A required to be filed along with it).

(3) * * *

(xvii) Section 1060(b) (relating to reporting requirements of transferors and transferees in certain asset acquisitions, generally reported on Form 8594, "Asset Acquisition Statement"), or section 1060(e) (relating to information required in the case of certain transfers of interests in entities);

(xviii) Section 4101(d) (relating to information reporting with respect to fuel oils);

* * *

(xxiv) Section 6055 (relating to information returns reporting minimum essential coverage);

(xxv) Section 6056 (relating to information returns reporting on offers of health insurance coverage by applicable large employer members); or

(xxvi) Section 6050Y (relating to returns relating to certain life insurance contract transactions).

(4) *Other items.*—The term information return also includes any form, statement, or schedule required to be filed with the Internal Revenue Service with respect to any amount from which tax is required to be deducted and withheld under chapter 3 of the Internal Revenue Code (or from which tax would be required to be so deducted and withheld but for an exemption under the Internal Revenue Code or any treaty obligation of the United States), generally Forms 1042–S, "Foreign Person's U.S. Source Income Subject to Withholding," and 8805, "Foreign Partner's Information Statement of Section 1446 Withholding Tax." The provisions of this paragraph (h)(4) referring to Form 8805, shall apply to partnership taxable years beginning after May 18, 2005, or such earlier time as the regulations under §§ 1.1446-1 through 1.1446-5 of this chapter apply by reason of an election under § 1.1446-7 of this chapter.

* * *

(6) *Filer.*—For purposes of this section the term "filer" means a person that is required to file an information return as defined in paragraph (h)(1) of this section under the applicable information reporting section described in paragraphs (h)(2) through (4) of this section.

(i) *Adjustment for inflation.*—Each of the dollar amounts under paragraphs (a), (b), (f) (other than (f)(2)), and (g) of this section and paragraphs (a), (b), (d) (other than paragraph (2)(A)), and (e) of section 6721 shall be adjusted for inflation pursuant to section 6721(f).

(j) *Applicability date.*—This section applies with respect to information returns required to be filed on or after January 1 of the calendar year immediately following the date of publication of a Treasury decision adopting these rules as final regulations in the **Federal Register**.

Estate and Person Acquiring Property from Decedent: Consistent Basis Reporting

Estate and Person Acquiring Property from Decedent: Consistent Basis Reporting.—Amendments to Reg. §§ 301.6721-1 and 301.6722-1, providing guidance regarding the requirement that a recipient's basis in certain property acquired from a decedent be consistent with the value of the property as finally determined for Federal estate tax purposes, are proposed (published in the Federal Register on March 4, 2016) (REG-127923-15).

Par. 8. Section 301.6721-1 is amended by removing the word "or" at the end of paragraph (g)(2)(x), removing the period and adding "; or" at the end of paragraph (g)(2)(xi), and adding paragraph (g)(2)(xii).

The addition reads as follows:

Reg. § 301.6721-1(g)(6)

§301.6721-1. Failure to file correct information returns.

* * *

(g) * * *

Par. 9. Section 301.6722-1 is amended by removing the word "or" at the end of paragraph (d)(2)(xxxiii), removing the period and adding a semi-colon in its place followed by the word "or" at the end of paragraph (d)(2)(xxxiv), and adding paragraph (d)(2)(xxxv). The addition reads as follows:

§301.6722-1. Failure to furnish correct payee statements.

* * *

(d) * * *

(2) * * *

(xii) Section 6035 (relating to basis of property acquired from decedents).

* * *

(2) * * *

(xxxv) Section 6035 (relating to basis of property acquired from decedents).

* * *

Information Returns: Using Magnetic Media

Information Returns: Using Magnetic Media.—Amendments to Reg. §301.6721-1, amending the rules for determining whether information returns must be filed using magnetic media (electronically), are proposed (published in the Federal Register on May 31, 2018) (REG-102951-16).

Par. 3. Section 301.6721-1 is amended as follows:

a. By removing the fifth through seventh sentences in paragraph (a)(2)(ii).

b. Adding paragraph (h).

The revisions and addition reads as follows:

§301.6721-1. Failure to file correct information returns.

* * *

(h) *Effective dates.*—Paragraph (a)(2)(ii) of this section is effective for information returns required to be filed after December 31, 2018.

Correct Payee Statements: Failure to File Correct Information: Penalties

Correct Payee Statements: Failure to File Correct Information: Penalties.—Amendments to Reg. §301.6722-1, relating to penalties for failure to file correct information returns or furnish correct payee statements, are proposed (published in the Federal Register on October 17, 2018) (REG-118826-16).

Par. 6. Section 301.6722-1 is amended by:

1. Revising paragraphs (a)(1), (a)(2)(ii), and (b)(2)(i).
2. In paragraphs (b)(2)(ii) and (iii), removing the comma at the end of each paragraph and adding a semicolon in its place.
3. Revising paragraph (b)(3) introductory text.
4. In paragraph (b)(3), designate *Examples 1* and *2* as paragraphs (b)(3)(i) and (ii).
5. Revising paragraph (c)(1).
6. Redesignating paragraphs (c)(2)(i), (ii), and (iii) as paragraphs (c)(2)(ii), (iii), and (iv).
7. Adding a new paragraph (c)(2)(i).
8. Revising newly redesignated paragraphs (c)(2)(ii) and (iii).
9. Redesignating paragraphs (d) and (e) as paragraphs (e) and (g).
10. Adding a new paragraph (d).
11. Revising newly redesignated paragraphs (e)(1), (e)(2) introductory text, and (e)(2)(xxxiii) and (xxxiv).
12. Adding paragraphs (e)(2)(xxxv), (xxxvi), and (xxxvii), (e)(4), and (f).
13. Revising newly redesignated paragraph (g).

The revisions and additions read as follows:

§301.6722-1. Failure to furnish correct payee statements.—(a) *Imposition of penalty.*—(1) *General rule.*—A penalty of $250 is imposed for each payee statement (as defined in section 6724(d)(2) and paragraph (e)(2) of this section) with respect to which a failure (as defined in section 6722(a) and paragraph (a)(2) of this section) occurs. No more than one penalty will be imposed under this paragraph (a) with respect to a single payee statement even though there may be more than one failure with respect to such statement. However, the penalty shall apply to failures on composite substitute payee statements as though each type of payment and other required information were furnished on separate statements. A "composite substitute payee statement" is a single document created by a filer to reflect several types of payments made to the same payee. The total amount imposed on any person for all failures during any calendar year with respect to all payee statements shall not exceed $3,000,000. See section 6722(e) and paragraph (c) of this section for higher penalties when a failure is due to intentional disregard of the requirement to furnish timely correct payee statements. See paragraph (d) of this section for a safe harbor exception for certain de minimis errors. See paragraph (f) of this section for inflation adjustments to penalty amounts. See §301.6724-1(a)(1) for a waiver of the penalty for a failure that is due to reasonable cause.

(2) * * *

(ii) A failure to include all of the information required to be shown on a payee statement or the inclusion of incorrect information ("failure to include correct information"). A failure to furnish timely includes a failure to furnish a written statement to the payee in a statement mailing as required under sections 6042(c), 6044(e), 6049(c), and 6050N(b), as well as a failure to furnish the statement on a form acceptable to the Internal Revenue Service. Except as provided in paragraph (b) or (d) of this section, a failure to include correct information encompasses a failure to include the information required by applicable information reporting statutes or by any administrative pronouncements issued thereunder (such as regulations,

revenue rulings, revenue procedures, or information reporting forms).

(b) * * *

(2) * * *

(i) A dollar amount, except as provided in paragraph (d) of this section;

* * *

(3) *Examples.*—The provisions of this paragraph (b) may be illustrated by the following examples which do not take into account any possible application of the penalty for intentional disregard under paragraph (c) of this section, the safe harbor exception for certain de minimis errors under paragraph (d) of this section, or the reasonable cause waiver under §301.6724-1(a):

* * *

(c) *Higher penalty for intentional disregard of requirement to furnish timely correct payee statements.*—(1) *Application of section 6722(e).*—If a failure is due to intentional disregard of the requirement to furnish timely correct payee statements, the amount of the penalty shall be determined under paragraph (c)(2) of this section. Whether a failure is due to intentional disregard of the requirement to furnish timely correct payee statements is based upon the facts and circumstances surrounding the failure. The facts and circumstances considered include those under §301.6721-1(g)(3), which shall apply in determining whether a failure under this section is due to intentional disregard.

(2) * * *

(i) Paragraph (d) of this section shall not apply;

(ii) The $3,000,000 limitation under paragraph (a) of this section shall not apply and the penalty under this paragraph (c)(2) shall not be taken into account in applying the $3,000,000 limitation to penalties not determined under this paragraph (c)(2);

(iii) The penalty imposed under paragraph (a) of this section shall be $500 or, if greater, the statutory percentage; and

Reg. §301.6722-1(c)(2)(iii)

* * *

(d) *Safe harbor exception for certain de minimis errors.*—(1) *In general.*—Except as provided in paragraphs (c) and (d)(3) of this section, the penalty under section 6722(a) and paragraph (a) of this section is not imposed for a failure described in section 6722(a)(2)(B) and paragraph (a)(2)(ii) of this section (failure to include correct information on payee statement) when the failure relates to an incorrect dollar amount and is a de minimis error. When this safe harbor applies to a payee statement and the payee statement was otherwise correct and timely furnished no correction is required and, for purposes of this section, the payee statement is treated as having been furnished with all of the correct required information.

(2) *Definition of de minimis error.*—For purposes of paragraph (d) of this section, an error in a dollar amount is de minimis if the difference between any single amount in error and the correct amount is not more than $100, and, if the difference is with respect to an amount of tax withheld, it is not more than $25. For purposes of this paragraph (d)(2), tax withheld includes any amount required to be shown on an information return or payee statement (as defined in section 6724(d)(1) and (d)(2), respectively) withheld under section 3402, as well as any such amount that is creditable under sections 27, 31, 33, or 1474.

(3) *Election to override the safe harbor exception.*—(i) *In general.*—Except as provided in paragraphs (d)(3)(vi) and (vii) of this section, the safe harbor exception provided for by this paragraph (d) does not apply to any payee statement if the person to whom the statement is required to be furnished (the payee) makes an election that the safe harbor not apply with respect to the statement.

(ii) *Timing of election.*—The payee must elect no later than the later of 30 days after the date on which the payee statement is required to be furnished to the payee, or October 15 of the calendar year, to receive a correct payee statement required to be furnished in that calendar year without having the safe harbor under paragraph (d)(1) of this section apply. The date of an election is the date the election is received by the filer. For purposes of this section, the provisions of section 7502 relating to timely mailing treated as timely delivery apply in determining the date an election is considered to be received by the filer, treating delivery to the filer as if the filer were an agency, officer, or office under such section. The election shall remain in effect for all subsequent years unless revoked under paragraph (d)(3)(vii) of this section.

(iii) *Manner for making the election.*—Except as provided in paragraph (d)(3)(v) of this section, the payee must make the election by delivering the election in writing to the filer. Except as provided in paragraph (d)(3)(v) of this section, the written election must be made in writing on paper. The payee may deliver the election in person, by mail by United States Postal Service, or by a designated delivery service as defined under section 7502(f)(2). If the filer has not otherwise provided an address under paragraph (d)(3)(v) of this section, the payee shall send the written election to the filer's address appearing on the payee statement furnished by the filer to the payee with respect to which the election is being made or as directed by that person upon appropriate inquiry by the payee. The written election must:

(A) Clearly state that the payee is making the election;

(B) Provide the payee's name, address, and taxpayer identification number (TIN) (as defined in section 7701(a)(41) of the Internal Revenue Code) to the filer;

(C) If the payee wants the election to apply only to specific types of statements, identify the type of payee statement(s) and account number(s), if applicable, to which the election applies (for example, Form 1099-DIV, "Dividends and Distributions"); and

(D) Provide any other information required by the Internal Revenue Service in forms, instructions, or publications.

(iv) *Payee statements to which the election applies.*—An election by a payee under paragraph (d)(3)(i) of this section applies to all types of payee statements the filer is required to furnish to the payee, unless the payee specifies otherwise on the election under paragraph (d)(3)(iii)(C) of this section.

(v) *Reasonable alternative manner for making the election in cases of notification by the filer.*—(A) *In general.*—If the filer satisfies the requirements of paragraph (d)(3)(v)(B) of this section, and provides for a reasonable alternative manner as described in paragraph (d)(3)(v)(E) of this section, a payee may decide to make the election under paragraph (d)(3)(i) of this section pursuant to that reasonable alternative manner.

(B) *Notification of payee of reasonable alternative manner for making election.*—The filer may elect to provide notification to the payee of a reasonable alternative manner to make the election under paragraph (d)(3)(i) of this section, as described in paragraph

(d)(3)(v)(E) of this section. To provide a valid notification under this paragraph (d)(3)(v)(B), the filer must provide notification to the payee that:

(1) Is in writing (either on paper or in electronic format);

(2) Is timely provided to the payee under paragraph (d)(3)(v)(D) of this section;

(3) Explains to the payee to whom that filer is required to furnish a payee statement of the payee's ability to elect, under paragraph (d)(3)(i) of this section, that the safe harbor exceptions for de minimis errors not apply, and of the payee's ability to choose to make the election using the default method under paragraph (d)(3)(iii) of this section;

(4) Provides an address to which the payee may send an election under paragraphs (d)(3)(i) and (iii) of this section;

(5) Provides any reasonable alternative manner or manners, as described in paragraph (d)(3)(v)(E) of this section, that the filer is making available for the payee to make the election under paragraph (d)(3)(i) of this section; and

(6) Describes the information required for making the election described by paragraphs (d)(3)(iii)(A) through (D) of this section. Solely for purposes of the reasonable alternative manner, the notification may provide that some or all of the information described in paragraph (d)(3)(iii)(B) of this section is not required and may provide that the provision of an account number as referenced in paragraph (d)(3)(iii)(C) of this section is required if the payee decides to use the reasonable alternative manner for the election.

(C) *Notification of revocation procedures.*—A notification under this paragraph (d)(3)(v) may also provide the procedures for making a revocation of an election under paragraph (d)(3)(vii) of this section. Solely for purposes of the reasonable alternative manner, the notification may provide that some or all of the information described in paragraph (d)(3)(vii)(B) of this section is not required and may provide that the provision of an account number as referenced in paragraph (d)(3)(vii)(E) of this section is required if the payee decides to use a reasonable alternative manner for making a revocation.

(D) *Time for providing notification of reasonable alternative manner for making payee election.*—A notification under this paragraph (d)(3)(v) will be timely under paragraph (d)(3)(v)(B)(2) of this section if:

(1) The notification is provided with, or at the time of, the furnishing of the payee statement; or

(2) The filer previously provided a valid notification under paragraph (d)(3)(v) of this section to the payee with, or at the time of, the furnishing of a payee statement associated with a particular account, in which case notification will be considered to have been timely provided with respect to subsequent payee statements associated with that particular account. If the filer wishes to provide for a different reasonable alternative manner than a previous reasonable alternative manner, the filer must provide new notification in compliance with the timeliness rule of paragraph (d)(3)(v)(D)(1) of this section, and must accept payee elections under the previous reasonable alternative manner for a period of at least 60 days after the receipt of the new notification by the payee.

(E) *Reasonable alternative manner.*—A reasonable alternative manner described in a notification under paragraph (d)(3)(v)(B) of this section may include that a payee election under paragraph (d)(3)(i) of this section may be made electronically (for example, via e-mail or web site) or telephonically. The reasonable alternative manner may not impose any prerequisite, condition, or time limitation on, or otherwise limit, the payee's ability to make an election under paragraph (d)(3)(i) of this section, except as described in paragraphs (d)(3)(ii) and (iii) of this section; it may only offer a reasonable alternative manner or manners for making this election under this paragraph (d)(3)(v).

(vi) *Election not available for certain information.*—The election to override the safe harbor exception provided for by paragraph (d)(3)(i) of this section is not available with respect to information that may not be altered under specific information reporting rules. See, for example, § 1.6045-4(i)(5) of this chapter.

(vii) *Revocation of election.*—The payee may revoke a prior election by submitting a revocation to the filer. The effect of a revocation of a prior election is that the safe harbor for certain de minimis errors will apply to the payee statements that the payee identifies and that are furnished or are due to be furnished after the revocation is received. The revocation will remain in effect until the payee makes a valid and timely election under paragraph (d)(3)(i) of this section. The date of a revocation is the date the revocation is received by the filer. For purposes of this section, the provisions of section 7502 relating to timely mailing treated as timely delivery apply in determining the date a revocation is considered to be received by the filer, treating delivery to the filer as if the filer were an agency, officer, or office under such section. The revocation must be made in the same manner or manners described for making the election, that is pursuant to either paragraph (d)(3)(iii) or (v) of this section, as the payee chooses if paragraph (d)(3)(v) of this section is applicable. Except as provided under paragraph (d)(3)(v)(B)(6) of this section, the revocation must:

(A) Clearly state that the payee is revoking the payee's prior election;

(B) Provide the payee's name, address, and TIN to the filer;

(C) Provide the name of the filer;

(D) Identify the type of payee statement(s) (for example, Form 1099-DIV)

to which the revocation applies;

(E) Identify the account number(s), if applicable, to which the revocation applies; and

(F) Provide any other information required by the Internal Revenue Service in forms, instructions or publications.

(viii) *Reasonable cause.*—See § 301.6724-1(h) for rules relating to waiver of the section 6722 penalty in cases where the safe harbor exception provided for by paragraph (d)(1) of this section does not apply because of an election under paragraph (d)(3)(i) of this section.

(4) *Record retention.*—To facilitate proof of compliance with reporting and other obligations under the internal revenue laws, filers must retain records of any election or revocation by the payee under paragraph (d)(3)(i) or (vii) of this section, respectively, and any notification made under paragraph (d)(3)(v) of this section for as long as the contents of the election, revocation, or notification may be material in the administration of any internal revenue law. For rules regarding record retention, see section 6001 and § 1.6001-1 of this chapter. For additional procedures applicable to record retention in the context of electronic storage, see Rev. Proc. 97-22, 1997-1 C.B. 652, Rev. Proc. 98-25, 1998-1 C.B. 689, and any subsequently published guidance.

(5) *Examples.*—The provisions of paragraphs (d)(1) through (4) of this section may be illustrated by the following examples, which do not address any possible application of the penalty for intentional disregard under paragraph (c) of this section or the reasonable cause waiver under § 301.6724-1(a):

(i) *Example 1.* (A) Filer W is required to file with the IRS by February 28, 2019, and furnish to Payee A by February 15, 2019, Form 1099-B "Proceeds From Broker and Barter Exchange Transactions," because Filer W is a broker who sold stocks on behalf of Payee A resulting in proceeds of $5000 during calendar year 2018. Filer W properly withheld an amount of $1736 under applicable backup withholding rules because Payee A failed to furnish Payee A's TIN to Filer W. On the Form 1099-B, Filer W reports as follows: Box 1d, Proceeds, $4900; and Box 4, Federal income tax withheld, $1761. Filer W otherwise correctly and timely files and furnishes the Form 1099-B. Payee A does not make an election under paragraph (d)(3)(i) of this section.

(B) The safe harbor exception for de minimis errors provided for by paragraph (d)(1) of this section applies, because the differences between each of the amounts reported in error and the correct amounts are not more than the applicable limits. The error in the dollar amount reported in Box 1d, Proceeds, is de minimis because the difference between the amount in error ($4900) and the correct amount ($5000) is not more than $100; it is exactly $100. The error in the dollar amount reported in Box 4, Federal income tax withheld, is de minimis because the $25 difference between the amount in error ($1761) and the correct amount ($1736) is not more than $25, the limit for an error with respect to an amount reported for tax withheld.

(ii) *Example 2.* (A) The facts are the same as in *Example 1* in paragraph (d)(5)(i) of this section, except that Filer W reports $1710 as the amount in Box 4, Federal income tax withheld.

(B) The safe harbor exception for de minimis errors provided for by paragraph (d)(1) of this section does not apply because the Form 1099-B contains a failure that is not a de minimis error. The difference between the amount in error ($1710) and the correct amount ($1736) is $26, which is more than the $25 limit for de minimis errors with respect to an amount reported for tax withheld.

(iii) *Example 3.* (A) In 2019, Filer X provides Payee B with valid notification of a reasonable alternative manner under paragraph (d)(3)(v) of this section for making the payee election under paragraph (d)(3)(i) of this section. Payee B timely elects pursuant to the reasonable alternative manner during 2019. Payee B elects with respect to all payee statements that Filer X is required to furnish to Payee B. In January 2020, Filer X decides to provide for a different, but also valid, reasonable alternative manner; Filer X provides notification of this different reasonable alternative manner to Payee B, and Payee B receives notification of this different reasonable alternative manner, pursuant to paragraph (d)(3)(v)(B) of this section, on January 16, 2020.

(B) Payee B decides to revoke Payee B's prior election, with respect to the Forms 1099-DIV that Filer X is required to furnish to Payee B. Under paragraph (d)(3)(vii) of this section, Payee B may provide the revocation to Filer X in any of three different manners. First, Payee B may provide the revocation to Filer X in the same manner as if Payee B were making an election under the default manner of paragraph (d)(3)(iii) of this section; Payee B may do so at any time. Second, having received notification from Filer X of the different reasonable alternative manner on January 16, 2020, Payee B may provide the revocation to Filer X in the same manner as if Payee B were making an election under the different reasonable alternative manner pursuant to paragraph (d)(3)(v) of this section. Third, because Filer X previously provided notification of a reasonable alternative manner (2019 alternative) before providing notification of a different reasonable alternative manner on January 16, 2020, (2020 alternative), Payee B may provide the revocation to Filer X in the same manner as if Payee B were making an election under the previous reasonable alternative manner (2019 alternative); Payee B may do so for a period of 60 days after January 16, 2020, pursuant to paragraph (d)(3)(v)(D)(2) of this section.

(e) *Definitions.*—(1) *Payee.*—See § 301.6721-1(h)(5) for the definition of "payee."

(2) *Payee statement.*—For purposes of this section the term "payee statement" has the same meaning as payee statement as defined by section 6724(d)(2), including any statement required to be furnished under—

* * *

(xxxiii) Section 6055 (relating to information returns reporting minimum essential coverage);

(xxxiv) Section 6056 (relating to information returns reporting on offers of health insurance coverage by applicable large employer members);

(xxxv) Section 6035, other than a statement described in section 6724(d)(1)(D), (relating to basis information with respect to property acquired from decedents, generally Schedule A of Form 8971, "Information Regarding Beneficiaries Acquiring Property From a Decedent"),

(xxxvi) Section 6050Y(a)(2), 6050Y(b)(2), or 6050Y(c)(2) (relating to certain life insurance contract transactions); or

(xxxvii) Section 6226(a)(2) (regarding statements relating to alternative to payment of imputed underpayment by a partnership) or under any other provision of this title which provides for the application of rules similar to section 6226(a)(2).

* * *

(4) *Filer.*—For purposes of this section the term "filer" means a person that is required to furnish a payee statement as defined in paragraphs (e)(2) and (3) of this section under the applicable information reporting section described in paragraphs (e)(2) and (3) of this section.

(f) *Adjustment for inflation.*—Each of the dollar amounts under paragraphs (a), (b), and (c) of this section and paragraphs (a), (b), (d)(1), and (e) of section 6722 shall be adjusted for inflation pursuant to section 6722(f).

(g) *Applicability date.*—This section applies with respect to payee statements required to be furnished on or after January 1 of the calendar year immediately following the date of publication of a Treasury decision adopting these rules as final regulations in the **Federal Register**.

Information Reporting: Waiver of Penalty: Prompt Correction

Information Reporting: Waiver of Penalty: Prompt Correction.—Amendments to Reg. § 301.6724-1, relating to waiver under Code Sec. 6724 of a penalty imposed by Code Sec. 6721 for failure to file a correct information return and providing guidance on the requirement of prompt correction of the failure to file or file correctly, are proposed (published in the Federal Register on July 9, 2003) (REG-141669-02).

☐ Par. 2. Section 301.6724-1 is amended by:

1. Revising paragraph (d)(1)(ii)(D).

2. Adding paragraph (d)(3).

The revision and addition read as follows:

§301.6724-1. Reasonable cause.

* * *

(d) * * *

(1) * * *

(ii) * * *

(D) Correcting the failure as promptly as possible upon removal of the impediment or discovery of the failure. A person may correct a failure by filing or correcting the information return, by furnishing or correcting the payee statement, or by providing or correcting the information to satisfy the specified information reporting requirement with respect to which the failure occurs. This paragraph (d)(1)(ii)(D) does not apply with respect to information that specific information reporting rules prohibit the filer from altering. See § 1.6045-4(i)(5) of this chapter. In the case of a waiver of a penalty imposed by section 6722 or 6723 of the Internal Revenue Code, correction is prompt if it is made within 30 days after the date of removal of the impediment or discovery of the failure. For purposes of section 6721 of the Internal Revenue Code, a correction is prompt if the Internal Revenue Service receives the correction—

(i) On or before 30 days after the required filing date;

(ii) On or before August 1 following that required filing date;

(iii) On or before the date or dates announced in guidance governing the electronic or magnetic filing of information returns;

(iv) On or before the date or dates announced in other guidance including forms and instructions; or

(v) Within 30 days after the date the impediment is removed or the failure is discovered if the correction is not submitted within the time frames set forth in paragraphs (d)(1)(ii)(D)(i) through (iv).

* * *

(3) [Reserved]For further guidance, see § 301.6724-1T(d)(3).

* * *

Catastrophic Health Coverage: Information Reporting

Catastrophic Health Coverage: Information Reporting.—Amendments to Reg. § 301.6724-1, relating to information reporting of minimum essential coverage under section 6055 of the Internal Revenue Code, are proposed (published in the Federal Register on August 2, 2016) (REG-103058-16).

Par. 4. Section 301.6724-1 is amended by adding a sentence to the end of paragraph (e)(1)(vi)(A) to read as follows:

§301.6724-1. Reasonable cause.

* * *

(e) * * *

(1) * * *

(vi) *Exceptions and limitations.*—(A) * * * See § 1.6055-1(h)(3) of this chapter, which provides rules on the time, form, and manner in which a TIN must be provided for information returns required to be filed and individual statements required to be furnished under section 6055.

* * *

Qualified Tuition: Related Expenses: Reporting

Qualified Tuition: Related Expenses: Reporting.—Amendments to Reg. § 301.6724-1, revising the rules for reporting qualified tuition and related expenses under section 6050S on a Form 1098-T, "Tuition Statement," and conforming the regulations to changes made to section 6050S by the Protecting Americans from Tax Hikes Act of 2015, are proposed (published in the Federal Register on August 2, 2016) (REG-131418-14).

Par. 9. Section 301.6724-1 is amended by adding a sentence at the end of paragraph (a)(1) to read as follows:

§301.6724-1. Reasonable cause.—(a) * * *

(1) * * * For waiver in the case of eligible educational institutions required to report information under section 6050S with respect to qualified tuition and related expenses, see § 1.6050S-1(f) of this chapter.

* * *

Correct Payee Statements: Failure to File Correct Information: Penalties

Correct Payee Statements: Failure to File Correct Information: Penalties.—Amendments to Reg. § 301.6724-1, relating to penalties for failure to file correct information returns or furnish correct payee statements, are proposed (published in the Federal Register on October 17, 2018) (REG-118826-16).

Par. 7. Section 301.6724-1 is amended by:

1. Revising paragraphs (a)(1) and (a)(2)(ii).

2. Designating the undesignated paragraph following paragraph (a)(2)(ii) as paragraph (a)(2)(iii) and revising newly designated paragraph (a)(2)(iii).

3. Revising paragraphs (b) introductory text and (b)(2)(i) and (ii).

4. Designating the undesignated paragraph following paragraph (b)(2)(ii) as paragraph (b)(3).

5. Revising paragraphs (c)(3)(ii), (e)(1) introductory text, (e)(1)(i), (e)(1)(vi)(E) and (F), (f)(1) introductory text, (f)(1)(i), (f)(5)(i) and (ii), (g), (h), (k), (m) introductory text, and (m)(1).

6. Adding paragraph (o).

The revisions and additions read as follows:

§301.6724-1. Reasonable cause.—(a) *Waiver of the penalty.*—(1) *General rule.*—The penalty for a failure relating to an information reporting requirement as defined in paragraph (j) of this section is waived if the failure is due to reasonable cause and is not due to willful neglect.

(2) * * *

(ii) The failure arose from events beyond the filer's control ("impediment"), as described in paragraph (c) of this section.

(iii) Moreover, the filer must establish that the filer acted in a responsible manner, as described in paragraph (d) of this section, both before and after the failure occurred. Thus, if the filer establishes that there are significant mitigating factors for a failure but is unable to establish that the filer acted in a responsible manner, the mitigating factors will not be sufficient to obtain a waiver of the penalty. Similarly, if the filer establishes that a failure arose from an impediment but is unable to establish that the filer acted in a responsible manner, the impediment will not be sufficient to obtain a waiver of the penalty. See paragraph (g) of this section for the reasonable cause safe harbor for persons who exercise due diligence. See paragraph (h) of this section for the reasonable cause safe harbor after an election under section 6722(c)(3)(B) and § 301.6722-1(d)(3).

(b) *Significant mitigating factors.*—In order to establish reasonable cause under this paragraph (b), the filer must satisfy paragraph (d) of this section and must show that there are significant mitigating factors for the failure. See paragraph (c)(5) of this section for the application of this paragraph (b) to failures attributable to the actions of a filer's agent. The applicable mitigating factors include, but are not limited to—

* * *

(2) * * *

(i) Whether the filer has incurred any penalty under § 301.6721-1, § 301.6722-1, or § 301.6723-1 in prior years for the failure; and

(ii) If the filer has incurred any such penalty in prior years, the extent of the filer's success in lessening its error rate from year to year.

* * *

(c) * * *

(3) * * *

(ii) The cost of filing on magnetic media was prohibitive as determined at least 45 days before the due date of the returns (without regard to extensions);

* * *

(e) *Acting in a responsible manner—special rules for missing TINs.*—(1) *In general.*—A filer that is seeking a waiver for reasonable cause under paragraph (c)(6) of this section will satisfy paragraph (d)(2) of this section with respect to establishing that a failure to include a TIN on an information return resulted from the failure of the payee to provide information to the filer (that is, a missing TIN) only if the filer makes the initial and, if required, the annual solicitations described in this paragraph (e) ("required solicitations"). For purposes of this section, a number is treated as a "missing TIN" if the number does not contain nine digits or includes one or more alpha characters (a character or symbol other than an Arabic numeral) as one of the nine digits. A solicitation means a request by the filer for the payee to furnish a correct TIN. See paragraph (f) of this section for the rules that a filer must follow to establish that the filer acted in a responsible manner with respect to providing incorrect TINs on information returns. See paragraph (e)(1)(vi)(A) of this section for alternative solicitation requirements. See paragraph (g) of this section for the safe harbor due diligence rules.

(i) *Initial solicitation.*—An initial solicitation for a payee's correct TIN must be made at the time an account is opened. The term "account" includes accounts, relationships, and other transactions. However, a filer is not required to make an initial solicitation under this paragraph (e)(1)(i) with respect to a new account if the filer has the payee's TIN and uses that TIN for all accounts of the payee. For example, see §31.3406(h)-3(a) of this chapter. If the account is opened in person, the initial solicitation may be made by oral or written request, such as on an account creation document. If the account is opened by mail, telephone, or other electronic means, the TIN may be requested through such communications. If the account is opened by the payee's completing and mailing an application furnished by the filer that requests the payee's TIN, the initial solicitation requirement is considered met. If a TIN is not received as a result of an initial solicitation, the filer may be required to make additional solicitations ("annual solicitations").

* * *

(vi) * * *

(E) A filer is not required to make annual solicitations by mail on accounts with respect to which the filer has an undeliverable address, that is, where other mailings to that address have been returned to the filer because the address was incorrect and no new address has been provided to the filer.

(F) Except as provided in paragraphs (e)(1)(vi) (A) and (C) of this section, no more than two annual solicitations are required under this paragraph (e) in order for a filer to establish reasonable cause.

* * *

(f) *Acting in a responsible manner—special rules for incorrect TINs.*—(1) *In general.*—A filer that is seeking a waiver for reasonable cause under paragraph (c)(6) of this section will satisfy paragraph (d)(2) of this section with respect to establishing that a failure resulted from incorrect information provided by the payee or any other person (that is, inclusion of an incorrect TIN) on an information return only if the filer makes the initial and annual solicitations described in this paragraph (f). See paragraph (e)(1) of this section for the definition of the term "solicitation." See paragraph (f)(5)(i) of this section for alternative solicitation requirements. See paragraph (g) of this section for the safe harbor due diligence rules.

(i) *Initial solicitation.*—An initial solicitation for a payee's correct TIN must be made at the time the account is opened. The term "account" includes accounts, relationships, and other transactions. However, a filer is not required to make an initial solicitation under this paragraph (f)(1)(i) with respect to a new account if the filer has the payee's TIN and uses that TIN for all accounts of the payee. For example, see §31.3406(h)-3(a) of this chapter. No additional solicitation is required after the filer receives the TIN unless the Internal Revenue Service or, in some cases, a broker notifies the filer that the TIN is incorrect. Following such notification the filer may be required to make an annual solicitation to obtain the correct TIN as provided in paragraphs (f)(1)(ii) and (iii) of this section.

* * *

(5) *Exceptions and limitations..*—(i) The solicitation requirements under this paragraph (f) do not apply to the extent that an information reporting provision under which a return, as defined in §301.6721-1(h), is filed provides specific requirements relating to the manner or the time period in which a TIN must be solicited. In that event, the requirements of this paragraph (f) will be satisfied only if the filer complies with the manner and time period requirement under the specific information reporting provisions and this paragraph (f), to the extent applicable.

(ii) An annual solicitation is not required to be made for a year under this paragraph (f) with respect to an account if no payments are made to the account for such year or if no return as defined in §301.6721-1(h) is required to be filed for the account for such year.

* * *

(g) *Due diligence safe harbor.*—(1) *In general.*—A filer may establish reasonable cause with respect to a failure relating to an information reporting requirement as described in paragraph (j) of this section if the filer exercises due diligence with respect to failures described in sections 6721 through 6723.

(2) *Special rules relating to TINs.*—(i) *Questions and answers.*—The following questions and answers provide guidance on the exercise of due diligence for an exception to a penalty under sections 6721 through 6723 for a failure to provide a correct TIN on any information return as defined in §301.6721-1(h), payee statement as defined in §301.6722-1(e), document as described in §301.6723-1(a)(4), or the failure merely to provide a TIN as described in §301.6723-1(a)(4)(ii).

(ii) *General rule.*—(A) Q–1.—Is a filer subject to a penalty for a failure to provide a correct TIN on an information return with respect to a reportable interest or dividend payment if the payee has certified, under penalties of perjury, that the TIN furnished to the filer is the payee's correct number, the filer provided that number on an information return, and the number is later determined not to be the payee's correct number?

(B) A–1.—A filer is not subject to a penalty for failure to provide the payee's correct TIN on an information return, if the payee has certified, under penalties of perjury, that the TIN provided to the filer was his correct number, and the filer included such number on the information return before being notified by the Internal Revenue Service (IRS) (or a broker) that the number is incorrect.

(iii) *Due Diligence Defined for Accounts Opened and Instruments Acquired After December 31, 1983.*—(A)(1) Q–2.—In order for a filer of a reportable interest or dividend payment (other than in a window transaction) to be considered to have exercised due diligence in furnishing the correct TIN of a payee with respect to an account opened or an instrument acquired after December 31, 1983, what actions must the filer take?

(2) A–2.—(i) In general, the filer of an account or instrument that is not a pre–1984 account nor a window transaction must use a TIN provided by the payee under penalties of perjury on information returns filed with the IRS to satisfy the due diligence requirement. Therefore, if a filer permits a payee to open an account without obtaining the payee's TIN under penalties of perjury and files an information return with the IRS with a missing or an incorrect TIN, the filer will be liable for the $250 penalty for the year with respect to which such information return is filed. However, in its administrative discretion, the IRS will not enforce the penalty with respect to a calendar year if the certified TIN is obtained after the account is opened and before December 31 of such year, provided that the filer exercises due diligence in processing such number, that is, the filer uses the same care in processing the TIN provided by the payee that a reasonably prudent filer would use in the course of the filer's business in handling account information such as account numbers and balances.

(ii) Once notified by the IRS (or a broker) that a number is incorrect, a filer is liable for the penalty for all prior years in which an information return was filed with that particular incorrect number if the filer has not exercised due diligence with respect to such years. A pre-existing certified TIN does not constitute an exercise of due diligence after the IRS or a broker notifies the filer that the number is incorrect unless the filer undertakes the actions described in §31.3406(d)-5(d)(2)(i) of this chapter with respect to accounts receiving reportable payments described in section 3406(b)(1) and reported on information returns described in sections 6724(d)(1)(A)(i) through (iv).

(B)(1) Q–3.—Is a filer as described in paragraph (g)(2)(iii)(A)(2) of this section liable for the penalty if the filer obtained a certified TIN from a payee but inadvertently processed the name or number incorrectly on the information return?

(2) A–3.—Yes. The filer is liable for the penalty unless the filer exercised that degree of care in processing the TIN and name and in furnishing it on the information return that a reasonably prudent filer would use in the course of the filer's business in handling account information, such as account numbers and account balances.

(iv) *Special rules.*—(A)(1) Q–4.—With respect to an instrument transferred without the assistance of a broker, is a filer liable for the penalty for filing an information return with a missing or an incorrect TIN if the filer records on its books a transfer of a readily tradable instrument in a transaction in which the filer was not a party?

(2) A–4.—Generally, a filer as described in paragraph (g)(2)(iv)(A)(1) of this section will be considered to have exercised due diligence with respect to a readily tradable instrument that is not part of a pre-1984 account with the filer if the filer records on its

books a transfer in which the filer was not a party. This exception applies until the calendar year in which the filer receives a certified TIN from the payee.

(B)(1) Q–5.—Is the filer described in paragraph (g)(2)(iv)(A)(2) of this section required to solicit the TIN of a payee of an account with a missing TIN in order to be considered as having exercised due diligence in a subsequent calendar year?

(2) A–5.—There is no requirement on the filer to solicit the TIN in order to be considered to have exercised due diligence in a subsequent calendar year under the rule set forth in paragraph (g)(2)(iv)(A)(2) of this section.

(C)(1) Q–6.—Is a filer as described in paragraph (g)(2)(iv)(A)(1) of this section considered to have exercised due diligence if the payee provides a TIN to the filer (whether or not certified), the filer uses that number on the information return filed for the payee, and the number is later determined to be incorrect?

(2) A–6.—A filer as described in paragraph (g)(2)(iv)(A)(1) of this section who records on its books a transfer in which it was not a party is considered to have exercised due diligence under the rule set forth in paragraph (g)(2)(iv)(A)(2) of this section where the transfer is accompanied with a TIN provided that the filer uses the same care in processing the TIN provided by a payee that a reasonably prudent filer would use in the course of the filer's business in handling account information, such as account numbers and account balances. Thus, a filer will not be liable for the penalty if the filer uses the TIN provided by the payee on information returns that it files, even if the TIN provided by the payee is later determined to be incorrect. However, a filer will not be considered as having exercised due diligence under paragraph (g)(2)(iv)(A)(2) of this section after the IRS or a broker notifies the filer that the number is incorrect unless the filer undertakes the required additional actions described in paragraph (g)(2)(iii)(A)(2)(ii) of this section.

(D)(1) Q–7.—Is a filer liable for a penalty for filing an information return with a missing or an incorrect TIN with respect to a post-1983 account or instrument if the filer could have met the due diligence requirements but for the fact that the filer incurred an undue hardship?

(2) A–7.—A filer of a post-1983 account or instrument is not liable for a penalty under section 6721(a) for filing an information return with a missing or an incorrect TIN if the IRS determines that the filer could have satisfied the due diligence requirements but for the fact that the filer incurred an undue hardship. An undue hardship is an extraordinary or unexpected event such as the destruction of records or place of business of the filer by fire or other casualty (or the place of business of the filer's agent who under a pre-existing written contract had agreed to fulfill the filer's due diligence obligations with respect to the account subject to the penalty and there was no means for the obligations to be performed by another agent or the filer). Undue hardship will also be found to exist if the filer could have met the due diligence requirements only by incurring an extraordinary cost.

(E)(1) Q–8.—How does a filer obtain a determination from the IRS that the filer has met the undue hardship exception to the penalty under section 6721(a) for the failure to include the correct TIN on an information return for the year with respect to which the filer is subject to the penalty?

(2) A–8.—A determination of undue hardship may be established only by submitting a written statement to the IRS signed under penalties of perjury that sets forth all the facts and circumstances that make an affirmative showing that the filer could have satisfied the due diligence requirements but for the occurrence of an undue hardship. Thus, the statement must describe the undue hardship and make an affirmative showing that the filer either was in the process of exercising or stood ready to exercise due diligence when the undue hardship occurred. A filer may request an undue hardship determination by submitting a written statement to the address provided with the notice proposing penalty assessment (for example, Notice 972CG) or the notice of penalty assessment (for example, CP15 or CP215), or as otherwise directed by the Internal Revenue Service in forms, instructions or publications.

(F)(1) Q–9.—Is a pre-1984 account or instrument of a filer that is exchanged for an account or instrument of another filer as a result of a merger of the other filer or acquisition of the accounts or instruments of such filer transformed into a post-1983 account or instrument if the merger or acquisition occurs after December 31, 1983?

(2) A–9.—No. A pre-1984 account or instrument that is exchanged for another account or instrument pursuant to a statutory merger or the acquisition of accounts or instruments is not transformed into a post-1983 account or instrument because the exchange occurs without the participation of the payee.

(G)(1) Q–10.—May the acquiring taxpayer described in paragraph (g)(2)(iv)(F)(2) of this section rely upon the business records and past procedures of the merged filer or the filer whose accounts or instruments were acquired in order to establish that due diligence has been exercised on the acquired pre-1984 and post-1983 accounts or instruments?

(2) A–10.—Yes. The acquiring filer may rely upon the business records and past procedures of the merged filer or of the filer whose accounts or instruments were acquired in order to establish due diligence to avoid the penalty under section 6721(a) with respect to information returns that have been or will be filed.

(H)(1) Q–11.—To what extent may a filer rely on the due diligence rules set forth in § § 35a.9999-1, 35a.9999-2, and 35a.9999-3 of this chapter in effect prior to January 1, 2001 (see § § 35a.9999-1, 35a.9999-2, and 35a.9999-3 as contained in 26 CFR part 35a, revised April 1, 1999).

(2) A–11.—A filer may rely on the due diligence rules set forth in § § 35a.9999-1, 35a.9999-2, and 35a.9999-3 of this chapter in effect prior to January 1, 2001 (see § § 35a.9999-1, 35a.9999-2, and 35a.9999-3 as contained in 26 CFR part 35a, revised April 1, 1999) solely for the definitions of terms or phrases used in this paragraph (g)(2).

(3) *Effective dates.*—This paragraph (g) is effective for information returns as defined in section 6724(d)(1) required to be filed, payee statements as defined in section 6724(d)(2) required to be furnished, and specified information as described in section 6724(d)(3) required to be reported on or after January 1 of the calendar year immediately following the date of publication of a Treasury decision adopting these rules as final regulations in the **Federal Register**. See § 301.6724-1(g) in effect prior to January 1 of the calendar year immediately following the date of publication of a Treasury decision adopting these rules as final regulations in the **Federal Register** for substantially similar rules applicable prior to January 1 of the calendar year immediately following the date of publication of a Treasury decision adopting these rules as final regulations in the **Federal Register**.

(h) *Reasonable cause safe harbor after election under section 6722(c)(3)(B).*—A filer may establish reasonable cause with respect to a failure relating to an information reporting requirement as described in paragraph (j) of this section under this paragraph (h) if the failure is a result of an election under § 301.6722-1(d)(3)(i) and the presence of a de minimis error or errors as described in sections 6721(c)(3) and 6722(c)(3) and § § 301.6721-1(e) and 301.6722-1(d) on a filed information return or furnished payee statement. This paragraph (h) applies only when the safe harbor exceptions provided for by § 301.6721-1(e)(1) or § 301.6722-1(d)(1) would have applied, but for an election under § 301.6722-1(d)(3)(i). To establish reasonable cause and not willful neglect under this paragraph (h), the filer must file a corrected information return or furnish a corrected payee statement, or both, as applicable, within 30 days of the date of the election under § 301.6722-1(d)(3)(i). Where specific rules provide for additional time in which to furnish a corrected payee statement and file a corrected information return, the 30-day rule does not apply and the specific rules will apply. See for example § § 31.6051-1(c) through (d) and 31.6051-2(b). If the filer rectifies the failure outside of this 30-day period, the determination of reasonable cause will be on a case-by-case basis.

* * *

(k) *Examples.*—The provisions of this section may be illustrated by the following examples:

(1) *Example 1.* (i) On August 1, 2015, Individual A, an independent contractor, establishes a relationship ("an account") with Institution L, which pays A amounts reportable under section 6041. When A opens the account L requests that A supply his TIN on the account creation document. A fails to provide his TIN. On October 1, 2015, L mails a solicitation for A's TIN that satisfies the requirement of paragraph (e)(1)(ii) of this section. A does not provide a TIN to L during 2015. L timely files an information return subject to section 6721, that does not contain A's TIN, for payments made during the 2015 calendar year with respect to A's account. A penalty is imposed on L pursuant to § 301.6721-1(a)(2) for L's failure to file a correct information return because A's TIN was not shown on the return. The penalty will be waived, however, if L establishes that the failure was due to reasonable cause as defined in this section.

(ii) To establish reasonable cause under this section, L must satisfy both paragraphs (c)(6) and (d) of this section. The criteria for obtaining a waiver under these paragraphs are as follows:

(A) L acted in a responsible manner in attempting to satisfy the information reporting requirement as described in paragraph (d) of this section; and

(B) L demonstrates that the failure arose from events beyond L's control, as described in paragraph (c)(6) of this section.

(iii) Pursuant to paragraph (d)(2) of this section, L may demonstrate that it acted in a responsible manner only by complying with paragraph (e) of this section. Paragraph (e) of this section requires a filer to request a TIN at the time the account is opened (the initial solicitation) and, if the filer does not receive the TIN at that time, to solicit the TIN on or before December 31 of the year the account is opened (for accounts opened before December) or January 31 of the following year (for accounts in the preceding December) (the annual solicitation). Because L has performed these solicitations within the time and in the manner prescribed by paragraph (e) of this section, L has acted in a responsible manner as described in paragraph (d) of this section. L satisfies paragraph (c)(6) of this section because under the facts, L can show that the failure was caused by A's failure to provide a TIN, an event beyond L's control. As a result, L has established reasonable cause under paragraph (a)(2) of this section. Therefore, the penalty imposed under § 301.6721-1(a)(2) for the failure on the 2015 information return is waived. See section 3406(a)(1)(A) which requires L to impose backup withholding on reportable payments to A if L has not received A's TIN.

(2) *Example 2.* (i) On August 1, 2015, Individual B opens an account with Bank M, which pays B interest reportable under section 6049. When B opens the account, M requests that B supply his TIN on the account creation document. B provides his TIN to M. On February 29, 2016, M includes the TIN that B provided on the Form 1099–INT for the 2015 calendar year. In October 2016 the Internal Revenue Service, pursuant to section 3406(a)(1)(B), notifies M that the 2015 return filed for B contains an incorrect TIN. In April 2017 a penalty is imposed on M pursuant to § 301.6721-1(a)(2) for M's failure to file a correct information return for the 2015 calendar year, that is, the return did not contain B's correct TIN. The penalty will be waived, however, if M establishes that the failure was due to reasonable cause as defined in this section.

(ii) To establish reasonable cause under this section, M must satisfy the criteria in both paragraphs (c)(6) and (d) of this section. Pursuant to paragraph (d)(2) of this section, M can demonstrate that it acted in a responsible manner only if M complies with paragraph (f) of this section. Paragraph (f) of this section requires a filer to request a TIN at the time the account is opened, an initial solicitation. Under paragraph (f)(4) of this section the initial solicitation relates to failures on returns filed for the year an account is opened. Because M performed the initial solicitation in 2015 in the time and manner prescribed in paragraph (f)(1)(i) of this section and reflected the TIN received from B on the 2015 return as required by paragraph (f)(1)(iv) of this section, M has acted in a responsible manner as described in paragraph (d) of this section. M satisfies paragraph (c)(6) of this section because, under the facts, M can show that the failure was caused by B's failure to provide a correct TIN, an event beyond M's control. As a result, M has established reasonable cause under paragraph (a)(2) of this section. Therefore, the penalty imposed under § 301.6721-1(a)(2) for the failure on the 2015 information return is waived. See section 3406(a)(1)(B) which requires M to impose backup withholding on reportable payments to B if M has not received B's correct TIN.

(3) *Example 3.* (i) *Table.*

Table 1 to Paragraph (k)(3)(i)

2015	2/2016	10/2016	2/2017
Account opened (solicits TIN)	2015 return	B-notice w/respect to 2015 return	2016 return filed.

4/2017	10/2017	2/2018	4/2018
6721 penalty notice for 2015 return	B-notice w/respect to 2016 return	2017 return filed	6721 penalty notice for 2016

(ii) The facts are the same as in Example 2 in paragraph (k)(2) of this section. Under § 31.3406(d)-5(d)(2)(i) of this chapter and paragraph (f)(3) of this section, within 15 days of the October 2016 notification of the incorrect TIN from the Internal Revenue Service, M solicits the correct TIN from B. B fails to respond. M timely files the return for 2016 with respect to the account setting forth B's incorrect TIN. In October 2017 the Internal Revenue Service notifies M pursuant to section 3406(a)(1)(B) that the 2016 return contains an incorrect TIN. In April 2018, a penalty is imposed on M pursuant to § 301.6721-1(a)(2) for M's failure to include B's correct TIN on the return for 2016. The penalty will be waived, if M establishes that the failure was due to reasonable cause as defined in this section.

(iii) M must satisfy the reasonable cause criteria in paragraphs (c)(6) and (d) of this section. M may demonstrate that it acted in a responsible manner as required under paragraph (d) of this section only by complying with paragraph (f) of this section. Paragraph (f) of this section requires a filer to make an initial solicitation for a TIN when an account is opened. Further, a filer must make an annual solicitation for a TIN by mail within 15 business days after the date that the Internal Revenue Service notifies the filer of an incorrect TIN pursuant to section 3406(a)(1)(B). M made the initial solicitation for the TIN in 2015 and, after being notified of the incorrect TIN in October 2016, the first annual solicitation within the time and manner prescribed by § 31.3406(d)-5(d)(2)(i) of this chapter and paragraphs (f)(1)(ii) and (f)(2) of this section. M acted in a responsible manner. M satisfies paragraph (c)(6) of this section because, under the facts, M can show that the failure was caused by B's failure to provide his correct TIN, an event beyond M's control. As a result M has established reasonable cause under paragraph (a)(2) of this section. Therefore, the penalty imposed under § 301.6721-1(a)(2) for the failure on the 2016 return is waived due to reasonable cause.

(4) *Example 4.* (i) *Table.*

Table 2 to Paragraph (k)(2)(i)

2015	2/2016	10/2016	2/2017
Account opened (solicits TIN)	2015 return filed	B-notice w/respect to 2015 return	2016 return filed.

4/2017	10/2017	2/2018	4/2018
6721 penalty notice for 2015 return	B-notice w/respect to 2016 return	2017 return filed	6721 penalty notice for 2016 return.

(ii) The facts are the same as in Example 3 in paragraph (k)(3) of this section. M timely solicits B's TIN in October 2017, which B fails to provide. M files the return for 2017 with the incorrect TIN. In April 2019 the Internal Revenue Service informs M that the 2017 return contains an incorrect TIN. M does not solicit a TIN from B in 2018 and files a return for 2018 with B's incorrect TIN. M seeks a waiver of the penalty under § 301.6721-1(a)(2) for reasonable cause. M must satisfy the reasonable cause criteria in paragraphs (c)(6) and (d) of this section. Because M made the initial and two annual solicitations as required by paragraph (f) of this section, M has demonstrated that it acted in a responsible manner and is not required to solicit B's TIN in 2018. See paragraph (f)(5)(iv) of this section. M satisfies paragraph (c)(6) of this section because, under the facts, M can show that the failure was caused by B's failure to provide his correct TIN, an event beyond M's control. Therefore, M has established reasonable cause under paragraph (a)(2) of this section.

(5) *Example 5.* In 2016, Mortgage Finance Company N lends money to C to purchase property in a transaction subject to reporting under section 6050H and to section 6721. As part of the transaction, C gives N a promissory note providing for repayment of principal and the payment of interest. At the time C incurs the obligation N requests C's TIN, as required under § 1.6050H-2(f) of this chapter. C fails to provide the TIN as required by § 1.6050H-2(f) of this chapter. N sends solicitations by mail in 2016 and 2017 for the missing TIN, which C fails to provide. However, for 2018 M fails to send the solicitation required by § 1.6050H–2(f) of this chapter. N files returns for the 2016, 2017, and 2018 calendar years pursuant to section 6050H without C's TIN. Although N made the initial and the first annual solicitations in 2016 and the second annual solicitation in 2017, N did not solicit the TIN in 2018 as required under section 6050H, which requires continued annual solicitations until the TIN is obtained. Therefore, under paragraph (e)(1)(vi)(A) of this section the penalty imposed under § 301.6721-1(a) for the 2018 information return is not waived.

(6) *Example 6.* (i) *Table.*

Table 3 to Paragraph (k)(6)(i)

10/2015	2/2016	10/2016	2/2017
Account opened. (solicits TIN)	2015 return filed	B-notice w/respect to 2015 return	2016 return filed.

4/2017	10/2017	02/2018	4/2018
6721 penalty notice for 2015 return	B-notice w/respect to 2016 return	2017 return filed	6721 penalty notice for 2016 return

(ii) On October 1, 2015, Individual E opens an account with Institution R, which pays E amounts reportable under section 6049. When E opens the account, R requests that E supply his TIN on an account creation document, which E does. Pursuant to paragraph (f)(1)(iv) of this section, R uses the TIN furnished by E on the information return filed for the 2015 calendar year. In October 2016 the Internal Revenue Service notifies R pursuant to section 3406(a)(1)(B) that the information return filed for the 2015 calendar year contained an incorrect TIN. At the time R receives this notification, E's account contains the incorrect TIN. On December 31, 2016, R telephones E pursuant to paragraphs (f)(2) and (e)(2)(ii) of this section and receives different TIN information from E. R uses this information on the return that it files timely for E for the 2016 calendar year, that is, in February 2017.

(iii) In April 2017, the Internal Revenue Service notifies R pursuant to §301.6721-1(a)(2) that the information return filed for the 2015 calendar year contains an incorrect TIN. The penalty will be waived, however, if R establishes the failure was due to reasonable cause as defined in this section.

(iv) To establish reasonable cause under this section, R must satisfy the criteria in both paragraphs (c)(6) and (d)(2) of this section. Pursuant to paragraph (d)(2) of this section, R can demonstrate that it acted in a responsible manner only if it complies with paragraph (f) of this section. R solicited E's TIN at the time the account was opened (initial solicitation). Under paragraphs (d)(2) and (f)(4) of this section, the initial solicitation relates to failures on returns filed for the year in which an account is opened (that is, 2015) and for subsequent years until the calendar year in which the filer receives a notification of an incorrect TIN pursuant to section 3406. Because E failed to provide the correct TIN upon request, the failure arose from events beyond R's control as described in paragraph (c)(6) of this section. Therefore, the penalty with respect to the failure on the 2015 calendar year information return is waived due to reasonable cause.

(7) *Example 7.* (i) The facts are the same as in Example 6 in paragraph (k)(6) of this section. In April 2018 the Internal Revenue Service notifies R pursuant to §301.6721-1(a)(2) that the information return filed for the 2016 calendar year for E contained an incorrect TIN.

(ii) To establish reasonable cause for the failure under this section, R must satisfy the criteria in both paragraphs (c)(6) and (d)(2) of this section. Pursuant to paragraph (d)(2) of this section R may establish that it acted in a responsible manner only by complying with paragraph (f) of this section. Pursuant to paragraph (f)(1)(ii) of this section, R must make an annual solicitation after being notified of an incorrect TIN if the payee's account contains the incorrect TIN at the time of the notification. Paragraph (f)(3) of this section provides that if the filer is notified pursuant to section 3406(a)(1)(B) the time and manner of making an annual solicitation is that required under §31.3406(d)-5(g)(1)(ii) of this chapter. Section 31.3406(d)-5(g)(1)(ii) of this chapter requires R to notify E by mail within 15 business days after the date of the notice from the Internal Revenue Service, which R failed to do. As a result, R has failed to act in a responsible manner with respect to the failure on the 2016 information return, and the penalty will not be waived due to reasonable cause.

(8) *Example 8.* (i) On January 31, 2017, Institution Q timely furnishes Form 1099-MISC to Individual F. Also on January 31, 2017, Q timely files a corresponding Form 1099-MISC with the Internal Revenue Service. On March 15, 2017, Q becomes aware of de minimis errors (within the meaning of §301.6722-1(d)(2)) made on the Form

1099-MISC furnished to F and filed with the Internal Revenue Service. On March 20, 2017, F makes an election under §301.6722-1(d)(3)(i) with respect to the Form 1099-MISC that Q furnished to F. Q furnishes a corrected Form 1099-MISC to F and files a corrected Form 1099-MISC with the Internal Revenue Service by April 19, 2017, which date is 30 days from March 20, 2017.

(ii) The election by F and the presence of de minimis errors on the Forms 1099-MISC make the penalties under sections 6721 and 6722 applicable to Q. See §§301.6721-1(e)(3) and 301.6722-1(d)(3). Q, however, rectified the failures within 30 days of March 20, 2017, the date F made the election under §301.6722-1(d)(3)(i) with respect to the Form 1099-MISC that Q furnished to F. Therefore, under paragraph (h) of this section, Q is considered to have established reasonable cause, and under section 6724 and paragraph (a)(1) of this section the penalties under sections 6721 and 6722 are inapplicable.

(9) *Example 9.* (i) The facts are the same as in Example 8 in paragraph (k)(8) of this section, except that Q does not become aware of de minimis errors made on the Form 1099-MISC furnished to F and filed with the Internal Revenue Service until June 28, 2017. Additionally, Q furnishes the corrected Form 1099-MISC to F and files the corrected Form 1099-MISC with the Internal Revenue Service after June 28, 2017, but by July 28, 2017, which date is 30 days from June 28, 2017.

(ii) As in the example in paragraph (k)(9)(i), the election by F and the presence of de minimis errors on the Forms 1099-MISC make the penalties under sections 6721 and 6722 applicable to Q. Additionally, because Q did not furnish a corrected Form 1099-MISC to F and file a corrected Form 1099-MISC with the Internal Revenue Service within 30 days of the date of F's election under §301.6722-1(d)(3)(i), paragraph (h) of this section does not apply. However, Q may be able to demonstrate reasonable cause under the provisions of paragraph (a) of this paragraph. As part of this demonstration, for example, Q may be able to demonstrate that Q acted in a responsible manner under paragraph (d)(1) of this section by rectifying the failure (the de minimis errors) within 30 days of discovery.

* * *

(m) *Procedure for seeking a waiver.*—In seeking an administrative determination that the failure was due to reasonable cause and not willful neglect, the filer must submit a written statement to the address provided with the notice proposing penalty assessment (for example, Notice 972CG) or the notice of penalty assessment (for example, CP15 or CP215), or as otherwise directed by the Internal Revenue Service in forms, instructions or publications. The statement must—

(1) State the specific provision under which the waiver is being requested, that is, paragraph (b) or under paragraphs (c)(2) through (6) or paragraph (h);

* * *

(o) *Applicability date.*—In general, this section applies with respect to information returns required to be filed and payee statements required to be furnished on or after January 1 of the calendar year immediately following the date of publication of a Treasury decision adopting these rules as final regulations in the **Federal Register**. See paragraph (g)(3) of this section for effective dates applicable to paragraph (g) of this section. Paragraph (h) of this section applies with respect to information returns required to be filed and payee statements required to be furnished on or after January 1, 2017. See I.R.C. section 7805(b)(1)(C) and section 4 of Notice 2017-09, IRB-2017-4 (January 23, 2017).

MISCELLANEOUS PROVISIONS

Taxable Year: Partnerships, S Corporations, Personal Service Corporations

Taxable Year: Election: Partnership: S Corporation: Personal Service Corporation.—Temporary Reg. §§1.7519-0T—1.7519-3T, relating to the election of a taxable year by a partnership, S corporation or personal service corporation, are also proposed as final regulations and, when adopted, would become Reg. §§1.7519-0—1.7519-3 (published in the Federal Register on May 27, 1988).

§1.7519-0. Table of contents.

§1.7519-1. Required payments for entities electing not to have required year.

§1.7519-2. Required payments—procedures and administration.

§1.7519-3. Effective date.

DISCOVERY OF LIABILITY AND ENFORCEMENT OF TITLE

Administrative Proceedings: Excluding Non-Government Attorneys

Administrative Proceedings: Excluding Non-Government Attorneys.—Amendments to Reg. §301.7602-1, relating to administrative proceedings by generally excluding non-government attorneys from receiving summoned books, paper, records, or other data or from participating in the interview of a witness summoned by the IRS to provide testimony under oath, are proposed (published in the Federal Register on March 28, 2018) (REG-132434-17).

Par. 2. Section 301.7602-1 is amended by revising paragraphs (b)(3) and (d) to read as follows:

§301.7602-1. Examination of books and witnesses.

* * *

(b) * * *

(3) *Participation of a person described in section 6103(n).*—(i) *In general.*—Except as provided in paragraph (b)(3)(ii) of this section, for purposes of this paragraph (b), a person authorized to receive returns or return information under section 6103(n) and §301.6103(n)-1(a) of the regulations may receive and review books, papers, records, or other data produced in compliance with a summons, and, in the presence and under the guidance of an IRS officer or employee, participate fully in the interview of a witness summoned by the IRS to provide testimony under oath. Fully participating in an interview includes, but is not limited to: receipt, review, and use of summoned books, papers, records, or other data; being present during summons interviews; and questioning the person providing testimony under oath.

(ii) *Exception for certain non-governmental attorneys.*—An attorney who is not an officer or employee of the United States may not be hired by the IRS to perform the activities described in paragraph (b)(3)(i) of this section unless the attorney is hired by the IRS as a specialist in foreign, state, or local law, including tax law, or in non-tax substantive law that is relevant to an issue in the examination, such as patent law, property law, or environmental law, or is hired for knowledge, skills, or abilities other than providing legal services as an attorney.

* * *

(d) *Applicability date.*—This section is applicable after September 3, 1982, except for paragraphs (b)(1) and (2) of this section which are applicable on and after April 1, 2005 and paragraph (b)(3) of this section which applies to examinations begun or administrative summonses served by the IRS on or after March 27, 2018. For rules under paragraphs (b)(1) and (2) of this section that are applicable to summonses issued on or after September 10, 2002 or under paragraph (b)(3) of this section that are applicable to summons interviews conducted on or after June 18, 2014 and before July 14, 2016, see 26 CFR 301.7602-1T (revised as of April 1, 2016). For rules under paragraph (b)(3) of this section that are applicable to administrative summonses served by the IRS before March 27, 2018, see 26 CFR 301.7602-1 (revised as of April 1, 2017).

Church Tax: Inquiries and Examinations: Questions and Answers

Church Tax: Inquiries and Examinations: Questions and Answers.—Amendments to Reg. §301.7611-1, relating to the questions and answers relating to church tax inquiries and examinations, are proposed (published in the Federal Register on August 5, 2009) (REG-112756-09).

☐ Par. 2. In §301.7611-1, each entry in the table, undesignated paragraphs in the "Old Paragraph" column are designated as new paragraphs in the "New Paragraph" column to read as follows:

§301.7611-1. Questions and answer relating to church tax inquiries and examinations.

Old Paragraph	New Paragraph
§301.7611-1 A-5 first undesignated paragraph	§301.7611-1 A-5 paragraph (a)
§301.7611-1 A-5 second undesignated paragraph	§301.7611-1 A-5 paragraph (b)
§301.7611-1 A-6 first undesignated paragraph	§301.7611-1 A-6 paragraph (a)
§301.7611-1 A-9 first undesignated paragraph	§301.7611-1 A-9 paragraph (a)
§301.7611-1 A-9 second undesignated paragraph	§301.7611-1 A-9 paragraph (b)
§301.7611-1 A-10 first undesignated paragraph	§301.7611-1 A-10 paragraph (a)
§301.7611-1 A-10 second undesignated paragraph	§301.7611-1 A-10 paragraph (b)
§301.7611-1 A-10 third undesignated paragraph	§301.7611-1 A-10 paragraph (c)
§301.7611-1 A-10 fourth undesignated paragraph	§301.7611-1 A-10 paragraph (d)
§301.7611-1 A-10 fifth undesignated paragraph	§301.7611-1 A-10 paragraph (e)
§301.7611-1 A-11 first undesignated paragraph	§301.7611-1 A-11 paragraph (a)
§301.7611-1 A-11 second undesignated paragraph	§301.7611-1 A-11 paragraph (b)
§301.7611-1 A-11 third undesignated paragraph	§301.7611-1 A-11 paragraph (c)
§301.7611-1 A-13 first undesignated paragraph	§301.7611-1 A-13 paragraph (a)
§301.7611-1 A-13a first undesignated paragraph	§301.7611-1 A-13a paragraph (a)
§301.7611-1 A-14 first undesignated paragraph	§301.7611-1 A-14 paragraph (a)
§301.7611-1 A-14 second undesignated paragraph	§301.7611-1 A-14 paragraph (b)

Old Paragraph	New Paragraph
§ 301.7611-1 A-15 first undesignated paragraph	§ 301.7611-1 A-15 paragraph (a)
§ 301.7611-1 A-15 second undesignated paragraph	§ 301.7611-1 A-15 paragraph (b)
§ 301.7611-1 A-15 third undesignated paragraph	§ 301.7611-1 A-15 paragraph (c)
§ 301.7611-1 A-15 fourth undesignated paragraph	§ 301.7611-1 A-15 paragraph (d)
§ 301.7611-1 A-15 fifth undesignated paragraph	§ 301.7611-1 A-15 paragraph (e)
§ 301.7611-1 A-15 sixth undesignated paragraph	§ 301.7611-1 A-15 paragraph (f)
§ 301.7611-1 A-15 seventh undesignated paragraph	§ 301.7611-1 A-15 paragraph (g)
§ 301.7611-1 A-16 first undesignated paragraph	§ 301.7611-1 A-16 paragraph (a)
§ 301.7611-1 A-17 first undesignated paragraph	§ 301.7611-1 A-17 paragraph (a)

Par. 3. For each section listed in the table, remove the language in the "Remove" column and add in its place the language in the "Add" column as set forth below:

Section	Remove	Add
§ 301.7611-1 A-1 first sentence	appropriate Regional Commissioner (or higher Treasury official)	Director, Exempt Organizations
§ 301.7611-1 A-7 first sentence	appropriate Internal Revenue Service Regional Commissioner	Director, Exempt Organizations
§ 301.7611-1 A-9 first sentence	appropriate Regional Commissioner	Director, Exempt Organizations
§ 301.7611-1 A-10 first sentence	appropriate Regional Counsel	Division Counsel/Associate Chief Counsel, Tax Exempt and Government Entities
§ 301.7611-1 A-10 paragraph (b) first sentence	At the time the notice of examination (second notice) is provided to the church, a copy of the same notice will be provided to the appropriate Regional Counsel.	Before the notice of examination (second notice) is provided to the church, a copy of the same notice will be provided to the Division Counsel / Associate Chief Counsel, Tax Exempt and Government Entities.
§ 301.7611-1 A-10 paragraph (b) second sentence	Regional Counsel	Division Counsel/Associate Chief Counsel, Tax Exempt and Government Entities
§ 301.7611-1 A-11 paragraph (c) first, second and third sentences	Regional Counsel	Division Counsel/Associate Chief Counsel, Tax Exempt and Government Entities
§ 301.7611-1 A-15 paragraph (c) first and third sentences	appropriate Regional Commissioner	Director, Exempt Organizations
§ 301.7611-1 A-15 paragraph (c) second sentence	Regional Commissioner	Director, Exempt Organizations
§ 301.7611-1 A-16 first sentence	Assistant Commissioner (Employee Plans and Exempt Organizations)	Commissioner, Tax Exempt and Government Entities or the Deputy Commissioner, Tax Exempt and Government Entities
§ 301.7611-1 A-16 second sentence	Assistant Commissioner's approval	approval of the Commissioner, Tax Exempt and Government Entities or the Deputy Commissioner, Tax Exempt and Government Entities
§ 301.7611-1 A-16 paragraph (a) second sentence	Assistant Commissioner (Employee Plans and Exempt Organizations)	Commissioner, Tax Exempt and Government Entities or the Deputy Commissioner, Tax Exempt and Government Entities
§ 301.7611-1 A-17 first sentence	Regional Commissioner	Director, Exempt Organizations
§ 301.7611-1 A-17 paragraph(a) third sentence	Regional Commissioner	Director, Exempt Organizations
§ 301.7611-1 A-17 paragraph (a) fourth sentence	appropriate Regional Commissioner's belief	belief of the Director, Exempt Organizations

DEFINITIONS

Gifts and Bequests from Covered Expatriates: Imposition of Tax

Gifts and Bequests from Covered Expatriates: Imposition of Tax.—Reg. § 28.7701-1, relating to a tax on United States citizens and residents who receive gifts or bequests from certain individuals who relinquished United States citizenship or ceased to be lawful permanent residents of the United States on or after June 17, 2008, is proposed (published in the Federal Register on September 10, 2015) (REG-112997-10).

Section 28.7701-1 is added to read as follows:

§ 28.7701-1. Tax return preparer.—For the definition of the term *tax return preparer*, see § 301.7701-15 of this chapter.

Classification: Cell Companies: Series LLCs

Classification: Cell Companies: Series LLCs.—Amendments to Reg. § 301.7701-1, regarding the classification for Federal tax purposes of a series of a domestic series limited liability company (LLC), a cell of a domestic cell company, or a foreign series or cell that conducts an insurance business, are proposed (published in the Federal Register on September 14, 2010) (REG-119921-09).

Par. 4. Section 301.7701-1 is amended by:

1. Adding paragraph (a)(5).
2. Revising paragraphs (e) and (f).
The additions and revisions read as follows:

§301.7701-1. Classification of organizations for Federal tax purposes.—(a) * * *

(5) *Series and series organizations.*—(i) *Entity status of a domestic series.*—For Federal tax purposes, except as provided in paragraph (a)(5)(ix) of this section, a series (as defined in paragraph (a)(5)(viii)(C) of this section) organized or established under the laws of the United States or of any State, whether or not a juridical person for local law purposes, is treated as an entity formed under local law.

(ii) *Certain foreign series conducting an insurance business.*—For Federal tax purposes, except as provided in paragraph (a)(5)(ix) of this section, a series organized or established under the laws of a foreign jurisdiction is treated as an entity formed under local law if the arrangements and other activities of the series, if conducted by a domestic company, would result in classification as an insurance company within the meaning of section 816(a) or section 831(c).

(iii) *Recognition of entity status.*—Whether a series that is treated as a local law entity under paragraph (a)(5)(i) or (ii) of this section is recognized as a separate entity for Federal tax purposes is determined under this section and general tax principles.

(iv) *Classification of series.*—The classification of a series that is recognized as a separate entity for Federal tax purposes is determined under paragraph (b) of this section.

(v) *Jurisdiction in which series is organized or established.*—A series is treated as created or organized under the laws of a State or foreign jurisdiction if the series is established under the laws of such jurisdiction. See §301.7701-5 for rules that determine whether a business entity is domestic or foreign.

(vi) *Ownership of series and the assets of series.*—For Federal tax purposes, the ownership of interests in a series and of the assets associated with a series is determined under general tax principles. A series organization is not treated as the owner for Federal tax purposes of a series or of the assets associated with a series merely because the series organization holds legal title to the assets associated with the series.

(vii) *Effect of Federal and local law treatment.*—To the extent that, pursuant to the provisions of this paragraph (a)(5), a series is a taxpayer against whom tax may be assessed under Chapter 63 of Title 26, then any tax assessed against the series may be collected by the Internal Revenue Service from the series in the same manner the assessment could be collected by the Internal Revenue Service from any other taxpayer. In addition, to the extent Federal or local law permits a debt attributable to the series to be collected from the series organization or other series of the series organization, then, notwithstanding any other provision of this paragraph (a)(5), and consistent with the provisions of Federal or local law, the series organization and other series of the series organization may also be considered the taxpayer from whom the tax assessed against the series may be administratively or judicially collected. Further, when a creditor is permitted to collect a liability attributable to a series organization from any series of the series organization, a tax liability assessed against the series organization may be collected directly from a series of the series organization by administrative or judicial means.

(viii) *Definitions.*—(A) *Series organization.*—A *series organization* is a juridical entity that establishes and maintains, or under which is established and maintained, a series (as defined in paragraph (a)(5)(viii)(C) of this section). A series organization includes a series limited liability company, series partnership, series trust, protected cell company, segregated cell company, segregated portfolio company, or segregated account company.

(B) *Series statute.*—A *series statute* is a statute of a State or foreign jurisdiction that explicitly provides for the organization or establishment of a series of a juridical person and explicitly permits—

(1) Members or participants of a series organization to have rights, powers, or duties with respect to the series;

(2) A series to have separate rights, powers, or duties with respect to specified property or obligations; and

(3) The segregation of assets and liabilities such that none of the debts and liabilities of the series organization (other than liabilities to the State or foreign jurisdiction related to the organization or operation of the series organization, such as franchise fees or administrative costs) or of any other series of the series organization are enforceable against the assets of a particular series of the series organization.

(C) *Series.*—A *series* is a segregated group of assets and liabilities that is established pursuant to a series statute (as defined in paragraph (a)(5)(viii)(B) of this section) by agreement of a series organization (as defined in paragraph (a)(5)(viii)(A) of this section). A series includes a series, cell, segregated account, or segregated portfolio, including a cell, segregated account, or segregated portfolio that is formed under the insurance code of a jurisdiction or is engaged in an insurance business. However, the term *series* does not include a segregated asset account of a life insurance company. See section 817(d)(1); §1.817-5(e). An election, agreement, or other arrangement that permits debts and liabilities of other series or the series organization to be enforceable against the assets of a particular series, or a failure to comply with the record keeping requirements for the limitation on liability available under the relevant series statute, will be disregarded for purposes of this paragraph (a)(5)(viii)(C).

(ix) *Treatment of series and series organizations under Subtitle C - Employment Taxes and Collection of Income Tax (Chapters 21, 22, 23, 23A, 24 and 25 of the Internal Revenue Code).*—[Reserved.]

(x) *Examples.*—The following examples illustrate the principles of this paragraph (a)(5):

Example 1. Domestic Series LLC. (i) *Facts.* Series LLC is a series organization (within the meaning of paragraph (a)(5)(viii)(A) of this section). Series LLC has three members (1, 2, and 3). Series LLC establishes two series (A and B) pursuant to the LLC statute of state Y, a series statute within the meaning of paragraph (a)(5)(viii)(B) of this section. Under general tax principles, Members 1 and 2 are the owners of Series A, and Member 3 is the owner of Series B. Series A and B are not described in §301.7701-2(b) or paragraph (a)(3) of this section and are not trusts within the meaning of §301.7701-4.

(ii) *Analysis.* Under paragraph (a)(5)(i) of this section, Series A and Series B are each treated as an entity formed under local law. The classification of Series A and Series B is determined under paragraph (b) of this section. The default classification under §301.7701-3 of Series A is a partnership and of Series B is a disregarded entity.

Example 2. Foreign Insurance Cell. (i) *Facts.* Insurance CellCo is a series organization (within the meaning of paragraph (a)(5)(viii)(A) of this section) organized under the laws of foreign Country X. Insurance CellCo has established one cell, Cell A, pursuant to a Country X law that is a series statute (within the meaning of paragraph (a)(5)(viii)(B) of this section). More than half the business of Cell A during the taxable year is the issuing of insurance or annuity contracts or the reinsuring of risks underwritten by insurance companies. If the activities of Cell A were conducted by a domestic company, that company would qualify as an insurance company within the meaning of sections 816(a) and 831(c).

(ii) *Analysis.* Under paragraph (a)(5)(ii) of this section, Cell A is treated as an entity formed under local law. Because Cell A is an insurance company, it is classified as a corporation under §301.7701-2(b)(4).

* * *

(e) *State.*—For purposes of this section and §§301.7701-2 and 301.7701-4, the term *State* includes the District of Columbia.

(f) *Effective/applicability dates.*—(1) *In general.*—Except as provided in paragraphs (f)(2) and (f)(3) of this section, the rules of this section are applicable as of January 1, 1997.

(2) *Cost sharing arrangements.*—The rules of paragraph (c) of this section are applicable on January 5, 2009.

(3) *Series and series organizations.*—(i) *In general.*—Except as otherwise provided in this paragraph (f)(3), paragraph (a)(5) of this section applies on and after the date final regulations are published in the **Federal Register**.

(ii) *Transition rule.*—(A) *In general.*—Except as provided in paragraph (f)(3)(ii)(B) of this section, a taxpayer's treatment of a series in a manner inconsistent with the final regulations will be respected on and after the date final regulations are published in the **Federal Register**, provided that—

(1) The series was established prior to September 14, 2010;

(2) The series (independent of the series organization or other series of the series organization) conducted business or investment activity, or, in the case of a series established pursuant to a foreign statute, more than half the business of the series was the issuing of insurance or annuity contracts or the reinsuring of risks

underwritten by insurance companies, on and prior to September 14, 2010;

    (3) If the series was established pursuant to a foreign statute, the series' classification was relevant (as defined in §301.7701-3(d)), and more than half the business of the series was the issuing of insurance or annuity contracts or the reinsuring of risks underwritten by insurance companies for all taxable years beginning with the taxable year that includes September 14, 2010;

    (4) No owner of the series treats the series as an entity separate from any other series of the series organization or from the series organization for purposes of filing any Federal income tax returns, information returns, or withholding documents in any taxable year;

    (5) The series and series organization had a reasonable basis (within the meaning of section 6662) for their claimed classification; and

    (6) Neither the series nor any owner of the series nor the series organization was notified in writing on or before the date final regulations are published in the **Federal Register** that classification of the series was under examination (in which case the series' classification will be determined in the examination).

    (B) Exception to transition rule.—Paragraph (f)(3)(ii)(A) of this section will not apply on and after the date any person or persons who were not owners of the series organization (or series) prior to September 14, 2010 own, in the aggregate, a fifty percent or greater interest in the series organization (or series). For purposes of the preceding sentence, the term interest means—

    (1) In the case of a partnership, a capital or profits interest; and

    (2) In the case of a corporation, an equity interest measured by vote or value.

Indian Tribal Governments

    Indian Tribal Governments: Treatment as States.—Temporary Reg. §305.7701-1, relating to the treatment of Indian tribal governments as states, is also proposed as a final regulation and, when adopted, would become Reg. §305.7701-1 (published in the Federal Register on May 7, 1984).

    §305.7701-1. Definition of Indian tribal government.

Employee Trusts: Effective Dates

    Employee Trusts: Tax Reform Act of 1984: Effective Dates.—Temporary Reg. §301.7701-17T is also proposed as a final regulation and, when adopted, would become Reg. §301.7701-17 (published in the Federal Register on February 4, 1986).

    §301.7701-17. Collective-bargaining plans and agreements.

Treaty-Based Return Positions

    Treaty-Based Return Positions: Dual Status Alien.—Reproduced below is the text of proposed amendments to Reg. §301.7701(b)-7, relating to treaty-based return positions (published in the Federal Register on April 27, 1992). The proposed amendment to Reg. §301.7701(b)-7(c)(2) was adopted by T.D. 8733 on October 6, 1997.

    ☐ Par. 3. Section 301.7701(b)-7 is amended as follows:

1. By adding text in paragraph (a)(4).
2. By adding text in paragraphs (c)(2) [see above regarding adoption of this amendment] and (3).
3. By adding a new *Example 5* to paragraph (e).
4. The additions read as follows.

    §301.7701(b)-7. Coordination with income tax treaties.—(a) * * *

    (4) Special rules for S corporations.—*(i) In general.*—Notwithstanding paragraph (a)(3) of this section, for purposes of determining whether a domestic corporation meets the definition of a small business corporation under section 1361(b)(1), the following rules in paragraphs (a)(4)(ii) through (v) of this section shall apply with respect to a dual resident taxpayer.

    (ii) Dual resident not claiming treaty benefits.—A dual resident taxpayer who does not claim any treaty benefits (as a nonresident of the United States) so as to reduce the individual's United States income tax liability shall be treated as a United States resident for purposes of section 1361(b)(1)(C). Accordingly, the dual resident taxpayer may be or become a shareholder in an S corporation without thereby causing the S corporation to have a nonresident alien as a shareholder for purposes of section 1361(b)(1)(C).

    (iii) Dual resident claiming treaty benefits.—A dual resident taxpayer who claims any treaty benefit (as a nonresident of the United States) so as to reduce the individual's United States income tax liability shall be treated as a nonresident alien of the United States for purposes of section 1361(b)(1)(C). Accordingly, if the dual resident taxpayer is a shareholder in an S corporation for any portion of a taxable year with respect to which the taxpayer claims a treaty benefit, then the corporation's election under section 1362(a) shall be terminated pursuant to section 1362(d)(2) effective as of the first day of the taxable year of the dual resident in which the dual resident is an S corporation shareholder and claims treaty benefits as a nonresident of the United States. See §301.7701(b)-7(b) and (c) for reporting requirements that apply to dual resident taxpayers.

    (iv) Special exception.—Notwithstanding paragraph (a)(4)(iii) of this section, a dual resident taxpayer who claims a treaty benefit (as a nonresident of the United States) shall be treated as a United States resident for purposes of section 1361(b)(1)(C) if the conditions of paragraphs (a)(4)(iv) (A), (B), and (C) of this section are satisfied. This paragraph (a)(4)(iv) shall not apply if the S corporation was a C corporation, the S corporation is a successor to a C corporation, or the S corporation is a successor to an S corporation that itself was a successor (direct or indirect) to a C corporation.

    (A) S corporation income.—*(1)* Except as otherwise provided in this section, in determining the dual resident taxpayer's United States income tax liability, in accordance with section 1366(b), the character and source of any item included in the dual resident's income shall be determined as if such item were realized by the dual resident taxpayer.

    (2) The dual resident taxpayer shall be considered as carrying on a business within the United States through a permanent establishment if the S corporation of which the dual resident taxpayer is a shareholder carries on such business. For this purpose, the S corporation shall be treated as a foreign corporation resident in the foreign country in which the dual resident is a resident.

    (3) Procedures similar to those provided under section 1446 relating to withholding requirements applicable to partnerships with foreign partners shall apply as if the S corporation were a partnership (other than a publicly traded partnership) and the dual resident taxpayer were a foreign partner in that partnership.

    (B) Dispositions of S corporation stock.—Except as otherwise provided in this section, for purposes of determining the taxation of the dual resident taxpayer on the disposition of the individual's shares in the S corporation, the S corporation shall be treated as a partnership (other than a publicly traded partnership) and the dual resident taxpayer shall be treated as a foreign partner in that partnership.

    (C) Withholding agreement.—The dual resident taxpayer and the S corporation of which the taxpayer is a shareholder must enter into an agreement, pursuant to procedures prescribed by the Commissioner, to withhold income tax with respect to the shareholder's pro rata share of items of income described in section 1366(a)(1) and gain from the disposition of his or her shares in the S corporation.

    (v) Effective date.—*(A) In general.*—The rules described in this paragraph (a)(4) shall be effective for taxable years of S corporations beginning on or after July 27, 1992.

    (B) Effect on prior years.—For taxable years of S corporations beginning before July 27, 1992, a dual resident S corporation shareholder that previously claimed or will claim a treaty benefit on a U.S. income tax return (as a nonresident of the United States) must either—

(1) Waive the treaty benefit claimed and file an amended return as a resident of the United States; or

(2) Determine the character of his or her pro rata share of S corporation items according to a reasonable method consistent with the principles of section 1366. A method that satisfies the requirements of paragraphs (a)(4)(iv)(A)(1) and (2) and (B) of this section is a reasonable method. A method under which the taxable income of the S corporation is not taxed to the dual resident shareholder under section 881 is not a reasonable method.

* * *

(c) * * *

(3) *S corporation shareholders.*—If the taxpayer who claims a treaty benefit as a nonresident of the United States is a shareholder in an S corporation (as defined in section 1361(a)(1)) then, for purposes of paragraph (c)(1) of this section, the statement shall also indicate that the taxpayer understands that claiming a treaty benefit as a nonresident of the United States shall, unless a withholding agreement is entered into pursuant to paragraph (a)(4)(iv) of this section and the procedures prescribed by the Commissioner, terminate the S corporation's election under section 1362(a).

* * *

(e) * * *

Example 5. D, an alien individual, is a resident of foreign country Z, under Z's internal law. D is also a resident of the United States under the Internal Revenue Code and a shareholder in Corp E, an S corporation within the meaning of section 1361(a)(1). Country Z is a party to an income tax convention with the United States. Under the convention D is considered to be a resident of country Z. If Corp E were a foreign corporation resident in country Z, Corp E (under the convention) would be deemed to be carrying on a business within the United States through a permanent establishment. D chooses to file in the United States as a nonresident in order to claim treaty benefits with respect to certain items of income covered by the convention. Pursuant to § 301.7701(b)-7(a)(4)(iii), D will be considered a nonresident of the United States for purposes of section 1361(b)(1)(C). Accordingly, Corp E will cease to qualify as a "small business corporation" within the meaning of section 1361(b)(1). However, if D and Corp E enter into a withholding agreement in accordance with the procedures prescribed by the Commissioner, Corp E will continue to qualify as a small business corporation. Pursuant to § 301.7701(b)-7(a)(4)(iv)(A), to the extent that Corp E's items of income, loss, deduction and credit would be considered to be attributable to a permanent establishment within the United States under the convention, D's pro rata share of Corp E items shall, pursuant to section 1366(b), be deemed to be attributable to a permanent establishment within the United States for purposes of determining D's United States tax liability.

Life Insurance Contracts: Reasonable Mortality Charges

Life Insurance Contracts: Reasonable Mortality Charges.—Reg. § 1.7702-1, relating to the required use of reasonable mortality charges in determining whether a contract qualifies as a life insurance contract, is proposed (published in the Federal Register on July 5, 1991).

§ 1.7702-1. Mortality charges. [1]—(a) *General rule.*—Reasonable mortality charges must be used in determining the "net single premium," the "guideline single premium," and the "guideline level premium" under section 7702 for a life insurance contract. For purposes of this paragraph, mortality charges are "reasonable mortality charges" if they do not exceed the lesser of (1) the charges described in paragraph (b) of this section or in one of the safe harbors contained in paragraph (c) of this section, or (2) the mortality charges specified in the contract.[1]

(b) *Reasonable mortality charges.*—(1) *Actually expected to be imposed.*—Except as limited by paragraph (b)(2) of this section, mortality charges described in this paragraph are those amounts that the insurance company actually expects to impose as consideration for its assuming the risk of the insured's death (regardless of the designation used for those charges), taking into account any relevant characteristics of the insured of which the company is aware. Every insurance company to which this paragraph applies must be prepared to establish to the satisfaction of the district director that the mortality charges are actually expected to be imposed, taking into account the likelihood of the surrender of the contract.

(2) *Limit on charges.*—If mortality charges described in paragraph (b)(1) of this section exceed the mortality charges derived from the prevailing commissioners' standard tables in effect as of the time the contract is issued, they are not described in this paragraph (b). Notwithstanding the preceding sentence, mortality charges that are imposed with regard to a substandard risk (as defined in paragraph (d)(2) of this section) or imposed with regard to a nonparticipating contract (as defined in paragraph (d)(3) of this section) do not fail to be described in this paragraph (b) solely on the grounds that the charges exceed the applicable mortality charges specified in the prevailing commissioners' standard tables as of the time the contract is issued.

(c) *Safe harbors.*—(1) *1980 C.S.O. Basic Mortality Tables.*—For contracts that provide a death benefit that is payable upon the death of one insured, mortality charges are reasonable mortality charges if they do not exceed the applicable mortality charges set forth in the 1980 Standard Ordinary Mortality Tables of the National Association of Insurance Commissioners for male or female insureds, without select factors (the "1980 C.S.O. Basic Mortality Tables").

(2) *Unisex tables and smoker/nonsmoker tables.*—Mortality charges exceeding those specified in the 1980 C.S.O. Basic Mortality Tables are reasonable mortality charges if the contract using the charges has only one insured and is issued under a plan of insurance (as defined in paragraph (d)(5) of this section) that meets the following requirements:

(i) The nonforfeiture values for all contracts issued under the plan of insurance are determined under either 1980 C.S.O. Gender-Blended Mortality Tables (unisex tables) or 1980 C.S.O. Smoker

and Nonsmoker Mortality Tables (smoker/nonsmoker tables), as appropriate; and

(ii) No contract issued under the plan of insurance calls for mortality charges which exceed the applicable charges specified in either the unisex or smoker/nonsmoker tables, as the case may be. That is, for any plan of insurance, if unisex tables are used to determine the mortality charges for female insureds, then the same tables must be used to determine the mortality charges for male insureds; if separate smoker tables are used to determine the mortality charges for smokers, then separate nonsmoker tables must be used to determine the mortality charges for nonsmokers.

(3) *Certain contracts based on 1958 C.S.O. table.*—Mortality charges exceeding those specified in the 1980 C.S.O. Basic Mortality Tables are reasonable mortality charges if the contract using the charges has only one insured and is issued under a plan of insurance that meets all of the following requirements:

(i) The mortality charge is imposed under a contract that is not a modified endowment contract, within the meaning of section 7702A, determined using the applicable mortality charges derived from the 1958 standard ordinary mortality and morbidity table of the National Association of Insurance Commissioners (1958 C.S.O. table);

(ii) The contract was issued on or before December 31, 1988, pursuant to a plan of insurance or policy blank that was based on the 1958 C.S.O. table;

(iii) The mortality charges for the contract do not exceed the charges specified in the 1958 C.S.O. table; and

(iv) The plan or policy blank was approved by the appropriate state regulatory authority on or before October 21, 1988.

(d) *Definitions.*—For purposes of this regulation the following terms have the following meaning.

(1) *Prevailing commissioners' standard tables.*—The term "prevailing commissioners' standard tables" means the tables containing the higher of—

(i) The charges in the tables defined by section 807(d)(5)(A), or

(ii) The charges in any other tables that sections 807(d)(5)(B) or 807(d)(5)(C) allow to be used with respect to the contract for purposes of section 807(d)(2)(C). For this purpose the limitation of section 807(d)(5)(E) shall not apply.

(2) *Substandard risk.*—"Substandard risk" means a risk of death that exceeds the standards set for normal or regular risks. Whether any particular insured person presents a substandard risk must be determined by taking into account all relevant facts and circumstances including the insured's medical history and laws that increase the potential unknown insurance risk with respect to an insured by limiting a company's ability to inquire into certain aspects of the insured's medical history.

---

[1] The tables referenced in this section are available for public inspection during normal business hours at the Internal Revenue Service FOIA Reading Room, Room 1569, 1111 Constitution Avenue, N.W., Washington, D.C. 20224.

(3) *Nonparticipating contract.*—"Nonparticipating contract" means a contract other than a "variable contract" defined in section 817(d) that provides no right to the policyholder to participate in the issuer's divisible surplus, if any, and that contains no charge reduction mechanism.

(4) *Charge reduction mechanism.*—"Charge reduction mechanism" means any dividend or similar distribution to the holder of the contract in his or her capacity as holder. A charge reduction mechanism includes—

(i) Any amount paid or credited (including an increase in benefits) if the amount is not fixed in the contract but depends on the experience of the company or the discretion of management,

(ii) Any amount in the nature of interest paid or credited to the extent the amount is in excess of interest determined at the minimum rate guaranteed under the contract,

(iii) Any amount by which the premium is reduced that (but for the reduction) would have been required to be paid under the contract, and

(iv) Any refund or credit based on the experience of the contract or group involved.

(5) *Plan of insurance.*—"Plan of insurance" refers to those life insurance contracts sold by the company to a targeted market group which is not defined, directly or indirectly, on the basis of either the gender or the smoking habits of the insureds.

(e) *Effective date.*—This section applies to life insurance contracts entered into on or after October 21, 1988. [Reg. § 1.7702-1.]

Life Insurance Contracts: Qualified Accelerated Death Benefits

Life Insurance Contracts: Qualified Accelerated Death Benefits.—Reproduced below are the texts of proposed Reg. §§1.7702-2 and 1.7702A-1, relating to the definition of a life insurance contract for federal tax purposes and the tax treatment of amounts received as qualified accelerated death benefits (published in the Federal Register on December 15, 1992).

☐ Par. 4. Sections 1.7702-2 and 1.7702A-1 are added to read as follows:

§1.7702-2. Definitions.—(a) *In general.*—Paragraphs (b) through (i) of this section provide definitions and other rules only for purposes of section 7702.

(b) *Cash value.*—(1) *In general.*—Except as otherwise provided in paragraph (b)(2) of this section, the cash value of a contract is the greater of—

(i) The maximum amount payable under the contract (determined without regard to any surrender charge or policy loan); or

(ii) The maximum amount that the policyholder can borrow under the contract.

(2) *Amounts excluded from cash value.*—The cash value of a contract does not include—

(i) The amount of any death benefit (as defined in paragraph (c) of this section);

(ii) The amount of any qualified additional benefit;

(iii) The amount of any other benefit described in paragraph (f) of this section;

(iv) An amount returned to the insured upon termination of a credit life insurance contract due to a full repayment of the debt covered by the contract; or

(v) A reasonable termination dividend not in excess of $35 for each $1,000 of the face amount of the contract.

(c) *Death benefit.*—(1) *In general.*—A death benefit is the amount payable by reason of the death of the insured (determined without regard to any qualified additional benefits).

(2) *Qualified accelerated death benefit treated as death benefit.*—For purposes of paragraph (b)(2)(i) of this section, the amount payable as a qualified accelerated death benefit as defined in paragraph (d) of this section (but determined without regard to any reduction for discounting) is treated as a death benefit.

(d) *Qualified accelerated death benefit.*—(1) *In general.*—A benefit payable prior to death (accelerated benefit) is a qualified accelerated death benefit if, under the contract, the following conditions are satisfied—

(i) The accelerated benefit is payable only if the insured becomes terminally ill (as defined in paragraph (e) of this section);

(ii) The amount of the accelerated benefit is equal to or more than the present value of the reduction in the death benefit otherwise payable in the event of the death of the insured (without regard to any qualified additional benefits); and

(iii) The ratio of the cash surrender value of the contract immediately after the payment of the accelerated benefit to the cash surrender value of the contract immediately before the payment of the accelerated benefit is equal to or greater than the ratio of the death benefit immediately after the payment of the accelerated benefit to the death benefit immediately before the payment of the accelerated benefit.

(2) *Determination of present value of the reduction in death benefit.*—For purposes of paragraph (d)(1)(ii) of this section, the present value of the reduction in death benefit occurring upon payment of an qualified accelerated death benefit must be determined by—

(i) Using as the discount rate the greater of—

(A) The applicable federal interest rate determined under section 846(c)(2); or

(B) The interest rate applicable to policy loans under the contract; and

(ii) Assuming that the death benefit (or the portion thereof) would have been paid 12 months after the date of the payment of the accelerated benefit.

(3) *Examples.*—The following examples illustrate the provisions of this paragraph (d).

Example 1. B owns an insurance contract with a death benefit of $100,000 and a cash value of $30,000. In 1994, the insured becomes terminally ill (as defined in paragraph (e) of this section). In 1994, B receives an accelerated benefit equal to forty percent of the death benefit under the contract (discounted in accordance with to the rules of paragraph (d)(2) of this section). As a result of the payment of the accelerated benefit, the amount that B is entitled to receive upon the surrender of the contract is reduced by $12,000 (forty percent of $30,000) to $18,000. The ratio of the cash surrender value of the contract immediately after the payment of the accelerated benefit to the cash surrender value of the contract immediately before the payment of the accelerated benefit (18:30) is equal to the ratio of the death benefit immediately after the payment of the accelerated benefit to the death benefit immediately before the payment of the accelerated benefit (60:100). The accelerated benefit constitutes a qualified accelerated death benefit.

Example 2. C owns an insurance contract with a death benefit of $100,000. In 1994, the insured becomes terminally ill (as defined in paragraph (e) of this section). The policy loan rate specified in the contract is 10 percent and exceeds the federal applicable rate determined under section 846(c). In 1994, C receives an accelerated benefit equal to the entire death benefit of the policy discounted by 10 percent for 12 months from the date of payment and the contract terminates. The accelerated benefit is a qualified accelerated death benefit.

Example 3. The facts are the same as in *Example 2* except that C receives an accelerated benefit equal to the entire death benefit of the policy discounted by 20 percent for 12 months from the date of payment and the contract terminates. The accelerated benefit is not a qualified accelerated death benefit.

(e) *Terminally ill defined.*—An individual is terminally ill if the insurer determines that the individual has an illness or physical condition that, notwithstanding appropriate medical care, is reasonably expected to result in death within 12 months from the date of payment of the accelerated death benefit.

(f) *Certain other additional benefits.*—(1) *In general.*—An additional benefit is described in this paragraph (f) if the following conditions are satisfied—

(i) The benefit is payable solely upon the occurrence of a morbidity risk;

(ii) The charges for the benefit are separately stated and currently imposed by the terms of the contract; and

(iii) The charges for the benefit are not included in premiums taken into account in the determination of the investment in the contract under section 72(c)(1) or 72(e)(6) and are not taken into account in the determination of premiums paid under section 7702(f)(1).

(2) *Examples.*—The following examples illustrate the provisions of this paragraph (f):

Example 1. A owns an insurance contract with a death benefit of $100,000. The contract contains a provision that upon the occurrence of a morbidity risk, the insurance company will pay to A a morbidity benefit equal to 70 percent of the contract's death benefit in complete termination of A's rights under the contract. Upon surrender of the contract prior to the occurrence of the morbidity risk, A currently would be entitled to receive $40,000. The morbidity benefit is payable solely upon the occurrence of a morbidity risk. The charges for the morbidity benefit are separately stated and currently imposed under the contract. The charges for the morbidity benefit are not included in premiums taken into account in the determination of the investment in the contract under section 72(c)(1) or 72(e)(6) and are not taken into account in the determination of premiums paid under section 7702(f)(1). The excess of the $70,000 (70 percent of $100,000) payable to A upon the occurrence of the morbidity risk over $40,000 is an additional benefit which is not a qualified additional benefit. The additional benefit is described in this paragraph (f). Under paragraph (b)(2)(iii) of this section, the amount of the additional benefit (the $30,000 payable by reason of the occurrence of a morbidity risk) is not included in the contract's cash value. Accordingly, $40,000 is treated as cash value payable upon complete surrender of the contract while the remaining $30,000 is treated as a morbidity benefit under the contract.

Example 2. The facts are the same as in *Example 1* except that the charges for the morbidity benefit are not separately stated and currently imposed. The benefit is not described in this paragraph (f) and consequently the benefit is not excluded from the cash value of the contract. Under paragraph (b)(2)(iii) of this section, the contract's cash value includes the amounts payable by reason of the occurrence of a morbidity risk.

Example 3. The facts are the same as in *Example 1* except that the charges for the morbidity benefit are included in premiums taken into account in the determination of the investment in the contract under section 72(c)(1) or 72(e)(6). The benefit is not described in this paragraph (f) and consequently the benefit is not excluded from the cash value of the contract. Under paragraph (b)(2)(iii) of this section, the contract's cash value includes the amounts payable by reason of the occurrence of a morbidity risk.

(g) *Adjustments under section 7702(f)(7).*—If a life insurance contract is not terminated upon the payment of a qualified accelerated death benefit or an additional benefit described in paragraph (f) of this section, any change in the benefits under (or in other terms of) the contract is a change not reflected in any previous determination or adjustment under section 7702 and is an adjustment event under section 7702(f)(7).

(h) *Cash surrender value.*—(1) *In general.*—Except as provided in paragraph (h)(2) of this section, cash surrender value of a contract is its cash value, as determined under paragraph (b) of this section.

(2) *For purposes of section 7702(f)(7).*—For purposes of determining the recapture ceiling under section 7702(f)(7), cash surrender value is the amount that would be payable under the contract (determined without regard to any surrender charge, policy loan, or reasonable termination dividends) if the contract were terminated immediately prior to the change in the benefits under (or in other terms of) the contract.

(i) *Net surrender value.*—For purposes of section 7702(g), the net surrender value of a contract at any time is the amount that would be payable under the contract (determined with regard to surrender charges but without regard to any policy loan) if the contract were terminated at that time.

(j) *Effective date and special rules.*—(1) *In general.*—Except as otherwise provided in this paragraph (j), this section applies only with respect to contracts issued or entered into after June 30, 1993.

(2) *Provision of certain benefits before July 1, 1993.*—(i) *Not treated as cash value.*—If a benefit or loan payable only in the event the insured becomes terminally ill (as defined in paragraph (e) of this section), or an additional benefit (other than a qualified additional benefit) or loan payable solely upon the occurrence of a morbidity risk, is provided in a life insurance contract before July 1, 1993, the benefit or loan is not treated as cash value under section 7702.

(ii) *No effect on date of issuance.*—If a benefit or loan provision described in paragraph (j)(2)(i) of this section is added to a life insurance contract before July 1, 1993, the addition of the benefit or loan has no effect on the date that the contract was issued or entered into for purposes of section 7702.

(iii) *Special rule for addition of benefit or loan provision after December 15, 1992.*—This paragraph (j)(2) applies with respect to a benefit or loan provision added to a life insurance contract after December 15, 1992, only if the insurer can demonstrate that the benefit or loan provision was available under a life insurance contract issued in the United States as of December 15, 1992.

(3) *Addition of qualified accelerated death benefit.*—If a qualified accelerated death benefit (as defined in paragraph (d) of this section) is added to a life insurance contract at any time—

(i) The addition of the benefit has no effect on the date that the contract was issued or entered into for purposes of section 7702; and

(ii) Paragraph (b)(2)(i) of this section shall apply to the qualified accelerated death benefit.

(4) *Addition of other additional benefits.*—If an additional benefit described in paragraph (f) of this section is added to a life insurance contract at any time—

(i) The addition of the benefit has no effect on the date that the contract was issued or entered into for purposes of section 7702; and

(ii) The benefit is not treated as cash value under section 7702. [Reg. § 1.7702-2.]

§ 1.7702A-1. Addition of certain benefits.—(a) *Addition of certain benefits before July 1, 1993.*—(1) *No effect on date of issuance.*—If a benefit or loan payable only in the event the insured becomes terminally ill (as defined in § 1.7702-2(e)), or an additional benefit (other than a qualified additional benefit) or loan payable solely upon the occurrence of a morbidity risk, is added to a life insurance contract before July 1, 1993, the addition of the benefit or loan provision has no effect on the date that the contract was issued or entered into for purposes of section 7702A.

(2) *No material change.*—If a benefit or loan provision described in paragraph (a)(1) of this section is added to a life insurance contract before July 1, 1993, the addition of the benefit is not treated as a material change under section 7702A(c)(3).

(3) *Special rule for addition of benefit or loan provision after December 15, 1992.*—This paragraph (a) applies with respect to a benefit or loan provision added to a life insurance contract after December 15, 1992, only if the insurer can demonstrate that the benefit or loan provision was available under a life insurance contract issued within the United States as of December 15, 1992.

(b) *Addition of qualified accelerated death benefit.*—If a qualified accelerated death benefit (as defined in § 1.7702-2(d)) is added to a life insurance contract at any time—

(1) The addition of the benefit has no effect on the date that the contract was issued or entered into for purposes of section 7702A; and

(2) The addition of the benefit is not treated as a material change under section 7702A(c)(3).

(c) *Addition of other additional benefits.*—If an additional benefit described in § 1.7702-2(f) is added to a life insurance contract at any time—

(1) The addition of the benefit has no effect on the date that the contract was issued or entered into for purposes of section 7702A; and

(2) The addition of the benefit is not treated as a material change under section 7702A(c)(3). [Reg. § 1.7702A-1.]

GENERAL RULES

Indian Tribal Governments

Indian Tribal Governments: Treatment as States.—Temporary Reg. § 305.7871-1, relating to the treatment of Indian tribal governments as states, is also proposed as a final regulation (published in the Federal Register on May 7, 1984).

§ 305.7871-1. Indian tribal governments treated as States for certain purposes.

Below Market Loans

Below Market Loans: Interest.—Reproduced below are the texts of proposed Reg. §§ 1.7872-1—1.7872-14, 20.7872-1 and 25.7872-1, relating to the tax treatment of both lender and borrower in certain below-market interest rate loan transactions (published in the Federal Register on August 20, 1985; proposed Reg. § 1.7872-4(e) was reproposed in the Federal Register on April 8, 1986).

☐ New § 1.7872-1 is added in the appropriate place. This new section reads as follows:

§1.7872-1. Introduction.—(a) *Statement of purpose.*—Section 7872 generally treats certain loans in which the interest rate charged is less than the applicable Federal rate as economically equivalent to loans bearing interest at the applicable Federal rate, coupled with a payment by the lender to the borrower sufficient to fund all or part of the payment of interest by the borrower. Such loans are referred to as "below-market loans." See § 1.7872-3 for detailed definitions of below-market loans and the determination of the applicable Federal rate.

Accordingly, section 7872 recharacterizes a below-market loan as two transactions:

(1) An arm's-length transaction in which the lender makes a loan to the borrower in exchange for a note requiring the payment of interest at the applicable Federal rate; and

(2) A transfer of funds by the lender to the borrower ("imputed transfer").

The timing and the characterization of the amount of the imputed transfer by the lender to the borrower are determined in accordance with the substance of the transaction. The timing and the amount of the imputed interest payment (the excess of the amount of interest required to be paid using the applicable Federal rate, *over* the amount of interest required to be paid according to the loan agreement) by the borrower to the lender depend on the character of the imputed transfer by the lender to the borrower and whether the loan is a term loan or a demand loan. If the imputed transfer by the lender is characterized as a gift, the provisions of chapter 12 of the Internal Revenue Code, relating to gift tax, also apply. All imputed transfers under section 7872 (*e.g.*, interest, compensation, gift) are characterized in accordance with the substance of the transaction, and, except as otherwise provided in the regulations under section 7872, are treated as so characterized for all purposes of the Code. For example, for purposes of section 170, an interest-free loan to a charity referred to in section 170 for which interest is imputed under section 7872, is treated as an interest bearing loan coupled with periodic gifts to the charity in the amount of the imputed transfer, for purposes of section 170. In addition, all applicable information and reporting requirements (*e.g.*, reporting on W-2 and Form 1099) must be satisfied.

(b) *Effective date.*—(1) *In general.*—The provisions of section 7872 generally apply, for periods after June 6, 1984, to demand loans outstanding after that date and to loans other than demand loans made after that date.

(2) *Demand loans repaid before September 17, 1984.*—If a demand loan which was outstanding on June 6, 1984, is repaid before September 17, 1984, section 7872 does not apply to the loan. For purposes of this paragraph (b)(2) only, a loan is treated as repaid if it is repaid, cancelled, forgiven, modified, or otherwise retired. For example, if the loan agreement for an interest-free demand loan, which is outstanding on June 6, 1984, is modified on September 10, 1984, to require the borrower to pay a 5 percent simple rate of interest, then for purposes of this paragraph (b)(2) the original loan is treated as repaid on September 10, 1984, and section 7872 applies to the modified loan beginning on that date.

(3) *Change in loan agreement.*—For purposes of section 7872, any loan which is renegotiated, extended, or revised after June 6, 1984, is treated as a loan made after June 6, 1984. Accordingly, for purposes of the effective date provisions of this paragraph (b) in the case of such a loan, the provisions of section 7872 apply as if the loan were a new loan made on the day the lender and borrower enter into a binding agreement to change the provisions of the loan.

(4) *Other Federal tax consequences.*—Section 7872 does not alter the law applicable to below-market loans for periods prior to the effective date of section 7872. Accordingly, below-market interest rate loans which are not subject to section 7872 by reason of the effective date provisions of this paragraph (b), including loans which are repaid under the rule described in paragraph (b)(2) of this section, may still have Federal tax consequences. See, *e.g.*, *Dickman v. Commissioner*, 465 U.S. — (1984), 104 S. Ct. 1086.

(c) *Key to Code provisions.*—The following key is intended to facilitate research with respect to specific Code provisions. The key identifies the regulations section in which the principal discussion of a particular Code provision appears. As a result of the interrelationship among Code provisions, other regulation sections may also discuss the particular Code provision. Section 1.7872-2 deals with the definition of the term "loan" for purposes of section 7872. The following table identifies the provisions of section 7872 that are dealt with in § § 1.7872-2 through 1.7872-14 and lists each provision of Code section 7872 below the regulation section in which it is covered.

§1.7872-2		
(f)	(8)	

§1.7872-3			§1.7872-4			§1.7872-5		
(e)	(1)		(c)	(1)		(g)	(1)	(C)
(f)	(2)		(f)	(3)				
(g)	(1)	(A)						

§1.7872-6			§1.7872-7			§1.7872-8		
(a)			(b)			(c)	(2)	
(d)	(2)		(d)	(2)		(d)	(1)	
			(f)	(1)				
			(f)	(4)				
			(f)	(10)				

§1.7872-9			§1.7872-10			§1.7872-11		
(c)	(3)		(f)	(5)		(f)	(7)	
(f)	(10)		(f)	(6)		(f)	(9)	
						(g)	(1)	(A)
						(g)	(1)	(B)

§1.7872-12			§1.7872-13			§1.7872-14		
(e)	(1)	(A)	(e)	(2)		(e)	(1)	(B)
						(f)	(1)	

See § 20.7872-1 for regulations under section 7872(g)(2).
See § 25.7872-1 for gift tax regulations.

See § 53.4941(d)-2 for interest-free loans between private foundations and disqualified persons. [Reg. § 1.7872-1.]

☐ New § 20.7872-1 is added in the appropriate place to read as follows:

§ 20.7872-1. Certain below-market loans.—For purposes of chapter 11 of the Internal Revenue Code, relating to estate tax, a gift term loan (within the meaning of § 1.7872-4(b)) that is made after June 6, 1984, shall be valued at the lesser of:

(a) the unpaid stated principal, plus accrued interest; or

(b) the sum of the present value of all payments due under the note (including accrual interest), using the applicable Federal rate for loans of a term equal to the remaining term of the loan in effect at the date of death.

No discount is allowed based on evidence that the loan is uncollectible unless the facts concerning collectibility of the loan have changed significantly since the time the loan was made. This section applies with respect to any term loan made with donative intent after June 6, 1984, regardless of the interest rate under the loan agreement, and regardless of whether that interest rate exceeds the applicable Federal rate in effect on the day on which the loan was made. [Reg. § 20.7872-1.]

☐ New § 25.7872-1 is added in the appropriate place to read as follows:

§ 25.7872-1. Certain below-market loans.—For purposes of Chapter 12 of the Internal Revenue Code, relating to gift tax, if a taxpayer makes a gift loan (within the meaning of § 1.7872-4(b)) that is a term loan (within the meaning of § 1.7872-10(a)(2)) and that is made after June 6, 1984, the excess of the amount loaned over the present value of all payments which are required to be made under the terms of the loan agreement shall be treated as a gift from the lender to the borrower on the date the loan is made. If a taxpayer makes a gift loan that is a demand loan (within the meaning of §1.7872-10(a)(1)) and that is outstanding during any calendar period after June 6, 1984, and not repaid before September 17, 1984, the amount of foregone interest (within the meaning of section 7872(e)(2)) attributable to that calendar period shall be treated as a gift from the lender to the borrower. The *de minimis* exception described in section 7872(c)(2) applies to the gift tax treatment of a gift loan. In the case of a term gift loan, however, once section 7872 applies to the loan, the *de minimis* exception will not apply to the loan at some later date regardless of whether the aggregate outstanding amount of loans does not continue to exceed the limitation amount. For a detailed analysis of section 7872, see the income tax regulations under section 7872, §1.7872-1 through §1.7872-14. [Reg. §25.7872-1.]

☐ New §§1.7872-2 through 1.7872-14 are added in the appropriate place. These new sections read as follows:

§1.7872-2. Definition of loan.—(a) *In general.*—(1) *"Loan" interpreted broadly.*—For purposes of section 7872, the term "loan" includes generally any extension of credit (including, for example, a purchase money mortgage) and any transaction under which the owner of money permits another person to use the money for a period of time after which the money is to be transferred to the owner or applied according to an express or implied agreement with the owner. The term "loan" is interpreted broadly to implement the anti-abuse intent of the statute. An integrated series of transactions which is the equivalent of a loan is treated as a loan. A payment for property, goods, or services under a contract, however, is not a loan merely because one of the payor's remedies for breach of the contract is recovery of the payment. Similarly, a bona fide prepayment made in a manner consistent with normal commercial practices for services, property, or the use of property, generally, is not a loan; see section 461 and the regulations thereunder for the treatment of certain prepaid expenses and for the special rules of sections 461(h) and (i). However, a taxpayer's characterization of a transaction as a prepayment or as a loan is not conclusive. Transactions will be characterized for tax purposes according to their economic substance, rather than the terms used to describe them. Thus, for example, receipt by a partner from a partnership of money is treated as a loan if it is so characterized under §1.731-1(c)(2).

(2) *Limitations on applicability of section 7872.*—(i) *In general.*—Section 7872 applies only to certain below-market loans (as defined in section 7872(e)(1)). Section 1.7872-4 lists the categories of below-market loans to which section 7872 generally applies. Certain below-market loans within these categories, however, are exempt from the provisions of section 7872. See §1.7872-5 for specific exemptions from the rules.

(ii) *Loans to which section 483 or 1274 applies.*—Generally, section 7872 does not apply to any loan which is given in consideration for the sale or exchange of property (within the meaning of section 1274(c)(1)) or paid on account of the sale or exchange of property (within the meaning of section 483(c)(1)), even if the rules of those sections do not apply by reason of exceptions or safe harbor provisions. Any transaction, however, which otherwise is described in section 7872(c)(1)(A), (B), or (C), and is—

(A) a debt instrument that is issued in exchange for property and that is payable on demand.

(B) A debt instrument described in section 1273(b)(3), or

(C) A debt instrument described in section 1275(b), unless the transaction is described in §1.7872-5(b)(1),

not subject to sections 483 and 1274 and is subject to section 7872.

(iii) *Relation to section 482.*—If a below-market loan subject to section 7872 would also be subject to section 482 if the Commissioner chose to apply section 482 to the loan transaction, then section 7872 will be applied first. If the Commissioner chooses to apply section 482, then the loan transaction is subject to section 482 in addition to section 7872.

(3) *Loan proceeds transferred over time.*—In general, each extension of credit or transfer of money by a lender to a borrower is treated as a separate loan. Accordingly, if the loan agreement provides that the lender will transfer the loan proceeds to the borrower in installments, each installment payment is treated as a separate loan. Similarly, in the case of a loan in which the transfer of the loan proceeds to the borrower is subject to a draw-down restriction, each draw-down of loan proceeds is treated as a separate loan.

(b) *Examples of transactions treated as loans.*—(1) *Refundable deposits.*—(i) *In general.*—If an amount is treated for Federal tax purposes as a deposit rather than as a prepayment or an advance payment, the amount is treated as a loan for purposes of section 7872.

(ii) *Partially refundable deposits.*—If an amount is treated for Federal tax purposes as a deposit rather than as a prepayment or an advance payment and the amount is refundable only for a certain period of time or is only partially refundable, then the deposit is treated as a loan only to the extent that it is refundable and only for the period of time that it is refundable.

(iii) *Exception.*—Paragraph (b)(1)(i) does not apply if the deposit is custodial in nature or is held in trust for the benefit of the transferor. The deposit is treated as custodial in nature if the transferee is not entitled to the beneficial enjoyment of the amount deposited including interest thereon (except as security for an obligation of the transferor). Thus, if an amount is placed in escrow to secure a contractual obligation of the transferor, and the escrow agreement provides that all interest earned is paid to the transferor and that the transferee has no rights to or interest in the escrowed amount unless and until the transferor defaults on the obligation, then, in the absence of any facts which indicate that the transaction was entered into for tax avoidance purposes, the deposit is not a loan.

(2) *Permitting agent or intermediary to retain funds.*—An agreement under which an agent or intermediary is permitted to retain possession of money for a period of time before transferring the money to his or her principal is treated as a loan for purposes of section 7872. For example, a taxpayer who enters into an agreement with a broker under which the broker may retain possession of the proceeds from the sale of the taxpayer's property (*e.g.*, securities issued by the taxpayer) for a period of time and uses or invests those funds (other than for the taxpayer's account) is treated as making a loan to the broker for the period of time that the broker retains possession of the proceeds.

(3) *Advances.*—An advance of money to a employee, salesman, or other similar person to defray anticipated expenditures is not treated as a loan for purposes of section 7872 if the amount of money advanced is reasonably calculated not to exceed the anticipated expenditures and if the advance of money is made on a day within a reasonable period of time of the day that the anticipated expenditure will be incurred. An advance or draw of money against a partner's distributive share of income which is treated in the manner described in §1.731-1(a)(1)(ii) is not a loan for purposes of section 7872. [Reg. §1.7872-2.]

§1.7872-3. Definition of below-market loans.—(a) *In general.*—Section 7872 does not impute interest on loans which require the payment of interest at the applicable Federal rate. This section defines the applicable Federal rate and provides rules for determining whether an interest-bearing loan provides sufficient stated interest to avoid classification as a below-market loan. The term "below-market loan" means any loan if—

(1) In the case of a demand loan, interest is payable at a rate less than the applicable Federal rate; or

(2) In the case of a term loan, the amount loaned exceeds the present value of all payments due under the loan, determined as of the day the loan is made, using a discount rate equal to the applicable Federal rate in effect on the day the loan is made.

Sections 1.7872-13 and 1.7872-14 contain the computations necessary for determining the amount of imputed interest on a below-market loan which is subject to section 7872.

(b) *Applicable Federal rate.*—(1) *In general.*—The applicable Federal rate is an annual stated rate of interest based on semiannual compounding. In addition, the Commissioner may prescribe equivalent rates based on compounding periods other than semiannual compounding (for example, annual compounding, quarterly compounding, and monthly compounding), to facilitate application of this section to loans other than those involving semiannual payments or compounding. Thus, loans providing for annual payments or annual compounding of interest over the entire life of the loan will use the applicable Federal rates based on annual compounding; loans providing for quarterly payments or quarterly compounding over the entire life of the loan will use the applicable Federal rates based on quarterly compounding; and loans providing for monthly payments or monthly compounding over the entire life of the loan will use the applicable Federal rates based on monthly compounding. The shorter of the compounding period or the payment interval determines which rate is appropriate. Loans providing for payments or compounding of interest at other intervals (*e.g.*, daily, weekly, bi-monthly) may use the applicable Federal rates published by the Commissioner based on the shortest compounding period that is longer than the shorter of the compounding period or the payment interval provided for over the entire life of the loan. Thus, loans providing for daily or weekly payments or compounding of interest may use the applicable Federal rate based on monthly compounding; loans providing for bi-monthly payments or compounding of interest will use the applicable Federal rates based on quarterly compounding; etc. Alternatively, taxpayers may compute and use interest rates other than those published by the Commissioner for other interest payment or compounding periods if such rates are equivalent to the applicable Federal rates. Any reference to the applicable Federal rate in the regulations under section 7872 includes the equivalent rates based on different compounding or payment periods.

(2) *Determination of applicable Federal rate.*—(i) *In general.*—The applicable Federal rate for loans described in paragraphs (b)(3), (4), and (5) of this section is defined by reference to Federal statutory rates and alternate Federal rates.

(ii) *Definition of Federal statutory rate.*—The Federal statutory rates are the short-, mid-, and long-term rates in effect under section 1274(d) and their equivalent rates based on different compounding assumptions. These rates are published by the Commissioner for each semiannual period January 1 through June 30 and July 1 through December 31.

(iii) *Definition of alternate Federal rate.*—The alternate Federal rates are the short-, mid-, and long-term rates established by the Commissioner on a monthly basis, and their equivalent rates based on different compounding assumptions. These rates are published by the Commissioner on a monthly basis.

(iv) *Definition of semiannual period.*—For purposes of section 7872 and the regulations thereunder, the first semiannual period means the period in any calendar year beginning on January 1 and ending on June 30, and the second semiannual period means the period in any calendar year beginning on July 1 and ending on December 31.

(3) *Demand loans.*—(i) *In general.*—In the case of a demand loan, the applicable Federal rate for a semiannual period (January 1 through June 30 or July 1 through December 31), is the lower of:

(A) The Federal statutory short-term rate in effect for the semiannual period; or

(B) The special rate for demand loans described in paragraph (b)(3)(ii) of this section.

(ii) *Special rate for demand loans.*—The special rate for demand loans is—

(A) For the semiannual period in which the loan is made, the alternate Federal short-term rate which is in effect on the day the loan is made; and

(B) For each subsequent semiannual period in which the loan is outstanding, the alternate Federal short-term rate which is in effect for the first month of that semiannual period (*i.e.*, January or July).

For a special safe harbor rule for certain variable interest rate demand loans, see paragraph (c)(2) of this section.

(4) *Term loans.*—In the case of a term loan, including a gift term loan or a term loan that is treated as a demand loan as provided in § 1.7872-10(a)(5), the applicable Federal rate is the lower of:

(i) The Federal statutory rate for loans of that term in effect on the day the loan is made; or

(ii) The alternate Federal rate for loans of that term in effect on the day the loan is made.

(5) *Loans conditioned on future services.*—In the case of a term loan that is treated as a demand loan as provided in § 1.7872-10(a)(5), on the date the condition to perform substantial services is removed or lapses, the demand loan is treated as terminated and a new term loan is created. The applicable Federal rate for the new term loan is the lower of the following:

(i) The applicable Federal rate in effect on the day the original loan was made; or

(ii) The applicable Federal rate in effect on the day the condition lapses or is removed.

(6) *Periods before January 1, 1985.*—For term loans made and demand loans outstanding after June 6, 1984, and before January 1, 1985, the applicable Federal rate under section 7872(f)(2) is as follows:

(i) 10.25 percent, compounded annually;

(ii) 10.00 percent, compounded semiannually;

(iii) 9.88 percent, compounded quarterly; and

(iv) 9.80 percent, compounded monthly.

(c) *Loans having sufficient stated interest.*—(1) *In general.*—Section 7872 does not apply to any loan which has sufficient stated interest. A loan has sufficient stated interest if it provides for interest on the outstanding loan balance at a rate no lower than the applicable Federal rate based on a compounding period appropriate for that loan. See paragraph (b)(1) of this section for a description of appropriate compounding periods. See § 1.7872-11(a) for rules relating to waiver of interest.

(2) *Safe harbor for demand loans.*—If the interest rate on a demand loan is changed, either under the terms of the original loan agreement, or subsequently, the loan will be treated as a new loan for purposes of determining the applicable Federal rate for that loan. Thus, the loan will have sufficient stated interest for the remainder of the semiannual period following such change of interest rate if the new interest rate is not less than the lower of the Federal statutory short-term rate in effect for the semiannual period or the alternate Federal short-term rate in effect on the day the new interest rate takes effect.

(3) *Examples.*—The provisions of this paragraph (c) may be illustrated by the following examples.

Example (1). On December 1, 1984, A makes a $100,000 5-year gift term loan to B, requiring 10 interest payments of $5,000 each, payable on May 31 and November 30 of each year the loan is outstanding. Since the loan requires semiannual interest payments, the appropriate compounding assumption is semiannual compounding. For term loans made during 1984, the applicable Federal rate based on semiannual compounding is 10 percent. The loan is not a below-market loan because it provides for interest at a rate of 10 percent, payable semiannually.

Example (2). Assume the same facts as in Example (1), except the loan requires 5 annual interest payments of $10,000 each, payable on November 30 of each year the loan is outstanding. Since the loan requires annual interest payments, the appropriate compounding assumption is annual compounding. The loan is a below-market loan because, although interest is stated at a rate of 10 percent, a rate that reflects semiannual compounding is not appropriate for a loan with annual payments.

Example (3). Assume the same facts as in Example (2), except that the loan requires 5 annual interest payments of $10,250 each, payable on November 30 of each year that the loan is outstanding. Since the loan requires annual interest payments, the appropriate compounding assumption is annual compounding. For term loans made during 1984, the applicable Federal rate based on annual compounding is 10.25 percent. The loan is not a below-market loan because it provides for interest at a rate of 10.25 percent, compounded annually.

Example (4). Assume the same facts as in Example (1), except that the loan requires 120 monthly interest payments of $816.67 each, payable on the last calendar day of each month that the loan is outstanding. Since the loan requires monthly interest payments, the appropriate compounding assumption is monthly compounding. The loan is not a below-market loan because it requires monthly payments of interest based on a rate of 9.80 percent, the applicable Federal rate of interest on monthly compounding.

Example (5). (i) A makes a demand loan to her son, B, on April 1, 1985. The loan requires quarterly interest payments due at the end of each calendar quarter at a rate of 10 percent. Assume that on April 1, 1985, the Federal statutory short-term rate in effect is 12 percent, compounded quarterly, and that the alternate Federal short-term rate in effect for the month of April is 10 percent, compounded quarterly. The loan is not a below-market loan for the period April 1, 1985, through June 30, 1985.

(ii) Assume that on July 1, 1985, the Federal sttutory short-term rate in effect is 11 percent, compounded quarterly, and the alternate Federal short-term rate in effect for the month of July is 10.20 percent, compounded quarterly. The loan no longer has sufficient stated interest. If A raises the interest rate to at least 10.20 percent, the loan will have sufficient stated interest and will not be a below-market loan for the period of July 1 through December 31, 1985.

(iii) Assume that on July 1, 1985, A increases the interest rate on the loan to 10.20 percent, a rate equal to the alternate Federal short-term rate in effect for July. Further assume that the alternate Federal short-term rate subsequently decreases so that such rate in effect for the month of August decreases to 10 percent. On August 1, 1985, A lowers the interest rate on this loan to 10 percent and does not change that rate for the remainder of the semiannual period. The loan has sufficient stated interest and will not be a below-market loan for the semiannual period beginning on July 1, 1985, even if the alternate Federal rate is greater than 10 percent for any or all of the four remaining months in the semiannual period ending on December 31, 1985.

(d) *Short periods.*—The rules for determining whether a loan has sufficient stated interest also apply to short periods (*e.g.*, a period that is shorter than the interval between interest payments or interest compounding under the loan which may occur at the beginning or end of the loan). For special computational rules and examples relating to short periods, see § 1.7872-12.

(e) *Variable rates of interest.*—(1) *In general.*—If a loan requires payments of interest calculated at a rate of interest based in whole or in part on an objective index or combination of indices of market interest rates (*e.g.,* a prime rate, the applicable Federal rate, the average yield on government securities as reflected in the weekly Treasury bill rate, the Treasury constant maturity series, or LIBOR (London interbank offered rate)), the loan will be treated as having sufficient stated interest if—

(i) In the case of a term loan, the rate fixed by the index or indices is no lower than the applicable Federal rate, as determined under paragraph (b)(4) of this section (as modified by paragraph (e)(2) of this section), on the date the loan is made; or

(ii) In the case of a demand loan, the interest rate fixed by the index or indices is no lower than the applicable Federal rate, as determined under paragraph (b)(3) of this section, for each semiannual period that the loan is outstanding. See paragraph (e)(2)(i) of this section for rules relating to variable interest rate demand loans the interest rates of which are tied to the applicable Federal rate.

(2) *Special rules.*—(i) *Demand loans tied to the applicable Federal rate.*—A variable rate demand loan will be treated as having sufficient stated interest if, by the terms of the loan agreement, the interest rate cannot be less than the lower of the Federal statutory short-term rate or the alternate Federal short-term rate in effect at the beginning (or, if the agreement so provides, at the end) of the payment or compounding period (whichever is shorter).

(ii) *Applicable Federal rate for variable interest rate term loans.*—For purposes of determining the applicable Federal rate, if a term loan requires payments or compounding of interest based on a variable rate (within the meaning of paragraph (e)(1) of this section), the term of the loan shall be treated as being equal to the longest period of time that exists between the dates that, under the loan agreement, the interest rate charged on the loan is required to be recomputed (whether or not the recomputation results in a rate different from the immediately preceding rate). Thus, for example, in the case of a 10 year term loan that charges interest at a variable rate equal to a rate 2 points above the prime rate, and that requires that the interest rate be adjusted every 18 months to reflect any changes in the prime rate, the applicable Federal rate is determined by treating the loan as having a term of 18 months rather than a term of 10 years. Accordingly, the applicable Federal short-term rate rather than the applicable Federal long-term rate shall apply.

(3) The provisions of paragraph (e)(1) of this section may be illustrated by the following examples:

Example (1). On April 1, 1985, A loans $200,000 to B, repayable on demand. The note calls for interest to be paid semiannually on September 30 and March 31 of each year at a rate equal to the alternate Federal short-term rate (based on semiannual compounding) for the month in which the payment is made. The loan has sufficient stated interest.

Example (2). Assume the same facts as in *Example (1)* except that the note calls for interest at a rate equal to the lower of the alternate Federal short-term rate or the statutory Federal short-term rate (in each case, based on semiannual compounding) for the month in which the payment is made. The loan has sufficient stated interest.

Example (3). Assume the same facts as in *Example (1)* except that interest is computed and compounded at the end of each month at a rate equal to the lower of the alternate Federal short-term rate or the statutory Federal short-term rate (in each case, based on monthly compounding) in effect for that month. Accrued interest is payable semiannually on September 30 and March 31 of each year. The loan has sufficient stated interest.

Example (4). Assume the same facts as in *Example (1)* except that interest is payable at the prime rate of a major lending institution at the time each payment is made. The prime rate is not an index which by its terms cannot be less than the lower of the statutory Federal short-term rate or the alternate Federal short-term rate. Therefore, the loan will be tested for sufficient stated interest in each semiannual period under the rules of paragraph (b)(3) of this section.

(f) *Contingent interest.*—[RESERVED] [Reg. § 1.7872-3.]

§1.7872-4. Types of below-market loans.—(a) *In general.*—Section 7872 applies only to certain categories of below-market loans. These categories are gift loans, compensation-related loans, corporation-shareholder loans, tax avoidance loans, and certain other loans classified in the regulations under section 7872 as significant tax effect loans (*i.e.,* loans whose interest arrangements have a significant effect on any Federal tax liability of the lender or the borrower).

(b) *Gift loans.*—(1) *In general.*—The term "gift loan" means any below-market loan in which the foregoing of interest is in the nature of a gift within the meaning of Chapter 12 of the Internal Revenue Code (whether or not the lender is a natural person).

(2) *Cross reference.*—See § 1.7872-8 for special rules limiting the application of section 7872 to gift loans. See paragraph (g) of this section for rules with respect to below-market loans which are indirectly gift loans.

(c) *Compensation-related loans.*—(1) *In general.*—A compensation-related loan is a below-market loan that is made in connection with the performance of services, directly or indirectly, between—

(i) An employer and an employee,

(ii) An independent contractor and a person for whom such independent contractor provides services, or

(iii) A partnership and a partner if the loan is made in consideration for services performed by the partner acting other than in his capacity as a member of the partnership.

The imputed transfer (amount of money treated as transferred) by the lender to the borrower is compensation. For purposes of this section, the term "in connection with the performance of services" has the same meaning as the term has for purposes of section 83. A loan from a qualified pension, profit-sharing, or stock bonus plan to a participant of the plan is not, directly or indirectly, a compensation-related loan.

(2) *Loan in part in exchange for services.*—Except as provided in paragraph (d)(2) of this section (relating to a loan from a corporation to an employee who is also a shareholder of the corporation), a loan which is made in part in exchange for services and in part for other reasons is treated as a compensation-related loan for purposes of section 7872(c)(3) only if more than 25 percent of the amount loaned is attributable to the performance of services. If 25 percent or less of the amount loaned is attributable to the performance of services, the loan is not subject to section 7872 by reason of being a compensation-related loan. The loan may, however, be subject to section 7872 by reason of being a below-market loan characterized other than as a compensation-related loan (*e.g.,* corporation-shareholder loan or tax avoidance loan). If—

(i) a loan is characterized as a "compensation-related" loan under this paragraph (c),

(ii) less than 100 percent of the amount loaned is attributable to the performance of services, and

(iii) the portion of the amount loaned that is not attributable to the performance of services is not subject to section 7872,

then the amounts of imputed transfer (as defined in § 1.7872-1(a)(2)) and imputed interest (as defined in § 1.7872-1(a)) are determined only with respect to that part of the loan which is attributable to services. All of the facts and circumstances surrounding the loan agreement and the relationship between the lender and the borrower are taken into account in determining the portion of the loan made in exchange for services.

(3) *Third-party lender as agent.*—A below-market loan by an unrelated third-party lender to an employee is treated as attributable to the performance of services if, taking into account all the facts and circumstances, the transaction is in substance a loan by the employer made with the aid of a third-party lender acting as an agent of the employer. Among the facts and circumstances which indicate whether such a loan has been made is whether the employer bears the risk of default at and immediately after the time the loan is made. The principles of this paragraph (c)(3) also apply with respect to a below-market loan by an unrelated third-party lender to an independent contractor.

(4) *Special rule for continuing care facilities.*—Any loan to a continuing care facility will not be treated, in whole or in part, as a compensation-related loan.

(5) *Cross-references.*—For a special rule in the case of a below-market loan that could be characterized as both a compensation-related loan and a corporation-shareholder loan, see paragraph (d)(2) of this section. See paragraph (g) of this section for rules with respect to below-market loans which are indirectly compensation-related loans.

(d) *Corporation-shareholder loans.*—(1) *In general.*—A below-market loan is a corporation-shareholder loan if the loan is made directly or indirectly between a corporation and any shareholder of the corporation. The amount of money treated as transferred by the lender to the borrower is a distribution of money (characterized according to section 301 or, in the case of an S corporation, section 1368) if the corporation is the lender, or a contribution to capital if the shareholder is the lender.

(2) *Special rule.*—A below-market loan—

(i) from a publicly held corporation to an employee of the corporation who is also a shareholder owning directly or indirectly more than 0.5 percent of the total voting power of all classes of stock entitled to vote or more than 0.5 percent of the total value of shares of all other classes of stock or 0.5 percent of the total value of shares of all other classes of stock or 5 percent of the total value of shares of all classes of stock (including voting stock) of the corporation; or

(ii) from a corporation that is not a publicly held corporation to an employee of the corporation who is also a shareholder owning directly or indirectly more than 5 percent of the total voting power of all classes of stock entitled to vote or more than 5 percent of the total number of shares of all other classes of stock or 5 percent of the total value of shares of all classes of stock (including voting stock) of the corporation;

will be presumed to be a corporation-shareholder loan, in the absence of clear and convincing evidence that the loan is made solely in connection with the performance of services. For purposes of determining the percentage of direct and indirect stock ownership, the constructive ownership rules of section 267(c) apply.

(3) *Cross-reference.*—See paragraph (g) of this section for rules with respect to below-market loans which are indirectly corporation-shareholder loans.

(e) *Tax avoidance loans.*—(1) *In general.*—A tax avoidance loan is any below-market loan one of the principal purposes for the interest arrangements of which is the avoidance of Federal tax with respect to either the borrower or the lender, or both. For purposes of this rule, tax avoidance is a principal purpose of the interest arrangements if a principal factor in the decision to structure the transaction as a below-market loan (rather than, for example, as a market interest rate loan and a payment by the lender to the borrower) is to reduce the Federal tax liability of the borrower or the lender or both. The purpose for entering into the transaction (for example, to make a gift or to pay compensation) is irrelevant in determining whether a principal purpose of the interest arrangements of the loan is the avoidance of Federal tax.

(2) *Certain loans incident to sales or exchanges.*—If, pursuant to a plan that is incident to a sale or exchange of property, a party who is related (within the meaning of section 168(e)(4)(D)) to the seller—

(i) Makes a below-market loan to the buyer of the property, or

(ii) Makes a below-market loan to the seller that is assumed by the buyer in connection with the sale or exchange,

then the loan shall be treated as a tax avoidance loan within the meaning of paragraph (e)(1) of this section. There shall be an irrebuttable presumption that such a plan exists if such a loan is made within one year of the sale or exchange.

(3) *Examples.*—The provisions of paragraph (e) of this section may be illustrated by the following examples:

Example (1). (i) S and T are each wholly-owned subsidiaries of P. S sells property to an individual, A, for cash of $3,000,000. Three months after the sale, T loans to A $2,000,000 for 10 years at an interest rate of 6%, payable semiannually. On the date the loan is made, the Federal long-term rate is 12%, compounded semiannually.

(ii) The loan from T to A is a tax avoidance loan pursuant to paragraph (e)(2) of this section. The issue price of the debt instrument given in exchange for the loan is $1,311,805, and the total amount of foregone interest is $688,195. On the date the loan is made, A is treated as having received a refund of $688,195 of the purchase price of the property from S, thereby reducing A's basis in the property by this amount. T is treated as having paid a dividend of $688,195 to P, and P is treated as having made a contribution to the capital of S in the same amount.

Example (2). The facts are the same as in example (1), except that T loans the $2,000,000 to S immediately before the sale. A purchases the property for cash of $1,000,000 and assumes S's debt to T. On the date of the sale, the Federal long-term rate is 12%, compounded semiannually. The loan from T to S is a tax-avoidance loan. The issue price of the debt instrument and the amount of foregone interest are the same as in example (1). A's basis in the property is limited to $2,311,805 (see § 1.1274-7(d)). T is treated as having paid a dividend of $688,195 to P, and P is treated as having made a contribution to the capital of S in the same amount.

(f) *Certain below-market loans with significant effect on tax liability* ("significant-effect" loans).—[RESERVED].

(g) *Indirect loans.*—(1) *In general.*—If a below-market loan is made between two persons and, based on all the facts and circumstances, the effect of the loan is to make a gift or a capital contribution or a distribution of money (under section 301 or in the case of an S corporation, section 1368), or to pay compensation to a third person ("indirect participant"), or is otherwise attributable to the relationship of the lender or borrower to the indirect participant, the loan is restructured as two or more successive below-market loans ("deemed loans") for purposes of section 7872, as follows:

(i) A deemed below-market loan made by the named lender to the indirect participant; and

(ii) A deemed below-market loan made by the indirect participant to the borrower.

Section 7872 is applied separately to each deemed loan, and each deemed loan is treated as having the same provisions as the original loan between the lender and the borrower. Thus, for example, if a father makes an interest-free loan to his daughter's corporation, the loan is restructured as a below-market loan from father to daughter (deemed gift loan) and a second below-market loan from daughter to corporation (deemed corporation-shareholder loan). Similarly, if a corporation makes an interest-free loan to another commonly controlled corporation, the loan is restructured as a below-market loan from the lending corporation to the common parent corporation and a second below-market loan from the parent corporation to the borrowing corporation.

(2) *Special rule for intermediaries.*—If a lender and a borrower use another person, such as an individual, a trust, a partnership, or a corporation, as an intermediary or middleman in a loan transaction and a purpose for such use is to avoid the application of section 7872(c)(1)(A), (B), or (C), the intermediary will be ignored and the loan will be treated as made directly between the lender and the borrower. Thus, for example, if a father and a son arrange their below-market loan transaction by having the father make a below-market loan to the father's partnership, followed by a second below-market loan (with substantially identical terms and conditions as the first loan) made by the partnership to the son, the two below-market loans will be restructured as one below-market loan from the father to the son. [Reg. § 1.7872-4.]

§ 1.7872-5. Exempted loans.—(a) *In general.*—(1) *General rule.*—Except as provided in paragraph (a)(2) of this section, notwithstanding any other provision of section 7872 and the regulations thereunder, section 7872 does not apply to the loans listed in paragraph (b) of this section because the interest arrangements do not have a significant effect on the Federal tax liability of the borrower or the lender.

(2) *No exemption for tax avoidance loans.*—If a taxpayer structures a transaction to be a loan described in paragraph (b) of this section and one of the principal purposes of so structuring the transaction is the avoidance of Federal tax, then the transaction will be recharacterized as a tax avoidance loan as defined in section 7872(c)(1)(D).

(b) *List of exemptions.*—Except as provided in paragraph (a) of this section, the following transactions are exempt from section 7872:

(1) Loans which are made available by the lender to the general public on the same terms and conditions and which are consistent with the lender's customary business practices;

(2) Accounts or withdrawable shares with a bank (as defined in section 581), or an institution to which section 591 applies, or a credit union, made in the ordinary course of its business;

(3) Acquisitions of publicly traded debt obligations for an amount equal to the public trading price at the time of acquisition;

(4) Loans made by a life insurance company (as defined in section 816(a)), in the ordinary course of its business, to an insured, under a loan right contained in a life insurance policy and in which the cash surrender values are used as collateral for the loans;

(5) Loans subsidized by the Federal, State (including the District of Columbia), or Municipal government (or any agency or instrumentality thereof), and which are made available under a program of general application to the public;

(6) Employee-relocation loans that meet the requirements of paragraph (c)(1) of this section;

(7) Obligations the interest on which is excluded from gross income under section 103;

(8) Obligations of the United States government;

(9) Loans to a charitable organization (described in section 170(c)), but only if at no time during the taxable year will the aggregate outstanding amount of loans by the lender to all such organizations exceed $10,000;

(10) Loans made to or from a foreign person that meet the requirements of paragraph (c)(2) of this section;

(11) Loans made by a private foundation or other organization described in section 170(c), the primary purpose of which is to accomplish one or more of the purposes described in section 170(c)(2)(B);

(12) Loans made prior to July 1, 1986, to the extent excepted from the application of section 482 for the 6-month (or longer) period referred to in § 1.482-2(a)(3);

(13) For periods prior to July 1, 1986, all money, securities, and property received by a futures commission merchant or by a clearing organization (i) to margin, guarantee or secure contracts for future delivery on or subject to the rules of a qualified board or exchange (as defined in section 1256(g)(7)), or (ii) to purchase, margin, guarantee or secure options contracts traded on or subject to the rules of a qualified board or exchange, and all money accruing to account holders as the result of such futures and options contracts;

(14) Loans where the taxpayer can show that the below market interest arrangements have no significant effect on any Federal tax liability of the lender or the borrower, as described in paragraph (c)(3) of this section; and

(15) Loans, described in revenue rulings or revenue procedures issued under section 7872(g)(1)(C), if the Commissioner finds that the factors justifying an exemption for such loans are sufficiently similar to the factors justifying the exemptions contained in this section.

(c) *Special rules.*—(1) *Employee-relocation loans.*—(i) *Mortgage loans.*—In the case of a compensation-related loan to an employee, where such loan is secured by a mortgage on the new principal residence (within the meaning of section 217 and the regulations thereunder) of the employee, acquired in connection with the transfer of that employee to a new principal place of work (which meets the requirements in section 217(c) and the regulations thereunder), the loan will be exempt from section 7872 if the following conditions are satisfied:

(A) The loan is a demand loan or is a term loan the benefits of the interest arrangements of which are not transferable by the employee and are conditioned on the future performance of substantial services by the employee;

(B) The employee certifies to the employer that the employee reasonably expects to be entitled to and will itemize deductions for each year the loan is outstanding; and

(C) The loan agreement requires that the loan proceeds be used only to purchase the new principal residence of the employee.

(ii) *Bridge loans.*—In the case of a compensation-related loan to an employee which is not described in paragraph (c)(1)(i) of this section, and which is used to purchase a new principal residence (within the meaning of section 217 and the regulations thereunder) of the employee acquired in connection with the transfer of that employee to a new principal place of work (which meets the requirements in section 217(c) and the regulations thereunder), the loan will be exempt from section 7872 if the following conditions are satisfied:

(A) The conditions contained in paragraphs (c)(1)(i)(A), (B), and (C) of this section;

(B) The loan agreement provides that the loan is payable in full within 15 days after the date of the sale of the employee's immediately former principal residence;

(C) The aggregate principal amount of all outstanding loans described in this paragraph (c)(1)(ii) to an employee is no greater than the employer's reasonable estimate of the amount of the equity of the employee and the employee's spouse in the employee's immediately former principal residence, and

(D) The employee's immediately former principal residence is not converted to business or investment use.

(2) *Below-market loans involving foreign persons.*—(i) Section 7872 shall not apply to a below-market loan (other than a compensation-related loan or a corporation-shareholder loan where the borrower is a shareholder that is not a C corporation as defined in section 1361(a)(2)) if the lender is a foreign person and the borrower is a U.S. person, unless the interest income imputed to the foreign lender (without regard to this paragraph) would be effectively connected with the conduct of a U.S. trade or business within the meaning of section 864(c) and the regulations thereunder and not exempt from U.S. income taxation under an applicable income tax treaty.

(ii) Section 7872 shall not apply to a below-market loan where both the lender and the borrower are foreign persons unless the interest income imputed to the lender (without regard to this paragraph) would be effectively connected with the conduct of a U.S. trade or business within the meaning of section 864(c) and the regulations thereunder and not exempt from U.S. income taxation under an applicable income tax treaty.

(iii) For purposes of this section, the term "foreign person" means any person that is not a U.S. person.

(3) *Loans without significant tax effect.*—Whether a loan will be considered to be a loan the interest arrangements of which have a significant effect on any Federal tax liability of the lender or the borrower will be determined according to all of the facts and circumstances. Among the factors to be considered are—

(i) whether items of income and deduction generated by the loan offset each other;

(ii) the amount of such items;

(iii) the cost to the taxpayer of complying with the provisions of section 7872 if such section were applied, and

(iv) any non-tax reasons for deciding to structure the transaction as a below-market loan rather than a loan with interest at a rate equal to or greater than the applicable Federal rate and a payment by the lender to the borrower. [Reg. § 1.7872-5.]

§ 1.7872-6. Timing and amount of transfers in connection with gift loans and demand loans.—(a) *In general.*—Section 7872(a) and the provisions of this section govern the timing and the amount of the imputed transfer by the lender to the borrower and the imputed interest payment by the borrower to the lender in the case of a below-market demand loan. Section 7872(a) and this section also govern the timing and the amount of the imputed transfer by the lender to the borrower and the imputed interest payment by the borrower to the lender for income tax purposes in the case of term gift loans. (See section 7872(b), 7872(d)(2), and § 1.7872-7 for rules governing the timing and the amount of the imputed transfer by the lender to the borrower in the case of term gift loans for gift tax purposes.) Section 7872(d)(1) and § 1.7872-8 limit the amount of the imputed interest payment with respect to certain gift loans. See § 1.7872-10(a) for rules for distinguishing demand loans from term loans. See § 1.7872-11(f) for special rules governing loans repayable in foreign currency, which apply notwithstanding any contrary rules set forth in this section.

(b) *Time of transfer.*—(1) *In general.*—Except as otherwise provided in paragraphs (b)(3), (4), and (5) of this section, the foregone interest (as defined in section 7872(e)(2) and paragraph (c) of this section) attributable to periods during any calendar year is treated as transferred by the lender to the borrower (and retransferred by the borrower to the lender) on December 31 of that calendar year and shall be treated for tax purposes in a manner consistent with the taxpayer's method of accounting.

(2) *Example.*—Paragraph (b)(1) of this section may be illustrated by the following example.

Example. On January 1, 1985, E makes a $200,000 interest-free demand loan to F, an employee of E. The loan remains outstanding for the entire 1985 calendar year. E has a taxable year ending September 30. F is a calendar year taxpayer. For 1985, the imputed compensation payment and the imputed interest payment (as computed under paragraph (c) of this section) are treated as made on December 31.

(3) *Gift loans between natural persons.*—In the case of gift loans directly between natural persons within the meaning of § 1.7872-8(a)(2), any imputed transfer and any imputed interest payment to which this section applies during the borrower's taxable year is treated, for both the lender and the borrower, as occurring on the last day of the borrower's taxable year.

(4) *Death, liquidation or termination of borrower.*—If the borrower dies (in the case of a borrower who is a natural person) or is liquidated or otherwise terminated (in the case of a borrower other than a natural person), any imputed transfer and any imputed interest payment arising during the borrower's final taxable year are treated, for both the lender and the borrower, as occurring on the last day of the borrower's final taxable year.

(5) *Repayment of loan.*—If a below-market loan is repaid, any imputed transfer and any imputed interest payment arising during the borrower's taxable year which includes the date of repayment is treated, for both the lender and the borrower, as occurring on the day the loan is repaid.

(c) *Amount of transfer.*—In the case of a below-market loan to which section 7872 applies and which is a demand loan (including a term loan that is treated as a demand loan as provided in § 1.7872-10(a)(5)) or a gift term loan, the foregone interest (as computed under the provisions of § 1.7872-13) with respect to the loan is treated as transferred by the lender to the borrower and retransferred as interest by the borrower to the lender. Generally, for any calendar year the term "foregone interest" means the excess of—

(1) The amount of interest that would have been payable in that year if interest had accrued at the applicable Federal rate (as determined in § 1.7872-13); over

(2) Any interest payable on the loan properly allocable to that year. The amount of foregone interest is computed for each day during the period for which section 7872(a) applies to the loan and is treated as transferred and retransferred on the date specified in paragraph (b) of this section. [Reg. § 1.7872-6.]

§ 1.7872-7. Timing and amount of transfers in connection with below-market term loans.—(a) *In general.*—This section governs the Federal income tax consequences of below-market term loans, other than gift term loans or term loans treated as demand loans under the provisions of § 1.7872-10(a)(5), to which section 7872 applies. It also governs the Federal gift tax consequences of below-market gift term loans. See § 1.7872-11(f) for special rules which govern loans repayable in foreign currency and which apply notwithstanding any contrary rules set forth in this section.

(1) *Timing and amount of transfer from lender to borrower.*—In the case of term loans to which this section applies, the amount of the imputed transfer by the lender to the borrower—

(i) is treated as transferred at the time the loan is made and is treated for tax purposes in a manner consistent with the taxpayer's method of accounting; and

(ii) is equal to the excess of—

(A) The amount loaned (as defined in paragraph (a)(4) of this section); over

(B) The present value (as determined in paragraph (a)(5) of this section and § 1.7872-14) of all payments which are required to be made under the terms of the loan agreement, whether express or implied.

(2) *Gift term loans.*—In the case of a gift term loan, the rules of paragraph (a)(1) of this section apply for gift tax purposes only. For rules governing the income tax consequences of gift term loans, see § 1.7872-6.

(3) *Treatment of amount equal to imputed transfer as original issue discount.*—(i) *In general.*—Any below-market loan to which paragraph (a)(1) of this section applies shall be treated as having original issue discount in an amount equal to the amount of the imputed transfer determined under paragraph (a)(1) of this section. This imputed original issue discount is in addition to any other original issue discount on the loan (determined without regard to section 7872(b) or this paragraph). For purposes of applying section 1272 to a loan described in this paragraph, the issue price shall be treated as equal to the stated principal reduced by the amount of the imputed transfer and the yield to maturity is the applicable Federal rate.

(ii) *Example.*—The provisions of this paragraph (a)(3) may be illustrated by the following example.

Example. (i) On June 10, 1984, L lends $45,000 to B, a corporation in which L is a shareholder, for five years in exchange for a $50,000 note bearing interest at a below-market rate. Assume that the present value of all payments that B must make to L is $42,000. This loan is a corporation-shareholder term loan under section 7872(c)(1)(C). Accordingly, the amount of the imputed transfer by L to B is determined under the provisions of section 7872(b).

(ii) On June 10, 1984, L is treated as transferring $3,000 (the excess of $45,000 (amount loaned) over $42,000 (present value of all payments)), in accordance with section 7872(b)(1). This imputed transfer is treated as a contribution to B's capital by L. An amount equal to the imputed transfer is treated as original issue discount. This original issue discount is in addition to the $5,000 ($50,000, the state redemption price, less $45,000, the issue price) of original issue discount otherwise determined under section 1273. As a result, the loan is treated as having a total $8,000 of original issue discount.

(4) *Amount loaned.*—The term "amount loaned" means the amount received by the borrower (determined without regard to section 7872). See § 1.7872-2(a)(3) for the treatment of the transfer of the loan proceeds to the borrower in installments or subject to drawdown restrictions.

(5) *Present value.*—The present value of all payments which are required to be made under the provisions of the loan agreement is computed as of the date the loan is made (or, if later, as of the day the loan first becomes subject to the provisions of section 7872). The discount rate for the present value computation is the applicable Federal rate as defined in § 1.7872-3(b) in effect on the day on which the loan is made. For rules governing the computation of present value, see § 1.7872-14. See also *Example (3)* in § 1.7872-8(b)(5).

(6) *Basis.*—In the case of a term loan the lender's basis in the note received in exchange for lending money is equal to the present value of all payments which are required to be made under the terms of the loan agreement, whether express or implied, with adjustments as provided for in section 1272(d)(2).

(b) *Special rule for the de minimis provisions.*—(1) *In general.*—If as a result of the application of the *de minimis* provisions of section 7872(c)(2) or (3), a loan becomes subject to section 7872 and this section on a day after the day on which the loan is made, the provisions of this section generally apply to the loan as if the loan were made on that later day. The applicable Federal rate applied to this loan (including for purposes of computing the present value of the loan), however, is the applicable Federal rate (as defined in § 1.7872-3(b)) in effect on the day on which the loan is first made. The present value computation described in paragraph (a)(1)(ii)(B) of this section is made as of the day on which section 7872 and this section first apply to the loan. For purposes of making this computation, the term of the loan is equal to the period beginning on the day that section 7872 first applies to the loan and ending on the day on which the loan is to be repaid according to the loan agreement. Any payments payable acording to the loan agreement before the day on which section 7872 and this section first apply to the loans are disregarded.

(2) *Continuing application of section 7872.*—Once section 7872 and this section apply to a term loan, they continue to apply to the loan regardless of whether the *de minimis* provisions of section 7872(c)(2) or (3) apply at some later date. In the case of a gift term loan, this paragraph applies only for gift tax purposes and does not apply for income tax purposes. [Reg. § 1.7872-7.]

§ 1.7872-8. Special rules for gift loans directly between natural persons.—(a) *Special rules for gift loans directly between natural persons.*—(1) *In general.*—Section 7872 (c)(2) and (d) apply special rules to gift loans directly between natural persons if the aggregate outstanding amount of loans (as determined in paragraph (b)(2) of this section) between those natural persons does not exceed specified limitations.

(2) *Loans directly between natural persons.*—(i) For purposes of this section, a loan is made directly between natural persons only if both the lender and borrower are natural persons. For this purpose, a loan by a natural person lender to the guardian (or custodian, in the case of a gift made pursuant to the Uniform Gift to Minors Act) of a natural person is treated as a loan directly between natural persons. If, however, a parent lends money to a trust of which the child is the sole beneficiary, the loan is not treated as directly between natural persons for purposes of this section.

(ii) A gift loan which results from restructuring an indirect loan as two or more loans (as described in § 1.7872-4(g)) and in which natural persons are deemed to be the lender and the borrower is treated as a loan directly between natural persons. Thus, for example, if an employer makes a below-market loan to an employee's child, the loan is restructured as one loan from the employer to the employee, and a second loan from the employee to his child. The deemed gift loan between the employee and the employee's child is treated as directly between natural persons.

(b) *De minimis exception.*—(1) *In general.*—Except as otherwise provided in paragraph (b)(3) of this section or in § 1.7872-7(a) (with respect to the gift tax consequences of a gift term loan to which the provisions of section 7872 have already been applied), in the case of any gift loan directly between natural persons, the provisions of section 7872 do not apply to any loan outstanding on any day in which the aggregate outstanding amount of loans between the lender and borrower does not exceed $10,000. The *de minimis* rule of this paragraph (b)(1) applies with respect to a gift loan even though that loan could also be characterized as a tax avoidance loan within the meaning of section 7872(c)(1)(D) and § 1.7872-4(e).

(2) *Aggregate outstanding amount of loans.*—The aggregate outstanding amount of loans between natural persons is the sum of the principal amounts of outstanding loans directly between the individuals, regardless of the character of the loans, regardless of the interest rate charged on the loans, and regardless of the date on which the loans were made. For this purpose, the principal amount of a loan which is also subject to section 1272 (without applying the limitation of section 1273(a)(3)) is the "adjusted issue price" as that term is defined in section 1272(a)(4). See § 1.7872-7(a)(3)(i) for the determination of the issue price of a loan which is also subject to section 1272.

(3) *Loans attributable to acquisition or carrying of income-producing assets.*—The *de minimis* exception described in paragraph (b)(1) of this section does not apply to any gift loan directly attributable to the purchase or carrying of the income-producing assets. A gift loan is directly attributable to the purchase or carrying of income-producing assets, for example, if the loan proceeds are directly traceable to the purchase of the income-producing assets, the assets are used as collateral for the loan, or there is direct evidence that the loan was made to avoid disposition of the assets.

(4) *Income-producing assets.*—For purposes of this paragraph (b), the term "income-producing asset" means (i) an asset of a type that generates ordinary income, or, (ii) a market discount bond issued before July 19, 1984. Accordingly, an income-producing asset includes, but is not limited to, a business, a certificate of deposit, a savings account, stock (whether or not dividends are paid), bonds and rental property.

(5) *Examples.*—The provisions of this paragraph (b) may be illustrated by the following examples.

Example (1). (i) As of January 1, 1985, the total aggregate outstanding amount of loans by Parent P, to child, C, is $6,000. None of these loans is a below-market loan. On February 1, 1985, P makes a $3,000 below-market demand loan to C. On March 1, 1985, P makes a $2,000 below-market demand loan to C. On November 1, 1985, C repays $1,500 of principal of the market-rate loans to P; all of the other loans remain outstanding as of December 31, 1985. The below-market loans are gift loans and are the only new loans between P and C for calendar year 1985.

(ii) For the periods January 1, 1985, through February 28, 1985, and November 1, 1985, through December 31, 1985, section 7872 does not apply to the loans between P and C because the outstanding loan balance between P and C does not exceed $10,000 during these periods. For the period beginning on March 1, 1985, and ending on October 31, 1985, however, the aggregate outstanding amount of loans directly between P and C exceeds $10,000. Accordingly, the provisions of section 7872(a) apply to the $3,000 gift loan and $2,000 gift loan during that period.

Example (2). (i) Assume the same facts as in Example (1) except that the $2,000 gift loan made on March 1, 1985, is a term loan for a period of five years. The Federal gift tax and income tax consequences of the $3,000 gift demand loan made on February 1, 1985, are the same as in Example (1).

(ii) With respect to the $2,000 gift term loan, section 7872(b)(1) applies beginning on March 1, 1985, for purposes of computing the amount of the imputed gift by P to C. For the period beginning on March 1, 1985, and ending on October 31, 1985, section 7872(a) applies to the $2,000 gift term loan for purposes of determining the amount and the timing of the imputed interest payment by C to P. For the two-monthly period beginning on November 1, 1985, section 7872(a) does not apply to the $2,000 loan for Federal income tax purposes because the outstanding loan balance between P and C does not exceed $10,000 during this period.

Example (3). (i) Assume the same facts as in Example (1) except that the $3,000 gift loan made on February 1, 1985, is a term loan for a period of five years. The Federal gift tax and income tax consequences of the $2,000 demand gift loan made on March 1, 1985, are identical to those in Example (1).

(ii) On February 1, 1985, section 7872 does not apply to the $3,000 loan because the outstanding loan balance between P and C does not exceed $10,000. On March 1, 1985, however, the aggregate outstanding amount of loans between P and C exceeds $10,000. For Federal gift tax purposes, section 7872(b)(1) applies to the $3,000 loan beginning on March 1, 1985. Under §1.7872-7(b), the provisions of section 7872 apply to the $3,000 loan for gift and income tax purposes as if the loan had been made on March 1, 1985. See §1.7872-7(a)(5) for special rules for computing the present value of payments due on the loan. For the eight-month period beginning on March 1, 1985, section 7872(a) applies to the $3,000 loan for purposes of determining the imputed interest payment by C to P. For the two-month period beginning on November 1, 1985, section 7872(a) does not apply to the $3,000 loan for Federal income tax purposes because of the application of the *de minimis* provisions.

Example (4). On June 10, 1984, parent, L, makes an $8,000 interest-free gift term loan to L's child, B. This is the only loan outstanding between L and B during 1984. On June 11, 1984, B invests the $8,000 in corporate stock. The $10,000 *de minimis* provision does not apply to the loan, because the loan proceeds are directly attributable to the purchase of corporate stock, an income-producing asset.

(c) *Limitation on amount of imputed interest payment.*—(1) *In general.*—In the case of a loan between a borrower and a lender both of whom are natural persons (within the meaning of paragraph (a)(2) of this section), for all days during the borrower's taxable year on which the aggregate outstanding amount of loans (within the meaning of paragraph (b)(2) of this section) between the borrower and the lender, is $100,000 or less, the amount of the imputed interest payment by the borrower to the lender with respect to any gift loan is limited to the borrower's net investment income (as determined under paragraph (c)(7) of this section) for the taxable year. This paragraph (c) does not affect the gift tax consequences of any loan under section 7872.

(2) *Tax avoidance loan.*—Paragraph (c)(1) of this section does not apply to any loan which is a tax avoidance loan within the meaning of §1.7872-4(e).

(3) *No limitation if investment income is manipulated.*—Paragraph (c)(1) of this section does not apply if a borrower can control the timing of the receipt of investment income and actually does manipulate the timing to accelerate or defer the receipt of investment income. For example, if the borrower can, and actually does, control the timing of dividends paid by a closely held corporation, the limitation on the amount of the imputed interest payment does not apply.

(4) *Net investment income of $1,000 or less disregarded.*—If paragraph (c)(1) of this section applies and if the borrower's net investment income (as determined under paragraph (c)(7) of this section) for a taxable year is $1,000 or less, the borrower's net investment income for that year is deemed to be zero for purposes of this paragraph (c).

(5) *No proration of net investment income.*—The entire amount of the borrower's net investment income for a taxable year (as determined under paragraph (c)(7) of this section) is taken into account in determining the maximum imputed interest payment for those days during the year on which the net investment income limitation applies. Accordingly, the amount of net investment income is not allocated among the days of the borrower's taxable year. Further, for a taxable year of a borrower which ends after June 6, 1984, and includes any day or days before June 7, 1984, the entire amount of net investment income for the taxable year is taken into account in determining the maximum imputed interest payment for the days during that year on which the limitation applies.

(6) *Allocation among gift loans.*—In the case of a borrower who has more than one gift loan outstanding during a taxable year, the borrower's net investment income for that year is allocated among the gift loans in proportion to the respective amounts which would be treated as imputed interest payments by the borrower to the lender or lenders with respect to those loans without regard to this paragraph (c). (See Example (2) of paragraph (c)(9) of this section.) No amount of the net investment income is allocable to any gift loan between the lender and the borrower for periods during which the aggregate outstanding amount of loans (within the meaning of paragraph (b)(2) of this section) between the borrower and that lender exceeds $100,000.

(7) *Amounts included in net investment income.*—For purposes of section 7872, net investment income for a taxable year equals the sum of—

(i) Net investment income for that year as determined under section 163(d)(3), excluding any item of income on a deferred payment obligation which is treated under section 7872(d)(1)(E)(iii) and paragraph (c)(7)(ii) of this section as interest received in a prior taxable year ending after June 6, 1984, and

(ii) The amount that is treated under section 7872(d)(1)(E)(iii) as interest received for that year on a deferred payment obligation.

(8) *Deferred payment obligation.*—The term "deferred payment obligation" means a market discount bond issued before July 18, 1984, or an obligation that, if held to maturity, would produce a predictable and regular flow of ordinary income which, under applicable tax rules, is not recognized until a subsequent period. Accordingly, deferred payment obligations include, but are not limited to, those obligations listed in section 7872(d)(1)(E)(iv).

(9) *Examples.*—The provisions of this paragraph (c) may be illustrated by the following examples.

Example (1). On January 1, 1985, parent P makes a $50,000 below-market gift loan to C, P's child, who uses the calendar year as the taxable year. On March 1, 1985, P makes an additional $75,000 market-rate loan to C. On October 1, 1985, C repays $30,000 of the market-rate loan. Assume that C's net investment income (as determined under paragraph (c)(7) of this section) for 1985 is $2,400. The limitation under section 7872(d)(1) on the amount of imputed interest payment applies to the $50,000 loan for the two-month period beginning on January 1, 1985, and the three-month period beginning on October 1, 1985. Accordingly, the imputed interest payment on the $50,000 loan for 1985 may not exceed $2,400.

Example (2). During 1985, natural person borrower B has three gift loans outstanding, each from a different lender. Each loan is eligible for the entire year for the special limitation on the amount of imputed interest payments under section 7872(d)(1) but none of the loans is eligible for the de minimis exception of paragraph (b) of this section. B's net investment income for 1985 is $6,000. The aggregate imputed interest payments on these loans (determined without regard to section 7872(d)(1)) would be $9,000. The amount of imputed interest payment attributable to each loan after application of section 7872(d)(1) is computed as follows:

Loan	Imputed interest payments (before application of section 7872(d)(1))	Relative share of net investment income (imputed interest payment after application of section 7872(d)(1))	
1	$3,000	$2,000	($6,000 × $3,000/$9,000)
2	4,000	2,667	(6,000 × 4,000/9,000)
3	2,000	1,333	(6,000 × 2,000/9,000)
Total	$9,000	$6,000	

Consequently, the imputed interest payment to lender 1 cannot exceed $2,000; the imputed interest payment to lender 2 cannot exceed $2,667; and, the imputed interest payment to lender 3 cannot exceed $1,333. [Reg. §1.7872-8.]

§1.7872-9. *De minimis* exception for compensation-related or corporation-shareholder loans.—(a) *In general.*—In the case of any demand loan described in section 7872(c)(1)(B) or (C), the provisions of section 7872 do not apply to any day on which the aggregate outstanding amount of loans between the lender and the borrower does not exceed $10,000. In the case of any term loan described in section 7872(c)(1)(B) or (C) (relating to the *de minimis* rules), the provisions of section 7872 apply to the loan as of the first day on which the aggregate outstanding amount of loans between the lender and the borrower exceeds $10,000. Once section 7872 applies to a term loan, section 7872 continues to apply to the loan regardless of whether the $10,000 limitation applies at some later date.

(b) *Aggregate outstanding amount of loans.*—The aggregate outstanding amount of loans between the lender and the borrower is the sum of the principal amounts of outstanding loans directly between the parties, regardless of the character of the loans, regardless of the interest rate charged on the loans, and regardless of the date on which the loans were made. For this purpose, the principal amount of a loan which is also subject to section 1272 (without applying the limitation of section 1273(a)(3)) is the "adjusted issue price" as that term is defined in section 1272(a)(4). See §1.7872-(a)(3)(i) for the determination of the issue price of a loan which is also subject to section 7872.

(c) *Tax avoidance loan.*—This section does not apply to any loan which is a tax avoidance loan within the meaning of §1.7872-4(e).

(d) *Example.*—The provisions of this section may be illustrated by the following example:

Example. (i) On January 1, 1985, L made a $4,000 four-year term loan to B, a corporation in which L is a shareholder. On October 15, 1986, L made a $7,000 five-year term loan to B. Both loans are interest-free and are payable on the last day of the loan term. There are no other outstanding loans between L and B. Neither loan is a tax avoidance loan.

(ii) For the period beginning on January 1, 1985 and ending on October 14, 1986, the provisions of section 7872 do not apply to the $4,000 loan because the outstanding loan balance between L and B does not exceed $10,000. On October 15, 1986, however, the aggregate amount of loans between L and B exceeds $10,000. Accordingly, the provisions of section 7872(b) apply to both loans. See §1.7872-4(d) for the proper Federal tax treatment of the imputed transfer by L to B. For purposes of computing the present value of all payments to be made under the loan agreements, the applicable Federal rate for the $4,000 loan is the applicable Federal rate in effect on January 1, 1985, for loans with a term of 4 years (even though less than three years remain before the loan ends). Under §1.7872-7(b), the present value of the payment to be made under the $4,000 loan agreement is determined as of October 15, 1986 (the date on which section 7872 first applies to the $4,000 loan) for a loan with a term which begins on October 15, 1986, and ends on January 1, 1989. [Reg. §1.7872-9.]

§1.7872-10. Other definitions.—(a) *"Term" and "demand" loans distinguished.*—For purposes of section 7872—

(1) *Demand loan.*—Any loan which is payable in full at any time on the demand of the lender (or within a reasonable time after the lender's demand), is a "demand loan."

(2) *Term loan.*—A loan is treated as a "term loan" if the loan agreement specifies an ascertainable period of time during which the loan is to be outstanding. For purposes of this rule, a period of time is treated as being ascertainable if the period may be determined actuarially. Thus, a loan agreement which provides that D loans E $16,000 for E's life will be treated as a term loan because the life expectancy of E may be determined actuarially.

(3) *Acceleration and extension clauses.*—Acceleration clauses and similar provisions that would make a loan due before the time otherwise specified including provisions permitting prepayment of a loan or accelerating the maturity date on disposition of collateral ("due on sale" clauses) are disregarded for purposes of section 7872. Thus, a loan for a term of 15 years is a term loan for 15 years even if it is subject to acceleration upon some action of the borrower. If the loan agreement specifies an ascertainable period of time during which the loan is to be outstanding but contains an extension clause or similar provision that would make the loan due after the time otherwise specified, the loan is a term loan during the ascertainable period and a second demand or term loan thereafter; the classification of the second loan as term or demand depends upon the terms of the extension clause.

(4) *Loans for a period of time not ascertainable.*—[Reserved]

(5) *Certain loans conditioned on future services.*—For all purposes of section 7872 other than determining the applicable Federal

rate (see, §1.7872-3(b)), if the benefits of the interest arrangements of a term loan are not transferable by the individual borrower and are conditioned on the future performance of substantial services by the individual borrower (within the meaning of section 83), the loan is treated as a demand loan. All facts and circumstances must be examined to determine whether the future services to be performed are substantial.

(6) *Revolving credit loans.*—For purposes of section 7872, an extension of credit by reason of the use of a credit card that is available to a broad segment of the general public is treated as a demand loan, and the provisions of section 7872 may apply if the loan is described in one of the categories set forth in §1.7872-4. The period during which the loan is outstanding begins on the first day on which a finance charge would be assessed if payment of the outstanding balance is not made. For rules governing the computation of foregone interest for demand loans with variable balances, see §1.7872-13(c).

(b) [Reserved for further definitions as needed.] [Reg. §1.7872-10.]

§1.7872-11. Special rules.—(a) *Waiver, cancellation or forgiveness of interest payments.*—If a loan is made requiring the payment of stated interest and the accrued but unpaid interest is subsequently waived, cancelled, or forgiven by the lender, such waiver, cancellation, or forgiveness is treated as if the interest had in fact been paid to the lender and then retransferred by the lender to the borrower but only if—

(1) the loan initially would have been subject to section 7872 had it been made without interest;

(2) the waiver, cancellation or forgiveness does not include in substantial part the loan principal; and

(3) a principal purpose of the waiver, cancellation, or forgiveness is to confer a benefit on the borrower, such as to pay compensation or make a gift, a capital contribution, a distribution of money under section 301, or a similar payment to the borrower.

The retransferred amount is characterized for Federal tax purposes in accordance with the substance of the transaction. The requisite purpose described in paragraph (a)(iii) of this section is presumed in the case of loans between family members, corporations and shareholders, employers and employees, or an independent contractor and a person for whom such independent contractor provides services unless the taxpayer can show by clear and convincing evidence that the interest obligation was waived, cancelled, or forgiven for a legitimate business purpose of the lender who is acting in the capacity as a creditor seeking to maximize satisfaction of a claim, such as in the case of a borrower's insolvency.

(b) *Disposition of interest or obligation in loan.*—[RESERVED]

(c) *Husband and wife treated as 1 person.*—Section 7872(f)(7) provides that a husband and wife shall be treated as 1 person. Accordingly, all loans to or from the husband will be combined with all loans to or from the wife for purposes of applying section 7872. All loans between a husband and a wife are disregarded for purposes of section 7872.

(d) *Withholding.*—In the case of any loan (term or demand) subject to section 7872, no amount is required to be withheld under chapter 24, relating to the collection of income tax at the source on wages and back-up withholding, with respect to any amount treated as transferred or retransferred under section 7872(a) or (b). Withholding is required where appropriate, however, for purposes of chapter 21, relating to the Federal Insurance Contributions Act, and Chapter 22, relating to the Railroad Retirement Tax Act, on any amount of money treated as transferred and retransferred between the lender and borrower because of the application of section 7872.

(e) *Treatment of renegotiations.*—[RESERVED]

(f) *Loans denominated in foreign currencies.*—(1) *Applicable rate.*—If a loan is denominated in a currency other than the U.S. dollar, then for purposes of section 7872 and the regulations thereunder, a rate that constitutes a market interest rate in the currency in which the loan is denominated shall be substituted for the applicable Federal rate.

(2) *Treatment of imputed transfer as interest.*—(i) *In general.*—If a loan is denominated in a currency other than the U.S. dollar then, notwithstanding section 7872(a)(1)(B), §1.7872-6, and §1.7872-7, the amount of imputed interest treated as retransferred by the borrower to the lender shall only be treated as interest to the extent consistent with other principles of tax law regarding foreign currency lending transactions and to the extent provided in this paragraph (f)(2).

(ii) *Loans denominated in appreciating currencies.*—[Reserved]

(iii) *Loans denominated in depreciating currencies.*—[Reserved]

(3) *Example.*—The provisions of this paragraph (f)(1) may be illustrated by the following example.

Example. A lends her daughter B thse sum of 100,000 foreign currency units, repayable in 5 years with interest payable semiannually at a rate of 12 percent. Assume that the market rate of interest for loans denominated in that foreign currency at the time of the transaction is 30 percent, compounded semiannually, and that the current exchange rate is 5 foreign currency units to the dollar. A has made a below-market gift loan to B. The amount of A's gift to B is the excess of 100,000 foreign currency units (or $20,000) over the present value of all payments to be made under the loan, using a discount rate of 30 percent, which is 54,831 foreign units (or $10,966). Thus, the amount of A's gift is $9,034.

(g) *Reporting requirements.*—(1) *Lender.*—A lender must attach a statement to the lender's income tax return for any taxable year in which the lender either has interest imputed under section 7872 or claims a deduction for an amount deemed to be transferred to a borrower under section 7872. The statement must—

(i) Explain that it relates to an amount includible in income or deductible by reason of section 7872,

(ii) Provide the name, address, and taxpayer identification number of each borrower.

(iii) Specify the amount of imputed interest income and the amount and character of any item deductible by reason of section 7872 attributable to each borrower.

(iv) Specify the mathematical assumptions used (*e.g.,* 360 day calendar year, the exact method or the approximate method for computing interest for a short period (see, § 1.7872-13)) for computing the amounts imputed under section 7872, and

(v) Include any other information required by the return or the instructions thereto.

(2) *Borrower.*—A borrower must attach a statement to the borrower's income tax return for any taxable year in which the borrower either has income from an imputed transfer under section 7872 or claims a deduction for an amount of interest expenst imputed under section 7872. The statement must—

(i) Explain that it relates to an amount includible in income or deductible by reason of section 7872,

(ii) Provide the name, address, and taxpayer identification number of each lender,

(iii) Specify the amount of imputed interest expense and the amount and character of any income imputed under section 7872 attributable to each lender,

(iv) Specify the mathematical assumptions used (*e.g.,* 360 day calendar year, the exact method or the approximate method for computing interest for a short period (see, § 1.7872-13)) for computing the amounts imputed under section 7872, and

(v) Include any other information required by the return or the instructions thereto.

(3) *Special rule for gift loans.*—In the case of a gift loan directly between natural persons, the lender must recognize the entire amount of interest income imputed under section 7872 (determined without regard to section 7872(d)(1)) unless the borrower notifies the lender, in a signed statement, of the amount of the borrower's net investment income properly allocable to the loan according to the provisions of section 7872(d)(1) and § 1.7872-8(c)(6).

(4) *Information and reporting.*—All amounts imputed under section 7872 (*e.g.,* interest, compensation, gift) are characterized in accordance with the substance of the transaction and, except as otherwise provided in the regulations under section 7872, are treated as so characterized for all purposes of the Code. Accordingly, all applicable information and reporting requirements (*e.g.,* reporting on Form W-2 and Form 1099) must be satisfied. [Reg. § 1.7872-11.]

§ 1.7872-12. Computational rules to determine sufficient stated interest for short periods.—(a) *Scope.*—This section provides computational rules only for the purpose of determining whether the interest payable on a loan during a short period is sufficient to prevent characterization of the loan as a below-market loan under § 1.7872-3. For rules for the calculation of the amount of interest to be imputed on a below-market loan, including rules for short periods, see § 1.7872-13 and § 1.7872-14.

(b) *Short period defined.*—(1) *In general.*—A short period (as referred to in § 1.7872-3(d)) for a loan is any period shorter than the regular compounding period or regular payment interval required under the loan agreement. Generally, a short period will arise at the beginning or the end of a loan (or at the time the loan first becomes subject to section 7872 because of the application of the *de minimis* provisions). For example, a loan made on January 17, 1985, and calling for semiannual payments of interest on June 30 and December 31 of each year will have a short period beginning on January 17, 1985, and ending on June 30, 1985.

(2) *Special short periods in the case of demand loans.*—In the case of a demand loan, in addition to any short periods described in paragraph (b)(1) of this section, additional short periods may also arise because of the need to adjust the applicable Federal rate on January 1 and July 1 of each year. These short periods arise in cases when the dates January 1 or July 1 fall within the compounding periods or payment intervals required under the loan agreement. For example, a below-market demand loan made on April 1, 1985, that is outstanding throughout 1985 and that calls for semiannual interest payments on September 30 and March 31 of each year will have 3 short periods in 1985. The first short period begins on April 1, 1985, and ends on June 30, 1985. The second short period begins on July 1, 1985, and ends on September 30, 1985. The third short period begins on October 1, 1985, and ends on December 31, 1985.

(c) *Interest payable for a short period.*—(1) *Exact method.*—The smallest amount of interest that must be paid for a short period in order to prevent the loan from being a below-market loan is determined by the exact method. The exact method assumes daily compounding of interest.

(2) *Approximate method.*—The approximate method is also provided for the convenience of taxpayers who do not wish to use the exact method. The approximate method assumes simple interest within any compounding period and will always produce an amount of interest for the short period that is slightly higher than that produced under the exact method. Under this method, a sufficient amount of interest for any short period is determined by multiplying the amount that would constitute sufficient stated interest for a full period by a fraction the numerator of which is equal to the length of the short period and the denominator of which is the length of a full period.

(3) *Counting convention.*—In computing the length of a short period, any reasonable convention may be used. Common conventions are "30 days per month/360 days per year", "actual days per month/actual days per year", and "actual days per month/360 days per year". The examples in the regulations under section 7872 all use the "30 days per month/360 days per year" convention.

(d) *Examples.*—This section may be illustrated by the following examples.

Example (1). On February 1, 1986, A makes a $100,000 loan to B for a term of 4 months. The loan is repaid on May 31, 1986. Assume that the applicable Federal rate on February 1, 1986, for a loan of this term is 10 percent, compounded semiannually. Using the exact method, the amount of interest that must be paid on May 31, 1986, if the loan is not to be a below-market loan is $3,306.16, calculated as follows:

$$\$100,000 \times [(1 + .10/2)^{4/6} - 1] = \$3,306.16$$

Example (2). Assume the same facts as in Example (1). Using the approximate method, a sufficient amount of interest is stated on the loan if $3,333.33 of interest is payable on May 31, 1986, calculated as follows:

$$\$100,000 \times [(.10/2) \times (4/6)] = \$3,333.33$$

[Reg. § 1.7872-12.]

§ 1.7872-13. Computation of foregone interest.—(a) *Demand loans outstanding for an entire calendar year.*—(1) *In general.*—In the case of a below-market demand loan of a fixed principal amount that remains outstanding for an entire calendar year, the amount of foregone interest (as referred to in § 1.7872-6(c)) shall be the excess of—

(i) The result produced when the "blended annual rate" is multiplied by the principal amount of the loan, over

(ii) The sum of all amounts payable as interest on the loan properly allocable to the calendar year (including all amounts of original issue discount allocated to that year under section 1272).

The "blended annual rate" will be published annually by the Commissioner and is determined generally by blending the applicable Federal rates for demand loans outstanding for the entire year.

(2) *Example.*—Paragraph (a)(1) may be illustrated by the following example.

Example. On January 1, 1985, A makes a $100,000 demand loan to B with stated interest equal to 9 percent. Interest is payable semiannually on June 30, and December 31. The loan remains outstanding for the entire year. On both June 30, and December 31, 1985, B makes a $4,500 payment of interest to A. Assume that the blended annual rate for 1985 is 10.45 percent. The amount of foregone interest is $1,450, computed as follows:

$$\$10,450 = \$100,000 \times 10.45 \text{ percent}$$
$$\$1,450 = \$10,450 - \$9,000$$

(b) *Demand loans outstanding for less than an entire calendar year.*—(1) *In general.*—In the case of any below-market demand loan outstanding for less than the calendar year, the amount of foregone interest shall be the excess of—

(i) The amount of interest ("I") which would have been payable on the loan for the year if interest accrued on the loan at the applicable Federal rate and were payable on the date specified in section 7872(a)(2) and §1.7872-6(b), over

(ii) The sum of all amounts payable as interest on the loan properly allocable to the calendar year (including all amounts of original issue discount allocated to that year under section 1272).

In general, "I" is determined by assuming daily compounding of interest. However, individual taxpayers who are parties to below-market loans in the aggregate of $250,000 or less may choose (see, §1.7872-11(g)) to compute and report foregone interest under the approximate method set forth in paragraph (b)(2) of this section. If the taxpayer chooses the approximate method but fails to properly compute the amount of foregone interest under that method, the correct amount of foregone interest will be recomputed under the approximate method.

(2) *Approximate method.*—Under the approximate method, "I" is calculated as follows:

(i) *Loan outstanding during one semiannual period only.*—If a loan is outstanding only during one semiannual period of a calendar year, to determine "I", multiply the principal amount of the loan by one-half the applicable Federal rate based on semiannual compounding in effect for that loan, then multiply the result by a fraction representing the portion of the semiannual period during which the loan was outstanding.

(ii) *Example.*—Paragraph (b)(2)(i) of this section may be illustrated by the following example.

Example. A $200,000 interest-free demand loan is outstanding on January 1, 1986, and is repaid on March 31, 1986. Assume that the applicable Federal rate (based on semiannual compounding) for demand loans made in January 1986 is 10 percent. The amount of interest that would have been payable on the loan for the year if the loan provided for interest at the applicable Federal rate determined under the approximate method is $5,000, computed as follows:

$5,000 = $200,000 \times (.10/2) \times (^3/_6)$

Because no interest is payable on the loan, this amount is also the amount of foregone interest.

(iii) *Loans outstanding during both semiannual periods.*—If a loan is outstanding for at least part of each semiannual period (but less than the full calendar year), then, under the approximate method, "I" must be calculated in two steps. First, calculate an amount of interest for the first semiannual period by treating the loan as if it were repaid on June 30, using the approach described in paragraph (b)(3)(i) of this section. Second, add this amount of interest to the principal of the loan, and then calculate an amount of interest for the second semiannual period as if the loan of this higher amount were made on July 1, again using the approach described in paragraph (b)(3)(i) of this section. The sum of these two interest amounts is the value for "I" calculated under the approximate method.

(3) *Examples.*—Paragraph (b)(2) of this section may be illustrated by the following examples.

Example (1). On March 1, 1986, A makes a $100,000 interest-free demand loan to B. The loan remains outstanding on December 31, 1986. Assume that the applicable Federal rate for a demand loan made in March 1986, based on semiannual compounding, for the first semiannual period in 1986 is 9.89 percent and that the applicable Federal rate, based on semiannual compounding, for a demand loan outstanding in July 1986 is 10.50 percent. The amount of foregone interest under the exact method is $8,691.76, calculated as follows:

$100,000 \times [(1 + .0989/2)^{4/6} (1 + .1050/2) - 1] = $8,691.76$

Example (2). (i) Assume the same facts as in Example (1). The amount of foregone interest under the approximate method is $8,719.92, calculated as follows:

(ii) For the short period March 1 to June 30, 1986, the amount of foregone interest is $3,296.67, calculated as follows:

$3,296.67 = $100,000 \times (.0989/2) \times (4/6)$

(iii) For the second semiannual period in 1986, the amount of foregone interest is computed by first adding the interest for the first semiannual period ($3,296.67) to the original principal amount to obtain a new principal amount of $103,296.67. Foregone interest for the second semiannual period is then $5,423.08, computed as follows:

$5,423.08 = $103,296.67 \times (.1050/2)$

(iv) Using the approximate method, the amount of foregone interest for 1986 is $8,719.75 ($3,296.67 + $5,423.08).

(c) *Demand loans with fluctuating loan balances.*—If a demand loan does not have a constant outstanding principal amount during a period, the amount of foregone interest shall be computed according to the principles set forth in paragraph (b) of this section, with each increase in the outstanding loan balance being treated as a new loan and each decrease being treated as first a repayment of accrued but unpaid interest (if any), and then a repayment of principal.

(d) *Examples.*—This provisions of paragraph (c) of this section may be illustrated by the following examples.

Example (1). (i) On October 1, 1984, C makes a $50,000 interest-free demand loan to D. On October 1, 1985, C makes an additional interest-free demand loan of $25,000 to D. Assume that section 7872 applies to both loans, that the blended annual rate for 1985 is 10.45 percent, and that the applicable Federal rate based on semiannual compounding for demand loans made in October 1985, is 10.50 percent. The amount of foregone interest for 1985 is calculated as follows:

(ii) $50,000 is outstanding for the entire year. The foregone interest on this amount is ($5,000 \times .1045) = $5,225.00.

(iii) $25,000 is outstanding for the last three months of 1985. Under the exact method, the amount of foregone interest on this portion of the loan is $647.86, computed as follows:

$25,000 \times [(1 + .1050/2)^{3/6} - 1] = 647.86

Under the approximate method, the amount of foregone interest is $656.25, computed as follows:

$25,000 \times (.1050/2) \times (3/6) = 656.25

(iv) The total amount of foregone interest is $5,872.86 ($5,225.00 + $647.86) under the exact method, and $5,881.25 ($5,225.00 + $656.25) under the approximate method.

Example (2). (i) On September 1, 1985, E makes a $100,000 interest-free demand loan to F. The loan agreement requires F to repay $10,000 of the principal amount of the loan at the end of each month that the loan is outstanding. Assume that section 7872 applies to the loan and that the applicable Federal rate based on semiannual compounding for demand loans made in September 1985, is 10.50 percent. The amount of foregone interest for 1985 is calculated as follows:

(ii) $70,000 is outstanding for four months. Under the exact method, the amount of foregone interest on this portion of the loan is $2,429.05, computed as follows:

$70,000 \times [(1 + .1050/2)^{4/6} - 1] = $2,429.05$

Under the approximate method, the amount of foregone interest on this protion of the loan is $2,450.00, computed as follows:

$70,000 \times (.1050/2) \times (4/6) = $2,450.00$

(iii) $10,000 is outstanding for 3 months. Under the exact method, the amount of foregone interest on this portion of the loan is $259.14, computed as follows:

$10,000 \times [(1 + .1050/2)^{3/6} - 1] = 259.14

Under the approximate method, the amount of foregone interest on this portion of the loan is $262.50, computed as follows:

$10,000 \times (.1050/2) \times (3/6) = 262.50

(iv) An additional $10,000 is outstanding 2 months. Under the exact method, the amount of foregone interest on this portion of the loan is $172.02, computed as follows:

$10,000 \times [(1 + .1050/2)^{2/6} - 1] = 172.02

Under the approximate method, the amount of foregone interest on this portion of the loan is $175.00, computed as follows:

$10,000 \times (.1050/2) \times (2/6) = 175.00

(v) A final $10,000 is outstanding for 1 month. Under the exact method, the amount of foregone interest on this portion of the loan is $85.65, computed as follows:

$10,000 \times [1 + 1050/2)^{1/6} - 1] = 85.65

Under the approximate method, the amount of foregone interest on this portion of the loan is $87.50, computed as follows:

$10,000 \times (.1050/2) \times (1/6) = 87.50

(vi) The total amount of foregone interest is $2,945.86 under the exact method, and $2,975.00 under the approximate method.

(e) *Gift term loans and certain loans conditioned on future services.*—(1) *In general.*—In the case of any gift term loan or any term loan that is treated as a demand loan as provided in §1.7872-10(a)(5), the amount of foregone interest for income tax purposes shall be computed as if the loan were a demand loan, except that:

(i) In applying paragraph (a)(1)(i), use the applicable Federal rate based on annual compounding in effect on the day the loan is made instead of the blended annual rate, and

(ii) In applying paragraph (b), use the applicable Federal rate based on semiannual compounding in effect on the day the loan is made instead of the applicable Federal rate for demand loans in effect during the period for which foregone interest is being computed.

(2) *Example.*—The provisions of this paragraph (e) may be illustrated by the following examples:

Example (1). On January 1, 1986, parent P makes a $200,000 gift term loan to child C. The loan agreement provides that the term of the loan is four years and that 5 percent simple interest is payable annually. Both P and C are calendar year taxpayers, and both are still living on December 31, 1986. Assume that the Federal mid-term rate based on annual compounding in effect on January 1, 1986, is 11.83 percent. The loan is a below-market loan. The amount of foregone interest for each year is $13,660.00, computed as follows:

($200,000) × .1183 = $23,660.00
$23,660.00 – $10,000.00 = $13,660.00

For gift tax purposes, an imputed gift is treated as made on January 1, 1986, and is equal to the excess of the amount loaned ($200,000) over the present value of all payments due under the loan, discounted at 11.83 percent compounded annually ($153,360.82), or $41,639.82. For rules for determining the computation of present value, see § 1.7872-14.

Example (2). Assume the same facts as in Example (1) except that C repays the loan on September 30, 1987, along with an interest payment of $7,500. For income tax purposes, the imputed payments are treated as transferred on December 31, 1986 and September 30, 1987. The amount of the imputed payments for 1986 are the same as in Example (1). For 1987, under the exact method the amount of foregone interest is $9,994.73, computed as follows:

$17,494.73 = $200,000 × [(1 + .1183) $^{9/12}$ – 1]

$17,494.73 – $ 7,500 = $9,994.73

For gift tax purposes, the imputed gift is treated as made January 1, 1986, and is the same as in Example (1).

(f) *Allocation of stated interest.*—If interest that is payable on a demand loan is properly allocable to a period which includes more than one calendar year, the amount of interest to be allocated to each calendar year is determined by using any reasonable method of allocation.

(g) *Counting conventions.*—(1) *Whole periods.*—All whole periods, whether expressed annually, semi-annually, quarterly, or monthly, shall be treated as having equal length. For example, a leap year shall be treated as having the same number of days as a non-leap year; all months shall be treated as having the same number of days.

(2) *Short periods.*—In computing the length of a short period, any reasonable convention may be used. See § 1.7872-12(c)(2) for a list of conventions commonly used. [Reg. § 1.7872-13.]

§ 1.7872-14. Determination of present value.—(a) *In general.*—This section provides rules for computing the present value of a payment (as referred to in § 1.7872-7(a)(1)) to be made in the future. In general, for purposes of section 7872, the present value of a loan payment to be made in the future is the amount of that payment discounted at the applicable Federal rate from the date in the future that the payment is due to the date on which the computation is made. For this purpose, the computation date is the date the loan first becomes subject to section 7872. To determine the present value of a payment, use the applicable Federal rate in effect on the day the loan is made that reflects the compounding assumption (*i.e.*, annual, semiannual, quarterly, or monthly) that is appropriate for the loan. See § 1.7872-3(b).

(b) *Examples.*—The provisions of this section may be illustrated by the following examples:

Example (1). (i) On July 1, 1984, corporation A makes a $200,000 interest-free three-year term loan to shareholder B. The applicable Federal rate is 10-percent, compounded semiannually.

(ii) The present value of this payment is $149,243.08, determined as follows:

$$149,243.08 = \frac{200,000}{[1 + (.10/2)]^6}$$

(iii) The excess of the amount loaned over the present value of all payments on the loan ($200,000 – $149,243.08), or $50,756.92, is treated as a distribution of property (characterized according to section 301) paid to B on July 1, 1984. The same amount, $50,756.92, is treated as original issue discount under sections 1272 and 163(e).

Example (2). (i) On July 1, 1984, Employer E makes a $3,000 interest-free three year compensation-related term loan to employee

W. On December 1, 1984, E makes an $9,000 interest-free compensation-related demand loan to W. The demand loan remains outstanding throughout December 1984. The two loans are the only loans outstanding between E and W during 1984, and neither is characterized under section 7872(c)(1)(D) as a tax avoidance loan. The applicable Federal rate for all loans for periods before January 1, 1985, is 10 percent, compounded semiannually.

(ii) For the period beginning on July 1, 1984, and ending on November 30, 1984, the provisions of section 7872 do not apply to the $3,000 loan because of the application of the *de minimis* rules of section 7872(c)(3).

(iii) On December 1, 1984, however, the aggregate amount of loans outstanding between E and W exceeds $10,000. As a result, section 7872 applies to both loans for December 1984. Both the imputed transfer and the imputed interest payment with respect to the $9,000 demand loan are determined under section 7872(a). The amount of the imputed transfer by E to W with respect to the $3,000 term loan is determined under section 7872(b)(1). An amount equal to the amount of the imputed transfer with respect to the $3,000 term loan is treated as original issue discount.

(iv) With respect to the $3,000 term loan, the amount of the imputed transfer is equal to the excess of the amount loaned, over the present value of all payments which are required to be made under the $3,000 two-year term loan agreement, determined as of December 1, 1984 (the day section 7872 first applies to the $3,000 loan). The present value of $3,000 payable on June 30, 1987, determined as of December 1, 1984, is $2,331.54, computed as follows:

$$2,331.54 = \frac{3,000}{(1 + .10/2)^{5+1/6}}$$

The imputed transfer on the $3,000 loan is $668.46 ($3,000.00 – $2,331.54).

(v) The foregone interest on the $9,000 demand loan is determined as of December 31, 1984, with respect to the one month during 1984 to which section 7872 applies to the loan. The amount of foregone interest for 1984 under the exact method is $73.48, computed as follows:

$73.48 = $9,000 × [(1 + .10/2) $^{1/6}$ – 1]

Example (3). (i) Assume the same facts as in Example (2) except that the provisions of the $3,000 three-year term loan require W to make annual payments of interest at a 5 percent simple rate and except that E makes W the $9,000 loan on November 27, 1985.

(ii) Under the agreement W pays $150 (5 percent of $3,000) on June 30, 1985, June 30, 1986, and June 30, 1987. Since the first of these payments is payable prior to November 27, 1985, only the second and third $150 payments are taken into account. W is treated as paying $150 on June 30, 1986 and $3,150 ($3,000 principal and $150 interest) on June 30, 1987.

(iii) The present value as of November 27, 1984 of the $150 payable on June 30, 1986, is $128.39, computed as follows:

$$128.39 = \frac{150.00}{(1 + .10/2)^{3+34/180}}$$

(iv) The present value as of November 27, 1984 of the $3,150 payable on June 30, 1987, is $2,445.47, computed as follows:

$$2,445.47 = \frac{3,150.00}{(1 + .10/2)^{5+34/180}}$$

The sum of these two present values is $2,573.86 ($128.39 + $2,445.47). Therefore, the amount of the imputed transfer with respect to the $3,000 loan is $426.14 ($3,000.00 – $2,573.86).

(v) The foregone interest on the $9,000 demand loan under the exact method is $83.33 ($9,000 × [(1 + .10/2) $^{34/180}$ – 1]). [Reg. § 1.7872-14.]

ELECTIONS UNDER ECONOMIC RECOVERY TAX ACT OF 1981

GST Exemption: Extension of Time

GST Exemption: Extension of Time.—Amendments to Reg. § 301.9100-3, describing the circumstances and procedures under which an extension of time will be granted under Code Sec. 2642(g)(1), are proposed (published in the Federal Register on April 17, 2008) (REG-147775-06).

☐ Par. 4. Section 301.9100-3 is amended by adding a newparagraph (g) to read as follows:

§301.9100-3. Other extensions.

* * *

(g) *Relief under section 2642(g)(1).*—(1) *Procedures.*—The procedures set forth in this section are not applicable for requests for relief

under section 2642(g)(1). For requests for reflief under section 2642(g)(1), see § 26.2642-7.

(2) *Effective/applicability date.*—Paragraph (g) of this section applies to requests for relief under section 2642(g)(1) filed on or after the date of publication of the Treasury decision adopting these rules as final regulations in the **Federal Register.**

Life Insurance Companies: Computation and Reporting of Reserves

Life Insurance Companies: Computation and Reporting of Reserves.—Amendments to Reg. §301.9100-6T, providing guidance on the computation of life insurance reserves and the change in basis of computing certain reserves of insurance companies, are proposed (published in the Federal Register on April 2, 2020) (REG-132529-17).

Par. 25. Section 301.9100-6T is amended by:

1. Removing from the table in paragraph (a)(1) the three entries for "211" and the entries for "216(c)(1)," "216(c)(2)," "217(i)," and "217(l)(2)(B)."

2. Removing and reserving paragraph (a)(2)(iii).

3. Removing paragraph (a)(3)(v).

4. In paragraph (a)(4):

i. Removing "211 (Code section 810(b)(3)), 216(c) (1) and (2), 217(l)," from the first sentence.

ii. Removing "211 (Code sections 806(d)(4), and 807(d)(4)(C)), 217(i)," from the second sentence.

iii. Removing the last sentence.

§301.9100-6T. Time and manner of making certain elections under the Deficit Reduction Act of 1984 (Temporary).

GROUP HEALTH PLAN REQUIREMENTS

Group Health Plans: Portability Requirements

Group Health Plans: Portability Requirements.—Reg. §54.9801-7 and amendments to Reg. §§54.9801-1, 54.9801-2, 54.9801-4, 54.9801-5 and 54.9801-6, clarifying certain portability requirements for group health plans and issuers of health insurance coverage offered in connection with a group health plans, are proposed (published in the Federal Register on December 30, 2004) (REG-130370-04).

☐ Par. 2. Section 54.9801-1 is amended in paragraph (a)(1) by removing the language "54.9801-6" and adding "54.9801-7" in its place.

§54.9801-1. Basis and scope.

☐ Par. 3. Section 54.9801-2 is amended in the first sentence by removing the language "54.9801-6" and adding "54.9801-7" in its place.

§54.9801-2. Definitions.

☐ Par. 4. Section 54.9801-4 is amended by:

a. Revising paragraphs (b)(2)(iii) and (b)(2)(iv).

b. Adding *Examples 4* and *6* in paragraph (b)(2)(v).

The revisions and additions read as follows:

§54.9801-4. Rules relating to creditable coverage.

* * *

(b) *Standard method.*—* * *

(2) *Counting creditable coverage.*—* * *

(iii) *Significant break in coverage defined.*—A *significant break in coverage* means a period of 63 consecutive days during each of which an individual does not have any creditable coverage, except that periods described in paragraph (b)(2)(iv) of this section are not taken into account in determining a significant break in coverage. (See section 731(b)(2)(iii) of ERISA and section 2723(b)(2)(iii) of the PHS Act, which exclude from preemption state insurance laws that require a break of more than 63 days before an individual has a significant break in coverage for purposes of state law.)

(iv) *Periods that toll a significant break.*—Days in a waiting period and days in an affiliation period are not taken into account in determining whether a significant break in coverage has occurred. In addition, for an individual who elects COBRA continuation coverage during the second election period provided under the Trade Act of 2002, the days between the date the individual lost group health plan coverage and the first day of the second COBRA election period are not taken into account in determining whether a significant break in coverage has occurred. Moreover, in the case of an individual whose coverage ceases, if a certificate of creditable coverage with respect to that cessation is not provided on or before the date coverage ceases, then the period that begins on the first date that an individual has no creditable coverage and that continues through the earlier of the following two dates is not taken into account in determining whether a significant break in coverage has occurred:

(A) The date that a certificate of creditable coverage with respect to that cessation is provided; or

(B) The date 44 days after coverage ceases.

(v) *Examples.*—* * *

Example 4. (i) *Facts.* Individual *B* terminates coverage under a group health plan, and a certificate of creditable coverage is provided 10 days later. *B* begins employment with Employer *R* and begins enrollment in *R*'s plan 60 days after the certificate is provided.

(ii) *Conclusion.* In this *Example 4*, even though *B* had no coverage for 69 days, the 10 days before the certificate of creditable coverage is provided are not taken into account in determining a significant break in coverage. Therefore, *B*'s break in coverage is only 59 days and is not a significant break in coverage. Accordingly, *B*'s prior coverage must be counted by *R*'s plan.

* * *

Example 6. (i) *Facts.* Employer *V* sponsors a group health plan. Under the terms of the plan, the only benefits provided are those provided under an insurance policy. Individual *D* works for *V* and has creditable coverage under *V*'s plan. *V* fails to pay the issuer the premiums for the coverage period beginning March 1. Consistent with applicable state law, the issuer terminates the policy so that the last day of coverage is April 30. *V* goes out of business on July 31. On August 15 *D* begins employment with Employer *W* and enrolls in *W*'s group health plan. *W*'s plan imposes a 12-month preexisting condition exclusion on all enrollees. *D* never receives a certificate of creditable coverage for coverage under *V*'s plan.

(ii) *Conclusion.* In this *Example 6*, the period from May 1 (the first day without coverage) through June 13 (the date 44 days after coverage under *V*'s plan ceases) is not taken into account in determining a 63-day break in coverage. This is because, in cases in which a certificate of creditable coverage is not provided by the date coverage is lost, the break begins on the date the certificate is provided, or the date 44 days after coverage ceases, if earlier. Therefore, even though *D*'s actual period without coverage was 106 days (May 1 through August 14), because the period from May 1 through June 13 is not taken into account, *D*'s break in coverage is only 62 days (June 14 through August 14). Thus, *D* has not experienced a significant break in coverage, and *D*'s prior coverage must be counted by *W*'s plan.

* * *

☐ Par. 5. Section 54.9801-5 is amended by:

a. Redesignating paragraphs (a)(3)(ii)(H)(5) and (6) as paragraphs (a)(3)(ii)(H)(6) and (7), respectively.

b. Adding a new paragraph (a)(3)(ii)(H)(5).

The addition reads as follows:

§ 54.9801-5. Evidence of creditable coverage.

(a) *Certificate of creditable coverage.*—* * *

(3) *Form and content of certificate.*—* * *

☐ Par. 6. Section 54.9801-6 is amended by:
a. Revising paragraph (a)(1).
b. Revising paragraph (a)(4).
c. Revising paragraph (b)(1).
d. Revising paragraph (b)(3).
e. Revising *Example* 2 in paragraph (b)(4).
f. Adding *Examples 3, 4,* and *5* in paragraph (b)(4).
The additions and revisions read as follows:

§ 54.9801-6. Special enrollment periods.—(a) *Special enrollment for certain individuals who lose coverage.*—(1) *In general.*—A group health plan is required to permit current employees and dependents (as defined in § 54.9801-2) who are described in paragraph (a)(2) of this section to enroll for coverage under the terms of the plan if the conditions in paragraph (a)(3) of this section are satisfied. Paragraph (a)(4) of this section describes procedures that a plan may require an employee to follow and describes the date by which coverage must begin. The special enrollment rights under this paragraph (a) apply without regard to the dates on which an individual would otherwise be able to enroll under the plan. (See section 701(f)(1) of ERISA and section 2701(f)(1) of the PHS Act, under which this obligation is also imposed on a health insurance issuer offering group health insurance coverage.)

* * *

(4) *Applying for special enrollment and effective date of coverage.*—(i) *Request.*—A plan must allow an employee a period of at least 30 days after an event described in paragraph (a)(3) of this section (loss of eligibility for coverage, termination of employer contributions, or exhaustion of COBRA continuation coverage) to request enrollment (for the employee or the employee's dependent). For this purpose, any written or oral request made to any of the following constitutes a request for enrollment —

(A) The plan administrator;

(B) An issuer offering health insurance coverage under the plan;

(C) A person who customarily handles claims for the plan (such as a third party administrator); or

(D) Any other designated representative.

(ii) *Tolling of period for requesting special enrollment.*—(A) In the case of an individual whose coverage ceases, if a certificate of creditable coverage with respect to that cessation is not provided on or before the date coverage ceases, then the period for requesting special enrollment described in paragraph (a)(4)(i) of this section does not end until 30 days after the earlier of —

(1) The date that a certificate of creditable coverage with respect to that cessation is provided; or

(2) The date 44 days after coverage ceases.

(B) For purposes of this paragraph (a)(4), if an individual's coverage ceases due to the operation of a lifetime limit on all benefits, coverage is considered to cease on the earliest date that a claim is denied due to the operation of the lifetime limit. (Nonetheless, the date of a loss of eligibility for coverage is determined under the rules of paragraph (a)(3) of this section, which provides that a loss of eligibility occurs when a claim that would meet or exceed a lifetime limit on all benefits is incurred, not when it is denied.)

(C) The rules of this paragraph (a)(4)(ii) are illustrated by the following examples:

Example 1. (i) *Facts.* Employer *V* provides group health coverage through a policy provided by Issuer *M.* Individual *D* works for *V* and is covered under *V's* plan. *V* fails to pay *M* the premiums for the coverage period beginning March 1. Consistent with applicable state law, *M* terminates the policy so that the last day of coverage is April 30. On May 15, *M* provides *D* with a certificate of creditable coverage with respect to *D's* cessation of coverage under *V's* plan.

(ii) *Conclusion.* In this *Example 1,* the period to request special enrollment ends no earlier than June 14 (which is 30 days after May 15, the day a certificate of creditable coverage is provided with respect to *D*).

Example 2. (i) *Facts.* Same facts as *Example 1,* except *D* is never provided with a certificate of creditable coverage.

(ii) *Conclusion.* In this *Example 2,* the period to request special enrollment ends no earlier than July 13. (July 13 is 74 days after April 30, the date coverage ceases. That is, July 13 is 30 days after the end of the 44-day maximum tolling period.)

(ii) *Required information.*—* * *
(H) * * *
(5) The interaction with the Family and Medical Leave Act;

* * *

Example 3. (i) *Facts.* Individual *E* works for Employer *W* and has coverage under *W's* plan. *W's* plan has a lifetime limit of $1 million on all benefits under the plan. On September 13, *E* incurs a claim that would exceed the plan's lifetime limit. On September 28, *W* denies the claim due to the operation of the lifetime limit and a certificate of creditable coverage is provided on October 3. *E* is otherwise eligible to enroll in the group health plan of the employer of *E's* spouse.

(ii) *Conclusion.* In this *Example 3,* the period to request special enrollment in the plan of the employer of *E's* spouse ends no earlier than November 2 (30 days after the date the certificate is provided) and begins not later than September 13, the date *E* lost eligibility for coverage.

(iii) *Reasonable procedures for special enrollment.* After an individual has requested enrollment under paragraph (a)(4)(i) of this section, a plan may require the individual to complete enrollment materials within a reasonable time after the end of the 30-day period described in paragraph (a)(4)(i) of this section. In these enrollment materials, the plan may require the individual only to provide information required of individuals who enroll when first eligible and information about the event giving rise to the special enrollment right. A plan may establish a deadline for receiving completed enrollment materials, but such a deadline must be extended for information that an individual making reasonable efforts does not obtain by that deadline.

(iv) *Date coverage must begin.* If the plan requires completion of additional enrollment materials in accordance with paragraph (a)(4)(iii) of this section, coverage must begin no later than the first day of the first calendar month beginning after the date the plan receives enrollment materials that are substantially complete. If the plan does not require completion of additional enrollment materials, coverage must begin no later than the first day of the first calendar month beginning after the date the plan receives the request for special enrollment under paragraph (a)(4)(i) of this section.

(b) *Special enrollment with respect to certain dependent beneficiaries.*—(1) *In general.*—A group health plan that makes coverage available with respect to dependents is required to permit individuals described in paragraph (b)(2) of this section to be enrolled for coverage in a benefit package under the terms of the plan. Paragraph (b)(3) of this section describes procedures that a plan may require an individual to follow and describes the date by which coverage must begin. The special enrollment rights under this paragraph (b) apply without regard to the dates on which an individual would otherwise be able to enroll under the plan. (See 29 CFR 2590.701-6(b) and 45 CFR 146.117(b), under which this obligation is also imposed on a health insurance issuer offering group health insurance coverage.)

* * *

(3) *Applying for special enrollment and effective date of coverage.*—(i) *Request.*—A plan must allow an individual a period of at least 30 days after the date of the marriage, birth, adoption, or placement for adoption (or, if dependent coverage is not generally made available at the time of the marriage, birth, adoption, or placement for adoption, a period of at least 30 days after the date the plan makes dependent coverage generally available) to request enrollment (for the individual or the individual's dependent). For this purpose, any written or oral request made to any of the following constitutes a request for enrollment —

(A) The plan administrator;

(B) An issuer offering health insurance coverage under the plan;

(C) A person who customarily handles claims for the plan (such as a third party administrator); or

(D) Any other designated representative.

(ii) *Reasonable procedures for special enrollment.*—After an individual has requested enrollment under paragraph (b)(3)(i) of this section, a plan may require the individual to complete enrollment materials within a reasonable time after the end of the 30-day period described in paragraph (b)(3)(i) of this section. In these enrollment materials, the plan may require the individual only to provide information required of individuals who enroll when first eligible and information about the event giving rise to the special enrollment right. A plan may establish a deadline for receiving completed enrollment materials, but such a deadline must be extended for information that an individual making reasonable efforts does not obtain by that deadline.

(iii) *Date coverage must begin.*—(A) *Marriage.*—In the case of marriage, if the plan requires completion of additional enrollment materials in accordance with paragraph (b)(3)(ii) of this section, coverage must begin no later than the first day of the first calendar month beginning after the date the plan receives enrollment materials that are substantially complete. If the plan does not require such additional enrollment materials, coverage must begin no later than the first day of the first calendar month beginning after the date the plan receives the request for special enrollment under paragraph (b)(3)(i) of this section.

(B) *Birth, adoption, or placement for adoption.*—Coverage must begin in the case of a dependent's birth on the date of birth and in the case of a dependent's adoption or placement for adoption no later than the date of such adoption or placement for adoption (or, if dependent coverage is not made generally available at the time of the birth, adoption, or placement for adoption, the date the plan makes dependent coverage available). If the plan requires completion of additional enrollment materials in accordance with paragraph (b)(3)(ii) of this section, the plan must provide benefits (including benefits retroactively to the date of birth, adoption, or placement for adoption) once the plan receives enrollment materials that are substantially complete.

(4) *Examples.*—* * *

Example 2. (i) *Facts.* Individual D works for Employer X. X maintains a group health plan with two benefit packages — an HMO option and an indemnity option. Self-only and family coverage are available under both options. D enrolls for self-only coverage in the HMO option. Then, a child, E, is placed for adoption with D. Within 30 days of the placement of E for adoption, D requests enrollment for D and E under the plan's indemnity option and submits completed enrollment materials timely.

(ii) *Conclusion.* In this *Example 2*, D and E satisfy the conditions for special enrollment under paragraphs (b)(2)(v) and (b)(3) of this section. Therefore, the plan must allow D and E to enroll in the indemnity coverage, effective as of the date of the placement for adoption.

Example 3. (i) *Facts.* Same facts as *Example 1*. On March 17 (two days after the birth of C), A telephones the plan administrator and requests special enrollment of A, B, and C. The plan administrator sends A an enrollment form. Under the terms of the plan, enrollment is denied unless a completed form is submitted within 30 days of the event giving rise to the special enrollment right (in this case, C's birth).

(ii) *Conclusion.* In this *Example 3*, the plan does not satisfy paragraph (b)(3) of this section. The plan may require only that A request enrollment during the 30-day period after C's birth. A did so by telephoning the plan administrator. The plan may not condition special enrollment on filing additional enrollment materials during the 30-day period. To comply with paragraph (b)(3) of this section, the plan must allow A a reasonable time after the end of the 30-day period to submit any additional enrollment materials. Once these enrollment materials are received, the plan must allow whatever coverage is chosen to begin on March 15, the date of C's birth.

Example 4. (i) *Facts.* Same facts as *Example 3*, except that A telephones the plan administrator to request enrollment on April 13 (29 days after C's birth). Also, under the terms of the plan, the deadline for submitting the enrollment form is 14 days after the end of the 30-day period for requesting special enrollment (thus, in this case, April 28, which is 44 days after C's birth). The form requests the same information for A, B, and C (name, date of birth, and place of birth) as well as a copy of C's birth certificate. A fills out the enrollment form and delivers it to the plan administrator on April 28. At that time A does not have a birth certificate for C but applies on that day for one from the appropriate government office. A receives the birth certificate on June 1 and furnishes a copy of the birth certificate to the plan administrator shortly thereafter.

(ii) *Conclusion.* In this *Example 4*, A, B, and C are entitled to special enrollment under the plan even though A did not satisfy the plan's requirement of providing a copy of C's birth certificate by the plan's 14-day deadline. While a plan may establish such a deadline, the plan must extend the deadline for information that an individual making reasonable efforts does not obtain by that deadline. A delivered the enrollment form to the plan administrator by the deadline and made reasonable efforts to furnish the birth certificate that the plan requires.

Example 5. (i) *Facts.* Same facts as *Example 4*. On May 3 (after A has delivered the enrollment form to the plan administrator but before A provides the birth certificate) A submits claims for all medical expenses incurred for B and C from the date of C's birth.

(ii) *Conclusion.* In this *Example 5*, the plan must pay all of the claims submitted by A. Because the plan requires that individuals seeking special enrollment complete additional enrollment materials, it is required to provide benefits once it receives enrollment materials that are substantially complete. The form that A submitted on April 28 was substantially complete. Because C's birth is the event giving rise to the special enrollment right, on April 28 A, B, and C become entitled to benefits under the plan retroactive to the date of C's birth.

* * *

☐ Par. 7. A new §54.9801-7 is added to read as follows:

§54.9801-7. Interaction with the Family and Medical Leave Act.—(a) *In general.*—The rules of §§54.9801-1 through 54.9801-6 apply with respect to an individual on leave under the Family and Medical Leave Act of 1993 (29 U.S.C. 2601) (FMLA), and apply with respect to a dependent of such an individual, except to the extent otherwise provided in this section.

(b) *Tolling of significant break in coverage during FMLA leave.*—In the case of an individual (or a dependent of the individual) who is covered under a group health plan, if the individual takes FMLA leave and does not continue group health coverage for any period of FMLA leave, that period is not taken into account in determining whether a significant break in coverage has occurred under §54.9801-4(b)(2)(iii).

(c) *Application of certification provisions.*—(1) *Timing of issuance of certificate.*—(i) In the case of an individual (or a dependent of the individual) who is covered under a group health plan, if the individual takes FMLA leave and the individual's group health coverage is terminated during FMLA leave, an automatic certificate must be provided in accordance with the timing rules set forth in §54.9801-5(a)(2)(ii)(B) (which generally require plans to provide certificates within a reasonable time after coverage ceases).

(ii) In the case of an individual (or a dependent of the individual) who is covered under a group health plan, if the individual takes FMLA leave and continues group health coverage for the period of FMLA leave, but then ceases coverage under the plan at the end of FMLA leave, an automatic certificate must be provided in accordance with the timing rules set forth in §54.9801-5(a)(2)(ii)(A) (which generally require plans to provide a certificate no later than the time a notice is required to be furnished for a qualifying event under a COBRA continuation provision).

(2) *Demonstrating FMLA leave.*—(i) A plan is required to take into account all information about FMLA leave that it obtains or that is presented on behalf of an individual. A plan must treat the individual as having been on FMLA leave for a period if —

(A) The individual attests to the period of FMLA leave; and

(B) The individual cooperates with the plan's efforts to verify the individual's FMLA leave.

(ii) Nothing in this section prevents a plan from modifying its initial determination of FMLA leave if it determines that the individual did not have the claimed FMLA leave, provided that the plan follows procedures for reconsideration similar to those set forth in §54.9801-3(f).

(d) *Relationship to loss of eligibility special enrollment rules.*—In the case of an individual (or a dependent of the individual) who is covered under a group health plan and who takes FMLA leave, a loss of eligibility for coverage under §54.9801-6(a) occurs when the period of FMLA leave ends if —

(1) The individual's group health coverage is terminated at any time during FMLA leave; and

(2) The individual does not return to work for the employer at the end of FMLA leave. [Reg. §54.9801-7.]

Expatriate Health Plans: Issuers: Excepted Benefits

Expatriate Health Plans: Issuers: Excepted Benefits.—Amendments to Reg. § 54.9801-2, relating to the rules for expatriate health plans, expatriate health plan issuers, and qualified expatriates under the Expatriate Health Coverage Clarification Act of 2014 (EHCCA), are proposed (published in the Federal Register on June 10, 2016) (REG-135702-15).

8. Section 54.9801-2 is amended by:

a. Adding in alphabetical order definitions for "expatriate health insurance issuer", "expatriate health plan", and "qualified expatriate;"

b. Revising the definition of "short-term, limited-duration insurance"; and

c. Adding in alphabetical order a definition for "travel insurance".

The additions and revisions read as follows:

§ 54.9801-2. Definitions.

* * *

Expatriate health insurance issuer means an expatriate health insurance issuer within the meaning of § 54.9831-1(f)(2).

Expatriate health plan means an expatriate health plan within the meaning of § 54.9831-1(f)(3).

* * *

Qualified expatriate means a qualified expatriate within the meaning of § 54.9831-1(f)(6).

* * *

[The definitions of *Short term, limited-duration insurance* and *Travel insurance* were adopted by T.D. 9791 on 10/28/2016.]

* * *

Group Health Plans: Genetic Information Nondiscrimination Act

Group Health Plans: Genetic Information Nondiscrimination Act.—Reg. § 54.9802-3, governing the provisions of the Genetic Information Nondiscrimination Act prohibiting discrimination based on genetic information for group health plans, is proposed (published in the Federal Register on October 7, 2009) (REG-123829-08).

Par. 2. Section 54.9802-3 is added to read as follows:

§ 54.9802-3. Additional requirements prohibiting discrimination based on genetic information.

[The text of proposed § 54.9802-3 is the same as the text of § 54.9802-3T as added by T.D. 9464.]

Group Health Plans: Cost-Sharing Information: Disclosure

Group Health Plans: Cost-Sharing Information: Disclosure.—Reg. § 54.9815-2715A, proposing requirements for group health plans and health insurance issuers in the individual and group markets to disclose cost-sharing information upon request, to a participant, beneficiary, or enrollee, including an estimate of such individual's cost-sharing liability for covered items or services furnished by a particular provider, is proposed (published in the Federal Register on November 27, 2019) (REG-118378-19).

Par. 2. Section 54.9815-2715A is added to read as follows:

§ 54.9815-2715A. Transparency in coverage.—(a) *Scope and definitions.*—(1) *Scope.*—This section establishes price transparency requirements for group health plans and health insurance issuers offering group health insurance coverage for the timely disclosure of information about costs related to covered items and services under a group health plan or health insurance coverage.

(2) *Definitions.*—For purposes of this section, the following definitions apply:

(i) *Accumulated amounts* means:

(A) The amount of financial responsibility a participant or beneficiary has incurred at the time a request for cost-sharing information is made, either with respect to a deductible or out-of-pocket limit. If an individual is enrolled in other-than-self-only coverage, these accumulated amounts would include the financial responsibility a participant or beneficiary has incurred toward meeting his or her individual deductible and/or out-of-pocket limit, as well as the amount of financial responsibility that the individuals enrolled under the plan or coverage have incurred toward meeting the other-than-self-only deductible and/or out-of-pocket limit, as applicable. Accumulated amounts include any expense that counts toward a deductible or out-of-pocket limit (such as a copayment or coinsurance), but excludes any expense that does not count toward a deductible or out-of-pocket limit (such as any premium payment, out-of-pocket expense for out-of-network services, or amount for items or services not covered under the group health plan or health insurance coverage); and

(B) To the extent a group health plan or health insurance issuer imposes a cumulative treatment limitation on a particular covered item or service (such as a limit on the number of items, days, units, visits, or hours covered in a defined time period) independent of individual medical necessity determinations, the amount that has accrued toward the limit on the item or service (such as the number of items, days, units, visits, or hours the participant or beneficiary has used).

(ii) *Beneficiary* has the meaning given the term under section 3(8) of the Employee Retirement Income Security Act of 1974 (ERISA).

(iii) *Billing code* means the code used by a group health plan or health insurance issuer or its in-network providers to identify health care items or services for purposes of billing, adjudicating, and paying claims for a covered item or service, including the Current Procedural Terminology (CPT) code, Healthcare Common Procedure Coding System (HCPCS) code, Diagnosis-Related Group (DRG) code, National Drug Code (NDC), or other common payer identifier.

(iv) *Bundled payment* means a payment model under which a provider is paid a single payment for all covered items and services provided to a patient for a specific treatment or procedure.

(v) *Cost-sharing liability* means the amount a participant or beneficiary is responsible for paying for a covered item or service under the terms of the group health plan or health insurance coverage. Cost-sharing liability generally includes deductibles, coinsurance, and copayments, but it does not include premiums, balance billing amounts for out-of-network providers, or the cost of items or services that are not covered under a group health plan or health insurance coverage.

(vi) *Cost-sharing information* means information related to any expenditure required by or on behalf of a participant or beneficiary with respect to health care benefits that are relevant to a determination of a participant's or beneficiary's out-of-pocket costs for a particular health care item or service.

(vii) *Covered items or services* means those items or services for which the costs are payable, in whole or in part, under the terms of a group health plan or health insurance coverage.

(viii) *In-network provider* means a provider that is a member of the network of contracted providers established or recognized under a participant's or beneficiary's group health plan or health insurance coverage.

(ix) *Items or services* means all encounters, procedures, medical tests, supplies, drugs, durable medical equipment, and fees (including facility fees), for which a provider charges a patient in connection with the provision of health care.

(x) *Machine-readable file* means a digital representation of data or information in a file that can be imported or read by a computer system for further processing without human intervention, while ensuring no semantic meaning is lost.

(xi) *Negotiated rate* means the amount a group health plan or health insurance issuer, or a third party on behalf of a group health plan or health insurance issuer, has contractually agreed to pay an in-network provider for covered items and services, pursuant to the terms of an agreement between the provider and the group health plan or health insurance issuer, or a third party on behalf of a group health plan or health insurance issuer.

(xii) *Out-of-network allowed amount* means the maximum amount a group health plan or health insurance issuer would pay for a covered item or service furnished by an out-of-network provider.

(xiii) *Out-of-network provider* means a provider that does not have a contract under a participant's or beneficiary's group health plan or health insurance coverage to provide items or services.

(xiv) *Out-of-pocket limit* means the maximum amount that a participant or beneficiary is required to pay during a coverage period

Reg. § 54.9815-2715A(a)(2)(xiv)

for his or her share of the costs of covered items and services under his or her group health plan or health insurance coverage, including for self-only and other-than-self-only coverage, as applicable.

(xv) *Participant* has the meaning given the term under section 3(7) of ERISA.

(xvi) *Plain language* means written and presented in a manner calculated to be understood by the average participant or beneficiary.

(xvii) *Prerequisite* means certain requirements relating to medical management techniques for covered items and services that must be satisfied before a group health plan or health insurance issuer will cover the item or service. Prerequisites include concurrent review, prior authorization, and step-therapy or fail-first protocols. The term prerequisite does not include medical necessity determinations generally or other forms of medical management techniques.

(b) *Required disclosures to participants or beneficiaries.*—At the request of a participant or beneficiary (or his or her authorized representative), a group health plan or health insurance issuer offering group or individual health insurance coverage must provide to the participant or beneficiary (or his or her authorized representative) the information required under paragraph (b)(1) of this section, in accordance with the method and format requirements set forth in paragraph (b)(2) of this section.

(1) *Required cost-sharing information.*—The information required under this paragraph (b)(1) is the following cost-sharing information, which is accurate at the time the request is made, with respect to a covered item or service and a particular provider or providers, to the extent relevant to the participant's or beneficiary's cost-sharing liability:

(i) An estimate of the participant's or beneficiary's cost-sharing liability for a requested covered item or service provided by a provider or providers that is calculated based on the information described in paragraphs (b)(1)(ii) through (iv) of this section;

(ii) Accumulated amounts the participant or beneficiary has incurred to date;

(iii) Negotiated rate, reflected as a dollar amount, for an in-network provider or providers for the requested covered item or service;

(iv) Out-of-network allowed amount for the requested covered item or service, if the request for cost-sharing information is for a covered item or service furnished by an out-of-network provider;

(v) If a participant or beneficiary requests information for an item or service subject to a bundled payment arrangement that includes the provision of multiple covered items and services, a list of the items and services for which cost-sharing information is being disclosed;

(vi) If applicable, notification that coverage of a specific item or service is subject to a prerequisite; and,

(vii) A notice that includes the following information in plain language:

(A) A statement that out-of-network providers may bill participants or beneficiaries for the difference between a provider's bill charges and the sum of the amount collected from the group health plan or health insurance issuer and from the patient in the form of a copayment or coinsurance amount (the difference referred to as balance billing), and that the cost-sharing information provided pursuant to this paragraph (b)(1) does not account for these potential additional amounts;

(B) A statement that the actual charges for a participant's or beneficiary's covered item or service may be different from an estimate of cost-sharing liability provided pursuant to paragraph (b)(1)(i) of this section, depending on the actual items or services the participant or beneficiary receives at the point of care;

(C) A statement that the estimate of cost-sharing liability for a covered item or service is not a guarantee that benefits will be provided for that item or service; and

(D) Any additional information, including other disclaimers, that the group health plan or health insurance issuer determines is appropriate, provided the additional information does not conflict with the information required to be provided by this paragraph (b)(1).

(2) *Required methods and formats for disclosing information to participants or beneficiaries (or their authorized representatives).*—The methods and formats for the disclosure required under this paragraph (b) are as follows:

(i) *Internet-based self-service tool.*—Information provided under this paragraph (b) must be made available in plain language, without subscription or other fee, through a self-service tool on an internet website that provides real-time responses based on cost-sharing information that is accurate at the time of the request Group health plans and health insurance issuers must ensure that the self-service tool allows users to:

(A) Search for cost-sharing information for a covered item or service provided by a specific in-network provider or by all in-network providers by inputting:

(1) A billing code (such as CPT code 87804) or a descriptive term (such as "rapid flu test"), at the option of the user;

(2) The name of the in-network provider, if the user seeks cost-sharing information with respect to a specific in-network provider; and

(3) Other factors utilized by the plan or issuer that are relevant for determining the applicable cost-sharing information (such as location of service, facility name, or dosage).

(B) Search for an out-of-network allowed amount for a covered item or service provided by out-of-network providers by inputting:

(1) A billing code or descriptive term, at the option of the user; and

(2) Other factors utilized by the plan or issuer that are relevant for determining the applicable out-of-network allowed amount (such as the location in which the covered item or service will be sought or provided).

(C) Refine and reorder search results based on geographic proximity of providers, and the amount of the participant's or beneficiary's estimated cost-sharing liability for the covered item or service, to the extent the search for cost-sharing information for covered items or services returns multiple results.

(ii) *Paper method.*—Information provided under this paragraph (b) must be made available in plain language, without a fee, in paper form at the request of the participant or beneficiary (or his or her authorized representative). The group health plan or health insurance issuer is required to:

(A) Provide the cost-sharing information in paper form pursuant to the individual's request, in accordance with the requirements in paragraphs (b)(2)(i)(A) through (C) of this section; and

(B) Mail the cost-sharing information no later than 2 business days after an individual's request is received.

(3) *Special rule to prevent unnecessary duplication with respect to group health coverage.*—To the extent coverage under a group health plan consists of group health insurance coverage, the plan satisfies the requirements of this paragraph (b) if the plan requires the health insurance issuer offering the coverage to provide the information pursuant to a written agreement. Accordingly, if a health insurance issuer and a plan sponsor enter into a written agreement under which the issuer agrees to provide the information required under this paragraph (b) in compliance with this section, and the issuer fails to do so, then the issuer, but not the plan, violates the transparency disclosure requirements of this paragraph (b).

(c) *Requirements for public disclosure of in-network provider negotiated rates and out-of-network allowed amounts for covered items and services.*—A group health plan or health insurance issuer must make available on an internet website the information required under paragraph (c)(1) of this section in two machine-readable files in accordance with the method and format requirements described in paragraph (c)(2) of this section and updated as required under paragraph (c)(3) of this section.

(1) *Required information.*—Machine-readable files required under this paragraph (c) that are made available to the public by a group health plan or health insurance issuer must include:

(i) Negotiated rate machine-readable file:

(A) The name and Employer Identification Number (EIN) or Health Insurance Oversight System (HIOS) identifier, as applicable, for each plan option or coverage offered by a health insurance issuer or group health plan;

(B) A billing code or other code used by the group health plan or health insurance issuer to identify covered items or services for purposes of claims adjudication and payment, and a plain language description for each billing code; and

(C) Negotiated rates that are:

(1) Reflected as dollar amounts, with respect to each covered item or service under the plan or coverage that is furnished by an in-network provider;

(2) Associated with the National Provider Identifier (NPI) for each in-network provider; and

(3) Associated with the last date of the contract term for each provider-specific negotiated rate that applies to each covered item or service, including rates for both individual items and services and items and services in a bundled payment arrangement.

(ii) Out-of-network allowed amount file:

(A) The name and Employer Identification Number (EIN) or Health Insurance Oversight System (HIOS) identifier, as applicable, for each plan option or coverage offered by a health insurance issuer or group health plan;

(B) A billing code or other code used by the group health plan or health insurance issuer to identify covered items or services for purposes of claims adjudication and payment, and a plain language description for each billing code; and

(C) Unique out-of-network allowed amounts with respect to covered items or services furnished by out-of-network providers during the 90-day time period that begins 180 days prior to the publication date of the machine-readable file (except that a group health plan or health insurance issuer must omit such data in relation to a particular item or service and provider when compliance with this paragraph (c)(1)(ii)(C) would require the group health plan or health insurance issuer to report payment of out-of-network allowed amounts in connection with fewer than 10 different claims for payments). Consistent with paragraph (d)(3) of this section, nothing in this paragraph (c)(1)(ii)(C) requires the disclosure of information that would violate any applicable health information privacy law. Each unique out-of-network allowed amount must be:

(1) Reflected as a dollar amount, with respect to each covered item or service under the plan or coverage that is furnished by an out-of-network provider; and

(2) Associated with the National Provider Identifier (NPI) for each out-of-network provider.

(2) *Required method and format for disclosing information to the public.*—The machine-readable files that must be made available under paragraph (c) of this section in a form and manner determined by the Department of Health and Human Services, the Department of Labor, and the Department of the Treasury. The first machine-readable file must include information regarding rates negotiated for in-network providers with each of the required elements described in paragraph (c)(1)(i) of this section. The second machine-readable file must include information related to the historical data showing allowed amounts for covered items and services furnished by out-of-network providers and include the required elements described in paragraph (c)(1)(ii) of this section. The machine-readable files must be publicly available and accessible to any person free of charge and without conditions, such as establishment of a user account, password, or other credentials, or submission of personally identifiable information to access the file.

(3) *Timing.*—A group health plan or health insurance issuer must update the machine-readable files and information required by this paragraph (c) monthly. The group health plan or health insurance issuer must clearly indicate the date that the files were most recently updated.

(4) *Special rules to prevent unnecessary duplication.*—(i) *Special rule for insured group health plans.*—To the extent coverage under a group health plan consists of group health insurance coverage, the plan satisfies the requirements of this paragraph (c) if the plan requires the health insurance issuer offering the coverage to provide the information pursuant to a written agreement. Accordingly, if a health insurance issuer and a group health plan sponsor enter into a written agreement under which the issuer agrees to provide the information required under this paragraph (c) in compliance with this section, and the issuer fails to do so, then the issuer, but not the plan, violates the transparency disclosure requirements of this paragraph (c).

(ii) *Other contractual arrangements.*—A group health plan or health insurance issuer may satisfy the requirements under this paragraph (c) by entering into a written agreement under which another party (such as a third-party administrator or health care claims clearinghouse) will provide the information required by this paragraph (c) in compliance with this section. Notwithstanding the preceding sentence, if a group health plan or health insurance issuer chooses to enter into such an agreement and the party with which it contracts fails to provide the information in compliance with this paragraph (c), the group health plan or health insurance issuer violates the transparency disclosure requirements of this paragraph (c).

(iii) *Aggregation permitted for out-of-network allowed amounts.*—Nothing in this section prohibits a group health plan or health insurance issuer from satisfying the disclosure requirement described in paragraph (c)(1)(ii) of this section by disclosing out-of-network allowed amounts made available by, or otherwise obtained from, a health insurance issuer, a service provider, or other party with which the plan or issuer has entered into a written agreement to provide the information. Under such circumstances, health insurance issuers, service providers, or other parties with which the group health plan or health insurance issuer has contracted may aggregate out-of-network allowed amounts for more than one group health plan or insurance policy or contract.

(d) *Applicability.*—(1) The provisions of this section apply for plan years beginning on or after [1 year after effective date of the final rule]. As provided under §54.9815-1251, this section does not apply to grandfathered health plans.

(2) This section does not apply to health reimbursement arrangements or other account-based group health plans defined in §54.9815-2711(d)(6).

(3) Nothing in the section alters or otherwise affects a group health plan's or health insurance issuer's duty to comply with requirements under other applicable state or Federal laws, including those governing the accessibility, privacy, or security of information required to be disclosed under this section, or those governing the ability of properly authorized representatives to access participant or beneficiary information held by group health plans and health insurance issuers.

(4) A group health plan or health insurance issuer will not fail to comply with this section solely because it, acting in good faith and with reasonable diligence, makes an error or omission in a disclosure required under paragraph (b) or (c) of this section, provided that the plan or issuer corrects the information as soon as practicable.

(5) A group health plan or health insurance issuer will not fail to comply with this section solely because, despite acting in good faith and with reasonable diligence, its internet website is temporarily inaccessible, provided that the plan or issuer makes the information available as soon as practicable.

(6) To the extent compliance with this section requires a group health plan or health insurance issuer to obtain information from any other entity, the plan or issuer will not fail to comply with this section because it relied in good faith on information from the other entity, unless the plan or issuer knows, or reasonably should have known, that the information is incomplete or inaccurate. [Reg. §54.9815-2715A.]

Group Health Plans: Portability Requirements

Group Health Plans: Portability Requirements.—Amendments to Reg. §54.9831-1, clarifying certain portability requirements for group health plans and issuers of health insurance coverage offered in connection with a group health plans, are proposed (published in the Federal Register on December 30, 2004) (REG-130370-04).

☐ Par. 8. Section 54.9831-1 is amended by:

a. Adding paragraph (a)(2).

b. Revising paragraph (b).

c. Adding paragraph (e).

d. Revising paragraph (c)(1).

The additions and revisions read as follows:

§54.9831-1. Special rules relating to group health plans.—(a) *Group health plan.*—* * *

(2) *Determination of number of plans.*—The number of group health plans that an employer or employee organization (including for this purpose a joint board of trustees of a multiemployer trust affiliated with one or more multiemployer plans) maintains is determined under the rules of this paragraph (a)(2).

(i) Except as provided in paragraph (a)(2)(ii) or (iii) of this section, health care benefits provided by a corporation, partnership, or other entity or trade or business, or by an employee organization, constitute one group health plan, unless —

(A) It is clear from the instruments governing the arrangement or arrangements to provide health care benefits that the benefits are being provided under separate plans; and

(B) The arrangement or arrangements are operated pursuant to such instruments as separate plans.

(ii) A multiemployer plan and a nonmultiemployer plan are always separate plans.

(iii) If a principal purpose of establishing separate plans is to evade any requirement of law, then the separate plans will be considered a single plan to the extent necessary to prevent the evasion.

(b) *General exception for certain small group health plans.*—The requirements of §§54.9801-1 through 54.9801-7, 54.9802-1, 54.9802-2,

54.9811-1T, 54.9812-1T, and 54.9833-1 do not apply to any group health plan for any plan year if, on the first day of the plan year, the plan has fewer than two participants who are current employees.

(c) *Excepted benefits.*—(1) *In general.*—The requirements of §§54.9801-1 through 54.9801-7, 54.9802-1, 54.9802-2, 54.9811-1T, 54.9812-1T, and 54.9833-1 do not apply to any group health plan in relation to its provision of the benefits described in paragraph (c)(2), (3), (4), or (5) of this section (or any combination of these benefits).

* * *

(e) *Determining the average number of employees.*—(1) *Scope.*—Whenever the application of a rule in this part depends upon the average number of employees employed by an employer, the determination of that number is made in accordance with the rules of this paragraph (e).

(2) *Full-time equivalents.*—The average number of employees is determined by calculating the average number of full-time equivalents on business days during the preceding calendar year.

(3) *Methodology.*—For the preceding calendar year, the average number of full-time equivalents is determined by —

(i) Determining the number of employees who were employed full-time by the employer throughout the entire calendar year;

(ii) Totaling all employment hours (not to exceed 40 hours per week) for each part-time employee, and for each full-time employee who was not employed full-time with the employer throughout the entire calendar year;

(iii) Dividing the total determined under paragraph (e)(3)(ii) of this section by a figure that represents the annual full-time hours under the employer's general employment practices, such as 2,080 hours (although for this purpose not more than 40 hours per week may be used); and

(iv) Adding the quotient determined under paragraph (e)(3)(iii) of this section to the number determined under paragraph (e)(3)(i).

(4) *Rounding.*—For purposes of paragraph (e)(3)(iv) of this section, all fractions are disregarded. For instance, a figure of 50.9 is deemed to be 50.

(5) *Employers not in existence in the preceding year.*—In the case of an employer that was in existence for less than the entire preceding calendar year (including an employer that was not in existence at all), a determination of the average number of employees that the employer employs is based on the average number of employees that it is reasonably expected the employer will employ on business days in the current calendar year.

(6) *Scope of the term "employer".*—For purposes of this paragraph (e), employer includes any predecessor of the employer. In addition, all persons treated as a single employer under section 414(b), (c), (m), or (o) are treated as one employer.

(7) *Special rule for multiemployer plans.*—(i) With respect to the application of a rule in this part to a multiemployer plan (as defined in section 3(37) of ERISA), each employer with at least one employee participating in the plan is considered to employ the same average number of employees. That number is the highest number that results by applying the rules of paragraphs (e)(1) through (6) of this section separately to each of the employers.

(ii) The rules of this paragraph (e)(7) are illustrated by the following example:

Example. (i) *Facts.* Twenty five employers have at least one employee who participates in Multiemployer Plan *M*. Among these 25 employers, Employer *K* has 51 employees, determined under the rules of paragraphs (e)(1) through (6) of this section. Each of the other 24 employers has fewer than 50 employees.

(ii) *Conclusion.* With respect to the application of a rule in this part to *M*, each of the 25 employers is considered to employ 51 employees.

Expatriate Health Plans: Issuers: Excepted Benefits

Expatriate Health Plans: Issuers: Excepted Benefits.—Amendments to Reg. §54.9831-1, relating to the rules for expatriate health plans, expatriate health plan issuers, and qualified expatriates under the Expatriate Health Coverage Clarification Act of 2014 (EHCCA), are proposed (published in the Federal Register on June 10, 2016) (REG-135702-15).

11. Section 54.9831-1 is amended:
a. In paragraph (c)(2)(vii) by removing "and" at the end;
b. In paragraph (c)(2)(viii) by adding "and" at the end;
c. Adding paragraph (c)(2)(ix);
d. Revising paragraph (c)(4)(i);
e. Adding paragraph (c)(4)(ii)(D);
f. Revising paragraphs (c)(4)(iii) and (c)(5)(i)(C); and
g. Adding paragraph (f).
The revisions and additions read as follows:

§54.9831-1. Special rules relating to group health plans.

* * *

(c) * * *

(2) * * *

(ix) [Amendment adopted by T.D. 9791 on 10/28/2016.]

* * *

(4) *Noncoordinated benefits.*—(i) *Excepted benefits that are not coordinated.*—Coverage for only a specified disease or illness (for example, cancer-only policies) or hospital indemnity or other fixed indemnity insurance is excepted only if the coverage meets each of the conditions specified in paragraph (c)(4)(ii) of this section.

(ii) * * *

(D) To be hospital indemnity or other fixed indemnity insurance, the insurance must pay a fixed dollar amount per day (or per other time period, such as per week) of hospitalization or illness (for example, $100/day) without regard to the amount of expenses incurred or the type of items or services received and —

(1) The plan or issuer must provide, in any application or enrollment materials provided to participants at or before the time participants are given the opportunity to enroll in the coverage, a notice that prominently displays in at least 14 point type the following language: "THIS IS A SUPPLEMENT TO HEALTH INSURANCE AND IS NOT A SUBSTITUTE FOR MAJOR MEDICAL COVERAGE. THIS IS NOT QUALIFYING HEALTH COVERAGE ('MINIMUM ESSENTIAL COVERAGE') THAT SATISFIES THE HEALTH COVERAGE REQUIREMENT OF THE AFFORDABLE CARE ACT. IF YOU DON'T HAVE MINIMUM ESSENTIAL COVERAGE, YOU MAY OWE AN ADDITIONAL PAYMENT WITH YOUR TAXES."

(2) If participants are required to reenroll (in either paper or electronic form) for renewal or reissuance, the notice described in paragraph (c)(4)(ii)(D)(1) of this section must be displayed in the reenrollment materials that are provided to the participants at or before the time participants are given the opportunity to reenroll in the coverage.

(3) If a notice satisfying the requirements of this paragraph (c)(4)(ii)(D) is timely provided to a participant, the obligation to provide the notice is satisfied for both the plan and the issuer.

(iii) *Examples.*—The rules of this paragraph (c)(4) are illustrated by the following examples:

Example 1. (i) *Facts.* An employer sponsors a group health plan that provides coverage through an insurance policy. The policy provides benefits only for hospital stays at a fixed percentage of hospital expenses up to a maximum of $100 a day.

(ii) *Conclusion.* In this *Example 1*, because the policy pays a percentage of expenses incurred rather than a fixed dollar amount per day (or per other time period, such as per week), the policy is not hospital indemnity or other fixed indemnity insurance that is an excepted benefit under this paragraph (c)(4). This is the result even if, in practice, the policy pays the maximum of $100 for every day of hospitalization.

Example 2. (i) *Facts.* An employer sponsors a group health plan that provides coverage through an insurance policy. The policy provides benefits for doctors' visits at $50 per visit, hospitalization at $100 per day, various surgical procedures at different dollar rates per procedure, and prescription drugs at $15 per prescription.

(ii) *Conclusion.* In this *Example 2*, for doctors' visits, surgery, and prescription drugs, payment is not made on a per-period basis, but instead is based on whether a procedure or item is provided, such as whether an individual has surgery or a doctor visit or is prescribed a drug, and the amount of payment varies based on the type of procedure or item. Because benefits related to office visits, surgery, and prescription drugs are not paid based on a fixed dollar amount per day (or per other time period, such as per week), as required under paragraph (c)(4) of this section, the policy is not hospital indemnity or other fixed indemnity insurance that is an excepted benefit under this paragraph (c)(4).

Example 3. (i) *Facts.* An employer sponsors a group health plan that provides coverage through an insurance policy. The policy provides benefits for certain services at a fixed dollar amount per day, but the dollar amount varies by the type of service.

(ii) *Conclusion.* In this *Example 3*, because the policy provides benefits in a different amount per day depending on the type of service, rather than one specific dollar amount per day regardless of the type of service, the policy is not hospital indemnity or other fixed indemnity insurance that is an excepted benefit under this paragraph (c)(4).

(5) * * *

(i) * * *

(C) [Amendment adopted by T.D. 9791 on 10/28/2016.]

* * *

(f) *Expatriate health plans and expatriate health insurance issuers.*—(1) *In general.*—With respect to coverage under an expatriate health plan, the requirements of section 9815 of the Code and implementing rules and regulations (incorporating sections 2701 through 2728 of the Public Health Service Act) do not apply to —

(i) An expatriate health plan (as defined in paragraph (f)(3) of this section),

(ii) An employer, solely in its capacity as plan sponsor of an expatriate health plan, and

(iii) An expatriate health insurance issuer (as defined in paragraph (f)(2) of this section) with respect to coverage under an expatriate health plan.

(2) *Definition of expatriate health insurance issuer.*—(i) *In general.*—Expatriate health insurance issuer means a health insurance issuer, within the meaning of § 54.9801-2, that issues expatriate health plans and that in the course of its normal business operations—

(A) Maintains network provider agreements that provide for direct claims payments, with health care providers in eight or more countries;

(B) Maintains call centers in three or more countries, and accepts calls from customers in eight or more languages;

(C) Processed at least $1 million in claims in foreign currency equivalents during the preceding calendar year, determined using the Treasury Department's currency exchange rate in effect on the last day of the preceding calendar year;

(D) Makes global evacuation/repatriation coverage available;

(E) Maintains legal and compliance resources in three or more countries; and

(F) Has licenses or other authority to sell insurance in more than two countries, including in the United States.

(ii) *Additional rules.*—For purposes of meeting the requirements of this paragraph (f)(2), two or more entities, including one entity that is the expatriate health insurance issuer, that are members of the expatriate health insurance issuer's controlled group (as determined under § 57.2(c) of this chapter) are treated as one expatriate health insurance issuer. Alternatively, the requirements of this paragraph (f)(2) may be satisfied through contracts between an expatriate health insurance issuer and third parties.

(3) *Definition of expatriate health plan.*—Expatriate health plan means a plan that satisfies the requirements of paragraphs (f)(3)(i) through (iii) of this section.

(i) *Substantially all qualified expatriates requirement.*—Substantially all primary enrollees in the expatriate health plan must be qualified expatriates. For purposes of this paragraph (f)(3)(i), the primary enrollee is the individual covered by the plan or policy whose eligibility for coverage is not due to that individual's status as the spouse, dependent, or other beneficiary of another covered individual. Notwithstanding the foregoing, an individual is not a primary enrollee if the individual is not a national of the United States and the individual resides in his or her country of citizenship. A plan satisfies the requirement of this paragraph (f)(3)(i) for a plan or policy year only if, on the first day of the plan or policy year, less than 5 percent of the primary enrollees (or less than 5 primary enrollees if greater) are not qualified expatriates.

(ii) *Substantially all benefits not excepted benefits requirement.*—Substantially all of the benefits provided under the plan or coverage must be benefits that are not excepted benefits described in § 54.9831-1(c).

(iii) *Additional requirements.*—To qualify as an expatriate health plan, the plan or coverage must also meet the following requirements:

(A) The plan or coverage provides coverage for inpatient hospital services, outpatient facility services, physician services, and emergency services (comparable to emergency services coverage that was described in and offered under section 8903(1) of title 5, United States Code for plan year 2009) in the following locations —

(1) In the case of individuals described in paragraph (f)(6)(i) of this section, in the United States and in the country or countries from which the individual was transferred or assigned, and such other country or countries the Secretary of Health and Human Services, in consultation with the Secretary of the Treasury and Secretary of Labor, may designate;

(2) In the case of individuals described in paragraph (f)(6)(ii) of this section, in the country or countries in which the individual is present in connection with his employment, and such other country or countries the Secretary of Health and Human Services, in consultation with the Secretary of the Treasury and Secretary of Labor, may designate; or

(3) In the case of individuals described in paragraph (f)(6)(iii) of this section, in the country or countries the Secretary of Health and Human Services, in consultation with the Secretary of the Treasury and Secretary of Labor, may designate.

(B) The plan sponsor reasonably believes that benefits provided by the plan or coverage satisfy the minimum value requirements of section 36B(c)(2)(C)(ii). For this purpose, a plan sponsor is permitted to rely on the reasonable representations of the issuer or administrator regarding whether benefits offered by the issuer or group health plan satisfy the minimum value requirements unless the plan sponsor knows or has reason to know that the benefits fail to satisfy the minimum value requirements.

(C) In the case of a plan or coverage that provides dependent coverage of children, such coverage must be available until an individual attains age 26, unless an individual is the child of a child receiving dependent coverage.

(D) The plan or coverage is:

(1) In the case of individuals described in paragraph (f)(6)(i) or (ii) of this section, a group health plan (including health insurance coverage offered in connection with a group health plan), issued by an expatriate health insurance issuer or administered by an expatriate health plan administrator. A group health plan will not fail to be an expatriate health plan merely because any portion of the coverage is provided through a self-insured arrangement.

(2) In the case of individuals described in paragraph (f)(6)(iii) of this section, health insurance coverage issued by an expatriate health insurance issuer.

(E) The plan or coverage offers reimbursements for items or services in local currency in eight or more countries.

(F) The plan or coverage satisfies the provisions of Chapter 100 and regulations thereunder as in effect on March 22, 2010. For this purpose, the plan or coverage is not required to comply with section 9801(e) (relating to certification of creditable coverage) and underlying regulations. However, to the extent the plan or coverage imposes a preexisting condition exclusion, the plan or coverage must ensure that individuals with prior creditable coverage who enroll in the plan or coverage have an opportunity to demonstrate that they have creditable coverage offsetting the preexisting condition exclusion.

(iv) *Example.*—The rule of paragraph (f)(3)(i) of this section is illustrated by the following example:

Example. (i) *Facts.* Business has health plan X for 250 U.S. citizens working outside of the United States in Country Y. All of the U.S. citizens working in Country Y satisfy the requirements to be qualified expatriates under § 54.9831-1(f)(6)(ii). In addition to the 250 U.S. citizens, Business employs 100 citizens of Country Y who reside in Country Y and do not satisfy the requirements to be qualified expatriates under § 54.9831-1(f)(6)(ii). Health plan X covers both the U.S. citizens and citizens of Country Y.

(ii) *Conclusion.* Health plan X satisfies the requirement of § 54.9831-1(f)(3)(i) that substantially all primary enrollees of an expatriate health plan be qualified expatriates because 100 percent of the primary enrollees are qualified expatriates. The 100 citizens of Country Y who reside in Country Y are not treated as primary enrollees for purposes of the substantially all requirement of § 54.9831-1(f)(3)(i) because they are not nationals of the United States and they reside in the country of their citizenship.

(4) *Definition of expatriate health plan administrator.*—(i) *In general.*—Expatriate health plan administrator means an administrator that in the course of its regular business operations—

(A) Maintains network provider agreements that provide for direct claims payments, with health care providers in eight or more countries,

(B) Maintains call centers, in three or more countries, and accepts calls from customers in eight or more languages,

(C) Processed at least $1 million in claims in foreign currency equivalents during the preceding calendar year, determined using the Treasury Department's currency exchange rate in effect on the last day of the preceding calendar year,

(D) Makes global evacuation/repatriation coverage available,

(E) Maintains legal and compliance resources in three or more countries, and

(F) Has licenses or other authority to sell insurance in more than two countries, including in the United States.

(ii) *Additional rules.*—For purposes of meeting the requirements of this paragraph (f)(4), two or more entities, including one entity that is the expatriate health plan administrator, that are members of the expatriate health plan administrator's controlled group (as determined under §57.2(c) of this chapter) are treated as one expatriate health plan administrator. Alternatively, the requirements of this paragraph (f)(4) may be satisfied through contracts between an expatriate health plan administrator and third parties.

(5) *Definition of group health plan.*—Group health plan, for purposes of this section, means a group health plan as defined in §54.9831-1(a).

(6) *Definition of qualified expatriate.*—Qualified expatriate, for purposes of this section, means an individual who is described in paragraph (f)(6)(i), (ii), or (iii) of this section.

(i) *Individuals transferred or assigned by their employer to work in the United States.*—An individual is described in this paragraph (f)(6)(i) only if such individual has the skills, qualifications, job duties, or expertise that has caused the individual's employer to transfer or assign the individual to the United States for a specific and temporary purpose or assignment that is tied to the individual's employment with such employer. This paragraph (f)(6)(i) applies only to an individual who the plan sponsor has reasonably determined requires access to health coverage and other related services and support in multiple countries, and is offered other multinational benefits on a periodic basis (such as tax equalization, compensation for cross-border moving expenses, or compensation to enable the individual to return to the individual's home country), and does not apply to any individual who is a national of the United States. For purposes of this paragraph (f)(6)(i), an individual who is not expected to travel outside the United States at least one time per year during the coverage period would not reasonably require access to health coverage and other related services and support in multiple countries. Furthermore, the offer of a one-time *de minimis* benefit would not meet the standard for the offer of other multinational benefits on a periodic basis.

(ii) *Individuals working outside the United States.*—An individual is described in this paragraph (f)(6)(ii) only if the individual is a national of the United States who is working outside the United States for at least 180 days in a consecutive 12-month period that overlaps with a single plan year, or across two consecutive plan years.

(iii) *Individuals within a group of similarly situated individuals.*—(A) An individual is described in this paragraph (f)(6)(iii) only if:

(1) The individual is a member of a group of similarly situated individuals that is formed for the purpose of traveling or relocating internationally in service of one or more of the purposes listed in section 501(c)(3) or (4), or similarly situated organizations or groups. For example, a group of students that is formed for purposes of traveling and studying abroad for a 6-month period is described in this paragraph (f)(6)(iii);

(2) In the case of a group organized to travel or relocate outside the United States, the individual is expected to travel or reside outside the United States for at least 180 days in a consecutive 12-month period that overlaps with the policy year (or in the case of a policy year that is less than 12 months, at least half the policy year);

(3) In the case of a group organized to travel or relocate within the United States, the individual is expected to travel or reside in the United States for not more than 12 months;

(4) The individual is not traveling or relocating internationally in connection with an employment-related purpose; and

(5) The group meets the test for having associational ties under section 2791(d)(3)(B) through (F) of the PHS Act (42 U.S.C. 300gg-91(d)(3)(B) through (F)).

(B) This paragraph (f)(6)(iii) does not apply to a group that is formed primarily for the sale or purchase of health insurance coverage.

(C) If a group of similarly situated individuals satisfies the requirements of this paragraph (f)(6)(iii), the Secretary of Health and Human Services, in consultation with the Secretary and the Secretary of Labor, has determined that the group requires access to health coverage and other related services and support in multiple countries.

(7) *Definition of United States.*—Solely for purposes of this paragraph (f), United States means the 50 States, the District of Columbia, and Puerto Rico.

(8) *National of the United States.*—For purposes of this paragraph (f), national of the United States, when referring to an individual, has the meaning used in the Immigration and Nationality Act (8 U.S.C. 1101 et. seq.) and includes U.S. citizens and non-citizen nationals. Thus, for example, an individual born in American Samoa is a national of the United States at birth.

STATEMENT OF PROCEDURAL RULES

Statement of Procedural Rules: Liability for Tax: Taxpayer Appeals

Statement of Procedural Rules: Liability for Tax: Taxpayer Appeals.—Amendments to Reg. §601.106, relating to how a taxpayer may appeal, without going to court, adjustments affecting a taxpayer's tax liability, are proposed (published in the Federal Register on September 20, 1993) (IA-85-91).

Par. 4. Section 601.106 is amended as follows:

1. Paragraphs (a) through (f) are revised.

2. Paragraph (g)(1) is revised.

3. Paragraph (h) is amended by:

  a. Redesignating the text of paragraph (h)(1) as paragraph (h)(1)(i).

  b. Adding paragraph headings for (h)(1) and newly designated paragraph (h)(1)(i).

  c. Redesignating the text of paragraph (h)(2) as paragraph (h)(1)(ii) and revising it.

  d. Redesignating the text of paragraph (h)(3) as paragraph (h)(2)(i).

  e. Adding headings for newly designated paragraphs (h)(2) and (h)(2)(i).

  f. Adding the word "original" immediately before the word "disposition" in newly designated paragraph (h)(2)(i).

  g. Redesignating the text of paragraph (h)(4) as paragraph (h)(2)(ii).

  h. Adding a heading to newly designated paragraph (h)(2)(ii).

4. Paragraph (i) is revised.

5. The revised and added provisions read as follows:

§601.106. Appeals functions.—(a) *General.*—(1) *Purpose.*—Appeals is the administrative appeals office of the Internal Revenue Service. Its purpose is to resolve tax controversies without litigation, to the extent possible. Appeals is to approach these controversies in a fair and impartial manner to both the taxpayer and the government.

(2) *Authorization.*—(i) *For the Appeals function.*—Appeals authority on non-docketed cases has been delegated by the Commissioner while Appeals authority on docketed cases has been delegated by the Chief Counsel.

(ii) *For an Appeals office.*—Each region contains Appeals offices with local office facilities within the region. An Appeals office has jurisdiction over cases originating in the office of any District Director, Service Center/Compliance Center Director, or the Assistant Commissioner (International) situated in the region, or in any case in which jurisdiction has been transferred to the region. A taxpayer residing or located outside the United States uses the facilities of the Washington, D.C. Appeals Office of the Mid-Atlantic Region or any other Appeals office that the taxpayer specifies when initiating the appeal.

(iii) *For settlement by Appeals personnel.*—Unless settlement authority has been delegated to other employees, settlements with a taxpayer must be approved by the Chief, an Associate Chief, or a Team Chief in the Appeals office.

(3) *Subject matter jurisdiction; in general.*—Appeals offices have exclusive settlement jurisdiction and final authority within the Internal Revenue Service for the determination of the following types of tax liability and other items—

(i) Federal income tax, estate tax (including extensions for payment under section 6161(a)(2) of the Internal Revenue Code), gift tax, generation-skipping transfer tax, or miscellaneous excise taxes under chapter 41, 42, 43, 44, or 45 of subtitle D of the Internal Revenue Code, all of which are subject to the deficiency procedures (Chapter 45 was repealed for oil removed on or after August 23, 1988.);

(ii) Any other tax which is subject to the deficiency procedures;

(iii) Employment tax or certain miscellaneous excise tax under subtitle D of the Internal Revenue Code (which are not subject to the deficiency procedures except as noted in paragraph (a)(3)(i)(A) of this section);

(iv) Liability for additions to the tax, additional amounts, and assessable penalties provided under chapter 68 of the Internal Revenue Code (collectively referred to in this section as penalties);

(v) The initial or continuing recognition of the tax exempt or foundation status of an organization;

(vi) The initial or continuing determination of employee plan qualification under subchapter D of chapter 1 of the Internal Revenue Code;

(vii) The adjustment or readjustment of partnership items;

(viii) Offers in compromise under section 7122 of the Internal Revenue Code;

(ix) Abatement of interest under section 6404(e)(1) of the Internal Revenue Code; and

(x) Any other disputed tax issues that the Internal Revenue Service determines are administratively appealable.

(4) *Limitations on authority.*—The authority described in paragraphs (a)(2) and (a)(3) of this section does not include the authority to:

(i)(A) Consider any case involving the qualification of an employee plan or the tax exempt or foundation status of an organization if such consideration has already been given in a National Office ruling or technical advice (but only to the extent the case involves qualification or the tax exempt or foundation status). In such a case the decision of the National Office is final. The plan or organization has no right of administrative appeal to Appeals or elsewhere;

(B) If a case is already under Appeals' jurisdiction and Appeals' proposed disposition is contrary to either a National Office ruling concerning tax exempt or foundation status, or a National Office technical advice concerning either qualification or tax exempt or foundation status (issued before the case went to Appeals), the Appeals determination is not final. In such a case Appeals' proposed disposition will be submitted to the Assistant Commissioner (Employee Plans and Exempt Organizations) through the Office of the Regional Director of Appeals. However, in a section 521 case, the proposed disposition will be submitted to the Associate Chief Counsel (Domestic) through the Office of the Regional Director of Appeals. The decision of the Assistant Commissioner or the Associate Chief Counsel will be followed by Appeals;

(ii) Consider any case that was docketed under section 6110 of the Internal Revenue Code concerning the public inspection of written documents or section 7428, 7476, 7477 (repealed after December 31, 1984) or 7478 of the Internal Revenue Code concerning declaratory judgements;

(iii) Eliminate the fraud penalty in a tax year or period for which criminal prosecution against the taxpayer (or related taxpayer involving the same transaction) has been recommended to the Department of Justice for a willful attempt to evade or defeat tax, or for a willful failure to file a return, except upon the recommendation or concurrence of Counsel. Similarly, an Appeals office has no authority to eliminate the fraud penalty in a tax year or period that relates to or affects the year or period described in this paragraph (4)(iii);

(iv) Consider any case in which a recommendation for criminal prosecution is pending, except with the concurrence of Counsel;

(v) Determine alcohol, tobacco, and certain other excise tax liability under subtitle E of the Internal Revenue Code or under subchapter D, chapter 78 of subtitle F of the Internal Revenue Code, insofar as subchapter D relates to taxes imposed under subtitle E;

(vi) Consider a Trust Fund Recovery Penalty case (formerly referred to as a 100 percent penalty case) if the assessment is to be made because of Chief Counsel's request to support a third-party action in a pending refund suit. See Rev. Proc. 84-78, 1984-2 C.B. 754;

(vii) Consider any case solely involving the failure or refusal to comply with the tax laws because of moral, religious, political, constitutional, conscientious, or similar grounds; or

(viii) Consider an issue or a case that is designated for litigation by Chief Counsel.

(b) *Appeal rights of the taxpayer.*—(1) *In general.*—The Appeals process is initiated at the request of the taxpayer. The procedures for initiating an appeal are described below.

(2) *When an organization, rather than each member, is treated as the taxpayer.*—Labor unions, trade associations, and other organizations whose members' dues have been disallowed as a deduction to each member because the organization spent amounts for lobbying, promoting or defeating legislation, political campaigning, or for propaganda related to those activities, are afforded rights of administrative appeal similar to those rights afforded to taxpayers generally.

(3) *Situations in which a taxpayer may request an appeal.*— (i) *Letter proposing adjustments.*—A taxpayer may request an appeal in any case in which a District Director, Service Center/Compliance Center Director, or the Assistant Commissioner (International) has issued a letter proposing adjustments (commonly referred to as the 30 day letter) concerning an item described in paragraph (a)(3) of this section. (The taxpayer will be informed of the right to an administrative appeal in this letter.)

(ii) *After issuance of a statutory notice of deficiency.*—A taxpayer who has been issued a statutory notice of deficiency (commonly referred to as the 90 day letter) will not be granted a conference by Appeals during the 90 day period (150 day period if the notice is addressed to a person outside the United States) following the mailing of the notice if the taxpayer had a conference or was offered a conference prior to the issuance, unless unusual circumstances exist.

(iii) *Penalties.*—Certain chapter 68 penalties that have been assessed may be appealed before payment is made. (These penalties may also be appealed after payment is made but before the filing of a claim for refund.) This post-assessment appeal procedure applies to all but the following chapter 68 penalties—

(A) Penalties that are not subject to a reasonable cause or reasonable basis determination (e.g., the penalty for failure to pay estimated income tax under section 6655 of the Internal Revenue Code);

(B) Penalties that are subject to the deficiency procedures of subchapter B of chapter 63 of the Internal Revenue Code (e.g., the accuracy-related penalty and the fraud penalty under sections 6662 and 6663 of the Internal Revenue Code, respectively). Taxpayers have the right to appeal these penalties prior to assessment;

(C) Penalties that are subject to an administratively granted pre-assessment appeal procedure (such as that provided in § 1.6694-2(a)(1) of this chapter for return preparers);

(D) The penalties provided in sections 6700 and 6701 of the Internal Revenue Code for promoting abusive tax shelters, and for aiding and abetting, respectively. These penalties are subject to the procedural rules of section 6703 of the Internal Revenue Code which provides for an extension of the period of collection of the penalty when a person pays not less than 15 percent of the amount of such penalty; and

(E) The Trust Fund Recovery Penalty (formerly referred to as the 100 percent penalty) provided under section 6672 of the Internal Revenue Code. The taxpayer generally has the opportunity to appeal this penalty prior to assessment.

(4) *Initiation of an appeal.*—(i) *General rules.*—An appeal is initiated by filing a protest. See paragraph (b)(4)(iii) of this section for a simplified procedure for small cases.

(ii) *Contents of a protest.*—A protest provides the reasons in writing why the taxpayer does not agree with the disputed adjustments to tax liability. In addition, a protest should contain identifying information, which is described in the letter (or in other information enclosed with the letter) that offers the taxpayer the opportunity to appeal. Examples of items that should be in a protest are as follows:

(A) If the disagreement concerns factual matters, the protest should include a statement in writing of the taxpayer's view of the facts. Factual matters concern, for example, evidence of the date when income was received and the existence of records proving the payment of an expense.

(B) If the disagreement concerns whether or how an item should be taxed, the protest should include a reason or reasons in writing for the taxpayer's position. Such disagreements concern, for example, whether the law requires that certain proceeds be included in gross income. The reasoning may be based simply on what the taxpayer believes is logical and fair. Inclusion of references to supporting authorities such as the Internal Revenue Code, Treasury regulations, court cases, revenue rulings and revenue procedures will facilitate consideration of the appeal. Reference may also be made to Internal Revenue Service publications.

(iii) *Small case request.*—(A) *In general.*—If the total amount (described in paragraph (b)(4)(iii)(B) of this section) is not more than $25,000 for any tax period, the taxpayer may initiate an appeal by requesting Appeals consideration, indicating the unagreed adjustments to tax liability and stating the reason for disagreement. A taxpayer may provide any additional information that he or she feels is pertinent.

(B) *Total amount defined.*—(1) *In general.*—The total amount includes the entire amount of additional tax and penalties proposed by the Internal Revenue Service, not just the portion of additional tax or penalties that the taxpayer disputes. The total amount also includes the entire amount of a refund or credit claimed by the taxpayer. Where the Service determines that an overassessment was made, the total amount is the amount proposed by the Internal Revenue Service. Interest is not included in any of these amounts.

(2) *Offer in compromise.*—In an offer in compromise, the total amount includes the assessed tax, penalties, and interest sought to be compromised.

(3) *Penalties.*—In the case of penalties that are assessed before a taxpayer is given the opportunity to dispute the penalties (a post-assessment penalty case), the total amount is the amount of the disputed penalties for any tax period.

(C) *Subjects always requiring a protest.*—A protest is required to obtain Appeals consideration in all employee plan and exempt organization cases. (If corporate or individual returns are adjusted in connection with employee plan or exempt organization cases, these returns are not subject to this paragraph (b)(4)(iii)(C).) A protest is also required in all partnership and S corporation cases.

(iv) *Where to file a protest or a small case request.*—Filing instructions are in the letter (or in other information enclosed with the letter) that offers the taxpayer the opportunity to appeal. The receiving office will review the protest or small case request for the purpose of deciding whether further development or action is required prior to referring the case to Appeals.

(c) *Nature of Appeals' proceedings.*—(1) *In general.*—Appeals' proceedings are informal. Testimony is not taken under oath, although matters alleged as facts may be required to be submitted later in the form of affidavits, or declared to be true under penalties of perjury.

(2) *Presentation of new information at Appeals.*—(i) *Newly discovered information.*—If newly discovered evidence is presented to Appeals in a case pending in non-docketed status, Appeals may send the new information to the originating function (the District Director, Service Center/Compliance Center Director, or Assistant Commissioner (International)) for consideration and comment.

(ii) *Withheld information.*—A taxpayer cannot withhold information from the District Director, Service Center/Compliance Center Director, or Assistant Commissioner (International) and expect to present it for the first time before Appeals at a conference in non-docketed status. If such information is presented to Appeals, generally, the case will be returned to the originating function for reconsideration.

(3) *Taxpayer representatives.*—Taxpayers may represent themselves or may designate a qualified representative to act for them. If a taxpayer engages a representative to present the appeal, the taxpayer and representative must follow the practice and conference procedures in Treasury Department Circular 230 as amended (31 CFR part 10), and in subpart E of this part.

(d) *Consideration of cases by Appeals.*—(1) *In general.*—Appeals will follow the law and the recognized standards of legal construction in determining facts and applying the law. Appeals will determine the correct amount of the tax with strict impartiality as between the taxpayer and the Government, and without favoritism or discrimination between taxpayers.

(2) *Factors considered by Appeals.*—Appeals will ordinarily consider the relative merits of the opposing views in light of the hazards which would exist if the case was litigated. However, no settlement will be made based upon the nuisance value of the case to either party. If the taxpayer makes an unacceptable settlement proposal under circumstances indicating a good faith attempt to reach an agreement on a basis that is fair to both the Government and the taxpayer, then, generally, the Appeals officer should indicate to the taxpayer the kind of settlement that the officer would recommend for acceptance. Appeals may defer action on, or may decline to settle,

certain cases or issues in order to achieve greater uniformity and enhance overall voluntary compliance with the tax laws.

(3) *Making a taxpayer's return.*—In cases under Appeals jurisdiction, the Appeals official has the authority to make and subscribe to a return under the provisions of section 6020 of the Internal Revenue Code where a taxpayer fails to make a required return.

(4) *When an Appeals officer's proposed settlement is not approved.*—An Appeals officer may recommend acceptance of the taxpayer's proposal of settlement, or may recommend other action favorable to the taxpayer. However, as stated in paragraph (a)(2)(iii) of this section, generally, settlements with a taxpayer must be approved by the Chief, an Associate Chief, or a Team Chief in the Appeals office. If the Appeals officer's recommendation is disapproved in whole or in part by a reviewing officer, then, generally, the reviewing officer will advise the taxpayer of the decision and will offer the taxpayer a conference (with the reviewing officer), which the taxpayer may accept by written confirmation. However, a conference will not be offered if the interest of the Government would be injured by delay, as, for example, in a case involving the imminent expiration of the period of limitations or the dissipation of assets.

(5) *Related taxpayer.*—The District Director, the Service Center/Compliance Center Director, and the Assistant Commissioner (International) are responsible for assembling the return of a related taxpayer for an examination. Ordinarily, a case concerning a related taxpayer is not requested from the examining office by Appeals unless this action is necessary to ensure consistency. If the action is necessary, Appeals contacts the examining office to determine what action should be taken by both offices. Appeals may assume jurisdiction in a related taxpayer case with the concurrence of the related taxpayer after the examining office has completed any necessary action. The related taxpayer does not have to file a protest. If the need for assuming jurisdiction over a related taxpayer case becomes apparent after a conference has been held, Appeals may contact the related taxpayer. In the absence of any objection, Appeals assumes jurisdiction after requesting that the examining office complete action on the case.

(6) *Assistance from Counsel.*—(i) *In general.*—Appeals may use Counsel as a resource on non-docketed cases when advice is needed concerning the hazards of litigation, interpretation of law, or evaluation of evidence. This advice will be provided through informal arrangements between each Counsel and Appeals office.

(ii) *Counsel attendance at conference.*—Appeals generally does not ask Counsel to attend settlement conferences. However, in certain cases Counsel may attend an appeals settlement conference. For example, Counsel may attend a conference for a case involving the fraud penalty for which criminal prosecution against the taxpayer (or a related taxpayer involving the same transaction) has been recommended to the Department of Justice for a willful attempt to evade or defeat tax, or for a willful failure to file a return.

(iii) *Technical advice from the National Office.*—(A) *Definition.*—Technical advice means advice or guidance as to the interpretation and proper application of internal revenue laws, related statutes, and regulations, to a specific set of facts, furnished by the National Office upon Appeals' request in connection with the processing and consideration of a non-docketed case. It is furnished as a means of assisting Internal Revenue Service personnel in closing cases and establishing and maintaining consistent holdings in the various regions. It does not include memoranda on matters of general technical application furnished to Appeals where the issues are not raised in connection with the consideration and handling of a specific taxpayer's case.

(B) *Procedures for technical advice.*—General procedures for technical advice are found in § 601.105(b)(5). In addition, the technical advice rules are not applicable to an appeal of penalties described in paragraph (b)(3)(iv) of this section.

(e) *Settlement of a case before Appeals.*—(1) *In general; new issue.*—During consideration of a case, the Appeals office should neither reopen an issue as to which the taxpayer and the office of the District Director, Service Center/Compliance Center Director, or Assistant Commissioner (International) are in agreement, nor raise a new issue, unless the ground for such action is a substantial one and the potential effect upon the tax liability is material. If Appeals raises a new issue, the taxpayer or the taxpayer's representative should be so advised and should be offered an opportunity for discussion before taking any formal action, such as the issuance of a statutory notice of deficiency (commonly referred to as the 90 day letter).

(2) *Case not docketed in the Tax Court.*—(i) *Agreed issues.*—If settlement of some or all of the issues is reached with the taxpayer by Appeals, the taxpayer will be requested to sign the appropriate agreement form for the agreed issue or issues.

(ii) *Unagreed Issues.*—(A) *In general.*—(1) *Case subject to the deficiency procedures.*—To the extent that the taxpayer does not agree with a proposed deficiency, a statutory notice of deficiency (commonly referred to as the 90 day letter) will be issued by Appeals as prescribed in sections 6212 and 6861 of the Internal Revenue Code. (The statutory notice is issued for deficiencies in income, estate, gift, generation-skipping transfer, or certain miscellaneous excise taxes (under chapter 41, 42, 43, 44, or 45 of the Internal Revenue Code). Each Chief, Associate Chief, or Team Chief of an Appeals office is authorized to issue the statutory notice of deficiency. The taxpayer may file a petition with the U.S. Tax Court for a redetermination of the deficiency. The petition must be filed within 90 days (150 days if the notice is addressed to a person outside of the United States) after the statutory notice of deficiency is mailed (not counting Saturday, Sunday, or a legal holiday in the District of Columbia as the last day).

(2) *Case not subject to the deficiency procedures.*—If the unagreed case is not subject to the deficiency procedures, the case and its administrative file will be forwarded to the appropriate Internal Revenue Service function with instructions to take action on the unagreed tax liability determined by Appeals.

(B) *Refund claimed by a Taxpayer.*—If a claim for refund is disallowed in full or in part by Appeals and the taxpayer does not sign Form 2297, Waiver of Statutory Notification of Claim Disallowance, Appeals will issue a statutory notice of claim disallowance.

(3) *Case docketed in Tax Court.*—(i) *Appeals jurisdiction.*—(A) *In general.*—Except in unusual cases, a docketed case is referred by Counsel to Appeals to reach a settlement with the taxpayer (even if Appeals issued the statutory notice of deficiency). If Appeals has the case under consideration at the time it is docketed, then it retains the case. See Rev. Proc. 87-24, 1987-1 C.B. 720.

(B) *Period of jurisdiction.*—(1) *Deficiency of more than $10,000.*—Appeals has exclusive jurisdiction of a docketed case involving a deficiency of more than $10,000 per period (including taxes and penalties) as long as Appeals believes there is a reasonable likelihood of settlement, or until the case appears on a trial calendar. Counsel may extend the period of Appeals consideration of the case when it appears on the trial calendar.

(2) *Deficiency of $10,000 or less.*—In general, Appeals has exclusive jurisdiction of a docketed case involving a deficiency of $10,000 or less per period (including tax and penalties) for a period of six months, except that jurisdiction ends one month before the trial calendar call. In a Small Tax Case (S case), Appeals' jurisdiction ends 15 days before the trial calendar call. Appeals and Counsel may agree to extend the period of consideration. A case is designated as an S case by the Court upon request of the petitioner and includes the letter S as part of the docket number. An S case is given expeditious consideration.

(C) *Exclusive jurisdiction.*—In general, Appeals has sole settlement authority over docketed cases referred to, or retained by, Appeals pursuant to these procedures until the case is returned to Counsel. However, a case or an issue in a case may be reserved by Counsel. Upon request, Appeals will return a case to Counsel to allow adequate trial preparation. Whenever a docketed case is returned to Counsel, sole authority to try or to settle the case will revert to Counsel, unless Counsel and Appeals agree that settlement authority over some or all of the issues will be retained by Appeals. Thus, in some situations Counsel will prepare a case for trial while Appeals simultaneously negotiates for a settlement.

(D) *Transfer of jurisdiction to and from Counsel.*—By agreement between Counsel and Appeals, any docketed case (or portions thereof) may be transferred from Counsel to Appeals or from Appeals to Counsel, notwithstanding the fact that the case was previously considered by the receiving function. This authority is to be utilized to promote more efficient disposition of the case.

(E) *Assisting Counsel.*—For cases or issues over which Counsel has jurisdiction, Appeals may assist Counsel with settlement negotiations, with trial preparation, or at trial.

(F) *Coordination of settlements in related cases.*—Unless both offices agree that the offer is acceptable, no settlement offer will be accepted by Appeals if there is a related case in Counsel. (Related cases may involve different tax years of the same taxpayer or different taxpayers engaging in a similar transaction.) Disagreements between Appeals and Counsel on whether the offer should be accepted will be resolved by the Regional Counsel, with the advice and assistance of the Regional Director of Appeals and the Deputy Regional Counsel (Tax Litigation).

(ii) *Agreed issues.*—If some or all of the issues in a docketed case are settled by the taxpayer and Appeals, Appeals generally prepares a document reflecting settlement of these issues. The agree-

ment is recorded in a decision document or stipulation of settlement. This document stipulates to the agreed deficiency or overpayment (or to the disposition of agreed issues if less than all issues are agreed) and is signed by the taxpayer. Appeals forwards the document, along with any necessary computations, to Counsel who signs and files the document with the Tax Court. If the court signs the document, it is entered as a decision of the court (or, if the settlement resolves only some of the issues in the case, as a part of the record of the case). No settlement of a docketed case is binding on either the taxpayer or the government until it is entered as a decision (or filed as part of the record in the case).

(iii) *Unagreed issues.*—To the extent issues in a docketed case remain unsettled after consideration and conference in Appeals, the case will be returned to Counsel.

(f) *Transfer of a case to another Appeals office.*—(1) *Non-docketed case.*—(i) *Routine.*—An Appeals office may transfer jurisdiction in a non-docketed case to an office that is closer to the taxpayer's residence or place of business if the taxpayer's books and records are available there.

(ii) *Hardship.*—An Appeals office may transfer jurisdiction in a non-docketed case to another office to relieve the taxpayer of hardship. The request is made to the transferring office which will determine whether hardship exists. If hardship exists, the transfer will be made if the taxpayer's books and records are available to the receiving office, and if both offices agree that the transfer is not an attempt to obtain a more favorable resolution of the disputed issues.

(iii) *Special situations.*—From time to time special transfer rules will be published in the Internal Revenue Manual for certain types of cases.

(iv) *Approval needed.*—Transfers within a region for reasons other than those listed in paragraphs (f)(1)(i), (ii) and (iii) of this section must be approved by both the transferring and receiving Regional Directors of Appeals. If the directors cannot agree, the proposed transfer may be referred to the National Director of Appeals for decision.

(2) *Docketed case.*—(i) *In general.*—A docketed case under Appeals jurisdiction will be transferred to the Appeals office serving the locality designated by the Tax Court for trial unless that locality is Washington, D.C. Docketed cases set for a Tax Court trial should be transferred to the Washington, D.C., office only if the taxpayer resides in the area and the books and records are available there. Otherwise the case should be transferred to the Appeals office serving the taxpayer's residence or place of business.

(ii) *Special situations.*—From time to time special transfer rules will be published in the Internal Revenue Manual for certain types of docketed cases.

(iii) *Approval needed.*—Transfers within a region for reasons other than those listed in paragraphs (f)(2)(i) and (ii) of this section must be approved by both the transferring and receiving Regional Directors of Appeals. If the directors cannot agree, the proposed transfer may be referred to the National Director of Appeals for decision.

(iv) *Coordination with Counsel.*—All transfers of docketed cases must be coordinated with Counsel.

(g) *Limitation on the jurisdiction and function of Appeals.*—(1) *Overpayment of more than $1,000,000.*—If Appeals determines that there is an overpayment of income, estate, generation-skipping transfer, gift or certain miscellaneous excise taxes (under chapter 41, 42, 43, 44, or 45 of the Internal Revenue Code), including penalties and interest, in excess of $1,000,000, such determination will be reviewed by the Joint Committee on Taxation. See § 601.108.

* * *

(h) * * *

(1) *Closed with mutual concessions.*—(i) *Service initiated opening.*—* * *

(ii) *Taxpayer initiated opening.*—Under certain unusual circumstances favorable to the taxpayer, such as retroactive legislation, a case not docketed in the Tax Court and closed by Appeals on the basis of concessions made by both Appeals and the taxpayer may be reopened upon written application from the taxpayer, and only with the approval of the Regional Director of Appeals. The processing of an application for a tentative carryback adjustment or a claim for refund or credit for an overassessment (for a year involved in the prior closing) attributable to a claimed deduction or credit for a carryback provided by law, and not included in a previous Appeals determination, does not constitute a reopening requiring approval. A subsequent assessment of an excessive tentative allowance also does not constitute such a reopening. The National Director of Appeals may authorize, in advance, the reopening of similar classes of cases if legislative enactments or compelling administrative reasons require such advance approval.

(2) *Closed without mutual concessions.*—(i) *Service initiated opening.*—* * *

(ii) *Taxpayer initiated opening.*—* * *

(i) *Effective dates.*—In general, the rules will be effective on the date of publication of the final rules in the Federal Register. The rules in § 601.106(b)(4), which describe how a taxpayer initiates an appeal, will be effective 60 days after the date of publication of the final rules in the Federal Register. However, if the letter (or other information enclosed with the letter) offering the taxpayer the opportunity to appeal refers to rules predating the rules in § 601.106(b)(4), then the taxpayer may follow either the old rules or new rules. [Reg. § 601.106.]

[The next page is 92,101.]

Proposed Regulations—Preambles

[¶ 49,003]   Proposed Regulations and Proposed Amendments of Regulations, published in the Federal Register on April 30, 1975.

Employee plans: Lump-sum distributions.—Reg. §§1.402(e)-2 and 1.402(e)-3 and amendments of Reg. §§1.72-4, 1.72-13, 1.101-2, 1.122-1, 1.402(a)-1, 1.403(a)-1, 1.403(a)-2, 1.652(b)-1, and 1.1304-2 (Code Sec. 1304 was repealed by the Tax Reform Act of 1986), relating to the treatment of lump-sum distributions, have been proposed. Reg. §§1.62-1 was removed 3/5/88 by T.D. 8189. Reg. §1.405-3 was removed by T.D. 9849 on 3/11/2019.

Notice is hereby given that the regulations set forth in tentative form in the attached appendix are proposed to be prescribed by the Commissioner of Internal Revenue, with the approval of the Secretary of the Treasury or his delegate. Prior to the final adoption of such regulations, consideration will be given to any comments pertaining thereto which are submitted in writing (preferably six copies) to the Commissioner of Internal Revenue, Attention: CC:LR:T, Washington, D.C. 20224, by June 16, 1975. Pursuant to 26 CFR 601.601(b), designations of material as confidential or not to be disclosed, contained in such comments, will not be accepted. Thus, a person submitting written comments should not include therein material that he considers to be confidential or inappropriate for disclosure to the public. It will be presumed by the Internal Revenue Service that every written comment submitted to it in response to this notice of proposed rule making is intended by the person submitting it to be subject in its entirety to public inspection and copying in accordance with the procedures of 26 CFR 601.702(d)(9). Any person submitting written comments who desires an opportunity to comment orally at a public hearing on these proposed regulations should submit his request, in writing, to the Commissioner by June 16, 1975. In such case, a public hearing will be held, and notice of the time, place, and date will be published in a subsequent issue of the FEDERAL REGISTER, unless the person or persons who have requested a hearing withdraw their requests for a hearing before notice of the hearing has been filed with the Office of the Federal Register. The proposed regulations are to be issued under the authority contained in sections 402(a)(2), 402(e), and 7805 of the Internal Revenue Code of 1954 (88 Stat. 990, 987 and 68A Stat. 917; 26 U.S.C. 402(a)(2), 402(e), 7805).

DONALD C. ALEXANDER,
Commissioner of Internal Revenue.

This document proposes amendments to the Income Tax Regulations (26 CFR Part 1) in order to conform the regulations under sections 62, 72, 101, 122, 402, 403, 405, 652, and 1304 of the Internal Revenue Code of 1954 to the provisions of section 2005 of the Employee Retirement Income Security Act of 1974 (Pub. L. 93-406, 88 Stat. 987), relating to taxation of certain lump sum distributions.

The amendments proposed relating to sections 62, 72, 101, 122, ¶ 403, ¶ 405, 652, and 1304 of the Code merely conform the regulations under those sections to the changes in the taxation of a lump sum distribution under section 402 of the Code, as amended by section 2005(a) of the Act.

Under section 402(a)(2) of the Code, as amended, a method of computing the capital gain portion of a lump sum distribution is provided. In general, the capital gain portion of a lump sum distribution will be an amount equal to the product of the total taxable amount of the lump sum distribution and a fraction, the numerator of which is the number of calendar years of active participation before January 1, 1974, and the denominator of which is the total number of calendar years of active participation.

Under section 402(e)(1) of the Code, as amended, a separate tax is imposed on the ordinary income portion of a lump sum distribution.

Under section 402(e)(2) of the Code, as amended, a special rule is provided for computing the separate tax on the ordinary income portion of a lump sum distribution if there have been one or more lump sum distributions after December 31, 1973, made with respect to the recipient within the 6-taxable-year period ending on the last day of the taxable year of the recipient in which the distribution is made.

Under section 402(e)(3) of the Code, as amended, a deduction is allowed from gross income equal to the amount of the ordinary income portion of the distribution included in the recipient's gross income.

Under section 402(e)(4) of the Code, as amended, definitions and special rules are provided for computing the separate tax, including the definition of a lump sum distribution and the computation of the ordinary income portion of a lump sum distribution.

Under proposed § 1.402(e)-2(c)(1), a special method for computing the separate tax on a distribution including an annuity contract is provided. In such a case, the adjusted total taxable amount must be determined. For taxable years beginning before January 1, 1975, the adjusted total taxable amount is defined as the sum of the total taxable amount of the lump sum distribution for the taxable year, and the current actuarial value of annuity contracts distributed to the recipient reduced by the portion of the net amount contributed by the employee which is allocable to the annuity contract. For taxable years beginning after December 31, 1974, the adjusted total taxable amount is defined as the sum of the total taxable amount of the lump sum distribution for the taxable year, and the current actuarial value of annuity contracts distributed to the recipient reduced by the excess of the net amount contributed by the employee over the cash and other property distributed.

Under proposed § 1.402(e)-2(d)(1), a distribution to multiple recipients (except a payment or distribution solely to two or more trusts) cannot qualify as a lump sum distribution unless the amount of the distribution is otherwise includible in the income of the individual in respect of whom the distribution was made under the judicial doctrines of assignment of income or constructive receipt of income.

Under proposed § 1.402(e)-2(d)(3), the term "active participation" is defined so that active participation commences with the first month in which an employee becomes a participant under the plan and ends with the earliest of (1) the month in which the employee receives a lump sum distribution under the plan, (2) in the case of an employee without regard to section 401(e)(1), the month in which the employee separates from the service of the employer, (3) the month in which the employee dies, or (4) in the case of a self-employed individual who receives a lump sum distribution on account of disability, the first month in which he becomes disabled.

It is contemplated that upon adoption of the proposed amendments the Temporary Income Tax Regulations under section 402(e)(4)(B)(§ 11.402(e)(4)(B)-1) will be revoked.

Proposed amendments to the regulations. In order to conform the Income Tax Regulations (26 CFR Part 1) to the provisions of section 2005 of the Employee Retirement Income Security Act of 1974 (Pub. L. 93-406, 88 Stat. 987), such regulations are amended.

[¶ 49,004]   Proposed Amendment of Regulations, published in the Federal Register on December 19, 1975.

Estates and trusts: Charitable remainder trusts.—An amendment of Reg. §1.664-1, relating to transfers for public, charitable and religious uses, is proposed.

Notice is hereby given that the regulations set forth in tentative form in the attached appendix are proposed to be prescribed by the Commissioner of Internal Revenue, with the approval of the Secretary of the Treasury or his delegate. Prior to the final adoption of such regulations, consideration will be given to any comments pertaining thereto which are submitted in writing (preferably six copies) to the Commissioner of Internal Revenue, Attention: CC:LR:T, Washington, D.C. 20224, by Jan. 23, 1976. Pursuant to 26 CFR 601.601(b), designations of material as confidential or not to be disclosed, contained in such comments, will not be accepted. Thus, persons submitting written comments should not include therein material that they consider to be confidential or inappropriate for disclosure to the public. It will be presumed by the Internal Revenue Service that every written comment submitted to it in response to this notice of proposed rule making is intended by the person submitting it to be subject in its entirety to public inspection and copying in accordance with the procedures of 26 CFR 601.702(d)(9). Any person submitting written comments who desires an opportunity to comment orally at a public hearing on these proposed regulations should submit a request, in writing, to the Commissioner by Jan. 23, 1976. In such case, a public hearing will be held, and notice of the time, place, and date will be published in a subsequent issue of the Federal Register, unless the person or persons who have requested a hearing withdraw their requests for a hearing before notice of the hearing has been filed with the Office of the Federal Register. The proposed regulations are to be issued under the authority contained in sections 2055(e)(3) and 7805 of the Internal Revenue Code of 1954 (68A Stat. 917; 26 U.S.C. 7805).

Preamble

This document contains proposed amendments to the Income Tax Regulations (26 CFR Part 1) and the Estate Tax Regulations (26 CFR Part 20) to conform such regulations to the provisions of section 2055(e)(3) as added by section 3, Act of Oct. 26, 1974 (P.L. 93-483).

Section 2055(e)(2)(A) of the Code disallows an estate tax deduction for certain transfers to charity if the transfer is not in the form either of a charitable remainder trust that complies with section 664 of the Code or a pooled income fund that complies with section 642(c)(5) of the Code.

The new amendment to section 2055 is a relief provision which, in certain limited cases, extends until December 31, 1975, the transitional period originally allowed under the Tax Reform Act of 1969 to amend or conform a trust to the provisions of section 664 of the Code.

The relief provision applies to any interest for charitable purposes which passes under a will executed before September 21, 1974, or by an intervivos trust created after July 31, 1969, and before September 21, 1974. The will or trust must be amended to meet the requirements of section 2055(e)(2)(A) by December 31, 1975, or judicial proceedings to amend the will or trust must be begun by that date.

The proposed regulations apply the relief provision to inter vivos transfers created after July 31, 1969, which are irrevocable at the date of death. However, in general, a trust amended pursuant to these temporary regulations is treated as a charitable remainder trust from the date it would be deemed created under section 664.

The proposed regulations make provision for judicial reformation as well as nonjudicial reformation by agreement of the parties provided the agreement is binding on all parties.

The proposed regulations provide that the amending procedure under section 2055(e)(3) is available only to charitable interests which, but for the disqualifying provisions of section 2055(e)(2)(A), qualify for a deduction under section 2055. A charitable interest cannot be created by the use of this relief provision.

[¶ 49,006] **Proposed Regulations,** filed in the Federal Register on February 24, 1977.

International boycotts: Loss of tax benefits: Computation of international boycott factor.—Reg. § 1.999-1, relating to the computation of the international boycott factor, is proposed.

The regulations set forth in tentative form in the attached appendix are proposed to be prescribed by the Secretary of the Treasury or his delegate. Prior to the final adoption of such regulations, consideration will be given to any comments that are submitted in writing (preferably six copies) to the Assistant Secretary for Tax Policy, U.S. Treasury Department, Washington, D.C. 20220, by April 15, 1977. Comments will be subject to public inspection and copying. Any person submitting written comments who desires an opportunity to comment orally at a public hearing on these proposed regulations should submit a request, in writing, to the Assistant Secretary for Tax Policy by April 15, 1977. In such case, a public hearing will be held, and notice of the time, place, and date will be published in a subsequent issue of the FEDERAL REGISTER, unless the persons who have requested a hearing withdraw their requests for a hearing before notice of the hearing has been filed with the Office of the Federal Register. The proposed regulations are to be issued under the authority contained in section 7805 of the Internal Revenue Code of 1954 (68A Stat. 917; 26 U.S.C. 7805).

Certain benefits of the foreign tax credit, deferral of earnings of foreign corporations, and DISC (Domestic International Sales Corporation) are denied if a person (or a member of a controlled group that includes that person) participates in or cooperates with an international boycott. The loss of tax benefits may be determined by multiplying the otherwise allowable tax benefits by the "international boycott factor".

The method of computing the international boycott factor is set forth in paragraph (c) of the regulations. The definitions of the terms used in the regulations are set forth in paragraph (b). A special rule for computing the international boycott factor of a person that is a member of two or more controlled groups is set forth in paragraph (d) of the regulations.

The regulations generally apply after November 3, 1976. However, in the case of binding contracts entered into before September 2, 1976, the regulations apply to such participation or cooperation after December 31, 1977. Transitional rules are set forth in paragraph (e) of the regulations.

The principal draftsperson of these regulations was John C. Holberton of the Office of International Tax Counsel. However, other personnel participated in developing the regulations, both on matters of substance and style. Mr. Holberton may be contacted at 202-566-8275 or at U.S. Treasury Department, Washington, D.C. 20220.

[¶ 49,007] **Proposed Regulations (LR-194-77),** published in the Federal Register on February 3, 1978.

Gross income: Deferred: Compensation reduction plans or arrangements.—Reg. § 1.61-16, relating to amounts of payments which are deferred under compensation reduction plans or arrangements, is proposed.

AGENCY: Internal Revenue Service, Treasury.

ACTION: Notice of proposed rulemaking.

SUMMARY: This document contains proposed regulations relating to the tax treatment of amounts of compensatory payments which are deferred under certain nonqualified compensation reduction plans or arrangements. The regulations would reflect a change in the Internal Revenue Service position relating to these plans or arrangements and provide the public with needed guidance.

DATES: Written comments and requests for a public hearing must be delivered or mailed by April 4, 1978. The amendments are proposed to be effective in the case of compensatory payments which the taxpayer has chosen to defer if the amount would have been payable, but for the taxpayer's exercise of the option to defer receipt, on or after a date 30 days following publication of this regulation as a Treasury Decision in the Federal Register.

ADDRESS: Send comments and requests for a public hearing to: Commissioner of Internal Revenue, Attention: CC:LR:T (LR-194-77), Washington, D.C. 20224.

FOR FURTHER INFORMATION CONTACT: William E. Mantle of the Legislation and Regulations Division, Office of the Chief Counsel, Internal Revenue Service, 1111 Constitution Avenue, NW., Washington D.C. 20224 (Attention: CC:LR:T) (202-566-3734).

SUPPLEMENTARY INFORMATION:

BACKGROUND

This document contains a proposed amendment to the Income Tax Regulations (26 CFR Part 1) under section 61 of the Internal Revenue Code of 1954. The amendment is proposed in order to change the Internal Revenue Service position on certain nonqualified compensation reduction plans or arrangements and is to be issued under the authority contained in section 7805 of the Internal Revenue Code of 1954 (68A Stat. 917; 26 U.S.C. 7805).

GENERAL RULE

The new regulation provides that if a taxpayer (whether or not an employee) individually chooses to have payment of some portion of his current compensation or an amount of an increase in compensation deferred and paid in a later year, the amount will nevertheless be treated as received by the taxpayer in the earlier taxable year. The taxpayer's exercise of the option to defer payment must be under a plan or arrangement other than one described in sections 401(a), 403(a) or (b), or 405(a) of the Internal Revenue Code of 1954 (relating respectively to qualified pension, profit-sharing, and stock bonus plans; taxation of employee annuities; and qualified bond purchase plans).

DEFINITION OF COMPENSATION

Under the proposed amendment, a taxpayer's compensation includes, in addition to basic or regular compensation fixed by contract, statute, or otherwise, a supplement, such as a bonus, and increases in basic or regular compensation.

EXCEPTION

An exception to the general rule is proposed to provide that it does not apply to the amount of any payment which the taxpayer has chosen to defer under an existing plan or arrangement if the amount would have been payable, but for the taxpayer's exercise of the option to defer receipt, before a date 30 days following publication of this regulation as a Treasury decision in the FEDERAL REGISTER.

EFFECT ON PRESENT IRS PUBLISHED POSITIONS

If this regulation is published as a Treasury decision, Rev. Rul. 67-449, 1967-2 C.B. 173, Rev. Rul. 68-86, 1968-1 C.B. 184, Rev. Rul. 69-650 1969-2 C.B. 106, and Rev. Rul. 71-419, 1971-2 C.B. 220 would no longer be applied and present Service acquiescences in the decisions in *James F. Oates*, 18 T.C. 570 (1952) and *Ray S. Robinson*, 44 T.C. 20 (1965) would be reconsidered. Further, it would be necessary to examine the facts and circumstances of cases similar to those described in several other published revenue rulings (such as Examples (1) and (3) of Rev. Rul. 60-31, 1960-1 C.B. 174, Rev. Rul. 68-99, 1968-1 C.B. 193, and Rev. Rul. 72-25, 1972-1 C.B. 127) to determine whether the deferral of payment of compensation was in fact at the individual option of the taxpayer who earned the compensation.

On September 7, 1977, the Service announced in IR-1881 that it had suspended the issuance of rulings dealing with the income tax treatment of certain non-qualified deferred compensation plans established by State and local governments and other employers pending completion of a review of this area. The plans reviewed permit the employee to individually elect to defer a portion of his or her salary. This proposed amendment represents conclusions reached as a result of this review.

COMMENTS AND REQUESTS FOR A PUBLIC HEARING

Before adopting these proposed regulations, consideration will be given to any written comments that are submitted (preferably six copies) to the Commissioner of Internal Revenue. All comments will be available for public inspection and copying. A public hearing will be held upon written request to the Commissioner by any person who has submitted written comments. If a public hearing is held, notice of the time and place will be published in the FEDERAL REGISTER.

DRAFTING INFORMATION

The principal author of these proposed regulations was William E. Mantle of the Legislation and Regulations Division of the Office of Chief Counsel, Internal Revenue Service. However, personnel from other offices of the Internal Revenue Service and Treasury Department participated in developing the regulation, both on matters of substance and style.

[¶ 49,008] **Proposed Regulations and Proposed Amendments of Regulations (EE-16-78),** published in the Federal Register on May 31, 1979.

Employee plans: Lump-sum distributions.—Reg. §1.402(e)-14 and amendments of Reg. §§1.402(a)-1, 1.402(e)-2 and 1.403(a)-2, relating to the election to treat no portion of a lump-sum distribution from an employee plan as long-term capital gain, are proposed.

AGENCY: Internal Revenue Service, Treasury.

ACTION: Notice of proposed rulemaking.

SUMMARY: This document contains proposed regulations relating to the election to treat no portion of a lump sum distribution from an employee benefit plan as long-term capital gain. Changes in the applicable tax law were made by the Tax Reform Act of 1976. The regulations would provide the public with the guidance needed to comply with that Act and would affect any recipient of a lump sum distribution.

DATES: Written comments and requests for a public hearing must be delivered or mailed by July 30, 1979. The amendments are proposed to be effective for distributions received in taxable years of the recipient beginning after December 31, 1975.

ADDRESS: Send comments and requests for a public hearing to: Commissioner of Internal Revenue, Attention: CC:LR:T:EE-16-78, Washington, D.C. 20224.

FOR FURTHER INFORMATION CONTACT: Richard L. Johnson of the Employee Plans and Exempt Organizations Division, Office of the Chief Counsel, Internal Revenue Service, 1111 Constitution Avenue, N.W., Washington, D.C. 20224. Attention: CC:LR:T, 202-566-3544 (not a toll-free number).

SUPPLEMENTARY INFORMATION:

BACKGROUND

On April 30, 1975, the Federal Register published at 40 F.R. 18798 proposed amendments to the Income Tax Regulations (26 CFR Part 1) under sections 402(a), 402(e), 403(a) and other sections of the Internal Revenue Code of 1954, relating to the taxation of lump sum distributions from qualified pension, profit-sharing, stock bonus and annuity plans. A correction notice was published in the Federal Register on May 23, 1975, at 40

F.R. 22548. The amendments were proposed to conform the regulations to section 2005 of the Employee Retirement Income Security Act of 1974 (88 Stat. 987). Proposed amendments contained in paragraphs 1 and 2 of the appendix to that notice of proposed rulemaking were adopted by Treasury decision 7399 published in the Federal Register on February 3, 1976, at 41 F.R. 5099. The remainder of the amendments proposed in the appendix to the notice of proposed rulemaking of April 30, 1975, have not yet been adopted.

This document contains further proposed amendments to the Income Tax Regulations (26 CFR Part 1) under Code sections 402(a)(2), ¶ 402(e) and ¶ 403(a)(2) to conform the regulations to Code section 402(e)(4)(L), as added by section 1512 of the Tax Reform Act of 1976 (90 Stat. 1742). The proposed regulations are to be issued under the authority contained in sections 402(e)(4)(L) and 7805 of the Internal Revenue Code of 1954 (90 Stat. 1742, 68A Stat. 917; 26 U.S.C. 402(e)(4)(L), 7805).

PRE-1974 AND POST-1973 PLAN PARTICIPATION

Under Code section 402(a)(2) or ¶ 403(a)(2), a portion of a lump sum distribution from a qualified pension, profit sharing, stock bonus or annuity plan is taxable as long-term capital gain. If the employee has been a participant in the plan for at least 5 years, and if the recipient is eligible to make the required election, the portion of the distribution not taxable as long-term capital gain is taxable under the 10-year averaging provisions of Code section 402(e). The portion of a lump sum distribution taxable as long-term capital gain is determined by taking into account the number of calendar years of participation by the employee in the plan before January 1, 1974. The portion taxable under Code section 402(e) represents participation in the plan after December 31, 1973.

ORDINARY INCOME ELECTION

Under Code section 402(e)(4)(L), a recipient may elect, under certain circumstances, to treat all calendar years of the employee's participation in all plans before January 1, 1974, as calendar years of participation after December 31, 1973. In such a case, no portion of the lump sum distribution is taxable as long-term capital gain. If the distribution is otherwise eligible for application of Code section 402(e), the total taxable amount of the distribution is taxable under the 10-year averaging provisions.

COMMENTS AND REQUESTS FOR A PUBLIC HEARING

Before adopting these proposed regulations, consideration will have to be given to any written comments that are submitted (preferably eight copies) to the Commissioner of Internal Revenue. All comments will be available for public inspection and copying. A public hearing will be held upon written request to the Commissioner by any person who has submitted written comments. If a public hearing is held, notice of the time and place will be published in the FEDERAL REGISTER.

DRAFTING INFORMATION

The principal author of these proposed regulations is Richard L. Johnson of the Employee Plans and Exempt Organizations Division of the Office of Chief Counsel, Internal Revenue Service. However, personnel from other offices of the Internal Revenue Service and Treasury Department participated in developing the regulation, both on matters of substance and style.

[¶ 49,009]   **Proposed Regulations (LR-168-76),** published in the Federal Register on June 5, 1979.

Deductions limited to amount at risk.—Reg. §§ 1.465-1—1.465-7, Reg. 1.465-9—1.469-13, 1.465-22—1.465-26, 1.465-38, 1.465-39, 1.465-41— 1.465-45, 1.465-66—1.465-69, 1.465-75—1.465-79 and 1.465-95, relating to determination of amounts at risk with respect to certain activities, are proposed. Proposed Reg. §§ 1.465-8 and 1.465-20 were adopted by T.D. 9124 on April 30, 2004.

AGENCY: Internal Revenue Service, Treasury.

ACTION: Notice of proposed rulemaking.

SUMMARY: This document contains proposed regulations relating to the determination of amounts at risk with respect to certain activities. Changes to the applicable tax law were made by the Tax Reform Act of 1976. The regulations would provide the public with the guidance needed to determine the amount of allowable deductions incurred with respect to activities covered by the at risk rules.

DATES: Written comments and requests for a public hearing must be delivered or mailed by August 6, 1979. The amendments are proposed to be effective for amounts paid or incurred in taxable years beginning after December 31, 1975, except as otherwise provided.

ADDRESS: Send comments and requests for a public hearing to: Commissioner of Internal Revenue, Attention: CC:LR:T (LR-168-76), Washington, D.C. 20224.

FOR FURTHER INFORMATION CONTACT: David Jacobson of the Legislation and Regulations Division, Office of the Chief Counsel, Internal Revenue Service, 1111 Constitution Avenue, N.W., Washington, D.C. 20224, 202-566-3923, not a toll-free call.

SUPPLEMENTARY INFORMATION:

BACKGROUND

This document contains proposed amendments to the Income Tax Regulations (26 CFR Part 1) and the Temporary Income Tax Regulations under the Tax Reform Act of 1976 (26 CFR Part 7) undersection 465 of the Internal Revenue Code of 1954. These amendments are proposed to conform the regulations to section 204 of the Tax Reform Act of 1976 (90 Stat. 1531) and are to be issued under the authority contained in section 7805 of the Internal Revenue Code of 1954 (68A Stat. 917; 26 U.S.C. 7805).

EXPLANATION OF THE REGULATIONS

Section 465 provides a limit on the amount of loss deductions taxpayers engaged in certain activities will be allowed. The activities for which the limits will apply are holding, producing or distributing motion picture films or videotapes; farming; leasing section 1245 property; and exploring for or exploiting oil and gas resources. Section 465 applies to all noncorporate taxpayers engaged in one or more of these activities. In addition, section 465 applies to electing small business corporations and personal holding companies if engaged in one or more of these activities.

Taxpayers to which section 465 applies are not permitted to deduct losses from the listed activities in excess of the amount they are at risk. The proposed regulations provide rules for determining the amount which a taxpayer is at risk. In general, a taxpayer is at risk for cash contributed to the activity as well as for amounts borrowed for use in the activity for which the taxpayer is personally liable. Amounts borrowed on a nonrecourse basis generally will not increase the amount a taxpayer is at risk. However, if property not used in the activity is pledged as security, the amount at risk may be increased to the extent of the net fair market value of the security.

Section 465 also provides that amounts borrowed from persons with an interest in the activity other than that of a creditor will not increase the amount at risk. The proposed regulations provide rules for determining who has an interest in the activity other than that of a creditor as well as providing other rules illustrating the applicability of section 465. The proposed regulations contain references to amendments to section 465 made by the Revenue Act of 1978 and the Energy Tax Act of 1978. These references have been added to the proposed regulations in order to alert taxpayers that section 465 has been amended since the time it was originally enacted. However, the proposed regulations do not provide guidance with respect to these amendments. This guidance will be provided in a later regulations project.

COMMENTS AND REQUESTS FOR A PUBLIC HEARING

Before adopting these proposed regulations, consideration will be given to any written comments that are submitted (preferably six copies) to the Commissioner of Internal Revenue. All comments will be available for public inspection and copying. A public hearing will be held upon written request to the Commissioner by any person who has submitted written comments. If a public hearing is held, notice of the time and place will be published in the FEDERAL REGISTER.

DRAFTING INFORMATION

The principal author of these proposed regulations is David Jacobson of the Legislation and Regulations Division of the Office of Chief Counsel, Internal Revenue Service. However, personnel from other offices of the Internal Revenue Service and Treasury Department participated in developing the regulation, both on matters of substance and style.

[¶ 49,009A]   **Proposed Regulations and Amendments of Proposed Regulations (EE-180-78),** published in the Federal Register on August 28, 1979.

Exempt organizations: Unrelated trade or business: Bingo games.—Amendments of Reg. §1.527-3, relating to the treatment of proceeds from bingo games, have been proposed. T.D. 7699, 5/20/80, adopted Reg. §1.513-5.

AGENCY: Internal Revenue Service, Treasury.

ACTION: Notice of proposed rulemaking.

SUMMARY: This document contains proposed regulations relating to the treatment of proceeds from bingo games. Changes to the applicable tax law were made by the Act of October 21, 1978. The regulations would provide the public with the guidance needed to comply with that Act and would affect exempt organizations and political organizations that conduct bingo games.

DATES: Written comments and requests for a public hearing must be delivered or mailed by October 29, 1979. The amendments are proposed to be effective for exempt organizations for taxable years beginning after December 31, 1969, and for political organizations for taxable years beginning after December 31, 1974.

ADDRESS: Send comments and request for a public hearing to: Commissioner of Internal Revenue, Attention: CC:LR:T:EE-180-78, Washington, D.C. 20224.

FOR FURTHER INFORMATION CONTACT: Charles Kerby of the Employee Plans and Exempt Organizations Division, Office of the Chief Counsel, Internal Revenue Service, 1111 Constitution Avenue, N.W., Washington, D.C. 20224, Attention: CC:LR:T:EE-180-78, 202-566-3422, (Not a toll-free call).

SUPPLEMENTARY INFORMATION:

BACKGROUND

This document contains proposed amendments to the Income Tax Regulations (26 CFR Part 1) under sections 513 and 527 of the Internal Revenue Code of 1954, as amended by sections 301 and 302 of the Act of October 21, 1978 (P.L. 95-502; Stat. 1702). The amendments are to be issued under the authority contained in section 7805 of the Internal Revenue Code of 1954 (68A Stat. 917; 26 U.S.C. 7805).

EXEMPT ORGANIZATIONS

A tax exempt organization is generally taxed on the income received from any "unrelated trade or business" conducted by the organization. Under prior law, a bingo game conducted by an exempt organization generally constituted an unrelated trade or business. Under Public Law 95-502, the term "unrelated trade or business" does not include the conducting of bingo games.

POLITICAL ORGANIZATIONS

A political organization is taxed on the income it receives that is not "exempt function income." Under prior law, proceeds from bingo games were not exempt function income and were, therefore, included in the taxable income of a political organization. Public Law 95-502 redefines the term "exempt function income" to include proceeds from bingo games.

COMMENTS AND REQUESTS FOR A PUBLIC HEARING

Before adopting these proposed regulations, consideration will be given to any written comments that are submitted (preferably six copies) to the Commissioner of Internal Revenue. All comments will be available for public inspection and copying. A public hearing will be held upon written request to the Commissioner by any person who has submitted written comments. If a public hearing is held, notice of the time and place will be published in the FEDERAL REGISTER.

DRAFTING INFORMATION

The principal author of these proposed regulations was Charles Kerby of the Employee Plans and Exempt Organizations Division of the Chief Counsel, Internal Revenue Service. However, personnel from other offices of the Internal Revenue Service and Treasury Department participated in developing the regulation, both on matters of substance and style.

[¶ 49,010]   **Proposed Regulations (EE-164-78),** published in the Federal Register on April 9, 1980.

Employee trusts: Vesting schedule: Discrimination.—Reg. §1.411(d)-1, relating to a determination if the vesting schedule of a qualified plan discriminates in favor of employees who are officers, shareholders, or highly compensated, is proposed.

AGENCY: Internal Revenue Service, Treasury.

ACTION: Notice of proposed rulemaking.

SUMMARY: This document contains proposed regulations prescribing rules for determining if the vesting schedule of a qualified plan discriminates in favor of employees who are officers, shareholders, or highly compensated. Changes to the applicable tax law were made by the

Employee Retirement Income Security Act of 1974. The regulations would provide the public with additional guidance needed to comply with the Act and would affect all employers maintaining qualified plans.

DATES: Written comments and requests for a public hearing must be delivered or mailed by June 9, 1980. The amendments are proposed to be effective for plan years beginning 30 days after the publication of this regulation in the FEDERAL REGISTER as a Treasury decision.

ADDRESS: Send comments and requests for a public hearing to: Commissioner of Internal Revenue, Attention: CC:LR:T (EE-164-78), Washington, D.C. 20224.

FOR FURTHER INFORMATION CONTACT: Kirk F. Maldonado of the Employee Plans and Exempt Organizations Division, Office of the Chief Counsel, Internal Revenue Service, 1111 Constitution Avenue, N.W., Washington, D.C. 20224 (Attention: CC:LR:T) (202-566-3430) (not a toll-free number).

SUPPLEMENTARY INFORMATION:

BACKGROUND

This document contains proposed amendments to the Income Tax Regulations (26 CFR Part 1) under section 411(d)(1) of the Internal Revenue Code of 1954. These amendments are proposed to conform the regulations to section 1012(a) of the Employee Retirement Income Security Act of 1974 (88 Stat. 901) and these regulations are to be issued under the authority contained in section 7805 of the Internal Revenue Code of 1954 (68A Stat. 917; 26 U.S.C. 7805).

STATUTORY PROVISIONS

Section 401(a)(4) of the Code provides that a plan which discriminates in favor of employees who are officers, shareholders, or highly compensated (hereinafter referred to as "prohibited group") is not a qualified plan under section 401(a). Section 411(d)(1) provides that the vesting schedule of a plan which satisfies the requirements of section 411 shall be considered as satisfying any vesting requirements resulting from the application of section 401(a)(4) except in two situations. One situation, as set forth in section 411(d)(1)(A) is a pattern of abuse under the plan which tends to discriminate in favor of the prohibited group (pattern of abuse). The other situation, as detailed in section 411(d)(1)(B)), is where there have been, or there is reason to believe there will be, an accrual of benefits or forfeitures tending to discriminate in favor of the prohibited group (hereinafter referred to as "discriminatory vesting").

PRIOR GUIDELINES

Initial guidelines under section 411(d)(1) were set forth in Revenue Procedure 75-49, 1975-2 C.B. 584. That procedure established several alternative tests, with respect to vesting, that a plan must satisfy to secure a favorable advance determination letter. If a plan fails to satisfy these tests, a favorable advance determination letter will not be issued unless the plan adopts accelerated vesting (so-called "4/40 vesting").

Revenue Procedure 75-49 was modified in Revenue Procedure 76-11, 1976-1 C.B. 550. That procedure adopted alternative ways of satisfying the requirements of section 411(d)(1) in order to secure a favorable advance determination letter, in addition to the tests contained in Revenue Procedure 75-49.

The tests of Revenue Procedures 75-49 and 76-11 were applied only with respect to whether a plan could receive a favorable advance determination letter. The determination letter by its terms provided that the approval of the plan's qualified status by the Service did not extend to the plan in operation. Therefore, separate tests for determining discrimination in vesting were necessary with respect to the issuance of a determination letter and with respect to testing the operation of the plan's vesting schedule.

In addition, the tests described in Revenue Procedures 75-49 and 76-11 were generally mechanical. Objections were raised by plan administrators and sponsors when they were required to accept 4/40 vesting as a minimum schedule, and yet 4/40 vesting did not reflect the policies of ERISA if applied as a maximum vesting schedule. At the same time, it is recognized that there is a value in allowing safe harbors for plan administrators who seek a determination letter with respect to the qualified status of a plan. Therefore, although a facts and circumstances test more accurately reflects the vesting antidiscrimination provisions of the Code, and the policies of ERISA, it is recognized that some forms of safe harbor are appropriate for certainty purposes.

The rules contained in the proposed regulations attempt to accommodate both goals. On the one hand, a facts and circumstances test is described. This description is amplified by a list of factors which may be included in applying the test. It is anticipated that these factors will offer substantial guidance to plan administrators in reviewing the vesting provisions applicable both with respect to a determination letter application and with respect to the status of a plan in operation. On the other hand, two safe harbor tests are provided which would insulate a plan against a finding of discriminatory vesting under the plan.

After this regulation is adopted, it is anticipated that the tests and vesting schedule contained in Revenue Procedures 75-49 and 76-11 will no longer be applied. While plans having determination letters based on 4/40 vesting need not apply for a new determination letter on the basis of the plan's vesting schedule, plan administrators should be aware that the tests included in these regulations will be applied in testing the operation of each plan's vesting schedule and are cautioned to review each plan accordingly. Because of the guidance to be provided by this regulation after it is adopted, the concerns voiced by plan administrators under prior rules regarding how a plan's operation with respect to vesting would be judged should be alleviated. In addition, when a plan is submitted to the Internal Revenue Service for a determination letter it is anticipated that the rules in these regulations will be applied for purposes of issuing such letters.

DISCRIMINATION IN VESTING

The proposed rules provide that the determination of whether there is a pattern of abuse or discriminatory vesting under a plan shall be determined on the facts and circumstances of each case. Several criteria are set forth as factors to be used in making such a determination.

Two safe harbors are provided against a finding of discriminatory vesting under the plan. One safe harbor requires full vesting after an employee has three years of service. The other safe harbor requires full vesting after ten years of service, and the sum of the vested percentages for the employee's service prior to the completion of ten years of service must equal or exceed 700.

COMMENTS AND REQUESTS FOR A PUBLIC HEARING

Before adopting these proposed regulations, consideration will be given to any written comments that are submitted (preferably eight copies) to the Commissioner of Internal Revenue. All comments will be available for public inspection and copying. A public hearing will be held upon written request to the Commissioner by any person who has submitted written comments. If a public hearing is held, notice of the time and place will be published in the FEDERAL REGISTER.

¶49,010

DRAFTING INFORMATION

The principal author of these proposed regulation is Kirk F. Maldonado of the Employee Plans and Exempt Organizations Division of the Office of Chief Counsel, Internal Revenue Service. However, personnel from other offices of the Internal Revenue Service and Treasury Department participated in developing these regulations, both on matters of substance and style.

[¶ 49,011]   Proposed Regulations (EE-5-78), published in the Federal Register on April 29, 1980.

Qualified group legal services plans.—Reg. §§1.120-1, 1.120-2 and 1.501(c)(20)-1, relating to qualified group legal services plans, are proposed.

AGENCY: Internal Revenue Service, Treasury.

ACTION: Notice of proposed rulemaking.

SUMMARY: This document contains proposed regulations relating to qualified group legal services plans. Changes to the applicable tax law were made by the Tax Reform Act of 1976. The regulations would provide the public with the guidance needed to comply with that Act and would affect both employers who establish group legal services plans and employees and their spouses and dependents who receive benefits under these plans.

DATES: Written comments and requests for a public hearing must be delivered or mailed by June 30, 1980. The amendments are generally proposed to be effective for taxable years beginning after December 31, 1976, and ending before January 1, 1982.

ADDRESS: Send comments and requests for a public hearing to: Commissioner of Internal Revenue, Attention: CC:LR:T: EE 5-78, Washington, D.C. 20224.

FOR FURTHER INFORMATION CONTACT: Richard L. Johnson of the Employee Plans and Exempt Organizations Division, Office of the Chief Counsel, Internal Revenue Service, 1111 Constitution Avenue, N.W., Washington, D.C. 20224, Attention: CC:LR:T:EE 5-78, 202-566-3544, (Not a toll-free number).

SUPPLEMENTARY INFORMATION:

BACKGROUND

This document contains proposed amendments to the Income Tax Regulations (26 CFR Part 1) under sections 120 and 501(c)(20) of the Internal Revenue Code of 1954, as added by section 2134 of the Tax Reform Act of 1976 (90 Stat. 1926). The amendments are to be issued under the authority contained in sections 120 and 7805 of the Internal Revenue Code of 1954 (90 Stat. 1926, 68A Stat. 917; 26 U.S.C. 120, 7805).

PREPAID LEGAL SERVICES

Code section 120(a) excludes from the gross income of an employee, and the employee's spouse or dependent, employer contributions made on their behalf to a qualified group legal services plan. The value of legal services provided, or amounts paid for legal services, under the plan are also excluded from gross income.

QUALIFIED GROUP LEGAL SERVICES PLAN

In order for a group legal services plan to be a qualified plan, the plan must satisfy certain requirements relating principally to nondiscrimination in employer contributions, plan benefits and eligibility for participation, the limitation on employer contributions for participants who are shareholders or owners, and the means by which the plan is funded. if the plan is funded by means of a trust, subject to certain requirements, the trust is exempt from tax.

DELETION OF REGULATIONS UNDER REPEALED CODE PROVISION

Existing §1.120-1 of the Income Tax Regulations provides regulations under Code section 120, relating to statutory subsistence allowance received by police, which was repealed by section 3 of the Technical Amendments Act of 1958 (72 Stat. 1607). This section is being deleted.

COMMENTS AND REQUESTS FOR A PUBLIC HEARING

Before adopting these proposed regulations, consideration will be given to any written comments that are submitted (preferably six copies) to the Commissioner of Internal Revenue. All comments will be available for public inspection and copying. A public hearing will be held upon written request to the Commissioner by any person who has submitted written comments. If a public hearing is held, notice of the time and place will be published in the FEDERAL REGISTER.

DRAFTING INFORMATION

The principal author of these proposed regulations is Richard L. Johnson of the Employee Plans and Exempt Organizations Division of the Office of Chief Counsel, Internal Revenue Service. However, personnel from other offices of the Internal Revenue Service and Treasury Department participated in developing the regulations, both on matters of substance and style.

[¶ 49,012]   Proposed Amendment of Regulation (EE-164-78), published in the Federal Register on June 12, 1980.

Employees' trusts: Antidiscrimination rules: Coordination of vesting and discrimination requirements.—An amendment of proposed Reg. §1.411(d)-1, relating to coordination of vesting and discrimination requirements for employees' trusts, is proposed.

AGENCY: Internal Revenue Service, Treasury.

ACTION: Notice of proposed rulemaking.

SUMMARY: This document contains modifications to proposed regulations, published in the FEDERAL REGISTER for April 9, 1980 (45 FR 24201), relating to coordination of vesting and discrimination requirements for qualified pension, etc. plans. These modifications to the proposed regulations have been prepared in response to the comments received on the proposed regulation. The test for determining the existence of discriminatory vesting is reproposed in modified form and the "safe harbors" against a finding of discriminatory vesting are withdrawn.

DATES: A public hearing on the notice of proposed rulemaking published April 9, 1980, has been scheduled for July 10, 1980. A notice of the public hearing was published in the FEDERAL REGISTER on May 2, 1980. Outlines of oral comments for the public hearing must be delivered or mailed by June 26, 1980. Written comments on the modifications set forth in this notice must be delivered or mailed by August 11, 1980.

ADDRESS: Send comments to: Commissioner of Internal Revenue, Attention: CC:LR:T (EE-164-78), Washington, D.C. 20224.

FOR FURTHER INFORMATION CONTACT: Kirk F. Maldonado of the Employee Plans and Exempt Organizations Division, Office of the Chief Counsel, Internal Revenue Service, 1111 Constitution Avenue, N.W., Washington, D.C. 20224 (Attention: CC:LR:T) (202-566-3430) (not a toll-free number).

SUPPLEMENTARY INFORMATION:

BACKGROUND

This document contains modifications to proposed regulations under section 411(d)(1) of the Internal Revenue Code of 1954. Section 411(d)(1) was added by section 1012(a) of the Employee Retirement Income Security Act of 1974 (88 Stat. 901). The amendments are to be issued under the authority contained in section 7805 of the Internal Revenue Code of 1954 (68A Stat. 917; 26 U.S.C. 7805).

STATUTORY PROVISIONS

Section 401(a)(4) of the Code provides that a plan which discriminates in favor of employees who are officers, shareholders, or highly compensated (hereinafter referred to as "prohibited group") is not a qualified plan under section 401(a). Section 411(d)(1) provides that the vesting schedule of a plan which satisfies the requirements of section 411 shall be considered as satisfying any vesting requirements resulting from the application of section 401(a)(4) except in two situations. One situation, as set forth in section ¶ 411(d)(1)(A), is a pattern of abuse under the plan which tends to discriminate in favor of the prohibited group (pattern of abuse). The other situation, as detailed in section 411(d)(1)(B), is where there have been, or there is reason to believe there will be, an accrual of benefits or forfeitures tending to discriminate in favor of the prohibited group (hereinafter referred to as "discriminatory vesting").

PRIOR DETERMINATION LETTERS

Initial guidelines under section 411(d)(1) were set forth in Revenue Procedure 75-49, 1975-2 C.B. 584. That Procedure established several alternative tests, with respect to vesting, that a plan must satisfy to secure a favorable advance determination letter. If a plan failed to satisfy these tests, a favorable determination letter was not issued unless the plan adopted the accelerated vesting schedule set forth in the Procedure (so-called "4/40 vesting").

Revenue Procedure 76-11, 1976-1 C.B. 550, was issued pending reconsideration of Revenue Procedure 75-49. That Procedure adopted two new alternative means of satisfying the requirements of section 411(d)(1) in order to secure a favorable advance determination letter, in addition to the tests contained in Revenue Procedure 75-49.

One of the new alternatives contained in Revenue Procedure 76-11 is to establish that the plan had previously received a favorable advance determination letter which had not been revoked, and that the percentage of vesting of each participant under the plan as amended is not less (at every point) than that provided under the vesting schedule of the plan when it received the most recent favorable prior determination letter.

The other new alternative contained in Revenue Procedure 76-11 is a demonstration, on the basis of all of the facts and circumstances that there has not been, and that there is no reason to believe there will be, any discriminatory accruals.

Revenue Procedure 76-11 also provided that a plan could secure a favorable determination letter without regard to whether the vesting is nondiscriminatory.

However, the determination letters processed in this manner contained a caveat to the effect that such letter is not a determination as to whether the vesting provisions of the plan satisfy the nondiscrimination requirements of section 401(a)(4).

The tests of Revenue Procedures 75-49 and 76-11 are applied only with respect to whether a plan could receive a favorable advance determination letter. The determination letter, by its terms, provided that the approval of the plan's qualified status by the Internal Revenue Service did not extend to the plan in operation. Therefore, separate tests for determining discrimination in vesting were necessary with respect to the issuance of a determination letter and with respect to testing the operation of the plan's vesting schedule.

Thus, an employer could receive a favorable advance determination letter, but would have no protection against a finding that the plan's vesting schedule was discriminatory in operation. The proposed rules remove this separate testing of form and operation, and provide that the test for discriminatory vesting shall be made, in both situations, on the basis of the facts and circumstances. Thus, if a plan has a favorable advance determination letter based on the facts and circumstances test of the proposed rules, this determination will protect the plan from a finding of discriminatory vesting in operation, provided the facts and circumstances have not materially changed since the determination letter was issued.

Additionally, plans which currently possess certain types of favorable determination letters will be treated as if their determination letter was processed under the facts and circumstances test contained in the proposed rules. The plans which will be given this treatment are those which received their favorable determination letter based on their satisfying one or more of the following tests:

1. the key employee and/or the turnover test of Revenue Procedure 75-49;

2. the prior letter test of Revenue Procedure 76-11; or

3. the facts and circumstances test of Revenue Procedure 76-11.

Thus, a plan described above would also be protected against a finding of discriminatory vesting in operation, based on its outstanding favorable determination letter, provided the facts and circumstances have not materially changed.

SAFE HARBORS

Paragraph (d) of proposed regulation § 1.411(d)-1, as published in the FEDERAL REGISTER on April 9, 1980, set forth two safe harbors against a finding of discriminatory vesting. Both of the safe harbors required the adoption of a vesting schedule substantially more rapid than 4/40 vesting. Many of the commentators viewed this as an attempt to require that all plans adopt either one of these accelerated vesting schedules. Because that was not the intent of those proposed rules, the portion of the proposed regulation containing the safe harbors is withdrawn.

However, this deletion should not be interpreted as meaning that 4/40 vesting is a safe harbor. Comments are requested from the public as to the desirability of reinstating a safe harbor and, if so, on what basis.

TEST FOR DISCRIMINATORY VESTING

Paragraph (c)(2) of proposed regulation § 1.411(d)-1, as published in the FEDERAL REGISTER on April 9, 1980, set forth certain factors to be considered in applying the facts and circumstances test for discriminatory vesting. These factors were included simply to reflect current Internal Revenue Service practice and to provide greater guidance to both employers and to Internal Revenue Service personnel. The factors were not intended to create new standards.

Nevertheless, many commentators interpreted the recital of specific factors as substantially increasing their burden of establishing that the plan's vesting schedule is nondiscriminatory. Accordingly, the list of specific factors is deleted in the reproposed test for discriminatory vesting.

The determination of whether the vesting schedule of a plan is discriminatory, under the reproposed rules, shall be made on the basis of the facts and circumstances of each case. The reproposed rules now specifically provide that a plan's vesting schedule is nondiscriminatory if the disparity between the vested benefits provided to the prohibited group and the vested benefits provided to all other employees is reasonable.

ADDITIONAL GUIDANCE

It is anticipated that additional guidance regarding the application of the facts and circumstances test for discriminatory vesting will be provided in revenue rulings and procedures issued at the time the regulations are published in final form. Accordingly, comments are requested as to whether the following examples are appropriate for this purpose:

Example 1. A plan has the "10 year cliff" vesting schedule described in section 411(a)(2)(A) for all employees. Employment turnover among members of the prohibited group is less than that for all other employees because the prohibited group tends to stay longer with the company. Nevertheless, the present value of the vested benefits for the officers and 5% shareholders (determined using the attribution rules of section 1563(e), without regard to section 1563(e)(3)(C)), is less than the present value of the vested benefits of all other employees. Because the vested benefits provided employees who are not officers or shareholders are greater than that provided officers and shareholders, the plan's vesting schedule is not considered to be discriminatory.

Example 2. The facts are the same as in *Example 1,* except that there has been no comparison of the present values of the vested benefits of each group of employees. However, it is clear that the class of employees who have vested benefits, considering those employees alone and not any nonvested employees, would satisfy the nondiscriminatory classification test of section 410(b)(1)(B) by covering a reasonable cross section. Because a reasonable cross section of all employees under the plan have vested benefits, the vesting schedule of the plan is not considered to be discriminatory. [When the example is published, specific facts along the lines of Revenue Ruling 70-200, 1970-1 C.B. 101, Revenue Ruling 74-255, 1974-1 C.B. 93, and Revenue Ruling 74-256, 1974-1 C.B. 94, will be included to illustrate the reasonable cross section test.]

Example 3. Company B has a plan that satisfies the minimum participation requirements of section 410. The plan provides for 4/40 vesting. In its six years of operation the plan has always covered five employees. Because of the high rate of employee turnover, the only employee, past or present, to earn a vested benefit under the plan is X. X is the sole shareholder of Company B. Absent a showing of other facts and circumstances, the vesting schedule of the plan is discriminatory.

COMMENTS AND PUBLIC HEARING

Before adopting these proposed regulations, consideration will be given to any written comments that are submitted (preferably eight copies) to the Commissioner of Internal Revenue. All comments will be available for public inspection and copying. As indicated above, a public hearing has already been scheduled on the proposed regulations published April 9, 1980. Anyone wishing to comment on these modifications may do so at that hearing.

DRAFTING INFORMATION

The principal author of this regulation is Kirk F. Maldonado of the Employee Plans and Exempt Organizations Division of the Office of Chief Counsel, Internal Revenue Service. However, personnel from other offices of the Internal Revenue Service and the Treasury Department participated in developing the regulation, both on matters of substance and style.

[¶ 49,013]   Proposed Regulations and Proposed Amendments of Regulations (LR-261-76), published in the Federal Register on August 7, 1980.

Business use or rental of dwelling unit.—Reg. §§1.280A-1—1.280A-3 and amendments of Reg. §§1.183-1, 1.212-1 and 1.262-1, relating to the deductibility of expenses in connection with the business use, or the rental to others, of a dwelling unit that the taxpayer is deemed to have used for personal purposes during the taxable year, are proposed.

AGENCY: Internal Revenue Service, Treasury.

ACTION: Notice of proposed rulemaking.

SUMMARY: This document contains proposed regulations relating to the deductibility of expenses in connection with the business use, or the rental to others, of a dwelling unit that the taxpayer is deemed to have used for personal purposes during the taxable year. The Tax Reform Act of 1976 established new conditions for the deductibility of such expenses. The regulations would provide the public with needed guidance in complying with the Act and would affect individuals, partnerships, trusts, estates, and electing small business corporations that incur business expenses for dwelling units which are deemed to have been used for personal purposes during the taxable year.

DATES: Written comments and requests for a public hearing must be delivered or mailed by October 6, 1980.

The amendments are proposed to be effective for taxable years beginning after 1975.

ADDRESS: Send comments and requests for a public hearing to: Commissioner of Internal Revenue, Attention: CC:LR:T (LR-261-76), Washington, D.C. 20224.

FOR FURTHER INFORMATION CONTACT: Paul A. Francis (202-566-6640).

SUPPLEMENTARY INFORMATION:

BACKGROUND

This document contains proposed amendments to the Income Tax Regulations (26 CFR Part 1) under sections 183, 212, 262, and 280A of the Internal Revenue Code of 1954. These amendments are proposed to provide regulations under section 280A which was added to the Code by section 601 of the Tax Reform Act of 1976 (90 Stat. 1569) and amended by section 306 of the Tax Reduction and Simplification Act of 1977 (91 Stat. 152) and section 701(h) of the Revenue Act of 1978 (92 Stat. 2904). The amendments to the regulations under sections 183, 212, and 262 provide for coordination of those sections with section 280A. These amendments are to be issued under the authority contained in section 7805 of the Internal Revenue Code of 1954 (68A Stat. 917; 26 U.S.C. 7805).

GENERAL RULE

Section 280A generally disallows business deductions for expenses with respect to the use of a dwelling unit used by the taxpayer as a residence during the taxable year, but there are several exceptions to this general rule. Section 280A prescribes certain criteria for determining whether a taxpayer who uses a dwelling unit for business purposes or rents a dwelling unit to others has used the dwelling unit as a residence during the taxable year. A dwelling unit may be a house, apartment, condominium, mobile home, boat, or similar property with basic living accommodations. Section 280A also applies to other property, such as a garage, which is closely related to the dwelling unit itself. If the taxpayer has used the dwelling unit as a residence, the taxpayer may deduct the expenses attributable to the business use or rental of the unit only to the extent provided in section 280A.

USE AS A RESIDENCE

A taxpayer uses a dwelling unit as a residence during a taxable year if the number of calendar days on which the taxpayer uses the unit for personal purposes exceeds the greater of 14 days or 10 percent of the number of calendar days on which the unit is rented at a fair rental (excluding days on which the taxpayer uses the unit for personal purposes). A special rule applies in certain situations in which the taxpayer is renting out a unit used by the taxpayer as a principal residence.

A taxpayer is treated as using a unit for personal purposes on any day on which the unit is used—

(1) for personal purposes by the taxpayer or any other person with an interest in the unit; or by certain relatives of either;

(2) by any person under an arrangement which enables the taxpayer to use another unit; or

(3) by any person (except certain employees) if fair rental has not been paid for the use of the unit for that day.

The proposed regulations explain how these rules apply to units in which entities, such as partnerships or trusts, have an interest. The proposed regulations also provide that an individual who works on repair or maintenance of the unit on a substantially full-time basis will not be treated as using the unit for personal purposes.

BUSINESS USE OF HOME

A taxpayer who uses a dwelling unit as a residence may deduct expenses for business use of the unit only if the use is within one of the exceptions enumerated in section 280A. No deductions are allowed unless the taxpayer uses the unit for a specified business purpose on a regular basis. Deductions are subject to the limitation explained below.

A taxpayer may deduct expenses allocable to the use of a portion of a dwelling unit as the taxpayer's principal place of business if the taxpayer makes no use of that portion of the unit other than for business purposes. The proposed regulations provide that this exception applies only if the unit is the principal place of the taxpayer's overall business activity. Use of a unit as the principal place of business for a secondary business does not qualify. The proposed regulations do not follow the decision of the Tax Court in *Curphey v. Commissioner*, 73 T.C. No. 61 (Feb. 4, 1980).

Expenses allocable to the use of a portion of a unit as a place of business used by patients, clients, or customers in meeting or dealing with the taxpayer are deductible if the taxpayer makes no use of that portion of the unit other than for business purposes.

A taxpayer who, in connection with a trade or business, uses a separate structure which is related to the dwelling unit but not attached to it may deduct expenses allocable to the use of the separate structure if the taxpayer makes no use of the structure other than for business purposes.

An employee may deduct expenses under the three exceptions just described only if the employee's use of the unit is for the convenience of the employer.

There is also an exception for expenses allocable to space within the unit in which the taxpayer stores inventory. The inventory must be held for use in the taxpayer's trade or business of selling products at wholesale or retail, and the unit must be the sole fixed location for that trade or business.

A taxpayer may deduct expenses allocable to the use of a unit in the taxpayer's trade or business of providing day care for children, for individuals who have attained age 65, or for individuals who are physically or mentally incapable of caring for themselves. The regulations distinguish day care services, which are primarily custodial, from educational activities.

There are two special rules that apply to the exception for day care services. The taxpayer may deduct expenses accruing after August, 1977, only if the taxpayer is taking, or has taken, whatever steps may be necessary to comply with applicable state laws such as licensing or registration requirements. The proposed regulations indicate when a taxpayer will be deemed to have satisfied this rule. If the taxpayer uses any portion of the unit for day care services and for some other purpose besides the purposes described in section 280A, the taxpayer must make a time allocation of the expenses attributable to that portion of the unit according to the formula specified in the proposed regulations.

LIMITATION ON DEDUCTIONS FOR BUSINESS USE

Deductions allowable under the five exceptions just described are subject to a special limitation. As the proposed regulations indicate, the first step necessary to apply the limitation is to determine the gross income derived from the use of the unit. If the taxpayer carries on the trade or business in more than one location, the taxpayer must allocate the income to the activity in the different locations. The gross income derived from the use of the unit equals the excess of the gross income allocable to the business activity in the unit over the expenses incurred in the activity but not allocable to the use of the unit itself, such as expenditures for supplies and compensation paid to assistants. The gross income derived from the use of the unit is the ceiling for all other deductions. The proposed regulations prescribe the sequence in which the deductions must be claimed.

RENTAL OF DWELLING UNIT

Section 280A prescribes several special rules with respect to the deductibility of expenditures in connection with the rental of dwelling units.

Section 280A(d)(3) provides that the days on which the taxpayer used the rental unit as a principal residence are disregarded in determining whether a taxpayer may deduct rental expenses in excess of income from a "qualified rental period." A "qualified rental period" is a consecutive period of 12 or more months, or a shorter period ending with the sale or exchange of the unit, during which the unit is rented to someone other than a family member, or is held for rental, at fair rental value.

Section 280A(f)(1)(B) excludes from the definition of "dwelling unit", and therefore from the general disallowance provision of section 280A(a), any portion of a unit "used exclusively as a hotel, motel, inn, or similar establishment". The proposed regulations state that this exception applies only if the portion of the unit is regularly available for occupancy by paying customers and only if no person with an interest in the property is deemed to have used it as a residence during the taxable year.

If a taxpayer uses a unit as a residence and actually rents it to others for less than 15 days during the year, the taxpayer disregards the rental use altogether for tax purposes. Thus, the taxpayer excludes the rental income from gross income for the year and may not deduct the rental expenses.

If a taxpayer who rents a dwelling unit to others makes any personal use of the unit during the taxable year, the taxpayer may not deduct more than a proportionate share of the expenses for the unit as rental expenses. The proposed regulations explain this limitation, which applies even if the personal use of the unit by the taxpayer is insufficient to constitute use as a residence.

A taxpayer who uses a unit as a residence and rents it to others for more than 14 days during the year may deduct rental expenses only to the extent of the gross rental income from the unit. The taxpayer must deduct expenses allocable to the rental use of the unit in the sequence prescribed in the proposed regulations. Items which are deductible without regard to any connection to a business activity, such as mortgage interest and taxes, are deducted first, then operating expenses, and finally items which affect basis, such as depreciation.

SPECIAL PROPERTY ARRANGEMENTS

The proposed regulations provide for the application of section 280A to two types of special property arrangements: rental pools and time sharing arrangements.

Rental pools are arrangements whereby a number of dwelling units are made available for rental and the owners of the units agree to share at least a portion of the rental receipts without regard to the actual rental of the individual units. The proposed regulations require each pool participant to include in gross income the amounts received from the pool. The limitation on the allocation of expenses to the rental use of a unit is applied by reference to the actual use of each unit.

A time sharing arrangement is an arrangement whereby two or more persons with interests in a dwelling unit agree to exercise control over the unit for different periods during a year. In general, the proposed regulations treat such arrangements as tenancies in common.

COMMENTS AND REQUESTS FOR A PUBLIC HEARING

Before adopting these proposed regulations, consideration will be given to any written comments that are submitted (preferably six copies) to the Commissioner of Internal Revenue. All comments will be available for public inspection and copying. A public hearing will be held upon written request to the Commissioner by any person who has submitted written comments. If a public hearing is held, notice of the time and place will be published in the FEDERAL REGISTER.

DRAFTING INFORMATION

The principal author of these proposed regulations was Paul A. Francis of the Legislation and Regulations Division of the Office of Chief Counsel, Internal Revenue Service. However, personnel from other offices of the Internal Revenue Service and Treasury Department participated in developing the regulations, both on matters of substance and style.

Evaluation of the effectiveness of the proposed regulations after issuance will be based upon comments received from offices within Treasury and the Internal Revenue Service, other governmental agencies, and the public.

[¶ 49,014] **Proposed Amendments of Regulations (LR-190-77),** published in the Federal Register on November 25, 1980.

Business expenses: Private foundations, excise taxes: Expenditures incurred in attempts to influence legislation.—Amendments of Reg. §§ 1.162-20 and 1.6033-2, relating to the treatment, for federal income tax purposes, of expenditures incurred in attempts to influence legislation, are proposed. The notice of proposed rulemaking issued on 12/23/88, EE-154-78 superseded the portion of this notice that proposed amendments to the regulations under Code Sec. 4945. T.D. 8308, 8/30/90, adopted the amendments in this notice to Reg. § 1.6001-1.

AGENCY: Internal Revenue Service, Treasury.

ACTION: Notice of proposed rulemaking.

SUMMARY: This document contains proposed regulations relating to the treatment, for tax purposes, of expenditures for attempts to influence legislation. There is a need for amendments to those regulations and especially for clearer guidelines for determining whether a communication constitutes an attempt to influence the public with respect to legislation. The proposed regulations set forth a three-factor test for making this determination, amend certain related rules, and provide for reporting by organizations making expenditures for purposes of influencing the public with respect to legislation. The proposed regulations will affect taxpayers and private foundations making expenditures of this kind directly or indirectly and the organizations through which taxpayers make the expenditures.

DATES: Written comments and requests for a public hearing must be delivered or mailed by January 26, 1981. The amendments generally are proposed to be effective for taxable years beginning after 1953 except that the new rules with respect to deductibility of dues, etc., and the reporting requirement for certain organizations are proposed to apply to expenditures made after 1980.

ADDRESS: Send comments and requests for a public hearing to: Commissioner of Internal Revenue, Attention: CC:LR:T (LR-190-77), Washington, D.C. 20224.

FOR FURTHER INFORMATION CONTACT: Paul A. Francis of the Legislation and Regulations Division, Office of the Chief Counsel, Internal Revenue Service, 1111 Constitution Avenue, N.W., Washington, D.C. 20224 (Attention: CC:LR:T) (202-566-6640).

SUPPLEMENTARY INFORMATION:

BACKGROUND

This document contains proposed amendments to the Income Tax Regulations (26 CFR Part 1) under sections 162, 6001, and 6033 of the Internal Revenue Code of 1954 and to the Regulations on Foundation Excise Taxes (26 CFR Part 53) under section 4945 of the Code. These amendments are proposed to provide clearer guidelines for determining whether a communication constitutes an attempt to influence the public with respect to legislation and to deal with certain related matters. The proposed regulations are to be issued under the authority contained in section 7805 of the Internal Revenue Code of 1954 (68A Stat. 917; 26 U.S.C. 7805).

Existing Rules With Respect to Business Taxpayers

Prior to 1962 the Income Tax Regulations under Code section 162 prohibited the deduction of expenditures for lobbying purposes. The prohibition applied both to expenditures for contacts with legislators and to expenditures for efforts to influence the general public with respect to legislation. Section 162(e), added to the Code in 1962, expressly permitted deduction of expenditures for contacts with legislators in certain circumstances but left standing the prohibition on deduction of expenditures to influence public opinion on legislation.

Three-factor Test

The proposed regulations establish a three-factor test for determining whether a communication constitutes an attempt to influence the public with respect to legislation. A communication will be treated as an attempt of that sort only if it—

(1) pertains to action by the legislative body;

(2) reflects a view on that legislative action, whether explicitly or implicitly; and

(3) is distributed in a manner so as to reach individuals as voters or constituents.

The proposed regulations provide definitions and examples to clarify the scope and application of this test.

Special Rule for Advertisements

Under the proposed regulations, no portion of an expenditure for an advertisement is deductible if any part of the advertisement constitutes an attempt to influence the general public with respect to legislation. This rule is consistent with the holding with respect to newspaper advertisements in *Consumers Power Co. v. United States*, 299 F. Supp. 1180, 1183 f. (E.D. Mich. 1969), *rev'd on other grounds*, 427 F. 2d 78 (6th Cir. 1970), *cert. denied*, 400 U.S. 925 (1970).

Certain Dues or Contributions

The proposed regulations also provide rules with respect to amounts paid to organizations that engage in political activities (including lobbying) within the scope of section 162(e)(2).

The existing regulations limit deductions for dues or other amounts paid to these organizations if the political activities of the organizations constitute a substantial part of their overall activities. The limitation does not apply if the political activities do not constitute a substantial part of the activities of an organization. Thus, the existing regulations allow taxpayers to deduct indirect expenditures for political activities in certain circumstances. The allowance of these deductions seems inconsistent with the disallowance of deductions for all direct expenditures for the same activities. Consequently, the proposed regulations limit deductions for dues or other payments if the recipient organization engages in any activities within the scope of section 162(e)(2), whether or not those activities constitute a substantial part of the organization's overall activities.

The proposed regulations also require organizations that receive dues or other payments for which the members or contributors may claim business deductions under section 162 to inform their members or contributors what percentage of their expenditures during a calendar year were expenditures for political activities. This information should assist taxpayers in determining what portion of their dues or contributions may be deductible. The proposed regulations provide certain exceptions to this requirement, which is to be effective for calendar years after 1980.

Rules With Respect to Private Foundations

The Tax Reform Act of 1969 added to the Code new section 4945 which imposes taxes on expenditures by private foundations for certain purposes. The committee reports indicate that the provisions in section 4945 that relate to attempts by private foundations to influence the public with respect to legislation were intended to be "substantially similar" to the rules applied to business taxpayers under section 162(e)(2). H.R. Rep. 91-413, 91st Cong., 1st Sess. 33 (1969); S. Rep. 91-552, 91st Cong., 1st Sess. 48 (1969).

The proposed regulations accordingly conform the general rules for private foundations with respect to attempts to influence the public to the rules proposed for business taxpayers. Thus, the three-factor test and the special rule for advertisements also apply to private foundations. Examples similar to those relating to business taxpayers illustrate the operation of the rules.

COMMENTS AND REQUESTS FOR A PUBLIC HEARING

Before adopting these proposed regulations, consideration will be given to any written comments that are submitted (preferably six copies) to the Commissioner of Internal Revenue. All comments will be available for public inspection and copying. A public hearing will be held upon written request to the Commissioner by any person who has submitted written comments. If a public hearing is held, notice of the time and place will be published in the FEDERAL REGISTER.

DRAFTING INFORMATION

The principal author of these proposed regulations was Paul A. Francis of the Legislation and Regulations Division of the Office of Chief Counsel, Internal Revenue Service. However, personnel from other offices of the Internal Revenue Service and Treasury Department participated in developing the regulations, both on matters of substance and style.

Evaluation of the effectiveness of the proposed regulations after issuance will be based upon comments received from officers within Treasury and the Internal Revenue Service, other governmental agencies, and the public.

[¶ 49,015]   Proposed Regulations (LR-173-80), published in the Federal Register on February 4, 1981.

Installment sales reporting: Sales occurring after October 19, 1980: General rules.—Reg. §§ 15A.453-0 and 15A.453-1, relating to installment sales or reporting of gain for sales occurring after October 19, 1980, are proposed.

AGENCY: Internal Revenue Service, Treasury.

ACTION: Proposed rulemaking cross-reference to temporary regulations.

SUMMARY: In the Rules and Regulations portion of this FEDERAL REGISTER, the Internal Revenue Service is issuing temporary income tax regulations relating to installment sales. The text of those temporary regulations also serves as the comment document for this proposed rulemaking.

DATES: Written comments and requests for a public hearing must be delivered or mailed by April 2, 1981.

ADDRESS: Send comments and a request for a public hearing to: Commissioner of Internal Revenue, Attention: CC:LR:T (LR-173-80), Washington, DC 20224.

FOR FURTHER INFORMATION CONTACT: Phoebe A. Mix of the Legislation and Regulations Division, Office of Chief Counsel, Internal Revenue Service, 1111 Constitution Avenue, N.W., Washington, DC 20224. (Attention: CC:LR:T) (202-566-3297).

SUPPLEMENTARY INFORMATION: The temporary regulations in the issue of the FEDERAL REGISTER amend part 15A of title 26 of the Code of Federal Regulations. The final regulations, which are proposed to be based on the temporary regulations, would amend 26 CFR Part 1.

For the text of the temporary regulations, see (T.D. 7768) published in the Rules and Regulations portion of this issue of the FEDERAL REGISTER.

Section 1.453-1, which will be deleted upon adoption of this document as a Treasury decision, contains material relating to installment sales by dealers in personal property. It is intended that eventually all of the regulations relating to installment sales will be amended to reflect the amendments to section 453 made by the Installment Sales Revision Act of 1980. Until those amendments are adopted, provisions in prior § 1.453-1 which relate to matters not covered in this document will remain in effect.

INITIAL REGULATORY FLEXIBILITY ANALYSIS

These proposed regulations are necessary to implement the provisions of section 453 of the Internal Revenue Code as amended by the Installment Sales Revision Act of 1980.

The objective of these regulations is to provide taxpayers with the guidance necessary to comply with the provisions of section 453 as amended by the Installment Sales Revision Act of 1980, and in particular, those provisions relating to contingent installment sales and to sales for which taxpayers did not elect to use installment method reporting. These regulations are promulgated under sections 453(i) and 7805 of the Internal Revenue Code of 1954.

These proposed regulations, if adopted, will affect small businesses but not other small entities, such as local governments or tax-exempt organizations, which do not pay taxes.

These proposed regulations, if adopted, will affect any small business making an installment sale of real property or a casual sale of personal property. It is anticipated that a significant number of small businesses will be affected. These regulations do not impose substantial reporting requirements beyond those already imposed by the tax laws generally nor record keeping requirements beyond those necessary to account for such sales in the ordinary course of business. The professional competence necessary to comply with these regulations is no greater than that already necessary for the conduct of a small business.

These regulations do not overlap with, conflict with or duplicate any existing federal regulations.

None of the significant alternatives considered in drafting these regulations would have significantly altered the economic impact of these regulations on small entities.

COMMENTS AND REQUESTS FOR A PUBLIC HEARING

Before adopting these proposed regulations, consideration will be given to any written comments that are submitted (preferably six copies) to the Commissioner of Internal Revenue. All comments will be available for public inspection and copying. A public hearing will be held upon written request to the Commissioner by any person who has submitted written comments. If a public hearing is held, notice of the time and place will be published in the FEDERAL REGISTER.

[¶ 49,016]   **Proposed Regulations (LR-222-78),** published in the Federal Register on May 21, 1981.

    Cost-sharing payments: Conservation payments: Exclusions: Recapture.—Reg. §§16A.126-0—16A.126-2, 16A.1255-1 and 16A.1255-2, relating to cost-sharing payments, are proposed.

AGENCY: Internal Revenue Service, Treasury.

ACTION: Proposed rulemaking cross-reference to temporary regulations.

SUMMARY: In the Rules and Regulations portion of this FEDERAL REGISTER, the Internal Revenue Service is issuing temporary income tax regulations relating to the exclusion for certain conservation cost-sharing payments. The text of those temporary regulations also serves as the comment document for this proposed rulemaking.

DATES: Written comments and requests for a public hearing must be delivered or mailed by [INSERT 60 DAYS AFTER THIS NOTICE IS PUBLISHED IN FEDERAL REGISTER]

ADDRESS: Send comments and requests for a public hearing to: Commissioner of Internal Revenue, Attention: CC:LR:T (LR-222-78), Washington, DC 20224.

FOR FURTHER INFORMATION CONTACT: Phoebe A. Mix of the Legislation and Regulations Division, Office of the Chief Counsel, Internal Revenue Service, 1111 Constitution Avenue, N.W., Washington, DC 20224 (Attention: CC:LR:T) (202-566-3297).

SUPPLEMENTARY INFORMATION:

The temporary regulations in the Rules and Regulations portion of this issue of the FEDERAL REGISTER amend part 153 of title 26 of the Code of Federal Regulations.

The final regulations which are proposed to be based on the temporary regulations would amend 26 CFR Part 1.

For the text of the temporary regulations, see FR Doc.—(T.D. 7778) published in the Rules and Regulations portion of this issue of the FEDERAL REGISTER.

REGULATORY FLEXIBILITY ACT

Although this document is a notice of proposed rulemaking which solicits public comment, the Internal Revenue Service has concluded that the regulations proposed are interpretative and that the notice and public procedure requirements of 5 U.S.C. 553 do not apply. Accordingly, these proposed regulations do not constitute regulations subject to the Regulatory Flexibility Act (5 U.S.C. chapter 6).

COMMENTS AND REQUEST FOR A PUBLIC HEARING

Before adopting these proposed regulations, consideration will be given to any written comments that are submitted (preferably six copies) to the Commissioner of Internal Revenue. All comments will be available for public inspection and copying. A public hearing will be held upon written request to the Commissioner by any person who has submitted written comments. If a public hearing is held, notice of the time and place will be published in the FEDERAL REGISTER.

[¶ 49,017]   **Proposed Regulations (LR-10-81),** published in the Federal Register on July 1, 1981.

    Interest on mortgage subsidy bonds: Exemption.—Reg. §§6a.103A-1—6a.103A-3, relating to the exemption of interest on mortgage subsidy bonds, are proposed.

AGENCY: Internal Revenue Service, Treasury.

ACTION: Notice of proposed rulemaking by cross-reference to temporary regulations.

SUMMARY: In the Rules and Regulations portion of this FEDERAL REGISTER, the Internal Revenue Service is issuing temporary income tax regulations that relate to mortgage subsidy bonds. The text of those temporary regulations also serves as the comment document for this proposed rulemaking.

DATES: Written comments and requests for a public hearing must be delivered or mailed by August 31, 1981. The regulations are proposed to be effective for obligations issued after April 24, 1979.

ADDRESS: Send comments and requests for a public hearing to: Commissioner of Internal Revenue, Attention: CC:LR:T (LR-10-81), Washington, D.C. 20224.

FOR FURTHER INFORMATION CONTACT: Harold T. Flanagan of the Legislation and Regulations Division, Office of the Chief Counsel, Internal Revenue Service, 1111 Constitution Avenue, N.W., Washington, D.C. 20224 (Attention: CC:LR:T) (202-566-3294).

SUPPLEMENTARY INFORMATION:

EXPLANATION

The temporary regulations in the Rules and Regulations portion of this issue of the FEDERAL REGISTER add a new Part 6a to Title 26 of the Code of Federal Regulations. The final regulations, which this document proposes to be based on those temporary regulations, would be added to Part 1 of Title 26 of the Code of Federal Regulations. Sections 6a.103A-1, 6a.103A-2 and 6a.103A-3 would become §§1.103A-1, 1.103A-2, and 1.103A-3, respectively. For the text of the temporary regulations, see FR Doc. (T.D. 7780) published in the Rules and Regulations portion of this issue of the FEDERAL REGISTER. The preamble to the temporary regulations explains the addition to the regulations.

The regulations interpret the provisions of section 103A of the Internal Revenue Code of 1954 which provides that a mortgage subsidy bond shall be treated as an obligation not described in section 103(a)(1) or (2) the interest on which shall not be excludable from gross income. Section 103A allows exceptions to this general rule for qualified mortgage bonds and qualified veterans' mortgage bonds.

These regulations are proposed to be issued under the authority contained in section 7805 of the Internal Revenue Code (26 U.S.C. 7805; 68A Stat. 917).

REGULATORY FLEXIBILITY ACT

Although this document is a notice of proposed rulemaking which solicits public comment, the Internal Revenue Service has concluded that the regulations proposed herein are interpretative and that the notice and public procedure requirements of 5 U.S.C. 553 do not apply. Accordingly, these proposed regulations do not constitute regulations subject to the Regulatory Flexibility Act (5 U.S.C. chapter 6).

COMMENTS AND REQUESTS FOR A PUBLIC HEARING

Before the adoption of these proposed regulations, consideration will be given to any written comments that are submitted (preferably six copies) to the Commissioner of Internal Revenue. All comments will be available for public inspection and copying. A public hearing will be held upon written request to the Commissioner by any person who has submitted written comments. If a public hearing is held, notice of the time and place will be published in the FEDERAL REGISTER.

[¶ 49,018]   **Proposed Regulations and Proposed Amendments of Regulations (EE-7-78)**, published in the Federal Register on July 14, 1981.

Individual retirement plans: Simplified employee pensions.—Reg. §§1.219-3, 1.220-1, 1.404(h)-1, 1.408-7, 1.408-8, 1.408-9 and 54.4973-1 and proposed amendments of Reg. §§1.219-1, 1.219-2, 1.408-2, 1.408-3, 1.408-4, 1.408-6, 54.4974-1 and 301.6693-1, relating to individual retirement plans and simplified employee pensions, are proposed. Reg. §1.62-1 was removed on 3/25/1988 by T.D. 8189 and Reg. §1.415-8 was removed on 4/4/2007 by T.D. 9319. Reg. §1.408-4(b)(4)(ii) was withdrawn on 7/11/2014 by REG-209459-78.

AGENCY: Internal Revenue Service, Treasury.

ACTION: Notice of proposed rulemaking.

SUMMARY: This document contains proposed regulations relating to individual retirement plans and simplified employee pensions. Changes to the applicable law were made by the Employee Retirement Income Security Act of 1974, the Tax Reform Act of 1976, the Revenue Act of 1978 and the Technical Corrections Act of 1979. The regulations would provide the public with the guidance needed to comply with these Acts and would affect institutions which sponsor individual retirement plans and simplified employee pensions. The regulations also affect employers and individuals who use these plans for retirement income.

DATES: Written comments and requests for a public hearing must be delivered or mailed by September 14, 1981. The amendments have varying effective dates. The provisions relating to spousal individual retirement plans are generally effective for taxable years beginning after December 31, 1976. The provisions relating to simplified employee pensions are generally effective for taxable years beginning after December 31, 1978. The provisions defining "active participant" for individuals covered by defined benefit offset plans are effective for taxable years beginning after December 31, 1980.

ADDRESS: Send comments and requests for a public hearing to: Commissioner of Internal Revenue, Attention: CC:LR:T (EE-7-78), Washington, D.C. 20224.

FOR FURTHER INFORMATION CONTACT: William D. Gibbs of the Employee Plans and Exempt Organizations Division, Office of the Chief Counsel, Internal Revenue Service, 1111 Constitution Avenue, N.W., Washington, D.C. 20224 (Attention: CC:LR:T) (202-566-3430) (not a toll-free number).

SUPPLEMENTARY INFORMATION:

BACKGROUND

This document contains proposed amendments to the Income Tax Regulations (26 CFR Part 1), the Gift Tax Regulations (26 CFR Part 25), the Employment Tax Regulations (26 CFR Part 31), the Regulations on Pension Excise Taxes (26 CFR Part 54) and the Procedure and Administration Regulations (26 CFR Part 301) under sections 62, 219, 220, 404, 408, 409, 2503, 3121, 3306, 4973, 4974, and 6693 of the Internal Revenue Code of 1954. These amendments are proposed to conform the regulations to section 2002(d) of the Employee Retirement Income Security Act of 1974 (88 Stat. 966), section 1501 of the Tax Reform Act of 1976 (90 Stat. 1734), sections 152, 156(c) and 157 of the Revenue Act of 1978 (92 Stat. 2797, 2802, 2803), and sections 101(a)(10), 101(a)(14)(A), 101(a)(14)(B), and 101(a)(14)(E)(ii) of the Technical Corrections Act of 1979 (94 Stat. 201-205). These regulations are to be issued under the authority contained in section 7805 of the Internal Revenue Code of 1954 (68A Stat. 917; 26 U.S.C. 7805).

On August 8, 1980, the Federal Register published final regulations relating to individual retirement plans under the Income Tax Regulations (26 CFR Part 1) under sections 219, 408, 409 and under the Pension Excise Taxes (26 CFR Part 54) under section 4974 (45 FR 52782). Also, because of subsequent statutory provisions, some of the proposed regulations published on February 21, 1975 (40 FR 7661) were withdrawn in connection with those final regulations. The preamble to those final regulations indicated that regulations under other statutory provisions relating to retirement plans would be reproposed at a later date. This document contains these reproposed amendments, other than those relating to the rollover rules under Code sections 402 and ¶403. The Service intends to repropose these rules at a later date in connection with the regulations under Code sections 402(a)(5), (6) and (7), and 403(a)(4), (6) and (8).

SPOUSAL INDIVIDUAL RETIREMENT PLANS

Internal Revenue Code section 220 allows an individual to deduct amounts contributed to an individual retirement plan maintained for the individual's benefit and an individual retirement plan maintained for the benefit of the individual's nonemployed spouse. The proposed regulations set forth the type of funding arrangements which must be used and additional limitations and restrictions the individual and spouse must meet in order for the individual to obtain this deduction.

SIMPLIFIED EMPLOYEE PENSIONS

Internal Revenue Code section 408(k) sets forth rules for simplified employee pension ("SEP's"). The proposed regulations, §§ 1.408-7 through -9, indicate to employers and sponsoring institutions what requirements these arrangements must meet. Section 1.404(h)-1 of the proposed regulations sets forth the special deduction limitations for employers under Code section 404(h). Sections 1.219-1(d)(4) and 1.219-3 of the proposed regulations set forth the rules governing the inclusion/deduction rules for employees for employer contributions to SEP's.

An employee will be allowed to deduct an employer contribution to a simplified employee pension. In general, the maximum amount the employee will be allowed to deduct is the lesser of 15 percent of compensation includible in gross income or $7,500. Proposed § 1.219-3 makes it clear that the deduction and the compensation are computed separately with respect to each employer's arrangement. Thus, an employee who has two or more employers can use only the compensation from the employer maintaining the simplified employee pension arrangement in computing the section 219(b)(7) limitation. On the other hand, if two or more employers of an employee each maintain a simplified employee pension arrangement, the employee will be allowed to deduct each employer's contribution, up to the compensation and dollar limit applied separately to each employer. Special limitations apply to certain related employers under Code section 414(b) and (c) and to self-employed individuals.

Certain rules have been included to make SEP arrangements more administrable by employers and the Service. Under proposed § 1.408-7(d)(1)(iii) an employer is not required to make a contribution to the SEP of an otherwise eligible employee who receives less than $200 compensation for a calendar year. This relieves employers of the burden of setting up SEP's to which very small amounts of money will be contributed (the maximum deductible contribution would equal $30 (15% of $200)). This rule was published by the Service in Announcement 80-112, 1980-36 I.R.B. 35.

Further, under proposed § 1.408-7(d)(2), employers may execute necessary documents on behalf of employees who are unwilling or unable to execute those documents or whom the employer is unable to locate. This remedial rule prevents an employer's SEP arrangement from being disqualified because of a recalcitrant employee or one who has left the employer's service and is unable to be located by the employer. (See also proposed § 1.408-9(c) for possible reporting requirements in this instance.) Comments are requested as to what alternative remedial action, in lieu of execution on behalf of employees, employers would wish to take to avoid disqualification of their SEP arrangements. Comments also are requested on this proposed rule as to whether in a particular State there is any law that would preclude this action by the employer on the employee's behalf.

Employer contributions which exceed the amounts called for under the written allocation formula for the SEP arrangement are treated as if made to the employee's individual retirement account or individual retirement annuity, maintained outside the employee's SEP. It is contemplated that the employer, when it discovers the erroneous contribution, will notify the employee of the amount of the non-SEP contribution made in excess of the allocation formula. Because this amount may result in an excess contribution when made the employee may wish to take appropriate action in order to avoid IRA penalties. The normal IRA rules under Code section 219 apply in such a situation. This rule is proposed in order to prevent the entire SEP arrangement from being disqualified due to an inadvertent error on the part of the employer, such as an incorrect calculation of employee compensation. Under Code section 408(k), the entire SEP arrangement could be disqualified on account of the excess contribution. This rule is proposed to provide relief in such cases. See proposed § 1.408-7(f) and the example of how the rule would operate in a particular case.

Proposed § 1.408-7(c)(2) contains a special rule clarifying the relationship between SEP's and salary reduction agreements. This rule makes it clear that employer contributions to an employee's individual retirement account or annuity that are made under a salary reduction agreement between the employer and employee are not treated as employer contributions to an employee's simplified employee pension. Thus, if the employee may elect either a contribution or current compensation, the contribution is treated as an employee contribution and, therefore, is not eligible for the favorable SEP arrangement rules.

Similarly, other contributions such as voluntary contributions made by the employee, or on behalf of the employee by the employer as the agent for the employee (such as by payroll withholding), are treated as employee contributions.

Even though the employer picks the institution or substantially influences the employee's choice of the institution to which the employer makes the SEP contribution and which serves as trustee or sponsor for the employee's SEP, the SEP arrangement remains qualified under the Code. Further, this action by the employer is not a prohibition on withdrawal of funds within the meaning of Code section 408(k)(4)(B). The employer should, however, be aware that the Department of Labor may require special reporting for such action. (See 29 C.F.R. § 2520.104-48 (1980) and 29 C.F.R. § 2520.104-49 (1981).)

Proposed § 1.408-9 contains reporting requirements for SEP's. Employers who use the Service's Model Simplified Employee Pension Arrangement (Form 5305-SEP) and furnish the Model to their employees will satisfy the disclosure requirements relating to adoption of the SEP arrangement. Further, if the employer reports the amount of the SEP contribution on an employee's W-2, the annual reporting requirements will be satisfied. The Department of Labor also has reporting requirements for SEP's, which are in addition to the requirements of the Internal Revenue Service. (See 29 C.F.R. § 2520.104-48 (1980) and 29 C.F.R. § 2520.104-49 (1981).)

Employers who failed to make required contributions on behalf of employees for calendar year 1979 because the employees were no longer employed at the end of the employer's taxable year may make such "make up" contributions before January 1, 1981. This conforms to Announcement 80-112, 1980-36 I.R.B. 35. This relief is given because employers may not have anticipated the rules contained in that announcement and § 1.408-7(d)(1), (2) and (3), relating to which employees are entitled to receive an allocation. It is expected that employers who make such contributions will comply with the reporting requirements of § 1.408-9(b) and file amended tax returns. Likewise, employees who receive such contributions are expected to file amended tax returns.

OTHER AMENDMENTS

Conforming and technical amendments made by the Tax Reform Act of 1976, the Revenue Act of 1978, and the Technical Corrections Act of 1979 have been made to the regulations under Code sections 62, 219, 220, 404, 408, 409, 415, 3121, 3306, 4973, 4974, and 6693.

Also, regulations are proposed which define "active participant" under section 219(b)(2) for individuals who are covered by defined benefit offset plans integrated with Federal or State benefits such as social security benefits. These rules were requested by commentators at the public hearing held July 19, 1979, on the reproposed active participant rules, and in other written comments on those proposed regulations published in the FEDERAL REGISTER on March 23, 1979 (44 FR 17754). This proposed rule allows employees to make IRA contributions when, in effect, they get no benefit from their employers' plans.

REGULATORY FLEXIBILITY ACT

Although this document is a notice of proposed rulemaking which solicits public comment, the Internal Revenue Service has concluded that the regulations proposed herein are interpretative and that the notice and public procedure requirements of 5 U.S.C. 553 do not apply. Accordingly, these proposed regulations do not constitute regulations subject to the Regulatory Flexibility Act (5 U.S.C. chapter 6).

COMMENTS AND REQUESTS FOR A PUBLIC HEARING

Before adopting these proposed regulations, consideration will be given to any written comments that are submitted (preferably six copies) to the Commissioner of Internal Revenue. All comments will be available for public inspection and copying. A public hearing will be held upon written request to the Commissioner by any person who has submitted written comments. If a public hearing is held, notice of the time and place will be published in the FEDERAL REGISTER.

DRAFTING INFORMATION

The principal author of these proposed regulations is William D. Gibbs of the Employee Plans and Exempt Organizations Division of the Office of Chief Counsel, Internal Revenue Service. However, personnel from other offices of the Internal Revenue Service and Treasury Department participated in developing the regulations, both on matters of substance and style.

§ 1.220-1.   **Deduction for retirement savings for certain married individuals** .—(a) *In general* .—Subject to the limitations and restrictions of paragraphs (c), (d) and (e) and the special rules of paragraph (f) of this section, there shall be allowed a deduction under section 62 from gross income of amounts paid for the taxable year of an individual by or on behalf of such individual for the benefit of himself and his spouse to an individual retirement account described in section 408(a), for an individual retirement annuity described in section 408(b), or for an individual retirement bond described in section 409. The amounts contributed to an individual retirement account, for an individual retirement annuity, or for an individual retirement bond by or on behalf of an individual for the benefit of himself and his spouse shall be deductible only by such individual. The first sentence of this paragraph shall apply only in the case of a contribution of cash; a contribution of property other than cash is not allowable as a deduction. In the case of an individual retirement bond, a deduction will not be allowed if the bond is redeemed within 12 months of its issue date.

(b) *Definitions* .—(1) *Compensation* .—For purposes of this section, the term "compensation" has the meaning set forth in § 1.219-1(c)(1).

(2) *Active participant* .—For purposes of this section, the term "active participant" has the meaning set forth in § 1.219-2.

(3) *Individual retirement subaccount* .—For purposes of this section, the term individual retirement subaccount is that part of an individual retirement account maintained for the exclusive benefit of the individual or the individual's spouse and which meets the following requirements:

(i) The individual or spouse for whom the subaccount is maintained has exclusive control over the subaccount after deposits have been made,

(ii) The subaccount, by itself, meets the requirements of section 408(a), except that it is not a separate trust,

(iii) The trustee or custodian maintains records indicating the ownership of the funds, and

(iv) The individual and spouse do not jointly own the individual retirement account of which the subaccount is a part.

(c) *Types of funding arrangements permitted* .—The deduction under paragraph (a) of this section shall be allowed only if one of the following types of funding arrangements is used:

(1) A separate individual retirement account, individual retirement annuity, or individual retirement bond is established or purchased for the benefit of the individual and a separate individual retirement account, individual retirement annuity or individual retirement bond is established or purchased for the individual's spouse.

(2) A single individual retirement account described in section 408 (a) is established or purchased and such account has an individual retirement subaccount for the benefit of the individual and an individual retirement subaccount for the benefit of the spouse. The single individual retirement account cannot be owned jointly by the husband and wife.

(3) An individual retirement account described in section 408(c) is maintained by an employer or employee association and such account has arrangements described in subparagraphs (1) or (2).

(d) *Maximum deduction* .—The amount allowable as a deduction under section 220(a) to an individual for any taxable year may not exceed—

(1) Twice the amount paid (including prior excess contributions) to the account, subaccount, annuity, or for the bond, established for the individual or for the spouse to or for which the lesser amount was paid for the taxable year,

(2) An amount equal to 15 percent of the compensation includible in the individual's gross income for the taxable year, or

(3) $1,750 whichever is the smallest amount.

(e) *Limitations and restrictions* .—(1) *Alternative deduction* .—No deduction is allowable under section 220(a) for the taxable year if the individual claims the deduction allowed by section 219(a) for the taxable year.

(2) *Individual or spouse covered by certain other plans* .—No deduction is allowable under section 220(a) to an individual for the taxable year if for any part of such year—

(i) He or his spouse was an active participant (as defined in § 1.219-2), or

(ii) Amounts were contributed by his employer, or his spouse's employer, on the individual's or spouse's behalf for an annuity contract described in section 403(b) (whether or not his, or his spouse's, rights in such contract are nonforfeitable).

(3) *Contributions after age 70 1/2* .—No deduction is allowable under section 220(a) with respect to any payment which is made for a taxable year of an individual if either the individual or his spouse has attained age 70$\frac{1}{2}$ before the close of such taxable year.

(4) *Recontributed amounts* .—No deduction is allowable under section 220(a) for any taxable year of an individual with respect to a rollover contribution described in section 402(a)(5), 402(a)(7), 403(a)(4), 403(b)(8), 408(d)(3), or 409(b)(3)(C).

(5) *Amounts contributed under endowment contracts* .—The rules for endowment contracts under section 220 are the same as the provisions for such contracts under § 1.219-1(b)(3).

(6) *Employed spouses* .—No deduction is allowable under section 220(a) if the spouse of the individual has any compensation (as defined in § 1.219-1(c)(1) determined without regard to section 911) for the taxable year of such spouse ending with or within the taxable year of the individual.

(f) *Special rules* .—(1) *Community property* .—Section 220 is to be applied without regard to any community property laws.

(2) *Time when contributions deemed made* .—The time when contributions are deemed made is determined in the same manner as under section 219(c)(3). See § 1.219-1(d).

(g) *Excess contributions treated as contribution made during subsequent year for which there is an unused limitation* .—(1) *In general* .—If for the taxable year the maximum amount allowable as a deduction under this section exceeds the amount contributed, then the taxpayer, whether or not a deduction is actually claimed, shall be treated as having made an additional contribution for the taxable year in an amount equal to the lesser of—

(i) The amount of such excess, or

(ii) The amount of the excess contributions for such taxable year (determined under section 4973(b)(2) without regard to subparagraph (C) thereof).

For purposes of computing the maximum deduction under section 220(b)(1), the excess contribution for a previous year shall be treated as made for the current year.

(2) *Amount contributed* .—For purposes of this paragraph, the amount contributed—

(i) Shall be determined without regard to this paragraph, and

(ii) Shall not include any rollover contribution.

(3) *Special rule where excess contribution was allowed for closed year* .—Proper reduction shall be made in the amount allowable as a deduction by reason of this paragraph for any amount allowed as a deduction under this section or section 219 for a prior taxable year for which the period for assessing a deficiency has expired if the amount so allowed exceeds the amount which should have been allowed for such prior taxable year.

(4) *Examples* .—The provisions of this paragraph may be illustrated by the following examples:

Example (1). (i) H, a calendar-year taxpayer, earns $10,000 in compensation includible in gross income for 1979. H is married to W, also a calendar-year taxpayer, who has no compensation for 1979. For 1979, neither H nor W is covered by certain other plans within the meaning of section 220(b)(3). On November 24, 1979, H establishes an individual retirement account (IRA) for himself and an individual retirement account for W. H contributes $850 to each account. Neither H nor W withdraws any money from either account after the initial contribution. Under section 220(b)(1) the maximum amount that H can deduct for 1979 is 15 percent of the compensation includible in his gross income or $1,500. H has made an excess contribution of $200 for 1979.

(ii) For 1980, H has compensation includible in gross income of $12,000. W has no compensation for 1980. For 1980, neither H nor W is covered by certain other plans within the meaning of section 220(b)(3). No contributions are made to the IRA of H or W for 1980.

(iii) Although H made no contributions to either his or W's IRA for 1980, under the rules contained in this paragraph, H is treated as having made an additional contribution of $100 to his IRA and $100 to W's IRA for 1980 and will be allowed to deduct $200 as his 1980 IRA contribution.

Example (2). (i) For 1979, the facts are the same as in *Example (1)*.

(ii) For 1980, H has compensation of $15,000 includible in gross income and is not covered by any other plans within the meaning of section 219(b)(2). W also goes to work in 1980 and has compensation of $6,000, but is not covered by certain other plans within the meaning of section 219(b)(2). H will not be treated as having made a deductible contribution of a previous year's excess contribution within the meaning of section 220(c)(6) because W has compensation for 1980. However, both H and W now meet the deduction standards of section 219 and each will be treated as having made a deductible contribution of $100 to their separate IRA's for 1980 under section 219(c)(5).

Example (3). (i) For 1979, the facts are the same as in *Example (1)*.

(ii) For 1980, H has compensation of $15,000 includible in gross income and is covered by certain other plans within the meaning of section 220(b)(3). W has no compensation for 1980 and is not covered by certain other plans within the meaning of section 220(b)(3). H will not be treated as having made a deductible contribution of a previous year's excess contribution within the meaning of section 219(c)(5) or 220(c)(6) because H is covered by other plans for 1980 and has no allowable deduction under section 219 or 220.

(iii) W will not be treated as having made a deductible contribution of a previous year's excess contribution within the meaning of section 219(c)(5) because W has no compensation for 1980 and thus no allowable deduction under section 219.

(h) *Effective date* .—(1) This section is effective for taxable years beginning after December 31, 1976.

(2) If, but for this subparagraph, an amount would be allowable as a deduction by reason of section 220(c)(6) and paragraph (g) for a taxable year beginning before January 1, 1978, such amount shall be allowable only for the taxpayer's first taxable year beginning in 1978. [Reg. § 1.220-1.]

* * *

[¶ 49,019]   Proposed Amendments of Regulations (LR-10-81), published in the Federal Register on November 10, 1981.

Interest on mortgage subsidy bonds: Exemption.—Amendments to Reg. §§6a.103A-1 and 6a.103A-2, relating to mortgage subsidy bonds, are proposed.

AGENCY: Internal Revenue Service, Treasury.

ACTION: Notice of proposed rulemaking by cross-reference to temporary regulations.

SUMMARY: In the Rules and Regulations portion of this FEDERAL REGISTER, the Internal Revenue Service is issuing amendments to temporary income tax regulations that relate to mortgage subsidy bonds. The text of those amendments also serves as the comment document for this proposed rulemaking.

DATES: Written comments and requests for a public hearing must be delivered or mailed by [60 DAYS AFTER PUBLICATION OF THIS DOCUMENT IN THE FEDERAL REGISTER]. The regulations are proposed to be effective for obligations issued after April 24, 1979.

ADDRESS: Send comments and requests for a public hearing to: Commissioner of Internal Revenue, Attention: CC:LR:T (LR-10-81), Washington, D.C. 20224.

FOR FURTHER INFORMATION CONTACT: Harold T. Flanagan of the Legislation and Regulations Division, Office of the Chief Counsel, Internal Revenue Service, 1111 Constitution Avenue, N.W., Washington, D.C. 20224 (Attention: CC:LR:T) (202-566-3294).

SUPPLEMENTARY INFORMATION:

BACKGROUND

The temporary regulations in the Rules and Regulations portion of this issue of the FEDERAL REGISTER amend the Temporary Regulations under Title 11 of the Omnibus Reconciliation Act of 1980 (26 CFR Part 6a) under section 103A of the Internal Revenue Code of 1954, which were published in the FEDERAL REGISTER for July 1, 1981 (46 FR 34311). The final regulations, which this document proposes to be based on amendments to the temporary regulations, would be added to Part 1 of Title 26 of the Code of Federal Regulations. For the text of the amendments to the temporary regulations, see FR Doc. (T.D. 7794) published in the Rules and Regulations portion of this issue of the FEDERAL REGISTER. The preamble to the temporary regulations explains the amendments to the regulations.

The temporary regulations as amended interpret the provisions of section 103A of the Internal Revenue Code of 1954 which provides that a mortgage subsidy bond shall be treated as an obligation not described in section 103(a)(1) or (2) the interest on which shall not be excludable from gross income. Section 103A allows exceptions to this general rule for qualified mortgage bonds and qualified veterans' mortgage bonds.

These regulations are proposed to be issued under the authority contained in section 7805 of the Internal Revenue Code (26 U.S.C. 7805; 68A Stat. 917).

REGULATORY FLEXIBILITY ACT

Although this document is a notice of proposed rulemaking which solicits public comment, the Internal Revenue Service has concluded that the regulations proposed herein are interpretative and that the notice and public procedure requirements of 5 U.S.C. 553 do not apply. Accordingly, these proposed regulations do not constitute regulations subject to the Regulatory Flexibility Act (5 U.S.C. chapter 6).

COMMENTS AND REQUESTS FOR A PUBLIC HEARING

Before the adoption of these proposed regulations, consideration will be given to any written comments that are submitted (preferably six copies) to the Commissioner of Internal Revenue. All comments will be available for public inspection and copying. A public hearing will be held upon written request to the Commissioner by any person who has submitted written comments. If a public hearing is held, notice of the time and place will be published in the FEDERAL REGISTER.

[¶ 49,020]   Proposed Amendment of Regulations (LR-176-80), published in the Federal Register on January 26, 1982.

Energy credits: Subsidized borrowings.—Amendment of Reg. §1.48-9, relating to the rule which reduces the energy credit where energy property is financed by subsidized energy financing or tax-exempt industrial development bonds, is proposed.

AGENCY: Internal Revenue Service, Treasury.

ACTION: Notice of proposed rulemaking.

SUMMARY: This document contains proposed regulations relating to the rule which reduces the energy credit where energy property is financed by subsidized energy financing or tax-exempt industrial development bonds. Changes to the applicable tax law were made by the Energy Tax Act of 1978 and the Crude Oil Windfall Profit Tax Act of 1980. These regulations will provide the public with the guidance needed to comply with the law.

DATES: Written comments and requests for a public hearing must be delivered or mailed by March 29, 1982. This amendment is proposed to be effective for certain periods after October 1, 1978.

ADDRESS: Send comments and requests for a public hearing to: Commissioner of Internal Revenue, Attn: CC:LR:T (LR-176-80) Washington, D.C. 20224.

FOR FURTHER INFORMATION CONTACT: Mary Frances Pearson of the Legislation and Regulations Division, Office of the Chief Counsel, Internal Revenue Service, 1111 Constitution Avenue, N.W., Washington, D.C. 20224 (Attn: CC:LR:T) (202-566-3458; not a toll-free number).

SUPPLEMENTAL INFORMATION:

BACKGROUND

This document contains a proposed amendment to the Income Tax Regulations (26 CFR Part 1) under section 48 of the Internal Revenue Code of 1954. This amendment is proposed to conform the regulations to changes made by section 301(b) of the Energy Tax Act of 1978 (Pub. L. 95-618, 92 Stat. 3195) and sections 221(b)(2) and 223(c) of the Crude Oil Windfall Profit Tax Act of 1980 (Pub. L. 96-223, 94 Stat. 229). The proposed regulations are to be issued under the authority contained in Code sections 7805 (68A Stat. 917, 26 U.S.C. 7805) and 38(b) (76 Stat. 962, 26 U.S.C. 38).

EXPLANATION OF PROVISIONS

In general, the energy percentage, as determined under section 46(a)(2)(C), is applied to the total amount of qualified investment in energy property to establish the amount of credit allowed. Section 301(b) of the Energy Tax Act of 1978 added section 48(1)(11) to the Code. This provision in effect reduces the energy credit percentage by one half if the energy property is financed in whole or in part with the proceeds of tax-exempt industrial development bonds within the meaning of section 103(b)(2) (exempt IDB's). Sections 221(b)(2) and 223(c) of the Crude Oil Windfall Profit Tax Act of 1980 amended section 48(1)(11) to reduce the qualified investment in energy property by the amount of financing attributable to the proceeds of exempt IDB's and subsidized energy financing.

The 1980 Act amendments apply for the period after December 31, 1979, in the case of property qualifying under the 1980 Act as energy property for the first time. This property is called "early application property" and is described in §1.48-9(o)(9) of the proposed amendments to the regulations. For all other energy property, the 1980 Act amendments apply for the period after December 31, 1982.

For example, assume a taxpayer acquires and places in service recycling equipment (which is not early application property) and finances the acquisition in part with exempt IDB's. If the equipment is acquired and placed in service before January 1, 1983, then to determine the credit for energy property, the energy percentage is reduced by one-half and then is multiplied against the total qualified investment in that property. If the equipment is acquired and placed in service after December 31, 1982, the qualified investment is reduced by the amount of the financing attributable to the exempt IDB's and the full energy credit is multiplied against the reduced qualified investment.

Subsidized energy financing

Section 48(1)(11), as amended by section 223(c) of the Crude Oil Windfall Profit Tax Act, defines subsidized energy financing as financing provided under a Federal, State, or local program a principal purpose of which is to provide subsidized financing for projects designed to conserve or produce energy.

The proposed regulations follow the Conference Report, which indicates that loan guarantees, credits against State and local income taxes, and taxable grants are not subsidized energy financing. See, H.R. Rep. No. 96-817, 96th Cong. 2d Sess. 136-137 (1980) (Conference Report). (For an example of a taxable energy grant, see, Rev. Rul. 79-356, 1979-2 C.B. 28). Non-taxable government grants also are not included within the definition of subsidized energy financing for purposes of the rule in section 48(1)(11). However, the same result is achieved for purposes of the energy credit since the basis of the property is determined with reference to cost under section 1012 and the amount of a non-taxable grant will not be taken into account in determining basis. Also, price guarantees and purchase commitments are not considered subsidized financing since these type of arrangements confer only a contingent benefit. However, if funds are advanced under a price guarantee or a purchase commitment agreement which, in effect, results in a loan (for example, where payments under the agreement are made before the project becomes operational), these advances are considered to be subsidized energy financing. The proposed regulations incorporate the substance of a colloquy between Senators Baker and Long on the Senate floor that subsidized energy financing does not include funds received by government owned utilities if the source of the funds is from rate-payers from the sale of services and no tax revenues are involved. See, 126 Cong. Rec. S. 3052 (daily ed. March 26, 1980); Rev. Rul. 81-52, 1981-7 I.R.B. 9.

Allocation

The statutory rule under Section 48(1)(11) multiplies qualified investment by a fraction to determine the amount of qualified investment taken into account for the energy credit. The fraction is one minus another fraction the numerator of which is the portion of qualified investment in the property which is allocable to subsidized financing or proceeds of exempt IDB's and the denominator of which is the total qualified investment in the property before the application of this rule. The proposed regulations achieve the same result as the statute by simply reducing qualified investment for the energy credit by the portion attributable to the energy financing or proceeds.

The proposed regulations allocate the proceeds according to the type of borrowings used to finance the energy property. Borrowings attributable to subsidized energy financing are directly applied to reduce the qualified investment in energy property. The reason is that subsidized energy loans, *e.g.*, loans granted pursuant to the Energy Security Act (Pub. L. 96-294, 94 Stat. 611), have legal restraints on the use of loans by taxpayers. For example, under section 509(a)(1)(B)(ii) of that Act, proceeds must be used to acquire a specific type of energy property, *i.e.*, solar energy systems. On the other hand, the proceeds of exempt IDB's are ratably allocated between energy property and other property and then, once the allocation is made, the qualified investment in the energy property is reduced by the portion of exempt IDB financing attributed to the energy property.

The reason for this ratable allocation approach is to prevent tax avoidance. In general, proceeds from exempt IDB's can be applied to all property in facility regardless of the mix of energy property or other property. In the absence of a ratable allocation rule, taxpayers in order to preserve the energy credit might attempt to allocate the proceeds first to non-energy property and only then, if any proceeds remain, to energy property.

COMMENTS AND REQUESTS FOR A PUBLIC HEARING

Before adopting these proposed regulations, consideration will be given to any written comments that are submitted (preferably six copies) to the Commissioner of Internal Revenue. All comments will be available for public inspection and copying. A public hearing will be held upon written request to the Commissioner by any person who has submitted written comments. If a public hearing is held, notice of the time and place will be published in the FEDERAL REGISTER.

REGULATORY FLEXIBILITY ACT

Although this document is a notice of proposed rulemaking which solicits public comment, the Internal Revenue Service has concluded that the regulations proposed herein are interpretative and that the notice and public procedure requirements of 5 U.S.C. 553 do not apply. Accordingly, these proposed regulations do not constitute regulations subject to the Regulatory Flexibility Act (5 U.S.C. chapter 6).

DRAFTING INFORMATION

The principal author of these proposed regulations is Mary Frances Pearson of the Legislation and Regulations Division of the Office of Chief Counsel, Internal Revenue Service. However, personnel from other offices of the Internal Revenue Service and Treasury Department participated in developing the regulations, both on matters of substance and style.

[¶ 49,021]   **Proposed Regulations (LR-255-82),** published in the Federal Register on November 15, 1982.

Obligations of the United States: Registration requirement: Deduction of interest.—Reg. §§ 5f.103-1 and 5f.163-1, relating to registration requirements with respect to debt obligations, are proposed. When adopted, Reg. § 5f.103-1 would become Reg. § 1.103-8(a)(7) and Reg. § 5f.163-1 would become Reg. § 1.163-5.

AGENCY: Internal Revenue Service, Treasury.

ACTION: Notice of proposed rulemaking by cross-reference to temporary regulations.

SUMMARY: In the Rules and Regulations portion of this FEDERAL REGISTER, the Internal Revenue Service is issuing temporary regulations that relate to registration requirements with respect to debt obligations. The text of those temporary regulations also serves as the comment document for this proposed rulemaking.

DATES: Written comments and requests to speak at the public hearing must be delivered by January 14, 1983. The regulations are proposed to be effective generally with respect to obligations issued after December 31, 1982.

ADDRESS: Send comments and requests to speak at the public hearing to: Commissioner of Internal Revenue, Attention: CC:LR:T (LR-255-82), Washington, D.C. 20224.

FOR FURTHER INFORMATION CONTACT: Diane L. Kroupa, Office of the Chief Counsel, Internal Revenue Service, 1111 Constitution Avenue, N.W., Washington, D.C. 20224 (Attention: CC:LR:T) (202-566-3590).

SUPPLEMENTARY INFORMATION:

BACKGROUND

The temporary regulations in the Rules and Regulations portion of this issue of the FEDERAL REGISTER add new part 5f to Title 26 of the Code of Federal Regulations. The final regulations, which this document proposes be based on those temporary regulations, would be added to Part 1 of

Title 26 of the Code of Federal Regulations. Section 5f.103-1 would become §1.103-8(a)(7), §5f.163-1 would become §1.163-5, and §§5f.103-1 and 5f.163-1 would be deleted.

GENERAL RULE

The regulations provide rules as to what obligations must be registered. The regulations define registration and provide rules for certain Federal tax consequences that will apply if obligations issued after December 31, 1982, are not issued in registered form. The regulations are necessary because of the additions made to sections 103 and 163 by the Tax Equity and Fiscal Responsibility Act of 1982 (Pub. L. 97-248, 96 Stat. 595). These regulations are proposed to be issued under the authority contained in sections 103(j), 163(f), and 7805 of the Internal Revenue Code (96 Stat. 596; 26 U.S.C. 103(j); 96 Stat. 596, 26 U.S.C. 163(f); 68A Stat. 917, 26 U.S.C. 7805), and in section 310 of the Tax Equity and Fiscal Responsibility Act of 1982 (96 Stat. 595).

NON-APPLICABILITY OF EXECUTIVE ORDER 12291

The Commissioner has determined that this proposed regulation is not subject to review under Executive Order 12291 or the Treasury and OMB implementation of the Order dated April 28, 1982.

REGULATORY FLEXIBILITY ACT

Pursuant to 5 U.S.C. 605(b), the Secretary of the Treasury has certified that the requirements of the Regulatory Flexibility Act do not apply to this notice of proposed rulemaking as it will not have a significant economic impact on a substantial number of small entities. The impact of the requirement that debt obligations be issued in registered form on both small and large issuers is due to requirements imposed directly by the statute. In the areas in which the Service has been given significant discretion under the statute, the Service has exercised its discretion so as to minimize the potential impact while ensuring compliance with the statute. For example, the requirement of registration of an obligation will be satisfied where the owner of the obligation can be ascertained through a book entry system. The regulations are liberal in permitting the use of book entry registration, thereby reducing the cost to issuers of issuing obligations in registered form.

LIST OF SUBJECTS IN 26 CFR PART 1

Income taxes, Exemptions, Deductions, Tax Equity and Fiscal Responsibility Act of 1982.

COMMENTS AND REQUESTS FOR A PUBLIC HEARING

Before adopting these proposed regulations, consideration will be given to any written comments that are submitted (preferably seven copies) to the Commissioner of Internal Revenue. All comments will be available for public inspection and copying. Notice of the time and place of the hearing appears in the notice of hearing section of this issue of the FEDERAL REGISTER.

[¶ 49,022]   Proposed Regulations and Proposed Amendments of Regulations (EE-99-78), published in the Federal Register on December 1, 1982.

Employees' trusts: Minimum funding requirements: Minimum funding excise taxes.—Reg. §§1.412(a)-1, 1.412(b)-1, 1.412(b)-4, 1.412(c)(2)-2, 1.412(c)(4)-1—1.412(c)(10)-1, 1.412(g)-1, and 54.4971-2—54.4971-3, amendments of Reg. §§1.413-1 and 1.413-2, and the deletions of Reg. §§11.412(c)-7, 11.412(c)-11, and 11.412(c)-12, relating to the minimum funding requirements for employee pension benefit plans, and to excise taxes for failure to meet the minimum funding standards, are proposed.

AGENCY: Internal Revenue Service, Treasury.

ACTION: Notice of proposed rulemaking.

SUMMARY: This document contains proposed regulations relating to the minimum funding requirements for employee pension benefit plans, and to excise taxes for failure to meet the minimum funding standards. Changes to the applicable tax law were made by the Employee Retirement Income Security Act of 1974. The regulations would provide the public with guidance needed to comply with that Act and would affect all pension plans subject to the provisions of the Act.

DATES: Written comments and requests for public hearing must be delivered or mailed by January 28, 1983. The proposed amendments would apply generally for plan years beginning after 1975, but earlier (or later) in the case of some plans as provided for meeting the minimum funding requirements under the Act. The proposed rules pertaining to the frequency of actuarial valuations, and to the time for making contributions, generally would not be effective prior to the publication of final regulations.

ADDRESS: Send comments and requests for a public hearing to: Commissioner of Internal Revenue, Attention: CC:LR:T (EE-99-78), Washington, D.C. 20224.

FOR FURTHER INFORMATION CONTACT: Eric A. Raps of the Employee Plans and Exempt Organizations Division, Office of the Chief Counsel, Internal Revenue Service, 1111 Constitution Avenue, N.W., Washington, D.C. 20224 (Attention: CC:LR:T) (202-566-6212, not a toll-free call).

SUPPLEMENTARY INFORMATION:

BACKGROUND

This document contains proposed amendments to the Income Tax Regulations (26 CFR Part 1) under section 412 of the Internal Revenue Code of 1954. These amendments are proposed to conform the regulations to section 1013(a) of the Employee Retirement Income Security Act of 1974 (ERISA) (88 Stat. 914). The proposed amendments would also apply for purposes of sections 302 and 305 of ERISA (88 Stat. 869, 873).

The proposed amendments would be issued under the authority of section 302(b)(4), (b)(5), (c)(2)(B), (c)(9) and (c)(10) of ERISA (88 Stat. 870, 871, and 872; 29 U.S.C. 1082) and sections 412(b)(4), (b)(5), (c)(2)(B), (c)(9) and (c)(10) and 7805 of the Internal Revenue Code of 1954 (88 Stat. 915, 916, and 917; 68A Stat. 917; 26 U.S.C. 412(b)(4), (b)(5), (c)(2)(B), (c)(9), and (c)(10) and 7805).

This document also contains proposed amendments to the Income Tax Regulations (26 CFR Part 1) and the Pension Excise Tax Regulations (26 CFR Part 54) under section 413(b)(6) and (c)(5) and section 4971 of the Internal Revenue Code of 1954. These regulations are proposed primarily to conform the regulations to section 1013(b) of the Employee Retirement Income Security Act of 1974 (ERISA) (88 Stat. 920). They are to be issued under the authority of section 413(b)(6) and (c)(5) and section 7805 of the Internal Revenue Code of 1954 (88 Stat. 924, 925, 68A Stat. 917; 26 U.S.C. 413(b)(6) and (c)(5), 7805).

The proposed regulations do not reflect changes to the second-level excise tax made by the Act of Dec. 24, 1980, Pub. L. 96-596 (94 Stat. 3469), or amendments to sections 412 and 4971 made by the Multiemployer Pension Plan Amendments Act of 1980, Pub. L. 96-364 (94 Stat. 1208).

PURPOSE AND SCOPE

The proposed amendments address the remaining statutory provisions not yet addressed by regulations relating to the minimum funding requirements with respect to which either regulatory guidance is required by law or interpretative assistance would be helpful in applying the law. These proposed amendments, together with proposed or final regulations previously issued under section 412 of the Code, generally constitute the regulatory guidance to be provided with respect to the minimum funding requirements, with the exception of rules relating to mergers. However, comments noting additional issues with respect to which regulatory guidance might be helpful will be considered along with comments addressing issues that arise under the proposed amendments.

The provisions under section 4971 of the Code contain sanctions for enforcing the minimum funding requirements. The sanctions are two excise taxes. The initial tax is 5 percent of an accumulated funding deficiency, and an additional tax of 100 percent is imposed if the deficiency is not corrected. Generally, the employer responsible for contributing to the plan is liable for these taxes.

Section 3002(b) of ERISA provides special rules regarding the section 4971 taxes and coordination of matters regarding these taxes with the Secretary of Labor.

FUNDING STANDARD ACCOUNT

Under section 412(b) of the Code, a plan must maintain a funding standard account. The mechanics for reflecting charges and credits to the account appear in section 412(b)(2) and (3). The proposed amendments address a number of key issues arising under the funding standard account provisions.

MONEY PURCHASE PLANS

Under the proposed amendments, a money purchase pension plan is, like other plans, required to maintain a funding standard account. However, the accounting under such a plan for funding purposes is limited to charges for the contribution required under the formula provided by the plan, credits for amounts actually contributed, and charges and credits to amortize certain bases.

Normally, the need to create an amortization base does not exist under a money purchase plan. However, such a base would be created, for example, with the issuance of a waiver of the minimum funding standard for a plan.

COMBINING AND OFFSETTING

The proposed amendments would provide rules, as required under section 412(b)(4) of the Code, for combining and offsetting amortization amounts determined under the funding standard account. The proposed method for combining and offsetting these amounts is described in the legislative history of ERISA. (See H.R. Rep. No. 93-807, 93d Cong., 2d Sess. 86-87 (1974), 1974-3 C.B. Supp. 321-322.)

TREATMENT OF INTEREST

The proposed amendments would provide rules, as required by section 412(b)(5) of the Code, for treating interest charges and credits under the funding standard account.

Generally under the proposed amendments, charges and credits are made as of an assumed accounting date under the plan. There must be an interest charge or credit, as the case may be, for the period between this assumed date and the end of the plan year.

A contribution made during the "grace period" between the last day of a plan year and the day determined under section 412(c)(10) is treated as having been made on the last day of the plan year.

RETROACTIVE CHANGES

The proposed amendments provide for reflecting in the funding standard account retroactive changes required by the Commissioner to adjust for the use of unreasonable assumptions or funding methods.

PLAN TERMINATION

The proposed amendments relating to the effect of plan termination on the funding standard account are substantially identical to the provisions of Rev. Rul. 79-237, 1979-2 C.B. 190.

BOND VALUATION ELECTION

The proposed amendments would provide rules, as required by section 412(c)(2)(B) of the Code, for the election of a special valuation rule applicable to bonds and other evidences of indebtedness. The proposed amendments would be substantially identical to temporary regulations published in 1974 with respect to the bond valuation election. However, the proposed amendments would clarify the temporary rules by providing that certain convertible debt instruments are treated as debt until converted into equity securities. The rules concerning valuation of convertible debt would be effective only for debt instruments acquired after the date on which the proposal is adopted as a final regulation. For debt instruments acquired before that date, a valuation method will be considered acceptable if it is applied on a consistent basis.

ACTUARIAL VALUATION

The proposed amendments would provide rules, as required by section 412(c)(9) of the Code, relating to the frequency of actuarial valuations for plans. These rules would identify situations in which valuations may be required more frequently than once every 3 years. Comments are requested as to the appropriateness of requiring more frequent valuations under the situations described in the proposed amendments. Comments are also requested as to any additional circumstances where valuations should be required more frequently than once every 3 years. The rules also would describe how the funding standard account is to be maintained for years when there is no valuation.

TIMING OF CONTRIBUTIONS

The proposed amendments would provide rules, as required by section 412(c)(10) of the Code, relating to the time for making contributions for purposes of section 412. Unlike the temporary regulations published in 1976, these rules would not contain an automatic six-month extension of the two and one-half month grace period set forth as a general rule under the statute for meeting the minimum funding requirements. The Commissioner may approve applications for an extension of the grace period of up to six months. This more restrictive approach would be applied prospectively from a date after the publication of final regulations. However, a transitional rule is provided to phase in the two and one-half month period over the first three plan years following a date after publication of final regulations, and extensions may be approved by the Commissioner.

ALTERNATIVE FUNDING STANDARD ACCOUNT

The proposed amendments contain rules that would apply to plans maintaining the alternative minimum funding standard account. These rules would reflect section 412(g)(1) by limiting the use of the alternative account to plans using a funding method that requires contributions in all years at least equal to those required under the entry age normal funding method. Thus, only plans that use the entry age normal funding method may use the alternative account.

ALLOCATION OF EXCISE TAX LIABILITY

The proposed amendments would contain rules to allocate excise tax liability under section 4971 of more than one employer, but they would permit allocation in a reasonable manner that is not inconsistent with the rules provided.

Under the proposed amendments, the tax liability of each employer would generally be based on the obligation of each employer to contribute to the plan. To the extent that a funding deficiency would be attributable to the delinquent contribution of an individual employer, that employer would be liable for the tax. To the extent that a funding deficiency is not attributable to a delinquent contribution, each employer would share liability in proportion to its share of required contributions to the plan.

ALLOCATIONS FOR RELATED EMPLOYERS

The general rules for allocating tax liability would not apply to certain related employers. To the extent that an accumulated funding deficiency is attributable to related employers, those employers would be jointly and severally liable for the excise tax with respect to that deficiency. This rule would apply to related employers maintaining a plan of their own or in conjunction with other employers.

EMPLOYER WITHDRAWAL

The proposed amendments would generally provide that an employer withdrawing from a plan remains liable for tax imposed with respect to the portion of an accumulated funding deficiency attributable to that employer for years before withdrawal. The remaining employers would be liable for the tax attributable to the accumulated funding deficiency for years after an employer's withdrawal, even if the deficiency is attributable to prior years.

TEMPORARY REGULATIONS SUPERSEDED

The proposed amendments contain rules that would supersede the following temporary regulations: § 11.412(c)-7, relating to the election to treat certain retroactive plan amendments as made on the first day of the plan year; § 11.412(c)-11, relating to the election with respect to bonds; and § 11.412(c)-12, relating to the extension of time to make contributions to satisfy requirements of section 412.

EXECUTIVE ORDER 12291 AND REGULATORY FLEXIBILITY ACT

The Commissioner of Internal Revenue has determined that this proposed regulation is not a major regulation for purposes of Executive Order 12291. Accordingly, a regulatory impact analysis is not required.

Although this document is a notice of proposed rulemaking which solicits public comments, the Internal Revenue Service has concluded that the regulations proposed herein are interpretative and that the notice and public procedure requirements of 5 U.S.C. 553 do not apply. Accordingly, these proposed regulations do not constitute regulations subject to the Regulatory Flexibility Act (5 U.S.C. chapter 6).

COMMENTS AND REQUESTS FOR A PUBLIC HEARING

Before adopting these proposed regulations, consideration will be given to any written comments that are submitted (preferably eight copies) to the Commissioner of Internal Revenue. It is requested that persons submitting comments use professional letterhead stationery only if the comment represents the position of the firm or a named client, rather than the views of the writer. All comments are available for public inspection and copying. A public hearing will be held upon written request to the Commission by any person who has submitted written comments. If a public hearing is held, notice of the time and place will be published in the Federal Register.

DRAFTING INFORMATION

The principal author of these proposed regulations is Joe E. Horowitz of the Employee Plans and Exempt Organizations Division of the Office of Chief Counsel, Internal Revenue Service. However, personnel from other offices of the Internal Revenue Service and Treasury Department participated in developing the regulations, both on matters of substance and style.

[¶ 49,023]   Proposed Regulations (LR-1-83), published in the Federal Register on January 26, 1983.

Subchapter S corporations: Elections, consents and refusals.—Reg. §§ 18.0, 18.1379-1 and 18.1379-2, relating to the time and manner of making certain elections, consents, and refusals under the Subchapter S Revision Act of 1982, are proposed. Reg. §§ 18.1362-1—18.1362-4 were removed 11/24/92 by T.D. 8449. Reg. § 18.1361-1 was removed 7/20/95 by T.D. 8600. Reg. § 18.1377-1 was removed 12/20/96 by T.D. 8696. Reg. § 18.1378-1 was removed 5/16/2002 by T.D. 8996.

AGENCY: Internal Revenue Service, Treasury.

ACTION: Notice of proposed rulemaking.

SUMMARY: In the Rules and Regulations section of this FEDERAL REGISTER, the Internal Revenue Service is issuing temporary regulations relating to (1) the time and manner of making certain elections, consents, and refusals under the Subchapter S Revision Act of 1982 and (2) the taxable year which a corporation may select in order to make the election to be an S corporation. The text of those temporary regulations also serves as the common document for this proposed rulemaking.

DATES: Written comments and requests for a public hearing must be delivered by March 28, 1983. The proposed regulations are proposed to have the same effective dates as the temporary regulations.

ADDRESS: Send comments and requests for a public hearing to: Commissioner of Internal Revenue, Attention: CC:LR:T (LR-1-83), Washington, D.C. 20224.

FOR FURTHER INFORMATION CONTACT: Robert H. Ginsburgh of the Legislation and Regulations Division, Office of Chief Counsel, Internal Revenue Service, 1111 Constitution Avenue, N.W., Washington, D.C. 20224 (Attention: CC:LR:T) (202-566-3297).

SUPPLEMENTARY INFORMATION: The temporary regulation in the Rules and Regulations section of this issue of the Federal Register retitles and revises 26 CFR Part 18. The final regulations which are proposed to be based on that temporary regulation would amend 26 CFR Part 1.

For the text of the temporary regulation, see FR Doc —(T.D.—) published in the Rules and Regulations section of this issue of the *FEDERAL REGISTER.*

COMMENTS AND REQUESTS FOR A PUBLIC HEARING

Before adopting these proposed regulations, consideration will be given to any written comments that are submitted (preferably six copies) to the Commissioner of Internal Revenue. All comments will be available for public inspection and copying. A public hearing will be held upon written request of any person who has submitted written comments. If a public hearing is held, notice of the time and place will be published in the *FEDERAL REGISTER.*

SPECIAL ANALYSES

The Commissioner of Internal Revenue has determined that this proposed regulation is not subject to review under Executive Order 12291 or the Treasury and OMB implementation of the Order dated April 28, 1980. Accordingly, a Regulatory Impact Analysis is not required.

Although this document is a notice of proposed rulemaking which solicits public comment, the Internal Revenue Service has concluded that the regulations proposed herein are interpretative and that the notice and public procedure requirements of 5 U.S.C. 553 do not apply. Accordingly, these proposed regulations do not constitute regulations subject to the Regulatory Flexibility Act (5 U.S.C. chapter 6).

[¶ 49,024] **Proposed Amendment of Regulation (LR-254-81),** published in the Federal Register on February 10, 1983.

Inventories: Last-in, first-out rule: Increase in value: Three-year averaging method.—Amendment of Reg. § 1.472-2, relating to three-year averaging for increases in inventory value, is proposed.

AGENCY: Internal Revenue Service, Treasury.

ACTION: Notice of proposed rulemaking.

SUMMARY: This document contains proposed regulations under section 472 of the Code relating to 3-year averaging for increases in inventory value. Changes in the applicable tax law were made by the Economic Recovery Tax Act of 1981. These regulations would provide the public with guidance needed to comply with the act and would affect taxpayers first adopting the LIFO inventory method for taxable years beginning after December 31, 1981.

DATES: Written comments and requests for a public hearing must be delivered or mailed by April 11, 1983. The amendments are proposed to be effective with respect to taxable years beginning after December 31, 1981.

ADDRESS: Send comments and requests for a public hearing to: Commissioner of Internal Revenue, Attention: CC:LR:T, (LR-254-81), Washington, D.C. 20224.

FOR FURTHER INFORMATION CONTACT: Mr. Gregory A. Roth of the Legislation and Regulations Division, Office of Chief Counsel, Internal Revenue Service, 1111 Constitution Avenue, N.W., Washington, D.C. 20224 (Attention: CC:LR:T) (202-566-3238, not a toll-free number).

SUPPLEMENTARY INFORMATION:

BACKGROUND

This document contains proposed amendments to the Income Tax Regulations (26 CFR Part 1) under section 472(d) of the Internal Revenue Code of 1954. These amendments are proposed to conform the regulations to section 236 of the Economic Recovery Tax Act of 1981 (95 Stat. 172) and are to be issued under the authority contained in sections 472(d) and 7805 of the Internal Revenue Code of 1954 (26 U.S.C. 472(d) and 7805).

INVENTORY VALUATION

Section 472(d) requires opening inventory of the taxable year for which the LIFO method is first used to be valued at cost. Restoration shall be made with respect to any writedown to market values resulting from the pricing of former inventories. Such restoration amount shall be taken into account ratably in each of the three taxable years beginning with the first taxable year for which the LIFO method is used.

COMMENTS AND REQUESTS FOR A PUBLIC HEARING

Before adopting these proposed regulations consideration will be given to any written comments that are submitted (preferably six copies) to the Commissioner of Internal Revenue. All comments will be available for public inspection and copying. A public hearing will be held on written request to the Commissioner by any person who has submitted written comments. If a public hearing is held, notice of the time and place will be published in the *FEDERAL REGISTER.*

SPECIAL ANALYSES

The Commissioner of Internal Revenue has determined that this proposed rule is not a major rule as defined in Executive Order 12291. Accordingly a Regulatory Impact Analysis is not required. Although this document is a notice of proposed rulemaking that solicits public comment, the Internal Revenue Service has concluded that the notice and public procedure requirements of 5 U.S.C. 553 do not apply because the rules proposed are interpretative. Accordingly, a Regulatory Flexibility Analysis is not required.

DRAFTING INFORMATION

The principal author of these proposed regulations is Gregory A. Roth of the Legislation and Regulations Division of the Office of Chief Counsel, Internal Revenue Service. However, personnel from other offices of the Internal Revenue Service and Treasury Department participated in developing the regulations, both on matters of substance and style.

[¶ 49,025] **Proposed Regulations and Amendments (EE-3-81),** published in the Federal Register on February 25, 1983.

Employees' trusts: Affiliated service groups.—Reg. §§ 1.414(m)-1—1.414(m)-4 and amendments of Reg. § 1.105-11, which prescribe rules for determining whether two or more separate service organizations constitute an affiliated group and which detail how certain requirements are satisfied by a qualified retirement plan maintained by a member of an affiliated service group, are proposed. Reg. § 1.415-8 was removed 4/4/2007 by T.D. 9319.

AGENCY: Internal Revenue Service, Treasury.

ACTION: Notice of proposed rulemaking.

SUMMARY: This document contains proposed regulations prescribing rules for determining whether two or more separate service organizations constitute an affiliated service group, and detailing how certain requirements are satisfied by a qualified retirement plan maintained by a member of an affiliated service group. Changes to the applicable tax law were made by the Miscellaneous Revenue Act of 1980. The regulations would provide the public with additional guidance needed to comply with that Act and would affect all employers that maintain qualified retirement plans and that are members of an affiliated service group.

DATES: Written comments and requests for a public hearing must be delivered or mailed by April 26, 1983. For plans that were not in existence on November 30, 1980, the amendments are effective for plan years ending after that date. For plans in existence on November 30, 1980, the amendments are effective for plan years beginning after that date.

ADDRESS: Send comments and requests for a public hearing to: Commissioner of Internal Revenue, Attention: CC:LR:T (EE-3-81), Washington, D.C. 20224.

FOR FURTHER INFORMATION CONTACT: Patricia K. Keesler of the Employee Plans and Exempt Organizations Division, Office of Chief Counsel, Internal Revenue Service, 1111 Constitution Avenue, N.W., Washington, D.C. 20224 (Attention: CC:LR:T) (202/566-3430) (not a toll-free number).

SUPPLEMENTARY INFORMATION:

BACKGROUND

This document contains proposed amendments to the Income Tax Regulations (26 CFR Part 1) under section 414(m) of the Internal Revenue Code of 1954. These amendments are proposed to conform the regulations to section 201 of the Miscellaneous Revenue Act of 1980 (94 Stat. 3526) and section 5 of Public Law 96-613 (94 Stat. 3580). These regulations do not reflect amendments made to section 414(m) under the Tax Equity and Fiscal Responsibility Act of 1982. These regulations are to be issued under the authority contained in section 414(m) and in section 7805 of the Internal Revenue Code of 1954 (94 Stat. 3526, 94 Stat. 3580, 68A Stat. 917; 26 U.S.C. 414(m), 7805).

STATUTORY PROVISIONS

Section 414(m)(1) of the Code provides that, for purposes of certain employee benefit requirements listed in section 414(m)(4), except to the extent otherwise provided in regulations, all employees of the members of an affiliated service group shall be treated as employed by a single employer.

Section 414(m)(2) defines an affiliated service group as a First Service Organization and one or more of the following: (A) any service organization (A Organization) that is a shareholder or partner in the First Service Organization and that regularly performs services for the First Service Organization or is regularly associated with the First Service Organization in performing services for third persons; and (B) any other organization (B Organization) if a significant portion of the business of that organization is the performance of services for the First Service Organization, for A Organizations, or both, of a type historically performed by employees in the service field of the First Service Organization or the A Organizations, and ten percent or more of the interests in the organization is held by persons who are officers, highly compensated employees, or owners of the First Service Organization or of the A Organizations.

Section 414(m)(3) defines a service organization as an organization the principal business of which is the performance of services.

Section 414(m)(5)(A) provides that the term "organization" means a corporation, partnership, or other organization. Section 414(m)(5)(B) provides that the principles of section 267(c) apply in determining ownership.

Section 414(m)(6) provides that the Secretary of the Treasury or his delegate shall prescribe such regulations as may be necessary to prevent the avoidance of the employee benefit requirements listed in section 414(m)(4) through the use of separate service organizations.

PRIOR GUIDELINES

Initial guidelines under section 414(m) were set forth in Revenue Ruling 81-105, 1981-1 C.B. 256. Rev. Rul. 81-105 provided illustrations of how the provisions of section 414(m) operate by way of three examples. The rules set forth in Rev. Rul. 81-105 remain operative and are not affected by the promulgation of these proposed regulations.

Revenue Procedure 81-12, 1981-1 C.B. 652, prescribes procedures for (1) obtaining a ruling on whether two or more organizations are members of an affiliated service group, and (2) obtaining determination letters on the qualification, under section 401(a) or 403(a), of an employees' pension, profit-sharing, stock bonus, annuity, or bond purchase plan established by a member of an affiliated service group.

ADMINISTRATIVE EXEMPTIONS

Several parties have expressed concern that aggregation may be required under the rules of section 414(m)(2)(A) and (B) in situations where there has been no attempt to avoid the employee benefit requirements listed in section 414(m)(4).

Those parties noted that an organization qualifies as an A Organization whenever it is a shareholder or partner in the First Service Organization and regularly performs services for the First Service Organization or is regularly associated with the First Service Organization in performing services for third persons. Thus, aggregation will be required regardless of how small the interest is that the A Organization holds in the First Service Organization, irrespective of whether the services performed by the A Organization are of a type historically performed by employees in the service field of the First Service Organization, and even if the services performed for the First Service Organization only constitute an insignificant portion of the business of the A Organization.

However, section 414(m)(1) grants authority to promulgate regulations that specify when all the employees of an affiliated service group will not be treated as employed by a single employer. Accordingly, proposed Treasury Regulation § 1.414(m)-1(c) provides that a corporation, other than a professional service corporation, will not be treated as a First Service Organization for purposes of section 414(m)(2)(A). Professional service corporations are not excepted from treatment as First Service Organizations for purposes of section 414(m)(2)(A) because the legislative history indicates that such corporations were intended to be covered. A special definition of professional service corporations is provided in the proposed regulation.

A corporation will still be treated as a First Service Organization for purposes of section 414(m)(2)(B). Thus, two corporations, neither of which is a professional service organization, will be aggregated only if one of the corporations satisfies the more stringent tests to be classified as a B Organization.

However, the Commissioner may determine that, in practice, the exception in the A Organization test for corporations, other than professional service corporations, results in an avoidance of the requirements of section 414(m) that circumvents Congressional intent. If such avoidance is found in a significant number of cases, this exception may be removed from the regulations.

Similarly, several parties have mentioned that aggregation may be required under section 414(m)(2)(B) whenever the owner of the potential B Organization acquires an interest in the First Service Organization (or in an A Organization), even though this interest is minimal and even though the owner does not have any other significant connection with the First Service Organization (*i.e.,* the owner is not an officer or highly compensated employee of the First Service Organization).

Pursuant to the authority contained in section 414(m)(1), a special rule is provided for determining whether ten percent or more of the interests in the potential B Organization is held by officers, highly compensated employees, or owners of the First Service Organization (or of an A Organization). For this purpose, the interests held by persons who are owners of the First Service Organization and the B Organization (but who are not also officers or highly compensated employees of the First Service Organization), will be taken into account as owners of the First Service Organization only if they hold, in the aggregate, three percent or more of the interests in such First Service Organization.

There may be other situations, not covered by the special rules of the regulations, where aggregation should not be required although the organizations are described in the literal language of either section 414(m)(2)(A) or (B). Comments are solicited from the public as to what these rules should be.

SIGNIFICANT PORTION

Proposed Treasury Regulation § 1.414(m)-2(c)(2) provides that the determination of whether providing services for the First Service Organization, for one or more A Organizations determined with respect to the First Service Organization, or for both, is a significant portion of the business of the potential B Organization will generally be based on the facts and circumstances. However, two specific rules are provided.

A safe harbor rule is provided under which the performance of services for the First Service Organization, for one or more A Organizations, or for both, will not be considered a significant portion of the business of a potential B Organization if the Service Receipts Percentage is less than five percent. The Service Receipts Percentage is the ratio of the gross receipts of the organization derived from performing services for the First Service Organization, for one or more A Organizations, or for both, to the total gross receipts of the organization derived from performing services. This ratio is the greater of the ratio for the year for which the determination is being made or for the three year period including that year and the two preceding years (or the period of existence of the organization, if less).

Except for a situation described in the preceding paragraph, the performance of services for the First Service Organization, for one or more A Organizations, or for both, will be considered a significant portion of the business of the potential B Organization if the Total Receipts Percentage is ten percent or more. The Total Receipts Percentage is calculated in the same manner as the Service Receipts Percentage, except that gross receipts in the denominator are determined without regard to whether they were derived from performing services.

Comments from the public are requested regarding these significant portion tests.

HISTORICALLY PERFORMED

Proposed Treasury Regulation § 1.414(m)-2(c)(3) provides that services will be considered of a type historically performed by employees in a particular service field if it was not unusual for the services to be performed by employees of organizations in that service field in the United States on December 13, 1980 (the date of enactment of section 414(m)).

CONSTRUCTIVE OWNERSHIP

Proposed Treasury Regulation § 1.414(m)-2(d)(2) provides that in determining ownership for purposes of section 414(m), an individual's interest under a plan that qualifies under section 401(a) will be taken into account. Comments from the public are requested concerning the appropriateness of this rule in cases in which the investment in employer securities by the plan results from an independent decision of the plan trustee.

ORGANIZATION

Proposed Treasury Regulation § 1.414(m)-2(e) provides that the term "organization" includes a sole proprietorship. The proposed regulations do not consider the impact of sections 414(b) (controlled group of corporations) or 414(c) (group of trades or businesses under common control) on the definition of "organization" in § 1.414(m)-2(e)(1). Specifically, the regulations do not consider the situation in which a particular organization is potentially part of both an affiliated service group and either a controlled group of corporations or a group of trades or businesses under common control. In such a situation, issues arise as to the order in which the determinations are made as to what constitutes a single employer. For example, whereas an individual corporation may be a service organization, the controlled group of which that corporation is a part may not be a service organization (or vice versa). Comments from the public are requested regarding the treatment of a controlled group of corporations or a group of trades or businesses under common control in this respect.

SERVICE ORGANIZATION

Proposed Treasury Regulation § 1.414(m)-2(f) provides that the principal business of an organization will be considered the performance of services if capital is not a material income-producing factor for the organization. The test for determining whether or not capital is a material income-producing factor is similar to the test in Treasury Regulation § 1.1348-3(a)(3)(ii), as in effect on February 25, 1983.

Numerous fields are listed in proposed Treasury Regulation § 1.414(m)-2(f) as being service fields. Organizations engaged in a field not listed therein and in which capital is a material income-producing factor will not be considered to be service organizations until the first day of the first plan year beginning at least 180 days after the date of the publication of an official document (such as a revenue ruling) giving notice to the contrary. The Commissioner of Internal Revenue is granted authority to determine that certain organizations, or types of organizations, should not be considered as being subject to the requirements of section 414(m) even though the organizations are engaged in a field listed in the proposed regulation. Comments are requested from the public as to examples of organizations that should or should not be considered as being service organizations subject to the provisions of section 414(m).

MULTIPLE AFFILIATED SERVICE GROUPS

Proposed Treasury Regulation § 1.414(m)-2(g) provides rules for multiple affiliated service groups. Two or more affiliated service groups will not be aggregated simply because an organization is an A Organization or a B Organization with respect to each affiliated service group. However, if an organization is a First Service Organization with respect to two or more A Organizations or two or more B Organizations, or both, all of the organizations will be considered to constitute a single affiliated service group.

SPECIAL QUALIFICATION REQUIREMENTS

Pursuant to the authority granted in section 414(m)(6), proposed Treasury Regulation § 1.414(m)-3(b) provides that if a plan maintained by a member of an affiliated service group covers an employee described in section 401(c)(1) (self-employed individual), an owner-employee (as described in section 401(c)(3)), or a shareholder-employee (as described in section 1379(d)) the plan must also satisfy the special requirements relating to plans that cover those types of employees, to the extent those requirements apply, even though that individual is not employed by the member maintaining the plan. This provision only applies if such an employee's earned income or compensation received as a shareholder-employee is taken into account in computing contributions or benefits under the plan.

MULTIPLE EMPLOYER PLANS

Proposed Treasury Regulation § 1.414(m)-3(c) provides that if a plan maintained by a member of an affiliated service group covers an individual who is not an employee of that member, but who is an employee of another member of that affiliated service group, the plan will be considered to be maintained by more than one employer for purposes of several provisions of section 413(c) (relating to plans maintained by more than one employer). This rule allows a member of the affiliated service group to deduct contributions on behalf of individuals who are not employed by that member.

However, this multiple employer plan rule does not apply in the case of a controlled group of corporations (as described in section 414(b)) or a group of trades or businesses under common control (as described in section 414(c)). Those situations will be governed by the special rules of section 414(b) or (c), respectively.

DISCRIMINATION

Proposed Treasury Regulation § 1.414(m)-3(d) provides that in testing for discrimination under section 401(a)(4) (requiring that contributions or benefits do not discriminate in favor of employees who are officers, shareholders, or highly compensated), all of the compensation paid to an individual must be considered in determining the contributions or benefits on behalf of the individual under a plan maintained by a member of an affiliated service group, without regard to the percentage of the organization employing the individual owned by the member maintaining the plan.

EFFECTIVE DATES

In the case of a plan that was not in existence on November 30, 1980, section 414(m) applies to plan years ending after that date. In the case of a plan that was in existence on November 30, 1980, section 414(m) applies to plan years beginning after that date.

Proposed Treasury Regulation § 1.414(m)-4(b)(1) provides that a defined contribution plan in existence on November 30, 1980 that fails to satisfy the requirements for qualification under section 401(a) solely because of the application of section 414(m) will be treated as continuing to satisfy the requirements of section 401(a) after the effective date of section 414(m) if the plan is terminated and all amounts are distributed to participants within 180 days after the latest of:

(i) [insert the date of the publication of this regulation in the Federal Register as a Treasury decision],

(ii) The date on which notice of the final determination with respect to a request for a determination letter is issued by the Internal Revenue Service, such request is withdrawn, or such request is finally disposed of by the Internal Revenue Service, provided the request for a determination letter was pending on [insert the date of the publication of this regulation in the Federal Register as a Treasury decision] or, in the case of a request for a determination letter on the plan termination, was made within 60 days after [insert the date of the publication of this regulation in the Federal Register as a Treasury decision], or

(iii) If a petition is timely filed with the United States Tax Court for a declaratory judgment under section 7476 with respect to the final determination (or the failure of the Internal Revenue Service to make a final determination) in response to such request, the date on which the decision of the United States Tax Court in such proceeding becomes final.

Proposed Treasury Regulation § 1.414(m)-4(b)(2) provides that a defined benefit plan in existence on November 30, 1980 that fails to satisfy the requirements for qualification under section 401(a) solely because of the application of section 414(m) will be treated as continuing to satisfy the requirements of section 401(a) after the effective date of section 414(m) if the plan is terminated and all amounts are distributed within the same period as that provided for defined contribution plans. However, deductions for contributions to the plan for plan years after the effective date of section 414(m) are limited to those necessary to satisfy the minimum funding standards of section 412.

RELIANCE ON PROPOSED REGULATIONS

Pending the adoption of final regulations, taxpayers may rely on the rules contained in this notice of proposed rulemaking and the Internal Revenue Service will issue determination, opinion, and ruling letters based on these rules. If any provisions of the final regulations are less favorable to taxpayers than these proposed rules, those provisions only will be effective for periods after adoption of the final regulations.

COMMENTS AND REQUESTS FOR A PUBLIC HEARING

Before adopting these proposed regulations, consideration will be given to any written comments that are submitted (preferably six copies) to the Commissioner of Internal Revenue. All comments will be available for public inspection and copying. A public hearing will be held upon written request to the Commissioner by any person who has submitted written comments. If a public hearing is held, notice of the time and place will be published in the FEDERAL REGISTER.

EXECUTIVE ORDER 12291 AND

REGULATORY FLEXIBILITY ACT

The Commissioner has determined that this proposed regulation is not a major regulation for purposes of Executive Order 12291. Accordingly, a regulatory impact analysis is not required.

Although this document is a notice of proposed rulemaking which solicits public comments, the Internal Revenue Service has concluded that the regulations proposed herein are interpretative and that the notice and public procedure requirements of 5 U.S.C. 553 do not apply. Accordingly, these proposed regulations do not constitute regulations subject to the Regulatory Flexibility Act (5 U.S.C. chapter 6).

DRAFTING INFORMATION

The principal authors of these proposed regulations are Kirk F. Maldonado and Mary M. Levontin of the Employee Plans and Exempt Organizations Division of the Office of Chief Counsel, Internal Revenue Service. However, personnel from other offices of the Internal Revenue Service and Treasury Department participated in developing these regulations, both on matters of substance and style.

[¶ 49,026]   **Proposed Regulations (LR-188-82)**, published in the Federal Register on March 31, 1983.

Personal service corporations: Allocation of income and deductions.—Reg. § 1.269A-1, relating to the reallocation of income, deductions, credits, and exclusions between a personal service corporation and its employee-owners if the corporation was formed or availed of primarily to evade or avoid federal income taxes, is proposed.

AGENCY: Internal Revenue Service, Treasury.

ACTION: Notice of proposed rulemaking.

SUMMARY: This document provides proposed regulations relating to the reallocation of income, deductions, credits, and exclusions between a personal service corporation and its employee-owners if the corporation was formed or availed of primarily to evade or avoid Federal income taxes. Changes to the applicable tax law were made by section 250 of the Tax Equity and Fiscal Responsibility Act of 1982 (TEFRA), which added new section 269A to the Internal Revenue Code of 1954. These regulations would affect all employee-owners and their personal service corporations if the personal service corporation provides substantially all of its services for or on behalf of one other entity, but only if the corporation was formed or availed of primarily to evade or avoid Federal income taxes. These regulations would provide affected persons with the guidance to comply with the law.

DATES: Written comments and requests for a public hearing must be delivered or mailed by May 31, 1983. The regulations provided by this document are proposed to be generally effective for taxable years of personal service corporations beginning after December 31, 1982.

ADDRESS: Send comments and requests for a public hearing to: Commissioner of Internal Revenue, Attention: CC:LR:T (LR-188-82) Washington, D.C. 20224.

FOR FURTHER INFORMATION CONTACT: Phoebe A. Mix or Philip R. Bosco of Legislation and Regulations Division, Office of Chief Counsel, Internal Revenue Service, 1111 Constitution Avenue, N.W., Washington, D.C. 20224, Attention: CC:LR:T, (202) 566-3238, not a toll-free call.

SUPPLEMENTARY INFORMATION:

BACKGROUND

Section 269A was added to the Internal Revenue Code by the Tax Equity and Fiscal Responsibility Act of 1982. Section 269A permits the Secretary to allocate all income, deductions, credits, exclusions, and other tax benefits between a personal service corporation and its employee-owners in order to prevent the avoidance or evasion of Federal income taxes or to reflect clearly the income of the personal service corporation or any of its employee-owners if substantially all of the services are performed for one other entity and if the principal purpose for forming, or availing of, the corporation is the avoidance or evasion of Federal income taxes. Avoidance or evasion of Federal income taxes may be either the reduction of income of an employee-owner through the use of the corporation or the securing of one or more tax benefits that would not otherwise be available. These regulations define benefits that would not otherwise be available as benefits that would not be available to a taxpayer providing services as an unincorporated individual.

These regulations also provide a safe-harbor, excluding from the application of section 269A those situations in which the Federal income tax liability of each employee-owner is reduced by not more than 10 percent or $2,500, whichever is less.

Prior to "parity" between qualified retirement plans of corporations and those of noncorporate employers (effective generally for taxable years beginning after December 31, 1983), an employee-owner can make larger contributions to a corporate qualified retirement plan than could have been made to a Keogh or H.R. 10 plan had the corporation not been in existence. For corporations in existence before the date of enactment of TEFRA (September 3, 1982), qualified retirement plans available to corporations generally will not be taken into account for purposes of determining the corporation's principal purpose. Thus, a corporation created principally to take advantage of the higher contributions to corporate plans may still have an impermissible purpose if its principal purpose (other than qualified retirement plan benefit) was to reduce income or secure one or more tax benefits. If a corporation is found to have an impermissible principal purpose, the contributions to the qualified retirement plan will neither be reallocated to the employee-owner nor reduced as a result of reallocation of other income to the employee-owner. For corporations formed after the date of enactment of TEFRA, this protection is not available for contributions or benefits that would not have been available to the employee-owner absent the corporation. In that case, contributions to a qualified retirement plan will be considered in determining the corporation's principal purpose and may be reallocated or reduced through application of section 269A.

Section 269A does not override other sections of the Code or existing tax law principles. Nothing in these regulations, including the safe-harbor provision, precludes application of any other Code section (e.g., sections 61 or 482) or principle of tax law (e.g., assignment of income doctrine) to reallocate or reapportion income, deductions, credits or any other tax benefits if such reallocation is necessary to reflect the true earner of the income.

The regulations provide guidance regarding certain specific section 269A issues determined to be of major interest. No inference should be drawn regarding issues not included in the regulations, or as to why some issues, and not others, are addressed.

SPECIAL ANALYSIS

The Commissioner of Internal Revenue has determined that these proposed regulations are not a major rule as defined in Executive Order 12291. Accordingly, a Regulatory Impact Analysis is not required. Although this document is a notice of proposed rulemaking that solicits public comment, the Internal Revenue Service has concluded that the notice and public procedure requirements of 5 U.S.C. 553 do not apply because the rules proposed are interpretative. Accordingly, a Regulatory Flexibility Analysis is not required.

COMMENTS AND REQUESTS FOR A PUBLIC HEARING

Before adopting these proposed regulations, consideration will be given to any written comments that are submitted (preferably seven copies) to the Commissioner of Internal Revenue. All comments will be available for public inspection and copying. A public hearing will be held upon written request to the Commissioner by any person who has submitted written comments. If a public hearing is held, notice of the time and place will be published in the Federal Register.

DRAFTING INFORMATION

The principal authors of these proposed regulations are Phoebe A. Mix and Philip R. Bosco of the Legislation and Regulations Division of the Office of Chief Counsel, Internal Revenue Service. However, personnel from other offices of the Internal Revenue Service and Treasury participated in developing the regulations, both on matters of substance and style.

[¶ 49,028] **Proposed Regulations (LR-261-76),** published in the Federal Register on July 21, 1983.

Business use or rental of dwelling unit.—Proposed Reg. §§ 1.280A-1, 1.280A-2 and 1.280A-3, relating to the deductibility of expenses in connection with the business use, or the rental to others, of a dwelling unit that the taxpayer is deemed to have used for personal purposes, are amended. Proposed Reg. § 1.280A-2(b)(2) and (3) were withdrawn on 5/20/94 by IA-023-93.

AGENCY: Internal Revenue Service, Treasury.

ACTION: Notice of proposed rulemaking.

SUMMARY: This document amends proposed regulations published on August 7, 1980, relating to the deductibility of expenses incurred in connection with the business use, or the rental to others, of a dwelling unit that the taxpayer is deemed to have used for personal purposes during the taxable year. The amendments in this document clarify and modify the earlier proposed regulations in several respects.

DATES: Written comments must be delivered or mailed by September 20, 1983. A public hearing on the August 7, 1980, notice of proposed rulemaking, as amended by this document, will be held on October 4, 1983; for further information, see the notice of public hearing published elsewhere in this issue of the FEDERAL REGISTER. The amendments are proposed to be effective for taxable years beginning after 1975.

ADDRESS: Send comments (and requests for copies of the August 7, 1980 notice of proposed rulemaking) to: Commissioner of Internal Revenue, Attention: CC:LR:T (LR-261-76), Washington, D.C. 20224.

FOR FURTHER INFORMATION CONTACT: Donald W. Stevenson (202-566-3297).

SUPPLEMENTARY INFORMATION

BACKGROUND

This document contains proposed amendments to a notice of proposed rulemaking that was published in the FEDERAL REGISTER on August 7, 1980 (45 F.R. 52399). This document will refer to that notice of proposed rulemaking as "the 1980 notice." The 1980 notice proposed to amend the Income Tax Regulations (26 CFR Part 1) under the Internal Revenue Code of 1954 to provide regulations under section 280A, which was added to the Code by section 601 of the Tax Reform Act of 1976 (90 Stat. 1569) and amended by section 306 of the Tax Reduction and Simplification Act of 1977 (91 Stat. 152) and by section 701(h) of the Revenue Act of 1978 (92 Stat. 2904). For more information regarding the 1980 notice, see the preamble to that notice.

Since publication of the 1980 notice, Code section 280A has been further amended by section 113 of the Black Lung Benefits Revenue Act of 1981 (95 Stat. 1641). The amendments in this document modify certain rules set out in the 1980 notice and conform that notice to the recent amendments to Code section 280A. These proposed regulations are to be issued under the authority contained in section 7805 of the Internal Revenue Code of 1954 (68A Stat. 917; 26 U.S.C. 7805).

REPAIR AND MAINTENANCE

The 1980 notice provided certain rules for determining whether the use of a dwelling unit by a taxpayer constituted use for purposes of repair and maintenance and consequently would not be treated as personal use by the taxpayer. In general, the 1980 notice required that both the taxpayer and all other individuals on the premises who were capable of working perform work on a substantially full-time basis in order to qualify the use as use for purposes of repair and maintenance.

Section 113(d) of the Black Lung Benefits Revenue Act of 1981 amended section 280A to provide that if the taxpayer is engaged in repair and maintenance on a substantially full-time basis for any day, the taxpayer will not be treated as having used the unit for personal purposes on that day merely because other individuals who are on the premises do not engage in repair and maintenance activities.

The amendment proposed in this document would incorporate this recent statutory change and substitute a "principal purpose" test for the rules set out in the 1980 notice. Under the proposed amendment, a taxpayer will not be treated as using a unit for personal purposes if the principal purpose of the use is to perform repair and maintenance work on the unit. Among the factors to be considered in determining whether repair and maintenance work is the principal purpose of the use of a unit are the following: the amount of time devoted to work on the unit, the frequency of the use of the unit for repair and maintenance purposes, and the presence and activities of companions.

PRINCIPAL PLACE OF BUSINESS

The interpretation of the phrase "the taxpayer's principal place of business" in section 280A(c)(1)(A) is important in determining the applicability of certain special rules. The 1980 notice provided that a taxpayer could have only one "principal place of business" regardless of the number of business activities in which the taxpayer was engaged.

The recent amendments to section 280A make clear that a taxpayer may have a principal place of business for each trade or business in which the taxpayer is engaged. This document conforms the 1980 notice to the statutory amendment.

LIMITATION ON DEDUCTIONS

The 1980 notice provided that deductions allowable with respect to the use of a dwelling unit for a qualifying use shall not exceed the gross income derived from that use of the unit. The proposed amendment makes clear that if a taxpayer uses a home office both for a business purpose for which an exception to the general disallowance rule is provided and for another business purpose for which no exception is provided, only the income from the first business may be considered in applying the limitation on deductions.

RENTAL TO FAMILY MEMBERS AND SHARED EQUITY AGREEMENTS

The 1980 notice provided that a taxpayer was deemed to have used a dwelling unit for personal purposes on any day on which the unit was used for personal purposes by any person who had an interest in the unit or by a close relative of the taxpayer or any co-owner.

Section 280A was amended to provide that the taxpayer will not be considered as having used the dwelling unit for personal purposes by reason of a rental arrangement on any day that the unit is rented at fair rental to any person (including a family member) as that person's principal residence. If the taxpayer actually makes personal use of the unit (other than for a brief visit as a guest) on any such day, however, that personal use is taken into account.

In the case of pass-thru entities such as partnerships, actual personal use of the unit by any beneficial owner is treated as actual personal use by the entity. However, this rule will not apply in the case of a partnership renting a unit to a partner for use as the partner's principal residence if there are no special allocations.

This new rule on rental of a unit as a principal residence applies to a rental to a person with an interest in the unit only if the rental is pursuant to a shared equity financing agreement. A shared equity financing agreement is an agreement under which two or more persons acquire qualified ownership interests in the unit and one or more of the persons is entitled to occupy the unit and is required to pay rent to one or more of the other persons holding a qualified ownership interest in the unit. A qualified ownership interest is an undivided interest for more than 50 years in the entire unit and appurtenant land.

RENTAL POOLS

The 1980 notice provided that, in the case of a rental pool, the number of days on which a unit is rented at fair rental and the number of days on which the unit is used for any purpose are to be determined by reference to the actual use of the unit.

The amendment proposed in this document permits rental pool participants to elect to average the rental use of their units. Under the proposed election, the number of days that a particular unit would be deemed to have been rented is determined by multiplying the aggregate number of days that all units in the rental pool were rented at fair rental during the pool season by a fraction, the numerator of which is the number of participation days of a particular unit and the denominator of which is the aggregate number of participation days of all units. The proposed amendment adds certain procedural rules necessary to administer this election and requires rental pool managers to furnish rental pool participants with the information needed to compute deductions for pool units.

PERMANENT PARTITION

The 1980 notice left unanswered the question of whether deductions incurred with respect to the use of a portion of a dwelling unit exclusively for business purposes would be disallowed if that portion of the dwelling unit is not separated by a permanent partition. The proposed amendment makes it clear that a permanent partition is not required.

USE BY PATIENTS, CLIENTS, ETC.

The 1980 notice did not expressly state that the exception provided for a portion of a unit used by patients, clients, or customers in meeting or dealing with the taxpayer applied only if the patients, clients or customers were physically present in the unit. This document makes clear that the patients, etc. must be physically present in the unit for purposes of this exception; telephone calls from other locations do not satisfy the requirement.

MISCELLANEOUS PROVISIONS

This document incorporates into the 1980 notice the new statutory provision with respect to the coordination of section 280A with the rules for travel expenses. This document also modifies the 1980 notice to make clear that a single building may contain more than one dwelling unit. Each apartment in an apartment building, for example, is a separate dwelling unit.

The 1980 notice did not explain how "fair rental" should be determined in the case of a unit owned by more than one person. This document makes clear that "fair rental" is determined by reference to the taxpayer's fractional interest in the unit. Thus, if a taxpayer with a one-half interest in a unit charges an occupant one-half of the fair rental for the entire unit, the taxpayer is charging fair rental regardless of the aggregate amount paid by the occupant.

The 1980 notice provided that the term "day" referred to a calendar day; consequently, use of a unit from Saturday afternoon through the following Saturday morning would constitute 8 days of use. Commenters objected to this construction of "day" on the grounds that it was inconsistent with the general usage of the term under rental agreements. This document provides that the term "day" means the period for which a day's rental is paid. This notice also amplifies the treatment in the 1980 notice of the exception for property used as a "hotel, motel, inn, or similar establishment."

COMMENTS AND PUBLIC HEARING

Before adoption of these proposed regulations, consideration will be given to any written comments that are submitted (preferably six copies) to the Commissioner of Internal Revenue. All comments will be available for public inspection and copying. A public hearing will be held on the 1980 notice, as amended by this document, on October 4, 1983.

For further information about the public hearing, see the notice of hearing that appears elsewhere in this issue of the FEDERAL REGISTER.

The collection of information requirements contained in this notice of proposed rulemaking have been submitted to the Office of Management and Budget (OMB) for review under section 3504(h) of the Paperwork Reduction Act. Comments on these requirements should be sent to the Office of Information and Regulatory Affairs of OMB, Attention: Desk Officer for Internal Revenue Service, New Executive Office Building, Washington, D.C. 20503. The Internal Revenue Service requests that persons submitting comments on these requirements to OMB also send copies of those comments to the Service.

SPECIAL ANALYSES

The Commissioner of Internal Revenue has determined that this proposed rule is not a major rule as defined in Executive Order 12291 and that a Regulatory Impact Analysis is therefore not required.

Although this document is a notice of proposed rulemaking which solicits public comment, the Internal Revenue Service has concluded that the regulations proposed herein are interpretative and that the notice and public comment requirements of 5 U.S.C. 553 do not apply. Accordingly, these proposed regulations do not constitute regulations subject to the Regulatory Flexibility Act (5 U.S.C. chapter 6).

DRAFTING INFORMATION

The principal author of these proposed regulations was Donald W. Stevenson of the Legislation and Regulations Division of the Office of Chief Counsel, Internal Revenue Service. However, personnel from other offices of the Internal Revenue Service and Treasury Department participated in developing the regulations, both on matters of substance and style.

Evaluation of the effectiveness of the proposed regulations after issuance will be based upon comments received from offices within Treasury and the Internal Revenue Service, other governmental agencies, and the public.

[¶ 49,029] **Proposed Regulations (LR-182-78)**, published in the Federal Register on July 26, 1983.

Transfers of securities under agreements.—Reg. §§1.1058-1, 1.1058-2, and 1.1223-2, relating to transfers of securities under certain agreements, are proposed.

AGENCY: Internal Revenue Service, Treasury.

ACTION: Notice of proposed rulemaking.

SUMMARY: This document contains proposed regulations relating to transfers of securities under certain agreements. Changes to the applicable tax law were made by the Act of August 15, 1978. The regulations would provide the public with the guidance needed to comply with that Act.

DATES: Written comments and requests for a public hearing must be delivered or mailed by September 26, 1983. The amendments are proposed to be effective for transfers of securities under agreements described in section 1058 of the Internal Revenue Code, occurring after December 31, 1976 and are proposed to be effective January 1, 1977.

ADDRESS: Send comments and requests for a public hearing to: Commissioner of Internal Revenue, Attention: CC:LR:T, [LR-182-78] Washington, D.C. 20224.

FOR FURTHER INFORMATION CONTACT: Howard A. Balikov of the Legislation and Regulations Division, Office of the Chief Counsel, Internal Revenue Service, 1111 Constitution Avenue, N.W., Washington, D.C. 20224, 202-566-3288, not a toll-free call.

SUPPLEMENTARY INFORMATION:

BACKGROUND

This document contains proposed amendments to the Income Tax Regulations (26 CFR Part 1) under sections 1058 and 1223 of the Internal Revenue Code of 1954. These amendments are proposed to conform the regulations to section 2 of the Act of August 15, 1978, Pub. L. 95-345 (92 Stat. 481) and are to be issued under the authority contained in section 1058(b) of the Internal Revenue Code of 1954 (92 Stat. 483; 26 U.S.C. 1058) and in section 7805 of the Code (68A Stat. 917; 26 U.S.C. 7805).

ADDITIONAL INFORMATION

Section 1058 and these regulations provide rules relating to the income tax treatment to be given to securities lending transactions. If the provisions of section 1058 and these regulations are met, the lender shall not recognize gain on the transfer of securities, or upon the return of identical securities.

COMMENTS AND REQUESTS FOR A PUBLIC HEARING

Before adopting these proposed regulations, consideration will be given to any written comments that are submitted (preferably seven copies) to the Commissioner of Internal Revenue. All comments will be available for public inspection and copying. A public hearing will be held upon written request to the Commissioner by any person who has submitted written comments. If a public hearing is held, notice of the time and place will be published in the FEDERAL REGISTER.

The collection of information requirements contained in this notice of proposed rulemaking have been submitted to the Office of Management and Budget (OMB) for review under section 3504(h) of the Paperwork Reduction Act. Comments on these requirements should be sent to the Office of Information and Regulatory Affairs of OMB, Attention: Desk Officer for Internal Revenue Service, New Executive Office Building, Washington, D.C. 20503. The Internal Revenue Service requests that persons submitting comments on these requirements to OMB also send copies of those comments to the Service.

SPECIAL ANALYSES

The Commissioner of Internal Revenue has determined that this proposed rule is not a major rule as defined in Executive Order 12291. Accordingly, a Regulatory Impact Analysis is not required. The Internal Revenue Service has concluded that although this document is a notice of proposed rulemaking that solicits public comment, the regulations proposed herein are interpretative and the notice and public procedure requirements of 5 U.S.C. 553 do not apply. Accordingly, no Regulatory Flexibility Analysis is required for this rule.

LIST OF SUBJECTS IN 26 CFR 1.1001-1—1.1102-3

Income taxes, Gain and Loss, Basis, Nontaxable exchanges.

LIST OF SUBJECTS IN 26 CFR 1.1201—1.1252-2

Income taxes, Capital gains and losses, Recapture.

DRAFTING INFORMATION

The principal author of these proposed regulations is Howard A. Balikov of the Legislation and Regulations Division of the Office of Chief Counsel, Internal Revenue Service. However, personnel from other offices of the Internal Revenue Service and Treasury Department participated in developing the regulations, both on matters of substance and style.

[¶ 49,030]   Proposed Regulations and Proposed Amendments of Regulations (LR-152-79), published in the Federal Register December 19, 1983.

Minimum addition to reserves for losses: Mutual savings banks.—Amendments of Reg. §§1.166-4, 1.581-2 and 1.591-1, relating to the minimum addition to reserves for losses on loans of mutual savings banks and other organizations, are proposed. Reg. §1.593-9 was removed on 4/26/93 by T.D. 8474. Reg. §§1.593-1—1.593-11 were removed by T.D. 9849 on 3/11/2019.

AGENCY: Internal Revenue Service, Treasury.

ACTION: Notice of proposed rulemaking.

SUMMARY: This document contains proposed regulations imposing a requirement of a minimum addition of reserve for losses on loans of mutual savings banks and other organizations to which section 593 of the Internal Revenue Code of 1954 applies. Certain of the proposed regulations reflect changes to the applicable law under the Economic Recovery Tax Act of 1981; others are intended to clarify existing regulations provisions. The proposed regulations would provide affected financial institutions with the necessary guidance in complying with the tax laws.

DATES: Written comments and requests for a public hearing must be delivered or mailed by February 17, 1984. Generally, the amendments are proposed to apply to taxable years beginning more than sixty days after publication of this notice as a final Treasury decision. With respect to certain distributions in redemption, the amendments are proposed to apply to certain distributions made on or after January 1, 1981. The amendments treating certain stock associations as mutual savings banks are proposed to be effective for taxable years ending after August 13, 1983.

ADDRESS: Send comments and requests for a public hearing to: Commissioner of Internal Revenue, Attention: CC:LR:T (LR-152-79), Washington, D.C. 20224.

FOR FURTHER INFORMATION CONTACT: Susan Thompson Baker or George T. Magnatta of the Legislation and Regulations Division, Office of the Chief Counsel, Internal Revenue Service, 1111 Constitution Avenue, N.W., Washington, D.C. 20224 (Attention: CC:LR:T) (202-566-3459).

SUPPLEMENTARY INFORMATION:

BACKGROUND

This document contains proposed amendments to clarify the Income Tax Regulations (26 CFR Part 1) under section 593 of the Internal Revenue Code of 1954. In addition, these amendments are proposed to conform the regulations to sections 243 and 245 of the Economic Recovery Tax Act of 1981 (95 Stat. 255). These amendments are to be issued under the authority contained in section 7805 of the Internal Revenue Code of 1954 (68A Stat. 917; 26 U.S.C. 7805).

NEW RULES

This notice of proposed rulemaking contains new rules applicable to mutual savings banks, domestic building and loan associations, and cooperative banks without capital stock organized and operated for mutual purposes and without profit (section 593 organizations). These new rules, which require that section 593 organizations make a minimum addition to their reserves for losses on qualifying real property loans and nonqualifying loans, are proposed in order to achieve consistency with the regulations under section 585, which contain a similar requirement with respect to other banking institutions.

CHANGES MADE BY THE ECONOMIC RECOVERY TAX ACT OF 1981

Section 243 of the Economic Recovery Tax Act of 1981 (ERTA) created an exception to the rule of section 593(e) that distributions from excess bad debt reserves of certain section 593 organizations are recaptured as ordinary income. Under the Act, this recapture rule does not apply to distributions to the Federal Savings and Loan Insurance Corporation in redemption of an interest in a section 593 organization originally received in exchange for financial assistance.

Additionally, ERTA provided that a bank (1) which has capital stock represented by shares, and (2) which is subject to, and operates under, Federal or State laws relating to mutual savings banks, is an organization that is eligible to compute its bad debt deduction under section 593. However, these organizations must compute their bad debt deduction under the percentage of taxable income method under the same rules applicable to building and loan associations (*i.e.*, 82 percent of their assets must be invested in qualified assets in order to receive the full 40-percent deduction and the reduction will be at three-fourths of one percent). ERTA also requires these stock organizations to recapture excess deductions to the extent required by section 593(e). Finally, ERTA provides the amounts paid to depositors of these organizations are deductible under section 591.

CLARIFYING AND CONFORMING CHANGES

These proposed amendments to the regulations also include clarifying changes to existing regulations. These changes include a renumbering of certain sections of the regulations under section 593 and the deletion of certain of those sections that pertained to taxable years beginning before January 1, 1963, or to taxable years beginning before July 12, 1969. These proposed amendments also clarify that section 593 organizations, like banking institutions subject to section 585, may adjust the amount of their addition to bad debt reserves, and thus change the amount of their bad debt deduction, within the applicable period of limitations, subject only to the maximum and minimum requirements set forth in these regulations.

COMMENTS AND REQUESTS FOR A PUBLIC HEARING

Before the adoption of these proposed regulations, consideration will be given to any written comments that are submitted (preferably seven copies) to the Commissioner of Internal Revenue. All comments will be available for public inspection and copying. A public hearing will be held upon written request to the Commissioner by any person who has submitted written comments. If a public hearing is held, notice of the time and place will be published in the FEDERAL REGISTER.

NON-APPLICATION OF EXECUTIVE ORDER 12291

The Treasury Department has determined that this proposed regulation is not subject to review under Executive Order 12291 or the Treasury and OMB implementation of the order dated April 29, 1983.

REGULATORY FLEXIBILITY ACT

Although this document is a notice of proposed rulemaking that solicits public comment, the Internal Revenue Service has concluded that the regulations proposed herein are interpretative and no general notice of proposed rulemaking is required by 5 U.S.C. 553(b). Accordingly, no Regulatory Flexibility Analysis is required.

PAPERWORK REDUCTION ACT

The collection of information requirements contained in this notice of proposed rulemaking have been submitted to the Office of Management and Budget (OMB) for review under section 3504(h) of the Paperwork Reduction Act. Comments on these requirements should be sent to the Office of Information and Regulatory Affairs of OMB, Attention: Desk Officer for Internal Revenue Service, New Executive Office Building, Washington, D.C. 20503. The Internal Revenue Service requests that persons submitting comments on these requirements to OMB also send copies of those comments to the Service.

DRAFTING INFORMATION

The principal authors of these proposed regulations are Susan Thompson Baker and George T. Magnatta of the Legislation and Regulations Division of the Office of Chief Counsel, Internal Revenue Service. However, personnel from other offices of the Internal Revenue Service and Treasury Department participated in developing the regulations, both on matters of substance and style.

[¶ 49,031]   **Proposed Regulations and Proposed Amendments of Regulations (EE-148-81),** published in the Federal Register on January 23, 1984.

Individual retirement plans: Simplified employee pensions: Qualified voluntary employee contributions.—Reg. §§ 1.219(a)-1—1.219(a)-6, 1.408-10 and 301.6652-4 and amendments of Reg. §§ 1.408-2 and 1.408-3, relating to individual retirement plans, simplified employee pensions and qualified voluntary employee contributions, are proposed. Reg. § 1.409-1 was withdrawn on 1/8/96 by EE-148-81. Reg. §§ 1.415-1, 1.415-2, 1.415-6 and 1.415-7 were removed 4/4/2007 by T.D. 9319.

AGENCY: Internal Revenue Service, Treasury.

ACTION: Notice of proposed rulemaking.

SUMMARY: This document contains proposed regulations relating to individual retirement plans, simplified employee pensions, and qualified voluntary employee contributions. Changes to the applicable law were made by the Economic Recovery Tax Act of 1981. The regulations would provide the public with the guidance needed to comply with the Act. The regulations would affect: institutions which sponsor individual retirement plans and simplified employee pensions, employers and individuals who use individual retirement plans and simplified employee pensions for retirement income, employers who maintain plans which accept qualified voluntary employee contributions and employees who make qualified voluntary employee contributions.

DATES: Written comments and requests for a public hearing must be delivered or mailed by March 23, 1984. The regulations are generally effective for taxable years beginning after December 31, 1981.

ADDRESS: Send comments and requests for a public hearing to: Commissioner of Internal Revenue, Attention: CC:LR:T (EE-148-81), Washington, D.C. 20224.

FOR FURTHER INFORMATION CONTACT: William D. Gibbs of the Employee Plans and Exempt Organizations Division, Office of the Chief Counsel, Internal Revenue Service, 1111 Constitution Avenue, N.W., Washington, D.C. 20224 (Attention: CC:LR:T) (202-566-3430) (not a toll-free number).

SUPPLEMENTARY INFORMATION:

BACKGROUND

This document contains proposed amendments to the Income Tax Regulations (26 CFR Part 1), the Estate Tax Regulations (26 CFR Part 20), the Gift Tax Regulations (26 CFR Part 25), and the Procedure and Administration Regulations (26 CFR Part 301) under sections 219, 408, 409, 415, 2039, 2517, and 6652 of the Internal Revenue Code of 1954. These amendments are proposed to conform the regulations to sections 311 (except subsection (b)) and 314(b) of the Economic Recovery Tax Act of 1981 (95 Stat. 274, 286). These regulations are to be issued under the authority contained in section 7805 of the Internal Revenue Code of 1954 (68A Stat. 917; 26 U.S.C. 7805).

INDIVIDUAL RETIREMENT PLANS

Section 219, as amended by the Economic Recovery Tax Act of 1981, allows an individual a deduction of up to the lesser of $2,000 or compensation includible in gross income for contributions to an individual retirement plan. Unlike old section 219, an individual is allowed this deduction whether or not he is an "active participant" in an employer's plan. The deduction for individual retirement plan contributions is reduced, however, by amounts which the employee contributes to an employer's plan and treats as qualified voluntary employee contributions. The remainder of the individual retirement plan rules are similar to those under prior law.

SPOUSAL INDIVIDUAL RETIREMENT ACCOUNTS

Code section 220 was deleted by the Economic Recovery Tax Act of 1981. In its place is new section 219(c), which allows an individual and his nonworking spouse to contribute up to the lesser of compensation includible in the working spouse's gross income or $2,250 to individual retirement accounts. The spouses must file a joint return to obtain this additional $250 deduction. No deduction is allowed if the spouse for whose benefit the individual retirement plan is maintained has attained age 70^1/$_2$ before the close of the taxable year.

There is no requirement, as under old law, that equal amounts be contributed to the individual retirement accounts of both spouses. However, no more than $2,000 may be contributed to the individual retirement account of either spouse.

SIMPLIFIED EMPLOYEE PENSIONS

The Economic Recovery Tax Act of 1981 increased the maximum deduction for contributions to simplified employee pensions to the lesser of 15% of compensation from the employer maintaining the simplified employee pension arrangement or the amount contributed by the employer to the simplified employee pension and included in gross income (but not in excess of $15,000). An employee may also contribute and deduct the lesser of $2,000 or compensation includible in gross income regardless of the employer's contribution to the simplified employee pension.

QUALIFIED VOLUNTARY EMPLOYEE CONTRIBUTIONS

Section 219, as amended by the Economic Recovery Tax Act of 1981, allows an individual a deduction for qualified voluntary employee contributions (QVEC's). QVEC's are voluntary contributions made by an individual as an employee under an employer's plan. The employer's plan must allow employees to make contributions which may be treated as QVEC's.

The maximum amount which can be deducted as a QVEC is the lesser of $2,000 or the compensation includible in gross income from the employer which maintains the plan which accepts the QVEC's.

Proposed § 1.219(a)-5(a) sets forth the type of plans which can accept qualified voluntary employee contributions.

Proposed § 1.219(a)-5(c) sets forth the rules a plan must follow to receive qualified voluntary employee contributions.

Additional rules for QVEC's are set forth in proposed § 1.219(a)-5(d), (e), and (f).

The reporting rules for qualified voluntary employee contributions are in proposed § 1.219(a)-5(g). This provision gives the Commissioner discretionary authority to modify the reporting requirements for these contributions. Any such modification of the reporting requirements would be subject to review by the Office of Management and Budget under the Paperwork Reduction Act of 1980.

OTHER AMENDMENTS

Conforming and technical amendments made by the Economic Recovery Tax Act of 1981 have been made to the regulations under Code sections 408, 409, 415, 2039, 2517, and 6652.

Although the Treasury Department stopped selling retirement bonds in early 1982, the regulations contain references to Code sections 405 and 409. These references apply to retirement bonds sold through early 1982 and to retirement bonds that may be sold subsequently.

These proposed regulations do not reflect amendments made to the Code by the Tax Equity and Fiscal Responsibility Act of 1982. These proposed regulations reflect changes in the applicable statutory provisions made by the Technical Corrections Act of 1982.

EXECUTIVE ORDER 12291 AND REGULATORY FLEXIBILITY ACT

The Commissioner has determined that this proposed regulation is not a major regulation for purposes of Executive Order 12291. Accordingly, a regulatory impact analysis is not required.

Although this document is a notice of proposed rulemaking which solicits public comment, the Internal Revenue Service has concluded that the regulations proposed herein are interpretative and that the notice and public procedure requirements of 5 U.S.C. 553 do not apply. Accordingly, these proposed regulations do not constitute regulations subject to the Regulatory Flexibility Act (5 U.S.C. chapter 6).

COMMENTS AND REQUESTS FOR A PUBLIC HEARING

Before adopting these proposed regulations, consideration will be given to any written comments that are submitted (preferably seven copies) to the Commissioner of Internal Revenue. All comments will be available for public inspection and copying. A public hearing will be held upon written request to the Commissioner by any person who has submitted written comments. If a public hearing is held, notice of the time and place will be published in the *Federal Register*.

The collection of information requirements contained in this notice of proposed rulemaking have been submitted to the Office of Management and Budget (OMB) for review under section 3504(h) of the Paperwork Reduction Act of 1980. Comments on these requirements should be sent to the Office of Information and Regulatory Affairs of OMB, Attention: Desk Office for Internal Revenue Service, New Executive Office Building, Washington, D.C. 20503. The Internal Revenue Service requests that persons submitting comments on these requirements to OMB also send copies of those comments to the Service.

DRAFTING INFORMATION

The principal author of these proposed regulations is William D. Gibbs of the Employee Plans and Exempt Organizations Division of the Office of Chief Counsel, Internal Revenue Service. However, personnel from other offices of the Internal Revenue Service and Treasury Department participated in developing the regulation, both on matters of substance and style.

[¶ 49,032]   **Proposed Regulations and Proposed Amendments of Regulations (LR-185-81),** published in the Federal Register on February 16, 1984.

Accelerated cost recovery system.—Reg. §§ 1.168-1—1.168-6 and amendments of Reg. §§ 1.167(a)-11, 1.178-1, 1.1016-3 and 1.1016-4, relating to the Accelerated Cost Recovery System for recovering capital costs of eligible property, are proposed. Reg. § 1.168-5(a) was adopted 12/23/86 by T.D. 8116. Reg. § 1.168-2(n) was withdrawn on 1/29/98.

AGENCY: Internal Revenue Service, Treasury.

ACTION: Notice of proposed rulemaking.

SUMMARY: This document contains proposed regulations relating to the Accelerated Cost Recovery System (hereinafter referred to as ACRS) for recovering capital costs of eligible property. Changes to the applicable tax law were made by the Economic Recovery Tax Act of 1981 (hereinafter referred to as ERTA), the Tax Equity and Fiscal Responsibility Act of 1982 (hereinafter referred to as TEFRA) and the Technical Corrections Act of 1982. Prior law allowed as a depreciation deduction a reasonable allowance for exhaustion, wear and tear, or obsolescence of eligible property. ERTA replaced this prior law depreciation system with ACRS. Generally, under ACRS cost recovery deductions are determined by the use of tables which reflect the use of accelerated methods of cost recovery over predetermined recovery periods. These recovery periods are generally unrelated to, and shorter than, prior law "useful lives." TEFRA repealed the more accelerated tables for personal property which were to be effective for property placed in service after 1984. These regulations would provide taxpayers with the guidance needed to comply with the Acts.

DATES: Written comments must be delivered or mailed by May 16, 1984. In general, these regulations apply to eligible property placed in service after December 31, 1980.

ADDRESS: Send comments to: Commissioner of Internal Revenue, Attention: CC:LR:T (LR-185-81), Washington, D.C. 20224.

FOR FURTHER INFORMATION CONTACT: John A. Tolleris (with respect to § 1.168-4 (202-566-3590)), Joseph M. Rosenthal (with respect to the repair allowance, § 1.167(a)-11(d)(2) (202-566-3288)), or George T. Magnatta (with respect to all other provisions (202-566-3294)), of the Legislation and Regulations Division, Office of the Chief Counsel, Internal Revenue Service, 1111 Constitution Avenue, N.W., Washington, D.C. 20224 (Attention: CC:LR:T).

SUPPLEMENTARY INFORMATION:

BACKGROUND

This document contains proposed amendments to the Income Tax Regulations (26 CFR Part 1) under sections 167, 168, 178, and 1016 of the Internal Revenue Code of 1954. These amendments are proposed to conform the regulations to sections 201 and 203 of the Economic Recovery Tax Act of 1981 (Pub. L. 97-34; 95 Stat. 203, 221), sections 205 and 206 of the Tax Equity and Fiscal Responsibility Act of 1982 (Pub. L. 97-248; 96 Stat. 427, 431), and section 102 of the Technical Corrections Act of 1982 (Pub. L. 97-448; 96 Stat. 2367). These amendments are to be issued under the authority contained in section 168 (95 Stat. 203; 26 U.S.C. 168) and section 7805 (68A Stat. 917; 26 U.S.C. 7805) of the Internal Revenue Code of 1954.

ACCELERATED COST RECOVERY SYSTEM

Section 168, as added by ERTA, is a replacement for the prior law depreciation system for recovering the capital costs of trade or business assets or investment assets. Generally, this new Accelerated Cost Recovery System (ACRS), added by section 168, provides for the recovery of capital costs of eligible property by the use of tables, which reflect the use of accelerated methods of cost recovery over predetermined recovery periods. These recovery periods are generally unrelated to, and shorter than, those under prior law. Unlike prior law, ACRS does not make any distinction between new and used property. This new capital cost recovery system is mandatory for all eligible property, hereinafter referred to as "recovery property." Recovery property includes both real and personal property. Generally, to be eligible for ACRS property must be (1) tangible property of a character subject to the allowance for depreciation, (2) used in a trade or business or held for the production of income, and (3) placed in service by the taxpayer after December 31, 1980. Recovery property does not include (1) tangible depreciable property the taxpayer properly elects to depreciate under a method not expressed in terms of years, (2) public utility property where the taxpayer does not use a normalization method of accounting, and (3) certain pre-1981 property involved in post-1980 "churning" transactions to obtain the benefits of ACRS.

In addition, recovery property does not include intangible property. The Internal Revenue Service is continuing to examine the extent to which certain types of property, such as computer software and master motion picture negatives, may constitute intangible property that is ineligible for ACRS. The Internal Revenue Service is also examining the manner in which other provisions of the Code (such as section 48(k)) may apply if such property is considered eligible for ACRS. Accordingly, these issues have been reserved in these proposed regulations and are the subject of a recently opened project, under which regulations will be issued as soon as possible. In the meantime, the Service will continue to administer the area in accordance with its current position. Comments on these questions from interested persons are welcome.

The allowable ACRS deduction is generally determined by multiplying the unadjusted basis of the property by the applicable percentage contained in the relevant ACRS tables. The prior law concept of salvage value is abolished in determining deductions under this new system. Thus, the entire cost or other basis of the property is recovered under ACRS. The proposed regulations provide rules for determining the allowable deduction when the basis of the property is redetermined (*e.g.*, where there is a readjustment of the purchase price).

Under ACRS, the cost of personal property must be recovered over a 3-year, 5-year, 10-year, or 15-year recovery period (unless the taxpayer elects a longer recovery period under rules described below). Real property is recovered over a 15-year recovery period (unless a longer period is elected). With respect to personal property, a full year's recovery deduction is allowed in the first recovery year regardless of when the asset is placed in service during that taxable year. No recovery deduction is allowed in the taxable year in which personal property is disposed of. The proposed regulations provide rules for computing the allowable deduction where the taxpayer has a taxable year of less than 12 months. In addition, for real property, the recovery for the year the asset is placed in service or is disposed of is based on the number of months the property is in service during the year, regardless of whether the taxpayer has a normal or short taxable year.

Taxpayers may elect to recover the cost of eligible property using the straight line method over the applicable recovery period or over a longer optional recovery period. For example, taxpayers may recover the capital costs of 5-year recovery property over a 5-year, 12-year, or 25-year period or the cost of real property over a 15-year, 35-year, or 45-year period, using the straight line method. Except for real property, the election applies to all recovery property of the particular class placed in service in the same taxable year. Generally, this election is irrevocable. The proposed regulations provide tables containing the applicable percentages when an optional straight line election is made.

Taxpayers may, under certain conditions, elect to recover the capital costs of certain recovery property in a mass asset account. If the election is made, mass assets which have the same asset depreciation range (ADR) midpoint life as of January 1, 1981, and which are placed in service in the same taxable year, will be accounted for in a single account. As a consequence of the election, upon the disposition of an asset from that account, the taxpayer will generally include in income the full amount realized on the disposition. The unadjusted basis of the asset disposed of will continue to be included in determining the recovery deduction for the account. The proposed regulations define mass assets, provide rules for determining when dispositions occur for purposes of investment tax credit recapture, and provide rules for recovering any increase in basis resulting from such recapture. The proposed regulations also provide rules relating to the recognition of gain or loss on the disposition of recovery property other than from a mass asset account.

Under ACRS, component cost recovery is not permitted. Thus, the same recovery period and method generally must be used for a building and all structural components. The recovery period for a component generally begins at the later of the time the component or the building is placed in service.

Under the proposed regulations, a building is considered placed in service when a significant portion is made available for use in a finished condition. The taxpayer at that time begins recovery of so much of the capitalized costs as are properly allocable to the portion of the building in service. Similarly, as portions of the building are later made available, recovery of the properly allocable costs will commence.

Capitalized expenditures, which are section 1250 property, paid or incurred after the building is completed are recovered under the same period and method as are used for the building, recovery beginning when the improvement is placed in service. However, if a capitalized expenditure qualifies as a "substantial improvement," a new recovery period and method are permitted, recovery beginning when the improvement is placed in service.

Similarly, with respect to personal property, amounts paid or incurred after the property is placed in service, which are properly chargeable to capital account, are treated as newly-purchased property for ACRS purposes. That property is assigned to the same recovery class as the property to which the expenditure relates. Any applicable recovery period and method may be selected for such improvement, recovery beginning when the improvement is placed in service.

Rules are also provided clarifying the results when a lessee makes improvements on leased property.

The proposed regulations clarify the rules which prevent taxpayers from converting pre-1981 property into post-1980 recovery property. Under those rules, if the taxpayer enters into certain "churning" transactions, the methods of cost recovery provided under ACRS are not available with respect to the property.

ACRS contains special rules for property which is used predominantly outside the United States. The proposed regulations define this type of property and also provide guidance for property which ceases or begins to be used predominantly outside the United States after having been placed in service in a prior taxable year.

Similarly, the proposed regulations provide rules for determining the deductions for other property which changes status under ACRS (*e.g.*, property which ceases to be used in connection with research and experimentation, property converted from personal to business use). Additionally, the proposed regulations provide rules for determining the deductions for property which is used both for personal and business purposes.

ACRS provides special rules for recovery property which is involved in certain nonrecognition and other transactions (section 168(f)(7),(10)). Generally, in these transactions the transferee is bound by the transferor's recovery period and method with respect to so much of the basis of the property in the hands of the transferee as does not exceed its basis in the hands of the transferor. The proposed regulations clarify the class of transactions subject to the rules and the manner of computing the deductions available to the transferor and transferee.

The proposed regulations also clarify the rules with respect to property involved in a transaction to which section 1031 or 1033 applies (section 168(f)(7)). Additionally, the proposed regulations clarify the deductions available with respect to property transferred by gift or bequest and with respect to partnership property to which basis adjustments are made.

The proposed regulations also provide the guidance necessary for making the various elections under section 168.

Since Congress made no change to certain provisions of the Code which require (or allow) a taxpayer to compute depreciation by use of the straight line method over the property's useful life (*e.g.*, section 163(d)(3)(C), 1016(a)(3)), the proposed regulations contain no special rules in that regard. As a result, the rules under prior law continue to apply.

Section 203(b) of ERTA terminated the class life asset depreciation range (ADR) system, authorized by section 167(m) of the Code, for recovery property placed in service after 1980. Additionally, section 201(c) of ERTA repealed the asset guideline class repair allowance, authorized by section 263(e), effective for property placed in service after December 31, 1980. The proposed regulations implement these statutory changes by amending § 1.167(a)-11(a)(1) and (d)(2) and by making other conforming amendments. The proposed regulations also clarify that the repair allowance is continued in effect for expenditures made after December 31, 1980, for the repair, maintenance, rehabilitation, or improvement of property placed in service before January 1, 1981.

The proposed regulations provide that the taxpayer may elect the repair allowance for a taxable year by (a) making the election to apply ADR for the taxable year (even if all the property placed in service during the taxable year is recovery property to which the ADR system does not apply), and (b) making an election to apply the asset guideline class repair allowance for the taxable year.

For periods after December 31, 1980, the proposed regulations provide that expenditures that are property improvements or excluded additions under the repair allowance rules shall generally be treated as separate items of recovery property, as described above.

These regulations concerning ACRS are effective for property placed in service after December 31, 1980. A taxpayer who has filed a return and who either did not claim allowable ACRS deductions, or did not claim the full amount allowable (*e.g.*, because the taxpayer used a different rule for years following a short taxable year than is provided in these regulations), should file an amended return.

NON-APPLICABILITY OF EXECUTIVE ORDER 12291

It has been determined that this notice of proposed rulemaking is not subject to review under Executive Order 12291 or the Treasury and OMB implementation of the order dated April 29, 1983.

REGULATORY FLEXIBILITY ACT

Although this document is a notice of proposed rulemaking which solicits public comment, the Internal Revenue Service has concluded that the regulations proposed herein are interpretative and that the notice and public procedure requirements of 5 U.S.C. 553 do not apply. Accordingly, these proposed regulations do not constitute regulations subject to the Regulatory Flexibility Act (5 U.S.C. chapter 6).

COMMENTS—PUBLIC HEARING

Before adopting these proposed regulations, consideration will be given to any written comments that are submitted (preferably seven copies) to the Commissioner of Internal Revenue. All comments will be available for public inspection and copying. A public hearing will be held in accordance with the notice of hearing published in this issue of the FEDERAL REGISTER.

PAPERWORK REDUCTION ACT

The collection of information requirements contained in this notice of proposed rulemaking have been submitted to the Office of Management and Budget (OMB) for review under section 3504(h) of the Paperwork Reduction Act. Comments on these requirements should be sent to the Office of Information and Regulatory Affairs of OMB, Attention: Desk Officer for Internal Revenue Service, New Executive Office Building, Washington, D.C. 20503. The Internal Revenue Service requests that persons submitting comments on these requirements to OMB also send copies of those comments to the Service.

DRAFTING INFORMATION

The principal authors of these regulations are John A. Tolleris, George T. Magnatta, Harold T. Flanagan, and Joseph M. Rosenthal of the Legislation and Regulations Division of the Office of Chief Counsel, Internal Revenue Service. However, personnel from other offices of the Internal Revenue Service and Treasury Department participated in developing the regulations, both on matters of substance and style.

[¶ 49,033] **Proposed Regulations and Proposed Amendments of Regulations (LR-228-82),** published in the Federal Register on March 26, 1984.

Estimated tax: Corporations.—Reg. §§1.6655-4 and 1.6655-5 and amendments of Reg. §§1.6152-1, 1.6164-4, 1.6164-8, 1.6654-2, 1.6655-1, 1.6655-2, 1.6655-3, 1.6655-6 and 301.6655-1, relating to estimated tax requirements for corporations, are proposed.

AGENCY: Internal Revenue Service, Treasury.

ACTION: Notice of proposed rulemaking.

SUMMARY: This document contains proposed regulations which provide guidance to corporations with respect to estimated tax requirements. Changes to the applicable tax law were made by the Omnibus Reconciliation Act of 1980, the Economic Recovery Tax Act of 1981, and the Tax Equity and Fiscal Responsibility Act of 1982. The regulations would provide corporations with the guidance needed to comply with applicable provisions of these acts.

DATES: Written comments and requests for a public hearing must be delivered by May 25, 1984. Generally, these regulations are proposed to be effective for taxable years beginning after December 31, 1982. The regulations providing guidance to "large corporations" are proposed to be effective for taxable years beginning after December 31, 1980.

ADDRESS: Send comments and requests for a public hearing to: Commissioner of Internal Revenue, Attention: CC:LR:T (LR-228-82), Washington, D.C. 20224.

FOR FURTHER INFORMATION CONTACT: George T. Magnatta of the Legislation and Regulations Division, Office of Chief Counsel, Internal Revenue Service, 1111 Constitution Avenue, NW., Washington, D.C. 20224 (Attention: CC:LR:T) (202-566-3294).

SUPPLEMENTARY INFORMATION:

BACKGROUND

This document contains proposed amendments to the Income Tax Regulations (26 CFR Part 1) under sections 6152, 6164, 6654, and 6655 of the Internal Revenue Code of 1954 and to the Regulations on Procedure and Administration (26 CFR Part 301) under section 6655 of the Code. These amendments are proposed to conform the regulations to section 1111 of the Omnibus Reconciliation Act of 1980 (Pub. L. 96-499; 94 Stat. 2681), section 731 of the Economic Recovery Tax Act of 1981 (Pub. L. 97-34; 95 Stat. 346), and section 234 of the Tax Equity and Fiscal Responsibility Act of 1982 (Pub. L. 97-248; 96 Stat. 503) and are to be issued under the authority contained in section 7805 of the Internal Revenue Code of 1954 (68A Stat. 917; 26 U.S.C. 7805).

GENERAL RULES

A corporation is required to make payments of estimated tax if it reasonably expects to have an estimated tax liability for the taxable year of $40 or more (*see* section 6154). Generally, a corporation is required to pay a percentage of its current year's tax liability in quarterly estimated tax installments. Under section 6655, if a corporation fails to pay its estimated tax installment when due and does not meet any exception to an underpayment, the corporation is subject to a penalty for underpayment of estimated taxes. The amount of the penalty is determined at the rate established under section 6621.

Under prior law, the penalty with respect to any underpayment of any installment was not imposed in any case where the total amount of all payments of estimated tax made on or before the last date prescribed for the payment of such installment equalled or exceeded the amount which would have been due had the estimated tax been based on any of the following: (1) the tax shown on the return for the preceding taxable year, if a return showing a tax liability was filed for the preceding taxable year and such preceding year was a taxable year of 12 months; (2) the tax computed at the rates applicable to the current taxable year but using the facts and law applicable to the preceding taxable year; or (3) 80 percent of the taxes which would have been due if the corporation's taxable income for specified preceding periods of the taxable year were annualized (annualization exception).

Additionally, for taxable years beginning prior to 1983, a corporation could elect under section 6152 to pay only half of its unpaid tax $2^{1}/_{2}$ months after the end of its taxable year and the remaining one-half 3 months later.

The Omnibus Reconciliation Act of 1980 amended section 6655 to provide that, in order to come within exception (1) (relating to the preceding year's tax) or (2) (relating to the preceding year's facts and law), described above, a large corporation's estimated tax payments must in no event be less than 60 percent of the current year's tax. The Economic Recovery Tax Act of 1981 further amended section 6655 to provide that for taxable years beginning in 1984 and thereafter exceptions (1) and (2) are no longer available to large corporations. A transitional rule provides that for taxable years beginning in 1981, 1982, or 1983, a large corporation's estimated tax payments shall in no event be less than 60 percent, 65 percent, and 75 percent, respectively, of the current year's tax in order to come within exception (1) or (2). Exception (3) (relating to the annualization of income) is still available to a large corporation.

For purposes of section 6655, a corporation is considered a large corporation if it (or its predecessor) had taxable income of at least $1 million or more in any of the 3 taxable years immediately preceding the taxable year involved ("testing period").

In determining a corporation's taxable income for any of the taxable years during the testing period, the proposed regulations provide that items which may be carried back under other Code provisions (*e.g.,* those described in sections 172 and 1212) from one of the years in the testing period to another year in the testing period are taken into account. Additionally, if a corporation's taxable income for a year during the testing period is redetermined during that testing period, by reason of an examination by the Internal Revenue Service or otherwise, such redetermination shall be taken into account in determining whether the corporation is "large" for its present taxable year. Any items that are carried forward under other Code provisions are also taken into account in determining a corporation's taxable income during the testing period.

In the case of component members of a controlled group of corporations (as defined in section 1563), the proposed regulations provide that the $1 million amount for any taxable year in the 3-year testing period is divided equally among the component members of such group unless all of such component members consent to an apportionment plan providing for an unequal allocation of such amount. There are special rules for the computation of taxable income for a year in the 3-year testing period where a transaction described in section 351 or section 381(a) occurs.

For taxable years beginning after December 31, 1982, the Tax Equity and Fiscal Responsibility Act of 1982 (TEFRA) increases from 80 percent to 90 percent the amount of a corporation's current tax liability that must be paid in installments. If a corporation makes estimated tax payments of at least 80 percent of its tax liability, the penalty for underpayment of estimated taxes is imposed at three-quarters of the full rate on underpayments determined under section 6621.

Similarly, TEFRA increases from 80 percent to 90 percent the amount of taxes that must be paid under the annualization exception.

An additional exception to the underpayment penalty is added by TEFRA. This new exception applies to a corporation with recurring seasonal income. Under this exception, income may be annualized by assuming that income earned in the current year is earned in the same pattern as in the 3 preceding taxable years. Thus, if a corporation pays its estimated tax installments as if taxable income for the taxable year is earned in the same seasonal pattern as in the preceding 3 years, no penalty for underpayment will be imposed. This exception is available to a large corporation.

TEFRA repealed section 6152 as it applies to corporations. The proposed regulations reflect this change.

Finally, the proposed regulations provide guidance with respect to how a corporation must compute its taxable income for a period of less than a full taxable year when using the annualization exceptions to the underpayment penalty.

REGULATORY FLEXIBILITY ACT

Although this document is a notice of proposed rulemaking which solicits public comment, the Internal Revenue Service has concluded that the regulations proposed herein are interpretative and that the notice and public procedure requirements of 5 U.S.C. 553 do not apply. Accordingly, these proposed regulations do not constitute regulations subject to the Regulatory Flexibility Act (5 U.S.C. chapter 6).

NON-APPLICATION OF EXECUTIVE ORDER 12291

The Treasury Department has determined that this proposed regulation is not subject to review under Executive Order 12291 or the Treasury and OMB implementation of the Order dated April 29, 1983.

COMMENTS AND REQUESTS FOR A PUBLIC HEARING

Before the adoption of these proposed regulations, consideration will be given to any written comments that are submitted (preferably seven copies) to the Commissioner of Internal Revenue. All comments will be available for public inspection and copying. A public hearing will be held upon written request to the Commissioner by any person who has submitted written comments. If a public hearing is held, notice of the time and place will be published in the FEDERAL REGISTER.

PAPERWORK REDUCTION ACT

The collection of information requirements contained in this notice of proposed rulemaking have been submitted to the Office of Management and Budget (OMB) for review under section 3504(h) of the Paperwork Reduction Act. Comments on these requirements should be sent to the Office of Information and Regulatory Affairs of OMB. Attention: Desk Officer for Internal Revenue Service. New Executive Office Building, Washington, D.C. 20503. The Internal Revenue Service requests that persons submitting comments on these requirements to OMB also send copies of those comments to the Service.

DRAFTING INFORMATION

The principal author of these proposed regulations is George T. Magnatta of the Legislation and Regulations Division of the Office of Chief Counsel, Internal Revenue Service. However, personnel from other offices of the Internal Revenue Service and Treasury Department participated in developing the regulations, on matters of both substance and style.

[¶ 49,034]   Proposed Amendments of Regulations (LR-186-80), published in the Federal Register on May 3, 1984.

Installment obligations: Nonrecognition transactions.—Reproduced below is the text of proposed amendments of Reg. § 1.453-1, relating to installment obligations received in certain nonrecognition transactions.

AGENCY: Internal Revenue Service, Treasury.

ACTION: Notice of proposed rulemaking.

SUMMARY: This document contains proposed regulations relating to installment obligations received in certain nonrecognition transactions. Changes to the applicable tax law were made by the Installment Sales Revision Act of 1980. These regulations would provide guidance to those taxpayers receiving installment obligations in certain nonrecognition exchanges and to personnel of the Internal Revenue Service who administer the installment sale provisions.

DATES: Written comments and requests for a public hearing must be delivered or mailed by July 2, 1984. Except as otherwise provided in this document, the amendments are proposed to apply to certain nonrecognition exchanges occurring after October 19, 1980.

ADDRESS: Send comments and a request for a public hearing to: Commissioner of Internal Revenue, Attention: CC:LR:T (LR-186-80), Washington, DC 20224.

FOR FURTHER INFORMATION CONTACT: Linda M. Kroening of the Legislation and Regulations Division, Office of Chief Counsel, Internal Revenue Service, 1111 Constitution Avenue, N.W., Washington, DC 20224. (Attention: CC:LR:T) (202-566-3288).

SUPPLEMENTARY INFORMATION:

BACKGROUND

This document contains proposed amendments to the Income Tax Regulations (26 CFR Part 1) under section 453(f)(6) of the Internal Revenue Code of 1954 relating to installment obligations received in certain nonrecognition exchanges. These amendments are proposed to reflect the amemdment of section 453 by section 2 of the Installment Sales Revision Act of 1980 (94 Stat. 2247). The amendments are to be issued under the authority contained in sections 453(j) and 7805 of the Code (94 Stat. 2247, 68A Stat. 917; 26 U.S.C. 453(j), 7805).

Under prior law, except as otherwise required by the 30-percent initial payment limitation, an installment obligation received as boot in an exchange of like-kind property described in section 1031 qualified for installment method reporting. The value of the like-kind property received by the seller was considered a payment in the year of the exchange and was taken into account in determining both the selling price and the contract price. The Installment Sales Revision Act of 1980 reverses this rule. The value of the like-kind property received is no longer considered a payment in the year of sale nor is it taken into account in determining either the selling price or the contract price. This change in the treatment of the receipt of like-kind property does not change the amount of gain which a taxpayer will recognize on the sale but does defer the time when the taxpayer reports the gain. Under prior law, a taxpayer reported gain upon receipt of the like kind property. Under the new law, the taxpayer does not report gain with respect to an installment obligation until he receives payment on or disposes of the installment obligation.

Under the Installment Sales Revision Act of 1980, the total contract price in a like-kind exchange in which an installment obligation is received as boot (property received in addition to the like-kind property) is the sum of cash received, the fair market value of other property (i.e., property other than like-kind property) received, and the face amount (less any discount required under section 483) of the installment obligation.

The basis of the like-kind property received (determined under section 1031(d)) will be determined as if the obligation had been satisfied at its face value less any discount for unstated interest. The taxpayer's basis in the transferred property is allocated first to the like-kind property received (but not in excess of its fair market value) and any remaining basis is used to determine the gross profit ratio.

The Act also provides that, under a plan of corporate reorganization, exchanges described in section 356(a) shall be treated similarly to section 1031(b) exchanges if the installment boot is not treated as a dividend. The Act excludes from installment method reporting any installment obligation which is treated as a dividend or would be treated as a dividend if the corporation had had sufficient earnings and profits to distribute a dividend.

These regulations also permit installment method reporting in certain nonrecognition exchanges (for example, section 351(b) exchanges) which are not explicitly dealt with in the Act. For these nonrecognition exchanges, the same basic rules apply: basis in the transferred property is first allocated to the nonrecognition property received, but not in excess of the fair market value of that property. Any excess basis is allocated to the installment note and any nonqualifying property.

Section 1.453-1 contains material relating to installment sales by dealers in personal property. It is intended that eventually all of the regulations relating to installment sales will be amended to reflect the amendments to section 453 made by the Installment Sales Revision Act of 1980. Until those amendments are adopted, provisions in §1.453-1 which relate to matters not covered in this document or other proposed regulations relating to installment method reporting will remain in effect.

SPECIAL ANALYSES

The Commissioner of Internal Revenue has determined that this proposed rule is not a major rule as defined in Executive Order 12291. Accordingly, a Regulatory Impact Analysis is not required.

Although this document is a notice of proposed rulemaking that solicits public comment, the Internal Revenue Service has concluded that the regulations proposed herein are interpretative and that the notice and public procedure requirements of 5 U.S.C. 553 do not apply. Accordingly, no Regulatory Flexibility Analysis is required by chapter 5 of title 5, United States Code.

COMMENTS AND REQUEST FOR A PUBLIC HEARING

Before adopting these proposed regulations, consideration will be given to any written comments that are submitted (preferably seven copies) to the Commissioner of Internal Revenue. All comments will be available for public inspection and copying. A public hearing will be held upon written request to the Commissioner by any person who has submitted written comments. If a public hearing is held, notice of the time and place will be published in the FEDERAL REGISTER.

DRAFTING INFORMATION

The principal author of this regulation is Phoebe A. Mix of the Legislation and Regulations Division of the Office of Chief Counsel, Internal Revenue Service. However, personnel from other offices of the Internal Revenue Service and Treasury Department participated in developing the regulations, on matters of both substance and style.

§1.453-1. **Installment method reporting for sales of real property and casual sales of personal property.—**

* * * * *

(f) *Installment obligations received in certain nonrecognition exchanges* .—(1) *Exchanges described in section 1031(b)* .—(i) *In general* .—The provisions of paragraph (f)(1) of this section apply to exchanges described in section 1031(b) ("section 1031(b) exchanges") in which the taxpayer receives as boot (property which is "other property" under section 1031(b)) an installment obligation issued by the other party to the exchange, as well as property with respect to which no gain or loss is recognized ("permitted property" for purposes of paragraph (f)(1) of this section). However, an exchange otherwise described in section 1036 in which the receipt of an installment obligation is treated as a dividend (or would be treated as a dividend if the issuing corporation had adequate earnings and profits) is not a section 1031(b) exchange for purposes of this section.

(ii) *Exclusion from payment* .—Receipt of permitted property will not be considered payment for purposes of paragraph (c) of this section.

(iii) *Installment method determinations* .—In a section 1031(b) exchange, the taxpayer's basis in the property transferred by the taxpayer, including nondeductible expenses of the exchange, will first be allocated to the permitted property received by the taxpayer up to, but not in excess of, the fair market value of such property. If the taxpayer's basis exceeds the fair market value of the permitted property, that excess amount of basis is "excess basis." In making all required installment method determinations, the exchange is treated as if the taxpayer had made an installment sale of appreciated property (with a basis equal to the amount of excess basis) in which the consideration received was the installment obligation and any other boot. In a section 1031(b) exchange, only net qualifying indebtedness is taken into account in determining the amount of qualifying indebtedness (as defined in §1.453-1A(b)(2)(iv)). For this purpose, net qualifying indebtedness is the excess of—

      (A) Liabilities of the taxpayer (or liabilities encumbering the property) assumed or taken subject to by the other party to the exchange as part of the consideration to the taxpayer, over

      (B) The sum of any net cash paid (cash paid less any cash received) by the taxpayer in the exchange and any liability assumed or taken subject to by the taxpayer in the exchange.

Therefore, for purposes of installment method determinations, the selling price is the sum of the face value of the installment obligation (reduced by any portion of the obligation characterized as interest by section 483 or 1232), any net qualifying indebtedness, any cash received (in excess of any cash paid) by the taxpayer, and the fair market value of any other boot. The basis is the excess basis. The total contract price is the selling price less any net qualifying indebtedness that does not exceed the excess basis. Finally, payment in the year of exchange includes any net qualifying indebtedness that exceeds the excess basis.

      (iv) *Examples* .—The provisions of paragraph (f)(1) of this section are illustrated by the following examples:

      Example (1). In 1981, A makes a section 1031(b) exchange of real property held for investment (basis $400,000) for permitted property worth $200,000, and an $800,000 installment obligation issued by the other party to the exchange bearing adequate stated interest. Neither the property transferred by A nor the property received in the exchange is mortgaged property. A's basis of $400,000 is allocated first to the permitted property received, up to the fair market value of $200,000. A's excess basis is $200,000 ($400,000 – $200,000). Since the installment obligation is the only boot received by A in the exchange, A's entire excess basis of $200,000 is allocable to it. Under the installment method, the selling price is $800,000 (the face amount of the installment obligation), and the contract price is also $800,000 (selling price less qualifying indebtedness, $800,000 – 0). The gross profit is $600,000 (selling price less excess basis allocated to the installment obligation, $800,000 – $200,000), and the gross profit ratio is 75% ($600,000/$800,000). A recognizes no gain until payments are received on the installment obligation. As A receives payments (exclusive of interest) on the installment obligation, 75% of each payment will be gain attributable to the exchange and 25% of each payment will be recovery of basis. A will hold the permitted property received in the exchange with a basis of $200,000.

      Example (2). The facts are the same as in example (1), except that in the exchange A receives permitted property worth $200,000, a $600,000 installment obligation, and $200,000 in cash. A is treated as having sold appreciated property (basis equal to the $200,000 excess basis) for $200,000 cash and a $600,000 installment obligation. As in example (1), the contract price and the selling price are $800,000, the gross profit is $600,000, and the gross profit ratio is 75%. Accordingly, A will recognize gain of $150,000 on receipt of the cash (75% of the $200,000 payment). A holds the permitted property with a basis of $200,000.

      Example (3). The facts are the same as in example (2), except that A does not receive $200,000 in cash. Instead, the property transferred by A in the exchange was subject to a mortgage (meeting the definition of qualifying indebtedness) of $200,000 to which the other party to the exchange took subject. The permitted property received by A in the exchange was not subject to a mortgage. A is treated as having sold appreciated property (basis equal to $200,000 excess basis) for $600,000 cash and $200,000 net relief of mortgage liability. The mortgage liability of which A is deemed relieved ($200,000), reduced by any cash paid by A and any mortgage liability encumbering the like-kind property received by A in the simultaneous exchange ($0), is treated as qualifying indebtedness. Since the qualifying indebtedness ($200,000) does not exceed A's excess basis ($200,000), B's taking subject to such indebtedness does not constitute payment to A in the year of exchange. Under the installment method, the selling price is $800,000 and the total contract price is $600,000 (selling price of $800,000 less $200,000 of qualifying indebtedness that does not exceed A's excess basis). Gross profit is also $600,000 (800,000 selling price less $200,000 excess basis), and the gross profit ratio is 1 ($600,000/600,000). A recognizes no gain until payments are received on the installment obligation. As A receives payment (exclusive of interest) in the $600,000 installment obligation, the full amount received will be gain attributable to the exchange. A holds the permitted property with a basis of $200,000.

      Example (4). The facts are the same as in example (2), except that A's basis in the property transferred by A was only $160,000. Since A's basis first must be allocated to permitted property received in the exchange up to the fair market value ($200,000) of that permitted property, there is no excess basis. Accordingly, A will recognize gain equal to the full amount of cash received ($200,000), and will hold the installment obligation at a basis of zero. A will hold the permitted property at a basis of $160,000.

      (2) *Certain exchanges described in section 356(a)* .—(i) *In general* .—The provisions of paragraph (f)(2) of this section apply to exchanges described in section 356(a)(1) ("section 356(a)(1) exchanges") in which the taxpayer receives as boot (property which is "other property" under section 356(a)(1)(B)) an installment obligation issued by a qualifying corporation which is not treated as a dividend to the taxpayer. For purposes of section 453(f)(6) and paragraph (f)(2) of this section, any such section 356(a)(1) exchange shall be treated as a disposition of property by the taxpayer to the qualifying corporation and an acquisition of such property by the qualifying corporation from the taxpayer. If section 354 would apply to the exchange but for the receipt of boot, the term "qualifying corporation" means a corpoation the stock of which could be received by the taxpayer in the exchange without recognition of gain or loss. If section 355 would apply to the exchange but for the receipt of boot, the term "qualifying corporation" means the distributing corporation (referred to in section 355(a)(1)(A)). Receipt of an installment obligation is treated as a dividend if section 356(a)(2) applies (determined without regard to the presence or absence of accumulated earnings and profits), or if section 356(e) (relating to certain exchanges for section 306 stock) applies to the taxpayer's receipt of the installment obligation.

      (ii) *Exclusion from payment* .—Receipt of permitted property shall not be considered payment for purposes of paragraph (c) of this section. For purposes of paragraph (f)(1) of this section, "permitted property" means property, the receipt of which does not result in recognition of gain under section 356(a)(1) (i.e., stock of a qualifying corporation).

      (iii) *Installment method determinations* .—Installment method determinations with respect to an installment obligation received in an exchange to which paragraph (f)(2) of this section applies shall be made in accordance with the rules prescribed in paragraph (f)(1)(iii) of this section. In applying such rules, a section 356(a)(1) exchange shall be treated as a section 1031(b) exchange and permitted property shall mean permitted property described in paragraph (f)(2) of this section.

      (iv) *Examples* .—The provisions of paragraph (f)(2) of this section are illustrated by the following examples:

      Example (1). T corporation and P corporation are unrelated closely held corporations. A owns 10% of the stock of T. A is not related to any other T stockholder or to any P stockholder. S corporation is a wholly-owned subsidiary of P. Pursuant to a plan of reorganization, T merges with and into S. In the merger, the T shares held by A are exchanged for shares of P worth $100,000 and a $300,000 installment obligation (bearing adequate interest) issued by P. In the merger the other stockholders of T exchange their T shares solely for P shares worth, in the aggregate, $3,600,000. The merger is a reorganization described in sections 368(a)(1)(A) and (a)(2)(D), and T, S, and P each is a party to the reorganization under section 368(b). P is a qualifying corporation and A is party to a section 356(a)(1) exchange in which receipt by A of the installment obligation will not be treated as a dividend to A. Because, for purposes of section 453(f)(6), this transaction is treated as a direct exchange between P and A, no gain or loss is recognized by S with respect to the P obligation. Assume A's basis in the T shares exchanged by A was $150,000. A's basis is allocated first to the permitted property (P shares) received, up to the fair market value of $100,000. A's excess basis is $50,000 ($150,000 – $100,000). Since the installment obligation is the only boot received by A in the exchange, the entire excess basis of $50,000 is allocable to it. Under the installment method, the contract price is $300,000 (face amount of the installment obligation), the gross profit is $250,000 (contract price less $50,000 excess basis allocated to the installment obligation), and the gross profit ratio is $^5/_6$ ($250,000/$300,000). A recognizes no gain until payments are received on the installment obligation. As A receives payments (exclusive of interest) on the installment obligation, $^5/_6$ths of each payment will be gain attributable to the exchange and $^1/_6$th of each payment will be recovery of basis. A will hold the permitted property (P stock) received in the exchange at a basis of $100,000.

Example (2). The facts are the same as in exmaple (1). B, who also owns 10% of the stock of T directly and owns no other stock by T by attribution within the meaning of 318(a), exchanges the T shares in the merger for $400,000 installment obligation issued by P (bearing adequate interest). Although section 356(a)(1) will not apply to this exchange because B receives no P stock in the transaction and the character of the gain is determined under section 302(a), for purposes of section 453 and paragraph (a) of this section, B is treated as having sold the T shares to P in exchange for P's installment obligation. B will report the installment sale on the installment method unless B elects under paragraph (e) of this section not to report the transaction on the installment method. If, by reason of constructive ownership of T shares under section 381(a) and failure to meet the requirements of section 302(c)(2), the character of the transaction as to B were determined under section 302(d), section 453 would not apply to the exchange by B.

Example (3). The facts are the same as in examples (1) and (2), except that the P stock is voting stock and S merges into T in a reorganization described in section 368(a)(2)(E). The results are the same as in examples (1) and (2).

Example (4) (i). T Corporation and larger P Corporation are unrelated public corporations the stock of each of which is widely held. A is a stockholder of T. S Corporation is a wholly owned subsidiary of P. On December 31, 1981, pursuant to a plan of reorganization which provides for a "note option" election, T merges with and into S. In the merger, A exercises the note option and the T shares held by A are exchanged for a $30,000 installment obligation (bearing adequate interest) issued by P, 1,000 P shares (worth $10 per share on the date of merger), and a non-negotiable certificate evidencing a right to receive (within 5 years from the date of merger) up to 1,000 additional P shares (plus adequate interest) if certain earnings conditions are satisfied. Neither the installment obligation nor the certificate evidencing the right to receive additional P shares is readily tradable within the meaning of §1.453-1A(c)(4)(iv)(C). There is a valid business reason for not issuing all of the P shares immediately. Certain of the other T shareholders exercise the note option and exchange their T shares for a similar package. Other T shareholders do not exercise the note option and receive in the merger P shares plus a non-negotiable right to receive up to an equal number of additional P shares (plus adequate interest) within 5 years. In the aggregate, the total outstanding T shares are exchanged for 20% P installment obligations, 40% P shares, and rights to receive an equal number of additional P shares within 5 years. The merger of T into S qualifies as a reorganization under section 368(a)(1)(A) and (a)(2)(D). P is a qualifying corporation, the P shares received and which may subsequently be received by A are permitted property, and the exchange to which A is a party is a section 356(a)(1) exchange.

(ii) Assume A's basis in the T shares exchanged by A was $25,000. A's basis is allocated first to permitted property (P shares) up to fair market value. In the exchange A has received 1,000 P shares (worth $10,000) and may receive up to an additional 1,000 P shares in the future. In allocating A's basis, it is assumed that all contingencies contemplated by the merger agreement will be met or otherwise resolved in a manner that will maximize the consideration A will receive. It is further assumed that each P share, when received, will have a fair market value equal to the fair market value ($10) of a P share at the date of merger. Accordingly, since A may receive a maximum of 2,000 P shares, $20,000 (2,000 × $10) of A's basis will be allocated to the 1,000 P shares A has received ($10 per share) and to A's right to receive up to an additional 1,000 P shares (at $10 per share). A's excess basis of $5,000 ($25,000 – $20,000) is allocated to the $30,000 P installment obligation.

(iii) In 1983 the earnings condition is fully satisfied and A receives an additional 1,000 P shares (plus adequate interest). Each P share held by A has a basis of $10.

(iv) Assume instead that the earnings condition is only partly satisfied and, by the close of 1986, A has received only an additional 600 P shares and is not entitled to receive any further P shares. Initially, each P share received by A was assigned a basis of $10. Of A's $25,000 basis in the T shares exchanged, $4,000 ($20,000 initially allocated to P shares received and to be received less $16,000 (1,600 P shares × $10)) now must be accounted for. The $4,000 of remaining basis will be assigned to the P shares than held by A. Thus, if A continues to hold all 1,600 P shares, A's basis in each P share will be increased by $2.50 ($4,000 divided by 1,600 P shares). If A previously sold 800 P shares and retains only 800 P shares, A's basis in each retained P share will be increased by $5 ($4,000 divided by 800 P shares). If A retains no P shares, and if all of the additional 600 P shares were issued to A and sold by A before the final year of the five year earn-out term (*i.e.*, by the end of 1985), A's remaining basis of $4,000 will be added to the basis at which A holds the unpaid portion of the P installment obligation (up to but not in excess of the maximum amount remaining payable under that obligation less A's remaining basis in the installment obligation determined immediately before the addition to basis). If A has previously disposed of the P installment obligation, so that A holds neither P shares nor the P installment obligation to which the remaining $4,000 of A's basis can be allocated, A will be allowed a $4,000 loss in 1986. Similarly, if A continues to hold the P installment obligation but the facts are such that the maximum amount thereafter payable under the obligation is only $3,000 in excess of A's basis in the obligation determined immediately before assignment of A's remaining $4,000 basis, $3,000 of that remaining basis would be assigned to the installment obligation and P would be allowed a $1,000 loss in 1986.

Example (5). Pursuant to a plan to acquire all the stock of T corporation, P purchases 90% of the T stock for cash. To acquire the remaining 10% of T stock P creates S corporation and transfers P stock and P's newly issued installment notes to S in exchange for all of S's stock. The P notes are not readily tradable. Thereafter S merges into T, and P stock and P's installment notes are distributed to the T minority shareholders, and the S stock held by P is automatically converted into T stock. Assume that for federal tax purposes the existence of S is disregarded and the transaction is treated as a sale of T stock to P in exchange for P stock and P's installment notes. The minority shareholders will report the gain realized on the receipt of the P installment notes on the installment method unless they elect otherwise. The receipt of P stock will be treated as a payment in the year of sale.

Example (6). The facts are the same as example (5) except P transferred only P's installment notes to S and only these notes were distributed to T minority shareholders. As in example (5) the transaction is treated as a sale of T stock to P in exchange for P's installment notes. Each minority shareholder realizing gain on the receipt of the installment notes will report the gain on the installment method unless electing otherwise.

(3) *Other partial recognition exchanges* .—(i) *In general* .—The provisions of paragraph (f)(3) of this section apply to exchanges not described in paragraph (f)(1) or (2) of this section in which a taxpayer, in exchange for appreciated property, receives both permitted property (*i.e.*,

property with respect to which no gain or loss would be recognized but which, in the hands of the taxpayer, would have as basis for determining gain or loss the same basis in whole or in part as the property exchanged) and boot that includes an installment obligation issued by the other party to the exchange. Ordinarily, the installment method rules set forth in paragraph (f)(1)(ii) and (iii) of this section will apply to an exchange described in paragraph (f)(3) of this section subject to such variations, if any, as may be required under the applicable provisions of the Code.

(ii) *Exchanges to which section 351 applies* .—If a taxpayer receives, in an exchange to which section 351(b) applies (a "section 351(b) exchange"), an installment obligation that is not a security within the meaning of section 351(a), the installment obligation is boot and the stock and securities (within the meaning of section 351(a)) are permitted property (within the meaning of paragraph (f)(1)(ii) of this section). The taxpayer will report the installment obligation on the installment method and any other boot received will be treated as a payment made in the year of the exchange. In applying the rules of paragraph (f)(1)(iii) of this section to a section 351(b) exchange the excess basis is the amount, if any, by which the taxpayer's basis in the property transferred (plus any cash transferred) by the taxpayer exceeds the sum of the transferred liabilities which are not treated as money received under section 357 plus the fair market value of permitted property received by the taxpayer. In determining selling price and total contract price, transferred liabilities which are not treated as money received under section 357 shall be disregarded. For purposes of paragraph (f)(3)(ii) of this section, transferred liabilities are liabilities described in section 357(a)(2). Solely for the purpose of applying section 358(a)(1), the taxpayer shall be treated as if the taxpayer elected not to report receipt of the installment obligation on the installment method. Under section 362(a)(1) the corporation's basis in the property received from the taxpayer is the taxpayer's basis in the property increased by the gain recognized by the taxpayer at the time of the exchange. As the taxpayer recognizes gain on the installment method, the corporation will increase its basis in the property by an amount equal to the amount of gain recognized by the taxpayer.

(iii) *Examples* .—The provisions of paragraph (f)(3) of this section are illustrated by the following examples. In each example, assume that adequate stated interest means both a reasonable rate of interest within the meaning of any applicable regulation promulgated under section 385 and a rate of interest not less than the test rate prescribed in the regulations under section 483, and that the debt to equity ratio of the issuing corporation is a permissible ratio under any applicable regulation promulgated under section 385.

Example (1). A owns Blackacre, unimproved real property, with a basis of $300,000. The fair market value of Blackacre is $700,000. Blackacre is encumbered by a longstanding mortgage of $200,000. A transfers Blackacre, subject to the mortgage, to a newly organized X corporation. A receives in exchange all of the stock of X, worth $400,000, and a $100,000 installment obligation (bearing adequate stated interest) issued by X. A realizes $400,000 of gain on the exchange. The installment obligation calls for a single payment of the full $100,000 face amount three years following the date of issue. The installment obligation is not a "security" within the meaning of section 351(a), and thus the exchange by A is a transaction described in section 351(b). The installment obligation is boot received by A in the exchange and the X stock is permitted property received by A in exchange. In applying the provisions of paragraph (f)(1)(ii) and (iii) of this section to a section 351(b) exchange, reference is required to section 357(a) under which the $200,000 mortgage liability is not treated as money or other property received by A in the exchange, and to section 358(a)(1) under which the basis of the X stock in the hands of A will be determined. These rules apply as follows: Neither receipt of the X stock nor relief of the mortgage encumbrance is treated as payment to A and thus A will recognize no gain in the year of the exchange. A's basis of $300,000 in Blackacre is reduced by the $200,000 mortgage from which A is deemed relieved in the exchange. The remaining basis of $100,000 is allocated to the X stock (but not in excess of the fair market value of the X stock); since the fair market value of the X stock is $400,000, the basis of the X stock in the hands of A is $100,000. Accordingly, in A's hands the installment obligation has a basis of zero. In the hands of X, the initial basis of Blackacre, determined under section 362(a), is $300,000 (the basis of the property in the hands of A), increased by the amount of gain recognized by A at the time of the transfer ($0)). As A receives payments on the installment obligation and recognizes gain, X's basis in Blackacre will be increased, at that time, in an amount equal to the gain recognized by A. Thus, if the $100,000 installment obligation is paid in full on the third anniversary date, A will recognize gain of $100,000 (because A's basis in the installment obligation is zero) and X at that time will increase the basis at which it holds Blackacre by $100,000. If in the third year X had sold the property for cash before making payment on the installment obligation, X would recognize a loss of $100,000 when X paid the obligation in that amount to A on the third anniversary date.

Example (2). B owns Whiteacre, unencumbered, unimproved real property, with a basis of $250,000. The fair market value of Whiteacre is $300,000. A transfers Whiteacre to newly organized Y corporation in exchange for all of the stock of Y corporation (worth $200,000) and a $100,000 installment obligation (bearing adequate interest). The installment obligation is payable in full on the second anniversary of the date of issue. The installment obligation is not a "security" within the meaning of section 351(a), and thus the transaction is a section 351(b) exchange. Applying the rules summarized in example (1) to the facts of this case, receipt of the installment obligation is not treated as payment to A, $200,000 of A's basis of $250,000 in Whiteacre is allocated to the Y stock (equal to the fair market value of the Y stock), and the excess basis of $50,000 is allocated to the installment obligation. In the hands of Y, the basis of Whiteacre initially is $250,000, and will be increased by $50,000 when the installment obligation is paid and A recognizes gain of $50,000.

Example (3). D owns a machine which is unencumbered 5-year recovery property with an adjusted basis of $500,000. The recomputed basis (as defined in section 1245(a)(2)) of the machine in the hands of D is $1 million. The fair market value of the machine also is $1 million. D transfers the machine to newly organized X corporation, and E, an unrelated individual, simultaneously transfers property worth $1 million to X corporation. D receives in exchange 400 shares of X common stock worth $400,000, a $400,000 15-year debenture issued by X (worth its face amount), and a $200,000 installment obligation (bearing adequate interest) issed by X. The installment obligation calls for a single payment of the full $200,000 face amount two years following the date of issue. E receives in the exchange 1,000 shares of X common stock worth $1 million. D and E are in control (as defined in section 368(c)) of X immediately after the exchange. The debenture received by D is a "security" within the meaning of section 351(a), but the installment obligation received by D is not a "security" within the meaning of that section and thus the exchange by D is a transaction described in section 351(b). The installment obligation is boot received by D in the exchange and the X stock and X debenture are permitted property received by D in the exchange. Since the aggregate fair market value ($800,000) of X stock ($400,000) and the X debenture ($400,000) received by D exceeds D's $500,000 adjusted basis in the machine, all of that basis is allocated proportionately among the items of permitted property. Thus, D will hold the X stock with a basis of $250,000 and the X debenture with a basis of $250,000. Since there is no excess basis, in the hands of D the installment obligation has a basis of zero. In the hands of X, the adjusted basis of the machine remains $500,000. When D receives payment from X on the $200,000 installment obligation, D will recognize gain of $200,000, all of which gain will be treated as ordinary income. See sections 1245(a)(1) and 453B(a). At that time, X's adjusted basis in the machine will be increased in an amount equal to the $200,000 gain recognized by D.

Example (4). In 1976 H and W purchased Blackacre as their principal residence for $50,000. In 1981 H and W, both of whom are less than 55 years of age, sold Blackacre to A for $90,000: $15,000 cash, A's assumption of the $40,000 mortgage, and A's promise to pay H and W $7,000 (with adequate stated interest) in each of the next 5 years. Within 2 years of the sale of Blackacre, H and W acquire Whiteacre, an unencumbered property, which will be their principal residence, for $80,000. Of the $40,000 gain that H and W realized upon the sale of Whiteacre, $30,000 will not be recognized pursuant to the provisions of section 1034. Unless H and W elect not to report the transaction on the installment method, they will treat the $10,000 gain to be recognized as the gross profit for purposes of calculating the gross profit ratio. Accordingly the gross profit ratio is $^{1}/_{5}$ ($10,000 gross profit/$50,000 contract price) and H and W will report as gain $3,000 ($^{1}/_{5} \times$ $15,000) in the year of the sale and $1,400 ($^{1}/_{5} \times$ $7,000) in each of the next five years.

(4) *Installment obligations received as distributions in redemptions of stock pursuant to section 302(a)* .—If a corporation redeems its stock and the redemption is treated as a distribution in part or full payment in exchange for the stock under section 302(a), then an installment obligation which meets the requirements of section 453 and is distributed in the redemption shall be reported on the installment method unless the taxpayer elects otherwise.

Example. A owns 10% of the stock of X corporation and is not considered as owning (under section 318(a)) any other shares of X corporation. X redeems all of A's X shares and distributes its installment obligation to A in full payment. The reduction is treated as a sale of the X shares by A under section 302(b)(3). A will report any gain realized in the redemption on the installment method unless A elects otherwise.

* * *

[¶ 49,035]   **Proposed Regulations (LR-221-83),** published in the Federal Register on May 7, 1984.

Indian tribal governments: Treatment as states.—Reg. §§ 305.7701-1 and 305.7871-1, relating to the treatment of Indian tribal governments as states, are proposed.

AGENCY: Internal Revenue Service, Treasury.

ACTION: Notice of proposed rulemaking by cross-reference to temporary regulations.

SUMMARY: In the Rules and Regulations portion of this FEDERAL REGISTER, the Internal Revenue Service is issuing temporary regulations that relate to the treatment of Indian tribal governments as States for certain purposes. The text of those temporary regulations also serves as the comment document for this proposed rulemaking.

DATES: Written comments and requests for a public hearing must be delivered by July 6, 1984. The amendments are proposed to be effective generally for taxable years beginning after December 31, 1982, and before January 1, 1985.

ADDRESS: Send comments and requests for a public hearing to: Commissioner of Internal Revenue,

Attention: CC:LR:T (LR-221-83), Washington, D.C. 20224.

FOR FURTHER INFORMATION CONTACT: Linda M. Kroening, Office of Chief Counsel, Internal Revenue Service, 1111 Constitution Avenue, N.W., Washington, D.C. 20224 (Attention: CC:LR:T) (202-566-3288) (not a toll-free call).

SUPPLEMENTARY INFORMATION:

BACKGROUND

The temporary regulations in the Rules and Regulations portion of this issue of the FEDERAL REGISTER add Part 305 to Title 26 of the Code of Federal Regulations. The final regulations, which this document proposes to base on those temporary regulations, would amend Part 301 of Title 26 of the Code of Federal Regulations.

The regulations provide guidance with respect to the treatment of Indian tribal governments as States for certain purposes under sections 7701(a)(40) and 7871 of the Internal Revenue Code of 1954, as added to the Code by sections 202 and 203 of the Indian Tribal Governmental Tax Status Act of 1982 (Pub. L. 97-473, 96 Stat. 2608, 2611). The regulations are to be issued under the authority contained in section 7805 of the Internal Revenue Code of 1954 (68A Stat. 917, 26 U.S.C. 7805). For the text of the temporary regulations, see FR Doc. (T.D. 7952) published in the Rules and Regulations portion of this issue of the FEDERAL REGISTER. The preamble to the temporary regulations provides a discussion of the rules.

SPECIAL ANALYSES

The Commissioner of Internal Revenue has determined that this proposed rule is not a major rule as defined in Executive Order 12291and that a Regulatory Impact Analysis is therefore not required.

Although this document is a notice of proposed rulemaking that solicits public comments, the Internal Revenue Service has concluded that the regulations proposed herein are interpretative and that the notice and public procedure requirements of 5 U.S.C. 553 do not apply. Accordingly, no Regulatory Flexibility Analysis is required by Chapter 6 of Title 5, United States Code.

COMMENTS AND REQUESTS FOR A PUBLIC HEARING

Before adopting these proposed regulations, consideration will be given to any written comments that are submitted (preferably seven copies) to the Commissioner of Internal Revenue. All comments will be available for public inspection and copying. A public hearing will be held upon written request to the Commissioner by any person who has submitted written comments. If a public hearing is held, notice of the time and place will be published in the FEDERAL REGISTER.

The collection of information requirements contained in this notice of proposed rulemaking have been submitted to the Office of Management and Budget (OMB) for review under section 3504(h) of the Paperwork Reduction Act. Comments on these requirements should be sent to the Office of Information and Regulatory Affairs of OMB, Attention: Desk Officer for Internal Revenue Service, New Executive Office Building, Washington, D.C. 20503. The Internal Revenue Service requests that persons submitting comments on these requirements to OMB also send copies of those comments to the Service.

DRAFTING INFORMATION

The principal author of these proposed regulations is Linda M. Kroening of the Legislation and Regulations Division of the Office of Chief Counsel, Internal Revenue Service. However, personnel from other offices of the Internal Revenue Service and Treasury Department participated in developing the regulations, on matters of both substance and style.

LIST OF SUBJECTS IN 26 CFR PART 301

Administrative practice and procedure, Bankruptcy, Courts, Crime, Employment taxes, Estate taxes, Excise taxes, Gift taxes, Income taxes, Investigations, Law enforcement, Penalties, Pensions, Statistics, Taxes, Disclosure of information filing requirements, Indian tribal governments.

[¶ 49,036]   **Proposed Regulations (LR-142-84),** published in the Federal Register on August 15, 1984.

Tax shelter registration.—Temporary Reg. § 301.6111-1T, relating to tax shelter registration, is proposed. Temporary Reg. § 301.6111-2T was removed on 4/17/1985 by T.D. 8020. Temporary Reg. § 301.6707-1T was removed on 7/30/2014 by T.D. 9686.

AGENCY: Internal Revenue Service, Treasury.

ACTION: Notice of proposed rulemaking by cross-reference to temporary regulations.

SUMMARY: In the Rules and Regulations portion of this issue of the *Federal Register,* the Internal Revenue Service is issuing temporary regulations relating to tax shelter registration. The text of those temporary regulations also serves as the comment document for this proposed rulemaking.

DATES: Written comments and requests for a public hearing must be delivered by October 15, 1984. The amendments are proposed to be effective generally with respect to tax shelters in which any interest is first sold after August 31, 1984.

ADDRESS: Send comments and requests for a public hearing to: Commissioner of Internal Revenue, Attention: CC:LR:T (LR-142-84), Washington, D.C. 20224.

FOR FURTHER INFORMATION CONTACT: Cynthia L. Clark, Office of Chief Counsel, Internal Revenue Service, 1111 Constitution Avenue, N.W., Washington, D.C. 20224 (Attention: CC:LR:T) (202-566-3828 not a toll-free call).

SUPPLEMENTARY INFORMATION:

BACKGROUND

The temporary regulations in the Rules and Regulations portion of this issue of the *Federal Register* amend Part 301 of Title 26 of the Code of Federal Regulations. The temporary regulations are designated by a "T" following their section citation. The final regulations, which this document proposes to base on those temporary regulations, would amend Part 301 of Title 26 of the Code of Federal Regulations.

The regulations provide rules relating to both tax shelter registration under section 6111 of the Internal Revenue Code of 1954 and the penalties imposed by section 6707 for failure properly to register tax shelters or to furnish the tax shelter registration number. The regulations reflect the addition of sections 6111 and 6707 to the Code by section 141 of the Tax Reform Act of 1984 (Pub. L. 98-369, 98 Stat. 678). The regulations are to be issued under the authority contained in sections 6111 and 7805 of the Internal Revenue Code of 1954 (98 Stat. 678, 26 U.S.C. 6111; 68A Stat. 917, 26 U.S.C. 7805). For the text of the temporary regulations, see FR Doc. (T.D. 7964) published in the Rules and Regulations portion of this issue of the *Federal Register.* The preamble to the temporary regulations provides a discussion of the rules.

EXECUTIVE ORDER 12291; REGULATORY FLEXIBILITY ACT

The Commissioner of Internal Revenue has determined that this proposed rule is not a major rule as defined in Executive Order 12291 and that a Regulatory Impact Analysis is therefore not required.

Although this document is a notice of proposed rulemaking that solicits public comments, the Internal Revenue Service has concluded that the regulations proposed herein are interpretative and that the notice and public procedure requirements of 5 U.S.C. 553 do not apply. Accordingly, these proposed regulations do not constitute regulations subject to the Regulatory Flexibility Act (5 U.S.C. Chapter 6).

COMMENTS AND REQUESTS FOR A PUBLIC HEARING

Before adopting these proposed regulations, consideration will be given to any written comments that are submitted (preferably seven copies) to the Commissioner of Internal Revenue. All comments will be available for public inspection and copying. A public hearing will be held upon written request to the Commissioner by any person who has submitted written comments. If a public hearing is held, notice of the time and place will be published in the *Federal Register.*

The collection of information requirements contained in this notice of proposed rulemaking have been submitted to the Office of Management and Budget (OMB) for review under section 3504(h) of the Paperwork Reduction Act. Comments on these requirements should be sent to the Office of Information and Regulatory Affairs of OMB, Attention: Desk Officer for Internal Revenue Service, New Executive Office Building, Washington, D.C. 20503. The Internal Revenue Service requests that persons submitting comments on these requirements to OMB also send copies of those comments to the Service.

DRAFTING INFORMATION

The principal author of these proposed regulations is Cynthia Clark of the Legislation and Regulations Division of the Office of Chief Counsel, Internal Revenue Service. However, personnel from other offices of the Internal Revenue Service and Treasury Department participated in developing the regulations, on matters of both substance and style.

[¶ 49,038]   **Proposed Amendments of Regulations (LR-190-78),** published in the Federal Register on August 22, 1984.

Industrial development bonds: Issuance to finance certain water facilities.—An amendment of Reg. § 1.103-8(h), relating to the income tax exemption for interest on industrial development bonds issued to finance certain water facilities, is proposed.

AGENCY: Internal Revenue Service, Treasury.

ACTION: Notice of proposed rulemaking.

SUMMARY: This document contains proposed regulations relating to the income tax exemption for interest on industrial development bonds issued to finance certain water facilities. Changes to the applicable tax law were made by the Revenue Act of 1978. The regulations would affect issuers, holders, and recipients of the proceeds of such obligations and provide them with the guidance needed to comply with the changed tax law.

DATES: Written comments and requests for a public hearing must be delivered or mailed by October 22, 1984. The amendments are proposed to be effective with respect to obligations issued by or on behalf of a State or local government after November 6, 1978.

ADDRESS: Send comments and requests for a public hearing to: Commissioner of Internal Revenue, 1111 Constitution Avenue, N.W., Washington, D.C. 20224, Attention: CC:LR:T (LR-190-78).

FOR FURTHER INFORMATION CONTACT: John A. Tolleris of the Legislation and Regulations Division, Office of the Chief Counsel, Internal Revenue Service, 1111 Constitution Avenue, N.W., Washington, D.C. 20224 (Attention: CC:LR:T) (202-566-3590).

SUPPLEMENTARY INFORMATION:

BACKGROUND

This document contains proposed amendments to the Income Tax Regulations (26 CFR Part 1) under section 103 of the Internal Revenue Code of 1954. These amendments are proposed to conform the regulations of section 333 of the Revenue Act of 1978 (92 Stat. 2840). They are to be issued under the authority contained in section 7805 of the Internal Revenue Code of 1954 (68A Stat. 917, 26 U.S.C. 7805).

EXPLANATION OF PROVISIONS

Section 333 of the Revenue Act of 1978 amended Code section 103(b)(4)(G) to expand the types of "facilities for the furnishing of water" that qualify for tax-exempt financing under section 103(b)(4)(G). The proposed regulations set out three principal requirements that facilities must meet to qualify for tax-exempt financing under Code section 103(b)(4)(G).

The first of these major requirements is that the facility must be a system that furnishes water or be a component of a system or project that furnishes water. Ordinarily, such a system or project would include only those components necessary for the collection, treatment, and distribution of water to a service area. The facility must not be a production facility.

The second major requirement is that the facility must make its water available to members of the general public, which may include agricultural, industrial, commercial, and electric utility users. Although a facility is not required to serve all segments of the general public within its service area in order to qualify for tax-exempt financing, it must grant access for residential users or municipal water districts to a substantial portion of its water in order to qualify. However, water is not made available to residential users merely because it is available for their recreational use.

The final major requirement is that the facility must be operated either by a governmental unit or by a regulated public utility. In order to meet this third major requirement, the governmental unit or regulated utility must be responsible for the repair and maintenance of the facility.

COMMENTS AND REQUESTS FOR A PUBLIC HEARING

Before adopting these proposed regulations, consideration will be given to any written comments that are submitted (preferably 8 copies) to the Commissioner of Internal Revenue. All comments will be available for public inspection and copying. A public hearing will be held upon written request to the Commissioner by any person who has submitted written comments. If a public hearing is held, notice of the time and place will be published in the *Federal Register*.

NON-APPLICABILITY OF EXECUTIVE ORDER 12291

The Treasury Department has determined that these proposed regulations are not subject to review under Executive Order 12291 or the Treasury and OMB implementation of the order dated April 29, 1983.

REGULATORY FLEXIBILITY ACT

The Internal Revenue Service has concluded that these proposed regulations are interpretative and that the notice and public procedure requirements of 5 U.S.C. 553 do not apply. Accordingly, these regulations do not constitute regulations subject to the Regulatory Flexibility Act (5 U.S.C. chapter 6).

DRAFTING INFORMATION

The principal author of these proposed regulations is John A. Tolleris of the Legislation and Regulations Division of the Office of Chief Counsel, Internal Revenue Service. However, personnel from other offices of the Internal Revenue Service and Treasury Department participated in developing the regulations, both on matters of substance and style.

[¶ 49,039] **Proposed Regulations (LR-149-84),** published in the Federal Register on August 29, 1984.

Tax shelters: List of investors.—Reg. § 301.6708-1T, relating to the requirement to maintain a list of investors in potentially abusive tax shelters, is proposed. Reg. § 301.6112-1T was removed 2/28/2003 by T.D. 9046.

AGENCY: Internal Revenue Service, Treasury.

ACTION: Notice of proposed rulemaking by cross-reference to temporary regulations.

SUMMARY: In the Rules and Regulations portion of this issue of the *Federal Register*, the Internal Revenue Service is issuing temporary regulations relating to the requirement to maintain a list of investors in potentially abusive tax shelters. The text of the temporary regulations also serves as the comment document for this notice of proposed rulemaking.

DATES: Written comments and requests for a public hearing must be delivered or mailed by October 29, 1984. The regulations are proposed to apply to any interest in a potentially abusive tax shelter other than an interest that was acquired by an investor before September 1, 1984.

ADDRESS: Send comments and requests for a public hearing to: Commissioner of Internal Revenue, Attention: CC:LR:T (LR-149-84), Washington, D.C. 20224.

FOR FURTHER INFORMATION CONTACT: Alice M. Bennett of the Legislation and Regulations Division, Office of Chief Counsel, Internal Revenue Service, 1111 Constitution Ave., N.W., Washington, D.C. 20224 (Attention: CC:LR:T) (202) 566-3918 (not a toll-free call).

BACKGROUND

The temporary regulations in the Rules and Regulations section to this issue of the *Federal Register* amend the Procedure and Administration Regulations (26 CFR Part 301) to provide rules under sections 6112 and 6708 of the Internal Revenue Code of 1954. The text of those temporary regulations serves as the comment document for this notice of proposed rulemaking.

Section 6112 provides that any person who organizes, or sells any interest in, a potentially abusive tax shelter must maintain a list of investors in that tax shelter. Any person who is required to maintain a list under section 6112 must make the list available for inspection upon request of the Secretary, and generally must retain any information required to be included on the list for 7 years.

Section 6708 provides that any person who fails to meet any requirement under section 6112 shall be subject to a penalty of $50 for each person with respect to whom there is such a failure, unless it is shown that the failure is due to reasonable cause and not to willful neglect. The penalty imposed by section 6708 on a person who fails to meet the requirements of section 6112 shall not exceed $50,000 for any calendar year. The penalty imposed by section 6708 is in addition to any other penalty provided by law.

The regulations under sections 6112 and 6708 are to be issued under the authority contained in sections 6112 and 7805 of the Internal Revenue Code of 1954 (98 Stat. 681, 68A Stat. 917; 26 U.S.C. 6112, 7805). For the text of the temporary regulations, see FR Doc. (T.D. 7969) published in the Rules and Regulations section of this issue of the *Federal Register*.

SPECIAL ANALYSES

The Commissioner of Internal Revenue has determined that this proposed rule is not a major rule as defined in Executive Order 12291 and that a regulatory impact analysis therefore is not required. Although this document is a notice of proposed rulemaking that solicits public comments, the Internal Revenue Service has concluded that the regulations proposed herein are interpretative and that the notice and public procedure requirements of 5 U.S.C. 553 do not apply. Accordingly, these proposed regulations do not constitute regulations subject to the Regulatory Flexibility Act (5 U.S.C. chapter 6).

COMMENTS AND REQUEST FOR A PUBLIC HEARING

Before these proposed regulations are adopted, consideration will be given to any written comments that are submitted (preferably seven copies) to the Commissioner of Internal Revenue. All comments will be available for public inspection and copying. A public hearing will be held upon written request to the Commissioner by any person who has submitted written comments. If a public hearing is held, notice of the time and place will be published in the *Federal Register*.

The collection of information requirements contained herein have been submitted to the Office of Management and Budget (OMB) for review under section 3504(h) of the Paperwork Reduction Act. Comments on the requirements should be sent to the Office of Information and Regulatory Affairs of OMB, Attention: Desk Officer for Internal Revenue Service, New Executive Office Building, Washington, D.C. 20503. The Internal Revenue Service requests persons submitting comments to OMB also to send copies of the comments to the Service.

DRAFTING INFORMATION

The principal author of these proposed regulations is Alice M. Bennett of the Legislation and Regulations Division of the Office of Chief Counsel, Internal Revenue Service. However, personnel from other offices of the Internal Revenue Service and Treasury Department participated in developing the regulations, on matters of both substance and style.

[¶ 49,040]   **Proposed Regulations (LR-181-84), published in the Federal Register on August 31, 1984.**

Information returns: Loan security: Abandonments, foreclosure and other acquisitions.—Reg. § 1.6050J-1T, relating to the requirement of reporting abandonments, foreclosures, and other acquisitions of property securing indebtedness, is proposed.

AGENCY: Internal Revenue Service, Treasury.

ACTION: Notice of proposed rulemaking by cross-reference to temporary regulations.

SUMMARY: In the Rules and Regulations portion of this issue of the Federal Register, the Internal Revenue Service is issuing temporary regulations relating to the requirement of reporting abandonments, foreclosures, and other acquisitions of property securing indebtedness. The text of those temporary regulations also serves as the comment document for this proposed rulemaking.

DATES: Written comments and requests for a public hearing must be delivered by October 30, 1984. The regulations are proposed to be effective for acquisitions and abandonments of property after December 31, 1984.

ADDRESS: Send comments and requests for a public hearing to: Commissioner of Internal Revenue, Attention: CC:LR:T (LR-181-84), Washington, D.C. 20224.

FOR FURTHER INFORMATION CONTACT: Annette J. Guarisco of the Legislation and Regulations Division, Office of Chief Counsel, Internal Revenue Service, 1111 Constitution Avenue, N.W., Washington, D.C. 20224, Attention: CC:LR:T, (202) 566-3238 (not a toll-free call).

SUPPLEMENTARY INFORMATION:

BACKGROUND

The regulations provide guidance concerning information returns relating to abandonments, foreclosures, and other acquisitions of property securing indebtedness under section 6050J of the Internal Revenue Code of 1954, as added to the Code by section 148 of the Tax Reform Act of 1984 (98 Stat. 687, 26 U.S.C. 6050J). The regulations are to be issued under the authority contained in section 7805 of the Internal Revenue Code of 1954 (68A Stat. 917, 26 U.S.C. 7805). For the text of the temporary regulations, see FR Doc. 84-23133 published in the Rules and Regulations portion of this issue of the FEDERAL REGISTER. The preamble to the temporary regulations provides a discussion of the rules. In the Proposed Rules section of this issue of the FEDERAL REGISTER is a notice of proposed rulemaking relating to information reporting of transfers of security to persons other than the lender under section 6050J(f) of the Internal Revenue Code of 1954, as added to the Code by section 148 of the Tax Reform Act of 1984 (98 Stat. 688, 26 U.S.C. 6050J(f)).

SPECIAL ANALYSES

The Commissioner of Internal Revenue has determined that this proposed rule is not a major rule as defined in Executive Order 12291. Accordingly, a Regulatory Impact Analysis is not required.

Although this document is a notice of proposed rulemaking that solicits public comments, the Internal Revenue Service has concluded that the regulations proposed herein are interpretative and that the notice and public procedure requirements of 5 U.S.C. 553 do not apply. Accordingly, no Regulatory Flexibility Analysis is required by Chapter 6 of Title 5, United States Code.

COMMENTS AND REQUESTS FOR A PUBLIC HEARING

Before adopting these proposed regulations, consideration will be given to any written comments that are submitted (preferably seven copies) to the Commissioner of Internal Revenue. All comments will be available for public inspection and copying. A public hearing will be held upon written request to the Commissioner by any person who has submitted written comments. If a public hearing is held, notice of the time and place will be published in the FEDERAL REGISTER.

The collection of information requirements contained in these regulations have been submitted to the Office of Management and Budget (OMB) in accordance with the requirements of the Paperwork Reduction Act of 1980. Comments on these requirements should be sent to the Office of Information and Regulatory Affairs of OMB, Attention: Desk Officer for Internal Revenue Service, New Executive Office Building, Washington, D.C. 20503. The Internal Revenue Service requests that persons submitting comments on these requirements to OMB also send copies to the Service.

DRAFTING INFORMATION

The principal author of these regulations is Annette J. Guarisco of the Legislation and Regulations Division of the Office of Chief Counsel, Internal Revenue Service. However, personnel from other offices of the Internal Revenue Service and Treasury Department participated in developing the regulations, on matters of both substance and style.

[¶ 49,041] Proposed Regulations (LR-153-84), published in the Federal Register on August 31, 1984.

Transfers: Alimony, separate maintenance, and dependency exemption.—Reg. §§ 1.71-1T, 1.215-1T and 1.1041-1T, relating to the treatment of transfers of property between spouses and former spouses, the tax treatments of alimony and separate maintenance payments, and the dependency exemption in the case of a child of divorced parents, are proposed. Temporary Reg. § 1.152-4T was removed by T.D. 9408 on July 1, 2008.

AGENCY: Internal Revenue Service, Treasury.

ACTION: Notice of proposed rulemaking and cross-reference to temporary regulations.

SUMMARY: In the Rules and Regulations portion of this issue of the FEDERAL REGISTER, the Internal Revenue Service is issuing temporary regulations relating to the treatment of transfers of property between spouses or former spouses, the tax treatment of alimony and separate maintenance payments, and the dependency exemption in the case of a child of divorced parents. The temporary regulations also serve as the text for this Notice of Proposed Rulemaking.

DATES: Written comments and requests for a public hearing must be delivered or mailed by October 30, 1984. These regulations are proposed to be effective for transfers of property between spouses or former spouses after July 18, 1984 (except as otherwise provided in § 1.1041-1T(f)), alimony or separate maintenance payments made with respect to divorce or separation instruments executed after December 31, 1984, and, to dependency exemptions released for tax years beginning after December 31, 1984.

ADDRESS: Send comments and requests for a public hearing to Commissioner of Internal Revenue, Attention: CC:LR:T (LR-153-84), Washington, D.C. 20224.

FOR FURTHER INFORMATION CONTACT: Ada S. Rousso of the Legislation and Regulations Division, Office of Chief Counsel, Internal Revenue Service, 1111 Constitution Avenue, N.W., Washington, D.C. 20224, Attention: CC:LR:T (LR-153-84) (202) 566-4336, not a toll free call.

SUPPLEMENTARY INFORMATION:

BACKGROUND

The temporary regulations in the Rules and Regulations portion of this issue of the FEDERAL REGISTER amend Part 1 of Title 26 of the Code of Federal Regulations. The temporary regulations are designated by a "T" following their section citation. The final regulations which are proposed to be based on the temporary regulations would amend Part 1 of Title 26 of the Code of Federal Regulations. The regulations provide rules relating to the treatment of transfers of property between spouses, or former spouses incident to divorce under section 1041 of the Internal Revenue Code of 1954 (Code) as added by section 421 of the Tax Reform Act of 1984 (Act) (P.L. 98-369, 98 Stat. 793), alimony or separate maintenance payments under sections 71 and 215 of the Code as amended by section 422 of the Act (P.L. 98-369, 98 Stat. 795) and the dependency exemption in the case of a child of divorced parents under section 152 of the Code, as amended by section 423 of the Act (P.L. 98-369, 98 Stat. 799). These regulations are to be issued under the authority contained in sections 1041(d)(4) (98 Stat. 798, 26 U.S.C. 1041(d)(4)), 152(e)(2)(A) (98 Stat. 802, 26 U.S.C. 152(e)(2)(A)), 215(c) (98 Stat. 800, 26 U.S.C. 215(c)) and 7805 (68A Stat. 917, 26 U.S.C. 7805) of the Code. For the text of the temporary regulations, see FR Doc. 84-23129 (T.D. 7973) published in the Rules and Regulations portion of this issue of the FEDERAL REGISTER. The preamble to the temporary regulations provides a discussion of the rules.

COMMENTS AND REQUESTS FOR A PUBLIC HEARING

Before adopting these proposed regulations, consideration will be given to any written comments that are submitted (preferably eight copies) to the Commissioner of Internal Revenue. All comments will be available for inspection and copying. A public hearing will be held upon written request to the Commissioner by any person who has submitted written comments. If a public hearing is held, notice of the time and place will be published in the FEDERAL REGISTER.

The collection of information requirements contained in this notice of proposed rulemaking have been submitted to the Office of Management and Budget (OMB) for review under section 3504(h) of the Paperwork Reduction Act. Comments on these requirements should be sent to the Office of Information and Regulatory Affairs of OMB, Attention: Desk Officer for Internal Revenue Service, New Executive Office Building, Washington, D.C. 20503. The Internal Revenue Service requests that persons submitting comments on these requirements to OMB also send copies of those comments to the Service.

SPECIAL ANALYSES

The Commissioner of Internal Revenue has determined that this proposed rule is not a major rule as defined in Executive Order 12291. Accordingly, a Regulatory Impact Analysis is not required. The Internal Revenue Service has concluded that although this document is a notice of proposed rulemaking that solicits public comment, the regulations proposed herein are interpretative and the notice and public procedure requirements of 5 U.S.C. 553 do not apply. Accordingly, no Regulatory Flexibility Analysis is required for this rule.

DRAFTING INFORMATION

The principal author of these temporary regulations is Ada S. Rousso of the Legislation and Regulations Division of the Office of Chief Counsel, Internal Revenue Service. However, personnel from other offices of the Internal Revenue Service and Treasury Department participated in developing the regulation, both on matters of substance and style.

[¶ 49,044] Proposed Regulations (LR-280-82), published in the Federal Register on October 9, 1984.

Modification of interest payments for certain periods.—Amendments of Reg. §§ 301.6601-1 and 301.6611-1, relating to the accrual of interest on overpayments and underpayments of tax, are proposed.

AGENCY: Internal Revenue Service, Treasury.

ACTION: Notice of proposed rulemaking.

SUMMARY: This document contains proposed regulations relating to the accrual of interest on overpayments and underpayments of tax. Changes to the applicable tax law were made by the Tax Equity and Fiscal Responsibility Act of 1982 and the Tax Reform Act of 1984. The proposed regulations provide guidance to taxpayers in determining when interest accrues on underpayments and overpayments of tax.

DATE: Written comments and requests for a public hearing must be delivered by December 10, 1984. Except as otherwise provided, the regulations are proposed to apply to returns filed, and interest accrued, after October 3, 1982, and are proposed to be effective on October 4, 1982.

ADDRESS: Send comments and request for a public hearing to: Commissioner of Internal Revenue, Attention: CC:LR:T (LR-280-82), Washington, D.C. 20224.

FOR FURTHER INFORMATION CONTACT: Howard A. Balikov of the Legislation and Regulations Division, Office of Chief Counsel, Internal Revenue Service, 1111 Constitution Avenue, N.W., Washington, D.C. 20224 (Attention: CC:LR:T) (202-566-3288), not a toll-free call.

SUPPLEMENTARY INFORMATION:

BACKGROUND

This document contains proposed amendments to the Regulations on Procedure and Administration (26 CFR Part 301) under sections 6601 and 6611 of the Internal Revenue Code of 1954. These amendments are proposed to conform the regulations to section 346 of the Tax Equity and Fiscal Responsibility Act of 1982 (96 Stat. 636) and section 714(n) of the Tax Reform Act of 1984 (98 Stat. 963) and are to be issued under the authority contained in section 7805 of the Internal Revenue Code of 1954 (68A Stat. 917; 26 U.S.C. 7805).

IN GENERAL

The proposed regulations provide rules with respect to the period during which interest accrues on underpayments of tax under sections 6601 and 6611. These rules will not affect the determination of when the statute of limitations begins to run. In general, taxpayers must pay interest at a rate established under section 6621 on any amount of unpaid tax during the period of time specified in section 6601(a). Section 6601(d) establishes the period during which interest accrues on an underpayment of tax that is reduced by a carryback of a subsequent net operating loss, net capital loss, or certain credits. Taxpayers are entitled to interest at a rate established under section 6621 on overpayments of tax for the period of time specified in section 6611.

PRIOR LAW

Under prior section 6601(d), the carryback of a net operating loss, net capital loss or certain credits to a year in which there was an underpayment of income tax reduced the underpayment, for purposes of computing interest on the underpayment, at the end of the taxable year in which the carryback arose.

Under prior section 6611, if an overpayment of tax was credited against other tax liability of the taxpayer, interest was generally allowed from the date of the overpayment (the date of payment of the first amount which, when added to previous payments, is in excess of the tax liability) to the due date of the amount against which the credit was taken. If an overpayment of tax was refunded to the taxpayer, interest was generally allowed from the date of the overpayment to a date preceding the date of the refund check by not more than 30 days. If, however, an overpayment of income tax was refunded within 45 days after the due date (determined without any extension of time) for filing a return (or, in the case of a return filed after the last date prescribed for filing, within 45 days after the return is filed), no interest was allowed on the payment. Furthermore, prior section 6611(f) stated that if a carryback of a net operating loss, net capital loss, or certain credits, caused an overpayment of income tax, the overpayment arose at the close of the taxable year in which the loss or credit arose.

TEFRA AMENDMENTS

The Tax Equity and Fiscal Responsibility Act of 1982 (TEFRA) amended section 6601(d) and section 6611. Section 6601(d), as amended, provides that the carryback of the loss or credit does not reduce the underpayment until the due date (without extensions) of the return for the taxable year in which the loss or credit arose.

Under section 6611(b)(3), as amended, if a return is filed after the due date (including extensions), no interest accrues on a credit or refund of an overpayment of tax until the return is filed. The return will not be treated as filed until it is filed in processible form. In addition, a return will not be treated as filed under section 6611(e), for the purpose of determining whether a refund has been made within 45 days after filing, until a return is filed in processible form. See section 6611(i). A return is filed in processible form if the return is filed on a permitted form and the return contains the taxpayer's name, address, and identification number, the required signature, and sufficient information to permit the mathematical verification of the tax liability shown on the return. The proposed regulations provide examples of what constitutes a return filed in processible form.

Section 6611(f), as amended by TEFRA, provides that the interest period for refunds of overpayments of income tax caused by a carryback of a net operating loss, net capital loss, or certain credits begins as of the due date (without extensions) of the return for the taxable year in which the loss or credit arises. Section 6611(f) further provides that the 45-day interest-free refund period of section 6611(e) is applied to refunds of overpayments resulting from a loss or credit carryback by treating the overpayment of tax as having occurred in the loss year and treating the return for the loss year as not being filed until the "claim" for the overpayment is filed. As a result, no interest is allowed on an overpayment resulting from a loss or credit carryback if the overpayment is refunded within 45 days of the later of the filing date for the loss year, or the date the claim is filed. Section 6611(f)(3)(B)(i)(II) in essence treats the claim as the return for purposes of the 45-day interest-free refund period under section 6611(c). The processible-form requirements of section 6611(i), therefore, apply to the claim for overpayment. Both the claim and the return must be in processible form. In addition, the proposed regulations treat a claim for a tentative carryback adjustment as a "claim" for purposes of section 6611(f)(3)(B)(i).

Section 6611(f)(3)(C), as amended by the Tax Reform Act of 1984, provides that if an application for a tentative carryback adjustment is filed after a claim for refund, the claim is treated as if it were filed on the date the application for a tentative carryback adjustment was filed. The effective date for the change made by the Tax Reform Act of 1984 is the same as the effective date for the changes made by TEFRA.

This regulation provides examples illustrating the determination of the interest period for: (1) interest accruing before and after October 3, 1982; and (2) returns and claims for refund filed before and after October 3, 1982.

COMMENTS AND REQUEST FOR A PUBLIC HEARING

Before adopting these proposed regulations, consideration will be given to any written comments that are submitted (preferably eight copies) to the Commissioner of Internal Revenue. All comments will be available for public inspection and copying. A public hearing will be held upon written request to the Commissioner by any person who has submitted written comments. If a public hearing is held, notice of the time and place will be published in the FEDERAL REGISTER.

The collection of information requirements contained in this notice of proposed rulemaking have been submitted to the Office of Management and Budget (OMB) for review under section 3504(h) of the Paperwork Reduction Act. Comments on these requirements should be sent to the Office of Information and Regulatory Affairs of OMB, Attention: Desk Officer for Internal Revenue Service, New Executive Office Building, Washington,

D.C. 20503. The Internal Revenue Service requests that persons submitting comments on these requirements to OMB also send copies of these comments to the Service.

SPECIAL ANALYSES

The Commissioner of Internal Revenue has determined that this proposed rule is not a major rule as defined in Executive Order 12291. Accordingly, a Regulatory Impact Analysis is not required. The Internal Revenue Service has concluded that although this document is a notice of proposed rulemaking that solicits public comment, the regulations proposed herein are interpretative and the notice and public procedure requirements of 5 U.S.C. 553 do not apply. Accordingly, no Regulatory Flexibility Analysis is required for this rule.

DRAFTING INFORMATION

The principal author of these regulations is Howard A. Balikov of the Legislation and Regulations Division of the Office of Chief Counsel, Internal Revenue Service. However, personnel from other offices of the Internal Revenue Service and Treasury Department participated in developing the regulations, both on matters of substance and style.

[¶ 49,045] Proposed Regulations (LR-145-84), published in the Federal Register on October 24, 1984.

Investment tax credit: Luxury automobiles: Limitation on amount of depreciation.—Reg. §§ 1.280F-1T—1.280F-5, relating to the limitations placed on the amount of cost recovery deductions and investment tax credit allowed for taxpayers who purchase passenger automobiles for use in a trade or business or for use in the production of income, are proposed. Temporary Reg. § 1.280F-6T was redesignated as Reg. § 1.280F-6 by T.D. 9133 on 6/24/2004.

AGENCY: Internal Revenue Service, Treasury.

ACTION: Notice of proposed rulemaking by cross-reference to temporary regulations.

SUMMARY: In the Rules and Regulations portion of this issue of the FEDERAL REGISTER, the Internal Revenue Service is issuing temporary income tax regulations under section 280F, added to the Code by the Tax Reform Act of 1984, and section 274. Those temporary regulations provide limitations on the amount of cost recovery deductions and investment tax credit allowed to taxpayers who purchase passenger automobiles for use in a trade or business or for use in the production of income. The temporary regulations also provide limitations on cost recovery deductions and the investment tax credit allowed to taxpayers who use "listed property" for both business and personal purposes. A person who leases "listed property" is similarly affected by those temporary regulations. Additionally, there are temporary regulations relating to substantiation requirements for "listed property." The text of those temporary regulations serves as the comment document for this notice of proposed rulemaking.

DATES:

PROPOSED EFFECTIVE DATES

The regulations relating to the limitations on the investment tax credit and recovery deductions are proposed to be effective in general for "listed property" placed in service or leased after June 18, 1984. Those regulations would not apply to certain property acquired or leased pursuant to a binding contract in effect on June 18, 1984. The regulations relating to substantiation requirements for the use of "listed property" are proposed to be effective for taxable years beginning after December 31, 1984.

DATES FOR COMMENTS AND REQUESTS FOR A PUBLIC HEARING

Written comments and requests for a public hearing must be delivered or mailed by December 24, 1984.

ADDRESS: Send comments and requests for a public hearing to: Commissioner of Internal Revenue, Attention: CC:LR:T (LR-145-84), Washington, D.C. 20224.

FOR FURTHER INFORMATION CONTACT: George T. Magnatta (with respect to cost recovery deduction questions) (202-566-6456), Michel A. Dazé (with respect to investment tax credit or leasing questions) (202-566-3458), or Cynthia E. Grigsby (with respect to definitional or substantiation questions) (202-566-3935), of the Legislation and Regulations Division, Office of the Chief Counsel, Internal Revenue Service, 1111 Constitution Avenue, N.W., Washington, D.C. 20224 (Attention: CC:LR:T).

SUPPLEMENTARY INFORMATION:

BACKGROUND

The temporary regulations published in the Rules and Regulations portion of this issue of the FEDERAL REGISTER amend the Income Tax Regulations (26 CFR Part 1) to reflect amendments to section 274 of the Internal Revenue Code of 1954, relating to substantiation requirements, and the addition to the Code of section 280F, relating to limitations on cost recovery deductions and the investment tax credit for certain property. The Code was amended by section 179 of the Tax Reform Act of 1984 (Pub. L. 98-369, 98 Stat. 494). The preamble to the temporary regulations contains an explanation of the provisions of these regulations. The temporary regulations will remain in effect until superseded by final regulations which are proposed to be based on the temporary regulations and issued under the authority contained in sections 280F and 7805 of the Internal Revenue Code of 1954 (98 Stat. 494, 26 U.S.C. 280F; 68A Stat. 917, 26 U.S.C. 7805).

COMMENTS AND REQUESTS FOR A PUBLIC HEARING

Before these proposed amendments are adopted, consideration will be given to any written comments that are submitted (preferably eight copies) to the Commissioner of Internal Revenue. All comments will be available for public inspection and copying.

Comments are invited on the means of determining the amount of compensation that would be included in gross income and subject to withholding as a result of the use of certain property provided as compensation (see § 1.280F-6T(d)(2)(ii)(A)(3) of the temporary regulations) and are also invited on the appropriate procedures to be established for employers to satisfy the withholding obligation. The Service is interested in providing further guidance so that employers will know their withholding obligations have been met.

Certain types of vehicles are excluded from the definition of "passenger automobile" including, *inter alia,* any truck or van, if the regulations so specify. Comments are invited as to the types of trucks or vans that could be excluded from the definition of "passenger automobile."

Finally, comments are invited with respect to the manner of allocating the use of "listed property" between the business and personal use of the property. Specifically, the Internal Revenue Service is interested in suggestions as to whether different measures of business and personal use than those provided in the temporary regulations are appropriate.

A public hearing will be held upon written request to the Commissioner by any person who has submitted written comments. If a public hearing is held, notice of the time and place will be published in the FEDERAL REGISTER.

The collection of information requirements contained in the temporary regulations have been submitted to the Office of Management and Budget (OMB) for review under section 3504(h) of the Paperwork Reduction Act. Comments on these requirements should be sent to the Office of Information and Regulatory Affairs of OMB, Attention: Desk Officer for Internal Revenue Service, New Executive Office Building, Washington, D.C. 20503. The Internal Revenue Service requests that persons submitting comments on the requirements to OMB also send copies of those comments to the Service.

EXECUTIVE ORDER 12291 AND REGULATORY FLEXIBILITY ACT

The Commissioner of Internal Revenue has determined that this proposed rule is not a major rule as defined in Executive Order 12291 and that a Reglatory Impact Analysis is therefore not required.

Although this document is a notice of proposed rulemaking which solicits public comment, the Internal Revenue Service has concluded that the regulations proposed herein are interpretative and that the notice and public procedure requirements of 5 U.S.C. 553 do not apply. Accordingly, these proposed regulations do not constitute regulations subject to the Regulatory Flexibility Act (5 U.S.C. Chapter 6).

[¶ 49,046]   **Proposed Regulations (LR-213-84),** published in the Federal Register on October 31, 1984.

Tax shelter registration: Lists of potential abusers.—Amendments to Reg. §301.6111-1T, relating to tax shelter registration and the requirement to maintain lists of investors in potentially abusive tax shelters, is proposed. Reg. §301.6112-1T was removed 2/28/2003 by T.D. 9046.

AGENCY: Internal Revenue Service, Treasury.

ACTION: Notice of proposed rulemaking by cross-reference to temporary regulations.

SUMMARY: In the Rules and Regulations portion of this issue of the FEDERAL REGISTER, the Internal Revenue Service is issuing temporary regulations relating to tax shelter registration, and the requirement to maintain lists of investors in potentially abusive tax shelters. The text of those temporary regulations also serves as the comment document for this proposed rulemaking.

DATES: Written comments and requests for a public hearing must be delivered by December 31, 1984. The amendments are proposed to apply to tax shelters in which any interest is first sold after August 31, 1984, and are proposed to be effective after August 31, 1984.

ADDRESS: Send comments and requests for a public hearing to: Commissioner of Internal Revenue, Attention: CC:LR:T (LR-213-84), Washington, D.C. 20224.

FOR FURTHER INFORMATION CONTACT: Cynthia L. Clark (with respect to tax shelter registration) or Alice M. Bennett (with respect to the requirement to maintain lists of investors) of the Legislation and Regulations Division, Office of Chief Counsel, Internal Revenue Service, 1111 Constitution Avenue, N.W., Washington, D.C. 20224 (Attention: CC:LR:T) (202-566-3828, not a toll-free call).

SUPPLEMENTARY INFORMATION:

BACKGROUND

The temporary regulations (designated by a "T" following the section citation) in the Rules and Regulations portion of this issue of the FEDERAL REGISTER amend Part 301 of Title 26 of the Code of Federal Regulations. These amendments change the rules relating to tax shelter registration under section 6111 of the Internal Revenue Code of 1954, as added by section 141 of the Tax Reform Act of 1984 (Pub. L. 98-369, 98 Stat. 678). These amendments also change the rules relating to the requirement to maintain lists of investors in potentially abusive tax shelters under section 6112 of the Internal Revenue Code of 1954, as added by section 142 of the Tax Reform Act of 1984 (Pub. L. 98-369, 98 Stat. 681). For the text of the temporary regulations, see FR Doc. (T.D. 7990) published in the Rules and Regulations portion of this issue of the FEDERAL REGISTER. The preamble to the temporary regulations provides a discussion of the rules. The final regulations, which this document proposes to base on those temporary regulations, would amend Part 301 of Title 26 of the Code of Federal Regulations. Those final regulations are to be issued under the authority contained in sections 6111, 6112 and 7805 of the Internal Revenue Code of 1954 (98 Stat. 678, 26 U.S.C. 6111; 98 Stat. 681, 26 U.S.C. 6112; 68A Stat. 917, 26 U.S.C. 7805).

EXECUTIVE ORDER 12291; REGULATORY FLEXIBILITY ACT

The Commissioner of Internal Revenue has determined that this proposed rule is not a major rule as defined in Executive Order 12291 and that a Regulatory Impact Analysis is therefore not required.

Although this document is a notice of proposed rulemaking that solicits public comments, the Internal Revenue Service has concluded that the regulations proposed herein are interpretative and that the notice and public procedure requirements of 5 U.S.C. 553 do not apply. Accordingly, these proposed regulations do not constitute regulations subject to the Regulatory Flexibility Act (5 U.S.C. Chapter 6).

COMMENTS AND REQUESTS FOR A PUBLIC HEARING

Before adopting these proposed regulations, consideration will be given to any written comments that are submitted (preferably seven copies) to the Commissioner of Internal Revenue. All comments will be available for public inspection and copying. A public hearing on these proposed regulations will be held in conjunction with the public hearing on the proposed regulations relating to tax shelter registration published in the FEDERAL REGISTER for Wednesday, August 15, 1984 (49 FR 32728), and the proposed regulations relating to the requirement to maintain lists of investors in potentially abusive tax shelters published in the FEDERAL REGISTER for Wednesday, August 29, 1984 (49 FR 34246). The public hearing on those proposed regulations scheduled for November 15, 1984, will be postponed and a notice of the new time and place will be published in the FEDERAL REGISTER.

The collection of information requirements contained in this notice of proposed rulemaking have been submitted to the Office of Management and Budget (OMB) for review under section 3504(h) of the Paperwork Reduction Act. Comments on these requirements should be sent to the Office of Information and Regulatory Affairs of OMB, Attention: Desk Officer for Internal Revenue Service, New Executive Office Building, Washington, D.C. 20503. The Internal Revenue Service requests that persons submitting comments on these requirements to OMB also send copies of those comments to the Service.

DRAFTING INFORMATION

The principal author of these proposed regulations is Cynthia L. Clark of the Legislation and Regulations Division of the Office of Chief Counsel, Internal Revenue Service. However, personnel from other offices of the Internal Revenue Service and Treasury Department participated in developing the regulations, on matters of both substance and style.

[¶ 49,047]   **Proposed Regulations (EE-65-83),** published in the Federal Register on November 16, 1984.

Individual retirement accounts: Annual information report: Trustees and issuers.—Reg. § 1.408-5, requiring annual reporting of information relating to individual retirement plans, is proposed.

AGENCY: Internal Revenue Service, Treasury.

ACTION: Notice of proposed rulemaking.

SUMMARY: This document contains proposed regulations that require annual reporting of information relating to individual retirement plans. The regulations reflect changes made to the applicable reporting requirements by both news release IR-83-88 and the Tax Reform Act of 1984. The regulations affect trustees of individual retirement accounts and issuers of individual retirement annuities (including accounts and annuities that are simplified employee pensions), and individuals who own or benefit from such individual retirement plans.

DATES: Written comments and requests for a public hearing must be delivered or mailed by January 15, 1985. The amendments are proposed to be effective for reports relating to calendar years beginning after 1982.

ADDRESS: Send comments and requests for a public hearing to: Commissioner of Internal Revenue, Attention: CC:LR:T (EE-65-83), 1111 Constitution Avenue, N.W., Washington, D.C. 20224.

FOR FURTHER INFORMATION CONTACT: Philip R. Bosco of the Employee Plans and Exempt Organizations Division, Office of the Chief Counsel, Internal Revenue Service, 1111 Constitution Avenue, N.W., Washington, D.C. 20224 (Attention: CC:LR:T), 202-566-3430 (not a toll-free number).

SUPPLEMENTARY INFORMATION:

BACKGROUND

Section 408 of the Internal Revenue Code of 1954 defines various individual retirement plans, including individual retirement accounts, individual retirement annuities, and simplified employee pensions. Section 408(i) of the Code provides that the trustee of an individual retirement account or the issuer of an individual retirement annuity (including an account or annuity that is a simplified employee pension) shall make such reports regarding the status of an account or annuity as the Secretary may require under regulations.

Section 1.408-5(c)(1) of the Income Tax Regulations (26 CFR Part 1) under section 408 of the Code requires that an annual report must be furnished to each participant, i.e., the individual for whose benefit the account was established or in whose name the annuity was purchased (or the beneficiary of such individual). The report must contain the following information for transactions occurring during the calendar year: the amount of contributions; the amount of distributions; in the case of an endowment contract, the amount of the premium paid allocable to the cost of life insurance; and the name and address of the trustee or issuer. The report must be furnished on or before June 30 following the calendar year for which the report is required. Paragraph (c)(2) of § 1.408-5 provides that the Commissioner may require the annual report to be filed with the Service at the time the Commissioner specifies.

On June 28, 1983, the Service issued news release IR-83-88 relating to the filing requirement permissible under § 1.408-5(c)(2). Beginning with the 1983 calendar year, the annual reports required by § 1.408-5 must also be filed with the Service. New Form 5498, Individual Retirement Arrangement Information, has been developed for this purpose. The form, a copy of which may be utilized to satisfy the existing reporting requirement of § 1.408-5, must contain the following information for transactions occurring during the calendar year: the amount of contributions (exclusive of rollover contributions for calendar years after 1983); the amount of rollover contributions (for calendar years after 1983); and the name and address of the trustee or issuer. For the 1983 calendar year, the form must be filed with the Service, and the annual report furnished to the participant, on or before June 30, 1984. Finally, IR-83-88 stated that, for calendar year 1984, the form must be filed with the Service on or before February 28, 1985, and the annual report must be furnished to the participant on or before June 30, 1985.

On July 18, 1984, section 147 of the Tax Reform Act of 1984 (Pub. L. 98-369) amended section 408(i) to provide that the information reports required by such section identify the taxable year to which individual retirement plan contributions relate. This amendment is effective for contributions made after December 31, 1984.

The proposed regulations contained in this document amend § 1.408-5 to conform such section to both the new filing requirements announced in news release IR-83-88 and the new reporting requirement added by the Tax Reform Act of 1984. The amendments are to be issued under the authority contained in sections 408(i) and 7805 of the Code (88 Stat. 964, 26 U.S.C. 408(i); 68A Stat. 917, 26 U.S.C. 7805, respectively).

As proposed, the regulations necessarily modify the requirements of IR-83-88 for calendar years 1984 and thereafter. Beginning with calendar year 1984, Form 5498 shall be filed with the Service and the statement to the participant shall be furnished to such person on or before May 31 following the calendar year for which such reports are required. For calendar year 1984, this is a change of the due dates originally announced in IR-83-88. Beginning with calendar year 1985, both Form 5498 and the statement to the participant must report, as the amount of contributions for the calendar year, the amount of contributions made during or after the calendar year that relate to such calendar year. Also beginning with calendar year 1985, both Form 5498 and the statement to the participant must report, in the case of an endowment contract premium allocable to the cost of life insurance, that amount of the premium paid either during or after the calendar year that relates to such calendar year.

Finally, the proposed regulations contain special transitional requirements for the 1985 calendar year reports. For that calendar year both Form 5498 and the statement to the participant must report, as a separate entry, the amount of contributions made during 1985 that relate to 1984. This requirement also applies to the statement to the participant in the case of an endowment contract premium allocable to the cost of life insurance paid during 1985 that relates to 1984.

SPECIAL ANALYSIS

The Commissioner of Internal Revenue has determined that these proposed rules are not major rules as defined in either Executive Order 12291 or the Treasury and OMB implementation of that Order dated April 29, 1983. Accordingly, a Regulatory Impact Analysis is not required.

Although this document is a notice of proposed rulemaking that solicits public comments, the Internal Revenue Service has concluded that the regulations proposed herein are interpretative and that the notice and public procedure requirements of 5 U.S.C. 553 do not apply. Accordingly, these proposed regulations do not constitute regulations subject to the Regulatory Flexibility Act (5 U.S.C. Chapter 6).

COMMENTS AND REQUEST FOR A PUBLIC HEARING

Before adopting these proposed regulations, consideration will be given to any written comments that are submitted (preferably eight copies) to the Commissioner of Internal Revenue. All comments will be available for public inspection and copying. A public hearing will be held upon written request to the Commissioner by any person who has submitted written comments. If a public hearing is held, notice of the time and place will be published in the FEDERAL REGISTER.

The collection of information requirements contained in this notice of proposed rulemaking have been submitted to the Office of Management and Budget (OMB) for review under section 3504(h) of the Paperwork Reduction Act of 1980. Comments on these requirements should be sent to the Office of Information and Regulatory Affairs of OMB, Attention: Desk Office for Internal Revenue Service, New Executive Office Building, Washington, D.C. 20503. The Internal Revenue Service requests that persons submitting comments on these requirements to OMB also send copies of those comments to the Service.

DRAFTING INFORMATION

The principal author of these proposed regulations is Philip R. Bosco of the Employee Plans and Exempt Organizations Division of the Office of Chief Counsel, Internal Revenue Service. However, personnel from other offices of the Internal Revenue Service and Treasury Department participated in developing the regulations, on matters of both substance and style.

[¶ 49,048]   **Proposed Regulations (LR-183-84),** published in the Federal Register on November 30, 1984.

Deductions: Losses: Interest: Transactions between related taxpayers.—Reg. §§1.267(a)-2 and 1.706-2, relating to deductions, timing of deductions and losses in transactions between certain related taxpayers, are proposed. Reg. §§1.267(f)-1T, 1.267(f)-2T and 1.1502-13T were removed by T.D. 8597 on 7/12/95.

AGENCY: Internal Revenue Service, Treasury.

ACTION: Notice of proposed rulemaking by cross-reference to temporary regulations.

SUMMARY: In the Rules and Regulations portion of this issue of the *Federal Register,* the Internal Revenue Service is issuing temporary regulations that provide guidance relating to changes in section 267 made by the Tax Reform Act of 1984. These changes relate to deductions, timing of deductions, and losses in certain transactions between related taxpayers. The text of §§1.267(a)-2T, 1.267(f)-1T, 1.267(f)-2T, and 1.1502-13T, as set forth in those temporary regulations, also serves as the comment document for this notice of proposed rulemaking.

DATES: Proposed effective date. The regulations are proposed to be effective, generally, for amounts otherwise allowable as deductions for taxable years beginning after 1983 and for losses on transactions after 1983.

Date for comments and requests for a public hearing: Written comments and requests for a public hearing must be delivered or mailed by January 29, 1985.

ADDRESS: Send comments and requests for a public hearing to: Commissioner of Internal Revenue, Attention: CC:LR:T (LR-183-84) Washington, D.C. 20224.

FOR FURTHER INFORMATION: Keith E. Stanley (for rules under section 267(f)) and John G. Schmalz or Robert H. Ginsburgh (for other rules) of the Legislation and Regulations Division, Office of Chief Counsel, Internal Revenue Service, 1111 Constitution Avenue, NW., Washington, D.C. 20224, Attention: CC:LR:T (Telephone: 202-566-3458 for Keith E. Stanley or 202-566-3297 for John G. Schmalz and Robert H. Ginsburgh; not a toll-free call).

SUPPLEMENTARY INFORMATION:

Background

Temporary regulations published in the Rules and Regulations portion of this issue of the *Federal Register* reflect amendments made to section 267 of the Internal Revenue Code of 1954 (relating to losses, expenses, and interest with respect to transactions between related taxpayers) by section 174 of the Tax Reform Act of 1984 (Pub. L. 98-369; 98 Stat. 494). More specifically, temporary regulations are added in question and answer form under section 267(a), (b), and (e), dealing with deferral of certain deductions generally and application of that deferral and the disallowance of certain losses to partnerships. The temporary regulations are added in standard format under section 267(f), dealing with losses between members of a controlled group of corporations. For the text of the amendments to the temporary regulations, see T.D. 7991, published in the Rules and Regulations portion of this issue of the *Federal Register.* The preamble to the temporary regulations explains the addition to the regulations.

Executive Order 12291 and Regulatory Flexibility Act

The Commissioner of Internal Revenue has determined that this proposed rule is not a major rule as defined in Executive Order 12291and that a Regulatory Impact Analysis is therefore not required. The Secretary of the Treasury has certified that the portion of this rule that is represented by §§1.267(f)-1T, 1.267(f)-2T, and §1.1502-13T will not have a significant impact on a substantial number of small entities because that portion of this rule applies only to a sale or exchange at a loss of property from one member of a controlled group of corporations to another member of that group and, if applicable, merely defers the loss until a later date. A regulatory flexibility analysis, therefore, is not required under the Regulatory Flexibility Act (5 U.S.C. chapter 6) for this portion of the rule. For the portion of this rule that is represented by §1.267(a)-2T, the Internal Revenue Service has concluded that, although this document is a notice of proposed rulemaking that solicits public comment, that portion of this rule is interpretative and that the notice and public procedure requirements of 5 U.S.C. 553 do not apply. Accordingly, that portion of this rule does not constitute a rule subject to this Regulatory Flexibility Act.

Comments and Requests for a Public Hearing

Before these proposed regulations are adopted, consideration will be given to any written comments that are submitted (preferably eight copies) to the Commissioner of Internal Revenue. All comments will be available for public inspection and copying. A public hearing will be held upon written request to the Commissioner by any person who has submitted written comments. If a public hearing is held, notice of the time and place will be published in the *Federal Register.* The collection of information requirements contained herein have been submitted to the Office of Management and Budget (OMB) for review under section 3504(h) of the Paperwork Reduction Act. Comments on the requirements should be sent to the Office of Information and Regulatory Affairs of OMB, Attention: Desk Officer for Internal Revenue Service, New Executive Office Building, Washington, D.C. 20503. The Internal Revenue Service requests persons submitting comments to OMB to also send copies of the comments to the Service.

Drafting Information

The principal author of these proposed regulations is Keith E. Stanley of the Legislation and Regulations Division of the Office of Chief Counsel, Internal Revenue Service. However, personnel from other offices of the Internal Revenue Service and Treasury Department participated in developing the regulations, both on matters of substance and style.

[¶ 49,049]   **Proposed Regulations (LR-180-84),** published in the Federal Register on December 28, 1984.

Interest rate: Overpayments and underpayments: Determination.—Reg. §301.6621-2T, relating to the increased rate of interest on substantial underpayments attributable to tax-motivated transactions, is proposed.

AGENCY: Internal Revenue Service, Treasury.

ACTION: Notice of proposed rulemaking by cross-reference to temporary regulations.

SUMMARY: In the Rules and Regulations portion of this FEDERAL REGISTER, the Internal Revenue Service is issuing temporary regulations relating to the increased rate of interest on substantial underpayments attributable to certain tax motivated transactions. The text of those temporary regulations also serves as the comment document for this proposed rulemaking.

DATES: Written comments and requests for a public hearing must be delivered by February 26, 1985. The amendments are proposed to be effective for interest accruing after December 31, 1984, on certain underpayments.

ADDRESS: Send comments and requests for a public hearing to: Commissioner of Internal Revenue, Attention: CC:LR:T (LR-180-84), Washington, D.C. 20224.

FOR FURTHER INFORMATION CONTACT: Linda M. Kroening, Office of Chief Counsel, Internal Revenue Service, 1111 Constitution Avenue, N.W., Washington, D.C. 20224 (Attention: CC:LR:T) (202-566-3238, not a toll-free call).

SUPPLEMENTARY INFORMATION:

BACKGROUND

The temporary regulations in the Rules and Regulations portion of this issue of the FEDERAL REGISTER amend Part 301 of Title 26 of the Code of Federal Regulations. The temporary regulations are designated by a "T" following their section citation. The final regulations, which this document proposes to base on those temporary regulations, would amend Part 301 of Title 26 of the Code of Federal Regulations.

The regulations provide rules relating to the increased rate of interest on substantial underpayments attributable to certain tax motivated transactions. The regulations reflect the addition of section 6621(d) to the Internal Revenue Code of 1954 by section 144 of the Tax Reform Act of 1984 (Pub. L. 98-369, 98. Stat. 682). The regulations are to be issued under the authority contained in section 6621(d) and 7805 of the Code (98 Stat. 682, 26 U.S.C. 6621(d); 68A Stat. 917, 26 U.S.C. 7805). For the text of the temporary regulations, see FR Doc. (T.D. 7998) published in the Rules and Regulations portion of this issue of the FEDERAL REGISTER. The preamble of the temporary regulations provides a discussion of the rules.

SPECIAL ANALYSES

The Commissioner of Internal Revenue has determined that this proposed rule is not a major rule as defined in Executive Order 12291. Accordingly, a Regulatory Impact Analysis is not required.

Although this document is a notice of proposed rulemaking that solicits public comment, the Internal Revenue Service has concluded that the regulations proposed herein are interpretative and that the notice and public procedure requirements of 5 U.S.C. 553 do not apply. Accordingly, a Regulatory Flexibility Analysis is not required (5 U.S.C. Chapter 6).

COMMENTS AND REQUESTS FOR A PUBLIC HEARING

Before adopting these proposed regulations, consideration will be given to any written comments that are submitted (preferably eight copies) to the Commissioner of Internal Revenue. All comments will be available for public inspection and copying. A public hearing will be held upon written request to the Commissioner by any person who has submitted written comments. If a public hearing is held, notice of the time and place will be published in the FEDERAL REGISTER.

DRAFTING INFORMATION

The principal author of these proposed regulations is Linda M. Kroening of the Legislation and Regulations Division of the Office of Chief Counsel, Internal Revenue Service. However, personnel from other offices of the Internal Revenue Service and Treasury Department participated in developing the regulations on matters of both substance and style.

[¶ 49,051]   **Proposed Regulations (LR-216-84),** published in the Federal Register on January 7, 1985.

Fringe benefits: Taxability.—Reg. §§1.162-25T, 31.3401(a)-1T, 31 .3501(a)-1T and 54.4977-1T, relating to the treatment of taxable and nontaxable fringe benefits, are proposed.

AGENCY: Internal Revenue Service, Treasury.

ACTION: Notice of Proposed Rulemaking by cross-reference to temporary regulations.

SUMMARY: In the Rules and Regulations portion of the FEDERAL REGISTER, the Internal Revenue Service is issuing temporary regulations relating to the taxation of fringe benefits. The text of those temporary regulations also serves as the comment document for this notice of proposed rulemaking.

DATES: Written comments and requests for a public hearing must be delivered by March 8, 1985. The regulations are proposed to be effective as of January 1, 1985.

ADDRESS: Send comments and requests for a public hearing to: Commissioner of Internal Revenue, Attention: CC:LR:T (LR-216-84), Washington, D.C. 20224.

FOR FURTHER INFORMATION CONTACT: Annette J. Guarisco of the Legislation and Regulations Division, Office of Chief Counsel, Internal Revenue Service, 1111 Constitution Avenue, N.W., Washington, D.C. 20224, Attention: CC:LR:T (202) 566-3918 (not a toll-free call).

SUPPLEMENTARY INFORMATION:

BACKGROUND

The temporary regulations in the Rules and Regulations portion of this issue of the FEDERAL REGISTER amend Parts 1, 31, and 54 of Title 26 of the Code of Federal Regulations. The temporary regulations are designated by a "T" following their section citation. The final regulations, which this document proposes to base on those temporary regulations, would amend Parts 1, 31, and 54 of Title 26 of the Code of Federal Regulations.

The regulations provide guidance on the treatment of taxable and nontaxable fringe benefits, including the valuation of taxable fringe benefits for purposes of income and employment tax withholding. In particular, the regulations provide special rules for valuing employer-provided automobiles, use of employer-provided automobiles for commuting, flights on employer-provided airplanes, and free or discounted flights on commercial airlines. In addition, the regulations provide guidance concerning when and in what manner employers must collect and pay income and employment taxes.

Sections 61, 3121, 3231, 3306, 3401, and 3501 of the Internal Revenue Code of 1954 (Code) were amended, and sections 132 and 4977 were added to the Code, by section 531 of the Tax Reform Act of 1984 (98 Stat. 877). The regulations are to be issued under the authority contained in sections 132 and 7805 of the Code (98 Stat. 878; 68A Stat. 917). For the text of the temporary regulations, see FR Doc. [T.D.] published in the Rules and Regulations portion of this issue of the FEDERAL REGISTER. The preamble to the temporary regulations contains a summary of the provisions of these regulations.

SPECIAL ANALYSES

The Commissioner of Internal Revenue has determined that this proposed rule is not a major rule as defined in Executive Order 12291. Accordingly, a Regulatory Impact Analysis is not required.

Although this document is a notice of proposed rulemaking that solicits public comments, the Internal Revenue Service has concluded that the regulations proposed herein are interpretative and that the notice and public procedure requirements of 5 U.S.C. 553 do not apply. Accordingly, no Regulatory Flexibility Analysis is required by Chapter 6 of Title 5, United States Code.

COMMENTS AND REQUESTS FOR A PUBLIC HEARING

Before adopting these proposed regulations, consideration will be given to any written comments that are submitted (preferably eight copies) to the Commissioner of Internal Revenue. All comments will be available for public inspection and copying. A public hearing will be held upon written request to the Commissioner by any person who has submitted written comments. If a public hearing is held, notice of the time and place will be published in the FEDERAL REGISTER.

Comments are invited concerning the administrability and appropriateness of the special rules contained in the temporary regulations relating to valuing employer-provided automobiles, use of employer-provided automobiles for commuting, flights on employer-provided airplanes, and free or discounted flights on commercial airlines. In particular, comments are requested on the manner in which employers and employees should elect to use these special valuation rules, including any necessary reporting requirements.

Comments are also requested relating to the need for other special rules for valuing taxable fringe benefits, such as the use of employer-operated eating facilities and athletic facilities, international flights on employer-provided airplanes, and use of employer-provided automobiles in foreign countries.

Comments are requested with respect to establishing a safe harbor for sales and service personnel that would elminate some of the record-keeping requirements for business use of automobiles for such persons.

On December 27, 1984, the Service announced its intention to exclude certain special-purpose farm vehicles, such as tractors and combines, from the definition of "other means of transportation" under section 280F. In addition, the Service announced that it is considering under what circumstances pick-up trucks used in the business of farming may be excluded from the definition of "passenger automobile" under section 280F. Comments are requested on these announcements.

Comments are also requested relating to the definition of "employee" for purposes of the section 4977 election concerning the line-of-business restriction in section 132. Specifically, comments are requested as to whether, and to what extent, retirees should be included in the definition of employee.

Comments are also requested concerning the circumstances under which retirees should be treated as officers, owners, or highly compensated employees for purposes of the nondiscrimination rules contained in section 132.

The collection of information requirements contained in these regulations have been submitted to the Office of Management and Budget (OMB) in accordance with the requirements of the Paperwork Reduction Act of 1980. Comments on those requirements should be sent to the Office of Information and Regulatory Affairs of OMB, Attention: Desk Officer for Internal Revenue Service, New Executive Office Building, Washington, D.C. 20503. The Internal Revenue Service requests that persons submitting comments on these requirements to OMB also send copies to the Service.

DRAFTING INFORMATION

The principal author of these regulations is Annette J. Guarisco of the Legislation and Regulations Division of the Office of Chief Counsel, Internal Revenue Service. However, personnel from other offices of the Internal Revenue Service and Treasury Department participated in developing the regulations, on matters of both substance and style.

[¶ 49,052]   **Proposed Regulations (LR-297-84),** published in the Federal Register on January 24, 1985.

Tax straddles: Loss deferral: Wash sales.—Reg. §§ 1.1092(b)-1T, 1.1092(b)-2T and 1.1092(b)-5T, relating to the application of the loss deferral and wash sale rules and treatment of holding periods and losses with respect to straddle positions, are proposed.

AGENCY: Internal Revenue Service, Treasury.

ACTION: Notice of proposed rulemaking by cross-reference to temporary regulations.

SUMMARY: In the Rules and Regulations portion of this issue of the *Federal Register*, the Internal Revenue Service is issuing Temporary Income Tax Regulations §§ 1.1092(b)-1T, 1.1092(b)-2T, and 1.1092(b)-5T relating to the application of the loss deferral and wash sale rules and treatment of holding periods and losses with respect to straddle positions. The text of those temporary regulations also serves as the text for a notice of proposed rulemaking for final income tax regulations.

DATES: Written comments and requests for a public hearing must be delivered or mailed before March 25, 1985. The regulations under § 1.1092(b)-1T are proposed to be effective for loss positions disposed of on or after January 24, 1985. Generally, the regulations under § 1.1092(b)-2T are proposed to be effective for positions established after June 23, 1981, in taxable years ending after such date. However, the regulations under § 1.1092(b)-2T(b)(2) are proposed to be effective for positions of mixed straddles established on or after January 1, 1984.

ADDRESS: Send comments and requests for a public hearing to: Commissioner of Internal Revenue, Attention: CC:LR:T (LR-297-84), Washington, D.C. 20224.

FOR FURTHER INFORMATION CONTACT: Neil W. Zyskind of the Legislation and Regulations Division, Office of the Chief Counsel, Internal Revenue Service, 1111 Consitution Avenue, N.W., Washington, D.C. 20224, Attention: CC:LR:T, 202-566-3287, not a toll-free call.

SUPPLEMENTARY INFORMATION

BACKGROUND

The temporary regulations in the Rules and Regulations portion of this issue of the *Federal Register* amends 26 CFR by adding new §§1.1092(b)-1T, 1.1092(b)-2T, and 1.1092(b)-5T. The final regulations would amend 26 CFR by adding new §§1.1092(b)-1, 1.1092(b)-2 and 1.1092(b)-5 to Part 1 (Income Tax; Taxable years beginning after December 31, 1953). The regulations are to be issued under the authority contained in sections 1092(b) and 7805 of the Internal Revenue Code of 1954 (68A Stat. 917, 95 Stat. 324; 26 U.S.C. 1092(b), 7805). For the text of the temporary regulations, see F.R. Doc. (T.D. 8007) published in the Rules and Regulations portion of this issue of the *Federal Register*.

SPECIAL ANALYSES

The Commissioner of Internal Revenue has determined that this proposed rule is not a major rule as defined in Executive Order 12291 and that a regulatory impact analysis is therefore not required. Although this document is a notice of proposed rulemaking which solicits public comment, the Internal Revenue Service has concluded that the regulations proposed herein are interpretative and that the notice and public procedure requirements of 5 U.S.C. 553 do not apply. Accordingly, these proposed regulations do not constitute regulations subject to the Regulatory Flexibility Act (5 U.S.C. chapter 6).

COMMENTS AND REQUESTS FOR A PUBLIC HEARING

Before adopting the temporary regulations referred to in this document as final regulations, consideration will be given to any written comments that are submitted (preferably eight copies) to the Commissioner of Internal Revenue. All comments will be available for public inspection and copying. A public hearing will be held upon written request to the Commissioner by any person who has submitted written comments. If a public hearing is held, notice of the time and place will be published in the *Federal Register.*

The collection of information requirements contained in this notice of proposed rulemaking has been submitted to the Office of Management and Budget (OMB) for review under section 3504(h) of the Paperwork Reduction Act. Comments on these requirements should be sent to the Office of Information and Regulatory Affairs of OMB, Attention: Desk Office of Internal Revenue Service, New Executive Office Building, Washington, D.C. 20503. The Internal Revenue Service requests that persons submitting comments on these requirements to OMB also send copies of those comments to the Service.

DRAFTING INFORMATION

The principal author of these proposed regulations is Neil W. Zyskind of the Legislation and Regulations Division of the Office of Chief Counsel, Internal Revenue Service. However, personnel from other offices of the Internal Revenue Service and Treasury Department participated in developing the regulations, both on matters of substance and style.

[¶ 49,053]   **Proposed Regulations (LR-299-84),** published in the Federal Register on January 24, 1985.

Tax straddles: Mixed straddles: Identification.—Reg. §§1.1092(b)-3T and 1.1092(b)-4T, relating to mixed straddles, are proposed.

AGENCY: Internal Revenue Service, Treasury.

ACTION: Notice of proposed rulemaking by cross-reference to temporary regulations.

SUMMARY: In the Rules and Regulations portion of this issue of the Federal Register, the Internal Revenue Service is issuing Temporary Income Tax Regulations §§1.1092(b)-3T and 1.1092(b)-4T relating to mixed straddles. The text of those temporary regulations also serves as the text for a notice of proposed rulemaking for final income tax regulations.

DATES: Written comments and request for a public hearing must be delivered or mailed before March 25, 1985. The regulations under §1.1092(b)-3T (relating to straddle-by-straddle identification) are proposed to be effective for straddles established on or after January 1, 1984. The regulations under §1.1092(b)-4T (relating to mixed straddle accounts) are proposed to be effective for positions held on or after January 1, 1984.

ADDRESS: Send comments and requests for a public hearing to: Commissioner of Internal Revenue, Attention: CC:LR:T (LR-299-84), Washington, D.C. 20224.

FOR FURTHER INFORMATION CONTACT: Neil W. Zyskind of the Legislation and Regulations Division, Office of the Chief Counsel, Internal Revenue Service, 1111 Constitution Avenue, N.W., Washington, D.C. 20224, Attention: CC:LR:T, 202-566-3287, not a toll-free call.

SUPPLEMENTARY INFORMATION:

BACKGROUND

The temporary regulations in the Rules and Regulations portion of this issue of the Federal Register amends 26 CFR by adding new §§1.1092(b)-3T and 1.1092(b)-4T. The final regulations would amend 26 CFR by adding new §§1.1092(b)-3 and 1.1092(b)-4 to Part 1 (Income Tax; Taxable years beginning after December 31, 1953). The regulations are to be issued under the authority contained in sections 1092(b)(1), 1092(b)(2), and 7805 of the Internal Revenue Code of 1954 (98 Stat. 627, 68A Stat. 917; 26 U.S.C. 1092(b)(1), 1092(b)(2), 7805). For the text of the temporary regulations, see F.R. Doc.—(T.D. 8008) published in the Rules and Regulations portion of this issue of the Federal Register.

SPECIAL ANALYSES

The Commissioner of Internal Revenue has determined that this proposed rule is not a major rule as defined in Executive Order 12291 and that a regulatory impact analysis is therefore not required. Although this document is a notice of proposed rulemaking which solicits public comment, the Internal Revenue Service has concluded that the regulations proposed herein are interpretative and that the notice and public procedure requirements of 5 U.S.C. 553 do not apply. Accordingly, these proposed regulations do not constitute regulations subject to the Regulatory Flexibility Act (5 U.S.C. chapter 6).

COMMENTS AND REQUESTS FOR A PUBLIC HEARING

Before adopting the temporary regulations referred to in this document as final regulations, consideration will be given to any written comments that are submitted (preferably eight copies) to the Commissioner of Internal Revenue. All comments will be available for public inspection and copying. A public hearing will be held upon written request to the Commissioner by any person who has submitted written comments. If a public hearing is held, notice of the time and place will be published in the FEDERAL REGISTER.

Comments are invited concerning other forms of independent verification that taxpayers may use to identify their section 1092(b)(2) identified mixed straddles.

The collection of information requirements contained in this notice of proposed rulemaking has been submitted to the Office of Management and Budget (OMB) for review under section 3504(h) of the Paperwork Reduction Act. Comments on these requirements should be sent to the Office of Information and Regulatory Affairs of OMB, Attention: Desk Office of Internal Revenue Service, New Executive Office Building, Washington, D.C. 20503. The Internal Revenue Service requests that persons submitting comments on these requirements to OMB also send copies of those comments to the Service.

DRAFTING INFORMATION

The principal author of these proposed regulations is Neil W. Zyskind of the Legislation and Regulations Division of the Office of Chief Counsel, Internal Revenue Service. However, personnel from other offices of the Internal Revenue Service and Treasury Department participated in developing the regulations, both on matters of substance and style.

[¶ 49,054] Proposed Regulations (LR-245-84), published in the Federal Register on May 8, 1985.

Mortgage credit certificates: Issuance: Penalties.—Reg. §§1.25-1T—1.25-8T, 1.163-6T and 1.6709-1T and amendments to Reg. §6a.103A-2, relating to the issuance of mortgage credit certificates, are proposed.

AGENCY: Internal Revenue Service, Treasury.

ACTION: Notice of proposed rulemaking by cross-reference to temporary regulations.

SUMMARY: This document provides proposed regulations that relate to mortgage credit certificates. Changes to the applicable tax law were made by the Tax Reform Act of 1984 (Pub. L. 98-369; 98 Stat. 905). These regulations affect all holders and issuers of mortgage credit certificates. In addition, in the Rules and Regulations portion of this *Federal Register*, the Internal Revenue Service is issuing temporary regulations that relate to mortgage credit certificates. The text of those temporary regulations also serves as the comment document for this proposed rulemaking.

DATES: Written comments and requests for a public hearing must be delivered or mailed by July 8, 1985. The regulations are proposed to be effective for interest paid or accrued after December 31, 1984, on indebtedness incurred after December 31, 1984, and for elections not to issue qualified mortgage bonds after 1983.

ADDRESS: Send comments and requests for a public hearing to: Commissioner of Internal Revenue, Attention: CC:LR:T (LR-245-84), Washington, D.C. 20224.

FOR FURTHER INFORMATION CONTACT: Mitchell H. Rapaport of the Legislation and Regulations Division, Office of the Chief Counsel, Internal Revenue Service, 1111 Constitution Avenue, N.W., Washington, D.C. 20224 (Attention: CC:LR:T) (202-566-3740).

SUPPLEMENTARY INFORMATION:

BACKGROUND

The temporary regulations in the Rules and Regulations portion of this issue of the *Federal Register* add new §§1.25-1T through 1.25-8T to Part 1 of Title 26 of the Code of Federal Regulations and amend Part 6a of Title 26. The final regulations, which this document proposes to be based on those temporary regulations, would be added to Part 1 of Title 26 of the Code of Federal Regulations. For the text of the temporary regulations, see FR Doc. (T.D. 8023) published in the Rules and Regulations portion of this issue of the *Federal Register*. The preamble to the temporary regulations explains the addition to the regulations.

The regulations interpret the provisions of section 25 of the Code, which provides that an issuing authority may issue mortgage credit certificates to individuals to be used in connection with the acquisition, qualified rehabilitation, or qualified home improvement of the taxpayer's principal residence. A qualified mortgage credit certificate entitles its recipient to claim a credit against his Federal income tax based on the amount of mortgage interest paid during the year.

The regulations permit great flexibility in the manner in which MCCs may be issued and programs administered. Examples are provided illustrating the manner in which certificates may be issued. Comments are requested with respect to other methods of issuing certificates and administering programs.

The proposed and temporary regulations provide, in general, that issuers may not limit the use of MCCs to indebtedness incurred from particular lenders. Thus, in general, a holder of an MCC must be free to take the certificate to any lender and use it to obtain any type of mortgage. A major exception permits an issuer to impose limitations on the use of MCCs to indebtedness incurred from particular lenders after demonstrating to the satisfaction of the Commissioner that the proposed limitations will result in significant economic benefits to the MCC holders. Comments on this provision and information on the types of limitations that issuers believe will result in significant economic benefits to MCC holders are requested.

These regulations are proposed to be issued under the authority contained in section 25 and section 7805 of the Internal Revenue Code (98 Stat. 905, 26 U.S.C. 25; 68A Stat. 917, 26 U.S.C. 7805).

NON-APPLICABILITY OF EXECUTIVE ORDER 12291

The Commissioner of Internal Revenue has determined that this proposed rule is not a major rule as defined in Executive Order 12291 and that a regulatory impact analysis therefore is not required.

REGULATORY FLEXIBILITY ACT

Although this document is a notice of proposed rulemaking that solicits public comment, the Internal Revenue Service has concluded that the regulations proposed herein are interpretative and that the notice and public procedure requirements of 5 U.S.C. 553 do not apply. Accordingly, these proposed regulations do not constitute regulations subject to the Regulatory Flexibility Act (5 U.S.C. Chapter 6).

DRAFTING INFORMATION

The principal author of these proposed regulations is Mitchell H. Rapaport of the Legislation and Regulations Division of the Office of Chief Counsel, Internal Revenue Service. However, personnel from other offices of the Internal Revenue Service and Treasury Department participated in developing the regulations, on matters of both substance and style.

COMMENTS AND REQUESTS FOR A PUBLIC HEARING

Before the adoption of these proposed regulations, consideration will be given to any written comments that are submitted (preferably seven copies) to the Commissioner of Internal Revenue. All comments will be available for public inspection and copying. A public hearing will be held upon written request to the Commissioner by any person who has submitted written comments. If a public hearing is held, notice of the time and place will be published in the *Federal Register*. The collection of information requirements contained herein have been submitted to the Office of

Management and Budget (OMB) for review under section 3504(h) of the Paperwork Reduction Act. Comments on the requirements should be sent to the Office of Information and Regulatory Affairs of OMB, Attention: Desk Officer for Internal Revenue Service, New Executive Office Building, Washington, D.C. 20503. The Internal Revenue Service requests persons submitting comments to OMB also to send copies of the comments to the Service.

[¶ 49,055]   Proposed Regulations (LR-31-85), published in the Federal Register on July 2, 1985.

Accelerated cost recovery system: Tax-exempt entity leasing.—Reg. §1.168(j)-1T, regarding tax-exempt entity leasing, is proposed. Temporary Reg. §1.48-12T was removed by T.D. 9040 on 1/30/2003. Temporary Reg. §1.168(f)(8)-1T was removed by T.D. 9849 on 3/11/2019.

AGENCY: Internal Revenue Service, Treasury.

ACTION: Notice of proposed rulemaking by cross reference to temporary regulations.

SUMMARY: This document provides proposed regulations regarding tax-exempt entity leasing. Changes to the applicable tax law were made by the Tax Reform Act of 1984. In the Rules and Regulations portion of this *Federal Register*, the Internal Revenue Service is issuing temporary regulations relating to tax-exempt entity leasing; the text of those temporary regulations also serves as the comment document for this notice of proposed rulemaking.

DATES: Written comments and requests for a public hearing must be delivered or mailed by [60 DAYS AFTER PUBLICATION OF THIS DOCUMENT IN THE Federal Register]. In general, the regulations are proposed to apply to leases involving tax-exempt entities entered into after May 23, 1983, and to property placed in service by the taxpayer after May 23, 1983. The revisions to the safe-harbor lease reporting requirements are proposed to apply to such lease agreements executed after June 30, 1985.

ADDRESS: Please mail or deliver comments to: Commissioner of Internal Revenue, Attention: CC:LR:T (LR-31-85), 1111 Constitution Avenue, N.W., Washington, D.C. 20224.

FOR FURTHER INFORMATION CONTACT: Robert Beatson of the Legislation and Regulations Division, Office of Chief Counsel, Internal Revenue Service, 1111 Consitution Avenue, N.W., Washington, D.C. 20224 (Attention: CC:LR:T) (202-566-3590).

SUPPLEMENTARY INFORMATION:

BACKGROUND

The temporary regulations in the Rules and Regulations portion of this issue of the *Federal Register* add new §§1.48-12T, 1.168(f)(8)-1T, and 1.168(j)-1T to Part 1 of Title 26 of the Code of Federal Regulations. When §1.48-12T is promulgated as a final regulation, it would be renumbered as §1.48-12 of Part 1 of Title 26 of the Code of Federal Regulations. When §1.168(f)(8)-1T is promulgated as a final regulation, it would be renumbered as §1.168(f)(8)-1 of Part 1 of Title 26 of the Code of Federal Regulations. When §1.168(j)-1T is promulgated as a final regulation, it would be renumbered as §1.168(j)-1 of Part 1 of Title 26 of the Code of Federal Regulations. For the text of the temporary regulations, see FR Doc. (T.D. 8033) published in the Rules and Regulations portion of this issue of the Federal Register. The preamble to the temporary regulations explains these additions to the Income Tax Regulations.

The proposed regulations provide needed guidance regarding the provisions of sections 168(j) and 7701(e) which were enacted by section 31 of the Tax Reform Act of 1984.

NON-APPLICABILITY OF EXECUTIVE ORDER 12291

The Commissioner of Internal Revenue has determined that this proposed rule is not a major rule as defined in Executive Order 12291and that a regulatory impact analysis therefore is not required.

REGULATORY FLEXIBILITY ACT

Although this document is a notice of proposed rulemaking that solicits public comment, the Internal Revenue Service has concluded that the regulations proposed herein are interpretative and that the notice and public procedure requirements of 5 U.S.C. 553 do not apply. Accordingly, these proposed regulations do not constitute regulations subject to the Regulatory Flexibility Act (5 U.S.C. chapter 6).

PAPERWORK REDUCTION ACT

The collection of information requirements contained in the temporary regulations have been submitted to the Office of Management and Budget (OMB) for review under Section 3504(h) of the Paperwork Reduction Act. Comments on these requirements should be sent to the Office of Information and Regulatory Affairs of OMB, Attention: Desk Officer for Internal Revenue Service, New Executive Office Building, Washington, D.C. 20503. The Internal Revenue Service requests that persons submitting comments on the requirements to OMB also send copies of those comments to the Service.

DRAFTING INFORMATION

The principal author of these proposed regulations is Robert Beatson of the Legislation and Regulations Division of the Office of the Chief Counsel, Internal Revenue Service. Personnel from other offices of the Internal Revenue Service and the Treasury Department participated, however, in developing the regulations on matters of both substance and style.

COMMENTS AND REQUESTS FOR A PUBLIC HEARING

Before adoption of these proposed regulations, consideration will be given to any written comments that are submitted (preferably seven copies) to the Commissioner of Internal Revenue. In particular, comments are invited concerning the rules for determining whether partnership allocations are qualified under section 168(j)(9)(B). All comments will be available for public inspection and copying. A public hearing will be held upon written request to the Commissioner by any person who has submitted written comments. If a public hearing is held, notice of the time and place will be published in the *Federal Register*.

[¶ 49,056]   Proposed Regulations (EE-66-84), published in the Federal Register on July 3, 1985.

Welfare benefit fund: Collective bargaining: Limits on contributions and reserves.—Reg. §1.419A-2T, relating to welfare benefit funds maintained pursuant to collective bargaining agreements, is proposed.

AGENCY: Internal Revenue Service, Treasury.

ACTION: Notice of proposed rulemaking by cross reference to temporary regulations.

SUMMARY: In the Rules and Regulations portion of this issue of the *Federal Register*, the Internal Revenue Service is issuing temporary regulations relating to contributions to and reserves of welfare benefit funds maintained pursuant to a collective bargaining agreement. The text of those temporary regulations also serves as the comment document for this notice of proposed rulemaking.

DATES: Written comments and requests for a public hearing must be delivered or mailed by September 3, 1985. The regulations are proposed to be effective for contributions paid or accrued after December 31, 1985.

ADDRESS: Send comments and requests for a public hearing to Commissioner of Internal Revenue, Attn: CC:LR:T (EE-66-84), 1111 Constitution Avenue NW., Washington, D.C. 20224.

FOR FURTHER INFORMATION CONTACT: John T. Ricotta of the Employee Plans and Exempt Organizations Division, Office of Chief Counsel, Internal Revenue Service, 1111 Constitution Avenue NW., Washington, D.C. 20224, Attention: CC:LR:T (EE-66-84), telephone: 202-566-4396 (not a toll-free number).

SUPPLEMENTARY INFORMATION:

Background

The temporary regulations provide guidance concerning the limits on contributions to and the reserves of welfare benefit funds maintained pursuant to a collective bargaining agreement under section 419A(f)(5) of the Internal Revenue Code of 1954 (Code), as added to the Code by section 511 of the Tax Reform Act of 1984 (26 U.S.C. 419A). The proposed regulations are issued under the authority contained in section 7805 of the Code (26 U.S.C. 7805). For the text of the temporary regulations, see FR Doc. 85-15940 published in the Rules and Regulations portion of this issue of the *Federal Register*.

Special Analyses

The Commissioner of Internal Revenue has determined that this proposed rule is not a major rule as defined in Executive Order 12291 and that a Regulatory Impact Analysis is therefore not required. Although this document is a notice of proposed rulemaking which solicits public comment, the Internal Revenue has concluded that the regulations proposed herein are interpretative and that the notice and public procedure requirements of 5 U.S.C. 553 do not apply. Accordingly, these proposed regulations do not constitute regulations subject to the Regulatory Flexibility Act (5 U.S.C. Chapter 6).

Comments and Requests for a Public Hearing

Before adopting the temporary regulations referred to in this document as final regulations, consideration will be given to any written comments that are submitted (preferably 8 copies) to the Commissioner of Internal Revenue. All comments will be available for public inspection and copying. A public hearing will be held upon written request to the Commissioner by any person who has submitted written comments. If a public hearing is held, notice of the time and place will be published in the *Federal Register*.

[¶ 49,057] Proposed Regulations (LR-165-84), published in the Federal Register on August 20, 1985.

Below-market loans: Interest.—Reg. §§ 1.7872-1—1.7872-14 and amendments to Reg. § 53.4941(d)-2, relating to the tax treatment of both lender and borrower in certain below-market interest rate loan transactions, are proposed.

AGENCY: Internal Revenue Service, Treasury.

ACTION: Notice of proposed rulemaking.

SUMMARY: This document contains proposed regulations relating to the Federal tax treatment of both the lender and the borrower in certain below-market interest rate loan transactions. Changes to the applicable tax law were made by the Tax Reform Act of 1984. These regulations would affect taxpayers who enter into certain below-market loans and provide them with guidance needed to comply with the law.

DATES: Written comments and requests for a public hearing must delivered or mailed by October 21, 1985. The regulations are generally proposed to be effective after June 6, 1984, for below-market term loans made after June 6, 1984, and below-market demand loans outstanding after June 6, 1984. Section 1.7872-1(c) provides special effective date rules for certain loan transactions.

ADDRESS: Send comments and requests for a public hearing to: Commissioner of Internal Revenue, Attention: CC:LR:T (LR-165-84), Washington, D.C. 20224.

FOR FURTHER INFORMATION CONTACT: Sharon L. Hall of the Legislation and Regulations Division, Office of Chief Counsel, Internal Revenue Service, 1111 Constitution Avenue, N.W., Washington, D.C. 20224, Attention: CC:LR:T, 202-566-3828 (not a toll-free call).

SUPPLEMENTARY INFORMATION:

BACKGROUND

This document contains proposed amendments to the Income Tax Regulations (26 CFR Part 1), the Estate Tax Regulations (26 CFR Part 20), the Gift Tax Regulations (26 CFR Part 25) and the Excise Tax Regulations (26 CFR Part 53) under section 7872 of the Internal Revenue Code of 1954. This document also amends the Table of OMB Control Numbers (26 CFR Part 602). These amendments are proposed to provide regulations under new section 7872, which was added to the Code by section 172 of the Tax Reform Act of 1984 (98 Stat. 699).

IN GENERAL

Prior to the enactment of section 7872, some taxpayers used interest-free loans or loans with an interest rate below the current market rate (in each case, "below-market loans") which purported to circumvent well-established rules of taxation. Thus, in family or similar situations, below-market loans have been used which purported to have the effect of avoiding taxation under the grantor trust rules and deflecting income to others. Corporations have made below-market loans to shareholders with the effect of avoiding taxation of income at the corporate level which is the economic equivalent of receiving a deduction for dividends paid to those shareholders. Employers have made below-market loans to employees with the effect of providing compensation which has not been subject to employment taxes. Interest-free loans have also been used to convert non-deductible expenses into the equivalent of deductible expenses.

Section 7872 addresses these and similar practices, generally, by treating certain below-market loans described in one of the categories specified in section 7872(c) as economically equivalent to loans bearing interest at the applicable Federal rate coupled with a payment by the lender to the borrower sufficient to fund the payment of interest by the borrower. Thus, the lender is treated as making (i) a loan to the borrower in exchange for a note requiring the payment of interest at the applicable Federal rate, and (ii) a transfer of funds to the borrower in an amount generally equal to the amount of interest imputed under section 7872. In the case of term gift loans, however, the amount of money treated as transferred by the lender to the borrower, which is subject to gift tax, and the amount of the imputed interest payment by the borrower to the lender are unequal because they are computed differently under the statute.

CHARACTER AND TIMING OF TRANSFERS

The character of the imputed transfer by the lender to the borrower is determined in accordance with the substance of the transaction. For example, the transfer is treated as a gift if the transaction is in substance a gift within the meaning of the gift tax provisions of the Code, and it is treated as compensation if the purpose of the transaction is the payment of compensation. This imputed transfer is computed annually and in the case of demand loans is treated as made, generally, on December 31. In the case of term loans, however, the imputed transfer is treated as made at the time the loan is made.

The timing and amount of the imputed interest payments by the borrower to the lender depend on the character of the amount transferred by the lender to the borrower and on whether the loan is a term loan or a demand loan. The imputed interest payment in the case of gift and demand loans is computed annually and generally is treated as transferred on December 31. The imputed interest payment in the case of term loans other than gift loans is computed on the date the loan is made and is subject to the original issue discount rules of section 1272.

DEFINITION OF LOAN

Because the purpose of section 7872 is to eliminate the use of below-market loans as a vehicle for tax avoidance, the term "loan" is interpreted broadly in the regulations. Accordingly, any extension of credit or any transaction under which the owner of money permits another person to use the money for a period of time after which the money is to be transferred back to the owner or applied according to an agreement with the owner, such as a refundable deposit, is a loan for purposes of section 7872. However, only those below-market loans that are gift loans, compensation-related loans, corporation-shareholder loans, tax avoidance loans or loans to be specified as significant-effect loans (see below), are subject to the provisions of section 7872. Proposed § 1.7872-4(g) provides a special rule for a below-market loan which is made between two persons and is attributable to the relationship of a third person to either the lender or the borrower (for example, a loan by an employer to the child of an employee). In this case, the loan is restructured as two successive "indirect" loans for purposes of section 7872. In addition, the regulations provide that if a lender and a borrower use another entity as an intermediary or middleman, such as in a "back-to-back" loan transaction, for the purpose of avoiding the application of section 7872, the intermediary will be ignored and the two loans will be restructured as one loan made directly between the lender and the borrower.

Section 7872(c)(1)(B)(ii) states that loans between an independent contractor and a person for whom the independent contractor provides services are subject to section 7872. In addition, the proposed regulations define a loan to include any transaction which would be treated as a refundable deposit under current law. Accordingly, if a taxpayer makes a refundable deposit to an independent contractor in connection with the performance of services, the deposit will be subject to the imputation rules of section 7872 (unless the de minimis rules are applicable). The Service is aware that cash amounts are frequently deposited with independent contractors in the ordinary course of business and characterized by the parties as prepayments rather than refundable deposits. Consequently, if this characterization is appropriate, those amounts would not be subject to section 7872. The proper distinction between refundable deposits and prepayments is a factual determination, and, to assist the Service in developing guidelines for drawing this distinction, interested parties are invited to comment on this issue.

PARTNERSHIPS AND PARTNERS

The Service is aware that some taxpayers have entered into below-market loans with partnerships and that other taxpayers have achieved the economic and tax result afforded a below-market loan transaction by utilizing partnerships and the tax laws under subchapter K. The proposed regulations provide that certain below-market loans made by a partnership to a partner that are made in consideration for services performed by the partner other than in his capacity as a member of the partnership will be treated as compensation-related loans for purposes of section 7872.

The final regulations under section 7872 will further address the relationship of section 7872 to partnership transactions, such as certain purported distributions which, under the facts and circumstances, may properly be characterized as loans. The Service is considering several proposals regarding the application of section 7872 to transactions between partners and partnerships and requests interested taxpayers to submit written comments on this point.

SIGNIFICANT EFFECT LOAN

In addition to the four enumerated categories of below-market loans, section 7872(c)(1)(E) provides regulatory authority for applying section 7872 to any other below-market loan if "the interest arrangements of such loan have a significant effect on any Federal tax liability of the lender or the borrower." The Conference Report accompanying the Tax Reform Act of 1984 states, among other things, that any loan that results in the conversion of a nondeductible expense into the equivalent of a deductible expense has an effect on the tax liability of the borrower or lender. The Conference Report further provides that whether an effect is significant is determined in light of all the facts and circumstances including:

(1) Whether the items of income and deduction generated by the loan offset each other;

(2) The amount of such items;

(3) The cost to the taxpayer of complying with the provision; and

(4) Any non-tax reasons for deciding to structure the transaction as a below-market loan rather than a loan with interest at a rate equal to or greater than the applicable Federal rate and a payment by the lender to the borrower.

The Service is aware of numerous situations in which below-market loans have the potential to convert nondeductible personal expenses into the equivalent of deductible expenses. This potential is particularly apparent where interest earned on the borrowed amount may be used to compensate (or provide additional compensation to) the borrower for services or property provided to the lender. Examples of these situations include:

(1) Loans to a membership organization in lieu of part or all of a membership fee;

(2) Loans to institutions providing meals, lodging, and/or medical services (e.g., continuing care facilities) in lieu of fees for such services;

(3) Loans to colleges and secondary schools in lieu of part or all of the tuition, room, and board that would otherwise be charged; and

(4) Loans to an employee or independent contractor by an employer in lieu of payment for a service provided to such employer by the employee (e.g., housing, life insurance coverage, health care).

Many of these transactions have a significant potential for distortion of tax liability, especially if the amounts loaned are relatively large. The Service has decided, however, not to propose regulations treating transactions as having a significant effect until further comment is received on how the facts and circumstances test should be applied, including the proper role of the factors cited by the Conference Report. The Service intends to hold a hearing after publication of these proposed regulations, if a public hearing is requested by any person who submits written comments. The Service urges taxpayers to submit written comments and to speak on this point at that hearing. No transaction will be treated under the regulations as a significant effect loan earlier than the date that future regulations under section 7872(c)(1)(E) are published in proposed form.

EXCLUSION FROM SECTION 7872

Proposed §§1.7872-7 and 1.7872-8 provide for the exclusion of certain below-market loans from the rules of section 7872. Generally, if the amount of loans between a lender and a borrower does not exceed $10,000, section 7872 does not apply. Furthermore, in the case of gift loans of less than $100,000, directly between natural persons, the imputed interest payment by the borrower to the lender each year generally is limited to the amount of the borrower's net investment income (as defined [in] section 7872(d)(1)(E)) for the taxable year.

In addition, section 7872(g)(1)(C) provides regulatory authority for exempting from the application of section 7872 any class of transactions if the application of section 7872 would not have a significant effect on any Federal tax liability of the lender or the borrower. Accordingly, proposed §1.7872-5 provides that certain below-market loans which are not structured as such for tax avoidance purposes are exempted from the provisions of section 7872. If, however, such a loan is structured as one of the exempted loans for tax avoidance purposes, the Service may recharacterize the transaction according to its economic substance and apply section 7872 in accordance with its terms. Interested taxpayers are invited to comment on whether other transactions should be exempted from section 7872, and on the proper tax treatment under section 7872 of private placements of convertible debt.

Section 7872(f)(8) provides that section 7872 does not apply to any loan to which section 483 or 1274 applies. The regulations clarify that generally section 7872 does not apply to any loan to which section 483 or 1274 could apply even though the rules of those sections do not apply because of exceptions or safe harbor provisions in one of those sections. The regulations further clarify that debt instruments issued for property and payable on demand, debt instruments described in section 1273(b)(3) and debt instruments described in section 1275(b) are not subject to sections 483 and 1274 and are subject to section 7872 if those instruments are described in section 7872(c)(1)(A), (B), or (C).

Certain loans subject to section 7872 are also described in section 482 of the Code (concerning the allocation of income and deductions among related taxpayers). These regulations provide for one limited exception to section 7872 in the case of a loan which is also described in §1.482-2(a)(3), concerning indebtedness arising in the ordinary course of business out of sales, leases, or the rendition of services by or between members of a group outstanding for six months or less (the "open accounts exception"). This limited exception will expire on June 30, 1986, by which time the Service plans to have completed its review of the commercial need for an exception from section 7872 in the case of certain "open account" transactions between parties described in section 7872. The Service invites written comments on this issue.

Where an employer makes a below-market term loan to an employee in certain circumstances, the loan is treated for purposes of section 7872 as a demand loan under section 7872(f)(5). In the case where the employer disposes of his interest in the loan by sale to a third party, questions have arisen regarding the proper tax treatment of the employer, employee and third-party purchaser. The Service is considering alternative ways to resolve the issues raised in these circumstances, consistent with the following principles:

(1) The employee should remain subject to section 7872(a)(1), so long as that section would be applicable if the employer had not sold his interest in the loan; and

(2) The disposition of the loan should not present opportunities for tax avoidance that would not arise had the employer not disposed of its interest in the loan.

When promulgated, these rules may also apply to certain loans, such as employee relocation loans, which are generally exempted from the statute under §1.7872-5. The Internal Revenue Service invites comments concerning this issue.

FOREIGN CURRENCY LOANS

The proposed regulations state that for purposes of applying the below-market loan rules to loans denominated in a foreign currency, a market rate of interest appropriate for that currency shall be used in lieu of the applicable Federal rate. However, the proposed regulations expressly leave open the question of how the imputed transfer from the borrower to the lender is to be treated for tax purposes. The Service is aware that high nominal rates of interest in currencies expected to depreciate with respect to the dollar may overstate the true cost of borrowing to a U.S. taxpayer if offsetting foreign currency gains are not taken into account. Conversely, low rates of interest in currencies expected to appreciate with respect to the dollar may understate true borrowing costs. The Service is studying this issue further, in the context of transactions governed by section 7872 as well as those governed by sections 1271 through 1275, and plans to address this issue in future regulations under these sections.

REQUEST FOR COMMENTS ON CERTAIN TRANSACTIONS

The Service is aware that numerous transactions which occur in the ordinary course of business in many industries may be characterized under section 7872(c)(1)(B) as compensation-related loans. (One example is a transaction in which a cash margin deposit is made pursuant to requirements of an exchange to a futures commission merchant or to the exchange as a condition for trading futures contracts. See §1.7872-5 for a special temporary rule pending comments.) In order to determine whether these transactions are subject to section 7872 and whether the interest arrangements of such transactions have a significant effect on the Federal tax liability of the lender or borrower, the Service requests that taxpayers submit written comments providing a full explanation of the transactions.

The Service is also aware that other persons subject to section 7872 may enter into numerous short-term demand loans for business-related or other purposes. (One example is short-term loans resulting from the extension of credit through the use of a credit card. See §1.7872-10(a)(6) for a special rule relating to revolving credit loans.) Because of the volume and the short-term nature of the loans in these situations, the Service is also considering whether special rules of convenience can be formulated in some circumstances to reduce the cost of compliance without creating opportunities for manipulation or tax avoidance. The Service invites comments and suggestions with respect to such possible rules of convenience, the circumstances in which they would be applicable, and any exceptions that may be necessary if such rules are adopted.

APPLICABLE FEDERAL RATE

Under the proposed regulations, the applicable Federal rate in effect at any time depends upon the Federal statutory rates established for semiannual periods and the alternate Federal rates established by the Commissioner on a monthly basis (see §1.1274-3T). The Federal statutory rates and the alternate Federal rates are published by the Commissioner along with equivalent rates which are based on different compounding periods. The choice of the appropriate Federal statutory rate or alternate Federal rate for any loan depends upon the payment intervals or compounding periods required under the loan agreement. The regulations provide special rules to permit use of the alternate Federal rate in the case of demand loans. In addition, the proposed regulations provide special rules for certain variable interest rate loans.

UNASCERTAINABLE TERM

The proposed regulations do not address the treatment of term loans in the case where the period for which the loan is outstanding is unascertainable. For example, a loan which must be repaid when the borrower marries is a term loan outstanding for an unascertainable period of time. In order to make the calculations required by section 7872(b), it is necessary to know the period of time that the term loan is outstanding. The Service invites comments on this issue.

OTHER ISSUES:

CONSISTENCY; ESTATE AND GIFT TAX RULES; PRIVATE FOUNDATIONS

Section 7872(g)(1)(B) provides regulatory authority for assuring that the positions of the lender and borrower are consistent as to the application or nonapplication of section 7872. Accordingly, proposed § 1.7872-11(f) provides that the lender and the borrower each must attach a statement to their income tax returns for any taxable year in which they either have imputed income or claim a deduction for an amount imputed under section 7872.

In addition, proposed § 20.7872-1 implements section 7872(g)(2) by prohibiting the discounting, at other than the applicable Federal rate, for estate tax purposes, of any term loan made by a decedent with donative intent after June 6, 1984. Proposed § 25.7872-1 implements section 7872(a) by providing that the amount transferred by the lender to the borrower and characterized as a gift is subject to the gift tax provisions. Finally, § 53.4941(d)-2 is amended to provide that the amount of interest on loans between a disqualified person and a private foundation is computed without regard to section 7872 for purposes of application of the excise tax imposed by that section.

EFFECTIVE DATES

In general, the provisions of section 7872 apply after June 6, 1984, to term loans made after June 6, 1984, and to demand loans outstanding after June 6, 1984. If, however, a demand loan that was outstanding after June 6, 1984, is retired before September 17, 1984, the provisions of section 7872 will not apply to the demand loan for the period ending on the date on which the loan is retired. For this purpose, the demand loan is retired by repayment, cancellation, forgiveness, modification of the interest arrangement, or some other similar action (see Internal Revenue Service News Release, IR-84-95, published August 28, 1984).

COMMENTS AND REQUESTS FOR A PUBLIC HEARING

Before adopting these proposed regulations, consideration will be given to any written comments that are submitted (preferably eight copies) to the Commissioner of Internal Revenue. All comments will be available for public inspection and copying. A public hearing will be held upon written request to the Commissioner by any person who has submitted written comments. If a public hearing is to be held, notice of the time and place will be published in the FEDERAL REGISTER.

The collection of information requirements contained in this notice of proposed rulemaking have been submitted to the Office of Management and Budget (OMB) for review under section 3504(h) of the Paperwork Reduction Act. Comments on these requirements should be sent to the Office of Information and Regulatory Affairs of OMB, Attention: Desk Officer for Internal Revenue Service, New Executive Office Building, Washington, D.C. 20503. The Internal Revenue Service requests that persons submitting comments on these requirements to OMB also send copies of those comments to the Service.

SPECIAL ANALYSES

The Commissioner of Internal Revenue has determined that this proposed rule is not a major rule as defined in Executive Order 12291. Accordingly, a Regulatory Impact Analysis is not required. Although this document is a notice of proposed rulemaking that solicits public comment, the Internal Revenue Service has concluded that the proposed regulations are interpretative and that the notice and public procedure requirements of 5 U.S.C. 553 do not apply. Accordingly, these proposed regulations do not constitute regulations subject to the Regulatory Flexibility Act (5 U.S.C. chapter 6).

DRAFTING INFORMATION

The principal author of these proposed regulations is Howard A. Balikov of the Legislation and Regulations Division of the Office of Chief Counsel, Internal Revenue Service. However, personnel from other offices of the Internal Revenue Service and Treasury Department participated in developing the regulations on matters of both substance and style.

[¶ 49,059]   Proposed Amendments to Regulations (LR-114-85), published in the Federal Register on September 3, 1985.

Mortgage credit certificates: Information reporting.—Amendments to Reg. § 1.25-4T, dealing with information reporting and policy statement requirements, are proposed.

AGENCY: Internal Revenue Service, Treasury.

ACTION: Notice of proposed rulemaking by cross-reference to temporary regulations.

SUMMARY: This document provides proposed regulations that relate to mortgage credit certificates. Changes to the applicable tax law were made by the Tax Reform Act of 1984. These regulations affect all holders and issuers of mortgage credit certificates. In addition, in the Rules and Regulations portion of this FEDERAL REGISTER, the Internal Revenue Service is issuing temporary regulations that relate to mortgage credit certificates. The text of those temporary regulations also serves as the comment document for this proposed rulemaking.

DATES: Written comments and requests for a public hearing must be delivered or mailed by November 4, 1985. These regulations are proposed to be effective with respect to mortgage credit certificates issued after September 30, 1985.

ADDRESS: Send comments and requests for a public hearing to: Commissioner of Internal Revenue, Attention: CC:LR:T (LR-114-85), Washington, D.C. 20224.

FOR FURTHER INFORMATION CONTACT: Mitchell H. Rapaport of the Legislation and Regulations Division, Office of Chief Counsel, Internal Revenue Service, 1111 Constitution Avenue, N.W., Washington, D.C. 20224 (Attention: CC:LR:T) (202-566-3740).

SUPPLEMENTARY INFORMATION:

BACKGROUND

The temporary regulations in the Rules and Regulations portion of this issue of the FEDERAL REGISTER amend § 1.25-4T of Title 26 of the Code of Federal Regulations. The final regulations, which this document proposes to be based on those temporary regulations, would be added to Part 1 of Title 26 of the Code of Federal Regulations. For the text of the Temporary Regulations, see FR Doc. (T.D. 8048) published in the Rules and Regulations portion of this issue of the FEDERAL REGISTER. The preamble to the temporary regulations explains the addition to the regulations.

On May 8, 1985, temporary and proposed regulations with respect to mortgage credit certificates were published in the FEDERAL REGISTER (50 FR 19344; 50 FR 19383). Those regulations reserved § 1.25-4T(e), relating to the information reporting requirement, and § 1.25-4T(f), relating to the policy statement requirement. The Service received numerous written comments responding to a notice of proposed rulemaking published in the FEDERAL REGISTER on December 12, 1984 (49 FR 48323), with respect to the reporting and policy statement requirements as they apply to qualified mortgage bonds and qualified veterans' mortgage bonds, and a public hearing was held on April 30, 1985. After consideration of all comments regarding those proposed regulations, temporary and proposed regulations relating to the information reporting and policy statement requirements applicable to mortgage credit certificates are being provided.

The regulations interpret the provisions of section 25(g) of the Code, which add certain information reporting requirements to the requirements that mortgage credit certificate programs must meet.

These regulations are proposed to be issued under the authority of section 25(g) and section 7805 of the Internal Revenue Code (98 Stat. 911, 26 U.S.C. 25(g); 68A Stat. 917, 26 U.S.C. 7805).

NON-APPLICABILITY OF EXECUTIVE ORDER 12291

The Commissioner of Internal Revenue has determined that this proposed rule is not a major rule as defined in Executive Order 12291and that a regulatory impact analysis therefore is not required.

REGULATORY FLEXIBILITY ANALYSIS

Although this document is a notice of proposed rulemaking that solicits public comment, the Internal Revenue Service has concluded that the regulations proposed herein are interpretative and that the notice and public procedure requirements of 5 U.S.C. 553 do not apply. Accordingly, these proposed regulations do not constitute regulations subject to the Regulatory Flexibility Act (5 U.S.C. chapter 6).

DRAFTING INFORMATION

The principal author of these proposed regulations is Mitchell H. Rapaport of the Legislation and Regulations Division of the Office of Chief Counsel, Internal Revenue Service. However, personnel from other offices of the Internal Revenue Service and Treasury Department participated in developing the regulations, on matters of both substance and style.

COMMENTS AND REQUESTS FOR A PUBLIC HEARING

Before the adoption of these proposed regulations, consideration will be given to any written comments that are submitted (preferably seven copies) to the Commissioner of Internal Revenue. All comments will be available for public inspection and copying. A public hearing will be held upon written request to the Commissioner by any person who has submitted written comments. If a public hearing is held, notice of the time and place will be published in the FEDERAL REGISTER. The collection of information requirements contained herein have been submitted to the Office of Management and Budget (OMB) for review under section 3504(h) of the Paperwork Reduction Act. Comments on the requirements should be sent to the Office of Information and Regulatory Affairs of OMB, Attention: Desk Officer for Internal Revenue Service, New Executive Office Building, Washington, D.C. 20503. The Internal Revenue Service requests persons submitting comments to OMB also to send copies of the comments to the Service.

[¶ 49,061]   **Proposed Regulations (LR-145-84), filed with the Federal Register on** November 1, 1985.

Business expenses: Substantiation: Recordkeeping requirements: Listed property.—Reg. §§1.274-5T and 1.274-6T and amendments to Reg. §§1.162-25T, 1.280F-1T, 1.280F-3T and 1.280F-5T, relating to the requirement that any deduction or credit with respect to certain business-related expenses be substantiated with adequate or sufficient evidence to corroborate a taxpayer's own statement and to the limitations on cost recovery deductions and the investment tax credit for listed property, are proposed. Portions of Reg. §1.274-5T were adopted by T.D. 8864 on 1/21/2000 and by T.D. 9483 on 5/18/2010. Temporary Reg. §1.280F-6T was redesignated as Reg. §1.280F-6 by T.D. 9133 on 6/24/2004.

AGENCY: Internal Revenue Service, Treasury.

ACTION: Notice of proposed rulemaking by cross-reference to temporary regulations.

SUMMARY: In the Rules and Regulations portion of this issue of the FEDERAL REGISTER, the Internal Revenue Service is issuing temporary income tax regulations under section 274 and amending other temporary regulations under sections 162 and 280F. The temporary regulations under section 274 provide rules for the substantiation of any deduction or credit claimed with respect to traveling away from home, certain entertainment expenditures, business-related gifts, and "listed property." The amendments to the temporary regulations under section 162 relate to the deductibility of certain expenses incurred by employers and employees with respect to noncash fringe benefits. The amendments to the temporary regulations under section 280F provide new limitations on the deductions of lessees of passenger automobiles. The text of the new and amended temporary regulations serves as the comment document for the notice of proposed rulemaking contained in this document.

DATES: Proposed effective dates: The regulations under section 162 are proposed to be effective as of January 1, 1985. The regulations under section 274 relating to the substantiation of deductions and credits claimed with respect to certain business expenditures are proposed to be effective generally for taxable years beginning after December 31, 1985. The amendments relating to the limitations on the deductions of lessees of passenger automobiles are proposed to be effective generally for automobiles leased after April 2, 1985.

Dates for comments and requests for a public hearing: Written comments and requests for a public hearing must be delivered or mailed by January 5, 1986.

ADDRESS: Send comments and requests for a public hearing to Commissioner of Internal Revenue, Attention: CC:LR:T (LR-145-84), Washington, D.C. 20224.

FOR FURTHER INFORMATION CONTACT: Michel A. Dazé of the Legislation and Regulations Division, Office of the Chief Counsel, Internal Revenue Service, 1111 Constitution Avenue, N.W., Washington, D.C. 20224 (202-566-6456, not a toll-free call).

SUPPLEMENTARY INFORMATION:

BACKGROUND

The temporary regulations published in the Rules and Regulations portion of this issue of the FEDERAL REGISTER amend the Income Tax Regulations (26 CFR Part 1) to reflect amendments to section 274 of the Internal Revenue Code of 1954, relating to substantiation requirements, and to section 280F relating to limitations on cost recovery deductions and the investment tax credit allowed for passenger automobiles. The temporary regulations issued under section 274 reflect amendments to section 274(d) by section 179 of the Tax Reform Act of 1984 (Pub. L. 98-369, 98 Stat. 494) and by sections 1(a) and 2 of the Repeal of Contemporaneous Recordkeeping Requirements (Pub. L. 99-44, 99 Stat. 77). The amendments to the temporary regulations under section 280F reflect amendments to that section by section 4 of Public Law 99-44. The preamble to the temporary regulations contains an explanation of the provisions of those regulations. The temporary regulations will remain in effect until superseded by final regulations which are proposed to be based on the temporary regulations.

Before amendment by the Tax Reform Act of 1984 and Public Law 99-44, section 274(d) required that any deduction for expenses incurred for (1) traveling away from home, (2) entertainment, amusement, or recreation activities or the use of a facility in connection with those activities, or (3) business-related gifts be substantiated by aequate records or sufficient evidence corroborating a taxpayer's own statement. Section 274(d) did not apply to vehicles when used in local travel. Instead, the more general substantiation standards under section 162 were applicable. As amended, section 274(d) requires, for taxable years beginning after December 31, 1985, that any deduction or credit claimed for the expenses described above and for expenses incurred with respect to "listed property" be substantiated by adequate records or sufficient evidence corroborating a taxpayer's own statement. Section 274(d) will then apply to vehicles used in local travel.

First adopted by Treasury decision in 1962, §1.274-5 of the Income Tax Regulations reflects the addition of section 274(d) to the Code. Amendments to §1.274-5 are proposed to conform the regulations to the 1984 Act and to Public Law 99-44. For the convenience of taxpayers who must comply with the section 274(d) substantiation requirements, the proposed amendments are incorporated into §1.274-5 and published in full in the format of a termporary regulation. New material is indicated by underlining.

COMMENTS AND REQUESTS FOR A PUBLIC HEARING

Before these proposed amendments are adopted, consideration will be given to any written comments that are submitted (preferably eight copies) to the Commissioner of Internal Revenue. All comments will be available for public inspection and copying.

Comments are invited, however, on only those portions of new temporary §1.274-5T that are amendments to §1.274-5 to reflect the recent legislation. Specifically, comments are invited on the following provisions that are included among those amendments:

Paragraph (b)(6), the elements of an expenditure or use with respect to listed property,

Paragraph (c)(2)(ii)(C), substantiation of business use,

Paragraph (c)(3)(ii), sampling rule for the substantiation of business use,

Paragraph (c)(6)(i)(C), aggregation of business use,

Paragraph (d)(2) and (3), disclosure on tax returns of certain information with respect to the use of listed property,

Paragraph (e), substantiation of working condition fringe exclusions and certain employee deductions, and

Paragraph (k), other vehicles that may be designated as qualified nonpersonal use vehicles.

Comments are also invited on the provisions of §1.162-25T and §1.274-6T and the amendments to the temporary regulations under section 280F. Comments have been received previously on the limitations applicable to lessees contained in §1.280F-5T of those temporary regulations. The comments have pointed out that separate limitations are not applicable to lessees to whom lessors have elected to pass through the investment credit. The Internal Revenue Service intends to issue an announcement in the near future providing separate limitations for these lessees.

In the case of a fleet of vehicles owned or leased by an employer and used by employees in connection with the employer's business, the Service is considering an alternative method for the employer to satisfy its substantiation requirements. An employer would be able to establish the business use of each vehicle in the fleet and the personal use by an employee by a method similar to the following:

(1) The employer would identify a class of at least 100 vehicles that are physically similar and that are used in a similar fashion,

(2) No vehicle in the class would have a fair market value greater than $16,500,

(3) At the beginning of each taxable year, the employer would select from the class a random sample using accepted sampling techniques,

(4) The sample size would preferably be at least 250 vehicles, or one-half the class in the case of fleets of less than 500 vehicles (but in no event less than 50 vehicles),

(5) The taxpayer would determine the business use of each vehicle in the sample from adequate records maintained for each vehicle, and

(6) The average of the business use of each vehicle in the sample would be the business use of each vehicle in the class.

Comments are invited with respect to this alternative method of satisfying the substantiation requirements of section 274(d).

A public hearing will be held upon written request to the Commissioner by any person who submits written comments. If a public hearing is held, notice of the time and place will be published in the FEDERAL REGISTER.

The collection of information requirements contained in the temporary regulations have been submitted to the Office of Management and Budget (OMB) for review under section 3504(h) of the Paperwork Reduction Act. Comments on these requirements should be sent to the Office of Information and Regulatory Affairs, Attention: Desk Officer for Internal Revenue Service, New Executive Office Building, Washington, D.C. 20503. The Internal Revenue Service requests that persons submitting comments on the requirements to OMB also send copies of those comments to the Service.

EXECUTIVE ORDER 12291 AND REGULATORY FLEXIBILITY ACT

The Commissioner of Internal Revenue has determined that the proposed rule is not a major rule as defined in Executive Order 12291and that a Regulatory Impact Analysis is therefore not required.

Although this document is a notice of proposed rulemaking which solicits public comment, the Internal Revenue Service has concluded that the regulations proposed herein are interpretative and that the notice and public procedure requirements of 5 U.S.C. 553 do not apply. Accordingly, these proposed regulations do not constitute regulations subject to the Regulatory Flexibility Act (5 U.S.C. Chapter 6).

DRAFTING INFORMATION

The principal author of this document is Michel A. Dazé of the Legislation and Regulations Division of the Office of Chief Counsel, Internal Revenue Service. However, personnel from other offices of the Internal Revenue Service and Treasury Department participated in developing the regulations on matters of both substance and style.

[¶ 49,062]   **Proposed Amendments to Regulations (LR-269-84), published in the Federal Register on** November 7, 1985.

Nontaxables: Government obligations: Tax-exempt industrial development bonds.—Amendments to Reg. §1.103-8(b), relating to the definition of low or moderate income made by the Tax Reform Act of 1984, are proposed.

AGENCY: Internal Revenue Service, Treasury.

ACTION: Notice of proposed rulemaking.

SUMMARY: This document provides proposed regulations that relate to the tax exempt status of industrial development bonds. Changes to the applicable tax law were made by the Tax Reform Act of 1984. These regulations affect all purchasers, beneficiaries, and government issuers of tax exempt industrial development bonds.

DATES: Written comments and requests for a public hearing must be delivered or mailed by January 6, 1986. Generally, the provisions permitting a residential rental project to be part of a mixed-use project are proposed to be effective for obligations issued after April 30, 1968. However, the provisions relating to the definition of low or moderate income are proposed to be effective for obligations issued after December 31, 1985.

ADDRESS: Send comments and requests for a public hearing to: Commissioner of Internal Revenue, Attention: CC:LR:T (LR-269-84), Washington, D.C. 20224.

FOR FURTHER INFORMATION CONTACT: Mitchell H. Rapaport of the Legislation and Regulations Division, Office of Chief Counsel, Internal Revenue Service, 1111 Constitution Avenue, N.W., Washington, D.C. 20224 (Attention: CC:LR:T) (202-566-3740).

SUPPLEMENTARY INFORMATION:

BACKGROUND

This document contains proposed amendments to the Income Tax Regulations (26 CFR Part 1) under Section 103(b) of the Internal Revenue Code of 1954. The proposed amendments reflect changes to section 103(b)(4) made by sections 614 and 628(e) of the Tax Reform Act of 1984 (Pub. L. 98-369; 98 Stat. 914, 932). The proposed amendments would also clarify the regulations under section 103(b)(12)(C), relating to the definition of individuals of low and moderate income.

EXPLANATION OF PROVISIONS

Section 103(a) provides that gross income does not include interest on the obligations of a State or political subdivision thereof. Section 103(b)(1) provides that any industrial development bond shall be treated as an obligation not described in section 103(a).

Section 103(b)(4)(A) and § 1.103-8(b)(1) provide that section 103(b)(1) shall not apply to an obligation issued as part of an issue substantially all of the proceeds of which are to be used to provide a residential rental project as defined in § 1.103-8(b)(4) in which 20 percent or more of the units provided with the proceeds of the issue are to be occupied by individuals or families of low or moderate income.

The notice of proposed rulemaking would amend § 1.103-8(b)(4) to provide that a residential rental project will not fail to qualify as such merely because part of the building or structure in which such property is located is used for purposes other than similarly constructed rental units, *e.g.,* commercial office space, owner-occupied residences. Thus, for example, a building the first floor of which is used for commercial purposes and the balance of which consists of rental units may qualify as a residential rental project.

In the case of such a mixed-use project, for purposes of determining whether substantially all of the proceeds are to be used to provide a residential rental project only the proceeds to be used to provide rental units that, in the aggregate, meet the low or moderate income occupancy requirement and other portions of the project allocable to such units are treated as providing a residential rental project. For this purpose, the cost of property benefitting, directly or indirectly, both the rental units qualifying for financing and the nonqualifying property must be properly allocated between the units and the nonqualifying property, with only the portion allocable to the units being treated as a cost of providing a residential rental project. In general, the proposed regulations provide that this allocation will be considered proper if made based on the ratio of the amount of floor space in the project to be used for nonqualifying property to the total floor space in the project. However, in those situations in which the use of this allocation method would not reasonably reflect the benefits to be received, directly or indirectly, from such property by the rental units and the nonqualifying property, the allocation may not be made under this method. In such circumstances the allocation may be made under any reasonable method. Comments are specifically requested concerning any other allocation methods that may be appropriate for this purpose.

Section 103(b)(4)(A) and § 1.103-8(b) provide that an obligation will be treated as being described in section 103(a) if substantially all of the proceeds of the issue of which such obligation is a part are to be used to provide a project for residential rental property in which at least 20 percent of the units (15 percent in targeted areas) are to be occupied by individuals or families of low or moderate income. Section 1.103-8(b)(8)(v) defines low or moderate income as 80 percent of the median gross income for the area. The proposed regulations would amend the definition of low or moderate income to make clear that median gross income for an area is to be determined with adjustments for family size.

The proposed regulations would amend § 1.103-8(b)(3), relating to the transitional rules provided in the Mortgage Subsidy Bond Tax Act of 1980, to reflect the amendments made to those rules by the Tax Reform Act of 1984, which terminated most of those transitional rules for obligations issued after December 31, 1984.

NON-APPLICABILITY OF EXECUTIVE ORDER 12291

The Commissioner of Internal Revenue has determined that this proposed rule is not a major rule as defined in Executive Order 12291 and that a regulatory impact analysis therefore is not required.

REGULATORY FLEXIBILITY ANALYSIS

Although this document is a notice of proposed rulemaking that solicits public comment, the Internal Revenue Service has concluded that the regulations proposed herein are interpretative and that the notice and public procedure requirements of 5 U.S.C. 553 do not apply. Accordingly, these proposed regulations do not constitute regulations subject to the Regulatory Flexibility Act (5 U.S.C. Chapter 6).

DRAFTING INFORMATION

The principal author of these proposed regulations is Mitchell H. Rapaport of the Legislation and Regulations Division of the Office of Chief Counsel, Internal Revenue Service. However, personnel from other offices of the Internal Revenue Service and Treasury Department participated in developing the regulations, on matters of both substance and style.

COMMENTS AND REQUESTS FOR A PUBLIC HEARING

Before the adoption of these proposed regulations, consideration will be given to any written comments that are submitted (preferably eight copies) to the Commissioner of Internal Revenue. All comments will be available for public inspection and copying. A public hearing will be held upon written request to the Commissioner by any person who has submitted written comments. If a public hearing is held, notice of the time and place will be published in the FEDERAL REGISTER.

[¶ 49,064]   **Proposed Regulations (LR-214-82), published in the Federal Register on** January 7, 1986.

Employment taxes: Real estate agents and direct sellers: Employer's liability.—Reg. §§ 31.3508-1, 31.3509-1 and 1.6041A-1, relating to the treatment of qualified real estate agents and direct sellers as nonemployees, to the determination of employer liability for income tax withholding and employee social security taxes where the employer treated an employee as a nonemployee for purposes of such taxes, and to information reporting of direct sales and payments of remuneration for services, are proposed.

AGENCY: Internal Revenue Service, Treasury

ACTION: Notice of proposed rulemaking.

SUMMARY: This document contains proposed amendments to the Employment Tax Regulations under sections 3508, relating to the treatment of qualified real estate agents and direct sellers as nonemployees for Federal income and employment tax purposes, and under section 3509, relating to the determination of employer liability for income tax withholding and employee social security taxes where the employer treated an employee as a nonemployee for purposes of such taxes. It also contains proposed amendments to the Income Tax Regulations under section 6041A, relating to information reporting of direct sales and payments of remuneration for services. Sections 3508, 3509, and 6041A were added to the tax law by sections 269, 270, and 312, respectively, of the Tax Equity and Fiscal Responsibility Act of 1982 (96 Stat. 551, 553, 601). The regulations would provide the public with the guidance needed to comply with the applicable tax law.

DATES: Written comments and requests for a public hearing must be delivered or mailed by March 10, 1986. The regulations under section 3508 are proposed to be effective for services performed after December 31, 1982, and the regulations under section 6041A are proposed to be effective for payments and sales made after December 31, 1982. The regulations under section 3509 are proposed to be effective for any income and employee social security taxes required to be deducted and withheld, except with respect to assessments made before January 1, 1983.

ADDRESS: Send comments and requests for a public hearing to: Commissioner of Internal Revenue, Attention: CC:LR:T (LR-214-82), Washington, D.C. 20224.

FOR FURTHER INFORMATION CONTACT: Robert E. Shaw of the Legislation and Regulations Division, Office of Chief Counsel, Internal Revenue Service, 1111 Constitution Avenue, N.W., Washington, D. C. 20224 (Attention: CC:LR:T) (202-566-3297, not a toll-free call).

SUPPLEMENTARY INFORMATION:

BACKGROUND

The determination of whether an individual is an employee or independent contractor for Federal tax purposes is important for several reasons. Wages paid to employees generally are subject to social security taxes imposed on the employer and the employee under the Federal Insurance Contributions Act (FICA) and to unemployment taxes imposed on the employer under the Federal Unemployment Tax Act (FUTA). Compensation paid to independent contractors is subject to the tax on self-employment income (SECA), but not to FICA or FUTA taxes. The SECA is generally paid only by self-employed individuals. In additon, Federal income tax must generally be withheld from compensation paid to employees but not from compensation paid to independent contractors.

Except for sections 3121(d)(3) and 3306(i), which establish categories of statutory employees for social security and Federal unemployment tax purposes, prior to the enactment of the Tax Equity and Fiscal Responsibility Act of 1982, the determination of an individual's status as an employee or independent contractor generally was made under common-law (i.e., nonstatutory) rules. Under the common-law test, an individual generally is an employee if the person for whom the individual performs services has the right to control and direct that individual, not only as to the result to be accomplished by the work but also as to the details and means by which that result is accomplished. Thus, the most important factor under the common law is the degree of control, or right of control, which the employer has over the manner in which the work is to be performed.

The Service applies various factors that have evolved from the common law to determine whether the requisite control exists. Because of the difficulty that often arises in applying these factors, several bills introduced in both the House and the Senate during 1982 set forth statutory "safe-harbor" tests which, if satisfied with respect to an individual, would result in that individual being classified as an independent contractor. The proposed safe-harbor requirements, generally applicable to post-1982 services, related to (1) control of hours worked, (2) place of business, (3) investment or income fluctuation, (4) written contract and notice of tax responsibilities, and (5) the filing of required returns. S.Rep. No. 97-494, 97 Cong., 2d Sess. 364 (1982). Workers who did not meet the safe-harbor tests still would have had their employment tax status determined under the common-law rules.

In enacting the Tax Equity and Fiscal Responsibility Act of 1982 (P.L. 97-248), Congress rejected the broader safe harbor tests proposed by these bills and instead partially resolved the employee-independent contractor controversy by creating two categories of statutory nonemployees— qualified real estate agents and direct sellers. Thus, notwithstanding the common-law rules, an individual is an independent contractor for services that satisfy the statutory requirements of section 3508. Other employment situations generally must continue to be evaluated under common-law principles.

In response to the serious tax deficiencies that may arise when a worker erroneously treated as an independent contractor is reclassified as an employee, Congress enacted section 3509, which fixes an employer's liability for income tax withholding and employee social security taxes generally at a fraction of the amount of taxes which should have been deducted and withheld. Section 3509 provides relief to employers who would otherwise be liable for the full amount of such taxes which should have been deducted and withheld and provides a sanction for an employer's erroneous treatment of a worker in situations in which the employer would otherwise be able to escape liability for such taxes under the statutory offset provisions of sections 3402(d) and 6521.

To assure increased compliance by direct sellers with the income tax law, Congress added section 6041A (section 312 of the Tax Equity and Fiscal Responsibility Act of 1982) which, in addition to other requirements, imposes an obligation on direct sellers of consumer products to report gross sales totalling $5,000 or more in a calendar year to any buyer for resale in the home or some place other than a permanent retail establishment. Congress also provided a penalty for failure to file this return (section 6652) and a penalty for failure to furnish certain statements (section 6678).

EXPLANATION OF PROVISIONS

In general

The proposed regulations provide that an individual performing services as a qualified real estate agent or a direct seller will not be treated as an employee and the service-recipient will not be treated as an employer for Federal income and employment tax purposes. In order to qualify for such treatment substantially all the remuneration paid by a service-recipient to an individual for services as a real estate agent or direct seller must be directly related to sales or other output and such services must be performed pursuant to a written contract providing that such individual will not be treated as an employee for Federal tax purposes.

The proposed regulations make clear that a statutory employee (that is, an individual treated as an employee under section 3121(d)(3) of the Code) who also qualifies as a nonemployee under section 3508 will be treated as a nonemployee for FICA, FUTA and Federal income tax withholding purposes with respect to services described in section 3508. For example, an agent-driver (statutory employee) who qualifies as a direct seller (statutory nonemployee) will be treated as a nonemployee for FICA, FUTA, and income tax withholding purposes with respect to services performed as a direct seller. The regulations also make clear that the written contract requirement is not met unless the contract specifically states that the individual will not be treated as an employee for Federal tax purposes. For this purpose, it is not sufficient that the contract merely states that the individual will not be treated as an employee.

"Substantially all" remuneration requirement

Section 3508 requires that in order for an individual to be treated as a qualified real estate agent or a direct seller substantially all of the remuneration received for services as a real estate agent or direct seller must be directly related to sales or other output. The proposed regulations provide that the "substantially all remuneration" test is satisfied with respect to services performed as a real estate agent or direct seller if at least 90 percent of the total remuneration received during the calendar year by the individual for services performed as a real estate agent or direct seller is directly related to sales or other output rather than to the number of hours worked. The proposed regulations also provide rules for applying the "directly related to sales or other output" requirement to pooled remuneration arrangements, remuneration received in advance of sales or performance, and remuneration dependent on the productivity of others.

Direct sellers

A direct seller is any salesperson who, in addition to meeting the "substantially all" remuneration and written contract requirements, sells consumer products, either directly or though a middleperson (*i.e.*, a buyer) for ultimate resale, in the home or in a place other than in a permanent retail establishment. The proposed regulations define "consumer product" as any tangible personal property which is distributed in commerce and which is normally used for personal, family, or household purposes (including any such property intended to be attached to or installed in any real property without regard to whether it is so attached or installed). This definition corresponds to the definition provided in 15 U.S.C. §2301, and the limitation to tangible property is consistent with other definitions of consumer products found in the United States Code (15 U.S.C. §2052; 18 U.S.C. §1365; 42 U.S.C. §6291). The proposed regulations define "permanent retail establishment" as any business operating in or from a structure or facility which remains stationary for a substantial period of time to which consumers go to purchase consumer goods. The proposed regulations also clarify that vendors operating within, or on the grounds of, a permanent structure or facility such as a sports arena or amusement park are considered to operate in a permanent retail establishment for purposes of section 3508. Thus, the term "direct seller" may include door-to-door salespersons of not only products traditionally thought of as consumer products (*e.g.*, personal toiletry items, vacuum cleaners, kitchen products) but also products which require installation or construction on the consumer's property (*e.g.*, residential swimming pools, aluminum siding, kitchen cabinets, storm windows, insulation, carpeting) and products not used in or around the home. The term also includes salespersons who sell consumer goods directly to consumers through an exchange medium other than a permanent retail establishment (*e.g.*, mobile meal wagons or street vendors). The term does not include door-to-door salespersons of intangible products (*e.g.*, insurance, cable television subscription).

Persons who provide services generally are not direct sellers. For example, persons who provide services that do not involve the use of a product (*e.g.*, polltakers) or services that involve parts or materials which are incidental to providing services (*e.g.*, painting, carpet cleaning, septic tank cleaning, lawn care, pest control services, or appliance repair) are considered service providers rather than direct sellers.

Services of real estate agent and direct seller

The proposed regulations provide that the services performed as a direct seller are activities generally associated with the sale of consumer products in the home or otherwise than in a permanent retail establishment. These services include activities that are necessary to increase the sales efforts of other individuals, such as providing motivation, encouragement, training, recruitment, or counseling. Installation services performed by a direct seller in connection with the sale of a consumer product generally are not services performed by a direct seller. However, the proposed regulations provide that installation services rendered by a seller in conjunction with the sale of a consumer product will be services performed as a direct seller if the value of the installation services is 10 percent or less of the purchase price of the product (including installation).

The services performed as a real estate agent are those activities generally associated with the sale of real property. Such services include appraising property, advertising and showing property, closing sales, acquiring a lease to the property, and recruiting, training and supervising other salespersons. The services performed as a real estate agent do not include the management of property.

Retirement plans for self-employed individuals

The proposed regulations make clear that the fact that an individual is treated as a nonemployee under section 3508 for employment tax purposes will not prevent the individual from being covered under a qualified retirement plan for self-employed individuals.

Employer liability under section 3509.

An employer's liability for failure to deduct and withhold income tax or employee social security taxes by reason of treating an employee as a nonemployee for purposes of such taxes is generally determined under section 3509. The employer's liability for income tax withholding is determined as if the amount required to be deducted and withheld was equal to 1.5 percent (3 percent where the employer disregards certain reporting requirements) of the wages paid to the individual erroneously treated as a nonemployee. The employer's liability for employee social security taxes is determined as if such taxes imposed were 20 percent (40 percent where the employer disregards certain reporting requirements) of the amount imposed without regard to section 3509. The increased percentages are applicable where an employer fails to timely file any return or statement under sections 6041 (a), 6041A, or 6051 that would be required consistent with the employer's treatment of the worker as a nonemployee.

The proposed regulations clarify that, for purposes of section 3509, an employer fails to withhold taxes when the employer fails to pay over the full amount of tax required to be deducted and withheld during a calendar year on or before the due date for the return relating to such taxes for the final quarter of such calendar year. Thus, section 3509 is generally applied with respect to each calendar year as a unit.

Under section 3509 and the proposed regulations, if an employer's liability for any tax is determined under section 3509 the employer (i) may not collect from the employee any amount of tax so determined, and (ii) is not entitled to any offset of liability under section 3402 (d) or 6521. An employee's liability for taxes is not affected by application of section 3509 to the employer and the offset provisions of section 6521 may, where applicable, apply with respect to the employee's liability for employee social security taxes. An employer's liability for employer social security taxes is not affected by section 3509.

Section 3509 does not apply where an employer deducts income tax but not employee social security taxes or where the employer intentionally disregards the requirements to withhold and deduct Federal income tax or employee social security taxes. Section 3509 does not apply to employee social security taxes with respect to statutory employees described in section 3121(d)(3). The proposed regulations clarify that if an employer's liability for any tax is determined under section 3509 the employer may still be liable for penalties with respect to his or her failure to deduct and withhold such tax. The amount of such penalties, however, is based on the amount of the employer's liability for such tax under section 3509.

The proposed regulations also clarify that the amount of an employer's liability for tax determined under section 3509 will be considered satisfied to the extent of the amount of such tax which was actually withheld and deducted from the employee and paid. If the amount withheld, deducted, and paid exceeds the employer's liability as computed under section 3509, however, the employer may not claim a refund or credit of such excess amount.

New reporting requirements

Section 6041A added two reporting requirements relating to payments as remuneration for services and gross sales of consumer products to a buyer for resale in the home or otherwise than in a permanent retail establishment. Section 6041A(a) requires that a service-recipient engaged in a trade or business, who, in the course of that trade or business, makes payments to a person as remuneration for services, report such payments if the total remuneration paid to that person by the service-recipient during the calendar year is $600 or more. The proposed regulations provide that such remuneration does not include any amounts which the service-recipient knows are excludable from the gross income of the person performing services (*e.g.*, qualified foster care payments under section 131). Section 6041A(b) requires a direct seller to report gross sales of consumer products totalling $5,000 or more in a calendar year to any buyer who resells the product in the home or any place other than a permanent retail establishment. All sales of consumer products to a buyer for resale to another person are taken into account in determining the aggregate amount of sales to that buyer during the calendar year, even if the buyer resells some of the products in a permanent retail establishment.

The proposed regulations clarify that the aggregate amount of sales of consumer products to a buyer during a calendar year includes the sale of products used by the buyer for the buyer's personal use or consumption (including products disposed of in a manner other than resale such as gifts to friends or relatives). However, the aggregate amount of sales does not include the sale of goods that cannot be resold, such as catalogs and samples.

The proposed regulations make clear that an information return is required with respect to any person who sells consumer products in the home or otherwise than in a permanent retail establishment regardless of whether that person purchases the product from the company and resells it to the consumer or is a company salesperson (other than an employee) who does not acquire title to a product before selling it.

The proposed regulations provide that the regulatory exceptions to the reporting requirement under section 6041, as set forth in §1.6041-3, are applicable to the reporting requirement under section 6041A(a).

COMMENTS AND PUBLIC HEARING

Before adoption of these proposed regulations, consideration will be given to any written comments that are submitted (preferably eight copies) to the Commissioner of Internal Revenue. All comments will be available for public inspection and copying. A public hearing will be held upon written request to the Commissioner by any person who has submitted written comments. If a public hearing is held, notice of the time and place will be published in the Federal Register.

The collection of information requirements contained in this notice of proposed rulemaking have been submitted to the Office of Management and Budget (OMB) for review under section 3504(h) of the Paperwork Reduction Act. Comments on these requirements should be sent to the Office of Information and Regulatory Affairs of OMB, Attention: Desk Officer for Internal Revenue Service, New Executive Office Building, Washington, D.C. 20530. The Internal Revenue Service requests that persons submitting comments on these requirements to OMB also send copies of those comments to the Service.

SPECIAL ANALYSES

The Commissioner of Internal Revenue has determined that this proposed rule is not a major rule as defined in Executive Order 12291and that a Regulatory Impact Analysis is therefore not required.

Although this document is a notice of proposed rulemaking which solicits public comment, the Internal Revenue Service has concluded that the regulations proposed herein are interpretative and that the notice and public comment requirements of 5 U.S.C. 553 do not apply. Accordingly, these proposed regulations do not constitute regulations subject to the Regulatory Flexibility Act (5 U.S.C. Chapter 6).

DRAFTING INFORMATION

The principal authors of these proposed regulations are Robert E. Shaw of the Legislation and Regulations Division of the Office of Chief Counsel, Internal Revenue Service, and Donald W. Stevenson, formerly of that Division. However, personnel from other offices of the Internal Revenue Service and Treasury Department participated in developing the regulations, both on matters of substance and style.

———————————

[¶ 49,065]   **Proposed Regulations (LR-106-77), published in the Federal Register on** January 21, 1986.

Possessions corporations credit: Qualified possession source investment income. Reg. §§1.936-2, 1.936-3 and 1.936-3A and amendments of Reg. §7.936-1, defining the term "qualified possession source investment income," are proposed.

AGENCY: Internal Revenue Service, Treasury.

ACTION: Notice of proposed rulemaking.

SUMMARY: This document contains proposed regulations defining the term "qualified possession source investment income" for purposes of the Puerto Rico and possession tax credit enacted by the Tax Reform Act of 1976.

DATES: Written comments and requests for a public hearing must be delivered or mailed by March 24, 1986. The regulations are proposed to apply generally to taxable years beginning after December 31, 1975.

ADDRESS: Send comments and requests for a public hearing to: Commissioner of Internal Revenue, Attention: CC:LR:T (LR-106-77), Washington, D.C. 20224.

FOR FURTHER INFORMATION CONTACT: Jacob Feldman of the Legislation and Regulations Division, Office of the Chief Counsel, Internal Revenue Service, 1111 Constitution Avenue, N.W., Washington, D.C. 20224, Attention: CC:LR:T, 202-566-3289, not a toll-free call.

SUPPLEMENTARY INFORMATION:

BACKGROUND

This document contains proposed amendments to the Income Tax Regulations (26 CFR Part 1) under section 936 of the Internal Revenue Code of 1954, and deletes Temporary Regulations (26 CFR Part 7) under section 936. Section 936 was added to the Code by section 1051(b) of the Tax Reform Act of 1976 and was amended by section 701(u)(11) of the Revenue Act of 1978.

EXPLANATION OF PROVISIONS

A domestic corporation that elects the application of section 936 may qualify for the Puerto Rico and possession tax credit. This credit is equal to the Federal income tax attributable to *inter alia* the corporation's qualified possession source investment income. Section 936(d)(2) defines qualified possession source investment income as gross income (less the properly apportioned or allocated deductions) that is—

(1) From sources within a possession of the United States in which a trade or business is actively conducted;

(2) Attributable to investment in that possession (for use therein); and

(3) Attributable to the investment of funds initially derived from the active conduct of a trade or business in that possession or from such investment.

Source of Income

Proposed §1.936-2(a) provides that generally the source of income for purposes of section 936 is to be determined in accordance with §1.863-6. Special rules are provided for determining the source of certain interest and dividends (proposed §1.936-2(b)).

Investment in a Possession (for use therein)

Proposed §1.936-3 takes the position that interest and certain dividends derived by a U.S. corporation which conducts an active trade or business in Puerto Rico will be treated as attributable to investment in Puerto Rico (for use therein) as required under section 936(d)(2) if the interest or certain dividends qualify for exemption from Puerto Rican income tax. To qualify for exemption from Puerto Rican income tax, a taxpayer must satisfy criteria in the Puerto Rican income tax statute and regulations thereunder that the funds invested are in fact used in Puerto Rico. This is the position taken in temporary regulation §7.936-1. The present proposed regulations, however, reflect the updating of the Puerto Rican regulations on April 17, 1984. In addition, for investments made by the U.S. corporation more than 30 days after publication of the regulation by Treasury decision, the U.S. corporation must obtain at the time it makes the investment the written agreement of the institution receiving the funds that the investment of the funds by the institution will qualify for the exemption under Puerto Rican regulations.

Reliance on the Puerto Rico regulatory system for satisfaction of this requirement is based on the rules in existence as a result of the April 17, 1984, amendments. Changes in those rules, or in the method of operation of the Puerto Rico government's regulatory or investment authority, may require the development and application of a separate set of rules for determining when investment income is attributable to investment in Puerto Rico (for use therein).

Proposed §1.936-3 deals only with the application of section 936(d)(2) to investment in Puerto Rico. The credit provided by section 936 is also available with respect to certain investment income derived from other possessions of the United States (not including the Virgin Islands), if such income is attributable to investment of funds in the possession "for use therein" and if the other requirements of section 936(d)(2) are met.

Initially Derived from a Possession

Proposed §1.936-3A takes the position that funds are treated as initially derived from a possession if such funds represent an investment of taxable income from sources without the United States derived from the active conduct of a trade or business in a possession or a reinvestment of qualified possession source investment income. Such funds are treated as qualified funds and the amount which may be invested is determined on an annual basis. Losses as well as distributions with respect to these funds will reduce the amount of qualified funds. Therefore, an investment which is treated as made from qualified funds in one year might no longer qualify if a loss or a distribution of income reduces the amount of qualified funds. The proposed regulation also takes the position that an investment of funds derived from a capital contribution does not qualify.

COMMENTS AND REQUESTS FOR A PUBLIC HEARING

Before adopting these proposed regulations, consideration will be given to any written comments that are submitted (preferably eight copies) to the Commissioner of Internal Revenue. All comments will be available for public inspection and copying. A public hearing will be held upon written request to the Commissioner by any person who has submitted written comments. If a public hearing is held, notice of the time and place will be published in the FEDERAL REGISTER.

REGULATORY FLEXIBILITY ACT AND EXECUTIVE ORDER 12291

Although this document is a notice of proposed rulemaking which solicits public comment, the Internal Revenue Service has concluded that the regulations proposed herein are interpretative and that the notice and public procedure requirements of 5 U.S.C. 553 do not apply. Accordingly, these proposed regulations do not constitute regulations subject to the Regulatory Flexibility Act (5 U.S.C. chapter 6). The Commissioner of Internal Revenue has determined that this proposed rule is not subject to Executive Order 12291, and, accordingly, a regulatory impact analysis is not required.

DRAFTING INFORMATION

The principal author of these proposed regulations is Jacob Feldman of the Legislation and Regulations Division of the Office of Chief Counsel, Internal Revenue Service. However, personnel from other offices of the Internal Revenue Service and Treasury Department participated in developing the regulation, both on matters of substance and style.

[¶ 49,066]   **Proposed Regulations (EE-96-85), published in the Federal Register on** February 4, 1986.

Employee trusts: Tax Reform Act of 1984: Effective dates.—Reg. §§1.72(e)-1T, 1.79-4T, 1.133-1T, 1.162-10T, 1.402(a)(5)-1T, 1.404(a)-1T, 1.404(b)-1T, 1.404(d)-1T, 1.404(k)-1T, 1.419-1T, 1.419A-1T, 1.505(c)-1T, 1.1042-1T, 54.4976-1T, 54.4978-1T and 301.7701-17T are proposed. The text of repealed Code Secs. 463, 4976 and 4978 no longer is reproduced in the compilations. The texts of these proposed regulations last appeared at 91(6) CCH ¶21,832 and 91(10) CCH ¶35,821 and ¶35,861. Temporary Reg. §1.463-1T was removed by T.D. 9138 on July 15, 2004. Temporary Reg. §1.125-2T was removed by T.D. 9349 on July 31, 2007. Proposed Reg. §1.512(a)-5 was withdrawn by REG-143874-10 on February 6, 2014. Temporary Reg. §1.404(a)(8)-1T was removed by T.D. 9849 on 3/11/2019.

AGENCY: Internal Revenue Service, Treasury.

ACTION: Notice of proposed rulemaking by cross reference to temporary regulations.

SUMMARY: In the Rules and Regulations portion of this issue of the Federal Register, the Internal Revenue Service is issuing temporary regulations relating to effective dates and certain other issues arising under the employee benefit provisions of the Tax Reform Act of 1984. The text of those temporary regulations also serves as the comment document for this notice of proposed rulemaking.

DATES: Written comments and requests for a public hearing must be delivered or mailed by April 7, 1986. The regulations are proposed to be effective on varying dates provided in the temporary regulations.

ADDRESS: Send comments and requests for a public hearing to Commissioner of Internal Revenue, Attn: CC:LR:T (EE-96-85), 1111 Constitution Avenue N.W., Washington, D.C. 20224. FOR FURTHER INFORMATION CONTACT: John T. Ricotta of the Employee Plans and Exempt Organizations Division, Office of Chief Counsel, Internal Revenue Service, 1111 Constitution Ave., N.W., Washington, D.C. 20224, Attention: CC:LR:T (EE-96-85), telephone: 202-566-3544 (not a toll-free number).

SUPPLEMENTARY INFORMATION:

BACKGROUND

The temporary regulations provide guidance concerning the economic performance requirement for certain employee benefits under section 461(h) of the Internal Revenue Code of 1954 (Code), as added by section 91 of the Tax Reform Act of 1984 (Act) (P.L. 98-369, 98 Stat. 598); the transitional rule for vested accrued vacation pay under section 463 of the Code, as amended by section 91(i) of the Act (P.L. 98-369, 98 Stat. 609); the treatment of group-term life insurance purchased for employees under section 79 of the Code, as amended by section 223 of the Act (P.L. 98-369, 98 Stat. 775); the treatment of funded welfare benefit plans under sections 419 and 419A of the Code, as added by section 511 of the Act (P.L. 98-369, 98 Stat. 854); the treatment of unfunded deferred benefits under sections 404(b) and 162 of the Code, as amended by section 512 of the Act (P.L. 98-369, 98 Stat. 862); additional requirements for tax-exempt status of certain organizations under section 505 of the Code, as added by section 513 of the Act (P.L. 98-369, 98 Stat. 863); rollovers of partial distributions under sections 402 and 403 of the Code, as amended by section 522 of the Act (P.L. 98-369, 98 Stat. 868); distributions where substantially all contributions are employee contributions under section 72 of the Code, as amended by section 523 of the Act (P.L. 98-369, 98 Stat. 871); repeal of the estate tax exclusion for qualified plan benefits under section 2039 of the Code, as amended by section 525 of the Act (P.L. 98-369, 98 Stat. 873); determination of whether there is a collective bargaining agreement under section 7701(a)(46) of the Code, as added by section 526(c) of the Act (P.L. 98-369, 98 Stat. 881); nonrecognition of gain on stock sold to an employee stock ownership plan (ESOP) under section 1042 of the Code, as added by section 541 of the Act (P.L. 98-369, 98 Stat. 887); deductibility of dividends relating to ESOPs under sections 404 and 3405 of the Code, as amended by section 542 of the Act (P.L. 98-369, 98 Stat. 890); exclusion of interest on ESOP loans under section 133 of the Code, as added by section 543 of the Act (P.L. 98-369, 98 Stat. 894); treatment of an employer and an employee benefit association as related under section 1239 of the Code, as amended by section 557 of the Act (P.L. 98-369, 98 Stat. 898); and technical corrections to the pension provisions of the Tax Equity and Fiscal Responsibility Act of 1982 under sections 713 and 715 of the Act (P.L. 98-369, 98 Stat. 955, 966). The proposed regulations are issued under the authority contained in section 7805 of the Code (26 U.S.C. §7805). For the text of the temporary regulations, see F.R. Doc. published in the Rules and Regulations portion of this issue of the FEDERAL REGISTER.

SPECIAL ANALYSES

The Commissioner of Internal Revenue has determined that this proposed rule is not a major rule as defined in Executive Order 12291and that a Regulatory Impact Analysis is therefore not required. Although this document is a notice of proposed rulemaking which solicits public comment, the Internal Revenue Service has concluded that the regulations proposed herein are interpretative and that the notice and public procedure requirements of 5 U.S.C. 553 do not apply. Accordingly, these proposed regulations do not constitute regulations subject to the Regulatory Flexibility Act (5 U.S.C. Chapter 6).

COMMENTS AND REQUESTS FOR A PUBLIC HEARING

Before the adoption of these proposed regulations, consideration will be given to any written comments that are submitted (preferably eight copies) to the Commissioner of Internal Revenue. All comments will be available for public inspection and copying. A public hearing will be held upon written request to the Commissioner by any person who has submitted written comments. If a public hearing is held, notice of the time and place will be published in the Federal Register. The collection of information requirements contained herein have been submitted to the Office of Management and Budget (OMB) for review under section 3504(h) of the Paperwork Reduction Act. Comments on the requirements should be sent to the Office of Information and Regulatory Affairs, of OMB, Attention: Desk Officer for Internal Revenue Service, New Executive Office Building, Washington, D.C. 20503. The Internal Revenue Service requests persons submitting comments to OMB also to send copies of the comments to the Service.

[¶ 49,067] **Proposed Amendments of Regulations (LR-59-74), published in the Federal Register on** February 21, 1986.

Interest received: Governmental obligations: Industrial development bonds: Principal user.—Amendment of Reg. §1.103-10, which would define the term "principal user" for purposes of Code Sec. 103(b)(6), (15), is proposed.

AGENCY: Internal Revenue Service, Treasury.

ACTION: Notice of proposed rulemaking.

SUMMARY: This document contains proposed regulations which would define the term "principal user" for purposes of paragraphs (6) and (15) of section 103(b) of the Internal Revenue Code of 1954. The regulations would affect issuers, holders, and recipients of the proceeds of industrial development bonds issued under section 103(b)(6) of the Code.

DATES: Written comments must be delivered or mailed by April 22, 1986. The amendments are proposed to be effective after August 20, 1986, in determining the tax-exempt status of obligations issued after August 20, 1986.

ADDRESS: Send comments to: Commissioner of Internal Revenue, Attention: CC:LR:T (LR-59-74), Washington, D.C. 20224.

FOR FURTHER INFORMATION CONTACT: John A. Tolleris of the Legislation and Regulations Division, Office of the Chief Counsel, Internal Revenue Service, 1111 Constitution Avenue, N.W., Washington, D.C. 20224 (Attention: CC:LR:T) (Telephone: 202-566-3590, not a toll-free number).

SUPPLEMENTARY INFORMATION:

BACKGROUND

This document contains proposed clarifying amendments to the Income Tax Regulations (26 CFR Part 1) under section 103(b)(6) of the Internal Revenue Code of 1954.

EXPLANATION OF PROVISIONS

The amendments clarify the term "principal user" for purposes of applying the provisions of Code section 103(b)(6) and (15) and the regulations thereunder with respect to small issues of industrial development bonds. Section 103(b)(6) provides, among other things, that an issue of $1 million or less of industrial development bonds financing the acquisition, construction, reconstruction, or improvement of land or property of a character subject to the depreciation allowance (or an issue to redeem such a prior issue) is not exempt from Federal taxation when the issue in question combined with the outstanding face amount of prior issues financing certain similar facilities exceeds $1 million; the facilities which are taken into account for this purpose are those the "principal user" of which is or will be the same or two or more related persons, and which are located within the same county or incorporated municipality.

Section 103(b)(6) also provides that, if an issuer makes the necessary election, the limit for an exempt small issue of industrial development bonds is increased from $1 million to $10 million. In such case, however, certain other amounts must also be aggregated with the issue of obligations in question for purposes of determining whether the $10 million limitation has been exceeded and whether the interest upon the issue of obligations in question is thus subject to Federal income taxation. The additional amounts to be taken into account are certain capital expenditures, made within a 6-year period beginning 3 years before the date of issue of the obligations in question and ending 3 years after the date of issue, with respect not only to the facility financed by the issue in question, but also with respect to other facilities within the same county or incorporated municipality of which the "principal user" is or will be the same person or a person related to the "principal user" of the facility financed with the issue of obligations in question.

The proposed regulations provide, in general, that the principal users are persons who for tax purposes currently hold more than a 10-percent ownership interest in a facility. In addition, lessees or sublessees who use a sufficiently valuable portion of the facility pursuant to a sufficiently long-term lease are also principal users. Persons with interests comparable to that of an owner or lessee who is a principal user and some purchasers of the output of certain facilities are also treated as principal users.

The proposed regulations provide that, when a facility has more than one principal user, certain issues of obligations with respect to all principal users must be aggregated with the issue of obligations in question for purposes of determining whether the $1 million or $10 million limitation has been exceeded. Similarly, if the $10 million limitation has been elected by the issuer, certain capital expenditures with respect to all principal users must also be aggregated to determine whether the $10 million limitation has been exceeded.

For purposes of aggregating issues of obligations or capital expenditures of persons who are principal users, only issues and capital expenditures with respect to persons who are principal users of the facility before the expiration of the test period described in section 103(b)(15)(D) are aggregated. Accordingly, if a person who is a principal user of a facility financed by an exempt small issue becomes the principal user of another facility financed by a second exempt small issue more than 3 years after the later of the date of the second issue or the date the facility financed by the second issue was placed in service, the two issues are not aggregated. Similarly, capital expenditures during the 6-year period described in section 103(b)(6)(D)(ii) with respect to a principal user are not taken into account if that person does not become a principal user of the facility until more than 3 years after the later of the date of the issue or the date the facility financed by the issue is first placed in service.

The test-period concept was adopted for purposes of section 103(b)(6) for reasons of administrative convenience. The statutory reference to a person who "is or will be" a principal user could be construed as referring to a person who at any time is a principal user; as referring only to a person who is or is about to be a principal user on the date of issuance; or as referring to a person who becomes a principal user within some intermediate time period. In adopting the test-period concept, the Service attempted to reach a result which gives effect to the statutory language while also being administrable. Adoption of the test period described in section 103(b)(15)(D) serves the additional function of limiting the period for determination of the principal user status to a single period for purposes of both paragraphs (6) and (15) of section 103(b).

The proposed regulations provide special rules for exempt persons, i.e., State and local governments and organizations that are tax-exempt under section 501(c)(3), that are principal users of facilities financed with exempt small issues of industrial development bonds. For purposes of determining whether the small-issue limitation has been exceeded with respect to any facility of which an exempt person is a principal user, certain industrial development bonds issued with respect to the exempt person and, for purposes of the $10 million limitation, certain capital expenditures must be aggregated with the issue in question. This does not include capital expenditures with respect to other facilities used by the exempt person in an activity other than an unrelated trade or business (as defined by section 513).

REGULATORY FLEXIBILITY ACT

The Secretary of the Treasury has certified that this proposed rule will not have a significant impact on a substantial number of small entities because the economic and any other secondary or incidental impact flows directly from the underlying statute. A regulatory flexibility analysis, therefore, is not required under the Regulatory Flexibility Act (5 U.S.C. chapter 6).

NON-APPLICABILITY OF EXECUTIVE ORDER 12291

The Commissioner of Internal Revenue has determined that this proposed rule is not a major rule as defined in Executive Order 12291 and that a regulatory impact analysis therefore is not required.

COMMENTS—PUBLIC HEARING

Before adoption of these proposed regulations, consideration will be given to any written comments that are submitted (preferably seven copies) to the Commissioner of Internal Revenue. All comments will be available for public inspection and copying. A public hearing will be held in accordance with the notice of hearing published in this issue of the FEDERAL REGISTER.

DRAFTING INFORMATION

The principal author of these proposed regulations is John A. Tolleris of the Legislation and Regulations Division of the Office of Chief Counsel, Internal Revenue Service. However, personnel from other offices of the Internal Revenue Service and Treasury Department participated in developing the regulations, both on matters of substance and style.

[¶ 49,068] **Proposed Amendments of Regulations (LR-157-84), published in the Federal Register on** February 21, 1986.

Interest received: Governmental obligations: Limitation on beneficiaries.—Amendments of Reg. § 1.103-10, relating to industrial development bonds and the beneficiaries of such bond issues, are proposed.

AGENCY: Internal Revenue Service, Treasury.

ACTION: Notice of proposed rulemaking.

SUMMARY: This document contains proposed regulations that relate to certain industrial development tax-exempt bonds and to certain beneficiaries of such bond issues. Changes to the applicable tax law were made by the Tax Reform Act of 1984 that generally deny Federal income tax exemption for a small issue of industrial development bonds if any of its test-period beneficiaries is allocated more than $40 million of outstanding industrial development bonds, including its allocated portion of the small issue in question. This provision restricts the amount of small issues of industrial development bonds that may be issued for a beneficiary when that person already benefits from a significant amount of tax-exempt industrial development bonds.

DATES: Written comments must be delivered or mailed by April 22, 1986. These regulations are proposed to be effective after August 20, 1986, in determining the tax-exempt status of obligations issued after August 20, 1986. However, these regulations would not apply to certain obligations described in section 631(f) of the Tax Reform Act of 1984 and to certain obligations with respect to facilities described in section 631(c)(3) of the Tax Reform Act of 1984. The provisions of § 1.103-10(i)(4)(vi) are generally proposed to be effective after December 31, 1983, in determining the tax-exempt status of obligations issued after December 31, 1983.

ADDRESS: Please mail or deliver comments to: Commissioner of Internal Revenue, Attention: CC:LR:T (LR-157-84), 1111 Constitution Avenue, N.W., Washington, D.C. 20224.

FOR FURTHER INFORMATION CONTACT: John A. Tolleris of the Legislation and Regulations Division, Office of Chief Counsel, 1111 Constitution Avenue, N.W., Washington, D.C. 20224 (Attention: CC:LR:T) (Telephone: 202-566-3590, not a toll-free number).

SUPPLEMENTARY INFORMATION:

BACKGROUND

This document contains proposed amendments to the Income Tax Regulations (26 CFR Part 1) under section 103(b)(15) of the Internal Revenue Code of 1954. These proposed amendments provide needed guidance regarding the provisions of section 103(b)(15) concerning the $40 million limitation which were enacted by section 623 of the Tax Reform Act of 1984 (Pub. L. 98-369; 98 Stat. 921).

EXPLANATION OF PROVISIONS

The $40 million limitation applicable to small issues of tax-exempt industrial development bonds was enacted in the Tax Reform Act of 1984. This limitation generally denies Federal income tax exemption for a small issue of industrial development bonds if any test-period beneficiary is allocated more than $40 million of outstanding industrial development bonds, including its allocated portion of the issue in question. A person is a "test-period beneficiary" of the bond-financed facility, if he is an owner or a principal user of a facility financed by the issue at any time during the 3-year period after the issue is issued, or after the facility is placed in service, whichever occurs later. A person who is related to a principal user at any time during the test period is also a test-period beneficiary, unless the principal user ceased using the facility before the two persons became related.

These proposed regulations provide guidance on the allocation of the proceeds of an issue of industrial development bonds among test-period beneficiaries. In determining whether the $40 million limitation has been exceeded with respect to a test-period beneficiary, the portions of the outstanding amounts of all industrial development bonds (not just small issues) allocable to the beneficiary are aggregated.

NONAPPLICABILITY OF EXECUTIVE ORDER 12291

The Commissioner of Internal Revenue has determined that this proposed rule is not a major rule as defined in Executive Order 12291and that a regulatory impact analysis therefore is not required.

REGULATORY FLEXIBILITY ACT

The Secretary of the Treasury has certified that this proposed rule will not have a significant impact on a substantial number of small entities because the economic and any other secondary or incidental impact flows directly from the underlying statute. A regulatory flexibility analysis, therefore, is not required under the Regulatory Flexibility Act (5 U.S.C. chapter 6).

DRAFTING INFORMATION

The principal author of these proposed regulations is John A. Tolleris of the Legislation and Regulations Division of the Office of Chief Counsel, Internal Revenue Service. However, personnel from other offices of the Internal Revenue Service and the Treasury Department participated in developing the regulations, on matters of both substance and style.

COMMENTS—PUBLIC HEARING

Before adoption of these proposed regulations, consideration will be given to any written comments that are submitted (preferably seven copies) to the Commissioner of Internal Revenue. All comments will be available for public inspection and copying. A public hearing will be held in accordance with the notice of hearing published in this issue of the FEDERAL REGISTER.

Income taxes, Taxable income, Deductions, Exemptions.

[¶ 49,069]   Proposed Amendment of Regulations (LR-66-85), published in the Federal Register on March 4, 1986.

Registration of tax shelters: Amended application.—Amendments of Reg. § 301.6111-1, relating to the registration of tax shelters, are proposed.

AGENCY: Internal Revenue Service, Treasury.

ACTION: Notice of proposed rulemaking by cross-reference to temporary regulations.

SUMMARY: In the Rules and Regulations portion of this issue of the FEDERAL REGISTER, the Internal Revenue Service is issuing temporary regulations relating to tax shelter registration. The text of those temporary regulations also serves as the comment document for this proposed rulemaking.

DATES: Written comments and requests for a public hearing must be delivered by [SIXTY DAYS AFTER PUBLICATION OF THIS DOCUMENT IN THE FEDERAL REGISTER]. The amendments are proposed to be effective generally with respect to tax shelters in which any interest is first sold after August 31, 1984.

ADDRESS: Send comments and requests for a public hearing to: Commissioner of Internal Revenue, Attention: CC:LR:T (LR-66-85), Washington, D.C. 20224.

FOR FURTHER INFORMATION CONTACT: Paulette Chernyshev, Office of Chief Counsel, Internal Revenue Service, 1111 Constitution Avenue, N.W., Washington, D.C. 20224 (Attention: CC:LR:T) telephone 202-566-3288 (not a toll-free call).

SUPPLEMENTARY INFORMATION:

BACKGROUND

The temporary regulations (designated by a "T" following the section citation) in the Rules and Regulations portion of this issue of the FEDERAL REGISTER amend Parts 301 and 602 of Title 26 of the Code of Federal Regulations. These amendments change the rules relating to tax shelter registration under section 6111 of the Internal Revenue Code of 1954, as added by section 141 of the Tax Reform Act of 1984 (Pub. L. 98-369, 98 Stat. 678). For the text of the temporary regulations, see FR Doc. (T.D. 8078) published in the Rules and Regulations portion of this issue of the FEDERAL REGISTER. The preamble to the temporary regulations provides a discussion of the rules. The final regulations, which this document proposes to base on those temporary regulations, would amend Parts 301 and 602 of Title 26 of the Code of Federal Regulations.

EXECUTIVE ORDER 12291; REGULATORY FLEXIBILITY ACT

The Commissioner of Internal Revenue has determined that this proposed rule is not a major rule as defined in Executive Order 12291and that a Regulatory Impact Analysis is therefore not required.

Although this document is a notice of proposed rulemaking that solicits public comments, the Internal Revenue Service has concluded that the regulations proposed herein are interpretative and that the notice and public procedure requirements of 5 U.S.C. 553 do not apply. Accordingly, these proposed regulations do not constitute regulations subject to the regulatory Flexibility Act (5 U.S.C. Chapter 6).

COMMENTS AND REQUESTS FOR A PUBLIC HEARING

Before adopting these proposed regulations, consideration will be given to any written comments that are submitted (preferably eight copies) to the Commissioner of Internal Revenue. All comments will be available for public inspection and copying. A public hearing will be held upon written request to the Commissioner by any person who has submitted written comments. If a public hearing is held, notice of the time and place will be published in the FEDERAL REGISTER.

The collection of information requirements contained in this notice of proposed rulemaking have been submitted to the Office of Management and Budget (OMB) for review under section 3504(h) of the Paperwork Reduction Act. Comments on these requirements should be sent to the Office of Information and Regulatory Affairs of OMB, Attention: Desk Officer for Internal Revenue Service, New Executive Office Building, Washington, D.C. 20503. The Internal Revenue Service requests that persons submitting comments on these requirements to OMB also send copies of those comments to the Service.

DRAFTING INFORMATION

The principal author of these regulations is Paulette Chernyshev of the Legislation and Regulations Division of the Office of Chief Counsel, Internal Revenue Service. However, personnel from other offices of the Internal Revenue Service and Treasury Department participated in developing the regulations on matters of both substance and style.

[¶ 49,070]   Proposed Regulations and Proposed Amendments of Regulations (LR-189-84), published in the Federal Register on April 8, 1986.

Imputed interest: Original issue discount: Safe haven interest rates.—Amendments of Reg. §§1.61-6, 1.61-7, 6a.103A-2, 1.163-4, 1.249-1, 1.582-1, 1.636-1, 1.818-3, 1.861-2, 1.993-1, 1.1012-2, 1.1016-5, 1.1037-1, 1.1232-1, 1.1232-2, 1.1232-3, 1.1232-3A, 1.6045-1, 1.6049-4—1.6049-6, 1.7872-4, 3.2 and 3.3, relating to (1) the tax treatment of debt instruments issued after July 1, 1982, that contain original issue discount, (2) the imputation of and the accounting for interest with respect to sales and exchanges of property occurring after December 31, 1984, and (3) safe haven interest rates for loans or advances between commonly controlled taxpayers and safe haven leases between such taxpayers, are proposed. Proposed Reg. §§1.163-7, 1.446-2, 1.483-3, 1.1271-1—1.1271-3, 1.1272-1, 1.1273-1, 1.1273-2, 1.1274-1, 1.1274-7, 1.1274A-1, 1.1275-1, 1.1275-2, 1.1275-3 and 1.1275-5 and proposed amendments of Reg. §§1.483-1, 1.483-2,1.1001-1 and 1.1012-1 were substantially revised on 12/22/92 by FI-189-84 and subsequently adopted on 1/27/94 by T.D. 8517. Proposed Reg. §1.1275-4, which was superseded on 12/16/94 by FI-59-91, was adopted on 6/11/96 by T.D. 8674.

AGENCY: Internal Revenue Service, Treasury.

ACTION: Notice of proposed rulemaking.

SUMMARY: This document contains proposed regulations relating to (1) the tax treatment of debt instruments issued after July 1, 1982, that contain original issue discount, (2) the imputation of and the accounting for interest with respect to sales and exchanges of property occurring after December 31, 1984, and (3) safe haven interest rates for loans or advances between commonly controlled taxpayers and safe haven leases between such taxpayers. Changes to the applicable law were made by the Tax Equity and Fiscal Responsibility Act of 1982 as amended by the Technical Corrections Act of 1982, and the Tax Reform Act of 1984 as amended by Pub. L. No. 98-612 and Pub. L. No. 99-121. The regulations would provide needed guidance to taxpayers who must comply with these provisions of the law.

DATES:

PROPOSED EFFECTIVE DATE

Generally, the regulations contained in this document are proposed to be effective as follows:

§1.163-7 §§1.1271-1—1.1273-2 §§1.1275-1—1.1275-5	Debt instruments issued after July 1, 1982
§§1.483-1—1.483-5 §§1.1274-1—1.1274-7	Sales or exchanges of property occurring after December 31, 1984
§1.1274A-1	Certain sales or exchanges of property occurring after June 30, 1985
§1.446-2	Lending transactions occurring after May 8, 1986, and certain sales or exchanges of property occurring after December 31, 1984
§1.482-2	Term loans and advances entered into after May 8, 1986, and demand loans and advances after such date

DATES FOR COMMENTS AND REQUEST FOR A PUBLIC HEARING

Written comments and request for a public hearing must be delivered or mailed by [60 DAYS AFTER THIS IS PUBLISHED IN THE FEDERAL REGISTER]. June 9, 1986.

ADDRESS: Send comments (preferably eight copies) and request for a public hearing to: Commissioner of Internal Revenue, Attention: CC:LR:T, (LR-189-84), 1111 Constitution Avenue, N.W., Washington, D.C. 20224.

FOR FURTHER INFORMATION CONTACT: Theresa E. Bearman (sections 163, 1271, 1272, 1273, 1275 and related matters), Ewan D. Purkiss (sections 446, 483, 1274 and related matters), Susan T. Baker (all matters other than those relating to sections 446, 482 and 483), or Joseph M. Rosenthal (section 482 and related matters) of the Legislation and Regulations Division, Office of Chief Counsel, Internal Revenue Service, 1111 Constitution Avenue, N.W., Washington, D.C. 20224 (Attention: CC:LR:T LR-189-84). Telephone 202-566-3829 (Bearman), 202-566-3238 (Purkiss), 202-566-3294 (Baker), 202-566-3289 (Rosenthal) (not a toll-free call).

SUPPLEMENTARY INFORMATION:

I. BACKGROUND

This document contains proposed amendments to the Income Tax Regulations (26 CFR Part 1) under sections 163(e), 446, 482, 483 and 1271 through 1275 of the Internal Revenue Code of 1954. With the exception of the amendments to the regulations under section 446, these amendments are proposed to conform the regulations to section 231 of the Tax Equity and Fiscal Responsibility Act of 1982 (96 Stat. 324, 496), as amended by section 306 of the Technical Corrections Act of 1982 (97 Stat. 448), and sections 41, 42 and 44 of the Tax Reform Act of 1984 (98 Stat. 494, 531) as amended by Pub. L. No. 98-612 (98 Stat. 3180) and Pub. L. No. 99-121 (99 Stat. 505). The amendments to the regulations under section 446 are proposed to provide rules to account for interest in transactions outside the scope of the original issue discount rules.

II. INTRODUCTION

The regulations under sections 163(e), 483, and 1271 through 1275 provide two principal sets of rules: the imputed interest rules and the original issue discount rules. The imputed interest rules are prescribed by sections 1274 and 483, and the original issue discount rules by sections 163(e), 1271, 1272, 1273 and 1275.

The imputed interest rules of sections 1274 and 483 relate to the measurement of interest and principal for tax purposes in a sale or exchange of property (other than publicly traded property) involving deferred payments. For transactions subject to the imputed interest rules, interest will be imputed to the transaction if a minimum amount of interest is not stated. If a transaction states at least the minimum amount of interest, it is said to provide for adequate stated interest. When interest is imputed to a transaction, a portion of the stated principal amount of the debt instrument is recharacterized as interest for tax purposes. The imputed interest rules do not require an increase in the total amount of payments agreed to by the parties to a transaction. These rules merely recharacterize as interest for Federal tax purposes a portion of the payments denominated as principal by the parties. In the case of transactions to which section 1274 applies, imputed interest is treated as original issue discount and is accounted for under those rules. In the case of transactions subject to section 483, imputed interest (and any stated interest) is subject to a new set of rules provided under section 446 and is accounted for under those rules.

In general, under the original issue discount rules, a portion of the original issue discount on a debt instrument is required to be included in income by the holder and deducted from income by the issuer annually without regard to their regular accounting methods. The total amount of original issue discount is defined as the difference between the debt instrument's stated redemption price at maturity and its issue price and arises in one of three ways. First, in the case of a debt instrument subject to section 1274 that does not provide for adequate stated interest, interest is imputed and is treated as original issue discount. Second, in the case of a debt instrument issued for cash or publicly traded property, original issue discount arises if the debt instrument is issued for less than its face amount. Third, in the case of all debt instruments, original issue discount arises if the debt instrument does not call for interest that is payable currently at a single constant rate over its entire term.

III. THE IMPUTED INTEREST RULES

A. APPLICABILITY

1. SECTION 1274

Section 1274 applies to any debt instrument issued in exchange for property if neither the debt instrument nor the property is publicly traded and if one or more of the payments under the debt instrument are due more than 6 months after the date of the sale or exchange. Section 1274, however, does not apply to the following:

(a) Certain sales or exchanges by an individual, estate, testamentary trust, or small corporation or partnership of a farm if the sales price of the farm does not exceed $1,000,000;

(b) Any sale or exchange by an individual of the individual's principal residence, regardless of the amount of the sales price;

(c) Any sale or exchange of property if the sum of all the payments (including principal and interest) under any debt instrument and the value of any other consideration does not exceed $250,000;

(d) Any debt instrument issued in a qualified sale within the meaning of section 483(e) if the stated principal amount of the debt instrument does not exceed $500,000; and

(e) Any cash method debt instrument within the meaning of section 1274A(c).

2. SECTION 483

Section 483 applies to sales or exchanges of nonpublicly traded property excepted from the provisions of section 1274. Thus, section 483 applies to: the sale or exchange of a farm if the sales price does not exceed $1,000,000, sales involving total payments of $250,000 or less, sales of principal residences, qualified sales of land, and cash method debt instruments. Unlike section 1274, however, section 483 applies only if the contract for the sale or exchange calls for payments due more than one year from the date of the sale or exchange. Section 483 does not apply to the following:

(a) Any sale or exchange of property if the sales price does not exceed $3,000; and

(b) In the case of a purchaser, any amount that is treated as containing interest under section 163(b).

3. EXCEPTIONS FROM BOTH SECTIONS 1274 AND 483

The imputed interest rules of sections 1274 and 483 do not apply to the following:

(a) Any transaction to the extent any amount is contingent upon the productivity, use, or disposition of property and entitled to capital gain treatment under section 1235, relating to sales or exchanges of patents.

(b) Any annuity under section 72 that is not a debt instrument within the meaning of section 1275(a).

(c) Any issuer (obligor) of a debt instrument issued for property that is personal use property in the hands of the issuer. The imputed interest rules, however, apply to any holder (obligee) of the debt instrument unless the loan incurred in the transaction is a below-market loan of the type described in section 7872(c)(1)(A)—(C). The treatment of the latter class of debt instruments is governed by the provisions of section 7872.

(d) Any debt instrument that evidences demand loan (within the meaning of section 7872(f)(5)) and is a below-market loan of the type described in section 7872(c)(1)(A)—(C). The treatment of these debt instruments is governed by the provisions of section 7872.

B. STATING ADEQUATE INTEREST TO AVOID THE IMPUTATION OF INTEREST

1. IN GENERAL

To prevent the imputation of interest, a debt instrument must provide for adequate stated interest. For this purpose, a debt instrument generally provides for adequate stated interest if it calls for interest over its entire term at a rate no lower than the test rate of interest applicable to the debt instrument. If a debt instrument does not provide for a fixed rate of interest at least equal to the test rate of interest, the adequacy of interest is determined by comparing the stated principal amount involved in the transaction with the sum of present values of all payments due under the debt instrument, determined by discounting the payments at a rate equal to the test rate of interest. A debt instrument generally has adequate stated interest if the stated principal amount of the debt instrument is less than or equal to the sum of these present values. However, in the case of a potentially abusive situation as discussed below, the debt instrument does not have adequate stated interest unless the stated principal amount is less than or equal to the fair market value of the property sold or exchanged.

The test rate of interest applicable to a debt instrument generally depends on the amount of seller financing (based on stated principal) involved in the transaction. For sales or exchanges of property (other than new section 38 property) involving seller financing of $2,800,000 or less, the test rate of interest is the lower of the applicable Federal rate or 9 percent, compounded semiannually (or an equivalent rate based on an appropriate compounding period). If the sales price is contingent, the 9 percent rate is not available unless the sales price cannot exceed $2,800,000. For sales or exchanges of property with seller financing in excess of $2,800,000, and all sales or exchanges of new section 38 property, the test rate of interest is 100 percent of the applicable Federal rate. For sales or exchanges of property involved in sale-leaseback transactions, the test rate of interest is 110 percent of the applicable Federal rate. These rules also apply to transactions subject to section 483. Sales or exchanges that are qualified sales, however, are subject to a special lower test rate of interest as discussed below. For sales or exchanges occurring before July 1, 1985, special test rates of interest apply.

The applicable Federal rate is either the Federal short-term rate (for debt instruments with terms not over 3 years), the Federal mid-term rate (for debt instruments with terms over 3 years but not over 9 years), or the Federal long-term rate (for debt instruments with terms over 9 years). The Federal rates are annual stated rates of interest based on semiannual compounding. The Federal rates are published monthly by the Commissioner in Revenue Rulings along with equivalent annual, quarterly and monthly rates. In general, the appropriate compounding period depends on the intervals between payments. In general, the applicable Federal rate is the lowest of the rates in effect for the first month in which there is a binding written contract or the two preceding two months.

The applicable Federal rates are determined monthly. The Federal rates are based on the yields to maturity of outstanding marketable obligations of the United States of similar maturities (for example, maturities up to 3 years for the Federal short-term rate) for the one-month period ending on the 14th day of the month preceding the month for which the rates are applicable. In certain cases, the applicable Federal rate may be a lower rate based on certain allowable Treasury index rates.

2. SPECIAL RULES

a. TEST RATE FOR INSTALLMENT OBLIGATIONS

The proposed regulations provide special rules for determining whether an installment obligation provides for adequate stated interest. For self-amortizing installment and level-principal obligations, tables are provided under which the test rate of interest may be computed as a blended rate equal to a weighted average of the Federal rates. In general, the rules are designed to allow taxpayers to receive the benefit of the short-term and mid-term rates (which are generally lower than the long-term rate) without having to provide three separate debt instruments.

b. CONTINGENT PAYMENTS

In general, contingent interest payments are not taken into account in applying the imputed interest rules. Thus, whether a debt instrument states adequate interest will be determined by ignoring any contingent interest payments.

Under a special rule proposed by the regulations, however, the stated principal amount of a debt instrument calling for contingent payments of interest will be respected in certain cases. To qualify for the special rule, the contingent payments of interest must be conditioned on a return from the use of the property. In addition, the debt instrument must call for fixed payments of interest equal to at least 80 percent of the test rate of interest applicable to the debt instrument, and it must be reasonable to expect that the payments of contingent interest will raise the yield on the debt instrument to at least the test rate of interest. If the property acquired for the debt instrument is depreciable or inventoriable property, then, in addition to the requirements noted above, the term of the debt instrument cannot exceed 4 years in the case of 3-year or 5-year property or inventoriable property, or 12 years in the case of any other depreciable property that is not inventoriable property.

The contingent payment rules do not affect whether rights to receive contingent payments constitute debt or equity for Federal tax purposes or whether an instrument evidences a valid indebtedness.

c. VARIABLE RATE DEBT INSTRUMENTS

For purposes of determining whether a debt instrument calling for variable interest based on current values of an objective interest index provides for adequate stated interest, the proposed regulations generally treat the debt instrument as if it called for interest at a fixed rate equal to the rate established by the index on the date the test rate of interest is determined. Examples of objective indices include the prime rate, the applicable Federal rate, the average yield on Treasury securities, and LIBOR (London Interbank Offered Rate). If the rate of interest determined by the index is no lower than the test rate of interest, the debt instrument has adequate stated interest. Interest payments based on an index other than an objective interest index are generally treated as contingent payments.

Under the proposed regulations, the applicable Federal rate for a variable rate debt instrument that calls for variable interest payments based on current values of an objective interest index is the Federal rate corresponding to the adjustment interval of the debt instrument. Thus, for example, if the interest rate on a debt instrument is tied to a bank's prime rate and adjusted annually, the adequacy of interest is determined by testing the rate of interest as determined by the index against the Federal short-term rate.

d. QUALIFIED SALES OF LAND

In the case of a debt instrument issued in a qualified sale of land and subject to the rules of section 483(e), the test rate of interest is 6 percent, compounded semiannually. A qualified sale is a sale or exchange of land by an individual to a member of the individual's family. A debt instrument issued in a qualified sale is subject to the rules of section 483(e) if the face amount (stated principal amount) of the debt instrument issued for the land does not exceed $500,000, regardless of the amount of the sales price, and if certain other conditions are satisfied. Thus, the parties are free to structure a sale with two debt instruments, the first having a face amount of $500,000 and a 6 percent interest rate, and the second subject to the rules of section 1274 or section 483, whichever is applicable. If, however, a single debt instrument is issued with a face amount in excess of $500,000, the 6 percent test rate does not apply.

The proposed regulations contain this rule because the Service is concerned with the complexity of rules that would be necessary to apply two different accounting rules to a single debt instrument. The Service invites comments on this proposed rule.

3. POTENTIALLY ABUSIVE TRANSACTIONS

Regardless of the amount of interest stated in a sale or exchange, if the transaction is a potentially abusive transaction, the adequacy of interest is determined by comparing the stated principal amount of the debt instrument with the fair market value of the property sold or exchanged as discussed above. A potentially abusive situation includes any transaction that is a tax shelter (within the meaning of section 6661(b)(2)(C)(ii)), and any situation involving recent sales transactions, nonrecourse financing, and financing with a term in excess of the economic life of the property. In addition, under regulatory authority, the proposed regulations categorize as potentially abusive situations transactions involving foreign currency. The potentially abusive situation rules also may apply to cash method debt instruments (which are described in greater detail below) subject to section 483.

4. ASSUMPTIONS AND MODIFICATIONS

Sections 1274 and 483 do not apply to a debt instrument assumed or taken subject to in a sale or exchange occurring after June 30, 1985, or a debt instrument issued before October 16, 1985, assumed or taken subject to in a sale or exchange involving a sales price of $100,000,000 or less occurring after December 31, 1984, and before July 1, 1985, unless the debt instrument is modified. The proposed regulations provide special rules for a debt instrument issued after October 15, 1984, or any debt instrument involved in a transaction with a sales price in excess of $100,000,000 that is assumed or taken subject to in a sale or exchange occurring after December 31, 1984, and before July 1, 1985, and that is not modified as part of the sale or exchange.

If a debt instrument assumed or taken subject to is modified, the modification is treated as a separate transaction. In general, a modified debt instrument is treated as a new debt instrument given in exchange for the old debt instrument in a transaction to which section 1274 applies. If a modification is attributable to the seller the modification is treated as occurring immediately before the sale or exchange, and the buyer is treated as assuming the modified debt instrument. Modifications are attributable to the seller unless the seller neither consents to nor participates in the modification. If a modification is attributable to the buyer, the modification is treated as occurring immediately after the sale or exchange.

With certain exceptions, sections 1274 and 483 apply to a debt instrument issued after October 15, 1984, or a debt instrument involved in a transaction with a sales price in excess of $100,000,000 that is assumed or taken subject to and that is not modified as part of a sale or exchange occurring after December 31, 1984, and before July 1, 1985. In these cases, sections 1274 and 483 apply only for purposes of determining the tax consequences of the sale or exchange to the buyer.

C. IMPUTATION OF INTEREST

Under section 1274, if a debt instrument does not provide for adequate stated interest, the issue price of the debt instrument is its imputed principal amount. Except in the case of potentially abusive situations, the imputed principal amount of a debt instrument is the sum of the present values of all the payments due under the instrument determined by discounting the payments at the imputed rate of interest. Generally, for purposes of imputing interest, the imputed rate of interest is the same as the test rate of interest. For sales or exchanges occurring before July 1, 1985, special imputed rates of interest apply.

When interest is imputed, the imputed principal amount becomes the issue price. This issue price is lower than the stated principal amount of the debt instrument, since it reflects the fact that a portion of the stated principal is recharacterized as interest. Thus, the imputed interest is treated as original issue discount. In potentially abusive situations, the imputed principal amount of the debt instrument is the fair market value of the property sold or exchanged.

Under section 483, imputed interest is referred to as unstated interest. Unstated interest is defined as the excess of the deferred payments (all payments of the sales price due more than 6 months after the date of the sale or exchange) over the sum of the present values of the deferred payments and any stated interest. For this purpose, the present values are determined by discounting the payments at the imputed rate of interest. In the case of cash method debt instruments to which the potentially abusive rules apply, the fair market value of the property sold or exchanged is used in place of the present value of the deferred payments and any stated interest.

IV. ACCOUNTING FOR ORIGINAL ISSUE DISCOUNT

A. IN GENERAL

Original issue discount is defined as the excess of a debt instrument's stated redemption price at maturity over its issue price. A portion of the original issue discount on a debt instrument is accounted for on a current basis by both the issuer and the holder. The amount of original issue discount that is accounted for on a current basis is the amount that accrues on a constant interest or economic accrual basis, regardless of whether the issuer or holder is an accrual basis taxpayer.

For purposes of determining the accrual of original issue discount, the term of a debt instrument generally is divided into accrual periods of equal length as discussed in greater detail below. Original issue discount is allocated to each accrual period according to a formula based upon the adjusted issue price of the debt instrument at the beginning of the accrual period, the yield of the debt instrument, and the actual interest payments (if any) for that period. To determine the holder's annual inclusion under section 1272, the original issue discount allocated to each accrual period is then apportioned ratably among the days within the accrual period to produce the daily portion of original issue discount for each day during that accrual period. The total amount of original issue discount includible for any taxable year is the sum of the daily portions of original issue discount for each day during the taxable year that the taxpayer held the debt instrument.

Debt instruments excepted from the current inclusion rule are debt instruments with a term of one year or less, tax-exempt obligations, debt instruments issued by a natural person before March 2, 1984, debt instruments purchased at a premium, U.S. savings bonds, certain loans made between natural persons, and debt instruments issued before January 1, 1985, which are not capital assets in the hands of the holder.

In general, the amount of original issue discount deductible by an issuer under section 163(e) is determined in the same manner as the amount includible by the holder under section 1272. The regulations contain several exceptions to this general rule.

B. PAYING INTEREST CURRENTLY AT CONSTANT RATE TO AVOID THE ORIGINAL ISSUE DISCOUNT RULES

In the case of any debt instrument subject to section 1274 that provides for adequate stated interest, or in the case of any debt instrument issued at par for cash of publicly traded property, the original issue discount rules do not apply if all interest is payable currently at a constant rate over the entire term of the debt instrument. For this purpose, interest is considered payable currently if the interest is payable unconditionally and at regular intervals of one year or less. Interest is not considered payable at a constant rate if the debt instrument involves deferred interest (if the debt instrument has a lower initial rate of interest or an interest holiday for an initial period) or prepaid interest (if it has a higher initial rate of interest).

C. DETERMINING THE TOTAL AMOUNT OF ORIGINAL ISSUE DISCOUNT

1. STATED REDEMPTION PRICE AT MATURITY

Except in the case of installment obligations, the stated redemption price at maturity of a debt instrument is defined as the amount fixed by the last modification of the purchase agreement including interest and other amounts payable at that time. The stated redemption price at maturity does not include any interest based on a fixed or variable rate that is actually and unconditionally payable at intervals of one year or less over the entire term of the debt instrument. These amounts are referred to as qualified periodic interest payments. In the case of an installment obligation, the stated redemption price at maturity equals the sum of all payments under the debt instrument less any qualified periodic interest payments.

2. DETERMINATION OF ISSUE PRICE

If a debt instrument subject to section 1274 states adequate interest, the issue price is the stated principal amount of the debt instrument. If the debt instrument does not state adequate interest as discussed above, the issue price is the imputed principal amount determined according to the provisions of section 1274.

The issue price of a debt instrument not subject to section 1274 is determined as follows:

(a) A debt instrument that is part of an issue of debt instruments publicly offered and issued for cash—the initial price at which a substantial portion of the issue is sold to the public;

(b) A debt instrument that is part of an issue of debt instruments not publicly offered and issued for cash—the price paid by the first buyer;

(c) A debt instrument that is issued for property and is part of an issue of debt instruments a portion of which is traded on an established securities market—the fair market value of that debt instrument determined as of the first trading date after the date of issue of the debt instrument;

(d) A nonpublicly traded debt instrument issued in exchange for publicly traded property—the fair market value of the property; and

(e) A debt instrument that does not fall within the first four categories set forth above and that is not governed by section 1274—its stated redemption price at maturity.

3. DE MINIMIS RULES

In the case of the holder, a debt instrument having a *de minimis* amount of original issue discount is treated as if the original issue discount were zero. Except in the case of an installment obligation, discount is considered *de minimis* if it is less than one-quarter of one percent of the stated redemption price at maturity multiplied by the number of complete years to maturity.

Special rules are provided for installment obligations. To compute the *de minimis* amount of original issue discount allowable on installment obligations generally, taxpayers must utilize a weighted average maturity in lieu of the number of full years from the issue date to final maturity. For debt instruments which are self-amortizing obligations, the proposed regulations provide a safe harbor which allows taxpayers to treat one-sixth of one percent of the stated redemption price at maturity multiplied by the number of complete years to final maturity as *de minimis* original issue discount.

D. ALLOCATION OF ORIGINAL ISSUE DISCOUNT TO AN ACCRUAL PERIOD

1. IN GENERAL

The amount of original issue discount allocable to an accrual period generally is equal to the product of the adjusted issue price at the beginning of the accrual period and the yield of the debt instrument, less amounts of stated interest payable during the accrual period. Each of the terms used in this calculation is defined under section 1272 and the proposed regulations as described in the succeeding discussion.

2. ACCRUAL PERIOD

Generally, for debt instruments issued after December 31, 1984, the accrual period is the interval between payment or compounding dates provided by the debt instrument (but in no event longer than one year), with the final accrual period ending on the maturity date of the debt instrument. Rules are provided for debt instruments with irregular payment or compounding intervals. For debt instruments that provide for a single payment at maturity and that have no other payment or compounding dates, the accrual period is the six-month period ending on the date in each calendar year that corresponds to the maturity date of the debt instrument or the date that is six months prior to that date. For debt instruments issued after July 1, 1982, and before January 1, 1985, the accrual period is the one-year period beginning on the issue date and on the corresponding day in each calendar year throughout the term of the debt instrument.

3. ADJUSTED ISSUE PRICE

The adjusted issue price at the beginning of the first accrual period is the issue price. The adjusted issue price at the beginning of each succeeding accrual period is equal to the adjusted issue price at the beginning of the immediately preceding accrual period increased by the amount of original issue discount accrued during that period. In the case of an installment obligation, the adjusted issue price at the beginning of an accrual period is reduced by any payments of principal or interest that are included in the stated redemption price at maturity and that are made during the immediately preceding accrual period.

4. YIELD

The yield of a debt instrument is that rate of interest that, when used to determine the present value of all payments of principal and interest to be made under the debt instrument, provides an amount equal to the issue price of the debt instrument. Yield is expressed as an annual interest rate and is determined by compounding at the end of the accrual period. Special rules are provided for certain debt instruments that provide a variable rate of interest with a resulting variable yield as discussed in greater detail below.

5. ACQUISITION PREMIUM

In determining the amount a holder must include in income, the daily portion of original issue discount is reduced by an appropriate share of any acquisition premium paid by that holder. Acquisition premium arises when a person purchases a debt instrument at a price which is in excess of the revised issue price on the date of purchase, but which is less than the stated redemption price at maturity. For debt instruments issued after July 1, 1982, and purchased before July 19, 1984, the daily portion is reduced ratably by an amount equal to the total acquisition premium divided by the number of days from the date of purchase up to (but not including) the stated maturity date. For debt instruments issued after July 1, 1982, and purchased after July 18, 1984, the daily portion is reduced by a constant fraction equal to the total acquisition premium divided by the total unaccrued original issue discount on the date of purchase.

E. SPECIAL RULES

1. SERIAL MATURITY AND INSTALLMENT OBLIGATIONS

Under regulations published under section 1232 of prior law, single obligations that provided for payments prior to maturity (other than payments of interest at fixed, periodic intervals of one year or less over the entire term of the obligation) were treated as a serial issue with each installment payment representing a separate obligation with its own issue price and stated redemption price at maturity. Original issue discount with respect to a serial issue, where independent issue prices could not be established for each individual series, was apportioned among the series based upon a linear ("bond-years") formula.

Because the OID rules now apply to a much broader class of obligations, including mortgages involving as many as 360 separate payments of principal, the proposed regulations eliminate the prior law treatment of each payment of principal under an installment obligations as a separate debt instrument. Instead, the regulations treat all installment obligations and certain serial maturity obligations as a single installment obligation for all purposes under sections 1271 through 1275. For this purpose, an installment obligation is defined as a debt instrument that provides for payments prior to maturity other than qualified periodic interest payments. Stated redemption price at maturity of an installment obligation is defined as the sum of all payments to be made under the obligation other than qualified periodic interest payments. This rule is effective for installment obligations issued after December 31, 1984 and for debt instruments maturing serially issued after May 8, 1986; the issuer and holder may, however, elect jointly to change this treatment.

2. VARIABLE RATE DEBT INSTRUMENTS

The proposed regulations provide rules for the determination of the amount of original issue discount on debt instruments that provide for a variable rate of interest based on current values of an objective interest rate index. Generally, original issue discount attributable to deferred payments of interest made under these debt instruments is accounted for based upon a variable yield equal to the variable rate fixed by the debt instrument. Any other original issue discount on these debt instruments is determined on the issue date by assuming that the interest rate in effect on that date remains constant over the entire term of the debt instrument and is accounted for on that basis, regardless of the actual interest rate under the debt instrument.

3. CONTINGENT PAYMENTS

Under the proposed regulations, contingent payments are generally not taken into account in applying the original issue discount and imputed interest rules. Instead, contingent payments are segregated from noncontingent payments and are accounted for separately. In determining whether a payment is contingent, the Commissioner may disregard remote and incidental contingencies. The parties to a transaction are, however, bound by its form and must treat a payment subject to a stated contingency as contingent. The contingent payment rules do not affect whether rights to receive contingent payments constitute debt or equity for Federal tax purposes or whether an instrument evidences a valid indebtedness.

Under the separate accounting rules for contingent payments, contingent payments may be recharacterized in certain situations. First, any payment of principal made on account of a sale or exchange of nonpublicly traded property that is not accompanied by a payment of adequate stated interest will be recharacterized in part as interest. Second, in the case of a debt instrument that does not provide for adequate stated interest and that accordingly has imputed interest, certain contingent interest payments may be recharacterized in part as principal to restore to basis amounts previously recharacterized as imputed interest. In these cases, a payment subject to recharacterization is treated as a payment of principal in an amount equal to the present value of the payment and as a payment of interest to the extent of the difference between the amount of the payment and the present value of the payment. The amount of all payments characterized as principal, however, cannot exceed the amount of the fixed or maximum stated principal amount under a debt instrument.

Third, a contingent payment made under a debt instrument issued for cash or publicly traded property may be recharacterized in a case in which the issue price of the debt instrument exceeds the sum of all the noncontingent payments due under the debt instrument. In such a case, the noncontingent payments under the debt instrument are treated entirely as principal. Each contingent payment is treated as a payment of interest to the extent of the total interest deemed accrued and not allocated to prior payments, and a payment of principal to the extent of the excess of the amount of the payment over the portion of the payment treated as interest. The total interest deemed accrued for any accrual period is based on an assumed yield to maturity equal to the applicable Federal rate which would have applied had the debt instrument been issued for nonpublicly traded property. Once the sum of all the portions of the contingent payments that are treated as principal under this rule reaches the difference between the issue price of the debt instrument and the sum of all the noncontingent payments under the debt instrument, any additional contingent payments are treated as interest.

If a contingent payment is paid within six months of the date it becomes fixed, the portion of the payment recharacterized as interest is accounted for by both the issuer and the holder when the payment becomes fixed. The proposed regulations provide, however, that if a contingent payment is not paid within six months of the date it becomes fixed, the buyer is treated as having issued a separate debt instrument on the date the payment becomes fixed. The issue price of this deemed debt instrument is determined under section 1274 (regardless of whether the payment arose under a debt instrument that was issued for cash or publicly traded property). An amount equal to the issue price is characterized as principal and interest as discussed above.

In the case of a debt instrument subject to section 1274, special rules are provided for the treatment of payments contingent only with respect to due date but which are payable within a fixed period. Under these rules, the buyer's initial basis and the allocation of interest to accrual periods are determined by assuming that all payments under the debt instrument are made at the latest possible date and in the smallest amount permitted. When payments are made before the end of the fixed period, basis and interest accrual adjustments are made.

4. PUT OR CALL OPTIONS

The proposed regulations provide a special rule for the determination of yield, maturity date, and stated redemption price at maturity of a debt instrument that provides for a put or call option or an option to extend the term of the debt instrument. Yield of such a debt instrument is determined as of the issue date by assuming that the holder of the particular option will act in accordance with his own economic interest (as viewed from the issue date) in deciding whether to exercise the option. For example, if the issuer of a debt instrument has a call right and if the yield to the call date (assuming exercise of the call option) would be less than the yield to maturity assuming no exercise of the call, it will be assumed as of the date of issue that the call option will be exercised. The maturity date and the stated redemption price at maturity are then determined according to the presumption of exercise. Special rules are provided for debt instruments issued in a transaction governed by section 1274 that contain such options.

5. REORGANIZATIONS

In the case of debt instruments issued after December 13, 1982, in exchange for other debt instruments in a reorganization (within the meaning of section 368(a)), a special rule limits the original issue discount created upon the exchange. If the issue price of the new debt instrument would be less than the adjusted issue price of the old debt instrument but for this rule, then the issue price of the new debt instrument is equal to the adjusted issue price of the old debt instrument.

F. INFORMATION REPORTING REQUIREMENTS

Section 1275(c)(1) requires an issuer of publicly offered debt instruments issued after the date of publication of these regulations in final form having original issue discount to set forth on the face of the debt instrument the amount of original issue discount and the issue date. In addition, the proposed regulations require the yield to maturity, the method selected to determine yield for a short accrual period, and the amount of original issue discount allocable to a short accrual period to be set forth on the face of the debt instrument. Similar requirements apply to the first holder of a nonpublicly offered debt instrument, if such holder disposes of the debt instrument before maturity.

Section 1275(c)(2) requires the issuer of a publicly offered debt instrument having original issue discount to furnish the Secretary with certain information. The temporary regulations issued under this section require certain additional items to be furnished to the Secretary and are proposed herein as a part of these regulations with the following amendment: Section 1275(c)(2) shall not apply to issuers of publicly offered debt instruments that are: (1) certificates of deposit, or (2) stripped bonds and coupons within the meaning of section 1286.

G. TREATMENT OF AMOUNTS RECEIVED ON SALE, EXCHANGE OR REDEMPTION OF DEBT INSTRUMENTS

Under the law in effect prior to the Tax Reform Act of 1984, amounts received upon retirement of certain debt instruments held as capital assets were considered to have been received in exchange therefor. Gain on sale, exchange, or retirement was treated as capital gain in the absence of an intention to call the bond before maturity. In the case of a short-term obligation, a portion of the gain was treated as ordinary interest income to the extent of accrued discount in the hands of the holder.

The rules of prior law relating to the characterization of gain upon sale, exchange or retirement of a debt instrument issued at a discount have been retained, except that the requirement that the debt instrument be a capital asset in the hands of the holder has been repealed for debt instruments issued at a discount after July 18, 1984.

V. ACCOUNTING FOR INTEREST

Under the revised section 483, unstated interest is required to be accounted for on an economic accrual basis consistent with the allocation of original issue discount under section 1272(a) and Rev. Rul. 83-84, 1983-1 C.B. 97. Unlike original issue discount, however, unstated interest is not subject to annual periodic inclusion or deduction. The proposed regulations prescribe rules under section 446 governing the method of accounting for interest in lending and deferred payment transactions outside the scope of the original issue discount rules. Thus, these rules apply to the accounting for unstated interest (and any stated interest) in transactions to which section 483 applies. Under the proposed section 446 regulations, interest accrues in generally the same manner as original issue discount. For purposes of determining how accrued interest is allocated to payments under a debt instrument, a payment is treated: first, as a payment of interest to the extent interest has accrued and remains unpaid as of the date of the payment; second, as a prepayment of interest to the extent the parties have allocated more interest to payments than the amount of interest that has accrued as of the date of the payment; and third, as a payment of principal to the extent of the excess of the payment over the sum of the accrued and the prepaid interest. In certain small transactions, however, the allocation of the parties of less interest to a payment than the amount of accrued interest that remains unpaid as of the date of the payment will be respected.

VI. CASH METHOD DEBT INSTRUMENTS

As noted above, section 483 rather than section 1274 applies to cash method debt instruments. Interest on a cash method debt instrument is accounted for under the cash receipts and disbursements method of accounting. In general, a debt instrument is a cash method debt instrument if the stated principal amount of the debt instrument does not exceed $2,000,000, the lender is neither an accrual method taxpayer nor a dealer with respect to the property, and the borrower and the lender jointly elect the cash method treatment. However, a debt instrument issued in exchange for new section 38 property or a debt instrument issued in a sale-leaseback transaction does not qualify for the cash method treatment. The cash method election is generally binding on successors of the lender and the borrower. If, however, the lender (or a successor thereof) transfers the cash method debt instrument to an accrual method taxpayer, the election does not apply to the successor for any period after the transfer and section 1272 will apply to the successor.

VII. AMENDMENTS TO SECTION 482 REGULATIONS

1. IN GENERAL

In section 44(b)(2) of the Tax Reform Act of 1984, Congress directed the Treasury to amend the safe haven interest rates under the section 482 regulations to provide floating rates consistent with the rates applicable under sections 483 and 1274. These proposed regulations are in response to that directive. In addition, these proposed regulations would make certain other changes to the section 482 regulations. The proposed regulations would reduce the interest-free period on certain intercompany balances between controlled taxpayers under existing §1.482-2(a)(3) from six months to 60 days. The proposed regulations would also delete the formula method for determining a safe-haven rental charge for leases of tangible depreciable property between related taxpayers under §1.482-2(c)(2)(ii).

2. EXPLANATION OF THE PROPOSED REGULATIONS

a. SAFE HAVEN INTEREST RATES

Section 1.482-2(a)(2)(iii) of the proposed regulations provides generally that the range of safe haven interest rates on loans or advances between controlled entities will be between 100 percent and 130 percent of the applicable Federal rate (AFR) corresponding to the term of the loan, with adjustments for inadequate interest made at 100 percent of the AFR, compounded semiannually, and adjustments for excessive interest made at 130 percent of the AFR, compounded semiannually. The upper limit of 130 percent of the AFR approximates the interest yield on bonds with a Moody's rating of BAA. Consistent with section 1274(e), the lower limit is 110 percent of the AFR in the case of sale-leaseback transactions. The effective dates of the proposed regulations are described in §1.482-2(a)(2)(iii)(A) of the proposed regulations.

The proposed regulations continue the rule of the existing regulations that controlled taxpayers may demonstrate that a rate outside the safe haven range is a more appropriate rate under all the facts and circumstances.

Section 1.482-2(a)(3) of the proposed regulations provides that where the interest rate on a loan or advance is subject to adjustment both under section 482 and some other Code section (for example, sections 467, 483, 1274, or 7872), the other Code section is to be applied first, and the provisions of section 482 may then be applied to the loan or advance, as adjusted by the other Code section. If the other Code section does not apply to the loan or advance because of an exception, limitation, or *de minimis* rule contained in the other Code section, the provisions of the section 482 regulations may still be applied to the loan or advance by the district director. Under this arrangement it would be unlikely that actual adjustments would be required under both section 482 and the other Code section. Under certain circumstances, however, both section 482 and the other Code section may apply. For example, if the AFR exceeds 9 percent, and if the related taxpayers use the special 9 percent rate prescribed in section 1274A(a), the transaction may be subject to further adjustment under section 482.

Under proposed §1.482-2(a)(1)(iii), the interest-free period on certain intercompany balances (six months under the existing regulations) is reduced to 60 days. The proposed regulations continue the rule of the existing regulations that the taxpayer is permitted to use a longer interest-free period if it can demonstrate that it regularly grants uncontrolled parties a longer interest-free period on similar transactions in its trade or business.

b. LEASES

Section 1.482-2(c) of the existing regulations provides a formula method for determining a safe haven rental charge for certain leases of tangible depreciable property between controlled entities. There is no minimum or maximum lease period for which the safe haven rental charge can be used. Under the existing regulation taxpayers are never required to use the safe haven formula rental if the taxpayer can establish a more appropriate rental charge. However, in cases where the taxpayer may use the safe haven rental amount, the IRS may not challenge the safe haven amount, even if the amount does not clearly reflect income. Because of these deficiencies in the operation of the safe haven formula, it would be deleted under the proposed regulations. The safe haven rule for subleases under §1.482-2(c)(2)(iii) would be retained. The effective dates of the proposed regulations are described in §1.482-2(c)(2)(ii).

VIII. QUESTIONS RESERVED

The proposed regulations do not revise the definition of intention to call before maturity nor do they address the application of the intention to call rules in the case of debt instruments with indefinite maturities. The Internal Revenue Service is actively considering and welcomes comments specifically directed toward these reserved issues, as well as those directed to the following:

1. How the original issue discount rules should apply to foreign currency transactions, and

2. Whether a portion of the issue price of a debt instrument providing for a conversion feature should properly be allocated to that conversion feature in a manner similar to the allocation of issue price for investment units under section 1273(c)(2).

REGULATORY FLEXIBILITY ACT

Although this document is a notice of proposed rulemaking that solicits public comment, the Internal Revenue Service has concluded that the regulations proposed herein are interpretative and that the notice and public procedure requirements of 5 U.S.C 553 do not apply. Accordingly, these proposed regulations do not constitute regulations subject to the Regulatory Flexibility Act (5 U.S.C. chapter 6).

NON-APPLICATION OF EXECUTIVE ORDER 12291

The Commissioner of Internal Revenue has determined that this proposed rule is not a major rule as defined in Executive Order 12291 and that a regulatory impact analysis therefore is not required.

COMMENTS AND REQUEST FOR A PUBLIC HEARING

Before these proposed regulations are adopted, consideration will be given to any written comments that are submitted (preferably eight copies) to the Commissioner of Internal Revenue. All comments will be available for public inspection and copying. A public hearing will be held upon written request to the Commissioner by any person who has submitted written comments. If a public hearing is held, notice of the time and place will be published in the FEDERAL REGISTER. The collection of information requirements contained herein have been submitted to the Office of Management and Budget (OMB) for review under section 3504(h) of the Paperwork Reduction Act. Comments on the requirements should be sent to the Office of Information and Regulatory Affairs of OMB, Attention: Desk Officer for Internal Revenue Service, New Executive Office Building, Washington, D.C. 20503. The Internal Revenue Service requests that persons submitting comments to OMB also send copies of the comments to the Service.

DRAFTING INFORMATION

The principal author of the proposed regulations under sections 163, 1271, 1272, 1273, and 1275 is Theresa E. Bearman of the Legislation and Regulations Division of the Office of Chief Counsel, Internal Revenue Service; the principal author of the regulations under sections 446, 483 and 1274 is Ewan D. Purkiss of the Legislation and Regulations Division of the Office of Chief Counsel, Internal Revenue Service; and the principal author of the regulations under section 482 is Joseph M. Rosenthal of the Legislation and Regulations Division of the Office of Chief Counsel, Internal Revenue Service. However, personnel from other offices of the Internal Revenue Service and the Treasury Department participated in developing the regulations on matters of both substance and style.

[¶ 49,071] Proposed Regulations (LR-3-86), published in the Federal Register on May 16, 1986.

Reorganizations: Foreign corporations: Transfer of property.—Reg. §§1.367(a)-1T, 1.367(a)-6T, 1.367(d)-1T and 1.6038B-1T, relating to transfers of property to foreign corporations, are proposed. Temporary Reg. §1.367(a)-3T was adopted as Reg. §1.367(a)-3 by T.D. 8702 on December 27, 1996. Temporary Reg. §§1.367(a)-2T and 1.367(a)-4T were adopted and Reg. §§1.367(a)-5T was removed by T.D. 9803 on December 15, 2016.

AGENCY: Internal Revenue Service, Treasury.

ACTION: Notice of proposed rulemaking cross-reference to temporary regulations.

SUMMARY: In the Rules and Regulations portion of this issue of the Federal Register, the Internal Revenue Service is issuing temporary regulations that add new §§1.367(a)-1T through 1.367(a)-6T, relating to transfers of property by U.S. persons to foreign corporations, new §1.367(d)-1T, relating to transfers of intangible property by U.S. persons to foreign corporations, and new §1.6038B-1T, relating to reporting of transactions described in section 367. The text of the new sections also serves as the comment document for this notice of proposed rulemaking.

DATES: Written comments and requests for a public hearing must be delivered or mailed before July 15, 1986. The regulations are proposed generally to apply to transfers made after December 31, 1984.

ADDRESS: Send comments and requests for a public hearing to: Commissioner of Internal Revenue, Attention: CC:LR:T [LR-3-86], Washington, DC 20224.

FOR FURTHER INFORMATION CONTACT: Charles W. Culmer of the Legislation and Regulations Division, Office of Chief Counsel, Internal Revenue Service, 1111 Constitution Avenue, N.W., Washington, DC 20224, (Attention: CC:LR:T) (202-566-4336, not a toll-free call).

SUPPLEMENTARY INFORMATION:

BACKGROUND

The temporary regulations published in the Rules and Regulations portion of this issue of the FEDERAL REGISTER add new §§1.367(a)-1T, 1.367(a)-2T, 1.367(a)-3T, 1.367(a)-4T, 1.367(a)-5T, 1.367(a)-6T, 1.367(d)-1T, and 1.6038B-1T to 26 CFR Part 1. The final regulations that are proposed to be based on these temporary regulations would amend 26 CFR Part 1 by adding these new temporary regulation sections as final regulation sections under sections 367 and 6038B of the Internal Revenue Code of 1954. For the text of the temporary regulations, see FR Doc.—[T.D. 8087]published in the Rules and Regulations portion of this issue of the FEDERAL REGISTER.

REGULATORY FLEXIBILITY ACT AND EXECUTIVE ORDER 12291

The Commissioner of Internal Revenue has determined that this proposed rule is not a major rule as defined in Executive Order 12291 and that a Regulatory Impact Analysis is therefore not required. The Secretary of the Treasury has certified that this rule will not have a significant impact on a substantial number of small entities. Few small entities would be affected by these regulations. A regulatory flexibility analysis, therefore, is not required under the Regulatory Flexibility Act (5 U.S.C. chapter 6).

COMMENTS AND REQUESTS FOR A PUBLIC HEARING

Before adopting these proposed regulations, consideration will be given to any written comments that are submitted (preferably eight copies) to the Commissioner of Internal Revenue. All comments will be available for public inspection and copying. A public hearing will be held upon written request to the Commissioner by any person who has submitted written comments. If a public hearing is held, notice of the time and place will be published in the FEDERAL REGISTER. The collection of information requirements contained herein have been submitted to the Office of Management and Budget (OMB) for review under section 3504(h) of the Paperwork Reduction Act. Comments on the requirements should be sent to the Office of Information and Regulatory Affairs of OMB, Attention: Desk Officer for Internal Revenue Service, New Executive Office Building, Washington, DC 20503. The Internal Revenue Service requests persons submitting comments to OMB to also send copies of the comments to the Service.

DRAFTING INFORMATION

The principal author of this regulation is Charles W. Culmer of the Legislation and Regulations Division of the Office of Chief Counsel, Internal Revenue Service. However, personnel from other offices of the Internal Revenue Service and Treasury Department participated in developing the regulations on matters of substance and style.

[¶ 49,072]   **Proposed Regulations (LR-144-85), published in the Federal Register on** December 17, 1986.

Information returns: Original issue discount: Brokers.—Reg. § 1.6049-5T, relating to reporting requirements for original issue discount debt instruments, is proposed.

AGENCY: Internal Revenue Service, Treasury.

ACTION: Notice of proposed rulemaking and cross-reference to temporary regulations.

SUMMARY: In the Rules and Regulations portion of this issue of the FEDERAL REGISTER, the Internal Revenue Service is issuing temporary regulations concerning the reporting requirements under section 6049 of the Internal Revenue Code of 1954 for original issue discount debt instruments. The temporary regulations also serve as the text for this notice of proposed rulemaking.

DATES: Written comments and requests for a public hearing must be delivered or mailed by February 17, 1987. The regulations are proposed to be effective on or after January 1, 1986.

ADDRESS: Send comments and requests for a public hearing to: Commissioner of Internal Revenue, Attention: CC:LR:T (LR-144-85), 1111 Constitution Avenue, N.W., Washington, D.C. 20224.

FOR FURTHER INFORMATION CONTACT: Susan T. Baker of the Legislation and Regulations Division, Office of the Chief Counsel, Internal Revenue Service, 1111 Constitution Avenue, N.W., Washington, D.C. 20224 (Attention: CC:LR:T) (LR-144-85) (202-566-3829, not a toll-free call).

SUPPLEMENTARY INFORMATION:

BACKGROUND

The temporary regulations published in the Rules and Regulations portion of this issue of the FEDERAL REGISTER amend 26 CFR Parts 1 and 602. The final regulations which are proposed to be based on the temporary regulations would amend 26 CFR Parts 1 and 602 to add new regulations under section 6049 of the Internal Revenue Code of 1954 relating to original issue discount reporting requirements as they apply to certain brokers and other middlemen.

DESCRIPTION OF PROPOSED REGULATIONS

For a description of the subject matter of these proposed regulations relating to the reporting requirements for brokers and other middlemen under section 6049 of the Internal Revenue Code of 1954, see the description and text of the temporary regulations incorporated in F.R. Doc. [T.D.—]published in the Rules and Regulations portion of this issue of the FEDERAL REGISTER.

NON-APPLICABILITY OF EXECUTIVE ORDER 12291

The Commissioner of Internal Revenue has determined that this proposed rule is not a major rule as defined in Executive Order 12291. Accordingly, a Regulatory Impact Analysis is not required.

REGULATORY FLEXIBILITY ACT

The Internal Revenue Service has concluded that although this document is a notice of proposed rulemaking that solicits public comment, the regulations proposed herein are interpretative and the notice and public procedure requirements of 5 U.S.C. 553 do not apply. Accordingly, no Regulatory Flexibility Analysis is required for this rule.

DRAFTING INFORMATION

The principal author of these proposed regulations is Theresa E. Bearman of the Legislation and Regulations Division of the Office of Chief Counsel, Internal Revenue Service. However, personnel from other offices of the Internal Revenue Service and Treasury Department participated in developing the regulations, on matters of both substance and style.

COMMENTS AND REQUESTS FOR A PUBLIC HEARING

Before these proposed regulations are adopted, consideration will be given to any written comments that are submitted (preferably eight copies) to the Commissioner of Internal Revenue. All comments will be available for public inspection and copying. A public hearing will be held upon written request to the Commissioner by any person who has submitted written comments. If a public hearing is held, notice of the time and place will be published in the FEDERAL REGISTER. The collection of information requirements contained herein have been submitted to the Office of Management and Budget (OMB) for review under section 3504(h) of the Paperwork Reduction Act. Comments on the requirements should be sent to the Office of Information and Regulatory Affairs of OMB, Attention: Desk Officer for Internal Revenue Service, New Executive Office Building, Washington, D.C. 20503. The Internal Revenue Service requests persons submitting comments to OMB to also send copies of the comments to the Service.

[¶ 49,073]   **Proposed Amendments of Regulations (INTL-53-86), published in the Federal Register on** December 19, 1986.

Registration-required obligations: Withholding.—Amendments of Reg. § 5f.103-1, relating to the definition of the term "registration-required" with respect to certain types of obligations and to the repeal of the 30 percent withholding tax on certain types of interest, are proposed. Reg. § 35a.9999-5 was removed by T.D. 8734 on October 6, 1997.

AGENCY: Internal Revenue Service, Treasury.

ACTION: Notice of proposed rulemaking by cross reference to temporary regulations.

SUMMARY: This document provides notice of proposed rulemaking relating to the definition of the term "registration-required" with respect to certain types of obligations, and relating to the repeal of the 30 percent withholding tax on certain types of interest by the Tax Reform Act of 1984. In the Rules and Regulations portion of this Federal Register, the Internal Revenue Service is issuing temporary income tax regulations relating to the definition of the term "registration-required" with respect to certain obligations, and the repeal of 30 percent withholding by the Tax Reform Act of 1984. The text of those temporary regulations serves as the comment document for this notice of proposed rulemaking.

DATE: Written comments and requests for a public hearing must be delivered or mailed before [DATE WHICH IS 60 DAYS AFTER PUBLICATION OF THIS DOCUMENT IN THE FEDERAL REGISTER].

ADDRESS: Send comments and requests for a public hearing to: Commissioner of Internal Revenue, Attention: CC:LR:T (INTL-53-86).

FOR FURTHER INFORMATION CONTACT: Carl Cooper of the Office of the Associate Chief Counsel (International) within the Office of Chief Counsel, Internal Revenue Service, 1111 Constitution Avenue, N.W., Washington, D.C. 20224, Attention: CC:LR:T [INTL-53-86], (202-566-3388).

SUPPLEMENTARY INFORMATION:

BACKGROUND

The temporary regulations published in the Rules and Regulations portion of this issue of the Federal Register amend existing temporary regulations. Section 5f.103-1 is amended by revising paragraph (c)(1), by adding a new paragraph (e), by revising example (2) of paragraph (f), and by adding examples to paragraph (f). Section 35a.9999-5 is amended by revising Q & As-1, 8, 18 and 20, by inserting new Q & As-19 and 22 through 28, and by renumbering existing Q & A-20 as Q & A-21. For the text of the temporary regulations, see FR Doc. [T.D. 8111] published in the rules and regulations portion of this issue of the Federal Register.

REGULATORY FLEXIBILITY ACT AND EXECUTIVE ORDER 12291

The Commissioner of Internal Revenue has determined that this proposed rule is not a major rule as defined in Executive Order 12291 and that a Regulatory Impact Analysis is therefore not required. Although this document is a notice of a proposed rulemaking which solicits public comment, the Internal Revenue Service has concluded that the regulations proposed herein are interpretative and that the notice and public procedure requirements of 5 U.S.C. 553 do not apply. Accordingly, these text of the temporary regulations, see FR Doc. [T.D. 8111]published in the rules and regulations portion of this issue of the Federal Register.

REGULATORY FLEXIBILITY ACT AND EXECUTIVE ORDER 12291

The Commissioner of Internal Revenue has determined that this proposed rule is not a major rule as defined in Executive Order 12291 and that a Regulatory Impact Analysis is therefore not required. Although this document is a notice of a proposed rulemaking which solicits public comment, the Internal Revenue Service has concluded that the regulations proposed herein are interpretative and that the notice and public procedure requirements of 5 U.S.C. 553 do not apply. Accordingly, these proposed regulations do not constitute regulations subject to the Regulatory Flexibility Act (5 U.S.C. chapter 6).

COMMENTS AND REQUESTS FOR A PUBLIC HEARING

Before adopting these proposed regulations as final regulations, consideration will be given to any written comments that are submitted (preferably eight copies) to the Commissioner of Internal Revenue. All comments will be available for public inspection and copying. A public hearing will be held upon written request to the Commissioner by any person who has submitted written comments. If a public hearing is held, notice of the time and place will be published in the Federal Register. The collection of information requirements contained herein have been submitted to OMB for review under the Paperwork Reduction Act, and comments on them should be sent to the Office of Information and Regulatory Affairs of OMB, Attn: Desk Officer for the Internal Revenue Service, New Executive Office Building, Washington, DC 20503. The Internal Revenue Service requests persons submitting comments to OMB to also send copies of the comments to the Service.

DRAFTING INFORMATION

The principal authors of this regulation are P. Ann Fisher and Carl Cooper of the Office of the Associate Chief Counsel (International) within the office of the Office of Chief Counsel, Internal Revenue Service. However, personnel from other Offices of the Internal Revenue Service and Treasury Department participated in developing the regulations on matters of substance and style.

[¶ 49,074] **Proposed Regulations and Amendments of Regulations (INTL-43-86), published in the Federal Register on** February 3, 1987.

Domestic International Sales Corporations: Taxation of income.—Reg. §§1.995-2A, 1.995-8, 1.995(f)-1 and 1.996-9 and amendments of Reg. §§1.921-1T, 1.991-1, 1.992-1, 1.992-2, 1.995-2, 1.995-7, 1.996-1 and 1.6011-2, relating to the taxation of income allocable to a DISC for taxable years beginning after 1984, are proposed. Reg. §1.995-7 was removed 1/5/96 by T.D. 8655.

AGENCY: Internal Revenue Service, Treasury.

ACTION: Notice of proposed rulemaking.

SUMMARY: This document contains proposed regulations relating to the taxation of income allocable to a Domestic International Sales Corporation (DISC) for taxable years beginning after 1984. Changes to the applicable tax law were made by the Tax Reform Act of 1984 and the Technical Corrections Title of the Tax Reform Act of 1986. The proposed regulations would provide DISCs and DISC shareholders with guidance needed to comply with the Act and would affect all DISCs and DISC shareholders.

DATES: Written comments and requests for a public hearing must be delivered or mailed by April 3, 1987. The regulations are proposed to be effective for transactions after December 31, 1984, in taxable years ending after December 31, 1984.

ADDRESS: Send comments and requests for a public hearing to: Commissioner of Internal Revenue, Attn: CC:LR:T (Intl-43-86), Washington, D.C. 20224.

FOR FURTHER INFORMATION CONTACT: Joseph M. Rosenthal of the Office of the Associate Chief Counsel (International), Internal Revenue Service, 1111 Constitution Avenue, N.W., Washington, D.C. 20224 (Attn: CC:LR:T). Telephone 202-566-6276 (not a toll-free call.)

SUPPLEMENTARY INFORMATION:

BACKGROUND

This document contains proposed amendments to the Income Tax Regulations (26 CFR Part 1) under sections 441, 991, 992, 995, 996 and 6011 of the Internal Revenue Code of 1954. These amendments are proposed to provide regulations under sections 441(h), 995(b)(1)(E), 995(f) and 996 which were added to the Code by sections 803 and 802 of the Tax Reform Act of 1984 (Pub. L. 98-369, 98 Stat. 672) or amended by the Technical Corrections Title of the Tax Reform Act of 1986 (Pub. L. 99-514, 100 Stat. 2085).

EXPLANATION OF THE PROPOSED REGULATIONS TERMINATION OF DISC ELECTION AND EXEMPTION OF DISC INCOME FROM TAX

Under section 805(b) of the Tax Reform Act of 1984, the last taxable year of each DISC which began before January 1, 1985, ended on December 31, 1984. The termination of a DISC's taxable year on that date is treated under §1.921-1T(a) as a revocation of the corporation's DISC election. All corporations which wish to be treated as a DISC for any period after 1984 must make a new DISC election on Form 4876A. Regulations providing for the time and manner of making the new DISC election were provided by §1.921-1T(b)(1) Q&A-1. Those regulations generally require that the election of a corporation to be treated as an interest charge DISC for the corporation's first taxable year beginning after December 31, 1984, must be filed on Form 4876A within 90 days after the beginning of such year. The Service has learned that many corporations which were DISCs on December 31, 1984, and which intended to continue to be treated as an interest charge DISC may have failed to re-elect DISC status in a timely manner. Accordingly, section 1.992-2(a)(3) of these proposed regulations extends the time for re-electing DISC status for 1985 and subsequent taxable years for corporations which were treated as a DISC for the taxable year ending December 31, 1984, to June 3, 1987. Forms 4876A filed by such corporations within this time will be accepted by the Service as a timely DISC election for the DISC's taxable year beginning January 1, 1985, based on these proposed regulations.

In addition, under section 805(b) of the Tax Reform Act of 1984, generally all corportions which qualified as DISCs on December 31, 1984, are permitted to treat their accumulated DISC income as previously taxed income when distributed after that date. Temporary regulations relating to the treatment of such distributions were provided by §1.921-1T and are contained in §1.996-9 of the proposed regulations. That section of the proposed regulations also provides that any net operating loss or capital loss carryforward of a DISC as of December 31, 1984, is to be reduced by the amount of accumulated DISC income that was exempted from tax. In addition, that section also provides that no foreign tax credit shall be allowed with respect to any foreign taxes paid with respect to the amount of accumulated DISC income that was exempted from tax.

NEW DISC RULES

The Tax Reform Act of 1984 also changed many of the rules applicable to DISCs effective for taxable years ending after 1984.

Taxable year of the DISC

A DISC is required to use the same taxable year as its principal shareholder. The same rule also applies to Foreign Sales Corporations (FSCs) and to small FSCs. Section 1.441-1(h) of the proposed regulations provides rules relating to this requirement. The DISC must change its taxable year if the principal shareholder changes its taxable year, or if a different shareholder having a different taxable year becomes the principal shareholder of the DISC. If the DISC must change its taxable year to conform to the taxable year of a new principal shareholder, §1.441-1(h)(3)(iii) of the proposed regulations provides that the short period required to effect the change shall end with the close of the new principal shareholder's taxable year within which the change in ownership occurs. This provision would amend the rule for determining the short period contained in §1.921-1T(b)(6) of the Temporary Regulations (under which the short period is the taxable year of the DISC following the DISC's taxable year in which the change of ownership occurs), and is proposed to be effective for changes in ownership occurring after 30 days after the date the proposed regulations are finalized.

Controlled groups

A DISC and a FSC or a small FSC cannot be members of the same greater-than-50-percent controlled group. Rules relating to this requirement are contained in §1.992-1(j) of the proposed regulations. In general, the DISC election of a corporation is treated as revoked if a FSC or a small FSC election becomes effective for any other member of the controlled group. A special transitional rule is provided if a DISC and a FSC or small FSC become members of the same controlled group by reason of an acquisition of a shareholder in either the DISC, the FSC or the small FSC.

Deemed distributions

The deemed distribution relating to base period export gross receipts (the incremental rule) is eliminated for taxable years beginning after 1984, and is replaced with a deemed distribution of the DISC's taxable income attributable to qualified export receipts that exceed $10 million. Section 1.995-8 of the proposed regulations provides rules relating to this new deemed distribution. In general, the $10 million amount may be allocated to qualified gross receipts on a transaction-by-transaction basis. Section 1.995-8(b)(2) of the proposed regulations provides a special rule for the allocation of qualified gross receipts attributable to related and subsidiary services. Section 1.995-8(f) of the proposed regulations provides a method for allocating the $10 million amount among DISCs which are members of the same controlled group. Under section 1.995-8(a), the $10 million amount is to be prorated on a daily basis in the case of a DISC having a short taxable year.

The deemed distribution of 50 percent of the DISC's taxable income to a non-C corporation DISC shareholder is eliminated, and the deemed distribution of 57.5 percent of the DISC's taxable income to a C corporation DISC shareholder is reduced to a deemed distribution of 1/17th of the amount of the DISC's taxable income for the taxable year in excess of the other deemed distributions. See §1.995-2A of the proposed regulations.

INTEREST CHARGE

In general

The Tax Reform Act of 1984 also provides for an annual interest charge on the shareholders of the DISC. Section 1.995(f)-1 of the proposed regulations provides rules relating to this requirement. In general, the amount of the interest charge is based on the additional income tax that would otherwise be due on the accumulated DISC income deferred by the DISC in taxable years beginning after 1984 computed as if the deferred income were distributed to the shareholder. The rate of interest charged is tied to the rate of interest on 52-week Treasury bills (the "base period T-bill rate"), as described below. The interest charge is not imposed on the accumulated DISC income for the taxable year in which it is earned. Thus, a DISC shareholder will not have an interest charge for the shareholder's taxable year ending with or including the last day of the DISC's first taxable year for which its new DISC election is made. Section 1.995(f)-1(f) contains rules for determining the amount of the deferred DISC income.

DISC-related deferred tax liability

The tax that would otherwise be due on the deferred DISC income, the "shareholder's DISC-related deferred tax liability", for a taxable year of the shareholder is the excess of the shareholder's tax liability computed as if the deferred DISC income were included in the shareholder's gross income over the shareholder's actual tax liability for the taxable year. Sections 1.995(f)-1(d) and (e) of the proposed regulations provide rules relating to this computation. Under section 995(f)(2), the computation is to be made without regard to carrybacks to the taxable year from a later taxable year. Under §1.995(f)-1(d)(4) of the proposed regulations, the computation is also to be made without regard to carryforwards to the taxable year or to any other item that may be carried by the shareholder to another taxable year. Thus, the treatment of carrybacks and carryovers of deductions and credits in the computation of the amount of the shareholder's DISC-related deferred tax liability is similar to the treatment of such items under section 644(a) of the Code. Section 644(a) provides a special rule for determining the tax imposed on a trust's gain on the sale of property contributed to the trust within two years by reference to the additional tax that would have been imposed on the grantor if the property had been sold by the grantor.

Base period T-bill rate

The rate of interest charged on the shareholder's DISC-related deferred tax liability for a taxable year is equal to the "base period T-bill rate." This rate is equivalent to the average investment yield on 52 week T-bills auctioned during the one-year period ending on September 30 of the calendar year ending with or within the taxable year of the shareholder. The base period T-bill rate, as determined above, is then compounded daily for the number of days in the shareholder's taxable year for which the interest charge is being determined. Under section 6622, the amount of any interest required to be paid under the Code is determined by daily compounding.

The base period T-bill rate for each one-year period ending September 30 shall be published in a revenue ruling in the Internal Revenue Bulletin. That revenue ruling shall also contain a table of factors reflecting daily compounding of the base period T-bill rate. Revenue Ruling 86-132, 1986-46 I.R.B. 5 published the base period T-bill rates for the periods September 30, 1984, 1985 and 1986, together with tables of factors reflecting daily compounding.

To compute the amount of the interest charge for the shareholder's taxable year, the shareholder shall multiply the DISC-related deferred tax liability by the base period T-bill rate factor corresponding to the number of days in the shareholder's taxable year for which the interest charge is being determined. Generally, the shareholder will use the base period T-bill rate factor for a 365 day year. The factor to be used will be other than the factor for 365 days if the shareholder's taxable year is a short taxable year, if the shareholder uses the 52-53 week taxable year, or if the shareholder's taxable year is a leap year.

Paragraph (g) of §1.995(f)-1 of the proposed regulations provides rules for determining the amount of the interest charge for a taxable year in which stock in the DISC is transferred. In general, the transferor and the transferee shareholders compute their DISC-related deferred tax liability as if they each held the stock for the entire taxable year and then multiply that amount by the base period T-bill rate factor for the number of days in the year that each shareholder held the stock. A reduction in the amount of deferred DISC income (and thus of the interest charge) is made for any gain recognized on the transfer under section 995(c).

Section 1.995(f)-1(h) of the proposed regulations provides for pass-through treatment of the interest charge in the case of DISC stock held by a partnership or an S corporation. If stock in a DISC is held by an estate or trust, however, the interest charge is imposed on the estate or trust.

Payment, collection and assessment of the interest charge

Section 995(f)(6) provides that the amount of the interest charge for a taxable year is treated as interest imposed on an underpayment of tax under section 6601. Thus, the interest charge may be deducted by the DISC shareholder only to the extent that the shareholder may deduct interest on an underpayment of tax. The interest charge is due at the same time the shareholder's income tax return for the taxable year is required to be filed, without regard to extensions. No payments of estimated tax under section 6154 or 6654 are required with respect to the interest charge.

The interest charge is to be computed on Form 8404. To assist the IRS in properly processing the shareholder's Form 8404 and crediting the payment to the shareholder's account, the Form 8404, together with the shareholder's payment of the interest charge, is *not* to be included with or attached to the shareholder's income tax return for the taxable year.

Technical corrections

The Technical Corrections Title of the Tax Reform Act of 1986 made several amendments to the DISC and FSC rules. The proposed regulations incorporate those amendments, but do not address any issues that may be raised by other substantive provisions of the Tax Reform Act of 1986.

EXECUTIVE ORDER 12291 AND REGULATORY FLEXIBILITY ACT

The Commissioner of Internal Revenue has determined that this proposed rule is not a major rule as defined in Executive Order 12291 and that a Regulatory Impact Analysis is therefore not required. Although this document is a notice of proposed rulemaking which solicits public comment, the Internal Revenue Service has determined that the regulations proposed herein are interpretative and that the notice and public procedure requirements of 5 U.S.C. §553 do not apply. Accordingly, these proposed regulations do not constitute regulations subject to the Regulatory Flexibility Act (5 U.S.C. Chapter 6).

COMMENTS AND REQUESTS FOR A PUBLIC HEARING

Before adopting these proposed regulations, consideration will be given to any written comments that are submitted (preferably eight copies) to the Commissioner of Internal Revenue. All comments will be available for public inspection and copying. A public hearing will be held upon written request to the Commissioner by any person who has submitted written comments. If a public hearing is held, notice of the time and place will be published in the FEDERAL REGISTER.

PAPERWORK REDUCTION ACT

The collection of information requirements contained in this notice of proposed rulemaking have been submitted to the Office of Management and Budget (OMB) for review under section 3504(h) of the Paperwork Reduction Act. Comments on these requirements should be sent to the Office of Regulatory Affairs of OMB, Attention: Desk Officer for Internal Revenue Service, New Executive Office Building, Washington, D.C. 20503. The Internal Revenue Service requests that persons submitting comments to these requirements to the OMB also send copies of those comments to the IRS.

DRAFTING INFORMATION

The principal author of the proposed regulations is Joseph M. Rosenthal of the Office of the Associate Chief Counsel (International), Internal Revenue Service. However, personnel from other offices of the Internal Revenue Service and the Treasury Department participated in developing these regulations on matters of substance and style.

[¶49,075]   Proposed Regulations (REG-209015-86) [originally issued as INTL-153-86], published in the Federal Register on March 3, 1987.

Foreign sales corporations.—Reg. §§1.927(a)-1T and 1.927(d)-2T, relating to foreign sales corporations, are proposed. Reg. §1.927(e)-1 was adopted 9/17/98 by T.D. 8782. Temporary Reg. §§1.921-3T, 1.923-1T, 1.924(a)-1T, 1.925(a)-1T, 1.925(b)-1T, 1.926(a)-1T, 1.927(b)-1T and 1.927(e)-2T were removed by T.D. 9849 on 3/11/2019.

AGENCY: Internal Revenue Service, Treasury.

ACTION: Notice of proposed rulemaking by cross-reference to temporary regulations.

SUMMARY: This document provides proposed Income Tax Regulations relating to rules for application of the foreign sales corporation (FSC) transfer pricing rules, for distributions from a FSC, for treatment of losses of a FSC, for sourcing and classification of a FSC's income, for computation of exempt foreign trade income, for computation of the FSC's and the FSC's United States shareholder's foreign tax credits, for definitions of foreign trading gross receipts, export property and gross receipts, for effect of boycott participation on FSC benefits, and for sourcing a related supplier's income if the transfer pricing rules are used to compute the FSC's profit. In the Rules and Regulations portion of this FEDERAL REGISTER, the Internal Revenue Service is issuing temporary regulations relating to these matters. The text of those temporary regulations also serves as the comment document for this proposed rulemaking.

DATES: Written comments and requests for a public hearing must be delivered or mailed before May 4, 1987. These rules would apply to taxable years beginning after December 31, 1984.

ADDRESS: Send comments and requests for a public hearing to Commissioner of Internal Revenue, Attention: CC: LR:T (INTL-153-86), Washington, D.C. 20224.

FOR FURTHER INFORMATION CONTACT: Richard Chewning, of the Office of Associate Chief Counsel (International), within the Office of Chief Counsel, Internal Revenue Service, 1111 Constitution Avenue, N.W., Washington, D.C. 20224 (Attention: CC:LR:T (INTL-153-86)) (202-566-6384, not a toll-free call).

SUPPLEMENTARY INFORMATION:

BACKGROUND

The temporary regulations published in the Rules and Regulations portion of this issue of the FEDERAL REGISTER add new §§1.921-3T, 1.923-1T, 1.924(a)-1T, 1.925(a)-1T, 1.925(b)-1T, 1.926(a)-1T, 1.927(a)-1T, 1.927(b)-1T, 1.927(d)-2T, 1.927(e)-1T and 1.927(e)-2T to 26 CFR Part 1. The final regulations that are proposed to be based on the temporary regulations would amend 26 CFR Part 1. For the text of the temporary regulations, see [INSERT FEDERAL REGISTER REFERENCE][T.D. 8126]published in the Rules and Regulations portion of this issue of the FEDERAL REGISTER.

EXECUTIVE ORDER 12291 AND REGULATORY FLEXIBILITY ACT

The Commissioner of Internal Revenue has determined that these proposed rules are not major rules as defined in Executive Order 12291 and that a Regulatory Impact Analysis is therefore not required. Although this document is a notice of a proposed rulemaking which solicits public comment, the Internal Revenue Service has concluded that the regulations proposed herein are interpretative and that the notice and public procedure requirements of 5 U.S.C. 553 do not apply. Accordingly, these proposed regulations do not constitute regulations subject to the Regulatory Flexibility Act (5 U.S.C. chapter 6).

PAPERWORK REDUCTION ACT

The collection of information requirements contained in this notice of proposed rulemaking have been submitted to the Office of Management and Budget (OMB) for review under section 3504(h) of the Paperwork Reduction Act. Comments on these collection of information requirements may be sent to the Office of Information and Regulatory Affairs of OMB, Attention: Desk Officer for Internal Revenue Service, New Executive Office Building, Washington, D.C. 20503. The Internal Revenue Service requests that persons submitting comments on these requirements to OMB also send copies of those comments to the Internal Revenue Service.

COMMENTS AND REQUESTS FOR A PUBLIC HEARING

Before adopting these proposed regulations, consideration will be given to any written comments that are submitted (preferably eight copies) to the Commissioner of Internal Revenue. All comments will be available for public inspection and copying. A public hearing will be held upon written request to the Commissioner by any person who has submitted written comments. If a public hearing is held, notice of the time and place will be published in the FEDERAL REGISTER.

DRAFTING INFORMATION

The principal author of these regulations is Richard Chewning, of the Office of Associate Chief Counsel (International), within the Office of Chief Counsel, Internal Revenue Service. Personnel from other offices of the Internal Revenue Service and Treasury Department participated in developing the regulations.

[¶ 49,076]   **Proposed Regulations (CO-23-87), published in the Federal Register on** March 18, 1987.

Consolidated returns: Alaska Native Corporations.—Reg. §1.1502-81T, relating to corporations included in a consolidated return with a Native Corporation established under the Alaska Native Claims Settlement Act, is proposed.

AGENCY: Internal Revenue Service, Treasury.

ACTION: Notice of proposed rulemaking by cross-reference to temporary regulations.

SUMMARY: In the Rules and Regulations portion of this issue of the FEDERAL REGISTER, the Internal Revenue Service is issuing temporary regulations that add new §1.1502-81T to provide rules relating to certain corporations included in a consolidated return with a Native Corporation established under the Alaska Native Claims Settlement Act. The text of the new section also serves as the comment document for this notice of proposed rulemaking.

PROPOSED EFFECTIVE DATE

The regulations are proposed to apply generally to taxable years beginning after December 31, 1984.

DATE FOR COMMENTS AND REQUESTS FOR A PUBLIC HEARING

Written comments and requests for a public hearing must be delivered or mailed by [60 DAYS AFTER DATE OF PUBLICATION OF THIS DOCUMENT IN THE FEDERAL REGISTER.]

ADDRESS: Send comments and requests for a public hearing to: Commissioner of Internal Revenue, Attention: CC:LR:T [LR-23-87], Washington, D.C. 20224.

FOR FURTHER INFORMATION CONTACT: Mark S. Jennings of the Legislation and Regulations Division, Office of Chief Counsel, Internal Revenue Service, 1111 Constitution Avenue, N.W., Washington, D.C. 20224 (Attention: CC:LR:T) or telephone 202-566-3458 (not a toll-free number).

SUPPLEMENTARY INFORMATION:

BACKGROUND

Temporary regulations published in the Rules and Regulations portion of this issue of the FEDERAL REGISTER add new temporary regulation § 1.1502-81T to Part 1 of Title 26 of the Code of Federal Regulations ("CFR"). The final regulations that are proposed to be based on the new temporary regulation would be added to Part 1 of Title 26 of the CFR. Those final regulations would make clear that the rules provided by section 60(b)(5) of the Tax Reform Act of 1984 and section 1804(e)(4) of the Tax Reform Act of 1986 result in no tax saving, tax benefit, or tax loss to any person, other than the use of the losses and credits of an Alaska Native Corporation and its wholly owned subsidiaries. For the text of the new temporary regulations, see T.D. 8130, published in the Rules and Regulations portion of this issue of the Federal Register. The preamble to the temporary regulations explains the additions to the regulations.

REGULATORY FLEXIBILITY ACT AND EXECUTIVE ORDER 12291

Although this document is a notice of proposed rulemaking that solicits public comment, the Secretary of the Treasury has certified that this rule will not have a significant impact on a substantial number of small entities because the economic and any other secondary or incidental impact flows directly from the underlying statute. A regulatory flexibility analysis is therefore not required under the Regulatory Flexibility Act (5 U.S.C. chapter 6). The Commissioner of Internal Revenue has determined that this proposed rule is not a major rule as defined in Executive Order 12291 and that a Regulatory Impact Analysis is therefore not required.

COMMENTS AND REQUESTS FOR A PUBLIC HEARING

Before these proposed regulations are adopted, consideration will be given to any written comments that are submitted (preferably eight copies) to the Commissioner of Internal Revenue. All comments will be available for public inspection and copying. A public hearing will be held upon written request to the Commissioner by any person who has submitted written comments. If a public hearing is held, notice of the time and place will be published in the FEDERAL REGISTER.

DRAFTING INFORMATION

The principal author of these proposed regulations is Mark S. Jennings of the Legislation and Regulations Division of the Office of Chief Counsel, Internal Revenue Service. However, personnel from other offices of the Internal Revenue Service and Treasury Department participated in developing the regulations, both on matters of substance and style.

[¶ 49,077] Proposed Regulations (EE-151-86), published in the Federal Register on April 3, 1987.

Excise tax: Retirement plans: Qualified plan assets: Reversion of.—Reg. §§ 54.6011-1T and 54.6071-1T, relating to the payment of excise tax by employers receiving reversions of qualified plan assets required by the Tax Reform Act of 1986, are proposed. Reg. § 54.6071-1T was withdrawn 4/26/93 by T.D. 8474.

AGENCY: Internal Revenue Service, Treasury.

ACTION: Notice of proposed rulemaking by cross reference to temporary regulations.

SUMMARY: This document provides regulations regarding the payment of the excise tax by employers receiving (directly or indirectly) reversions of qualified plan assets required by the Tax Reform Act of 1986. In the Rules and Regulations portion of this FEDERAL REGISTER, the Internal Revenue Service is issuing temporary regulations relating to the payment of the excise tax; the text of these temporary regulations also serves as the comment document for this notice of proposed rulemaking.

DATES: Written comments and requests for a public hearing must be delivered or mailed by June 2, 1987. These amendments are proposed to be applicable to reversions occurring after December 31, 1985.

ADDRESS: Please mail or deliver comments to: Commissioner of Internal Revenue, Attention: CC:LR:T (EE-151-86), 1111 Constitution Avenue, N.W., Washington, D.C. 20224.

FOR FURTHER INFORMATION CONTACT: Suzanne K. Tank of the Employee Plans and Exempt Organizations Division, Office of Chief Counsel, Internal Revenue Service, 1111 Constitution Avenue, N.W., Washington, D.C. 20224 (Attention: CC:LR:T) (202-566-3938, not a toll-free number).

SUPPLEMENTARY INFORMATION:

BACKGROUND

The temporary regulations in the Rules and Regulations portion of this issue of the FEDERAL REGISTER amend Part 54 of the Code of Federal Regulations. New § 54.6011-1T and new § 54.6071-1T are added to Part 54 of Title 26 of the Code of Federal Regulations. When § 54.6011-1T is promulgated as final regulations, § 54.6011-1 will be revised to reflect the new provision. For the text of the temporary regulations, see FR Doc. (TD 8133) published in the Rules and Regulations portion of this issue of the FEDERAL REGISTER. The preamble to the temporary regulations explains this addition to the Pension Excise Tax Regulations.

NONAPPLICABILITY OF EXECUTIVE ORDER 12291

The Commissioner of Internal Revenue has determined that this proposed rule is not a major rule as defined in Executive Order 12291 and that a regulatory impact analysis therefore is not required.

REGULATORY FLEXIBILITY ACT

The Secretary of the Treasury has certified that this rule will not have a significant impact on a substantial number of small entities. First, most small businesses maintain defined contribution plans. The regulations do not generally affect defined contribution plans. Hence, small businesses would not generally be affected by the regulation. Second, very few businesses with defined benefit plans will be terminating their plans and receiving a reversion in any calendar quarter or year. A Regulatory Flexibility Analysis, therefore, is not required under the Regulatory Flexibility Act (5 U.S.C. 605(b)).

PAPERWORK REDUCTION ACT

The collection of information requirements contained in this regulation have been submitted to the Office of Management and Budget (OMB) for review under section 3504(h) of the Paperwork Reduction Act of 1980. Comments on these requirements should be sent to the Office of Information and Regulatory Affairs of OMB, Attention: Desk Officer for Internal Revenue Service, New Executive Office Building, Washington, D.C. 20503. The

Internal Revenue Service requests that persons submitting comments on the requirements to OMB also send copies of these comments to the Service.

DRAFTING INFORMATION

The principal author of these proposed regulations is Suzanne K. Tank of the Employee Plans and Exempt Organizations Division of the Office of Chief Counsel, Internal Revenue Service. However, personnel from other offices of the Internal Revenue Service and the Treasury Department participated in developing the regulations, on matters of both substance and style.

COMMENTS AND REQUESTS FOR A PUBLIC HEARING

Before adoption of these proposed regulations, consideration will be given to any written comments that are submitted (preferably eight copies) to the Commissioner of Internal Revenue. All comments will be available for public inspection and copying. A public hearing will be held upon written request to the Commissioner by any person who has submitted written comments. If a public hearing is held, notice of the time and place will be published in the FEDERAL REGISTER.

[¶ 49,078]   **Proposed Regulations and Amendments of Regulations (EE-143-86), published in the Federal Register on** June 15, 1987.

Business expenses: Sickness and disability payments: Group health plan.—Amendments of Reg. § 1.106-1, relating to the requirement that a group health plan offer continuation coverage to people who would otherwise lose coverage as a result of certain events, are proposed. Reg. § 1.162-26 was adopted by T.D. 8812 (see Reg. § § 54.4980B-0—54.4980B-8), applicable to qualifying events occurring in plan years beginning on or after January 1, 2000.

AGENCY: Internal Revenue Service, Treasury.

ACTION: Notice of proposed rulemaking.

SUMMARY: This document contains proposed regulations relating to the requirement that a group health plan offer continuation coverage to people who would otherwise lose coverage as a result of certain events. They reflect changes made by the Consolidated Omnibus Budget Reconciliation Act of 1985 (COBRA) and the Tax Reform Act of 1986. The regulations will generally affect sponsors of and participants in group health plans, and they provide plan sponsors with guidance necessary to comply with the law.

DATES: Written comments and requests for a public hearing must be delivered or mailed [60 DAYS AFTER DATE OF PUBLICATION OF NOTICE OF PROPOSED RULEMAKING]. These regulations are proposed to be effective when final regulations are published in the FEDERAL REGISTER as a Treasury decision.

ADDRESS: Send comments and requests for a public hearing to: Commissioner of Internal Revenue, Attention: CC:LR:T (EE-143-86) Washington, D.C. 20224.

FOR FURTHER INFORMATION CONTACT: Mark Schwimmer of the Employee Plans and Exempt Organizations Division, Office of Chief Counsel, Internal Revenue Service, 1111 Constitution Avenue, N.W., Washington, D.C. 20224 (Attention: CC:LR:T). Telephone 202-566-6212 (not a toll-free number).

SUPPLEMENTARY INFORMATION:

BACKGROUND

This document contains proposed amendments to the Income Tax Regulations (26 CFR Part 1) under sections 106(b), 162(i)(2), and 162(k) of the Internal Revenue Code of 1986 (Code). The proposed regulations conform the regulations to section 10001 of the Consolidated Omnibus Budget Reconcilation Act of 1985 (COBRA) (100 Stat. 222) and to section 1895(d) of the Tax Reform Act of 1986 (100 Stat. 2936), which made technical corrections to the COBRA provisions.

COBRA added a new section 162(k) of the Code to specify continuation coverage requirements for employer-provided group health plans. In general, a group health plan must offer each "qualified beneficiary" who would otherwise lose coverage under the plan as a result of a "qualifying event" an opportunity to elect continuation of the coverage being received immediately before the qualifying event. A qualified beneficiary who properly elects continuation coverage can be charged an amount no greater than 102 percent of the "applicable premium." The "applicable premium" is based on the plan's cost of providing coverage.

If a group health plan fails to comply with these continuation coverage requirements, the employer will be unable to deduct contributions made to that or any other group health plan (section 162(i)(2)), and certain highly compensated individuals will be unable to exclude from income any employer-provided coverage under that or any other group health plan (section 106(b)).

In addition, there may be non-tax consequences if a group health plan fails to comply with parallel requirements that section 10002 of COBRA added to Title I of the Employee Retirement Income Security Act of 1974 (ERISA). Title I of ERISA is administered by the Department of Labor. Governmental plans (as defined in section 414(d) of the Code) are exempt from both the tax and ERISA provisions. However, State and local governmental group health plans are subject to parallel requirements that section 10003 of COBRA added to the Public Health Service Act, which is administered by the Department of Health and Human Services.

The proposed regulations do not reflect section 9501 of the Omnibus Budget Reconciliation Act of 1986, which extended the COBRA continuation coverage requirements to certain individuals receiving retiree medical benefits from employers that are involved in bankruptcy proceedings. The changes made by that act will be addressed in a later issuance.

The proposed regulations clarify which plans must offer COBRA continuation coverage and the tax consequences of failing to do so. They also provide guidance on a variety of details, including the scope of the continuation coverage, who is a qualified beneficiary, what is a qualifying event, how elections are made, and when payment must be made. Rules regarding computation of the applicable premium under section 162(k)(4) will be addressed in a later issuance.

Section 414(t) as added by the Tax Reform Act of 1986 extends the employer aggregation rules of sections 414(b), (c), (m), and (o) to a variety of employee benefit provisions. The list of those provisions includes section 106 (denying an income exclusion to highly compensated employees of an employer maintaining a group health plan that fails to comply with section 162(k)), but does not include section 162(i)(2) (denying deductions to such an employer) or section 162(k) itself. A technical correction to add sections 162(i)(2) and 162(k) to the list was included in H.Con.Res. 395. Although the 99th Congress adjourned without enacting that concurrent resolution, the correction was identical in both House and Senate versions. Accordingly, the proposed regulations set forth employer aggregation rules that anticipate a similar technical correction with retroactive effect being enacted in the current session of Congress.

There is no connection between the proposed regulations and section 89 of the Code. For example, the definitions set forth in the proposed regulations will not affect the meaning of "core benefits," "non-core benefits," or any other terms for purposes of section 89. Also, the computation of applicable premiums for COBRA continuation coverage will not affect the determination of the value of group health plan benefits for purposes of section 89.

EFFECTIVE DATE

The regulations are proposed to be effective when final regulations are published in the FEDERAL REGISTER as a Treasury decision. Group health plans become subject to the COBRA continuation coverage requirements at different times, however, depending on the plan year of a plan and whether the plan is a collectively bargained plan. With respect to qualifying events that occur on or after the date that a plan became or becomes subject to those requirements and before the effective date of final regulations, the plan and the employer must operate in good faith compliance with a reasonable interpretation of the statutory requirements (i.e., title X of COBRA). For the period before the effective date of final regulations, the Internal Revenue Service will consider compliance with the terms of these proposed regulations to constitute good faith compliance with a reasonable interpretation of the statutory requirements (other than the statutory requirements regarding the computation of the applicable premium or the treatment, under section 9501 of the Omnibus Budget Reconciliation Act of 1986, of certain bankruptcies as qualifying events, which are not addressed in these proposed regulations). Moreover, plans and employers will be considered to be in compliance with the terms of these proposed regulations if, between [DATE OF PUBLICATION OF NOTICE OF PROPOSED RULEMAKING] and [90 DAYS AFTER DATE OF PUBLICATION OF NOTICE OF PROPOSED RULEMAKING], they operate in good faith compliance with a reasonable interpretation of the statutory requirements and, from [91 DAYS AFTER DATE OF PUBLICATION OF NOTICE OF PROPOSED RULEMAKING] until the effective date of final regulations, they operate in compliance with the terms of these proposed regulations. In addition, the Internal Revenue Service will not consider actions inconsistent with the terms of these proposed regulations necessarily to constitute a lack of good faith compliance with a reasonable interpretation of the statutory requirements; whether there has been good faith compliance with a reasonable interpretation of the statutory requirements will depend on all the facts and circumstances of each case.

SPECIAL ANALYSES

The Commissioner of Internal Revenue has determined that this proposed rule is not a major rule as defined in Executive Order 12291. Therefore, a Regulatory Impact Analysis is not required. Although this document is a notice of proposed rulemaking which solicits public comment, the Internal Revenue Service has concluded that the regulations proposed herein are interpretative and that the notice and public procedure requirements of 5 U.S.C. 553 do not apply. Accordingly, these proposed regulations do not constitute regulations subject to the Regulatory Flexibility Act (5 U.S.C. chapter 6).

COMMENTS AND REQUESTS FOR PUBLIC HEARING

Before adopting these proposed regulations, consideration will be given to any written comments that are submitted (preferably eight copies) to the Commissioner of Internal Revenue. All comments will be available for public inspection and copying. A public hearing will be held upon written request to the Commissioner by any person who has submitted written comments. If a public hearing is held, notice of the time and place will be published in the FEDERAL REGISTER.

DRAFTING INFORMATION

The principal author of these proposed regulations is Mark Schwimmer of the Employee Plans and Exempt Organizations Division of the Office of Chief Counsel, Internal Revenue Service. However, personnel from other offices of the Internal Revenue Service and Treasury Department participated in developing the regulations, both on matters of substance and style.

§ 1.162-26 **Continuation coverage requirements of group health plans.—**
TABLE OF CONTENTS

COBRA in general: Q&A-1 to Q&A-6
Which plans must comply and when: Q&A-7 to Q&A-14
Qualified beneficiaries: Q&A-15 to Q&A-17
Qualifying events: Q&A-18 to Q&A-21
COBRA continuation coverage: Q&A-22 to Q&A-31
Electing COBRA continuation coverage: Q&A-32 to Q&A-37
Duration of COBRA continuation coverage: Q&A-38 to Q&A-43
Paying for COBRA continuation coverage: Q&A-44 to Q&A-48
LIST OF QUESTIONS
COBRA IN GENERAL

Q-1: What are the new health care continuation coverage requirements added to the Internal Revenue Code by the Consolidated Omnibus Budget Reconciliation Act of 1985 ("COBRA")?

Q-2: What is the effect of a group health plan's failure to comply with section 162(k)?

Q-3: How are employer deductions affected by a group health plan's failure to comply with section 162(k)?

Q-4: How is the gross income of certain individuals affected by a group health plan's failure to comply with section 162(k)?

Q-5: What is the employer?

Q-6: How does COBRA apply to group health plan before the effective date of this section?

WHICH PLANS MUST COMPLY AND WHEN

Q-7: What is a group health plan?

Q-8: What group health plans are subject to COBRA?

Q-9: What is a small-employer plan?

Q-10: When is an arrangement considered to be two or more separate group health plans rather than a single group health plan?

Q-11: When must group health plans comply with section 162(k)?

Q-12: What is a collectively bargained group health plan?

Q-13: What is the plan year of a group health plan?

Q-14: How do the COBRA continuation coverage requirements apply to cafeteria plans and other flexible benefit arrangements?

QUALIFIED BENEFICIARIES

Q-15: Who is a qualified beneficiary?

Q-16: Who is a covered employee?

Q-17: Other than those individuals who are qualified beneficiaries as of the day before a qualifying event, can any other person (such as a newborn or adopted child or a new spouse) obtain qualified beneficiary status for COBRA continuation coverage purposes?

QUALIFYING EVENTS

Q-18: What is a qualifying event?

Q-19: Can a qualifying event result from a voluntary termination of employment?

Q-20: Can a qualifying event occur before the effective date of section 162(k) (as described in Q&A-11 of this section)?

Q-21: Can a qualifying event occur while a group health plan is excepted from COBRA (see Q&A-8 of this section)?

COBRA CONTINUATION COVERAGE

Q-22: What is COBRA continuation coverage?

Q-23: How is COBRA continuation coverage affected by changes in the coverage that is provided to similarly situated beneficiaries with respect to whom a qualifying event has not occurred?

Q-24: Can a group health plan require a qualified beneficiary who wishes to receive COBRA continuation coverage to elect to receive a continuation of all of the coverage that he or she was receiving under the plan immediately before the qualifying event?

Q-25: What is core coverage?

Q-26: Must a qualified beneficiary be given an opportunity to elect core coverage plus only one of two non-core coverages that the qualified beneficiary had under the plan immediately before the qualifying event?

Q-27: Must a qualified beneficiary who is covered under a single plan providing both core coverage and non-core coverage be offered the opportunity to elect non-core coverage only?

Q-28: What deductibles apply if COBRA continuation coverage is elected?

Q-29: How do a plan's limits apply to COBRA continuation coverage?

Q-30: Can a qualified beneficiary who elects COBRA continuation coverage ever change from the coverage received by that individual immediately before the qualifying event?

Q-31: Aside from open enrollment periods, can a qualified beneficiary who has elected COBRA continuation coverage choose to cover individuals (such as newborn children, adopted children, or new spouses) who join the qualified beneficiary's family on or after the date of the qualifying event?

ELECTING COBRA CONTINUATION COVERAGE

Q-32: What is the minimum period during which a group health plan must allow a qualified beneficiary to elect COBRA continuation coverage (i.e., the election period)?

Q-33: Must a covered employee or qualified beneficiary inform the employer or plan administrator of the occurrence of a qualifying event?

Q-34: During the election period and before the qualified beneficiary has made an election, must coverage be provided?

Q-35: Is a waiver before the end of the election period effective to end a qualified beneficiary's election rights?

Q-36: Can an employer withhold money or other benefits owed to a qualified beneficiary until the qualified beneficiary either waives COBRA continuation coverage, elects and pays for such coverage, or allows the election period to expire?

Q-37: Can each qualified beneficiary make an independent election under COBRA?

DURATION OF COBRA CONTINUATION COVERAGE

Q-38: How long must COBRA continuation coverage be available to a qualified beneficiary?

Q-39: When does the maximum coverage period end?

Q-40: Can the maximum coverage period ever be expanded?

Q-41: If coverage is provided to a qualified beneficiary after a qualifying event without regard to COBRA continuation coverage (e.g., as a result of State or local law, industry practice, a collective bargaining agreement, or plan procedure), will such alternative coverage extend the maximum coverage period?

Q-42: How can an event that occurs before a group health plan becomes subject to section 162(k) affect the maximum coverage period when a later, qualifying event occurs?

Q-43: Must a qualified beneficiary be given the right to enroll in a conversion health plan at the end of the maximum coverage period for COBRA continuation coverage?

PAYING FOR COBRA CONTINUATION COVERAGE

Q-44: Can a qualified beneficiary be required to pay for COBRA continuation coverage?

Q-45: After a qualified beneficiary has elected COBRA continuation coverage under a group health plan, can the plan increase the amount that the qualified beneficiary must pay for COBRA continuation coverage?

Q-46: Must a qualified beneficiary be allowed to pay for COBRA continuation coverage in installments?

Q-47: Can a qualified beneficiary choose to have the first payment for COBRA continuation coverage applied prospectively only?

Q-48: What is timely payment for COBRA continuation coverage?

COBRA IN GENERAL

Q-1: What are the new health care continuation coverage requirements added to the Internal Revenue Code by the Consolidated Omnibus Budget Reconciliation Act of 1985 ("COBRA")?

A-1: Section 10001 of COBRA added a new section 162(k) to the Code to provide generally that a group health plan must offer each qualified beneficiary who would otherwise lose coverage under the plan as a result of a qualifying event an opportunity to elect, within the applicable election period, continuation coverage under the plan. That continuation coverage is referred to in this section as "COBRA continuation coverage" and a group health plan that is subject to section 162(k) is referred to as being "subject to COBRA" (see Q&A-8 of this section). A qualified beneficiary can be required to pay for COBRA continuation coverage. A qualified beneficiary is defined in Q&A-15 of this section. A qualifying event is defined in Q&A-18 of this section. The election procedures are described in Q&A-32 through Q&A-37 of this section. COBRA continuation coverage is described in Q&A-22 through Q&A-31 of this section. Payment for COBRA continuation coverage is addressed in Q&A-44 through Q&A-48 of this section. Unless otherwise specified, any reference in this section to "COBRA" refers to section 10001 of COBRA and to section 162(k) of the Code as added by COBRA (as amended).

Q-2: What is the effect of a group health plan's failure to comply with section 162(k)?

A-2: If a group health plan subject to COBRA fails to comply with section 162(k), certain deductions are disallowed to the employer under section 162(i)(2) (see Q&A-3 of this section) and the income exclusion under section 106(a) is denied to certain highly compensated employees of the employer under section 106(b)(1) (see Q&A-4 of this section). There may be additional non-tax consequences if the plan fails to comply with parallel requirements that were added by section 10002 of COBRA to Title I of the Employee Retirement Income Security Act of 1974 (ERISA), which is administered by the Department of Labor. Although governmental plans are not subject to section 162(k) because they are not "subject to COBRA" (see Q&A-8 of this section), certain governmental plans are subject to parallel requirements that were added by section 10003 of COBRA to the Public Health Service Act, which is administered by the Department of Health and Human Services.

Q-3: How are employer deductions affected by a group health plan's failure to comply with section 162(k)?

A-3: (a) Under section 162(i)(2), if a group health plan subject to COBRA fails to comply with section 162(k), each employer maintaining the plan is denied a deduction for any contributions or other expenses paid or incurred in connection with any group health plan that it maintains. The deduction is denied for any taxable year of the taxpayer during which there are one or more days on which plan is not in compliance with section 162(k). Thus, if a failure to comply with section 162(k) arises in one taxable year of a taxpayer and is not corrected until after the beginning of the following taxable year, the deduction for contributions or expenses for both of those taxable years is denied. Section 162(i)(2) operates each taxable year to permanently deny a deduction for amounts paid or incurred in that year, and is applied before applying any provision of the Code that governs the timing of an otherwise available deduction. Examples of such provisions include sections 263A (capitalization and inclusion in inventory costs), 419 (treatment of funded welfare benefit plans), and 460 (special rules for long-term contracts). In addition, section 162(i)(2) operates with respect to each employer maintaining the group health plan, without regard to whether the employers are treated as a single employer (see Q&A-5 of this section) and without regard to whether the failure to satisfy section 162(k) occurs with respect to only an employee of one of the employers. See Q&A-10 of this section regarding when an arrangement is treated as two or more separate group health plans.

(b) A failure of a group health plan to comply with section 162(k) that occurs before, and is not corrected by, the date that an employer maintaining the plan and another entity are first treated as a single employer under Q&A-5 of this section ("the combination date") will not result in a denial of a deduction to the other entity under paragraph (a) of this Q&A-3, so long as (1) the other entity did not also maintain the plan before the combination date, and (2) the failure is corrected before the end of the first taxable year of the other entity that begins after the combination date.

(c) The rules of this Q&A-3 are illustrated by the following examples:

Example 1: Plan A is a group health plan subject to COBRA that is maintained by two unrelated employers, X and Y. Section 162(k) became effective with respect to plan A before April 1, 1988. The taxable year of employer X ends on March 31, and the taxable year of employer Y ends on April 30. If plan A fails to comply with section 162(k) on April 1, 1988, by not offering COBRA continuation coverage to a qualified beneficiary of an employee of employer X, and the failure is not corrected until June 1, 1988, both employers X and Y are disallowed deductions for their contributions and other expenses relating to all their group health plans (including any group health plan that is maintained only by employer X or only by employer Y) for each taxable year that includes one or more days of noncompliance. Thus, the disallowance applies to employer X for its taxable year ending March 31, 1989, and to employer Y for both its taxable year ending April 30, 1988, and its taxable year ending April 30, 1989. (However, see Q&A-10 of this section regarding when an arrangement is considered to be two or more separate group health plans.)

Example 2: Assume that companies Z and W are treated as a single employer under section 414(b) at all relevant times (see Q&A-5 of this section), that Z maintains group health plans P and Q, that W maintains group health plans R and S, and that none of these plans is excepted from COBRA (see Q&A-8 of this section). Assume further that the taxable year of company Z ends on May 31, that the taxable year of company W ends on July 31, and that section 162(k) becomes effective with respect to the group health plans as follows: for plan P on February 1, 1987; for plan Q on April 1, 1987; and for plans R and S on June 1, 1987. If at any time during February through May of 1987 plan P is not in compliance with section 162(k), then company Z is disallowed all deductions with respect to plans P and Q for its taxable year ending May 31, 1987, and company W is disallowed all deductions with respect to plans R and S for its taxable year ending July 31, 1987.

Example 3: Assume that a group health plan maintained only by M, a calendar year employer, is subject to COBRA and fails to comply with section 162(k) during February of 1988, that the failure is corrected during April of 1988, and that on June 1, 1988 employer M becomes a wholly owned subsidiary of N, a previously unrelated corporation with a taxable year ending July 31. For 1988, M is disallowed a deduction for all its contributions with respect to any group health plan. Because M and N were not treated as a single employer (see Q&A-5 of this section) during the period of noncompliance by M's plan (i.e., February to April of 1988), the failure of M's plan to comply with section 162(k) during that period will not result in a disallowance of any deductions to N, the new parent corporation. Even if the failure to comply that arises in February of 1988 is not corrected until after June 1, 1988, it will not result in a disallowance of any deductions to N, so long as the failure to comply is corrected by July 31, 1989 (the end of N's first taxable year that begins after June 1, 1988). However, if the failure is not corrected until August of 1989, N will be disallowed a deduction for all its contributions with respect to any group health plan for its taxable years ending on July 31 of 1988, 1989, and 1990. Also, if another failure of M's plan to comply with section 162(k) arises on or after June 1, 1988, that second failure will result in a disallowance of deductions to N.

Example 4: Assume that a calendar year employer maintaining a group health plan through a welfare benefit fund contributes $800,000 to the fund in 1988 and $500,000 in 1989. Assume further that only $600,000 of the 1988 contribution would be deductible under section 419 for 1988, and that the remaining $200,000 would be deemed to be contributed in 1989 and deductible under section 419 for 1989 along with the $500,000 actually contributed in that year. However, the deduction under section 419 is only available if these amounts are otherwise deductible under section 162. Therefore, if at any time during 1988 the group health plan is not in compliance with section 162(k), the $800,000 contributed in 1988 is disallowed in full as a deduction for 1988 and for all later years. However, if the plan does comply with section 162(k) throughout 1988 but at some time during 1989 is not in compliance, the $600,000 deduction for 1988 is unaffected while the $700,000 otherwise deductible for 1989 is permanently disallowed.

Q-4: How is the gross income of certain individuals affected by a group health plan's failure to comply with section 162(k)?

A-4: (a) Under section 106(a), employer-provided coverage under an accident or health plan is generally excluded from the gross income of an employee. Under section 106(b), however, if a group health plan that is subject to COBRA fails to comply with section 162(k), certain individuals shall have certain employer-provided coverage included in their gross income for each of their taxable years during which the plan is not in compliance, even if the coverage would otherwise be excludable from income under section 106(a). The individuals referred to in the preceding sentence consist of each person who is, at any time during which the plan is not in compliance with section 162(k), a highly compensated employee (within the meaning of section 414(q) and the regulations under that section) of any employer maintaining the plan. The coverage included in the individual's gross income for each such taxable year shall consist of all coverage provided by the employer to the individual and his or her spouse and dependent children during that taxable year under any group health plan (other than a plan that is excepted from COBRA—see Q&A-8 of this section). For purposes of section 106(b) and this Q&A-4, whether an individual is a highly compensated employee shall be determined on the basis of plan years or any alternative period permitted under section 414(q) and the regulations under that section. As used in the preceding sentence, "plan year" means the plan year as defined in Q&A-13 of this section.

(b) A failure of a group health plan to comply with section 162(k) that occurs before, and is not corrected by, the date that an employer maintaining the plan and another entity are first treated as a single employer under Q&A-5 of this section ("the combination date") will not result in an income inclusion for highly compensated employees of the other entity under paragraph (a) of this Q&A-4, so long as (1) the other entity did not also maintain the plan before the combination date, and (2) the failure is corrected before the end of the first taxable year of the other entity that begins after the combination date.

(c) The rules of this Q&A-4 are illustrated by the following examples, in which it is assumed that all individuals are calendar year taxpayers:

Example 1: Employer Z maintains group health plan T, and maintains no other group health plans. If plan T fails to comply with section 162(k) on November 10, 1988, and the failure is not corrected until February 15, 1989, each individual who is a highly compensated employee of Z at any time from November 10, 1988, through February 15, 1989, shall have coverage included in gross income for that individual's 1988 and 1989 taxable years. If the individual was covered under plan T throughout those years, the coverage included in 1988 is all coverage provided by employer Z under plan T on behalf of the individual and the individual's family during 1988, and the coverage included in 1989 is all coverage provided by employer Z under plan T on behalf of the individual and the individual's family during 1989.

Example 2: The facts are the same as in Example 1, except that employer Z's highly compensated employees are covered under plan U. Even if plan U complies with section 162(k) at all times, each individual who is a highly compensated employee of Z at any time from November 10, 1988, through February 15, 1989 (the period of plan T's noncompliance), shall have coverage included in gross income for that individual's 1988 and 1989 taxable years. If the individual was covered under plan U throughout those years, the coverage included in 1988 is all coverage provided by employer Z under plan U on behalf of the individual and the individual's family during 1988, and the coverage included in 1989 is all coverage provided by employer Z under plan U on behalf of the individual and the individual's family during 1989.

Example 3: The facts are the same as in Example 1, except that the failure to comply with section 162(k) is corrected on December 20, 1988, rather than on February 15, 1989. The income inclusion for highly compensated employees applies only for the 1988 taxable year and only to those individuals who are highly compensated employees of Z at some time from November 10 to December 20, 1988.

Example 4: The facts are the same as in Example 1. In addition, employer W maintains group health plan V, and maintains no other group health plans. Employer W's taxable year ends on May 31. Employer W becomes a wholly-owned subsidiary of employer Z on December 1, 1988. Plan T's failure to comply with section 162(k) that arises on November 10, 1988, does not result in an income inclusion to any of employer W's highly compensated employees because the failure is corrected on February 15, 1989, which is before May 31, 1990 (the end of employer W's first taxable year that begins after December 1, 1988). However, if another failure of Plan T to comply with section 162(k) arises on December 15, 1988, and that failure to comply is also corrected on February 15, 1989, each employee of employer W who is a highly compensated employee at any time from December 15, 1988, through February 15, 1989, is also subject to the income inclusion set forth in this Q&A-4.

Q-5: What is the employer?

A-5: For purposes of this § 1.162-26 and sections 106(b), 162(i), and 162(k), the term "employer" refers to the employer and any entity that is a member of a group described in section 414(b), (c), (m), or (o) that includes the employer, and to any successor of either the employer or such an entity. However, the rule of this Q&A-5 does not apply for purposes of determining whether a group health plan is a small-employer plan (see Q&A-9 of this section).

Q-6: How does COBRA apply to a group health plan before the effective date of this section?

A-6: This section is proposed to be effective when final regulations that include it are published in the FEDERAL REGISTER as a Treasury decision. Group health plans become subject to the COBRA continuation coverage requirements at different times, however, as set forth in Q&A-11 of this section. With respect to qualifying events that occur on or after the date that a plan became or becomes subject to those requirements and before the effective date of final regulations, the plan and the employer must operate in good faith compliance with a reasonable interpretation of the statutory requirements (i.e., title X of COBRA). For the period before the effective date of final regulations, the Internal Revenue Service will consider compliance with the terms of these proposed regulations to constitute good faith compliance with a reasonable interpretation of the statutory requirements (other than the statutory requirements regarding the computation of the applicable premium or the treatment, under section 9501 of the Omnibus Budget Reconciliation Act of 1986, of certain bankruptcies as qualifying events, which are not addressed in these proposed regulations). Moreover, plans and employers will be considered to be in compliance with the terms of these proposed regulations if, between June 15, 1987, and September 14, 1987, they operate in good faith compliance with a reasonable interpretation of the statutory requirements and, from September 15, 1987, until the effective date of final regulations, they operate in compliance with the terms of these proposed regulations. In addition, the Internal Revenue Service will not consider actions inconsistent with the terms of these proposed regulations necessarily to constitute a lack of good faith compliance with a reasonable interpretation of the statutory requirements; whether there has been good faith compliance with a reasonable interpretation of the statutory requirements will depend on all the facts and circumstances of each case.

WHICH PLANS MUST COMPLY AND WHEN

Q-7: What is a group health plan?

A-7: (a) A group health plan is any plan maintained by an employer to provide medical care (as defined in section 213(d)) to the employer's employees, former employees, or the families of such employees or former employees, whether directly or through insurance, reimbursement, or otherwise, and whether or not provided through an on-site facility (except as set forth in paragraph (e) of this Q&A-7), or through a cafeteria plan (as defined in section 125) or other flexible benefit arrangement. For purposes of this Q&A-7, insurance includes not only group insurance policies but also one or more individual insurance policies in any arrangement that involves the provision of medical care to two or more employees. A plan "maintained by an employer" is any plan of, or contributed to (directly or indirectly) by, an employer. Thus, a group health plan is "maintained by an employer," regardless of whether the employer contributes to it, if coverage under the plan would not be available at the same cost to an employee in the event that he or she were not employed by the employer. However, a plan that is maintained by an employee representative is not "maintained by an employer" if the employer does not contribute to the plan and has no involvement (e.g., payroll checkoff) in the operation of the plan. See Q&A-10 of this section for rules governing when a single arrangement is considered to be two or more separate group health plans.

(b) Medical care (as defined in section 213(d)) includes the diagnosis, cure, mitigation, treatment, or prevention of disease, and any other undertaking for the purpose of affecting any structure or function of the body. Medical care also includes transportation primarily for and essential to medical care as described in the preceding sentence. However, medical care does not include anything that is merely beneficial to the general health of an individual, such as a vacation. Thus, if an employer maintains a program that furthers general good health, but the program does not relate to the relief or alleviation of health or medical problems and is generally accessible to and used by employees without regard to their physical condition or state of health, that program is not considered a program that provides medical care and so is not a group health plan for purposes of this section.

(c) For example, if an employer maintains a spa, swimming pool, or exercise/fitness program that is normally accessible to and used by employees for reasons other than relief of health or medical problems, such a facility would not constitute medical care. In contrast, if the employer maintains a drug or alcohol treatment program or a health clinic, or any other facility or program that is intended to relieve or alleviate a physical condition or health problem (whether the condition or problem is chronic or acute), the facility or program is considered to be the provision of medical care and so is considered a group health plan for purposes of this section.

(d) Whether a benefit provided to employees constitutes medical care is not affected by whether the benefit is excludable from income under section 132 (relating to certain fringe benefits). For example, if a department store provides its employees discounted prices on all merchandise, including health care items such as drugs or eyeglasses, the mere fact that the discounted prices also apply to health care items will not cause the program to be a plan providing medical care, so long as the discount program would normally be accessible to and used by employees without regard to health needs or physical condition. If, however, the employer maintaining the discount program is a health clinic, so that the program is used exclusively by employees with health or medical needs, the program is considered as a plan providing medical care and so is considered a group health plan for purposes of this section.

(e) The provision of medical care at a facility that is located on the premises of an employer does not constitute a group health plan if (1) the medical care consists primarily of first aid that is provided during the employer's working hours for treatment of a health condition, illness, or injury that occurs during those working hours, (2) the medical care is available only to the employer's current employees, and (3) employees are not charged for the use of the facility.

Q-8: What group health plans are subject to COBRA?

A-8: (a) All group health plans are subject to COBRA (i.e., subject to section 162(k)) except group health plans described in section 106(b)(2). However, a group health plan is not subject to COBRA before the effective date prescribed for that plan in Q&A-11 of this section.

(b) The following group health plans are described in section 106(b)(2): (1) small-employer plans (see Q&A-9 of this section), (2) church plans (within the meaning of section 414(e)), and (3) governmental plans (within the meaning of section 414(d)). Plans that are described in section 106(b)(2) are referred to in this §1.162-26 as "excepted from COBRA." The income inclusion rule of section 106(b)(1), the deduction denial rule of section 162(i), and the continuation coverage requirements of section 162(k) do not apply with respect to group health plans that are excepted from COBRA. Certain governmental plans, however, are governed by parallel requirements that were added by section 10003 of COBRA to the Public Health Service Act, which is administered by the Department of Health and Human Services.

Q-9: What is a small-employer plan?

A-9: (a) A "small-employer plan" is a group health plan maintained by one or more employers where each of the employers maintaining the plan for a calendar year normally employed fewer than 20 employees during the preceding calendar year. For purposes of this definition, each employer maintaining the plan shall, in combination with all other entities under common control with that employer (as determined under section 52(a) and (b)), be considered a single employer. See Q&A-10 of this section for rules governing when a single arrangement is considered to be two or more separate group health plans.

(b) An employer is considered as having normally employed fewer than 20 employees during a particular calendar year if, and only if, it had fewer than 20 employees on at least 50 percent of its working days during that year.

(c) In determining the number of its employees, an employer shall treat as employees all full-time and part-time employees, and all employees within the meaning of section 401(c)(1). For example, partners in a law firm are treated as employees for this purpose. An employer shall also treat as employees for this purpose all agents and independent contractors (and their employees, agents, and independent contractors, if any), and all directors (in the case of a corporation), but only if such individuals are eligible to participate in a group health plan maintained by the employer.

(d) The determination of whether a plan is a small-employer plan on any particular date depends on which employers are maintaining the plan on that date and on the workforce of those employers during the preceding calendar year. If a plan that is otherwise subject to COBRA ceases to be a small-employer plan because of the addition during a calendar year of an employer that did not normally employ fewer than 20 employees on a typical business day during the preceding calendar year, the plan ceases to be excepted from COBRA and section 162(k) becomes effective with respect to it immediately upon the addition of the new employer. In contrast, if the plan ceases to be a small-employer plan by reason of an increase during a calendar year in the workforce of an employer maintaining the plan, the plan ceases to be excepted from CORBA and section 162(k) becomes effective with respect to it on the January 1 immediately following the calendar year in which the employer's workforce increased. However, a plan described in the preceding sentence will be treated as not having become subject to section 162(k) on that January 1 (i.e., still excepted from COBRA) if all the employers who did not normally employ fewer than 20 employees in the preceding calendar year have ceased to maintain the plan by the February 1 immediately following that January 1. For example, if each employer maintaining a group health plan normally employs fewer than 20 employees during each of 1986 and 1987 but two of the employers do not normally employ fewer than 20 employees during 1988, the entire plan becomes subject to COBRA and must begin to comply with section 162(k) on January 1, 1989, even if the plan year is not a calendar year, unless those two employers depart from the plan before February 1, 1989.

Q-10: When is an arrangement considered to be two or more separate group health plans rather than a single group health plan?

A-10: (a) The rules below in paragraphs (b) through (g) of this Q&A-10 determine when an arrangement is considered to be two or more separate group health plans. If more than one of those paragraphs applies to a particular arrangement, the paragraphs are applied in succession to break the arrangement into the smallest possible group health plans. For example, if an arrangement offers high option and low option benefit schedules (see paragraph (c)) and constitutes a multiple employer welfare arrangement maintained by three different employers (see paragraph (d)), the arrangement consists of six separate group health plans: three high-option plans (one for each employer) and three low-option plans (one for each employer).

(b) The rules in this Q&A-10 apply without regard to whether the arrangement is maintained by one or more than one employer. Moreover, the fact that a particular arrangement has been traditionally referred to as a single plan or has reported as a single plan (e.g., by filing a single Form 5500) is not controlling in the determination of whether the arrangement will be considered as two or more separate plans for purposes of section 162(k). All references elsewhere in this section to a "group health plan" are references to a separate group health plan as determined under this Q&A-10. The identification of separate group health plans is relevant to determinations such as those involving which coverage must be separately electable, the effective date of section 162(k), which employers will be denied deductions in the event of a failure to comply with section 162(k), the cost of a continuation coverage, and the availability of the exception for small-employer plans (see Q&A-9 of this section). The relevance of treating an arrangement as two or more separate group health plans is illustrated by the following examples:

Example 1: If an employee is covered under more than one group health plan at the time of a qualifying event, the qualified beneficiaries must be offered an opportunity to elect COBRA continuation coverage with respect to each of the plans. In contrast, if the arrangement in which the employee participates is treated as a single group health plan with several features, no individual feature of the plan would have to be made available to a qualified beneficiary unless the qualified beneficiary elects coverage under the entire plan. (But see Q&A-24 of this section regarding the election to receive only core coverage.)

Example 2: If an arrangement that involves many employers is considered to be a single group health plan, that plan will fail to qualify for the small-employer plan exception if any one of those employers had too many employees during the preceding calendar year. However, if the arrangement is considered to be a separate plan with respect to each employer, then the exception would be available for each of those particular employers that normally employed fewer than 20 employees during the preceding calendar year.

Example 3: An arrangement covering the employees of unrelated employers A and B fails to comply with section 162(k) by failing to offer COBRA continuation coverage to an employee of employer A, but complies with section 162(k) in all other respects. If the arrangement consists of two separate group health plans, one covering the employees of A and one covering the employees of B, employer A will lose deductions under section 162(i) and A's highly compensated employees will lose the benefit of the section 106(a) exclusion, but employer B and its employees will be unaffected. In contrast, if the arrangement consists of a single group health plan, the consequences of failing to comply with section 162(k) will apply to both employers A and B.

(c) Each different benefit package or option offered under an arrangement is treated as a separate group health plan. For this purpose, self-only coverage and self-and-family coverage are not considered to be separate packages or options. The rule of this paragraph (c) is illustrated by the following examples:

Example 1: If an arrangement offers "high option" and "low option" benefit schedules and the alternatives of self-only and self-and-family coverage, the arrangement is considered to be two separate plans: one offering high option coverage (whether self-only or self-and-family), and one offering low option coverage (whether self-only or self-and-family).

Example 2: If two types of coverage differ only because one has a $100 deductible and the other has a $250 deductible, or because one has a $1,500 catastrophic limit and the other has a $2,500 catastrophic limit, each type of coverage is a different benefit package and so is treated as a separate group health plan.

Example 3: An arrangement has a deductible equal to 1 percent of compensation, but consists of a single plan in all other respects. The fact that employees with different levels of compensation will have different deductibles will not cause the arrangement to be treated as separate group health plans for each resulting deductible.

Example 4: If an arrangement consists of a single plan in all respects except that an employee can choose to have either hospital benefits or hospital benefits combined with mental health benefits, there are two separate plans: one providing hospital coverage, and one providing hospital-and-mental-health coverage. If an employee could instead choose independently whether to have hospital benefits and whether to have mental-health benefits, there would also be two separate plans: one providing hospital-only coverage and one providing mental-health-only coverage. In such a case an employee receiving both hospital and mental-health benefits would be covered under two separate group health plans and would have separate COBRA election rights under each plan.

(d) An arrangement that constitutes a multiple employer welfare arrangement as defined in section 3(40) of the Employee Retirement Income Security Act of 1974 (ERISA) is considered a separate group health plan with respect to each employer maintaining the arrangement. Solely for purposes of this paragraph (d), the rules of section 3(40)(B) of ERISA (regarding trades or businesses under common control) shall apply in determining whether two or more employers are treated as a single employer.

(e) In the case of an insured arrangement, if two or more groups of employees are covered under separate contracts between a participating employer or employers and an insurer or insurers, each separate contract is considered a separate group health plan, even if the coverage under the separate contracts is identical.

(f) In the case of a self-funded arrangement, each segregated portion of the arrangement shall be considered a separate group health plan. A portion of an arrangement is a segregated portion if and only if (1) assets available to pay benefits under that portion are unavailable to pay benefits under any other portion, and (2) assets available to pay benefits under any other portion are unavailable to pay benefits out of that portion. For example, if several employers contribute to a trust that provides medical benefits but each employee's benefits are payable only out of contributions (and earnings on contributions) made by that employee's employer, each employer's portion of the arrangement is considered a separate group health plan. The rule of this paragraph (f) shall apply whether or not a trust is used, and whether or not the arrangement is partially insured through stop-loss insurance, insurance for some but not all benefits, or some other method.

(g) Arrangements providing medical benefits are broken down as described in Q&A-12 of this section into their collectively bargained portion (if any) and non-collectively bargained portion (if any), each of which is considered a separate group health plan.

Q-11: When must group health plans comply with section 162(k)?

A-11: (a) Non-collectively bargained plans: For plans that are not excepted from COBRA (see Q&A-8 of this section) and that do not constitute collectively bargained group health plans (see Q&A-12 of this section), the requirements of section 162(k) apply as of the first day of the first plan year beginning on or after July 1, 1986. For example, if such a plan has a February 1 to January 31 plan year, it must begin to comply with section 162(k) by February 1, 1987.

(b) Collectively bargained plans: For plans that are not excepted from COBRA and that constitute collectively bargained group health plans (see Q&A-12 of this section), the requirements of section 162(k) apply as of the first day of the first plan year beginning on or after the later of (1) January 1, 1987, or (2) the date on which the last of the collective bargaining agreements relating to the plan terminates (determined without regard to any extension thereof agreed to after April 7, 1986). This rule is illustrated by the following example:

Example: Assume that the plan year of a collectively bargained group health plan is the calendar year and that, as of April 7, 1986, the plan is maintained pursuant to three collective bargaining agreements having expiration dates in October 1987, February 1988, and July 1988. The plan must comply with section 162(k) beginning on January 1, 1989. Of course, the plan must begin to comply by January 1, 1987, with respect to a collective bargaining unit that was not, as of April 7, 1986, covered by one of those three agreements.

Q-12: What is a collectively bargained group health plan?

A-12: (a) A collectively bargained group health plan is a group health plan covering only employees and former employees (and their families) who are covered by an agreement that is a collective bargaining agreement entered into between employee representatives and one or more employers (as determined under section 7701(a)(46)). Thus, if an arrangement that would otherwise be considered to be a single group health plan under the standards set out in Q&A-10 of this section covers both (1) employees and former employees (and their families) who are covered by a collective bargaining agreement described in the preceding sentence and (2) employees and former employees (and their families) who are not covered by such an agreement, the arrangement consists of two separate group health plans: one plan that is a collectively bargained group health plan and one that is not. The plan that is collectively bargained will have an effective date determined under paragraph (b) of Q&A-11 of this section, and the other plan will have an effective date determined under paragraph (a) of Q&A-11 of this section. For example, if the plan year is the calendar year and the only collective bargaining agreement in effect as of April 7, 1986, expires March 31, 1988, the effective date of section 162(k) is January 1, 1989, for the plan covering bargaining-unit employees and their families, and January 1, 1987, for the plan covering the other employees and their families.

(b) For purposes of this Q&A-12, employees of an employee representative that is a party to a collective bargaining agreement described in paragraph (a) of this Q&A-12, and employees of a trust or fund maintained to pay benefits to individuals covered by the collective bargaining agreement, are considered to be employees covered by that collective bargaining agreement. Thus, a plan that is otherwise considered a single, collectively bargained plan will not fail to be a single, collectively bargained plan merely because it also covers employees or former employees (and their families) of the employee representative or of a trust or fund from which the benefits are paid.

Q-13: What is the plan year of a group health plan?

A-13: (a) For purposes of determining when a group health plan must begin to comply with section 162(k) (see Q&A-11 of this section), the plan year of a group health plan is the year that is designated as the plan year in the plan document. However, if the plan document does not designate a plan year, or if there is no plan document, the plan year is determined under paragraph (b) of this Q&A-13. The designation of a plan year on a Form 5500 filed by a group health plan is not controlling in the determination of the plan year under this Q&A-13.

(b) If the plan year of a group health plan is determined under this paragraph (b), the plan year is the plan's limit/deductible year except that (1) in the case of an insured group health plan, the plan year is the policy year if that is later than the limit/deductible year or if the plan has no limit/deductible year, and (2) in the case of a self-funded group health plan having no limit/deductible year, the plan year is the later of the calendar year or the employer's taxable year. For purposes of this paragraph (b), a plan's "limit/deductible year" means the year that is used by the plan in applying benefit limits and deductibles, except that if different years are used for benefit limits and for deductibles, it means the later of those years. For purposes of this paragraph (b), one year is "later" than another if it begins later in relation to the underlying date from which the effective date of section 162(k) is determined for the plan under Q&A-11 of this section. Compare, for example, a year that begins on March 1 with a year that begins on December 1. The March 1 year is later than a December 1 year in the case of a non-collectively bargained plan, because the first March 1 occurring on or after July 1, 1986, is March 1, 1987, which is later than December 1, 1986 (the first December 1 occurring on or after July 1, 1986). If, however, the plan is a collectively bargained plan and becomes subject to section 162(k) for the first plan year beginning on or after February 1, 1987, a December 1 year is later than a March 1 year.

Q-14: How do the COBRA continuation coverage requirements apply to cafeteria plans and other flexible benefit arrangements?

A-14: The provision of medical care through a cafeteria plan (as defined in section 125) or other flexible benefit arrangement constitutes a group health plan. However, the COBRA continuation coverage requirements of section 162(k) apply only to those medical benefits under the cafeteria plan or other arrangement that a covered employee has actually chosen to receive (if any). The application of this rule to a cafeteria plan is illustrated by the following examples:

Example 1: Under the terms of a cafeteria plan, employees can choose among life insurance coverage, membership in a Health Maintenance Organization (HMO), coverage for medical expenses under an indemnity arrangement, and cash compensation. Of these available choices, the HMO and the indemnity arrangement constitute separate group health plans. Assume that these group health plans are subject to COBRA (see Q&A-8 of this section) and that the employer does not provide any group health plan outside of the cafeteria plan. Assume further that B and C are unmarried employees, that B has chosen the life insurance coverage, and that C has chosen the indemnity arrangement. B does not have to be offered COBRA continuation coverage upon terminating employment, nor must a subsequent open enrollment period for active employees be made available to B. However, if C terminates employment and the termination constitutes a qualifying event, C must be offered an opportunity to elect COBRA continuation coverage under the indemnity arrangement. If C makes such an election and an open enrollment period for active employees occurs while C is still receiving the COBRA continuation coverage, C must be offered the opportunity to switch from the indemnity arrangement to the HMO (but not to the life insurance coverage because that does not constitute a group health plan).

Example 2: An employer maintains a group health plan under which all employees receive employer-paid coverage. Employees can arrange to cover their families by paying an additional amount. The employer also maintains a cafeteria plan, under which one of the options is to pay part or all of the charge for family coverage under the group health plan. Thus, an employee might pay for family coverage under the group health plan partly with before-tax dollars and partly with after-tax dollars. If an employee's family is receiving coverage under the group health plan when a qualifying event occurs, each of the qualified beneficiaries must be offered an opportunity to elect COBRA continuation coverage, regardless of how that qualified beneficiary's coverage was paid for before the qualifying event.

Example 3: One of the choices available under a cafeteria plan is an individual medical expense reimbursement arrangement. At the beginning of each calendar year, an employee can choose, instead of being paid a specified dollar amount of compensation, to have that amount placed in an account to be used for reimbursement of medical expenses incurred during the year by the employee or the employee's spouse or dependent children. Any amount remaining in the account as of the end of the year is forfeited. The reimbursement of medical expenses through these arrangements constitutes a group health plan.

QUALIFIED BENEFICIARIES

Q-15: Who is a qualified beneficiary?

A-15: (a) Except as set forth in paragraphs (b) through (d) of this Q&A-15, a qualified beneficiary is any individual who, on the day before a qualifying event, is covered under a group health plan maintained by the employer of a covered employee by virtue of being on that day either (1) the covered employee, (2) the spouse of the covered employee, or (3) the dependent child of the covered employee.

(b) An individual is not a qualified beneficiary if, on the day before the qualifying event referred to in paragraph (a) of this Q&A-15, the individual (1) is covered under the group health plan by reason of another individual's election of COBRA continuation coverage and is not already a qualified beneficiary by reason of a prior qualifying event, or (2) is entitled to Medicare benefits under Title XVIII of the Social Security Act.

(c) A covered employee can be a qualified beneficiary only in connection with a qualifying event that consists of the termination (other than by reason of the covered employee's gross misconduct), or reduction of hours, of the covered employee's employment.

(d) An individual is not a qualified beneficiary if the individual's status as a covered employee is attributable to a period in which the individual was a nonresident alien who received no earned income (within the meaning of section 911(d)(2)) from the individual's employer that constituted income from sources within the United States (within the meaning of section 861(a)(3)). If, pursuant to the preceding sentence, an individual is not a qualified beneficiary, then a spouse or dependent child of the individual shall not be considered a qualified beneficiary by virtue of the relationship to the individual.

Q-16: Who is a covered employee?

A-16: (a) A covered employee is any individual who is (or was) provided coverage under a group health plan (other than a plan that is excepted from COBRA on the date of the qualifying event; see Q&A-8 of this section) by virtue of the individual's employment or previous employment with an employer. For example, a retiree or former employee who is covered by such a group health plan is a covered employee if the coverage results in whole or in part from his or her previous employment. An individual (whether a present or former employee) who is merely eligible for coverage under a group health plan is not a covered employee if the individual is not and has not been actually covered under the plan. The reason for an individual's lack of actual coverage (such as the individual's having declined participation in the plan or failed to satisfy the plan's conditions for participation) is not relevant for this purpose.

(b) The following individuals are also covered employees, but only if they are (or were) actually covered under a group health plan by virtue of their relationship to an employer maintaining the plan, and only if that plan or some other group health plan maintained by the employer covers one or more common-law employees of the employer: (1) employees within the meaning of section 401(c)(1), (2) agents and independent contractors (and their employees, agents, and independent contractors), and (3) directors (in the case of a corporation). The rule of this paragraph (b) is illustrated by the following example:

Example: A law firm maintains a group health plan for its common-law employees. If the firm also provides group health coverage for its partners, the partners are covered employees regardless of whether their coverage is provided under the same group health plan as the common-law employees or under a separate plan. In contrast, if the partners are the only individuals who receive any health coverage, they are not covered employees.

Q-17: Other than those individuals who are qualified beneficiaries as of the day before a qualifying event, can any other person (such as a newborn or adopted child or a new spouse) obtain qualified beneficiary status for COBRA continuation coverage purposes?

A-17: (a) No. The group of qualified beneficiaries entitled to elect COBRA continuation coverage as a result of a qualifying event is closed as of the day before the qualifying event. Thus, newborn children, adopted children, and spouses who join the family of a qualified beneficiary after that day do not become qualified beneficiaries. The new family members do not themselves become qualified beneficiaries even if they become covered under the plan. (For situations in which a plan is required to make coverage available to new family members of a qualified beneficiary who is receiving COBRA continuation coverage, see Q&A-31 of this section and paragraph (c) of Q&A-30 of this section.)

(b) A qualified beneficiary who fails to elect COBRA continuation coverage in connection with a qualifying event ceases to be a qualified beneficiary at the end of the election period (see Q&A-32 of this section). Thus, for example, if such a former qualified beneficiary is later added to a covered employee's coverage (e.g., during an open enrollment period) and then another qualifying event occurs with respect to the covered employee, the former qualified beneficiary will not be treated as a qualified beneficiary.

(c) The rules of this Q&A-17 are illustrated by the following examples:

Example 1: Assume that A is a single employee who voluntarily terminates employment and properly elects COBRA continuation coverage under a group health plan. Under the terms of the plan, a covered employee who marries can choose to have his or her spouse covered under the plan as of the date of marriage. One month after electing COBRA continuation coverage, A marries and chooses to cover A's spouse under the plan. A's spouse is not a qualified beneficiary. Thus, if A dies during the period of COBRA continuation coverage, the plan does not have to offer A's surviving spouse an opportunity to elect COBRA continuation coverage.

Example 2: Assume that B is a married employee who terminates employment, B properly elects COBRA continuation coverage for B but not B's spouse, and B's spouse declines to elect such coverage. B's spouse thus ceases to be a qualified beneficiary. Later, at the next open enrollment period, B adds the spouse as a beneficiary under the plan. The addition of the spouse during the open enrollment period does not make the spouse a qualified beneficiary. The plan will thus not have to offer the spouse an opportunity to elect COBRA continuation coverage upon a later divorce from or death of B.

Example 3: Assume that, under the terms of a group health plan, a covered employee's child ceases to be a dependent eligible for coverage upon attaining age 18. At that time, the child must be offered an opportunity to elect COBRA continuation coverage. If the child elects COBRA continuation coverage, the child marries during the period of the COBRA continuation coverage, and the child's spouse becomes covered under the group health plan, the child's spouse would not become a qualified beneficiary upon a later qualifying event as a result of that coverage.

Example 4: Assume that C is a single employee who, upon retirement, is given the opportunity to elect COBRA continuation coverage but declines it in favor of an alternative offer of 12 months of employer-paid retiree health benefits. C ceases to be a qualified beneficiary and will not have to be given another opportunity to elect COBRA continuation coverage at the end of those 12 months. Assume further that C marries D during the period of retiree health coverage and, under the terms of that coverage, D becomes covered under the plan. If a divorce from or death of C will result in D's losing coverage, D will be a qualified beneficiary because D's coverage under the plan on the day before the qualifying event (i.e., the divorce) will have been by reason of C's acceptance of 12 months of employer-paid coverage after the prior qualifying event (C's retirement) rather than by reason of an election of COBRA continuation coverage.

Example 5: Assume the same facts as in Example 4 except that, under the terms of the plan, the divorce or death does not cause D to lose coverage so that D continues to be covered for the balance of the original 12-month period. D does not have to be allowed to elect COBRA continuation coverage because the divorce or death does not constitute a qualifying event. See Q&A-18 of this section.

QUALIFYING EVENTS

Q-18: What is a qualifying event?

A-18: (a) A qualifying event is an event that satisfies paragraphs (b), (c), and (d) of this Q&A-18.

(b) An event satisfies this paragraph (b) if the event is either (1) the death of a covered employee, (2) the termination (other than by reason of the employee's gross misconduct), or reduction of hours, of a covered employee's employment, (3) the divorce or legal separation of a covered employee from the employee's spouse, (4) a covered employee becoming entitled to Medicare benefits under Title XVIII of the Social Security Act, or (5) a dependent child ceasing to be a dependent child of the covered employee under the generally applicable requirements of the plan. In the case of a covered employee who is not a common-law employee, termination of "employment" for this purpose means termination of the relationship (e.g., directorship of a corporation or membership in a partnership) giving rise to the individual's treatment as a covered employee under paragraph (b) of Q&A-16 of this section.

(c) An event satisfies this paragraph (c) if, under the terms of the group health plan, the event causes the covered employee, or the spouse or a dependent child of the covered employee, to lose coverage under the plan. For this purpose, to "lose coverage" means to cease to be covered under the same terms and conditions as in effect immediately before the qualifying event. If coverage is reduced or eliminated in anticipation of an event, the reduction or elimination is disregarded in determining whether the event causes a loss of coverage. Moreover, for purposes of this paragraph (c), a loss of coverage need not occur immediately after the event, so long as the loss of coverage will occur before the end of the maximum coverage period (see Q&A-39 and Q&A-40 of this section). However, if neither the covered employee nor the spouse or a dependent child of the covered employee will lose coverage before the end of what would be the maximum coverage period, the event does not satisfy this paragraph (c).

(d) An event satisfies this paragraph (d) if it occurs while the plan is subject to COBRA. Thus, an event will not satisfy this paragraph (d) if it occurs before the plan becomes subject to section 162(k) (see Q&A-11 of this section) or while the plan is excepted from COBRA (see Q&A-8). See Q&A-20 and Q&A-21 of this section.

(e) The rules of this Q&A-18 are illustrated by the following examples, each of which assumes that paragraph (d) is satisfied:

Example 1: If an employee who is covered by a group health plan terminates employment (other than by reason of the employee's gross misconduct) and, as of the date of separation, is given 3 months of employer-paid coverage under the same terms and conditions as before that date, the termination is a qualifying event because it satisfies both paragraphs (b) and (c) of this Q&A-18.

Example 2: Upon the retirement of an employee who, along with the employee's spouse, has been covered under a group health plan, the employee is given identical coverage for life but the spousal coverage will not be continued beyond 6 months unless premiums are then paid by the employee or spouse. The spouse will "lose coverage" 6 months after the employee's retirement when the premium requirement takes effect, so the retirement is a qualifying event and the spouse must be given an opportunity to elect COBRA continuation coverage.

Example 3: F is a covered employee who is married to G, and both are covered under a group health plan maintained by F's employer. F and G are divorced and, under the terms of the plan, the divorce will cause G to lose coverage. The divorce is a qualifying event. If G elects COBRA continuation coverage and then remarries during the period of COBRA continuation coverage, G's new spouse might become covered under the plan. (See Q&A-31 of this section and paragraph (c) of Q&A-30 of this section.) However, G's later death or divorce from G's new spouse will not be a qualifying event because G is not a covered employee.

Q-19: Can a qualifying event result from a voluntary termination of employment?

A-19: Yes. Apart from gross misconduct, the facts surrounding a termination or reduction of hours are irrelevant. It does not matter whether the employee voluntarily terminated or was discharged. For example, a strike or walkout is a termination or reduction of hours that constitutes a qualifying event if the strike or walkout results in a loss of coverage as described in paragraph (c) of Q&A-18 of this section. Similarly, a layoff that results in such a loss of coverage is a qualifying event.

Q-20: Can a qualifying event occur before the effective date of section 162(k) (as described in Q&A-11 of this section)?

A-20: No. An event that occurs before section 162(k) becomes effective for a group health plan does not satisfy paragraph (d) of the definition of qualifying event in Q&A-18 of this section. A group health plan does not have to offer individuals whose coverage ends as a result of such an event the opportunity to elect COBRA continuation coverage. For example, if an employee terminated employment on July 15, 1986, and the plan covering the employee had a November 1, to October 31 plan year (so that the plan became subject to section 162(k) on November 1, 1986), the plan docs not have to permit the employee to elect COBRA continuation coverage. Even if that employee is given 6 months of additional coverage from the July 15, 1986, termination date (whether merely as a result of the terms of the plan, or pursuant to state or local law or otherwise) so that the coverage extends beyond the November 1 effective date, the employee does not have to be given the opportunity to elect COBRA continuation coverage at the end of the 6 months' coverage because there will be no qualifying event at that time. In contrast, if the employee's spouse is covered by the 6 months' coverage and, as a result of the employee's death after the November 1 effective date and before the end of the 6-month period, the spouse will lose coverage for the balance of the 6-month period, the death will constitute a qualifying event and the spouse will be a qualified beneficiary entitled to elect COBRA continuation coverage. See Q&A-42 of this section regarding the maximum coverage period in such a case.

Q-21: Can a qualifying event occur while a group health plan is excepted from COBRA (see Q&A-8 of this section)?

A-21: No. An event that occurs while a group health plan is excepted from COBRA does not satisfy paragraph (d) of the definition of qualifying event in Q&A-18 of this section. Even if the plan later becomes subject to COBRA, it does not have to provide COBRA election rights to anyone whose coverage ends as a result of such an event. For example, if a group health plan is excepted from COBRA as a small-employer plan during 1988 (see Q&A-9 of this section) and an employee terminates employment on December 31, 1988, the termination is not a qualifying event and the plan does not have to permit the employee to elect COBRA continuation coverage. This is the case even if the plan ceases to be a small-employer plan as of January 1, 1989. Also, the same result will follow even if the employee is given 3 months of coverage beyond December 31 (i.e., through March of 1989), because there will be no qualifying event as of the termination of coverage in March. However, if the employee's spouse is initially provided with the 3-month coverage through March 1989, but the spouse divorces the employee before the end of the 3 months and loses coverage as a result of the divorce, the divorce will constitute a qualifying event during 1989 and so entitle the spouse to elect COBRA continuation coverage. See Q&A-42 of this section regarding the maximum coverage period in such a case.

COBRA CONTINUATION COVERAGE

Q-22: What is COBRA continuation coverage?

A-22: If a qualifying event occurs, each qualified beneficiary (other than a qualified beneficiary for whom the qualifying event will not result in any immediate or deferred loss of coverage) must be offered an opportunity to elect to continue to receive the group health plan coverage that he or she received immediately before the qualifying event. This continued coverage is "COBRA continuation coverage." Except as set forth in Q&A-23 through Q&A-31 of this section, if the continuation coverage offered differs in any way from the coverage enjoyed immediately before the qualifying event, the coverage offered does not constitute COBRA continuation coverage and the group health plan is not in compliance with section 162(k) unless other coverage that does constitute COBRA continuation coverage is also offered. Any elimination or reduction of coverage in anticipation of a qualifying event is disregarded for purposes of this Q&A-22 and for purposes of any other reference in this section to coverage in effect immediately before (or on the day before) a qualifying event. COBRA continuation coverage must not be conditioned upon, or discriminate on the basis of lack of, evidence of insurability.

Q-23: How is COBRA continuation coverage affected by changes in the coverage that is provided to similarly situated beneficiaries with respect to whom a qualifying event has not occurred?

A-23: COBRA continuation coverage must generally be the same as the group health plan coverage enjoyed by the qualified beneficiary immediately before the qualifying event. However, if the coverage provided to similarly situated active employees is changed or eliminated but the employer continues to maintain one or more group health plans (so that the qualified beneficiary's COBRA continuation coverage cannot be terminated at that time—see Q&A-37 of this section), the employer must permit the qualified beneficiary receiving COBRA continuation coverage to elect to be covered under any of the remaining group health plans maintained by the employer for similarly situated active employees. If the coverage of the qualified beneficiary was subject to deductibles and the change in coverage occurs before the end of the prescribed period for accumulating such deductibles, the new coverage selected by the qualified beneficiary must credit him or her with the amounts incurred under the original coverage. The rule in the preceding sentence also applies to those limits that are in the nature of deductibles, such as copayment limits or catastrophic limits on a covered individual's out-of-pocket expenses. The qualified beneficiary can be charged the amount determined under Q&A-44 of this section for the coverage selected.

Q-24: Can a group health plan require a qualified beneficiary who wishes to receive COBRA continuation coverage to elect to receive a continuation of all of the coverage that he or she was receiving under the plan immediately before the qualifying event?

A-24: (a) In general, no. A qualified beneficiary who, immediately before the qualifying event, is covered by a plan that provides both core coverage and non-core coverage must be able to elect to receive either (1) the coverage that he or she had immediately before the qualifying event (including the core coverage and any non-core coverage), or (2) the core coverage only. However, there are two exceptions to this rule, as set forth in paragraphs (b) and (c) of this Q&A-24.

(b) If the applicable premium for core coverage would be at least 95 percent of the applicable premium for core coverage and non-core coverage combined, the plan does not have to offer qualified beneficiaries the opportunity to elect core coverage only. (See Q&A-44 of this section regarding the applicable premium.)

(c) If an employer maintaining a group health plan that includes non-core coverage also maintains at least one other group health plan for similarly situated active employees that does not provide any non-core coverage, the plan that includes non-core coverage does not have to offer a qualified beneficiary an opportunity to elect core coverage only. However, the qualified beneficiary must instead be offered the opportunity to elect coverage under any other group health plan maintained by the employer for similarly situated active employees.

Q-25: What is core coverage?

A-25: (a) "Core coverage" means all of the coverage that a qualified beneficiary was receiving under the group health plan immediately before a qualifying event that gives rise to the qualified beneficiary's COBRA election rights, other than "non-core coverage." "Non-core coverage" means coverage for vision benefits and dental benefits. However, coverage for vision benefits or dental benefits that must be provided under applicable law is core coverage.

(b) For purposes of this Q&A-25, vision benefits include only those benefits related to vision care of a type that is not required under local law to be performed by a physician.

(c) For purposes of this Q&A-25, dental benefits does not include any benefits for dental care or oral surgery in connection with an accidental injury.

(d) The definitions in this Q&A-25 apply only for purposes of this § 1.162-26 and sections 106, 162(i)(2), and 162(k) of the Code.

Q-26: Must a qualified beneficiary be given an opportunity to elect core coverage plus only one of two non-core coverages that the qualified beneficiary had under the plan immediately before the qualifying event?

A-26: No. A group health plan is required only to offer qualified beneficiaries the right to elect (a) core coverage, or (b) core coverage plus all non-core coverages that the qualified beneficiary had immediately before the qualifying event. Thus, a qualified beneficiary who has core coverage plus vision and dental coverage upon the occurrence of a qualifying event must be offered the opportunity to continue either the core coverage or the core coverage and both dental and vision coverage. Such a qualified beneficiary would not have to be offered the opportunity to elect core coverage plus vision coverage only or core coverage plus dental coverage only. Of course, if the vision and dental coverage are provided under two separate plans that are independent of the core plan, a qualified beneficiary would be able to continue one or both of the coverages. Assume, for example, that an employer maintains three group health plans—a core plan, a vision plan, and a dental plan—and that each active employee can elect to be covered under one or more of the three plans. (Thus, an employee could have vision-only, dental-only, or core-only coverage, or any combination of the three.) A qualified beneficiary who is covered under all three plans at the time of a qualifying event would have separate election rights with respect to each plan, and so would be able to elect coverage under the dental-only and core-only plans.

Q-27: Must a qualified beneficiary who is covered under a single plan providing both core coverage and non-core coverage be offered the opportunity to elect non-core coverage only?

A-27: No. A qualified beneficiary who is covered by a single plan providing both core coverage and non-core coverage need not be offered the opportunity to elect only non-core coverage. Of course, if immediately before the qualifying event the qualified beneficiary is covered by a group health plan that provides non-core coverage but no core coverage, the qualified beneficiary must be offered the opportunity to continue that non-core coverage. Moreover, such an individual generally would not have to be given the opportunity to elect core coverage. (But see Q&A-30 of this section regarding open enrollment periods.)

Q-28: What deductibles apply if COBRA continuation coverage is elected?

A-28: (a) Qualified beneficiaries electing COBRA continuation coverage are generally subject to the same deductibles as similarly situated employees for whom a qualifying event has not occurred. If a qualified beneficiary's COBRA continuation coverage begins before the end of the prescribed period for accumulating amounts toward deductibles, the qualified beneficiary must retain credit for expenses incurred toward those deductibles before the beginning of COBRA continuation coverage as though the qualifying event had not occurred. The specific application of this rule depends on the type of deductible, as set forth in paragraphs (b) through (d) of this Q&A-28. Special rules are set forth in paragraphs (e) and (f), and examples appear in paragraph (g).

(b) If a deductible is computed separately for each individual receiving coverage under the plan, each individual's remaining deductible amount (if any) on the date that COBRA continuation coverage begins is equal to that individual's remaining deductible amount immediately before that date.

(c) If a deductible is computed on a family basis, the deductible for each new family unit after the beginning of COBRA continuation coverage (or the existing family unit, in the case of a qualifying event that does not result in there being more than one family unit) is computed as follows: On the date that COBRA continuation coverage begins, the remaining deductible amount for each new family unit (or the remaining number of individual deductibles, in the case of a family deductible that is satisfied by completing a specified number of individual deductibles) is equal to the preexisting family unit's remaining deductible amount (or remaining number of individual deductibles, as applicable) immediately before that date. This rule applies regardless of whether the plan provides that the family deductible is an alternative to individual deductibles or an additional requirement.

(d) Deductibles that are not described in paragraphs (b) or (c) of this Q&A-28 must be treated in a manner consistent with the principles set forth in those paragraphs.

(e) If a deductible is computed on the basis of a covered employee's compensation instead of being a fixed dollar amount, the plan can treat the employee's compensation as frozen for the duration of the COBRA continuation coverage at the level that was used to compute the deductible in effect immediately before the COBRA continuation coverage began.

(f) If a single deductible is prescribed for core coverage and non-core coverage and a qualified beneficiary electing COBRA continuation coverage elects to receive core coverage only, the treatment of expenses for non-core coverage depends on when the expenses were incurred, as follows: if the expenses were incurred before the beginning of COBRA continuation coverage, they must continue to be counted toward satisfaction of the deductible, but they need not be counted if they were incurred after the beginning of COBRA continuation coverage.

(g) The rules of this Q&A-28 are illustrated by the following examples; in each example it is assumed that deductibles are determined on a calendar year basis:

Example 1: A group health plan applies a separate $100 annual deductible to each individual whom it covers. The plan provides that the spouse and dependent children of a covered employee will lose coverage on the last day of the month after the month of the covered employee's death. A covered employee dies on June 11, 1988. The spouse and the two dependent children elect COBRA continuation coverage, which will begin on August 1, 1988. As of July 31, 1988, the spouse has incurred $80 of covered expenses, the older child has incurred no covered expenses, and the younger one has incurred $120 (i.e., already satisfied the deductible). At the beginning of COBRA continuation coverage on August 1, the spouse has a remaining deductible of $20, the older child still has the full $100 deductible, and the younger one has no further deductible.

Example 2: A group health plan applies a separate $200 annual deductible to each individual whom it covers, except that each family member will be treated as having satisfied the individual deductible once the family has incurred $500 of covered expenses during the year. The plan provides that upon the divorce of a covered employee, coverage will end immediately for the employee's spouse and any children who do not remain in the employee's custody. Assume that a covered employee with four dependent children is divorced, that the spouse obtains custody of the two oldest children, and that the spouse and those children all elect COBRA continuation coverage to begin immediately. Assume also that the family had accumulated $420 of covered expenses before the divorce, as follows: $70 by each parent, $200 by the oldest child, $80 by the youngest child, and none by the other two children. Each new family unit after the divorce (i.e., the employee plus two children, still receiving regular coverage under the plan, and the spouse plus two children, receiving COBRA continuation coverage) has a remaining family deductible amount of $80 ($500 minus $420).

Example 3: The facts are the same as in Example 2, except that the family deductible is defined as two individual $200 deductibles instead of a $500 aggregate (i.e., the plan disregards all remaining individual deductibles after the satisfaction of any two individual deductibles). Before the divorce, the family has satisfied one individual deductible (the oldest child's). At the beginning of COBRA continuation coverage, therefore, each new family unit is treated as having already satisfied one individual deductible even though the oldest child is included in only one of the new family units.

Example 4: Each year a group health plan pays 70 percent of the cost of an individual's psychotherapy after that individual's first three visits. A qualified beneficiary who elects COBRA continuation coverage beginning August 1, 1988, and has already made two visits as of that date need only pay for one more visit before the plan must begin to pay 70 percent of the cost of the remaining visits during 1988.

Example 5: A group health plan has a $250 annual deductible per covered individual. The plan provides that if the deductible is not satisfied in a particular year, expenses incurred during October through December of that year are credited toward satisfaction of the deductible in the next year. A qualified beneficiary who has incurred covered expenses of $150 from January through September of 1988 and $40 during October elects COBRA continuation coverage beginning November 1, 1988. The remaining deductible amount for this qualified beneficiary is $60 at the beginning of the COBRA continuation coverage. If this individual incurs covered expenses of $50 in November and December of 1988 combined (so that the $250 deductible for 1988 is not satisfied), the $90 incurred from October through December of 1988 are credited toward satisfaction of the deductible amount for 1989.

Q-29: How do a plan's limits apply to COBRA continuation coverage?

A-29: (a) Limits are treated in the same way as deductibles (see Q&A-28 of this section). This rule applies both to limits on plan benefits (e.g., a maximum number of hospital days or dollar amount of reimbursable expenses) and limits that are in the nature of deductibles (e.g., a copayment limit, or a catastrophic limit on a covered employee's out-of-pocket expenses). This rule applies equally to annual and lifetime limits.

(b) The rule of this Q&A-29 is illustrated by the following examples; in each example it is assumed that limits are determined on a calendar year basis:

Example 1: A group health plan pays for a maximum of 150 days of hospital confinement per individual per year. A covered employee who has had 20 days of hospital confinement as of May 1, 1989, terminates employment and elects COBRA continuation coverage as of that date. During the remainder of 1989 the plan need only pay for a maximum of 130 days of hospital confinement for this individual.

Example 2: A group health plan reimburses a maximum of $20,000 of covered expenses per family per year, and the same $20,000 limit applies to unmarried covered employees. A covered employee and spouse who have no children divorce on May 1, 1989, and the spouse elects COBRA continuation coverage as of that date. If the employee and spouse together incurred $15,000 of reimbursable expenses during January through April of 1989, each of these individuals has a $5,000 maximum benefit for the remainder of 1989, regardless who incurred what portion of the $15,000.

Example 3: A group health plan pays for 80 percent of covered expenses after satisfaction of a $100-per-individual deductible, and 100 percent of them after a family has incurred out-of-pocket costs of $2,000. An employee and spouse with three dependent children divorce on June 1, 1989, and one of the children remains with the employee. The spouse elects COBRA continuation coverage as of that date for the spouse and the other two children. During January through May of 1989, all five individual deductibles were satisfied and the family incurred $4,000 of covered expenses, resulting in out-of-pocket expenses totalling $1,200 (five $100 deductibles, plus the non-reimbursed 20 percent of the other $3,500, or $700). For the remainder of 1989, each new family unit has an out-of-pocket limit of $800.

Q-30: Can a qualified beneficiary who elects COBRA continuation coverage ever change from the coverage received by that individual immediately before the qualifying event?

A-30: (a) In general, a qualified beneficiary need only be given an opportunity to continue the coverage that he or she was receiving immediately before the qualifying event. This is true regardless of whether the coverage received by the qualified beneficiary before the qualifying event ceases to be of value to the qualified beneficiary, such as in the case of a qualified beneficiary covered under a region-specific Health Maintenance Organization (HMO) who leaves the HMO's service region. The only situations in which a qualified beneficiary must be allowed to change from the coverage received immediately before the qualifying event are as set forth in paragraphs (b) and (c) of this Q&A-30, in Q&A-24 of this section (regarding core coverage), and in Q&A-23 of this section (regarding changes to or elimination of the coverage provided to similarly situated active employees).

(b) If a qualified beneficiary participates in a region-specific plan (such as an HMO or an on-site clinic) that will not service his or her health needs in the area to which he or she is relocating (regardless of the reason for the relocation) and the employer has employees in the area to which the qualified beneficiary relocates, the qualified beneficiary must be given an opportunity to elect alternative coverage if (and on the same basis as) a similarly situated active employee who transfers to that new location while continuing to work for the employer would be given the opportunity to elect alternative coverage at the time of transfer.

(c) If an employer maintains more than one group health plan and an open enrollment period is available to similarly situated active employees with respect to whom a qualifying event has not occurred, the same open enrollment period rights must be available to each qualified beneficiary receiving COBRA continuation coverage. An open enrollment period means a period during which an employee covered under a plan can choose to be covered under another group health plan, or to add or eliminate coverage of family members.

(d) The rules of this Q&A-30 are illustrated by the following examples:

Example 1: Assume that (1) E is an employee who works for an employer that maintains several group health plans; (2) under the terms of the plans, if an employee chooses to cover any family members under a plan, all family members must be covered by the same plan and that plan must be the same as the plan covering the employee; (3) immediately before E's termination of employment (for reasons other than gross misconduct), E is covered along with E's spouse and children by a plan that provides only core coverage, and (4) the coverage under that plan will end as a result of the termination of employment. Upon E's termination of employment, each of the four family members is a qualified beneficiary. Even though the employer maintains various other plans and options, it is not necessary for the qualified beneficiaries to be allowed to switch to a new plan when E terminates employment. Assume further that none of the four family members declines to elect COBRA continuation coverage, and that 3 months after E's termination of employment there is an open enrollment period during which similarly situated active employees are offered an opportunity to choose to be covered under a new plan or to add or eliminate family coverage. During the open enrollment period, each of the four qualified beneficiaries must be offered the opportunity to switch to another plan (as though each beneficiary were an individual employee). For example, each member of E's family could choose coverage under a separate plan, even though the family members of employed individuals could not choose coverage under separate plans. Of course, if each family member chooses COBRA continuation coverage under a separate plan, each family member can be required to pay an amount for that coverage that is based on the applicable premium for individual coverage under that separate plan. See Q&A-44 of this section.

Example 2: The facts are the same as in Example 1, except that E's family members are not covered under E's group health plan when E terminates employment. Although the family members do not have to be given an opportunity to elect COBRA continuation coverage, E must be allowed to add them to E's COBRA continuation coverage during the open enrollment period. This is true even though the family members are not, and cannot become, qualified beneficiaries (see Q&A-17 of this section).

Q-31: Aside from open enrollment periods, can a qualified beneficiary who has elected COBRA continuation coverage choose to cover individuals (such as newborn children, adopted children, or new spouses) who join the qualified beneficiary's family on or after the date of the qualifying event?

A-31: If the plan covering the qualified beneficiary provides that such new family members of active employees can become covered (either automatically or upon an appropriate election) before the next open enrollment period, then the same right must be extended to the new family members of a qualified beneficiary. Of course, if the addition of a new family member will result in a higher applicable premium (e.g., if the qualified beneficiary was previously receiving COBRA continuation coverage as an individual, or if the applicable premium for family coverage depends on family size), the plan can require the qualified beneficiary to pay a correspondingly higher amount for the COBRA continuation coverage. See Q&A-44 of this section.

ELECTING COBRA CONTINUATION COVERAGE

Q-32: What is the minimum period during which a group health plan must allow a qualified beneficiary to elect COBRA continuation coverage (i.e., the election period)?

A-32: A group health plan can condition the availability of COBRA continuation coverage upon a qualified beneficiary's timely election of such coverage. An election of COBRA continuation coverage is a timely election if it is made during the election period. The election period must begin on or before the date that the qualified beneficiary would lose coverage on account of the qualifying event. (See paragraph (c) of Q&A-18 of this section for the meaning of "lose coverage.") The election period must not end before the date that is 60 days after the later of (a) the date that the qualified beneficiary would lose coverage on account of the qualifying event, or (b) the date that the qualified beneficiary is sent notice of his or her right to elect COBRA continuation coverage. An election is considered to be made on the date that it is sent to the employer or plan administrator. The rules of this Q&A-32 are illustrated by the following example:

Example: An unmarried employee who is receiving employer-paid coverage under a group health plan voluntarily terminates employment on June 1, 1988. *Case 1:* If the plan provides that the employer-paid coverage ends immediately upon the termination of employment, the election period must begin on or before June 1, 1988, and must not end earlier than July 31, 1988. If notice of the right to elect COBRA continuation coverage is not sent to the employee until June 15, 1988, the election period must not end earlier than August 14, 1988. *Case 2:* If the plan provides that the employer-paid coverage does not end until 6 months after the termination of employment, the employee does not lose coverage until December 1, 1988. The election period can therefore begin as late as December 1, 1988, and must not end before January 30, 1989. *Case 3:* If employer-paid coverage for 6 months after the termination of employment is offered only to those qualified beneficiaries who waive COBRA continuation coverage, the employee "loses coverage" on June 1, 1988, so the election period is the same as in Case 1. The difference between Case 2 and Case 3 is that in Case 2 the employee can receive 6 months of employer-paid coverage and then elect to pay for up to an additional 12 months of COBRA continuation coverage, while in Case 3 the employee must choose between 6 months of employer-paid coverage and paying for up to 18 months of COBRA continuation coverage. In all three cases, COBRA continuation coverage need not be provided for more than 18 months after the termination of employment (see Q&A-39 of this section), and in certain circumstances might be provided for a shorter period (see Q&A-38 of this section).

Q-33: Must a covered employee or qualified beneficiary inform the employer or plan administrator of the occurrence of a qualifying event?

A-33: In general, the employer or plan administrator must determine when a qualifying event has occurred. However, each covered employee or qualified beneficiary is responsible for notifying the employer or other plan administrator of the occurrence of a qualifying event that is either a dependent child ceasing to be a dependent child of the covered employee or a divorce or legal separation of a covered employee. If the notice is not sent to the employer or other plan administrator within 60 days after the later of (a) the date of the qualifying event, or (b) the date that the qualified beneficiary would lose coverage on account of the qualifying event, the group health plan does not have to offer the qualified beneficiary an opportunity to elect COBRA continuation coverage. For purposes of this Q&A-33, if more than one qualified beneficiary would lose coverage on account of a divorce or legal separation of a covered employee, a timely notice of the divorce or legal separation that is sent by the covered employee or any one of those qualified beneficiaries will be sufficient to preserve the election rights of all of the qualified beneficiaries.

Q-34: During the election period and before the qualified beneficiary has made an election, must coverage be provided?

A-34: (a) In general, each qualified beneficiary has until at least 60 days after the date that the qualifying event would cause him or her to lose coverage to decide whether to elect COBRA continuation coverage. If the election is made during that period, coverage must be provided from the date that coverage would otherwise have been lost (but see Q&A-35 of this section). This can be accomplished as described in paragraph (b) or (c) of this Q&A-34.

(b) In the case of an indemnity or reimbursement arrangement, the employer can provide for plan coverage during the election period or, if the plan allows retroactive reinstatement, the employer can drop the qualified beneficiary from the plan and reinstate him or her when the election is made. Of course, claims incurred by a qualified beneficiary during the election period do not have to be paid before the election (and, if applicable, payment for the coverage) is made.

(c) In the case of a group health plan that provides health services (such as a Health Maintenance Organization or a walk-in clinic), the plan can require that a qualified beneficiary who has not yet elected and paid for COBRA continuation coverage choose between (1) electing and paying for the coverage or (2) paying the reasonable and customary charge for the plan's services, but only if a qualified beneficiary who chooses to pay for the services will be reimbursed for that payment within 30 days after electing COBRA continuation coverage (and, if applicable, paying any balance due for the coverage). In the alternative, the plan can provide continued coverage and treat the qualified beneficiary's use of the facility as a constructive election. In such a case, the qualified beneficiary is obligated to pay any applicable charge for the coverage, but only if the qualified beneficiary is informed of the meaning of the constructive election before using the facility.

Q-35: Is a waiver before the end of the election period effective to end a qualified beneficiary's election rights?

A-35: A qualified beneficiary who, during the election period, waives COBRA continuation coverage can revoke the waiver at any time before the end of the election period. However, if a qualified beneficiary who waives COBRA continuation coverage later revokes the waiver, coverage need not be provided retroactively (i.e., from the date of the loss of coverage until the waiver is revoked). Waivers and revocations of waivers are considered made on the date that they are sent to the employer or plan administrator, as applicable.

Q-36: Can an employer withhold money or other benefits owed to a qualified beneficiary until the qualified beneficiary either waives COBRA continuation coverage, elects and pays for such coverage, or allows the election period to expire?

A-36: No. An employer must not withhold anything to which a qualified beneficiary is otherwise entitled (by operation of law or other agreement) in order to compel payment for COBRA continuation coverage or to coerce the qualified beneficiary to give up rights to COBRA continuation coverage (including the right to use the full election period to decide whether to elect such coverage). Such a withholding constitutes a failure to comply with section 162(k), and any purported waiver obtained by means of such a withholding is invalid.

Q-37: Can each qualified beneficiary make an independent election under COBRA?

A-37: Yes. Each qualified beneficiary must be offered the opportunity to make an independent election to receive COBRA continuation coverage and, if applicable, an independent election (a) to receive COBRA continuation coverage that is limited to core coverage and (b) to switch to another group health plan during an open enrollment period. However, if a qualified beneficiary who is either a covered employee or the spouse of a covered employee makes an election to provide any other qualified beneficiary with COBRA continuation coverage (whether for core coverage only or core plus non-core coverage), the election shall be binding on that other qualified beneficiary. An election on behalf of a minor child can be made by the child's parent or legal guardian. An election on behalf of a qualified beneficiary who is incapacitated or dies can be made by the legal representative of the qualified beneficiary or the qualified beneficiary's estate, as determined under applicable state law, or by the spouse of the qualified beneficiary. The rules of this Q&A-37 are illustrated by the following examples:

Example 1: Assume that employee H and H's spouse are covered under a group health plan immediately before H's termination of employment (for reasons other than gross misconduct), the plan provides only core coverage, and the coverage under the plan will end as a result of the termination of employment. Upon H's termination of employment both H and H's spouse are qualified beneficiaries and each must be allowed to elect COBRA continuation coverage. Thus, H might elect COBRA continuation coverage while the spouse declines to elect such coverage. However, if H elects to provide COBRA continuation coverage for both of them, that election is binding on the spouse, and the spouse cannot decline COBRA continuation coverage. In contrast, H cannot decline COBRA continuation coverage on behalf of H's spouse. Thus, if H does not elect COBRA continuation coverage on behalf of the spouse, the spouse must still be allowed to elect COBRA continuation coverage.

Example 2: The facts are the same in Example 1, except that coverage under the plan includes both core coverage and non-core coverage, and H and H's spouse have two dependent children who are also covered under the plan immediately before H's termination of employment. All four family members are qualified beneficiaries, each of whom must be offered the opportunity to elect COBRA continuation coverage either with or without non-core coverage. One possible result, therefore, is for the children to continue their full coverage while the parents continue only core coverage. This result can be achieved in a variety of ways, including separate elections by each family member, or a single election by H that binds the entire family.

DURATION OF COBRA CONTINUATION COVERAGE

Q-38: How long must COBRA continuation coverage be available to a qualified beneficiary?

A-38: Except for an interruption of coverage in connection with a waiver as described in Q&A-35 of this section, COBRA continuation coverage that has been elected by a qualified beneficiary must extend for at least the period beginning on the date of the qualifying event and ending not before the earliest of the following dates: (a) the last day of the maximum coverage period (see Q&A-39 of this section); (b) the first day for which timely payment is not made to the plan with respect to the qualified beneficiary (see Q&A-48 of this section); (c) the date upon which the employer ceases to maintain any group health plan (including successor plans); (d) the first date after the date of the election upon which the qualified beneficiary is covered (i.e., actually covered, rather than merely eligible to be covered) under any other group health plan that is not maintained by the employer, even if that other coverage is less valuable to the qualified beneficiary than COBRA continuation coverage (e.g., if the other coverage provides no benefits for preexisting conditions); or (e) the date that the qualified beneficiary is entitled to Medicare benefits under Title XVIII of the Social Security Act. However, a group health plan can terminate for cause the coverage of a qualified beneficiary receiving COBRA continuation coverage on the same basis that the plan terminates for cause the coverage of similarly situated active employees with respect to whom a qualifying event has not occurred. For purposes of the preceding sentence, termination for cause does not include termination based on a failure to make timely payment to the plan. (See Q&A-48 of this section regarding timely payment.)

Q-39: When does the maximum coverage period end?

A-39: The maximum coverage period ends (a) 18 months after the qualifying event, if the qualifying event that gives rise to COBRA continuation coverage election rights is a termination or reduction of hours; and (b) 36 months after the qualifying event, for any other type of qualifying event. The end of the maximum coverage period is measured from the date of the qualifying event even if the qualifying event does not result in a loss of coverage under the plan until some later date. See also Q&A-40 of this section in the case of multiple qualifying events. Nothing in section 162(k) or this section prohibits a group health plan from providing coverage that continues beyond the end of the maximum coverage period.

Q-40: Can the maximum coverage period ever be expanded?

A-40: No, with one exception. The exception involves a qualifying event that gives rise to an 18-month maximum coverage period and is followed, within that 18-month period, by a second qualifying event (e.g., a death or divorce). In such a case, the original 18-month period is expanded to 36 months, but only for those individuals who were qualified beneficiaries under the group health plan as of the first qualifying event and were covered under the plan at the time of the second qualifying event. No qualifying event can give rise to a maximum coverage period that ends more than 36 months after the date of the first qualifying event. For example, if an employee covered by a group health plan that is subject to COBRA terminates employment (for reasons other than gross misconduct) on December 31, 1987, the termination is a qualifying event giving rise to a maximum coverage period that extends for 18 months to June 30, 1989. If the employee dies after the employee and the employee's spouse and dependent children have elected COBRA continuation coverage and before June 30, 1989, the spouse and children (exempt anyone among them whose COBRA continuation coverage had already ended for some other reason) will be able to elect COBRA continuation coverage through December 31, 1990.

Q-41: If coverage is provided to a qualified beneficiary after a qualifying event without regard to COBRA continuation coverage (e.g., as a result of state or local law, industry practice, a collective bargaining agreement, or plan procedure), will such alternative coverage extend the maximum coverage period?

A-41: (a) The alternative coverage will not extend the maximum coverage period. The end of the maximum coverage period is measured solely from the date of the qualifying event, as described in Q&A-39 and Q&A-40 of this section.

(b) If the alternative coverage does not satisfy all the requirements for COBRA continuation coverage, the group health plan covering the qualified beneficiary immediately before the qualifying event is not in compliance with section 162(k) unless the qualified beneficiary receiving the alternative coverage was also offered the opportunity to elect COBRA continuation coverage and rejected COBRA continuation coverage in favor of the alternative coverage. At the end of that alternative coverage, the individual need not be offered a COBRA election. However, if the individual is a covered employee and the spouse or a dependent child of the individual would lose that alternative coverage as a result of a qualifying event (such as the death of the covered employee), the spouse or dependent child must be given an opportunity to elect to continue that alternative coverage, with a maximum coverage period of 36 months measured from the date of that qualifying event.

(c) If the alternative coverage does satisfy the requirements for COBRA continuation coverage, it can be credited toward satisfaction of the 18- or 36-month maximum coverage period. Moreover, in the case of a covered employee who receives more than 18 months of alternative coverage that satisfies the requirements for COBRA continuation coverage, if the spouse or a dependent child of the covered employee loses coverage as a result of a second qualifying event (such as the death of the covered employee) that occurs after the 18-month period, that spouse or dependent child need not be given an election to continue coverage.

Q-42: How can an event that occurs before a group health plan becomes subject to section 162(k) affect the maximum coverage period when a later, qualifying event occurs?

A-42: (a) If there are two events that satisfy the conditions set forth in paragraph (b) of this Q&A-42, then the first event is treated as though it were a qualifying event that occurred on the date that the plan became subject to section 162(k) (i.e., with a maximum coverage period that began on that date), so that the second event is not merely a qualifying event but a second qualifying event. This treatment applies solely for purposes of determining the maximum coverage period under Q&A-39 through Q&A-41 of this section in connection with that second qualifying event. It does not give rise to any right to elect COBRA continuation coverage in connection with the first event.

(b) The conditions referred to in paragraph (a) of this Q&A-42 are as follows: (1) the first event is listed in paragraph (b) of Q&A-18 of this section (regarding what is a qualifying event) but occurs before the date that the plan becomes subject to section 162(k), (2) the plan provides coverage to a qualified beneficiary after the first event that continues to or beyond the date that the plan becomes subject to section 162(k), and (3) a second event then occurs and is a qualifying event.

(c) The rule of this Q&A-42 is illustrated by the following examples:

Example 1: Assume that a group health plan became subject to section 162(k) on January 1, 1987. Employee F, who was covered by the plan, voluntarily terminated employment on January 1, 1986, and was given employer-paid coverage that would continue for 5 more years. F's spouse was also to be covered for the 5 years, except that the spouse's coverage would terminate upon divorce or F's death. F dies on January 1, 1988. F's death is a qualifying event, so F's spouse can elect COBRA continuation coverage (unless the election is precluded for some independent reason, such as the spouse's entitlement to Medicare benefits). F's termination of employment on January 1, 1986, is treated as though it were a qualifying event that occurred on January 1, 1987. F's death is thus a *second* qualifying event, for which the spouse's maximum coverage period ends on January 1, 1990 (i.e., 36 months after the first qualifying event). The spouse can thus elect up to 24 months of COBRA continuation coverage.

Example 2: Assume the same facts as in Example 1, except that F's death occurs after January 1, 1990. The plan does not have to give F's spouse an opportunity to elect COBRA continuation coverage.

Q-43: Must a qualified beneficiary be given the right to enroll in a conversion health plan at the end of the maximum coverage period for COBRA continuation coverage?

A-43: If a qualified beneficiary's COBRA continuation coverage under a group health plan ends as a result of the expiration of the maximum coverage period, the group health plan must, during the 180-day period that ends on that expiration date, provide the qualified beneficiary the option of enrolling under a conversion health plan if such an option is otherwise generally available to similarly situated active employees under the group health plan. If such a conversion option is not otherwise generally available, COBRA does not require that it be made available to qualified beneficiaries.

PAYING FOR COBRA CONTINUATION COVERAGE

Q-44: Can a qualified beneficiary be required to pay for COBRA continuation coverage?

A-44: Yes. For any period of COBRA continuation coverage, a group health plan can require a qualified beneficiary to pay an amount that does not exceed 102 percent of the applicable premium for that period. The "applicable premium" is defined in section 162(k)(4) of the Code. A group health plan can terminate a qualified beneficiary's COBRA continuation coverage as of the first day of any period for which timely payment is not made to the plan with respect to that qualifed beneficiary (see Q&A-38 of this section). For the meaning of "timely payment," see Q&A-48 of this section.

Q-45: After a qualified beneficiary has elected COBRA continuation coverage under a group health plan, can the plan increase the amount that the qualified beneficiary must pay for COBRA continuation coverage?

A-45: Yes, if the applicable premium increases. However, the applicable premium for each determination period must be computed and fixed by the plan before the determination period begins. A determination period is any 12-month period selected by the plan, but it must be applied consistently from year to year. Thus, each qualified beneficiary does not have a separate determination period beginning on the date (or anniversaries of the date) that COBRA continuation coverage begins for that qualified beneficiary.

Q-46: Must a qualified beneficiary be allowed to pay for COBRA continuation coverage in installments?

A-46: Yes. A group health plan must allow a qualified beneficiary to pay for COBRA continuation coverage in monthly installments. A group health plan can also allow qualified beneficiaries the alternative of paying for COBRA continuation coverage at other intervals (e.g., quarterly or semiannually).

Q-47: Can a qualified beneficiary choose to have the first payment for COBRA continuation coverage applied prospectively only?

A-47: No. The first payment for COBRA continuation coverage is applied to the period of coverage beginning immediately after the date that coverage under the plan would have been lost on account of the qualifying event. Of course, if the group health plan allows a qualified beneficiary to waive COBRA continuation coverage for any period before electing to receive COBRA continuation coverage, the first payment is not applied to period of the waiver.

Q-48: What is timely payment for COBRA continuation coverage?

A-48: (a) If a qualified beneficiary's election of COBRA continuation coverage is made after the date of the qualifying event, timely payment for any COBRA continuation coverage during the period before the date of the election means payment that is made to the plan within 45 days after the date of the election. Timely payment for any other period of COBRA continuation coverage is governed by paragraph (b) of this Q&A-48.

(b) In general, timely payment for a period of COBRA continuation coverage under a group health plan means payment that is made to the plan by the date that is 30 days after the first day of that period. However, payment that is made to the plan by a later date is also considered timely payment if either (1) under the terms of the plan, covered employees or qualified beneficiaries are allowed until that later date to pay for their coverage during the period, or (2) under the terms of an arrangement between the employer and an insurance company, Health Maintenance Organization, or other entity that provides plan benefits on the employer's behalf, the employer is allowed until that later date to pay for coverage of similarly situated employees during the period. [Reg. § 1.162-26.]

[¶ 49,079]   Proposed Regulations (LR-122-86), published in the Federal Register on June 16, 1987.

Accounting methods: Cash method: Limitations.—Reg. § § 1.448-1T, relating to the limitation on the use of the cash method of accounting, is proposed. Reg. § 1.448-2T was adopted on 8/31/2006 by T.D. 9285.

AGENCY: Internal Revenue Service, Treasury.

ACTION: Notice of proposed rulemaking by cross-reference to temporary regulations.

SUMMARY: In the Rules and Regulations portion of this issue of the FEDERAL REGISTER, the Internal Revenue Service is issuing temporary amendments to the income tax regulations relating to the limitation on the use of the cash method of accounting. Changes to the law were made by the Tax Reform Act of 1986. The text of those temporary regulations also serves as the comment document for this proposed rulemaking.

DATES: Written comments and requests for a public hearing must be delivered or mailed by [60 DAYS AFTER PUBLICATION OF THIS PROPOSED RULE IN THE FEDERAL REGISTER].

ADDRESS: Send comments and requests for public hearing to: Commissioner of Internal Revenue, Attention: CC:LR:T (LR-122-86), Washington, D.C. 20224.

FOR FURTHER INFORMATION CONTACT: Ewan D. Purkiss of the Legislation and Regulations Division, Office of Chief Counsel, Internal Revenue Service, 1111 Constitution Avenue, N.W., Washington, D.C. 20224 (Attention: CC:LR:T) (202-566-3238, not a toll-free call).

SUPPLEMENTARY INFORMATION:

BACKGROUND

The temporary regulations (designated by a T following the section citation) in the Rules and Regulations portion of this issue of the FEDERAL REGISTER amend Part 1 of Title 26 of the Code of Federal Regulations. These amendments reflect the provisions of section 448 of the Internal Revenue Code of 1986 as added by section 801 of the Tax Reform Act of 1986 (Pub. L. 99-514, 100 Stat. 2085). For the text of the temporary regulations, see FR Doc. (T.D. 8143) published in the Rules and Regulations portion of this issue of the FEDERAL REGISTER. A general discussion of the temporary regulations is contained in the preamble to the regulations. The final regulations, which this document proposes to base on the temporary regulations, would amend Part 1 of Title 26 of the Code of Federal Regulations.

SPECIAL ANALYSIS

The Commissioner of Internal Revenue has determined that this proposed rule is not a major rule as defined in Executive Order 12291. Accordingly, a Regulatory Impact Analysis is not required. Although this document is a notice of proposed rulemaking that solicits public comments, the Internal Revenue Service has concluded that the proposed regulations are interpretative and that the notice and public procedure requirements of 5 U.S.C. 553 do not apply. Accordingly, a regulatory flexibility analysis is not required under the Regulatory Flexibility Act (5 U.S.C. chapter 6).

COMMENTS AND REQUESTS FOR A PUBLIC HEARING

Before adopting these proposed regulations, consideration will be given to any written comments that are submitted (preferably eight copies) to the Commissioner of Internal Revenue. All comments will be available for public inspection and copying. A public hearing will be held upon written request to the Commissioner by any person who submitted comments. If a public hearing is held, notice of the time and place will be published in the FEDERAL REGISTER.

The collection of information requirements contained in this notice of proposed rulemaking have been submitted to the Office of Management and Budget (OMB) for review under section 3504(h) of the Paperwork Reduction Act. Comments on the requirements should be sent to the Office of Information and Regulatory Affairs of OMB, Attention: Desk Officer for Internal Revenue Service, New Executive Office Building, Washington, D.C. 20503. The Internal Revenue Service requests that persons submitting comments on these requirements to OMB also send copies of those comments to the Service.

DRAFTING INFORMATION

The principal author of these proposed regulations is Ewan D. Purkiss of the Legislation and Regulations Division, Office of Chief Counsel, Internal Revenue Service. However, personnel from other offices of the Internal Revenue Service and Treasury participated in developing the regulations on matters of both substance and style.

[¶ 49,080]   **Proposed Regulations (LR-83-86), published in the Federal Register on** June 22, 1987.

Low-income housing credit.—Reg. §1.42-1T, relating to the low-income housing credit, is proposed.

AGENCY: Internal Revenue Service, Treasury.

ACTION: Notice of proposed rulemaking by cross reference to temporary regulations.

SUMMARY: In the Rules and Regulations portion of this issue of the FEDERAL REGISTER, the Internal Revenue Service is issuing temporary regulations relating to the low-income housing credit under section 42 of the Internal Revenue Code of 1986, as enacted by the Tax Reform Act of 1986 (Pub. L. 99-514). The text of those temporary regulations also serves as the comment document for this notice of proposed rulemaking.

DATES: Written comments and requests for a public hearing must be delivered or mailed by August 21, 1987. In general, the regulations are proposed to be effective after December 31, 1986, for buildings placed in service after December 31, 1986, in taxable years ending after that date.

ADDRESS: Send comments and requests for a public hearing to: Commissioner of Internal Revenue, Attention: CC:LR:T (LR-83-86), 1111 Constitution Avenue, N.W., Washington, D.C. 20224.

FOR FURTHER INFORMATION CONTACT: Robert Beatson of the Legislation and Regulations Division, Office of Chief Counsel, Internal Revenue Service, 1111 Constitution Avenue N.W., Washington, D.C. 20224 (Attention: CC:LR:T) (202-566-3829, not a toll-free call).

SUPPLEMENTARY INFORMATION:

BACKGROUND

The temporary regulations in the Rules and Regulations portion of this issue of the FEDERAL REGISTER amend 26 CFR Parts 1 and 602. The temporary regulations add new §1.42-1T to Part 1 of Title 26 of the Code of Federal Regulations. The final regulations, which this document proposes to be based on those temporary regulations, would amend 26 CFR Parts 1 and 602 and would add new §1.42-1 to Part 1 of Title 26 of the Code of Federal Regulations. For the text of the temporary regulations, see FR Doc. (T.D. 8144) published in the Rules and Regulations portion of this issue of the FEDERAL REGISTER. The preamble to the temporary regulations explains the additions to the Income Tax Regulations.

The proposed regulations provide needed guidance regarding the provisions of section 42, as enacted by section 252 of the Tax Reform Act of 1986.

NON-APPLICABILITY OF EXECUTIVE ORDER 12291

The Commissioner of Internal Revenue has determined that this proposed rule is not a major rule as defined in Executive Order 12291 and that a regulatory impact analysis therefore is not required.

REGULATORY FLEXIBILITY ACT

Although this document is a notice of proposed rulemaking that solicits public comment, the Internal Revenue Service has concluded that the regulations proposed herein are interpretative and that the notice and public procedure requirements of 5 U.S.C. 553 do not apply. Accordingly, this proposed regulation does not constitute a regulation subject to the Regulatory Flexibility Act (5 U.S.C. chapter 6).

DRAFTING INFORMATION

The principal author of these proposed regulations is Robert Beatson of the Legislation and Regulations Division of the Office of Chief Counsel, Internal Revenue Service. However, personnel from other offices of the Internal Revenue Service and the Treasury Department participated in developing the regulations both on matters of substance and style.

COMMENTS AND REQUESTS FOR A PUBLIC HEARING

Before adoption of these proposed regulations, consideration will be given to any written comments that are submitted (preferably eight copies) to the Commissioner of Internal Revenue. Comments are encouraged both with respect to the matters addressed in these proposed regulations and any other issues arising under section 42 with respect to which guidance is needed. All comments will be available for public inspection and copying. A public hearing will be held upon written request to the Commissioner by any person who has submitted written comments. If a public hearing is held, notice of the time and place will be published in the FEDERAL REGISTER. The collection of information requirements contained herein have been submitted to the Office of Management and Budget (OMB) for review under section 3504(h) of the Paperwork Reduction Act. Comments on the requirements should be sent to the Office of Information and Regulatory Affairs of OMB, Attention: Desk Officer for Internal Revenue Service, New Executive Office Building, Washington, DC 20503. The Internal Revenue Service requests persons submitting comments to OBM to also send copies of the comments to the Service.

[¶ 49,081]   **Proposed Regulations (LR-10-87), published in the Federal Register on** July 2, 1987.

Interest paid or payable: Allocation.—Reg. §1.163-8T, relating to the allocation of interest expense among a taxpayer's expenditures, is proposed.

AGENCY: Internal Revenue Service, Treasury.

ACTION: Notice of proposed rulemaking by cross-reference to temporary regulations.

SUMMARY: In the Rules and Regulations portion of this issue of the FEDERAL REGISTER, the Internal Revenue Service is issuing temporary regulations relating to the allocation of interest expense among expenditures. The text of those temporary regulations also serves as the comment document for this proposed rulemaking.

DATE: The amendments to the regulations are proposed to be effective with respect to interest expense paid or accrued in taxable years beginning after December 31, 1986. Written comments and requests for a public hearing must be delivered or mailed by August 31, 1987.

ADDRESS: Send comments and requests for a public hearing to:

Commissioner of Internal Revenue, Attention: CC:LR:T (LR-10-87), Washington, D.C. 20224.

FOR FURTHER INFORMATION CONTACT: Michael J. Grace of the Legislation and Regulations Division, Office of Chief Counsel, Internal Revenue Service, 1111 Constitution Avenue, N.W., Washington, D.C. 20224, Attention: CC:LR:T, (202) 566-3288 (not a toll-free call).

SUPPLEMENTARY INFORMATION:

BACKGROUND

The temporary regulations (designated by a T following the section citation) in the Rules and Regulations portion of this issue of the FEDERAL REGISTER amend the Income Tax Regulations (26 CFR Part 1) to provide rules relating to the allocation of interest expense for purposes of applying the limitations on passive activity losses and credits, investment interest, and personal interest. The temporary regulations reflect the amendment of the Internal Revenue Code of 1986 by sections 501 and 511 of the Act (100 Stat. 2233 and 2244), which added sections 469 (relating to the limitation on passive activity losses and credits) and 163(h) (relating to the disallowance of deductions for personal interest) and amended section 163(d) (relating to the limitation on investment interest). This document proposes to adopt the temporary regulations as final regulations. Accordingly, the text of the temporary regulations serves as the comment document for this notice of proposed rulemaking. In addition, the preamble to the temporary regulations explains the proposed and temporary rules.

For the text of the temporary regulations, see FR Doc. (T.D.) published in the Rules and Regulations portion of this issue of the FEDERAL REGISTER.

SPECIAL ANALYSES

The Commissioner of Internal Revenue has determined that this proposed rule is not a major rule as defined in Executive Order 12291 and that a regulatory impact analysis is not required. Although this document is a notice of proposed rulemaking that solicits public comments, the Internal Revenue Service has concluded that the proposed regulations are interpretative and that the notice and public procedure requirements of 5 U.S.C. 553 do not apply. Accordingly, these proposed regulations are not subject to the Regulatory Flexibility Act (5 U.S.C. chapter 6).

COMMENTS AND REQUESTS FOR A PUBLIC HEARING

Before these proposed regulations are adopted, consideration will be given to any written comments that are submitted (preferably eight copies) to the Commissioner of Internal Revenue. All comments will be available for public inspection and copying. A public hearing will be held upon written request to the Commissioner by any person who submitted comments. If a public hearing is held, notice of the time and place will be published in the FEDERAL REGISTER.

The collection of information requirements contained herein have been submitted to the Office of Management and Budget (OMB) for review under section 3504(h) of the Paperwork Reduction Act. Comments on the requirements should be sent to the Office of Information and Regulatory Affairs of OMB, Attention: Desk Officer for Internal Revenue Service, New Executive Office Building, Washington, D.C. 20503. The Internal Revenue Service requests that persons submitting comments to OMB also send copies of the comments to the Service.

DRAFTING INFORMATION

The principal author of these proposed regulations is Michael J. Grace of the Legislation and Regulations Division, Office of Chief Counsel, Internal Revenue Service. However, personnel from other offices of the Internal Revenue Service and Treasury participated in developing the regulations on matters of both substance and style.

[¶ 49,083]   **Proposed Regulations (LR-106-86), published in the Federal Register on** August 11, 1987.

   Carryforwards: Ownership change: Limitations.—Reg. § 1.382-2T, relating to the limitation on net operating loss carryforwards and certain built-in losses following ownership changes, is proposed. Reg. § 1.382-1T was redesignated as Reg. § 1.382-1 on 10/2/92 by T.D. 8440.

AGENCY: Internal Revenue Service, Treasury.

ACTION: Notice of proposed rulemaking by cross-reference to temporary regulations.

SUMMARY: In the Rules and Regulations portion of this issue of the FEDERAL REGISTER, the Internal Revenue Service is adding temporary regulations pertaining to section 382 of the Internal Revenue Code of 1986 ("Code"), which was amended by section 621 of the Tax Reform Act of 1986. The temporary regulations provide the necessary guidance for determining when there is an ownership change resulting in a limitation on corporate net operating loss carryforwards under section 382. The text of the temporary regulations also serves as the comment document for this notice of proposed rulemaking.

DATES FOR COMMENTS AND REQUESTS FOR A PUBLIC HEARING

Written comments and requests for a public hearing must be delivered or mailed by [60 DAYS AFTER DATE OF PUBLICATION OF THIS DOCUMENT IN THE FEDERAL REGISTER].

ADDRESS: Send comments or requests for a public hearing to: Commissioner of Internal Revenue, Attention: CC:LR:T [LR-106-86], 1111 Constitution Avenue, N.W., Washington, D.C. 20224.

FOR FURTHER INFORMATION CONTACT: Keith E. Stanley of the Legislation and Regulations Division, Office of Chief Counsel, Internal Revenue Service, 1111 Constitution Avenue, N.W., Washington, D.C. 20224 (Attention: CC:LR:T) or telephone (202) 566-3458 (not a toll-free number).

SUPPLEMENTARY INFORMATION:

BACKGROUND

Temporary regulations published in the Rules and Regulations portion of this issue of the FEDERAL REGISTER add temporary regulations §§ 1.382-1T and 1.382-2T to Part 1 of Title 26 of the Code of Federal Regulations ("CFR"). The final regulations which are proposed to be based on the temporary regulations would be added to Part 1 of Title 26 of the CFR. The final regulations would provide the necessary guidance with respect to the determination of when there is an ownership change that results in a limitation on corporate net operating loss carryforwards under section 382. Section 382 of the Code was amended by section 621 of the Tax Reform Act of 1986 (Pub. L. No. 99-514, 100 Stat. 2085). For the text of the temporary regulations, see T.D. 8149 published in the Rules and Regulations portion of this issue of the FEDERAL REGISTER. The preamble to the temporary regulations explains the added regulations.

REGULATORY FLEXIBILITY ACT AND EXECUTIVE ORDER 12291

Although this document is a notice of proposed rulemaking that solicits public comment, the Internal Revenue Service has concluded that the notice and public procedure requirements of 5 U.S.C. 553 do not apply because the rules provided herein are interpretative. Accordingly, these proposed regulations do not constitute regulations subject to the Regulatory Flexibility Act (5 U.S.C. chapter 6). The Commissioner of Internal Revenue has determined that this proposed rule is not a major rule as defined in Executive Order 12291 and that a Regulatory Impact Analysis therefore is not required.

COMMENTS AND REQUESTS FOR A PUBLIC HEARING

Before adopting these proposed regulations, consideration will be given to any written comments that are submitted (preferably eight copies) to the Commissioner of Internal Revenue. All comments will be available for public inspection and copying. A public hearing will be held upon written request to the Commissioner by any person who has submitted written comments. If a public hearing is held, notice of time and place will be published in the FEDERAL REGISTER. The collection of information requirements contained herein have been submitted to the Office of Management and Budget (OMB) for review under section 3504(h) of the Paperwork Reduction Act. Comments on the requirements should be sent to the Office of Information and Regulatory Affairs of OMB, Attention: Desk Officer for Internal Revenue Service, New Executive Office Building, Washington, D.C. 20503. The Internal Revenue Service requests persons submitting comments to OMB also send copies of the comments to the Service.

DRAFTING INFORMATION

The principal author of these regulations is Keith E. Stanley of the Legislation and Regulations Division of the Office of Chief Counsel, Internal Revenue Service. However, personnel from other offices of the Internal Revenue Service and Treasury Department participated in developing the regulations, both in matters of substance and style.

[¶ 49,084]   **Proposed Regulations (EE-111-82), published in the Federal Register on** August 27, 1987.

Employee trusts: Affiliated service groups, employee leasing and other arrangements.—Reg. §1.414(o)-1, relating to affiliated service groups, employee leasing and other arrangements, is proposed. Reg. §§1.414(m)-5, 1.414(m)-6, 1.414(n)—1.414(n)-4 and portions of Reg. §1.414(o)-1 were withdrawn 4/27/93 by CO-53-92.

AGENCY: Internal Revenue Service, Treasury.

ACTION: Notice of proposed rulemaking.

SUMMARY: This document provides proposed regulations prescribing rules for determining: (1) when a management organization and the organization for which the management organization performs management services constitute an affiliated service group; (2) when leased employees are treated as employees of the lessee organization for purposes of certain employee benefit provisions; and (3) when arrangements involving separate organizations, employee leasing, or other arrangements will be ignored in order to prevent the avoidance of certain employee benefit requirements.

Changes to the applicable tax law were made by the Tax Equity and Fiscal Responsibility Act of 1982, the Tax Reform Act of 1984, and the Tax Reform Act of 1986. The regulations provide the public with guidance needed to comply with those Acts and would affect employers that maintain, and participants in, qualified plans.

DATES: Written comments and requests for a public hearing must be delivered or mailed by October 26, 1987. The regulations provided by this document are proposed to be generally effective for tax years beginning after December 31, 1983.

ADDRESS: Send comments and requests for a public hearing to: Commissioner of Internal Revenue, Attention: CC:LR:T (EE-111-82), Washington, D.C. 20224.

FOR FURTHER INFORMATION CONTACT: Michael Garvey of the Employee Plans and Exempt Organizations Division, Office of Chief Counsel, Internal Revenue Service, 1111 Constitution Avenue, N.W., Washington, D.C. 20224, Attention: CC:LR:T, (202) 566-3903, not a toll-free call.

SUPPLEMENTARY INFORMATION:

BACKGROUND

This document contains proposed amendments to the Income Tax Regulations (26 CFR Part 1) under sections 414(m)(5), 414(n), and 414(o) of the Internal Revenue Code. These amendments are proposed to conform the regulations to sections 246 and 248 of the Tax Equity and Fiscal Responsibility Act of 1982 (26 USC §§414(m)(5), 414(n)), section 526 of the Tax Reform Act of 1984 (26 USC §§414(n)(2), 414 (o)), and section 1146 of the Tax Reform Act of 1986 (26 USC §§414(n), 414(o)). Other sections of the Tax Reform Act of 1986 that relate to section 414(n) are not reflected in this document.

ORGANIZATIONS PERFORMING MANAGEMENT FUNCTIONS

Section 414(m)(5) of the Code expands the definition of an affiliated service group that is to be treated as a single employer under section 414(m) for purposes of certain employee benefit requirements. Pursuant to section 414(m)(5), an affiliated service group includes a management organization and a recipient organization (i.e., the organization (and related organizations) for which the management organization performs management functions). An organization is a management organization if the principal business of the organization is the performing of, on a regular and continuing basis, management functions for a recipient organization.

EMPLOYEE LEASING

Section 414(n) provides that, under certain circumstances, an individual ("leased employee") who performs services for a person ("recipient") through another person ("leasing organization") shall be treated as the employee of the recipient for purposes of certain employee benefit requirements. If the services being provided by an individual to a recipient are pursuant to an agreement between the recipient and the leasing organization, and the individual performs such services for the recipient on a substantially full-time basis for a period of at least one year, and the services are of a type historically performed by employees, then the individual is a leased employee and, therefore, shall be treated as an employee of the recipient.

Section 414(n)(5) provides, however, that if the leasing organization maintains a safe-harbor plan with respect to a leased employee, such individual will generally not be treated as an employee of the recipient. Section 414(n)(5), as originally enacted, required that a safe-harbor plan must be a qualified money purchase pension plan with provision for nonintegrated employer contributions of at least 7$\frac{1}{2}$ percent, immediate participation, and full and immediate vesting.

The Tax Reform Act of 1986 amended several provisions relating to sections 414(n) and 414(o). These amendments include the following.

(1) The definition of a safe-harbor plan under section 414(n)(5) has been amended to require a contribution rate of 10 percent and to require that the plan must cover all employees of the leasing organization (other than employees who perform substantially all of their services for the leasing

organization (and not for recipients) and employees whose compensation from the leasing organization is less than $1,000 during the plan year and during each of the 3 prior plan years).

(2) Under section 414(n)(5), a leased employee will be treated as an employee of the recipient, regardless of the existence of a safe-harbor plan, if more than 20 percent of the recipient's nonhighly compensated workforce are leased employees (as specially defined for this purpose).

(3) A recordkeeping exception from the section 414(n) employee leasing provisions is provided under section 414(o) in the case of an employer that has no section 416(g) top-heavy plans and that uses the services of nonemployees only for an insignificant percentage of the employer's total workload.

(4) The scope of the section 414(n) employee leasing provisions has been expanded to include a number of non-pension employee benefit requirements (listed under section 414(n)(3)), including group-term life insurance, accident and health plans, qualified group legal services, cafeteria plans, etc. In addition, the employee leasing provisions will apply to these non-pension employee benefit requirements regardless of the existence of a safe-harbor plan.

Except for the amendments relating to the non-pension employee benefit requirements, the proposed regulations reflect the Tax Reform Act of 1986 amendments described above. Guidance relating to the non-pension employee benefit requirements, and other relevant amendments made by the Tax Reform Act of 1986, will be forthcoming.

AVOIDANCE OF CERTAIN EMPLOYEE BENEFITS REQUIREMENTS

Section 414(o) provides that the Secretary shall prescribe such regulations as may be necessary to prevent the avoidance of any employee benefit requirement listed in sections 414(m)(4) or 414(n)(3) through the use of separate organizations, employee leasing, or other arrangements. Specifically, the Secretary has the authority to provide rules in addition to the rules contained in sections 414(m) and 414(n).

Pursuant to section 414(o), the proposed regulations provide rules relating to several arrangements that may result in the avoidance of the listed employee benefit requirements. These arrangements include the leasing of certain owners, the leasing of certain managers, the creation of successive organizations in time, expense sharing arrangements, plans maintained by certain corporate directors, and plans covering certain five-percent owners.

EFFECTIVE DATES

The amendments made to section 414 by the Tax Equity and Fiscal Responsibility Act of 1982 are effective for tax years of a recipient or of a member of an affiliated service group that begin after December 31, 1983.

The amendments made to section 414 by the Tax Reform Act of 1984 are effective as of July 18, 1984. The regulations promulgated under section 414(o), however, are variously effective for (1) plan years beginning more than six months after this document is published in the FEDERAL REGISTER, (2) plan years beginning more than sixty days after this document is published in the FEDERAL REGISTER as a Treasury decision, and (3) plan years beginning during or after the first tax year of a recipient beginning after December 31, 1983. (To the extent that the regulations under section 414(o) aggregate plans for purposes of section 415 that were not previously aggregated, the rules of § 1.415-10 apply.)

The amendments made to section 414 by the Tax Reform Act of 1986 are generally effective with respect to services performed after December 31, 1986. The recordkeeping exception from section 414(n), provided under section 414(o), and certain clarifying amendments under section 414(n) are effective as if originally enacted as part of the section 414 amendments made by the Tax Equity and Fiscal Responsibility Act of 1982. The section 414(n)(3) amendments relating to the non-pension employee benefit requirements are generally effective when section 89 applies to such non-pension employee benefits (see section 1151(k) of the Tax Reform Act of 1986).

SPECIAL ANALYSIS

The Commissioner of Internal Revenue has determined this rule is not a major rule as defined in Executive Order 12291. Therefore, a Regulatory Impact Analysis is not required. Although this document is a notice of proposed rulemaking that solicits public comment, the Internal Revenue Service has concluded that the regulations proposed are interpretative and that the notice and public procedure requirements of 5 USC 553(b) do not apply. Accordingly, these proposed regulations do not constitute regulations subject to the Regulatory Flexibility Act (5 USC chapter 6).

COMMENTS AND REQUESTS FOR A PUBLIC HEARING

Before adopting these proposed regulations, consideration will be given to any written comments that are submitted (preferably eight copies) to the Commissioner of Internal Revenue. All comments will be available for public inspection and copying. A public hearing will be held upon written request to the Commissioner by any person who has submitted written comments. If a public hearing is held, notice of the time and place will be published in the FEDERAL REGISTER.

DRAFTING INFORMATION

The principal author of these proposed regulations is Philip R. Bosco of the Employee Plans and Exempt Organizations Division of the Office of Chief Counsel, Internal Revenue Service. However, personnel from other offices of the Internal Revenue Service and Treasury participated in developing the regulations, both on matters of substance and style.

[¶ 49,086]   **Proposed Regulations (LR-45-870), published in the Federal Register on** December 23, 1987.

Personal service corporations: Partnerships: S corporations: Taxable years.—Reg. § 1.702-3T is proposed. Reg. § 18.1366-5 was removed by **T.D. 8600 on July 20, 1995. Reg. § § 1.441-1T, 1.441-2T and 1.441-4T were removed by T.D. 8996 on May 16, 2002.**

AGENCY: Internal Revenue Service, Treasury.

ACTION: Notice of proposed rulemaking by cross-reference to temporary regulations.

SUMMARY: In the Rules and Regulations portion of this issue of the *Federal Register*, the Internal Revenue Service is issuing temporary regulations relating to taxable years of personal service corporations, partnerships and S corporations (and owners of those entities). Changes to the applicable law were made by the Tax Reform Act of 1986. The text of those temporary regulations also serves as the comment document for this proposed rulemaking.

DATES: Written comments and requests for a public hearing must be mailed or delivered by February 22, 1988. The amendments are proposed to be effective for taxable years beginning after December 31, 1986.

ADDRESS: Send comments and requests for public hearing to: Commissioner of Internal Revenue, Attention: CC:LR:T (LR-45-87) Washington, D.C. 20224.

FOR FURTHER INFORMATION CONTACT: Arthur E. Davis III of the Legislation and Regulations Division, Office of Chief Counsel, Internal Revenue Service, 1111 Constitution Avenue, N.W., Washington, D.C. 20224 (Attention: CC:LR:T), (202) 566-3238, not a toll-free call.

SUPPLEMENTARY INFORMATION:

BACKGROUND

The temporary regulations (designated by a "T" following the section citation) in the Rules and Regulations portion of this issue of the Federal Register amend Part 1 of Title 26 of the Code of Federal Regulations. These amendments are proposed to conform the regulations to the requirements of section 806 of the Tax Reform Act of 1986 (Pub. L. 99-514), 100 Stat. 2362. For the text of the temporary regulations, see FR Doc. (T.D. 8167) published in the Rules and Regulations portion of this issue of the *Federal Register*. The preamble to the temporary regulations provides a discussion of the rules. The final regulations, which this document proposes to base on those temporary regulations, would amend Part 1 of Title 26 of the Code of Federal Regulations.

SPECIAL ANALYSES

The Commissioner of Internal Revenue has determined that this proposed rule is not a major rule as defined in Executive Order 12291. Accordingly, a Regulatory Impact Analysis is not required. Although this document is a notice of proposed rulemaking that solicits public comments, the Internal Revenue Service has concluded that the regulations proposed herein are interpretative and that the notice and public procedure requirements of 5 U.S.C. 553 do not apply. Accordingly, a regulatory flexibility analysis is not required under the Regulatory Flexibility Act (5 U.S.C. chapter 6).

COMMENTS AND REQUESTS FOR A PUBLIC HEARING

Before adopting these proposed regulations, consideration will be given to any written comments that are submitted (preferably eight copies) to the Commissioner of Internal Revenue. All comments will be available for public inspection and copying. A public hearing will be held upon written request to the Commissioner by any person who has submitted comments. If a public hearing is held, notice of the time and place will be published in the *Federal Register.*

DRAFTING INFORMATION

The principal author of these regulations is Arthur E. Davis III of the Legislation and Regulations Division, Office of Chief Counsel, Internal Revenue Service. However, personnel from other offices of the Internal Revenue Service and Treasury Department participated in developing the regulations on matters of both substance and style.

[¶ 49,087]   **Proposed Regulations (LR-137-86), published in the Federal Register on** December 22, 1987.

Personal interest: Paid or accrued: Qualified residence interest.—Reg. §§1.163-9T and 1.163-10T, relating to the treatment of personal interest and the treatment and determination of qualified residence interest, are proposed.

AGENCY: Internal Revenue Service, Treasury.

ACTION: Notice of proposed rulemaking by cross-reference to temporary regulations.

SUMMARY: In the Rules and Regulations portion of this issue of the *Federal Register,* the Internal Revenue Service is issuing temporary amendments to the income tax regulations relating to the treatment of personal interest and the treatment and determination of qualified residence interest. Changes to the law were made by the Tax Reform Act of 1986. The text of those temporary regulations also serves as the comment document for this proposed rulemaking.

DATES: The regulations contained in this document are proposed to be effective for taxable years beginning after December 31, 1986. Written comments and requests for a public hearing must be delivered or mailed by [60 DAYS AFTER PUBLICATION OF THIS PROPOSED RULE IN THE FEDERAL REGISTER].

ADDRESS: Send comments and requests for public hearing to: Commissioner of Internal Revenue, Attention: CC:LR:T (LR-137-86), Washington, D.C. 20224.

FOR FURTHER INFORMATION CONTACT: Sharon L. Hall of the Legislation and Regulations Division, Office of Chief Counsel, Internal Revenue Service, 111 Constitution Avenue, N.W., Washington, D.C. 20224 (Attention: CC:LR:T) (202-566-3288, not a toll-free call).

SUPPLEMENTARY INFORMATION:

BACKGROUND

The temporary regulations (designated by a T following the section citation) in the Rules and Regulations portion of this issue of the Federal Register amend Part 1 of Title 26 of the Code of Federal Regulations. These amendments reflect the provisions of section 163(h) of the Internal Revenue Code of 1986 as added by section 511(b) of the Tax Reform Act of 1986 (Pub. L. 99-514, 100 Stat. 2246). For the text of the temporary regulations, see FR Doc. (T.D. 8168) published in the Rules and Regulations portion of this issue of the *Federal Register*. A general discussion of the temporary regulations is contained in the preamble to the regulations. The final regulations, which this document proposes to base on the temporary regulations, would amend Part 1 of Title 26 of the Code of Federal Regulations.

SPECIAL ANALYSES

The Commissioner of Internal Revenue has determined that this proposed rule is not a major rule as defined in Executive Order 12291. Accordingly, a Regulatory Impact Analysis is not required. Although this document is a notice of proposed rulemaking that solicits public comments, the Internal Revenue Service has concluded that the proposed regulations are interpretative and that the notice and public procedure requirements of 5 U.S.C. 553 do not apply. Accordingly, a regulatory flexibility analysis is not required under the Regulatory Flexibility Act (5 U.S.C. chapter 6).

The collection of information requirements contained in this notice of proposed rulemaking have been submitted to the Office of Management and Budget (OMB) for review under section 3504(h) of the Paperwork Reduction Act. Comments on the requirements should be sent to the Office of Information and Regulatory Affairs of OMB, Attention: Desk Officer for Internal Revenue Service, New Executive Office Building, Washington, D.C. 20503. The Internal Revenue Service requests that persons submitting comments on these requirements to OMB also send copies of those comments to the Service.

COMMENTS AND REQUESTS FOR A PUBLIC HEARING

Before adopting these proposed regulations, consideration will be given to any written comments that are submitted (preferably eight copies) to the Commissioner of Internal Revenue. All comments will be available for public inspection and copying. A public hearing will be held upon written request to the Commissioner by any person who submitted comments. If a public hearing is held, notice of the time and place will be published in the *Federal Register*.

DRAFTING INFORMATION

The principal author of these proposed regulations is Sharon L. Hall of the Legislation and Regulations Division, Office of Chief Counsel, Internal Revenue Service. However, personnel from other offices of the Internal Revenue Service and Treasury participated in developing the regulations on matters of both substance and style.

[¶ 49,088]   **Proposed regulations (EE-167-86), published in the Federal Register on** January 6, 1988.

Qualified employee plans: Minimum vesting standards.—Reg. §§ 1.410(a)-3, 1.410(a)-8, 1.410(a)-9, 1.411(a)-3, 1.411(a)-4 and 1.411(a)-8, relating to minimum vesting standards for qualified employee plans, are proposed.

AGENCY: Internal Revenue Service, Treasury.

ACTION: Notice of proposed rulemaking by cross-reference to temporary regulations.

SUMMARY: This document provides proposed regulations relating to the minimum vesting standards for qualified employee plans. Changes to the applicable laws were made by the Tax Reform Act of 1986. These proposed regulations amend the current regulations to reflect the changes. In the Rules and Regulations portion of this issue of the FEDERAL REGISTER, the Internal Revenue Service is issuing temporary regulations relating to the minimum vesting standards. The text of these temporary regulations also serves as the comment document for this notice of proposed rulemaking.

DATES: Written comments and requests for a public hearing must be delivered or mailed by March 7, 1988. The amendments are proposed to be generally effective for plan years beginning after December 31, 1988.

ADDRESS: Send comments and requests for a public hearing to: Commissioner of Internal Revenue, Attention: CC:LR:T (EE-167-86), 1111 Constitution Avenue, N.W., Washington, D.C. 20224.

FOR FURTHER INFORMATION CONTACT: V. Moore of the Employee Plans and Exempt Organizations Division, Office of Chief Counsel, Internal Revenue Service, 1111 Constitution Avenue, N.W., Washington, D.C. 20224 (Attention: CC:LR:T) (202-566-3938, not a toll-free call).

SUPPLEMENTARY INFORMATION:

BACKGROUND

The temporary regulations in the Rules and Regulations portion of this issue of the FEDERAL REGISTER amend Part 1 of the Code of Federal Regulations. New § 1.410(a)-3T, § 1.410(a)-8T, § 1.410(a)-9T, § 1.411(a)-3T, § 1.411(a)-4T, and § 1.411(a)-8T are added to Part 1 of Title 26 of the Code of Federal Regulations. When these temporary regulations are promulgated as final regulations, § 1.410(a)-3, § 1.410(a)-5, § 1.410(a)-7, § 1.411(a)-3, § 1.411(a)-4, and § 1.411(a)-8 will be revised to reflect the new provisions. For the text of the temporary regulations, see T.D. 8170 published in the Rules and Regulations portion of this issue of the FEDERAL REGISTER. The preamble to the temporary regulations explains the amendments to the Income Tax Regulations.

REGULATORY FLEXIBILITY ACT AND EXECUTIVE ORDER 12291

Although this document is a notice of proposed rulemaking which solicits public comment, the Internal Revenue Service has concluded that the regulations proposed herein are interpretative and that the notice and public procedure requirements of 5 U.S.C. 553 do not apply. Accordingly, these proposed regulations do not constitute regulations subject to the Regulatory Flexibility Act (5 U.S.C. chapter 6).

The Commissioner of Internal Revenue has determined that this proposed rule is not a major rule as defined in Executive Order 12291 and that a regulatory impact analysis therefore is not required.

COMMENTS AND REQUESTS FOR A PUBLIC HEARING

Before adopting these proposed regulations, consideration will be given to any written comments that are submitted (preferably eight copies) to the Commissioner of Internal Revenue. All comments will be available for public inspection and copying. A public hearing will be held upon written request to the Commissioner by any person who has submitted written comments. If a public hearing is held, notice of the time and place will be published in the FEDERAL REGISTER.

DRAFTING INFORMATION

The principal author of these proposed regulations is V. Moore of the Employee Plans and Exempt Organizations Division of the Office of Chief Counsel. Other offices of the Internal Revenue Service and Treasury Department participated in developing the regulations, both on matters of substance and style.

[¶ 49,089]   **Proposed regulations (EE-129-86), published in the Federal Register on February 19, 1988.**

Employee benefit plans: Highly compensated employee: Compensation: Definition.—Reg. § 1.414(q)-1T, relating to the scope and meaning of the terms "highly compensated employee" and "compensation," are proposed.

AGENCY: Internal Revenue Service, Treasury.

ACTION: Notice of proposed rulemaking by cross-reference to temporary regulations.

SUMMARY: In the Rules and Regulations portion of this issue of the Federal Register, the Internal Revenue Service is issuing temporary regulations relating to the scope and meaning of the terms "highly compensated employee" in section 414(q) and "compensation" in section 414(s) of the Internal Revenue Code of 1986. They reflect changes made by the Tax Reform Act of 1986 (TRA '86). The text of those temporary regulations also serves as the text for this Notice of Proposed Rulemaking. These regulations will provide the public with guidance necessary to comply with the law and would affect sponsors of, and participants in, pension, profit-sharing and stock bonus plans, and certain other employee benefit plans.

DATES: Written comments and requests for a public hearing must be delivered or mailed April 19, 1988. In general, these regulations apply to years beginning on or after January 1, 1987, except as otherwise specified in TRA '86.

ADDRESS: Send comments and requests for a public hearing to: Commissioner of Internal Revenue, Attention: CC:LR:T (EE-129-86) Washington, D.C. 20224.

FOR FURTHER INFORMATION CONTACT: Nancy J. Marks of the Employee Plans and Exempt Organizations Division, Office of the Chief Counsel, Internal Revenue Service, 1111 Constitution Avenue, N.W., Washington, D.C. 20224 (Attention: CC:LR:T). (202-566-3938) (not a toll-free number).

SUPPLEMENTARY INFORMATION:

BACKGROUND

The temporary regulations in the Rules and Regulations portion of this issue of the Federal Register amend 26 CFR by adding a new section 1.414(q)-1T under Part 1 to provide guidance with respect to the definitions of highly compensated employee and compensation within the meaning of Code section 414(q) and (s). The regulations are proposed to be issued under the authority contained in sections 414(s) and 7805 of the Code (100 Stat. 2453, 68A Stat. 917; 26 U.S.C. 414(s), 7805). For the text of the temporary regulations, see F.R. Doc. (T.D.) published in the Rules and Regulations portion of this issue of the Federal Register.

SPECIAL ANALYSES

The Commissioner of Internal Revenue has determined that this proposed rule is not a major rule as defined in Executive Order 12291 and that a regulatory impact analysis is not required.

Although this document is a notice of proposed rulemaking which solicits public comment, the Internal Revenue Service has concluded that the regulations proposed herein are interpretative and that the notice and public procedure requirements of 5 U.S.C. 553 do not apply. Accordingly, these proposed regulations do not constitute regulations subject to the Regulatory Flexibility Act (5 U.S.C. chapter 6).

COMMENTS AND REQUESTS FOR PUBLIC HEARING

Before adopting these proposed regulations, consideration will be given to any written comments that are submitted (preferably eight copies) to the Commissioner of Internal Revenue. All comments will be available for public inspection and copying. A public hearing will be held upon written request to the Commissioner by any person who has submitted written comments. If a public hearing is held, notice of the time and place will be published in the FEDERAL REGISTER.

DRAFTING INFORMATION

The principal author of these proposed regulations is Nancy J. Marks of the Employee Plans and Exempt Organizations Division of the Office of Chief Counsel, Internal Revenue Service. However, personnel from other offices of the Internal Revenue Service and Treasury Department participated in developing the regulations, both on matters of substance and style.

[¶ 49,090] **Proposed Regulations (LR-14-88), published in the Federal Register on** February 24, 1988.

Passive activity losses and credits: Limitations.—Reg. §§1.469-1T, 1.469-2T, 1.469-3T, and 1.469-5T, relating to the limitations on passive activity losses and passive activity credits, are proposed. Reg. §1.469-11T was adopted 5/11/92 by T.D. 8417.

AGENCY: Internal Revenue Service, Treasury.

ACTION: Notice of proposed rulemaking by cross-reference to temporary regulations.

SUMMARY: In the Rules and Regulations portion of this issue of the Federal Register, the Internal Revenue Service is issuing temporary regulations relating to the limitations on passive activity losses and passive activity credits. Changes to the applicable tax law were made by the Tax Reform Act of 1986. The text of those temporary regulations also serves as the comment document for this notice of proposed rulemaking.

DATE: Except as otherwise provided in §1.469-11T, the amendments to the regulations are proposed to be effective for taxable years beginning after December 31, 1986. Written comments and requests for a public hearing must be delivered or mailed by [60 DAYS AFTER PUBLICATION OF THIS PROPOSED RULE IN THE FEDERAL REGISTER].

ADDRESS: Send comments and requests for a public hearing to: Commissioner of Internal Revenue, Attention: CC:LR:T (LR-14-88), Washington, D.C. 20224.

FOR FURTHER INFORMATION CONTACT: Michael J. Grace of the Legislation and Regulations Division, Office of Chief Counsel, Internal Revenue Service, 1111 Constitution Avenue, N.W., Washington, D.C. 20224, Attention: CC:LR:T, (202) 566-3288 (not a toll-free call).

SUPPLEMENTARY INFORMATION:

BACKGROUND

The temporary regulations (designated by a T following the section citations) in the Rules and Regulations portion of this issue of the Federal Register amend the Income Tax Regulations (26 CFR Part 1) to provide rules relating to the limitations on passive activity losses and passive activity credits. The temporary regulations reflect the amendment of the Internal Revenue Code of 1986 by sections 501 and 502 of the Tax Reform Act of 1986 (Pub. L. 99-514, 100 Stat. 2233 and 2241), which added section 469 (relating to the limitations on passive activity losses and passive activity credits). This document proposes to adopt the temporary regulations as final regulations. Accordingly, the text of the temporary regulations serves as the comment document for this notice of proposed rulemaking. In addition, the preamble to the temporary regulations explains the proposed and temporary rules.

For the text of the temporary regulations, see FR Doc. (T.D. 8175) published in the Rules and Regulations portion of this issue of the Federal Register.

SPECIAL ANALYSES

The Commissioner of Internal Revenue has determined that this proposed rule is not a major rule as defined in Executive Order 12291 and that a regulatory impact analysis is not required. Although this document is a notice of proposed rulemaking that solicits public comments, the Internal Revenue Service has concluded that the proposed regulations are interpretative and that the notice and public procedure requirements of 5 U.S.C. 553 do not apply. Accordingly, these proposed regulations are not subject to the Regulatory Flexibility Act (5 U.S.C. chapter 6).

COMMENTS AND REQUESTS FOR A PUBLIC HEARING

Before these proposed regulations are adopted, consideration will be given to any written comments that are submitted (preferably eight copies) to the Commissioner of Internal Revenue. All comments will be available for public inspection and copying. A public hearing will be held upon written request to the Commissioner by any person who submitted comments. If a public hearing is held, notice of the time and place will be published in the Federal Register.

DRAFTING INFORMATION

The principal author of these proposed regulations is Michael J. Grace of the Legislation and Regulations Division, Office of Chief Counsel, Internal Revenue Service. However, personnel from other offices of the Internal Revenue Service and Treasury Department participated in developing the regulations on matters of both substance and style.

[¶ 49,091] Proposed Regulations (INTL-941-86), published in the Federal Register on March 2, 1988.

Passive foreign investment companies: Elections.—Reg. §§ 1.1291-0T, 1.1294-1T and 1.1297-3T, relating to requirements for making certain elections by passive foreign investment companies and their shareholders that are United States persons, are proposed. Reg. § 1.1295-1T was removed 3/31/92 by T.D. 8404. Reg. § 1.1291-10 was adopted 12/26/96 by T.D. 8701.

AGENCY: Internal Revenue Service, Treasury.

ACTION: Notice of proposed rulemaking by cross-reference to temporary regulations.

SUMMARY: In the Rules and Regulations portion of this issue of the FEDERAL REGISTER, the Internal Revenue Service is issuing temporary income tax regulations relating to elections by passive foreign investment companies and their shareholders who are United States persons. The text of the temporary regulations also serves as the comment document for this notice of proposed rulemaking.

DATES: The regulations are proposed to be effective for taxable years beginning after December 31, 1986. Written comments and requests for a public hearing must be delivered or mailed by May 5, 1988.

ADDRESS: Send comments and requests for a public hearing to Commissioner of Internal Revenue, Attention: CC:LR:T (CC:INTL-941-86), Washington, DC 20224.

FOR FURTHER INFORMATION CONTACT: Gayle E. Novig of the Office of the Associate Chief Counsel (International), within the Office of Chief Counsel, Internal Revenue Service, 1111 Constitution Avenue N.W., Washington, DC 20224 (Attention: CC:LR:T) (202-634-5423, not a toll free number).

SUPPLEMENTARY INFORMATION:

BACKGROUND

This document provides proposed income tax regulations (26 CFR Part 1) under sections 1291(d)(2), 1294, 1295, and 1297(b)(1) of the Internal Revenue Code of 1986. These provisions were added to the Internal Revenue Code by section 1235 of the Tax Reform Act of 1986 (Pub. L. 99-514). The regulations will be effective for taxable years beginning after 1986. For the text of the temporary regulations, see T.D. 8178 published in the Rules and Regulations portion of this FEDERAL REGISTER. The preamble to the temporary regulations provides a discussion of the rules.

SPECIAL ANALYSES

It has been determined that this proposed rule is not a major rule as defined in Executive Order 12291. Therefore, a Regulatory Impact Analysis is not required and has not been prepared. Although this document is a notice of proposed rulemaking that solicits public comment, it has been concluded that the notice and public procedure requirements of 5 U.S.C. 553 do not apply. Accordingly, these proposed regulations do not constitute regulations subject to the Regulatory Flexibility Act (5 U.S.C. chapter 6).

COMMENTS AND REQUESTS FOR A PUBLIC HEARING

Before these temporary and proposed regulations are adopted as final regulations, consideration will be given to any written comments that are submitted (preferably seven copies) to the Commissioner of Internal Revenue. All comments will be available for public inspection and copying. A public hearing will be held upon written request to the Commissioner by any person who has submitted written comments. If a public hearing is held, notice of the time and place will be published in the FEDERAL REGISTER. The collection of information requirements contained herein have been submitted to the Office of Management and Budget (OMB) for review under section 3504(h) of the Paperwork Reduction Act. Comments on the requirements should be sent to the Office of Information and Regulatory Affairs of OMB,

Attention: Desk Officer for Internal Revenue Service, New Executive Office Building, Washington, DC 20503. The Internal Revenue Service requests persons submitting comments to OMB to also send copies of the comments to the Service.

DRAFTING INFORMATION

The principal author of these temporary regulations is Gayle E. Novig of the Office of the Associate Chief Counsel (International), within the Office of Chief Counsel, Internal Revenue Service. However, personnel from other offices of the Internal Revenue Service and Treasury Department participated in developing the regulations, on matters of both substance and style.

[¶ 49,092] Proposed Regulations (LR-97-86), published in the Federal Register on March 28, 1988.

Itemized deductions: Two-percent floor.—Reg. §§ 1.62-1T, 1.67-1T and 1.67-2T, relating to the two-percent floor on miscellaneous itemized deductions, are proposed.

AGENCY: Internal Revenue Service, Treasury.

ACTION: Notice of proposed rulemaking by cross-reference to temporary regulations.

SUMMARY: In the Rules and Regulations portion of this issue of the FEDERAL REGISTER, the Internal Revenue Service is issuing temporary income tax regulations relating to the 2-percent floor on miscellaneous itemized deductions. The text of the temporary regulations also serves as the comment document for this notice of proposed rulemaking.

DATES:

PROPOSED EFFECTIVE DATE

The regulations are proposed to be effective for taxable years beginning after December 31, 1986.

DATES FOR COMMENTS AND REQUESTS FOR A PUBLIC HEARING

Written comments and requests for a public hearing must be delivered or mailed by May 27, 1988.

ADDRESS: Send comments and requests for a public hearing to: Commissioner of Internal Revenue, Attention: CC:LR:T (LR-97-86) Washington, D.C. 20224.

FOR FURTHER INFORMATION CONTACT: Beverly A. Baughman of the Legislation and Regulations Division, Office of Chief Counsel, Internal Revenue Service, 1111 Constitution Ave., N.W., Washington, D.C. 20224 (Attention: CC:LR:T) (202-566-3297, not a toll-free call).

SUPPLEMENTARY INFORMATION:

BACKGROUND

The temporary regulations in the Rules and Regulations portion of this issue of the FEDERAL REGISTER amend the Income Tax Regulations (26 CFR Part 1) to provide rules under section 67.

For the text of the temporary regulations, see T.D. 8189, published in the Rules and Regulations portion of this issue of the FEDERAL REGISTER. The preamble to the temporary regulations explains the addition to the regulations.

SPECIAL ANALYSES

The Commissioner of Internal Revenue has determined that this proposed rule is not a major rule as defined in Executive Order 12291 and that a Regulatory Impact Analysis is therefore not required. Although this document is a notice of proposed rulemaking that solicits public comment, the Internal Revenue Service has concluded that the regulations proposed herein are interpretative and that the notice and public procedure requirements of 5 U.S.C. 553 do not apply. Accordingly, these proposed regulations do not constitute regulations subject to the Regulatory Flexibility Act (5 U.S.C. chapter 6).

COMMENTS AND REQUESTS FOR A PUBLIC HEARING

Before adopting these proposed regulations, consideration will be given to any written comments that are submitted (preferably seven copies) to the Commissioner of Internal Revenue. All comments will be available for public inspection and copying. A public hearing will be held upon written request to the Commissioner by any person who has submitted written comments. If public hearing is held, notice of time and place will be published in the FEDERAL REGISTER. The collection of information requirements contained herein have been submitted for OMB review under the Paperwork Reduction Act, and comments on them should be sent to the Office of Information and Regulatory Affairs of OMB, ATTN: Desk Office for Internal Revenue Service, New Executive Office Bldg., Washington, D.C. 20503. The Internal Revenue Service requests persons submitting comments to OMB to also send copies of the comments to the Service.

DRAFTING INFORMATION

The principal author of these proposed regulations is Beverly A. Baughman of the Legislation and Regulations Divisions of the Office of Chief Counsel, Internal Revenue Service. However, personnel from other offices of the Internal Revenue Service and Treasury Department participated in developing the regulations, both on matters of substance and style.

———————————

[¶ 49,093]   **Proposed Regulations and Amendments of Regulations (EE-184-86), published in the Federal Register on** April 11, 1988.

Pension plans: Accruals: Retirement age.—Reg. §§1.410(a)-4A and 1.411(b)-2 and amendments of Reg. §§1.411(a)-1, 1.411(a)-7 and 1.411(c)-1, relating to the requirement for continued accruals beyond normal retirement age under employee pension plans, are proposed.

AGENCY: Internal Revenue Service, Treasury.

ACTION: Notice of proposed rulemaking.

SUMMARY: This document contains proposed regulations relating to the requirement for continued accruals beyond normal retirement age under employee pension benefit plans. Changes to the applicable tax law were made by the Omnibus Budget Reconciliation Act of 1986. These regulations will provide the public with guidance needed to comply with the minimum participation and vesting standards and affect employers maintaining employee retirement plans.

DATES: Written comments and requests for a public hearing must be delivered or mailed by [60 DAYS AFTER PUBLICATION OF NOTICE OF PROPOSED RULEMAKING]. These amendments generally apply to plan years beginning after December 31, 1987, except as otherwise specified in the Omnibus Budget Reconciliation Act of 1986.

ADDRESS: Send comments and requests for a public hearing to: Commissioner of Internal Revenue, Attention: CC:LR:T (EE-184-86) Washington, D.C. 20224.

FOR FURTHER INFORMATION CONTACT: Michael C. Garvey of the Employee Benefits and Exempt Organizations Division, Office of Chief Counsel, Internal Revenue Service, 1111 Constitution Avenue, N.W., Washington, D.C. 20224 (Attention: CC:LR:T) (202-566-6271) (not a toll-free number).

SUPPLEMENTARY INFORMATION:

BACKGROUND

This document contains proposed amendments to the Income Tax Regulations (26 CFR Part 1) under sections 410 and 411 of the Internal Revenue Code of 1986. These amendments are proposed to conform the regulations to sections 9201 through 9204, Subtitle C (Older Americans Pension Benefits) of Title IX of the Omnibus Budget Reconciliation Act of 1986 (Pub. L. 99-509) (OBRA 1986) (100 Stat. 1874, 1973).

EXPLANATION OF PROVISIONS

Section 9202(b)(1) of OBRA 1986 added subparagraph (H) to section 411(b)(1) of the Internal Revenue Code (Code) to provide rules for continued benefit accruals under defined benefit plans without regard to the attainment of any age. Section 9202(b)(2) of OBRA 1986 redesignated paragraphs (2) and (3) of Code section 411(b) as paragraphs (3) and (4) and added a new paragraph (2) to Code section 411(b) to provide rules for allocations to the accounts of employees in defined contribution plans without regard to the attainment of any age.

Effective with respect to plan years beginning after December 31, 1987, section 411(b)(1)(H)(i) provides the general rule that a defined benefit plan will not be treated as meeting the minimum vesting standards of section 411 (and, accordingly, will not constitute a qualified plan under section 401(a)) if under the plan an employee's benefit accrual is ceased, or the rate of an employee's benefit accrual is reduced, because of the attainment of any age. Effective for plan years beginning after December 31, 1987, section 411(b)(2) provides that a defined contribution plan will not be treated as satisfying the minimum vesting standards of section 411 (and, accordingly, will not constitute a qualified plan under section

401(a)) if allocations to an employee's account are ceased, or the rate of allocations to an employee's account is reduced, because of the attainment of any age.

The proposed regulations provide that reductions or cessations of account allocations or benefit accruals that are based on factors other than age will not affect the qualification of the plan under section 411(b)(1)(H) or (b)(2). The proposed regulations also provide that benefits under a defined benefit plan may accrue at different rates without violating section 411(b)(1)(H), provided the difference in the rate of benefit accrual is determined without regard to the attainment of any age.

Section 411(b)(1)(H)(ii) provides that a plan will not be treated as failing to satisfy the general rule in section 411(b)(1)(H)(i) merely because the plan contains a limitation (determined without regard to age) on the maximum number of years of service or participation that are taken into account in determining benefits under the plan or merely because the plan contains a limitation on the amount of benefits an employee will receive under the plan. The proposed regulations provide that these limitations are permitted in both defined benefit plans and defined contribution plans (including target benefit plans).

Section 411(b)(1)(H)(iii) provides that, with respect to an employee who, as of the end of a plan year, has attained normal retirement age under a defined benefit plan, certain adjustments may be made to the benefit accrual for the plan year if the plan distributes benefits to the employee or if the plan adjusts the amount of the benefits payable to take into account delayed payment. The continued benefit accrual rules of section 411(b)(1)(H) operate in conjunction with the suspension of benefit payment rules under section 203(a)(3)(B) of the Employee Retirement Income Security Act of 1974 (ERISA) and the proposed regulations do not change the rules relating to the suspension of pension benefit payments under section 203(a)(3)(B) of ERISA and the regulations thereunder issued by the Department of Labor. However, the proposed regulations provide rules under which benefit accruals required under section 411(b)(1)(H)(i) may be reduced or offset either by the value of actuarial adjustments in an employee's normal retirement benefit or by the value of benefit distributions made to an employee.

Section 411(b)(1)(H)(iv) provides that a defined benefit plan will not be treated as failing to satisfy the general rule of section 411(b)(1)(H)(i) merely because the subsidized portion of an early retirement benefit provided under the plan (whether provided on a permanent or temporary basis) is disregarded in determining benefit accruals under the plan. The proposed regulations also provide that a plan will not be treated as failing to satisfy the general rule of section 411(b)(1)(H)(i) merely because a social security supplemental benefit or a qualified disability benefit is disregarded in determining benefit accruals under the plan.

The proposed regulations provide that the rate of an employee's benefit accrual under a defined benefit plan or the rate of allocations to an employee's account under a defined contribution plan will be considered to be reduced on account of the attainment of a specified age if optional forms of benefits, ancillary benefits or other benefits, rights or features under a plan that are provided with respect to benefits or allocations prior to such age are not provided (on terms that are at least as favorable to employees) with respect to benefits or allocations after such age. Thus, for example, under the proposed regulations, a plan may not make a lump sum option available only with respect to benefits or allocations attributable to service prior to a specified age. Similarly, a plan may not use actuarial assumptions that are less favorable to employees for determining lump sum benefits payable after a specified age than are used for determining lump sum benefits payable prior to such age. However, the proposed regulations provide that the accrual rate under a defined benefit plan will not be considered to be reduced merely because the subsidized portion of an early retirement benefit, a qualified disability benefit or a social security supplemental benefit provided under the plan ceases to be provided to an employee or is provided on a reduced basis to an employee by a plan on account of the employee's attainment of a specified age.

Section 411(b)(1)(H)(v) and (b)(2)(D) provide that the Secretary shall prescribe regulations coordinating the requirements of section 411(b)(1)(H) and (b)(2) with the requirements of sections 411(a), 404, 410, 415 and the antidiscrimination provisions of subchapter D of Chapter 1 (Code sections 401 through ¶425). The proposed regulations provide that no allocation to the account of an employee in a defined contribution plan and no benefit accrual on behalf of an employee in a defined benefit plan are required under section 411(b)(1)(H) or (b)(2) if such allocation or benefit accrual would cause the plan to (1) exceed the section 415 limitations on benefits and contributions, or (2) discriminate in favor of highly compensated employees within the meaning of section 401(a)(4).

Section 9203(a)(2) of OBRA 1986 amended Code section 410(a)(2) to provide that a plan will not constitute a qualified plan under section 401(a) if the plan excludes from participation (on the basis of age) an employee who has attained a specified age. The proposed regulations provide that, effective for plan years beginning after December 31, 1987, a plan may not apply a maximum age provision to any employee who has at least one hour of service for the employer on or after January 1, 1988, regardless of when the employee first performed an hour of service for the employer.

In the case of an employee who was ineligible to participate in a plan before the effective date of amended Code section 410(a)(2) because of a maximum age condition and who is eligible to participate in the plan on or after the effective date of such section, hours of service and years of service credited to the employee before the first plan year beginning on or after January 1, 1988, shall be taken into account in accordance with section 411 and the regulations thereunder and in accordance with 29 CFR Part 2530 for purposes of determining the employee's nonforfeitable right to the employee's accrued benefit. However, with respect to an employee described in the preceding sentence, hours of service and years of service credited to the employee before the first plan year beginning on or after January 1, 1988, are not required to be taken into account for purposes of determining the employee's accrued benefit under the plan for plan years beginning on or after January 1, 1988. See, also, section 411(a)(4) and §1.411(a)-5 for rules relating to service that must be taken into account in determining an employee's nonforfeitable right to the employee's accrued benefit.

Section 9203(b)(2) of OBRA 1986 amended Code section 411(a)(8)(B) to provide rules relating to the determination of a participant's normal retirement age under a defined benefit plan and a defined contribution plan. Because section 203(e) of the pending Technical Corrections Act of 1987 (H.R. 2636) would change the definition of normal retirement age from the definition now set forth in section 411(a)(8)(B) (as amended by OBRA 1986), the proposed regulations do not set forth any rules under section 411(a)(8)(B) (as amended by OBRA 1986).

Section 9202(b) of OBRA 1986 amended Code section 411(b)(2)(C) to require the Secretary to provide by regulations for the application of the continued allocation rules of section 411(b)(2) to target benefit plans. The proposed regulations do not provide detailed special rules applicable to target benefit plans. Target benefit plans are subject to the rules applicable to defined contribution plans. The Commissioner will prescribe such additional rules relating to the continued allocation of contributions and accrual of benefits under target benefit plans as may be necessary or appropriate.

EFFECTIVE DATE

Section 9204(a)(1) of OBRA 1986 provides that the amendments made with regard to section 411(b)(1)(H) and (b)(2) "shall apply only with respect to plan years beginning on or after January 1, 1988, and only to employees who have 1 hour of service in any plan year to which such amendments apply." The proposed regulations provide that section 411(b)(1)(H) and (b)(2) does not apply to an employee who does not have at least 1 hour of service for the employer in a plan year beginning on or after January 1, 1988.

However, the proposed regulations provide that section 411(b)(1)(H) and (b)(2) applies with respect to all years of service completed by an employee who has at least 1 hour of service in a plan year beginning on or after January 1, 1988. Accordingly, under section 411(b)(1)(H)(i), the proposed regulations provide that, for plan years beginning on or after January 1, 1988, in determining the benefit payable under a defined benefit plan to a participant who has at least 1 hour of service in a plan year beginning on or after January 1, 1988, the plan does not satisfy section 411(a) if the plan disregards, because of the participant's attainment of any age, any year of service completed by the participant or any compensation earned by the participant after attaining such age, including years of service completed and compensation earned before the first plan year beginning on or after January 1, 1988. Under the proposed regulations, section 411(b)(2) does not require allocations to the accounts of employees under a defined contribution plan for any plan year beginning before January 1, 1988. However, the proposed regulations provide that, for plan years beginning on or after January 1, 1988, in determining the allocation to the account of a participant (who has at least 1 hour of service in a plan year beginning on or after January 1, 1988) under a defined contribution plan that determines allocations under a service related allocation formula, the plan does not satisfy section 411(a) if the plan disregards, because of the participant's attainment of any age, any year of service completed by the participant.

Under the proposed regulations, a defined benefit plan and a defined contribution plan will not be treated as impermissibly disregarding, because of the participant's attainment of any age, a year of service completed by the participant before the first plan year beginning before January 1, 1988, merely because the participant was not eligible under the plan to make mandatory or voluntary employee contributions (as well as contributions under a cash or deferred arrangement described in section 401(k)) for such year.

TITLE I OF ERISA AND OBRA 1986

Under section 101 of Reorganization Plan No. 4 of 1978 (43 FR 47713), the Secretary of the Treasury has jurisdiction over the subject matter addressed in the OBRA 1986 regulations. Therefore, under section 104 of the Reorganization Plan, these regulations apply when the Secretary of Labor exercises authority under Title I of ERISA (as amended, including the amendments made by Title IX of OBRA 1986 and the amendments by the Tax Reform Act of 1986). Thus, the requirements also apply to employee plans subject to Part 2 of Title I of ERISA.

Under section 9201 of OBRA 1986, these regulations also apply for purposes of applying comparable provisions under section 4(i)(7) of the Age Discrimination in Employment Act of 1967 (29 U.S.C. 623) as amended. No inference is intended under the proposed regulations as to the application of the Age Discrimination in Employment Act of 1967, as in effect prior to its amendment by OBRA 1986, to employees who are not credited with at least 1 hour of service in a plan year beginning on or after January 1, 1988.

RELIANCE ON THESE PROPOSED REGULATIONS

Taxpayers may rely on these proposed regulations for guidance pending the issuance of final regulations. Because these regulations are generally effective for plan years beginning after 1987, the Service will apply these proposed regulations in issuing rulings and in examining returns with respect to taxpayers and plans. If future guidance is more restrictive, such guidance will be applied without retroactive effect.

TIME OF PLAN AMENDMENTS

The proposed regulations provide rules relating to the postponement of the deadline for amending plans to comply with the provisions of OBRA 1986. Plan amendments required to conform the plan to the changes contained in OBRA 1986 need not be made until the dates specified in section 1140 of the Tax Reform Act of 1986 (in general, the last day of the first plan year commencing on or after January 1, 1989). This deferred amendment date is available only if: (1) the plan is operated in accordance with the applicable provisions of OBRA 1986 for the period beginning with the effective date of the provision with respect to the plan; (2) the plan amendments adopted are retroactive to such effective date; and (3) the plan amendments adopted are consistent with plan operation during the retroactive effective period.

SPECIAL ANALYSES

The Commissioner of Internal Revenue has determined that this proposed rule is not a major rule as defined in Executive Order 12291 and that a regulatory impact analysis is not required.

Although this document is a notice of proposed rulemaking which solicits public comments, the Internal Revenue Service has concluded that the regulations proposed herein are interpretative and that the notice and public procedure requirements of 5 U.S.C. 553 do not apply. Accordingly, these proposed regulations do not constitute regulations subject to the Regulatory Flexibility Act (5 U.S.C. Chapter 6).

COMMENTS AND REQUESTS FOR A PUBLIC HEARING

Before adopting these proposed regulations, consideration will be given to any written comments that are submitted (preferably eight copies) to the Commissioner of Internal Revenue. All comments will be available for public inspection and copying. A public hearing will be held upon written request to the Commissioner by any person who has submitted comments. If a public hearing is held, notice of the time and place will be published in the FEDERAL REGISTER.

DRAFTING INFORMATION

The principal author of these proposed regulations is Michael C. Garvey of the Employee Benefits and Exempt Organizations Division of the Office of Chief Counsel, Internal Revenue Service. However, personnel from other offices of the Internal Revenue Service and Treasury Department participated in developing the regulations, both on matters of substance and style.

[¶ 49,095]   **Proposed Regulations (REG-209039-87) [originally issued as INTL-491-87], published in the Federal Register on** May 5, 1988.

Nonresident aliens and foreign corporations: Disposition of investment in U.S. real property.—Reg. §§ 1.897-4AT, 1.897-5T, 1.897-6T, 1.897-7T, 1.897-8T, 1.897-9T, 1.1445-10T and 1.1445-11T, relating to dispositions of U.S. real property interests by nonresident aliens and foreign corporations, are proposed. Temporary Reg. § 1.1445-9T was removed by T.D. 9082.

AGENCY: Internal Revenue Service, Treasury.

ACTION: Notice of proposed rulemaking by cross-reference to temporary regulations.

SUMMARY: In the Rules and Regulations portion of this issue, the Internal Revenue Service is issuing temporary regulations that add new §§ 1.897-4AT, 1.897-5T, 1.897-6T, 1.897-7T, 1.897-8T and 1.897-9T relating to corporate distributions and certain nonrecognition exchanges, and new §§ 1.1445-9T and 1.1445-10T relating to certain withholding provisions, all in the context of the Foreign Investment in Real Property Tax Act (FIRPTA). In addition, the regulations provide rules with respect to the treatment of interests in publicly traded corporations. The text of the temporary regulations also serves as the comment document for this notice of proposed rulemaking.

DATES: Written comments and requests for a public hearing must be delivered or mailed before July 5, 1988. Except as otherwise specifically provided, these rules are proposed to apply to exchanges, distributions, or transfers of U.S. real property interests occurring after June 18, 1980. Although these regulations are proposed to be applied as of June 18, 1980, it is anticipated that any taxpayer desiring to apply the temporary regulations in lieu of the final regulations for the period prior to the adoption of the final regulations will be allowed to so choose. All changes and additions to portions of the existing regulations under sections 897 and 1445 are proposed to be generally effective after June 6, 1988. Paragraph (e) of §1.897-9T dealing with foreign governments and international organizations is effective July 1, 1986. The special rules under section 1445 for section 1034 nonrecognition are effective after August 3, 1988.

ADDRESS: Send comments and requests for a public hearing to Commissioner of Internal Revenue, Attention: CC:LR:T (INTL-491-87), Washington, DC 20224.

FOR FURTHER INFORMATION CONTACT: Charles P. Besecky of the Office of Associate Chief Counsel (International) within the Office of Chief Counsel, Internal Revenue Service, 1111 Constitution Avenue, N.W., Washington, DC 20224 (Attn: CC:LR:T). Telephone 202-566-3319, (not a toll-free call).

SUPPLEMENTARY INFORMATION:

BACKGROUND

The temporary regulations published in the Rules and Regulations portion of this issue of the Federal Register add §§1.897-4AT, 1.897-5T, 1.897-6T, 1.897-7T, 1.897-8T, 1.897-9T, 1.1445-9T and 1.1445-10T to 26 CFR Part 1. The final regulations that are proposed to be based on these temporary regulations would amend 26 CFR Part 1 by adding these temporary regulations sections as final regulations under section 897(c), (d), (e), (g), and (j), under the authority of section 367(e)(2), and under section 1445 of the Internal Revenue Code of 1986. For the text of the temporary regulations, see FR Doc.—[T.D. 8198] published in the Rules and Regulations portion of this issue of the Federal Register.

SPECIAL ANALYSES

It has been determined that this proposed rule is not a major rule as defined in Executive Order 12291 and that a Regulatory Impact Analysis is therefore not required. It has also been determined that this rule will not have a significant impact on a substantial number of small entities. Few small entities would be affected by these regulations. A regulatory flexibility analysis, therefore, is not required under the Regulatory Flexibility Act (5 U.S.C. chapter 6).

COMMENTS AND REQUESTS FOR A PUBLIC HEARING

Before adopting these proposed regulations, consideration will be given to any written comments that are submitted (preferably eight copies) to the Commissioner of Internal Revenue. All comments will be available for public inspection and copying. A public hearing will be held upon written request to the Commissioner by any person who has submitted written comments. If a public hearing is held, notice of the time and place will be published in the FEDERAL REGISTER.

The collection of information requirements contained herein have been submitted to the Office of Management and Budget (OMB) for review under section 3504(h) of the Paperwork Reduction Act. Comments on the requirements should be sent to the Office of Information and Regulatory Affairs of OMB, Attention: Desk Office for Internal Revenue Service, New Executive Office Building, Washington, DC 20503. The Internal Revenue Service requests persons submitting comments to OMB to also send copies of the comments to the Service.

DRAFTING INFORMATION

The principal author of this regulation is Charles P. Besecky of the Office of Associate Chief Counsel, (International), within the Office of Chief Counsel, Internal Revenue Service. However, personnel from other offices of the Internal Revenue Service and Treasury Department participated in developing the regulations on matters of substance and style.

[¶49,096] **Proposed Amendments of Regulations (LR-83-87)**, published in the Federal Register on May 5, 1988.

Charitable contributions: Substantiation requirements.—Amendments of Reg. §§1.642(c)-1 and 1.642(c)-2, relating to deductions in excess of $5,000 claimed for charitable contributions of property, are proposed. Proposed amendments of Reg. §1.170A-13 was withdrawn on August 7, 2008 by REG-140029-07.

AGENCY: Internal Revenue Service, Treasury.

ACTION: Notice of proposed rulemaking.

SUMMARY: This document contains proposed amendments to the income tax regulations relating to deductions in excess of $5,000 claimed for charitable contributions of certain property. The proposed regulations would provide substantiation requirements with which all donors must comply with respect to charitable contributions of certain property if the amount claimed or reported as a deduction with respect to the contribution exceeds $5,000.

DATES:

PROPOSED EFFECTIVE DATES

The regulations are proposed to be effective for certain charitable contributions of property made after the date that is 30 days after a Treasury decision on this subject is published in the FEDERAL REGISTER.

DATES FOR COMMENTS AND REQUESTS FOR A PUBLIC HEARING

Written comments and requests for a public hearing must be delivered or mailed by July 6, 1988.

ADDRESS: Send comments and requests for a public hearing to: Commissioner of Internal Revenue, Attention: CC:LR:T (LR-83-87), Washington, D.C. 20224.

FOR FURTHER INFORMATION CONTACT: Beverly A. Baughman of the Legislation and Regulations Division, Office of Chief Counsel, Internal Revenue Service, 1111 Constitution Ave., N.W., Washington, D.C. 20224 (Attention: CC:LR:T) (202-566-3297, not a toll-free call.)

SUPPLEMENTARY INFORMATION:

BACKGROUND

On December 31, 1984, the FEDERAL REGISTER published proposed amendments to the Income Tax Regulations (26 CFR Part 1) under sections 170(a) and 6050L of the Internal Revenue Code of 1954, as well as temporary regulations (T.D. 8003) containing the same rules. The temporary regulations set forth substantiation requirements with which individuals, closely held corporations, personal service corporations, partnerships, and S corporations must comply with respect to charitable contributions of certain property made after December 31, 1984, if the amount claimed or reported as a deduction with respect to the contribution exceeds $5,000. Treasury decision [8199], which is contained in the Rules and Regulations portion of this issue of the FEDERAL REGISTER, finalizes the temporary and proposed regulations. The final regulations add the requirement that C corporations (as defined in section 1361 (a)(2)) must comply with some of the substantiation requirements contained in the regulations with respect to contributions of certain property made after June 6, 1988.

This document contains proposed amendments to § 1.170A-13 of the Income Tax Regulations (26 CFR Part 1), as amended by T.D. [INSERT T.D. NUMBER]

EXPLANATION OF PROVISIONS

The proposed regulations would apply all the substantiation requirements contained in § 1.170A-13 (c) to all donors (including C corporations, trusts, estates, and pooled income funds) with respect to contributions of certain property made after the date that is 30 days after a Treasury decision on the subject of this notice of proposed rulemaking is published in the FEDERAL REGISTER.

SPECIAL ANALYSES

The Commissioner of Internal Revenue has determined that this proposed rule is not a major rule as defined in Executive Order 12291 and that a Regulatory Impact Analysis is therefore not required. Although this document is a notice of proposed rulemaking that solicits public comment, the Internal Revenue Service has concluded that the regulations proposed herein are interpretative and that the notice and public procedure requirements of 5 U.S.C. 553 do not apply. Accordingly, the proposed regulations do not constitute regulations subject to the Regulatory Flexibility Act (5 U.S.C. chapter 6).

COMMENTS AND REQUESTS FOR A PUBLIC HEARING

Before adopting these proposed regulations consideration will be given to any written comments that are submitted (preferably seven copies) to the Commissioner of Internal Revenue. All comments will be available for public inspection and copying. A public hearing will be held upon written request to the Commissioner by any person who has submitted written comments. If a public hearing is held, notice of the time and place will be published in the FEDERAL REGISTER. The collection of information requirements contained herein have been submitted to the Office of Management and Budget (OMB) for review under section 3504 (h) of the Paperwork Reduction Act. Comments on the requirements should be sent to the Office of Information and Regulatory Affairs for OMB, Attention: Desk Officer for Internal Revenue Service, New Executive Office Building, Washington, D.C. 20503. The Internal Revenue Service requests persons submitting comments to OMB to also send copies of the comments to the Service.

DRAFTING INFORMATION

The principal author of there proposed regulations is Beverly A. Baughman of the Legislation and Regulations Division of the Office of Chief Counsel, Internal Revenue Service. However, personnel from other offices of the Internal Revenue Service and Treasury Department participated in developing the regulations, on matters of both substance and style.

[¶ 49,097]   **Proposed Regulations (INTL-990-86), published in the Federal Register on** May 19, 1988.

Interest paid: Pass-through certificates: Registration requirements.—Reg. § 1.163-5T, relating to registration requirements with respect to certain debt obligations and sanctions on issuers of registration-required obligations not in registered form, is proposed.

AGENCY: Internal Revenue Service, Treasury.

ACTION: Notice of proposed rulemaking by cross-reference to temporary regulations.

SUMMARY: This document provides a notice of proposed rulemaking relating to the definition of the term "registration-required obligations" with respect to pass-through certificates and the application of the sanctions on issuers of "registration-required obligations" not in registered form to the issuers of such certificates. In the Rules and Regulations portion of this Federal Register, the Internal Revenue Service is issuing temporary income tax regulations with respect to this subject. The text of these temporary regulations serves as the comment document for this notice of proposed rulemaking.

DATE: Written comments and requests for a public hearing must be delivered or mailed by July 18, 1988.

ADDRESS: Send comments and requests for public hearing to: Commissioner of Internal Revenue, Attention: CC:LR:T (INTL-990-86), Washington, D.C. 20224.

FOR FURTHER INFORMATION CONTACT: Carl M. Cooper of the Office of Associate Chief Counsel (International), within the Office of Chief Counsel, Internal Revenue Service, 1111 Constitution Avenue, N.W., Washington, D.C. 20224, Attention: CC:LR:T [INTL-990-86], telephone 202-566-3388, (not a toll-free number).

SUPPLEMENTARY INFORMATION:

BACKGROUND

Section 1.163-5T(d) was deleted by T.D. 8110, which was published on December 19, 1986, in the Federal Register at 51 FR 45453 when all of § 1.163-5T was removed. Paragraph (d) is being replaced retroactively into the regulations as § 1.163-5T(d) (with prior paragraphs reserved) through temporary regulations published in the Rules and Regulations portion of this issue of the Federal Register.

REGULATORY FLEXIBILITY ACT AND EXECUTIVE ORDER 12291

The Commissioner of Internal Revenue has determined that this proposed rule is not a major rule as defined in Executive Order 12291 and that a Regulatory Impact Analysis is therefore not required. Although this document is a notice of proposed rulemaking which solicits public comment, the Internal Revenue Service has concluded that the regulations proposed herein are interpretative and that the notice and public procedure requirements of 5 U.S.C. 553 do not apply. Accordingly, these proposed regulations do not constitute regulations subject to the Regulatory Flexibility Act (5 U.S.C. chapter 6).

COMMENTS AND REQUESTS FOR A PUBLIC HEARING

Before adopting these proposed regulations as final regulations, consideration will be given to any written comments that are submitted (preferably eight copies) to the Commissioner of Internal Revenue. All comments will be available for public inspection and copying. A public hearing will be held **upon written request to the Commissioner by any person who has submitted written comments. If a public hearing is held, notice of the time and place will be published in the Federal Register.**

DRAFTING INFORMATION

The principal author of this regulation is Carl M. Cooper of the Office of Associate Chief Counsel (International), within the Office of Chief Counsel, Internal Revenue Service. However, personnel from other offices of the Internal Revenue Service and Treasury Department participated in developing the regulations on matters of substance and style.

LIST OF SUBJECTS IN 26 CFR 1.61 through 1.281-4

Income taxes, Taxable income, Deductions, Exemptions

Proposal of Regulations

The temporary regulations, FR Doc. [T.D. 8202] published in the Rules and Regulations portion of this issue of the Federal Register, are hereby also proposed as final regulations under section 163 of the Internal Revenue Code of 1954.

[¶ 49,098]   Proposed Amendment of Regulations (INTL-905-87), published in the Federal Register on May 19, 1988.

Interest paid: Pass-through certificates: Registration requirements.—Amendments of Reg. § 1.163-5T, relating to registration requirements with respect to certain debt obligations and sanctions on issuers of registration-required obligations not in registered form, are proposed.

AGENCY: Internal Revenue Service, Treasury.

ACTION: Notice of proposed rulemaking.

SUMMARY: This document provides a notice of proposed rulemaking relating to the application of the sanctions on issuers of registration required obligations not in registered form. These regulations would provide the public with guidance necessary to comply with the Tax Equity and Fiscal Responsibility Act of 1982.

DATES: Written comments and requests for a public hearing must be delivered or mailed before July 18, 1988. These regulations are proposed to be applicable to the transfers of obligations occurring after August 17, 1988.

ADDRESS: Send comments and request for a public hearing to: Commissioner of Internal Revenue, Attention: CC:LR:T (INTL-905-87), Washington, DC 20224.

FOR FURTHER INFORMATION CONTACT: Carl M. Cooper of the Office of Associate Chief Counsel (International), within the Office of Chief Counsel, Internal Revenue Service, 1111 Constitution Avenue, N.W., Washington, DC 20224 (Attn: CC:LR:T). Telephone 202-566-3388, (not a toll-free call).

SUPPLEMENTARY INFORMATION:

BACKGROUND

Section 4701 imposes a tax on issuers of "registration-required obligations" not in registered form. Section 5f.103-1(c)(1) provides generally that an obligation is in registered form if it is registered with the issuer (or its agent) and may be transferred by surrender and reissuance by the issuer (or its agent), or through a book entry system maintained by the issuer (or its agent), or through both of these methods.

EXPLANATION OF PROVISIONS

An issuer or its agent may have no knowledge or control over the method of transfer of an obligation that is held by a nominee. A new paragraph (d)(7) of § 1.163-5T has been proposed to provide explicitly for the application of section 4701 to circumstances in which a holder transfers an obligation through a method not described in § 5f.103-1(c)(1).

Section 1.163-5T(d)(7) of these proposed regulations provides, pursuant to § 46.4701-1(a)(5), that any person who holds a registration required obligation that is in registered form within the meaning of § 5f.103-1(c)(1) and who transfers the obligation through a method not described in § 5f.103-1(c)(1) is considered the issuer of the obligations transferred for purposes of section 4701. Such transferor is therefore subject to the tax imposed under section 4701, even though he may not be the person whose interest deduction would be disallowed by reason of section 163(f)(1). Such transferor is considered to have issued the obligation on the date of the transfer in the principal amount of the obligation transferred. Section 1.163-5T(d)(7) would apply to transfers occurring after August 17, 1988.

SPECIAL ANALYSES

It has been determined that this proposed rule is not a major rule as defined in Executive Order 12291 and that a Regulatory Impact Analysis is therefore not required. Although this document is a notice of proposed rulemaking that solicits public comments, it has been determined that the regulations proposed herein are interpretative and that the notice and public procedure requirements of 5 U.S.C. 553 do not apply. Accordingly, these proposed regulations do not constitute regulations subject to the Regulatory Flexibility Act (5 U.S.C. chapter 6) and a Regulatory Flexibility Analysis has not been prepared.

COMMENTS AND REQUESTS FOR A PUBLIC HEARING

Before adopting final regulations, consideration will be given to any written comments that are submitted (preferably eight copies) to the Commissioner of Internal Revenue. All comments will be available for public inspection and copying. A public hearing will be held upon written request to the Commissioner by any person who has submitted written comments. If a public hearing is held, notice of the time and place will be published in the FEDERAL REGISTER.

DRAFTING INFORMATION

The principal author of these regulations is Carl M. Cooper of the Office of Associate Chief Counsel (International), within the Office of Chief Counsel, Internal Revenue Service. However, personnel from other offices of the Internal Revenue Service and the Treasury Department participated in developing these regulations, both in matters of substance and style.

[¶ 49,099]   Proposed Regulations (LR-53-880), published in the Federal Register on May 27, 1988.

Taxable year: Election: Partnership: S corporation: Personal service corporation.—Reg. §§ 1.280H-0T, 1.280H-1T, 1.444-0T—1.444-3T and 1.7519-0T—1.7519-3T, relating to the election of a taxable year by a partnership, S corporation or personal service corporation, are proposed. Reg. § 1.706-1T was removed by T.D. 8996 on 5/16/2002. Reg. § 1.706-3T was adopted as amendments to Reg. § 1.706-1 by T.D. 9009 on 7/22/2002.

AGENCY: Internal Revenue Service, Treasury.

ACTION: Notice of proposed rulemaking.

SUMMARY: In the rules and regulations portion of this issue of the FEDERAL REGISTER, the Internal Revenue Service is issuing temporary regulations relating to the election of a taxable year other than the required year by a partnership, S corporation or personal service corporation. Changes to the applicable law were made by the Revenue Act of 1987. In addition, the regulations include conforming and clarifying rules regarding the determination of the taxable year of a partnership undersection 706. The text of these temporary regulations also serves as the comment document for this notice of proposed rulemaking.

DATES: The amendments to the regulations are proposed to be effective generally for taxable years beginning after December 31, 1986. Written comments and requests for a public hearing must be delivered or mailed by July 26, 1988.

ADDRESS: Send comments and requests for a public hearing to: Commissioner of Internal Revenue, Attention: CC:LR:T (LR-53-88), Washington, D.C. 20224.

FOR FURTHER INFORMATION CONTACT: Arthur E. Davis III of the Legislation and Regulations Division, Office of Chief Counsel, Internal Revenue Service, 1111 Constitution Avenue N.W., Washington, D.C. 20224, Attention: CC:LR:T, (202) 566-3918 (not a toll-free call).

SUPPLEMENTARY INFORMATION:

BACKGROUND

The temporary regulations (designated by a "T" following the section citations) in the Rules and Regulations portion of this issue of the FEDERAL REGISTER amend the Income Tax Regulations (26 CFR Part 1) to provide temporary rules relating to the election by a partnership, S corporation, or personal service corporation to use a taxable year other than the year required (the "required year") under the applicable provision of the Internal Revenue Code of 1986 (the "Code"). The temporary regulations reflect the amendment of the Code by section 10206 of the Revenue Act of 1987 (Pub. L. 100-203, 101 Stat. 1330), which added sections 444, 7519 and 280H. Section 444 provides for the election (a "section 444 election") to use a taxable year other than the required year. A partnership or S corporation that makes or continues a section 444 election must make the payment required by section 7519. A personal service corporation that makes or continues a section 444 election is subject to the deduction limitations imposed by section 280H. This document proposes to adopt the temporary regulations as final regulations. Accordingly, the text of the temporary regulations serves as the comment document for this notice of proposed rulemaking. In addition, the preamble to the temporary regulations explains the proposed and temporary rules.

For the text of the temporary regulations, see FR Doc. (T.D. 8205) published in the Rules and Regulations portion of this issue of the FEDERAL REGISTER.

SPECIAL ANALYSES

The Commissioner of Internal Revenue has determined that this proposed rule is not a major rule as defined in Executive Order 12291 and that a regulatory impact analysis therefore is not required. Although this document is a notice of proposed rulemaking that solicits public comments, the Internal Revenue Service has concluded that the proposed regulations are interpretative and that the notice and public procedure requirements of 5 U.S.C. 553 do not apply. Accordingly, these proposed regulations are not subject to the Regulatory Flexibility Act (5 U.S.C. chapter 6).

The reporting requirements contained in this notice of proposed rulemaking have been submitted in accordance with the requirements of the Paperwork Reduction Act of 1980 to the Office of Management and Budget (OMB) for review. OMB has approved these requirements (control number 1545-1036).

COMMENTS AND REQUESTS FOR A PUBLIC HEARING

Before these proposed regulations are adopted, consideration will be given to any written comments that are submitted (preferably eight copies) to the Commissioner of Internal Revenue. All comments will be available for public inspection and copying. A public hearing will be held upon written request to the Commissioner by any person who submitted written comments. If a public hearing is held, notice of the time and place will be published in the Federal Register.

DRAFTING INFORMATION

The principal author of these proposed regulations is Arthur E. Davis III of the Legislation and Regulations Division of the Office of Chief Counsel, Internal Revenue Service. However, personnel from other offices of the Internal Revenue Service and Treasury Department participated in developing the regulations on matters of both substance and style.

[¶ 49,100]   **Proposed Regulations and Amendments of Regulations (LR-3-87), published in the Federal Register on** June 9, 1988.

Exclusions: Scholarships: Payment for services.—Reg. §§ 1.117-0 and 1.117-6 and amendments of Reg. §§ 1.117-1—1.117-5, relating to the exclusion from gross income of qualified scholarships, are proposed. On 10/6/97, T.D. 8734 adopted the proposal to withdraw amendments to § 1.6041-3.

AGENCY: Internal Revenue Service, Treasury.

ACTION: Notice of proposed rulemaking.

SUMMARY: This document contains proposed regulations relating to the exclusion from gross income of qualified scholarships. Changes to the applicable law were made by the Tax Reform Act of 1986. These regulations would provide necessary guidance to Internal Revenue Service personnel who administer the Internal Revenue Code and members of the public who are subject to these laws.

DATES: Written comments and requests for a public hearing must be delivered or mailed by [SIXTY DAYS AFTER DATE OF PUBLICATION IN THE FEDERAL REGISTER]. These amendments are proposed to be generally effective for taxable years beginning after December 31, 1986.

ADDRESS: Send comments and requests for a public hearing to: Commissioner of Internal Revenue, Attention: CC:LR:T (LR-3-87) Washington, D.C. 20224.

FOR FURTHER INFORMATION CONTACT: Ruth Hoffman of the Legislation and Preambles Division, Office of Chief Counsel, Internal Revenue Service, 1111 Constitution Avenue, N.W., Washington, D.C. 20224 (Attention CC:LR:T) (202-566-3287) (not a toll-free number).

SUPPLEMENTARY INFORMATION:

BACKGROUND

This document contains proposed amendments to the Income Tax Regulations (26 CFR Part 1) under sections 117 and 6041 of the Internal Revenue Code of 1986 (Code). These amendments are proposed to conform the regulations under section 117 and section 6041 to the changes made by section 123(a) of the Tax Reform Act of 1986 (1986 Act) (Pub. L. 99-514, 100 Stat. 2112).

IN GENERAL

The 1986 Act amended section 117 of the Code, relating to the exclusion from gross income of scholarships or fellowship grants. Section 117(a) provides that gross income does not include any amount received as a qualified scholarship by an individual who is a candidate for a degree at an educational organization described in section 170(b)(1)(A)(ii). An individual who is not a candidate for a degree must include in gross income any amount received as a scholarship or fellowship grant. Proposed § 1.117-6(c)(4) defines the term candidate for a degree. Proposed § 1.117-6(c)(1) provides that a qualified scholarship is any amount received by an individual as a scholarship or fellowship grant and used for qualified tuition and related expenses. As defined in proposed § 1.117-6(c)(2), qualified tuition and related expenses are tuition and fees required for enrollment or attendance at an educational organization, and fees, books, supplies, and equipment required for courses of instruction. Qualified tuition and related expenses do not include any amount received as a scholarship or fellowship grant and used for room and board or incidental expenses such as travel, research, or clerical help. Thus, any such amount is not excludable from gross income.

Under proposed § 1.117-6(h), any amount of a scholarship or fellowship grant in excess of the amount permitted to be excluded from gross income under proposed § 1.117-6(b) is considered earned income for purposes of section 63(c)(5) (relating to the standard deduction for dependents) and section 6012(a)(1)(C)(i) (relating to dependents required to make returns of income).

Section 117(d) provides that gross income does not include any amount received as a qualified tuition reduction. This document does not provide proposed regulations with respect to section 117(d). Proposed regulations addressing matters relating to section 117(d) are expected to be provided by another regulations project.

SCHOLARSHIPS REPRESENTING PAYMENT FOR SERVICES

The general rule providing for an exclusion from gross income of qualified scholarships is limited under section 117(c) to qualified scholarship amounts that do not represent payment for teaching, research, or other services by the recipient required as a condition to receiving the qualified scholarship. Section 117(c) also applies to qualified tuition reductions (as defined under section 117(d)).

Under proposed § 1.117-6(d)(1), that portion of a scholarship or fellowship grant that represents payment for services is included in gross income, regardless of whether such services are required of all candidates for the degree as a condition to receiving the degree.

Proposed § 1.117-6(d)(2) provides that a scholarship or fellowship grant represents payment for services when the grantor requires the recipient to perform services in return for the granting of the scholarship or fellowship. A requirement that the recipient pursue studies, research, or other activities primarily for the benefit of the grantor is treated as a requirement to perform services. The granting of a scholarship or fellowship is considered to be in return for services whether such services are required to be performed before, concurrent with, or after receiving the scholarship or fellowship grant.

If only a portion of a scholarship or fellowship grant represents payment for services, the grantor must determine the amount of the scholarship or fellowship grant (including any reduction in tuition or related expenses) to be allocated to payment for services. Proposed § 1.117-6(d)(3) provides rules for determining what portion of the scholarship or fellowship grant must be allocated by the grantor to payment for services, and indicates some of the factors to be considered in making that allocation. If the recipient includes in gross income the amount allocated by the grantor to payment for services and such amount represents reasonable compensation for those services, then any additional amount of a scholarship or fellowship grant received from the same grantor that meets the requirements of proposed § 1.117-6(b) is excludable from gross income.

EFFECTIVE DATE RULES

Section 117, as amended by the 1986 Act, generally applies to taxable years beginning on or after January 1, 1987. However, under proposed § 1.117-6(f), section 117, as in effect prior to its amendment by the 1986 Act, continues to apply to a scholarship or fellowship granted before August 17, 1986, whenever received. In addition, section 117, as in effect prior to its amendment by the 1986 Act, applies in the case of a scholarship or fellowship granted after August 16, 1986, and before January 1, 1987, to the extent of any amount received prior to January 1, 1987, that is attributable to expenditures incurred before January 1, 1987.

For purposes of the effective date rules, proposed § 1.117-6(f)(2) provides that a scholarship or fellowship is granted when the grantor either notifies the recipient of the award or notifies an organization or institution acting on behalf of a specified recipient of the award to be provided to such recipient. If the notification is sent by mail, notification occurs as of the date the notice is postmarked. If evidence of a postmark does not exist, the date on the award letter is treated as the notification date.

Under proposed § 1.117-6(f)(3), a scholarship or fellowship is considered granted before August 17, 1986, to the extent that, in a notice of award made before that date, the grantor made a firm commitment to provide the recipient with a fixed cash amount or a readily determinable amount. For purposes of this section, a condition that the recipient remain in good standing or maintain a specific grade point average, or a requirement that the recipient show continuing financial need is not taken into account in determining whether the grantor made a firm commitment to provide the scholarship or fellowship grant for more than one academic period.

Under proposed § 1.117-6(f)(3)(i), amounts treated as a scholarship or fellowship granted before August 17, 1986, must be applied against qualified tuition and related expenses before any amount treated as a scholarship or fellowship granted after August 16, 1986, may be eligible for exclusion as a qualified scholarship.

In addition, proposed § 1.117-6(f)(3)(i) provides that if a scholarship or fellowship initially awarded before August 17, 1986, is granted for a period exceeding one academic period (for example, a semester), amounts received in subsequent academic periods are treated as granted before August 17, 1986, only if: (a) the amount awarded for the first academic period is described in the original notice of award as a fixed cash amount or readily determinable amount; (b) the original notice of award contains a firm commitment by the grantor to provide the scholarship or fellowship grant for more than one academic period; and (c) the recipient is not required to reapply to the grantor in order to receive the scholarship or fellowship grant in future academic periods.

Proposed § 1.117-6(f)(3)(ii) provides that amounts received in subsequent academic periods that were not initially described in the notice of award as either fixed cash amounts or readily determinable amounts are treated as granted before August 17, 1986, but only to the extent of the amount granted for the initial academic period.

REPORTING AND WITHHOLDING REQUIREMENTS

Under proposed § 1.6041-3(q), unless a scholarship or fellowship grant represents payment for services by the recipient, neither the grantor nor the educational organization attended by the recipient is required to file a return of information with respect to such grant. However, there are reporting and withholding requirements for scholarship or fellowship grants to nonresident aliens under section 1441 of the Code.

Under proposed § 1.117-6(d)(4), any amount of a scholarship or fellowship grant that represents payment for services is considered wages for purposes of section 3401(a). Therefore, such amounts are subject to section 3402 (relating to withholding for income taxes) and the grantor is subject to section 6051 (relating to reporting wages of employees) and is required to file Form W-2 with respect to scholarship or fellowship amounts representing payment for services. However, according to the rules set forth in sections 3121(b), 3306(c), and the regulations thereunder, the application of sections 3101 and 3111 (relating to the Federal Insurance Contributions Act (FICA)), or section 3301 (relating to the Federal Unemployment Tax Act (FUTA)) depends upon the nature of the employment and the status of the organization. When only a portion of a scholarship or fellowship grant represents payment for services, the grantor is subject to the reporting and withholding requirements only with respect to the portion that represents such payments.

SPECIAL ANALYSES

The Commissioner of Internal Revenue has determined that this proposed rule is not a major rule as defined in Executive Order 12291 and that a Regulatory Impact Analysis is therefore not required. Although this document is a notice of proposed rulemaking that solicits public comment, the Internal Revenue Service has concluded that the notice and public procedure requirements of 5 U.S.C. 553 do not apply. Accordingly, these proposed regulations do not constitute regulations subject to the Regulatory Flexibility Act (5 U.S.C. chapter 6).

COMMENTS AND REQUEST FOR A PUBLIC HEARING

Before adopting these proposed regulations, consideration will be given to any written comments that are submitted (preferably eight copies) to the Commissioner of Internal Revenue. All comments will be available for public inspection and copying. A public hearing will be held upon written request to the Commissioner by any person who has submitted written comments. If a public hearing is held, notice of the time and place will be published in the FEDERAL REGISTER. The collection of information requirements contained herein have been submitted to the Office of Management and Budget (OMB) for review under section 3504(h) of the Paperwork Reduction Act. Comments on the requirements should be sent to the Office of Information and Regulatory Affairs of OMB, Attention: Desk Officer for Internal Revenue Service, New Executive Office Building, Washington, D.C. 20503. The Internal Revenue Service requests that persons submitting comments to OMB also send copies of those comments to the Service.

DRAFTING INFORMATION

The principal author of these proposed regulations is Ruth Hoffman of the Legislation and Regulations Division of the Office of Chief Counsel, Internal Revenue Service. However, personnel from other offices of the Internal Revenue Service and Treasury Department participated in developing the regulations, on matters of both substance and style.

[¶ 49,101]   **Proposed Regulations and Amendments of Regulations (REG-209001-86) [originally issued as INTL-49-86], published in the Federal Register on** June 14, 1988.

Controlled foreign corporations: Investment of earnings in U.S. property: Related person factoring income.—Reg. § 1.864-8T and amendments to Reg. §§ 1.956-1T and 1.956-2T, relating to the treatment of related person factoring income, are proposed. Reg. § 1.304-4T was reproposed by REG-132232-08 on December 30, 2009. Reg. § 1.956-3 adopted by T.D. 9792 on November 2, 2016. Proposed Reg. §§ 1.956-1(b)(4), 1.956-2(d)(2) and 1.956-3(b)(2)(ii) withdrawn by REG-122387-16 on November 3, 2016.

AGENCY: Internal Revenue Service, Treasury.

ACTION: Notice of proposed rulemaking by cross-reference to temporary regulations.

SUMMARY: This document provides proposed regulations relating to the treatment of related person factoring income, as well as proposed changes to regulations relating to the determination of the amount of earnings of a controlled foreign corporation invested in United States property. Also included is a proposed regulation relating to redemptions of stock through the use of related corporations. In the Rules and Regulations portion of this issue of the FEDERAL REGISTER, the Internal Revenue Service is issuing temporary Income Tax Regulations relating to the treatment of related person factoring income, investments in United States property and redemptions through the use of related corporations. The text of the temporary regulations also serves as the comment document for this notice of proposed rulemaking.

DATES: The regulations under §§ 1.864-8T and 1.956-3T are proposed to be effective July 14, 1988, and are proposed to be applicable, as of their dates of transfer, with respect to accounts receivable and evidences of indebtedness transferred after March 1, 1984. The regulations under §§ 1.956-1T, and 1.956-2T are proposed to be effective July 14, 1988, with respect to investments in U.S. property made on or after June 14, 1988. The regulations under § 1.304-4T are proposed to be effective June 14, 1988, with respect to acquisitions of stock occurring on or after June 14, 1988.

Written comments and requests for a public hearing must be delivered or mailed by August 15, 1988.

ADDRESS: Send comments and requests for a public hearing to: Commissioner of Internal Revenue, Attention: CC:LR:T (INTL-49-86), Washington, D.C. 20224.

FOR FURTHER INFORMATION CONTACT: Regarding §§ 1.864-8T and 1.956-3T, contact Barbara Allen Felker of the Office of the Associate Chief Counsel (International) within the Office of Chief Counsel, Internal Revenue Service, 1111 Constitution Avenue, N.W., Washington, D.C. 20224, Attention: CC:LR:T (INTL-49-86). Telephone (202) 634-5406 (not a toll-free call). Regarding §§ 1.304-4T, 1.956-1T, and 1.956-2T, contact Riea M. Lainoff of the Office of the Associate Chief Counsel (International), within the Office of Chief Counsel, Internal Revenue Service, 1111 Constitution Avenue, N.W., Washington, D.C. 20224, Attention: CC:LR:T (INTL-49-86). Telephone (202) 566-6645 (not a toll-free call).

SUPPLEMENTARY INFORMATION:

BACKGROUND

The temporary regulations published in the Rules and Regulations portion of this issue of the FEDERAL REGISTER add new §§ 1.864-8T and 1.956-3T to Part 1 of the Title 26 of the Code of Federal Regulations. These regulations implement sections 864(d) and 956(b)(3), which were added to the Internal Revenue Code of 1954 by section 123 of the Tax Reform Act of 1984 (Pub. L. 98-369, 98 Stat. 644, 646) and amended by sections 1201(d)(4), 1221(a)(2),1223(b)(1),1275(c)(7) and 1810(c) of the Tax Reform Act of 1986 (Pub. L. 99-514, 100 Stat. 2085, 2525, 2550, 2558, 2599, 2824). New §§ 1.956-1T, and 1.956-2T amend §§ 1.956-1(b)(4), 1.956-1(e), and § 1.956-2(d)(2), respectively, under section 956 of the Internal Revenue Code of 1986. The temporary regulations published in the Rules and Regulations portion of this issue of the FEDERAL REGISTER also add new

§ 1.304-4T to Part 1 of Title 26 of the Code of Federal Regulations. The preamble to the temporary regulations explains these additions to the Income Tax Regulations.

COMMENTS AND REQUESTS FOR A PUBLIC HEARING

Before adopting these proposed regulations, consideration will be given to any written comments that are submitted (preferably eight copies) to the Commissioner of Internal Revenue. All comments will be available for public inspection and copying. A public hearing will be held upon written request to the Commissioner by any person who has submitted written comments. If a public hearing is held, notice of the time and place will be published in the FEDERAL REGISTER.

SPECIAL ANALYSES

It has been determined that these proposed rules are not major rules as defined in Executive Order 12291 and that a Regulatory Impact Analysis is therefore not required. Although this document is a notice of a proposed rulemaking which solicits public comment, the Internal Revenue Service has concluded that the regulations proposed herein are interpretative and that the notice and public procedure requirements of 5 U.S.C. § 553 do not apply. Accordingly, these proposed regulations do not constitute regulations subject to the Regulatory Flexibility Act (5 U.S.C. chapter 6).

DRAFTING INFORMATION

The principal authors of these proposed regulations are Barbara Allen Felker, Riea M. Lainoff, Marnie J. Carro, and Ann Zukas of the Office of the Associate Chief Counsel (International) within the Office of Chief Counsel, Internal Revenue Service. However, personnel from other offices of the Internal Revenue Service and Treasury Department participated in developing the regulations on matters of both substance and style.

[¶ 49,102]   Proposed Regulations (REG-209020-86) [originally issued as INTL-061-86], published in the Federal Register on June 23, 1988.

Foreign tax credits: Foreign tax redeterminations: Notification.—Reg. § § 1.905-4T, 1.905-5T and 301.6689-1T, relating to a taxpayer's obligation to file notification of a foreign tax redetermination, to make adjustments to a taxpayer's pools of foreign taxes and earnings and profits, and the imposition of the civil penalty for failure to file such notice or report such adjustments, are proposed. Reg. § 1.905-3T is adopted by T.D. 9882.

AGENCY: Internal Revenue Service, Treasury.

ACTION: Notice of proposed rulemaking by cross-reference to temporary regulations.

SUMMARY: This document provides proposed Income Tax Regulations and Regulations on Procedure and Administration relating to a taxpayer's obligation under section 905(c) of the Internal Revenue Code of 1986 to file notification of a foreign tax redetermination, to make adjustments to a taxpayer's pools of foreign taxes and earnings and profits, and the imposition of the civil penalty for failure to file such notice or report such adjustments. In the Rules and Regulations portion of this issue of the FEDERAL REGISTER, the Internal Revenue Service is issuing temporary regulations relating to these matters. The text of those temporary regulations also serves as the comment document for this proposed rulemaking.

DATES: Written comments and requests for a public hearing must be delivered or mailed before August 22, 1988. These rules would generally apply to taxable years beginning after December 31, 1986.

ADDRESS: Send comments and requests for a public hearing to Commissioner of Internal Revenue, Attention: CC:LR:T (INTL-061-86), Washington, D.C. 20224.

FOR FURTHER INFORMATION CONTACT: Eli J. Dicker, of the Office of Associate Chief Counsel (International), within the Office of Chief Counsel, Internal Revenue Service, 1111 Constitution Avenue, N.W., Washington, D.C. 20224 (Attention: CC:LR:T (INTL-061-86)) (202-566-3490, not a toll-free call).

SUPPLEMENTARY INFORMATION:

PAPERWORK REDUCTION ACT

The collection of information contained in this notice of proposed rulemaking has been submitted to the Office of Management and Budget for review in accordance with the Paperwork Reduction Act of 1980 (44 U.S.C. 3504(h)). Comments on the collection of information should be sent to the Office of Information and Regulatory Affairs, Office of Management and Budget, Washington, D.C. 20503, Attention: Desk Officer for Internal Revenue Service, with copies to the Internal Revenue Service, Washington, D.C. 20224, Attention: IRS Reports Clearance Officer TR:FP.

The collection of information in this regulation is in § § 1.905-3T, 1.905-4T, and 1.905-5T. This information is required by the Internal Revenue Service to enable it to effectively administer the provisions of section 905(c). The information is needed by the Service to verify pooling adjustments to account for the effect of foreign tax redeterminations and to recompute a United States taxpayer's United States tax liability when a foreign tax redetermination requires such a recomputation. The likely respondents are individuals, households, businesses, and other for-profit institutions. Estimated total annual reporting burden: 10,000 hours. Estimated average annual burden per respondent: one hour. Estimated number of respondents: 10,000. Estimated annual frequency of responses: as necessary to comply with the provisions of section 905(c).

BACKGROUND

The temporary regulations published in the Rules and Regulations portion of this issue of the FEDERAL REGISTER add new § § 1.905-3T, 1.905-4T, and 1.905-5T to 26 CFR Part 1. They also add § 301.6689-1T to 26 CFR Part 301. The final regulations that are proposed to be based on the temporary regulations would amend 26 CFR Parts 1, 301, and 602. For the text of the temporary regulations, see [T.D. 8210]published in the Rules and Regulations portion of this issue of the FEDERAL REGISTER.

SPECIAL ANALYSES

These proposed rules are not major rules as defined in Executive Order 12291. Therefore, a Regulatory Impact Analysis is not required. Although this document is a notice of proposed rulemaking that solicits public comments, the notice and public procedure requirements of 5 U.S.C. § 553 do not apply because the regulations proposed herein are interpretative. Therefore, an initial Regulatory Flexibility Analysis is not required by the Regulatory Flexibility Act (5 U.S.C. Chapter 6).

COMMENTS AND REQUESTS FOR A PUBLIC HEARING

Before adopting these proposed regulations, consideration will be given to any written comments that are submitted (preferably eight copies) to the Commissioner of Internal Revenue. All comments will be available for public inspection and copying. A public hearing will be held upon written request to the Commissioner by any person who has submitted written comments. If a public hearing is held, notice of the time and place will be published in the FEDERAL REGISTER.

DRAFTING INFORMATION

The principal author of these regulations is Eli J. Dicker, of the Office of Associate Chief Counsel (International), within the Office of Chief Counsel, Internal Revenue Service. Other personnel from offices of the Internal Revenue Service and Treasury Department participated in developing the regulations both on matters of substance and style.

[¶ 49,103]   **Proposed Regulations (REG-209024-88) [originally issued as INTL-285-88],** published in the Federal Register on June 27, 1988.

Income of foreign governments and international organizations.—Reg. §§ 1.892-1T—1.892-7, relating to current taxation of income of **foreign governments from investment sources within the United States, are proposed. Reg. § 1.1441-8T was adopted as Reg. § 1.1441-8 by T.D. 8734, effective 1/1/2001 (per T.D. 8856).**

Income of Foreign Governments and International Organizations

AGENCY: Internal Revenue Service, Treasury.

ACTION: Notice of proposed rulemaking by cross-reference to temporary regulations.

SUMMARY: This document contains proposed income tax regulations relating to current taxation of income of foreign governments from investment sources within the United States. This action is necessary because of changes to the applicable tax law made by the Tax Reform Act of 1986. In the Rules and Regulations portion of this FEDERAL REGISTER, the Internal Revenue Service is issuing temporary regulations relating to these matters. The text of those temporary regulations also serves as the comment document for this proposed rulemaking.

DATES: These regulations are proposed to be effective for taxable years beginning after June 30, 1986. Written comments and request for a public hearing must be delivered or mailed by August 26, 1988.

ADDRESS: Send comments and requests for a public hearing to: Commissioner of Internal Revenue, (Attention: CC:LR:T, INTL-285-88), Washington, DC 20224.

FOR FURTHER INFORMATION CONTACT: David A. Juster of the Office of Associate Chief Counsel (International), within the Office of Chief Counsel, Internal Revenue Service, 1111 Constitution Avenue, N.W., Washington, DC 20224 (Attention: CC:LR:T (INTL-285-88)) (202-566-6384, not a toll-free call).

SUPPLEMENTARY INFORMATION:

PAPERWORK REDUCTION ACT

The collection of information contained in this notice of proposed rulemaking has been submitted to the Office of Management and Budget for review in accordance with the Paperwork Reduction Act of 1980 (44 U.S.C. 3504(h)). Comments on the collection of information should be sent to the Office of Information and Regulatory Affairs, Office of Management and Budget, Washington, D.C. 20503, attention: Desk Officer for Internal Revenue Service, with copies to the Internal Revenue Service, Washington, D.C. 20224, Attention: IRS Reports Clearance Officer TR:FP.

The collection of information in this regulation is in § 1.1441-8T(b). This information is required by Internal Revenue Service to avoid withholding of tax at source with regard to specific types of income received by foreign governments and international organizations. This information will be used by withholding agents to verify that specific items of income received by such foreign governments or international organizations are excluded from gross income by reason of section 892 and are therefore exempt from withholding under section 1441. The likely respondents are foreign governments or international organizations.

Estimated total annual reporting burden: 45,000 hours.

Estimated average annual burden per respondent: 15 hours.

Estimated number of respondents: 3000.

Estimated annual frequency of responses: Annually.

BACKGROUND

The temporary regulations published in the Rules and Regulations portion of this issue of the FEDERAL REGISTER add new §§ 1.892-1T through 1.892-7T and 1441-8T. The final regulations that are proposed to be based on the temporary regulations would amend 26 CFR Parts 1 and 602. For the text of the temporary regulations, see [T.D. 8277] published in the Rules and Regulations portion of this issue of the FEDERAL REGISTER.

SPECIAL ANALYSES

These proposed rules are not major rules as defined in Executive Order 12291. Therefore, a Regulatory Impact Analysis is not required. Although this document is a notice of proposed rulemaking that solicits public comments, the notice and public procedure requirements of 5 U.S.C. § 553 do not apply because the regulations proposed herein are interpretative. Therefore, an initial Regulatory Flexibility Analysis is not required by the Regulatory Flexibility Act (5 U.S.C. Chapter 6).

COMMENTS AND REQUEST FOR A PUBLIC HEARING

Before adopting as final regulations these proposed regulations, consideration will be given to any written comments that are submitted (preferably a signed original and seven copies) to the Commissioner of Internal Revenue. All comments will be available for public inspection and copying. A public hearing will be held upon written request to the Commissioner by any person who has submitted written comments. If a public hearing is to be held, notice of the time and place will be published in the FEDERAL REGISTER.

DRAFTING INFORMATION

The principal author of these regulations is David A. Juster of the Office of Associate Chief Counsel (International), within the Office of Chief Counsel, Internal Revenue Service. However, personnel from other offices of the Internal Revenue Service and Treasury Department participated in developing the regulations on matters of substance and style.

[¶ 49,105]   **Proposed Regulations and Amendments of Regulations (LR-119-86),** published in the Federal Register on July 18, 1988.

Gains and losses: Asset acquisitions: Allocation rules.—Reg. §§ 1.167(a)-5T and 1.1031(d)-1T, relating to allocation rules for certain asset acquisitions under Code Sec. 1060, are proposed. Reg. § 1.1060-1T was removed 2/12/2001 by T.D. 8940 and Reg. § 1.755-2T was removed 6/6/2003 by T.D. 9059.

AGENCY: Internal Revenue Service, Treasury.

ACTION: Notice of proposed rulemaking by cross-reference to temporary regulations.

SUMMARY: In the Rules and Regulations portion of this issue of the FEDERAL REGISTER, the Internal Revenue Service is issuing temporary regulations to provide guidance to taxpayers concerning the application of the allocation rules for certain asset acquisitions under section 1060 to taxpayers generally and to partnerships. The text of the new sections also serves as the comment document for this notice of proposed rulemaking.

DATES:

PROPOSED EFFECTIVE DATE

The regulations are proposed to apply generally to any applicable asset acquisition made after May 6, 1986, unless such acquisition is pursuant to a binding contract which was in effect on May 6, 1986, and at all times thereafter. The reporting requirements apply to asset acquisitions (and to certain adjustments of consideration) occurring in a taxable year for which the due date (including extensions of time) of the income tax return or return of income is on or after September 13, 1988.

DATE FOR COMMENTS AND REQUESTS FOR A PUBLIC HEARING

Written comments and requests for a public hearing must be delivered or mailed by September 16, 1988.

ADDRESS: Send comments and requests for a public hearing to: Commissioner of Internal Revenue, Attention: CC:LR:T [LR-119-86], Washington, D.C. 20224.

FOR FURTHER INFORMATION CONTACT: Judith C. Winkler of the Legislation and Regulations Division, Office of Chief Counsel, Internal Revenue Service, 1111 Constitution Avenue, N.W., Washington, D.C. 20224 (Attention: CC:LR:T) or telephone 202-566-3458 (not a toll-free number). For information concerning the temporary regulations under section 755, contact Robert E. Shaw of the Legislation and Regulations Division, Office of Chief Counsel, Internal Revenue Service, 1111 Constitution Avenue, N.W., Washington, D.C. 20224, (Attention: CC:LR:T) or telephone 202-566-3297 (not a toll-free number).

SUPPLEMENTARY INFORMATION:

PAPERWORK REDUCTION ACT

The collection of information contained in this notice of proposed rulemaking has been submitted to the Office of Management and Budget for review in accordance with the Paperwork Reduction Act of 1980 (44 U.S.C. 3504(h)). Comments on the collection of information should be sent to the Office of Information and Regulatory Affairs, Office of Management and Budget, Washington, D.C. 20503, Attention: Desk Officer for the Internal Revenue Service, with copies to the Internal Revenue Service at the address previously specified.

The collection of information in this regulation is in section 26 CFR 1.1060-1T(h). This information is required by the Internal Revenue Service pursuant to section 1060. This information will be used to verify that the purchaser and the seller are complying with section 1060 by allocating the consideration among the assets pursuant to the residual method of allocation. The likely respondents are businesses or other for-profit institutions and small businesses or organizations.

Estimated total annual reporting and/or recordkeeping burden: 21,053 hours.

Estimated average annual burden hours per respondent and/or recordkeeper: 1.05 hours.

Estimated number of respondents and/or recordkeepers: 20,000.

Estimated annual frequency of responses: One time generally.

BACKGROUND

Temporary regulations published in the Rules and Regulations portion of this issue of the FEDERAL REGISTER add new temporary regulations §§1.167(a)-5T, 1.755-2T, 1.1031(d)-1T, and 1.1060-1T, to Part 1 of Title 26 of the Code of Federal Regulations (CFR), and amend §1.338(b)-3T. The final regulations that are proposed to be based on these temporary regulations would be added to Part 1 of Title 26 of the CFR. Those final regulations would provide guidance on the allocation of consideration among the assets transferred in an applicable asset acquisition. Section 1060 was added by section 641 of the Tax Reform Act of 1986 (Pub. L. No. 99-514; 100 Stat. 2085). For the text of the new temporary regulations, see T.D. 8215, published in the Rules and Regulations portion of this issue of the FEDERAL REGISTER. The preamble to the temporary regulations explains the regulations.

SPECIAL ANALYSES

Although this document is a notice of proposed rulemaking that solicits public comment, the Internal Revenue Service has concluded that the regulations proposed herein are interpretative and the notice and public procedure requirements of 5 U.S.C. 553 do not apply. Accordingly, these proposed regulations do not constitute regulations subject to the Regulatory Flexibility Act (5 U.S.C. chapter 6). The Commissioner of Internal Revenue has determined that this proposed rule is not a major rule as defined in Executive Order 12291 and that a Regulatory Impact Analysis therefore is not required.

COMMENTS AND REQUESTS FOR A PUBLIC HEARING

Before these proposed regulations are adopted, consideration will be given to any written comments that are submitted (preferably eight copies) to the Commissioner of Internal Revenue. All comments will be available for public inspection and copying. A public hearing will be held upon written request to the Commissioner by any person who has submitted written comments. If a public hearing is held, notice of the time and place will be published in the FEDERAL REGISTER.

DRAFTING INFORMATION

The principal author of the proposed regulations under sections 167, 338, 1031 and 1060 is Judith C. Winkler of the Legislation and Regulations Division of the Office of Chief Counsel, Internal Revenue Service. The principal author of the proposed regulations under section 755 is Robert Shaw of the Legislation and Regulations Division of the Office of Chief Counsel, Internal Revenue Service. However, personnel from other offices of the Internal Revenue Service and Treasury Department participated in developing the regulations, on matters of both substance and style.

[¶49,106] **Proposed Regulations (INTL-934-86),** published in the Federal Register on September 2, 1988.

Foreign corporations: Branch profits tax.—Reg. §§1.884-0T—1.884-5T, relating to the branch profits tax, are proposed. Reg. §§1.884-0, 1.884-1, 1.884-4 and 1.884-5 were adopted 9/10/92 by T.D. 8432.

AGENCY: Internal Revenue Service, Treasury.

ACTION: Notice of proposed rulemaking by cross-reference to temporary regulations.

SUMMARY: This document contains proposed Income Tax Regulations relating to the branch tax. In the Rules and Regulations portion of this FEDERAL REGISTER, the Internal Revenue Service is issuing temporary regulations relating to these matters. The text of these temporary regulations also serves as the comment document for this proposed rulemaking.

DATES: These regulations are proposed to be effective for taxable years beginning after December 31, 1986. Written comments and requests for a public hearing must be delivered or mailed by November 1, 1988.

ADDRESS: Send comments and requests for a public hearing to: Commissioner of Internal Revenue, (Attention: CC:LR:T, INTL-934-86), Washington, DC 20224.

FOR FURTHER INFORMATION CONTACT: Richard M. Elliott of the Office of Associate Chief Counsel (International), within the Office of the Chief Counsel, Internal Revenue Service, 1111 Constitution Avenue, N.W., Washington, DC 20224 (Attn: CC:LR:T, INTL-934-86) (202-566-6457, not a toll-free call).

SUPPLEMENTARY INFORMATION:

PAPERWORK REDUCTION ACT

The collection of information contained in this notice of proposed rulemaking has been submitted to the Office of Management and Budget for review in accordance with the Paperwork Reduction Act of 1980 (44 U.S.C. 3504(h)). Comments on the collection of information should be sent to the Office of Information and Regulatory Affairs, Office of Management and Budget, Washington, DC 20503, Attention: Desk Officer for Internal Revenue Service, with copies to the Internal Revenue Service, Washington, DC 20224, Attention: IRS Reports Clearance Officer TR:FP.

The collection of information in this regulation is in §§1.884-1T(d)(11), 1.884-2T(a)(2), 1.884-2T(b), 1.884-2T(c)(2), 1.884-2T(d)(1), 1.884-2T(d)(4), 1.884-2T(d)(5), 1.884-4T(b)(7), 1.884-4T(c)(1), 1.884-5T(b)(3) through (7), 1.884-5T(d)(6), and 1.884-5T(f). This information is required by the Internal Revenue Service to ensure the correct computation of tax under section 884. This information will be used in audits of taxpayers. The likely respondents are business or other for-profit institutions.

Estimated total annual reporting and/or recordkeeping burden: 20,500 hours.

The estimated annual burden per respondent/recordkeeper varies from .5 to 10.5 hours depending on individual circumstances, with an estimated average of 6.5 hours.

Estimated number of respondents and/or recordkeepers: 3000.

Estimated annual frequency of responses: Annually.

BACKGROUND

The temporary regulations published in the Rules and Regulations portion of this issue of the FEDERAL REGISTER add new §§1.884-0T through 1.884-2T, 1.884-4T, and 1.884-5T. The final regulations that are proposed to be based on the temporary regulations would amend 26 CFR Parts 1 and 602. For the text of the temporary regulations, see [INSERT FEDERAL REGISTER REFERENCE][T.D. 8223] published in the Rules and Regulations portion of this issue of the FEDERAL REGISTER.

SPECIAL ANALYSES

These proposed rules are not major rules as defined in Executive Order 12291. Therefore, a Regulatory Impact Analysis is not required. Although this document is a notice of proposed rulemaking that solicits public comments, the notice and public procedure requirements of 5 U.S.C. §553 do not apply because the regulations proposed herein are interpretative. Therefore, an initial Regulatory Flexibility Analysis is not required by the Regulatory Flexibility Act (5 U.S.C. Chapter 6).

COMMENTS AND REQUEST FOR A PUBLIC HEARING

Before adopting as final regulations these proposed regulations, consideration will be given to any written comments that are submitted (preferably a signed original and seven copies) to the Commissioner of Internal Revenue. All comments will be available for public inspection and copying. A public hearing will be held upon written request to the Commissioner by any person who has submitted written comments. If a public hearing is to be held, notice of the time and place will be published in the FEDERAL REGISTER.

DRAFTING INFORMATION

The principal author of these regulations is Richard M. Elliott of the Office of the Associate Chief Counsel (International), within the Office of the Chief Counsel, Internal Revenue Service. However, personnel from other offices of the Internal Revenue Service and Treasury Department participated in developing the regulations.

[¶49,107] **Proposed Regulations (LR-156-86),** published in the Federal Register on September 6, 1988.

Returns: Partnerships: Partnership information.—Reg. §§1.6031(b)-1T and 1.6031(c)-1T, relating to partnership statements and nominee reporting of partnership information, are proposed.

AGENCY: Internal Revenue Service, Treasury.

ACTION: Notice of proposed rulemaking by cross-reference to temporary regulations.

SUMMARY: In the Rules and Regulations portion of this issue of the FEDERAL REGISTER, the Internal Revenue Service is issuing temporary regulations relating to partnership statements and nominee reporting of partnership information. The text of the temporary regulations serves as the comment document for this notice of proposed rulemaking.

DATES: Written comments and requests for a public hearing must be delivered or mailed by [60 DAYS AFTER DATE OF PUBLICATION OF THIS DOCUMENT IN THE FEDERAL REGISTER]. Except as otherwise provided, the text of §1.6031(b)-1T is proposed to be effective for partnership taxable years beginning after September 3, 1982. Except as otherwise provided, the text of §1.6031(c)-1T is proposed to be effective for partnership taxable years beginning after October 22, 1986.

ADDRESS: Send comments and requests for a public hearing to: Commissioner of Internal Revenue, 1111 Constitution Avenue, N.W., Attention: CC:LR:T (LR-156-86), Washington, D.C. 20224.

FOR FURTHER INFORMATION CONTACT: Stuart G. Wessler of the Legislation and Regulations Division, Office of the Chief Counsel, Internal Revenue Service, 1111 Constitution Avenue, N.W., Washington, D.C. 20224 (Attention: CC:LR:T LR-1556-86). Telephone 202-566-3297 (not a toll-free call).

SUPPLEMENTARY INFORMATION:

PAPERWORK REDUCTION ACT

The collection of information contained in this notice of proposed rulemaking has been submitted to the Office of Management and Budget for review in accordance with the Paperwork Reduction Act of 1980 (44 U.S.C. 3504(h)). Comments on the collection of information should be sent to the Office of Information and Regulatory Affairs, Office of Management and Budget, Washington, D.C. 20503, attention: Desk Officer for the Internal Revenue Service, with copies to the Internal Revenue Service at the address previously specified.

The collection of information in this regulation are in §§ 1.6031(b)-1T (a) and 1.6031(c)-1T (a) and (h). This information is required by the Internal Revenue Service pursuant to section 6031. This information will be used to verify that a taxpayer is reporting the correct amount of income or gain or claiming the correct amount of losses, deductions, or credits with respect to that taxpayer's interest in the partnership. The likely respondents are individuals or households, State or local governments, farms, business or other for-profit institutions, non-profit institutions, and small businesses or organizations.

These estimates are an approximation of the average time expected to be necessary for a collection of information. They are based on such information as is available to the Internal Revenue Service. Individual respondents/recordkeepers may require greater or less time, depending on their particular circumstances.

Estimated total annual reporting and recordkeeping burden: 6,374 hours.

Estimated average annual burden hours per respondent and recordkeeper varies from .02 to .627 hours, depending on individual circumstances, with an estimated average of .06 hours.

Estimated number of respondents and recordkeepers: 105,000.

Estimated annual frequency of response: On occasion.

BACKGROUND

The temporary regulations (designated by a "T" following the section citation) in the Rules and Regulations section of this issue of the FEDERAL REGISTER amend Part 1 of Title 26 of the Code of Federal Regulations to provide rules under section 6031(b) of the Internal Revenue Code of 1986, as added by section 403 of the Tax Equity end Fiscal Responsibility Act of 1982 (96 Stat. 669) and amended by sections 1501(c)(16) and 1811(b)(1)(A)(i) of the Tax Reform Act of 1986 (100 Stat. 2740, 2832), and under section 6031(c), as added by section 1811(b)(1)(A)(ii) of the Tax Reform Act of 1986 (100 Stat. 2832). This document proposes to adopt those temporary regulations as final regulations; accordingly, the text of the temporary regulations serves as the comment document for this notice of proposed rulemaking. In addition, the preamble to the temporary regulations provides a discussion of the proposed and temporary rules.

For the text of the temporary regulations, see T.D. 8225 published in the Rules and Regulations section of this issue of the FEDERAL REGISTER.

SPECIAL ANALYSES

The Commissioner of Internal Revenue has determined that the proposed rule is not a major rule as defined in Executive Order 12291 and that a Regulatory Impact Analysis is therefore not required.

The Secretary of the Treasury has certified that this rule will not have a significant impact on a substantial number of small entities because the number of significantly affected small entities is not substantial. A regulatory flexibility analysis, therefore, is not required under the Regulatory Flexibility Act (5 U.S.C. chapter 6).

COMMENTS AND REQUESTS FOR A PUBLIC HEARING

Before adopting these proposed regulations, consideration will be given to any written comments that are submitted (preferably eight copies) to the Commissioner of Internal Revenue. All comments will be available for public inspection and copying. A public hearing will be held upon written request of any person who has submitted written comments. If a public hearing is held, notice of the time and place will be published in the FEDERAL REGISTER.

DRAFTING INFORMATION

The principal author of these proposed regulations is Stuart G. Wessler of the Legislation and Regulations Division of the Office of Chief Counsel, Internal Revenue Service. However, personnel from other offices of the Internal Revenue Service and Treasury Department participated in developing the regulations, both on matters of substance and style.

[¶ 49,109]   **Proposed Regulations (INTL-952-86),** published in the Federal Register on September 14, 1988.

Income from U.S. sources: Allocation and apportionment of expenses.—Reg. §§ 1.861-8T—1.861-12T, 1.861-14T and 1.863-3T (redesignated as Temporary Reg. § 1.863-3AT by T.D. 8687), relating to the allocation and apportionment of interest expense and certain other expenses for purposes of the foreign tax credit rules and certain other international tax provisions, are proposed. Temporary Reg. § 1.861-9T(e)(2) and (e)(3) were adopted on 7/15/2014 by T.D. 9676.

AGENCY: Internal Revenue Service, Treasury.

ACTION: Notice of proposed rulemaking by cross-reference to temporary regulations.

SUMMARY: This document provides proposed Income Tax Regulations relating to the allocation and apportionment of interest expense and certain other expenses for purposes of the foreign tax credit rules and certain other international tax provisions. In the rules and regulations portion of this FEDERAL REGISTER, the Internal Revenue Service is issuing temporary regulations relating to these matters. The text of those temporary regulations also serves as the comment document for this notice of proposed rulemaking. This document also withdraws the notice of proposed rulemaking relating to the same subject that appeared in the FEDERAL REGISTER on September 11, 1987 (52 FR 34580).

DATES: In general, these regulations would be applicable to the allocation and apportionment of interest expense and certain other expenses for taxable years beginning after December 31, 1986. Comments and requests for a public hearing must be delivered or mailed before December 13, 1988.

ADDRESS: Send comments and requests for a public hearing to: Commissioner of Internal Revenue, (Attention: CC:LR:T, INTL-952-86), Washington, D.C. 20224.

FOR FURTHER INFORMATION CONTACT: David Merrick, regarding the allocation and apportionment of interest expense, and Carl Cooper, regarding the allocation and apportionment of other expenses, both of the Office of Associate Chief Counsel (International), within the Office of Chief Counsel, Internal Revenue Service, 1111 Constitution Avenue, NW, Washington, D.C. 20224 (Attention: CC:LR:T (INTL-952-86)) (David Merrick 202-566-6276, Carl Cooper 202-634-5406, not a toll-free call).

SUPPLEMENTARY INFORMATION:

PAPERWORK REDUCTION ACT

The collection of information contained in this notice of proposed rulemaking has been submitted to the Office of Management and Budget for review in accordance with the Paperwork Reduction Act of 1980 (44 U.S.C. § 3504(h)). Comments on the collection of information should be sent to the Office of Information and Regulatory Affairs, Office of Management and Budget, Washington, DC 20503, Attention: Desk Officer for Internal Revenue Service, with copies to the Internal Revenue Service at the address previously specified.

The affirmative elections in this regulation are in § 1.861-9T(g)(1)(ii), which requires taxpayers affirmatively to elect either the gross income or the asset method of apportionment in the case of a controlled foreign corporation, and in § 1.861-12T(c)(4)(ii), which permits taxpayers to elect under certain circumstances to reallocate interest expense that is allocated to a noncontrolled section 902 corporation. This information will be used in audits of taxpayers. The likely respondents are businesses and other for-profit institutions.

Estimated total annual reporting burden: 2,500 hours.

Estimated annual burden per respondent: 10 minutes.

Estimated number of respondents: 15,000.

Estimated annual frequency of responses: On occasion.

BACKGROUND

The temporary regulations published in the rules and regulations portion of this issue of the FEDERAL REGISTER add new temporary regulations §§ 1.861-8T through 1.861-14T. For the text of the temporary regulations, see [INSERT FEDERAL REGISTER REFERENCE]

[T.D. 8228] published in the rules and regulations portion of this issue of the FEDERAL REGISTER.

SPECIAL ANALYSES

It has been determined that these proposed rules are not major rules as defined in Executive Order 12291. Therefore, a Regulatory Impact Analysis is not required. Although this document is a notice of proposed rulemaking that solicits public comment, the notice and public procedure requirements of 5 U.S.C. § 553 do not apply because it has been determined that these proposed regulations will not have a significant impact on a substantial number of small entities. Therefore, an initial Regulatory Flexibility Analysis is not required by Regulatory Flexibility Act (5 U.S.C. Chapter 6).

COMMENTS AND REQUESTS FOR A PUBLIC HEARING

Before adopting these proposed regulations, consideration will be given to any written comments that are submitted (preferably a signed original and seven copies) to the Commissioner of Internal Revenue. All comments will be available for public inspection and copying. A public hearing will be held upon written request by any person who submits written comments on the proposed rules. Notice of the time and place for the hearing will be published in the FEDERAL REGISTER.

DRAFTING INFORMATION

The principal author of the proposed regulations relating to the allocation and apportionment of interest expense is David Merrick, and the principal author of the proposed regulations relating to the allocation and apportionment of other expenses is Carl Cooper, both of the Office of Associate Chief Counsel (International), within the Office of Chief Counsel, Internal Revenue Service. Other personnel from offices of the Internal Revenue Service and Treasury Department participated in developing these regulations.

[¶ 49,110]   **Proposed Regulations and Amendments (IA-111-86),** published in the Federal Register on January 9, 1989.

Exclusions: Prizes and awards: Employee achievement awards.—Reg. §§ 1.74-2 and 1.274-8 and amendments of Reg. §§ 1.74-1, 1.102-1, 1.274-1 and 1.274-3, relating to prizes and awards and employee achievement awards, are proposed.

AGENCY: Internal Revenue Service.

ACTION: Notice of proposed rulemaking.

SUMMARY: This document contains proposed amendments to the regulations relating to the excludability of certain prizes and awards and to the deductibility of certain employee awards. Changes to the applicable tax law were made by the Tax Reform Act of 1986. These amendments, if adopted, will provide the public with the guidance needed to comply with this Act.

DATES: Written comments and requests for a public hearing must be delivered or mailed by Mar. 10, 1989. The amendments are proposed to be effective after December 31, 1986.

ADDRESS: Send comments and requests for a public hearing to: Commissioner of Internal Revenue, Internal Revenue Service, 1111 Constitution Avenue, N.W., Washington, D.C. 20224; Attention: CC:CORP:T:R, IA-111-86.

FOR FURTHER INFORMATION CONTACT: Johnnel St. Germain of the Office of Assistant Chief Counsel (Income Tax and Accounting), Internal Revenue Service, 1111 Constitution Avenue, N.W., Washington, D.C. 20224; Attention: CC:CORP:T:R, IA-111-86. Telephone 202-566-4509 (not a toll-free call).

SUPPLEMENTARY INFORMATION:

PAPERWORK REDUCTION ACT

The collections of information contained in this notice of proposed rulemaking have been submitted to the Office of Management and Budget for review in accordance with the Paperwork Reduction Act of 1980 (44 U.S.C. 3504(h)). Comments on the collections of information should be sent to the Office of Information and Regulatory Affairs, Office of Management and Budget, Washington, D.C. 20503, attention: Desk Officer for the Internal Revenue Service. Copies of comments should also be sent to the Internal Revenue Service at the address previously specified.

The collections of information in this regulation are in 26 CFR §§ 1.74-1(c). This information is required by the Internal Revenue Service in order to verify that the proper amount of income is reported by taxpayers on their returns of tax. The likely respondents are individuals

Estimated total annual reporting burden: 1,275 hours.

Estimated average annual burden per respondent: 15 minutes.

Estimated number of respondents: 5,100.

BACKGROUND

This document contains proposed amendments to the Income Tax Regulations (26 CFR Part 1) under sections 74, 102, and 274 of the Internal Revenue Code (Code). The amendments are proposed to conform the regulations to section 122 of the Tax Reform Act of 1986 (Pub. L. 99-514). The proposed amendments, if adopted, will be issued under the authority contained in section 7805 of the Code (68A Stat. 917; 26 U.S.C. 7805).

GENERAL INFORMATION

Prior to the 1986 Code, section 74 stated that prizes and awards, other than certain types of fellowship grants and scholarships, were includible in gross income unless they were made primarily in recognition of religious, charitable, scientific, educational, artistic, literary, or civic achievement. To qualify for the exclusion, the recipient must have been selected without any action on his part and could not be required to render substantial services as a condition to receiving the prize or award.

Within the context of a business relationship, prizes and awards that would otherwise be includible in a recipient's gross income were excludable if they qualified as gifts under section 102. In general, section 274(b) disallowed an employer a business deduction for gifts to an employee to the extent that the total cost of all gifts of cash, tangible personal property, and other items to the same individual during the taxable year exceeded $25. A special exception to the $25 limitation was allowed for items of tangible personal property awarded to an employee for length of service, safety achievement, or productivity. The employer could deduct the cost of such an award up to $400. If the item was provided under a qualified award plan, the deductibility limitation was increased to $1600, provided the average cost of all plan awards made during the year did not exceed $400. A de minimis fringe benefit under section 132(e) was, and continues to be, excludable from gross income and is not subject to the requirements imposed upon prizes and awards under sections 74 and 274.

EXPLANATION OF PROVISIONS

These proposed amendments relate to the excludability of certain prizes and awards and to the deductibility of certain employee awards and reflect the substantial changes made by the Tax Reform Act of 1986 (the Act) to sections 74, 102 and 274 of the Internal Revenue Code (Code). Changes to the applicable sections of the Code and regulations, amended or newly incorporated by this document, are effective for awards made after December 31, 1986.

Under the Act, the section 74(b) exclusion for prizes or awards received in recognition of charitable achievement is available only if the payor transfers the prize or award to one or more entities described in paragraph (1) and/or (2) of section 170(c), pursuant to the direction of the recipient.

Section 1.74-1(c) of the proposed regulations requires that recipients of prizes and awards clearly designate, in writing, within 45 days of the date the item is granted that they wish to have the prize or award transferred to one or more qualifying donee organizations. The proposed regulations set forth requirements which, in certain instances, determine whether a qualifying designation has been made.

Section 1.74-1(d) of the proposed regulations clarifies that the exclusion under section 74(b) will not be available unless the prize or award is transferred by the payor to one or more qualified donee organizations before the recipient, or any person other than the grantor or a qualified donee organization, uses the item. In general, a transfer may be accomplished by any method that results in receipt of the prize or award by, or on behalf of, one or more qualified donee organizations.

Section 1.74-1(e) further clarifies the requirements of section 74(b) by defining certain terms. Definitions are included which determine what constitutes a "qualified donee organization," when a "disqualifying use" has taken place, and when an item is considered "granted."

Section 1.74-1(f) provides that neither the payor nor the recipient of the prize or award may claim a charitable contribution deduction for the value of any prize or award for which an exclusion is allowed under section 74(b).

All of the requirements of section 74(b) in existence prior to passage of the Act remain in effect and must be met in order for the award recipient to be eligible for the exclusion. Accordingly, rules and regulations governing these additional requirements, to the extent they are not inconsistent with the proposed regulations, will remain in effect.

New Code section 74(c) excludes certain employee achievement awards from gross income. The exclusion applies, subject to certain limitations, to the value of awards made by the employer for safety achievement or length of service achievement. The amount of the exclusion generally corresponds with the deduction given the employer under new section 274(j) for these "employee achievement awards." Thus, in general, the employee must include these awards in income to the extent that the fair market value of the award, or, if greater, the cost of the award to the employer, exceeds the amount deductible under section 274(j). The exclusion allows an employee to exclude the full fair market value of the award where the cost of the award is fully deductible by the employer.

Section 1.74-2(d) of the proposed regulations provides special rules for employee achievement awards applicable to sole-proprietors and tax-exempt employers.

Section 1.74-2(e) clarifies that an employee award, whether or not an employee achievement award, may be excludible from gross income as a de minimis fringe benefit under section 132(e).

Section 102(c) of the Code clarifies that, with the exception of employee achievement awards under section 74(c) and de minimis fringe benefits under section 132(e), an employee shall not exclude from gross income any amount transferred to the employee (or for the employee's benefit) by, or on behalf of, the employer in the form of a gift, bequest, devise, or inheritance. Therefore, while awards satisfying the requirements of section 74(c) and de minimis fringe benefits qualifying under section 132(e) will be excluded from gross income under those sections, no amounts (except in certain narrowly defined circumstances) transferred by, or on behalf of, an individual's employer will be excludable from gross income under section 102.

Section 1.102-1(f)(2) of the proposed regulations provides that for purposes of section 102(c), extraordinary transfers to the natural objects of one's bounty will not be considered transfers to an employee if it can be shown that the transfer was not made in recognition of the transferee's employment. Thus, the rules set out in *Comm. v. Duberstein*, 363 U.S. 278 (1960), formerly applicable in the determination of whether all property transferred inter-vivos from an employer to an employee constitutes a gift, will only be applicable where the transferee employee would be the natural object of the employer's bounty.

From an employer's perspective, the Act substantially modifies an employer's ability to deduct the cost of certain employee awards. New section 274(j) defines deductible "employee achievement awards" to include only those awards made for length of service achievement award or safety achievement. In addition, an employee achievement award must be an item of tangible personal property awarded as part of a meaningful presentation and made under conditions and circumstances that do not create a significant likelihood of the payment of disguised compensation.

Section 274(j) also establishes a limit on the amount that may be deducted by an employer. The annual deduction limitation per employee is $400 for employee achievement awards that are not awarded as part of a qualified award plan. The annual deduction limitation per employee is $1,600 for employee achievement awards that are awarded as part of a qualified award plan. In no event may an employer deduct more than $1,600 per employee for all employee achievement awards made during the year. An award is not a qualified plan award where the average cost of all employee achievement awards made by the employer pursuant to a plan exceeds $400 during the taxable year.

Section 1.274-8(b) of the proposed regulations clarifies that the $1,600 deduction limitation applies in the aggregate, so that the $1,600 limitation for qualified plan awards and the $400 limitation for employee achievement awards that are not qualified plan awards cannot be added together to allow deductions exceeding $1,600 for employee achievement awards made to an employee in a taxable year.

Section 1.274-8(c)(2) of the proposed regulations provides that tangible personal property does not include cash or any gift certificate other than a nonnegotiable gift certificate conferring only the right to receive tangible personal property. The proposed regulations also give examples of what will be considered to create a significant likelihood of the payment of disguised compensation. For example, the providing of employee achievement awards in a manner that discriminates in favor of highly paid employees will be considered to be payment of disguised compensation.

Section 1.274-8(c)(5) of the proposed regulations defines a "qualified plan award" as an employee achievement award presented pursuant to an established written award plan or program of the employer that does not discriminate as to eligibility or benefits.

Section 1.274-8(d)(1) of the proposed regulations states that the deduction limitations shall apply to a partnership as well as to each member of the partnership. Paragraph (d)(2) provides that the cost of length of service achievement awards (other than awards excludable under section 132(e)) may only be deducted by the employer if the employee has at least 5 years of service with the employer and has not received a length of service achievement award during that year or any of the 4 prior years. In addition, this paragraph clarifies that although a retirement award will be treated as having been provided for length of service achievement, it may also qualify for treatment as a de minimis fringe benefit under § 132(e) of the Code. Paragraph (d)(3) provides guidance with respect to safety achievement awards. An employer may deduct the cost of safety achievement awards only when presented to no more than 10% of an employer's eligible employees. Eligible employees include any employee who has worked for the employer in a full time capacity for at least one year and who is not a manager, administrator, clerical employee, or other professional employee. Special rules clarify that in the case where more than 10% of an employer's eligible employees receive a safety achievement award, no award will be considered to be awarded for safety achievement if it cannot be determined that that award was presented before the 10% limitation was exceeded.

The Act specifically excludes awards qualifying as de minimis fringe benefits under section 132(e) from the requirements for length of service achievement and safety achievement. As a result, employers are not required to consider section 132(e) awards in determining whether employee achievement awards comply with the 5 year limitations for length of service achievement and the 10% eligible employee limitations for safety achievement.

SPECIAL ANALYSES

The Commissioner of Internal Revenue has determined that this proposed rule is not a major rule as defined in Executive Order 12291. Accordingly, a Regulatory Impact Analysis is not required. The Internal Revenue Service has concluded that although this document is a notice of proposed rulemaking that solicits public comment, the regulations proposed herein are interpretative and the notice and public procedure requirements of 5 U.S.C. 553 do not apply. Accordingly, no Regulatory Flexibility Analysis is required for this rule.

COMMENTS AND REQUESTS FOR A PUBLIC HEARING

Before adopting these proposed regulations, consideration will be given to any written comments that are submitted (preferably eight copies) to the Commissioner of Internal Revenue. All comments will be available for public inspection and copying. A public hearing will be held upon written request to the Commissioner by any person who has submitted written comments. If a public hearing is held, notice of time and place will be published in the FEDERAL REGISTER.

DRAFTING INFORMATION

The principal author of these proposed regulations is Christopher J. Wilson, formerly of the Legislation and Regulations Division of the Office of Chief Counsel, Internal Revenue Service. However, personnel from other offices of the Internal Revenue Service and Treasury Department participated in developing the regulations, on matters of both substance and style.

[¶ 49,111]   **Proposed Regulations (INTL-304-89),** published in the Federal Register on August 2, 1989.

Income from source: Interest expense allocation.—Reg. §§ 1.861-9T and 1.861-13T, relating to transition rules for the allocation and apportionment of interest expense for the purposes of the foreign tax credit rules and certain other international tax provisions, are proposed.

AGENCY: Internal Revenue Service, Treasury.

ACTION: Notice of proposed rulemaking by cross-reference to temporary regulations.

SUMMARY: This document provides proposed Income Tax Regulations relating to transition rules for the allocation and apportionment of interest expense for purposes of the foreign tax credit rules and certain other international tax provisions. This document also provides rules concerning the treatment of financial products that alter effective interest expense. Changes to the transition rules were made by the Technical and Miscellaneous Revenue Act of 1988. These regulations are necessary to provide guidance needed by taxpayers engaging in international transactions in order to comply with these changes. In the rules and regulations portion of this FEDERAL REGISTER, the Internal Revenue Service is issuing temporary regulations relating to these matters. The text of those temporary regulations also serves as the comment document for this notice of proposed rulemaking. Certain additional regulations are also proposed by this document.

DATES: These regulations are proposed to be effective for taxable years beginning after December 31, 1986. These regulations would be applicable to the allocation and apportionment of interest expense for taxable years beginning after December 31, 1986, except for § 1.861-9T(b)(6), which is effective for transactions entered into after September 14, 1988. Comments and requests for a public hearing must be delivered or mailed before August 31, 1989.

ADDRESS: Send comments and requests for a public hearing to: Commissioner of Internal Revenue, Attention: CC:CORP:T:R (INTL-952-86), Room 4429, Washington, D.C. 20224.

FOR FURTHER INFORMATION CONTACT: Charles Plambeck of the office of Associate Chief Counsel (International), within the Office of Chief Counsel, Internal Revenue Service, 1111 Constitution Avenue, NW, Washington, D.C. 20224 (Attention: CC:CORP:T:R. (INTL-952-86)) (202-566-6284), not a toll-free call).

SUPPLEMENTARY INFORMATION:

BACKGROUND

The temporary regulations published in the rules and regulations portion of this issue of the FEDERAL REGISTER add new temporary regulations § 1.861-13T and a new paragraph (b)(6) to § 1.861-9T. For the text of the temporary regulations, see T.D. 8257 published in the rules and regulations portion of this issue of the FEDERAL REGISTER. Certain additional regulations are also proposed by this document.

SPECIAL ANALYSES

It has been determined that these rules are not major rules as defined in Executive Order 12291. Therefore, a Regulatory Impact Analysis is not required. It has also been determined that section 553(b) of the Administrative Procedure Act (5 U.S.C. Chapter 5) and the Regulatory Flexibility Act (5 U.S.C. Chapter 6) do not apply to these regulations, and, therefore, an initial Regulatory Flexibility Analysis is not required. Pursuant to section 7805(f) of the Internal Revenue Code, the notice of proposed rulemaking for the regulations was submitted to the Administrator of the Small Business Administration for comment on their impact on small business.

COMMENTS AND REQUESTS FOR A PUBLIC HEARING

Before adopting these proposed regulations, consideration will be given to any written comments that are submitted (preferably a signed original and eight copies) to the Commissioner of Internal Revenue. All comments will be available for public inspection and copying. A public hearing will be held upon written request by any person who submits written comments on the proposed rules. Notice of the time and place for the hearing will be published in the FEDERAL REGISTER.

DRAFTING INFORMATION

The principal author of these proposed regulations is David Merrick of the Office of Associate Chief Counsel (International), within the Office of Chief Counsel, Internal Revenue Service. Other personnel from offices of the Internal Revenue Service and Treasury Department participated in developing these regulations.

[¶ 49,112]   Proposed Regulations and Amendments of Regulations (CO-69-87), published in the Federal Register on September 20, 1989.

Carryovers: Excess credits: Use of pre-change attributes.—Amendments of Reg. § 1.382-2T, relating to the manner and method of absorbing the Code Sec. 382 limitation with respect to certain capital losses and excess credits after there has been an ownership change of a corporation, are proposed. Reg. §§ 1.383-1 and 1.383-2 were adopted by T.D. 8352 on 6/26/91.

AGENCY: Internal Revenue Service, Treasury.

ACTION: Notice of proposed rulemaking by cross-reference to temporary regulations.

SUMMARY: In the Rules and Regulations portion of this issue of the Federal Register, the Internal Revenue Service is adding temporary regulations pertaining to section 383 of the Internal Revenue Code of 1986 ("Code"), which was amended by the Tax Reform Act of 1986. The temporary regulations provide guidance under section 383 relating to the manner and method of absorbing the section 382 limitation with respect to certain capital losses and excess credits after there has been an ownership change of a corporation within the meaning of section 382. The temporary regulations also contain amendments to the temporary regulations under section 382. The text of the temporary regulations also serves as the comment document for this notice of proposed rulemaking.

DATES: Written comments and requests for a public hearing must be mailed by Nov 20, 1989. The proposed regulations would apply generally to any ownership change, as defined under section 382, occurring after December 31, 1986.

ADDRESS: Send comments or requests for a public hearing to: Internal Revenue Service, Attention: CC:CORP:T:R [CO-69-87], Room 4429, 1111 Constitution Avenue, N.W., Washington, D.C. 20224.

FOR FURTHER INFORMATION CONTACT: Lori J. Jones of the Office of Assistant Chief Counsel (Corporate), Office of Chief Counsel, (202) 566-3205 (not a toll-free number).

SUPPLEMENTARY INFORMATION:

Paperwork Reduction Act

The collections of information contained in this notice of proposed rulemaking have been submitted to the Office of Management and Budget for review in accordance with the Paperwork Reduction Act of 1980 (44 U.S.C. 3504(h)). Comments on the collections of information should be sent to the Office of Management and Budget, Paperwork Reduction Project, Washington, D.C. 20503, with copies to the Internal Revenue Service, ATTN: IRS Reports Clearances Officer TR:FP, Washington, D.C. 20224.

The collections of information in this regulation are in 26 CFR 1.382-2T(a) and 1.383-1T(j). This information is required by the Internal Revenue Service to help ensure that loss corporations report the proper amount of certain capital losses and excess credits on their income tax returns. The information will be used by the Internal Revenue Service to more readily verify compliance with sections 382 and 383.

These estimates are an approximation of the average time expected to be necessary for a collection of information. They are based on such information as is available to the Internal Revenue Service. Individual respondents may require greater or less time, depending on their particular circumstances. Estimated total annual reporting burden: 247,500 hours. The estimated annual burden per respondent varies from 6 minutes to 30 minutes, depending on individual circumstances, with an estimated average of 18 minutes.

Estimated number of respondents: 750,000

Estimated frequency of respondents: annually.

Background

Temporary regulations published in the Rules and Regulations portion of this issue of the Federal Register add temporary regulations § 1.383-1T and 2T to Part 1 of Title 26 of the Code of the Federal Regulations ("CFR") and amend § 1.382-2T of that part. The final regulations which are proposed to be based on the temporary regulations would be added to Part 1 of Title 26 of CFR. The final regulations would provide guidance under sections 382 and 383 relating to the manner and method of absorbing the section 382 limitation with respect to certain capital losses and excess credits after there has been an ownership change of a corporation within the meaning of section 382. Sections 382 and 383 of the Code were amended by section 621 of the Tax Reform Act of 1986 (Pub. L. No. 99-514, 100 Stat. 2085). Section 382 was further amended by section 10225 of the Revenue Act of 1987 (Pub. L. No. 100-203; 101 Stat. 1330-413) and by sections 1006, 4012, and 5077 of the Technical and Miscellaneous Revenue Act of 1988 (Pub. L. No. 100-647). For the text of the temporary regulations, see T.D. [8264] published in the Rules and Regulations portion of this issue of the Federal Register. The preamble to the temporary regulations explains the added regulations.

Special Analyses

It has been determined that these proposed rules are not major rules as defined in Executive Order 12291. Therefore, a Regulatory Impact Analysis is not required. It has also been determined that section 553(b) of the Administrative Procedure Act (5 U.S.C. Chapter 5) and the Regulatory Flexibility Act (5 U.S.C. Chapter 6) do not apply to these regulations and, therefore, an initial Regulatory Flexibility Analysis is not required. Pursuant to section 7805(f) of the Internal Revenue Code, these regulations will be submitted to the Administrator of the Small Business Administration for comment on their impact on small business.

Comments and Requests for a Public Hearing

Before adopting these proposed regulations, consideration will be given to any written comments that are submitted (preferably eight copies) to the Internal Revenue Service. All comments will be available for public inspection and copying. A public hearing will be held upon written request by any person who has submitted written comments. If a public hearing is held, notice of time and place will be published in the Federal Register.

Drafting Information

The principal author of these proposed regulations is Lori J. Jones, Office of the Assistant Chief Counsel (Corporate), Office of Chief Counsel, Internal Revenue Service. However, personnel from other offices of the Internal Revenue Service and Treasury Department participated in developing the regulations, in matters of both substance and style.

[¶ 49,115]   **Proposed Regulations and Amendments of Regulations (INTL-704-87),** published in the Federal Register on January 16, 1990.

Corporate distributions: Foreign corporation.—Amendments of Reg. § 1.367(a)-1T, relating to the distribution of stock and securities by a domestic corporation to a person who is not a United States person, and also relating to a liquidating distribution of property by a domestic or foreign corporation to a foreign corporation, are proposed as final. Reg. §§ 1.367(e)-0 and 1.367(e)-1 were adopted 1/15/93 by T.D. 8472 and removed 8/9/96 by T.D. 8682. Reg. § 1.367(e)-2 was adopted 8/6/99 by T.D. 8834. Reg. § 7.367(b)-1 was removed 1/21/2000 by T.D. 8862.

AGENCY: Internal Revenue Service, Treasury.

ACTION: Notice of proposed rulemaking by cross-reference to temporary regulations.

SUMMARY: In the Rules and Regulations portion of this issue, the Internal Revenue Service is issuing temporary Income Tax Regulations that add new sections necessary to implementing section 367(e)(1) and (2) of the Internal Revenue Code of 1986, relating to certain corporate distributions to foreign shareholders. These provisions affect the taxability of both corporate distributors and shareholder distributees. The regulations also add certain provisions under section 367(a) and (b) concerning reorganizations under section 368(a)(1)(F) involving foreign corporations. The text of the temporary regulations also serves as the comment document for this notice of proposed rulemaking.

DATES: Written comments and requests for a public hearing must be delivered or mailed before March 19, 1990.

Except as set forth below, these regulations are proposed to be effective with respect to distributions after July 31, 1986. The following provisions have the following special proposed effective dates:

§ 1.367(a)-1(e)	April 1, 1987
§ 1.367(a)-1(f)	January 1, 1985
§ 1.367(e)-1	February 16, 1990
§ 1.367(b)-1(e)	April 1, 1987
§ 1.367(b)-1(f)	January 1, 1985

ADDRESS: Send comments and requests for a public hearing to Commissioner of Internal Revenue, (Attention: CC:CORP:T:R INTL-704-87), Room 4429, Washington, DC 20224.

FOR FURTHER INFORMATION CONTACT: Charles P. Besecky of the Office of Associate Chief Counsel (International) within the Office of Chief Counsel, Internal Revenue Service, 1111 Constitution Avenue, N.W., Washington, DC 20224 (Attention: CC:LR:T) (202-566-6444, not a toll-free call).

SUPPLEMENTARY INFORMATION:

PAPERWORK REDUCTION ACT

The collection of information contained in this notice of proposed rulemaking has been submitted to the Office of Management and Budget for review in accordance with the Paperwork Reduction Act of 1980 (44 U.S.C. § 3504(h)). Comments on the collection of information should be sent to the Office of Management and Budget, Paperwork Reduction Project (1545-1124), Washington, D.C. 20503, with copies to the Internal Revenue Service, Attention: IRS Reports Clearance Officer TR:FP, Washington, DC 20224.

The collection of information in this regulation is in section 1.367(e)-1T(c)(2) and section 1.367(e)-2T(b)(2)(i) and (c)(2)(i). This information is required by the Internal Revenue Service to ensure that gains recognized by the distributing and distributee corporations are reported on the appropriate income tax return. This information will be used to assure compliance with the provisions of the regulation. The likely respondents are business or other for-profit institutions.

These estimates are an approximation of the average time expected to be necessary for a collection of information. They are based on such information as is available to the Internal Revenue Service. Individual respondents/recordkeepers may require greater or less time, depending upon their particular circumstances.

Estimated total annual reporting and/or recordkeeping burden: 3,200 hours.

Estimated average annual burden per respondent: 8 hours.

Estimated number of respondents: 400.

Estimated annual frequency of responses: 1.

BACKGROUND

The temporary regulations published in the Rules and Regulations portion of this issue of the FEDERAL REGISTER add §§ 1.367(a)-1T(e) and (f), 1.367(a)-0T, 1.367(e)-1T, and 1.367(e)-2T to 26 CFR Part 1, and add new paragraphs (e) and (f) to § 7.367(b)-1 of 26 CFR Part 7. The final regulations that are proposed to be based on these temporary regulations would amend 26 CFR Parts 1, 7 and 602 by adding these temporary regulations as final regulations under section 367(a), (b) and (e) of the Internal Revenue Code of 1986. For the text of the temporary regulations, see T.D. 8280 published in the Rules and Regulations portion of this issue of the FEDERAL REGISTER.

SPECIAL ANALYSES

It has been determined that this proposed rule is not a major rule as defined in Executive Order 12291. Therefore, a Regulatory Impact Analysis is not required. It is hereby certified that the proposed rule will not have a significant impact on a substantial number of small entities. Few small entities would be affected by these regulations. A regulatory flexibility analysis, therefore, is not required under the Regulatory Flexibility Act (5 U.S.C. chapter 6). Pursuant to section 7805(f) of the Internal Revenue Code, these regulations will be submitted to the Administrator of the Small Business Administration for comment on their impact on small business.

COMMENTS AND REQUESTS FOR A PUBLIC HEARING

Before adopting these proposed regulations, consideration will be given to any written comments that are submitted (preferably a signed original and eight copies) to the Commissioner of Internal Revenue. All comments will be available for public inspection and copying. A public hearing will be held upon written request to the Commissioner by any person who has submitted written comments. If a public hearing is held, notice of the time and place will be published in the FEDERAL REGISTER.

DRAFTING INFORMATION

The principal author of these regulations is Charles P. Besecky of the Office of Associate Chief Counsel (International), within the Office of Chief Counsel, Internal Revenue Service. However, personnel from other offices of the Internal Revenue Service and Treasury Department participated in developing the regulations on matters of substance and style.

[¶ 49,118] **Proposed Regulations and Proposed Amendments of Regulations (IL-868-89),** published in the Federal Register on December 10, 1990.

Foreign-owned corporations: Information returns: Records.—Reg. §1.6038C-1, relating to foreign-owned corporations, is proposed. Reg. §§1.6038A-0—1.6038A-7 are adopted.

AGENCY: Internal Revenue Service, Treasury.

ACTION: Notice of proposed rulemaking.

SUMMARY: This document contains proposed Income Tax Regulations relating to information which must be reported and records which must be maintained by certain foreign-owned corporations under sections 6038A and 6038C of the Internal Revenue Code. These regulations will provide appropriate guidance for affected reporting corporations and related parties. The regulations will affect any reporting corporation, that is, certain domestic corporations or foreign corporations, as well as certain related parties of the reporting corporation.

DATES: Written comments, requests to appear, and outlines of oral comments to be presented at a public hearing scheduled for Friday, February 22, 1991, at 10:00 a.m., must be received by Friday, February 8, 1991. See notice of hearing published elsewhere in this issue of the Federal Register.

FOR FURTHER INFORMATION CONTACT: Concerning the hearing on the proposed rulemaking, Felicia Daniels, Regulations Unit, 202-566-3935 (not a toll-free call); concerning a particular regulation section, Carol P. Tello or Grace Perez-Navarro of the Office of Associate Chief Counsel (International), within the Office of Chief Counsel, (202-377-9493 (Ms. Tello), 202-287-4851 (Ms. Perez-Navarro), not toll-free calls).

SUPPLEMENTARY INFORMATION:

Paperwork Reduction Act

The collection of information contained in this notice of proposed rulemaking has been submitted to the Office of Management and Budget in accordance with the Paperwork Reduction Act of 1980 (44 U.S.C. 3504(h)). Comments on the collection of information should be sent to the Office of Management and Budget, Attention: Desk Officer for the Department of the Treasury, Office of Information and Regulatory Affairs, Washington, D. C. 20503, with copies to the Internal Revenue Service, Attention: IRS Reports Clearance Officer T.FP, Washington, D. C. 20224. The collection of information in this regulation is in §§1.6038A-2 and 1.6038A-3. This information is required by the Internal Revenue Service to determine the correct tax treatment of transactions between 25-percent foreign-owned corporations engaged in a U.S. trade or business and related parties. The likely respondents for Form 5472 are corporations.

These estimates are an approximation of the average time expected to be necessary for record maintenance and collection of information. They are based upon such information as is available to the Internal Revenue Service. Individual respondents and recordkeepers may require greater or less time, depending on their particular circumstances.

Estimated total annual reporting and recordkeeping burden: 1,539,000 hours

The estimated average annual reporting burden per respondent is 14 hours and 26 minutes.

The estimated average annual recordkeeping burden per recordkeeper is 10 hours.

Estimated number of respondents/recordkeepers: 63,000.

Estimated annual frequency of responses: 1.

Background

This document contains proposed Income Tax Regulations (26 CFR Part 1) under sections 6038A and 6038C of the Internal Revenue Code of 1986. These regulations are generally proposed to be effective for taxable years beginning after July 10, 1989. However, special effective date rules are proposed to provide that certain provisions sections will be effective as of, except as follows:

§ 1.6038A-1(c)	July 10, 1989
§ 1.6038A-2	July 10, 1989
§ 1.6038A-3	March 20, 1990
§ 1. 6038A-4	July 10, 1989
§ 1. 6038A-6	November 5, 1990

Explanation of Provisions

Prior Law

Prior to the enactment of the Revenue Reconciliation Act of 1989, section 6038A required an annual filing of an information return, Form 5472, by a domestic corporation (or a foreign corporation engaged in trade or business within the United States) that is controlled by a foreign person. A person controlled a corporation if that person owned stock possessing more than 50 percent of the total voting power of all classes of stock entitled to vote or more than 50 percent of the total value of shares of all classes of stock. If a corporation failed to furnish the information required under the statute, a penalty of $1000 was imposed for each taxable year with respect to which such failure occurred. An additional penalty of $1000 was imposed for each 30-day period during which such failure continued after the expiration of a 90-day period following the mailing of a notice of failure. The increase in the additional penalty was limited to $24,000.

Statutory Provision

The Revenue Reconciliation Act of 1989 amended section 6038A in several significant ways. First, the threshold of foreign ownership subjecting a corporation to the application of section 6038A was lowered from 50 percent to 25 percent. Second, amended section 6038A requires the maintenance of records as prescribed by regulations.

The penalty for the failure either to file timely the annual information return or to maintain (or to cause another to maintain) the prescribed records is $10,000 for each taxable year with respect to which such failure occurs. The former maximum additional penalty of $24,000 has been deleted. If the failure continues for more than 90 days after the day on which notice is given by the Service of such failure, an additional penalty of $10,000 is assessed for each 30-day period or part thereof that the failure continues.

In addition to the above changes, the 1989 Act added a new section, section 6038A(e)(1), requiring a foreign related party that engages in transactions with a reporting corporation to authorize the reporting corporation to act as its agent solely for purposes of sections 7602, 7603, and 7604.

If the related party does not authorize the reporting corporation to act as its agent, the Secretary shall apply the noncompliance penalty with respect to transactions between the related party and the reporting corporation.

If the noncompliance penalty applies, the amount allowed as a deduction for amounts paid or incurred to the related party and for the cost of goods purchased from the related party or sold by the reporting corporation to the related party is determined by the Secretary in his sole discretion based upon such probative information as the Secretary may choose to obtain. See H.R. Conf. Rep. 386, 101st Cong., 1st Sess. 593-595 (1989).

The noncompliance penalty may also be applied to a transaction between the related party and the reporting corporation if the reporting corporation does not substantially comply with a summons for records or testimony relating to such transaction.

The Omnibus Budget Reconciliation Act of 1990 (the 1990 Act) added section 6038C to the Internal Revenue Code. Foreign corporations engaged in U.S. trade or business are subject to the provisions of section 6038C, which are similar to the provisions of section 6038A. Additional regulations under section 6038C will be issued at a later time which will reflect the 1990 Act changes with respect to such corporations.

Comments

Comments are solicited with respect to ways to permit related foreign corporations to file a single agency designation, in a manner similar to the rules contained in paragraph (g) of §1.6038A-1 regarding the ability of the common parent of an affiliated group to file a consolidated Form 5472 for all related party transactions of the U.S. consolidated return group and to be designated as agent for related parties.

The de minimis rule of §1.6038A-1(h) was developed after consideration of case studies submitted by international examiners. Comments from taxpayers are solicited.

Comments and case studies are also solicited on whether the various tests for determining material profit and loss statements under §1.6038A-3(c)(3) are appropriate. In particular, comments regarding the existing accounting and business practices for maintaining profit and loss statements are requested. Objections to the profit and loss statement standards set forth in these regulations should be accompanied by proposed alternatives. Comments also are solicited on when a profit margin analysis, rather than a return on assets analysis, might be appropriate for the high profit test under paragraph (c)(6) of section 1.6038A-3.

Explanation of Proposed Regulations

General requirement and definitions

Section 1.6038A-1 provides the general rule that certain foreign-owned U.S. corporations and foreign corporations engaged in trade or business within the United States (reporting corporations) must furnish certain information annually on an information return, Form 5472, and maintain records relating to transactions between the reporting corporation and a foreign related party as described in §1.6038A-3. Definitions are provided for the terms reporting corporation, 25-percent foreign-owned, 25-percent foreign shareholder, related party, foreign person, and foreign related party. Special rules are provided for U.S. consolidated return groups.

Requirement of return

Section 1.6038A-2 describes the information that must be furnished annually on Form 5472. Reporting corporations whose sole trade or business in the United States is a banking, financing, or similar business as defined in §1.864-4(c)(5)(i) (formerly excepted from filing Form 5472) will be subject to the information filing requirement of §1.6038A-2.

Record maintenance

Section 1.6038A-3 provides the general rule that records to be maintained by a reporting corporation are those records sufficient to establish the correctness of the federal income tax return (including the correct treatment of transactions with related parties) of the reporting corporation. Records prepared, maintained, or possessed by a foreign related party relating to transactions between the reporting corporation and any related parties must be maintained in the United States, except where an election is in effect under paragraph (f) of §1.6038A-3. A record may be maintained in the United States by a party other than the reporting corporation; however, the reporting corporation remains liable for the proper compilation and maintenance of such records.

The regulations generally are based upon the view that the requirement to "maintain" records does not require their creation. However, basic accounting records and material profit and loss statements must be created if they are not otherwise maintained. In connection with record maintenance and production, labels placed upon documents by the taxpayer shall not control.

Some reporting corporations may be unfamiliar with record maintenance practices generally adopted in the United States under the guidance of section 6001, its regulations, and longstanding administrative practice developed thereunder. In addition, such corporations may not be aware of the specific information that would be relevant to an examination of their related party transactions. In the absence of detailed guidance, such reporting corporations might not retain the information that is required for U.S. tax purposes. Therefore, six general categories of records with respect to related party transactions are provided as a safe harbor. Reporting corporations that maintain records in the categories that apply to the particular industry or business of the reporting corporation, to the extent such records may be relevant to the correct U.S. tax treatment of the transactions between related parties, are deemed to meet the record maintenance requirements of section 6038A.

Reporting corporations may enter into agreements with the District Director or the Assistant Commissioner (International) specifying what records must be maintained to satisfy the maintenance requirements for such reporting corporations under this section. Agreements with respect to retention of machine-sensible records under Rev. Proc. 86-19 may also be executed. An annual election to maintain records outside the United States is provided if the reporting corporation agrees to produce the records as prescribed by the regulations. The District Director or the Assistant Commissioner (International) may invalidate the election to maintain records outside the United States under certain circumstances.

Monetary penalty

Section 1.6038A-4 provides for the imposition of a monetary penalty of $10,000 for each taxable year in which a reporting corporation fails to timely file Form 5472, fails to maintain or cause another to maintain the records described in § 1.6038A-3, or fails to produce the records within the time prescribed in § 1.6038A-3. A rule permitting a reporting corporation to show reasonable cause as to why the failure occurred is provided. The reasonable cause exception is to be interpreted in accordance with the legislative history. *See* S. Prt. 101- [ ], 101st Cong., 1st Sess. 117 (1989) and H. Conf. Rep. No. 386, 101st Cong., 1st Sess. 593 (1989). Failure to maintain records is determined upon the basis of the overall compliance with the records maintenance requirement by a reporting corporation. Finally, rules relating to the increase in the penalty where the failure continues after notification are provided.

Authorization of agent

Section 1.6038A-5 provides that the noncompliance penalty in § 1.6038A-7 shall apply to any transaction between a related party and a reporting corporation, unless the related party authorizes the reporting corporation to act as its limited agent solely for purposes of sections 7602, 7603, and 7604. When the proposed regulations become final, a related party annually shall authorize the reporting corporation to act as its limited agent on Form 5472 or within 30 days of a request from the Service. Until official Internal Revenue Service forms are available, the authorization as set forth in the regulations should be utilized. A procedure is provided for the retroactive authorization of an agent with respect to inadvertent transactions with related parties when the relationship is attenuated and certain other requirements are met. Additionally, a provision allows for the authorization by a foreign related party to be deemed under certain circumstances. A deemed authorization is effective only for transactions entered into prior to the time when the reporting corporation knew or had reason to know that the related party was in fact related.

Failure to furnish information

Section 1.6038A-6 provides that the noncompliance penalty contained in § 1.6038A-7 may be applied under certain circumstances when information requested by the Service is not produced. A special rule permits the District Director or the Assistant Commissioner (International) to choose not to apply the noncompliance penalty when, in the discretion of the District Director or the Assistant Commissioner (International), the failure to furnish information is *de minimis*.

Noncompliance penalty

Section 1.6038A-7 provides that if a foreign related party does not authorize the reporting corporation to act as its agent as required by § 1.6038A-5 or, if following a failure to furnish information as required by § 1.6038A-6, the District Director or the Assistant Commissioner (International) determines that § 1.6038A-7 should apply, the District Director or the Assistant Commissioner (International) shall determine the amount of deductions allowed for any amount paid or incurred by the reporting corporation to the related party in connection with such transaction and the cost to the reporting corporation of any property acquired in such transaction from the related party or transferred to the related party. The amount of the deduction or cost to the reporting corporation shall be determined in the sole discretion of the District Director or the Assistant Commissioner (International). *See* H. Conf. Rep. 386, 101st Cong., 1st Sess. 593-95 (1989).

Section 6038C

Corporations subject to section 6038C generally will be subject to the rules contained in § § 1.6038A-1 through 1.6038A-7.

Special Analyses

It has been determined that these proposed rules are not major rules as defined in Executive Order 12291. Therefore, a Regulatory Impact Analysis is not required. It also has been determined that section 553(b) of the Administrative Procedure Act (5 U.S.C. Chapter 5) and the Regulatory Flexibility Act (5 U.S.C. Chapter 6) do not apply to these regulations, and, therefore, a final Regulatory Flexibility Analysis is not required. Pursuant to section 7805(f) of the Internal Revenue Code, these regulations will be submitted to the Administrator of the Small Business Administration for comments on their impact on small business.

Comments and Request for a Public Hearing

Before adopting these proposed regulations, consideration will be given to any written comments that are submitted (preferably a signed original and eight copies) to the Internal Revenue Service. All comments will be available for public inspection and copying. A public hearing will be held on Friday, February 22, 1991.

Drafting Information

The principal authors of these regulations are Carol P. Tello and Grace Perez-Navarro of the Office of Associate Chief Counsel (International), within the Office of Chief Counsel, Internal Revenue Service. Other personnel from the Internal Revenue Service and Treasury Department participated in developing these regulations.

[¶ 49,119] **Proposed Regulations and Proposed Amendments of Regulations (REG-208289-86) [originally issued as INTL-939-86]**, published in the Federal Register on April 17, 1991.

Controlled foreign corporations: Insurance income: Tax years after 1986.—Reg. § § 1.953-0—1.953-7 and amendments to Reg. § § 1.953-1—1.953-6, 1.954-1T, 1.964-1, 1.1248-1 and 1.6046-1, relating to the definition and computation of the insurance income of controlled foreign corporations, have been proposed.

AGENCY: Internal Revenue Service, Treasury.

ACTION: Notice of proposed rulemaking.

SUMMARY: This document contains proposed Income Tax Regulations relating to the definition and computation of the insurance income of a controlled foreign corporation. The proposed regulations also contain definitions and rules applicable to certain captive insurance companies. This action is necessary because of changes to the applicable tax law made by the Tax Reform Act of 1986 and by the Technical and Miscellaneous Revenue Act of 1988. These regulations would provide guidance needed to comply with these changes and would affect controlled foreign corporations with income derived from insurance operations.

DATES: Written comments must be received by June 17, 1991.

A public hearing on these proposed regulations will be held Monday, June 24, 1991, beginning at 10 a.m. See the notice of public hearing on these proposed regulations elsewhere in this issue of the Federal Register.

ADDRESSES: Send comments to: Commissioner of Internal Revenue, P.O. Box 7604, Ben Franklin Station, Attention: CC:CORP:T:R (INTL-939-86), Room 4429, Washington, DC 20044.

FOR FURTHER INFORMATION CONTACT: David R. Cooper of the Office of Associate Chief Counsel (International), within the Office of Chief Counsel, Internal Revenue Service, 1111 Constitution Avenue, N.W., Washington, DC 20224, Attention: CC:INTL:Br2 (INTL-939-86) (202-566-6645, not a toll-free call).

SUPPLEMENTARY INFORMATION:

Paperwork Reduction Act

The collection of information contained in this notice of proposed rulemaking has been submitted to the Office of Management and Budget for review in accordance with the Paperwork Reduction Act of 1980 (44 U.S.C. §3504(h)). Comments on the collection of information should be sent to the Office of Management and Budget, Attention: Desk Officer for the Department of the Treasury, Office of Information and Regulatory Affairs, Washington, DC 20503, with copies to the Internal Revenue Service, Attention: IRS Reports Clearance Officer T:FP, Washington, DC 20224.

The collection of information in these regulations is in §§ 1.953-2(e)(3)(iii), 1.953-4(b), 1.953-5(a), 1.953-6(a), 1.953-7(c)(8), 1.6046-1(a)(2)(i)(c), and 1.6046-1(c)(1)(iii). This information is required by the Internal Revenue Service in order for taxpayers to elect to locate risks with respect to movable property by reference to the location of the property in a prior period; to allocate investment income to a particular category of insurance income; to allocate deductions to a particular category of insurance income; to determine the amount of those items, such as reserves, which are computed with reference to an insurance company's annual statement; to elect to have related person insurance income treated as income effectively connected with the conduct of a United States trade or business; and to collect the information required by section 6046 relating to controlled foreign corporations as defined in section 953(c). The information will be used to verify that locating movable property on the basis of where the property is located in a prior period does not result in a material distortion when compared to where the property is actually located during a current period; to verify the connection between certain items of investment income and a specific category of insurance income; to verify the connection between deductions and a specific category of insurance income; to verify the accuracy of those items which are determined by reference to an insurance company's annual statement; to permit related person insurance income to be taxed at the corporate level as income effectively connected with the conduct of a United States trade or business rather than at the shareholder level as subpart F income; and to ensure compliance with the Internal Revenue Code as it relates to controlled foreign corporations as defined in section 953(c). The likely respondents are business or other for-profit institutions.

These estimates are an approximation of the average time expected to be necessary for a collection of information. They are based on information as is available to the Internal Revenue Service. Individual respondents/recordkeepers may require greater or less time, depending on their particular circumstances.

Estimated total annual reporting and recordkeeping burden: 14,100 hours.

The estimated annual burden per respondent and/or recordkeeper varies from 20 to 60 hours, depending on individual circumstances, with an estimated average of 28.2 hours.

Estimated number of respondents and/or recordkeepers: 500.

Estimated annual frequency of responses: Annually.

Background

This document contains proposed amendments to the Income Tax Regulations (26 CFR Part 1) under sections 953, 954, 964, 1248, and 6046 of the Internal Revenue Code of 1986. These amendments are proposed to conform the regulations to section 1221(b) of the Tax Reform Act of 1986 (Pub. L. 99-514, 100 Stat. 2085, 2551) and to section 1012(i) of the Technical and Miscellaneous Revenue Act of 1988 (Pub. L. 100-647, 102 Stat. 3342).

Explanation of Provisions

Statutory Provisions

A United States shareholder of a controlled foreign corporation is subject to current United States taxation on the subpart F income of the foreign corporation. Subpart F income is defined under section 952 and consists of several types of income, one of which is "insurance income," as defined in section 953. Insurance income exists only with respect to bona fide contracts of insurance (or reinsurance) or annuity contracts. This regulation does not address the issue of what constitutes insurance. Whether a payment is considered an insurance premium or a contribution to capital can, however, affect both the characterization of receipts as "insurance income" and the value of stock in a controlled foreign corporation owned by United States persons. Therefore, the characterization of payments as insurance premiums or contributions to capital must be considered carefully.

Insurance income is income (including investment income) attributable to the issuing or reinsuring of any insurance or annuity contract in connection with risks located in a country other than the country under the laws of which the controlled foreign corporation is created or organized and which would be taxed under subchapter L of the Code if the income were the income of a domestic insurance company. Although not within the definition of insurance income under section 953, the investment income attributable to insurance, reinsurance, or annuity contracts covering risks located in the controlled foreign corporation's country of incorporation may be subject to subpart F as foreign personal holding company income under sections 954(a)(1) and 954(c) of the Code.

Section 953(c) provides special definitions of the terms "United States shareholder" and "controlled foreign corporation" for the purpose of taking into account related person insurance income. Related person insurance income is any insurance income attributable to a policy of insurance or reinsurance under which the insured is a United States shareholder of the controlled foreign corporation or a related person to such a shareholder. For purposes of taking into account related person insurance income, the term "United States shareholder" means any United States person (as defined in section 957(c)) who owns, within the meaning of section 958(a), any stock of the foreign corporation, and the term "controlled foreign corporation" means any foreign corporation if 25 percent or more of the total combined voting power of all classes of stock of the foreign corporation entitled to vote, or 25 percent or more of the total value of the stock of the foreign corporation, is owned (within the meaning of section 958(a)), or is considered as owned by applying the rules of ownership of section 958(b), by United States shareholders on any day during the taxable year of the foreign corporation. A person is related to a United States shareholder if such person is related within the meaning of section 954(d)(3) to the United States shareholder. In addition, in the case of a policy covering liabilities arising from services performed as a director, officer, or employee of a corporation, or as a partner or employee of a partnership, the person performing the services and the entity for which the services are performed are related persons.

Section 953(c) contains certain exceptions which, if applicable, relieve United States shareholders (other than United States shareholders as defined in section 951(b)) from having to include related person insurance income in their gross income. Section 953(c) also provides special rules for determining a United States shareholder's pro rata share of related person insurance income and provides for the application of section 1248 to persons who are United States shareholders solely by virtue of section 953(c)(1)(A).

Finally, the statute provides for certain rules preventing the application of certain provisions of subchapter L of the Code in computing insurance income, and provides regulatory authority to prescribe rules for the allocation and apportionment of income, expenses, losses, and deductions, as well as rules to carry out the purpose of the related person insurance income provisions of section 953(c).

The proposed regulations do not address section 953(d), which permits a foreign insurance company that is a controlled foreign corporation to elect to be treated as a domestic corporation, or section 964(d), which permits a qualified insurance branch of a controlled foreign corporation to be treated as a separate foreign corporation created under the laws of the foreign country. Guidance will be provided under those sections as part of another regulation project. *See* Notice 89-79, 1989-2 C.B. 392, for interim guidance under section 953(d).

Consideration has been given to whether the definition of the term "life insurance contract" under section 7702(a), the diversification requirements for variable contracts under section 817(h), and the distribution requirements of section 72(s) should be considered applicable for subpart F purposes to contracts issued by controlled foreign corporations conducting insurance operations with nonresident aliens. The proposed regulations contain a reservation on these issues. Comments are invited on them.

Summary of Regulations

Because of the substantial modification of the provisions of section 953 by the Tax Reform Act of 1986, the proposed regulations redraft the current regulations under section 953 in their entirety. In addition, several conforming modifications in the form of proposed regulations are made to the final regulations under sections 954, 964(a), 1248(a), and 6046(a). The regulations are proposed to be applicable to taxable years of controlled foreign corporations beginning after December 31, 1986. However, the amendments to sections 953(c)(2) and 953(c)(3) by sections 1012(i)(3)(A) and 1012(i)(3)(B)(i) and (ii) of the Technical and Miscellaneous Revenue Act of 1988 are proposed to apply to taxable years beginning after December 31, 1987 to the extent such amendments add the phrase "(directly or indirectly)." Further, the rsisk location rules of § 1.953-2 are proposed to apply only to periods of coverage that begin on or after June 17, 1991. Prior to the effective date of § 1.953-2, taxpayers may determine the location of risks by using the principles of § 1.953-2 of the current regulations, but those principles shall be applied to determine whether risks are located in or outside the controlled foreign corporation's country of incorporation rather than in or outside the United States. Comments are invited on whether other transitional rules would be appropriate.

Upon adoption of the proposed regulations as temporary or final regulations, the current regulations under section 953 will be retained (although redesignated as § § 1.953-1A through 1.953-6A) because they remain applicable with respect to taxable years of controlled foreign corporations beginning before January 1, 1987. Similarly, several conforming modifications in the form of proposed regulations are made to the final regulations under sections 954, 964(a), 1248(a), and 6046(a).

Section 1.953-1(a) provides definitions of the different categories of insurance income of a controlled foreign corporation that issues insurance, reinsurance, or annuity contracts. Income from a contract covering risks outside the controlled foreign corporation's country of incorporation (the "home country") constitutes insurance income within the meaning of section 953. Income from a contract covering risks in the controlled foreign corporation's home country is income within the same-country insurance category (the "SCI category"). Premiums within the SCI category are generally not considered to be section 953 insurance income and are not includable in the gross income of United States shareholders of a controlled foreign corporation. However, investment income within the SCI category may be subject to inclusion in the gross income of United States shareholders of the controlled foreign corporation as foreign personal holding company income under sections 954(a)(1) and 954(c). Section 1.953-1(a) also defines two categories of section 953 insurance income: income within the RPII category, which is income that constitutes related person insurance income, and income within the nonRPII category, which is all section 953 insurance income other than related person insurance income.

Section 1.953-1(b) provides the procedures that are used to determine the amount of a controlled foreign corporation's section 953 insurance income and its foreign personal holding company income derived from insurance, reinsurance, and annuity contracts. The first step in the procedure is to determine whether premiums constitute section 953 insurance income or SCI income. The second step is to determine whether premiums that constitute section 953 insurance income are attributable to the RPII or nonRPII categories. The third step is to allocate and apportion investment income to the RPII, nonRPII, and SCI categories. The last step is to allocate and apportion expenses, losses, and other deductions among the RPII, nonRPII, and SCI categories, and to allocate and apportion deductions within the SCI category, and in certain circumstances within the RPII category, between premium and investment income.

Section 1.953-2 provides rules for determining whether premiums are attributable to the section 953 insurance income or SCI income categories. That determination is made by locating the risks covered by an insurance, reinsurance, or annuity contract during the period of coverage to which the premiums under the contract relate. Premiums written before the first taxable year of a controlled foreign corporation beginning after December 31, 1986 that become earned under section 832(b)(4) in such taxable year or succeeding taxable years must be classified as either section 953 insurance income or SCI income.

Section 1.953-2(d) provides general rules of allocation and apportionment of premiums to or between the section 953 insurance income category and the SCI income category where an insurance, reinsurance, or annuity contract covers risks both in and outside the home country. Section 1.953-2(d) also provides that if 80 percent or more of the premiums under a contract of insurance or reinsurance or an annuity contract are apportioned to risks in or outside the home country, then all of the premiums are attributed to risks in or outside the home country, respectively.

Section 1.953-2(e) sets forth specific rules for locating risks in connection with property. Such risks are generally located where the property is located during the period or periods of coverage under the contract of insurance or reinsurance that are applicable to a taxable year. Specific rules are provided for determining the location of commercial transportation property, noncommercial transportation property, property exported or imported by railroad or motor vehicle, property exported or imported by ship or aircraft, and shipments originating and terminating in or outside the home country. Specific rules are also provided for allocating and apportioning premiums when the contract of insurance or reinsurance covers many related items of property, such as inventory, which may be both in and outside the home country. In order to aid a controlled foreign corporation that is not able to determine the location of moveable property as of the close of its taxable year, a specific rule is also set forth for locating risks in connection with such property.

Section 1.953-2(f) provides specific rules for locating risks in connection with liability arising out of activities. Generally, such risks are located where the activities that could give rise to the liability are performed. Specific rules are provided for locating activities with respect to liabilities arising from the use or consumption of property that is manufactured, produced, constructed, or assembled by the insured. Specific rules are also provided for determining the location of activities in connection with transportation property and selling activities.

Section 1.953-2(g) sets forth rules for locating risks in connection with contracts of insurance or reinsurance covering life or health. This section also covers the location of risks under annuity contracts, whether life annuities or annuities certain. Such risks are generally located in the country of the residence of the person with the "determining life." For a contract of insurance or reinsurance providing protection against loss of life or health, the determining life is the person whose life or health is covered by the contract. For a life annuity, or a contract reinsuring life annuities, the determining life is the person by whose life the annuity payments are measured. For an annuity certain, or a contract reinsuring annuities certain, both the purchaser of the annuity and the beneficiary of the annuity payments are the appropriate determining lives. If either the purchaser or beneficiary of an annuity certain resides outside the home country, the premiums received with respect to the annuity constitute section 953 insurance income. The residence of the person with the determining life is generally determined by the address of such person that is provided to the insurer. Finally, section 1.953-2(h) provides rules for determining the location of risks in certain direct or indirect cross-insurance arrangements.

Section 1.953-3 contains the rules for distinguishing RPII premiums from non-RPII premiums. Section 1.953-3(a) states that RPII premiums are section 953 insurance income premiums that constitute related person insurance income.

Section 1.953-3(b) defines related person insurance income. Related person insurance income is included within the meaning of the term "insurance income" as that term is used in section 953 of the Code. Related person insurance income is defined as premium and investment income attributable to a policy of insurance or reinsurance that provides insurance coverage to a related insured on risks located outside the controlled foreign corporation's country of incorporation, or premium and investment income attributable to any annuity contract that is purchased by, or for the benefit of, a related insured if the determining life is located outside the controlled foreign corporation's country of incorporation. For this purpose, a related insured is any insured, purchaser of an annuity contract, or beneficiary under an annuity contract that is a United States shareholder of the controlled foreign corporation or a related person (within the meaning of section 954(d)(3)) to a United States shareholder. In addition, in the case of any policy of insurance covering liability arising from services performed as a director, officer, or employee of a corporation, or as a partner or employee of a partnership, the person performing such services and the entity for which such services are performed shall be treated as related persons. Related person insurance income also includes income attributable to contracts reinsuring and contracts indirectly insuring related insureds if the risks under the contract are located outside the controlled foreign corporation's country of incorporation.

For purposes only of taking related person insurance income into account, the terms "United States shareholder" and "controlled foreign corporation" are specially defined in §1.953-3(b). An exception from the modified definition of United States shareholder is provided for persons who would be United States shareholders of an insuring foreign corporation as a result of their ownership of stock in another foreign corporation if the stock of the other foreign corporation is publicly traded, the United States person owns less than five percent of such foreign corporation's stock and the stock of the insuring foreign corporation constitutes less than five percent of the total value of all assets of such foreign corporation. Section 1.953-3(b) also provides that related person insurance income includes insurance income attributable to certain direct or indirect cross-insurance arrangements.

Section 1.953-3(b) also provides rules for determining whether premiums constitute related person insurance premiums under certain specific circumstances. Premiums received prior to December 31, 1986 which become earned in the controlled foreign corporation's first taxable year beginning after December 31, 1986, or any succeeding taxable year, may constitute related person insurance income. Rules are also provided for computing RPII premiums when the related insured owns stock for less than the entire taxable year. An anti-abuse rule states that capital contributions may be recharacterized as premiums in certain circumstances.

Section 1.953-4 provides guidance concerning the allocation and apportionment of items of investment income to or among the RPII, nonRPII, and SCI categories. An item of investment income is allocated to a particular category of income if it directly relates to a contract which gives rise to premiums allocable to that category. An item of investment income is considered directly related to a contract which gives rise to premiums within a particular category if the income is derived from an asset which is identified on the controlled foreign corporation's books and records as an asset relating to RPII, nonRPII, or SCI contracts and the controlled foreign corporation separately accounts for the various income, exclusion, deduction, reserve, and other liability items properly attributable to such contracts. If investment income cannot be allocated, it is apportioned among the various categories of income in accordance with apportionment formulas provided in §1.953-4(c).

Section 1.953-5(a) provides rules for allocating expenses, losses, and other deductions among the RPII, nonRPII, and SCI categories. Allocation of deductions generally is made in accordance with §§1.861-8, 1.861-8T, 1.861-9T, 1.861-10T, and 1.861-12T of the regulations. Specific rules are provided to allocate reserve deductions and deductions for claims, benefits, and losses. Deductions that cannot be allocated are apportioned among the various categories in accordance with the rules provided in §1.953-5(b), which are generally consistent with the principles of §§1.861-8, 1.861-8T, 1.861-9T, 1.861-10T, and 1.861-12T. Under §1.953-5(b), deductions that are allocated or apportioned to investment income pursuant to the regulations under section 861 are apportioned among the various income categories in the same manner as investment income. Other deductions that are not allocated or apportioned to investment income pursuant to the regulations under section 861 are apportioned among the various income categories in accordance with the amount of premium income, adjusted by increases or decreases in reserves, in each category.

Section 1.953-5(c) provides rules for allocating and apportioning deductions to or between premium and investment income within the SCI and, in certain circumstances, within the RPII categories. Although deductions other than those for reserves, losses, and specified policy acquisition expenses are allocated and apportioned between investment and premium income by following the principles of §§1.861-8, 1.861-8T, 1.861-9T, 1.861-10T, and 1.861-12T, specific rules are provided under §1.953-5(c)(3) for apportioning reserves, losses, and specified policy acquisition expenses between investment and premium income for taxable years beginning on or after April 17, 1991. The method prescribed for apportioning reserves between premium and investment income is based on the assumptions that premiums are received and losses paid at mid-year, and that the investment income portion of the increase in reserves can be calculated by assuming the reserves earn investment income at the interest rate used to calculate tax reserves. For taxable years beginning prior to April 17, 1991, taxpayers may use a reasonable apportionment formula. However, in most cases, a method that apportions reserves and losses between premium and investment income based on the ratio of premium or investment income to total income will not be considered a reasonable apportionment.

Section 1.953-6 contains provisions relating to the application of subchapter L and certain sections of subchapter N of the Code. Section 1.953-6(a) states that the provisions of subchapter L are generally applicable in determining the amount of a controlled foreign corporation's section 953 insurance income and SCI investment income to be included in gross income. Section 1.953-6(b) lists the provisions of subchapter L which are not applicable. Section 1.953-6(c) contains rules for making the election under section 831(b) to be taxed on investment income only. A section 831(b) election is a corporate level election and therefore can be made only by a controlled foreign corporation that has made the election under §1.953-7(c) to have its related person insurance income taxed as income effectively connected with the conduct of a trade or business within the United States. Section 1.953-6(d) contains rules necessary to determine whether a controlled foreign corporation is subject to the rules of part I of subchapter L of the Code relating to life insurance companies. Section 1.953-6(e) provides specific rules relating to the computation of the reserves of a controlled foreign corporation. Section 1.953-6(f) states that a controlled foreign corporation that would not be taxable as an insurance company if it were a domestic corporation is nevertheless subject to section 953 and prescribes rules for determining the insurance income of such a corporation. Section 1.953-6(g) describes the relationship between sections 953 and 954. Section 1.953-6(h) provides rules for computing a United States shareholder's pro rata share of section 953 insurance income. Section 1.953-6(i) states that section 959 (exclusion from gross income of previously taxed earnings and profits), section 961 (adjustment to basis in stock in controlled foreign corporations and of other property), and section 1248 (gains from certain sales or exchanges of stock in certain foreign corporations) are applicable to persons who would not be United States shareholders but for section 953(c) and §1.953-3(b)(2)(i). Section 1.953-6(k) provides that income that is subject to subpart F solely by virtue of the full inclusion rule of section 954(b)(3)(B) is not considered related person insurance income and need not be included in the gross income of persons that are not United States shareholders within the meaning of section 951(b),

Section 1.953-7 sets forth the exceptions to inclusion of related person insurance income by persons who are not United States shareholders under section 951(b). Section 1.953-7(a) provides rules relating to the exception that applies if less than 20 percent of the stock of a controlled foreign corporation is owned by insureds. Section 1.953-7(b) relates to the exception for a controlled foreign corporation with a de minimis amount of related person insurance income. Section 1.953-7(c) provides rules and procedures for an election by a corporation that is a controlled foreign corporation solely by virtue of section 953(c) to have its related person insurance income treated as if it were effectively connected with a United States trade or business. To make an election, the controlled foreign corporation must waive treaty benefits, except for benefits with respect to section 884, must timely file an election statement, must enter a closing agreement with the Internal Revenue Service, and must provide an adequate letter of credit.

These proposed regulations would amend the temporary regulations under §1.954-1T(c) to state that a controlled foreign corporation with foreign base company income derived from insurance operations allocates and apportions deductions in accordance with §1.953-5. These proposed regulations also would amend §1.964-1(c)(5) to identify those shareholders who are the controlling United States shareholders of a foreign corporation that is a controlled foreign corporation solely by virtue of section 953(c)(1) for purposes of making elections on behalf of the controlled foreign corporation. In addition, these proposed regulations would amend the final regulations under section 1248(a) to make clear the application of section 1248 to persons that are United States shareholders by virtue of section 953(c). Finally, these proposed regulations also would amend the regulations under section 6046(a) to make the reporting requirements of that section applicable to persons that are United States shareholders by virtue of section 953(c).

With certain exceptions, the proposed regulations do not draw a distinction between mutual insurance companies and stock insurance companies. However, the Internal Revenue Service is interested in receiving comments relating to application of the rules of this regulation with respect to mutual insurance companies and, in particular, whether certain mutual insurance companies should be excluded from the provisions of section 953 and the criteria for such an exclusion.

Special Analyses

It has been determined that these proposed rules are not major rules as defined in Executive Order 12291. Therefore, a Regulatory Impact Analysis is not required. It has also been determined that section 553(b) of the Administrative Procedure Act (5 U.S.C. Chapter 5) and the Regulatory Flexibility Act (5 U.S.C. Chapter 6) do not apply to these regulations, and, therefore, an initial Regulatory Flexibility Analysis is not required. Pursuant to section 7805(f) of the Internal Revenue Code, these regulations will be submitted to the Chief Counsel for Advocacy of the Small Business Administration for comment on their impact on small business.

Comments and Public Hearing

Before adopting these proposed regulations, consideration will be given to any written comments that are submitted (preferably a signed original and eight copies) to the Internal Revenue Service. All comments will be available for public inspection and copying.

A public hearing will be held on Monday, June 24, 1991, beginning at 10 a.m., in the Internal Revenue Service Auditorium, Seventh Floor, 7400 Corridor, Internal Revenue Building, 1111 Constitution Avenue, N.W., Washington, DC. For further information, see the notice of public hearing on these proposed regulations in the Proposed Rules section of this issue of the Federal Register.

Drafting Information

The principal author of these proposed regulations is Philip L. Garlett, formerly of the Office of Associate Chief Counsel (International), within the Office of Chief Counsel, Internal Revenue Service. Other personnel from the Internal Revenue Service and Treasury Department participated in developing the regulations.

[¶49,120] **Proposed Amendments of Regulations (REG-209014-89) [originally issued as INTL-088-89]**, published in the Federal Register on May 13, 1991.

Qualified Caribbean Basin Countries: Investments: Requirements.—Amendments to Reg. §1.936-10, relating to the use of Code Sec. 936 funds to finance an investment that qualifies as a privatization, are proposed.

AGENCY: Internal Revenue Service, Treasury.

ACTION: Notice of proposed rulemaking.

SUMMARY: This document contains proposed regulations relating to the use of section 936 funds to finance an investment that qualifies as a privatization. The regulations prescribe conditions for such an investment to qualify as for use in Puerto Rico under section 936(d)(4). These regulations are necessary to give guidance as to whether the use of section 936 funds in a privatization transaction will qualify as for use in Puerto Rico under section 936(d)(4).

DATES: Written comments, requests to appear, and outlines of oral comments to be presented at a public hearing scheduled for Friday, July 12, 1991, at 10:00 a.m., must be received by Friday, June 28, 1991. See notice of hearing published elsewhere in this issue of the Federal Register.

Addresses: Send comments, requests to appear and outline of oral comments to be presented to: Internal Revenue Service, P. O. Box 7604, Ben Franklin Station, Atten: CC:CORP:T:R (INTL-88-89), Room 5228, Washington, D.C. 20044.

FOR FURTHER INFORMATION CONTACT: Concerning the hearing on the proposed rulemaking, Felicia Daniels, Regulations Unit, 202-566-3935; concerning a particular provision of this proposed regulation, Christine Halphen (202-377-9493, not a toll-free call) or W. Edward Williams (202-287-4851, not a toll-free call) of the Office of Associate Chief Counsel (International) within the Office of Chief Counsel, Internal Revenue Service.

SUPPLEMENTARY INFORMATION:

Background

This document contains proposed amendments to the Income Tax Regulations (26 CFR Part 1). These regulations are proposed to be issued under the authority contained in section 7805 of the Internal Revenue Code of 1986 (68A Stat. 917, 26 U.S.C. 7805).

On September 22, 1989, the Federal Register published proposed and temporary Income Tax Regulations (26 CFR part 1) [T.D. 8268, 1989-2 C.B. 134] under section 936(d)(4) of the Internal Revenue Code of 1986, which section was enacted by section 1231(c) of the Tax Reform Act of 1986 (100 Stat. 2085). The proposed and temporary regulations reserved on the issue of privatization. The final regulations published in the Rules and Regulations portion of this Federal Register also reserve on this issue.

Explanation of Provision

In general, the proposed regulations provide that a financing transaction effecting a privatization will be a qualified investment for purposes of section 936(d)(4) if the investment involves a transfer of ownership from a government entity to the private sector and has a positive developmental impact on the economy of a qualified CBI country. Section 1.936-10(c)(5)(v) of the proposed regulations lists six requirements for a qualified privatization. One of these requirements is that the United States Agency for International Development, or the Overseas Private Investment Corporation if it is sponsoring a transaction, certifies that the acquisition is expected to have a significant positive developmental impact in the qualified Caribbean Basin country where the privatization occurs. The regulations are proposed to be effective 30 days after their publication in the Federal Register as final regulations.

Regulatory Flexibility Act and Executive Order 12291

Although this document is a notice of proposed rulemaking which solicits public comment, it has been determined that the regulations proposed herein are interpretative and that the notice and public procedure requirements of 5 U.S.C. 553 do not apply. Accordingly, these proposed regulations do not constitute regulations subject to the Regulatory Flexibility Act (5 U.S.C. chapter 6).

It has also been determined that this proposed rule is not a major rule as defined in Executive Order 12291 and that a regulatory impact analysis therefore is not required.

Drafting Information

The principal authors of these proposed regulations are Christine Halphen and W. Edward Williams of the Office of the Associate Chief Counsel (International) within the Office of Chief Counsel, Internal Revenue Service. Other personnel from offices of the Internal Revenue Service and the Treasury Department participated in developing these proposed regulations.

———————————

[¶ 49,122] Proposed Regulations (FI-069-89), published in the Federal Register on July 5, 1991.

Life insurance contracts: Reasonable mortality charges.—Proposed Reg. §1.7702-1, relating to the required use of reasonable mortality charges in determining whether a contract qualifies as a life insurance contract, are proposed. Reg. §1.7702 was adopted by T.D. 9287 on September 12, 2006.

AGENCY: Internal Revenue Service, Treasury.

ACTION: Notice of proposed rulemaking.

SUMMARY: This document provides proposed regulations relating to the required use of reasonable mortality charges in determining whether a contract qualifies as a life insurance contract and, by cross-reference, whether the contract is a modified endowment contract for federal tax purposes. Changes were made to this requirement by the Technical and Miscellaneous Revenue Act of 1988. These regulations are necessary to provide guidance to insurance companies attempting to qualify their products as life insurance contracts.

DATES: Written comments must be received by September 4, 1991. Requests to speak (with outlines of oral comments) at a public hearing scheduled for September 25, 1991, at 10 a.m. must be received by September 11, 1991. See notice of hearing published elsewhere in this issue of the Federal Register.

ADDRESSES: Send comments, requests to appear at the public hearing, and outlines of comments to be presented to: Internal Revenue Service, P.O. Box 7604, Ben Franklin Station, Atten: CC:CORP:T:R (FI-69-89), Room 5228, Washington, D.C. 20044.

FOR FURTHER INFORMATION CONTACT: Concerning the regulations, Donald J. Drees, Jr., 202-566-3350 (not a toll-free number). Concerning the hearing, Carol Savage of the Regulations Unit, 202-377-9236 (not a toll-free number).

SUPPLEMENTARY INFORMATION:

Background

This document sets forth proposed income tax regulations under section 7702(c)(3)(B)(i) of the Internal Revenue Code relating to the required use of reasonable mortality charges in determining whether a contract qualifies as a life insurance contract for purposes of the Code. Section 7702(c)(3)(B)(i) was amended by the Technical and Miscellaneous Revenue Act of 1988, 102 Stat. 3342. In Notice 88-128, 1988-2 C.B. 540, the Internal Revenue Service provided interim rules interpreting the reasonable mortality charge requirement.

Explanation of Provisions

Section 7702, which was enacted by the Tax Reform Act of 1984, section 221(a), defines the term "life insurance contract" for purposes of the Code as any contract that is a life insurance contract under applicable law, but only if the contract either (1) meets the cash value accumulation test of section 7702(b), or (2) both meets the guideline premium requirements of section 7702(c) and falls within the cash value corridor of section 7702(d).

Section 7702(c)(3)(B)(i) provides that reasonable mortality charges are those which meet the requirements (if any) prescribed in regulations and which (except as provided in regulations) do not exceed the mortality charges specified in the prevailing commissioners' standard tables (as defined in section 807(d)(5)) as of the time the contract is issued. The mortality charges specified in section 7702(c)(3)(B)(i) are used to determine the "net single premium" (for the cash value accumulation test) and the "guideline single premium" and the "guideline level premium" (for the guideline premium test). *See* sections 7702(b)(2)(B) and 7702(c)(4).

These proposed regulations define "reasonable mortality charges" as those amounts that an insurance company actually expects to impose as consideration for assuming the risk of the insured's death (regardless of the designation used for those charges), taking into account any relevant characteristics of the insured of which the company is aware. Except as provided in the proposed regulations, reasonable mortality charges cannot exceed the lesser of the applicable mortality charges specified in the prevailing commissioners' standard tables in effect at the time the contract is issued or the mortality charges specified in the contract at issuance.

The proposed regulations provide three safe harbors under which mortality charges for contracts with only one insured are deemed to be reasonable mortality charges. The first safe harbor provides that mortality charges that do not exceed the applicable charges set forth in the Commissioners' 1980 Standard Ordinary Mortality Table for male or female insureds ("1980 C.S.O. Basic Mortality Tables") are treated as reasonable mortality charges. (These tables are gender specific but do not contain other selection factors.) There is statistical evidence that mortality charges provided in these tables exceed charges actually proposed by insurance companies. As a result, contracts qualifying as life insurance under the safe harbor can be more investment-oriented than contracts that are tested under an "actually imposed" mortality charge standard. Nevertheless, this safe harbor is created in recognition of state minimum nonforfeiture laws which may require cash values based on these higher mortality charges.

The second safe harbor treats mortality charges that do not exceed the applicable charges in certain variations of the 1980 C.S.O. Mortality Tables as reasonable mortality charges, provided certain requirements are satisfied. Thus, if a state permits minimum nonforfeiture values for all contracts issued under a plan of insurance to be determined using the 1980 C.S.O. Gender-Blended Mortality Tables ("unisex tables"), then the applicable mortality charges in those tables are treated as reasonable mortality charges for female insureds (provided the same tables are used to determine mortality charges for male insureds) even though the charges exceed the charges applicable for female insureds specified in the 1980 C.S.O. Basic Mortality Tables. Similarly, if a state permits minimum nonforfeiture values for all contracts issued under a plan of insurance to be determined using the 1980 C.S.O. Smoker and Nonsmoker Mortality Tables ("smoker/nonsmoker tables"), then the applicable mortality charges in those tables for smoker insureds are treated as reasonable mortality charges (provided nonsmoker tables are used to determine nonsmoker mortality charges) even though the charges exceed the applicable charges specified in the 1980 C.S.O. Basic Mortality Tables. The third safe harbor treats mortality charges as reasonable if they are not in excess of the applicable charges specified in the 1958 C.S.O. Mortality Table provided that the applicable contracts are not "modified endowment contracts" and were issued on or before December 31, 1988, pursuant to a plan of insurance or policy blank that was based on the 1958 C.S.O. Mortality Tables and that was approved by the appropriate state regulatory authority on or before October 21, 1988.

The proposed regulations also provide special rules for contracts involving substandard risks and for nonparticipating contracts. Although reasonable mortality charges generally may not exceed the applicable charges specified in the prevailing commissioners' standard tables, the special rules permit mortality charges for contracts involving substandard risks and for nonparticipating contracts to exceed the charges set forth in the prevailing tables if the insurance company actually expects to impose those higher charges. For this purpose, the term "substandard risk" is defined to mean a risk of death that exceeds the standards set for normal or regular risks. In determining whether any particular insured presents a substandard risk, a company must take into account relevant facts and circumstances such as the insured person's medical history and any law that prohibits or limits the company's inquiry into some or all aspects of the insured's medical history (thereby increasing the potential unknown insurance risk with respect to insureds). The term "nonparticipating contract" is defined as a contract that contains no right to participate in the issuer's divisible surplus, if any, and that contains no "charge reduction mechanism."

The proposed regulations define the term "prevailing commissioners' standard tables" to mean the tables containing the higher of the charges in the tables described in section 807(d)(5)(A) or the charges in any other tables that section 807(d)(5) allows to be used with respect to contracts for purposes of section 807(d)(2)(C) (relating to the computation of life insurance reserves). (For this purpose, the limitation of section 807(d)(5)(E) does not apply.) Thus, for example, if the prevailing commissioners' standard tables as of the beginning of any calendar year (hereinafter referred to as the year of change) is different from the prevailing commissioners' standard tables as of the beginning of the preceding calendar year, then except as provided in the temporary regulations, the reasonable mortality charges for contracts issued after the change and before the close of the 3-year period beginning on the first day of the year of change cannot exceed the higher of the applicable mortality charges specified in the old tables or those specified in the new tables.

The proposed regulations apply to life insurance contracts entered into on or after October 21, 1988.

Special Analyses

It has been determined that these proposed rules are not major rules as defined in Executive Order 12291. Therefore, a Regulatory Impact Analysis is not required. It has also been determined that section 553(b) of the Administrative Procedure Act (5 U.S.C. chapter 5) and the Regulatory Flexibility Act (5 U.S.C. chapter 6) do not apply to these regulations, and, therefore, an initial Regulatory Flexibility Analysis is not required. Pursuant to section 7805(f) of the Internal Revenue Code, the proposed regulations will be submitted to the Chief Counsel for Advocacy of the Small Business Administration for comment on their impact on small business.

Comments and Request for a Public Hearing

Before the adoption of these proposed regulations, consideration will be given to any written comments that are submitted (preferably a signed original and eight copies) to the Internal Revenue Service. Comments are specifically requested on the appropriateness of using mortality charges that are less than those in the 1980 C.S.O. tables either to define reasonable mortality charges or to establish a safe harbor. Comments are also specifically requested on (1) whether or not the 1980 C.S.O. tables, which are a safe harbor under these proposed regulations, generally contain mortality charges high enough to cover the charges actually imposed with respect to the most common substandard risk cases, and (2) any appropriate safe harbors or methodologies for computing mortality charges for contracts involving more than one insured.

All comments will be available for public inspection and copying in their entirety. A public hearing has been scheduled for September 25, 1991. See notice of hearing published elsewhere in this issue of the Federal Register.

Drafting Information

The principal author of these proposed regulations is Donald J. Drees, Jr., Office of the Assistant Chief Counsel (Financial Institutions and Products), Office of Chief Counsel, Internal Revenue Service. However, personnel from other offices of the Service and the Treasury Department participated in developing the regulations, in matters of both substance and style.

[¶ 49,123]   Proposed Regulations and Proposed Amendments of Regulations (FI-16-89), published in the Federal Register on July 10, 1991.

Notional principal contracts: Timing of income and deductions.—Reg. §1.446-3 relating to notional principal contracts, is proposed. T.D. 8491 adopted Reg §§1.446-3 (except (e)(4)(iv)) and 1.1092(d)-1 and amendments of Reg. §§1.61-14, 1.162-1, 1.451-1, 1.461-4 and 1.988-2 on October 8, 1993. On October 14, 1993, proposed Reg. §1.446-4 was withdrawn. On December 16, 1994, proposed Reg. §1.1275-4 was superseded.

AGENCY: Internal Revenue Service, Treasury.

ACTION: Notice of proposed rulemaking.

SUMMARY: These proposed regulations relate to the timing of income and deductions with respect to notional principal contracts. The regulations will provide taxpayers and Internal Revenue Service personnel with guidance necessary to account for notional principal contracts. The proposed regulations also permit dealers and traders in derivative financial instruments to elect, subject to certain conditions, to mark those instruments to market. Finally, the proposed regulations define actively traded personal property under section 1092(d).

DATES: Written comments, requests to appear, and outlines of oral comments to be presented at the public hearing scheduled for October 7, 1991 must be received by September 23, 1991. See notice of hearing published elsewhere in this issue of the Federal Register.

ADDRESSES: Send comments, requests to appear, and outlines of oral comments to: Internal Revenue Service, P.O. Box 7604, Ben Franklin Station, Attn: CC:CORP:T:R (FI-16-89), Room 5228, Washington, D.C. 20044.

FOR FURTHER INFORMATION CONTACT: Karl T. Walli, (202) 566-3516 (not a toll-free number).

SUPPLEMENTARY INFORMATION:

Background

This document contains proposed amendments to the Income Tax Regulations (26 CFR part 1) under sections 446(b) (relating to general rules for methods of accounting) and 1092(d) (relating to definitions and special rules with respect to straddles) of the Internal Revenue Code of 1986. These regulations are cross-referenced in new proposed regulations § § 1.61-14, 1.162-1, 1.451-1, 1.461-4, 1.988-2T, and 1.1275-4, which are also added to part 1 of title 26 of the CFR.

Except as noted below, these regulations are proposed to be effective for notional principal contracts entered into after the date a Treasury Decision based on these proposed regulations is published in the Federal Register. For contracts entered into prior to the effective date of the proposed regulations, the Commissioner generally will treat a method of accounting as clearly reflecting income if it takes payments into account over the life of the contract under a reasonable amortization method, whether or not the method satisfies the rules in the proposed regulations. See Notice 89-21, 1989-1 C.B. 651, 652. Proposed regulation section 1.446-4 is proposed to be effective for taxable years ending on or after the date a Treasury Decision based on these proposed regulations is published in the Federal Register. Proposed regulation section 1.1092(d)-1 is proposed to be effective for notional principal contracts entered into on or after July 8, 1991.

Explanation of Provisions

A. Overview

The term "notional principal contract" generally describes an agreement between two parties to exchange payments calculated by reference to a notional principal amount. The term typically encompasses interest rate swap agreements, commodity swap agreements, interest rate cap and floor agreements, currency swap agreements, and other similar contracts. Financial institutions and corporations use these products to minimize exposure to adverse changes in interest rates, commodity prices, and currency exchange rates.

In a typical interest rate swap agreement, one party agrees to make periodic payments based on a fixed rate while the counterparty agrees to make periodic payments based on a floating rate. Payments are calculated on the basis of a hypothetical or "notional" principal amount, and payment amounts are typically netted when payments are due on common dates. A commodity swap is like an interest rate swap except that a commodity price index is used instead of an interest rate index, and the notional principal amount is measured in units of a commodity, rather than in dollars. A typical interest rate cap agreement involves an initial cash payment by one party (the purchaser) to a counterparty (the seller, usually a financial institution) in exchange for an agreement by the seller to make cash payments to the purchaser at specified future times if interest rates (as determined by a specified interest rate index) exceed a specified level. Under an interest rate floor agreement, the seller of the floor agrees to pay the purchaser if interest rates fall below a specified level.

Because the notional principal amount is not exchanged by the parties, the payments due under a typical interest rate swap, cap, or floor are not compensation for the use or forbearance of money and therefore are not "interest." On the other hand, a lump-sum payment under one of these contracts may be economically identical to a loan. In this case, the party making the lump-sum payment receives a return, part of which is properly characterized as interest under section 61(a)(4) because it represents compensation for the use or forbearance of money.

A notional principal contract may be entered into directly with another principal end-user. More commonly, however, the counterparty to the contract is a commercial or investment bank that acts as a "dealer" in such contracts. The dealer typically creates a portfolio of notional principal contracts and seeks to maintain a balanced market position. Notional principal contract dealers provide liquidity for the market by standing ready to enter into these contracts with any qualified party at any time.

As described in part B below, these proposed regulations prescribe rules for the timing of income and deductions with respect to notional principal contracts. Except in limited circumstances where amounts are recharacterized as interest, these regulations do not address the character of income, loss, or deductions with respect to notional principal contracts.

The Service is aware of the fact that many notional principal contracts are used to hedge assets or liabilities, and it is considering whether to permit taxpayers to account for a notional principal contract and the asset or liability that the notional principal contract hedges on an integrated basis. Comments on this subject are welcome. At this time, however, the proposed regulations do not permit taxpayers to determine the timing of income or deductions with respect to a notional principal contract by integrating that contract with any other asset or liability.

B. Specific Provisions

Section 1.446-3(b) states that the purpose of these proposed regulations is to clearly reflect the income and deductions from notional principal contracts. The Internal Revenue Service believes that the income from a notional principal contract can only be reflected clearly by applying accounting methods that reflect the economic substance of that contract. The proposed regulations prescribe accounting methods that are intended to reflect the economic substance of notional principal contracts without creating unnecessary complexity.

Section 1.446-3(c) defines a notional principal contract as a financial instrument that provides for payments by one party to another at specified intervals calculated by reference to a specified index upon a notional principal amount in exchange for specified consideration or a promise to pay similar amounts. The term "specified index" includes fixed interest rates and prices, interest rate indices, stock indices, and commodity indices, as well as amounts derived from arithmetic operations on these indices, such as fixed multiples and averages. Thus, notional principal contracts governed by this section include interest rate swaps, basis swaps, interest rate caps and floors, commodity swaps, equity swaps, equity index swaps, and similar agreements. The Internal Revenue Service is currently considering whether equity and equity index swaps should be treated in the same manner as interest rate and commodity swaps for sourcing and withholding tax purposes.

Section 1.446-3(d) describes several of the common notional principal contracts that are governed by the regulations, including interest rate swaps, interest rate caps, interest rate floors, and commodity swaps. Options and forwards that entitle or obligate a party to enter into, extend, cancel, or change the terms of a notional principal contract are not notional principal contracts, although a payment made or received in connection with such an agreement is treated as a nonperiodic payment with respect to a notional principal contract if and when the notional principal contract is entered into.

Section 1.446-3(e)(1) provides that net income or deduction from a notional principal contract for a taxable year is included in or deducted from gross income for that taxable year. The net income or deduction from a notional principal contract for a taxable year equals the sum of all of the periodic payments that are recognized from that contract for the taxable year and all of the nonperiodic payments that are recognized from that contract for the taxable year.

A periodic payment is defined in section 1.446-3(e)(2) as a payment that generally is payable at fixed periodic intervals of one year or less during the entire term of a notional principal contract. Periodic payments are included in income or deducted in the taxable year to which they relate.

Section 1.446-3(e)(3) defines a nonperiodic payment as any payment made or received pursuant to a notional principal contract that is not a periodic payment or a termination payment. Nonperiodic payments must be included in income or deducted over the life of the notional principal contract in a manner that reflects the economic substance of the payment. Thus, a nonperiodic payment for a swap must be amortized in a manner consistent with the values of a series of cash-settled forward contracts that reflect the specified index and the notional principal amount. In the case of an interest rate swap, the taxpayer may elect to amortize nonperiodic payments over the term of the swap assuming a constant yield to maturity. The premium paid for a cap or floor must be amortized in a manner consistent with the values of a series of cash-settled options that reflect the specified index and the notional principal amount.

Because the Service is concerned that some taxpayers may not have access to information or expertise about option pricing, the Service intends to issue a revenue procedure to provide taxpayers with an alternative method of amortizing payments for interest rate caps and floors. The revenue procedure will be issued at the time of publication of the Treasury Decision that promulgates final regulations based upon these proposed regulations. The proposed text of this revenue procedure is set out below. Comments are requested concerning the factors contained in Tables 1 and 2 of this proposed revenue procedure, and concerning the feasibility of, and need for, similar revenue procedures covering other notional principal contracts, such as commodity caps and floors.

Rev. Proc. **-**

SECTION 1. PURPOSE

This revenue procedure sets out optional amortization tables to compute the amount of a nonperiodic payment that is to be included in income or deducted over the life of an interest rate cap or floor agreement under section 1.446-3(e)(3)(ii)(D)(2) of the Income Tax Regulations.

SEC. 2. BACKGROUND AND OBJECTIVE

Section 1.446-3(e)(3)(ii)(A) of the regulations provides that premium payments made to purchase caps and floors are to be amortized in a manner that reflects the economic substance of the instruments. Section 1.446-3(e)(3)(ii)(D)(2) provides that the Commissioner may prescribe by revenue procedure an alternative method for allocating the premium paid or received for an interest rate cap or floor to each year of the agreement. Pursuant to that section, this revenue procedure sets out tables that taxpayers may use to amortize interest rate cap and floor premiums if they so elect. The tables set out in section 4 are derived from standard option pricing formulas, incorporating volatility assumptions that are intended to be consistent with representative pricing for interest rate caps and floors.

SEC. 3. SCOPE

.01 *In general.* The election provided in this revenue procedure applies only to interest rate caps and floors that are based on a specified index that—

(1) meets the conditions in section 1.446-3(c)(2)(ii) or (iii) of the regulations,

(2) is an average of specified indices described in paragraph (1) above, or

(3) is a specified index described in paragraph (1) or (2) above plus or minus a fixed number of basis points.

Taxpayers may not make the election for any interest rate cap or floor with a cap or floor rate that, at the inception of the contract, falls outside of the range of rates specified in the cap table or the floor table, respectively.

.02 *Dealers and traders.* This election is not available for any taxpayer that is a dealer or trader in any derivative financial instruments within the meaning of section 1.446-4(b) of the regulations.

SEC. 4. PROCEDURE

.01 *Annual election.* For each taxable year in which the taxpayer enters into an interest rate cap or floor agreement, the taxpayer may elect to use the method provided in this revenue procedure for all interest rate cap and floor agreements entered into in that year. As to those agreements, the election is irrevocable.

.02 *Method of election.* The election is made by attaching to the timely filed (including extensions) federal income tax return a statement that the taxpayer is making an election under this revenue procedure for the taxable year that the cap or floor agreement is entered into.

SEC. 5. USE OF THE TABLES

The amortization tables set forth in section 6 below may be used to derive a schedule of annual amortization rates to be applied to the unadjusted amount of the premium paid or received for an interest rate cap or floor agreement. Table 1 lists a series of factors corresponding to the years covered by the interest rate cap agreement and the number of basis points by which the cap rate differs from the specified interest rate index. Table 2 lists a series of factors corresponding to the years covered by the interest rate floor agreement and the number of basis points by which the specified interest rate index differs from the floor rate. The annual amortization amount for a year covered by an interest rate cap or floor agreement is calculated as follows:

First, obtain the sum of the factors for all years covered by the agreement.

Second, divide that year's factor by the sum of the factors for all years covered by the agreement.

Third, multiply that result by the premium to be amortized.

Taxpayers may use any reasonable method of interpolation to determine the appropriate factors for a particular cap or floor if a period covered by the agreement is less than 12 months long or the number of basis points by which the current rate differs from the cap or floor rate is between two amounts that are shown on the table.

SEC. 6. CAP AND FLOOR TABLES

TABLE 1
Factors to Be Used in Amortizing Interest Rate Cap Agreements

Excess of cap rate over current rate in basis points	Term of interest rate cap agreement in years				
	1	2	3	4	5
500	0.0	2.7	15.8	31.3	50.1
450	0.0	4.4	19.8	41.3	60.0
400	0.0	8.1	26.8	49.2	70.7
350	0.3	11.5	37.2	64.3	83.7
300	0.9	19.4	52.4	80.3	104.5
250	2.6	28.3	67.9	100.7	124.7
200	5.4	45.1	88.9	122.9	151.4
150	11.8	68.3	121.2	157.2	183.8

Excess of cap rate over current rate in basis points	Term of interest rate cap agreement in years				
	1	2	3	4	5
100	25.3	101.3	159.2	195.2	224.1
50	53.1	158.5	207.3	242.6	256.7
0	100.0	216.8	264.0	295.2	311.4
(25)	139.5	261.8	301.5	322.7	341.7
	6	7	8	9	10
500	64.8	79.4	91.2	100.9	109.8
450	77.0	91.1	104.5	115.6	121.8
400	90.1	103.5	115.8	128.3	135.5
350	105.8	120.9	134.7	144.1	152.2
300	124.5	139.9	152.0	161.0	168.4
250	146.9	162.1	173.6	181.7	189.5
200	173.6	187.9	196.8	206.5	210.2
150	203.2	217.8	223.3	229.9	234.6
100	239.4	249.8	251.4	256.1	256.4
50	271.5	283.2	287.4	288.2	288.8
0	320.4	326.6	327.3	327.7	323.9
(25)	349.6	351.6	353.1	347.2	341.7

TABLE 2
Factors to Be Used in Amortizing Interest Rate Floor Agreements

Excess of current rate over floor rate in basis points	Term of interest rate floor agreement in years				
	1	2	3	4	5
350	0.0	0.1	1.9	6.3	11.4
300	0.0	1.0	7.0	16.0	26.2
250	0.1	5.5	19.1	33.2	48.2
200	0.9	16.4	41.9	61.6	79.3
150	4.9	39.4	73.7	102.2	126.1
100	18.1	79.1	125.8	155.1	180.6
50	46.6	140.9	190.6	219.7	235.0
0	100.0	216.8	264.0	295.2	311.4
(25)	143.1	267.2	308.5	339.1	352.8
	6	7	8	9	10
350	17.9	23.3	28.3	33.2	37.4
300	34.9	42.4	49.7	55.9	59.6
250	60.0	69.6	76.6	83.8	89.2
200	95.0	105.9	114.5	120.7	126.7
150	140.6	151.7	160.8	163.6	167.4
100	194.4	205.5	211.6	209.6	210.5
50	250.6	260.0	264.1	266.4	264.6
0	320.4	326.6	327.3	327.7	323.9
(25)	361.1	364.9	363.4	360.3	353.2

SEC. 7. EXAMPLE

At a time when the three-month London Interbank Offered Rate ("LIBOR") is 8%, a taxpayer purchases a three year interest rate cap agreement under which a bank is obligated to make quarterly payments to the taxpayer equal to a $25 million notional principal amount times one-quarter of the excess, if any, of three-month LIBOR over 9%. The taxpayer pays the bank a premium of $600,000 at the inception of the contract, and elects to amortize the cap premium using the method provided in this revenue procedure.

An interest rate cap agreement using LIBOR as an interest rate index qualifies under section 3.01 of this revenue procedure, and the taxpayer makes the election as required in section 4.01 of this revenue procedure for all interest rate caps and floors entered into during that taxable year.

Table 1 applies to interest rate cap agreements. Table 1 lists the following factors for a three year interest rate cap that is 100 basis points over the current LIBOR rate: 25.3, 101.3, and 159.2, for years 1, 2, and 3, respectively. The sum of these three factors is 285.8. Thus, the amortization ratio for the first 12-month period covered by the agreement is 8.85% (the ratio of the first year factor, 25.3, to the total of all factors, 285.8). The amortization ratio for the second 12-month period is 35.44% (101.3/285.8), and the amortization ratio for the third 12-month period is 55.71% (159.2/285.8). Applying these amortization ratios to the $600,000 cap premium, the taxpayer's deductions with respect to this nonperiodic payment are $53,100 for the first period (8.85% × $600,000), $212,640 for the second period (35.44% × $600,000), and $334,260 for the third period (55.71% × $600,000).

SEC. 8. EFFECTIVE DATE

The election provided by this revenue procedure may be made for interest rate cap and floor agreements entered into in tax years ending on or after [Insert date a Treasury Decision based on these proposed regulations is published in the Federal Register].

Section 1.446-3(e)(4) of the proposed regulations provides special rules for compound and disguised notional principal contracts, notional principal contracts that are hedged with other financial instruments, swaps with significant nonperiodic payments, and caps and floors that are significantly in-the-money. Because swaps with significant nonperiodic payments and caps and floors that are significantly in-the-money include a significant loan component, income is not clearly reflected unless the parties to these contracts account for the interest income and expense. The Service is aware of the withholding tax consequences that may arise from interest recharacterization. These rules are not intended to disrupt typical market transactions, and the Service solicits comments on the standards for recharacterization set out in the proposed regulations (including the examples).

Section 1.446-3(e)(5) treats payments made with respect to options and forward contracts that entitle or obligate a person to enter into a notional principal contract as nonperiodic payments if and when the notional principal contract is entered into.

Section 1.446-3(e)(6) requires all parties to a notional principal contract to recognize gain or loss from the termination of a notional principal contract in the year of termination. A termination includes both an extinguishment and an assignment of a notional principal contract.

Section 1.446-3(f) sets forth an anti-abuse rule that is intended to prevent a taxpayer from applying the accounting methods that are prescribed by the proposed regulations to a notional principal contract that is not a customary commercial transaction if applying those methods to that contract would produce a material distortion of income and the taxpayer would not have entered into the transaction but for that material distortion of income. In such a case, the Commissioner has the discretion to apply accounting methods that reflect the economic substance of the transaction. This anti-abuse rule is included so that the overall purpose of the proposed regulations, which is to clearly reflect the income from a transaction by prescribing accounting methods that reflect the economic substance of the transaction, can be fulfilled with respect to all notional principal contracts.

Subject to certain conditions, section 1.446-4 permits dealers and traders in derivative financial instruments to elect a mark-to-market method of accounting in computing their taxable income. The mark-to-market election is invalid if the dealer or trader or any related party uses a lower-of-cost-or-market method (LCM) to account for securities or commodities held in a capacity as a dealer or trader (or as hedges of such securities or commodities). A "derivative financial instrument" includes notional principal contracts as well as futures, forwards, options, and short positions in commodities and securities.

The mark-to-market election is proposed to be available for taxable years ending on or after the date a Treasury Decision based on these proposed regulations is published in the Federal Register. The Service anticipates issuing a revenue procedure that will waive the 180-day rule contained in section 1.446-1(e)(3)(i) of the regulations so that dealers and traders can change their method of accounting for derivative financial instruments by making the mark-to-market election for their first taxable year ending on or after publication of the Treasury Decision. The Service anticipates issuing a second revenue procedure for electing taxpayers that are required to change their method of accounting for securities and commodities from the LCM method. The revenue procedures will describe how to obtain the Commissioner's consent for these changes and will set forth the terms and conditions that will be imposed for consent to be granted.

The Service anticipates that the revenue procedure governing the mark-to-market election under section 1.446-4 for derivative financial instruments will impose terms and conditions (including the section 481(a) adjustment period) similar to those applicable to Category B methods of accounting. See Rev. Proc. 84-74, 1984-2 C.B. 736. The Service further anticipates that the revenue procedure governing the change from the LCM method for securities and commodities will employ a cut-off transition. Under this cut-off transition, the taxpayer's old method of accounting will continue to apply to inventory acquired prior to the year of change. The Service invites comments on appropriate terms and conditions for these revenue procedures.

Section 1.1092(d)-1(a) of the proposed regulations clarifies the definition of "actively traded" personal property. Generally, actively traded personal property includes any personal property for which brokers or dealers provide regular pricing information in an established financial market. Section 1.1092(d)-1(b) enumerates several categories of established financial markets.

The proposed regulations under section 1092 also address the application of that section to notional principal contracts. There has been some question whether a financial product such as an interest rate swap, which may be either an asset or a liability depending upon the movement of interest rates, constitutes an interest in personal property that is subject to section 1092 and section 1234A. Under section 1.1092(d)-1(c)(1), notional principal contracts are generally actively traded personal property. Thus, under the proposed regulations, a loss realized with respect to a notional principal contract would not be recognized under section 1092(a) to the extent the taxpayer has an unrecognized gain in one or more offsetting positions. Further, the gain or loss realized through the termination (through extinguishment or assignment) of a taxpayer's rights and obligations under a notional principal contract would generally be treated as gain or loss from the sale of a capital asset under section 1234A.

Special Analyses

It has been determined that these proposed rules are not major rules as defined in Executive Order 12291. Therefore, a Regulatory Impact Analysis is not required. Although this document is a notice of proposed rulemaking that solicits public comments, the notice and public comment procedure requirements of 5 U.S.C. section 553(b) do not apply because the regulations proposed herein are interpretative. Therefore, an initial Regulatory Flexibility Analysis is not required by the Regulatory Flexibility Act (5 U.S.C. chapter 6). Pursuant to section 7805(f)(1) of the Internal Revenue Code, these regulations will be submitted to the Chief Counsel for Advocacy of the Small Business Administration for comment on their impact on small business.

Comments and Public Hearing

Before adopting these proposed regulations, consideration will be given to any written comments that are submitted (preferably a signed original and eight copies) to the Internal Revenue Service. All comments will be available for public inspection and copying in their entirety. A public hearing is scheduled for October 7, 1991. See Notice of Public Hearing published elsewhere in this issue of the Federal Register.

Drafting Information

The principal author of these proposed regulations is Karl T. Walli, Office of the Assistant Chief Counsel (Financial Institutions and Products), Office of Chief Counsel, Internal Revenue Service. However, other personnel from the Service and the Treasury Department participated in their development.

[¶ 49,124] **Proposed Regulations and Proposed Amendments of Regulations (FI-38-91)**, published in the Federal Register on September 30, 1991.

REMICs: Reporting information: Extension of time.—Reg. §§1.67-3T, 1.860F-4 and 1.6049-7, relating to real estate mortgage investment conduits, are proposed.

AGENCY: Internal Revenue Service, Treasury

ACTION: Notice of proposed rulemaking.

SUMMARY: This document contains proposed income tax regulations relating to real estate mortgage investment conduits (REMICs). The relevant provisions in the Internal Revenue Code were added or amended by the Tax Reform Act of 1986 and by the Technical and Miscellaneous Revenue Act of 1988. These regulations extend the time for REMICs and certain other issuers to provide financial information to brokers, middlemen, and certain holders of REMIC interests or other debt instruments.

DATES: Written comments must be received by (*Insert date that is 45 days after date of publication in the Federal Register*). A public hearing has been scheduled for December 5, 1991. Requests to speak at the hearing, along with outlines of oral comments, must be received by (*Insert date that is 45 days after date of publication in the Federal Register*). See the notice of hearing published elsewhere in this issue of the Federal Register.

ADDRESSES: Send comments and requests to speak at the public hearing, along with outlines of oral comments, to: Internal Revenue Service, P.O. Box 7604, Ben Franklin Station, Attention: CC:CORP:T:R (FI-38-91), Room 5228, Washington, D.C. 20044.

FOR FURTHER INFORMATION CONTACT: Felicia Daniels, with respect to the public hearing, telephone 202-566-3935, and James W.C. Canup, with respect to the proposed regulations, telephone 202-566-6624. These are not toll-free numbers.

SUPPLEMENTARY INFORMATION:

Background

Section 671 of the Tax Reform Act of 1986 (the 1986 Act) added to the Internal Revenue Code (Code) new sections 860A through 860G to provide rules relating to real estate mortgage investment conduits. Section 674 of the 1986 Act amended section 6049 to impose certain information reporting requirements with respect to REMIC interests and certain other debt instruments. Section 1006(t) of the Technical and Miscellaneous Revenue Act of 1988 (TAMRA) amended certain provisions in sections 860A through 860G and section 6049.

In the Rules and Regulations portion of this Federal Register, the Internal Revenue Service is issuing final and temporary regulations under sections 67, 860D, 860F, and 6049 of the Code. Those regulations generally govern the filing of REMIC tax returns and require notice of income and other information to be provided to investors in REMICs and other collateralized debt obligations. This document proposes amendments to those final and temporary regulations.

Explanation of Provisions

Sections 1.67-3T(f), 1.860F-4(e)(2), and 1.6049-7(e)(3) and (f)(7) generally require certain financial information concerning REMIC interests and collateralized debt obligations to be furnished on or before the 30th day after the close of a calendar quarter or calendar year (the 45th day in the case of a non-calendar year taxpayer requesting information from a broker or middleman). The information must be furnished to persons specified in § 1.6049-7(e)(4), which includes certain brokers and middlemen. These brokers and middlemen are required by § 1.6049-7(b)(2) to file information returns with the Internal Revenue Service by February 28 of the following year (absent any extensions of time) and by § 1.6049-7(f) to furnish the holder with a written statement by March 15 of the following year.

Commentators have indicated that in many instances the 30-day time period allotted for REMICs and issuers of collateralized debt obligations to obtain, process, and report the financial information on the underlying mortgages or obligations is not sufficient.

In response to this concern, the proposed regulations would amend the existing regulations to require the financial information to be reported on or before the 41st day after the close of a calendar quarter or calendar year (the 55th day in the case of a non-calendar year taxpayer requesting information from a broker or middleman). The dates by which brokers and middlemen must report to the Service and holders, however, would not be extended. The proposed regulations would not change the information to be reported.

These regulations are proposed to be effective for calendar quarters and calendar years ending after (*Insert date that is 60 days after the date a Treasury Decision based on these proposed regulations is published in the Federal Register*).

Special Analyses

It has been determined that these proposed regulations will not be major regulations as defined in Executive Order 12291. Therefore, a Regulatory Impact Analysis is not required. It has also been determined that section 553(b) of the Administrative Procedure Act (5 U.S.C. chapter 5) and the Regulatory Flexibility Act (5 U.S.C. chapter 6) do not apply to these regulations, and, therefore, an initial Regulatory Flexibility Analysis is not required. Pursuant to section 7805(f) of the Internal Revenue Code, the proposed regulations are being sent to the Chief Counsel for Advocacy of the Small Business Administration for comment on their impact on small business.

Comments and Requests to Appear at the Public Hearing

Before adopting these proposed regulations, consideration will be given to any written comments that are submitted (preferably a signed original and eight copies) to the Internal Revenue Service. All comments will be available for public inspection and copying in their entirety. A public hearing has been scheduled for December 5, 1991. See the notice of hearing published elsewhere in this issue of the Federal Register.

Drafting Information

The principal author of these proposed regulations is James W.C. Canup, Office of the Assistant Chief Counsel (Financial Institutions and Products), Internal Revenue Service. However, personnel from other offices of the IRS and Treasury Department participated in their development.

[¶ 49,125]   **Proposed Amendments of Regulations (REG-208202-91) [originally issued as INTL-0015-91]**, published in the Federal Register on March 17, 1992.

Gain or loss: Nonfunctional currency transactions.—Amendments of Reg. §§ 1.988-1, 1.988-2 and 1.988-5, relating to the taxation of gain or loss from certain foreign currency transactions, are proposed. Amendments of Reg. § 1.988-2(b)(15), (d)(5), (e)(3)(iv) and (e)(7) were adopted 1/12/2000 by T.D. 8860. Amendments of Reg. § 1.6045-1 were adopted 10/6/97 by T.D. 8734. Proposed amendments of Reg. § 1.988-1(a)(3), (4) and (5) were withdrawn 8/29/2003.

AGENCY: Internal Revenue Service, Treasury.

ACTION: Notice of proposed rulemaking.

SUMMARY: This document contains proposed Income Tax Regulations relating to the taxation of gain or loss from certain foreign currency transactions and applies to taxpayers engaging in such transactions. This action is necessary because of changes to the applicable tax law made by the Tax Reform Act of 1986.

DATES: Comments and requests for a public hearing must be received by May 18, 1992.

ADDRESSES: Send comments and requests for a public hearing to: Internal Revenue Service, P.O. Box 7604, Ben Franklin Station, Attention: CC:CORP:T:R (INTL-O015-91), Room 5228, Washington, D.C. 20044.

FOR FURTHER INFORMATION CONTACT: Jeffrey L. Dorfman of the Office of Associate Chief Counsel (International), within the Office of Chief Counsel, Internal Revenue Service, 1111 Constitution Avenue, N. W., Washington, DC 20224 (Attention: CC:CORP:T:R (INTL-O015-91) (202-377-9059 (Dorfman), not toll-free calls).

SUPPLEMENTARY INFORMATION:

Paperwork Reduction Act

The collection of information contained in this notice of proposed rulemaking has been submitted to the Office of Management and Budget for review in accordance with the Paperwork Reduction Act of 1980 (44 U.S.C. 3504(h)). Comments on the collection of information should be sent to the Office of Management and Budget, Attn: Desk Officer for the Department of the Treasury, Office of Information and Regulatory Affairs, Washington, D.C. 20503, with copies to the Internal Revenue Service, Attention: IRS Reports Clearance Officer T:FP, Washington, DC 20224.

The collection of information in these regulations is in §1.988-5(d) and (f). This information is required by the Internal Revenue Service to verify various elections made by the taxpayer. The likely respondents are businesses or other for-profit institutions.

These estimates are an approximation of the average time expected to be necessary for a collection of information. They are based on information as is available to the Internal Revenue Service. Individual respondents/recordkeepers may require greater or less time, depending on their particular circumstances.

Estimated total annual reporting and/or recordkeeping burden: 1,000 hours.

The estimated annual burden per respondent/recordkeeper varies from 30 minutes to 60 minutes, depending on individual circumstances, with an estimated average of 40 minutes.

Estimated number of respondents and/or recordkeepers: 1,500.

Background

This document contains proposed amendments to the Income Tax Regulations (26 CFR part 1) under section 988 of the Internal Revenue Code.

Explanation of Provisions

Section 1.988-1.

Section 1.988-1(a)(3) coordinates section 988 with §1.1275-4(g) of the proposed regulations. Section 1.988-1(a)(3) provides that §1.1275-4(g) applies prior to section 988 to separate a contingent payment debt instrument into contingent and noncontingent components. To the extent applicable, section 988 applies to the distinct components.

Section 1.988-1(a)(4) provides rules for the treatment of dual currency debt instruments. Section 1.988-1(a)(4) provides that a dual currency debt instrument is separated into two hypothetical instruments—a zero coupon bond denominated in the currency of the stated redemption price at maturity (discounted as provided in §1.1273-2(d)(2)(iv) of the proposed regulations), and an installment obligation, as defined in §1.1273-1(b)(2) of the proposed regulations, denominated in the currency of the qualified periodic interest payments of the dual currency debt instrument. To the extent applicable, section 988 applies to the distinct instruments.

Section 1.988-1(a)(5) provides rules for multi-currency debt instruments similar to the rules applicable to dual currency debt instruments.

Section 1.988-2.

Pursuant to section 989(c)(5), §1.988-2(b)(14) provides special rules regarding nonfunctional currency related person debt. If a debt instrument denominated in a nonfunctional currency is entered into between related persons as defined in sections 267(b) and 707(b), and the taxpayer disposes of or terminates such instrument prior to maturity in a transaction in which exchange gain or loss would be recognized, the District Director or the Assistant Commissioner (International) may defer such gain or loss if he determines that the debt has in effect been replaced with debt denominated in a different currency (replacement debt) entered into with a related person (regardless of whether the replacement currency is the taxpayer's functional currency). Such deferral, however, shall not exceed the earlier of the date the replacement debt is terminated in a transaction in which gain or loss is recognized or the maturity date of the replacement debt (so long as such debt is not replaced with related person debt denominated in a different currency). The rule set forth in §1.988-2(b)(14) does not apply to debt for debt exchanges in the same nonfunctional currency. The Service solicits comments regarding issues raised by debt for debt exchanges in the same nonfunctional currency.

Section 1.988-2(b)(15) provides rules addressing debt instruments denominated in hyperinflationary currencies. Generally, exchange gain or loss is recognized at the close of each taxable year and is treated as a offset to interest income or expense.

Section 1.988-2(d)(4) and (e)(7) provides rules addressing forward contracts, futures contracts, option contracts and currency swaps where payments to be made or received are denominated in hyperinflationary currencies (hereafter referred to as hyperinflationary contracts). Section 1.988-2(d)(4) and (e)(7) generally provides that a taxpayer's position in a hyperinflationary contract is to be marked to market on the last day of the taxable year and any exchange gain or loss realized on such date.

Section 1.988-2(e)(3)(iv) coordinates section 988 with the rules of §1.446-3(e)(4)(iii) of the proposed regulations regarding currency swaps with significant nonperiodic payments.

Section 1.988-5.

Section 1.988-5(d) provides integration rules for hedged qualified payments patterned after the rules in §1.988-5(b) of the final regulations regarding hedged executory contracts. A qualified payment is—(1) a declared but unpaid dividend denominated in a nonfunctional currency with respect to the recipient of such dividend, or (2) an unaccrued rent or royalty payment denominated in a nonfunctional currency of the taxpayer the amount of which is fixed on the date the hedge is entered into. The term hedge is defined in §1.988-5(d)(2)(iii). If a qualified payment and a hedge satisfy the rules of §1.988-5(d)(2)(i), the qualified payment and hedge are integrated. The effect of integrating a qualified payment and hedge is to treat amounts paid or received under the hedge as paid or received under the qualified payment or any subsequent account payable or receivable, or that portion thereof to which the hedge relates.

Mark to market method of accounting.

Pursuant to §1.988-5(f), certain taxpayers may elect to realize for the taxable year exchange gain or loss on section 988 transactions that results from changes in exchange rates between the date a financial accounting period begins and the date a financial accounting period closes (but no less frequently than quarterly), provided such treatment is consistent with the taxpayer's method of accounting for financial reporting purposes (and that method conforms to U.S. generally accepted accounting principles). If a taxpayer makes the mark to market election under §1.988-5(f), it must use the mark to market method to account for all section 988 transactions, other than those subject to the special hedging rules of §1.988-5. Designation of a transaction as a hedging transaction for financial accounting (which generally precludes such transaction from being marked to market under the financial accounting rules) is irrelevant.

The time and manner of making a mark to market election is prescribed in §1.988-5(f)(4). Such election cannot be revoked without the consent of the Commissioner and related person conformity rules apply.

If there is a Treasury Decision based on these proposed regulations, the Service anticipates issuing a revenue procedure setting forth the terms and conditions under which a change of method of accounting will be granted. The Service solicits comments regarding the terms and conditions of the revenue procedure, including the character of the adjustments for purposes of sections 904 and 954, and the appropriate period during which the section 481(a) adjustment should be taken into account.

§ 1.6045-1(d)(6)(iii)

Proposed § 1.6045-1(d)(6)(iii) is in response to a comment which suggested conforming the section 6045 broker reporting rules and section 988(d) hedging rules where the sale of stock or securities for nonfunctional currency and the hedge are effected through the same broker.

Special Analyses

It has been determined that these rules are not major rules as defined in Executive Order 12291. Therefore, a Regulatory Impact Analysis is not required. It also has been determined that section 553(b) of the Administrative Procedure Act (5 U.S.C. chapter 5) and the Regulatory Flexibility Act (5 U.S.C. chapter 6) do not apply to these regulations, and, therefore, an initial Regulatory Flexibility Analysis is not required. Pursuant to section 7805(f) of the Internal Revenue Code, these regulations will be submitted to the Chief Counsel for Advocacy of the Small Business Administration for comment on their impact on small business.

Comments and Request for a Public Hearing

Before adopting these regulations, consideration will be given to any written comments that are submitted (preferably a signed original and eight copies) to the Internal Revenue Service. All comments will be available for public inspection and copying. A public hearing will be held upon written request by any person who submits timely written comments on the proposed rules. Notice of the time, place and date for the hearing will be published in the Federal Register.

Drafting Information

The principal authors of these regulations are Jeffrey Dorfman and Charles T. Plambeck. Messrs. Dorfman and Plambeck are of the Office of Chief Counsel, Internal Revenue Service. Other personnel from the Internal Revenue Service and Treasury Department participated in developing the regulations.

[¶ 49,126]   **Proposed Regulations and Proposed Amendments of Regulations (INTL-941-86, INTL-656-87, INTL-704-87)**, published in the Federal Register on April 1, 1992.

Passive foreign investment companies: Qualified electing funds: Shareholders.—Reg. §§ 1.1291-1—1.1291-7, 1.1293-1 and 1.1295-1, relating to the taxation of shareholders of certain passive foreign investment companies (PFICs) upon payment of distributions by such companies or upon the disposition of stock of such companies, are proposed. Reg. §§ 1.1291-0, 1.1291-9 and 1.1291-10 were adopted 12/26/1996 by T.D. 8701. Reg. § 1.1291-8 was withdrawn on 2/1/1999. Reg. § 1.367(e)-1T was adopted as Reg. § 1.367(e)-1 on 1/15/1993 by T.D. 8472 and removed on 8/9/1996 by T.D. 8682. Reg. § 1.367(e)-2T was removed on 8/6/1999 by T.D. 8834. Reg. § 1.1291-1(b)(2)(ii), (b)(2)(v), (b)(7), (b)(8), and (i) was withdrawn on 12/31/2013 by REG-113350-13.

AGENCY: Internal Revenue Service, Treasury.

ACTION: Notice of proposed rulemaking.

SUMMARY: This document contains proposed income tax regulations concerning the taxation of shareholders of certain passive foreign investment companies (PFICs) upon payment of distributions by such companies or upon disposition of the stock of such companies. These rules were enacted by the Tax Reform Act of 1986, and amended by the Technical and Miscellaneous Revenue Act of 1988.

DATES: Written comments and requests for a public hearing must be received by July 30, 1992.

ADDRESSES: Send written comments and requests for a public hearing to Internal Revenue Service, P.O. Box 7604, Ben Franklin Station, Attention: CC:CORP:T:R (INTL-656-87), room 5228, Washington, DC 20044.

FOR FURTHER INFORMATION CONTACT: Gayle E. Novig of the Office of Associate Chief Counsel (International), within the Office of Chief Counsel, Internal Revenue Service, 1111 Constitution Avenue, NW, Washington, DC 20224 (Attention: CC:CORP:T:R (INTL-656-87)) (202-377-9059, not a toll free number).

SUPPLEMENTARY INFORMATION:

Paperwork Reduction Act

The collections of information contained in this notice of proposed rulemaking have been submitted to the Office of Management and Budget for review in accordance with the Paperwork Reduction Act of 1980 (44 U.S.C. 3504(h)). Comments on the collections of information should be sent to the Office of Management and Budget, Attention: Desk Officer for the Department of the Treasury, Office of Information and Regulatory Affairs, Washington, DC 20503, with copies to the Internal Revenue Service, Attention: IRS Reports Clearance Officer T:FP, Washington, DC 20224.

The collections of information in these regulations are in 26 CFR sections 1.1291-1(i), 1.1291-2(f)(2)(ii), 1.1291-3(e)(5)(iii), 1.1291-6(g), 1.1291-8(g), 1.1291-9(d), and 1.1291-10(d)(2)(vii). The collections of information found in 26 CFR section 1.1291-9(d) and 1.1291-10(d)(2)(vii) are also being published as temporary rules in the Rules and Regulations section of this issue of the Federal Register. This information is required by the Internal Revenue Service to identify PFICs and their shareholders, administer shareholder elections, verify amounts reported, and track transfers of stock of certain PFICs. The likely respondents and/or recordkeepers are individuals or households, business or other for-profit institutions, non-profit institutions, and small businesses or organizations.

These estimates are an approximation of the average time expected to be necessary for a collection of information. They are based on such information as is available to the Internal Revenue Service. Individual respondents/recordkeepers may require greater or less time, depending on their particular circumstances.

Estimated total annual reporting and/or recordkeeping burden for filing Form 8621 reported in OMB No. 1545-1002: 31,680 hours.

The estimated total annual burden per respondent/recordkeeper for the other requirements in this regulation is 8,750 hours, with an estimated average of one hour.

Estimated number of respondents and/or recordkeepers: 8,750.

Estimated frequency of responses: Annually.

Background

This document contains proposed Income Tax Regulations (26 CFR part 1) under sections 1291, 1293, 1295, and 1297 of the Internal Revenue Code of 1986. These provisions were added to the Internal Revenue Code of 1986 by section 1235 of the Tax Reform Act of 1986 (Pub. L. 99-514, 100

Stat. 2320), and amended by section 1012(p) of the Technical and Miscellaneous Revenue Act of 1988 (Pub. L. 100-647, 102 Stat. 3342). With the exceptions of different effective dates for the rules concerning certain pledges of PFIC stock outstanding on the effective date of the statute (§ 1.1291-3(d)(6)), and the mark-to-market election available to regulated investment companies (§ 1.1291-8), these regulations are proposed to be effective April 1, 1992. However, as sections 1291 through 1297 of the Code are effective for taxable years of foreign corporations beginning after 1986, shareholders of PFICs are subject to those provisions with respect to transactions occurring during those taxable years.

Explanation of Provisions

Overview of Statute

The Tax Reform Act of 1986, as amended by the Technical and Miscellaneous Revenue Act of 1988, established special rules for the taxation of U.S. persons that are shareholders of PFICs. For taxable years beginning after December 31, 1986, a foreign corporation will be classified as a PFIC if either 75 percent or more of its gross income for the taxable year is passive, or the average percentage of its assets (by value) for the taxable year that produce passive income or are held for the production of passive income is at least 50 percent. Subject to certain exceptions, passive income for these purposes generally is foreign personal holding company income as defined in section 954(c) of the Internal Revenue Code of 1986.

Sections 1291 through 1297 provide two different and sometimes overlapping sets of rules for taxing U.S. persons that are shareholders of a PFIC. In general, shareholders are subject to a special tax regime under section 1291 that applies to distributions by the PFIC and dispositions of PFIC stock. In the proposed regulations, if section 1291 applies to a particular shareholder with respect to a PFIC, the PFIC is referred to as a section 1291 fund with respect to the shareholder. A significant consequence of being treated as a section 1291 fund is that the foreign corporation will continue to be treated as a PFIC, and therefore the shareholder will continue to be subject to section 1291, even after the corporation ceases to satisfy either the income or the asset test for PFIC status under section 1296.

Each shareholder, however, may elect under section 1295 to treat a PFIC as a qualified electing fund (QEF); if such an election is made, the shareholder will be taxed currently under section 1293 on its pro rata share of the earnings of the QEF. A shareholder that makes a QEF election may or may not continue to be subject to the special tax regime under section 1291. Stated differently, a PFIC that is a QEF with respect to a particular shareholder may or may not continue to be a section 1291 fund with respect to that shareholder. If the shareholder makes the QEF election for the foreign corporation's first taxable year as a PFIC that is included in the shareholder's holding period for the stock of the PFIC, section 1291 will not apply to the shareholder. If the shareholder makes the QEF election at a later time, but also makes an election under section 1291(d)(2) to purge the PFIC stock that it holds of its taint as a section 1291 fund, the shareholder will accelerate the application of section 1291 to the PFIC stock that it holds, and section 1291 will not apply to the shareholder thereafter. In both cases, the proposed regulations refer to such a PFIC as a pedigreed QEF with respect to the electing shareholder, and the PFIC is not considered to be a section 1291 fund with respect to that shareholder.

On the other hand, if the shareholder makes the QEF election at a later time and does not make a purging election, section 1291 will continue to apply to the shareholder notwithstanding the application of section 1293. The proposed regulations refer to such a PFIC as an unpedigreed QEF in respect of the shareholder. Because section 1291 applies to the shareholder of an unpedigreed QEF, the QEF continues to be a section 1291 fund.

Pursuant to section 1291, a U.S. person that is a shareholder of a section 1291 fund pays tax and an interest charge on receipt of certain distributions and upon disposition of stock of the section 1291 fund. Under this rule, gain from a disposition or the portion of any distribution that is an excess distribution (defined in section 1291(b)) is treated as ordinary income earned ratably over the shareholder's holding period of the stock of the section 1291 fund. The portion allocated to the current year, and to years when the corporation was not a PFIC, are included in the shareholder's gross income for the year of the distribution; the remainder is not included in gross income, but the shareholder must pay a deferred tax amount (defined in section 1291(c)) with respect to that portion. The deferred tax amount is, in general, the amount of tax that would have been owed if the allocated amount had been included in income in the earlier year, plus interest.

Section 1291(f) provides regulatory authority for taxing transfers of stock of a section 1291 fund notwithstanding an otherwise applicable nonrecognition provision of the Code or regulations. Accordingly, gifts, transfers at death, and exchanges of stock pursuant to nonrecognition provisions will be taxable to the extent provided in the regulations.

Section 1297(a) provides attribution rules for determining whether a U.S. person is an indirect shareholder of a PFIC. Section 1297(b)(5) provides that, under regulations, a U.S. person treated as an indirect shareholder of a PFIC under section 1297(a) will be taxable on any distribution paid by the PFIC to the actual owner of the PFIC stock (indirect distribution), and on any disposition by the U.S. person or the actual owner if, as a result of the disposition, the U.S. person is no longer treated under section 1297(a) as owning the stock of the PFIC (indirect disposition).

Section 1297(d) grants authority to the Secretary to prescribe such regulations as may be necessary or appropriate to carry out the purposes of sections 1291 through 1297.

Explanation of Proposed Regulations

Definitions and general rules

Section 1.1291-1(b) defines the terms PFIC, QEF, pedigreed QEF, unpedigreed QEF, nonqualified fund, and section 1291 fund. As explained above, whether a corporation is a PFIC, QEF (pedigreed or unpedigreed), nonqualified fund, or section 1291 fund is determined on a shareholder by shareholder basis. In general, section 1291 and the proposed regulations under that section do not apply to determine the taxation of a shareholder of a pedigreed QEF with respect to a distribution paid by the pedigreed QEF or a disposition of its stock.

It should be noted that the definition of the term nonqualified fund in the proposed regulations differs from the definition of the same term in the current Form 8621, Return by a Shareholder of a Passive Foreign Investment Company or Qualified Electing Fund. (In the form, the term has the same meaning as the term section 1291 fund in the proposed regulations.) The form will be revised to eliminate this difference.

Section 1.1291-1(b)(3), (4), and (5) define the terms prePFIC year, prior PFIC year, and current shareholder year, terms relevant to the determination of the tax consequences under section 1291 of a distribution by, or a disposition of, a section 1291 fund. A prePFIC year is a taxable year (or portion thereof) of the shareholder included wholly or partly in the shareholder's holding period, either before the shareholder became a United States person (within the meaning of section 7701(a)(30)), or before the section 1291 fund qualified as a PFIC. A prior PFIC year is a taxable year (or portion thereof), other than the current shareholder year, included in the shareholder's holding period during which the section 1291 fund was a PFIC. The term current shareholder year refers to the shareholder's taxable year in which the taxable event occurs.

The term shareholder includes any person that owns an equity interest in the PFIC directly or indirectly, as provided in § 1.1291-1(b)(8). Section 1.1291-1(b)(8) defines the term indirect shareholder as a U.S. person that indirectly owns stock of a PFIC, and provides attribution rules for ownership of a PFIC through a person other than an individual.

Stock directly or indirectly owned by a U.S. person generally is not attributed to another U.S. person. However, pursuant to section 1297(a) and (d), stock owned directly or indirectly by an S corporation or domestic partnership, trust or estate is treated as owned proportionately by its shareholders, partners or beneficiaries. Moreover, stock may be attributed through a domestic C corporation in some circumstances if, absent such attribution, the stock of a PFIC would not be treated as owned by any U.S. person.

As described above, under the proposed regulations a beneficiary of a trust or estate is a shareholder of a proportionate amount of the PFIC stock owned directly or indirectly by the trust or estate. Comment is solicited whether different attribution rules, such as the indirect ownership rules in § 25.2701-6 (relating to special valuation rules for purposes of estate and gift taxes), should be adopted for purposes of determining whether a beneficiary of a trust or estate is an indirect shareholder of a PFIC.

Stock of a section 1291 fund owned directly or indirectly by a regulated investment company (RIC) or a real estate investment trust (REIT) is not attributed to the shareholders of the RIC or REIT. A RIC or REIT that is a shareholder of a section 1291 fund is taxable on direct or indirect distributions and dispositions. For a special mark-to-market rule applicable to RICs, see § 1.1291-8.

Under section 1297(a)(4) and the regulations, a person that holds an option to acquire PFIC stock is treated as a shareholder of PFIC stock. Section 1.1291-1(d) provides that such a person will be treated as a shareholder of a section 1291 fund subject to section 1291 on a disposition (other than by exercise) of that option. For purposes of sections 1291 through 1297, the holding period of stock of a PFIC acquired upon exercise of an option will include the period that the option was held. If the shareholder elects to treat the PFIC as a QEF, the PFIC will be an unpedigreed QEF because of the PFIC years in the shareholder's holding period attributable to the period the person held the option. The shareholder may make a section 1291(d)(2) election to purge those years from its holding period in order for the PFIC to be a pedigreed QEF.

In limited circumstances, an exempt organization that is a direct or indirect shareholder of a section 1291 fund may be subject to tax under section 1291 and these regulations. Section 1.1291-1(e) provides that an exempt organization will be taxable under section 1291 and the regulations with respect to a distribution from a section 1291 fund or a disposition of its stock if a dividend from that corporation would be taxable to the exempt organization pursuant to subchapter F.

With certain exceptions, the general Code and regulatory rules apply for purposes of determining a shareholder's holding period of PFIC stock. The proposed regulations also provide that generally, unless a shareholder previously held the stock directly, an indirect shareholder's holding period of stock of a PFIC begins on the first day that ownership of the stock of the PFIC is attributed to the person under section 1297(a). A shareholder will get a new holding period in the stock of a PFIC only after the shareholder recognizes all the gain with respect to the stock. If stock of a section 1291 fund is acquired in a transaction to which section 1223(1) or 1223(2) applies, the character of the years in the shareholder's tacked holding period as prePFIC or prior PFIC is determined by reference to the character of the holding period of the property transferred in the exchange (section 1223(1)) or received from the transferor (section 1223(2)).

Section 1.1291-1(i) sets forth the annual reporting requirements of direct and indirect shareholders of all PFICs.

Section 1.1291-2—Taxation of Excess Distributions

In general. Section 1.1291-2 provides rules for taxing a direct or indirect shareholder of a section 1291 fund on a distribution by the fund. Section 1.1291-2(b) defines the term distribution for purposes of section 1291. The term does not include a nontaxable distribution that qualifies under section 305(a) or 355(a). In addition, distributions that are treated as in exchange for stock, such as liquidation distributions and section 302(a) redemptions, are not distributions to which § 1.1291-2 applies. Those distributions are treated as dispositions subject to § 1.1291-3.

The proposed regulations at § 1.1291-2(b)(3) provide that the shareholder has an excess distribution to the extent section 304(b)(2) treats the distribution as being paid out of the earnings and profits of an issuing corporation that is a section 1291 fund. In addition, the section 304 transaction will be a taxable disposition of stock of a section 1291 fund to the extent the shareholder's interest in the issuing corporation that is a section 1291 fund is reduced as a result of the transaction. Finally, the regulations provide that an amount paid by an acquiring corporation that is a section 1291 fund will be an excess distribution. It is possible that there may be multiple taxation under these rules. Comments are therefore solicited about how to better coordinate sections 304 and 1291, without permitting avoidance of section 1291.

Section 1.1291-2(c) provides rules for determining the nonexcess distribution and the total excess distribution for the current shareholder year. These amounts are calculated on a per share basis without regard to the earnings and profits of the section 1291 fund. The total excess distribution is the amount by which the total distribution for the current shareholder year, with certain adjustments, exceeds the nonexcess distribution. The nonexcess distribution is defined as the portion of the total distribution that does not exceed 125 percent of the average of the distributions made with respect to the stock during the preceding three taxable years included in the shareholder's holding period. For purposes of calculating the excess distribution, the portion of a prior year's excess distribution that was not included in income (the portion subject to the deferred tax amount) is not considered a distribution made in a prior year. If the section 1291 fund makes more than one distribution during the current shareholder year, and there is a total excess distribution for the year, a ratable portion of each distribution is an excess distribution.

Section 1.1291-2(c)(3)(ii) provides that the total excess distribution is zero in the taxable year of the shareholder in which the shareholder's holding period begins. This rule applies only to distributions, and not to excess distributions arising from dispositions of section 1291 fund stock.

The excess distribution is calculated using the U.S. dollar. In general, each distribution in a foreign currency is converted into U.S. dollars at the spot rate on the date of the distribution. However, if all relevant distributions have been made in a single foreign currency, the excess distribution is calculated in that currency and then converted into the U.S. dollar at the spot rate on the date of the current shareholder year distribution.

The earnings and profits of a section 1291 fund are generally irrelevant for purposes of section 1291. For that reason, as stated above, the excess distribution is calculated without regard to the earnings and profits of the section 1291 fund. If the earnings and profits can be calculated, the shareholder can avoid the interest charge and other disadvantages under section 1291 by making the QEF election.

However, the earnings and profits of a section 1291 fund are relevant for purposes of claiming the foreign tax credit for deemed paid taxes and determining the taxation of a nonexcess distribution. For these purposes, § 1.1291-2(e)(3) provides that earnings and profits are allocated proportionately between the nonexcess distribution and the total excess distribution.

Special rules. Pursuant to proposed § 1.1291-2(b)(2), neither an inclusion of income under section 951(a)(1), 551(b) or 1293(a), nor an actual distribution of an amount previously taxed under one of those sections, is a distribution for purposes of section 1291. Accordingly, an inclusion in income under section 951, 551 or 1293 is neither subject to section 1291 in the year of inclusion nor treated as a distribution made in a prior year when calculating a nonexcess distribution. In addition, distributions of previously taxed amounts are not taken into account when calculating the nonexcess distribution. Therefore, the total distribution for the current year is first reduced by the amount that is not included in gross income by reason of section 959, 551(d), or 1293(c). In developing these rules, treatment of inclusions in income under section 951, 551, or 1293 in prior years as distributions was considered. However, such a rule was not adopted because such amounts were not subject to section 1291 in the year of inclusion.

Proposed regulation § 1.1291-2(d)(1) provides that, for purposes of calculating the average of distributions made during the preceding three taxable years, a shareholder whose holding period begins after the first day of the shareholder's taxable year may take into account distributions paid during that year but before the shareholder's holding period began. Consideration was given to other methods of annualizing distributions (for example, extrapolation from distributions actually received), but such methods were rejected because they tended to produce distorted results.

Pursuant to section 1291(b)(3)(G), § 1.1291-2(d)(5) provides rules for adjusting an excess distribution received by a trust that is entitled to deduct the amount of its fixed annual charitable obligation from gross income under section 642(c).

The proposed regulations at § 1.1291-2(d)(6) provide a rule for calculating the excess distribution in a taxable year of the shareholder during which the foreign corporation was a PFIC for only part of that year. Under this rule, all distributions paid during the year with respect to the stock owned or treated as owned by the shareholder are taken into account for purposes of calculating the excess distribution, but only those distributions made after the foreign corporation became a PFIC are taxed under section 1291.

Taxation of a distribution. Section 1.1291-2(e) provides the rules for the taxation of a nonexcess distribution and an excess distribution. A nonexcess distribution is taxed according to the general rules applicable to corporate distributions. To determine the taxation of an excess distribution, the excess distribution is allocated pro rata to each day in the shareholder's holding period (treated as ending on the date of the distribution) without regard to whether the corporation actually derived earnings and profits during the years to which the excess distribution is allocated.

The portions of an excess distribution allocated to the current shareholder year and to the prePFIC years are included in the shareholder's ordinary income and are not subject to the deferred tax amount. The portions of an excess distribution allocated to the prior PFIC years are not included, or treated as included, in gross income for any purpose. Therefore, any losses in the current shareholder year or prior years may not offset the portions of an excess distribution allocated to the prior PFIC years. The amounts allocated to prior PFIC years are subject to the deferred tax amount, determined under § 1.1291-4, which includes an interest charge.

Indirect distributions. An indirect distribution is a distribution by a section 1291 fund to the actual shareholder of stock of a section 1291 fund that a shareholder is considered to own under § 1.1291-1(b)(8). Generally, a shareholder is taxable on its pro rata share of the total distribution paid by the section 1291 fund. The nonexcess distribution and total excess distribution are calculated at the indirect shareholder level.

The proposed regulations provide an exception to the general rule that all indirect distributions are taxable. A shareholder is not taxable on an indirect distribution paid by a section 1291 fund to its sole shareholder that is a section 1291 fund owned directly by the shareholder, provided the distributing fund has distributed all its earnings each year included in the shareholder's holding period of the distributing fund. Comment is solicited on whether there are additional circumstances in which an indirect shareholder of a section 1291 fund should not be taxed on distributions by, or dispositions of the stock of, a section 1291 fund.

The proposed regulations require partnerships and S corporations to provide information to their partners and shareholders. This information is intended to assist the indirect shareholders in calculating their excess distributions. Information reporting obligations of trusts and estates are reserved.

Other than the guidance provided in § 1.1291-2(f)(6) (adjustments for trusts permitted to take the section 642(c) deduction) and § 1.1291-6(d)(3) (section 643(e)(3) election), the regulations do not provide explicit rules for determining the tax consequences to a trust or estate (or a beneficiary thereof) that directly or indirectly owns stock of a section 1291 fund. Until such rules are issued, the shareholder must apply the PFIC rules and subchapter J in a reasonable manner that triggers or preserves the interest charge. Comments are invited about the manner in which excess distributions paid with respect to stock directly or indirectly owned by trusts or estates should be taxed under section 1291.

Dispositions of stock of section 1291 funds

Section 1.1291-3 provides general rules for determining the tax consequences of transfers of stock of section 1291 funds. Unless otherwise provided, gain recognized on a direct or indirect disposition of a share of stock of a section 1291 fund is taxed as an excess distribution in the manner provided in § 1.1291-2(e)(2).

A loss that is recognized on the disposition of a share of stock of a section 1291 fund does not offset the gain recognized on another share. The general rules applicable to losses recognized on a disposition of stock apply to losses realized and recognized on the disposition of stock of a section 1291 fund.

Definition of disposition. Section 1.1291-3(b)(1) defines the term disposition for purposes of section 1291. A disposition includes a gift, a transfer by reason of death, and a transfer that qualifies for nonrecognition treatment under another provision of the Code. Paragraphs (b)(2) and (d) of proposed § 1.1291-3 contain special rules providing that the change of residence or citizenship status of a U.S. resident alien or citizen to nonresident alien status, and a pledge of section 1291 fund stock constitute dispositions. Under § 1.1291-3(c), (d), and (e), dispositions of stock of a section 1291 fund are generally taxable unless an exception applies.

Indirect dispositions. An indirect disposition includes a disposition of the stock of a section 1291 fund by its actual owner and a disposition by the indirect shareholder or other person of any interest in a person if by virtue of such interest a U.S. person is treated as an owner of the stock of the section 1291 fund. The former rule applies without regard to whether the disposition reduces or terminates the shareholder's interest in the PFIC. The latter rule, however, does not apply if the transaction does not affect the shareholder's interest in the PFIC or the actual owner's basis in the PFIC. The proposed regulations also provide that an indirect disposition includes a transaction that reduces or eliminates the indirect shareholder's interest in the PFIC.

The scope of the indirect disposition rules in the proposed regulations is broader than the scope of the rule in section 1297(b)(5). The rules have been expanded under the authority of section 1297(d) to prevent avoidance of section 1291 (for example, through transactions between affiliated foreign companies).

In the case of an indirect disposition, the gain that is treated as an excess distribution to the indirect shareholder is the shareholder's proportionate share of the actual owner's gain with respect to the stock of the fund (whether or not such gain is realized by the actual owner). Thus, the amount taxable to the indirect shareholder is determined without regard to the amount the shareholder would recognize on a disposition of the interest through which the shareholder is considered to own the stock of the section 1291 fund.

Generally, the excess distribution is allocated over the indirect shareholder's holding period. However, § 1.1291-1(h)(4)(iii) provides that an S corporation shareholder uses the holding period of the S corporation if the S corporation directly or indirectly owned the stock of the PFIC prior to its election under section 1362. In addition, the deferred tax amount owed by the S corporation shareholders is calculated using the applicable rate of tax under section 1, even for years during which the S corporation was a C corporation that are included in the shareholders' holding period, pursuant to § 1.1291-4(c)(2).

The S corporation also may be taxable on a disposition of section 1291 fund stock as provided in section 1374. If the S corporation pays built-in gain tax pursuant to section 1374 on the disposition of the section 1291 fund, the S corporation shareholders' excess distribution, pursuant to section 1366(f)(2), does not include the built-in gain tax paid by the S corporation. However, the proposed regulations provide that the section 1366(f)(2) deduction is disregarded when calculating the aggregate amount of interest under section 1291(c)(3).

Transfers within a consolidated group. Proposed regulation § 1.1291-3(f) provides a special rule for transfers of stock of a section 1291 fund between members of a consolidated return group. Comments are solicited on how to coordinate this rule with the consolidated return regulations.

Installment sales. Section 1.1291-3(g) provides rules for applying section 1291 to installment sales of section 1291 fund stock. The gain portion of each installment is an excess distribution. For purposes of allocating each excess distribution under § 1.1291-2(e), the holding period of the transferred stock is treated as ending on the date the installment payment is received. A deferred tax amount is owed for each installment received. This rule applies section 1291(a)(3), which provides that the holding period ends on the date of each excess distribution.

Coordination with sections 1246 and 1248. Section 1.1291-3(i) provides that neither section 1246 nor section 1248 applies to the disposition of stock of a section 1291 fund. However, as provided in §1.1291-5(e), a shareholder may calculate a foreign tax credit on a disposition of stock of a section 1291 fund taking into account the indirect foreign tax credits to which the shareholder would have been entitled if section 1248 would have applied to the disposition of the section 1291 fund stock but for section 1291.

Deferred Tax Amount

Section 1.1291-4 provides the rules for determining the deferred tax amount. The deferred tax amount is calculated with respect to that portion of the excess distribution that is allocated to prior PFIC years and not included in income. It is the sum of the aggregate increases in taxes and the aggregate amount of interest determined with respect to the increases in taxes.

An increase in tax is calculated for each portion of an excess distribution allocated to a prior PFIC year. It is the product of the portion of the excess distribution allocated to a prior PFIC year and the highest rate of tax in effect in that prior year under section 1 or 11, as applicable. The aggregate increases in taxes are the sum of all increases in tax calculated with respect to an excess distribution. The aggregate increases in taxes are additional taxes owed in the current shareholder year regardless of the shareholder's tax position in that year or any of the prior PFIC years. Therefore, if unpaid, they will result in penalties and interest in the same manner as other taxes on income.

The aggregate amount of interest, the interest charge component of the deferred tax amount, is interest under section 6601 for the underpayment of tax. Interest is owed on each increase in tax calculated for a prior PFIC year (reduced by foreign tax credits pursuant to §1.1291-5) as if the portion of the excess distribution allocated to that prior PFIC year was distributed in that year but the tax thereon was not paid until the return due date for the current shareholder year. The interest charge is calculated, using the rates and method provided in section 6621, for the period beginning on the due date (without regard to extensions) for the shareholder's return for the prior PFIC year, and ending on the due date (without regard to extensions) for the shareholder's return for the current shareholder year.

Coordination with the Foreign Tax Credit Rules

Section 1.1291-5 provides the steps for determining the foreign tax credit a shareholder may claim against the increases in tax on an excess distribution, including in certain cases the excess distribution on a disposition of stock of a section 1291 fund. The foreign tax credit under these steps is determined separately for distributions received from different section 1291 funds and for each excess distribution. Excess foreign tax credits calculated with respect to an increase in tax may not be used to offset any other increase in tax or any other federal income tax. The calculation of the foreign tax credit for foreign taxes paid on the portion of the excess distribution subject to the deferred tax amount is separate from the calculation of the credit for other foreign taxes paid during the current shareholder year.

Nonrecognition Transfers of Stock of Section 1291 funds

In general. Section 1.1291-6 provides rules for the recognition of gain by a shareholder on a direct or indirect disposition of stock of a section 1291 fund that results from a transaction in which, but for section 1291(f), there would not be full recognition of gain. The general rule of §1.1291-6 is that the U.S. person recognizes gain unless an exception set forth in §1.1291-6(c) applies. Gain from the disposition therefore is generally recognized and taxed as an excess distribution notwithstanding any other provision of the Code or regulations.

Exceptions to the gain recognition rule. Generally, a shareholder will not be required to recognize gain if the shareholder receives a direct or indirect interest of equivalent value in a PFIC in exchange for the PFIC stock transferred. In addition, a shareholder will not be required to recognize gain if, immediately after the transfer, the transferred stock is owned by a U.S. person (the U.S. transferee) that will be taxed under section 1291 on subsequent distributions and dispositions of the transferred stock, provided the U.S. transferee's adjusted basis in the stock is less than or equal to the shareholder's basis, and the U.S. transferee's holding period of the stock is at least as long as the shareholder's holding period.

Nothing in §1.1291-6 is to be interpreted as overriding any other provision of the Code or regulations requiring recognition of gain or loss. If, under §1.1291-6(c), an exception to the gain recognition rule applies to a transfer that is taxable under another provision, such as section 367 and the regulations under that section, the gain is taxable as a distribution or disposition, as appropriate, under section 1291. Section 1.1291-6 also does not require or permit the recognition of loss unless the loss is recognized under another section of the Code or regulations.

Basis and holding period rules. If gain is recognized under the gain recognition rule of §1.1291-6, the basis of the transferred stock and the basis of any stock received in exchange therefor are increased by the amount of gain recognized. If all gain realized is recognized, the holding period of such stock begins on the day after the transfer. If a shareholder realizes a loss on a transfer to which the gain recognition rule would have applied had a gain been realized, the shareholder does not recognize the loss, but the shareholder's holding period begins on the day after the transfer. If stock is transferred at death to a U.S. person and gain is not recognized, the basis of the transferred stock is the lower of the fair market value or adjusted basis of the transferred stock in the hands of the decedent shareholder on the date of death. The U.S. beneficiary's holding period of that stock includes the period the decedent held the stock. The days in the holding period of stock received by a shareholder or transferee in a transfer to which an exception to the gain recognition rule applies retain the PFIC character those days had with respect to the stock transferred.

Mark-to-market election by a regulated investment company

In general. Section 1.1291-8 of the proposed regulations permits a RIC to make a mark-to-market election with respect to the stock of section 1291 funds of which it is a direct or indirect shareholder. Because RICs in many instances have not been able to obtain the information necessary to make the QEF election under section 1295, the election under §1.1291-8 is needed as a means to coordinate the rules of section 1291 with the rules of sections 851 through 855.

The deferred tax amount generally will be avoided with respect to stock of section 1291 funds because stock that was marked to market at the end of a year gets a new holding period at the beginning of the following year. Any excess distribution with respect to stock subject to the election thereafter will be allocated under §1.1291-2(e)(2) only to days in the current year.

Nothing in the proposed regulation precludes a RIC from electing under section 1295 to treat as a QEF a section 1291 fund whose stock was previously marked to market under §1.1291-8.

Scope. The mark-to-market election is only available to a RIC that is either an open-end RIC or a closed-end RIC that determines and publishes weekly its net asset value. In such cases, the election will apply to all section 1291 fund stock of which the RIC is a shareholder. Comment is solicited on whether, and how, the election should be extended to other RICs.

Effect of the election. The election applies to the year in which made and to each succeeding year unless revoked with the consent of the Commissioner. At the end of each of the RIC's taxable years to which the election applies, the RIC recognizes, on a share-by-share basis, the amount by which the fair market value of the section 1291 fund stock exceeds its adjusted basis. No loss may be recognized as a result of making the election. The holding period of stock that was marked to market, including stock of a section 1291 fund with respect to which there was no mark-to-market gain, begins on the first day of each taxable year of the RIC. The proposed regulations also provide for basis adjustments to avoid double taxation of the mark-to-market gain

Except as provided in §1.1291-8, the election otherwise has no effect on the manner in which a distribution by a section 1291 fund or a disposition of its stock is taxed to the electing RIC. Accordingly, distributions by a section 1291 fund will be taxable to the RIC pursuant to the general rules of the proposed regulations. Similarly, gain from the disposition of stock of the section 1291 fund will be treated as an excess distribution.

The proposed regulations provide a transition rule pursuant to which a RIC that makes the mark-to-market election in the first taxable year ending after [INSERT DATE THIS DOCUMENT IS PUBLISHED AS FINAL REGULATIONS] must include as ordinary income in that year all appreciation in the section 1291 fund stock as of the beginning of that year and pay a nondeductible interest charge. In addition, if the RIC failed to make a mark-to-market election in a prior year because it reasonably believed that it was not a shareholder of a section 1291 fund or did not apply a previously made election to a corporation because it reasonably believed that the corporation was not a section 1291 fund, the proposed regulations permit the RIC to elect to recognize the mark-to-market gains for the prior years with respect to the discovered stock in the year of discovery. All the mark-to market gain is included in income in the year of discovery, subject to a nondeductible interest charge.

Although the objective of the mark-to-market election is to eliminate the RIC's liability for the deferred tax amount, the RIC may nevertheless owe such tax in the first year in which the election applies with respect to stock with a holding period that includes a prior PFIC year if it did not make the election in the first year in which it is permitted to do so. In that case, the transition rule will not apply to the RIC if it makes the election in a subsequent year; any gain recognized will be allocated over the entire holding period, triggering the deferred tax amount. Similarly, if the RIC does not elect the remedy in §1.1291-8(e) of the proposed regulations in the year of discovery, the RIC may be liable for the deferred tax amount arising from excess distributions with respect to the discovered stock.

Purging Elections

Deemed Dividend Election. Section 1.1291-9 specifies the time and manner for making the election under section 1291(d)(2)(B). This election may be made by a U.S. person that is a direct or indirect shareholder of an unpedigreed QEF that also is a CFC. A shareholder that makes the section 1291(d)(2)(B) election is treated as receiving a dividend on the first day of its taxable year in which it makes the QEF election (qualification date).

The fact that the qualification date falls on a day other than the first day of the CFC's first taxable year as a QEF will have no effect on the amount that the shareholder must include in income pursuant to section 1293(a) for that first QEF year. As provided in section 1293, the shareholder includes in income its pro rata share of the ordinary earnings and net capital gain of the QEF for the taxable year of the QEF that ends during the shareholder's taxable year. However, the amount of the deemed dividend will not include the portion of the current earnings that the shareholder demonstrates are included in the shareholder's income that year under section 1293(a).

Section 1.1291-9(h)(2) provides that a shareholder may not make the deemed dividend election of section 1291(d)(2)(B) if the CFC will not qualify as a PFIC under section 1296(a) for the first taxable year for which the QEF election was made. In that case, the shareholder of an unpedigreed QEF that no longer qualifies as a PFIC under section 1296(a) may make only the deemed sale election provided in section 1297(b)(1) and §1.1297-3T.

Deemed sale election. The proposed regulations differ from §1.1291-10, as proposed, in two significant respects. First, the proposed regulations change the qualification date for deemed sale elections made after May 1, 1992. This change is consistent with the definition of qualification date for the deemed dividend election described above.

Secondly, the proposed regulations clarify the amount of gain a shareholder recognizes when it makes a deemed sale election with respect to a PFIC of which it is an indirect shareholder. An indirect shareholder recognizes the amount of gain the actual shareholder of the stock would realize if the actual owner sold or otherwise disposed of the PFIC stock that the shareholder is considered to own.

Section 1293

Proposed §1.1293-1(a) provides that section 1293 applies to pedigreed QEF shareholders only with respect to taxable years of the QEF in which the QEF satisfies either the income test or the asset test of section 1296(a). The proposed regulation also provides that if the PFIC is an unpedigreed QEF with respect to the shareholder, section 1293 applies to the shareholder in all years that the PFIC is a section 1291 fund, including those years in which the corporation does not satisfy either the income or asset test.

Application of section 1295 election

Section 1.1295-1 of the proposed regulations provides specific rules concerning the application of the section 1295 election to the electing shareholder, transferees of the shareholder, stock acquired after the election was made, stock received in exchange for the QEF stock, and corporations that are successors of QEFs. The proposed regulations, however, do not provide guidance for making the section 1295 election. Until publication of regulations providing such guidance, taxpayers wishing to make the section 1295 election may continue to rely on Notice 88-125, 1988-2 C.B. 535.

The QEF election applies only to the shareholder that makes the election and not to any other shareholder of the PFIC or to a transferee of the QEF stock. Furthermore, the QEF election only applies to the corporation for which the shareholder makes the election and not to a successor corporation. Nevertheless, proposed regulation §1.1295-1(b)(2)(i) permits a shareholder who transferred stock of a QEF in a nonrecognition transaction before a certain date to make a retroactive section 1295 election to treat the successor corporation as a QEF.

Distributions described in section 367(e)

The proposed regulations amend proposed §§1.367(e)-1 and 1.367(e)-2 to provide that §1.1291-3 and, in certain cases, §1.1291-6 apply to determine the taxation of distributions of stock of a section 1291 fund described in section 367(e)(1) and (2). The proposed regulations also amend proposed §1.367(e)-2(c)(3)(iv) to cross-reference to the rule that provides that the liquidation of a section 1291 fund may be an indirect disposition taxable to the indirect shareholder.

Effective dates. Proposed §1.1291-1(j) provides that, with certain exceptions, the regulations are effective April 1, 1992. Although the regulations are proposed to be effective prospectively, sections 1291 through 1297 are nevertheless effective for taxable years of foreign corporations beginning after December 31, 1986. Shareholders of corporations that qualified as PFICs after that date therefore must apply the statute in determining the tax consequences of distributions by section 1291 funds and dispositions of stock of section 1291 funds that were effected before the effective date of the proposed regulations. Such shareholders must apply reasonable interpretations of the Code. The Department of the Treasury and the Internal Revenue Service regard these regulations as a reasonable interpretation of the Code.

Certain provisions of the proposed regulations have other effective dates. Section 1.1291-3(d)(6) of the proposed regulations, which concerns pledges of PFIC stock outstanding on the effective date of the statute, will be effective retroactively to taxable years of PFICs beginning after December 31, 1986. Section 1.1291-8 permits regulated investment companies to make a mark-to-market election with respect to their section 1291 fund stock in taxable years ending after [INSERT DATE THIS DOCUMENT IS PUBLISHED AS A FINAL REGULATION].

Special Analyses

It has been determined that these proposed rules are not major rules as defined in Executive Order 12291. Therefore, a Regulatory Impact Analysis is not required. It has also been determined that section 553(b) of the Administrative Procedure Act (5 U.S.C. chapter 5) and the Regulatory Flexibility Act (5 U.S.C. chapter 6) do not apply to these regulations, and, therefore, an initial Regulatory Flexibility Analysis is not required. Pursuant to section 7805(f) of the Internal Revenue Code, these regulations will be submitted to the Chief Counsel for Advocacy of the Small Business Administration for comment on their impact on small business.

Comments and Request for a Public Hearing

Before adopting these proposed regulations, consideration will be given to any written comments that are submitted timely (preferably a signed original and eight copies) to the Internal Revenue Service. All comments will be available for public inspection and copying. A public hearing will be held upon written request by any person who submits written comments as prescribed in the proposed rules. Notice of the time and place for the hearing will be published in the Federal Register.

Drafting Information

The principal author of these proposed regulations is Gayle E. Novig of the Office of Associate Chief Counsel (International), within the Office of Chief Counsel, Internal Revenue Service. Other personnel from the IRS and Treasury Department participated in developing the regulations.

[¶ 49,127] Proposed Amendments of Regulations (INTL-121-90), published in the Federal Register on April 27, 1992.

Treaty-based return positions: Dual status alien.—Amendments of Reg. §301.7701(b)-7 (except (c)(2)), relating to treaty-based return positions, are proposed. Amendments to Reg. §§301.6114-1 and 301.7701(b)-7(c)(2) were adopted 10/6/97 by T.D. 8733.

AGENCY: Internal Revenue Service, Treasury.

ACTION: Notice of proposed rulemaking.

SUMMARY: This document contains proposed Income Tax Regulations relating to sections 6114 and 7701(b) of the Internal Revenue Code of 1986 (the Code). The proposed regulations under section 6114 provide that reporting is specifically required if the residency of an individual is determined under a treaty and apart from the Code. This action is necessary to implement section 6114 of the Internal Revenue Code of 1986 in cases in which a resident alien, who claims treaty benefits as a resident of the other treaty partner's country ("dual status alien"), fails to file a statement as required by the regulations under section 7701(b). The proposed regulations under section 7701(b) provide that for purposes of determining the U.S. income tax liability of a dual status alien who is a shareholder of an S corporation, the trade or business or permanent establishment of the S corporation shall be passed through to the dual status alien pursuant to section 1366(b).

DATES: Written comments and requests for a public hearing must be received by June 26, 1992.

ADDRESSES: Send comments and requests for a public hearing to: Internal Revenue Service, P. O. Box 7604, Ben Franklin Station, Attn: CC:CORP:T:R, (INTL-121-90), room 5228, Washington, DC 20044.

FOR FURTHER INFORMATION CONTACT: David A. Juster of the Office of Associate Chief Counsel (International), within the Office of Chief Counsel, Internal Revenue Service, 1111 Constitution Avenue, N.W., Washington, DC 20224, Attention: CC:CORP:T:R (INTL-121-90) (202-566-3452, not a toll-free call).

SUPPLEMENTARY INFORMATION:

Paperwork Reduction Act

The collections of information contained in this notice of proposed rulemaking has been submitted to the Office of Management and Budget for review in accordance with the Paperwork Reduction Act of 1980 (44 U.S.C. 3504(h)). Comments on the collections of information should be sent to the Office of Management and Budget, Attn: Desk Officer for the Department of the Treasury, Office of Information and Regulatory Affairs, Washington, DC 20503, with copies to the Internal Revenue Service, Attention: IRS Reports Clearance Officer T:FP, Washington, D.C. 20224.

The collections of information in these regulations are in §§301.6114-1(b)(8) and 301.7701(b)-7(a)(4)(iv)(C). The information required by §301.6114-1(b)(8) will be used by the Internal Revenue Service to identify taxpayers taking a treaty-based return position and the specific income for which such treaty-position is taken. The information required by §301.7701(b)-7(a)(4)(iv)(C) will be used by the Internal Revenue Service to identify dual resident S corporation shareholders taking treaty-based return positions in order to ensure that at least one level of U.S. tax is paid on an S corporation's earnings.

These estimates are an approximation of the average time expected to be necessary for a collection of information. They are based on such information as is available to the Internal Revenue Service. Individual respondents may require greater or less time, depending on their particular circumstances.

§301.6114-1(b)(8) Reporting requirement.

Estimated total annual reporting burden: 1,000 hours.

The estimated annual burden per respondent varies from 1/2 hour to 3 hours, depending on individual circumstances, with an estimated average of 1 hour.

Estimated number of respondents: 1,000.

Estimated frequency of responses: Annually.

§301.7701(b)-7(a)(4)(iv)(C) Reporting requirement.

Estimated total annual reporting burden: 15 hours.

The estimated annual burden per respondent varies from 1/2 hour to 1 hour, depending on individual circumstances, with an estimated average of 3/4 hour.

Estimated number of respondents: 20.

Estimated frequency of responses: Annually

Background

This document contains proposed amendments to the final Income Tax Regulations (26 CFR §301.6114-1), published in the Federal Register on March 14, 1990 (55 FR 9438) and on July 12, 1990 (55 FR 28608). The proposed amendments relate to paragraphs (b) and (c) of §301.6114-1. The regulations under section 6114 are proposed to be effective after [insert the date that is 60 days after the date these regulations are published in the Federal Register as final regulations]. Also contained in this document are proposed amendments to the final Income Tax Regulations (26 CFR 301.7701(b)-7), published elsewhere in this issue of the Federal Register. The proposed amendments which relate to paragraphs (a)(4) and (c)(3) of §301.7701(b)-7 are proposed to be effective for S corporation taxable years beginning on or after July 27, 1992. The proposed amendments to paragraph (c)(2) of §301.7701(b)-7 are proposed to be effective after [insert the date that is 60 days after the date these regulations are published in the Federal Register as final regulations].

Explanation of Provisions

Section 6114 requires each taxpayer who, with respect to any tax imposed by the Code, takes a position that a treaty of the United States overrules, or modifies, an internal revenue law of the United States to disclose that position on a return of tax for that tax or in such other form as the Secretary may prescribe. Section 6712 provides penalties for the failure to comply with the disclosure requirement of section 6114.

Currently, paragraph (c)(2) of §301.6114-1 provides that if the residency of an individual is determined under a treaty and apart from the Code, then the section 6114 treaty-based return reporting requirement is waived. The waiver was originally provided because it was contemplated, at the time of the promulgation of regulations under section 6114, that the regulations under section 7701(b), being drafted at that time, would include a reporting requirement and penalty provision. In the process of completing the regulations under section 7701(b), the Service concluded that the rules of section 6114 should apply to individuals determining their residence under a treaty.

This document contains proposed regulations which add new paragraph (b)(8) and amend paragraph (c) of §301.6114-1. New paragraph (b)(8) of §301.6114-1 is proposed to provide that, for returns relating to taxable years for which the due date for filing returns (without extensions) is after [the date that is 60 days after the date these regulations are published in the Federal Register as final regulations], reporting is required under section 6114 if the residency of an individual is determined under a treaty and apart from the Code. Proposed paragraph (b)(8) also provides that the taxpayer shall disclose the treaty-based return position on a statement (in the form required by §301.7701(b)-7(c)) attached to his or her return. This proposed change will not result in duplicative reporting under section 6114 because a statement in the form required in §301.7701(b)-7(c) will be considered disclosure for purposes of section 6114 and the regulations thereunder. The proposed amendment to paragraph (c)(2) of §301.6114-1 provides that, for returns relating to earlier taxable years not subject to this change, reporting is waived under section 6114 if the residency of an individual is determined under a treaty and apart from the Code. In addition, a proposed amendment to the end flush language of paragraph (c) provides that the reporting requirements under new paragraph (b)(8) of §301.6114-1, are waived if payments or income items received by the individual during the course of the taxable year do not exceed $100,000 in the aggregate.

This document also contains proposed revisions to §301.7701(b)-7 of the final regulations published elsewhere in this issue of the Federal Register. Section 301.7701(b)-7 of the regulations provides, in general, that if a dual resident taxpayer (an alien individual who is a resident of both the United States and a foreign country with which the United States has an income tax convention) claims a treaty benefit as a nonresident alien with respect to an item of income covered by the treaty, the individual will be treated as a nonresident for purposes of computing the individual's United States income tax liability under the Internal Revenue Code. Congress has made it clear (by the enactment of section 1361(b)(2)(C)) that nonresident aliens may not be shareholders of an S corporation. In order to ensure that at least one level of U.S. tax is paid on an S corporation's earnings, paragraph (a)(4)(iii) of §301.7701(b)-7 is proposed to provide that for purposes of determining whether a domestic corporation meets the definition of an S corporation under section 1361(a)(1), a dual resident taxpayer who claims a treaty benefit (as a nonresident of the United States) so as to reduce the individual's United States income tax liability shall be treated as a nonresident alien of the United States. Accordingly, if the dual resident taxpayer is a shareholder in an S corporation for any portion of a taxable year with respect to which the taxpayer claims a treaty benefit, then the corporation's election under section 1362(a) shall be terminated pursuant to section 1362(d)(2) effective on the first day of the dual resident's taxable year with respect to which the dual resident taxpayer claims a treaty benefit. A dual resident who does not claim treaty benefits to reduce U.S. tax will not be subject this rule, and thus, may be or become a shareholder in an S corporation.

Proposed paragraph (a)(4)(iv) of §301.7701(b)-7 provides a special exception (if certain specified conditions are satisfied) that permits a dual resident taxpayer to be treated as United States resident for purposes of section 1361(a)(1) even if the taxpayer claims treaty benefits. The special exception will apply if a dual resident S corporation shareholder and the S corporation enter into an agreement to be subject to tax and withholding as if the dual resident were a nonresident alien partner in a partnership. The character and source of the S corporation items included in the dual resident shareholder's income will be determined as if realized by the shareholder. The dual resident shareholder will be considered as carrying on a business within the United States through a permanent establishment if the S corporation carries on such a business. The Service intends to publish a revenue procedure that will provide additional detail concerning the manner of applying these rules and the contents of the withholding agreement. For example, the revenue procedure will prescribe the withholding requirements on current income (income attributable to a permanent establishment, income that is fixed or determinable, annual or periodical income, and income attributable to U.S. real property interests), and gain on sale of S corporation stock (including gain attributable to U.S. real property interests). A dual resident shareholder of an S corporation that was a C corporation, or a successor to a C corporation or a successor to an S corporation that itself was a successor (direct or indirect) to a C corporation is not eligible for the exception.

For years to which this special exception does not apply, an individual who has claimed treaty benefits so as to reduce his or her United States income tax liability will not be considered a nonresident alien for purposes of section 1361(b)(1)(C) provided the individual has reasonably taken into account for United States income tax purposes his or her share of S corporation income, gain, loss, deduction, and credit in accordance with section 1366 of the Code.

Under paragraph (b) of §301.7701(b)-7, a dual resident taxpayer who claims a treaty benefit as a nonresident alien must attach a statement (in the form required by paragraph (c)) to his or her Form 1040NR. Proposed paragraph (c)(3) of §301.7701(b)-7 provides that an additional declaration must be included in the statement disclosing a treaty-based return position that is filed by a dual resident taxpayer who is a shareholder in an S corporation.

Proposed paragraph (c)(2) of §301.7701(b)-7 also provides that for purposes of stating the approximate amount of subpart F income to be included in the statement filed by a dual resident taxpayer who is a shareholder in a controlled foreign corporation (as defined in section 957), the approximate amount of income may be based on the audited foreign financial statements of the CFC if there are no other United States shareholders in that CFC.

Special Analyses

It has been determined that these rules are not major rules as defined in Executive Order 12291. Therefore, a Regulatory Impact Analysis is not required. It has also been determined that §553(b) of the Administrative Procedure Act (5 U.S.C. chapter 5) and the Regulatory Flexibility Act (5 U.S.C. chapter 6) do not apply to these regulations, and therefore, an initial Regulatory Flexibility Analysis is not required. Pursuant to section 7805(f) of the Internal Revenue Code, these regulations will be submitted to the Chief Counsel for Advocacy of the Small Business Administration for comment on their impact on small business.

Comments and Request for a Public Hearing

Before adopting these proposed regulations, consideration will be given to any written comments that are timely submitted (preferably a signed original and eight copies) to the Internal Revenue Service. All comments will be available for public inspection and copying. A public hearing will be held upon written request by any person who submits timely written comments on the proposed rules. Notice of the time, place and date for the hearing will be published in the Federal Register.

Drafting Information

Various personnel from the Office of Associate Chief Counsel (International), within the Office of Chief Counsel, Internal Revenue Service and the Treasury Department participated in developing the regulations.

[¶ 49,129] Proposed Amendments of Regulations (EE-23-92), published in the Federal Register on August 7, 1992.

Exemption from tax: VEBA: Geographic locale restriction.—Amendments to Reg. § 1.501(c)(9)-2, relating to the qualification of voluntary employees' beneficiary associations under Code Sec. 501(c)(9), are proposed.

AGENCY: Internal Revenue Service, Treasury.

ACTION: Notice of proposed rulemaking and notice of public hearing.

SUMMARY: This document contains proposed regulations about the qualification of voluntary employees' beneficiary associations (VEBAs) under section 501(c)(9) of the Internal Revenue Code (Code). The proposed regulations supplement the existing regulations with rules for determining whether the membership of an organization consists of employees of employers engaged in the same line of business in the same geographic locale. The proposed regulations will provide the public with guidance necessary to comply with the law in the case of an organization that does not consist exclusively of the employees of a single employer or the members of a single labor union. They will affect entities seeking to sponsor VEBAs covering the employees of more than one unrelated employer, as well as those employees.

DATES: Written comments must be received by October 6, 1992. Requests to speak (with outlines of oral comments) at a public hearing scheduled for December 3, 1992, at 1:00 p.m. must be received by November 12, 1992.

ADDRESSES: Send all submissions to: Internal Revenue Service, P.O. Box 7604, Ben Franklin Station, Attention: CC:CORP:T:R (EE-23-92) Washington, D.C. 20044.

FOR FURTHER INFORMATION CONTACT: Michael J. Roach at 202-622-6060 concerning the regulations; Carol Savage at 202-622-8452 concerning the hearing (not toll-free numbers).

SUPPLEMENTARY INFORMATION:

Background

The existing regulations at § 1.501(c)(9)-2(a)(1) contain general rules for determining when an association qualifies as a voluntary employees' beneficiary association (VEBA) eligible for exemption from income tax under section 501(c)(9) of the Internal Revenue Code. Under those regulations, the members of the association must share an employment-related common bond. The members are deemed to share an employment-related common bond if membership in the association is open only to persons whose eligibility for membership is based on employment by a single employer or affiliated group of employers, or is based on membership in one or more locals of a national or international labor union, or is based on coverage under one or more collective bargaining agreements. In addition, under the existing regulations, employees of one or more employers engaged in the same line of business in the same geographic locale are considered to share an employment-related common bond.

Questions have arisen about the geographic extent of a single "geographic locale." In its report on the Deficit Reduction Act of 1984, Pub. L. No. 98-369, 98 Stat. 494, the House Ways and Means Committee described the effect of the geographic locale restriction affecting VEBAs as follows:

Under [the] standards [prescribed in the regulations], for example, a group of car dealers in the same city or other similarly restricted geographical locale could form a VEBA to provide permissible benefits to their employees.

H.R. Rep. No. 432, Part II, 98th Cong., 2d Sess. 1285.

Administratively, the Internal Revenue Service has treated employers located in any one state as located in the same geographic locale. The Service has also treated a single standard metropolitan statistical area (SMSA), as defined by the Bureau of the Census, as a single geographic locale, even though the boundaries of some SMSAs include portions of more than one state.

In 1986, the United States Court of Appeals for the Seventh Circuit held the geographic locale restriction invalid in *Water Quality Association Employees' Benefit Corp. v. United States*, 795 F.2d 1303 (7th Cir. 1986). The court agreed with the Government's argument that the existence of an employment-related common bond is the essential factor that distinguishes a tax-exempt VEBA from a taxable insurance company, but concluded that restricting VEBAs covering employees of unrelated employers to those employers located in the same geographic locale did not enhance the employment-related bond of the employees participating in the organization.

The preamble to the final regulations published as T.D. 7750, 1981-1 C.B. 338 (46 F. R. 1719 (January 7, 1981)), explains the reason why the Secretary decided to retain the geographic locale restriction despite comments from the public requesting its deletion from the final regulations. In relevant part, the preamble states:

First, section 501(c)(9) provides for the exemption of associations of employees who enjoy some employment related bond. Allowing section 501(c)(9) to be used as a tax-exempt vehicle for offering insurance products to unrelated individuals scattered throughout the country would undermine those provisions of the Internal Revenue Code that prescribe the income tax treatment of insurance companies. Second, it is the position of the Internal Revenue Service that where an organization such as a national trade association or business league exempt from taxation under section 501(c)(6) operates a group insurance program for its members, the organization is engaged in an unrelated trade or business. *See* Rev. Rul. 66-151, 1966-1 C.B. 152; Rev. Rul. 73-386, 1973-2 C.B. 191; Rev. Rul. 78-52, 1978-1 C.B. 166. To allow trade associations to provide insurance benefits through a trust exempt under section 501(c)(9) would simply facilitate circumvention of the unrelated trade or business income tax otherwise applicable to such organizations.

These restrictions are consistent with the history of section 501(c)(9) of the Code. As Kenneth W. Gideon, then Assistant Secretary of the Treasury for Tax Policy, said in testimony before the Subcommittee on Taxation of the Senate Finance Committee on September 10, 1991, the VEBA tax exemption was originally intended to benefit associations formed and managed by employees of a single employer, or of small local groups of employers, to provide certain welfare benefits to their members in situations where such benefits would not otherwise have been available. *Tax Simplification Bills: Hearings on S. 1364, S. 1394, and H.R. 2777 Before the Subcommittee on Taxation of the Senate Committee on Finance*, 102d Cong., 1st Sess., 260-261. In 1928, when the predecessor of section 501(c)(9) of the Code was enacted as section 103(16) of the Revenue Act of 1928, 45 Stat; 791, the prevalent form of "mutual benefit association" that provided welfare benefits to employees was an organization providing benefits to the employees of a single establishment, such as an industrial plant. National Industrial Conference Board, *The Present Status of Mutual Benefit Associations*, 1-2, 50-51 (1931). At the time, there was concern that, although these organizations performed valuable social functions, they might not be able to continue to exist without a tax exemption. By contrast, larger associations covering employees of unrelated employers in different geographic areas are more likely to be viable without a tax exemption, and the benefits they provide are more likely to be available through commercial insurance. *Tax Simplification Bills, supra*, at 260. In general, when Congress exempts a class of organizations from income tax, it is deemed to have referred to the existing organizations of that class at the time the exemption was adopted. *United States v. Cambridge Loan and Building Co.*, 278 U.S. 55, 58 (1928). Thus, the absence of large regional or national organizations among the class of organizations known as VEBAs or "mutual benefit associations" that were dedicated to providing welfare benefits to employees in 1928 is relevant in determining the proper scope of the exemption granted by section 501(c)(9) of the Code.

The factors cited in the preamble to the 1981 regulations for imposing a geographic locale restriction on the membership of VEBAs that include employees of unrelated employers are matters of continuing concern today. Because of these factors and the history of section 501(c)(9), the proposed regulations limit the geographic region within which unrelated employers must be engaged in the same line of business in order for employees of those lines of business to participate in a single VEBA to the minimum area that is consistent with enabling all employees of employers engaged in a particular line of business to participate in an economically feasible VEBA. If VEBA participation were always limited to employees of employers located in the same state or SMSA, however, the diversity of regional population density and employment patterns in the United States could make it infeasible in many cases for benefits to be provided through a VEBA. Accordingly, the proposed regulations afford a safe harbor that treats any three contiguous states as a single geographic locale, and they authorize the Commissioner of Internal Revenue to recognize larger areas as a single geographic locale on a case-by-case basis upon application by an organization seeking recognition as a VEBA. Thus, the Commissioner may recognize an organization as a VEBA under section 501(c)(9), even though its members are employed by unrelated employers engaged in the same line of business located in any number of states, whether or not contiguous. To obtain recognition as a VEBA under this discretionary authority, the applicant must show (1) that it would not be economically feasible to cover employees of employers engaged in that line of business in the states to be included in the proposed VEBA under two or more separate VEBAs, and (2) either that the states to be included are all contiguous, or that there are legitimate reasons supporting the inclusion of those particular states.

During the drafting of these proposed regulations consideration was given to a rule that would allow an area to be treated as a single geographic locale even though it included areas outside the United States. It is not clear, however, whether it is necessary or desirable to include such a rule. Comments are invited about the extent, if any, to which the regulations should allow the inclusion of areas outside the United States in a single geographic locale.

Proposed Effective Date

These regulations are proposed to be effective on August 7, 1992; however, taxpayers may treat the rules as applicable to prior years.

Special Analyses

It has been determined that these rules are not major rules as defined in Executive Order 12291. Therefore, a Regulatory Impact Analysis is not required. It has also been determined that section 553(b) of the Administrative Procedure Act (5 U.S.C. chapter 5) and the Regulatory Flexibility Act (5 U.S.C. chapter 6) do not apply to these proposed regulations and, therefore, an initial Regulatory Flexibility Analysis is not required. Pursuant to section 7805(f) of the Internal Revenue Code, these regulations will be submitted to the Chief Counsel for Advocacy of the Small Business Administration for comment on their impact on small business.

Comments and Public Hearing

Before these proposed regulations are adopted as final regulations, consideration will be given to any written comments that are submitted timely (preferably an original and eight copies) to the Internal Revenue Service. All comments will be available for public inspection and copying.

A public hearing will be held on Thursday, December 3, 1992, at 1:00 p.m. in the Internal Revenue Service Auditorium, Internal Revenue Building, 1111 Constitution Avenue, N.W. Washington, DC. The rules of § 601.601(a)(3) of the "Statement of Procedural Rules" (26 CFR part 601) shall apply to the public hearing.

Persons who have submitted written comments by October 6, 1992, and who also desire to present oral comments at the hearing on the proposed regulations, should submit, not later than November 12, 1992, a request to speak and an outline of the oral comments to be presented at the hearing stating the time they wish to devote to each subject.

Each speaker (or group of speakers representing a single entity) will be limited to 10 minutes for an oral presentation exclusive of the time consumed by the questions from the panel for the government and answers thereto.

Because of controlled access restrictions, attendees cannot be admitted beyond the lobby of the Internal Revenue Building before 12:45 p.m.

An agenda showing the scheduling of the speakers will be made after outlines are received from the persons testifying. Copies of the agenda will be available free of charge at the hearing.

Drafting Information

The principal author of these proposed regulations is Michael J. Roach, Office of the Associate Chief Counsel (Employee Benefits and Exempt Organizations), Internal Revenue Service. However, personnel from other offices of the Service and the Treasury Department participated in their development.

[¶ 49,130] **Proposed Regulations (PS-55-89)**, published in the Federal Register on August 31, 1992.

MACRS: General asset accounts.—Amendments to Reg. § 1.56(g)-1, relating to the election to maintain general asset accounts for depreciable assets to which Code Sec. 168 applies, are proposed. Reg. § § 1.168(i)-0 and 1.168(i)-1 adopted by T.D. 8566 on October 7, 1994.

AGENCY: Internal Revenue Service, Treasury.

ACTION: Notice of proposed rulemaking.

SUMMARY: This document contains proposed regulations on the election to maintain general asset accounts for depreciable assets to which section 168 of the Internal Revenue Code applies. Changes to the applicable tax law were made by the Tax Reform Act of 1986. The regulations will simplify certain depreciation calculations.

DATES: Written comments must be received by October 15, 1992. Requests to speak (with outlines of oral comments to be presented) at a public hearing scheduled for 10 a.m. on November 4, 1992, must be received by October 14, 1992.

ADDRESSES: Send comments and requests to speak (with outlines of oral comments to be presented) at the public hearing to: Internal Revenue Service, P.O. Box 7604, Ben Franklin Station, Washington, D.C. 20044 (Attn: CC:CORP:T:R (PS-55-89), Room 5228)

FOR FURTHER INFORMATION CONTACT: Concerning the hearing, Carol Savage at (202) 622-8452 (not a toll-free number); concerning the regulations, Kathleen Reed at (202) 622-3110 (not a toll-free number).

SUPPLEMENTARY INFORMATION:

Paperwork Reduction Act

The collection of information requirement contained in this notice of proposed rulemaking has been submitted to the Office of Management and Budget for review in accordance with the Paperwork Reduction Act of 1980 (44 U.S.C 3504(h)). Comments on the collection of information should be sent to the Office of Management and Budget, Attention: Desk Officer for the Department of the Treasury, Office of Information and Regulatory Affairs, Washington, D.C. 20503, with copies to the Internal Revenue Service, Attention: IRS Reports Clearance Officer T:FP, Washington, D.C. 20224.

The collection of information in this regulation is in proposed regulation § 1.168(i)-1(g)(3). This information is required by the Internal Revenue Service to monitor compliance with the election requirement of section 168(i)(4) of the Internal Revenue Code. The likely respondents or recordkeepers are individuals, businesses, and other for-profit institutions.

These estimates are an approximation of the average time expected to be necessary for a collection of information. They are based on such information as is available to the Internal Revenue Service. Individual respondents or recordkeepers may require more or less time depending on their particular circumstances. Estimated total annual reporting and recordkeeping burden: 250 hours.

The estimated annual burden per respondent or recordkeeper varies from .20 to .30 hours, depending on individual circumstances, with an estimated average of .25 hours. Estimated number of respondents and recordkeepers: *1,000.*

Estimated annual frequency of responses: One.

Background

This document contains proposed amendments to the Income Tax Regulations (26 CFR 1) under section 168(i)(4) of the Internal Revenue Code (Code) reflecting amendments made by section 201 of the Tax Reform Act of 1986. The amendments are to be issued under the authority contained in sections 168(i)(4) and 7805 of the Code.

Explanation of Provisions

The proposed regulations would simplify the computation of depreciation by allowing taxpayers to elect to group assets in one or more general asset accounts under section 168(i)(4) of the Code. The assets in any particular general asset account are depreciated as a single asset.

The proposed regulations provide that a general asset account includes assets that have the same asset class, depreciation method, recovery period, and convention and that are placed in service in the same taxable year. Assets subject to the general depreciation system of section 168(a) of the Code or the alternative depreciation system of section 168(g) may be accounted for in general asset accounts. Unlike the rules under section 168 as in existence before enactment of the Tax Reform Act of 1986, general asset account treatment is not limited to "mass assets."

An asset may not be placed in a general asset account if a credit is determined under section 47 or 48 of the Code or if the asset initially is used both in a trade or business (or for the production of income) and in a personal activity. If investment credit assets were included, additional rules would be required to redetermine the basis of the general asset account for any recapture amount determined under section 50. The Service concluded that the added complexity of these rules is not warranted under the circumstances; however, taxpayers are invited to comment on this matter.

In addition, assets that are used predominantly outside the United States or that give rise to depreciation deductions that are apportioned in whole or in part to foreign source income may not be placed in a general asset account. The inclusion of such assets would present substantial difficulties in applying other provisions of the Code, such as the rules of section 864(e) of the Code for apportioning the deduction for interest expense and the rules of section 865(c) for determining the source of gain from the disposition of depreciable personal property. The Service invites comments on how the issues presented by including such assets in a general asset account might be resolved in a manner that would not be unduly burdensome.

As required by section 168(i)(4) of the Code, the proposed regulations provide generally that the amount realized upon the disposition of an asset from a general asset account is recognized as ordinary income. The ordinary income treatment, however, is limited to the unadjusted depreciable basis of the account (determined by disregarding any election made under section 179 or 190 with respect to assets in the account) less any amounts previously recognized as ordinary income at the time of disposition. Any excess amount realized is subject to all other applicable provisions of the Code relating to recognition and character of gain (except the recapture provisions). In computing the depreciation allowance for the account, the unadjusted depreciable basis and the depreciation reserve of the general asset account are not reduced as a result of the disposition.

A special rule is provided for the disposition of all the assets or the last asset from the general asset account. Moreover, the taxpayer may terminate general asset account treatment for a particular asset if the asset is disposed of as the result of a casualty, a charitable contribution, the cessation of a business, or in transactions to which certain nonrecognition sections of the Code apply. For transactions described in section 168(i)(7)(B) of the Code, the transferee generally is bound by the transferor's general asset account election.

The proposed regulations include an anti-abuse rule providing that if an asset in a general asset account is disposed of in certain transactions one of the principal purposes of which is to avoid the limitations imposed under the Code with respect to a net operating loss deduction or the utilization of any credit, the disposition of the asset is treated as though an election under section 168(i)(4) of the Code had never been made for the asset.

The proposed regulations further provide the time and manner in which to make the election to establish general asset accounts. The election generally is irrevocable and is binding on the taxpayer for computing taxable income as well as computing alternative minimum taxable income.

Finally, the proposed regulations provide that these regulations apply to assets placed in service in taxable years ending on or after [the date of publication of the final regulations in the Federal Register]. For prior taxable years, the Service will allow the use of any reasonable method that clearly reflects income and is consistently applied to the general asset accounts.

Special Analyses

It has been determined that these proposed rules are not major rules as defined in Executive Order 12291. Therefore, a Regulatory Impact Analysis is not required. It has also been determined that section 553(b) of the Administrative Procedure Act (5 U.S.C. chapter 5) and the Regulatory Flexibility Act (5 U.S.C. chapter 6) do not apply to these proposed regulations. Therefore, an initial Regulatory Flexibility Analysis is not required. Pursuant to section 7805(f) of the Code, a copy of the rules will be submitted to the Chief Counsel for Advocacy of the Small Business Administration for comment on their impact on small business.

Written Comments and Public Hearing

Before adopting these proposed regulations, consideration will be given to any written comments that are submitted (preferably a signed original and eight copies) to the Internal Revenue Service. All comments will be available for public inspection and copying. The public hearing will be held at 10 a.m. on November 4, 1992. See the notice of public hearing published elsewhere in this issue of the Federal Register.

Drafting Information

The principal author of these proposed regulations is Kathleen Reed, Office of Assistant Chief Counsel (Passthroughs and Special Industries), Internal Revenue Service. However, personnel from other offices of the Internal Revenue Service and Treasury Department participated in their development and style.

[¶49,131]   Proposed Regulations (FI-61-91), published in the Federal Register on September 3, 1992.

REMICs: Reporting requirements: Allocable investment expenses.—Reg. §1.67-3T, relating to reporting requirements with respect to real estate mortgage investment conduits, is proposed.

AGENCY: Internal Revenue Service, Treasury.

ACTION: Notice of proposed rulemaking.

SUMMARY: On March 9, 1988, the Internal Revenue Service issued temporary regulations [T.D. 8186]under section 67 of the Internal Revenue Code relating to reporting requirements with respect to Real Estate Mortgage Investment Conduits (REMICs) that were published in the Rules and Regulations portion of the Federal Register (53 FR 7504). These regulations propose to adopt as final regulations that portion of the temporary regulations under §1.67-3T(a) through (e) (as contained in the CFR edition revised as of April 1, 1992), relating to reporting requirements under section 67 with respect to REMICs. The text of the temporary regulations serves as the comment document for this notice of proposed rulemaking.

DATES: Written comments and requests to speak (with outlines of oral comments) at the public hearing that is scheduled for November 9, 1992, must be received by October 19, 1992. See notice of hearing published elsewhere in this issue of the Federal Register.

ADDRESSES: Send comments, requests to speak at the public hearing, and outlines of oral comments, to: Internal Revenue Service, P.O. Box 7604, Ben Franklin Station, Washington, D.C. 20044, Attn: CC:CORP:T:R (FI-61-91), Room 5228.

FOR FURTHER INFORMATION CONTACT: James W.C. Canup, 202-622-3950 (not a toll-free number).

SUPPLEMENTARY INFORMATION:

Background

On March 9, 1988, temporary regulations [T.D. 8186] under section 67 were published in the Federal Register (53 FR 7504). Section 1.67-3T(f) of those regulations was amended on September 7, 1989 [T.D. 8259](54 FR 37098). Section 1.67-3T(f) of those regulations was also revised on September 30, 1991 [T.D. 8366] (56 FR 49512). In the Rules and Regulations portion of this issue of the Federal Register, the Internal Revenue Service is issuing final regulations under §1.67-3(f). These regulations propose to adopt as final regulations that portion of the temporary regulations under §1.67-3T(a) through (e) (as contained in the CFR edition revised as of April 1, 1992).

Section 132 of the Tax Reform Act of 1986 (the 1986 Act) added to the Internal Revenue Code section 67, which disallows certain miscellaneous itemized deductions in computing the taxable income of an individual to the extent that the aggregate of those deductions does not exceed two percent of the individual's adjusted gross income. Section 67(c) directs that regulations be issued to prohibit the indirect deduction through pass-through entities of amounts that are not allowable as a deduction if paid or incurred directly by an individual. Section 67(c) also directs that regulations provide any necessary reporting requirements. The regulations under section 67 that are contained in this document fulfill the requirements of section 67(c) as it applies to REMICs.

Explanation of Provisions

In general, a REMIC is a fixed pool of mortgages in which multiple classes of interests are held by investors and which elects to be taxed as a REMIC. The regulations under section 67 require notice of income and other information to be provided to REMIC investors and the Internal Revenue Service.

Treatment of allocable investment expenses

Section 1.67-3T(a)(1) requires a REMIC to allocate to each of its pass-through interest holders the holder's proportionate share of the aggregate amount of allocable investment expenses of the REMIC for the calendar quarter. In general, a pass-through interest holder (as defined in §1.67-3T(a)(2)(i)(A)) is any holder of a residual interest that is either an individual (other than certain nonresident aliens), a person that computes its taxable income in the same manner as would an individual, or a pass-through entity, interests in which are owned by either an individual or a person that computes its taxable income in the same manner as would an individual.

The term "pass-through entity" includes, pursuant to §1.67-2T(g), a grantor trust, a partnership, an S corporation, a common trust fund, a nonpublicly offered regulated investment company, and a REMIC. It does not include an estate, a nongrantor trust, a cooperative, a real estate investment trust, or other entities such as a qualified pension plan, an individual retirement account, or an insurance company holding assets in a separate asset account to fund certain variable contracts. The term "allocable investment expenses" (as defined in §1.67-3T(a)(3)) means the aggregate amount of the expenses paid or accrued in the calendar quarter for which a deduction is allowable under section 212 in determining the taxable income of the REMIC for the calendar quarter.

Pursuant to §1.67-3T(b)(1) a pass-through interest holder is treated both as having received or accrued income and as having paid or incurred an expense described in section 212 (or section 162 in the case of a pass-through interest holder that is a regulated investment company) in an amount equal to the pass-through interest holder's proportionate share of the allocable investment expenses of the REMIC.

Under §1.67-3T(b)(1)(i), a pass-through interest holder whose taxable year is the calendar year or ends with a calendar quarter takes into account the amounts in those calendar quarters that fall within the holder's taxable year. Separate inclusion rules apply under §1.67-3T(b)(1)(ii) to a holder whose taxable year does not end with a calendar quarter. An interest holder in a REMIC that is not a pass-through interest holder does not take into account in computing its taxable income any amount of its proportionate share of allocable investment expenses. Under §1.67-3T(c)(1), a REMIC generally computes a pass-through interest holder's proportionate share of its allocable investment expenses by determining the daily amount of such expenses and allocating this daily amount to the pass-through interest holder in proportion to its respective holdings on that day. Generally, a pass-through interest holder's proportionate share of the daily amount of the allocable investment expenses is determined by taking into account all holders of REMIC residual interests, whether or not those holders are pass-through interest holders.

Single-class REMICs

In the case of a single-class REMIC (as described in §1.67-3T(a)(2)(ii)), the term "pass-through interest holder" is defined more broadly to include any regular or residual interest holder that is either an individual (other than certain nonresident aliens), a person that computes its taxable income in the same manner as would an individual, or a pass-through entity, interests in which are owned by certain types of holders. Under §1.67-3T(c)(3), a single-class REMIC allocates its investment expenses for a calendar quarter to each holder in proportion to the amount of income that accrues to the holder for that quarter.

Special Analyses

It has been determined that these proposed rules are not major rules as defined in Executive Order 12291. Therefore, a Regulatory Impact Analysis is not required. It has also been determined that section 553(b) of the Administrative Procedure Act (5 U.S.C. chapter 5) and the Regulatory Flexibility Act (5 U.S.C. chapter 6) do not apply to this regulation, and, therefore, an initial Regulatory Flexibility Analysis is not required. Pursuant to section 7805(f) of the Internal Revenue Code, this regulation will be submitted to the Chief Counsel for Advocacy of the Small Business Administration for comment on its impact on small business.

Comments and Requests to Appear at the Public Hearing

Before this proposed regulation is adopted, consideration will be given to any written comments that are timely submitted (preferably a signed original and eight copies) to the Internal Revenue Service. All comments will be available for public inspection and copying in their entirety. A public hearing will be held on November 9, 1992. See the notice of public hearing published elsewhere in this issue of the Federal Register.

Drafting Information

The principal author of the proposed regulation is James W. C. Canup, Office of the Assistant Chief Counsel (Financial Institutions and Products), Internal Revenue Service. However, other personnel from the Service and Treasury Department participated in their development.

Proposal of Regulations

The portion of the temporary regulations (T.D. 8186) under §1.67-3T(a) through (e) (as contained in the CFR edition revised as of April 1, 1992), is hereby also proposed as final regulations under section 67 of the Internal Revenue Code of 1986.

[¶ 49,132]   **Proposed Amendments of Regulations (EE-101-91)**, published in the Federal Register on October 9, 1992.

Fringe benefits: Employer-provided vehicle and fuel: Lease valuation rule.—Amendments to Reg. §1.61-21, relating to the valuation of an employee's personal use of employer-provided fuel when an employer-provided automobile is valued pursuant to the automobile lease valuation rule, are proposed.

AGENCY: Internal Revenue Service, Treasury.

ACTION: Notice of proposed rulemaking

SUMMARY: This document contains proposed amendments relating to the taxation and valuation of fringe benefits under section 61 of the Internal Revenue Code. These proposed amendments update previous guidance concerning the valuation of an employee's personal use of employer-provided fuel when an employer-provided automobile is valued pursuant to the automobile lease valuation rule. The proposed regulations affect employees receiving this fringe benefit and provide guidance to employers and employees to help determine their federal tax liability.

DATES: Written comments and requests for a public hearing must be received by November 9, 1992.

ADDRESSES: Send comments and requests for a public hearing to: Internal Revenue Service, P.O. Box 7604, Ben Franklin Station, Attention: CC:CORP:T:R (EE-lOl-91), Room 5228, Washington, D.C. 20044.

FOR FURTHER INFORMATION CONTACT: Marianna Dyson, at 202-622-4606 (not a toll-free number).

SUPPLEMENTARY INFORMATION:

Background

This document contains proposed amendments to the Income Tax Regulations (26 CFR part 1) under section 61 of the Internal Revenue Code of 1986 (Code). The amendments pertain to the valuation of employer-provided fuel under the automobile lease valuation rule of §1.61-21(d) of the regulations.

Explanation of Provisions

The final fringe benefit regulations issued in July 1989 and effective for benefits furnished on or after January 1, 1989, provide that in valuing the personal use of automobiles under §1.61-21(d) of the regulations, the Annual Lease Values do not include the fair market value of fuel provided by the employer. Thus, fuel consumed for any personal miles driven must be valued separately for inclusion in income. Section 1.61-21(d)(3)(ii)(A).

Under §1.61-21(d)(3)(ii)(B), employer-paid fuel provided *in kind* to employees for personal use may be valued at fair market value or, in the alternative, at 5.5 cents per mile. If the cost of the fuel is reimbursed by or charged to an employer, the value of the fuel is its fair market value, which is generally the amount of the actual reimbursement or amount charged, provided the purchase of the fuel is at arm's-length. Section 1.61-21(d)(3)(ii)(C).

For employers with fleets of at least 20 automobiles, §1.61-21(d)(3)(ii)(D) sets forth two additional methods for valuing fuel for personal use. The general method provides that employers who reimburse employees for the cost of fuel or allow employees to charge the employer for the cost of fuel may value the fuel by reference to the employer's "fleet-average cents-per-mile fuel cost." The fleet-average cents-per-mile fuel cost is equal to the fleet-average per-gallon fuel cost divided by the fleet-average miles-per-gallon rate. The average per-gallon fuel cost and the miles-per-gallon rate are determined by averaging the per-gallon fuel costs and miles-per-gallon rates of a representative sample of the automobiles in the fleet equal to the greater of ten percent of the automobiles in the fleet or 20 automobiles for a representative period. Section 1.61-21(d)(3)(ii)(D).

In lieu of calculating the "fleet-average cents-per-mile fuel cost" under the general method of paragraph (d)(3)(ii)(D) of §1.61-21, employers with fleets of at least 20 automobiles that use the fleet-average valuation rule of paragraph (d)(5)(D) may use the 5.5 cents-per-mile option of paragraph (d)(3)(ii)(B), if determining the amount of the actual reimbursement or the amount charged for the purchase of fuel would impose unreasonable administrative burdens on the employer ("the alternative method").

In no event, however, may an employer with a fleet of at least 20 automobiles use either the general or alternative method of paragraph (d)(3)(ii)(D) of §1.61-21 unless the requirements of paragraph (d)(5)(v)(D) are also met. This paragraph contains the rules for using a fleet-average value in calculating the Annual Lease Values of the automobiles in the fleet. In particular, it specifies that the fair market value of each vehicle in the fleet may not exceed $16,500 (as adjusted pursuant to section 280F(d)(7) of the Code).

For calendar years prior to 1991, Notice 89-110, 1989-2 C.B. 447, expanded the availability of the 5.5 cents-per-mile option to employers with fleets of at least 20 automobiles that satisfy the requirements of paragraph (d)(5)(v)(D), regardless of whether they are actually using the fleet-average valuation rule of paragraph (d)(5)(v). Notice 91-41, 1991-51 I.R.B. 63, provides that the 5.5 cents-per-mile option as provided in Notice 89-110 is available in calendar year 1991.

Notice 89-110 did not eliminate the requirement that the employer must demonstrate that it is using the 5.5 cents-per-mile option because determining the amount of the actual reimbursement or the amount charged for the purchase of fuel would impose unreasonable administrative burdens on the employer. As a practical matter, however, it is believed that fleet operators with at least 20 automobiles would have little difficulty in demonstrating the existence of unreasonable administrative burdens.

The proposed amendments to §1.61-21(d)(3)(ii) provide that, for calendar year 1992, employers with fleets of at least 20 automobiles may continue to use the 5.5 cents-per-mile rate as provided in Notice 89-110 and extended in Notice 91-41. In addition, the proposed amendments provide that employers with fleets of at least 20 automobiles may value fuel that is reimbursed by or charged to the employer by reference to the alternative cents-per-mile rate without regard to the rules in paragraph (d)(5)(v)(D) concerning the value of automobiles in the fleet, and without the necessity of demonstrating the existence of administrative burdens.

Finally, the proposed amendments provide that for calendar years subsequent to 1992 the Service will announce the appropriate cents-per-mile rate for valuing fuel that is provided in kind or that is reimbursed by or charged to employers with fleets of at least 20 automobiles. The announcement will appear in the annual revenue procedure concerning the optional standard mileage rates used in computing deductible costs of operating a passenger automobile for business.

The rules under paragraph (d)(3)(ii) of §1.61-21, as amended by this Notice, will enable employers with fleets of at least 20 automobiles to value the personal use of employer-paid fuel in any of the following ways: (1) fuel provided in kind may be valued at fair market value based on all the facts and circumstances; (2) fuel that is provided in kind may be valued at the cents-per-mile rate applicable to the particular year; (3) fuel, the cost of which is reimbursed by or charged to the employer, may be valued based on the amount of the actual reimbursement or the amount charged; (4) fuel, the cost of which is reimbursed by or charged to the employer, may be valued based on the fleet-average cents-per-mile fuel cost; or (5) fuel, the cost of which is reimbursed by or charged to the employer, may be valued based on the applicable cents-per-mile rate without regard to the fair market value of any automobile in the fleet or the administrative burdens requirement.

The amendments are proposed to be effective for benefits provided in calendar years beginning after December 31, 1992. However, because of the number of inquiries the Service has received from taxpayers expressing uncertainty as to the scope of the guidance in Notice 89-110 concerning employer-provided fuel, the amendments may be relied upon as if they had been included in the final regulations published on July 6, 1989.

Special Analyses

It has been determined that these rules are not major rules as defined in Executive Order 12291. Therefore, a Regulatory Impact Analysis is not required. It has also been determined that section 553(b) of the Administrative Procedure Act (5 U.S.C. chapter 5) and the Regulatory Flexibility Act (5 U.S.C. chapter 6) do not apply to these regulations, and, therefore, an initial Regulatory Flexibility Analysis is not required. Pursuant to section 7805(f) of the Internal Revenue Code, these regulations will be submitted to the Chief Counsel for Advocacy of the Small Business Administration for comment on their impact on small business.

Comments and Requests to Appear at a Public Hearing

Before adopting these proposed regulations, consideration will be given to any written comments that are submitted (preferably a signed original and eight copies) to the Internal Revenue Service. All comments will be available for public inspection and copying in their entirety. A public hearing will be held upon written request to the Commissioner by any person who has submitted written comments. Written comments and requests for a hearing must be received by November 9, 1992. If a public hearing is held, notice of the time and place will be published in the Federal Register.

Drafting Information

The principal author of these regulations is Marianna Dyson, Office of the Associate Chief Counsel (Employee Benefits and Exempt Organizations), Internal Revenue Service. However, personnel from other offices of the Service and Treasury Department participated in their development.

[¶49,134] **Proposed Regulations (FI-25-92)**, published in the Federal Register on December 15, 1992.

Life insurance contracts: Qualified accelerated death benefits.—Reg. §§1.101-8, 1.7702-0, 1.7702-2, and 1.7702A-1, relating to the definition of a life insurance contract for federal tax purposes and the tax treatment of amounts received as qualified accelerated death benefits, are **proposed.**

AGENCY: Internal Revenue Service, Treasury.

ACTION: Notice of proposed rulemaking.

SUMMARY: This document provides proposed regulations relating to the definition of a life insurance contract for federal tax purposes and to the federal income tax treatment of amounts received as qualified accelerated death benefits. These proposed regulations are necessary to provide guidance to insurance companies and their policyholders.

DATES: Written comments, requests to speak, and outlines of oral arguments to be presented at the hearing scheduled for March 19, 1993, at 10:00 a.m. in the Internal Revenue Service Auditorium, must be received by February 26, 1993. See notice of hearing published elsewhere in this issue of the **Federal Register.**

ADDRESSES: Send submissions to: Internal Revenue Service, P.O. Box 7604, Ben Franklin Station, Attention: CC:CORP:T:R (FI-25-92), Room 5228, Washington, D.C. 20044.

FOR FURTHER INFORMATION CONTACT: Concerning the regulations, Ann H. Logan, 202-622-3970 (not a toll-free number). Concerning the hearing, Mike Slaughter of the Regulations Unit, 202-622-7190 (not a toll-free number).

SUPPLEMENTARY INFORMATION:

Background

This document sets forth proposed amendments to the Income Tax Regulations (26 CFR part 1) under sections 101, 7702, and 7702A of the Internal Revenue Code (Code). The proposed rules relate to the definition of a life insurance contract under section 7702 of the Internal Revenue Code, to the treatment of a life insurance contract under section 7702A, and to the federal income tax treatment of amounts received as qualified accelerated death benefits under section 101. The proposed regulations reflect the addition of section 7702 to the Code by section 221(a) of the Tax Reform Act of 1984, Pub. L. 98-369, and the addition of section 7702A to the Code by section 5012 of the Technical and Miscellaneous Revenue Act of 1988, Pub. L. 100-647.

Purpose of Regulations

The proposed regulations provide insurers with the standards needed to design and market insurance contracts that provide both death benefits and morbidity benefits without subjecting policyholders to taxation on the inside build-up of the life insurance contracts.

In recognition of the needs of individuals who become terminally ill, the proposed regulations also allow the payment of benefits prior to death without any income tax liability to the recipient if death is expected to occur within 12 months.

For insurance contracts that, prior to July 1, 1993, provide for a benefit or loan for terminally ill individuals or a morbidity benefit, the proposed regulations provide transition rules that prevent the benefit or loan from resulting in adverse federal tax consequences to the policyholders and avoid the reporting and withholding requirements that would be imposed upon the insurers if the contracts were to fail to qualify as life insurance contracts. *See* Rev. Rul. 91-17, 1991-1 C.B. 190.

Summary of Relevant Statutory Provisions

Section 7702 defines a "life insurance contract" as any contract that is a life insurance contract under applicable law, but only if the contract either (1) meets the cash value accumulation test of section 7702(b), or (2) meets the guideline premium requirements of section 7702(c) and falls within the cash value corridor of section 7702(d).

The cash value accumulation test of section 7702(b) requires that, by the terms of the contract, the cash surrender value of the contract may not at any time exceed the net single premium that would have to be paid at that time to fund the future benefits under the contract. "Cash surrender value" for purposes of section 7702 is defined in section 7702(f)(2)(A) as the cash value of the contract determined without regard to any surrender charge, policy loan, or reasonable termination dividends. The "net single premium" must be determined using the assumptions, computational rules, definitions, and special rules contained in section 7702.

The guideline premium limitation of section 7702(c) provides that the premiums paid under the contract at any time must not exceed the greater of the guideline single premium or the sum of the guideline level premiums to that date. Contracts qualifying as life insurance under the guideline premium test also must satisfy the cash value corridor of section 7702(d). The corridor specifies a minimum ratio of death benefits to cash surrender values.

Section 7702(f)(7) provides for adjustments in determinations made under section 7702 if there is a change in the benefits under (or in other terms of) the contract which was not reflected in any previous determination or adjustment. A reduction in death benefits is an adjustment event under section 7702(f)(7). Qualification as a life insurance contract after an adjustment event requires redetermination of values under the contract, including the net single premium, the guideline premium limitation, and the cash value corridor, depending on the test under which the contract qualifies as life insurance.

Section 7702(g) governs the federal income tax treatment of a life insurance contract under applicable law that fails to meet the definition of a life insurance contract under section 7702(a), either at inception or at a later date. In general, under section 7702(g)(1)(A), the "income on the contract" is treated as ordinary income that is received or accrued annually by the policyholder.

Section 7702A(a) defines a modified endowment contract as a life insurance contract meeting the requirements of section 7702 which is entered into on or after June 21, 1988 and which fails to meet the 7-pay test of section 7702A(b) or a life insurance contract which is received in exchange for a modified endowment contract.

Section 7702A(c)(3)(A)(i) provides that, if there is a "material change" within the meaning of section 7702A(c)(3) to a life insurance contract that is subject to section 7702A, the contract is treated as entered into on the day that the material change takes effect. A material change in the benefits under (or in other terms of) the contract includes any increase in the death benefit under the contract or any increase in, or addition of, a qualified additional benefit under the contract.

Section 101(a) provides in part that gross income does not include amounts received (whether in a single sum or otherwise) under a life insurance contract, if the amounts are paid by reason of the death of the insured.

Section 72(c)(1) defines investment in the contract for purposes of determining the exclusion ratio for amounts received as an annuity under an annuity, endowment, or life insurance contract. Section 72(e)(6) defines investment in the contract for amounts received under an annuity, endowment, or life insurance contract if the amount is not received as an annuity and no other income tax provision applies. *See* Rev. Rul. 55-349, 1955-1 C.B. 232, (premiums for supplementary benefits excluded from the investment in the contract).

New Insurance Contracts

Insurance companies have developed insurance contracts which provide both death benefits and "living benefits" designed to assist policyholders with the rising costs of medical care, particularly medical care in the later years of life. Living benefits generally may be divided into two types of benefits. The first type of living benefit, an "accelerated death benefit," addresses the needs of terminally ill individuals who may incur substantial medical and living expenses prior to death. This benefit allows the policyholder, under a life insurance contract insuring a terminally ill individual, to "accelerate" the death benefit paid under the contract. Generally, the accelerated death benefit is equal to all or a portion of the death benefit discounted for the remaining life expectancy (generally 12 months or less) of the terminally ill individual. The payment of a benefit is conditioned upon the policyholder surrendering all or a portion of the policyholder's rights under the life insurance contract.

A second type of living benefit provides accident and health benefits upon the occurrence of certain morbidity risks, for example, a condition requiring a long-term stay in a nursing home or certain dread diseases. The living benefit is a specified amount which is determined by reference to all or a portion of the death benefit otherwise payable. As with accelerated death benefits, the payment of a benefit is conditioned upon the policyholder surrendering all or a portion of the policyholder's rights under the life insurance contract.

Explanation of Provisions

The proposed regulations are being promulgated to provide guidance concerning the tax treatment to the owners and issuers of insurance contracts that provide living benefits by addressing the application of sections 72, 101, 7702, and 7702A to those insurance contracts.

The proposed regulations allow qualified accelerated death benefits under an insurance contract to be treated as amounts paid by reason of the death of the insured for purposes of sections 101(a) and 7702. This proposed treatment allows an insurance contract including these benefits to continue to meet the definition of a life insurance contract under section 7702. The proposed regulations also permit a person who receives a qualified accelerated death benefit to exclude, under section 101(a), the benefit from gross income.

A qualified accelerated death benefit is defined in the proposed regulations as a benefit payable under a contract on the life of an insured who becomes terminally ill, where the amount of the death benefit made available cannot be discounted by more than 12 months at the rate of interest specified in the regulations. Under the proposed regulations an individual is terminally ill if the individual has an illness or physical condition that, notwithstanding appropriate medical care, is reasonably expected to result in death within 12 months from the date of payment of the accelerated death benefit. As the 12 month determination is necessarily subjective to some extent, it is expected that the insurer will act prudently in its determination of whether the person is terminally ill. The Service is considering whether to develop further guidance that would create a presumption of terminal illness in certain circumstances.

The proposed regulations also address the treatment, under section 7702, of other living benefits that provide payments upon the occurrence of a morbidity risk of an amount determined by reference to all or a portion of the death benefit otherwise payable under an insurance contract. For purposes of section 7702, the benefit could be viewed as an amount paid upon surrender of a contract and accordingly would be included in the cash surrender value of the contract. The impact of this characterization would be to disqualify as life insurance under section 7702 many contracts providing these benefits. Contracts with large cash surrender values would no longer qualify under the cash value accumulation test of section 7702(b) while contracts qualifying under the guideline premium test of section 7702(c) would fail the cash value corridor test of section 7702(d). For example, a policyholder, age 37, might own an insurance contract with a $100,000 face amount, that also provides for a payment of $70,000 upon surrender of the contract if the policyholder is hospitalized for a specified number of days. The $70,000 hospital benefit could result in the failure of the contract to qualify as a life insurance contract under section 7702.

To enable policyholders to avoid this result, the proposed regulations adopt an approach which assumes that a life insurance contract and an accident and health insurance contract which could be sold separately should be allowed to be sold together without endangering the qualification of the contract offering both benefits as a life insurance contract under section 7702. To preserve qualification of the contract offering both benefits as a life insurance contract, the proposed regulations exclude amounts payable as additional benefits (other than qualified additional benefits) from cash value if the following conditions are satisfied: (1) the benefits are paid solely upon the occurrence of a morbidity risk, (2) the charges for the benefits are separately stated and currently imposed by the insurer, and (3) the charges are not included in premiums taken into account in the determination of the investment in the contract under section 72 and are not taken into account in the determination of premiums paid under section 7702(f)(1).

If the three conditions are met, the proposed regulations treat a life insurance contract with an additional accident and health benefit as providing both a potential death benefit and a potential living benefit which is paid upon the occurrence of a morbidity risk. The living benefit is treated as being comprised of two elements: (1) a payment upon the partial or full surrender of the life insurance contract for part or all of the cash value, and (2) a payment upon the occurrence of a morbidity event of an additional accident and health benefit equal to the difference between the total payment received and the amount received by the policyholder on the full or partial surrender of the contract. If, however, the three conditions are not satisfied, the additional benefit will not be excluded from cash value under section 7702.

The requirement that morbidity risk charges for living benefits be separately stated and currently imposed by the terms of the life insurance contract is necessary if section 7702 is to operate in the manner intended by Congress. Providing for the proper allocation and treatment of charges for these contracts assures the appropriate treatment of amounts paid into the contract and benefits paid.

The approach in the proposed regulations is intended to level the playing field between contracts that provide accident and health benefits in conjunction with life insurance benefits and contracts that provide only accident and health benefits. Thus, the approach of the proposed regulations will allow a contract providing both accident and health and life insurance benefits to continue to qualify as a life insurance contract under section 7702 so long as the contract provides appropriate treatment of the charges for the accident and health benefits.

The proposed regulations also exclude from cash value qualified additional benefits, certain amounts returned upon termination of a credit life insurance contract, and reasonable termination dividend.

The proposed regulations define cash surrender value, net surrender value, and death benefit for purposes of section 7702.

Proposed Effective Dates

The proposed regulations under section 7702, relating to the definition of cash value and the tax treatment of certain benefits, would be effective generally for contracts issued or entered into after June 30, 1993.

Under the proposed regulations, the provision of certain benefits or loans in a life insurance contract before July 1, 1993, does not increase the cash value of the contract. The proposed regulations also provide that the addition to a life insurance contract, before July 1, 1993, of certain benefits or loans has no effect on the date that the contract was issued or entered into for purposes of section 7702 and 7702A, and does not cause a material change in the contract under section 7702A.

The addition of a qualified accelerated death benefit (or an additional benefit satisfying the three conditions specified in proposed § 1.7702-2(f)) to a life insurance contract at any time has no effect on the date that the contract was issued or entered into for purposes of section 7702 and 7702A, and does not cause a material change in the contract under section 7702A.

The section 101 exclusion provided by the proposed regulations for qualified accelerated death benefits would be effective for amounts received on or after the date on which final regulations defining a qualified accelerated death benefit are published in the Federal Register.

Special Analyses

It has been determined that these proposed rules are not major rules as defined in Executive Order 12291. Therefore, a Regulatory Impact Analysis is not required. It has also been determined that section 553(b) of the Administrative Procedure Act (5 U.S.C. chapter 5) and the Regulatory Flexibility Act (5 U.S.C. chapter 6) do not apply to these regulations, and, therefore, an initial Regulatory Flexibility Analysis is not required. Pursuant to section 7805(f) of the Internal Revenue Code, the proposed regulations will be submitted to the Chief Counsel for Advocacy of the Small Business Administration for comment on their impact on small business.

Comments and Request for a Public Hearing

Before the adoption of these proposed regulations, consideration will be given to any written comments that are timely submitted (preferably a signed original and eight copies) to the Internal Revenue Service.

Comments are specifically requested on the need for special rules under section 7702(f)(7) for contracts that do not terminate upon payment of a morbidity benefit or a qualified accelerated death benefit. Comments are also requested on whether the proposed regulations treat additional benefits insuring morbidity risks that are attached to a life insurance contract in the same fashion as contracts which provide similar benefits that are not attached to a life insurance contract. Finally, comments are requested on whether the regulations should specify how premiums and charges should be allocated among the various benefits provided under a life insurance contract.

All comments will be available for public inspection and copying in their entirety. A public hearing has been scheduled for March 19, 1993. See notice of hearing published elsewhere in this issue of the Federal Register.

Drafting Information

The principal author of these proposed regulations is Ann H. Logan, Office of the Assistant Chief Counsel (Financial Institutions and Products), Office of Chief Counsel, Internal Revenue Service. However, personnel from other offices of the Service and the Treasury Department participated in developing the regulations, in matters of both substance and style.

[¶ 49,136]   Proposed Regulations and Proposed Amendments of Regulations (FI-189-84), published in the Federal Register on December 22, 1992.

Debt instruments: Imputed interest: Original issue discount: Sale or exchange of property.—Reg. §§1.163-7, 1.446-2, 1.483-1—1.483-3, 1.1271-1, 1.1272-1, 1.1272-2, 1.1272-3, 1.1273-1, 1.1273-2, 1.1274-1, 1.1274-2, 1.1274-3, 1.1274-4, 1.1274-5, 1.1274A-1, 1.1275-1, 1.1275-2, 1.1275-3 and 1.1275-5, and amendments of Reg. §§1.1001-1 and 1.1012-1, relating to the tax treatment of debt instruments with original issue discount and the imputation of interest on deferred payments under certain contracts for the sale or exchange of property, were adopted on 1/27/94 by T.D. 8517. Reg. §1.446-2(e)(3) is still proposed.

AGENCY: Internal Revenue Service, Treasury.

ACTION: Notice of proposed rulemaking.

SUMMARY: This document contains proposed regulations relating to the tax treatment of debt instruments with original issue discount and the imputation of interest on deferred payments under certain contracts for the sale or exchange of property. The proposed regulations in this document revise some of the proposed regulations that were published in the Federal Register on April 8, 1986. The proposed regulations would provide needed guidance to holders and issuers of debt instruments with original issue discount and to buyers and sellers of property.

DATES: A public hearing on these proposed regulations is scheduled for 10:00 a.m. on February 16, 1993, in room 3313 at 1111 Constitution Ave., N.W., Washington, D.C. Requests to appear at the public hearing and outlines of oral comments must be received by January 26, 1993. Written comments must be received by January 26, 1993. See notice of hearing published elsewhere in this issue of the Federal Register.

ADDRESSES: Send comments, requests to appear, and outlines of oral comments to: Internal Revenue Service, P.O. Box 7604, Ben Franklin Station, Attn: CC:CORP:T:R (FI-189-84), Room 5228, Washington, D.C. 20044.

FOR FURTHER INFORMATION CONTACT: Frederick S. Campbell-Mohn, 202-622-3940 (not a toll-free number), William E. Blanchard, 202-622-3950 (not a toll-free number), or Andrew C. Kittler, 202-622-3940 (not a toll-free number).

SUPPLEMENTARY INFORMATION:

Paperwork Reduction Act

The collection of information requirements contained in this notice of proposed rulemaking has been submitted to the Office of Management and Budget for review in accordance with the Paperwork Reduction Act of 1980 (44 U.S.C. 3504(h)). Comments on the collection of information should be sent to the Office of Management and Budget, Attn: Desk Officer for the Department of the Treasury, Office of Information and Regulatory Affairs, Washington, D.C. 20503, with copies to the Internal Revenue Service, Attn: IRS Reports Clearance Officer T:FP, Washington, D.C. 20224.

The required collections of information in this regulation are in §§1.1272-1(d)(2)(iii), 1.1272-3, 1.1273-2(f)(2), 1.1274-3(d), 1.1274-5(b), 1.1274A-1(c), and 1.1275-3(b). This information is required by the Internal Revenue Service in connection with tracking the accrual of original issue discount. This information will be used for audit and examination purposes. The likely respondents are businesses or other for-profit institutions.

These estimates are an approximation of the average time expected to be necessary for a collection of information. They are based on such information as is available to the Internal Revenue Service. Individual respondents may require more or less time, depending on their particular circumstances.

Estimated total reporting burden: 289,500 hours.

The estimated burden per respondent varies from .3 to .5 hours, depending on individual circumstances, with an estimated average of .4 hours.

Estimated number of respondents: 750,000.

Estimated annual frequency of responses: 1.

Background

On April 8, 1986, the Federal Register published a notice of proposed rulemaking (51 FR 12022) relating to original issue discount (OID) under section 163(e) and sections 1271 through 1275, unstated interest under section 483, and the accrual of interest under section 446. The notice also included proposed amendments to the regulations under related provisions of the Internal Revenue Code. The proposed regulations were subsequently amended on September 7, 1989 (54 FR 37125), February 28, 1991 (56 FR 8308), May 7, 1991 (56 FR 21112) and July 12, 1991 (56 FR 31887). The proposed regulations that were issued in 1986, as amended in 1989 and 1991, are hereinafter referred to as the 1986 proposed regulations.

Explanation of Provisions

Numerous written comments were made on the 1986 proposed regulations. In addition, on November 17, 1986, the Internal Revenue Service held a public hearing on the 1986 proposed regulations. In general, commentators criticized the complexity and length of the 1986 proposed regulations, as well as the narrow definitions of certain terms, including the definitions of accrual period, qualified periodic interest payment, variable rate debt instrument, and de minimis OID.

In response to these comments, the proposed regulations simplify the rules that were in the 1986 proposed regulations and, as explained below, provide more flexible definitions of certain terms for purposes of these rules. The proposed regulations attempt to conform the rules to normal commercial practices and to exclude from their application debt instruments with limited potential to defer or accelerate interest.

The proposed regulations are significantly shorter in length than the 1986 proposed regulations. The shorter length is generally attributable to the simplification of the rules and the elimination of rules that are also in the statute. In addition, because the proposed regulations are proposed to be effective for debt instruments issued on or after the date that is 60 days after the date the regulations are finalized, the proposed regulations do not include the numerous transitional rules that were in the 1986 proposed regulations.

The proposed regulations do not amend the rules for contingent payments that are in §1.1275-4 of the 1986 proposed regulations. These rules will be addressed in future regulations.

In general, the major changes from the 1986 proposed regulations are noted as follows:

Section 1.163-7 Deduction for OID on certain debt instruments.

The proposed regulations allow the issuer of a debt instrument with a de minimis amount of OID to deduct the OID using a straight line method rather than a constant yield method. In addition, if an issuer redeems a debt instrument for the issuer's newly issued debt instrument, the proposed regulations provide rules to determine the amount of the repurchase premium, if any, on the redemption and the timing of the issuer's deduction for the repurchase premium. To determine the amount of the repurchase premium, the issuer's repurchase price for the debt instrument is the issue price of the newly issued debt instrument (reduced by any unstated interest). However, if the issue price of the newly issued debt instrument is determined under either section 1273(b)(4) or section 1274, any repurchase premium on the redemption is amortized by the issuer over the term of the newly issued instrument in the same manner as if it were OID on the instrument.

Section 1.446-2 Method of accounting for interest.

The proposed regulations clarify that unstated interest, as determined under section 483, is taken into account by the buyer and the seller based on their respective methods of accounting for stated interest.

Request for comments: In general, the proposed regulations require the use of the constant yield method to determine interest accruals. However, the proposed regulations generally respect the allocation of payments under a lending or sales contract if (1) the aggregate amount of payments due under the contract does not exceed $250,000, (2) the contract does not have unstated interest, and (3) the debt instrument evidencing the contract is not issued at a discount. This small transaction exception was also in the 1986 proposed regulations. The exception, however, has a limited scope, and taxpayers must still determine whether interest is prepaid under their allocation. Comments are requested as to whether the final regulations should keep this exception. Comments are also requested as to whether the final regulations should allow the use of the Rule of 78's (or any other method) to allocate interest on consumer loans that are not within the small transaction exception, including loans issued for cash.

Section 1.483-1 through 1.483-3 Unstated interest.

For purposes of the lower test rate under section 483(e) for certain sales or exchanges of land between related individuals, the proposed regulations allow the use of the lower rate for a single debt instrument to the extent the stated principal amount of the instrument does not exceed $500,000. For example, if the stated principal amount of the debt instrument is $700,000, the proposed regulations treat the instrument as two instruments: a $500,000 debt instrument, which is eligible for the lower test rate, and a $200,000 debt instrument. The 1986 proposed regulations only allowed the lower rate if a separate debt instrument was issued for the principal amount in excess of $500,000.

Sections 1.1001-1(g) and 1.1012-1(g) Amount realized and basis.

The proposed regulations provide that the issue price of a debt instrument issued in a sale or exchange of property determines the seller's amount realized and the buyer's basis in the property. However, the proposed regulations provide that if the issue price of the debt instrument equals the instrument's stated redemption price at maturity under section 1273(b)(4), the issue price is reduced by any unstated interest for purposes of sections 1001 and 1012.

Section 1.1271-1 Special rules applicable to amounts received on retirement, sale or exchange of debt instruments.

Under section 1271, if there is an intention to call a debt instrument prior to maturity, the gain on the sale, exchange, or retirement of the debt instrument is treated as ordinary income to the extent of any unaccrued OID. The proposed regulations add rules to determine when there is an intention to call the debt instrument prior to maturity. An intention to call exists only if there is an agreement not provided for in the debt instrument that the issuer will redeem the instrument prior to maturity. For example, a mandatory sinking fund provision or call option is not evidence of an intention to call under section 1271. The proposed regulations also provide that the intention to call rules do not apply to publicly offered debt instruments or to debt instruments subject to section 1272(a)(6).

Section 1.1272-1 Current inclusion in income of OID.

The proposed regulations provide that the amount of OID that accrues during an accrual period is determined using the constant yield method. For purposes of this determination, the 1986 proposed regulations required that all accrual periods on a debt instrument (other than a short initial or final accrual period) be of equal length. The proposed regulations, however, allow the use of accrual periods of different lengths of not more than one year. In determining the amount of OID accruals, the yield of the debt instrument must be adjusted to take into account the length of the particular accrual period if accrual periods of different lengths are used.

The proposed regulations also provide new rules to determine the yield and maturity of a debt instrument with a stated contingency that could result in the acceleration or deferral of payments if the amounts payable upon the occurrence of the contingency are fixed. In general, the contingency is ignored. However, if, based on all the facts and circumstances, the contingency is more likely than not to occur, it is assumed that the contingency will occur. In addition, special rules that were in the 1986 proposed regulations for a debt instrument with a put option, call option, or option to extend are retained, and extended to a debt instrument with an option to pay interest in the form of additional debt instruments of the issuer.

If a debt instrument is partially prepaid, the proposed regulations provide that the payment is subject to the payment ordering rule under § 1.1275-2. In general, the payment reduces the adjusted issue price of the debt instrument. For purposes of OID accruals after the prepayment, the yield of the debt instrument is not adjusted for the prepayment. However, any shortfall created as a result of the prepayment is treated as OID and allocated to the final accrual period. *See* § 1.1272-1(c)(2).

Section 1.1272-2 Treatment of debt instruments purchased at a premium.

The proposed regulations define the term purchase as any acquisition of a debt instrument. In addition, the proposed regulations provide new rules to determine the adjusted basis of a debt instrument for purposes of determining whether a holder has acquired a debt instrument at a premium or at an acquisition premium.

Section 1.1272-3 Election by accrual method holder to treat all interest on a debt instrument as OID.

Under the proposed regulations, a holder that uses an accrual method of accounting may elect to treat all interest on a debt instrument as OID. For purposes of the election, interest includes stated interest, OID, market discount, de minimis OID and market discount, acquisition discount, and unstated interest, as adjusted for any acquisition premium or amortizable bond premium. In effect, the election simplifies the calculation of interest income for the holder by applying a single method (constant yield method) to determine the timing and amount of interest income on the debt instrument (*e.g.*, a holder that acquires a debt instrument with acquisition premium need not calculate and use the acquisition premium fraction).

Request for comments: The proposed regulations impose certain conditions on the use of the election. In general, the conditions are similar to those in the market discount and amortizable bond premium rules. For example, if the election is made for a debt instrument with amortizable bond premium or with market discount, the holder becomes subject to the conformity requirements of section 171 or section 1278(b), whichever is applicable. Comments are requested as to whether the final regulations should retain the conformity requirements and other conditions.

Section 1.1273-1 Definition of OID.

OID is defined as the excess of a debt instrument's stated redemption price at maturity over the instrument's issue price. Under the 1986 proposed regulations, a debt instrument's stated redemption price at maturity was defined as the sum of all payments due under the instrument other than qualified periodic interest payments. In general, qualified periodic interest payments were defined as a series of payments equal to the product of the outstanding principal balance of the debt instrument and a single fixed rate of interest that is actually and unconditionally payable at fixed periodic intervals of one year or less during the entire term of the debt instrument (including short periods).

The proposed regulations, by providing a more flexible approach to the treatment of stated interest, generally exclude from their application debt instruments with limited potential to defer or accelerate interest. Under the proposed regulations, "qualified stated interest" is the term used to refer to stated interest that is not includible in the debt instrument's stated redemption price at maturity. Qualified stated interest for a fixed-rate debt instrument is stated interest that is unconditionally payable in cash or in property (other than debt instruments of the issuer) at least annually at a single fixed rate. Interest is payable at a single fixed rate only if the rate appropriately takes into account the length of the interval between payments.

The proposed regulations provide that no stated interest on a short-term obligation is qualified stated interest. Therefore, all stated interest payments on a short-term obligation are included in its stated redemption price at maturity. In response to comments made on the 1986 proposed regulations, which had the same rule, the rule applies for purposes of sections 871 and 881.

The proposed regulations provide an additional rule to determine when a debt instrument with an interest holiday or a teaser rate has a de minimis amount of OID. Under this rule, the amount of OID resulting from an interest holiday or a teaser rate is generally the amount of interest foregone during the holiday or teaser period. The instrument is then tested under the general de minimis rules to determine whether the debt instrument has de minimis OID. For example, under this rule, a 30-year self-amortizing mortgage loan with a fixed interest rate of 8.5 percent, compounded monthly, but a 2-year teaser rate of 6 percent, compounded monthly, would have only a de minimis amount of OID.

The proposed regulations also add rules for the treatment of de minimis OID by the holder. A holder includes de minimis OID in income on a pro rata basis as principal payments are made on the debt instrument. In addition, any gain attributable to de minimis OID that is recognized upon the sale or exchange of a debt instrument is capital gain if the instrument is a capital asset in the hands of the holder. A similar rule was provided in § 1.1232-3(b)(1)(ii).

Section 1.1273-2 Determination of issue price.

The proposed regulations provide new rules to determine when a debt instrument is publicly traded or is issued for property that is publicly traded for purposes of determining the issue price of the debt instrument. In general, a debt instrument or property (stock, security, contract, commodity, or currency) is publicly traded if, at any time during a 60-day period ending 30 days after the issue date of the debt instrument, the debt instrument or property is traded on an established market. A debt instrument or property is traded on an established market if (1) it is listed on certain securities exchanges, interdealer quotation systems, or designated foreign exchanges or boards of trade, (2) it is traded on a designated contract market or an interbank market, (3) it appears on a system of general circulation that provides a reasonable basis to determine fair market value by disseminating either recent price quotations of identified brokers and dealers or actual prices of recent sales transactions, or (4) price quotations with respect to the debt instrument are readily available from dealers and brokers. Price quotations are deemed not readily available if (1) no other outstanding debt of the issuer is traded on an established market, (2) the original stated principal amount of the issue is less than $25 million, (3) all other issues of the issuer's debt that are traded on an established market impose materially more restrictive covenants or conditions on the issuer, or (4) the maturity date of the debt instrument is more than 3 years after the latest maturity date of all other issues of the issuer that are traded on an established market.

The proposed regulations allocate the issue price of an investment unit between the components of the unit based on their relative fair market values. The 1986 proposed regulations provided allocation rules that generally restated common law valuation principles. Unlike the 1986 proposed regulations, the proposed regulations do not provide specific allocation rules. Under the proposed regulations, however, the holder of an investment unit must use the issuer's allocation unless the holder discloses on its Federal income tax return that it plans to use an allocation that is inconsistent with the issuer's allocation.

The 1986 proposed regulations provided that no portion of the issue price of a debt instrument is allocated to a right to convert the instrument into stock of the issuer. However, after the amendments proposed on February 28, 1991, if the conversion right could be satisfied in cash, the 1986 proposed regulations allocated a portion of the issue price of the debt instrument to the conversion right. The proposed regulations modify these rules by providing that no portion of the issue price of a debt instrument is allocated to a right to convert the instrument into stock of the issuer or a party related to the issuer, even if the conversion right may be satisfied in cash.

The proposed regulations change the lender's treatment of a payment of points made incident to a lending transaction. Under the proposed regulations, a payment of points (including a payment of points that is deductible by the borrower under section 461(g)(2)) reduces the issue price of the debt instrument, thereby creating OID on the instrument. If the amount of OID created under this rule is de minimis, the proposed regulations treat the OID in the same manner as any other amount of de minimis OID. By contrast, the 1986 proposed regulations required that the lender include the payment in income when received, regardless of the lender's method of accounting. *See* § 1.446-2(e) of the 1986 proposed regulations.

Sections 1.1274-1 through 1.1274-5 Determination of issue price in the case of certain debt instruments issued for property.

The proposed regulations restructure and simplify the rules that were in § § 1.1274-1 through 1.1274-7 of the 1986 proposed regulations.

The proposed regulations modify the 1986 proposed regulations by providing that the issue price of a debt instrument issued for nonpublicly traded property in a potentially abusive situation is the fair market value of the property. In addition, the proposed regulations treat a debt instrument with clearly excessive interest as issued in a potentially abusive situation. The proposed regulations also provide that, for purposes of the potentially abusive rules, the term nonrecourse financing does not include a sale or exchange of a real property interest financed by a nonrecourse debt instrument, if, in addition to the instrument, the purchaser provides a down payment that is at least 20 percent of the total stated purchase price of the interest.

The proposed regulations provide new rules to determine the imputed principal amount of a debt instrument if the instrument provides for contingent payments. Under the proposed regulations, the imputed principal amount generally is the sum of the present values of the noncontingent payments and the fair market value of the contingent payments. If the fair market value of the contingent payments cannot be determined when separated from the noncontingent payments, the imputed principal amount is the fair market value of the debt instrument. Only in rare and extraordinary cases will the fair market value of the debt instrument be treated as not reasonably ascertainable.

The proposed regulations provide new rules to determine the test rate of interest for an installment obligation. Unlike the 1986 proposed regulations, which had three alternative rules, the proposed regulations use a single rule that uses the weighted average maturity of the debt instrument to determine the test rate.

The proposed regulations no longer contain the transitional rule in the 1986 proposed regulations that provided that section 1274 applied to a modified debt instrument only if the original debt instrument was subject to section 1274.

The proposed regulations limit the use of a test rate that is lower than the applicable Federal rate to debt instruments having a maturity of six months or less (or to debt instruments with a qualified floating rate of interest that is reset at least every six months). For debt instruments having a maturity of less than three months, the proposed regulations modify the 1986 proposed regulations and provide that the allowable Treasury index rate is the market yield on U.S. Treasury bills with the same maturity as the debt instrument.

The proposed regulations provide new rules for debt instruments that are materially modified in connection with an assumption of a debt instrument as part of a sale or exchange of property. In general, the modification is treated as a separate transaction that takes place immediately before the sale or exchange and is attributed to the seller. The seller and buyer, however, may jointly elect to treat the transaction as one in which the buyer first assumed the unmodified debt instrument and subsequently modified the debt instrument.

Request for comments: The proposed regulations provide rules to determine the issue price of a debt instrument subject to an option that allows a holder or issuer the unconditional right to accelerate or defer payments (including a put option, call option, or option to extend the maturity of an instrument). These rules are similar to rules contained in the 1986 proposed regulations. Comments are requested regarding the appropriateness of these rules and regarding whether these rules should be extended to options subject to contingencies that affect the right to exercise or the amounts payable in the event of exercise.

The proposed regulations do not provide any limitations on "recent sales transactions" that are subject to the potentially abusive situation rules. Comments are requested on the limitations, if any, that should be included in the final regulations.

Section 1.1274A-1 Special rules for certain transactions where stated principal amount does not exceed $2,800,000.

The proposed regulations revise the rules for making a cash method election. The proposed regulations also allow a cash method election for a debt instrument that was issued in a debt-for-debt exchange, subject to an anti-abuse rule, if the instrument otherwise qualifies as a cash method debt instrument. The 1986 proposed regulations only allowed the election if the "old" debt instrument was a cash method debt instrument. In addition, the proposed regulations disallow interest deductions for a debt instrument that is incurred or continued to purchase or carry a cash method debt instrument.

Section 1.1275-1 Definitions.

The term "debt instrument" is defined as any instrument or contractual arrangement that constitutes indebtedness under general principles of Federal income tax law. Based on this definition, the proposed regulations treat a payment of stock pursuant to a contingent stock payout under section 483, rather than under the OID provisions. *See Example 3* in § 1.446-2(h).

Section 1.1275-2 Special rules relating to debt instruments.

The proposed regulations revise the aggregation rules that were in the 1986 proposed regulations. In general, only debt instruments that are issued by a single issuer to a single holder are aggregated. The Commissioner, however, may aggregate debt instruments that are issued by more than one issuer or that are issued to more than one holder if the debt instruments are issued in an arrangement that is designed to avoid the aggregation rule. In addition, if under the terms of a debt instrument the holder may receive one or more additional debt instruments of the issuer, the additional debt instruments are aggregated with the original debt instrument.

The proposed regulations also provide a specific payment ordering rule for purposes of the OID provisions. In addition, the proposed regulations add rules for qualified reopenings of Treasury securities.

Section 1.1275-3 OID information reporting requirements.

The 1986 proposed regulations generally required an issuer of a debt instrument with OID to legend the instrument with certain information. The proposed regulations provide that debt instruments do not have to be legended if the instruments are publicly offered or are issued by individuals. In addition, the proposed regulations except a debt instrument from legending if the instrument is not evidenced by a physical document. In the case of a debt instrument that has to be legended, the proposed regulations provide new rules that should simplify compliance with the legending requirement. As an alternative to detailed legending of OID information, the proposed regulations permit the issuer to provide the address or telephone number of a representative of the issuer who will promptly give the OID information to the holder upon request.

Section 1.1275-5 Variable rate debt instruments.

The proposed regulations substantially expand the definition of the term "variable rate debt instrument." In general, a variable rate debt instrument is a debt instrument that provides for stated interest (compounded or paid at least annually) at a qualified floating rate, an objective rate, a fixed rate followed by a qualified floating rate, or a qualified floating rate followed by another qualified floating rate. A qualified floating rate generally is an interest-like rate, such as the applicable Federal rate or LIBOR. An objective rate generally is a rate based on the price of property that is actively traded (other than foreign currency) or an index of the prices of such property. An objective rate is also a rate that is based on one or more qualified floating rates (unless the rate itself is a qualified floating rate). For example, a multiple of a qualified floating rate is an objective rate.

For purposes of determining whether a variable rate debt instrument has OID, the proposed regulations generally treat all stated interest on the instrument that is unconditionally payable at least annually as qualified stated interest. If, however, the debt instrument provides for stated interest at a fixed rate followed by a qualified floating rate or a qualified floating rate followed by a different qualified floating rate, the instrument may have accelerated or deferred interest, which is not qualified stated interest. For example, if a ten-year debt instrument provides for annual interest payments for the first five years equal to the value of one-year LIBOR on each payment date and for the last five years equal to the value of one-year LIBOR on each payment date plus 200 basis points, the 200 basis points in the last five years is deferred interest.

The proposed regulations also provide rules for the accrual of OID on variable rate debt instruments. In general, if the OID is attributable to accelerated or deferred interest or to "true discount" (the excess of a debt instrument's stated principal amount over its issue price), the OID is allocated to an accrual period under the rules of section 1272. The allocation, however, is determined by assuming that the debt instrument provided for qualified stated interest payments at the end of each accrual period based on a reasonable fixed rate.

The proposed regulations provide a special rule for certain tax-exempt debt instruments that provide for stated interest at an objective rate. If the issuer of a tax-exempt debt instrument, contemporaneously with the issuance, enters into one or more financial contracts that substantially offset the variations in the objective rate, the debt instrument is not a variable rate debt instrument. The Treasury Department and the Internal Revenue Service are considering the appropriate treatment of tax-exempt debt instruments with embedded options, forwards, and swaps.

Request for comments: The 1986 proposed regulations did not provide clear guidance on the treatment of a debt instrument that provided for one or more variable interest rates or a combination of a fixed and a variable interest rate. The proposed regulations provide guidance for the treatment of these debt instruments. In general, the proposed regulations attempt to provide rules that reflect the economics of these debt instruments and limit the acceleration or deferral of interest. Comments are requested on the appropriateness of these rules, including the rules for accelerated and deferred interest.

As noted above, the proposed regulations provide a special rule for certain tax-exempt debt instruments with stated interest at an objective rate. Comments are requested on the appropriateness of this rule.

Comments are requested on whether there should be a consistency rule for debt instruments with accelerated interest or deferred interest.

Effective dates

The proposed regulations are proposed to be effective for debt instruments issued on or after the date that is 60 days after the date the regulations are finalized. The proposed regulations are also proposed to be effective for lending transactions, sales and exchanges that occur on or after the date that is 60 days after the date the regulations are finalized. The rules for qualified reopenings of Treasury securities, however, will be effective for reopenings on or after March 25, 1992.

The Internal Revenue Service intends to treat the 1986 proposed regulations that are withdrawn in this document as authority under section 6662 for debt instruments issued prior to their withdrawal and for lending transactions, sales and exchanges that occurred prior to their withdrawal.

Special Analyses

It has been determined that these proposed rules are not major rules as defined in Executive Order 12291. Therefore, a Regulatory Impact Analysis is not required. It also has been determined that section 553(b) of the Administrative Procedure Act (5 U.S.C. chapter 5) and the Regulatory Flexibility Act (5 U.S.C. chapter 6) do not apply to these regulations, and, therefore, an initial Regulatory Flexibility Analysis is not required. Pursuant to section 7805(f) of the Internal Revenue Code, these proposed regulations will be submitted to the Chief Counsel for Advocacy of the Small Business Administration for comment on their impact on small business.

Comments and Public Hearing

Before these proposed regulations are adopted, consideration will be given to any written comments that are timely submitted (preferably a signed original and eight copies) to the Internal Revenue Service. All comments will be available for public inspection and copying in their entirety.

A public hearing on these proposed regulations will be held on February 16, 1993, at 10:00 a.m. See the notice of public hearing published elsewhere in this issue of the Federal Register.

Drafting Information

The principal authors of these regulations are Frederick S. Campbell-Mohn, William E. Blanchard, and Andrew C. Kittler of the Office of Assistant Chief Counsel (Financial Institutions and Products), Internal Revenue Service. However, other personnel from the Service and Treasury Department participated in their development.

[¶49,138]   **Proposed Regulations and Proposed Amendments of Regulations (IA-57-89)**, published in the Federal Register on December 30, 1992.

     Consolidated returns: Alternative minimum tax.—Reg. §§1.1502-55 and amendments of Reg. §§1.56(g)-1, 1.1502-1, 1.1502-5, 1.1502-33 and 1.1552-1, relating to the computation of the alternative minimum tax by consolidated groups, are proposed. Proposed amendments of Reg. §1.1502-2 is withdrawn on December 13, 2018 by REG-104259-18.

AGENCY: Internal Revenue Service, Treasury.

ACTION: Notice of Proposed Rulemaking.

SUMMARY: This document proposes regulations under sections 53 through 59, 1502, and 1552 of the Internal Revenue Code relating to the computation of the alternative minimum tax by consolidated groups. The regulations also provide rules for allocating items such as the consolidated alternative minimum tax liability and the consolidated minimum tax credit among the members of a consolidated group. In addition, certain conforming amendments are proposed for related regulations dealing with the computation of adjusted current earnings.

DATES: Written comments and requests to speak (with outlines of oral comments to be presented) at the public hearing scheduled for April 6, 1993, at 10:00 a.m., must be received by March 1, 1993.

ADDRESSES: Send submissions to: Internal Revenue Service, P.O. Box 7604, Ben Franklin Station, Attn: CC:CORP:TR (IA-57-89), Room 5228, Washington, D.C. 20044.

FOR FURTHER INFORMATION CONTACT: Martin Scully, Jr. of the Office of the Assistant Chief Counsel, Income Tax and Accounting, (202) 622-4960 (not a toll-free number).

SUPPLEMENTARY INFORMATION:

Background

For taxable years beginning after December 31, 1986, corporations are subject to both the regular tax and the alternative minimum tax (AMT). These proposed regulations apply the AMT to consolidated groups. The Internal Revenue Service recognizes that application of the statutory AMT provisions to consolidated groups is complex and requests comments on how these proposed regulations might be further simplified.

Explanation of Provisions

I. *Computation of Consolidated AMT*

   A. *In general*

The Service believes that Congress generally intended the AMT and adjusted current earnings (ACE) systems to be separate from, and parallel to, the regular tax system. *See, e.g.,* §1.56(g)-1(a)(5). Accordingly, under the separate and parallel principle, all of the provisions of the Internal Revenue Code (Code) and regulations apply in determining consolidated alternative minimum taxable income (AMTI) and consolidated ACE unless the Service provides otherwise in regulations or other guidance.

The proposed regulations apply the separate and parallel principle to consolidated groups. They do not, however, illustrate how this principle applies in all cases. For example, although not discussed in the regulations, the loss disallowance rules of §1.1502-20 and the life/non-life consolidation rules of §1.1502-47 apply to consolidated groups under the AMT and ACE systems. Unless an exception to the separate and parallel principle is provided, the separate and parallel principle governs the treatment of all consolidated AMT and ACE items.

The proposed regulations provide rules for (a) computing the AMT liability of a consolidated group (consolidated AMT) and (b) allocating various consolidated AMT attributes to members as necessary (e.g., to determine the allocation of the attributes when a corporation ceases to be a member). The statutory scheme and definitions in sections 53 through 59 of the Code generally apply in determining consolidated AMT, as modified in the proposed regulations to clarify their application to consolidated groups. Thus, consolidated AMT is the excess of consolidated tentative minimum tax (TMT) for the taxable year over consolidated regular tax for the taxable year. Consolidated TMT is determined by first computing 20 percent of the excess of consolidated AMTI for the taxable year over a consolidated exemption amount. That amount is then reduced by the consolidated AMT foreign tax credit in arriving at consolidated TMT. Consolidated regular tax is computed in accordance with the principles of section 55(c) of the Code.

Consolidated AMTI is equal to consolidated pre-adjustment AMTI, increased or decreased by the consolidated ACE adjustment, and then decreased by the consolidated alternative tax net operating loss (ATNOL) deduction, which is the consolidated NOL deduction taking into account the AMT adjustments and preferences.

Under the separate and parallel principle, a consolidated group generally computes its AMT liability in much the same way as its regular tax liability. For example, consolidated pre-adjustment AMTI is computed in accordance with §§1.1502-11 and 1.1502-12 principles. The separate pre-adjustment AMTI of each member is calculated under §1.1502-12, determined by taking into account the adjustments and preferences in sections 56 (excluding the ACE adjustment under section 56(g)), 57, and 58. The separate pre-adjustment AMTIs of the members are then aggregated under §1.1502-11 principles. Next, the consolidated items listed in §1.1502-11 (other than the consolidated NOL deduction), determined by taking into account the adjustments and preferences of sections 56 (excluding the section 56(g) ACE adjustment), 57, and 58, are added to that aggregate amount to arrive at consolidated pre-adjustment AMTI. Consolidated ACE is calculated in a similar manner.

Under the method proposed for calculating consolidated AMT, separate member data will be available to calculate each member's allocable share of the group's consolidated AMT for purposes of determining annual stock basis adjustments under proposed §§1.1502-19 and 1.1502-32 and annual adjustments to earnings and profits under §1.1502-33. In addition, the proposed method will provide groups with the separate corporation data necessary for various other computations required under the consolidated return regulations. See, e.g., proposed §1.1502-76(b) (allocating a subsidiary's income between separate and consolidated returns). Finally, because the proposed method parallels the computation of consolidated regular taxable income, it should be familiar to taxpayers.

To implement the proposed approach to the computation of consolidated AMT, certain conforming amendments are necessary. At present, §1.56(g)-1(n)(3) of the ACE regulations provides that consolidated pre-adjustment AMTI is the consolidated taxable income (as defined in §1.1502-11) of a consolidated group determined with appropriate adjustments and preferences. The Service proposes to amend the ACE regulations to specify that under the separate and parallel principle a consolidated group computes its consolidated ACE in accordance with the rules for computing consolidated regular taxable income in §§1.1502-11 and 1.1502-12, as modified in these proposed regulations.

B. Treatment of adjustments and preferences

In most cases, the amount of a preference or adjustment is not affected by whether the item is computed separately by each member or on a consolidated basis. The Service has, however, identified three preference items that are affected by whether they are computed on a consolidated basis: (a) the preference for excess intangible drilling costs (IDCs); (b) the preference for charitable contributions of appreciated property; and (c) the preference for bad debt reserves of financial institutions. As discussed below, the proposed regulations apply a consolidated approach to compute the preferences for excess IDCs and charitable contributions, and a separate member approach to compute the preference for bad debt reserves.

1. Section 57(a)(2) preference for excess IDCs

Section 57(a)(2) provides a preference equal to the amount by which excess IDCs are greater than 65 percent of net income from all oil, gas, and geothermal properties of the taxpayer. Because section 57(a)(2) applies with respect to all such properties of the taxpayer, "excess net income" from one property (i.e., where 65 percent of the property's net income is greater than the excess IDCs) can offset a section 57(a)(2) preference that would otherwise be generated by other properties held by the taxpayer. Similarly, the proposed regulations provide that the section 57(a)(2) IDC preference is computed using a consolidated approach. Thus, one member's section 57(a)(2) preference may be offset by another member's excess net income from oil, gas, and geothermal properties.

Although the IDC preference is computed using a consolidated approach, it is nevertheless allocated back to the members and included in the computation of separate pre-adjustment AMTI. This treatment is consistent with the regular tax treatment of the limitation on percentage depletion deductions under §1.1502-44, which is computed using a consolidated approach but is included in separate taxable income under §1.1502-12(p).

2. Section 57(a)(6) preference for charitable contributions of appreciated property

Section 57(a)(6) provides a preference equal to the amount by which the section 170 charitable contribution deduction would be reduced if all capital gain property (as defined in section 57 (a)(6)(B)) were taken into account at its adjusted basis. Under §§1.1502-11(a)(5) and 1.1502-24, a consolidated section 170 deduction is computed. Therefore, to be consistent with the single entity principles of §§1.1502-11 and 1.1502-24, the section 57(a)(6) preference is computed on a consolidated basis. The proposed regulations provide that the consolidated section 57(a)(6) preference is the amount by which the consolidated charitable contribution deduction would be reduced if all capital gain property of the group were taken into account at its adjusted basis.

3. Section 57(a)(4) preference for bad debt reserves of financial institutions

Section 57(a)(4) provides a preference equal to the amount by which a financial institution's allowable section 593 deduction for a reasonable addition to a reserve for bad debts (the section 593 deduction) exceeds the amount that would have been allowable under section 585(b) had the financial institution maintained its bad debt reserve for all taxable years on the basis of actual experience (the hypothetical section 585 deduction).

Section 593 does not specifically set forth the amount to be deducted. For example, for qualifying real property loans, a financial institution subject to section 593 may generally deduct an amount equal to the amount determined under section 593(b)(2) (the percentage of taxable income method), an amount equal to the amount determined under section 585(b), or some lesser amount. Thus, each section 593 financial institution makes an election regarding its reasonable addition to its reserve for bad debts for the taxable year. The Service believes that, because each member's section 593 deduction is determined separately based on elections made and methods of accounting employed by that member, the section 57(a)(4) preference should also be determined separately by each member.

In addition, if the section 57(a)(4) preference were computed on a consolidated basis, an undue double benefit to taxpayers could result. If a financial institution chooses under section 593 to deduct an amount that is less than its hypothetical section 585(b) deduction, the next year's hypothetical section 585(b) deduction is increased by the difference between the institution's hypothetical section 585(b) deduction and its section 593 deduction. This increase in the hypothetical section 585(b) deduction in the next year potentially lowers the section 57(a)(4) preference in that year. If, in addition to lowering the next year's preference, the difference between the institution's hypothetical section 585(b) deduction and its section 593 deduction were to offset the current year preferences of other group members, the group could obtain a double benefit.

C. *Rules relating to separate return limitation years*

The proposed regulations do not limit a consolidated group's use of net positive ACE adjustments arising in a separate return limitation year (SRLY). Although a negative ACE adjustment may be used only to the extent of prior net positive ACE adjustments, the Service has concluded that the increased compliance burden of applying the SRLY rules to net positive ACE adjustments is not warranted.

The proposed regulations reserve, however, on other applications of the SRLY limitations.

D. *Carryovers and carrybacks of consolidated AMT items to separate return years*

The proposed regulations provide rules for the carryover and carryback of consolidated AMT items—items for which there are regular tax counterparts, as well as the consolidated ACE adjustment—to separate return years of a member. In the case of consolidated AMT items for which there are regular tax counterparts (*e.g.*, consolidated ATNOLs and consolidated AMT and ACE net capital losses), the portion of the item that is allocated to a corporation ceasing to be a member and carried to its separate return years is determined in accordance with the regular tax principles relating to the parallel regular tax item. In general, a consolidated item is allocated to a member based on its proportionate share of the separately determined items of all members. *See, e.g.*, proposed § 1.1502-21(b)(2) (carryovers and carrybacks of consolidated net operating losses to separate return years).

The proposed regulations also provide rules for allocating consolidated positive ACE adjustments (*i.e.*, the increases in consolidated AMTI of the group in prior years due to the consolidated ACE adjustment) to members. Because a current year negative ACE adjustment is allowable only to the extent that prior year positive ACE adjustments exceed prior year negative ACE adjustments, positive ACE adjustments from prior years could be valuable to a corporation ceasing to be a member.

The proposed regulations provide that a member's portion of the consolidated positive ACE adjustments is taken into account in the member's separate return years under the principles of § 1.56(g)-1(a)(2) and proposed § 1.1502-21(b). The member's portion of the consolidated positive ACE adjustments is based on the member's proportionate share of the separate cumulative ACE adjustments of all members (the consolidated cumulative ACE adjustment taking into account only the member's items). Because of the potentially burdensome nature of the cumulative allocation method, and the required recordkeeping, the Service considered not allocating the consolidated ACE adjustment to departing members. Under this alternative approach, the group's prior consolidated ACE adjustments would remain entirely with the group even when corporations responsible for that adjustment cease to be members. However, each member already must calculate its separate ACE and its separate pre-adjustment AMTI in computing consolidated AMTI. Further, even corporations filing separate returns must track their cumulative ACE history to determine whether a negative ACE adjustment may offset AMTI. The proposed regulations, therefore, do not adopt this non-allocation approach. The Service, however, solicits comments on whether the final regulations should provide that no allocations of the consolidated ACE adjustment should be made to departing members. These comments should address issues that would arise if no allocations were made, including acquisitions of groups and groups ceasing to exist as consolidated groups.

E. *Deferral and restoration of AMT items*

The proposed regulations provide rules relating to the deferral and restoration of AMT items. Under the separate and parallel approach, the regular tax principles used in computing consolidated taxable income are applied in computing consolidated pre-adjustment AMTI and consolidated ACE. *See, e.g.*, § 1.1502-13.

F. *Stock basis adjustments*

Proposed regulations modifying the determination of stock basis adjustments under § 1.1502-32 (and excess loss accounts under § 1.1502-19) were filed with the Federal Register on November 10, 1992. *See* CO-30-92 (57 FR 53634, 1992-48 I.R.B. 27). Based on those proposed regulations, this document proposes rules for adjusting stock basis (and excess loss accounts) in computing consolidated pre-adjustment AMTI and consolidated ACE. Under the separate and parallel approach, the principles of proposed § § 1.1502-19 and 1.1502-32 for determining the regular tax basis in (or the regular tax excess loss account with respect to) a member's stock are generally applied in computing consolidated pre-adjustment AMTI and consolidated ACE.

Certain modifications to the general principles are provided, however. For example, while recently-issued proposed regulations ordinarily require basis adjustments to be determined as of the close of each consolidated return year and as of any other time necessary to determine the tax liability of any person, basis adjustments in computing consolidated pre-adjustment AMTI and consolidated ACE are required only if a difference between the regular tax and AMT or ACE basis in a member's stock will affect the tax liability of any person (*e.g.*, on the sale of the stock). Thus, the annual reporting requirements of proposed § 1.1502-32(g) are not applied under the AMT system.

II. *Consolidated Minimum Tax Credit*

A. *General rules*

Under the proposed regulations, a group's consolidated minimum tax credit (MTC) is equal to the sum of (a) the consolidated return year MTC, and (b) the separate return year MTC. The proposed regulations provide rules for computing the consolidated return year MTC and the separate return year MTC. The consolidated MTC allowable for any consolidated return year is limited to the excess (if any) of modified consolidated regular tax for the year, over consolidated TMT for the year. Modified consolidated regular tax is the consolidated regular tax determined under the principles of section 26(b) reduced by all allowable credits (other than the consolidated MTC).

B. *Carryover of consolidated MTC to separate return years*

The proposed regulations provide rules for the carryover of the consolidated MTC to the separate return years of corporations that cease to be members. Specifically, the portion of the consolidated MTC that is allocated to a member and carried over to a separate return year is determined in accordance with the principles of section 53, § 1.1502-3(c), and proposed § 1.1502-21(b).

The amount of the consolidated MTC allocated to a member is generally the member's share of the group's consolidated adjusted net minimum tax for each consolidated return year, reduced by the member's share of the consolidated adjusted net minimum tax allowable as a consolidated MTC during consolidated return years for which the member was included in the group. A member's allocable share of the consolidated adjusted net minimum tax is based on its proportionate share of the separate adjusted AMT of the members for the year. The separate adjusted AMT of a member is, in general, the excess of the consolidated AMT for the year over the consolidated AMT for the year computed by excluding the member's items.

The method provided in the proposed regulations for computing the separate adjusted AMT of each member takes into account not only the member's separate AMT, but also other contributions the member makes to consolidated AMT. For example, if a member has a regular tax net operating loss (NOL) on a separate basis that reduces consolidated regular tax, the NOL may increase consolidated AMT (unless the member's corresponding ATNOL reduces consolidated TMT by at least the same amount). Under the proposed regulations, if the member's NOL (considering its relationship to the ATNOL) increases consolidated AMT, that increase is taken into account in allocating consolidated MTC.

The Service is aware that, under the proposed allocation method, it is possible for a member with regular tax in excess of TMT on a separate company basis to receive an allocation of the consolidated MTC. Consider the following example:

	P	S	Consolidated
Taxable income	$(100)	$100	$- 0 -
AMTI	100	50	150
TMT	20	10	30
Regular tax (34% rate)	- 0 -	34	- 0 -
AMT	$20	$0	$30

Consolidated AMT computed with S's items is $30, but consolidated AMT computed without S's items is only $20. Thus, under the proposed allocation method S would be allocated consolidated MTC even though S's regular tax exceeded its TMT on a separate basis. This result is appropriate because S's $100 of taxable income did not increase the consolidated regular tax, while its $50 of AMTI did increase consolidated TMT by $10. The inclusion of S's items therefore increased consolidated AMT by $10.

The Service considered other methods for allocating the consolidated MTC. Under one alternative, the group's consolidated MTC would be allocated to each member based on that member's proportionate share of the group's total adjustments and preferences. This method was rejected because it takes into account only one component that contributes to the consolidated MTC and it could lead to distortions. For example, a member with adjustments and preferences may actually reduce consolidated AMT if the member's items increase consolidated regular tax more than they increase consolidated TMT. Nevertheless, the member would be allocated an amount of the consolidated MTC under this method.

Another alternative would allocate consolidated MTC based on the separate AMT liability of each member. The separate AMT liability of a member would be the consolidated AMT taking into account only that member's items. Under this method, each member with a separate AMT liability would be allocated a proportionate share of the consolidated MTC. This method was also rejected because it could lead to inappropriate results and would fail to make any allocation of the consolidated MTC in certain cases. For example, a group could have an AMT liability, even though none of its members has a separate AMT liability. In such a case, no member of the group would receive an allocation under this method.

The Service invites suggestions about other ways to allocate the consolidated MTC that are either simpler or more accurate than the method in the proposed regulations.

III. *Proposed amendments to the existing consolidated return regulations*

The proposed regulations generally provide that references in the consolidated return regulations to the tax liability of a consolidated group are to the tax liability determined under § 1.1502-2(a). Under § 1.1502-2(a), as proposed to be amended by these regulations, consolidated tax liability is the sum of (a) the consolidated regular tax, (b) the consolidated AMT, (c) the consolidated environmental tax, and (d) the aggregate of the additional taxes provided under section 26(b)(2) (other than the taxes under sections 55 and 59A) imposed on members. However, references to the consolidated tax liability (or the tax liability of a consolidated group) in § 1.1552-1(a) through (f) are generally references to the group's regular tax liability determined in accordance with section 26(b). Similar references in § 1.1502-33(d) have already been clarified in recently-issued proposed regulations. *See* CO-30-92 (57 FR 53634, 1992-48 I.R.B. 27).

Section 1.1502-5, dealing with estimated tax payments by a consolidated group, is amended to reflect recent law changes with respect to the estimated tax underpayment exceptions and to add the consolidated AMT to the estimated tax payment requirements.

Comments are solicited as to additional conforming changes to the existing consolidated return regulations that should be included in the final regulations to take into account the definition of the term "tax" under these proposed regulations.

IV. *Allocations in determining earnings and profits*

A. *Allocation of consolidated AMT*

The proposed regulations allocate consolidated AMT among the members for purposes of determining earnings and profits. Additionally, if modified consolidated regular tax exceeds consolidated TMT, the proposed regulations require that the earnings and profits of a member be increased for the member's allocable share of any consolidated MTC allowable.

The proposed regulations provide only one method for determining the amount of consolidated AMT allocated to each member of a consolidated group. The method selected for allocating the consolidated AMT among members considers the benefits that one member's AMT and ACE attributes provide in offsetting the consolidated AMT liability that would otherwise result if the member were not included in the consolidated group. For this reason, and because each member's decrease in earnings and profits based on its allocable share of the consolidated AMT is ultimately reversed by the member's allocable share of any consolidated MTC allowable in a consolidated return year, the proposed regulations do not provide for § 1.1502-33(d) AMT liability allocations.

The Service invites comments regarding its conclusion that § 1.1502-33(d) allocation rules are not necessary given the method provided in the proposed regulations for allocating the consolidated AMT liability. Comments should recommend any specific alternatives to the approach taken in the proposed regulations and should consider the appropriate treatment of departing group members under any such alternatives.

B. *Allocation of consolidated environmental tax*

The proposed regulations allocate the consolidated environmental tax based on a member's proportionate share of the separate modified AMTI of the members for the year. Separate modified AMTI is the consolidated modified AMTI taking into account only the member's items of income, gain, deduction, and loss.

C. *Allocation of consolidated additional taxes*

The proposed regulations provide that the consolidated additional taxes (defined in § 1.1502-2(b)) are allocated to members in accordance with any reasonable method used by the group. *See, e.g.*, the taxes under sections 531 and 541.

V. *References to proposed regulations*

References in the amendatory paragraphs of this Notice of Proposed Rulemaking to § § 1.1502-19, 1.1502-21, 1.1502-22, 1.1502-32, and 1.1502-33, (or any of the paragraphs thereunder) are intended as references to those sections, as proposed to be amended by previously issued Notices of Proposed Rulemaking.

Special Analyses

It has been determined that these proposed rules are not major rules as defined in Executive Order 12291. Therefore, a Regulatory Impact Analysis is not required. It has also been determined that section 553(b) of the Administrative Procedure Act (5 U.S.C. chapter 5) and the Regulatory Flexibility Act (5 U.S.C. chapter 6) do not apply to these proposed rules, and therefore, an initial Regulatory Flexibility Analysis is not required. Pursuant to section 7805(f) of the Internal Revenue Code, these proposed rules will be submitted to the Chief Counsel for Advocacy of the Small Business Administration for comment on their impact on small businesses.

Written Comments and Public Hearing

Before these proposed regulations are adopted, consideration will be given to any written comments that are submitted timely (preferably a signed original and eight copies) to the Internal Revenue Service. All comments will be available for public inspection and copying in their entirety. Written comments, requests to appear at the public hearing, and outlines of oral comments to be presented at a public hearing scheduled for April 6, 1993, must be received by March 16, 1993. See notice of hearing published elsewhere in this issue of the Federal Register.

Drafting Information

The principal author of these proposed regulations is Martin Scully, Jr. of the Office of Assistant Chief Counsel, Income Tax and Accounting, Internal Revenue Service. However, other personnel from the Service and the Treasury assisted in their development.

[¶ 49,139] Proposed Regulations and Proposed Amendments of Regulations (REG-208985-89) [originally issued as INTL-0848-89], published in the Federal Register on January 5, 1993.

Foreign corporations: Tax years.—Reg. §§1.563-3 and 1.898-0—1.898-4, and amendments of Reg. §§1.442-1, and 1.563-3, relating to the required taxable year of those foreign corporations beginning after July 10, 1989, are proposed. Amendments to Proposed Reg. §1.898-4 were proposed on 6/13/2001. Reg. §§1.441-1T and 1.442-2T were removed by T.D. 8996 on May 16, 2002.

AGENCY: Internal Revenue Service, Treasury.

ACTION: Notice of proposed rulemaking.

SUMMARY: This document contains proposed Income Tax Regulations setting forth the required taxable year for specified foreign corporations for taxable years of those foreign corporations beginning after July 10, 1989. This action is necessary because of changes to the applicable tax law made by the Omnibus Budget Reconciliation Act of 1989, which added section 898 to the Internal Revenue Code. The regulations will give guidance on which foreign corporations must change their taxable year and how to effect the change in taxable year.

DATES: Written comments and requests for a public hearing must be received by March 8, 1993.

ADDRESSES: Send written comments and requests for a public hearing to: Internal Revenue Service, P.O. Box 7604, Ben Franklin Station, Attention: CC:CORP:T:R (INTL-0848-89), room 5228, Washington, DC 20044.

FOR FURTHER INFORMATION CONTACT: Bill Lundeen of the Office of Associate Chief Counsel (International), within the Office of Chief Counsel, Internal Revenue Service, 1111 Constitution Avenue, N.W., Washington, DC 20224 (Attention: CC:CORP:T:R (202-622-3870 (INTL-0848-89), not a toll-free call).

SUPPLEMENTARY INFORMATION:

A. *Paperwork Reduction Act*

The collection of information contained in this notice of proposed rulemaking has been submitted to the Office of Management and Budget for review in accordance with the Paperwork Reduction Act of 1980 (44 U.S.C. 3504(h)). Comments on the collection of information should be sent to the Office of Management and Budget, Attn: Desk Officer for the Department of the Treasury, Office of Information and Regulatory Affairs, Washington, D.C. 20503, with copies to the Internal Revenue Service, Attn: IRS Reports Clearance Officer, T:FP, Washington, DC 20224.

The collection of information in these proposed regulations is in §§1.563-3, 1.898-3 and 1.898-4. The Internal Revenue Service requires this information to verify compliance with section 898 of the Internal Revenue Code. The respondents will be certain United States shareholders of specified foreign corporations.

The estimates are an approximation of the average time expected to be necessary for a collection of information.

They are based on information as is available to the Internal Revenue Service. Individual respondents may require greater or lesser time, depending on their particular circumstances.

Estimated total annual reporting burden: 600 hours.

Estimated burden per respondent varies from .5 hours to 1.5 hour, depending on individual circumstances, with an estimated average of 1 hour.

Estimated number of respondents: 600.

Estimated frequency of responses: Once every three years.

B. *Background*

This document contains proposed regulations under sections 441, 442, 563 and 898 of the Internal Revenue Code (Code). Sections 1.898-1 through 1.898-4 are proposed to be effective for taxable years of specified foreign corporations beginning after July 10, 1989. However, §§1.898-3 (a)(4)(regarding situations in which inconsistent majority U.S. shareholder years exist) and 1.898-3 (a)(5)(iii)(regarding situations in which additional testing days are required) are proposed to be effective for taxable years beginning after [INSERT DATE 120 DAYS AFTER DATE OF PUBLICATION OF FINAL REGULATIONS IN THE FEDERAL REGISTER], and section 1.898-4 (b) is proposed to be effective for changes in the required year of a specified foreign corporation subsequent to its first taxable year beginning after July 10, 1989.

C. *Explanation of Provisions*

Introduction

Section 7401(a) of the Omnibus Budget Reconciliation Act of 1989, Pub. L. No. 101-239, 103 Stat. 2106 ("the Act"), added section 898 to the Code. The purpose of section 898 is to eliminate the deferral of income and, therefore, the understatement in income, by United States shareholders of certain controlled foreign corporations and foreign personal holding companies, referred to in the statute as specified foreign corporations. Deferral results when certain income earned by these corporations is subject to United States income tax in a taxable year of the United States shareholder subsequent to the taxable year during which it was earned. The elimination of deferral is accomplished by requiring a specified foreign corporation to conform its taxable year to the required year, which is generally the majority U.S. shareholder year, for taxable years of specified foreign corporations beginning after July 10, 1989.

Section 1.898-1.

Section 1.898-I provides the general rule that, for purposes of the Internal Revenue Code, the taxable year of any specified foreign corporation shall be the required year determined under section 898(c) and §1.898-3. In addition, §1.898-1 (b) sets forth the effective dates of the regulations under section 898.

The regulations at paragraph (c) exempt certain specified foreign corporations from section 898 in three circumstances. First, a specified foreign corporation is exempt from section 898 so long as its United States shareholders do not have any amount includible in gross income pursuant to section 951(a) and do not receive any actual or deemed distributions attributable to amounts described in section 553 with respect to that corporation. Once any United States shareholder has such amounts, however, section 898 applies to the specified foreign corporation. Second, a specified foreign corporation that is a foreign insurance company and elects to be treated as a domestic corporation pursuant to section 953(d) is exempt from section 898. Likewise, a specified foreign corporation described in section 1504(d) for which an election has been made to treat it as a domestic corporation is exempt from section 898.

Section 1.898-2.

Section 1.898-2(a) defines specified foreign corporation. Generally, a specified foreign corporation is defined to include controlled foreign corporations and foreign personal holding companies. However, specified foreign corporations include only those controlled foreign corporations and foreign personal holding companies that meet certain ownership requirements. Paragraphs (b)(1) and (b)(2) set forth the ownership requirements of a specified foreign corporation and paragraph (b)(3) defines United States shareholder for purposes of these rules. Paragraph (c) provides a special rule for foreign personal holding companies that are specified foreign corporations.

There is an inconsistency in the legislative history of section 898 between the Senate Print and the Conference Report. The conference agreement generally follows the Senate amendment, but misstates the Senate amendment in reporting that section 898 applies only to a controlled foreign corporation or foreign personal holding company, more than 50 percent of the total voting power or value of the *U.S.-owned* stock of which is treated as owned by a United States shareholder, and that section 898 takes into account only the taxable years of those United States shareholders (and certain related persons) in determining the majority U.S. shareholder year. The words "U.S.-owned" did not appear in the Senate amendment, which is the version of the bill that Congress enacted and which became public law. Accordingly, specified foreign corporations include controlled foreign corporations and foreign personal holding companies in which a United States shareholder owns (or is considered to own) more than 50 percent of the voting power of all classes of stock of the corporation entitled to vote, or more than 50 percent of the total value of all classes of stock of the corporation.

Section 1.898-3.

Section 1.898-3(a)(1) provides the general rule that the required year of a specified foreign corporation means the majority U.S. shareholder year. Paragraph (a)(2) provides that a specified foreign corporation that is a controlled foreign corporation may elect, in lieu of the required year, a taxable year beginning one month earlier than the majority U.S. shareholder year. Paragraph (a)(3) defines majority U.S. shareholder year, and paragraph (a) (4) provides rules for situations in which more than one majority U.S. shareholder year exists. Paragraph (a)(5) defines testing days which are the days on which a specified foreign corporation must determine whether it is using the required year. Paragraph (b) provides special rules for foreign personal holding companies that are specified foreign corporations.

Section 1.898-4.

Section 1.898-4 provides special rules applicable to specified foreign corporations. Paragraph (a) sets forth rules for changes to the required year of a specified foreign corporation for its first taxable year beginning after July 10, 1989, and paragraph (b) provides rules for changes in the required year of a specified foreign corporation during a taxable year subsequent to its first taxable year beginning after July 10, 1989.

Paragraph (c) provides rules for situations in which a specified foreign corporation maintains a foreign taxable year (for purposes of computing income tax liabilities due a foreign country) that is different from its required year, including rules relating to the computation of income and earnings and profits of the corporation and rules for the situation in which the U.S. majority shareholder year is a 52-53-week taxable year and the specified foreign corporation's taxable year is not, or in which the specified foreign corporation's taxable year is a 52-53-week taxable year and the U.S. majority shareholder year is not.

A foreign income tax accrues only when the liability for it is fixed and the amount of the liability can be determined. This event generally occurs at the end of the foreign taxable year with respect to a foreign income tax that is imposed on that year's income. Consequently, with the enactment of section 898, a mismatch may arise between the income that comprises a subpart F or foreign personal holding company inclusion and the creditable foreign taxes related to the inclusion when the foreign taxable year of a specified foreign corporation ends later than the corporation's United States taxable year.

Adherence to the foreign tax accrual rule in the context of section 898 may result in income being taxed under subpart F without the associated foreign income taxes being available as a credit under section 960. While we considered several options to address the effect of the foreign tax accrual rule in this context, we believe that adherence to the foreign tax accrual rule is justified for several reasons. First, unlike section 338(i), there is no direct authority in section 898 to modify the rule. Second, rules that require the pooling of post-1986 undistributed earnings and foreign taxes mitigate the effect of the foreign tax accrual rule. Third, determining the foreign taxes on a specified foreign corporation's taxable income prior to the end of the foreign taxable year may not be possible, especially where that foreign taxable year has not ended by the filing date of the applicable U.S. tax return. Accordingly, modifying the foreign tax accrual rule for specified foreign corporations that have foreign taxable years which differ from their required year would result in speculative foreign tax accruals, necessitating a corrective mechanism, and would result in a set of highly complex rules which would be difficult to administer. Such an approach would place additional pressure on the foreign tax credit rules, in particular, on the section 905(c) rules. Finally, the potential mismatch resulting from adherence to the foreign tax accrual rule is mitigated by the rule, discussed below, that applies to the first taxable year after section 898 was enacted and that spreads over four taxable years the recognition of certain income otherwise required to be recognized in one year as a result of section 898.

Section 1.898-4(d) provides rules to implement section 7401(d)(2)(C) of the Act. That section of the Act provides that if, because of the change in taxable year, any United States person would be required to include in gross income for its taxable year amounts attributable to two taxable years of the specified foreign corporation, the amount of income reported for the short taxable year of the specified foreign corporation shall be included in the United States person's gross income ratably over its next four taxable years beginning with its taxable year in which amounts attributable to two taxable years of the specified foreign corporation would have been included.

The foregoing four-year rule applies only when a United States person would otherwise be required to include deemed distributions of income from more than one taxable year of the specified foreign corporation in any one of its own taxable years, and only if the short taxable year of the specified foreign corporation was its first taxable year beginning after July 10, 1989. If a specified foreign corporation that changed its taxable year in accordance with section 898 derived subpart F income in its first taxable year, but not in its second (short) taxable year, which ended within the one taxable year of the United States person, then the ratable four-year inclusion would not be applicable. Finally, any United States person who would otherwise be subject to the four-year rule may not waive that rule and accelerate an income inclusion due to the application of section 898.

Section 1.563-3.

Section 7401(b)(1) of the Act amended section 563 of the Code by adding a new subsection (c) which generally requires that, in determining the dividends paid deduction for purposes of the foreign personal holding company provisions of the Code, a dividend paid after the close of any taxable year, and on or before the 15th day of the third month following the close of that taxable year, will be considered as paid during that taxable year to the extent the foreign personal holding company designates the dividend as being taken into account under section 563(c). Section 1.563-3 provides rules to implement section 7401(b)(1).

D. *Special Analyses*

It has been determined that these rules are not major rules as defined in Executive Order 12291. Therefore, a Regulatory Impact Analysis is not required. It has also been determined that section 553(b) of the Administrative Procedure Act (5 U.S.C. chapter 5) and the Regulatory Flexibility Act (5 U.S.C. chapter 6) do not apply to these regulations, and therefore, an initial Regulatory Flexibility Analysis is not required. Pursuant to section 7805(f) of the Internal Revenue Code, these regulations will be submitted to the Chief Counsel for Advocacy of the Small Business Administration for comment on the impact of the rules on small business.

E. *Comments and Requests for a Public Hearing*

Before adopting these regulations, consideration will be given to any written comments that are submitted (preferably a signed original and eight copies) to the Internal Revenue Service. All comments will be available for public inspection and copying. A public hearing will be held upon written request by any person who submits timely written comments on the proposed rules. Notice of the time, place and date for the hearing will be published in the Federal Register.

F. *Drafting Information*

The principal author of this regulation is Bill Lundeen of the Office of Associate Chief Counsel (International), within the Office of Chief Counsel, Internal Revenue Service. Other personnel from the Internal Revenue Service and Treasury Department participated in developing the regulations.

[¶ 49,142]   Proposed Regulations (REG-245935-96) [originally issued as EE-14-81], published in the Federal Register on May 7, 1993.

Foreign deferred compensation plans: Limitations: Deductions: Adjustments: Earnings and profits.—Reg. §§ 1.404A-0—1.404A-7, relating to the limitations on deductions and adjustments to earnings and profits with respect to certain foreign deferred compensation plans, are proposed. The proposed regulations issued under Code Sec. 404A on April 8, 1985, have been withdrawn.

AGENCY: Internal Revenue Service, Treasury.

ACTION: Withdrawal of previous proposed rules and notice of proposed rulemaking.

SUMMARY: This document contains proposed regulations relating to the limitations on deductions and adjustments to earnings and profits (or accumulated profits) with respect to certain foreign deferred compensation plans. These new proposed regulations reflect changes to the applicable law made by the Act of December 28, 1980, as amended by the Technical Corrections Act of 1982, by the Tax Reform Act of 1986, and by the Technical and Miscellaneous Revenue Act of 1988. The new proposed regulations will affect employers (and shareholders of employers) that provide deferred compensation directly or indirectly to foreign employees and will provide the public and Internal Revenue Service personnel with the guidance needed to comply with section 404A of the Internal Revenue Code of 1986. These new proposed regulations supersede the prior proposed regulations published in the Federal Register on April 8, 1985 (50 FR 13821).

DATES: Written comments must be received by [*INSERT DATE THAT IS 60 DAYS AFTER THE DATE OF PUBLICATION OF THESE PROPOSED REGULATIONS IN THE FEDERAL REGISTER*]. Requests to speak (with outlines of oral comments) at a public hearing scheduled for October 5, 1993, at 10:00 a.m., must be received by September 14, 1993. See notice of hearing published elsewhere in this issue of the Federal Register.

ADDRESSES: Send comments, requests to appear at the public hearing, and outlines of comments to be presented to: Internal Revenue Service, P.O. Box 7604, Ben Franklin Station, Attention: CC:CORP:T:R (EE-14-81), Room 5228, Washington, D.C. 20044.

FOR FURTHER INFORMATION CONTACT: Concerning the proposed regulations, Elizabeth A. Purcell, Office of the Associate Chief Counsel (Employee Benefits and Exempt Organizations) at (202) 622-6080 (not a toll-free number). Concerning the hearing, Carol Savage, Regulations Unit, at (202) 622-8452 (not a toll-free number).

SUPPLEMENTARY INFORMATION:

Statutory Authority.

This document contains proposed amendments to the Income Tax Regulations (26 CFR part 1) under sections 404A and 7805(a) of the Internal Revenue Code (Code).

Paperwork Reduction Act.

The collection of information requirement contained in this notice of proposed rulemaking has been submitted to the Office of Management and Budget for review in accordance with the Paperwork Reduction Act of 1980 (44 U.S.C. 3504(h)). Comments on the collection of information should be sent to the Office of Management and Budget, Attention: Desk Officer for the Department of the Treasury, Office of Information and Regulatory Affairs, Washington, D.C. 20503, with copies to the Internal Revenue Service, Attention: IRS Reports Clearance Officer T:FP, Washington, D.C. 20224.

The collection of information requirement in these regulations is in §§ 1.404A-5, 1.404A-6 and 1.404A-7. This information is required by the Internal Revenue Service to determine accurately the correct deductions and reductions in earnings and profits for foreign deferred compensation. The likely respondents are businesses or other for-profit institutions.

These estimates are an approximation of the average time expected to be necessary for a collection of information. They are based on such information as is available to the Internal Revenue Service. Individual respondents may require greater or less time, depending on their particular circumstances. The estimated total annual reporting burden is 633,200 hours. The estimated annual reporting burden per respondent varies from 5 hours to 1,000 hours, depending on individual circumstances, with an estimated average of 506 hours. The estimated number of respondents is 1,250. The estimated annual frequency: once.

Background.

On April 8, 1985, the Internal Revenue Service published in the Federal Register proposed amendments to the Income Tax Regulations under section 404A of the Internal Revenue Code of 1954 (now 1986) (50 FR 13821). Comments were requested and received, and a public hearing was held on September 20, 1985. After consideration of the comments received, the Service has determined that, rather than promulgate final regulations, it is more appropriate to withdraw the original proposed regulations and propose new regulations. This determination is based on a number of factors, including the number of significant substantive changes made to the prior proposed rules, changes to the underlying statute and other relevant Code provisions, and a need to reorganize the regulations. For a general discussion of section 404A and description of the prior proposed regulations, see the preamble to the prior proposed regulations published in the Federal Register on April 8, 1985.

The significant differences (or, where appropriate, the significant similarities) between these new proposed regulations and the prior proposed regulations are discussed, section by section, in the remainder of this preamble. Prior proposed §1.404A-1 remains new proposed §1.404A-1. However, the rules found in §1.404A-2 of the prior proposed regulations are now incorporated in new proposed §§1.404A-6 and 1.404A-7. Prior proposed §§1.404A-3, 1.404A-4, 1.404A-5 and 1.404A-6 are redesignated §§1.404A-2, 1.404A-3, 1.404A-4 and 1.404A-5, respectively.

Section 1.404A-1: General rules concerning deductions and adjustments to earnings and profits for foreign deferred compensation plans.

90-percent test

As a condition to electing treatment as a qualified foreign plan, section 404A(e)(2) requires that 90 percent or more of the amounts taken into account for a taxable year under the plan be attributable to services performed by nonresident aliens, the compensation for which is not subject to United States federal income tax. Prior proposed §1.404A-1(c) provided that, in determining whether the 90-percent test is satisfied, accrued benefits may be calculated under any reasonable method. It also provided that the rules for calculating the present value of accrued benefits at normal retirement age (except for the actuarial assumption safe harbor) under §1.416-1 (concerning the determination whether a retirement plan is top-heavy) are presumed to be reasonable for this purpose.

Many commentators suggested that these rules for calculating accrued benefits for purposes of the 90-percent test are extremely burdensome and disproportionately expensive. They also suggested that the calculations require a degree of precision and accuracy that in many cases is unwarranted by the circumstances (i.e., where very few plan participants are United States citizens or residents and little compensation of the plan participants is subject to United States federal income tax). To give taxpayers in those cases a less burdensome and less expensive means of demonstrating compliance with the 90-percent requirement, a safe harbor provision has been provided in paragraph (c)(2) of new proposed §1.404A-1. It provides that the 90-percent requirement of §1.404A-1(a)(3) will be deemed satisfied with respect to a plan if the participants' benefits under the plan increase generally in proportion to their compensation taken into account under the plan, and the sum of (1) the compensation of United States citizens and residents taken into account under the plan, and (2) any other compensation subject to United States federal income tax taken into account under the plan, does not exceed five percent of all compensation taken into account under the plan for the plan year. This safe harbor provision does not apply, however, if the Commissioner determines that a significant purpose of the plan is to provide benefits not otherwise eligible for tax benefits under the Internal Revenue Code for participants who are United States citizens or residents. An example is provided in new proposed §1.404A-1(c)(4) to illustrate the application of this safe harbor provision.

Termination indemnity plans

Many commentators suggested that the regulations be revised to provide specifically that certain termination indemnity plans are considered deferred compensation plans for purposes of section 404A. The laws of many countries require employers to maintain termination indemnity plans to pay termination benefits. Some of these termination indemnities are payable solely upon involuntary discharge (other than by reason of mandatory retirement) and thus may be viewed as dismissal wage plans under United States tax principles. However, other termination indemnity plans are akin to deferred compensation plans. For example, one commentator noted that, in one European country, employers are required by law to provide severance benefits equal to one month's pay (final pay) for each year of service. These benefits are fully vested and payable upon all events of termination, including retirement.

Because the provisions of termination indemnity plans may vary widely, paragraph (iii) of the definition of deferred compensation in paragraph (e) of new proposed §1.404A-1 provides guidelines for determining whether such a plan provides deferred compensation. A termination indemnity plan is considered to provide deferred compensation if: (1) a major purpose of the plan is to provide for the payment of retirement benefits, (2) it has a benefit formula providing for payment based at least in part upon length of service, (3) it provides for the payment of benefits to employees (or their beneficiaries) after the employee's retirement, death or other termination of employment, and (4) it meets such other requirements as may be prescribed by the Commissioner with respect to termination indemnity plans. An example is provided under the definition of deferred compensation in paragraph (e) of new proposed §1.404A-1 to illustrate this provision. Any plan that meets these requirements is treated as providing deferred compensation, whether or not it is called a termination indemnity plan.

Equivalent of a trust

Section 404A(b)(5)(A) provides that, in order for a contribution to be taken into account in the case of a qualified funded plan, it must be paid to a trust or the "equivalent of a trust". The reference to the equivalent of a trust recognizes that, in some foreign countries, the common law concept of a trust does not exist. Thus, in those countries, the arrangement used to fund deferred compensation benefits for purposes of section 404A(b)(5)(A) must be functionally equivalent to a trust. The essential function of a trust in the context of a United States deferred compensation plan is to provide an entity separate from an employer through which deferred compensation benefits may be secured and liabilities funded. The four elements necessary to accomplish this function are provided in the definition of "equivalent of a trust" in paragraph (e) of new proposed §1.404A-1. These elements have been revised to allow an employer some latitude to insulate corpus and income from the claims of an employer's creditors, and to remove the concept of legal and beneficial ownership. Finally, the concept of fiduciary duty has been replaced with legally enforceable duty.

Some commentators urged the Service to endorse as the equivalent of a trust the so-called "Security Contract" or "Security Concept" developed in Germany. As explained by those commentators, the Security Contract combines a book reserve commitment by an employer with a pledge and guaranty. First, an employer establishes a book reserve for its pension liabilities for which it receives a tax deduction under German law. It then establishes a wholly-owned subsidiary to which it transfers assets to fund its pension liabilities. As such, the corpus and income of the subsidiary are separately identifiable from an employer's general assets. This arrangement, without more, would not satisfy the requirements of the equivalent of a trust because the assets held by the subsidiary are not protected from the claims of an employer's creditors in the event of bankruptcy or receivership. Under the Security Contract concept, however, the subsidiary also pledges its assets irrevocably to a custodian who then gives a guaranty to the employees to pay the benefits up to the assets pledged to the custodian in the event an employer declares bankruptcy or goes into receivership. The custodian's guaranty is intended to place a prior lien on the assets pledged and protect them from the claims of an employer's creditors in the event of bankruptcy or receivership.

As one commentator asserted, however, it is unclear under German law that the arrangement provides such protection. According to that commentator, in the event of bankruptcy or receivership, the German Pension Guaranty Corporation is required by law to settle an employer's book reserve commitment. The Pension Guaranty Corporation then becomes a non-privileged creditor in the bankruptcy process and exercises any rights the employees have under the plan. As a non-privileged creditor, the Pension Guaranty Corporation is not entitled to all the assets pledged to the custodian, but is limited to a percentage of employer assets that is consistent with its general bankruptcy quota. Thus, it appears that the subsidiary's assets may be subject to the claims of an employer's creditors before all claims of the Pension Guaranty Corporation, exercising the rights of the employees under the plan, are settled.

Until the Service is satisfied that the corpus and income of the subsidiary are to be used to satisfy the claims of the employees and their beneficiaries (or those exercising their rights under the plan) before those of an employer's creditors, the Service cannot endorse this arrangement as the equivalent of a trust.

Exclusive means for deduction or reduction in earnings and profits

For foreign plans that fail to satisfy the requirements of section 404A, section 404 governs deductions for deferred compensation expense. For plans that are not qualified under section 401, section 404(a)(5) generally provides that the employer's deduction for contributions is delayed until amounts attributable to the employer's contribution are includible in the plan participant's gross income. In addition, under section 404(a)(5), deductions are denied altogether unless separate accounts are maintained for each participant. The Service took this position with respect to a foreign plan in Private Letter Ruling 7904042 (Oct. 25, 1978), available in the Freedom of Information Reading Room, Room 1569, Internal Revenue Service, 1111 Constitution Avenue, N.W., Washington, D.C. 20224. This position is reflected, in part, in paragraph (a) of new proposed §1.404A-1.

Prior proposed §1.404A-1(e) provided that earnings and profits (or accumulated profits) may be reduced with respect to payments by an employer to a funded foreign deferred compensation plan that are not deductible under section 404(a) even where an election under section 404A has not been made. Upon reexamination of the Congressional intent underlying the enactment of section 404A, however, the Service now believes that the position reflected in the prior proposed regulations is inconsistent with the purposes of section 404A (and the limitations thereunder). Thus, in accordance with the Secretary's section 404A(h) authority to prescribe regulations necessary to carry out the purposes of section 404A, paragraph (a) of new proposed §1.404A-1 provides that section 404A provides the exclusive means by which an employer may reduce earnings and profits for deferred compensation in situations other than those in which a reduction of earnings and profits is permitted under section 404. See also the discussion below of the relevance of sections 61, 671 through 679, and 1001 in this context.

Request for comments concerning foreign corporations that are not controlled

The Service is considering whether simplified or alternative methods of determining allowable earnings and profits reductions under section 404A might be appropriate for foreign corporations that are not controlled. Suggestions are invited on this matter.

Section 1.404A-2: Rules for qualified funded plans.

Substantiality of payments to trust

A commentator suggested that the focus of the flush language of paragraph (b) of prior proposed §1.404A-3 (requiring a trust to have "substantiality") should be on the substantiality of payments to a trust (or the equivalent of a trust) rather than on the substantiality of a trust (or the equivalent of a trust), because the determination with respect to the latter can be made under the standards set forth in prior proposed §1.404A-1(g)(9). Accordingly, new proposed §1.404A-2(b)(2)(i) provides that employer contributions must have substance. For example, contributions may not be made in the form of a promissory note. This also means that the contributions must be accumulated in the trust (or the equivalent of a trust) in order to be distributed as benefits under a deferred compensation plan. Whether contributions are being accumulated in the trust (or the equivalent of a trust) to be distributed as benefits will depend on the facts and circumstances. The example in paragraph (b)(5) of new proposed §1.404A-2 reflects this change.

Exclusive benefit rule

Section 404A(b)(5)(A) provides that, in the case of a qualified funded plan, a contribution is taken into account only if it is paid to a trust (or the equivalent of a trust) that meets the requirements of section 401(a)(2). Section 401(a)(2) provides generally that it must be impossible, at any time prior to the satisfaction of all liabilities with respect to employees and their beneficiaries under the trust, for any part of the corpus or income to be used for, or diverted to, purposes other than the exclusive benefit of the employees or their beneficiaries. Thus, in effect, section 404A(b)(5)(A) reemphasizes, with regard to qualified funded plans, the general rule found in section 404A(e) that any "qualified foreign plan" must be for the exclusive benefit of an employer's employees or their beneficiaries. (As stated in the Senate Finance Committee Report, "[f]irst, the plan must be for the exclusive benefit of an employer's employees or their beneficiaries." S. Rep. No. 1039, 96th Cong., 2d Sess. 13 (1980).)

To reflect this emphasis, new proposed §1.404A-2(b)(2) provides that one important factor that is taken into account in determining whether a trust has or has not been operated in a manner consistent with the exclusive benefit rule is whether it has not or has been involved in a transaction that would be described in section 4975(c)(1) if the plan were the type of plan subject to those rules. For example, a loan from the trust to an employer, on any terms, ordinarily would be a circumstance that strongly suggests noncompliance with section 404A(b)(5)(A). Similarly, a sale, exchange, or lease of any property between the trust and an employer would generally violate this provision. These rules, as set forth in new proposed §1.404A-2(b)(2), apply prospectively.

Contributions deemed made before payment

Paragraph (c) of new proposed §1.404A-2 clarifies the circumstances under which a payment made after the last day of an employer's taxable year is deemed to have been made on that last day.

Frequency of actuarial valuations

The new proposed regulations generally continue the requirement in the prior proposed regulations that an actuarial valuation be made no less frequently than once every three years for a qualified funded plan. However, for interim years, they require a reasonable actuarial determination to be made of whether the full funding limit in §1.404A-5(c)(2) applies to the plan, and provide that the Commissioner may require an actuarial valuation in interim years under appropriate circumstances. It is anticipated that the Commissioner will not exercise this authority except in situations similar to those described in §1.412(c)(9)-1(d) of the proposed regulations.

Shareholder-level consequences

A sentence in paragraph (d)(1) of prior proposed §1.404A-3 provided that, where a foreign corporation maintained a qualified funded plan, the deductible amount was taken into account for the shareholder's taxable year in which or with which an employer's taxable year ended. This sentence has been deleted because section 404A does not govern the time at which adjustments to earnings and profits of a foreign employer corporation for a particular year are taken into account at the shareholder level.

Section 1.404A-3: Rules for qualified reserve plans.

The new proposed regulations have modified in several ways the guidance on the calculation of the amount that may be taken into account under a qualified reserve plan. First, the presentation has been changed in order to parallel the components of net periodic pension cost used in Statement of Financial Accounting Standards No. 87 "Employer's Accounting for Pensions" (1985), available from the Financial Accounting Standards Board, 401 Merritt 7, Norwalk, CT 06856. Thus, the amount taken into account for a year is based on the sum of a type of "service cost", "interest cost" and the amortization of the increase or decrease in the reserve from other sources. As part of this change, the steps for determining the actuarial gain or loss have been made explicit. In addition, as discussed below, certain increases or decreases in the reserve that were subject to amortization under the old proposed regulations are now included in the reasonable addition to the reserve.

Ten-Year amortization

Section 404A(c)(4) provides for the spreading over ten years of certain increases and decreases in reserves on account of various events including a catch-all category of "such other factors as may be prescribed by regulations". The Senate Finance Committee Report includes two suggestions of possible items that could be included in this category: "adjustments in the reserve resulting from changes in levels of compensation on which benefits depend or the vesting in one year of a benefit which was accrued in a prior year." S. Rep. No. 1039, 96th Cong. 2d. Sess. 14 (1980).

Some commentators criticized the rule in paragraph (d) of prior proposed §1.404A-4 providing for the amortization of changes in the reserve arising from these two sources. They suggested that the ten-year amortization requirement for increases or decreases to the reserve on account of changes in the level of compensation upon which plan benefits depend, and for vesting of benefits accrued in prior years, was unnecessary because those items are ongoing costs of the plan that are specifically contemplated by the plan and will arise periodically as each participant's circumstances dictate. Thus, those increases or decreases can be expected to occur regularly in the aggregate and will not create the "bunching" that section 404A(c)(4) was designed to avoid.

The new proposed regulations respond to commentators' concerns by incorporating certain increases in the reserve (as described below) into the definition of the reasonable addition to a reserve, subject to an anti-abuse rule. The effect of this change is to allow immediate recognition, rather than ten-year amortization, of these changes. Under normal circumstances this immediate recognition will not result in significant bunching of income or deductions. Further, to the extent bunching occurs, abuse potential is limited because the bunching is the result of a deferral of deductions rather than the recognition of these items. Finally, as discussed below, for taxable years beginning after December 31, 1986, the indirect foreign tax credit is determined using post-1986 earnings and profits (i.e., aggregated for all post-1986 years). Use of a multi-year earnings and profits pool diminishes the effect of bunching on the foreign tax credit.

The increases in reserve that are now included in the reasonable addition to the reserve are those increases that result from expected changes in compensation and from the increase in vesting for employees whose liabilities were included in the reserve as of the beginning of the year. Thus, for example, the reasonable addition to the reserve may reflect an expected increase in compensation of five percent and expected changes in the vesting percentage in the current year for all employees in the reserve as of the beginning of the year. By contrast, any increase in reserve that results from compensation changes that are greater than expected or from the inclusion of newly-vested employees who were not included in the prior year's reserve are categorized as actuarial losses subject to ten-year amortization.

Section 1.404A-4: United States and foreign law limitations on amounts taken into account for qualified foreign plans.

Section 404A(d) limitation—pooling of earnings and profits

Section 404A(d)(3) provides that, in determining the earnings and profits (and accumulated profits) of any foreign corporation with respect to a qualified foreign plan, the amount determined under section 404A with respect to any plan for any taxable year must not exceed the amount allowed as a deduction under the appropriate foreign law for such taxable year. As the legislative history makes clear, this limitation was imposed in response to "the possibilities for distortion of a taxpayer's indirect foreign tax credit which are presented by the present annual system for determining the amount of the foreign taxes paid by a subsidiary which are attributable to dividends paid to U.S. shareholders." S. Rep. No. 1039, 96th Cong., 2d Sess. 15 (1980). The legislative history further makes clear that "[t]his potential for distortion might be eliminated if the indirect credit were computed with reference to the subsidiary's accumulated foreign taxes and undistributed accumulated profits for all years." *Id.*

Section 1202(a) of the Tax Reform Act of 1986 amended section 902 to provide for computation of the indirect foreign tax credit by pooling all post-1986 earnings and profits and all post-1986 creditable foreign taxes. These amendments to section 902 prevent the distortion at which section 404A(d)(3) was aimed. Section 1012(b)(4) of the Technical and Miscellaneous Revenue Act of 1988 added specific regulatory authority to section 404A(d)(3) (retroactive to enactment of the Tax Reform Act of 1986), to take this change in the law into account. Accordingly, pursuant to that grant of regulatory authority, new proposed §1.404A-4 provides that, for taxable years beginning after December 31, 1986, the reduction of earnings and profits of a foreign corporation with respect to a qualified foreign plan is determined without regard to the tax deduction under foreign law for that year. This new rule allows any amount that is disallowed for a year (because the foreign tax deduction for that year is greater than the amount allowed under section 404A(b) or (c)) to be carried forward to a future year, in which it may increase the amount allowable under section 404A.

Section 404A(d) limitation

Section 404A(d)(1) provides that the annual amount allowable under section 404A "shall equal" the lesser of the cumulative United States amount or the cumulative foreign amount, reduced by the aggregate amount. Prior proposed §1.404A-5 (a) provided that the annual amount allowable "shall not exceed" these cumulative amounts. The new proposed regulations adopt the language of the statute. See new proposed §1.404A-4 (b).

Foreign currency rules

One commentator requested guidance with respect to a number of foreign currency issues. Sections 985-989 were subsequently enacted by the Tax Reform Act of 1986. These sections, effective for taxable years beginning after December 31, 1986, address many of the problems identified by the commentator. Paragraph (d)(1) in new proposed §1.404A-4 clarifies that, for taxable years beginning after December 31, 1986, income or loss of foreign branches and earnings and profits (or deficits in earnings and profits) of foreign corporations are determined in functional currency as defined in section 985. For taxable years beginning before January 1, 1987, paragraph (d)(2) in new proposed §1.404A-4 provides that the rules in effect for those taxable years determine the amount of income or loss or earnings and profits (or deficit in earnings and profits) for the foreign branch or subsidiary. A new paragraph (d)(3) provides special rules for those circumstances where the net worth method of accounting is used.

Section 1.404A-5: Additional limitations on amounts taken into account for qualified foreign plans.

New proposed §1.404A-5 clarifies the evidentiary requirements and rules on actuarial assumptions. No significant changes are made to the rules in prior proposed §1.404A-6, which are now contained in new proposed §1.404A-5.

Section 1.404A-6: Elections under section 404A and other changes in accounting method.

Time and manner for making elections

Paragraph (b)(5) of prior proposed §1.404A-2 provided that elections made under section 404A must be made no later than the time prescribed by law for filing the United States tax return for a United States taxpayer's taxable year. For a qualified foreign plan maintained by a foreign corporation, the regulations have been modified to conform the filing requirements to the general rules applicable to tax accounting elections on behalf of foreign corporations under section 964. For example, under the new proposed regulations, a section 404A election need not be made before the United States shareholder's tax liability is affected by the earnings and profits of the foreign corporation. Such an effect on the United States shareholder's tax liability may occur as the result of any of the following: a dividend distribution, an income inclusion under section 951(a), a section 1248 transaction, a section 864(e) basis adjustment by earnings and profits, or an inclusion in income of the earnings of a qualified electing fund under section 1293(a)(1).

The prior proposed regulations provided that, in order for "protective" or "Method (2)" elections to be effective, taxpayers who made those elections had to file amended returns no later than 90 days after the date on which the final regulations were published in the Federal Register. See Ann. 81-114, Ann. 81-148 and Ann. 82-128, reproduced as an appendix to this preamble. Otherwise, the elections would have no effect. Numerous commentators suggested that the 90-day period is inadequate for taxpayers to evaluate the final regulations, collect the required data, make the appropriate actuarial calculations, decide whether the election is beneficial, and file the required returns. Thus, the deadlines for perfecting retroactive elections and making or perfecting certain other elections in new proposed §1.404A-7 have generally been extended to 365 days after the publication of final regulations.

Single plan

As originally proposed, §1.404A-2(b)(6)(i) provided that an election may be made with respect to each plan that qualifies as a "single plan". The term "single plan" has for this purpose the same definition as it has in §1.414(l)-1(b). Commentators asked for an illustration of the application of this single plan rule to an existing deferred compensation plan that is split into two single plans for purposes of section 404A. Thus, a new example has been added in paragraph (a)(2) of new proposed §1.404A-6.

Section 481(a) adjustment

New proposed §1.404A-6(a) addresses the adoption of methods of accounting and changes in methods of accounting with respect to a foreign deferred compensation plan for which an election under section 404A has been made. It clarifies, for example, that an initial election with respect to a pre-existing plan, termination of an election, revocation of an election, and a change in actuarial funding method, constitute changes in methods of accounting under section 446(e) and section 481(a). To compute the section 481(a) adjustment upon a change in method of accounting under section 404A, §1.404A-6(f)(6) of the prior proposed regulations required a historical computation. Taxpayers were to compute contributions, deductions or reductions in earnings and profits from the establishment of the plan to the first day of the first year in which a section 404A election was made. Commentators argued that this historical approach was unduly burdensome.

The new proposed regulations respond to commentators' concerns by generally replacing the historical computation requirement with a "snapshot" approach to determining the amount of the section 481(a) adjustment for purposes of section 404A. As illustrated below, the snapshot approach is adopted in the proposed regulations in an effort to reduce substantially taxpayers' recordkeeping and compliance burdens.

The snapshot approach is generally intended to compare (i) the extent to which an employer has accelerated deductions (or reductions in earnings and profits) under its old method of accounting for deferred compensation with (ii) the acceleration (if any) that would have been allowed under its new method of accounting. In the interest of avoiding historical calculations and other complexities, the snapshot approach generally attempts to compare the old and new methods of accounting based, to the extent possible, on actual reserve or fund balances existing at the time of the change. These balances generally have been reduced for amounts actually paid to plan participants and beneficiaries. However, amounts actually paid to participants and beneficiaries would be the same under both an employer's old method and its new method of accounting. Therefore, deductions attributable to such payments can be eliminated from consideration in determining both the old and the new method amounts that are compared.

In other words, in the case of both the old method and the new method of accounting, the extent of acceleration is measured by reference to a common baseline: the amount actually paid to plan participants and beneficiaries (i.e., a pay-as-you-go method). Thus, the snapshot approach generally measures the extent to which an employer, under its old method of accounting, has claimed deductions (or reductions in earnings and profits) that exceed the amount actually paid to plan participants and beneficiaries as of the change in accounting method. This amount (generally referred to as the "Old Method Closing Amount") is then compared to the deductions (or reductions in earnings and profits) in excess of the amount actually paid to plan participants and beneficiaries that the employer would have claimed for the same period under its new method of accounting (generally referred to as the "New Method Opening Amount"). The section 481(a) adjustment is equal to the difference between the Old Method Closing Amount and the New Method Opening Amount. The comparison is based on the status of the plan as of the beginning of the year of a change in accounting method.

To illustrate, if the employer has used a funded method of accounting for deferred compensation, the Old Method Closing Amount equals the amount of the fund balance as of the beginning of the year that the accounting method is changed. In determining the amount of the section 481(a) adjustment for purposes of section 404A, this fund balance is compared with a New Method Opening Amount. The New Method Opening Amount will depend on which new method of accounting the employer elects. If the employer makes a qualified funded plan election, the New Method Opening Amount generally will equal the amount of the fund balance, adjusted as appropriate to reflect the limitations in section 404A(b) and (d) on prior contributions to the fund that could have been taken into account under section 404A. If, however, the employer makes a qualified reserve plan election, the New Method Opening Amount generally will be the amount of the reserve under section 404A(c). Alternatively, if the new method of accounting is a non-section 404A method (i.e., a pay-as-you-go method), the New Method Opening Amount generally will be zero.

As the foregoing discussion indicates, the new method will not necessarily be a section 404A method (a qualified funded plan method or qualified reserve plan method), and the old method will not necessarily be a non-section 404A method. The section 481(a) adjustment and the proposed snapshot approach to computing the adjustment apply whether the employer is changing to or from a section 404A method or from one section 404A method to another. For example, assume that a foreign branch has a qualified funded plan with a trust fund balance of 15 of functional currency (as defined in section 985(b)). Assume that this fund balance resulted from FC10 of deductible contributions to the fund under section 404A, plus FC5 of net investment income earned within the fund. Under the snapshot approach, the Old Method Closing Amount upon a change to qualified reserve plan treatment is FC15. Assuming that the reserve under the qualified reserve plan method is FC20 as of the date of the method change, the New Method Opening Amount is FC20, and the amount of the section 481(a) adjustment under section 404A is a negative FC5.

By using the amount of the fund balance in determining both the Old Method Closing Amount and the New Method Opening Amount, the proposed regulations require consideration of both the deductions previously taken by the employer and the accumulated net income (or inside build-up) of a fund in calculating the amount of the section 481(a) adjustment for purposes of section 404A. The Service believes that, in addition to permitting the adoption of a simplified method for determining the section 481(a) adjustment, consideration of a fund's accumulated net income under the snapshot approach avoids additional complexities that might result from the application of sections 61 and 1001 at the time of an election under section 404A. For example, consider an employer that makes a qualified funded plan election after having used a funded method of accounting for a foreign deferred compensation plan that is not a qualified funded plan. Ordinarily, the value of the fund (which is used to satisfy the employer's plan liabilities) will exceed the employer's contributions to the fund (net of the fund's previous payments to plan participants and beneficiaries). If the snapshot method were not applied, arguably sections 61 and 1001 would result in a recognition of income (or increase in earnings and profits) by the employer at the time of the election equal to the excess of the value of the fund over the employer's basis in the fund. This result is consistent with the treatment of a change in method of accounting that consists of a qualified funded plan election as involving a change in the status of the fund from a grantor trust (defined and treated in accordance with sections 671 through 679) to a non-grantor trust (treated in a manner analogous to the treatment of a trust under a section 401(a) tax-qualified plan). The Service solicits comments from interested parties on this analysis and on the utility of the snapshot approach in reducing taxpayer burden.

Effect of section 404A(d)(1) limits on section 481(a) adjustment computation

Since the limitations of section 404A(d)(1) are part of the section 404A method of accounting under the new proposed regulations, the snapshot section 481(a) adjustment calculation must take into account the cumulative foreign amount limitation in section 404A(d) and new proposed §1.404A-4. This is a departure from §1.404A-6(f)(9) in the prior proposed regulations. The snapshot approach includes a simplified method to make this adjustment in computing the section 481(a) adjustment. More specifically, paragraph (g) of new proposed §1.404A-6 allows taxpayers to use the snapshot approach to compute the initial cumulative United States and foreign law limitations under section 404A(d) as of the beginning of a year of change in method of accounting. The rules to initialize the cumulative United States amount, cumulative foreign amount and the aggregate amount rely on the constant relationship between these three amounts (i.e., the aggregate amount always equals the lesser of the two cumulative amounts).

Section 481(a) adjustment period

As required by section 404A(g)(5), the period for taking into account the section 481(a) adjustment arising from an election or a re-election under section 404A is 15 years. Additionally, new proposed § 1.404A-6(e)(2)(iii) provides for a six-year section 481(a) adjustment period for a change in method of accounting arising from the termination or revocation of an election under section 404A, and for any other change in accounting method under section 404A. This new paragraph also requires netting of any section 481(a) adjustment remaining from a previous change in method in determining the amount to be taken into account during the six-year section 481(a) adjustment period. The example in new proposed § 1.404A-6(e)(4) illustrates this netting rule.

Examples in the new proposed regulations illustrate the principle under section 446(e) and its underlying administrative procedures that the District Director may modify a taxpayer's calculated section 481(a) adjustment under section 404A if the District Director (1) determines that the taxpayer used an erroneous method of accounting in an open year prior to the year in which the taxpayer's qualified funded plan or qualified reserve plan election is effective, and (2) requires the taxpayer to change its erroneous method of accounting in that earlier open year. For example, if a taxpayer erroneously deducted FC100 for amounts accrued under a reserve plan in an open year prior to the effective date of a qualified reserve plan election under section 404A, the District Director could require the taxpayer to change its method of accounting in that earlier open year and to take a positive FC100 section 481(a) adjustment into account entirely in that earlier open year (rather than permitting the positive FC100 amount to be netted against any New Method Opening Amount under the snapshot approach and spread prospectively over a 15-year section 481(a) adjustment period). See section 2.02 of Rev. Proc. 92-20, 1992-1 C.B. 685.

Section 1.404A-7: Effective date and retroactive application.

Prior proposed § 1.404A-2(c), relating to retroactive elections, has been moved to § 1.404A-7. This change was made because the rules relating to retroactive elections are relatively discrete and thus logically should be set apart from the general election rules. Because the importance of these rules will greatly diminish within a few years, their placement at the end of the regulations will improve the clarity of the remainder of the regulations for the future. Other specific changes to the retroactive election rules are discussed below.

All-or-nothing rule

Many commentators criticized the rule in paragraph (c)(2)(ii) of prior proposed § 1.404A-2 as an improper interpretation of section 2(e)(2) of the Act of December 28, 1980 (Pub. L. 96-603). Prior proposed § 1.404A-2(c)(2)(i) provided that a taxpayer could elect, during its "open period," for section 404A to apply to a qualified foreign plan maintained by a foreign subsidiary. However, prior proposed § 1.404A-2(c)(2)(i) conditioned that election for any plan on a taxpayer electing to apply section 404A with respect to all written plans of every foreign subsidiary (whether or not wholly owned) that defer the receipt of compensation and that satisfy the requirements of section 404A(e)(1) and (2). Commentators argued that the "all-or-nothing rule" of section 2(e)(2) of the Act of December 28, 1980, simply provides that a taxpayer may elect to have section 404A apply for certain prior years, and that such an election must be made for all of a taxpayer's foreign subsidiaries. It does not, however, require that a taxpayer make an election under section 404A for any of its foreign subsidiaries' plans. According to this view, once the election is made to have section 404A apply to the foreign subsidiaries for prior years, the consequences of making or not making an election under section 404A will be determined as though section 404A had been in effect for those years.

After further consideration, the proposed regulations adopt the commentators' view of section 2(e)(2) of the Act of December 28, 1980. Thus, if a taxpayer makes an election to have section 404A apply retroactively to its foreign subsidiaries during its open period, the election to have section 404A apply must be made for all of a taxpayer's foreign subsidiaries (whether or not wholly owned) during a taxpayer's open period. Accordingly, if a taxpayer elects to have section 404A apply during a taxpayer's open period, it may not rely on any other law or rule of law to reduce earnings and profits (or accumulated profits) of any foreign subsidiary with respect to deferred compensation expenses, regardless of whether the taxpayer elects to apply section 404A to any specific deferred compensation plan. Paragraph (b) of new § 1.404A-7 reflects this view, and paragraph (c)(5) illustrates this rule with an example.

Making, perfecting and revoking retroactive elections

New proposed § 1.404A-7 provides rules for making, perfecting and revoking retroactive effective date elections as well as retroactive plan by plan elections for qualified foreign plans maintained by foreign subsidiaries and for qualified funded plans maintained by foreign branches. Taxpayers are afforded 365 days after publication of the final regulations to decide whether to perfect or revoke retroactive elections or to make, revoke or re-elect in intervals of six or more years, effective for taxable years in the open period (as defined in new proposed § 1.404A-7(g)(6)) and continuing after taxable years beginning after December 31, 1979. Taxpayers must file amended returns and attach statements in order to perfect a retroactive election and to conform all items to the treatment consistent with election or revocation. If the amended returns and statements are not timely filed, the retroactive elections will be deemed revoked.

Alternative to contemporaneous evidence requirement

Many commentators criticized the rule in prior proposed § 1.404A-2(c)(4)(iii) prohibiting a retroactive election if a taxpayer was unable to calculate the requisite section 481(a) adjustment based upon actual data, because, in effect, it unduly restricted taxpayers' ability to make retroactive elections. The commentators were concerned that many taxpayers would lack "actual data", and thus be unable to make the election, and that, even if such data were technically available, its retrieval would be prohibitively burdensome. After further consideration, the Service has altered this requirement. Accordingly, new proposed § 1.404A-7(f) provides that the section 481(a) adjustment must be made based upon contemporaneous substantiation quality data. If contemporaneous substantiation quality data is not readily available, however, the adjustment may be based on data which are combinations of actual contemporaneous evidence and reasonable actuarial backward projections of substantiation quality data.

For the convenience of taxpayers, Ann. 81-114, 1981 I.R.B. 21, Ann. 81-148, 1981-39 I.R.B. 15, and Ann. 82-128, 1982-39 I.R.B. 103, concerning Method (1) and Method (2) elections, are reproduced below.

APPENDIX

ANNOUNCEMENT 81-114, 1981-28 I.R.B. 21

This announcement provides guidance relating to section 404A of the Internal Revenue Code. Until proposed regulations are published, taxpayers may rely on the guidance provided below.

Section 404A, added by the Act of December 28, 1980, Pub. L. 96-603 (1981-5 I.R.B. 31), allows taxpayers to make certain elections concerning deductions for amounts paid or accrued by an employer under qualified foreign plans. The two types of qualified foreign plans are qualified funded plans and qualified reserve plans. A qualified foreign plan is any written plan which defers the receipt of compensation and which satisfies two requirements. First, the plan must be for the exclusive benefit of the employer's employees or their beneficiaries. Second, 90 percent or more of the amounts taken into account for the taxable year under the plan must be attributable to services performed by nonresident aliens, the compensation for which is not subject to federal income tax. In addition, the employer must properly elect to have section 404A apply to such plan. If an employer does not make such an election, deductions (or reductions in earnings and profits) are allowed only as provided under section 404 for plans and trusts meeting the requirements of that section.

The rules of section 404A are applicable for taxable years beginning after December 31, 1979, and for certain prior years to the extent the taxpayer elects to have the provisions of section 404A of the Code apply retroactively. Pending the issuance of regulations relating to such elections, the elections referred to in section 404A(e)(3) and (f)(2) of the Code may be made either by (1) claiming the permissible deduction or credit on the taxpayer's income tax return for the first taxable year ending on or after December 31, 1980, including extensions (or an amended return that is filed no later than the end of the extended time period prescribed in section 6081, whether or not such time is actually extended for filing the taxpayer's return), or (2) attaching a statement of election to the taxpayer's income tax return within the time period described in the first method. If the election is made by attaching a statement of election under method (2), the taxpayer's current return would not include deductions or in the case of foreign subsidiaries, take into account reductions in earnings and profits that relate to foreign deferred compensation plans. Deductions or credits consistent with the election would be included on an amended return, to be filed no later than the deadline (described below) for revoking the election. Under either method, the taxpayer must attach to the return a list of plans with respect to which the elections are made. Method (1) or method (2) may also be used for the elections described in section 2(e) of Pub. L. 96-603. When method (2) is used in connection with section 2(e) of Pub. L. 96-603, taxpayers need not amend past returns until regulations are issued.

A taxpayer must determine the amount deductible under section 404A(d) based, in part, on the cumulative foreign amount as defined in section 404A(d)(2)(B). No deduction is allowable under section 404A unless the cumulative foreign amount is established in one of the documents described in section 404A(g)(2)(A)(i), (ii) or (iii) of the Code. Section 404A(g)(2)(A)(iii) authorizes the Secretary to promulgate regulations that would accept certain unspecified statements or evidence as being sufficient to establish the amount of the deduction under foreign law. Until such time as regulations are promulgated under section 404A(g)(2)(A)(iii), the requirements of that section will be considered to be satisfied by a statement prepared at or before the time the return is filed, which lists separately for each plan the cumulative foreign amount and which states that such cumulative foreign amount has been determined pursuant to the requirements of the appropriate foreign tax law. The statement must be prepared by the U.S. taxpayer or a person authorized to practice before the Service. While a taxpayer need not attach any of these documents to its tax return, the taxpayer must furnish the documents for examination upon request of the Internal Revenue Service.

Taxpayers that have made the elections described in section 404A and/or section 2 (e) of Pub. L. 96-603 under method (2) need not prepare the statement, described in the immediately preceding paragraph, until they amend their returns. In addition, taxpayers that have made the election described in section 404A for taxable years beginning after December 31, 1979, under Method (1), and have made the election described in section 2 (e) of Pub. L. 96-603 under method (2) will satisfy section 404A(g)(2)(A)(iii) if the cumulative foreign amount in the statement reflects the aggregate foreign deductions allowed under foreign law for taxable years commencing after December 31, 1979.

Taxpayers that have already made an election, referred to in this announcement, that does not conform with the requirements stated herein may perfect that election on an amended return filed by the later of September 23, 1981 or by the due date of the taxpayer's income tax return for the first taxable year beginning after December 31, 1979, including extensions. These taxpayers may also satisfy section 404A(g)(2)(A)(iii), to the extent applicable as previously described in this announcement, by preparing the required statement within the same time limits for perfecting the elections under sections 404A(e)(3) and (f)(2).

The qualified reserve plan election, including any retroactive election described in section 2(e)(2) of Pub. L. 96-603, may be revoked on an amended return for the first taxable year ending on or after December 31, 1980, without the consent of the Commissioner until 90 days after the publication of final regulations regarding such elections. Similarly, the qualified foreign plan election and the retroactive election described in section 2(e)(3) may be revoked within the same period.

It is anticipated that the effective date of the final regulations generally will be for taxable years beginning after December 31, 1979, and such prior years as may be affected by an election under section 2(e) of Pub. L. 96-603. Accordingly, taxpayers may be required to amend their tax returns to the extent that deductions or credits claimed are inconsistent with final regulations.

ANNOUNCEMENT 81-148, 1981-39 I.R.B. 15

On June 24, 1981, the Internal Revenue Service issued Announcement 81-114, 1981-28 I.R.B. 21. The announcement was intended to provide pre-regulation guidance to taxpayers concerning recent legislation under section 404A. Taxpayers have expressed concern with respect to a statement in that announcement, with respect to reductions of earnings and profits if section 404A is not elected. Announcement 81-114 is clarified as follows:

The decision not to elect section 404A will not affect the computation of earnings and profits with respect to contributions to plans as allowed under prior law. In the case of an accrued liability to a reserve plan, however, such accrued liability reduces earnings and profits only as provided in section 404A with respect to the taxable years described in section 2 (e) of Pub. L. 96-603, 1980-2 C.B. 684.

ANNOUNCEMENT 82-128, 1982-39 I.R.B. 103

Taxpayers that are interested in making the elections referred to in section 404A(e)(3) and (f)(2) of the Internal Revenue Code may continue to use the "method (1)" or "method (2)" election described in Announcement 81-114, 1981-28 I.R.B. 21 for taxable years beginning after December 31, 1979, until further guidance is made available. Pending the issuance of regulations under section 404A, qualified foreign plans must comply with the reporting requirements and other rules contained in Announcement 81-114.

Effective dates.

The amendments are proposed generally to apply to taxable years beginning after December 31, 1979. The prohibited transaction rules in §1.404A-2 (a) are proposed to be effective May 6, 1993. If a taxpayer elected pursuant to section 2(e)(2) of the Act of December 28, 1980, the amendments are proposed to apply to certain prior taxable years beginning after December 31, 1970.

Special Analyses.

It has been determined that these proposed rules are not major rules as defined in Executive Order 12291. Therefore, a Regulatory Impact Analysis is not required. It has also been determined that section 553(b) of the Administrative Procedure Act (5 U.S.C. chapter 5) and the Regulatory Flexibility Act (5 U.S.C. chapter 6) do not apply to these proposed regulations and, therefore, an initial Regulatory Flexibility Analysis is not required. Pursuant to section 7805(f) of the Internal Revenue Code, these proposed regulations will be submitted to the Chief Counsel for Advocacy of the Small Business Administration for comment on their impact on small business.

Comments and Requests to Appear at the Public Hearing.

Before adopting these proposed regulations, consideration will be given to any written comments that are submitted (preferably a signed original and eight copies) to the Commissioner of Internal Revenue. All comments will be available for public inspection and copying in their entirety. Because the Treasury Department expects to issue final regulations on this matter as soon as possible, a public hearing will be held at 10:00 a.m. on October 5, 1993, in Room 2615, Internal Revenue Building, 1111 Constitution Ave., N.W., Washington, D.C. Written comments must be received by July 6, 1993. Requests to speak (with outlines of oral comments) at the public hearing must be received by September 14, 1993. See notice of hearing published elsewhere in this issue of the Federal Register.

Drafting Information.

The principal author of these proposed regulations is Elizabeth A. Purcell of the Office of the Associate Chief Counsel (Employee Benefits and Exempt Organizations), Internal Revenue Service. However, personnel from other offices of the Service and Treasury Department participated in their development.

[¶ 49,143]   Proposed Amendments of Regulation (IA-85-91), published in the Federal Register on September 20, 1993.

Statement of Procedural Rules: Liability for tax: Taxpayer appeals.—Amendments to Reg. § 601.106, relating to how a taxpayer may appeal, without going to court, adjustments affecting a taxpayer's tax liability, are proposed.

AGENCY: Internal Revenue Service (IRS), Treasury.

ACTION: Proposed Amendments to Statement of Procedural Rules and Notice of Public Hearing.

SUMMARY: This document proposes to amend the Statement of Procedural Rules relating to how a taxpayer may appeal, without going to court, adjustments affecting a taxpayer's tax liability. This document clarifies, updates, reorders, and revises the existing rules.

DATES: Written comments, requests to speak and outlines of oral comments to be presented at the public hearing scheduled for November 23, 1993, must be received by November 4, 1993.

ADDRESSES: Send submissions to: Internal Revenue Service, P.O. Box 7604, Ben Franklin Station, Attn: CC:DOM:CORP:T:R (IA-85-91), room 5228, Washington, DC 20044. In the alternative, submissions may be hand delivered to: CC:DOM:CORP:T:R (IA-85-91), room 5228, Internal Revenue Service, 1111 Constitution Avenue, NW, Washington, DC 20224. The public hearing will be held in room 2615, Internal Revenue Service Building, 1111 Constitution Avenue, NW, Washington, DC.

FOR FURTHER INFORMATION CONTACT: Cheryl Revier at telephone (202) 401-5202 (not a toll-free number).

SUPPLEMENTARY INFORMATION:

Paperwork Reduction Act

The collection of information contained in this proposed amendment is not subject to the Paperwork Reduction Act of 1980 (44 U.S.C. 3504(h)) because it concerns information collected during an administrative action.

Background

Statements of Procedural Rules inform the public of the procedures to be followed by a government agency and the public in their dealings with each other. Government agencies are required to file Statements of Procedural Rules in the Federal Register by the Administrative Procedure Act of 1946, 5 U.S.C. 552(a)(1)(c). The Statement of Procedural Rules for the Appeals function of the Internal Revenue Service is codified in § 601.106 of title 26 of the Code of Federal Regulations.

This document concerns the subpart of the Statement of Procedural Rules that describes how a taxpayer may appeal, without going to court, adjustments affecting a taxpayer's tax liability. These adjustments generally result from letters from the Internal Revenue Service, office interviews or field examinations. The appeal is made to the taxpayer's local Appeals Office of the Internal Revenue Service, which is independent of the local District Director, Service Center/Compliance Center Director, or Assistant Commissioner (International) that made the adjustments.

This document, for the most part, simply clarifies, updates, and reorders the existing rules. However, this document also changes the rules in § 601.106(b)(4) prescribing the information that a taxpayer provides to initiate an appeal (the protest rules). This document also revises the rules in § 601.106(e)(3) for disposition and settlement of cases docketed in the Tax Court to reflect Rev. Proc. 87-24, 1987 1 C.B. 720.

These rules are procedural, and, therefore, are exempt from the general notice of rulemaking requirements (5 U.S.C. 553(b)(3)(A)). However, public comment is being sought on the procedural rules because of the change in the protest rules. Comments are particularly sought on the protest rules to ensure they are both simple and effective.

Explanation of Provision

Information that a taxpayer provides to initiate an appeal

Presently, the information a taxpayer must provide to initiate an appeal varies depending on which Internal Revenue Service function has proposed the adjustments to the taxpayer's tax liability. Under the proposed general protest rule, the information would not vary in this manner.

Under proposed § 601.106(b)(4) the information to be provided to initiate an appeal varies only with the dollar amount of the adjustments to the taxpayer's liability. If the proposed change in tax for the period is not more than $25,000, a "small case request" is used to initiate an appeal. For greater amounts, a "protest" is used to initiate the appeal. (In certain cases described in § 601.106(b)(4)(iii)(C) involving $25,000 or less, however, a protest was required under the old rules and continues to be required.) A small case request should indicate the unagreed adjustments and provide the reasons for the disagreement. Generally, more detail and formality is required in a protest than in a small case request. In addition to the items in a small case request, a protest should provide the taxpayer's view of any disputed facts. The protest should also provide references to any materials the taxpayer would like to bring to Appeal's attention in support of the reasons for disagreement. Complete protest requirements are described in Publication 5, the Internal Revenue Service publication concerning taxpayers' appeal rights and protest rules.

Disposition and settlement of cases docketed in the Tax Court

Rev. Proc. 87-24, 1987-1 C.B. 720, facilitates the effective use of Appeals in Tax Court cases and the earlier development and disposition of such cases either by settlement or by trial. These rules are now fully reflected in § 601.106(e)(3).

Among other items, the following items have been clarified or have been updated in the statement of procedural rules to reflect current Appeals practice:

• Certain references to offices or positions have been changed to reflect various reorganizations within the Service.

• The positions to whom settlement authority in Appeals has been or could be delegated are clarified by specific references to the Chief, an Associate Chief, or a Team Chief in the Appeals office and to other employees specifically delegated such authority.

• The list of items for Appeals' subject matter jurisdiction is updated to include, among others, the following items: (1) any tax that is subject to the deficiency procedures; (2) partnership items that are adjusted or readjusted; (3) offers in compromise under section 7122 of the Internal Revenue Code; (4) abatement of interest under section 6404(e)(1) of the Internal Revenue Code; and (5) any other disputed tax issues that the Internal Revenue Service determines are administratively appealable.

• The regulations clarify that Appeals' may accept jurisdiction of the following docketed cases: (1) cases for which Appeals issued the notice of deficiency, liability, or other determination, and (2) cases for which the Employee Plans/Exempt Organization function issued such notice after all petitioned issues were considered by Appeals.

• The regulations make clear that Appeals' authority does not extend to include issues designated for litigation by Chief Counsel.

• Because the technical advice procedures are published annually in a revenue procedure the technical advice rules have been removed from these regulations. See, Rev. Proc. 93-2, 1993-1 I.R.B. 50.

• The procedure for settlement of docketed cases is clarified to provide that no settlement of a docketed case is binding on either the government or the taxpayer until it is entered as a decision.

• The procedure for transferring a case to another Appeals office is updated to reflect that a case may be transferred to relieve the taxpayer of hardship.

Proposed effective dates

In general, the rules will be effective on the date of publication of the final rules in the Federal Register. The rules in §601.106(b)(4), which describe how a taxpayer initiates an appeal, will be effective 60 days after the date of publication of the final rules in the Federal Register. However, if the letter (or other information enclosed with the letter) offering the taxpayer the opportunity to appeal refers to rules predating the rules in §601.106(b)(4), then the taxpayer may follow either the old rules or new rules.

Special Analyses

It has been determined that these proposed rules are not major rules as defined in Executive Order 12291. Therefore, a Regulatory Impact Analysis is not required. It has also been determined that section 553(b) of the Administrative Procedure Act (5 U.S.C. chapter 5) and the Regulatory Flexibility Act (5 U.S.C. chapter 6) do not apply to these rules, and, therefore, a Regulatory Flexibility Analysis is not required. Pursuant to section 7805(f) of the Internal Revenue Code, a copy of these proposed amendments will be submitted to the Chief Counsel for Advocacy of the Small Business Administration for comment on their impact on small business.

Comments and Public Hearing

Before these proposed amendments are adopted as final, consideration will be given to any written comments that are timely submitted (preferably an original and eight copies) to the Internal Revenue Service. All comments will be available for public inspection and copying in their entirety.

A public hearing will be held on Tuesday, November 23, 1993, at 10:00 a.m. in Room 2615, Internal Revenue Service Building, 1111 Constitution Avenue, NW, Washington, DC. The rules of §601.601(a)(3) of the Statement of Procedural Rules apply to the public hearing.

Any person who has submitted timely written comments, and who desires to present oral comments at the public hearing on the proposed amendments, should submit, not later than November 4, 1993, a request to speak and an outline of the oral comments to be presented at the hearing stating the time the person wishes to devote to each subject.

Each speaker (or group of speakers representing a single entity) will be limited to 10 minutes for an oral presentation exclusive of the time consumed by questions from the panel for the government and answers thereto.

Because of controlled access restrictions, attendees cannot be admitted beyond the lobby of the Internal Revenue Service Building before 9:45 a.m.

An agenda showing the scheduling of the speakers will be made after the outlines are received from persons testifying. Copies of the agenda will be available free of charge at the hearing.

Drafting Information

The principal author of these rules is Cheryl Revier, Office of Field Services, National Director of Appeals, Internal Revenue Service. However, personnel from other offices of the Internal Revenue Service participated in their development.

———————————

[¶ 49,144]   **Proposed Regulations (PS-55-93)**, published in the Federal Register on March 15, 1994.

Deductions: Elections: Depreciation: Intangible property.—Reg. §§ 1.167(a)-13 and 1.197-1, relating to the procedures for making elections under the intangibles provisions of the Omnibus Budget Reconciliation Act of 1993 (P.L. 103-66), are proposed.

AGENCY: Internal Revenue Service (IRS), Treasury.

ACTION: Notice of proposed rulemaking by cross-reference to temporary regulations.

SUMMARY: In the Rules and Regulations section of this issue of the Federal Register, the IRS is issuing temporary regulations relating to the procedures for making elections regarding the amortization of certain intangible property. The temporary regulations reflect changes to the law made by the Omnibus Budget Reconciliation Act of 1993 (OBRA '93) and affect electing taxpayers who acquired intangible property after July 25, 1991, or who acquired intangibles under a written binding contract in effect on August 10, 1993. The text of the temporary regulations also serves as the text of these proposed regulations.

DATES: Written comments must be received by May 16, 1994.

ADDRESSES: Send submissions to: CC:DOM:CORP:T:R (PS-55-93), room 5228, Internal Revenue Service, P.O. Box 7604, Ben Franklin Station, Washington, DC 20044. In the alternative, comments and requests may be hand delivered to: CC:DOM:CORP:T:R (PS-55-93), Internal Revenue Service, room 5228, 1111 Constitution Avenue NW, Washington, DC 20224.

FOR FURTHER INFORMATION CONTACT: John Huffman, (202) 622-3110 (not toll-free number).

SUPPLEMENTARY INFORMATION:

Paperwork Reduction Act

The collection of information contained in this notice of proposed rulemaking has been submitted to the Office of Management and Budget for review in accordance with the Paperwork Reduction Act (44 U.S.C. 3504(h)). Comments on the collection of information should be sent to the Office of Management and Budget, Attn: Desk Officer for the Department of the Treasury, Office of Information and Regulatory Affairs, Washington, DC 20503, with copies to the Internal Revenue Service, Attn: IRS Reports Clearance Officer, PC:FP, Washington, DC 20224.

The collection of information is in §1.197-1T(e). This information is required by the IRS in order to verify that electing taxpayers have properly determined amortization and depreciation deductions allowable under sections 167(f) and 197. The likely reporting entities are businesses and other for-profit institutions.

Estimated total annual reporting burden: 10,000 hours.

The estimated annual burden per respondent varies from 30 minutes to 75 minutes, depending on individual circumstances, with an estimated average of 1 hour.

Estimated number of respondents: 10,000.

Estimated annual frequency of responses: One time.

Background

Temporary regulations in the Rules and Regulations section of this issue of the Federal Register amend the Income Tax Regulations (26 CFR part 1) relating to sections 167(f) and 197 by adding §§1.167(a)-13T and 1.197-1T. The temporary regulations contain rules relating to the depreciation and amortization of certain intangible property.

The text of those temporary regulations also serves as the text of these proposed regulations. The preamble to the temporary regulations explains the temporary and proposed regulations.

Special Analyses

It has been determined that this notice of proposed rulemaking is not a significant regulatory action as defined in Executive Order 12866. Therefore, a regulatory assessment is not required. It also has been determined that section 553(b) of the Administrative Procedure Act (5 U.S.C. chapter 5) and the Regulatory Flexibility Act (5 U.S.C. chapter 6) do not apply to these regulations, and, therefore, a Regulatory Flexibility Analysis is not required. Pursuant to section 7805(f) of the Internal Revenue Code, this notice of proposed rulemaking will be submitted to the Chief Counsel for Advocacy of the Small Business Administration for comment on its impact on small business.

Comments and Requests for a Public Hearing

Before these proposed regulations are adopted as final regulations, consideration will be given to any written comments that are submitted timely (preferably a signed original and eight copies) to the IRS. All comments will be available for public inspection and copying. A public hearing may be scheduled if requested in writing by a person that timely submits written comments. If a public hearing is scheduled, notice of the date, time, and place for the hearing will be published in the Federal Register.

Drafting Information

The principal author of these regulations is John Huffman, Office of Assistant Chief Counsel (Passthroughs and Special Industries). However, other personnel from the IRS and Treasury Department participated in their development.

[¶ 49,145] Proposed Regulations and Proposed Amendments of Regulations (REG-209724-94) [originally issued as FI-42-94], published in the Federal Register on January 4, 1995.

Methods of accounting: Mark-to-market method: Dealers in securities.—Reg. §§1.475(a)-1, 1.475(a)-2 and 1.475(b)-3, relating to the mark-to-market method of accounting for securities that is required to be used by a dealer in securities, are proposed. Reg. §1.475-0, 1.475(a)-3 and 1.475(b)-4 and amendments of Reg. §§1.475(c)-1, 1.475(c)-2 and 1.475(e)-1 were adopted 12/23/96 by T.D. 8700.

AGENCY: Internal Revenue Service (IRS), Treasury.

ACTION: Notice of proposed rulemaking and notice of public hearing.

SUMMARY: This document contains proposed regulations relating to the mark-to-market method of accounting for securities that is required to be used by a dealer in securities. The proposed regulations address the relationship between mark-to-market accounting and the accrual of stated interest and discount and the amortization of premium and between mark-to-market accounting and the tax treatment of bad debts. They also provide rules relating to certain dispositions and acquisitions of securities required to be marked to market, the exemption from mark-to-market treatment of securities in certain securitization transactions, and the identification requirements for obtaining exemption from mark-to-market treatment. Finally, these proposed regulations provide guidance relating to the exclusion of REMIC residual interests from the definition of security and to the relationship between the mark-to-market provisions and the integrated transaction rules in the proposed regulations on debt instruments with contingent payments. This document also provides notice of a public hearing on these proposed regulations.

DATES: Written comments must be received by April 3, 1995. Outlines of oral comments to be presented at a public hearing scheduled for May 3, 1995, at 10 a.m. must be received by April 3, 1995.

ADDRESSES: Send submissions to: CC:DOM:CORP:T:R (FI-42-94), room 5228, Internal Revenue Service, POB 7604, Ben Franklin Station, Washington, DC 20044. In the alternative, submissions may be hand delivered between the hours of 8 a.m. and 5 p.m. to: CC:DOM:CORP:T:R (FI-42-94), Courier's Desk, Internal Revenue Service, 1111 Constitution Avenue NW, Washington, DC.

The public hearing will be held in the Internal Revenue Auditorium, 7400 corridor, Internal Revenue Building, 1111 Constitution Avenue NW, Washington, DC 20224.

FOR FURTHER INFORMATION CONTACT: Concerning §1.475(c)-2(a)(4), Carol A. Schwartz, (202) 622-3920; concerning other sections of the regulations, Robert B. Williams, (202) 622-3960, or JoLynn Ricks, (202) 622-3920; concerning submissions and the hearing, Michael Slaughter, (202) 622-7190 (not toll-free numbers).

SUPPLEMENTARY INFORMATION:

Paperwork Reduction Act

The collection of information contained in this notice of proposed rulemaking has been submitted to the Office of Management and Budget for review in accordance with the Paperwork Reduction Act (44 U.S.C. 3504(h)). Comments on the collection of information should be sent to the Office of Management and Budget, Attn: Desk Officer for the Department of the Treasury, Office of Information and Regulatory Affairs, Washington, DC 20503, with copies to the Internal Revenue Service, Attn: IRS Reports Clearance Officer, PC:FP, Washington, DC 20224.

The collection of information is in §1.475(b)-4. The information required to be recorded under §1.475(b)-4 is required by the IRS to determine whether exemption from mark-to-market treatment is properly claimed. This information will be used to make that determination upon audit of taxpayers' books and records. The likely recordkeepers are businesses or other for-profit institutions.

Estimated total annual recordkeeping burden: 2,500 hours.

The estimated annual burden per recordkeeper varies from 15 minutes to 3 hours, depending on individual circumstances, with an estimated average of 1 hour.

Estimated number of recordkeepers: 2,500.

Background

Section 475 of the Internal Revenue Code requires mark-to-market accounting for dealers in securities, broadly defined. Section 475 was added by section 13223 of the Revenue Reconciliation Act of 1993, Pub. L. 103-66, 107 Stat. 481, and is effective for all taxable years ending on or after December 31, 1993.

On December 29, 1993, temporary regulations (T.D. 8505, 58 FR 68747) and cross-reference proposed regulations (FI-72-93, 58 FR 68798) were published to furnish guidance on several issues, including the scope of exemptions from the mark-to-market requirements, certain transitional issues relating to the scope of exemptions, and the meaning of the statutory terms "dealer in securities" and "held for investment." This notice contains proposed regulations that supplement, and in a few cases revise, the proposed regulations that were published last December.

Explanation of Provisions

Stated Interest, Discount, and Premium

The proposed regulations contained in this notice provide rules for taking into account interest (including original issue discount (OID) and market discount), premium, and certain gains and losses on securities that are debt instruments. In general, immediately before a debt instrument is marked to market, Code provisions related to calculating interest must be applied, and basis must be correspondingly adjusted. The mark-to-market computations do not affect either the amount treated as interest earned from a debt instrument or the taxable years in which that interest is taken into account.

For example, immediately before a debt instrument is marked to market, accruals of unpaid qualified stated interest (QSI) must be taken into account, and basis must be correspondingly increased. This is true regardless of the taxpayer's regular method of accounting. Marking a debt instrument to market under section 475(a) precludes the deferral that a cash-basis taxpayer might have experienced in the absence of the statutory provision, and the current accrual under the proposed regulations is needed in order to preserve the interest character of the QSI.

For debt instruments acquired with original issue discount or market discount, the proposed regulations require that, immediately before the mark-to-market gain or loss is computed under section 475(a), any OID or market discount accrued through the date of computation must be taken into account, and basis must be correspondingly increased. The amount of discount attributable to a particular period of time is computed under sections 1272 through 1275 (in the case of OID) and sections 1276 through 1278 (in the case of market discount). Thus, for example, the computation of OID attributable to a particular period takes into account any reduction for acquisition premium under section 1272(a)(7).

As indicated in the preceding paragraph, the proposed regulations provide that, in the case of a market discount bond to which section 475(a) applies, the holder must take market discount into account as it accrues, regardless of whether the holder elected under section 1278(b) to do so for all of its bonds. This rule is necessary to prevent market discount from producing gain on the mark instead of interest income. This provision, however, does not impose a section 1278(b) election on the taxpayer, because it does not apply to bonds that are not marked to market under section 475.

For taxable debt instruments acquired with amortizable bond premium, the proposed regulations provide that, if a dealer has made an election to amortize premium under section 171, any amortization for the taxable year (or for the portion of the taxable year during which the instrument is held by the dealer) must be taken into account (and basis must be appropriately reduced) before the mark-to-market gain or loss is computed under section 475. Because section 171 applies only to instruments not held primarily for sale to customers in the ordinary course of the taxpayer's trade or business, this proposed regulatory provision is applicable only to premium instruments described in section 475(b)(1) for which the taxpayer has not made the identification described in section 475(b)(2).

In the case of tax-exempt bonds, the proposed regulations require basis to be reduced as required by section 1016(a)(5) or (6) before mark-to-market gain or loss is computed.

If a dealer acquires a bond with premium and a section 171 election first applies to the bond in a taxable year after the year of acquisition, the proposed regulations require the dealer to amortize premium based on the original basis, without regard to any mark-to-market adjustments that may have been taken into account before the section 171 election became effective, but with regard to the adjustments required under section 171(b)(1). Thus, for example, if a dealer acquires in year 1 an instrument that is subject to section 475(a) and that has $10 of amortizable premium and if the dealer makes an election to amortize premium that is first effective in year 4 (when unamortized premium attributable to years 1 through 3 is $4), the dealer takes into account the appropriate portion of the remaining $6 of amortizable bond premium (as required under section 171(b)(3)) each taxable year before computing the mark-to-market adjustment on the instrument. Any mark-to-market basis adjustments in taxable years 1 through 3 are ignored in determining the amount of amortizable bond premium to which the election applies.

Under section 475(a)(2), a dealer in securities recognizes mark-to-market gain or loss on a security, other than inventory, as if the security were sold on the last business day of the taxable year. Although there may be circumstances under which marking a security to market produces results similar to the actual sale of the security, the statutory reference to the deemed sale prescribes the amount of gain or loss to be taken into account and does not trigger all of the consequences of a sale and reacquisition under the Code. For example, when a dealer in securities marks a bond (or other security) to market and takes recognized gain or loss into account, the dealer has not actually sold and reacquired the bond. Thus, under the proposed regulations, marking a debt instrument does not create, increase, or reduce market discount, acquisition premium, or bond premium.

The proposed regulations also contain a special rule to provide the proper character for mark-to-market gains or losses on a market discount instrument that was originally identified as held for investment by the dealer. This rule is necessary to ensure that all market discount is ultimately characterized as interest income and not as gain from the sale of a security.

Worthless Debts

The proposed regulations provide rules for marking a partially or wholly worthless debt to market. These rules coordinate the mark-to-market rules with the bad debt rules under the Code. The amount of gain or loss recognized under section 475(a)(2) when a debt instrument is marked to market generally is the difference between the adjusted basis and the fair market value of the debt. Under the proposed regulations, if a debt becomes partially or wholly worthless during a taxable year, the amount of any gain or loss required to be taken into account under section 475(a) is determined using a basis that reflects the worthlessness. The basis of the marked-to-market debt is treated as having been reduced by the amount of any book or regulatory charge-off (including the establishment of a specific allowance for a loan loss) for which a deduction could have been taken, without regard to whether any portion of the charge-off is, in fact, deducted or charged to a tax reserve for bad debts. The difference between this adjusted basis and the fair market value of the debt is the amount of gain or loss to be taken into account under section 475(a)(2). Thus, if the debt is wholly worthless, its basis would be reduced to zero and no gain or loss would be taken into account under section 475(a)(2).

This proposed treatment preserves the longstanding distinctions between losses due to the worthlessness of debts and other losses on debt instruments held by a taxpayer. See §1.166-1(a), which requires bad debts to be taken into account either as a specific deduction in respect of debts or as a deduction for a reasonable addition to a reserve for bad debts. See also §§1.585-3 and 1.593-7(c), which require a reserve-method taxpayer to charge bad debts to the reserve for bad debts. In addition, computing the mark-to-market adjustment as if the debt's basis had been adjusted to reflect worthlessness preserves a taxpayer's ability to postpone claiming a deduction for partial worthlessness until the debt becomes wholly worthless. To the extent that a debt has been previously charged off, mark-to-market gain is treated as a recovery.

The rules that are provided for bad debts in the proposed regulations do not apply to debts accounted for by a dealer as inventory under section 475(a)(1). Although it is possible for a debt that is in inventory to become partially worthless prior to sale, the likelihood or frequency of such an occurrence is difficult to ascertain given the speed with which inventory is sold. Comments are requested, however, concerning whether similar rules are necessary for partially worthless debt that is accounted for as inventory of the dealer.

Dispositions

Section 475(a) states that regulations may provide for securities held by a dealer to be marked to market at times other than the end of the dealer's taxable year. In general, the proposed regulations provide that, if a dealer in securities ceases to be the owner of a security for tax purposes, and if the security would have been marked to market under section 475(a) if the dealer's taxable year had ended immediately before the dealer ceases to own it, then (whether or not the security is inventory in the hands of the dealer) the dealer must recognize gain or loss as if the security had been sold for its fair market value immediately before the dealer ceases to own it. Any gain or loss so recognized is taken into account at that time.

In the absence of a mark upon disposition, a gain on a security held by a dealer could be deferred by transferring the security before the end of the taxable year to a related non-dealer in an intercompany transaction or in a non-recognition, carry-over-basis transaction. This potential for abuse is avoided if marking to market is required in every case in which a dealer ceases to be the owner of a security for tax purposes. The proposed requirement is analogous to the requirement that applies to dispositions of securities that are required to be marked to market under section 1256.

Transfers to which the proposed rule applies include the following: (a) Transfers to a controlled corporation under section 351; (b) Transfers to a trust (other than a grantor trust); (c) Transfers by gift to a charitable or non-charitable donee; (d) Transfers to other members of the same controlled group; (e) Transfers to a partnership under section 721; and (f) Transfers of mortgages to a REMIC under section 860F(b).

In the case of a transfer by a dealer to a partnership, the basis of a security transferred is generally its fair market value, because the security is marked to market immediately before the transfer. Thus, no special allocation issues arise. If there is any difference between a transferred security's basis after the mark and its fair market value (because, for example, the security transferred had been properly identified as held for investment but ceased to be so held at some time prior to the date of transfer), any special allocation of built-in gain or loss with respect to that security in the hands of the partnership will be made under section 704 and the regulations thereunder.

The mark to market immediately before disposition is separate and distinct from the disposition transaction. Thus, for example, the gain or loss from the mark is not gain or loss from a deferred intercompany transaction under §1.1502-13.

Securities Acquired with Substituted Basis

The proposed regulations provide rules for situations where a dealer in securities receives a security with a basis in its hands that is determined, in whole or in part, either by reference to the basis of the security in the hands of the transferor or by reference to other property held at any time by the dealer. In these cases, section 475(a) applies only to post-acquisition gain and loss with respect to the security. That is, section 475(a) applies only to changes in value of the security occurring after its acquisition. See section 475(b)(3). The character of the mark-to-market gain or loss is determined as provided under section 475(d)(3). The character of pre-acquisition gain or loss (that is, the built-in gain or loss at the date the dealer acquires the security) and the time for taking that gain or loss into account are determined without regard to section 475. The fact that a security has a substituted basis in the dealer's hands does not affect the security's date of acquisition for purposes of determining the timeliness of an identification under section 475(b).

The proposed regulations provide rules for the identification of securities contributed and received in securitization transactions. Under the proposed regulations, a taxpayer that expects to contribute securities to a trust or other entity in exchange for interests therein may identify the contributed securities as held for investment (within the meaning of section 475(b)(1)(A)) or not held for sale (within the meaning of section 475(b)(1)(B)) only if it expects each of the interests received (whether or not a security within the meaning of section 475(c)(2)) to be either held for investment or not held for sale to customers in the ordinary course of the taxpayer's business. Thus, for example, if a mortgage banker securitizes its loans and does not intend to hold for investment (or for other than sale to customers) all of the interests received in the securitization transaction, the mortgage banker will be required to account for its inventory of mortgages at fair market value under section 475(a)(1), regardless of whether the mortgages are to be sold to a trust or contributed to a REMIC.

Under the proposed regulations, if a dealer engages in a securitization transaction that results in dispositions of only partial interests in the contributed securities, the dealer is not permitted to identify the contributed securities as exempt under section 475(b)(1)(A) or (B). As a result, all of the contributed securities must be accounted for under section 475(a). Moreover, under the mark-on-disposition rule of these proposed regulations, the dealer is required to mark the securities to market immediately before the securitization transaction. The Service invites comments on whether there are other administrable approaches that reflect the fact that only a partial disposition of the securities has occurred.

In other securitization transactions, a taxpayer transfers securities to a trust (or other entity) in a transaction that is not a disposition of the securities for tax purposes. The trust issues certificates (or other forms of interest) that represent secured debt of the taxpayer rather than debt of the trust or ownership of the underlying securities. In these cases, if the taxpayer retains the full ownership of the contributed securities for tax purposes and if the contributed securities otherwise qualify to be identified as held for investment or not held for sales then the taxpayer may identify the securities as held for investment or not held for sale notwithstanding the transfer.

Further, if a transfer of securities is a disposition, a taxpayer may identify the interests received in a securitization transaction as exempt from mark-to-market if the interests are described in section 475(b)(1) and are not treated for tax purposes as continuing ownership of the securities transferred. This identification is permitted even if the securitized assets were marked to market under section 475. For example, a taxpayer may identify some of the REMIC regular interests received on the transfer of mortgage securities to a REMIC, even if the mortgages were subject to section 475(a). Conversely, a taxpayer that has marked mortgages to market but subsequently contributes those mortgages to a grantor trust and receives beneficial interests therein may not identify the beneficial interests as exempt from mark-to-market treatment, because the beneficial interests represent continued ownership of the contributed securities, whose eligibility for exemption was determined when they were acquired.

The proposed regulations clarify that an identification of a security as exempt must specify the subparagraph of section 475(b)(1) under which the exemption is claimed and that the time by which a dealer must identify a security as exempt is not affected by whether the dealer has a substituted basis in the security. The proposed regulations also provide rules for determining whether an identification of a security as exempt is timely where a dealer engages in certain integrated transactions described in §1.1275-6 as proposed on December 16, 1994 (FI-59-91, 59 FR 64884, 64905).

Definition of Dealer in Securities

Section 475(c)(1) defines a dealer in securities as a taxpayer who regularly purchases securities from, or sells securities to, customers in the ordinary course of a trade or business or who regularly offers to enter into, assume, offset, assign or otherwise terminate positions in securities with customers in the ordinary course of a trade or business.

The proposed regulations provide that whether a taxpayer is transacting business with customers is determined based on all of the facts and circumstances.

Under section 475(c)(1)(B) and the proposed regulations, the term dealer in securities includes a taxpayer that, in the ordinary course of its trade or business, regularly holds itself out as being willing and able to enter into either side of a transaction enumerated in section 475(c)(1)(B). For instance, if a taxpayer regularly holds itself out as being willing to enter a swap in which it is either the fixed or the floating payor, the taxpayer is a swaps dealer.

The proposed regulations clarify that a life insurance company does not become a dealer in securities solely by selling annuity, endowment, or life insurance policies to its customers. Under the temporary regulations published on December 29, 1993 (T.D. 8505), a contract that is treated for federal income tax purposes as an annuity, endowment, or life insurance contract is deemed to have been identified as held for investment, and is therefore not marked to market by the policy holder. This was necessary because variable life and annuity products fall within the literal language of section 475(c)(2)(E). Because many life insurance companies sell these insurance contracts to their customers, some commentators asked whether these life insurance companies were dealers in securities. There is no indication that Congress intended for a life insurance company that was not otherwise a dealer in securities to be characterized as a dealer merely because it sells life insurance policies to its customers. These proposed regulations provide the appropriate clarification.

Definition of Security

The temporary regulations that were published on December 29, 1993 (T.D. 8505), exclude certain items from the definition of security. Among the excluded items are liabilities of the taxpayer and negative value residual interests (NVRIs) in a REMIC and other arrangements that are determined to have substantially the same economic effect as NVRIs (for example, a widely held partnership that holds noneconomic REMIC residual interests). Those rules are needed to carry out the purposes of section 475 and other Code provisions, including section 860E.

These proposed regulations clarify that a liability of the taxpayer means a debt issued by the taxpayer. Also, for the reasons given below, these proposed regulations exclude all REMIC residual interests from the definition of security.

A typical REMIC holds a pool of long-term, real estate mortgages originated at a "blended" interest rate. These mortgages are used to support the issuance of regular interests, which are treated as debt, with varied maturities and interest rates. The REMIC takes cash flows on the mortgages and redirects them to holders of the regular interests. As a result, there is generally a mismatch in the recognition of interest income from the mortgages and the interest expense attributable to the regular interests. This mismatch of interest income and interest deductions results in taxable income or loss that does not represent economic gain or loss. Some commentators refer to this as "phantom" income or loss.

Phantom income or loss is allocated to the holders of the residual interests in a REMIC even though that income or loss does not represent any economic benefit or detriment to those holders. Further, sections 860C and 860E require a residual interest holder to pay taxes on a portion of phantom income (called "excess inclusion") and to increase the basis of the residual interest by the amount of phantom income. Because this basis increase does not represent economic value, a subsequent mark to market is likely to result in a loss. Permitting taxpayers to take this loss into account currently under the mark-to-market provisions effectively undermines the Congressional mandate embodied in section 860E to require current taxation of phantom income.

Although the adverse effect of section 475 on section 860E is most apparent when the residual interests being considered are NVRIs, residual interests with positive value present the same issue. Many residual interests with positive value, in spite of being entitled to REMIC distributions, have substantially the same economic effect as NVRIs and thus are already excluded by the temporary regulations from the definition of "security." The IRS is concerned, however, that residual interests may be structured in a way that avoids embodying substantially the same economic effects as an NVRI but that still undermines the purposes of section 860E. The proposed regulations, therefore, contain a rule that would remove from the category of securities subject to section 475 all residual interests that are acquired after January 4, 1995. Also removed are arrangements that are acquired after that date and are determined to have substantially the same economic effect as a REMIC residual interest (for instance, an interest in a widely held partnership holding residual interests). The temporary regulations continue to apply to all residual interests described therein for all taxable years ending on or after December 31, 1993.

In addition, the Commissioner has determined that, if a residual interest, or an interest or arrangement that has substantially the same economic effect, is not a security within the meaning of section 475, it should not be treated as inventory under other provisions. Additional guidance on this matter will be issued.

Comments are requested concerning whether there are any residual interests that do not undermine section 860E upon being marked to market. If comments are received that describe any such interests, subsequent guidance may provide that they are included in the mark-to-market regime. In this regard, it is important that any mechanism for identifying these interests not impose an undue burden on either taxpayers or the IRS.

Additional Comments Requested

The provisions of section 475 generally apply in determining the taxable income of a dealer that may also be subject to various international provisions of the Code. The Service is considering the possibility of using the definitions contained in section 475 and the regulations thereunder for purposes of various international provisions, except where a modification of the provisions is necessary to carry out the purposes of those international provisions. Comments on this issue also are welcome.

Finally, the Service is considering whether there are additional situations in which securities should not be accounted for under section 475(a). (The temporary and proposed regulations that were published on December 29, 1993, listed some such situations.) For example, a dealer in securities may acquire at original issue and in exchange for property certain non-interest-bearing debt instruments that are not subject to the interest imputation provisions of section 1274 or 483. Because these instruments will seldom appreciate in value, it may be inappropriate to subject them to the mark-to-market regime.

Dates of Applicability

The proposed regulations will apply to identifications made, securities acquired, or events occurring, on or after January 4, 1995, or to taxable years beginning on or after January 1, 1995, as appropriate.

Special Analyses

It has been determined that this notice of proposed rulemaking is not a significant regulatory action as defined in EO 12066. Therefore, a regulatory assessment is not required. It also has been determined that section 553(b) of the Administrative Procedure Act (5 U.S.C. chapter 5) and the Regulatory Flexibility Act (5 U.S.C. chapter 6) do not apply to these regulations, and, therefore, a Regulatory Flexibility Analysis is not required.

Pursuant to section 7805(f) of the Code, this notice of proposed rulemaking will be submitted to the Chief Counsel for Advocacy of the Small Business Administration for comment on its impact on small business.

Comments and Public Hearing

Before these proposed regulations are adopted as final regulations, consideration will be given to any written comments (a signed original and eight (8) copies) that are submitted timely to the IRS. All comments will be available for public inspection and copying.

A public hearing has been scheduled for Wednesday, May 3, 1995 at 10 a.m. The public hearing will be held in the Internal Revenue Auditorium, 7400 corridor, Internal Revenue Building, 1111 Constitution Avenue NW, Washington, DC 20224. Because of access restrictions, visitors will not be admitted beyond the Internal Revenue Building lobby more than 15 minutes before the hearing starts.

The rules of 26 CFR 601.601(a)(3) apply to the hearing.

Persons that wish to present oral comments at the hearing must submit written comments by April 3, 1995, and submit an outline of the topics to be discussed and the time to be devoted to each topic (signed original and eight (8) copies) by April 3, 1995.

A period of 10 minutes will be allotted to each person for making comments.

An agenda showing the scheduling of the speakers will be prepared after the deadline for receiving outlines has passed. Copies of the agenda will be available free of charge at the hearing.

Drafting Information

The principal authors of these regulations are Robert B. Williams and JoLynn Ricks, Office of Assistant Chief Counsel (Financial Institutions & Products). However, other personnel from the IRS and Treasury Department participated in their development.

[¶ 49,147]   **Proposed Regulations and Proposed Amendments of Regulations (INTL-65-93)**, published in the Federal Register on April 28, 1995.

Passive foreign investment companies: Passive income characterization: Certain foreign banks and securities dealers: Exceptions to.—Reg. §§1.1296-4 and 1.1296-6 and amendments of Reg. §1.1291-0, relating to the application of the exceptions to passive income contained in section 1296(b) for foreign banks, securities dealers and brokers, are proposed. On 1/2/98, amendments of proposed Reg. §1.1296-4 were proposed (¶ 49,242). A public hearing on this proposal is scheduled for August 31, 1995.

AGENCY: Internal Revenue Service (IRS), Treasury.

ACTION: Notice of proposed rulemaking and notice of public hearing.

SUMMARY: This document provides guidance concerning the application of the exceptions to passive income contained in section 1296(b) for foreign banks, securities dealers and brokers. This document affects persons who own direct or indirect interests in certain foreign corporations. This document also provides notice of a public hearing on these proposed regulations.

DATES: Written comments must be received by August 10, 1995. Outlines of oral comments to be presented at the public hearing scheduled for August 31, 1995 at 10 a.m. must be received by August 10, 1995.

ADDRESSES: Send submissions to: CC:DOM:CORP:T:R (INTL-0065-93), room 5228, Internal Revenue Service, POB 7604, Ben Franklin Station, Washington, DC 20044. In the alternative, submissions may be hand delivered between the hours of 8 a.m. and 5 p.m. to: CC:DOM:CORP:T:R (INTL-0065-93), Courier's Desk, Internal Revenue Building, 1111 Constitution Avenue, NW, Washington, DC.

FOR FURTHER INFORMATION CONTACT: Concerning the regulations, Ramon Camacho at (202) 622-3870; concerning submissions and the hearing, Ms. Christina Vasquez, (202) 622-7180 (not toll-free numbers).

SUPPLEMENTARY INFORMATION

Background

A passive foreign investment company (PFIC) is any foreign corporation that satisfies either the income test or asset test in section 1296(a) of the Internal Revenue Code (Code). Under the income test, a foreign corporation is a PFIC if 75 percent or more of its gross income for the year is passive income. Sec. 1296(a)(1). Alternatively, a foreign corporation is a PFIC if 50 percent or more of the average value of its assets for the taxable year produce passive income or are held for the production of passive income. Sec. 1296(a)(2). Under section 1296(b)(1), passive income is foreign personal holding company income as defined in section 954(c) of the Code, and includes dividends, interest, certain rents and royalties, and gain from certain property transactions, including gain from the sale of assets that produce passive income.

Under section 1296(b)(2)(A), income earned in the active conduct of a banking business by a foreign corporation licensed to do business as a bank in the United States and, to the extent provided in regulations, by other corporations engaged in the banking business is not passive. Notice 89-81, 1989-2 CB 399, (Notice) described rules to be incorporated into subsequent regulations that would expand this exception to certain foreign banks not licensed to do a banking business in the United States. The rules contained in §1.1296-4 of the proposed regulations would implement section 1296(b)(2)(A) for banking activities conducted by foreign corporations.

In 1993, Congress added section 1296(b)(3)(A) to the Code, effective for taxable years beginning after September 30, 1993. See Omnibus Budget Reconciliation Act of 1993 (1993 Act), Pub. L. 103-66, section 13231(d), 107 Stat. 312, 499. The provision treats as nonpassive any income derived in the active conduct of a securities business by a controlled foreign corporation (CFC) if the CFC is a U.S. registered dealer or broker and, to the extent provided in regulations, a CFC not so registered. The rules contained in §1.1296-6 would implement section 1296(b)(3)(A).

Section 956A, added by the 1993 Act, requires each U.S. shareholder of a CFC to include in income its pro rata share of the CFC's excess passive assets. Under section 956A(c)(2), a passive asset is any asset that produces passive income as defined in section 1296(b). An asset that generates nonpassive income under §1.1296-4 or §1.1296-6 of the proposed regulations will be nonpassive for purposes of section 956A.

Explanation of Provisions.

I. *Description of Proposed Rules for Foreign Banks.*

A. *General Rule.*

Section 1.1296-4(a) of the proposed regulations provides generally that, for purposes of section 1296(a)(1), passive income does not include banking income earned by an active bank or by a qualified affiliate of such a bank. For this purpose, an active bank is either a corporation that possesses a license issued under federal or state law to do business as a bank in the United States, or a foreign corporation that meets the licensing, deposit-taking, and lending requirements of paragraphs (c), (d), and (e), respectively, of §1.1296-4.

The proposed rules generally adopt the deposit, lending, and licensing standards contained in the Notice. These standards are consistent with the provisions of the Code that define a bank as an institution that accepts deposits from and makes loans to the public and is licensed under state or federal law to conduct banking activities. See e.g., sec. 581. The IRS and Treasury believe that Congress intended to grant the banking exception only to corporations that conform to a traditional U.S. banking model.

However, the proposed rules liberalize the approach taken in the Notice in several ways. Most significantly, the proposed rules adopt subjective tests to measure whether the corporation meets the deposit-taking and lending requirements. The IRS and Treasury rejected reliance on objective tests such as those in the Notice after learning, through several ruling requests pursuant to the Notice, that objective standards may cause legitimate banks to be treated as nonbanks.

Because of the rigidity of the objective tests, the Notice permitted the IRS to rule in rare and unusual circumstances that a foreign corporation was an active bank even though it failed to satisfy the requirements of the Notice. The proposed regulations do not adopt this procedure because the IRS and Treasury believe that the enhanced flexibility of the proposed rules should permit all foreign corporations actively conducting a licensed banking business (whether directly or through affiliates) to qualify for the bank exception.

B. *Licensing Requirement*

A foreign corporation that is not licensed in the United States satisfies the licensing requirements of §1.1296-4(c) if it is licensed or authorized to accept deposits from residents of the country in which it is chartered or incorporated, and to conduct, in such country, any of the banking activities described in the proposed regulations. However, a corporation fails this licensing test if one of the principal purposes for its obtaining a license was compliance with the requirements of this section.

The IRS and Treasury believe that being licensed as a bank by a bank regulatory authority is strong evidence that a corporation is a bank. The proposed regulations therefore adopt a licensing test to distinguish banks from investment funds.

C. *Deposit-taking Test.*

A foreign corporation satisfies the deposit-taking test of §1.1296-4(d) if it regularly accepts deposits in the ordinary course of its trade or business from customers who are residents of the country in which it is licensed or authorized. In addition, the amount of deposits shown on the corporation's balance sheet must be substantial. Section 1.1296-4(d)(3) provides that whether the amount of deposits on a corporation's balance sheet is substantial depends on all the facts and circumstances, including whether the capital structure and funding of the bank as a whole are similar to that of comparable banking institutions engaged in the same types of activities and subject to regulation by the same banking authorities.

The proposed regulations adopt this deposit-taking test in part to distinguish banks from finance companies, which do not accept deposits. This distinction between finance companies and banks is required by Congress. H.R. Conf. Rep. No. 213, 103d Cong., 1st Sess. 641 (1993) (noting that the banking, insurance, and securities exemptions "do not apply to income derived in the conduct of financing and credit services businesses"). Although the IRS and Treasury believe that deposit-taking is a key attribute of all active banks, they also recognize that subjective tests will better accommodate the various types of banks that have developed as a result of different banking systems and regulatory frameworks.

The proposed regulations introduce flexibility to the deposit-taking requirements in several ways. First, the requirement that the amount of deposits be substantial is more flexible than the Notice requirement that deposits constitute at least 50 percent of the total liabilities of the bank. The IRS and Treasury recognize that a bank's funding preferences may be affected by market conditions and regulatory requirements and believes that an institution may be properly treated as an active bank even if deposits do not constitute the institution's primary source of funding.

Second, unlike the Notice, the proposed regulations do not include any special rules for interbank deposits but treat them like any other deposit, regardless of whether they are received from persons who are members of a related group as defined in §1.1296-4(i)(4). The IRS and Treasury believe this change is appropriate because the acceptance of interbank deposits from related or unrelated persons on an arm's length basis is a banking activity normally engaged in by banks. In addition, the impact of a rule that distinguishes between interbank deposits received from related persons and those received from unrelated persons is diminished where deposit-taking activity is not measured with a bright-line test.

Finally, the proposed rules change the Notice requirement that a corporation must hold deposits from at least 1,000 persons who are bona fide residents of the country that issued the corporation's banking license because this requirement proved troublesome for certain private banks with clientele from several countries. The requirement was intended to address cases where a bank is licensed by a country but not allowed to accept deposits from its residents. In the IRS and Treasury's view, such an entity should not be treated as an active bank for purposes of section 1296 because it is not accorded full bank status by the bank authorities that issued its banking license. However, the IRS and Treasury believe that a bright-line deposit standard is not necessary to address this concern. Instead, the proposed regulations require that a corporation regularly accept deposits from residents of the country in which it is licensed.

D. *Lending Test.*

A foreign corporation satisfies the lending test of §1.1296-4(e) if it regularly makes loans to customers in the ordinary course of its trade or business. This is a change from the Notice's requirement that loans to unrelated persons make up more than 50 percent of the corporation's loan portfolio. The lending test is necessary to distinguish banks, which extend credit to customers, from corporations that merely invest. However, such a distinction can be drawn without relying on a bright-line standard such as that contained in the Notice.

In order to distinguish loans from investments for purposes of these rules, the proposed regulations provide that a note, bond, debenture or other evidence of indebtedness is a loan only if it is received by the corporation on an extension of credit made pursuant to a loan agreement entered into in the ordinary course of the corporation's banking business. Debt instruments treated as securities for purposes of the corporation's financial statements generally are not loans.

E. *Banking Income and Activities.*

Section 1.1296-4(f)(1) provides that banking income is gross income derived from the active conduct of any banking activity as defined in §1.1296-4(f)(2). These activities include all of the activities treated as banking activities in the Notice, with no material changes, except that finance leasing is included as a banking activity.

The proposed regulations do not adopt the Notice's rule that all of the U.S. effectively connected income earned by a foreign corporation in the active conduct of a trade or business pursuant to a U.S. bank license automatically is nonpassive. One effect of this rule was that effectively connected income earned by a U.S.-licensed bank from transactions with related parties would have been banking income, while income earned by non-U.S.-licensed banks from similar related-party transactions would not have been banking income. Because the proposed regulations generally do not differentiate between related party and non-related party transactions in the same way as the Notice, the only effect of the rule would have been to treat, in the case of U.S. licensed banks only, as banking income the income earned on transactions with related parties who are not customers and income earned from activities (such as securities activities) that are not banking activities described in §1.1296-4(f). The IRS and Treasury believe that the standards for determining whether income is derived in the active conduct of a banking business should be the same for all corporations that are either active banks or qualified bank affiliates.

The IRS and Treasury are aware that many bank activities may also be considered securities activities. Under the proposed regulations, an entity that performs an activity that is both a banking activity and a securities activity must satisfy only the requirements of the bank rules to treat income from such activity as nonpassive. For example, an entity that derives income from dealing in foreign exchange may treat such income as nonpassive if it is an active bank (or a qualified bank affiliate) even though it is not a controlled foreign corporation.

Dealing in securities, however, is not included as both a banking activity and a securities activity. The IRS and Treasury believe that Congress intended that income from dealing in securities should be nonpassive only if it is earned by a controlled foreign corporation that actively conducts a securities business and meets the other requirements of section 1296(b)(3)(A).

The IRS and Treasury have become aware that certain developing country economies impose high deposit reserve requirements as a tool for implementing monetary policy. Because the central banks of these countries require the maintenance of such reserves as a prerequisite to conducting a banking business, the earnings on such assets, if any, should appropriately be excluded from passive income.

F. *Customer Relationship.*

Under the proposed regulations, a bank satisfies the deposit and lending tests only if it carries on such activities with customers. Moreover, only the income from its banking activities (and those of its qualified bank affiliates) conducted with, or for, customers will produce nonpassive income. This is a change from the Notice requirement, under which activities qualified only if they were conducted with unrelated parties. Under the proposed regulations, a customer may be any person, related or unrelated, if that person has a customer relationship with the bank. Whether such a relationship exists depends on all the facts and circumstances. However, persons who are related to, or who are shareholders, officers, directors, or other employees of, the corporation will not be treated as customers of the corporation if one of the principal purposes for the corporation's transacting business with such persons was to qualify the corporation as an active bank or qualified bank affiliate.

G. *Affiliates of Active Banks*

The IRS and Treasury recognize that many active banks conduct one or more banking activities through separately incorporated affiliates that may not individually qualify as active banks. Accordingly, the proposed regulations provide rules under which income from banking activities may be treated as nonpassive if earned by a corporation that does not qualify as an active bank but is a member of a related group of which an active bank is also a member. However, such income is nonpassive only for purposes of determining whether any member of the related group is a passive foreign investment company or for purposes of applying the excess passive asset rules of section 956A(c)(2)(A). In addition, such income remains passive with respect to persons who own stock in the affiliate but who are not members of the related group of which the affiliate is a member.

For purposes of these rules, a related group is any group of persons related within the meaning of section 954(d)(3), substituting person for controlled foreign corporation. This definition is a departure from the affiliated group definition of the Notice because it permits noncorporate entities (such as partnerships) to count as members of the group for purposes of satisfying the groupwide gross income test.

Section 1.1296-4(i)(2) requires the bank affiliate to generate more than 60 percent of its income from banking, insurance and securities activities (but not other financial services). For purposes of this test, the look-through rules of sections 1296(c) and 1296(b)(2)(C) do not apply. This requirement ensures that a bank affiliate's eligibility for the bank exception depends upon the business activities conducted directly by the affiliate, and is not influenced by activities conducted by related persons. However, a bank affiliate may nevertheless apply sections 1296(c) and 1296(b)(2)(A) to determine whether it is a PFIC under the income or asset tests of section 1296(a).

In addition, the related group must meet two gross income tests for the exception to apply. First, under § 1.1296-4(i)(3)(i), income from banking activities derived by active banks must constitute at least 30 percent of the financial services income earned by group members. Second, under § 1.1296-4(i)(3)(ii), income earned by group members from banking activities, securities activities, and insurance activities must constitute at least 70 percent of the financial services income earned by group members that are financial services entities. The regulations adopt the definition of financial services income contained in § 1.904-4(e), which includes only income earned by financial services entities.

These affiliate rules are structurally similar to the affiliate rules contained in the Notice, but have been modified in several respects to respond to taxpayer comments. For example, the 80 percent stock ownership threshold of the Notice caused many corporations to be treated as PFICs solely because the gross income of subsidiaries in which the group owned less than an 80 percent interest was excluded for purposes of the Notice's gross income tests, even though the group had voting control of such subsidiaries. The adoption of a lower 50 percent ownership threshold for group membership in the proposed regulations recognizes that international groups are not organized to meet the 80 percent threshold required for consolidation under U.S. tax law.

In addition, the gross income tests were changed in several ways to deal with problems encountered by diversified affiliated groups. First, the denominators of the fractions now include only financial services income, which by its terms includes only income earned by financial services entities. This change prevents foreign corporations that are part of a banking group from being disqualified solely because the group is a subgroup of a larger group that does not perform solely financial services.

Second, the numerator of the fraction for the groupwide gross income test now includes gross income from securities and insurance activities in addition to banking activities. This change prevents a foreign corporation engaged in banking activities that is part of a banking subgroup from being disqualified solely because it is part of a larger group that provides a broad range of financial services.

Finally, the proposed rules drop the Notice requirement that an active bank be a group member for 5 years before its income may count towards satisfaction of the gross income tests. Since PFIC status is determined annually, the IRS and Treasury believe that whether a group is a banking group should depend only on its status during the current taxable year.

H. *Income from Nonbanking Activities.*

As in the Notice, § 1.1296-4(j) of the proposed regulations provides that income derived from the conduct of activities other than banking activities described in § 1.1296-4(f)(2) and income from assets held for the conduct of such activities are nonpassive only to the extent provided in section 1296.

J. *Effective Date.*

Section 1.1296-4 is proposed to be effective for all taxable years beginning after December 31, 1994. However, taxpayers may apply § 1.1296-4 to a taxable year beginning after December 31, 1986, but must consistently apply § 1.1296-4 to such taxable year and all subsequent years. While application of § 1.1296-4 to a year beginning after December 31, 1986, cannot affect the tax liability of a taxpayer for any closed taxable year, a taxpayer may apply § 1.1296-4 to a closed taxable year for the purpose of determining whether a foreign corporation is a PFIC in calculating the taxpayer's liability for an open taxable year.

II. *Exception for Income Earned in a Securities Business.*

A. *General Rule.*

Section 1.1296-6(a) of the proposed regulations provides generally that securities income earned by an active securities dealer, active securities broker or qualified securities affiliate is nonpassive. As required by section 1296(b)(3)(C), the rules apply only for purposes of determining whether a controlled foreign corporation (as defined in section 957(a)) is a PFIC with respect to its United States shareholders (as defined in section 951(b)), or for purposes of determining whether an asset is passive under section 956A(c)(2).

B. *Active Securities Dealer and Active Securities Broker.*

Under § 1.1296-6(b)(1), an active dealer or broker is a dealer or broker that meets certain licensing requirements. Section 1.1296-6(c) defines a securities dealer as a dealer in securities within the meaning of section 475(c)(1). Under § 1.1296-6(d), a securities broker is a foreign corporation that stands ready to effect transactions in securities and other financial instruments for the account of customers in the ordinary course of its trade or business during the taxable year. A securities dealer or broker is licensed under § 1.1296-6(b) if it possesses a U.S. license to do business as a securities dealer or broker in the United States or if it is licensed or authorized in the country in which it is chartered or incorporated to conduct one or more securities activities described in § 1.1296-6(e)(2) with residents of that country. The conduct of such activities must be subject to bona fide regulation, including appropriate reporting, monitoring and prudential requirements, by a Securities regulatory authority that regularly enforces compliance with such standards.

C. *Securities Income & Securities Activities.*

Section 1.1296-6(e)(1) provides generally that securities income means the gross income derived from the active conduct of any securities activity that constitutes a trade or business. The list of securities activities contained in § 1.1296-6(e)(2) generally is consistent with the legislative history to section 1296(b)(3)(A). See H.R. Rep. No. 111, 103d Cong., 1st Sess. 704 (1993).

Section 1.1296-6(e)(2)(iv) includes as an additional securities activity the maintenance of a capital deposit required under foreign law as a prerequisite to acting as a broker in that jurisdiction. Without this rule, a broker that is not also a dealer could be a PFIC under section 1296(a)(2) even though the majority of its income is commission income. This rule applies only if significant restrictions exist on the use of its capital. Thus, working capital will not qualify as a deposit for purposes of this rule.

In general, only income from transactions entered into with, or on behalf of, persons with whom the corporation has a dealer-customer relationship may be treated as nonpassive. Section 1.1296-6(g) adopts without change the definition of dealer-customer relationship contained in the bank rules.

Under § 1.1296-6(h) of the proposed regulations, income and gain from a security identified as held for investment under section 475(b)(1)(A) or which is not held for sale within the meaning of section 475(b)(1)(B) is passive. Because the identification rules of sections 475(b) and 1.475(b)-1T and 1.475(b)-2T apply, the rules governing identification of inventory securities in Notice 88-22, 1988-1 CB 489 and Notice 89-81, 1989-2 CB 399 do not apply with respect to taxable years beginning after September 30, 1993. However, the inventory identification rules of Notice 89-81 and Notice 88-22 will continue to apply for taxable years beginning before October 1, 1993.

D. *Matched Book Income*

Section 1.1296-6(i) of the proposed regulations provides special rules for determining a securities dealer's income from certain matched transactions. These rules are adopted in order to eliminate a potential opportunity for abuse that arises from the manner in which a matched book repo business is conducted by securities dealers.

A matched transaction is defined as a sale and repurchase agreement with respect to the same security, entered into by the controlled foreign corporation in the active conduct of its trade or business and properly treated as offsetting agreements in a matched book. In a typical repurchase agreement a taxpayer sells a security and, at the same time, agrees to repurchase an identical security from the purchaser at a price in excess of the taxpayer's sales price. In a reverse repurchase agreement, a taxpayer purchases a security and concurrently agrees to sell an identical security to the seller at a price in excess of the taxpayer's purchase price. A taxpayer who keeps a matched book generally enters into offsetting repurchase and reverse repurchase agreements involving identical securities. Such taxpayers act as intermediaries by matching persons who need cash for a short period with those who need securities for the same period.

Under the proposed regulations, securities income includes only the net (not gross) income from matched transactions. Without the proposed regulation's netting rule, related groups that are predominantly engaged in passive activities could easily meet the gross income tests contained in the qualified affiliate rules because a CFC conducting a matched book business will earn large amounts of gross income, even though net economic income from matched book activities is comparatively small.

E. *Affiliates of Dealers or Brokers.*

Like banks, securities dealers and brokers frequently operate through separately incorporated subsidiaries that may not qualify independently as active securities dealers or brokers but which form part of an integrated securities business conducted by an active dealer or broker. Accordingly, the proposed regulations contain rules that extend the securities dealer/broker exception to certain qualified affiliates of active securities dealers or brokers. These rules generally mirror the qualified bank affiliate rules contained in § 1.1296-4(i), except that they extend the securities dealer/broker exception only to qualified securities affiliates that are CFCs, as required by section 1296(b)(3)(A).

F. *Income from Nonsecurities Activities.*

Section 1.1296-6(k) of the proposed regulations provides that income derived from the conduct of activities other than securities activities described in § 1.1296-6(e)(2) and income from assets held for the conduct of such activities are nonpassive only to the extent provided in section 1296.

G. *Effective Date.*

The rules contained in § 1.1296-6 are proposed to be effective for taxable years beginning after September 30, 1993.

III. *Look-Through Rules.*

The proposed regulations do not contain guidance regarding the look-through rules of sections 1296(c) and 1296(b)(2)(C) or the grouping rules of section 956A(d). In general, the proposed regulations also do not address whether, and to what extent, look-through principles may apply to characterize income from a partnership as nonpassive and an interest in a partnership as a nonpassive asset, except to the extent that section 475 may treat a partnership as a securities dealer. Because these issues are not unique to financial institutions, the IRS and Treasury will address them in future regulations of more general application. The IRS and Treasury solicit comments on the proper scope and application of look-through and grouping concepts to banks, securities dealers and securities brokers.

Special Analyses

It has been determined that this notice of proposed rulemaking is not a significant regulatory action as defined in EO 12866. Therefore, a regulatory assessment is not required. It also has been determined that section 553(b) of the Administrative Procedure Act (5 U.S.C. chapter 5) and the Regulatory Flexibility Act (5 U.S.C. chapter 6) do not apply to these regulations, and, therefore, a Regulatory Flexibility Analysis is not required. Pursuant to section 7805(f) of the Internal Revenue Code, this notice of proposed rulemaking will be submitted to the Chief Counsel for Advocacy of the Small Business Administration for comment on its impact on small business.

Comments and Public Hearing

Before these proposed regulations are adopted as final regulations, consideration will be given to any written comments (a signed original and eight (8) copies) that are submitted timely to the IRS. All comments will be available for public inspection and copying.

A public hearing has been scheduled for August 31, 1995, at 10 a.m., in the Internal Revenue Service Auditorium, 7400 corridor. Because of access restrictions, visitors will not be admitted beyond the Internal Revenue Building lobby more than 15 minutes before the hearing starts.

The rules of 26 CFR 601.601(a)(3) apply to the hearing.

Persons that wish to present oral comments at the hearing must submit written comments and an outline of the topics to be discussed and the time to be devoted to each topic (signed original and eight (8) copies) by August 10, 1995.

A period of 10 minutes will be allotted to each person for making comments.

An agenda showing the scheduling of the speakers will be prepared after the deadline for receiving outlines has passed. Copies of the agenda will be available free of charge at the hearing.

Drafting Information

The principal author of these regulations is Ramon Camacho, Office of the Associate Chief Counsel (International). However, other personnel from the IRS and Treasury Department participated in their development.

[¶ 49,148]   **Proposed Amendments of Regulations (FI-21-95)**, published in the Federal Register on May 2, 1995.

Straddles: Personal property defined.—Amendments of Reg. § 1.1092(d)-2, relating to the definition of personal property for purposes of the straddle rules, are proposed. A public hearing on this proposal is scheduled for August 30, 1995.

AGENCY: Internal Revenue Service (IRS), Treasury.

ACTION: Notice of proposed rulemaking and notice of public hearing.

SUMMARY: This document contains proposed regulations relating to the definition of personal property for purposes of the straddle rules. This action is necessary to reflect changes in the law made by the Tax Reform Act of 1984. The regulations provide guidance to persons who enter into straddle transactions.

DATES: Written comments must be received by July 31, 1995. Requests to appear and outlines of topics to be discussed at the public hearing scheduled for August 30, 1995, must be submitted by August 9, 1995.

ADDRESSES: Send submissions to: CC:DOM:CORP:T:R (FI-21-95), room 5228, Internal Revenue Service, POB 7604, Ben Franklin Station, Washington, DC 20044. In the alternative, submissions may be hand delivered between the hours of 8 a.m. and 5 p.m. to: CC:DOM:CORP:T:R (FI-21-95), Courier's Desk, Internal Revenue Service, 1111 Constitution Avenue, NW., Washington, DC. A public hearing has been scheduled for Wednesday, August 30, 1995, at 10 a.m. in the Auditorium, Internal Revenue Building, 1111 Constitution Avenue, NW., Washington, DC.

FOR FURTHER INFORMATION CONTACT: Concerning the regulations, Robert B. Williams, (202) 622-3960; concerning submissions and the hearing, Michael Slaughter, (202) 622-7190 (not toll-free numbers).

SUPPLEMENTARY INFORMATION:

Background

Section 1092(d) of the Internal Revenue Code provides definitions and special rules relating to straddles. Under section 1092(d)(3)(B)(i)(II), an ownership interest in stock, which generally is not treated as personal property subject to the straddle rules, may be personal property if it is part of a straddle at least one of the offsetting positions of which is, under regulations, a position with respect to substantially similar or related property (other than stock). On March 20, 1995, the IRS published final regulations (§ 1.1092(d)-2) under section 1092(d)(3)(B). Those regulations generally apply the rules of § 1.246-5 to determine whether an offsetting position is a position with respect to substantially similar or related property (other than stock) within the meaning of section 1092(d)(3)(B)(i)(II).

Explanation of Provisions

The proposed regulations clarify the definition of the term *personal property* under section 1092(d)(1) as it applies to stock. The proposed regulations provide that personal property includes any stock of a type that is actively traded and that is part of a straddle at least one of the offsetting positions of which is a position with respect to substantially similar or related property (other than stock). For this purpose, a position with respect to substantially similar or related property (other than stock) does not include direct ownership of stock or a short sale of stock but includes any other position with respect to substantially similar or related property. These proposed regulations thus clarify that, for example, stock and an equity swap with respect to property that is substantially similar or related to that stock can constitute a straddle for purposes of section 1092.

The proposed regulations also address the scope of section 1092(d)(3)(B)(i), which provides that stock that is offset by an option with respect to that stock or substantially identical stock or by a position with respect to substantially similar or related property (other than stock) is treated as personal property under section 1092(d)(3)(B). Although this provision does not contain an explicit active trading requirement, the legislative history of the Tax Reform Act of 1984 indicates that Congress contemplated that the stock would be treated as personal property under this test only if it is of a type that is actively traded. H.R. Conf. Rep. No. 861, 98th Cong., 2d Sess. 907 (1984). The regulations, therefore, include this requirement. In contrast, the regulations clarify that, for purposes of section 1092(d)(3)(B)(ii), if a corporation is formed or availed of to take positions in personal property that offset positions taken by any shareholder, stock of the corporation may be treated as personal property under section 1092(d)(3)(B) even if it is not actively traded.

The proposed regulations generally are effective for positions established on or after May 1, 1995. The IRS believes, however, that the regulations merely clarify the rule that applied once § 1.1092(d)-2 was promulgated. There is no implication that the results reached under these proposed regulations would not also be reached for positions established on or after March 17, 1995, and before May 1, 1995.

Special Analyses

It has been determined that this notice of proposed rulemaking is not a significant regulatory action as defined in EO 12866. Therefore, a regulatory assessment is not required. It also has been determined that section 553(b) of the Administrative Procedure Act (5 U.S.C. chapter 5) and the Regulatory Flexibility Act (5 U.S.C. chapter 6) do not apply to these regulations, and, therefore, a Regulatory Flexibility Analysis is not required. Pursuant to section 7805(f) of the Internal Revenue Code, this notice of proposed rulemaking will be submitted to the Chief Counsel for Advocacy of the Small Business Administration for comment on its impact on small business.

Comments and Public Hearing

Before these proposed regulations are adopted as final regulations, consideration will be given to any written comments (a signed original and eight (8) copies) that are submitted timely to the IRS. All comments will be available for public inspection and copying.

A public hearing has been scheduled for Wednesday, August 30, 1995, at 10 a.m. The public hearing will be held in the IRS Auditorium, 7th Floor, 1111 Constitution Avenue, NW, Washington DC 20224. Because of access restrictions, visitors will not be admitted beyond the Internal Revenue Building lobby more than 15 minutes before the hearing starts.

The rules of 26 CFR 601.601(a)(3) apply to the hearing.

Persons that wish to present oral comments at the hearing must submit written comments by July 31, 1995, and submit an outline of the topics to be discussed and the time to be devoted to each topic (signed original and eight (8) copies) by August 9, 1995.

A period of 10 minutes will be allotted to each person for making comments.

An agenda showing the scheduling of the speakers will be prepared after the deadline for receiving outlines has passed. Copies of the agenda will be available free of charge at the hearing.

Drafting Information

The principal author of these regulations is Robert B. Williams, Office of Assistant Chief Counsel (Financial Institutions and Products). However, other personnel from the IRS and Treasury Department participated in their development.

[¶ 49,151] Proposed Amendments of Regulations (EE-35-95), published in the Federal Register on December 26, 1995.

Employers-Employees: Retirement plans: Contributions: Allocation: Accrued benefits.—Amendments of Reg. §1.411(c)-1, relating to guidance on calculation of an employee's accrued benefit derived from the employee's contributions to a qualified defined benefit pension plan, is proposed.

AGENCY: Internal Revenue Service (IRS), Treasury.

ACTION: Notice of proposed rulemaking.

SUMMARY: This document contains proposed regulations that provide guidance on calculation of an employee's accrued benefit derived from the employee's contributions to a qualified defined benefit pension plan. These regulations are issued to reflect changes to the applicable law made by the Omnibus Budget Reconciliation Act of 1987 (OBRA `87) and the Omnibus Budget Reconciliation Act of 1989 (OBRA '89). OBRA '87 and OBRA '89 amended the law to change the accumulation of employee contributions and the conversion of those accumulated contributions to employee-derived accrued benefits.

DATES: Written comments and requests for a public hearing must be received by March 21, 1996.

ADDRESSES: Send submissions to: CC:DOM:CORP:R (EE-35-95), room 5228, Internal Revenue Service, POB 7604, Ben Franklin Station, Washington, DC 20044. In the alternative, submissions may be hand delivered between the hours of 8 a.m. and 5 p.m. to: CC:DOM:CORP:R (EE-35-95), Courier's Desk, Internal Revenue Service, 1111 Constitution Avenue, NW., Washington, DC.

FOR FURTHER INFORMATION CONTACT: Concerning the regulations, Janet A. Laufer, (202) 622-4606, concerning submissions, Michael Slaughter, (202) 622-7190 (not toll-free numbers).

SUPPLEMENTARY INFORMATION:

Background

This document contains proposed amendments to regulations containing rules for computing an employee's accrued benefit derived from the employee's contributions to a qualified defined benefit pension plan. The proposed amendments reflect changes made to section 411(c)(2) by the Omnibus Budget Reconciliation Act of 1987, Public Law 100-203 (OBRA `87), and the Omnibus Budget Reconciliation Act of 1989, Public Law 101-239 (OBRA `89). OBRA `87 and OBRA `89 changed the interest rates used to accumulate an employee's contributions to normal retirement age. OBRA `89 also changed the manner in which the accumulated contributions are converted to an annual benefit payable at normal retirement age, and removed a limitation on the employee-derived accrued benefit contained in prior law.

Section 411(c)(1) provides that an employee's accrued benefit derived from employer contributions as of any applicable date is the excess, if any, of the accrued benefit for the employee as of that date over the accrued benefit derived from contributions made by the employee as of that date. Section 411(c)(2)(B) provides that in the case of a defined benefit plan, the accrued benefit derived from contributions made by an employee as of any applicable date is the amount equal to the employee's contributions accumulated to normal retirement age using the interest rate(s) specified in section 411(c)(2)(C), expressed as an actuarially equivalent annual benefit commencing at normal retirement age using an interest rate which would be used by the plan under section 417(e)(3), as of the determination date. If the employee-derived accrued benefit is determined with respect to a benefit other than an annual benefit in the form of a single life annuity (without ancillary benefits) commencing at normal retirement age, section 411(c)(3) requires that the employee-derived accrued benefit be the actuarial equivalent of the benefit determined under section 411(c)(2).

Under section 411(c)(2)(C)(iii)(I), effective for plan years beginning after December 31, 1987, the interest rate used to accumulate an employee's contributions until the determination date is 120 percent of the Federal mid-term rate under section 1274 of the Internal Revenue Code (Code). For the period between the determination date and normal retirement age, section 411(c)(2)(C)(iii)(II) provides that the interest rate used to accumulate an employee's contributions is the interest rate which would be used under the plan under section 417(e)(3) as of the determination date. As noted above, section 411(c)(2)(B) provides that the interest rate which would be used under the plan under section 417(e)(3) as of the determination date also applies for purposes of converting the accumulated contributions to an annual benefit commencing at normal retirement age. The Retirement Protection Act of 1994, Public Law 103-465 (RPA `94) amended section 417(e) to change the applicable interest rate under section 417(e)(3) and to specify the applicable mortality table under that section. Examples contained in §1.411(c)-1(c)(6) of these proposed regulations reflect a plan that has been amended to comply with the interest rate and mortality table specifications enacted in RPA '94.

Explanation of Provisions

1. *Conversion calculation*

Prior to OBRA `89, section 411(c)(2)(B) specified that the conversion factor to be used for purposes of computing the employee-derived accrued benefit was 10 percent for a straight life annuity commencing at normal retirement age of 65 (i.e., multiply the accumulated contributions by .10), and that for other normal retirement ages the conversion factor was to be determined in accordance with regulations prescribed by the Secretary. Section 1.411(c)-1(c)(2) of the existing regulations provides that for normal retirement ages other than age 65, the conversion factor shall be the factor as determined by the Commissioner.

Rev. Rul. 76-47 (1976-1 C.B. 109) sets forth in tabular form the conversion factors to be used for determining the accrued benefit derived from employee contributions when the normal retirement age under the plan is other than age 65 or when the normal form of benefit is other than a single life annuity (without ancillary benefits). Rev. Rul. 76-47 further provides that where no standard factor is available, a conversion factor must be determined using an interest rate of 5 percent and the UP-1984 mortality table (without age setback).

OBRA `89 deleted the ten percent conversion factor in section 411(c)(2)(B) and replaced it with the requirement that the accumulated contributions at normal retirement age be expressed as an annual benefit commencing at normal retirement age using an interest rate which would be used under the plan under section 417(e)(3) (as of the determination date). This change was effective retroactively to the effective date of the OBRA '87 provision relating to section 411(c)(2)(C) (the first day of the first plan year beginning after December 31, 1987).

To reflect the OBRA `89 amendments, these proposed regulations define *appropriate conversion factor* with respect to an accrued benefit expressed in the form of an annual benefit that is nondecreasing for the life of the participant as the present value of an annuity in the form of that annual benefit commencing at normal retirement age at a rate of $1 per year. This amount is to be computed using the interest rate and mortality table which would be used under the plan under section 417(e)(3) and §1.417(e)-1T. To reflect the post-OBRA '89 conversion factor definition and to conform to common actuarial practice, these proposed regulations would change the *multiplied by* language in §1.411(c)-1(c)(1) to *divided by*.

2. *Accumulated contributions*

As added by the Employee Retirement Income Security Act of 1974 (ERISA), section 411(c)(2)(C) provided that employee contributions were to be accumulated using a standard interest rate of 5 percent for years beginning on or after the effective date of that section. OBRA `87 changed the interest rate under section 411(c)(2)(C) to 120 percent of the applicable Federal mid-term rate under section 1274 for plan years after 1987. OBRA '89 again amended section 411(c)(2)(C) to provide that 120 percent of the applicable Federal mid-term rate under section 1274 is to be used for accumulating contributions only up to the *determination date*. For the period from the determination date to normal retirement age, the interest rate which would be used under the plan under section 417(e)(3) (as of the determination date) must be used for accumulating contributions for the period from the determination date to normal retirement age. Accordingly, these proposed regulations would amend paragraph (3) of §1.411(c)-1(c) to reflect those rates. As stated above, RPA '94 amended section 417(e)(3) to change the applicable interest rate. See §1.417(e)-1T.

3. *Determination date*

Section 1.411(c)-1(c)(5)(i) defines the term determination date for purposes of section 411(c)(2)(C)(iii), in a case in which a participant will receive his or her entire accrued benefit derived from employee contributions in any one of the following forms (described in paragraph (c)(5)(ii)): an annuity that is substantially nonincreasing, substantially nonincreasing installment payments for a fixed number of years, or a single sum distribution. In such a case, the term determination date means the date on which distribution of such benefit commences. For this purpose, an annuity that is nonincreasing except for automatic increases to reflect increases in the consumer price index is considered to be an annuity that is substantially nonincreasing.

Thus, for example, for purposes of section 411(c)(2)(C)(iii), in the case of a distribution of the employee's entire accrued benefit (or the employee's entire employee-derived accrued benefit) in the form of a nonincreasing single life annuity payable commencing either at normal retirement age or at early retirement age, the determination date is the date the annuity commences. Similarly, in the case of a single sum distribution of accumulated employee contributions (i.e., employee contributions plus interest computed at or above the section 411(c) required rates) upon termination of employment with a deferred annuity benefit derived solely from employer contributions, the determination date is the date of distribution of the single sum of accumulated employee contributions.

Alternatively, the plan may provide that the determination date is the annuity starting date, as defined in §1.401(a)-20, Q&A-10.

Under §1.411(c)-1(c)(5)(iii) of these regulations, where a participant will receive a distribution that is not described in paragraph (c)(5)(i), the determination date will be as provided by the Commissioner.

4. *Elimination of limitation on employee-derived accrued benefit*

Prior to OBRA `89, section 411(c)(2)(E) of the Code limited the accrued benefit derived from employee contributions to the greater of (1) the employee's accrued benefit under the plan, or (2) the sum of the employee's mandatory contributions, without interest. Section 7881(m)(1)(C) of OBRA `89 deleted that provision. Section 7881(m)(1)(D) of OBRA '89 added section 411(a)(7)(D) to the Code, which provides that the accrued benefit of an employee shall not be less than the amount determined under section 411(c)(2)(B) with respect to the employee's accumulated contributions. Accordingly, these proposed regulations delete the rule included in §1.411(c)-1(d) of the existing regulations, which reflects the pre-OBRA `89 rule.

5. *Delegation of authority*

Section 1.411(c)-1(d) of these proposed regulations provides that the Commissioner may prescribe additional guidance on calculating the accrued benefit derived from employer or employee contributions under a defined benefit plan.

Effective Date

These amendments are proposed to be effective for plan years beginning on or after January 1, 1997. For example, assume that under a plan the employee's date of termination of employment is treated as the determination date, and distribution of the employee's entire employee-derived accrued benefit (as determined under the terms of the plan then in effect) occurs or commences prior to the first day of the plan year beginning in 1997. In that case, with respect to interest credits under section 411(c)(2)(C)(iii) for plan years beginning after 1987, the Service will not treat the plan as having failed to satisfy the requirements of section 411(c), nor will it require that additional amounts be credited in the calculation of the employee-derived accrued benefit in order to satisfy the requirements of section 411(c) after final regulations become effective, merely because the date the employee's employment terminated was treated as the determination date, provided that interest is credited in accordance with section 411(c)(2)(C)(iii)(I) for the period before the date the employee terminated employment and in accordance with section 411(c)(2)(C)(iii)(II) thereafter.

Once amendments to the regulations under §1.411(c)-1 are adopted in final form, the Service will obsolete or modify Rev. Rul. 76-47, Rev. Rul. 78-202 (1978-2 C.B. 124) and Rev. Rul. 89-60 (1989-1 C.B. 113) as necessary or appropriate.

Taxpayers may rely on these proposed regulations for guidance pending the issuance of final regulations.

Special Analyses

It has been determined that this notice of proposed rulemaking is not a significant regulatory action as defined in EO 12866. Therefore, a regulatory assessment is not required. It also has been determined that section 553(b) of the Administrative Procedure Act (5 U.S.C. chapter 5) and the Regulatory Flexibility Act (5 U.S.C. chapter 6) do not apply to these regulations, and, therefore, a Regulatory Flexibility Analysis is not required. Pursuant to section 7805(f) of the Internal Revenue Code, this notice of proposed rulemaking will be submitted to the Chief Counsel for Advocacy of the Small Business Administration for comment on its impact on small business.

Comments and Requests for a Public Hearing

Before these proposed regulations are adopted as final regulations, consideration will be given to any written comments (a signed original and eight (8) copies) that are submitted timely to the IRS. All comments will be available for public inspection and copying. A public hearing may be scheduled if requested in writing by a person that timely submits written comments. If a public hearing is scheduled, notice of the date, time, and place for the hearing will be published in the Federal Register.

Drafting Information

The principal author of these regulations is Janet A. Laufer, Office of the Associate Chief Counsel (Employee Benefits and Exempt Organizations). However, other personnel from the IRS and Treasury Department participated in their development.

[¶ 49,152]   **Proposed Amendments of Regulations (INTL-0054-95)**, published in the Federal Register on March 8, 1996.

Foreign corporations: Determination of interest expense deduction: Branch profits tax.—Amendments of Reg. §§1.882-5 and 1.884-1, relating to the determination of the interest expense deduction of foreign corporations and the branch profits tax, are proposed. A public hearing on this proposal is scheduled for June 6, 1996.

AGENCY: Internal Revenue Service (IRS), Treasury.

ACTION: Notice of proposed rulemaking and notice of public hearing.

SUMMARY: This document contains proposed Income Tax Regulations relating to the determination of the interest expense deduction of foreign corporations under section 882 and the branch profits tax under section 884 of the Internal Revenue Code of 1986. These proposed regulations are necessary to provide guidance that coordinates with guidance provided in final regulations under sections 882 and 884 published elsewhere in this issue of the Federal Register. These regulations will affect foreign corporations engaged in a U.S. trade or business. This document also provides notice of a public hearing on these proposed regulations.

DATES: Written comments must be received by June 6, 1996. Outlines of topics to be discussed at the public hearing scheduled for Thursday, June 6, 1996, at 10:00 a.m. must be received by May 23, 1996.

ADDRESSES: Send submissions to: CC:DOM:CORP:R (INTL-0054-95), room 5228, Internal Revenue Service, POB 7604, Ben Franklin Station, Washington DC 20044. In the alternative, submissions may be hand delivered between the hours of 8 a.m. and 5 p.m. to CC:DOM:CORP:R (INTL-0054-95), Courier's Desk, Internal Revenue Service, 1111 Constitution Avenue NW., Washington DC. The public hearing will be held in the Auditorium, Internal Revenue Building, 1111 Constitution Avenue NW., Washington DC.

FOR FURTHER INFORMATION CONTACT: Concerning the regulations, Ahmad Pirasteh or Richard Hoge, (202) 622-3870; and the hearing, Michael Slaughter (202) 622-7190 (not toll-free numbers).

SUPPLEMENTARY INFORMATION:

Background

This document contains proposed regulations amending the Income Tax Regulations (26 CFR Part 1) under sections 882 and 884 of the Internal Revenue Code. In final regulations under sections 882 and 884, published elsewhere in this issue of the Federal Register, various sections were reserved. These proposed regulations would provide guidance under those reserved sections, as well as amend other sections, to coordinate with the final regulations.

Explanation of the Provisions

I. *Financial products.*

The proposed regulations include several provisions that take into account recent developments in the tax treatment of financial instruments, such as the enactment of section 475, the development of hedging rules and the introduction of profit split methodologies in global trading Advance Pricing Agreements. The IRS and Treasury intend to issue regulations under section 864 that will address these recent developments as they affect the determination of a foreign corporation's effectively connected income. Comments are solicited on these proposed regulations as they relate to financial products and on their interaction with the determination of effectively connected income.

A. *"Split asset" rule for section 475 securities and section 1256 contracts.* Currently §1.884-1(d)(2)(vii) provides a "split asset" rule for certain securities described in §1.864-4(c)(5)(ii)(b)(3) that produce income only a portion of which is treated as effectively connected with the conduct of a U.S. trade or business. Since other securities may also produce income split between effectively connected and non-effectively connected income, the rule has been broadened to cover all financial instruments that meet the definition of a security under section 475(c)(2), as well as section 1256 contracts, that may produce such split income. Accordingly, a foreign corporation that, under an Advance Pricing Agreement, is permitted to apply a "profit split" methodology to determine the portion of its income from a portfolio of securities that is effectively connected with the conduct of a U.S. trade or business would apply this rule. This rule will also apply to determine the portion of a foreign corporation's portfolio of securities that is a U.S. asset for purposes of §1.882-5.

B. *Hedging transactions.* Proposed §1.884-1(c)(2)(ii) introduces a new rule for hedging transactions for purposes of section 884. The new rule requires that a taxpayer increase or decrease, as the case may be, the amount of its U.S. assets by the amount of any gain or loss on any transaction that hedges the U.S. assets. If the hedging transaction is undertaken outside the United States, perhaps as part of a global hedging strategy of the foreign corporation, then the hedging transaction is only taken into account to the extent that income from the transaction would be treated as income effectively connected with the U.S. trade or business of the taxpayer. If, however, the hedging transaction is entered into by the U.S. branch, it will only affect the amount of U.S. assets if it is contemporaneously identified as a hedging transaction in accordance with the provisions of §1.1221-2.

In response to comments, hedging rules also have been added to the interest allocation rules of §1.882-5. These rules provide that a transaction that hedges a U.S. booked liability will be taken into account in determining the amount, currency denomination, and interest rate associated with that liability for purposes of performing the second and third steps of the interest expense calculation.

C. *Securities marked-to-market.* Section 1.884-1(d)(6), which provides "E&P basis" rules for specific types of U.S. assets, has been clarified to provide rules for securities subject to mark-to-market accounting. The new provision in §1.884 1(d)(6)(v) specifies that securities subject to section 475, as well as section 1256 contracts, have an E&P basis equal to their mark-to-market value as of the determination date. Proposed §1.882-5(b)(2)(iv) provides a basis adjustment rule under which such assets are treated as having been marked-to-market on each determination date. Examples are contained in the proposed regulations that illustrate the effect of these rules on the calculation of worldwide assets and liabilities.

II. *Transactions between partners and partnerships.*

Example 4 in proposed § 1.882-5(c)(5) would clarify that an obligation of a partnership to make payments to its partner for the use of capital, which gives rise to guaranteed payments under section 707(c), is not a liability for purposes of § 1.882-5. The Service and Treasury solicit comments on the treatment of loans between partners and partnerships as part of Treasury's review of the international tax aspects of pass-through entities.

Special Analyses

It has been determined that this notice of proposed rulemaking is not a significant regulatory action as defined in EO 12866. Therefore, a regulatory assessment is not required. It has also been determined that section 553(b) of the Administrative Procedures Act (5 U.S.C. chapter 5) and the Regulatory Flexibility Act (5 U.S.C. chapter 6) do not apply to these regulations, and, therefore, a Regulatory Flexibility Analysis is not required. Pursuant to section 7805(f) of the Internal Revenue Code, this notice of proposed rulemaking will be submitted to the Chief Counsel for Advocacy of the Small Business Administration for comment on its impact on small business.

Comments and Request for a Public Hearing

Before these proposed regulations are adopted as final regulations, consideration will be given to any written comments (signed original and eight (8) copies) that are timely submitted to the IRS. All comments will be available for public inspection and copying.

A public hearing has been scheduled for Thursday, June 6, 1996, at 10:00 a.m. in the Auditorium, Internal Revenue Building, 1111 Constitution Avenue NW., Washington, DC. Because of access restrictions, visitors will not be admitted beyond the building lobby more than 15 minutes before the hearing starts.

The rules of 26 CFR 601.601(a)(3) apply to the hearing. Persons that wish to present oral comments at the hearing must submit written comments by June 6, 1996, and submit an outline of topics to be discussed and time to be devoted to each topic (signed original and eight (8) copies) by May 23, 1996.

A period of 10 minutes will be allotted to each person for making comments.

An agenda showing the scheduling of the speakers will be prepared after the deadline for receiving outlines has passed. Copies of the agenda will be available free of charge at the hearing.

Drafting Information

Several persons from the Office of Chief Counsel and the Treasury Department participated in drafting these regulations.

[¶ 49,154]   Proposed Regulations and Proposed Amendments of Regulations (REG-209826-96), published in the Federal Register on September 27, 1996.

Trusts: Nonexempt employees': Grantor trust rules: Application of.—Reg. § 1.1297-4 and amendments of Reg. §§ 1.671-1 and 1.671-2, relating to the application of the grantor trust rules to nonexempt employees' trusts, are proposed. A public hearing on this proposal is scheduled for January 15, 1997.

AGENCY: Internal Revenue Service (IRS), Treasury.

ACTION: Notice of proposed rulemaking and notice of public hearing.

SUMMARY: This document contains proposed regulations relating to the application of the grantor trust rules to nonexempt employees' trusts. The proposed regulations clarify that the grantor trust rules generally do not apply to domestic nonexempt employees' trusts, and clarify the interaction between the grantor trust rules, the rules generally governing the taxation of nonqualified deferred compensation arrangements, and the antideferral rules for United States persons holding interests in foreign entities. The proposed regulations affect nonexempt employees' trusts funding deferred compensation arrangements, as well as U.S. persons holding interests in certain foreign corporations and foreign partnerships with deferred compensation arrangements funded through foreign nonexempt employees' trusts. In addition, the proposed regulations affect U.S. persons that have deferred compensation arrangements funded through certain foreign nonexempt employees' trusts. This document also provides notice of a public hearing on these proposed regulations.

DATES: Written comments must be received by December 26, 1996. Requests to speak (with outlines of oral comments to be discussed) at the public hearing scheduled for January 15, 1997, at 10:00 a.m. must be submitted by December 24, 1996.

ADDRESSES: Send submissions to: CC:DOM:CORP:R (REG-209826-96), room 5226, Internal Revenue Service, POB 7604, Ben Franklin Station, Washington, DC 20044. Submissions may be hand delivered between the hours of 8 a.m. and 5 p.m. to: CC:DOM:CORP:R (REG-209826-96), Courier's Desk, Internal Revenue Service, 1111 Constitution Avenue, NW., Washington, DC. The public hearing will be held in room 2615, Internal Revenue Building, 1111 Constitution Avenue, NW., Washington, DC. Alternatively, taxpayers may submit comments electronically via the Internet by selecting the "Tax Regs" option on the IRS Home Page, or by submitting comments directly to the IRS Internet site at http://www.irs.ustreas.gov/prod/tax>regs/comments.html.

FOR FURTHER INFORMATION CONTACT: Concerning the regulations, James A. Quinn, (202) 622-3060; Linda S. F. Marshall, (202) 622-6030; Kristine K. Schlaman (202) 622-3840; and M. Grace Fleeman (202) 622-3850; concerning submissions and the hearing, Michael Slaughter, (202) 622-7190 (not toll-free numbers).

SUPPLEMENTARY INFORMATION:

Paperwork Reduction Act

The collection of information contained in this notice of proposed rulemaking has been submitted to the Office of Management and Budget for review in accordance with the Paperwork Reduction Act of 1995 (44 U.S.C. 3507(d)). Comments on the collection of information should be sent to the Office of Management and Budget, Attn: Desk Officer for the Department of the Treasury, Office of Information and Regulatory Affairs, Washington, DC 20503, with copies to the Internal Revenue Service, Attn: IRS Reports Clearance Officer, T:FP, Washington, DC 20224. Comments on the collection of information should be received by November 26, 1996. Comments are specifically requested concerning:

Whether the proposed collection of information is necessary for the proper performance of the functions of the Internal Revenue Service, including whether the information will have practical utility;

The accuracy of the estimated burden associated with the proposed collection of information (see below);

How the quality, utility, and clarity of the information to be collected may be enhanced;

How the burden of complying with the proposed collection of information may be minimized, including through the application of automated collection techniques or other forms of information technology; and

Estimates of capital or start-up costs and costs of operation, maintenance, and purchase of services to provide information.

The collection of information in this proposed regulation is in §1.671-1(h)(3)(iii). This information is required by the IRS to determine accurately the portion of certain foreign employees' trusts properly treated as owned by the employer. This information will be used to notify the Commissioner that certain entities are relying on an exception for reasonable funding. The collection of information is mandatory. The likely respondents are businesses or other for-profit organizations.

Estimated total annual reporting burden: 1,000 hours.

The estimated annual burden per respondent varies from .5 hours to 1.5 hours, depending on individual circumstances, with an estimated average of 1 hour.

Estimated number of respondents: 1,000.

Estimated annual frequency of responses: On occasion.

An agency may not conduct or sponsor, and a person is not required to respond to, a collection of information unless the collection of information displays a valid control number assigned by the Office of Management and Budget.

Books or records relating to a collection of information must be retained as long as their contents may become material in the administration of any internal revenue law. Generally, tax returns and tax return information are confidential, as required by 26 U.S.C. 6103.

Background

On May 7, 1993, the IRS issued proposed regulations under section 404A (58 FR 27219). The section 404A proposed regulations provide that section 404A is the exclusive means by which an employer may take a deduction or reduce earnings and profits for amounts used to fund deferred compensation in situations other than those in which a deduction or reduction of earnings and profits is permitted under section 404 (the "exclusive means" rule).

The section 404A proposed regulations do not provide rules regarding the treatment of income and ownership of assets of foreign trusts established to fund deferred compensation arrangements, but refer to "other applicable provisions," including the grantor trust rules of subpart E of the Internal Revenue Code of 1986, as amended. Thus, the 1993 proposed section 404A regulations imply that, if an employer cannot or does not elect section 404A treatment for a foreign trust established to fund the employer's deferred compensation arrangements, the employer may be treated as the owner of the entire trust for purposes of subtitle A of the Code under sections 671 through 679 even though all or part of the trust assets are set aside for purposes of satisfying liabilities under the plan. Conversely, some commentators believe that, for U.S. tax purposes, a foreign employer would not be treated as the owner of any portion of a foreign trust established to fund a section 404A qualified foreign plan even though all or part of the trust assets might be used for purposes other than satisfying liabilities under the plan. A number of different rules, in addition to the grantor trust rules, potentially affect the taxation of foreign trusts established to fund deferred compensation arrangements. These rules include: the nonexempt deferred compensation trust rules of sections 402(b) and 404(a)(5); the partnership rules of subchapter K; and the antideferral rules, which include subpart F and the passive foreign investment company (PFIC) rules (sections 1291 through 1297).

Following publication of the proposed 1993 regulations and enactment of section 956A in August of 1993, comments were received concerning both the asset ownership rules for foreign employees' trusts and the "exclusive means" rule for deductions or reductions in earnings and profits. These proposed regulations address only comments concerning income and asset ownership rules for foreign employees' trusts for federal income tax purposes. A foreign employees' trust is a nonexempt employees' trust described in section 402(b) that is part of a deferred compensation plan, and that is a foreign trust within the meaning of section 7701(a)(31). Comments concerning the "exclusive means" rule will be addressed in future regulations.

Statutory Background

1. Transfers of Property Not Complete for Tax Purposes

In certain situations, assets that are owned by a trust as a legal matter may be treated as owned by another person for tax purposes. Thus, assets may be treated as owned by a pension trust for non-tax legal purposes but not for tax purposes. This occurs, for example, if the person who has purportedly transferred assets to the trust retains the benefits and burdens of ownership. *See, e.g., Frank Lyon Co. v. United States*, 435 U.S. 561 (1978); *Corliss v. Bowers*, 281 U.S. 376 (1930); *Grodt & McKay Realty, Inc. v. Commissioner*, 77 T.C. 1221 (1981); Rev. Proc. 75-21 (1975-1 C.B. 715). If, under these principles, no assets have been transferred to an employees' trust for federal tax purposes, these proposed regulations do not apply.

2. Subpart E—Grantors and others treated as substantial owners

Even if there has been a completed transfer of trust assets, the subpart E rules may apply to treat the grantor as the owner of a portion of the trust for federal income tax purposes. Subpart E of part I of subchapter J, chapter 1 of the Code (sections 671 through 679) taxes income of a trust to the grantor or another person notwithstanding that the grantor or other person may not be a beneficiary of the trust. Under section 671, a grantor or another person includes in computing taxable income and credits those items of income, deduction, and credit against tax that are attributable to or included in any portion of a trust of which that person is treated as the owner.

Sections 673 through 679 set forth the rules for determining when the grantor or another person is treated as the owner of a portion of a trust for federal income tax purposes. Under sections 673 through 678, the grantor trust rules apply only if the grantor or other person has certain powers or interests. For example, section 676 provides that the grantor is treated as the owner of a portion of a trust where, at any time, the power to revest in the grantor title to that portion is exercisable by the grantor or a nonadverse party, or both. A grantor who is the owner of a trust under subpart E is treated as the owner of the trust property for federal income tax purposes. See Rev. Rul. 85-13 (1985-1 C.B. 184). This document is made available by the Superintendent of Documents, U.S. Government Printing Office, Washington, DC 20402.

Section 679 generally applies to a U.S. person who directly or indirectly transfers property to a foreign trust, subject to certain exceptions described below. Section 679 generally treats a U.S. person transferring property to a foreign trust as the owner of the portion of the trust attributable to the transferred property for any taxable year of that person for which there is a U.S. beneficiary of any portion of the trust. In general, a trust is treated as having a U.S. beneficiary for a taxable year of the U.S. transferor unless, under the terms of the trust, no part of the income or corpus of the trust may be paid or accumulated during the taxable year to or for the benefit of a U.S. person, and unless no part of the income or corpus of the trust could be paid to or for the benefit of a U.S. person if the trust were terminated at any time during the taxable year. A U.S. person is treated as having made an indirect transfer to the foreign trust of property if a non-U.S. person acts as a conduit with respect to the transfer or if the U.S. person has sufficient control over the non-U.S. person to direct the transfer by the non-U.S. person rather than itself.

Section 679(a) provides several exceptions from the application of section 679 for certain compensatory trusts. Under these exceptions, section 679 does not apply to a trust described in section 404(a)(4) or section 404A. Pursuant to amendments made in section 1903(b) of the Small Business Job Protection Act of 1996 (SBJPA), section 679 also does not apply to any transfer of property after February 6, 1995, to a trust described in section 402(b).

3. Taxability of beneficiary of nonexempt employees' trust

Section 402(b) provides rules for the taxability of beneficiaries of a nonexempt employees' trust. Under section 402(b)(1), employer contributions to a nonexempt employees' trust generally are included in the gross income of the employee in accordance with section 83. Section 402(b)(2) provides that amounts distributed or made available from a nonexempt employees' trust generally are taxable to the distributee under the rules of section 72 in the taxable year in which distributed or made available. Section 402(b)(4) provides that, under certain circumstances, a highly compensated employee is taxed each year on the employee's vested accrued benefit (other than the employee's investment in the contract) in a nonexempt employees' trust. Under section 402(b)(3), a beneficiary of a nonexempt employees' trust generally is not treated as the owner of any portion of the trust under subpart E. The rules of section 402(b) apply to a beneficiary of a nonexempt employees' trust regardless of whether the trust is a domestic trust or a foreign trust.

4. Employer deduction for contributions to a nonexempt employees' trust

Section 404(a)(5) provides rules regarding the deductibility of contributions to a nonqualified deferred compensation plan. Under section 404(a)(5), any contribution paid by an employer under a deferred compensation plan, if otherwise deductible under chapter 1 of the Code, is deductible only in the taxable year in which an amount attributable to the contribution is includible in the gross income of employees participating in the plan, and only if separate accounts are maintained for each employee. Section 1.404(a)-12(b)(1) clarifies that an employer's deduction for contributions to a nonexempt employees' trust is restricted to the amount of the contribution, and excludes any income received by the trust with respect to contributed amounts.

5. The partnership rules of subchapter K

A partnership is not subject to income taxation. However, a partner must take into account separately on its return its distributive share of the partnership's income, gain, loss, deduction, or credit. A U.S. partner of a foreign partnership is subject to U.S. tax on its distributive share of partnership income. In addition, a foreign partnership may have a controlled foreign corporation (CFC) partner which must take into account its distributive share of partnership income, gain, loss, or deduction in determining its taxable income. These distributive share inclusions of the CFC may result in subpart F income and thus income to a U.S. shareholder of the CFC. If the grantor trust rules do not apply to any portion of a foreign employees' trust, a foreign partnership could fund a foreign employees' trust in excess of the amount needed to meet its obligations to its employees under its deferred compensation plan and yet retain control over the excess amount. As a result, the foreign partnership would not have to include items in taxable income attributable to the excess amount, and consequently the U.S. partner or CFC would not have to include those items in its income.

6. The antideferral rules of subpart F, including section 956A, and PFIC

A U.S. person that owns stock in a foreign corporation generally pays no U.S. tax currently on income earned by the foreign corporation. Instead, the United States defers taxation of that income until it is distributed to the U.S. person. The antideferral rules, however, which include subpart F and the PFIC rules, limit this deferral in certain situations.

Subpart F of part III of Subchapter N (sections 951 through 964) applies to CFCs. A foreign corporation is a CFC if more than 50 percent of the total voting power of all classes of stock entitled to vote, or the total value of the stock in the corporation, is owned by "U.S. shareholders" (defined as U.S. persons who own ten percent or more of the voting power of all classes of stock entitled to vote) on any day during the foreign corporation's taxable year. The United States generally taxes U.S. shareholders of the CFC currently on their pro rata share of the CFC's subpart F income and sections 956 and 956A amounts. In effect, the U.S. shareholders are treated as having received a distribution out of the earnings and profits (E&P) of the CFC.

The types of income earned by a foreign employees' trust (dividends, interest, income equivalent to interest, rents and royalties, and annuities) are generally subpart F income. The inclusion under section 956 is based on the CFC's investment in U.S. property, which generally includes stock of a U.S. shareholder of the CFC. A U.S. shareholder's section 956A amount for a taxable year is the lesser of two amounts. The first amount is the excess of the U.S. shareholder's pro rata share of the CFC's "excess passive assets" over the portion of the CFC's E&P treated as previously included in gross income by the U.S. shareholder under section 956A. For purposes of section 956A, "passive asset" includes any asset which produces (or is held for the production of) passive income, and generally includes property that produces dividends, interest, income equivalent to interest, rents and royalties, and annuities, subject to exceptions that generally are not relevant in this context. The second amount is the U.S. shareholder's pro rata share of the CFC's "applicable earnings" to the extent accumulated in taxable years beginning after September 30, 1993.

Section 1501(a)(2) of SBJPA repeals section 956A. The repeal is effective for taxable years of foreign corporations beginning after December 31, 1996, and for taxable years of U.S. shareholders with or within which such taxable years of foreign corporations end.

If a CFC employer is not treated for federal income tax purposes as the owner of any portion of a foreign employees' trust under the grantor trust rules, then to the extent that passive assets contributed by a CFC to a nonexempt employees' trust would otherwise result in subpart F consequences for the CFC and its shareholders, the CFC's contribution could allow those consequences to be avoided. For example, a contribution by a CFC of passive assets to its foreign employees' trust could reduce the CFC's subpart F earnings and profits, and its applicable earnings or passive assets for section 956A purposes, and could affect the CFC's increase in investment in U.S. property for purposes of section 956, all of which could affect a U.S. shareholder's pro rata subpart F inclusions for the taxable year.

In contrast to the subpart F rules, the PFIC rules apply to any U.S. person who directly or indirectly owns any stock in a foreign corporation that is a PFIC under either an income or asset test. A foreign corporation, including a CFC, is a PFIC if either (1) 75 percent or more of its gross income for the taxable year is passive income or (2) at least 50 percent of the value of the corporation's assets produce passive income or are held for the production of passive income. For this purpose, passive income generally is the same type of income (dividends, interest, income equivalent to interest, rents and royalties, and annuities) that would be earned by a foreign employees' trust.

Under the PFIC rules, a U.S. person who is a direct or indirect shareholder of a PFIC is subject to a special tax regime upon either disposition of the PFIC's stock or receipt of certain distributions (excess distributions) from the PFIC. A shareholder, however, may avoid the application of this special regime by electing to include its pro rata share of certain of the PFIC's passive income in the year in which the foreign corporation earns it.

If the grantor trust rules did not apply to any portion of a foreign employees' trust, a contribution by a foreign corporation of passive assets to a nonexempt employees' trust would enable a U.S. person to avoid the PFIC rules if those assets would otherwise generate PFIC consequences for the foreign corporation and its shareholders. For example, by transferring passive assets to its nonexempt employees' trust in excess of the amount needed to meet obligations to its employees under its deferred compensation plan while retaining control over the excess amount, a foreign corporation could divest itself of a sufficient amount of passive assets and the passive income they produce to avoid meeting the income and asset tests. Furthermore, a foreign corporation that is a PFIC could minimize income inclusions for a U.S. shareholder that has made an election to include PFIC income currently by transferring income-producing assets to a foreign employees' trust.

Overview of proposed regulations

Under the proposed regulations, an employer is not treated as an owner of any portion of a domestic nonexempt employees' trust described in section 402(b) for federal income tax purposes. Section 404(a)(5) and §1.404(a)-12(b) provide a deduction to the employer solely for contributions to a nonexempt employees' trust, and not for any income of the trust. This rule is inconsistent with treating the employer as owning any portion of a nonexempt employees' trust, which would require the employer to recognize the trust's income that it may not deduct under section 404(a)(5). Accordingly, such a trust is treated as a separate taxable trust that is taxed under the rules of section 641 et seq. The rule in the proposed regulations is consistent with the holdings of a number of private letter rulings with respect to nonexempt employees' trusts and with the Service's treatment of trusts that no longer qualify as exempt under 501(a) (because they are no longer described in section 401(a)) as separate taxable trusts rather than as grantor trusts. See also Rev. Rul. 74-299 (1974-1 C.B. 154). This document is made available by the Superintendent of Documents, U.S. Government Printing Office, Washington, DC 20402.

Under the proposed regulations, an employer generally is not treated as the owner of any portion of a foreign nonexempt employees' trust for federal income tax purposes, except as provided under section 679. The proposed regulations, however, also provide that the grantor trust rules apply to determine whether an employer that is a CFC or a U.S. employer is treated as the owner of a specified "fractional interest" in a foreign employees' trust. This rule applies whether or not the employer elects section 404A treatment for the trust. Under the proposed regulations, this rule also applies in the case of an employer that is a foreign partnership with one or more partners that are U.S. persons or CFCs (U.S.- related partnership). Such an employer is treated as the owner of a portion of a foreign employees' trust under these proposed regulations only if the employer retains a grantor trust power or interest over a foreign employees' trust and has a specified "fractional interest" in the trust.

Under these proposed regulations, the grantor trust rules of subpart E do not apply to a foreign employees' trust with respect to a foreign employer other than a CFC or a U.S.-related foreign partnership, except for cases in which assets are transferred to a foreign employees' trust with a principal purpose of avoiding the PFIC rules. The IRS and Treasury will continue to consider whether these regulations should provide additional antiabuse rules that may be necessary for other purposes, including for purposes of calculating earnings and profits, determining the foreign tax credit limitation, and applying the interest allocation rules of §1.882-5.

Explanation of provisions

1. §1.671-1(g): Domestic nonexempt employees' trusts

The proposed regulations provide that an employer is not treated for federal income tax purposes as an owner of any portion of a nonexempt employees' trust described in section 402(b) that is part of a deferred compensation plan, and that is not a foreign trust within the meaning of section 7701(a)(31), regardless of whether the employer has a power or interest described in sections 673 through 677 over any portion of the trust. This rule is analogous to the rule set forth in §1.641(a)-0, which provides that subchapter J, including the grantor trust rules, does not apply to tax-exempt employees' trusts.

2. §1.671-1(h): Subpart E rules for certain foreign employees' trusts

The proposed regulations provide Subpart E rules for foreign employees' trusts of CFCs, foreign partnerships, and U.S. employers that apply for all federal income tax purposes. Under the proposed regulations, except as provided under section 679 or the proposed regulations (as described below), an employer is not treated as an owner of any portion of a foreign employees' trust for federal income tax purposes. If an employer is treated as the owner of a portion of a foreign employees' trust for federal income tax purposes as described below, then the employer is considered to own the trust assets attributable to that portion of the trust for all federal income tax purposes. Thus, for example, if an employer is treated as the owner of a portion of a foreign employees' trust for federal income tax purposes as described below, then income of the trust that is attributable to that portion of the trust increases the employer's earnings and profits for purposes of sections 312 and 964.

A foreign employees' trust is a nonexempt employees' trust described in section 402(b) that is part of a deferred compensation plan, and that is a foreign trust within the meaning of section 7701(a)(31). The proposed regulations apply to any foreign employees' trust of a CFC or U.S.-related foreign partnership, whether or not a trust funds a qualified foreign plan (as defined in section 404A(e)). The proposed regulations clarify that the income inclusion and asset ownership rules apply to the entity whose employees or independent contractors are covered under the deferred compensation plan.

A. Plan of CFC employer

The proposed regulations provide that, if a CFC maintains a deferred compensation plan funded through a foreign employees' trust, then, with respect to the CFC, the provisions of subpart E apply to the portion of the trust that is the fractional interest of the trust described in the proposed regulations.

B. Plan of U.S. employer

The proposed regulations provide that if a U.S. person maintains a deferred compensation plan funded through a foreign employees' trust, then, with respect to the U.S. person, the provisions of subpart E apply to the portion of the trust that is the fractional interest of the trust described in the proposed regulations.

C. Plan of U.S.-related foreign partnership employer

The proposed regulations provide that, if a U.S.-related foreign partnership maintains a deferred compensation plan funded through a foreign employees' trust, then, with respect to the U.S.-related foreign partnership, the provisions of subpart E apply to the portion of the trust that is the fractional interest of the trust described in the proposed regulations. The IRS and Treasury solicit comments on whether these regulations should provide a safe harbor rule for a U.S.-related foreign partnership that maintains a deferred compensation plan funded through a foreign employees' trust if U.S. or CFC partnership interests are de minimis. The IRS and Treasury specifically solicit comments concerning the amount of U.S. or CFC partnership interests that would qualify as "de minimis."

D. Plan of non-CFC foreign employer

The proposed regulations provide that a foreign employer that is not a CFC is treated as an owner of a portion of a foreign employees' trust only as provided in the antiabuse rule of §1.1297-4.

E. Fractional interest

The fractional interest of a foreign employees' trust described above is defined in the proposed regulations as an undivided fractional interest in the trust for which the fraction is equal to the relevant amount determined for the employer's taxable year divided by the fair market value of trust assets determined for the employer's taxable year.

F. Relevant amount

The relevant amount for the employer's taxable year is defined in the proposed regulations as the amount, if any, by which the fair market value of trust assets, plus the fair market value of any assets available to pay plan liabilities (including any amount held under an annuity contract that exceeds the amount that is needed to satisfy the liabilities provided for under the contract) that are held in the equivalent of a trust within the meaning of section 404A(b)(5)(A), exceed the plan's accrued liability, determined using a projected unit credit funding method.

The relevant amount is reduced to the extent the taxpayer demonstrates to the Commissioner that the relevant amount is attributable to amounts that were properly contributed to the trust pursuant to a reasonable funding method, or experience that is favorable relative to any actuarial assumptions used that the Commissioner determines to be reasonable. In addition, if an employer that is a controlled foreign corporation otherwise would be treated as the owner of a fractional interest in a foreign employees' trust, the taxpayer may rely on this rule only if it so indicates on a statement attached to a timely filed Form 5471. The IRS and Treasury solicit comments regarding the most appropriate way in which to extend a filing requirement to partners in U.S.-related foreign partnerships and other affected taxpayers.

G. Plan's accrued liability

Under the proposed regulations, the plan's accrued liability for a taxable year of the employer is computed as of the plan's measurement date for the employer's taxable year. The plan's accrued liability is determined using a projected unit credit funding method, taking into account only liabilities relating to services performed for the employer or a predecessor employer. In addition, the plan's accrued liability is reduced (but not below zero) by any liabilities that are provided for under annuity contracts held to satisfy plan liabilities.

Because CFCs generally are required to determine their taxable income by reference to U.S. tax principles, the definition of a plan's "accrued liability" refers to §1.412(c)(3)-1. This definition generally is intended to track the method used for calculating pension costs under Statement of Financial Accounting Standards No. 87, Employers' Accounting for Pensions (FAS 87), available from the Financial Accounting Standards Board, 401 Merritt 7, Norwalk, CT 06856. Under the method required to be used to calculate FAS 87's projected benefit obligation (PBO), plan costs are based on projected salary levels. Because many taxpayers already compute PBO annually to determine the pension costs of their nonexempt employees' trusts for financial reporting, the timing, interval and method to compute plan liabilities under §1.671-1(h) should minimize taxpayer burden. The IRS and Treasury solicit comments regarding the extent to which the proposed regulations conform to existing procedures under FAS 87 and applicable foreign law, and regarding appropriate conforming adjustments.

H. Fair market value of trust assets

Under the proposed regulations, for a taxable year of the employer, the fair market value of trust assets, and the fair market value of retirement annuities or other assets held in the equivalent of a trust, equals the fair market value of those assets, as of the measurement date for the employer's taxable year. The fair market value of these assets is adjusted to include contributions made between the measurement date and the end of the employer's taxable year.

I. De minimis exception

The proposed regulations provide an exception to the general rule for determining the relevant amount. If the relevant amount would not otherwise be greater than the plan's normal cost for the plan year ending with or within the employer's taxable year, then the relevant amount is considered to be zero.

J. Proposed effective date and transition rules

The proposed regulations are proposed to be prospective. For taxable years ending prior to September 27, 1996, employers generally would not be treated for federal income tax purposes as owning the assets of foreign nonexempt employees' trusts (except as provided under section 679), consistent with the rules applying to domestic nonexempt employees' trusts. A transition rule, for purposes of §1.671-1(h), exempts certain amounts from the application of the proposed regulations. This exemption is phased out over a ten-year period. There is a special transition rule for any foreign corporation that becomes a CFC after September 27, 1996. In addition, there is a special transition rule for certain entities that become U.S.-related foreign partnerships after September 27, 1996.

3. §1.671-2: General asset ownership rules

The proposed regulations provide that a person who is treated as the owner of any portion of a trust under subpart E is considered to own the trust assets attributable to that portion of the trust for all federal income tax purposes.

4. §1.1297-4: Subpart E rules for foreign employers that are not controlled foreign corporations

Under the proposed regulations, a foreign employer other than a CFC is not treated as the owner of any portion of a foreign nonexempt employees' trust for purposes of sections 1291 through 1297, except for cases in which a principal purpose for transferring property to the trust is to avoid classification of a foreign corporation as a PFIC (as defined in section 1296) or, if the foreign corporation is classified as a PFIC, in cases in which a principal purpose for transferring property to the trust is to avoid or to reduce taxation of U.S. shareholders of the PFIC under section 1291 or 1293. The effective date of this rule is September 27, 1996.

Income inclusion and related asset ownership rules for foreign welfare benefit plans

The IRS and Treasury solicit comments on the need for (and content of) income inclusion and asset ownership rules for foreign welfare benefit trusts.

Special Analyses

It has been determined that this notice of proposed rulemaking is not a significant regulatory action as defined in Executive Order 12866. Therefore, a regulatory assessment is not required. It is hereby certified that these regulations do not have a significant economic impact on a substantial number of small entities. This certification is based on the fact that these regulations will primarily affect U.S. owners of significant interests in foreign entities, which owners generally are large multinational corporations. This certification is also based on the fact that the burden imposed by the collection of information in the regulation, which is a requirement that certain entities may rely on an exception for reasonable funding only if they indicate such reliance on a statement attached to a timely filed Form 5471, is minimal, and, therefore, the collection of information will not impose a significant economic impact on such entities. Therefore, a Regulatory Flexibility Analysis under the Regulatory Flexibility Act (5 U.S.C. chapter 6) is not required. Pursuant to section 7805(f) of the Internal Revenue Code, this notice of proposed rulemaking will be submitted to the Chief Counsel for Advocacy of the Small Business Administration for comment on its impact on small business.

Comments and Public Hearing

Before these proposed regulations are adopted as final regulations, consideration will be given to any written comments (a signed original and eight (8) copies) that are submitted timely to the IRS. All comments will be available for public inspection and copying.

A public hearing has been scheduled for January 15, 1997, at 10:00 a.m. in room 2615, Internal Revenue Building, 1111 Constitution Avenue, NW., Washington DC. Because of access restrictions, visitors will not be admitted beyond the Internal Revenue Building lobby more than 15 minutes before the hearing starts.

The rules of 26 CFR 601.601(a)(3) apply to the hearing.

Persons that wish to present oral comments at the hearing must submit written comments by December 26, 1996, and submit an outline of the topics to be discussed and the time to be devoted to each topic (signed original and eight (8) copies) by December 24, 1996.

A period of 10 minutes will be allotted to each person for making comments.

An agenda showing the scheduling of the speakers will be prepared after the deadline for receiving outlines has passed. Copies of the agenda will be available free of charge at the hearing.

Drafting Information

The principal authors of these regulations are James A. Quinn of the Office of Assistant Chief Counsel (Passthroughs and Special Industries), Linda S. F. Marshall of the Office of Associate Chief Counsel (Employee Benefits and Exempt Organizations), and Kristine K. Schlaman and M. Grace Fleeman of the Office of Associate Chief Counsel (International). However, other personnel from the IRS and Treasury Department participated in their development.

[¶ 49,155] **Proposed Regulations (REG-209040-88)**, published in the Federal Register on December 24, 1996.

PFICs: Shareholders: Qualified electing fund elections.—Reg. §§ 1.1293-2 and 1.1295-2, relating to permitting certain shareholders to make a special election under Code Sec. 1295, in lieu of the election currently provided for under that section, with respect to certain preferred shares of a passive foreign investment company (PFIC), are proposed. A public hearing has been scheduled for May 8, 1997.

AGENCY: Internal Revenue Service (IRS), Treasury

ACTION: Notice of proposed rulemaking and notice of public hearing.

SUMMARY: This document contains proposed regulations permitting certain shareholders to make a special election under section 1295, in lieu of the election currently provided for under that section, with respect to certain preferred shares of a passive foreign investment company (PFIC). A shareholder that makes a special election must account for dividend income on the shares subject to the special election under special income inclusion rules, rather than under the general income inclusion rules of section 1293. This document also provides notice of a public hearing on these proposed regulations.

DATES: Written comments must be received by March 24, 1997. Requests to speak and outlines of oral comments to be discussed at the public hearing scheduled for May 8, 1997, at 10:00 a.m. must be received by April 17, 1997.

ADDRESSES: Send submissions to: CC:DOM:CORP:R (REG-209040-88), room 5226, Internal Revenue Service, POB 7604, Ben Franklin Station, Washington, DC 20044. Submissions may be hand delivered between the hours of 8 a.m. and 5 p.m. to: CC:DOM:CORP:R (REG-209040-88), Courier's Desk, Internal Revenue Service, 1111 Constitution Avenue, NW., Washington, DC. Alternatively, taxpayers may submit comments electronically via the Internet by selecting the "Tax Regs" option on the IRS Home Page, or by submitting comments directly to the IRS Internet site at http://www.irs.ustreas.gov/prod/tax>regs/comments.html. The public hearing will be held in room 3313, Internal Revenue Building, 1111 Constitution Avenue, NW., Washington, DC.

FOR FURTHER INFORMATION CONTACT: Concerning the regulations, Judith Cavell Cohen, (202) 622-3880; concerning submissions and the hearing, Evangelista Lee, (202) 622-7190 (not toll-free numbers).

SUPPLEMENTARY INFORMATION:

Paperwork Reduction Act

The collection of information contained in this notice of proposed rulemaking has been submitted to the Office of Management and Budget for review in accordance with the Paperwork Reduction Act of 1995 (44 U.S.C. 3507(d)). Comments on the collection of information should be sent to the Office of Management and Budget, Attn: Desk Officer for the Department of the Treasury, Office of Information and Regulatory Affairs, Washington, DC 20503, with copies to the Internal Revenue Service, Attn: IRS Reports Clearance Officer, T:FP, Washington, DC 20224. Comments on the collection of information should be received by February 24, 1997. Comments are specifically requested concerning:

Whether the proposed collection of information is necessary for the proper performance of the functions of the Internal Revenue Service, including whether the information will have practical utility;

The accuracy of the estimated burden associated with the proposed collection of information (see below);

How the quality, utility, and clarity of the information to be collected may be enhanced;

How the burden of complying with the proposed collection of information may be minimized, including through the application of automated collection techniques or other forms of information technology; and

Estimates of capital or start-up costs and costs of operation, maintenance, and purchase of services to provide information.

The collection of information in this proposed regulation is in proposed regulation § 1.1295-2(c)(3) and proposed regulation § 1.1295-2(e) and (f). This information will notify the Commissioner that certain shareholders have made the special election. In addition, this information will enable the IRS to determine if a shareholder qualifies for the special election and is satisfying the income inclusion requirements of proposed regulation § 1.1293-2. The collection of information is mandatory. The likely respondents are individuals, businesses, and other for-profit organizations.

Estimated total annual reporting/recordkeeping burden: 600 hours. The estimated annual burden per respondent varies from 21 minutes to 8.3 hours, depending on individual circumstances, with an estimated average of 35 minutes.

Estimated number of respondents: 1030.

Estimated annual frequency of responses: On occasion.

An agency may not conduct or sponsor, and a person is not required to respond to, a collection of information unless the collection of information displays a valid control number assigned by the Office of Management and Budget.

Books or records relating to a collection of information must be retained as long as their contents may become material in the administration of any internal revenue law. Generally, tax returns and tax return information are confidential, as required by 26 U.S.C. 6103.

Background

This document contains proposed Income Tax Regulations (26 CFR part 1) under sections 1293 and 1295 of the Internal Revenue Code. Sections 1293 and 1295 were added by the Tax Reform Act of 1986 (the Act) and were amended by the Technical and Miscellaneous Revenue Act of 1988 (TAMRA). The sections, as amended, were effective for taxable years of foreign corporations beginning after December 31, 1986. Section 1293 also was amended by the Omnibus Reconciliation Act of 1993 (OBRA). Guidance for making the section 1295 election was provided in proposed regulation § 1.1295-1 and Notice 88-125, 1988-2 C.B. 535. Guidance regarding the annual income inclusion rule for shareholders making a section 1295 election was provided in proposed regulation § 1.1293-1.

Explanation of Provisions

Special Preferred Section 1295 Election

1. Introduction.

The passive foreign investment company (PFIC) rules of the Code are designed to eliminate potential tax deferral opportunities associated with equity investments by United States persons in foreign corporations that have substantial levels of passive income or assets. The PFIC rules eliminate tax deferral opportunities by applying the section 1291 interest charge regime to PFIC shareholders that fail to make a section 1295 annual income inclusion election (section 1295 election). In general, the section 1291 interest charge regime applies to the "extraordinary" portion of any distribution received by the shareholder, and any gain recognized on a disposition of shares.

The PFIC rules apply to investments in both common and preferred shares of a PFIC. Preferred shares, unlike common shares, generally provide for limited dividend and liquidation or redemption rights, and thus do not participate significantly in corporate growth. Accordingly, preferred shares of a PFIC generally do not afford U.S. investors with the same potential for U.S. tax deferral as common shares of a PFIC.

Preferred shareholders, like common shareholders, may make the section 1295 election to avoid the interest charge regime of section 1291. Shareholders that make the section 1295 election are required under section 1293 to include in income annually, as ordinary income, their pro rata share of the PFIC's ordinary earnings and, as long-term capital gain, their pro rata share of the PFIC's net capital gain for the year. In order to determine their pro rata share of ordinary earnings and net capital gain, shareholders that have made a section 1295 election must obtain certain U.S. tax accounting information from the PFIC regarding the PFIC's earnings. If this information is not available, the shareholders cannot make the section 1295 election. If the requisite information is available, the annual information reporting and collection requirements associated with the section 1295 election may render the election impractical for smaller investors. Because preferred shares often do not afford investors with significant tax-deferral opportunity, commenters have suggested that the current section 1295 election regime should be simplified for certain types of preferred shares.

The proposed regulations adopt a special section 1295 election regime that would require holders of certain preferred shares of a PFIC that elect to be subject to the regime to accrue annually ordinary dividend income with respect to the preferred shares regardless of the holder's pro rata share of ordinary earnings or net capital gain of the PFIC for the year. Because shareholders would accrue income regardless of the earnings and net capital gain of the PFIC, shareholders that elect to be subject to the regime would not have to report and collect any U.S. tax accounting information regarding the PFIC in order to make the special section 1295 election.

The proposed regulations are issued under two sections of the Code. Section 1.1295-2 of the proposed regulations provides rules for making a QEF election under the special proposed section 1295 election regime (special preferred QEF election). Section 1.1293-2 describes the annual income inclusion rules for shareholders that have made the special preferred QEF election. The proposed regulations would apply only with respect to qualifying preferred shares issued after the date the proposed regulations are finalized.

2. Rules for making the special preferred QEF election.

Under proposed regulation § 1.1295-2(a), the special preferred QEF election may be made in lieu of the section 1295 election described in proposed regulation § 1.1295-1 and Notice 88-125, 1988-2 C.B. 535 (regular section 1295 election), with respect to certain types of preferred shares (qualified preferred shares) by certain holders satisfying prescribed ownership requirements.

The special preferred QEF election may only be made with respect to qualified preferred shares as defined in proposed regulation § 1.1295-2(b). To ensure that the special preferred QEF election cannot be used for tax avoidance purposes and to reduce complexity, the proposed regulations define qualified preferred shares narrowly to include only a limited class of preferred shares likely to be marketed to U.S. retail investors. Although the definition of qualified preferred shares includes both cumulative and non-cumulative preferred shares, the definition excludes various types of preferred shares, including preferred shares denominated in a foreign currency and preferred shares issued at a significant discount to their liquidation or redemption amounts. The PFIC issuing the preferred shares must represent that it intends to pay dividends currently. Proposed regulation § 1.1295-2(b) provides additional restrictions with respect to preferred shares acquired in secondary market transactions.

Proposed regulation § 1.1295-2(c) describes shareholders who may make the election. Under proposed regulation § 1.1295-2(c)(1), any United States person that acquires qualified preferred shares for cash or in certain nonrecognition transactions and that holds such shares directly may make the election. United States persons that are pass-through entities, including partnerships, S corporations, trusts and estates, may qualify as shareholders.

The special preferred QEF election regime is narrowly targeted to eliminate certain of the information reporting and collection requirements associated with the existing section 1295 election and annual inclusion rules for U.S. retail investors in preferred shares of PFICs. Treasury and the Service believe that the special preferred QEF election regime should only apply with respect to foreign corporations that are not expected to be in a position to provide U.S. tax accounting information to shareholders. Accordingly, proposed regulation § 1.1295-2(c)(2) provides that the special preferred QEF election does not apply to holders of preferred shares in a PFIC that is a controlled foreign corporation. Further, proposed regulation § 1.1295-2(c)(3) provides that the special preferred QEF election does not apply to holders that own 5 percent or more of the vote or value of any class of shares of the PFIC. Holders of five percent or more of the vote or value of any class of shares are not the type of retail investor that the proposed regulations are designed to assist. Such holders may only make the section 1295 election provided under current rules.

Proposed regulation § 1.1295-2(c)(3) requires the corporation to provide to electing shareholders a statement, directly or in a disclosure document generally available to all U.S. shareholders, either that it is or that it reasonably believes that it is a PFIC and that it is not a controlled foreign corporation. Shareholders that fail to receive such a statement are not permitted to make a special preferred QEF election

Proposed regulation § 1.1295-2(d) describes the effect of the special preferred QEF election. Proposed regulation § 1.1295-2(d)(1) provides that shares subject to a special preferred QEF election will be treated as shares of a pedigreed QEF (as defined in proposed regulation § 1.1291-1(b)(2)(ii)) for all taxable years of the foreign corporation that are included wholly or partly in the shareholder's holding period of the shares. Under the proposed regulations, the election will apply to all qualified preferred shares of a foreign corporation owned directly by the shareholder that are acquired in the taxable year with respect to which the election is made. Although a special preferred QEF election will not apply automatically to qualified preferred shares acquired in subsequent taxable years of a shareholder, the proposed regulations permit the shareholder to make separate special preferred QEF elections with respect to qualified preferred shares acquired in later years.

Proposed regulation § 1.1295-2(d)(2) provides that the special preferred QEF election regime applies whether or not the foreign corporation is a PFIC in any year subsequent to the year of the election. Accordingly, shareholders that make the special preferred QEF election must make annual § 1.1293-2 income inclusions, as provided in proposed regulation § 1.1295-2(d)(3), even if the foreign corporation does not qualify as a PFIC for a particular year.

Proposed regulation § 1.1295-2(e) specifies the time and manner of making the special preferred QEF election. In order to make the special preferred QEF election, a shareholder files Form 8621 (Return by a Shareholder of a Passive Foreign Investment Company or Qualified Electing Fund), for the taxable year of the election, checking the appropriate box in Form 8621, Part I, for making the section 1295 election, and indicating in the margin of Part I that the shareholder is making a special preferred QEF election with respect to certain specified shares. In addition, the shareholder must attach to Form 8621 a brief statement containing the information and representations contained in proposed regulation § 1.1295-2(e)(2)(ii). Under proposed regulation § 1.1295-2(f), in subsequent years, the shareholder must file Form 8621 with respect to the foreign corporation but need not attach any statement to the form. For all taxable years covered by the election, the shareholder must report on Line 6a of Part II of Form 8621 the amount includible under proposed regulation § 1.1293-2 with respect to qualified preferred shares subject to a special preferred QEF election.

Proposed regulation § 1.1293-2(g) states that a sale, exchange or other disposition of shares subject to a special preferred QEF election terminates the election with respect to those shares. Also, the Commissioner may terminate or invalidate an election if a shareholder fails to satisfy the initial or ongoing requirements of the election. For example, the Commissioner may terminate or invalidate a special preferred QEF election if the shareholder owns five percent or more of the vote or value of any class of shares of the PFIC at any time during the period that the shareholder owns qualified preferred shares subject to the election. A shareholder may not itself terminate a special preferred QEF election.

3. Annual inclusion rules for electing shareholders.

Under proposed regulation § 1.1293-2(a), a shareholder that has made a special preferred QEF election must make annual income inclusions with respect to qualified preferred shares subject to the election. Unlike the annual income inclusions provided under section 1293 and proposed regulation § 1.1293-1, the annual inclusions under the special preferred QEF election regime are determined without regard to the shareholder as pro rata share of the foreign corporation's ordinary earnings or net capital gains.

Proposed regulation § 1.1293-2(b) provides rules for determining the amount that a shareholder must include in income annually under the special preferred QEF election regime. Under the proposed regulations, this annual amount consists of two components. The first component is an annual inclusion amount based on a ratable daily portion of dividend income that accrues on the qualified preferred shares (annual dividend amount). This ratable inclusion rule for the annual dividend amount is analogous to the rule for inclusion of income with respect to periodic payments on notional principal contracts under § 1.446-3. The second component of the preferred QEF amount arises only in respect of fixed term preferred shares, as described proposed regulation § 1.1295-2(b)(vii), acquired in a secondary market transaction, and is calculated based on the ratable inclusion of the excess, if any, of the redemption price of the shares over the acquisition cost of the shares (preferred discount amount). This ratable inclusion rule for the preferred discount amount is analogous to the rule for the ratable inclusion of market discount on certain debt under section 1276(b)(1). The Service and Treasury solicit comments regarding the income inclusion rules of the proposed regulations, including comments as to whether foreign corporations and their agents could effectively assist holders in complying with the income inclusion rules applicable to preferred discount.

Proposed regulation § 1.1293-2(c) provides certain special rules regarding the annual income inclusion required under proposed regulation § 1.1293-2(a). Under § 1.1293-2(c)(1), annual amounts are included in income by shareholders irrespective of the PFIC's earnings and profits. In this regard, the special preferred QEF election differs from the regular section 1295 election in that shareholders making the special preferred QEF election must accrue the annual amount as ordinary income even if the amount exceeds the shareholder's pro rata share of the foreign corporation's earnings and profits. Proposed regulation § 1.1293-2(c)(3) requires the shareholder to include the annual dividend amount as ordinary income regardless of whether any portion of the PFIC's earnings for the year represents net capital gain. Proposed regulation § 1.1293-2(c)(4) provides rules for the tax-free distribution of previously taxed amounts. Proposed regulation § 1.1293-2(c)(5) provides certain basis adjustment rules similar to the basis adjustment rule of section 1293(d). Finally, proposed regulation § 1.1293-2(c)(6) provides rules intended to limit the effect of a special preferred QEF election to the shareholder making the election. Accordingly, a special preferred QEF election will not affect the foreign corporation's calculation of its earnings and profits, and will have no consequences for shareholders that have not made a special preferred QEF election.

Special Analyses

It has been determined that this notice of proposed rulemaking is not a significant regulatory action as defined in Executive Order 12866. Therefore, a regulatory assessment is not required. It is hereby certified that these regulations do not have a significant economic impact on a substantial number of small entities. This certification is based on the fact that these regulations represent a wholly elective simpler alternative to the section 1295 election described in § 1.1295-1 and Notice 88-125, 1988-2 C.B. 535, and impose a lighter collection of information burden. Further, the requirement that electing shareholders indicate their special election on Form 8621 annually and attach a statement, providing certain information in the first year of the election only, is minimal and will not impose a significant economic impact on electing shareholders. Therefore, a Regulatory Flexibility Analysis under the Regulatory Flexibility Act (5 U.S.C. chapter 6) is not required. Pursuant to section 7805(f) of the Internal Revenue Code, this notice of proposed rulemaking will be submitted to the Chief Counsel for Advocacy of the Small Business Administration for comment on its impact on small business.

Comments and Public Hearing

Before these proposed regulations are adopted as final regulations, consideration will be given to any written comments (a signed original and eight (8) copies) that are submitted timely to the IRS. All comments will be available for public inspection and copying.

A public hearing has been scheduled for May 8, 1997, at 10:00 a.m. in room 3313, Internal Revenue Building, 1111 Constitution Avenue, NW., Washington DC. Because of access restrictions, visitors will not be admitted beyond the Internal Revenue Building lobby more than 15 minutes before the hearing starts.

The rules of 26 CFR 601.601(a)(3) apply to the hearing.

Persons that wish to present oral comments at the hearing must submit written comments by March 24, 1997, and submit an outline of the topics to be discussed and the time to be devoted to each topic (signed original and eight (8) copies) by April 17, 1997.

A period of 10 minutes will be allotted to each person for making comments.

An agenda showing the schedule of speakers will be prepared after the deadline for receiving outlines has passed. Copies of the agenda will be available free of charge at the hearing.

Drafting Information

The principal author of these regulations is Judith Cavell Cohen of the Office of Associate Chief Counsel (International). However, other personnel from the IRS and Treasury Department participated in their development.

[¶ 49,156]   Proposed Amendments of Regulations (REG-246018-96), published in the Federal Register on January 2, 1997.

Life insurance companies: Property and casualty insurance companies: Life insurance reserves.—Amendments of Reg. § 1.801-4, permitting the recomputation of certain life insurance reserves if such reserves were initially computed or estimated on other than an actuarial basis, are proposed. A public hearing on this proposal is scheduled for April 17, 1997.

AGENCY: Internal Revenue Service (IRS), Treasury.

ACTION: Notice of proposed rulemaking and notice of public hearing.

SUMMARY: This document contains proposed regulations relating to the definition of life insurance reserves. The proposed regulations permit the taxpayer or the IRS to recompute certain reserves if those reserves were initially computed or estimated on other than an actuarial basis. The proposed regulations affect both life insurance companies and property and casualty insurance companies. This document also contains a notice of a public hearing on the proposed regulations.

DATES: Written comments must be received by April 2, 1997. Requests to speak and outlines of oral comments to be discussed at the public hearing scheduled for Thursday, April 17, 1997, at 10 a.m. must be received by Thursday, March 27, 1997.

ADDRESSES: Send submissions to: CC:DOM:CORP:R (REG-246018-96), room 5226, Internal Revenue Service, POB 7604, Ben Franklin Station, Washington, DC 20044. Submissions may be hand delivered between the hours of 8 a.m. and 5 p.m. to: CC:DOM:CORP:R (REG-246018-96), Courier's Desk, Internal Revenue Service, 1111 Constitution Avenue NW, Washington, DC. Alternatively, taxpayers may submit comments electronically via the Internet by selecting the "Tax Regs" option on the IRS Home Page, or by submitting comments directly to the IRS Internet site at http://www.irs.ustreas.gov/prod/tax>regs/comments.html. The public hearing will be held in the Commissioner's conference room, room 3313, Internal Revenue Service Building, 1111 Constitution Avenue, N.W. Washington, D.C.

FOR FURTHER INFORMATION CONTACT: Concerning the regulations, Ann Cammack, (202) 622-3970; concerning submissions and the hearing, Evangelista Lee, (202) 622-7190 (not toll-free numbers).

SUPPLEMENTARY INFORMATION:

Background

To qualify as a life insurance reserve for purposes of Part I of subchapter L of the Internal Revenue Code, a reserve must satisfy various requirements, including the requirement in section 816(b)(1)(A) and § 1.801-4(a)(1) that it be "computed or estimated on the basis of recognized mortality or morbidity tables and assumed rates of interest." Qualifying as a life reserve under section 816(b) has various consequences. Life reserves are included in the numerator and denominator of the reserve ratio test of section 816(a), which is used to determine when an insurance company is taxed as a life insurance company under Part I of subchapter L. Increases in life reserves as defined in section 816(b) are taken into account under section 807(c)(1). In addition, life reserves as defined in section 816(b) are considered part of a nonlife company's unearned premiums under section 832(b)(4).

Two circuits have construed former section 801(b)(1)(A), which was recodified as section 816(b)(1)(A) in 1984, to prevent reserves held with respect to life, annuity or noncancellable accident and health policies but not computed or estimated using actuarial tables from qualifying as life reserves. The IRS also has held that life reserves must be computed or estimated using actuarial tables under former section 801(b)(1)(A). See, e.g., Rev. Rul. 69-302 (1969-2 C.B. 186). The Claims Court, in contrast, has concluded that the statute and regulation do not necessarily require the insurance company to compute its life reserves using actuarial tables, when a different method results in reserves that "reasonably approximate" actuarial reserves.

Rev. Rul. 69-302 held that not only were life reserves required to be computed or estimated on the basis of recognized mortality or morbidity tables and assumed rates of interest, but that reserves for credit life insurance contracts could not be retroactively recomputed in a manner that would enable them to qualify as life reserves. Neither of the cases cited in Rev. Rul. 69-302, however, addressed the question of whether taxpayers or the Commissioner could recompute reserves based on information that was available at the end of the applicable taxable year. Two subsequent cases came to opposite conclusions on this issue.

The reserve ratio test of section 816(a) was intended to distinguish between life and nonlife insurance companies based on the nature of each company's business, as measured by its reserves. This purpose is not achieved, however, if a company that only issues life insurance, annuity or noncancellable accident and health contracts can elect to be taxed as a nonlife company by failing to use mortality and morbidity tables and assumed rates of interest in computing or estimating its reserves for some of those contracts.

Explanation of Provisions

Proposed § 1.801-4(g)(1) provides that if an insurance company does not compute or estimate its reserves for certain contracts on the basis of mortality or morbidity tables and assumed rates of interest, then the taxpayer or the Commissioner may recompute those reserves on the basis of mortality or morbidity tables and assumed rates of interest. This regulation will apply to reserves for contracts involving, at the time with respect to which the reserves are computed, life, accident or health contingencies, if such reserves were not initially computed in accordance with the requirements of section 816(b)(1)(A).

Proposed § 1.801-4(g)(2) provides that if the taxpayer or the Commissioner recomputes reserves pursuant to § 1.801-4(g)(1), the reserves satisfy the section 816(b)(1)(A) requirement that a life reserve be computed or estimated using actuarial tables and assumed rates of interest. Assuming that these amounts satisfy the other requirements of section 816(b), the recomputed amounts will be considered life insurance reserves under section 816(b), and the recomputed reserves will be included in both the numerator and the denominator of the reserve ratio test under section 816(a). In addition, the reserves for such contracts will be taken into account under section 807(c)(1) and will be used to compute a nonlife company's unearned premiums under section 832(b)(4).

Proposed § 1.801-4(g)(3) provides that for purposes of section 816(b)(4) and § 1.801-3(i), which provide that the mean of the beginning and end of year reserves will be used for purposes of section 816(a), (b) and (c), the reserves on a life insurance, annuity or noncancellable accident and health contract must be recomputed for both the beginning and the end of the year.

Proposed § 1.801-4(g)(4) requires that no information acquired after the date as of which the beginning of year reserves were initially computed or estimated may be taken into account in recomputing those reserves under paragraph (g)(1). It also requires that no information acquired after the date as of which the end of year reserves were initially computed or estimated may be taken into account in recomputing those reserves under paragraph (g)(1).

The IRS is considering whether to issue guidance under section 816, including regulations regarding the definition of "total reserves" under section 816(c) as well as redesignating and revising the regulations issued under prior law section 801. The IRS invites comments on this matter.

Proposed Effective Date

Proposed §1.801-4(g) would be effective with respect to returns filed for taxable years beginning after the publication of the final regulations.

Effect on Other Documents

The IRS will modify, clarify, or obsolete publications as necessary to conform with this regulation as of the date of publication in the Federal Register of the final regulations. *See e.g.*, Rev. Rul. 69-302 (1969-2 C.B. 186). The IRS solicits comments as to whether other publications should be modified or obsoleted.

Special Analyses

It has been determined that this notice of proposed rulemaking is not a significant regulatory action as defined in EO 12866. Therefore, a regulatory assessment is not required. It also has been determined that section 553(b) of the Administrative Procedure Act (5 U.S.C. chapter 5) does not apply to these regulations, and because the regulations do not impose a collection of information on small entities, the Regulatory Flexibility Act (5 U.S.C. chapter 6) does not apply. Pursuant to section 7805(f) of the Internal Revenue Code, this notice of proposed rulemaking will be submitted to the Chief Counsel for Advocacy of the Small Business Administration for comment on its impact on small business.

Comments and Public Hearing

Before these proposed regulations are adopted as final regulations, consideration will be given to any written comments (a signed original and 8 copies) that are submitted timely to the IRS. All comments will be available for public inspection and copying.

A public hearing has been scheduled for Thursday, April 17, 1997 in the Commissioner's conference room, room 3313, Internal Revenue Service Building at 10:00 a.m. Because of access restrictions, visitors will not be admitted beyond the Internal Revenue Building lobby more than 15 minutes before the hearing starts.

The rules of 26 CFR 601.601(a)(3) apply to the hearing.

Persons that wish to present oral comments at the hearing must submit written comments by March 27, 1997 and submit an outline of the topics to be discussed and the time to be devoted to each topic (a signed original and 8 copies) by March 27, 1997.

A period of 10 minutes will be allotted to each person for making comments.

An agenda showing the scheduling of the speakers will be prepared after the deadline for receiving outlines has passed. Copies of the agenda will be available free of charge at the hearing.

Drafting Information

The principal author of this regulation is Ann B. Cammack, Office of Assistant Chief Counsel (Financial Institutions and Products). However, other personnel from the IRS and Treasury Department participated in their development.

[¶ 49,157] **Proposed Amendments of Regulations (REG-209824-96)**, published in the Federal Register on January 13, 1997.

Limited partner for self-employment tax purposes: Definition of.—Amendments of Reg. §1.1402(a)-2, relating to the self-employment income tax imposed under Code Sec. 1402, are proposed. A public hearing on this proposal is scheduled for May 21, 1997.

AGENCY: Internal Revenue Service (IRS), Treasury.

ACTION: Notice of proposed rulemaking and notice of public hearing.

SUMMARY: This document contains proposed amendments to the regulations relating to the self-employment income tax imposed under section 1402 of the Internal Revenue Code of 1986. These regulations permit individuals to determine whether they are limited partners for purposes of section 1402(a)(13), eliminating the uncertainty in calculating an individual's net earnings from self-employment under existing law. This document also contains a notice of public hearing on the proposed regulations.

DATES: Written comments must be received by April 14, 1997. Requests to speak and outlines of oral comments to be discussed at the public hearing scheduled for May 21, 1997, at 10 a.m. must be received by April 30, 1997.

ADDRESSES: Send submissions to: CC:DOM:CORP:R (REG-209824-96), room 5226, Internal Revenue Service, POB 7604, Ben Franklin Station, Washington, DC 20044. Submissions may be hand delivered between the hours of 8 a.m. and 5 p.m. to: CC:DOM:CORP:R (REG-209824-96), Courier's Desk, Internal Revenue Service, 1111 Constitution Avenue, NW, Washington, DC. Alternatively, taxpayers may submit comments electronically via the Internet by selecting the "Tax Regs" option on the IRS Home Page, or by submitting comments directly to the IRS Internet site at http://www.irs.ustreas.gov/prod/tax>regs/comments.html. The public hearing will be held in the Auditorium, Internal Revenue Service building, 1111 Constitution Avenue, NW, Washington, DC.

FOR FURTHER INFORMATION CONTACT: Concerning the regulation, Robert Honigman, (202) 622-3050; concerning submissions and the hearing, Christina Vasquez, (202) 622-6808 (not toll-free numbers).

SUPPLEMENTARY INFORMATION:

Background

This document contains proposed amendments to the Income Tax Regulations (26 CFR part 1) under section 1402 of the Internal Revenue Code and replaces the notice of proposed rulemaking published in the Federal Register on December 29, 1994, at 59 FR 67253, that treated certain members of a limited liability company (LLC) as limited partners for self-employment tax purposes. Written comments responding to the proposed regulations were received, and a public hearing was held on June 23, 1995.

Under the 1994 proposed regulations, an individual owning an interest in an LLC was treated as a limited partner if (1) the individual lacked the authority to make management decisions necessary to conduct the LLC's business (the management test), and (2) the LLC could have been formed as a limited partnership rather than an LLC in the same jurisdiction, and the member could have qualified as a limited partner in the limited partnership under applicable law (the limited partner equivalence test). The intent of the 1994 proposed regulations was to treat owners of an LLC interest in the same manner as similarly situated partners in a state law partnership.

Public comments on the 1994 proposed regulations were mixed. While some commentators were pleased with the proposed regulations for attempting to conform the treatment of LLCs with state law partnerships, others criticized the 1994 proposed regulations based on a variety of arguments.

A number of commentators discussed administrative and compliance problems with the 1994 proposed regulations. For example, it was noted that both the management test and the limited partner equivalence test depend upon legal or factual determinations that may be difficult for taxpayers or the IRS to make with certainty.

Another commentator pointed out that basing the self-employment tax treatment of LLC members on state law limited partnership rules would lead to disparate treatment between members of different LLCs with identical rights based solely on differences in the limited partnership statutes of the states in which the members form their LLC. For example, State A's limited partnership act may allow a limited partner to participate in a partnership's business while State B's limited partnership act may not. Thus, an LLC member, who is not a manager, that participates in the LLC's business would be a limited partner under the proposed regulations if the LLC is formed in State A, but not if the LLC is formed in State B. Commentators asserted that this disparate treatment is inherently unfair for federal tax purposes.

Some commentators argued for a "material participation" test to determine whether an LLC member's distributive share is included in the individual's net earnings from self-employment. The proposed regulations did not contain a participation test. Commentators advocating a participation test stressed that such a test would eliminate uncertainty concerning many LLC members' limited partner status and would better implement the self-employment tax goal of taxing compensation for services.

Other commentators argued for a more uniform approach, stating that a single test should govern all business entities (i.e., partnerships, LLCs, LLPs, sole proprietorships, et al.) whose members may be subject to self-employment tax. These commentators generally recognized, however, that a change in the treatment of a sole proprietorship or an entity that is not characterized as a partnership for federal tax purposes would be beyond the scope of regulations to be issued under section 1402(a)(13).

Finally, some commentators focused on whether the Service would respect the ownership of more than one class of partnership interest for self-employment tax purposes (bifurcation of interests). The proposed regulations treated an LLC member as a limited partner with respect to his or her entire interest (if the member was not a manager and satisfied the limited partner equivalence test), or not at all (if either the management test or limited partner equivalence test was not satisfied). Commentators, however, pointed to the legislative history of section 1402(a)(13) to support their argument that Congress only intended to tax a partner's distributive share attributable to a general partner interest. Under this argument, a partner that holds both a general partner interest and a limited partner interest is only subject to self-employment tax on the distributive share attributable to the partner's general partner interest. This intent also may be inferred from the statutory language of section 1402(a)(13) that the self-employment tax does not apply to " . . . the distributive share of any item of income or loss of a limited partner, as such . . . ." Based on this evidence, these commentators requested that the proposed regulations be revised to allow the bifurcation of interests for self-employment tax purposes.

After considering the comments received, the IRS and Treasury have decided to withdraw the 1994 notice of proposed rulemaking and to re-propose amendments to the Income Tax Regulations (26 CFR part 1) under section 1402 of the Code.

Explanation of Provisions

The proposed regulations contained in this document define which partners of a federal tax partnership are considered limited partners for section 1402(a)(13) purposes. These proposed regulations apply to all entities classified as a partnership for federal tax purposes, regardless of the state law characterization of the entity. Thus, the same standards apply when determining the status of an individual owning an interest in a state law limited partnership or the status of an individual owning an interest in an LLC. In order to achieve this conformity, the proposed regulations adopt an approach which depends on the relationship between the partner, the partnership, and the partnership's business. State law characterizations of an individual as a "limited partner" or otherwise are not determinative.

Generally, an individual will be treated as a limited partner under the proposed regulations unless the individual (1) has personal liability (as defined in § 301.7701-3(b)(2)(ii) of the Procedure and Administration Regulations) for the debts of or claims against the partnership by reason of being a partner; (2) has authority to contract on behalf of the partnership under the statute or law pursuant to which the partnership is organized; or, (3) participates in the partnership's trade or business for more than 500 hours during the taxable year. If, however, substantially all of the activities of a partnership involve the performance of services in the fields of health, law, engineering, architecture, accounting, actuarial science, or consulting, any individual who provides services as part of that trade or business will not be considered a limited partner.

By adopting these functional tests, the proposed regulations ensure that similarly situated individuals owning interests in entities formed under different statutes or in different jurisdictions will be treated similarly. The need for a functional approach results not only from the proliferation of new business entities such as LLCs, but also from the evolution of state limited partnership statutes. When Congress enacted the limited partner exclusion found in section 1402(a)(13), state laws generally did not allow limited partners to participate in the partnership's trade or business to the extent that state laws allow limited partners to participate today. Thus, even in the case of a state law limited partnership, a functional approach is necessary to ensure that the self-employment tax consequences to similarly situated taxpayers do not differ depending upon where the partnership organized.

The proposed regulations allow an individual who is not a limited partner for section 1402(a)(13) purposes to nonetheless exclude from net earnings from self-employment a portion of that individual's distributive share if the individual holds more than one class of interest in the partnership. Similarly, the proposed regulations permit an individual that participates in the trade or business of the partnership to bifurcate his or her distributive share by disregarding guaranteed payments for services. In each case, however, such bifurcation of interests is permitted only to the extent the individual's distributive share is identical to the distributive share of partners who qualify as limited partners under the proposed regulation (without regard to the bifurcation rules) and who own a substantial interest in the partnership. Together, these rules exclude from an individual's net earnings from self-employment amounts that are demonstrably returns on capital invested in the partnership.

Proposed Effective Date

These regulations are proposed to be effective beginning with the individual's first taxable year beginning on or after the date these regulations are published as final regulations in the Federal Register.

Special Analyses

It has been determined that this notice of proposed rulemaking is not a significant regulatory action as defined in EO 12866. Therefore, a regulatory assessment is not required. It also has been determined that section 553(b) of the Administrative Procedure Act (5 U.S.C. chapter 5) does not apply to these regulations, and, because the regulations do not impose a collection of information on small entities, the Regulatory Flexibility Act (5 U.S.C. chapter 6) does not apply. Pursuant to section 7805(f) of the Internal Revenue Code, this notice of proposed rulemaking will be submitted to the Chief Counsel for Advocacy of the Small Business Administration for comment on its impact on small business.

Comments and Public Hearing

Before these proposed regulations are adopted as final regulations, consideration will be given to any written comments (a signed original and eight (8) copies) that are submitted timely to the IRS. All comments will be available for public inspection and copying.

A public hearing has been scheduled for Wednesday, May 21, 1997, at 10 a.m. in the Auditorium, Internal Revenue Service building, 1111 Constitution Avenue, NW, Washington, DC. Because of access restrictions, visitors will not be admitted beyond the Internal Revenue Service building lobby more than 15 minutes before the hearing starts.

The rules of 26 CFR 601.601(a)(3) apply to the hearing.

Persons that wish to present oral comments at the hearing must submit written comments by April 14, 1997, and submit an outline of the topics to be discussed and the time to be devoted to each topic (signed original and eight (8) copies) by April 30, 1997.

A period of 10 minutes will be allotted to each person for making comments.

An agenda showing the scheduling of the speakers will be prepared after the deadline for receiving outlines has passed. Copies of the agenda will be available free of charge at the hearing.

Drafting Information

The principal author of these regulations is Robert Honigman of the Office of Assistant Chief Counsel (Passthroughs & Special Industries). However, other personnel from the IRS and Treasury Department participated in their development.

[¶ 49,160]   **Proposed Amendments of Regulations (REG-107872-97),** published in the Federal Register on October 14, 1997.

Withholding: Nonresident aliens: Form W-8: Electronic transmission.—Amendments of Reg. §1.1441-1, relating to the establishment by withholding agents and payors of an electronic system for use by beneficial owners or payees in furnishing Form W-8 (Certificate of Foreign Status), are proposed.

AGENCY: Internal Revenue Service (IRS), Treasury.

ACTION: Notice of proposed rulemaking.

SUMMARY: This document contains proposed regulations relating to the submission of Form W-8, a withholding certificate, needed for purposes of chapters 3 and 61 of the Internal Revenue Code (Code) and other withholding or reporting provisions of the Code, such as section 3402, 3405, or 3406. The proposed regulations provide guidance to withholding agents and payors who wish to establish an electronic system for use by beneficial owners or payees in furnishing Form W-8. The proposed regulations state the general requirements that such an electronic system must satisfy so that a withholding agent or payor may rely on a Form W-8 transmitted through such a system. These regulations affect withholding agents and payors that establish electronic systems and beneficial owners and payees who use these systems.

DATES: Written comments and requests for a public hearing must be received by [INSERT DATE 90 DAYS AFTER DATE OF PUBLICATION OF THIS DOCUMENT IN THE FEDERAL REGISTER].

ADDRESSES: Send submissions to: CC:DOM:CORP:R (REG-107872-97), room 5228, Internal Revenue Service, POB 7604, Ben Franklin Station, Washington, DC 20044. Submissions may be hand delivered between the hours of 8 a.m. and 5 p.m. to: CC:DOM:CORP:R (REG-107872-97), Courier's Desk, Internal Revenue Service, 1111 Constitution Avenue, NW., Washington, DC. Alternatively, taxpayers may submit comments electronically via the Internet by selecting the "Tax Regs" option on the IRS Home Page, or by submitting comments directly to the IRS Internet site at www.irs.ustreas.gov/prod/tax_regs/comments.html.

FOR FURTHER INFORMATION CONTACT: Concerning the regulations, Lilo Hester, 202-622-3840; concerning submissions, Evangelista Lee, 202-622-8452 (not toll-free numbers).

SUPPLEMENTARY INFORMATION:

Background

This document contains proposed amendments to the Income Tax Regulations (26 CFR part 1) under section 1441 of the Internal Revenue Code (Code). These amendments are proposed to provide general procedures for withholding agents and payors to establish acceptable electronic systems.

Final regulations published in the Rules and Regulations section of this issue of the Federal Register add §1.1441-1(e)(4)(iv) which authorizes the electronic transmission of a Form W-8 described in §1.1441-1(e)(1)(i). In addition, by cross-reference contained in §1.6049-5(c)(2) (published as a final rule in the Rules and Regulations section of this issue of the Federal Register), the regulation authorizes electronic transmission of a Form W-8 furnished for purposes of chapter 61 of the Code (i.e., information reporting) or for purposes of another income tax withholding provision of the Code, such as section 3406.

Pursuant to chapter 3 (or, in certain cases, chapter 61) of the Code, a beneficial owner or a payee (i.e., a person who receives a payment) must furnish a withholding certificate to a withholding agent or payor in order to establish its status as a foreign person and entitlement to a reduced rate of withholding. By establishing foreign status, and other relevant characteristics, a beneficial owner or payee may be entitled to a reduction or exemption in the amount of withholding under chapter 3 of the Code or an exemption from information reporting under chapter 61 of the Code or from backup withholding under section 3406. The receipt of a withholding certificate affects the amount of tax that the withholding agent or payor may be required to withhold from the payment, and the type and form of information that it must provide to the IRS. The regulations under sections 1441 and 1443 specifically identify Form W-8 (or an acceptable substitute form) as the required form of the withholding certificate.

These proposed regulations apply to electronic transmission of Forms W-8. The regulations do not apply to Form 8233 for use by individuals who claim a reduced rate of withholding under an income tax convention for services performed in the United States. See §1.1441-4(b)(2). In addition, the regulations do not apply to documentary evidence (described in §1.6049-5(c)(1)) that may be substituted for the Form W-8 with respect to certain payments made to accounts maintained outside of the United States. However, the IRS and Treasury invite comments on any computer technology (e.g., imaging) that could make electronic transmission of documentary evidence possible.

Explanation of Provisions

1. Type and Design of System Determined by Withholding Agent or Payor Subject to Specific Requirements.

Under the proposed regulations, a withholding agent or payor may choose to establish an electronic system to receive or transmit Forms W-8 (or such other form as the IRS may prescribe), including a payor or withholding agent that is an intermediary. The withholding agent or payor may determine the type of system (such as telephone or computer) available for that purpose. The system must, however, (1) reliably identify the user,

(2) ensure that the information received is the information sent, and (3) document occasions of user access that result in a submission, renewal, or modification of the withholding certificate. The proposed regulations envision that implementation of these specific requirements necessitates a direct relationship between the withholding agent or payor and the beneficial owner or payee. The proposed regulations reserve on applicable standards for systems used by intermediaries to transmit forms received from another payor or withholding agent. The IRS and Treasury recognize the importance of allowing the electronic transmission of Forms W-8 through one or more intermediaries (i.e., persons not acting for their own account). Therefore, comments are solicited regarding the logistical operation of an electronic transmission system for use by an intermediary satisfying the IRS requirements that the integrity, accuracy, and reliability of the original electronic transmission through an intermediary system is adequately protected.

2. Relationship Between Paper and Electronic Withholding Certificate.

The electronic transmission must contain exactly the same information as the paper Form W-8 (or such other form as the IRS may prescribe). Any guidance, such as regulations or instructions, that applies to the paper Form W-8 also applies to electronically transmitted forms.

3. Electronic Filing Optional.

Section 1.1441-1(e)(4)(iv) authorizing the use of electronic systems was promulgated to assist in reducing burdens (in terms of cost and time) on withholding agents, payors, payees, and beneficial owners. The use of an electronic system for the transmission of Form W-8 is merely an alternative to the use of a paper form. Electronic transmission of Form W-8 is not mandatory. A withholding agent or payor may not mandate the use of electronic systems to receive or transmit the forms. Thus, a payee or beneficial owner may furnish a Form W-8 to the withholding agent or payor on paper.

4. Signature Under Penalties of Perjury.

Section 6061 generally provides that any return, statement, or other document required to be made under any provision of the internal revenue laws or regulations shall be signed in accordance with forms or regulations prescribed by the Secretary. Section 301.6061-1(b) provides that the Secretary may prescribe in forms, instructions, or other appropriate guidance the method of signing any return, statement, or other document required to be made under any provision of the internal revenue laws or regulations. Section 6065 provides that, except as provided by the Secretary, any return, statement or other document shall contain or be verified by a written declaration that it is made under the penalties of perjury. These requirements apply to a Form W-8 (or such other form as the Internal Revenue Service may prescribe), including one that is filed electronically, as provided in § 1.1441-1(e)(2)(ii), (3)(ii), (3)(iii), and (3)(v), and § 1.1441-5(c)(2)(iv) and (3)(iii) of the final regulations. The proposed regulations, therefore, include guidance on the perjury statement and the signature requirements for Forms W-8 that are filed electronically.

5. IRS Requests for Electronic Data.

Upon request by the IRS in the course of an examination, a withholding agent or payor must supply a hard copy of the information contained on the electronically transmitted Form W-8 and a statement that, to the best of the withholding agent's knowledge, the electronic Form W-8 was furnished by the person whose name is on the form. The printout of the Form W-8 information must be provided to the IRS in English.

Proposed Effective Date

These regulations are proposed to become effective January 1, 1999.

Special Analyses

It has been determined that this Treasury decision is not a significant regulatory action as defined in EO 12866. Therefore, a regulatory assessment is not required. It also has been determined that section 553(b) of the Administrative Procedure Act (5 U.S.C. chapter 5) does not apply to these regulations, and, because the proposed regulations do not impose a collection of information on small entities, the Regulatory Flexibility Act (5 U.S.C. chapter 6) does not apply. Pursuant to section 7805(f) of the Code, this notice of proposed rulemaking will be submitted to the Small Business Administration for comment on its impact on small business.

Comments and Requests for a Public Hearing

Before these proposed regulations are adopted as final regulations, consideration will be given to any written comments (a signed original and eight copies) that are submitted timely (in the manner described in the ADDRESSES portion of this preamble) to the IRS. All comments will be available for public inspection and copying.

A public hearing may be scheduled if requested in writing by any person that submits written comments. If a public hearing is scheduled, notice of the date, time, and place for the hearing will be published in the Federal Register.

Drafting Information

The principal author of these regulations is Lilo A. Hester, Office of the Associate Chief Counsel (International), IRS. However, other personnel from the IRS and Treasury Department participated in their development.

[¶ 49,161]   Proposed Amendments of Regulations (REG-114000-97), published in the Federal Register on October 14, 1997.

Withholding: Nonresident aliens: Sale of obligations: Interest: Between interest payment dates.—Amendments of Reg. § 1.1441-3, relating to the obligation to withhold on interest paid with respect to obligations in the case of sales of obligations between interest payment dates, are proposed. A public hearing on this proposal is scheduled for January 26, 1998.

AGENCY: Internal Revenue Service (IRS), Treasury.

ACTION: Notice of proposed rulemaking and notice of public hearing.

SUMMARY: This notice of proposed rulemaking provides guidance regarding the obligation to withhold on interest paid with respect to obligations in the case of the sale of obligations between interest payment dates. These regulations would affect United States and foreign withholding agents and recipients. This document also provides notice of a public hearing on these proposed regulations.

DATES: Comments and outlines of oral comments to be presented at the public hearing scheduled for January 26, 1998, at 10 a.m. must be received by January 5, 1998.

ADDRESSES: Send submission to: CC:DOM:CORP:R (REG-114000-97), room 5226, Internal Revenue Service, POB 7604, Ben Franklin Station, Washington DC 20224. Submissions may be hand delivered between the hours of 8 a.m. and 5 p.m. to: CC:DOM:CORP:R (Reg-114000-97), Courier desk, Internal Revenue Service, 1111 Constitution Avenue, NW., Washington DC. Alternatively, taxpayers may submit comments electronically via the internet by selecting the "Tax Regs" option on the IRS Home Page, or by submitting comments directly to the IRS internet site at http://

www.irs.ustreas.gov/prod/tax>regs/comments.html. The hearing scheduled for January 26, 1998, will be held in the Commissioner's Conference Room, room 3313, Internal Revenue Service, 1111 Constitution Avenue, NW., Washington, DC.

FOR FURTHER INFORMATION CONTACT: Concerning the regulations, Lilo Hester at (202) 622-3840 (not a toll-free number); concerning submissions and the hearing, Evangelista Lee, (202) 622-7180 (not a toll-free number).

SUPPLEMENTARY INFORMATION

Background

In this issue of the Federal Register, the IRS and Treasury are publishing final withholding and reporting regulations under chapter 3 of the Internal Revenue Code (Code) and other sections of the Code. Section 1.1441-3(b)(2) of the final regulations provides that no withholding is required upon interest accrued on the date of a sale of debt obligations when the sale occurs between two interest payment dates, even though the amount is treated as interest under §1.61-7(c) or (d) and is subject to tax under section 871 or 881. In contrast, §1.1441-2(b)(3) of the final regulations provides that withholding is required on amounts of original issue discount in the event of a sale of an original issue discount obligation or a payment on such an obligation, subject to certain exceptions. The IRS and Treasury believe that, in view of these provisions, the exemption from withholding on non-OID amounts is no longer justified. A withholding agent that pays amounts to a foreign person in connection with the sale of an obligation between interest payments dates is in the same position as a withholding agent that pays amounts to a foreign person in connection with the sale of an original issue discount obligation. The withholding exemption for sale of debt obligations between interest payment dates provides an easy avenue for the avoidance of the documentation requirements imposed under sections 871(h) and 881(c) for purposes of qualifying interest on registered debt obligations as portfolio interest. For this reason, and in order to create parity with the tax treatment of original issue discount obligations under chapter 3 of the Code, it is no longer appropriate to continue this exemption.

Under §1.1441-2(b)(3), a withholding agent must withhold on an amount of original issue discount to the extent that it has actual knowledge of the proportion of the amount of the payment that is taxable to the beneficial owner under section 871(a)(1)(C) or 881(a)(3)(A). A withholding agent has actual knowledge if it knows how long the beneficial owner has held the obligation, the terms of the obligation, and the extent to which the beneficial owner purchased the obligation at a premium. A withholding agent is treated as having knowledge if the information is reasonably available. Special rules are provided for withholding agents with which the beneficial owner does not maintain a direct account relationship. Further, the regulations under §1.1441-2(b)(3) dealing with original issue discount provide that, in the case of an obligation that would qualify as portfolio interest if documentation were provided to the withholding agent, withholding is required on the entire amount of stated interest, if any, and original issue discount, if no such documentation is provided, irrespective of whether the withholding agent has knowledge of the portion of the payment representing taxable original issue discount. For this purpose, the withholding agent may rely upon the IRS List of Original issue Discount Instruments contained in IRS Publication 1212 (available from the IRS Distribution Centers).

In response to comments, the provisions in §1.1441-3(b)(1) are proposed to be modified to reduce the amount upon which withholding is required. No obligation to withhold is imposed under current law on the payment of stated interest on an obligation that was purchased between interest payment dates. Under §1.61-7(c), interest received on the interest payment date is treated as a return of basis to the extent it represents accrued unpaid interest as of the date of purchase as reflected in the new holder's basis for the obligation. Therefore, when the new holder receives a payment of the stated interest, the holder's tax liability is limited to the amount of interest accrued after the date of purchase (subject to additional adjustments reflecting possible acquisition premiums or market discounts). Because of the difficulty for a withholding agent to determine the amount accrued to the holder and other adjustments affecting the actual amount taxable to the holder, withholding on the entire amount of stated interest is required under the current withholding regulations under §1.1441-3(b)(1).

Commentators have asked that the withholding agent be permitted to withhold on the amount that it knows is taxable. The final withholding regulations did not modify the proposed regulations on this point because the Treasury and IRS consider that withholding on the entire amount is justified if withholding on sales of obligations between interest payment dates is not required. However, because these proposed regulations require withholding, the regulations permit a withholding agent to adjust the amount of withholding at the time of payment of stated interest to account for earlier withholding.

Special Analyses

It has been determined that this notice of proposed rulemaking is not a significant regulatory action as defined in EO 12866. Therefore, a regulatory assessment is not required. It also has been determined that section 553(b) of the Administrative Procedure Act (5 U.S.C. chapter 5) does not apply to these regulations, and because the regulation does not impose a collection of information on small entities, the Regulatory Flexibility Act (5 U.S.C. chapter 6) does not apply. Pursuant to section 7805(f) of the Internal Revenue Code, this notice of proposed rulemaking will be submitted to the Chief Counsel for Advocacy of the Small Business Administration for comment on its impact on small business.

Comments and Public Hearing

Before these proposed regulations are adopted as final regulations, consideration will be given to any comments that are submitted timely to the IRS. All comments will be available for public inspection and copying.

A public hearing has been scheduled for January 26, 1998, at 10 a.m. in the Commissioner's Conference Room, room 3313, Internal Revenue Building, 1111 Constitution Ave, NW., Washington DC. Because of access restrictions, visitors will not be admitted beyond the Internal Revenue Building lobby more than 15 minutes before the hearing starts.

The rules of 26 CFR 601.601(a)(3) apply to the hearing.

Persons who wish to present oral comments at the hearing must submit comments and an outline of the topics to be discussed and the time to be devoted to each topic by January 5, 1998.

A period of 10 minutes will be allotted to each person for making comments.

An agenda showing the scheduling of the speakers will be prepared after the deadline for receiving outlines has passed. Copies of the agenda will be available free of charge at the hearing.

[¶ 49,164]   **Proposed Regulations and Proposed Amendments of Regulations (REG-115795-97)**, published in the Federal Register on January 2, 1998.

     Passive foreign investment companies. Shareholders: Qualified electing fund election.—Amendments of proposed Reg. §1.1296-4 (as proposed on 4/28/95 by INTL-65-93 (¶ 49,203)) and Reg. §1.1297-3, relating to rules for a passive foreign investment company shareholder that makes the election under Code Sec. 1295 to treat the passive foreign investment company as a qualified electing fund, are proposed. Reg. §§1.1291-1, 1.1293-1, 1.1295-1 and 1.1295-3 were adopted 2/4/2000 by T.D. 8870.

AGENCY: Internal Revenue Service (IRS), Treasury

ACTION: Notice of proposed rulemaking by cross-reference to temporary regulations and notice of public hearing.

SUMMARY: In the Rules and Regulations section of this issue of the Federal Register, the IRS is issuing temporary regulations that provide guidance to a passive foreign investment company (PFIC) shareholder that makes the election under section 1295 (section 1295 election) to treat the PFIC as a qualified electing fund (QEF). The temporary regulations also provide guidance for shareholders that wish to make a section 1295 election that will apply on a retroactive basis (retroactive election). The temporary regulations also include a rule concerning the taxation under section 1291 of an exempt organization that is a shareholder of a PFIC that is not a pedigreed QEF. This rule was originally proposed in 1992. The text of the temporary regulations also serves as the text of these proposed regulations. In addition, this document proposes amendments to proposed regulation § 1.1296-4(e), concerning the treatment of interbank deposits as loans for purposes of the exception to passive income characterization of income derived in the active conduct of a banking business. This document also provides notice of a public hearing on these proposed regulations.

DATES: Written comments must be received by April 2, 1998. Requests to speak and outlines of oral comments to be discussed at the public hearing scheduled for April 16, 1998, must be received by March 26, 1998.

ADDRESSES: Send submissions to: CC:DOM:CORP:R (REG-115795-97), room 5226, Internal Revenue Service, POB 7604, Ben Franklin Station, Washington, DC 20044. Submissions may be hand delivered between the hours of 8 a.m. and 5 p.m. to: CC:DOM:CORP:R (REG-115795-97), Courier's Desk, Internal Revenue Service, 1111 Constitution Avenue, NW, Washington, DC. Alternatively, taxpayers may submit comments electronically via the Internet by selecting the "Tax Regs" option on the IRS Home Page, or by submitting comments directly to the IRS Internet site at http://www.irs.ustreas.gov/prod/tax>regs/comments.html. The public hearing will be held in Room 3313, Internal Revenue Service, 1111 Constitution Avenue, NW, Washington, DC.

FOR FURTHER INFORMATION CONTACT: Concerning the regulations, Gayle Novig, (202) 622-3840; concerning submissions and the hearing, Evangelista Lee, (202) 622-7190 (not toll-free numbers).

SUPPLEMENTARY INFORMATION:

Paperwork Reduction Act

The collection of information contained in this notice of proposed rulemaking has been submitted to the Office of Management and Budget for review in accordance with the Paperwork Reduction Act of 1995 (44 U.S.C. 3507(d)).

Comments on the collection of information should be sent to the Office of Management and Budget, Attn: Desk Officer for the Department of the Treasury, Office of Information and Regulatory Affairs, Washington, DC 20503, with copies to the Internal Revenue Service, Attn: IRS Reports Clearance Officer, T:FP, Washington, DC 20224. Comments on the collection of information should be received by March 3, 1998. Comments are specifically requested concerning:

Whether the proposed collection of information is necessary for the proper performance of the functions of the Internal Revenue Service, including whether the information will have practical utility;

The accuracy of the estimated burden associated with the proposed collection of information (see below);

How the quality, utility, and clarity of the information to be collected may be enhanced;

How the burden of complying with the proposed collection of information may be minimized, including through the application of automated collection techniques or other forms of information technology; and

Estimates of capital or start-up costs and costs of operation, maintenance, and purchase of services to provide information.

The collection of information in this proposed regulation is in proposed regulation § § 1.1295-1(f), 1.1295-1(g), 1.1295-3(c), and 1.1295-3(g). The information required in § 1.1295-1(f) and (g) will notify the Internal Revenue Service that certain shareholders have made the section 1295 election, and will enable the Internal Revenue Service to determine if a shareholder is satisfying the election and annual reporting requirements and is reporting income as required under section 1293.

The information required in proposed regulation § 1.1295-3(c) will notify the IRS that certain shareholders of foreign corporations have filed a Protective Statement to preserve their ability to make a retroactive section 1295 election, and that those shareholders have extended the periods of limitations for their taxable years to which the Protective Statement will apply. The information will enable the IRS to verify that the shareholders filing the Protective Statement had the requisite reasonable belief at the time they filed the statement. The information required in proposed regulation § 1.1295-3(g) will notify the IRS that a shareholder has made the retroactive election and, in the case of a shareholder that filed a Protective Statement, that the shareholder's waiver of the periods of limitations will terminate within three years of making the election. The information will enable the Service to verify that the requirements for making a retroactive election have been satisfied.

The collection of information and responses to these collections of information are mandatory. The likely respondents are individuals, businesses, and other for-profit organizations.

An agency may not conduct or sponsor, and a person is not required to respond to, a collection of information unless the collection of information displays a valid control number assigned by the Office of Management and Budget.

Books or records relating to a collection of information must be retained as long as their contents may become material in the administration of any internal revenue law. Generally, tax returns and tax return information are confidential, as required by 26 U.S.C. 6103.

Estimated total annual reporting/recordkeeping burden: 623 hours. The estimated annual burden per respondent varies from 15 minutes to three hours, depending on individual circumstances, with an estimated average of 29 minutes.

Estimated number of respondents: 1,290.

Estimated annual frequency of responses: Annually or one time only.

Background

Sections 1291, 1293, 1295, and 1297.

Temporary regulations in the Rules and Regulations section of this issue of the Federal Register amend the Income Tax Regulations (26 CFR part 1) relating to sections 1291, 1293, 1295, and 1297. The temporary regulations contain rules concerning the taxation of exempt organizations under section 1291, elections under section 1295 to treat passive foreign investment companies as qualified electing funds (QEFs), the calculation of net capital gain for purposes of section 1293, and the inclusion of the pro rata shares of the earnings and profits of QEFs held through pass through entities. The temporary regulations amend § 1.1297-3T, permitting in certain cases the application of the rules of section 1291(d)(2)(B) to an election made under section 1297(b)(1).

The text of those temporary regulations also serves as the text of these proposed regulations. The preamble to the temporary regulations explains the temporary regulations.

Section 1296.

On April 28, 1995, proposed regulations were published providing guidance for the exceptions to passive income characterization of certain income derived by active foreign banks and foreign security dealers provided in section 1296(b)(2)(A) and (b)(3), respectively. The proposed section 1296 regulations reflect comments received with respect to Notice 89-81, 1989-2 C.B. 399. That notice established tests for determining whether a foreign corporation qualified for the active foreign bank exception. The notice specifically stated that interbank deposits would not be treated as loans made in the ordinary course of a banking business.

After consideration of the comments received with respect to the Notice, the IRS and Treasury determined that interbank deposits were made and accepted in the ordinary course of a banking business, and therefore should be treated as such for purposes of section 1296(b)(2)(A). Accordingly, proposed regulation § 1.1296-4(d)(3) specifically includes interbank deposits with other deposits for purposes of determining whether the foreign corporation satisfies the deposit-taking requirements of § 1.1296-4(d). Also in response to comments, proposed regulation § 1.1296-4(e) is clarified to specifically provide that interbank deposits made with banks in the ordinary course of business constitute loans for purposes of § 1.1296-4. This clarification is favorable to taxpayers, and is proposed to be effective for taxable years beginning after December 31, 1994. It is also proposed that taxpayers may apply it to a taxable year beginning after December 31, 1986, provided it is consistently applied to that taxable year and all subsequent taxable years. The dates for applying proposed regulation § 1.1296-4(e) coincide with the dates for which § 1.1296-4 is proposed to be effective. See proposed regulation § 1.1296-4(k).

Special Analyses

It has been determined that this notice of proposed rulemaking is not a significant regulatory action as defined in Executive Order 12866. Therefore, a regulatory assessment is not required. Pursuant to section 7805(f) of the Internal Revenue Code, this notice of proposed rulemaking will be submitted to the Chief Counsel for Advocacy of the Small Business Administration for comment on its impact on small business. It has been determined that an initial regulatory flexibility analysis is required for the collection of information in this notice of proposed rulemaking under 5 U.S.C. § 603. This analysis is set forth below under the heading 'Initial Regulatory Flexibility Analysis.'

Initial Regulatory Flexibility Analysis. This initial analysis is provided pursuant to the Regulatory Flexibility Act (5 U.S.C. chapter 6). The major objective of the proposed regulations is to provide guidance to PFIC shareholders that wish to elect under section 1295 to treat their PFICs as QEFs, and provide guidance to those PFICs about the requirements imposed on them. The legal basis for these requirements is contained in sections 1293, 1294, and 1295. The IRS and Treasury are not aware of any federal rules that duplicate, overlap, or conflict with the proposed regulations.

The recordkeeping and reporting requirements of the proposed regulations enable the Internal Revenue Service to identify those taxpayers that are treating their PFICs as QEFs; to verify that those U.S. taxpayers are currently including their shares of QEF earnings in income, as required in section 1293 of the Internal Revenue Code; to be informed of those QEF shareholders that are not paying their section 1293 tax liability because they made the section 1294 election to defer the time for payment; to identify those shareholders of foreign corporations that are preserving their right to make a retroactive section 1295 election; to identify those shareholders making retroactive elections and verify that they are satisfying the requirements of a retroactive election; and, in the case of shareholders that have filed Protective Statements, the dates by which the shareholders' extensions of periods of limitations will terminate.

These proposed regulations will affect those small entities that are PFICs, at least one shareholder of which makes the section 1295 election. The proposed regulations also will affect those small entities that are PFIC shareholders that make the section 1295 election. The IRS and Treasury believe that affected small entities generally will be small businesses, as local governments are not likely to invest in PFICs. Also, few, if any, affected small entities likely will be tax exempt organizations, because only a tax exempt entity that is taxable under subchapter F on dividends received from the PFIC generally would need to consider making the section 1295 election.

The collections of information in these proposed regulations would impact a small entity that is treated as a QEF principally by requiring the entity to calculate annually its ordinary earnings and net capital gain according to federal income tax accounting principles, as required by section 1293, and report that information to its shareholders that are U.S. persons. With the enactment of section 1(h), the QEF also must calculate each type of long term capital gain that it derived and the applicable rates of tax for proper inclusion of the QEF's net capital gain by the QEF shareholders. Alternatively, the regulations permit the QEF to provide its shareholders with its books, records and other documents necessary for the shareholders to calculate the ordinary earnings and net capital gain amounts. This alternative will enable a small entity that is a QEF to avoid the burden of calculating its net capital gain by providing its shareholders with information with which the shareholders can make the calculations.

The economic impact of other collections of information contained in these proposed regulations would fall on a small entity that is a shareholder of a PFIC for which it has made the section 1295 election or that is a pass through entity to which an interest holder transferred stock subject to a section 1295 election. The economic impact would result primarily from the reporting and recordkeeping requirements pertaining to (1) the manner for making the section 1295 election and the annual election requirements; (2) the calculation by the shareholder (rather than the QEF) of the QEF's ordinary earnings and net capital gain according to federal income tax principles, and its pro rata shares thereof; (3) a request for consent to revoke a section 1295 election; (4) the preservation of the right to make a retroactive election under section 1295; (5) a request for consent to make a retroactive election; (6) making a retroactive election, including filing amended returns for the affected taxable years; and (7) providing interest holders with PFIC statements and other information received by an intermediary shareholder.

The proposed regulations reduce the burden under existing rules for making the section 1295 election for all taxpayers, including small businesses and other small entities. Unlike the current requirements provided in Notice 88-125, the proposed regulations only require electing shareholders to file Form 8621 to make the section 1295 election, thereby eliminating the shareholder election statement as well as the requirement to file a copy of the PFIC Annual Information Statement. The proposed regulations only require shareholders to retain the PFIC Annual Information Statement or the Annual Intermediary Statement received as well as a copy of their filings for each year to which the section 1295 election applies. In addition, the proposed regulations impose a lesser burden on small shareholders, typically individuals and small entities, to preserve their right to make a retroactive election and a lesser burden of making a retroactive election. A small entity that owns less than five percent of each class of stock of a foreign corporation and satisfies other requirements is not required to file a Protective Statement to preserve its right to make a retroactive election with respect to the foreign corporation. Similarly, a small entity potentially has fewer amended returns to file to make a retroactive election than a shareholder that filed a Protective Statement. These changes in election requirements are illustrative of IRS efforts to minimize burden, particularly with respect to small entities.

An estimate of the number of small entities that would be affected by these regulations is unavailable. In any event, the enactment in 1997 of the mark-to-market election for PFIC shareholders and the elimination of the overlap in certain cases of subpart F and the PFIC provisions, will reduce the number of small entities that would be affected by these regulations.

None of the significant alternatives considered in drafting these regulations would have significantly altered the economic impact of the collections of information on small entities. In considering the significant alternatives that would be permissible under the Code and would enable the IRS to ensure compliance with the Code, the IRS and Treasury concluded that the alternatives generally would impose equal or greater burdens.

Comments and Public Hearing

Before these proposed regulations are adopted as final regulations, consideration will be given to any written comments (a signed original and eight (8) copies) that are submitted timely to the IRS. All comments will be available for public inspection and copying.

A public hearing has been scheduled for April 16, 1998, at 10 a.m., in room 2615, Internal Revenue Building, 1111 Constitution Avenue, NW, Washington, DC. Because of access restrictions, visitors will not be admitted beyond the Internal Revenue lobby more than 15 minutes before the hearing starts.

The rules of 26 CFR 601.601(a)(3) apply to the hearing.

Persons that wish to present oral comments at the hearing must submit written comments by April 2, 1998, and submit an outline of the topics to be discussed and the time to be devoted to each topic (signed original and eight (8) copies) by March 26, 1998.

A period of 10 minutes will be allotted to each person for making comments.

An agenda showing the schedule of speakers will be prepared after the deadline for receiving outlines has passed. Copies of the agenda will be available free of charge at the hearing.

Drafting Information

The principal authors of the proposed regulations are Gayle Novig and Judith Cavell Cohen, of the Office of the Associate Chief Counsel (International). Other personnel from the IRS and Treasury Department also participated in the development of these regulations.

[¶ 49,165]   Proposed Regulations and Proposed Amendments of Regulations (REG-208299-90), published in the Federal Register on March 6, 1998 (corrected 4/21/98).

Global dealing operations: Allocation and sourcing of income and deductions.—Reg. §§ 1.475(g)-2 and 1.482-8 and amendments of Reg. §§ 1.482-0—1.482-2, 1.482-8, 1.863-3, 1.863-7, 1.864-4, 1.864-6, 1.894-1 and 1.988-4, relating to the allocation and sourcing of income, deductions, gains and losses from a global dealing operation, are proposed. A public hearing on this proposal is scheduled for July 14, 1998.

AGENCY: Internal Revenue Service (IRS), Treasury.

ACTION: Notice of proposed rulemaking and notice of public hearing.

SUMMARY: This document contains proposed rules for the allocation among controlled taxpayers and sourcing of income, deductions, gains and losses from a global dealing operation; rules applying these allocation and sourcing rules to foreign currency transactions and to foreign corporations engaged in a U.S. trade or business; and rules concerning the mark-to-market treatment resulting from hedging activities of a global dealing operation. These proposed rules affect foreign and domestic persons that are participants in such operations either directly or indirectly through subsidiaries or partnerships. These proposed rules are necessary to enable participants in a global dealing operation to determine their arm's length contribution to a global dealing operation. This document also provides notice of a public hearing on these proposed regulations.

DATES: Written comments must be received by June 4, 1998. Outlines of oral comments to be discussed at the public hearing scheduled for July 14, 1998, must be received by June 18, 1998.

ADDRESSES: Send submissions to: CC:DOM:CORP:R (REG-208299-90), room 5226, Internal Revenue Service, POB 7604, Ben Franklin Station, Washington, DC 20044. Submissions may be hand delivered between the hours of 8 a.m. and 5 p.m. to: CC:DOM:CORP:R (REG-208299-90), Courier's Desk, Internal Revenue Service, 1111 Constitution Avenue, N.W., Washington, D.C. Alternatively, taxpayers may submit comments electronically via the Internet by selecting the "Tax Regs" option on the IRS Home Page, or by submitting comments directly to the IRS Internet site at http://www.irs.ustreas.gov/prod/tax>regs/comments.html. The public hearing will be held in room 2615, Internal Revenue Building, 1111 Constitution Avenue, NW, Washington, DC.

FOR FURTHER INFORMATION CONTACT: Concerning the regulations in general, Ginny Chung of the Office of Associate Chief Counsel (International), (202) 622-3870; concerning the mark-to-market treatment of global dealing operations, Richard Hoge or JoLynn Ricks of the Office of Assistant Chief Counsel (Financial Institutions & Products), (202) 622-3920; concerning submissions and the hearing, Michael Slaughter, (202) 622-7190 (not toll-free numbers).

SUPPLEMENTARY INFORMATION:

Paperwork Reduction Act

The collections of information contained in this notice of proposed rulemaking have been submitted to the Office of Management and Budget for review in accordance with the Paperwork Reduction Act of 1995 (44 U.S.C. 3507(d)). Comments on the collections of information should be sent to the Office of Management and Budget, Attn: Desk Officer for the Department of the Treasury, Office of Information and Regulatory Affairs, Washington, DC 20503, with copies to the Internal Revenue Service, Attn: IRS Reports Clearance officer, T:FS:FP, Washington, DC 20224. Comments on the collections of information should be received by May 5, 1998.

Comments are specifically requested concerning:

Whether the proposed collections of information are necessary for the proper performance of the functions of the Internal Revenue Service, including whether the information will have practical utility;

The accuracy of the estimated burden associated with the proposed collections of information (see below);

How the quality, utility, and clarity of the information to be collected may be enhanced;

How the burden of complying with the proposed collections of information may be minimized, including through the application of automated collection techniques or other forms of information technology; and

Estimates of capital or start-up costs and costs of operation, maintenance, and purchase of services to provide information.

The collections of information in these proposed regulations are in §§ 1.475(g)-2(b), 1.482-8(b)(3), 1.482-8(c)(3), 1.482-8(d)(3), 1.482-8(e)(5), 1.482-8(e)(6), and 1.863-3(h). The information is required to determine an arm's length price. The collections of information are mandatory. The likely recordkeepers are business or other for-profit institutions.

An agency may not conduct or sponsor, and a person is not required to respond to, a collection of information unless the collection of information displays a valid control number assigned by the Office of Management and Budget.

Books or records relating to a collection of information must be retained as long as their contents may become material in the administration of any internal revenue law. Generally, tax returns and tax return information are confidential, as required by 26 U.S.C. 6103.

Estimated total annual recordkeeping burden: 20,000 hours. Estimated average annual burden per recordkeeper is 40 hours. Estimated number of recordkeepers: 500.

Background

In 1990, the IRS issued Announcement 90-106, 1990-38 IRB 29, requesting comments on how the regulations under sections 482, 864 and other sections of the Internal Revenue Code could be improved to address the taxation issues raised by global trading of financial instruments. Section 482 concerns the allocation of income, deductions, credits and allowances among related parties. Section 864 provides rules for determining the income of a foreign person that is "effectively connected" with the conduct of a U.S. trade or business and therefore can be taxed on a net income basis in the United States. Provisions under sections 864(c)(2) and (3) provide rules for determining when U.S. source income is effectively connected income (ECI); section 864(c)(4) provides rules for determining when foreign source income is ECI.

The rules for determining the source of income generally are in sections 861, 862, 863 and 865, and the regulations promulgated under those sections. Section 1.863-7 provides a special rule for income from notional principal contracts, under which such income will be treated as U.S.-source ECI if it arises from the conduct of a U.S. trade or business under principles similar to those that apply under section 864(c)(2). An identical rule applies for determining U.S. source ECI under §1.988-4(c) from foreign exchange gain or loss from certain transactions denominated in a foreign currency.

Because no regulations were issued in response to the comments that were received after Announcement 90-106, there remain a number of uncertainties regarding the manner in which the existing regulations described above apply to financial institutions that deal in financial instruments through one or more entities or trading locations. Many financial institutions have sought to resolve these problems by negotiating advance pricing agreements (APAs) with the IRS. In 1994, the IRS published Notice 94-40, 1994-1 CB 351, which provided a generic description of the IRS's experience with global dealing operations conducted in a functionally fully integrated manner. Notice 94-40 specified that it was not intended to prescribe rules for future APAs or for taxpayers that did not enter into APAs. Moreover, Notice 94-40 provided no guidance of any kind for financial institutions that do not conduct their global dealing operations in a functionally fully integrated manner.

Explanation of Provisions

1. Introduction

This document contains proposed regulations relating to the determination of an arm's length allocation of income among participants engaged in a global dealing operation. For purposes of these regulations, the terms "global dealing operation" and "participant" are specifically defined. The purpose of these regulations is to provide guidance on applying the arm's length principle to transactions between participants in a global dealing operation. The general rules in the final regulations under section 482 that provide the best method rule, comparability analysis, and the arm's length range are generally adopted with some modifications to conform these principles to the global dealing environment. In addition, the proposed regulations contain new specified methods with respect to global dealing operations that replace the specified methods in §§1.482-3 through 1.482-6.

This document also contains proposed regulations addressing the source of income earned in a global dealing operation and the circumstances under which such income is effectively connected to a foreign corporation's U.S. trade or business. The regulations proposed under section 863 generally source income earned in a global dealing operation by reference to the residence of the participant. For these purposes, residence is defined under section 988(a)(3)(B) such that global dealing income may be sourced between separate qualified business units (QBUs) of a single taxpayer or among separate taxpayers who are participants, as the case may be. Exceptions to this general rule are discussed in further detail below.

Proposed amendments to the regulations under section 864 provide that the principles of the proposed section 482 regulations may be applied to determine the amount of income, gain or loss from a foreign corporation's global dealing operation that is effectively connected to a U.S. trade or business of a participant. Similar rules apply to foreign currency transactions that are part of a global dealing operation.

The combination of these allocation, sourcing, and effectively connected income rules is intended to enable taxpayers to establish and recognize on an arm's length basis the contributions provided by separate QBUs to a global dealing operation.

This document also contains proposed regulations under section 475 to coordinate the accounting rules governing the timing of income with the allocation, sourcing, and effectively connected income rules proposed in this document and discussed above.

2. Explanation of Specific Provisions

A. §1.482-1(a)(1)

Section 1.482-1(a)(1) has been amended to include expressly transactions undertaken in the course of a global dealing operation between controlled taxpayers within the scope of transactions covered by section 482. The purpose of this amendment is to clarify that the principles of section 482 apply to evaluate whether global dealing transactions entered into between controlled taxpayers are at arm's length.

B. §1.482-8(a)—General Requirements

Section 1.482-8(a)(1) lists specified methods that may be used to determine if global dealing transactions entered into between controlled taxpayers are at arm's length. The enumerated methods must be applied in accordance with all of the provisions of §1.482-1, including the best method rule of §1.482-1(c), the comparability analysis of §1.482-1(d), and the arm's length range rule of §1.482-1(e). The section further requires that any modifications or supplemental considerations applicable to a global dealing operation set forth in §1.482-8(a)(3) be taken into account when applying any of the transfer pricing methods. Specific modifications to the factors for determining comparability and the arm's length range rule are provided in §1.482-8(a)(3). These modifications and special considerations are discussed in more detail under their respective headings below.

C. §1.482-8(a)(2)—Definitions Applicable to a Global Dealing Operation

Section 1.482-8(a)(2) defines "global dealing operation," "participant," "regular dealer in securities," and other terms that apply for purposes of these regulations. These definitions supplement the general definitions provided in §1.482-1(i).

The rules of §1.482-8 apply only to a global dealing operation. A "global dealing operation" consists of the execution of customer transactions (including marketing, sales, pricing and risk management activities) in a particular financial product or line of financial products, in multiple tax jurisdictions and/or through multiple participants. The taking of proprietary positions is not included within the definition of a global dealing operation unless the proprietary positions are entered into by a regular dealer in securities in connection with its activities as such a dealer. Thus, a hedge fund that does not have customers is not covered by these regulations. Positions held in inventory by a regular dealer in securities, however, are covered by these regulations even if the positions are unhedged because the dealer is taking a view as to future market changes.

Similarly, lending activities are not included within the definition of a global dealing operation. However, if a person makes a market in, by buying and selling, asset-backed securities, the income from that activity may be covered by these regulations, regardless of whether the dealer was a party to the loans backing the securities. Therefore, income earned from such lending activities or from securities held for investment is not income from a global dealing operation and is not governed by this section. A security may be held for investment for purposes of this section even though it is not identified as held for investment under section 475.

Activities unrelated to the conduct of a global dealing operation are not covered by these regulations, even if they are accounted for on a mark-to-market basis. Accordingly, income from proprietary trading that is not undertaken in connection with a global dealing operation, and other financial transactions that are not entered into in a dealing capacity are not covered by these proposed regulations. The regulations require that participants engaged in dealing and nondealing activities and/or multiple dealing activities segregate income and expense attributable to each separate dealing operation so that the best method may be used to evaluate whether controlled transactions entered into in connection with a particular dealing activity are priced at arm's length. The regulations also require that taxpayers segregate their dealer activities from their lending, proprietary trading or other investment activities not entered into in connection with a global dealing operation. Comments are solicited on whether the proposed regulations issued under section 475 in this notice of proposed rulemaking are sufficient to facilitate identification of the amount of income that should be subject to allocation under the global dealing regulations.

The term "participant" is defined as a controlled taxpayer that is either a regular dealer in securities within the meaning of § 1.482-8(a)(2)(iii), or a member of a group of controlled taxpayers which includes a regular dealer in securities, so long as that member conducts one or more activities related to the activities of such dealer. For these purposes, such related activities are the marketing, sales, pricing, and risk management activities necessary to the definition of a global dealing operation. Additionally, brokering is a related activity that may give rise to participant status. Related activities do not include credit analysis, accounting services, back office services, or the provision of a guarantee of one or more transactions entered into by a regular dealer in securities or other participant. This definition is significant because the transfer pricing methods contained in this section can only be used by participants, and only to evaluate whether compensation attributable to a regular dealer in securities or a marketing, sales, pricing, risk management or brokering function is at arm's length. Whether the compensation paid for other functions performed in the course of a global dealing operation (including certain services and development of intangibles) is at arm's length is determined under the appropriate section 482 regulations applicable to those transactions.

The definition of a global dealing operation does not require that the global dealing operation be conducted around the world or on a twenty-four hour basis. These regulations will apply if the controlled taxpayers, or QBUs of a single taxpayer, operate in the aggregate in more than one tax jurisdiction. It is not necessary, however, for the participants to conduct the global dealing operation in more than one tax jurisdiction. For example, a participant that is resident in one tax jurisdiction may conduct its participant activities in the global dealing operation through a trade or business in another jurisdiction that is the same jurisdiction where the dealer activity of a separate controlled taxpayer takes place. In this situation, the rules of this section apply to determine the allocation of income, gain or loss between the two controlled taxpayers even if all of the income, gain or loss is allocable within the same tax jurisdiction.

The term "regular dealer in securities" is specifically defined in this regulation consistently with the definition of a regular dealer under § 1.954-2(a)(4)(iv). Under these proposed regulations, a dealer in physical securities or currencies is a regular dealer in securities if it regularly and actively offers to, and in fact does, purchase securities or currencies from and sell securities or currencies to customers who are not controlled taxpayers in the ordinary course of a trade or business. In addition, a dealer in derivatives is a regular dealer in securities if it regularly and actively offers to, and in fact does, enter into, assume, offset, assign or otherwise terminate positions in securities with customers who are not controlled entities in the ordinary course of a trade or business. The IRS solicits comments on whether these regulations should be extended to cover dealers in commodities and/or persons trading for their own account that are not dealers.

D. Best Method and Comparability

Consistent with the general principles of section 482, the best method rule applies to evaluate the most appropriate method for determining whether the controlled transactions are priced at arm's length. New specified methods which replace the specified methods of §§ 1.482-2 through 1.482-6 for a global dealing operation are set forth in §§ 1.482-8(b) through 1.482-8(f). The comparable profits method of § 1.482-5 has been excluded as a specified method for a global dealing operation because of the high variability in profits from company to company and year to year due to differences in business strategies and fluctuations in the financial markets.

The proposed regulations do not apply specific methods to certain trading models, such as those commonly referred to in the financial services industry as "separate enterprise," "natural home," "centralized product management," or "integrated trading." Rather, the proposed regulations adopt the best method rule of § 1.482-1(c) to determine the most appropriate transfer pricing methodology, taking into account all of the facts and circumstances of a particular taxpayer's trading structure. Consistent with the best method rule, there is no priority of methods.

Application of the best method rule will depend on the structure and organization of the individual taxpayer's global dealing operation and the nature of the transaction at issue. Where a taxpayer is engaged in more than one global dealing operation, it will be necessary to segregate each activity and determine on a transaction-by-transaction basis within each activity which method provides the most reliable measure of an arm's length price. It may be appropriate to apply the same method to multiple transactions of the same type within a single business activity entered into as part of a global dealing operation. For example, if a taxpayer operates its global dealing activity in notional principal contracts differently than its foreign exchange trading activity, then the income from notional principal contracts may be allocated using a different methodology than the income from foreign exchange trading. Moreover, the best method rule may require that different methods be used to determine whether different controlled transactions are priced at arm's length even within the same product line. For example, one method may be the most appropriate to determine if a controlled transaction between a global dealing operation and another business activity is at arm's length, while a different method may be the most appropriate to determine if the allocation of income and expenses among participants in a global dealing operation is at arm's length.

Section 1.482-8(a)(3) reiterates that the principle of comparability in § 1.482-1(d) applies to transactions entered into by a global dealing operation. The comparability factors provided in § 1.482-8(a)(3) (functional analysis, risk, and economic conditions), however, must be applied in place of the comparability factors discussed in § 1.482-1(d)(3). The comparability factors for contractual terms in § 1.482-8(a)(3) supplement the comparability factors for contractual terms in § 1.482-1(d)(3)(ii). The comparability factors in this section have been included to provide guidance on the factors that may be most relevant in assessing comparability in the context of a global dealing operation.

E. Arm's Length Range

In determining the arm's length range, § 1.482-1(e) will apply except as modified by these proposed regulations. In determining the reliability of an arm's length range, the IRS believes that it is necessary to consider the fact that the market for financial products is highly volatile and participants in a global dealing operation frequently earn only thin profit margins. The reliability of using a statistical range in establishing a comparable price of a financial product in a global dealing operation is based on facts and circumstances. In a global dealing operation, close proximity in time between a controlled transaction and an uncontrolled transaction may be a relevant factor in determining the reliability of the uncontrolled transaction as a measure of the arm's length price. The relevant time period will depend on the price volatility of the particular product.

The district director may, notwithstanding §1.482-1(e)(1), adjust a taxpayer's results under a method applied on a transaction-by-transaction basis if a valid statistical analysis demonstrates that the taxpayer's controlled prices, when analyzed on an aggregate basis, provide results that are not arm's length. See §1.482-1(f)(2)(iv). This may occur, for example, when there is a pattern of prices in controlled transactions that are higher or lower than the prices of comparable uncontrolled transactions.

Comments are solicited on the types of analyses and factors that may be relevant for pricing controlled financial transactions in a global dealing operation. Section 1.482-1(e) continues to apply in its entirety to transactions among participants that are common to businesses other than a global dealing operation. In this regard, the existing rules continue to apply to pricing of certain services from a participant to a regular dealer in securities other than services that give rise to participant status.

F. *Comparable Uncontrolled Financial Transaction Method*

The comparable uncontrolled financial transaction (CUFT) method is set forth in §1.482-8(b). The CUFT method evaluates whether controlled transactions satisfy the arm's length standard by comparing the price of a controlled financial transaction with the price of a comparable uncontrolled financial transaction. Similarity in the contractual terms and risks assumed in entering into the financial transaction are the most important comparability factors under this method.

Ordinarily, in global dealing operations, proprietary pricing models are used to calculate a financial product's price based upon market data, such as interest rates, currency rates, and market risks. The regulations contemplate that indirect evidence of the price of a CUFT may be derived from a proprietary pricing model if the data used in the model is widely and routinely used in the ordinary course of the taxpayer's business to price uncontrolled transactions, and adjustments are made to the amount charged to reflect differences in the factors that affect the price to which uncontrolled taxpayers would agree. In addition, the proprietary pricing model must be used in the same manner to price transactions with controlled and uncontrolled parties. If a taxpayer uses its internal pricing model as evidence of a CUFT, it must, upon request, furnish the pricing model to the district director in order to substantiate its use.

G. *Gross Margin Method*

The gross margin method is set forth in §1.482-8(c) and should be considered in situations where a taxpayer performs only a routine marketing or sales function as part of a global dealing operation. Frequently, taxpayers that perform the sales function in these circumstances participate in the dealing of a variety of, rather than solely identical, financial products. In such a case, the variety of financial products sold within a relevant time period may limit the availability of comparable uncontrolled financial transactions. Where the taxpayer has performed a similar function for a variety of products, however, the gross margin method can be used to determine if controlled transactions are priced at arm's length by reference to the amount earned by the taxpayer for performing similar functions with respect to uncontrolled transactions.

The gross margin method determines if the gross profit realized on sales of financial products acquired from controlled parties is at arm's length by comparing that profit to the gross profit earned on uncontrolled transactions. Since comparability under this method depends on the similarity of functions performed and risks assumed, adjustments must be made for differences between the functions performed in the disposition of financial products acquired in controlled transactions and the functions performed in the disposition of financial products acquired in uncontrolled transactions. Although close product similarity will tend to improve the reliability of the gross margin method, the reliability of this method is not as dependent on product similarity as the CUFT method.

Participants in a global dealing operation may act simply as brokers, or they may participate in structuring complex products. As the role of the participant exceeds the brokerage function, it becomes more difficult to find comparable functions because the contributions made in structuring one complex financial product are not likely to be comparable to the contributions made in structuring a different complex financial product. Accordingly, the regulations provide that the reliability of this method is decreased where a participant is substantially involved in developing a financial product or in tailoring the product to the unique requirements of a customer prior to resale.

H. *Gross Markup Method*

Like the gross margin method, the gross markup method set forth in §1.482-8(d) should generally be considered in situations where a taxpayer performs only a routine marketing or sales function as part of a global dealing operation, and, as is often the case, handles a variety of financial products within a relevant time period. The gross markup method is generally appropriate in cases where the taxpayer performs a routine sales function in buying a financial product from an uncontrolled party and reselling or transferring the product to a controlled party.

The gross markup method determines if the gross profit earned on the purchase of financial products from uncontrolled parties and sold to controlled taxpayers is at arm's length by comparing that profit to the gross profit earned on uncontrolled transactions. Like the gross margin method, comparability under this method depends on the similarity of the functions performed and risks assumed in the controlled and uncontrolled transactions. Accordingly, adjustments should be made for differences between the functions performed in the sale or transfer of financial products to controlled parties, and the functions performed with respect to the sale or transfer of financial products to uncontrolled parties. Although close product similarity will tend to improve the reliability of the gross markup method, the reliability of this method is not as dependent on product similarity as the CUFT method.

As in the gross margin method, the regulations provide that the reliability of this method generally is decreased where a participant is substantially involved in developing a financial product or in tailoring the product to the unique requirements of a customer prior to resale.

I. *Profit Split Methods*

New profit split methods are proposed for global dealing participants under §1.482-8(e). Global dealing by its nature involves a certain degree of integration among the participants in the global dealing operation. The structure of some global dealing operations may make it difficult to apply a traditional transactional method to determine if income is allocated among participants on an arm's length basis. Two profit split methods, the total profit split method and the residual profit split method, have been included as specified methods for determining if global dealing income is allocated at arm's length.

Profit split methods may be used to evaluate if the allocation of operating profit from a global dealing operation compensates the participants at arm's length for their contribution by evaluating if the allocation is one which uncontrolled parties would agree to. Accordingly, the reliability of this method is dependent upon clear identification of the respective contributions of each participant to the global dealing operation.

In general, the profit split methods must be based on objective market benchmarks that provide a high degree of reliability, i.e., comparable arrangements between unrelated parties that allocate profits in the same manner and on the same basis. Even if such comparable uncontrolled transactions are not available, however, the taxpayer may be able to demonstrate that a total profit split provides arm's length results that reflect the economic value of the contribution of each participant, by reference to other objective factors that provide reliability due to their arm's length nature. For example, an allocation of income based on trader bonuses may be reliable, under the particular facts and circumstances of a given case, if the taxpayer can demonstrate that such bonuses are based on the value added by the individual traders. By contrast, an allocation based on headcount or gross expenses may be unreliable, because the respective participants might, for example, have large differences in efficiency or cost control practices, which would tend to make such factors poor reflections of the economic value of the functions contributed by each participant.

The proposed regulations define gross profit as gross income earned by the global dealing operation. Operating expenses are those not applicable to the determination of gross income earned by the global dealing operation. The operating expenses are global expenses of the global dealing operation and are subtracted from gross profit to determine the operating profit. Taxpayers may need to allocate operating expenses that relate to more than one global dealing activity.

The regulations state that in appropriate circumstances a multi-factor formula may be used to determine whether an allocation is at arm's length. Use of a multi-factor formula is permitted so long as the formula allocates the operating profit or loss based upon the factors that uncontrolled taxpayers would consider. The regulations do not prescribe specific factors to be used in the formula since the appropriateness of any one factor will depend on all the facts and circumstances associated with the global dealing operation. However, the regulations require that the multi-factor formula take into account all of the functions performed and risks assumed by a participant, and attribute the appropriate amount of income or loss to each function. The IRS also solicits comments concerning which factors may be appropriate (for example, initial net present value of derivatives contracts) and the circumstances under which specific factors may be appropriately applied.

The purpose of the factors is to measure the relative value contributed by each participant. Thus, adjustments must be made for any circumstances other than the relative value contributed by a participant that influence the amount of a factor so that the factor does not allocate income to a participant based on circumstances that are not relevant to the value of the function or activity being measured. For example, if trader compensation is used to allocate income among participants, and the traders in two different jurisdictions would be paid different amounts (for example, due to cost of living differences) to contribute the same value, adjustments should be made for the difference so that the factors accurately measure the value contributed by the trading function. The IRS solicits comments regarding the types of adjustments that should be made, how to make such adjustments, and the need for further guidance on this point.

The total profit split method entails a one step process whereby the operating profit is allocated among the participants based on their relative contributions to the profitability of the global dealing operation. No distinction is made between routine and nonroutine contributions. The total profit split method may be useful to allocate income earned by a highly integrated global dealing operation where all routine and nonroutine dealer functions are performed by each participant in each location. Accordingly, total profit or loss of the global dealing operation may be allocated among various jurisdictions based on the relative performance of equivalent functions in each jurisdiction.

The residual profit split method entails a two step process. In the first step, the routine functions are compensated with a market return based upon the best transfer pricing method applicable to that transaction. Routine functions may include, but are not limited to, functions that would not give rise to participant status and which should be evaluated under §§1.482-3 through 1.482-6. After compensating the routine functions, the remaining operating profit (the "residual profit") is allocated among the participants based upon their respective nonroutine contributions.

It should be noted that, while in appropriate cases a profit split method may be used to determine if a participant is compensated at arm's length, use of the profit split method does not change the contractual relationship between participants, nor does it affect the character of intercompany payments. For example, if a controlled taxpayer provides solely trading services to a global dealing operation in a particular jurisdiction, any payment it receives as compensation for services retains its character as payment for services and, under the regulations, is not converted into a pro rata share of each item of gross income earned by the global dealing operation.

J. Unspecified Methods

Consistent with the principles underlying the best method rule, the regulations provide the option to use an unspecified method if it is determined to be the best method. The IRS solicits comments on the extent to which the variety of methods on which specific guidance has been provided is adequate.

Guidance on the use of a comparable profits method has specifically not been included as a specified method in the proposed regulations because use of that method depends on the existence of arrangements between uncontrolled taxpayers that perform comparable functions and assume comparable risks. Global dealing frequently involves the use of unique intangibles such as trader know-how. Additionally, anticipated profit is often influenced by the amount of risk a participant is willing to bear. Accordingly, the IRS believes it is unlikely that the comparability of these important functions can be measured and adjusted for accurately in a global dealing operation.

K. Source of Global Dealing Income

Under current final regulations in §1.863-7(a), all of the income attributable to a notional principal contract is sourced by reference to the taxpayer's residence. Exceptions are provided for effectively connected notional principal contract income, and for income earned by a foreign QBU of a U.S. resident taxpayer if the notional principal contract is properly reflected on the books of the foreign QBU. Attribution of all of the income from a notional principal contract to a single location has generally been referred to as the "all or nothing" rule. The current final regulations do not provide for multi-location sourcing of notional principal contract income among the QBUs that have participated in the acquisition or risk management of a notional principal contract and therefore do not recognize that significant activities, including structuring or risk managing derivatives, often occur through QBUs in more than one jurisdiction.

Recognizing the need for multi-location sourcing of income earned in a global dealing operation, the proposed regulations provide a new rule under §1.863-3(h) which sources income from a global dealing operation in the same manner as the income would be allocated under §1.482-8 if each QBU were a separate entity. However, the rules must be applied differently to take into account the economic differences between acting through a single legal entity and through separate legal entities.

Accordingly, income from a single transaction may be split-sourced to more than one location, so long as the allocation methodology satisfies the arm's length standard. The all or nothing rule of §1.863-7(a) continues to apply to notional principal contract income attributable to activities not related to a global dealing operation. Corresponding changes have been made in proposed §1.988-4(h) to exclude exchange gain or loss derived in the conduct of a global dealing operation from the general source rules in §1.988-4(b) and (c).

These special source rules apply only with respect to participants that perform a dealing, marketing, sales, pricing, risk management or brokering function. Moreover, these rules do not apply to income, such as fees for services, for which a specific source rule is provided in section 861, 862 or 865 of the Code. Accordingly, if a controlled taxpayer provides back office services, the amount and source of an intercompany payment for such services is determined under existing transfer pricing and sourcing rules applicable to those services without regard to whether the controlled taxpayer is also a participant in a global dealing operation.

If an entity directly bears the risk assumed by the global dealing operation, it should be compensated for that function. In providing, however, that the source (and effectively connected status) of global dealing income is determined by reference to where the dealing, marketing, sales, pricing, risk management or brokering function that gave rise to the income occurred, the regulations effectively provide that compensation for risk bearing should be sourced by reference to where the capital is employed by traders, marketers and salespeople, rather than the residence of the capital provider. This principle applies where a taxpayer directly bears risk arising from the conduct of a global dealing operation, such as when it acts as a counterparty without performing other global dealing functions. A special rule provides that the activities of a dependent agent may give rise to participant status through a deemed QBU that performs its participant functions in the same location where the dependent agent performs its participant functions. The deemed QBU may be created without regard to the books and records requirement of § 1.989-1(b).

As indicated, accounting, back office, credit analysis, and general supervision and policy control functions do not give rise to participant status in a global dealing operation but are services that should be remunerated and sourced separately under existing rules. This principle also applies where a taxpayer bears risk indirectly, such as through the extension of a guarantee. Accordingly, the sourcing rule of § 1.863-3(h) does not apply to interest, dividend, or guarantee fee income received by an owner or guarantor of a global dealing operation that is conducted by another controlled taxpayer. The source of interest, dividend and guarantee fee income, substitute interest and substitute dividend payments sourced under §§ 1.861-2(a)(7) and 1.861-3(a)(6), and other income sourced by section 861, 862 or 865 continues to be governed by the source rules applicable to those transactions.

The proposed regulations provide, consistent with U.S. tax principles, that an agreement between two QBUs of a single taxpayer does not give rise to a transaction because a taxpayer cannot enter into nor profit from a "transaction" with itself. See, e.g., § 1.446-3(c)(1). The IRS believes, however, that these agreements between QBUs of a single taxpayer may provide evidence of how income from the taxpayer's transactions with third parties should be allocated among QBUs. It is a common practice for taxpayers to allocate income or loss from transactions with third parties among QBUs for internal control and risk management purposes. Accordingly, the proposed regulations specifically provide that such allocations may be used to source income to the same extent and in the same manner as they may be used to allocate income between related persons. Conversely, such transactions may not be used to the extent they do not provide an arm's length result.

L. *Determination of Global Dealing Income Effectively Connected with a U.S. Business*

After determining the source of income, it is necessary to determine the extent to which such income is ECI. Under current law, the general rule is that all of the income, gain or loss from a global dealing operation is effectively connected with a U.S. trade or business if the U.S. trade or business materially participates in the acquisition of the asset that gives rise to the income, gain or loss, or property is held for use in the active conduct of a U.S. trade or business, or the business activities conducted by the U.S. trade or business are a material factor in the realization of income, gain or loss. As noted above, the current final regulations do not permit the attribution of income, gain or loss from a global dealing operation that is allocated and sourced to a U.S. trade or business under § 1.863-3(h) shall be effectively connected. In this regard, an asset used in a global dealing operation is treated as an asset used in a U.S. trade or business to the extent that an allocation is made to a U.S. QBU. Similarly, the U.S. trade or business is also treated as a material factor in the realization of income, gain or loss for which an allocation is made to a U.S. QBU. A special rule for U.S. source interest and dividend income, including substitute interest and substitute dividends, earned by a foreign banking or similar financial institution in a global dealing operation treats such income as attributable to a U.S. trade or business to the extent such income would be sourced to the United States under § 1.863-3(h). Any foreign source income allocated to the United States under the principles of § 1.863-3(h) is also treated as attributable to the U.S. trade or business.

The proposed regulations also limit an entity's effectively connected income from a global dealing operation to that portion of an item of income, gain or loss that would be sourced to the U.S. trade or business if the rules of § 1.863-3(h) were to apply. These rules are intended to ensure that income for which a specific source rule is provided in section 861, 862 or 865 does not produce effectively connected income unless it was earned through functions performed by a U.S. QBU of the taxpayer.

With respect to notional principal contract income and foreign exchange gain or loss, proposed §§ 1.863-3(h) and 1.988-4(h) also provide that such income, gain or loss is effectively connected with the conduct of a U.S. trade or business to the extent that it is sourced to the United States under § 1.863-3(h).

In certain circumstances, the global dealing activities of an entity acting as the agent of a foreign taxpayer in the United States may cause the foreign taxpayer to be engaged in a U.S. trade or business. Any income effectively connected with the U.S. trade or business must be reported by the foreign corporation on a timely filed U.S. tax return in order for the foreign corporation to be eligible for deductions and credits attributable to such income. See § 1.882-4. In addition, the agent must also report any income earned in its capacity as agent on its own tax return. The provisions governing the time and manner for foreign corporations to make elections under §§ 1.882-5 and 1.884-1 remain in force as promulgated. Under current rules, these formalities must be observed even if all of the global dealing income would be allocated between a U.S. corporation and a foreign corporation's U.S. trade or business. The IRS believes that these requirements are justified because of potential differences that might occur with respect to the realization of losses and between actual dividend remittances of a U.S. corporation and deemed dividend remittances under the branch profits tax. The IRS, however, solicits comments regarding whether these filing requirements can be simplified, taking into consideration the policies underlying the filing requirements of § 1.882-4.

The Business Profits article contained in U.S. income tax treaties requires the United States to attribute to a permanent establishment that portion of the income earned by the entity from transactions with third parties that the permanent establishment might be expected to earn if it were an independent enterprise. Because the proposed regulations contained in this document allocate global trading income among permanent establishments under the arm's length principle of the Associated Enterprises article of U.S. income tax treaties, such rules are consistent with our obligations under the Business Profits article. Accordingly, a proposed rule under section 894 provides that, if a taxpayer is engaged in a global dealing operation through a U.S. permanent establishment, the proposed regulations will apply to determine the income attributable to that U.S. permanent establishment under the applicable U.S. income tax treaty.

M. *Relationship to Other Regulations*

The allocation rules contained herein do not apply to the allocation of interest expense. As discussed in the preamble to § 1.882-5 (TD 8658, 1996-1 CB 161, 162, 61 FR 9326, March 5, 1996), the rules contained in § 1.882-5 are the exclusive rules for allocating interest expense, including under U.S. income tax treaties.

Proposed regulations have been issued under sections 882 and 884 (INTL-0054-95, 1996-1 CB 844, 61 FR 9377, March 5, 1996) for purposes of allocating interest expense and determining the U.S. assets and/or liabilities reflected on the books of a foreign corporation's U.S. trade or business that are attributable to its activities as a dealer under section 475. The proposed regulations (and similar final regulations) under section 884 address the treatment of assets which give rise to both effectively connected and non-effectively connected income. Those rules thus address a situation analogous to the split-sourcing situation addressed in these proposed regulations. The IRS anticipates issuing proposed regulations under section 861 that provide a similar rule for purposes of allocating interest expense of a U.S. corporation that has assets that give rise to split-sourced income. Comments are solicited on the compatibility of the proposed regulations contained in this document with the principles of the proposed regulations that address a foreign corporation's allocation of interest expense, including its computation of U.S. assets included in step 1 of the § 1.882-5 formula and component liabilities included in steps 2 and 3 of the § 1.882-5 formula.

The IRS believes that the transfer pricing compliance issues associated with a global dealing operation are substantially similar to those raised by related party transactions generally. The IRS also believes that the existing regulations under section 6662 adequately address these issues. Accordingly, amendments have not been proposed to the regulations under section 6662. Section 6662 may not in certain circumstances, however, apply to the computation of effectively connected income in accordance with proposed regulations under section 475, 863, 864 or 988 contained in this document. The IRS will propose regulations under section 6038C regarding the information reporting and recordkeeping requirements applicable to foreign corporations engaged in a global dealing operation. It is anticipated that these regulations will coordinate the application of sections 6662 and 6038C where necessary.

No inference should be drawn from the examples in these proposed regulations concerning the treatment or significance of liquidity and creditworthiness or the effect of such items on the valuation of a security. The purpose of the proposed regulations under section 482 is not to provide guidance on the valuation of a security, but rather to determine whether the prices of controlled transactions satisfy the arm's length standard. Section 475 and the regulations thereunder continue to govern exclusively the valuation of securities.

N. *Section 475*

A dealer in securities as defined in section 475 is generally required to mark its securities to market. Securities are exempt from mark-to-market accounting if the securities are held for investment or not held for sale to customers and are properly identified on the taxpayer's books and records. Additionally, securities that hedge positions that are not subject to mark-to-market accounting are exempt from mark-to-market accounting if they are properly identified.

Under the current regulations, a taxpayer may not take into account an agreement between separate business units within the same entity that transfers risk management responsibility from a non-dealing business unit to a dealing business unit. Moreover, such an agreement may not be used to allocate income, expense, gain or loss between activities that are accounted for on a mark-to-market basis and activities that are accounted for on a non-mark-to-market basis. In contrast, the regulations proposed in this document under sections 482, 863, 864, 894, and 988 allow a taxpayer to take into account records of internal transfers when allocating global dealing income earned from third parties for purposes of determining source and effectively connected income. This may cause a mismatch in the timing of income, expense, gain, or loss.

For example, if a taxpayer's lending desk enters into a third-party transaction that exposes the lending desk to currency or interest rate risk, the lending desk may transfer responsibility for managing the risk for that particular transaction to another business activity that can manage the risk more efficiently (e.g., the desk that deals in currency or interest rate derivatives). The dealing desk then, in the ordinary course of its business, may enter into a transaction such as a swap with a third party to hedge the aggregate risk of the dealing desk and, indirectly, the risk incurred by the lending desk with respect to the original transaction. Where, as is generally the case, the dealing desk has a large volume of transactions, it is not possible as a practical matter to associate the aggregate hedge with the risk of the lending desk. Since the transactions entered into by the dealing desk must generally be marked to market, the third-party transaction that hedges the aggregate risk of the dealing desk (which includes the risk transferred from the lending desk) must generally also be marked. To the extent that a portion of the income, expense, gain, or loss from the aggregate hedging transaction is allocated to the lending desk under the proposed global dealing regulations, the potential timing mismatch described above will occur if the lending desk accounts for its positions on a non-mark-to-market basis. This mismatch could occur because the portion of the income, expense, gain, or loss from the hedging transaction, although allocated to the lending desk for sourcing and effectively connected income purposes, will be accounted for on a mark-to-market basis under the dealing desk's method of accounting. Entirely exempting the aggregate hedging transaction from mark-to-market accounting does not adequately solve this problem, because it results in the portion of the income, expense, gain or loss from the aggregate hedging transaction that is allocated to the dealing desk being accounted for on other than a mark-to-market method.

As the example shows, respecting records of internal transfers for purposes of sourcing without respecting these same records for purposes of timing could produce unpredictable and arbitrary results. Accordingly, the proposed regulations permit participants in a global dealing operation to respect records of internal transfers in applying the timing rules of section 475. Because the need to reconcile sourcing and timing exists only in the context of a cross-border operation, the proposed regulations have a limited scope. In particular, for the proposed regulations to apply, income of the global dealing desk must be subject to allocation among two or more jurisdictions or be sourced to two or more jurisdictions.

The purpose of the proposed regulations under section 475 is to coordinate section 475 with the proposed global dealing regulations and to facilitate identification of the amount of income, expense, gain or loss from third party transactions that is subject to mark-to-market accounting. This rule is not intended to allow a shifting of income inconsistent with the arm's length standard.

Under the proposed section 475 regulations, an interdesk agreement or "risk transfer agreement" (RTA) includes a transfer of responsibility for risk management between a business unit that is hedging some of its risk (the hedging QBU) and another business unit of the same taxpayer that uses mark-to-market accounting (the marking QBU). If the marking QBU, the hedging QBU, and the RTA satisfy certain requirements, the RTA is taken into account for purposes of determining the timing of income allocated by the proposed global dealing regulations to the separate business units of a taxpayer.

The proposed amendments to the section 475 regulations require that the marking QBU must be a dealer within the meaning of proposed § 1.482-8(a)(2)(iii) and that its income must be allocated to at least two jurisdictions under proposed § 1.482-8 or sourced to at least two jurisdictions under proposed § 1.863-3(h). Additionally, the RTA qualifies only if the marking QBU would mark its side of the RTA to market under section 475 if the transaction were with an unrelated third party. Thus, if the marking QBU were to identify the RTA as a hedge of a position that is not subject to mark-to-market accounting (such as debt issued by the marking QBU), the RTA would not qualify. The IRS requests comments on whether the marking QBU should ever be able to exempt its position in the RTA from mark-to-market treatment and account for its position in the RTA.

The proposed amendments to the section 475 regulations are intended to address situations where the hedging QBU transfers responsibility for the management of risk arising from a transaction with a third party. Accordingly, the proposed regulations require that the hedging QBU's position in the RTA would be a hedge within the meaning of § 1.1221-2(b) if the transaction were entered into with an unrelated entity. The IRS solicits comments on whether this requirement is broad enough to address the business needs of entities engaged in global dealing and nondealing activities. Comments suggesting that the requirement should be broadened (e.g., to include risk reduction with respect to capital assets) should address how such a regime could be coordinated with other relevant rules (e.g., the straddle rules). Additionally, if a taxpayer suggests changes to the section 475 rules proposed in this notice, the IRS requests additional comments addressing whether or not corresponding changes should be made to § 1.1221-2(d).

The proposed regulations also require that the RTA be recorded on the books and records of the QBU no later than the time the RTA is effective. RTAs that are not timely recorded do not qualify under the proposed regulations. Additionally, the RTA must be accounted for in a manner that is consistent with the QBU's usual accounting practices.

If all of the requirements of the proposed regulations are satisfied, then for purposes of determining the timing of income, expense, gain, or loss allocated to a QBU under the global dealing regulations, the marking QBU and the hedging QBU account for their respective positions in the RTA as if the position were entered into with an unrelated third part.

Special Analyses

It has been determined that this notice of proposed rulemaking is not a significant regulatory action as defined in Executive Order 12866. Therefore, a regulatory impact analysis is not required. It is hereby certified that these regulations do not have a significant economic impact on a substantial number or small entities. This certification is based upon the fact that these regulations affect entities who participate in cross-border global dealing of stocks and securities. These regulations affect the source of income and allocation of income, deductions, credits, and allowances among such entities. The primary participants who engage in cross-border global dealing activities are large regulated commercial banks and brokerage firms, and investment banks. Accordingly, the IRS does not believe that a substantial number of small entities engage in cross-border global dealing activities covered by these regulation. Therefore, a Regulatory Flexibility Analysis under the Regulatory Flexibility Act (5 U.S.C. Chapter 6) is not required. Pursuant to section 7805(f) of the Code, this notice of proposed rulemaking will be submitted to the Chief Counsel for Advocacy of the Small Business Administration for comment on their impact on small business.

Comments and Public Hearing

Before these proposed regulations are adopted as final regulations, consideration will be given to any written. comments that are submitted timely to the IRS (a signed original and eight (8) copies). All comments will be available for public inspection and copying.

A public hearing has been scheduled for July 14, 1998, at 10 a.m. in room 2615, Internal Revenue Building, 1111 Constitution Avenue NW, Washington, DC. Because of access restrictions, visitors will not be admitted beyond the Internal Revenue Building lobby more than 15 minutes before the hearing starts.

The rules of 26 CFR 601.601(a)(3) apply to the hearing.

Persons that wish to present oral comments at the hearing must submit written comments by June 4, 1998, and submit an outline of the topics to be discussed and the time to be devoted to each topic by June 18, 1998.

A period of 10 minutes will be allotted to each person for making comments.

An agenda showing the scheduling of the speakers will be prepared after the deadline for receiving outlines has passed. Copies of the agenda will be available free of charge at the hearing.

Proposed Effective Date

These regulations are proposed to be effective for. taxable years beginning after the date final regulations are published in the Federal Register.

Drafting Information

The principal authors of these regulations are Ginny Chung of the Office of Associate Chief Counsel (International) and Richard Hoge of the Office of Assistant Chief Counsel (Financial Institutions & Products). However, other personnel from the IRS and Treasury Department participated in their development.

[¶ 49,166]   Proposed Regulation (REG-106031-98), published in the Federal Register on June 12, 1998.

Foreign taxpayers: Derivative financial instruments: Safe harbors.—Reg. §1.864(b)-1, providing that foreign taxpayers who effect transactions in derivative financial instruments for their own accounts are not thereby engaged in a trade or business in the United States if they are not dealers in stocks, securities, commodities or derivatives, is proposed. A public hearing on this proposal is scheduled for September 9, 1998.

ACTION: Notice of proposed rulemaking and notice of public hearing.

SUMMARY: This document contains proposed rules for the treatment of foreign taxpayers trading in derivative financial instruments for their own account. These proposed rules provide that foreign taxpayers who effect transactions in derivative financial instruments for their own accounts are not thereby engaged in a trade or business in the United States if they are not dealers in stocks, securities, commodities or derivatives. These proposed rules affect foreign persons that conduct such trading for their own account either directly through U.S. offices or indirectly through partnerships or other agents. This document also provides notice of a public hearing on these proposed regulations.

DATES: Written comments must be received by September 10, 1998. Outlines of oral comments to be discussed at the public hearing scheduled for September 9, 1998, must be received by August 19, 1998.

ADDRESSES: Send submissions to: CC:DOM:CORP:R (REG-106031-98), room 5226, Internal Revenue Service, POB 7604, Ben Franklin Station, Washington, DC 20044. Submissions may be hand delivered between the hours of 8 a.m. and 5 p.m. to: CC:DOM:CORP:R (REG-106031-98), Courier's Desk, Internal Revenue Service, 1111 Constitution Avenue NW., Washington, DC. Alternatively, taxpayers may submit comments electronically via the Internet by selecting the "Tax Regs" option on the IRS Home Page, or by submitting comments directly to the IRS Internet site at http://www.irs.ustreas.gov/prod/tax>regs/comments.html. The public hearing will be held in room 2615, Internal Revenue Building, 1111 Constitution Avenue NW., Washington, DC.

FOR FURTHER INFORMATION CONTACT: Milton Cahn of the Office of Associate Chief Counsel (International), (202) 622-3870; concerning submissions and the hearing, LaNita Van Dyke, (202) 622-7190 (not toll-free numbers).

SUPPLEMENTARY INFORMATION:

Background

Section 864(b) of the Code provides that the phrase "trade or business within the United States" generally includes the performance of personal services within the United States at any time during the taxable year but, under certain circumstances, does not include trading in stocks, securities, or commodities through an independent agent or for a taxpayer's own account (the "trading safe harbors").

Regulations regarding certain aspects of the trading safe harbors were promulgated in 1968. Since the promulgation of these regulations, the use of derivative financial instruments has increased significantly. This is due in large measure to the overall expansion and growing sophistication of global capital markets. Although guidance concerning the tax treatment of derivatives and notional principal contracts has been issued under other provisions of the Code (see, e.g., §§ 1.446-3, 1.863-7(b)), the section 864(b) regulations have not been modernized to take into account the manner in which taxpayers customarily use derivative transactions.

Explanation of Provisions

1. *In General*

These proposed regulations provide that foreign taxpayers who are not dealers with respect to any derivative transactions, who are not otherwise dealers in stocks, securities, or commodities, and who enter into derivative transactions for their own accounts are not engaged in trade or business within the United States solely by reason of those transactions. The term "derivative" is defined as an interest rate, currency, equity or commodity notional principal contract or an evidence of an interest in, or derivative financial instrument in, any commodity, currency, or any of the items described in Code section 475(c)(2)(A)-(D).

For purposes of these proposed regulations, the term "currency" is limited to those currencies that are of a kind customarily dealt in on an organized commodity exchange. No inference is intended, however, as to whether currencies that are not traded on an organized commodity exchange are "of a kind" customarily dealt in on an organized commodity exchange. Comments are solicited on this issue.

Under the statutory safe harbors, taxpayers who are dealers in stocks and securities but not commodities may avail themselves of the commodities trading safe harbor of section 864(b)(2)(B)(ii), and likewise, dealers in commodities but not stocks and securities may avail themselves of the stocks and securities trading safe harbor of section 864(b)(2)(A)(ii). The proposed regulations, however, do not specify into which statutory safe harbor any particular derivative transaction falls. Accordingly, dealers in stocks, securities, commodities, or derivatives may not avail themselves of the benefits of these proposed regulations.

Treasury and the IRS are considering the appropriate application of both the stocks and securities safe harbor of section 864(b)(2)(A)(ii) and the commodities safe harbor of section 864(b)(2)(B)(ii) with respect to a dealer in a derivative which arguably might be classified as both a security and a commodity. Treasury and the IRS are also considering the appropriate application of the section 864(b)(2)(A)(ii) and (B)(ii) safe harbors to dealers in either stocks and securities or commodities who enter into a derivative transaction which arguably might be classified within both sections. Comments are solicited on these points including the classification of specific derivatives for purposes of the safe harbors.

Comments are also solicited regarding whether the final regulations should include derivative transactions in either the stocks and securities, or commodities trading safe harbors under sections 864(b)(2)(A)(i) and (B)(i). In particular, the IRS solicits comments as to whether certain dealers could inappropriately avoid the limitations of section 864(b)(2)(C) with respect to derivative transactions effected through independent agents in the United States.

2. Eligible Nondealer

Until Treasury and the IRS determine whether particular derivative transactions should be classified under the stocks and securities or commodities safe harbors, the proposed regulations provide that derivative transactions (including hedging transactions) do not constitute a U.S. trade or business if the taxpayer meets the newly proposed definition of an "eligible nondealer."

An eligible nondealer is defined as a foreign resident taxpayer who is not a dealer in stocks, securities, commodities or derivatives at any time during the taxable year. Dealer status is determined on a worldwide basis and disqualifies a taxpayer from the safe harbor of the proposed regulations even if no dealing activities are conducted in the United States. For example, if a taxpayer is a dealer in commodities through its home country office and conducts no dealing activities through its U.S. office, but enters into derivative transactions for its own account through the U.S. office, the taxpayer fails to be an eligible nondealer.

Under the proposed regulations, the definition of dealer in stocks or securities refers to §1.864-2(c)(2)(iv) and the definition of dealer in commodities refers to the use of that term in §1.864-2(d). The definition of eligible nondealer contains language based on the definition of dealer in securities in section 475(c)(1)(B), including regularly holding oneself out, in the ordinary course of one's trade or business, as being willing and able to enter into either side of a derivative transaction. See §1.475(c)-1(a)(2).

Treasury and the IRS are considering issuing additional guidance with respect to the definition of a dealer for purposes of applying the trading safe harbors generally. Comments are solicited regarding the definition of a dealer, including the adequacy of the present rules in §1.864-2(c)(2)(iv) and §1.864-2(d), possible rules for identifying derivative transactions entered into with customers in the "ordinary course," and the appropriateness of adopting a definition similar to that provided in section 475(c)(1).

3. Swaps on U.S. Equities

Treasury and the IRS are aware that in order to avoid the tax imposed on U.S. source dividends under sections 871 and 881 and Chapter 3 of the Code, some foreign investors use notional principal contract transactions based on U.S. equities ("U.S. based equity swaps"). Accordingly, Treasury and the IRS are considering whether rules should be developed to preserve the withholding tax with respect to such transactions. Specifically, Treasury and the IRS are evaluating whether conduit (e.g., section 7701(l)) or other principles should be invoked in regulations, to characterize payments made with respect to U.S. based equity swaps as subject to U.S. withholding tax.

Treasury and the IRS are considering whether or not finalization of the proposed regulations as they relate to U.S. based equity swaps should await guidance concerning the application of the withholding rules to such transactions. Broadening the section 864(b)(2)(A)(ii) and (B)(ii) safe harbors to include derivatives could impair the ability of the United States to tax U.S. source dividend payments.

Congress enacted the stocks and securities trading safe harbor in 1936 to provide certainty that foreign persons who merely trade stocks and securities would not be subject to the net income tax regime. Section 211(b), Revenue Act of 1936, Pub. L. 74-740, 49 Stat. 1648, 1714-15 (1936); S. Rep. No. 2156, 74th Cong., 2d Sess. 21 (1936). Congress' decision to include the safe harbor was premised on the fundamental assumption that ordinary income from U.S. stocks and securities would be appropriately subject to U.S. taxation through the withholding tax on fixed and determinable or annual and periodic income ("FDAP"), and that activities beyond the scope of the safe harbor would remain subject to net tax if the taxpayer was engaged in a trade or business or had an office in the United States. Id. The Foreign Investors Tax Act of 1966, which expanded the trading safe harbors to include trading activities conducted by or on behalf of a non-U.S. resident taxpayer through a U.S. office for the foreign taxpayer's own account, built upon the same principles reflected in the Revenue Act of 1936. See Section 102(d), Foreign Investors Tax Act of 1966, Pub. L. 89-809, 80 Stat. 1539, 1544 (1966); S. Rep. No. 1701, 99th Cong., 2d Sess. 16-17, 22-23, 32-33 (1966).

Treasury and the IRS request comments regarding the U.S. taxation of non-U.S. persons investing in derivatives generally in addition to the treatment of derivatives under the trading safe harbors. Comments are also solicited concerning the appropriate source of payments made pursuant to U.S. based equity swaps and whether conduit or other principles should be invoked for purposes of sections 871, 881 and Chapter 3 of the Code, including the circumstances under which such payments between non-U.S. resident counterparties (i.e., foreign-to-foreign payments) may be included in such regulations. In addition, comments are also solicited concerning the appropriate treatment of swaps or other derivative transactions on property (other than stocks and securities) that produce FDAP income, e.g., rents and royalties.

Special Analyses

It has been determined that this notice of proposed rulemaking is not a significant regulatory action as defined in EO 12866. Therefore, a regulatory impact analysis is not required. It also has been determined that section 553(b) of the Administrative Procedure Act (5 U.S.C. chapter 5) does not apply to these regulations, and because the regulation does not impose a collection of information on small entities, the Regulatory Flexibility Act (5 U.S.C. chapter 6) does not apply. Therefore, a Regulatory Flexibility Analysis under the Regulatory Flexibility Act (5 U.S.C. Chapter 6) is not required. Pursuant to section 7805(f) of the Code, this notice of proposed rulemaking will be submitted to the Chief Counsel for Advocacy of the Small Business Administration for comment on their impact on small business.

Comments and Public Hearing

Before these proposed regulations are adopted as final regulations, consideration will be given to any written comments that are submitted timely to the IRS (a signed original and eight (8) copies). All comments will be available for public inspection and copying.

A public hearing has been scheduled for September 9, 1998, at 10:00 A.M., in room 2615, Internal Revenue Building, 1111 Constitution Avenue NW, Washington, DC. Because of access restrictions, visitors will not be admitted beyond the Internal Revenue Building lobby more than 15 minutes before the hearing starts.

The rules of 26 CFR 601.601(a)(3) apply to the hearing. Persons that wish to present oral comments at the hearing must submit written comments by September 10, 1998, and submit an outline of the topics to be discussed and the time to be devoted to each topic by August 19, 1998.

A period of 10 minutes will be allotted to each person for making comments.

An agenda showing the scheduling of the speakers will be prepared after the deadline for receiving outlines has passed. Copies of the agenda will be available free of charge at the hearing.

Proposed Effective Date

These regulations are proposed to be effective for taxable years beginning 30 days after the date final regulations are published in the Federal Register. Taxpayers may elect to apply the provisions of the final regulations to taxable years beginning before the date which is 30 days after these regulations are published as final in the Federal Register. No inference is intended regarding the treatment of derivative transactions under sections 864(b)(2)(A)(ii) and (B)(ii) and the current regulations. For periods prior to the effective date, taxpayers engaged in derivative transactions may take any reasonable position with regard to the section 864(b)(2)(A)(ii) and (B)(ii) safe harbors. Positions consistent with these proposed regulations will be considered reasonable.

Drafting Information

The principal author of these regulations is Milton Cahn of the Office of Associate Chief Counsel (International). However, other personnel from the IRS and Treasury Department participated in their development.

[¶ 49,167]   **Proposed Regulations (REG-106177-97)**, published in the Federal Register on August 24, 1998.

Qualified state tuition programs: Distributions: Reporting requirements.—Reg. §§ 1.529-0—1.529-6, relating to qualified state tuition programs (QSTPs) and affecting QSTPs established and maintained by a state, or an agency or instrumentality of a state, and individuals receiving distributions from QSTPs, are proposed. A public hearing on this proposal has been scheduled for January 6, 1999.

AGENCY: Internal Revenue Service (IRS), Treasury.

ACTION: Notice of proposed rulemaking and notice of public hearing.

SUMMARY: This document contains proposed regulations relating to qualified State tuition programs (QSTPs). These proposed regulations reflect changes to the law made by the Small Business Job Protection Act of 1996 and the Taxpayer Relief Act of 1997. The proposed regulations affect QSTPs established and maintained by a State or agency or instrumentality of a State, and individuals receiving distributions from QSTPs. This document also provides notice of a public hearing on these proposed regulations.

DATES: Written comments must be received by November 23, 1998. Outlines of topics to be discussed at the public hearing scheduled for Wednesday, January 6, 1999, at 10 a.m. must be received by December 16, 1998.

ADDRESSES: Send submissions to CC:DOM:CORP:R (REG-106177-97), room 5226, Internal Revenue Service, POB 7604, Ben Franklin Station, Washington, DC 20044. Submissions may be hand delivered between the hours of 8 a.m. and 5 p.m. to: CC:DOM:CORP:R (REG106177-97), Courier's Desk, Internal Revenue Service, 1111 Constitution Avenue, NW., Washington DC. Alternatively, taxpayers may submit comments electronically via the Internet by selecting the "Tax Regs" option on the IRS Home Page, or by submitting comments directly to the IRS Internet site at http://www.irs.ustreas.gov/prod/tax>regs/comments.html. The public hearing will be held in room 2615, Internal Revenue Building, 1111 Constitution Avenue, NW., Washington, DC.

FOR FURTHER INFORMATION CONTACT: Concerning the proposed regulations, Monice Rosenbaum, (202) 622-6070; concerning the proposed estate and gift tax regulations, Susan Hurwitz (202) 622-3090; concerning submissions and the hearing, Michael Slaughter, (202) 622-7190 (not toll-free numbers).

SUPPLEMENTARY INFORMATION:

Paperwork Reduction Act

The collection of information contained in this notice of proposed rulemaking has been submitted to the Office of Management and Budget for review in accordance with the Paperwork Reduction Act of 1995 (44 U.S.C. 3507(d)). Comments on the collection of information should be sent to the Office of Management and Budget, Attn: Desk Officer for the Department of the Treasury, Office of Information and Regulatory Affairs, Washington DC 20503, with copies to the Internal Revenue Service, Attn: IRS Reports Clearance Officer, OP:FS:FP, Washington, DC 20224. Comments on the collection of information should be received by October 23, 1998. Comments are specifically requested concerning:

Whether the proposed collection of information is necessary for the proper performance of the functions of the Internal Revenue Service, including whether the information will have practical utility;

The accuracy of the estimated burden associated with the proposed collection of information;

How the quality, utility, and clarity of the information to be collected may be enhanced;

How the burden of complying with the proposed collection of information may be minimized, including through the application of automated collection techniques or other forms of information technology; and

Estimates of capital or start-up costs and costs of operation, maintenance, and purchase or services to provide information.

The collection of information in this proposed regulation is in §§ 1.529-2(e)(4), 1.529-2(f) and (i), 1.529-4, and 1.529-5(b)(2). This information is required by the IRS to verify compliance with sections 529(b)(3), (4), (7) and (d). This information will be used by the IRS and individuals receiving distributions from QSTPs to determine that the taxable amount of the distribution has been computed correctly. The collection of information is required to obtain the benefit of being a QSTP described in section 529. The likely respondents and/or recordkeepers are state governments and distributees who receive distributions under the programs. The burden for reporting distributions is reflected in the burden for Form 1099-G, Certain Government Payments. The burden for electing to take certain contributions to a QSTP into account ratably over a five year period in determining the amount of gifts made during the calendar year is reflected in the burden for Form 709, Federal Gift Tax Return.

Estimated total annual reporting/recordkeeping burden: 705,000 hours

Estimated average annual burden per respondent/recordkeeper: 35 hours, 10 minutes

Estimated number of respondents/recordkeepers: 20,051

Estimated annual frequency of responses: On occasion

An agency may not conduct or sponsor, and a person is not required to respond to, a collection of information unless it displays a valid control number assigned by the Office of Management and Budget.

Books or records relating to a collection of information must be retained as long as their contents may become material in the administration of any internal revenue law. Generally, tax returns and tax return information are confidential, as required by 26 U.S.C. 6103.

Background

This document contains proposed amendments to the Income Tax Regulations (26 CFR part 1) relating to qualified State tuition programs described in section 529. Section 529 was added to the Internal Revenue Code by section 1806 of the Small Business Job Protection Act of 1996, Public Law 104-188, 110 Stat. 1895. Section 529 was modified by sections 211 and 1601(h) of the Taxpayer Relief Act of 1997, Public Law 105-34, 111 Stat. 810 and 1092.

Section 529 provides tax-exempt status to qualified State tuition programs (QSTPs) established and maintained by a State (or agency or instrumentality thereof) under which persons may (1) purchase tuition credits or certificates on behalf of a designated beneficiary entitling the beneficiary to a waiver or payment of qualified higher education expenses, or (2) contribute to an account established exclusively for the purpose of meeting qualified higher education expenses of the designated beneficiary. Qualified higher education expenses, for purposes of section 529, are tuition, fees, books, supplies, and equipment required for enrollment or attendance at an eligible educational institution, as well as certain room and board expenses for students who attend an eligible educational institution at least half-time. An eligible educational institution is an accredited post-secondary educational institution offering credit toward a bachelor's degree, an associate's degree, a graduate-level or professional degree, or another recognized post-secondary credential. The institution must be eligible to participate in Department of Education student aid programs.

QSTPs established and maintained by a State (or agency or instrumentality thereof) must require all contributions to the program be made only in cash. Neither contributors nor designated beneficiaries may direct the investment of any contributions or any earnings on contributions. No interest in the program may be pledged as security for a loan. A separate accounting must be provided to each designated beneficiary in the program. A program must impose a more than de minimis penalty on refunds that are not used for qualified higher education expenses, not made on account of death or disability of the designated beneficiary, or not made on account of a scholarship or certain other educational allowances. A program must provide adequate safeguards to prevent contributions in excess of those necessary to provide for the qualified higher education expenses of the beneficiary. A specified individual must be designated as the beneficiary at the commencement of participation in a QSTP, unless the interests in the program are purchased by a State or local government or a tax-exempt organization described in section 501(c)(3) as part of a scholarship program operated by such government or organization under which beneficiaries to be named in the future will receive the interests as scholarships.

Distributions under a QSTP are includible in the gross income of the distributee in the manner as provided under section 72 to the extent not excluded from gross income under any other provision. Distributions include in-kind benefits furnished to a designated beneficiary under a QSTP. Any distribution, or portion of a distribution, that is transferred within 60 days under a QSTP to the credit of a new designated beneficiary who is a member of the family of the old designated beneficiary shall not be treated as a distribution. A change in the designated beneficiary of an interest in a QSTP shall not be treated as a distribution if the new beneficiary is a member of the family of the old beneficiary. A member of the family means the spouse of the designated beneficiary or an individual who is related to the designated beneficiary as described in section 152(a)(1) through (8) or is the spouse of any of these individuals.

Section 529, as added to the Code by the Small Business Job Protection Act of 1996 (1996 Act), contained provisions addressing the estate, gift, and generation-skipping transfer tax. The provisions were significantly revised, effective prospectively, by the Taxpayer Relief Act of 1997 (1997 Act).

A contribution on behalf of a designated beneficiary to a QSTP which is made after August 20, 1996, and before August 6, 1997, is not treated as a taxable gift. Rather, the subsequent waiver (or payment) of qualified higher education expenses of a designated beneficiary by (or to) an educational institution under the QSTP is treated as a qualified transfer under section 2503(e) and is not treated as a transfer of property by gift for purposes of section 2501. As such, the contribution is not subject to the generation-skipping transfer tax imposed by section 2601.

In contrast, under section 529 as amended by the 1997 Act, a contribution on behalf of a designated beneficiary to a QSTP after August 5, 1997, is a completed gift of a present interest in property under section 2503(b) from the contributor to the designated beneficiary and is not a qualified transfer within the meaning of section 2503(e). The portion of a contribution excludible from taxable gifts under section 2503(b) also satisfies the requirements of section 2642(c)(2) and, therefore, is also excludible for purposes of the generation-skipping transfer tax imposed under section 2601. For purposes of the annual exclusion, a contributor may elect to take certain contributions to a QSTP into account ratably over a five-year period in determining the amount of gifts made during the calendar year. Under section 529 as amended by the 1997 Act, a transfer which occurs by reason of a change in the designated beneficiary of a QSTP, or a rollover from the account of one beneficiary to the account of another beneficiary in a QSTP, is not a taxable gift if the new beneficiary is a member of the family, as defined in section 529(e)(2), of the old beneficiary, and is assigned to the same generation, as defined in section 2651, as the old beneficiary. If the new beneficiary is assigned to a lower generation than the old beneficiary, the transfer is a taxable gift from the old beneficiary to the new beneficiary regardless of whether the new beneficiary is a member of the family of the old beneficiary. In addition, the transfer will be subject to the generation-skipping transfer tax if the new beneficiary is assigned to a generation which is two or more levels lower than the generation assignment of the old beneficiary. The five-year averaging election for purposes of the gift tax annual exclusion may be applied to the transfer.

Regarding the application of the estate tax, the value of any interest in any QSTP which is attributable to contributions made by a decedent who died after August 20, 1996, and before June 9, 1997, is includible in the decedent's gross estate. In contrast, pursuant to the 1997 Act amendments to section 529, the value of such an interest is not includible in the gross estate of a decedent who dies after June 8, 1997, unless the decedent had elected the five-year averaging rule for purposes of the gift tax annual exclusion and died before the close of the five-year period. In that case, the portion of the contribution allocable to calendar years beginning after the decedent's date of death is includible in his gross estate.

Also, pursuant to the 1997 Act amendments to section 529, the value of any interest in a QSTP held for a designated beneficiary who dies after June 8, 1997, is includible in the designated beneficiary's gross estate.

The Federal estate and gift tax treatment of QSTP interests has no effect on the actual rights and obligations of the parties pursuant to the terms of the contracts under State law. In addition, the estate and gift tax treatment of contributions to a QSTP and interests in a QSTP is generally different from the treatment that would otherwise apply under generally applicable estate and gift tax principles. For example, under most contracts, the contributor may retain the right to change the designated beneficiary of an account, to designate any person other than the designated beneficiary to whom funds may be paid from the account, or to receive distributions from the account if no such other person is designated. Such rights would ordinarily cause the transfer to the account to fail to be a completed gift and mandate inclusion of the value of the undistributed interest in the QSTP in the gross estate of the contributor under sections 2036 and/or 2038. However, under section 529, the gross estate of a contributor who dies after June 8, 1997, does not include the value of any interest in a QSTP attributable to contributions from the contributor (except amounts attributable to calendar years after death where the five-year averaging rule has been elected). Also, because a contribution after August 5, 1997, is a completed gift from the contributor to the designated beneficiary, any subsequent transfer which occurs by reason of a change in the designated beneficiary or a rollover from the account of the original designated beneficiary to the account of another beneficiary is treated, to the extent it is subject to the gift and/or generation-skipping transfer tax, as a transfer from the original designated beneficiary to the new beneficiary. This is the result even though the change in beneficiary or the rollover is made at the direction of the contributor under the terms of the contract.

Comments from Notice 96-58

In Notice 96-58, 1996-2 C.B. 226, the Internal Revenue Service invited comments on section 529 including the requirements for reporting distributions by QSTPs, the requirements for qualification and operation of programs, and the treatment of distributions made by programs for federal tax purposes. Eighteen comments were received. The comments addressed a broad range of issues, including but not limited to, those outlined by Notice 96-58, the concept of account ownership and gift tax rules, enforcement of penalties, accounting and recordkeeping, and transition relief for programs in existence on August 20, 1996. The summary below is not intended to be a complete discussion of the comments. However, all matters presented in the comments were considered in the drafting of this notice of proposed rulemaking.

One commenter discussed in detail the requirements that a QSTP be "established and maintained" by a State or agency or instrumentality of a State. The commenter recommended a list of factors to be considered in determining whether a State maintains the program. This commenter and others urged that the use of outside contractors or the holding of program deposits at a private financial institution selected by the State not be determinative of whether the program was maintained by the State.

One commenter was endorsed by several others for suggesting two specific safe harbors to satisfy the requirement that a program impose more than a de minimis penalty on refunds. The first safe harbor was a 5 percent of earnings penalty on refunds of earnings prior to the designated beneficiary matriculating, reduced to at least a 1 percent penalty on refunds of earnings only after the age of matriculation. The second safe harbor was a fixed-rate safe harbor equal to the lesser of $50 or 1 percent of the assets distributed. Another commenter suggested an additional safe harbor based on the return of Series EE savings bonds. That commenter also suggested that safe harbors are not necessarily the minimum acceptable penalties and that all facts and circumstances should be taken into account in determining the adequacy of penalties that are less than the safe harbor penalties.

Commenters urged that regulations limit or avoid rules requiring programs to enforce penalties or require substantiation to ensure that disbursements are used to pay for qualified higher education expenses. Recognizing however that there may be some misuse in this area, commenters recommended that checks from QSTPs be marked with a special endorsement or be payable to both the educational institution and the designated beneficiary.

Commenters suggested that the prohibition on investment direction not include a choice between a prepaid tuition program and a savings program (established and maintained in one State), a choice among options in a prepaid tuition program, a choice among options for the initial contribution to the program, or an opportunity to change investment strategies. One commenter suggested that the prohibition on investment direction not apply to prevent participation in the program by program board and staff members.

Commenters suggested several approaches for satisfying the prohibition on excess contributions. Two safe harbors were proposed; one was based upon eight times the average annual undergraduate tuition and required fees at private four-year universities; the other was based upon five years of tuition, fees, books, supplies, and equipment at the highest cost institution allowed by the State's program. Other approaches proposed allowing the provision of adequate safeguards to prevent excess contributions to be left to the discretion of the program or allowing the contributor to certify that no attempt would be made to overfund the account.

Commenters made suggestions and raised concerns regarding: separate accounting rules including, but not limited to, the valuation and tracking of tuition units; the operating rules treating all programs in which an individual is a designated beneficiary as one program, and treating all distributions during a taxable year as one distribution; the application of section 72 to calculate distributions; and, income tax consequences relating to account ownership, penalties, and withholding.

The modifications made to section 529 by the Taxpayer Relief Act of 1997 have addressed, in large part, the issues raised by commenters concerning transition relief for programs in existence on August 20, 1996, estate and gift tax consequences for contributors and designated beneficiaries, and definitions pertaining to family members and eligible educational institutions.

Explanation of Provisions

Qualification as Qualified State Tuition Program (QSTP): Unrelated Business Income Tax and Filing Requirements

The proposed regulations provide guidance on the requirements a program must satisfy in order to be a QSTP described in section 529. A program that meets these requirements generally is exempt from income taxation. However, a QSTP is subject to the taxes imposed by section 511 relating to imposition of tax on unrelated business income. For purposes of section 529 and these regulations, an interest in a QSTP shall not be treated as debt for purposes of section 514; consequently, investment income earned on contributions to the program by purchasers will not constitute debt-financed income subject to the unrelated business income tax. However, investment income of the QSTP shall be subject to the unrelated business income tax to the extent the program incurs indebtedness when acquiring or improving income-producing property. Earnings forfeited on educational contracts or savings, amounts collected as penalties on refunds or excess contributions, and certain administrative and other fees are not unrelated business income to the QSTP. A QSTP is not required to file Form 990, Return of Organization Exempt From Income Tax, however, this does not affect the obligation of a QSTP to file Form 990-T, Exempt Organization Business Income Tax Return.

Established and Maintained

The proposed regulations provide that a program is established by a State or agency or instrumentality of the State if the program is initiated by State statute or regulation, or by an act of a State official or agency with the authority to act on behalf of the State. A program is maintained by a State or agency or instrumentality of a State if all the terms and conditions of the program are set by the State or agency or instrumentality and the State or agency or instrumentality is actively involved on an ongoing basis in the administration of the program, including supervising all decisions relating to the investment of assets contributed to the program. The proposed regulations set forth factors that are relevant in determining whether a State, agency or instrumentality is actively involved in the administration of the program. Included in the factors is the manner and extent to which it is permissible for the program to contract out for professional and financial services.

Penalties and Substantiation—Safe Harbors

As required by section 529(b)(3), a more than de minimis penalty must be imposed on the earnings portion of any distribution from the program that is not used for the qualified higher education expenses of the designated beneficiary, not made on account of the death or disability of the designated beneficiary, or not made on account of a scholarship or certain other payments described in sections 135(d)(1)(B) and (C) that are received by the designated beneficiary to the extent the amount of the refund does not exceed the amount of the scholarship, allowance, or payment. The penalty shall also not apply to rollover distributions described in section 529(c)(3)(C) which are discussed in the section titled *Income Tax Treatment of Distributees*, below. The proposed regulations provide that a penalty is more than de minimis if it is consistent with a program intended to assist individuals in saving exclusively for qualified higher education expenses. Whether any penalty is more than de minimis will depend upon the facts and circumstance of the particular program, including the extent to which the penalty offsets the federal income tax benefit from having deferred income tax liability on the earnings portion of any distribution. The proposed regulations provide a safe harbor penalty that a program may adopt for satisfying this requirement. For purposes of the safe harbor, a penalty imposed on the earnings portion of a distribution is more than de minimis if it is equal to or greater than 10 percent of the earnings.

To be treated as imposing a more than de minimis penalty as required by section 529(b)(3) a program must implement practices and procedures for identifying whether a distribution is subject to a penalty and collecting any penalty that is due. The proposed regulations, in the form of a safe harbor, set forth practices and procedures that may be implemented by a program. The safe harbor provides that distributions are treated as payments of qualified higher education expenses if the distribution is made directly to an eligible educational institution; the distribution is made in the form of a check payable to both the designated beneficiary and the eligible educational institution; the distribution is made after the designated beneficiary submits substantiation showing that the qualified higher education expenses were paid and the program reviews the substantiation; or the designated beneficiary certifies prior to distribution the amount to be used for qualified higher education expenses and the program requires substantiation of payment within 30 days of making the distribution, the program reviews the substantiation, and the program retains an amount necessary to collect the penalty owed on the distribution if valid substantiation is not produced.

The safe harbor procedure provides that a penalty be collected on all other distributions except where prior to distribution the program receives written third party confirmation that the designated beneficiary has died or become disabled or has received a scholarship or allowance or payment described in section 135(d)(1)(B) or (C). Alternatively, distributions may be made upon the certification of the account owner that the designated beneficiary has died or become disabled or has received a scholarship or allowance or payment described above, if the program withholds a portion of the distribution as a penalty. The penalty may be refunded after receipt of third party confirmation of the certification made by the account owner.

The safe harbor procedure provides that a program may document amounts refunded from eligible educational institutions that were not used for qualified higher education expenses by requiring a signed written statement from the distributee identifying the amount of any refund received from an eligible educational institution at the end of each year in which distributions for qualified higher education expenses were made and of the next year. A program must also have procedures to collect the penalty either by retaining a sufficient balance in the account to pay the penalty, withholding an amount equal to the penalty from a distribution, or collecting the penalty on a State income tax return.

Other Requirements for QSTP Qualification

As described in section 529(b)(1)(A), the proposed regulations provide that contributions to the program can be placed into either a prepaid educational arrangement or contract, or an educational savings account, or both, but cannot be placed into any other type of account. Contributions may be made only in cash and not in property as provided in section 529(b)(2), however, the proposed regulations provide that a program may accept payment in cash, or by check, money order, credit card, or similar methods.

Section 529(b)(4) requires that a program provide separate accounting for each designated beneficiary. Separate accounting requires that contributions for the benefit of a designated beneficiary and earning attributable to those contributions are allocated to the appropriate account. The proposed regulations provide that if a program does not ordinarily provide each account owner an annual account statement showing the transactions related to the account, the program must give this information to the account owner or designated beneficiary upon request.

Section 529(b)(5) states that a program shall not be treated as a QSTP unless it provides that any contributor to, or designated beneficiary under, such program may not directly or indirectly direct the investment of any contributions to the program or any earnings thereon. A program will not violate the requirement of this paragraph if it permits a person who establishes an account to select between a prepaid educational services account and an educational savings account, or to select among different investment strategies designed exclusively by the program, at the time that an educational savings account is established. However, the proposed regulations clarify that a program will violate this requirement if, after an account with the program initially is established, the account owner, a contributor, or the designated beneficiary subsequently is permitted to select among different investment options or strategies. A program will not violate this requirement merely because it permits its board members, its employees, or the board members or employees of a contractor it hires to perform administrative services to purchase tuition credits or certificates or make contributions.

Section 529(b)(6) provides that a program may not allow any interest in the program, or any portion of an interest in the program, to be used as security for a loan. The proposed regulations clarify that this restriction includes, but is not limited to, a prohibition on the use of any interest in the program as security for a loan used to purchase the interest in the program.

Section 529(b)(7) requires a program to establish adequate safeguards to prevent contributions for the benefit of a designated beneficiary in excess of those necessary to provide for the qualified higher education expenses of the designated beneficiary. The proposed regulations provide a safe harbor that permits a program to satisfy this requirement if the program will bar any additional contributions to an account as soon as the account reaches a specified limit applicable to all accounts of designated beneficiaries with the same expected year of enrollment. The total contributions may not exceed the amount determined by actuarial estimates that is necessary to pay tuition, required fees, and room and board expenses of the designated beneficiary for five years of undergraduate enrollment at the highest cost institution allowed by the program. The safe harbor in the proposed regulations applies only to the program. Despite the fact that a program has met the safe harbor, a particular account established under the program may have a balance that exceeds the amount actually needed to cover the particular designated beneficiary's qualified higher education expenses. Distributions made that are not used for qualified higher education expenses of the designated beneficiary are subject to the penalty provisions of section 529(b)(3).

Income Tax Treatment of Distributees

In accordance with section 529(c)(3), the proposed regulations provide that distributions made by a QSTP, including any benefit furnished in-kind, must be included in the gross income of the distributee to the extent that the distribution consists of earnings. The proposed regulations clarify that term "distributee" refers to the designated beneficiary or the account owner who receives or is treated as receiving a distribution from a QSTP. As required by section 529(c)(3)(A), distributions under a QSTP must be included in income in the manner as provided under section 72. Therefore, deposits or contributions made into an account under a QSTP are recovered ratably over the period of time distributions are made. The amount of taxable earnings shall be determined by applying an earnings ratio, generally the earnings allocable to the account as of the close of the calendar year divided by the total account balance as of the close of the calendar year, to the distribution. In the case of a prepaid educational services account, this method of calculating taxable earnings utilizes an average value for each unit of education (e.g., credit, hour, semester, or other unit of education) that is distributed rather than the recovery of the cost of any particular unit of education.

In accordance with section 529(c)(3)(C), the proposed regulations permit nontaxable rollover distributions. A rollover consists of a distribution or transfer from an account of a designated beneficiary that is transferred to or deposited within 60 days of the distribution into an account of another individual who is a member of the family of the designated beneficiary. A distribution is not a rollover distribution unless there is a change in beneficiary. The new designated beneficiary's account may be in a QSTP established or maintained by the same State or by another State. A transfer from the designated beneficiary to himself or herself, regardless of whether the transfer is to an account within the same QSTP or another QSTP in the same or another State, is not a rollover distribution and is taxable under the general rule. The Internal Revenue Service is concerned about the use of multiple rollovers to circumvent the restriction on investment direction. In particular, the Internal Revenue Service requests comments on this issue, including whether limits should be placed on the number of rollovers permitted within a certain time period or rollovers back to the original designated beneficiary. No taxable distribution will result from a change in designated beneficiary of an interest in a QSTP purchased by a State or local government or an organization described in section 501(c)(3) as part of a scholarship program.

Reporting Requirements

The proposed regulations set forth recordkeeping and reporting requirements. A QSTP must maintain records that enable the program to produce an annual account balance for each account. See, requirements related to section 529(b)(4) above. A QSTP must report taxable earnings on Form 1099-G, Certain Government Payments, to distributees. Any reporting requirements promulgated under section 529(d) apply in lieu of any other reporting requirement for a program that may apply with respect to information returns or payee statements or distributions. The proposed regulations contain more detail on how the information must be reported.

Estate and Gift Tax

The proposed regulations provide guidance on the gift and generation-skipping transfer tax consequences of contributions to a QSTP, a change in the designated beneficiary of a QSTP, and a rollover from the account of one beneficiary to the account of another beneficiary under a QSTP. The proposed regulations also provide guidance on whether and to what extent the value of an interest in a QSTP is includible in the gross estate of a contributor to a QSTP or the gross estate of a designated beneficiary of a QSTP. Because of the amendments to section 529 made by the Taxpayer Relief Act of 1997, different gift tax rules apply to contributions made after August 20, 1996, and before August 6, 1997, than apply to contributions made after August 5, 1997. Also, estates of decedents dying after August 20, 1996, and before June 9, 1997, are treated differently from estates of decedents dying after June 8, 1997. Comments are requested specifically on whether there is a need for more detailed guidance with respect to the estate, gift, and generation-skipping transfer tax provisions.

Transition Rules

In accordance with section 1806(c) of the Small Business Job Protection Act of 1996 and section 1601(h) of the Taxpayer Relief Act of 1997, special transition rules apply to programs in existence on August 20, 1996. The proposed regulations provide that no income tax liability will be asserted against a QSTP for any period before the program meets the requirements of section 529 and these regulations if the program qualifies for the transition relief. A program shall be treated as meeting the transition rule if it conforms to the requirements of section 529 and these regulations by the date of final regulations.

The proposed regulations provide transition rules that grandfather certain provisions in contracts issued and accounts opened before August 20, 1996. These contracts may be honored without regard to the definitions of "member of the family" and "eligible educational institution" used in section 529(e)(2) and (3), and without regard to section 529(b)(6) which prohibits the pledging of a QSTP interest as security for a loan. However, regardless of the terms of any agreement executed before August 20, 1996, distributions made by the QSTP are subject to tax according to the rules of § 1.529-3 and subject to the reporting requirements of § 1.529-4.

Proposed Effective Date

These regulations are proposed to be effective on the date they are published in the Federal Register as final regulations. Taxpayers may, however, rely on the proposed regulations for taxable years ending after August 20, 1996. Programs that were in existence on August 20, 1996, may also rely upon the transition rules provided.

Special Analyses

It has been determined that this notice of proposed rulemaking is not a significant regulatory action as defined in Executive Order 12866. Therefore, a regulatory assessment is not required. It has also been determined that section 553(b) of the Administrative Procedure Act (5 U.S.C. chapter 5) does not apply to these regulations, and, because the regulations do not impose a collection of information on small entities, the Regulatory Flexibility Act (5 U.S.C. chapter 6) does not apply. Pursuant to section 7805(f) of the Internal Revenue Code, this notice of proposed rulemaking will be submitted to the Chief counsel for Advocacy of the Small Business Administration for comment on its impact on small business.

Comments and Public Hearing

Before these proposed regulations are adopted as final regulations, consideration will be given to any written comments (a signed original and eight (8) copies) that are submitted timely to the IRS. All comments will be available for public inspection and copying.

A public hearing has been scheduled for Wednesday, January 6, 1999, beginning at 10 a.m. in room 2615 of the Internal Revenue Building, 1111 Constitution Avenue, NW., Washington, DC. Because of access restrictions, visitors will not be admitted beyond the Internal Revenue Building lobby more than 15 minutes before the hearing starts.

The rules of 26 CFR 601.601(a)(3) apply to the hearing.

Persons who wish to present oral comments at the hearing must submit written comments and an outline of the topics to be discussed and the time to be devoted to each topic (signed original and eight (8) copies) by December 16, 1998.

A period of 10 minutes will be allotted to each person for making comments.

An agenda showing the scheduling of the speakers will be prepared after the deadline for receiving outlines has passed. Copies of the agenda will be available free of charge at the hearing.

Drafting Information

The principal authors of these proposed regulations are Monice Rosenbaum, Office of Associate Chief Counsel (Employee Benefits and Exempt Organizations) and Susan Hurwitz, Office of the Associate Chief Counsel (Passthroughs and Special Industries). However, other personnel from the IRS and Treasury Department participated in their development.

[¶ 49,169] **Proposed Regulations and Proposed Amendments of Regulations (REG-104924-98)**, published in the Federal Register on January 28, 1999.

Commodities: Securities: Mark-to-market accounting.—Reg. §§ 1.471-12, 1.475(e)-1, 1.475(f)-1 and 1.475(f)-2 and amendments of Reg. §§ 1.446-1, 1.475(c)-1, 1.475(c)-2, 1.475(e)-1 and 1.475(g)-1, regarding the election to use the mark-to-market method of accounting for dealers in commodities and traders in securities or commodities, are proposed. A public hearing on this proposal has been scheduled for June 3, 1999.

AGENCY: Internal Revenue Service (IRS), Treasury.

ACTION: Notice of proposed rulemaking and notice of public hearing.

SUMMARY: This document contains proposed regulations for dealers in commodities and traders in securities or commodities regarding the election to use the mark-to-market method of accounting for their businesses. Section 1001(b) of the Taxpayer Relief Act of 1997 amended the applicable tax law for these taxpayers. This document also contains proposed regulations providing guidance on statutory changes to section 475 contained in the Internal Revenue Service Restructuring and Reform Act of 1998 (IRS Restructuring Act). This guidance is necessary because section 7003 of the IRS Restructuring Act generally prohibited the application of mark-to-market accounting to nonfinancial customer paper. Among other things, the proposed regulations provide guidance to taxpayers who are using mark-to-market accounting for nonfinancial customer paper. This document also provides notice of a public hearing on these proposed regulations.

DATES: Written comments and outlines of topics to be discussed at the public hearing scheduled for June 3, 1999, at 10 a.m. must be received by May 13, 1999.

ADDRESSES: Send submissions to CC:DOM:CORP:R (REG-104924-98), room 5226, Internal Revenue Service, POB 7604, Ben Franklin Station, Washington, DC 20044. Submissions may be hand delivered Monday through Friday between the hours of 8 a.m. and 5 p.m. to: CC:DOM:CORP:R (REG-104924-98), Courier's Desk, Internal Revenue Service, 1111 Constitution Avenue, NW., Washington, DC. Alternatively, taxpayers may submit comments electronically via the Internet by selecting the "Tax Regs" option on the IRS Home Page, or by submitting comments directly to the IRS Internet site at http://www.irs.ustreas.gov/prod/tax>regs/comments.html. The public hearing will be held in room 2615, Internal Revenue Building, 1111 Constitution Avenue, NW., Washington, DC.

FOR FURTHER INFORMATION CONTACT: Concerning the regulations about elections by commodities dealers and securities and commodities traders, Jo Lynn Ricks, 202-622-3920; concerning the regulations about nonfinancial customer paper, Pamela Lew, 202-622-3950; concerning submissions and the hearing, Michael L. Slaughter, Jr., 202-622-7190 (not toll-free numbers).

SUPPLEMENTARY INFORMATION:

Paperwork Reduction Act

The collection of information contained in this notice of proposed rulemaking has been submitted to the Office of Management and Budget for review in accordance with the Paperwork Reduction Act of 1995 (44 U.S.C. 3507(d)). Comments on the collection of information should be sent to the Office of Management and Budget, Attn: Desk Officer for the Department of Treasury, Office of Information and Regulatory Affairs, Washington, DC, 20503, with copies to the Internal Revenue Service, Attn: IRS Reports Clearance Officer, OP:FS:FP, Washington, DC 20224. Comments concerning the collection of information must be received by March 29, 1999.

The first collection of information in this proposed regulation is described in the Explanation of Provisions section of this document (rather than being included in the text of the proposed regulations). That description indicates that the elections under section 475(e)(1) and (f)(1) and (2) may be required to be made on a form to be developed by the IRS. This burden will be reflected on that new form.

The second collection of information in this proposed regulation is in §§ 1.475(e)-1 and 1.475(f)-2. The information required to be recorded under §§ 1.475(e)-1 and 1.475(f)-2 is required by the IRS to determine whether an exemption from mark-to-market accounting is properly claimed. This information will be used to make that determination upon audit of taxpayers' books and records. The likely recordkeepers are businesses or other for-profit institutions.

Estimated total annual recordkeeping burden: 1,000 hours.

The estimated annual burden per recordkeeper varies from 15 minutes to 3 hours, depending on individual circumstances, with an estimated average of 1 hour.

Estimated number of recordkeepers: 1,000.

An agency may not conduct or sponsor, and a person is not required to respond to, a collection of information unless it displays a valid control number assigned by the Office of Management and Budget.

Books or records relating to a collection of information must be retained as long as their contents may become material in the administration of any internal revenue law. Generally, tax returns and tax return information are confidential, as required by 26 U.S.C. 6103.

Background

Section 475 provides that dealers in securities generally must use mark-to-market accounting for all securities. Exceptions from the mark-to-market requirement are generally provided for securities not held for sale to customers and certain securities held as a hedge, provided that the securities are identified as exempt in a proper and timely manner.

For purposes of section 475, a security includes any note, bond, debenture, or other evidence of indebtedness. Revenue Ruling 97-37 (1997-39 I.R.B. 4), clarified that "other evidence of indebtedness" includes customer paper, commonly referred to as trade accounts receivable. The IRS provided procedures for a taxpayer to change its method of accounting for customer paper in Revenue Procedure 97-43 (1997-39 I.R.B. 12).

The IRS Restructuring Act modified the definition of security for purposes of section 475 to exclude nonfinancial customer paper. For this purpose, nonfinancial customer paper is any receivable arising out of the sale of nonfinancial goods or services by a person the principal activity of which is the selling or providing of nonfinancial goods or services if the receivable is held by that person (or a related person) at all times since its issuance. Section 475(c)(4), added by the IRS Restructuring Act, precludes a taxpayer from using mark-to-market accounting under section 475 for nonfinancial customer paper. In addition, the legislative history of the IRS Restructuring Act indicates that taxpayers may not account for nonfinancial customer paper using a mark-to-market or lower-of-cost-or-market method of accounting under other sections of the Code. See H.R. Conf. Rep. No. 599, 105th Cong., 2d Sess. 353-54 (1998). Congress, however, authorized the Secretary to issue regulations describing situations where taxpayers must use mark-to-market accounting for nonfinancial customer paper in order to prevent taxpayers from using the exclusion in section 475(c)(4) to avoid marking to market receivables that are inventory in the hands of the taxpayer or a related person.

Section 475(e) and (f), added by section 1001(b) of the Taxpayer Relief Act of 1997, allows securities traders and commodities traders and dealers to elect mark-to-market accounting similar to that currently required for securities dealers. These provisions are effective for all taxable years ending after August 5, 1997, the date of enactment of the Taxpayer Relief Act. The proposed regulations clarify several issues relating to these elections, including the identification of securities and commodities as exempt from mark-to-market accounting, the character of marked securities and commodities, and the time and manner for making the elections.

Explanation of Provisions

Nonfinancial Customer Paper

Sections 1.446-1(c)(2)(iii), 1.471-12, and 1.475(c)-2(d) of the proposed regulations provide that taxpayers may not use mark-to-market or lower-of-cost-or-market accounting for any nonfinancial customer paper unless a regulation affirmatively provides that the nonfinancial customer paper is to be marked to market as inventory.

The remaining proposed regulations pertaining to section 475(c)(4) are cross references or minor technical changes required by the addition of § 1.475(c)-2(d).

Dealers in Commodities

The proposed regulations generally provide that, except as provided in guidance prescribed by the Commissioner, the rules for mark-to-market accounting for securities dealers apply to commodities dealers that make an election under section 475(e)(1) (electing commodities dealers). Comments are requested whether there are circumstances where the specific rules applicable to securities dealers should not be applied to electing commodities dealers.

Under the proposed regulations, unless the Commissioner otherwise provides in a revenue ruling, revenue procedure, or letter ruling, the exemption from mark-to-market accounting for assets held for investment does not apply to a commodity derivative held by an electing dealer in commodities. If the rule described in the preceding sentence applies (and consequently requires a commodity derivative to be marked to market), the gain or loss is ordinary. The IRS and the Treasury Department believe that it would be extremely rare for a commodity derivative held by a commodities derivative dealer to be acquired other than in a dealer capacity. See § 1.475(c)-1(a)(2). Moreover, the IRS and the Treasury Department believe that a dealer in physical commodities generally engages in derivatives activities that are virtually indistinguishable from its dealings in physical commodities. This situation invokes many of the practical concerns that led Congress to enact section 475(b)(4). The IRS and the Treasury Department welcome comments on whether, and under what circumstances, it may be appropriate for a dealer in physical commodities to identify commodity derivatives as held for investment.

The proposed regulations also provide that, in all cases, if a dealer in commodities identifies a commodity as exempt from mark-to-market accounting under section 475(b)(2), the identification is ineffective unless it is made before the close of the day on which the commodity was acquired, originated, or entered into. Thus, a rule similar to the 30-day identification rule for certain securities in Holding 8 of Rev. Rul. 97-39 (1997-39 I.R.B. 4), does not apply to commodities dealers.

Traders in Securities or Commodities

The proposed regulations provide that the principles underlying the rules and administrative interpretations applicable to securities dealers also apply to electing traders, unless the proposed regulations or the Commissioner provides otherwise. The IRS and the Treasury Department request comments on whether there are circumstances under which a specific rule applicable to securities dealers should not apply to electing securities traders.

The proposed regulations provide rules for the identification of investment securities as exempt from mark-to-market accounting. The proposed regulations clarify that a trader in securities who elects mark-to-market accounting under section 475(f)(1) for its trading business (an electing trader) must identify, in accordance with section 475(f)(1)(B)(ii), any security held other than in connection with the trading business. If the electing trader is also a dealer in securities, the trader need only identify under section 475(f)(1)(B)(ii) securities that are not held in connection with the trading business and that are also described in section 475(b)(1) (without regard to section 475(b)(2)). That is, the trader need not identify securities that could not properly be identified as being exempt from section 475(a).

The IRS and the Treasury Department believe that in making the section 475 election available to securities traders, Congress did not want taxpayers selectively to mark to market some securities but selectively to identify other securities as exempt from this treatment. Congress addressed this concern by establishing a higher burden of proof for electing securities traders to identify securities as not subject to section 475 than is applicable to securities dealers. The IRS and the Treasury Department share this concern, particularly because it traditionally has been easier to distinguish investment securities from dealer securities than to distinguish investment securities from trading securities. Accordingly, the proposed regulations provide that in no event is the requirement of section 475(f)(1)(B)(i) satisfied unless the electing trader demonstrates by clear and convincing evidence that a security has no connection to its trading activities. The IRS and Treasury Department request comments on whether any trader of securities could meet this burden and under what circumstances.

In addition, the IRS and the Treasury Department seek comments on the manner in which securities are identified as not held in connection with trading activities and, in particular, comments that focus on the administrability of rules in this area.

Because of the fungible nature of certain securities, the proposed regulations provide a special rule for identifying securities held other than in connection with the electing trader's trading business when the electing trader also trades other of the same or substantially similar securities. In this circumstance, the electing trader does not satisfy section 475(f)(1)(B)(i) unless the security is held in a separate, nontrading account maintained with a third party. The IRS and the Treasury Department are considering extending this special identification rule to all securities, rather than solely to those that are fungible, and request comments on the advisability of doing so.

Under the proposed regulations, all identifications under section 475(f)(1)(B)(ii) must be made on the same day the electing trader acquires, originates, or enters into the security. Thus, a rule similar to the 30-day identification rule for certain securities in Holding 8 of Rev. Rul. 97-39 does not apply to electing traders.

Because the principles of the rules and administrative interpretations applicable to securities dealers apply to electing traders, if an electing trader improperly identifies as exempt a security that is actually held in connection with that business, the gain or loss with respect to the security is ordinary, and the consequences described in section 475(d)(2) apply to the security (i.e., the security is marked to market and any losses realized with respect to the security prior to its disposition are recognized only to the extent of gain previously recognized with respect to the security). Similarly, under the proposed regulations, if an electing trader fails to identify a security that is not held in connection with its trading business, the consequences of section 475(d)(2) apply to the security, and the gain or loss with respect to the security is ordinary. Moreover, in the event of this failure, the Commissioner may nevertheless treat the security as if the requirements for exemption from mark-to-market accounting were satisfied.

The proposed regulations further provide that the gain or loss with respect to a security that is marked to market under section 475(f)(1)(A) is ordinary. Under this rule, if an electing trader disposes of a security before the close of the taxable year, proposed § 1.475(a)-2 applies, and the gain or loss is ordinary income or loss. See sections 475(f)(1)(D) and 475(d)(3) and the legislative history to section 475(f). H.R. Rep. No. 148, 105th Cong., 1st Sess. 445 (1997).

Under the proposed regulations, the above rules for electing securities traders also apply to electing commodities traders. In addition, the proposed regulations provide a special character rule for traders in section 1256 commodity contracts who elect mark-to-market accounting for their businesses. For these traders, the proposed regulations clarify that the capital character rule of section 1256 does not apply to these contracts and, thus, the gain or loss with respect to such contracts is ordinary.

Making the Elections

The proposed regulations clarify that if a dealer in securities also has a securities or commodities trading business or a commodities dealing business, the dealer may make an election for that business.

The proposed regulations also provide that the mark-to-market elections for dealers in commodities and for traders in securities or commodities must be made in the time and manner prescribed by the Commissioner. The IRS and the Treasury Department anticipate requiring taxpayers to make the election by filing a form, to be developed by the IRS, not later than 22 months after the beginning of the taxable year for which the election is made. (See the Paperwork Reduction Act section of this preamble, which requests comments on the burden that may be imposed by this requirement.) Interim procedures are being provided in a revenue procedure.

Proposed Effective Dates

The proposed regulations in §1.475(c)-2(d)(1) apply to every taxpayer who is required by section 475(c)(4) to cease using mark-to-market accounting for nonfinancial customer paper. These regulations are applicable for all taxable years ending after July 22, 1998. Proposed §§1.446-1(c)(2)(iii), 1.471-12, and 1.475(c)-2(d)(2) are applicable for all taxable years ending on or after January 28, 1999. The proposed regulations in §§1.475(e)-1 and 1.475(f)-2 generally apply to securities or commodities acquired on or after March 1, 1999. The rules concerning the time and manner for making the mark-to-market elections for commodities dealers and securities and commodities traders are generally applicable for taxable years ending on or after January 28, 1999.

Special Analyses

It has been determined that this notice of proposed rulemaking is not a significant regulatory action as defined in EO 12866. Therefore, a regulatory impact analysis is not required. It is hereby certified that the collection of information in these regulations will not have a significant economic impact on a substantial number of small entities. As previously noted, in those instances where a small entity elects to apply the rules in these regulations, the burden of the collection of information is not significant. Accordingly, a Regulatory Flexibility Analysis is not required. Pursuant to section 7805(f), this notice of proposed rulemaking will be submitted to the Chief Counsel for Advocacy of the Small Business Administration for comment on its impact on small business.

Comments and Public Hearing

Before these proposed regulations are adopted as final regulations, consideration will be given to any written comments (a signed original and eight (8) copies) that are submitted timely to the IRS. The IRS and the Treasury Department specifically request comments on the clarity of the proposed regulations and how they can be made easier to understand. All comments will be available for public inspection and copying.

A public hearing has been scheduled for June 3, 1999, beginning at 10 a.m. in room 2615 of the Internal Revenue Building, 1111 Constitution Avenue, NW., Washington, DC. Due to building security procedures, visitors must enter at the 10th Street entrance, located between Constitution and Pennsylvania Avenues, NW. In addition, all visitors must present photo identification to enter the building. Because of access restrictions, visitors will not be admitted beyond the immediate entrance area more than 15 minutes before the hearing starts. For information about having your name placed on the building access list to attend the hearing, see the "FOR FURTHER INFORMATION CONTACT" section of this preamble.

The rules of 26 CFR 601.601(a)(3) apply to the hearing. Persons who wish to present oral comments at the hearing must submit written comments and an outline of the topics to be discussed and the time to be devoted to each topic (signed original and eight (8) copies) by May 13, 1999. A period of 10 minutes will be allotted to each person for making comments. An agenda showing the scheduling of the speakers will be prepared after the deadline for receiving outlines has passed. Copies of the agenda will be available free of charge at the hearing.

Drafting Information

The principal authors of these regulations are Jo Lynn Ricks and Pamela Lew of the Office of Assistant Chief Counsel (Financial Institutions & Products). However, other personnel from the IRS and the Treasury Department participated in their development.

[¶ 49,170] **Proposed Regulation and Proposed Amendments of Regulations (REG-113909-98)**, published in the Federal Register on July 13, 1999.

Controlled foreign corporations: Hybrid branches: Subpart F income.—Reg. §1.954-9 and amendments of Reg. §§1.904-5 and 1.954-0—1.954-2, relating to the treatment under subpart F of certain payments involving branches of a controlled foreign corporation that are treated as separate entities for foreign tax purposes or partnerships in which controlled foreign corporations are partners, are proposed. Proposed regulations (REG-104537-97) published on March 26, 1998, are withdrawn. A public hearing on this proposal is scheduled for December 1, 1999.

AGENCY: Internal Revenue Service (IRS), Treasury.

ACTION: Withdrawal; Notice of proposed rulemaking; and notice of public hearing.

SUMMARY: This document withdraws the notice of proposed rulemaking and notice of proposed rulemaking by cross-reference to temporary regulations that was published in the Federal Register on March 26, 1998, providing guidance under subpart F relating to partnerships and branches. This document contains new proposed regulations relating to the treatment under subpart F of certain transactions involving hybrid branches. These regulations are necessary to provide guidance on transactions relating to such entities. This document also provides notice of a public hearing on these proposed regulations.

DATES: Written comments, and outlines of oral comments to be discussed at the public hearing scheduled for December 1, 1999, must be received by November 10, 1999.

ADDRESSES: Send submissions to: CC:DOM:CORP:R (REG-113909-98), room 5226, Internal Revenue Service, POB 7604, Ben Franklin Station, Washington DC 20044. Submissions may be hand delivered Monday through Friday between the hours of 8 a.m. and 5 p.m. to: CC:DOM:CORP:R (REG-113909-98), Courier's Desk, Internal Revenue Service, 1111 Constitution Avenue, NW., Washington DC. Alternatively, taxpayers may submit comments electronically via the Internet by selecting the "Tax Regs" option on the IRS Home Page, or by submitting comments directly to the IRS Internet site at http://www.irs.ustreas.gov/prod/tax>regs/regslist.html. The public hearing will be held in room 2615, Internal Revenue Building, 1111 Constitution Avenue NW., Washington, DC 20224.

FOR FURTHER INFORMATION CONTACT: Concerning the regulations, Valerie Mark, (202) 622-3840; concerning submissions of comments, the hearing, and/or to be placed on the building access list to attend the hearing, LaNita Van Dyke (202) 622-7180 (not toll-free numbers).

SUPPLEMENTARY INFORMATION:

Background

On March 23, 1998 (63 FR 14669, March 26, 1998), the IRS issued proposed regulations (REG-104537-97) relating to the treatment under subpart F of certain partnership and hybrid branch transactions. The provisions of the proposed regulations relating to hybrid branch transactions were also issued as temporary regulations (TD 8767) (63 FR 14613, March 26, 1998). Certain members of Congress and taxpayers raised concerns about the proposed and temporary regulations relating to hybrid branch transactions. On June 19, 1998, the Treasury announced in Notice 98-35 (1998-27 I.R.B. 35) that the temporary regulations would be removed and that the proposed regulations relating to hybrid transactions would be re-proposed with new dates of applicability to give Congress the opportunity to consider in greater depth the issues raised by hybrid transactions.

As provided in Notice 98-35, these proposed regulations substantially restate the regulations relating to hybrid transactions issued in March of 1998. These proposed regulations, however, contain certain clarifications requested by taxpayers. Further, as described in greater detail below, unlike the effective date rules announced in Notice 98-35, these regulations are proposed to be effective only for payments made in taxable years commencing after the date that is five years after the date of finalization of these regulations. The permanent grandfather relief described in Notice 98-35 remains unchanged.

These proposed regulations represent the IRS and Treasury's views of how current law should be enforced. Treasury is currently undertaking a comprehensive study of subpart F. These proposed regulations will not control the results of the study. For example, an objective analysis of the policies and goals of subpart F may lead to the conclusion that subpart F should be significantly restructured.

To the extent, however, that Congress does not restructure subpart F in a manner that would alter the rules enforced by these regulations, Treasury and the IRS believe that these regulations will be necessary to preserve the integrity of the current statutory scheme. The use of hybrid arrangements, which is greatly facilitated by the "check-the-box" entity classification regulations (§§ 301.7701-1 through 301.7701-3), would otherwise give rise to the following inconsistency: if sales income is shifted from one CFC to a related CFC in a different jurisdiction, subpart F income may arise; if sales income is shifted from one CFC to its branch in a different jurisdiction, subpart F income may arise; if income is shifted through interest payments from one CFC to a related CFC in a different jurisdiction, subpart F income may arise; however, if income is shifted through interest payments from one CFC to its hybrid branch in a different jurisdiction, subpart F income will not arise. This final result does not seem an appropriate policy outcome within the framework of current subpart F, and is almost certainly inconsistent with the Congressional intent underlying the rules being interpreted here.

Treasury anticipates that taxpayers will comment both on the appropriateness of these proposed regulations under current law, and on the contents of its subpart F study, including any conclusions that the study might draw about potential changes to subpart F. To allow proper time to consider all these issues, Treasury and the IRS have significantly modified and liberalized the effective date rules set forth in Notice 98-35. New regulations regarding the treatment of a controlled foreign corporation's distributive share of partnership income will be proposed at a later date.

Explanation of Provisions

I. *In General*

In these proposed regulations, Treasury and the IRS set forth a framework for dealing with issues arising under subpart F (sections 951 through 964) that relate to the use of certain entities that are regarded as fiscally transparent for purposes of U.S. tax law.

II. *Hybrid Branches*

Treasury and the IRS understand that certain taxpayers are using arrangements involving hybrid branches to circumvent the purposes of subpart F. These arrangements generally involve the use of deductible payments to reduce the taxable income of a CFC under foreign law, thereby reducing that CFC's foreign tax and, also under foreign law, the corresponding creation in another entity of low-taxed, passive income of the type to which subpart F was intended to apply. Because of the structure of these arrangements, however, taxpayers take the position that this income is not taxed under subpart F. Treasury and the IRS have concluded that use of these hybrid branch arrangements is contrary to the policies and rules of subpart F.

Under these proposed regulations, hybrid branch payments, as defined in the regulations, between a CFC and its hybrid branch, or between hybrid branches of the CFC may give rise to subpart F income. When certain conditions are present, the non-subpart F income of the CFC, in the amount of the hybrid branch payment, is recharacterized as subpart F income of the CFC. Those conditions include that: the hybrid branch payment reduces the foreign tax of the payor; the hybrid branch payment would have been foreign personal holding company income if made between separate CFCs; and there is a disparity between the effective rate of tax on the payment in the hands of the payee and the hypothetical rate of tax that would have applied if the payment had been taxed in the hands of the payor.

The proposed regulations would make clear that the CFC and the hybrid branch, or the hybrid branches, are treated as separate corporations only to recharacterize non-subpart F income as subpart F income in the amount of the hybrid branch payment, and to apply the tax disparity rule of § 1.954-9(a)(5)(iv). For all other purposes (e.g., for purposes of the earnings and profits limitation of section 952), a CFC and its hybrid branch, or hybrid branches, would not be treated as separate corporations.

The proposed regulations would provide that the amount recharacterized as subpart F income is the gross amount of the hybrid branch payment limited by the amount of the CFC's earnings and profits attributable to non-subpart F income. This amount is the excess of current earnings and profits over subpart F income, determined after the application of the rules of sections 954(b) and 952(c) and before the application of these proposed regulations. To the extent that the full amount required to be recharacterized under this provision cannot be recharacterized because it exceeds earnings and profits attributable to non-subpart F income, there is no requirement to carry such amounts back or forward to another year.

The proposed regulations would provide that, under certain circumstances, the recharacterization rules will also apply to a CFC's proportionate share of any hybrid branch payment made between a partnership in which the CFC is a partner and a hybrid branch of the partnership, or between hybrid branches of such a partnership. When the partnership is treated as fiscally transparent by the CFC's taxing jurisdiction, the recharacterization rules are applied by treating the hybrid branch payment as if it had been made directly between the CFC and the hybrid branch, or as though the hybrid branches of the partnership had been hybrid branches of the CFC, as applicable. If the partnership is treated as a separate entity by the CFC's taxing jurisdiction, the recharacterization rules are applied to the partnership as if it were a CFC.

The proposed regulations would provide that income will not be recharacterized unless there is a disparity between the effective rate at which the hybrid branch payment is taxed to the payee and a hypothetical tax rate that measures the tax savings to the payor from the deductible payment. This provision is similar to the rule in § 1.954-3(b), and adopts the same percentage tests as contained in that provision. The regulations also provide a special high tax exception applicable to the hybrid branch payment that is similar to the one contained in section 954(b)(4).

For purposes of determining the amount of taxes deemed paid under section 960, the amount of non-subpart F income recharacterized as subpart F income is treated as attributable to income in separate foreign tax credit baskets in proportion to the ratio of non-subpart F income in each basket to the total amount of non-subpart F income of the CFC for the taxable year.

III. *Related Provisions*

These proposed regulations would provide rules, contained in § 1.954-1(c)(1)(i)(B), to prevent expenses, including related person interest expense that would normally be allocable under section 954(b)(5) to subpart F income of a CFC, from being allocated to a payment from which the expense arises. The allocation limit applies: (i) to the extent such payment is included in the subpart F income of the CFC; (ii) if the expense arises from any payment between the CFC and ahybrid partnership in which the CFC is a partner; and (iii) if the payment reduces foreign tax and there is a significant disparity in tax rates between the payor and payee jurisdictions.

These proposed regulations also would address the application of the related person exceptions to the foreign personal holding company income rules in the context of partnership distributive shares and transactions involving hybrid branches. Under section 954(c)(3), foreign personal holding company income does not include certain interest, dividends, rents and royalties received from related corporations. These exceptions apply, in the case of interest and dividends, when the related corporate payor is organized in the country in which the CFC is organized and uses a substantial part of its assets in a trade or business in that country and, in the case of rents and royalties, when the rent or royalty payment is made for the use or privilege of using property within the CFC's country of incorporation.

Under these proposed regulations, if the partnership receives an item of income that reduces the foreign income tax of the payor, the related person exceptions of section 954(c)(3) would apply to exclude the income from the foreign personal holding company income of the CFC partner only where: the exception would have applied if the CFC earned the income directly (testing relatedness and country of incorporation at the CFC partner level); and either the partnership is organized and operates in the CFC's country of incorporation, the partnership is treated as fiscally transparent in the CFC's countries of incorporation and operation, or there is no significant disparity between the effective rate of tax imposed on the income and the rate of tax that would be imposed on the income if earned directly by the CFC partner.

In addition, these proposed regulations contain rules that would apply the related person exceptions to certain payments involving hybrid branches. These rules would apply to payments by a CFC to a hybrid branch of a related CFC. Under these rules, the related person exceptions would apply to exclude the payments from the foreign personal holding company income of the recipient CFC only if the payment would have qualified for the exception if the hybrid branch had been a separate CFC incorporated in the jurisdiction in which the payment is subject to tax (other than a withholding tax).

IV. *Request for Comments*

Comments on policy issues that relate to subpart F and deferral, generally, including comments on legislative modifications to the current rules, and comments solicited on the broad policy issues mentioned in Notice 98-35, can be submitted in response to the study mentioned above. Treasury and the IRS invite comments on the appropriateness of these regulations under the current subpart F rules.

Proposed Effective Date

These proposed regulations will not be finalized before July 1, 2000. It is proposed that, when finalized, these regulations would be effective only for payments made in taxable years of a controlled foreign corporation commencing after the date that is five years after the date of finalization of these regulations. These regulations would not, however, apply to any payments made under hybrid arrangements entered into before June 19, 1998. This exception is permanent so long as the arrangement is not substantially modified on or after June 19, 1998. An illustrative list of events that would and would not constitute "substantial modification" of an arrangement is included in these regulations.

Special Analyses

It has been determined that this notice of proposed rulemaking is not a significant regulatory action as defined in Executive Order 12866. Therefore, a regulatory assessment is not required. It has also been determined that section 553(b) of the Administrative Procedures Act (5 U.S.C. chapter 5) does not apply to these regulations, and, because the regulation does not impose a collection of information on small entities, the Regulatory Flexibility Act (5 U.S.C. chapter 6) does not apply. Pursuant to section 7805(f) of the Internal Revenue Code, this notice of proposed rulemaking will be submitted to the Chief Counsel for Advocacy of the Small Business Administration for comment on its impact on small business.

Request for Comments

Before these proposed regulations are adopted as final regulations, consideration will be given to any written comments (a signed original and eight (8) copies) that are submitted timely to the IRS. The IRS and Treasury specifically request comments on the clarity of these proposed regulations and how they may be made easier to understand. All comments will be available for public inspection and copying.

A public hearing has been scheduled for December 1, 1999, at 10 a.m., in room 2615, Internal Revenue Building, 1111 Constitution Avenue NW., Washington, DC. Due to building security procedures, visitors must enter at the 10th Street entrance, located between Constitution and Pennsylvania Avenues, NW. In addition, all visitors must present photo identification to enter the building. Because of access restrictions, visitors will not be admitted beyond the immediate entrance area more than 15 minutes before the hearing starts. For information about having your name placed on the building access list to attend the hearing, see the "FOR FURTHER INFORMATION CONTACT" section of this preamble.

The rules of 26 CFR 601.601(a)(3) apply to the hearing.

Persons that wish to present oral comments at the hearing must submit written comments and an outline of topics to be discussed and time to be devoted to each topic (signed original and eight (8) copies) by November 10, 1999.

A period of 10 minutes will be allotted to each person for making comments.

An agenda showing the scheduling of the speakers will be prepared after the deadline for receiving outlines has passed. Copies of the agenda will be available free of charge at the hearing.

Drafting Information

The principal author of these regulations is Valerie Mark, of the Office of the Associate Chief Counsel (International). Other personnel from the IRS and Treasury Department also participated in the development of these regulations.

[¶ 49,172]   **Proposed Amendments of Regulation (REG-103882-99)**, published in the Federal Register on February 8, 2000.

Depletion: Lease of mineral property: Uniform capitalization rules: Delay rental, treatment of.—Amendments of Reg. § 1.612-3, conforming regulations relating to delay rental to the requirements of Code Sec. 263A relating to capitalization and inclusion in inventory of costs of certain expenses, are proposed. A public hearing on this proposal is scheduled for May 26, 2000.

AGENCY: Internal Revenue Service (IRS), Treasury.

ACTION: Notice of proposed rulemaking and notice of public hearing.

SUMMARY: This document contains proposed amendments conforming regulations relating to delay rental to the requirements of section 263A relating to capitalization and inclusion in inventory of costs of certain expenses. Changes to the applicable law were made by the Tax Reform Act of 1986 and the Technical and Miscellaneous Revenue Act of 1988. The proposed regulations provide the public with guidance concerning the application of section 263A to delay rental.

DATES: Written comments must be received by May 8, 2000. Outlines of topics to be discussed at the public hearing scheduled for May 26, 2000, at 10 a.m. must be received by May 5, 2000.

ADDRESSES: Send submissions to: CC:DOM:CORP:R (REG-103882-99), room 5226, Internal Revenue Service, POB 7604, Ben Franklin Station, Washington, DC 20044. Submissions may be hand delivered between the hours of 8 a.m. and 5 p.m. to: CC:DOM:CORP:R (REG-103882-99), Courier's Desk, Internal Revenue Service, 1111 Constitution Avenue, NW., Washington, DC. Alternatively, taxpayers may submit comments electronically via the Internet by selecting the "Tax Regs" option on the IRS Home Page, or by submitting comments directly to the IRS Internet site at http://www.irs.ustreas.gov/prod/tax_regs/regslist.html. The public hearing will be held in room 2615, Internal Revenue Building, 1111 Constitution Avenue, NW., Washington, DC.

FOR FURTHER INFORMATION CONTACT: Concerning the regulation, Brenda M. Stewart, (202) 622-3120; concerning submissions and the hearing, LaNita Van Dyke, (202) 622-7180 (not toll-free numbers).

SUPPLEMENTARY INFORMATION:

Background

This document contains proposed amendments to the Income Tax Regulations (26 CFR part 1) under section 612 to conform them to the requirements of section 263A. Section 263A was enacted by the Tax Reform Act of 1986, Public Law 99-514 (100 Stat. 2085), and amended by the Technical and Miscellaneous Revenue Act of 1988, Public Law 100-647 (102 Stat. 3342).

Explanation of Provisions

Under the terms of a lease of mineral property, the lessee acquires, for a stated term, the right and obligation to obtain production of minerals from the property. A lease may provide that for each year that the lessee fails to make efforts to obtain production, the lessee must pay a "delay rental" to the lessor.

Section 1.612-3(c)(1) of the final regulations defines a delay rental as an amount paid for the privilege of deferring development of the property and which could have been avoided by abandonment of the lease, or by commencement of development operations, or by obtaining production. Section 1.612-3(c)(2) of the final regulations provides that since a delay rental is in the nature of rent, it is ordinary income to the payee and not subject to depletion. The payor may at his election deduct the delay rental as an expense, or charge it to depletable capital account under section 266.

Section 263A was enacted subsequent to the issuance of §1.612-3(c) of the final regulations. The uniform capitalization rules of section 263A generally require the capitalization of all direct costs and certain indirect costs properly allocable to property produced by the taxpayer. Capitalization may be required even though production (development) has not yet begun. §1.263A-2(a)(3)(ii). In some situations, a delay rental may be required to be capitalized under section 263A. Accordingly, the proposed regulation clarifies that subsequent to the enactment of section 263A, the payor of a delay rental may elect to expense currently the delay rental or charge it to depletable capital account under section 266 to the extent that the delay rental is not required to be capitalized under section 263A and the regulations thereunder.

Special Analyses

It has been determined that this notice of proposed rulemaking is not a significant regulatory action as defined in Executive Order 12866. Therefore, a regulatory assessment is not required. It has also been determined that section 553(b) of the Administrative Procedure Act (5 U.S.C. chapter 5) does not apply to these regulations, and because the regulations do not impose a collection of information on small entities, a Regulatory Flexibility Analysis is not required. Pursuant to section 7805(f) of the Internal Revenue Code, this notice of proposed rulemaking will be submitted to the Chief Counsel for Advocacy of the Small Business Administration for comment on its impact on small business.

Comments and Public Hearing

Before these proposed regulations are adopted as final regulations, consideration will be given to any written comments that are submitted timely (a signed original and eight copies) to the IRS. The IRS and Treasury request comments on the clarity of the proposed regulations and they may be made easier to understand. All comments will be made available for public inspection and copying.

A public hearing has been scheduled for May 26, 2000, at 10 a.m. in room 2615, Internal Revenue Building, 1111 Constitution Avenue NW., Washington, DC. Because of access restrictions, visitors will not be admitted beyond the Internal Revenue Building lobby more than 15 minutes before the hearing starts.

The rules of 26 CFR 601.601(a)(3) apply to the hearing.

Persons that wish to present oral comments at the hearing must submit written comments (a signed original and eight (8) copies) by May 8, 2000. The outline of topics to be discussed at the hearing must be received by May 5, 2000.

A period of 10 minutes will be allotted for each person for making comments.

An agenda showing the scheduling of the speakers will be prepared after the deadline for receiving outlines has passed. Copies of the agenda will be available free of charge at the hearing.

Drafting Information

The principal author of this proposed regulation is Brenda M. Stewart of the Office of Assistant Chief Counsel (Passthroughs and Special Industries), Internal Revenue Service. However, other personnel from the IRS and Treasury Department participated in its development.

[¶ 49,175] **Proposed Regulations and Proposed Amendments of Regulations (REG-116050-99)**, published in the Federal Register on November 15, 2000.

Corporate reorganizations: Foreign corporations: Stock transfer rules: Carryovers.—Reg. §1.367(b)-8 and amendments of Reg. §§1.312-10, 1.367(b)-5 and 1.367(e)-1, addressing the carryover of certain tax attributes such as earnings and profits and foreign income tax accounts when

two corporations combine in a section 367(b) transaction, are proposed. Reg. §§1.367(b)-7 and 1.367(b)-9 and amendments to Reg. §§1.367(b)-0—1.367(b)-6 and 1.381(a)-1 were adopted by T.D. 9273 on August 7, 2006.

AGENCY: Internal Revenue Service (IRS), Treasury.

ACTION: Notice of proposed rulemaking and notice of public hearing.

SUMMARY: This document contains proposed regulations addressing transactions described in section 367(b) of the Internal Revenue Code (section 367(b) transactions). A section 367(b) transaction includes a corporate reorganization, liquidation, or division involving one or more foreign corporations. The proposed regulations address the carryover of certain tax attributes, such as earnings and profits and foreign income tax accounts, when two corporations combine in a section 367(b) transaction. The proposed regulations also address the allocation of certain tax attributes when a corporation distributes stock of another corporation in a section 367(b) transaction. This document also provides notice of a public hearing on the proposed regulations.

DATES: Written or electronic comments and requests to speak (with outlines of oral comments) at a public hearing scheduled for March 13, 2001 must be received by February 20, 2001.

ADDRESSES: Send submissions to: CC:M&SP:RU (REG-116050-99), room 5226, Internal Revenue Service, POB 7604, Ben Franklin Station, Washington, DC 20044. Submissions may be hand delivered Monday through Friday between the hours of 8 a.m. and 5 p.m. to: CC:M&SP:RU (REG-116050-99), Courier's Desk, Internal Revenue Service, 1111 Constitution Avenue, NW., Washington, DC. Alternatively, taxpayers may submit comments electronically via the Internet by selecting the "Tax Regs" option on the IRS Home Page, or by submitting comments directly to the IRS Internet site at http://www.irs.gov/tax>regs/regslist.html. The public hearing will be held in room 7218, Internal Revenue Building, 1111 Constitution Avenue, NW., Washington DC.

FOR FURTHER INFORMATION CONTACT: Concerning the proposed regulations, Anne O'Connell Devereaux, at (202) 622-3850; concerning submissions of comments, the hearing, and/or to be placed on the building access list to attend the hearing, Guy Traynor, at (202) 622-7180 (not toll-free numbers).

SUPPLEMENTARY INFORMATION:

Paperwork Reduction Act

The collection of information contained in this notice of proposed rulemaking has been submitted to the Office of Management and Budget for review in accordance with the Paperwork Reduction Act of 1995 (44 U.S.C. 3507(d)). Comments on the collection of information should be sent to the Office of Management and Budget, Attn: Desk Officer for the Department of the Treasury, Office of Information and Regulatory Affairs, Washington, DC 20503, with copies to the Internal Revenue Service, Attn: IRS Reports Clearance Officer, W:CAR:MP:FP:S:O, Washington, DC 20224. Comments on the collection of information should be received by January 16, 2001. Comments are specifically requested concerning:

—Whether the proposed collection of information is necessary for the proper performance of the functions of the IRS, including whether the information will have practical utility;

—The accuracy of the estimated burden associated with the proposed collection of information (see below);

—How the quality, utility, and clarity of the information to be collected may be enhanced;

—How the burden of complying with the proposed collection of information may be minimized, including through the application of automated collection techniques or other forms of information technology; and

—Estimates of capital or start-up costs and costs of operation, maintenance, and purchase of services to provide information.

The collection of information in this proposed regulation is in §1.367(b)-1. This collection of information is required by the IRS to verify compliance with the regulations under section 367(b) relating to exchanges described therein. The likely respondents are corporations that are affected by such exchanges.

Estimated total annual reporting burden: 1,800 hours.

The estimated annual burden per respondent: 3 hours.

Estimated number of respondents: 600.

Estimated annual frequency of responses: One.

An agency may not conduct or sponsor, and a person is not required to respond to, a collection of information unless it displays a valid control number assigned by the Office of Management and Budget.

Books or records relating to a collection of information must be retained as long as their contents may become material in the administration of any internal revenue law. Generally, tax returns and tax return information are confidential, as required by 26 U.S.C. 6103.

Background

On December 27, 1977, the IRS and Treasury issued proposed and temporary regulations under section 367(b) of the Code. Subsequent guidance updated and amended the 1977 temporary regulations several times over the next 14 years. On August 26, 1991, the IRS and Treasury issued proposed regulations §§1.367(b)-1 through 1.367(b)-6 (the 1991 proposed regulations). Final regulations under section 367(b) of the Internal Revenue Code (Code) were issued in June 1998 and January 2000 and the 1977 temporary regulations and the 1991 proposed regulations were generally removed. The preamble to the January 2000 final regulations refers to proposed regulations that would be issued at a later date to address the carryover of certain corporate tax attributes in transactions involving one or more foreign corporations. Those proposed regulations are set forth in this document.

Overview

A. General Policies of Section 367(b)

In general, section 367 governs corporate restructurings under sections 332, 351, 354, 355, 356, and 361 (Subchapter C nonrecognition transactions) in which the status of a foreign corporation as a "corporation" is necessary for the application of the relevant nonrecognition provisions. Other provisions in Subchapter C (Subchapter C carryover provisions) apply to such transactions in conjunction with the enumerated provisions and detail additional consequences that occur in connection with the transactions. For example, sections 362 and 381 govern the carryover of basis and earnings and profits from the transferor corporation to the transferee corporation in applicable transactions and section 312 governs the allocation of earnings and profits from a distributing corporation in a transaction described in section 355.

The Subchapter C carryover provisions generally have been drafted to apply to domestic corporations and U.S. shareholders, and thus do not fully take into account the cross-border aspects of U.S. taxation. For example, sections 381 and 312 do not take into account source and foreign tax credit issues that arise when earnings and profits move from one corporation to another.

Congress enacted section 367(b) to ensure that international tax considerations in the Code are adequately addressed when the Subchapter C provisions apply to an exchange involving a foreign corporation in order to prevent the avoidance of U.S. taxation. Because determining the proper interaction of the Code's international and Subchapter C provisions is "necessarily highly technical," Congress granted the Secretary broad regulatory authority to provide the "necessary or appropriate" rules rather than enacting a complex statutory regime. H.R. Rep. No. 658, 94th Cong., 1st Sess. 241 (1975). Thus, section 367(b)(2) provides in part that the regulations "shall include (but shall not be limited to) regulations . . . providing . . . the extent to which adjustments shall be made to earnings and profits, basis of stock or securities, and basis of assets."

The proposed regulations provide rules regarding the movement of certain corporate tax attributes between corporations in a Subchapter C nonrecognition transaction involving one or more foreign corporations. Generally, the regulations continue to apply the principles of the Subchapter C carryover provisions with modifications as necessary or appropriate to preserve international tax policies of the Code and to prevent material distortions of income.

The remainder of the Overview section is divided by specific categories of section 367(b) transactions and describes the relevant Subchapter C and international policies and provisions. The "Details of Provisions" portion of this preamble describes the proposed regulations' principal operative rules that implement the policies and reconcile the provisions described in the Overview portion of this preamble. The IRS and Treasury welcome comments regarding both the general approach and the specific provisions of the proposed regulations.

B. *Specific Policies Related to Inbound Nonrecognition Transactions (Prop. Reg. §1.367(b)-3)*

Proposed § 1.367(b)-3 addresses acquisitions by a domestic corporation (domestic acquiring corporation) of the assets of a foreign corporation (foreign acquired corporation) in a section 332 liquidation or an asset acquisition described in section 368(a)(1), such as a C, D, or F reorganization (inbound nonrecognition transaction).

The preamble to the January 2000 final regulations generally describes international policy issues that can arise in an inbound nonrecognition transaction. The preamble states that the "principal policy consideration of section 367(b) with respect to inbound nonrecognition transactions is the appropriate carryover of attributes from foreign to domestic corporations. This consideration has interrelated shareholder-level and corporate-level components." The final regulations address the carryover of certain attributes, such as the carryover of foreign taxes, earnings and profits, and basis. However, the carryover of earnings and profits, and basis are addressed only to the extent attributable to earnings and profits accumulated during a U.S. shareholder's holding period, i.e., "the all earnings and profits amount," as defined in § 1.367(b)-2(d).

The preamble to the final regulations also notes that it would be consistent with the policy considerations of section 367(b) for future regulations to provide further rules with respect to the extent to which attributes carry over from a foreign corporation to a U.S. corporation. The proposed regulations do not comprehensively address this issue. Compare Modify Treatment of Built-In Losses and Other Attribute Trafficking, General Explanations of the Administration's Fiscal Year 2001 Revenue Proposals at 205. However, the proposed regulations do provide additional rules concerning several attributes, specifically net operating loss and capital loss carryovers, and earnings and profits that are not included in income as an all earnings and profits amount (or a deficit in earnings and profits). The proposed regulations generally provide that these tax attributes carry over from a foreign acquired corporation to a domestic acquiring corporation only to the extent that they are effectively connected to a U.S. trade or business (or attributable to a permanent establishment, in the case of an applicable U.S. income tax treaty).

C. *Specific Policies Related to Foreign 381 Transactions (Prop. Reg. §1. 367(b)-7)*

Proposed regulation § 1.367(b)-7 applies to an acquisition by a foreign corporation (foreign acquiring corporation) of the assets of another foreign corporation (foreign target corporation) in a transaction described in section 381 (foreign 381 transaction) and addresses the manner in which earnings and profits and foreign income taxes of the foreign acquiring corporation and foreign target corporation carry over to the surviving foreign corporation (foreign surviving corporation). This would include, for example, a C, D, or F reorganization or a section 332 liquidation between two foreign corporations.

The international provisions of the Code distinguish between categories of foreign corporations. A foreign acquiring, target, or surviving corporation can be a controlled foreign corporation as defined in section 953 or 957 (CFC), a noncontrolled section 902 corporation as defined in section 904(d)(2)(E) after 2003, the effective date of section 1105(b) of Public Law 105-34 (111 Stat. 788) (the 1997 Act) (look-through 10/50 corporation and, together with CFCs, look-through corporations), a noncontrolled section 902 corporation before 2003 (non-look-through 10/50 corporation and, together with look-through 10/50 corporations, 10/50 corporations), or a foreign corporation that is neither a CFC nor a 10/50 corporation (less-than-10%-U.S.-owned foreign corporation).

The principal Code sections implicated by the carryover of earnings and profits and foreign income taxes in a foreign 381 transaction are sections 381, 902, 904, and 959. Section 381 generally permits earnings and profits (or deficit in earnings and profits) to carry over to a surviving corporation, thus enabling "the successor corporation to step into the 'tax shoes' of its predecessor . . . . [and] represents the economic integration of two or more separate businesses into a unified business enterprise." H. Rep. No. 1337, 83rd Cong., 2nd Sess. 41 (1954). However, a deficit in earnings and profits of either the transferee or transferor corporation can only be used to offset earnings and profits accumulated after the date of transfer (hovering deficit rule). Section 381(c)(2)(B). The hovering deficit rule is a legislative mechanism designed to deter the trafficking in favorable tax attributes that the IRS and courts had repeatedly encountered. See, e.g., *Commissioner v. Phipps*, 336 U.S. 410 (1949). The proposed regulations adopt the principles of section 381 but adapt its operation in consideration of the international provisions that address foreign corporations' earnings and profits and their related foreign income taxes, such as sections 902, 904, and 959.

Section 902 generally provides that a deemed paid foreign tax credit is available to a domestic corporation that receives a dividend from a foreign corporation in which it owns 10 percent or more of the voting stock (i.e., a look-through corporation or non-look-through 10/50 corporation). The Code modifies the general last-in, first-out (LIFO) rule of section 316 and provides that look-through corporations and non-look-through 10/50 corporations pay dividends out of multi-year pools of earnings and profits and foreign income taxes for earnings and profits accumulated (and related foreign income taxes paid or deemed paid) in taxable years beginning after December 31, 1986, or the first day after which a domestic corporation owns 10 percent or more of the voting stock of a foreign corporation, whichever is later. Section 902(c). (The Code and regulations refer to pooled earnings and profits and foreign income taxes as post-1986 undistributed earnings and post-1986 foreign income taxes even though a particular corporation may begin to pool after 1986. Sections 902(c)(1) and (2), § 1.902-1(a) (8) and (9).)

Congress enacted the pooling rules because it believed that averaging of foreign income taxes was fairer than distributions out of annual layers. Joint Committee on Taxation, General Explanation of the Tax Reform Act of 1986 (Public Law 99-514) (1986 Bluebook) at 870. Averaging prevents taxpayers from inflating their foreign income tax rate for a particular year in order to obtain artificially enhanced foreign tax credits. Id. Averaging also prevents the trapping of foreign income taxes in years in which a taxpayer may have no earnings and profits. Id.

However, Congress enacted pooling on a limited basis. Earnings and profits accumulated (and related foreign income taxes paid or deemed paid) while a foreign corporation is a less-than-10%-U.S.-owned foreign corporation and pre-1987 earnings and profits accumulated (and related foreign income taxes paid or deemed paid) by a look-through corporation or non-look-through 10/50 corporation are not pooled. Rather, such earnings and profits (and related foreign income taxes) are maintained in separate annual layers. Section 902(c)(6). (The Code and regulations refer to earnings and profits and foreign income taxes in annual layers as pre-1987 accumulated profits and pre-1987 foreign income taxes even though a particular corporation may have annual layers for years after 1986. Section 902(c)(6); § 1.902-1(a)(10).)

A distribution of earnings and profits is first out of pooled earnings and profits and then, only after all pooled earnings and profits have been distributed, out of annual layers of earnings and profits on a LIFO basis. Section 902(a) and (c). The retention of annual layers beneath pooled earnings and profits limits the need to recreate tax histories, an administrative burden that is more significant for periods during which a corporation had limited nexus to the U.S. taxing jurisdiction and for pre-1987 earnings and profits when pooling was not required.

The section 904 foreign tax credit limitation ensures that taxpayers can use foreign tax credits only to offset U.S. tax on foreign source income. The limitation is computed separately with respect to different categories of income (baskets). The purpose of the baskets is to limit taxpayers' ability to cross-credit taxes from different categories of foreign source income. Congress was concerned that, without separate limitations, cross-crediting opportunities would distort economic incentives to invest in the United States versus abroad. 1986 Bluebook at 862.

A dividend received by a U.S. shareholder that owns less than 10 percent of the stock of a foreign corporation is categorized as passive income because such a dividend is in the nature of a portfolio investment. 1986 Bluebook at 866.

A dividend received by a U.S. shareholder that owns 10 percent or more of a foreign corporation is subject to other limitations. Dividends paid by a non-look-through 10/50 corporation to a 10 percent or greater U.S. corporate shareholder are currently subject to a separate basket limitation on a corporation-by-corporation basis. Congress initially separately basketed dividends from each 10/50 corporation because it believed a minority investment in a foreign corporation did not create sufficient identity of interest to justify look-through treatment and that cross-crediting of taxes among investments in 10/50 corporations was inappropriate because the foreign companies were not parts of a single economic unit. 1986 Bluebook at 868. In addition, Congress was concerned about the administrability of applying the look-through rules to 10/50 corporations. 1986 Bluebook at 868.

In 1997, Congress amended the Code's treatment of dividends from 10/50 corporations to provide that dividends paid after taxable years beginning after December 31, 2002 by a look-through 10/50 corporation out of earnings and profits accumulated before 2003 are subject to a single separate basket limitation for all 10/50 corporations, while dividends paid out of earnings and profits accumulated after 2003 are treated as income in a basket based on the ratio of the earnings and profits attributable to income in such basket to the foreign corporation's total earnings and profits (the so-called "look-through" approach). Earnings and profits accumulated after 2003 by a look-through 10/50 corporation are distributed before earnings and profits accumulated by that same foreign corporation before 2003. Joint Committee on Taxation, General Explanation of Tax Legislation Enacted in 1997 (1997 Bluebook) at 303.

The legislative history indicates that Congress changed its view with respect to 10/50 corporations because the separate basket limitation for dividends from each 10/50 corporation imposed a substantial recordkeeping burden and discouraged minority investments in foreign joint ventures. 1997 Bluebook at 302. However, as described above, the 1997 Act enacted look-through treatment for 10/50 corporation dividends only on a limited basis. Furthermore, Congress provided regulatory authority regarding the treatment of distributions out of earnings and profits for periods prior to a taxpayer's acquisition of stock in a look-through 10/50 corporation because of concerns that look-through treatment could provide inappropriate opportunities to traffic in foreign taxes.

Dividends paid by a CFC out of earnings and profits accumulated while the corporation was not a CFC are treated as a distribution from a 10/50 corporation while dividends paid out of earnings and profits accumulated while the corporation was a CFC are eligible for look-through treatment. Section 904(d)(2)(E)(i) and (d)(3). As in the case of a look-through 10/50 corporation, pooled earnings and profits of a CFC that are eligible for look-through treatment are distributed before other pooled earnings and profits. Prop. Reg. § 1.904-4(g)(3)(iii). Congress provided look-through treatment for dividends paid by CFCs in order to provide greater parity between the treatment of income earned through a branch and a subsidiary. 1986 Bluebook at 866.

Before 1997, except as otherwise provided in regulations, dividend distributions to a 10 percent U.S. shareholder of a CFC did not obtain look-through treatment unless the distributed earnings and profits accrued while the shareholder was a 10 percent U.S. shareholder and the corporation was a CFC. Section 904(d)(2)(E)(i), as in effect before the 1997 Act. This rule was intended to prevent trafficking in foreign income taxes related to preacquisition earnings and profits. However, because of the administrative issues presented by maintaining shareholder-level earnings and profits accounts, Congress modified the rule in 1997 to provide that look-through treatment applies with respect to CFC earnings and profits without regard to whether a 10 percent U.S. shareholder was a shareholder at the time accumulated. However, pre-CFC earnings and profits continue to be treated as earnings and profits of a 10/50 corporation because of foreign tax credit trafficking concerns.

The section 904 basketing rules reflect Congress' concern with respect to cross-crediting opportunities and its intent to limit the benefit of look-through treatment to appropriate circumstances. Where Congress determined that look-through is inappropriate, a dividend is treated as passive income or is subject to a separate limitation for 10/50 corporations (whether separately or collectively). Regulations have not yet been issued with respect to preacquisition earnings and profits of a look-through 10/50 corporation and the effect, if any, on the treatment of pre-CFC earnings and profits described in section 904(d)(2)(E)(i). The IRS and Treasury solicit comments as to the appropriate treatment of such earnings and profits after 2003 in light of Congress' anti-trafficking concerns, as well as the impact that such rules should have on the section 367(b) regulations.

Another international provision implicated by the movement of earnings and profits in foreign 381 transactions is section 959. Section 959 governs the distribution of earnings and profits that have been previously taxed to U.S. shareholders under section 951(a) (PTI). After studying the interaction of section 367(b) and the PTI rules, the IRS and Treasury determined that more guidance under section 959 would be useful before issuing regulations to address PTI issues that arise under section 367(b). Accordingly, the IRS and Treasury have opened a separate regulations project under section 959 and expect to issue regulations that address PTI issues under section 959 as well as section 367(b) in the future. The fundamental issue under consideration in that project is whether earnings and profits that are treated as PTI should be distributable to another shareholder, as well as the various implications that result from that determination. The IRS and Treasury invite comments with respect to these issues. Accordingly, the proposed regulations reserve on section 367(b) issues related to PTI.

Other sections may have also applied to characterize pre-transaction earnings of a foreign acquiring corporation or a foreign target corporation for certain purposes of the Code. For example, certain earnings may have been subject to characterization as U.S. source earnings under section 904(g), effectively connected earnings and profits under section 884, or post-1986 undistributed U.S. earnings under section 245. The characterization of such earnings carry over to the foreign surviving corporation for purposes of applying the relevant Code sections. See *Georday Enterprises v. Commissioner*, 126 F.2d 384 (4th Cir. 1942).

D. *Specific Policies Related to Foreign Divisive Transactions (Prop. Req. § 1.367(b)-8)*

Proposed regulation § 1.367(b)-8 addresses the allocation of earnings and profits and foreign income taxes in a transaction described in section 312(h) (that is, a section 355 distribution whether or not in connection with a section 368(a)(1)(D) reorganization) in which either or both the distributing or the controlled corporation is a foreign corporation (foreign divisive transaction). The scope of proposed § 1.367(b)-8 thus encompasses three situations: a domestic distributing corporation that distributes stock of a foreign controlled corporation, a foreign distributing corporation that distributes stock of a domestic controlled corporation, and a foreign distributing corporation that distributes stock of a foreign controlled corporation. The proposed regulations generally adopt the principles embodied in the regulations under section 312(h) but modify their application in consideration of the international provisions such as the source and foreign tax credit rules.

Regulations under section 312(h) reflect the principle that a pro rata portion of a distributing corporation's earnings and profits should be reduced to account for the distribution of a portion of its assets. §1.312-10. Furthermore, the earnings and profits of a controlled corporation should include the portion of the distributing corporation's earnings and profits allocable to any assets transferred to the controlled corporation in connection with a section 368(a)(1)(D) reorganization (D reorganization) that immediately precedes the section 355 distribution (together with a D reorganization, a D/355 distribution). §1.312-10(a). If a section 355 distribution is not preceded by a D reorganization, the earnings and profits of the controlled corporation are at least equal to the amount of the reduction in the distributing corporation's earnings and profits. §1.312-10(b). It is likely that this rule was included to prevent taxpayers from using a section 355 distribution as a device to facilitate a bailout of earnings and profits through the controlled corporation. (The §1.312-10 rules are derived from the Senate's directions to the IRS and Treasury in implementing the regulatory authority in section 312(h); the Senate Report does not, however, explain its reasons for these rules. Senate Finance Committee, Report on H.R. 8300 (1954), at 249.)

The application of the §1.312-10 rules to foreign divisive transactions implicates the Code's international provisions because earnings and profits are moving in the cross-border context and because the earnings and profits of controlled foreign corporations are being adjusted. In transactions involving a domestic distributing corporation and a foreign controlled corporation, the foreign controlled corporation may succeed to earnings and profits of the domestic distributing corporation. A post-transaction distribution by the foreign controlled corporation out of earnings and profits it receives from the domestic distributing corporation is generally eligible for the dividends received deduction and treated as U.S. source income under sections 243(e) and 861(a)(2)(C). This treatment is appropriate because the earnings and profits have already been subject to U.S. corporate taxation and should not be subject to a second level of U.S. corporate tax upon repatriation if the earnings and profits would have qualified for the dividends received deduction if distributed before the section 355 distribution. H.R. Rep. No. 2101, at 3 (1960). In addition, such earnings and profits should not increase a domestic distributee's foreign tax credit limitation under section 904.

In circumstances where the foreign controlled corporation makes a post-transaction distribution to foreign shareholders, the foreign divisive transaction should not alter the character of earnings and profits allocated from the domestic distributing corporation. Otherwise, the section 355 distribution may serve as a vehicle to avoid U.S. tax, including U.S. withholding tax. Accordingly, the proposed regulations provide that a post-transaction distribution out of earnings and profits of a distributing corporation that carry over to a foreign controlled corporation is generally treated as a U.S. source dividend for purposes of Chapter 3 of subtitle A of the Code. See *Georday Enterprises v. Commissioner*, 126 F.2d 384 (4th Cir. 1942).

Foreign divisive transactions involving a foreign distributing corporation and a domestic controlled corporation are similar to inbound nonrecognition transactions to the extent the domestic controlled corporation receives assets of a foreign corporation. Current regulations under §1.367(b)-3 require direct and indirect U.S. shareholders in an inbound asset reorganization to include an all earnings and profits amount in income in order to ensure, in part, that the bases of assets repatriated to the United States reflect an after-tax amount. Section 1.367(b)-3(d) and proposed §1.367(b)-3(f) provide further rules regarding the carryover of earnings and profits and foreign income taxes from a foreign corporation to a domestic corporation. Those rules should also apply to a section 355 distribution involving a foreign distributing corporation and a domestic controlled corporation. These transactions also implicate the current rules under §1.367(b)-5, because a reduction in a foreign distributing corporation's earnings and profits can directly affect the post-transaction application of section 1248 with respect to U.S. shareholders of the distributing corporation.

Foreign divisive transactions involving a foreign distributing corporation and a foreign controlled corporation raise issues similar to those raised in the context of a foreign 381 transaction described in §1.367(b)-7, to the extent the controlled corporation succeeds to earnings and profits (and related foreign income taxes) of the distributing corporation. Accordingly, the proposed regulations adopt the principles of §1.367(b)-7 to determine the manner in which the foreign controlled corporation succeeds to the earnings and profits (and related foreign income taxes) of a foreign distributing corporation. These transactions also implicate the §1.367(b)-5 rules concerning diminutions in U.S. shareholders' section 1248 amounts.

The proposed regulations under §1.367(b)-8 balance the §1.312-10 rules and policies with the interests and concerns of the relevant international provisions of the Code. However, the IRS and Treasury recognize that the mechanics of §1.312-10 as applied in the international context can be cumbersome and complex. The IRS and Treasury solicit comments as to whether the mechanical difficulties of applying the section 312 rules in the cross-border context outweigh the benefits and, if so, whether there are simpler alternative regimes that would address the international policy concerns without compromising the Subchapter C policies embodied in §1.312-10.

Details of Provisions

A. *Prop. Reg. §1.367(b)-1*

The proposed regulations supplement the current §1.367(b)-1 notice requirements in consideration of the transactions addressed by proposed §§1.367(b)-7 and 1.367(b)-8. Accordingly, foreign surviving corporations described in proposed §1.367(b)-7 and distributing and controlled corporations involved in transactions described in proposed §1.367(b)-8 are included within the scope of the §1.367(b)-1 notice requirement.

B. *Prop. Reg. §1.367(b)-3*

The proposed regulations address the carryover of net operating loss and capital loss carryovers, and earnings and profits that are not included in income as an all earnings and profits amount (or a deficit in earnings and profits). The proposed regulations generally provide that these tax attributes do not carry over from a foreign acquired corporation to a domestic acquiring corporation unless they are effectively connected to a U.S. trade or business (or attributable to a permanent establishment, in the context of a relevant U.S. income tax treaty).

The limitations on the carryover of these attributes prevent inappropriate or anomalous results. For example, net operating loss and capital loss carryovers are eligible to carry over from a foreign acquired corporation to a domestic acquiring corporation only to the extent the underlying deductions or losses were allowable under Chapter 1 of subtitle A of the Code. Thus, only a net operating loss or capital loss carryover that is effectively connected to a U.S. trade or business (or attributable to a permanent establishment) may carry over. Inappropriate or anomalous results are thus avoided because losses incurred by a foreign acquired corporation outside the U.S. taxing jurisdiction should not be available to offset the future U.S. tax liability of a domestic acquiring corporation. Otherwise, a taxpayer would have an incentive to import losses into the United States in order to shelter future income from U.S. tax.

The carryover of earnings and profits (or a deficit in earnings and profits) of the foreign acquired corporation can create similarly inappropriate results. For example, the policies underlying the section 243(a) dividends received deduction are not present with respect to a subsequent distribution by the domestic acquiring corporation out of earnings and profits accumulated by the foreign acquired corporation because those earnings and profits are not generally subject to a U.S. corporate level of tax. On the other hand, if the foreign acquired corporation has PTI, those earnings should not be taxed again when distributed to U.S. shareholders to whom the PTI is attributable regardless of whether or not the U.S. shareholder is eligible for the dividends received deduction. A deficit in earnings and profits can also be used to avoid tax, such as in the case of a foreign shareholder of a domestic acquiring corporation that imports a deficit and therefore is not subject to U.S. withholding tax on subsequent corporate distributions.

As a result of the issues raised by a carryover of earnings and profits and given that §1.367(b)-3 already requires U.S. shareholders to include in income as a deemed dividend the all earnings and profits amount, the proposed regulations provide that earnings and profits (or deficit in earnings and profits) of the foreign acquired corporation do not carry over to the domestic acquiring corporation except to the extent effectively connected to a U.S. trade or business (or attributable to a permanent establishment, in the context of a relevant U.S. income tax treaty).

C. Prop. Reg. §1.367(b)-7

Proposed §1.367(b)-7 provides the manner in which a foreign surviving corporation succeeds to and takes into account the earnings and profits and foreign income taxes of a foreign acquiring corporation and a foreign target corporation. The proposed regulation attempts to preserve the character of earnings and profits and foreign income taxes to the extent possible in light of the applicable statutory limitations, as well as the relevant policy and administrative concerns. Compare §1.381(c)(2)-1(a)(3) (ensuring that earnings and profits accumulated before March 1, 1913 retain their character as pre-1913 earnings and profits after a section 381 transaction). Accordingly, the proposed rules provide that, to the extent possible, pooled earnings and profits (and foreign income taxes) remain pooled, earnings and profits (and foreign income taxes) in annual layers remain in annual layers, foreign income taxes trapped before the transaction remain trapped after the transaction, and earnings and profits (and foreign income taxes) remain in the same basket before and after the transaction.

The proposed regulation also respects the section 902 preference for distributing pooled earnings and profits before earnings and profits in annual layers. Accordingly, proposed §1.367(b)-7 provides that a foreign surviving corporation's pooled earnings and profits are distributed first (even though earnings and profits in the annual layers may have been accumulated after earnings and profits in the pool) and annual layers are distributed on a LIFO basis. Similarly, the proposed regulation also incorporates the section 904 preference for distributing pooled earnings and profits eligible for look-through before other pooled earnings and profits.

However, in certain cases, an overriding statutory policy requires that the proposed regulation modify the character of earnings and profits (and related foreign income taxes). For example, if a CFC combines with a non-look-through 10/50 corporation in a foreign 381 transaction and the foreign surviving corporation is a non-look-through 10/50 corporation, dividends paid by the surviving non-look-through 10/50 corporation are required to be separately basketed and do not obtain the benefit of look-through. Thus, earnings and profits of a CFC that would have obtained the benefit of look-through if distributed before the foreign 381 transaction are not eligible for look-through after the transaction. (The loss of look-through in connection with this type of foreign 381 transaction is somewhat ameliorated by a U.S. shareholder's section 1248 amount inclusion under §1.367(b)-4 with respect to earnings and profits that accrued during its holding period.)

Proposed regulation §1.367(b)-7 also provides rules regarding the carryover of deficits in earnings and profits from one foreign corporation to another. The purpose of the hovering deficit rule in the domestic context is to prevent the trafficking of deficits in earnings and profits. Otherwise, a corporation with positive earnings and profits may acquire or be acquired by another corporation with a deficit in earnings and profits and make distributions out of capital rather than earnings and profits.

In transactions involving foreign corporations, similar concerns exist regarding the trafficking of deficits in earnings and profits. The ability to benefit from combining positive and deficit earnings and profits among foreign corporations is different than in the domestic context, however, because of the nature of the foreign tax credit rules. In a reorganization involving two domestic corporations, the hovering deficit rule applies to a corporation with a net accumulated deficit in earnings and profits because the relevant statutory rules do not distinguish among classes of earnings and profits. In contrast, the foreign tax credit rules require further subcategorization of earnings and profits according to the pooling and basketing rules. Because of these distinctions, taxpayers may inappropriately benefit by trafficking in an earnings and profits deficit in a basket, pool, or particular annual layer, even though a corporation may have net positive earnings and profits. Accordingly, the proposed regulations apply the hovering deficit principle to the relevant subcategories of earnings and profits and provide that foreign income taxes related to the deficit are not added to the foreign surviving corporation's foreign income tax accounts until all of the deficit has been offset with post-transaction earnings. (Under proposed §1.367(b)-9 (which is described below), these hovering deficit rules do not apply to F reorganizations and foreign 381 transactions in which either the foreign target corporation or the foreign acquiring corporation is newly created.)

Because the treatment of distributions by a foreign surviving corporation depends on whether it is a look-through corporation, a non-look-through 10/50 corporation, or a less-than-10%-U.S.-owned foreign corporation, proposed §1.367(b)-7 is divided according to these categories. The proposed regulation uses the term surviving corporation in order to prevent confusion between the acquiring corporation and the foreign surviving entity. In addition, the term highlights the proposed regulation's general approach that provides the same results regardless of whether a corporation is the ostensible acquiring or target corporation.

1. Look-through surviving corporation

Where the foreign surviving corporation is a look-through corporation, the proposed regulation generally preserves the character of earnings and profits and foreign income taxes. For example, if a CFC (CFC1) acquires the assets of another CFC (CFC2) in a foreign 381 transaction and the surviving corporation is a CFC, then the corporations' positive amounts of earnings and profits and foreign income taxes would carry over in a manner that combines the look-through earnings and profits pools (and related foreign income taxes) of each corporation on a basket-by-basket basis. Thus, for example, CFC1's passive basket would be combined with CFC2's passive basket, CFC1's general basket would be combined with CFC2's general basket, and so forth.

If CFC1 or CFC2 has pooled earnings and profits or foreign income taxes that do not qualify for look-through treatment (non-look-through pool) (for example, earnings and profits accumulated during a period when the corporation was not a CFC and that are subject to a separate 10/50 limitation), such earnings and profits and foreign income taxes would be distributed only after all of the look-through earnings and profits pool has been distributed. This rule is consistent with the ordering rule in Prop. Reg. §1.904-4(g)(3)(iii), which provides that when a 10/50 corporation becomes a CFC, pooled earnings and profits accumulated and foreign income taxes paid or accrued while the corporation is a CFC are distributed before pooled earnings and profits accumulated and foreign income taxes paid or accrued while the corporation was a 10/50 corporation. (If the foreign surviving corporation is instead a look-through 10/50 corporation, this rule is also consistent with the earnings and profits in the look-through pool being distributed before earnings and profits in the non-look-through pool.)

When earnings and profits from the non-look-through pool are distributed, the earnings and profits will be distributed pro rata out of the non-look-through pools of CFC1 and CFC2 (if any) and placed in two separate baskets under section 904(d)(1)(E). This preserves the character of the earnings and profits and related foreign income taxes and is consistent with the policy of section 904(d)(1)(E) to maintain separate baskets for each 10/50 corporation. After 2003, these earnings and profits will continue to be distributed pro rata from separate non-look-through pools but will be combined into a single 10/50 basket in the hands of the distributee. Maintaining separate pools prevents the refreshing of foreign income taxes that would have been trapped had the foreign 381 transaction not occurred. (The same rules apply in the case of a foreign surviving corporation that is a look-through 10/50 corporation.)

If CFC1 or CFC2 has pre-1987 accumulated profits (i.e., annual layers of earnings and profits) or foreign income taxes, then those earnings and profits are distributed only after the distribution of all pooled earnings and profits and taxes, regardless of whether those earnings and profits may have been accumulated after the pooled earnings and profits of the other corporation. Such earnings and profits are distributed on a LIFO basis and pro rata out of the respective corporation's annual layers if both companies have earnings and profits in the same year that are treated as pre-1987 accumulated profits and foreign income taxes. This rule respects two international policies. First, pooled earnings and profits are distributed before earnings and profits in annual layers. Second, earnings and profits in annual layers should not be pooled unless they are distributed to an upper-tier entity. Compare § 1.902-1(a)(8)(ii) (providing that distributions out of pre-1987 earnings and profits by a lower-tier corporation are included in the post-1986 earnings and profits of an upper-tier corporation). This rule is also consistent with the section 902 rule that traps foreign income taxes in annual layers in which there are no earnings and profits.

These results preserve the character of earnings and profits and taxes because pooled earnings and profits and taxes remain pooled, earnings and profits and taxes retain the same character under the look-through provisions, and foreign income taxes that were trapped before the foreign 381 transaction remain trapped. The rules are also consistent with concerns about limiting the administrative burden of requiring taxpayers to recreate tax histories.

Because of the foreign tax credit considerations presented by foreign 381 transactions, § 1.367(b)-7 applies the hovering deficit rule to subcategories of earnings and profits. Thus, deficits in the look-through pool, non-look-through pool, and net deficits in annual layers can offset only future earnings and profits of the foreign surviving corporation. In addition, a hovering deficit cannot be used to reduce current earnings and profits of the foreign surviving corporation and, as a result, does not reduce subpart F income. Foreign income taxes related to a hovering deficit do not enter the foreign income tax accounts of the surviving corporation until the entire hovering deficit offsets post-transaction earnings and profits. However, foreign income taxes related to the post-transaction earnings that are offset by the hovering deficit immediately enter the foreign income tax accounts of the foreign surviving corporation.

2. Non-look-through 10/50 surviving corporation

The proposed regulation's rules with respect to a non-look-through 10/50 corporation apply if the foreign surviving corporation is a 10/50 corporation before 2003. The principal statutory limitation of a non-look-through 10/50 corporation is that a dividend distribution is not eligible for look-through treatment and is instead separately basketed for each 10/50 corporation. As a result, earnings and profits of an acquiring or target corporation that would have been eligible for look-through (assuming the corporation qualified under the look-through rule) if distributed before the foreign 381 transaction lose their look-through character after the transaction.

For example, suppose a CFC combines with a non-look-through 10/50 corporation in a foreign 381 transaction in 2001 and the surviving entity is a non-look-through 10/50 corporation. Prior to the transaction, the CFC maintained earnings and profits and foreign income tax accounts expecting that the look-through rules would apply on a distribution of earnings and profits to U.S. shareholders. However, after the foreign 381 transaction, section 904(d)(1)(E) requires that a distribution from the surviving 10/50 corporation will be deemed to be paid out of a single pool of earnings and profits that will be separately basketed. In order to address the carryover of attributes to a non-look-through 10/50 corporation in a manner consistent with section 904(d)(1)(E), the proposed regulations combine the net positive earnings and profits and foreign income taxes in the respective pools of the acquiring and target corporations. (Thus, the separate baskets of pooled earnings and profits and foreign income taxes of the CFC would be netted into a single pool along with the non-look-through 10/50 corporation's pooled earnings and profits and foreign income taxes.)

Annual layers of the acquiring and target corporations are carried over to the foreign surviving corporation under the same rules as described above with respect to look-through corporations. Hovering deficit rules similar to those described with respect to a look-through corporation's non-look-through pool and annual layers also apply to surviving non-look-through 10/50 corporations.

Look-through treatment of earnings and profits and foreign income taxes does not re-emerge if the corporation later becomes a look-through corporation. For example, if the surviving non-look-through 10/50 corporation becomes a CFC, all of the earnings and profits and foreign income taxes of the surviving non-look-through 10/50 corporation remain as earnings and profits to which the look-through rules do not apply. Look-through only applies to earnings and profits accumulated after the corporation becomes a CFC. The IRS and Treasury believe that this rule is appropriate because of the administrative difficulties posed by recreating tax histories. In addition, earnings and profits and foreign income taxes of a CFC accumulated during a U.S. shareholder's holding period are generally deemed distributed (and the look-through rules apply) if a U.S. shareholder includes a section 1248 amount in income under § 1.367(b)-4 in connection with the foreign 381 transaction.

3. Less-than-10%-U.S.-owned foreign surviving corporation

Proposed § 1.367(b)-7 also determines the manner in which earnings and profits and foreign income taxes of the acquiring and target corporation are combined if the foreign surviving corporation is a less-than-10%-U.S.-owned foreign corporation. Generally, rules similar to the rules provided for annual layers of look-through corporations and non-look-through 10/50 corporations apply with respect to the annual layers of the acquiring and target corporation, but the rules take into account the possibility that one of the corporations may have been a CFC or 10/50 corporation immediately prior to the foreign 381 transaction.

If either the acquiring or target corporation is a CFC or a 10/50 corporation, its pooled earnings and profits and foreign income taxes are treated as earnings and profits and foreign income taxes accumulated in the annual layer of the applicable corporation immediately before the foreign 381 transaction. For example, suppose a less-than-10%-U.S.-owned foreign corporation combines with a 10/50 corporation and the foreign surviving corporation is a less-than-10%-U.S.-owned foreign corporation. The foreign surviving corporation is an entity that has never been required to pool earnings and profits and foreign income taxes under section 902(c)(3). Accordingly, distributions from the foreign surviving corporation are out of annual layers on a LIFO basis. Rather than recreating the tax history of the acquired 10/50 corporation for each year, the proposed regulation places all pooled earnings and profits and foreign income taxes of the 10/50 corporation into a single annual layer that closes immediately before the foreign 381 transaction. This rule is intended to ameliorate administrative burdens while respecting the policy that earnings and profits and foreign income taxes are distributed from annual layers for a less-than-10%-U.S.-owned foreign corporation. Because of concerns about neutrality, the same result applies regardless of whether the 10/50 corporation is the ostensible acquiring or target corporation.

If the surviving less-than-10%-U.S.-owned foreign corporation later becomes a non-look-through 10/50 corporation or a look-through corporation, earnings and profits and foreign income taxes that were pooled or obtained the benefit of look-through prior to the foreign 381 transaction are not recreated. Instead, those earnings and profits and foreign income taxes remain as earnings and profits accumulated and foreign income taxes paid or deemed paid while the corporation was a less-than-10%-U.S.-owned foreign corporation. As in the case of a surviving non-look-through 10/50 corporation that later becomes a look-through corporation, this rule is provided because of administrative issues associated with recreating tax histories. In addition, earnings and profits and foreign income taxes of a CFC accumulated during a shareholder's holding period generally would have been deemed distributed (and the look-through rules would have applied) if the shareholder was required to include a section 1248 amount in income under § 1.367(b)-4 in connection with the foreign 381 transaction.

D. Prop. Reg. § 1.367(b)-8

Section 1.367(b)-8 provides rules applicable to foreign divisive transactions. The regulation is divided into four sections. Section 1.367(b)-8(b) provides rules that are generally applicable to foreign divisive transactions. The other three sections describe the application of the general rules to specific situations. Section 1.367(b)-8(c) applies to a distribution by a domestic distributing corporation of the stock of a foreign controlled corporation, §1.367(b)-8(d) applies to a distribution by a foreign distributing corporation of the stock of a domestic controlled corporation, and §1.367(b)-8(e) applies to a distribution by a foreign distributing corporation of the stock of a foreign controlled corporation.

1. General rules applicable to foreign divisive transactions

Section 1.367(b)-8(b) provides that the rules of §1.312-10 generally apply to determine the allocation of earnings and profits between a distributing and a controlled corporation, as well as to determine the reduction in the earnings and profits of a distributing corporation. The rules of §1.312-10 are, however, subject to certain modifications.

In a D/355 distribution involving a controlled corporation that is newly created as part of the transaction, §1.312-10(a) allocates the pre-transaction earnings and profits of the distributing corporation between the distributing and controlled corporations based upon a comparison of the fair market values of the assets received by the controlled corporation and the assets retained by the distributing corporation after the D reorganization. Section 1.312-10(a) provides that, "in a proper case," this allocation should be based on the relative net bases of the assets transferred and retained by the distributing corporation, or based on another "appropriate" method.

The proposed regulations generally adopt the rule of §1.312-10(a), except that the allocation is based upon relative net adjusted bases of assets transferred and retained in all cases. This rule reflects the view that net basis is the most accurate measure of the appropriate amount of earnings and profits that should be allocated to the assets transferred by a distributing corporation in the D reorganization. For example, in cases where the controlled corporation recognizes gain on a later sale or distribution of appreciated property that it receives from the distributing corporation an allocation based upon relative bases prevents a misallocation of earnings and profits to the controlled corporation.

In a section 355 distribution that is not preceded by a D reorganization, §1.312-10(b) provides that the earnings and profits of the distributing corporation are decreased by an amount equal to the lesser of (i) the amount by which the earnings and profits of the distributing corporation would have been decreased if it had transferred the stock of the controlled corporation to a new corporation in a D/355 distribution, and (ii) the net worth of the controlled corporation. For this purpose, net worth is defined as "the sum of the bases of all of the properties plus cash minus all liabilities." If "the earnings and profits of the controlled corporation immediately before the transaction are less than the amount of the decrease in earnings and profits of the distributing corporation . . . the earnings and profits of the controlled corporation, immediately after the transaction, shall be equal to the amount of such decrease. If the earnings and profits of the controlled corporation immediately before the transaction are more than the amount of the decrease in the earnings and profits of the distributing corporation, they shall remain the same."

Section 1.312-10(b) reflects the principle that a pro rata portion of a distributing corporation's earnings and profits should be reduced to account for the distribution of the controlled corporation. In addition, the requirement that the earnings and profits of the controlled corporation at least equal the reduction in the distributing corporation's earnings and profits appears intended to prevent a bailout of earnings and profits through the controlled corporation, while preventing the potential double counting of earnings and profits in situations where the distributing corporation did not organize the controlled corporation.

In consideration of the complexities raised by the cross-border application of the §1.312-10(b) adjustment to the controlled corporation's earnings and profits, taken together with the current rules that prevent the potential bailout of earnings and profits in the international context (such as the §1.367(b)-5 requirement that a shareholder include in income a reduction in its section 1248 amount), the IRS and Treasury have concluded that the §1.312-10(b) rules should be modified when applied to section 367(b) transactions. Accordingly, the proposed regulations provide that the earnings and profits of the distributing corporation are decreased in an amount equal to the amount by which the earnings and profits of the distributing corporation would have been decreased if it had transferred the stock of the controlled corporation to a new corporation in a D/355 distribution. However, the earnings and profits of the controlled corporation are not increased or replaced. The reduction in earnings and profits (and related foreign income taxes) of the distributing corporation disappears unless otherwise included in income, such as under §1.367(b)-5.

Section 1.312-10 does not specifically address the allocation and reduction of earnings and profits in connection with a D/355 distribution that involves a preexisting controlled corporation. The proposed regulations provide that, in such a case, the distributing corporation's earnings and profits are reduced in a manner that incorporates both the rules applicable to a D/355 distribution with a newly created controlled corporation and a section 355 distribution that is not preceded by a D reorganization. The rule thus accounts for a decrease in earnings and profits attributable to assets transferred to the controlled corporation as part of the D reorganization as well as a decrease in earnings and profits attributable to the distribution of stock of a preexisting controlled corporation (without regard to the D reorganization). The controlled corporation succeeds only to those earnings and profits allocable to the property it receives in the D reorganization.

In consideration of the international provisions' distinctions among classes and categories of earnings and profits, proposed §1.367(b)-8(b) specifically addresses the determination of which earnings and profits of the distributing corporation are affected by a foreign divisive transaction. The proposed regulation provides that an allocation or reduction in earnings and profits shall generally be pro rata out of a cross-section of the distributing corporation's tax history (except to the extent it is included in income as a deemed dividend such as under §1.367(b)-3 or §1.367(b)-5). This rule determines the earnings and profits (and related foreign income taxes, where applicable) that remain in the distributing corporation after the transaction as well as any earnings and profits (and related foreign income taxes, where applicable) to which the controlled corporation succeeds in a D reorganization.

The proposed §1.367(b)-8(b) cross-section rule decreases the earnings and profits of a distributing corporation without regard to the type of income generated by the assets of the controlled corporation. This is consistent with the general assumption in §1.312-10 and the proposed regulations that the earnings and profits of the distributing corporation should be decreased proportionately to reflect the transfer or distribution of assets, rather than by some other measure, such as by determining the earnings and profits attributable to the income generated by assets transferred or distributed (a tracing model) or by decreasing most recently accumulated earnings and profits to the extent of assets transferred or distributed (a dividend model).

2. Branch profits tax considerations

Notwithstanding the above-described rules, the proposed regulations provide that an allocation or reduction in a distributing corporation's earnings and profits shall not reduce the distributing corporation's effectively connected earnings and profits or non-previously taxed accumulated effectively connected earnings and profits, as defined in the branch profits rule in section 884 (branch earnings). Both a domestic or foreign distributing corporation can potentially have branch earnings that are subject to the branch profits tax.

In the case of a foreign divisive transaction that does not include a D reorganization, a U.S. branch of a foreign distributing corporation would be retained by the foreign distributing corporation. Accordingly, §1.367(b)-8 should not reduce the foreign distributing corporation's branch earnings because such a reduction would improperly decrease the earnings subject to the branch profits tax upon the section 355 distribution (which would trigger the branch profits tax under section 884). The same issues arise in the case of a D/355 distribution in which a foreign distributing corporation transfers the assets that are not part of a U.S. branch to a controlled corporation. The IRS and Treasury do not believe that it is appropriate to reduce the earnings that could give rise to a subsequent branch profits tax under these circumstances.

Different issues arise in a foreign divisive transaction in which a foreign distributing corporation transfers the assets of a U.S. branch to a controlled corporation as part of a D/355 distribution. While the branch profits rules permit a deferral of the branch profits tax in certain instances (by allowing branch earnings to be allocated to the domestic transferee in proportion to the assets transferred when a branch is incorporated in a section 351 exchange in a domestic corporation (see §1.884-2T(d)(1)), the branch profits tax is triggered in any event if stock of the incorporated branch is later distributed to its shareholders. See §1.884-2T(d)(5). Accordingly, because foreign divisive transactions include a section 355 distribution immediately following the D reorganization, it would be unnecessary and inappropriate to attribute branch earnings to a domestic controlled corporation under proposed §1.367(b)-8.

Similar branch profits issues can arise with respect to a domestic distributing corporation. While branch earnings are accumulated by a foreign corporation, such earnings may have been carried over to a domestic corporation in a prior section 351 or 381 transaction. See §1.884-2T(c)(4). Accordingly, the proposed regulations treat domestic distributing corporation in the same manner as foreign distributing corporations with respect to branch earnings.

3. Domestic corporation distributes stock of a foreign corporation

In foreign divisive transactions involving a domestic distributing corporation and a foreign controlled corporation, the foreign controlled corporation may succeed to earnings and profits of the domestic distributing corporation. The regulations provide that sections 243(e) and 861(a)(2)(C) apply to earnings and profits allocated to the foreign controlled corporation that were accumulated by a domestic corporation. In addition, a post-transaction distribution out of earnings and profits allocated to the foreign controlled corporation is generally treated as a U.S. source dividend under section 904(g) and for purposes of Chapter 3 of subtitle A of the Code. See *Georday Enterprises v. Commissioner*, 126 F.2d 384 (4th Cir. 1942).

4. Foreign corporation distributes stock of a domestic corporation

In foreign divisive transactions involving a foreign distributing corporation and a domestic controlled corporation, two issues arise in determining the appropriate reduction in the foreign distributing corporation's earnings and profits and its effects on the earnings and profits of the domestic controlled corporation. First, it should be determined whether it is appropriate to reduce PTI of the foreign distributing corporation and, if so, in what manner (e.g., if the foreign distributing corporation has earnings and profits that are PTI and not PTI, should the reduction in earnings and profits be out of PTI first, last, pro rata, or depending on the identity of the controlled corporation's shareholders). As in the case of §1.367(b)-7, §1.367(b)-8 reserves on PTI issues, and the IRS and Treasury solicit comments with respect to the appropriate treatment of these amounts.

Second, a domestic corporation succeeds to the earnings and profits of a foreign corporation if the section 355 distribution is preceded by a D reorganization. Because earnings and profits are allocable from foreign corporate solution to U.S. corporate solution, U.S. shareholders are required to include in income the all earnings and profits amount attributable to earnings and profits that carry over to the controlled corporation. The proposed regulations provide rules that coordinate the proposed §1.367(b)-8 and the current §1.367(b)-3 regimes. The regulations, however, reserve with respect to the treatment of U.S. persons that own foreign distributing corporation stock after a non pro rata distribution. The IRS and Treasury invite comments as to whether U.S. shareholders should have an all earnings and profits amount inclusion in connection with a non pro rata foreign divisive transaction in which they do not receive stock of the domestic controlled corporation.

5. Foreign corporation distributes stock of a foreign corporation

In foreign divisive transactions involving a foreign distributing corporation and a foreign controlled corporation, the foreign controlled corporation may succeed to earnings and profits of the foreign distributing corporation. Because such earnings and profits are allocated from one foreign corporation to another foreign corporation, the transaction raises issues similar to those in a foreign 381 transaction. Accordingly, the proposed regulations adopt and apply the principles in proposed regulation §1.367(b)-7 to these transactions.

E. Prop. Reg. §1.367(b)-9

Proposed §1.367(b)-9 provides special rules applicable to foreign-to-foreign F reorganizations and foreign 381 transactions in which either the foreign target corporation or the foreign acquiring corporation is newly created. Proposed §1.367(b)-9 also applies to foreign divisive transactions that involve a foreign distributing and a foreign controlled corporation, either of which is newly created.

Under proposed §1.367(b)-9, a foreign surviving corporation succeeds to earnings and profits, deficits in earnings and profits, and foreign income taxes without regard to the proposed §1.367(b)-7 hovering deficit rules. See section 1.381(b)-1(a)(2) (providing an analogous rule with respect to domestic F reorganizations).

This rule prevents inappropriate tax consequences. For example, under the generally applicable hovering deficit rules, a foreign corporation with significant deficits in earnings and profits could combine with a newly created foreign corporation and thereafter distribute dividends (along with deemed paid foreign income taxes under section 902), despite the presence of a significant deficit that would have precluded a dividend distribution before the transaction. Proposed §1.367(b)-7 provides the Commissioner discretion to apply the principles of proposed §1.367(b)-9 to circumstances where a principal purpose of the foreign 381 transaction is to affirmatively use the hovering deficit rule in order to gain a tax benefit.

Proposed Effective Dates

These regulations are proposed to apply to section 367(b) exchanges that occur on or after 30 days after these regulations are published as final regulations in the Federal Register.

Special Analyses

It has been determined that this notice of proposed rulemaking is not a significant regulatory action as defined in Executive Order 12866. Therefore, a regulatory assessment is not required. It has also been determined that section 553(b) of the Administrative Procedure Act (5 U.S.C. chapter 5) does not apply to these regulations, and because the regulation does not impose a collection of information on small entities, the Regulatory Flexibility Act (5 U.S.C. chapter 6) does not apply.

Comments and Public Hearing

Before these proposed regulations are adopted as final regulations, consideration will be given to any electronic or written comments (a signed original and eight (8) copies) that are submitted timely to the IRS. The IRS and Treasury Department request comments on the clarity of the proposed rules and how they can be made easier to understand. All comments will be available for public inspection and copying.

A public hearing has been scheduled for March 13, 2001, beginning at 10 a.m., in room 7218 of the Internal Revenue Building, 1111 Constitution Avenue, NW., Washington, DC. Due to building security procedures, visitors must enter at the 10th Street entrace, located between Constitution and Pennsylvania Avenues, NW. In addition, all visitors must present photo identification to enter the building. Because of access restrictions, visitors will not be admitted beyond the immediate entrance area more than 15 minutes before the hearing starts. For information about having your name placed on the building access list to attend the hearing, see the "FOR FURTHER INFORMATION CONTACT" section of this preamble.

The rules of 26 CFR 601.601(a)(3) apply to the hearing. Persons who wish to present oral comments at the hearing must submit electronic or written comments and an outline of the topics to be discussed and the time to be devoted to each topic (signed original and eight (8) copies) by

February 20, 2001. A period of 10 minutes will be allotted to each person for making comments. An agenda showing the scheduling of the speakers will be prepared after the deadline for receiving outlines has passed. Copies of the agenda will be available free of charge at the hearing.

Drafting Information

The principal author of these regulations is Anne O'Connell Devereaux, Office of Associate Chief Counsel (International). However, other personnel from the IRS and Treasury Department participated in their development.

[¶ 49,181]   **Proposed Amendments of Regulations (REG-105801-00)**, published in the Federal Register on January 18, 2001.

Straddle rules: Capitalization of interest: Carrying charges: Personal property.—Reg. §§ 1.263(g)-1—1.263(g)-5, clarifying the application of the straddle rules to a variety of financial instruments, are proposed. A public hearing on this proposal is scheduled for May 22, 2001. Proposed amendments of Reg. § 1.1092(d)-1 adopted as Temporary Reg. § 1.1092(d)-1T by T.D. 9635 on 9/4/2013.

AGENCY: Internal Revenue Service (IRS), Treasury.

ACTION: Notice of proposed rulemaking and notice of public hearing.

SUMMARY: This document contains proposed regulations that clarify the application of the straddle rules to a variety of financial instruments. The proposed regulations clarify what constitutes interest and carrying charges and when interest and carrying charges are properly allocable to personal property that is part of a straddle. The proposed regulations also clarify that a taxpayer's obligation under a debt instrument can be a position in personal property that is part of a straddle. The proposed regulations provide guidance to taxpayers that enter into straddle transactions. This document provides notice of a public hearing on these proposed regulations.

DATES: Written and electronic comments and requests to appear and outlines of topics to be discussed at the public hearing scheduled for May 22, 2001, at 10 a.m., must be submitted by May 1, 2001.

ADDRESSES: Send submissions to: CC:M&SP:RU (REG-105801-00), room 5226, Internal Revenue Service, POB 7604, Ben Franklin Station, Washington, DC 20044. Submissions may be hand delivered between the hours of 8 a.m. and 5 p.m. to: CC:M&SP:RU (REG-105801-00), Courier's Desk, Internal Revenue Service, 1111 Constitution Avenue NW., Washington, DC. Alternatively, taxpayers may submit comments electronically via the Internet by submitting comments directly to the IRS Internet site at http://www.irs.gov/tax_regs/regslist.html. The public hearing will be held in the Auditorium, Internal Revenue Building, 1111 Constitution Avenue, NW., Washington, DC.

FOR FURTHER INFORMATION CONTACT: Concerning the proposed regulations, Kenneth Christman (202) 622-3950; concerning submission and delivery of comments and the public hearing, Treena Garrett, (202) 622-7180 (not toll-free numbers).

SUPPLEMENTARY INFORMATION:

Background

Sections 501 and 502 of the Economic Recovery Tax Act of 1981 (Public Law 97-34, 95 Stat. 172) added sections 1092 and 263(g), respectively, to the Internal Revenue Code to address certain deferral and conversion strategies involving economically offsetting positions in actively traded personal property. These economically offsetting positions are called straddles. Section 1092(c)(1).

In general, under section 1092, a taxpayer that realizes a loss on a position in actively traded personal property must defer the recognition of the loss to the extent the taxpayer has unrecognized gain on an economically offsetting position in the property. This deferral rule matches the recognition of loss with the recognition of the economically offsetting income. Section 263(g) addresses interest and carrying charges properly allocable to personal property that is part of a straddle. Under this section, these otherwise deductible expenses are not currently deductible. Instead, they must be capitalized into the basis of the property. By requiring capitalization, section 263(g) prevents: (1) a taxpayer from gaining a timing advantage by accruing deductions associated with carrying the straddle transaction before recognizing income from a position in personal property that is part of the straddle; and (2) the deductions from having a character different from that of the income.

These proposed regulations provide certain rules with respect to the application of section 263(g) and section 1092.

Explanation of Provisions

The proposed regulations consist of § 1.263(g)-1, which provides a general introduction, and §§ 1.263(g)-2, 1.263(g)-3, 1.263(g)-4, and 1.263(g)-5, described below. The proposed regulations also include a new paragraph 1.1092(d)-1(d).

The proposed regulations generally address four issues: (1) the definition of *personal property* as such term is used in section 263(g) (in § 1.263(g)-2); (2) the type of payments that are subject to the capitalization rules of section 263(g) (in § 1.263(g)-3); (3) the operation of the capitalization rules of section 263(g) (in § 1.263(g)-4); and (4) the circumstances under which an issuer's obligation under a debt instrument can be a position in actively traded personal property and, therefore, part of a straddle (in § 1.1092(d)-1(d)). These issues are discussed in more detail below.

Definition of the Term Personal Property for Purposes of Section 263(g)

Section 263(g)(1) requires capitalization of interest and carrying charges properly allocable to personal property that is part of a straddle (as defined in section 1092(c)). Section 1092(d)(1) defines personal property for purposes of section 1092, as personal property of a type that is actively traded. Commentators have suggested that because sections 263(g) and 1092 were enacted at the same time, the term *personal property* as used in section 263(g) should be given the same definition under section 1092(d)(1). This would limit the definition of personal property in section 263(g) to personal property of a type that is actively traded.

Despite this suggestion, the proposed regulations provide that personal property has its common law meaning in section 263(g) for two reasons. First, the definition in section 1092(d)(1) by its terms applies only for purposes of section 1092. Second, the broader, common law interpretation of personal property more closely accords with the purposes of section 263(g). Application of the limited definition in section 1092(d)(1) for purposes of section 263(g) could result in dissimilar tax treatment of economically similar transactions. For example, adoption of the narrower definition would cause section 263(g) to apply to a transaction in which a taxpayer borrows to purchase actively traded personal property that is a part of a straddle but not to a similar transaction in which the taxpayer borrows to purchase a derivative instrument that is not itself actively traded but is a position in actively traded property.

Consequently, proposed § 1.263(g)-2 defines personal property as a property right, whether or not actively traded, other than a right in real property. This definition includes both financial positions that provide substantial rights but do not impose substantial obligations on the holder (e.g., common stock or a purchased option) and executory contracts that impose both rights and obligations on the holder (e.g., notional principal contracts (NPC's) and forward transactions). However, the definition excludes straddles comprised only of financial positions that impose only obligations on the holder (e.g., the obligor's position in a debt instrument or a writer's position in an option).

Payments That Are Subject to the Capitalization Rules of Section 263(g)

Section 263(g)(1) provides for the capitalization of interest and carrying charges. For this purpose, *interest and carrying charges* are collectively defined in section 263(g)(2) as "interest incurred or continued to purchase or carry the personal property" and "all other amounts (including charges to insure, store, or transport) paid or incurred to carry the personal property," less certain types of income from the personal property.

The phrase "incurred or continued to purchase or carry" also appears in section 265(a)(2), which disallows interest expense on indebtedness incurred or continued to purchase or carry tax-exempt debt. Rev. Proc. 72-18 (1972-1 C.B. 740) sets out rules for determining when this standard is met for purposes of section 265(a)(2). Under that revenue procedure, indebtedness issued by a taxpayer that is not a dealer in tax-exempt obligations meets this standard if (1) the proceeds of the indebtedness are directly traceable to the purchase of the tax-exempt obligations, (2) the tax-exempt obligations are used as collateral for the borrowing, or (3) the totality of the facts and circumstances supports a reasonable inference that the purpose of the borrowing was to purchase or carry tax-exempt obligations. In general, the facts-and-circumstances test is met if there is a "sufficiently direct relationship" between the borrowing and the investment in the tax-exempt obligations. Similarly, the proposed regulations provide that a sufficiently direct relationship between indebtedness or other financing and personal property that is part of a straddle exists if payments on the indebtedness or other financing are determined by reference to the value or change in value of the personal property. See § 1.263(g)-3(c).

Section 263(g) also applies to "all other amounts (including charges to insure, store or transport the personal property)" paid or incurred to carry personal property that is part of a straddle. As noted by one commentator, "taxpayers should not be permitted to deduct items incurred in connection with protecting or preserving the value of assets" that are part of a straddle. Therefore, the term, *to carry* in the context of section 263(g) includes the reduction of the risk of holding an asset. Because straddles necessarily involve positions that offset each other, the positions "carry" each other.

Accordingly, under § 1.263(g)-3(b) of the proposed regulations, interest and carrying charges subject to capitalization under section 263(g) include: (I) otherwise deductible payments or accruals (including interest and original issue discount) on indebtedness or other financing issued or continued to purchase or carry personal property that is part of a straddle; (2) otherwise deductible fees or expenses paid or incurred in connection with the taxpayer's acquiring or holding personal property that is part of a straddle, including, but not limited to, fees or expenses incurred to purchase, insure, store, maintain, or transport the personal property; and (3) other otherwise deductible payments or accruals on financial instruments that are part of a straddle or that carry part of a straddle.

Section 263(g) requires capitalization of interest and carrying charges that exceed certain specified income inclusions (allowable offsets) listed in section 263(g)(2)(B). Section 1.263(g)-3(e) sets forth the allowable offsets, including amounts that are receipts or accruals on financial instruments that are part of a straddle or carry part of a straddle. The Treasury Department and the IRS solicit comments regarding whether other amounts should be treated as allowable offsets for purposes of section 263(g).

Operation of the Capitalization Rules of Section 263(g)

Generally, section 263(g) coordinates the character and timing of items of income and loss attributable to a taxpayer's position in a straddle by allocating interest and carrying charges to the capital account of a position in personal property that is part of the straddle. Proposed regulation § 1.263(g)-4 provides a set of allocation rules governing the "capitalization" of interest and carrying charges.

In many cases, certain allocation rules readily suggest themselves.

Congress was aware of "cash and carry" transactions in adopting section 263(g). See H.R. Rep. No. 201, 97th Cong. 1st Sess. 203-04 (1981). In a typical transaction, a taxpayer borrows to purchase personal property and sells the property forward. The debt instrument generates ordinary deductions (interest expense) that precede predictable (and approximately equal) capital gains on the sale of the personal property. Coordination of the amount and timing of income and loss in a cash and carry transaction is achieved under the proposed regulation by allocating the interest expense to the capital account of the personal property. This rule applies to all transactions in which a taxpayer has borrowed to purchase personal property that is part of a straddle.

If the proceeds of a borrowing are not used to purchase personal property, a second allocation rule allocates interest expense to personal property when the personal property collateralizes the borrowing. See Rev. Proc. 72-18, § 3.03 (disallowing interest deduction for debt secured by tax-exempt obligations); Rev. Rul. 78-348 (1978-2 C.B. 95) (applying yield restrictions to investments pledged by person benefitting from tax-exempt bond financing).

A third allocation rule of the proposed regulations allocates interest on indebtedness to personal property when payments on the indebtedness are determined by reference to the value, or change in value, of the personal property that is part of a straddle.

Fees and charges related to the maintenance of the personal property, such as charges to insure, store, or transport the personal property, are allocated to the capital account of that personal property. See S. Rep. No. 144, 97th Cong. 1st Sess. 154 (1981).

In other cases, the appropriate method for allocating capitalized interest and carrying charges is less obvious. This may be true of payments or accruals on a financial instrument, such as a NPC, described in proposed § 1.263(g)-3(d). For example, the proposed rules would apply to a taxpayer that holds stock and enters into an equity swap that is a short position with respect to the stock. In such a case, both the stock and the equity swap may be personal property that is part of a straddle, and payments on the equity swap could be capitalized with respect to the capital account of either the stock or the equity swap. However, it may not be clear how a capitalization rule would apply in conjunction with the rules under § 1.446-3 with respect to payments on NPCs. Accordingly, the proposed rules provide that, in cases to which a specific allocation rule is not applicable, interest and carrying charges will be allocated to personal property that is part of a straddle in the manner that is most appropriate under all the facts and circumstances. Proposed regulations § 1.263(g)-4(c) *Example 7* (relating to a straddle consisting of stock and an equity swap) illustrate one application of this facts and circumstances rule. The Treasury Department and the IRS invite comments and suggestions regarding both the proposed specific allocation rules and the general facts and circumstances allocation rule.

The regulations under section 263(g) are proposed to be effective for expenses paid, incurred, or accrued after the date the regulations are adopted as final for straddles established on or after January 18, 2001. See § 1.263(g)-5.

Obligation Under a Debt Instrument as a Position in Personal Property

If a taxpayer is the obligor under a debt instrument that provides for one or more payments linked to the value of actively traded personal property, the value of the taxpayer's obligation under the debt instrument changes as the value of the referenced property changes. For this reason, the taxpayer's position as obligor under the debt instrument functions as a position in the referenced property.

Some commentators have suggested that a debt instrument (other than one denominated in an actively traded foreign currency) cannot be a position of the obligor in personal property that is part of a straddle. Section 1092(d)(7) provides that an obligor's interest in a nonfunctional-currency-denominated debt instrument is treated under section 1092(d)(2) as a position in the nonfunctional currency. From this, the commentators infer that an obligor's interest in a debt instrument may never be treated as an interest in personal property other than a nonfunctional currency.

However, neither the legislative history nor the express language of section 1092(d)(7) indicates that Congress intended to exclude interests in personal property from the definition of *position* in section 1092(d)(2). A rule that a debt instrument can be a position in currency does not establish that a debt instrument is a position only in currency. This interpretation of section 1092(d)(7) has already been rejected by the IRS and Treasury in § 1.1275-4(b)(9)(vi), which provides that increased interest expense on a contingent payment debt instrument issued by a taxpayer may be a straddle loss subject to section 1092 deferral.

To clarify the definition of *position* under section 1092(d)(2), § 1.1092(d)-1(d) of the proposed regulations explicitly provides that an obligation under a debt instrument may be a position in personal property that is part of a straddle. This provision is proposed to be effective for straddles established on or after January 18, 2001. However, no inference is intended with respect to straddles established prior to January 18, 2001. Thus, in appropriate cases, the IRS may take the position under section 1092(d)(2) that, even in the absence of a regulation, an obligation under a debt instrument was part of a straddle prior to the effective date of § 1.1092(d)-1(d) if the debt instrument functioned economically as an interest in actively traded personal property.

In 1995, the IRS published proposed regulation § 1.1092(d)-(2). See 60 F.R.21482; FI-21-95, 1995-1 C.B. 935. The proposed regulations clarify the circumstances in which common stock may be personal property for the purposes of section 1092. Because proposed regulation § § 1.1092(d)-2 and 1.1092(d)-1(d) address similar issues, the IRS proposes to finalize both regulations simultaneously. The Treasury Department and the IRS, therefore, invite additional comment on proposed § 1.1092(d)-(2).

In addition, in 1985, the Treasury Department and the IRS adopted Temporary Regulation § 1.1092(d)-5T(d), which defines the term *loss* for purposes of § § 1.1092(b)-1T through 1.1092(b)-4T as a loss otherwise allowable under section 165(a). The Treasury Department and the IRS request comments on whether that definition should be expanded to include expenses such as interest and carrying charges or payments on notional principal contracts. If so, how should such a change be coordinated with the proposed regulations in this document?

Special Analyses

It has been determined that this notice of proposed rulemaking is not a significant regulatory action as defined in Executive Order 12866. Therefore, a regulatory assessment is not required. It also has been determined that section 553(b) of the Administrative Procedure Act (5 U.S.C. chapter 5) does not apply to these regulations, and because the regulation does not impose a collection of information on small entities, the Regulatory Flexibility Act (5 U.S.C. chapter 6) does not apply. Pursuant to section 7805(f) of the Internal Revenue Code, this notice of proposed rulemaking will be submitted to the Chief Counsel for Advocacy of the Small Business Administration for comment on its impact on small business.

Comments and Public Hearing

Before these proposed regulations are adopted as final regulations, consideration will be given to any written or electronic comments (a signed original and eight (8) copies, if written) that are submitted timely (in the manner described in the ADDRESSES portion of this preamble) to the IRS. The IRS and Treasury request comments on the clarity of the proposed regulations and how they may be made easier to understand. All comments will be available for public inspection and copying.

A public hearing has been scheduled for May 22, 2001, at 10 a.m. in the Auditorium, Internal Revenue Building, 1111 Constitution Avenue NW., Washington DC. Due to building security procedures, visitors must enter at the 10th Street entrance located between Constitution and Pennsylvania Avenues, NW. In addition, all visitors must present photo identifications to enter the building. Because of access restrictions, visitors will not be admitted beyond the immediate entrance area more than 15 minutes before the hearing starts. For information about having your name placed on the building access list to attend the hearing, see the "FOR FURTHER INFORMATION CONTACT" section of this preamble.

The rules of 26 CFR 601.601(a)(3) apply to the hearing. Persons who wish to present oral comments at the hearing must submit and an outline of the topics to be discussed and the time to be devoted to each topic (signed original and eight (8) copies) by May 1, 2001. A period of 10 minutes will be allotted to each person for making comments. An agenda showing the scheduling of the speakers will be prepared after the deadline for receiving outlines has passed. Copies of the agenda will be available free of charge at the hearing.

Drafting Information

The principal author of these regulations is Kenneth Christman, Office of Associate Chief Counsel (Financial Institutions and Products). However, other personnel from the IRS and Treasury Department participated in their development.

[¶ 49,183]   Proposed Amendments of Regulation (REG-137519-01), published in the Federal Register on November 14, 2001.

Consolidated returns: Applicability of other provisions of law: Non-applicability of Code Sec. 357(c).—Amendments of Reg. § 1.1502-80, relating to the consolidated return regulations dealing with the non-applicability of Code Sec. 357(c) in a consolidated group, are proposed. A public hearing on this proposal is scheduled for March 21, 2002.

AGENCY: Internal Revenue Service (IRS), Treasury.

ACTION: Notice of proposed rule-making and notice of public hearing.

SUMMARY: This document proposes amendments relating to the consolidated return regulations dealing with the non-applicability of section 357(c) in a consolidated group. The proposed amendments clarify that, in certain transfers described in section 351 between members of a consolidated group, a transferee's assumption of certain liabilities described in section 357(c)(3) will not reduce the transferor's basis in the transferee's stock received in the transfer. This document also provides notice of a public hearing on these proposed regulations.

DATES: Written or electronic comments and requests to speak (with outlines of oral comments to be discussed) at the public hearing scheduled for March 21, 2002, must be submitted by February 28, 2002.

ADDRESSES: Send submissions to: CC:ITA:RU (REG-137519-01), room 5226, Internal Revenue Service, POB 7604, Ben Franklin Station, Washington, DC 20044. Submissions may be hand delivered Monday through Friday between the hours of 8 a.m. and 5 p.m. to: CC:ITA:RU (REG-137519-01), Courier's Desk, Internal Revenue Service, 1111 Constitution Avenue, NW., Washington, DC. Alternatively, taxpayers may submit comments electronically via the internet by selecting the "Tax Regs" option on the IRS Home Page, or by submitting comments directly to the IRS internet site at *http://www.irs.ustreas.gov/tax_regs/reglist.html*. The public hearing will be held in room 4718, Internal Revenue Building, 1111 Constitution Avenue, NW., Washington, DC.

FOR FURTHER INFORMATION CONTACT: Concerning the regulations, T. Ian Russell of the Office of Associate Chief Counsel (Corporate), (202) 622-7930; concerning submissions, the hearing, and/or to be placed on the building access list to attend the hearing, Donna M. Poindexter (202-622-7180) (not toll-free numbers).

SUPPLEMENTARY INFORMATION:

Background

Section 357(c)(1) generally provides that, in the case of certain exchanges described in section 351, if the sum of the amount of the liabilities assumed by the transferee corporation exceeds the total of the adjusted basis of the property transferred pursuant to such exchange, then such excess shall be considered as gain from the sale or exchange of a capital asset or of property that is not a capital asset. Section 357(c)(3), however, excludes from the computation of liabilities assumed liabilities the payment of which would give rise to a deduction, provided that the incurrence of such liabilities did not result in the creation of, or an increase in, the basis of any property.

Section 358(a) generally provides that, in the case of an exchange to which section 351 applies, the basis of the property permitted to be received without the recognition of gain or loss is decreased by the amount of any money received by the transferor. For this purpose, under section 358(d)(1), the transferee's assumption of a liability of the transferor is treated as money received by the transferor on the exchange. Section 358(d)(2), however, provides an exception for liabilities excluded under section 357(c)(3).

On August 15, 1994, final regulations (TD 8560) adding paragraph (d) to §1.1502-80 were published in the Federal Register (59 FR 41666). A correcting amendment adding a sentence to the end of paragraph (d) of §1.1502-80 was published in the Federal Register for March 14, 1997 (62 FR 12096). As currently in effect, §1.1502-80(d) provides that "[s]ection 357(c) does not apply to any transaction to which §1.1502-13, §1.1502-13T, §1.1502-14, or §1.1502-14T applies, if it occurs in a consolidated return year beginning on or after January 1, 1995." The example in that regulation contemplates that, to the extent that the transferor does not recognize gain under section 357(c) by reason of the rule of §1.1502-80(d), the transferor's basis in the stock of the transferee that it receives in the exchange is reduced, with the result that an excess loss account may arise.

A concern has been raised that, as currently drafted, §1.1502-80(d) may produce an unintended basis result in certain intragroup transfers described in section 351. In particular, it is possible that one might conclude that, because §1.1502-80(d) provides that section 357(c) does not apply to certain intragroup section 351 exchanges, no liabilities can technically be excluded under section 357(c)(3). If that analysis were correct, in the case of a transfer described in section 351 between members of a consolidated group, the transferor's basis in the stock of the transferee received in the transfer would be reduced by liabilities assumed by the transferee, including those liabilities described in section 357(c)(3) that would not have reduced basis had section 357(c) applied. Assuming the transferor and the transferee are members of the consolidated group at the time the liability does in fact give rise to a deduction on the part of the transferee and is taken into account on the consolidated return, the transferor's basis in the stock of the transferee would be reduced a second time under the principles of §1.1502-32. This duplicated basis reduction, i.e., once at the time of the transfer described in section 351 and again at the time the liability is taken into account by the consolidated group, may ultimately cause the transferor to recognize an amount of gain on the sale of the stock of the transferee that does not clearly reflect income.

Explanation of Provisions

These proposed regulations clarify that, in certain transfers described in section 351 between members of a consolidated group, a transferee's assumption of liabilities described in section 357(c)(3)(A), other than those also described in section 357(c)(3)(B), will not reduce the transferor's basis in the transferee's stock received in the exchange.

Proposed Effective Date

These regulations are proposed to apply to transactions occurring in consolidated return years beginning on or after the date these regulations are published as final regulations in the Federal Register.

Special Analyses

It has been determined that this notice of proposed rulemaking is not a significant regulatory action as defined in Executive Order 12866. Therefore, a regulatory assessment is not required. It is hereby certified that these regulations do not have a significant economic impact on a substantial number of small entities. This certification is based on the fact that these regulations will affect affiliated groups of corporations that have elected to file consolidated returns, which tend to be larger businesses. Therefore, a Regulatory Flexibility Analysis under the Regulatory Flexibility Act (5 U.S.C. chapter 6) is not required. Pursuant to section 7805(f) of the Internal Revenue Code, these regulations will be submitted to the Chief Counsel for Advocacy of the Small Business Administration for comment on their impact on small business.

Comments and Public Hearing

Before these proposed regulations are adopted as final regulations, consideration will be given to any written comments (preferably a signed original and eight (8) copies) that are submitted timely to the IRS. The IRS and Treasury request comments on the clarity of the proposed regulations and how it may be made easier to understand. All comments will be available for public inspection and copying.

A public hearing has been scheduled for March 21, 2002, beginning at 10 a.m., in room 4718, Internal Revenue Building, 1111 Constitution Avenue NW., Washington, DC.

Because of access restrictions, visitors will not be admitted beyond the Internal Revenue Building lobby more than 15 minutes before the hearing starts.

The rules of 26 CFR 601.601(a)(3) apply to the hearing.

Persons that wish to present oral comments at the hearing must submit timely written comments and an outline of the topics to be discussed and the time to be devoted to each topic (preferably a signed original and eight (8) copies) by February 28, 2002.

A period of 10 minutes will be allotted to each person for making comments.

An agenda showing the scheduling of the speakers will be prepared after the deadline for receiving outlines has passed. Copies of the agenda will be available free of charge at the hearing.

Drafting Information

The principal author of these regulations is T. Ian Russell, Office of Associate Chief Counsel (Corporate). However, other personnel from the IRS and Treasury Department participated in their development.

[¶49,187] Proposed Amendments of Regulation (REG-165706-01), published in the Federal Register on April 10, 2002.

Tax-exempt bonds: Refunding issue, definition of.—Amendments of Reg. §1.150-1, modifying to the definition of refunding issue applicable to tax-exempt bonds issued by States and local governments, are proposed. A public hearing on this proposal is scheduled for July 30, 2002.

AGENCY: Internal Revenue Service (IRS), Treasury.

ACTION: Notice of proposed rulemaking and notice of public hearing.

SUMMARY: This document contains proposed regulations on the definition of refunding issue applicable to tax-exempt bonds issued by States and local governments. This document provides a notice of public hearing on these proposed regulations.

DATES: Written or electronic comments must be received by July 9, 2002. Outlines of topics to be discussed at the public hearing scheduled for July 30, 2002, at 10 a.m., must be received by July 9, 2002.

ADDRESSES: Send submissions to: CC:ITA:RU (REG-165706-01), room 5226, Internal Revenue Service, POB 7604, Ben Franklin Station, Washington, DC 20044. Submissions may be hand delivered between the hours of 8 a.m. and 5 p.m. to: CC:ITA:RU (REG-165706-01), courier's desk, Internal Revenue Service, 1111 Constitution Avenue NW., Washington, DC. Alternatively, submissions may be made electronically to the IRS Internet site at www.irs.gov/regs. The public hearing will be held in the Auditorium, Internal Revenue Building, 1111 Constitution Avenue NW., Washington, DC.

FOR FURTHER INFORMATION CONTACT: Concerning the regulations, Michael P. Brewer, (202) 622-3980; concerning submissions and the hearing, Treena Garrett, (202) 622-7190 (not toll-free numbers).

SUPPLEMENTARY INFORMATION:

Background

   Section 150 of the Internal Revenue Code (Code) provides certain definitions and special rules for purposes of applying the tax-exempt bond limitations contained in sections 103 and 141 through 150. On June 18, 1993, final regulations (TD 8476) under section 150 were published in the Federal Register (58 FR 33510). On May 9, 1997, additional final regulations (TD 8718) under section 150 were published in the Federal Register (62 FR 25502). This document proposes to modify the definition of refunding issue under § 1.150-1(d).

Explanation of Provisions

   Section 1.150-1(d) of the current regulations provides a definition of *refunding issue*. In general, a refunding issue is an issue of obligations the proceeds of which are used to pay principal, interest, or redemption price on another issue. The current regulations contain certain exceptions to this general rule. One exception (the *change in obligor exception*) provides that an issue is not a refunding issue to the extent that the obligor of one issue is neither the obligor of the other issue nor a related party with respect to the obligor of the other issue. Another exception (the *six-month exception*) provides that if a person assumes (including taking subject to) obligations of an unrelated party in connection with an asset acquisition (other than a transaction to which section 381(a) applies if the person assuming the obligation is the acquiring corporation within the meaning of section 381(a)), and the assumed issue is refinanced within six-months before or after the date of the debt assumption, the refinancing issue is not treated as a refunding issue.

   Section 1.150-1(b) of the current regulations provides that the term *related party* means, in reference to a governmental unit or a 501(c)(3) organization, any member of the same controlled group. Section 1.150-1(e) of the current regulations provides that the term *controlled group* means a group of entities controlled directly or indirectly by the same entity or group of entities. The determination of control is made on the basis of all the relevant facts and circumstances. One entity or group of entities (the *controlling entity*) generally controls another entity or group of entities (the *controlled entity*) if the controlling entity possesses either of the following rights or powers and the rights or powers are discretionary and non-ministerial: (i) the right or power both to approve and to remove without cause a controlling portion of the governing body of the controlled entity; or (ii) the right or power to require the use of funds or assets of the controlled entity for any purpose of the controlling entity.

   Recently, questions have arisen regarding the application of these provisions with respect to certain issuances of bonds for 501(c)(3) organizations that operate hospital systems. In question generally is whether bonds issued in connection with the combination of two or more 501(c)(3) organizations to refinance outstanding bonds should be characterized as refunding bonds. One question is how the change in obligor exception and the six-month exception should be applied when the obligor of the new issue becomes related to the obligor of the other issue as part of the refinancing transaction. Another question is whether the acquisition by a 501(c)(3) organization of the sole membership interest in another 501(c)(3) organization should be treated as an asset acquisition for purposes of the six-month exception. A third question is what assets should be treated as financed by the new bonds under both the change in obligor exception and the six-month exception.

   In general, the proposed regulations retain the change in obligor exception and the six-month exception, with certain modifications. The proposed regulations clarify that the determination of whether persons are related for purposes of the change in obligor exception and the six-month exception is generally made immediately before the transaction. However, a refinancing issue is a refunding issue under the proposed regulations if the obligor of the refinanced issue (or any person that is related to the obligor of the refinanced issue immediately before the transaction) has or obtains in the transaction the right to appoint the majority of the members of the governing body of the obligor of the refinancing issue (or any person that controls the obligor of the refinancing issue).

   The proposed regulations state that the six-month exception applies to *acquisition transactions*. An acquisition transaction is a transaction is a transaction in which a person acquires from an unrelated party: (i) assets, other than an equity interest in an entity, if the acquirer is treated as acquiring such assets for all Federal income tax purposes; (ii) stock of a corporation with respect to which a valid election under section 338 is made; or (iii) control of a governmental unit or a 501(c)(3) organization through the acquisition of stock, membership interests or otherwise.

   The proposed regulations retain the exclusion under which the six-month exception does not apply to transactions to which section 381(a) applies, and broaden its scope. In particular, under the proposed regulations the exclusion may apply even if the person assuming the obligations is not the acquiring corporation within the meaning of section 381(a) (for example, a transaction in which a corporation assumes the obligations of a target corporation in a transaction to which section 381(a) applies and then contributes all of the assets of the target corporation to a controlled subsidiary). The proposed regulations also extend the application of this rule for section 381(a) transactions to the change in obligor exception.

   The proposed regulations provide two new, additional requirements for purposes of the change in obligor exception and the six-month exception. In certain circumstances where the obligors of the issues are affiliated before the transaction or become affiliated as part of the transaction, the proposed regulations provide that an issue will be treated as a refunding issue unless: (i) the refinanced issue is redeemed on the earliest date on which the issue may be redeemed, and (ii) the new issue is treated as being used to finance the assets that were financed with the proceeds of the refinanced issue. These new requirements are intended to further the Congressional policy against overburdening the tax-exempt bond market, as expressed in sections 148 and 149(d). In particular, they are intended to prevent overburdening in the case of transactions between affiliated persons that contain certain economic characteristics of a refunding.

Proposed Effective Date

   The proposed regulations will apply to bonds sold on or after the date of publication of final regulations in the Federal Register. However, issuers may apply the proposed regulations in whole, but not in part, to any issue that is sold on or after the date the proposed regulations are published in the Federal Register and before the applicability date of the final regulations.

Special Analyses

It has been determined that this notice of proposed rulemaking is not a significant regulatory action as defined in Executive Order 12866. Therefore, a regulatory assessment is not required. It has also been determined that section 553(b) of the Administrative Procedure Act (5 U.S.C. chapter 5) does not apply to these regulations, and because the regulations do not impose a collection of information on small entities, the Regulatory Flexibility Act (5 U.S.C. chapter 6) does not apply. Pursuant to section 7805(f) of the Internal Revenue Code, this notice of proposed rulemaking will be submitted to the Chief Counsel for Advocacy of the Small Business Administration for comment on its impact on small business.

Comments and Public Hearing

Before these proposed regulations are adopted as final regulations, consideration will be given to any written comments that are submitted timely (preferably a signed original and eight copies) to the IRS. All comments will be available for public inspection and copying.

A public hearing has been scheduled for July 30, 2002, at 10:00 a.m. in the Auditorium, Internal Revenue Building, 1111 Constitution Avenue, NW., Washington, DC. Because of access restrictions, visitors will not be admitted beyond the lobby more than 15 minutes before the hearing starts.

The rules of 26 CFR 601.601(a)(3) apply to the hearing.

Persons who wish to present oral comments at the hearing must submit written comments by July 9, 2002, and submit an outline of the topics to be discussed and the amount of time to be devoted to each topic by July 9, 2002.

A period of 10 minutes will be allotted to each person for making comments.

An agenda showing the scheduling of the speakers will be prepared after the deadline for receiving outlines has passed. Copies of the agenda will be available free of charge at the hearing.

Drafting Information

The principal authors of these regulations are Bruce M. Serchuk, Office of Chief Counsel (Tax-exempt and Government Entities), Internal Revenue Service and Stephen J. Watson, Office of Tax Legislative Counsel, Department of the Treasury. However, other personnel from the IRS and Treasury Department participated in their development.

[¶ 49,189] Proposed Amendments of Regulation (REG-122564-02), published in the Federal Register on May 31, 2002.

Consolidated returns: Net operating losses: 5-year carryback period.—Amendments of Reg. §1.1502-21, permitting certain acquiring consolidated groups to elect to waive all or a portion of the pre-acquisition portion of the 5-year carryback period under Code Sec. 172(b)(1)(H) for certain losses attributable to certain acquired members, are proposed.

AGENCY: Internal Revenue Service (IRS), Treasury.

ACTION: Notice of proposed rulemaking.

SUMMARY: This document contains proposed regulations under section 1502 that affect corporations filing consolidated returns. In the Rules and Regulations section of this issue of the Federal Register, the IRS is issuing temporary regulations permitting certain acquiring consolidated groups to elect to waive all or a portion of the pre-acquisition portion of the 5-year carryback period under section 172(b)(1)(H) for certain losses attributable to certain acquired members. The text of those regulations also serves as the text of these proposed regulations.

DATES: Written or electronic comments and requests for a public hearing must be received by July 30, 2002.

ADDRESSES: Send submissions to: CC:ITA:RU, room 5226 (REG-122564-02), Internal Revenue Service, POB 7604, Ben Franklin Station, Washington, DC 20044. Submissions may also be hand delivered Monday through Friday between the hours of 8 a.m. and 5 p.m. to: CC:ITA:RU, room 5226 (REG-122564-02), Courier's Desk, Internal Revenue Service, 1111 Constitution Avenue, NW, Washington, DC. Alternatively, taxpayers may submit comments electronically via the Internet directly to the IRS Internet site at www.irs.gov/regs.

FOR FURTHER INFORMATION CONTACT: Concerning the regulation, Marie C. Milnes-Vasquez (202) 622-7770; concerning submissions and/or requests for a public hearing, Guy Traynor, (202) 622-7180 (not toll-free numbers).

SUPPLEMENTARY INFORMATION:

Paperwork Reduction Act

The collection of information contained in this notice of proposed rulemaking has been submitted to the Office of Management and Budget for review in accordance with the Paperwork Reduction Act of 1995 (44 U.S.C. 3507(d)). Comments on the collection of information should be sent to the **Office of Management and Budget,** Attn: Desk Officer for the Department of the Treasury, Office of Information and Regulatory Affairs, Washington, DC 20503, with copies to the **Internal Revenue Service,** Attn: IRS Reports Clearance Officer, W:CAR:MP:FP:S, Washington, DC 20224. Comments on the collection of information should be received by July 30, 2002. Comments are specifically requested concerning:

Whether the proposed collection of information is necessary for the proper performance of the functions of the Internal Revenue Service, including whether the information will have practical utility;

The accuracy of the estimated burden associated with the proposed collection of information (see below);

How the quality, utility, and clarity of the information to be collected may be enhanced;

How the burden of complying with the proposed collections of information may be minimized, including through the application of automated collection techniques or other forms of information technology; and

Estimates of capital or start-up costs and costs of operation, maintenance, and purchase of service to provide information.

The collection of information in this proposed regulation is in §1.1502-21(b)(3)(ii)(C). This information is required to document the taxpayer's election to relinquish portions of its carryback period for 2001 and 2002 losses attributable to acquired members. The data will be used by the Internal Revenue Service to ensure that taxpayers are preparing their returns in accordance with their elections. The collection of information is required to obtain a benefit. The likely respondents are businesses.

Estimated total annual reporting burden: 1,000 hours.

Estimated average annual burden hours per respondent: 15 minutes.

Estimated number of respondents: 4,000.

Estimated annual frequency of responses: Once.

An agency may not conduct or sponsor, and a person is not required to respond to, a collection of information unless it displays a valid control number assigned by the Office of Management and Budget.

Books or records relating to a collection of information must be retained as long as their contents may become material in the administration of any internal revenue law. Generally, tax returns and tax return information are confidential, as required by 26 U.S.C. 6103.

Background and Explanation

Temporary regulations in the Rules and Regulations section of this issue of the Federal Register amend the Income Tax Regulations (26 CFR part 1) relating to section 1502. The temporary regulations provide rules permitting certain acquiring consolidated groups to elect to waive all or a portion of the pre-acquisition portion of the 5-year carryback period under section 172(b)(1)(H) for certain losses attributable to certain acquired members. The text of those regulations also serves as the text of these proposed regulations. The preamble to the temporary regulations explains the amendments.

Special Analyses

It has been determined that this notice of proposed rulemaking is not a significant regulatory action as defined in Executive Order 12866. Therefore, a regulatory assessment is not required. It is hereby certified that these regulations do not have a significant economic impact on a substantial number of small entities. This certification is based on the fact that these regulations principally affect persons filing consolidated Federal income tax returns. Available data indicates that most consolidated return filers are large companies (not small businesses). Therefore, a Regulatory Flexibility Analysis under the Regulatory Flexibility Act (5 U.S.C. chapter 6) is not required. Pursuant to section 7805(f) of the Internal Revenue Code, these regulations will be submitted to the Chief Counsel for Advocacy of the Small Business Administration for comment on their impact on small business.

Comments and Public Hearing

Before these proposed regulations are adopted as final regulations, consideration will be given to any written comments (a signed original and eight (8) copies) or electronic comments that are timely submitted to the IRS. All comments will be made available for public inspection and copying. A public hearing may be scheduled if requested in writing by any person that timely submits written comments. If a public hearing is scheduled, notice of the date, time, and place for the hearing will be published in the Federal Register.

Drafting Information

The principal author of these proposed regulations is Marie C. Milnes-Vasquez, Office of the Associate Chief Counsel (Corporate). However, other personnel from the IRS and Treasury Department participated in their development.

[¶ 49,190]   Proposed Regulations (REG-103823-99), published in the Federal Register on May 31, 2002.

Depreciation methods: Income forecast method: Cost recovery.—Reg. §§ 1.167(n)-0—1.167(n)-7, relating to deductions available to taxpayers using the income forecast method of depreciation under Code Sec. 167(g), are proposed. A public hearing on this proposal is scheduled for September 4, 2002.

AGENCY: Internal Revenue Service (IRS), Treasury.

ACTION: Notice of proposed rulemaking and notice of public hearing.

SUMMARY: This document contains proposed regulations relating to deductions available to taxpayers using the income forecast method of depreciation under section 167(g). These proposed regulations reflect changes to the law made by the Small Business Job Protection Act of 1996 and the Taxpayer Relief Act of 1997 and affect taxpayers that produce, own, or license films, videos, sound recordings, books, copyrights, patents, and certain other similar properties. This document also provides notice of a public hearing on these regulations.

DATES: Written comments must be received by August 29, 2002. Requests to speak and outlines of topics to be discussed at the public hearing scheduled for September 4, 2002, at 10 a.m., must be received by August 13, 2002.

ADDRESSES: Send submissions to: CC:IT&A:RU (REG-103823-99), room 5226, Internal Revenue Service, POB 7604, Ben Franklin Station, Washington, DC 20044. Submissions may be hand delivered between the hours of 8 a.m. and 5 p.m. to: CC:IT&A:RU (REG-103823-99), Courier's Desk, Internal Revenue Service, 1111 Constitution Avenue NW., Washington, DC. Alternatively, taxpayers may submit comments directly to the IRS Internet site at www.irs.gov/regs. A public hearing will be held in room 2615, Internal Revenue Building, 1111 Constitution Avenue NW., Washington, DC.

FOR FURTHER INFORMATION CONTACT: Concerning the regulations, Bernard P. Harvey, (202) 622-3110; concerning submissions and, the hearing and/or to be placed on the building access list to attend the hearing, Guy R. Traynor, (202) 622-7180 (not toll-free numbers).

SUPPLEMENTARY INFORMATION:

Background

This document contains proposed amendments to 26 CFR part 1 to provide regulations under section 167(g) of the Internal Revenue Code of 1986 (Code). Section 167(g) was added to the Code by the Small Business Job Protection Act of 1996, Public Law 104-188, 1604 (110 Stat. 1755, 1836) (Aug. 20, 1996), and significant amendments were made to the provision by the Taxpayer Relief Act of 1997, Public Law 105-34, 1086 (111 Stat. 788, 957) (Aug. 5, 1997).

Explanation of Provisions

The income forecast method of depreciation has been a permissible method for certain properties since the early 1960s. The income forecast method permits taxpayers to recover the depreciable basis in property over the anticipated income to be earned from the property. The income forecast method is available for interests (including interests involving limited rights in property) in motion picture films, video tapes, sound recordings, copyrights, books, and patents. See Rev. Rul. 60-358 (1960-2 C.B. 68); Rev. Rul. 64-273 (1964-2 C.B. 62); Rev. Rul. 79-285 (1979-2 C.B. 91); and Rev. Rul. 89-62 (1989-1 C.B. 78). The income forecast method is appropriate for these types of property because they possess unique income earning characteristics (for example, the income earning potential of a film may vary as a direct result of the film's popularity) and, therefore, the economic usefulness of these properties cannot be measured adequately by the property's physical condition or by the passage of time. In 1996, Congress enacted statutory income forecast rules to ensure that, for certain properties, the allowances for depreciation appropriately match the basis of an income forecast property with the income derived therefrom. In 1997, Congress placed limitations on the type of property that could be depreciated using the income forecast method.

Computation of Allowances for Depreciation

The proposed regulations provide that, under the income forecast method, a taxpayer's allowance for depreciation for a given year for an income forecast property generally is an amount that bears the same relationship to the depreciable basis of the property that the "current year income" for that year bears to the "forecasted total income" for the property. The proposed regulations provide a revised computation for computing a taxpayer's allowance for depreciation in years when conditions necessitate using a revised forecasted total income that differs from the forecasted total income used in computing depreciation allowances in previous years. Pursuant to these rules, taxpayers may revise forecasted total income and use the revised computation in taxable years after income forecast property is placed in service when information becomes available that indicates that forecasted total income (or revised forecasted total income) previously used to compute income forecast depreciation is inaccurate. Under the revised computation, a taxpayer's allowance for depreciation for the current and all future years for an income forecast property is an amount that bears the same relationship to the unrecovered depreciable basis of the property that the current year income for that year bears to the result obtained by subtracting from revised forecasted total income for the property the amounts of current year income for prior taxable years. Taxpayers are required to use the revised computation in certain situations (discussed in this preamble under the heading of *Income From the Property*).

The proposed regulations also provide several special rules for computing allowances for depreciation under the income forecast method. A special rule applies for certain basis redeterminations whereby an additional "catch up" allowance for depreciation is allowed in the year that basis is redetermined. Under this special rule, the additional depreciation allowance is an amount equal to the cumulative allowances for depreciation that would have been permitted in previous years had the basis redetermination amount been included in basis in the year the property was placed in service. It is intended that this additional allowance will ameliorate the potential back-loading of depreciation deductions that may otherwise occur if the additional amount were taken into account over the remaining income from the property and diminish the amount of look-back interest that may otherwise accrue. This special rule does not apply if the additional basis is treated as separate property.

Pursuant to section 167(g)(1)(C), a taxpayer's adjusted basis in an income forecast property is to be recovered by the end of the tenth taxable year following the taxable year in which the income forecast property is placed in service. The proposed regulations also provide that generally a taxpayer may deduct the adjusted basis in income forecast property in the year income from the property ceases completely and permanently (unless the income cessation arises in connection with the disposition of income forecast property). If additional amounts are paid or incurred with respect to income forecast property in taxable years after either of these special rules is applied, the additional amounts may be deducted when paid or incurred unless such amounts give rise to separate property.

Use of the income forecast method is elected on a property-by-property basis. Once elected, the income forecast method is a method of accounting that may not be changed without the consent of the Commissioner. Modifications to forecasted total income to take into account information that becomes available after the property is placed in service in accordance with these proposed regulations is not a change in a method of accounting requiring the Commissioner's consent.

Section 167(g) sets forth rules for the use of the income forecast method and any similar method. Thus, any method that calculates depreciation based on the flow of income generated by a property (or group of properties) is a "similar method" subject to the requirements of this regulation, including, e.g., the requirement that the look-back method be applied in certain circumstances. Congress did not identify any method that should be treated as a similar method. Treasury and the IRS seek comments on other methods that should be treated as coming within the scope of the term *any similar method*.

Commentators suggested that we specifically approve a method of depreciation based on the application of percentages derived from historical patterns of income for similar properties as a similar method because to do so would simplify the computation of depreciation deductions for large groupings of properties. This suggestion has not been adopted because it is not clear that the historical patterns of income used to apply the suggested approach will accurately reflect the income from any particular income forecast property. Moreover, this suggested approach is not predicated upon the unique income earning characteristics of an income forecast property.

Basis Rules

The cost of producing income forecast property is capitalized and recovered through an allowance for depreciation. The proposed regulations follow the general principles set forth in the regulations under sections 263, 263A, 446, and 461 for determining the basis of income forecast property. Commentators have written to Treasury and the IRS requesting guidance on various issues involving the timing of inclusion in basis of direct costs of income forecast property that are contingent upon the amount of income earned from the property (or other similar factors) and the means by which those costs may be deducted. In accordance with these requests, and in light of section 167(g)(1)(B), the proposed regulations address certain basis issues that are peculiar to the income forecast method of computing depreciation allowances.

Section 263A applies to income forecast property produced by the taxpayer. Section 1.263A-1(c)(2)(ii) provides that an amount required to be capitalized under section 263A may not be included in basis any earlier than the taxable year during which the amount is incurred within the meaning of § 1.446-1(c)(1)(ii). Section 1.446-1(c)(1)(ii) provides that under an accrual method of accounting a liability is incurred, and generally is taken into account for Federal income tax purposes, in the taxable year in which the "all events test" is satisfied. Sections 1.446-1(c)(1)(ii) and 1.461-1(a)(2) set forth the "all events test" which provides that a liability is incurred in the taxable year in which: (1) all the events have occurred that establish the fact of liability; (2) the amount of the liability can be determined with reasonable accuracy; and (3) economic performance has occurred with respect to the liability. Because section 167(g)(1)(B) provides that the adjusted basis of income forecast property depreciated using the income forecast method includes only amounts with respect to which the requirements of section 461(h) are satisfied, these rules are specifically restated in the proposed regulations.

The proposed regulations reiterate that contingent amounts that are either direct costs of the production of income forecast property or indirect costs properly allocable to the production of income forecast property are not added to basis until the taxable year in which the all events test, including the economic performance requirement of section 461(h), is satisfied. Under the proposed rules, the timing of the inclusion of certain of these costs in basis may be affected by § 1.461-1(a)(2)(iii)(A), § 1.461-1(a)(2)(iii)(D) and section 404.

Thus, the proposed regulations provide that contingent basis amounts that are either direct costs of income forecast property or indirect costs properly allocable to income forecast property are generally treated as basis redetermination amounts which increase the basis of income forecast property in the year paid or incurred. As noted above, the proposed regulations provide a special allowance applicable to certain basis redetermination amounts.

Commentators have also suggested that *Transamerica Corp. v. United States*, 999 F.2d 1362 (9th Cir. 1993), supports including contingent amounts in the basis of income forecast property beginning in the year the property is placed in service. In *Transamerica*, the Ninth Circuit interpreted Rev. Rul. 60-358, supra, as it applied in taxable years prior to the enactment of section 167(g), the economic performance requirements of section 461(h), the uniform capitalization requirement of section 263A, and other changes. The Ninth Circuit held that contingent basis amounts may be included in the basis of income forecast property in the year that the property is placed in service so long as the forecasted total income used in the computation of depreciation under the income forecast method includes an amount of income from the property sufficient to indicate that the contingency will be satisfied. Commentators urge the continuing application of the *Transamerica* approach because this approach matches most closely the costs of creating an income forecast property with the income earned therefrom. Treasury and the IRS recognize that it may appear to be reasonable to include estimated amounts in the basis of income forecast property when the operation of the income forecast formula requires the use of estimated amounts in the forecasts of income that are used to determine the amount of income forecast depreciation, particularly where the income forecasts indicate that the contingencies will be resolved, and resolved relatively quickly, after the property is placed in service. Treasury and the IRS also recognize that the historic operation of the income forecast formula deters taxpayers from increasing their forecast of income in order to increase the contingent basis amounts includible in the basis of income forecast property because the increases in forecasted total income operate to increase the denominator of the income forecast formula and thus diminish the amount of depreciation of the income forecast property. This deterrent effect operates in most (but not all) situations to prevent the cumulative amount of income forecast depreciation deductions in any given taxable year from exceeding the total amount actually incurred in any given taxable year, which is the primary concern with the inclusion of contingent amounts in basis. However, because Congress specifically provided in section 167(g)(1)(B) that the adjusted basis of income forecast property includes only those amounts which satisfy the requirements of section 461(h) and because all events that establish the fact of the liability for contingent amounts have not occurred, the proposed regulations do not follow the *Transamerica* approach.

Commentators have also argued that *Associated Patentees, Inc. v. Commissioner*, 4 T.C. 979 (1945), supports an immediate deduction for contingent basis amounts arising from the provision of either property or services in the production of income forecast property that are paid or incurred in years after the year in which income forecast property is placed in service. The proposed regulations do not adopt this interpretation of *Associated Patentees* because providing a more favorable cost recovery rule for contingent basis amounts than for fixed amounts would create an unwarranted incentive for characterizing costs as contingent amounts. Contingent basis amounts arising from the provision of either property or services in the production of income forecast property must be capitalized into the basis of income forecast property in accordance with § 1.263A-1(e).

Salvage Value

The proposed regulations do not provide that the basis upon which depreciation is computed under the income forecast method is reduced for salvage value. The unique statutory scheme Congress adopted for income forecast property requires this departure from the rules generally applicable to property depreciated under section 167, and from the provisions of Rev. Rul. 60-358, supra, which had governed income forecast depreciation prior to the enactment of section 167(g). Based on the provisions of section 167(g), Congress intended that taxpayers be able to recover their entire basis in income forecast property within the period beginning with the year income forecast property is placed in service and ending with the 10th taxable year after the year the property is placed in service and that basis be recovered over the total income earned in connection with the property within that same time frame.

Section 167(g)(1)(C) requires taxpayers to recover the adjusted basis of income forecast property as of the beginning of the 10th taxable year after the property is placed in service as an allowance for depreciation in such year. The term *adjusted basis* refers to the basis of property for purposes of determining gain or loss, which is determined generally by adjusting the cost or other basis in property prescribed by section 1012 by the adjustments required by section 1016. See § 1.1011-1. The use of this term in section 167(g)(1)(C) indicates that Congress intended that the entire basis of an income forecast property be recovered within the period beginning with the year income forecast property is placed in service and ending with the 10th taxable year after the year the property is placed in service. The legislative history confirms this reading of the provision, stating that "(a)ny costs that are not recovered by the end of the tenth taxable year after the property was placed in service may be taken into account as depreciation in such year." H.R. Conf. Rep. No. 737, 104th Cong., 2d Sess. 299 (1996).

Consistent with this rule, the estimated income from the property is all the income projected to be earned over the first eleven taxable years the property is used by any taxpayer. Under section 167(g)(1)(A), the adjusted basis of income forecast property is to be recovered through allowances for income forecast depreciation over the "amount of income earned in connection with the property" through the end of the tenth taxable year after the year in which the income forecast property is placed in service. The legislative history to section 167(g)(1)(A) states that "income to be taken into account under the income forecast method includes all estimated income generated by the property." H.R. Conf. Rep. No. 737, at 297. By referring to income generated by the property, and not to income to be earned by the taxpayer, Congress established a regime whereby a taxpayer using the income forecast method must include within forecasted total income amounts that are to be earned not only by the taxpayer, but also by any subsequent owner during the eleven year period.

Income From the Property

The income forecast formula uses the ratio of current year income to forecasted total income from the property to determine the current allowance for depreciation. Both current year income and forecasted total income are to be computed in accordance with a taxpayer's method of accounting. Pursuant to Code section 167(g)(1)(A) and (g)(5)(C), forecasted total income is to include all anticipated income from any source through the end of the tenth taxable year following the year in which the income forecast property is placed in service (except, as discussed below, in the year of disposition of income forecast property). Thus, for example, in the case of a film, such income includes income from foreign and domestic theatrical, television, and other releases and syndications; income from video tape releases, sales, rentals, and syndications; and incidental income associated with the property such as income from the financial exploitation of characters, designs, titles, scripts, and scores, but only to the extent that such incidental income is earned in connection with the ultimate use of such items by, or the ultimate sale of merchandise to, persons who are not related to the taxpayer (within the meaning of section 267(b)). Apportionment rules are provided for situations when income from the exploitation of characters, designs, titles, scripts, scores, and other incidental income may relate to more than one income forecast property.

Under the proposed regulations, taxpayers are required at the end of the taxable year in which income forecast property is placed in service to make an accurate projection of all anticipated income to be earned from the income forecast property based on the conditions known to exist at that time. This estimate is referred to as forecasted total income. As discussed above, forecasted total income includes not only the income that the taxpayer forecasts it will earn by the end of the tenth taxable year after the year in which the income forecast property is placed in service, but also income that may be earned by other owners of the income forecast property during that same period.

The proposed regulations also require taxpayers to evaluate the accuracy of their forecasts annually. In order to perform these evaluations of forecasted total income, taxpayers must compute revised forecasted total income. Revised forecasted total income is the sum of current year income for the current taxable year and all prior taxable years, plus all income from the income forecast property that the taxpayer reasonably believes will be includible in current year income in taxable years after the current taxable year up to and including the 10th taxable year after the year in which the income forecast property is placed in service. Taxpayers are required to use the revised computation if forecasted total income in the immediately preceding taxable year falls outside a range bounded on the low end by 90 percent of revised forecasted total income for the current taxable year, and on the upper end by 110 percent of revised forecasted total income for the current taxable year. (In the situation where revised forecasted total income was used to compute income forecast depreciation in the immediately preceding taxable year, this comparison is made by comparing the revised forecasted total income for the current taxable year to revised forecasted total income for the immediately preceding taxable year.) Taxpayers may elect to alter their computations of income forecast depreciation (using the revised computation detailed below) when revised forecasted total income differs from forecasted total income.

Pursuant to Code section 167(g)(5)(B), income from the syndication of a television series need not be included in the income forecast computation prior to the fourth taxable year beginning after the date the first episode of the series is placed in service, unless an arrangement relating to future syndication exists. In such a case, syndication income is included in the income forecast computation at the time the arrangement relating to future syndication is made. This special rule also applies for purposes of applying the look-back method.

Special rules apply if income forecast property is disposed of prior to the end of the 10th taxable year after the year the property is placed in service. In such a case, section 167(g)(5)(E) requires that for purposes of applying the look-back method, income from the disposition of the property is to be taken into account. Failure to apply a similar rule for purposes of computing income forecast depreciation in the year of disposition may permit a depreciation differential that would not be corrected through the operation of the look-back method (because the differential would arise in a year for which the period of time to which look-back interest would apply would be zero). Accordingly, the proposed regulations require taxpayers to take income from the disposition of income forecast property into account in the year of disposition in computing revised forecasted total income both for purposes of computing its income forecast depreciation and for purposes of applying the look-back method.

Income Forecast Property

Section 167(g)(6) limits the types of property for which the income forecast method may be utilized. The income forecast method is available for interests (including interests involving limited rights in property) in motion picture films, video tapes, sound recordings, copyrights, books, and patents. In addition, section 167(g)(6)(E) provides the authority for Treasury and the IRS to extend the income forecast method to other types of property. The proposed regulations extend the method to theatrical productions and authorize the Commissioner to publish guidance designating other properties.

The proposed regulations generally require the income forecast method to be applied on a property-by-property basis. In certain limited circumstances, interests in multiple properties may be grouped together and treated as a single income forecast property. The ability to treat multiple income forecast properties as a single property for purposes of applying the income forecast method of depreciation is limited, however, to certain episodes of a television series or to multiple interests in specified income forecast properties acquired for broadcast pursuant to a single contract. The special allowance applicable to certain basis redetermination amounts is not available to basis redetermination amounts associated with interests in multiple income forecast properties treated as a single income forecast property under these rules. Commentators have requested that broad groupings of dissimilar properties be permitted in accordance with historic financial accounting practices. Because it is not clear that income would be clearly reflected if broader groupings of properties were permitted, this suggestion has not been incorporated into the proposed regulations. Treasury and the IRS request comments on whether the proposed permitted groupings are appropriate and whether additional groupings should be allowed.

Under section 167(g)(5)(A)(ii), an amount incurred after income forecast property is placed in service that is significant and that gives rise to a significant increase in income when compared to the previous amount of forecasted total income is treated as a separate income forecast property and depreciated accordingly. Under the proposed regulations, an amount that does not exceed the lesser of 5 percent of the depreciable basis of the income forecast property with which the amount is associated or $100,000 is not considered significant for this purpose. An amount incurred after income forecast property is placed in service that is not significant or that does not give rise to a significant increase in income is subject to the general rules and is treated as a basis redetermination amount.

In addition, a cost incurred in a taxable year following the year in which the taxpayer has recovered through depreciation the entire adjusted basis of an income forecast property is treated as a separate income forecast property. If it is expected to give rise to a significant increase in income, the amount of the cost is treated as income forecast property that is newly placed in service. Otherwise, it is deductible in the year paid or incurred.

Look-back

In general, the look-back method applies any time property is depreciated using the income forecast method. A taxpayer using the income forecast method is required to pay, or is entitled to receive, interest computed under the look-back method for any year to which the look-back requirement applies. A taxpayer must pay look-back interest if deductions are accelerated due to the underestimation of total income expected to be earned with respect to the property. Conversely, a taxpayer is entitled to receive look-back interest if deductions are delayed as a result of overestimating total income expected to be earned with respect to the property. The look-back method applies separately to each income forecast property, unless properties are aggregated pursuant to special rules contained in the proposed regulations.

Generally, the look-back method is applied in the third and tenth taxable years following the year in which the income forecast property is placed in service. The look-back method also applies in the year income from the income forecast property ceases with respect to the taxpayer (and with respect to all persons who would be treated as a single taxpayer with the taxpayer under rules similar to those in section 41(f)(1)).

The look-back method does not apply to any income forecast property the basis of which is $100,000 or less in the year the look-back method would otherwise apply (redetermined without any reduction for depreciation allowed or allowable). In addition, the look-back method is not applicable for any year which would otherwise be a recomputation year if a 10 percent test is satisfied. The 10 percent test is met if forecasted total income (and, if applicable, revised forecasted total income) for each prior year is greater than 90 percent of revised forecasted total income for the year which would otherwise be a recomputation year and is less than 110 percent of revised forecasted total income for the year which would otherwise be a recomputation year. If the look-back method is applied for the third taxable year following the year in which income forecast property is placed in service, a special rule applies in determining whether the 10 percent test is satisfied in any subsequent year. Under the special rule, the amount of the forecasted total income or the revised forecasted total income for each taxable year up to and including the third taxable year following the year in which income forecast property is placed in service is deemed to be equal to the revised forecasted total income that was used for purposes of applying the look-back method in the third taxable year following the year in which income forecast property is placed in service.

In order to apply the look-back method, prior year allowances for depreciation for income forecast property are recomputed using revised forecasted total income for the recomputation year in lieu of forecasted total income (or, if appropriate, revised forecasted income) from the property that was used in the computation of depreciation under the income forecast method in the prior year. If a taxpayer sells or otherwise disposes of income forecast property, the amount realized upon the disposition of the property is included in determining revised forecasted total income from the property in the year of disposition. These recomputed depreciation allowances are then used to determine either a hypothetical overpayment of tax or a hypothetical underpayment of tax.

Generally, taxpayers must determine the hypothetical overpayment or underpayment of tax arising from the change in depreciation allowances by recomputing their tax liability. Thus, a taxpayer's tax liability for each prior year is recomputed by substituting the recomputed depreciation allowances for the depreciation allowances originally claimed. The recomputed tax liability is then compared to the taxpayer's actual liability. For purposes of this comparison, the taxpayer must determine the actual tax liability for each prior year based on the information available on the later of (1) the due date of the return, including extensions, (2) the date of an amended return, (3) the date a return is adjusted by examination, or (4) the date of any previous application of the look-back requirement for the income forecast property. The result of this comparison is a hypothetical overpayment or underpayment of tax for each prior year in which allowances for depreciation were claimed for income forecast property subject to the look-back method.

Pass-through entities that are not closely-held pass-through entities must use a simplified method to compute their hypothetical overpayment or underpayment for each prior year in which allowances for depreciation were claimed for income forecast property subject to the look-back method. Under the simplified method, taxpayers apply a set rate (i.e., the highest rate applicable under section 1 or 11) to the net changes in depreciation allowances for each year. Treasury and the IRS considered, but did not provide, an election for other taxpayers to use the simplified method similar to the election set forth in § 1.460-6(d)(4)(ii). Treasury and the IRS request comments on whether the use of the simplified method should be extended to taxpayers other than those required to use the simplified method, and if so, whether additional safeguards beyond the consistency rules for related taxpayers, the rules precluding changes from the simplified method without permission, and the overpayment ceiling would be appropriate.

Regardless of the method used, the resulting hypothetical overpayments or underpayments are then used to compute interest that is to be charged or credited on each of these amounts. Interest is generally computed from the due date of the return (not including extensions) for the years in which changes in depreciation allowances occur to the due date of the recomputation year (not including extensions). Special rules are provided for taxpayers who do not use the simplified method where changes in depreciation allowances affect tax liability in years other than the year in which the changes in depreciation allowances occur. Interest is computed using the overpayment rate under section 6621. The amounts resulting from these computations are netted to arrive at look-back interest due to the taxpayer or payable to the government for the recomputation year. For purposes of computing taxable income, look-back interest is treated as interest on an overpayment or underpayment of tax. Under section 167(g)(5)(D), look-back interest required to be paid is treated as a tax liability for penalty purposes.

Proposed Effective Date

The regulations are proposed to apply to property placed in service on or after the date that final regulations are published in the Federal Register.

Special Analyses

It has been determined that this Treasury decision is not a significant regulatory action as defined in Executive Order 12866. Therefore, a regulatory assessment is not required. It also has been determined that section 553(b) of the Administrative Procedure Act (5 U.S.C. chapter 5) does not apply to these regulations and, because these regulations do not impose on small entities a collection of information requirement, the Regulatory Flexibility Act (5 U.S.C. chapter 6) does not apply. Therefore, a Regulatory Flexibility Analysis is not required. Pursuant to section 7805(f) of the Code, this notice of proposed rulemaking will be submitted to the Chief Counsel for Advocacy of the Small Business Administration for comment on its impact on small business.

Comments and Public Hearing

Before these proposed regulations are adopted as final regulations, consideration will be given to any written or electronic comments (a signed original and eight (8) copies, if written) that are submitted timely (in the manner described in the ADDRESSES portion of this preamble) to the IRS. The IRS and the Treasury Department specifically request comments on the clarity of the proposed regulations and how they may be made easier to understand. All comments will be available for public inspection and copying.

A public hearing has been scheduled for September 4, 2002, at 10 a.m. in the Internal Revenue Service Auditorium, Internal Revenue Building, 1111 Constitution Avenue NW, Washington, DC. All visitors must present photo identification to enter the building. Because of access restrictions, visitors will not be admitted beyond the immediate entrance area more than 30 minutes before the hearing starts at the Constitution Avenue entrance. For information about having your name placed on the building access list to attend the hearing, see the "FOR FURTHER INFORMATION CONTACT" section of this preamble.

The rules of 26 CFR 601.601(a)(3) apply to this hearing. Persons that wish to present oral comments at the hearing must submit timely written comments and an outline of the topics to be discussed and the time to be devoted to each topic (preferably a signed original and eight (8) copies) by August 13, 2002.

A period of 10 minutes will be allotted to each person for making comments.

An agenda showing the scheduling of the speakers will be prepared after the deadline for receiving outlines has passed. Copies of the agenda will be available free of charge at the hearing.

Drafting Information

The principal author of these regulations is Bernard P. Harvey, Office of Associate Chief Counsel (Passthroughs and Special Industries). However, other personnel from the IRS and Treasury Department participated in their development.

[¶ 49,206]   **Proposed Amendments of Regulations (REG-141669-02)**, published in the Federal Register on July 9, 2003.

Penalties, civil: Failure to file a correct information return: Waiver.—Amendments of Reg. § 301.6724-1, relating to waiver of a penalty imposed by Code Sec. 6721 for failure to file a correct information return, are proposed. A public hearing on this proposal is scheduled for October 21, 2003.

AGENCY: Internal Revenue Service (IRS), Treasury.

ACTION: Notice of proposed rulemaking and notice of public hearing.

SUMMARY: This document contains proposed regulations relating to waiver under section 6724 of the Internal Revenue Code (Code) of a penalty imposed by section 6721 for failure to file a correct information return. The proposed regulations provide guidance on the requirement of prompt correction of the failure to file or file correctly. The proposed regulations provide that the IRS will deem information returns promptly corrected if corrected within 30 days of the required filing date, or by August 1 following that required filing date. After August 1, a correction is prompt if made by the time announced by the IRS in published guidance. The proposed regulations do not change the rules for determining reasonable cause for waiving the penalty for failure to furnish correct payee statements under section 6722 or the time to comply with other information reporting requirements under section 6723.

DATES: Written and electronic comments are due by October 7, 2003. Requests to speak (with outlines of topics to be discussed) at the public hearing scheduled for October 21, 2003, are due by September 30, 2003.

ADDRESSES: Send submissions to: CC:PA:RU (REG-141669-02), Room 5526, Internal Revenue Service, POB 7604, Ben Franklin Station, Washington, DC 20044. Commenters may hand deliver submissions Monday through Friday between the hours of 8 a.m. and 4 p.m. to: CC:PA:RU (REG-141669-02), Courier's Desk, Internal Revenue Service, 1111 Constitution Avenue, NW., Washington, DC. Alternatively, commenters may submit comments electronically to the IRS Internet site at *www.irs.gov/regs*. The public hearing will be held in the IRS Auditorium, Internal Revenue Building, 1111 Constitution Avenue, NW., Washington, DC.

FOR FURTHER INFORMATION CONTACT: Concerning the proposed regulations, contact Robert A. Desilets, Jr. at (202) 622-4910; concerning submissions of comments, the hearing, and/or to be placed on the building access list to attend the hearing, Treena Garrett at (202) 622-7180 (not toll-free numbers).

SUPPLEMENTARY INFORMATION:

Background

This document contains proposed amendments to the Procedure and Administration Regulations (26 CFR part 301) under section 6724(a) of the Code. Section 301.6724-1(d)(1)(ii)(D) of the proposed regulations will clarify when a correction of an information return is prompt for purposes of establishing reasonable cause to waive the penalty under section 6721 of the Code. Existing § 301.6724-1(d)(1)(ii)(D), adopted on December 31, 1991 (56 FR 67178), provides in pertinent part that a correction is prompt if it occurs on the earliest date of a regular submission of corrections, defining regular submissions as occurring at intervals of 30 or fewer days. Many information return filers have urged the IRS to replace the 30-day correction interval with an interval corresponding to the schedule for tiered penalties.

Explanation of Provisions

I. Section 6721

Section 6721 imposes penalties on failures to file, or file correct, information returns. Section 6721 creates a threetiered penalty structure to encourage timely filing and prompt correction of errors in previously filed returns. Congress enacted the three-tiered penalty structure in the Omnibus Budget Reconciliation Act of 1989 (Public Law 101-239, 103 Stat. 2388, 2389). Section 6721 generally imposes a penalty in the amount of $50 for each return with respect to which a failure occurs, but not to exceed $250,000 per person per calendar year. However, if a filer corrects a failure within 30 days after the required filing date, the penalty with respect to such return shall be $15 in lieu of $50, but not to exceed $75,000 per filer per calendar year. Moreover, if a filer corrects a failure more than 30 days after the required filing date, but before August 1 of the calendar year in which the required filing date occurs, the penalty with respect to each return shall be $30 in lieu of $50, but not to exceed $150,000 per filer per calendar year. Section 6721 provides these penalties to encourage prompt corrections of failures to file, or file correct, information returns. H.R. Rep. 101-386, at 648-649 (1989).

II. Section 6724

Section 6724(a) provides for a waiver of information reporting penalties under sections 6721 through 6723 if the failure giving rise to such penalties was due to reasonable cause and not willful neglect. Under § 301.6724-1(a) of the regulations, to prove reasonable cause for a failure, the filer must establish either that there are significant mitigating factors with respect to the failure or that the failure arose from an event beyond the filer's control (an impediment). In addition, the filer must have acted in a responsible manner both before and after the failure.

Under § 301.6724-1(d) of the regulations, a filer is considered as acting in a responsible manner if the filer exercises reasonable care, i.e., the care that a reasonably prudent person would use under the circumstances in the course of business in determining filing obligations and in handling account information such as account numbers and balances. Section 301.6724-1(d) of the regulations also refers to the promptness of correction, i.e., when the filer undertook significant steps to avoid or mitigate the failure.

Section 301.6724-1(d)(1)(ii)(D) currently provides, in part, that a correction is considered prompt if it is made within 30 days after the date of removal of an impediment or discovery of a failure, or on the earliest date thereafter on which a regular submission of corrections occurs. Submissions are regular only if they occur at intervals of 30 days or fewer. Under the 30-day rule, a filer of a large number of information returns that discovers errors over a period of several months would be required to submit multiple corrections in a series of filings. Information return filers have urged the IRS to allow filers to "bundle" their corrections, i.e., submit the corrected information returns less frequently according to a defined timetable. The IRS agrees that the current rule may be burdensome and that bundling should be permitted.

The proposed regulations provide that a correction of an information return is prompt if the filer makes the correction within 30 days of the required filing date, or by August 1 following that required filing date. After August 1, a correction is prompt if the filer makes the correction by the date or dates announced in guidance governing the electronic or magnetic filing of information returns, or in other guidance including forms and instructions. It is anticipated that the date or dates will be in November and/or December of the calendar year in which the required filing date occurs. After the dates announced in the guidance, the proposed regulations provide that a correction is prompt if it is made within 30 days after the date the impediment is removed or the failure is discovered.

The proposed regulations apply solely for the purpose of determining whether there is reasonable cause for waiving the penalty for failure to file correct information returns imposed by section 6721. The proposed regulations do not apply for the purpose of determining whether there is reasonable cause for waiving the penalties imposed by sections 6722 and 6723. The IRS and Treasury Department believe that a filer should correct promptly a failure to furnish a correct payee statement or a failure to satisfy the reporting requirements described in section 6724(d)(2) and (3) with regard to sections 6722 and 6723, respectively. Therefore, the proposed regulations retain the 30-day correction period for waiving the penalties imposed by sections 6722 and 6723.

The proposed regulations do not affect or alter the tiered penalty rate schedule of section 6721. To ensure that a reduced penalty amount under section 6721 will apply, in the event that the IRS does not grant a reasonable cause waiver, a filer should file correct information returns with the IRS within 30 days after the required filing date, or before August 1 of the calendar year in which the required filing date occurs.

Proposed Effective Date

The proposed regulations apply to corrections of information returns made after the date of publication of a Treasury decision adopting the proposed regulations as final regulations in the **Federal Register**. However, filers may cite these rules for purposes of requesting a reasonable cause waiver prior to the date that the proposed regulations become final.

Special Analyses

It has been determined that this notice of proposed rulemaking is not a significant regulatory action as defined in Executive Order 12866. Therefore, a regulatory assessment is not required. It has also been determined that section 553(b) of the Administrative Procedure Act (5 U.S.C. chapter 5) does not apply to these proposed regulations, and because the proposed regulations do not impose a collection of information on small entities, the Regulatory Flexibility Act (5 U.S.C. chapter 6) does not apply. Pursuant to section 7805(f) of the Code, this notice of proposed rulemaking will be submitted to the Chief Counsel for Advocacy of the Small Business Administration for comment on its impact on small business.

Comments and Public Hearing

Before adoption of these proposed regulations as final regulations, the IRS will consider any electronic or written comments (a signed original and eight (8) copies) that a commenter submits timely (in the manner described in the ADDRESSES portion of this preamble) to the IRS. The IRS and the Treasury Department request comments on the clarity of the proposed regulations and how they can be easier to understand. All comments will be available for public inspection and copying. Written comments on the proposed regulations are due by October 7, 2003.

A public hearing has been scheduled for October 21, 2003, beginning at 10 a.m. in the IRS Auditorium, Internal Revenue Building, 1111 Constitution Avenue, NW., Washington, DC. All visitors must present photo identification to enter the building. Because of access restrictions, visitors will not be admitted beyond the immediate entrance area more than 30 minutes before the hearing starts. For information about having your name placed on the building access list to attend the hearing, see the FOR FURTHER INFORMATION CONTACT portion of this preamble.

The rules of 26 CFR 601.601(a)(3) apply to the hearing. Persons who wish to present oral comments must submit electronic or written comments and an outline of the topics for discussion and the time for each topic (a signed original and eight (8) copies) by September 30, 2003. Each person making comments will have 10 minutes to present comments. The IRS will prepare an agenda showing the scheduling of the speakers after the deadline for reviewing outlines has passed. Copies of the agenda will be available free of charge at the hearing.

Drafting Information

The principal author of these proposed regulations is Robert A. Desilets, Jr., Office of the Associate Chief Counsel (Procedure and Administration), Administrative Provisions and Judicial Practice Division. However, other personnel from the IRS and the Treasury Department participated in their development.

———————————

[¶ 49,208]   **Proposed Amendments of Regulations (REG-121122-03)**, published in the Federal Register on July 9, 2003.

Proposed regulations: Nonrecognition of gain on stock sold to employee organizations: Reporting requirements: Notarized statement of purchase requirements.—Amendments of Reg. §1.1042-1T, relating to notarized statements of purchase and taxpayers making an election to defer recognition of gain on the sale of stock to an employee stock ownership plan, are proposed.

AGENCY: Internal Revenue Service (IRS), Treasury.

ACTION: Notice of proposed rulemaking.

SUMMARY: This document contains proposed amendments to the temporary regulations relating to notarized statements of purchase under section 1042 of the Internal Revenue Code of 1986. The proposed regulations would affect taxpayers making an election to defer the recognition of gain under section 1042 on the sale of stock to an employee stock ownership plan. The proposed regulations provide guidance on the notarization requirements of the temporary regulations.

DATES: Written and electronic comments and requests for a public hearing must be received by October 8, 2003.

ADDRESSES: Send submissions to: CC:PA:RU (REG-121122-03), room 5226, Internal Revenue Service, POB 7604, Ben Franklin Station, Washington, DC 20044. Submissions may be hand delivered Monday through Friday between the hours of 8 a.m. and 4 p.m. to: CC:PA:RU (REG-121122-03), Courier's Desk, Internal Revenue Service, 1111 Constitution Avenue, NW., Washington, DC. Alternatively, taxpayers may submit comments electronically directly to the IRS Internet site at *www.irs.gov/regs*.

FOR FURTHER INFORMATION CONTACT: Concerning the regulations, John T. Ricotta at (202) 622-6060 (not a toll-free number); concerning submissions or hearing requests, Sonya Cruse, (202) 622-7180 (not a toll-free number).

SUPPLEMENTARY INFORMATION:

Background

This document contains proposed amendments to the requirement of §1.1042-1T, A-3(b) of the Temporary Income Tax regulations that a statement of purchase for qualified replacement property be notarized within 30 days of the date of purchase of the property (30-day notarization requirement).

The temporary regulations under section 1042 were published in TD 8073 on February 4, 1986 (EE-63-84) (51 FR 4312) as part of a package of temporary regulations addressing effective dates and other issues under the Tax Reform Act of 1984. The text of the temporary regulations also served as a notice of proposed rulemaking (EE-96-85) (51 FR 4391). A public hearing was held on June 26, 1986, concerning the proposed regulations.

Explanation of Provisions

Overview

Section 1042(a) provides that a taxpayer or executor may elect in certain cases not to recognize long-term capital gain on the sale of *qualified securities* to an employee stock ownership plan (ESOP) (as defined in section 4975(e)(7)) or eligible worker owned cooperative (as defined in section 1042(c)(2)) if the taxpayer purchases *qualified replacement property* (as defined in section 1042(c)(4)) within the replacement period of section 1042(c)(3) and the requirements of section 1042(b) and §1.1042-1T of the Temporary Income Tax Regulations are satisfied.

Section 1042(c)(1) provides that the term *qualified securities* means employer securities (as defined in section 409(l)) which are issued by a domestic C corporation that has no stock outstanding that is readily tradable on an established securities market and which were not received by the taxpayer in a distribution from a plan described in section 401(a) or in a transfer pursuant to an option or other right to acquire stock to which section 83, 422, or 423 applied.

A sale of *qualified securities* meets the requirements of section 1042(b) if: (1) the qualified securities are sold to an ESOP (as defined in section 4975(e)(7)), or an eligible worker owned cooperative; (2) the plan or cooperative owns (after application of section 318(a)(4)), immediately after the sale, at least 30 percent of (a) each class of outstanding stock of the corporation (other than stock described in section 1504(a)(4)) which issued the securities or (b) the total value of all outstanding stock of the corporation (other than stock described in section 1504(a)(4)); (3) the taxpayer files with the Secretary a verified written statement of the employer whose employees are covered by the ESOP or an authorized officer of the cooperative consenting to the application of sections 4978 and 4979A (which provide for excise taxes on certain dispositions or allocations of securities acquired in a sale to which section 1042 applies) with respect to such employer or cooperative; and (4) the taxpayer's holding period with respect to the qualified securities is at least three years (determined as of the time of the sale).

The taxpayer must purchase *qualified replacement property* within the *replacement period*, which is defined in section 1042(c)(3) as the period which begins three months before the date on which the sale of qualified securities occurs and ends 12 months after the date of such sale.

Section 1042(c)(4)(A) defines *qualified replacement property* as any security issued by a domestic operating corporation which did not, for the taxable year preceding the taxable year in which such security was purchased, have passive investment income (as defined in section 1362(d)(3)(C)) in excess of 25 percent of the gross receipts of such corporation for such preceding taxable year, and is not the corporation which issued the qualified securities which such security is replacing or a member of the same controlled group of corporations (within the meaning of section 1563(a)(1)) as such corporation.

Section 1042(c)(4)(B) defines an *operating corporation* as a corporation more than 50 percent of the assets of which, at the time the security was purchased or before the close of the replacement period, were used in the active conduct of a trade or business.

Section 1.1042-1T A-3(a) of the Temporary Income Tax Regulations states that the election is to be made in a *statement of election* attached to the taxpayer's income tax return filed on or before the due date (including extensions of time) for the taxable year in which the sale occurs.

Section 1.1042-1T A-3(b) states that the *statement of election* must provide that the taxpayer elects to treat the sale of securities as a sale of qualified securities under section 1042(a) and must contain the following information: (1) A description of the qualified securities sold, including the type and number of shares; (2) The date of the sale of the qualified securities; (3) The adjusted basis of the qualified securities; (4) The amount realized upon the sale of the qualified securities; (5) The identity of the ESOP or eligible worker-owned cooperative to which the qualified securities were sold; and (6) If the sale was part of a single interrelated transaction under a prearranged agreement between taxpayers involving other sales of qualified securities, the names and taxpayer identification numbers of the other taxpayers under the agreement and the number of shares sold by the other taxpayers.

Section 1.1042-1T, A-3(b) further provides that, if the taxpayer has purchased qualified replacement property at the time of the election, the taxpayer must attach as part of the statement of election a *statement of purchase* describing the qualified replacement property, the date of the purchase, and the cost of the property, and declaring such property to be qualified replacement property with respect to the sale of qualified securities.

The statement of purchase must be notarized no later than 30 days after the purchase. The purpose of the statement of purchase is to identify qualified replacement property with respect to a sale of qualified securities. The qualified replacement property will have its cost basis reduced under section 1042(d) to reflect the gain on the sale of qualified securities that is being deferred by the taxpayer. Upon subsequent disposition of the qualified replacement property by the taxpayer, the deferred gain will be recognized by the taxpayer under section 1042(e). Under section 1042(f), the filing of the statement of purchase of qualified replacement property (or a statement of the taxpayer's intention not to purchase replacement property) will begin the statutory period for assessment of any deficiency with respect to gain arising from the sale of the qualified securities. The purpose of the 30-day notarization requirement is to provide a contemporaneous identification of replacement property.

However, the 30-day notarization requirement leads to frequent mistakes by taxpayers and their advisors. Taxpayers are often unaware of this requirement and become aware of it only when they prepare their tax returns for the year of sale to the ESOP. By this time, the 30-day period is typically past because purchases of replacement property may have been made up to one year before. A number of private letter rulings have been issued granting relief to taxpayers in these situations as long as the statements were notarized shortly after the taxpayer became aware of the requirement and it was represented that the property listed was the only replacement property purchased for this sale.

A number of commentators on the temporary and proposed regulations criticized this requirement as without statutory authority, a trap for the unwary, and inconsistent with the definition of the qualified replacement period in section 1042(c)(3).

Proposed Amendment to the Regulations

In order to facilitate taxpayer compliance with the temporary regulations concerning identification of qualified replacement property through notarization of the statements of purchase, the proposed amendment to the temporary regulations would modify § 1.1042-1T, A-3(b) to provide that the notarization requirements for the *statement of purchase* are satisfied if the taxpayer's statement of purchase is notarized not later than the time the taxpayer files the income tax return for the taxable year in which the sale of qualified securities occurred in any case in which any qualified replacement property was purchased by such time and during the qualified replacement period. If qualified replacement property was purchased after such filing date and during the qualified replacement period, the statement of purchase must be notarized not later than the time the taxpayer's income tax return is filed for the taxable year following the year for which the election under section 1042(a) was made.

Proposed Effective Date

The proposed amendments to the temporary regulations would apply to taxable years of sellers ending on or after the date of publication of the Treasury decision adopting these amendments as final regulations in the **Federal Register**. However, taxpayers may rely upon these proposed regulations for guidance with respect to all open taxable years pending the issuance of final regulations. If, and to the extent, future guidance is more restrictive than the guidance in these proposed regulations, the future guidance will be applied without retroactive effect.

Special Analyses

It has been determined that this notice of proposed rulemaking is not a significant regulatory action as defined in Executive Order 12866. Therefore, a regulatory assessment is not required. It also has been determined that section 553(b) of the Administrative Procedure Act (5 U.S.C. chapter 5) does not apply to these regulations, and because these regulations do not impose a collection of information on small entities, the Regulatory Flexibility Act (5 U.S.C. chapter 6) does not apply. Pursuant to section 7805(f) of the Internal Revenue Code, these proposed regulations will be submitted to the Chief Counsel for Advocacy of the Small Business Administration for comment on its impact on small business.

Comments and Public Hearing

Before these proposed regulations are adopted as final regulations, consideration will be given to any written (a signed original and 8 copies) or electronic comments that are submitted timely to the IRS. The IRS and Treasury Department request comments on the clarity of the proposed rules and how they can be made easier to understand. All comments will be available for public inspection and copying. A public hearing will be scheduled if requested in writing by any person that timely submits written comments. If a public hearing is scheduled, notice of the date, time, and place for the public hearing will be published in the **Federal Register**.

Drafting Information

The principal author of these regulations is John T. Ricotta of the Office of the Division Counsel/Associate Chief Counsel (Tax Exempt and Government Entities). However, other personnel from The IRS and Treasury participated in their development.

[¶ 49,216]   **Proposed Regulations and Proposed Amendments of Regulations (REG-166012-02)**, published in the Federal Register on February 26, 2004.

    Sales or exchanges: Notional principal contracts: Contingent nonperiodic payments: Inclusion in income: Deduction: Accounting methods: Proposed regulations.—Reg. §§ 1.162-30 and 1.1234A-1 and amendments of Reg. §§ 1.212-1 and 1.446-3, relating to the inclusion into income or deduction of a contingent nonperiodic payment provided for under a notional principal contract (NPC), are proposed. A public hearing on this proposal is scheduled for May 25, 2004.

AGENCY: Internal Revenue Service (IRS), Treasury.

ACTION: Notice of proposed rulemaking and notice of public hearing.

SUMMARY: This document contains proposed regulations relating to the inclusion into income or deduction of a contingent nonperiodic payment provided for under a notional principal contract (NPC). This document also provides guidance relating to the character of payments made pursuant to an NPC. These regulations will affect taxpayers that enter into NPCs. This document also provides a notice of a public hearing on these proposed regulations.

DATES: Written or electronically transmitted comments and requests to speak (with outlines of oral comments to be discussed) at the public hearing scheduled for May 25, 2004, at 10 a.m., must be received by May 4, 2004. Comments on the collection of information should be received by April 26, 2004.

ADDRESSES: Send submissions to CC:PA:LPD:PR (REG-166012-02), room 5203, Internal Revenue Service, POB 7604, Ben Franklin Station, Washington, DC 20044. Submissions may be hand-delivered Monday through Friday between the hours of 8 a.m. and 4 p.m. to CC:PA:LPD:PR (REG-166012-02), Courier's Desk, Internal Revenue Service, 1111 Constitution Avenue, NW., Washington, DC. Alternatively, taxpayers may submit electronic comments directly to the IRS Internet site at: *www.irs.gov/regs*. The public hearing will be held in the IRS Auditorium, Seventh Floor, Internal Revenue Service, 1111 Constitution Avenue, NW., Washington, DC.

FOR FURTHER INFORMATION CONTACT: Concerning submissions of comments, the hearing, or to be placed on the building access list to attend the hearing, Sonya Cruse, (202) 622-7180; concerning the regulations, Kate Sleeth, (202) 622-3920 (not toll-free numbers).

SUPPLEMENTARY INFORMATION:

Paperwork Reduction Act

The collection of information contained in this notice of proposed rulemaking has been submitted to the Office of Management and Budget for review in accordance with the Paperwork Reduction Act of 1995 (44 U.S.C. 3507(d)). Comments on the collection of information should be sent to the **Office of Management and Budget,** Attn: Desk Officer for the Department of the Treasury, Office of Information and Regulatory Affairs, Washington, DC 20503, with copies to the **Internal Revenue Service**, Attn: IRS Reports Clearance Officer, SE:W:CAR:MP:T:T:SP, Washington, DC 20224. Comments on the collection of information should be received by April 26, 2004. Comments are specifically requested concerning:

Whether the proposed collection of information is necessary for the proper performance of the functions of the IRS, including whether the information will have practical utility;

The accuracy of the estimated burden associated with the proposed collection of information (see below);

How the quality, utility, and clarity of the information to be collected may be enhanced;

How the burden of complying with the proposed collection of information may be minimized, including through the application of automated collection techniques or other forms of information technology; and

Estimates of capital or start-up costs and costs of operation, maintenance, and purchase of services to provide information.

The collection of information in these proposed regulations is in § 1.446-3(g)(6)(vii). This information is required by the IRS to verify compliance with section 446 and the method of accounting described in § 1.446-3(g)(6). This information will be used to determine whether the amount of tax has been calculated correctly. The collection of information is required to properly determine the amount of income or deduction to be taken into account. The respondents are sophisticated investors that enter into notional principal contracts with contingent nonperiodic payments.

Estimated total annual recordkeeping burden: 25,500 hours.

Estimated average annual burden per recordkeeper: 6 hours.

Estimated number of recordkeepers: 4,250.

An agency may not conduct or sponsor, and a person is not required to respond to, a collection of information unless it displays a valid control number assigned by the Office of Management and Budget.

Books or records relating to a collection of information must be retained as long as their contents may become material in the administration of any internal revenue law. Generally, tax returns and tax return information are confidential, as required by 26 U.S.C. 6103.

Background

This document contains proposed amendments to 26 CFR Part 1 under section 446(b) of the Internal Revenue Code (Code). This document also contains proposed amendments under sections 162, 212 and 1234A of the Code.

In 1989, the IRS issued Notice 89-21 (1989-1 C.B. 651), to provide guidance with respect to the tax treatment of lump-sum payments received in connection with NPCs. The Notice stated that a method of accounting that properly recognizes a lump-sum payment over the life of the contract clearly reflects income and indicated that regulations would be issued to provide specific rules regarding the manner in which a taxpayer must take into account over the life of an NPC payments made or received with respect to the contract. The Notice further stated that "for contracts entered into prior to the effective date of the regulations, the Commissioner will generally treat a method of accounting as clearly reflecting income if it takes such payments into account over the life of the contract under a reasonable amortization method, whether or not the method satisfies the specific rules in the forthcoming regulations." (1989-1 C.B. 652).

On October 14, 1993, the IRS published in the **Federal Register** final regulations (TD 8491; 1993-2 C.B. 215 [58 FR 53125]) under section 446(b) relating to the timing of income and deductions for amounts paid or received pursuant to NPCs. § 1.446-3. In this preamble, the final regulations published in 1993 are referred to as the 1993 Treasury regulations.

The 1993 Treasury regulations define an NPC as a "financial instrument that provides for the payment of amounts by one party to another at specified intervals calculated by reference to a specified index upon a notional principal amount in exchange for specified consideration or a promise to pay similar amounts." § 1.446-3(c)(1)(i). Payments made pursuant to NPCs are divided into three categories (periodic, nonperiodic, and termination payments), and the 1993 Treasury regulations provide timing regimes for each. The 1993 Treasury regulations require all taxpayers, regardless of their method of accounting, to recognize the ratable daily portion of a nonperiodic payment for the taxable year to which that portion relates. Nonperiodic payments generally must be recognized over the term of an NPC in a manner that reflects the economic substance of the contract. § 1.446-3(f)(2)(i). Although § 1.446-3 does not distinguish between noncontingent and contingent nonperiodic payments, the specific rules and examples in the 1993 Treasury regulations address only noncontingent nonperiodic payments. The Preamble to the 1993 Treasury regulations states that "the IRS expects to address contingent payments in future regulations, and welcomes comment on the treatment of those payments." (1993-2 C.B. 216). In addition, neither § 1.446-3 nor any other section provides specific rules governing the character of the various types of NPC payments.

On July 23, 2001, the IRS published Notice 2001-44 (2001-2 C.B. 77), soliciting comments on the appropriate method for the inclusion or deduction of contingent nonperiodic payments made pursuant to NPCs and the proper character treatment of payments made pursuant to an NPC. The Notice set forth four different methods under consideration by the IRS and Treasury and asked the public to comment on the extent to which each method reflects certain fundamental tax policy principles, including certainty, clarity, administrability, and neutrality. Several comments were received from the public, which expressed diverse views regarding the relative advantages and disadvantages of the different methods. Included in the four methods were the noncontingent swap method and a mark-to-market method, versions of which are adopted in the proposed regulations.

The Notice also solicited comments on the proper character of payments on NPCs and bullet swaps. The comments received on this issue also reflected differing views.

Explanation of Provisions

A. *Overview*

The IRS and Treasury understand that some taxpayers take into account contingent nonperiodic payments on an NPC only when the payment becomes fixed and determinable (the open transaction or wait-and-see method of accounting). The wait-and-see method, however, is inconsistent with the existing specific timing rules for periodic and nonperiodic payments and with the general rule in § 1.446-3(f)(2)(i) respecting recognition of nonperiodic payments over the term of the contract. For example, if the amount of a periodic payment is set in arrears at the end of an accrual period that spans taxable years, the parties cannot use a wait-and-see method for the portion of the accrual period in the first taxable year. Instead, the parties must use a reasonable estimate of the payment for determining taxable income in the year before the payment is fixed. § 1.446-3(e)(2)(ii). In addition, some NPCs are structured to provide for nonperiodic payments consisting of a noncontingent component and a contingent component, which the parties to the contract treat as a single contingent payment that they account for under the wait-and-see method. The attempted application of the wait-and-see method to these contracts highlights the potential for abuse present in the method. See Rev. Rul. 2002-30 (2002-1 C.B. 971).

The back-loaded timing of tax consequences that results from the wait-and-see method is also inconsistent with the timing regime that § 1.1275-4(b) provides for contingent debt instruments subject to the noncontingent bond method. Under the noncontingent bond method, the parties to a contingent payment debt instrument must determine the yield at which a comparable noncontingent debt instrument would be issued and then project a fixed amount for each contingent payment and each noncontingent payment. The projected amounts are accounted for over the term of the debt instrument. The difference, if any, between the projected amount of a contingent payment and the actual amount of the payment generally is accounted for when payment is made.

The proposed regulations adopt a variation on the noncontingent swap regime described in Notice 2001-44, as well as an elective mark-to-market regime. The 1993 Treasury regulations reflect an underlying principle that nonperiodic payments should be spread over the term of an NPC in a manner that properly reflects the economic substance of the contract. The proposed regulations build upon this principle. Furthermore, the IRS and Treasury believe that the proposed regulations provide a timing regime for contingent nonperiodic payments that clearly reflects the economics of the underlying contracts. The requirement that nonperiodic payments be spread over the term of an NPC results in substantially similar treatment for all NPCs without regard to whether payment obligations are settled on a current basis through periodic payments or are either pre-paid or deferred through nonperiodic payments. Adopting this approach for contingent payment NPCs achieves symmetry between fixed payment NPCs and contingent payment NPCs.

The proposed noncontingent swap method requires taxpayers to project the expected amount of contingent payments, to take into account annually the appropriate portions of the projected contingent amounts, to reproject the contingent amounts annually, and to reflect the differences between projected amounts and reprojected amounts through adjustments. The IRS and Treasury recognize that annual reprojections will require additional effort by taxpayers and the IRS. The IRS and Treasury believe, however, that the annual reprojection requirement is essential to ensure clear reflection of income with respect to NPCs with one or more contingent nonperiodic payments. Moreover, reprojections, and the resulting adjustments to current inclusion and deduction amounts, are especially important for the income and deductions generated by these types of contracts because otherwise, taxpayers might be more likely to attempt to manipulate the character of the income or deductions from the contract.

In developing the proposed regulations, the IRS and Treasury have taken into account comments received in response to Notice 2001-44, as well as the following considerations. First, although many comments advocated the wait-and-see method of accounting for contingent nonperiodic payments, this method encourages the creation of NPCs that provide such payments. As a result of the adoption of guidelines for taking contingent nonperiodic payments into account over the term of an NPC, the tax treatment of payments with respect to an NPC should no longer provide an incentive for structuring payments in a particular manner. Second, taxpayers using swaps with contingent nonperiodic payments are sophisticated investors. Many of these taxpayers will be making similar projections and reprojections for their own purposes in evaluating the results of their derivative investments and taking actions to manage the risks created by their derivative investments. Third, the proposed regulations also provide an elective mark-to-market method as an alternative to the noncontingent swap method. Taxpayers who use a mark-to-market method for financial reporting purposes may adopt the elective mark-to-market method to reduce their tax and accounting administrative burden for NPCs.

The IRS and Treasury understand that similar timing issues exist for other types of derivative investments, like bullet swaps and prepaid forward contracts. Although the application of the proposed regulations to these types of transactions may achieve appropriate timing, the application of these rules to investments other than NPCs could present a number of issues not directly addressed by the rules contained in these proposed regulations. The expansion of the scope of these proposed regulations to contracts other than NPCs is not being proposed at this time so as not to delay the publication of the proposed regulations.

With respect to character, the proposed regulations under sections 162 and 212 provide that both periodic and nonperiodic payments with respect to NPCs are generally ordinary in character. This is because neither periodic nor nonperiodic payments (whenever made) involve a sale or exchange within the meaning of section 1222, and no other section of the Code provides otherwise. The proposed regulations issued under section 1234A provide capital treatment for termination payments. Under the proposed regulations, however, even nonperiodic payments made at the maturity of an NPC are not termination payments under section 1234A.

Because of their recurring nature, periodic payments should be treated as ordinary income items, whether or not the payments are made at the expiration of an NPC. The same rationale applies to nonperiodic payments, which are required to be spread over the term of an NPC. Even if a nonperiodic payment is made at the expiration or termination of an NPC, only the final portion is taken into account on the termination date for the contract, and that portion should be treated in the same way as a periodic payment.

B. *Specific Provisions*

Adjustments

Paragraph (d) (2) of the proposed regulations provides for adjustments to be made in the gain or loss realized on the sale, exchange, or termination of an NPC, to account for inclusions into income and deductions provided for in the 1993 Treasury regulations and the proposed regulations, as well as for any payments made or received on the NPC. These adjustments are expected to produce consequences similar to the consequences that would result if basis were increased or decreased for these items. Using adjustments for this purpose avoids the issue of negative basis.

Significant nonperiodic payments

Paragraph (g)(4) of the proposed regulations clarifies the rules for the treatment of an NPC with a significant upfront nonperiodic payment and provides additional rules for the treatment of a significant nonperiodic payment that is not paid upfront. The 1993 Treasury regulations provide that a significant nonperiodic payment on an NPC is treated as two separate transactions - an on-market level payment NPC and a loan. § 1.446-3(g)(4). The proposed regulations clarify that the parties to an NPC with one or more significant nonperiodic payments must treat the contract as two or more separate transactions consisting of an on-market NPC and one or more loans. In some cases, the on-market NPC payments for a party making a significant nonperiodic upfront payment will be level payments that may be constructed through a combination of the actual payments on the NPC and level payments computed under the level payment method described in § 1.446-3(f)(2)(iii)(A).

The proposed regulations also provide that an NPC with a significant nonperiodic payment that is not paid upfront is treated as if the party receiving the significant nonperiodic payment paid a series of annual level payment loan advances, equal to the present value of the nonperiodic payment, to the party owing the significant nonperiodic payment. The interest component of the level payments is treated as interest for all purposes of the Code and is not taken into account in determining the income and deductions on the NPC. The principal component of the level payments is calculated solely to determine the interest amount. The party owing the significant nonperiodic payment is then treated as using the level payment loan advances to make annual level payment NPC payments, which are included in income and deducted as provided in § 1.446-3(d).

Contingent nonperiodic payments

The 1993 Treasury regulations define both periodic and nonperiodic payments but do not distinguish between contingent and noncontingent nonperiodic payments. Paragraph (g)(6)(i)(B) of the proposed regulations defines a contingent nonperiodic payment as any nonperiodic payment other than a noncontingent nonperiodic payment. A noncontingent nonperiodic payment is defined in paragraph (g)(6)(i)(A) of the proposed regulations as a nonperiodic payment that either is fixed on or before the end of the taxable year in which a contract commences or is equal to the sum of amounts that would be periodic payments if they are paid when they become fixed, including amounts determined as interest accruals.

Paragraph (g)(6)(ii) of the proposed regulations sets forth the noncontingent swap method for the inclusion into income and deduction of contingent nonperiodic payments. The noncontingent swap method requires taxpayers to project the reasonably expected amount of the contingent nonperiodic payment and to apply the level payment method and, as appropriate, the rules for significant nonperiodic payments, to the projected amount as if it were a noncontingent nonperiodic payment. The risk-free rate of return, which is defined in the proposed regulations, is used in applying the level payment method.

Paragraphs (g)(6)(iii)(A) through (C) of the proposed regulations provide the methods for projecting the reasonably expected amount. If the contingent payment is determined by reference to the value of a specified index at a designated future date, the projected amount may be determined by reference to the future value of the specified index in actively traded futures or forward contracts providing for delivery or settlement on the designated future date. If no actively traded contract exists for the designated future date, the value may be derived from actively traded futures or forward contracts providing for delivery or settlement within three months of the designated future date.

The projected amount may also be determined based on the projected future value of the current market price of the specified index. The future value is determined using a constant yield method at the risk-free interest rate with appropriate compounding and making appropriate adjustments for expected cash payments on the property underlying the specified index. The proposed regulations use the applicable federal rate under section 1274(d)(1) as the risk-free rate for this purpose. Comments are requested on whether this rate is appropriate.

If neither of the two methods described above results in a reasonable estimate of the future value of the specified index, the taxpayer must use another method that does result in a reasonable estimate of the amount of the contingent payment and that is based on objective financial information, and must consistently use the method from year to year.

The proposed regulations require annual adjustments to the projected amounts of the contingent payment. Paragraphs (g)(6)(iv) through (vi) of the proposed regulations provide rules for the redetermination of the projected amount of the contingent payment and the subsequent adjustments to the recognition of income and deductions under a contract based on the reprojected amount.

Paragraph (g)(6)(iv) of the proposed regulations provides that the projected amount must be redetermined on each successive anniversary date (redetermination date) and on each special redetermination date as described below. On each redetermination date, the taxpayer must reproject the amount of the contingent payment using the same method used at the commencement of the NPC but applied to the new current value of the specified index. Once the contingent payment is reprojected, the level payment method (and the rules for significant nonperiodic payments, if applicable) are applied again using the new projected amount.

Comments are requested as to how the reprojection process should respond to changes in the availability of market data during the life of an NPC. Suppose, for example, that the initial projection is made when there are no actively traded futures or forward contracts in the specified index but that these contracts come into existence before the time of one of the reprojections. Should the reprojections be made using the newly available futures data rather than the method employed for the first projection?

Paragraph (g)(6)(v) of the proposed regulations provides rules for adjustments following the redetermination of the projected amount of the contingent payment. The amounts determined for the redetermined projected amount under the level payment method and, as applicable, the rules for significant nonperiodic payments, are recognized in the current and subsequent taxable years. In addition, any difference between the newly determined amounts for prior periods and the amounts determined and previously taken into account using the previously projected contingent payment are recognized ratably over the one-year period beginning with the redetermination date. Any difference in amounts that would have been treated as interest under the rules for significant nonperiodic payments is also treated as interest for all purposes of the Code.

Paragraph (g)(6)(iv)(B) of the proposed regulations provides a special rule for a contingent nonperiodic payment that is fixed more than six months before it is due. If the date on which the payment becomes fixed is in a different taxable year from the date it is due, the date on which the payment becomes fixed is a special redetermination date. In such a case, the fixed amount is treated as the reprojected amount, and the rules described above for redeterminations and adjustments apply.

In general, under paragraph (g)(6)(vi) of the proposed regulations, when a contingent payment is made, the parties must make appropriate adjustments to the amount of income or deduction attributable to the NPC for any differences between the projected amount of the contingent payment and the actual amount of the contingent payment.

Paragraph (g)(6)(vii) of the proposed regulations provides a recordkeeping requirement with respect to the noncontingent swap method. Taxpayers must maintain in their books and records a description of the method used to determine the projected amount of the contingent payment, the projected payment schedules, and the adjustments taken into account under the proposed regulations.

The IRS and Treasury are considering whether to provide an alternative to the noncontingent swap method that would permit a taxpayer to use a current inclusion method for certain NPCs that provide for periodic calculations of amounts due under the terms of the NPC, but provide for deferred payment of the amounts. The IRS and Treasury are considering permitting current inclusion of income and deduction for the amounts so calculated, provided the NPC also provides for accrual of interest at a qualified rate until the periodically determined amounts are paid or offset against other amounts due under the NPC. The purpose of providing a current inclusion method for the deferred payment NPC described above is to provide tax treatment for NPCs with contingent nonperiodic payments that is economically equivalent to the tax treatment of NPCs providing only for periodic payments while avoiding the necessity of using projected amounts for contingent payments. The IRS and Treasury request comments concerning whether an NPC like the deferred payment NPC described above would be a viable transaction for market participants, whether a current inclusion method would be an appropriate substitute for the noncontingent swap method for deferred payment NPCs, and whether that method should require separate computation of interest accruals.

Elective mark-to-market methodology

Paragraph (i) of the proposed regulations provides an elective mark-to-market methodology for certain NPCs providing for nonperiodic payments. If an election is made, the specific accounting rules for nonperiodic payments in §1.446-3(f)(2) (other than (f)(2)(i)) are not applicable. Instead, for any contract that is held at the close of the taxable year, the taxpayer determines income inclusions and deductions by reference to the gain or loss that would be realized if the contract were sold for its fair market value on the last business day of the taxable year. Because the determination of fair market value takes into account the expected value of future nonperiodic payments, the mark-to-market methodology constitutes a reasonable basis for amortizing the nonperiodic payments over the term of the contract as required by §1.446-3(f)(2)(i).

Proper adjustments are made in the amount of gain or loss subsequently realized (or calculated) for income inclusions and deductions taken into account in marking the contract to fair market value. Furthermore, under paragraph (i)(5) of the proposed regulations, if an election is made for a contract providing for a significant nonperiodic payment, paragraph (g)(4) continues to apply and proper adjustments must be made to the income inclusions and deductions recognized under the mark-to-market methodology to take into account amounts recognized as interest and the payment or receipt of the significant nonperiodic payment, subject to the special rule set forth below.

The proposed regulations set forth a special rule for contracts providing for significant contingent nonperiodic payments that are subject to the mark-to-market election. If a contract provides for a significant contingent nonperiodic payment, the taxpayer must apply the noncontingent swap method to determine the amounts recognized as interest under paragraph (g)(4). However, the taxpayer is not required to reproject the amount of the contingent payment each year. The interest amounts for subsequent years are the interest amounts as determined using the initial projection of the contingent payment. Furthermore, an alternative deemed equivalent value method may be used to determine the projected amount of the contingent payment. The deemed equivalent value method may be applied when the contract fixes the timing and amount of all of the payments under the contract, except for the significant contingent nonperiodic payment. The amount of the significant contingent nonperiodic payment is deemed to be the amount that causes the present value of all the payments by the taxpayer to equal the present value of all of the payments of the counterparty to the contract.

The inclusion of an elective mark-to-market methodology is intended to provide taxpayers with an alternative to the provisions of paragraphs (f) of the 1993 Treasury regulations and (g)(6) of the proposed regulations respecting nonperiodic payments. With respect to significant nonperiodic payments, however, the proposed regulations preserve certain features of those provisions for purposes of computing an interest component of swap payments. Such a calculation is necessary to preserve the characterization of an accrual as interest. The IRS and Treasury request comments on the appropriateness of requiring taxpayers to compute an interest amount for significant nonperiodic payments under the elective mark-to-market methodology and, in particular, on any effect that requirement may have on the relative usefulness and administrability of the mark-to-market methodology.

Paragraph (i)(2) of the proposed regulations provides the scope of the election. The election is available to contracts that are: (1) actively traded within the meaning of §1.1092(d)-1(c) (determined without regard to the limitation in §1.1092(d)-1(c)(2)); (2) marked to market for purposes of the taxpayer's financial statements provided the taxpayer satisfies the requirements in paragraph (i)(4) of the proposed regulations; (3) subject to an agreement by a party to the contract that is a person to whom section 475 applies to supply to the taxpayer the value that it uses in applying section 475(a)(2); or (4) marked to market by a regulated investment company (RIC) described in section 1296(e)(2). Paragraphs (i)(3)(i) through (iv) of the proposed regulations provide the acceptable methods for determining fair market value. If the contract is actively traded, the fair market value is determined based on the mean between the bid and asked prices quoted for the contract. If a contract is not actively traded, but is marked to market for financial statement purposes, and the valuations used for those purposes comply with the requirements of paragraph (i)(4), the fair market value is deemed to be the value used for the financial statements. For a contract that is subject to an agreement with a dealer in securities to provide a value, the value that is provided by the dealer is the fair market value. Finally, for a contract marked to market by a RIC, the fair market value is equal to the value used for purposes of determining the RIC's net asset value.

Paragraph (i)(6) of the proposed regulations provides that the mark-to-market election shall be made in the time and manner prescribed by the Commissioner and is effective for the taxable year in which it is made and all subsequent years unless revoked with the consent of the Commissioner.

The proposed regulations indicate that a taxpayer will be permitted to elect the mark-to-market method for NPCs that are marked to market for purposes of the taxpayer's financial statements and that the values used on the financial statements may be used as fair market value under the mark-to-market election. However, the proposed regulations also indicate that an election to use financial statement values will be subject to further requirements. On May 5, 2003, the IRS and Treasury published in the **Federal Register** an Advance Notice of Proposed Rule Making (REG-100420-03) requesting comments regarding appropriate rules for the use of financial statement values under the mark-to-market provisions of section 475 applicable to securities dealers and electing commodities dealers and securities and commodities traders. The IRS and Treasury will take into account the comments received in response to that Advance Notice in developing the rules to be established for use of financial statement values under the mark-to-market method set forth in paragraph (i) of the proposed regulations. In addition, unlike other mark-to-market regimes, the mark-to-market method proposed in paragraph (i) does not require a mark immediately before disposition in either a recognition or nonrecognition context. *Cf.* section 1256(c) and proposed regulations §1.475(a)-2. The IRS and Treasury request comments regarding this aspect of the proposed regulations and whether taxpayers who are eligible to elect a mark-to-market method under section 475 but do not do so should be eligible to make the paragraph (i) election for NPCs.

Anti-abuse rule

Paragraph (i) of the 1993 Treasury regulations provides that if a taxpayer "enters into a transaction with a principal purpose of applying the rules of [§1.446-3] to produce a material distortion of income," the IRS may depart from those rules "as necessary to reflect the appropriate timing of income and deductions from the transaction." In light of the comprehensive rules in the proposed regulations prescribing methods of accounting for NPCs, the IRS and Treasury have determined that a general anti-abuse rule is not necessary to prevent these methods being used in a manner that fails to clearly reflect income. Accordingly, the proposed regulations delete this rule.

Proposed dates of applicability

These proposed regulations contain both new substantive rules as well as clarifying changes to the 1993 Treasury regulations. The new substantive rules, which are contained in paragraph (g)(6) (the noncontingent swap method) (except (g)(6)(i)) and paragraph (i) (the mark-to-market election), are proposed to apply to NPCs entered into on or after 30 days after the date of publication of the final regulations in the **Federal Register**. Paragraphs (c) (definitions), (d) (taxable year of inclusion and deduction), (f) (nonperiodic payments), (g)(4) (significant nonperiodic payments), and (g)(6)(i) (definition of contingent and noncontingent nonperiodic payments) are proposed to be integrated into the 1993 Treasury regulations which apply to NPCs entered into on or after December 13, 1993. Because of their purely clarifying nature, these proposed changes will apply to the same transactions that are governed by the 1993 Treasury regulations.

With respect to NPCs that provide for contingent nonperiodic payments and that are in effect or entered into on or after 30 days after the date of publication of these proposed regulations in the **Federal Register**, if a taxpayer has not adopted a method of accounting for those NPCs, the taxpayer must adopt a method that takes contingent nonperiodic payments into account over the life of the contract under a reasonable amortization method, which may be, but need not be, a method that satisfies the specific rules in these proposed regulations. If a taxpayer has adopted a method of accounting for these NPCs, the Commissioner generally will not require a change in the accounting method earlier than the first year ending on or after 30 days after the date of publication of the final regulations in the **Federal Register**. The preceding sentence does not apply to transactions described in Rev. Rul. 2002-30 (2002-1 C.B. 971) or other published guidance.

The proposed regulations do not contain a specific consistency requirement. Nevertheless, under the general rules governing accounting methods, once a taxpayer adopts a method of accounting for an item, the taxpayer must use the same method from year to year unless the taxpayer obtains the Commissioner's consent to change to another method of accounting.

Character

The proposed regulations under §1.162-30 provide that in general, the net periodic and nonperiodic payments (including mark-to-market deductions) are deductible by the payor under section 162 as ordinary and necessary business expenses. However, payments representing interest under the rules for significant nonperiodic payments as well as termination payments are not deductible under section 162. A similar rule is provided for individuals in the proposed regulations under §1.212-1(q). These regulations under sections 162 and 212 are proposed to apply to NPCs entered into on or after 30 days after the date of publication of the final regulations in the **Federal Register**.

Any gain or loss arising from a termination payment, however, is treated as capital gain or loss pursuant to the proposed regulations under section 1234A. These proposed regulations clarify that periodic payments, noncontingent nonperiodic payments, and contingent nonperiodic payments are not termination payments.

The proposed regulations under section 1234A also apply to any gain or loss arising from the settlement of obligations under a bullet swap or forward contract. A payment in settlement of obligations under a bullet swap or forward contract, including a payment pursuant to the terms of the bullet swap or forward contract, is treated as gain or loss from a termination of the bullet swap or forward contract.

For purposes of these proposed regulations, a bullet swap is defined as a financial instrument that is not an excluded contract as defined in §1.446-3(c)(1)(ii), that provides for the computation of an amount or amounts due from one party to another by reference to a specified index upon a notional principal amount, and that provides for settlement of all the parties' obligations at or close to maturity of the contract, rather than for the payment of the specified amounts at specific intervals. The definition of bullet swap is intended to cover a contract that obligates each party to make a payment at the end of the contract, although only one net payment will actually be paid. For example, party A is obligated to pay at the end of three years a fixed rate multiplied by the notional amount. Also at the end of three years, party B is obligated to pay a variable rate multiplied by the same notional amount. At the end of three years, only one party makes a net payment equal to the difference between the fixed rate multiplied by the notional amount and the variable rate multiplied by the notional amount.

These regulations under section 1234A are proposed to apply to NPCs entered into on or after 30 days after the date of publication of the final regulations in the **Federal Register**.

Special Analyses

It has been determined that this notice of proposed rulemaking is not a significant regulatory action as defined in Executive Order 12866. Therefore, a regulatory assessment is not required. It is hereby certified that these regulations will not have a significant economic impact on a substantial number of small entities. This certification is based on the fact that very few small businesses enter into NPCs with contingent nonperiodic payments because these contracts are costly and complex and because they require constant monitoring and a sophisticated understanding of the capital markets. Therefore, a Regulatory Flexibility Analysis is not required. Pursuant to section 7805(f) of the Code, this notice of proposed rulemaking will be submitted to the Chief Counsel for Advocacy of the Small Business Administration for comment on its impact on small businesses.

Comments and Public Hearing

Before these proposed regulations are adopted as final regulations, consideration will be given to any written comments (a signed original and eight (8) copies) or electronic comments that are submitted timely to the IRS. The IRS and Treasury specifically request comments on the clarity of the proposed rules and how they may be made easier to understand. All comments will be available for public inspection and copying.

A public hearing has been scheduled for May 25, 2004, beginning at 10 a.m., in the IRS Auditorium, Seventh Floor, Internal Revenue Building, 1111 Constitution Avenue, NW., Washington, DC. Due to building security procedures, visitors must enter at the Constitution Avenue entrance. In addition, all visitors must present photo identification to enter the building. Because of access restrictions, visitors will not be admitted beyond the immediate entrance area more than 30 minutes before the hearing starts. For information about having your name placed on the building access list to attend the hearing, see "FOR FURTHER INFORMATION CONTACT" section of this preamble.

The rules of 26 CFR 601.601(a)(3) apply to the hearing. Persons who wish to present oral comments at the hearing must submit written comments or electronic comments and an outline of topics to be discussed and the time to be devoted to each topic (a signed original and eight (8) copies) by May 4, 2004. A period of 10 minutes will be allotted to each person making comments. An agenda showing the scheduling of the speakers will be prepared after the deadline for receiving outlines has passed. Copies of the agenda will be available free of charge at the hearing.

Drafting Information

The principal author of these regulations is Kate Sleeth, Office of the Associate Chief Counsel (Financial Institutions and Products). However, other personnel from the IRS and Treasury participated in their development.

[¶ 49,217]   **Proposed Amendments of Regulations (REG-153172-03),** published in the Federal Register on March 18, 2004.

Consolidated returns: Regulations covering consolidated returns: Losses: Disposition of subsidiary stock: Proposed regulations.—Amendments of Reg. §1.1502-80, relating to the deductibility of losses recognized on dispositions of subsidiary stock by members of a consolidated group, the consequences of treating subsidiary stock as worthless, and when stock of a member of a consolidated group may be treated as worthless, are proposed. Amendments of Reg. §1.337(d)-2 were adopted by T.D. 9187 on 3/2/2005. Amendments of Reg. §1.1502-35 were adopted by T.D. 9254 on 3/9/2006.

AGENCY: Internal Revenue Service (IRS), Treasury.

ACTION: Notice of proposed rulemaking by cross-reference to temporary regulations.

SUMMARY: In the Rules and Regulations section of this issue of the **Federal Register**, the IRS is issuing temporary regulations under sections 337(d) and 1502 of the Internal Revenue Code relating to the deductibility of losses recognized on dispositions of subsidiary stock by members of a consolidated group, the consequences of treating subsidiary stock as worthless, and when stock of a member of a consolidated group may be treated as worthless. The temporary regulations apply to corporations filing consolidated returns. The text of the temporary regulations published in this issue of the **Federal Register** also serves as the text of these proposed regulations.

DATES: Written or electronic comments must be received by June 16, 2004.

ADDRESSES: Send submissions to: CC:PA:LPD:PR (REG-153172-03), room 5203, Internal Revenue Service, POB 7604, Ben Franklin Station, Washington, DC 20044. Submissions may be hand delivered Monday through Friday between the hours of 8 a.m. and 4 p.m. to CC:PA:LPD:PR (REG-153172-03), Courier's Desk, Internal Revenue Service, 1111 Constitution Avenue, NW., Washington, DC 20044. Alternatively, taxpayers may submit electronic comments directly to the IRS Internet site at *www.irs.gov/regs*.

FOR FURTHER INFORMATION CONTACT: Regarding the regulations under section 337(d), Mark Weiss (202-622-7790) of the Office of Associate Chief Counsel (Corporate), and regarding the regulations under section 1502, Lola L. Johnson (202-622-7550) of the Office of Associate Chief Counsel (Corporate); regarding submission of comments and/or requests for a hearing, Sonya M. Cruse (202-622-4693) of the Office of Procedure and Administration (not toll-free numbers).

SUPPLEMENTARY INFORMATION:

Background and Explanation of Provisions

Temporary regulations in the Rules and Regulations section of this issue of the **Federal Register** amend the Income Tax Regulations (26 CFR part 1) relating to section 337(d) and section 1502. The text of those regulations also serves as the text of these proposed regulations. The preamble to the temporary regulations explains the amendments.

Special Analyses

It has been determined that this notice of proposed rulemaking is not a significant regulatory action as defined in Executive Order 12866. Therefore, a regulatory assessment is not required. It is hereby certified that these regulations will not have a significant economic impact on a substantial number of small entities. This certification is based on the fact that these regulations will primarily affect affiliated groups of corporations, which tend to be larger businesses. Therefore a Regulatory Flexibility Analysis is not required. Pursuant to section 7805(f) of the Internal Revenue Code, this notice of proposed rulemaking will be submitted to the Chief Counsel for Advocacy of the Small Business Administration for comment on its impact on small business.

Comments and Requests for a Public Hearing

Before these proposed regulations are adopted as final regulations, consideration will be given to any written comments (a signed original and eight (8) copies) or electronic comments that are submitted timely to the IRS. The IRS and the Treasury Department request comments on the clarity of the proposed regulations and how they may be made easier to understand. All comments will be available for public inspection and copying. A public hearing may be scheduled if requested by any person who timely submits comments. If a public hearing is scheduled, notice of the date, time and place for the hearing will be published in the **Federal Register**.

Drafting Information

The principal author of the regulations under section 337(d) is Mark Weiss, Office of Associate Chief Counsel (Corporate). The principal author of the regulations under section 1502 is Lola L. Johnson, Office of Associate Chief Counsel (Corporate). However, other personnel from the IRS and Treasury participated in their development.

[¶ 49,219] Proposed Amendments of Regulations (REG-128590-03), published in the Federal Register on May 7, 2004.

Deductions: Expenses: Interest: Tax-exempt obligations: Related entities: Consolidated groups: Income exclusion.—Amendments of Reg. §§ 1.265-2 and 1.1502-13, affecting corporations filing consolidated returns and providing special rules for the treatment of certain intercompany transactions involving interest on intercompany obligations, are proposed.

AGENCY: Internal Revenue Service (IRS), Treasury.

ACTION: Notice of proposed rulemaking.

SUMMARY: This document contains proposed regulations under section 265(a)(2) that affect corporations filing consolidated returns. These regulations provide special rules for the treatment of certain intercompany transactions involving interest on intercompany obligations.

DATES: Written or electronic comments and requests for a public hearing must be received by August 5, 2004.

ADDRESSES: Send submissions to: CC:PA:LPD:PR (REG-128590-03), room 5203, Internal Revenue Service, POB 7604, Ben Franklin Station, Washington, DC 20044. Submissions may be hand delivered Monday through Friday between the hours of 8 a.m. and 4 p.m. to CC:PA:LPD:PR (REG-128590-03), Courier's Desk, Internal Revenue Service, 1111 Constitution Avenue, NW., Washington, DC. Alternatively, taxpayers may submit comments electronically via the IRS Internet site at *www.irs.gov/regs* or via the Federal eRulemaking Portal at *www.regulations.gov* (indicate IRS and REG-128590-03).

FOR FURTHER INFORMATION CONTACT: Concerning the proposed regulations, Frances L. Kelly, (202) 622-7770; concerning submissions of comments and/or requests for a public hearing, Guy Traynor, (202) 622-7180 (not toll-free numbers).

SUPPLEMENTARY INFORMATION:

Background

Section 265(a)(2)

Section 163(a) generally allows a deduction for all interest paid or accrued within the taxable year on indebtedness. Under section 265(a)(2), however, no deduction is allowed for interest on indebtedness incurred or continued to purchase or carry obligations the interest on which is wholly exempt from Federal income taxes.

Rev. Proc. 72-18 (1972-1 C.B. 740) provides guidelines for the application of section 265(a)(2) to taxpayers holding tax-exempt obligations. Section 3.01 of the revenue procedure states that the application of section 265(a)(2) requires a determination, based upon all the facts and circumstances, of the taxpayer's purpose in incurring or continuing each item of indebtedness. Such purpose may be established by either direct or circumstantial evidence. Direct evidence includes direct tracing of borrowed funds to investments in tax-exempt obligations and the pledging of tax-exempt obligations as security for the indebtedness. To the extent that there is direct evidence establishing a purpose to purchase or carry tax-exempt obligations, the interest paid or incurred on such indebtedness may not be deducted. In certain other cases when an interest deduction is disallowed (for example, when amounts borrowed by a dealer in tax-exempt obligations are not directly traceable to tax-exempt obligations), section 7 of Rev. Proc. 72-18 sets forth a formula to calculate the disallowed interest deduction. That formula provides that the amount of the disallowed interest deduction is determined by multiplying the total interest on the indebtedness by a fraction, the numerator of which is the average amount during the taxable year of the taxpayer's tax-exempt obligations (valued at their adjusted bases), and the denominator of which is the average amount during the taxable year of the taxpayer's total assets (valued at their adjusted bases) minus the amount of any indebtedness the interest deduction on which is not subject to disallowance to any extent under Rev. Proc. 72-18.

In *H Enterprises International, Inc. v. Commissioner*, 75 T.C.M. (CCH) 1948 (1998), *aff'd*, 183 F.3d 907 (8th Cir. 1999), a parent and a subsidiary were members of the same consolidated group of corporations. The subsidiary declared a dividend and, a few days later, borrowed funds and immediately used part of those funds to make the dividend distribution to the parent. A portion of the distributed funds was disbursed to two investment divisions of the parent, which used the funds to acquire investments including tax-exempt obligations.

The court held that a portion of the subsidiary's indebtedness was incurred for the purpose of purchasing or carrying tax-exempt obligations (held in the parent's investment divisions) and, therefore, no deduction was allowed for the interest on this portion of the indebtedness under section 265(a)(2). To establish the required purposive connection under section 265(a)(2), the court reasoned that the activities of the parent corporation were relevant in determining the subsidiary's purpose for borrowing the funds. The court stated that if the analysis only focused on the borrower and not the transferee, then the purpose of the borrower corporation would always be acceptable, frustrating the legislative intent of section 265(a)(2).

Rev. Rul. 2004-47 (2004-21 I.R.B.) provides guidance on the application of section 265(a)(2) in a number of situations in which a member of an affiliated group borrows money from an unrelated party and transfers funds to another member of the group that is a dealer in tax-exempt obligations. In *Situation 4*, P and S are members of the same affiliated group but file separate tax returns. P borrows funds from L, an unrelated bank, and lends the borrowed funds to S, a dealer in tax-exempt obligations. S uses the borrowed funds in its business. The ruling examines the obligation from L to P and the obligation from P to S for the application of section 265(a)(2). With regard to the loan from L to P, P uses the borrowed funds to make a loan to S, and P separately accounts for the taxable interest income from the obligation. The ruling concludes that P does not have a purpose of using the borrowed funds to purchase or carry tax-exempt obligations within the meaning of section 265(a)(2). With regard to the loan from P to S, although the borrowed funds are not directly traceable to S's purchase or carry of tax-exempt obligations, the ruling concludes that section 265(a)(2) applies to disallow a deduction for a portion of S's interest expense. The portion of S's interest deduction that is disallowed is determined pursuant to the formula of section 7 of Rev. Proc. 72-18.

The Intercompany Transaction Regulations

Section 1.1502-13 prescribes rules relating to the treatment of transactions between members of a consolidated group. With respect to intercompany obligations, the intercompany transaction rules generally operate to match the debtor member's items with the lending member's items from the intercompany obligation.

Under §1.1502-13(c)(6)(i), if section 265(a)(2) permanently and explicitly disallows a debtor member's interest deduction with respect to a debt to another member, the lending member's interest income is treated as excluded from gross income. See §1.1502-13(g)(5), *Example* 1(d). In cases when a member of the group borrows from another member to purchase or carry tax-exempt obligations, and the lending member has not borrowed from sources outside of the group to fund the intercompany obligation, the result reached under the §1.1502-13(c)(6)(i) exclusion rule is appropriate in that it reflects that intercompany lending transactions do not alter the net worth of the group and, thus, should not affect consolidated taxable income.

However, when the lending member borrows from a nonmember, the lending member lends those funds to the debtor member, and the debtor member uses those funds to purchase or carry tax-exempt obligations, the application of the §1.1502-13(c)(6)(i) exclusion rule may produce inappropriate results. For example, assume P borrows $100 from L, a nonmember, for the purpose of lending the $100 to S under the same terms, and S's purpose for borrowing $60 of the intercompany loan from P is to purchase $60 of tax-exempt obligations. Under section 265(a)(2), a deduction would be disallowed for a portion of S's interest expense on the intercompany obligation and a portion of P's interest income would be excluded from P's gross income under §1.1502-13(c)(6)(i). Accordingly, section 265(a)(2) may have no effect on the group's taxable income, even though the group has borrowed to purchase tax-exempt obligations.

Explanation of Provisions

The IRS and Treasury Department believe that, when a member's indebtedness to a nonmember is directly traceable to an intercompany obligation and another member of the group uses the funds borrowed from the nonmember to purchase or carry tax-exempt obligations, the net tax effect of these transactions for the group should be a disallowance of a deduction for interest under section 265(a)(2).

These proposed regulations reflect that when a member (P) borrows funds from a nonmember and lends all of those funds to another member (S) that uses those funds to purchase tax-exempt obligations, section 265(a)(2) will apply to disallow a deduction for the interest on S's obligation to P, not P's obligation to the nonmember. These proposed regulations provide that, if a member of a consolidated group incurs or continues indebtedness to a nonmember, that indebtedness to the nonmember is directly traceable to all or a portion of an intercompany obligation extended to a member of the group (the borrowing member) by another member of the group (the lending member), and section 265(a)(2) applies to disallow a deduction for all or a portion of the borrowing member's interest expense incurred with respect to the intercompany obligation, then §1.1502-13(c)(6)(i) will not apply to exclude an amount of the lending member's interest income with respect to the intercompany obligation that equals the amount of the borrowing member's disallowed interest deduction. This override of the exclusion rule is subject, however, to a limitation. In particular, the amount of interest income not excluded cannot exceed the interest expense on the portion of the nonmember indebtedness that is directly traceable to the intercompany obligation. This limitation ensures that applying section 265(a)(2) to disallow an interest deduction with respect to an intercompany obligation that can be directly traced to nonmember indebtedness does not result in a worse overall tax position for the group than applying section 265(a)(2) to disallow a deduction for the interest paid to the nonmember.

Therefore, subject to the limitation discussed above, if the proceeds of P's borrowing from a nonmember can be directly traced to a P-S intercompany obligation and all or a portion of S's interest expense on the P-S intercompany obligation is disallowed as a deduction under section 265(a)(2), these proposed regulations require that all or a portion of P's interest income on the intercompany obligation not be excluded under §1.1502-13(c)(6)(i).

In an Advance Notice of Proposed Rulemaking (REG-128572-03) in this issue of the **Federal Register**, the IRS and Treasury Department are soliciting comments regarding whether regulations under section 7701(f) should address the application of sections 265(a)(2) and 246A in transactions involving related parties, pass-thru entities, or other intermediaries, and suggestions as to the approach that should be taken by those regulations. It is possible that those comments and any regulations proposed under section 7701(f) will result in amendments to the rules set forth in these proposed regulations.

Proposed Effective Date

These regulations are proposed to apply to taxable years beginning on or after the date these regulations are published as final regulations in the **Federal Register**.

Special Analysis

It has been determined that this notice of proposed rulemaking is not a significant regulatory action as defined in Executive Order 12866. Therefore, a regulatory assessment is not required. It is hereby certified that these regulations will not have a significant economic impact on a substantial number of small entities. This certification is based upon the fact that these regulations will primarily affect affiliated groups of corporations that have elected to file consolidated returns, which tend to be larger businesses. Therefore, a Regulatory Flexibility Analysis under the Regulatory Flexibility Act (5 U.S.C. chapter 6) is not required. Pursuant to section 7805(f) of the Internal Revenue Code, these regulations will be submitted to the Chief Counsel for Advocacy of the Small Business Administration for comment on their impact on small business.

Comments and Requests for a Public Hearing

Before these proposed regulations are adopted as final regulations, consideration will be given to any written (a signed original and eight (8) copies) or electronic comments that are submitted timely to the IRS. The IRS and Treasury Department request comments on the clarity of the proposed rules and how they can be made easier to understand. All comments will be available for public inspection and copying. A public hearing will be scheduled if requested in writing by any person that timely submits written comments. If a public hearing is scheduled, notice of the date, time, and place for the public hearing will be published in the **Federal Register.**

Drafting Information

The principal author of these proposed regulations is Frances L. Kelly, Office of the Associate Chief Counsel (Corporate). However, other personnel from the IRS and Treasury Department participated in their development.

[¶ 49,226]   **Proposed Amendments of Regulations (REG-108637-03)**, published in the Federal Register on August 25, 2004.

Original issue discount: Accrual: REMICs.—Amendments of Reg. §§1.1271-0 and 1.1275-2, relating to the accrual of original issue discount (OID) on certain real estate mortgage investment conduit (REMIC) regular interests, are proposed. A public hearing on this proposal is scheduled for November 17, 2004.

AGENCY: Internal Revenue Service (IRS), Treasury.

ACTION: Notice of proposed rulemaking and notice of public hearing.

SUMMARY: This document contains proposed regulations relating to the accrual of original issue discount (OID) on certain real estate mortgage investment conduit (REMIC) regular interests. The proposed regulations are necessary to provide guidance to REMICs, REMIC regular interest holders and information reporters regarding the accrual of OID. This document also provides notice of a public hearing on the proposed regulations.

DATES: Written or electronic comments must be received by November 23, 2004. Outlines of topics to be discussed at the public hearing scheduled for November 17, 2004, must be received by October 27, 2004.

ADDRESSES: Send submissions to: CC:PA:LPD:PR (REG-108637-03), room 5203, Internal Revenue Service, PO Box 7604, Ben Franklin Station, Washington, DC 20044. Submissions may be hand-delivered Monday through Friday between the hours of 8 a.m. and 4 p.m. to CC:PA:LPD:PR (REG-108637-03), Courier's Desk, Internal Revenue Service, 1111 Constitution Avenue, NW., Washington, DC, or sent electronically, via the IRS Internet site at *www.irs.gov/regs* or via the Federal eRulemaking Portal at *www.regulations.gov* (IRS—REG-108637-03). The public hearing will be held in the Auditorium, Internal Revenue Building, 1111 Constitution Avenue, NW., Washington, DC.

FOR FURTHER INFORMATION CONTACT: Concerning the regulations, contact Rebecca Asta at (202) 622-3930. To be placed on the building access list for the hearing, contact Sonya Cruse at (202) 622-7180.

SUPPLEMENTARY INFORMATION:

Background and Explanation of Provisions

1. *General Background*

A debt instrument may provide for qualified stated interest (QSI) (that is, certain periodic payments of stated interest), OID, or both. Sections 163(e) and 1271 through 1275 provide rules for the treatment of OID on debt instruments. In general, the holder of a debt instrument includes OID in income as it accrues, even if the holder generally uses a cash method of accounting. A holder of a REMIC regular interest includes QSI in income under an accrual method of accounting because section 860B(b) requires that amounts includible in gross income with respect to a REMIC regular interest be determined under an accrual method.

For many debt instruments, only one or two days separate the date on which the holder becomes entitled to a payment (the record date) from the date on which the holder receives payment (the payment date). For REMIC regular interests, however, the record date may precede the payment date by 15 to 30 days.

2. *Current REMIC Accrual Practice*

Under the governing contract provisions, REMIC regular interests generally accrue interest from the issue date to the final record date, and holders become entitled to receive interest payments based on month-end record dates. The IRS and the Treasury Department understand, however, that, in general, REMIC servicers have interpreted the OID rules to require or permit holders' OID to accrue for tax purposes over the period from payment date to payment date and have treated QSI as accruing over the same periods. To compensate for accruing QSI and OID beyond the final record date to the final payment date, the servicers have treated QSI and OID on REMIC regular interests as not accruing from the date of issue for a period equal to the number of days between the record date and payment date. In effect, for tax purposes, the tax accrual of QSI and OID lags the legal accrual of interest by the delayed payment period.

For tax purposes, as of the date a REMIC regular interest is purchased in the secondary market, the purchaser begins to accrue QSI and OID, and the seller ceases to accrue QSI and OID. A purchaser that holds the instrument until the final payment date or redemption accrues QSI and OID past the final record date as long as it holds the instrument. A purchaser that begins to accrue QSI and OID on the purchase date gives up the benefit of the lag in the beginning of the accrual period. As a result, the delayed accrual system causes the last secondary market purchaser of a REMIC regular interest to accrue for tax purposes an additional number of days of QSI and OID equal to the number of days between the record and payment dates, and too much QSI and OID is allocated to the last secondary purchaser of the REMIC regular interest. Moreover, because of principal payments, the holder will earn interest on a declining principal balance, while the lagging tax accruals will be based on a higher principal amount between record dates and payment dates in many instances. Consequently, a secondary market purchaser that is not the last secondary market purchaser will experience tax accruals in excess of legal entitlements if the regular interest has significant stated principal and bears interest at a stated rate.

3. *Overview of the Proposed Regulations*

The proposed rules address the misallocation of QSI and OID by creating a special rule for accruing OID on REMIC regular interests that provide for a delay between record and payment dates. Under the proposed regulations, the period over which OID accrues generally coincides with the period over which the holder's right to interest payments accrues under the governing contract provisions.

Generally, under the proposed regulations, if the terms of a REMIC regular interest provide for a delay between the record and payment dates, the initial accrual period begins on the date of issuance of the regular interest, and the final accrual period ends on the final record date of that REMIC regular interest. By shifting the entire tax accrual schedule, this special rule allocates all QSI and OID to the period between the issue date and the final record date of the instrument and none to the period between the final record date and final payment date. For purposes of calculating OID in the final accrual period with the methodology described in section 1272(a)(6), but for no other purpose, payments on the REMIC regular interest after the end of that accrual period that are included in the stated redemption price at maturity of the instrument (such as the payment on the final payment date) are treated as being made during the final accrual period.

The IRS and Treasury Department recognize that, although the proposed regulations result in a more accurate allocation of QSI and OID among REMIC regular interest holders, some economic accuracy may be sacrificed by ending the accrual of OID before final payments are made on the regular interests. Therefore, the proposed regulations are limited to REMIC regular interests with delayed payment periods of fewer than 32 days. The regulation regarding REMIC regular interests with delayed payment periods of more than 31 days is reserved. The IRS and Treasury Department request comments on whether additional guidance is needed for these REMIC regular interests.

4. *Accrual of Qualified Stated Interest*

Section 1.1272-1(a) requires a holder to include QSI in income under the holder's regular method of accounting. Section 1.446-2(b) requires a holder, as well as the issuer, to accrue QSI ratably over the accrual period to which it is attributable. In addition, section 860B(b) requires a holder of a regular interest to accrue amounts into gross income regardless of the holder's overall method of accounting. The amounts that must be so accrued include QSI. The Treasury Department and the IRS understand that many REMIC servicers have accrued QSI over the same period as OID. It is intended that, with respect to the accrual periods referenced in §1.446-2(b), the initial accrual period for QSI will begin on the date of issuance and the final accrual period for QSI will end on the final record date. As a result, the QSI accrues over the same period as the OID.

Proposed Effective Date

These regulations are proposed to apply to any REMIC regular interest issued after the date the final regulations are published in the **Federal Register.** The proposed regulations provide automatic consent for the holder of a REMIC regular interest to change its method of accounting for OID under the final regulations. The change is proposed to be made on a cut-off basis and, thus, does not affect REMIC regular interests issued before the date the final regulations are published in the **Federal Register.**

The Treasury Department and the IRS are concerned regarding the extent to which holders of REMIC regular interests will be aware that changes in accounting methods for QSI may be necessary to comply with the special rule in the proposed regulations. If a holder of REMIC regular interests relies on data provided on behalf of the REMIC rather than performing its own computations, the holder may be unaware that these rules will have required newly issued REMICs to alter the accrual periods over which interest reported to holders is computed. The Treasury Department and the IRS request comments on the way in which a change in accounting method for QSI should be effected.

The Treasury Department and the IRS request comments concerning the extent to which any other debt instruments provide for a significant delay between record and payment dates and, if some do, whether rules like those in the proposed regulations should be extended to them. Any comments received will be considered in connection with the publication of final regulations in the **Federal Register.**

Special Analyses

It has been determined that this notice of proposed rulemaking is not a significant regulatory action as defined in Executive Order 12866. Therefore, a regulatory flexibility assessment is not required. It has also been determined that section 553(b) of the Administrative Procedures Act (5 U.S.C. chapter 5) does not apply to these regulations, and because the regulation does not impose a collection of information on small entities, the Regulatory Flexibility Act (5 U.S.C. chapter 6) does not apply. Pursuant to section 7805(f) of the Internal Revenue Code, this notice of proposed rulemaking will be submitted to the Chief Counsel for Advocacy of the Small Business Administration for comment on its impact on small businesses.

Comments and Public Hearing

Before these proposed regulations are adopted as final regulations, consideration will be given to any written comments (a signed original and eight (8) copies) or electronic comments that are submitted timely to the IRS. The Treasury Department and IRS specifically request comments on the clarity of the proposed rules and how they may be made easier to understand. All comments will be available for public inspection and copying.

A public hearing has been scheduled for November 17, 2004, beginning at 10 a.m. in the Auditorium of the Internal Revenue Building, 1111 Constitution Avenue, NW., Washington, DC. Due to building security procedures, visitors must enter at the Constitution Avenue entrance. All visitors must present photo identification to enter the building. Because of access restrictions, visitors will not be admitted beyond the immediate entrance area more than 30 minutes before the hearing starts. For information about having your name placed on the building access list to attend the hearing, see the "FOR FURTHER INFORMATION CONTACT" section of this preamble.

The rules of 26 CFR 601.601(a)(3) apply to the hearing. Persons who wish to present oral comments at the hearing must submit written or electronic comments by November 23, 2004, and an outline of the topics to be discussed and the time to be devoted to each topic (signed original and eight (8) copies) by October 27, 2004. A period of 10 minutes will be allotted to each person for making comments. An agenda showing the schedule of speakers will be prepared after the deadline for receiving outlines has passed. Copies of the agenda will be available free of charge at the hearing.

Drafting Information

The principal author of these proposed regulations is Rebecca Asta of the Office of Associate Chief Counsel (Financial Institutions and Products). However, other personnel from the IRS and Treasury Department participated in their development.

[¶49,228]   **Proposed Regulation and Proposed Amendments of Regulations (REG-114726-04),** published in the Federal Register on November 10, 2004 (corrected 12/28/2004).

Pension plans: Phased retirement: Partial retirement: Benefits paid: Benefit accrual: Testing: Retirement age.—Reg. §1.401(a)-3 and amendments of Reg. §1.401(a)-1, providing rules permitting distributions to be made from a pension plan under a phased retirement program, are proposed. Amendments to Reg. §1.401(a)-1 were adopted 5/21/2007 by T.D. 9325.

AGENCY: Internal Revenue Service (IRS), Treasury.

ACTION: Notice of proposed rulemaking.

SUMMARY: This notice of proposed rulemaking contains proposed amendments to the Income Tax Regulations under section 401(a) of the Internal Revenue Code. These proposed regulations provide rules permitting distributions to be made from a pension plan under a phased retirement program and set forth requirements for a bona fide phased retirement program. The proposed regulations will provide the public with guidance regarding distributions from qualified pension plans and will affect administrators of, and participants in, such plans.

DATES: Written or electronic comments and requests for a public hearing must be received by February 8, 2005.

ADDRESSES: Send submissions to: CC:PA:LPD:PR (REG-114726-04), room 5203, Internal Revenue Service, PO Box 7604, Ben Franklin Station, Washington, DC 20044. Submissions may be hand-delivered Monday through Friday between the hours of 8 a.m. and 4 p.m. to CC:PA:LPD:PR (REG-114726-04), Courier's Desk, Internal Revenue Service, 1111 Constitution Avenue, NW., Washington, DC, or sent electronically, via the IRS Internet site at *www.irs.gov/regs* or via the Federal eRulemaking Portal at *www.regulations.gov* (indicate IRS and REG-114726-04).

FOR FURTHER INFORMATION CONTACT: Concerning the regulations, Cathy A. Vohs, 202-622-6090; concerning submissions and requests for a public hearing, contact Sonya Cruse, 202-622-7180 (not toll-free numbers).

SUPPLEMENTARY INFORMATION:

Background

As people are living longer, healthier lives, there is a greater risk that individuals may outlive their retirement savings. In addition, employers have expressed interest in encouraging older, more experienced workers to stay in the workforce. One approach that some employers have implemented is to offer employees the opportunity for phased retirement."

While there is no single approach to phased retirement, these arrangements generally provide employees who are at or near eligibility for retirement with the opportunity for a reduced schedule or workload, thereby providing a smoother transition from full-time employment to retirement. These arrangements permit the employer to retain the services of an experienced employee and provide the employee with the opportunity to continue active employment at a level that also allows greater flexibility and time away from work.

During such a transition arrangement, employees may wish to supplement their part-time income with a portion of their retirement savings. However, phased retirement can also increase the risk of outliving retirement savings for employees who begin drawing upon their retirement savings before normal retirement age. Even though the annuity distribution options offered by defined benefit plans preclude outliving benefits, early distribution of a portion of the employee's benefit will reduce the benefits available after full retirement. On the other hand, phased retirement also can provide employees additional time to save for retirement because employees continue working while they are able to do so, and can accrue additional benefits and reduce or forgo early spending of their retirement savings.

In light of this background, Treasury and the IRS issued Notice 2002-43 in the Cumulative Bulletin (2002-27 C.B. 38 (July 8, 2002)), in which comments were requested regarding phased retirement. Notice 2002-43 specifically requested comments on a wide variety of issues, including the following:

! Under what circumstances, if any, would permitting distributions from a defined benefit plan before an employee attains normal retirement age be consistent with the requirement that a defined benefit plan be established and maintained primarily for purposes of providing benefits after retirement, such as the extent to which an employee has actually reduced his or her workload?

! If there are such circumstances, how should any early retirement subsidy be treated?

Comments Received

Sixteen written comments were formally submitted in response to Notice 2002-43. These comments are in addition to the substantial number of articles and other published materials addressing phased retirement.[1]

While some of the comments expressed concerns over the potential for both dissipation of retirement funds and violation of age discrimination laws, commentators generally responded favorably to the proposal to provide guidance on facilitating phased retirement arrangements. These commentators noted that permitting pension distributions during phased retirement would be attractive to both employers and employees. Commentators also indicated that any guidance issued should provide that establishment of phased retirement arrangements be optional on the part of the employer and that participation in any such arrangement be voluntary on the part of the employee.

Most of the comments recommended that eligibility to participate in a phased retirement program be limited to employees who are eligible for immediately commencing retirement benefits under the plan (including those eligible for early retirement benefits). Other comments recommended that retirement benefits be permitted to start at a specific age or combination of age and service; however, they noted that current legislative constraints, notably the section 72(t) 10 percent additional income tax on early distributions, may limit the desirability of this option.

Some commentators advocated that any phased retirement arrangement should be cost neutral and not create additional funding obligations for employers. Others recommended that any early retirement subsidy available to an employee upon full retirement continue to be available if the employee participates in phased retirement. For example, one such commentator recommended not only that any early retirement subsidy be available upon phased retirement, but also that the subsidy so paid not be permitted to be applied to reduce the remainder of the benefit that is earned by the employee, particularly if the employee continues working past normal retirement age.

The comments were divided over what constituted phased retirement. Several recommended that phased retirement benefits be limited to cases in which there is a reduction in hours worked. Others recommended that a reduction in hours not be required and that a transition to a less stressful job also be considered phased retirement or that the full retirement benefit be payable after the attainment of a specified age or years of service without regard to any change in work.

The commentators who recommended that phased retirement benefits be limited to cases in which there is a reduction in hours worked generally recommended that the phased retirement benefits payable be proportionate to the reduction in work, based on a "dual status" approach. Under this dual status approach, an employee who reduces his or her work schedule to, for example, 80 percent of full-time would be considered to be 20 percent retired and thus entitled to 20 percent of his or her retirement benefit. The employee would continue to accrue additional benefits based on the actual hours he or she continues to work.

---

[1] See, for example, Pension & Welfare Benefits Administration, U.S. Department of Labor, "Report on Working Group on Phased Retirement to the Advisory Council on Employee Welfare & Pension Benefit Plans," 2000; Forman, Jonathan Barry, "How Federal Pension Laws Influence Individual Work and Retirement Decisions," 54 Tax Law. 143 (2000); Littler Mendelson, "Employers Consider 'Phased Retirement' to Retain Employees," Maryland Employment Law Letter, Vol 10, Issue 6 (April, 2000); Geisel, Jerry, "Rethinking Phased Retirement; IRS Call for Comment May Signal Pension Law Changes," Business Insurance (June 24, 2002); Flahaven, Brian, "Please Don't Go! Why Phased Retirement May Make Sense For Your Government," 18 Gov't Finance Review 24 (Oct. 1, 2002); NPR, Morning Edition, "Older Workers Turn to 'Phased' Retirement," (May 18, 2004) at *www.npr.org/features/feature.php?wfld=1900465*

Several of the commentators discussed the implications of phased retirement benefits for purposes of the nondiscrimination rules of section 401(a)(4) and the anti-cutback rules of section 411(d)(6). Many of the comments said that phased retirement arrangements must be flexible and that it would be important for employers to be able to adopt a phased retirement arrangement on a temporary (even experimental basis).

Many commentators expressed concern over the effect that a reduction in hours and the corresponding reduction in compensation would have on the final average pay of an individual for purposes of the benefit calculation when the employee fully retires. These comments generally requested guidance on this issue, including clarification as to whether an employee's final average pay is permitted to decline as a result of the employee's reduction in hours pursuant to participation in a phased retirement arrangement.

Explanation of Provisions

Overview

The proposed regulations would amend § 1.401(a)-1(b) and add § 1.401(a)-3 in order to permit a pro rata share of an employee's accrued benefit to be paid under a bona fide phased retirement program. The pro rata share is based on the extent to which the employee has reduced hours under the program. Under this pro rata approach, an employee maintains a dual status (i.e., partially retired and partially in service) during the phased retirement period. This pro rata or dual status approach to phased retirement was one of the approaches recommended by commentators.

While all approaches suggested by commentators were considered, the pro rata approach is the most consistent with the requirement that benefits be maintained primarily for retirement. Other approaches, such as permitting benefits to be fully available if an employee works reduced hours as part of phased retirement or permitting distributions of the entire accrued benefit to be paid as of a specified age prior to normal retirement age, are fundamentally inconsistent with the § 1.401(a)-1(b) principle that benefits be paid only after retirement. In addition, although a number of commentators suggested that guidance address the practice of terminating an employee with a prearranged rehiring of the employee (or similar sham transactions), the proposed regulations do not address this topic because it involves additional issues outside the scope of this project.

Rules Relating to Phased Retirement

Under the proposed regulations, a plan would be permitted to pay a pro rata portion of the employee's benefits under a bona fide phased retirement program before attainment of normal retirement age. The proposed regulations define a bona fide phased retirement program as a written, employer-adopted program pursuant to which employees may reduce the number of hours they customarily work beginning on or after a retirement date specified under the program and receive phased retirement benefits. Payment of phased retirement benefits is permitted only if the program meets certain conditions, including that employee participation is voluntary and the employee and employer expect the employee to reduce, by 20 percent or more, the number of hours the employee works during the phased retirement period.

Consistent with the pro rata approach discussed above, the maximum amount that is permitted to be paid is limited to the portion of the employee's accrued benefit equal to the product of the employee's total accrued benefit on the date the employee commences phased retirement (or any earlier date selected by the plan for administrative ease) and the employee's reduction in work. The reduction in work is based on the employee's work schedule fraction, which is the ratio of the hours that the employee is reasonably expected to work during the phased retirement period to the hours that would be worked if the employee were full-time. Based in part on commentators' concerns regarding early retirement subsidies, the proposed regulations generally require that all early retirement benefits, retirement-type subsidies, and optional forms of benefit that would be available upon full retirement be available with respect to the phased retirement accrued benefit. However, the proposed regulations would not permit payment to be made in the form of a single-sum distribution (or other eligible rollover distribution) in order to prevent the premature distribution of retirement benefits. The phased retirement benefit is an optional form of benefit protected by section 411(d)(6) and the election of a phased retirement benefit is subject to the provisions of section 417, including the required explanation of the qualified joint and survivor annuity.

Some comments suggested that phased retirement be limited to employees who have attained an age or service (or combination thereof) that is customary for retirement, e.g., where the employer has reasonably determined in good faith that participants who cease employment with the employer after that age or service combination are typically not expected to continue to perform further services of a generally comparable nature elsewhere in the workforce. Such a retirement age might be considerably lower than age 65 in certain occupations (such as police or firefighters). As discussed further below (under the heading *Application to Plans Other Than Qualified Pension Plans*), the Treasury and IRS have concluded that they do not have the authority to permit payments to begin from a section 401(k) plan under a bona fide phased retirement program before the employee attains 59 $^1/_2$ or has a severance from employment.[2] Further, section 72(t)(3)(B) provides an additional income tax on early distributions if annuity distributions are made before the earlier of age 59 $^1/_2$ or separation from service. Accordingly, in lieu of a customary retirement age, the proposed regulations adopt a rule that is consistent with section 401(k) and section 72(t)(3)(B), under which phased retirement benefits may not be paid before an employee attains age 59 $^1/_2$.

Additional Accruals During Phased Retirement

The regulations provide that, during the phased retirement period, in addition to being entitled to the phased retirement benefit, the employee must be entitled to participate in the plan in the same manner as if the employee were still maintaining a full-time work schedule (including calculation of average earnings) and must be entitled to the same benefits (including early retirement benefits, retirement-type subsidies, and optional forms of benefits) upon full retirement as a similarly situated employee who has not elected phased retirement, except that the years of service credited under the plan for any plan year during the phased retirement period is multiplied by the ratio of the employee's actual hours of service during the year to the employee's full-time work schedule, or by the ratio of the employee's compensation to the compensation that would be paid for full-time work. Thus, for example, under a plan with a 1,000 hours of service requirement to accrue a benefit, an employee participating in a phased retirement program will accrue proportionate additional benefits, even if the employee works fewer than 1,000 hours of service.

The requirement that full-time compensation be imputed, with a proportionate reduction based on an employee's actual service, is intended to ensure that a participant is not disadvantaged by reason of choosing phased retirement. This rule precludes the need for extensive disclosure requirements, e.g., disclosure to alert participants to rights that may be lost as a result of participating in a phased retirement program. To be consistent with the requirement to use full-time compensation, the proposed regulations require an employee who was a highly compensated employee before commencing phased retirement to be treated as a highly compensated employee during phased retirement. See also § 1.414(q)-1T, A-4 & A-5.

Under the proposed regulations, the employee's final retirement benefit is comprised of the phased retirement benefit and the balance of the employee's accrued benefit under the plan (i.e., the excess of the total plan formula benefit over the portion of the accrued benefit paid as a phased retirement benefit). Upon full retirement, the phased retirement benefit can continue unchanged or the plan is permitted to offer a new election with respect to that benefit.

---

[2] Cf., *Edwards v. Commissioner*, T.C. Memo. 1989-409, aff'd, 906 F.2d 114 (4th Cir. 1990).

This bifurcation is consistent with commentators' recommendation that an employee who is in a phased retirement program has a dual status, under which the employee is treated as retired to the extent of the reduction in hours and is treated as working to the extent of the employee's continued work with the employer. This approach also ensures that a phased retirement program offers an early retirement subsidy to the extent the employee has reduced his or her hours, and that the remainder of the employee's benefit rights is not adversely affected by participation in the phased retirement program.

Testing and Adjustment of Payments

Subject to certain exceptions, the proposed regulations require periodic testing to ensure that employees in phased retirement are in fact working at the reduced schedule, as expected. Thus, unless an exception applies, a plan must provide for an annual comparison between the number of hours actually worked by an employee during a testing period and the number of hours the employee was reasonably expected to work. If the actual hours worked during the testing period are materially greater than the expected number of hours, then the employee's phased retirement benefit must be reduced prospectively. For this purpose, the employee's hours worked are materially greater than the employee's work schedule if they exceed either $133^1/_3$ percent of the work schedule or 90 percent of the hours that the employee would work under a full-time schedule.

This annual comparison is not required after the employee is within 3 months of attaining normal retirement age or if the amount of compensation paid to the employee by the employer during the phased retirement testing period does not exceed the compensation that would be paid to the employee if he or she had worked full time multiplied by the employee's work schedule fraction. Further, no comparison is required during the first year of an employee's phased retirement or if the employee has entered into an agreement with the employer that the employee will retire within 2 years.

In the event that the employer and employee agree to increase prospectively the hours that the employee will work, then the employee's phased retirement benefit must be adjusted based on a new work schedule. The date of the agreement to increase the employee's hours is treated as a comparison date for testing purposes.

In calculating the employee's benefit at full retirement, if an employee's phased retirement benefits have been reduced during phased retirement, the employee's accrued benefit under the plan is offset by an amount that is actuarially equivalent to the additional payments made before the reduction. The potential for this offset, like other material features of the phased retirement optional form of benefit, must be disclosed as part of the QJSA explanation as required under § 1.401(a)-20, Q&A-36, and § 1.417(a)(3)-1(c)(1)(v) and (d)(1).

If the employee's phased retirement benefit is less than the maximum amount permitted or the employee's work schedule is further reduced at a later date, the proposed regulations allow a plan to provide one or more additional phased retirement benefits to the employee. The additional phased retirement benefit, commencing at a later annuity starting date, provides flexibility to reflect future reductions in the employee's work hours.

Provisions Relating to Payment After Normal Retirement Age

The proposed regulations clarify that a pension plan (i.e., a defined benefit plan or money purchase pension plan) is permitted to pay benefits upon an employee's attainment of normal retirement age. However, normal retirement age cannot be set so low as to be a subterfuge to avoid the requirements of section 401(a), and, accordingly, normal retirement age cannot be earlier than the earliest age that is reasonably representative of a typical retirement age for the covered workforce.[3]

Application to Plans Other Than Qualified Pension Plans

The regulations that limit distributions that are modified by these proposed regulations only apply to pension plans (i.e., defined benefit or money purchase pension plans). Other types of plans may be subject to less restrictive rules regarding in-service distributions, including amounts held in or attributable to: (1) qualified profit sharing and stock bonus plans to the extent not attributable to elective deferrals under section 401(k); (2) insurance annuities under section 403(b)(1), and retirement income accounts under section 403(b)(9), to the extent not attributable to elective deferrals; (3) custodial accounts under section 403(b)(7) to the extent not attributable to elective deferrals; and (4) elective deferrals under section 401(k) or 403(b). In general, these types of plans are permitted to provide for distributions after attainment of age 59 $^1/_2$, without regard to whether the employee has retired or had a severance from employment. Accordingly, they may either provide for the same phased retirement rules that are proposed in these regulations or may provide for other partial or full in-service distributions to be available after attainment of age 59 $^1/_2$. However, eligible governmental plans under section 457(b) are not generally permitted to provide for payments to be made before the earlier of severance from employment or attainment of age 70 $^1/_2$. See generally § 1.457-6.

Other Issues

The proposed regulations also authorize the Commissioner to issue additional rules in guidance of general applicability regarding the coordination of partial retirement under a phased retirement program and the plan qualification rules under section 401(a).

These proposed regulations do not address all of the issues that commentators raised in response to Notice 2002-43. Thus, as noted above, the proposed regulations do not address when a full retirement occurs and specifically do not endorse a prearranged termination and rehire as constituting a full retirement. Further, the proposed regulations only address certain tax issues. For example, although commentators pointed out that the continued availability of health coverage would be an important feature for employees in deciding whether to participate in phased retirement, the proposed regulations do not include any rules relating to health coverage. Similarly, the proposed regulations do not address any potential age discrimination issues, other than through the requirement that participation in a bona fide phased retirement program be voluntary.

Proposed Effective Date

The rules in these regulations are proposed to apply to plan years beginning on or after the date of publication of the Treasury decision adopting these rules as final regulations in the **Federal Register**. These proposed regulations cannot be relied on before they are adopted as final regulations.

Special Analyses

It has been determined that this notice of proposed rulemaking is not a significant regulatory action as defined in Executive Order 12866. Therefore, a regulatory assessment is not required. It also has been determined that section 553(b) of the Administrative Procedure Act (5 U.S.C. chapter 5) does not apply to these proposed regulations, and, because these regulations do not impose a collection of information on small entities, the Regulatory Flexibility Act (5 U.S.C. chapter 6) does not apply. Pursuant to section 7805(f) of the Internal Revenue Code, this notice of proposed rulemaking will be submitted to the Chief Counsel for Advocacy of the Small Business Administration for comment on its impact on small business.

---

[3] While a low normal retirement age may have a significant cost effect on a traditional defined benefit plan, this effect is not as significant for defined contribution plans or for hybrid defined benefit plans.

Comments and Requests for a Public Hearing

Before these proposed regulations are adopted as final regulations, consideration will be given to any written comments (a signed original and eight (8) copies) or electronic comments that are submitted timely to the IRS. All comments will be available for public inspection and copying.

Comments are specifically requested on the following issues:

- Should eligibility to participate in a phased retirement program be extended to employees that reduce their workload using a standard, other than counting hours, to identify the reduction, and, if so, are there administrable methods for measuring the reduction?

- The proposed regulations require periodic testing of the hours an employee actually works during phased retirement, and if the hours are materially greater than the employee's phased retirement work schedule, the phased retirement benefit must be adjusted. As discussed above (under the heading *Testing*), there are a number of exceptions to this requirement. Are there other, less complex alternatives that also would ensure that phased retirement benefits correspond to the employee's reduction in hours?

- The proposed regulations require an offset for the actuarial value of additional payments made before a reduction in phased retirement benefits. Should the regulations permit this offset to be calculated without regard to any early retirement subsidy and, if so, how should a subsidy be quantified?

- The proposed regulations clarify that the right to receive a phased retirement benefit as a partial payment is a separate optional form of benefit for purposes of section 411(d)(6) and, thus, is a benefit, right, or feature for purposes of the special nondiscrimination rules at § 1.401(a)(4)-4. Comments are requested on whether there are facts and circumstances under which the age and service conditions for a particular employer's phased retirement program should be disregarded in applying § 1.401(a)(4)-4 (even if the program may only be in place for a temporary period), or under which the rules at § 1.401(a)(4)-4 should otherwise be modified with respect to phased retirement.

- Should any special rules be adopted to coordinate the rules regarding distributions and continued accruals during phased retirement with a plan's provisions regarding employment after normal retirement age, such as suspension of benefits?

A public hearing may be scheduled if requested in writing by a person that timely submits written comments. If a public hearing is scheduled, notice of the date, time and place for the hearing will be published in the **Federal Register**.

Drafting Information

The principal author of these proposed regulations is Cathy A. Vohs of the Office of the Division Counsel/Associate Chief Counsel (Tax Exempt and Government Entities). However, other personnel from the IRS and Treasury participated in their development.

[¶ 49,234]   **Proposed Regulations (REG-130370-04)**, published in the Federal Register on December 30, 2004.

Group health plan requirements: Portability: Regulations.—Reg. § 54.9801-7 and amendments of Reg. §§ 54.9801-1, 54.9801-2, 54.9801-4—54.9801-6 and 54.9831-1, relating to the portability requirements for group health plans and issuers of health insurance coverage offered in connection with a group health plan, are proposed.

AGENCIES: Internal Revenue Service, Department of the Treasury; Employee Benefits Security Administration, Department of Labor; Centers for Medicare & Medicaid Services, Department of Health and Human Services.

ACTION: Notice of proposed rulemaking and request for comments.

SUMMARY: These proposed rules would clarify certain portability requirements for group health plans and issuers of health insurance coverage offered in connection with a group health plan. These rules propose to implement changes made to the Internal Revenue Code, the Employee Retirement Income Security Act, and the Public Health Service Act enacted as part of the Health Insurance Portability and Accountability Act of 1996.

DATES : Written comments on this notice of proposed rulemaking are invited and must be received by the Departments on or before March 30, 2005.

ADDRESSES: Written comments should be submitted with a signed original and three copies (except for electronic submissions) to any of the addresses specified below. Any comment that is submitted to any Department will be shared with the other Departments.

Comments to the IRS can be addressed to:

CC:PA:LPD:PR (REG-130370-04)

Room 5203

Internal Revenue Service

POB 7604, Ben Franklin Station

Washington, DC 20044

In the alternative, comments may be hand-delivered between the hours of 8 a.m. and 4 p.m. to:

CC:PA:LPD:PR (REG-130370-04)

Courier's Desk

Internal Revenue Service

1111 Constitution Avenue, NW.

Washington, DC 20224

Alternatively, comments may be transmitted electronically via the IRS Internet site at: *www.irs.gov/regs* or via the Federal eRulemaking Portal at *www.regulations.gov* (IRS - REG-130370-04).

Comments to the Department of Labor can be addressed to:

U.S. Department of Labor

Employee Benefits Security Administration

200 Constitution Avenue NW., Room C-5331

Washington, DC 20210

Attention : Proposed Portability Requirements

Alternatively, comments may be hand-delivered between the hours of 9:00 a.m. and 5:00 p.m. to the same address. Comments may also be transmitted by e-mail to: e-ohpsca.ebsa@dol.gov.

Comments to HHS can be submitted as described below:

In commenting, please refer to file code CMS-2158-P. Because of staff and resource limitations, we cannot accept comments by facsimile (FAX) transmission.

You may submit comments in one of three ways (no duplicates, please):

1. *Electronically.* You may submit electronic comments on specific issues in this regulation to *http://www.cms.hhs.gov/regulations/ecomments*. (Attachments should be in Microsoft Word, WordPerfect, or Excel; however, we prefer Microsoft Word.)

2. *By mail.* You may mail written comments (one original and two copies) to the following address ONLY:

Centers for Medicare & Medicaid Services,

Department of Health and Human Services,

Attention: CMS-2158-P,

P.O. Box 8017,

Baltimore, MD 21244-8010.

Please allow sufficient time for mailed comments to be received before the close of the comment period.

3. *By hand or courier.* If you prefer, you may deliver (by hand or courier) your written comments (one original and two copies) before the close of the comment period to one of the following addresses. If you intend to deliver your comments to the Baltimore address, please call telephone number (410) 786-7195 in advance to schedule your arrival with one of our staff members.

Room 445-G, Hubert H. Humphrey Building,

200 Independence Avenue, SW.,

Washington, DC 20201; or

7500 Security Boulevard,

Baltimore, MD 21244-1850.

(Because access to the interior of the HHH Building is not readily available to persons without Federal Government identification, commenters are encouraged to leave their comments in the CMS drop slots located in the main lobby of the building. A stamp-in clock is available for persons wishing to retain a proof of filing by stamping in and retaining an extra copy of the comments being filed.)

Comments mailed to the addresses indicated as appropriate for hand or courier delivery may be delayed and received after the comment period.

Submission of comments on paperwork requirements. You may submit comments on this document's paperwork requirements by mailing your comments to the addresses provided at the end of the "Collection of Information Requirements" section in this document.

All submissions to the IRS will be open to public inspection and copying in room 1621, 1111 Constitution Avenue, NW., Washington, DC from 9 a.m. to 4 p.m.

All submissions to the Department of Labor will be open to public inspection and copying in the Public Disclosure Room, Employee Benefits Security Administration, U.S. Department of Labor, Room N-1513, 200 Constitution Avenue, NW., Washington, DC from 8:30 a.m. to 4:30 p.m.

All submissions timely submitted to HHS will be available for public inspection as they are received, generally beginning approximately three weeks after publication of a document, at the headquarters for the Centers for Medicare & Medicaid Services, 7500 Security Boulevard, Baltimore, MD 21244, Monday through Friday of each week from 8:30 a.m. to 4:00 p.m. To schedule an appointment to view public comments, phone 410-786-7195.

FOR FURTHER INFORMATION CONTACT: Dave Mlawsky, Centers for Medicare & Medicaid Services (CMS), Department of Health and Human Services, at 1-877-267-2323 ext. 61565; Amy Turner, Employee Benefits Security Administration, Department of Labor, at (202) 693-8335; or Russ Weinheimer, Internal Revenue Service, Department of the Treasury, at (202) 622-6080.

SUPPLEMENTARY INFORMATION:

Customer Service Information

To assist consumers and the regulated community, the Departments have issued questions and answers concerning HIPAA. Individuals interested in obtaining copies of Department of Labor publications concerning changes in health care law may call a toll free number, 1-866-444-EBSA (3272), or access the publications on-line at www.dol.gov/ebsa, the Department of Labor's website. These regulations as well as other information on the new health care laws are also available on the Department of Labor's interactive web pages, Health E laws. In addition, CMS's publication entitled "Protecting Your Health Insurance Coverage" is available by calling 1-800-633-4227 or on the Department of Health and Human Services' website (www.cms.hhs.gov/hipaa1), which includes the interactive webpages, HIPAA Online. Copies of the HIPAA regulations, as well as notices and press releases related to HIPAA and other health care laws, are also available at the above-referenced websites.

A. Background

The Health Insurance Portability and Accountability Act of 1996 (HIPAA), Public Law 104-191, was enacted on August 21, 1996. HIPAA amended the Internal Revenue Code of 1986 (Code), the Employee Retirement Income Security Act of 1974 (ERISA), and the Public Health Service Act (PHS Act) to provide for, among other things, improved portability and continuity of health coverage. Interim final regulations implementing the HIPAA provisions were first made available to the public on April 1, 1997 (published in the **Federal Register** on April 8, 1997, 62 FR 16894) (April 1997 interim rules). On December 29, 1997, the Departments published a clarification of the April 1997 interim rules as they relate to excepted benefits. On October 25, 1999, the Departments published a notice in the **Federal Register** (64 FR 57520) soliciting additional comments on the portability requirements based on the experience of plans and issuers operating under the April 1997 interim rules.

After consideration of all the comments received on the portability provisions, the Departments are publishing final regulations elsewhere in this issue of the **Federal Register**. These proposed rules address additional and discrete issues for which the Departments are soliciting further comment before promulgating final regulations.

B. Overview of the Proposed Regulations

1. *Rules Relating to Creditable Coverage - 26 CFR 54.9801-4, 29 CFR 2590.701-4, 45 CFR 146.113*

Tolling of the 63-day break-in-coverage rule

These proposed rules would modify the 63-day break-in-coverage rules with one significant substantive change. Under the proposed rules, the beginning of the period that is used for determining whether a significant break in coverage has occurred (generally 63 days) is tolled in cases in which a certificate of creditable coverage is not provided on or before the day coverage ceases. In those cases, the significant-break-in-coverage period is tolled until a certificate is provided but not beyond 44 days after the coverage ceases.

The Departments have fashioned this tolling rule (and a similar tolling rule for the 30-day period for requesting special enrollment) in an effort to address the inequity of individuals' losing coverage without being aware that the coverage has ended while minimizing the burdens on subsequent plans and issuers that are not responsible for providing the missing or untimely certificates. Numerous situations have come to the attention of the Departments in which an individual's health coverage is terminated but in which the individual does not learn of the termination of coverage until well after it occurs. The statute generally requires that a certificate of creditable coverage be provided at the time an individual ceases to be covered under a plan. The statute, the April 1997 interim rules, and the final regulations (published elsewhere in this issue of the **Federal Register**) all permit a plan or issuer to provide the certificate at a later date if it is provided at a time consistent with notices required under a COBRA continuation provision. The statute also directs the Secretaries to establish rules to prevent a plan or issuer's failure to provide a certificate timely from adversely affecting the individual's subsequent coverage. If a plan or issuer chooses to provide a certificate later than the date an individual loses coverage, as the regulations permit in certain circumstances, these proposed rules provide that an individual should not suffer from this rule of convenience for the plan or issuer. However, to prevent the abuse that might result from an open-ended tolling rule, an outside limit of 44 days is placed on this relief. This reflects the fact that, in most cases, plans and issuers are required to provide certificates within 44 days (although some plans and issuers may be required to provide certificates sooner than 44 days after coverage ceases and some entities are not required to provide certificates at all). The Departments have adopted this uniform limit on the tolling rule for purposes of consistency. New examples have been added to illustrate the tolling rule.

2. *Evidence of Creditable Coverage - 26 CFR 54.9801-5, 29 CFR 2590.701-5, 45 CFR 146.115*

Information in certificate and model certificate

These proposed rules would modify the required elements for the educational statement in certificates of creditable coverage to require a disclosure about the Family and Medical Leave Act. Use of the first model certificate below by group health plans and group health insurance issuers, or use of the appropriate model certificate that appears in the preamble to the related final regulations published elsewhere in this issue of the **Federal Register**, will satisfy the requirements of paragraph (a)(3)(ii) in this section of the final regulations. Similarly, for purposes of complying with those final regulations, State Medicaid programs may use the second version below, or may use the appropriate model certificate that appears in the preamble to those final regulations. Thus, until this proposed regulation is published as a final regulation, entities may use either the model certificates published below, or those published elsewhere in this issue of the **Federal Register**. For entities that choose not to use the model certificates below until this proposed regulation is published as a final regulation, we welcome comments as to the applicability date for using them.

CERTIFICATE OF GROUP HEALTH PLAN COVERAGE

1. Date of this certificate:_____

2. Name of group health plan:_____

_____

3. Name of participant:_____

4. Identification number of participant:_____

5 Name of individuals to whom this certificate applies:_____

_____

6. Name, address, and telephone number of plan administrator or issuer responsible for providing this certificate:_____

7. For further information, call:_____

8. If the individual(s) identified in line 5 has (have) at least 18 months of creditable coverage (disregarding periods of coverage before a 63-day break), check here and skip lines 9 and 10:_____

9. Date waiting period or affiliation period (if any) began:_____

10. Date coverage began:_____

11. Date coverage ended (or if coverage has not ended, enter "continuing"):_____

[Note: separate certificates will be furnished if information is not identical for the participant and each beneficiary.]

Statement of HIPAA Portability Rights

IMPORTANT—KEEP THIS CERTIFICATE. This certificate is evidence of your coverage under this plan. Under a federal law known as HIPAA, you may need evidence of your coverage to reduce a preexisting condition exclusion period under another plan, to help you get special enrollment in another plan, or to get certain types of individual health coverage even if you have health problems.

Preexisting condition exclusions. Some group health plans restrict coverage for medical conditions present before an individual's enrollment. These restrictions are known as "preexisting condition exclusions." A preexisting condition exclusion can apply only to conditions for which medical advice, diagnosis, care, or treatment was recommended or received within the 6 months before your "enrollment date." Your enrollment date is your first day of coverage under the plan, or, if there is a waiting period, the first day of your waiting period (typically, your first day of work). In addition, a preexisting condition exclusion cannot last for more than 12 months after your enrollment date (18 months if you are a late enrollee). Finally, a preexisting condition exclusion cannot apply to pregnancy and cannot apply to a child who is enrolled in health coverage within 30 days after birth, adoption, or placement for adoption.

If a plan imposes a preexisting condition exclusion, the length of the exclusion must be reduced by the amount of your prior creditable coverage. Most health coverage is creditable coverage, including group health plan coverage, COBRA continuation coverage, coverage under an individual health policy, Medicare, Medicaid, State Children's Health Insurance Program (SCHIP), and coverage through high-risk pools and the Peace Corps. Not all forms of creditable coverage are required to provide certificates like this one. If you do not receive a certificate for past coverage, talk to your new plan administrator.

You can add up any creditable coverage you have, including the coverage shown on this certificate. However, if at any time you went for 63 days or more without any coverage (called a break in coverage) a plan may not have to count the coverage you had before the break.

—Therefore, once your coverage ends, you should try to obtain alternative coverage as soon as possible to avoid a 63-day break. You may use this certificate as evidence of your creditable coverage to reduce the length of any preexisting condition exclusion if you enroll in another plan.

Right to get special enrollment in another plan. Under HIPAA, if you lose your group health plan coverage, you may be able to get into another group health plan for which you are eligible (such as a spouse's plan), even if the plan generally does not accept late enrollees, if you request enrollment within 30 days. (Additional special enrollment rights are triggered by marriage, birth, adoption, and placement for adoption.)

—Therefore, once your coverage ends, if you are eligible for coverage in another plan (such as a spouse's plan), you should request special enrollment as soon as possible.

Prohibition against discrimination based on a health factor . Under HIPAA, a group health plan may not keep you (or your dependents) out of the plan based on anything related to your health. Also, a group health plan may not charge you (or your dependents) more for coverage, based on health, than the amount charged a similarly situated individual.

Right to individual health coverage. Under HIPAA, if you are an "eligible individual," you have a right to buy certain individual health policies (or in some states, to buy coverage through a high-risk pool) without a preexisting condition exclusion. To be an eligible individual, you must meet the following requirements:

• You have had coverage for at least 18 months without a break in coverage of 63 days or more;

• Your most recent coverage was under a group health plan (which can be shown by this certificate);

• Your group coverage was not terminated because of fraud or nonpayment of premiums;

• You are not eligible for COBRA continuation coverage or you have exhausted your COBRA benefits (or continuation coverage under a similar state provision); and

• You are not eligible for another group health plan, Medicare, or Medicaid, and do not have any other health insurance coverage.

The right to buy individual coverage is the same whether you are laid off, fired, or quit your job.

—Therefore, if you are interested in obtaining individual coverage and you meet the other criteria to be an eligible individual, you should apply for this coverage as soon as possible to avoid losing your eligible individual status due to a 63-day break.

Special information for people on FMLA leave. If you are taking leave under the Family and Medical Leave Act (FMLA) and you drop health coverage during your leave, any days without health coverage while on FMLA leave will not count towards a 63-day break in coverage. In addition, if you do not return from leave, the 30-day period to request special enrollment in another plan will not start before your FMLA leave ends.

—Therefore, when you apply for other health coverage, you should tell your plan administrator or health insurer about any prior FMLA leave.

State flexibility . This certificate describes minimum HIPAA protections under federal law. States may require insurers and HMOs to provide additional protections to individuals in that state.

For more information. If you have questions about your HIPAA rights, you may contact your state insurance department or the U.S. Department of Labor, Employee Benefits Security Administration (EBSA) toll-free at 1-866-444-3272 (for free HIPAA publications ask for publications concerning changes in health care laws). You may also contact the CMS publication hotline at 1-800-633-4227 (ask for "Protecting Your Health Insurance Coverage"). These publications and other useful information are also available on the Internet at: *http://www.dol.gov/ebsa*, the DOL's interactive web pages - Health *E* laws, or *http://www.cms.hhs.gov/hipaa1*.

CERTIFICATE OF MEDICAID COVERAGE

1. Date of this certificate:_____
2. Name of state Medicaid program:_____

3. Name of recipient:_____
4. Identification number of recipient:_____
5 Name of individuals to whom this certificate applies:_____

6. Name, address, and telephone number of state Medicaid agency responsible for providing this certificate:_____

7. For further information, call:_____
8. If the individual(s) identified in line 5 has (have) at least 18 months of creditable coverage (disregarding periods of coverage before a 63-day break), check here and skip line 9._____
9. Date coverage began:_____
10. Date coverage ended (or if coverage has not ended, enter "continuing"):_____

[Note: separate certificates will be furnished if information is not identical for the recipient and each dependant]

Statement of HIPAA Portability Rights

IMPORTANT—KEEP THIS CERTIFICATE. This certificate is evidence of your coverage under this state Medicaid program. Under a federal law known as HIPAA, you may need evidence of your coverage to reduce a preexisting condition exclusion period under a group health plan, to help you get special enrollment in a group health plan, or to get certain types of individual health coverage even if you have health problems.

Preexisting condition exclusions. Some group health plans restrict coverage for medical conditions present before an individual's enrollment. These restrictions are known as "preexisting condition exclusions." A preexisting condition exclusion can apply only to conditions for which medical advice, diagnosis, care, or treatment was recommended or received within the 6 months before your "enrollment date." Your enrollment date is your first day of coverage under the plan, or, if there is a waiting period, the first day of your waiting period (typically, your first day of work). In addition, a preexisting condition exclusion cannot last for more than 12 months after your enrollment date (18 months if you are a late enrollee). Finally, a preexisting condition exclusion cannot apply to pregnancy and cannot apply to a child who is enrolled in health coverage within 30 days after birth, adoption, or placement for adoption.

If a plan imposes a preexisting condition exclusion, the length of the exclusion must be reduced by the amount of your prior creditable coverage. Most health coverage is creditable coverage, including group health plan coverage, COBRA continuation coverage, coverage under an individual health policy, Medicare, Medicaid, State Children's Health Insurance Program (SCHIP), and coverage through high-risk pools and the Peace Corps. Not all forms of creditable coverage are required to provide certificates like this one. If you do not receive a certificate for past coverage, talk to your new plan administrator.

You can add up any creditable coverage you have, including the coverage shown on this certificate. However, if at any time you went for 63 days or more without any coverage (called a break in coverage) a plan may not have to count the coverage you had before the break.

—Therefore, once your coverage ends, you should try to obtain alternative coverage as soon as possible to avoid a 63-day break. You may use this certificate as evidence of your creditable coverage to reduce the length of any preexisting condition exclusion if you enroll in a group health plan.

Right to get special enrollment in another plan. Under HIPAA, if you lose your group health plan coverage, you may be able to get into another group health plan for which you are eligible (such as a spouse's plan), even if the plan generally does not accept late enrollees, if you request enrollment within 30 days. (Additional special enrollment rights are triggered by marriage, birth, adoption, and placement for adoption.)

—Therefore, once your coverage in a group health plan ends, if you are eligible for coverage in another plan (such as a spouse's plan), you should request special enrollment as soon as possible.

Prohibition against discrimination based on a health factor . Under HIPAA, a group health plan may not keep you (or your dependents) out of the plan based on anything related to your health. Also, a group health plan may not charge you (or your dependents) more for coverage, based on health, than the amount charged a similarly situated individual.

Right to individual health coverage. Under HIPAA, if you are an "eligible individual," you have a right to buy certain individual health policies (or in some states, to buy coverage through a high-risk pool) without a preexisting condition exclusion. To be an eligible individual, you must meet the following requirements:

• You have had coverage for at least 18 months without a break in coverage of 63 days or more;

• Your most recent coverage was under a group health plan;

• Your group coverage was not terminated because of fraud or nonpayment of premiums;

• You are not eligible for COBRA continuation coverage or you have exhausted your COBRA benefits (or continuation coverage under a similar state provision); and

• You are not eligible for another group health plan, Medicare, or Medicaid, and do not have any other health insurance coverage.

The right to buy individual coverage is the same whether you are laid off, fired, or quit your job.

—Therefore, if you are interested in obtaining individual coverage and you meet the other criteria to be an eligible individual, you should apply for this coverage as soon as possible to avoid losing your eligible individual status due to a 63-day break.

Special information for people on FMLA leave. If you are taking leave under the Family and Medical Leave Act (FMLA) and you drop health coverage during your leave, any days without health coverage while on FMLA leave will not count towards a 63-day break in coverage. In addition, if you do not return from leave, the 30-day period to request special enrollment in another plan will not start before your FMLA leave ends.

—Therefore, when you apply for other health coverage, you should tell your plan administrator or health insurer about any prior FMLA leave.

State flexibility . This certificate describes minimum HIPAA protections under federal law. States may require insurers and HMOs to provide additional protections to individuals in that state.

For more information. If you have questions about your HIPAA rights, you may contact your state insurance department or the U.S. Department of Labor, Employee Benefits Security Administration (EBSA) toll-free at 1-866-444-3272 (for free HIPAA publications ask for publications concerning changes in health care laws). You may also contact the CMS publication hotline at 1-800-633-4227 (ask for "Protecting Your Health Insurance Coverage"). These publications and other useful information are also available on the Internet at: *http://www.dol.gov/ebsa* or *http://www.cms.hhs.gov/hipaa1.*

3. *Special Enrollment Periods - 26 CFR 54.9801-6, 29 CFR 2590.701-6, 45 CFR 146.117*

Tolling of the special enrollment period

Under HIPAA, the April 1997 interim rules, and the final regulations, an individual wishing to special enroll following a loss of coverage is generally required to request enrollment not later than 30 days after the loss of eligibility, termination of employer contributions, or exhaustion of COBRA continuation coverage. For individuals whose coverage ceases and a certificate of creditable coverage is not provided on or before the date coverage ceases, this regulation provides for proposed tolling rules similar to those described above for determining a significant break. That is, the special enrollment period terminates at the end of the 30-day period that begins on the first day after the earlier of the date that a certificate of creditable coverage is provided or the date 44 days after coverage ceases.

Modification of special enrollment procedures and when coverage begins under special enrollment

The April 1997 interim rules did not establish procedures for processing requests for special enrollment beyond affirming the statutory requirement that requests be made not later than 30 days after the event giving rise to the special enrollment right and providing that the same requirements could be imposed on special enrollees that were imposed on other enrollees (e.g., that the request be made in writing). Some examples in the April 1997 interim rules could be read to suggest that plans and issuers could require individuals requesting special enrollment to file completed applications for health coverage by the end of the special enrollment period.

It has been brought to the Departments' attention that some plans and issuers were imposing application requirements that could not reasonably be completed within the special enrollment period (for example, requiring the social security number of a newborn within 30 days of the birth), effectively denying individuals their right to special enroll their dependents. In this regard, the statute merely requires an employee to request special enrollment, or an individual to seek to enroll, during the special enrollment period. These proposed regulations preserve individuals' access to special enrollment by clarifying that during the special enrollment period individuals are only required to make an oral or written request for special enrollment.

The proposed regulations provide further that after a timely request, the plan or issuer may require the individual to complete all enrollment materials within a reasonable time after the end of the special enrollment period. However, the enrollment procedure may only require information required from individuals who enroll when first eligible and information about the event giving rise to the special enrollment right. While a plan can impose a deadline for submitting the completed enrollment materials, the deadline must be extended for information that an individual making reasonable efforts cannot obtain within that deadline.

Thus, even where a plan requires social security numbers from individuals who enroll when first eligible, the plan must provide an extended deadline for receiving the social security number in the case of a newborn. In no event could a plan deny special enrollment for newborns because an employee could not provide a social security number for the newborn within the special enrollment period.

As regards the effective date of coverage for special enrollments, the proposed rules generally follow the statute, the April 1997 interim final rules, and the final regulations being published elsewhere in this issue of the **Federal Register**. However clarifications of the effective date of coverage are added to conform to the clarification of the special enrollment procedures. Where the special enrollment right results from a loss of eligibility for coverage or marriage, coverage generally must begin no later than the first day of the first calendar month after the date the plan or issuer receives the request for special enrollment. However, if the plan or issuer requires completion of additional enrollment materials, coverage must begin no later than the first day of the first calendar month after the plan or issuer receives enrollment materials that are substantially complete.

Where the special enrollment right results from a birth, coverage must begin on the date of birth. In the case of adoption or placement for adoption, coverage must begin no later than the date of such adoption or placement for adoption. If a plan or issuer requires completion of additional enrollment materials, the plan or issuer must provide benefits once the plan or issuer receives substantially complete enrollment materials. However, the benefits provided at that time must be retroactive to the date of birth, adoption, or placement for adoption.

The Departments welcome comments on these aspects of the proposed rule.

4. *Interaction with the Family and Medical Leave Act -26 CFR 54.9801-7, 29 CFR 701-8, 45 CFR 146.120*

The proposed rules address how the HIPAA portability requirements apply in situations where a person is on leave under the Family and Medical Leave Act of 1993 (FMLA). A general principle of FMLA is that an employee returning from leave under FMLA should generally be in the same position the employee was in before taking leave. At issue is how to reconcile that principle of FMLA with the HIPAA rights and requirements that are triggered by an individual ending coverage under a group health plan. These proposed regulations provide specific rules that clarify how HIPAA and FMLA interact when the coverage of an employee or an employee's dependent ends in connection with an employee taking leave under FMLA.

With respect to the rules concerning a significant break in coverage, if an employee takes FMLA leave and does not continue group health coverage for any part of the leave, the period of FMLA leave without coverage is not taken into account in determining whether a significant break in coverage has occurred for the employee or any dependents. To the extent an individual needs to demonstrate that coverage ceased in connection with FMLA leave (which would toll any significant break with respect to another plan or issuer), these regulations provide that a plan or issuer must take into account all information that it obtains about an employee's FMLA leave. Further, if an individual attests to the period of FMLA leave and the individual cooperates with a plan's or issuer's efforts to verify the individual's FMLA leave, the plan or issuer must treat the individual as having been on FMLA leave for the period attested to for purposes of determining if the individual had a significant break in coverage. Nonetheless, a plan or issuer is not prevented from modifying its initial determination of FMLA leave if it determines that the individual did not have the claimed FMLA leave, provided that the plan or issuer follows procedures for reconsideration similar to those set forth in the final rules governing determinations of creditable coverage.

The question has arisen whether it would be appropriate to waive the general requirement to provide automatic certificates of creditable coverage in the case of an individual who declines coverage when electing FMLA leave if the individual will be reinstated at the end of FMLA leave. At the time an employee elects FMLA leave, the employer (as well as the employee) may not know if the employee will later return from FMLA leave and elect to be reinstated. Requiring plans and issuers to provide certificates when individuals cease health coverage in connection with FMLA leave may result in some certificates being issued when individuals ceasing coverage will not need the certificates as evidence of coverage (because of later reinstatement). However, automatic issuance likely imposes less burden because the plan or issuer does not need to determine whether a certificate is required. Moreover, automatic issuance eliminates the need for remedial measures if an individual expected to be reinstated in fact is not later reinstated. Thus, these proposed regulations clarify there is no exception to the general rule requiring automatic certificates when coverage ends and provide that if an individual covered under a group health plan takes FMLA leave and ceases coverage under the plan, an automatic certificate must be provided.

With respect to the special enrollment rules, an individual (or a dependent of the individual) who is covered under a group health plan and who takes FMLA leave has a loss of eligibility that results in a special enrollment period if the individual's group health coverage is terminated at any time during FMLA leave and the individual does not return to work for the employer at the end of FMLA leave. This special enrollment period begins when the period of FMLA leave ends. Moreover, the rules that delay the start of the special enrollment period until the receipt of a certificate of creditable coverage continue to operate.

5. *Special rules—Excepted plans and excepted benefits—26 CFR 54.9831-1, 29 CFR 2590.732, 45 CFR 146.145*

Determination of number of plans

Various provisions in Chapter 100 of the Code, Part 7 of Subtitle B of Title I of ERISA, and Title XXVII of the PHS Act apply when an individual commences coverage or terminates coverage under a group health plan. For example, a certificate of creditable coverage must be provided when an individual ceases to be covered under a group health plan. Under the April 1997 interim rules, it was not always clear whether an individual changing benefit elections among those offered by an employer or employee organization was merely switching between benefit packages under a single plan or was switching from one plan to another. These proposed regulations add rules to remove this uncertainty.

Under these proposed regulations, all medical care benefits made available by an employer or employee organization (including a board of trustees of a multiemployer trust) are generally considered to constitute one group health plan (the default rule). However, the employer or employee organization can establish more than one group health plan if it is clear from the instruments governing the arrangements to provide medical care benefits that the benefits are being provided under separate plans and if the arrangements are operated pursuant to the instruments as separate plans. A multiemployer plan and a nonmultiemployer plan are always separate plans. Under an anti-abuse rule, separate plans are aggregated to the extent necessary to prevent the evasion of any legal requirement.

These rules provide plan sponsors great flexibility while minimizing the burden of making decisions about how many plans to maintain. For example, many employers may wish to minimize the number of certificates of creditable coverage required to be furnished to continuing employees. Under the default rule, because all health benefits provided by an employer are considered a single group health plan, there is no need to furnish a certificate of creditable coverage when an employee merely switches coverage among the options made available by the employer. This need would arise only if the employer designated separate benefit packages as separate plans in the plan documents and only if the benefit packages were also operated pursuant to the plan documents as separate plans.

The anti-abuse rule limits the flexibility of these rules to prevent evasions. For example, a plan sponsor might design an arrangement under which the participation of each of many employees in the arrangement would be considered a separate plan. On the face of it, such an arrangement might appear to satisfy the requirement for a plan being exempt from the requirements of Chapter 100 of the Code, Part 7 of ERISA, and Title XXVII of the PHS Act because on the first day of the plan year each plan would have fewer than two participants who are current employees. This would give the impression that the plans would not have to comply with the prohibitions against discriminating based on one or more health factors, with the restrictions on preexisting condition exclusions, nor with any of the other requirements of Chapter 100 of the Code, Part 7 of ERISA, and Title XXVII of the PHS Act. The anti-abuse rule would require the aggregation of plans under such an arrangement to the extent necessary to make the plans subject to the requirements of Chapter 100 of the Code, Part 7 of ERISA, and Title XXVII of the PHS Act. The anti-abuse rule would apply in similar fashion to prevent the evasion of any other law that applies to group health plans or to the parties administering them or providing benefits under them.

Counting the average number of employees

These proposed regulations add rules for counting the average number of employees employed by an employer during a year.[1] Various rules in Chapter 100 of the Code, Part 7 of ERISA, and Title XXVII of the PHS Act require the determination of such an average number, including the Mental Health Parity Act provisions, the guaranteed access provisions under the PHS Act for small employers, and the exemption from the excise tax under the Code for certain small employers.

Under these proposed regulations, the average number of employees employed by an employer is determined by using a full-time equivalents method. Each full-time employee employed for the entire previous calendar year counts as one employee. Full-time employees employed less than the entire previous calendar year and part-time employees are counted by totaling their employment hours in the previous calendar year (but not to exceed 40 hours for any week) and dividing that number by the annual full-time hours under the employer's general employment practices (but not exceeding 40 hours per week). Any resulting fraction is disregarded. For example, if these calculations produce a result of 50.9, the average number of employees is considered to be 50. If an employer existed for less than the entire previous calendar year (including not being in existence at all), then the determination of the average number of employees is made by estimating the average number of employees that it is reasonably expected that the employer will employ on business days in the current calendar year. For a multiemployer plan, the number of employees employed by the employer with the most employees is attributed to each employer with at least one employee participating in the plan.

C. Economic Impact and Paperwork Burden

Summary—Department of Labor and Department of Health and Human Services

HIPAA's group market portability provisions, which limit the scope and application of preexisting condition exclusions and establish special enrollment rights, provide a minimum standard of protection designed to increase access to health coverage. The Departments crafted these proposed regulations to secure these protections under certain special circumstances, consistent with the intent of Congress, and to do so in a manner that is economically efficient. The Departments are unable to quantify the regulations' economic benefits and costs, but believe that their benefits will justify their costs.

HIPAA's primary economic effects ensue directly from its statutory provisions. HIPAA's statutory group market portability provisions extend coverage to certain individuals and preexisting conditions not otherwise covered. This extension of coverage entails both benefits and costs. Individuals enjoying expanded coverage will realize benefits, sometimes including improvements in health and relief from so-called "job lock." The costs of HIPAA's portability provisions generally include the cost of extending coverage, as well as certain attendant administrative costs. The Departments believe that the benefits of HIPAA are concentrated in a relatively small population, while the costs are distributed broadly across group plan enrollees. The economic effects of HIPAA's statutory portability provisions are discussed in detail in the preamble to the final regulation under the "Effects of the Statute" of the "Basis for Assessment of Economic Impact" section, published elsewhere in this issue of the **Federal Register**.

By clarifying and securing HIPAA's statutory portability protections, these proposed regulations will help ensure that HIPAA rights are fully realized. The result is likely to be a small increase at the margin in the economic effects of HIPAA's statutory portability provisions.

These proposed regulations are intended to secure and implement HIPAA's group market portability and special enrollment provisions under certain special circumstances. The regulations will secure HIPAA's portability rights for individuals who are not timely notified that their coverage has ended and for individuals whose coverage ends in connection with the taking of leave that is guaranteed under FMLA. The regulations also will clarify and thereby secure individuals' special enrollment rights under HIPAA, and clarify the methodologies to be used by employers to determine the number of plans offered and the average number of individuals employed during a given year.

Additional economic benefits derive from the regulations' clarifications of HIPAA requirements. The regulations will reduce uncertainty and costly disputes between employees, employers and issuers, and promote confidence among employees in health benefits' value, thereby promoting labor market efficiency and fostering the establishment and continuation by employers of group health plans.

Benefits under these regulations will be concentrated among a small number of affected individuals while costs will be spread thinly across group plan enrollees.

Affected individuals will generally include those who would have lost access to coverage for needed medical care after being denied HIPAA portability and/or special enrollment rights due to time spent without coverage prior to receiving a certificate or while on FMLA-guaranteed leave. The benefits of these regulations for any particular affected individual may be significant. As noted above and under "Effects of the Statute" in the "Basis for Assessment of Economic Impact" section of the preamble to the final regulation, published elsewhere in this issue of the **Federal Register**, access to coverage for needed medical care is important to individuals' health and productivity. However, the number of affected individuals, and therefore the aggregate cost of extended access to coverage under these regulations, is expected to be small, for several reasons. First, these regulations extend HIPAA rights only in instances where individuals are not timely notified that their coverage has ended or their coverage ends in connection with the taking of FMLA-guaranteed leave. Second, the period over which this regulation extends rights will often be short, insofar as certificates are often provided promptly after coverage ends and many family leave periods are far shorter than the guaranteed 12 weeks. Third, it is generally in individuals' interest to minimize periods of uninsurance. Individuals are likely to exercise their portability and special enrollment rights as soon as possible after coverage ends, which will often be before any extension of such rights under these regulations becomes effective. Fourth, only a portion of individuals who enroll in health plans in circumstances where these regulations alone guarantee their special enrollment or portability rights would otherwise have been denied such rights. Fifth, only a small minority of individuals who avoid a significant break in coverage as a direct result of these regulations would otherwise have lost coverage for needed medical care. (The affected minority would be those who suffer from preexisting conditions, join health plans that exclude coverage for such conditions, and require treatment of such conditions during the exclusion periods.)

Affected individuals may also include some who would have been denied special enrollment rights if plans or issuers failed to recognize their requests for special enrollment or imposed unreasonable deadlines or requirements for completion of enrollment materials.

As noted above, the Departments expect that these regulations will increase at the margin the economic effects of HIPAA's statutory portability provisions. For the reasons stated immediately above, the Departments believe that these increases will be small on aggregate, adding only a small increment to the costs attributable to HIPAA's statutory portability provisions, which themselves amount to a small fraction of one percent of health plan expenditures. Additionally, as with the cost of HIPAA's statutory portability provisions, the majority of these costs will be borne by group plan enrollees. The Departments expect these regulations to have little or no perceptible negative impact on employers' propensity to offer health benefit plans or on the generosity of those plans. In sum, the Departments expect that the benefits of these regulations, which can be very large for a particular affected individual, will justify their costs. The basis for the Departments' conclusions is detailed below.

---

[1] The rules for determining the average number of employees employed by an employer during a year are not used for counting the number employed by the employer on a given day, such as the first day of a plan year.

The Departments solicit comments on their conclusions and their basis for them, and empirical data or other information that would support a fuller or more accurate analysis.

Executive Order 12866—Department of Labor and Department of Health and Human Services

Under Executive Order 12866 (58 FR 551735, Oct. 4, 1993), the Departments must determine whether a regulatory action is "significant" and therefore subject to the requirements of the Executive Order and subject to review by the Office of Management and Budget (OMB). Under section 3(f), the order defines a "significant regulatory action" as an action that is likely to result in a rule: (1) having an annual effect on the economy of $100 million or more, or adversely and materially affecting a sector of the economy, productivity, competition, jobs, the environment, public health or safety, or state, local or tribal governments or communities (also referred to as "economically significant"); (2) creating serious inconsistency or otherwise interfering with an action taken or planned by another agency; (3) materially altering the budgetary impacts of entitlement grants, user fees, or loan programs or the rights and obligations of recipients thereof; or (4) raising novel legal or policy issues arising out of legal mandates, the President's priorities, or the principles set forth in the Executive Order.

Pursuant to the terms of the Executive Order, the Departments have determined that this action raises novel policy issues arising out of legal mandates. Therefore, this notice is "significant" and subject to OMB review under Section 3(f)(4) of the Executive Order. Consistent with the Executive Order, the Departments have assessed the costs and benefits of this regulatory action. The Departments' assessment, and the analysis underlying that assessment, is detailed below. The Departments performed a comprehensive, unified analysis to estimate the costs and benefits attributable to the regulations for purposes of compliance with Executive Order 12866, the Regulatory Flexibility Act, and the Paperwork Reduction Act.

Statement of need for proposed action

These proposed regulations clarify and interpret the HIPAA portability provisions under Section 701 of the Employee Retirement Income Security Act of 1974 (ERISA), Section 2701 of the Public Health Service Act, and Section 9801 of the Internal Revenue Code of 1986. The regulations are needed to secure and implement HIPAA's portability rights for individuals who are not timely notified that their coverage has ended and for individuals whose coverage ends in connection with the taking of leave that is guaranteed under FMLA, and to clarify and secure individuals' special enrollment rights under HIPAA.

Economic effects

As noted above, HIPAA's primary economic effects ensue directly from its statutory provisions. HIPAA's statutory group market portability provisions extend coverage to certain individuals and preexisting conditions not otherwise covered. This extension of coverage entails both benefits and costs. The economic effects of HIPAA's statutory portability provisions is summarized above and discussed in detail under the "Basis for Assessment of Economic Impact" section of the preamble to the final regulation, published elsewhere in this issue of the **Federal Register**

Also as noted above, by clarifying and securing HIPAA's statutory portability protections, these regulations will help ensure that HIPAA rights are fully realized. The result is likely to be a small increase at the margin in the economic effects of HIPAA's statutory portability provisions. The benefits of these regulations will be concentrated among a small number of affected individuals, while their costs will be spread thinly across plans and issuers. The regulations also will reduce uncertainty about health benefits' scope and value, thereby promoting employee health benefit coverage and labor market efficiency. The Departments believe that the regulations' benefits will justify their cost. The Departments assessment of the expected economic effects of the regulation are summarized above and discussed in detail below.

Regulatory Flexibility Act—The Department of Labor and Department of Health and Human Services

The Regulatory Flexibility Act (5 U.S.C. 601 *et seq.*) (RFA), imposes certain requirements with respect to Federal rules that are subject to the notice and comment requirements of section 553(b) of the Administrative Procedure Act (5 U.S.C. 551 *et seq.*) and which are likely to have a significant economic impact on a substantial number of small entities. Section 603 of the RFA stipulates that an agency, unless it certifies that a proposed rule will not have a significant economic impact on a substantial number of small entities, must present an initial regulatory flexibility analysis at the time of publication of the notice of proposed rulemaking that describes the impact of the rule on small entities and seeks public comment on such impact. Small entities include small businesses, organizations, and governmental jurisdictions.

For purposes of analysis under the RFA, the Departments consider a small entity to be an employee benefit plan with fewer than 100 participants. The basis for this definition is found in section 104(a)(2) of ERISA, which permits the Secretary of Labor to prescribe simplified annual reports for pension plans which cover fewer than 100 participants. Under section 104(a)(3), the Secretary may also provide for simplified annual reporting and disclosure if the statutory requirements of part 1 of Title I of ERISA would otherwise be inappropriate for welfare benefit plans. Pursuant to the authority of section 104(a)(3), the Department of Labor has previously issued at 29 CFR 2520.104-20, 2520.104-21, 2520.104-41, 2520.104-46 and 2520.104b-10 certain simplified reporting provisions and limited exemptions from reporting and disclosure requirements for small plans, including unfunded or insured welfare plans covering fewer than 100 participants and which satisfy certain other requirements.

Further, while some small plans are maintained by large employers, most are maintained by small employers. Both small and large plans may enlist small third party service providers to perform administrative functions, but it is generally understood that third party service providers transfer their costs to their plan clients in the form of fees. Thus, the Departments believe that assessing the impact of this rule on small plans is an appropriate substitute for evaluating the effect on small entities. The definition of small entity considered appropriate for this purpose differs, however, from a definition of small business based on size standards promulgated by the Small Business Administration (SBA) (13 CFR 121.201) pursuant to the Small Business Act (5 U.S.C. 631 *et seq.*). The Department of Labor solicited comments on the use of this standard for evaluating the effects of the proposal on small entities. No comments were received with respect to the standard. Therefore, a summary of the initial regulatory flexibility analysis based on the 100 participant size standard is presented below.

The economic effects of HIPAA's statutory provisions on small plans are discussed extensively under the "Regulatory Flexibility Act— Department of Labor and Department of Health and Human Services" section of the preamble to the final regulation, published elsewhere in this issue of the **Federal Register**.

By clarifying and securing HIPAA's statutory portability protections, these regulations will help ensure that these benefits are fully realized. The result is likely to be a small increase in the economic effects of HIPAA's statutory provisions. The Departments were unable to estimate the amount of this increase. However, the direct financial value of coverage extensions pursuant to HIPAA's statutory portability provisions are estimated to be approximately $180 million for small plans, or a small fraction of one percent of total small plan expenditures.[2]

The regulations also will reduce uncertainty about health benefits' scope and value, thereby promoting employee health benefit coverage, including coverage under small plans, and labor market efficiency.

---

[2] Computer runs using Medical Expenditure Survey Household Component (MEPS-HC) and the Robert Wood Johnson Employer Health Benefits Survey determined that the share of covered private-sector job leavers at small firms average 35 percent of all covered private sector job leavers. From this, we inferred that the financial burden borne by small plans is approximately 35 percent of the total expenditures by private-sector group health plans which was estimated to be $515 million.

The benefits of these regulations will be concentrated among a small number of affected small group plan enrollees, while their costs will be spread thinly across small group plans enrollees. The benefits of these regulations for any particular affected individual, which may include improved health and productivity, may be significant. However, as previously noted, the number of affected individuals, and therefore the aggregate cost of these regulations, is expected to be small. The Departments believe that the benefits to affected individuals of the application of these regulations to small plans justify the cost to small plans of such application. The basis for the Departments' conclusions is detailed below.

The Departments generally expect the impact of the regulations on any particular small plan to be small. A very large majority of small plans are fully insured, so the cost will fall nominally on issuers rather than from plans. Issuers are expected to pass this cost back to plans and enrollees, but will spread much of it across a large number of plans, thereby minimizing the impact on any particular plan. However, it is possible that small plans that self-insure, or fully insured small plans whose premiums are tied closely to their particular claims experience, might bear all or most of the cost associated with extensions of coverage attributable directly to these regulations. The Departments have no way to quantify the incidence or magnitude of such costs, and solicit comments on such incidence and magnitude, and on whether these regulations would have a significant impact on a substantial number of small plans.

Special Analyses—Department of the Treasury

Notwithstanding the determinations of the Departments of Labor and of Health and Human Services, for purposes of the Department of the Treasury this notice of proposed rulemaking is not a significant regulatory action. Because this notice of proposed rulemaking does not impose a collection of information on small entities and is not subject to section 553(b) of the Administrative Procedure Act (5 U.S.C. chapter 5), the Regulatory Flexibility Act (5 U.S.C. chapter 6) does not apply pursuant to 5 U.S.C. 603(a), which exempts from the Regulatory Flexibility Act's requirements certain rules involving the internal revenue laws. Pursuant to section 7805(f) of the Internal Revenue Code, this notice of proposed rulemaking will be submitted to the Chief Counsel for Advocacy of the Small Business Administration for comment on its impact on small business.

Paperwork Reduction Act

Department of Labor

These final regulations include three separate collections of information as that term is defined in the Paperwork Reduction Act of 1995 (PRA 95), 44 U.S.C. 3502(3): the Notice of Enrollment Rights, Notice of Preexisting Condition Exclusion, and Certificate of Creditable Coverage. Each of these disclosures is currently approved by the Office of Management and Budget (OMB) through October 31, 2006 in accordance with PRA 95 under control numbers 1210-0101, 1210-0102, and 1210-0103.

Department of the Treasury

These final regulations include a collection of information as that term is defined in PRA 95: the Notice of Enrollment Rights, Notice of Preexisting Condition Exclusion, and Certificate of Creditable Coverage. Each of these disclosures is currently approved by OMB under control number 1545-1537.

Department of Health and Human Services

These final regulations include three separate collections of information as that term is defined in PRA 95: the Notice of Enrollment Rights, Notice of Preexisting Condition Exclusion, and Certificate of Creditable Coverage. Each of these disclosures is currently approved by OMB through June 30, 2006 in accordance with PRA 95 under control number 0938-0702.

Small Business Regulatory Enforcement Fairness Act

The rule being issued here is subject to the provisions of the Small Business Regulatory Enforcement Fairness Act of 1996 (5 U.S.C. 801 *et seq.*) and, if finalized, will be transmitted to Congress and the Comptroller General for review. The rule is not a "major rule" as that term is defined in 5 U.S.C. 804, because it is not likely to result in (1) an annual effect on the economy of $100 million or more; (2) a major increase in costs or prices for consumers, individual industries, or federal, state, or local government agencies, or geographic regions; or (3) significant adverse effects on competition, employment, investment, productivity, innovation, or on the ability of United States-based enterprises to compete with foreign-based enterprises in domestic or export markets.

Unfunded Mandates Reform Act

Section 202 of the Unfunded Mandates Reform Act of 1995 requires that agencies assess anticipated costs and benefits before issuing any rule that may result in an expenditure in any 1 year by state, local, or tribal governments, in the aggregate, or by the private sector, of $100 million. These proposed regulations have no such mandated consequential effect on state, local, or tribal governments, or on the private sector.

Federalism Statement Under Executive Order 13132—Department of Labor and Department of Health and Human Services

Executive Order 13132 outlines fundamental principles of federalism. It requires adherence to specific criteria by federal agencies in formulating and implementing policies that have "substantial direct effects" on the States, the relationship between the national government and States, or on the distribution of power and responsibilities among the various levels of government. Federal agencies promulgating regulations that have these federalism implications must consult with State and local officials, and describe the extent of their consultation and the nature of the concerns of State and local officials in the preamble to the regulation.

In the Departments' view, these proposed regulations have federalism implications because they may have substantial direct effects on the States, the relationship between the national government and States, or on the distribution of power and responsibilities among the various levels of government. However, in the Departments' view, the federalism implications of these proposed regulations are substantially mitigated because, with respect to health insurance issuers, the vast majority of States have enacted laws which meet or exceed the federal HIPAA portability standards.

In general, through section 514, ERISA supersedes State laws to the extent that they relate to any covered employee benefit plan, and preserves State laws that regulate insurance, banking or securities. While ERISA prohibits States from regulating a plan as an insurance or investment company or bank, HIPAA added a new section to ERISA (as well as to the PHS Act) narrowly preempting State requirements for issuers of group health insurance coverage. Specifically, with respect to seven provisions of the HIPAA portability rules, states may impose stricter obligations on health insurance issuers.[3] Moreover, with respect to other requirements for health insurance issuers, states may continue to apply state law requirements except to the extent that such requirements prevent the application of HIPAA's portability, access, and renewability provisions.

---

[3] States may shorten the six-month look-back period prior to the enrollment date; shorten the 12-month and 18-month maximum preexisting condition exclusion periods; increase the 63-day significant break in coverage period; increase the 30-day period for newborns, adopted children, and children placed for adoption to enroll in the plan with no preexisting condition exclusion; further limit the circumstances in which a preexisting condition exclusion may be applied (beyond the federal exceptions for certain newborns, adopted children, children placed for adoption, pregnancy, and genetic information in the absence of a diagnosis; require additional special enrollment periods;

In enacting these new preemption provisions, Congress intended to preempt State insurance requirements only to the extent that they prevent the application of the basic protections set forth in HIPAA. HIPAA's conference report states that the conferees intended the narrowest preemption of State laws with regard to health insurance issuers. H.R. Conf. Rep. No. 736, 104\th/ Cong. 2d Session 205 (1996). State insurance laws that are more stringent than the federal requirements are unlikely to "prevent the application of" the HIPAA portability provisions, and be preempted. Accordingly, States have significant latitude to impose requirements on health insurance insurers that are more restrictive than the federal law.

Guidance conveying this interpretation of HIPAA's preemption provisions was published in the Federal Register on April 8, 1997, 62 F.R. 16904. These proposed regulations clarify and implement the statute's minimum standards and do not significantly reduce the discretion given the States by the statute. Moreover, the Departments understand that the vast majority of States have requirements that meet or exceed the minimum requirements of the HIPAA portability provisions.

HIPAA provides that the States may enforce the provisions of HIPAA as they pertain to issuers, but that the Secretary of Health and Human Services must enforce any provisions that a State fails to substantially enforce. To date, CMS enforces the HIPAA portability provisions in only one State in accordance with that State's specific request to do so. When exercising its responsibility to enforce the provisions of HIPAA, CMS works cooperatively with the State for the purpose of addressing the State's concerns and avoiding conflicts with the exercise of State authority. CMS has developed procedures to implement its enforcement responsibilities, and to afford the States the maximum opportunity to enforce HIPAA's requirements in the first instance. CMS's procedures address the handling of reports that States may not be enforcing HIPAA's requirements, and the mechanism for allocating responsibility between the States and CMS. In compliance with Executive Order 13132's requirement that agencies examine closely any policies that may have federalism implications or limit the policymaking discretion of the States, the Department of Labor and CMS have engaged in numerous efforts to consult and work cooperatively with affected State and local officials.

For example, the Departments sought and received input from State insurance regulators and the National Association of Insurance Commissioners (NAIC). The NAIC is a non-profit corporation established by the insurance commissioners of the 50 States, the District of Columbia, and the four U.S. territories. In most States the Insurance Commissioner is appointed by the Governor, in approximately 14 States, the insurance commissioner is an elected official. Among other activities, it provides a forum for the development of uniform policy when uniformity is appropriate. Its members meet, discuss and offer solutions to mutual problems. The NAIC sponsors quarterly meetings to provide a forum for the exchange of ideas and in-depth consideration of insurance issues by regulators, industry representatives and consumers. CMS and the Department of Labor staff have consistently attended these quarterly meetings to listen to the concerns of the State Insurance Departments regarding HIPAA portability issues. In addition to the general discussions, committee meetings, and task groups, the NAIC sponsors the standing CMS/DOL meeting on HIPAA issues for members during the quarterly conferences. This meeting provides CMS and the Department of Labor with the opportunity to provide updates on regulations, bulletins, enforcement actions, and outreach efforts regarding HIPAA.

The Departments received written comments on the interim regulation from the NAIC and from ten States. In general, these comments raised technical issues that the Departments considered in conjunction with similar issues raised by other commenters. In a letter sent before issuance of the interim regulation, the NAIC expressed concerns that the Departments interpret the new preemption provisions of HIPAA narrowly so as to give the States flexibility to impose more stringent requirements. As discussed above, the Departments address this concern in the preamble to the interim regulation.

In addition, the Departments specifically consulted with the NAIC in developing these proposed regulations. Through the NAIC, the Departments sought and received the input of State insurance departments regarding certain insurance industry definitions, enrollment procedures and standard coverage terms. This input is generally reflected in the discussion of comments received and changes made in Section B - Overview of the Regulations of the preamble to the final regulations published elsewhere in this issue of the **Federal Register**.

The Departments have also cooperated with the States in several ongoing outreach initiatives, through which information on HIPAA is shared among federal regulators, State regulators and the regulated community. In particular, the Department of Labor has established a Health Benefits Education Campaign with more than 70 partners, including CMS, NAIC and many business and consumer groups. CMS has sponsored conferences with the States - the Consumer Outreach and Advocacy conferences in March 1999 and June 2000, and the Implementation and Enforcement of HIPAA National State-Federal Conferences in August 1999, 2000, 2001, 2002, and 2003. Furthermore, both the Department of Labor and CMS websites offer links to important State websites and other resources, facilitating coordination between the State and federal regulators and the regulated community.

Throughout the process of developing these regulations, to the extent feasible within the specific preemption provisions of HIPAA, the Departments have attempted to balance the States' interests in regulating health insurance issuers, and the Congress' intent to provide uniform minimum protections to consumers in every State. By doing so, it is the Departments' view that they have complied with the requirements of Executive Order 13132.

Pursuant to the requirements set forth in Section 8(a) of Executive Order 13132, and by the signatures affixed to proposed final regulations, the Departments certify that the Employee Benefits Security Administration and the Centers for Medicare & Medicaid Services have complied with the requirements of Executive Order 13132 for the attached proposed regulation, Notice of Proposed Rulemaking for Health Coverage Portability: Tolling and Certain Time Periods and Interaction with the Family and Medical Leave Act under HIPAA Titles I & IV (RIN 1210-AA54 and RIN 0938-AL88), in a meaningful and timely manner.

Basis for Assessment of Economic Impact—Department of Labor and Department of Health and Human Services

As noted above, the primary economic effects of HIPAA's portability provisions ensue directly from the statute. The Department's assessment of the economic effects of HIPAA's statutory portability provisions and the basis for the assessment is presented in detail under the "Basis for Assessment of Economic Impact" section of the preamble to the final regulation, published elsewhere in this issue of the **Federal Register**. By clarifying and securing HIPAA's statutory portability protections, these regulations will help ensure that HIPAA rights are fully realized. The result is likely to be a small increase in the economic effects of HIPAA's statutory portability provisions.

Additional economic benefits derive from the regulations' clarifications of HIPAA's portability requirements. The regulations provide clarity through both their provisions and their examples of how those provisions apply in various circumstances. By clarifying employees' rights and plan sponsors' obligations under HIPAA's portability provisions, the regulations will reduce uncertainty and costly disputes over these rights and obligations. They will promote employers' and employees' common understanding of the value of group health plan benefits and confidence in the security and predictability of those benefits, thereby improving labor market efficiency and fostering the establishment and continuation of group health plans by employers.[4]

(Footnote Continued)

and reduce the HMO affiliation period to less than 2 months (3 months for late enrollees).

[4] The voluntary nature of the employment-based health benefit system in conjunction with the open and dynamic character of labor markets make explicit as well as implicit negotiations on compensation a key determinant of the prevalence of employee benefits coverage. It is likely that 80% to 100% of the cost of employee benefits is borne by

workers through reduced wages (see for example Jonathan Gruber and Alan B. Krueger, "The Incidence of Mandated Employer-Provided Insurance: Lessons from Workers Compensation Insurance," in, David Bradford, ed., *Tax Policy and Economy*, pp:111-143 (Cambridge, MA: MIT Press, 1991); Jonathan Gruber, "The Incidence of Mandated Maternity Benefits," *American Economic Review*, Vol. 84 no. 3 (June 1994), pp. 622-641; Lawrence H. Summers, "Some Simple Economics of Mandated Benefits," *American*

These proposed regulations are intended to secure and implement HIPAA's group market portability provisions under certain special circumstances. The regulations will secure HIPAA's portability rights for individuals who are not timely notified that their coverage has ended and for individuals whose coverage ends in connection with the taking of leave that is guaranteed under FMLA. The regulations also will clarify and thereby secure individuals' special enrollment rights under HIPAA, and clarify the methodologies to be used by employers to determine the number of plans offered and the average number of individuals employed during a given year.

The benefits of these regulations will be concentrated among a small number of affected individuals.

Affected individuals will generally include those who would have lost access to coverage for needed medical care after forfeiting HIPAA portability and/or special enrollment rights due to time spent without coverage prior to receiving a certificate or while on FMLA-guaranteed leave. Affected individuals may also include some who would have been denied special enrollment rights if plans or issuers failed to recognize their requests for special enrollment or imposed unreasonable deadlines or requirements for completion of enrollment materials. The benefits of these regulations for any particular affected individual may be large. As noted above, access to coverage for needed medical care is important to individuals' health and productivity. However, the number of affected individuals, and therefore the aggregate cost of extended access to coverage under these regulations, is expected to be small, for several reasons.

First, these regulations extend HIPAA rights only in instances where individuals do not receive certificates immediately when coverage ends or their coverage ends in connection with the taking of FMLA-guaranteed leave. The Departments know of no source of data on the timeliness with which certificates are typically provided. The final regulations that accompany these proposed regulations permit plans to provide certificates with COBRA notices, up to 44 days after coverage ends. Plans, however, often do have the option of providing certificates immediately when coverage ends or even in advance, for example as part of exit packages given to terminating employees or in mailings to covered dependents in advance of birthdays that will end their eligibility for coverage. With respect to FMLA-protected leave, data provided in a 1996 report to Congress suggests that the number of employees who lose coverage in connection with FMLA-protected leave is likely to be small. The report notes that over an 18-month period just 1.2 percent of surveyed employees took what they reported to be FMLA leave. A similar survey of employers found that 3.6 percent of employees took such leave. Nearly all of those taking leave continued their health coverage. (This is not surprising, given that FMLA requires covered employers to extend eligibility for health insurance to employees on FMLA-protected leave on the same terms that applied when the employees were not on leave.) Just 9 percent of leave-takers reported that they lost some kind of employee benefit, with one-third of these reporting that they lost health insurance.[5] Putting these numbers together and converting to an annual basis, in a given year between 0.02 percent and 0.07 percent of employees, or well under one in one thousand, might lose health coverage in connection with FMLA-protected leave. Many of these will ultimately exercise their right to be reinstated in the job from which they took leave and to exercise their FMLA-guaranteed right to resume their previous health coverage. Therefore, the number of employees who will lose coverage and then, later and at the conclusion of FMLA-protected leave, enjoy extended portability rights under HIPAA as a result of these regulations, is likely to be very small.

Second, the period over which this regulation extends rights will often be short, insofar as certificates are often provided promptly after coverage ends and many family leave periods are far shorter than the guaranteed 12 weeks. As noted above, plans generally are required to provide certificates no later than 44 days after coverage ends and may provide them sooner. According to the aforementioned report to Congress on FMLA-protected leave, 41 percent of employees taking FMLA-protected leave did so for less than 8 days. Fifty-eight percent were on leave for less than 15 days, and two-thirds were on leave for less than 29 days. (FMLA protects leaves of up to 12 weeks, or 84 days.)

Third, it is generally in individuals' interest to minimize periods of uninsurance. Individuals are likely to exercise their portability and special enrollment rights as soon as possible after coverage ends, which will often be before any extension of such rights under these regulations becomes effective. Over one 36-month period prior to HIPAA, 71 percent of Americans had continuous coverage - that is, incurred not even a single, one-month break in coverage. Just 4 percent were uninsured for the entire period. About one-half of observed spells without insurance lasted less than 5 months. As noted above, few employees taking FMLA-protected leave had a lapse in health coverage.

Fourth, only a portion of individuals who enroll in health plans in circumstances where these regulations alone guarantee their special enrollment or portability rights would otherwise have been denied such rights. HIPAA special enrollment and portability requirements, both as specified under the final regulations and as modified under these proposed regulations, are minimum standards. Plans are free to provide additional enrollment opportunities.

Fifth, only a small minority of individuals who avoid a significant break in coverage solely as a direct result of these regulations would otherwise have lost coverage for needed medical care. The affected minority would be those who suffer from preexisting conditions, join health plans that exclude coverage for such conditions, and require treatment of such conditions during the exclusion periods. GAO estimated that HIPAA could ensure continued coverage for up to 25 million Americans.[6] More recent estimates suggest that the number of individual policy holders and their dependents which could be helped by HIPAA's portability provisions are in the 14 million range.[7] As noted above, however, the number of workers and dependents actually gaining coverage for a preexisting condition due to credit for prior coverage following a job change under HIPAA will be smaller than this. Both GAO's and our estimates of people who could benefit include all job changers with prior coverage and their dependents, irrespective of whether their new employer offers a plan, whether their new plan imposed a preexisting condition exclusion period, and whether they actually suffer from a preexisting condition. Accounting for these narrower criteria, CBO estimated that, at any point in time, about 100,000 individuals would have a preexisting condition exclusion reduced for prior creditable coverage. An additional 45,000 would gain added coverage in the individual market. The CBO estimate demonstrates that the number of individuals actually gaining coverage for needed medical services will be a small fraction of all those whose right to such coverage HIPAA's portability provisions guarantee. Accordingly, the Departments expect that the number gaining coverage for needed services as a direct result of these regulations will be a small fraction of the already small number whose right to such coverage these regulations would establish.

(Footnote Continued)

Economic Review, Vol. 79, No. 2 (May 1989), pp:177-183; Louise Sheiner, "Health Care Costs, Wages, and Aging," Federal Reserve Board of Governors working paper, April 1999; Mark Pauly and Brad Herring, *Pooling Health Insurance Risks* (Washington, DC: AEI Press, 1999), Gail A. Jensen and Michael A. Morrisey, "Endogenous Fringe Benefits, Compensating Wage Differentials and Older Workers," *International Journal of Health Care Finance and Economics* Vol 1, No. 3-4 (forthcoming), and Edward Montgomery, Kathryn Shaw, and Mary Ellen Benedict, "Pensions and Wages: An Hedonic Price Theory Approach," *International Economic Review*, Vol. 33 No. 1 (Feb. 1992.), pp:111-128.) The prevalence of benefits is therefore largely dependent on the efficacy of this exchange. If workers perceive that there is the potential for inappropriate denial of benefits they will discount their value to adjust for this risk. This discount drives a wedge in the compensation negotiation, limiting its efficiency. With workers unwilling to bear the full cost of the benefit, fewer benefits will be provided. The extent to which workers perceive a federal regulation supported by enforcement authority to improve the security and quality of benefits, the differential between the employers costs and workers willingness top accept wage offsets is minimized.

[5] Commission on Family and Medical Leave and U.S. Department of Labor, *A Workable Balance: Report to Congress on Family and Medical Leave Policies*, transmitted April 30, 1996.

[6] U.S. General Accounting Office, Report HEHS-95-257, "Health Insurance Portability: Reform Could Ensure Continued Coverage for up to 25 Million Americans," September 1995.

[7] We calculated these estimates using internal runs off the MEPS-HC. These runs gave the number of total job changers, total job changers that had employer-sponsored insurance (ESI), and whether this coverage had been for less than 12 months or not. Estimates for dependents were based off the ratio of policy-holders to total dependents from the March 2003 Current Population Survey (March CPS). It should be noted, however, that the EBSA estimate of 14 million does not include estimate of individuals no longer eligible for COBRA continuation coverage or individuals facing job lock, while the GAO numbers do.

The Departments attempted to estimate the number of individuals who might avoid a break in coverage because of the provision of these proposed regulations that tolls the break until the individual receives a certification but not more than 44 days. The Departments examined coverage patterns evident in the Survey of Income and Program Participation (SIPP), a longitudinal household survey that tracks transitions in coverage. SIPP interviews households once every four months. The Departments estimate that, in a given year, about 7 million individuals have breaks in coverage lasting 4 months or less. The survey data suffer from so-called "seam bias" - respondents tend to report that status as unchanged over 4-month increments. Of the 7 million reporting breaks of 4 months or less, 6.5 million report breaks of exactly 4 months. This finding is consistent with the more general finding that breaks of 4 months or less are far more common than longer breaks. It seems likely that the 7 million breaks of 4 months or less actually included proportionate or disproportionately large share of breaks of 1 or 2 months. Assuming the breaks are actually distributed evenly by length between 1 day and 4 months, then about one-half of the breaks, or 3.5 million breaks, would have lasted less than 63 days and therefore would not have constituted breaks for purposes of HIPAA's portability protections even without reference to the provision of this proposed regulation that tolls the break until the individual receives a certification but not more than 44 days. Approximately three-fourths of the remaining breaks or about 2.6 million breaks, would have lasted between 1 and 44 additional days and thereby potentially have been tolled until the individuals received their certifications but not more than 44 days. Thus 2.6 million provides a reasonable upper bound on the number of individuals who might avoid a break in coverage in a given year because of this tolling provision. It is not known what fraction of these would subsequently join group health plans that include preexisting condition exclusions while suffering from and requiring additional care for preexisting conditions. Comparing GAO's (20 million or more) and our (14 million) estimates of the number of individuals who could potentially benefit from HIPAA's portability protections (individuals with prior creditable coverage who join new health plans in a given year) with the CBO estimate of the number who might actually have added group coverage for needed care (100,000) produces a ratio of about 1 percent. If this proportion holds for group health plan enrollees who avoid breaks because of this tolling provision, then an upper bound of about 26,000 individuals annually might gain coverage for needed care under the proposed regulation's provision treating coverage under such programs as creditable coverage.

The Departments considered whether certain individuals whose HIPAA portability rights these proposed regulations would extend may be disproportionately likely to be in (or have dependents who are in) poor health. Specifically, individuals taking FMLA-protected leave, especially those who elect not to be reinstated in their prior jobs following FMLA-protected leave, may be so likely. On the other hand, individuals in such circumstances are also particularly unlikely to allow their health insurance from their prior job to lapse while they are on leave. Accordingly, most such individuals' special enrollment periods and countable breaks in coverage (if any) would probably have begun at the conclusion of the FMLA-protected leave even in absence of these proposed regulations. The Departments are therefore uncertain whether individuals who would exercise HIPAA portability rights extended solely by these regulations would be more costly to insure than others exercising HIPAA portability rights, and solicit comments on this question.

Affected individuals may also include some who would have been denied special enrollment rights if plans or issuers failed to recognize their requests for special enrollment or imposed unreasonable deadlines or requirements for completion of enrollment materials.

As noted above, the Departments expect that these regulations will result in a small increase the economic effects of HIPAA's statutory provisions. For the reasons stated immediately above, the Departments believe that this increase will be small on aggregate, adding only a small increment to the cost attributable to HIPAA's statutory portability provisions, which themselves amount to a small fraction of one percent of health plan expenditures. Thus the increase will be negligible relative to typical year-to-year increases in premiums charged by issuers, which can amount to several percentage points or more. Therefore, the Departments expect these regulations to have little or no perceptible negative impact on employers' propensity to offer health benefit plans or on the generosity of those plans. In sum, the Departments expect that the benefits of these regulations, which can be very large for a particular affected individual, will justify their costs.

[¶ 49,239]   **Proposed Regulations and Proposed Amendments of Regulations (REG-102144-04),** published in the Federal Register on May 24, 2005.

Consolidated returns: Dual consolidated losses: Dual resident corporation: Separate unit.—Amendments of Reg. §1.6043-4T, relating to dual consolidated losses, are proposed. A public hearing on this proposal is scheduled for September 7, 2005. Reg. §§1.1503(d)-0—1.1503(d)-6 and amendments of Reg. §§1.1502-21, are adopted.

AGENCY: Internal Revenue Service (IRS), Treasury.

ACTION: Notice of proposed rule making and notice of public hearing.

SUMMARY: This document contains proposed regulations under section 1503(d) of the Internal Revenue Code (Code) regarding dual consolidated losses. Section 1503(d) generally provides that a dual consolidated loss of a dual resident corporation cannot reduce the taxable income of any other member of the affiliated group unless, to the extent provided in regulations, such loss does not offset the income of any foreign corporation. Similar rules apply to losses of separate units of domestic corporations. The proposed regulations address various dual consolidated loss issues, including exceptions to the general prohibition against using a dual consolidated loss to reduce the taxable income of any other member of the affiliated group.

DATES: Written and electronic comments and outlines of topics to be discussed at the public hearing scheduled for September 7, 2005, at 10:00 a.m., must be received by May 24, 2005

ADDRESSES: Send submissions to CC:PA:LPD:PR (REG-102144-04), room 5203, Internal Revenue Service, P.O. Box 7604, Washington, DC 20044. Submissions may be hand delivered between the hours of 8 a.m. and 4 p.m. to CC:PA:LPD:PR (REG-102144-04), Courier's Desk, Internal Revenue Service, 1111 Constitution Avenue, NW., Washington, DC, or sent electronically via the IRS Internet site at *www.irs.gov/regs* or via the Federal eRulemaking Portal at *www.regulations.gov/* (IRS and REG-102144-04). The public hearing will be held in the Auditorium of the Internal Revenue Building, 1111 Constitution Avenue, NW., Washington, DC.

FOR FURTHER INFORMATION CONTACT: Concerning the proposed regulations, Kathryn T. Holman, (202) 622-3840 (not a toll-free number); concerning submissions and the hearing, Robin Jones, (202) 622-3521 (not a toll-free number).

SUPPLEMENTARY INFORMATION:

Paperwork Reduction Act

The collection of information contained in this notice of proposed rulemaking has been submitted to the Office of Management and Budget in accordance with the Paperwork Reduction Act of 1995 (44 USC 3507(d)). Comments on the collection of information should be sent to the **Office of Management and Budget,** Attn: Desk Officer for the Department of the Treasury, Office of Information and Regulatory Affairs, Washington, DC 20503, with copies to the **Internal Revenue Service,** Attn: IRS Reports Clearance Officer, W:CAR:MP:FP:S Washington, DC 20224. Comments on the collection of information should be received by July 22, 2005. Comments are specifically requested concerning:

Whether the proposed collection of information is necessary for the proper performance of the functions of the IRS, including whether the information will have practical utility;

The accuracy of the estimated burden associated with the proposed collection of information (see below);

How the quality, utility, and clarity of the information to be collected may be enhanced;

How the burden of complying with the proposed collection of information may be minimized, including through the application of automated collection techniques or other forms of information technology; and

Estimates of capital or start-up costs and costs of operation, maintenance, and purchase of service to provide information.

The collections of information in these proposed regulations are in §§1.1503(d)-1(b)(14), 1.1503(d)-1(c)(1), 1.1503(d)-2(d), 1.1503(d)-4(c)(2), 1.1503(d)-4(d), 1.1503(d)-4(e)(2), 1.1503(d)-4(f)(2), 1.1503(d)-4(g), 1.1503(d)-4(h) and 1.1503(d)-4(i). The various information is required. First, it notifies the IRS when the taxpayer asserts that it had reasonable cause for failing to comply with certain filing requirements under the regulations. Second, it indicates when the taxpayer attempts to rebut the amount of presumed tainted income. Finally, it provides the IRS various information regarding exceptions to the domestic use limitation, including domestic use elections, domestic use agreements, triggering events and recapture.

The collection of information is in certain cases required and in certain cases voluntary. The likely respondents will be domestic corporations with foreign operations that generate losses.

Estimated total annual reporting and/or recordkeeping burden: 2,665 hours.

Estimated average annual burden hours per respondent and/or recordkeeper: 1.5 hours.

Estimated number of respondents and/or recordkeepers: 1,765.

Estimated annual frequency of responses: Annually.

An agency may not conduct or sponsor, and a person is not required to respond to, a collection of information unless it displays a valid control number assigned by the Office of Management and Budget.

Books or records relating to a collection of information must be retained as long as their contents may become material in the administration of any internal revenue law. Generally, tax returns and tax return information are confidential, as required by 26 USC 6103.

Background

The United States taxes the worldwide income of domestic corporations. A domestic corporation is a corporation created or organized in the United States or under the law of the United States or of any State. The United States allows certain domestic corporations to file consolidated returns with other affiliated domestic corporations. When two or more domestic corporations file a consolidated return, losses that one corporation incurs generally may reduce or eliminate tax on income that another corporation earns.

Some countries use criteria other than place of incorporation or organization to determine whether corporations are residents for tax purposes. For example, some countries treat corporations as residents for tax purposes if they are managed or controlled in that country. If one of these countries determines a corporation to be a resident, the corporation is generally subject to income tax of that foreign country on a residence basis. As a result, if such a corporation is a domestic corporation for U.S. tax purposes, it is a dual resident corporation and is subject to the income tax of both the foreign country and the United States on a residence basis.

Prior to the Tax Reform Act of 1986, if a corporation was a resident of both a foreign country and the United States, and the foreign country permitted the losses of the corporation to be used to offset the income of another person (for example, as a result of consolidation), then the dual resident corporation could use any losses it generated twice: once to offset income that was subject to U.S. tax, but not foreign tax, and a second time to offset income subject to foreign tax, but not U.S. tax (double-dip).

Congress was concerned that this double-dip of a single economic loss could result in an undue tax advantage to certain foreign investors that made investments in domestic corporations, and could create an undue incentive for certain foreign corporations to acquire domestic corporations and for domestic corporations to acquire foreign rather than domestic assets. Staff of Joint Committee on Taxation, 99th Cong., 2nd Sess., General Explanation of the Tax Reform Act of 1986, at 1064 - 1065 (1987). Through such double-dipping, worldwide economic income could be rendered partially or fully exempt from current taxation. Moreover, even if the foreign income against which the loss was used would eventually be subject to U.S. tax (upon a repatriation of earnings), there were timing benefits of double dipping that the statute was intended to prevent. Congress responded to this concern by enacting section 1503(d) as part of the Tax Reform Act of 1986.

Section 1503(d) provides that a dual consolidated loss of a corporation cannot reduce the taxable income of any other member of the corporation's affiliated group. The statute defines a dual consolidated loss as a net operating loss of a domestic corporation that is subject to an income tax of a foreign country on its income without regard to the source of its income, or is subject to tax on a residence basis. The statute authorizes the issuance of regulations permitting the use of a dual consolidated loss to offset the income of a domestic affiliate if the loss does not offset the income of a foreign corporation under foreign law.

Section 1503(d) further states that, to the extent provided in regulations, similar rules apply to any loss of a *separate unit* of a domestic corporation as if such unit were a wholly owned subsidiary of the corporation. Although the statute does not define the term separate unit, the legislative history to the provision refers to the loss of any separate and clearly identifiable unit of a trade or business of a taxpayer and cites as an example a foreign branch of a domestic corporation. See H.R. Rep. No. 795, 100th Cong., 2d Sess. July 26, 1988) at 293.

The IRS and Treasury issued temporary regulations under section 1503(d) in 1989 (TD 8261, 1989-2 C.B. 220). The temporary regulations generally provided that, unless one of three limited exceptions applied, a dual consolidated loss of a dual resident corporation could not offset the income of any other member of the dual resident corporation's affiliated group. The temporary regulations contained similar rules for losses incurred by separate units.

In response to comments that the temporary regulations were unnecessarily restrictive, the IRS and Treasury issued final regulations under section 1503(d) in 1992 (TD 8434, 1992-2 C.B. 240). These final regulations were updated and amended over the next 11 years (current regulations). The current regulations apply the section 1503(d) limitation more narrowly than the temporary regulations. The current regulations adopt an *actual use* standard for permitting a dual consolidated loss to offset income of members of the affiliated group. This standard, which applies to both dual resident corporations and separate units, requires taxpayers to certify that no portion of the dual consolidated loss has been or will be used to offset the income of any other person under the income tax laws of a foreign country. If such a certification is made and a subsequent *triggering event* occurs, the dual consolidated loss must be recaptured in the year of the event (plus an applicable interest charge).

This document proposes amendments to the current regulations under section 1503(d). Conforming amendments are also proposed to related regulations under sections 1502 and 6043.

Overview

In general, the proposed regulations address three fundamental concerns that arise in connection with the current regulations. First, the IRS and Treasury believe that the scope of application of the current regulations should be modified. For example, the current regulations may apply to certain structures where there is little likelihood of a double-dip. Moreover, the IRS and Treasury understand that some taxpayers have taken the position that the current regulations do not apply to certain structures that provide taxpayers the benefits of the type of double-dip that section 1503(d) is intended to deny. Accordingly, the proposed regulations are designed to minimize these cases of potential over- and under-application.

Second, the IRS and Treasury recognize that there are many unresolved issues that arise when applying the current regulations, particularly in light of the adoption of the entity classification regulations under §§ 301.7701-1 through 301.7701-3. Thus, the proposed regulations modernize the dual consolidated loss regime to take into account the entity classification regulations and to resolve the related issues so that the rules can be applied by taxpayers and the Commissioner with greater certainty.

Finally, the IRS and Treasury believe that, in many cases, the current regulations are administratively burdensome to both taxpayers and the Commissioner. Accordingly, the proposed regulations reduce, to the extent possible, the administrative burden imposed on taxpayers and the Commissioner.

Explanation of Provisions

A. *Structure of the Proposed Regulations*

The proposed regulations are set forth in six sections. Section 1.1503(d)-1 contains definitions and special rules for filings. Section 1.1503(d)-2 sets forth operating rules, which include the general rule that prohibits the domestic use of a dual consolidated loss (subject to certain exceptions discussed below), a rule that limits the use of dual consolidated losses following certain transactions, an anti-avoidance provision that prevents dual consolidated losses from offsetting income from assets acquired in certain nonrecognition transactions or contributions to capital, and rules for computing foreign tax credit limitations. Section 1.1503(d)-3 contains special rules for accounting for dual consolidated losses. These special rules determine the amount of a dual consolidated loss, determine the effect of a dual consolidated loss on domestic affiliates, and provide special basis adjustments. Section 1.1503(d)-4 provides exceptions to the general rule that prohibits the domestic use of a dual consolidated loss, including a domestic use election. Section 1.1503(d)-5 contains examples that illustrate the application of the proposed regulations. Finally, § 1.1503(d)-6 contains the proposed effective date of the proposed regulations.

In addition to the proposed regulatory amendments under section 1503(d), the proposed regulations also include conforming proposed amendments to § 1.1502-21 and § 1.6043-4T.

B. *Definitions and Special Rules for Filings under Section 1503(d)—§ 1.1503(d)-1*

1. *Treatment of a separate unit as a domestic corporation and a dual resident corporation*

Section 1.1503-2(c)(3) and (4) of the current regulations defines a separate unit of a domestic corporation as a foreign branch, within the meaning of § 1.367(a)-6T(g), (foreign branch separate unit) and an interest in a partnership, trust or hybrid entity. The current regulations also provide that any separate unit of a domestic corporation is treated as a separate domestic corporation for purposes of applying the dual consolidated loss rules. Section 1.1503-2(c)(2). In addition, the current regulations provide that, unless otherwise indicated, any reference to a dual resident corporation refers also to a separate unit. As a result of these rules, certain provisions of the current regulations only refer to dual resident corporations, and therefore apply to separate units because they are treated as domestic corporations and dual resident corporations. However, other provisions of the current regulations refer to both dual resident corporations and separate units (for example, see § 1.1503-2(g)(2)(iii)(A)).

The IRS and Treasury believe that, in certain cases, treating separate units as domestic corporations creates uncertainty in applying the current regulations. This may occur, for example, as a result of certain rules applying to separate units because they are treated as domestic corporations or dual resident corporations, while other rules apply explicitly to separate units themselves. Accordingly, the proposed regulations do not contain a general rule that treats separate units as domestic corporations or dual resident corporations for all purposes of applying the dual consolidated loss regulations. Instead, the proposed regulations explicitly refer to dual resident corporations and separate units where appropriate, treat separate units as domestic corporations only for limited purposes, and modify the operative rules where necessary to take into account differences between dual resident corporations and separate units.

2. *Application of section 1503(d) to S corporations*

Section 1.1503-2(c)(2) of the current regulations provides that an S corporation, as defined in section 1361, is not a dual resident corporation. The preamble to the current regulations explains that S corporations are so excluded because an S corporation cannot have a domestic corporation as one of its shareholders. The current regulations do not, however, explicitly exclude separate units owned by an S corporation from the definition of a dual resident corporation. As a result, the current regulations can be read to provide that an S corporation, although it cannot itself be a dual resident corporation, could own a separate unit that would be a dual resident corporation.

The IRS and Treasury believe that such a result is inappropriate because an S corporation cannot have a domestic corporation as one of its shareholders and generally is not taxable at the entity level. Accordingly, the proposed regulations provide that for purposes of the dual consolidated loss rules, an S corporation is not treated as a domestic corporation. This modification clarifies that the dual consolidated loss regulations do not apply to the S corporation itself, or to foreign branches or interests in certain flow-through entities owned by an S corporation.

The IRS and Treasury request comments as to whether regulated investment companies (as defined in section 851) or real estate investment trusts (as defined in section 856) should be similarly excluded from the application of the dual consolidated loss rules.

3. *Losses of a foreign insurance company treated as a domestic corporation*

Section 953(d) generally provides that a foreign corporation that would qualify to be taxed as an insurance company if it were a domestic corporation may, under certain circumstances, elect to be treated as a domestic corporation. Section 953(d)(3) provides that if a corporation elects to be treated as a domestic corporation pursuant to section 953(d) and is treated as a member of an affiliated group, any loss of such corporation is treated as a dual consolidated loss for purposes of section 1503(d), without regard to section 1503(d)(2)(B) (grant of regulatory authority to exclude losses which do not offset the income of foreign corporations from the definition of a dual consolidated loss). Therefore, losses of such corporations are treated as dual consolidated losses regardless of whether the corporation is subject to an income tax of a foreign country on its worldwide income or on a residence basis.

The current regulations do not address the application of section 953(d)(3). However, the definition of a dual resident corporation contained in the proposed regulations includes a foreign insurance company that makes an election to be treated as a domestic corporation pursuant to section 953(d) and is a member of an affiliated group, regardless of how such entity is taxed by the foreign country.

4. *Definition of a separate unit*

(a) *Interests in Non-Hybrid Entity Partnerships and Interests in Non-Hybrid Entity Grantor Trusts*

Section 1.1503-2(c)(4) of the current regulations defines a separate unit to include an interest in a hybrid entity (hybrid entity separate unit). The current regulations define a hybrid entity as an entity that is not taxable as an association for U.S. income tax purposes, but is subject to income tax in a foreign jurisdiction as a corporation (or otherwise at the entity level) either on its worldwide income or on a residence basis. This definition includes an interest in such an entity that is treated for U.S. tax purposes as a partnership (hybrid entity partnership) or as a grantor trust (hybrid entity grantor trust). An interest in an entity that is treated as a partnership or a grantor trust for both U.S. and foreign tax purposes (non-hybrid entity partnership and non-hybrid entity grantor trust, respectively) also is treated as a separate unit under the current regulations. § 1.1503-2(c)(3)(i).

The current regulations also apply to a separate unit owned indirectly through a partnership or grantor trust. Thus, for example, if a partnership owns a foreign branch within the meaning of § 1.367(a)-6T(g), a domestic corporate partner's interest in such partnership, and its indirect interest in a portion of the foreign branch owned through the partnership, each constitutes a separate unit.

Under the current regulations, an interest in a non-hybrid entity partnership or a non-hybrid entity grantor trust is also treated as a separate unit, regardless of whether the partnership or grantor trust has any nexus with a foreign jurisdiction. This rule can result in the application of the dual consolidated loss rules when there may be little opportunity for a double-dip. For example, if two domestic corporations each own 50 percent of a domestic partnership that generates losses attributable to activities conducted solely in the United States, the corporate partners would be technically subject to the dual consolidated loss rules and therefore would not be allowed to offset their income with such losses, unless an exception applied. In such a case, however, it may be unlikely that the losses would be available to offset income of another person under the income tax laws of a foreign country.

The IRS and Treasury believe that including an interest in a non-hybrid entity partnership and an interest in a non-hybrid entity grantor trust in the definition of a separate unit may not be necessary and is administratively burdensome. In such cases, it may be unlikely that deductions and losses solely attributable to activities of the partnership or grantor trust, that do not rise to the level of a taxable presence in a foreign jurisdiction, can be used to offset income of another person under the income tax laws of a foreign country. As a result, the proposed regulations eliminate from the definition of a separate unit an interest in a non-hybrid entity partnership and an interest in a non-hybrid entity grantor trust. It should be noted, however, that the proposed regulations retain the rule contained in the current regulations that a domestic corporation can own a separate unit indirectly through both hybrid entity and non-hybrid entity partnerships, and through both hybrid entity and non-hybrid entity grantor trusts.

(b) *Separate Unit Combination Rule*

Section 1.1503-2(c)(3)(ii) of the current regulations provides that if two or more foreign branches located in the same foreign country are owned by a single domestic corporation and the losses of each branch are made available to offset the income of the other branches under the tax laws of the foreign country, then the branches are treated as one separate unit. The combination rule in the current regulations does not apply to interests in hybrid entity separate units or to dual resident corporations.

Although a disregarded entity is treated as a branch of its owner for various purposes of the Code, the current regulations distinguish a hybrid entity separate unit that is disregarded as an entity separate from its owner from a foreign branch separate unit. Compare § 1.1503-2(c)(3)(i)(A) and (c)(4); see also § 1.1503-2(g)(2)(vi)(C). Accordingly, the combination rule under the current regulations does not apply to an interest in a hybrid entity separate unit, even if the hybrid entity is disregarded as an entity separate from its owner.

The combination rule in the current regulations also requires the foreign branches to be owned by a single domestic corporation. Thus, for example, the current regulations do not permit the combination of foreign branches owned by different domestic corporations, even if such corporations are members of the same consolidated group. In addition, in some cases the current regulations do not allow the combination of foreign branches that are owned indirectly by a single domestic corporation through other separate units because, as discussed above, such other separate units are generally treated as domestic corporations for purposes of applying the dual consolidated loss regulations. As a result, such foreign branches are not treated as being owned by a single domestic corporation.

The IRS and Treasury believe that the application of the combination rule should not be restricted to foreign branch separate units. In addition, the IRS and Treasury believe that the combination rule should not be limited to those cases where the domestic corporation owns the separate units directly. Therefore, provided certain requirements are satisfied, the proposed regulations adopt a broader combination rule that combines all separate units that are directly or indirectly owned by a single domestic corporation.

In order for separate units to be combined under the proposed regulations, the losses of each separate unit must be made available to offset the income of the other separate units under the tax laws of a single foreign country. In addition, if the separate unit is a foreign branch separate unit, it must be located in the foreign country that allows its losses to be made available to offset income of each separate unit; if the separate unit is a hybrid entity separate unit, the hybrid entity must be subject to tax in the foreign country that allows losses to be made available to each separate unit either on its worldwide income or on a residence basis.

The combination rule in the proposed regulations does not combine separate units owned by different domestic corporations, even if the domestic corporations are included in the same consolidated group. The IRS and Treasury believe this approach is consistent with section 1503(d)(3), which provides that, to the extent provided in regulations, a loss of a separate unit of a domestic corporation is subject to the dual consolidated loss rules as if it were a wholly owned subsidiary of such domestic corporation. In addition, the combination rule contained in the proposed regulations only applies to separate units and therefore does not apply to dual resident corporations.

The IRS and Treasury, however, request comments as to whether there is authority to expand the combination rule and, if so, whether the combination rule should be expanded to include separate units that are owned directly or indirectly by domestic corporations that are members of the same consolidated group. Similarly, comments are requested as to whether the combination rule should be extended to apply to dual resident corporations. Further, the IRS and Treasury request comments on the application of the operative provisions of the proposed regulations to combined separate units owned by different domestic corporations (for example, the SRLY limitation under § 1.1503(d)-3(c)).

5. *Exception to the definition of a dual consolidated loss*

Section 1.1503-2(c)(5)(ii)(A) of the current regulations provides a very limited exception to the definition of a dual consolidated loss where the income tax laws of a foreign country do not permit the dual resident corporation to either: (1) use its losses, expenses, or deductions to offset the income of any other person in the same taxable year; or (2) carry over or carry back its losses, expenses, or deductions to be used, by any means, to offset the income of any other person in other taxable years. This exception only applies in rare and unusual cases where the income tax laws of the foreign country do not allow any portion of the dual consolidated loss to be used to offset income of another person under any circumstances.

The IRS and Treasury understand that some taxpayers have improperly interpreted this provision in a manner inconsistent with the policies of the dual consolidated loss rules. As a result, the proposed regulations eliminate this exception to the definition of a dual consolidated loss. As discussed below, however, the proposed regulations contain a new exception to the general rule restricting the use of a dual consolidated loss to offset income of a domestic affiliate. In general, this new exception applies when there is no possibility that any portion of the dual consolidated loss can be double-dipped, and operates in a manner that is similar to the manner in which the exception to the definition of a dual consolidated loss contained in the current regulations operates.

6. *Partnership special allocations*

Section 1.1503-2(c)(5)(iii) of the current regulations reserves on the treatment of dual consolidated losses of separate units that are partnership interests, including interests in hybrid entities. The preamble to the current regulations explains that the reservation was principally the result of concerns regarding partnership special allocations.

The proposed regulations no longer reserve on the treatment of separate units that are partnership interests. However, the IRS will continue to challenge structures that attempt to use special allocations in a manner that is inconsistent with the principles of section 1503(d).

7. *Domestic use of a dual consolidated loss*

Section 1.1503-2(b)(1) of the current regulations states that, except as otherwise provided, a dual consolidated loss cannot offset the taxable income of any domestic affiliate, regardless of whether the loss offsets income of another person under the income tax laws of a foreign country, and regardless of whether the income that the loss may offset in the foreign country is, has been, or will be subject to tax in the United States. Section 1.1503-2(c)(13) defines the term domestic affiliate to mean any member of an affiliated group, without regard to exceptions contained in section 1504(b) (other than section 1504(b)(3)) relating to includible corporations.

The proposed regulations retain the general prohibition against using a dual consolidated loss to offset income of domestic affiliates contained in the current regulations, with modifications, and refer to such usage as a *domestic use* of a dual consolidated loss. This general prohibition is subject to a number of exceptions, discussed below. In addition, because the proposed regulations do not treat separate units as domestic corporations and dual resident corporations (other than for limited purposes) the proposed regulations expand the definition of a domestic affiliate to include separate units. This expanded definition is necessary for purposes of applying the domestic use limitation rule.

8. *Foreign use of a dual consolidated loss*

(a) *General Rule*

Section 1.1503-2T(g)(2)(i) of the current regulations provides that, in order to elect relief from the general limitation on the use of a dual consolidated loss to offset income of a domestic affiliate with respect to a dual consolidated loss ((g)(2)(i) election), the taxpayer must, among other things, certify that no portion of the losses, expenses, or deductions taken into account in computing the dual consolidated loss has been, or will be, used to offset the income of any other person under the income tax laws of a foreign country. If, contrary to this certification, there is such a *use*, the dual consolidated loss subject to the (g)(2)(i) election generally must be recaptured and reported as gross income.

The IRS and Treasury understand that issues arise involving the application of the use rule contained in the current regulations. For example, issues may arise where items of income, gain, deduction and loss are treated as being generated or incurred by different persons under U.S. and foreign law. Similarly, issues may arise due to different definitions of a *person* under U.S. and foreign law. These issues have become more prevalent since the adoption of the entity classification regulations under § § 301.7701-1 through 301.7701-3.

The IRS and Treasury also understand that taxpayers have taken positions under the current regulations regarding the use of a dual consolidated loss that are inconsistent with the policies underlying section 1503(d). On the other hand, the IRS and Treasury believe that, under the current regulations, a use can be deemed to occur in certain cases where there may be little likelihood of the type of double-dip that section 1503(d) was intended to prevent.

For the reasons discussed above, the proposed regulations modify the definition of *use* and provide a rule based on *foreign use*. These modifications are intended to minimize the potential over- and under-application of the dual consolidated loss rules that can occur under the current regulations. Under the proposed regulations, the foreign use definition is intended to minimize the opportunity for a double-dip. However, the new definition is also intended to minimize the situations in which a foreign use will occur in cases where there may be little likelihood of a double-dip.

The proposed regulations provide that a foreign use is deemed to occur only if two conditions are satisfied. The first condition is satisfied if any portion of a loss or deduction taken into account in computing the dual consolidated loss is made available under the income tax laws of a foreign country to offset or reduce, directly or indirectly, any item that is recognized as income or gain under such laws (including items of income or gain generated by the dual resident corporation or separate unit itself), regardless of whether income or gain is actually offset, and regardless of whether such items are recognized under U.S. tax principles. This condition ensures that there will not be a foreign use unless all or a portion of the dual consolidated loss offsets or reduces, or is made available to offset or reduce, income or gain for foreign tax purposes.

The second condition is satisfied if items that are (or could be) offset pursuant to the first condition are considered, under U.S. tax principles, to be items of: (1) a foreign corporation; or (2) a direct or indirect (for example, through a partnership) owner of an interest in a hybrid entity, provided such interest is not a separate unit. This condition is intended to limit a foreign use to situations where the foreign income that is (or could be) offset by the dual consolidated loss is not currently subject to U.S. corporate income tax. In general, if the foreign income that is offset is currently subject to U.S. corporate income tax, there is no double-dip of the dual consolidated loss.

(b) *Exception to Foreign Use if no Dilution of an Interest in a Separate Unit*

Section 1.1503-2(c)(15) of the current regulations employs a so-called *actual use* standard for determining whether there has been a use of a dual consolidated loss to offset the income of another person under the laws of a foreign country. Although referred to as an *actual use* standard, this rule provides that a use is considered to occur in the year in which a loss, expense or deduction taken into account in computing the dual consolidated loss is made available for such an offset, unless an exception applies. The fact that the other person does not have sufficient income in that year to benefit from such an offset is not taken into account.

The *available* component of the actual use standard was adopted because of the administrative complexity that would result from having a use occur only when income is actually offset. For example, if in the year that a portion of the dual consolidated loss is made available to be used by another person, the other person itself generates a loss (or has a loss carryover), then in many cases the portion of the dual consolidated loss would become part of the loss carryover. Such loss therefore would be available to be carried forward or carried back to offset income in different taxable years. Under this approach, the portion of the loss carryforward or carryback that was taken into account in computing the dual consolidated loss would need to be identified and tracked, which would require detailed ordering rules for determining when such losses were used. Timing and base differences between the U.S. and foreign jurisdiction would further complicate such an approach.

Because of the administrative complexities discussed above, the foreign use definition contained in the proposed regulations retains the available for use standard. However, because the available for use standard is retained, there are many cases in which a foreign use of a dual consolidated loss attributable to interests in hybrid entity partnerships and hybrid entity grantor trusts, and separate units owned indirectly through partnerships and grantor trusts, occurs, even though no portion of any item of deduction or loss comprising the dual consolidated loss is double-dipped. In the case of interests in hybrid entity partnerships and hybrid entity grantor trusts, a portion of the dual consolidated loss attributable to an interest in such entity in many cases would be made available to offset income or gain of a direct or indirect owner of an interest in such hybrid entity, provided such interest is not a separate unit. This typically would occur because under foreign law the hybrid entity is taxed as a corporation (or otherwise at the entity level) and its net losses may be carried forward or carried back. A similar result may occur in the case of a separate unit owned indirectly through a non-hybrid entity partnership or a non-hybrid entity grantor trust because of timing and base differences between the laws of the United States and the foreign jurisdiction.

The IRS and Treasury believe this is an inappropriate result in many cases. For example, the IRS and Treasury believe that if there is no dilution of the domestic owner's interest in the separate unit, it is unlikely that any portion of the dual consolidated loss attributable to such separate unit can be put to a foreign use (other than through an election to consolidate or similar method, discussed below). Therefore, the proposed regulations include three new exceptions to the definition of a foreign use where there is no dilution of an interest in a separate unit. The new exceptions to foreign use apply to dual consolidated losses attributable to two types of separate units: (1) interests in hybrid entity partnerships and interests in hybrid entity grantor trusts; and (2) separate units owned indirectly through partnerships and grantor trusts.

The first exception to foreign use provides that, in general, no foreign use shall be considered to occur with respect to a dual consolidated loss attributable to an interest in a hybrid entity partnership or a hybrid entity grantor trust, solely because an item of deduction or loss taken into account in computing such dual consolidated loss is made available, under the income tax laws of a foreign country, to offset or reduce, directly or indirectly, any item that is recognized as income or gain under such laws and is considered under U.S. tax principles to be an item of the direct or indirect owner of an interest in such hybrid entity that is not a separate unit.

The second exception to foreign use provides that, in general, no foreign use shall be considered to occur with respect to a dual consolidated loss attributable to or taken into account by a separate unit owned indirectly through a partnership or grantor trust solely because an item of deduction or loss taken into account in computing such dual consolidated loss is made available, under the income tax laws of a foreign country, to offset or reduce, directly or indirectly, any item that is recognized as income or gain under such laws and is considered under U.S. tax principles to be an item of a direct or indirect owner of an interest in such partnership or trust.

Finally, the proposed regulations provide a similar exception for combined separate units that include individual separate units to which one of the other dilution exceptions would apply, but for the separate unit combination rule.

The new exceptions to foreign use are subject to certain limitations, however. First, the exceptions will not apply if there has been a dilution of the interest in the separate unit. That is, the exception will not apply if during any taxable year the domestic owner's percentage interest in the separate unit, as compared to its interest in the separate unit as of the last day of the taxable year in which such dual consolidated loss was incurred, is reduced as a result of another person acquiring through sale, exchange, contribution or other means an interest in such partnership or grantor trust, unless the taxpayer demonstrates, to the satisfaction of the Commissioner, that the other person that acquired the interest in the partnership or grantor trust was a domestic corporation. The exceptions to foreign use should not apply when a person (other than a domestic corporation) acquires an interest in the separate unit because the dilution would typically result in an actual foreign use.

Second, the exceptions do not apply if the availability does not arise solely from the ownership in such partnership or trust and the allocation of the item of deduction or loss, or the offsetting by such deduction or loss, of an item of income or gain of the partnership or trust. For example, the exception does not apply in the case where the item of loss or deduction is made available through a foreign consolidation regime.

The IRS and Treasury request comments on the issues discussed above in connection with the availability component of the foreign use definition. Comments are specifically requested as to whether the dilution rules are appropriate and, if so, whether a *de minimis* exception should be provided.

9. *Mirror legislation rule*

Section 1.1503-2(c)(15)(iv) of the current regulations contains a *mirror legislation rule* that addresses legislation enacted by foreign jurisdictions that operates in a manner similar to the dual consolidated loss rules. This rule was designed to prevent the revenue gain resulting from the disallowance of the double-dip benefit of a dual consolidated loss from inuring solely to the foreign jurisdiction (to the detriment of the United States). Staff of the Joint Committee on Taxation, General Explanation of the Tax Reform Act of 1986, at 1065-66 (J. Comm. Print 1987).

Congress recognized that mirror legislation in a foreign jurisdiction, in conjunction with a mirror legislation rule such as that contained in the current regulations, could result in the disallowance of a dual consolidated loss in both the United States and in the foreign jurisdiction. In such a case, Congress intended that Treasury pursue with the appropriate authorities in the foreign jurisdiction a bilateral agreement that would allow the use of the loss of a dual resident corporation to offset income of an affiliate in only one country. Staff of the Joint Committee on Taxation, General Explanation of the Tax Reform Act of 1986, at 1066. The mirror rule was specifically held to be valid by the Court of Appeals for the Federal Circuit. *British Car Auctions, Inc. v. United States*, 35 Fed. Cl. 123 (1996), *aff'd without op.*, 116 F.3d 1497 (Fed. Cir. 1997).

The mirror legislation rule contained in the current regulations provides that if the laws of a foreign country deny the use of a loss of a dual resident corporation (or separate unit) to offset the income of another person because the dual resident corporation (or separate unit) is also subject to tax by another country on its worldwide income or on a residence basis, the loss is deemed to be used against the income of another person in such foreign country such that no (g)(2)(i) election can be made with respect to such loss. This rule is intended to prevent the foreign jurisdiction from enacting legislation that gives taxpayers no choice but to use the dual consolidated loss to offset income in the United States. This result is contrary to the general policy underlying the structure of the current regulations that provides taxpayers the choice of using the dual consolidated loss to either offset income in the United States or income in the foreign jurisdiction (but not both).

As a result of the consistency rule (discussed below), the deemed use of a dual consolidated loss pursuant to the mirror legislation rule may also restrict the ability to use other dual consolidated losses to offset the income of domestic affiliates, even if such losses are not subject to the mirror legislation.

Subsequent to the issuance of the current regulations, several foreign jurisdictions enacted various forms of mirror legislation that, absent the mirror legislation rule, would have the effect of forcing certain taxpayers to use dual consolidated losses to offset income of domestic affiliates.

Given the relevant legislative history and *British Car Auctions*, the IRS and Treasury believe that the mirror legislation rule remains necessary. This is particularly true in light of the prevalence of mirror legislation in foreign jurisdictions. As a result, the proposed regulations retain the mirror legislation rule. The proposed regulations modify the mirror legislation rule, however, to address its proper application with respect to mirror legislation enacted subsequent to the issuance of the current regulations, and to modify its application to better take into account the policies underlying the consistency rule.

In general, the mirror legislation rule contained in the proposed regulations applies when the opportunity for a foreign use is denied because: (1) the loss is incurred by a dual resident corporation that is subject to income taxation by another country on its worldwide income or on a residence basis; (2) the loss may be available to offset income other than income of the dual resident corporation or separate unit under the laws of another country; or (3) the deductibility of any portion of a loss or deduction taken into account in computing the dual consolidated loss depends on whether such amount is deductible under the laws of another country.

The IRS and Treasury understand that there may be uncertainty as to the application of the mirror legislation rule in a given case when the mirror legislation is limited in its application. Mirror legislation may or may not apply to a particular dual resident corporation or separate unit depending on various factors, including the type of entity or structure that generates the loss, the ownership of the operation or entity that generates the loss, the manner in which the operation or entity is taxed in another jurisdiction, or the ability of the losses to be deducted in another jurisdiction. As a result, the proposed regulations clarify that the mere existence of mirror legislation, regardless of whether it applies to the particular dual resident corporation, may not result in a deemed foreign use. For example, see § 1.1503(d)-5(c) *Example 23.*

The proposed regulations also clarify that the absence of an affiliate in the foreign jurisdiction, or the failure to make an election to enable a foreign use, does not prevent the opportunity for a foreign use. Thus, for example, the mirror legislation rule may apply even if there are no affiliates of the dual resident corporation in the foreign jurisdiction or, even where there is such an affiliate, no election is made to consolidate.

As discussed below, the consistency rule is intended to promote uniformity and reduce administrative burdens. The IRS and Treasury believe that these concerns may not be significant, however, where there is only a deemed foreign use of a dual consolidated loss as a result of the mirror legislation rule. Accordingly, the mirror legislation rule contained in the proposed regulations provides that a deemed foreign use is not treated as a foreign use for purposes of applying the consistency rule.

10. *Reasonable cause exception*

The current regulations require various filings to be included on a timely filed tax return. In addition, taxpayers that fail to include such filings on a timely filed tax return must request an extension of time to file under § 301.9100-3.

The IRS and Treasury believe that requiring taxpayers to request relief for an extension of time to file under § 301.9100-3 results in an unnecessary administrative burden on both taxpayers and the Commissioner. The IRS and Treasury believe that a reasonable cause standard, similar to that used in other international provisions of the Code (such as sections 367(a) and 6038B), is a more appropriate and less burdensome means for taxpayers to cure compliance defects under section 1503(d). As a result, the proposed regulations adopt a reasonable cause standard. Moreover, extensions of time under § 301.9100-3 will not be granted for filings under these proposed regulations. See § 301.9100-1(d).

Under the reasonable cause standard, if a person that is permitted or required to file an election, agreement, statement, rebuttal, computation, or other information under the regulations fails to make such a filing in a timely manner, such person shall be considered to have satisfied the timeliness requirement with respect to such filing if the person is able to demonstrate, to the satisfaction of the Director of Field Operations having jurisdiction of the taxpayer's tax return for the taxable year, that such failure was due to reasonable cause and not willful neglect. Once the person becomes aware of the failure, the person must make this demonstration and comply by attaching all the necessary filings to an amended tax return (that amends the tax return to which the filings should have been attached), and including a written statement explaining the reasons for the failure to comply.

In determining whether the taxpayer has reasonable cause, the Director of Field Operations shall consider whether the taxpayer acted reasonably and in good faith. Whether the taxpayer acted reasonably and in good faith will be determined after considering all the facts and circumstances. The Director of Field Operations shall notify the person in writing within 120 days of the filing if it is determined that the failure to comply was not due to reasonable cause, or if additional time will be needed to make such determination.

C. *Operating Rules—§ 1.1503(d)-2*

1. *Application of rules to multiple tiers of separate units*

Section 1.1503-2(b)(3) of the current regulations provides that if a separate unit of a domestic corporation is owned indirectly through another separate unit, limitations on the dual consolidated losses of the separate units apply as if the upper-tier separate unit were a subsidiary of the domestic corporation, and the lower-tier separate unit were a lower-tier subsidiary. In light of changes made to other provisions of the proposed regulations, this rule is no longer necessary. As a result, the proposed regulations do not contain this provision.

2. *Tainted income*

Section 1.1503-2(e) of the current regulations prevents the dual consolidated loss of a dual resident corporation that ceases being a dual resident corporation from offsetting tainted income of such corporation. Subject to certain exceptions, tainted income is defined as income derived from assets that are acquired by a dual resident corporation in a nonrecognition transaction, or as a contribution to capital, at any time during the three taxable years immediately preceding the tax year in which the corporation ceases to be a dual resident corporation, or at any time thereafter. The current regulations also contain a rule that, absent proof to the contrary, presumes an amount of income generated during a taxable year as being tainted income. Such amount is the corporation's taxable income for the year multiplied by a fraction, the numerator of which is the fair market value of the tainted assets at the end of the year, and the denominator of which is the fair market value of the total assets owned by each domestic corporation at the end of each year.

The tainted income rule is intended to prevent taxpayers from obtaining a double-dip with respect to a dual consolidated loss by stuffing assets into a dual resident corporation after, or in certain cases before, it terminates its status as a dual resident corporation. A double-dip may be obtained in such case because the income that offsets the dual consolidated loss generally would not be subject to tax in the foreign jurisdiction after the dual resident status of the corporation terminates.

The proposed regulations retain the tainted income rule, subject to the following modifications. The proposed regulations clarify that tainted income includes both income or gain recognized on the sale or other disposition of tainted assets and income derived as a result of holding tainted assets. The proposed regulations also modify the rule defining the amount of income presumed to be tainted income. The proposed regulations clarify that the presumptive rule only applies to income derived as a result of holding tainted assets; income or gain recognized on the sale or other disposition of tainted assets should be readily determinable such that the presumptive rule need not apply. The proposed regulations also provide that the numerator in the presumptive income fraction is the fair market value of tainted assets determined at the time such assets were acquired by the corporation, as opposed to being determined at the end of the taxable year. The IRS and Treasury believe that this approach is more administrable because value should be more readily determinable on the acquisition date. In addition, this approach does not require tainted assets to be traced over time.

D. *Special Rules for Accounting for Dual Consolidated Losses—§ 1.1503(d)-3*

1. *Items attributable to a separate unit*

(a) *Overview*

Section 1.1503-2(d)(1)(ii) of the current regulations provides a rule for determining whether a separate unit has a dual consolidated loss. Under this rule, the separate unit must compute its taxable income as if it were a separate domestic corporation that is a dual resident corporation, using only those items of income, expense, deduction, and loss that are *otherwise attributable to* such separate unit.

The current regulations do not provide any guidance for determining the items of income, gain, deduction and loss that are otherwise attributable to a separate unit. The IRS and Treasury understand that the absence of such guidance has resulted in considerable uncertainty. For example, commentators have questioned whether all or any portion of the interest expense of a domestic owner is attributable to a separate unit.

It is also unclear the extent to which a separate unit is treated as a separate domestic corporation under this rule. For example, commentators have questioned whether a transaction between a separate unit and its owner that is generally disregarded for federal tax purposes (for example, interest paid by a disregarded entity on an obligation held by its owner) can create an item of income, gain, deduction or loss for purposes of calculating a dual consolidated loss.

Commentators have also questioned whether each separate unit in a tiered separate unit structure (that is, where one separate unit owns another separate unit) must separately determine whether it has a dual consolidated loss, or whether such separate units are combined for this purpose.

The proposed regulations provide more definitive rules for determining the amount of a dual consolidated loss (or income) of a separate unit. These rules apply solely for purposes of section 1503(d) and, therefore, do not apply for other purposes of the Code (for example, section 987). The proposed regulations first provide general rules that apply for purposes of calculating dual consolidated losses (or income) for both foreign branch separate units and hybrid entity separate units. The proposed regulations provide additional rules for calculating the dual consolidated losses (or income) of foreign branch separate units, hybrid entity separate units, and separate units owned indirectly through other separate units, non-hybrid entity partnerships, or non-hybrid entity grantor trusts. Finally, the proposed regulations provide special rules that apply to tiered separate units, combined separate units, dispositions of separate units, and the treatment of certain income inclusions on stock.

(b) General Rules

The proposed regulations clarify that only existing tax accounting items of income, gain, deduction and loss (translated into U.S. dollars) should be taken into account for purposes of calculating the dual consolidated loss of a separate unit. In other words, treating a separate unit as a separate domestic corporation does not cause items that are disregarded for U.S. tax purposes (for example, interest paid by a disregarded entity on an obligation held by its owner) to be regarded for purposes of calculating a separate unit's dual consolidated loss.

The proposed regulations also clarify that in the case of tiered separate units, each separate unit must calculate its own dual consolidated loss and no item of income, gain, deduction and loss may be taken into account in determining the taxable income or loss of more than one separate unit. Similarly, the proposed regulations clarify that items of one separate unit cannot offset or otherwise be taken into account by another separate unit for purposes of calculating a dual consolidated loss (unless the separate unit combination rule applies). These rules ensure that the dual consolidated loss calculation is computed separately for each separate unit, which is necessary to prevent deductions and losses from being double-dipped.

(c) Foreign Branch Separate Unit

The proposed regulations provide that the asset use and business activities principles of section 864(c) apply for purposes of determining the items of income, gain, deduction (other than interest) and loss that are taken into account in determining the taxable income or loss of a foreign branch separate unit. For this purpose, the trading safe harbors of section 864(b) do not apply for purposes of determining whether a trade or business exists within a foreign country or whether income may be treated as effectively connected to a foreign branch separate unit. In addition, the limitations on effectively connected treatment of foreign source related-party income under section 864(c)(4)(D) do not apply.

The proposed regulations further provide that the principles of §1.882-5, as modified, apply for purposes of determining the items of interest expense that are taken into account in determining the taxable income or loss of a foreign branch separate unit. The rules provide that a taxpayer must use U.S. tax principles to determine both the classification and amounts of the assets and liabilities when the actual worldwide ratio is used. The valuation of assets must be determined under the same methodology the taxpayer uses under §1.861-9T(g) for purposes of allocating and apportioning interest expense under section 864(e). Further, and solely for these purposes, the domestic owner of the foreign branch separate unit is treated as a foreign corporation, the foreign branch separate unit is treated as a trade or business within the United States, and assets other than those of the foreign branch separate unit are treated as assets that are not U.S. assets. Accordingly, only the interest expense of the domestic owner of the foreign branch separate unit is subject to allocation for purposes of computing the dual consolidated loss. The IRS and Treasury believe that the application of these principles will better harmonize the borrowing rate and effective interest costs that both the United States and the foreign country take into account in determining the dual consolidated loss, as compared to the use of §1.861-9T.

The IRS and Treasury believe that taking items into account in determining the taxable income or loss of a foreign branch separate unit under these standards is administrable because of the existing guidance provided under these provisions. In addition, the IRS and Treasury believe that this approach furthers the policy underlying section 1503(d) because it serves as a reasonable approximation of the items that the foreign jurisdiction may recognize as being taken into account in determining the taxable income or loss of a branch or permanent establishment of a non-resident corporation in such jurisdiction. Nevertheless, the IRS and Treasury solicit comments on these provisions and whether other administrable approaches (that approximate the items taken into account by the foreign jurisdiction) should be considered.

(d) Hybrid Entity

The proposed regulations provide rules for attributing items of income, gain, deduction and loss to a hybrid entity. These rules are necessary to determine the items that are attributable to an interest in a hybrid entity that constitutes a separate unit.

The proposed regulations provide that, in general, the items of income, gain, deduction and loss that are attributable to a hybrid entity are those items that are properly reflected on its books and records, as adjusted to conform to U.S. tax principles. The principles of §1.988-4(b)(2) apply for purposes of making this determination. These principles generally provide that the determination is a question of fact and must be consistently applied. These principles also provide that the Commissioner may allocate items of income, gain, deduction and loss between the domestic corporation (and intervening entities, if any) that own the hybrid entity separate unit, and the hybrid entity separate unit, if such items are not properly reflected on the books and records of the hybrid entity.

The proposed regulations also provide that if a hybrid entity owns an interest in either a non-hybrid entity partnership or a non-hybrid entity grantor trust, items of income, gain, deduction and loss that are properly reflected on the books and records of such partnership or grantor trust (under the principles of §1.988-4(b)(2), as adjusted to conform to U.S. tax principles), are treated as being properly reflected on the books and records of the hybrid entity. However, such items are treated as being properly reflected on the books and records of the hybrid entity only to the extent they are taken into account by the hybrid entity under principles of subchapter K, chapter 1 of the Code, or the principles of subpart E, subchapter J, chapter 1 of the Code, as the case may be.

The IRS and Treasury believe that attributing items to a hybrid entity under this standard is administrable because it is generally consistent with the accounting treatment of the items. The IRS and Treasury also believe that this standard furthers the policy underlying section 1503(d) because the items that are properly reflected on the books and records of the hybrid entity (as adjusted to conform to U.S. tax principles) represent the best approximation of items that the foreign jurisdiction would recognize as being attributable to the entity. For example, it is likely that a foreign jurisdiction would recognize and take into account as being attributable to a hybrid entity the interest expense properly reflected on the books and records of the hybrid entity; however, it is unlikely that a foreign jurisdiction would recognize, and take into account as being attributable to a hybrid entity, interest expense of a domestic corporation that owns an interest in the hybrid entity.

(e) *Interest in a Disregarded Hybrid Entity*

The proposed regulations provide that, except to the extent otherwise provided under special rules (discussed below), items that are attributable to an interest in a hybrid entity that is disregarded as an entity separate from its owner are those items that are attributable to such hybrid entity itself.

(f) *Interests in Hybrid Entity Partnerships, Interests in Hybrid Entity Grantor Trusts, and Separate Units Owned Indirectly Through Partnerships and Grantor Trusts*

The proposed regulations provide rules for determining the extent to which: (1) items of income, gain, deduction and loss that are attributable to a hybrid entity that is a partnership are attributable to an interest in such hybrid entity partnership; and (2) items of income, gain, deduction and loss of a separate unit that is owned indirectly through a partnership are taken into account by a partner in such partnership. These items are taken into account to the extent they are includible in the partner's distributive share of the partnership income, gain, deduction or loss, as determined under the rules and principles of subchapter K, chapter 1 of the Code.

The proposed regulations also provide rules for determining the extent to which: (1) items of income, gain, deduction and loss attributable to a hybrid entity that is a grantor trust are attributable to an interest in such hybrid entity grantor trust; and (2) the items of income, gain, deduction and loss of a separate unit owned indirectly through a grantor trust are taken into account by an owner of such grantor trust. These items are taken into account to the extent they are attributable to trust property that the holder of the trust interest is treated as owning under the rules and principles of subpart E, subchapter J, chapter 1 of the Code.

(g) *Allocation of Items Between Certain Indirectly Owned Separate Units*

The proposed regulations provide special rules for allocating items of income, gain, deduction and loss to foreign branch separate units that are owned, directly or indirectly (other than through a hybrid entity separate unit) by hybrid entities. In such a case, only items that are attributable to the hybrid entity that owns such separate unit (and intervening entities, if any, that are not themselves separate units) are taken into account.

This rule is intended to minimize the items taken into account by a foreign branch separate unit that the foreign jurisdiction would not recognize as being so taken into account. This may occur in these cases because the foreign jurisdiction taxes the hybrid entity as a corporation (or otherwise at the entity level) and therefore likely would not take into account items of its owner. For example, if a domestic corporation indirectly owns a Country X foreign branch separate unit through a Country Y hybrid entity, Country X likely would take into account items of the Country Y hybrid entity as being items of the Country X branch. It is unlikely, however, that Country X would take into account items of the domestic corporation as items of the Country X branch because Country X views the owner of the Country X branch (the Country Y hybrid entity) as a corporation. Therefore, only the items of income, gain, deduction and loss of the Country Y hybrid entity (and not items of the domestic corporation) should be taken into account for purposes of determining the dual consolidated loss of the Country X branch.

The proposed regulations also provide that only income and assets of such hybrid entity are taken into account for purposes of applying the principles of section 864(c) and §1.882-5, as modified, in determining the items taken into account by the foreign branch separate unit; thus, other income and assets of the domestic owner, for example, are not taken into account for these purposes. This rule is also intended to ensure that the principles under these provisions are applied in a way that best approximates the items that the foreign jurisdiction would recognize as being taken into account by a taxable presence in such jurisdiction.

Finally, the proposed regulations provide that items generally attributable to an interest in a hybrid entity are not taken into account to the extent they are taken into account by a foreign branch separate unit owned, directly or indirectly (other than through a hybrid entity separate unit), by the hybrid entity. This rule prevents two or more separate units from taking into account the same item of income, gain, deduction or loss under different rules.

(h) *Combined Separate Units*

As discussed above, the proposed regulations combine separate units owned, directly or indirectly, by a single domestic corporation, provided certain requirements are satisfied. Because different rules may apply for purposes of attributing items to individual separate units that may be combined into a single separate unit, special rules are necessary to attribute items to combined separate units.

The proposed regulations provide that in the case of a combined separate unit, items are first attributable to, or otherwise taken into account by, the individual separate units composing the combined separate unit, without regard to the combination rule. The combined separate unit then takes into account all of the items attributable to, or taken into account by, the individual separate units that compose such combined separate unit.

(i) *Gain or Loss Recognized on Dispositions of Separate Units*

The current regulations do not indicate whether items of income, gain, deduction and loss recognized on the sale or disposition of a separate unit, or of an interest in a partnership or grantor trust through which a separate unit is indirectly owned, is attributable to or taken into account by such separate unit for purposes of calculating the dual consolidated loss of the separate unit for the year of the sale (or for purposes of reducing the amount of recapture as a result of a triggering event).

The IRS and Treasury believe that it is appropriate to take into account items of income, gain, deduction and loss recognized on these dispositions. Thus, the proposed regulations provide that items of income, gain, deduction and loss recognized on the disposition of a separate unit (or an interest in a partnership or grantor trust that directly or indirectly owns a separate unit), are attributable to or taken into account by the separate unit to the extent of the gain or loss that would have been recognized had such separate unit sold all its assets in a taxable exchange, immediately before the disposition of the separate unit, for an amount equal to their fair market value. The proposed regulations clarify that for this purpose items of income and gain include loss recapture income or gain under section 367(a)(3)(C) or 904(f)(3).

The proposed regulations also address situations where more than one separate unit is disposed of in the same transaction and items of income, gain, deduction and loss recognized on such disposition are attributable to more than one separate unit. In such a case, items of income, gain, deduction and loss are attributable to or taken into account by each such separate unit based on the gain or loss that would have been recognized by each separate unit if it had sold all of its assets in a taxable exchange, immediately before the disposition of the separate unit, for an amount equal to their fair market value.

(j) *Income Inclusion on Stock*

The current regulations do not indicate whether an amount included in income arising from the ownership of stock in a foreign corporation (income inclusion) is attributable to or taken into account by a separate unit that owns the stock that gave rise to the income inclusion. For example, if a domestic corporation has a section 951(a) inclusion attributable to stock of a controlled foreign corporation that is owned by a hybrid entity separate unit, it is not clear under the current regulations whether such income inclusion is taken into account for purposes of calculating the dual consolidated loss of the hybrid entity separate unit.

The IRS and Treasury believe that, solely for purposes of applying the dual consolidated loss rules, it is appropriate to treat income inclusions arising from the ownership of stock in the same manner that dividend income is treated. Accordingly, the proposed regulations provide that income inclusions are taken into account for purposes of calculating the dual consolidated loss of a separate unit if an actual dividend from such foreign corporation would have been so taken into account.

(k) *Section 987 Gain or Loss*

Section 987 provides that if a taxpayer has one or more qualified business units with a functional currency other than the dollar, the taxpayer must make proper adjustments to take into account foreign currency gain or loss on certain transfers of property between such qualified business units.

In 1991, the IRS and Treasury issued proposed regulations under section 987 that included rules for determining the amount of foreign currency gain or loss recognized on certain transfers of property between qualified business units. On April 3,2000, the IRS and Treasury issued Notice 2000-20 (2000-14 I.R.B. 851) announcing that the IRS and Treasury intend to review and possibly replace the proposed regulations issued under section 987. The IRS and Treasury have opened a regulations project under section 987 and expect to issue new section 987 regulations in the future.

The current regulations do not provide specific rules that indicate whether section 987 gains or losses of a domestic owner are attributable to, or taken into account by, a separate unit for purposes of calculating the separate unit's dual consolidated loss. Because the IRS and Treasury have an open regulations project under section 987 and expect to issue new regulations under section 987, the IRS and Treasury do not believe it is appropriate to address this issue in the proposed regulations. The IRS and Treasury request comments on whether section 987 gains and losses of a domestic owner should be attributable to, or taken into account by, a separate unit, particularly with respect to section 987 gains and losses attributable to, or taken into account by, separate units owned indirectly through hybrid entity separate units.

2. *Effect of a dual consolidated loss*

Section 1.1503-2(d)(2) of the current regulations provides that if a dual resident corporation has a dual consolidated loss that is subject to the general rule restricting it from offsetting the income of a domestic affiliate, the consolidated group of which the dual resident corporation is a member must compute its taxable income without taking into account the items of income, gain, deduction or loss taken into account in computing the dual consolidated loss. The current regulations contain a similar rule for separate units.

These rules do not exclude only the dual consolidated loss in computing taxable income, but instead provide that none of the gross tax accounting items that compose the dual consolidated loss are taken into account. While this approach has the same effect on net income as would excluding only the dual consolidated loss, removing all gross items of income, gain, deduction and loss may have a distortive effect on other federal tax calculations.

The IRS and Treasury believe that this distortive effect will be minimized if only the dual consolidated loss itself is not taken into account. Accordingly, the proposed regulations provide that only a pro rata portion of each item of deduction and loss taken into account in computing the dual consolidated loss are excluded in computing taxable income. In addition, to the extent that a dual consolidated loss is carried over or carried back and, subject to §1.1502-21(c) (as modified in the proposed regulations), is made available to offset income generated by the dual resident corporation or separate unit, the proposed regulations treat items composing the dual consolidated loss as being used on a pro rata basis.

3. *Basis adjustments*

Section 1.1503-2(d)(3) of the current regulations contains special basis adjustment rules that override the normal investment adjustment rules under §1.1502-32 for stock of affiliated dual resident corporations or affiliated domestic owners owned by other members of the consolidated group. These rules provide that stock basis is reduced by a dual consolidated loss, even though such loss is subject to the general limitation on the use of a dual consolidated loss to offset income of a domestic affiliate. To avoid reducing the stock basis a second time for the same dual consolidated loss, the rules also provide that no negative adjustment shall be made for the amount of dual consolidated loss subject to the general limitation that is subsequently absorbed in a carryover or carryback year. Finally, the rules provide that there is no basis increase for recapture income recognized as a result of a triggering event. Similar rules apply to separate units arising from ownership of an interest in a partnership. These special basis adjustment rules are generally intended to prevent an indirect deduction of a dual consolidated loss.

The proposed regulations retain the special stock basis adjustment rules, as modified, to prevent the indirect use of a dual consolidated loss. In addition, the proposed regulations retain the rules addressing the effect of a dual consolidated loss on a partner's adjusted basis in its partnership interest in cases where the partnership interest is a separate unit, or a separate unit is owned indirectly through a partnership. These rules require the partner to adjust its basis in accordance with the principles of section 705, subject to certain modifications.

The IRS and Treasury recognize that these rules may lead to harsh results, particularly in light of the fact that the indirect use of the dual consolidated loss would only arise through the disposition of the stock of a dual resident corporation (or a partnership interest) that may not occur for many years after the dual consolidated loss is incurred. In addition, upon such subsequent disposition the resulting deduction or loss would generally be capital in nature, and the definition of a dual consolidated loss excludes capital losses incurred by the dual resident corporation or separate unit. As a result, the IRS and Treasury request comments regarding concerns over these types of indirect uses and whether the special basis rules should be retained. These comments should consider whether the policies underlying section 1503(d) require basis adjustment rules that differ from other basis adjustment rules that apply to non-capital, non-deductible expenses (for example, rules under sections 705 and 1367, and §1.1502-32(b))

E. *Exceptions to the Domestic Use Limitation Rule—§1.1503(d)-4*

1. *No possibility of foreign use*

The proposed regulations provide a new exception to the general rule prohibiting the domestic use of a dual consolidated loss. To qualify under this exception, the consolidated group, unaffiliated dual resident corporation, or unaffiliated domestic owner must: (1) demonstrate, to the satisfaction of the Commissioner, that there can be no foreign use of the dual consolidated loss at any time; and (2) prepare a statement and attach it to its tax return for the taxable year in which the dual consolidated loss is incurred. This statement must include an analysis, in reasonable detail and specificity, supported with an official or certified English translation of the relevant provisions of foreign law, of the treatment of the losses and deductions composing the dual consolidated loss, and the reasons supporting the conclusion that there cannot be a foreign use of the dual consolidated loss by any means at any time.

This exception is intended to replace the exception to the definition of a dual consolidated loss contained in §1.1503-2(c)(5)(ii)(A) of the current regulations. Thus, under the proposed regulations the question of foreign use is not relevant to the definition of a dual consolidated loss; the issue will instead be whether an exception to the domestic use limitation applies. Consistent with the exception to the definition of a dual consolidated loss contained in the current regulations, the IRS and Treasury believe that this new exception to the domestic use limitation rule contained in the proposed regulations will apply only in rare and unusual circumstances due to the definition of foreign use and general principles of foreign law. For example, if the foreign jurisdiction recognizes any item of deduction or loss composing the dual consolidated loss (regardless of whether recognized currently or deferred, for example, by being reflected in the basis of assets), and such item is available for foreign use through a form of consolidation, carryover or carryback, or a transaction (for example, a merger, basis carryover transaction, or entity classification election), then the exception will not apply.

2. *Domestic use election and agreement*

As discussed above, the current regulations provide an exception to the general rule prohibiting the use of a dual consolidated loss to offset the income of a domestic affiliate if a (g)(2)(i) election is made. Under this exception, the consolidated group, unaffiliated dual resident corporation, or unaffiliated domestic owner must enter into an agreement ((g)(2)(i) agreement) certifying, among other things, that no portion of the deductions or losses taken into account in computing the dual consolidated loss have been, or will be, used to offset the income of any other person under the income tax laws of a foreign country.

The proposed regulations retain this elective exception, with modifications, and refer to it as a *domestic use election*. In addition, the proposed regulations refer to the consolidated group, unaffiliated dual resident corporation, or unaffiliated domestic owner, as the case may be, that makes a domestic use election as an *elector*. In order to elect relief under this exception, the proposed regulations require the elector to enter into a domestic use agreement, which is similar to the (g)(2)(i) agreement required by the current regulations.

3. *Certification period*

Under the current regulations, a (g)(2)(i) agreement generally provides that if there is a triggering event during the 15-year period following the year in which the dual consolidated loss was incurred (certification period), the taxpayer must recapture and report as income the amount of the dual consolidated loss, and pay an interest charge. See § 1.1503-2(g)(2)(iii)(A).

Commentators have questioned whether under the current regulations the 15-year certification period applies only to the use triggering event, or whether it applies to all triggering events. These commentators note that, under this interpretation, triggering events other than use could occur after the expiration of the certification period. The IRS and Treasury believe that the certification period applies to all triggering events. Accordingly, the proposed regulations clarify that all triggering events are subject to the certification period and, therefore, a triggering event cannot occur after the expiration of the certification period.

The IRS and Treasury also believe that a 15-year certification period is not required to deter and monitor double-dipping of losses and deductions. Moreover, the IRS and Treasury believe that requiring taxpayers to comply with the dual consolidated loss regulations, including the need to monitor potential triggering events and to comply with the various filing requirements, for a 15-year period is unnecessarily burdensome to both taxpayers and the Commissioner. As a result, the proposed regulations reduce the certification period from 15 years to seven years with respect to a domestic use election.

4. *Consistency rule*

Section 1.1503-2(g)(2)(ii) of the current regulations contains a consistency rule. Under this rule, if any losses, expenses, or deductions taken into account in computing the dual consolidated loss of a dual resident corporation or separate unit are used to offset the income of another person under the laws of a single foreign country while the dual resident corporation or separate unit is owned by the domestic owner or member of the consolidated group, the losses, expenses, or deductions taken into account in computing the dual consolidated losses of other dual resident corporations or separate units owned by the same consolidated group (or other separate units owned by the unaffiliated domestic owner of the first separate unit) in that year are deemed to offset income of another person in the same foreign country. This rule only applies, however, if such losses, expenses, or deductions are recognized in the foreign country in the same taxable year. Moreover, this rule does not apply if, under foreign law, the other dual resident corporation or separate unit cannot use its losses, expenses, or deductions to offset income of another person in such taxable year.

The consistency rule is intended to ensure that a consolidated group or domestic owner treats uniformly all dual consolidated losses of dual resident corporations or separate units that it owns that are available for use in a foreign country in a given year. The rule is also intended to minimize the administrative burden associated with identifying the items of loss or deduction of a particular dual consolidated loss that are used to offset income of another person under the income tax laws of a foreign country.

Commentators have questioned the need for the consistency rule, noting that it can lead to harsh results.

The IRS and Treasury believe that, despite concerns raised by commentators, the consistency rule continues to be necessary to promote the uniform treatment of dual consolidated losses of dual resident corporations and separate units owned by the consolidated group or domestic owner, and to minimize administrative burdens. As a result, the proposed regulations retain the consistency rule, as modified.

In addition, the proposed regulations clarify that the consistency rule only applies to a dual consolidated loss that is subject to a domestic use agreement (other than a new domestic use agreement). In other words, the proposed regulations clarify that the consistency rule does not apply to a foreign use of a dual consolidated loss that occurs subsequent to a triggering event that terminates the domestic use agreement filed with respect to such dual consolidated loss.

5. *Restrictions on domestic use elections*

The current regulations do not explicitly address situations where a triggering event (discussed below) with respect to a dual consolidated loss occurs in the year in which the dual consolidated loss is incurred. The proposed regulations, however, make clear that a domestic use election cannot be made for a dual consolidated loss incurred in the same year in which a triggering event with respect to such loss occurs.

The current regulations also do not explicitly address the application of section 953(d)(3) (limiting losses of foreign insurance companies that elect to be treated as domestic corporations). The proposed regulations, however, provide that a foreign insurance company that has elected to be treated as a domestic corporation pursuant to section 953(d) may not make a domestic use election. This rule is consistent with section 953(d)(3), which broadly prohibits regulatory exceptions to the general prohibition on the domestic use of dual consolidated losses in such cases.

6. *Triggering events*

(a) *In General*

Section 1.1503-2(g)(2)(iii) of the current regulations provides rules relating to certain events which require the recapture of previously allowed dual consolidated losses. Under these rules, if a consolidated group, unaffiliated dual resident corporation, or unaffiliated domestic owner, as the case may be, makes a (g)(2)(i) election, the dual resident corporation or separate unit must recapture, and the consolidated group, unaffiliated dual resident corporation or unaffiliated domestic owner must report as income the amount of the dual consolidated loss (and pay an interest charge) if a triggering event occurs during the certification period. Taxpayers may, however, rebut these triggering events upon making certain showings to the satisfaction of the Commissioner.

The proposed regulations generally retain the triggering event rules contained in the proposed regulations, as modified, if a taxpayer makes a domestic use election.

(b) Carryover of Losses, Deductions, and Basis

Under the current regulations, certain asset transfers by a dual resident corporation that result, under the laws of a foreign country, in a carryover of losses, expenses, or deductions are triggering events. The current regulations contain a similar rule for such transfers by separate units. See § 1.1503-2(g)(2)(iii)(A)(4), and (5).

The proposed regulations retain these triggering events, as modified, and combine them into a single triggering event. The proposed regulations also clarify that certain asset transfers that result in the carryover of basis in assets under the laws of a foreign country also qualify as triggering events. This is the case because asset basis generally will, at some point in the future, be converted into a loss or deduction as a result of the depreciation, amortization or disposition of the asset. Accordingly, under foreign law, a transaction that results in the carryover of asset basis generally has the same effect as a transaction that results in the carryover of losses or deductions and therefore should be treated similarly.

(c) Disposition by a Separate Unit or Dual Resident Corporation of an Interest in a Separate Unit or Stock of a Dual Resident Corporation

The current regulations provide that certain sales or other dispositions of 50 percent or more of the assets of a separate unit or dual resident corporation are deemed to be triggering events. See § 1.1503-2(g)(2)(iii)(A)(4) and (5). For this purpose, an interest in a separate unit and stock of a dual resident corporation are treated as assets of the separate unit or dual resident corporation. One commentator stated that, as a result of this rule, the disposition of an interest in one separate unit by another separate unit may inappropriately result in a triggering event for both separate units. Accordingly, the commentator suggested that the disposition of the interest in the lower-tier separate unit should not result in a triggering event with respect to dual consolidated losses of the separate unit that disposed of such interest.

The IRS and Treasury believe that the disposition of an interest in a lower-tier separate unit (or the shares of a dual resident corporation) by an upper-tier separate unit (or dual resident corporation) typically will not result in the carryover of the dual consolidated loss of the upper-tier separate unit (or dual resident corporation) under the laws of the foreign jurisdiction such that it could be put to a foreign use. Therefore, the proposed regulations provide that for purposes of determining whether 50 percent or more of the separate unit's or dual resident corporation's assets is disposed of, an interest in a separate unit and the stock of a dual resident corporation shall not be treated as assets of the separate unit or dual resident corporation making such disposition. The IRS and Treasury request comments as to other assets the disposition of which should be excluded from the 50 percent test under this triggering event.

(d) Fifty Percent Threshold for Asset Transfer Triggering Events

Section 1.1503-2(g)(2)(iii)(A)(7) of the current regulations provides that a triggering event occurs if, within a 12-month period, the domestic owner of a separate unit disposes of 50 percent or more (by voting power or value) of the interest in the separate unit that was owned by the domestic owner on the last day of the taxable year in which the dual consolidated loss was incurred. As noted above, the current regulations also provide that a triggering event occurs if a domestic owner of a separate unit transfers assets of the separate unit in a transaction that results, under the laws of a foreign country, in a carryover of the separate unit's losses, expenses, or deductions. Section 1.1503-2(g)(2)(iii)(A)(5). Moreover, the current regulations deem such an asset transfer to be a triggering event if 50 percent or more of the separate unit's assets (measured by fair market value at the time of transfer) are disposed of within a 12-month period.

One commentator noted that the two triggering events discussed above operate differently in that any transfer of assets of a separate unit may constitute a triggering event, while the transfer of an interest in a separate unit constitutes a triggering event only if a 50 percent threshold is met.

The IRS and Treasury believe that these two triggering events should operate in a consistent manner. As a result, the proposed regulations provide that both the asset transfer triggering event and the separate unit interest transfer triggering event occur only if a 50 percent threshold is satisfied. It should be noted, however, that transfers of assets of a dual resident corporation or separate unit, and transfers of interests of separate units, in many cases will subsequently result in a foreign use triggering event, even though the 50 percent threshold for the asset transfer triggering event and the separate unit interest transfer triggering event are not satisfied. For example, if a domestic owner of an interest in a hybrid entity separate unit transfers 25 percent of its interest in the hybrid entity separate unit to a foreign corporation, all or a portion of a dual consolidated loss attributable to such separate unit in a prior year may be available to offset subsequent income of the owner of the transferred interest (that is not a separate unit after such transfer because it is held by a foreign corporation) and therefore may result in a foreign use triggering event.

(e) S Corporation Conversion

Under the current regulations, if either an affiliated dual resident corporation or an affiliated domestic owner that has filed a (g)(2)(i) agreement with respect to a dual consolidated loss elects to be an S corporation pursuant to section 1362(a), such election results in a triggering event because it terminates the consolidated group and the affiliated dual resident corporation or affiliated domestic owner ceases to be a member of a consolidated group. See § 1.1503-2(g)(2)(iii)(A)(2). The current regulations do not, however, address an election to be an S corporation by either an unaffiliated dual resident corporation or an unaffiliated domestic owner that has made a (g)(2)(i) election.

The IRS and Treasury believe that the election by an unaffiliated dual resident corporation or unaffiliated domestic owner to be an S corporation should be treated in the same manner as an election by an affiliated dual resident corporation or affiliated domestic owner that is a member of a consolidated group. Accordingly, the proposed regulations add as a new triggering event the election of either an unaffiliated dual resident corporation or unaffiliated domestic owner to be an S corporation.

(f) Consolidated Group Remains in Existence

As stated above, and subject to exceptions, the current regulations provide that a triggering event occurs with respect to a dual consolidated loss of an affiliated dual resident corporation or affiliated domestic owner if such dual resident corporation or affiliated domestic owner ceases to be a member of the consolidated group of which it was a member when the dual consolidated loss was incurred. The current regulations also provide that an affiliated dual resident corporation or affiliated domestic owner is considered to cease to be a member of a consolidated group if the consolidated group ceases to exist (group termination triggering event) because, for example, the common parent is no longer in existence. Section 1.1503-2(g)(2)(iii)(A)(2).

One commentator stated that language contained in Revenue Procedure 2000-42 (2000-2 C.B. 394) may imply that there is a group termination triggering event if the common parent of a consolidated group that made a (g)(2)(i) election ceases to exist, or is a party to a reverse acquisition, even though the consolidated group remains in existence. This interpretation is contrary to the principles underlying the triggering events. Accordingly, the proposed regulations clarify that such transactions do not constitute group termination triggering events. See § 1.1503(d)-5(c) Example 47.

7. Rebuttal of triggering events

Under the current regulations, taxpayers may rebut all but two of the triggering events such that there is no dual consolidated loss recapture (or related interest charge) as a result of a putative triggering event. In general, under the current regulations, a triggering event is rebutted if the taxpayer demonstrates to the satisfaction of the Commissioner that, depending on the triggering event, either: (1) the losses, expenses or deductions of the dual resident corporation (or separate unit) cannot be used to offset income of another person under the laws of a foreign country or; (2) the transfer of assets did not result in a carryover under foreign law of the losses, expenses, or deductions of the dual resident corporation (or separate unit) to the transferee of the assets. See § 1.1503-2(g)(2)(iii)(A)(2) through (7). The policies underpinning the dual consolidated loss rules do not require recapture or an interest charge in such cases because there is no opportunity for any portion of the dual consolidated loss to be used to offset income of any other person under the income tax laws of a foreign country.

The rebuttal rules impose a standard of proof on taxpayers that in many cases is difficult and burdensome to meet, even though there may be little likelihood that any portion of the dual consolidated loss could be used to offset the income of any other person under the income tax laws of a foreign country. For example, demonstrating that no portion of the dual consolidated loss can be used by another person as a result of typical loss carryover transactions under foreign law may not satisfy the burden if there is some potential that any portion of losses or deductions composing the dual consolidated loss could be so used as a result of a transaction that is rare, commercially impractical, or not reasonably foreseeable. In addition, because there are often significant differences between U.S. and foreign law, ruling out the various types of transactions that under U.S. law would allow all or a portion of the dual consolidated loss to be used by another person also may not be sufficient to rebut a triggering event.

Commentators have noted that under the current regulations it may not be possible to rebut certain triggering events if the tax basis of a single asset carries over to another person under foreign law, even though as a result of the transaction recognized losses and accrued deductions generally do not carry over to another person under foreign law. This is the case because the person that receives the carryover asset basis may at some point in the future enjoy the benefit of a loss or deduction as a result of the depreciation, amortization or disposition of the asset. As a result, the carryover of a nominal amount of asset tax basis causes the entire dual consolidated loss to be recaptured. Similar issues arise in connection with assumptions of liabilities that, for example, result in deductions for U.S. tax purposes on an accrual basis, but are deductible under the laws of the foreign jurisdiction at a later time when paid. This result is consistent with the *all or nothing* principle, discussed below.

The IRS and Treasury recognize that in some of these cases the use of a portion of a dual consolidated loss may be denied in both the United States and the foreign jurisdiction. Further, commentators have stated that denying a loss or deduction from offsetting income in both the United States and the foreign jurisdiction generally is inconsistent with the principles underlying section 1503(d) because the statute's purpose is to prevent the use of the same loss or deduction to offset income in multiple jurisdictions.

The proposed regulations retain the rebuttal standard contained in the current regulations, with modifications. Taxpayers may rebut a triggering event under the proposed regulations if it can be demonstrated, to the satisfaction of the Commissioner, that there can be no foreign use of the dual consolidated loss. In addition, unlike the current regulations that have different standards for different triggering events, the proposed regulations apply the same standard to all triggering events (other than a foreign use triggering event, which cannot be rebutted).

The IRS and Treasury believe that when the proposed regulations are finalized the number of transactions undertaken by taxpayers that result in triggering events will be significantly reduced, as compared to the current regulations, because of the significant reduction in the term of the certification period. Nevertheless, the IRS and Treasury believe that the current rebuttal standard may exceed that required to address adequately the concern that all or a portion of a dual consolidated loss could be put to a foreign use. Moreover, the IRS and Treasury believe that more definitive and administrable rebuttal rules should be provided to assist taxpayers and the Commissioner in determining whether the triggering event has been rebutted, and to minimize situations where there is recapture of a dual consolidated loss even though it may be unlikely that a significant portion of the dual consolidated loss could be put to a foreign use. Therefore, it is anticipated that, prior to the finalization of these proposed regulations, a revenue procedure will be issued that will provide safe harbors whereby triggering events will be deemed to be rebutted if the taxpayer satisfies various conditions. The revenue procedure may be issued in proposed form and then made final contemporaneously with these regulations.

It is anticipated that the conditions contained in the revenue procedure would include the requirement that taxpayers demonstrate, to the satisfaction of the Commissioner, that there can be no foreign use of any significant portion of the dual consolidated loss as a result of certain enumerated transactions. It is also anticipated that the revenue procedure will address, and in some cases provide relief for, transactions that result in a *de minimis* carry over of asset basis under foreign law and are difficult or impossible to rebut under the current regulations. Finally, the revenue procedure may provide relief for triggering events resulting from the assumption of liabilities in connection with the acquisition of a trade or business as a result of liabilities incurred in the ordinary course of business being deductible at different times under U.S. law and the law of the foreign jurisdiction.

The IRS and Treasury request comments regarding the transactions that should be included in the revenue procedure, approaches to address basis carryover transactions and liabilities assumed in the ordinary course of business, and other ways to minimize the administrative burden associated with rebutting the triggering events, while ensuring that there is little or no likelihood that a significant portion of the dual consolidated loss can be put to a foreign use.

8. Triggering event exception for acquisition by an unaffiliated domestic corporation or a new consolidated group

Section 1.1503-2(g)(2)(iv)(B)(1) of the current regulations provides that if certain requirements are satisfied, the following events do not constitute triggering events: (1) an affiliated dual resident corporation or affiliated domestic owner becomes an unaffiliated domestic corporation or a member of a new consolidated group (unless such transaction also qualifies under another exception); (2) assets of a dual resident corporation or a separate unit are acquired by an unaffiliated domestic corporation or a member of a new consolidated group; or (3) a domestic owner of a separate unit transfers its interest in the separate unit to an unaffiliated domestic corporation or to a member of a new consolidated group.

The first requirement necessary for this exception to apply is that the consolidated group, unaffiliated dual resident corporation, or unaffiliated domestic owner that made the (g)(2)(i) election, and the unaffiliated domestic corporation or new consolidated group must enter into a closing agreement with the IRS providing that both parties will be jointly and severally liable for the total amount of the recapture of the dual consolidated loss and interest charge upon a subsequent triggering event. Second, the unaffiliated domestic corporation or new consolidated group must agree to treat any potential recapture as unrealized built-in gain for purposes of section 384, subject to any applicable exceptions thereunder. Finally, the unaffiliated domestic corporation or new consolidated group must file with its timely filed income tax return for the year in which the event occurs a (g)(2)(i) agreement (new (g)(2)(i) agreement), whereby it assumes the same obligations with respect to the dual consolidated loss as the corporation or consolidated group that filed the original (g)(2)(i) agreement with respect to that loss.

On July 30, 2003, the IRS and Treasury issued final regulations (2003 regulations), published in the **Federal Register** at 68 FR 44616, that limited the need for closing agreements to avoid triggering events to only those three transactions described above. The preamble to the 2003 regulations explained that in certain cases the requirement for a closing agreement resulted in an unnecessary administrative burden because the several liability imposed by § 1.1502-6, in conjunction with the original (g)(2)(i) agreement and a new (g)(2)(i) agreement, provided for liability sufficiently comparable to that imposed under a closing agreement. Accordingly, the 2003 regulations provided that if a new (g)(2)(i) agreement is filed by the unaffiliated domestic corporation or new consolidated group, a closing agreement is not required in the following two instances: (1) an unaffiliated dual resident corporation or unaffiliated domestic owner that filed a (g)(2)(i) agreement becomes a member of a consolidated group; and (2) a consolidated group that filed a (g)(2)(i) agreement ceases to exist as a result of a transaction described in § 1.1502-13(j)(5)(i) (unless a member of the terminating group, or successor-in-interest of such member, is not a member of the surviving group immediately after the terminating group ceases to exist).

The preamble to the 2003 regulations noted that the IRS and Treasury were continuing to consider other alternatives to further reduce the administrative and compliance burdens under section 1503(d). After further consideration, the IRS and Treasury believe that, as a result of various requirements contained in the proposed regulations, there are sufficient protections, independent of a closing agreement, in all cases in which a closing agreement is otherwise required under the current regulations. As a result, the proposed regulations eliminate the closing agreement requirement contained in the current regulations and provide an exception to triggering events in all such cases (subsequent elector events) if: (1) the unaffiliated domestic corporation or new consolidated group (subsequent elector) enters into a domestic use agreement (new domestic use agreement); and (2) the corporation or consolidated group that filed the original domestic use agreement (original elector) files a statement with its tax return for the year of the event.

Pursuant to the new domestic use agreement, the subsequent elector must: (1) agree to assume the same obligations with respect to the dual consolidated loss as the original elector had pursuant to its domestic use agreement; (2) agree to treat any potential recapture of the dual consolidated loss at issue as unrealized built-in gain pursuant to section 384, subject to any applicable exceptions thereunder; (3) agree to be subject to the successor elector rules, discussed below; and (4) identify the original elector (and subsequent electors, if any). Pursuant to the statement filed by the original elector, the original elector must agree to be subject to the subsequent elector rules and must identify the subsequent elector.

9. Triggering event exception—private letter ruling and closing agreement option

Under the current regulations, only specific triggering events can qualify for an exception as a result of the parties entering into a closing agreement. Therefore, the IRS will not consider entering into a closing agreement in other circumstances, even though the government's interests may be adequately protected in such circumstances such that recapture may not be necessary.

Although the proposed regulations eliminate the need for a closing agreement to qualify for an exception to triggering events, discussed above, the IRS and Treasury are considering whether in limited cases it may be appropriate for the Commissioner, in its sole discretion and subject to the taxpayer satisfying conditions specified by the Commissioner, to enter into closing agreements with taxpayers such that certain other events would not be triggering events. Comments are requested as to the specific and limited types of triggering events that may be suitable for this exception, taking into account the policies underlying section 1503(d), administrative burdens, and the general interests of the U.S. government.

10. Annual certification reporting requirement

Section 1.1503-2T(g)(2)(vi)(B) of the current regulations provides that if a (g)(2)(i) election is made with respect to a dual consolidated loss of a dual resident corporation or a hybrid entity separate unit, the consolidated group, unaffiliated dual resident corporation, or unaffiliated domestic owner, as the case may be, must file with its tax return an annual certification during the certification period. This filing certifies that the losses or deductions that make up the dual consolidated loss have not been used to offset the income of another person under the tax laws of a foreign country. The filing also warrants that arrangements have been made to ensure that there will be no such use of the dual consolidated loss and that the taxpayer will be informed if any such use were to occur. The current regulations do not, however, require annual certifications for dual consolidated losses of foreign branch separate units.

The IRS and Treasury believe that annual certifications of dual consolidated losses improve taxpayer compliance with the dual consolidated loss rules and are beneficial to the Commissioner in monitoring such compliance. The IRS and Treasury also believe that foreign branch separate units, hybrid entity separate units, and dual resident corporations should, to the extent possible, be treated consistently to reduce complexity. As a result, the proposed regulations expand the annual certification requirement to include dual consolidated losses of foreign branch separate units. However, the reduction in the certification period from 15 years to seven years should substantially reduce the overall compliance burden of this requirement.

11. Amount of recapture

As stated above, under the current regulations a triggering event (other than a foreign use) generally can be rebutted only if no portion of the dual consolidated loss can be used by (or carries over to) another person under foreign law. See § 1.503-2(g)(2)(iii)(A)(2) through (7). Thus, if even a *de minimis* portion of the dual consolidated loss can be used by (or carries over to) another person, the triggering event cannot be rebutted. Similarly, § 1.1503-2(g)(2)(vii)(A) of the current regulations provides that if a triggering event occurs, the entire dual consolidated loss subject to the (g)(2)(i) agreement (reduced by income earned subsequently by the dual resident corporation or separate unit) is recaptured and reported as income, regardless of the amount of the dual consolidated loss used by the other person. Thus, even a *de minimis* foreign use will cause the entire amount of the dual consolidated loss to be recaptured and reported as income.

This so-called *all or nothing* principle is included in the current regulations primarily due to administrative concerns. In many cases, the exact amount of the dual consolidated loss that is used by another person cannot be readily determined. This inability is due, in part, to differences between U.S. and foreign law. For example, there may be temporary and permanent differences in the treatment of items of income, gain, deduction and loss. There may also be differences in loss carryover provisions. These concerns are exacerbated by the principle that certain deductions are fungible and, therefore, cannot easily be traced to a particular loss incurred in a particular year.

Commentators have noted that in some cases the *all or nothing* principle results in a disallowance of deductions in both the United States and the foreign jurisdiction. Nevertheless, the IRS and Treasury believe that making a precise determination as to the amount of the dual consolidated loss put to a foreign use would require the Commissioner and taxpayers to analyze foreign law in great detail and, in some cases, compare the treatment of items under foreign law with their treatment under U.S. law. Such an analysis, however, is inconsistent with the principle underlying the regulations that, to the extent possible, the Commissioner and taxpayers should not be required to analyze foreign law. Moreover, departing from the *all or nothing* principle would likely require detailed ordering, stacking, and tracing rules to determine the amount and nature of dual consolidated losses that are recaptured upon a use. Such rules would add considerable complexity to the regulations. As a result, the proposed regulations retain the *all or nothing* rule contained in the current regulations. However, the IRS and Treasury request comments regarding administrable alternatives to the *all or nothing* rule that would not involve substantial analyses of foreign law. For example, comments are requested as to whether a pro rata recapture rule with respect to dispositions of separate units would be consistent with the general framework of the proposed regulations and would be administrable.

12. Subsequent elector rules

Neither the current regulations nor Rev. Proc. 2000-42 (2000-2 C.B. 394) explicitly address the consequences resulting from a triggering event (to which no exception applies) with respect to a dual consolidated loss that was not recaptured due to an earlier triggering event as a result of the parties entering into a closing agreement. In such a case, both parties are jointly and severally liable for the total amount of the recapture of the dual consolidated loss and interest charge resulting from such a subsequent triggering event. However, it is unclear which taxpayer must report the recapture income (and related interest charge) on its tax return upon the subsequent triggering event. In addition, there is little or no procedural guidance outlining how, pursuant to a closing agreement, the IRS would collect recapture tax and the related interest charge from the parties to the closing agreement.

Accordingly, the proposed regulations contain rules regarding subsequent electors. These rules apply when, subsequent to an event that is not a triggering event because the unaffiliated domestic corporation or new consolidated group enters into a new domestic use agreement and satisfies other requirements (excepted event), a triggering event occurs, and no exception applies to such event (subsequent triggering event). The proposed regulations also provide rules that apply in the case of multiple subsequent electors (when subsequent to an excepted event, another excepted event occurs).

The proposed regulations first provide that, except to the extent provided under the subsequent elector rules, the original elector (and in the case of multiple excepted events, any prior subsequent elector) is not subject to the general recapture and interest charge rules provided under the regulations. As a result, only the subsequent elector that owns the dual resident corporation or separate unit at the time of the subsequent triggering event is subject to the general recapture and interest charge rules.

The proposed regulations also provide that, upon a subsequent triggering event to which no exception applies, the subsequent elector must calculate the recapture tax amount with respect to the dual consolidated loss subject to the new domestic use agreement and include it, along with an identification of the dual consolidated losses at issue and the original elector, on a statement attached to its tax return. The subsequent elector calculates the recapture tax amount based on a *with and without* calculation. The recapture tax amount equals the excess (if any) of the income tax liability of the subsequent elector for the taxable year of the subsequent triggering event, over the income tax liability of the subsequent elector for such taxable year computed by excluding the amount of recapture and related interest charge with respect to the dual consolidated losses at issue.

In addition, the proposed regulations provide rules regarding tax assessment and collection procedures. The proposed regulations provide that an assessment identifying an income tax liability of the subsequent elector is considered an assessment of the recapture tax amount where such amount is part of the income tax liability being assessed and the recapture tax amount is reflected in the statement attached to the subsequent elector's tax return. The recapture tax amount is considered to be properly assessed as an income tax liability of the original elector, and each prior subsequent elector, if any, on the same date the income tax liability of the subsequent elector was properly assessed. This liability is joint and several.

The proposed regulations also provide procedures pursuant to which any unpaid balance of the recapture tax amount may be collected from the original elector and the prior subsequent elector, if any. Such amounts may be collected from the original elector, and/or any prior subsequent elector, if each of the following conditions is satisfied: (1) the Commissioner has properly assessed the recapture amount; (2) the Commissioner has issued a notice and demand for payment of the recapture tax amount to the subsequent elector; (3) the subsequent elector has failed to pay all of the recapture tax amount by the date specified in such notice and demand; and (4) the Commissioner has issued a notice and demand for payment of the unpaid portion of the recapture tax amount to the original elector and prior subsequent electors, if any. If the subsequent elector's income tax liability for a taxable period includes a recapture amount, and if such income tax liability is satisfied in part by payment, credit, or offset, such amount shall be allocated first to that portion of the income tax liability that is not attributable to the recapture tax amount, and then to that portion of the income tax liability that is attributable to the recapture tax amount.

Finally, the proposed regulations contain rules regarding the refund of an income tax liability that includes a recapture tax amount.

13. *Character and source of recapture income*

Section 1.1503-2(g)(2)(vii)(D) of the current regulations provides that recapture income is treated as ordinary income having the same source and falling within the same separate category under section 904 as the dual consolidated loss being recaptured. The current regulations do not, however, provide an explicit rule to identify the items that compose the dual consolidated loss. As a result, it is unclear under the current regulations how to determine the source and separate category of recapture income. In addition, the current regulations do not explicitly state how the recapture income is treated for purposes of the Code other than section 904.

The proposed regulations clarify that the character (to the extent consistent with the recapture income being ordinary income in all cases) and source of the recapture income is determined based on the character and source of a pro rata portion of the deductions that were taken into account in calculating the dual consolidated loss. As discussed above, the dual consolidated loss is composed of a pro rata portion of all items of deduction and loss that are taken into account in computing such dual consolidated loss. Moreover, the proposed regulations clarify that the determination of the character and source of such income is not limited to section 904, but applies for all purposes of the Code (for example, section 856(c)(2) and (3)).

Under the proposed regulations, the character and source of losses and deductions composing the dual consolidated loss should be identified during the year in which they are incurred, rather than the year in which they are ultimately used to offset income or gain. This approach attempts to simplify the rules and make them more administrable, rather than providing comprehensive stacking, ordering, and tracing rules that track the ultimate use of such items, which would be complex.

14. *Failure to comply with recapture provisions*

Under the current regulations, if the taxpayer fails to comply with the recapture provisions upon the occurrence of a triggering event, the dual resident corporation or separate unit that incurred the dual consolidated loss (or successor-in-interest) is not eligible to enter into a (g)(2)(i) agreement with respect to any dual consolidated losses incurred in the five taxable years beginning with the taxable year in which recapture is required. The current regulations contain two exceptions to this rule that apply unless the triggering event is an actual use of the dual consolidated loss. Under the first exception, the rule does not apply if the failure to comply is due to reasonable cause. Under the second exception, the rule does not apply if the taxpayer unsuccessfully attempted to rebut the triggering event by timely filing a rebuttal statement with its tax return.

This provision is intended to encourage taxpayers to carefully monitor potential triggering events and properly comply with the recapture provisions upon the occurrence of a triggering event.

The IRS and Treasury believe that the failure to comply penalty contained in the current regulations often does not operate in a manner that encourages compliance with the dual consolidated loss regulations. For example, if a taxpayer sells a dual resident corporation to a third party that is treated as a triggering event, but the taxpayer fails to comply with the recapture rules, the rule contained in the current regulations prevents the purchaser of the dual resident corporation from entering into a (g)(2)(i) agreement with respect to dual consolidated losses of the dual resident corporation for five years; it does not adversely affect the taxpayer that failed to properly comply with the recapture provisions. As a result, the proposed regulations do not include this penalty provision.

Although the proposed regulations do not retain this penalty provision, the Commissioner may consider applying other applicable penalty provisions in appropriate circumstances; for example, the Commissioner may consider applying the accuracy-related penalty of section 6662. In addition, the IRS and Treasury will continue to consider whether a penalty provision, similar to the one contained in the current regulations, is appropriate, especially in cases of repeated non-compliance.

F. *Effective Date—§ 1.1503(d)-6*

The proposed regulations are proposed to apply to dual consolidated losses incurred in taxable years beginning after the date that these proposed regulations are published as final regulations in the Federal Register.

The IRS and Treasury request comments on the application of the regulations, including comments as to whether the proposed regulations, when finalized, should contain an election that would allow taxpayers to apply all or a portion of the regulations retroactively. In addition, comments are requested as to possible transition rules that may apply, including the application of the proposed regulations, when finalized, to existing (g)(2)(i) agreements.

Effect on Other Documents

When these proposed regulations are adopted as final regulations, Rev. Proc. 2000-42 (2000-2 C.B. 394), will be obsolete with respect to dual consolidated losses incurred in taxable years beginning after the date that these proposed regulations are published as final regulations in the **Federal Register.**

Special Analyses

It has been determined that this notice of proposed rule making is not a significant regulatory action as defined in Executive Order 12866. Therefore, a regulatory assessment is not required. It is hereby certified that these regulations will not have a significant economic impact on a substantial number of small entities. This certification is based on the fact that these regulations will primarily affect affiliated groups of corporations that also have a foreign affiliate, which tend to be larger businesses. Moreover, the number of taxpayers affected and the average burden are minimal. Therefore, a Regulatory Flexibility Analysis is not required. Pursuant to section 7805(f) of the Code, these regulations will be submitted to the Chief Counsel for Advocacy of the Small Business Administration for comment on their impact on small business.

Comments and Public Hearing

A public hearing has been scheduled for September 7, 2005, at 10 a.m., in the Auditorium of the Internal Revenue Building, 1111 Constitution Avenue, NW., Washington, DC. Because of access restrictions, visitors must enter at the main entrance, located at 1111 Constitution Avenue, NW. All visitors must present photo identification to enter the building. Because of access restrictions, visitors will not be admitted beyond the immediate entrance more than 30 minutes before the hearing starts. For information about having your name placed on the building access list to attend hearing, see the "FOR FURTHER INFORMATION CONTACT" portion of this preamble.

The rules of 26 CFR 601.601(a)(3) apply to the hearing. Persons who wish to present oral comments must submit written or electronic comments and an outline of the topic to be discussed and time to be devoted to each topic (preferably a signed original and eight (8) copies) by August 22, 2005. A period of 10 minutes will be allotted to each person for making comments. An agenda showing the scheduling of the speakers will be prepared after the deadline for receiving outlines has passed. Copies of the agenda will be available free of charge at the hearing.

Drafting Information

The principal author of these regulations is Kathryn T. Holman of the Office of Associate Chief Counsel (International). However, other personnel from the IRS and Treasury Department participated in their development.

[¶ 49,242] Proposed Regulations, Proposed Amendments of Regulations and Partial Withdrawal of Proposed Regulations (REG-105346-03), published in the Federal Register on May 23, 2005.

Partners and partnerships: Transfers of partnership equity: Performance of service: Capital interest v. partnership profit: Elections.—Reg. §1.706-3 and amendments of Reg. §§1.83-3, 1.83-6, 1.704-1, 1.707-1, 1.721-1 and 1.761-1, relating to the tax treatment of certain transfers of partnership equity in connection with the performance of services, are proposed. Previously proposed amendments of Reg. §1.721-1 were withdrawn. A public hearing on this proposal is scheduled for October 5, 2005.

AGENCY: Internal Revenue Service (IRS), Treasury.

ACTION: Partial withdrawal of notice of proposed rulemaking, notice of proposed rulemaking, and notice of public hearing.

SUMMARY: This document withdraws the remaining portion of the notice of proposed rulemaking published in the **Federal Register** on June 3, 1971 (36 FR 10787) and contains proposed regulations relating to the tax treatment of certain transfers of partnership equity in connection with the performance of services. The proposed regulations provide that the transfer of a partnership interest in connection with the performance of services is subject to section 83 of the Internal Revenue Code (Code) and provide rules for coordinating section 83 with partnership taxation principles. The proposed regulations also provide that no gain or loss is recognized by a partnership on the transfer or vesting of an interest in the transferring partnership in connection with the performance of services for the transferring partnership. This document also provides a notice of public hearing on these proposed regulations.

DATES: Written or electronic comments must be received by August 22, 2005.

Outlines of topics to be discussed at the public hearing scheduled for October 5, 2005, at 10 a.m. must be received by September 14, 2005.

ADDRESSES: Send submissions to: CC:PA:LPD:PR (REG-105346-03), room 5203, Internal Revenue Service, PO Box 7604, Ben Franklin Station, Washington, DC 20044. Submissions may be hand-delivered Monday through Friday between the hours of 8 a.m. and 4 p.m. to CC:PA:LPD:PR (REG-105346-03), Courier's Desk, Internal Revenue Service, 1111 Constitution Avenue, NW., Washington, DC, or sent electronically, via the IRS Internet site at *www.irs.gov/regs* or via the Federal eRulemaking Portal at *www.regulations.gov* (IRS REG-105346-03).

FOR FURTHER INFORMATION CONTACT: Concerning the section 83 regulations, Stephen Tackney at (202) 622-6030; concerning the subchapter K regulations, Audrey Ellis or Demetri Yatrakis at (202) 622-3060; concerning submissions, the hearing, and/or to be placed on the building access list to attend the hearing, Robin Jones, (202) 622-7180 (not toll free numbers).

SUPPLEMENTARY INFORMATION:

Paperwork Reduction Act

The collection of information contained in this notice of proposed rulemaking has been submitted to the Office of Management and Budget for review in accordance with the Paperwork Reduction Act of 1995 (44 U.S.C. 3507(d)). Comments on the collection of information should be sent to the **Office of Management and Budget,** Attn: Desk Officer for the Department of the Treasury, Office of Information and Regulatory Affairs, Washington, DC 20503, with copies to the **Internal Revenue Service,** Attn: IRS Reports Clearance Officer, SE:W:CAR:MP:T:T:SP, Washington, DC 20224. Comments on the collection of information should be received by July 25, 2005. Comments are specifically requested concerning:

Whether the proposed collection of information is necessary for the proper performance of the functions of the IRS, including whether the information will have practical utility;

The accuracy of the estimated burden associated with the proposed collection of information (see below);

How the quality, utility, and clarity of the information to be collected may be enhanced;

How the burden of complying with the proposed collection of information may be minimized, including through the application of automated collection techniques or other forms of information technology; and

Estimates of capital or start-up costs and costs of operation, maintenance, and purchase of services to provide information.

The following collections of information in this proposed regulation are in § 1.83-3(1):

(1) Requirement that electing partnerships submit an election with the partnership tax return.

(2) Requirement that certain partners submit a document to the partnership;

(3) Requirement that such documents be retained; and

(4) Requirement that partnerships submit a termination document with the partnership tax return as one method of terminating the election.

These collections of information are required by the IRS to determine whether the amount of tax has been calculated correctly. The respondents are partnerships and partners or other service providers.

The estimated total annual reporting and/or recordkeeping burden is 112,500 hours.

The estimated annual burden per respondent/recordkeeper varies from .10 hours to 10 hours, depending on individual circumstances, with an estimated average of 1 hour for partnerships and .25 hour for a partner or service provider. The estimated number of respondents and/or recordkeepers is 100,000 partnerships and 50,000 partners or other service providers.

The estimated annual frequency of responses (used for reporting requirements only) is on occasion.

An agency may not conduct or sponsor, and a person is not required to respond to, a collection of information unless it displays a valid control number assigned by the **Office of Management and Budget.**

Books or records relating to a collection of information must be retained as long as their contents may become material in the administration of any internal revenue law. Generally, tax returns and tax return information are confidential as required by 26 U.S.C. 6103.

Background

Partnerships issue a variety of instruments in connection with the performance of services. These instruments include interests in partnership capital, interests in partnership profits, and options to acquire such interests (collectively, partnership equity). On June 5, 2000, the Treasury Department and the IRS issued Notice 2000-29 (2000-1 C.B. 1241), inviting public comment on the Federal income tax treatment of the exercise of an option to acquire a partnership interest, the exchange of convertible debt for a partnership interest, and the exchange of a preferred interest in a partnership for a common interest in that partnership. On January 22, 2003, the Treasury Department and the IRS published in the **Federal Register** (REG-103580-02) (68 FR 2930), proposed regulations regarding the Federal income tax consequences of noncompensatory partnership options, convertible equity, and convertible debt. In the preamble to those proposed regulations, the Treasury Department and the IRS requested comments on the proposed amendment to § 1.721-1(b)(1) that was published in the **Federal Register** on June 3, 1971 (36 FR 10787), and on the Federal income tax consequences of the issuance of partnership capital interests in connection with the performance of services and options to acquire such interests. In response to the comments received, the Treasury Department and the IRS are withdrawing the proposed amendment to § 1.721-1(b)(1) and issuing these proposed regulations, which prescribe rules on the application of section 83 to partnership interests and the Federal income tax consequences associated with the transfer, vesting, and forfeiture of partnership interests transferred in connection with the performance of services.

Explanation of Provisions

1. Application of Section 83 to Partnership Interests

Section 83 generally applies to a transfer of property by one person to another in connection with the performance of services. The courts have held that a partnership capital interest is property for this purpose. See *Schulman v. Commissioner*, 93 T.C. 623 (1989) (section 83 governs the issuance of an option to acquire a partnership interest as compensation for services provided as an employee); *Kenroy, Inc. v. Commissioner*, T.C. Memo 1984-232. Therefore, the proposed regulations provide that a partnership interest is property within the meaning of section 83, and that the transfer of a partnership interest in connection with the performance of services is subject to section 83.

The proposed regulations apply section 83 to all partnership interests, without distinguishing between partnership capital interests and partnership profits interests. Although the application of section 83 to partnership profits interests has been the subject of controversy, see, e.g., *Campbell v. Commissioner*, T.C. Memo 1990-162, aff'd in part and rev'd in part, 943 F.2d 815 (8th Cir. 1991), n. 7; *St. John v. U.S.*, 84-1 USTC 9158 (C.D. III. 1983), the Treasury Department and the IRS do not believe that there is a substantial basis for distinguishing among partnership interests for purposes of section 83. All partnership interests constitute personal property under state law and give the holder the right to share in future earnings from partnership capital and labor. Moreover, some commentators have suggested that the same tax rules should apply to both partnership profits interests and partnership capital interests. These commentators have suggested that taxpayers may exploit any differences in the tax treatment of partnership profits interests and partnership capital interests. The Treasury Department and the IRS agree with these comments. Therefore, all of the rules in these proposed regulations and the accompanying proposed revenue procedure (described below) apply equally to partnership capital interests and partnership profits interests. However, a right to receive allocations and distributions from a partnership that is described in section 707(a)(2)(A) is not a partnership interest. In section 707(a)(2)(A), Congress directed that such an arrangement should be characterized according to its substance, that is, as a disguised payment of compensation to the service provider. See S. Rep. No. 98-169, 98 Cong. 2d Sess., at 226 (1984).

Section 83(b) allows a person who receives substantially nonvested property in connection with the performance of services to elect to include in gross income the difference between: (A) the fair market value of the property at the time of transfer (determined without regard to a restriction other than a restriction which by its terms will never lapse); and (B) the amount paid for such property. Under section 83(b)(2), the election under section 83(b) must be made within 30 days of the date of the transfer of the property to the service provider.

Consistent with the principles of section 83, the proposed regulations provide that, if a partnership interest is transferred in connection with the performance of services, and if an election under section 83(b) is not made, then the holder of the partnership interest is not treated as a partner until the interest becomes substantially vested. If a section 83(b) election is made with respect to such an interest, the service provider will be treated as a partner for purposes of Subtitle A of the Code. These rules are similar to the current rules pertaining to substantially nonvested stock in a subchapter S corporation. See § 1.1361-1(b)(3) (upon an election under section 83(b), the service provider becomes a shareholder for purposes of subchapter S).

These principles differ from Rev. Proc. 2001-43. Under that revenue procedure, if a partnership profits interest is transferred in connection with the performance of services, then the holder of the partnership interest may be treated as a partner even if no section 83(b) election is made, provided that certain conditions are met.

Certain changes to the regulations under both subchapter K and section 83 are needed to coordinate the principles of subchapter K with the principles of section 83. Among the changes that are proposed in these regulations are: (1) conforming the subchapter K rules to the section 83 timing rules; (2) revising the section 704(b) regulations to take into account the fact that allocations with respect to an unvested interest may be forfeited; and (3) providing that a partnership generally recognizes no gain or loss on the transfer of an interest in the partnership in connection with the performance of services for that partnership. In addition, Rev. Procs. 93-27 (1993-2 C.B. 343), and 2001-43 (2001-2 C.B. 191), which generally provide for nonrecognition by both the partnership and the service provider on the transfer of a profits interest in the partnership for services performed for that partnership, must be modified to be consistent with these proposed regulations. Accordingly, in conjunction with these proposed regulations, the IRS is issuing Notice 2005-43 (2005-24 I.R.B.). That Notice contains a proposed revenue procedure that, when finalized, will obsolete Rev. Procs. 93-27 and 2001-43. The Treasury Department and the IRS intend for these proposed regulations and the proposed revenue procedure to become effective at the same time. The proposed amendments to the regulations under section 83 and subchapter K, as well as the Notice, are described in further detail below.

The proposed revenue procedure and certain parts of the proposed regulations (as described below) only apply to a transfer by a partnership of an interest in that partnership in connection with the performance of services for that partnership (compensatory partnership interests). The Treasury Department and the IRS request comments on the income tax consequences of transactions involving related persons, such as, for example, the transfer of an interest in a lower-tier partnership in exchange for services provided to the upper-tier partnership.

2. Timing of Partnership's Deduction

Except as otherwise provided in §1.83-6(a)(3), if property is transferred in connection with the performance of services, then the service recipient's deduction, if any, is allowed only for the taxable year of that person in which or with which ends the taxable year of the service provider in which the amount is included as compensation. See section 83(h). In contrast, under section 706(a) and §1.707-1(c), guaranteed payments described in section 707(c) are included in the partner's income in the partner's taxable year within or with which ends the partnership's taxable year in which the partnership deducted the payments. Under §1.721-1(b)(2) of the current regulations, an interest in partnership capital issued by the partnership as compensation for services rendered to the partnership is treated as a guaranteed payment under section 707(c). Some commentators suggested that the proposed regulations should resolve the potential conflict between the timing rules of section 83 and the timing rules of section 707(c).

Under the proposed regulations, partnership interests issued to partners for services rendered to the partnership are treated as guaranteed payments. Also, the proposed regulations provide that the section 83 timing rules override the timing rules of section 706(a) and §1.707-1(c) to the extent they are inconsistent. Accordingly, if a partnership transfers property to a partner in connection with the performance of services, the timing and the amount of the related income inclusion and deduction is determined by section 83 and the regulations thereunder.

In drafting these regulations, the Treasury Department and the IRS considered alternative approaches for resolving the timing inconsistency between section 83 and section 707(c). One alternative approach considered was to provide that the transfer of property in connection with the performance of services is not treated as a guaranteed payment within the meaning of section 707(c). This approach was not adopted in the proposed regulations due to, among other things, concern that such a characterization of these transfers could have unintended consequences on the application of provisions of the Code outside of subchapter K that refer to guaranteed payments. The Treasury Department and the IRS request comments on alternative approaches for resolving the timing inconsistency between section 83 and section 707(c).

3. Allocation of Partnership's Deduction

The proposed regulations provide guidance regarding the allocation of the partnership's deduction for the transfer of property in connection with the performance of services. Some commentators suggested that the proposed regulations require that the partnership's deduction be allocated among the partners in accordance with their interests in the partnership prior to the transfer.

Section 706(d)(1) provides generally that, if, during any taxable year of a partnership, there is a change in any partner's interest in the partnership, each partner's distributive share of any item of income, gain, loss, deduction, or credit of the partnership for such taxable year shall be determined by the use of any method prescribed by regulations which takes into account the varying interests of the partners in the partnership during the taxable year. Regulations have not yet been issued describing the rules for taking into account the varying interests of the partners in the partnership during a taxable year. Section 1.706-1(c)(2)(ii) provides that, in the case of a sale, exchange, or liquidation of a partner's entire interest in a partnership, the partner's share of partnership items for the taxable year may be determined by either: (1) closing the partnership's books as of the date of the transfer (closing of the books method); or (2) allocating to the departing partner that partner's pro rata part of partnership items that the partner would have included in the partner's taxable income had the partner remained a partner until the end of the partnership taxable year (proration method). The Treasury Department and the IRS believe that section 706(d)(1) adequately ensures that partnership deductions that are attributable to the portion of the partnership's taxable year prior to a new partner's entry into the partnership are allocated to the historic partners.

Section 706(d)(2), however, places additional limits on how partnerships may allocate these deductions. Under section 706(d)(2)(B), payments for services by a partnership using the cash receipts and disbursements method of accounting are allocable cash basis items. Under section 706(d)(2)(A), if during any taxable year of a partnership there is a change in any partner's interest in the partnership, then (except to the extent provided in regulations) each partner's distributive share of any allocable cash basis item must be determined under the proration method. To allow partnerships to allocate deductions with respect to property transferred in connection with the performance of services under a closing of the books method, the proposed regulations provide that section 706(d)(2)(A) does not apply to such a transfer.

4. Accounting for Compensatory Partnership Interests

A. Transfer of compensatory partnership interest

Under the proposed regulations, the service provider's capital account is increased by the amount the service provider takes into income under section 83 as a result of receiving the interest, plus any amounts paid for the interest. Some commentators suggested that the amount included in the service provider's income under section 83, plus the amount paid for the interest, may differ from the amount of capital that the partnership has agreed to assign to the service provider. These commentators contend that the substantial economic effect safe harbor in the section 704(b) regulations should be amended to allow partnerships to reallocate capital between the historic partners and the service provider to accord with the economic agreement of the parties.

The reallocation of partnership capital in these circumstances is not consistent with the policies underlying the substantial economic effect safe harbor and the capital account maintenance rules. The purpose of the substantial economic effect safe harbor is to ensure that, to the extent that there is an economic benefit or burden associated with a partnership allocation, the partner to whom the allocation is made receives the economic benefit or bears the economic burden. Under section 83, the economic benefit of receiving a partnership interest in connection with the performance of services is the amount that is included in the compensation income of the service provider, plus the amount paid for the interest. This is the amount by which the service partner's capital account should be increased.

As explained in section 6 below, a proposed revenue procedure issued concurrently with these proposed regulations would allow a partnership, its partners, and the service provider to elect to treat the fair market value of a partnership interest as equal to the liquidation value of that interest. If such an election is made, the capital account of a service provider receiving a partnership interest in connection with the performance of services is increased by the liquidation value of the partnership interest received.

B. Forfeiture of certain compensatory partnership interests

If an election under section 83(b) has been made with respect to a substantially nonvested interest, the holder of the nonvested interest may be allocated partnership items that may later be forfeited. For this reason, allocations of partnership items while the interest is substantially nonvested cannot have economic effect. Under the proposed regulations, such allocations will be treated as being in accordance with the partners' interests in the partnership if: (a) the partnership agreement requires that the partnership make forfeiture allocations if the interest for which the section 83(b) election is made is later forfeited; and (b) all material allocations and capital account adjustments under the partnership agreement not pertaining to substantially nonvested partnership interests for which a section 83(b) election has been made are recognized under section 704(b). This safe harbor does not apply if, at the time of the section 83(b) election, there is a plan that a substantially nonvested interest will be forfeited. All of the facts and circumstances (including the tax status of the holder of the substantially nonvested interest) will be considered in determining whether there is a plan that the interest will be forfeited. In such a case, the partners' distributive shares of partnership items shall be determined in accordance with the partners' interests in the partnership under § 1.704-1(b)(3).

Generally, forfeiture allocations are allocations to the service provider of partnership gross income and gain or gross deduction and loss (to the extent such items are available) that offset prior distributions and allocations of partnership items with respect to the forfeited partnership interest. These rules are designed to ensure that any partnership income (or loss) that was allocated to the service provider prior to the forfeiture is offset by allocations on the forfeiture of the interest. Also, to carry out the prohibition under section 83(b)(1) on deductions with respect to amounts included in income under section 83(b), these rules generally cause a forfeiting partner to be allocated partnership income to offset any distributions to the partner that reduced the partner's basis in the partnership below the amount included in income under section 83(b).

Forfeiture allocations may be made out of the partnership's items for the entire taxable year. In determining the gross income of the partnership in the taxable year of the forfeiture, the rules of § 1.83-6(c) apply. As a result, the partnership generally will have gross income in the taxable year of the forfeiture equal to the amount of the allowable deduction to the service recipient partnership upon the transfer of the interest as a result of the making of the section 83(b) election, regardless of the fair market value of the partnership's assets at the time of forfeiture.

In certain circumstances, the partnership will not have enough income and gain to fully offset prior allocations of loss to the forfeiting service provider. The proposed revenue procedure includes a rule that requires the recapture of losses taken by the service provider prior to the forfeiture of the interest to the extent that those losses are not recaptured through forfeiture allocations of income and gain to the service provider. This rule does not provide the other partners in the partnership with the opportunity to increase their shares of partnership loss (or reduce their shares of partnership income) for the year of the forfeiture by the amount of loss that was previously allocated to the forfeiting service provider.

In other circumstances, the partnership will not have enough deductions and loss to fully offset prior allocations of income to the forfeiting service provider. It appears that, in such a case, section 83(b)(1) may prohibit the service provider from claiming a loss with respect to partnership income that was previously allocated to the service provider. However, a forfeiting partner is entitled to a loss for any basis in a partnership that is attributable to contributions of money or property to the partnership (including amounts paid for the interest) remaining after the forfeiture allocations have been made. See § 1.83-2(a).

Comments are requested as to whether the regulations should require or allow partnerships to create notional tax items to make forfeiture allocations where the partnership does not have enough actual tax items to make such allocations. Comments are also requested as to whether section 83(b)(1) should be read to allow a forfeiting service provider to claim a loss with respect to partnership income that was previously allocated to the service provider and not offset by forfeiture allocations of loss and deduction and, if so, whether it is appropriate to require the other partners in the partnership to recognize income in the year of the forfeiture equal to the amount of the loss claimed by the service provider. In particular, comments are requested as to whether section 83 or another section of the Code provides authority for such a rule.

5. Valuation of Compensatory Partnership Interests

Commentators requested guidance regarding the valuation of partnership interests transferred in connection with the performance of services. Section 83 generally provides that the recipient of property transferred in connection with the performance of services recognizes income equal to the fair market value of the property, disregarding lapse restrictions. See *Schulman v. Commissioner*, 93 T.C. 623 (1989). However, some authorities have concluded that, under the particular facts and circumstances of the case, a partnership profits interest had only a speculative value or that the fair market value of a partnership interest should be determined by reference to the liquidation value of that interest. See § 1.704-1(e)(1)(v); *Campbell v. Commissioner*, 943 F.2d 815 (8th Cir. 1991); *St. John v. U.S.*, 1984-1 USTC 9158 (C.D. Ill. 1983). But see *Diamond v. Commissioner*, 492 F.2d 286 (7th Cir. 1974) (holding under pre-section 83 law that the receipt of a profits interest with a determinable value at the time of receipt resulted in immediate taxation); *Campbell v. Commissioner*, T.C. Memo 1990-162, aff'd in part and rev'd in part, 943 F.2d 815 (8th Cir. 1991).

The Treasury Department and the IRS have determined that, provided certain requirements are satisfied, it is appropriate to allow partnerships and service providers to value partnership interests based on liquidation value. This approach ensures consistency in the treatment of partnership profits interests and partnership capital interests, and accords with other regulations issued under subchapter K, such as the regulations under section 704(b).

In accordance with these proposed regulations, the revenue procedure proposed in Notice 2005-43 (2005-24 I.R.B.) will, when finalized, provide additional rules that partnerships, partners, and persons providing services to the partnership in exchange for interests in that partnership would be required to follow when electing under § 1.83-3(l) of these proposed regulations to treat the fair market value of those interests as being equal to the liquidation value of those interests. For this purpose, the liquidation value of a partnership interest is the amount of cash that the holder of that interest would receive with respect to the interest if, immediately after the transfer of the interest, the partnership sold all of its assets (including goodwill, going concern value, and any other intangibles associated with the partnership's operations) for cash equal to the fair market value of those assets, and then liquidated.

6. Application of Section 721 to Partnership on Transfer

There is a dispute among commentators as to whether a partnership should recognize gain or loss on the transfer of a compensatory partnership interest. Some commentators believe that, on the transfer of such an interest, the partnership should be treated as satisfying its compensation obligation with a fractional interest in each asset of the partnership. Under this deemed sale of assets theory, the partnership would recognize gain or loss equal to the excess of the fair market value of each partial asset deemed transferred to the service provider over the partnership's adjusted basis in that partial asset. Other commentators believe that a partnership should not recognize gain or loss on the transfer of a compensatory partnership interest. They argue, among other things, that the transfer of such an interest is not properly treated as a realization event for the partnership because no property owned by the partnership has changed hands. They also argue that taxing a partnership on the transfer of such an interest would result in inappropriate gain acceleration, would be difficult to administer, and would cause economically similar transactions to be taxed differently.

Generally, when appreciated property is used to pay an obligation, gain on the property is recognized. The Treasury Department and the IRS are still analyzing whether an exception to this general rule is appropriate on the transfer of an interest in the capital or profits of a partnership to satisfy certain partnership obligations (such as the obligations to pay interest or rent). However, the Treasury Department and the IRS believe that partnerships should not be required to recognize gain on the transfer of a compensatory partnership interest. Such a rule is more consistent with the policies underlying section 721—to defer recognition of gain and loss when persons join together to conduct a business—than would be a rule requiring the partnership to recognize gain on the transfer of these types of interests. Therefore, the proposed regulations provide that partnerships are not taxed on the transfer or substantial vesting of a compensatory partnership interest. Under § 1.704-1(b)(4)(i) (reverse section 704(c) principles), the historic partners generally will be required to recognize any income or loss attributable to the partnership's assets as those assets are sold, depreciated, or amortized.

The rule providing for nonrecognition of gain or loss does not apply to the transfer or substantial vesting of an interest in an eligible entity, as defined in § 301.7701-3(a) of the Procedure and Administration Regulations, that becomes a partnership under § 301.7701-3(f)(2) as a result of the transfer or substantial vesting of the interest. See *McDougal v. Commissioner*, 62 T.C. 720 (1974) (holding that the service recipient recognized gain on the transfer of a one-half interest in appreciated property to the service provider, immediately prior to the contribution by the service recipient and the service provider of their respective interests in the property to a newly formed partnership).

7. Revaluations of Partnership Property

The proposed regulations concerning noncompensatory partnership options published on January 22, 2003, contained special rules regarding the revaluations of partnership property while noncompensatory partnership options were outstanding. Specifically, the regulations proposed modifications to § 1.704-1(b)(2)(iv)(*f*) and (*h*) to provide that any revaluation during the period in which there are outstanding noncompensatory options generally must take into account the fair market value, if any, of outstanding options. These proposed regulations do not contain similar provisions, because under recently proposed modifications to the regulations under § 1.704-1(b)(2)(iv), the obligation to issue a partnership interest in satisfaction of an option agreement is a liability that is taken into account in determining the fair market value of partnership assets as a result of a revaluation. See REG-106736-00, 68 FR 37434 (June 24, 2003) (relating to the assumption of certain obligations by partnerships from partners).

8. Characterization Rule

The proposed regulations concerning noncompensatory partnership options published on January 22, 2003 contained a rule (§ 1.761-3) providing that the holder of a noncompensatory option is treated as a partner under certain circumstances. However, the Treasury Department and the IRS have concluded that these proposed regulations should not contain a similar rule for partnership options transferred in connection with the performance of services because of the possibility that constructive transfers of property, subject to section 83, may occur under circumstances other than those described in the proposed rules for treating the holder of a noncompensatory option as a partner. The Treasury Department and the IRS request comments on whether anti-abuse rules are necessary to prevent taxpayers from using the rules in these proposed regulations or the rules in Notice 2005-43 to inappropriately shift items of partnership income or loss between the service provider and the other partners.

9. Retroactive Allocations

Section 761(c) generally allows a partnership to modify its agreement at any time on or prior to the due date for the partnership's return for the taxable year (without regard to extensions). Thus, for example, a partnership could, at the end of its taxable year, amend its partnership agreement to provide that a service provider was entitled to a substantially vested or nonvested interest in partnership profits and losses from the beginning of the partnership's taxable year. It is expected that, if a substantially vested compensatory partnership interest is transferred to an employee or independent contractor (or an election under section 83(b) is made with respect to the transfer of a substantially nonvested compensatory partnership interest to an employee or independent contractor), the partnership will report the transfer on Form W-2, "Wage and Tax Statement," or Form 1099-MISC, "Miscellaneous Income," as appropriate. The Form W-2 or Form 1099-MISC would be issued to the service provider by the partnership by January 31 of the year following the calendar year in which the partnership interest is transferred, and the partnership would file such forms with the Social Security Administration or IRS, respectively, by February 28 (March 31 if filed electronically) of the year following the calendar year in which the partnership interest is transferred. The service provider would be required to report any income recognized on the transfer of the partnership interest on the service provider's return for the taxable year (of the service provider) in which the transfer occurs.

It is unclear whether the retroactive commencement date of such an interest should be treated as the date of the transfer of the interest for purposes of section 83 and other provisions of the Code outside of subchapter K. If the retroactive effective date of the interest is treated as the transfer date for all purposes, a number of administrative concerns arise. For example, the partnership may not, by the January 31 deadline, have the information necessary to issue Form W-2 or Form 1099-MISC to the service provider. Also, the service provider may not, by the due date for filing the section 83(b) election, have the information necessary to file the election. The Treasury Department and the IRS request comments on the timing for section 83 purposes of retroactive transfers of partnership interests and on any actions that may be appropriate to address the associated administrative concerns.

10. Information Reporting to Partners

As explained above, the proposed regulations treat the transfer of a partnership interest to a partner in connection with the performance of services as a guaranteed payment. To ensure that the service provider partner has the information necessary to include the transfer in income for the taxable year in which the transfer occurs (rather than the taxable year in which or with which ends the partnership taxable year in which the transfer occurs), the Treasury Department and the IRS are considering the possibility of amending the section 6041 regulations to provide that this type of guaranteed payment must be reported by the partnership on Form 1099-MISC, which is required to be issued to the service provider on or before January 31 of the year following the calendar year of such transfer. The Treasury Department and the IRS request comments on whether such a requirement is appropriate and administrable.

Proposed Effective Date

These regulations are proposed to apply to transfers of property on or after the date final regulations are published in the **Federal Register**.

Special Analyses

It has been determined that this notice of proposed rulemaking is not a significant regulatory action as defined in Executive Order 12866. Therefore, a regulatory assessment is not required. It also has been determined that section 553(b) of the Administrative Procedure Act (5 U.S.C. chapter 5) does not apply to these regulations. It is hereby certified that the collection of information in these regulations will not have a significant economic impact on a substantial number of small entities. This certification is based upon the fact that the reporting burden, as discussed earlier in this preamble, is not expected to be significant. Partnerships with partnership agreements that contain the binding provisions referred to in § 1.83-3(l) only will be required to submit a single election form in order to rely on the safe harbor described in that paragraph. Partnerships that desire to elect to use the safe harbor described in § 1.83-3(l), but which do not have partnership agreements containing these provisions, are required to obtain partner-level consents to the election. However, these partnerships are expected to be rare. Moreover, in most cases the partners in such partnerships are not expected to be small businesses. Therefore, a Regulatory Flexibility Analysis under the Regulatory Flexibility Act (5 U.S.C. chapter 6) is not required. Pursuant to section 7805(f) of the Code, this notice of proposed rulemaking will be submitted to the Chief Counsel for Advocacy of the Small Business Administration for comment on its impact on small business.

Comments and Public Hearing

Before these proposed regulations are adopted as final regulations, consideration will be given to any electronic or written comments (a signed original and eight copies) that are submitted timely to the IRS. The IRS and the Treasury Department request comments on the clarity of the proposed rules and how they can be made easier to understand. All comments will be available for public inspection and copying.

A public hearing has been scheduled for October 5, 2005, beginning at 10 a.m. in the IRS Auditorium, Internal Revenue Building, 1111 Constitution Avenue, NW., Washington, DC. Due to building security procedures, visitors must enter at the Constitution Avenue entrance. In addition, all visitors must present photo identification to enter the building. Because of access restrictions, visitors will not be admitted beyond the immediate entrance area more than 30 minutes before the hearing starts. For information about having your name placed on the building access list to attend the hearing, see the "FOR FURTHER INFORMATION CONTACT" portion of this preamble.

The rules of 26 CFR 601.601(a)(3) apply to the hearing. Persons who wish to present oral comments must submit written comments and an outline of the topics to be discussed and the time to be devoted to each topic (a signed original and eight (8) copies) by September 14, 2005. A period of 10 minutes will be allotted to each person for making comments. An agenda showing the scheduling of the speakers will be prepared after the deadline for reviewing outlines has passed. Copies of the agenda will be available free of charge at the hearing.

Drafting Information

The principal authors of these regulations are Audrey Ellis and Demetri Yatrakis of the Office of Associate Chief Counsel (Passthroughs and Special Industries), and Stephen Tackney of the Office of Associate Chief Counsel (Tax Exempt and Government Entities). However, other personnel from the IRS and Treasury Department participated in their development.

———————

[¶ 49,247]   **Proposed Regulations (REG-133578-05)**, published in the Federal Register on August 24, 2005.

    Corporations: Dividends paid deduction: Employee stock ownership plans (ESOPs): Applicable dividends: Payments to reacquire stock.—Reg. §1.404(k)-2, concerning which corporation is entitled to the deduction for applicable dividends under Code Sec. 404(k) and clarifying that a payment in redemption of employer securities held by an employee stock ownership plan (ESOP) is not deductible, is proposed. Reg. §§1.162(k)-1 and 1.404(k)-3 were adopted by T.D. 9282 on August 29, 2006. The text is at ¶18,370C.

AGENCY: Internal Revenue Service (IRS), Treasury.

ACTION: Notice of proposed rulemaking.

SUMMARY: This document contains proposed regulations under sections 162(k) and 404(k) of the Internal Revenue Code (Code) relating to employee stock ownership plans (ESOPs). The regulations provide guidance concerning which corporation is entitled to the deduction for applicable dividends under section 404(k). These regulations also clarify that a payment in redemption of employer securities held by an ESOP is not deductible. These regulations will affect administrators of, employers maintaining, participants in, and beneficiaries of ESOPs. In addition, they will affect corporations that make distributions in redemption of stock held in an ESOP.

DATES: Written or electronic comments and requests for a public hearing must be received by November 23, 2005.

ADDRESSES: Send submissions to: CC:PA:LPD:PR (REG-133578-05), room 5203, Internal Revenue Service, POB 7604, Ben Franklin Station, Washington, DC 20044. Submissions may be hand-delivered Monday through Friday between the hours of 8 a.m. and 4 p.m. to: CC:PA:LPD:PR (REG-133578-05), Courier's Desk, Internal Revenue Service, 1111 Constitution Avenue, NW., Washington D.C. Alternatively, taxpayers may submit comments electronically directly to the IRS Internet site at *www.irs.gov/regs*, or via the Federal eRulemaking Portal at *www.regulations.gov* (IRS-REG-133578-05).

FOR FURTHER INFORMATION CONTACT: Concerning the regulations, John T. Ricotta at (202) 622-6060 with respect to section 404(k) or Martin Huck at (202) 622-7750 with respect to section 162(k); concerning submission of comments or to request a public hearing, Robin Jones at (202) 622-7180 (not toll-free numbers).

SUPPLEMENTARY INFORMATION:

Background and Explanation of Provisions

This document contains proposed regulations under sections 162(k) and 404(k) of the Internal Revenue Code (Code). These regulations address two issues that have arisen in the application of these sections. The first issue arises in a case in which the applicable employer securities held in an employee stock ownership plan (ESOP) are not securities of the corporation or corporations that maintain the plan. The issue is which corporation is entitled to the deduction under section 404(k) for certain dividends paid with respect to the stock held in the ESOP. The second issue is whether payments in redemption of stock held by an ESOP are deductible.

Code and Regulations

Section 404(a) provides that contributions paid by an employer to or under a stock bonus, pension, profit sharing, or annuity plan are deductible under section 404(a), if they would be otherwise deductible, within the limitations of that section. Section 404(k)(1) provides that, in the case of a C corporation, there is allowed as a deduction for a taxable year the amount of any applicable dividend paid in cash by such corporation during the taxable year with respect to applicable employer securities held by an ESOP. The deduction under section 404(k) is in addition to the deductions allowed under section 404(a).

Section 4975(e)(7) provides, in relevant part, that an ESOP is a defined contribution plan that is a stock bonus plan qualified under section 401(a) and designed to invest primarily in qualifying employer securities. Section 4975(e)(8) states that the term *qualifying employer security* means any employer security within the meaning of section 409(l). Section 409(l) generally provides that the term *employer security* means common stock issued by the employer (or a corporation that is a member of the same controlled group) that is readily tradable on an established securities market, if the corporation (or a member of the controlled group) has common stock that is readily tradable on an established securities market. Section 409(l)(4)(A) provides that, for purposes of section 409(l), the term *controlled group of corporations* has the meaning given to that term by section 1563(a) (determined without regard to subsections (a)(4) and (e)(3)(C) of section 1563). Section 409(l)(4)(B) provides that, for purposes of section 409(l)(4)(A), if a common parent owns directly stock possessing at least 50 percent of the voting power of all classes of stock and at least 50 percent of each class of nonvoting stock in a first tier subsidiary, such subsidiary (and all corporations below it in the chain which would meet the 80 percent test of section 1563(a) if the first tier subsidiary were the common parent) are treated as includible corporations.

Section 404(k)(2), for taxable years beginning on or after January 1, 2002, generally provides that the term *applicable dividend* means any dividend which, in accordance with the plan provisions—(i) is paid in cash to the participants in the plan or their beneficiaries, (ii) is paid to the plan and is distributed in cash to participants in the plan or their beneficiaries not later than 90 days after the close of the plan year in which paid, (iii) is, at the election of such participants or their beneficiaries—(I) payable as provided in clause (i) or (ii), or (II) paid to the plan and reinvested in qualifying employer securities, or (iv) is used to make payments on a loan described in section 404(a)(9), the proceeds of which were used to acquire the employer securities (whether or not allocated to participants) with respect to which the dividend is paid. Under section 404(k)(4), the deduction is allowable in the taxable year of the corporation in which the dividend is paid or distributed to a participant or beneficiary.

Prior to 2002, section 404(k)(5)(A) provided that the Secretary may disallow the deduction under section 404(k) for any dividend if the Secretary determines that such dividend constitutes, in substance, an evasion of taxation. Section 662(b) of the Economic Growth and Tax Relief Reconciliation Act of 2001 (115 Stat. 38, 2001) amended section 404(k)(5)(A) to provide that the Secretary may disallow a deduction under section 404(k) for any dividend the Secretary determines constitutes, in substance, an avoidance or evasion of taxation. The amendment is effective for tax years after December 31, 2001.

Section 162(k)(1) generally provides that no deduction otherwise allowable under chapter 1 of the Code is allowed for any amount paid or incurred by a corporation in connection with the reacquisition of its stock or the stock of any related person (as defined in section 465(b)(3)(C)). The legislative history of section 162(k) states that the phrase "in connection with" is "intended to be construed broadly." H.R. Conf. Rep. No. 99-841, at 168 (1986).

Corporation Entitled to Section 404(k) Deduction

An ESOP may benefit employees of more than one corporation. In addition, an ESOP may be maintained by a corporation other than the payor of a dividend. In these cases, the issue arises as to which entity is entitled to the deduction provided under section 404(k). Assume, for example, that a publicly traded corporation owns all of the stock of a subsidiary. The subsidiary operates a trade or business with employees in the U.S. and maintains an ESOP that holds stock of its parent for its employees. If the parent distributes a dividend with respect to its stock held in the ESOP maintained by the subsidiary, questions have arisen as to whether the parent or subsidiary is entitled to the deduction under section 404(k). This question arises in cases in which the parent and subsidiary file a consolidated return as well as in cases in which the parent and subsidiary do not file a consolidated return.

The IRS and Treasury Department believe that the statutory language of section 404(k) clearly provides that only the payor of the applicable dividend is entitled to the deduction under section 404(k), regardless of whether the employees of multiple corporations benefit under the ESOP and regardless of whether another member of the controlled group maintains the ESOP. Therefore, in the example above, the parent, not the subsidiary, is entitled to the deduction under section 404(k).

Treatment of Payments Made to Reacquire Stock

Some corporations have claimed deductions under section 404(k) for payments in redemption of stock held by an ESOP that are used to make benefit distributions to participants or beneficiaries, including distributions of a participant's account balance upon severance from employment. These taxpayers have argued that the payments in redemption qualify as dividends under sections 301 and 316 and, therefore, are deductible under section 404(k).

In Rev. Rul. 2001-6 (2001-1 C.B. 491), the IRS concluded that section 162(k) bars a deduction for payments made in redemption of stock from an ESOP. This conclusion was based on the fact that section 162(k)(1) disallows a deduction for payments paid in connection with the reacquisition of an issuer's stock and that the redemption payments are such payments. The IRS also concluded that such payments were not applicable dividends under section 404(k)(1). The IRS reasoned that allowing a deduction for redemption amounts would vitiate important rights and protections for recipients of ESOP distributions, including the right to reduce taxes by utilizing the return of basis provisions under section 72, the right to make rollovers of ESOP distributions received upon separation from service, and the protection against involuntary cash-outs. Finally, the IRS stated that a deduction under section 404(k)(1) for such amounts would constitute, in substance, an evasion of tax.

In *Boise Cascade Corporation v. United States*, 329 F.3d 751 (9th Cir. 2003), the Court of Appeals for the Ninth Circuit held that payments made by a corporation to redeem its stock held by its ESOP were deductible as dividends paid under section 404(k), and that the deduction was not precluded by section 162(k). The court reasoned that the distribution by the ESOP of the redemption proceeds to the participants was a transaction separate from the redemption transaction. Therefore, the court concluded that the distribution did not constitute a payment *in connection with* the corporation's reacquisition of its stock, and section 162(k) did not bar the deduction of such payments.

For the reasons stated in Rev. Rul. 2001-6, the IRS and Treasury Department continue to believe that allowing a deduction for amounts paid to reacquire stock is inconsistent with the intent of, and policies underlying, section 404. In addition, the IRS and Treasury Department believe that allowing such a deduction would constitute, in substance, an avoidance or evasion of taxation within the meaning of section 404(k)(5)(A) because it would allow a corporation to claim two deductions for the same economic cost: once for the value of the stock originally contributed to the ESOP and again for the amount paid to redeem the same stock. See *Charles Ilfeld Co. v. Hernandez*, 292 U.S. 62 (1934). Moreover, despite the Ninth Circuit's conclusion in *Boise Cascade*, the IRS and Treasury Department continue to believe that, even if a payment in redemption of stock held by an ESOP were to qualify as an applicable dividend, section 162(k) would disallow a deduction for that amount because such payment would be in connection with the reacquisition of the corporation's stock.

This notice of proposed rulemaking, therefore, includes proposed regulations under section 404(k) that confirm that payments made to reacquire stock held by an ESOP are not deductible under section 404(k) because such payments do not constitute applicable dividends under section 404(k)(2) and a deduction for such payments would constitute, in substance, an avoidance or evasion of taxation within the meaning of section 404(k)(5). It also includes proposed regulations under section 162(k) that provide that section 162(k), subject to certain exceptions, disallows any deduction for amounts paid or incurred by a corporation in connection with the reacquisition of its stock or the stock of any related person (as defined in section 465(b)(3)(C)). The proposed regulations also provide that amounts paid or incurred in connection with the reacquisition of stock include amounts paid by a corporation to reacquire its stock from an ESOP that are then distributed by the ESOP to its participants (or their beneficiaries) or otherwise used in a manner described in section 404(k)(2)(A).

Proposed Effective Date

These regulations are proposed to be effective on the date of issuance of final regulations. However, before these regulations become effective, the IRS will continue to assert in any matter in controversy outside of the Ninth Circuit that sections 162(k) and 404(k) disallow a deduction for payments to reacquire employer securities held by an ESOP. See Chief Counsel Notice 2004-038 (October 1, 2004) available at *www.irs.gov/foia* through the *electronic reading room*.

Special Analyses

It has been determined that this notice of proposed rulemaking is not a significant regulatory action as defined in Executive Order 12866. Therefore, a regulatory assessment is not required. It has also been determined that section 553(b) of the Administrative Procedure Act (5 U.S.C. chapter 5) does not apply to these regulations, and, because the regulations do not impose a collection of information on small entities, the Regulatory Flexibility Act (5 U.S.C. chapter 6) does not apply. Pursuant to section 7805(f) of the Code, this notice of proposed rulemaking will be submitted to the Chief Counsel for Advocacy of the Small Business Administration for comment on its impact on small business.

Comments and Public Hearing

Before these proposed regulations are adopted as final regulations, consideration will be given to any written (a signed original and eight (8) copies) or electronic comments that are submitted timely to the IRS. The IRS and Treasury Department specifically request comments on the clarity of the proposed regulations and how they may be made easier to understand. All comments will be available for public inspection and copying. A public hearing will be scheduled if requested in writing by any person that timely submits written comments. If a public hearing is scheduled, notice of the date, time, and place for the public hearing will be published in the **Federal Register**.

Drafting Information

The principal authors of these regulations are John T. Ricotta, Office of Division Counsel/Associate Chief Counsel (Tax Exempt and Government Entities) and Martin Huck of Office of Associate Chief Counsel (Corporate). However, other personnel from the IRS and Treasury participated in the development of these regulations.

[¶ 49,277] **Proposed Amendments of Regulations (REG-121509-00)**, published in the Federal Register on August 29, 2006 (corrected 12/8/2006).

[Code Secs. 959, 961 and 1502]

Controlled foreign corporations: Previously taxed income: Basis adjustments: Consolidated returns.—Reg. §§ 1.961-3 and 1.961-4, and amendments of Reg. §§ 1.959-1, 1.959-2, 1.959-3, 1.959-4, 1.961-1, 1.961-2, 1.1502-12 and 1.1502-32, relating to the exclusion from gross income of previously taxed earnings and profits under section 959 of the Internal Revenue Code and related basis adjustments under 961 of the Code, are proposed.

AGENCY: Internal Revenue Service (IRS), Treasury.

ACTION: Notice of proposed rulemaking.

SUMMARY: This document contains proposed regulations that provide guidance relating to the exclusion from gross income of previously taxed earnings and profits under section 959 of the Internal Revenue Code (Code) and related basis adjustments under section 961 of the Code. These regulations reflect relevant statutory changes made in years subsequent to 1983. These regulations also address a number of issues that the current section 959 and section 961 regulations do not clearly answer. These regulations, in general, will affect United States shareholders of controlled foreign corporations and their successors in interest.

DATES: Written or electronic comments and requests for a public hearing must be received by November 27, 2006.

ADDRESSES: Send submissions to: CC:PA:LPD:PR (REG-121509-00), Internal Revenue Service, PO Box 7604, Ben Franklin Station, Washington, DC 20044 or send electronically, via the IRS Internet site at *www.irs.gov/regs* or via the Federal eRulemaking Portal at *www.regulations.gov* (IRS REG-121509-00).

FOR FURTHER INFORMATION CONTACT: Concerning the proposed regulations, Ethan Atticks, (202) 622-3840; concerning submissions of comments, Kelly Banks, (202) 622-0392 (not toll-free numbers).

SUPPLEMENTARY INFORMATION:

Background

This document contains proposed amendments to 26 CFR Part 1 under sections 959, 961 and 1502. Section 959(a)(1) generally provides an exclusion from the gross income of a United States shareholder for distributions of earnings and profits of a foreign corporation attributable to amounts which are, or have been, included in a United States shareholder's gross income under section 951(a). Section 959(a)(2) excludes from the gross income of a United States shareholder earnings and profits attributable to amounts which are, or have been, included in the gross income of a United States shareholder under section 951(a) which would, but for section 959(a)(2), be again included in gross income of a United States shareholder under section 951(a)(1)(B) as an amount determined under section 956 (section 956 amounts). Earnings and profits of a foreign corporation included in a United States shareholder's gross income under section 951(a) are referred to as previously taxed earnings and profits or previously taxed income (PTI).

Section 959(b) generally provides that for purposes of section 951(a), PTI shall not, when distributed through a chain of ownership described in section 958(a), be included in the gross income of a controlled foreign corporation (CFC) in such chain for purposes of the application of section 951(a) to such CFC.

Section 959(c) generally provides for the allocation of distributions by a foreign corporation to three different categories of the corporation's earnings and profits: (1) PTI attributable to section 956 amounts that are included in the gross income of a United States shareholder under section 951(a)(1)(B) and section 956 amounts that would have been so included but for section 959(a)(2), (2) PTI attributable to amounts included in gross income under section 951(a)(1)(A), and (3) other earnings and profits (non-PTI). Section 959(f) provides for the allocation of section 956 amounts first to PTI arising from a United States shareholder's income inclusions under section 951(a)(1)(A) and then to non-PTI. In addition, section 959(f) provides a priority rule under which actual distributions of earnings and profits are taken into account before section 956 amounts.

Certain amounts are treated as amounts included in the gross income of a United States shareholder under section 951(a)(1)(A) for purposes of section 959. For example, section 959(e) generally provides that any amount included in the gross income of any person as a dividend by reason of subsection (a) or (f) of section 1248 is treated for purposes of section 959 as an amount included in the gross income of such person under section 951(a)(1)(A).

Section 961 authorizes the Secretary of the Treasury to promulgate regulations adjusting the basis of stock in a foreign corporation, as well as the basis of other property by reason of which a United States person is considered under section 958(a) to own stock in a foreign corporation. Section 961(a) generally provides for an increase in a United States shareholder's basis in its CFC stock, or in the property by reason of which it is considered to own such stock, by the amount required to be included in its gross income under section 951(a) with respect to such stock.

Under section 961(b), and the regulations thereunder, when a United States person receives an amount which is excluded from gross income under section 959(a), the adjusted basis of the foreign corporation stock or the property by reason of which the shareholder is considered to own such stock is reduced by the amount of the exclusion. In addition, section 961(c) generally provides for regulations under which adjustments similar to those provided for under section 961(a) and (b) are made to the basis of stock in a CFC which is owned by another CFC (and certain other CFCs in the chain) for the purpose of determining the amount included under section 951 in the gross income of a United States shareholder.

Section 959 was enacted so that PTI is excluded from gross income and, thus, not taxed again when distributed by the foreign corporation. Moreover, section 959 effects the relevant gross income exclusion at the earliest possible point. Thus, the "allocation of distribution" rules of section 959(c) ensure that distributions from the foreign corporation are to be paid first out of earnings and profits attributable to amounts that have been previously included in income by the United States shareholders. Accordingly, as a result of its section 951(a)(1) inclusion, a United States shareholder is made whole by receiving, without further U.S. tax, PTI attributable to its stock in a foreign corporation before it receives any taxable distributions from the foreign corporation. Section 961, which adjusts basis in the stock in a foreign corporation for PTI attributable to such stock, also ensures that PTI is not taxed twice if the stock in the foreign corporation is sold before the PTI is distributed.

The existing regulations under sections 959 and 961 were published in 1965. See TD 6795 (1965-1 CB 287). Minor amendments were made to the regulations in 1974, 1978, and 1983. See TD 7334 (1975-1 CB 246); TD 7545 (1978-1 CB 245); TD 7893 (1983-1 CB 132). The regulations have not been updated since 1983 to reflect relevant statutory changes in subsequent years. For example, section 959(e) (described above) was added by the Deficit Reduction Act of 1984 (Public Law 98-369). Section 304(b)(6) was enacted by the IRS Restructuring and Reform Act of 1998 (Public Law 105-206) and provides that in the case of a section 304 transaction in which the acquiring corporation or the issuing corporation is a foreign corporation, the Secretary of the Treasury is to prescribe regulations providing rules to prevent the multiple inclusion of any item in income and to provide appropriate basis adjustments, including rules modifying the application of sections 959 and 961. The determination of the amount includible in a United States shareholder's gross income as a result of a CFC's investments in United States property under section 956 was modified by the Omnibus Budget Reconciliation Act of 1993 (Public Law 103-66). Congress enacted section 961(c) (described in this preamble) as part of the Taxpayer Relief Act of 1997 (Public Law 105-34) and further modified the provision in the Gulf Opportunity Zone Act of 2005 (Public Law 109-135). Section 986 was added to the Code by the Tax Reform Act of 1986 (Public Law 99-514) and provides that earnings and profits of foreign corporations are maintained in the foreign corporation's functional currency and translated into United States dollars when taken into account by a United States person at the appropriate exchange rate specified in section 989.

Further, in addition to raising issues about the complexities of section 959 in cross-chain stock sales subject to section 304(a)(1), commentators and taxpayers have raised a number of other issues that the current section 959 regulations do not clearly answer. For example, issues have been raised about distributions of PTI through a chain of CFCs and the status of PTI when a United States shareholder's stock in a foreign corporation is sold to a foreign person. There are numerous other examples where the existing section 959 regulations simply do not provide sufficient guidance. As a result, additional regulatory guidance is needed to address these and other section 959 issues. In addition, the IRS and Treasury Department are currently studying the new section 954(c)(6) rule enacted by the Tax Increase Prevention and Reconciliation Act of 2005 (Public Law 109-222), which generally provides for look-through treatment of payments between related CFCs under the foreign personal holding company rules of section 954(c), to determine whether that rule requires any additional regulatory guidance under section 959. Any such guidance will be included in a subsequent project.

Explanation of Provisions

These proposed regulations provide guidance with respect to a number of issues that are not specifically addressed in the current regulations and also resolve some of the complexities raised regarding the application of sections 959 and 961. The guidance needed to answer open issues under sections 959 and 961 is intended to be consistent with the legislative intent of avoiding double taxation and allowing United States persons to receive the full benefit of their PTI at the earliest possible time.

In order to carry out this legislative intent, these regulations propose new rules that are primarily based on maintaining shareholder accounts for PTI. As described in this preamble, maintaining shareholder accounts for PTI will better ensure that taxpayers are able to receive distributions of PTI before receiving taxable distributions, provide consistency for treatment of PTI by taxpayers and also, provide more rational and clear rules for resolving many of the issues that have been raised by taxpayers since the current section 959 regulations were issued. Under the proposed rules, earnings and profits will still be maintained at the foreign corporation level in the PTI and non-PTI categories described in section 959(c) on an aggregate basis with respect to all of the foreign corporation's outstanding shares.

The proposed rules also would modify the current regulations to reflect amendments to the law since 1965, such as the addition of section 959(e) and section 961(c), and the modification of sections 304 and 956. Minor changes have also been proposed to reflect changes in IRS titles and organizational units used in the current regulations.

A. Shareholder-level Exclusion Under Section 959(u)

1. In general

Section 959 provides rules for the exclusion from gross income of PTI. Prop. Reg. §1.959-1 describes the scope and purpose of the proposed regulations under section 959 in paragraph (a), and provides definitions in paragraph (b). Paragraph (c) generally provides for the exclusion from a covered shareholder's gross income of a distribution or section 956 amount based upon the amount of adjustments made to a shareholder's PTI accounts with respect to the relevant stock under Prop. Reg. §1.959-3 because of that distribution or section 956 amount, as discussed below. A covered shareholder is defined to mean a person who is (1) a United States person who owns stock (within the meaning of section 958(a)) in a foreign corporation and who has had a section 951(a) inclusion with respect to its stock in such corporation, (2) a "successor in interest" (defined in this preamble), or (3) a corporation that is not described in (1) or (2) and that owns stock (within the meaning of section 958(a)) in a foreign corporation in which another corporation is a covered shareholder described in (1) or (2), if both corporations are members of the same consolidated group.

2. Shareholder PTI accounts

Prop. Reg. §1.959-1(d)(1) requires each covered shareholder of a foreign corporation to maintain a PTI account for each share of stock in a foreign corporation that the shareholder owns directly or indirectly under section 958(a). Although the PTI account is share specific, as a matter of administrative convenience, Prop. Reg. §1.959-1(d)(1) permits a shareholder to maintain the account with respect to an entire block of stock in foreign corporation if the PTI attributable to each share in the block is the same. For a discussion of the rules for maintaining a PTI account, see Part C of this discussion.

3. Successors in interest

Section 959(a) extends the exclusion from gross income for PTI to any United States person who acquires from any person any portion of the interest of a United States shareholder (as the term is defined in section 951(b) or section 953(c)(1)(A)) in a foreign corporation, but only to the extent of that portion and subject to such proof of the identity of such interest as the Secretary of the Treasury may by regulations prescribe. Consequently, Prop. Reg. §1.959-1(d)(2)(i) provides that a transferee of stock in a foreign corporation acquires the PTI account of the transferor for such stock and may exclude PTI from gross income under section 959(a) by reference to the PTI account for the stock acquired, if the transferee is a United States person that can prove the right to the exclusion (successor in interest).

In order to establish a United States person's right to the exclusion, the proposed regulations provide that a person must attach a statement to its return that provides that it is excluding amounts from gross income because it is a successor in interest and that provides the name of the foreign corporation. Further, a person must be prepared to provide, within 30 days upon the request of the Director of Field Operations, certain additional information (e.g., evidence showing that the earnings and profits for which an exclusion is claimed are PTI and that such amounts were not previously excluded from the gross income of a United States person). The information that may be required under these proposed regulations remains substantially unchanged from the information that is currently required to be included in a statement with the United States person's return under §1.959-1(d).

Moreover, Prop. Reg. §1.959-1(d)(2)(ii) provides that the amount of the PTI account for stock that is transferred to someone who is not a successor in interest (e.g., a foreign person) is preserved unchanged during the period of such person's ownership of such stock. However, section 959(a) extends the section 959(a) exclusion to a United States person who acquires a United States shareholder's interest in a foreign corporation from any person. Accordingly, Prop. Reg. §1.959-1(d)(2)(i) provides that if a United States person acquires stock in a foreign corporation from any person, including a person who is not a successor in interest, such as a foreign person, and the United States person qualifies as a successor in interest, the United States person acquires the PTI account attributable to the foreign corporation stock acquired and may exclude PTI from gross income under section 959(a) by reference to the PTI account for such stock.

B. *CFC-level Exclusion Under Section 959(b)*

Section 959(b) provides an exclusion pursuant to which the earnings and profits of a CFC (lower-tier CFC) attributable to amounts which are, or have been, included in the gross income of a United States shareholder under section 951(a) shall not, when distributed through a chain of ownership described in section 958(a), be also included in the gross income of the CFC receiving the distribution (upper-tier CFC) in such chain for purposes of the application of section 951(a) to such upper-tier CFC with respect to such United States shareholder. Prop. Reg. §1.959-2 contains rules relating to the section 959(b) exclusion. These rules are intended to reflect the holding of Rev. Rul. 82-16 (1982-1 CB 106) as well as to provide guidance regarding cross-chain sales of stock in a foreign corporation by a CFC subject to section 304(a)(1).

In Rev. Rul. 82-16, an upper-tier CFC, 70 percent owned by a United States shareholder (USP) and 30 percent owned by a foreign person, received a distribution of $200x of earnings and profits from a lower-tier CFC wholly-owned by the upper-tier CFC. The lower-tier CFC had earned $100x of subpart F income for the year of the distribution ($70x of which was included in USP's gross income under section 951(a)) and a $100x of non-subpart F income. The ruling held that $100x, rather than $70x, was excluded from the gross income of the upper-tier CFC under section 959(b). If only $70x were excluded, USP would be required to include in gross income $21x of subpart F income with respect to the remaining $30x included in the upper-tier CFC's gross income, resulting in a total inclusion in USP's gross income of $91x ((70% ×$30x) + (70% × $100x)).

Prop. Reg. §1.959-2(a) addresses the issue raised in Rev. Rul. 82-16, and accordingly, provides that the amount of the exclusion provided under section 959(b) is the entire amount distributed by the lower-tier CFC to the upper-tier CFC that gave rise (in whole or in part) to an adjustment of the United States shareholder's PTI accounts with respect to the stock it owns (within the meaning of section 958(a)) in the lower- and upper-tier CFC under Prop. Reg. §1.959-3(e)(3) (discussed in this preamble). This amount shall not exceed the earnings and profits of the distributor CFC attributable to amounts described in section 951(a). Such amount is not limited to the amount of the adjustment to the United States shareholder's PTI account.

For example, under the facts of Rev. Rul. 82-16, the amount excluded from the upper-tier CFC's gross income for purposes of applying section 951(a) to USP under Prop. Reg. §1.959-2(a) is $100x. That is, the entire amount of the earnings and profits distributed by the lower-tier CFC that were attributable to amounts described in section 951(a) and that caused an adjustment to USP's PTI accounts in both the upper-and lower-tier CFCs under Prop. Reg. §1.959-3(e)(3).

Prop. Reg. §1.959-2(a) produces results consistent with Rev. Rul. 82-16, while ensuring that section 959(b) does not inappropriately prevent taxation under section 951(a) of a United States shareholder that has acquired stock in a CFC from a person that was not taxed on the subpart F income of a lower-tier CFC in the year such income was earned (e.g., a foreign person). For example, assume the same facts as those of Rev. Rul. 82-16, except that: (1) the subpart F income was earned by the lower-tier CFC in year 1, (2) another United States shareholder (DC) acquired the 30 percent interest in the upper-tier CFC in year 2 from the foreign person with a zero PTI account, and (3) the lower-tier CFC did not distribute any property until year 3. Under Prop. Reg. §1.959-2(a), the section 959(b) exclusion for the upper-tier CFC for purposes of calculating USP's section 951(a) inclusion is still $100x. In contrast, Prop. Reg. §1.959-2(a) provides that the section 959(b) exclusion for the upper-tier CFC for purposes of determining DC's section 951(a) inclusion is zero because none of the earnings and profits distributed were attributable to amounts included in income under section 951(a) with respect to DC or the person to whom DC is a successor in interest. Therefore, DC may have an income inclusion under section 951(a).

In addition, Prop. Reg. §1.959-2(b) provides guidance with respect to the application of section 959(b) in the context of stock sales subject to section 304(a)(1) where the selling corporation is a CFC. The proposed regulations clarify that in the case of a deemed redemption resulting from a transaction described in section 304(a)(1) in which earnings and profits of an acquiring foreign corporation or an acquired foreign corporation or both are deemed distributed to a selling CFC, the selling CFC is deemed for purposes of section 959(b) to receive such distributions through a chain of ownership described under section 958(a).

C. *Maintenance of PTI Accounts*

The proposed regulations contain detailed rules regarding the maintenance of shareholder PTI accounts and the maintenance of pools of PTI and non-PTI earnings and profits with respect to a foreign corporation, including rules for adjusting PTI accounts as a result of certain transactions. In addition, the proposed regulations provide rules for covered shareholders that have more than one share of stock in a foreign corporation and covered shareholders that are members of a consolidated group.

1. *Shareholder-level accounting of PTI*

The proposed regulations provide that a covered shareholder's PTI account with respect to its stock in a foreign corporation shall identify the amounts included in gross income by a United States shareholder under section 951(a)(1)(A) with respect to the stock (PTI described in section 959(c)(2)), and amounts that are included in the gross income of a United States shareholder under section 951(a)(1)(B) and section 956 amounts that would have been so included but for section 959(a)(2) (PTI described in section 959(c)(1)) by such shareholder that owns the stock or by a successor in interest. A shareholder account must also reflect these amounts in the functional currency of the foreign corporation and the annual dollar basis of each category of PTI in the account.

2. *Corporate-level accounting of PTI*

The proposed regulations also provide that separate aggregate categories (with respect to all of the shareholders of a foreign corporation) of PTI described in section 959(c)(1) and section 959(c)(2) and non-PTI shall be maintained with respect to foreign corporations. These categories of earnings and profits of a foreign corporation shall be maintained in the functional currency of the foreign corporation.

The proposed regulations reflect the basic allocation rules under section 959(c) and (e). Those rules provide that distributions are considered to be made on a last-in first-out basis under section 316(a), first from any PTI described in section 959(c)(1), then from PTI described in section 959(c)(2), and finally from non-PTI earnings and profits. In addition, section 956 amounts are allocated first to section 959(c)(2) earnings and profits and then to non-PTI earnings and profits. Consequently, PTI resulting from section 956 amounts in a prior year cannot exclude section 956 amounts in a later year from otherwise being included in a United States shareholder's gross income under section 951(a)(1)(B).

The proposed regulations also provide that these allocations to PTI are made in conjunction with the shareholder-level adjustments to shareholder-level PTI accounts. In addition, any adjustments to earnings and profits required under section 312 or other sections of the Code or Treasury regulations shall generally be made only to non-PTI.

3. *Foreign currency and foreign tax credit rules*

The proposed regulations also contain several rules that reflect the significant changes made to the foreign currency translation rules since the existing section 959 regulations were issued. The proposed regulations also contain rules regarding the foreign tax credit rules relating to PTI.

a. *Dollar basis pooling election*

The proposed regulations provide that a shareholder account must reflect the annual dollar basis of each category of PTI in the account. However, Prop. Reg. § 1.959-3(b)(2)(ii) allows taxpayers to elect to treat distributions as being made from a single pool of post-1986 PTI for purposes of computing foreign currency gain or loss under section 986(c) and basis adjustments under section 961 with respect to distributions of PTI. Thus, the reduction of the basis of shares in a foreign corporation and the foreign currency gain (or loss) attributable to a PTI distribution may both be determined by assigning a pro rata portion of the shareholder's aggregate dollar basis in its PTI account to a distribution of PTI. The proposed regulations make this pooled approach available to taxpayers for purposes of section 986(c) at the taxpayer's election. The proposed regulations provide that the election is made by using a dollar basis pool to compute foreign currency gain or loss under section 986(c) with respect to distributions of PTI of a foreign corporation, or to compute gain or loss with respect to its stock in the foreign corporation, whichever occurs first. Any subsequent change in the taxpayer's method of assigning dollar basis may only be made with the consent of the Commissioner.

b. *Taxes and other expenses attributable to PTI*

Prop. Reg. § 1.959-3(c) provides that the corporate-level and shareholder-level PTI accounts are reduced by the functional currency amount of any income, war profits, or excess profits taxes imposed by any foreign country or a possession of the United States on or with respect to PTI as it is distributed by a foreign corporation to another foreign corporation through a chain of ownership described in section 958(a). The proposed regulations further provide that such taxes are not added to the foreign corporation's post-1986 foreign income taxes pool, which is maintained with respect to the foreign corporation's post-1986 undistributed earnings. Rather, such taxes are maintained in a separate account and allowed as a credit pursuant to section 960(a)(3) when the associated PTI is distributed to a United States shareholder (or its successor in interest). This rule ensures that amounts previously included in income that are used to pay creditable foreign taxes and so are unavailable for distribution to covered shareholders reduce the amount of PTI available for distribution but may be claimed as a foreign tax credit at the appropriate time. The proposed regulations also provide for corresponding adjustments to the covered shareholder's dollar basis of the PTI account.

Prop. Reg. § 1.959-3(d) provides that no expenses of a foreign corporation, other than creditable foreign income taxes described in Prop. Reg. § 1.959-3(c), shall be allocated and apportioned to reduce PTI. By allocating all such expenses to non-PTI, this rule preserves the amount of PTI that may be distributed to a United States shareholder (or its successor in interest) in a non-taxable manner.

4. *Adjustment of shareholder PTI accounts*

The proposed regulations generally provide rules for the adjustment of a covered shareholder's PTI account upon an inclusion of income by the shareholder under section 951, an actual distribution of earnings and profits to the shareholder, or a determination of a section 956 amount with respect to the shareholder. The proposed regulations provide that the adjustment of PTI accounts occur according to the ordering rules of section 959 to determine the tax consequences of the various events. For purposes of determining the tax consequences to a covered shareholder in a foreign corporation, the proposed regulations provide that with respect to a foreign corporation's taxable year, and for the taxable year of the covered shareholder in which or with which such taxable year of the foreign corporation ends, the following events are taken into account in the following order: (1) the covered shareholder's inclusion of subpart F income or other amounts in gross income under section 951(a)(1)(A) for a taxable year, (2) any actual distributions of current or accumulated earnings and profits by a foreign corporation during the year, including redemptions treated as distributions of property to which section 301 applies pursuant to section 302(d); and (3) any investments in United States property by a CFC during the year resulting in a section 956 amount for one or more United States shareholders for the year. For purposes of the proposed regulations, amounts included in the gross income of any person as a dividend under section 1248(a) or (f) are generally treated as section 951(a)(1)(A) inclusions.

Thus, under Prop. Reg. § 1.959-3(e)(2), at the end of the foreign corporation's taxable year, a shareholder's PTI account is first adjusted upward by the amount of any subpart F income included in gross income by the shareholder under section 951(a) with respect to the shareholder's stock in the foreign corporation. Second, a shareholder's PTI account is adjusted downward by the amount of any distributions of PTI to the shareholder with respect to the stock during the year. However, a PTI account can never be reduced below zero. Third, to the extent that any section 956 amount for the year is equal to (or less than) the amount of PTI described in section 959(c)(2), an amount of such PTI equal to the section 956 amount is reclassified as PTI described in section 959(c)(1), but does not decrease the shareholder's PTI account. Finally, the shareholder's PTI account is adjusted upward by any section 956 amount in excess of the PTI described in section 959(c)(2) for the year. Corresponding adjustments are made to the dollar basis of the PTI account.

This sequence of adjustments may be affected by the PTI sharing rules discussed below. Although the sharing rules are described in greater detail in Prop. Reg. § § 1.959-3(f) and (g), the order of the adjustments described in these sections are provided for in the steps described in Prop. Reg. § 1.959-3(e)(2).

The amount of a downward adjustment to the covered shareholder's PTI account under the second step described above is excluded from the shareholder's gross income under section 959(a)(1) and Prop. Reg. § 1.959-1(c)(1). Similarly, the amount of section 959(c)(2) PTI which is reclassified as section 959(c)(1) PTI under the third step described above is excluded from the covered shareholder's gross income under section 959(a)(2) and Prop. Reg. § 1.959-1(c)(2).

5. *Adjustment to PTI accounts upon distributions to intermediary CFCs*

Where stock in a lower-tier CFC is owned indirectly by a United States shareholder (or successor in interest) through one or more upper-tier CFCs in a chain of ownership under section 958(a), the shareholder's PTI accounts with respect to stock in the relevant foreign corporations in the chain must be adjusted when the lower-tier CFC makes a distribution of PTI to an upper-tier CFC in the chain. Prop. Reg. § 1.959-3(e)(3) provides that the shareholder's PTI account with respect to stock in the distributing foreign corporation is decreased by the amount of PTI distributed with respect to such stock, and the shareholder's PTI account with respect to stock in the recipient foreign corporation is increased by the same amount (in addition to being increased by any non-PTI portion of the distribution that results in an inclusion in the shareholder's gross income under section 951(a) as subpart F income of the receiving CFC). Prop. Reg. § 1.959-3(e)(3) provides a spot rate translation convention for cases in which the distributing and receiving corporations use different functional currencies.

6. *Effect of deficits in earnings and profits*

Prop. Reg. § 1.959-3(e)(5) provides that a shareholder's PTI account is not adjusted to take into account any deficit in earnings and profits of the corporation for the taxable year. Deficits will reduce only the non-PTI of the corporation under section 312.

7. *Distribution in excess of the PTI account*

Under Prop. Reg. § 1.959-3(e)(5), when a foreign corporation distributes to a shareholder an amount exceeding the PTI account with respect to the relevant stock, the treatment of the excess amount depends on the facts and circumstances. Subject to the PTI sharing rules discussed below, the excess amount of a distribution generally is treated as a dividend under section 316 to the extent of the distributing corporation's non-PTI, and thereafter as a return of capital (reducing the shareholder's basis in its stock in the foreign corporation) under section 301(c)(2). Any portion of the distribution remaining after the shareholder's basis of the stock in the foreign corporation is reduced to zero is treated as capital gain under section 301(c)(3).

8. *PTI sharing rules*

The purpose of section 959 is to prevent double taxation of amounts that have been previously included in gross income by a United States shareholder under section 951(a) and, importantly, to prevent such double taxation at the earliest possible time. Section 951 subjects a United States shareholder to tax on undistributed income of a CFC, so the ordering rule of section 959(c) effectuates this statutory purpose by treating actual distributions to the shareholder as coming first out of PTI. As one of the goals of section 959 is to treat distributions as first coming from PTI, the IRS and Treasury Department believe that a United States shareholder (or successor in interest) should be entitled to exclude from gross income under section 959(a) all of a foreign corporation's distributions of earnings and profits and section 956 amounts to the extent of PTI associated with any of the United States person's stock in the foreign corporation, before that person is required to include additional distributions of earnings and profits or section 956 amounts of the foreign corporation in gross income.

The IRS and Treasury Department believe that similar rules should apply with respect to members of a consolidated group. Although the taxation of a consolidated group represents a hybrid of single and separate entity treatment, consolidated attribute utilization is generally based on single entity treatment. For example, when determining consolidated taxable income for a given year, subject to certain limitations, the group is entitled to offset its income with any consolidated net operating losses that are carried forward to such year (regardless of which member or members recognized the income or incurred the losses). Given the broad regulatory authority of section 1502 and the statutory mandate in section 959 to allow United States shareholders (or successors in interest) to recover PTI at the earliest possible time, the IRS and Treasury Department believe that PTI is an attribute for which single entity treatment of United States consolidated groups is appropriate. As a result, the IRS and Treasury Department have concluded that a shareholder of a foreign corporation that is a member of a consolidated group should be entitled to exclude from gross income under section 959(a) all of a foreign corporation's distributions of earnings and profits, and section 956 amounts, to the extent of PTI associated with any stock in the foreign corporation owned by any member of the consolidated group (with appropriate adjustments). Therefore, the proposed regulations provide for sharing of PTI between accounts of different members of a consolidated group in a manner similar to the sharing of PTI between multiple accounts of a single shareholder, as described below.

a. *Shareholder with multiple PTI accounts*

Prop. Reg. § 1.959-3(f) provides a special rule that applies when a United States shareholder has more than one PTI account with respect to stock in a foreign corporation, and during its taxable year, the foreign corporation distributes earnings and profits in an amount that exceeds one or more of such PTI accounts. In that case, the shareholder's PTI accounts with respect to all of its other stock in the foreign corporation that it owns at the end of the foreign corporation's taxable year shall be reduced, in the aggregate, by the amount of the excess, on a pro rata basis by reference to the level of such PTI accounts (after such PTI accounts have first been adjusted to reflect any distributions of earnings and profits with respect to those blocks of stock).

The aggregate reduction in such PTI accounts produces a corresponding increase in the PTI account that would have been exceeded by the amount distributed but for the operation of this sharing rule. That PTI account is then reduced to zero to reflect the amount of earnings and profits distributed with respect to that block of stock during the year.

Similarly, if the section 959(c)(2) portion of a PTI account for a share in a foreign corporation is exceeded by the section 956 amount attributable to the share, the aggregate amount of the section 959(c)(2) portion of the PTI accounts for all other stock of the foreign corporation owned by the shareholder on the last day of the foreign corporation's taxable year is available for purposes of excluding the section 956 amount from gross income under section 959(a)(2).

b. *Shareholder that is a member of a consolidated group*

Prop. Reg. § 1.959-3(g) provides similar sharing rules where stock in a foreign corporation is owned by two or more members of a consolidated group. For purposes of administrative convenience, however, this rule focuses on whether the shareholders are members of the same consolidated group at the end of the foreign corporation's taxable year and not at the time the PTI in question was generated. Specifically, if the total amount of a United States shareholder's PTI account or accounts for stock in a foreign corporation is exceeded by the amount of earnings and profits distributed by the corporation to the shareholder during the year, the PTI accounts of other members of the shareholder's consolidated group that own stock in the corporation are decreased on a pro rata basis (after adjustment) and the shareholder's PTI accounts or account, as the case may be, will be correspondingly increased and then adjusted downward to zero.

Similarly, if the total amount of the section 959(c)(2) portion of a shareholder's PTI account or accounts for stock in a foreign corporation is exceeded by the shareholder's section 956 amount for the year, the aggregate amount of the section 959(c)(2) portions of the PTI accounts of other member's of the shareholder's consolidated group at the end of the foreign corporation's taxable year that own stock in the foreign corporation will be available to the shareholder for purposes of excluding the section 956 amount from gross income under section 959(a)(2).

9. *Redemptions, including section 304 transactions*

The proposed regulations provide rules for the adjustment of PTI accounts and the effect on the corporation's non-PTI when a foreign corporation redeems its stock. The effect of a distribution in redemption of stock (redemption distribution) depends on whether the redemption distribution is treated as a payment in exchange for the stock under sections 302(a) or 303, or as a distribution of property to which section 301 applies pursuant to section 302(d).

a. *Redemptions treated as sales or exchanges*

If a redemption distribution is treated as a sale or exchange, generally the amount chargeable to the earnings and profits of the redeeming corporation is limited by section 312(n)(7) to a ratable share of the earnings and profits. Where the redeeming corporation is a foreign corporation and there is a PTI account with respect to the redeemed stock, the proposed regulations provide that section 312(n)(7) is applied by limiting the reduction of the redeeming corporation's earnings and profits to an amount which does not exceed the sum of (1) the amount in the PTI account for the redeemed stock and (2) a ratable share of the corporation's non-PTI attributable to the redeemed shares, if any. This sum first reduces the PTI account with respect to the redeemed stock and then reduces the corporation's non-PTI.

The IRS and Treasury Department believe that, in the case where a foreign corporation redeems stock in a transaction treated as a sale or exchange for an amount that is less than the PTI account for that stock, it would be inappropriate to transfer the remainder of the PTI account to any other PTI accounts with respect to stock in the foreign corporation. Under section 961(a) and the regulations thereunder, the basis of stock in a foreign corporation is increased by the amount included in the shareholder's gross income under section 951(a), which is reflected in the PTI account with respect to such stock. The shareholder recovers this increase in basis upon a sale of the stock, preventing the shareholder from suffering double taxation on gain attributable to PTI (or in appropriate cases enabling the shareholder to recognize a loss). Consequently, under the proposed regulations, the remainder of the PTI account in the situation described above is not transferred to any other PTI account because it was already accounted for in the treatment of the redemption as a sale or exchange. Any corporate-level PTI attributable to the redeemed stock that remains after the reduction under section 312(n)(7) loses its character as PTI and is reclassified as non-PTI of the corporation. The IRS and Treasury Department believe that because the redeemed shareholder is able to use the loss resulting from the redemption to offset other income, its excess PTI must become other earnings and profits that remain with the foreign corporation so that those earnings and profits can be subject to tax.

b. *Redemptions treated as section 301 distributions*

If, under section 302(d), a redemption distribution is treated as a distribution of property to which section 301 applies, the proposed regulations provide that the rules of Prop. Reg. § § 1.959-1 and -3 shall apply in the same manner as they do to any other distribution to which section 301(c) applies. The PTI account with respect to the redeemed stock is reduced by the amount of the redemption distribution. If the redemption distribution exceeds such PTI account, the sharing rules described above regarding nonredemptive distributions of earnings and profits will be applicable. If, instead, the PTI account with respect to the redeemed shares exceeds the amount of the redemption distribution, the excess PTI is reallocated to the PTI accounts with respect to the remaining stock in the foreign corporation in a manner consistent with, and in proportion to, the proper adjustments of the basis in the remaining shares of the foreign corporation pursuant to § 1.302-2(c). Accordingly, the proposed regulations also require proper adjustment of the basis of the shareholder's remaining stock in the redeeming corporation, and of stock in the redeeming corporation held by related persons (not limited to members of the shareholder's consolidated group).

c. *Deemed redemptions under section 304*

With respect to amounts paid to acquire stock in a transaction described in section 304(a)(1) and to which section 301(c) applies, the rules of Prop. Reg. § § 1.959-1 and -3 shall apply in the same manner as they do to any other distribution to which section 301(c) applies. As discussed below, the sharing rules described above are applicable to such redemption distributions that are treated as distributions of property to which section 301 applies. In addition, a covered shareholder receiving such a distribution of earnings and profits shall have a PTI account with respect to the stock of each foreign corporation deemed to have distributed its earnings and profits under section 304(b)(2).

The Senate Report on the IRS Restructuring and Reform Act of 1998 states with respect to the Secretary's authority to prescribe regulations resulting from the enactment of section 304(b)(6), "It is expected that such regulations will provide for an exclusion from income for distributions from earnings and profits of the acquiring corporation and the issuing corporation that represent previously taxed income under subpart F. It further is expected that such regulations will provide for appropriate adjustments to the basis of stock held by the corporation treated as receiving the distribution or by the corporation that had the prior inclusion with respect to the previously taxed income." S. Rep. No. 105-174 at 179 (1998). The Conference agreement on the Act follows the Senate amendment. H.R. Conf. Rep. No. 105-599 (1998).

In the case where members of a United States consolidated group own stock in the issuing corporation and the acquiring corporation in a section 304(a)(1) transaction, the PTI accounting and sharing rules are intended to prevent double taxation of PTI, as intended by Congress in enacting sections 304(b)(6) and 959. A lower-tier, cross-chain acquisition of stock is generally subject to section 304(a)(1) and the transferor is treated as having transferred the stock in the issuing corporation to the acquiring corporation in exchange for stock in the acquiring corporation in a transaction to which section 351(a) applies. The acquiring corporation is treated as having redeemed those shares pursuant to a redemption distribution to which section 301 applies. As a result, in accordance with these regulations, a PTI account with respect to the stock in the foreign corporation that is treated as redeemed under section 304(a)(1) would be considered to arise at the time of the transaction. Any PTI accounts with respect to stock in the foreign corporation owned by other members of the shareholder's consolidated group would be reduced, and the PTI account of the redeemed shareholder increased (and then reduced to zero), under the PTI sharing rules described above.

D. *Basis Adjustments*

The proposed regulations contain corresponding amendments to the regulations under section 961. These proposed regulations generally provide for increases and reductions in the basis of foreign corporation stock or other property through which foreign corporation stock is owned which match the increases and reductions in the PTI account with respect to such stock under the section 959 proposed regulations. The proposed regulations provide translation conventions for determining dollar basis adjustments under section 961 as a result of inclusions under section 951(a), distributions, and the foreign income taxes imposed on PTI as it is distributed through tiers of foreign corporations.

The proposed regulations also implement section 961(c) by providing for adjustments to the basis of stock in a CFC that is held by another CFC in a chain of ownership described in section 958(a) for the purpose of determining the amount properly includible in gross income under section 951(a) by a United States shareholder upon a sale of stock in a lower-tier CFC.

The regulations also contain rules describing basis adjustments resulting from cross-chain sales of foreign corporation stock under section 304(a)(1).

E. *Basis Adjustments of Consolidated Group Members*

In the case where there is sharing of PTI among members of a U.S. consolidated group, the proposed regulations also clarify the interaction of the investment adjustment provisions in the consolidated return regulations with the section 961 basis adjustment provisions. Accordingly, the proposed regulations clarify that a consolidated group member who utilizes PTI of another member shall treat the increase in its PTI account as the receipt of tax exempt income under Prop. Reg. § 1.1502-32(b)(3)(ii)(D), and a member whose PTI is utilized shall treat the reduction in its PTI account as a noncapital nondeductible expense under Prop. Reg. § 1.1502-32(b)(3)(iii)(B) for purposes of making the investment adjustments required by § 1.1502-32.

F. *Proposed Effective Date and Transition Rule*

These regulations are proposed to apply to taxable years of foreign corporations beginning on or after the date these regulations are published as final regulations in the **Federal Register**, and taxable years of U.S. shareholders with or within which such taxable years of foreign corporations end. After these regulations become effective, foreign corporations and shareholders who are currently accounting for PTI in a manner other than that which is provided in these regulations may use any reasonable method to conform their current accounting of PTI to the rules provided in these regulations.

Request for Comments

A. *Coordination of Shareholder-level and Corporate-level Accounts*

Prop. Reg. § 1.959-3(e)(4) requires aggregate categories of PTI to be maintained at the corporate level and to be adjusted in accordance with adjustments made to the individual shareholder-level PTI accounts. No explicit rules are provided for how shareholder-level and corporate-level

PTI information is to be shared among the shareholders of a foreign corporation. Comments are requested on whether such information sharing rules are necessary and, if so, how they should operate to ensure conformity between shareholder-level and corporate-level PTI accounting.

B. *PTI and Consolidated Groups*

The application of the PTI sharing rules in the proposed regulations result in corresponding adjustments to the basis of stock in the sharing member corporations (and potentially higher tier members) held by other members of the shareholder's consolidated group. As noted above, the IRS and Treasury Department believe that the PTI sharing rules result in the corresponding basis adjustments under the current investment adjustment provisions. There is some tension between single and separate entity treatment of a consolidated group regarding the PTI sharing rules, and the IRS and Treasury Department are continuing to study how to balance the policy in favor of minimizing multiple income inclusions with the policy of preserving the location of attributes within a consolidated group. In particular, the IRS and Treasury Department are concerned about the potential basis shifting that may occur as a result of the PTI sharing rules. The IRS and Treasury Department request comments on the proposed rules and whether there are more appropriate rules for determining the basis of: (1) the stock in a member of the consolidated group that transfers PTI to another member of the consolidated group under the proposed regulations, (2) the stock in the member of the consolidated group that receives the transferred PTI under the proposed regulations and (3) the stock in the higher tier members of the consolidated group that directly or indirectly own the stock in the members of the consolidated group whose PTI accounts are affected by the sharing rules in the proposed regulations.

The proposed regulations do not limit the application of the PTI sharing rules between members of a consolidated group to PTI earned by a foreign corporation while the member with excess PTI was a member of such group. The IRS and Treasury Department did not adopt such a limitation out of concern that it would be overly complex and concern that such a limitation might not be consistent with the successor in interest rule. However, the IRS and Treasury Department recognize that some may believe that such a limitation might be more consistent with other attribute sharing rules in the consolidated group context. Consequently, the IRS and Treasury Department request comments as to whether a limitation on PTI sharing between members of a consolidated group similar to those of § 1.1502-21(c) is appropriate.

The IRS and Treasury Department believe that transactions described in section 304 are generally covered by the PTI sharing rules contained in Prop. Reg. § § 1.959-3(h)(1) through (3) that are applicable to typical redemptions. However, a specific rule has also been provided in Prop. Reg. § 1.959-3(h)(4) that makes the PTI sharing rules explicitly applicable to transactions described in section 304(a)(1) that are treated as distributions of property to which section 301 applies. The IRS and Treasury Department request comments regarding whether the PTI sharing rules should also be made explicitly applicable to transactions described in section 304(a)(1) that are treated as sales or exchanges or to transactions described in section 304(a)(2). In addition, comments are requested on whether rules should be provided to address the proper allocation of PTI after a transaction described in section 355.

C. *PTI and Section 367(b) Transactions.*

On November 15, 2000, the IRS and Treasury Department issued proposed regulations in the **Federal Register** (65 FR 69138) (REG-116050-99) addressing (1) the carryover of certain tax attributes, such as earnings and profits and foreign income tax accounts, when two corporations combine in a section 367(b) transaction described in section 381, and (2) the allocation of certain tax attributes when a corporation distributes stock in another corporation in a section 367(b) transaction (a foreign divisive transaction). In the preamble to those proposed regulations, the IRS and Treasury Department indicated that further guidance under section 959 would be required prior to addressing PTI issues that arise under section 367(b). At that time the IRS and Treasury Department requested comments with respect to proposed § 1.367(b) regarding whether PTI should be transferable and retain its character as PTI for section 959 purposes, as well as the various implications that result from that determination. Additionally, in the 2000 proposed regulations, the IRS and Treasury Department requested comments with respect to § 1.367(b)-8 of the proposed regulations regarding the proper adjustment of the PTI of a CFC following a foreign divisive transaction.

On August 8, 2006, the IRS and Treasury Department issued final regulations under § § 1.367(b)-3 and -7 with respect to the carryover of non-PTI amounts, among other things, while reserving final regulations under § 1.367(b)-8 with respect to the allocation of tax attributes in foreign divisive transactions.

The IRS and Treasury Department invite comments regarding the proper extension of the principles in these proposed regulations (including shareholder-level accounting of PTI and the PTI sharing rules) to § § 1.367(b)-3 and -7, as well as Prop. Reg. § 1.367(b)—8.

D. *Foreign Currency Gain or Loss and Foreign Tax Credits With Respect to PTI Distributions*

Under section 986(c) of the Code, foreign currency gain or loss with respect to distributions of PTI that is attributable to movements in exchange rates between the date(s) of the income inclusion that created the PTI and the distribution of such PTI shall be recognized and treated as ordinary income or loss from the same source as the associated income inclusion. The IRS and Treasury Department invite comments regarding additional guidance that may be needed under section 986(c) in light of the proposed regulations under section 959. The IRS and Treasury Department also invite comments regarding additional guidance that is needed to ensure that section 960(a)(3) provides appropriate foreign tax credit rules with respect to taxes imposed on PTI that is distributed through tiers of foreign corporations.

E. *Section 962*

The IRS and Treasury Department have not determined how the proposed accounting rules and basis rules should apply to a United States individual shareholder who has elected to be taxed as a corporation under section 962. Therefore, those rules are reserved for future study. The IRS and Treasury Department, however, invite comments about how the PTI rules and basis rules should apply for purposes of section 962.

F. *Section 961(c) Basis Adjustments*

Section 961(c) is only applicable for purposes of determining the amount included under section 951 in gross income of a United States shareholder. Consequently, the IRS and Treasury Department have so limited the application of Prop. Reg. § 1.961-3. In the event of a sale of a lower-tier CFC by an upper-tier CFC for which the rules of section 961(c) are implicated in determining the gain on the sale, the basis created in the lower-tier CFC stock for purposes of applying section 951 would not apply, for example, to determine the earnings and profits of the upper-tier CFC. However, the IRS and Treasury Department are concerned about the potential double taxation that may result in the event of the later distribution of these earnings and profits to a United States person.

G. *Transition Rule*

These regulations are proposed to apply to taxable years of foreign corporations beginning on or after the date these regulations are published as final regulations in the **Federal Register**, and taxable years of U.S. shareholders with or within which such taxable years of foreign corporations end. After these regulations become effective, foreign corporations and shareholders who are currently accounting for PTI in a manner other than that which is provided in these regulations may use any reasonable method to conform their current accounting of PTI to the rules provided in these regulations. Comments are requested on whether more detailed transition rules should be provided, and, if so, how such transition rules should operate to conform existing methods of PTI accounting with the method of PTI accounting required by these regulations.

Special Analyses

It has been determined that this notice of proposed rulemaking is not a significant regulatory action as defined in Executive Order 12866. Therefore, a regulatory assessment is not required. It has also been determined that section 553(b) of the Administrative Procedure Act (5 U.S.C. chapter 5) does not apply to these regulations and because the proposed regulation does not impose a collection of information on small entities, the Regulatory Flexibility Act (5 U.S.C. Ch. 6) does not apply. Pursuant to section 7805(f) of the Code, this notice of proposed rulemaking will be submitted to the Chief Counsel for Advocacy of the Small Business Administration for comment on its impact on small business.

Comments and Requests for Public Hearing

Before these proposed regulations are adopted as final regulations, consideration will be given to any written (a signed original and eight (8) copies) or electronic comments that are submitted timely to the IRS. The IRS and Treasury Department request comments on the clarity of the proposed rules and how they can be made easier to understand. All comments will be available for public inspection and copying. A public hearing will be scheduled if requested in writing by any person that timely submits written comments. If a public hearing is scheduled, notice of the date, time, and place for the public hearing will be published in the **Federal Register**.

Drafting Information

The principal author of these regulations is Ethan Atticks, Office of Associate Chief Counsel (International). However, other personnel from the IRS and Treasury Department participated in their development.

[¶ 49,280] **Proposed Amendments of Regulations (REG-141901-05)**, published in the Federal Register on October 18, 2006.

[Code Secs. 72 and 1001]

Sales and exchanges: Annuities: Gain or loss recognition.—Amendments of Reg. §§1.72-6 and 1.1001-1, providing guidance on the taxation of the exchange of property for an annuity contract, are proposed.

AGENCY: Internal Revenue Service (IRS), Treasury.

ACTION: Notice of proposed rulemaking and notice of public hearing.

SUMMARY: This document contains proposed regulations that provide guidance on the taxation of the exchange of property for an annuity contract. These regulations are necessary to outline the proper taxation of these exchanges and will affect participants in transactions involving these exchanges. This document also provides notice of public hearing.

DATES: Written or electronic comments must be received by January 16, 2007. Outlines of topics to be discussed at the public hearing scheduled for February 16, 2007, at 10 a.m. must be received by January 16, 2007.

ADDRESSES: Send submissions to: CC:PA:LPD:PR (REG-141901-05), room 5203, Internal Revenue Service, PO Box 7604, Ben Franklin Station, Washington, DC 20044. Submissions may be hand delivered to CC:PA:LPD:PR (REG-141901-05), Courier's Desk, Internal Revenue Service, Crystal Mall 4 Building, 1901 S. Bell St., Arlington, VA, or sent electronically, via the IRS internet site at www.irs.gov/regs or via the Federal eRulemaking Portal at www.regulations.gov (IRS and REG141901-05).

FOR FURTHER INFORMATION CONTACT: Concerning the proposed regulations, James Polfer, at (202) 622-3970; concerning submissions of comments, the hearing, and/or to be placed on the building access list to attend the hearing, Kelly Banks, at (202) 622-0392 (not toll-free numbers).

SUPPLEMENTARY INFORMATION:

Background

This document contains proposed amendments to the Income Tax Regulations.

Section 1001 of the Internal Revenue Code (Code) provides rules for determining the amount of gain or loss recognized. Gain from the sale or other disposition of property equals the excess of the amount realized therefrom over the adjusted basis of the property; loss from the sale or other disposition of property equals the excess of the adjusted basis of the property over the amount realized. Section 1.1001-1(a) of the Income Tax Regulations provides further that the exchange of property for other property differing materially either in kind or in extent is treated as income or as loss sustained. Under section 1001(b), the amount realized from the sale or other disposition of property is the sum of any money received plus the fair market value of any property (other than money) received. Except as otherwise provided in the Code, the entire amount of gain or loss on the sale or exchange of property is recognized.

Under section 72(a), gross income includes any amount received as an annuity (whether for a period certain or for the life or lives of one or more individuals) under an annuity, endowment, or life insurance contract. Section 72(b) provides that gross income does not include that part of any amount received as an annuity which bears the same ratio to such amount as the investment in the contract bears to the expected return under the contract. Under section 72(e), amounts received under an annuity contract before the annuity starting date are included in gross income to the extent allocable to income on the contract, and are excluded from gross income to the extent allocable to the investment in the contract. Investment in the contract is defined in section 72(c) as the aggregate amount of premiums or other consideration paid, reduced by amounts received before the annuity starting date that were excluded from gross income.

In *Lloyd v. Commissioner*, 33 B.T.A. 903 (1936), *nonacq.*, XV-2 CB 39 (1936), *nonacq. withdrawn and acq.*, 1950-2 CB 3, the Board of Tax Appeals considered the taxation of gain from a father's sale of property to his son for an annuity contract. The Board concluded that the annuity contract had no fair market value within the meaning of the predecessor of section 1001(b) because of the uncertainty of payment from the son. Because the annuity contract had no fair market value under that provision, the Board held that the gain from the sale of the property was not required to be recognized immediately but rather would be included in income only when the annuity payments exceeded the property's basis. In reaching its holding, the Board applied the open transaction doctrine articulated by the Supreme Court in *Burnet v. Logan*, 283 U.S. 404 (1931). Under this doctrine, if an amount realized from a sale cannot be determined with certainty, the seller recovers the basis of the property sold before any income is realized on the sale.

In Rev. Rul. 69-74, 1969-1 CB 43, a father transferred a capital asset having an adjusted basis of $20,000 and a fair market value of $60,000 to his son in exchange for the son's legally enforceable promise to pay him a life annuity of $7,200 per year, in equal monthly installments of $600. The present value of the life annuity was $47,713.08. The ruling concluded that: (1) the father realized capital gain based on the difference between the father's basis in the property and the present value of the annuity; (2) the gain was reported ratably over the father's life expectancy; (3) the investment in the contract for purposes of computing the exclusion ratio was the father's basis in the property transferred; (4) the excess of the fair market value of the property transferred over the present value of the annuity was a gift from the father to the son; and (5) the prorated capital gain reported annually was derived from the portion of each annuity payment that was not excludible.

In *Estate of Bell v. Commissioner*, 60 T.C. 469 (1973), *acq. in part and nonacq. in part*, 1974 WL 36039 (Jan. 8, 1974), *acq.*, AOD No. 1979-184 (August 15, 1979), a husband and wife transferred stock in two closely held corporations to their son and daughter and their spouses in exchange for an annuity contract. The fair market value of the stock substantially exceeded the value of the annuity contract. The stock transferred was placed in escrow to secure the promise of the transferees. As further security, the annuity agreement provided for a cognovit judgment against the transferees in the event of default. Because of the secured nature of the annuity, the tax court held that (i) the difference between the value of the stock and the value of the annuity contract constituted a gift; (ii) the difference between the adjusted basis of the stock and the value of the annuity contract constituted gain that was taxable in the year of the transfer (which was not before the court); and (iii) the investment in the annuity contract equaled the present value of the annuity. Similarly, in *212 Corp. v. Commissioner*, 70 T.C. 788 (1978), the tax court held that the entire amount of gain realized from the exchange of appreciated real property for an annuity contract was fully taxable in the year of the exchange because the annuity contract was secured by (i) an agreement that the annuity payments would be considered a charge against the rents from the property, (ii) an agreement not to mortgage or sell the property without written consent of the transferors, and (iii) the authorization of a confession of judgment against the transferee in the event of default.

The Treasury Department and the IRS have learned that some taxpayers are inappropriately avoiding or deferring gain on the exchange of highly appreciated property for the issuance of annuity contracts. Many of these transactions involve private annuity contracts issued by family members or by business entities that are owned, directly or indirectly, by the annuitants themselves or by their family members. Many of these transactions involve a variety of mechanisms to secure the payment of amounts due under the annuity contracts.

The Treasury Department and the IRS believe that neither the open transaction approach of *Lloyd v. Commissioner* nor the ratable recognition approach of Rev. Rul. 69-74 clearly reflects the income of the transferor of property in exchange for an annuity contract. Contrary to the premise underlying these authorities, an annuity contract - whether secured or unsecured - may be valued at the time it is received in exchange for property. See generally section 7520 (requiring the use of tables to value any annuity contract for federal income tax purposes, except for purposes of any provision specified in regulations); §1.1001-1(a) ("The fair market value of property is a question of fact, but only in rare and unusual circumstances will property be considered to have no fair market value."). The Treasury Department and the IRS believe that the transferors should be taxed in a consistent manner regardless of whether they exchange property for an annuity or sell that property and use the proceeds to purchase an annuity.

Explanation of Provisions

These proposed amendments provide that, if an annuity contract is received in exchange for property (other than money), (i) the amount realized attributable to the annuity contract is the fair market value (as determined under section 7520) of the annuity contract at the time of the exchange; (ii) the entire amount of the gain or loss, if any, is recognized at the time of the exchange, regardless of the taxpayer's method of accounting; and (iii) for purposes of determining the initial investment in the annuity contract under section 72(c)(1), the aggregate amount of premiums or other consideration paid for the annuity contract equals the amount realized attributable to the annuity contract (the fair market value of the annuity contract). Thus, in situations where the fair market value of the property exchanged equals the fair market value of the annuity contract received, the investment in the annuity contract equals the fair market value of the property exchanged for the annuity contract.

In order to apply the proposed regulations to an exchange of property for an annuity contract, taxpayers will need to determine the fair market value of the annuity contract as determined under section 7520. In the case of an exchange of property for an annuity contract that is in part a sale and in part a gift, the proposed regulations apply the same rules that apply to any other such exchange under section 1001.

The proposed regulations provide that, for purposes of determining the investment in the annuity contract under section 72(c)(1), the aggregate amount of premiums or other consideration paid for the annuity contract is the portion of the amount realized on the exchange that is attributable to the annuity contract (which is the fair market value of the annuity contract at the time of the exchange). This rule is intended to ensure that no portion of the gain or loss on the exchange is duplicated or omitted by the application of section 72 in the years after the exchange. The annuitant's investment in the contract would be reduced in subsequent years under section 72(c)(1)(B) for amounts already received under the contract subsequent to the exchange and excluded from gross income when received as a return of the annuitant's investment in the contract.

The proposed regulations do not distinguish between secured and unsecured annuity contracts, or between annuity contracts issued by an insurance company subject to tax under subchapter L and those issued by a taxpayer that is not an insurance company. Instead, the proposed regulations provide a single set of rules that leave the transferor and transferee in the same position before tax as if the transferor had sold the property for cash and used the proceeds to purchase an annuity contract. The same rules would apply whether the exchange produces a gain or loss. The regulations do not, however, prevent the application of other provisions, such as section 267, to limit deductible losses in the case of some exchanges. The proposed regulations apply to exchanges of property for an annuity contract, regardless of whether the property is exchanged for a newly issued annuity contract or whether the property is exchanged for an already existing annuity contract.

Existing regulations in §1.1011-2 govern the tax treatment of an exchange of property that constitutes a bargain sale to a charitable organization (including an exchange of property for a charitable gift annuity). Example 8 in section 2(c) of those regulations provides that any gain on such an exchange is reported ratably, rather than entirely in the year of the exchange. This notice of proposed rulemaking does not propose to change the existing regulations in §1.1011-2. However, comments are requested as to whether a change should be made in the future to conform the tax treatment of exchanges governed by §1.1011-2 to the tax treatment prescribed in these proposed regulations.

The Treasury Department and the IRS are aware that property is sometimes exchanged for an annuity contract, including a private annuity contract, for valid, non-tax reasons related to estate planning and succession planning for closely held businesses. The proposed regulations are not intended to frustrate these transactions, but will ensure that income from the transactions is accounted for in the appropriate periods. In section 453, Congress set forth rules permitting the deferral of income from a transaction that qualifies as an installment sale. Taxpayers retain the ability to structure transactions as installment sales within the meaning of section 453(b), provided the other requirements of section 453 are met. The Treasury Department and IRS request comments as to the circumstances, if any, in which an exchange of property for an annuity contract should be treated as an installment sale, and as to any changes to the regulations under section 453 that might be advisable with regard to those circumstances.

Proposed Effective Date

The Treasury Department and the IRS propose §1.1001-1(j) to be effective generally for exchanges of property for an annuity contract after October 18, 2006. Thus, the regulations would not apply to amounts received after October 18, 2006, under annuity contracts that were received in exchange for property before that date. For a limited class of transactions, however, §1.1001-1(j) is proposed to be effective for exchanges of property for an annuity contract after April 18, 2007.

The Treasury Department and the IRS propose §1.72-6(e) to be effective generally for annuity contracts received in such exchanges after October 18, 2006. For a limited class of transactions, however, §1.72-6(e) is proposed to be effective for annuity contracts received in exchange for property after April 18, 2007. The Treasury Department and the IRS also propose to declare Rev. Rul. 69-74 obsolete effective contemporaneously with the effective date of these regulations. Thus, the obsolescence would be effective April 18, 2007, for exchanges described in §1.1001-1(j)(2)(ii) and §1.72-6(e)(2)(ii), and effective October 18, 2006, for all other exchanges of property for an annuity contract.

In both regulations, the effective date is delayed for six months for transactions in which (i) the issuer of the annuity contract is an individual; (ii) the obligations under the annuity contract are not secured, either directly or indirectly; and (iii) the property transferred in the exchange is not subsequently sold or otherwise disposed of by the transferee during the two-year period beginning on the date of the exchange. The Treasury Department and the IRS believe that the later proposed effective date for these transactions provides ample notice of the proposed rules for taxpayers currently planning transactions that present the least opportunity for abuse.

Special Analyses

It has been determined that this notice of proposed rulemaking is not a significant regulatory action as defined in Executive Order 12866. Therefore, a regulatory assessment is not required. It is hereby certified that these regulations will not have a significant economic impact on a substantial number of small entities. Accordingly, a regulation flexibility analysis is not required. This certification is based on the fact that typically only natural persons within the meaning of section 72(u) exchange property for an annuity contract. In addition, these regulations do not impose new reporting, recordkeeping, or other compliance requirements on taxpayers. Pursuant to section 7805(f) of the Code, the notice of proposed rulemaking will be submitted to the Chief Counsel for Advocacy of the Small Business Administration for comment on their impact on small business.

Comments and Public Hearing

Before these proposed regulations are adopted as final regulations, consideration will be given to any written (a signed original and eight (8) copies) or electronic comments that are timely submitted to the IRS. In addition to comments on the proposed regulations more generally, the Treasury Department and the IRS specifically request comments on (i) the clarity of the proposed regulations and how they can be made easier to understand; (ii) what guidance, if any, is needed in addition to Rev. Rul. 55-119, 1955-1 CB 352, see § 601.601(d)(2), on the treatment of the issuer of an annuity contract that is not taxed under the provisions of subchapter L of the Code; (iii) whether any changes to § 1.1011-2 (concerning a bargain sale to a charitable organization in exchange for an annuity contract), conforming those regulations to the proposed regulations, would be appropriate; (iv) circumstances (and corresponding changes to the regulations under section 453, if any) in which it might be appropriate to treat an exchange of property for an annuity contract as an installment sale; (v) circumstances, if any, in which the fair market value of an annuity contract for purposes of § 1.1001-1(j) should be determined other than by tables promulgated under the authority of section 7520; and (vi) additional transactions, if any, for which the six month delayed effective date would be appropriate. All comments will be available for public inspection and copying.

A public hearing has been scheduled for February 16, 2007, at 10 a.m., in the auditorium, Internal Revenue Service, New Carrollton Building, 5000 Ellin Road, Lanham, MD 20706. All visitors must present photo identification to enter the building. Because of access restrictions, visitors will not be admitted beyond the immediate entrance area lobby more than 30 minutes before the hearing starts. For information about having your name placed on the access list to attend the hearing, see the "FOR FURTHER INFORMATION CONTACT" portion of this preamble.

The rules of 26 CFR 601.601(a)(3) apply to the hearing.

Persons who wish to present oral comments at the hearing must submit written comments by January 16, 2007, and submit an outline of the topics to be discussed and the time to be devoted to each topic (a signed original and eight (8) copies) by that same date.

A period of 10 minutes will be allotted to each person making comments. An agenda showing the scheduling of the speakers will be prepared after the deadline for receiving outlines has passed. Copies of the agenda will be available free of charge at the hearing.

Drafting Information

The principal author of these proposed regulations is James Polfer, Office of the Associate Chief Counsel (Financial Institutions and Products), Internal Revenue Service.

[¶ 49,293]   **Proposed Amendments of Regulations (REG-156779-06)**, published in the Federal Register on March 30, 2007 (corrected 5/10/2007).

[Code Sec. 901]

Foreign tax credit: Foreign tax payments: Structured passive investment arrangements: Noncompulsory payments: U.S-owned foreign entities: Loss transfers: Combined settlements.—Amendments of Reg. § 1.901-2, which affect taxpayers that claim direct and indirect foreign tax credits, are proposed. Amendments to Reg. § 1.901-2(e)(5)(iv) adopted as Temporary Reg. § 1.901-2T(e)(5)(iv) by T.D. 9416 on July 15, 2008.

AGENCY: Internal Revenue Service (IRS), Treasury.

ACTION: Notice of proposed rulemaking and notice of public hearing

SUMMARY: These proposed regulations provide guidance relating to the determination of the amount of taxes paid for purposes of section 901.

The proposed regulations affect taxpayers that claim direct and indirect foreign tax credits. This document also provides notice of a public hearing.

DATES: Written or electronic comments must be received by June 28, 2007. Outlines of topics to be discussed at the public hearing scheduled for July 30, 2007, at 10 a.m. must be received by July 9, 2007.

ADDRESSES: Send submissions to CC:PA:LPD:PR (REG-156779-06), Room 5203, Internal Revenue Service, P.O. Box 7604, Ben Franklin Station, Washington, DC 20044. Submissions may be hand delivered Monday through Friday between the hours of 8 a.m. and 4 p.m. to CC:PA:LPD:PR (REG-156779-06), Courier's Desk, Internal Revenue Service, 1111 Constitution Avenue, N.W., Washington, DC, or sent electronically via the Federal eRulemaking Portal at http://www.regulations.gov (IRS REG-156779-06). The public hearing will be held in the Auditorium of the Internal Revenue Building, 1111 Constitution Avenue, NW., Washington, DC.

FOR FURTHER INFORMATION CONTACT: Concerning submission of comments, the hearing, and/or to be placed on the building access list to attend the hearing, Kelly Banks (202) 622-7180; concerning the regulations, Bethany A. Ingwalson, (202) 622-3850 (not toll-free numbers).

SUPPLEMENTARY INFORMATION:

Background

Section 901 of the Internal Revenue Code (Code) permits taxpayers to claim a credit for income, war profits, and excess profits taxes paid or accrued (or deemed paid) during the taxable year to any foreign country or to any possession of the United States.

Section 1.901-2(a) of the regulations defines a tax as a compulsory payment pursuant to the authority of a foreign country to levy taxes, and further provides that a tax is an income, war profits, or excess profits tax if the predominant character of the tax is that of an income tax in the U.S. sense. Section 1.901-2(e) provides rules for determining the amount of tax paid by a taxpayer for purposes of section 901. Section 1.901-2(e)(5) provides that an amount paid is not a compulsory payment, and thus is not an amount of tax paid, to the extent that the amount paid exceeds the amount of liability under foreign law for tax. For purposes of determining whether an amount paid exceeds the amount of liability under foreign law for tax, § 1.901-2(e)(5) provides the following rule:

An amount paid does not exceed the amount of such liability if the amount paid is determined by the taxpayer in a manner that is consistent with a reasonable interpretation and application of the substantive and procedural provisions of foreign law (including applicable tax treaties) in such a way as to reduce, over time, the taxpayer's reasonably expected liability under foreign law for tax, and if the taxpayer exhausts all effective and practical remedies, including invocation of competent authority procedures available under applicable tax treaties, to reduce, over time, the taxpayer's liability for foreign tax (including liability pursuant to a foreign tax audit adjustment).

Section 1.901-2(e)(5) provides further that if foreign tax law includes options or elections whereby a taxpayer's liability may be shifted, in whole or part, to a different year, the taxpayer's use or failure to use such options or elections does not result in a noncompulsory payment, and that a settlement by a taxpayer of two or more issues will be evaluated on an overall basis, not on an issue-by-issue basis, in determining whether an amount is a compulsory amount. In addition, it provides that a taxpayer is not required to alter its form of doing business, its business conduct, or the form of any transaction in order to reduce its liability for tax under foreign law.

A. U.S.-Owned Foreign Entities

Commentators have raised questions regarding the application of § 1.901-2(e)(5) to a U.S. person that owns one or more foreign entities. In particular, commentators have raised questions concerning the application of the regulation when one foreign entity directly or indirectly owned by a U.S. person transfers, pursuant to a group relief type regime, a net loss to another foreign entity, which may or may not also be owned by the U.S. person. Certain commentators have expressed concern that foreign taxes paid by the transferor in a subsequent tax year might not be compulsory payments to the extent the transferor could have reduced its liability for those foreign taxes had it chosen not to transfer the net loss in the prior year. This concern arises because the current final regulations apply on a taxpayer-by-taxpayer basis, obligating each taxpayer to minimize its liability for foreign taxes over time, even though the net effect of the loss surrender may be to minimize the amount of foreign taxes paid in the aggregate by the controlled group over time.

Similar questions and concerns arise when one or more foreign subsidiaries of a U.S. person reach a combined settlement with a foreign taxing authority that results in an increase in the amount of one foreign subsidiary's foreign tax liability and a decrease in the amount of a second foreign subsidiary's foreign tax liability.

B. Certain Structured Passive Investment Arrangements

The IRS and Treasury Department have become aware that certain U.S. taxpayers are engaging in highly structured transactions with foreign counterparties in order to generate foreign tax credits. These transactions are intentionally structured to create a foreign tax liability when, removed from the elaborately engineered structure, the basic underlying business transaction generally would result in significantly less, or even no, foreign taxes. In particular, the transactions purport to convert what would otherwise be an ordinary course financing arrangement between a U.S. person and a foreign counterparty, or a portfolio investment of a U.S. person, into some form of equity ownership in a foreign special purpose vehicle (SPV). The transaction is deliberately structured to create income in the SPV for foreign tax purposes, which income is purportedly subject to foreign tax. The parties exploit differences between U.S. and foreign law in order to permit the U.S. taxpayer to claim a credit for the purported foreign tax payments while also allowing the foreign counterparty to claim a foreign tax benefit. The U.S. taxpayer and the foreign counterparty share the cost of the purported foreign tax payments through the pricing of the arrangement.

Explanation of Provisions

The proposed regulations address the application of § 1.901-2(e)(5) in cases where a U.S. person directly or indirectly owns one or more foreign entities and in cases in which a U.S. person is a party to a highly structured passive investment arrangement described in this preamble. The proposed regulations would treat as a single taxpayer for purposes of § 1.901-2(e)(5) all foreign entities with respect to which a U.S. person has a direct or indirect interest of 80 percent or more. The proposed regulations would treat foreign payments attributable to highly structured passive investment arrangements as noncompulsory payments under § 1.901-2(e)(5) and, thus, would disallow credits for such amounts.

A. U.S.-Owned Foreign Entities

Section 1.901-2(e)(5) requires a taxpayer to interpret and apply foreign law reasonably in such a way as to reduce, over time, the taxpayer's reasonably expected liability under foreign law for tax. This requirement ensures that a taxpayer will make reasonable efforts to minimize its foreign tax liability even though the taxpayer may otherwise be indifferent to the imposition of foreign tax due to the availability of the foreign tax credit. The purpose of this requirement is served if all foreign entities owned by such person, in the aggregate, satisfy the requirements of the regulation. Accordingly, for purposes of determining compliance with § 1.901-2(e)(5), the proposed regulations would treat as a single taxpayer all foreign entities in which the same U.S. person has a direct or indirect interest of 80 percent or more. For this purpose, an interest of 80 percent or more means stock possessing 80 percent or more of the vote and value (in the case of a foreign corporation) or an interest representing 80 percent or more of the income (in the case of non-corporate foreign entities).

The proposed regulations provide that if one 80 percent-owned foreign entity transfers or surrenders a net loss for the taxable year to a second such entity pursuant to a foreign law group relief or similar regime, foreign tax paid by the transferor in a different tax year does not fail to be a compulsory payment solely because such tax would not have been due had the transferor retained the net loss and carried it over to such other year. Similarly, it provides that if one or more 80 percent-owned foreign entities enter into a combined settlement under foreign law of two or more issues, such settlement will be evaluated on an overall basis, not on an issue-by-issue or entity-by-entity basis, in determining whether an amount is a compulsory amount. The proposed regulations include examples to illustrate the proposed rule.

The IRS and Treasury Department intend to monitor structures involving U.S.-owned foreign groups, including those that would be covered by the proposed regulations, to determine whether taxpayers are utilizing such structures to separate foreign taxes from the related income. The IRS and Treasury Department may issue additional regulations in the future in order to address arrangements that result in the inappropriate separation of foreign tax and income.

B. Certain Structured Passive Investment Arrangements

The structured arrangements discovered and identified by the IRS and the Treasury Department can be grouped into three general categories: (1) U.S. borrower transactions, (2) U.S. lender transactions, and (3) asset holding transactions. The transactions, including the claimed U.S. tax results, are described in section B.1 of this preamble. Section B.2 of this preamble discusses the purpose of the foreign tax credit regime and explains why allowing a credit in the transactions is inconsistent with this purpose. Section B.3 of this preamble discusses comments the IRS and the Treasury Department have received on the transactions and describes the proposed regulations. The IRS is continuing to scrutinize the transactions under current law and intends to utilize all tools available to challenge the claimed U.S. tax results in appropriate cases.

1. Categories of structured passive investment arrangements

(a) U.S. borrower transactions. The first category consists of transactions in which a U.S. person indirectly borrows funds from an unrelated foreign counterparty. If a U.S. person were to borrow funds directly from a foreign person, the U.S. person generally would make nondeductible principal payments and deductible interest payments. The U.S. person would not incur foreign tax. The foreign lender generally would owe foreign tax on its interest income. In a structured financing arrangement, the U.S. borrower attempts to convert all or a portion of its deductible interest payments and, in certain cases, its nondeductible principal payments into creditable foreign tax payments. The U.S. borrower's foreign tax credit benefit is shared by the parties through the pricing of the arrangement. See Example 1 of proposed § 1.901-2(e)(5)(iv)(D).

In a typical structured financing arrangement, the loan is made indirectly through an SPV. The foreign lender's interest income (and, in many cases, other income) is effectively isolated in the SPV. The U.S. borrower acquires a direct or indirect interest in the SPV and asserts that it has a direct or indirect equity interest in the SPV for U.S. tax purposes. The U.S. borrower claims a credit for foreign taxes imposed on the income derived by the SPV. The U.S. borrower's purported equity interest may be treated as debt for foreign tax purposes or it may be treated as an equity interest that is owned by the foreign lender for foreign tax purposes. In either case, the foreign lender is treated as owning an equity interest in the SPV for foreign tax purposes, which entitles the foreign lender to receive tax-free distributions from the SPV.

For example, assume that a U.S. person seeks to borrow $1.5 billion from a foreign person. Instead of borrowing the funds directly, the U.S. borrower forms a corporation (SPV) in the same country as the foreign counterparty. The U.S. borrower contributes $1.5 billion to SPV in exchange for 100 percent of the stock of SPV. SPV, in turn, loans the entire $1.5 billion to a corporation wholly owned by the U.S. borrower. The U.S. borrower recovers its $1.5 billion by selling its entire interest in SPV to the foreign counterparty, subject to an obligation to repurchase the interest in five years for $1.5 billion. Each year, SPV earns $120 million of interest income from the U.S. borrower's subsidiary. SPV pays $36 million of foreign tax and distributes the remaining $84 million to the foreign counterparty.

The U.S. borrower takes the position that, for U.S. tax purposes, the sale-repurchase transaction is a borrowing secured by the SPV stock. Accordingly, the U.S. borrower asserts that it owns the stock of SPV for U.S. tax purposes and has an outstanding debt obligation to the foreign counterparty. It reports the distribution from SPV as dividend income and claims indirect credits under section 902 for the $36 million of foreign taxes paid by SPV. It includes in income the cash dividend of $84 million paid to the foreign counterparty, plus a section 78 gross-up amount of $36 million, for a total of $120 million. The U.S. borrower claims a deduction of $84 million as interest on its debt obligation to the foreign counterparty. In addition, the U.S. borrower's subsidiary claims an interest deduction of $120 million. In the aggregate, the U.S. borrower and its subsidiary claim a foreign tax credit of $36 million and an interest expense deduction (net of income inclusions) of $84 million.

For foreign tax purposes, the foreign counterparty owns the equity of SPV and is not subject to additional foreign tax upon receipt of the dividend. Thus, the net result is that the foreign jurisdiction receives foreign tax payments attributable to what is in substance the lender's interest income, which is consistent with the foreign tax results that would be expected from a direct borrowing.

Both parties benefit from the arrangement. The foreign lender obtains an after-foreign tax interest rate that is higher than the after-foreign tax interest rate it would earn on a direct loan. The U.S. borrower's funding costs are lower on an after-U.S. tax basis (though not on a pre-U.S. tax basis) because it has converted interest expense into creditable foreign tax payments.

The benefit to the parties is solely attributable to the reduction in the U.S. borrower's U.S. tax liability resulting from the foreign tax credits claimed by the U.S. borrower. The foreign jurisdiction benefits from the arrangement because the amount of interest received by SPV exceeds the amount of interest that would have been received by the foreign lender if the transaction had been structured as a direct loan. As a result, the amount paid by SPV to the foreign jurisdiction exceeds the amount of foreign tax the foreign jurisdiction would have imposed on the foreign lender's interest income in connection with a direct loan.

(b) U.S. lender transactions. The second category consists of transactions in which a U.S person indirectly loans funds to an unrelated foreign counterparty. If a U.S. person were to loan the funds directly to the foreign person, the U.S. person generally would be subject to U.S. tax on its interest income and the borrower would receive a corresponding deduction for the interest expense. The U.S. person generally would not be subject to foreign tax other than, in certain circumstances, a gross basis withholding tax.

In a typical structured financing arrangement, the U.S. person advances funds to a foreign borrower indirectly through an SPV. The U.S. person asserts that its interest in the SPV is equity for U.S. tax purposes. Income of the foreign borrower (or another foreign counterparty) is effectively shifted into the SPV. The U.S. person receives cash payments from the SPV and claims a credit for foreign taxes imposed on the income recognized by the SPV for foreign tax purposes. The foreign tax credits eliminate all or substantially all of the U.S. tax the U.S. person would otherwise owe on its return and, in many cases, U.S. tax the U.S. person would otherwise owe on unrelated foreign source income. The economic cost of the foreign taxes is shared through the pricing of the arrangement. See Example 4 of proposed § 1.901-2(e)(5)(iv)(D).

For example, assume a U.S. person seeks to loan $1 billion to a foreign person. In lieu of a direct loan, the U.S. lender contributes $1 billion to a newly-formed corporation (SPV). The foreign counterparty contributes $2 billion to SPV, which is organized in the same country as the foreign counterparty. SPV contributes the total $3 billion to a second special purpose entity (RH), receiving a 99 percent equity interest in RH in exchange. The foreign counterparty owns the remaining 1 percent of RH. RH loans the funds to the foreign counterparty in exchange for a note that pays interest currently and a second zero-coupon note. RH is a corporation for U.S. tax purposes and a flow-through entity for foreign tax purposes.

Each year, the foreign counterparty pays $92 million of interest to RH, and RH accrues $113 million of interest on the zero-coupon note. RH distributes the $92 million of cash it receives to SPV. Because RH is a partnership for foreign tax purposes, SPV is required to report for foreign tax purposes 99 percent ($203 million) of the income recognized by RH. Because RH is a corporation for U.S. tax purposes, SPV recognizes only the cash distributions of $92 million for U.S. tax purposes. SPV pays foreign tax of $48 million on its net income (30 percent of $159 million, or $203 interest income less $44 million interest deduction) and distributes its remaining cash of $44 million to the U.S. lender.

The U.S. lender takes the position that it has an equity interest in SPV for U.S. tax purposes. It claims an indirect credit for the $48 million of foreign taxes paid by SPV. It includes in income the cash dividend of $44 million, plus a section 78 gross-up amount of $48 million. For foreign tax purposes, the U.S. lender's interest in SPV is debt, and the foreign borrower owns 100 percent of the equity of SPV. The foreign counterparty and SPV, in the aggregate, have a net deduction of $44 million for foreign tax purposes.

Both parties benefit from the transaction. The foreign borrower obtains "cheap financing" because the $44 million of cash distributed to the U.S. lender is less than the amount of interest it would have to pay on a direct loan with respect to which the U.S. lender would owe U.S. tax. The U.S. lender is better off on an after-U.S. tax basis because of the foreign tax credits, which eliminate the U.S. lender's U.S. tax on the "dividend" income.

The benefit to the parties is solely attributable to the reduction in the U.S. lender's U.S. tax liability resulting from the foreign tax credits claimed by the U.S. lender. The foreign jurisdiction benefits because the aggregate foreign tax result is a deduction for the foreign borrower that is less than the amount of the interest deduction the foreign borrower would have had upon a direct loan.

(c) Asset holding transactions. The third category of transactions ("asset holding transactions") consists of transactions in which a U.S. person that owns an income-producing asset moves the asset into a foreign taxing jurisdiction. For example, assume a U.S. person owns passive-type assets (such as debt obligations) generating an income stream that is subject to U.S. tax. In an asset holding transaction, the U.S. person transfers the assets to an SPV that is subject to tax in a foreign jurisdiction on the income stream. Ordinarily, such a transfer would not affect the U.S. person's after-tax position since the U.S. person could claim a credit for the foreign tax paid and, thereby, obtain a corresponding reduction in the amount of U.S. tax it would otherwise owe. In the structured transactions, however, the cost of the foreign tax is shared by a foreign person who obtains a foreign tax benefit by participating in the arrangement. Thus, the U.S. person is better off paying the foreign tax instead of U.S. tax because it does not bear the full economic burden of the foreign tax.

In a typical structured transaction, a foreign counterparty participates in the arrangement with the SPV. For example, the foreign counterparty may be considered to own a direct or indirect interest in the SPV for foreign tax purposes. The foreign counterparty's participation in the arrangement allows it to obtain a foreign tax benefit that it would not otherwise enjoy. The foreign counterparty compensates the U.S. person for this benefit in some manner. This compensation, which can be viewed as a reimbursement for a portion of the foreign tax liability resulting from the transfer of the assets, puts the U.S. person in a better after-U.S. tax position. See Example 7 of proposed § 1.901-2(e)(5)(iv)(D).

The benefit to the parties is solely attributable to the reduction in the U.S. taxpayer's U.S. tax liability resulting from the foreign tax credits claimed by the U.S. taxpayer. The foreign jurisdiction benefits because the foreign taxes purportedly paid by the SPV exceed the amount by which the foreign counterparty's taxes are reduced.

2. Purpose of the Foreign Tax Credit

The purpose of the foreign tax credit is to mitigate double taxation of foreign source income. Because the foreign tax credit provides a dollar-for-dollar reduction in U.S. tax that a U.S. person would otherwise owe, the U.S. person generally is indifferent, subject to various foreign tax credit limitations, as to whether it pays foreign tax on its foreign source income (if fully offset by the foreign tax credit) or whether it pays U.S. (and no foreign) tax on that income.

The structured arrangements described in section B.1 of this preamble violate this purpose. A common feature of all these arrangements is that the U.S. person and a foreign counterparty share the economic cost of the foreign taxes claimed as credits by the U.S. person. This creates an incentive for the U.S. person to subject itself voluntarily to the foreign tax because there is a U.S. tax motivation to do so. The result is an erosion of the U.S. tax base in a manner that is not consistent with the purpose of the foreign tax credit provisions.

Although the foreign counterparty derives a foreign tax benefit in these arrangements, the foreign jurisdiction generally is made whole because of the payments to the foreign jurisdiction made by the special purpose vehicle. In fact, the aggregate amount of payments to the foreign jurisdictions in connection with these transactions generally exceeds the amount of foreign tax that would have been imposed in the ordinary course. Only the U.S. fisc experiences a reduction in tax payments as a result of the structured arrangements.

The IRS and Treasury Department recognize that often there is a business purpose for the financing or portfolio investment underlying the otherwise elaborately engineered transactions. However, it is inconsistent with the purpose of the foreign tax credit to permit a credit for foreign taxes that result from intentionally structuring a transaction to generate foreign taxes in a manner that allows the parties to obtain duplicate tax benefits and share the cost of the tax payments. The result in these structured arrangements is that both parties as well as the foreign jurisdiction benefit at the expense of the U.S. fisc.

3. Comments and Proposed Regulations

The IRS and Treasury Department have determined that it is not appropriate to allow a credit in connection with these highly engineered transactions where the U.S. taxpayer benefits by intentionally subjecting itself to foreign tax. The proposed regulations would revise § 1.901-2(e)(5) to provide that an amount paid to a foreign country in connection with such an arrangement is not an amount of tax paid. Accordingly, under the proposed regulations, a taxpayer would not be eligible to claim a foreign tax credit for such a payment. For periods prior to the effective date of final regulations, the IRS will continue to utilize all available tools under current law to challenge the U.S. tax results claimed in connection with such arrangements, including the substance over form doctrine, the economic substance doctrine, debt-equity principles, tax ownership principles, existing § 1.901-2(e), section 269, and the partnership anti-abuse rules of § 1.701-2.

Certain commentators recommended that the IRS and Treasury Department adopt a broad anti-abuse rule that would deny a foreign tax credit in any case where allowance of the credit would be inconsistent with the purpose of the foreign tax credit regime. Other commentators recommended a narrower approach that would only deny foreign tax credits attributable to transactions that include particular features. The IRS and Treasury Department are concerned that a broad anti-abuse rule would create uncertainty for both taxpayers and the IRS. The IRS and Treasury Department have concluded that, at this time, a targeted rule denying foreign tax credits in arrangements similar to the arrangements described in section B.1 of this preamble is more appropriate.

For periods after the effective date of final regulations, the IRS and Treasury Department will continue to scrutinize other arrangements that are not covered by the regulations but are inconsistent with the purpose of the foreign tax credit. Such arrangements may include arrangements that are similar to arrangements described in the proposed regulations, but that do not meet all of the conditions included in the proposed regulations. The IRS will utilize all available tools, including those described above, to challenge the claimed U.S. tax results in appropriate cases. In addition, the IRS and Treasury Department may issue additional regulations in the future in order to address such other arrangements.

The proposed regulations would retain the general rule in the existing regulations that a taxpayer need not alter its form of doing business or the form of any transaction in order to reduce its foreign tax liability. However, the proposed regulations would provide that, notwithstanding the general rule, an amount paid to a foreign country (a "foreign payment") is not a compulsory payment, and thus is not an amount of tax paid, if the foreign payment is attributable to a structured passive investment arrangement. For this purpose, the proposed regulations would define a structured passive investment arrangement as an arrangement that satisfies six conditions. The six conditions consist of features that are common to the three types of arrangements identified in section B.1 of this preamble. The IRS and Treasury Department believe it is appropriate to treat foreign payments attributable to these arrangements as voluntary payments because such arrangements are intentionally structured to generate the foreign payment.

The first condition is that the arrangement utilizes an entity that meets two requirements (an "SPV"). The first requirement is that substantially all of the gross income (for United States tax purposes) of the entity is attributable to passive investment income and substantially all of the assets of the entity are assets held to produce such passive investment income. The second requirement is that there is a purported foreign tax payment attributable to income of the entity. The purported foreign tax may be paid by the entity itself, by the owner(s) of the entity (if the entity is treated as a pass-through entity under foreign law) or by a lower-tier entity (if the lower-tier entity is treated as a pass-through entity under U.S. law).

For purposes of this first requirement, passive investment income is defined as income described in section 954(c), with two modifications. The first modification is that if the entity is a holding company that owns a direct equity interest (other than a preferred interest) of 10 percent or more in another entity (a lower-tier entity) that is predominantly engaged in the active conduct of a trade or business (or substantially all the assets of which consist of qualifying equity interests in other entities that are predominantly engaged in the active conduct of a trade or business), passive investment income does not include income attributable to the interest in such lower-tier entity. This exception does not apply if there are arrangements under which substantially all of the opportunity for gain and risk of loss with respect to such interest in the lower-tier entity are borne by either the U.S. party or the counterparty (but not both). Accordingly, a direct equity interest in any such lower-tier entity is not held to produce passive investment income provided there are no arrangements under which substantially all of the entity's opportunity for gain and risk of loss with respect to the lower-tier entity are borne by either the U.S. party or the counterparty (but not both). This modification is based on the notion that an entity is not a passive investment vehicle of the type targeted by these regulations if the entity is a holding company for one or more operating companies. This modification ensures that a joint venture arrangement between a U.S. person and a foreign person is not treated as a passive investment arrangement solely because the joint venture is conducted through a holding company structure.

The second modification is that passive investment income is determined by disregarding sections 954(c)(3) and (c)(6) and by treating income attributable to transactions with the counterparties (described in this preamble) as ineligible for the exclusions under sections 954(h) and (i). Sections 954(c)(3) and (c)(6) provide exclusions for certain related party payments of dividends, interest, rents, and royalties. Those exclusions are not appropriate for these transactions because these transactions can be structured utilizing related party payments. The modifications to the application of sections 954(h) and (i) are intended to ensure that income derived from the counterparty cannot qualify for the exclusion from passive investment income, but will not prevent other income from qualifying for those exclusions. The IRS and Treasury Department intend that the structured financing arrangements described in this preamble do not qualify for the active banking, financing or insurance business exceptions to the definition of passive investment income. Comments are requested on whether further modifications or clarifications to the proposed regulations' definition of passive investment income are appropriate to ensure this result.

The requirement that substantially all of the assets of the entity produce passive investment income is intended to ensure that an entity engaged in an active trade or business is not treated as an SPV solely because, in a particular year, it derives only passive investment income.

The second overall condition is that a person (a "U.S. party") would be eligible to claim a credit under section 901(a) (including a credit for foreign taxes deemed paid under section 902 or 960) for all or a portion of the foreign payment if such payment were an amount of tax paid. Such eligibility to claim the credit could arise because the U.S. party would be treated as having paid or accrued the foreign payment for purposes of section 901 if it were an amount of tax paid. Alternatively, the U.S. party's eligibility to claim the credit could arise because the U.S. party owns an equity interest in the SPV or another entity that would be treated as having paid or accrued the foreign payment for purposes of section 901 if it were an amount of tax paid.

The third overall condition is that the foreign payment or payments are (or are expected to be) substantially greater than the amount of credits, if any, that the U.S. party would reasonably expect to be eligible to claim under section 901(a) if such U.S. party directly owned its proportionate share of the assets owned by the SPV other than through a branch, a permanent establishment or any other arrangement (such as an agency arrangement) that would subject the income generated by its share of the assets to a net basis foreign tax. For example, if the SPV owns a note that generates interest income with respect to which a foreign payment is made, but foreign law (including an applicable treaty) provides for a zero rate of withholding tax on interest paid to non-residents, the U.S. party would not reasonably expect to pay foreign tax for which it could claim foreign tax credits if it directly owned the note and directly earned the interest income.

The fourth condition is that the arrangement is structured in such a manner that it results in a foreign tax benefit (such as a credit, deduction, loss, exemption or a disregarded payment) for a counterparty or for a person that is related to the counterparty, but not related to the U.S. party.

The fifth condition is that the arrangement involves a counterparty. A counterparty is a person (other than the SPV) that is unrelated to the U.S. party and that (i) directly or indirectly owns 10 percent or more of the equity of the SPV under the tax laws of a foreign country in which such person is subject to tax on the basis of place of management, place of incorporation or similar criterion or otherwise subject to a net basis foreign tax or (ii) acquires 20 percent or more of the assets of the SPV under the tax laws of a foreign country in which such person is subject to tax on the basis of place of management, place of incorporation or similar criterion or otherwise subject to a net basis foreign tax.

The sixth condition is that the U.S. and an applicable foreign country treat the arrangement differently under their respective tax systems. For this purpose, an applicable foreign country is any foreign country in which either the counterparty, a person related to the counterparty (but not related to the U.S. party) or the SPV is subject to net basis tax. To provide clarity and limit the scope of this factor, the proposed regulations provide that the arrangement must be subject to one of four specified types of inconsistent treatment. Specifically, the U.S. and the foreign country (or countries) must treat one or more of the following aspects of the arrangement differently, and the U.S. treatment of the inconsistent aspect must materially affect the amount of foreign tax credits claimed, or the amount of income recognized, by the U.S. party to the arrangement: (i) The classification of an entity as a corporation or other entity subject to an entity-level tax, a partnership or other flow-through entity or an entity that is disregarded for tax purposes; (ii) the characterization as debt, equity or an instrument that is disregarded for tax purposes of an instrument issued in the transaction, (iii) the proportion of the equity of the SPV (or an entity that directly or indirectly owns the SPV) that is considered to be owned directly or indirectly by the U.S. party and the counterparty; or (iv) the amount of taxable income of the SPV for one or more tax years during which the arrangement is in effect.

Under the proposed regulations, a foreign payment would not be a compulsory payment if it is attributable to an arrangement that meets the six conditions. The proposed regulations would treat a foreign payment as attributable to such an arrangement if the foreign payment is attributable to income of the SPV. Such foreign payments include a payment by the SPV, a payment by the owner of the SPV (if the SPV is a pass-through entity under foreign law) and a payment by a lower-tier entity that is treated as a pass-through entity under U.S. law. For this purpose, a foreign payment is not treated as attributable to the income of the SPV if the foreign payment is a gross basis withholding tax imposed on a distribution or payment from the SPV to the U.S. party. Such taxes could be considered to be noncompulsory payments because the U.S. party intentionally subjects itself to the taxes as part of the arrangement. However, the IRS and Treasury Department have determined that such taxes should not be treated as attributable to the arrangement because, among other reasons, the foreign counterparty generally does not derive a duplicative foreign tax benefit and, therefore, generally does not share the economic cost of such taxes.

The IRS and Treasury Department considered excluding all foreign payments with respect to which the economic cost is not shared from the definition of foreign payments attributable to the arrangement, but determined that such a rule would be difficult to administer. The IRS and Treasury Department request comments on whether it would be appropriate to exclude certain foreign payments from the definition of foreign taxes attributable to the structured passive investment arrangement. Comments should address the rationale and administrable criteria for identifying any such exclusions.

Certain commentators recommended that the proposed regulations include a requirement that the foreign tax credits attributable to the arrangement be disproportionate to the amount of taxable income attributable to the arrangement. This recommendation has not been adopted for three reasons. First, the IRS and Treasury Department were concerned that such a requirement would create too much uncertainty and would be unduly burdensome for taxpayers and the IRS. Second, the extent to which interest and other expenses, as well as returns on borrowed funds and capital, should be considered attributable to a particular arrangement is not entirely clear. A narrow view could present opportunities for manipulation, especially for financial institutions having numerous alternative placements of leverage for use within the group, while an expansive view could undercut the utility of such a test. Third, the fundamental concern in these transactions is that they create an incentive for taxpayers voluntarily to subject themselves to foreign tax. This concern exists irrespective of whether the particular arrangement generates a disproportionate amount of foreign tax credits.

The IRS and Treasury Department considered whether it would be appropriate to permit a taxpayer to treat a foreign payment attributable to an arrangement that meets the definition of a structured passive investment arrangement as an amount of tax paid, if the taxpayer can show that tax considerations were not a principal purpose for the structure of the arrangement. Alternatively, the IRS and Treasury Department considered whether it would be appropriate to treat a foreign payment as an amount of tax paid if a taxpayer shows that there is a substantial business purpose for utilizing a hybrid instrument or entity, which would not include reducing the taxpayer's after-tax costs or enhancing the taxpayer's after-tax return through duplicative foreign tax benefits. The IRS and Treasury Department determined not to include such a rule in these proposed regulations due to administrability concerns. Comments are requested, however, on whether the final regulations should include such a rule as well as how such a rule could be made to be administrable in practice, including what reasonably ascertainable evidence would be sufficient to establish such a substantial non-tax business purpose, or the lack of a tax-related principal purpose. Comments should also address whether it would be appropriate to adopt a broader anti-abuse rule and permit a taxpayer to demonstrate that it should not apply.

C. Effective Date

The regulations are proposed to be effective for foreign taxes paid or accrued during taxable years of the taxpayer ending on or after the date on which the final regulations are published in the Federal Register. No inference is intended regarding the U.S. tax consequences of structured passive investment arrangements prior to the effective date of the regulations.

Special Analyses

It has been determined that this notice of proposed rulemaking is not a significant regulatory action as defined in Executive Order 12866. Therefore, a regulatory assessment is not required. It also has been determined that section 553(b) of the Administrative Procedure Act (5 U.S.C. chapter 5) does not apply to these regulations, and because the regulations do not impose a collection of information on small entities, the Regulatory Flexibility Act (5 U.S.C. chapter 6), does not apply. Pursuant to section 7805(f) of the Internal Revenue Code, this regulation has been submitted to the Chief Counsel for Advocacy of the Small Business Administration for comment on its impact on small businesses.

Comments and Public Hearing

Before these proposed regulations are adopted as final regulations, consideration will be given to any written (a signed original and eight (8) copies) or electronic comments that are submitted timely to the IRS. The IRS and Treasury Department request comments on the clarity of the proposed regulations and how they can be made easier to understand. All comments will be available for public inspection and copying.

A public hearing has been scheduled for July 30, 2007, at 10 a.m. in the Internal Revenue Building, 1111 Constitution Avenue, NW., Washington, DC. All visitors must present photo identification to enter the building. Because of access restrictions, visitors will not be admitted beyond the immediate entrance area more than 30 minutes before the hearing starts. For information about having your name placed on the building access list to attend the hearing, see the FOR FURTHER INFORMATION CONTACT section of this preamble.

The rules of 26 CFR 601.601(a)(3) apply to the hearing. Persons who wish to present oral comments must submit electronic or written comments and an outline of the topics to be discussed and time to be devoted to each topic (a signed original and eight (8) copies) by July 9, 2007. A period of 10 minutes will be allotted to each person for making comments. An agenda showing the scheduling of the speakers will be prepared after the deadline for receiving outlines has passed. Copies of the agenda will be available free of charge at the hearing.

Drafting Information

The principal author of these regulations is Bethany A. Ingwalson, Office of Associate Chief Counsel (International). However, other personnel from the IRS and the Treasury Department participated in their development.

[¶ 49,297]   Proposed Amendments of Regulations (REG-123365-03), published in the Federal Register on May 8, 2007 (corrected 6/5/2007).

[Code Sec. 355]

Corporate distributions: Section 355 distribution: Active trade or business requirement: Acquisition of trade or business: Affiliated group members: Pre-distribution period: Multi-step acquisitions.—Amendments of Reg. §§ 1.355-0, 1.355-1 and 1.355-3, providing guidance regarding the active trade or business requirement under section 355(b) of the Internal Revenue Code, are proposed.

AGENCY: Internal Revenue Service (IRS), Treasury.

ACTION: Notice of proposed rulemaking.

SUMMARY: This document contains proposed regulations that provide guidance regarding the active trade or business requirement under section 355(b) of the Internal Revenue Code. These proposed regulations provide guidance on issues involving the active trade or business requirement under section 355(b), including guidance resulting from the enactment of section 355(b)(3). These proposed regulations will affect corporations and their shareholders.

DATES: Written or electronic comments and requests for a public hearing must be received by August 8, 2007.

ADDRESSES: Send submissions to: CC:PA:LPD:PR (REG-123365-03), room 5203, Internal Revenue Service, PO Box 7604, Ben Franklin Station, Washington, DC 20044. Submissions may be hand-delivered Monday through Friday between the hours of 8 a.m. and 4 p.m. to CC:PA:LPD:PR (REG-123365-03), Courier's Desk, Internal Revenue Service, 1111 Constitution Avenue, NW., Washington, DC, or sent electronically via the Federal eRulemaking Portal at *www.regulations.gov* (IRS REG-123365-03).

FOR FURTHER INFORMATION CONTACT: Concerning the proposed regulations, Russell P. Subin, (202) 622-7790; concerning submissions and the hearing, Kelly Banks, (202) 622-7180 (not toll-free numbers).

SUPPLEMENTARY INFORMATION:

Background and Explanation of Provisions

A. Background and Overview of the Key Aspects of the Proposed Regulations

1. Background

Section 355(a) of the Internal Revenue Code (Code) provides that, under certain circumstances, a corporation may distribute stock and securities of a corporation it controls to its shareholders and security holders without causing either the corporation or its shareholders and security holders to recognize income, gain or loss. Sections 355(a)(1)(C) and 355(b)(1) generally require that the distributing corporation (distributing) and controlled corporation (controlled) each be engaged, immediately after the distribution, in the active conduct of a trade or business. Section 355(b)(2)(A) provides that a corporation shall be treated as engaged in the active conduct of a trade or business if and only if it is engaged in the active conduct of a trade or business, or substantially all of its assets consist of stock and securities of a corporation controlled by it (immediately after the distribution) which is so engaged. For this purpose, control is defined under section 368(c). All references to control in this preamble are references to control as defined in section 368(c).

Section 202 of the Tax Increase Prevention and Reconciliation Act of 2005, Public Law 109-222 (120 Stat. 345, 348) (TIPRA) amended section 355(b) by adding section 355(b)(3). Section 355(b)(3)(A), as amended by Division A, Section 410 of the Tax Relief and Health Care Act of 2006, Public Law

109-432 (120 Stat. 2922, 2963), provides that in the case of any distribution made after May 17, 2006, a corporation shall be treated as meeting the requirement of section 355(b)(2)(A) if and only if such corporation is engaged in the active conduct of a trade or business. Section 355(b)(3)(B) provides that for purposes of section 355(b)(3)(A) (and, consequently, section 355(b)(2)(A)), all members of such corporation's separate affiliated group (SAG) shall be treated as one corporation (SAG rule). For purposes of the preceding sentence, a corporation's SAG is the affiliated group which would be determined under section 1504(a) if such corporation were the common parent and section 1504(b) did not apply.

Thus, the separate affiliated group of distributing (DSAG) is the affiliated group that consists of distributing as the common parent and all corporations affiliated with distributing through stock ownership described in section 1504(a)(1)(B) (regardless of whether the corporations are includible corporations under section 1504(b)). The separate affiliated group of controlled (CSAG) is determined in a similar manner (with controlled as the common parent). Accordingly, unlike prior law, a corporation is not treated as engaged in the active conduct of a trade or business solely as a result of substantially all of its assets consisting of stock, or stock and securities, of one or more corporations that are merely controlled by it (immediately after the distribution) each of which is engaged in the active conduct of a trade or business.

Section 355(b)(2)(B) requires that the trade or business have been actively conducted throughout the five-year period ending on the date of the distribution (pre-distribution period). Section 355(b)(2)(C) provides that the trade or business must not have been acquired in a transaction in which gain or loss was recognized, in whole or in part, within the pre-distribution period. Section 355(b)(2)(D), as amended in 1987 and 1988, provides that control of a corporation which (at the time of acquisition of control) was conducting the trade or business must not have been directly or indirectly acquired by any distributee corporation or by distributing during the pre-distribution period in a transaction in which gain or loss was recognized, in whole or in part. See Public Law 100-203 (101 Stat. 1330, 1330-411 (1987)) and Public Law 100-647 (102 Stat. 3342, 3605 (1988)). For purposes of section 355(b)(2)(D), all distributee corporations which are members of the same affiliated group (as defined in section 1504(a) without regard to section 1504(b)) shall be treated as one distributee corporation. The requirements under section 355(b) are collectively referred to in this preamble as either the active trade or business requirement or the requirements of section 355(b).

Accordingly, the requirements of section 355(b) are generally satisfied if distributing and controlled each have engaged in the active conduct of a trade or business throughout the pre-distribution period, are so engaged immediately after the distribution, and there have been no acquisitions of control of distributing or controlled during such period.

The active trade or business requirement is one of several requirements that must be satisfied in order for a distribution to qualify under section 355. For example, section 355(a)(1)(B) states that a transaction must not be used principally as a device for distributing the earnings and profits of distributing, controlled, or both. In addition, § 1.355-2(b)(1) provides that section 355 will apply to a transaction only if it is carried out for one or more corporate business purposes.

The active trade or business requirement, in tandem with the device prohibition and business purpose requirement, limits a corporation's ability to convert dividend income into capital gain through the use of a section 355 distribution. See S. Rep. No. 83-1622, at 50-51 (1954) and *Coady v. Commissioner*, 33 TC 771, 777 (1960), *acq.*, 1965-2 CB 4, *aff'd*, 289 F.2d 490 (6th Cir. 1961). In *Coady*, the Tax Court stated that one purpose of section 355(b) is "to prevent the tax-free separation of *active* and *inactive* assets into *active* and *inactive* corporate entities." The court also stated that a tax-free separation under section 355 "will involve the separation only of those assets attributable to the carrying on of an active trade or business . . . ." *Coady*, 33 TC at 777.

The IRS and Treasury Department are aware of a number of issues that have arisen regarding the active trade or business requirement, including issues arising as a result of the enactment of section 355(b)(3). The following sections describe the active trade or business requirement and the significant issues that are addressed in these proposed regulations. No inference should be drawn from these proposed regulations regarding the definition of trade or business or active trade or business under any other provision of the Code or Treasury regulations, even if such provision specifically references section 355. Comments are requested as to whether or the extent to which these proposed regulations should apply to other provisions that specifically reference section 355.

2. *Overview of the key aspects of the proposed regulations*

Principally, these proposed regulations provide guidance regarding the application of section 355(b)(3), the application of the acquisition rules in section 355(b)(2)(C) and (D) and the impact thereon of section 355(b)(3), and the determination of whether a corporation is engaged in a trade or business through the attribution of trade or business assets and activities from a partnership.

As discussed in section A. 1. of this preamble, section 355(b)(3) treats all SAG members as one corporation. Accordingly, as discussed in detail in section B. of this preamble, these proposed regulations provide that subsidiary SAG members (SAG members that are not the common parent of such SAG) are treated like divisions of distributing or controlled, as the case may be. These proposed regulations also clarify that controlled may be a DSAG member during the pre-distribution period. Most significantly, these provisions treat a stock acquisition that results in a corporation becoming a subsidiary SAG member as an asset acquisition. As a result, the applicability of section 355(b)(2)(D) is substantially reduced. Further, as discussed in section E. of this preamble, this treatment alters the analysis regarding whether an existing business may be expanded as a result of a stock acquisition.

Notwithstanding that these proposed regulations provide that certain stock acquisitions may be treated as asset acquisitions under section 355(b)(3), purchases of stock of controlled during the pre-distribution period may be subject to section 355(a)(3)(B). See section F. of this preamble.

As discussed in detail in section C. and section D. of this preamble, these proposed regulations interpret section 355(b)(2)(C) and (D) to mean that a corporation generally cannot use its assets to acquire a trade or business to be relied on to facilitate a distribution under section 355. Accordingly, these proposed regulations generally prohibit acquisitions made in exchange for distributing's assets even if no gain or loss is recognized in connection with the acquisition. Further, these proposed regulations provide certain exceptions to the literal application of section 355(b)(2)(C) and (D) for acquisitions in which gain or loss is recognized where the purposes of that section are not violated. However, these proposed regulations do not disregard the recognition of gain or loss in transactions between affiliates unless the affiliates are members of the same SAG. See section G. of this preamble.

Section I. of this preamble explains how these proposed regulations clarify a corporation's ability to be attributed the trade or business assets and activities of a partnership. Most significantly, these partnership provisions yield results similar to the rules regarding the satisfaction of the continuity of business enterprise requirement, and thus allow a partner to be attributed the partnership's trade or business assets and activities where the partner owns a significant interest in the partnership.

B. *TIPRA*

Congress enacted section 355(b)(3) because it was concerned that, prior to a distribution under section 355, corporate groups conducting business in separate corporate entities often had to undergo elaborate restructurings to place active businesses in the proper entities to satisfy the active trade or business requirement. See, for example, H.R. Rep. No. 109-304, at 53, 54 (2005). By treating a SAG as one corporation, Congress believed that it would greatly reduce the need for such restructurings. However, the introduction of the affiliation-based SAG rule into the active trade or business requirement significantly impacts the application of section 355(b)(2) in certain situations.

Accordingly, consistent with congressional intent, these proposed regulations provide several rules interpreting section 355(b)(3) in a manner that diminishes the need for pre-distribution restructurings while fully integrating the various provisions in section 355(b). These rules are intended to more closely reflect the way corporate groups structure their businesses while, at the same time, ensuring that the purposes underlying section 355(b)(2)(C) and (D) are not circumvented.

Specifically, to accomplish these objectives the IRS and Treasury Department believe that it is appropriate to apply the SAG rule by disregarding the separate existence of all subsidiary SAG members for purposes of determining whether distributing and controlled satisfy the requirements of section 355(b).

1. *SAG rule applicable during the pre-distribution period*

The IRS and Treasury Department believe that it is appropriate to apply the SAG rule for purposes of determining whether the trade or business was actively conducted throughout the pre-distribution period and whether the requirements of section 355(b)(2)(C) or (D) have been violated.

The SAG rule applies for purposes of determining whether distributing and controlled are engaged in the active conduct of a trade or business immediately after the distribution. Specifically, the legislative history to section 355(b)(3) describes the corporations included in the DSAG and CSAG by reference to post-distribution affiliation. See H.R. Rep. No. 109-455, at 88 (2006) (Conf. Rep.); H.R. Rep. No. 109-304, at 54 (2005). However, there is nothing in the statute or legislative history that precludes the SAG rule from applying throughout the pre-distribution period.

The IRS and Treasury Department believe that applying the SAG rule throughout the pre-distribution period is consistent with the single-entity approach. If the SAG rule is not applied during the pre-distribution period, there may be unintended consequences. For example, assume that an active trade or business is segmented among the SAG members in a manner that precludes any one member from individually being treated as engaged in an active trade or business. Under the SAG rule the segments are aggregated and may be treated as a single active trade or business immediately after the distribution. However, if the SAG rule is not applied throughout the pre-distribution period, there would be no five-year active trade or business because no one member would be engaged in that trade or business. The IRS and Treasury Department do not believe there is any policy reason to apply the SAG rule in such a disparate manner. Accordingly, these proposed regulations apply the SAG rule throughout the pre-distribution period. This approach is consistent with Congressional intent to view SAGs as an aggregate for purposes of the active trade or business requirement.

Because the SAG rule treats all SAG members as one corporation, the separate existence of subsidiary SAG members is disregarded and all assets (and activities) owned (and performed) by SAG members are treated as owned (and performed) by distributing or controlled, as the case may be, for purposes of determining whether distributing or controlled is engaged in a five-year active trade or business. Therefore, where one DSAG or CSAG member satisfies the active trade or business requirement, distributing or controlled, as the case may be, satisfies the active trade or business requirement.

Consistent with the foregoing, these proposed regulations provide that the SAG rule also applies for purposes of determining whether there has been an impermissible acquisition, as discussed in section C. of this preamble, of a trade or business during the pre-distribution period under section 355(b)(2)(C) or (D). Because the SAG rule disregards the separate existence of subsidiary SAG members, these proposed regulations generally treat stock acquisitions that result in a corporation becoming a subsidiary SAG member as a direct acquisition of any assets (or activities) owned (or performed) by the acquired corporation. Further, these proposed regulations generally disregard transfers of assets (or activities) that are owned (or performed) by the SAG immediately before and immediately after the transfer. Such transfers cannot result in an acquisition. Under the SAG rule, such transfers have the effect of a transfer between divisions of a single corporation.

2. *The DSAG may include CSAG members throughout the pre-distribution period*

The IRS and Treasury Department believe that it is appropriate to include the CSAG members in the DSAG during the pre-distribution period if the applicable affiliation requirements are satisfied. The IRS and Treasury Department believe this approach is consistent with the purposes of section 355(b)(3) and the SAG rule's general single-entity approach, and provides flexibility for the division of SAG members between distributing and controlled.

For example, assume that during the pre-distribution period, segments or portions of the business to be conducted by controlled are held by distributing (or other subsidiaries that are not directly or indirectly owned by controlled) and that distributing intends to transfer those portions of the business to controlled immediately prior to the distribution. If the DSAG does not include the CSAG members throughout the pre-distribution period, it is possible that neither SAG would be engaged in the active conduct of that trade or business throughout the pre-distribution period, because neither SAG would have all the appropriate segments of that business to satisfy the active trade or business requirement. The IRS and Treasury Department believe that such a result is inconsistent with the purposes of section 355(b)(3). Accordingly, by including the CSAG members in the DSAG throughout the pre-distribution period if the ownership requirements are satisfied, these proposed regulations give appropriate credit to five-year active trades or businesses regardless of how the assets and activities may be owned (and performed) by the SAG members throughout the pre-distribution period.

3. *Acquisitions of stock in subsidiary SAG members*

Section 355(b)(3) treats SAG members as one corporation for purposes of satisfying the requirements of section 355(b). As a result, the SAG rule alters the application of section 355(b)(2)(C) and (D) with respect to the acquisition of stock of a corporation that is or becomes a subsidiary SAG member. Further, because section 355(b)(3) supplanted the holding company rule in section 355(b)(2)(A), section 355(b)(2)(D) is now only applicable to certain acquisitions of stock of distributing and certain acquisitions of stock of controlled.

The SAG rule alters the application of section 355(b)(2)(C) and (D) with respect to the acquisition of stock of a corporation that is or becomes a subsidiary SAG member. Section 355(b)(3) treats SAG members as one corporation for purposes of satisfying section 355(b). Consequently, a transaction that results in a corporation — including controlled — becoming a subsidiary SAG member is treated as a direct acquisition of all the assets (and activities) owned (and performed) by the acquired corporation at the time of the acquisition. Thus, such an acquisition is tested under section 355(b)(2)(C) rather than section 355(b)(2)(D). Nevertheless, as discussed in sections B.4. and C.3.a.ii. of this preamble, section 355(b)(2)(D) has continuing limited application.

In addition, an acquisition that results in a corporation becoming a subsidiary SAG member in a transaction in which gain or loss is recognized might satisfy the requirements of section 355(b)(2)(C) as an expansion of one of the acquiring SAG's existing businesses, as discussed in section E. of this preamble. Finally, because the SAG rule treats subsidiary SAG members like divisions, the acquisition of additional stock of a current subsidiary SAG member has no effect for purposes of applying section 355(b)(2)(C).

4. *Acquisitions of control of controlled where it is not a DSAG member*

While section 355(b)(2)(D) is not applicable to acquisitions of stock of subsidiary SAG members, the requirements of section 355(b)(2)(D) must be satisfied where the DSAG acquires control of controlled where controlled is not and does not become a DSAG member prior to the distribution. This rule applies where distributing acquires stock constituting control of controlled but not stock meeting the requirements of section 1504(a)(2).

C. *Acquisitions of a Trade or Business*

Section 355(b)(2)(C) and (D) generally provides that a trade or business acquired, directly or indirectly, during the pre-distribution period will not satisfy the active trade or business requirement unless it was acquired in a transaction in which no gain or loss was recognized. The IRS and Treasury Department believe that these provisions have been and should continue to be interpreted and applied in a manner consistent with the overall purposes of section 355. For example, in certain situations, transactions in which gain or loss is recognized have been found not to violate the purposes of section 355(b)(2)(C) and (D). See, for example, *C.I.R. v. Gordon*, 382 F.2d 499 (2d Cir.1967), *rev'd on other grounds*, 391 US 83 (1968) (discussed in section C.2. of this preamble). Additionally, while the enactment of section 355(b)(3) substantially revised how distributing and controlled may satisfy the active trade or business requirement, TIPRA did not contain conforming amendments to section 355(b)(2)(C) and (D). As such, the IRS and Treasury Department also believe that a purpose-based interpretation of section 355(b)(2) is essential to harmonize these provisions. Accordingly, these proposed regulations interpret and apply section 355(b)(2)(C) and (D), and section 355(b)(3), in a manner consistent with their purpose, even if not always consistent with the literal language of the statute.

1. *Purpose of section 355(b)(2)(C) and (D)*

Section 355 "contemplates that a tax-free separation shall involve only the separation of assets attributable to the carrying on of an active business." S. Rep. No. 83-1622, at 50 (1954). The active trade or business requirement is intended to ensure that only these types of separations qualify under section 355. Further, it operates as an additional safeguard to the device prohibition (a prohibition against disguised dividends) in section 355(a)(1)(B).

As discussed in section A. of this preamble, the active trade or business requirement is designed to limit the potential for the conversion of dividend income into capital gain through a section 355 distribution. Specifically, section 355(b)(2)(C) and (D) is intended to prevent dividend avoidance otherwise available through the purchase of a new business in order to facilitate a tax-free distribution under section 355. See *Gordon*, 382 F.2d at 506-507 (stating that "[t]o safeguard against this possibility, subsections (b)(2)(C) and (D) prohibit acquisition of a trade or business, or of a corporation, in a transaction in which gain or loss was recognized."). Thus, the statute prohibits acquisitions of a trade or business in which gain or loss is recognized. Nevertheless, the recognition of gain or loss, in and of itself, does not violate the purposes of section 355. Rather, recognition of gain or loss is generally indicative of the type of consideration used in the transaction. Typically, a transaction in which gain or loss is recognized consists of an acquisition in exchange for assets. On the other hand, a transaction in which no gain or loss is recognized typically consists of an acquisition in exchange for the corporation's equity.

Accordingly, the IRS and Treasury Department believe that the common purpose of section 355(b)(2)(C) and (D) is to prevent distributing from using assets — instead of its stock or stock of a corporation in control of distributing — to acquire a new trade or business in anticipation of distributing that trade or business (or facilitating the distribution of another trade or business) to its shareholders in a tax-free distribution. A distribution of a corporation holding assets that would have been used to effect a purchase generally would be treated as a dividend and section 355 was not intended to allow a tax-free separation of such assets. Acquiring a new trade or business using these assets and distributing it (or an existing trade or business) would effectively accomplish such a separation, and should not qualify under section 355.

Complementing the principle that the common purpose of section 355(b)(2)(C) and (D) is to prevent distributing from using its assets — instead of its stock, or stock of a corporation in control of distributing — to acquire a new trade or business is the notion that section 355 is intended to apply to separations of active trades or businesses with which the participants have a historic relationship. Section 355, like the reorganization provisions, involves the maintenance by the shareholders of a continuing interest in their business or businesses in modified corporate forms. For section 355 to apply to a divisive transaction, it is essential that distributing and its shareholders have a historic relationship with the active trades or businesses in the two resulting corporations. See, for example, § 1.355-1(b) ("[section 355] applies only to the separation of existing businesses that have been in active operation for at least five years . . . and which, in general, have been owned, directly or indirectly, for at least five years by the distributing corporation"). These requirements ensure that the historic owners of the acquired trade or business are participants in the divisive transaction and minimize the potential for transactions that violate the common purpose of section 355(b)(2)(C) and (D).

Where distributing issues its own equity (or uses the equity of a corporation in control of distributing) to acquire an active trade or business in a transaction in which no gain or loss is recognized, distributing is not acquiring the trade or business in exchange for its assets and the historic owners of the trade or business will be participants in the divisive transaction. In such cases, the common purpose of section 355(b)(2)(C) and (D) is carried out.

Finally, an additional purpose of section 355(b)(2)(D) is to prevent a distributee corporation from acquiring control of distributing in anticipation of a distribution to which section 355 would otherwise apply, enabling the disposition of controlled without the proper recognition of corporate level gain. See H.R. Rep. No. 100-391, at 1080, 1082-1083 (1987).

2. *Current law and the § 1.355-3(b)(4) regulations*

Under current law, several authorities depart from the literal language of section 355(b)(2)(C) and (D) in order to carry out the common purpose underlying section 355(b)(2)(C) and (D). For example, in *Gordon*, gain was recognized when distributing transferred a trade or business to controlled. The Second Circuit concluded that, even though gain was recognized, section 355(b)(2)(C) was not violated because new assets were not brought within the combined corporate shells of distributing and controlled. Therefore, the common purpose of section 355(b)(2)(C) and (D) was not violated. Furthermore, Rev. Rul. 69-461 (1969-2 CB 52) held that a first-tier subsidiary's taxable distribution of stock of a second-tier subsidiary to its parent did not violate section 355(b)(2)(D). The ruling stated that section 355(b)(2)(D) is intended to prevent the acquisition of control of a corporation from a party not within the direct or indirect control of distributing. In addition, Rev. Rul. 78-442 (1978-2 CB 143) held that gain under section 357(c) on the transfer from distributing to controlled does not violate section 355(b)(2)(C). Rev. Rul. 78-442 stated that section 355(b)(2)(C) is intended to prevent the acquisition of a trade or business by distributing or controlled from an outside party in a taxable transaction within five years of a distribution.

Similarly, § 1.355-3(b)(4) (generally applicable to distributions on or before December 15, 1987, but applied in various situations by the IRS administratively to distributions occurring after that date) provides an exception from the literal language of section 355(b)(2)(C) and (D) for the direct or indirect acquisition of a trade or business by one member of an affiliated group from another member of the group, stating that an acquisition from another member of the affiliated group "is not the type of transaction to which section 355(b)(2)(C) and (D) is intended to apply." See § 1.355-3(b)(4)(iii).

Section 1.355-3(b)(4) also departs from the literal language of section 355(b) in providing that a trade or business acquired, directly or indirectly, within the pre-distribution period in a transaction in which the basis of the assets acquired was not determined in whole or in part by reference to the transferor's basis does not qualify under section 355(b)(2), even though no gain or loss was recognized by the transferor. See § 1.355-3(b)(4)(i). The reason for this departure is that in some circumstances a transaction in which no gain or loss is recognized may nevertheless constitute a prohibited acquisition of a trade or business in exchange for assets.

3. *The proposed regulations*

Consistent with current law (and § 1.355-3(b)(4)), these proposed regulations generally prohibit acquisitions in which gain or loss was recognized but apply section 355(b)(2)(C) and (D) in a manner consistent with their purposes. Accordingly, these proposed regulations provide for certain exceptions for acquisitions in which gain or loss is recognized, and prohibit certain transactions in which no gain or loss is recognized. a. Certain Transactions in Which Recognized Gain or Loss is Disregarded

Under these proposed regulations, certain acquisitions are excepted from the general rule under section 355(b)(2)(C) and (D) that a trade or business, or control of a corporation engaged in a trade or business, cannot satisfy the active trade or business requirement if it was acquired during the pre-distribution period in a transaction in which gain or loss was recognized. These transactions are so excepted because they do not violate the purposes of section 355(b)(2)(C) and (D).

i. Certain Acquisitions By the DSAG or CSAG

These proposed regulations provide a number of exceptions to the application of section 355(b)(2)(C) and (D) not contained in the current regulations (or § 1.355-3(b)(4)). One of these exceptions disregards any gain or loss recognized in connection with an acquisition by the CSAG from the DSAG of a trade or business, an interest in a partnership engaged in a trade or business, or stock of a corporation engaged in a trade or business. This exception is appropriate because it is not a use of distributing's assets to acquire the trade or business.

Another exception disregards gain or loss recognized in an acquisition solely as a result of the payment of cash to shareholders for fractional shares where the cash paid represents a mere rounding off of the fractional shares in the exchange and is not separately bargained for consideration. The IRS and Treasury Department believe that this is not the type of transaction to which section 355(b)(2)(C) or (D) is intended to apply. Although such a transaction involves a small use of assets, these proposed regulations except such acquisitions because the small amount of assets are not separately bargained for and are used merely to simplify the exchange. Other authorities reach similar conclusions in the context of reorganizations. See Rev. Rul. 66-365 (1966-2 CB 116), amplified by Rev. Rul. 81-81 (1981-1 CB 122) (concluding that cash in lieu of fractional shares does not violate the solely for voting stock requirement of section 368(a)(1)(B) and (C) because it was merely a mathematical rounding off for simplicity, and the transaction "was for all practical purposes 'solely in exchange for voting stock'").

In addition, as discussed in section G. of this preamble, these proposed regulations provide a limited exception for taxable acquisitions from affiliates that are members of the same SAG. Specifically, acquisitions between SAG members (where the assets (or activities) are owned (or performed) by the SAG immediately before and immediately after the transfer) are disregarded whether they are taxable or not.

Like the current regulations, these proposed regulations provide that acquisitions that expand a pre-existing business are generally exempted from the nonrecognition requirement. See § 1.355-3(b)(3)(ii). While these transactions may involve the use of the DSAG's or CSAG's assets, they are not acquisitions of a new or different trade or business. Because the DSAG or CSAG, as the case may be, is already in the business, such transactions are not considered acquisitions of a trade or business under section 355(b)(2)(C) and (D).

ii. Certain Acquisitions By a Distributee Corporation

Consistent with the principles of Rev. Rul. 74-5 (1974-1 CB 82), obsoleted by Rev. Rul. 89-37 (1989-1 CB 107), these proposed regulations disregard the recognition of gain or loss in applying section 355(b)(2)(D) to certain acquisitions of the stock of distributing by a distributee corporation. Prior to the 1987 and 1988 amendments noted in section A.1. of this preamble, section 355(b)(2)(D) was not violated in a case where distributing distributed the stock of controlled even though a purchaser acquired distributing's stock during the pre-distribution period in a transaction in which gain or loss was recognized. See Rev. Rul. 74-5 (reasoning that the purpose of section 355(b)(2)(D) was to prevent distributing, rather than the shareholder of distributing, from accumulating excess funds to purchase the stock of a corporation engaged in an active trade or business). However, Rev. Rul. 74-5 held that the purchaser could not then further distribute the stock of controlled until five years after such purchase, reasoning that the purchaser, the distributing corporation in the second distribution, indirectly acquired the stock of controlled through another corporation, the distributing corporation in the first distribution.

The 1987 and 1988 amendments to section 355(b)(2)(D) prohibited such transactions because of a concern that such acquisitions were similar to transactions that permitted a corporation to dispose of an appreciated subsidiary without the proper recognition of gain contrary to the repeal of the *General Utilities* doctrine. For example, assume P, a corporation, acquired the stock of D in a transaction in which gain or loss was recognized and D immediately distributed the stock of C to P in a section 355 transaction. P would allocate its basis in the newly acquired D stock between the D stock and the C stock received in the distribution. P could then potentially sell the C stock without the appropriate recognition of gain. See H.R. Rep. No. 100-391, at 1080, 1082-1083 (1987).

However, there are transactions that violate the literal requirements of section 355(b)(2)(D) but do not violate the purpose of the 1987 and 1988 amendments. For example, assume that for more than five years, T, a corporation, owned all of the stock of D, which in turn owned all the stock of C. Throughout this period, D and C have each engaged in the active conduct of a trade or business. In year 6, P acquires the stock of T in a transaction in which gain or loss is recognized, and holds the T stock with a cost basis determined under section 1012. In year 7, P liquidates T in a transaction to which section 332 applies and in which no gain or loss is recognized, thereby eliminating its cost basis in the T stock. Thereafter, P holds the D stock with a basis equal to T's basis in the D stock. In year 8, D distributes the C stock to P. Under these facts, P cannot dispose of the D or C stock without recognizing the same amount of gain or loss that T would have recognized.

Similarly, assume the same facts as the previous example, except that in year 6 P acquires all of T's assets, including the D stock, in exchange for P stock and cash in a reorganization described in section 368(a)(1)(A). Because all of the cash is distributed to the T shareholders, T does not recognize any gain, and P's basis in the D stock is equal to T's basis in the D stock. See section 362(b). In year 7, D distributes the C stock to P. Under these facts, P cannot dispose of the D or C stock without recognizing the same amount of gain or loss that T would have recognized.

The IRS and Treasury Department believe that the distributee corporation language in section 355(b)(2)(D)(i) is intended only to prevent transactions that are contrary to the repeal of the *General Utilities* doctrine. In both of the examples just described, neither the D stock nor C stock can be disposed of in a manner that is contrary to the repeal of the *General Utilities* doctrine. Accordingly, these proposed regulations provide that section 355(b)(2)(D) is not violated where there is a direct or indirect acquisition by a distributee corporation of control of distributing in one or more transactions in which gain or loss is recognized where the basis of the acquired distributing stock in the hands of the distributee corporation is determined in whole by reference to the transferor's basis. However, consistent with the principles of Rev. Rul. 74-5, this rule is only applicable with respect to a distribution by the acquired distributing, and does not apply for purposes of any subsequent distribution by any distributee corporation.

b. Certain Nonrecognition Transactions Treated as Recognition Transactions

Because the IRS and Treasury Department believe that acquisitions made in exchange for assets violate the common purpose of section 355(b)(2)(C) and (D) even if no gain or loss is recognized, these proposed regulations provide that such transactions are treated as transactions in which gain or loss is recognized.

i. Acquisitions in Exchange for Assets

As discussed in section C.1. of this preamble, the common purpose underlying section 355(b)(2)(C) and (D) is that distributing generally should not be able to use its assets to acquire a new trade or business in anticipation of distributing that trade or business (or facilitating the distribution of another trade or business) to its shareholders in a tax-free transaction. Similarly, and also discussed in section C.1. of this preamble, section 355(b), by permitting the use of distributing stock to acquire a trade or business, ensures a historic relationship between the distributing shareholders and the trades or businesses relied upon to satisfy the active trade or business requirement.

The following examples illustrate distributing's use of its assets to acquire a new trade or business.

First, assume that D, a corporation that does not directly conduct a five-year active trade or business, owns all of the stock of C, a corporation with a five-year active trade or business. D wishes to spin-off C to its shareholders, but to do so D must satisfy the active trade or business requirement. Accordingly, D contributes assets to an unrelated partnership that is engaged in a five-year active trade or business in a transaction to which section 721 applies in exchange for an interest in the partnership that otherwise satisfies the requirements for D to be attributed the trade or business assets and activities of the partnership, as discussed in section I. of this preamble. Two years after the transfer, when D's only active trade or business is the business conducted by the partnership, D distributes the C stock pro rata to the D shareholders.

Alternatively, assume that D, a corporation with a five-year active trade or business, transfers assets to unrelated T, a corporation with a five-year active trade or business, in a transaction to which section 351 applies in exchange for an amount of T stock constituting control. Two years after the transfer, when T's only active trade or business is the business T conducted before D's transfer, D distributes the T stock pro rata to the D shareholders.

Similarly, assume that D, a corporation with a five-year active trade or business, owns all of the stock of C, a corporation that does not have a five-year active trade or business but has other assets. To cause C to satisfy the active trade or business requirement, D arranges for C to acquire a five-year active trade or business from T, an unrelated corporation, in a reorganization described in section 368(a)(1)(A). In the reorganization, the shareholders of T receive solely common stock of C representing 20 percent or less of the voting power of all classes of C stock. Two years after the reorganization, D distributes the C stock pro rata to the D shareholders.

In each of these examples, D has directly or indirectly acquired a trade or business in exchange for assets. See and compare Situation 2 of Rev. Rul. 2002-49 (2002-2 CB 288) (corporation's use of appreciated securities to acquire a trade or business of a partnership in a transaction to which section 721 applies is treated as an acquisition in which gain or loss was recognized); section 4.01(29) of Rev. Proc. 2007-3 (2007-1 IRB 108) (the IRS will not ordinarily rule where distributing acquires control of controlled by transferring inactive assets in a transaction meeting the requirements of section 351(a) or section 368(a)(1)(D) and in which no gain or loss is recognized). While these transactions satisfy the literal requirements of section 355(b)(2)(C) or (D), the underlying common purpose of those provisions has been violated. In each case, distributing has acquired in exchange for distributing's assets, either directly or indirectly through the issuance of controlled stock the trade or business to be relied on by distributing or controlled.

Furthermore, in each of these examples, the historic owners have supplied a trade or business for distributing or controlled, but they are not participants in the divisive transaction. Not being shareholders of D, the position of the historic owners of the acquired business is not altered by the distribution of the controlled stock. Accordingly, neither distributing nor the distributing shareholders have a historic relationship with the separated businesses, and the distribution of the controlled stock is not the type of transaction to which section 355 was intended to apply.

By contrast, had D issued its own stock in the reorganization in the last example, the substance of the transaction would be different. D would not have indirectly acquired a trade or business in exchange for assets but rather for its own equity. Because D would not be purchasing a business for its shareholders, the distribution is not a substitute for a taxable distribution of the consideration that would have been used in the purchase. Furthermore, where D stock is used as the consideration the former T shareholders would have joined D's shareholder base, and become participants in the divisive reorganization.

These proposed regulations prohibit the acquisition of a trade or business directly or indirectly in exchange for assets in order to ensure that the common purpose of section 355(b)(2)(C) and (D) is satisfied. Such an acquisition also would include a swap of an interest in an existing five-year active trade or business for an interest in a new active trade or business. This type of an acquisition could occur through the formation of a joint venture structure.

For example, assume D and X form a partnership joint venture in which D contributes a five-year active trade or business (ATBD) and X contributes a different five-year active trade or business (ATBX). D and X each receive a 50-percent interest in the partnership. D's interest is sufficient to satisfy the requirements for D to be attributed the partnership's trade or business assets and activities (as discussed in section I. of this preamble). Prior to a potential section 355 distribution by D, and within five years of the contribution, the partnership sells ATBD.

D cannot rely on ATBX until five years after the acquisition of its interest in the partnership because, in effect, at the time of the contributions D exchanged a 50-percent undivided interest in ATBD for a 50-percent undivided interest in ATBX. Therefore, D acquired its interest in ATBX in exchange for its assets. While this was a transaction in which no gain or loss was recognized, the exchange of assets violates the common purpose of section 355(b)(2)(C) and (D). Further, the historic owner of ATBX would not participate in any distribution of controlled stock by D. Accordingly, such a distribution would not be the type of transaction to which section 355 was intended to apply.

Similarly, a corporation can effectively swap its assets through the issuance of stock of a subsidiary (including controlled). Accordingly, these proposed regulations provide a specific rule to address tax-free acquisitions involving the issuance of subsidiary stock. These proposed regulations provide that if a SAG directly or indirectly owns stock of a subsidiary (including a subsidiary SAG member) and the subsidiary directly or indirectly acquires a trade or business, an interest in a partnership engaged in a trade or business, or stock of a corporation engaged in a trade or business from a person other than such SAG in exchange for stock of such subsidiary in a transaction in which no gain or loss is recognized (the acquisition), solely for purposes of applying section 355(b)(2)(C) or (D) with respect to the trade or business, partnership interest, or stock acquired by the subsidiary in the acquisition, the subsidiary's stock directly or indirectly owned by the SAG immediately after the acquisition is treated as acquired at the time of the acquisition in a transaction in which gain or loss is recognized.

This rule reflects the fact that although the acquiring subsidiary did not make the acquisition in exchange for its assets (it issued its own stock), the SAG that owns stock of the subsidiary has exchanged an indirect interest in the subsidiary's assets for an indirect interest in the trade or business acquired by the subsidiary in the acquisition. Thus, the SAG has indirectly acquired a portion of the subsidiary's newly acquired trade or business (equal to the shareholder's stock interest in the subsidiary immediately after the acquisition) in exchange for assets. Further, the IRS and Treasury Department believe that it would be inappropriate to allow such acquired trade or business to be relied on to satisfy the active trade or business requirement within five years of its acquisition because the historic owners of that trade or business would not participate in any distribution of controlled stock.

However, because such a transaction does not result in an acquisition of any pre-existing trade or business of the subsidiary, this rule merely treats the SAG's stock in the subsidiary immediately after the acquisition as acquired in a gain or loss transaction for purposes of applying section 355(b)(2)(C) or (D) to the newly acquired trade or business. Further, the impact of such a transaction on the ability to rely on the newly acquired trade or business to satisfy the requirements of section 355(b) depends upon how much subsidiary stock the SAG owns immediately after the transaction.

For example, assume D owns all of the sole class of stock of S, a corporation that does not conduct a five-year active trade or business. T, an unrelated corporation with a five-year active trade or business (ATBT), merges into S in a reorganization described in section 368(a)(1)(A) and (D) solely in exchange for 80 percent of the S stock, and no gain or loss is recognized. Immediately after the merger, D owns only 20 percent of the sole class of S stock. Solely for purposes of determining whether ATBT can be relied on to satisfy the active trade or business requirement, D is treated as having acquired its 20 percent of the S stock at the time of the merger of T into S in a transaction in which gain or loss was recognized. Accordingly, as described in section D.2.a. of this preamble regarding certain multi-step acquisitions of a subsidiary SAG member, if D subsequently acquired the 80 percent of the S stock held by the other shareholders solely in exchange for D voting stock in a reorganization described in section 368(a)(1)(B) in which no gain or loss was recognized, S would become a DSAG member and D could rely on ATBT to satisfy the active trade or business requirement.

Accordingly, in light of all of these concerns, these proposed regulations generally provide that acquisitions paid for in whole or in part, directly or indirectly, with assets of the DSAG will be treated as acquisitions in which gain or loss is recognized. However, if a DSAG member or controlled acquires the trade or business solely in exchange for distributing stock, distributing acquires control of controlled solely in exchange for distributing stock, or controlled acquires the trade or business from distributing solely in exchange for stock of controlled, in a transaction in which no gain or loss is recognized, the requirements of section 355(b)(2)(C) and (D) are satisfied. Such acquisitions are not made in exchange for assets of the DSAG.

An additional question arising under section 355(b)(2)(C) and (D) is whether the assumption of liabilities is treated as a payment of money or other property, and hence the use of assets. See *United States v. Hendler*, 303 US 564, reh'g denied, 304 US 588 (1938) (viewing an assumption of a liability by a transferee as in substance a payment to the transferor). Congress has indicated that the assumption of liabilities is not to be treated as the payment of money or other property in certain transactions in which no gain or loss is recognized. For example, the assumption of liabilities is not treated as the payment of money or other property in certain exchanges to which section 351 or 361 applies. See section 357(a). Further, the assumption of liabilities does not violate the solely for voting stock requirement in a reorganization described in section 368(a)(1)(C) where the acquiring corporation does not otherwise exchange money or other property. See section 368(a)(1)(C) and (a)(2)(B). Because Congress has granted this special treatment for liability assumptions in certain nonrecognition transactions, the IRS and Treasury Department believe that similar treatment is generally appropriate for purposes of section 355(b)(2)(C) and (D). Accordingly, these proposed regulations provide that the assumption by the DSAG or CSAG of liabilities of a transferor shall not, in and of itself, be treated as the payment of assets if such assumption is not treated as the payment of money or other property under any other applicable provision.

Finally, these proposed regulations clarify that an acquisition to which section 304(a)(1) applies does not satisfy the requirements of section 355(b)(2)(C) or (D). The IRS and Treasury Department believe that a stock acquisition to which section 304 applies is a transaction in which gain or loss is recognized for purposes of section 355(b)(2)(C) and (D) even if it merely results in the transferor's receipt of dividend income. These proposed regulations clarify that, regardless of the tax consequences to the transferor, such a transaction is an acquisition made in exchange for assets, and therefore does not satisfy the requirements of section 355(b)(2)(C) and (D).

ii. Partnership Distributions

These proposed regulations provide that an acquisition consisting of a distribution from a partnership is generally treated as a transaction in which gain or loss is recognized because it constitutes an acquisition in exchange for assets. That is, the distributee partner is generally exchanging an indirect interest in all the assets of the partnership for a direct interest in the property distributed. However, these proposed regulations provide that if the corporation is already attributed the trade or business assets and activities of a partnership, the corporation's acquisition of such trade or business assets and activities from the partnership is not, in and of itself, the acquisition of a new trade or business. Further, these proposed regulations provide that an acquisition consisting of a pro rata distribution from a partnership of stock or an interest in a lower-tier partnership is not an acquisition in exchange for assets to the extent the distributee partner did not acquire the interest in the distributing partnership during the pre-distribution period in a transaction in which gain or loss was recognized and to the extent the distributing partnership did not acquire the distributed stock or partnership interest within such period. In such a case, the distributee partner has merely exchanged an indirect interest for a direct interest in the distributed stock or partnership interest, and continues to possess the same indirect interest in the remaining assets of the partnership.

iii. Lack of Transferred Basis

Section 1.355-3(b)(4)(i) provides that a trade or business acquired, directly or indirectly, within the pre-distribution period in a transaction in which the basis of the assets acquired was not determined in whole or in part by reference to the transferor's basis does not qualify under section 355(b)(2), even though no gain or loss was recognized by the transferor. These proposed regulations do not include a similar provision. The IRS and Treasury Department believe that the prohibition against acquisitions in exchange for assets fully addresses such acquisitions.

c. Application of Section 355(b)(2)(C) and (D) to Predecessors

Unlike § 1.355-3(b)(4)(i), which only took "a predecessor in interest" into account for purposes of applying section 355(b)(2)(D), these proposed regulations provide that any reference to a corporation includes a reference to a predecessor of such corporation in applying both section 355(b)(2)(C) and (D). The IRS and Treasury Department believe that predecessors should be taken into account in applying both section 355(b)(2)(C) and (D) because the same policy concerns exist regardless of whether the transaction involves the acquisition of assets or stock. For this purpose, the proposed regulations define a predecessor of a corporation as a corporation that transfers its assets to such corporation in a transaction to which section 381 applies. The IRS and Treasury Department believe that it is appropriate to take predecessors into account in applying these provisions in order to appropriately minimize the significance of which corporation is the acquiror and which corporation is the target.

Further, because the SAG rule effectively treats SAG members as a single-entity for purposes of section 355(b), these proposed regulations also apply section 355(b)(2)(C) and (D) to acquisitions during the pre-distribution period by corporations that later become DSAG or CSAG members. These types of acquisitions are similar to predecessor asset acquisitions.

4. *Requests for comments regarding exceptions to section 355(b)(2)(C) and (D)*

The IRS and Treasury Department request comments regarding whether any additional exceptions to section 355(b)(2)(C) and (D) are appropriate. In particular, the IRS and Treasury Department request comments regarding whether acquisitions in which gain is recognized solely as a result of the application of section 367 should be treated as violating section 355(b)(2)(C) or (D). The IRS and Treasury Department also request comments regarding whether an exception should exist for taxable acquisitions made by distributing solely in exchange for distributing stock because such acquisitions are not made in exchange for distributing's assets and do not appear to violate the common purpose of section 355(b)(2)(C) and (D).

In addition, the IRS and Treasury Department request comments regarding whether a redemption of stock should be a transaction to which section 355(b)(2)(C) or (D) applies. Under current law, no relief is provided for such transactions. See *McLaulin v. Commissioner*, 276 F.3d 1269 (11th

Cir. 2001) (concluding that section 355(b)(2)(D) applies when distributing acquires control of a subsidiary through a redemption of subsidiary stock). Compare Rev. Rul. 57-144 (1957-1 CB 123). Specifically, comments are requested on whether all types of redemptions should be subject to the same rule, whether the treatment of redemptions should be determined by the source of payment, whether the redemption constitutes an indirect exchange for assets of distributing or controlled, and the method of making these determinations. Alternatively, the IRS and Treasury Department request comments on whether an exception should be provided for redemptions of shareholders that exercise dissenters' rights. Compare Rev. Rul. 68-285 (1968-1 CB 147) (concluding that cash paid to dissenting target corporation shareholders by the target corporation does not violate the solely for voting stock requirement of section 368(a)(1)(B)) with Rev. Rul. 73-102 (1973-1 CB 186) (concluding that cash paid to dissenting target corporation shareholders by the acquiring corporation is treated as money or other property paid by the acquiring corporation for the properties of the target corporation in a reorganization under section 368(a)(1)(C)). These proposed regulations do not include an exception for redemptions generally or for those in connection with the exercise of dissenters' rights.

Finally, the IRS and Treasury Department request comments regarding whether a transaction in which a distributee corporation acquires in a transaction in which no gain or loss is recognized newly issued stock of distributing in exchange for money or property previously acquired for cash during the pre-distribution period should be treated as a transaction in which gain or loss is recognized. For example, assume D and C have each engaged in the active conduct of a trade or business for more than five years. During the pre-distribution period, P, an unrelated corporation, purchases trucks and transfers them to D in exchange for D stock meeting the requirements of section 368(c) in a transaction to which section 351 applies. No gain or loss is recognized. D subsequently distributes all the C stock to P in a separate transaction within five years of P's acquisition of the D stock. Notwithstanding that this transaction satisfies the literal requirements of section 355(b)(2)(D), it appears to violate the *General Utilities* doctrine because it permits the distributee corporation, P, to receive a fair market value basis (or close to a fair market value basis) in the distributing stock, enabling the potential sale of controlled stock without the appropriate recognition of gain. Additionally, the IRS and Treasury Department are studying whether the principles of the foregoing rule should be extended to any distributee in regulations under section 355(d), and request comments on this point.

D. *Treatment of Certain Multi-step Acquisitions*

These proposed regulations provide specific rules regarding the application of section 355(b)(2)(C) and (D) to certain multi-step acquisitions. Based on the interpretation of section 355(b)(2)(D), and the enactment of section 355(b)(3), the IRS and Treasury Department believe that it is appropriate to apply section 355(b)(2)(C) and (D) to multi-step acquisitions in a consistent manner. Further, the IRS and Treasury Department believe that it is appropriate to treat certain multi-step acquisitions of target corporation stock as satisfying the requirements of section 355(b)(2)(C) or (D) (as applicable) notwithstanding that some portion of the stock may have been acquired in a separate transaction in which gain or loss was recognized.

1. *Multi-step acquisition of control of distributing or controlled*

a. Direct Acquisitions

Section 355(b)(2)(D) provides that control of distributing or controlled may be acquired within the pre-distribution period provided that "in each case in which such control was so acquired, it was so acquired, only by reason of transactions in which gain or loss was not recognized in whole or in part, or only by reason of such transactions combined with acquisitions before the beginning of such period." The IRS and Treasury Department interpret this language to mean that at the time control is first acquired, the acquiring corporation (or its SAG) is required to own stock meeting the requirements of section 368(c) that was acquired in one or more transactions in which no gain or loss was recognized or by reason of such transactions combined with acquisitions before the beginning of the pre-distribution period. Thus, at the time an acquiring corporation (or its SAG) first satisfies the section 368(c) control requirement, the acquiring corporation (or its SAG) must possess section 368(c) control without relying on any stock acquired in a transaction in which gain or loss was recognized during the pre-distribution period.

For example, assume that C has two classes of stock outstanding. X owns all 95 shares of the class A stock of C representing 95 percent of the voting power and 70 percent of the value and Y owns all of the class B stock of C representing five percent of the voting power and 30 percent of the value. In year 1, unrelated D acquires 10 shares of the class A C stock from X in a transaction in which gain or loss is recognized. In year 2, D acquires an additional 80 shares of class A C stock from X in a separate transaction in which no gain or loss is recognized. In year 3, D acquires the remaining five shares of class A C stock from X in a separate transaction in which gain or loss is recognized. In year 4, D distributes the 95 shares of class A C stock to the D shareholders. Assuming all of the other requirements of section 355(b) are satisfied, the requirements of section 355(b)(2)(D)(ii) are satisfied because at the time D first acquired control of C (immediately after the year 2 acquisition), D owned an amount of C stock constituting control that was acquired in a transaction in which no gain or loss was recognized (the 80 shares of class A C stock acquired in year 2). (However, the 10 shares of class A C stock acquired in year 1 and the five shares of class A C stock acquired in year 3 may be treated as boot under section 355(a)(3)(B).)

On the other hand, assume the same facts as the previous example, except that, in year 2, D acquires only 75 shares of class A C stock from X. The requirements of section 355(b)(2)(D)(ii) are not satisfied because at the time D first acquired control of C (immediately after the year 2 acquisition), D did not own an amount of C stock constituting control that was acquired in one or more transactions in which no gain or loss was recognized or acquired prior to the pre-distribution period. D only owns C voting stock representing 75 percent of the total voting power that was acquired in a transaction in which no gain or loss was recognized. The result would be the same if the year 3 acquisition was also a transaction in which no gain or loss was recognized.

b. Indirect Acquisitions

These proposed regulations also provide that the principles of this rule will be applied with respect to an indirect acquisition of distributing or controlled stock. For example, assume T corporation owns stock of C (an unaffiliated subsidiary) constituting control (and no more). Unrelated D acquires 10 percent of the sole outstanding class of stock of T in a transaction in which gain or loss is recognized. In a separate transaction, T merges into D solely in exchange for D stock in a transaction in which no gain or loss is recognized. In applying this multi-step acquisition rule to D's subsequent acquisition of control of C in the merger, the prior acquisition of T stock in the transaction in which gain or loss was recognized is treated as an acquisition of 10 percent of the C stock owned by T (representing 8 percent of the total combined voting power of the C stock) in a transaction in which gain or loss is recognized. Accordingly, the requirements of section 355(b)(2)(D)(ii) are not satisfied because at the time D first acquires control of C, D does not own an amount of C stock constituting control that was acquired in one or more transactions in which no gain or loss is recognized or acquired prior to the pre-distribution period. At that time, D had only acquired C stock representing 72 percent of the total combined voting power of the C stock in a transaction in which no gain or loss is recognized.

2. *Other multiple-step acquisitions*

As discussed in sections A.1., B.1., and B.3. of this preamble, if D acquires section 1504(a)(2) stock of a corporation, the acquired corporation will become a DSAG member and the corporation will be treated like a division of D for purposes of the active trade or business requirement. As such, D is treated as if it acquired the assets and activities of the new subsidiary SAG member, and the acquisition must satisfy the requirements of section 355(b)(2)(C) rather than section 355(b)(2)(D). If D subsequently acquires the remaining stock of the corporation in a separate transaction, such acquisition is disregarded for purposes of satisfying the active trade or business requirement (regardless of whether gain or loss was recognized in the separate transaction) because the subsidiary is already treated as a division of D for this purpose. The IRS and Treasury Department believe that the order of these acquisitions should not be determinative in applying section 355(b)(2)(C), provided that at the time the corporation first becomes a subsidiary SAG member, the SAG owns section 1504(a)(2) stock in the corporation without relying on any stock acquired in a transaction in which gain or loss was recognized during the pre-distribution period.

a. Direct SAG Acquisitions

Consistent with the treatment of multi-step acquisitions of control of a corporation discussed in section D.1. of this preamble, these proposed regulations provide that multi-step acquisitions of stock resulting in a corporation becoming a subsidiary SAG member will satisfy the requirements of section 355(b)(2)(C), provided that at the time the corporation first becomes a subsidiary SAG member, the SAG owns section 1504(a)(2) stock in the corporation without relying on any stock acquired in a transaction in which gain or loss was recognized during the pre-distribution period.

For example, assume that in year 1, D does not conduct an active trade or business and has owned control of C for more than five years. C and T, an unrelated corporation, have each engaged in the active conduct of a trade or business for more than five years. In year 1, D acquires 10 percent of T's sole outstanding class of stock in a transaction in which gain or loss was recognized. In year 2, D acquires an additional 80 percent of T's stock in a separate transaction in which no gain or loss was recognized. T becomes a DSAG member as a result of the year 2 stock acquisition. In year 3, D distributes the C stock to the D shareholders. Assuming all of the other requirements of section 355(b) are satisfied, the requirements of section 355(b)(2)(C) are satisfied because at the time T first became a DSAG member (immediately after the year 2 acquisition), D owned an amount of T stock meeting the requirements of section 1504(a)(2) that was acquired in a transaction in which no gain or loss was recognized (the T stock acquired in year 2).

On the other hand, assume the same facts as the previous example except that, in year 2, D only acquires an additional 75 percent of T's stock. The requirements of section 355(b)(2)(C) are not satisfied because at the time T first became a DSAG member (immediately after the year 2 acquisition), D did not own an amount of T stock meeting the requirements of section 1504(a)(2) that was acquired in one or more transactions in which no gain or loss was recognized or acquired prior to the pre-distribution period. D owns only 75 percent of T's stock that was acquired in a transaction in which no gain or loss was recognized. The result would be the same even if, in year 3 prior to the distribution of the C stock, D acquired the remaining 15 percent of the T stock in a transaction in which no gain or loss is recognized.

b. Indirect SAG Acquisitions

Similar to the rule regarding multi-step acquisitions of control of distributing or controlled, these proposed regulations also provide that the principles of this rule will be applied with respect to an indirect acquisition by the SAG of stock of a corporation that becomes a SAG member. For example, assume a DSAG member acquires 25 percent of the sole outstanding class of stock of T, a corporation that wholly owns S, in a transaction in which gain or loss is recognized. In a separate transaction, another DSAG member acquires all of the stock of S from T solely in exchange for D voting stock in a reorganization described in section 368(a)(1)(B) in which no gain or loss is recognized. As a result, S becomes a DSAG member. In applying this multi-step acquisition rule to the DSAG's subsequent acquisition of S stock, the acquisition of 25 percent of the T stock in the transaction in which gain or loss was recognized will be treated as an acquisition of 25 percent of the S stock in a transaction in which gain or loss is recognized. Accordingly, the requirements of section 355(b)(2)(C) are not satisfied because at the time S first becomes a DSAG member, the DSAG does not own section 1504(a)(2) stock of S that was acquired in one or more transactions in which no gain or loss is recognized or acquired prior to the pre-distribution period.

c. Multi-step Asset Acquisitions

Because stock acquisitions that result in a corporation becoming a subsidiary SAG member are treated as direct acquisitions of the target corporation's assets for purposes of applying section 355(b), these proposed regulations apply a comparable multi-step acquisition rule to acquisitions of stock in non-SAG members where such non-members' assets are subsequently directly acquired by a SAG member. Specifically, these proposed regulations provide that if immediately before a SAG's direct acquisition of a trade or business (or an interest in a partnership engaged in a trade or business) held by a corporation (owner) in a transaction to which section 381 applies and in which no gain or loss is recognized, the SAG owns an amount of stock of the owner that it acquired in one or more transactions during the pre-distribution period in which gain or loss was recognized such that all of the other stock of the owner does not meet the requirements of section 1504(a)(2), such direct acquisition shall be treated as a transaction in which gain or loss was recognized. Thus, these proposed regulations apply section 355(b)(2)(C) to multi-step acquisitions in the same manner regardless of whether the separate steps result in the target corporation becoming a subsidiary SAG member or result in a direct acquisition of the target corporation's assets.

For example, assume that in year 1, D does not conduct an active trade or business, and has owned control of C for more than five years. C and T, an unrelated corporation, have each engaged in the active conduct of a trade or business for more than five years. In year 1, D acquires 10 percent of T's sole outstanding class of stock in a transaction in which gain or loss was recognized. In year 2, in a separate reorganization described in section 368(a)(1)(A), T merges into D and the T shareholders receive solely D stock in exchange for their T stock. No gain or loss is recognized in the merger. In year 3, D distributes the stock of C to the D shareholders. Assuming all of the other requirements of section 355(b) are satisfied, the requirements of section 355(b)(2)(C) are satisfied because, at the time D acquires T's active trade or business, D did not own an amount of T stock that was acquired in one or more transactions during the pre-distribution period in which gain or loss was recognized such that all of the other T stock does not meet the requirements of section 1504(a)(2).

On the other hand, assume the same facts as the previous example except that in year 1 D acquires 21 percent of T's stock. The requirements of section 355(b)(2)(C) are not satisfied because, at the time D acquires T's active trade or business, D owned an amount of T stock that was acquired in one or more transactions during the pre-distribution period in which gain or loss was recognized such that all of the other T stock does not meet the requirements of section 1504(a)(2).

These proposed regulations also provide that the principles of this rule will be applied with respect to an indirect acquisition of the target corporation's stock by the SAG.

E. *Expansion Acquisitions*

The legislative history, the courts, and the current regulations acknowledge that a trade or business can undergo many changes during the pre-distribution period and still satisfy the requirements of section 355(b). See H.R. No. 83-2543, at 37, 38 (1954) (Conf. Rep.); *Estate of Lockwood v. Commissioner*, 350 F.2d 712 (8th Cir. 1965); and § 1.355-3(b)(3)(ii). Furthermore, § 1.355-3(b)(3)(ii) provides "if a corporation engaged in the active conduct of one trade or business during that five-year period purchased, created, or otherwise acquired another trade or business in the same line of business, then the acquisition of that other business is ordinarily treated as an expansion of the original business, all of which is treated as having been actively conducted during that five-year period, unless that purchase, creation, or other acquisition effects a change of such a character as to constitute the acquisition of a new or different business." Therefore, an acquired trade or business that is an expansion of the original trade or business inherits the business history of the expanded business.

None of these authorities, however, addresses whether an existing trade or business can be expanded by acquiring the stock of a corporation engaged in a trade or business in the same line of business as the acquiror. Because the SAG rule causes a stock acquisition in which the acquired corporation becomes a subsidiary SAG member to be treated as an asset acquisition, a corporation engaged in a trade or business should be able to expand its existing trade or business by acquiring stock of a corporation (including controlled) engaged in a trade or business in the same line of business provided the acquisition results in the acquired corporation becoming a subsidiary SAG member.

On the other hand, section 355(b)(3) does not allow a corporation to rely on the trade or business of a non-SAG subsidiary — even if the corporation controls the subsidiary — to satisfy the active trade or business requirement. As such, it effectively precludes stock expansions where the acquired corporation does not become a subsidiary SAG member. The IRS and Treasury Department believe that section 355(b)(3) is the exclusive means by which a corporation is attributed the assets (or activities) owned (or conducted) by another corporation. Accordingly, a stock acquisition that does not result in the acquired corporation becoming a subsidiary SAG member should not be an expansion of the SAG's original business.

In addition, these proposed regulations provide certain facts and circumstances to be considered in determining whether one trade or business is in the same line of business as another trade or business. The inclusion of these facts and circumstances in these proposed regulations is not intended to be a substantive change, but merely to clarify and restate the current law regarding expansions. See Rev. Rul. 2003-18 (2003-1 CB 467) and Rev. Rul. 2003-38 (2003-1 CB 811). Some of the examples from the current regulations have been altered in these proposed regulations to reflect this inclusion (as well as certain stylistic changes).

F. *Rules Related to Hot Stock*

Section 355(a)(3)(B) provides that stock of controlled acquired by distributing during the Treasury pre-distribution period in a transaction in which gain or loss is recognized is treated as boot. Section 1.355-2(g) provides guidance regarding the application of section 355(a)(3)(B). The IRS and Treasury Department request comments regarding whether §1.355-2(g) should be amended to adopt rules under section 355(a)(3)(B) similar to those provided in these proposed regulations for determining whether an acquisition is one in which gain or loss is recognized for purposes of section 355(b)(2)(C) or (D).

In particular, the IRS and Treasury Department request comments concerning the application of section 355(a)(3)(B) to acquisitions of stock of controlled in gain or loss transactions that, under these proposed regulations, are not treated as violating the requirements of section 355(b). For example, where distributing acquires stock of controlled in a gain or loss transaction that is treated as an expansion of distributing's existing trade or business (because controlled is in distributing's line of business and becomes a DSAG member), what portion, if any, of the acquired stock should be subject to section 355(a)(3)(B)?

The current authorities may suggest a linkage between the interpretation of sections 355(a)(3)(B) and 355(b). See §1.355-2(g)(1) (not applying section 355(a)(3)(B) to a taxable acquisition from an affiliate); Rev. Rul. 78-442 (stating "[l]ikewise, for the same reasons [that section 355(b)(2)(C) does not apply], section 355(a)(3)[(B)]of the Code is not applicable"). However, section 355(b)(3) by its literal terms does not appear to apply for purposes section 355(a)(3)(B).

The IRS and Treasury Department continue to study how to coordinate the application of these provisions and request comments in this regard. Accordingly, these proposed regulations contain no proposal to change §1.355-2(g) at this time.

G. *Limited Affiliate Exception*

Other than with respect to transfers of assets (or activities) that are owned (or performed) by the SAG immediately before and immediately after the transfer, these proposed regulations do not include the special treatment accorded affiliated group members in §1.355-3(b)(4)(iii). Thus, these proposed regulations treat non-SAG member affiliates of distributing or controlled in the same manner as unrelated persons for purposes of applying section 355(b)(2)(C) and (D). While distributing is the common parent of its SAG, distributing may be a subsidiary member of a larger affiliated group. Therefore, not all members of distributing's affiliated group are DSAG members.

Section 1.355-3(b)(4)(iii) provides that acquisitions by one member of an affiliated group from another member of the group are disregarded in applying section 355(b)(2)(C) and (D), even if gain or loss is recognized. Section 1.355-3(b)(4)(iii) provides for this treatment for affiliates because although "[t]he requirements of section 355(b)(2)(C) and (D) are intended to prevent the direct or indirect acquisition of a trade or business by a corporation in anticipation of a distribution by the corporation of that trade or business in a distribution to which section 355 would otherwise apply[,]" acquisitions from affiliates are not the type of transaction to which these provisions were intended to apply. Section 1.355-3(b)(4)(iv) defines the term "affiliated group" as an affiliated group as defined in section 1504(a) (without regard to section 1504(b)), except that the term "stock" includes nonvoting stock described in section 1504(a)(4).

The IRS and Treasury Department believe that limiting this special treatment to transfers in which the assets (or activities) remain in the SAG (as opposed to the larger affiliated group) is more consistent with the purposes of section 355(b)(3). As discussed in section A.1. of this preamble, section 355(b)(3) states, in effect, that in determining whether distributing or controlled is engaged in a trade or business all DSAG or CSAG members, as the case may be, are treated as one corporation. Therefore, a transfer of trade or business assets (or activities) from one SAG member to another SAG member is disregarded, and is not an acquisition for purposes of section 355(b)(2)(C) (or section 355(b)(2)(D) in the case of stock of controlled that is not a DSAG member). The SAG rule implies a corollary, which is that if the trade or business assets (or activities) are not owned (or performed) by the SAG, such assets (or activities) should generally not be able to be acquired from outside the SAG in a transaction in which gain or loss is recognized. Thus, these proposed regulations generally do not permit taxable acquisitions of an active trade or business from outside the SAG.

The IRS and Treasury Department recognize that not providing this special treatment for non-SAG member affiliates is a change from how the law has been administered in various situations. Further, the IRS and Treasury Department recognize that this change can represent a relaxing or tightening of the law in this area, depending upon the circumstances. For example, under these proposed regulations the requirements of section 355(b)(2)(C) are satisfied where P, a higher-tier affiliate of distributing, purchases a trade or business for cash and contributes it to distributing solely in exchange for distributing stock in a transaction in which no gain or loss is recognized. On the other hand, under these proposed regulations, the requirements of section 355(b)(2)(C) are not satisfied where P has actively conducted a trade or business for more than five years and sells it to D in exchange for cash.

H. *Activities Performed by Certain Related Parties*

Current §1.355-3(b)(2)(iii) provides, in part, that to satisfy the active trade or business requirement, the corporation itself generally is required to perform active and substantial management and operational functions. That regulation further provides that activities performed by the corporation itself generally do not include activities performed by independent contractors. In this regard, "a corporation must engage in entrepreneurial endeavors of such a nature and to such an extent as to qualitatively distinguish its operations from mere investments [, and] . . . there should be objective indicia of such corporate operations." *Rafferty v. Commissioner*, 452 F.2d 767, 772 (1st Cir. 1971) *cert. denied* 408 US 922 (1972) (concluding that a corporation that did not pay salaries or rent, did not employ independent contractors, and merely collected rent, paid taxes, and kept separate books, failed to satisfy these requirements). The IRS and Treasury Department believe that a corporation may rely on the activities performed by certain related parties in conducting its "entrepreneurial endeavors," and such activities can constitute "objective indicia" of corporate operations.

While section 355(b)(3) treats all SAG members as one corporation, the IRS and Treasury Department are aware that affiliated groups of corporations that include non-SAG member affiliates might use employees of one member of the group to perform management or operational functions for another member of the group. The IRS and the Treasury Department believe that a corporation can satisfy the active trade or business requirement even if all the management and operational functions are performed by employees of affiliates that are not members of either the DSAG or CSAG. In other words, the DSAG or CSAG can be engaged in "entrepreneurial endeavors" that are distinguishable from mere passive investment even if the management and operational functions are performed for the DSAG or CSAG by employees of non-SAG affiliates. Such individuals bear a close enough relationship to the DSAG or CSAG to be distinguished from mere independent contractors for purposes of the active trade or business requirement. The IRS and Treasury Department believe that this treatment is appropriate and consistent with previously published guidance.

Issued prior to the enactment of section 355(b)(3), Rev. Rul. 79-394 (1979-2 CB 141), amplified by Rev. Rul. 80-181 (1980-2 CB 121), concludes that controlled satisfies the active trade or business requirement even though all of the operational activities of its business are conducted by an affiliate's employees before the distribution. The IRS and Treasury Department believe that extending the principles of Rev. Rul. 79-394 and Rev. Rul. 80-181 to the performance of management (in addition to operational) functions by employees of an affiliate is consistent with the purposes underlying the active trade or business requirement. Accordingly, these proposed regulations provide that, in determining whether a corporation is engaged in the active conduct of a trade or business, activities (including management and operational functions) performed by employees of the corporation's affiliates (including non-SAG members) are taken into account.

Furthermore, the IRS and Treasury Department believe that a corporation can satisfy the active trade or business requirement even if all the management and operational functions are performed by shareholders of the corporation if it is closely held. The shareholders of closely held corporations possess a close relationship with the corporation, similar to employees of affiliates. Accordingly, these proposed regulations provide that, in determining whether a corporation is engaged in the active conduct of a trade or business, activities (including management and operational functions) performed by shareholders of a closely held corporation are taken into account in certain cases.

The IRS and Treasury Department do not believe that the absence of an exception for acquisitions from non-SAG member affiliates is inconsistent with concluding that a corporation can satisfy the active trade or business requirement by relying on the management and operational functions performed by employees of non-SAG member affiliates. Relying on the activities of such employees does not involve the acquisition of a trade or business. As such, it is not the type of transaction or arrangement section 355(b)(2) was intended to address. Accordingly, the IRS and Treasury Department believe it is appropriate to apply a broader standard with respect to relying on employees of non-SAG member affiliates.

While it is appropriate to consider the management and operational activities of employees of all affiliates in determining whether a corporation satisfies the active trade or business requirement, the IRS and Treasury Department believe that a corporation should satisfy the active trade or business requirement only if it (or another SAG member, or a partnership from which the trade or business assets and activities are attributed) is the principal owner of the goodwill and significant assets of the trade or business for Federal income tax purposes. Accordingly, a corporation will be treated as engaged in the active conduct of a trade or business only if, for Federal income tax purposes, it (or its SAG member, or a partnership from which the trade or business assets and activities are attributed) is the principal owner of the goodwill and significant assets of the trade or business. Accordingly, some of the examples from the current regulations have been altered in these proposed regulations to reflect this goodwill and significant asset standard (as well as certain stylistic changes).

I. *Activities Conducted by a Partnership*

Revenue Ruling 92-17 (1992-1 CB 142) and Rev. Rul. 2002-49 (2002-2 CB 288) address in a number of fact situations whether a corporation that is a partner in a partnership can satisfy the active trade or business requirement by reason of its ownership of the partnership interest where the partnership conducts a trade or business. Those rulings illustrate that a corporation owning a 20-percent interest in a state law partnership or limited liability company (LLC) that is classified as a partnership for Federal income tax purposes can be treated as engaged in the active conduct of the trade or business of the partnership if the corporation performs active and substantial management functions for the partnership's business. In addition, Rev. Rul. 2002-49 concludes that such a corporation can be treated as engaged in the active conduct of a partnership's trade or business, even if another partner also performs active and substantial management functions for the partnership's trade or business.

Consistent with the principles set forth in Rev. Rul. 92-17 and Rev. Rul. 2002-49 regarding satisfying the active trade or business requirement through an interest in a partnership, these proposed regulations provide that for purposes of section 355(b) a partner will be attributed the trade or business assets and activities of a partnership if the partner (1) performs active and substantial management functions for the partnership with respect to the trade or business assets or activities (for example, makes decisions regarding significant business issues of the partnership and regularly participates in the overall supervision, direction, and control of the employees performing the operational functions for the partnership), and (2) owns a meaningful interest in the partnership. Further, because a partnership might only conduct a portion of a trade or business, the IRS and Treasury Department believe that a partner that satisfies these requirements can be attributed the portions of a trade or business (or assets and activities) that are conducted by a partnership. Under these circumstances the IRS and Treasury Department believe that it is appropriate to aggregate the partnership's trade or business assets and activities with those of the partner for purposes of determining whether the partner satisfies the active trade or business requirement. However, the stock of a corporation held by the partnership is not attributed to a partner.

The IRS and Treasury Department understand that the facts presented in Rev. Rul. 92-17 and Rev. Rul. 2002-49 do not necessarily reflect the exclusive methods by which corporations engage in a trade or business through a partnership. In particular, the IRS and Treasury Department understand that both the management and operational activities of an LLC are often conducted by the LLC itself, rather than by its members, to protect its members from liability for the LLC's activities. In these cases, Rev. Rul. 92-17 and Rev. Rul. 2002-49 do not explicitly support the conclusion that a corporation may rely on the trade or business assets and activities of an LLC to satisfy the active trade or business requirement, since no activities are performed by the corporate partner.

The IRS and Treasury Department believe that, in certain cases, a partner that owns a significant interest in an entity that is treated as a partnership for Federal income tax purposes should be attributed the trade or business assets and activities of a partnership, even if the partner does not directly conduct any activities relating to the business of the partnership. By comparison, the IRS and Treasury Department have promulgated regulations regarding the treatment of acquired assets held by a partnership for purposes of satisfying the continuity of business enterprise requirement applicable to reorganizations. Those regulations provide that a partner will be treated as owning the acquired target business assets used in the business of a partnership in satisfaction of the continuity of business enterprise requirement if the members of the qualified group, in the aggregate, own an interest in the partnership representing a significant interest in that partnership business. See § 1.368-1(d)(4)(iii)(B)(*1*). Those regulations include an example concluding that the continuity of business enterprise requirement is satisfied where a partner owns a one-third interest in a partnership that continues the business of the target corporation, even though the partner performs no management or operational functions for that business. See § 1.368-1(d)(5) *Example 9*.

These proposed regulations yield results similar to the continuity of business enterprise rule in determining whether the active trade or business requirement is satisfied when a corporation conducts a trade or business or portions of a trade or business through a partnership but does not participate in the partnership's activities. Specifically, these proposed regulations provide that for purposes of section 355(b) a partner will be attributed the trade or business assets and activities of a partnership provided the partner owns a significant interest in the partnership. The IRS and Treasury Department intend that the term "significant interest" requires an ownership interest that is greater than that suggested by the term "meaningful interest," which is the level of ownership required for a partner to be attributed the trade or business assets and activities of a partnership in cases where the partner performs active and substantial management functions for the partnership.

However, a partner will be attributed the trade or business assets and activities of a partnership only during the period it owns a significant interest or alternatively owns a meaningful interest and performs active and substantial management functions.

J. *Additional Requests for Comments*

The IRS and Treasury Department request comments regarding whether the regulations should include a rule that would treat an acquisition in which no gain or loss is recognized as an acquisition in which gain or loss is recognized if that would be the treatment had the transaction been executed in the opposite direction. For example, assume that, in year 1, P, a corporation not engaged in an active trade or business, acquires 50 percent of all of the outstanding stock of D (which is engaged in an active trade or business, and owns control of C, which is also engaged in an active trade or business) in a transaction in which gain or loss is recognized, and then, in a separate transaction in year 3, D merges into P solely in exchange for P stock in a transaction described in section 368(a)(1)(A) in which no gain or loss is recognized. P then distributes the C stock to its shareholders in year 4. Under these proposed regulations, P is treated as having acquired D's trade or business and control of C during the pre-distribution period in a transaction in which gain or loss is recognized because P acquired more than 20 percent of D's stock during the pre-distribution period in a transaction in which gain or loss was recognized (see sections D.1.b. and D.2.c. of this preamble). However, if P merges downstream into D solely in exchange for D stock in a reorganization described in section 368(a)(1)(A) and (D) in which no gain or loss is recognized, there literally is not an acquisition in which gain or loss is recognized under these proposed regulations, because D did not acquire any interest in an active trade or business from P. Comments are requested regarding whether the result should differ depending upon the direction of the merger. See and compare §1.355-3(b)(4)(ii) (predecessor of distributing acquiring control of distributing).

Further, the IRS and Treasury Department request comments regarding the appropriate methods of measuring indirect acquisitions of stock for purposes of the rules regarding multi-step acquisitions, as discussed in section D. of this preamble. Specifically, comments are requested regarding how the indirect acquisition should be measured where the acquired corporation has multiple classes of stock outstanding, or where the acquired entity is a partnership. For example, assume T is a corporation that owns all of the stock of a subsidiary, S, and T has class A common stock, class B common stock, and preferred stock outstanding. If D acquires 10 percent of the T class A common stock, how should one determine what percentage of S stock D has indirectly acquired? Should it be based on the value of the T stock D acquired relative to the value of all of the T stock or other factors? How should the voting power of the acquired T stock be taken into account in applying these rules to potential indirect acquisitions of control?

In addition, the IRS and Treasury Department request comments regarding whether the parameters of the good faith and inadvertence exceptions in Notice 2004-37 (2004-1 CB 947) regarding the value requirement in section 1504(a)(2)(B) should apply for purposes of determining whether corporations are SAG members even if they are not members of a consolidated group. That is, the IRS and Treasury Department request comments regarding whether the policies underlying the SAG rule and the reference to section 1504(a) in section 355(b)(3)(B) suggest that the good faith and inadvertence exceptions should apply and be interpreted in the same way for SAG membership as for affiliation for purposes of filing consolidated returns.

The IRS and Treasury Department also request comments regarding whether the regulations should clarify the circumstances under which the separation of a segment of an active trade or business should be treated as a separate active trade or business after it is spun off and, if so, what the governing principle should be. See, for example, §1.355-3(c) *Example 9* (separation of a corporation's research department from the rest of its manufacturing business).

Although these regulations are generally proposed to be applicable to distributions that occur after the date these regulations are published as final regulations in the **Federal Register,** the IRS and Treasury Department invite comments regarding whether it would be appropriate and desirable to allow taxpayers to elect to apply these provisions retroactively (subject to the applicability of section 355(b)(3)).

Proposed Effective Date

These proposed regulations are proposed to apply to distributions that occur after the date these regulations are published as final regulations in the **Federal Register.**

Special Analyses

It has been determined that this notice of proposed rulemaking is not a significant regulatory action as defined in Executive Order 12866. Therefore, a regulatory assessment is not required. It has also been determined that section 553(b) of the Administrative Procedure Act (5 U.S.C. chapter 5) does not apply to these regulations, and, because these regulations do not impose a collection of information on small entities, the Regulatory Flexibility Act (5 U.S.C. chapter 6) does not apply. Pursuant to section 7805(f) of the Code, these regulations have been submitted to the Chief Counsel for Advocacy of the Small Business Administration for comment on its impact on small businesses.

Comments and Requests for Public Hearing

Before these proposed regulations are adopted as final regulations, consideration will be given to any written (a signed original and eight (8) copies) or electronic comments that are submitted timely to the IRS. The IRS and Treasury Department request comments on the clarity of the proposed rules and how they can be made easier to understand. All comments will be available for public inspection and copying. A public hearing will be scheduled if requested in writing by any person that timely submits written comments. If a public hearing is scheduled, notice of the date, time, and place for the public hearing will be published in the **Federal Register.**

Drafting Information

The principal author of these proposed regulations is Russell P. Subin of the Office of Associate Chief Counsel (Corporate). However, other personnel from the IRS and Treasury Department participated in their development.

Availability of IRS Documents

IRS revenue rulings, procedures, and notices cited in this preamble are made available by the Superintendent of Documents, U.S. Government Printing Office, Washington, DC 20402.

[¶49,315]   Proposed Regulations (REG-142695-05), published with the Federal Register on August 6, 2007 (corrected 9/20/2007).

[Code Sec. 125]

Employers: Compensation and benefits: Cafeteria plans: Proposed regulations.—Reg. §§ 1.125-0, 1.125-1, 1.125-2, 1.125-5, 1.125-6 and 1.125-7, providing guidance on cafeteria plans, are proposed. Proposed Reg. § 1.125-1 and § 1.125-2 are withdrawn.

AGENCY: Internal Revenue Service (IRS), Treasury.

ACTION: Withdrawal of prior notices of proposed rulemaking, notice of proposed rulemaking and notice of public hearing.

SUMMARY: This document contains new proposed regulations providing guidance on cafeteria plans. This document also withdraws the notices of proposed rulemaking relating to cafeteria plans under section 125 that were published on May 7, 1984, December 31, 1984, March 7, 1989, November 7, 1997 and March 23, 2000. In general, these proposed regulations would affect employers that sponsor a cafeteria plan, employees that participate in a cafeteria plan, and third-party cafeteria plan administrators.

DATES: Written or electronic comments must be received by November 5, 2007. Outlines of topics to be discussed at the hearing scheduled for November 15, 2007, at 10 a.m., must be received by October 25, 2007.

ADDRESSES: Send submissions to: CC:PA:LPD:PR (REG-142695-05), room 5203, Internal Revenue Service, P.O. Box 7604, Ben Franklin Station, Washington, DC 20044. Submissions may be hand delivered Monday through Friday between the hours of 8 a.m. and 4 p.m. to CC:PA:LPD:PR (REG-142695-05), Courier's Desk, Internal Revenue Service, 1111 Constitution Avenue, NW., Washington, DC or sent electronically via the Federal eRulemaking Portal at *www.regulations.gov* (IRS REG-142695-05). The public hearing will be held at the IRS Auditorium, Internal Revenue Building, 1111 Constitution Avenue, NW, Washington, DC.

FOR FURTHER INFORMATION CONTACT: Concerning the proposed regulations, Mireille T. Khoury at (202) 622-6080; concerning submissions of comments, the hearing, and/or to be placed on the building access list to attend the hearing, Oluwafunmilayo Taylor of the Publications and Regulations Branch at (202) 622-7180 (not toll-free numbers).

SUPPLEMENTARY INFORMATION

Paperwork Reduction Act

The collections of information contained in this notice of proposed rulemaking have been submitted to the Office of Management and Budget for review in accordance with the Paperwork Reduction Act of 1995 (44 U.S.C. 3507(d)). Comments on the collections of information should be sent to the **Office of Management and Budget**, Attn: Desk Officer for the Department of Treasury, Office of Information and Regulatory Affairs, Washington, DC 20503, with copies to the **Internal Revenue Service**, Attn: IRS Reports Clearance Officer, SE:W:CAR:MP:T:T:SP, Washington, DC 20224. Comments on the collections of information should be received by October 5, 2007. Comments are specifically requested concerning:

Whether the proposed collections of information is necessary for the proper performance of the functions of the Internal Revenue Service, including whether the information will have practical utility;

The accuracy of the estimated burden associated with the proposed collection of information;

How the quality, utility, and clarity of the information to be collected may be enhanced;

How the burden of complying with the proposed collections of information may be minimized, including through the application of automatic collection techniques or other forms of information technology; and

Estimates of the capital or start-up costs and costs of operation, maintenance, and purchase of service to provide information.

The collection of information in this proposed regulation is in § 1.125-2 (cafeteria plan elections); § 1.125-6(b)-(g) (substantiation of expenses); and § 1.125-7 (cafeteria plan nondiscrimination rules). This information is required to file employment tax returns and Forms W-2. The collection of information is voluntary to obtain a benefit. The likely respondents are Federal, state or local governments, business or other for-profit institutions, nonprofit institutions, and small businesses or organizations.

Estimated total annual reporting burden: 34,000,000 hours.

Estimated average annual burden per respondent: 5 hours.

Estimated annual frequency of responses: once.

An agency may not conduct or sponsor, and a person is not required to respond to, a collection of information unless it displays a valid control number assigned by the Office of Management and Budget.

Books or records relating to a collection of information must be retained as long as their contents may become material in the administration of any internal revenue law. Generally, tax returns and tax return information are confidential, as required by 26 U.S.C. 6103.

Background

This document contains proposed Income Tax Regulations (26 CFR Part 1) under section 125 of the Internal Revenue Code (Code). On May 7, 1984, December 31, 1984, March 7, 1989, November 7, 1997, and March 23, 2000, the IRS and Treasury Department published proposed amendments to 26 CFR Part 1 under section 125 in the **Federal Register** (49 FR 19321, 49 FR 50733, 54 FR 9460, 62 FR 60196 and 65 FR 15587). These 1984, 1989, 1997 and 2000 proposed regulations are hereby withdrawn. Also, the temporary regulations under section 125 that were published on February 4, 1986 in the **Federal Register** (51 FR 4318) are being withdrawn in a separate document. The new proposed regulations that are published in this document replace those proposed regulations.

Explanation of Provisions

Overview

The new proposed regulations are organized as follows: general rules on qualified and nonqualified benefits in cafeteria plans (new proposed § 1.125-1), general rules on elections (new proposed § 1.125-2), general rules on flexible spending arrangements (new proposed § 1.125-5), general rules on substantiation of expenses for qualified benefits (new proposed § 1.125-6) and nondiscrimination rules (new proposed § 1.125-7). The new proposed regulations, new Proposed §§ 1.125-1, 1.125-2, 1.125-5, 1.125-6 and § 1.125-7, consolidate and restate Proposed § 1.125-1 (1984, 1997, 2000), § 1.125-2 (1989, 1997, 2000) and § 1.125-2T (1986). Unless otherwise indicated, references to "new proposed regulations" or "these proposed regulations" mean the proposed section 125 regulations being published in this document.

The new proposed regulations reflect changes in tax law since the prior regulations were proposed, including: the change in the definition of dependent (section 152) and the addition of the following as qualified benefits: adoption assistance (section 137), additional deferred compensation benefits described in section 125(d)(1)(B), (C) and (D), Health Savings Accounts (HSAs) (sections 223, 125(d)(2)(D) and 4980G), and qualified HSA distributions from health FSAs (section 106(e)). Other changes include the prohibition against long-term care insurance and long-term care services (section 125(f)) and the addition of the key employee concentration test in section 125(b)(2).

The prior proposed regulations, §§ 1.125-1 and 1.125-2, provide the basic framework and requirements for cafeteria plans and elections under cafeteria plans. The prior proposed regulations also outlined the most significant rules for benefits under a health flexible spending arrangement (health FSA) offered by a cafeteria plan - the requirement that the maximum reimbursement be available at all times during the coverage period (the uniform coverage rule), the requirement of a 12-month period of coverage, the requirement that the health FSA only reimburse medical expenses, the requirement that all medical expenses be substantiated by a third party before reimbursement, the requirement that expenses be incurred during the period of coverage, and the prohibition against deferral of compensation (including the use-or-lose rule). The prior proposed regulations also provided guidelines for dependent care FSAs, and the application of section 125 to paid vacation days offered under a cafeteria plan. These remain substantially unchanged in the new proposed regulations, with certain clarifications. Finally, the prior proposed regulations included a number of Q & As addressing transitional issues relating to the enactment of section 125, as well as the application of the now-repealed section 89 (special nondiscrimination rules with respect to certain employee benefit plans). These provisions are omitted from the new proposed regulations.

I. New Proposed § 1.125-1—Qualified and nonqualified benefits in cafeteria plans Section 125 exclusive noninclusion rule

Section 125 provides that, except in the case of certain discriminatory benefits, no amount shall be included in the gross income of a participant in a cafeteria plan (as defined in section 125(d)) solely because, under the plan, the participant may choose among the benefits of the plan. The new proposed regulations clarify and amplify the general rule in the prior proposed regulations that section 125 is the exclusive means by which an employer can offer employees a choice between taxable and nontaxable benefits without the choice itself resulting in inclusion in gross income by the employees. When employees may elect between taxable and nontaxable benefits, this election results in gross income to employees, unless a specific Internal Revenue Code (Code) section (such as section 125) intervenes to prevent gross income inclusion. Thus, except for an election made through a cafeteria plan that satisfies section 125 or another specific Code section (such as section 132(f)(4)), any opportunity to elect among taxable and nontaxable benefits results in inclusion of the taxable benefit regardless of what benefit is elected and when the election is made. This interpretation of section 125 is consistent with the legislative history of section 125. The legislative history begins with the interim ERISA rules for cafeteria plans:

Under . . . ERISA, an employer contribution made before January 1, 1977, to a cafeteria plan in existence on June 27, 1974, is required to be included in an employees' gross income only to the extent that the employee actually elects taxable benefits. In the case of a plan not in existence on June 27, 1974, the employer contribution is required to be included in an employee's gross income to the extent the employee could have elected taxable benefits. S. Rep. No. 1263, 95th Cong., 2d Sess. 74 (1978), reprinted in 1978 U.S.C.C.A.N. 6837; H. R. Rep. No. 1445, 95th Cong., 2d Sess. 63 (1978); H.R. Conf. Rep. No. 1800, 95th Cong., 2d Sess. 206 (1978).

The legislative history also provides:

[G]enerally, employer contributions under a written cafeteria plan which permits employees to elect between taxable and nontaxable benefits are excluded from the gross income of an employee to the extent that nontaxable benefits are elected.

S. Rep. No. 1263, 95th Cong., 2d Sess. 75 (1978), reprinted in 1978 U.S.C.C.A.N. 6838; H. R. Rep. No. 1445, 95th Cong., 2d Sess. 63 (1978). See also H.R. Conf. Rep. No. 1800, 95th Cong., 2d Sess. 206 (1978).

The legislative history to the 1984 amendments to section 125 continues:

The cafeteria plan rules of the Code provide that a participant in a nondiscriminatory cafeteria plan will not be treated as having received a taxable benefit offered under the plan solely because the participant has the opportunity, before the benefit becomes available, to choose among the taxable and nontaxable benefits under the plan.

H.R. Conf. Rep. No. 861, 98th Cong., 2d Sess. 1173 (1984), reprinted in 1984 U.S.C.C.A.N. 1861. See also H.R. Conf. Rep. No. 736, 104th Cong., 2d Sess. 295, reprinted in 1996 U.S.C.C.A.N. 2108.

The new proposed regulations provide that unless a plan satisfies the requirements of section 125 and the regulations, the plan is not a cafeteria plan. Reasons that a plan would fail to satisfy the section 125 requirements include: offering nonqualified benefits; not offering an election between at least one permitted taxable benefit and at least one qualified benefit; deferring compensation; failing to comply with the uniform coverage rule or use-or-lose rule; allowing employees to revoke elections or make new elections during a plan year, except as provided in § 1.125-4; failing to comply with substantiation requirements; paying or reimbursing expenses incurred for qualified benefits before the effective date of the cafeteria plan or before a period of coverage; allocating experience gains (forfeitures) other than as expressly allowed in the new proposed regulations; and failing to comply with grace period rules.

Definition of a cafeteria plan

The new proposed regulations provide that a cafeteria plan is a separate written plan that complies with the requirements of section 125 and the regulations, that is maintained by an employer for employees and that is operated in compliance with the requirements of section 125 and the regulations. Participants in a cafeteria plan must be permitted to choose among at least one permitted taxable benefit (for example, cash, including salary reduction) and at least one qualified benefit. A plan offering only elections among nontaxable benefits is not a cafeteria plan. Also, a plan offering only elections among taxable benefits is not a cafeteria plan. See Rev. Rul. 2002-27, Situation 2 (2002-1 CB 925), see § 601.601(d)(2)(ii)(b). Finally, a cafeteria plan must not provide for deferral of compensation, except as specifically permitted in section 125(d)(2)(B), (C), or (D).

Written plan

Section 125(d)(1) requires that a cafeteria plan be in writing. The cafeteria plan must be operated in accordance with the written plan terms. The new proposed regulations require that the written plan specifically describe all benefits, set forth the rules for eligibility to participate and the procedure for making elections, provide that all elections are irrevocable (except to the extend that the plan includes the optional change in status rules in § 1.125-4), and state how employer contributions may be made under the plan (for example, salary reduction or nonelective employer contributions), the maximum amount of elective contributions, and the plan year. If the plan includes a flexible spending arrangement (FSA), the written plan must include provisions complying with the uniform coverage rule and the use-or-lose rule. Because section 125(d)(1)(A) states that a cafeteria plan is a written plan under which "all participants are employees," the new proposed regulations require that the written cafeteria plan specify that only employees may participate in the cafeteria plan. The new proposed regulations also require that all provisions of the written plan apply uniformly to all participants.

Individuals who may participate in a cafeteria plan

All participants in a cafeteria plan must be employees. See section 125(d)(1)(A). These proposed regulations provide that employees include common law employees, leased employees described in section 414(n), and full-time life insurance salesmen (as defined in section 7701(a)(20)). These proposed regulations further provide that former employees (including laid-off employees and retired employees) may participate in a plan, but a plan may not be maintained predominantly for former employees. See Rev. Rul. 82-196 (1982-2 CB 53); Rev. Rul. 85-121 (1985-2 CB 57), see

§ 601.601(d)(2)(ii)(*b*). All employees who are treated as employed by a single employer under section 414(b), (c) or (m) are treated as employed by a single employer for purposes of section 125. See section 125(g)(4). A participant's spouse or dependents may receive benefits through a cafeteria plan although they cannot participate in the cafeteria plan.

Self-employed individuals are not treated as employees for purposes of section 125. Accordingly, the new proposed regulations make clear that sole proprietors, partners, and directors of corporations are not employees and may not participate in a cafeteria plan. In addition, the new proposed regulations clarify that 2-percent shareholders of an S corporation are not employees for purposes of section 125. The new proposed regulations provide rules for dual status individuals and individuals moving between employee and non-employee status. A self-employed individual may, however, sponsor a cafeteria plan for his or her employees.

Election between taxable and nontaxable benefits

The new proposed regulations require that a cafeteria plan offer employees an election among only permitted taxable benefits (including cash) and qualified nontaxable benefits. See section 125(d)(1)(B). For purposes of section 125, cash means cash from current compensation (including salary reduction), payment for annual leave, sick leave, or other paid time off, severance pay, property, and certain after-tax employee contributions. Distributions from qualified retirement plans are not cash or taxable benefits for purposes of section 125. See Rev. Rul. 2003-62 (2003-1 CB 1034) (distributions to former employees from a qualified employees' trust, applied to pay health insurance premiums, are includible in former employees' gross income under section 402), see § 601.601(d)(2)(ii)(*b*).

Qualified benefits

In general, in order for a benefit to be a qualified benefit for purposes of section 125, the benefit must be excludible from employees' gross income under a specific provision of the Code and must not defer compensation, except as specifically allowed in section 125(d)(2)(B), (C) or (D). Examples of qualified benefits include the following: group-term life insurance on the life of an employee (section 79); employer-provided accident and health plans, including health flexible spending arrangements, and accidental death and dismemberment policies (sections 106 and 105(b)); a dependent care assistance program (section 129); an adoption assistance program (section 137); contributions to a section 401(k) plan; contributions to certain plans maintained by educational organizations, and contributions to HSAs. Section 125(f), (d)(2)(B), (C), (D). See Notice 97-9 (1997-2 CB 35) (adoption assistance), see § 601.601(d)(2)(ii)(*b*); Notice 2004-2, Q & A-33 (2004-1 CB 269) (HSAs), see § 601.601(d)(2)(ii)(*b*). A cafeteria plan may also offer long-term and short-term disability coverage as a qualified benefit (see section 106). However, see paragraph (q) in § 1.125-1 for nonqualified benefits.

Group-term life insurance

An employer may provide group-term life insurance through a combination of methods. Generally, under section 79(a), the cost of $50,000 or less of group-term life insurance on the life of an employee provided under a policy (or policies) carried directly or indirectly by an employer is excludible from the employee's gross income. (Special rules apply to key employees if the group-term life insurance plan does not satisfy the nondiscrimination rules in section 79(d)). However, if the group-term life insurance provided to an employee by an employer or employers exceeds $50,000 (taking into account all coverage provided both through a cafeteria plan and outside a cafeteria plan), the cost of coverage exceeding coverage of $50,000 is includible in the employee's gross income. For this purpose, the cost of group-term life insurance is shown in § 1.79-3(d)(2), Table I (Table I). The Table I cost of the excess group-term life insurance (minus all after-tax contributions by the employee for group-term life insurance coverage) is includible in each covered employee's gross income. The new proposed regulations provide that the cost of group-term life insurance on the life of an employee, that either is less than or equal to the amount excludible from gross income under section 79(a) or provides coverage in excess of that amount, but not combined with any permanent benefit, is a qualified benefit that may be offered in a cafeteria plan. The new proposed regulations also provide that the entire amount of salary reduction and employer flex-credits for group-term life insurance coverage on the life of an employee is excludible from an employee's gross income.

The rule in the new proposed regulations differs from Notice 89-110 (1989-2 CB 447), see § 601.601(d)(2)(ii)(*b*). Notice 89-110 provides that an employee includes in gross income the greater of the Table I cost of group-term life insurance coverage exceeding $50,000 or the employee's salary reduction and employer flex-credits for excess group-term life insurance coverage. The new proposed regulations provide instead that the employee includes in gross income the Table I cost of the excess coverage (minus all after-tax contributions by the employee for group-term life insurance coverage) and that the entire amount of salary reduction and employer flex-credits for group-term life insurance coverage on the life of the employee is excludible from the employee's gross income. As noted in this preamble, taxpayers may rely on the new proposed regulations for guidance pending the issuance of final regulations.

Employer-provided accident and health plan

Coverage under an employer-provided accident and health plan that satisfies the requirements of section 105(b) may be provided as a qualified benefit through a cafeteria plan and is excludible from employees' gross income. Section 106; § 1.106-1. The nondiscrimination rules under section 105(h) apply to self-insured medical reimbursement arrangements (including health FSAs).

The new proposed regulations specifically permit a cafeteria plan (but not a health FSA) to pay or reimburse substantiated individual accident and health insurance premiums. See Rev. Rul. 61-146 (1961-2 CB 25), see § 601.601(d)(2)(ii)(*b*). In addition, a cafeteria plan may provide for payment of COBRA premiums for an employee.

For employer-provided accident and health plans and medical reimbursement plans, the definition of dependents is the definition in section 105(b) as amended by the Working Families Tax Relief Act of 2004 (WFTRA), Public Law 108-311, section 207(9) (118 Stat. 1166) (that is, a dependent as defined in section 152, determined without regard to section 152(b)(1), (b)(2), or (d)(1)(B)). See Notice 2004-79 (2004-2 CB 898), see § 601.601(d)(2)(ii)(*b*). For purposes of the exclusion from employees' gross income for accident and health plans and for medical reimbursement under sections 105(b) and 106, the spouse or dependent of a former employee (including a retired employee or a laid-off employee) or of a deceased employee is treated as a spouse or dependent. See Rev. Rul. 82-196 (1982-2 CB 53); Rev. Rul. 85-121 (1985-2 CB 57), see § 601.601(d)(2)(ii)(*b*).

Dependent care assistance programs and adoption assistance programs

If the requirements of section 129 are satisfied, up to $5,000 of employer-provided assistance for amounts paid or incurred by employees for dependent care is excludible from employees' gross income. The new proposed regulations outline the general requirements for providing dependent care assistance programs and adoption assistance programs under section 137 through a cafeteria plan. See Notice 97-9, section II (1997-2 CB 35), see § 601.601(d)(2)(ii)(*b*).

Cafeteria plan year

The new proposed regulations require that a cafeteria plan year must be 12 consecutive months and must be set out in the written cafeteria plan. A short plan year (or a change in plan year resulting in a short plan year) is permitted only for a valid business purpose. A change in plan year resulting in a short plan year, for other than a valid business purpose, is disregarded. If a principal purpose of a change in plan year is to circumvent the rules of section 125, the change in plan year is ineffective.

No deferral of compensation

Qualified benefits must be current benefits. In general, a cafeteria plan may not offer benefits that defer compensation or operate to defer compensation. Section 125(d)(2)(A). In general, benefits may not be carried over to a later plan year or used in one plan year to purchase benefits to be provided in a later plan year. For example, life insurance with a cash value build-up or group-term life insurance with a permanent benefit (within the meaning of §1.79-0) defers the receipt of compensation and thus is not a qualified benefit.

The new proposed regulations clarify whether certain benefits and plan administration practices defer compensation. For example, the regulations permit an accident and health insurance policy to provide certain benefit features that apply for more than one plan year, such as reasonable lifetime limits on benefits, level premiums, premium waiver during disability, guaranteed renewability of coverage, coverage for specified accidental injury or specific diseases, and the payment of a fixed amount per day for hospitalization. But these insurance policies must not provide an investment fund or cash value to pay premiums, and no part of the premium may be held in a separate account for any beneficiary. The new proposed regulations also provide that the following benefits and practices do not defer compensation: a long-term disability policy paying benefits over more than one plan year; reasonable premium rebates or policy dividends; certain two-year lock-in vision and dental policies; certain advance payments for orthodontia; salary reduction contributions in the last month of a plan year used to pay accident and health insurance premiums for the first month of the following plan year; reimbursement of section 213(d) expenses for durable medical equipment; and allocation of experience gains (forfeitures) among participants.

Paid time off

Under the prior proposed regulations, permitted taxable benefits included various forms of paid leave. Since the prior proposed regulations were issued, many employers have recharacterized and combined vacation days, sick leave and personal days into a single category of "paid time off." The new proposed regulations use the term "paid time off" to refer to vacation days and other types of paid leave. The new proposed regulations contain the same ordering rule for elective and nonelective paid time off as set forth in Prop. §1.125-1, Q & A-7 (1984). A plan offering an election solely between paid time off and taxable benefits is not a cafeteria plan.

Grace period

The new proposed regulations allow a written cafeteria plan to provide an optional grace period immediately following the end of each plan year, extending the period for incurring expenses for qualified benefits. A grace period may apply to one or more qualified benefits (for example, health FSA or dependent care assistance program) but in no event does it apply to paid time off or contributions to section 401(k) plans. Unused benefits or contributions for one qualified benefit may only be used to reimburse expenses incurred during the grace period for that same qualified benefit. The amount of unused benefits and contributions available during the grace period may be limited by the employer. A grace period may extend to the fifteenth day of the third month after the end of the plan year (but may be for a shorter period). Benefits or contributions not used as of the end of the grace period are forfeited under the use-or-lose rule. The grace period applies to all employees who are participants (including through COBRA), as of the last day of the plan year. Grace period rules must apply uniformly to all participants. The grace period rules in these proposed regulations are based on Notice 2005-42 (2005-1 CB 1204), modified in Notice 2007-22 (2007-10 IRB 670), see §601.601(d)(2)(ii)(*b*), amplified in Notice 2005-86 (2005-2 CB 1075), amplified in Notice 2007-22 (2007-10 IRB 670), see §601.601(d)(2)(ii)(*b*). For eligibility to contribute to a Health Savings Account (HSA) during a grace period, see Notice 2005-86 (2005-2 CB 1075), see §601.601(d)(2)(ii)(*b*). For Form W-2 reporting for unused dependent care assistance used for expenses incurred during a grace period, see Notice 2005-61 (2005-2 CB 607), see §601.601(d)(2)(ii)(*b*).

Contributions to section 401(k) plans through a cafeteria plan

A cafeteria plan may include contributions to a section 401(k) plan. Section 125(d)(2)(B). The new proposed regulations clarify the interactions between section 125 and section 401(k). Contributions to a section 401(k) plan expressed as a percentage of compensation are permitted. Pursuant to §1.401(k)-1(a)(3)(ii), elective contributions to a section 401(k) plan may be made through automatic enrollment (that is, when the employee does not affirmatively elect cash, the employee's compensation is reduced by a fixed percentage, which is contributed to a section 401(k) plan).

Nonqualified benefits

A cafeteria plan must not offer any of the following benefits: scholarships (section 117); employer-provided meals and lodging (section 119); educational assistance (section 127); fringe benefits (section 132); long-term care insurance. See section 125(f). Long-term care services are nonqualified benefits, H.R. Conf. Rep. No. 736, 104th Cong., 2d Sess. 296, reprinted in 1996 U.S.C.C.A.N. 2109. (An HSA funded through a cafeteria plan may, however, be used to pay premiums for long-term care insurance or for long-term care services.) The new proposed regulations clarify that contributions to Archer Medical Savings Accounts (sections 220, 106(b)), group term life insurance for an employee's spouse, child or dependent, and elective deferrals to section 403(b) plans are also nonqualified benefits. A plan offering any nonqualified benefit is not a cafeteria plan. A cafeteria plan may not offer a health FSA that provides for the carryover of unused benefits. See Notice 2002-45, Part I (2002-2 CB 93); Rev. Rul. 2002-41 (2002-2 CB 75), see §601.601(d)(2)(ii)(*b*).

After-tax employee contributions

The new proposed regulations allow a cafeteria plan to offer after-tax employee contributions for qualified benefits or paid time off. A cafeteria plan may only offer the taxable benefits specifically permitted in the new proposed regulations. Nonqualified benefits may not be offered through a cafeteria plan, even if paid with after-tax employee contributions.

Employer contributions through salary reduction

Employees electing a qualified benefit through salary reduction are electing to forego salary and instead to receive a benefit which is excludible from gross income because it is provided by employer contributions. Section 125 provides that the employee is treated as receiving the qualified benefit from the employer in lieu of the taxable benefit. A cafeteria plan may also impose reasonable fees to administer the cafeteria plan which may be paid through salary reduction. A cafeteria plan is not required to allow employees to pay for any qualified benefit with after-tax employee contributions.

II. *New Prop. §1.125-2 - Elections in cafeteria plans*

Making, revoking and changing elections

Generally, a cafeteria plan must require employees to elect annually between taxable benefits and qualified benefits. Elections must be made before the earlier of the first day of the period of coverage or when benefits are first currently available. The determination of whether a taxable benefit is currently available does not depend on whether it has been constructively received by the employee for purposes of section 451. Annual elections generally must be irrevocable and may not be changed during the plan year. However, §1.125-4 permits a cafeteria plan to provide for changes in elections based on certain changes in status. An employer that wishes to permit such changes in elections must incorporate the rules in §1.125-4 in its written cafeteria plan. These proposed regulations omit the rule in Q & A-6(b) in Prop. §1.125-2 (1989) (cessation of required contributions), because the change in status rules in §1.125-4 superseded this provision of the 1989 proposed regulations.

If HSA contributions are made through salary reduction under a cafeteria plan, employees may prospectively elect, revoke or change salary reduction elections for HSA contributions at any time during the plan year with respect to salary that has not become currently available at the time of the election.

A cafeteria plan is permitted to include an automatic election for new employees or current employees. Rev. Rul. 2002-27 (2002-1 CB 925), see § 601.601(d)(2)(ii)(b). A new rule also permits a cafeteria plan to provide an optional election for new employees between cash and qualified benefits. New employees avoid gross income inclusion if they make an election within 30 days after the date of hire even if benefits provided pursuant to the election relate back to the date of hire. However, salary reduction amounts used to pay for such an election must be from compensation not yet currently available on the date of the election. Also, this special election rule for new employees does not apply to any employee who terminates employment and is rehired within 30 days after terminating employment (or who returns to employment following an unpaid leave of absence of less than 30 days).

New elections and revocations or changes in elections can be made electronically. The safe harbor for electronic elections in § 1.401(a)-21 is available. Only an employee can make an election or revoke or change his or her election. An employee's spouse or dependent may not make an election under a cafeteria plan and may not revoke or change an employee's election.

III. *New Prop. § 1.125-5-Flexible spending arrangements*

Overview

In general, a flexible spending arrangement (FSA) is a benefit designed to reimburse employees for expenses incurred for certain qualified benefits, up to a maximum amount not substantially in excess of the salary reduction and employer flex-credits allocated for the benefit. The maximum amount of reimbursement reasonably available must be less than five times the value of the coverage. Employer flex-credits are non-elective employer contributions that an employer makes available for every employee eligible to participate in the cafeteria plan, to be used at the employee's election only for one or more qualified benefits (but not as cash or other taxable benefits). The three types of FSAs are dependent care assistance, adoption assistance and medical care reimbursements (health FSA).

Uniform coverage rule

The new proposed regulations retain the rule that the maximum amount of reimbursement from a health FSA must be available at all times during the period of coverage (properly reduced as of any particular time for prior reimbursements). The uniform coverage rule does not apply to FSAs for dependent care assistance or adoption assistance.

Use-or-lose rule

An FSA must satisfy all the requirements of section 125, including the prohibition against deferring compensation. In general, as discussed under "No deferral of compensation", in order to satisfy this requirement of section 125, all benefits and contributions must be used by the end of the plan year (or grace period, if applicable), or are forfeited. The new proposed regulations continue the use-or-lose rule.

Period of coverage

The required period of coverage for all FSAs continues to be twelve months, with an exception for short plan years that satisfy the conditions in the new proposed regulations. The period of coverage and the plan year need not be the same. The beginning and end of a period of coverage is clarified. The new proposed regulations also clarify that FSAs for different qualified benefits need not have the same coverage period. See also "Grace period", discussed in this preamble. The new proposed regulations also continue to provide that expenses are incurred when services are provided. Expenses incurred before or after the period of coverage may not be reimbursed.

Health FSA

A health FSA may only reimburse certain substantiated section 213(d) medical care expenses incurred by the employee, or by the employee's spouse or dependents. A health FSA may be limited to a subset of permitted section 213(d) medical expenses (for example, a health FSA is permitted to exclude reimbursement of over-the-counter drugs described in Rev. Rul. 2003-102 (2003-2 CB 559), see § 601.601(d)(2)(ii)(b)). Similarly, a health FSA may be an HSA-compatible limited-purpose health FSA or post-deductible health FSA. Rev. Rul. 2004-45 (2004-1 CB 971), see § 601.601(d)(2)(ii)(b), amplified, Notice 2005-86 (2005-2 CB 1075). A health FSA may not reimburse premiums for accident and health insurance or long-term care insurance. See section 125(f).

A health FSA must satisfy all requirements of section 105(b), §§ 1.105-1 and 1.105-2. The section 105(h) nondiscrimination rules apply to health FSAs. All medical expenses must be substantiated before expenses are reimbursed. See *Incurring and reimbursing expenses for qualified* benefits, discussed in this preamble. The new proposed regulations also clarify when medical expenses are incurred.[1] A cafeteria plan may limit enrollment in a health FSA to those employees who participate in the employer's accident and health plan.

Qualified HSA distributions

Section 106(e), enacted in section 302 of the Health Opportunity Patient Empowerment Act of 2006, Public Law 109-432 (120 Stat. 2922 (2006)) allows "qualified HSA distributions" from health FSAs to HSAs. Section 106(e) applies to distributions between December 20, 2006 and December 31, 2011. The proposed regulations incorporate the rules on qualified HSA distributions set forth in Notice 2007-22 (2007-10 IRB 670). See § 601.601(d)(2)(ii)(b).

Dependent care assistance after termination

A new optional rule permits an employer to reimburse a terminated employee's qualified dependent care expenses incurred after termination through a dependent care FSA, if all section 129 requirements are otherwise satisfied.

Experience gains

If an employee fails to use all contributions and benefits for a plan year before the end of the plan year (and the grace period, if applicable), those unused contributions and benefits are forfeited under the use-or-lose rule. Unused amounts are also known as experience gains. The new proposed regulations retain the forfeiture allocation rules in the 1989 proposed regulations, and clarify that the employer sponsoring the cafeteria plan may retain forfeitures, use forfeitures to defray expenses of administering the plan or allocate forfeitures among employees contributing through salary reduction on a reasonable and uniform basis.

---

[1] See Rev. Rul. 2005-55 (2005-2 CB 284) and Rev. Rul. 2005-24 (2005-1 CB 892), see § 601.601(d)(2)(ii)(b) (section 105(b) exclusion only applicable to reimbursements for medical expenses incurred by employee, or by the employee's spouse or dependents); Rev. Rul. 2002-3 (2002-1 CB 316) (purported reimbursements to employees of health insurance premiums not paid by employees and therefore impermissible); Rev. Rul. 2002-80 (2002-2 CB 925), see § 601.601(d)(2)(ii)(b) (so-called advance reimbursements and purported loans are impermissible); Rev. Rul. 2003-43 (2003-1 CB 935), see § 601.601(d)(2)(ii)(b); Notice 2006-69 (2006-31 IRB 107) (substantiation requirements for debit cards), amplified in Notice 2007-2 (2007-2 IRB 254), see § 601.601(d)(2)(ii)(b).

FSA Administrative rules

Salary reduction contributions may be made at whatever interval the employer selects, including ratably over the plan year based on the employer's payroll periods or in equal installments at other regular intervals (for example, quarterly installments). These rules must apply uniformly to all participants.

IV. New Prop. §1.125-6-Substantiation of expenses for all cafeteria plans Incurring and reimbursing expenses for qualified benefits

The new proposed regulations provide that only expenses for qualified benefits incurred after the later of the effective date or the adoption date of the cafeteria plan are permitted to be reimbursed under the cafeteria plan. Similarly, if a plan amendment adds a new qualified benefit, only expenses incurred after the later of the effective date or the adoption date are eligible for reimbursement.[2] This rule applies to all qualified benefits. Similarly, a cafeteria plan may pay or reimburse only expenses for qualified benefits incurred during a participant's period of coverage.

Substantiation and reimbursement of expenses for qualified benefits

The new proposed regulations provide, after an employee incurs an expense for a qualified benefit during the coverage period, the expense must first be substantiated before the expense may be paid or reimbursed. All expenses must be substantiated (substantiating only a limited number of total claims, or not substantiating claims below a certain dollar amount does not satisfy the requirements in the new proposed regulations). See § 1.105-2; Rul. 2003-80; Rev. Rul. 2003-43 (2002-1 CB 935), see § 601.601(d)(2)(ii)(*b*); Notice 2006-69 (2006-31 IRB 107), Notice 2007-2 (2007-2 IRB 254). FSAs for dependent care assistance and adoption assistance must follow the substantiation procedures applicable to health FSAs.

Debit cards

The new proposed regulations incorporate previously issued guidance on substantiating, paying and reimbursing expenses for section 213(d) medical care incurred at a medical care provider when payment is made with a debit card. Rev. Rul. 2003-43 (2003-1 CB 935), amplified, Notice 2006-69 (2006-31 IRB 107), Notice 2007-2 (2007-2 IRB 254); Rev. Proc. 98-25 (1998-1 CB 689), see § 601.601(d)(2)(ii)(*b*). Among the permissible substantiation methods are copayment matches, recurring expenses, and real-time substantiation. The new proposed regulations also allow point-of-sale substantiation through matching inventory information with a list of section 213(d) medical expenses. The employer is responsible for ensuring that the inventory information approval system complies with the new regulations and with the recordkeeping requirements in section 6001. Rev. Rul. 2003-43 (2003-1 CB 935), amplified, Notice 2006-69 (2006-31 IRB 107), Notice 2007-2 (2007-2 IRB 254); Rev. Proc. 98-25 (1998-1 CB 689), see § 601.601(d)(2)(ii)(*b*). The new proposed regulations also provide rules under which an FSA may pay or reimburse dependent care expenses using debit cards.

Pursuant to prior guidance (in Notice 2006-69 (2006-31 IRB 107), amplified, Notice 2007-2 (2007-2 IRB 254)), for plan years beginning after December 31, 2006, the recordkeeping requirements described in paragraph (f) in §1.125-6 apply (that is, responsibility of employers relying on the inventory information approval system for health FSA debit cards to ensure that the system complies with the new proposed recordkeeping requirements, including Rev. Proc. 98-25 (1998-1 CB 689), Notice 2006-69 (2006-31 IRB 107), amplified, Notice 2007-2 (2007-2 IRB 254). For health FSA debit card transactions occurring on or before December 31, 2007, all supermarkets, grocery stores, discount stores and wholesale clubs that do not have a medical care merchant category code (as described in Rev. Rul. 2003-43 (2003-2 CB 935) are nevertheless deemed to be an "other medical provider" as described in Rev. Rul. 2003-43. (For a list of merchant category codes, see Rev. Proc. 2004-43 (2004-2 CB 124).) During this time period, mail-order vendors and web-based vendors that sell prescription drugs are also deemed to be an "other medical provider" as described in Rev. Rul. 2003-43. After December 31, 2008, health FSA debit cards may not be used at stores with the Drug Stores and Pharmacies merchant category code unless (1) the store participates in the inventory information approval system described in Notice 2006-69, or (2) on a store location by store location basis, 90 percent of the store's gross receipts during the prior taxable year consisted of items which qualify as expenses for medical care under section 213(d) (including nonprescription medications described in Rev. Rul. 2003-102 (2003-2 CB 559)). Notice 2006-69 (2006-31 IRB 107), amplified, Notice 2007-2 (2007-2 IRB 254).

V. New Prop. §1.125-7-Nondiscrimination rules

Discriminatory benefits provided to highly compensated participants and individuals and key employees are included in these employees' gross income. See section 125(b), (c). The new proposed regulations reflect changes in tax law since Prop. §1.125-1, Q & A-9 through 13 and 19 were proposed in 1984, including the key employee concentration test, statutory nontaxable benefits (enacted in the Deficit Reduction Act of 1984 (DEFRA), Public Law 98-369, section 531(b), (98 Stat. 881(1984)), and the change in definition of dependent in WFTRA.

The new proposed regulations provide additional guidance on the cafeteria plan nondiscrimination rules, including definitions of key terms, guidance on the eligibility test and the contributions and benefits tests, descriptions of employees allowed to be excluded from testing and a safe harbor nondiscrimination test for premium-only-plans.

Specifically, the new proposed regulations define several key terms, including highly compensated individual or participant (consistent with the section 414(q) definition of highly compensated employee), officer, five percent shareholder, key employee and compensation. The new proposed regulations also provide guidance on the nondiscrimination as to eligibility requirement by incorporating some of the rules under section 410(b) (specifically the rules under §1.410(b)-4(b) and (c) dealing with reasonable classification, the safe harbor percentage test and the unsafe harbor percentage component of the facts and circumstances test).

The new proposed regulations also provide additional guidance on the contributions and benefits test and, unlike the prior proposed regulations, the new proposed regulations provide an objective test to determine when the actual election of benefits is discriminatory. Specifically, the new proposed regulations provide that a cafeteria plan must give each similarly situated participant a uniform opportunity to elect qualified benefits, and that highly compensated participants must not actually disproportionately elect qualified benefits. Finally, the new rules provide guidance on the safe harbor for cafeteria plans providing health benefits and create a safe harbor for premium-only-plans that satisfy certain requirements.

The example in Prop. §1.125-1, Q & A-11 (1984) is deleted because it concerns a qualified legal services plan, which is no longer a qualified benefit.

Other issues

These proposed regulations provide guidance under section 125 (26 U.S.C. 125). Other statutes may impose additional requirements (for example, the Employee Retirement Income Security Act of 1974 (ERISA) (29 U.S.C. 1000), the Health Insurance Portability and Accountability Act of 1996 (HIPAA), (sections 9801-9803); and the continuation coverage requirements under the Consolidated Omnibus Budget Reconciliation Act of 1985 (COBRA) (section 4980B).

---

[2] See *American Family Mut. Ins. Co. v. United States*, 815 F. Supp. 1206 (W.D. Wis. 1992); *Wollenberg v. United States*, 75 F. Supp.2d 1032 (D. Neb. 1999); Rev. Rul. 2002-58 (2002-2 CB 541), see § 601.601(d)(2)(ii)(*b*); Notice 97-9, section II (adoption assistance).

Proposed Effective Date

With the exceptions noted in the "Effect on other documents" section of this preamble and under the "Debit cards" section of the preamble, it is proposed that these regulations apply for plan years beginning on or after January 1, 2009. Taxpayers may rely on these regulations for guidance pending the issuance of final regulations. Prior published guidance on qualified benefits under sections 79, 105, 106, 129, 137 and 223 that is affected by these proposed regulations remains applicable through the effective date of the final regulations (except as modified in "Effect on other documents" section of this preamble).

Effect on Other Documents

Notice 89-110 (1989-2 CB 447), see § 601.601(d)(2)(ii)(*b*), states that where group-term life insurance provided to an employee by an employer exceeds $50,000, the employee includes in gross income the greater of the cost of group-term life insurance shown in § 1.79-3(d)(2), Table I (Table I) on the excess coverage or the employee's salary reduction and employer flex-credits for excess coverage. Notice 89-110 is modified, effective as of the date the proposed regulations are published in the **Federal Register**.

Published guidance under § 105(b) states that if any person has the right to receive cash or any other taxable or nontaxable benefit under a health FSA other than the reimbursement of section 213(d) medical expenses of the employee, employee's spouse or employee's dependents, then all distributions made from the arrangement are included in the employee's gross income, even amounts paid to reimburse medical care. See Rev. Rul. 2006-36 (2006-36 IRB 353); Rev. Rul. 2005-24 (2005-1 CB 892); Rev. Rul. 2003-102 (2003-2 CB 559); Notice 2002-45 (2002-2 CB 93); Rev. Rul. 2002-41 (2002-2 CB 75); Rev. Rul. 69-141 (1969-1 CB 48). New section 106(e) provides that a health FSA will not fail to satisfy the requirements of sections 105 or 106 merely because the plan provides for a qualified HSA distribution. Amounts rolled into an HSA may be used for purposes other than reimbursing the section 213(d) medical expenses of the employee, spouse or dependents. Accordingly, Rev. Rul. 2006-36, Rev. Rul. 2005-24, Rev. Rul. 2003-102, Notice 2002-45, Rev. Rul. 2002-41, and Rev. Rul. 69-141 are modified with respect to qualified HSA distributions described in section 106(e). See Notice 2007-22 (2007-10 IRB 670), see § 601.601(d)(2)(ii)(*b*).

Special Analyses

It has been determined that this notice of proposed rulemaking is not a significant regulatory action as defined in Executive Order 12866. Therefore, a regulatory assessment is not required. It also has been determined that section 553(b) of the Administrative Procedure Act (5 U.S.C. chapter 5) does not apply to this regulation. It is hereby certified that the collection of information in this regulation will not have a significant economic impact on a substantial number of small entities. This certification is based on the fact that the regulations will only minimally increase the burdens on small entities. The requirements under these regulations relating to maintaining a section 125 cafeteria plan are a minimal additional burden independent of the burdens encompassed under existing rules for underlying employee benefit plans, which exist whether or not the benefits are provided through a cafeteria plan. In addition, most small entities that will maintain cafeteria plans already use a third-party plan administrator to administer the cafeteria plan. The collection of information required in these regulations, which is required to comply with the existing substantiation requirements of sections 105, 106, 129 and 125, and the recordkeeping requirements of section 6001, will only minimally increase the third-party administrator's burden with respect to the cafeteria plan. Therefore, an analysis under the Regulatory Flexibility Act (5 U.S.C. chapter 6) is not required. Pursuant to section 7805(f) of the Internal Revenue Code, this proposed regulation has been submitted to the Chief Counsel for Advocacy of the Small Business Administration for comment on its impact on small business.

Comments and Public Hearing

Before these proposed regulations are adopted as final regulations, consideration will be given to any written comments (a signed original and eight (8) copies) or electronic comments that are submitted timely to the IRS. The IRS and Treasury Department specifically request comments on the clarity of the proposed rules and how they can be made easier to understand. In addition, comments are requested on the following issues:

1. Whether, consistent with section 125 of the Internal Revenue Code, multiple employers (other than members of a controlled group described in section 125(g)(4)) may sponsor a single cafeteria plan;

2. Whether salary reduction contributions may be based on employees' tips and how that would work;

3. For cafeteria plans adopting the change in status rules in § 1.125-4, when a participant has a change in status and changes his or her salary reduction amount, how should the participant's uniform coverage amount be computed after the change in status.

All comments will be available for public inspection and copying.

A public hearing has been scheduled for November 15, 2007, beginning at 10 a.m. in the Auditorium, Internal Revenue Service, 1111 Constitution Avenue, NW., Washington, DC. Due to building security procedures, visitors must enter at the Constitution Avenue entrance. In addition, all visitors must present photo identification to enter the building. Because of access restrictions, visitors will not be admitted beyond the immediate entrance area more than 30 minutes before the hearing starts. For information about having your name placed on the building access list to attend the hearing, see the "FOR FURTHER INFORMATION CONTACT" section of this preamble.

The rules of 26 CFR 601.601(a)(3) apply to the hearing. Persons who wish to present oral comments at the hearing must submit written or electronic comments and an outline of the topics to be discussed and the amount of time to be devoted to each topic (a signed original and eight (8) copies) by October 25, 2007. A period of 10 minutes will be allotted to each person for making comments. An agenda showing the scheduling of the speakers will be prepared after the deadline for receiving outlines has passed. Copies of the agenda will be available free of charge at the hearing.

Drafting Information

The principal author of these proposed regulations is Mireille T. Khoury, Office of Division Counsel/Associate Chief Counsel (Tax Exempt and Government Entities), Internal Revenue Service. However, personnel from other offices of the IRS and Treasury Department participated in their development.

[¶ 49,318]   **Proposed Amendments of Regulations (REG-143397-05)**, published in the Federal Register on August 22, 2007 (corrected 11/6/2007).

[Code Secs. 704 and 737]

Partnerships: Distributions: Allocation of pre-contribution gain and loss: Assets-over partnership merger.—Amendments of Reg. §§ 1.704-3, 1.704-4, 1.737-1, 1.737-2 and 1.737-5, relating to the applications of Code Secs. 704(c)(1)(B) and 737 to distributions of property after two partnerships engage in an assets-over merger, are proposed.

AGENCY: Internal Revenue Service (IRS), Treasury.

ACTION: Notice of proposed regulations **and notice** of public hearing

SUMMARY: This document contains regulations that provide rules concerning the application of sections 704(c)(1)(B) and 737 to distributions of property after two partnerships engage in an assets-over merger. The proposed regulations affect partnerships and their partners. This document also provides a notice of public hearing on these proposed regulations.

DATES: Written or electronic comments must be received by November 20, 2007. Outlines of the topic to be discussed at the public hearing scheduled for December 5, 2007 at 10 a.m. must be received by November 21, 2007.

ADDRESSES: Send submissions to: CC:PA:LPD:PR (REG-143397-05), room 5203, Internal Revenue Service, PO Box 7604, Ben Franklin Station, Washington DC 20044. Submissions may be hand delivered Monday through Friday, between the hours of 8 a.m. and 4 p.m. to CC:PA:LPD:PR (REG-143397-05), Courier's Desk, Internal Revenue Service, 1111 Constitution Avenue, NW., Washington, DC or sent electronically via the Federal eRulemaking Portal at *http://www.regulations.gov* (IRS REG-143397-05). The public hearing will be held in the Auditorium, Internal Revenue Building, 1111 Constitution Avenue NW, Washington, DC.

FOR FURTHER INFORMATION CONTACT: Concerning the proposed regulations, Jason Smyczek or Laura Fields (202) 622-3050, concerning submissions of comments, the hearing, and/or to be placed on the building access list to attend the hearing, Richard Hurst, *Richard.A.Hurst@irscounsel.treas.gov*, (202) 622-7180 (not toll-free numbers).

SUPPLEMENTAL INFORMATION:

Background

Section 704(c)(1)(B) provides that a partner that contributes section 704(c) property to a partnership must recognize gain or loss on the distribution of such property to another partner within seven years of its contribution to the partnership in an amount equal to the gain or loss that would have been allocated to such partner under section 704(c) if the distributed property had been sold by the partnership to the distributee partner for its fair market value at the time of the distribution.

Section 737(a) provides that a partner that contributes section 704(c) property to the partnership and then receives a distribution of property (other than money) within seven years of its contribution must recognize gain in an amount equal to the lesser of (1) the excess (if any) of (A) the fair market value of property (other than money) received in the distribution over (B) the adjusted basis of the partner's interest in the partnership immediately before the distribution reduced (but not below zero) by the amount of money received in the distribution, or (2) the net precontribution gain of the partner.

Section 737(b) provides that for purposes of section 737, the term "net precontribution gain" means the net gain (if any) which would have been recognized by the distributee partner under section 704(c)(1)(B) if all property which (1) had been contributed to the partnership by the distributee partner within seven years of the distribution, and (2) is held by the partnership immediately before the distribution, had been distributed by the partnership to another partner.

Rev. Rul. 2004-43, 2004-1 CB 842, (see § 601.601(d)(2) of this chapter) issued on April 12, 2004, addressed the application of sections 704(c)(1)(B) and 737 in an assets-over partnership merger described in § 1.708-1(c)(3)(i). Rev. Rul. 2004-43 held that section 704(c)(1)(B) applies to newly created section 704(c) gain or loss in property contributed by the transferor partnership to the transferee partnership in an assets-over partnership merger. The revenue ruling also held that for purposes of section 737(b), net precontribution gain includes newly created section 704(c) gain or loss in property contributed by the transferor partnership to the transferee partnership in an assets-over partnership merger. In addition, the revenue ruling held that section 704(c)(1)(B) will not apply to, and, for purposes of section 737, net precontribution gain will not include, reverse section 704(c) gain or loss resulting from a revaluation of property of the transferee partnership.

Some commentators argued that Rev. Rul. 2004-43 was not consistent with the existing regulations under sections 704(c)(1)(B) and 737, and that the conclusions contained in the ruling should not be applied retroactively. In response to these comments, the Treasury Department and the IRS issued Notice 2005-15, 2005-7 IRB 527, (see § 601.601(d)(2) of this chapter) indicating their intent to issue regulations under sections 704(c)(1)(B) and 737 implementing the principles of the ruling, and issued Rev. Rul. 2005-10, 2005-7 IRB 492, (see § 601.601(d)(2) of this chapter) officially revoking Rev. Rul. 2004-43. The Notice provided that any such regulations would be effective for distributions made after January 19, 2005.

Explanation of Provisions

A. Assets-Over Partnership Mergers

These proposed regulations implement the principles articulated in Rev. Rul. 2004-43. The proposed regulations under § 1.704-4(c)(4) and § 1.737-2(b) provide that in an assets-over merger, sections 704(c)(1)(B) and 737 do not apply to the transfer by a partnership (the transferor partnership) of all of its assets and liabilities to another partnership (the transferee partnership), followed by a distribution of the interests in the transferee partnership in liquidation of the transferor partnership as part of the same plan or arrangement.

The proposed regulations, however, provide that section 704(c)(1)(B) applies to a subsequent distribution by the transferee partnership of section 704(c) property contributed in the assets-over merger by the transferor partnership to the transferee partnership. The proposed regulations also provide that section 737 applies when a partner of the transferor partnership receives a subsequent distribution of property (other than money) from the transferee partnership.

The proposed regulations provide that for property contributed to the transferor partnership (original contribution), the amount of original section 704(c) gain or loss is the difference between the property's fair market value and the contributing partner's adjusted basis at the time of contribution to the extent such difference has not been eliminated by section 704(c) allocations, prior revaluations, or in connection with the merger. In the case of property contributed with original section 704(c) loss, section 704(c)(1)(C) which was added by the American Jobs Creation Act of 2004 provides special rules for determining the basis of the property contributed. The Treasury Department and IRS are currently developing guidance that will implement the provisions of section 704(c)(1)(C). Thus, the proposed regulations do not address the impact of section 704(c)(1)(C) in applying these rules. However, when finalized, these regulations will clarify the application of section 704(c)(1)(C) to these rules.

The proposed regulations provide that the seven year period will not restart with respect to the original section 704(c) gain or loss as a result of the merger. Accordingly, a subsequent distribution by the transferee partnership of property with original section 704(c) gain or loss is subject to sections 704(c)(1)(B) and 737 if the distribution occurs within seven years of the contribution of the property to the transferor partnership (original contribution). However, with respect to new section 704(c) gain or loss, the regulations provide that the seven-year period in sections 704(c)(1)(B) and 737 begins on the date of merger. Thus, a subsequent distribution by the transferee partnership of property with new section 704(c) gain or loss is subject to sections 704(c)(1)(B) and 737 if the distribution occurs within seven years of the merger.

The regulations further provide that no original section 704(c) gain or loss will be recognized under section 704(c)(1)(B) or section 737 if property that was originally contributed to the transferor partnership is distributed to the original contributor. If property has new section 704(c) gain or loss, then a subsequent distribution of such property within seven years of the merger to one of the former partners of the transferor partnership (former partner) is subject to section 704(c)(1)(B) only to the extent of the other former partners' shares of such gain or loss.

New section 704(c) gain or loss shall be allocated among the partners of the transferor partnership in a manner consistent with the principles of §§ 1.704-3(a)(7) and newly designated 1.704-3(a)(10) (previously § 1.704-3(a)(9)). In addition, the partners of the transferor partnership are deemed to have contributed an undivided interest in the assets of the partnership. The proposed regulations provide that the determination of the partners' undivided interest for this purpose shall be made by the transferor partnership using any reasonable method. The Treasury Department and the IRS request comments on methods that should be considered reasonable for this purpose.

The proposed regulations also provide that if less than all of a section 704(c) property is distributed, then a proportionate amount of original and new section 704(c) gain or loss must be recognized under section 704(c)(1)(B). Similarly, if gain is required to be recognized under section 737, a proportionate amount of original and new section 704(c) gain must be recognized under section 737. Each partner must recognize its respective proportionate share of gain or loss required to be recognized.

The proposed regulations further provide a subsequent merger rule. This rule provides that if the transferee partnership is subsequently merged (a subsequent merger) the new section 704(c) gain or loss that resulted from the original merger shall be subject to section 704(c)(1)(B) for seven years from the time of the original merger and the new section 704(c) gain or loss that resulted from the subsequent merger will be subject to section 704(c)(1)(B) for seven years from the time of the subsequent merger.

In addition, the proposed regulations provide an identical ownership and a de minimis change in ownership exception to sections 704(c)(1)(B) and 737 with regard to assets-over partnership mergers. Under the identical ownership exception, section 704(c)(1)(B) will not apply to, and section 737 net precontribution gain will not include, new section 704(c) gain or loss in any property contributed in an assets-over partnership merger where the ownership of both partnerships is identical. In order for merging partnerships to qualify for the identical ownership exception, each partner must own identical interests in book capital and in each item of income, gain, loss, deductions and credit, and identical shares of distributions and liabilities in each of the transferor and transferee partnerships. Where ownership of both partnerships is identical, the merger more accurately represents a change in form, and should have no substantive tax consequences. The same principles apply where the change in ownership is de minimis. For purposes of the de minimis exception, a difference in ownership is de minimis if ninety seven percent of the interests in book capital, items of income, gain, loss, deduction and credit and share of distributions and liabilities of the transferor partnership and transferee partnership are owned by the same owners in the same proportions.

Proposed regulations under § 1.704-3(c)(9) provide that taxpayers may distinguish between the original and new portions of section 704(c) gain or loss. The proposed regulations provide that the transferee partnership may continue to use the section 704(c) allocation method adopted by the transferor partnership with respect to original section 704(c) property, or it may adopt another reasonable section 704(c) method. In addition, the transferee partnership may adopt any reasonable section 704(c) method with respect to new section 704(c) gain or loss. With respect to both the original and the new section 704(c) gain or loss, the transferee partnership must use a reasonable method that is consistent with the purpose of sections 704(b) and 704(c).

B. Miscellaneous Provisions

As part of this proposed regulation, the Treasury Department and the IRS are also making certain regulatory changes to reflect statutory changes that occurred as part of the Taxpayer Relief Act of 1997 (Public Law 105-34). Effective June 8, 1997, Congress lengthened the period of time from five years to seven for accounting for section 704(c) gain or loss with respect to distributions. Consistent with the statutory changes, various provisions in § 1.704-4 and § 1.737-1 have been amended.

Effective Dates

Except as otherwise provided, these proposed regulations will be effective for any distributions of property after January 19, 2005, if such property was contributed in an assets-over merger after May 3, 2004. Provisions relating to the change in the regulations in § 1.704-4 and § 1.737-1 from the previous five-year rule to the seven-year rule will be effective August 22, 2007.

Special Analyses

It has been determined that this notice of proposed rulemaking is not a significant regulatory action as defined in Executive Order 12866. Therefore, a regulatory assessment is not required. It has also been determined that section 553(b) of the Administrative Procedure Act (5 U.S.C. chapter 5) does not apply to these regulations, and because the regulation does not impose a collection of information on small entities, the Regulatory Flexibility Act (5 U.S.C. chapter 6) does not apply. Pursuant to section 7805(f) of the Code, this notice of proposed rulemaking will be submitted to the Chief Counsel for Advocacy of the Small Business Administration for comment on its impact on small business.

Comments and Public Hearing

Before these proposed regulations are adopted as final regulations, consideration will be given to any written comments (a signed original and eight (8) copies) or electronic comments that are submitted timely to the IRS. The Treasury Department and IRS request comments on the clarity of the proposed rules and how they may be made easier to understand. All comments will be available for public inspection and copying.

A public hearing has been scheduled for **December 5, 2007**, 10 a.m. in the Auditorium, Internal Revenue Building, 1111 Constitution Avenue, N.W., Washington, DC. Due to building security procedures, visitors must enter at the Constitution Avenue entrance. In addition, all visitors must present photo identification to enter the building. Because of access restrictions, visitors will not be admitted beyond the immediate entrance area more than 15 minutes before the hearing starts. For information about having your name placed on the building access list to attend the hearing, see the "FOR FURTHER INFORMATION CONTACT" section of this preamble.

The rules of 26 CFR 601.601(a)(3) apply to the hearing. Persons who wish to present oral comments at the hearing must submit written or electronic comments by November 20, 2007, and an outline of the topics to be discussed and time to be devoted to each topic (a signed original and eight (8) copies) by November 21, 2007. A period of 10 minutes will be allotted to each person for making comments. An agenda showing the scheduling of the speakers will be prepared after the deadline for receiving outlines has passed. Copies of the agenda will be available free of charge at the hearing.

Drafting Information

The principal authors of these proposed regulations are Jason Smyczek and Laura Fields, Office of the Associate Chief Counsel (Passthroughs and Special Industries), IRS. However, other personnel from the IRS and the Treasury Department participated in their development.

[¶ 49,322] Proposed Amendments of Regulations (REG-129916-07), published in the Federal Register on September 26, 2007.

[Code Secs. 6011 and 6111]

Proposed regulations: Patenting of tax advice or tax strategies: Reportable transactions: Disclosure: List maintenance.—Amendments of Regs. § 1.6011-4 and 301.6111-3, relating to the disclosure of reportable transactions under Code Secs. 6011 and 6111, are proposed.

AGENCY: Internal Revenue Service (IRS), Treasury.

ACTION: Notice of proposed rulemaking.

SUMMARY: This document contains proposed regulations that provide rules relating to the disclosure of reportable transactions under sections 6011 and 6111 of the Internal Revenue Code (Code). These regulations propose to add the patented transactions category of reportable transaction to the regulations under § 1.6011-4 of the Income Tax Regulations. The regulations also include conforming changes to the rules relating to the disclosure of reportable transactions by material advisors under section 6111. The regulations affect taxpayers participating in reportable transactions under section 6011, material advisors responsible for disclosing reportable transactions under section 6111, and material advisors responsible for keeping lists under section 6112.

DATES: Written or electronic comments and requests for a public hearing must be received by December 26, 2007.

ADDRESSES: Send submissions to: CC:PA:LPD:PR (REG-129916-07), room 5203, Internal Revenue Service, PO Box 7604, Ben Franklin Station, Washington, DC 20044. Submissions may be hand-delivered Monday through Friday between the hours of 8 a.m. and 4 p.m. to CC:PA:LPD:PR (REG-129916-07), Courier's Desk, Internal Revenue Service, 1111 Constitution Avenue, NW., Washington, DC, or sent electronically, via the Federal eRulemaking Portal at www.regulations.gov (IRS-REG-129916-07).

FOR FURTHER INFORMATION CONTACT: Concerning the proposed regulations, Michael H. Beker or Charles D. Wien, (202) 622-3070; concerning the submissions of comments and requests for hearing, Richard Hurst at Richard.A.Hurst@irscounsel.treas.gov or (202) 622-7180 (not toll-free numbers).

SUPPLEMENTARY INFORMATION:

Background

This document proposes to amend 26 CFR parts 1 and 301 by adding the patented transactions category of reportable transaction to the rules under section 6011 and by making conforming changes to the rules relating to the disclosure of reportable transactions by material advisors under section 6111.

On November 1, 2006, the IRS and Treasury Department issued a notice of proposed rulemaking and temporary and final regulations under sections 6011, 6111, and 6112 (REG-103038-05, REG-103039-05, REG-103043-05, TD 9295) (the November 2006 regulations). The November 2006 regulations were published in the **Federal Register** (71 FR 64488, 71 FR 64496, 71 FR 64501, 71 FR 64458) on November 2, 2006. In the preamble to those proposed regulations, the IRS and Treasury Department expressed concern, shared by many commentators, regarding the patenting of tax advice or tax strategies that have the potential for tax avoidance. A patent for tax advice or a tax strategy might be interpreted by taxpayers as approval by the IRS and Treasury Department of the transaction, which might impede the efforts of the IRS and Treasury Department to obtain information regarding tax avoidance transactions and have an impact on effective tax administration. Consequently, the IRS and Treasury Department requested comments regarding the creation of a new category of reportable transaction to address these concerns.

The IRS and Treasury Department received written public comments responding to the proposed regulations and held a public hearing regarding the proposed rules on March 20, 2007. After consideration of the comments received, the IRS and Treasury Department are issuing these proposed regulations with respect to patented transactions. Upon publication of final regulations, these regulations will be effective for transactions entered into on or after the date of publication of this notice of proposed rulemaking.

Explanation of Provisions

In response to the request for comments, the IRS and Treasury Department received five comments regarding the creation of a new category of reportable transaction to address the patenting of tax advice or tax strategies. One commentator suggested that the patenting of tax advice or tax strategies should not be addressed through the addition of a new category of reportable transaction. The commentator suggested that the IRS should require a form of notification or have a disclosure requirement informing the IRS when the United States Patent and Trademark Office (USPTO) issues a tax strategy patent. The commentator suggested that this could be accomplished through cooperation between the IRS and the USPTO. To the extent cooperation does not result in the necessary disclosures, the commentator suggested that the current reportable transaction regime or another mechanism could provide the necessary notifications and disclosures.

One commentator suggested that the patenting of tax advice or tax strategies should be addressed through the transaction of interest category of reportable transaction under § 1.6011-4(b)(6). The commentator suggested that each application for, or grant of a patent be automatically included within the scope of a transaction of interest, thereby requiring anyone who "participated" in the transaction to file a disclosure statement. In addition, the commentator suggested that the party who files an application for a patent, or for whom a patent is granted, be considered a material advisor, as defined in § 301.6111-3(b) of the Procedure and Administration Regulations. The commentator noted that treating the patent applicant or holder as a material advisor would obligate that party to file a disclosure statement under § 301.6111-3 and also to maintain an investor list under § 301.6112-1. Further, the commentator proposed that each material advisor should be required to disclose to each taxpayer on that material advisor's list of investors that the transaction is a transaction of interest and that the taxpayer is required to disclose the transaction.

Two commentators suggested the creation of a new category of reportable transaction for taxpayers who participate in a transaction that uses a patented tax strategy for each year in which the taxpayer's return reports items attributable to such transaction. The two commentators both suggested treating the patent holder as a material advisor within the meaning of section 6111. One of the two commentators suggested lowering the gross income threshold amounts for material advisors in § 301.6111-3(b)(3). One of the commentators recommended that a material advisor should only include the owner of the patent and advisors who pay fees directly or indirectly for the patented tax strategy or advice. This commentator also recommended that the disclosure obligations be narrowly construed so as not to apply to those taxpayers and material advisors who implement patented tax strategies and provided advice without any knowledge that the tax strategy or advice has been patented.

Another commentator also recommended limiting the scope of a category of reportable transaction for patents so that the category applies only to those taxpayers and material advisors who have a legal right to use the patented tax strategy or tax advice. Finally, commentators recommended excluding from the category of reportable transaction the use of patented tax methods or processes for complying with return preparation and filing and other administrative requirements.

After careful consideration of the comments received, the IRS and Treasury Department continue to be concerned about the patenting of tax advice or tax strategies and believe that adding a new category of reportable transaction to the section 6011 regulations for patented transactions will assist the IRS and Treasury Department in obtaining disclosures of tax avoidance transactions and in providing effective tax administration. Under the new category of reportable transactions, the "patented transaction" is a transaction for which a taxpayer pays (directly or indirectly) a fee in any amount to a patent holder or the patent holder's agent for the legal right to use a tax planning method that the taxpayer knows or has reason to know is the subject of the patent. A patented transaction also is a transaction for which a taxpayer (the patent holder or the patent holder's agent) has the right to payment for another person's use of a tax planning method that is the subject of the patent.

The proposed regulations exclude mathematical calculations or mechanical assistance in the preparation of tax returns from the patented transaction category of reportable transactions. Thus, a patented transaction does not include patent-protected tax preparation software or other tools used to perform or model mathematical calculations or to provide mechanical assistance in the preparation of tax or information returns.

For purposes of the new patented transaction category, a taxpayer has participated in a patented transaction if the taxpayer's tax return reflects a tax benefit from the transaction (including a deduction for fees paid in any amount to the patent holder or patent holder's agent). A taxpayer also has participated in a patented transaction if the taxpayer is the patent holder or patent holder's agent and the taxpayer's tax return reflects a tax benefit in relation to obtaining a patent for a tax planning method (including any deduction for amounts paid to the United States Patent and Trademark Office as required by title 35 of the United States Code and attorney's fees) or reflects income from a payment received from another person for the use of the tax planning method that is the subject of the patent.

These regulations also describe when a person is a material advisor with respect to a patented transaction under section 6111. Because of the nature of patented transactions and how those transactions are marketed, the threshold amount as described in section 6111(b) is reduced from $50,000 to $250 and from $250,000 to $500. A person who is a material advisor with respect to a patented transaction will have a list maintenance obligation under section 6112.

Special Analyses

It has been determined that these regulations are not a significant regulatory action as defined in Executive Order 12866. Therefore, a regulatory assessment is not required. It has also been determined that section 553(b) of the Administrative Procedure Act (5 U.S.C. chapter 5) does not apply to these regulations. It is hereby certified that the collection of information in these regulations will not have a significant economic impact on a substantial number of small entities. This certification is based on the fact that most information is already required to be reported on the disclosure statement referenced in the regulation and approved under OMB control number 1545-0074; the new information required by these proposed regulations add little or no new burden to the existing requirements. Therefore, a Regulatory Flexibility Analysis under the provisions of the Regulatory Flexibility Act (5 U.S.C. chapter 6) is not required. Pursuant to section 7805(f) of the Code, this notice of proposed rulemaking will be submitted to the Chief Counsel for Advocacy of the Small Business Administration for comment on its impact on small business.

Comments and Requests for a Public Hearing

Before these proposed regulations are adopted as final regulations, consideration will be given to any written comments (a signed original and eight (8) copies) or electronic comments that are submitted timely to the IRS. The IRS and Treasury Department specifically request comments on the clarity of the proposed rules, how they can be made easier to understand, and the administrability of the rules in the proposed regulations. All comments will be available for public inspection and copying. A public hearing will be scheduled if requested in writing by any person that submits timely written or electronic comments. If a public hearing is scheduled, notice of the date, time, and place for the public hearing will be published in the **Federal Register**.

Drafting Information

The principal authors of these regulations are Michael H. Beker and Charles D. Wien, Office of the Associate Chief Counsel (Passthroughs and Special Industries). However, other personnel from the IRS and Treasury Department participated in their development.

[¶ 49,326]   **Proposed Amendments of Regulations (REG-140206-06)**, published in the Federal Register on October 17, 2007 (corrected 11/7/2007).

[Code Sec. 1441]

Withholding of tax: Corporate distributions: Procedures.—Amendments of Reg. §1.1441-3, regarding a withholding agent's obligation to withhold and report tax under Chapter 3 of the Internal Revenue Code when there is a distribution in redemption of stock of a corporation that is actively traded on an established financial market, are proposed.

AGENCY: Internal Revenue Service (IRS), Treasury.

ACTION: Notice of proposed rulemaking and notice of public hearing.

SUMMARY: This document contains proposed regulations regarding a withholding agent's obligation to withhold and report tax under Chapter 3 of the Internal Revenue Code when there is a distribution in redemption of stock of a corporation that is actively traded on an established financial market. Specifically, the proposed regulations provide an escrow procedure that a withholding agent must apply while making the determination under section 302 as to whether the distribution in redemption of the stock held by a foreign shareholder is treated as a dividend subject to withholding, or a distribution in part or full payment in exchange for stock. These regulations would affect corporations that are actively traded on an established financial market and their shareholders. This document also provides a notice of public hearing on these proposed regulations.

DATES: Written or electronic comments must be received by January 16, 2008. Outlines of topics to be discussed at the public hearing scheduled for February 6, 2008 at 10 a.m. must be received by January 16, 2008.

ADDRESSES: Send submissions to CC:PA:LPD:PR (REG-140206-06), room 5203, Internal Revenue Service, PO Box 7604, Ben Franklin Station, Washington, DC 20044. Submissions may be hand delivered Monday through Friday between the hours of 8 a.m. and 4 p.m. to CC:PA:LPD:PR (REG-140206-06), Courier's Desk, Internal Revenue Service, 1111 Constitution Avenue, NW., Washington, DC or sent electronically, via the Federal eRulemaking Portal at www.regulations.gov (IRS REG-140206-06). The public hearing will be held in room 2140, Internal Revenue Building, 1111 Constitution Avenue, NW., Washington, DC.

FOR FURTHER INFORMATION CONTACT: Concerning the proposed regulations, Kathryn Holman, (202) 622-3840 (not a toll-free number); concerning submissions of comments, the hearing, and/or to be placed on the building access list to attend the hearing, e-mail Richard.A.Hurst@irscounsel.treas.gov.

SUPPLEMENTARY INFORMATION:

Paperwork Reduction Act

The collections of information contained in this notice of proposed rulemaking have been submitted to the Office of Management and Budget for review in accordance with the Paperwork Reduction Act of 1995 (44 U.S.C. 3507(d)). Comments on the collections of information should be sent to the Office of Management and Budget, Attn: Desk Office for the Department of the Treasury, Office of Information and Regulatory Affairs, Washington, DC 20503, with copies to the Internal Revenue Service, Attn: IRS Reports Clearance Officer, SE:W:CAR:MP:T:T:SP, Washington, DC 20224. Comments on the collection of information should be received by January 16, 2008. Comments are specifically requested concerning:

Whether the proposed collection of information is necessary for the proper performance of the functions of the Internal Revenue Service, including whether the information will have practical utility;

The accuracy of the estimated burden associated with the proposed collection of information;

How the quality, utility, and clarity of the information to be collected may be enhanced;

How the burden of complying with the proposed collections of information may be minimized, including through the application of automated collection techniques or other forms of information technology; and

Estimates of capital or start-up costs and costs of operation, maintenance and purchase of service to provide information.

The collection of information in these proposed regulations is in § 1.1441-3(c)(5)(iii). This information is required to allow a U.S. financial institution that is applying the escrow procedure to properly comply with its withholding and reporting obligations under sections 1441, 1442 and 1443 in the case of a distribution made by a corporation with respect to its stock that is actively traded on an established financial market and that requires a determination under section 302 as to whether the distribution is treated as a dividend or a distribution in part or full payment in exchange for stock. The collection of information is mandatory and the respondents are nonresident aliens and foreign corporations.

Estimated total annual reporting burden: 1400 hours.

The estimated annual burden per respondent: 2 hours.

Estimated number of respondents: 700.

Estimated annual frequency of responses: 5 times.

An agency may not conduct or sponsor, and a person is not required to respond to, a collection of information unless it displays a valid control number assigned by the Office of Management and Budget.

Books or records relating to a collection of information must be retained as long as their contents may become material in the administration of any internal revenue law. Generally, tax returns and tax return information are confidential as required by 26 U.S.C. 6103.

Background

These proposed regulations, REG-140206-06, provide guidance regarding the withholding and reporting obligations of a withholding agent under Chapter 3 of the Internal Revenue Code (Code) in the case of a distribution in redemption of the stock of a corporation that is actively traded on an established financial market within the meaning of § 1.1092(d)-1 (publicly traded). In general the proposed regulations contemplate a transaction where a publicly traded corporation offers to purchase stock from its shareholders (a self tender), where the amount of stock purchased and the shareholders involved in the transaction (the participating shareholders) depend on a number of factors, including each shareholder's willingness to sell some or all of its stock, and the terms set forth in the offer. The regulations would also apply to transactions described in section 304(a)(2).

In the case of a self-tender, a corporation may purchase stock from some or all of its shareholders and, as a result, each participating shareholder's percentage ownership interest in the corporation may increase, decrease, or remain the same. Although the corporation's self tender offer is denominated as an offer to purchase shares, the tax consequences to the corporation and any participating shareholder of the payment to such a shareholder, as described in this preamble, depend on several factors. Further, where the participating shareholder is a foreign person, withholding under Chapter 3 of the Code may or may not be required.

Sections 1441 and 1442 and § 1.1441-1(b)(1) generally require a person that makes a payment of an "amount subject to withholding" to a beneficial owner that is a foreign person to deduct and withhold 30 percent of the payment unless the payor can reliably associate the payment with documentation upon which the payor can rely to treat the payment as made to a beneficial owner that is a U.S. person or as made to a beneficial owner that is a foreign person entitled to a reduced rate of withholding under the Code, regulations or an income tax treaty.

Section 1.1441-2(a) provides that the term amounts subject to withholding means amounts from sources within the United States that constitute fixed or determinable annual or periodical income (FDAP) described in § 1.1441-2(b) or other amounts subject to withholding described in § 1.1441-2(c).

Section 1.1441-2(b)(1) provides that FDAP includes all income described in section 61 of the Code, unless the item of income is described in § 1.1441-2(b)(2). Section 1.1441-2(b)(2)(i) generally excludes from FDAP gains derived from the sale of property. Thus, a distribution to a shareholder that is treated as gain from the sale of stock is excluded from FDAP. Further, to the extent a distribution is a return of capital, it is not gross income under section 61, and thus also is not FDAP.

Section 302 provides rules for determining when a distribution in redemption of stock is treated as a distribution in part or full payment in exchange for stock. That section generally requires a comparison of a shareholder's overall interest in the corporation before the distribution and its overall interest in such corporation after the distribution. See section 302(b). In conducting the comparison, the constructive ownership rules of section 318 generally apply. If the shareholder's interest in the corporation has been sufficiently reduced, then the distribution is treated as a payment in exchange for the shareholder's stock under section 302(a). If the shareholder's interest in the corporation has not been sufficiently reduced, the tax consequences of the distribution are determined under section 301, and such distribution is a dividend to the shareholder to the extent the distribution is out of the distributing corporation's earnings and profits, then applied against and reduce the adjusted basis of the stock, and finally treated as gain from the sale or exchange of property. See section 301(c).

When a publicly held corporation makes a distribution in redemption of its stock, a determination must be made under section 302 with respect to each shareholder as to whether the redemption is treated as a distribution of property to which section 301 applies (potentially constituting a dividend in whole or in part) or as a distribution in part or full payment in exchange for stock. However, the information necessary for each shareholder to make such a determination generally is not available until after the transaction is completed because the redemption of stock held by other shareholders must be taken into account. Further, because of the application of the constructive ownership rules of section 318, when a distribution is made to a foreign shareholder, a withholding agent will often not be in the best position to make a determination as to whether the distribution to the foreign shareholder should be treated as a payment in exchange for the shareholder's stock or a dividend.

There are two revenue rulings that consider the issue of whether the interest of a shareholder in a publicly held corporation has been sufficiently reduced as a result of a distribution to effect exchange treatment under section 302(a).

In Rev. Rul. 76-385, 1976-2 CB 92, See § 601.601(d)(2)(ii)(b), the IRS ruled that a shareholder who actually and constructively owned 0.0001118% of a publicly traded corporation's stock before a redemption, but only constructively owned 0.0001081% after the redemption, had experienced a "meaningful reduction in proportionate interest" in the corporation under the principles of United States v. Davis, 397 U.S. 301 (1970), rehearing denied, 397 U.S. 107 (1970). The shareholder's interest in the corporation after the redemption therefore was approximately 96.7% of the shareholder's interest before the redemption, taking constructive ownership into account. Nevertheless, the reduction was considered meaningful, and so the distribution to the shareholder was treated as not essentially equivalent to a dividend under section 302(b)(1) and as a payment in exchange for the shareholder's stock under section 302(a).

Consistent with Rev. Rul. 76-385, in Rev. Rul. 81-289, 1981-2 CB 82, See § 601.601(d)(2)(ii)(b), the IRS ruled that a shareholder who owned 0.2% of the common stock of a publicly traded company before a redemption, and 0.2% of the common stock in the company after the redemption, did not satisfy the "meaningful reduction" standard of United States v. Davis, and that the redemption did not qualify for exchange treatment under section 302(a).

Under the analysis adopted in these revenue rulings, each minority shareholder who participates in a self tender must compute its percentage ownership of the total outstanding stock of the corporation before and after the transaction. If after the transaction the shareholder's percentage ownership is less than it was before the transaction, the shareholder generally has experienced a "meaningful reduction" in the shareholder's proportionate interest in the corporation, and the transaction, at least with respect to that shareholder, is considered a distribution in exchange for the stock under section 302(a) and not a distribution of property to which section 301 applies. This result occurs even if another participating shareholder in the same self tender experiences no change or an increase in its percentage ownership of the corporation, and, therefore, is considered to receive a distribution of property to which section 301 applies. See also section 302(b)(2), (3), and (4).

Section 1.1441-3(c) requires a corporation making a distribution with respect to its stock to a foreign shareholder, as well as any intermediary (such as a broker) making a payment of such a distribution, to withhold on the entire amount of the distribution, unless it elects to reduce the amount of withholding under §1.1441-3(c). Section 1.1441-3(c)(2)(i)(B) provides that a distributing corporation or intermediary may elect to not withhold on a distribution to the extent it represents a distribution in part or full payment in exchange for stock. Section 1.1441-3(c)(2)(i) provides that a corporation or intermediary makes the election by reducing the amount of withholding at the time that the payment is made. However, a withholding agent cannot avail itself of this election unless it knows the extent to which a distribution represents a payment in exchange for stock under section 302(a). As previously noted, in the context of a distribution in redemption of stock held in a publicly traded corporation, the withholding agent generally will not have this information unless, at the time of the redemption, it has obtained information from each participating shareholder regarding actual and constructive ownership of stock for purposes of the foregoing analysis.

The Treasury Department and the IRS are aware that, in the context of transactions involving distributions in redemption of stock held by foreign persons where such stock is actively traded on an established financial market, the means of compliance with sections 1441, 1442, and 1443 is varied. The Treasury Department and the IRS believe that the discretion permitted by the current regulations, and the resulting different treatment of similar transactions is not appropriate. Accordingly, these proposed regulations provide the procedure ("escrow procedure") to be followed by U.S. withholding agents to satisfy the withholding, reporting and deposit requirements of the regulations under sections 1441, 1442, and 1443 with respect to any payment of a corporate distribution in redemption of stock made to a foreign account holder with respect to certain self tenders.

Explanation of Provisions

The proposed regulations set forth an escrow procedure for withholding agents to follow in the case of a payment made after December 31, 2008 of a corporate distribution in redemption of stock that is actively traded on an established financial market within the meaning of §1.1092(d)-1 (section 302 payment).

In general, the proposed regulations require a U.S. financial institution (withholding agent) to set aside in an escrow account 30 percent (or the applicable dividend rate provided under a treaty) of the amount of the section 302 payment. The withholding agent is then required to provide information to the foreign beneficial owner regarding the distribution, including the total number of the distributing corporation's shares outstanding before and after the distribution. The withholding agent must also provide a written statement explaining the conditions under which the section 302 payment will be treated as a dividend or a payment in exchange for stock (including an explanation of the constructive ownership rules under section 318). In the written explanation provided to the foreign beneficial owner, the withholding agent must request that the beneficial owner provide a written certification to the withholding agent within 60 days as to whether the distribution is either a dividend or a payment in exchange for stock.

The certification to be provided by the foreign beneficial owner must contain, among other requirements, the beneficial owner's name and account number, a certification that the distribution is a payment in exchange for stock or is a dividend, and the number of shares actually and constructively owned by the beneficial owner before and after the distribution. The beneficial owner's certification must be signed under penalties of perjury.

A withholding agent may generally rely on a certification received from a foreign beneficial owner in determining its section 1441 obligations with respect to payments for such beneficial owner's stock. However, if the withholding agent knows or has reason to know that the certification is unreliable or incorrect, or the withholding agent does not receive a certification from a foreign beneficial owner, the withholding agent is required to treat the amount set aside in escrow as tax withheld on the 61st day, and deposit that amount pursuant to the applicable regulations.

Although a qualified intermediary (QI) may, and a withholding foreign partnership and a withholding foreign trust (WP/WT) must, assume primary withholding responsibility under section 1441 and receive payments without any withholding by the U.S. financial institution, under the proposed regulations, in the case of a section 302 payment, the QI or WP/WT cannot assume primary withholding responsibility and receive the payment in gross. The QI or WP/WT must apply the procedure described in this preamble and provide the U.S. financial institution with a withholding statement that details the appropriate rate of withholding and information reporting for amounts paid to the QI or WP/WT. In addition, if there is a chain of QIs or WPs/WTs this procedure must be followed at each level in the chain. The U.S. financial institution shall treat beneficial owners that are U.S. non-exempt recipients, and that hold stock in the distributing corporation through QIs, WPs/WTs, NQIs and flow-throughs, in accordance with the section 302 payment certifications obtained from those U.S. non-exempt recipients and shall instruct foreign intermediaries and foreign flow-through entities to do the same.

These proposed regulations would apply for redemptions of stock that are made after December 31, 2008. However, a withholding agent may, at its option, rely on these proposed regulations for a redemption of stock that occurs before January 1, 2009.

The Treasury Department and the IRS are aware that withholding agents serve various customer bases: some may maintain accounts for a small number of account holders, others may maintain accounts for a much greater number of account holders. Comments are requested on alternatives to the escrow procedure described in this proposed regulation for withholding agents that maintain accounts for large numbers of customers.

Special Analyses

It has been determined that this notice of proposed rulemaking is not a significant regulatory action as defined in Executive Order 12866. Therefore, a regulatory assessment is not required.

It has been determined that section 553(b) of the Administrative Procedure Act (5 U.S.C. chapter 5) does not apply to these regulations.

These regulations impose a collection of information on small entities, and the Regulatory Flexibility Act (5 U.S.C. chapter 6) applies. This rule regulates securities brokerages that have foreign customers that respond to a tender offer by a U.S. publicly traded corporation to purchase some of its stock from its shareholders. The Small Business Administration (SBA) has established size standards for types of economic activities which are classified based on the North American Industry Classification Codes (NAICS). The regulations specifying size standards are set forth in Title 13, Code of Federal Regulations, part 121 (13 CFR part 121), Small Business Size Regulations. The NAICS Code for a small securities brokerage is specified at 13 CFR 121.201. Pursuant to subsector 523120 of the NAICS, a small securities brokerage is one with receipts of less than 6.5 million dollars. According to NAICS 523120, U.S. Census Bureau, Statistics of U.S. Business (2002), there are a total of 7,886 securities brokerages of which 7,113 generate revenue less than $5 million and 224 generate revenue between $5 million and $10 million. It is estimated that 7,213 of the securities brokerages are considered small businesses. The IRS requests information regarding the number of transactions these small securities brokerages engage in each year involving self tenders by public corporations. In the case of a tender offer by a publicly held corporation, it is estimated that a brokerage clerk would spend two hours preparing the paperwork and verifying the computations required to accurately withhold with respect to foreign customers. According to the Bureau of Labor Statistics, the mean hourly wage of a brokerage clerk is $18.34, so it is estimated that it will cost a small securities brokerage $36.68 per transaction. This cost is not significant when compared to the annual revenue of the small securities brokerage. Pursuant to section 605(b) of the Regulatory Flexibility Act, 5 U.S.C. 605, the Chief Counsel certifies that this rule will not have a significant economic impact on a substantial number of small entities. The IRS invites specific comments on the economic impact of compliance from members of the public who believe there will be a significant economic impact on small businesses that are regulated by this rule. Pursuant to section 7805(f) of the Internal Revenue Code, this regulation has been submitted to the Chief Counsel for Advocacy of the Small Business Administration for comment on its impact on small businesses.

Comments and Public Hearing

Before these proposed regulations are adopted as final regulations, consideration will be given to any written (a signed original and eight (8) copies) or electronic comments that are submitted timely to the IRS. The IRS and the Treasury Department request comments on the clarity of the proposed rules and how they can be made easier to understand. All comments will be available for public inspection and copying.

A public hearing has been scheduled for February 6, 2008, beginning at 10 a.m. in room 2140 of the Internal Revenue Building, 1111 Constitution Avenue, NW., Washington, DC. Due to building security procedures, visitors must enter at the 12th street entrance. In addition, all visitors must present photo identification to enter the building. Because of access restrictions, visitors will not be admitted beyond the immediate entrance area more than 30 minutes before the hearing starts. For information about having your name placed on the building access list to attend the hearing, see the FOR FURTHER INFORMATION CONTACT section of this preamble.

The rules of 26 CFR 601.601(a)(3) apply to the hearing. Persons who wish to present oral comments at the hearing must submit electronic or written comments, and an outline of the topics to be discussed, and the time to be devoted to each topic (signed original and eight (8) copies) by January 16, 2008. A period of 10 minutes will be allotted to each person for making comments. An agenda showing the scheduling of the speakers will be prepared after the deadline for receiving outlines has passed. Copies of the agenda will be available free of charge at the hearing.

Drafting Information

The principal author of these proposed regulations is Kathryn Holman, Office of Associate Chief Counsel (International). However, other personnel from the IRS and Treasury Department participated in their development.

[¶ 49,327]   **Proposed Amendments of Regulations (REG-114125-07)**, published in the Federal Register on October 17, 2007.

[Code Sec. 861]

International tax: Compensation: Source: United States v. foreign.—Amendments of Reg. §1.861-4, regarding clarification of the determination of source of compensation of a person, including an artist or athlete, who is compensated for labor or personal services performed at specific events, are proposed.

AGENCY: Internal Revenue Service (IRS), Treasury.

ACTION: Notice of proposed rulemaking.

SUMMARY: This document contains proposed changes to existing final regulations regarding the source of compensation for labor or personal services. The proposed changes are needed to clarify the determination of source of compensation of a person, including an artist or athlete, who is compensated for labor or personal services performed at specific events. These proposed regulations affect such an individual.

DATE: Written or electronic comments and requests for a public hearing must be received by January 15, 2008.

ADDRESSES: Send submissions to: CC:PA:LPD:PR (REG-114125-07), room 5203, Internal Revenue Service, PO Box 7604, Ben Franklin Station, Washington, DC 20044. Submissions may be hand-delivered Monday through Friday between the hours of 8 a.m. and 4 p.m. to: CC:PA:LPD:PR (REG-114125-07), Courier's Desk, Internal Revenue Service, 1111 Constitution Avenue, NW, Washington, DC, or sent electronically via the Federal eRulemaking Portal at http://www.regulations.gov (IRS-REG-114125-07).

FOR FURTHER INFORMATION CONTACT: Concerning the proposed regulations, David Bergkuist at (202) 622-3850; concerning the submissions of comments and requests for a hearing, Regina Johnson at (202) 622-7180 (not toll free numbers).

SUPPLEMENTARY INFORMATION

Background

This document contains proposed amendments under 26 CFR part 1 under section 861 of the Internal Revenue Code (Code). On July 14, 2005, final regulations that revised and amended §1.861-4 were published in the Federal Register (70 FR 40663) as TD 9212. In these final regulations, §1.861-4(b)(2)(ii)(C)(3) was reserved with respect to compensation for labor or personal services performed partly within and partly without the United States by an artist or an athlete who is an employee.

Section 861(a)(3) of the Internal Revenue Code provides that, subject to certain exceptions, compensation for labor or personal services performed in the United States is gross income from sources within the United States. See also §1.861-4(a) of the regulations. Section 862(a)(3) of the Code provides that compensation for labor or personal services performed without the United States is gross income from sources without the United States. Section 1.861-4(b) provides rules for determining the source of compensation for labor or personal services performed partly within and partly without the United States. Section 1.861-4(b)(2)(i) provides rules for determining the source of compensation for labor or personal services performed partly within and partly without the United States by an individual other than as an employee. Section 1.861-4(b)(2)(ii) provides rules for determining the source of compensation for labor or personal services performed partly within and partly without the United States by an individual as an employee.

Under §1.861-4(b)(2)(ii), if an individual performs labor or personal services as an employee, the source of the individual's compensation is generally determined on a time basis, with certain fringe benefits sourced on a geographic basis. An individual may determine the source of his or her compensation as an employee for labor or personal services performed partly within and partly without the United States under an alternative basis if the individual establishes to the satisfaction of the Commissioner that, under the facts and circumstances of the particular case, the alternative basis more properly determines the source of the compensation than the general rules of §1.861-4(b)(2)(ii). See §1.861-4(b)(2)(ii)(C)(1)(i). In addition, the Commissioner may, under the facts and circumstances of the particular case, determine the source of compensation that is received by an individual as an employee under an alternative basis if such compensation is not for a specific time period, provided that the Commissioner's alternative basis determines the source of compensation in a more reasonable manner than the basis used by the individual.

The final regulations at §1.861-4(b)(2)(ii)(C)(3) provided a reservation with respect to the source of compensation for labor or personal services performed partly within and partly without the United States by an artist or athlete who is an employee. The preamble of TD 9212 indicated that it was intended that the rule for artists and athletes who are employees, when issued, would require such individuals to determine the proper source of their compensation for labor or personal services on the basis that most correctly reflects the proper source of income under the facts and circumstances of the particular case, consistent with current law.

Explanation of Provisions

The proposed regulations would set forth a new "events basis" rule in §1.861-4(b)(2)(ii)(G) and make certain other clarifying changes to the existing final regulations. The proposed regulations also would remove §1.861-4(b)(2)(ii)(C)(3), which reserved with respect to artists and athletes.

The amount of income received by a person, including an individual who is an artist or an athlete, that is properly treated as compensation from the performance of labor or personal services is determined based on all of the facts and circumstances of the particular case. Proposed §1.861-4(b)(2)(ii)(G) specifies that the amount of compensation for labor or personal services determined on an event basis is the amount of the person's compensation which, based on the facts and circumstances, is attributable to the labor or personal services performed at the location of a specific event.

The IRS and the Treasury Department have determined that the proper source of compensation received by a person, including an individual who is an artist or athlete, specifically for performing labor or personal services at an event is the location of the event. A basis that purports to determine the source of compensation from the performance of labor or personal services at a specific event, whether on a time basis or otherwise, by taking into account the location of labor or personal services performed in preparation for the performance of labor or personal services at the specific event will generally not be the basis that most correctly determines the source of the compensation. This rule applies to situations covered by §1.861-4(a) and (b).

Under §1.861-4(a), the source of compensation for labor or personal services performed wholly within the United States is generally from sources within the United States. Therefore, if a person, including an individual who is an artist or an athlete, is specifically compensated for performing labor or personal services at an event in the United States, the source of such compensation is wholly within the United States because the labor or personal services were performed wholly at an event within the United States. The proposed regulations state that a basis that purports to determine the source of such income on a time basis by taking into account the location of labor or personal services performed in preparation for the performance of labor or personal services at the specific event will generally not be a more reasonable basis for determining source of the compensation. The proposed regulations add an example to §1.861-4(c) to illustrate the application of this rule.

Section 1.861-4(b) applies to instances in which a person is compensated for performing labor or personal services at multiple events, only some of which are within the United States, and at least a portion of the person's compensation cannot be specifically attributed to the person's performance of labor or personal services at a specific location. If the person is not an individual who is compensated as an employee, the source of compensation for labor or personal services is determined on the basis that most correctly reflects the proper source of that income under the facts and circumstances of the particular case. See §1.861-4(b)(1) and (2)(i). If a person is compensated specifically for labor or personal services performed at multiple events, the basis that most correctly reflects the proper source of that income under the facts and circumstances of the particular case will generally be the location of the events. In addition, a basis that purports to determine the source of such income on a time basis by taking into account the location of labor or personal services performed in preparation for the performance of labor or personal services at the specific event will generally not be the basis that most correctly reflects the proper source of the compensation under proposed §1.861-4(b)(2)(ii)(G).

The Commissioner may, under the facts and circumstances of the particular case, determine the source of compensation that is received by an individual as an employee under an alternative basis if such compensation is not for a specific time period, provided that the Commissioner's alternative basis determines the source of compensation in a more reasonable manner than the basis used by the individual. Compensation specifically for labor or personal services performed at a specific event is not compensation for a specific time period. The basis that most correctly reflects the proper source of that income will generally be the location of the event under proposed §1.861-4(b)(2)(ii)(G). In addition, a basis that purports to determine the source of such income on a facts and circumstances basis by taking into account the location of labor or personal services performed in preparation for the performance of labor or personal services at the specific event will generally not more properly determine the source of the compensation under proposed §1.861-4(b)(2)(ii)(G).

These proposed regulations provide examples to illustrate the event basis for determining the source of compensation of an individual, including an artist or athlete, who is compensated specifically for performing labor or personal services at an event.

The revisions to §1.861-4(b)(1), (b)(2)(i), and (b)(ii)(C)(1)(i) and (ii) which refer to the event basis; the revisions in §1.861-4(b)(2)(ii)(C)(3), (b)(2)(ii)(E), and (b)(2)(ii)(F), (b)(2)(ii)(G), and (c); and new Examples 7 through 11 of §1.861-4(c) would be effective for taxable years beginning after the date final regulations are published in the Federal Register.

Special Analysis

It has been determined that this notice of proposed rulemaking is not a significant regulatory action as defined in Executive Order 12866. Therefore, a regulatory assessment is not required. It has also been determined that section 553(b) of the Administrative Procedure Act (5 U.S.C. chapter 5) does not apply to these regulations. Because these regulations do not impose a collection of information on small entities, the provisions of the Regulatory Flexibility Act (5 U.S.C. chapter 6) do not apply. Pursuant to section 7805(f) of the Internal Revenue Code, this notice of proposed rulemaking has been submitted to the Chief Counsel for Advocacy of the Small Business Administration for comment on its impact on small business.

Comments and Requests for a Public Hearing

Before these proposed regulations are adopted as final regulations, consideration will be given to any written (a signed original and eight (8) copies) or electronic comment that is submitted timely to the IRS. The Treasury Department and the IRS request comments on the clarity of the proposed rules and how they can be made easier to understand. All comments will be available for public inspection and copying. A hearing will be scheduled if requested in writing by any person that timely submits written comments. If a public hearing is scheduled, notice of the date, time, and place for a public hearing will be published in the Federal Register.

Drafting Information

The principal author of these proposed regulations is David Bergkuist, Office of the Associate Chief Counsel (International). However, other personnel from the IRS and the Treasury Department participated in their development.

[¶ 49,329] Proposed Amendments of Regulations (REG-209020-86), published in the Federal Register on November 7, 2007 (corrected 12/18/2007).

[Code Secs. 905 and 6689]

Foreign taxes: Penalties, civil: Foreign tax credit: Redetermination of tax: Notification to IRS.—Reg. §§ 1.905-4, 1.905-5 and 301.6689-1, relating to Code Sec. 905(c) and Code Sec. 6689, are proposed. Amendments of Reg. 1.905-3(d)(2)(iii)-(iv) and 1.905-3(d)(4) are withdrawn. Reg. § 1.905-3 is adopted by T.D. 9882.

AGENCY: Internal Revenue Service (IRS), Treasury.

ACTION: Partial withdrawal of notice of proposed rulemaking and notice of proposed rulemaking by cross-reference to temporary regulations.

SUMMARY: This document withdraws portions of the notice of proposed rulemaking published on June 23, 1988, relating to sections 905(c) and 6689 (the 1988 proposed regulations). In addition, in the Rules and Regulations section of this issue of the Federal Register, the IRS and the Treasury Department are issuing temporary regulations relating to a taxpayer's obligation under section 905(c) of the Internal Revenue Code to notify the IRS of a foreign tax redetermination. The IRS and the Treasury Department are also issuing temporary regulations on Procedure and Administration under section 6689 relating to the civil penalty for failure to notify the IRS of a foreign tax redetermination as required under section 905(c). These temporary regulations affect taxpayers that have paid foreign taxes which have been redetermined and provide guidance needed to comply with statutory changes made to the applicable law by the Taxpayer Relief Act of 1997 and the American Jobs Creation Act of 2004. The text of those temporary regulations also serves as the text of these proposed regulations.

DATES: Written or electronic comments and requests for a public hearing must be received by February 5, 2008.

ADDRESSES: Send submissions to: CC:PA:LPD:PR (REG-209020-86), room 5203, Internal Revenue Service, PO Box 7604, Ben Franklin Station, Washington, DC 20044. Submissions may be hand-delivered between the hours of 8 a.m. and 4 p.m. to CC:PA:LPD:PR (REG-209020-86), Courier's Desk, Internal Revenue Service, 1111 Constitution Ave., NW., Washington, DC or sent electronically via the Federal eRulemaking Portal at www.regulations.gov (IRS REG-209020-86).

FOR FURTHER INFORMATION CONTACT: Concerning the proposed regulations, Teresa Burridge Hughes, (202) 622-3850 (not a toll-free number); concerning the submission of comments, Kelly Banks, (202) 622-7180 (not a toll-free number).

SUPPLEMENTARY INFORMATION:

Paperwork Reduction Act

The collections of information contained in this notice of proposed rulemaking have been submitted to the Office of Management and Budget for review in accordance with the Paperwork Reduction Act of 1995 (44 U.S.C. 3507(d)). Comments on the collection of information should be sent to the Office of Management and Budget, Attn: Desk Officer for the Department of Treasury, Office of Information and Regulatory-Affairs, Washington, DC 20503, with copies to the Internal Revenue Service, Attn: IRS Reports Clearance Officer, SE:W:CAR:MP:T:T:SP, Washington, DC 20224. Comments on the collection of information should be received by January 7, 2008. Comments are specifically requested concerning:

Whether the proposed collections of information is necessary for the proper performance of the functions of the IRS, including whether the information will have practical utility;

The accuracy of the estimated burden associated with the proposed collections of information;

How the quality, utility, and clarity of the information to be collected may be enhanced;

How the burden of complying with the proposed collections of information may be minimized, including through the application of automated collection techniques or other forms of information technology; and

Estimates of capital or start-up costs and costs of operation, maintenance, and purchase of service to provide information.

The collections of information in this notice of proposed rulemaking are in § 1.905-4. This information is required to enable the IRS to verify the amounts of the foreign tax redeterminations and to determine the amount of the penalty under section 6689, if a taxpayer fails to notify the IRS of a foreign tax redetermination. This information will be used by the IRS for examination purposes. The collections of information are mandatory. The likely respondents are individuals and business or other for-profit institutions.

Estimated total annual reporting: 54,000 hours.

The estimated annual burden per respondent varies from 3 hours to 8 hours, depending on individual circumstances, with an estimated average of 4.2 hours.

Estimated number of respondents: 13,000.

Estimated frequency of responses: Annually.

An agency may not conduct or sponsor, and a person is not required to respond to, a collection of information unless it displays a valid control number assigned by the Office of Management and Budget.

Books or records relating to a collection of information must be retained as long as their contents may become material in the administration of any internal revenue law. Generally, tax returns and tax return information are confidential, as required by 26 U.S.C. 6103.

Background and Explanation of Provisions

On June 23, 1988, the IRS published in the Federal Register a notice of proposed rulemaking (53 FR 23659) (INTL-061-86) (the 1988 proposed regulations) that would have provided rules with respect to the time and manner of reporting a foreign tax redetermination and to the penalty under section 6689. Written comments were received; however, no hearing was requested or held. Subsequently, section 1102(a)(1) and 1102(a)(2) of the Taxpayer Relief Act of 1997, Public Law 105-34 (111 Stat. 788, 963-966 (1997)), amended section 905(c), effective for taxes paid or accrued in taxable years beginning after December 31, 1997. Subsequently, section 408(a) of the American Jobs Creation Act of 2004, Public Law 108-357 (118 Stat. 1418, 1499 (2004)), modified section 986(a), effective for taxable years beginning after December 31, 2004. In light of the comments received on the 1988 proposed regulations and the statutory changes to sections 905(c) and 986(a), sections of the 1988 proposed regulations are revised and other sections are withdrawn. The preamble to the temporary regulations explains the temporary regulations and these proposed regulations.

Special Analyses

It has been determined that this notice of proposed rulemaking is not a significant regulatory action as defined in Executive Order 12866. Therefore, a regulatory assessment is not required. It also has been determined that section 553(b) of the Administrative Procedure Act (5 U.S.C. chapter 5) does not apply to the following regulations, §§ 1.905-3, 1.905-4, 1.905-5, and 301.6689-1. With respect to § 1.905-4, it is hereby certified that this regulation will not have a significant economic impact on a substantial number of small entities. This certification is based on the fact that the collection of information requirement under § 1.905-4 that is imposed on small entities flows directly from section 905(c), which states that, "[T]he taxpayer shall notify the Secretary," of a foreign tax redetermination that may result in a redetermination of the taxpayer's United States tax liability. In order for the taxpayer to satisfy this notification requirement, information with respect to all foreign tax redeterminations must be collected. Therefore, a regulatory flexibility analysis is not required. Pursuant to section 7805(f) of the Internal Revenue Code, this regulation has been submitted to the Chief Counsel for Advocacy of the Small Business Administration for comment on their impact on small businesses.

Comments and Requests for a Public Hearing

Before these proposed regulations are adopted as final regulations, consideration will be given to any written (a signed original and eight (8) copies) or electronic comments that are submitted timely to the IRS. All comments will be available for public inspection and copying. A public hearing may be scheduled if requested in writing by any person that timely submits written or electronic comments. If a public hearing is scheduled, notice of the date, time, and place for the public hearing will be published in the Federal Register.

Drafting Information

The principal author of this document is Teresa Burridge Hughes, Office of Associate Chief Counsel (International). However, other personnel from the IRS and the Treasury Department participated in its development.

[¶ 49,357]   Proposed Regulations (REG-151135-07), published in the Federal Register on March 18, 2008 (corrected 4/9/2008).

[Code Sec. 432]

Multiemployer retirement plans: Determination of critical or endangered status: Certification of status: Notice of status.—Reg. §§1.432(a)-1 and 1.432(b)-1, providing additional rules for certain multiemployer defined benefit plans that are in effect on July 16, 2006, are proposed.

AGENCY: Internal Revenue Service (IRS), Treasury

ACTION: Notice of proposed rulemaking.

SUMMARY: This document contains proposed regulations under section 432 of the Internal Revenue Code (Code). These proposed regulations provide additional rules for certain multiemployer defined benefit plans that are in effect on July 16, 2006. These proposed regulations affect sponsors and administrators of, and participants in multiemployer plans that are in either endangered or critical status. These regulations are necessary to implement the new rules set forth in section 432 that are effective for plan years beginning after 2007. The proposed regulations reflect changes made by the Pension Protection Act of 2006.

DATES: Written or electronic comments and requests for public hearing must be received by June 16, 2008.

ADDRESSES: Send submissions to: CC:PA:LPD:PR (REG-151135-07), room 5203, Internal Revenue Service, PO Box 7604, Ben Franklin Station, Washington, DC 20044. Submissions may be hand-delivered Monday through Friday between the hours of 8 a.m. and 4 p.m. to CC:PA:LPD:PR (REG-151135-07), Courier's Desk, Internal Revenue Service, 1111 Constitution Avenue, NW, Washington, DC 20224, or sent electronically via the Federal eRulemaking Portal at *www.regulations.gov* (IRS REG-151135-07).

FOR FURTHER INFORMATION CONTACT: Concerning the regulations, Bruce Perlin, (202) 622-6090; concerning submissions and requests for a public hearing, *Richard.A.Hurst@irscounsel.treas.gov* or at (202) 622-7180 (not toll-free numbers).

SUPPLEMENTARY INFORMATION:

Paperwork Reduction Act

The collection of information contained in this notice of proposed rulemaking have been submitted to the Office of Management and Budget for review in accordance with the Paperwork Reduction Act of 1995 (44 U.S.C. 3507(d). Comments on the collection of information should be sent to the **Office of Management and Budget,** Attn: Desk Officer for the Department of the Treasury, Office of Information and Regulatory Affairs, Washington, DC 20503, with copies to the **Internal Revenue Service,** Attn: IRS Reports Clearance Officer, SE:CAR:MP:T:T:SP, Washington, DC 20224. Comments on the collection of information should be received by May 19, 2008.

Comments are specifically requested concerning:

Whether the proposed collection of information is necessary for the proper performance of the functions of the Internal Revenue Service, including whether the information will have practical utility;

The accuracy of the estimated burden associated with the collection of information;

How the quality, utility, and clarity of the information to be collected may be enhanced;

How the burden of complying with the collection of information may be minimized, including through the application of automated collection techniques or other forms of information technology; and

Estimates of capital or start-up costs and costs of operation, maintenance, and purchase of service to provide information.

The collection of information in this regulation is in §1.432(b)-1(d) and (e). This information is required in order for a qualified multiemployer defined benefit plan's enrolled actuary to provide a timely certification of the plan's funding status. In addition, if it is certified that a plan is or will be in critical or endangered status, the plan sponsor is required to notify the Department of Labor, the Pension Benefit Guaranty Corporation, the bargaining parties, participants, and beneficiaries of the status designation. For plans in critical status, the plan sponsor is required to include in the notice an explanation of the possibility that adjustable benefits may be reduced at a later date and that certain benefits are restricted as of the date the notice is sent. The annual certification by the enrolled actuary for the plan will be used to provide an accurate determination and certification of the plan's funded status and to provide notice to the required parties of the status designation. The collection of information is mandatory. The likely respondents are multiemployer plan sponsors and enrolled actuaries.

Estimated total annual reporting burden: 1,200 hours.

Estimated average annual burden hours per respondent: 0.75 hours.

Estimated number of respondents: 1,600.

Estimated annual frequency of responses: occasional.

An agency may not conduct or sponsor, and a person is not required to respond to, a collection of information unless it displays a valid control number assigned by the Office of Management and Budget.

Books or records relating to a collection of information must be retained as long as their contents may become material in the administration of any internal revenue law. Generally, tax returns and tax return information are confidential, as required by 26 U.S.C. 6103.

Background

This document contains proposed Income Tax Regulations (26 CFR part 1) under section 432, as added to the Internal Revenue Code by the Pension Protection Act of 2006 (PPA '06), Public Law 109-280, 120 Stat 780.

Section 412 contains minimum funding rules that generally apply to pension plans. Section 431 sets forth the funding rules that apply specifically to multiemployer defined benefit plans. Section 432 sets forth additional rules that apply to multiemployer plans in effect on July 16, 2006, that are in endangered or critical status[1].

Section 432 generally provides for a determination by the enrolled actuary for a multiemployer plan as to whether the plan is in endangered status or in critical status for a plan year. In the first year that the actuary certifies that the plan is in endangered status, section 432(a)(1) requires that the plan sponsor adopt a funding improvement plan. The funding improvement plan must meet the requirements of section 432(c) and the plan must apply the rules of section 432(d) during the period that begins when the plan is certified to be in endangered status and ends when the plan is no longer in that status. In the first year that the actuary certifies that the plan is in critical status, section 432 (a)(2) requires that the plan sponsor adopt a rehabilitation plan. The rehabilitation plan must meet the requirements of section 432(e) and the plan must apply the rules of section 432(f) during the period that begins when the plan is certified to be in critical status and ends when the plan is no longer in that status. In addition, section 432(f)(2) requires that the plan suspend certain actions as described more fully in this preamble.

Section 432(b)(3)(A) requires an actuarial certification of whether or not a multiemployer plan is in endangered status, and whether or not a multiemployer plan is or will be in critical status, for each plan year. This certification must be completed by the 90th day of the plan year and must be provided to the Secretary of the Treasury and to the plan sponsor. If the certification is with respect to a plan year that is within the plan's funding improvement period or rehabilitation period arising from a prior certification of endangered or critical status, the actuary must also certify whether or not the plan is making scheduled progress in meeting the requirements of its funding improvement or rehabilitation plan. Failure of the plan's actuary to certify the status of the plan is treated as a failure to file the annual report under section 502(c)(2) of the Employee Retirement Income Security Act of 1974 (ERISA). Thus, a penalty of up to $1,100 per day applies.

Under section 432(b)(1), a multiemployer plan is in endangered status if the plan is not in critical status and, as of the beginning of the plan year, (1) the plan's funded percentage for the plan year is less than 80 percent, or (2) the plan has an accumulated funding deficiency for the plan year or is projected to have an accumulated funding deficiency in any of the six succeeding plan years (taking into account amortization extensions under section 431(d)). Under section 432(i), a plan's funded percentage is the percentage determined by dividing the value of the plan's assets by the accrued liability of the plan.

Under section 432(b)(2), a multiemployer plan is in critical status for a plan year if it meets any of four specified tests. Under section 432(b)(2)(A), a plan is in critical status if, as of the beginning of the plan year: (1) the funded percentage of the plan is less than 65 percent and (2) the sum of (A) the market value of plan assets, plus (B) the present value of reasonably anticipated employer contributions for the current plan year and each of the six succeeding plan years is less than the present value of all nonforfeitable benefits projected to be payable under the plan during the current plan year and each of the six succeeding plan years (plus administrative expenses). For this purpose, employer contributions are determined assuming that the terms of all collective bargaining agreements pursuant to which the plan is maintained for the current plan year continue in effect for succeeding plan years.

Under section 432(b)(2)(B), a plan is in critical status if the plan has an accumulated funding deficiency for the current plan year or is projected to have an accumulated funding deficiency for any of the three succeeding plan years. For purposes of this test, the determination of accumulated funding deficiency is made not taking into account any amortization extension under section 431(d). In addition, if a plan has a funded percentage of 65 percent or less, the three-year period for projecting whether the plan will have an accumulated funding deficiency is extended to four years.

Under section 432(b)(2)(C), a plan is in critical status for the plan year if (1) the plan's normal cost for the current plan year, plus interest for the current plan year on the amount of unfunded benefit liabilities under the plan as of the last day of the preceding year, exceeds the present value of the reasonably anticipated employer and employee contributions for the current plan year, (2) the present value of nonforfeitable benefits of inactive participants is greater than the present value of nonforfeitable benefits of active participants, and (3) the plan has an accumulated funding deficiency for the current plan year, or is projected to have an accumulated funding deficiency for any of the four succeeding plan years (not taking into account amortization period extensions under section 431(d)).

Under section 432(b)(2)(D), a plan is in critical status for a plan year if the sum of (A) the market value of plan assets, and (B) the present value of the reasonably anticipated employer contributions for the current plan year and each of the four succeeding plan years is less than the present value of all benefits projected to be payable under the plan during the current plan year and each of the four succeeding plan years (plus administrative expenses). For this purpose, employer contributions are determined assuming that the terms of all collective bargaining agreements pursuant to which the plan is maintained for the current plan year continue in effect for succeeding plan years.

In making the determinations and projections applicable under the endangered and critical status rules, the plan actuary must make projections for the current and succeeding plan years of the current value of the assets of the plan and the present value of all liabilities to participants and beneficiaries under the plan for the current plan year as of the beginning of such year. The actuary's projections must be based on reasonable actuarial estimates, assumptions, and methods that offer the actuary's best estimate of anticipated experience under the plan. An exception to this rule applies in the case of projected industry activity. Any projection of activity in the industry or industries covered by the plan, including future covered employment and contribution levels, must be based on information provided by the plan sponsor, and the plan sponsor must act reasonably and in good faith. The projected present value of liabilities as of the beginning of the year must be based on either the most recent actuarial statement required with respect to the most recently filed annual report or the actuarial valuation for the preceding plan year.

Under section 432(b)(3)(B)(ii), any actuarial projection of plan assets must assume (1) reasonably anticipated employer contributions for the current and succeeding plan years, assuming that the terms of one or more collective bargaining agreements pursuant to which the plan is maintained for the current plan year continue in effect for the succeeding plan years, or (2) that employer contributions for the most recent plan year will continue indefinitely, but only if the plan actuary determines that there have been no significant demographic changes that would make continued application of such terms unreasonable.

The first year that an actuary certifies that a plan is in endangered or critical status establishes a timetable for a number of actions. Under section 432(b)(3)(D), within 30 days after the date of certification, the plan sponsor must notify the participants and beneficiaries, the bargaining parties, the PBGC and the Secretary of Labor of the plan's endangered or critical status. If it is certified that a plan is or will be in critical status, the plan sponsor must include in the notice an explanation of the possibility that (1) adjustable benefits (as defined in section 432(e)(8)) may be reduced and

---

[1] Section 302 and section 304 of the Employee Retirement Income Security Act of 1974, as amended (ERISA) sets forth funding rules that are parallel to those in section 412 and section 431 of the Code. Section 305 of ERISA sets forth additional rules for multiemployer plans that are parallel to those in section 432 of the Code. Under section 101 of Reorganization Plan No. 4 of 1978 (43 FR 47713) and section 302 of ERISA, the Secretary of the Treasury has interpretive jurisdiction over the subject matter addressed in these proposed preambles for purposes of ERISA, as well as the Code. Thus, these Treasury Department regulations issued under section 432 of the Code apply as well for purposes of ERISA section 305.

(2) such reductions may apply to participants and beneficiaries whose benefit commencement date is on or after the date such notice is provided for the first plan year in which the plan is in critical status.

If a plan is certified to be in critical status, the plan must take certain actions after notifying the plan participants of the critical status. Specifically, section 432(f)(2) restricts the payment of benefits that are in excess of a single life annuity (plus any social security supplement) effective on the date the notice is sent. Section 432(f)(2)(B) provides that this restriction does not apply to amounts that may be immediately distributed without the consent of the employee under section 411(a)(11) and to any makeup payment in the case of a retroactive annuity starting date or a similar payment of benefits owed with respect to a prior period. In addition, the plan sponsor must refrain from making any payment for the purchase of an irrevocable commitment from an insurer to pay benefits.

Sections 432(c)(1) and 432(e)(1) provide that in the first year that a plan is certified to be in endangered or critical status, the plan sponsor must adopt a funding improvement plan (in the case of a plan that is in endangered status) or a rehabilitation plan (in the case of a plan that is in critical status). The deadline for adoption of the funding improvement plan or rehabilitation plan is 240 days after the deadline for the certification. Accordingly, if the actuarial certification is made after the 90-day deadline, the amount of time for adopting the funding improvement plan or rehabilitation plan is shortened.

Section 432(c)(3) defines a funding improvement plan as a plan which consists of the actions, including options or a range of options, to be proposed to the bargaining parties, formulated to provide, based on reasonably anticipated experience and reasonable actuarial assumptions, for the attainment by the plan of certain requirements. Those requirements are based on a statutorily specified improvement in the plan's funding percentage from the percentage that applied on the first day of the funding improvement period. The first day of the funding improvement period is defined in section 432(c)(4) as the first day of the first plan year beginning after the earlier of (1) the second anniversary of the date of the adoption of the funding improvement plan or (2) the expiration of the collective bargaining agreements in effect on the due date for the actuarial certification of endangered status for the initial endangered year and covering, as of such due date, at least 75 percent of the active participants in such multiemployer plan.

Section 432(d)(1) sets forth rules that apply after the certification of endangered status and before the first day of the funding improvement period. After the adoption of the funding improvement plan, section 432(d)(2) prohibits any amendments that are inconsistent with the funding improvement plan. In addition, section 432(d)(2) provides special rules for acceptance of collective bargaining agreements and plan amendments that increase benefits.

A rehabilitation plan is a plan which consists of the actions, including options or a range of options, to be proposed to the bargaining parties, formulated to provide, based on reasonably anticipated experience and reasonable actuarial assumptions, for the attainment by the plan of certain requirements. Generally, the rehabilitation plan should enable the plan to emerge from critical status by the end of a 10-year period that begins after the earlier of (1) the second anniversary of the date of the adoption of the rehabilitation plan or (2) the expiration of the collective bargaining agreements in effect on the due date for the actuarial certification of critical status for the initial critical year and covering, as of such due date, at least 75 percent of the active participants in such multiemployer plan. For this purpose a plan emerges from critical status when the plan actuary certifies that the plan is not projected to have an accumulated funding deficiency for the plan year or any of the nine succeeding plan years, without regard to the use of the shortfall method and taking into account amortization period extensions under section 431(d). As an alternative, if the plan sponsor determines that, based on reasonable actuarial assumptions and upon exhaustion of all reasonable measures, the plan cannot reasonably be expected to emerge from critical status by the end of the 10-year period, the requirements for a rehabilitation plan are that the plan include reasonable measures to emerge from critical status at a later time or to forestall possible insolvency (within the meaning of section 4245 of ERISA).

Section 432(e)(8) allows a rehabilitation plan for a plan that is in critical status to provide for a reduction of certain "adjustable" benefits that would otherwise be protected by section 411(d)(6). These adjustable benefits include early retirement benefits and retirement-type subsidies within the meaning of section 411 (d)(6)(B)(i). Under section 432(e)(8)(A)(ii), no reduction will apply to a participant whose benefit commencement date is before the date the notice under section 432(b)(3)(D) for the initial critical year is provided. Under section 432(e)(8)(B), except with respect to certain benefit increases described in 432(e)(8)(A)(iv)(III), a plan is not permitted to reduce the level of a participant's accrued benefit payable at normal retirement age. Furthermore, section 432(e)(8)(C) prohibits any reduction until 30 days after plan participants and beneficiaries, employers and employee organizations are notified of the reduction.

In years after the initial critical year or initial endangered year, sections 432(c)(6) and 432(e)(3)(B) provide that the plan sponsor must annually update the funding improvement or rehabilitation plan. This includes updating the schedule of contribution rates. Updates are required to be filed with the plan's annual report.

Section 432(f)(4) sets forth rules that apply after the certification of critical status and before the first day of the rehabilitation period. After the adoption of the rehabilitation plan, section 432(f)(1) prohibits any amendments that are inconsistent with the rehabilitation plan.

Section 432(h) provides rules for the treatment of employees who participate in the plan even though they are not covered by a collective bargaining agreement.

Section 432(i) provides a number of definitions that apply for purposes of section 432. For example, under section 432(i)(8), the actuary's determination with respect to a plan's normal cost, actuarial accrued liability, and improvements in a plan's funded percentage must be based on the unit credit funding method (whether or not that method is used for the plan's actuarial valuation).

Section 432 is effective for plan years beginning on or after January 1, 2008. Section 212(e)(2) of PPA '06 provides a special rule permitting a plan to provide the notice described in section 432(b)(3)(D) on an early basis. Specifically, if the plan actuary certifies that the plan is reasonably expected to be in critical status for the first plan year beginning after 2007, the plan is permitted to provide the notice described in section 432(b)(3)(D) at any time between the enactment of PPA '06 and the date the notice is otherwise required to be provided.

Explanation of Provisions

Overview

These regulations provide guidance with respect to certain of the provisions of section 432. Specifically, these regulations provide guidance regarding the determination of when a plan is in endangered status or critical status and the associated notices. These regulations do not provide guidance with respect to all issues relating to a multiemployer plan that is in endangered or critical status. For example, no guidance is provided on the parameters for the adoption of a funding improvement plan or rehabilitation plan. Guidance with respect to additional issues will be included in a second set of regulations that are expected to be issued this year.

§ 1.432(a)-1 General rules relating to section 432

Section 1.432(a)-1 provides general rules relating to section 432, including definitions of certain terms used for purposes of section 432 and the special rules that apply to participants in multiemployer plans who are not participating pursuant to a collective bargaining agreement.

The regulations provide that effective on the date that a notice of critical status for the initial critical year is sent to the plan participants, the plan must not pay any benefit in excess of the monthly amount paid under a single life annuity (plus any social security supplement) and is not permitted to purchase an irrevocable commitment from an insurer to pay benefits. The restriction does not apply to the small-dollar cash-outs allowed under section 411(a)(11) nor to the make-up payments under a retroactive annuity starting date.

The regulations provide that if the notice described in section 432(b)(3)(D) has been sent and the restrictions provided under section 432(f)(2) have been applied, and it is later determined that the restrictions should not have been applied, then the plan must correct any benefit payments that were restricted in error. The regulations provide two examples of situations requiring this correction, each of which involves an actuary certifying that the plan is reasonably expected to be in critical status for the first plan year beginning after 2007, followed by an early notification of critical status that is made to employees under the rules of section 212(e)(2) of PPA '06. In one example of a plan taking actions that require correction, the plan restricts benefits before the first plan year beginning after 2007 (the effective date of section 432). In the second such example, the plan is not in critical status for the first plan year beginning after 2007 (even though the enrolled actuary for the plan had certified that it is reasonably expected that the plan will be in critical status with respect to that year).

The regulations incorporate a number of definitions listed in section 432(i) along with other definitions that are located in sections 432(c) and (e). The regulations do not include the broad provision under section 432(i)(8) to use the unit credit funding method for purposes of the plan's "normal cost, actuarial accrued liability, and improvements in a plan's funded percentage." Instead, consistent with the intended scope of section 432(i)(8), the regulations require the use of this funding method solely for purposes of determining a plan's funded percentage and the section 432(b)(2)(C)(i) comparison of contributions with the sum of the plan's normal cost and interest on the amount of unfunded liability. Thus, the determination of whether a plan is projected to have an accumulated funding deficiency in the determination of a plan's status under section 432 is based on the plan's actual funding method, rather than the unit credit funding method. The regulations substitute the term "initial endangered year" for the statutory term "initial determination year."

In addition, the regulations provide guidance for plans that change their status in subsequent years. For example, a plan that is in critical status may emerge from that status and later reenter critical status. In such a circumstance, the year of reentry into critical status is treated as the initial critical year. Similarly, a plan that is in endangered status may have a status change and at a later date reenter endangered status. In such a circumstance, the year of reentry into endangered status is treated as the initial endangered year.

§1.432(b)-1 Determination of status and adoption of a plan

The regulations provide rules for the determination of whether a plan is in endangered status or critical status within the meaning of section 432(b)(1) and (2). These rules reflect the different ways a plan can be in endangered status under section 432(b)(1)(A) or (B) and in critical status under section 432(b)(2)(A), (B), (C), or (D). The regulations also provide that a plan is in critical status for a plan year if it was in critical status in the immediately preceding year and the plan does not meet the emergence from critical status rule of section 432(e)(4)(B). Thus, a plan that was in critical status for the prior year will remain in critical status if the enrolled actuary for the plan certifies that the plan is projected to have an accumulated funding deficiency for the plan year or any of the 9 succeeding plan years, without regard to the use of the shortfall funding method, but taking into account any extensions of the amortization periods under section 431(d).

The regulations provide limited guidance on the actuarial projections that are used for purposes of the certification of status by the enrolled actuary for the plan. The projections must generally be based on reasonable actuarial assumptions and methods that, as under section 431(c)(3), offer the actuary's best estimate of anticipated experience under the plan. The actuarial projection of future contributions and assets must assume either that the terms of the one or more collective bargaining agreements pursuant to which the plan is maintained for the current plan year continue in effect for succeeding plan years, or that the dollar amount of employer contributions for the most recent plan year will continue indefinitely. If the actuarial projections assume the continued maintenance of the collective bargaining agreements, the plan sponsor must provide a projection of activity in the industry, including future covered employment, to the plan actuary, and the actuary is permitted to rely on those projections. In making these projections, the plan sponsor must act reasonably and in good faith. The alternative assumption that the dollar amount of contributions remains unchanged into the future is only available if the enrolled actuary for the plan determines there have been no significant demographic changes that would make such assumption unreasonable. In addition, the regulations provide that the alternative assumption is not available for purposes of determining whether the plan is in critical status under the tests in section 432(b)(2)(A) and (D).

The projected present value of liabilities as of the beginning of such year is determined based on the most recent information reported on the most recent of either the actuarial statement required under section 103(d) of ERISA that has been filed with respect to the most recent year, or the actuarial valuation for the preceding plan year.

The regulations provide that, for purposes of section 432, if the plan received an extension of any amortization period under section 412(e), the extension is treated the same as an extension under section 431(d). Thus, such an extension is taken into account in determining endangered status under section 432(b)(1)(B) and emergence from critical status under section 432(e)(4)(B). In contrast, such an extension is not taken into account in determining whether a plan has or will have an accumulated funding deficiency for purposes of determining critical status under section 432(b)(2)(B) and (C).

The regulations describe the content of the annual certification required under section 432(b)(3) that must be sent to the plan sponsor and the IRS. The annual certification must be provided regardless of whether the plan is in endangered or critical status. If the plan is certified to be in endangered or critical status, then the certification must identify the plan, the plan sponsor, and the enrolled actuary who signs the certification; provide contact information for the plan sponsor and actuary; state whether or not the plan is in endangered or critical status for the plan year; and, if the certification is for a year other than the initial endangered year or the initial critical year, whether the plan is making the scheduled progress described in the plan's funding improvement plan or rehabilitation plan. The regulations also provide an IRS address to which the certification is to be mailed.

The regulations also provide that the content of the annual certification and the IRS address to which it is mailed may be added to or modified in guidance of general applicability to be published in the Internal Revenue Bulletin. Such additional information may include, for instance, which endangered status or critical status standard(s) applies to the plan; supporting information for the classification; a description of the actuarial assumptions used in making the certification; and a projection of the plan's funded percentage for future years. The guidance may also require additional supporting information for certifications made prior to the issuance of the guidance.

The regulations provide guidance on the notice required under section 432(b)(3)(D).[2] In particular the regulations require that, in the case of a plan that is in critical status and which provides for benefits that would be restricted under section 432(f)(2), the notice for the initial critical year must tell participants about the restriction. A plan sponsor that sends the model notice provided by the Secretary of Labor pursuant to section 432(b)(3)(D)(iii) satisfies this requirement.

If a section 432(b)(3)(D) notice for such a plan was sent prior to the deadline in that section and the notice did not contain the disclosure regarding the immediate restriction on benefits under section 432(f)(2), then the regulations provide that the notice does not satisfy the requirements for notice under section 432(b)(3)(D). Accordingly, the restrictions under section 432(f)(2) do not apply as a result of the issuance of such a notice and the plan will not be treated as having issued the notice for purposes of the section 432(e)(8)(A)(ii) restriction on reducing

---

[2] Under section 432(b)(3)(D)(ii), the Secretary of Labor is to prescribe a model notice that a multiemployer plan may use to satisfy this notice requirement.

adjustable benefits for participants whose benefit commencement dates are prior to the issuance of that notice. However, if additional notice that includes all of the information required under the regulations is provided prior to the required date for notice for the initial critical year under section 432(b)(3)(D) (that is, 30 days after the certification for the plan year), then the notice requirements of section 432(b)(3)(D) are satisfied as of the date of the later notice. In such a case, if the earlier notice contained the information described in section 432(b)(3)(D)(ii), then the date of that earlier notice will apply for purposes of the section 432(e)(8)(A)(ii) restriction.

The regulations reflect the rules of section 212(e)(2) of PPA under which a plan sponsor is permitted to send an early notice to plan participants. This early notice, which applies solely to the first plan year beginning after 2007, is only available if the plan actuary certifies to the plan sponsor that the plan is reasonably expected to be in critical status for that initial plan year. This preliminary certification that the plan is reasonably expected to be in critical status is different from the annual certification that the plan actuary must make; accordingly, the plan actuary must still certify whether the plan is in critical or endangered status (or in neither critical nor endangered status) for that plan year by the normal 90-day deadline for the certification.

Proposed legislation

As of the date of the issuance of these proposed regulations, bills have been introduced in the House of Representatives and the Senate that would exclude from the section 432(f)(2) limitation on accelerated benefits a distribution with an annuity starting date that is before the date that the notice under section 432(b)(3)(D) is provided.[3] Section 1.432(a)-1(a)(3)(iii)(C) has been reserved in order to accommodate any enacted changes.

Effective/Applicability Dates

These regulations apply to plan years ending after March, 18, 2008, but only with respect to plan years that begin on or after January 1, 2008. These regulations do not address the sunset provision provided by PPA '06 section 221(c).

Special Analyses

It has been determined that this notice of proposed rulemaking is not a significant regulatory action as defined in Executive Order 12866. Therefore, a regulatory assessment is not required. It has also been determined that section 553(b) of the Administrative Procedure Act (5 U.S.C. chapter 5) does not apply to these regulations. It is hereby certified that the collection of information imposed by these proposed regulations will not have a significant economic impact on a substantial number of small entities. Accordingly, a regulatory flexibility analysis is not required. The estimated burden imposed by the collection of information contained in these proposed regulations is 0.75 hours per respondent. Moreover, most of this burden is attributable to the requirement for a qualified multiemployer defined benefit plan's enrolled actuary to provide a timely certification of the plan's funding status. In addition, if a plan is certified that it is or will be in critical or endangered status, the plan sponsor is required to notify the Department of Labor, the Pension Benefit Guaranty Corporation, the bargaining parties, participants, and beneficiaries of the status designation. For plans in critical status, the plan sponsor is required to include an explanation of the possibility that adjustable benefits may be reduced and that certain benefits are restricted as of the date the notice is sent. Pursuant to section 7805(f) of the Internal Revenue Code, this regulations has been submitted to the Chief Counsel for Advocacy of the Small Business Administration for comment on its impact on small business.

Comments and Requests for a Public Hearing

Before these proposed regulations are adopted as final regulations, consideration will be given to any written (one signed and eight (8) copies) or electronic comments that are submitted timely to the IRS. The IRS and the Treasury Department request comments on the clarity of the proposed rules and how they may be made easier to understand. All comments will be available for public inspection and copying. A public hearing will be scheduled if requested in writing by any person who timely submits written comments. If a public hearing is scheduled, notice of the date, time, and place of the public hearing will be published in the **Federal Register.**

Drafting Information

The principal author of this regulation is Bruce Perlin, Office of Division Counsel/Associate Chief Counsel (Tax Exempt and Government Entities). However, other personnel from the IRS and the Treasury Department participated in their development.

[¶ 49,363]   **Proposed Amendments of Regulations (REG-147775-06)**, published in the Federal Register on April 17, 2008.

[Code Sec. 2642]

Generation-skipping transfer tax: Allocation of exemption: Elections: Extension of time.—Amendments of Reg. § 301.9100-3, describing the circumstances and procedures under which an extension of time will be granted under Code Sec. 2642(g)(1), are proposed. A hearing for this proposal has been scheduled for August 5, 2008.

AGENCY: Internal Revenue Service (IRS), Treasury.

ACTION: Notice of proposed rulemaking and notice of public hearing.

SUMMARY: This document contains proposed regulations providing guidance under section 2642(g)(1). The proposed regulations describe the circumstances and procedures under which an extension of time will be granted under section 2642(g)(1). The proposed guidance affects individuals (or their estates) who failed to make a timely allocation of generation-skipping transfer (GST) exemption to a transfer, and individuals (or their estates) who failed to make a timely election under section 2632(b)(3) or (c)(5). This document also provides notice of a public hearing.

DATES: Written or electronic comments must be received by July 17, 2008.

Outlines of topics to be discussed at the public hearing scheduled for August 5, 2008, must be received by July 15, 2008.

ADDRESSES: Send submissions to: CC:PA:LPD:PR (REG-147775-06), Internal Revenue Service, Room 5203, PO Box 7604, Ben Franklin Station, Washington, DC 20044. Submissions may be hand delivered Monday through Friday between the hours of 8 a.m. and 4 p.m. to CC:PA:LPD:PR (REG-147775-06), 1111 Constitution Avenue NW., Washington, DC 20224; or sent electronically via the Federal eRulemaking Portal at *www.regulations.gov* (IRS-REG-147775-06). The public hearing will be held in the IRS auditorium.

FOR FURTHER INFORMATION CONTACT: Concerning the proposed regulations, Theresa M. Melchiorre, (202) 622-3090; concerning submissions of comments, the hearing, and/or to be placed on the building access list to attend the hearing, Richard Hurst at *Richard.A.Hurst @irscoun-sel.treas.gov* or (202) 622-7180 (not toll-free numbers).

---

[3] See H.R. 3361 (August 3, 2007) and S. 1974 (August 2, 2007) at sections 3(b)(1)(E) and 3(b)(2)(E)(ii). However, S. 1974, as amended and passed by the Senate on December 19, 2007, did not include this provision

SUPPLEMENTARY INFORMATION:

Paperwork Reduction Act

The collections of information contained in this notice of proposed rulemaking have been submitted to the Office of Management and Budget for review in accordance with the Paperwork Reduction Act of 1995 (44 U.S.C. 3507(d)). Comments on the collections of information should be sent to the **Office of Management and Budget**, Attn: Desk Officer for the Department of the Treasury, Office of Information and Regulatory Affairs, Washington, DC 20503, with copies to the **Internal Revenue Service**, Attn: IRS Reports Clearance Officer, SE:W:CAR:MP:T:T:SP, Washington, DC 20224. Comments on the collection of information should be received by June 17, 2008.

Comments are specifically requested concerning:

Whether the proposed collection of information is necessary for the proper performance of the functions of the IRS, including whether the information will have practical utility;

The accuracy of the estimated burden associated with the proposed collection of information;

How the quality, utility, and clarity of the information to be collected may be enhanced;

How the burden of complying with the proposed collection of information may be minimized, including through the application of automated collection techniques or other forms of information technology; and

Estimates of capital or start-up costs and costs of operation, maintenance, and purchase of service to provide information.

The reporting requirement in these proposed regulations is in § 26.2642-7(h)(2) and (3). This information must be reported by transferors or the executors of transferors' estates requesting relief under section 2642(g)(1). This information will be used by the IRS to determine whether to grant a transferor or a transferor's estate an extension of time to: (1) allocate GST exemption, as defined in section 2631, to a transfer; (2) elect under section 2632(b)(3) (the election not to have the deemed allocation of GST exemption apply to a direct skip); (3) elect under section 2632(c)(5)(A)(i) (the election not to have the deemed allocation of GST exemption apply to an indirect skip or transfers made to a particular trust); and (4) elect under section 2632(c)(5)(A)(ii) (the election to treat any trust as a GST trust for purposes of section 2632(c)).

The following estimates are an approximation of the average time expected to be necessary for a collection of information. They are based on the information that is available to the IRS. Individual respondents may require greater or less time, depending on their particular circumstances.

Estimated total annual reporting burden: 1800 hours.

Estimated average annual burden: 2 hours.

Estimated number of respondents: 900.

Estimated annual frequency of response: When relief is requested.

An agency may not conduct or sponsor, and a person is not required to respond to, a collection of information unless it displays a valid control number assigned by the Office of Management and Budget.

Books or records relating to a collection of information must be retained as long as their contents may become material in the administration of any internal revenue law. Generally, tax returns and tax return information are confidential, as required by 26 U.S.C. 6103.

Background

The proposed regulations provide guidance on the application of section 2642(g)(1). Congress added section 2642(g)(1) to the Internal Revenue Code (Code) in section 564 of the Economic Growth and Tax Relief Reconciliation Act of 2001 (EGTRRA), (Public Law 107-16, § 564, 115 Stat. 91). This section directs the Secretary to issue regulations describing the circumstances and procedures under which an extension of time will be granted to: (1) allocate GST exemption, as defined in section 2631(a), to a transfer; (2) elect under section 2632(b)(3) (the election not to have the deemed allocation of GST exemption apply to a direct skip); (3) elect under section 2632(c)(5)(A)(i) (the election not to have the deemed allocation of GST exemption apply to an indirect skip or transfers made to a particular trust); and (4) elect under section 2632(c)(5)(A)(ii) (the election to treat any trust as a GST trust for purposes of section 2632(c)). In determining whether to grant relief, section 2642(g)(1) directs that all relevant circumstances be considered including evidence of intent contained in the trust instrument or the instrument of transfer.

The legislative history accompanying section 2642(g)(1) indicates that Congress believed that, in appropriate circumstances, an individual should be granted an extension of time to allocate GST exemption regardless of whether any period of limitations had expired. Those circumstances include situations in which the taxpayer intended to allocate GST exemption and the failure to allocate the exemption was inadvertent. H.R. Conf. Rep. No. 107-84, 202 (2001).

After the enactment of section 2642(g)(1), the IRS issued Notice 2001-50 (2001-2 CB 189), which announced that transferors may seek an extension of time to make an allocation of GST exemption. The Notice provides, generally, that relief will be granted under § 301.9100-3 of the Procedure and Administration Regulations if the taxpayer satisfies the requirements of those regulations and establishes to the satisfaction of the Commissioner that the taxpayer acted reasonably and in good faith and that a grant of the requested relief will not prejudice the interests of the Government. If relief is granted under § 301.9100-3 and the allocation is made, the amount of GST exemption allocated to the transfer is the Federal gift or estate tax value of the property as of the date of the transfer and the allocation is effective as of the date of the transfer. (Notice 2001-50 will be made obsolete upon the publication of the Treasury decision adopting these proposed regulations as final regulations in the **Federal Register**.)

On August 2, 2004, the IRS issued Rev. Proc. 2004-46 (2004-2 CB 142), which provides an alternate simplified method to obtain an extension of time to allocate GST exemption in certain situations. Generally, this method is available only with regard to an inter vivos transfer to a trust from which a GST may be made and only if each of the following requirements is met: (1) the transfer qualified for the gift tax annual exclusion under section 2503(b); (2) the sum of the amount of the transfer and all other gifts by the transferor to the donee in the same year did not exceed the applicable annual exclusion amount for that year; (3) no GST exemption was allocated to the transfer; (4) the taxpayer has unused GST exemption to allocate to the transfer as of the filing of the request for relief; and (5) no taxable distributions or taxable terminations have occurred as of the filing of the request for relief.

To date, the IRS has issued numerous private letter rulings under § 301.9100-3 granting an extension of time to timely allocate GST exemption in situations in which transferors (or their executors) failed to allocate GST exemption to a trust on a timely filed Federal gift or estate tax return. These proposed regulations are intended to replace § 301.9100-3 with regard to relief under section 2642(g)(1).

Accordingly, § 301.9100-3 will be amended to provide that relief under section 2642(g)(1) cannot be obtained through the provisions of §§ 301.9100-1 and 301.9100-3 after the date of publication of the Treasury decision adopting these rules as final regulations in the **Federal Register**. Relief under § 301.9100-2(b) (the automatic 6-month extension) will continue to be available to transferors or transferor's estates qualifying for that relief. In addition, the procedures contained in Revenue Procedure 2004-46 will remain effective for transferors within the scope of that Revenue Procedure.

Explanation of Provisions

The proposed regulations identify the standards that the IRS will apply in determining whether to grant a transferor or a transferor's estate an extension of time to: (1) allocate GST exemption, as defined in section 2631, to a transfer; (2) elect under section 2632(b)(3) (the election not to have the deemed allocation of GST exemption apply to a direct skip); (3) elect under section 2632(c)(5)(A)(i) (the election not to have the deemed allocation of GST exemption apply to an indirect skip or transfers made to a particular trust); and (4) elect under section 2632(c)(5)(A)(ii) (the election to treat any trust as a GST trust for purposes of section 2632(c)). The proposed regulations also identify situations with facts that do not satisfy the standards for granting relief and in which, as a result, an extension of time will not be granted.

If an extension of time to allocate GST exemption is granted under section 2642(g)(1), the allocation of GST exemption will be considered effective as of the date of the transfer, and the value of the property transferred for purposes of chapter 11 or chapter 12 will determine the amount of GST exemption to be allocated. If an extension of time to elect out of the automatic allocation of GST exemption under section 2632(b)(3) or (c)(5)(A)(i) is granted under section 2642(g)(1), the election will be considered effective as of the date of the transfer. If an extension of time to elect to treat any trust as a GST trust under section 2632(c)(5)(A)(ii) is granted under section 2642(g)(1), the election will be considered effective as of the date of the first (or each) transfer covered by that election.

The amount of GST exemption that may be allocated to a transfer pursuant to an extension granted under section 2642(g)(1) is limited to the amount of the transferor's unused GST exemption under section 2631(c) as of the date of the transfer. Thus, if the amount of GST exemption has increased since the date of the transfer, no portion of the increased amount may be applied by reason of the grant of relief under section 2642(g)(1) to a transfer taking place in an earlier year and prior to the effective date of that increase.

Requests for relief under section 2642(g)(1) will be granted when the taxpayer establishes to the satisfaction of the IRS that the taxpayer acted reasonably and in good faith, and that the grant of relief will not prejudice the interests of the Government. For purposes of section 2642(g)(1), the following nonexclusive list of factors will be used to determine whether a transferor or the executor of a transferor's estate acted reasonably and in good faith: (1) the intent of the transferor or the executor of the transferor's estate to timely allocate GST exemption or to timely make an election under section 2632(b)(3) or (c)(5) as evidenced in the trust instrument, instrument of transfer, or contemporaneous documents, such as Federal gift or estate tax returns or correspondence; (2) the occurrence of intervening events beyond the control of the transferor as defined in section 2652(a), or of the executor of the transferor's estate as defined in section 2203, that caused the failure to allocate GST exemption to a transfer or the failure to elect under section 2632(b)(3) or (c)(5); (3) the lack of awareness by the transferor or the executor of the transferor's estate of the need to allocate GST exemption to a transfer after exercising reasonable diligence, taking into account the experience of the transferor or the executor of the transferor's estate and the complexity of the GST issue; (4) evidence of consistency by the transferor in allocating (or not allocating) the transferor's GST exemption, although evidence of consistency may be less relevant if there is evidence of a change of circumstances or change of trust beneficiaries that would otherwise support a deviation from prior GST tax exemption allocation practices; and (5) reasonable reliance by the transferor or the executor of the transferor's estate on the advice of a qualified tax professional retained or employed by either (or both) of them, and the failure of the transferor or executor, in reliance on or consistent with that advice, to allocate GST exemption to the transfer or to make an election described in section 2632(b)(3) or (c)(5). The IRS will consider all relevant facts and circumstances in making this determination.

For purposes of section 2642(g)(1), the following nonexclusive list of factors will be used to determine whether the interests of the Government would be prejudiced: (1) the grant of requested relief would permit the use of hindsight to produce an economic advantage or other benefit that either would not have been available if the allocation or election had been timely made, or that results from the selection of one out of a number of alternatives (other than whether or not to make an allocation or election) that were available at the time the allocation or election could have been made timely; (2) if the transferor or the executor of the transferor's estate delayed the filing of the request for relief with the intent to deprive the IRS of sufficient time (by reason of the expiration or the impending expiration of the applicable statute of limitations or otherwise) to challenge the claimed identity of the transferor, the value of the transferred property that is the subject of the requested relief, or any other aspect of the transfer that is relevant for transfer tax purposes; and (3) a determination by the IRS that, in the event of a grant of relief under section 2642(g)(1), it would be unreasonably disruptive or difficult to adjust the GST tax consequences of a taxable termination or a taxable distribution that occurred between the time for making a timely allocation of GST exemption or a timely election described in section 2632(b)(3) or (c)(5) and the time at which the request for relief under section 2642(g)(1) was filed. The IRS will consider all relevant facts and circumstances in making this determination.

Relief under section 2642(g)(1) will not be granted when the standard of reasonableness, good faith and lack of prejudice to the interests of the Government is not met. This standard is not met in the following situations: (1) the transferor or the executor of the transferor's estate made an allocation of GST exemption as described in § 26.2632-1(b)(4)(ii)(A)(*1*), or an election under section 2632(b)(3) or (c)(5), on a timely filed Federal gift or estate tax return, and the relief requested would decrease or revoke that allocation or election; (2) the transferor or the transferor's executor delayed in requesting relief in order to preclude the IRS, as a practical matter, from challenging the identity of the transferor, the value of the transferred interest on the Federal estate or gift tax return, or any other aspect of the transaction that is relevant for Federal estate or gift tax purposes; (3) the action or inaction that is the subject of the request for relief reflected or implemented the decision with regard to the allocation of GST exemption or an election described in section 2632(b)(3) or (c)(5) that was made by the transferor or executor of the transferor's estate who had been accurately informed in all material respects by a qualified tax professional retained or employed by either (or both) of them; or (4) the IRS determines that the transferor's request is an attempt to benefit from hindsight.

A request for relief under section 2642(g)(1) does not reopen, suspend or extend the period of limitations on assessment of any estate, gift, or GST tax under section 6501. Thus, the IRS may request that the transferor or the transferor's executor consent under section 6501(c)(4) to extend the period of limitations on assessment of any or all gift and GST taxes on the transfer(s) for which relief under section 2642(g)(1) has been requested. The transferor or the transferor's executor has the right to refuse to extend the period of limitations, or to limit such extension to particular issues or to a particular period of time. See section 6501(c)(4)(B).

If the grant of relief under section 2642(g)(1) results in a potential tax refund claim, no refund will be paid or credited to the taxpayer or the taxpayer's estate if, at the time of filing the request for relief, the period of limitations for filing a claim for a credit or refund of Federal gift, estate, or GST tax under section 6511 on the transfer for which relief is granted has expired.

Relief provided under section 2642(g)(1) will be granted through the IRS letter ruling program.

Proposed Effective Date

Section 26.2642-7 applies to requests for relief filed on or after the date of publication of the Treasury decision adopting these rules as final regulations in the **Federal Register**.

Availability of IRS Documents

The IRS notice and revenue procedure cited in this preamble are published in the Cumulative Bulletin and are available at www.irs.gov.

Special Analyses

It has been determined that this notice of proposed rulemaking is not a significant regulatory action as defined in Executive Order 12866. Therefore, a regulatory assessment is not required. Pursuant to the Regulatory Flexibility Act (RFA) (5 U.S.C. chapter 6), it is hereby certified that this regulation will not have a significant economic impact on a substantial number of small entities. The applicability of this rule is limited to individuals (or their estates) and trusts, which are not small entities as defined by the RFA (5 U.S.C. 601). Although it is anticipated that there may be a beneficial economic impact for some small entities, including entities that provide tax and legal services that assist individuals in the private letter ruling program, any benefit to those entities would be indirect. Further, this indirect benefit will not affect a substantial number of these small entities because only a limited number of individuals (or their estates) and trusts would submit a private letter ruling request under this rule. Therefore, only a small fraction of tax and legal services entities would generate business or benefit from this rule. Accordingly, a regulatory flexibility analysis is not required. Pursuant to section 7805(f) of the Code, this regulation has been submitted to the Chief Counsel for Advocacy of the Small Business Administration for comment on its impact on small entities.

Comments and Public Hearing

Before these proposed regulations are adopted as final regulations, consideration will be given to any written (a signed original and eight (8) copies) or electronic comments that are submitted timely to the IRS. The IRS and Treasury Department request comments on the clarity of the proposed rules and also on how they can be made easier to understand. All comments will be available for public inspection and copying.

A public hearing has been scheduled for August 5, 2008 in the IRS auditorium. Due to building security procedures, visitors must enter at the Constitution Avenue entrance. In addition, all visitors must present photo identification to enter the building. Because of access restrictions, visitors will not be admitted beyond the immediate entrance area more than 30 minutes before the hearing starts. For more information about having your name placed on the list to attend the hearing, see the "FOR FURTHER INFORMATION CONTACT" section of this preamble.

The rules of 26 CFR 601.601(a)(3) apply to the hearing. Persons who wish to present oral comments at the hearing must submit written (a signed original and eight (8) copies) or electronic comments by July 17, 2008 and an outline of the topics to be discussed and the time to be devoted to each topic by July 15, 2008. A period of 10 minutes will be allotted to each person for making comments. An agenda showing the scheduling of the speakers will be prepared after the deadline for receiving outlines has passed. Copies of the agenda will be available free of charge at the hearing.

Drafting Information

The principal author of these regulations is Theresa M. Melchiorre, Office of Chief Counsel, IRS.

[¶ 49,374] Proposed Regulations (REG-100464-08), published with the Federal Register on June 18, 2008.

[Code Sec. 411]

Retirement plans: Defined benefit plans: Accrued benefits testing: Greatest of two or more separate formulas.—Amendments of Reg. §1.411(b)-1, providing guidance on the application of the accrual rule for defined benefit plans under Code Sec. 411(b)(1)(B) in cases where plan benefits are determined on the basis of the greatest of two or more separate formulas, are proposed.

AGENCY: Internal Revenue Service (IRS), Treasury.

ACTION: Notice of proposed rulemaking and notice of public hearing.

SUMMARY: This document contains proposed regulations providing guidance on the application of the accrual rule for defined benefit plans under section 411(b)(1)(B) of the Internal Revenue Code (Code) in cases where plan benefits are determined on the basis of the greatest of two or more separate formulas. These regulations would affect sponsors, administrators, participants, and beneficiaries of defined benefit plans. This document also provides a notice of a public hearing on these proposed regulations.

DATES: Written or electronic comments must be received by September 18, 2008. Outlines of topics to be discussed at the public hearing scheduled for October 15, 2008, at 10 a.m. must be received by September 24, 2008. ADDRESSES: Send submissions to: CC:PA:LPD:PR (REG 100464-08), room 5203, Internal Revenue Service, PO Box 7604, Ben Franklin Station, Washington, DC 20044. Submissions may be hand-delivered Monday through Friday between the hours of 8 a.m. and 4 p.m. to CC:PA:LPD:PR (REG 100464-08), Courier's Desk, Internal Revenue Service, 1111 Constitution Avenue NW., Washington, DC., or sent electronically via the Federal eRulemaking Portal at www.regulations.gov (IRS REG-100464-08). The public hearing will be held in the IRS Auditorium, Internal Revenue Building, 1111 Constitution Avenue NW., Washington, DC.

FOR FURTHER INFORMATION CONTACT: Concerning the regulations, Lauson C. Green or Linda S. F. Marshall at (202) 622-6090; concerning submissions of comments, the hearing, and/or being placed on the building access list to attend the hearing, Richard A. Hurst at Richard.A.Hurst@irscounsel.treas.gov or at (202) 622-7180 (not toll-free numbers).

SUPPLEMENTARY INFORMATION:

Background

This document contains proposed Income Tax Regulations (26 CFR part 1) under section 411(b) of the Code.[1]

Section 401(a)(7) provides that a trust is not a qualified trust under section 401 unless the plan of which such trust is a part satisfies the requirements of section 411 (relating to minimum vesting standards).

Section 411(a) requires a qualified plan to provide that an employee's right to the normal retirement benefit is nonforfeitable upon attainment of normal retirement age and that an employee's right to his or her accrued benefit is nonforfeitable upon completion of the specified number of years of service under one of the vesting schedules set forth in section 411(a)(2). Section 411(a)(7)(A)(i) defines a participant's accrued benefit under a defined benefit plan as the employee's accrued benefit determined under the plan, expressed in the form of an annual benefit commencing at normal retirement age, subject to an exception in section 411(c)(3) under which the accrued benefit is the actuarial equivalent of the annual benefit commencing at normal retirement age in the case of a plan that does not express the accrued benefit as an annual benefit commencing at normal retirement age.

Section 411(a) also requires that a defined benefit plan satisfy the requirements of section 411(b)(1). Section 411(b)(1) provides that a defined benefit plan must satisfy one of the three accrual rules of section 411(b)(1)(A), (B), and (C) with respect to benefits accruing under the plan. The three accrual rules are the 3 percent method of section 411(b)(1)(A), the 133$\frac{1}{3}$ percent rule of section 411(b)(1)(B), and the fractional rule of section 411(b)(1)(C).

Section 411(b)(1)(A) provides that a defined benefit plan satisfies the requirements of the 3 percent method if, under the plan, the accrued benefit payable upon the participant's separation from service is not less than (A) 3 percent of the normal retirement benefit to which the participant would

---

[1] Section 204(b) of the Employee Retirement Income Security Act of 1974, Public Law 93-406 (88 Stat. 829), as amended (ERISA), sets forth rules that are parallel to those in section 411(b) of the Code. Under section 101 of Reorganization Plan No. 4 of 1978 (43 FR 47713), the Secretary of the Treasury has interpretive jurisdiction over the subject matter addressed in these proposed regulations for purposes of ERISA, as well as the Code. Thus, these proposed Treasury regulations issued under section 411(b)(1)(B) of the Code would apply as well for purposes of section 204(b)(1)(B) of ERISA.

be entitled if the participant commenced participation at the earliest possible entry age under the plan and served continuously until the earlier of age 65 or the normal retirement age under the plan, multiplied by (B) the number of years (not in excess of 33 1/3 years) of his or her participation in the plan. Section 411(b)(1)(A) provides that, in the case of a plan providing retirement benefits based on compensation during any period, the normal retirement benefit to which a participant would be entitled is determined as if the participant continued to earn annually the average rate of compensation during consecutive years of service, not in excess of 10, for which his or her compensation was highest. Section 411(b)(1)(A) also provides that Social Security benefits and all other relevant factors used to compute benefits are treated as remaining constant as of the current plan year for all years after the current year.

Section 411(b)(1)(B) provides that a defined benefit plan satisfies the requirements of the 133 1/3 percent rule for a particular plan year if, under the plan, the accrued benefit payable at the normal retirement age is equal to the normal retirement benefit, and the annual rate at which any individual who is or could be a participant can accrue the retirement benefits payable at normal retirement age under the plan for any later plan year is not more than 133 1/3 percent of the annual rate at which the individual can accrue benefits for any plan year beginning on or after such particular plan year and before such later plan year.

For purposes of applying the 133 1/3 percent rule, section 411(b)(1)(B)(i) provides that any amendment to the plan which is in effect for the current year is treated as in effect for all other plan years. Section 411(b)(1)(B)(ii) provides that any change in an accrual rate which does not apply to any individual who is or could be a participant in the current plan year is disregarded. Section 411(b)(1)(B)(iii) provides that the fact that benefits under the plan may be payable to certain participants before normal retirement age is disregarded. Section 411(b)(1)(B)(iv) provides that Social Security benefits and all other relevant factors used to compute benefits are treated as remaining constant as of the current plan year for all years after the current year.

Section 411(b)(1)(C) provides that a defined benefit plan satisfies the fractional rule if the accrued benefit to which any participant is entitled upon his or her separation from service is not less than a fraction of the annual benefit commencing at normal retirement age to which the participant would be entitled under the plan as in effect on the date of separation if the participant continued to earn annually until normal retirement age the same rate of compensation upon which the normal retirement benefit would be computed under the plan, determined as if the participant had attained normal retirement age on the date on which any such determination is made (but taking into account no more than 10 years of service immediately preceding separation from service). This fraction, which cannot exceed 1, has a numerator that is the total number of the participant's years of participation in the plan (as of the date of separation from service) and a denominator that is the total number of years the participant would have participated in the plan if the participant separated from service at normal retirement age. Section 411(b)(1)(C) also provides that Social Security benefits and all other relevant factors used to compute benefits are treated as remaining constant as of the current plan year for all years after the current year.

Section 1.411(a)-7(a)(1) of the Income Tax Regulations provides that, for purposes of section 411 and the regulations under section 411, the accrued benefit of a participant under a defined benefit plan is either (A) the accrued benefit determined under the plan if the plan provides for an accrued benefit in the form of an annual benefit commencing at normal retirement age, or (B) an annual benefit commencing at normal retirement age which is the actuarial equivalent (determined under section 411(c)(3) and §1.411(c)-1)) of the accrued benefit under the plan if the plan does not provide for an accrued benefit in the form of an annual benefit commencing at normal retirement age.

Section 1.411(b)-1(a)(1) provides that a defined benefit plan is not a qualified plan unless the method provided by the plan for determining accrued benefits satisfies at least one of the alternative methods in §1.411(b)-1(b) for determining accrued benefits with respect to all active participants under the plan. The three alternative methods are the 3 percent method, the 133 1/3 percent rule, and the fractional rule. A defined benefit plan may provide that accrued benefits for participants are determined under more than one plan formula. Section 1.411(b)-1(a)(1) provides that, in such a case, the accrued benefits under all such formulas must be aggregated in order to determine whether or not the accrued benefits under the plan for participants satisfy one of these methods. Under §1.411(b)-1(a)(1), a plan may satisfy different methods with respect to different classifications of employees, or separately satisfy one method with respect to the accrued benefits for each such classification, provided that such classifications are not so structured as to evade the accrued benefit requirements of section 411(b) and §1.411(b)-1.

Section 1.411(b)-1(b)(2)(i) provides that a defined benefit plan satisfies the 133 1/3 percent rule for a particular plan year if (A) under the plan the accrued benefit payable at the normal retirement age (determined under the plan) is equal to the normal retirement benefit (determined under the plan), and (B) the annual rate at which any individual who is or could be a participant can accrue the retirement benefits payable at normal retirement age under the plan for any later plan year cannot be more than 133 1/3 percent of the annual rate at which the participant can accrue benefits for any plan year beginning on or after such particular plan year and before such later plan year.

Section 1.411(b)-1(b)(2)(ii)(A) through (D) sets forth a series of rules that correspond to the rules of section 411(b)(1)(B)(i) through (iv). For example, §1.411(b)-1(b)(2)(ii)(A) sets forth a special plan amendment rule for purposes of satisfying the 133 1/3 percent rule that corresponds to section 411(b)(1)(B)(i). Under that rule, any amendment to a plan that is in effect for the current year is treated as if it were in effect for all other plan years.

Section 1.411(b)-1(b)(2)(ii)(E) provides that a plan is not treated as failing to satisfy the requirements of §1.411(b)-1(b)(2) for a plan year merely because no benefits under the plan accrue to a participant who continues service with the employer after the participant has attained normal retirement age.[2] Section 1.411(b)-1(b)(2)(ii)(F) provides that a plan does not satisfy the requirements of §1.411(b)-1(b)(2) if the base for the computation of retirement benefits changes solely by reason of an increase in the number of years of participation.

Rev. Rul. 2008-7 (2008-7 IRB 419), see §601.601(d)(2)(ii)(b), describes the application of the accrual rules of section 411(b)(1)(A) through (C) and the regulations under section 411(b)(1)(A) through (C) to a defined benefit plan that was amended to change the plan's benefit formula from a traditional formula based on highest average compensation to a new lump sum-based benefit formula. Under the terms of the plan described in the revenue ruling, for an employee who was employed on the day before the change, a hypothetical account was established equal to the actuarial present value of the employee's accrued benefit as of that date, and that account was also to be credited with subsequent pay credits and interest credits. Under transition rules set forth in the plan, the accrued benefit of certain participants is the greater of the accrued benefit provided by the hypothetical account balance at the age 65 normal retirement age and the accrued benefit determined under the traditional formula as in effect on the day before the change, but taking into account post-amendment compensation and service for a limited number of years.

Revenue Ruling 2008-7 describes how the accrued benefits of different participant groups satisfy, or fail to satisfy, the accrual rules under section 411(b)(1)(A) through (C), taking into account the requirement in §1.411(b)-1(a)(1) that a plan that determines a participant's accrued benefits under more than one formula must aggregate the accrued benefits under all of those formulas in order to determine whether or not the accrued benefits under the plan satisfy one of the alternative methods under section 411(b)(1)(A) through (C). However, Revenue Ruling 2008-7 explains that, in the case of a plan amendment that replaces the benefit formula under the plan for all periods after the amendment, pursuant to section 411(b)(1)(B)(i) and §1.411(b)-1(b)(2)(ii)(A), the rule that would otherwise require aggregation of the multiple formulas does not apply. Under section

---

[2] However, section 411(b)(1)(H), which was added to the Code after the issuance of §1.411(b)-1, generally requires the continued accrual of benefits after attainment of normal retirement age.

411(b)(1)(B)(i) and § 1.411(b)-1(b)(2)(ii)(A), any amendment to the plan which is in effect for the current plan year is treated as if it were in effect for all other plan years (including past and future plan years).

Revenue Ruling 2008-7 illustrates the application of this rule with respect to participants who only accrue benefits under the new formula (who in the ruling are referred to as participants who are not "grandfathered"). For these participants, the plan amendment completely ceases accruals under a traditional pension benefit formula that provides an annuity at normal retirement age based on service and average pay and, for all periods after the amendment, provides for the greater of the section 411(d)(6) protected benefit under the pre-amendment formula and the benefit under a new post-amendment lump sum-based benefit formula. In such a case, as stated in Revenue Ruling 2008-7, the section 411(d)(6) protected benefit under the pre-amendment formula is not aggregated with the post-amendment formula, but rather is entirely disregarded, for purposes of applying the 133 $^1/_3$ percent rule because the new formula is treated under section 411(b)(1)(B)(i) and § 1.411(b)-1(b)(2)(ii)(A) as having been in effect for all plan years. This analysis was reflected in *Register v. PNC Fin. Servs. Group, Inc.*, 477 F.3d 56 (3d Cir. 2007).

In addition to satisfying the requirements of section 411(b)(1)(B), a defined benefit plan must also satisfy the age discrimination rules of section 411(b)(1)(H), taking into account section 411(b)(5), as added to the Code by the Pension Protection Act of 2006, Public Law 109-280 (120 Stat. 780) (PPA '06). In the case of a conversion of a plan to a statutory hybrid plan pursuant to an amendment that is adopted after June 29, 2005 (a "post-PPA conversion plan"), the conversion amendment must satisfy the rule of section 411(b)(5)(B)(iii) that prohibits wearaway of benefits upon conversion. In the case of a plan converted to a statutory hybrid plan pursuant to an amendment that is adopted on or before June 29, 2005 (a "pre-PPA conversion plan"), as provided in Notice 2007-6, the IRS will not consider and will not issue determination letters with respect to whether such a pre-PPA conversion plan satisfies the requirements of section 411(b)(1)(H) (as in effect prior to the addition of section 411(b)(5) by PPA '06), including the effect of any wearaway. Thus, although wearaway upon conversion is expressly prohibited with respect to post-PPA conversion plans pursuant to section 411(b)(5), the IRS will not address and will not issue determination letters with respect to whether a conversion that results in wearaway with respect to a pre-PPA conversion plan violates the age discrimination rules of section 411(b)(1)(H). See § 601.601(d)(2)(ii)(*b*).

Revenue Ruling 2008-7 provides a different analysis as to whether a plan with wearaway fails to satisfy the accrual rules of section 411(b)(1)(B) when the preamendment formula continues in place after the amendment for a group of participants. In such a case, where an amendment has gone into effect but continues the prior formula for some period of time with respect to one or more participants, the application of the rule in section 411(b)(1)(B)(i) and § 1.411(b)-1(b)(2)(ii)(A) does not result in a disregard of the prior plan formula (which remains in effect after the amendment). Instead, the 133 $^1/_3$ percent rule must be applied with respect to those participants based on the combined effect of the two ongoing formulas.[3]

Revenue Ruling 2008-7 provides relief from disqualification under the Internal Revenue Code (under the authority of section 7805(b)) for a limited class of plans under which a group of employees specified under the plan receives a benefit equal to the greatest of the benefits provided under two or more formulas (an applicable "greater-of" benefit), provided that each such formula standing alone would satisfy an accrual rule of section 411(b)(1)(A), (B), or (C) for the years involved. Under the relief set forth in Rev. Rul. 2008-7, for plan years beginning before January 1, 2009, the IRS will not treat a plan eligible for the relief as failing to satisfy the accrual rules of section 411(b)(1)(A), (B), and (C) solely because the plan provides an applicable "greater-of" benefit, where the separate formulas, standing alone, would satisfy an accrual rule of section 411(b)(1)(A), (B), and (C).

Explanation of Provisions

The fact pattern described in Revenue Ruling 2008-7 has occurred in a number of situations over the past few years. Employers sponsoring these plans have suggested that their plans should satisfy the accrual rules of section 411(b)(1)(A), (B), and (C), contending that any technical violation of the accrual rules is directly because the participant has higher frontloaded accruals under one formula when compared to the other formula that will ultimately provide the larger benefit under the plan. While the relief under section 7805(b) that is provided under Revenue Ruling 2008-7 addresses the situation for past years, the relief does not apply for the parallel accrual rules of section 204(b)(1)(A), (B) and (C) of ERISA and only applies to plan years beginning before January 1, 2009.

The proposed regulations would provide a limited exception to the existing requirement under § 1.411(b)-1(a)(1) to aggregate the accrued benefits under all formulas in order to determine whether or not the accrued benefits under the plan for participants satisfy one of the alternative methods under section 411(b)(1)(A) through (C). Under this limited exception, certain plans that determine a participant's benefits as the greatest of the benefits determined under two or more separate formulas would be permitted to demonstrate satisfaction of the 133 $^1/_3$ percent rule of section 411(b)(1)(B) by demonstrating that each separate formula satisfies the 133 $^1/_3$ percent rule of section 411(b)(1)(B).[4]

A plan would be eligible for this exception only if each of the separate formulas uses a different basis for determining benefits. For example, a plan would be eligible for this special rule if it provides a benefit equal to the greater of the benefits under two formulas, one of which determines benefits on the basis of highest average compensation and the other of which determines benefits on the basis of career average compensation. As another example, a traditional defined benefit plan which determined benefits based on highest average compensation that is amended to add a cash balance formula (as in the facts of Rev. Rul. 2008-7) would be eligible for this exception where, in order to provide a better transition for longer service active participants, the plan provides that a group of participants is entitled to the greater of the benefit provided by the hypothetical account balance and the benefit determined under the continuing traditional formula. In each of the above two examples, each separate formula under the plan uses a different basis for determining benefits and, therefore, both of those plans would be eligible to utilize this exception. Accordingly, both plans would be permitted to demonstrate satisfaction of the 133 $^1/_3$ percent rule of section 411(b)(1)(B) by demonstrating that each separate formula under the plan satisfies the 133 $^1/_3$ percent rule of section 411(b)(1)(B).

The utility of this exception can be seen from the following example of a plan that provides a benefit equal to the greater of two formulas. One formula provides a benefit of 1 percent of average compensation for the 3 consecutive years of service with the highest such average multiplied by the number of years of service at normal retirement age (not in excess of 25 years of service), and the other formula provides a benefit that is the accumulation of 1.5 percent of compensation for each year of service. Under the existing final regulations, the 133 $^1/_3$ percent rule of section 411(b)(1)(B) is applied by reference to the annual rate of accrual for each year from the year of the test through normal retirement age. If the participant's accrued benefit currently is determined using the 1 percent formula (because the high-3 average compensation is significantly higher than the effective career average compensation that is used under the 1.5 percent formula), but the participant's normal retirement benefit will ultimately be determined using the 1.5 percent formula if service continues to normal retirement age (because the 25-year service cap will apply to the 1 percent formula, but not the 1.5 percent formula), then the annual rate of accrual will have to be determined for testing purposes on a consistent basis for each year, either using each year's compensation or high-3 average compensation. Thus, in order to test the plan under the 133 $^1/_3$ percent rule, the existing final regulations would require that either the accruals under the 1 percent formula be expressed in terms of a single

---

[3] Two federal courts have taken a position contrary to this interpretation of section 411(b)(1)(B)(i) and § 1.411(b)-1(b)(2)(ii)(A) as set forth in Revenue Ruling 2008-7. See *Tomlinson v. El Paso Corp.*, 2008 WL 762456 (D. Colo. Mar. 19, 2008); *Wheeler v. Pension Value Plan for Employees of Boeing Corp.*, 2007 WL 2608875 (S.D. Ill. Sept. 6, 2007).

[4] These proposed regulations would only apply for purposes of the 133 $^1/_3$ percent rule of section 411(b)(1)(B) (and the parallel rule of section 204(b)(1)(B) of ERISA). Neither Rev. Rul. 2008-7 nor these proposed regulations are relevant to (and thus they do not affect) the application of the age discrimination rules of section 411(b)(1)(H) (or the parallel age discrimination rules of section 204(b)(1)(H) of ERISA).

year's pay or the accruals under the 1.5 percent formula be expressed in terms of high-3 average compensation. In either case, the annual rates of accrual would differ from the stated rates under the plan formulas. In addition, the annual rates of accrual for the accumulation formula when those rates are expressed in terms of high-3 average compensation could be negative in some cases. In contrast, using the exception set forth in the proposed regulation would enable the plan to be tested using the annual rates of accrual expressed in the plan formulas.

The proposed regulations would also provide an extension of this exception in the case of a plan that provides benefits based on the greatest of three or more benefit formulas. In such a case, the plan would be eligible for a modified version of the formula-by-formula testing under the proposed regulations. Under this modification, the accrued benefits determined under all benefit formulas that have the same basis are first aggregated and then those aggregated formulas are treated as a single formula for purposes of applying the separate testing rule under the proposed regulations.

Eligibility for separate testing under the proposed regulations would be constrained by an anti-abuse rule. The proposed regulations would provide that a plan is not eligible for separate testing if the Commissioner determines that the plan's use of separate formulas with different bases is structured to evade the general requirement to aggregate formulas under §1.411(b)-1(a)(1) (for example, if the differences between the bases of the separate formulas are minor).

Proposed Effective/Applicability Date

These regulations are proposed to be effective for plan years beginning on or after January 1, 2009.

Special Analyses

It has been determined that this notice of proposed rulemaking is not a significant regulatory action as defined in Executive Order 12866. Therefore, a regulatory assessment is not required. It also has been determined that section 553(b) of the Administrative Procedure Act (5 U.S.C. chapter 5) does not apply to these regulations, and because the regulations do not impose a collection of information on small entities, the Regulatory Flexibility Act (5 U.S.C. chapter 6) does not apply. Pursuant to section 7805(f) of the Code, this regulation has been submitted to the Chief Counsel for Advocacy of the Small Business Administration for comment on its impact on small business.

Comments and Public Hearing

Before these proposed regulations are adopted as final regulations, consideration will be given to any written (a signed original and eight (8) copies) or electronic comments that are submitted timely to the IRS. The IRS and the Treasury Department specifically request comments on the clarity of the proposed regulations and how they may be made easier to understand. All comments will be available for public inspection and copying.

Under these proposed regulations, a plan eligible for the separate testing option would not violate the accrual rules merely because the plan provides higher frontloaded accruals under one formula when compared to the other formula that will ultimately provide the larger benefit under the plan. Some commentators have suggested a broader rule that would modify the regulations to provide that a plan does not violate the accrual rules where the plan provides a pattern of accruals that affords higher benefits in earlier years (that is, benefit accruals are frontloaded) relative to a pattern of accruals that satisfies the accrual rules. The 3 percent method of section 411(b)(1)(A) and the fractional rule of section 411(b)(1)(C) automatically achieve this result because they are cumulative tests that test on the basis of the total accrued benefit compared to the projected normal retirement benefit. By contrast, the 133 1/3 percent rule is based on a comparison of the "annual rate at which any individual who is or could be a participant can accrue the retirement benefits payable at normal retirement age" for a later plan year with the annual rate for an earlier plan year. The existing final regulations include an example (§1.411(b)-1(b)(2)(iii), Example (3)) that demonstrates how a plan fails the 133 1/3 percent rule where it provides accruals in earlier years that are frontloaded relative to accruals that apply in later years. The proposed regulations do not include a provision under the 133 1/3 percent rule that recognizes prior frontloading of benefits. However, commentators who would suggest such a provision under the 133 1/3 percent rule should describe how that provision would fit within the statutory language of section 411(b)(1)(B), including the application of section 411(b)(1)(B)(i) (which requires that an amendment to the plan that is in effect for the current year be treated as in effect for all other plan years).

A public hearing has been scheduled for October 15, 2008, beginning at 10 a.m. in the Auditorium, Internal Revenue Service, 1111 Constitution Avenue, NW., Washington, DC. Due to building security procedures, visitors must enter at the Constitution Avenue entrance. In addition, all visitors must present photo identification to enter the building. Because of access restrictions, visitors will not be admitted beyond the immediate entrance area more than 30 minutes before the hearing starts. For information about having your name placed on the building access list to attend the hearing, see the **FOR FURTHER INFORMATION CONTACT** section of this preamble.

The rules of 26 CFR 601.601(a)(3) apply to the hearing. Persons who wish to present oral comments at the hearing must submit written or electronic comments by September 18, 2008, and an outline of topics to be discussed and the amount of time to be devoted to each topic (a signed original and eight (8) copies) by September 24, 2008. A period of 10 minutes will be allotted to each person for making comments. An agenda showing the scheduling of the speakers will be prepared after the deadline for receiving outlines has passed. Copies of the agenda will be available free of charge at the hearing.

Drafting Information

The principal authors of these regulations are Lauson C. Green and Linda S. F. Marshall, Office of Division Counsel/Associate Chief Counsel (Tax Exempt and Government Entities). However, other personnel from the IRS and the Treasury Department participated in the development of these regulations.

[¶ 49,376]   **Proposed Amendments of Regulations (REG-143453-05)**, published in the Federal Register on June 26, 2008.

[Code Sec. 179B]

Qualified capital costs: Diesel fuel: Sulfur control: Deduction.—Reg. §1.179B-1, relating to the deduction for qualified capital costs paid or incurred by a small business refiner to comply with the highway diesel fuel sulfur control requirements of the Environmental Protection Agency, is proposed.

AGENCY: Internal Revenue Service (IRS), Treasury.

ACTION: Notice of proposed rulemaking by cross-reference to temporary regulations and notice of public hearing.

SUMMARY: In the Rules and Regulations section of this issue of the **Federal Register**, the IRS is issuing temporary regulations under section 179B of the Internal Revenue Code (Code) relating to the deduction for qualified capital costs paid or incurred by a small business refiner to comply with the highway diesel fuel sulfur control requirements of the Environmental Protection Agency (EPA). The temporary regulations implement changes to the law made by the American Jobs Creation Act of 2004, the Energy Policy Act of 2005, and the Tax Technical Corrections Act of 2007. The text of those temporary regulations also serves as the text of these proposed regulations. This document also provides notice of a public hearing on these proposed regulations.

DATES: Written or electronic comments must be received by September 25, 2008. Outlines of topics to be discussed at the public hearing scheduled for October 28, 2008, at 10 a.m. must be received by September 22, 2008.

ADDRESSES: Send submissions to: CC:PA:LPD:PR (REG-143453-05), room 5203, Internal Revenue Service, PO Box 7604, Ben Franklin Station, Washington, DC 20044. Submissions may be hand-delivered Monday through Friday between the hours of 8 a.m. and 4 p.m. to CC:PA:LPD:PR (REG-143453-05), Courier's Desk, Internal Revenue Service, 1111 Constitution Avenue NW., Washington, DC, or sent electronically via the Federal eRulemaking Portal at http://www.regulations.gov (IRS REG-143453-05). The public hearing will be held in the IRS Auditorium, Internal Revenue Building, 1111 Constitution Avenue, NW, Washington, DC.

FOR FURTHER INFORMATION CONTACT: Concerning the proposed regulations, Nicole Cimino, (202) 622-3110; concerning submissions of comments, the hearing, and/or to be placed on the building access list to attend the hearing, Oulwafunmilayo Taylor, (202) 622-7180 (not toll-free numbers).

SUPPLEMENTARY INFORMATION:

Paperwork Reduction Act

The collection of information contained in this notice of proposed rulemaking has been submitted to the Office of Management and Budget for review in accordance with the Paperwork Reduction Act of 1995 (44 U.S.C. 3507(d)). Comments on the collection of information should be sent to the **Office of Management and Budget** , Attn: Desk Officer for the Department of the Treasury, Office of Information and Regulatory Affairs, Washington, DC 20503, with copies to the **Internal Revenue Service** , Attn: IRS Reports Clearance Officer, SE:W:CAR: MP:T:T:SP, Washington, DC 20224. Comments on the collection of information should be received by August 26, 2008. Comments are specifically requested concerning:

Whether the proposed collection of information is necessary for the proper performance of the functions of the IRS, including whether the information will have practical utility;

The accuracy of the estimated burden associated with the proposed collection of information;

How the quality, utility, and clarity of the information to be collected may be enhanced;

How the burden of complying with the proposed collection of information may be minimized, including through the application of automated collection techniques or other forms of information technology; and

Estimates of capital or start-up costs and costs of operation, maintenance, and purchase of service to provide information.

The collection of information in this proposed regulation is in section 1.179B-1T(d) and section 1.179B-1T(e). This information collected under section 1.179B-1T(d) relates to the election under section 179B(a) by a small business refiner to deduct a portion of the qualified capital costs paid or incurred. The information collected under section 1.179B-1T(e) relates to the election under section 179B(e) by a cooperative small business refiner to allocate all or some of its section 179B(a) deduction to its cooperative owners and to notify those cooperative owners of the allocated amount. This information will be used by the IRS for examination purposes. The collection of information is required to obtain a benefit. The likely respondents are small business refiners.

Estimated total annual reporting burden: 50 hours.

The estimated annual burden per respondent varies from .75 to 1.5 hours, depending on individual circumstances, with an estimated average of 1 hour.

Estimated number of respondents: 50.

Estimated frequency of responses: Annually.

An agency may not conduct or sponsor, and a person is not required to respond to, a collection of information unless it displays a valid control number assigned by the Office of Management and Budget.

Books or records relating to a collection of information must be retained as long as their contents may become material in the administration of any internal revenue law. Generally, tax returns and tax return information are confidential, as required by 26 U.S.C. 6103.

Background

Temporary regulations in the Rules and Regulations section of this issue of the **Federal Register** amend 26 CFR part 1 by adding regulations under section 179B of the Code. The temporary regulations contain rules relating to the deduction provided under section 179B for qualified costs paid or incurred by a small business refiner to comply with the highway diesel fuel sulfur control requirements of the EPA. The text of those temporary regulations also serves as the text of these proposed regulations. The preamble to the temporary regulations explains the temporary regulations and these proposed regulations.

Special Analyses

It has been determined that this notice of proposed rulemaking is not a significant regulatory action as defined in Executive Order 12866. Therefore, a regulatory assessment is not required. It also has been determined that section 553(b) of the Administrative Procedure Act (5 U.S.C. chapter 5) does not apply to these regulations. It is hereby certified that the collection of information in these regulations will not have a significant economic impact on a substantial number of small entities. This certification is based upon the fact, as discussed earlier in this preamble, that the amount of time necessary to record and retain the required information is estimated to average one hour for those taxpayers electing to deduct qualified capital costs and electing to allocate all or some of that deduction to certain owners. Therefore, a Regulatory Flexibility Analysis under the Regulatory Flexibility Act (5 U.S.C. chapter 6) is not required. Pursuant to section 7805(f) of the Code, this notice of proposed rulemaking has been submitted to the Chief Counsel for Advocacy of the Small Business Administration for comment on its impact on small business.

Comments and Public Hearing

Before these proposed regulations are adopted as final regulations, consideration will be given to any written comments (a signed original and eight (8) copies) or electronic comments that are submitted timely to the IRS. The IRS and the Treasury Department specifically request comments on the clarity of the proposed rules and how they may be made easier to understand. All comments will be available for public inspection and copying.

A public hearing has been scheduled for October 28, 2008, beginning at 10:00 a.m. in the IRS Auditorium, Internal Revenue Building, 1111 Constitution Avenue, NW., Washington, DC. Due to building security procedures, all visitors must enter at the Constitution Avenue entrance. In addition, all visitors must present photo identification to enter the building. Because of access restrictions, visitors will not be admitted beyond the immediate entrance area more than 30 minutes before the hearing starts. For information about having your name placed on the building access list to attend the hearing, see the **FOR FURTHER INFORMATION CONTACT** section of this preamble.

The rules of 26 CFR 601.601(a)(3) apply to the hearing. Persons who wish to present oral comments at the hearing must submit written or electronic comments by September 25, 2008 and an outline of the topics to be discussed and the time to be devoted to each topic (signed original and eight (8) copies) by September 22, 2008. A period of 10 minutes will be allotted to each person for making comments. An agenda showing the scheduling of the speakers will be prepared after the deadline for receiving outlines has passed. Copies of the agenda will be available free of charge at the hearing.

Drafting Information

The principal author of these regulations is Nicole R. Cimino, Office of Associate Chief Counsel (Passthroughs and Special Industries). However, other personnel from the IRS and the Treasury Department participated in their development.

[¶ 49,389]   Proposed Amendments of Regulations (REG-155087-05), published in the Federal Register on July 29, 2008.

[Code Secs. 40 and 40A]

Excise tax: Fuel credits: Alcohol mixtures: Biodiesel mixtures: Renewable diesel mixtures: Alternative fuel mixtures: Alternative fuel.—Amendments of Reg. §§ 1.40-1, 1.40-2 and 1.40A-1 relating to credits and payments for alcohol mixtures, biodiesel mixtures, renewable diesel mixtures, alternative fuel mixtures, and alternative fuel sold of use or used as a fuel, are proposed.

AGENCY: Internal Revenue Service (IRS), Treasury.

ACTION: Notice of proposed rulemaking.

SUMMARY: This document contains proposed regulations relating to credits and payments for alcohol mixtures, biodiesel mixtures, renewable diesel mixtures, alternative fuel mixtures, and alternative fuel sold for use or used as a fuel, as well as proposed regulations relating to the definition of gasoline and diesel fuel. These regulations reflect changes made by the American Jobs Creation Act of 2004, the Energy Policy Act of 2005, the Safe, Accountable, Flexible, Efficient Transportation Equity Act: A Legacy for Users, and the Tax Technical Corrections Act of 2007. These regulations affect producers of alcohol, biodiesel, and renewable diesel; producers of alcohol, biodiesel, renewable diesel, and alternative fuel mixtures; sellers and users of alternative fuel; and certain persons liable for the tax on removals, entries, or sales of gasoline or diesel fuel.

DATES: Written or electronic comments and requests for a public hearing must be received by October 28, 2008.

ADDRESSES: Send submissions to CC:PA:LPD:PR (REG-155087-05), room 5203, Internal Revenue Service, PO Box 7604, Ben Franklin Station, Washington, DC 20044. Submissions may be hand delivered Monday through Friday between the hours of 8 a.m. and 4 p.m. to CC:PA:LPD:PR (REG-155087-05), Courier's Desk, Internal Revenue Service, 1111 Constitution Avenue, NW, Washington, DC, or sent electronically, via the Federal eRulemaking Portal at *http://www.regulations.gov* (IRS REG-155087-05).

FOR FURTHER INFORMATION CONTACT: Concerning the proposed regulations, Stephanie Bland, Taylor Cortright, or DeAnn Malone, all of whom can be reached at (202) 622-3130 (not a toll-free call); concerning the submission of comments or requests for a public hearing, Oluwafunmilayo Taylor at (202) 622-7180 (not a toll-free call).

SUPPLEMENTARY INFORMATION:

Paperwork Reduction Act

The collections of information contained in this notice of proposed rulemaking have been submitted to the Office of Management and Budget for review in accordance with the Paperwork Reduction Act of 1995 (44 U.S.C. 3507(d)). Comments on the collection of information should be sent to the **Office of Management and Budget**, Attn: Desk Officer for the Department of the Treasury, Office of Information and Regulatory Affairs, Washington, DC 20503, with copies to the Internal Revenue Service, Attn: IRS Reports Clearance Officer, SE:W:CAR:MP:T:T:SP, Washington, DC 20224. Comments on the collection of information should be received by September 28, 2008. Comments are specifically requested concerning:

Whether the proposed collection of information is necessary for the proper performance of the functions of the Internal Revenue Service, including whether the information will have practical utility;

The accuracy of the estimated burden associated with the proposed collection of information;

How the quality, utility, and clarity of the information to be collected may be enhanced;

How the burden of complying with the proposed collection of information may be minimized, including through the application of automated collection techniques or other forms of information technology; and

Estimates of capital or start-up costs and costs of operation, maintenance, and purchase of service to provide information.

The collection of information in this proposed regulation is in § 48.6426-3(e), describing the certificate the biodiesel producer must give to the claimant of a biodiesel mixture credit or biodiesel credit; § 48.6426-3(f), describing the statement a biodiesel reseller must give to the claimant of a biodiesel mixture credit or biodiesel credit; § 48.6426-4(e), describing the certificate the renewable diesel producer must give to the claimant of a renewable diesel mixture credit or renewable diesel credit; § 48.6426-4(f), describing the statement a renewable diesel reseller must give to the claimant of a renewable diesel mixture credit or renewable diesel credit; and § 48.6426-6(c), describing the statement given to a seller of liquefied natural gas. This information is required to obtain a tax benefit. This information will be used by the IRS to substantiate claims for the tax benefits. The likely recordkeepers are business or other for-profit institutions and small businesses or organizations.

Estimated total annual reporting burden: 17,710 hours.

Estimated average annual burden hours per respondent varies from 2.5 hours to 25 hours, depending on individual circumstances, with an estimated average of 22 hours.

Estimated number of respondents: 756.

Estimated annual frequency of responses: On occasion.

An agency may not conduct or sponsor, and a person is not required to respond to, a collection of information unless it displays a valid control number assigned by the Office of Management and Budget.

Books or records relating to a collection of information must be retained as long as their contents may become material in the administration of any internal revenue law. Generally, tax returns and tax return information are confidential, as required by 26 U.S.C. 6103.

Background

The Internal Revenue Code (Code) provides incentives for certain renewable and alternative fuels. Before January 1, 2005, a reduced rate of tax applied to most alcohol-blended fuels. The American Jobs Creation Act of 2004 (Public Law 108-357) replaced the reduced rate of tax for alcohol-blended fuels with credits or payments for alcohol and alcohol mixtures that are sold for use or used as a fuel. The Act also added credits and payments for biodiesel and biodiesel mixtures sold for use or used as a fuel. Credit and payment provisions for renewable diesel, renewable diesel mixtures, alternative fuel, alternative fuel mixtures, and diesel-water fuel emulsions were added to the Code by the Energy Policy Act of 2005 (Public Law 109-58) and the Safe, Accountable, Flexible, Efficient Transportation Equity Act: A Legacy for Users (Public Law 109-59) (SAFETEA). Technical corrections to SAFETEA were made by the Tax Technical Corrections Act of 2007 (Public Law 110-172).

The incentives include a credit under section 6426 for alcohol fuel mixtures, biodiesel mixtures, renewable diesel mixtures (incorporated into section 6426 by section 40A(f)), and alternative fuel mixtures sold for use or used as a fuel and alternative fuel sold for use or used as a fuel in a motor vehicle or motorboat. The credit under section 6426 is allowed against the claimant's fuel tax liability. The incentives for these fuels also include a payment under section 6427(e) and a refundable income tax credit under section 34. The amount allowed as a payment or credit under these provisions is reduced by the claimant's excise tax liability against which a credit is allowed under section 6426. Section 40 provides a nonrefundable income tax credit for alcohol fuel mixtures, alcohol that is sold for use or used as a fuel, and for the production of alcohol by certain small ethanol producers; section 40A provides similar rules relating to biodiesel and renewable diesel. The Code includes coordination rules that limit the maximum incentive that may be claimed for any particular gallon of alcohol, biodiesel, renewable diesel, and alternative fuel. Generally, for alcohol that is ethanol, the benefit is $0.51 per gallon; for biodiesel, the incentive is $0.50 per gallon ($1.00 per gallon in the case of agri-biodiesel); for renewable diesel, the incentive is $1.00 per gallon; and, for alternative fuel, the incentive is $0.50 per gallon. In the case of small ethanol producers and small agri-biodiesel producers, however, the Code allows an additional income tax credit of $0.10 per gallon.

Notice 2005-4 (2005-1 CB 289) describes the alcohol and biodiesel credits and payments and provides general guidance for these incentives. Comments received after the publication of Notice 2005-4 requested additional guidance with regard to the biodiesel producer certificates in the case of resale, commingled biodiesel, the definition of agri-biodiesel, and the definition of a biodiesel mixture. Guidance on these issues was provided in Notice 2005-62 (2005-2 CB 443). Notice 2005-80 (2005-2 CB 953) describes the registration requirements related to diesel-water fuel emulsions. Notice 2006-92, (2006-43 IRB. 774) describes the alternative fuel credits and payments. Notice 2007-37 (2007-17 IRB 1002) provides guidance on renewable diesel. Notice 2007-97 (2007-49 IRB 1092) provides guidance on liquid hydrocarbons for purposes of the definition of alternative fuel. Comments were received in response to these notices and have been considered in the development of this notice of proposed rulemaking.

Renewable and alternative fuels; currently applicable rules.

The IRS has received numerous inquiries about the proper steps that must be taken to comply with the tax laws and to take full advantage of the tax incentives for certain renewable and alternative fuels. The following are general rules that are currently applicable and would not be changed by these proposed regulations.

Registration.

Registration by the IRS is required for each person that produces alcohol, biodiesel, renewable diesel, or blended taxable fuel or claims credits or payments with respect to alternative fuel.

Application for registration is made on Form 637, "Application for Registration (For Certain Excise Tax Activities)." A person generally may not engage in an activity for which registration is required until the IRS has approved the person's registration with respect to the activity.

Imposition of tax.

Tax is imposed on the removal of a biodiesel mixture that is diesel fuel from the terminal at the terminal rack. In the case of blended taxable fuel, tax is imposed on a blender's sale or removal of the fuel and the blender is liable for the tax. Blended taxable fuel includes diesel fuel or gasoline produced outside of the bulk transfer/terminal system by mixing an untaxed liquid, such as biodiesel or alcohol, with a taxable fuel, such as diesel fuel or gasoline, that has been previously taxed (even if only at the Leaking Underground Storage Tank Trust Fund financing rate). Thus, for example, if a person produces, outside the bulk transfer/terminal system, a biodiesel mixture that is diesel fuel, that person is liable for tax on its removal or sale of the mixture. Further, tax generally is imposed on the delivery of fuel that has not been taxed into the fuel supply tank of a motor vehicle or diesel-powered train and on the delivery of alternative fuel (liquid fuel other than gas oil, fuel oil, or taxable fuel) into the fuel supply tank of a motorboat unless the delivery of the fuel or alternative fuel is for a nontaxable purpose.

Liability for these excise taxes is reported on Form 720, "Quarterly Federal Excise Tax Return." Persons that are liable for excise taxes may also be required to make semi-monthly deposits. See Form 720 for more information on deposits.

Tax incentives for mixtures.

The excise tax credits for mixtures containing alcohol, biodiesel, renewable diesel, or alternative fuel must be claimed on Form 720, Schedule C. These credits are allowed to the extent of certain fuel tax liability. The credits are claimed by the person producing the mixture.

The mixture producer may also claim payments (or refundable income tax credits) for incentives that exceed tax liability; that is, for the amount by which the maximum incentive allowable for the mixture exceeds the credit allowed on the Form 720. Notice 2005-62 contains guidance on the computation of payment limitations. Claims for payment are made either on Form 8849, "Claim for Refund of Excise Taxes," or Schedule C, Form 720, "Quarterly Federal Excise Tax Return." (Thus, claims on Form 720 may be for both an excise tax credit and a payment.) Claims for the refundable income tax credit are made on Form 4136, "Credit for Federal Tax Paid on Fuel," which is attached to the claimant's income tax return.

Tax incentives for neat fuels.

A nonrefundable general business tax credit may be claimed for alcohol, biodiesel, and renewable diesel fuels that are not in a mixture and are used as a fuel. This is the only credit or payment allowed with respect to the use of these neat fuels as a fuel. Claims for the credit are made by the person using the renewable fuel in a trade or business or by the person that sold the fuel at retail and delivered it into a vehicle. The small ethanol producer credit and the small agri-biodiesel producer credit are also nonrefundable general business credits. Claims for nonrefundable general business credits are made on Form 6478, "Credit for Alcohol Used as Fuel," and Form 8864, "Biodiesel and Renewable Diesel Fuels Credit," attached to the claimant's income tax return.

An excise tax credit may be claimed for alternative fuel that is not in a mixture and is used as a fuel. The excise tax credit is claimed on Form 720, Schedule C. The credit is allowed to the extent of certain fuel excise tax liability. The credit is claimed by the alternative fueler (unmixed fuel). If the incentive for unmixed alternative fuel exceeds the applicable excise tax liability the excess may be claimed as a payment on Form 8849 or as a refundable income tax credit on Form 4136.

Explanation of Provisions

The proposed regulations add provisions relating to registration requirements and excise tax credits or payments for alcohol, biodiesel, renewable diesel and alternative fuel mixtures and for alternative fuel and dieselwater fuel emulsions. The regulations provide definitions and prescribe rules for claiming a credit or payment. Specifically, the regulations prescribe the conditions to allowance of a credit or payment, the content of claims for credit or payment, and the form of applicable certificates. The proposed regulations also remove obsolete regulations relating to gasohol and other alcohol fuels.

The proposed regulations generally adopt the rules of Notices 2005-4, 2005-62, 2005-80, 2006-92, 2007-37, and 2007-97. Differences between the notices and the proposed regulations are described in this preamble.

Biodiesel mixtures and liability for tax.

Notice 2005-62 provides that *biodiesel mixture* means a mixture of biodiesel and diesel fuel that contains at least 0.1 percent (by volume) of diesel fuel. That rule is unchanged by these proposed regulations.

Under existing regulations, diesel fuel does not include "excluded liquid"; biodiesel mixtures with a high concentration of biodiesel typically are classified as an excluded liquid. The definition of "excluded liquid" predates the biodiesel incentives and was intended to ensure that the diesel fuel tax was not imposed on certain liquids typically not used as fuel. The proposed regulations revise the definition of "excluded liquid" so that all biodiesel mixtures, which are generally used as a substitute for diesel fuel, will be classified as diesel fuel for tax purposes. As a result, under the proposed regulations, tax is imposed on a biodiesel mixture when it is removed from the bulk transfer/terminal system. If a biodiesel mixture is produced outside the bulk transfer/terminal system, tax is imposed on the sale or removal of the mixture by the mixture producer. The mixture producer is liable for the tax and must be registered as a blender of taxable fuel. The tax incentive for the biodiesel mixture generally must be taken as a credit against the producer's fuel tax liability and any excess over the fuel tax liability is allowable as either a payment or an income tax credit.

Also, the de minimis exception to the definition of "blended taxable fuel" is removed. Under this exception, a mixture is not blended fuel if the person creating the mixture adds less than 400 gallons of untaxed liquid to previously taxed fuel during the quarter and the operator of the vehicle using the mixture is liable for the tax on the untaxed liquid. Thus, in cases in which the untaxed liquid is alcohol, biodiesel, or alternative fuel, the exception prevents the credit for which the mixture producer is eligible from being used to offset the tax. With the removal of this exception, the same person (the producer of the mixture) will be liable for the tax and eligible for the credit that can be used to offset the tax.

Biodiesel and EPA registration requirements.

The Code defines *biodiesel* as monoalkyl esters of long chain fatty acids derived from plant or animal matter that meet (1) the registration requirements of the Environmental Protection Agency (EPA) for fuel and fuel additives and, (2) ASTM D6751. Under the proposed regulations, a product meets the EPA registration requirements if the EPA does not require the product to be registered. Thus, for example, if a biodiesel mixture is to be sold only at a marina for use in boats, the biodiesel in the mixture meets the EPA registration requirement because EPA registration requirements do not apply to fuels or fuel additives sold for use in boats.

Biodiesel certificates.

The Code provides that a claim relating to a biodiesel mixture is not allowed unless, among other conditions, the claimant obtains the prescribed certificate from the biodiesel producer. Under existing rules, as well as the proposed regulations, this certificate must be attached to the claim that is filed with the IRS. However, the proposed regulations do not require a separate certificate to accompany the claim filed by a mixture producer that is also the producer of the biodiesel in the mixture. Further, the proposed regulations require, as a condition to allowance of an excise tax credit or a payment, that the claimant obtain the certificate from a registered biodiesel producer. If the claim is for a nonrefundable general business credit, the certificate may be from the registered producer or importer.

Erroneous biodiesel certificates.

Under the Code, a claim relating to a biodiesel mixture is not allowed if the mixture does not actually contain biodiesel. Guidance was requested on whether a claim would be allowed if the claimant attached a certificate for biodiesel and the information on the certificate proved to be incorrect. The proposed regulations make clear that such a claim is not allowed even if the claim is based on a biodiesel certificate that the claimant accepted in good faith. In such a case, however, the proposed regulations generally provide that reliance on the certificate will be treated as reasonable cause for purposes of the penalties imposed by sections 6651 (relating to failure to pay) and 6675 (relating to excessive claims).

Alternative fuel.

The Code allows a credit or payment for alternative fuel that is not in a mixture if the alternative fuel is sold for use or used as a fuel in a motor vehicle or motorboat. If the claim is based on a sale, the claimant must deliver the fuel into the fuel supply tank of the motor vehicle or motorboat or, in the case of a bulk sale, obtain the statement described in § 48.4041-5(a)(2), § 48.4041-21(b), or proposed § 48.6426-6(c).

Registration of alternative fuelers.

A person must be registered by the IRS before claiming the alternative fuel or alternative fuel mixture credit or payment. Section 34 allows a refundable income tax credit with respect to alternative fuel or an alternative fuel mixture. This credit is claimed on Form 4136 filed with the claimant's Federal income tax return. Because partnerships do not file federal income tax returns, the refundable income tax credit allowable with respect to a partnership's sale or use of alternative fuel is made by its partners. The partners may file Form 4136 with their income tax returns to claim a credit based on the information provided them on the partnership's Schedule K-1.

The proposed regulations provide that a partner in a partnership is treated as a registered alternative fueler for purposes of claims on Form 4136 if the partnership is registered for purposes of claims for an excise tax credit or payment. A partner that is treated as registered under this rule is to provide the partnership's registration number on Form 4136. These rules also apply for purposes of ultimate vendor claims by partners in partnerships that are ultimate vendors of diesel fuel or kerosene.

Small ethanol producer credit.

Section 40(a)(3) provides an income tax credit for ethanol produced by eligible small ethanol producers. The amount of ethanol that is eligible for the credit during any taxable year cannot exceed 15,000,000 gallons for any producer. A small ethanol producer generally means a person whose productive capacity for all alcohol, including alcohol for which a credit is not allowable under section 40, does not exceed 60,000,000 gallons at any time during the taxable year. Section 40(g)(5) authorizes the Secretary to prescribe regulations to prevent the credit from benefiting a person that directly or indirectly has a productive capacity for alcohol in excess of 60,000,000 gallons and to prevent any person from directly or indirectly benefiting with respect to more than 15,000,000 gallons during the taxable year. Section 40A provides similar rules with respect to the small agri-biodiesel producer credit.

The proposed regulations provide that *producer* means the person that has title to the ethanol immediately after the ethanol is created. Also, the producer must use a feedstock other than ethanol to produce the ethanol. The proposed regulations do not allow the credit for ethanol produced at the facilities of a contract manufacturer if the contract manufacturer has a direct or indirect productive capacity of more than 60,000,000 gallons of alcohol during the taxable year. Similarly, if the manufacturer does not have a productive capacity of more than 60,000,000 gallons but more than 15,000,000 gallons of ethanol is produced at the manufacturer's facilities during the taxable year, the proposed regulations allow the credit with respect to only the first 15,000,000 gallons of ethanol produced at the facilities during the taxable year. These rules apply to small agribiodiesel producers also.

Gasoline and gasoline blends.

The Code defines gasoline as including gasoline blends. The proposed regulations generally define a gasoline blend as any liquid that contains at least 0.1 percent (by volume) of finished gasoline and that is suitable for use as a fuel in a motor vehicle or motorboat. Thus, for example, E-85 (a mixture of 85 percent ethanol made from corn or other agricultural products and 15 percent gasoline) is treated as a gasoline blend. Tax is imposed on the gasoline blend when it is removed from the bulk transfer/terminal system or, if it is blended taxable fuel, when it is sold or removed by the blender. The proposed regulations also classify leaded gasoline as gasoline. Thus, for example, gasoline products that are sold as "racing gasoline" generally are treated as gasoline even though their lead content make them unsuitable for highway use.

Excise tax returns.

The privilege to file consolidated returns under section 1501 applies only to income tax returns and not to excise tax returns. The proposed regulations note this rule and also reflect the rules of § 301.7701-2(c)(2)(v), which was added by TD 9356 (72 FR 45891, August 16, 2007), relating to the excise tax treatment of certain business entities that are treated as separate from their owner for income tax purposes.

Proposed effective/applicability date.

The amendments to the regulations generally are proposed to be effective on the date they are published as final regulations in the **Federal Register**.

Future regulations projects.

Future proposed regulations will address other fuel-related provisions in the American Jobs Creation Act, the Energy Policy Act, and SAFETEA. These include provisions related to kerosene used in aviation, the Leaking Underground Storage Tank Trust Fund tax, the tax on alternative fuel, and two-party exchanges.

Availability of IRS documents

IRS notices cited in this preamble are published in the Internal Revenue Bulletin or Cumulative Bulletin and are available at IRS.gov.

Special Analyses

It has been determined that this notice of proposed rulemaking is not a significant regulatory action as defined in Executive Order 12866. Therefore, a regulatory assessment is not required. It also has been determined that section 553(b) of the Administrative Procedure Act (5 U.S.C. chapter 5) does not apply to these proposed regulations. It is hereby certified that this regulation will not have a significant economic impact on a substantial number of small entities. This certification is based on IRS estimates that less than 700 small entities will be required to provide certificates each year, such certificates will be provided only on occasion, and the average annual burden per respondent will be 22 hours. The economic impact of the collection of information is limited to completing a certificate in the form prescribed by the regulations. The certificate can be completed by filling in a small number of fields with information that is readily available to the taxpayer, and completion of a certificate should generally take less than 15 minutes. Accordingly, the time and resources required to prepare and provide these certificates is minimal and will not have a significant effect on those entities providing them. Therefore, an analysis under the Regulatory Flexibility Act (5 U.S.C. chapter 6) is not required. Pursuant to section 7805(f) of the Internal Revenue Code, this notice of proposed rulemaking has been submitted to the Chief Counsel for Advocacy of the Small Business Administration for comment on its impact on small business.

Comments and Requests for a Public Hearing

Before these proposed regulations are adopted as final regulations, consideration will be given to any written (a signed original and eight (8) copies) or electronic comments that are submitted timely to the IRS. The IRS and the Treasury Department request comments on the clarity of the proposed regulations and how they may be made easier to understand. All comments will be available for public inspection and copying. A public hearing will be scheduled if requested in writing by any person that timely submits written comments. If a public hearing is scheduled, notice of the date, time, and place for the hearing will be published in the **Federal Register**.

Drafting Information

The principal authors of these regulations are Taylor Cortright and Frank Boland, Office of Associate Chief Counsel (Passthroughs and Special Industries). However, other personnel from the IRS and the Treasury Department participated in their development.

[¶ 49,390] Proposed Amendments of Regulations (REG-120844-07), published in the Federal Register on August 4, 2008.

[Code Sec. 460]

Long-term contracts: Construction contracts: Home construction contracts.—Amendments of Reg. §§ 1.460-3, 1.460-4, 1.460-5 and 1.460-6, providing guidance to taxpayers in the home construction industry regarding accounting for certain long-term construction contracts that qualify as home construction contracts, are proposed.

AGENCY: Internal Revenue Service (IRS), Treasury.

ACTION: Notice of proposed rulemaking and Notice of Public Hearing.

SUMMARY: This document contains proposed regulations amending the regulations under § 1.460 to provide guidance to taxpayers in the home construction industry regarding accounting for certain long-term construction contracts that qualify as home construction contracts under section 460(e)(6) of the Internal Revenue Code (Code) and to provide guidance to taxpayers with long-term contracts under section 460(f) regarding certain changes in method of accounting for long-term contracts. This document also provides a notice of a public hearing on these proposed regulations.

DATES: Written comments must be received by November 3, 2008. Outlines of topics to be discussed at the public hearing scheduled for December 5, 2008, at 10:00 a.m. must be received by November 13, 2008.

ADDRESSES: Send submissions to CC:PA:LPD:PR (REG-120844-07), room 5203, Internal Revenue Service, POB 7604 Ben Franklin Station, Washington, DC 20224. Submissions may be hand delivered Monday through Friday between the hours of 8 a.m. and 4 p.m. to CC:PA:LPD:PR (REG-120844-07), Courier's Desk, Internal Revenue Service, 1111 Constitution Avenue, NW., Washington, DC. Alternatively, taxpayers may submit comments electronically via the Federal eRulemaking Portal at www.regulations.gov (IRS REG-120844-07). The public hearing will be held in the auditorium, Internal Revenue Service Building, 1111 Constitution Avenue, NW., Washington, DC.

FOR FURTHER INFORMATION CONTACT: Concerning the proposed regulations, Brendan P. O'Hara, (202) 622-4920; concerning submission of comments, the hearing, or to be placed on the building access list to attend the hearing, Richard Hurst, (202) 622-7180 (not toll-free numbers).

SUPPLEMENTARY INFORMATION:

Background and Explanation of Provisions

This document contains a proposed amendment to the Income Tax Regulations, 26 CFR Part 1, under section 460 and §§ 1.460-3, 1.460-4, 1.460-5 and 1.460-6 of the Income Tax Regulations. In general, section 460(a) requires taxpayers to use the percentage of completion method (PCM) to account for taxable income from any long-term contract. Section 460(e) exempts home construction contracts from the general requirement to use the percentage of completion method of accounting. Section 460(e)(6) defines a home construction contract to be any construction contract if 80 percent or more of the total estimated contract costs are reasonably expected to be attributable to the construction of (i) dwelling units contained in buildings containing 4 or fewer dwelling units, and (ii) improvements to real property directly related to such dwelling units and located on the site of such dwelling units. Section 460(e)(4) defines a construction contract to be any contract for the building, construction, reconstruction, or rehabilitation of, or the installation of any integral component to, or improvement of, real property.

These proposed regulations expand the types of contracts eligible for the home construction contract exemption and amend the rules for how taxpayer-initiated changes in methods of accounting to comply with the regulations under section 460 may be implemented.

Definition of a Home Construction Contract

Improvements to real property

The definition of a *construction contract* under section 460(e) includes many transactions involving land developers and construction service providers in the home construction industry. For example, a construction contract under section 460(e) includes a contract for the provision of land by the taxpayer if the estimated total allocable contract costs attributable to the taxpayer's construction activities (not including the cost of the land provided to the customer) are 10 percent or more of the contract's total contract price.

As noted, section 460(a) requires that the income from any long-term contract be recognized using the percentage of completion method. However, taxpayers with contracts that meet the definition of a "home construction contract" are not required to use the percentage of completion method for those contracts and may use an exempt method. Exempt methods commonly used to account for home construction contracts include the completed contract method (CCM) and the accrual method.

Under section 460, a home construction contract includes any construction contract if 80 percent of the total estimated contract costs are reasonably expected to be attributable to the construction of improvements to real property directly related to qualifying dwelling units and located on the site of such dwelling units. Commentators have suggested that many contracts entered into by land developers in the home construction industry should fall within the definition of a home construction contract.

The proposed regulations expand the scope of the home construction contract exemption by providing that a contract for the construction of common improvements is considered a contract for the construction of improvements to real property directly related to the dwelling unit(s) and located on the site of such dwelling unit(s), even if the contract is not for the construction of any dwelling unit. Therefore, under the proposed regulations, a land developer that is selling individual lots (and its contractors and subcontractors) may have long-term construction contracts that qualify for the home construction contract exemption.

Townhouses, rowhouses, and condominiums

Under section 460, a home construction contract also includes any construction contract if 80 percent of the total contract costs are reasonably expected to be attributable to the construction of dwelling units contained in buildings containing four or fewer dwelling units. Section 460(e)(6) states that each townhouse or rowhouse shall be treated as a separate building, regardless of the number of townhouses or rowhouses physically attached to each other. In certain circumstances, the terms condominium and townhouse are used interchangeably to describe similar structures. Individual condominium units possess many of the characteristics generally associated with townhouses and rowhouses such as private ownership, shared portions of their structures, residential housing, and the economics of the underlying purchase transactions.

The proposed regulations expand what is considered a townhouse or rowhouse, for purposes of the home construction contract exemption, to include an individual condominium unit. This will have the effect of allowing each condominium unit to be treated as a separate building for purposes of determining whether the underlying contract qualifies as a home construction contract.

Completed contract method

Under the current regulations under section 460, the appropriate severing of a home construction contract requires a facts and circumstances analysis based upon certain factors that are neither specific nor always relevant to home construction contracts. Likewise, the date a home construction contract is considered completed and accepted is determined using a facts and circumstances analysis.

The IRS and Treasury Department are aware of controversies related to the application of the existing facts and circumstances analyses for determining the appropriate severance and final completion and acceptance of home construction contracts accounted for using the completed contract method. Expanding the definition of a home construction contract as provided in these proposed regulations may heighten the significance of these issues. As a result, the IRS and Treasury Department expect to propose specific severing and completion rules for home construction contracts accounted for using the completed contract method. Taxpayers are encouraged to submit comments on the types of severing and completion rules that would result in the clear reflection of income for home construction contracts accounted for using the completed contract method. Specifically, the IRS and the Treasury Department request comments on the circumstances (if any) in which it would not be appropriate to require severing and completion of a home construction contract to be determined on a dwelling unit by dwelling unit or lot by lot basis or, when a contract is not for the sale of a dwelling unit or lot, on the basis of when the taxpayer receives payment(s) under the contract.

Method of accounting

Currently, the regulations under section 460 provide that a taxpayer that uses the percentage-of-completion method (PCM), the exempt-contract percentage-of-completion method (EPCM), or elects the 10-percent method or special alternative minimum taxable income (AMTI) method, or that adopts or elects a cost allocation method of accounting (or changes to another method of accounting with the Commissioner's consent) must apply the method(s) consistently for all similarly classified contracts until the taxpayer obtains the Commissioner's consent under section 446 to change to another method of accounting. The regulations further provide that a taxpayer-initiated change in method of accounting will be permitted only on a cut-off basis (that is, for contracts entered into on or after the year of change), and thus, a section 481(a) adjustment will not be permitted nor required. The proposed regulations continue this cut-off method of implementation but only for taxpayer-initiated changes from a permissible PCM method to another permissible PCM method for long-term contracts for which PCM is required and for taxpayer-initiated changes from a cost allocation method of accounting that complies with the cost allocation rules of §1.460-5 to another cost allocation method of accounting that complies with the cost allocation rules of §1.460-5. Under the proposed regulations all other taxpayer-initiated changes in method of accounting under section 460 will be made with a section 481(a) adjustment.

The proposed regulations provide that in determining the hypothetical underpayment or overpayment of tax for any year as part of the look-back computation, amounts reported as section 481(a) adjustments shall generally be taken into account in the tax year or years they are reported. For purposes of determining whether there is a hypothetical underpayment or overpayment of tax under the look-back computation, a taxpayer would use amounts reported under its old method for the years the old method was used and would use amounts reported under its new method for the years the new method was used, netted against the amount of any section 481(a) adjustments required to be taken into account. Thus, a look-back computation would not be required upon contract completion simply because the taxpayer has changed its method of accounting. However, a look-back computation would be required upon contract completion if actual costs or the contract price differ from the estimated amounts notwithstanding the fact a change in method of accounting occurred. For example, if a taxpayer using PCM changed its method of accounting for construction costs incurred in a contract reported under PCM, the section 460 look-back would be computed using the costs recognized prior to the year of change (reported under the taxpayer's old method of accounting) and the costs recognized in subsequent years using the new method of accounting, netted against any applicable section 481(a) adjustment. Similarly, for changes in methods of accounting where no costs were recognized under the old method of accounting (for example, a change in method of accounting from CCM to PCM), look-back would effectively only apply to years in which the taxpayer's new method of accounting was used to the extent that no costs were recognized prior to the year of change under the old method of accounting. This approach to the look-back computation is consistent with the underlying purpose of look-back as well as the general accounting method change procedures. Comments are specifically requested with respect to issues that taxpayers may foresee with respect to the rules provided in these proposed regulations for taking into account section 481(a) adjustments in the year reported for purposes of the look-back computation.

Proposed Effective/Applicability Date

These regulations are proposed to apply to taxable years beginning on or after the date the final regulations are published in the **Federal Register**. The final regulations will provide rules applicable to taxpayers that seek to change a method of accounting to comply with the rules contained in the final regulations. Taxpayers may not change or otherwise use a method of accounting in reliance upon the rules contained in these new proposed regulations until the rules are published as final regulations in the **Federal Register**.

Special Analyses

It has been determined that this proposed regulation is not a significant regulatory action as defined in Executive Order 12866. Therefore, a regulatory assessment is not required. It has also been determined that section 553(b) of the Administrative Procedure Act (5 U.S.C. chapter 5) does not apply, and because the regulations do not impose a collection of information on small entities, the Regulatory Flexibility Act (5 U.S.C. chapter 6) does not apply. Pursuant to section 7805(f) of the Code, this notice of proposed rulemaking will be submitted to the Chief Counsel for Advocacy of the Small Business Administration for comment on its impact on small businesses.

Comments and Public Hearing

Before these proposed regulations are adopted as final regulations, consideration will be given to any written comments (a signed original with eight (8) copies) or electronic comments that are submitted timely to the IRS. The IRS and Treasury Department request comments on the clarity of the proposed regulations and how they may be made easier to understand. All comments will be available for public inspection and copying.

A public hearing has been scheduled for December 5, 2008, beginning at 10:00 a.m., in the auditorium of the Internal Revenue Building, 1111 Constitution Avenue, NW., Washington, DC. Due to building security procedures, visitors must enter at the Constitution Avenue entrance. In addition, all visitors must present photo identification to enter the building. Because of access restrictions, visitors will not be admitted beyond the immediate entrance area more than 30 minutes before the hearing starts. For information about having your name placed on the building access list to attend the hearing, see the "FOR FURTHER INFORMATION CONTACT" section of this preamble.

The rules of 26 CFR 601.601(a)(3) apply to the hearing. Persons who wish to present oral comments at the hearing must submit electronic or written comments and an outline of the topics to be discussed and the time to be devoted to each topic (signed original and eight (8) copies) by November 13, 2008. A period of 10 minutes will be allotted to each person for making comments. An agenda showing the scheduling of the speakers will be prepared after the deadline for receiving outlines has passed. Copies of the agenda will be available free of charge at the hearing.

Drafting Information

The principal author of these regulations is Brendan P. O'Hara, Office of Associate Chief Counsel (Income Tax and Accounting). However, other personnel from the IRS and Treasury Department participated in their development.

[¶ 49,393]   **Proposed Amendments of Regulations (REG-149404-07)**, published in the Federal Register on August 11, 2008.

[Code Sec. 45D]

Credits: Business related credits: New markets tax credit.—Amendments of Reg. §1.45D-1, relating to the new markets tax credit under section 45D of the Internal Revenue Code, are proposed.

AGENCY: Internal Revenue Service (IRS), Treasury.

ACTION: Notice of proposed rulemaking and notice of public hearing.

SUMMARY: This document contains proposed regulations relating to the new markets tax credit under section 45D of the Internal Revenue Code (Code). The proposed regulations revise and clarify certain rules relating to recapture of the new markets tax credit and will affect certain taxpayers claiming the new markets tax credit. This document also provides a notice of a public hearing on these proposed regulations.

DATES: Written or electronic comments must be received by November 10, 2008. Outlines of topics to be discussed at the public hearing scheduled for December 12, 2008, at 10:00 a.m. must be received by November 3, 2008.

ADDRESSES: Send submissions to: CC:PA:LPD:PR (REG-149404-07), room 5203, Internal Revenue Service, PO Box 7604, Ben Franklin Station, Washington, DC 20044. Submissions may be hand delivered Monday through Friday between the hours of 8 a.m. and 4 p.m. to: CC:PA:LPD:PR (REG-149404-07), Courier's Desk, Internal Revenue Service, 1111 Constitution Avenue, NW, Washington, DC, or sent electronically, via the Federal eRulemaking Portal at http://www.regulations.gov (IRS REG-149404-07). The public hearing will be held in the IRS Auditorium, Internal Revenue Building, 1111 Constitution Avenue, NW, Washington, DC.

FOR FURTHER INFORMATION CONTACT: Concerning the proposed regulations, Julie Hanlon-Bolton, (202) 622-7028; concerning submission of comments, the hearing, and/or to be placed on the building access list to attend the hearing, Regina Johnson, (202) 622-7180 (not toll-free numbers).

SUPPLEMENTARY INFORMATION:

Background

This document amends 26 CFR part 1 to provide and clarify rules relating to the new markets tax credit under section 45D of the Code. Section 45D was added to the Code by section 121 of the Community Renewal Tax Relief Act of 2000, Public Law 106-554 (114 Stat. 2763 (2000)) and amended by section 221 of the American Jobs Creation Act of 2004, Public Law 108-357 (118 Stat. 1418 (2004)), section 101 of the Gulf Opportunity Zone Act of 2005, Public Law 109-135 (119 Stat. 25 (2005)), and Division A, section 102 of the Tax Relief and Health Care Act of 2006, Public Law 109-432 (120 Stat. 2922 (2006)). On December 28, 2004, the IRS and the Treasury Department published final regulations under section 45D (69 FR 77625), with corrections on January 28, 2005 (70 FR 4012).

Groups and organizations representing investors, qualified community development entities, businesses, and other entities involved with the new markets tax credit program have since submitted comments requesting further guidance on the recapture of the credit. The commentators suggested that revising the final regulations to reduce recapture uncertainty would encourage investors to bring increased amounts of capital to low-income communities.

General Overview

Section 45D(a)(1) provides a new markets tax credit on a taxpayer's qualified equity investment (QEI) in a qualified community development entity (CDE). To qualify for the credit, among other requirements, substantially all of the taxpayer's cash must be used by the CDE to make qualified low-income community investments (QLICIs) pursuant to section 45D(b)(1)(B).

A CDE is any domestic corporation or partnership if, among other requirements, the primary mission of the entity is serving, or providing investment capital for, lowincome communities or low-income persons pursuant to section 45D(c)(1). Section 45D(d)(1) provides that a QLICI is: (A) any capital or equity investment in, or loan to, any qualified active low-income community business (QALICB); (B) the purchase from another CDE of any loan made by the entity that is a QLICI; (C) financial counseling and other services to businesses located in, and residents of, low-income communities; and (D) any equity investment in, or loan to, any CDE. A QALICB is any corporation or partnership in which at least 50 percent of the total gross income of the entity is derived from the active conduct of a qualified business within any low-income community, provided certain other requirements are met pursuant to section 45D(d)(2).

Section 45D(g)(1) provides that, if there is a recapture event at any time during the 7-year period beginning on the date of the original issue of a QEI in a CDE, then the tax imposed by this chapter for the taxable year in which the event occurs must be increased by the credit recapture amount. Section 45D(g)(3) provides that a recapture event occurs with respect to an equity investment in a CDE if (A) such entity ceases to be a CDE, (B) the proceeds of the investment cease to be used to make QLICIs as required by section 45D(b)(1)(B), or (C) the QEI is redeemed by the CDE.

Explanation of Provisions

Redemption Safe Harbor for Partnership CDEs

Section 1.45D-1(e)(3)(iii) provides that, in the case of an equity investment that is a capital interest in a CDE that is a partnership for Federal tax purposes, a pro rata cash distribution by the CDE to its partners based on each partner's capital interest in the CDE during the taxable year will not be treated as a redemption for purposes of §1.45D-1(e)(2)(iii) if the distribution does not exceed the CDE's operating income for the taxable year. In addition, a non-pro rata *de minimis* cash distribution by a CDE to a partner or partners during the taxable year will not be treated as a redemption provided the distribution does not exceed the lesser of 5 percent of the CDE's operating income for that taxable year or 10 percent of the partner's capital interest in the CDE.

Commentators expressed the concern that a CDE may not be able to calculate its operating income in time to make a distribution during the taxable year. Because most CDEs will make a low estimate of operating income in order to lessen the risk of not satisfying the requirements of the redemption safe harbor, many CDEs may not distribute the entire amount of operating income during the taxable year. In response to this concern, the proposed regulations provide that, in the case of an equity investment that is a capital interest in a CDE that is a partnership for Federal tax purposes, a pro rata cash distribution by the CDE to its partners based on each partner's capital interest in the CDE during the taxable year will not be treated as a redemption for purposes of §1.45D-1(e)(2)(iii) if the distribution does not exceed the sum of the CDE's operating income for the taxable year and the CDE's undistributed operating income (if any) for the prior taxable year.

Additionally, for purposes of the redemption safe harbor for partnership CDEs, §1.45D-1(e)(3)(iii) defines *operating income* as the sum of (A) the CDE's taxable income as determined under section 703 (except that (1) the items described in section 703(a)(1) shall be aggregated with the non-separately stated tax items of the partnership; and (2) any gain resulting from the sale of a capital asset under section 1221(a) or section 1231 property shall not be included in taxable income); (B) deductions under section 165 (but only to the extent the losses were realized from QLICIs under §1.45D-1(d)(1)); (C) deductions under sections 167 and 168 (including the additional first-year depreciation under section 168(k)); (D) start-up expenditures amortized under section 195; and (E) organizational expenses amortized under section 709. The proposed regulations add tax-exempt income under section 103 and any other depreciation and amortization deductions under the Code to the list of Code sections that determine the amount of operating income.

Commentators have indicated that some CDEs are adding their distributive share of the deductions listed in §1.45D-1(e)(3)(iii) from another partnership to the CDE's calculation of operating income. For example, some CDEs are adding their distributive share of the amortization and depreciation deductions under sections 167 and 168 from another partnership to the CDE's calculation of operating income. The proposed regulations clarify that a CDE may rely on §1.704-1(b)(1)(vii) to determine its allocable share of the deductions listed in §1.45D-1(e)(3)(iii) from another partnership to the CDE's calculation of its operating income. Therefore, §1.704-1(b)(1)(vii) applies to treat an allocation to a partner of its share of partnership net or "bottom line" taxable income or loss as an allocation to such partner of the same share of each item of income, gain, loss, and deduction that is taken into account in computing the partner's net or "bottom line" taxable income or loss.

Termination of a Partnership CDE under Section 708(b)(1)(B)

Under section 708(b)(1)(B), a partnership is considered as terminated if within a twelve-month period there is a sale or exchange of 50 percent or more of the total interest in partnership capital and profits. Section 1.708-1(b)(4) provides, in part, that if a partnership is terminated by a sale or exchange of an interest, the following is deemed to occur: the partnership contributes all of its assets and liabilities to a new partnership in exchange for an interest in the new partnership; and, immediately thereafter, the terminated partnership distributes interests in the new partnership to the purchasing partner and the other remaining partners in proportion to their respective interests in the terminated partnership in liquidation of the terminated partnership, either for the continuation of the business by the new partnership or for its dissolution and winding up.

If the terminating partnership is a CDE, because of the deemed distribution of interests in that new partnership to the purchasing partner and the other remaining partners, a recapture event may be triggered under section 45D(g)(3)(C) and §1.45D-1(e)(2)(iii). However, because the sale of a QEI is not a recapture event under section 45D(g)(3) and because the remaining partner or partners are not being cashed out, the IRS and the Treasury Department do not believe that the sale of a QEI that causes the termination of a CDE partnership under section 708(b)(1)(B) should trigger recapture. Accordingly, the proposed regulations provide that a termination under section 708(b)(1)(B) of a CDE partnership is not a recapture event.

Reasonable Expectations

Section 1.45D-1(d)(6)(i) provides that an entity is generally treated as a QALICB for the duration of the CDE's investment in the entity if the CDE reasonably expects, at the time the CDE makes the capital or equity investment in, or loan to, the entity, that the entity will satisfy the requirements to be a QALICB under §1.45D-1(d)(4)(i) throughout the entire period of the investment or loan. The proposed regulations clarify how the reasonable expectations rule of §1.45D-1(d)(6)(i) applies when a CDE makes an investment in or loan to another CDE.

The proposed regulations provide that a CDE may rely on §1.45D-1(d)(6)(i) to treat an entity as a QALICB even if the CDE's investment in or loan to the entity is made through other CDEs under §1.45D-1(d)(1)(iv)(A).

Commentators indicated that some CDEs are unsure whether they may rely on §1.45D-1(d)(6)(i) if their investments involve the portions of business rule under section 45D(d)(2)(C), the rental to others of real property under sections 45D(d)(3)(A), and the exclusions from the definition of a qualified business under §1.45D-1(d)(5)(iii). Section 1.45D-1(d)(6)(i) already applies to all of these rules in determining whether an entity meets the requirements to be a QALICB under §1.45D-1(d)(4)(i). Nevertheless, the proposed regulations clarify that CDEs may rely on these rules when applying §1.45D-1(d)(6)(i).

Proposed Effective Date

The rules contained in these regulations are proposed to apply to taxable years ending on or after the date of publication of the Treasury decision adopting these rules as final regulations in the **Federal Register**.

Request for Comments

The IRS and the Treasury Department invite taxpayers to submit comments on issues relating to this notice of proposed rulemaking. In particular, the IRS and the Treasury Department encourage taxpayers to submit comments on how to define, under §1.45D-1(d)(2)(i), the dollar amounts received by a CDE "in payment of, or for, capital, equity, or principal" that are set aside either for financial counseling and other services, for an equity investment, or as principal received on a loan. Section 1.45D-1(d)(2)(i) provides that such amounts must be reinvested by the CDE in a QLICI no later than twelve months from the date of receipt to be treated as continuously invested in a QLICI. Commentators suggested defining amounts received "in payment of, or for, capital, equity, or principal" by using the same rules and redemption safe harbor in §1.45D-1(e)(3), which defines when an investment is redeemed or otherwise cashed out by a CDE. The proposed regulations do not adopt this suggestion. The IRS and the Treasury Department believe this approach may be inappropriate because redeeming one dollar of an equity investment is a recapture event under section 45D(g)(3)(C), while failing to reinvest one dollar in a QLICI under §1.45D-1(d)(2)(i) lowers the dollar amount treated as meeting the substantially-all requirement by one dollar.

Special Analyses

It has been determined that this notice of proposed rulemaking is not a significant regulatory action as defined in Executive Order 12866. Therefore, a regulatory assessment is not required. It also has been determined that section 553(b) of the Administrative Procedure Act (5 U.S.C. chapter 5) does not apply to these regulations, and because the regulations do not impose a collection of information on small entities, the Regulatory Flexibility Act (5 U.S.C. chapter 6) does not apply. Pursuant to section 7805(f) of the Code, this notice of proposed rulemaking has been submitted to the Chief Counsel for Advocacy of the Small Business Administration for comment on its impact on small business.

Comments and Public Hearing

Before these proposed regulations are adopted as final regulations, consideration will be given to any written comments (a signed original and eight (8) copies) or electronic comments that are submitted timely to the IRS. Comments are requested on all aspects of the proposed regulations. All comments will be available for public inspection and copying.

A public hearing has been scheduled for December 12, 2008, beginning at 10:00 a.m. in the IRS Auditorium, Internal Revenue Building, 1111 Constitution Avenue, NW, Washington, DC. Due to building security procedures, visitors must enter at the Constitution Avenue entrance. In addition, all visitors must present photo identification to enter the building. Because of access restrictions, visitors will not be admitted beyond the immediate entrance area more than 30 minutes before the hearing starts. For information about having your name placed on the building access list to attend the hearing, see the FOR FURTHER INFORMATION CONTACT section of this preamble.

The rules of 26 CFR 601.601(a)(3) apply to the hearing. Persons who wish to present oral comments at the hearing must submit electronic or written comments by November 10, 2008. Outline of the topics to be discussed and the time to be devoted to each topic (a signed original and eight (8) copies) by November 3, 2008. A period of 10 minutes will be allotted to each person for making comments. An agenda showing the scheduling of the speakers will be prepared after the deadline for receiving outlines has passed. Copies of the agenda will be available free of charge at the hearing.

Drafting Information

The principal author of these regulations is Julie Hanlon-Bolton with the Office of the Associate Chief Counsel (Passthroughs and Special Industries). However, other personnel from the IRS and the Treasury Department participated in their development.

[¶ 49,401]   Proposed Amendments of Regulations (REG-107318-08), published in the Federal Register on October 9, 2008.

[Code Secs. 401, 402, 411 and 417]

Retirement plans: Notice: Deferral: Immediately distributable benefit: Election period: Waiver of joint and survivor annuity: Notice timing.—Amendments of Reg. §§1.401(a)-13, 1.401(a)-20, 1.402(f)-1, 1.411(a)-11 and 1.417(e)-1, providing that the notice required under section 411(a)(11) to be provided to a participant of his or her right, if any, to defer receipt of an immediately distributable benefit must also describe the consequences of failing to defer receipt of the distribution, are proposed.

AGENCY: Internal Revenue Service (IRS), Treasury.

ACTION: Notice of Proposed Rulemaking and notice of public hearing.

SUMMARY: This document contains proposed regulations under sections 402(f), 411(a)(11), and 417 of the Internal Revenue Code (Code). The proposed regulations would provide that the notice required under section 411(a)(11) to be provided to a participant of his or her right, if any, to defer receipt of an immediately distributable benefit must also describe the consequences of failing to defer receipt of the distribution. The proposed regulations would also provide that the applicable election period for waiving the qualified joint and survivor annuity form of benefit under section 417 is the 180-day period ending on the annuity starting date, and that a notice required to be provided under section 402(f), section 411(a)(11), or section 417 may be provided to a participant as much as 180 days before the annuity starting date (or, for a notice under section 402(f), the distribution date). These regulations would affect administrators of, employers maintaining, participants in, and beneficiaries of tax-favored retirement plans.

DATES: Written or electronic comments and requests to speak at the public hearing must be received by January 7, 2009.

ADDRESSES: Send submissions to: CC:PA:LPD:PR (REG-107318-08), room 5203, Internal Revenue Service, PO Box 7604, Ben Franklin Station, Washington D.C. 20044. Submissions may be hand-delivered Monday through Friday between the hours of 8 a.m. and 4 p.m. to: CC:PA:LPD:PR (REG-107318-08), Courier's Desk, Internal Revenue Service, 1111 Constitution Avenue, N.W., Washington, D.C., or sent electronically via the Federal eRulemaking Portal at *http://www.regulations.gov* (IRS REG-107318-08).

FOR FURTHER INFORMATION CONTACT: Concerning the regulations, Michael P. Brewer at (202) 622-6090; concerning submission of comments or to request to speak at the public hearing, Funmi Taylor at (202) 622-7180 (not toll-free numbers).

SUPPLEMENTARY INFORMATION:

Paperwork Reduction Act

The collection of information contained in this notice of proposed rulemaking has been submitted to the Office of Management and Budget for review in accordance with the Paperwork Reduction Act of 1995 (44 U.S.C. 3507(d)). Comments on the collection of information should be sent to the **Office of Management and Budget**, Attn: Desk Officer for the Department of the Treasury, Office of Information and Regulatory Affairs, Washington, DC 20503, with copies to the **Internal Revenue Service**, Attn: IRS Reports Clearance Officer, SE:W:CAR:MP:T:T:SP; Washington, DC 20224. Comments on the collection of information should be received by December 8, 2008. Comments are specifically requested concerning:

Whether the proposed collection of information is necessary for the proper performance of the functions of the Internal Revenue Service, including whether the information will have practical utility;

The accuracy of the estimated burden associated with the proposed collection of information;

How the quality, utility, and clarity of the information to be collected may be enhanced;

How the burden of complying with the proposed collections of information may be minimized, including through the application of automated collection techniques or other forms of information technology; and

Estimates of capital or start-up costs and costs of operation, maintenance, and purchase of service to provide information.

The collection of information in these proposed regulations is in § 1.411(a)-11(c)(2) of the Income Tax Regulations. This collection of information is required to comply with the statutory notice requirements of section 411(a), and is expected to be included in the notices currently provided to employees that inform them of their rights and benefits under the plan. The likely recordkeepers are businesses or other forprofit institutions and nonprofit institutions and organizations.

Estimated total annual recordkeeping burden: 100,000 hours.

Estimated average annual burden hours per recordkeeper: 1 hour.

Estimated number of recordkeepers: 100,000.

An agency may not conduct or sponsor, and a person is not required to respond to, a collection of information unless it displays a valid control number assigned by the Office of Management and Budget.

Books or records relating to a collection of information must be retained as long as their contents may become material in the administration of any internal revenue law. Generally, tax returns and tax return information are confidential, as required by 26 U.S.C. 6103.

Background

A. Notice of Consequences of Failing to Defer

Section 411(a)(11)(A) provides that, if the present value of any nonforfeitable accrued benefit exceeds $5,000, a qualified plan must provide that such benefit may not be immediately distributed without the consent of the participant. Similarly, section 203(e) of the Employee Retirement Income Security Act of 1974, as amended (ERISA), provides that if the present value of any nonforfeitable accrued benefit with respect to a participant in a plan exceeds $5,000, the benefit may not be immediately distributed without the consent of the participant.

Section 1102(b)(1) of the Pension Protection Act of 2006 (PPA '06), 109 Public Law 280, 120 Stat. 780, instructs the Secretary of the Treasury to modify the regulations under section 411(a)(11) of the Code "to provide that the description of a participant's right, if any, to defer receipt of a distribution shall also describe the consequences of failing to defer such receipt." Section 1102(b)(2)(A) of PPA '06 provides that the modifications required by section 1102(b)(1) of PPA '06 shall apply to years beginning after December 31, 2006. Section 1102(b)(2)(B) of PPA '06, however, states that a plan shall not be treated as failing to meet the requirements of section 411(a)(11) with respect to any description of the consequences of failing to defer provided "within 90 days after the Secretary of the Treasury issues the modifications required by [section 1102(b)(1) of PPA '06]if the plan administrator makes a reasonable attempt to comply with such requirements."

Section 1.411(a)-11(c)(2)(i) states that, in order for a plan to obtain valid consent under section 411(a)(11), "so long as a benefit is immediately distributable, a participant must be informed of the right, if any, to defer receipt of the distribution." Section 1.411(a)-11(c)(4) states that a distribution is immediately distributable prior to the later of the time a participant has attained normal retirement age or age 62.

Q&A-32 of Notice 2007-7, 2007-5 I.R.B. 395, provides that a plan administrator is required to revise the notice required under section 411 to reflect the modifications made by section 1102(b) of PPA '06 for notices provided in plan years beginning after December 31, 2006. Notice 2007-7 further provides that, pursuant to section 1102(b)(2)(B) of PPA '06, a plan will not be treated as failing to meet the new requirements of section 1102(b) of PPA '06 if the plan administrator makes a reasonable attempt to comply with the new requirements with respect to a notice that is provided prior to the 90th day after the issuance of regulations reflecting the modifications required by such section 1102(b) of PPA '06. See § 601.601 (b) (2) (ii) (*b*).

Q&A-33 of Notice 2007-7 includes a safe harbor that would be considered a reasonable attempt to comply with the requirement in section 1102(b)(1) of PPA '06 that a description of a participant's right to defer receipt of a distribution include a description of the consequences of failing to defer. In particular, Q&A-33 provides that a description that is written in a manner reasonably calculated to be understood by the average participant and that includes the following information is a reasonable attempt to comply with the requirements of section 1102(b)(2)(B) of PPA '06: (a) in the case of a defined benefit plan, a description of how much larger benefits will be if the commencement of distributions is deferred; (b) in the case of a defined contribution plan, a description indicating the investment options available under the plan (including fees) that will be available if distributions are deferred; and (c) the portion of the summary plan description that contains any special rules that might materially affect a participant's decision to defer. For purposes of clause (a), a plan administrator can use a description that includes the financial effect of deferring distributions, as described in § 1.417(a)(3)-1(d)(2)(i), based solely on the normal form of benefit.

Q&A-31 of Notice 2007-7 provides that the provisions of section 1102 apply to plan years that begin after December 31, 2006. Q&A-31 explains that this means that the new rules relating to the content of the notices apply only to notices issued in those plan years, without regard to the annuity starting date for the distributions.

B. Expansion of Applicable Election Period

Section 401(a)(11)(A)(i) provides that, except as provided in section 417, a plan that is qualified under section 401(a) must provide the accrued benefit payable to a vested participant who does not die before the annuity starting date in the form of a qualified joint and survivor annuity.

Section 417(a)(1)(A) provides that, in general, a plan satisfies section 401(a)(11) only if each participant may elect at any time during the "applicable election period" to waive the qualified joint and survivor annuity form of benefit (and to revoke the waiver), and certain other requirements are satisfied. Before PPA '06, section 417(a)(6)(A) provided that the "applicable election period" for a participant to waive the qualified joint and survivor annuity form of distribution was the 90-day period ending on the annuity starting date.

Section 1102(a)(1)(A) of PPA '06 amended section 417(a)(6)(A) by changing the 90-day "applicable election period" for electing a distribution subject to the qualified joint and survivor annuity (QJSA) rules of sections 401(a)(11) and 417 in a form other than a QJSA to a 180-day applicable election period. Section 1102(a)(2)(A) of PPA '06 made a parallel amendment to section 205(c)(7)(A) of ERISA by striking "90-day" and inserting "180-day".

Sections 1102(a)(1)(B) and 1102(a)(2)(B) of PPA '06 provide that the Secretary of the Treasury shall modify the regulations relating to section 417 of the Code and section 205 of ERISA by substituting "180 days" for "90 days" each place it appears.

Section 1102(a)(3) of PPA '06 provides that the amendments to the applicable election period apply to years beginning after December 31, 2006.

C. Expansion of Period for Notices

Section 417(a)(3)(A) of the Code and section 205(c)(3)(A) of ERISA provide that a plan must provide to each participant, "within a reasonable period of time before the annuity starting date" and consistent with such regulations as the Secretary of the Treasury may prescribe, a written explanation that describes the terms and conditions of the qualified joint and survivor annuity and certain other information. Similarly, section 402(f)(1) provides that a plan administrator must, "within a reasonable period of time" before making an eligible rollover distribution, provide to recipients an explanation of certain tax consequences of the distribution.

Section 1102(a)(1)(B) of PPA '06 provides that the Secretary of the Treasury shall modify the regulations under sections 402(f), 411(a)(11), and 417 by substituting "180 days" for "90 days" each place it appears in §§ 1.402(f)-1, 1.411(a)-11(c), and 1.417(e)-1(b). Similarly, section 1102(a)(2)(B) of PPA '06 provides that the Secretary of the Treasury shall modify the regulations relating to sections 203(e) and 205 of ERISA by substituting "180 days" for "90 days" each place it appears.

Section 1102(a)(3) provides that the amendments to the notice periods apply to years beginning after December 31, 2006. Q&A-31 of Notice 2007-7 explains that the 180-day period for distributing notices applies to notices distributed in a plan year that begins after December 31, 2006.

D. Requirements under ERISA

ERISA section 203(e) is the parallel provision to section 411(a)(11) of the Code and ERISA section 205 is the ERISA parallel to section 417 of the Code. Pursuant to section 101 of Reorganization Plan No. 4 of 1978, 29 U.S.C. 1001nt (the Reorganization Plan), the Secretary of the Treasury generally has authority to issue regulations under parts 2 and 3 of subtitle B of title I of ERISA, including sections 203(e) and 205 of ERISA. Thus, the changes required by section 1102 of PPA '06 would apply as well for purposes of ERISA sections 203(e) and 205.

Explanation of Provisions

A. Notice of Consequences of Failing to Defer

These proposed regulations would provide that the notice required by section 411(a)(11) advising a participant of the right, if any, to defer receipt of a distribution must also inform the participant of the consequences of failing to defer such receipt. The proposed regulations would also provide guidance on the relevant information that must be provided to a participant in order to satisfy the requirement that the participant be notified of the consequences of failing to defer.

Specifically, these proposed regulations would require that the participant be provided a description of specified federal tax implications of failing to defer and, in the case of a defined benefit plan, a statement of the amount payable to the participant under the normal form of benefit both upon immediate commencement and when the benefit is no longer immediately distributable (that is, the later of age 62 or attainment of normal retirement age). Section 1.417(a)(3)-1(c)(2)(ii) permits a plan to provide participants with a QJSA explanation, which does not vary based on the participant's marital status, of the relative value of optional forms of benefit compared to the value of a QJSA. These proposed regulations would permit the statement of the amount payable to not be based on the participant's marital status, to the extent the plan is permitted under § 1.417(a)(3)-1(c)(2)(ii) to use a QJSA explanation that does not vary based on whether the participant is married or unmarried.

The proposed regulations would also require the information in the notice to include, in the case of a defined contribution plan, a statement that some currently available investment options in the plan may not be generally available on similar terms outside the plan and contact information for obtaining additional information on the general availability outside the plan of currently available investment options in the plan. In addition, the proposed regulations would require the notice to include, in the case of a defined contribution plan, a statement that fees and expenses (including administrative or investment-related fees) outside the plan may be different from fees and expenses that apply to the participant's account and contact information for obtaining information on such fees.

The proposed regulations also include an additional category of information that must be provided relating to any provisions of the plan (and provisions of any accident or health plan maintained by the employer) that could reasonably be expected to materially affect a participant's decision whether to defer receipt of the distribution. Thus, for example, the proposed regulations would require a description of the eligibility requirements for retiree health benefits if such benefits are limited to participants who have an undistributed benefit under the employer's retirement plan.

In general, the proposed regulations would also provide that the required information regarding the consequences of a participant's failing to defer receipt of a distribution must appear together. However, the proposed regulations would permit a cross-reference to where the required information may be found in notices or other information provided or made available to the participant, as long as the notice of consequences of failing to defer includes a statement of how the referenced information may be obtained without charge and explains why the referenced information is relevant to a decision whether to defer.

B. Expansion of Applicable Election Period and Period for Notices

Consistent with sections 1102(a)(1)(A) and (1)(B) and 1102(a)(2)(A) and (2)(B) of PPA '06, the proposed regulations would both (1) expand the definition of applicable election period to up to 180 days, and (2) expand the time period for notices issued under sections 402(f), 411(a)(11), and 417 to allow the notices to be issued up to 180 days prior to the annuity starting date (or, in the case of a notice under section 402(f), the date of distribution). Specifically, the proposed regulations would substitute "180 days" for "90 days" and "180-day" for "90-day" each place those terms appear in § 1.401(a)-13(g)(4)(ii), § 1.401(a)-20, A-3(b)(1), A-4, A-10(a), A-16, and A-24(a)(1), § 1.402(f)-1, § 1.411(a)-11(c), and § 1.417(e)-1(b).

Pursuant to section 101 of the Reorganization Plan, the Secretary of Treasury has the authority to issue regulations under ERISA sections 203(e) and 205. Thus, these proposed regulations that apply to sections 402(f), 411(a)(11), and 417 of the Code would apply as well for purposes of sections 203(e) and 205 of ERISA.

Proposed Effective/Applicability Date

These regulations are proposed to become effective for notices provided (and election periods beginning) on or after the first day of the first plan year beginning on or after January 1, 2010. However, in no event will the regulations become effective for notices provided (and election periods beginning) earlier than the first day of the first plan year beginning 90 days after publication of final regulations in the **Federal Register**.

With respect to the regulations relating to the notice of consequences of failing to defer the receipt of distributions, until these regulations become effective, a plan will be treated as complying if: (1) the plan complies either with these proposed regulations or with Q&A-32 and Q&A-33 in Notice 2007-7; or (2) if the plan administrator makes a reasonable attempt to comply with the requirement that the description of a participant's right, if any, to defer receipt of a distribution shall also describe the consequences of failing to defer such receipt.

With respect to the proposed regulations relating to the expanded applicable election period and the expanded period for notices, plans may rely on these proposed regulations for notices provided (and election periods beginning) during the period beginning on the first day of the first plan year beginning on or after January 1, 2007 and ending on the effective date of final regulations.

Special Analyses

It has been determined that this notice of proposed rulemaking is not a significant regulatory action as defined in Executive Order 12866. Therefore, a regulatory assessment is not required. It also has been determined that section 553(b) of the Administrative Procedure Act (5 U.S.C. chapter 5) does not apply to these regulations.

It is hereby certified that the collection of information contained in this regulation will not have a significant economic impact on a substantial number of small entities. This certification is based on several factors, including that the regulation merely provides guidance to implement a statutorily-required notice, and that the incremental burden in the regulation would be minimal because it only requires including additional information in notices already provided by all of the affected entities. Accordingly, a Regulatory Flexibility Analysis under the Regulatory Flexibility Act (5 U.S.C. chapter 6) is not required. Pursuant to section 7805(f) of the Code, this notice of proposed rulemaking will be submitted to the Chief Counsel for Advocacy of the Small Business Administration for comment on its impact on small business.

Comments and Public Hearing

Before these proposed regulations are adopted as final regulations, consideration will be given to any written (one signed and eight (8) copies) or electronic comments that are submitted timely to the IRS. All comments will be available for public inspection and copying.

A public hearing has been scheduled for Friday, February 20, 2009, at 10 a.m. in the IRS Auditorium, Internal Revenue Building, 1111 Constitution Avenue, N.W., Washington, DC. Due to building security procedures, visitors must enter at the Constitution Avenue entrance. In addition, all visitors must present photo identification to enter the building. Because of access restrictions, visitors will not be admitted beyond the immediate entrance area more than 30 minutes before the hearing starts. For information about having your name placed on the building access list to attend the hearing, see the FOR FURTHER INFORMATION CONTACT section of this preamble.

Persons who wish to present oral comments at the hearing must submit written or electronic comments by January 7, 2008 and submit an outline of the topics to be discussed and the amount of time to be devoted to each topic (a signed original and eight (8) copies) by January 16, 2009. A period of 10 minutes will be allotted to each person for making comments.

An agenda showing the scheduling of the speakers will be prepared after the deadline for receiving outlines has passed. Copies of the agenda will be available free of charge at the hearing.

Drafting Information

The principal author of these regulations is Michael P. Brewer, Office of Division Counsel/Associate Chief Counsel (Tax Exempt and Government Entities). However, other personnel from the Office of Chief Counsel, IRS, and the Department of Treasury participated in the development of these regulations.

———————————

[¶ 49,406]   **Proposed Regulations, NPRM REG-148326-05**, published in the Federal Register on December 8, 2008 (corrected 2/18/2009).

[Code Sec. 409A]

Retirement plans: Nonqualified deferred compensation: Plan compliance failure: Calculating income to include in year of failure: Calculating additional income tax.—Reg. § 1.409A-4 and amendments of Reg. § 1.409A-0, relating to the calculation of amounts includible in income under Code Sec. 409A and the additional taxes imposed by such section with respect to service providers participating in certain nonqualified deferred compensation plants, are proposed.

AGENCY: Internal Revenue Service (IRS), Treasury.

ACTION: Notice of proposed rulemaking and notice of public hearing.

SUMMARY: This document contains proposed regulations on the calculation of amounts includible in income under section 409A(a) and the additional taxes imposed by such section with respect to service providers participating in certain nonqualified deferred compensation plans. The regulations would affect such service providers and the service recipients for whom the service providers provide services. This document also provides a notice of public hearing on these proposed regulations.

DATES: Written or electronic comments must be received by March 7, 2009.

Outlines of topics to be discussed at the public hearing scheduled for April 2, 2009, must be received by March 9, 2009.

ADDRESSES: Send submissions to: CC:PA:LPD:PR (REG-148326-05), room 5203, Internal Revenue Service, PO Box 7604, Ben Franklin Station, Washington, DC 20044. Submissions may be hand-delivered Monday through Friday between the hours of 8 a.m. and 4 p.m. to CC:PA:LPD:PR

(REG-148326-05), Courier's Desk, Internal Revenue Service, 1111 Constitution Avenue, NW., Washington, DC or sent electronically, via the Federal eRulemaking Portal at *www. Regulations.gov* (IRS REG-148326-05). The public hearing will be held in the auditorium, Internal Revenue Building, 1111 Constitution Avenue, NW., Washington, DC.

FOR FURTHER INFORMATION CONTACT: Concerning the proposed regulations, Stephen Tackney, at (202) 927-9639; concerning submissions of comments, the hearing, and/or to be placed on the building access list to attend the hearing, Funmi Taylor at (202) 622-3628 (not toll-free numbers).

SUPPLEMENTARY INFORMATION:

Background

Section 409A was added to the Internal Revenue Code (Code) by section 885 of the American Jobs Creation Act of 2004, Public Law 108-357 (118 Stat. 1418). Section 409A generally provides that if certain requirements are not met at any time during a taxable year, amounts deferred under a nonqualified deferred compensation plan for that year and all previous taxable years are currently includible in gross income to the extent not subject to a substantial risk of forfeiture and not previously included in gross income. Section 409A also includes rules applicable to certain trusts or similar arrangements associated with nonqualified deferred compensation.

On December 20, 2004, the IRS issued Notice 2005-1 (2005-2 CB 274), setting forth initial guidance on the application of section 409A, and providing transition guidance in accordance with the terms of the statute. On April 10, 2007, the Treasury Department and the IRS issued final regulations under section 409A. (72 FR 19234, April 17, 2007). The final regulations are applicable for taxable years beginning after December 31, 2008. See Notice 2007-86 (2007-46 IRB 990). Notice 2005-1 and the final regulations do not address the calculation of the amount includible in income under section 409A if a plan fails to meet the requirements of section 409A and the calculation of the additional taxes applicable to such income. On November 30, 2006, the Treasury Department and the IRS issued Notice 2006-100 (2006-51 IRB 1109) providing interim guidance for taxable years beginning in 2005 and 2006 on the calculation of the amount includible in income if the requirements of section 409A were not met, and requesting comments on these issues for use in formulating future guidance. On October 23, 2007, the Treasury Department and the IRS issued Notice 2007-89 (2007-46 IRB 998) providing similar interim guidance for taxable years beginning in 2007. See § 601.601(d)(2)(ii)(*b*).

Commentators submitted a number of comments addressing the topics covered by these proposed regulations in response to Notice 2005-1, Notice 2006-100, Notice 2007-89, and the regulations, all of which were considered by the Treasury Department and the IRS in formulating these proposed regulations.

Explanation of Provisions

I. *Scope of Proposed Regulations*

These proposed regulations address the calculation of amounts includible in income under section 409A(a), and related issues including the calculation of the additional taxes applicable to such income. Section 409A(a) generally provides that amounts deferred under a nonqualified deferred compensation plan in all years are includible in income unless certain requirements are met. The requirements under section 409A(a) generally relate to the time and form of payment of amounts deferred under the plan, including the establishment of the time and form of payment through initial deferral elections and restrictions on the ability to change the time and form of payment through subsequent deferral elections or the acceleration of payment schedules. As provided in the regulations previously issued under section 409A, a nonqualified deferred compensation plan must comply with the requirements of section 409A(a) both in form and in operation.

Taxpayers may also be required to include amounts in income under section 409A(b). Section 409A(b) generally applies to a transfer of assets to a trust or similar arrangement, or to a restriction of assets, for purposes of paying nonqualified deferred compensation, if such trust or assets are located outside the United States, if such assets are transferred during a restricted period with respect to a single-employer defined benefit plan sponsored by the service recipient, or if such assets are restricted to the provision of benefits under a nonqualified deferred compensation plan in connection with a change in the service recipient's financial health. These proposed regulations do not address the application of section 409A(b), including the calculation of amounts includible in income if the requirements of section 409A(b) are not met. For guidance on the calculation of such amounts for taxable years beginning on or before January 1, 2007, including the application of the Federal income tax withholding requirements, see Notice 2007-89. The Treasury Department and the IRS anticipate issuing further interim guidance for later taxable years on the calculation of the amount includible in income under section 409A(b) and the application of the Federal income tax withholding requirements to such an amount.

II. *Effect of a Failure to Comply with Section 409A(a) on Amounts Deferred in Subsequent Years*

Commentators asked how section 409A(a) applies if a plan fails to comply with section 409A(a) during a taxable year and the service provider continues to have amounts deferred under the plan in subsequent years during which the plan otherwise complies with section 409A(a) both in form and in operation. The statutory language may be construed to provide that a failure is treated as continuing during taxable years beyond the year in which the initial failure occurred, if the failure continues to affect amounts deferred under the plan. For example, if an amount has been improperly deferred under the plan, the statutory language could be construed to provide that the plan fails to comply with section 409A(a) during all taxable years during which the improperly deferred amounts remain deferred. However, this position could cause harsh results and would add administrative complexity. For example, a service provider could be required to include in income, and pay additional taxes on, amounts deferred over a number of taxable years even if the sole failure to comply with section 409A(a) occurred many years earlier. In addition, even if there were no failure in the current year, to determine a taxpayer's liability for income taxes with respect to nonqualified deferred compensation for a particular year, the taxpayer and the IRS would need to examine the plan's form and operation for every year in which the service provider had an amount deferred under the plan to determine if there was a failure to comply with section 409A(a) during any of those years.

For these reasons, the proposed regulations do not adopt this interpretation and instead generally would apply the adverse tax consequences that result from a failure to comply with section 409A(a) only with respect to amounts deferred under a plan in the year in which such noncompliance occurs and all previous taxable years, to the extent such amounts are not subject to a substantial risk of forfeiture and have not previously been included in income. Therefore, under the proposed regulations, a failure to meet the requirements of section 409A(a) during a service provider's taxable year generally would not affect the taxation of amounts deferred under the plan for a subsequent taxable year during which the plan complies with section 409A(a) in form and in operation with respect to all amounts deferred under the plan. This would apply even though the amount deferred under the plan as of the end of such subsequent taxable year includes amounts deferred in earlier years during which the plan failed to comply with section 409A(a) (including, for example, amounts deferred pursuant to an untimely deferral election in the earlier year), as long as there was no failure under the plan in a later year. Because there would be no continuing or permanent failure with respect to a plan that fails to comply with section 409A(a) during an earlier year, each taxable year would be analyzed independently to determine if there was a failure. As a result, assessment of tax liabilities due to a plan's failure to comply with the requirements of section 409A(a) in a closed year would be time-barred. But, if a service provider fails to properly include amounts in income under section 409A for a taxable year during which there was a failure to comply with section 409A(a), and assessment of taxes with respect to such year becomes barred by the statute of limitations, then the taxpayer's duty of consistency would prevent the service provider from claiming a tax benefit in a later year with respect to such amount (such as, for example, by claiming any type of "basis" or "investment in the contract" in the year the service recipient paid such amount to the service provider pursuant to the plan's terms).

Under the general rule in the proposed regulations, if all of a taxpayer's deferred amounts under a plan are nonvested and the taxpayer makes an impermissible deferral election or accelerates the time of payment with respect to some or all of the nonvested deferred amount, the nonvested deferred amount generally would not be includible in income under section 409A(a) in the year of the impermissible change in time and form of payment (although if there were vested amounts deferred under the plan, such amounts would be includible in income under section 409A(a)). In the subsequent taxable year in which the service provider becomes vested in the deferred amount, the plan might comply with section 409A(a) in form and in operation, so that under the general rule no income inclusion would be required and no additional taxes would be due for that year as a result of the late deferral election or acceleration of payment. In proposing to adopt this interpretation of the statute, the Treasury Department and the IRS do not intend to create an opportunity for taxpayers who ignore the requirements of section 409A(a) with respect to nonvested amounts to avoid the payment of taxes that would otherwise be due as a result of such a failure to comply. To ensure that this rule does not become a means for taxpayers to disregard the requirements of the statute, the proposed regulations would disregard a substantial risk of forfeiture for purposes of determining the amount includible in income under section 409A[1] with respect to certain nonvested deferred amounts, if the facts and circumstances indicate that the service recipient has a pattern or practice of permitting such impermissible changes in the time and form of payment with respect to nonvested deferred amounts (regardless of whether such changes also apply to vested deferred amounts). If such a pattern or practice exists, an amount deferred under a plan that is otherwise subject to a substantial risk of forfeiture is not treated as subject to a substantial risk of forfeiture if an impermissible change in the time and form of payment (including an impermissible initial deferral election) applies to the amount deferred or if the facts and circumstances indicate that the amount deferred would be affected by such pattern or practice.

III. *Calculation of the Amount Deferred under a Plan for the Taxable Year in which the Plan Fails to Meet the Requirements of Section 409A(a) and all Preceding Taxable Years*

A. *In general*

Section 409A(a)(1)(A) generally provides that if at any time during a taxable year a nonqualified deferred compensation plan fails to meet the requirements of section 409A(a)(2) (payments), section 409A(a)(3) (the acceleration of payments), or section 409A(a)(4) (deferral elections), or is not operated in accordance with such requirements, all compensation deferred under the plan for the taxable year and all preceding taxable years is includible in gross income for the taxable year to the extent not subject to a substantial risk of forfeiture and not previously included in gross income. Accordingly, to calculate the amount includible in income upon a failure to meet the requirements of section 409A(a), the first step is to determine the total amount deferred under the plan for the service provider's taxable year and all preceding taxable years. The second step is to calculate the portion of the total amount deferred for the taxable year, if any, that is either subject to a substantial risk of forfeiture (nonvested) or has been included in income in a previous taxable year. The last step is to subtract the amount determined in step two from the amount determined in step one. The excess of the amount determined in step one over the amount determined in step two is the amount includible in income and subject to additional income taxes for the year as a result of the plan's failure to comply with section 409A(a). Sections III.B through III.D of this preamble explain how the proposed regulations would address the first step in the process of determining the amount includible in income under section 409A, calculating the total amount deferred for the taxable year.

B. *Total amount deferred*

1. In General

In general, under the proposed regulations, the amount deferred under a plan[2] for a taxable year and all preceding taxable years would be referred to as the total amount deferred for a taxable year and would be determined as of the last day of the taxable year. Therefore, for calendar year taxpayers, such as most individuals, the relevant calculation date would be December 31. Determining the total amount deferred for the taxable year as of the last day of the taxable year during which a plan fails to comply with section 409A(a) would allow taxpayers to avoid the administrative burden of tracking amounts deferred under a plan on a daily basis, because adjustments would not be made to reflect notional earnings or losses or other fluctuations in the amount payable under the plan as they occur during the taxable year, but would be applied only on a net basis as of the last day of the taxable year. For example, if a service provider has a calendar year taxable year, and if the service provider's account balance under a plan is $105,000 as of July 1, but is only $100,000 as of December 31 of the same year, due solely to deemed investment losses (with no payments made under the plan during the year), the total amount deferred under the plan for that taxable year would be $100,000.

Similarly, the total amount deferred for a taxable year would not necessarily be the greatest total amount deferred for any previous year, even if no amount has been paid under the plan. For example, if a service provider has a calendar year taxable year, and if the service provider's account balance under a plan as of December 31, 2010 is $105,000, as of December 31, 2011 is $100,000, and as of December 31, 2012 is $95,000, and if those decreases are due solely to deemed investment losses (and no payments were made under the plan in 2011 or 2012), then the total amount deferred for 2011 would be $100,000 and the total amount deferred for 2012 would be $95,000.

2. Treatment of Payments

If a service recipient pays an amount deferred under a plan during a taxable year, the amount remaining to be paid to (or on behalf of) the service provider under the plan as of the last day of the taxable year will have been reduced as a result of such payment. To reasonably reflect the effect of payments made during a taxable year, the proposed regulations provide that the sum of all payments of amounts deferred under a plan during a taxable year, including all payments that are substitutes for an amount deferred, would be added to the amounts deferred outstanding as of the last day of the taxable year (determined in accordance with the regulations) to calculate the total amount deferred for such taxable year. To lower the administrative burden of the calculation, the proposed regulations provide that the addition of such payments to the total amount deferred for the taxable year would not be increased by any interest or other amount to reflect the time value of money. The total amount deferred for a taxable year would include all payments, regardless of whether the service recipient made some or all of the payments in accordance with the requirements of section 409A(a). For example, if during a taxable year an employee receives a single sum payment of the entire amount deferred under a plan, the employee would have a total amount deferred under the plan for the taxable year equal to the amount paid.

3. Treatment of Deemed Losses

Because the total amount deferred would be determined as of the last day of the taxable year, losses that occur during a taxable year (due to losses on deemed investments, actuarial losses, and other similar reductions in the amount payable under a plan) generally would be netted with any gains that occur during the same taxable year (due to deemed investment or actuarial gains, additional deferrals, or other additions to the amount payable under the plan). To that extent, deemed investment losses, actuarial losses, or other similar reductions could offset deemed investment or actuarial gains, additional deferrals, or other increases in the amount deferred under the plan for purposes of determining the total

---

[1] Under section 409A(e)(5), the Treasury Department and the IRS have the authority to disregard a substantial risk of forfeiture where necessary to carry out the purposes of section 409A.

[2] For this purpose, the term plan refers to a plan as defined under §1.409A-1(c), including any applicable plan aggregation rules.

amount deferred for the taxable year. This would apply regardless of whether a deemed loss occurs before or after the date of any specific failure to comply with section 409A(a). For example, assume a service provider begins a taxable year with a $10,000 balance under an account balance plan. During the year, the service provider has an additional deferral to the plan of $5,000 and incurs net deemed investment losses of $2,000. No payments are made pursuant to the plan during the year, the employee has no vested legally binding right to further deferrals to the plan, and there are no other changes to the account balance. The total amount deferred for the taxable year would equal the $13,000 account balance ($10,000 + $5,000 - $2,000) as of the last day of the taxable year.

4. Treatment of Rights to Deemed Earnings on Amounts Deferred

Under section 409A(d)(5), income (whether actual or notional) attributable to deferred compensation constitutes deferred compensation for purposes of section 409A. See §1.409A-1(b)(2). For example, if a service provider must include a deferred amount in income because an account balance plan in which the service provider participates fails to satisfy the requirements of section 409A(a), notional earnings credited with respect to such amount constitute deferred compensation and are subject to section 409A. If the plan also fails to comply with the requirements of section 409A(a) during a subsequent taxable year, the notional earnings must be included in income and are subject to the additional taxes under section 409A(a), notwithstanding that the "principal" amount of deferred compensation has already been included in income under section 409A(a) for a previous year.

In this respect, the treatment of earnings on nonqualified deferred compensation for purposes of section 409A is significantly different from the treatment of such earnings for purposes of section 3121(v)(2) (application of Federal Insurance Contributions Act (FICA) tax to nonqualified deferred compensation). As a result, notional earnings ordinarily are deferred compensation that is subject to section 409A even if such earnings would not constitute wages for purposes of the FICA tax when paid to the service provider because of the special timing rule under section 3121(v)(2) and §31.3121(v)(2)-1(a)(2). Accordingly, the proposed regulations provide that earnings that are credited with respect to deferred compensation during a taxable year or that were credited in previous taxable years, and earnings with respect to deferred compensation that are paid during such taxable year, must be included in determining the total amount deferred for the taxable year.

5. Total Amount Deferred for a Taxable Year Relates to the Entire Taxable Year, Regardless of Date or Period of Failure

Section 409A(a)(1)(A)(i) states that if at any time during a taxable year a nonqualified deferred compensation plan fails to meet the requirements of section 409A(a), all compensation deferred under the plan for the taxable year and all preceding years shall be includible in gross income for the taxable year to the extent not subject to a substantial risk of forfeiture (vested) and not previously included in gross income. The statutory reference to the deferred compensation required to be included in income under section 409A(a) does not distinguish between amounts deferred in a taxable year before a failure to meet the requirements of section 409A(a), and amounts deferred in the same taxable year after such failure. Accordingly, under the proposed regulations the total amount deferred under a plan for a taxable year would refer to the total amount deferred as of the last day of the taxable year, regardless of the date upon which a failure occurs. For example, if a plan is amended during a service provider's taxable year to add a provision that fails to meet the requirements of section 409A(a), the total amount deferred as of the last day of the taxable year would be includible in income under section 409A(a). This would include all payments under the plan during the taxable year, including payments made before the amendment (regardless of whether such payments are made in accordance with the requirements of section 409A(a)). Similarly, if the plan in operation fails to meet the requirements of section 409A(a) during the taxable year, the total amount deferred for the taxable year would include all payments under the plan during the taxable year, including payments made before and after the date the failure occurred.

The proposed regulations provide that amounts deferred under a plan during a taxable year in which a failure occurs must be included in income under section 409A(a) even if such deferrals occur after the failure and are otherwise made in compliance with section 409A(a). For example, salary deferrals for periods during a taxable year after an impermissible accelerated payment under the same plan during the same taxable year would be required to be included in the total amount deferred for the taxable year and included in income under section 409A(a), regardless of whether the salary deferrals are made in accordance with an otherwise compliant deferral election.

6. Treatment of Short-Term Deferrals

Under §1.409A-1(b)(4), an arrangement may not provide for deferred compensation if the amount is payable, and is paid, during a limited period of time following the later of the date the service provider obtains a legally binding right to the payment or the date such right is no longer subject to a substantial risk of forfeiture (generally referred to as the applicable 2 1/2 month period). Whether an amount will be treated as a short-term deferral or as deferred compensation may not be determinable as of the last day of the service provider's taxable year, because it may depend upon whether the amount is paid on or before the end of the applicable 2 1/2 month period. For purposes of calculating the total amount deferred for a taxable year, the proposed regulations provide that the right to a payment that, under the terms of the arrangement and the facts and circumstances as of the last day of the taxable year, may or may not be a short-term deferral, is not included in the total amount deferred. In addition, even if such amount is not paid by the end of the applicable 2 1/2 month period so that the amount would be deferred compensation, the amount would not be includible in the total amount deferred until the service provider's taxable year in which the applicable 2 1/2 month period expired. For example, assume that as of December 31, 2010, an employee whose taxable year is the calendar year is entitled to an annual bonus that is scheduled to be paid on March 15, 2011, and that the bonus would qualify as a short-term deferral if paid on or before the end of the applicable 2 1/2 month period, which ends on March 15, 2011. The bonus would not be included in the total amount deferred for 2010. This would be true regardless of whether the bonus is paid on or before March 15, 2011. However, the bonus would be includible in the total amount deferred for 2011 if the bonus is not paid on or before March 15, 2011.

C. Calculation of total amount deferred - general principles

1. General Rule

Generally, the proposed regulations provide that the total amount deferred under a plan for a taxable year is the present value as of the close of the last day of a service provider's taxable year of all amounts payable to the service provider under the plan, plus amounts paid to the service provider during the taxable year. For this purpose, present value generally would mean the value as of the close of the last day of the service provider's relevant taxable year of the amount or series of amounts due thereafter, where each such amount is multiplied by the probability that the condition or conditions on which payment of the amount is contingent would be satisfied (subject to special treatment for certain contingencies), discounted according to an assumed rate of interest to reflect the time value of money. A discount for the probability that the service provider will die before commencement of payments under the plan would be permitted to the extent that the payments would be forfeited upon the service provider's death. The proposed regulations provide that the present value cannot be discounted for the probability that payments will not be made (or will be reduced) because of the unfunded status of the plan, the risk associated with any deemed investment of amounts deferred under the plan, the risk that the service recipient or another party will be unwilling or unable to pay amounts deferred under the plan when due, the possibility of future plan amendments, the possibility of a future change in the law, or similar risks or contingencies. The proposed regulations further provide that restrictions on payment that will or may lapse with the passage of time, such as a temporary risk of forfeiture that is not a substantial risk of forfeiture, are not taken into account in determining present value. However, any potential additional deferrals contingent upon a bona fide requirement that the service provider perform services after the taxable year, such as potential salary deferrals, service credits or additions due to increases in compensation, would not be taken into account in determining the total amount deferred for the taxable year.

For purposes of calculating the present value of the benefit, the proposed regulations require the use of reasonable actuarial assumptions and methods. Whether assumptions and methods are reasonable for this purpose would be determined as of each date the benefit is valued for purposes of determining the total amount deferred.

The proposed regulations also provide certain rules relating to the crediting of earnings, generally providing that the schedule for crediting earnings will be respected if the earnings are credited at least once a year. In general, if the rules with respect to the crediting of earnings are met, any additional earnings that would be credited after the end of the taxable year only if the service provider continued performing services after the end of the year would not be includible in the total amount deferred for the year. If the right to earnings is based on an unreasonably high interest rate, the proposed regulations generally would characterize the unreasonable portion of earnings as a current right to additional deferred compensation. In addition, if earnings are based on a rate of return that does not qualify as a predetermined actual investment or a reasonable interest rate, the proposed regulations provide that the general calculation rules as applied to formula amounts would apply.

The proposed regulations provide other general rules that address issues such as plan terms under which amounts may be payable when a triggering event occurs, rather than on a fixed date, or plan terms under which the amount payable is determined in accordance with a formula, rather than being set at a fixed amount. In addition, the proposed regulations provide specific rules under which the total amounts deferred under certain types of nonqualified deferred compensation plans would be determined. The rules applicable to specific types of plans would apply in conjunction with the general rules. As a result, under the proposed regulations, an amount of deferred compensation may be includible in income under section 409A(a) even if the same amount would not yet be includible in wages under section 3121(v)(2).

2. Rules Regarding Alternative Times and Forms of Payment

To calculate the total amount deferred under a nonqualified deferred compensation plan, it is necessary to determine the time and form of payment pursuant to which the amount will be paid. Under the proposed regulations, if an amount deferred under a plan could be payable pursuant to more than one time and form of payment under the plan, the amount would be treated as payable in the available time and form of payment that has the highest present value. For this purpose, a time and form of payment generally would be an available time and form of payment to the extent a deferred amount under the plan could be payable pursuant to such time and form of payment under the plan's terms, provided that if there is a bona fide requirement that the service provider continue to perform services after the end of the taxable year to be eligible for the time and form of payment, the time and form of payment would not be treated as available. If an alternative time and form of payment is available only at the service recipient's discretion, the time and form of payment would not be treated as available unless the service provider has a legally binding right under the principles of §1.409A-1(b)(1) to any additional value that would be generated by the service recipient's exercise of such discretion. If a service provider has begun receiving payments of an amount deferred under a plan and neither the service provider nor the service recipient can change the time and form of payment of such deferred amount without the other party's approval, then no other time and form of payment under the plan would be treated as available if such approval requirement has substantive significance.

In certain instances, a service provider will be eligible for an alternative time and form of payment only if the service provider has a certain status as of a future date. For example, a time and form of payment may be available only if the service provider is married at the time the payment commences. The proposed regulations generally provide that for purposes of determining whether the service provider will meet the eligibility requirements so that an alternative time and form of payment is available, the service provider is assumed to continue in the service provider's status as of the last day of the taxable year. However, if the eligibility requirement is not bona fide and does not serve a bona fide business purpose, the eligibility requirement would be disregarded and the service provider would be treated as eligible for the alternative time and form of payment. For this purpose, an eligibility condition based upon the service provider's marital status, parental status, or status as a U.S. citizen or lawful permanent resident would be presumed to be bona fide and to serve a bona fide business purpose.

If the calculation of the present value of the amount payable to a service provider under a plan requires assumptions relating to the timing of the payment because the payment date is, or could be, a triggering event rather than a specified date, the proposed regulations specify certain assumptions that must be applied to make such calculation. First, the possibility that a particular payment trigger would occur generally would not be taken into account if the right to the payment would be subject to a substantial risk of forfeiture if that payment trigger were the only specified payment trigger. For example, if an amount is payable upon the earlier of the attainment of a specified age or an involuntary separation from service (as defined in the §1.409A-1(n)), the present value of the amount payable upon involuntary separation from service would not be taken into account if the payment would be subject to a substantial risk of forfeiture if that were the only payment trigger. However, if multiple triggers with respect to the same payment would, applied individually, constitute substantial risks of forfeiture, such triggers would not be disregarded under this rule unless all such triggers, applied in the aggregate, would also constitute a substantial risk of forfeiture. Second, the possibility that an unforeseeable emergency, as defined in §1.409A-3(i)(3), would occur and result in a payment also would not be taken into account for purposes of calculating the amount deferred.

If an amount is payable upon a service provider's death, it generally would not be necessary to make assumptions concerning when the service provider would die because any additional value due to the amount becoming payable upon the service provider's death generally would be treated as an amount payable under a death benefit plan, and amounts payable under a death benefit plan are not deferred compensation for purposes of section 409A(a). Similarly, such assumptions generally would not be necessary for an amount payable upon a service provider's disability, because any additional value due to the amount becoming payable upon the service provider's disability generally would be payable under a disability plan, and amounts payable under a disability plan are not deferred compensation for purposes of section 409A. See §1.409A-1(a)(5).

In other cases where it is necessary to make assumptions concerning when a payment trigger would occur to determine the amount deferred under a plan, taxpayers generally would be required to assume that the payment trigger would occur at the earliest possible time that the conditions under which the amount would become payable reasonably could occur, based on the facts and circumstances as of the last day of the taxable year. However, the proposed regulations provide a special rule for amounts payable due to the service provider's separation from service, termination of employment, or other event requiring the service provider's reduction or cessation of services for the service recipient. In such a case, the total amount deferred would be calculated as if the service provider had met the required reduction or cessation of services as of the close of the last day of the service provider's taxable year for which such calculation was being made. These rules would apply regardless of whether the payment trigger has or has not occurred as of any future date upon which the amount deferred for a prior taxable year was being determined.

The Treasury Department and the IRS recognize that for some service providers, the earliest possible time that a payment trigger reasonably could occur will not be the most likely time the trigger will occur. Similarly, the Treasury Department and the IRS recognize that for many service providers, the assumption that the service provider ceases providing services as of the end of the taxable year may not be realistic. The Treasury Department and the IRS request comments on alternative standards that could be utilized for these payment triggers.

An alternative approach might presume a date upon which the service provider will separate from service such as, for example, 100 months after the last day of the service provider's taxable year for which the amount deferred is being calculated. Cf. §1.280G-1 Q&A 24(c)(4). Such a standard, however, would not reflect the value of additional deferred compensation that would be paid only if the service provider separates from service before the end of the 100-month period, such as an early retirement subsidy or a window benefit, unless special rules were developed to address such situations. Another issue that arises is whether such a standard should apply if the service provider is likely to retire during the next 100 months, such as if a service provider has attained a certain age, number of years of service, or level of financial independence. However, the

Treasury Department and the IRS are concerned whether an approach involving the application of individualized standards to determine the probability that a particular service provider will separate from service will be administrable in practice.

3. Treatment of Rights to Formula Amounts

Once the date that a payment will occur has been fixed (either as a specified date under the plan's terms or through application of the rules in the proposed regulations), it is necessary to quantify the amount of the payment to which the service provider will be entitled to calculate the total amount deferred under a nonqualified deferred compensation plan. However, certain plans may define the amount payable by a formula or other method that is based on factors that may vary in future years. In general, if, at the end of the service provider's taxable year, the amount to be paid in a future year is a formula amount, the proposed regulations provide that the amount payable in the future year for purposes of calculating the total amount deferred must be determined using reasonable assumptions.

A deferred amount generally would be a formula amount subject to the reasonable assumptions standard if calculating the payment amount is dependent upon factors that are not determinable after taking into consideration all of the assumptions and other calculation rules provided in the proposed regulations. For example, a future payment equal to one percent of a corporation's net profits over five calendar years generally would be a formula amount until the last day of the fifth year, because the corporation's net profits over the five calendar years could not be determined by applying the assumptions and rules set out in the proposed regulations until the end of the fifth calendar year.

A deferred amount would not be a formula amount at the end of the taxable year merely because the information necessary to determine the amount is not readily available, if such information exists at the end of such taxable year. For example, if a deferred amount is based upon the service recipient's profits for its taxable year that coincides with the service provider's taxable year, the amount would be considered a non-formula amount at the end of the taxable year because the information necessary to determine the service recipient's profits exists, although such information may not be immediately accessible.

The right to have a deferred amount credited with reasonable earnings that may vary, for example because the earnings are based on the value of a deemed investment, would not affect whether the right to the underlying deferred amount is a formula amount. In addition, the amount of earnings to which the service provider has become entitled at the end of a particular taxable year would not be treated as a formula amount, regardless of whether such earnings could subsequently be reduced by future losses. For example, assume a service provider has a $10,000 account under an account balance plan, to be paid out in three years subject to earnings based on a mutual fund designed to replicate the performance of the S&P 500 index. At the end of Year 1, the account balance is $10,500. For Year 1, the service provider would have a total amount deferred equal to $10,500, notwithstanding that the amount could be reduced by future losses based on losses in the mutual fund.

D. Calculation of total amounts deferred - specific types of plans

1. Account Balance Plans

Under the proposed regulations, the amount deferred under an account balance plan for a taxable year generally equals the aggregate balance of all accounts under the plan as of the close of the last day of the taxable year, plus any amounts paid from such plan during the taxable year, so long as the aggregate account balance is determined using not more than a reasonable interest rate or the return on a predetermined actual investment. This rule would apply regardless of whether the applicable interest rate used to determine the earnings was higher or lower than the applicable Federal rate (AFR) under section 1274(d), provided that the interest rate was no more than a reasonable rate of interest. For a description of the proposed rules on how to calculate the total amount deferred if the right to earnings is based on an unreasonably high interest rate, see section III.C.1 of this preamble.

2. Nonaccount Balance Plans

Under the proposed regulations, the total amount deferred for a taxable year under a nonaccount balance plan generally is calculated under the general calculation rule. See section III.C of this preamble. For example, if a service provider has the right to be paid on a specified future date a fixed amount that is not credited with earnings, the total amount deferred for a year generally would be the present value as of the last day of the service provider's taxable year of the amount to which the service provider has a right to be paid in the future year (assuming no payments were made under the plan during the year). Increases in the present value of the payment in subsequent years due to the passage of time would be treated as earnings in the years in which such increases occur. For example, a right to a payment of $10,000 in Year 3 may have a present value in Year 1 equal to $8,900, and a present value in Year 2 equal to $9,434, so that the total amount deferred in Year 1 would be $8,900, the total amount deferred in Year 2 would be $9,434, and the total amount deferred in Year 3 would be $10,000 (assuming no payments were made during any year except Year 3). Any potential additional service credits or increases in compensation after the end of the taxable year for which the calculation is being made would not be taken into account in determining the total amount deferred for the taxable year.

3. Stock Rights

In general, the proposed regulations provide that the total amount deferred under an outstanding stock right is the amount of money and the fair market value of the property that the service provider would receive by exercising the right on the last day of the taxable year, reduced by the amount (if any) the service provider must pay to exercise the right and any amount the service provider paid for the right, which is commonly referred to as the spread. Accordingly, for an outstanding stock option, the total amount deferred generally would equal the underlying stock's fair market value on the last day of the taxable year, less the sum of the exercise price and any amount paid for the stock option. For an outstanding stock appreciation right, the total amount deferred generally would equal the underlying stock's fair market value on the last day of the taxable year, less the sum of the exercise price and any amount paid for the stock appreciation right. For this purpose, the stock's fair market value would be determined applying the principles set forth in § 1.409A-1(b)(5).

The Treasury Department and the IRS recognize that the spread generally is less than the fair market value of the stock right, which is used for purposes of determining the amount taxable under other Code provisions such as section 83 (if a stock option has a readily ascertainable fair market value), section 4999, and section 457(f). However, because these types of stock rights typically will fail to comply with section 409A(a) in multiple years, a taxpayer who holds such a stock right generally will be required to include amounts in income under section 409A in more than one taxable year. Therefore, the Treasury Department and the IRS believe that it is more appropriate to use the spread for purposes of applying section 409A(a) to stock rights.

4. Separation Pay Arrangements

A deferred amount that is payable only upon an involuntary separation from service generally will be treated as subject to a substantial risk of forfeiture until the service provider involuntarily separates from service. Accordingly, under the proposed regulations the amount of deferred compensation generally would not be required to be calculated until the service provider has involuntarily separated from service. In addition, if the amount were payable upon either an involuntary separation from service or some other trigger, such as a fixed date, the possibility of payment upon an involuntary separation from service generally would be ignored for purposes of determining the total amount deferred under the arrangement. See section III.C.2 of this preamble. Once an involuntary separation from service has occurred, the amount deferred under the plan would be determined using the rules that would apply to the schedule of payments if the right to payment were not contingent upon an involuntary separation from service. For example, if the amounts payable are installment payments and the remaining installment payments include interest credited at a reasonable rate, the total amount deferred under the plan would be determined under the rules governing account balance plans. If more than one type of deferred compensation arrangement were provided under the separation pay agreement, the amount deferred under each arrangement would be determined using the rules applicable to that type of arrangement. The total amount deferred for the taxable year would be the sum of all of the amounts deferred under the various arrangements constituting the plan.

5. Reimbursement Arrangements

The proposed regulations provide a method of calculating the amount deferred under a reimbursement arrangement, including an arrangement where the benefit is provided as an in-kind benefit from the service recipient or the service recipient will pay directly the third-party provider of the goods or services to the service provider. For example, the amount deferred under an arrangement providing a specified number of hours of financial planning services after a service provider's separation from service would be determined using the rules applicable to reimbursement arrangements, regardless of whether the service recipient reimburses the service provider for the service provider's expenses in purchasing such services, provides the financial planning services directly to the service provider, or pays a third-party financial planner to provide such services. The rules for reimbursement arrangements would apply to all such types of arrangements, including arrangements that would not be disaggregated from a nonaccount balance plan under §1.409A-1(c)(2)(i)(E) because the amounts subject to reimbursement exceed the applicable limits.

The proposed calculation rules provide that if a service provider has a right to reimbursements but only up to a specified maximum amount, it is presumed that the taxpayer will incur the maximum amount of expenses eligible for reimbursement, at the earliest possible time such expenses may be incurred and payable at the earliest possible time the amount may be reimbursed under the plan's terms. The service provider could rebut the presumption if the service provider demonstrates by clear and convincing evidence that it is unreasonable to assume that the service provider would expend (or would have expended) the maximum amount of expenses eligible for reimbursement. For example, if a service provider is entitled to the reimbursement of country club dues the service provider incurs in the next taxable year, not to exceed $30,000, if the service provider can demonstrate that the most expensive country club within reasonable geographic proximity of the service provider's residence and work location will cost $20,000 per year, and that the service provider's level of compensation and financial resources make it unreasonable to assume that the service provider would travel periodically to the locales of other, more expensive country clubs, the service provider can calculate the amount deferred based upon the $20,000 being eligible for reimbursement. The presumption of maximum utilization of expenses eligible for reimbursement generally would not apply if the expenses subject to reimbursement are medical expenses.

If a right to reimbursement is not subject to a maximum amount, the taxpayer would be treated as having deferred a formula amount, provided that the taxpayer would be required to calculate the amount based on the maximum amount that reasonably could be expended and reimbursed. The amount would be considered a nonformula amount as soon as the taxpayer incurs the expense that is subject to reimbursement, in an amount equal to the reimbursement to which the taxpayer is entitled. For example, a right to the reimbursement of half of the expenses the service provider incurs to purchase a boat without any limitation with respect to the cost would be treated as a deferral of a formula amount, until such time as the service provider purchases the boat.

6. Split-Dollar Life Insurance Arrangements

The amount deferred under a split-dollar life insurance arrangement would be determined based upon the amount that would be required to be included in income in a future year under the applicable split-dollar life insurance rules. Determination of the amount includible in income would depend upon the Federal tax regime and guidance applicable to such arrangement. If the split-dollar life insurance arrangement is not subject to §1.61-22 or §1.7872-15 due to application of the effective date provisions under §1.61-22(j), the amount payable would be determined by reference to Notice 2002-8 (2002-1 CB 398) and any other applicable guidance. If the split-dollar life insurance arrangement is subject to §1.61-22 or §1.7872-15, the amount payable would be determined by reference to such regulations, based upon the type of arrangement. For this purpose, the amount includible in income generally would be determined by applying the split-dollar life insurance rules to the arrangement in conjunction with the general rules providing assumptions on payment dates of deferred amounts. However, in the case of an arrangement subject to §1.7872-15, to the extent the rules regarding time and form of payment and other payment assumptions under these proposed regulations conflict with the provisions of §1.7872-15, the provisions of §1.7872-15 would apply instead of the conflicting rules under these proposed regulations. As provided in Notice 2007-34 (2007-17 IRB 996), the portion of the benefit provided under the split-dollar life insurance arrangement consisting of the cost of current life insurance protection is not treated as deferred compensation for this purpose. See §601.601(d)(2)(ii)(*b*).

7. Foreign Arrangements

Although certain foreign arrangements are a separate category under the plan aggregation rules (§1.409A-1(c)(2)(i)(G)), the amounts deferred under such arrangements would be determined using the same rules that would apply if the arrangements were not foreign arrangements. For example, the total amount deferred by a United States citizen participating in a salary deferral arrangement in France that meets the requirements of §1.409A-1(c)(2)(i)(G), but that otherwise would constitute an elective account balance plan under §1.409A-1(c)(2)(i)(A), would be determined using the rules applicable to account balance plans.

8. Other Plans

The calculation of the total amount deferred under a plan that does not fall into any of the enunciated categories (and accordingly is treated as a separate plan under §1.409A-1(c)(2)(i)(I)), would be determined by applying the general calculation rules.

E. *Calculation of amounts includible in income.*

This section III.E of the preamble addresses the second step in determining the amount includible in income under section 409A for a taxable year - the determination of the portion of the total amount deferred for a taxable year that was either subject to a substantial risk of forfeiture or had previously been included in income. That portion of the total amount deferred for the taxable year would not be includible in income under section 409A.

1. Determination of the Portion of the Total Amount Deferred for a Taxable Year that is Subject to a Substantial Risk of Forfeiture

In general, the proposed regulations provide that the portion of the total amount deferred for a taxable year that is subject to a substantial risk of forfeiture (nonvested) is determined as of the last day of the service provider's taxable year. Accordingly, all amounts that vest during the taxable year in which a failure occurs would be treated as vested for purposes of section 409A(a), regardless of whether the vesting event occurs before or after the failure to meet the requirements of section 409A(a). For example, if a plan fails to comply with section 409A(a) due to an operational failure on July 1 of a taxable year, and the substantial risk of forfeiture applicable to an amount deferred under the plan lapses as of October 1 of the same taxable year, that amount would be treated as a vested amount for purposes of determining the amount includible in income for the taxable year.

2. Determination of the Portion of the Total Amount Deferred for a Taxable Year that has been Previously Included in Income

For a deferred amount to be treated as previously included in income, the proposed regulations would require that the service provider actually and properly have included the amount in income in accordance with a provision of the Internal Revenue Code. This would include amounts reflected on an original or amended return filed before expiration of the applicable statute of limitations on assessment and amounts included in income as part of an audit or closing agreement process. In addition, a deferred amount would be treated as an amount previously included in income only until the amount is paid. Accordingly, if a deferred amount is paid in the same taxable year in which an amount is included in income under section 409A, or all or a portion of an amount previously included in income is allocable to a payment made under the plan (see section VI.A of this preamble), in subsequent taxable years that amount would not be treated as an amount previously included in income. For example, if an employee includes $100,000 in income under section 409A(a), and $10,000 of the amount includible in income consists of a payment under the plan during the taxable year, only $90,000 would remain to be treated as a deferred amount previously included in income. Similarly, if in the next year the employee receives a payment, to the extent any or all of that $90,000 amount previously included in income is allocated to that payment so that all or a portion of the payment is not includible in gross income, the amount allocated would no longer be treated as an amount previously included in income.

F. *Treatment of failures continuing during more than one taxable year*

A plan term that fails to meet the requirements of section 409A(a) may be retained in the plan over multiple taxable years. In addition, operational failures may occur in multiple years. This section III.F of the preamble discusses how section 409A(a) applies in such cases.

Each of the service provider's taxable years would be analyzed independently to determine if amounts were includible in income under section 409A(a). See section II of this preamble. Thus, for any taxable year during which a failure occurs, all amounts deferred under the plan would be includible in income unless the amount has previously been included in income or is subject to a substantial risk of forfeiture. Generally, this means that a service provider who includes in income under section 409A(a) all amounts deferred under a plan for a taxable year would not be relieved of the requirement to include amounts in income for an earlier taxable year in which a failure also occurred. It would undermine the statutory purpose to allow a service provider to include an amount in income under section 409A(a) (or otherwise) on a current basis with respect to a failure that occurred in a prior taxable year and thereby eliminate the taxes owed for the earlier year, especially if intervening payments of deferred amounts have reduced the total amount deferred as of the end of such current year. In addition, this rule generally would prohibit a service provider from selecting from among several previous taxable years the most favorable year in which to include income. However, if an amount was actually and properly included in income under section 409A(a) in a previous year, the amount would be treated as an amount previously in income for purposes of all subsequent years. Accordingly, this rule would never make the same amount includible in income twice under section 409A(a).

For example, assume an employee participates in a nonqualified deferred compensation plan and defers $10,000 each year, credited annually with interest at 5 percent (assumed to be reasonable for purposes of this example), and receives no payments under the plan. The employee's total amount deferred would be $10,500 for Year 1, $21,525 for Year 2, and $33,101 for Year 3. If the nonqualified deferred compensation plan fails to meet the requirements of section 409A(a) in each year, the employee would be required to include $10,500 in income under section 409A(a) for Year 1, $11,025 in income for Year 2, and $11,576 in income for Year 3. If the employee includes $33,101 in income under section 409A(a) for Year 3, the employee would not have properly reported income for Year 1 and Year 2. However, an amount included in income for Year 3 would be treated as previously included in income for purposes of any further failures in subsequent years. In addition, if the employee subsequently properly includes amounts in income for Year 1 and Year 2 on amended returns, the employee could claim a refund of the tax paid on the excess amounts included in income for Year 3. Similar consequences apply to the employer. If the employer fails to report and withhold on amounts includible in income under section 409A(a) in Year 1 and Year 2, the employer could not avoid liability for the failure to withhold in Year 1 and Year 2 by reporting the full amount and withholding in Year 3.

Because each taxable year would be analyzed independently, the IRS could elect to audit and assess with respect to a single taxable year, and require inclusion of all amounts deferred under the plan through that taxable year (even if failures also occurred in prior taxable years). Under those circumstances, the taxpayer could simply include amounts in income under section 409A(a) for that taxable year. However, before expiration of the applicable statute of limitations, the taxpayer could amend returns for previous taxable years and include in income amounts required to be included under section 409A(a), lowering the amount includible in income under section 409A(a) for the audited taxable year because, for purposes of that taxable year, those amounts would have been included in income in previous years. For example, an audit of Year 3 in the example above could result in an adjustment requiring $33,101 to be included in income under section 409A(a). However, before expiration of the applicable statute of limitations, the employee could amend the employee's Year 1 and Year 2 Federal tax returns to include $10,500 in income under section 409A(a) for Year 1, and $11,025 in income under section 409A(a) for Year 2, and accordingly include only $11,576 in income under section 409A(a) for Year 3. However, the employee would be required to pay the additional section 409A(a) taxes for Year 1 and Year 2, including the premium interest tax. In addition, if amounts deferred under the plan had been paid in Year 1 or Year 2, the employee would be required to include those additional amounts in income under section 409A(a) for the year paid (meaning, if the payment had been included in income for the year in which it was paid, the employee would be required to amend the previously filed tax returns to pay the additional section 409A(a) taxes on such income).

IV. *Application of Additional 20 Percent Tax*

Section 409A(a)(1)(B)(i)(II) provides that if compensation is required to be included in gross income under section 409A(a)(1)(A) for a taxable year, the income tax imposed is increased by an amount equal to 20 percent of the compensation that is required to be included in gross income. This amount is an additional income tax, subject to the rules governing the assessment, collection, and payment of income tax, and is not an excise tax.

V. *Application of Premium Interest Tax*

A. *In general*

Section 409A(a)(1)(B)(i)(I) provides that if compensation is required to be included in gross income under section 409A(a)(1)(A) for a taxable year, the income tax imposed is increased by an amount equal to the amount of interest determined under section 409A(a)(1)(B)(ii). This amount is an additional income tax, subject to the rules governing assessment, collection, and payment of income tax, and is not an excise tax or interest on an underpayment. Section 409A(a)(1)(B)(ii) provides that this premium interest tax is determined as the amount of interest at the underpayment rate (established under section 6621) plus one percentage point on the underpayments that would have occurred had the deferred compensation been includible in gross income for the taxable year in which first deferred or, if later, the first taxable year in which such deferred compensation is not subject to a substantial risk of forfeiture (vested). Thus, section 409A(a)(1)(B) requires that the premium interest tax be applied to hypothetical underpayments where the hypothetical underpayments are determined by first allocating the amounts deferred under the plan required to be included in income under section 409A(a) to the initial year (or years) the amount was deferred or vested, then determining the hypothetical underpayment that would have resulted had such amounts been includible in income at that time, and then determining the interest that would be due upon that hypothetical underpayment based upon a premium interest rate equal to the underpayment rate plus one percentage point.

B. *Amounts to which the premium interest tax applies*

Section 409A(a)(1)(B)(ii) provides for an additional tax based upon the interest that would be applied to the resulting underpayments of tax if the deferred compensation includible in income under section 409A(a) had been includible in income in previous years. Because the total amount deferred for the taxable year in which a failure occurs (the current year) may be less than the amounts deferred under the same plan in a previous year due to payments or deemed investment or other losses in the previous years, so that a portion of the amount deferred in the previous year would not be includible in income under section 409A(a) for the current year, commentators have asked what amounts deferred under the plan must be taken into account in determining the premium interest tax. Section 409A(a)(1)(B)(i) refers first to the compensation required to be included in gross income under section 409A(a)(1)(A). Accordingly, under the proposed regulations the amount required to be included in income under section 409A(a) for the taxable year is the only deferred amount required to be allocated to previous taxable years for purposes of determining the premium interest tax under section 409A(a)(1)(B)(i)(I).

For example, assume an employee who participates in a plan has a total amount deferred in Year 1 of $100,000 and a total amount deferred in Year 2 of $80,000 due to deemed investment losses in Year 2. If the plan fails to meet the requirements of section 409A(a) in Year 2 (and not Year 1), the employee is required to include $80,000 in income under section 409A(a). In calculating the premium interest tax, the employee must allocate only the $80,000 required to be included in income under section 409A(a) to the year or years the amount was first deferred or vested, even though additional amounts were deferred under the plan in previous taxable years.

C. *Identification of initial years of deferral for includible amounts*

1. Identification of Amounts Deferred in a Particular Taxable Year - General Principles

To calculate the premium underpayment interest tax, the taxable year or years during which the amount required to be included in income was first deferred or first vested must be determined. The proposed regulations provide that the amount deferred during a particular taxable year generally is the excess (if any) of the vested total amount deferred for that taxable year over the vested total amount deferred for the immediately preceding taxable year. For example, if a service provider first participated in a plan in the taxable year 2010 and has a vested total amount deferred under the plan for 2010 of $10,000, a vested total amount deferred for 2011 of $15,000, and a vested total amount deferred for 2012 of $25,000, then the service provider would be treated as having first deferred $10,000 during 2010, $5,000 during 2011, and $10,000 during 2012.

2. Identification of Initial Years of Deferral -Treatment of Amounts Previously Included in Income, Payments, and Investment Losses

The general rule would apply in cases where during previous taxable years there have been no payments under the plan, no net deemed investment or other losses, and no amounts otherwise included in income. If a service provider has received a payment, incurred net deemed losses, or included an amount in income, the general rule would need to be modified. For example, assume that the vested total amount deferred for Year 1 is $100,000, for Year 2 is $200,000 (including a $50,000 payment), and for Year 3 is $250,000. If there is a failure to meet the requirements of section 409A(a) in Year 3, the service provider would be required to include $250,000 in income. The service provider would also need to determine the year or years during which the $250,000 was first deferred and vested for purposes of calculating the premium interest tax. The issue then arises whether the $50,000 payment in Year 2 was a payment of an amount first deferred and vested in Year 1 or Year 2. If the $50,000 payment is treated as a payment of an amount first deferred and vested in Year 1, then only $50,000 of the $100,000 deferred in Year 1 would remain to be treated as part of the $250,000 includible in income in Year 3. In contrast, if the $50,000 payment is treated as a payment of an amount first deferred in Year 2, then the entire $100,000 deferred in Year 1 would remain to be treated as part of the $250,000. Similar issues arise with respect to the treatment of deemed investment losses and amounts previously included in income.

Under the calculation method set forth in the proposed regulations, payments, deemed investment or other losses, and amounts included in income during taxable years before the year in which the failure occurs, generally are attributed to amounts deferred and vested in the earliest year or years in which there are amounts deferred. The proposed calculation method generally achieves this result by reducing the amount deferred for each year preceding the payment or deemed investment or other loss, and treating only the remaining deferred amounts as the source of the outstanding deferrals and payments includible in income under section 409A for the year in which the failure occurs. This proposed rule generally should result in the lowest possible amount of premium interest tax, because deferred amounts includible in income under section 409A would be treated as first deferred and vested in the latest possible years, resulting in less premium interest on the hypothetical underpayments.

D. *Calculation of the hypothetical underpayment*

The hypothetical underpayment would be calculated as if the amount were paid to the service provider as a cash payment of compensation during the taxable year. Further, the hypothetical underpayment would be calculated based on the taxpayer's taxable income, credits, filing status, and other tax information for the year, based on the original return the taxpayer filed for such year, as adjusted as a result of any examination for such year or any amended return the taxpayer filed for such year that was accepted by the IRS. The hypothetical underpayment would reflect the effect that such additional compensation would have had on the amount of Federal income tax owed by the taxpayer for such year, including the continued availability of any deductions taken, and the use of any carryovers such as carryover losses. For purposes of calculating a hypothetical underpayment in a subsequent year (whether or not a portion of the deferred amount was first deferred and vested in the subsequent year), any changes to the taxpayer's Federal income tax liability for the subsequent year that would have occurred if the portion of the deferred amount that was first deferred and vested during the previous taxable year had been included in the taxpayer's income for the previous year would be taken into account. For example, if in calculating the hypothetical underpayment for one year, an additional amount of unused charitable contribution deductions is absorbed, the use of the additional charitable contributions would be reflected in determining the hypothetical underpayment for a subsequent year (meaning that the same portion of the charitable contribution could not be deducted twice in determining the hypothetical underpayments for more than one year).

Calculation of the premium interest tax would take into account only the consequences the additional income would have had on the Federal income tax due based on items of income and deduction, credits, filing status and similar information existing as of the end of the taxable year at issue. Other potential effects of the additional compensation payment on service provider or service recipient actions or elections would not be taken into account, including how such additional compensation could have affected participation in an employee benefit plan or other arrangement. For example, the impact such additional compensation would have had on contributions to a qualified plan, even if the additional compensation would have affected the amount the service provider would have been permitted or required to contribute, would be disregarded.

E. *Potential safe harbor calculation methods*

The Treasury Department and the IRS recognize that calculation of the premium underpayment interest tax may be cumbersome, potentially involving the recalculation of several years' tax returns. In response, the Treasury Department and the IRS are considering whether safe harbor calculation methods could be devised that would reduce the calculation burden but still result in an appropriate amount of tax applicable to the amount includible in income under section 409A(a). Specifically, the Treasury Department and the IRS request comments on calculation methods that would more easily identify the taxable year or years during which an amount includible in income under section 409A(a) was first deferred and vested, and that would more easily determine the hypothetical underpayments applicable to such year or years. Comments should consider both how the safe harbor method would be applied by taxpayers, and the extent to which such methods could be applied by the IRS in the examination context.

VI. *Treatment of Payments, Forfeitures, or Permanent Losses of Deferred Amounts in Taxable Years after the Amount is Included in Income under Section 409A(a)*

A. *Payments of deferred compensation in taxable years after the inclusion of such amounts in income under section 409A(a)*

Section 409A(c) provides that any amount included in gross income under section 409A is not required to be included in gross income under any other provision of the Code or any other rule of law later than the time provided in section 409A. Accordingly, if a service provider includes an amount in income under section 409A, the proposed regulations provide for a type of deemed "basis" or "investment in the contract" such that the amount would not be required to be included in income again (for example, when the amount was actually paid). For this purpose, the amount previously included in income would be treated as the inclusion in income of an amount deferred under the plan, but would not be allocated to any specific amount deferred under the plan. Accordingly, if an amount under the plan would be includible in income if section 409A were disregarded (for example, because an amount is paid under the plan), the amount previously included in income would be immediately applied to the amount paid under the plan such that the amount paid would not be required to be included in gross income a second time.

For example, assume that in Year 1 an employee defers $10,000 under a salary deferral elective account balance plan and is required to include that amount in income under section 409A. Assume that in Year 2 the employee defers $15,000 under the same salary deferral elective account balance plan, and an additional $5,000 under a bonus deferral elective account balance plan, both of which are compliant with section 409A. Assume that in Year 3 the employee receives a payment of $5,000 under the bonus deferral elective account balance plan. Because the payment would be treated for purposes of section 409A as made from a single elective account balance plan in which the employee participated, and because the employee has already included $10,000 in income under section 409A due to participation in the plan, the employee would apply $5,000 of the $10,000 that was previously included in income to the $5,000 payment and not include the $5,000 payment in gross income in Year 3 (or any subsequent year). The remaining amount previously included in income would be $5,000.

The employee could not elect the extent to which the amount previously included in income would be applied in this context. Rather, the amount previously included in income would be required to be applied immediately to the extent an amount deferred under the same plan would otherwise become includible in income under a Code section other than section 409A. The inclusion of any amount in income and the resulting amount previously included in income for subsequent years would not affect the potential for earnings related to such amounts to be subject to section 409A or to be required to be included in income under section 409A.

B. *Permanent forfeiture or loss of a deferred amount previously included in income under section 409A(a)*

The application of section 409A(a) may require inclusion in income of amounts that the service provider ultimately never receives. This result may occur under four different circumstances. First, because a nonqualified deferred compensation plan generally involves an unfunded, unsecured promise of a service recipient to pay compensation in a future year, the funds to pay the deferred amount may not be available in the future year. For example, the service recipient may be insolvent, bankrupt or have ceased to exist at the time the payment is due.

Second, some amounts of deferred compensation may be included in income under section 409A(a) if the amounts are subject to a risk of forfeiture, but the risk of forfeiture does not qualify as a substantial risk of forfeiture. For example, a deferred amount payable only if the service provider does not compete with the service recipient for a defined period is not subject to a substantial risk of forfeiture. However, if the service provider actually competes with the service recipient, the service provider may forfeit the right to the amount.

Third, the deferred amount may be subject to deemed investment losses. If losses occur after the deferred amount has been included in income under section 409A(a), the amount paid to the service provider may be less than the amount included in income.

Fourth, in the case of a formula amount, the calculation of the deferred amount may result in the inclusion in income under section 409A(a) of an amount that is greater than the amount ultimately paid. For example, if a service provider receives a right to a certain percentage of the service recipient's profits payable at separation from service, and determines that the total amount deferred under the plan is $100,000, once the profits are calculated the service provider may be entitled to a lesser amount.

1. Effect on Service Provider

The proposed regulations provide that a service provider who is required to include an amount in income under section 409A(a) with respect to a deferred amount under a nonqualified deferred compensation plan is entitled to a deduction at the time the service provider's legally binding right to all deferred compensation under the plan (including all arrangements treated as a single plan under the aggregation rules) is permanently forfeited under the plan's terms, or the right to such compensation is otherwise permanently lost. The available deduction would equal the excess of the amount included in income under section 409A(a) in a previous year over any amount actually or constructively received by the service provider. A right to an amount would not be treated as permanently lost merely because the deferred amount had decreased, for example due to deemed investment losses, if the service provider retains a right to an amount deferred under the plan. In addition, a right to an amount would not be treated as permanently forfeited or otherwise lost if the obligation to make such payment is substituted for another deferred amount or obligation to make a payment in a future year. However, the right to an amount would be treated as permanently lost if the right to the payment of the amount becomes wholly worthless. A service provider would not be entitled to a deduction with respect to an amount previously included in income under section 409A(a) if the service provider retains a right to any amount deferred under all arrangements treated as a single plan under § 1.409A-1(c)(2). However, if the entire deferred amount payable under the plan has been paid out and the service recipient has no remaining liability to the service provider under the plan, any remaining unpaid deferred amount that had previously been included in income would be treated as permanently lost.

For example, if at the end of Year 1 an employee has an account balance of $100,000 which is required to be included in income under section 409A, and at the end of Year 2 an employee has an account balance of $90,000 due to notional investment losses, the employee would not be entitled to a deduction for Year 2. However, if in Year 3 the entire account balance of $95,000 is paid to the employee, so there no longer are any amounts deferred under the plan (determined after applying applicable aggregation rules) and nothing remains to be paid to the employee, the employee would be entitled to a $5,000 deduction for Year 3.

In the case of a service provider that is an employee, the available deduction generally would be treated as a miscellaneous itemized deduction, subject to the deduction limitations applicable to such expenses. Section 1341 would not be applicable to such deduction because inclusion of an amount in income as a result of noncompliance with section 409A(a) would not constitute receipt of an amount to which it appeared that the taxpayer had an unrestricted right in the taxable year of inclusion. In the first circumstance listed above, a service provider that does not receive payment of deferred compensation because of the bankruptcy or insolvency of the service recipient retains the legal right to the income even though the income is not collectible. In each of the three other circumstances in which such a deduction becomes available, the deferred compensation is not paid because of an event that occurred after the taxable year in which the amount deferred was included in income under section 409A, rather than from the absence of a right to the deferred compensation in the year in which it was includible in gross income. Finally, certain of such circumstances, such as the actual amount received differing from the amount included in income because the amount deferred was a formula amount, result from the inherent uncertainties in valuing rights to such amounts, rather than from a lack of a claim of right to income.

2. Effect on Service Recipient

If a service provider is entitled to a deduction with respect to a deferred amount included in income under section 409A(a) that is subsequently permanently forfeited or otherwise lost, to the extent the service recipient has benefited from a deduction or increased the basis of an asset because the deferred amount was included in the service provider's gross income, or such inclusion by the service provider has otherwise reduced or could otherwise reduce the service recipient's gross income, the service recipient may be required to recognize income under the tax benefit rule and section 111, or make other appropriate adjustments to reflect that the deferred amount included in income by the service provider under section 409A(a) has been permanently forfeited or otherwise lost, and thus will not be paid by the service recipient.

VII. *Service Provider Income Inclusion and Additional Taxes and Service Recipient Reporting and Withholding Obligations*

A. *Service provider income inclusion*

The Treasury Department and the IRS anticipate issuing interim guidance during 2008 addressing the extent to which taxpayers may rely on the proposed regulations with respect to the calculation of the amounts includible in income under section 409A(a) and the calculation of the additional taxes under section 409A(a). The interim guidance is also expected to address the calculation of the amounts includible in income and additional taxes under section 409A(b) and service recipient reporting and withholding obligations with respect to amounts includible in income under section 409A(a) or (b) for taxable years beginning before the final regulations become applicable. The Treasury Department and the IRS anticipate that such interim guidance will provide that taxpayers may rely upon the proposed regulations in their entirety (but that taxpayers may not rely on part, but not all, of the proposed regulations).

B. *Annual deferral reporting*

Section 885(b) of the Act amended sections 6041 and 6051 to require that an employer or payer report all deferrals for the year under a nonqualified deferred compensation plan on a Form W-2, "Wage and Tax Statement" or a Form 1099-MISC, "Miscellaneous Income", regardless of whether such deferred compensation is includible in gross income under section 409A(a) (annual deferral reporting). Notice 2007-89 permanently waives this requirement for 2007 Forms W-2 and Forms 1099. Notice 2006-100 permanently waives this requirement for 2005 and 2006 Forms W-2 and Forms 1099. The Treasury Department and the IRS anticipate that this reporting will be implemented beginning with the first taxable year for which these proposed regulations are finalized and effective. The Treasury Department and the IRS further anticipate that the annual deferral reporting rules will be based upon the principles set forth in these regulations as finalized, except that taxpayers will not be required to report deferred amounts that are not reasonably ascertainable (as defined in §31.3121(v)(2)-1(e)(4)(i)(B)) until such amounts become reasonably ascertainable. The Treasury Department and the IRS anticipate that the deferred amounts required to be reported will reflect earnings on the amounts deferred in previous years, if the amount of such earnings is reasonably ascertainable, because section 409A specifically treats earnings on deferred amounts as additional deferred amounts. The Treasury Department and the IRS request comments on the potential application of the standards set forth in these regulations to this reporting requirement, including suggestions for possible adaptations or modifications that may decrease the administrative burden of compliance while maintaining the integrity of the information reported.

C. *Income inclusion reporting and income tax withholding*

Section 885(b) of the Act also amended section 3401(a) to provide that the term "wages" includes any amount includible in the gross income of an employee under section 409A, and amended section 6041 to require that a payer report amounts includible in gross income under section 409A that are not treated as wages under section 3401(a) (income inclusion reporting). Notice 2005-1 provides that an employer should report amounts includible in gross income under section 409A and in wages under section 3401(a) in box 1 of Form W-2 as wages paid to the employee during the year and subject to income tax withholding, and that the employer should also report such amounts in box 12 of Form W-2 using code Z. Notice 2005-1 also provides that a payer should report amounts includible in gross income under section 409A and not treated as wages under section 3401(a) as nonemployee compensation in box 7 of Form 1099-MISC, and should also report such amounts in box 15b of Form 1099-MISC. Notice 2006-100 provided guidance on income inclusion reporting for the 2005 and 2006 Forms W-2 and Forms 1099. Notice 2007-89 provided guidance on income inclusion reporting for the 2007 Forms W-2 and Forms 1099. The Treasury Department and the IRS anticipate issuing further interim guidance during 2008 on income inclusion reporting for 2008 Forms W-2 and Forms 1099 for taxable years beginning before the final regulations become applicable. The Treasury Department and the IRS anticipate that such interim guidance will provide that taxpayers may rely upon the proposed regulations in their entirety (but that taxpayers may not rely on part, but not all, of the proposed regulations).

Amounts includible in an employee's income under section 409A also are treated as wages for purposes of section 3401. Notice 2007-89 provides guidance on a service recipient's income tax withholding obligations for 2007. The Treasury Department and the IRS anticipate issuing further interim guidance during 2008 on a service recipient's income tax withholding obligations for calendar years beginning before the final regulations become applicable. The Treasury Department and the IRS anticipate that such interim guidance will provide that taxpayers may rely upon the proposed regulations in their entirety (but that taxpayers may not rely on part, but not all, of the proposed regulations).

Proposed Effective Date

These regulations are proposed to be generally applicable for taxable years beginning on or after the issuance of final regulations. Before the applicability date of the final regulations, taxpayers may rely on these proposed regulations only to the extent provided in further guidance.

Special Analyses

It has been determined that this notice of proposed rulemaking is not a significant regulatory action as defined in Executive Order 12866. Therefore, a regulatory assessment is not required. It has also been determined that section 553(b) of the Administrative Procedure Act (5 U.S.C. chapter 5) does not apply to these regulations, and because the regulation does not impose a collection of information on small entities, the Regulatory Flexibility Act (5 U.S.C. chapter 6) does not apply. Pursuant to section 7805(f) of the Code, this notice of proposed rulemaking will be submitted to the Chief Counsel for Advocacy of the Small Business Administration for comment on its impact on small business.

Comments and Public Hearing

Before these proposed regulations are adopted as final regulations, consideration will be given to any written (a signed original and eight (8) copies) or electronic comments that are submitted timely to the IRS. The IRS and Treasury Department request comments on the clarity of the proposed rules and how they can be made easier to understand. All comments will be available for public inspection and copying.

A public hearing has been scheduled for April 2, 2009 at 10:00 a.m., in the auditorium. Due to building security procedures, visitors must enter at the Constitution Avenue entrance. In addition, all visitors must present photo identification to enter the building. Because of access restrictions, visitors will not be admitted beyond the immediate entrance area more than 30 minutes before the hearing starts. For information about having your name placed on the building access list to attend the hearing, see the "FOR FURTHER INFORMATION CONTACT" section of this preamble.

The rules of 26 CFR 601.601(a)(3) apply to the hearing. Persons who wish to present oral comments at the hearing must submit written or electronic comments and an outline of the topics to be discussed and the time to be devoted to each topic (a signed original and eight (8) copies) by March 9, 2009. A period of 10 minutes will be allotted to each person for making comments. An agenda showing the scheduling of the speakers will be prepared after the deadline for receiving outlines has passed. Copies of the agenda will be available free of charge at the hearing.

Drafting Information

The principal author of these regulations is Stephen Tackney of the Office of Division Counsel/Associate Chief Counsel (Tax Exempt and Government Entities). However, other personnel from the IRS and the Treasury Department participated in their development.

[¶ 49,415]   Proposed Amendments of Regulations (REG-147636-08), published in the Federal Register on February 11, 2009.

[Code Secs. 367 and 1248]

Foreign corporation: Distribution of property: Stock: Sale or exchange: Gain.—Reg. § 1.367(a)-9, concerning transfers of stock to a foreign corporation that are described in Code Sec. 351 by reason of Code Sec. 304(a)(1) and recognized by a shareholder under Code Sec. 301(c)(3) in connection with the receipt of a distribution of property from a foreign corporation with respect to its stock shall be treated as gain from the sale or exchange of the stock of such foreign corporation, is proposed. Amendments of Reg. § 1.1248-1 were adopted on 4/23/2012 by T.D. 9585. Amendments of Reg. § 1.367(b)-4 were withdrawn and then re-proposed by REG-135734-14 on April 8, 2016 (see ¶ 49,693).

AGENCY: Internal Revenue Service (IRS), Treasury.

ACTION: Notice of proposed rulemaking by cross-reference to temporary regulations.

SUMMARY: In the Rules and Regulations section of this issue of the **Federal Register**, the IRS and Treasury Department are issuing temporary regulations under sections 304 and 1248 of the Internal Revenue Code (Code). The temporary regulations provide rules under section 367(a) and (b) that apply to certain transfers of stock by a United States person to a foreign corporation described in section 304(a)(1). The temporary regulations under section 1248(a) provide that, for purposes of section 1248(a), gain recognized by a shareholder under section 301(c)(3) in connection with the receipt of a distribution of property from a foreign corporation with respect to its stock shall be treated as gain from the sale or exchange of the stock of such foreign corporation. The temporary regulations affect certain shareholders that transfer stock in a corporation to a foreign corporation in a transaction to which section 304(a)(1) applies, or that receive a distribution from a foreign corporation described in section 301(c)(3). The text of the temporary regulations also serves as the text of these proposed regulations. The preamble to the temporary regulations explains the temporary regulations and these proposed regulations.

DATES: Written or electronic comments and requests for a public hearing must be received by May 12, 2009.

ADDRESSES: Send submissions to: CC:PA:LPD:PR (REG-147636-08), room 5205, Internal Revenue Service, PO Box 7604, Ben Franklin Station, Washington, DC 20044. Submissions may be hand-delivered Monday through Friday between the hours of 8 a.m. and 4 p.m. to CC:PA:LPD:PR (REG-147636-08), Courier's Desk, Internal Revenue Service, 1111 Constitution Avenue NW., Washington, DC, or sent electronically via the Federal eRulemaking Portal at *www.regulations.gov* (IRS REG-147636-08).

FOR FURTHER INFORMATION CONTACT: Concerning the proposed regulations, Sean W. Mullaney, (202) 622-3860; concerning submissions of comments or requests for a public hearing, Richard.A.Hurst@irscounsel.treas.gov; at (202) 622-7180 (not tollfree numbers).

SUPPLEMENTARY INFORMATION:

Background and Explanation of Provisions

Temporary regulations in the Rules and Regulations section of this issue of the **Federal Register** amend the Income Tax Regulations (26 CFR part 1) relating to sections 304 and 1248 of the Code. The text of those regulations also serves as the text of these proposed regulations. The preamble to the temporary regulations explains the temporary regulations and these proposed regulations.

Special Analyses

It has been determined that this notice of proposed rulemaking is not a significant regulatory action as defined in Executive Order 12866. Therefore, a regulatory assessment is not required. These regulations are necessary to ensure that the appropriate amount of income (dividend income, capital gain or both) is recognized currently in the transactions described in the explanation of provisions section in this preamble. Accordingly, good cause is found for dispensing with notice and public comment pursuant to 5 U.S.C. 553(b) and (c) and with a delayed effective date pursuant to 5 U.S.C. 553(d). For applicability of the Regulatory Flexibility Act, see the cross-referenced notice of proposed rulemaking published elsewhere in this **Federal Register**. Pursuant to section 7805(f) of the Code, these regulations have been submitted to the Chief Counsel for Advocacy of the Small Business Administration for comment on its impact on small business.

Comments and Requests for a Public Hearing

Comments are also requested regarding whether IRS and Treasury Department should exercise the regulatory authority under section 304(b)(6) to permit an increase to the basis of the transferred stock in a section 304(a)(1) transaction to the extent the distribution in redemption of the shares deemed issued by the acquiring corporation is treated as a dividend from the earnings and profits of the issuing corporation.

Before these proposed regulations are adopted as final regulations, consideration will be given to any written comments (a signed original and eight (8) copies) or electronic comments that are submitted timely to the IRS. The IRS and Treasury Department specifically request comments on the clarity of the proposed rules and how they can be made easier to understand. All comments will be available for public inspection and copying. A public hearing will be scheduled if requested in writing by any person that timely submits written comments. If a public hearing is scheduled, notice of the date, time, and place for the public hearing will be published in the **Federal Register**.

Drafting Information

The principal author of these proposed regulations is Sean W. Mullaney of the Office of Associate Chief Counsel (International). However, other personnel from the IRS and the Treasury Department participated in their development.

[¶ 49,426]   Proposed Amendments of Regulations (REG-112756-09), published in the Federal Register on August 5, 2009.

[Code Sec. 7611]

Exempt organizations: Church tax inquiries: IRS restructuring.—Amendments of Reg. § 301.7611-1, amending the questions and answers relating to church tax inquiries and examinations, are proposed.

AGENCY: Internal Revenue Service ("IRS"), Treasury.

ACTION: Notice of proposed rulemaking.

SUMMARY: This document contains proposed regulations amending the questions and answers relating to church tax inquiries and examinations. These proposed regulations replace references to positions that were abolished by the Internal Revenue Service Restructuring and Reform Act of 1998 with references that are consistent both with the statute and the IRS's current organizational structure.

DATES: Written or electronic comments and requests for a public hearing must be received by November 3, 2009.

ADDRESSES: Send submissions to: CC:PA:LPD:PR (REG-112756-09), room 5205, Internal Revenue Service, PO Box 7604, Ben Franklin Station, Washington, DC 20044. Submissions may be hand-delivered Monday through Friday between the hours of 8 a.m. and 4 p.m. to CC:PA:LPD:PR (REG-112756-09), Courier's Desk, Internal Revenue Service, 1111 Constitution Avenue, NW, Washington, DC, or sent electronically, via the Federal eRulemaking Portal at *www.regulations.gov* (IRS-REG-112756-09).

FOR FURTHER INFORMATION CONTACT: Concerning these proposed regulations, Benjamin Akins at (202) 622-1124 or Monice Rosenbaum at (202) 622-6070; concerning submission of comments and requests for a public hearing, Richard Hurst, *Richard.A.Hurst@irscounsel.treas.gov*, (202) 622-7180 (not a toll-free numbers).

SUPPLEMENTARY INFORMATION:

Background

Restrictions on Church Tax Inquiries and Examinations

This document contains amendments to the regulations on Procedure and Administration (26 CFR part 301) under section 7611 of the Internal Revenue Code. Section 7611 was enacted by section 1033 of the Deficit Reduction Act of 1984 (Public Law 98-369, 98 Stat. 1034-1039) ("DRA 1984").

Prior to the enactment of section 7611, section 7605(c) imposed special requirements that the IRS had to meet before it could examine church books of account, but there were no special requirements imposed before the IRS could commence an investigation or inquiry into a church's tax liabilities. As explained in the Conference Report accompanying DRA 1984, H.R. Rep. No. 98-861, 98th Cong., 2d Sess. 1101 (1984), 1984-3 CB Vol. 2 355, Congress sought to address certain problems that arise when the IRS examines the records of a church. Thus, Congress expanded the requirements relating to IRS interactions with churches. Although prior law imposed limitations on the examination of church records, those limitations were somewhat vague and relied on internal IRS procedures to protect the rights of a church in the examination process. Additionally, there was some uncertainty regarding the scope of the investigations to which prior law applied and the nature of the records protected by the law. The enactment of section 7611 attempted to resolve these competing considerations by providing detailed rules for the IRS to follow in making tax inquiries to churches, both as to tax-exempt status and as to the existence of unrelated business income.

Section 7611(a)(2) permits the IRS to begin an inquiry into whether a church qualifies for exemption from income tax as an organization described in section 501(c)(3) or whether a church has a liability for unrelated business income tax only if an appropriate high-level Treasury official first reasonably believes on the basis of facts and circumstances, recorded in writing, that the church may not be exempt under section 501(a), or that the church may be carrying on an unrelated trade or business, or may be otherwise engaged in activities subject to tax. Section 7611(h)(7) provides that the term "appropriate high-level Treasury official" means the Secretary of the Treasury or any delegate of the Secretary whose rank is no lower than that of a principal Internal Revenue officer for an internal revenue region. The legislative history of section 7611 interprets the term "appropriate high-level Treasury official" to mean an IRS Regional Commissioner (or higher official). H.R. Rep. No. 98-861, 98th Cong. 2d Sess. 1101 (1984), 1984-3 CB Vol. 2 355. Final regulations under section 7611, which were published on February 21, 1986, 50 Fed. Reg. 6219, also interpret the term to mean an IRS Regional Commissioner. See Treas. Reg. § 301.7611 Q1-A1.

Section 7611(b)(2)(A) provides that at least 15 days before the beginning of a church tax examination, the IRS must provide notice of the examination to both the church and the appropriate regional counsel. Section 7611(b)(3)(C) provides that any regional counsel who receives notice under section 7611(b)(2)(A) may submit to a regional commissioner an advisory objection to the examination within 15 days after the notice of examination is provided.

Section 7611(c)(1)(A) provides that the IRS must make a final determination as to any church tax inquiry or examination within two years of the date the notice of examination is provided to the church under section 7611(b). In instances where no examination follows a church tax inquiry, section 7611(c)(1)(B) requires the IRS to make a final determination as to the inquiry no later than 90 days after the date the notice of inquiry is provided to the church under section 7611(a). Section 7611(c)(2) suspends the periods described in section 7611(c)(1) (that is, 2 year period and 90 day period) while certain judicial proceedings are pending or being appealed, including proceedings brought by the IRS against a church seeking to compel compliance with a reasonable request to examine church records or religious activities.

Section 7611(d)(1) prohibits the IRS from making certain final determinations (that is, revocation of tax-exempt status, notice of deficiency, or assessment) regarding a church until after the appropriate regional counsel determines in writing that there has been substantial compliance with the requirements of section 7611. Section 7611(d)(1) further requires the appropriate regional counsel's written approval of such final determination before the IRS can make the determination.

Section 7611(e)(1) provides that if the IRS has not substantially complied with the requirements of section 7611, any proceeding to compel compliance with a summons shall be stayed until the court finds that the IRS has taken all practicable steps to correct the noncompliance. Section 7611(e)(2) states that the remedy provided in subsection (e)(1) shall be the exclusive remedy for a church in regard to any noncompliance by the IRS with the requirements of section 7611.

Under section 7611(f), the IRS may not commence an inquiry or examination of a church if, within the previous five years, the IRS completed an inquiry or examination regarding the church that did not result in a revocation, notice of deficiency, assessment, or a request for a significant change in the church's operating practices. An exception exists where the Secretary or his delegate approves the second inquiry or examination in writing. There is also an exception where the issues involved in the subsequent inquiry or examination are not the same or similar to issues involved in the preceding inquiry or examination. Prior to the Internal Revenue Service Restructuring and Reform Act of 1998, Public Law 105-206 ("RRA 1998"), discussed below, section 7611(f) required the Assistant Commissioner (Employee Plans and Exempt Organizations), instead of the Secretary or his delegate, to approve subsequent inquiries and examinations for the exception to apply.

Reorganization of the IRS

Section 1001 of RRA 1998 requires the Commissioner of Internal Revenue to develop and implement a plan to reorganize the IRS. The congressional mandate provides that the plan shall "eliminate or substantially modify the existing organization of the IRS which is based on a national, regional, and district structure; [and] establish organizational units serving particular groups of taxpayers with similar needs . . . ." Under the reorganized IRS, four nationwide operating divisions were established to serve different types of taxpayers. One of these operating divisions serves tax-exempt and government entities, including churches.

Section 1102(e)(3) of RRA 1998 amended section 7611(f)(1), relating to second inquiries and examinations within five years of a previous inquiry or examination, by replacing Assistant Commissioner (Employee Plans and Exempt Organizations) with Secretary. Under section 7701(a)(11)(B), Secretary is defined to refer to the Secretary of the Treasury or his delegate. RRA 1998 did not amend other portions of section 7611, such as references to "appropriate high-level Treasury official" and "appropriate regional counsel."

In mandating the restructuring of the IRS under RRA 1998, Congress realized that certain positions within the IRS would be eliminated as a result of transitioning from a geographic structure to a structure based on nationwide jurisdiction of similar types of taxpayers. Accordingly, Congress included a savings provision in RRA 1998. Section 1001(b) provides, "All orders, determinations, rules, regulations . . . and other administrative actions . . . which are in effect at the time this section takes effect . . . shall continue in effect according to their terms until modified, terminated, superseded, set aside or revoked in accordance with law by . . . the Secretary of the Treasury [or] the Commissioner of Internal Revenue . . . ." This provision keeps in effect regulations that make reference to officers whose positions no longer exist. The legislative history of RRA 1998 at H.R. Conf. Rep. No. 105-599, 105th Cong., 2d Sess. 195 (1998) explains that "[t]he legality of IRS actions will not be affected pending further appropriate statutory changes relating to such a reorganization (e.g., eliminating statutory references to obsolete positions)." Accordingly, the Treasury Regulations under section 7611 have remained in effect notwithstanding their references to the positions of Regional Commissioner, Regional Counsel, and Assistant Commissioner (Employee Plans and Exempt Organizations), positions that were eliminated by the reorganization. Delegation Order 193 (Rev. 6) (11/08/2000) provides in part that actions previously delegated to Regional Commissioners by Treasury Regulations (par. 7) are now delegated to "Assistant Deputy Commissioners, Division Commissioners; Chiefs; and Directors, Submission Processing Field, Compliance Services Field, and Accounts Management Field." In the Internal Revenue Manual ("IRM"), the IRS designated the Director, Exempt Organizations Examinations as the appropriate high-level Treasury official for purposes of section 7611. See IRM § 4.76.7.

Recent litigation has challenged the IRS's interpretation of the term "appropriate high-level Treasury official" following the reorganization. See *United States v. Living Word Christian Center*, Civil No. 08-mc-37, D.C. Minn. (Jan. 30, 2009) ("*LWCC*"). In particular, concern has been expressed about the need for an update to the regulations in light of the statutorily mandated reorganization and the elimination of internal revenue regions.

In *LWCC*, the District Court for the District of Minnesota ruled that the Director, Exempt Organizations Examinations is not an appropriate high-level Treasury official to make the "reasonable belief" determination required before the IRS may commence a church tax inquiry under section 7611. *LWCC* at 2. The district court concluded that the Director, Exempt Organizations Examinations is not an appropriate high-level Treasury official within the meaning of section 7611(h) because that official does not have a comparable breadth of responsibility to a regional commissioner nor as high a position within the IRS. Although the IRS disagrees with the district court's reasoning and conclusion in *LWCC*, the IRS acknowledges that it would be beneficial to revise the regulations in light of the changes in IRS organization made in the wake of RRA 1998 to clarify who is an appropriate high-level Treasury official for purposes of section 7611. Further, the IRS recognizes the significance of the special procedural requirements for church tax inquiries and examinations. These proposed regulations assign responsibility for making the determinations required under section 7611(a) to the Director, Exempt Organizations.

Explanation of Provisions

These proposed regulations eliminate references to the positions of Regional Commissioner and Regional Counsel under the existing regulations and give responsibilities formerly assigned to these now defunct positions to the Director, Exempt Organizations and the Division Counsel / Associate Chief Counsel, Tax Exempt and Government Entities, respectively. In addition, these proposed regulations eliminate references to the position of Assistant Commissioner (Employee Plans and Exempt Organizations) under the existing regulations and give responsibilities formerly assigned to that position to the Commissioner, Tax Exempt and Government Entities or the Deputy Commissioner, Tax Exempt and Government Entities.

Reasonable Belief and Inquiry Notice Requirement

With respect to the initiation of the church tax inquiry process, Treas. Reg. § 301.7611-1 Q1-A1 provides that a "Regional Commissioner (or higher Treasury official)" is the appropriate high-level Treasury official for purposes of this reasonable belief requirement. Similarly, Treas. Reg. § 301.7611-1 Q7-A7 states, "Repeated (two or more) failures by a church or its agents to reply to routine requests . . . will be considered by the appropriate Internal Revenue Service Regional Commissioner to be a reasonable basis for commencement of a church tax inquiry under the church tax inquiry and examination procedures of section 7611." In addition, Treas. Reg. § 301.7611 Q9-A9 requires a Regional Commissioner to provide written notice to the church of the beginning of an inquiry.

These proposed regulations eliminate references to the Regional Commissioner and instead provide that the Director, Exempt Organizations is the "appropriate high-level Treasury official" for purposes of the reasonable belief and inquiry notice requirements of Treas. Reg. § 301.7611-1 Q1-A1, Q7-A7, and Q9-A9. The Director, Exempt Organizations is a senior executive who reports to the Commissioner / Deputy Commissioner, Tax Exempt and Government Entities Division, and who is responsible for planning, managing, directing and executing nationwide activities for Exempt Organizations. See IRM § 1.1.23.5 for a comprehensive description of these activities.

Examination Notice Requirement

Under section 7611(b)(2) and Treas. Reg. § 301.7611-1 Q10-A10, a church tax examination cannot be commenced without first providing written notice of such examination to the church and to the "appropriate Regional Counsel" at least 15 days before the IRS begins the church tax examination. The regulation allows the Regional Counsel to file an advisory objection to the examination within this same 15-day period.

These proposed regulations amend Treas. Reg. § 301.7611-1 Q10-A10 by substituting Division Counsel / Associate Chief Counsel, Tax Exempt and Government Entities, for each occurrence of Regional Counsel. These proposed regulations further specify that before the notice of examination is provided to the church, a copy of the notice must be provided to the Division Counsel / Associate Chief Counsel, Tax Exempt and Government Entities.

Revocation of Exemption or of Church Status

Section 7611(d)(1) and Treas. Reg. § 301.7611-1 Q11-A11 require the Regional Counsel to approve, in writing, certain final determinations that are within the scope of section 7611 and adversely affect the tax-exempt status or increase any tax liability of a church. Further, prior to such adverse action, section 7611(d) requires Regional Counsel to determine, in writing, that there has been substantial compliance with the requirements of section 7611, when applicable.

These proposed regulations amend Treas. Reg. § 301.7611-1 Q11-A11 by providing that the Division Counsel / Associate Chief Counsel, Tax Exempt and Government Entities, is the official responsible for complying with the written determination and approval requirements of section 7611(d)(1).

Limitations on Period of Assessment

Section 7611(d)(2) and Treas. Reg. § 301.7611-1 Q15-A15 provide special limitation periods for church tax liabilities. These special rules are not to be construed to increase an otherwise applicable limitation period. Treas. Reg. § 301.7611-1 Q15-A15 states that, for purposes of section 7611(d)(2)(A), that is, the statute of limitations applicable to liabilities arising from church tax examinations, a church is determined not to be a church exempt from tax when the appropriate Regional Commissioner approves, in writing, the completed findings of the examining agent that the organization is not a church exempt from tax for one or more of the three most recently completed taxable years ending before the examination notice date. The regulation also states that the Regional Commissioner cannot delegate this approval to a subordinate official. Further, the completed findings of the examining agent, which are approved by the appropriate Regional Commissioner, are not considered a final revenue agent's report (defined in section 7611(g)).

These proposed regulations substitute the Director, Exempt Organizations for the appropriate Regional Commissioner for purposes of Treas. Reg. §301.7611-1 Q15-A15.

Multiple Examinations

Consistent with the language of section 7611(f)(1) prior to enactment of RRA 1998, Treas. Reg. §301.7611-1 Q16-A16 provides that the Assistant Commissioner (Employee Plans and Exempt Organizations) is responsible for providing the written approval necessary to begin a second inquiry or examination of a church. These proposed regulations provide that the Commissioner, Tax Exempt and Government Entities or the Deputy Commissioner, Tax Exempt and Government Entities is responsible for approving second inquiries and examinations under section 7611(f).

Remedies for Violation of Section 7611

Section 7611(e) and Treas. Reg. §301.7611-1 Q17-A17 provide that, if there has not been substantial compliance with certain requirements in section 7611, including the notice requirements of section 7611(a) and (b), the exclusive remedy for such noncompliance is a stay in an enforcement proceeding to compel compliance with a summons with respect to the inquiry or examination. The stay continues until the court finds that all practicable steps to correct the noncompliance have been taken. Treas. Reg. §301.7611-1 Q17-A17 further states that failure of the Regional Commissioner to approve an inquiry may not be raised as a defense or as an affirmative ground for relief in a summons proceeding or any other judicial proceeding other than as specifically set forth in the regulation.

These proposed regulations amend Treas. Reg. §301.7611-1 Q17-A17 to replace each reference to Regional Commissioner with Director, Exempt Organizations.

Special Analyses

It has been determined that this notice of proposed rulemaking is not a significant regulatory action as defined in Executive Order 12866. Therefore, a regulatory assessment is not required. It has also been determined that section 553(b) of the Administrative Procedure Act (5 U.S.C. chapter 5) does not apply to these proposed regulations and because the regulation does not impose a collection of information on small entities, the Regulatory Flexibility Act (5 U.S.C. 601) does not apply.

Pursuant to section 7805(f) of the Code, these proposed regulations have been submitted to the Chief Counsel for Advocacy of the Small Business Administration for comment on its impact on small business.

Comments and Requests for a Public Hearing

Before these proposed regulations are adopted as final regulations, consideration will be given to any written comments (a signed original and eight (8) copies) or electronic comments that are submitted timely to the IRS. Comments are requested on all aspects of the proposed regulations. All comments will be available for public inspection and copying. A public hearing will be scheduled if requested in writing by any person that timely submits written or electronic comments. If a public hearing is scheduled, notice of the date, time, and place for the public hearing will be published in the **Federal Register**.

Drafting Information

The principal authors of these proposed regulations are Benjamin Akins and Monice Rosenbaum of the Office of Division Counsel / Associate Chief Counsel (Tax Exempt and Government Entities). However, other personnel from the IRS and the Treasury Department participated in their development.

[¶ 49,435]   **Proposed Regulations (REG-123829-08)**, published in the Federal Register on October 7, 2009.

[Code Sec. 9802]

Group health plans: Genetic information nondiscrimination regulations: Proposed regulations.—Reg. §54.9802-3, providing guidance to employers and group health plans relating to the group health plan genetic nondiscrimination requirements, is proposed.

AGENCY: Internal Revenue Service (IRS), Treasury.

ACTION: Notice of proposed rulemaking by cross-reference to temporary regulations.

SUMMARY: Elsewhere in this issue of the **Federal Register**, the IRS is issuing temporary and final regulations governing the provisions of the Genetic Information Nondiscrimination Act (GINA) prohibiting discrimination based on genetic information for group health plans. The IRS is issuing the temporary and final regulations at the same time that the Employee Benefits Security Administration of the U.S. Department of Labor and the Centers for Medicare & Medicaid Services of the U.S. Department of Health and Human Services are issuing substantially similar interim final regulations with respect to GINA for group health plans and issuers of health insurance coverage offered in connection with a group health plan under the Employee Retirement Income Security Act of 1974 and the Public Health Service Act. The temporary regulations provide guidance to employers and group health plans relating to the group health plan genetic nondiscrimination requirements. The text of those temporary regulations also serves as the text of these proposed regulations.

DATES: Written or electronic comments and requests for a public hearing must be received by January 5, 2010.

ADDRESSES: Send submissions to: CC:PA:LPD:PR (REG-123829-08), room 5205, Internal Revenue Service, P.O. Box 7604, Ben Franklin Station, Washington, DC 20044. Submissions may be hand-delivered to: CC:PA:LPD:PR (REG-123829-08), Courier's Desk, Internal Revenue Service, 1111 Constitution Avenue, NW, Washington DC 20224. Alternatively, taxpayers may submit comments electronically via the Federal eRulemaking Portal at *http://www.regulations.gov* (IRS REG-123829-08).

FOR FURTHER INFORMATION CONTACT: Concerning the regulations, Russ Weinheimer at 202-622-6080; concerning submissions of comments, Oluwafumilayo Taylor at (202) 622-7180 (not toll-free numbers).

SUPPLEMENTARY INFORMATION:

Paperwork Reduction Act

The collection of information referenced in this notice of proposed rulemaking has been submitted to the Office of Management and Budget for review in accordance with the Paperwork Reduction Act of 1995 (44 U.S.C. 3507(d)). Comments on the collection of information should be sent to the **Office of Management and Budget**, Attn: Desk Officer for the Department of the Treasury, Office of Information and Regulatory Affairs, Washington, DC 20503, with copies to the **Internal Revenue Service**, Attn: IRS Reports Clearance Officer, SE:W:CAR:MP:T:T:SP, Washington, DC 20224. Comments on the collection of information should be received by December 7, 2009. Comments are specifically requested concerning:

- Whether the proposed collection of information is necessary for the proper performance of the functions of the Internal Revenue Service, including whether the information will have practical utility;

- The accuracy of the estimated burden associated with the proposed collection of information (see the preamble to the temporary regulations published elsewhere in this issue of the **Federal Register**);

- How to enhance the quality, utility, and clarity of the information to be collected;

- How to minimize the burden of complying with the proposed collection of information, including the application of automated collection techniques or other forms of information technology; and

- Estimates of capital or start-up costs and costs of operation, maintenance, and purchase of services to provide information.

The collection of information is in §54.9802-3 (see the temporary regulations published elsewhere in this issue of the **Federal Register**). The collection of information is required so that the IRS can be apprised when a group health plan is conducting research with respect to genetic information of plan participants or beneficiaries to ensure that all the requirements of the research exception to GINA are being complied with. The likely respondents are business or other for-profit institutions, and nonprofit institutions. Responses to this collection of information are required if a plan wishes to conduct genetic research with respect to participants or beneficiaries of the plan.

An agency may not conduct or sponsor, and a person is not required to respond to, a collection of information unless it displays a valid control number assigned by the Office of Management and Budget.

Books or records relating to a collection of information must be retained as long as their contents may become material in the administration of any internal revenue law. Generally tax returns and tax return information are confidential, as required by 26 U.S.C. 6103.

Background

The temporary regulations published elsewhere in this issue of the **Federal Register** add a new §54.9802-3T to the Miscellaneous Excise Tax Regulations. In the same document, certain conforming changes are also being made to the final regulations under §§54.9801-1, 54.9801-2, 54.9802-1, and 54.9831-1. The proposed, temporary, and final regulations are being published as part of a joint rulemaking with the Department of Labor and the Department of Health and Human Services (the joint rulemaking). The text of those temporary regulations also serves as the text of these proposed regulations. The preamble to the temporary regulations explains the temporary regulations.

Special Analyses

It has been determined that this notice of proposed rulemaking is not a significant regulatory action as defined in Executive Order 12866. Therefore, a regulatory assessment is not required. It has also been determined that section 553(b) of the Administrative Procedure Act (5 U.S.C. chapter 5) does not apply to this proposed regulation. It is hereby certified that the collection of information contained in this notice of proposed rulemaking will not have a significant impact on a substantial number of small entities. Accordingly, a regulatory flexibility analysis is not required. GINA requires group health plans claiming the research exception to GINA to notify the Secretary of the Treasury when the exception is being claimed. This notice of proposed rulemaking does not add to the reporting requirement imposed by the statute. Moreover, it is anticipated that very few and only the largest group health plans are likely to claim the research exception to GINA and thus be subject to the reporting requirement. For this reason, the burden imposed by the reporting requirement of the statute and this notice of proposed rulemaking on small entities is expected to be near zero. For further information and for analyses relating to the joint rulemaking, see the preamble to the joint rulemaking. Pursuant to section 7805(f) of the Internal Revenue Code, this notice of proposed rulemaking will be submitted to the Chief Counsel for Advocacy of the Small Business Administration for comment on its impact on small business.

Comments and Requests for a Public Hearing

Before these proposed regulations are adopted as final regulations, consideration will be given to any written comments (a signed original and eight (8) copies) or electronic comments that are submitted timely to the IRS. Comments are specifically requested on the clarity of the proposed regulations and how they may be made easier to understand. All comments will be available for public inspection and copying. A public hearing may be scheduled if requested in writing by a person that timely submits written comments. If a public hearing is scheduled, notice of the date, time, and place for the hearing will be published in the **Federal Register**.

Drafting Information

The principal author of these proposed regulations is Russ Weinheimer, Office of the Division Counsel/Associate Chief Counsel (Tax Exempt and Government Entities), IRS. The proposed regulations, as well as the temporary and final regulations, have been developed in coordination with personnel from the U.S. Department of Labor and the U.S. Department of Health and Human Services.

[¶ 49,439] Proposed Amendments of Regulations, NPRM REG-101896-09, published in the Federal Register on December 17, 2009 (corrected 1/21/2010).

[Code Secs. 408, 1012, 3406, 6039, 6042, 6044, 6045, 6045A, 6045B, 6049, 6051, 6721 and 6722]

Information reporting: Return of brokers: Basis and other reporting obligations: Proposed regulations.—Amendments of Reg. §31.3406(b)(3)-2, relating to reporting sales of securities by brokers and determining the basis of securities, are proposed. Reg. §§1.6045A-1 and 1.6045B-1, and amendments of Reg. §§1.408-7, 1.1012-1, 1.6039-2, 1.6042-4, 1.6044-5, 1.6045-1, 1.6045-2, 1.6045-3, 1.6045-4, 1.6045-5, 1.6049-6, 31.6051-4, 301.6721-1 and 301.6722-1 were adopted by T.D. 9504 on October 12, 2010.

AGENCY: Internal Revenue Service (IRS), Treasury.

ACTION: Notice of proposed rulemaking and notice of public hearing.

SUMMARY: This document contains proposed regulations relating to reporting sales of securities by brokers and determining the basis of securities. The proposed regulations reflect changes in the law made by the Energy Improvement and Extension Act of 2008 that require brokers when reporting the sale of securities to the IRS to include the customer's adjusted basis in the sold securities and to classify any gain or loss as longterm or short-term. This document also contains proposed regulations reflecting changes in the law that alter how taxpayers compute basis when averaging the basis of shares acquired at different prices and that expand the ability of taxpayers to compute basis by averaging. The document also proposes regulations that provide brokers and others until February 15 to furnish certain information statements to customers. This document also contains proposed regulations that implement new reporting requirements imposed upon persons that transfer custody of stock and upon issuers of stock regarding organizational actions that affect the basis of the issued stock. This document also contains proposed regulations reflecting changes in the law that alter how brokers report short sales of securities. Finally, this document provides for a notice of a public hearing on these proposed regulations.

DATES: Written or electronic comments must be received by February 8, 2010. Outlines of topics to be discussed at the public hearing scheduled for February 17, 2010 must be received by February 8, 2010.

ADDRESSES: Send submissions to: CC:PA:LPD:PR (REG-101896-09), room 5203, Internal Revenue Service, PO Box 7604, Ben Franklin Station, Washington, DC 20044. Submissions may be hand-delivered Monday through Friday between the hours of 8 a.m. and 4 p.m. to CC:PA:LPD:PR (REG-101896-09), Courier's Desk, Internal Revenue Service, 1111 Constitution Avenue, NW., Washington, DC, or sent electronically via the Federal eRulemaking Portal at *www.regulations.gov* (IRS REG-101896-09). The public hearing will be held in the auditorium of the IRS New Carrollton Federal Building, 5000 Ellin Road, Lanham, Maryland 20706.

FOR FURTHER INFORMATION CONTACT: Concerning the proposed regulations under section 1012, Edward C. Schwartz of the Office of Associate Chief Counsel (Income Tax and Accounting) at (202) 622-4960; concerning the proposed regulations under sections 3406, 6045, 6045A, 6045B, 6721, and 6722, Stephen Schaeffer of the Office of Associate Chief Counsel (Procedure and Administration) at (202) 622-4910; concerning submissions of comments, the public hearing, and/or to be placed on the building access list to attend the public hearing, Funmi Taylor of the Office of Associate Chief Counsel (Procedure and Administration) at (202) 622-7180 (not toll-free numbers).

SUPPLEMENTARY INFORMATION:

Paperwork Reduction Act

The collection of information contained in this notice of proposed rulemaking related to the furnishing of information in connection with the transfer of securities has been submitted to the Office of Management and Budget in accordance with the Paperwork Reduction Act of 1995 (44 U.S.C. 3507(d)). Comments on the collection of information should be sent to the **Office of Management and Budget**, Attn: Desk Officer for the Department of the Treasury, Office of Information and Regulatory Affairs, Washington, DC 20503, with copies to the **Internal Revenue Service**, Attn: IRS Reports Clearance Officer, SE:W:CAR:MP:T:T:SP, Washington, DC 20224. Comments on the collection of information should be received by February 16, 2010. Comments are specifically requested concerning:

Whether the proposed collection of information is necessary for the proper performance of the functions of the IRS, including whether the information will have practical utility;

The accuracy of the estimated burden associated with the proposed collection of information;

How the quality, utility, and clarity of the information to be collected may be enhanced;

How the burden of complying with the proposed collection of information may be minimized, including through the application of automated collection techniques or other forms of information technology; and

Estimates of capital or start-up costs and costs of operation, maintenance, and purchase of services to provide information.

The collection of information in these proposed regulations in §§ 1.6045-1(c)(3)(xi)(C) and 1.6045A-1 concerning furnishing information in connection with a transfer of securities is necessary to allow brokers that effect sales of transferred covered securities to determine and report the adjusted basis of the securities and whether any gain or loss with respect to the securities is long-term or short-term in compliance with section 6045(g) of the Internal Revenue Code (Code). The collection of information is required to comply with the provisions of section 403 of the Energy Improvement and Extension Act of 2008, Division B of Public Law 110-343 (122 Stat. 3765, 3854 (2008)). The likely respondents are brokers of securities and issuers, transfer agents, and professional custodians of securities that do not effect sales.

Estimated total annual reporting burden: 240,000 hours.

Estimated average annual burden per respondent: 8 hours.

Estimated average burden per response: 4 minutes.

Estimated number of respondents: 30,000.

Estimated frequency of responses: 4,000,000.

The burden for the collection of information contained in proposed regulation § 1.6045-1 except for § 1.6045-1(c)(3)(xi)(C) will be reflected in the burden on Form 1099-B, "Proceeds from Broker and Barter Exchange Transactions," when revised to request the additional information in that proposed regulation. The burden for the collection of information contained in proposed regulation § 1.6045B-1 will be reflected in the burden on the form that the IRS will create to request the information in that proposed regulation.

An agency may not conduct or sponsor, and a person is not required to respond to, a collection of information unless it displays a valid control number assigned by the Office of Management and Budget.

Background

This document contains proposed amendments to the Income Tax Regulations (26 CFR part 1), the Regulations on Employment Tax and Collection of Income Tax at the Source (26 CFR part 31), and the Regulations on Procedure and Administration (26 CFR part 301) relating to information reporting by brokers and others as required by section 6045. The document also contains proposed amendments relating to the scope and computation of basis by the average basis method under section 1012 and to new information reporting requirements by brokers, custodians, and issuers of securities under sections 6045A and 6045B. These sections were amended or added by section 403 of the Energy Improvement and Extension Act of 2008, Division B of Public Law 110-343 (122 Stat. 3765, 3854 (2008)) (the Act). These proposed regulations are proposed to be issued under the authority contained in sections 1012, 3406, 6045, 6045A, 6045B, and 7805.

1. *Returns of Brokers*

Section 6045(g) provides that every broker that is required to file a return with the IRS under section 6045(a) showing the gross proceeds from the sale of a covered security must include in the return the customer's adjusted basis in the security and whether any gain or loss with respect to the security is long-term or short-term. Thus, a broker that is currently subject to gross proceeds reporting under section 6045(a) with respect to the sale of a covered security is also subject to the reporting of adjusted basis of that security and whether any gain or loss with respect to that security is long-term or short-term under section 6045(g).

Section 1.6045-1(a)(1) provides that the term *broker* generally means any U.S. or foreign person that, in the ordinary course of a trade or business, stands ready to effect sales to be made by others. However, with respect to a sale (including a redemption or retirement) effected at an office outside the United States, a broker includes only a person described as a U.S. payor or U.S. middleman in § 1.6049 5(c)(5). Additionally, under § 1.6045-1(g)(1), reporting is not required with respect to certain holders of securities that are exempt foreign persons. U.S. and foreign brokers that are subject to gross proceeds reporting under the existing rules will also be subject to reporting under the rules of section 6045(g).

a. *Covered security*

For purposes of reporting under section 6045(g), section 6045(g)(3)(A) provides that a covered security is any specified security acquired on or after the applicable date if the security: (1) was acquired through a transaction in the account in which the security was held; or (2) was transferred to that account from an account in which the security was a covered security, but only if the broker receiving custody of the security receives a statement under section 6045A (described later in this preamble) with respect to the transfer.

b. *Specified security*

Section 6045(g)(3)(B) provides that a specified security is any: (1) share of stock in a corporation; (2) note, bond, debenture, or other evidence of indebtedness; (3) commodity, or a contract or a derivative with respect to the commodity, if the Secretary determines that adjusted basis reporting is appropriate; and (4) other financial instrument with respect to which the Secretary determines that adjusted basis reporting is appropriate.

c. *Applicable date*

The applicable date of the reporting requirements under section 6045(g) depends on the type of specified security that is sold. For stock in or of a corporation (other than stock in a regulated investment company (RIC) or stock acquired in connection with a dividend reinvestment plan (DRP)), section 6045(g)(3)(C)(i) provides that the applicable date is January 1, 2011. For stock in a RIC (RIC stock) or stock acquired in connection with a DRP (DRP stock) (for which additional rules are described later in this preamble), section 6045(g)(3)(C)(ii) provides that the applicable date is January 1, 2012. For any other specified security, section 6045(g)(3)(C)(iii) provides that the applicable date is January 1, 2013, or a later date determined by the Secretary. The reporting rules related to options transactions apply only to options granted or acquired on or after January 1, 2013, as provided in section 6045(h)(3).

d. *Reporting method*

A broker must report a customer's adjusted basis under the following statutory rules. Under section 6045(g)(2)(B)(i)(I), a broker must report the adjusted basis of any security (other than RIC stock or DRP stock) using the first-in, first-out (FIFO) basis determination method unless the customer notifies the broker of the specific stock to be sold or transferred by means of making an adequate identification of the stock sold or transferred at the time of sale or transfer. Under section 6045(g)(2)(B)(i)(II), a broker must report the adjusted basis of RIC stock or DRP stock in accordance with the broker's default method under section 1012 unless the customer notifies the broker that the customer elects another permitted method.

2. *Determination of Basis*

a. *In general*

For any sale, exchange, or other disposition of a specified security on or after the applicable date, section 1012(c) provides that the conventions prescribed by regulations under section 1012 for determining adjusted basis apply on an account by account basis.

b. *RIC stock*

Section 1012(c)(2) provides that RIC stock acquired before January 1, 2012, is treated as held in a separate account from RIC stock acquired on or after that date. However, a RIC may elect (at the time and in the form and manner prescribed by the Secretary), on a stockholder by stockholder basis, to treat all stock in the RIC held by the stockholder as one account without regard to when the stock was acquired (single-account election). When this election applies, the average basis of a customer's stock is computed by averaging the basis of shares of identical stock acquired before, on, and after January 1, 2012, and all the shares are treated as covered securities. If a broker holds RIC stock as a nominee of the beneficial owner of the shares, the broker makes the election.

c. *DRP stock*

If stock is acquired on or after January 1, 2011, in connection with a DRP, section 1012(d)(1) provides that the basis of that stock is determined under one of the basis computation methods permissible for RIC stock. Accordingly, the average basis method may be used for determining the basis of DRP stock. This special rule for DRP stock, however, applies only while the stock is held as part of the DRP. If the stock is transferred to another account, under section 1012(d)(2), each share of stock has a cost basis in that other account equal to its basis in the DRP immediately before the transfer (with adjustment for charges connected with the transfer).

Section 1012(d)(4)(A) provides that a DRP is any arrangement under which dividends on stock are reinvested in stock identical to the stock on which the dividends are paid. Stock is treated as acquired in connection with a DRP if the stock is acquired pursuant to the DRP or if the dividends paid on the stock are subject to the DRP. Under section 1012(d)(3), in determining basis under this rule, the account by account rules of section 1012(c), including the single-account election available to RICs, apply.

3. *Other Broker Reporting Provisions*

a. *Wash sales*

Section 6045(g)(2)(B)(ii) provides that, unless the Secretary provides otherwise, a customer's adjusted basis in a covered security generally is determined for reporting purposes without taking into account the effect on basis of the wash sale rules of section 1091 unless the purchase and sale transactions resulting in a wash sale occur in the same account and are in identical securities (rather than substantially identical securities as required by section 1091).

b. *S corporations*

Section 6045(g)(4) provides that, for purposes of section 6045, an S corporation (other than a financial institution) is treated in the same manner as a partnership. This rule applies to any sale of a covered security acquired by an S corporation (other than a financial institution) after December 31, 2011. When this rule takes effect, brokers generally will be required to report gross proceeds and basis information to customers that are S corporations for securities purchased on or after January 1, 2012.

c. *Short sales*

In the case of a short sale, section 6045(g)(5) provides that gross proceeds and basis reporting under section 6045 generally is required for the year in which the short sale is closed (rather than, as under the present rule for gross proceeds reporting, the year in which the short sale is entered into).

d. *Options*

Section 6045(h)(1) provides that if a covered security is acquired or disposed of pursuant to the exercise of an option that was granted or acquired in the same account as the covered security, the amount received with respect to the grant or paid with respect to the acquisition of such option must be treated for reporting purposes as an adjustment to gross proceeds or as an adjustment to basis, as the case may be. Section 6045(h)(2) provides that gross proceeds and basis reporting is required when there is a lapse of, or a closing transaction with respect to, an option on a specified security or an exercise of a cash-settled option on a specified security. Section 6045(h)(3) provides that section 6045(h)(1) and (h)(2) do not apply to any option granted or acquired before January 1, 2013.

e. Time for furnishing statements

The Act amended section 6045(b) to extend the due date from January 31 to February 15 for furnishing certain information statements to customers, effective for statements required to be furnished after December 31, 2008. Section 6045(b) provides that the statements to which the new February 15 due date applies are statements required under section 6045 and statements with respect to other reportable items that are furnished with these statements in a consolidated reporting statement (as defined in regulations under section 6045). See Notice 2009-11 (2009-5 IRB 420), providing that, with respect to reportable items from calendar year 2008, brokers had until February 17, 2009, to report all items that they customarily reported on their annual composite form recipient statements. See § 601.601(d)(2).

4. Transfer Statements

The Act added section 6045A, which provides that a broker and any other person specified in Treasury regulations (applicable person) that transfers to a broker a security that is a covered security in the hands of the transferring person must furnish to the broker receiving custody of the security (receiving broker) a written statement that allows the receiving broker to satisfy the basis reporting requirements of section 6045(g). Section 6045A(c) provides that, unless the Secretary provides otherwise, the statement required by this rule must be furnished to the receiving broker not later than fifteen days after the transfer of the covered security.

5. Issuer Reporting

The Act added section 6045B, which provides that an issuer of specified securities must file a return according to forms or regulations prescribed by the Secretary describing any organizational action (such as a stock split, merger, or acquisition) that affects the basis of the specified security, the quantitative effect on the basis of that specified security, and any other information the Secretary requires. Section 6045B(b) provides that this return must be filed within forty-five days after the date of the organizational action, unless the action occurs in December, in which case the return must be filed by January 15th of the following year.

Section 6045B(c) provides that an issuer must furnish, according to forms or regulations prescribed by the Secretary, to each nominee with respect to that security (or to each certificate holder if there is no nominee) a written statement showing: (1) the name, address, and telephone number of the information contact of the person required to file the return; (2) the information required to be included on the return with respect to the security; and (3) any other information required by the Secretary. This statement must be furnished to the nominee or certificate holder on or before January 15th of the year following the calendar year in which the organizational action took place.

Section 6045B(e) provides that the Secretary may waive the return filing and information statement requirements if the person to which the requirements apply makes publicly available, in the form and manner determined by the Secretary, the name, address, telephone number, and e-mail address of the information contact of that person, and the information about the organizational action and its effect on basis otherwise required to be included in the return.

6. Penalties

The Act amended the list of returns and statements in section 6724(d) for which sections 6721 and 6722 impose penalties for any failure to file or furnish complete and correct returns and statements. This section imposes a penalty on brokers for a failure to file returns or furnish complete and correct statements after a sale of securities as required by section 6045. Section 6724(d) now also imposes penalties with respect to the returns and statements required by sections 6045A and 6045B.

7. Request for Comments

Notice 2009-17 (2009-8 IRB 575), published by the IRS on February 23, 2009, invited public comments regarding guidance under the new reporting requirements in sections 6045, 6045A, and 6045B and for determining the basis of certain securities under section 1012. In particular, Notice 2009-17 requested comments on the applicability of the reporting requirements, basis method elections, DRPs, reconciliation with customer reporting, special rules and mechanical issues, transfer reporting, issuer reporting, and broker practices and procedures. Many comments were received in response to Notice 2009-17. The comments were considered in developing the proposed regulations. See § 601.601(d)(2).

Explanation of the Provisions and Summary of Comments

The proposed regulations provide rules for determining basis and for reporting adjusted basis and whether any gain or loss on a sale is long-term or short-term. The proposed regulations also address the new reporting requirements imposed upon persons transferring custody of stock and upon issuers of stock.

The proposed regulations do not address rules regarding reporting for options, compensatory options, or other equity-based compensation arrangements, or reporting of adjusted basis for indebtedness, because indebtedness is only subject to the requirements of section 6045(g) if acquired on or after January 1, 2013, and options are only subject to the requirements of section 6045(g) and (h) if granted or acquired on or after January 1, 2013. These rules are expected to be addressed in future guidance.

The proposed regulations generally are limited to the amendments to the Internal Revenue Code (Code) under the Act in sections 1012, 6045, 6045A, 6045B, and 6724 and do not address requests from commentators regarding changes to substantive rules in other areas such as the rules regarding allocation of a return of capital. The proposed regulations also do not address technical issues related to information reporting such as electronic delivery of returns by brokers to customers. These comments are outside the scope of the proposed regulations.

1. Returns of Brokers

Section 1.6045-1(c) requires brokers to make a return of information with respect to each sale by a customer of the broker effected by the broker in the ordinary course of a trade or business in which the broker stands ready to effect sales to be made by others. Section 1.6045-1(d) sets forth the information that the broker must include on the return.

The proposed regulations amend the definition of *broker* in § 1.6045-1(a)(1) to modify the exception for non-U.S. payors and non-U.S. middlemen. Under the revised rule, a non-U.S. payor or non-U.S. middleman would be a broker to the extent provided in a withholding agreement described in § 1.1441-1(e)(5)(iii) between a qualified intermediary and the IRS or similar agreement with the IRS. The Treasury Department and IRS expect that such agreements generally will provide that the broker that is party to such agreement will be subject to the broker reporting requirements under section 6045 to the same extent as U.S. payors and U.S. middlemen. The Treasury Department and IRS request comments regarding the usefulness of information received from non-U.S. payors and non-U.S. middlemen, the costs to non-U.S. payors and non-U.S. middlemen of complying with such a requirement, and other potential effects of such a requirement in a withholding or reporting agreement with the IRS.

a. *Form and manner of new broker reporting requirements*

The proposed regulations provide that brokers must report adjusted basis and whether any gain or loss with respect to the security is long-term or short-term on Form 1099-B, "Proceeds from Broker and Barter Exchange Transactions," or any successor form under section 6045(a) when reporting the sale of a covered security. They clarify that the basis reported by a broker is the total amount paid by a customer or credited against a customer's account as a result of the acquisition of securities adjusted for commissions and the effects of other transactions occurring within the account. The proposed regulations also require brokers to adjust the basis they report to take into account the information received on a transfer statement in connection with the transfer of a covered security (including transfers from a decedent and gift transfers) as well as information received from issuers of stock about the quantitative effect on basis from corporate actions. The proposed regulations generally do not require a broker to adjust the reported basis for transactions, elections, or events occurring outside the account. For example, with respect to wash sales (discussed in more detail later in this preamble), the proposed regulations require that a broker adjust the reported basis in accordance with section 1091 if both the purchase and sale transactions occur with respect to identical securities in the same account.

Commentators suggested that brokers be required to report certain warnings or indicators to a customer about potential discrepancies between the broker-reported basis and the basis the customer must report on the customer's income tax return. For example, commentators suggested that a flag be added to the information return that would alert a customer that a foreign issuer may not have reported to the broker all issuer actions affecting basis. The proposed regulations do not adopt these suggestions but, as discussed with respect to wash sales later in this preamble, require a broker to report to customers engaging in wash sales the amount of any disallowed loss. Brokers may communicate additional information on other statements furnished to customers if desired. The Treasury Department and IRS request further comments regarding whether additional information items should be required on the information return. A draft of the 2011 Form 1099-B is available for viewing and comment on the IRS web site at *http://www.irs.gov/pub/irs-dft/f1099b--dft.pdf*.

For a sale of securities that were acquired on different dates or at different prices, some commentators requested that brokers be permitted to report the sale on a single information return. Other commentators asked that the proposed regulations require separate reporting of the sale of securities acquired on different dates or at different prices. The proposed regulations generally maintain the current requirement that brokers report a sale of securities within an account on one return, even if the sale involves multiple acquisitions, to limit the number of separate returns filed with the IRS and statements furnished to customers. However, because brokers must report whether any gain or loss on the sale of a covered security is short-term or long-term, and because noncovered securities must be reported separately from covered securities to avoid treatment as covered securities, a single sale in an account could necessitate as many as three returns if the sale included covered securities held more than a year, covered securities held one year or less, and noncovered securities.

b. *Scope of covered securities and treatment of noncovered securities*

The proposed regulations clarify that a broker is not required to report adjusted basis and whether any gain or loss on a sale is long-term or short-term for securities that are excepted from all reporting under section 6045 at the time of their acquisition. For example, the new basis reporting requirements do not apply to a security purchased by an organization that is tax-exempt even if the organization later loses its tax-exempt status and becomes subject to gross proceeds reporting on the sale of securities under section 6045(a).

With respect to a security transferred into an account in a non-sale transaction, the security is a covered security under the proposed regulations if it was a covered security prior to transfer and the broker receives the statement required under section 6045A for the transfer (the transfer statement, discussed in more detail later in this preamble) indicating that the security is a covered security. Conversely, a security is a noncovered security if the broker receives a transfer statement indicating that the security is a noncovered security. A transferred security will be presumed to be a covered security unless the transfer statement expressly states that the security is a noncovered security.

If the receiving broker does not receive a transfer statement or receives a transfer statement that does not contain all of the required information, the proposed regulations permit the broker to treat the security as a noncovered security if, as suggested by commentators, the broker notifies the person that effected the transfer and requests a complete statement, and no complete statement is provided in response to this request before the broker reports the sale or subsequent transfer of the security. The proposed regulations do not require brokers to make this request more than once.

If a broker receives the information required on the transfer statement after reporting the sale of the security, the proposed regulations require the broker to file a corrected Form 1099-B if the reporting was incorrect or incomplete. Similarly, if an issuer furnishes the return required by section 6045B concerning corporate organizational actions (the issuer statement, discussed in more detail later in this preamble) after the broker has reported the sale of the security, the proposed regulations require the broker to file a corrected Form 1099-B to report any adjustments to basis not reflected previously. Commentators requested that corrected reporting not be required for de minimis adjustments or for statements furnished beyond a specific period after the close of the calendar year. The proposed regulations do not adopt either suggestion. The Treasury Department and IRS request further comments regarding corrected reporting.

Commentators expressed concern regarding the difficulty, in some cases, of determining whether a security is stock (for which basis must be reported for acquisitions beginning in January 2011 or January 2012) or indebtedness or another financial instrument (for which basis does not need to be reported for acquisitions in 2011 or 2012). Some commentators suggested that the proposed regulations classify each security or require issuers to file a classification report with the IRS to permit the IRS to publish a report identifying each security. The proposed regulations do not adopt this approach. Instead, the proposed regulations provide that, solely for purposes of determining the applicable date for basis reporting, any security an issuer classifies as stock is treated as stock. If no issuer classification has been made, the security is not treated as stock unless the broker knows, or has reason to know, that the security is reasonably classified as stock under general tax principles.

Some commentators expressed a desire to report adjusted basis and whether any gain or loss on a sale is long-term or short-term for noncovered securities. Other commentators requested that the regulations prohibit such reporting on Form 1099-B and permit reporting only of adjusted basis and whether any gain or loss on a sale is long-term or short-term to the customer on statements not filed with the IRS. In order to encourage more reporting of information and simplify reporting by taxpayers on their income tax returns, the proposed regulations allow brokers the option of reporting adjusted basis and whether any gain or loss on a sale is long-term or short-term for noncovered securities on a security by security basis. Therefore, a broker may choose to report this information for any given noncovered security. The proposed regulations also provide that a broker that chooses to report this information with respect to a noncovered security is not subject to penalties under section 6721 or 6722 for any failure to report such information correctly, provided that the broker indicates on Form 1099-B that the sale reported is a sale of a noncovered security. The instructions to the tax return will inform taxpayers of their duty to verify the information reported by brokers and to adjust the reported information when necessary to reflect the taxpayer's correct information. This duty applies equally to covered and noncovered securities.

c. *Determination of basis required to be reported*

Section 6045(g)(2)(B)(i)(I) provides that, except for RIC stock or DRP stock, a broker must report using the FIFO basis determination method unless the customer notifies the broker of the specific security to be sold or transferred by means of making an adequate identification of the security sold or transferred at the time of sale or transfer. With respect to RIC stock or DRP stock, section 6045(g)(2)(B)(i)(II) provides that a broker must report adjusted basis in accordance with the broker's default method under section 1012 unless the customer notifies the broker that the customer elects another permitted method.

The proposed regulations clarify that, when a customer sells less than the entire position of a security in an account, the selling broker must follow the customer's instruction, if any, adequately identifying the security sold or, when applicable, requesting that average basis be used to compute the basis of eligible stock. Thus, under the proposed regulations, a broker must report basis using any permitted lot identification and basis determination method the customer chooses when the customer provides a valid instruction (discussed in more detail later in this preamble). Absent a valid instruction from the customer, the proposed regulations clarify that a broker must report basis of a security (other than stock eligible for averaging) using the FIFO basis determination method when reporting the sale. The proposed regulations also clarify that, absent a valid instruction to use another method, a broker must report basis for stock eligible for averaging using the broker's default basis determination method.

Commentators requested that brokers and customers be permitted to report basis by different methods and that brokers be permitted to report basis for all sales using only one of the permitted basis determination methods, for example, the average basis method. The proposed regulations do not adopt these requests because section 1012 permits customers to report basis by a different permissible method than the default method selected by the broker and section 6045 requires brokers to follow instructions from customers regarding this selection. The requested rules are inconsistent with the goal of conforming broker reporting with taxpayer basis determination method elections to facilitate and promote compliance in taxpayer reporting of income.

2. *Average Basis Method*

Section 1.1012-1(e) provides rules for computing the basis of RIC stock by averaging the cost of all shares in the account (the average basis method). Taxpayers may elect to use the average basis method for RIC stock acquired at different prices and maintained by a custodian or agent in an account for the periodic acquisition, redemption, sale, or other disposition of the stock.

Consistent with section 1012(d)(1), the proposed regulations extend the average basis method to shares of stock acquired after December 31, 2010, in connection with a DRP, and clarify that shares are eligible for averaging only if they are identical.

Commentators suggested that stock should be eligible for averaging together if it has the same Committee on Uniform Security Identification Procedures (CUSIP) number. The proposed regulations adopt this suggestion and define *identical shares of stock* as stock with the same CUSIP number (or other security identifier number as permitted in additional guidance of general applicability, see § 601.601(d)(2)). However, for purposes of defining a DRP, the proposed regulations provide that the stock of a successor entity or entities that result from certain corporate actions such as mergers, consolidations, split-offs, or spinoffs, is identical to the stock of the predecessor entity. Thus, corporate actions will not cause stock acquired in connection with a DRP to become ineligible for averaging because, for example, a dividend declared before the action and paid after the action is completed is not reinvested in stock with the same CUSIP number. The proposed regulations further provide, however, that shares of stock acquired in connection with a DRP are not identical to shares of stock with the same CUSIP number that are not acquired in connection with a DRP.

3. *Broker's Default Basis Determination Method*

Consistent with section 6045(g)(2)(B)(i)(II), the proposed regulations provide that the basis of RIC stock and DRP stock is determined in accordance with a broker's default method, unless a taxpayer elects another permitted method.

a. *Consistency in use of average basis method*

Commentators suggested that the proposed regulations should not require brokers to compute basis for a DRP using the average basis method for taxpayers electing this method. The proposed regulations do not adopt this recommendation because it is inconsistent with the statutory requirement that the average basis method be available to any taxpayer that desires to use it for a DRP, as well as with the goal of conforming broker reporting with taxpayer basis determination method elections to facilitate and promote compliance in taxpayer reporting of income. The proposed regulations specify that a broker must compute basis using the basis determination method the taxpayer elects. The proposed regulations also provide that the taxpayer must report gain or loss on its return using the method the taxpayer elects or, if the taxpayer fails to make an election, the broker's default method.

b. *Default method*

Commentators suggested that a broker should be allowed to determine a default basis determination method when a taxpayer fails to elect a method for determining the basis of RIC stock or DRP stock. Consistent with section 6045(g)(2)(B)(i)(II), the proposed regulations do not prescribe a broker default method, which each broker may determine.

c. *Communicating default method to taxpayers*

A commentator suggested that the proposed regulations should require that a broker notify a taxpayer of the broker's default method by the earlier of opening a new account or January 1 of the year the average basis method election is effective. Other commentators suggested, however, that the proposed regulations should not specify how brokers communicate their default basis determination method to taxpayers. The proposed regulations do not require a specific method or time for this communication.

4. *Definition of Dividend Reinvestment Plan*

a. *Issuer and non-issuer plans*

A commentator requested that the proposed regulations broadly define *dividend reinvestment plan* to include both broker administered plans and issuer, or corporate, administered plans. Other commentators suggested, however, that if brokers are required to use the average basis method, the definition should include only issueradministered plans. The proposed regulations define dividend reinvestment plan to include a written arrangement, plan, or program administered by an issuer or non-issuer of stock. Neither the statute nor the legislative history indicates any Congressional intent to limit the average basis method to issuer-administered plans.

b. *Reinvestment of dividends*

A commentator suggested that a plan requiring reinvestment of only a portion of the dividends paid should qualify as a DRP under the proposed regulations. The proposed regulations provide that a plan qualifies as a DRP if the plan documents require that at least 10 percent of any dividend paid be reinvested in identical stock. Assuming this 10 percent requirement is met, a plan may reinvest different percentages of dividends in different stocks.

A commentator opined that a plan should not be considered a DRP if the stock is not paying dividends when the issuer offers the plan. Another commentator verbally stated that the proposed regulations should provide that a plan may qualify as a DRP even if the stock has never issued dividends or ceases to pay dividends. This commentator noted that the stock of a start-up company may be included in a DRP in the expectation of paying dividends in the future, and that a company that traditionally pays dividends may be required to temporarily suspend dividends, for example in the case of bankruptcy reorganization. The proposed regulations provide that a stock may be held in a DRP even if no dividends have ever been declared or paid or the issuer has ceased paying dividends.

A commentator suggested that the term *dividends* should include all income from stock for purposes of a DRP. The proposed regulations do not define dividends. Specific comments are requested on whether and how the regulations should define dividends, such as whether the regulations should define the term by reference to section 316, or more broadly to include any payment or distribution from stock, including ordinary dividends, capital gains dividends or distributions, non-taxable returns of capital, and cash dividends in lieu of fractional shares. Comments may address industry practices that relate to this definition.

c. Acquired in connection with a DRP

Commentators suggested that subsequent additions to a DRP, such as purchases or transfers of stock, be eligible for the average basis method. A commentator recommended that subsequent additions be separated into separate averaging pools. Another commentator suggested that a single averaging pool should be allowed for all post-effective date identical stock. One commentator stated that brokers have difficulty distinguishing non-DRP purchases of stock from purchases of stock with the same CUSIP number in a DRP, and therefore brokers should be allowed to apply the same basis determination method to all stock with the same CUSIP number in an account.

Consistent with section 1012(d)(4), the proposed regulations provide that stock is acquired in connection with a DRP if the stock is acquired under the DRP or the dividends paid are subject to the DRP. Stock acquired in connection with a DRP includes the initial purchase of stock in the DRP, subsequent transfers of identical stock into the DRP, additional periodic purchases of identical stock through the DRP, and all identical stock acquired through reinvestment of dividends paid under the DRP.

d. Withdrawal from or termination of a DRP

A commentator asked about the consequences if a DRP is terminated or a taxpayer transfers shares from a DRP at one broker to a broker that does not offer a DRP. The proposed regulations provide that, if a taxpayer withdraws from a DRP or the plan administrator terminates the DRP, shares of identical stock acquired after the withdrawal or termination are not acquired in connection with a DRP. After the withdrawal or termination, the taxpayer may no longer use the average basis method for the stock, but the basis of each share of stock immediately after the change is the same as the basis immediately before the change.

5. Computing Average Basis

a. Elimination of double-category method

Under § 1.1012-1(e)(3) and (4), taxpayers compute average basis using either a double-category method, which divides stock by holding period and averages long-term shares separately from short-term shares, or a single-category method, which averages all shares together regardless of holding period.

Commentators suggested that the proposed regulations eliminate the doublecategory method and noted that it is not widely used. One commentator stated that problems may occur when shares are transferred between accounts that use different methods. The proposed regulations adopt this suggestion and eliminate the doublecategory method. The proposed regulations provide that average basis is computed by averaging the basis of all identical stock in an account regardless of holding period and include a transition rule that requires taxpayers using the double-category method to average the basis of all identical stock in an account on the date of publication of final regulations. Specific comments are requested on whether the double-category method should be retained.

Section 1.1012-1(e)(4)(iii) provides that the single-category method may not be used if it appears that the taxpayer's purpose is to convert long-term gain or loss into short-term gain or loss, or vice versa. Consistent with the elimination of the doublecategory method, the proposed regulations remove this provision. The proposed regulations include ordering rules that specify that the holding period of stock to which the average basis method applies is determined on a FIFO basis.

b. Wash sales

Section 1.1012-1(e)(4)(iv) provides that section 1091(d) and the associated regulations apply to wash sales of stock from an account using the single-category method of computing average basis. Commentators suggested that brokers should not be required to apply these rules to stock held in separate accounts.

Section 6045(g)(2)(B)(ii) provides that, for purposes of reporting, brokers must apply the wash sale rules only to acquisition and sale transactions in the same account and for identical securities. The rules for brokers are discussed later in this preamble.

For a taxpayer using the average basis method, the proposed regulations provide that the taxpayer must apply section 1091 and the associated regulations (dealing with wash sales of substantially identical securities) in computing average basis regardless of whether the stock or security sold or otherwise disposed of and the stock acquired are in the same account or in different accounts.

c. Basis after change from average basis method

The proposed regulations provide that, except for a revocation of the average basis method election (discussed later in this preamble), if a taxpayer changes from the average basis method to another basis determination method for any reason, the basis of each share of stock immediately after the change is the same as the basis immediately before the change.

6. Time and Manner of Making the Average Basis Method Election

Section 1.1012-1(e)(6) provides that a taxpayer elects to use the average basis method on an income tax return for the first taxable year the taxpayer wants the election to apply.

a. Manner of making the average basis method election

Under the proposed regulations, a taxpayer elects the average basis method for covered securities by notifying the custodian or other agent for the taxpayer's account in writing. The taxpayer makes a separate election for each account holding stock for which the average basis method is permissible. A taxpayer uses the procedures under the current regulations to elect the average basis method for noncovered securities.

Commentators requested that the proposed regulations provide guidance on how taxpayers must inform brokers of their basis determination method. Commentators suggested that brokers may obtain this information through documents provided to a taxpayer opening an account and urged that the rules be flexible and allow electronic communication. The proposed regulations require that a taxpayer must notify a custodian or agent in writing of an average basis method election, but otherwise do not specify how a taxpayer must communicate a basis determination method.

b. *Time for making the average basis method election*

Some commentators suggested that taxpayers should be allowed or required to choose a basis determination method when opening an account or when acquiring stock for which the average basis method is permitted. Other commentators stated that taxpayers should choose a method by the date of a sale. The proposed regulations provide that taxpayers may elect the average basis method at any time, effective for sales after the date of the election.

c. *Revocation of average basis method election*

A commentator asked for clarification on how long brokers must retain basis information. Another commentator suggested that any revocation period should end by the earlier of the date of first sale, the end of the calendar year, or one year from the first purchase of stock.

In order to minimize broker recordkeeping requirements, the proposed regulations provide that a taxpayer may revoke the average basis method election by the earlier of one year from the date of making the election or the first sale or other disposition of the stock following the election. A broker may extend the one-year period but no longer than the first sale. A revocation applies to all identical stock in an account and is effective when the taxpayer notifies the broker or other custodian of the revocation. If a taxpayer revokes the election, the basis of each share of stock in the account is determined using another permissible method.

d. *Change from average basis method*

Section 1.1012-1(e)(6)(ii) provides that a taxpayer that elects to use the average basis method may not revoke the election without the consent of the Commissioner. Under Rev. Proc. 2008-52 (2008-36 IRB 587), Section 30 of the Appendix, a taxpayer within the scope of Rev. Proc. 2008-52 uses the automatic consent procedures to change to the basis determination method described in § 1.1012-1(c)(1) (FIFO or specific identification, discussed later in this preamble). The revenue procedure provides that the automatic consent procedures do not apply to RIC stock or to a change from FIFO to specific identification or vice versa, which is not a change in method of accounting. See § 601.601(d)(2).

A commentator recommended that taxpayers should not be able to change from the average basis method except by opening a new account. Other commentators opined that taxpayers should have broad discretion to change from the average basis method. Several commentators suggested that brokers should not be required to recreate a stock's original basis if a taxpayer changes from the average basis method.

The proposed regulations provide that a taxpayer may change from the average basis method to another permissible method at any time. A taxpayer's change in basis determination method applies to stock acquired on or after January 1, 2012, in a different manner than to stock acquired before January 1, 2012. Consistent with the account by account rules, discussed later in this preamble, a change in basis determination method applies to identical stock a taxpayer acquires on or after January 1, 2012, that the taxpayer holds in the same account. By contrast, a taxpayer's change in basis determination method applies to all identical stock the taxpayer acquires before January 1, 2012, that the taxpayer holds in any account. Unless the taxpayer revokes the average basis method election, discussed earlier in this preamble, the taxpayer must change from the average basis method prospectively. Thus, the basis of each share of stock to which the change applies is the basis immediately before the change.

A commentator requested clarification on how often a taxpayer may change a basis method election. Commentators suggested that changes should be limited, for example to once per year. The proposed regulations do not limit the number of times or frequency a taxpayer may change basis determination methods.

A commentator suggested that the proposed regulations should require taxpayers to obtain the Commissioner's permission to change basis determination methods. Another commentator recommended that taxpayers be allowed to change from the average basis method without the Commissioner's permission. The proposed regulations clarify that a change in basis determination method is a change in method of accounting to which the provisions of sections 446 and 481 and the associated regulations apply. A taxpayer may change its basis determination method by obtaining the consent of the Commissioner under applicable administrative procedures. The IRS may publish additional guidance of general applicability, see § 601.601(d)(2), that provides broad consent for taxpayers to change basis determination methods.

7. *Applying Average Basis Method Account by Account*

Section 1.1012-1(e)(2) provides that a taxpayer must use the same basis determination method for all of the taxpayer's accounts in the same RIC. Section 1.1012-1(e)(6)(ii) provides that a taxpayer must apply an average basis method election to all shares (except certain gift shares) of a particular RIC that the taxpayer holds in any account.

a. *Definition of account*

Commentators requested that the proposed regulations define the term "account." Commentators noted that each fund of a RIC is treated as a single account, while a broker may hold other securities with different CUSIP numbers in a single account. Commentators suggested that accounts should be treated as separate accounts if they have different account numbers, and that subaccounts such as cash and margin accounts should not be treated as separate accounts.

The proposed regulations do not define the term account. Instead, the proposed regulations provide rules prescribing when stock must be treated as held in separate accounts and the result of that treatment.

b. *Basis determination methods applied account by account*

Commentators suggested that the proposed regulations allow a taxpayer to make separate basis calculations for the same stock held in two separate accounts, even if held by the same broker. The proposed regulations adopt this suggestion. Consistent with section 1012(c), the proposed regulations provide that the average basis method election applies to all identical RIC stock or DRP stock in an account. For sales or other dispositions of stock after 2011, a taxpayer may use different basis determination methods for identical stock held in two separate accounts, even if held by the same broker. A taxpayer also may use different basis determination methods for shares of stock held in the same account that are not identical.

For sales or other dispositions before 2012 of RIC stock or DRP stock for which a taxpayer has used the average basis method, the proposed regulations retain the rules requiring that the taxpayer use the average basis method for identical stock held in separate accounts. However, a taxpayer may use different basis determination methods for shares of stock held in the same account that are not identical.

c. *Separate accounts*

Consistent with section 1012(c)(2)(A), the proposed regulations provide that, absent a single-account election (explained later in this preamble), RIC stock or DRP stock that a taxpayer acquires before January 1, 2012, is treated as held in a separate account from any stock acquired on or after that date. The proposed regulations further provide that any stock that is a covered security (within the meaning of section 6045(g)(3)) is treated as held in a separate account from any stock that is a noncovered security regardless of when acquired, as is consistent with Congressional intent. The proposed regulations include an example in which a security acquired on or after January 1, 2012, is a noncovered security.

8. Single-account Election

Section 1012(c)(2) provides that, with respect to RIC stock, a RIC may elect (at the time and in the form and manner prescribed by the Secretary), on a stockholder by stockholder basis, to treat all stock in the RIC held by the stockholder as one account without regard to when the stock was acquired (single-account election). Section 1012(d)(3) provides that the account by account rules of section 1012(c), including the single-account election available to RICs, also apply to DRP stock.

a. Application and scope of election

The proposed regulations provide that a RIC or DRP may make a single-account election to treat identical RIC stock or identical DRP stock held in separate accounts for which the taxpayer has elected to use the average basis method as held in a single account. If a broker holds the stock as a nominee, the broker, and not the RIC or DRP, makes the election. The single-account election is irrevocable. Commentators opined that a single-account election should not encompass stock a taxpayer acquires before January 1, 2012, if the basis information is unreliable. A commentator requested that the proposed regulations include a standard of reliability or, alternatively, allow brokers to exclude stock for which reliable basis information is not available from the singleaccount election. Another commentator requested penalty relief if reliable basis information is not available for pre-effective date shares.

The proposed regulations provide that a RIC, DRP, or broker may make a singleaccount election only for stock for which it has accurate basis information. A RIC, DRP, or broker has accurate basis information if the RIC, DRP, or broker neither knows nor has reason to know that the basis information is inaccurate. See also section 6724 and the regulations thereunder regarding standards for relief from information reporting penalties. Stock for which accurate basis information is unavailable may not be included in the single-account election and must be treated as held in a separate account.

The proposed regulations provide that, once the single-account election is made, it applies to all identical stock that is a covered security a taxpayer later acquires in an account. If a taxpayer acquires identical stock that is a noncovered security in an account, a RIC, DRP, or broker may make another single-account election if the RIC, DRP, or broker has accurate basis information. In addition to allowing a RIC, DRP, or broker to make a single-account election for some taxpayers and not others, consistent with section 1012(c)(2)(B), the proposed regulations allow a RIC, DRP, or broker to make the election for some identical stocks held for a taxpayer and not for other stocks.

b. Time and manner for making the single-account election

The proposed regulations provide that a RIC, DRP, or broker makes the singleaccount election by clearly noting it on its books and records. The books and records must reflect the date of the election; the taxpayer's name, account number, and taxpayer identification number; the stock subject to the election; and the taxpayer's basis in the stock. The books and records reflecting the election must be provided to the taxpayer upon request. The proposed regulations provide that the single-account election may be made at any time and more than once for a specific stock.

The proposed regulations require a RIC, DRP, or broker to use reasonable means to notify a taxpayer of a single-account election. Reasonable means include mailings, circulars, and electronic mail. The notification may be sent separately to the taxpayer or included with the taxpayer's account statement, or by other means calculated to provide actual notice. The notice must identify the securities subject to the election and advise the taxpayer that the stock will be treated as covered securities without regard to the date acquired.

9. FIFO and Specific Identification Methods

Section 1.1012-1(c)(1) provides that if a taxpayer acquires shares of stock on different dates or at different prices and sells or transfers some of those shares, and does not adequately identify the lot from which the shares are sold or transferred, the shares deemed sold or transferred are the earliest acquired shares (the FIFO rule). If a taxpayer makes an adequate identification of the shares sold under §1.1012-1(c)(2), (3), or (4), the shares treated as sold are the shares the taxpayer identified.

a. FIFO rule

A commentator verbally requested that the proposed regulations clarify how the FIFO rule of §1.1012-1(c)(1) applies to stock splits. The commentator asked whether shares acquired from the split are treated as acquired on the date of the purchase of the original shares or on the date of the split. In general, the shares that are first acquired are the shares with the longest holding period. Therefore, this question is addressed by rules under sections 307 and 1223 and the associated regulations and is outside the scope of these regulations.

A commentator requested clarification on whether the FIFO rule applies to stock that is part of a stock certificate that includes multiple lots. In response to this comment, the proposed regulations clarify that the FIFO rule also applies to multiple lots represented by a single stock certificate.

b. Timing of lot selection

Commentators suggested that taxpayers that wish to identify a specific lot of stock to be sold should be required to do so at the time of trade. Some commentators recommended that taxpayers should be allowed to wait to identify stock until the settlement date or until the end of the year. Other commentators opined that post-sale changes to specific identification of stock should not be allowed.

Rev. Rul. 67-436 (1967-2 CB 266) holds that an identification of stock by the time of delivery, which was within four days of the sale date, complied with the requirement to identify stock at the time of the sale or transfer. Consistent with Rev. Rul. 67-436, the proposed regulations provide that a taxpayer makes an adequate identification of stock at the time of sale, transfer, delivery, or distribution if the taxpayer identifies the stock no later than the earlier of the settlement date or the time for settlement under Securities and Exchange Commission regulations. Rev. Rul. 67-436 will be obsoleted when these regulations are published as final regulations. See §601.601(d)(2).

c. Standing lot selection orders

Several commentators recommended that the proposed regulations allow taxpayers to specify a lot selection method to their brokers through standing orders such as last-in-first-out or highest-in-first-out. In response to these comments, the proposed regulations clarify that taxpayers may establish a lot selection method by standing order.

d. Method of communicating lot selection

To provide maximum flexibility, the proposed regulations do not designate how taxpayers must communicate lot selection to brokers. Any reasonable method of communication, including electronic and oral communication, is permissible.

e. Confirmation of sales

Section 1.1012-1(c)(3)(i)(b) and (ii)(b) requires a broker or agent to provide written confirmation of the sale of stock a taxpayer has specifically identified within a reasonable time after sale. Commentators suggested that the broker or agent should determine whether to provide a confirmation and its form, and that current technology renders the confirmation requirement obsolete. Another commentator suggested that the proposed regulations allow brokers to provide lot information to taxpayers either by trade confirmation, monthly statements, or year-end reports.

The proposed regulations do not amend the current confirmation requirement, which ensures that taxpayers receive necessary information in a timely manner. What is reasonable depends on the facts and circumstances.

f. Writing in electronic format

Commentators suggested that the proposed regulations specifically authorize electronic written confirmation or recordkeeping. In response to these comments, the proposed regulations clarify that a written confirmation, record, document, instruction, or advice includes a writing in electronic format.

g. Identification by trustee or executor

Section 1.1012-1(c)(4) provides that a trustee of a trust or executor or administrator of an estate makes an adequate identification if the trustee, executor, or administrator specifies the stock in writing in the books and records of the trust or estate. If the stock is distributed, the trustee, executor, or administrator must identify the stock in writing to the distributee.

A commentator verbally noted that this rule does not require a trustee, executor, or administrator to identify stock to a broker or other agent selling the stock. The proposed regulations add the requirement that the trustee, executor, or administrator identify the stock to the broker or agent.

10. Reporting of Wash Sales

Section 6045(g)(2)(B)(ii) provides that, unless the Secretary instructs otherwise, a broker is required to report the adjusted basis of a covered security without taking into account the effect on basis of the wash sale rules of section 1091 unless the purchase and sale transactions resulting in a wash sale occur in the same account and are for identical securities (rather than substantially identical securities).

The proposed regulations provide that a broker is required to report adjusted basis in accordance with section 1091 only if both the purchase and sale transactions occur with respect to covered securities in the same account with the same CUSIP number (or other security identifier number that the Secretary may designate by publication in the **Federal Register** or in the Internal Revenue Bulletin). If a broker is required to apply section 1091 for reporting purposes, the broker must report the amount of the disallowed loss in addition to adjusted basis and gross proceeds for the sold security. The proposed regulations further provide that the broker must adjust the basis of the purchased security by the amount of the disallowed loss when reporting the eventual sale of the purchased security.

Commentators requested exceptions from reporting wash sales resulting in de minimis adjustments and wash sales triggered by scheduled periodic investments such as in an employee stock purchase plan or by automatic dividend reinvestment. Because the underlying substantive rules disallow losses in these situations, the proposed regulations do not adopt these recommendations. In addition, commentators requested an exception from reporting for wash sales for high frequency traders such as day traders based on the belief that high frequency traders generally make timely and valid elections to use the mark-to-market method of accounting under section 475(e) or (f) and that section 475(d)(1) therefore exempts them from the wash sale rules. Commentators also requested that the regulations provide a general exception from basis reporting for high frequency traders based on the belief that section 475 makes basis reporting superfluous for most high frequency traders. The proposed regulations do not adopt these recommendations, in part because the proposed regulations provide generally that reporting should occur without regard to the mark-to-market method of accounting. The Treasury Department and IRS request further comments on the treatment of high frequency traders, including specifics about the burden that basis reporting may impose, and how brokers can identify customers that have made valid and timely mark-to-market accounting method elections under section 475(e) or (f) and which transactions by these persons are subject to the provisions of section 475.

Commentators asserted that identical securities could have separate CUSIP numbers, potentially after a change to the name of the issuer. To facilitate administration of wash sale reporting, the proposed regulations interpret identical securities to mean securities with the same CUSIP number (or other security identifier number that the Secretary may designate by publication in the **Federal Register** or in the Internal Revenue Bulletin).

11. Reporting of Short Sales

In the case of a short sale, section 6045(g)(5) provides that gross proceeds and basis reporting under section 6045 is generally required for the year in which the short sale is closed rather than, as under the present law rule for gross proceeds reporting, the year in which the short sale is entered into.

The proposed regulations implement this change to reporting of short sales by requiring brokers to report all short sales opened on or after January 1, 2010, for the year in which the short sale is closed. For sales that are opened and closed in 2010, the proposed regulations require brokers to report only gross proceeds information with respect to the securities sold to open the short sale, which is consistent with how brokers currently report short sale transactions. For sales closed on or after January 1, 2011, using covered securities, however, the proposed regulations require brokers to report both the information concerning the securities sold to open the short sale and the information concerning the securities acquired to close the short sale on a single return of information. For sales closed on or after January 1, 2011, using noncovered securities, the proposed regulations require brokers to report only the information concerning the securities sold to open the short sale and permit, but do not require, brokers to report adjusted basis for the securities acquired to close the short sale and whether any gain or loss on the short sale is long-term or short-term. The proposed regulations provide that reporting adjusted basis and whether any gain or loss on the short sale is long-term or short-term is not subject to penalty under section 6721 or 6722 if the Form 1099-B indicates that the sale reported is a sale of a noncovered security. These requirements are in line with the reporting beginning with calendar year 2011 of both adjusted basis and gross proceeds on Form 1099-B.

Under section 1233, satisfaction of a short sale obligation through other borrowed property does not close a short sale. The proposed regulations address this situation and provide that, if an obligation arising from a short sale is satisfied by the receipt of transferred securities that themselves are borrowed from or through the person effecting the transfer, the receiving broker should not file a Form 1099-B but should instead provide the information regarding the short sale of the borrowed securities to the person effecting the transfer. Under the proposed regulations, the person effecting the transfer must file Form 1099-B when the obligation is finally satisfied and the short sale is closed.

The proposed regulations modify the backup withholding rules for short sales to provide that backup withholding can occur only at the time the short sale is closed and becomes subject to reporting under section 6045(g)(5).

Commentators requested that brokers not be responsible for the additional reporting requirements related to short sales that are opened before January 2011 but also requested clear guidance on how to implement reporting for short sales opened prior to January 2011 to prevent duplicate reporting. The proposed regulations prevent duplicate reporting by requiring brokers to report short sales opened prior to January 2011 under current rules except for short sales opened in 2010 that remain open into 2011. Instead of reporting the sale for calendar year 2010, the proposed regulations require that brokers report these sales for the year in which the sale is closed.

Finally, commentators requested that the reporting of short sales not require brokers to apply the constructive sale rules of section 1259, which can trigger the recognition of gain if the investor also holds or acquires an appreciated position in the same securities, or the rules under section 1233(h) concerning limitations imposed on investors that own property substantially identical to the short sale property. The proposed regulations provide for these exclusions from reporting.

12. *Reporting of Sales by S Corporations*

Under §1.6045-1(c)(3)(i)(B)(*1*), a broker currently is not required to report sales of securities by corporations. Section 1.6045-1(c)(3)(i)(C) currently permits a broker to treat a customer as a corporation if the broker has actual knowledge that the customer is a corporation, if the customer files a Form W-9, "Request for Taxpayer Identification Number and Certification," exemption certificate claiming an exemption as a corporation, or, absent knowledge to the contrary, if the name of the customer contains an unambiguous expression of corporate status such as "Corporation" or "Incorporated."

To comply with the new requirement under section 6045(g)(4) that brokers report sales by customers that are S corporations of covered securities acquired on or after January 1, 2012, the proposed regulations exclude S corporations from the list of exempt Form 1099-B recipients, but only for sales of covered securities acquired on or after January 1, 2012. The proposed regulations also curtail the ability of brokers to rely solely on the name of the customer to determine whether the customer is a corporation exempt from reporting, but only for sales of covered securities acquired on or after January 1, 2012. Commentators requested that the proposed regulations retain this rule because its removal potentially requires brokers to seek a certification from all corporate customers. The proposed regulations do not adopt this recommendation, however, because brokers cannot infer from a customer's name whether the customer is taxed as an S corporation or C corporation. Commentators also requested that accounts opened by corporations before January 2012 be excepted from reporting. The proposed regulations do not adopt this request as contrary to the statute.

Commentators requested that Form W-9 be updated to facilitate a customer's statement to its broker of its current election to be taxed as an S corporation and that the proposed regulations require brokers to solicit or re-solicit Form W-9 from each existing corporate customer. The IRS is currently considering the requested modification to Form W-9. The proposed regulations do not impose a requirement to solicit or re-solicit Form W-9 from all existing corporate customers because, under §1.6045-1(c)(3)(i)(C), Form W-9 is only one method by which brokers may determine whether a corporate customer is exempt from all reporting beginning in 2012. However, if a broker does not have actual knowledge that a corporate customer is taxed as a C corporation or is otherwise exempt (for example, because it is a bank or organization exempt from tax under section 501(a)), a broker must request a Form W-9 exemption certificate or else must make a return of information for any sales by the corporation of covered securities acquired on or after January 1, 2012. A broker also may be required to backup withhold on gross proceeds paid to the customer.

Commentators requested that brokers be permitted to report other Form 1099 information such as interest and dividends for S corporations because reporting of the sales of securities is done on composite statements containing all such information. The proposed regulations do not address this topic directly because no penalty is imposed for the act of filing a nonrequired return.

13. *Reporting to Trust Interest Holders in a WHFIT*

Commentators requested that the proposed regulations except trustees and middlemen from any requirement to report information under sections 6045(g) to trust interest holders in a widely held fixed investment trust (WHFIT) with respect to both the securities held by a WHFIT and trust interests in a WHFIT because the WHFIT rules in §1.671-5 already provide a framework for communicating similar information to trust interest holders. These proposed regulations clarify that the sale of a trust interest in a WHFIT by a trust interest holder is required to be reported under section 6045(a). However, to the extent that a trustee or middleman has a requirement to provide information under section 6045(g), the trustee or middleman is deemed to meet those requirements by complying with the WHFIT rules in §1.671-5. The Treasury Department and IRS request additional comments on whether any basis reporting rules are needed in addition to those provided under §1.671-5 to accommodate trust interest holders in a WHFIT.

14. *Due date for Payee Statements Furnished in a Consolidated Reporting Statement*

Section 6045(b) extends the due date to furnish all of the payee statements required under section 6045 to customers from January 31 to February 15, effective for statements required to be furnished after December 31, 2008. Thus, in addition to Form 1099-B, "Proceeds from Broker and Barter Exchange Transactions," the February 15 due date applies to Form 1099-S, "Proceeds from Real Estate Transactions," and, when reporting payments to attorneys or substitute payments by brokers in lieu of dividends or interest, Form 1099-MISC, "Miscellaneous Income." This February 15 due date also applies to any other statement required to be furnished on or before January 31 of a calendar year if furnished with a statement required under section 6045 in a consolidated reporting statement. The Act did not define consolidated reporting statement but provided that the term would be defined in regulations. See Notice 2009-11 (2009-5 IRB 420), providing that, with respect to reportable items from calendar year 2008, brokers had until February 17, 2009, to report all items that they customarily reported on their annual composite form recipient statements. See §601.601(d)(2).

The proposed regulations define *consolidated reporting statement* as a grouping of statements furnished to the same customer or same group of customers on the same date whether or not the statements are furnished with respect to the same or different accounts or transactions. Importantly, the proposed regulations require that the grouping of statements be limited to those furnished to the customer based on the same relationship as the statement furnished under section 6045 (for example, broker, payor, or real estate settlement agent), and not as a result of any other relationship between the parties such as debtor to creditor or employer to employee. Based on this limitation, the following forms may be furnished in a consolidated reporting statement with a statement required under section 6045: Form 1099-DIV, "Dividends and Distributions"; Form 1099-INT, "Interest Income"; Form 1099-MISC, "Miscellaneous Income"; Form 1099-OID, "Original Issue Discount"; Form 1099-PATR, "Taxable Distributions Received From Cooperatives"; Form 1099-Q, "Payments From Qualified Education Programs (Under Sections 529 and 530)"; Form 1099-R, "Distributions From Pensions, Annuities, Retirement or Profit-Sharing Plans, IRAs, Insurance Contracts, etc."; Form 3921, "Exercise of an Incentive Stock Option Under Section 422(b)" (in development); Form 3922, "Transfer of Stock Acquired Through an Employee Stock Purchase Plan Under Section 423(c)" (in development); and Form 5498, "IRA Contribution Information." The Treasury Department and IRS request further comments regarding whether any other forms should be included in the definition of consolidated reporting statement.

For statements filed by brokers with respect to sales, the proposed regulations acknowledge that a customer may not sell securities in an account in every year and, thus, may not receive Form 1099-B every year. The proposed regulations provide that a broker may treat any customer as receiving a required statement under section 6045 if the customer has an account for which a statement would be required to be furnished under section 6045 had a sale occurred during the year.

15. *Reporting Required in Connection with Transfers of Securities*

Under new section 6045A, a broker and any other person specified in Treasury regulations (applicable person) that transfers to a broker a security that is a covered security in the hands of the applicable person must furnish to the receiving broker a written statement for purposes of enabling the receiving broker to satisfy the reporting requirements of section 6045(g). Section 6045A(c) provides that, unless the Secretary provides otherwise, the statement required by this rule must be furnished to the receiving broker not later than fifteen days after the transfer of the covered security.

a. *Transfer reporting generally*

The proposed regulations create a presumption that every transfer of custody effected by an applicable person to a broker or other professional custodian of any share of stock in a corporation on or after January 1, 2011, that is not a sale is a transfer of a covered security subject to reporting.

Thus, the proposed regulations provide that a transfer statement must be furnished for every such transfer. This duty applies even if the security transferred is a noncovered security or is treated as a noncovered security because it was excepted from all reporting under section 6045 (for example, because the customer was an exempt recipient) at the time of its acquisition. In either situation, the transfer statement is not required to include any other required information provided that the transfer statement indicates that the security transferred is a noncovered security. This presumption that all transferred securities are covered securities and the requirement to provide a transfer statement for noncovered or excepted securities solely for the purpose of establishing that the security is a noncovered or excepted security will reduce uncertainty for receiving brokers and custodians. The person initiating the transfer of custody is permitted, but not required, to provide other information about the noncovered or excepted security.

The proposed regulations place the duty to furnish the transfer statement on the person effecting the transfer of custody if the person is an applicable person. Under the proposed regulations, an *applicable person* is a broker within the meaning of §1.6045-1(a)(1), any person that acts as a custodian of securities in the ordinary course of a trade or business, any issuer of securities, and any agent of these persons. An applicable person does not include the beneficial owner of the securities, any governmental unit or agency or instrumentality of a governmental unit with respect to escheated securities, or any person that acts solely as a clearing house for the transfer.

Under the proposed regulations, an applicable person has a duty to furnish a transfer statement if that person effects the transfer of custody of the securities. For securities held by direct registration with the issuer, including certificated shares, the person effecting the transfer is the issuer or its transfer agent. For securities held in street name, the person effecting the transfer is the broker or other firm carrying the securities.

Although the person responsible for providing a transfer statement will often be a broker or other applicable person that effects sales, the proposed regulations also impose this duty on issuers, transfer agents, professional custodians, and other applicable persons that may not effect sales. For these applicable persons, this duty is limited to a duty to receive the statement when receiving custody of transferred securities and then to retransmit the information on the statement when transferring custody of those securities to a broker (or, if no statement is received, to furnish a statement that the securities are noncovered securities). The proposed regulations regarding transfer statements do not impose a duty on those that do not effect sales to update basis in response to adjustments announced by issuers under section 6045B or to compute basis by average cost under section 1012. These computations apply only to basis reporting at the time of sale under section 6045 and, thus, apply only to brokers effecting sales. The Treasury Department and IRS request further comments regarding the scope of the transfer statement requirement.

Because the transfer statement is not filed with the IRS, no official form or format will be required. Instead, the proposed regulations specify the information required on the statement. At the request of commentators, the proposed regulations permit flexibility in the format and method by which the information is furnished pursuant to agreement of the parties. The Treasury Department and IRS request further comments about the form and format for the transfer statement and any substitutes thereto.

Under the proposed regulations, the transfer statement must identify the applicable person furnishing the statement, the broker receiving the statement, the owner or owners transferring the securities, and, if different, the owner or owners of the securities after any transfer other than a sale, such as a transfer of gifted or inherited securities. The transfer statement must also identify the securities being transferred and information about the transfer such as the date the transfer was initiated and the settlement date of the transfer (if known when reporting).

Under the proposed regulations, a transfer statement must include the total adjusted basis of the securities, the original date of acquisition, and the date for determining whether any gain or loss with respect to the security would be long-term or short-term at the time of sale. The transfer statement must also indicate the extent to which the reported basis amount has been adjusted to reflect any corporate actions that affect the basis of the security by reporting the number from the issuer statement required under section 6045B (discussed later in this preamble) of the most recent corporate action that is reflected on the transfer statement. Additionally, if the average basis method is used to determine basis, the proposed regulations permit reporting an original acquisition date of "VARIOUS" for securities owned at least five years.

Commentators suggested that additional information items be required on the statement such as the original purchase amount, the reason why the securities are (or are treated as) noncovered securities (if applicable), and the basis method used by the taxpayer immediately prior to the transfer. The proposed regulations do not require this additional information on the statement because the proposed regulations do not require this information to be reported on Form 1099-B. Additional information may be communicated with the statement, even if not required.

If an applicable person furnishing a transfer statement later receives a statement for an earlier transfer that reports that the transferred securities are covered securities and includes information inconsistent with the subsequent transfer statement, the proposed regulations require that a corrected statement be furnished to correct the inconsistent information within fifteen days following the receipt of the prior transfer statement.

b. *Reporting required in connection with transfers of gifted and inherited securities*

Under section 6045(g)(3)(A)(ii), a covered security includes stock or indebtedness acquired on or after the applicable date if the security is transferred from an account in which the security was a covered security (but only if the receiving broker or other professional custodian receives a transfer statement). Therefore, under the proposed regulations, gifted and inherited securities that were covered securities in the account of the donor or decedent remain covered securities when transferred to the recipient's account and accompanied by a transfer statement.

Under the proposed regulations, when covered securities are transferred from a decedent, the transfer statement must indicate that the securities are inherited. The transfer statement must also report the date of death as the acquisition date and must report adjusted basis in accordance with the instructions and valuations provided by an authorized representative of the estate. The proposed regulations require that the selling broker take these basis adjustments into account in reporting adjusted basis upon the subsequent sale or other disposition of these securities.

When covered securities are transferred to a different owner as a gift, the proposed regulations require the statement to indicate that the transfer consists of gifted securities and to state the adjusted basis of the securities in the hands of the donor and the donor's original acquisition date of the securities. The transfer statement must also report the date of the gift (if known when furnishing the statement) and the fair market value of the gift on that date (if known or readily ascertainable). Upon the subsequent sale or other disposition of these securities, the selling broker must apply the relevant basis rules for gifts when reporting adjusted basis.

Commentators opposed subjecting transfers of gifted and inherited securities to the requirements of transfer reporting because the substantive rules governing basis computation for these securities are complex. The proposed rules do not exclude transfers of gifted and inherited securities, however, because these transfers fall within the plain language of the statute. The proposed regulations provide workable rules to minimize complexity.

Issuers and transfer agents commented that they often do not know the reason for the transfer of shares from one owner to another. The proposed regulations provide that, if the request to transfer ownership between different people is silent as to the reason for the transfer, the transfer should generally be treated as a gift.

Commentators expressed concern regarding gifted and inherited securities about the potential burden to value privately traded securities or other securities for which fair market value is not easily determined. For inherited securities, the proposed regulations allow the applicable person effecting the transfer to rely on the authorized estate representative to provide the instructions and valuations necessary to report correct basis for any transferred securities. If the applicable person effecting the transfer does not receive instructions and valuations from the authorized estate representative, the applicable person must request this information from the authorized estate representative before preparing the transfer statement. If this information is not provided before the transfer statement is prepared, then the transfer statement must indicate that the transfer consists of an inherited security but must report the security as a noncovered security. If this information is provided after the transfer statement is sent, the applicable person effecting the transfer must send a corrected transfer statement.

For gifted securities, the proposed regulations only require the applicable person effecting the gift transfer to report the date of the gift if known at the time the transfer statement is prepared and the fair market value of the securities on the date of the gift if known or readily ascertainable at that time. However, the proposed regulations provide that, if the gifted securities are subsequently transferred to a different account of the same owner, the applicable person must include the date of the gift on the subsequent transfer statement and, if known or readily ascertainable at the time the subsequent transfer statement is prepared, the fair market value of the securities as of the date of the gift. The proposed regulations provide a special reporting rule for brokers that applies on the sale of a gifted security when the security's adjusted basis depends upon its fair market value as of the date of the gift but the transfer statement received by the selling broker does not report this amount and this amount is not readily ascertainable by the broker. Under these circumstances, the proposed regulations provide that the broker must report adjusted basis equal to the gross proceeds from the sale.

c. *Reporting required in connection with transfers of borrowed securities*

To facilitate the correct reporting of short sales involving transfers of borrowed securities, the proposed regulations require the transfer statement to indicate that the transferred securities are borrowed and provide instructions on how the receiving broker can provide information to the applicable person effecting the transfer about any short position potentially being closed by the transfer or other sale of the securities. This information is required to alert the receiving broker that, if the transferred securities are used to satisfy a short sale obligation, the short sale remains open and should not be reported as closed to the IRS or to the customer.

16. *Reporting by Issuers of Actions Affecting Basis of Securities*

If an organizational action (such as a stock split or a merger or acquisition) by an issuer affects the basis of a specified security, new section 6045B requires the issuer to file a return with the IRS and furnish to each nominee (or to each certificate holder if there is no nominee) a written statement regarding the action. The return filing and information statement requirements may be waived under section 6045B(e) if the issuer makes the information about the action publicly available, in the form and manner determined by the Secretary.

The proposed regulations require a reporting issuer to identify itself and the security on the return and provide information about the organizational action and the quantitative effect on the basis resulting from the action. The proposed regulations also require the issuer to assign and report a sequential number determined separately by security for each information report the issuer files.

The proposed regulations require a domestic or foreign issuer to furnish a written statement to each holder of record that is not an exempt recipient as defined in § 1.6045B-1(b)(5) as of the record date of the corporate action and all subsequent holders of record through the date the issuer furnishes the statement. The Treasury Department and IRS request comments as to the extent to which foreign issuers will be able to comply with such a reporting requirement, and whether it may be appropriate to limit foreign issuers' reporting requirements (such as, for example, limiting foreign issuers' reporting requirements to securities that are traded on a securities exchange in the United States).

If the security is held in the name of someone other than the holder of record on the books of the issuer, the proposed regulations require the issuer to furnish the statement to the nominee listed on its books unless such nominee is the issuer or the issuer's agent. For example, an issuer must furnish statements to the participants of the issuer's direct stock purchase plan even if the plan is listed as a nominee for the participants. The proposed regulations permit an issuer to furnish to its holders and nominees a copy of the return that it files with the IRS.

The proposed regulations provide that both the return filing and information statement requirements under section 6045B are waived if an issuer posts a statement with the required information in a readily accessible format in an area of its primary public website dedicated to this purpose by the same due date for reporting the organizational action to the IRS and keeps the form accessible to the public. Under the proposed regulations, this public reporting relieves the issuer of its duty both to file the return with the IRS and to furnish the statement to its nominees and certificate holders.

Commentators have questioned how issuers could report the effect on basis within 45 days of a corporate action when the effect may not be determinable until the conclusion of other events such as the end of the issuer's fiscal year. Any request to extend the due date was not adopted as inconsistent with the 45-day statutory due date. The proposed regulations provide that an issuer may make reasonable assumptions about facts that cannot be determined prior to this due date and must file a corrected return once the facts are determined if necessary to report the correct quantitative effect on basis. Under the proposed regulations, it is expected that an issuer will treat a payment that may be a dividend consistently with its treatment of the payment under section 6042(b)(3) and § 1.6042-3(c).

Some commentators suggested that the IRS establish a central repository on its website for posting information statements from issuers that wish to report publicly in lieu of filing returns. This suggestion was not adopted in the proposed regulations due to IRS resource and system constraints. The Treasury Department and IRS request comments on the definition of public reporting including rules about retaining the returns on the website and alternatives other than the use of a central repository.

Commentators requested that the proposed regulations except actions by S corporations from reporting under section 6045B because adjustments are specific to the shareholder and are reported on Schedule K-1 (Form 1120S), "Shareholder's Share of Income, Deductions, Credits, etc." The proposed regulations do not except reporting by S corporations, but deem an S corporation to satisfy the requirements under section 6045B if it reports the effect of the organizational action on the proper Schedule K-1 for each shareholder, timely files the schedules with the IRS, and timely furnishes the schedules to all proper parties.

17. *Penalty Provisions*

The current regulations impose penalties on brokers for failing to file or furnish complete and correct returns and statements after the sale of a security. The proposed regulations expand the list of required statements and returns filed with the IRS in § 301.6721-1 and the list of required statements furnished to payees in § 301.6722-1 to include the new penalties associated with the new transfer statements and issuer statements. The proposed regulations also update the full list of returns and statements included in section 6724(d).

Commentators expressed concern that the IRS would assert penalties against a broker for reporting an incorrect adjusted basis or incorrectly reporting whether any gain or loss on a sale is long-term or short-term after relying on incorrect information provided by others. Under the proposed regulations, brokers generally must adjust basis reported for covered securities to reflect: (1) information received on any transfer statement under section 6045A; and (2) information reported by the issuer under section 6045B regarding the effect on basis of any organizational actions. The proposed regulations provide that any failure to report correct information that arises solely from this reliance is deemed to be due to reasonable cause with respect to the penalties under sections 6721 and 6722.

The proposed regulations permit, but do not require, a broker to adjust the reported basis in accordance with information that is not reflected on a transfer statement or issuer statement, including any information the broker has about securities held by the same customer in other accounts with the broker. The proposed regulations deem that a broker that takes into account information received from a customer or third party other than information reflected on a transfer statement or issuer statement relies upon such information in good faith in accordance with existing rules found in § 301.6724-1(c)(6) if the broker neither knows nor has reason to know that the information is incorrect.

Proposed Effective and Applicability Dates

These regulations are proposed to take effect when published in the **Federal Register** as final regulations except as follows. The regulations regarding reporting basis and whether any gain or loss on a sale is long-term or short-term under section 6045(g) are proposed to apply to: (1) any share of stock other than RIC stock or DRP stock acquired on or after January 1, 2011; and (2) any share of RIC stock or DRP stock acquired on or after January 1, 2012. The regulations regarding the determination of basis under section 1012 are proposed to apply for taxable years beginning after the date the regulations are published as final regulations in the **Federal Register**. However, the rules in § 1.1012-1(e)(1)(i), in part, apply to stock acquired on or after January 1, 2011, the rules in § 1.1012-1(e)(2) and (e)(9), in part, apply to stock acquired on or after January 1, 2012, and the rules in § 1.1012-1(e)(7)(i), in part, and in § 1.1012-1(e)(10), in part, apply to sales, exchanges, or other dispositions of stock on or after January 1, 2012.

The regulations regarding transfer statement reporting under section 6045A are proposed to apply to: (1) transfers of stock other than RIC stock or DRP stock that occur on or after January 1, 2011; and (2) transfers of RIC stock or DRP stock that occur on or after January 1, 2012. The regulations regarding issuer reporting under section 6045B are proposed to apply to: (1) organizational actions affecting basis of stock other than RIC stock that occur on or after January 1, 2011; and (2) organizational actions affecting basis of RIC stock that occur on or after January 1, 2012. The regulations regarding the timing for reporting short sales of securities under section 6045 and for collecting backup withholding in connection with short sales under section 3406 are proposed to apply to short sales opened on or after the date the final regulations are published in the **Federal Register** but no earlier than January 1, 2010.

Effect on Other Documents

Rev. Rul. 67-436 will be obsoleted as of the date these regulations are published as final regulations in the **Federal Register**.

Special Analyses

It has been determined that this notice of proposed rulemaking is not a significant regulatory action as defined in Executive Order 12866. Therefore, a regulatory assessment is not required. It also has been determined that section 553(b) of the Administrative Procedure Act (5 U.S.C. chapter 5) does not apply to this regulation.

Pursuant to the Regulatory Flexibility Act (5 U.S.C. chapter 6), it is hereby certified that this regulation will not have a significant economic impact on a substantial number of small entities, because any effect on small entities by the rules proposed in this document flows directly from section 403 of the Energy Improvement and Extension Act of 2008, Division B of Public Law 110-343 (122 Stat. 3765, 3854 (2008)).

Section 403(a) of the Act modifies section 6045 to require that brokers report the adjusted basis of the securities and whether any gain or loss with respect to the securities is long-term or short-term when reporting the sale of a covered security. It is anticipated that this statutory requirement will fall only on financial services firms with annual receipts greater than $7 million and, therefore, on no small entities. Further, in implementing the statutory requirement, the regulation proposes to limit reporting to the information described in the Act: adjusted basis and whether any gain or loss with respect to the securities is long-term or short-term.

Section 403(c) of the Act adds new section 6045A, which requires applicable persons to furnish a transfer statement in connection with the transfer of custody of a covered security. In implementing this statutory requirement, the regulation proposes to define applicable person to include brokers, professional custodians of securities, and issuers of securities. This definition effectuates the Act by giving the broker who receives the transfer statement the information necessary to determine and report adjusted basis and whether any gain or loss with respect to the security is long-term or short-term as required by section 6045 when the security is subsequently sold. Consequently, the regulation does not add to the impact on small entities imposed by the statutory scheme. Instead, it limits reporting to only these necessary entities. It also limits the information to be reported to only those items necessary to effectuate the statutory scheme.

Section 403(d) of the Act adds new section 6045B, which requires issuer reporting by all issuers of specified securities regardless of size and even when the securities are not publicly traded. In implementing this statutory requirement, the regulation proposes to limit reporting to those items necessary to meet the Act's requirements. Additionally, the regulation proposes to mitigate the burden imposed by the Act by providing rules to permit issuers to report each action publicly as permitted by the Act instead of filing a return and furnishing each nominee or holder a statement about the action. The regulation therefore does not add to the statutory impact on small entities but instead eases this impact to the extent the statute permits.

Therefore, because this regulation will not have a significant economic impact on a substantial number of small entities, a regulatory flexibility analysis is not required. The Treasury Department and IRS request comments on the accuracy of this statement. Pursuant to section 7805(f) of the Code, this regulation has been submitted to the Chief Counsel for Advocacy of the Small Business Administration for comment on its impact on small business.

Comments and Public Hearing

Before these proposed regulations are adopted as final regulations, consideration will be given to any written (a signed original and eight (8) copies) or electronic comments that are timely submitted to the IRS. The Treasury Department and IRS request comments on the clarity of the proposed regulations and how they can be made easier to understand. All comments will be available for public inspection and copying.

A public hearing has been scheduled for February 17, 2010, beginning at 10 a.m., in the auditorium of the IRS New Carrollton Federal Building, 5000 Ellin Road, Lanham, Maryland 20706. All visitors must present photo identification to enter the building. Because of access restrictions, visitors will not be admitted beyond the immediate entrance area more than 30 minutes before the hearing starts. For information about having your name placed on the building access list to attend the hearing, see the "FOR FURTHER INFORMATION CONTACT" section of this preamble.

The rules of 26 CFR 601.601(a)(3) apply to the hearing. Persons who wish to present oral comments at the hearing must submit written or electronic comments by February 8, 2010 and an outline of the topics to be discussed and the time to be devoted to each topic (a signed original and eight (8) copies) by February 8, 2010. A period of ten minutes will be allotted to each person for making comments. An agenda showing the scheduling of speakers will be prepared after the deadline for receiving outlines has passed. Copies of the agenda will be available free of charge at the hearing.

Drafting Information

The principal authors of these proposed regulations are Edward C. Schwartz, Amy J. Pfalzgraf, and William L. Candler, Office of Associate Chief Counsel (Income Tax and Accounting), and Stephen Schaeffer, Office of Associate Chief Counsel (Procedure and Administration). However, other personnel from the IRS and the Treasury Department participated in their development.

[¶ 49,450]   Proposed Amendments of Regulations (REG-151605-09), published in the Federal Register on June 23, 2010.

[Code Sec. 1502]

Consolidated returns: Net operating loss: Extended carryback period.—Amendments of Reg. § 1.1502-21, providing guidance to consolidated groups that implements the revisions to section 172(b)(1)(H), are proposed.

AGENCY: Internal Revenue Service (IRS), Treasury.

ACTION: Notice of proposed rulemaking by cross-reference to temporary regulations.

SUMMARY: In the Rules and Regulations section of this issue of the **Federal Register**, the IRS is issuing temporary regulations that provides guidance to consolidated groups that implements the revisions to section 172(b)(1)(H). The text of those regulations also serves as the text of these proposed regulations.

DATES: Written or electronic comments and a request for a public hearing must be received by September 21, 2010.

ADDRESSES: Send submissions to: CC:PA:LPD:PR (REG-151605-09), Room 5203, Internal Revenue Service, P.O. Box 7604, Ben Franklin Station, Washington, DC 20044. Submissions may be hand-delivered Monday through Friday between the hours of 8 a.m. and 4 p.m. to CC:PA:LPD:PR (REG-151605- 09), Courier's Desk, Internal Revenue Service, 1111 Constitution Avenue NW, Washington, DC, or sent electronically via the Federal eRulemaking Portal at *http://www.regulations.gov* (IRS REG-151605-09).

FOR FURTHER INFORMATION CONTACT: Concerning the proposed regulations, Grid Glyer, (202) 622-7930, concerning submissions of comments, Regina Johnson (202) 622-7180 (not toll-free numbers).

SUPPLEMENTARY INFORMATION:

Paperwork Reduction Act

The collection of information contained in this notice of proposed rulemaking has been submitted to the Office of Management and Budget for review in accordance with the Paperwork Reduction Act of 1995 (44 U.S.C. 3507(d) under control number 1545-2171). Comments on the collection of information should be sent to the **Office of Management and Budget**, Attn: Desk Officer for the Department of the Treasury, Office of Information and Regulatory Affairs, Washington, D.C. 20503, with copies to the **Internal Revenue Service**, Attn: IRS Reports Clearance Officer, SE:W:CAR:MP:T:T:SP, Washington, D.C. 20224. Comments on the collection of information should be received by August 23, 2010. Comments are specifically requested concerning:

Whether the proposed collection of information is necessary for the proper performance of the functions of the **Internal Revenue Service**, including whether the information will have practical utility;

The accuracy of the estimated burden associated with the proposed collection of information;

How the quality, utility and clarity of the information to be collected may be enhanced;

How the burden of complying with the proposed collection of information may be minimized, including through the application of automated collection techniques or other forms of information technology; and

Estimates of capital or start-up costs and costs of operation, maintenance and purchase of service to provide information.

The collection of information in these proposed regulations is in § § 1.1502-21(b)(3)(ii)(C)(2) and 1.1502-21(b)(3)(ii)(C)(3).

The proposed regulations provide guidance to consolidated groups that implements the revisions to section 172(b)(1)(H).

The collection of information is required in order to obtain a benefit. The likely respondents are corporations that are members of consolidated groups.

Estimated total annual reporting burden: 1,000 hours.

Estimated average annual burden hours per respondent: 0.25 hours.

Estimated number of respondents: 4,000.

Estimated frequency of responses: Once.

An agency may not conduct or sponsor, and a person is not required to respond to, a collection of information unless it displays a valid control number assigned by the Office of Management and Budget.

Books or records relating to a collection of information must be retained as long as their contents may become material in the administration of any internal revenue law. Generally, tax returns and tax return information are confidential, as required by 26 U.S.C. 6103.

Background and Explanation of Provisions

Temporary regulations in the Rules and Regulations section of this issue of the **Federal Register** amend 26 CFR Part 1 to revise § 1.1502-21T. The text of those temporary regulations also serves as the text of these proposed regulations. The preamble to the temporary regulations explains the amendments.

Special Analyses

It has been determined that this notice of proposed rulemaking is not a significant regulatory action as defined in Executive Order 12866. Therefore, a regulatory assessment is not required. With respect to the proposed regulation, § 1.1502-21, it is hereby certified that this provision will not have a significant economic impact on a substantial number of small entities. This certification is based on the fact that these regulations primarily affect large corporations that are members of consolidated groups and will provide a benefit if the election is made. Therefore, a regulatory flexibility analysis is not required. Pursuant to section 7805(f) of the Internal Revenue Code, these regulations have been submitted to the Chief Counsel for Advocacy of the Small Business Administration for comment on their impact on small business.

Comments and Requests for a Public Hearing

Before these proposed regulations are adopted as final regulations, consideration will be given to any written comments (a signed original and eight (8) copies) or electronic comments that are submitted timely to the IRS. All comments will be available for public inspection and copying. A public hearing may be scheduled if requested in writing by any person that timely submits written comments. If a public hearing is scheduled, notice of the date, time, and place for the public hearing will be published in the **Federal Register**.

Drafting Information

The principal author of these regulations is Grid Glyer of the Office of Associate Chief Counsel (Corporate). Other personnel from the Treasury Department and the IRS participated in their development.

[¶ 49,462]   Proposed Amendments of Regulations (REG-119921-09), published in the Federal Register on September 14, 2010.

[Code Secs. 6011, 6071 and 7701]

Series limited liability companies: Cell companies: Entity classification.—Reg. §§ 301.6011-6 and 301.6071-2, and amendments of Reg. § 301.7701-1, regarding the classification for Federal tax purposes of a series of a domestic series limited liability company (LLC), a cell of a domestic cell company, or a foreign series or cell that conducts an insurance business, are proposed. The texts are at ¶ 35,129N, ¶ 36,706C and ¶ 43,081A.

AGENCY: Internal Revenue Service (IRS), Treasury.

ACTION: Notice of proposed rulemaking.

SUMMARY: This document contains proposed regulations regarding the classification for Federal tax purposes of a series of a domestic series limited liability company (LLC), a cell of a domestic cell company, or a foreign series or cell that conducts an insurance business. The proposed regulations provide that, whether or not a series of a domestic series LLC, a cell of a domestic cell company, or a foreign series or cell that conducts an insurance business is a juridical person for local law purposes, for Federal tax purposes it is treated as an entity formed under local law. Classification of a series or cell that is treated as a separate entity for Federal tax purposes generally is determined under the same rules that govern the classification of other types of separate entities. The proposed regulations provide examples illustrating the application of the rule. The proposed regulations will affect domestic series LLCs; domestic cell companies; foreign series, or cells that conduct insurance businesses; and their owners.

DATES: Written or electronic comments and requests for a public hearing must be received by December 13, 2010.

ADDRESSES: Send submissions to: CC:PA:LPD:PR (REG-119921-09), Room 5203, Internal Revenue Service, PO Box 7604, Ben Franklin Station, Washington, DC 20044. Submissions may be hand-delivered Monday through Friday between the hours of 8 a.m. and 4 p.m. to CC:PA:LPD:PR (REG-119921-09), Courier's Desk, Internal Revenue Service, 1111 Constitution Avenue, NW, Washington, DC, or sent electronically, via the Federal eRulemaking portal at *www.regulations.gov* (IRS REG-119921-09).

FOR FURTHER INFORMATION CONTACT: Concerning the proposed regulations, Joy Spies, (202) 622-3050; concerning submissions of comments, Oluwafunmilayo (Funmi) Taylor, (202) 622-7180 (not toll-free numbers).

SUPPLEMENTARY INFORMATION:

Background

1. Introduction

A number of states have enacted statutes providing for the creation of entities that may establish series, including limited liability companies (series LLCs). In general, series LLC statutes provide that a limited liability company may establish separate series. Although series of a series LLC generally are not treated as separate entities for state law purposes and, thus, cannot have members, each series has "associated" with it specified members, assets, rights, obligations, and investment objectives or business purposes. Members' association with one or more particular series is comparable to direct ownership by the members in such series, in that their rights, duties, and powers with respect to the series are direct and specifically identified. If the conditions enumerated in the relevant statute are satisfied, the debts, liabilities, and obligations of one series generally are enforceable only against the assets of that series and not against assets of other series or of the series LLC.

Certain jurisdictions have enacted statutes providing for entities similar to the series LLC. For example, certain statutes provide for the chartering of a legal entity (or the establishment of cells) under a structure commonly known as a protected cell company, segregated account company or segregated portfolio company (cell company). A cell company may establish multiple accounts, or cells, each of which has its own name and is identified with a specific participant, but generally is not treated under local law as a legal entity distinct from the cell company. The assets of each cell are statutorily protected from the creditors of any other cell and from the creditors of the cell company.

Under current law, there is little specific guidance regarding whether for Federal tax purposes a series (or cell) is treated as an entity separate from other series or the series LLC (or other cells or the cell company, as the case may be), or whether the company and all of its series (or cells) should be treated as a single entity.

Notice 2008-19 (2008-5 IRB 366) requested comments on proposed guidance concerning issues that arise if arrangements entered into by a cell constitute insurance for Federal income tax purposes. The notice also requested comments on the need for guidance concerning similar segregated arrangements that do not involve insurance. The IRS received a number of comments requesting guidance for similar arrangements not involving insurance, including series LLCs and cell companies. These comments generally recommended that series and cells should be treated as separate entities for Federal tax purposes if they are established under a statute with provisions similar to the series LLC statutes currently in effect in several states. The IRS and Treasury Department generally agree with these comments. See § 601.601(d)(2)(ii)(*b*).

2. Entity Classification for Federal Tax Purposes

A. Regulatory framework

Sections 301.7701-1 through 301.7701-4 of the Procedure and Administration Regulations provide the framework for determining an organization's entity classification for Federal tax purposes. Classification of an organization depends on whether the organization is treated as: (i) a separate entity under § 301.7701-1, (ii) a "business entity" within the meaning of § 301.7701-2(a) or a trust under § 301.7701-4, and (iii) an "eligible entity" under § 301.7701-3.

Section 301.7701-1(a)(1) provides that the determination of whether an entity is separate from its owners for Federal tax purposes is a matter of Federal tax law and does not depend on whether the organization is recognized as an entity under local law. Section 301.7701-1(a)(2) provides that a joint venture or other contractual arrangement may create a separate entity for Federal tax purposes if the participants carry on a trade, business, financial operation, or venture and divide the profits therefrom. However, a joint undertaking merely to share expenses does not create a separate entity for Federal tax purposes, nor does mere co-ownership of property where activities are limited to keeping property maintained, in repair, and rented or leased. *Id.*

Section 301.7701-1(b) provides that the tax classification of an organization recognized as a separate entity for tax purposes generally is determined under §§ 301.7701-2, 301.7701-3, and 301.7701-4. Thus, for example, an organization recognized as an entity that does not have associates or an objective to carry on a business may be classified as a trust under § 301.7701-4.

Section 301.7701-2(a) provides that a business entity is any entity recognized for Federal tax purposes (including an entity with a single owner that may be disregarded as an entity separate from its owner under § 301.7701-3) that is not properly classified as a trust or otherwise subject to special treatment under the Internal Revenue Code (Code). A business entity with two or more members is classified for Federal tax purposes as a corporation or a partnership. See § 301.7701-2(a). A business entity with one owner is classified as a corporation or is disregarded. See § 301.7701-2(a). If the entity is disregarded, its activities are treated in the same manner as a sole proprietorship, branch, or division of the owner. However, § 301.7701-2(c)(2)(iv) and (v) provides for an otherwise disregarded entity to be treated as a corporation for certain Federal employment tax and excise tax purposes.

Section 301.7701-3(a) generally provides that an eligible entity, which is a business entity that is not a corporation under § 301.7701-2(b), may elect its classification for Federal tax purposes.

B. *Separate entity classification*

The threshold question for determining the tax classification of a series of a series LLC or a cell of a cell company is whether an individual series or cell should be considered an entity for Federal tax purposes. The determination of whether an organization is an entity separate from its owners for Federal tax purposes is a matter of Federal tax law and does not depend on whether the organization is recognized as an entity under local law. Section 301.7701-1(a)(1). In *Moline Properties, Inc. v. Commissioner*, 319 U.S. 436 (1943), the Supreme Court noted that, so long as a corporation was formed for a purpose that is the equivalent of business activity or the corporation actually carries on a business, the corporation remains a taxable entity separate from its shareholders. Although entities that are recognized under local law generally are also recognized for Federal tax purposes, a state law entity may be disregarded if it lacks business purpose or any business activity other than tax avoidance. See *Bertoli v. Commissioner*, 103 T.C. 501 (1994); *Aldon Homes, Inc. v. Commissioner*, 33 T.C. 582 (1959).

The Supreme Court in *Commissioner v. Culbertson*, 337 U.S. 733 (1949), and *Commissioner v. Tower*, 327 U.S. 280 (1946), set forth the basic standard for determining whether a partnership will be respected for Federal tax purposes. In general, a partnership will be respected if, considering all the facts, the parties in good faith and acting with a business purpose intended to join together to conduct an enterprise and share in its profits and losses. This determination is made considering not only the stated intent of the parties, but also the terms of their agreement and their conduct. *Madison Gas & Elec. Co. v. Commissioner*, 633 F.2d 512, 514 (7th Cir. 1980); *Luna v. Commissioner*, 42 T.C. 1067, 1077-78 (1964).

Conversely, under certain circumstances, arrangements that are not recognized as entities under state law may be treated as separate entities for Federal tax purposes. Section 301.7701-1(a)(2). For example, courts have found entities for tax purposes in some co-ownership situations where the co-owners agree to restrict their ability to sell, lease or encumber their interests, waive their rights to partition property, or allow certain management decisions to be made other than by unanimous agreement among co-owners. *Bergford v. Commissioner*, 12 F.3d 166 (9th Cir. 1993); *Bussing v. Commissioner*, 89 T.C. 1050 (1987); *Alhouse v. Commissioner*, T.C. Memo. 1991-652. However, the Internal Revenue Service (IRS) has ruled that a co-ownership does not rise to the level of an entity for Federal tax purposes if the owner employs an agent whose activities are limited to collecting rents, paying property taxes, insurance premiums, repair and maintenance expenses, and providing tenants with customary services. Rev. Rul. 75-374 (1975-2 CB 261). See also Rev. Rul. 79-77 (1979-1 CB 448), (see § 601.601(d)(2)(ii)(*b*)).

Rev. Proc. 2002-22 (2002-1 CB 733), (see § 601.601(d)(2)(ii)(*b*)), specifies the conditions under which the IRS will consider a request for a private letter ruling that an undivided fractional interest in rental real property is not an interest in a business entity under § 301.7701-2(a). A number of factors must be present to obtain a ruling under the revenue procedure, including a limit on the number of co-owners, a requirement that the co-owners not treat the co-ownership as an entity (that is, that the co-ownership may not file a partnership or corporate tax return, conduct business under a common name, execute an agreement identifying any or all of the co-owners as partners, shareholders, or members of a business entity, or otherwise hold itself out as a partnership or other form of business entity), and a requirement that certain rights with respect to the property (including the power to make certain management decisions) must be retained by co-owners. The revenue procedure provides that an organization that is an entity for state law purposes may not be characterized as a co-ownership under the guidance in the revenue procedure.

The courts and the IRS have addressed the Federal tax classification of investment trusts with assets divided among a number of series. In *National Securities Series-Industrial Stocks Series v. Commissioner*, 13 T.C. 884 (1949), *acq.*, 1950-1 CB 4, several series that differed only in the nature of their assets were created within a statutory open-end investment trust. Each series regularly issued certificates representing shares in the property held in trust and regularly redeemed the certificates solely from the assets and earnings of the individual series. The Tax Court stated that each series of the trust was taxable as a separate regulated investment company. See also Rev. Rul. 55-416 (1955-1 CB 416), (see § 601.601(d)(2)(ii)(*b*)). But see *Union Trusteed Funds v. Commissioner*, 8 T.C. 1133 (1947), (series funds organized by a state law corporation could not be treated as if each fund were a separate corporation).

In 1986, Congress added section 851(g) to the Code. Section 851(g) contains a special rule for series funds and provides that, in the case of a regulated investment company (within the meaning of section 851(a)) with more than one fund, each fund generally is treated as a separate corporation. For these purposes, a fund is a segregated portfolio of assets the beneficial interests in which are owned by holders of interests in the regulated investment company that are preferred over other classes or series with respect to these assets.

C. *Insurance company classification*

Section 7701(a)(3) and § 301.7701-2(b)(4) provide that an arrangement that qualifies as an insurance company is a corporation for Federal income tax purposes. Sections 816(a) and 831(c) define an insurance company as any company more than half the business of which during the taxable year is the issuing of insurance or annuity contracts or the reinsuring of risks underwritten by insurance companies. See also § 1.801-3(a)(1), ("[T]hough its name, charter powers, and subjection to State insurance laws are significant in determining the business which a company is authorized and intends to carry on, it is the character of the business actually done in the taxable year which determines whether a company is taxable as an insurance company under the Internal Revenue Code."). Thus, an insurance company includes an arrangement that conducts insurance business, whether or not the arrangement is a state law entity.

3. *Overview of Series LLC Statutes and Cell Company Statutes*

A. *Domestic statutes*

Although § 301.7701-1(a)(1) provides that state classification of an entity is not controlling for Federal tax purposes, the characteristics of series LLCs and cell companies under their governing statutes are an important factor in analyzing whether series and cells generally should be treated as separate entities for Federal tax purposes.

Series LLC statutes have been enacted in Delaware, Illinois, Iowa, Nevada, Oklahoma, Tennessee, Texas, Utah and Puerto Rico. Delaware enacted the first series LLC statute in 1996. Del. Code Ann. Tit. 6, section 18-215 (the Delaware statute). Statutes enacted subsequently by other states are similar, but not identical, to the Delaware statute. All of the statutes provide a significant degree of separateness for individual series within a series LLC, but none provides series with all of the attributes of a typical state law entity, such as an ordinary limited liability company. Individual series generally are not treated as separate entities for state law purposes. However, in certain states (currently Illinois and Iowa), a series is treated as a separate entity to the extent provided in the series LLC's articles of organization.

The Delaware statute provides that a limited liability company may establish, or provide for the establishment of, one or more designated series of members, managers, LLC interests or assets. Under the Delaware statute, any such series may have separate rights, powers, or duties with respect to specified property or obligations of the LLC or profits and losses associated with specified property or obligations, and any such series may have a separate business purpose or investment objective. Additionally, the Delaware statute provides that the debts, liabilities, obligations, and expenses of a particular series are enforceable against the assets of that series only, and not against the assets of the series LLC generally or any other series of the LLC, and, unless the LLC agreement provides otherwise, none of the debts, liabilities, obligations, and expenses of the series LLC generally or of any other series of the series LLC are enforceable against the assets of the series, provided that the following requirements are met: (1) the LLC agreement establishes or provides for the establishment of one or more series; (2) records maintained for any such series account for the assets of the series separately from the other assets of the series LLC, or of any other series of the series LLC; (3) the LLC agreement so provides; and (4) notice of the limitation on liabilities of a series is set forth in the series LLC's certificate of formation.

Unless otherwise provided in the LLC agreement, a series established under Delaware law has the power and capacity to, in its own name, contract, hold title to assets, grant liens and security interests, and sue and be sued. A series may be managed by the members of the series or by a manager. Any event that causes a manager to cease to be a manager with respect to a series will not, in itself, cause the manager to cease to be a manager of the LLC or of any other series of the LLC.

Under the Delaware statute, unless the LLC agreement provides otherwise, any event that causes a member to cease to be associated with a series will not, in itself, cause the member to cease to be associated with any other series or with the LLC, or cause termination of the series, even if there are no remaining members of the series. Additionally, the Delaware statute allows a series to be terminated and its affairs wound up without causing the dissolution of the LLC. However, all series of the LLC terminate when the LLC dissolves. Finally, under the Delaware statute, a series generally may not make a distribution to the extent that the distribution will cause the liabilities of the series to exceed the fair market value of the series' assets.

The series LLC statutes of Illinois, 805 ILCS 180/37-40 (the Illinois statute), and Iowa, I.C.A. § 489.1201 (the Iowa statute) provide that a series with limited liability will be treated as a separate entity to the extent set forth in the articles of organization. The Illinois statute provides that the LLC and any of its series may elect to consolidate their operations as a single taxpayer to the extent permitted under applicable law, elect to work cooperatively, elect to contract jointly, or elect to be treated as a single business for purposes of qualification to do business in Illinois or any other state.

In addition, under the Illinois statute, a series' existence begins upon filing of a certificate of designation with the Illinois secretary of state. A certificate of designation must be filed for each series that is to have limited liability. The name of a series with limited liability must contain the entire name of the LLC and be distinguishable from the names of the other series of the LLC. If different from the LLC, the certificate of designation for each series must list the names of the members if the series is member-managed or the names of the managers if the series is manager-managed. The Iowa and Illinois statutes both provide that, unless modified by the series LLC provisions, the provisions generally applicable to LLCs and their managers, members, and transferees are applicable to each series.

Some states have enacted series provisions outside of LLC statutes. For example, Delaware has enacted series limited partnership provisions (6 Del. C. § 17-218). In addition, Delaware's statutory trust statute permits a statutory trust to establish series (12 Del. C. § 3804). Both of these statutes contain provisions that are nearly identical to the corresponding provisions of the Delaware series LLC statute with respect to the ability of the limited partnership or trust to create or establish separate series with the same liability protection enjoyed by series of a Delaware series LLC.

All of the series LLC statutes contain provisions that grant series certain attributes of separate entities. For example, individual series may have separate business purposes, investment objectives, members, and managers. Assets of a particular series are not subject to the claims of creditors of other series of the series LLC or of the series LLC itself, provided that certain record-keeping and notice requirements are observed. Finally, most series LLC statutes provide that an event that causes a member to cease to be associated with a series does not cause the member to cease to be associated with the series LLC or any other series of the series LLC.

However, all of the state statutes limit the powers of series of series LLCs. For example, a series of a series LLC may not convert into another type of entity, merge with another entity, or domesticate in another state independent from the series LLC. Several of the series LLC statutes do not expressly address a series' ability to sue or be sued, hold title to property, or contract in its own name. Ordinary LLCs and series LLCs generally may exercise these rights. Additionally, most of the series LLC statutes provide that the dissolution of a series LLC will cause the termination of each of its series.

B. *Statutes with respect to insurance*

The insurance codes of a number of states include statutes that provide for the chartering of a legal entity commonly known as a protected cell company, segregated account company, or segregated portfolio company. See, for example, Vt. Stat. Ann. tit. 8, chap.141, §§ 6031-6038 (sponsored captive insurance companies and protected cells of such companies); S.C. Code Ann. tit. 38, chap. 10, §§ 38-10-10 through 39-10-80 (protected cell insurance companies). Under those statutes, as under the series LLC statutes described above, the assets of each cell are segregated from the assets of any other cell. The cell may issue insurance or annuity contracts, reinsure such contracts, or facilitate the securitization of obligations of a sponsoring insurance company. Rev. Rul. 2008-8 (2008-1 CB 340), (see § 601.601(d)(2)(ii)(*b*)), analyzes whether an arrangement entered into between a protected cell and its owner possesses the requisite risk shifting and risk distribution to qualify as insurance for Federal income tax purposes. Under certain domestic insurance codes, the sponsor may be organized under a corporate or unincorporated entity statute.

Series or cell company statutes in a number of foreign jurisdictions allow series or cells to engage in insurance businesses. See, for example, The Companies (Guernsey) Law, 2008 Part XXVII (Protected Cell Companies), Part XXVIII (Incorporated Cell Companies); The Companies (Jersey) law, 1991, Part 18D; Companies Law, Part XIV (2009 Revision) (Cayman Isl.) (Segregated Portfolio Companies); and Segregated Accounts Companies Act (2000) (Bermuda).

Explanation of Provisions

1. *In General*

The proposed regulations provide that, for Federal tax purposes, a domestic series, whether or not a juridical person for local law purposes, is treated as an entity formed under local law.

With one exception, the proposed regulations do not apply to series or cells organized or established under the laws of a foreign jurisdiction. The one exception is that the proposed regulations apply to a foreign series that engages in an insurance business.

Whether a series that is treated as a local law entity under the proposed regulations is recognized as a separate entity for Federal tax purposes is determined under § 301.7701-1 and general tax principles. The proposed regulations further provide that the classification of a series that is recognized as a separate entity for Federal tax purposes is determined under § 301.7701-1(b), which provides the rules for classifying organizations that are recognized as entities for Federal tax purposes.

The proposed regulations define a *series organization* as a juridical entity that establishes and maintains, or under which is established and maintained, a series. A series organization includes a series limited liability company, series partnership, series trust, protected cell company, segregated cell company, segregated portfolio company, or segregated account company.

The proposed regulations define a *series statute* as a statute of a State or foreign jurisdiction that explicitly provides for the organization or establishment of a series of a juridical person and explicitly permits (1) members or participants of a series organization to have rights, powers, or duties with respect to the series; (2) a series to have separate rights, powers, or duties with respect to specified property or obligations; and (3) the segregation of assets and liabilities such that none of the debts and liabilities of the series organization (other than liabilities to the State or foreign jurisdiction related to the organization or operation of the series organization, such as franchise fees or administrative costs) or of any other series of the series organization are enforceable against the assets of a particular series of the series organization. For purposes of this definition, a "participant" of a series organization includes an officer or director of the series organization who has no ownership interest in the series or series organization, but has rights, powers, or duties with respect to the series.

The proposed regulations define a series as a segregated group of assets and liabilities that is established pursuant to a series statute by agreement of a series organization. A series includes a cell, segregated account, or segregated portfolio, including a cell, segregated account, or segregated portfolio that is formed under the insurance code of a jurisdiction or is engaged in an insurance business. However, the term "series" does not include a segregated asset account of a life insurance company, which consists of all assets the investment return and market value of which must be allocated in an identical manner to any variable life insurance or annuity contract invested in any of the assets. See § 1.817-5(e). Such an account is accorded special treatment under subchapter L. See generally section 817(a) through (c).

Certain series statutes provide that the series liability limitation provisions do not apply if the series organization or series does not maintain records adequately accounting for the assets associated with each series separately from the assets of the series organization or any other series of the series organization. The IRS and the Treasury Department considered whether a failure to elect or qualify for the liability limitations under the series statute should affect whether a series is a separate entity for Federal tax purposes. However, limitations on liability of owners of an entity for debts and obligations of the entity and the rights of creditors to hold owners liable for debts and obligations of the entity generally do not alter the characterization of the entity for Federal tax purposes. Therefore, the proposed regulations provide that an election, agreement, or other arrangement that permits debts and liabilities of other series or the series organization to be enforceable against the assets of a particular series, or a failure to comply with the record keeping requirements for the limitation on liability available under the relevant series statute, will not prevent a series from meeting the definition of "series" in the proposed regulations. For example, a series generally will not cease to be an entity under the proposed regulations simply because it guarantees the debt of another series within the series organization.

The proposed regulations treat a series as created or organized under the laws of the same jurisdiction in which the series is established. Because a series may not be a separate juridical entity for local law purposes, this rule provides the means for establishing the jurisdiction of the series for Federal tax purposes.

Under § 301.7701-1(b), § 301.7701-2(b) applies to a series that is recognized as a separate entity for Federal tax purposes. Therefore, a series that is itself described in § 301.7701-2(b)(1) through (8) would be classified as a corporation regardless of the classification of the series organization.

The proposed regulations also provide that, for Federal tax purposes, ownership of interests in a series and of the assets associated with a series is determined under general tax principles. A series organization is not treated as the owner of a series or of the assets associated with a series merely because the series organization holds legal title to the assets associated with the series. For example, if a series organization holds legal title to assets associated with a series because the statute under which the series organization was organized does not expressly permit a series to hold assets in its own name, the series will be treated as the owner of the assets for Federal tax purposes if it bears the economic benefits and burdens of the assets under general Federal tax principles. Similarly, for Federal tax purposes, the obligor for the liability of a series is determined under general tax principles.

In general, the same legal principles that apply to determine who owns interests in other types of entities apply to determine the ownership of interests in series and series organizations. These principles generally look to who bears the economic benefits and burdens of ownership. See, for example, Rev. Rul. 55-39 (1955-1 CB 403), (see § 601.601(d)(2)(ii)(*b*)). Furthermore, common law principles apply to the determination of whether a person is a partner in a series that is classified as a partnership for Federal tax purposes under § 301.7701-3. See, for example, *Commissioner v. Culbertson*, 337 U.S. 733 (1949); *Commissioner v. Tower*, 327 U.S. 280 (1946).

The IRS and the Treasury Department considered other approaches to the classification of series for Federal tax purposes. In particular, the IRS and the Treasury Department considered whether series should be disregarded as entities separate from the series organization for Federal tax purposes. This approach would be supported by the fact that series are not generally considered entities for local law purposes (except, for example, potentially under the statutes of Illinois and Iowa, where a series may be treated as a separate entity to the extent set forth in the articles of organization). Additionally, while the statutes enabling series organizations grant series significant autonomy, under no current statute do series possess all of the attributes of independence that entities recognized under local law generally possess. For example, series generally cannot convert into another type of entity, merge with another entity, or domesticate in another jurisdiction independent of the series organization. In addition, the dissolution of a series organization generally will terminate all of its series.

The IRS and the Treasury Department believe that, notwithstanding that series differ in some respects from more traditional local law entities, domestic series generally should be treated for Federal tax purposes as entities formed under local law. Because Federal tax law, and not local law, governs the question of whether an organization is an entity for Federal tax purposes, it is not dispositive that domestic series generally are not considered entities for local law purposes. Additionally, the IRS and the Treasury Department believe that, overall, the factors supporting separate entity status for series outweigh the factors in favor of disregarding series as entities separate from the series organization and other series of the series organization. Specifically, managers and equity holders are "associated with" a series, and their rights, duties, and powers with respect to the series are direct and specifically identified. Also, individual series may (but generally are not required to) have separate business purposes and investment objectives. The IRS and the Treasury Department believe these factors are sufficient to treat domestic series as entities formed under local law.

Although some statutes creating series organizations permit an individual series to enter into contracts, sue, be sued, and/or hold property in its own name, the IRS and the Treasury Department do not believe that the failure of a statute to explicitly provide these rights should alter the treatment of a domestic series as an entity formed under local law. These attributes primarily involve procedural formalities and do not appear to affect the substantive economic rights of series or their creditors with respect to their property and liabilities. Even in jurisdictions where series may not possess these attributes, the statutory liability shields would still apply to the assets of a particular series, provided the statutory requirements are satisfied.

Furthermore, the rule provided in the proposed regulations would provide greater certainty to both taxpayers and the IRS regarding the tax status of domestic series and foreign series that conduct insurance businesses. In effect, taxpayers that establish domestic series are placed in the same position as persons that file a certificate of organization for a state law entity. The IRS and the Treasury Department believe that the approach of the proposed regulations is straightforward and administrable, and is preferable to engaging in a case by case determination of the status of each series that would require a detailed examination of the terms of the relevant statute. Finally, the IRS and the Treasury Department believe that a rule generally treating domestic series as local law entities would be consistent with taxpayers' current ability to create similar structures using multiple local law entities that can elect their Federal tax classification pursuant to §301.7701-3.

The IRS and the Treasury Department believe that domestic series should be classified as separate local law entities based on the characteristics granted to them under the various series statutes. However, except as specifically stated in the proposed regulations, a particular series need not actually possess all of the attributes that its enabling statute permits it to possess. The IRS and the Treasury Department believe that a domestic series should be treated as a separate local law entity even if its business purpose, investment objective, or ownership overlaps with that of other series or the series organization itself. Separate state law entities may have common or overlapping business purposes, investment objectives and ownership, but generally are still treated as separate local law entities for Federal tax purposes.

The proposed regulations do not address the entity status for Federal tax purposes of a series organization. Specifically, the proposed regulations do not address whether a series organization is recognized as a separate entity for Federal tax purposes if it has no assets and engages in no activities independent of its series.

Until further guidance is issued, the entity status of a foreign series that does not conduct an insurance business will be determined under applicable law. Foreign series raise novel Federal income tax issues that continue to be considered and addressed by the IRS and the Treasury Department.

2. Classification of a Series that is Treated as a Separate Entity for Federal Tax Purposes

If a domestic series or a foreign series engaged in an insurance business is treated as a separate entity for Federal tax purposes, then §301.7701-1(b) applies to determine the proper tax classification of the series. However, the proposed regulations do not provide how a series should be treated for Federal employment tax purposes. If a domestic series is treated as a separate entity for Federal tax purposes, then the series generally is subject to the same treatment as any other entity for Federal tax purposes. For example, a series that is treated as a separate entity for Federal tax purposes may make any Federal tax elections it is otherwise eligible to make independently of other series or the series organization itself, and regardless of whether other series (or the series organization) do not make certain elections or make different elections.

3. Entity Status of Series Organizations

The proposed regulations do not address the entity status or filing requirements of series organizations for Federal tax purposes. A series organization generally is an entity for local law purposes. An organization that is an entity for local law purposes generally is treated as an entity for Federal tax purposes. However, an organization characterized as an entity for Federal income tax purposes may not have an income or information tax filing obligation. For example, §301.6031(a)-(1)(a)(3)(i) provides that a partnership with no income, deductions, or credits for Federal income tax purposes for a taxable year is not required to file a partnership return for that year. Generally, filing fees of a series organization paid by series of the series organization would be treated as expenses of the series and not as expenses of the series organization. Thus, a series organization characterized as a partnership for Federal tax purposes that does not have income, deductions, or credits for a taxable year need not file a partnership return for the year.

4. Continuing Applicability of Tax Law Authority to Series

Notwithstanding that a domestic series or a foreign series engaged in an insurance business is treated as an entity formed under local law under the proposed regulations, the Commissioner may under applicable law, including common law tax principles, characterize a series or a portion of a series other than as a separate entity for Federal tax purposes. Series covered by the proposed regulations are subject to applicable law to the same extent as other entities. Thus, a series may be disregarded under applicable law even if it satisfies the requirements of the proposed regulations to be treated as an entity formed under local law. For example, if a series has no business purpose or business activity other than tax avoidance, it may be disregarded under appropriate circumstances. See *Bertoli v. Commissioner*, 103 T.C. 501 (1994); *Aldon Homes, Inc. v. Commissioner*, 33 T.C. 582 (1959). Furthermore, the anti-abuse rule of §1.701-2 is applicable to a series or series organization that is classified as a partnership for Federal tax purposes.

5. Applicability to Organizations that Qualify as Insurance Companies

Notice 2008-19 requested comments on proposed guidance setting forth conditions under which a cell of a protected cell company would be treated as an insurance company separate from any other entity for Federal income tax purposes. Those who commented on the notice generally supported the proposed guidance, and further commented that it should extend to non-insurance arrangements as well, including series LLCs. Rather than provide independent guidance for insurance company status setting forth what is essentially the same standard, the proposed regulations define the term *series* to include a cell, segregated account, or segregated portfolio that is formed under the insurance code of a jurisdiction or is engaged in an insurance business (other than a segregated asset account of a life insurance company).

Although the proposed regulations do not apply to a series organized or established under the laws of a foreign jurisdiction, an exception is provided for certain series conducting an insurance business. Under this exception, a series that is organized or established under the laws of a foreign jurisdiction is treated as an entity if the arrangements and other activities of the series, if conducted by a domestic company, would result in its being classified as an insurance company. Thus, a foreign series would be treated as an entity if more than half of the series' business is the issuing or reinsuring of insurance or annuity contracts. The IRS and the Treasury Department believe it is appropriate to provide this rule even though the proposed regulations otherwise do not apply to a foreign series because an insurance company is classified as a per se corporation under section 7701(a)(3) regardless of how it otherwise would be treated under §§301.7701-1, 301.7701-2, or 301.7701-3.

The IRS and the Treasury Department are aware that insurance-specific guidance may still be needed to address the issues identified in §3.02 of Notice 2008-19 and insurance-specific transition issues that may arise for protected cell companies that previously reported in a manner inconsistent with the regulations. See §601.601(d)(2)(ii)(b).

6. Effect of Local Law Classification on Tax Collection

The IRS and Treasury Department understand that there are differences in local law governing series (for example, rights to hold title to property and to sue and be sued are expressly addressed in some statutes but not in others) that may affect how creditors of series, including state taxing authorities, may enforce obligations of a series. Thus, the proposed regulations provide that, to the extent Federal or local law permits a creditor to collect a liability attributable to a series from the series organization or other series of the series organization, the series organization and other series of the series organization may also be considered the taxpayer from whom the tax assessed against the series may be collected pursuant to administrative or judicial means. Further, when a creditor is permitted to collect a liability attributable to a series organization from any series of the series organization, a tax liability assessed against the series organization may be collected directly from a series of the series organization by administrative or judicial means.

7. Employment Tax and Employee Benefits Issues

A. *In general*

The domestic statutes authorizing the creation of series contemplate that a series may operate a business. If the operating business has workers, it will be necessary to determine how the business satisfies any employment tax obligations, whether it has the ability to maintain any employee benefit plans and, if so, whether it complies with the rules applicable to those plans. Application of the employment tax requirements will depend principally on whether the workers are employees, and, if so, who is considered the employer for Federal income and employment tax purposes. In general, an employment relationship exists when the person for whom services are performed has the right to control and direct the individual who performs the services, not only as to the result to be accomplished by the work but also as to the details and means by which that result is accomplished. See § § 31.3121(d)-1(c)(2), 31.3306(i)-1(b), and 31.3401(c)-1(b).

B. *Employment tax*

An entity must be a person in order to be an employer for Federal employment tax purposes. See sections 3121(b), 3306(a)(1), 3306(c), and 3401(d) and § 31.3121(d)-2(a). However, status as a person, by itself, is not enough to make an entity an employer for Federal employment tax purposes. The entity must also satisfy the criteria to be an employer under Federal employment tax statutes and regulations for purposes of the determination of the proper amount of employment taxes and the party liable for reporting and paying the taxes. Treatment of a series as a separate person for Federal employment tax purposes would create the possibility that the series could be an "employer" for Federal employment tax purposes, which would raise both substantive and administrative issues.

The series structure would make it difficult to determine whether the series or the series organization is the employer under the relevant criteria with respect to the services provided. For example, if workers perform all of their services under the direction and control of individuals who own the interests in a series, but the series has no legal authority to enter into contracts or to sue or be sued, could the series nonetheless be the employer of the workers? If workers perform services under the direction and control of the series, but they are paid by the series organization, would the series organization, as the nominal owner of all the series assets, have control over the payment of wages such that it would be liable as the employer under section 3401(d)?

The structure of a series organization could also affect the type of employment tax liability. For example, if a series were recognized as a distinct person for Federal employment tax purposes, a worker providing services as an employee of one series and as a member of another series or the series organization would be subject to FICA tax on the wages paid for services as an employee and self-employment tax on the member income. Note further that, if a domestic series were classified as a separate entity that is a business entity, then, under § 301.7701-3, the series would be classified as either a partnership or a corporation. While a business entity with one owner is generally classified as a corporation or is disregarded for Federal tax purposes, such an entity cannot be disregarded for Federal employment tax purposes. See § 301.7701-2(c)(2)(iv).

Once the employer is identified, additional issues arise, including but not limited to the following: How would the wage base be determined for employees, particularly if they work for more than one series in a common line of business? How would the common paymaster rules apply? Who would be authorized to designate an agent under section 3504 for reporting and payment of employment taxes, and how would the authorization be accomplished? How would the statutory exceptions from the definitions of employment and wages apply given that they may be based on the identity of the employer? Which entity would be eligible for tax credits that go to the employer such as the Work Opportunity Tax Credit under section 51 or the tip credit under section 45B? If a series organization handles payroll for a series and is also the nominal owner of the series assets, would the owners or the managers of the series organization be responsible persons for the Trust Fund Recovery Penalty under section 6672?

Special administrative issues might arise if the series were to be treated as the employer for Federal employment tax purposes but not for state law purposes. For example, if the series were the employer for Federal employment tax purposes and filed a Form W-2, "Wage and Tax Statement," reporting wages and employment taxes withheld, but the series were not recognized as a juridical person for state law purposes, then administrative problems might ensue unless separate Forms W-2 were prepared for state and local tax purposes. Similarly, the IRS and the states might encounter challenges in awarding the FUTA credit under section 3302 to the appropriate entity and certifying the amount of state unemployment tax paid.

In light of these issues, the proposed regulations do not currently provide how a series should be treated for Federal employment tax purposes.

C. *Employee benefits*

Various issues arise with respect to the ability of a series to maintain an employee benefit plan, including issues related to those described above with respect to whether a series may be an employer. The proposed regulations do not address these issues. However, to the extent that a series can maintain an employee benefit plan, the aggregation rules under section 414(b), (c), (m), (o) and (t), as well as the leased employee rules under section 414(n), would apply. In this connection, the IRS and Treasury Department expect to issue regulations under section 414(o) that would prevent the avoidance of any employee benefit plan requirement through the use of the separate entity status of a series.

8. Statement Containing Identifying Information about Series

As the series organization or a series of the series organization may be treated as a separate entity for Federal tax and related reporting purposes but may not be a separate entity under local law, the IRS and Treasury Department believe that a new statement may need to be created and required to be filed annually by the series organization and each series of the series organization to provide the IRS with certain identifying information to ensure the proper assessment and collection of tax. Accordingly, these regulations propose to amend the Procedure and Administration Regulations under section 6011 to include this requirement and a cross-reference to those regulations is included under § 301.7701-1. The IRS and Treasury Department are considering what information should be required by these statements. Information tentatively being considered includes (1) the name, address, and taxpayer identification number of the series organization and each of its series and status of each as a series of a series organization or as the series organization; (2) the jurisdiction in which the series organization was formed; and (3) an indication of whether the series holds title to its assets or whether title is held by another series or the series organization and, if held by another series or the series organization, the name, address, and taxpayer identification number of the series organization and each series holding title to any of its assets. The IRS and Treasury Department are also considering the best time to require taxpayers to file the statement. For example, the IRS and Treasury Department are considering whether the statement should be filed when returns, such as income tax returns and excise tax returns, are required to be filed or whether it should be a stand-alone statement filed separately by a set date each year, as with information returns such as Forms 1099. A cross-reference to these regulations was added to the Procedure and Administration regulations under section 6071 for the time to file returns and statements. The proposed regulations under section 6071 provide that the statement will be a stand-alone statement due March 15th of each year. In addition, the IRS and Treasury Department are considering revising Form SS-4, "Application for Employer Identification Number," to include questions regarding series organizations.

Proposed Effective Date

These regulations generally apply on the date final regulations are published in the **Federal Register**. Generally, when final regulations become effective, taxpayers that are treating series differently for Federal tax purposes than series are treated under the final regulations will be required to change their treatment of series. In this situation, a series organization that previously was treated as one entity with all of its series may be required to begin treating each series as a separate entity for Federal tax purposes. General tax principles will apply to determine the consequences of the conversion from one entity to multiple entities for Federal tax purposes. See, for example, section 708 for rules relating to partnership divisions in the case of a series organization previously treated as a partnership for Federal tax purposes converting into multiple partnerships upon recognition of the series organization's series as separate entities. While a division of a partnership may be tax-free, gain may be recognized in certain situations under section 704(c)(1)(B) or section 737. Sections 355 and 368(a)(1)(D) provide rules that govern certain divisions of a corporation. The division of a series organization into multiple corporations may be tax-free to the corporation and to its shareholders; however, if the corporate division does not satisfy one or more of the requirements in section 355, the division may result in taxable events to the corporation, its shareholders, or both.

The regulations include an exception for series established prior to publication of the proposed regulations that treat all series and the series organization as one entity. If the requirements for this exception are satisfied, after issuance of the final regulations the series may continue to be treated together with the series organization as one entity for Federal tax purposes. Specifically, these requirements are satisfied if (1) The series was established prior to September 14, 2010; (2) The series (independent of the series organization or other series of the series organization) conducted business or investment activity or, in the case of a foreign series, more than half the business of the series was the issuing of insurance or annuity contracts or the reinsuring of risks underwritten by insurance companies, on and prior to September 14, 2010; (3) If the series was established pursuant to a foreign statute, the series' classification was relevant (as defined in § 301.7701-3(d)), and more than half the business of the series was the issuing of insurance or annuity contracts or the reinsuring of risks underwritten by insurance companies for all taxable years beginning with the taxable year that includes September 14, 2010; (4) No owner of the series treats the series as an entity separate from any other series of the series organization or from the series organization for purposes of filing any Federal income tax returns, information returns, or withholding documents for any taxable year; (5) The series and series organization had a reasonable basis (within the meaning of section 6662) for their claimed classification; and (6) Neither the series nor any owner of the series nor the series organization was notified in writing on or before the date final regulations are published in the **Federal Register** that classification of the series was under examination (in which case the series' classification will be determined in the examination).

This exception will cease to apply on the date any person or persons who were not owners of the series organization (or series) prior to September 14, 2010 own, in the aggregate, a 50 percent or greater interest in the series organization (or series). For this purpose, the term *interest* means (i) in the case of a partnership, a capital or profits interest and (ii) in the case of a corporation, an equity interest measured by vote or value. This transition rule does not apply to any determination other than the entity status of a series, for example, tax ownership of a series or series organization or qualification of a series or series organization conducting an insurance business as a controlled foreign corporation.

Special Analyses

It has been determined that this notice of proposed rulemaking is not a significant regulatory action as defined in Executive Order 12866. Therefore, a regulatory assessment is not required. It also has been determined that section 553(b) of the Administrative Procedure Act (5 U.S.C. chapter 5) does not apply to these regulations.

Pursuant to the Regulatory Flexibility Act (5.U.S.C. chapter 6), it is hereby certified that the regulations will not have a significant economic impact on a substantial number of small entities. The regulations require that series and series organizations file a statement to provide the IRS with certain identifying information to ensure the proper assessment and collection of tax. The regulations affect domestic series LLCs, domestic cell companies, and foreign series and cells that conduct insurance businesses, and their owners. Based on information available at this time, the IRS and the Treasury Department believe that many series and series organizations are large insurance companies or investment firms and, thus, are not small entities. Although a number of small entities may be subject to the information reporting requirement of the new statement, any economic impact will be minimal. The information that the IRS and the Treasury Department are considering requiring on the proposed statement should be known by or readily available to the series or the series organization. Therefore, it should take minimal time and expense to collect and report this information. For example, the IRS and the Treasury Department are considering requiring the following information: (1) The name, address, and taxpayer identification number of the series organization and each of its series and status of each as a series of a series organization or as the series organization; (2) The jurisdiction in which the series organization was formed; and (3) An indication of whether the series holds title to its assets or whether title is held by another series or the series organization and, if held by another series or the series organization, the name, address, and taxpayer identification number of the series organization and each series holding title to any of its assets. The IRS and the Treasury Department request comments on the accuracy of the statement that the regulations in this document will not have a significant economic impact on a substantial number of small entities. Pursuant to section 7805(f) of the Code, this notice of proposed rulemaking has been submitted to the Chief Counsel for Advocacy of the Small Business Administration for comment on its impact on small businesses.

Comments and Requests for a Public Hearing

Before these proposed regulations are adopted as final regulations, consideration will be given to any written comments (a signed original and eight (8) copies) that are submitted timely to the IRS. Alternatively, taxpayers may submit comments electronically directly to the Federal eRulemaking portal at *www.regulations.gov*.

The IRS and the Treasury Department request comments on the proposed regulations. In addition, the IRS and the Treasury Department request comments on the following issues:

(1) Whether a series organization should be recognized as a separate entity for Federal tax purposes if it has no assets and engages in no activities independent of its series;

(2) The appropriate treatment of a series that does not terminate for local law purposes when it has no members associated with it;

(3) The entity status for Federal tax purposes of foreign cells that do not conduct insurance businesses and other tax consequences of establishing, operating, and terminating all foreign cells;

(4) How the Federal employment tax issues discussed and similar technical issues should be resolved;

(5) How series and series organizations will be treated for state employment tax purposes and other state employment-related purposes and how that treatment should affect the Federal employment tax treatment of series and series organizations (comments from the states would be particularly helpful);

(6) What issues could arise with respect to the provision of employee benefits by a series organization or series; and

(7) The requirement for the series organization and each series of the series organization to file a statement and what information should be included on the statement.

All comments will be available for public inspection and copying. A public hearing may be scheduled if requested in writing by a person who timely submits comments. If a public hearing is scheduled, notice of the date, time and place for the hearing will be published in the **Federal Register**.

Drafting Information

The principal author of these proposed regulations is Joy Spies, IRS Office of the Associate Chief Counsel (Passthroughs and Special Industries). However, other personnel from the IRS and the Treasury Department participated in their development.

[¶ 49,475]   Proposed Amendments of Regulations (REG-140108-08), published in the Federal Register on March 15, 2011.

[Code Sec. 6104]

Disclosure of information to state officials: Tax-exempt organizations: Obtaining and inspecting returns and return information.— Amendments of Reg. § 301.6104(c)-1, amending existing regulations to reflect changes to Code Sec. 6104(c) made by the Pension Protection Act of 2006 (PPA) (P.L. 109-280), are proposed.

AGENCY: Internal Revenue Service (IRS), Treasury.

ACTION: Notice of proposed rulemaking.

SUMMARY: This document contains proposed regulations that amend existing regulations to reflect changes to section 6104(c) of the Internal Revenue Code (Code) made by the Pension Protection Act of 2006 (PPA). These rules provide guidance to states regarding the process by which they may obtain or inspect certain returns and return information (including information about final and proposed denials and revocations of tax-exempt status) for the purpose of administering state laws governing certain tax-exempt organizations and their activities. These regulations will affect such exempt organizations, as well as those state agencies choosing to obtain information from the Internal Revenue Service (IRS) under section 6104(c).

DATES: Written or electronic comments and requests for a public hearing must be received by June 13, 2011.

ADDRESSES: Send submissions to: CC:PA:LPD:PR (REG-140108-08), Room 5203, Internal Revenue Service, P.O. Box 7604, Ben Franklin Station, Washington, DC 20044. Submissions may be hand-delivered Monday through Friday between the hours of 8 a.m. and 4 p.m. to CC:PA:LPD:PR (REG-140108-08), Courier's Desk, Internal Revenue Service, 1111 Constitution Avenue, NW, Washington, DC, or sent electronically via the Federal eRulemaking Portal at *www.regulations.gov* (IRS REG-140108-08).

FOR FURTHER INFORMATION CONTACT: Concerning submission of comments, Oluwafunmilayo Taylor, (202) 622-7180 (not a toll-free number); concerning the proposed regulations, Casey Lothamer, (202) 622-6070 (not a toll-free number).

SUPPLEMENTARY INFORMATION:

Background

I. In general

This document contains proposed amendments to 26 CFR part 301 under section 6104(c), which will replace current § 301.6104(c)-1 in its entirety. Section 6104(c) governs when the IRS may disclose to state officials certain information about organizations described in section 501(c)(3) ("charitable organizations"), organizations that have applied for recognition as organizations described in section 501(c)(3) ("applicants"), and certain other exempt organizations. Section 6104(c) was added to the Code by section 101(e) of the Tax Reform Act of 1969 (Public Law 91-172, 83 Stat. 523) and significantly amended by section 1224(a) of the PPA (Public Law 109-280, 120 Stat. 1091).

Section 501(c)(3) organizations may be affected by the expanded disclosures to state officials authorized under the statute and proposed regulations. First, the IRS is now authorized (under new section 6104(c)(2), as added by the PPA) to disclose information about certain proposed revocations and proposed denials before an administrative appeal has been made and a final revocation or denial has been issued. For those organizations that have received a determination letter stating that they are described in section 501(c)(3), the IRS may disclose a proposed revocation (before any administrative appeal) to an appropriate state officer (ASO). This broader authority applies both where the organization was required under section 508 to apply for the determination letter and where the organization elected to apply for a determination letter even though it was not required to do so. The IRS continues to be authorized to disclose final revocations and final denials issued after any administrative appeal has been concluded for any section 501(c)(3) organization.

Second, under the authority of new section 6104(c)(2)(D), as added by the PPA, the IRS may disclose returns or return information of any section 501(c)(3) organization to ASOs on its own initiative, regardless of whether it has initiated an examination, if it determines that the information may be evidence of noncompliance with state laws under the jurisdiction of the ASO. Thus, if the IRS believes these conditions are met, it may, for example, disclose to ASOs a proposed revocation of exemption for a section 501(c)(3) organization that does not have a determination letter. All disclosures authorized under section 6104(c) may be made only if the state receiving the information is following applicable disclosure, recordkeeping and safeguard procedures.

The statute and proposed regulations also permit disclosure of information to state officials about all applicants for section 501(c)(3) status.

Exempt organizations other than section 501(c)(3) organizations also may be affected by the disclosures to state officials authorized under the statute and proposed regulations. The IRS is authorized to disclose returns and return information of these organizations to ASOs upon written request, but only to the extent necessary to administer state laws regulating the solicitation or administration of charitable funds or charitable assets. Again, all such disclosures may be made only if the state receiving the information is following applicable disclosure, recordkeeping and safeguard procedures.

Section 6104(c)(1), which is unchanged by the PPA, directs the IRS to share certain information with ASOs regarding charitable organizations and applicants. Specifically, section 6104(c)(1) provides that the IRS is to notify the ASO of the following final determinations: (1) a refusal to recognize an entity as an organization described in section 501(c)(3); (2) the operation of a section 501(c)(3) organization in a manner not meeting, or no longer meeting, the requirements of its exemption; and (3) the mailing of a notice of deficiency for any tax imposed under section 507, chapter 41, or chapter 42. See section 6104(c)(1)(A) and (c)(1)(B). The directive under section 6104(c)(1)(A) to notify ASOs of an organization no longer meeting the requirements for exemption under section 501(c)(3) includes not only notice of a revocation of exemption, but also notice (when the IRS is so informed) that a charitable organization is terminating or has dissolved in accordance with its governing documents. Upon request, an ASO may inspect and copy the returns, filed statements, records, reports, and other information relating to a final determination as described in this paragraph, as are relevant to any determination under state law. See section 6104(c)(1)(C).

II. PPA changes to section 6104(c)

The PPA amended section 6104(c) by striking paragraph (2) and inserting new paragraphs (2) through (6) as follows.

(1) The IRS may disclose to an ASO proposed refusals to recognize organizations as charitable organizations, and proposed revocations of such recognition. The PPA also allows disclosure of notices of proposed deficiencies of excise taxes imposed by section 507 and chapters 41 and 42

relating to charitable organizations. See section 6104(c)(2)(A)(i) and (c)(2)(A)(ii). Previously, only final determinations of this kind (denials of recognition, revocations, and notices of deficiency) could be disclosed under section 6104(c).

(2) The IRS may disclose to an ASO the names, addresses, and taxpayer identification numbers of applicants. See section 6104(c)(2)(A)(iii). Previously, information on applicants, other than information relating to a denial of recognition, could not be disclosed under section 6104(c).

(3) The IRS may disclose to an ASO the returns and return information of organizations with respect to which information is disclosed as described in paragraphs (1) and (2) of this section II (proposed determinations and applicant identifying information). See section 6104(c)(2)(B). Prior law allowed for disclosure under section 6104(c) only of returns and return information related to final determinations.

(4) Proposed determinations, identifying information, and the related returns and return information with respect to charitable organizations and applicants may be disclosed to an ASO only upon the ASO's written request and only as necessary to administer state laws regulating charitable organizations, such as laws governing tax-exempt status, charitable trusts, charitable solicitation, and fraud. See section 6104(c)(2)(C). Prior law provided for automatic disclosure (without a request), but only of final determinations and their related returns and return information.

(5) The IRS may disclose to an ASO on its own initiative (without a written request) returns and return information with respect to charitable organizations and applicants if the IRS determines that this information might constitute evidence of noncompliance with the laws under the jurisdiction of the ASO. See section 6104(c)(2)(D). There was no such provision under section 6104(c) previously.

(6) The IRS may disclose returns and return information of section 501(c) organizations other than those described in section 501(c)(1) or (c)(3) to an ASO upon the ASO's written request, but only to the extent necessary in administering state laws relating to the solicitation or administration of charitable funds or charitable assets of such organizations. See section 6104(c)(3). Previously, only information relating to charitable organizations or applicants was disclosed under section 6104(c).

(7) Returns and return information of organizations and taxable persons disclosed under section 6104(c) may be disclosed in civil administrative and civil judicial proceedings pertaining to the enforcement of state laws regulating such organizations, under procedures prescribed by the IRS similar to those under section 6103(h)(4). See section 6104(c)(4). There was no such provision under section 6104(c) previously.

(8) No return or return information may be disclosed under section 6104(c) to the extent the IRS determines that such disclosure would seriously impair federal tax administration. See section 6104(c)(5). This disclosure prohibition, though new in the PPA, was provided previously by regulation. See current § 301.6104(c)-1(b)(3)(ii).

(9) The IRS may disclose returns and return information under section 6104(c) to a state officer or employee designated by the ASO to receive such information on the ASO's behalf. See section 6104(c)(2)(C) (flush language) and (c)(3). Prior law did not provide for IRS disclosures to persons other than ASOs.

(10) An ASO is defined as the state attorney general, state tax officer, any state official charged with overseeing charitable organizations (in the case of charitable organizations and applicants), and the head of the state agency charged with the primary responsibility for overseeing the solicitation of funds for charitable purposes (in the case of section 501(c) organizations other than those described in section 501(c)(1) or (c)(3)). See section 6104(c)(6)(B). Before its amendment by the PPA, section 6104(c)(2) defined ASO as the state attorney general, state tax officer, or any state official charged with overseeing organizations of the type described in section 501(c)(3).

III. Related PPA provisions

The PPA amended section 6103(p) to make the disclosure of returns and return information under section 6104(c) subject to the disclosure, recordkeeping, and safeguard provisions of section 6103. These provisions include—

(1) section 6103(a), which is the general prohibition on the disclosure of returns and return information, except as authorized by Title 26 of the United States Code;

(2) section 6103(p)(3), which requires the IRS to maintain permanent standardized records of all requests for inspection or disclosure of returns or return information under section 6104(c) and of all such information inspected or disclosed pursuant to those requests; and

(3) section 6103(p)(4), which requires an ASO, as a condition for receiving returns or return information under section 6104(c), to establish and maintain certain safeguards, such as keeping permanent standardized records of all requests and disclosures, maintaining a secure information storage area, restricting access to the information, and providing whatever other safeguards the IRS deems necessary to protect the confidentiality of the information. See § 301.6103(p)(4)-1 and IRS Publication 1075, Tax Information Security Guidelines for Federal, State and Local Agencies and Entities. Publication 1075 can be found at www.irs.gov/formspubs.

The PPA also included amendments to sections 7213, 7213A, and 7431 to impose civil and criminal penalties for the unauthorized disclosure or inspection of section 6104(c) information.

IV. IRS disclosure procedures

In general, before any federal or state agency may receive returns and return information from the IRS under a particular Code provision, it must file with the IRS a report detailing the physical, administrative, and technical safeguards implemented by the agency to protect this information from unauthorized inspection or disclosure. Only upon approval of these safeguards by the IRS, as well as satisfaction of any other statutory requirements (such as submission of a written request), may an agency receive the information to which it is entitled under the Code, and then only for the use specified by the relevant statute. See section 6103(p)(4).

Under various disclosure programs, the IRS and other federal and state agencies often execute agreements detailing the responsibilities of the parties and the terms and parameters of the disclosure arrangement. For example, under section 6103(d), the IRS executes a disclosure agreement (the "Basic Agreement") with each state tax agency to which it discloses information. The Basic Agreement, which serves as the written request required by section 6103(d), has been the foundation of the state tax disclosure program under this provision of the Code for over 30 years. See Internal Revenue Manual Exhibit 11.3.32-1 (sample Basic Agreement).

After the PPA, the IRS revised its disclosure procedures under section 6104(c) to model them after the highly successful section 6103(d) program. The section 6104(c) program uses a disclosure agreement patterned after the Basic Agreement but tailored to the specific requirements and restrictions of section 6104(c).

Explanation of Provisions

These proposed regulations provide guidance regarding disclosures under section 6104(c), as amended by the PPA. The PPA amendments to sections 6104(c) and 6103 expand the scope of information the IRS may disclose to an ASO, but make such disclosures contingent on the ASO adopting the safeguard standards and procedures of section 6103 that apply to federal and state agencies that receive returns and return information under other provisions of the Code. Accordingly, these proposed regulations provide that, without prior safeguard approval, the IRS will not give automatic notification of any determinations or other information that may be disclosed under section 6104(c).

Under these proposed regulations, the IRS may (and currently does) require an ASO to enter into a disclosure agreement with the IRS, which will stipulate the procedures for disclosure under section 6104(c), as well as the restrictions on use and redisclosure. These proposed regulations provide that this agreement, or any similar document, satisfies the requirement under section 6104(c) for a written request for disclosure.

An ASO who meets the safeguard and other procedural requirements of section 6103(p)(4) may receive information from the IRS to be used in the administration of state laws governing charitable organizations, as well as laws governing the solicitation or administration of charitable funds or charitable assets of certain noncharitable exempt organizations. The information available to ASOs under these proposed regulations not only is greater in scope than what was available under section 6104(c) before its amendment by the PPA, but comes at an earlier stage in the IRS administrative and enforcement processes. Thus, the IRS may disclose such information as whether an organization has applied for recognition as a charitable organization and, if so, whether the IRS proposes to deny such recognition, or the organization has withdrawn its application; whether an organization's charitable status has terminated; whether the IRS proposes to assess any chapter 42 excise taxes (for example, the tax on excess benefit transactions under section 4958); and whether the IRS has revoked an organization's exemption, or proposes to revoke the recognition of its exemption.

Without a written request, but still subject to the safeguard requirements of section 6103(p)(4), the IRS has the authority under section 6104(c)(2)(D) to disclose returns and return information of charitable organizations and applicants if it determines that such information may constitute evidence of noncompliance with the laws under the ASO's jurisdiction. The IRS may make these disclosures on its own initiative. These proposed regulations clarify that the IRS' authority under section 6104(c)(2)(D) is in addition to its disclosure authority under other provisions of section 6104(c)(1) and (c)(2), to the effect that discretionary disclosures may be made before the IRS issues a proposed determination or takes other action. The proposed regulations also make clear that the determination required by the statute concerns possible noncompliance with state laws regulating charitable organizations and not just any state law violation.

The disclosure provisions of section 6104(c), as amended by the PPA, offer significant advantages to states in their enforcement efforts. The ability of the IRS to disclose returns and return information early in its own administrative and enforcement processes, as well as the IRS' authority under section 6104(c)(2)(D) to disclose information on its own initiative, greatly enhance the administration and enforcement of state laws, both tax and nontax, governing charitable activities, funds, and assets.

These proposed regulations define certain key terms for purposes of section 6104(c), including "appropriate state officer", "return", "return information", and "taxable person."

Special Analyses

It has been determined that this notice of proposed rulemaking is not a significant regulatory action as defined in Executive Order 12866; therefore, a regulatory assessment is not required. It also has been determined that section 553(b) of the Administrative Procedure Act (5 U.S.C. chapter 5) and the Regulatory Flexibility Act (5 U.S.C. chapter 6) do not apply to the proposed regulations; therefore, a regulatory flexibility analysis is not required. Pursuant to section 7805(f) of the Internal Revenue Code, the proposed regulations have been submitted to the Chief Counsel for Advocacy of the Small Business Administration for comments regarding their impact on small businesses.

Comments and Requests for a Public Hearing

Before these proposed regulations are adopted as final, any written (signed original and 8 copies) or electronic comments timely submitted to the IRS will be considered. The IRS and Treasury Department request comments on the clarity of these proposed regulations and how they might be made easier to understand. Of particular interest are comments on whether paragraph (e) of these proposed regulations, describing the organizations to which disclosure applies, lists all the organizations with respect to which ASOs might legitimately need information. All comments will be available for public inspection and copying. A public hearing will be scheduled if requested in writing by any person who timely submits written comments. If a public hearing is scheduled, notice of the date, time, and place for the public hearing will be published in the **Federal Register**.

Drafting Information

The principal author of these regulations is Casey Lothamer of the Office of Division Counsel/Associate Chief Counsel (Tax Exempt and Government Entities), though other persons in the IRS and Treasury Department participated in their development.

[¶ 49,493] Proposed Amendments of Regulations (REG-111283-11), published in the Federal Register on September 16, 2011.

[Code Secs. 446, 512, 863, 954, 988 and 1256]

Swap contracts: Notional principal contracts: Section 1256 contracts: Qualified board or exchange.—Reg. §§1.1256(b)-1 and 1.1256(g)-1, and amendments of Reg. §§1.446-3, 1.512(b)-1, 1.863-7, 1.954-2 and 1.988-1, describing swaps and similar agreements that fall within the meaning of Code Sec. 1256(b)(2)(B), are proposed. The texts are at ¶20,613E, ¶22,835B, ¶27,172A, ¶28,535D, ¶28,902D, ¶31,102 and ¶31,105.

AGENCY: Internal Revenue Service (IRS), Treasury.

ACTION: Notice of proposed rulemaking and notice of public hearing.

SUMMARY: This document contains proposed regulations that describe swaps and similar agreements that fall within the meaning of section 1256(b)(2)(B) of the Internal Revenue Code (Code). This document also contains proposed regulations that revise the definition of a notional principal contract under §1.446-3 of the Income Tax Regulations. This document provides a notice of public hearing on these proposed regulations.

DATES: Written or electronic comments must be received by December 15, 2011. Outlines of topics to be discussed at the public hearing scheduled for January 19, 2012, must be received by December 14, 2011.

ADDRESSES: Send submissions to: CC:PA:LPD:PR (REG-111283-11), room 5203, Internal Revenue Service, POB 7604, Ben Franklin Station, Washington DC 20044. Submissions may be hand delivered Monday through Friday, between the hours of 8 a.m. and 4 p.m. to CC:PA:LPD:PR (REG-111283-11), Courier's Desk, Internal Revenue Service, 1111 Constitution Avenue, N.W., Washington, DC. Alternatively, taxpayers may submit comments electronically via the Federal eRulemaking Portal at *www.regulations.gov/* (IRS-REG-111283-11). The public hearing will be held in the Auditorium, Internal Revenue Building, 1111 Constitution Avenue, N.W., Washington, DC.

FOR FURTHER INFORMATION CONTACT: Concerning the proposed regulations, K. Scott Brown (202) 622-7454; concerning submissions of comments, the hearing, and/or to be placed on the building access list to attend the hearing, Richard Hurst, (202) 622-7180 (not toll-free numbers).

SUPPLEMENTARY INFORMATION:

Background

This document contains proposed amendments to the Income Tax Regulations (26 CFR 1) under sections 1256 and 446 of the Code. Section 1256(b)(2)(B) was added to the Code by section 1601 of the Dodd-Frank Wall Street Reform and Consumer Protection Act (Public Law No. 111-203,

§1601, 124 Stat. 1376, 2223 (2010)) (the Dodd-Frank Act). Section 1256(b)(2)(B) provides that certain swaps and similar agreements are not subject to section 1256 of the Code. These proposed regulations provide guidance on the category of swaps and similar agreements that are within the scope of section 1256(b)(2)(B). These proposed regulations also revise the definition and scope of a notional principal contract under §1.446-3 of the Income Tax Regulations.

Explanation of Provisions

A. *Section 1256(b)(2)(B) Language and Legislative History*

Section 1256 provides that contracts classified as section 1256 contracts are marked to market and any gain or loss is generally treated as 60 percent long-term capital gain or loss and 40 percent short-term capital gain or loss. Section 1256(b)(1) defines the term "section 1256 contract" as a regulated futures contract, foreign currency contract, nonequity option, dealer equity option, and dealer securities futures contract. With the exception of a foreign currency contract, a section 1256 contract must be traded on or subject to the rules of a "qualified board or exchange" as defined in section 1256(g)(7).

Section 1601 of the Dodd-Frank Act added section 1256(b)(2)(B), which excludes swaps and similar agreements from the definition of a section 1256 contract. Section 1256(b)(2)(B) provides that the term "section 1256 contract" shall not include—

any interest rate swap, currency swap, basis swap, interest rate cap, interest rate floor, commodity swap, equity swap, equity index swap, credit default swap, or similar agreement.

Congress enacted section 1256(b)(2)(B) to resolve uncertainty under section 1256 for swap contracts that are traded on regulated exchanges. The specific uncertainty addressed by the enactment of section 1256(b)(2)(B) was described in the Conference Report:

The title contains a provision to address the recharacterization of income as a result of increased exchange-trading of derivatives contracts by clarifying that section 1256 of the Internal Revenue Code does not apply to certain derivatives contracts transacted on exchanges.

H.R. Conf. Rep. No. 111-517, at 879 (2010).

Section 1256(b)(2)(B) contemplates that a swap contract, even if traded on or subject to the rules of a qualified board or exchange, will not be a section 1256 contract.

B. *Scope of Swaps Excluded by Section 1256(b)(2)(B)*

1. *Notional principal contracts and credit default swaps*

Congress incorporated into section 1256(b)(2)(B) a list of swaps that parallels the list of swaps included under the definition of a notional principal contract in §1.446-3(c) with the addition of credit default swaps. The parallel language suggests that Congress was attempting to harmonize the category of swaps excluded under section 1256(b)(2)(B) with swaps that qualify as notional principal contracts under §1.446-3(c), rather than with the contracts defined as "swaps" under section 721 of the Dodd-Frank Act. Accordingly, §1.1256(b)-1(a) of the proposed regulations provides that a section 1256 contract does not include a contract that qualifies as a notional principal contract as defined in proposed §1.446-3(c). As discussed herein, the proposed regulations under §1.446-3 also expressly provide that a credit default swap is a notional principal contract.

2. *Option on a notional principal contract*

Section 1256(b)(2)(B) raises questions as to whether an option on a notional principal contract that is traded on a qualified board or exchange would constitute a "similar agreement" or would instead be treated as a nonequity option under section 1256(g)(3). Since an option on a notional principal contract is closely connected with the underlying contract, the Treasury Department and the IRS believe that such an option should be treated as a similar agreement within the meaning of section 1256(b)(2)(B). Accordingly, §1.1256(b)-1(a) of the proposed regulations also provides that a section 1256 contract does not include an option on any contract that is a notional principal contract defined in §1.446-3(c) of the proposed regulations.

3. *Ordering rule*

The proposed regulations provide an ordering rule for a contract that trades as a futures contract regulated by the Commodity Futures Trading Commission (CFTC), but that also meets the definition of a notional principal contract. The Treasury Department and the IRS believe that such a contract is not a commodity futures contract of the kind envisioned by Congress when it enacted section 1256. Accordingly, §1.1256(b)-1(a) of the proposed regulations provides that section 1256 does not include any contract, or option on such contract, that is both a section 1256 contract and a notional principal contract as defined in §1.446-3(c) of the proposed regulations.

C. *Definition of Regulated Futures Contract*

Section 1256(g)(1) defines a regulated futures contract as "a contract (A) with respect to which the amount required to be deposited and the amount which may be withdrawn depends on a system of marking to market, and (B) which is traded on or subject to the rules of a qualified board or exchange." The apparent breadth of section 1256(g)(1) has raised questions in the past as to whether a contract other than a futures contract can be a regulated futures contract. The Treasury Department and the IRS have historically limited the scope of a regulated futures contract to those futures contracts that have the characteristics of traditional futures contracts. Under the Dodd-Frank Act, a "designated contract market" may trade both futures contracts and swap contracts, although there will be specific reporting rules for swap contracts. In order to properly limit section 1256 to futures contracts that trade on designated contract markets, §1.1256(b)-1(b) of the proposed regulations provides that a regulated futures contract is a section 1256 contract only if the contract is a futures contract that is not required to be reported as a swap under the Commodity Exchange Act (7 U.S.C. 1) (the CEA). The reporting provisions for swaps under the CEA will not be effective until the CFTC has published final rules implementing such provisions. It is anticipated that swap reporting rules will be in effect before these regulations are finalized. If, however, these proposed income tax regulations are finalized before the swap reporting provisions become effective, the Treasury Department and the IRS will evaluate whether the provisions of §1.1256(b)-1(b) need to be adjusted.

Questions have also been raised as to whether the requirement that a regulated futures contract be "traded on or subject to the rules of" a qualified board or exchange includes off-exchange transactions such as an exchange of a futures contract for a cash commodity, or an exchange of a futures contract for a swap, that are carried out subject to the rules of a CFTC designated contract market. The phrase "traded on or subject to the rules of" appears to have originated under the CEA. Section 4(a) of the CEA provides, in part, that it is unlawful to engage in any transaction in, or in connection with, a commodity futures contract unless such transaction is conducted on or subject to the rules of a board of trade which has been designated as a contract market and such contract is executed or consummated by or through a contract market. Section 5(d) of the CEA, as amended by section 735 of the Dodd-Frank Act, provides that the rules of a designated contract market may authorize, for bona fide business purposes, transfer trades or office trades, or an exchange of (i) futures in connection with a cash commodity transaction, (ii) futures for cash commodities, or (iii) futures for swaps. As such, the Treasury Department and the IRS believe that a futures contract that results from one of these transactions is a regulated futures contract under section 1256(g)(1) because the contract is traded subject to the rules of a designated contract market.

D. *Qualified Board or Exchange*

Section 1256(g)(7)(C) provides that a qualified board or exchange includes any other exchange, board of trade, or other market which the Secretary determines has rules adequate to carry out the purposes of section 1256. Section 1.1256(g)-1(a) of the proposed regulations specifies that such determinations are only made through published guidance in the **Federal Register** or in the Internal Revenue Bulletin.

Since section 1256(g)(7) was adopted, the Treasury Department and the IRS have issued determinations for six entities, all of them foreign futures exchanges. See Rev. Rul. 2010-3 (2010-1 CB 272 (London International Financial Futures and Options Exchange)), Rev. Rul. 2009-24 (2009-2 CB 306 (ICE Futures Canada)), Rev. Rul. 2009-4 (2009-1 CB 408 (Dubai Mercantile Exchange)), Rev. Rul. 2007-26 (2007-1 CB 970 (ICE Futures)), Rev. Rul. 86-7 (1986-1 CB 295 (The Mercantile Division of the Montreal Exchange)), and Rev. Rul. 85-72 (1985-1 CB 286 (International Futures Exchange (Bermuda))). The IRS has followed a two step process for making each of the six qualified board or exchange determinations under section 1256(g)(7). See § 601.601(d)(2)(ii)(b).

In the first step, the exchange submitted a private letter ruling to the IRS requesting a determination that the exchange is a qualified board or exchange within the meaning of section 1256(g)(7)(C). Once the IRS determined that the exchange had rules sufficient to carry out the purposes of section 1256, the Treasury Department and the IRS published a revenue ruling announcing that the named exchange was a qualified board or exchange. The revenue rulings apply to commodity futures contracts and futures contract options of the type described under the CEA that are entered into on the named exchange. The revenue ruling does not apply to contracts that are entered into on another exchange that is affiliated with the named exchange.

In determining whether a foreign exchange is a qualified board or exchange under section 1256(g)(7)(C), the Treasury Department and the IRS have looked to whether the exchange received a CFTC "direct access" no-action relief letter permitting the exchange to make its electronic trading and matching system available in the United States, notwithstanding that the exchange was not designated as a contract market pursuant to section 5 of the CEA. Section 738 of the Dodd-Frank Act, however, provides the CFTC with authority to adopt rules and regulations that require registration of a foreign board of trade that provides United States participants direct access to the foreign board of trade's electronic trading system. In formulating these rules and regulations, the CFTC is directed to consider whether comparable supervision and regulation exists in the foreign board of trade's home country. Pursuant to section 738, the CFTC has proposed a registration system to replace the direct access no-action letter process. Under the proposed registration system, a foreign board of trade operating pursuant to an existing direct access no-action relief letter must apply through a limited application process for an "Order of Registration" which will replace the foreign board of trade's existing direct access no-action letter. Many of the proposed requirements for and conditions applied to a foreign board of trade's registration will be based upon those applicable to the foreign board of trade's currently granted direct access no-action relief letter.

The IRS has conditioned a foreign exchange's qualified board or exchange status under section 1256(g)(7)(C) on the exchange continuing to satisfy all CFTC conditions necessary to retain its direct access no-action relief letter. Consequently, if the CFTC adopts the proposed registration system, an exchange that has previously received a qualified board or exchange determination under section 1256(g)(7)(C) must obtain a CFTC Order of Registration in order to maintain its qualified board or exchange status. The IRS will continue to evaluate the CFTC's rules in this regard to determine if any changes to the IRS's section 1256(g)(7)(C) guidance process are warranted.

E. *Definition and Scope of a Notional Principal Contract*

1. *Payments under a notional principal contract*

In 1993, the IRS promulgated § 1.446-3(c) which defines a notional principal contract as a financial instrument that provides for the payment of amounts by one party to another at specified intervals calculated by reference to a specified index upon a notional principal amount in exchange for specified consideration or a promise to pay similar amounts. Questions have arisen as to the proper interpretation of this requirement. Sections 1.446-3(c)(1)(i) and (ii) of the proposed regulations expressly provide that a notional principal contract requires one party to make two or more payments to a counterparty. For this purpose, the fixing of an amount is treated as a payment, even if the actual payment reflecting that amount is to be made at a later date. Thus, for example, a contract that provides for a settlement payment referenced to the appreciation or depreciation on a specified number of shares of common stock, adjusted for actual dividends paid during the term of the contract, is treated as a contract with more than one payment with respect to that leg of the contract.

2. *Credit default swaps*

In Notice 2004-52 (2004-2 CB 168), the Treasury Department and the IRS described four possible characterizations of a credit default swap. See § 601.601(d)(2)(ii)(b). These proposed regulations resolve this uncertainty by adding credit default swaps to the list of swaps categorized as notional principal contracts governed by the rules of § 1.446-3.

3. *Weather-related and other non-financial index based swaps*

Since the time that the § 1.446-3 regulations were promulgated, markets have developed for contracts based on non-financial indices. Many of these contracts are structured as swaps, and payments are calculated based on indices such as temperature, precipitation, snowfall, or frost. For example, payments made under a weather derivative may be based on heating degree days and cooling degree days. As a technical matter, a weather-related swap currently is not a notional principal contract because a weather index does not qualify as a "specified index" under § 1.446-3(c)(2) of the current regulations, which generally require that such index be a financial index.

The Treasury Department and the IRS believe that swaps on non-financial indices should be treated as notional principal contracts. Accordingly, § 1.446-3(c)(2)(ii) of the proposed regulations expands a specified index to include non-financial indices that are comprised of any objectively determinable information that is not within the control of any of the parties to the contract and is not unique to one of the parties' circumstances, and that cannot be reasonably expected to front-load or back-load payments accruing under the contract.

4. *Excluded contracts*

Section 1.446-3(c)(1)(ii) currently provides that a contract described in section 1256(b) and a futures contract are not notional principal contracts. In order to remove the circularity that would otherwise exist between excluded contracts under § 1.446-3(c)(1)(ii) and proposed § 1.1256(b)-1, a contract described in section 1256(b) and a futures contract have been deleted from excluded contracts under proposed § 1.446-3(c)(1)(iv).

5. *Conforming Amendments*

The definition of a notional principal contract in § 1.446-3(c) of the proposed regulations is intended to be the operative definition for all Federal income tax purposes, except where a different or more limited definition is specifically prescribed. Thus, the regulations under sections 512, 863, 954, and 988 have been amended to reference the definition of a notional principal contract in § 1.446-3(c).

Proposed Effective/Applicability Date

These regulations are proposed to apply to contracts entered into on or after the date the final regulations are published in the **Federal Register**.

Special Analyses

It has been determined that this notice of proposed rulemaking is not a significant regulatory action as defined in Executive Order 12866. Therefore, a regulatory assessment is not required. It has also been determined that section 553(b) of the Administrative Procedure Act (5 U.S.C. chapter 5) does not apply to these regulations, and because the regulation does not impose a collection of information on small entitles, the Regulatory Flexibility Act (5 U.S.C. chapter 6) does not apply. Pursuant to section 7805(f) of the Code, this notice of proposed rulemaking will be submitted to the Chief Counsel for Advocacy of the Small Business Administration for comment on its impact on small business.

Comments and Public Hearing

Before these proposed regulations are adopted as final regulations, consideration will be given to any written comments (a signed original and eight (8) copies) or electronic comments that are submitted timely to the IRS. The Treasury Department and IRS invite comments on the clarity of the proposed rules and how they can be made easier to understand. All comments will be available at *www.regulations.gov* or upon request.

A public hearing has been scheduled for January 19, 2012, beginning at 10 a.m. in the Auditorium, Internal Revenue Building, 1111 Constitution Avenue, N.W., Washington, DC. Due to building security procedures, visitors must enter at the Constitution Avenue entrance. In addition, all visitors must present photo identification to enter the building. Because of access restrictions, visitors will not be admitted beyond the immediate entrance area more than 30 minutes before the hearing starts. For information about having your name placed on the building access list to attend the hearing, see the "FOR FURTHER INFORMATION CONTACT" section of this preamble.

The rules of 26 CFR 601.601(a)(3) apply to the hearing. Persons who wish to present oral comments at the hearing must submit written or electronic comments by December 15, 2011 and an outline of the topics to be discussed and the time to be devoted to each topic (a signed original and eight (8) copies) by December 14, 2011. A period of 10 minutes will be allotted to each person for making comments. An agenda showing the scheduling of the speakers will be prepared after the deadline for receiving outlines has passed. Copies of the agenda will be available free of charge at the hearing.

Drafting Information

The principal author of these proposed regulations is K. Scott Brown, Office of the Associate Chief Counsel (Financial Institutions and Products). However, other personnel from the IRS and Treasury Department participated in their development.

[¶ 49,499]   Proposed Amendments of Regulations (REG-133002-10), published in the Federal Register on October 24, 2011.

[Code Sec. 1502]

Corporations: Consolidated returns: Net unrealized built-in gains: Net unrealized built-in losses.—Amendments of Reg. §1.1502-91, relating to corporations filing consolidated returns, are proposed.

AGENCY: Internal Revenue Service (IRS), Treasury.

ACTION: Notice of proposed rulemaking.

SUMMARY: This document contains proposed regulations under section 1502 of the Internal Revenue Code. The regulations will apply to corporations filing consolidated returns. The regulations will require a loss group or loss subgroup to redetermine its consolidated net unrealized built-in gain and loss in certain circumstances. This document also invites comments from the public regarding these proposed regulations.

DATES: Written or electronic comments and requests for a public hearing must be received by January 23, 2012.

ADDRESSES: Send submissions to: CC:PA:LPD:PR (REG-133002-10), room 5205, Internal Revenue Service, PO Box 7604, Ben Franklin Station, Washington, DC 20044. Submissions may be hand-delivered Monday through Friday between the hours of 8 a.m. and 4 p.m. to CC:PA:LPD:PR (REG-133002-10), Courier's Desk, Internal Revenue Service, 1111 Constitution Avenue, NW, Washington, DC, or sent electronically, via the Federal eRulemaking Portal at *http://www.regulations.gov* (IRS REG-133002-10).

FOR FURTHER INFORMATION CONTACT: Concerning the proposed regulations, Grid Glyer (202) 622-7930; concerning submissions of comments and requests for a public hearing, Oluwafunmilayo Taylor (202) 622-7180 (not toll-free numbers).

SUPPLEMENTARY INFORMATION:

Background

To prevent loss trafficking, section 382 imposes a limitation (the section 382 limitation) on a loss corporation's ability to use net operating losses that arose prior to an ownership change. Section 382(b)(1). In addition, if a loss corporation has a net unrealized built-in loss (NUBIL) at the time of an ownership change, built-in losses will be subject to the section 382 limitation as if they were pre-change losses of the loss corporation if they are recognized during the five-year period following the ownership change (the recognition period). Section 382(h)(1)(B). If a corporation has a net unrealized built-in gain (NUBIG) at the time of its ownership change, recognized built-in gains will increase the section 382 limitation if they are recognized during the recognition period. Section 382(h)(1)(A). Rules for determining whether a loss corporation has a NUBIG or NUBIL are found in section 382(h)(3).

Sections 1.1502-90 through 1.1502-99 provide guidance for applying section 382 with respect to a consolidated loss group or loss subgroup. In this preamble, the term loss group refers to both loss groups and loss subgroups. See §§1.1502-91(c)(1) and 1.1502-91(d).

Section 1.1502-91(g) provides rules for determining whether a loss group has a NUBIG or NUBIL. Section 1.1502-91(g)(1) provides that the determination of whether a loss group has a consolidated NUBIG or NUBIL is based on the aggregate amount of the separately determined NUBIGs and NUBILs of each member included in the loss group. Under this rule, unrealized gain or loss with respect to the stock of a member of the loss group (an included subsidiary) is disregarded in determining the separately determined NUBIG or NUBIL.

Explanation of Provisions

The current regulations under §1.1502-91(g) are premised upon the observation that unrecognized gain or loss on included subsidiary stock generally reflects the same economic gain or loss reflected in the subsidiary's assets and that the consolidated return regulations generally prevent the group from taking that duplicative gain or loss into account more than once. This is the case because, if the subsidiary first recognizes the duplicated gain or loss on its assets, §1.1502-32 eliminates the duplicative gain or loss reflected in stock basis. Conversely, if a member first recognizes duplicated loss on the subsidiary stock, §1.1502-36 eliminates the duplicative asset loss. Although the regulations do not specifically address the recognition of duplicative gain on subsidiary stock, taxpayers generally avoid duplicative gain recognition, for example, through actual and section 338 deemed asset sales and through stock elimination transactions, such as section 332 liquidations. Because duplicative gain and loss is expected to be taken into account only once, the determination of NUBIG and NUBIL would be distorted if it included such amounts more than once.

To illustrate, assume P, the common parent of a consolidated group, contributes $100 to S in exchange for S's sole share of stock. S uses the $100 to purchase a truck. The value of the truck then declines to $70. At this point, the stock has a basis of $100 and a value of $70, reflecting a $30 loss. In addition, the truck has a basis of $100 and value of $70, also reflecting a $30 loss. Thus, it would appear the group has $60 of loss available. However, if S sells the truck and the group absorbs the $30 loss, P will reduce its basis in the S stock by $30 under § 1.1502-32, and the duplicative stock loss will be eliminated. On the other hand, if P sells its S share before the loss on the truck is recognized and absorbed, the duplicated loss (on either the truck or the stock, as P chooses) will be eliminated by § 1.1502-36. As a result, the group takes into account a single $30 economic loss, and the inclusion of both the unrecognized stock loss and the unrecognized asset loss in the NUBIL determination would overstate the amount of loss actually available to the group.

However, if an unrecognized gain or loss on subsidiary stock exceeds the included subsidiary's gain or loss on its assets, disregarding this unduplicated gain or loss on the stock understates the amount that the group may take into account.

To illustrate, assume the same facts as in the previous example except that P originally purchased the S stock for $150 (S's basis in the truck is still $100). In this case, there is $80 of loss available to the group, the $30 loss that is duplicated (reflected in the bases of both the stock and the truck), as well as the $50 unduplicated stock loss. Disregarding P's loss in its S stock causes the group's NUBIL to be understated by $50. These proposed regulations are intended to prevent such understatement.

The current rule is administratively less burdensome to taxpayers and the government than a rule that would require taxpayers to identify and take into account all unduplicated gain and loss on stock of included subsidiaries when determining NUBIG and NUBIL. Nevertheless, the IRS and the Treasury Department believe that the purpose of section 382(h) would be better served by a rule that does not wholly disregard such gain and loss. A rule that takes into account unduplicated gain or loss on stock would avoid both the understating of loss available to the group (when there is unduplicated stock loss) and the overstating of loss trafficking potential (when there is unduplicated stock gain).

The IRS and the Treasury Department are concerned, however, that requiring all consolidated NUBIG and NUBIL determinations to include all unduplicated stock gains and losses would significantly increase the administrative burden on both taxpayers and the government.

Accordingly, the IRS and the Treasury Department propose to modify the current regulations to take into account the unduplicated gain or loss on stock of included subsidiaries, but only to the extent that such gain or loss is taken into account by the group during the recognition period. This will generally be the case only if, within the recognition period, such stock is sold to a nonmember or becomes worthless, or a member takes an intercompany item into account with respect to such stock.

More specifically, the proposed regulations would revise § 1.1502-91(g) by adding a rule that would apply when any member of the consolidated group directly or indirectly (for example, through a partnership) takes any amount of gain or loss into account with respect to a share of stock of an included subsidiary (S), whether or not such amount is absorbed. When the rule applies, the loss group would be required to redetermine NUBIG or NUBIL to include any unduplicated built-in gain or loss with respect to the share. As used in these proposed regulations, the term unduplicated built-in stock gain or loss refers to the portion of the built-in stock gain or loss that was not originally reflected in the loss group's NUBIG or NUBIL as unrealized gain or loss on the assets of a lower-tier included subsidiary. The proposed regulations identify unduplicated built-in stock gain or loss by treating the separate NUBIG or NUBIL of each included subsidiary that is lower-tier to S as having been taken into account and absorbed immediately before the change date. These amounts are then deemed to tier-up to tentatively adjust the basis in the S shares under the principles of § 1.1502-32. The difference between the tentatively adjusted change-date basis in a share of S stock and the fair market value of the share (as of the change date) is the unduplicated gain or loss in the S share. However, if, immediately before the change date, a member of the loss group has a deferred gain or loss on S stock and that gain or loss is taken into account during the recognition period, the unduplicated portion of such gain or loss is determined as of the date of the transaction in which the deferred gain or loss was recognized, notwithstanding that such date would be prior to the change date.

The loss group then redetermines its NUBIG or NUBIL by including its unduplicated gain or loss on the S share (or shares) with respect to which an amount is taken into account. Under the proposed regulations, the redetermined NUBIG or NUBIL is given effect only immediately before the gain or loss on the stock is taken into account. It has no effect on the treatment of built-in gain or loss that is recognized and taken into account prior to the time that built-in stock gain or loss is taken into account. Thus, for example, the fact that a NUBIL group was redetermined to be a NUBIG group, or that a NUBIL that exceeded the 15 percent threshold amount in section 382(h)(3)(B) no longer exceeds such amount, has no effect on the tax treatment of amounts taken into account prior to the redetermination of NUBIG or NUBIL.

The proposed regulations also reorganize § 1.1502-91(g) and revise § 1.1502-91(h)(2) and (h)(4) without substantive change.

Effective/Applicability Date

These proposed regulations will apply to amounts taken into account with respect to a share of stock of an included subsidiary on or after the date that final regulations are published in the **FEDERAL REGISTER**, but only with respect to ownership changes occurring on or after October 24, 2011.

Special Analyses

It has been determined that this notice of proposed rulemaking is not a significant regulatory action as defined in Executive Order 12866, as supplemented by Executive Order 13565. Therefore, a regulatory assessment is not required. Pursuant to the Regulatory Flexibility Act (5 U.S.C. chapter 6), it is hereby certified that these proposed regulations would not have a significant economic impact on a substantial number of small entities. This certification is based on the fact that these proposed regulations would primarily affect members of consolidated groups which tend to be large corporations. Accordingly, a regulatory flexibility analysis is not required. Pursuant to section 7805(f) of the Internal Revenue Code, these regulations have been submitted to the Chief Counsel for Advocacy of the Small Business Administration for comment on their impact on small business.

Comments and Requests for a Public Hearing

Before these proposed regulations are adopted as final regulations, consideration will be given to any written (a signed original and eight (8) copies) or electronic comments that are submitted timely to the IRS. All comments will be available for public inspection and copying. A public hearing may be scheduled if requested in writing by any person that timely submits written or electronic comments. If a public hearing is scheduled, notice of the date, time, and place for the public hearing will be published in the **Federal Register**.

Drafting Information

The principal author of these regulations is Grid Glyer of the Office of Associate Chief Counsel (Corporate). However, other personnel from the IRS and the Treasury Department participated in its development.

[¶ 49,503] **Proposed Amendments of Regulations (REG-146537-06)**, published in the Federal Register on November 3, 2011 (corrected 11/23/2011).

[Code Sec. 892]

International taxation: Foreign governments: International organizations: Income from U.S. sources.—Reg. §1.892-4 and amendments of Reg. §1.892-5, relating to the taxation of the income of foreign governments from investments in the United States under Code Sec. 892, are proposed.

AGENCY: Internal Revenue Service (IRS), Treasury.

ACTION: Notice of proposed rulemaking.

SUMMARY: This document contains proposed Income Tax Regulations that provide guidance relating to the taxation of the income of foreign governments from investments in the United States under section 892 of the Internal Revenue Code of 1986 (Code). The regulations will affect foreign governments that derive income from sources within the United States.

DATES: Written or electronic comments and requests for a public hearing must be received by February 1, 2012.

ADDRESSES: Send submissions to: CC:PA:LPD:PR (REG-146537-06), Room 5205, Internal Revenue Service, PO Box 7604, Ben Franklin Station, Washington, DC 20044. Submissions may be hand-delivered Monday through Friday between the hours of 8 a.m. and 4 p.m. to CC:PA:LPD:PR (REG-146537-06), Courier's Desk, Internal Revenue Service, 1111 Constitution Avenue, NW, Washington, DC, or sent electronically, via the Federal eRulemaking Portal at *www.regulations.gov* (IRS REG-146537-06).

FOR FURTHER INFORMATION CONTACT: Concerning the proposed regulations, David A. Juster, (202) 622-3850 (not a toll-free number); concerning submission of comments, contact Richard A. Hurst at *Richard.A.Hurst@irscounsel.treas.gov*.

SUPPLEMENTARY INFORMATION:

Paperwork Reduction Act

The collections of information contained in this notice of proposed rulemaking have been submitted to the Office of Management and Budget (OMB) for review and approval under OMB approval number 1545-1053 in accordance with the Paperwork Reduction Act of 1995 (44 U.S.C. 3507(d)). Comments on the collections of information should be sent to the **Office of Management and Budget**, Attn: Desk Officer for the Department of the Treasury, Office of Information and Regulatory Affairs, Washington, DC 20503, with copies to the **Internal Revenue Service**, Attn: IRS Reports Clearance Officer, SE:CAR:MP:T:T:SP, Washington, DC 20224. Comments on the collections of information should be received by January 3, 2012. Comments are specifically requested concerning:

Whether the proposed collections of information are necessary for the proper performance of the functions of the Internal Revenue Service, including whether the information will have practical utility;

The accuracy of the estimated burden associate with the proposed collections of information;

How the quality, utility, and clarity of the information to be collected may be enhanced;

How the burden of complying with the proposed collections of information may be minimized, including through the application of automated collection techniques or other forms of information technology; and

Estimates of capital or start-up costs and costs of operation, maintenance, and purchase of services to provide information.

The collections of information in this proposed regulations are in §§1.892-5(a)(2)(ii)(B) and 1.892-5(a)(2)(iv). This information is required to determine if taxpayers qualify for exemption from tax under section 892. The collections of information are voluntary to obtain a benefit. The likely respondents are foreign governments.

Estimated total annual reporting burden: 975 hours.

Estimated average annual burden hours per respondent: 5 hours.

Estimated number of respondents: 195.

Estimated annual frequency of responses: 1.

An agency may not conduct or sponsor, and a person is not required to respond to, a collection of information unless it displays a valid control number assigned by the Office of Management and Budget.

Books or records relating to a collection of information must be retained as long as their contents may become material in the administration of any internal revenue law. Generally, tax returns and tax return information are confidential, as required by 26 U.S.C. 6103.

Background

This document contains proposed amendments to 26 CFR part 1 and to 26 CFR part 602. On June 27, 1988, temporary regulations under section 892 (TD 8211, 53 FR 24060) (1988 temporary regulations) with a cross-reference notice of proposed rulemaking (53 FR 24100) were published in the **Federal Register** to provide guidance concerning the taxation of income of foreign governments and international organizations from investments in the United States. The proposed regulations contained herein supplement the cross-reference notice of proposed rulemaking to provide additional guidance for determining when a foreign government's investment income is exempt from U.S. taxation.

Explanation of Provisions

The Treasury Department and the IRS have recently received numerous written comments on the 1988 temporary regulations. The proposed regulations are issued in response to those comments.

Treatment of Controlled Entities

Section 892 exempts from U.S. income taxation certain qualified investment income derived by a foreign government. Section 1.892-2T defines the term foreign government to mean only the integral parts or controlled entities of a foreign sovereign. The exemption from U.S. income tax under section 892 does not apply to income (1) derived from the conduct of any commercial activity, (2) received by a controlled commercial entity or received (directly or indirectly) from a controlled commercial entity, or (3) derived from the disposition of any interest in a controlled commercial entity. Section 892(a)(2)(B) defines a controlled commercial entity as an entity owned by the foreign government that meets certain ownership or control thresholds and that is engaged in commercial activities anywhere in the world. Accordingly, an integral part of a foreign sovereign that derives income from both qualified investments and from the conduct of commercial activity is eligible to claim the section 892 exemption with respect to the income from qualified investments, but not with respect to the income derived from the conduct of commercial activity. In contrast, if a controlled entity (as defined in §1.892-2T(a)(3)) engages in commercial activities anywhere in the world, it is treated as a controlled commercial entity, and none of its income (including income from otherwise qualified investments) qualifies for exemption from tax under section 892. In addition, none of the income derived from the controlled entity (e.g., dividends), including the portion attributable to qualified investments of the controlled entity, will be eligible for the section 892 exemption. Several comments raised concerns that this so-called "all or nothing" rule represents an unnecessary administrative and operational burden for foreign governments and a trap for unwary foreign governments that inadvertently conduct a small level of commercial activity. These comments have requested that the Treasury Department and the IRS revise § 1.892-5T(a) to provide for a de minimis exception under which an entity would not be treated as a controlled commercial entity as a result of certain inadvertent commercial activity.

In response to these comments, the proposed regulations at § 1.892-5(a)(2) provide that an entity will not be considered to engage in commercial activities if it conducts only inadvertent commercial activity. Commercial activity will be treated as inadvertent commercial activity only if: (1) the failure to avoid conducting the commercial activity is reasonable; (2) the commercial activity is promptly cured; and (3) certain record maintenance requirements are met. However, none of the income derived from such inadvertent commercial activity will qualify for exemption from tax under section 892.

In determining whether an entity's failure to avoid conducting a particular commercial activity is reasonable, due regard will be given to the number of commercial activities conducted during the taxable year, as well as the amount of income earned from, and assets used in, the conduct of the commercial activity in relationship to the entity's total income and assets. However, a failure to avoid conducting commercial activity will not be considered reasonable unless adequate written policies and operational procedures are in place to monitor the entity's worldwide activities. The proposed regulations include a safe harbor at § 1.892-5(a)(2)(ii)(C) under which, provided that there are adequate written policies and operational procedures in place to monitor the entity's worldwide activities, the controlled entity's failure to avoid the conduct of commercial activity during a taxable year will be considered reasonable if: (1) the value of the assets used in, or held for use in, the activity does not exceed five percent of the total value of the assets reflected on the entity's balance sheet for the taxable year as prepared for financial accounting purposes; and (2) the income earned by the entity from the commercial activity does not exceed five percent of the entity's gross income as reflected on its income statement for the taxable year as prepared for financial accounting purposes.

Comments also requested further guidance on the duration of a determination that an entity is a controlled commercial entity. In response to these comments, the proposed regulations at § 1.892-5(a)(3) provide that the determination of whether an entity is a controlled commercial entity within the meaning of section 892(a)(2)(B) will be made on an annual basis. Accordingly, an entity will not be considered a controlled commercial entity for a taxable year solely because the entity engaged in commercial activities in a prior taxable year.

Definition of Commercial Activity

Section 1.892-4T of the 1988 temporary regulations provides rules for determining whether income is derived from the conduct of a commercial activity, and specifically identifies certain activities that are not commercial, including certain investments, trading activities, cultural events, non-profit activities, and governmental functions. Several comments have expressed uncertainty about the applicable U.S. standard for determining when an activity will be considered a commercial activity, a non-profit activity, or governmental function for purposes of section 892 and § 1.892-4T.

Section 1.892-4(d) of the proposed regulations restates the general rule adopted in the 1988 temporary regulations that, subject to certain enumerated exceptions, all activities ordinarily conducted for the current or future production of income or gain are commercial activities. Section 1.892-4(d) of the proposed regulations further provides that only the nature of an activity, not the purpose or motivation for conducting the activity, is determinative of whether the activity is a commercial activity. This standard also applies for purposes of determining whether an activity is characterized as a non-profit activity or governmental function under § 1.892-4T(c)(3) and (c)(4). In addition, § 1.892-4(d) of the proposed regulations clarifies the rule in the 1988 temporary regulations by providing that an activity may be considered a commercial activity even if the activity does not constitute a trade or business for purposes of section 162 or does not constitute (or would not constitute if undertaken in the United States) the conduct of a trade or business in the United States for purposes of section 864(b).

Section 1.892-4T(c) lists certain activities that will not be considered commercial activities. One such activity is investments in financial instruments, as defined in § 1.892-3T(a)(4), which, if held in the execution of governmental financial or monetary policy, are not commercial activities for purposes of section 892. Several comments have requested that the condition that financial instruments be "held in the execution of governmental financial or monetary policy" be eliminated to more closely conform the treatment of investments in financial instruments, including derivatives, with investments in physical stocks and securities, which under the 1988 temporary regulations generally are not commercial activities regardless of whether they are held in the execution of governmental financial or monetary policy. Section 1.892-4(e)(1)(i) of the proposed regulations modifies the rules in § 1.892-4T(c)(1)(i) by providing that investments in financial instruments will not be treated as commercial activities for purposes of section 892, irrespective of whether such financial instruments are held in the execution of governmental financial or monetary policy. In addition, § 1.892-4(e)(1)(ii) of the proposed regulations expands the existing exception in § 1.892-4T(c)(1)(ii) from commercial activity for trading of stocks, securities, and commodities to include financial instruments, without regard to whether such financial instruments are held in the execution of governmental financial or monetary policy. These revisions address only the definition of commercial activity for purposes of determining whether a government will be considered to derive income from the conduct of a commercial activity, or whether an entity will be considered to be engaged in commercial activities. They do not address whether income from activities that are not commercial activities will be exempt from tax under section 892. Pursuant to § 1.892-3T(a), only income derived from investments in financial instruments held in the execution of governmental financial or monetary policy will qualify for exemption from tax under section 892.

Comments have requested clarification as to whether an entity that disposes of a United States real property interest (USRPI) as defined in section 897(c) will be deemed to be engaged in commercial activities solely by reason of this disposition. Section 897(a)(1) requires that a nonresident alien or foreign corporation take into account gain or loss from the disposition of a USRPI as if the taxpayer were engaged in a trade or business within the United States during the taxable year and as if such gain or loss were effectively connected with that trade or business. The Treasury Department and the IRS believe that an entity that only holds passive investments and is not otherwise engaged in commercial activities should not be deemed to be engaged in commercial activities solely by reason of the operation of section 897(a)(1). Accordingly, § 1.892-4(e)(1)(iv) of the proposed regulations provides that a disposition, including a deemed disposition under section 897(h)(1), of a USRPI, by itself, does not constitute the conduct of a commercial activity. However, as provided in § 1.892-3T(a), the income derived from the disposition of the USRPI described in section 897(c)(1)(A)(i) shall in no event qualify for the exemption from tax under section 892.

After the 1988 temporary regulations were published, section 892(a)(2)(A) was amended by the Technical and Miscellaneous Revenue Act of 1988 (TAMRA), Public Law No. 100-647, 102 Stat. 3342 to provide that income derived from the disposition of any interest in a controlled commercial entity does not qualify for the exemption under section 892. The proposed regulations revise § 1.892-5(a) to reflect the amendment of section 892 by TAMRA.

Treatment of Partnerships

Section 1.892-5T(d)(3) provides a general rule that commercial activities of a partnership are attributable to its general and limited partners ("partnership attribution rule") and provides a limited exception to this rule for partners of publicly traded partnerships (PTPs). Several comments have requested that the Treasury Department and the IRS modify the partnership attribution rule to provide that the activities of a partnership will not be attributed to a foreign government partner if that government: (i) holds a minority interest, as a limited partner, in the partnership; and (ii) has no greater rights to participate in the management and conduct of the partnership's business than would a minority shareholder in a corporation conducting the same activities as the partnership. The comments assert that the partnership attribution rule causes many controlled entities of foreign sovereigns to forego making investments in foreign partnerships or other foreign entities that do not invest in the United States out of concern that such investments might cause those controlled entities to be treated as controlled commercial entities.

In response to these comments, §1.892-5(d)(5)(iii) of the proposed regulations modifies the existing exception to the partnership attribution rule for PTP interests by providing a more general exception for limited partnership interests. Under this revised exception, an entity that is not otherwise engaged in commercial activities will not be treated as engaged in commercial activities solely because it holds an interest as a limited partner in a limited partnership, including a publicly traded partnership that qualifies as a limited partnership.

For this purpose, an interest as a limited partner in a limited partnership is defined as an interest in an entity classified as a partnership for federal tax purposes if the holder of the interest does not have rights to participate in the management and conduct of the partnership's business at any time during the partnership's taxable year under the law of the jurisdiction in which the partnership is organized or under the governing agreement. This definition of an interest as a limited partner in a limited partnership applies solely for purposes of this exception, and no inference is intended that the same definition would apply for any other provision of the Code making or requiring a distinction between a general partner and a limited partner.

Although the commercial activity of a limited partnership will not cause a controlled entity of a foreign sovereign limited partner meeting the requirements of the exception for limited partnerships to be engaged in commercial activities, the controlled entity partner's distributive share of partnership income attributable to such commercial activity will be considered to be derived from the conduct of commercial activity, and therefore will not be exempt from taxation under section 892. Additionally, in the case of a partnership that is a controlled commercial entity, no part of the foreign government partner's distributive share of partnership income will qualify for exemption from tax under section 892.

Comments also assert that disparity in tax treatment exists under the temporary regulations regarding foreign government trading activity described in §1.892-4T(c)(1)(ii) because trading for a foreign government's own account does not constitute a commercial activity but no similar rule applies in the case of trading done by a partnership of which a foreign government is a partner. The comments note that this disparity is not generally present in determining whether an activity is a trade or business within the United States under section 864(b). See §1.864-2(c)(2)(i) and (d)(2)(i). In response to these comments, §1.892-5(d)(5)(ii) of the proposed regulations provides that an entity that is not otherwise engaged in commercial activities will not be considered to be engaged in commercial activities solely because it is a member of a partnership that effects transactions in stocks, bonds, other securities, commodities, or financial instruments for the partnership's own account. However, this exception does not apply in the case of a partnership that is a dealer in stocks, bonds, other securities, commodities, or financial instruments. For this purpose, whether a partnership is a dealer is determined under the principles of §1.864-2(c)(2)(iv)(a).

Proposed Effective/Applicability Date

These regulations are proposed to apply on the date of publication of the Treasury decision adopting these rules as final regulations in the **Federal Register**. For rules applicable to periods prior to the publication date, see the corresponding provisions in §§1.892-4T and 1.892-5T in the 1988 temporary regulations and in §1.892-5(a) as issued under TD 9012 (August 1, 2002).

Reliance on Proposed Regulations

Taxpayers may rely on the proposed regulations until final regulations are issued.

Special Analyses

It has been determined that this notice of proposed rulemaking is not a significant regulatory action as defined in Executive Order 12866. Therefore, a regulatory assessment is not required. It has also been determined that section 553(b) of the Administrative Procedure Act (5 U.S.C. chapter 5) does not apply to these regulations and because the proposed regulations do not impose a collection of information on small entities, the Regulatory Flexibility Act (5 U.S.C. chapter 6) does not apply. Pursuant to section 7805(f) of the Code, this notice of proposed rulemaking has been submitted to the Chief Counsel for Advocacy of the Small Business Administration for comment on its impact on small business.

Comments and Requests for Public Hearing

Before the proposed regulations are adopted as final regulations, consideration will be given to any written (a signed original and eight (8) copies) or electronic comments, that are submitted timely to the IRS. The Treasury Department and the IRS request comments on the clarity of the proposed regulations and how they can be made easier to understand. All comments will be available for public inspection and copying. A public hearing will be scheduled if requested in writing by any person that timely submits written comments. If a public hearing is scheduled, notice of the date, time, and place for the public hearing will be published in the **Federal Register**.

Drafting Information

The principal author of these regulations is David A. Juster of the Office of Associate Chief Counsel (International), within the Office of Chief Counsel, IRS. Other personnel from the Treasury Department and the IRS participated in developing the regulations.

[¶ 49,504] Proposed Amendments of Regulations (REG-114749-09) and Withdrawal of Notice of Proposed Rulemaking (INTL-0018-92/REG-209545-92), published in the Federal Register on November 4, 2011.

[Code Sec. 964]

Foreign income: Controlled foreign corporations: Domestic shareholders: Elections: Method of accounting: Tax year.—Amendments of Reg. §1.964-1, relating to clarify the rules for controlling domestic shareholders to adopt or change a method of accounting or tax year on behalf of a foreign corporation, are proposed. The notice of proposed rulemaking published on July 1, 1992, is withdrawn.

AGENCY: Internal Revenue Service (IRS), Treasury.

ACTION: Withdrawal of notice of proposed rulemaking and notice of proposed rulemaking.

SUMMARY: These proposed regulations would clarify the rules for controlling domestic shareholders to adopt or change a method of accounting or taxable year on behalf of a foreign corporation. The regulations affect United States persons that own stock in certain foreign corporations.

DATES: Written or electronic comments and requests for a public hearing must be received by February 2, 2012.

ADDRESSES: Send submissions to CC:PA:LPD:PR (REG-114749-09), Room 5203, Internal Revenue Service, PO Box 7604, Ben Franklin Station, Washington, DC 20044. Submissions may be hand-delivered between the hours of 8 a.m. and 4 p.m. to CC:PA:LPD:PR (REG-114749-09), Courier's

Desk, Internal Revenue Service, 1111 Constitution Avenue NW; Washington DC, 20224 or sent electronically via the Federal Rulemaking Portal at *www.regulations.gov* (IRS REG-114749-09).

FOR FURTHER INFORMATION CONTACT: Concerning submission of comments, Oluwafunmilayo (Funmi) Taylor (202) 622-7180; concerning the regulations, Joseph W. Vetting (202) 622-3402 (not toll-free numbers).

SUPPLEMENTARY INFORMATION:

Background

On April 17, 1991, a notice of proposed rulemaking (INTL-939-86) under sections 953, 954, 964, 1248, and 6046 of the Internal Revenue Code (Code) was published in the **Federal Register** (56 FR 15540) (the 1991 proposed regulations). No comments were received with respect to the proposed amendments under section 964, which would provide a special definition of controlling domestic shareholders for certain controlled foreign corporations with insurance income. Comments were received on other provisions of the 1991 proposed regulations, but no public hearing was requested and none was held.

On July 1, 1992, a notice of proposed rulemaking (INTL-0018-92) under sections 952 and 964 of the Code was published in the **Federal Register** (57 FR 29246). A correction to the notice of proposed rulemaking was published on October 8, 1992, in the **Federal Register** (57 FR 46355). The proposed regulations would modify the regulations relating to required book-to-tax adjustments in respect of depreciation and inventory accounting. Comments were received. A public hearing was not requested and none was held.

Final regulations published on June 10, 2009 (TD 9452) provided guidance for shareholders of certain foreign corporations to elect or change a method of accounting or a taxable year on behalf of the foreign corporation under section 964 of the Code.

Explanation of Provisions

These proposed regulations provide clarification of the required book-to-tax adjustments, including those in respect of depreciation and amortization, and additional examples illustrating the application of §1.964-1(a) and (c). The proposed regulations also would delete §1.964-1(b)(3), *Example 2*. The example refers to section 963, which was repealed for taxable years beginning after December 31, 1975. Additionally, the proposed regulations provide rules regarding IRS-initiated method changes.

The Treasury Department and the IRS again request comments on whether the special control group definition contained in the 1991 proposed regulations should be adopted.

Special Analyses

It has been determined that this notice of proposed rulemaking is not a significant regulatory action as defined in Executive Order 12866. Therefore, a regulatory assessment is not required. It also has been determined that section 553(b) of the Administrative Procedure Act (5 U.S.C. chapter 5) does not apply to these regulations, and because the regulations do not impose a collection of information on small entities, the Regulatory Flexibility Act (5 U.S.C. chapter 6) does not apply. Pursuant to section 7805(f) of the Internal Revenue Code, these regulations will be submitted to the Chief Counsel for Advocacy of the Small Business Administration for comment on their impact on small businesses.

Comments and Request for a Public Hearing

Before these proposed regulations are adopted as final regulations, consideration will be given to any written (a signed original and eight (8) copies) or electronic comments that are submitted timely to the IRS. The IRS and Treasury Department request comments on the clarity of the proposed regulations and how they can be made easier to understand. All comments will be available for public inspection and copying at *www.regulations.gov* or upon request. A public hearing may be scheduled if requested in writing by a person who timely submits comments. If a public hearing is scheduled, notice of the date, time, and place for the hearing will be published in the **Federal Register**.

Drafting Information

The principal author of these regulations is Joseph W. Vetting, Office of Associate Chief Counsel (International). However, other personnel from the IRS and Treasury Department participated in their development.

[¶ 49,509]   **Proposed Amendments of Regulations (REG-109369-10)**, published in the Federal Register on November 28, 2011.

[Code Sec. 469]

Partners and partnerships: Limited partners: Limited partnerships: Definition of limited partner: Material participation: Business activity: Passive activity losses.—Amendments of Reg. §§1.469-0, 1.469-5, 1.469-9 and Temporary Reg. §1.469-5T, regarding the definition of an "interest in a limited partnership as a limited partner" for purposes of determining whether a taxpayer materially participates in an activity under Code Sec. 469, are proposed.

AGENCY: Internal Revenue Service (IRS), Treasury.

ACTION: Notice of proposed rulemaking.

SUMMARY: This document contains proposed regulations regarding the definition of an "interest in a limited partnership as a limited partner" for purposes of determining whether a taxpayer materially participates in an activity under section 469 of the Internal Revenue Code (Code). These proposed regulations affect individuals who are partners in partnerships.

DATES: Written or electronic comments and requests for a public hearing must be received by February 27, 2012.

ADDRESSES: Send submissions to: CC:PA:LPD:PR (REG-109369-10), Room 5203, Internal Revenue Service, P.O. Box 7604, Ben Franklin Station, Washington, DC 20044. Submissions may be hand-delivered Monday through Friday between the hours of 8 a.m. and 4 p.m. to: CC:PA:LPD:PR (REG-109369-10), Courier's Desk, Internal Revenue Service, 1111 Constitution Avenue NW., Washington, DC, or sent electronically, via the Federal eRulemaking Portal at *http://www.regulations.gov/*(IRS REG-109369-10).

FOR FURTHER INFORMATION CONTACT: Concerning the proposed regulations, Michala Irons, (202) 622-3050; concerning submissions of comments and requests for public hearing, Oluwafunmilayo Taylor, (202) 622-7180 (not toll free numbers).

SUPPLEMENTARY INFORMATION:

Background

Section 469(a)(1) limits the ability of certain taxpayers to deduct losses from passive activities. Section 469(b) permits passive losses disallowed in one year to be carried over to the next year. Section 469(c)(1) provides that a passive activity means any activity which involves the conduct of any trade or business, and in which the taxpayer does not materially participate. Section 469(h)(1) provides that a taxpayer shall be treated as materially participating in an activity only if the taxpayer is involved in the operations of the activity on a basis which is regular, continuous, and substantial. The Treasury Department and the IRS promulgated temporary regulations under section 469 in 1988. See TD 8175, 53 FR 5686 (February 25, 1988). Section 1.469-5T(a) provides that an individual taxpayer shall be treated as materially participating in an activity for the taxable year if and only if:

(1) The individual participates in the activity for more than 500 hours during such year;

(2) The individual's participation in the activity for the taxable year constitutes substantially all of the participation in such activity of all individuals (including individuals who are not owners of interests in the activity) for such year;

(3) The individual participates in the activity for more than 100 hours during the taxable year, and such individual's participation in the activity for the taxable year is not less than the participation in the activity of any other individual (including individuals who are not owners of interests in the activity) for such year;

(4) The activity is a significant participation activity (within the meaning of §1.469-5T(c)) for the taxable year, and the individual's aggregate participation in all significant participation activities during such year exceeds 500 hours;

(5) The individual materially participated in the activity (determined without regard to §1.469-5T(a)(5)) for any five taxable years (whether or not consecutive) during the ten taxable years that immediately precede the taxable year;

(6) The activity is a personal service activity (within the meaning of §1.469-5T(d)), and the individual materially participated in the activity for any three taxable years (whether or not consecutive) preceding the taxable year; or

(7) Based on all of the facts and circumstances (taking into account the rules in §1.469-5T(b)), the individual participates in the activity on a regular, continuous, and substantial basis during such year.

Section 469(h)(2) presumptively treats losses from interests in limited partnerships as passive. Section 469(h)(2) provides that, except as provided in regulations, no interest in a limited partnership as a limited partner shall be treated as an interest with respect to which a taxpayer materially participates. Section 1.469-5T(e)(2) permits an individual taxpayer to establish material participation in a limited partnership but constrains the individual taxpayer to only three of the seven regulatory tests in §1.469-5T(a), (§1.469-5T(a)(1), (a)(5), or (a)(6)).

Section 1.469-5T(e)(3)(i) generally provides that a partnership interest shall be treated as a limited partnership interest if (A) such interest is either designated as a limited partnership interest in the limited partnership agreement or the certificate of limited partnership, without regard to whether the liability of the holder of such interest for obligations of the partnership is limited under applicable State law; or (B) the liability of the holder of such interest for obligations of the partnership is limited, under the law of the State in which the partnership is organized, to a determinable fixed amount (for example, the sum of the holder's capital contributions to the partnership and contractual obligations to make additional capital contributions to the partnership). However, even if the interest is characterized as a limited partnership interest under §1.469-5T(e)(3)(i), an exception under §1.469-5T(e)(3)(ii) applies if the individual is a general partner in the partnership at all times during the partnership's taxable year ending with or within the individual's taxable year (or portion of the partnership's taxable year during which the individual (directly or indirectly) owns such limited partnership interest) (the "general partner exception"). If the general partner exception applies, the limited partnership interest will not be treated as such for the year in which the individual taxpayer is a general partner in the partnership. This allows the individual taxpayer to demonstrate material participation through any of the seven regulatory tests in §1.469-5T(a).

Courts have concluded, in certain instances, that the holder of a limited liability company (LLC) interest is not treated as holding an interest in a limited partnership as a limited partner for purposes of applying the section 469 material participation tests. In *Gregg v. U.S.*, 186 F.Supp.2d 1123 (D. Or. 2000), an Oregon district court concluded that, in the absence of regulations to the effect that an LLC member should be treated as a limited partner, the limited partner exception in section 469(h)(2) was not applicable to LLC members. In *Garnett v. Comm'r*, 132 T.C. 368 (2009), the Tax Court found that the taxpayers' ownership interests in limited liability partnerships and LLCs were not interests in limited partnerships because their interests fit within the general partner exception in §1.469-5T(e)(3)(ii). Shortly thereafter, in *Thompson v. U.S.*, 87 Fed. Cl. 728 (2009), the Court of Federal Claims concluded that the regulations under section 469(h)(2) require the taxpayer's ownership interest to be in a partnership under State law rather than a partnership under Federal income tax law. Accordingly, because an LLC member is not a limited partner under State law, the court concluded that section 469(h)(2) did not apply to an LLC member. Most recently, the Tax Court in *Newell v. Comm'r*, T.C. Memo. 2010-23, concluded that section 469(h)(2) did not apply to the managing member of an LLC and that the member fell within the general partner exception in §1.469-5T(e)(3)(ii). On April 5, 2010, the IRS issued an Action on Decision acquiescing in the result only in *Thompson v. U.S.*, AOD 2010-02, 2010-14 I.R.B. 515.

Explanation of Provisions

The proposed regulations provide that an interest in an entity will be treated as an interest in a limited partnership under section 469(h)(2) if (A) the entity in which such interest is held is classified as a partnership for Federal income tax purposes under §301.7701-3; and (B) the holder of such interest does not have rights to manage the entity at all times during the entity's taxable year under the law of the jurisdiction in which the entity was organized and under the governing agreement. Rights to manage include the power to bind the entity. The proposed regulations provide rules concerning an interest in a limited partnership based on the purposes for which section 469 was enacted, and the manner in which the provision is structured and operates within the Code. Accordingly, the rules concerning an interest in a limited partnership in the proposed regulations are provided solely for purposes of section 469 and no inference is intended that the same rules would apply for any other provisions of the Code requiring a distinction between a general partner and a limited partner.

In *Garnett v. Comm'r, supra*, the Tax Court noted that Congress enacted section 469(h)(2) to address the limitations on a limited partner's ability to participate in the control of the partnership's business. Under the Uniform Limited Partnership Act of 1916, limited partners could lose their limited liability protection if they participated in the control of the partnership. The regulations under section 469(h)(2) were drafted with these constraints in mind. Today, many states have adopted a variation of the Revised Uniform Limited Partnership Act of 1985 (RULPA). Under RULPA, limited partners may participate in the management and control of the partnership without losing their limited liability. As a consequence, limited partners under RULPA are now more akin to general partners and LLC members with respect to their rights in the management of the entity. Under the Uniform Limited Liability Company Act of 1996, LLC members of member-managed LLCs do not lose their limited liability by participating in the management and conduct of the company's business. In *Newell v. Comm'r, supra*, the Tax Court noted that the managing member of the LLC at issue managed the day-to-day operations of the LLC and was the "substantial equivalent" of a general partner. Recognizing that the original presumptions regarding the limitations on a limited partner's participation in the activities of the entity are no longer valid today, and also recognizing the emergence of LLCs, the proposed regulations eliminate the current regulations' reliance on limited liability for purposes of determining whether an interest is an interest in a limited partnership as a limited partner under section 469(h)(2) and instead adopt an approach that relies on the individual partner's right to participate in the management of the entity.

The regulations are proposed to apply to taxable years beginning on or after the date of publication of the Treasury decision adopting these regulations as final regulations in the **Federal Register.**

Special Analyses

It has been determined that this notice of proposed rulemaking is not a significant regulatory action as defined in Executive Order 12866, as supplemented by Executive Order 13563. Therefore, a regulatory assessment is not required. It has also been determined that section 553(b) of the Administrative Procedure Act (5 U.S.C. chapter 5) does not apply to this regulation, and because the regulation does not impose a collection of information on small entities, the Regulatory Flexibility Act (5 U.S.C. chapter 6) does not apply. Pursuant to section 7805(f) of the Code, these regulations will be submitted to the Chief Counsel for Advocacy of the Small Business Administration for comment on its impact on small business.

Comments and Requests Public Hearing

Before these proposed regulations are adopted as final regulations, consideration will be given to any written (a signed original and eight (8) copies) or electronic comments that are submitted timely to the IRS. All comments will be available for public inspection and copying. A public hearing will be scheduled if requested in writing by any person that timely submits written comments. If a public hearing is scheduled, notice of the date, time, and place for the public hearing will be published in the **Federal Register.**

Drafting Information

The principal author of these proposed regulations is Michala Irons, Office of the Associate Chief Counsel (Passthroughs and Special Industries). However, other personnel from the Treasury Department and the IRS participated in their development.

[¶ 49,524]   Proposed Amendments of Regulations (REG-124791-11), published in the Federal Register on February 15, 2012.

[Code Sec. 6109]

Identifying numbers: Obtaining identifying numbers: Tax return preparers: Preparers tax identification number (PTIN).—Amendments of Reg. §1.6109-2, providing guidance on the eligibility of tax return preparers to obtain a preparer tax identification number (PTIN), are proposed.

AGENCY: Internal Revenue Service (IRS), Treasury.

ACTION: Notice of proposed rulemaking.

SUMMARY: This document contains proposed regulations that provide guidance on the eligibility of tax return preparers to obtain a preparer tax identification number (PTIN). These proposed regulations expand the list of tax return preparers who may obtain and renew a PTIN. The proposed regulations additionally provide guidance concerning those tax forms submitted to the Internal Revenue Service that are considered returns of tax or claims for refund of tax for purposes of the requirement to obtain a PTIN and related provisions. This document also invites comments from the public regarding these proposed regulations.

DATES: Written or electronic comments and requests for a public hearing must be received by May 15, 2012.

ADDRESSES: Send submissions to: CC:PA:LPD:PR (REG-124791-11), room 5205, Internal Revenue Service, P.O. Box 7604, Ben Franklin Station, Washington, DC 20044. Submissions may be hand-delivered Monday through Friday between the hours of 8 a.m. and 4 p.m. to CC:PA:LPD:PR (REG-124791-11), Courier's Desk, Internal Revenue Service, 1111 Constitution Avenue, NW., Washington, DC 20224, or sent electronically via the Federal eRulemaking Portal at *www.regulations.gov* (IRS REG-124791-11).

FOR FURTHER INFORMATION CONTACT: Concerning the proposed regulations, Stuart Murray at (202) 622-4940; concerning submissions of comments and requests for a hearing, Oluwafunmilayo (Funmi) Taylor at (202) 622-7180 (not a toll-free numbers).

SUPPLEMENTARY INFORMATION:

Background

This document contains proposed amendments to regulations under section 6109 of the Internal Revenue Code (Code) relating to the identifying number of a tax return preparer and furnishing a tax return preparer's identifying number on tax returns and claims for refund of tax. The Department of Treasury and the Internal Revenue Service published in the **Federal Register** on September 30, 2010 (75 FR 60309) final regulations under section 6109 that prescribe certain requirements relating to the identifying number of tax return preparers.

In particular, the final regulations provided that for tax returns or claims for refund of tax filed after December 31, 2010, the identifying number of a tax return preparer is a PTIN or other identifying number that the IRS prescribes in forms, instructions, or other guidance. The final regulations also provided that after December 31, 2010, a tax return preparer must have a PTIN that is applied for and renewed in the manner the IRS prescribes. The final regulations added §1.6109-2(d) to the regulations under title 26, providing that to obtain a PTIN or other prescribed identifying number, a tax return preparer must be an attorney, certified public accountant, enrolled agent, or registered tax return preparer authorized to practice before the IRS under Treasury Department Circular No. 230, 31 CFR Part 10 (which Treasury and the IRS amended in final regulations published in the **Federal Register** on June 3, 2011 (76 FR 32286)). For purposes of these requirements, a *tax return preparer* means any individual who is compensated for preparing, or assisting in the preparation of, all or substantially all of a tax return or claim for refund of tax. The final regulations under section 6109 additionally added §1.6109-2(f), which provides that the IRS may conduct a Federal tax compliance check on a tax return preparer who applies for or renews a PTIN or other prescribed identifying number.

Although the rules in the final regulations under section 6109 went into effect on January 1, 2011, §1.6109-2(h) allows Treasury and the IRS to prescribe, through forms, instructions, or other appropriate guidance, exceptions to the rules in §1.6109-2, as necessary, in the interest of effective tax administration. Section 1.6109-2(h) also provides that the IRS may specify through other appropriate guidance "specific returns, schedules, and other forms that qualify as tax returns or claims for refund for purposes of these regulations."

After §1.6109-2 was amended, Treasury and the IRS issued Notice 2011-6 (2011 IRB 315 January 17, 2011) (see §601.601(d)(2)(ii)(*b*) of this chapter), which provides additional guidance on the implementation of §1.6109-2. Specifically, Notice 2011-6, in part, provides further guidance as to tax return preparers who may obtain a PTIN. As explained in Notice 2011-6, the IRS "decided to allow certain individuals who are not attorneys, certified public accountants, enrolled agents, or registered tax return preparers to obtain a PTIN and prepare, or assist in the preparation of, all or substantially all of a tax return in certain discrete circumstances." Pursuant to the authority in §1.6109-2(h), Notice 2011-6 established two additional categories of tax return preparers who may obtain a PTIN: (1) tax return preparers supervised by attorneys, certified public accountants, enrolled agents, enrolled retirement plan agents, and enrolled actuaries (see §1.02a of Notice 2011-6); and (2) tax return preparers who prepare tax returns not covered by a competency examination applicable to registered tax return preparers (see §1.02b of Notice 2011-6). Notice 2011-6 prescribes the requirements an individual must satisfy under each of these two categories, including passing a Federal tax compliance check and a suitability check (when available). Individuals who obtain or renew a PTIN under either of these categories are not registered tax return preparers. Registered tax return preparers are subject to separate, more extensive requirements in Circular 230, including continuing education.

Also pursuant to the authority in §1.6109-2(h), the IRS in Notice 2011-6 specified that all tax returns, claims for refund, and other tax forms submitted to the IRS are considered tax returns or claims for refund of tax for purposes of §1.6109-2 unless the IRS provides otherwise. Section 1.03 of Notice 2011-6 explains that the IRS interprets the term "tax forms" broadly for this purpose, and a tax return preparer must obtain a PTIN to prepare for compensation, or to assist in preparing for compensation, all or substantially all of "any form" except those forms that the IRS explicitly excludes. Notice 2011-6 lists the forms by number and title that are currently excluded.

Explanation of Provisions

Treasury and the IRS propose to incorporate the relevant provisions of Notice 2011-6 discussed earlier in this preamble in §1.6109-2. The proposed regulations provide for two additional categories of tax return preparers to obtain a PTIN (or other identifying number the IRS prescribes), namely, certain supervised tax return preparers and tax return preparers who prepare tax returns and claims for refund that are not covered by a competency examination. As to the first category, the proposed regulations provide that any individual 18 years of age or older is eligible for a PTIN if the individual is supervised as a tax return preparer by an attorney, certified public accountant, enrolled agent, enrolled retirement plan agent, or enrolled actuary authorized to practice before the IRS under Circular 230. The proposed regulations provide that the supervision must be in accordance with any requirements the IRS may prescribe; these requirements are currently set forth in §1.02a of Notice 2011-6.

As to the second category, the proposed regulations provide that any individual 18 years of age or older is eligible for a PTIN if the individual exclusively prepares tax returns and claims for refund that are not covered by any minimum competency test or tests that the IRS prescribes for registered tax return preparers. To be eligible for a PTIN, an individual must certify, at the time and in whatever manner the IRS may prescribe, that the individual only prepares tax returns and claims for refund that are not covered by a minimum competency test. Under the proposed regulations, the individual must also comply with any other eligibility requirements that the IRS may prescribe; these requirements are currently set forth in §1.02b of Notice 2011-6.

The proposed regulations provide that for purposes of §1.6109-2, the terms *tax return* and *claim for refund of tax* include all tax forms submitted to the IRS except forms that the IRS specifically excludes in other appropriate guidance. Notice 2011-6 (§1.03) is the current guidance specifying the excluded tax forms. The proposed regulations also amend §1.6109-2(f) to clarify that the IRS may conduct a suitability check, in addition to a Federal tax compliance check, on certain tax return preparers who apply for or renew a PTIN or other prescribed identifying number. This clarification is consistent with the provisions in both the final Circular 230 regulations and Notice 2011-6 stating that certain individuals who apply to obtain or renew a PTIN or to become a registered tax return preparer will be subject to a suitability check, as well as a tax compliance check.

Proposed Effective/Applicability Date

These regulations are effective on the date that final regulations are published in the **Federal Register**. For proposed dates of applicability, see §1.6109-2(i).

Special Analyses

It has been determined that this notice of proposed rulemaking is not a significant regulatory action as defined in Executive Order 12866, as supplemented by Executive Order 13563. Therefore, a regulatory assessment is not required. It has also been determined that section 553(b) of the Administrative Procedure Act (5 U.S.C. chapter 5) does not apply to these regulations, and because the regulation does not impose a collection of information on small entities, the Regulatory Flexibility Act (5 U.S.C. chapter 6) does not apply. Pursuant to section 7805(f) of the Code, this notice of proposed rulemaking has been submitted to the Chief Counsel for Advocacy of the Small Business Administration for comment on its impact on small business.

Comments and Requests for Public Hearing

Before these proposed regulations are adopted as final regulations, consideration will be given to any written comments (a signed original and eight (8) copies) or electronic comments that are submitted timely to the IRS. Treasury and the IRS request comments on all aspects of the proposed rules. All comments that are submitted by the public will be available for public inspection and copying. A public hearing will be scheduled if requested in writing by any person who timely submits comments. If a public hearing is scheduled, notice of the date, time, and place for the public hearing will be published in the **Federal Register**.

Drafting Information

The principal author of these proposed regulations is Stuart Murray of the Office of the Associate Chief Counsel, Procedure and Administration.

[¶ **49,539**] **Proposed Amendments of Regulations (REG-153627-08)**, published in the Federal Register on June 21, 2012 (corrected 7/19/2012).

[Code Secs. 6057 and 6081]

Pension plans: Annual registration: Information returns: When to file: Automatic extension to file.—Amendments of Reg. §§301.6057-1, 301.6057-2 and 1.6081-11, providing guidance relating to automatic extensions of time for filing certain employee plan returns by adding the Form 8955-SSA, "Annual Registration Statement Identifying Separated Participants With Deferred Vested Benefits," to the list of forms that are covered by the Income Tax Regulations on automatic extensions, are proposed.

AGENCY: Internal Revenue Service (IRS), Treasury

ACTION: Notice of proposed rulemaking.

SUMMARY: This document contains proposed regulations that would provide guidance relating to automatic extensions of time for filing certain employee plan returns by adding the Form 8955-SSA, "Annual Registration Statement Identifying Separated Participants With Deferred Vested Benefits," to the list of forms that are covered by the Income Tax Regulations on automatic extensions. The proposed regulations would also provide guidance on applicable reporting and participant notice rules that require certain plan administrators to file registration statements and provide notices that set forth information for deferred vested participants. These regulations would affect administrators of, employers maintaining, participants in, and beneficiaries of plans that are subject to the reporting and participant notice requirements.

DATES: Comments and requests for a public hearing must be received by September 19, 2012.

ADDRESSES: Send submissions to CC:PA:LPD:PR (REG-153627-08), room 5205, Internal Revenue Service, PO Box 7604, Ben Franklin Station, Washington D.C. 20044. Submissions may be hand-delivered Monday through Friday between the hours of 8 a.m. and 4 p.m. to CC:PA:LPD:PR (REG-153627-08), Courier's Desk, Internal Revenue Service, 1111 Constitution Avenue, N.W., Washington, DC, 20224, or sent electronically via the Federal eRulemaking Portal at *www.regulations.gov* (IRS REG-153627-08).

FOR FURTHER INFORMATION CONTACT: Concerning the proposed regulations, William Gibbs, Sarah Bolen, or Pamela Kinard at (202) 622-6060; concerning the submission of comments or to request a public hearing, Oluwafunmilayo Taylor, (202) 622-7180 (not toll-free numbers).

SUPPLEMENTARY INFORMATION:

Paperwork Reduction Act

The collection of information contained in this notice of proposed rulemaking has been approved by the Office of Management and Budget for review in accordance with the Paperwork Reduction Act of 1995 (44 U.S.C. 3507(d)) under 1545-2187 and 1545-0212. Comments on the collection of information should be sent to the **Office of Management and Budget**, Attn: Desk Officer for the Department of the Treasury, Office of Information and Regulatory Affairs, Washington D.C. 20503, with copies to the **Internal Revenue Service**, Attn: IRS Reports Clearance Officer, SE:CAR:MP:T:T:SP; Washington DC 20224. Comments on the collection of information should be received by August 20, 2012. Comments are specifically requested concerning:

Whether the proposed collection of information is necessary for the proper performance of the functions of the Internal Revenue Service, including whether the information will have practical utility;

The accuracy of the estimated burden associated with the proposed collection of information;

How the quality, utility, and clarity of the information to be collected may be enhanced;

How the burden of complying with the proposed collection of information may be minimized, including through the application of automated collection techniques or other forms of information technology; and

Estimates of capital or start-up costs and costs of operation, maintenance, and purchase of service to provide information.

The collection of information in these proposed regulations is in §§ 301.6057-1 and 1.6081-11. This information is required in order to comply with the reporting and notice requirements of section 6057 and to provide automatic extensions of time for filing certain employee plan returns under section 6081. Information relating to these proposed regulations will be collected through Form 8955-SSA and Form 5558. This information relates to plan participants who separate from service covered under the plan and who are entitled to deferred vested retirement benefits under the plan. Any burden relating to these proposed regulations will be included and reported in the next revisions of Form 8955-SSA and Form 5558, after these proposed regulations are accepted as final.

An agency may not conduct or sponsor, and a person is not required to respond to, a collection of information, unless it displays a valid control number assigned by the Office of Management and Budget.

Books or records relating to a collection of information must be retained as long as their contents may become material in the administration of any internal revenue law. Generally, tax returns and tax return information are confidential, as required by 26 U.S.C. 6103.

Background

Section 6057(a) of the Internal Revenue Code (Code) requires the administrator of a plan that is subject to the vesting standards of section 203 of the Employee Retirement Income Security Act of 1974 (ERISA) to file, within the time prescribed by regulations, a registration statement with the Secretary of the Treasury. The registration statement sets forth certain information relating to the plan, plan participants who separate from service covered by the plan and are entitled to deferred vested retirement benefits, and the nature, amount, and form of deferred vested retirement benefits to which the plan participants are entitled.

Section 6057(b) provides that any plan administrator required to register under section 6057(a) shall, within the time prescribed by regulations, also notify the Secretary of any change in the name of the plan or the name and address of the plan administrator, the termination of the plan, or the merger or consolidation of the plan with any other plan or its division into two or more plans.

Section 6057(c) provides that, to the extent provided in regulations prescribed by the Secretary, the administrator of a plan not subject to the reporting requirements of section 6057(a) (including a governmental plan within the meaning of section 414(d) or a church plan within the meaning of section 414(e)) may at its option file such information as the plan administrator may wish to file with respect to the deferred retirement vested benefit rights of any plan participant separated from service covered by the plan.

Section 6057(d) requires the Secretary to transmit copies of any statements, notifications, reports, or other information obtained by the Secretary under section 6057 to the Commissioner of Social Security.

Section 6057(e) of the Code and section 105(c) of ERISA require each plan administrator that is subject to the reporting requirements of section 6057 to furnish to each deferred vested participant an individual statement setting forth the information required by section 6057(a)(2). The individual statement required by section 6057(e) must also notify each participant of any benefits that are forfeitable if the participant dies before a certain date. The individual statement must be furnished no later than the date for filing the registration statement required under section 6057(a).

Section 6057(f)(1) provides that the Secretary, after consultation with the Commissioner of Social Security, may issue such regulations as may be necessary to carry out the provisions of this section.

Since the enactment of ERISA, the Schedule SSA, a schedule to the Form 5500, "Annual Return/Report of Employee Benefit Plan," has been the form used by plan administrators to comply with the reporting requirements of section 6057. On July 21, 2006, the Department of Labor (DOL) published a final rule in the **Federal Register** (71 FR 41359) requiring electronic filing of the Form 5500 series for plan years beginning after January 1, 2008. On November 16, 2007, the DOL published a final rule in the **Federal Register** (72 FR 64710) postponing the effective date of the electronic filing mandate to apply to plan years beginning on or after January 1, 2009. See 29 CFR § 2520.104a-2.

In order to implement the DOL's mandate for electronic filing of the Form 5500, the IRS-only schedules to the Form 5500, including the Schedule SSA, were eliminated from the Form 5500. One result of the elimination of the Schedule SSA is that Form 5500 filings that include Schedule SSA information regarding participants are now subject to rejection (even for late or amended filings for plan years before 2009). The Schedule SSA was replaced by Form 8955-SSA, "Annual Registration Statement Identifying Separated Participants With Deferred Vested Benefits," an IRS-only stand-alone form. Announcement 2011-21 (2011-12 IRB 567), see § 601.601(d)(2), designates Form 8955-SSA as the form to be used to satisfy the reporting requirements of section 6057 for plan years beginning on or after January 1, 2009. Announcement 2011-21 also established an annual due date for the filing of the Form 8955-SSA. In general, if a Form 8955-SSA must be filed for a plan year, it must be filed by the last day of the 7th month following the last day of that plan year (plus extensions).

Section 6081(a) provides that the Secretary may grant a reasonable extension of time for filing any required return, declaration, statement, or other document. Except for certain taxpayers, the extension of time shall not exceed 6 months.

Section 1.6081-1(a) of the Income Tax Regulations provides that the Commissioner is authorized to grant a reasonable extension of time for filing any return, declaration, statement, or other document that relates to any tax imposed under subtitle A of the Code. Under § 1.6081-1(b), the application must be in writing, be signed by the taxpayer or his representative, and set forth the reason for requesting an extension.

Section 1.6081-11 of the regulations provides that a plan administrator or sponsor of an employee benefit plan required to file a Form 5500 will be allowed an automatic extension of the time to file the Form 5500. To receive an automatic extension of time to file, the plan administrator or sponsor must complete a Form 5558, "Application for Extension of Time to File Certain Employee Plan Returns,"and file the application with the Internal Revenue Service on or before the date that the Form 5500 series return must be filed.

Form 5558 is used to request an automatic extension of time to file a Form 5500 return or Form 8955-SSA. In accordance with § 1.6081-11 and Form 5558 (including instructions), an application for an extension of time to file a Form 5500 series return need not be signed. However, in accordance with § 1.6081-1, Form 5558 provides that an application for an extension of time to file Form 8955-SSA must be signed.

Explanation of Provisions

After the current version of the Form 5558 was issued, several comments were received that questioned the need for a signature to extend the time for filing Form 8955-SSA, particularly since a signature is not required to extend the time to file a Form 5500 series return. The commentators noted that, like its predecessor, the Schedule SSA, the Form 8955-SSA is generally prepared in conjunction with the preparation of a plan's Form 5500. They also stated that a signature requirement for the Form 8955-SSA is likely to cause confusion and missed deadlines because of the different rule for the Form 5500. Finally, the commentators contended that the signature requirement is burdensome for both filers and the IRS because the requirement complicates the extension request process.

The proposed regulations would amend § 1.6081-11, relating to automatic extensions of time for filing certain employee plan returns, by adding the Form 8955-SSA to the list of forms that are covered by the automatic 2^1/$_2$ month extension that applies by filing Form 5558. This will permit a plan administrator to receive an automatic extension of 2^1/$_2$ months by submitting, on or before the general due date of the Form 8955-SSA, a Form 5558 indicating that an extension is being requested for filing the Form 8955-SSA. Thus, under the proposed regulations, the same rules that apply to request an extension of time to file the Form 5500 series would also apply to request an extension of time to file Form 8955-SSA. In addition, the proposed regulations would amend § 1.6081-11 to provide that a signature would not be required to request an extension of time to file Form 5500 and Form 8955-SSA. It is anticipated that the Form 5558 and instructions will be revised to reflect this change for the Form 8955-SSA.

In addition, pursuant to section 6011(a), these proposed regulations would formally designate the Form 8955-SSA as the form used to satisfy the reporting requirements of section 6057. These proposed regulations would retain the general reporting requirements that applied to the Schedule SSA with certain minor modifications.

As discussed in the background section of this preamble, section 6057(a) requires the plan administrator (within the meaning of section 414(g)) of a plan that is subject to the vesting standards of section 203 of ERISA to file, within the time prescribed by regulations, a registration statement that sets forth certain information on deferred vested participants. Under existing § 301.6057-1(c)(1) of the Procedure and Administration regulations, the plan administrator of an employee benefit plan described in § 301.6057-1(a)(3), or any other employee retirement benefit plan (including a governmental or church plan), may at its option file on the Schedule SSA information relating to the deferred vested retirement benefit of any plan participant who separates at any time from service covered under the plan. These proposed regulations would retain the ability of such plans to report deferred vested information on a voluntary basis but require that the information be submitted to the IRS on Form 8955-SSA. The proposed regulations would also delegate authority to the Commissioner of the Internal Revenue Service to provide special rules under section 6057 (including designating the form used to comply with section 6057) in revenue rulings, notices, or other guidance published in the Internal Revenue Bulletin (see § 601.601(d)(2)(ii)(b) of this chapter). Finally, the proposed regulations would delete certain obsolete transition rules and update cross-references in § § 1.6057-1 and 1.6057-2.

Proposed Effective Date

These regulations are generally proposed to be effective on or after June 21, 2012. Taxpayers may rely on these proposed regulations for guidance pending the issuance of final regulations. If, and to the extent, the final regulations are more restrictive than the guidance in these proposed regulations, those provisions of the final regulations will be applied without retroactive effect.

Special Analyses

It has been determined that this notice of proposed rulemaking is not a significant regulatory action as defined in Executive Order 12866. Therefore, a regulatory assessment is not required. It has been determined that 5 U.S.C. 533(b) of the Administrative Procedure Act (5 U.S.C. chapter 5) does not apply to these regulations. It is hereby certified that the collection of information in these proposed regulations will not have a significant economic impact on a substantial number of small entities. This certification is based on the fact that most small entities that maintain employee retirement income benefit plans use third party administrators to perform their recordkeeping function. Therefore, an analysis under the Regulatory Flexibility Act (5 U.S.C. chapter 6) is not required. Pursuant to section 7805(f) of the Internal Revenue Code, these regulations have been submitted to the Office of Chief Counsel for Advocacy of the Small Business Administration for comments on its impact on small business.

Comments and Requests for Public Hearing

Before these proposed regulations are adopted as final regulations, consideration will be given to any comments that are submitted timely to the IRS as prescribed in this preamble under the "Addresses" heading. The IRS and Treasury Department request comments on all aspects of the proposed rules. All comments are available at *www.regulations.gov* or upon request. A public hearing will be scheduled if requested in writing by any person who timely submits written comments. If a public hearing is scheduled, notice of the date, time, and place of the public hearing will be published in the **Federal Register**.

Drafting Information

The principal authors of these regulations are Sarah R. Bolen and Pamela R. Kinard, Office of Division Counsel/Associate Chief Counsel (Tax Exempt and Government Entities). However, other personnel from the IRS and the Treasury Department participated in the development of these regulations.

[¶ 49,542] Proposed Amendments of Regulations (REG-134935-11), published in the Federal Register on June 25, 2012.

[Code Sec. 904]

Foreign tax credit: Limitations on credit: Categories of income: Recapture: Foreign losses: Property dispositions: Ordering rules.— Amendments of Reg. § § 1.904-4 and 1.904(g)-3, providing guidance regarding the coordination of the rules for determining high-taxed income with capital gains adjustments and the allocation and recapture of overall foreign losses and overall domestic losses, as well as the coordination of the recapture of overall foreign losses on certain dispositions of property and other rules concerning overall foreign losses and overall domestic losses, are adopted.

[¶ 49,548] Proposed Amendments of Regulations (REG-140668-07), published in the Federal Register on September 17, 2012 (corrected 10/23/2012).

[Code Secs. 172 and 1502]

Corporations: Consolidated returns: Corporate equity reduction transactions (CERTs): Consolidated net operating losses (CNOLs): Election to carry back CNOLs.—Reg. §§ 1.172(h)-0—1.172(h)-5 and 1.1502-72 and amendments of Reg. § 1.1502-21, regarding the treatment of corporate equity reduction transactions (CERTs), including the treatment of multiple-step plans for the acquisition of stock and CERTs involving members of a consolidated group, are proposed.

AGENCY: Internal Revenue Service (IRS), Treasury.

ACTION: Notice of proposed rulemaking.

SUMMARY: This document contains proposed regulations under section 172(h) and section 1502 of the Internal Revenue Code. These proposed regulations provide guidance regarding the treatment of corporate equity reduction transactions (CERTs), including the treatment of multiple step plans for the acquisition of stock and CERTs involving members of a consolidated group. These proposed regulations also provide guidance regarding certain elections relating to the carryback of consolidated net operating losses (CNOLs) to separate return years. These proposed regulations will affect C corporations and corporations filing consolidated returns.

DATES: Written or electronic comments and requests for a public hearing must be received by December 17, 2012.

ADDRESSES: Send submissions to: CC:PA:LPD:PR (REG-140668-07), Room 5203, Internal Revenue Service, P.O. Box 7604, Ben Franklin Station, Washington, DC 20044. Submissions may be hand-delivered Monday through Friday between the hours of 8 a.m. and 4 p.m. to CC:PA:LPD:PR (REG-140668-07), Courier's Desk, Internal Revenue Service, 1111 Constitution Avenue, NW, Washington, DC, or sent electronically, via the Federal eRulemaking Portal at *www.regulations.gov* (IRS REG-140668-07).

FOR FURTHER INFORMATION CONTACT: Concerning the proposed regulations, Amie Colwell Breslow or Marie C. Milnes-Vasquez at (202) 622-7530; concerning submissions of comments and request for public hearing, Oluwafunmilayo Taylor at Oluwafunmilayo.P.Taylor@irscounsel.treas.gov or (202) 622-7180 (not toll-free numbers).

SUPPLEMENTARY INFORMATION:

Paperwork Reduction Act

The collection of information contained in this notice of proposed rulemaking has been submitted to the Office of Management and Budget for review in accordance with the Paperwork Reduction Act of 1995 (44 U.S.C. 3507(d)) under control number 1545-2171. Comments on the collection of information should be sent to the **Office of Management and Budget**, Attn: Desk Officer for the Department of the Treasury, Office of Information and Regulatory Affairs, Washington, D.C. 20503, with copies to the **Internal Revenue Service**, Attn: IRS Reports Clearance Officer, SE:W:CAR:MP:T:T:SP, Washington, D.C. 20224. Comments on the collection of information should be received by November 16, 2012. Comments are specifically requested concerning:

Whether the proposed collection of information is necessary for the proper performance of the functions of the **Internal Revenue Service**, including whether the information will have practical utility;

The accuracy of the estimated burden associated with the proposed collection of information;

How the quality, utility and clarity of the information to be collected may be enhanced;

How the burden of complying with the proposed collection of information may be minimized, including through the application of automated collection techniques or other forms of information technology; and

Estimates of capital or start-up costs and costs of operation, maintenance, and purchase of service to provide information.

The collection of information in these proposed regulations is in §§ 1.1502-21(b)(3)(ii)(B) and 1.1502-72(e).

The proposed regulations provide guidance regarding application of section 172(b)(1)(E) and (h) and section 1502.

The collection of information is required in order to obtain a benefit. The likely respondents are corporations that are members of consolidated groups.

Estimated total annual reporting burden: 120,000 hours.

Estimated average annual burden hours per respondent: 15 hours.

Estimated number of respondents: 8,000.

Estimated frequency of responses: Once.

An agency may not conduct or sponsor, and a person is not required to respond to, a collection of information unless it displays a valid control number assigned by the Office of Management and Budget.

Books or records relating to a collection of information must be retained as long as their contents may become material in the administration of any internal revenue law. Generally, tax returns and tax return information are confidential, as required by 26 U.S.C. 6103.

Background

Section 172 provides rules relating to net operating loss (NOL) carrybacks and carryovers. Section 172(b)(1)(A) states that the NOL for any taxable year generally is carried back to each of the 2 years preceding the taxable year of the loss and carried over to each of the 20 years following the taxable year of the loss.

The corporate equity reduction transaction rules of section 172(b)(1)(E) and (h) were enacted in 1989 in response to the use of NOL carrybacks to finance leveraged buyout transactions. Congress enacted these rules to limit a corporation's ability to obtain tax refunds as the result of the carryback of NOLs that were attributable to interest deductions allocable to such transactions. See Explanation of Corporate Tax Refund Restriction Bill, 135 Cong. Rec. S9936-01, at S9944 (1989); 1989 WL 193512.

Section 172(h)(3)(A) defines a *corporate equity reduction transaction* (CERT) as a "major stock acquisition" (MSA) or an "excess distribution" (ED). Section 172(h)(3)(B) defines *major stock acquisition* as the acquisition by a corporation, pursuant to a plan of such corporation (or any group of persons acting in concert with such corporation), of stock in another corporation representing 50 percent or more (by vote or value) of the stock in such other corporation. Section 172(h)(3)(C) defines *excess distribution* as the excess (if any) of the aggregate distributions (including redemptions) made during a taxable year by a corporation with respect to its stock over the greater of: 150 percent of the average of such distributions during the 3 taxable years immediately preceding such taxable year, or 10 percent of the fair market value of the stock of the corporation at the beginning of such taxable year. Thus, the total of distributions that may be treated as an ED is limited to the amount that exceeds the greater of two baselines: one tied to a historical, three-year average and the other based on the fair market value of the distributor.

If an MSA or ED occurs, section 172(b)(1)(E) and (h) limit the carryback of the portion of an NOL that constitutes a "corporate equity reduction interest loss" (CERIL) of an "applicable corporation" in any "loss limitation year." See section 172(b)(1)(E)(i). Section 172(b)(1)(E)(iii) defines an *applicable corporation* as a C corporation that acquires stock, or the stock of which is acquired, in an MSA; a C corporation making distributions with respect to, or redeeming, its stock in connection with an ED; or a C corporation that is a successor to one of the other types of applicable corporations. Section 172(b)(1)(E)(ii) defines *loss limitation year* as the taxable year in which a CERT occurs and each of the two succeeding taxable years. Section 172(h)(1) defines *corporate equity reduction interest loss* as the excess of (1) the total NOL for a loss limitation year, over (2) the NOL for the loss limitation year computed without regard to the allocable interest deductions that are otherwise taken into account in computing the NOL. Section 172(h)(2)(A) defines *allocable interest deductions* as deductions allowed on the portion of any indebtedness allocable to a CERT.

Under section 172(h)(2)(B), except as provided in regulations or section 172(h)(2)(E), indebtedness is allocable to a CERT in the manner prescribed under section 263A(f)(2)(A) without regard to paragraph (i) thereof (relating to traced debt). Thus, a portion of the taxpayer's total interest expense is allocable to the CERT. See H.R. Rep. No. 101-247, at 1251 (Conf. Rep.). However, section 172(h)(2)(C) limits the amount of allocable interest deductions for any loss limitation year to (1) the amount allowable as a deduction for interest paid or accrued by the taxpayer during the loss limitation year, less (2) the average of deductions allowed for interest paid or accrued by the taxpayer for the three taxable years preceding the taxable year in which the CERT occurred. Therefore, the allocable interest deductions are limited to the increase in interest deductions over a historical, three-year baseline.

Section 172(h)(3)(C) and (E) sets forth specific rules for determining whether an ED has occurred. For purposes of determining a corporation's aggregate distributions for a taxable year under section 172(h)(3)(C)(i) and the average of such distributions during the three taxable years preceding the relevant taxable year under section 172(h)(3)(C)(ii)(I), section 172(h)(3)(E)(ii) provides that the distributions taken into account are reduced by the aggregate amount of stock issued by the corporation during the applicable period in exchange for money or property other than stock in the corporation. However, section 172(h)(3)(E)(i) provides that stock described in section 1504(a)(4) (certain preferred stock) and distributions (including redemptions) with respect to such stock are disregarded.

For purposes of applying section 172(b)(1)(E) and (h), an applicable corporation and all members of its consolidated group are treated as a single taxpayer. See section 172(h)(4)(C).

Currently, there are no regulations under section 172(b)(1)(E) and (h). Section 172(h)(5) grants the Secretary the authority to prescribe such regulations as may be necessary to carry out the purposes of section 172(h), including regulations: (A) for applying section 172(h) to successor corporations and to cases in which a taxpayer becomes (or ceases to be) a member of a consolidated group; (B) to prevent the avoidance of section 172(h) through the use of related parties, pass-through entities, and intermediaries; and (C) for applying section 172(h) when more than one corporation is involved in a CERT. In addition, section 172(h)(2)(B) grants the Secretary authority to issue regulations prescribing a method for allocating indebtedness to a CERT other than the method contained in section 263A(f)(2)(A). Section 1502 provides the Secretary with broad authority to prescribe rules applicable to corporations that file consolidated returns that are different from the income tax provisions that would apply if those corporations filed separate returns.

These proposed regulations provide general rules addressing whether a CERT has occurred, the computation of a CERIL, and the treatment of successors. The proposed regulations also address issues specific to the application of section 172(b)(1)(E) and (h) to consolidated groups, including: (1) treatment of the consolidated group as a single taxpayer; (2) determination of the group's three-year average that is relevant to a particular consolidated return loss limitation year; (3) application of these rules if the corporation participating in a CERT becomes a member of a consolidated group; (4) application of these rules if a group member deconsolidates after the group has participated in (or is treated as having participated in) a CERT; (5) apportionment of a CERIL (and other special status CNOLs) to members of a consolidated group for carryback or carryover to separate return years; and (6) application of section 172(b)(1)(E) and (h) to a life-nonlife group. The proposed regulations also provide rules that would amend the loss carryback waivers available to deconsolidating group members.

At this time, the Department of Treasury and the IRS are not providing rules addressing the application of section 172(h) to related parties, pass-through entities, or intermediaries. However, the Department of Treasury and the IRS continue to study the circumstances under which these persons should be subject to section 172(b)(1)(E) and (h). For example, the purposes of the statute may be furthered if section 172(b)(1)(E) and (h) apply to the acquisition of 100 percent of the stock of a target by a partnership in which a corporation (or consolidated group) holds a controlling interest. On the other hand, the purposes of the statute may not be advanced if 100 percent of the stock of a target is acquired in a single transaction, but the percentage of target stock indirectly attributable to corporate acquirers is relatively small. The Department of Treasury and the IRS request comments regarding the parameters for applying section 172(b)(1)(E) and (h) to indirect corporate acquirers, and what special computational rules, if any, would be needed to implement its application.

The Department of Treasury and the IRS considered inclusion of an anti-avoidance rule to prevent taxpayers from engaging in section 381 transactions to shorten loss limitation years. However, the Department of Treasury and the IRS believe that the detrimental effects of shortening tax years make it unlikely that taxpayers will attempt to undertake such transactions as a planning technique. For example, shortening a loss limitation year will reduce the income in that year, and, accordingly, will limit the ability to carry back any losses to that year. The Department of Treasury and the IRS continue to study whether an anti-abuse rule is needed and request comments on this issue.

In addition, the Department of Treasury and the IRS are not providing rules addressing the application of section 172(b)(1)(E) and (h) to transactions occurring before these rules are adopted as final regulations (transitional issues). However, the Department of Treasury and the IRS continue to study, and request comments on, transitional issues. For example, the Department of Treasury and the IRS request comments regarding the application of section 172(b)(1)(E) and (h) if a taxable year constitutes a loss limitation year with regard to more than one CERT, one occurring before and the other occurring after the adoption of these proposed regulations as final regulations.

Explanation of Provisions

1. *General CERT Rules*

A. *Determination of existence of a CERT*

As discussed, a CERT is either an MSA or an ED. The statute does not exclude tax-free transactions from treatment as an MSA or an ED. In addition, the concerns targeted by Congress in enacting section 172(b)(1)(E) and (h) can exist in the context of both taxable and tax-free transactions. Accordingly, the proposed regulations provide that a tax free transaction that meets the statutory definition of an MSA or an ED must be tested as a CERT under section 172(b)(1)(E) and (h) and these proposed regulations (collectively, the "CERT rules"). For example, a section 355 transaction, a corporate organization under section 351, or a stock acquisition that qualifies for reorganization treatment under section 368(a)(1)(A) and (a)(2)(E) must be tested under the CERT rules.

These proposed regulations also provide that an integrated plan of stock acquisition including multiple steps will be tested as a single potential MSA for purposes of determining the consequences of the transaction under the CERT rules. This treatment applies even if a step in the plan might separately constitute an ED, or might so qualify in conjunction with other distributions in the same taxable year.

Section 172(h)(3)(C)(ii) limits the amount of distributions in a taxable year that may be treated as an ED. Under one prong of this limitation, the taxpayer's distributions are treated as an ED only to the extent that they exceed 150 percent of the taxpayer's average of distributions (three-year distribution average) made in the three taxable years preceding the taxable year in which a potential ED occurs (the distribution lookback period). These proposed regulations provide that, to the extent that a distribution is part of an integrated plan that is treated as an MSA, the distribution is excluded from the computation of the taxpayer's three-year distribution average that is relevant to any other potential ED. These proposed regulations provide additional rules for calculating the taxpayer's three-year distribution average under section 172(h)(3)(C)(ii)(I) relevant to potential EDs that occur in taxable years that are not full 12-month years.

B. *Loss limitation years*

The proposed regulations generally provide that the taxable year in which a CERT occurs and each of the two succeeding taxable years constitute loss limitation years with regard to the CERT. The proposed regulations also provide special rules addressing loss limitation years of successors, consolidated groups, and former members of consolidated groups.

C. *Computation of a CERIL*

Under section 172(h)(1), the term *CERIL* means, with respect to any loss limitation year, the excess (if any) of (1) the NOL for such taxable year, over (2) the NOL for such taxable year determined without regard to any allocable interest deductions otherwise taken into account in computing such loss. Section 172(h)(2)(A) defines *allocable interest deductions* as deductions allowed for interest on any indebtedness allocable to a CERT. Section 172(h)(2)(B) states that, except as provided in regulations and section 172(h)(2)(E), the indebtedness allocable to a CERT is determined under the avoided cost methodology of section 263A(f)(2)(A), with certain adjustments.

Under section 263A(f)(2)(A) and the regulations thereunder, allocable interest deductions are computed by multiplying the "weighted average interest rate" by "average excess expenditures" as those terms are defined in §1.263A-9(c)(5)(ii) and (iii). Because section 263A contemplates transactions that are very different in nature from CERTs, it is often difficult to identify the costs associated with a CERT that are analogous to average excess expenditures. To ameliorate this difficulty, these proposed regulations provide MSA- and ED-specific rules for computing costs associated with a CERT (CERT costs). Further, these proposed regulations identify additional CERT costs by looking to the capitalization rules under section 263(a). Specifically, the proposed regulations treat as CERT costs amounts paid or incurred to facilitate an MSA or ED to the extent that those amounts are required to be capitalized under section 263(a) (with certain modifications), and any amounts disallowed under section 162(k). Because most CERTs occur under circumstances that already require application of section 263(a), invoking those rules should result in greater administrability. Once the CERT costs are identified, the interest allocable to those costs is computed under the principles of section 263A(f)(2)(A) and the regulations thereunder (with adjustments). The avoided cost methodology of section 263A(f)(2)(A) effectively allocates interest to a CERT to the extent that the taxpayer's interest costs could have been reduced if the taxpayer had not engaged in the CERT. For purposes of applying the avoided cost rules of section 263A(f)(2)(A), all CERT costs are treated as if they were cash expenditures.

Under the proposed regulations, *CERT costs* with regard to an MSA include the fair market value of the stock acquired, whether that stock is acquired in exchange for cash, stock of the acquirer, or other property. The inclusion of the fair market value of stock acquired in stock-for-stock exchanges ensures that such transactions are treated similarly to an issuance of acquirer's stock for cash followed by an MSA funded with the cash proceeds. Further, inclusion of the fair market value of stock acquired is consistent with the avoided cost methodology applied under section 172(h)(2) because the CERT statute rejects tracing and assumes that debt is used to fund all CERT costs.

In addition, CERT costs of an MSA include the fair market value of any distribution that is part of an integrated transaction constituting the MSA. CERT costs also include amounts paid or incurred to facilitate any step of the MSA to the extent that those amounts are required to be capitalized under section 263(a), and any amounts disallowed under section 162(k).

Under the proposed regulations, CERT costs associated with an ED include the fair market value of distributions to shareholders that are determined to be EDs during the year in which the CERT occurs. CERT costs also include a portion of amounts paid or incurred to facilitate the distributions to the extent that those amounts are required to be capitalized under section 263(a), and any amounts disallowed under section 162(k). However, if neither section 263(a) nor section 162(k) applies or if only section 162(k) applies to a distribution included in an ED, additional CERT costs associated with the distribution are determined under the principles of §1.263(a)-4(e) (relating to the capitalization of costs that facilitate the acquisition or creation of intangibles), applied as if the ED were a transaction within the scope of §1.263(a)-4.

As discussed, the rules of section 263(a) are applied in the CERT context with certain modifications. For the purpose of identifying CERT costs under these proposed regulations, modifications to the operation of §1.263(a)-4 and -5 include treating certain borrowing costs as facilitative of an MSA or ED. Therefore, CERT costs will include these borrowing costs. Congress objected to the carryback of NOLs resulting from leveraging that directly or indirectly enables CERTs; therefore, the Department of Treasury and the IRS believe that it is appropriate to include borrowing costs in total CERT costs. However, the Department of Treasury and the IRS request comments regarding the extent to which borrowing costs should be included in CERT costs.

The computation of interest allocable to CERTs under the rules of section 263A(f)(2)(A) involves the time-weighted average of costs incurred as of various dates in the taxable year. Therefore, these proposed regulations set forth rules for determining when CERT costs should be taken into account. Under these proposed regulations, accumulated CERT costs as of a particular date are the total CERT costs that have been taken into account as of that date under the applicable corporation's method of accounting. A special proration rule is provided to determine accumulated CERT costs related to an ED. Finally, CERT costs incurred in any year prior to the year in which the CERT occurs are included in accumulated CERT costs beginning on the first day of the year in which the CERT occurs.

Section 172(h)(2)(E) requires that the allocation of interest to a CERT be reduced if an unforeseeable extraordinary adverse event occurs during a loss limitation year but after the CERT. The proposed regulations do not provide guidance with regard to unforeseeable extraordinary adverse events. However, the Department of Treasury and the IRS request comments regarding whether rules are necessary and, if so, what type of events should constitute unforeseeable extraordinary adverse events.

D. *Limitation on interest deductions*

The CERT rules generally provide that the portion of an NOL for any loss limitation year that is attributable to the interest deductions allocable to a CERT (that is, a CERIL) may not be carried back to any year prior to the year in which the CERT occurred. As discussed, section 172(h)(2)(C) limits the amount of interest treated as an allocable interest deduction to the excess of the amount allowable as a deduction for interest paid or accrued by the taxpayer during the loss limitation year, over the average of amounts allowable as a deduction for interest paid or accrued (the three-year average) during the three taxable years preceding the taxable year in which the CERT occurred (the lookback period). These proposed regulations provide special rules for computing the three-year average in special situations, such as if an applicable corporation is not in existence for the entire lookback period. Further, the proposed regulations adjust the three-year average if the relevant loss limitation year is not a full

12-month taxable period. These proposed regulations also set forth special rules for any taxable year that constitutes a loss limitation year with regard to multiple CERTs.

The legislative history indicates that Congress expected the Department of Treasury and the IRS to write rules that provide that increases attributable solely to fluctuations in interest rates would not be taken into account for purposes of applying the three-year average. Out of concern that the additional complexities of such rules would outweigh the benefit, these proposed regulations do not include rules that factor out increases in interest deductions attributable solely to fluctuations in interest rates. However, the Department of Treasury and the IRS are studying a rule that, for purposes of applying the three-year average, would factor out interest deductions that are attributable to increases in a taxpayer's interest rate that occur after the date of a CERT. Under the rule being considered, the measurement of a baseline interest rate after the CERT occurs would take into account the fact that CERT activity will often decrease a taxpayer's creditworthiness and increase its average cost of borrowing, and accordingly that the existence of the CERT, in and of itself, will increase a taxpayer's borrowing expenses. The Department of Treasury and the IRS request comments on whether such a baseline would effectively account for fluctuations in interest rates or whether an alternative measure would be more appropriate.

E. *Predecessor and successor*

As discussed, the CERT rules apply only to applicable corporations. Under section 172(b)(1)(E)(iii)(III), an applicable corporation includes any corporation that is a successor of: a corporation that acquires stock in an MSA; a corporation the stock of which is acquired in an MSA; or a corporation making a distribution with respect to, or redeeming, its stock in connection with an ED. For purposes of applying the CERT rules, these proposed regulations define *successor* as a transferee or distributee in a transaction to which section 381(a) applies. Further, if a successor to a previous applicable corporation with regard to a CERT itself transfers assets to a further successor, the further successor corporation is treated as an applicable corporation with regard to that CERT. In addition, these proposed regulations set forth special rules for computing a successor's CERIL.

F. *Operating rules*

The proposed regulations include special rules regarding the prohibition on carryback of a CERIL. These rules provide that no CERIL may be carried back to any taxable year that includes solely dates that precede the date on which the CERT at issue occurred. In applying this rule to multi-step MSAs and to EDs that include multiple distributions, the date on which the CERT occurs is the earliest date on which the requirements for CERT status have been satisfied. These proposed regulations also provide that, for purposes of determining whether an ED has occurred, the computation of any three-year distribution average under section 172(h)(3)(C)(ii)(I) will be reduced by the average of the stock issuances made by the applicable corporation during the three years of the distribution lookback period.

The principles of the proposed regulations apply to the computation of the alternative minimum tax net operating loss under section 56(d).

2. *Special CERT Rules Applicable to Consolidated Groups*

A. *Single entity treatment*

Section 172(h)(4)(C) states that, except as provided by regulation, all members of a consolidated group are treated as a single taxpayer for purposes of section 172(b)(1)(E) and (h). These proposed regulations provide further guidance regarding the application of single entity principles. These proposed regulations affirm that transactions and expenditures undertaken by a particular member are not separately tracked; rather, the entire group is treated as a single applicable corporation. For example, if multiple members of a group acquire in total 50 percent or more (by vote or value) of the stock of another corporation, the group has engaged in an MSA. Likewise, the computation of a group's CERIL under section 172(h)(1) for any loss limitation year that is a consolidated return year includes the debt of all members and all interest deductions that are allowed on the group's consolidated return.

Intercompany transactions (including interest accruals and payments on intercompany obligations) are generally disregarded under the proposed regulations. However, these proposed regulations provide that a transaction will not be disregarded if a party to the transaction becomes a non-member as a part of the same plan or arrangement.

The most difficult issues in the CERT area arise from the application of single entity concepts if different corporations join and deconsolidate from a group within the same three-year period. The fungibility of money and the ease of moving cash and debt within a consolidated group may provide a consolidated group with an unwarranted ability to manipulate the application of the CERT rules, further complicating the analysis. After considering different approaches, the Department of Treasury and the IRS have determined that application of single entity principles, under which corporations cease to be separately tracked for CERT purposes after their inclusion in a group, will limit complexity and promote administrability. Furthermore, single entity treatment is consistent with the statutory default of treating the consolidated group as a single taxpayer.

Consistent with single entity treatment, these proposed regulations provide that, if an applicable corporation with regard to a CERT occurring in a separate return year (pre-existing CERT member) joins a consolidated group, the group is treated as a single applicable corporation with regard to that CERT in the consolidated return year of the acquisition and any relevant succeeding year. The pre-existing CERT member will no longer have separate status as an applicable corporation. Beginning on the day the pre-existing CERT member is first included in the group, the only CERIL computation will be that of the group.

These proposed regulations also provide that, in the consolidated return context, both the debt of a new member acquired in a CERT and the corresponding interest expenses are included in the group's CERIL computation, even if the group would not have been in a position to pay off the debt of the acquired corporation if the CERT had not occurred. For example, if a target corporation acquired by a consolidated group has debt outstanding prior to the acquisition, the group takes into account interest incurred by the group that is attributable to the target's pre-existing debt, despite the fact that the group would have had no reason to satisfy the target's debt if the acquisition had not occurred. If the acquisition had not occurred, the debt of the target would not have become a liability of the applicable corporation (the group), and the associated interest expense would not have been deducted by the group. As will be discussed, the historical interest expense of the target is also included in the group's computation of the three-year average applied to limit the interest allocated to the CERT.

B. *Applicable corporation status and allocation of CERT costs following deconsolidation from a group*

These proposed regulations provide that, if a member deconsolidates from a group on or after (1) the date on which the group engages in a CERT, or (2) the date on which the group acquires a pre-existing CERT member, then, following the deconsolidation, both the deconsolidating member and the group generally will be treated as applicable corporations with regard to the CERT. The deconsolidating member will be apportioned a pro rata share of the group's CERT costs incurred through the date of the deconsolidation. The proration is based on the relative fair market values of the deconsolidating corporation (immediately after its deconsolidation) and the entire group (immediately before the deconsolidation). This rule applies regardless of whether any particular corporation would have constituted an applicable corporation with regard to the CERT without the application of the single entity treatment. The Department of Treasury and the IRS request comments regarding alternatives for allocating CERT costs following deconsolidation from a group.

The CERT costs that are allocated and apportioned to the deconsolidating member are subtracted from the group's CERT costs and will not attract allocable interest in any loss limitation year of the group (or any separate return loss limitation year of another group member) after the year of deconsolidation. Therefore, the group may have less CERIL in the years following the deconsolidation. Apportionment of CERT costs to the deconsolidating member may result in that corporation having a CERIL in the period following its deconsolidation.

Under these proposed regulations, the deconsolidating member (or the common parent of any group that the deconsolidating member joins immediately after deconsolidation) may elect out of the general rule of apportionment. In making this election, the member or common parent permanently waives all carrybacks of losses allocable to the deconsolidating member to years of the former group and any preceding taxable years. If this election is made, the deconsolidating member will not be treated as an applicable corporation with regard to the CERT, and it will not be allocated any CERT costs. Applicable corporation status and CERT costs will remain with the former group. This is true even if the deconsolidating member directly engaged in the CERT. Further, none of the interest history of the group will be allocated to the deconsolidating member for CERT purposes, including determining the CERIL related to any future CERT. The resulting lack of interest history may increase the amount of a CERIL in future taxable years associated with other CERTs of the deconsolidating corporation. This election is available to any deconsolidating member, even if the former group is not an applicable corporation with regard to any CERT at the time of the deconsolidation.

C. Loss limitation years

Because all members of a consolidated group are treated as a single taxpayer under section 172(h)(4)(C), a consolidated group is treated as the "applicable corporation" with regard to a CERT. These proposed regulations provide special rules for determining loss limitation years of consolidated groups and former members of consolidated groups. Under these proposed regulations, the taxable year in which a CERT actually occurs is a loss limitation year. Any other taxable year (potential loss limitation year) of any applicable corporation (including a consolidated group) will constitute a loss limitation year with regard to the CERT only if, under the carryover rules of sections 172(b)(1)(A)(ii) and 381(c)(1), the potential loss limitation year would constitute the first or second taxable year following the taxable year of the corporation or consolidated group that actually engaged in the CERT, which includes the date of the CERT. For purposes of tracking taxable years, sections 172 and 381 are applied as if the inclusion of any corporation in a consolidated group or the deconsolidation of any member from a group were a transaction described in section 381(a).

The proposed regulations provide that the separate return years of a corporation that deconsolidates from a consolidated group may be loss limitation years with regard to a CERT of the former group. This may occur only if the consolidated return year of the deconsolidation is a first or second loss limitation year with regard to that CERT. The taxable years of more than one applicable corporation (including a consolidated group) may be loss limitation years with regard to the same CERT, even if those taxable years include the same dates.

The special rules for determining loss limitation years can be illustrated as follows: T corporation maintains a calendar taxable year and does not join in the filing of a consolidated return. The X group holds 60 percent of the only class of T stock. On July 1, Year 5, T engages in a CERT. The X group, which includes member S, maintains a calendar taxable year. On December 31, Year 5, the X group acquires all of the remaining T stock. T is first included in the X group on January 1, Year 6. On June 30, Year 6, S deconsolidates from the X group, and thereafter S maintains a calendar taxable year. The first loss limitation year with respect to the T CERT is T's calendar Year 5. Pursuant to these proposed regulations, as a result of acquiring T, the X group is treated as an applicable corporation with respect to the T CERT. The X group's loss limitation years with respect to the T CERT are its calendar Years 6 and 7. Because no election is made with respect to the deconsolidation of S, following the deconsolidation, S is also treated as an applicable corporation with regard to the T CERT. Because consolidated return Year 6 (the year of the deconsolidation) is a second loss limitation year with regard to the CERT, S's short year ending December 31, Year 6 will be S's only loss limitation year with regard to the T CERT.

D. Determining the three-year average of a group

As discussed in section 1.D. of this preamble, under section 172(h)(2)(C), the interest deductions treated as allocable to a CERT are limited to the difference between the interest paid or accrued in the loss limitation year at issue and the average of the interest paid or accrued in the three years preceding the year of the CERT (three-year average). These proposed regulations adopt single entity concepts intended, in part, to decrease the complexity of the computation of the three-year average resulting from the entry of corporations into, and the deconsolidation of corporations from, a consolidated group. Under these proposed regulations, with regard to a corporation joining a group, the interest history of that corporation is combined with that of the acquiring group. For purposes of the CERT rules, this interest is thereafter generally treated as having been paid or accrued by the group and is no longer separately traced to the acquired corporation. Similarly, with regard to the deconsolidation of a member from a group, a portion of the group's entire interest history is generally apportioned to the deconsolidating member for purposes of the CERT rules. The apportionment is based on the relative fair market values of the deconsolidating corporation (immediately after its deconsolidation) and the entire group (immediately before the deconsolidation). Under these proposed regulations, the allocated and apportioned history is subtracted from the group's interest history solely for purposes of the CERT rules and is unavailable to the group with regard to any loss limitation year of the group (or any separate return loss limitation year of another group member) after the year of deconsolidation. Consistent with single entity treatment and rejection of a tracing regime, the interest allocated to a particular deconsolidating member is not tied to that member's actual interest history.

These proposed regulations also provide special rules relevant to any loss limitation year during which a corporation (partial-year member) becomes a member of, or ceases to be a member of, a group (transitional year). For purposes of computing any three-year average of a group that is relevant to a transitional year, these rules require proration of the interest history that is attributable to the partial-year member so that a group that includes a particular member for only a portion of a loss limitation year includes only a pro rata portion of that member's three-year interest history. These proposed regulations also provide special rules for computing the three-year average if a group is not in existence for three taxable years prior to the consolidated return year in which the CERT occurs (the lookback period) and for determining the lookback period if a group acquires a corporation that previously engaged in a CERT.

E. Excess distributions in groups

These proposed regulations contain rules pertaining to the computation of EDs of consolidated groups and of corporations that have been consolidated group members. Consistent with single entity treatment under section 172(h)(4)(C), the proposed regulations provide that the distributions relevant for purposes of computing an ED of a consolidated group generally include only non-intercompany distributions. However, this general rule does not apply if a party to the transaction deconsolidates as part of the same plan or arrangement. Under those circumstances, the distribution will be tested on a separate entity basis as a potential CERT.

As discussed in section 1.A. of this preamble, section 172(h)(3)(C)(ii) places a limitation on the amount of distributions in a taxable year that may be treated as ED, and the limitation is based in part on 150 percent of the taxpayer's average of distributions (three-year distribution average) made in the three taxable years preceding the taxable year of the potential ED. These proposed regulations provide that single entity principles generally apply to the computation of the three-year distribution average of a consolidated group or a corporation that has been a consolidated group member. That is, the only distributions taken into account are those made to non-member shareholders. However, in computing the three-year distribution average of a consolidated group that includes a member for less than the entire consolidated return year of a potential ED, the group takes into account only a pro rata portion of the actual distribution history of that member. Further, a corporation that deconsolidates from a group takes into account its actual history of non-intercompany distributions for purposes of applying the CERT rules in future separate return years. The corporation is not apportioned a pro rata share of the total distribution history of the group.

Additional rules apply with regard to computation of stock issuances and valuation of the group, which are intended to ensure that the rules in those areas are applied on a single entity basis. Specifically, the proposed regulations provide that, in applying section 172(h)(3)(E)(ii) to determine the offset of stock issuances against distributions, only stock that is issued to non-members is taken into account. Further, the proposed regulations provide that the value of the group, computed pursuant to section 172(h)(3)(C)(ii)(II), equals the value of the stock of all members other than stock that is owned directly or indirectly by another member.

F. *Reverse acquisitions*

These proposed regulations address the application of the MSA rules to reverse acquisitions, as defined in §1.1502-75(d)(3). The proposed regulations provide that, if a reverse acquisition occurs, the CERT rules will be applied by treating the acquirer in form as the target corporation, and treating the target in form as the acquiring corporation. They also provide special rules regarding the computation of the CERT costs in a reverse acquisition.

G. *Life-nonlife groups*

These proposed regulations provide rules for applying the CERT rules to a group that elects under section 1504(c)(2) to file a consolidated return (life-nonlife group). As with consolidated groups generally, the fungibility of money and the ease of moving cash and debt within a life-nonlife group may provide an unwarranted ability to manipulate the application of the CERT rules. Accordingly, these proposed regulations generally apply the CERT rules and the consolidated return CERT rules to a life-nonlife group on a single entity basis, and not on a subgroup basis. Under the proposed regulations, a single CERIL is computed with regard to any loss limitation year of a life-nonlife group, which includes all life-nonlife group members' CERT costs, debt, and interest paid or accrued for that year. However, for purposes of determining the CERIL of a life-nonlife group under section 172(h)(1) for any loss limitation year, the sum of the nonlife consolidated net operating loss (nonlife CNOL) (if any) and the life consolidated loss from operations (LO) (if any) for that year is treated as a notional "NOL" of the group. For this purpose, nonlife consolidated taxable income does not offset any LO, and consolidated partial life insurance company taxable income (as used in §1.1502-47(g)) does not offset any nonlife CNOL.

If a CERIL exists for a loss limitation year of a life-nonlife group, that CERIL is allocated on a pro rata basis between the nonlife CNOL and the LO of the group, based on the relative sizes of the two attributes.

3. *Specialized CNOL Carryback Rules*

These proposed regulations provide rules regarding the apportionment of CNOLs that contain a component portion of special status loss, such as a CERIL or a specified liability loss. See section 172(h)(1) and (f)(1). Under these rules, a special status loss is apportioned to each group member, separately from the remainder of the CNOL, under the method provided in §1.1502-21(b)(2)(iv). This apportionment occurs without separate entity inquiry into whether a particular member incurred the specific expenses or engaged in the particular activities required by the provisions governing the special status loss.

The proposed regulations also amend and expand the current election under §1.1502-21(b)(3)(ii)(B), informally referred to as the "split-waiver" election. That election is currently available to any group that acquires one or more members from another group. By making the election, the acquiring group relinquishes, with respect to all CNOLs attributable to the newly-acquired corporation, the portion of the carryback period during which that corporation was a member of another group. The current rule does not allow a group to waive the portion of the carryback period for which a newly-acquired corporation was not a member of a consolidated group. The current election is a one-time election and must be made with the acquiring group's timely-filed original return for the year of the acquisition.

The proposed regulations amend the split waiver election to make the election available to any group that acquires a corporation, regardless of whether such corporation was acquired from another group. An election results in the waiver of the entire carryback period with regard to CNOLs allocable to the acquired corporation, not only the period during which the corporation was a member of another group. Further, any election that is made with regard to a newly-acquired member that had been a member of another group at the time of its acquisition must include all members acquired from the same group during the taxable year of the acquiring group.

In addition, the proposed regulations give the electing group a choice of making the one-time election or making the split-waiver election on an annual basis with regard to the CNOL of a particular consolidated return year. Any annual split-waiver election must be filed with the group's timely filed original return for the year of the CNOL. The one-time election and the annual split-waiver election that are available under proposed §1.1502-21(b)(3)(ii)(B) apply generally with respect to losses attributable to the acquired corporation. These split-waiver elections are in addition to the one-time election available under the CERT rules to elect out of the general rule of apportionment for CERT costs and interest history to a deconsolidating member, which also results in the waiver of all carrybacks of losses allocable to the deconsolidating member to any prior taxable years. As a result, under these proposed regulations, corporations may have three, mutually exclusive, irrevocable elections to waive carryback of CNOLs to separate return years: an annual election, a one-time election, and a special CERT election.

Proposed Effective Date

Sections 1.172(h)-1 through 1.172(h)-5 and §1.1502-72 (except §1.1502-72(e)) are effective for CERTs occurring on or after the date of publication of the Treasury decision adopting these rules as final regulations in the **Federal Register**, except that they do not apply to any CERTs occurring pursuant to a written agreement that is binding prior to the date of publication of the Treasury decision adopting these rules as final regulations in the **Federal Register**. The amendments to §1.1502-21(b)(2) are effective for taxable years for which the due date of the original return (without extensions) is on or after the date of publication of the Treasury decision adopting these rules as final regulations in the **Federal Register**. Section 1.1502-72(e) and the amendments to §1.1502-21(b)(3) are effective for acquisitions or deconsolidations, as appropriate, occurring on or after the date of publication of the Treasury decision adopting these rules as final regulations in the **Federal Register**, except that they do not apply to any acquisition or deconsolidations, as appropriate, occurring pursuant to a written agreement that is binding before the date of publication of the Treasury decision adopting these rules as final regulations in the **Federal Register**.

Special Analyses

It has been determined that this notice of proposed rulemaking is not a significant regulatory action as defined in Executive Order 12866, as supplemented by Executive Order 13563. Therefore, a regulatory assessment is not required. Pursuant to the Regulatory Flexibility Act (5 U.S.C. chapter 6), it is hereby certified that these proposed regulations will not have a significant economic impact on a substantial number of small entities. This certification is based on the fact that these proposed regulations will primarily affect C corporations and members of consolidated groups, which tend to be large corporations. Accordingly, a regulatory flexibility analysis is not required. Pursuant to section 7805(f) of the Internal Revenue Code, these regulations have been submitted to the Chief Counsel for Advocacy of the Small Business Administration for comment on their impact on small business.

Comments and Requests for Public Hearing

Before these proposed regulations are adopted as final regulations, consideration will be given to any written (a signed original and eight (8) copies) or electronic comments that are submitted timely to the IRS. The Department of Treasury and the IRS request comments on all aspects of the proposed regulations. All comments will be available for public inspection and copying. A public hearing will be scheduled if requested in writing by any person that timely submits written comments. If a public hearing is scheduled, notice of the date, time, and place for the public hearing will be published in the **Federal Register.**

Drafting Information

The principal authors of these proposed regulations are Rebecca J. Holtje and Marie C. Milnes-Vasquez of the Office of Associate Chief Counsel (Corporate). However, other personnel from the Department of Treasury and the IRS participated in their development.

[¶ 49,564]　**Proposed Amendments of Regulations (REG-106918-08)**, published in the Federal Register on February 5, 2013.

[Code Secs. 761 and 1234]

Partnerships: Options: Recognition of gain or loss: Noncompensatory partnership options: Characterization rule measurement event.— Amendments of Reg. §§ 1.761-3 and 1.1234-3, relating to the tax treatment of noncompensatory options and convertible instruments issued by a partnership, are proposed.

AGENCY: Internal Revenue Service (IRS), Treasury.

ACTION: Notice of proposed rulemaking.

SUMMARY: This document contains proposed regulations relating to the tax treatment of noncompensatory options and convertible instruments issued by a partnership. Specifically, the proposed regulations expand the characterization rule measurement events to include certain transfers of interests in the issuing partnership and other lookthrough entities, and provide additional guidance in determining the character of the grantor's gain or loss as a result of a closing transaction with respect to, or a lapse of, an option on a partnership interest. The proposed regulations will affect partnerships that issue noncompensatory options, the partners of such partnerships, and the holders of such options.

DATES: Written or electronic comments and requests for a public hearing must be received by May 6, 2013.

ADDRESSES: Send submissions to: CC:PA:LPD:PR (REG-106918-08), room 5203, Internal Revenue Service, PO Box 7604, Ben Franklin Station, Washington, DC 20044. Submissions may be hand-delivered Monday through Friday between the hours of 8 a.m. and 4 p.m. to CC:PA:LPD:PR (REG-106918-08), Courier's Desk, Internal Revenue Service, 1111 Constitution Avenue, NW., Washington, DC, or sent electronically via the Federal eRulemaking Portal at *www.regulations.gov* (IRS REG-106918-08).

FOR FURTHER INFORMATION CONTACT: Concerning the proposed regulations under § 1.761-3, Benjamin Weaver at (202) 622-3050; concerning the proposed regulations under § 1.1234-3, Shawn Tetelman at (202) 622-3930; concerning submissions of comments and requests for a public hearing, Oluwafunmilayo (Funmi) Taylor, (202) 622-7180 (not toll free numbers).

SUPPLEMENTARY INFORMATION:

Background

This document contains proposed amendments to 26 CFR part 1 under sections 761 and 1234 of the Internal Revenue Code (Code). On January 22, 2003, proposed regulations (REG-103580-02) relating to the tax treatment of noncompensatory options and convertible instruments issued by a partnership (noncompensatory partnership option regulations) were published in the **Federal Register** (68 FR 2930). Final regulations in the Rules and Regulations section of this issue of the **Federal Register** contain amendments to the Income Tax Regulations (26 CFR Part 1), which finalize the proposed regulations. However, the Treasury Department and the IRS have decided to propose amendments to the regulations expanding the characterization rule measurement events to include certain transfers of interests in the issuing partnership and other look-through entities.

Additionally, the Treasury Department and the IRS received comments on the proposed regulations expressing uncertainty as to whether section 1234(b) applies to the grantor of an option on a partnership interest on the lapse or repurchase of the option. The comments indicated that it was unclear whether the term "securities," as used in section 1234(b)(2)(B), includes partnership interests. After consideration of all comments received, the IRS and Treasury Department believe that it is appropriate to propose an amendment to the regulations under section 1234(b) to expressly treat partnership interests as securities for purposes of section 1234(b).

Explanation of Provisions

1. *Proposed Additions to the Noncompensatory Partnership Option Characterization Rule Measurement Events*

The final regulations being published elsewhere in this issue of the **Federal Register**, relating to the tax treatment of noncompensatory partnership options, contain a characterization rule providing that the holder of a noncompensatory option is treated as a partner under certain circumstances. Under the characterization rule, a noncompensatory option is treated as a partnership interest if, on the date of a measurement event (1) the noncompensatory option provides the option holder with rights that are substantially similar to the rights afforded a partner, and (2) there is a strong likelihood that the failure to treat the holder of the noncompensatory option as a partner would result in a substantial reduction in the present value of the partners' and noncompensatory option holder's aggregate Federal tax liabilities. The final regulations define a measurement event as: (1) issuance of the noncompensatory option; (2) an adjustment of the terms (modification) of the noncompensatory option or of the underlying partnership interest (including an adjustment pursuant to the terms of the noncompensatory option or the underlying partnership interest); or (3) transfer of the noncompensatory option if either (A) the option may be exercised (or settled) more than 12 months after its issuance, or (B) the transfer is pursuant to a plan in existence at the time of the issuance or modification of the noncompensatory option that has as a principal purpose the substantial reduction of the present value of the aggregate Federal tax liabilities of the partners and the noncompensatory option holder.

The Treasury Department and the IRS believe it is appropriate to expand the list of measurement events to include certain transfers of interests in the issuing partnership and look-through entities. The proposed regulations add three measurement events to the list above, but apply only if those measurement events are pursuant to a plan in existence at the time of the issuance or modification of the noncompensatory option that has as a principal purpose the substantial reduction of the present value of the aggregate Federal tax liabilities of the partners and the noncompensatory option holder. The three additional measurement events are: (1) issuance, transfer, or modification of an interest in, or liquidation of, the issuing partnership; (2) issuance, transfer, or modification of an interest in any look-through entity that directly, or indirectly through one or more look-through entities, owns the noncompensatory option; and (3) issuance, transfer, or modification of an interest in any look-through entity that directly, or indirectly through one or more look-through entities, owns an interest in the issuing partnership. The Treasury Department and the IRS believe that the first of these measurement events is necessary because it is inconsistent to test a noncompensatory option under the characterization rule upon transfer of the noncompensatory option, but not upon transfer of an interest in the issuing partnership, because either type of transfer may change the analysis of whether there is a strong likelihood that the failure to treat the option holder as a partner would result in a substantial reduction in the present value of the partners' and option holder's aggregate tax liabilities. The Treasury Department and the IRS believe that the second and third measurement events are necessary to prevent avoidance of the characterization rule through the use of look-through entities.

Like the measurement events in the final regulations, the three measurement events in the proposed regulations are subject to exceptions in § 1.761-3(c)(2). The Treasury Department and the IRS believe that the limitations on these measurement events will reduce the administrative burden associated with testing under the characterization rule upon these events.

The Treasury Department and the IRS request comments on the appropriate procedures for notifying the partners and the partnership upon the occurrence of a measurement event.

2. *Character of Gain or Loss on Lapse, Sale, or Exchange of Partnership Options*

A. *Character of gain or loss to the grantor of the option*

In response to comments, the proposed regulations address the application of section 1234(b) to the grantor of an option on a partnership interest on the lapse or repurchase of the option. Section 1234(b) provides that, in the case of the grantor of an option, gain or loss from any closing transaction with respect to, and gain on lapse of, an option in property shall be treated as gain or loss from the sale or exchange of a capital asset held not more than one year. Section 1234(b)(2)(B) defines the term property to mean stock and securities (including stocks and securities dealt with on a when issued basis), commodities, and commodity futures. Accordingly, for section 1234(b) to apply to a closing transaction with respect to, or lapse of, an option on a partnership interest, a partnership interest would have to be a security and, thus, property within the meaning of section 1234(b)(2)(B). The proposed regulations provide that the term "securities" as used in section 1234(b)(2)(B) includes partnership interests. As a result, in the case of the grantor of an option on a partnership interest, gain or loss from any closing transaction with respect to, and gain on lapse of, the option is generally treated under the proposed regulations as gain or loss from the sale or exchange of a capital asset held not more than 1 year.

B. *Character of gain or loss to the option holder*

With respect to an option holder, under section 1234(a), gain or loss on the sale or exchange of, or loss on failure to exercise, an option is considered gain or loss from the sale or exchange of property that has the same character as the property to which the option relates would have in the hands of the taxpayer. Although a partnership interest is generally considered a capital asset, section 751(a) may apply to recharacterize a portion of a partner's gain on the sale or exchange of a partnership interest as ordinary. A number of commenters on the noncompensatory partnership option proposed regulations questioned whether section 751 applies to the lapse, repurchase, sale, exchange, or other termination of a noncompensatory option.

The Treasury Department and the IRS continue to study this issue and request comments on (1) if section 751(a) applies to the lapse, repurchase, sale, or exchange of a noncompensatory option, (a) how the option holder's share of income or loss from section 751 property would be determined under § 1.751-1(a)(2), and (b) how a partner in the issuing partnership that transfers its partnership interest while the option is outstanding would determine its share of income or loss from section 751 property under § 1.751-1(a)(2) (that is, should it be reduced by the amount of income or loss from section 751 property attributable to the option holder); and (2) if section 751(a) does not apply to the lapse, repurchase, sale, or exchange of a noncompensatory option, what measures, if any, should be taken to ensure that ordinary income is not permanently eliminated.

Effective/Applicability Date

To coordinate the proposed regulations with the final noncompensatory partnership option regulations, the proposed regulations are proposed to have the same effective date as the final noncompensatory partnership option regulations. Therefore, the proposed regulations are proposed to apply to options issued on or after February 5, 2013.

Special Analyses

It has been determined that this notice of proposed rulemaking is not a significant regulatory action as defined in Executive Order 12866, as supplemented by Executive Order 13563. Therefore, a regulatory assessment is not required. It also has been determined that section 553(b) of the Administrative Procedure Act (5 U.S.C. chapter 5) does not apply to this regulation, and because the regulation does not impose a collection of information requirement on small entities, the Regulatory Flexibility Act (5 U.S.C. chapter 6) does not apply. Pursuant to section 7805(f) of the Code, this regulation has been submitted to the Chief Counsel for Advocacy of the Small Business Administration for comment on its impact on small business.

Comments and Requests for Public Hearing

Before these proposed regulations are adopted as final regulations, consideration will be given to any written (a signed original and eight (8) copies) or electronic comments that are submitted timely to the IRS. The Treasury Department and the IRS request comments on all aspects of the proposed rules. All comments are available at *www.regulations.gov* or upon request. A public hearing may be scheduled if requested in writing by any person that timely submits written comments. If a public hearing is scheduled, notice of the date, time, and place for the public hearing will be published in the **Federal Register**.

Drafting Information

The principal authors of these proposed regulations are Benjamin Weaver of the Office of Associate Chief Counsel (Passthroughs and Special Industries) and Shawn Tetelman of the Office of Associate Chief Counsel (Financial Institutions and Products). However, other personnel from the IRS and Treasury Department participated in their development.

[¶ 49,574]   **Proposed Amendments of Regulations (REG-125398-12)**, published in the Federal Register on May 3, 2013.

[Code Secs. 36B and 6011]

Credits: Health insurance premium tax credit: Qualified health plan.—Amendments of Reg. §§ 1.36B-0, 1.36B-1, 1.36B-2, 1.36B-3, 1.36B-6 and 1.6011-8, relating to the health insurance premium tax credit enacted by the Patient Protection and Affordable Care Act (P.L. 111-148) and the Health Care and Education Reconciliation Act of 2010 (P.L. 111-152), as amended by the Medicare and Medicaid Extenders Act of 2010 (P.L. 111-309), the Comprehensive 1099 Taxpayer Protection and Repayment of Exchange Subsidy Overpayments Act of 2011 (P.L. 112-9), and the Department of Defense and Full-Year Continuing Appropriations Act, 2011 (P.L. 112-10) and providing guidance on determining whether health coverage under an eligible employer-sponsored plan provides minimum value and affect employers that offer health coverage and their employees, are adopted. NOTE: Only some of the amendments to proposed Reg. § 1.36B-6 were adopted by T.D. 9745. The text is at ¶ 4196U.

AGENCY: Internal Revenue Service (IRS), Treasury.

ACTION: Notice of proposed rulemaking.

SUMMARY: This document contains proposed regulations relating to the health insurance premium tax credit enacted by the Patient Protection and Affordable Care Act and the Health Care and Education Reconciliation Act of 2010, as amended by the Medicare and Medicaid Extenders Act of 2010, the Comprehensive 1099 Taxpayer Protection and Repayment of Exchange Subsidy Overpayments Act of 2011, and the Department of Defense and Full-Year Continuing Appropriations Act, 2011. These proposed regulations affect individuals who enroll in qualified health plans through Affordable Insurance Exchanges (Exchanges) and claim the premium tax credit, and Exchanges that make qualified health plans available to individuals and employers. These proposed regulations also provide guidance on determining whether health coverage under an eligible employer-sponsored plan provides minimum value and affect employers that offer health coverage and their employees.

DATES: Written (including electronic) comments and requests for a public hearing must be received by July 2, 2013.

ADDRESSES: Send submissions to: CC:PA:LPD:PR (REG-125398-12), Room 5203, Internal Revenue Service, PO Box 7604, Ben Franklin Station, Washington, DC 20044. Submissions may be hand-delivered Monday through Friday between the hours of 8 a.m. and 4 p.m. to CC:PA:LPD:PR (REG-125398-12), Courier's Desk, Internal Revenue Service, 1111 Constitution Avenue, NW., Washington, DC, or sent electronically via the Federal eRulemaking Portal at *www.regulations.gov* (IRS REG-125398-12).

FOR FURTHER INFORMATION CONTACT: Concerning the proposed regulations, Andrew S. Braden, (202) 622-4960; concerning the submission of comments and/or requests for a public hearing, Oluwafunmilayo Taylor, (202) 622-7180 (not toll-free calls).

SUPPLEMENTARY INFORMATION:

Background

Beginning in 2014, under the Patient Protection and Affordable Care Act, Public Law 111-148 (124 Stat. 119 (2010)), and the Health Care and Education Reconciliation Act of 2010, Public Law 111-152 (124 Stat. 1029 (2010)) (collectively, the Affordable Care Act), eligible individuals who purchase coverage under a qualified health plan through an Affordable Insurance Exchange may receive a premium tax credit under section 36B of the Internal Revenue Code (Code). Section 36B was subsequently amended by the Medicare and Medicaid Extenders Act of 2010, Public Law 111-309 (124 Stat. 3285 (2010)); the Comprehensive 1099 Taxpayer Protection and Repayment of Exchange Subsidy Overpayments Act of 2011, Public Law 112-9 (125 Stat. 36 (2011)); and the Department of Defense and Full-Year Continuing Appropriations Act, 2011, Public Law 112-10 (125 Stat. 38 (2011)).

Notice 2012-31 (2012-20 IRB 910) requested comments on methods for determining whether health coverage under an eligible employer-sponsored plan provides minimum value (MV). Final regulations under section 36B (TD 9590) were published on May 23, 2012 (77 FR 30377). The final regulations requested comments on issues to be addressed in further guidance. The comments have been considered in developing these proposed regulations.

Minimum Value

Individuals generally may not receive a premium tax credit if they are eligible for affordable coverage under an eligible employer-sponsored plan that provides MV. An applicable large employer (as defined in section 4980H(c)(2)) may be liable for an assessable payment under section 4980H if a full-time employee receives a premium tax credit.

Under section 36B(c)(2)(C)(ii), a plan fails to provide MV if the plan's share of the total allowed costs of benefits provided under the plan is less than 60 percent of the costs. Section 1302(d)(2)(C) of the Affordable Care Act provides that, in determining the percentage of the total allowed costs of benefits provided under a group health plan, the regulations promulgated by the Secretary of Health and Human Services (HHS) under section 1302(d)(2) apply.

HHS published final regulations under section 1302(d)(?) on February 25, 2013 (78 FR 12834). The HHS regulations at 45 CFR 156.20 define the percentage of the total allowed costs of benefits provided under a group health plan as (1) the anticipated covered medical spending for essential health benefits (EHB) coverage (as defined in 45 CFR 156.110(a)) paid by a health plan for a standard population, (2) computed in accordance with the plan's cost-sharing, and (3) divided by the total anticipated allowed charges for EHB coverage provided to a standard population. In addition, 45 CFR 156.145(c) provides that the standard population used to compute this percentage for MV (as developed by HHS for this purpose) reflects the population covered by typical self-insured group health plans.

The HHS regulations describe several options for determining MV. Under 45 CFR 156.145(a)(1), plans may use the MV Calculator (available at *http://cciio.cms.gov/resources/regulations/index.html*). Alternatively, 45 CFR 156.145(a)(2) provides that a plan may determine MV through a safe harbor established by HHS and IRS. For plans with nonstandard features that are incompatible with the MV Calculator or a safe harbor, 45 CFR 156.145(a)(3) provides that the plan may determine MV through an actuarial certification from a member of the American Academy of Actuaries after performing an analysis in accordance with generally accepted actuarial principles and methodologies. Finally, 45 CFR 156.145(a)(4) provides that a plan in the small group market satisfies MV if it meets the requirements for any of the levels of metal coverage defined at 45 CFR 156.140(b) (bronze, silver, gold, or platinum).

Miscellaneous Provisions Under Section 36B

To be eligible for a premium tax credit, an individual must be an applicable taxpayer. Under section 36B(c)(1), an applicable taxpayer is a taxpayer whose household income for the taxable year is between 100 percent and 400 percent of the federal poverty line (FPL) for the taxpayer's family size.

Section 36B(b)(1) provides that the premium assistance credit amount is the sum of the premium assistance amounts for all coverage months in the taxable year for individuals in the taxpayer's family. The premium assistance amount for a coverage month is the lesser of (1) the premiums for the month for one or more qualified health plans that cover a taxpayer or family member, or (2) the excess of the adjusted monthly premium for the second lowest cost silver plan (as described in section 1302(d)(1)(B) of the Affordable Care Act (42 U.S.C. 18022(d)(1)(B)) (the benchmark plan) that applies to the taxpayer over 1/12 of the product of the taxpayer's household income and the applicable percentage for the taxable year. The adjusted monthly premium, in general, is the premium an insurer would charge for the plan adjusted only for the ages of the covered individuals.

Under section 36B(c)(2)(A), a coverage month is any month for which the taxpayer or a family member is covered by a qualified health plan enrolled in through an Exchange and the premium is paid by the taxpayer or through an advance credit payment. Section 36B(c)(2) provides that a month is not a coverage month for an individual who is eligible for other minimum essential coverage. If the other coverage is eligible employer-sponsored coverage, however, it is treated as minimum essential coverage only if it is affordable and provides MV. Eligible employer-sponsored coverage is affordable for an employee and related individuals if the portion of the annual premium the employee must pay for self-only coverage does not exceed the required contribution percentage (9.5 percent for taxable years beginning before January 1, 2015) of the taxpayer's household income. The MV requirement is discussed in the Explanation of Provisions.

Any arrangement under which employees are required, as a condition of employment or otherwise, to be enrolled in an employer-sponsored plan that does not provide minimum value or is unaffordable, and that does not give the employees an effective opportunity to terminate or decline the coverage, raises a variety of issues. Proposed regulations under section 4980H indicate that if an employer maintains such an arrangement it would not be treated as having made an offer of coverage. As a result, an applicable large employer could be subject to an assessable payment under that section. See Proposed § 54.4980H-4(b), 78 FR 250 (January 2, 2013). Such an arrangement would also raise additional concerns. For example, it is questionable whether the law permits interference with an individual's ability to apply for a section 36B premium tax credit by seeking to involuntarily impose coverage that does not provide minimum value. (See, for example, the Fair Labor Standards Act, as amended by section 1558 of the Affordable Care Act, 29 U.S.C. 218c(a).) If an employer sought to involuntarily impose on its employees coverage that did not provide minimum value or was unaffordable, the IRS and Treasury, as well as other relevant departments, may treat such arrangements as impermissible interference with an employee's ability to access premium tax credits, as contemplated by the Affordable Care Act.

Explanation of Provisions and Summary of Comments

1. *Minimum Value*

a. *In general*

The proposed regulations refer to the proportion of the total allowed costs of benefits provided to an employee that are paid by the plan as the plan's MV percentage. The MV percentage is determined by dividing the cost of certain benefits (described in paragraph b.) the plan would pay for a standard population by the total cost of certain benefits for the standard population, including amounts the plan pays and amounts the employee pays through cost-sharing, and then converting the result to a percentage.

b. *Health benefits measured in determining MV*

Commentators sought clarification of the health benefits considered in determining the share of benefit costs paid by a plan. Some commentators maintained that MV should be based on the plan's share of the cost of coverage for all EHBs, including those a plan does not offer. Other commentators suggested that the MV percentage should be based on the plan's share of the costs of only those categories of EHBs the plan covers.

The proposed regulations do not require employer-sponsored self-insured and insured large group plans to cover every EHB category or conform their plans to an EHB benchmark that applies to qualified health plans. The preamble to the HHS regulations (see 78 FR 12833) notes that employer-sponsored group health plans are not required to offer EHBs unless they are health plans offered in the small group market subject to section 2707(a) of the Public Health Service Act. The preamble also states that, under section 1302(d)(2) of the Affordable Care Act, MV is measured based on the provision of EHBs to a standard population and plans may account for any benefits covered by the employer that also are covered in any one of the EHB-benchmark plans. See 45 CFR 156.145(b)(2).

Consistent with 45 CFR 156.135(a)-(c) and the assumptions described in Notice 2012-31, these proposed regulations provide that MV is based on the anticipated spending for a standard population. The plan's anticipated spending for benefits provided under any particular EHB-benchmark plan for any State counts towards MV.

c. *Health reimbursement arrangements, health savings accounts, and wellness program incentives*

i. Arrangements that Reduce Cost-Sharing

Some commentators suggested that current year health savings account (HSA) contributions and amounts newly made available under a health reimbursement arrangement (HRA) should be fully counted toward the plan's share of costs included in calculating MV. Some commentators suggested that only HRA contributions that may be used to pay for cost sharing and not HRAs restricted to other uses should be counted in the MV calculation.

Consistent with 45 CFR 156.135(c), the proposed regulations provide that all amounts contributed by an employer for the current plan year to an HSA are taken into account in determining the plan's share of costs for purposes of MV and are treated as amounts available for first dollar coverage. Amounts newly made available under an HRA that is integrated with an eligible employer-sponsored plan for the current plan year count for purposes of MV in the same manner if the amounts may be used only for cost-sharing and may not be used to pay insurance premiums. It is anticipated that regulations will provide that whether an HRA is integrated with an eligible employer-sponsored plan is determined under rules that apply for purposes of section 2711 of the Public Health Service Act (42 U.S.C. 300gg-11). Commentators offered differing opinions about how nondiscriminatory wellness program incentives that may affect an employee's cost sharing should be taken into account for purposes of the MV calculation. Some commentators noted that the rules governing wellness incentives require that they be available to all similarly situated individuals. These commentators suggested that because eligible individuals have the opportunity to reduce their cost-sharing if they choose, a plan's share of costs should be based on the costs paid by individuals who satisfy the terms of the wellness program. Other commentators expressed concern that, despite the safeguards of the regulations governing wellness incentives, certain individuals inevitably will face barriers to participation and fail to qualify for rewards. These commentators suggested that a plan's share of costs should be determined without assuming that individuals would qualify for the reduced cost-sharing available under a wellness program.

The proposed regulations provide that a plan's share of costs for MV purposes is determined without regard to reduced cost-sharing available under a nondiscriminatory wellness program. However, for nondiscriminatory wellness programs designed to prevent or reduce tobacco use, MV may be calculated assuming that every eligible individual satisfies the terms of the program relating to prevention or reduction of tobacco use. This exception is consistent with other Affordable Care Act provisions (such as the ability to charge higher premiums based on tobacco use) reflecting a policy about individual responsibility regarding tobacco use.

ii. Arrangements that Reduce Premiums

Section 36B(c)(2)(C)(i)(II) and the final regulations provide that eligible employer-sponsored coverage is affordable only if an employee's required contribution for self-only coverage does not exceed 9.5 percent of household income. The preamble to the final regulations indicated that rules for determining how HRAs and wellness program incentives are counted in determining the affordability of eligible employer-sponsored coverage would be provided in later guidance.

Some commentators asserted that an employer's entire annual contribution to an HRA plus prior year contributions should be taken into account in determining affordability. The proposed regulations provide that amounts newly made available under an HRA that is integrated with an eligible employer-sponsored plan for the current plan year are taken into account only in determining affordability if the employee may use the amounts only for premiums or may choose to use the amounts for either premiums or cost-sharing. Treating amounts that may be used either for premiums or cost-sharing only towards affordability prevents double counting the HRA amounts when assessing MV and affordability of eligible employer-sponsored coverage.

It is anticipated that regulations under section 5000A will provide that amounts newly made available under an HRA that is integrated with an eligible employer-sponsored plan for the current plan year are also taken into account for purposes of the affordability exemption under section 5000A(e)(1) if the employee may use the amounts only for premiums or for either premiums or cost-sharing.

The final regulations requested specific comments on the nature of wellness incentives and how they should be treated for determining affordability. Commentators expressed similar views about the treatment of wellness incentives that affect the cost of premiums as about the treatment of wellness incentives that affect cost-sharing.

Like the rule for determining MV, the proposed regulations provide that the affordability of an employer-sponsored plan is determined by assuming that each employee fails to satisfy the requirements of a wellness program, except the requirements of a nondiscriminatory wellness program related to tobacco use. Thus, the affordability of a plan that charges a higher initial premium for tobacco users will be determined based on the premium that is charged to non-tobacco users, or tobacco users who complete the related wellness program, such as attending smoking cessation classes.

In many circumstances these rules relating to the effect of premium-related wellness program rewards on affordability will have no practical consequences. They matter only when the employer sets the level of the employee's required contribution to self-only premium, and establishes a wellness program that provides for a level of premium discount, in such a manner that the employee's required contribution to premium would exceed 9.5 percent of household income (or wages, under an affordability safe harbor under the section 4980H proposed regulations) but for the potential premium discount under the wellness program. If, for example, the employee's household income was at least $25,000, and the employee's required contribution for self-only coverage did not exceed $2,375 (9.5 percent of $25,000), the coverage would be affordable whether or not a wellness premium discount was taken into account to reduce the $2,375 required contribution.

It is anticipated that regulations under section 5000A will provide that nondiscriminatory wellness programs that affect premiums will be treated for purposes of the affordability exemption under section 5000A(e)(1) in the same manner as they are treated for purposes of determining affordability under section 36B.

Solely for purposes of applying section 4980H and solely for plan years of an employer's group health plan beginning before January 1, 2015, with respect to an employee described in the next sentence, an employer will not be subject to an assessable payment under section 4980H(b) with respect to an employee who received a premium tax credit because the offer of coverage was not affordable or did not satisfy MV, if the offer of coverage to the employee under the employer's group health plan would have been affordable or would have satisfied MV based on the total required employee premium and cost-sharing for that group health plan that would have applied to the employee if the employee satisfied the requirements of any wellness program described in the next sentence, including a wellness program with requirements unrelated to tobacco use. The rule in the preceding sentence applies only (1) to the extent of the reward as of May 3, 2013, expressed as either a dollar amount or a fraction of the total required employee contribution to the premium (or the employee cost-sharing, as applicable), (2) under the terms of a wellness program as in effect on May 3, 2013, and (3) with respect to an employee who is in a category of employees eligible under the terms of the wellness program as in effect on May 3, 2013 (regardless of whether the employee was hired before or after that date). Any required employee contribution to premium determined based upon assumed satisfaction of the requirements of a wellness program available under this transition relief may be applied to the use of an affordability safe harbor provided in the proposed regulations under section 4980H.

d. Standard population and utilization

Consistent with 45 CFR 156.145(c), the proposed regulations provide that the standard population used to determine MV reflects the population covered by self-insured group health plans. HHS has developed the MV standard population and described it through summary statistics (for example, continuance tables). MV continuance tables and an explanation of the MV Calculator methodology and the health claims data HHS has used to develop the continuance tables are available at http://cciio.cms.gov/resources/regulations/index.html.

e. Methods for determining minimum value

Notice 2012-31 and 45 CFR 156.145(a) describe several methods for determining MV: the MV Calculator, a safe harbor, actuarial certification, and, for small group market plans, a metal level. Some commentators requested that plans be allowed to choose one of the four methods in determining MV. Other commentators favored requiring employers to use the most precise method for plans that may be close to the 60 percent threshold.

The proposed regulations provide that taxpayers may determine whether a plan provides MV by using the MV Calculator made available by HHS and the IRS. Taxpayers must use the MV Calculator to measure standard plan features (unless a safe harbor applies), but the percentage may be adjusted based on an actuarial analysis of plan features that are outside the parameters of the calculator.

Certain safe harbor plan designs that satisfy MV will be specified in additional guidance under section 36B or 4980H, see § 601.601(d). It is anticipated that the guidance will provide that the safe harbors are examples of plan designs that clearly would satisfy the 60 percent threshold if measured using the MV Calculator. The safe harbors are intended to provide an easy way for sponsors of typical employer-sponsored group health plans to determine whether a plan meets the MV threshold without having to use the MV Calculator.

Plan designs meeting the following specifications are proposed as safe harbors for determining MV if the plans cover all of the benefits included in the MV Calculator: (1) a plan with a $3,500 integrated medical and drug deductible, 80 percent plan cost-sharing, and a $6,000 maximum out-of-pocket limit for employee cost-sharing; (2) a plan with a $4,500 integrated medical and drug deductible, 70 percent plan cost-sharing, a $6,400 maximum out-of-pocket limit, and a $500 employer contribution to an HSA; and (3) a plan with a $3,500 medical deductible, $0 drug deductible, 60 percent plan medical expense cost-sharing, 75 percent plan drug cost-sharing, a $6,400 maximum out-of-pocket limit, and drug co-pays of $10/$20/$50 for the first, second and third prescription drug tiers, with 75 percent coinsurance for specialty drugs. Comments are requested on these and other common plan designs that would satisfy MV and should be designated as safe harbors.

Consistent with 45 CFR 156.145(a), the proposed regulations require plans with nonstandard features that cannot determine MV using the MV Calculator or a safe harbor to use the actuarial certification method. The actuary must be a member of the American Academy of Actuaries and must perform the analysis in accordance with generally accepted actuarial principles and methodologies and any additional standards that subsequent guidance requires.

f. Other issues

Commentators suggested a de minimis exception to the MV 60 percent level of coverage, noting that similar de minimis variations are permitted in determining actuarial value for qualified health plans. However, as other commentators noted, permitting a de minimis exception would have the effect of lowering the minimum level of coverage to a percentage below 60 percent. Under section 36B(c)(2)(C)(ii), coverage below 60 percent does not provide MV. Accordingly, the proposed regulations do not provide for a de minimis exception.

2. Miscellaneous Issues Under Section 36B

a. Definition of modified adjusted gross income

Section 36B(d)(2) provides that the term household income means the modified adjusted gross income of the taxpayer plus the modified adjusted gross income of all members of the taxpayer's family required to file a tax return under section 1 for the taxable year. The final regulations provide that the determination of whether a family member is required to file a return is made without regard to section 1(g)(7). Under section 1(g)(7), a parent may, if certain requirements are met, elect to include in the parent's gross income, the gross income of his or her child. If the parent makes the election, the child is treated as having no gross income for the taxable year.

The proposed regulations remove "without regard to section 1(g)(7)" from the final regulations because that language implies that the child's gross income is included in both the parent's adjusted gross income and the child's adjusted gross income in determining household income. Thus, the proposed regulations clarify that if a parent makes an election under section 1(g)(7), household income includes the child's gross income included on the parent's return and the child is treated as having no gross income.

b. *Rating area*

Section 36B(b)(3)(B) determines the applicable benchmark plan by reference to the rating area where a taxpayer resides. The final regulations reserved the definition of *rating area*. The proposed regulations provide that the term *rating area* has the same meaning as used in section 2701(a)(2) of the Public Health Service Act (42 U.S.C. 300gg) and 45 CFR 156.255.

c. *Retiree coverage*

The section 36B final regulations provide that an individual who may enroll in continuation coverage required under Federal law or a State law that provides comparable continuation coverage is eligible for minimum essential coverage only for months that the individual is enrolled in the coverage. These proposed regulations apply this rule to former employees only. Active employees eligible for continuation coverage as a result of reduced hours should be subject to the same rules for eligibility of affordable employer-sponsored coverage offering MV as other active employees. The proposed regulations add a comparable rule for health coverage offered to retired employees (retiree coverage). Accordingly, an individual who may enroll in retiree coverage is eligible for minimum essential coverage under the coverage only for the months the individual is enrolled in the coverage.

d. *Coverage month for newborns and new adoptees*

Under section 36B(c)(2)(A)(i) and the final regulations, a month is a coverage month for an individual only if, as of the first day of the month, the individual is enrolled in a qualified health plan through an Exchange. A child born or adopted during the month is not enrolled in coverage on the first day and therefore would not be eligible for the premium tax credit or cost-sharing reductions for that month. Accordingly, the proposed regulations provide that a child enrolled in a qualified health plan in the month of the child's birth, adoption, or placement with the taxpayer for adoption or in foster care, is treated as enrolled as of the first day of the month.

e. *Adjusted monthly premium for family members enrolled for less than a full month*

Under section 36B(c), the premium assistance amount for a coverage month is computed by reference to the adjusted monthly premium for an applicable benchmark plan. The final regulations provide that the applicable benchmark plan is the plan that applies to a taxpayer's coverage family. The final regulations do not address whether changes to a coverage family, for example as the result of the birth and enrollment of a child or the disenrollment of another family member, that occur during the month affect the premium assistance amount. The proposed regulations provide that the adjusted monthly premium is determined as if all members of the coverage family for that month were enrolled in a qualified health plan for the entire month.

f. *Premium assistance amount for partial months of coverage*

The final regulations do not address the computation of the premium assistance amount if coverage under a qualified health plan is terminated during the month. The proposed regulations provide that when coverage under a qualified health plan is terminated before the last day of a month and, as a result, the issuer reduces or refunds a portion of the monthly premium the premium assistance amount for the month is prorated based on the number of days of coverage in the month.

g. *Family members residing at different locations.*

The final regulations reserved rules on determining the premium for the applicable benchmark plan if family members are geographically separated and enroll in separate qualified health plans. The proposed regulations provide that the premium for the applicable benchmark plan in this situation is the sum of the premiums for the applicable benchmark plans for each group of family members residing in a different State.

h. *Correction to applicable percentage table*

The applicable percentage table in the final regulations erroneously states that the 9.5 percentage applies only to taxpayers whose household income is less than 400 percent of the FPL. The proposed regulations clarify that the 9.5 percentage applies to taxpayers whose household income is not more than 400 percent of the FPL.

i. *Additional benefits and applicable benchmark plan*

Under section 36B(b)(3)(D) and the final regulations, only the portion of the premium for a qualified health plan properly allocable to EHBs determines a taxpayer's premium assistance amount. Premiums allocable to benefits other than EHBs (additional benefits) are disregarded. The final regulations do not address, however, whether a taxpayer's benchmark plan is determined before or after premiums have been allocated to additional benefits. The proposed regulations provide that premiums are allocated to additional benefits before determining the applicable benchmark plan. Thus, only essential health benefits are considered in determining the applicable benchmark plan, consistent with the requirement in section 36B(b)(3)(D) that only essential health benefits are considered in determining the premium assistance amount. In addition, allocating premium to benefits that exceed EHBs before determining the applicable benchmark plan results in a more accurate determination of the premium assistance amount.

j. *Requirement to file a return to reconcile advance credit payments*

The final regulations provided that a taxpayer who receives advance credit payments must file an income tax return for that taxable year on or before the fifteenth day of the fourth month following the close of the taxable year. Under the proposed regulations, a taxpayer who receives advance credit payments must file an income tax return on or before the due date for the return (including extensions).

Effective/Applicability Date

These regulations are proposed to apply for taxable years ending after December 31, 2013. Taxpayers may apply the proposed regulations for taxable years ending before January 1, 2015.

Special Analyses

It has been determined that this notice of proposed rulemaking is not a significant regulatory action as defined in Executive Order 12866, as supplemented by Executive Order 13563. Therefore, a regulatory assessment is not required. It has also been determined that section 553(b) of the Administrative Procedure Act (5 U.S.C. chapter 5) does not apply to these regulations and, because the regulations do not impose a collection of information on small entities, the Regulatory Flexibility Act (5 U.S.C. chapter 6) does not apply. Pursuant to section 7805(f) of the Code, this notice of proposed rulemaking has been submitted to the Chief Counsel for Advocacy of the Small Business Administration for comment on its impact on small business.

Comments and Requests for Public Hearing

Before these proposed regulations are adopted as final regulations, consideration will be given to any comments that are submitted timely to the IRS as prescribed in this preamble under the "Addresses" heading. Treasury and the IRS request comments on all aspects of the proposed rules. All comments will be available at *www.regulations.gov* or upon request. A public hearing will be scheduled if requested in writing by any person who timely submits written comments. If a public hearing is scheduled, notice of the date, time and place for the hearing will be published in the **Federal Register**.

Drafting Information

The principal authors of these proposed regulations are Andrew S. Braden, Frank W. Dunham III, and Stephen J. Toomey of the Office of Associate Chief Counsel (Income Tax and Accounting). However, other personnel from the IRS and the Treasury Department participated in the development of the regulations.

[¶ 49,580]   Proposed Amendments of Regulations (REG-132251-11), published in the Federal Register on August 13, 2013.

[Code Secs. 66 and 6015]

Joint and several liability: Community property laws: Innocent spouse relief: When to request relief: How to request relief.—Amendments of Reg. §§1.66-4, 1.66-5, 1.6015-0, 1.6015-5 and 1.6015-9, relating to relief from joint and several tax liability under Code Sec. 6015 and relief from the federal income tax liability resulting from the operation of state community property laws under Code Sec. 66, are proposed.

AGENCY: Internal Revenue Service (IRS), Treasury.

ACTION: Notice of proposed rulemaking.

SUMMARY: This document contains proposed regulations relating to relief from joint and several tax liability under section 6015 of the Internal Revenue Code (Code) and relief from the Federal income tax liability resulting from the operation of state community property laws under section 66. The proposed regulations provide guidance to taxpayers on when and how to request relief under sections 66 and 6015. This document also invites comments from the public regarding these proposed regulations.

DATES: Written or electronic comments and requests for a public hearing must be received by November 12, 2013.

ADDRESSES: Send submissions to: CC:PA:LPD:PR (REG-132251-11), room 5205, Internal Revenue Service, P.O. Box 7604, Ben Franklin Station, Washington, DC 20044. Submissions may be hand-delivered Monday through Friday between the hours of 8 a.m. and 4 p.m. to CC:PA:LPD:PR (REG-132251-11), Courier's Desk, Internal Revenue Service, 1111 Constitution Avenue, N.W., Washington, DC; or sent electronically via the Federal eRulemaking Portal at *www.regulations.gov* (IRS REG-132251-11).

FOR FURTHER INFORMATION CONTACT: Concerning the proposed regulations, Mark Shurtliff at (202) 622-4910; concerning submissions of comments and requests for a hearing, Oluwafunmilayo (Funmi) Taylor at (202) 622-7180 (not toll-free numbers).

SUPPLEMENTARY INFORMATION:

Background

Section 6013(a) of the Code permits taxpayers who are husband and wife to file a joint Federal income tax return. Married individuals who choose to file a joint income tax return are each jointly and severally liable under section 6013(d)(3) for the tax arising from that return, which, pursuant to sections 6601(e)(1) and 6665(a)(2), includes any additions to tax, additional amounts, penalties, and interest. Because the liability is joint and several, the IRS is authorized to collect the entire amount from either spouse, without regard to which spouse the items of income, deduction, credit, or basis that gave rise to the liability are attributable.

Section 6015 was enacted in 1998 to provide relief from joint and several liability in certain circumstances. Section 6015 sets forth three bases for relief from joint and several liability. First, section 6015(b) allows a taxpayer to elect relief from understatements of tax attributable to erroneous items of the other spouse if the taxpayer had no reason to know of the understatement and, taking into account all the facts and circumstances, it is inequitable to hold the taxpayer liable. Second, section 6015(c) allows a taxpayer who is divorced or legally separated from, or no longer living with, the spouse or former spouse with whom the joint return was filed to elect to allocate a deficiency (or a portion of a deficiency) to the other spouse, as if the spouses had filed separate tax returns. Third, section 6015(f) provides that a taxpayer may request, under "procedures prescribed by the Secretary," relief from a tax understatement or underpayment when the taxpayer does not qualify for relief under the other two subsections and it would be inequitable to hold the taxpayer liable considering all the facts and circumstances.

Section 6015(h) directs the Treasury Department and the IRS to prescribe such regulations as are necessary to carry out the provisions of section 6015. The Treasury Department and the IRS exercised that authority by promulgating regulations under section 6015 on July 18, 2002 (TD 9003, 67 FR 47278). Sections 1.6015-2, 1.6015-3, and 1.6015-4 of the final regulations provide guidance on the bases for relief in section 6015(b), (c), and (f), respectively. Section 1.6015-5 provides rules on the time and manner to request section 6015 relief.

By their terms, paragraphs (b) and (c) of section 6015 impose a two-year deadline for a taxpayer to elect the application of either subsection. Under the deadline, a taxpayer must make the election no later than two years after the date of the IRS's first collection activity with respect to the taxpayer. See section 6015(b)(1)(E) and (c)(3)(B). In contrast, paragraph (f) of section 6015 does not contain an explicit deadline to request relief. In accordance with the authority in section 6015(f) to prescribe procedures for the administration of equitable relief, the Treasury Department and the IRS, beginning in 1998, prescribed in published guidance a two-year deadline to request equitable relief under section 6015(f) to be consistent with the statutory time limit to claim relief under section 6015(b) and (c). The two-year deadline to request equitable relief was first prescribed in Notice 98-61 (1998-2 CB 758 (December 21, 1998)) (see § 601.601(d)(2)(ii)(b) of this chapter). The two-year deadline was reiterated in Rev. Proc. 2000-15 (2000-1 CB 447), which was superseded by Rev. Proc. 2003-61 (2003-2 CB 296), and ultimately adopted in the regulations under section 6015, which were issued on July 18, 2002, as § 1.6015-5(b)(1).

Besides establishing when and how to request relief from joint and several liability, § 1.6015-5 also defines key terms, such as "collection activity," sets forth examples illustrating the time and manner provisions, and explains the effect of a final administrative determination.

In *Lantz v. Commissioner*, 132 T.C. 131 (2009), the Tax Court considered for the first time whether the two-year deadline to request equitable relief was valid. After analyzing the issue under the standard for judicial review of an agency regulation, the Tax Court held the two-year deadline for equitable relief in § 1.6015-5(b)(1) invalid. The *Lantz* decision was reversed on appeal by the United States Court of Appeals for the Seventh Circuit in an opinion upholding the validity of the deadline to request equitable relief. *Lantz v. Commissioner*, 607 F.3d 479 (7th Cir. 2010). After *Lantz*, the

Tax Court continued to find the two-year deadline invalid in cases not appealable to the Seventh Circuit but the deadline was upheld again in *Mannella v. Commissioner*, 631 F.3d 115 (3d Cir. 2011), and *Jones v. Commissioner*, 642 F.3d 459 (4th Cir. 2011).

Notwithstanding the validity of the regulation setting the two-year deadline, the Treasury Department and the IRS considered whether to retain the deadline and determined, in the interest of tax administration, that the time period to request equitable relief under section 6015(f) should be extended. As announced in Notice 2011-70 (2011-32 IRB 135 (Aug. 8, 2011)), the two-year deadline no longer applies to requests for equitable relief under section 6015(f). In place of the prior two-year deadline, Notice 2011-70 provides that, to be considered for equitable relief, a request must be filed with the IRS within the period of limitation for collection of tax in section 6502 or, for any credit or refund of tax, within the period of limitation in section 6511. Notice 2011-70 explains that the regulations under section 6015 will be revised to reflect the change. These proposed regulations reflect the changes made by Notice 2011-70. Notice 2011-70 has no effect on the two-year deadline to elect relief under section 6015(b) (and § 1.6015-2) or section 6015(c) (and § 1.6015-3).

Notice 2011-70 specifies transitional rules that apply until the Treasury Department and the IRS amend the regulations under section 6015. Under the transitional rules, the two-year deadline does not apply to any request for equitable relief filed on or after July 25, 2011 (the date Notice 2011-70 was issued) or any request already filed and pending with the IRS as of that date. The transitional rules provide that the IRS will consider these current and future requests for equitable relief if they were filed within the applicable limitation period under section 6502 or 6511. As for past requests for equitable relief—requests that the IRS denied as untimely under the two-year deadline—the notice allows the individuals who filed those requests to reapply for equitable relief, unless the individual litigated the denial or the denial included a determination that the individual was not entitled to equitable relief on the merits. In addition, Notice 2011-70 provides separate rules for claiming equitable relief with respect to litigated cases.

A similar rule is added to § 1.66-4 for claims for equitable relief under section 66(c). Section 66(c) provides two avenues for married taxpayers who do not file a joint Federal income tax return in a community property state to request relief from the operation of the state community property laws. Under state law, each spouse generally is responsible for the tax on one-half of all the community income for the year. Traditional relief under section 66(c) allows the requesting spouse to avoid liability for tax on community income of which the requesting spouse did not know and had no reason to know. If a requesting spouse does not satisfy the requirements for traditional relief, the Secretary may grant equitable relief. The IRS uses the same procedures for determining eligibility for equitable relief under section 66(c) as it does for equitable relief under section 6015(f). As a result, it is appropriate for the IRS to use the same timing rules for consideration of requests for equitable relief, whether under section 66(c) or section 6015(f).

Explanation of Provisions

The Treasury Department and the IRS propose to amend the provisions of § 1.6015-5 on the time and manner for requesting relief from joint and several liability under section 6015. A similar rule is added to § 1.66-4(j)(2)(ii) for claims for equitable relief from the Federal income tax liability resulting from the operation of state community property law.

1. *Requesting Relief as Part of Collection Due Process*

The proposed regulations revise § 1.6015-5(a) to reflect that a requesting spouse (defined in § 1.6015-1(h)(1)) may elect the application of section 6015(b) [§ 1.6015-2] or section 6015(c) [§ 1.6015-3] or request equitable relief under section 6015(f) [§ 1.6015-4] as part of the collection due process (CDP) hearing procedures under sections 6320 and 6330. A corresponding change is made to § 1.6015-5(c)(1) to clarify that, although section 6015 relief may be raised in a CDP proceeding, a requesting spouse may not request section 6015 relief in the course of a CDP hearing if the requesting spouse previously requested section 6015 relief and the IRS ruled on that request by issuing a final administrative determination. These proposed regulations do not change existing CDP hearing procedures. See § 301.6330-1(e)(2). Rather, these changes make the regulations under section 6015 consistent with the regulations under section 6330.

2. *Time to Request Relief*

Section 1.6015-5(b) of the proposed regulations retains the two-year deadline, measured from the date of the first collection activity, to elect the application of § 1.6015-2 (describing the circumstances in which a taxpayer may be eligible for relief under section 6015(b)) or 1.6015-3 (describing the circumstances in which a taxpayer may be eligible for relief under section 6015(c)). In accordance with Notice 2011-70, the deadline is removed for a request for equitable relief under § 1.6015-4 (describing the circumstances in which a taxpayer may be eligible for relief under section 6015(f)) and replaced with a requirement that a request for equitable relief must be filed with the IRS within the period of limitation in section 6502 for collection of tax or the period of limitation in section 6511 for credit or refund of tax, as applicable to the specific request. A similar rule is added to § 1.66-4(j)(2)(ii) for claims for equitable relief from the Federal income tax liability resulting from the operation of state community property law.

Under section 6502(a)(1), the period of limitation on collection of tax is normally ten years after the date of assessment of the tax, although it may be extended by other provisions of the Code. Under section 6511(a), the period of limitation to claim a credit or refund of tax is generally the later of three years after the date a tax return for the taxable period was filed or two years after the date the tax was paid. If no return was filed, the two-year period applies.

Section 1.6015-5(b)(2) of the proposed regulations explains that if a requesting spouse files a request for equitable relief under § 1.6015-4 within the limitation period on collection of tax, the IRS will consider the request, but any relief in the form of a tax credit or refund depends on whether the limitation period for credit or refund was also open as of the date the claim for relief was filed and the other requirements relating to credits or refunds are satisfied. In cases in which the limitation period for credit or refund happens to be the longer of the two periods and is open when a request for equitable relief is filed, the request can be considered for a potential refund or credit of any amounts collected or otherwise paid by the requesting spouse during the applicable look-back period of section 6511(b)(2), even if the collection period is closed.

If a request for equitable relief is filed after the expiration of the limitation period for collection of a joint tax liability, the IRS is barred from collecting any remaining unpaid tax from the requesting spouse. Similarly, if a request for equitable relief under § 1.6015-4 is filed after the expiration of the limitation period for a credit or refund of tax, section 6511(b)(1) bars the IRS from allowing, and a taxpayer from receiving, a credit or refund. The proposed regulations provide, therefore, that the IRS will not consider an individual's request to be equitably relieved from a tax that is no longer legally collectible.

3. *Collection Activity*

The proposed regulations clarify what constitutes collection activity for purposes of starting the two-year deadline that continues to apply to §§ 1.6015-2 and 1.6015-3.

A notice of intent to levy and right to request a CDP hearing (section 6330 notice) is a type of collection activity that starts the two-year period applicable to applications to elect relief under §§ 1.6015-2 and 1.6015-3. The proposed regulations at § 1.6015-5(b)(3)(ii) clarify that the two-year period will start irrespective of a requesting spouse's actual receipt of the section 6330 notice, if the notice was sent by certified or registered mail to the requesting spouse's last known address. This clarification is consistent with the holding in *Mannella v. Commissioner*, 132 T.C. 196 (2009), *rev'd on other grounds*, 631 F.3d 115 (3d Cir. 2011).

4. *Examples*

Section 1.6015-5 in its current form contains several examples intended to illustrate how the timing rules for requesting relief under section 6015 operate. The proposed regulations update these examples to reflect the proposed changes to the timing rules. Thus, *Example 1* is revised to explicitly limit it to elections under § 1.6015-2 or 1.6015-3. *Example 2* illustrates the operation of both the two-year deadline for purposes of § § 1.6015-2 and 1.6015-3 and the periods of limitation that apply to equitable relief requests under § 1.6015-4, including a situation in which the requesting spouse will still be considered for relief for unpaid amounts even though the limitation period for credit or refund had expired when the request was filed as discussed in § 1.6015-5(b)(2). *Example 3* is principally intended to illustrate that collection activity against a nonrequesting spouse (defined in § 1.6015-1(h)(2)) does not begin the time in which a requesting spouse must elect the application of § 1.6015-2 or 1.6015-3. *Example 4* illustrates the rule of § 1.6015-5(c)(3)(i) that a section 6330 notice sent to a requesting spouse's last known address, even if not actually received by the requesting spouse, is a collection activity for purposes of the timing rules, but the issuance of the notice, or the time between the mailing of the notice and the filing of a request for relief, does not affect the IRS's consideration of equitable relief under § 1.6015-4 as no two-year deadline applies. *Example 5* illustrates the timing rules in § 1.6015-5(b)(2) under which if a requesting spouse has paid some or all of a joint tax liability, or if the IRS has collected all or a part of the liability from a requesting spouse, the requesting spouse will be considered for equitable relief under § 1.6015-4 if the requesting spouse filed for relief within the limitation period for a credit or refund of tax, even though the limitation period for collection of tax was expired when the request was filed. The example further illustrates that in a case of payments or collection activity over time, a requesting spouse is eligible for a credit or refund only for amounts of tax for which the period of limitation allows a credit or refund as of when the request for relief was filed. The last example, *Example 6*, builds off of *Example 5* and illustrates a situation in which the IRS will not consider a request for equitable relief under § 1.6015-4 because both the limitation period for a credit or refund of tax and the limitation period for collection of tax had expired as of the date the claim for relief was filed.

5. *Reconsideration and Effect of a Final Administrative Determination*

The proposed regulations also revise § 1.6015-5(c), which prescribes the effect of a final administrative determination. Under § 1.6015-5(c)(1), a requesting spouse generally is entitled to submit only one request for relief under section 6015 from a joint tax liability (except as provided in § 1.6015-1(h)(5)), and the IRS will issue only one final administrative determination. The proposed regulations clarify in § 1.6015-5(c)(1) that after a final administrative determination, a requesting spouse may not, even under the procedures for a CDP hearing, again request relief under section 6015 with respect to the same joint tax liability.

Consistent with the general restriction, but to provide flexibility within that framework, the IRS has developed procedures in the Internal Revenue Manual (Chapter 25.15.17 (Rev. 03/08/2013)) to reconsider a final administrative determination if a requesting spouse submits additional information not previously submitted and considered and the requesting spouse did not petition the Tax Court from the prior final administrative determination. If the requesting spouse did petition the Tax Court, then the requesting spouse is not eligible for reconsideration unless the Tax Court case was dismissed for lack of jurisdiction. A reconsideration process allows for relief in situations where a requesting spouse was unable to initially provide the information, such as the requesting spouse not fully understanding how to file a complete request for relief under section 6015. The reconsideration process, however, does not replace the IRS's final administrative determination for purposes of determining whether Tax Court review is available or whether a Tax Court petition was timely filed. A request for reconsideration is not a qualifying election ("the first timely claim for relief from joint and several liability for the tax year for which relief is sought") under § 1.6015-2 or 1.6015-3, or request under § 1.6015-4, for purposes of § 1.6015-1(h)(5), and does not trigger the restrictions on collection pursuant to section 6015(e)(1)(B) or the suspension of the collection period of limitation under section 6015(e)(2). A reconsideration letter (formerly Letter 4277C and currently either Letter 5186C, Letter 5187C, or Letter 5188C)) is not a final determination letter for purposes of section 6015(e) and § 1.6015-7. Accordingly, a requesting spouse who receives a reconsideration letter may not petition the Tax Court to challenge a denial of relief following the IRS's reconsideration even if the requesting spouse provided new information not previously considered. The proposed regulations add a new provision to § 1.6015-5(c) acknowledging the reconsideration process but also providing that the reconsideration letter is not the IRS's final determination and is not subject to review by the Tax Court.

The general restriction in the regulations to one request for relief under section 6015 per tax liability and one final administrative determination of that request does not prohibit a requesting spouse from reapplying for equitable relief under § 1.6015-4 pursuant to the terms of Notice 2011-70 if the requesting spouse's request for relief under § 1.6015-4 was denied solely for being untimely and that denial was not litigated. The notice allows individuals who filed requests for equitable relief that were denied by the IRS solely on the basis of the two-year deadline and were not litigated to reapply to the IRS for equitable relief. A Form 8857, "Request for Innocent Spouse Relief," or substitute written statement, signed under the penalties of perjury, filed as a reapplication for equitable relief under Notice 2011-70 is not considered a second request, and the resulting determination will be the final administrative determination for purposes of the regulations. A reapplication under Notice 2011-70 is not a reconsideration under the IRS's reconsideration process, and a denial of equitable relief on reapplication may be timely petitioned to the Tax Court for review.

Proposed Effective/Applicability Date

Except as provided below, these proposed regulations are effective as of the date that final regulations are published in the **Federal Register**. For proposed dates of applicability, see § 1.6015-9.

Notice 2011-70 announced that the Treasury Department and the IRS intended to amend the regulations under section 6015 to remove the requirement that taxpayers request equitable relief under section 6015(f) and § 1.6015-4 within two years of the first collection activity. Under section 7805(b)(1)(C), the proposed regulations provide that § 1.6015-5(b)(1) and (b)(2) will be effective as of July 25, 2011, the date that Notice 2011-70 was issued to the public.

Statement of Availability for IRS Documents

For copies of recently issued Revenue Procedures, Revenue Rulings, Notices and other guidance published in the Internal Revenue Bulletin or Cumulative Bulletin, please visit the IRS website at *http://www.irs.gov*.

Special Analyses

It has been determined that this notice of proposed rulemaking is not a significant regulatory action as defined in Executive Order 12866, as supplemented by Executive Order 13563. Therefore, a regulatory assessment is not required. It has also been determined that section 553(b) of the Administrative Procedure Act (5 U.S.C. chapter 5) does not apply to these regulations. In addition, because the regulation does not impose a collection of information on small entities, the Regulatory Flexibility Act (5 U.S.C. chapter 6) does not apply. Accordingly, a regulatory flexibility analysis is not required under the Regulatory Flexibility Act (5 U.S.C. chapter 6). Pursuant to section 7805(f) of the Code, this notice of proposed rulemaking has been submitted to the Chief Counsel for Advocacy of the Small Business Administration for comment on its impact on small business.

Comments and Requests for Public Hearing

Before these proposed regulations are adopted as final regulations, consideration will be given to any written comments (a signed original and eight (8) copies) or electronic comments that are submitted timely to the IRS. The Treasury Department and the IRS request comments on all aspects of the proposed rules. All comments submitted by the public will be made available for public inspection and copying at *http://www.regulations.gov* or upon request. A public hearing may be scheduled if requested in writing by any person who timely submits comments. If a public hearing is scheduled, notice of the date, time, and place for the public hearing will be published in the **Federal Register**.

Drafting Information

The principal authors of these proposed regulations are Stuart Murray and Mark Shurtliff of the Office of the Associate Chief Counsel, Procedure and Administration.

[¶ 49,587]   Proposed Amendments of Regulations (REG-132455-11), published in the Federal Register on September 9, 2013.

[Code Secs. 6011, 6055, 6081, 6721 and 6722]

Patient Protection and Affordable Care Act (PPACA): Minimum essential health coverage: Information reporting: Employers: Insurers: Coverage providers.—Reg. §301.6011-8, providing guidance to providers of minimum essential health coverage that are subject to the information reporting requirements of section 6055 of the Internal Revenue Code (Code), enacted by the Affordable Care Act, is proposed. Reg. §§1.6055-1, 1.6055-2 and amendments of Reg. §§1.6081-8, 301.6721-1 and 301.6722-1 were adopted by T.D. 9660 on March 5, 2014.

AGENCY: Internal Revenue Service (IRS), Treasury.

ACTION: Notice of proposed rulemaking and notice of public hearing.

SUMMARY: This document contains proposed regulations providing guidance to providers of minimum essential health coverage that are subject to the information reporting requirements of section 6055 of the Internal Revenue Code (Code), enacted by the Affordable Care Act. Health insurance issuers, certain employers, and others that provide minimum essential coverage to individuals must report to the IRS information about the type and period of coverage and furnish related statements to covered individuals. These proposed regulations affect health insurance issuers, employers, governments, and other persons that provide minimum essential coverage to individuals.

DATES: Written or electronic comments must be received by November 8, 2013. Requests to speak and outlines of topics to be discussed at the public hearing scheduled for November 19, 2013, at 10 a.m., must be received by November 8, 2013.

ADDRESSES: Send submissions to: CC:PA:LPD:PR (REG-132455-11), Room 5203, Internal Revenue Service, PO Box 7604, Ben Franklin Station, Washington, DC 20044. Submissions may be hand-delivered Monday through Friday between the hours of 8 a.m. and 4 p.m. to CC:PA:LPD:PR (REG-132455-11), Courier's Desk, Internal Revenue Service, 1111 Constitution Avenue, NW, Washington, DC, or sent electronically via the Federal eRulemaking Portal at *http://www.regulations.gov* (IRS REG-132455-11).

FOR FURTHER INFORMATION CONTACT: Concerning the proposed regulations, Andrew Braden, (202) 622-4960; concerning the submission of comments and/or to be placed on the building access list to attend the public hearing, Oluwafunmilayo (Funmi) Taylor, (202) 622-7180 (not toll-free calls).

SUPPLEMENTARY INFORMATION:

Paperwork Reduction Act

The collection of information contained in this notice of proposed rulemaking has been submitted to the Office of Management and Budget in accordance with the Paperwork Reduction Act of 1995 (44 U.S.C. 3507(d)). Comments on the collection of information should be sent to the **Office of Management and Budget**, Attn: Desk Officer for the Department of the Treasury, Office of Information and Regulatory Affairs, Washington, DC 20503, with copies to the **Internal Revenue Service**, Attn: IRS Reports Clearance Officer, SE:W:CAR:MP:T:T:SP, Washington, DC 20224. Comments on the collection of information should be received by November 8, 2013. Comments are specifically requested concerning:

Whether the proposed collection of information is necessary for the proper performance of the functions of the IRS, including whether the information will have practical utility;

How the quality, utility, and clarity of the information to be collected may be enhanced;

How the burden of complying with the proposed collection of information may be minimized, including through the application of automated collection techniques or other forms of information technology; and

Estimates of capital or start-up costs and costs of operation, maintenance, and purchase of services to provide information.

The collection of information in these proposed regulations is in §§1.6055-1 and 1.6055-2. The collection of information will be used to determine whether an individual has minimum essential coverage under section 1501(b) of the Patient Protection and Affordable Care Act (26 U.S.C. 5000A(f)). The collection of information is required to comply with the provisions of section 6055 of the Code. The likely respondents are health insurers, self-insured employers or other sponsors of self-insured health plans, and governments that provide minimum essential coverage.

The burden for the collection of information contained in these proposed regulations will be reflected in the burden on Form 1095-B or another form that the IRS designates, which will request the information in the proposed regulation.

An agency may not conduct or sponsor, and a person is not required to respond to, a collection of information unless it displays a valid control number assigned by the Office of Management and Budget.

Background

Beginning in 2014, under the Patient Protection and Affordable Care Act, Public Law 111-148 (124 Stat. 119 (2010)), and the Health Care and Education Reconciliation Act of 2010, Public Law 111-152 (124 Stat. 1029 (2010)) (collectively, the Affordable Care Act), nonexempt individuals have the choice of maintaining minimum essential coverage (as defined in section 5000A(f)) or paying an individual shared responsibility payment with their income tax returns. Minimum essential coverage may be health insurance coverage offered in the individual market (such as a qualified health plan offered through an Affordable Insurance Exchange (Exchange, also known as a Marketplace)), an employer-sponsored plan, or a government-sponsored program. Section 5000A(f)(1)(A) specifies that Medicare Part A, Medicaid, the Children's Health Insurance Program established under title XXI of the Social Security Act (42 U.S.C. 1397aa et seq.) (CHIP), TRICARE, certain health care programs for veterans and other individuals under chapter 17 or 18 of Title 38 U.S.C., coverage for Peace Corps volunteers under 22 USC 2504(e), and coverage under the Nonappropriated Fund Health Benefits Program under section 349 of Public Law 103-337, are government-sponsored programs that qualify as minimum essential coverage.

Section 1401 of the Affordable Care Act enacted section 36B, allowing certain taxpayers a refundable premium tax credit that will make minimum essential coverage in qualified health plans offered in the individual market through an Exchange more affordable.

Section 1502 of the Affordable Care Act enacted section 6055 regarding information reporting by any person that provides minimum essential coverage to an individual. Section 6055(b)(1)(B) requires providers of minimum essential coverage to report (1) the name, address, and taxpayer identification number (TIN) of the primary insured, (2) the name, dates of coverage, and TIN of each individual covered under a policy, (3) whether health insurance coverage is a qualified health plan offered through an Exchange, (4) for a qualified health plan, the amount of any advance payments of the premium tax credit under section 1412 of the Affordable Care Act and cost-sharing reductions under section 1402 of the Affordable Care Act, and (5) other information the Secretary requires.

Section 6055(b)(2) requires, for coverage through an employer's group health plan, reporting (1) the name, address, and employer identification number (EIN) of the employer maintaining the plan, (2) the portion of the premium (if any) paid by the employer, and (3) any other information that the Secretary requires for administering the credit under section 45R (the tax credit for employee health insurance expenses of small employers).

Section 6055(c) directs a person filing an information return under section 6055 to provide a written statement to each individual listed on the return that shows the name, address, and contact phone number of the reporting entity and information reported to the IRS for that individual. The statement must be furnished to the individual by January 31 of the year following the coverage year.

The information reported under section 6055 will allow taxpayers to establish and the IRS to verify that the taxpayers were covered by minimum essential coverage and their months of enrollment during a calendar year.

Under section 6724(d), as amended by the Affordable Care Act, a reporting entity that fails to comply with the filing and statement furnishing requirements of section 6055 may be subject to penalties for failure to file a correct information return (section 6721) and failure to furnish correct payee statements (section 6722). However, these penalties may be waived if the failure was due to reasonable cause and not to willful neglect (section 6724(a)).

Section 1514 of the Affordable Care Act enacted section 6056, which requires applicable large employers (generally employers with 50 or more full-time employees) to report to the IRS information about the coverage that they offer to their full-time employees and requires them to furnish related statements to employees.

Notice 2012-32 (2012-20 IRB 910) requested public comments on issues to be addressed in regulations under section 6055. In addition, Notice 2012-33 (2012-20 IRB 912) requested public comments on issues to be addressed in regulations under section 6056. As described later in this preamble, the written comments in response to Notice 2012-32 and other written comments have been considered in connection with the development of these proposed regulations.

As discussed in Notice 2013-45 (2013-31 IRB 116), Treasury and the IRS have engaged in dialogue with stakeholders in an effort to simplify section 6055 (and section 6056) reporting consistent with effective implementation of the law. This process has included discussions with stakeholders representing a wide range of interests to assist in the consideration of effective information reporting rules that will be as streamlined, simple, and workable as possible. The effort to develop these proposed information reporting rules has reflected a considered balancing of the importance of (1) providing individuals the information to complete their tax returns accurately, including with respect to the individual responsibility provisions and eligibility for the premium tax credit, (2) minimizing cost and administrative tasks for the reporting entities and individuals, and (3) providing the IRS with information needed for effective and efficient tax administration. As noted elsewhere in this preamble, the proposed regulations will be the subject of public comments, including comments that are specifically invited regarding particular issues identified in the preamble.

Notice 2013-45 provides as transition relief that section 6055 information reporting will be optional for 2014. The IRS will not impose penalties for failure to timely and accurately report under section 6055 for coverage in 2014. As stated in Notice 2013-45, the IRS encourages voluntary section 6055 reporting for coverage in 2014.

Explanation of Provisions and Summary of Comments

1. *Persons Subject to Information Reporting Requirement*

a. *Plans in the individual market*

Under section 36B(f)(3) and § 1.36B-5, an Exchange must report information relating to enrollment in qualified health plans in the individual market to the IRS and taxpayers. This information includes the period coverage was in effect, the names and TINs of each individual covered, the amount of advance credit payments relating to the coverage, and the amount of premiums for the coverage. This reporting facilitates compliance with and administration of the premium tax credit under section 36B. A commenter suggested that issuers of qualified health plans should not be required to report under section 6055 regarding minimum essential coverage that they provide in the individual market through the Exchange because the Exchange reporting provides the IRS and taxpayers with the necessary information about this coverage.

In response to this comment and to reduce the burden associated with reporting under section 6055, the proposed regulations provide that issuers are not required to submit section 6055 information returns for coverage under a qualified health plan in the individual market enrolled in through an Exchange. For individuals enrolled in this coverage, the IRS and individuals will receive information necessary to administer or comply with the individual shared responsibility provision through information reporting by Exchanges under section 36B(f)(3). Issuers must report, however, on qualified health plans in the small group market enrolled in through the Small Business Health Options Program (SHOP), because annual information reporting by Exchanges under section 36B(f)(3) does not include these plans.

b. *Employer-sponsored insured group health plans*

Commenters recommended that the proposed regulations require employers rather than health insurance issuers to report under section 6055 for insured coverage under an employer-sponsored group health plan. The commenters suggested that employers have more direct access to information required to be reported for an employee enrolled in a group health plan.

Because section 6055(a) requires reporting by the entities providing the coverage, which for insured coverage is the issuer, the proposed regulations provide that health insurance issuers are responsible for reporting under section 6055 for all insured coverage, except coverage under certain government-sponsored programs (such as Medicaid and Medicare) that provide coverage through a health insurance issuer and coverage under qualified health plans in the individual market enrolled in through an Exchange.

Reporting entities are permitted to use third parties to facilitate filing returns and furnishing statements to comply with reporting requirements, including those under section 6055. These arrangements do not, however, transfer the potential liability for failure of the reporting entity to report and furnish under the regulations.

A party preparing returns or statements required under section 6055 that is a tax return preparer will be subject to the requirements that generally apply to return preparers.

c. *Self-insured group health plans*

The proposed regulations provide that sponsors of self-insured health coverage are responsible for reporting under section 6055. The proposed regulations identify the employer as the plan sponsor and reporting entity for a self-insured group health plan established or maintained by a single employer. This rule is consistent with section 3(16)(B)(i) of the Employee Retirement Income Security Act of 1974 (ERISA), which states that the term "plan sponsor" means the employer in the case of an employee benefit plan established or maintained by a single employer.

Commenters noted that individuals may be covered under a self-insured arrangement that is a multiemployer plan and offered suggestions for identifying the entity responsible for reporting. Some commenters stated that employers that participate in a multiemployer plan do not have access to the information required to be reported under section 6055 and that the multiemployer plan or its administrator, for example, the joint board of trustees, should report for the participating employers. Another commenter suggested that labor unions report for multiemployer plans. Other commenters asserted that a plan's administrator or trustees generally are in the best position to report minimum essential coverage funded under a collective bargaining agreement unless the plan is funded by a single employer. A commenter asserted that each participating employer should be responsible for reporting under section 6055 for a multiple employer welfare arrangement (MEWA) under section 3(40) of ERISA (29 U.S.C. 1002(40)).

In response to these comments, the proposed regulations identify the sponsor and reporting entity for various types of self-insured arrangements (for example, the joint board of trustees for a multiemployer plan). For these purposes, the section 414 employer aggregation rules do not apply. Accordingly, a self-insured group health plan or arrangement covering employees of related corporations is treated as sponsored by more than one employer and each employer must report for its employees. However, one member of the group may assist the other members by filing returns and furnishing statements on behalf of all members.

Section 6055(d) provides that an appropriately designated person may report under section 6055 on behalf of a government employer. Accordingly, the proposed regulations allow a government employer providing self-insured coverage for its employees to report under section 6055 on its own behalf or to designate as the reporting entity another governmental unit or agency or instrumentality of a governmental unit that is part of or related to the same governmental unit as the government employer. If the designation is made before the filing deadline and the designee accepts it, the designated governmental unit, agency, or instrumentality is the sponsor responsible for section 6055 reporting. Comments are requested on issues specific to government employer plans and arrangements.

As noted, section 6056 requires applicable large employers to report information about the coverage that they offer to their full-time employees and to furnish related statements to employees. Commenters suggested that applicable large employers with self-insured health plans that must report under both sections 6055 and 6056 should be allowed to combine that reporting.

The general rules described in the proposed regulations assume separate reporting, but include other rules that reduce duplicative reporting and otherwise simplify reporting. For example, the proposed regulations allow the use of substitute forms and statements to individuals, which may permit self-insured health plans to furnish a single substitute statement to covered individuals for both sections 6055 and 6056.

In addition, the preamble to proposed regulations under section 6056 advises that the IRS and the Treasury Department are considering permitting applicable large employers with self-insured plans that provide mandatory, minimum value coverage to employees, and offer that coverage to spouses and dependents, all with no employee contribution, to forgo providing section 6056 statements to those covered employees. Because the section 6055 return would provide the individual taxpayers information to accurately file the taxpayers' income tax returns, and would provide the IRS the information concerning those employees to administer the premium tax credit and employer shared responsibility provisions, Treasury and the IRS are considering whether for those employees the employer could file and furnish only the return required under section 6055 and include a code on the employees' Forms W-2.

Comments are requested on other ways to simplify and combine reporting.

d. *Foreign employers that provide minimum essential coverage*

Section 6055(b)(2)(A) requires that reporting for coverage under a group health plan include the employer's EIN. A commenter noted that a foreign employer may provide minimum essential coverage but may not have an EIN. Comments are requested on rules for reporting by foreign employers without EINs that sponsor self-insured plans and on any other issues specific to reporting coverage provided by foreign employers.

e. *Government-sponsored programs*

The proposed regulations provide that the executive department or agency of a governmental unit that provides coverage under a government-sponsored program (within the meaning of section 5000A(f)(1)(A)) is responsible for reporting under section 6055. For example, the Department of Defense is responsible for reporting coverage under the TRICARE program. The proposed regulations identify the State agency that administers the Medicaid or CHIP program, rather than the Department of Health and Human Services, as the reporting entity for these programs. Additionally, under the proposed regulations, the responsible government department or agency, and not the issuer, is the reporting entity for coverage under a government-sponsored program provided through a health insurance issuer (such as some Medicaid, CHIP, and Medicare programs). Comments are requested on issues specific to reporting coverage under government-sponsored programs.

f. *Other arrangements designated as minimum essential coverage*

Section 5000A(f)(1)(E) provides that the Secretary of Health and Human Services (HHS), in coordination with the Secretary of the Treasury, may recognize other health benefits coverage as minimum essential coverage. On July 1, 2013, HHS published final regulations designating certain coverage as minimum essential coverage and outlining substantive and procedural requirements that other types of coverage must fulfill to be recognized as minimum essential coverage. Patient Protection and Affordable Care Act: Exchange Functions: Eligibility for Exemptions; Miscellaneous Minimum Essential Coverage Provisions, 78 FR 39494 (HHS MEC regulations). These regulations designate as minimum essential coverage (1) self-funded student health coverage for plan or policy years beginning on or before December 31, 2014, (2) Refugee Medical Assistance supported by the Administration for Children and Families, (3) Medicare Advantage plans, and (4) State high risk pools for plan or policy years beginning on or before December 31, 2014.

The proposed rule that designates the government department or agency as the reporting entity for coverage under a government-sponsored program provided through a health insurance issuer applies to Medicare Advantage plans. Comments are requested on appropriate rules for identifying the reporting entity for other arrangements recognized as minimum essential coverage under section 5000A(f)(1)(E).

2. *Information Required to Be Reported*

a. *In general*

The proposed regulations provide that the section 6055 information return must include the name of each individual enrolled in minimum essential coverage and the name and address of the primary insured or other related person (for example, a parent or spouse) who submits the application for coverage (the responsible individual). The proposed regulations use the term *responsible individual* rather than the term *primary insured* because minimum essential coverage may not be insured coverage (for example, health coverage provided by the Department of Veterans

Affairs). The return also must report the TIN and months of coverage for each individual who is covered under the policy or program and other information specified in forms, instructions, or published guidance, see §§601.601(d) and 601.602. For employer-provided coverage, the proposed regulations require reporting the name, address, and EIN of the employer maintaining the plan and whether coverage was enrolled in through the SHOP.

As part of the effort to minimize the cost and administrative steps associated with the reporting requirements, the proposed regulations do not require reporting information that would not be needed by individual taxpayers or the IRS for purposes of administering the individual shared responsibility provisions or the credit for small employers. Accordingly, the proposed regulations do not require reporting the portion of the premium paid by an employer, which the IRS does not need to determine if an individual is covered by minimum essential coverage. The proposed regulations require reporting the months of coverage rather than the specific dates of coverage, because minimum essential coverage applies month by month. The proposed regulations do not require reporting the amount of any cost-sharing reductions, which are not administered by the IRS. Finally, the proposed regulations do not require reporting the amount of advance payments or on coverage in a qualified health plan in the individual market enrolled in through an Exchange, since in both cases this information is reported to the IRS and provided to individuals by the Exchanges under section 36B(f)(3).

b. *Identifying information*

Health insurance issuers and employers with self-funded plans expressed concern that they do not typically collect TINs from dependents covered under their policies and that they may have difficulty obtaining TINs for some covered individuals. Other commenters suggested allowing alternative means of identifying individuals, such as unique enrollee identification numbers similar to the method used by the Massachusetts Health Connector (the State-based exchange), or allowing reporting without TINs for individuals who enroll in coverage but decline to provide a TIN. Some commenters suggested simplifying reporting requirements for dependents or providing alternatives in reporting TINs for new beneficiaries and others who may not provide TINs at the time of enrollment.

The proposed regulations adopt TIN reporting, consistent with the statute. Section 6055 reporting allows individuals to confirm their coverage and the IRS to verify that coverage without the need to contact the individuals. The use of TINs to cross-check individuals against coverage months is the most efficient way for individuals and the IRS to avoid the need for follow-up. Accordingly, covered individuals have an interest in providing TINs to reporting entities.

Federal tax records for individuals for all purposes are maintained by TIN and individual taxpayers identify themselves on their returns by TIN. Establishing another method of identifying individuals for sections 5000A and 6055 purposes would require the IRS to create, and taxpayers to adapt to, an entire parallel identification system solely for this purpose.

While section 6055 and the proposed regulations require TINs for administering section 5000A, reporting entities that make reasonable efforts to collect TINs but do not receive them will not be subject to penalties under sections 6721 and 6722 for failure to timely and accurately report. In particular, section 6055 reporting is governed by the same procedures, limitations, and protections as other information reporting that requires obtaining and reporting TINs. Section 6724 and the regulations under that section waive penalties on reporting entities for a reasonable failure to include correct TIN information on a return or statement, including those required under section 6055. Penalties are waived if the reporting entity demonstrates that it acted in a responsible manner both before and after the failure occurred, and that the failure was due to significant mitigating factors or events beyond the reporting entity's control. In general, a reporting entity acts responsibly in attempting to solicit a TIN if after an initial, unsuccessful request for a TIN (for example, at the time of enrollment), the reporting entity makes two consecutive annual TIN solicitations. No section 6724 penalty is imposed unless the reporting entity fails to make the two additional solicitations. Accordingly, section 6055 reporting entities will not be unduly penalized for failing to report a TIN.

As a backstop to reporting a TIN, the proposed regulations allow reporting entities to report date of birth if a TIN is not available. This alternative should not be used, however, unless the reporting entity has made reasonable efforts to obtain the information by requesting that a covered individual provide the TIN.

A commenter requested that the proposed regulations provide rules authorizing reporting entities to request TINs. This authority exists under section 6109(a)(2) and §301.6109-1(b)(1) of the Procedure and Administration Regulations, which require individuals to furnish TINs to persons that must file information returns.

A commenter noted that issuers and employers may have difficulty obtaining overseas addresses for individuals living abroad. The proposed regulations provide that only the last known address for the responsible individual must be reported.

c. *Coverage dates*

For purposes of section 5000A, an individual who has coverage on any day in a month is treated as having minimum essential coverage for the entire month. See proposed §1.5000A-1(b) (78 FR 7314). As a result, the specific coverage dates are not necessary for administering and complying with rules relating to minimum essential coverage. Accordingly, the proposed regulations do not require reporting of the specific dates of coverage. Instead, the proposed regulations generally require reporting of the months during which an individual is treated as having minimum essential coverage.

A commenter noted that coverage dates may be inaccurate because coverage may be terminated or reinstated after the reporting date for periods occurring before the reporting date. Under section 6724 and the regulations under that section, the IRS may waive penalties if there is reasonable cause for the failure to correct an information return for retroactive terminations or reinstatements that are determined after the calendar year in which coverage was terminated or reinstated.

A commenter recommended permitting separate returns or creating special forms to report coverage for individuals who change their coverage during the year to a different health plan with the same issuer. Although the proposed regulations do not adopt a rule addressing this situation, additional procedures that are responsive to this comment may be provided in IRS forms and instructions, see §601.602.

A commenter noted that employers face challenges in determining coverage dates for employees and dependents, including seasonal and temporary workers whose term of employment changes during the year. The commenter recommended that the rules allow reporting an individual's enrollment in minimum essential coverage as of a fixed date each year to accommodate an employer's administrative, payroll, and recordkeeping procedures. The individual responsibility payment under section 5000A applies to individuals on a monthly basis, so reporting based on one day during the year would not be sufficient. Additionally, varying reporting dates would be difficult to administer and would produce information less useful to taxpayers, who generally file their tax returns and must determine their coverage based on a calendar year. Accordingly, the proposed regulations do not adopt this suggestion. Comments are welcome on potential alternative ways to address the challenges associated with determining coverage dates when employment changes.

d. *Supplemental coverage arrangements*

A commenter asked whether an employer and an issuer must coordinate section 6055 reporting for an employer-sponsored group health plan that consists of an insured high-deductible health plan (HDHP) and additional health benefits provided through a contribution to a health savings account. Health savings accounts are not minimum essential coverage, and therefore section 6055 reporting is not required for them. Additionally, the proposed regulations provide that reporting is not required for arrangements such as health reimbursement arrangements that supplement minimum essential coverage.

3. Time and Manner of Filing

a. Form of return

The proposed regulations provide that the return under section 6055 may be made on Form 1095-B or another form the IRS designates, or on a substitute form. A substitute form must comply with revenue procedures or other published guidance, see § 601.601(d)(2), that apply to substitute forms. The proposed regulations require that information returns be submitted to the IRS with a transmittal form, Form 1094-B. In accordance with usual procedure, these forms will be made available in draft form at a later date.

b. Time for filing returns

The proposed regulations provide for reporting entities to file the return and transmittal form on or before February 28 (or March 31 if filed electronically) of the year following the calendar year in which they provided minimum essential coverage. Commenters suggested that the proposed regulations provide different reporting deadlines for fiscal year health plans to avoid calendar year reporting of data from multiple plan years. Since most individuals file calendar year returns, permitting fiscal year reporting would interfere with return preparation and processing for individuals potentially subject to the section 5000A individual shared responsibility payment. Therefore, the proposed regulations do not adopt this comment.

c. Electronic reporting

Commenters recommended permitting electronic reporting under section 6055. Section 6011(e) and § 301.6011-2 require high-volume filers (those who file 250 or more returns during the calendar year) to file electronically. The proposed regulations provide that these electronic filing requirements apply to information returns under section 6055, but do not limit electronic filing to high-volume filers. Accordingly, any reporting entity may file electronically under section 6055.

4. Combined Reporting

As discussed earlier in this preamble, applicable large employers that provide minimum essential coverage on a self-insured basis are subject to the reporting requirements of sections 6055 and 6056, as well as the requirement under section 6051 to file Form W-2, Wage and Tax Statement, showing wages paid to employees and taxes withheld. Notices 2012-32 and 2012-33 requested comments on how to minimize duplication in reporting under these provisions.

Several commenters recommended that the regulations allow combined information reporting under sections 6055 and 6056 for applicable large employers that sponsor self-insured group health plans and must report under both sections. Other commenters recommended that employers be permitted to use a single information return to report under sections 6051 and 6055, for example by adding the information required under section 6055 to Form W-2.

As discussed elsewhere in this preamble, these proposed regulations seek to simplify reporting and reduce duplication through a number of approaches. In particular, the proposed regulations provide that issuers need not report under section 6055 for individual market qualified health plans enrolled in through an Exchange. The proposed regulations also provide relief from the requirement to report several items of information that are unnecessary for tax administration or are available from other reporting, and they allow the use of substitute forms and statements to individuals, which, under future guidance, may include furnishing a single substitute statement to covered individuals for both sections 6055 and 6056.

Accordingly, while the rules for section 6055 reporting in the proposed regulations do not assume full combined reporting under sections 6055, 6056 and 6051, they reflect other means of avoiding duplication and simplifying reporting. We continue to seek comments on other ways to streamline the reporting methods that would be permissible under the statute.

5. Statements Furnished to Individuals

The proposed regulations provide that a reporting entity must furnish a statement to the covered individual providing the policy number and the name, address, and a contact number for the reporting entity, and the information required to be reported to the IRS. The proposed regulations permit substitute statements that include the information required to be shown on the return filed with the IRS and comply with applicable requirements in published guidance relating to substitute statements. See § 601.601(d)(2) of this chapter. A substitute statement that includes the information required by both sections 6055 and 6056 in a single statement may be permitted by future guidance.

Commenters recommended permitting electronic delivery of statements to individuals. A commenter suggested that the regulations provide rules for electronic delivery of statements to individuals that are similar to the rules under section 2715 of the Public Health Service Act for providing a summary of benefits and coverage. The commenter suggested that these reporting regulations permit the furnishing of one electronic statement per home address rather than multiple statements per household. Another commenter requested guidance on procedures when an email notice is returned due to an incorrect address.

The proposed regulations permit electronic delivery of statements to individuals if the recipient consents. In response to concerns about the need to furnish a statement to each individual, the proposed regulations also permit furnishing only one statement per address. Comments are requested on whether and under what circumstances the regulations should direct reporting entities to provide a statement to another individual (who may, for example, need the statement to determine his or her tax liability).

Commenters expressed concern about protecting the privacy of individuals who provide TINs and about disclosure of the TINs to other parties. The regulations provide that section 6055 information reporting will be included in the IRS truncated TIN program. Accordingly, to protect the privacy of covered individuals, statements furnished to individuals under section 6055 are not required to disclose their complete TINs.

A commenter recommended that the statement to individuals should explain minimum essential coverage and advise taxpayers that they may be subject to a penalty for months in which they do not have minimum essential coverage. The proposed regulations do not include rules addressing educational content in the statement. However, information on the section 5000A individual shared responsibility payment may be included in IRS forms, instructions, and publications.

6. Penalties

Commenters recommended providing procedures for correcting errors in reporting and a safe harbor from penalties for an issuer that fails to report information that another entity fails to provide to the issuer. The proposed regulations provide that the provisions of section 6724(a) providing relief for a failure due to reasonable cause apply to reporting under section 6055. Because the procedures described in § 301.6721-1(b), which provide for reduced penalties for reporting errors that are timely corrected, will apply to corrections of errors in reporting under section 6055 that are not due to reasonable cause, the proposed regulations do not prescribe separate rules for correcting errors.

Proposed Effective/Applicability Date

These regulations are proposed to apply for calendar years beginning after December 31, 2014. Consistent with Notice 2013-45, reporting entities will not be subject to penalties for failure to comply with the section 6055 reporting requirements for coverage in 2014, which would have resulted in reporting in 2015 and furnishing statements to covered individuals in 2015. Accordingly, a reporting entity will not be subject to penalties if it first reports beginning in 2016 for 2015, including the furnishing of statements to covered individuals in 2016 with respect to 2015. Taxpayers are encouraged, however, to voluntarily comply with section 6055 information reporting for minimum essential coverage provided in 2014 by applying these regulations once finalized.

Special Analyses

It has been determined that this notice of proposed rulemaking is not a significant regulatory action as defined in Executive Order 12866, as supplemented by Executive Order 13563. Therefore, a regulatory assessment is not required. It has also been determined that section 553(b) of the Administrative Procedure Act (5 U.S.C. chapter 5) does not apply to these regulations.

It is hereby certified that these regulations will not have a significant economic impact on a substantial number of small entities. This certification is based on the fact that the information collection required under these regulations is imposed under section 6055. Consistent with the statute, the proposed regulations require a person that provides minimum essential coverage to an individual to file a return with the IRS reporting certain information and to furnish a statement to the responsible individual who enrolled an individual or family in the coverage. These regulations primarily provide the method of filing and furnishing returns and statements under section 6055. Moreover, the proposed regulations attempt to minimize the burden associated with this collection of information by limiting reporting to the information that the IRS will use to verify minimum essential coverage and administer tax credits.

Based on these facts, a Regulatory Flexibility Analysis under the Regulatory Flexibility Act (5 U.S.C. chapter 6) is not required.

Pursuant to section 7805(f) of the Code, this notice of proposed rulemaking has been submitted to the Chief Counsel for Advocacy of the Small Business Administration for comment on its impact on small business.

Comments and Public Hearing

Before these proposed regulations are adopted as final regulations, consideration will be given to any comments that are submitted timely to the IRS as prescribed in this preamble under the "Addresses" heading. The IRS and Treasury Department request comments on all aspects of the proposed rules. All comments will be available at www.regulations.gov or upon request.

A public hearing has been scheduled for November 19, 2013, at 10 a.m., in the auditorium, Internal Revenue Building, 1111 Constitution Avenue NW., Washington, DC. Due to building security procedures, visitors must enter at the Constitution Avenue entrance. All visitors must present photo identification to enter the building. Because of access restrictions, visitors will not be admitted beyond the immediate entrance more than 30 minutes before the hearing starts. For information about having your name placed on the building access list to attend the hearing, see the "**FOR FURTHER INFORMATION CONTACT**" section of this preamble.

The rules of 26 CFR 601.601(a)(3) apply to the hearing. Persons who wish to present oral comments at the hearing must submit written or electronic comments by November 8, 2013, an outline of topics to be discussed and the time to be devoted to each topic by (signed original and eight (8) copies by November 8, 2013. A period of 10 minutes will be allotted to each person for making comments.

An agenda showing the scheduling of the speakers will be prepared after the deadline for receiving outlines has passed. Copies of the agenda will be available free of charge at the hearing.

Drafting Information

The principal authors of these proposed regulations are Andrew Braden and Frank W. Dunham III of the Office of Associate Chief Counsel (Income Tax and Accounting). However, other personnel from the IRS and the Treasury Department participated in the development of the regulations.

[¶ 49,588]   Proposed Amendments of Regulations (REG-136630-12), published in the Federal Register on September 9, 2013.

[Code Secs. 6011 and 6056]

Patient Protection and Affordable Care Act (PPACA): Minimum essential health coverage: Information reporting: Employers: Insurers: Coverage providers.—Reg. §301.6011-9, providing guidance to employers that are subject to the information reporting requirements under section 6056 of the Internal Revenue Code (Code), enacted by the Affordable Care Act, is proposed. Reg. §§301.6056-1 and 301.6056-2 were adopted by T.D. 9661 on March 5, 2014.

AGENCY: Internal Revenue Service (IRS), Treasury.

ACTION: Notice of proposed rulemaking and notice of public hearing.

SUMMARY: This document contains proposed regulations providing guidance to employers that are subject to the information reporting requirements under section 6056 of the Internal Revenue Code (Code), enacted by the Affordable Care Act. Section 6056 requires those employers to report to the IRS information about their compliance with the employer shared responsibility provisions of section 4980H of the Code and about the health care coverage they have offered employees. Section 6056 also requires those employers to furnish related statements to employees so that employees may use the statements to help determine whether, for each month of the calendar year, they can claim on their tax returns a premium tax credit under section 36B of the Code (premium tax credit). In addition, that information will be used to administer and ensure compliance with the eligibility requirements for the employer shared responsibility provisions and the premium tax credit. The proposed regulations affect applicable large employers (generally meaning employers with 50 or more full-time employees, including full-time equivalent employees, in the prior year), employees and other individuals.

This document also provides notice of a public hearing on these proposed rules. DATES: Written or electronic comments must be received by November 8, 2013. Requests to speak and outlines of topics to be discussed at the public hearing scheduled for November 18, 2013, at 10 a.m., must be received by November 8, 2013.

ADDRESSES: Send submissions to: CC:PA:LPD:PR (REG-136630-12), room 5205, Internal Revenue Service, PO Box 7604, Ben Franklin Station, Washington, DC 20044. Submissions may be hand-delivered Monday through Friday between the hours of 8 a.m. and 4 p.m. to CC:PA:LPD:PR (REG-136630-12), Courier's Desk, Internal Revenue Service, 1111 Constitution Avenue, NW, Washington, DC, or sent electronically, via the Federal eRulemaking Portal at www.regulations.gov (IRS REG-136630-12). The public hearing will be held in the Auditorium, Internal Revenue Building, 1111 Constitution Avenue, NW, Washington, DC.

FOR FURTHER INFORMATION CONTACT: Concerning the proposed regulations, Ligeia Donis (202) 927-9639; concerning submission of comments, the hearing, and/or to be placed on the building access list to attend the hearing, please contact Oluwafunmilayo (Funmi) Taylor at (202) 622-7180 (not toll-free numbers).

SUPPLEMENTARY INFORMATION

Paperwork Reduction Act

The collection of information contained in this notice of proposed rulemaking has been submitted to the Office of Management and Budget for review in accordance with the Paperwork Reduction Act of 1995 (44 U.S.C. 3507(d)). Comments on the collection of information should be sent to the **Office of Management and Budget,** Attn: Desk Officer for the Department of the Treasury, Office of Information and Regulatory Affairs, Washington, DC 20503, with copies to the **Internal Revenue Service**, Attn: IRS Reports Clearance Officer, SE:W:CAR:MP:T:T:SP, Washington, DC 20224. Comments on the collection of information should be received by November 8, 2013. Comments are specifically requested concerning:

Whether the proposed collection of information is necessary for the proper performance of the functions of the IRS, including whether the information will have practical utility;

How the quality, utility, and clarity of the information to be collected may be enhanced;

How the burden of complying with the proposed collection of information may be minimized, including through the application of automated collection techniques or other forms of information technology; and

Estimates of capital or start-up costs and costs of operation, maintenance, and purchase of services to provide information.

The collection of information in these proposed regulations is in proposed regulation §§ 301.6011-9, 301.6056-1, and 301.6056-2. This information will be used by the IRS to verify compliance with the return and employee statement requirements under section 6056 for purposes of section 4980H, and with the eligibility requirements for the premium tax credit. This information will be used to determine whether the information has been reported and calculated correctly for purposes of section 4980H and section 6056, and whether claims for the premium tax credit are correct. The likely respondents are employers that are applicable large employers, as defined under section 4980H(c)(2).

An agency may not conduct or sponsor, and a person is not required to respond to, a collection of information unless it displays a valid control number assigned by the Office of Management and Budget.

Books or records relating to a collection of information must be retained as long as their contents may become material in the administration of any internal revenue law. Generally, tax returns and tax return information are confidential, as required by 26 U.S.C. 6103.

Background

Sections I through V of the preamble ("Background") describe the statutory provisions governing the information reporting requirements, as well as related statutory provisions. Sections VI through XIII of the preamble ("Explanation of Provisions and Summary of Comments") describe and explain how these regulations propose to implement the statutory provisions of section 6056 and include a discussion of a variety of potential simplified reporting methods that are under consideration. As is typical with regulations on information reporting, these proposed regulations refer generally to additional information that may be required under the applicable forms and instructions. Sections IX.B and C of this preamble set forth the specific data elements that Treasury and the IRS anticipate will be included with the reporting, including the data elements that Treasury and the IRS anticipate will be provided through the use of an indicator code.

Section 6056[1] requires applicable large employers, as defined in section 4980H(c)(2), to file returns at the time prescribed by the Secretary with respect to each full-time employee and furnish a statement to each full-time employee by January 31 of the calendar year following the calendar year for which the return must be filed. Section 6056 specifies certain information that must be reported on the section 6056 return and related statement, and authorizes the Secretary to require additional information and determine the form of the return. Section 6056 is effective for periods beginning after December 31, 2013; however, Notice 2013-45 (2013-31 IRB 116) provides transition relief for 2014 from the section 6056 information reporting requirements (as well as the section 6055 information reporting requirements relating to the section 5000A individual shared responsibility provisions and the section 4980H employer shared responsibility provisions).

I. *Shared Responsibility for Employers (Section 4980H)*

One of the purposes of section 6056 reporting is to assist with the administration of the employer shared responsibility provisions added by the Affordable Care Act as section 4980H of the Code. Section 4980H imposes an assessable payment on applicable large employers if certain requirements relating to the provision of health care coverage to full-time employees are not met and one or more full-time employees claim a premium tax credit. On December 28, 2012, Treasury and the IRS released proposed regulations under section 4980H. The proposed regulations under section 4980H were published in the **Federal Register** on January 2, 2013 (REG-138006-12 [78 FR 218]). Section 4980H is effective for months after December 31, 2013; however, Notice 2013-45, issued on July 9, 2013, provides transition relief for 2014 from the section 4980H employer shared responsibility provisions.

The reporting requirements under section 6056 apply only to employers that are subject to section 4980H (which the statute refers to as "applicable large employers"). Section 4980H(c)(2) defines the term "applicable large employer" as, with respect to a calendar year, an employer that employed an average of at least 50 full-time employees on business days during the preceding calendar year. Generally, for purposes of determining applicable large employer status, a full-time employee includes any employee who was employed on average at least 30 hours of service per week and any full-time equivalents determined pursuant to section 4980H(c)(2)(E). All employers treated as a single employer under section 414(b), (c), (m), or (o) are treated as one employer for purposes of determining applicable large employer status. Section 4980H contains rules for determining whether an employer qualifies as an applicable large employer, including special rules addressing an employer's first year of existence and predecessor and successor employers. See section 4980H(c)(2)(C) and proposed § 54.4980H-2. Proposed regulations under section 4980H provide guidance on determining applicable large employer status and determining full-time employee status, including defining and providing rules for calculating hours of service. See proposed §§ 54.4980H-1(a)(21) (definition of hours of service), 54.4980H-2 (determination of applicable large employer status), and 54.4980H-3 (determination of full-time employee status).

II. *Premium Tax Credit (Section 36B)*

Section 6056 reporting will also be used for the administration of the premium tax credit, which was added by the Affordable Care Act as section 36B of the Code. Section 36B allows an advanceable and refundable premium tax credit to help individuals and families afford health insurance

---

[1] Section 6056 was enacted by section 1514(a) of the Patient Protection and Affordable Care Act, Public Law 111-148 (124 Stat. 119 (2010)), amended by the Health Care and Education Reconciliation Act of 2010, Public Law 111-152 (124 Stat. 1029 (2010)), and further amended by the Department of Defense and Full-Year Continuing Appropriations Act of 2011, Public Law 112-10 (125 Stat. 38 (2011)) (collectively, the Affordable Care Act).

coverage purchased through an Affordable Insurance Exchange (Exchange). An employee is not eligible for a premium tax credit to subsidize the cost of Exchange coverage if the employee is offered affordable coverage under an employer-sponsored plan that provides minimum value, or if the employee enrolls in an employer-sponsored plan. For this purpose, an employer-sponsored plan is affordable if the employee's required contribution for the lowest-cost self-only minimum value coverage offered does not exceed 9.5% of the employee's household income. Thus, an employee (and in the case of an employer-sponsored plan that offers coverage to an employee's spouse or dependents, the employee's spouse and dependents) who does not accept an offer of affordable minimum value coverage under an employer-sponsored plan and who purchase coverage on an Exchange may not be eligible for a premium tax credit. Individuals and the IRS will use the information on the cost of the lowest-cost employer-sponsored self-only coverage that provides minimum value to verify the individual's eligibility for the premium tax credit.[2]

III. *Individual Shared Responsibility (Section 5000A)*

In addition, the Affordable Care Act added section 5000A to the Code. Section 5000A provides nonexempt individuals with a choice: maintain minimum essential coverage for themselves and any nonexempt family members, or include an additional payment with their Federal income tax return. Section 5000A(f)(1)(B) provides that minimum essential coverage includes coverage under an eligible employer-sponsored plan. Under section 5000A(f)(2), an eligible employer-sponsored plan is, with respect to an employee, a group health plan or group health insurance coverage offered by an employer to the employee that is (1) a governmental plan, within the meaning of section 2791(d)(8) of the Public Health Service Act (42 U.S.C. 300gg-91(d)(8)), or (2) any other plan or coverage offered in the small or large group market within a State. An eligible employer-sponsored plan also includes a grandfathered health plan, as defined in section 5000A(f)(1)(D), offered in a group market. Group health plans within the meaning of section 1301(b)(3) of the Affordable Care Act (42 U.S.C. 18021(b)(3)) include both insured health plans and self-insured health plans. Accordingly, a self-insured group health plan is an eligible employer-sponsored plan. See the Questions and Answers on the Individual Shared Responsibility Provision available on the IRS website at www.irs.gov.

IV. *Information Reporting By Providers of Coverage (Issuers, Self-Insuring Employers, and Sponsors of Certain Government-Sponsored Programs) (Section 6055)*

The Affordable Care Act also added section 6055 to the Code, providing for information reporting for the administration of section 5000A. The section 6055 reporting requirements are effective for years beginning after December 31, 2013; however, Notice 2013-45 provides transition relief for 2014 from the section 6055 reporting requirements. Section 6055 requires information reporting by any person that provides minimum essential coverage to an individual during a calendar year, including coverage provided under an eligible employer-sponsored plan, and the furnishing to taxpayers of a related statement covering each individual listed on the section 6055 return. The information reported under section 6055 can be used by individuals and the IRS to verify the months (if any) in which they were covered by minimum essential coverage. Treasury and the IRS are issuing proposed regulations under section 6055 (REG-132455-11) concurrently with these proposed regulations.

V. *Reporting Requirements for Applicable Large Employers (Section 6056)*

Section 6056 directs an applicable large employer (within the meaning of section 4980H(c)(2)) to file a return with the IRS that reports for each employee who was a full-time employee for one or more months during the calendar year certain information described in section 6056(b) about the health care coverage the employer offered to that employee (or, if applicable, that the employer did not offer health care coverage to that employee). Section 6056 also requires such employers to furnish by January 31 of the calendar year following the calendar year for which the return must be filed a related statement described in section 6056(c) to each full-time employee for whom information is required to be included on the return.

Section 6056(b) describes the return required to be filed with the IRS under section 6056. It states that a return meets the requirements of section 6056 if the return is in such form as the Secretary may prescribe and contains (1) the name, date, and employer's employer identification number (EIN), (2) a certification as to whether the employer offers to its full-time employees (and their dependents) the opportunity to enroll in minimum essential coverage under an eligible employer-sponsored plan (as defined in section 5000A(f)(2)), (3) the number of full-time employees for each month during the calendar year, and (4) the name, address, and taxpayer identification number of each full-time employee during the calendar year and the months, if any, during which that employee (and any dependents) were covered under any such health benefits plans.

If the applicable large employer certifies that it offered to its full-time employees (and their dependents) the opportunity to enroll in minimum essential coverage under an eligible employer-sponsored plan (as defined in section 5000A(f)(2)), section 6056 specifies that the return must also include (1) the length of any waiting period (as defined in section 2701(b)(4) of the Public Health Service Act (42 USC 300gg(b)(4)) with respect to that coverage,[3] (2) the months during the calendar year for which coverage under the plan was available, (3) the monthly premium for the lowest cost option in each of the enrollment categories under the plan, and (4) the employer's share of the total allowed costs of benefits provided under the plan. Section 6056(b)(2)(F) provides that the return must include such other information as the Secretary may require. See section IX of this preamble for a discussion of the information proposed to be included in these proposed regulations as part of the reporting requirements, as well as additional information that may be required under the applicable forms and instructions, as is typical with regulations on information reporting.

Section 6056(c) requires that every person required to make a return under section 6056(a) furnish to each full-time employee whose name is required to be set forth in the return a written statement showing (1) the name and address of the person required to make that return and the phone number of the information contact for that person, and (2) the information required to be shown on the return with respect to that individual. The written statement must be furnished on or before January 31 of the year following the calendar year for which the return under section 6056(a) was required to be made.

As discussed in section IX.B of this preamble, the approach contemplated by these proposed regulations would give effect to these statutory provisions by limiting the information elements listed and other information that would be provided annually to those that are needed by individual taxpayers to accurately complete their tax returns or by the IRS to effectively administer other provisions of the Affordable Care Act. Treasury and the IRS seek comments on ways to achieve these goals efficiently and effectively.

Section 6056(d) provides that to the maximum extent feasible, the Secretary may permit combined reporting under section 6056, section 6051 (employers filing and furnishing Forms W-2, Wage and Tax Statement, with respect to employees) or section 6055, and in the case of an applicable

---

[2] In connection with providing advance payment of the premium tax credit, the Exchanges will employ a verification process. Because the information concerning household income and other relevant factors that are known to the individual and the Exchanges at that time may differ from the information used to file the tax return after the close of the coverage year, an individual who receives an advance payment of the premium tax credit will also need to calculate the appropriate amount of the credit when filing his or her tax return, and the credit may be more or less than the advance payment.

[3] While section 6056(b)(2)(C)(i) refers to the term "waiting period" as defined in section 2701(b)(4) of the PHS Act, amendments made by section 1201 of the Affordable Care Act moved this definition from section 2701(b)(4) of the PHS Act to section 2704(b)(4). Separately, section 2708 of the PHS Act prohibits a group health plan and a health insurance issuer offering group health insurance coverage from applying any waiting period that exceeds 90 days. The Affordable Care Act adds section 715(a)(1) to the Employee Retirement Income Security Act (ERISA) and section 9815(a)(1) to the Code to incorporate the provisions of part A of title XXVII of the PHS Act (specifically, PHS Act sections 2701 through 2728) into ERISA and the Code, and to make them applicable to group health plans and health insurance issuers providing health insurance coverage in connection with group health plans.

large employer offering health insurance coverage of a health insurance issuer, the employer may enter into an agreement with the issuer to include information required under section 6056 with the return and statement required to be provided by the issuer under section 6055.

Section 6056(e) generally permits governmental units, or any agency or instrumentality thereof, to designate a person to comply with the section 6056 requirements on behalf of the governmental unit, agency or instrumentality.

Under section 6724(d), as amended by the Affordable Care Act, an applicable large employer that fails to comply with the filing and statement furnishing requirements of section 6056 may be subject to penalties for failure to file a correct information return (section 6721) and failure to furnish correct payee statements (section 6722). However, these penalties may be waived if the failure is due to reasonable cause and not to willful neglect (section 6724).

Notice 2012-32 (2012-20 IRB 910) requested public comments on issues to be addressed in regulations under section 6055. Notice 2012-33 (2012-20 IRB 912) requested public comments on issues to be addressed in regulations under section 6056. In developing these proposed regulations and the proposed regulations under section 6055, including the potential further simplified reporting methods described in section XI of this preamble, Treasury and the IRS have considered the written comments submitted in response to these notices and other written comments received.

In addition, consistent with Notice 2013-45, Treasury and the IRS have engaged in further dialogue with stakeholders in an effort to simplify section 6056 and section 6055 reporting consistent with effective implementation of the law. This process has included discussions with stakeholders representing a wide range of interests to assist in the consideration of effective information reporting rules that will be as streamlined, simple, and workable as possible. The effort to develop these proposed information reporting rules has reflected a considered balancing of the importance of (1) providing individuals the information to complete their tax returns accurately, including with respect to the individual responsibility provisions and eligibility for the premium tax credit, (2) minimizing cost and administrative tasks for the reporting entities and individuals, and (3) providing the IRS with information to use for effective and efficient tax administration. As noted elsewhere in this preamble, the proposed regulations will be the subject of public comments, including comments that are specifically invited regarding particular issues identified in the preamble.

Explanation of Provisions and Summary of Comments

VI. *Introduction*

The Explanation of Provisions that follows (Sections VII through XIII of the preamble) describes the regulatory provisions proposed to implement the statutory reporting provisions described in the Background portion of the preamble. Specifically, this section includes the following:

Section VII . . . . Key Terms

Section VIII . . . . ALE Member Subject to Section 6056 Requirements With Respect to Full-Time Employees

Section IX . . . . General Method -Content, Manner, and Timing of Information Required to be Reported to the IRS and Furnished to Full-Time Employees

Section X . . . . Combined Reporting Under Section 6056 and Section 6051 or 6055

Section XI . . . . Potential Simplified Methods for Section 6056 Information Reporting

Section XII . . . . Person Responsible for Section 6056 Reporting

Section XIII . . . . Applicability of Information Return Requirements

VII. *Key Terms*

These proposed regulations under section 6056 use a number of terms that are defined in other Code provisions or regulations. For example, section 6056(f) provides that any term used in section 6056 that is also used in section 4980H shall have the same meaning given to the term by section 4980H. Relevant terms include the following:

A. *Applicable Large Employer*

The proposed regulations provide that the term applicable large employer has the same meaning as in section 4980H(c)(2) and any applicable guidance. See proposed § 54.4980H-1(a)(4).

B. *ALE Member*

All persons treated as a single employer under section 414(b), (c), (m), or (o) are treated as one employer for purposes of determining applicable large employer status.[4] Under the proposed regulations, the section 6056 filing and furnishing requirements are applied separately to each person comprising the applicable large employer consistent with the approach taken in the section 4980H proposed regulations (REG-138006-12 [78 FR 218]) with respect to the determination of any assessable payment under section 4980H. The person or persons that comprise the applicable large employer are referred to as ALE members. The proposed regulations define the term *ALE member* as a person that, together with one or more other persons, is treated as a single employer that is an applicable large employer. For this purpose, if a person, together with one or more other persons, is treated as a single employer that is an applicable large employer on any day of a calendar month, that person is an ALE member for that calendar month. This definition is the same as the definition provided in the proposed regulations under section 4980H. See § 54.4980H-1(a)(5).

C. *Dependent*

The proposed regulations provide that the term *dependent* has the same meaning as in section 4980H(a) and (b) and any applicable guidance. See proposed § 54.4980H-1(a)(11).

D. *Eligible Employer-Sponsored Plan*

The proposed regulations provide that the term eligible *employer-sponsored plan* has the same meaning as in section 5000A(f)(2) and any applicable guidance.

E. *Full-time Employee*

The proposed regulations provide that the term *full-time employee* has the same meaning as in section 4980H(c)(4) and any applicable guidance as applied to the determination and calculation of liability under section 4980H(a) and (b) with respect to any individual employee. See proposed § 54.4980H-1(a)(18).

---

[4] As explained in section 1.A.2 of the preamble to the proposed regulations under section 4980H (REG-138006-12 [78 FR 218]), until further guidance is issued, government entities, churches, and a convention or association of churches may apply a reasonable, good faith interpretation of section 414(b), (c), (m), and (o) in determining whether a person or group of persons is an applicable large employer and whether a particular entity is an applicable large employer member. See proposed § 54.4980H-1(a)(5).

F. *Governmental Unit and Agency or Instrumentality of a Governmental Unit*

The proposed regulations define the term *governmental* unit as the government of the United States, any State or political subdivision thereof, or any Indian tribal government (as defined in section 7701(a)(40)) or subdivision of an Indian tribal government (as defined in section 7871(d)). The proposed regulations do not define the term *agency or instrumentality of a governmental unit*, but rather reserve on the issue.

G. *Minimum Essential Coverage*

The proposed regulations provide that the term *minimum essential coverage* has the same meaning as in section 5000A(f)(1) and any applicable guidance.

H. *Minimum Value*

The proposed regulations provide that the term minimum value has the same meaning as in section 36B and any applicable guidance. See proposed § 1.36B-6.

I. *Person*

The proposed regulations provide that the term *person* has the same meaning as provided in section 7701(a)(1) and the regulations thereunder.

VIII. *ALE Member Subject to Section 6056 Requirements with Respect to Full-Time Employees*

As discussed earlier in section VII.B of this preamble, an ALE member is any person that is an applicable large employer or a member of an aggregated group (determined under section 414(b), 414(c), 414(m) or 414(o)) that is determined to be an applicable large employer. Under the proposed regulations, the section 6056 filing and statement furnishing requirements apply on a member-by-member basis to each ALE member, even though the determination of whether an entity is an applicable large employer is made at the aggregated group level. For example, if an applicable large employer is comprised of a parent corporation and 10 wholly-owned subsidiary corporations, there are 11 ALE members (the parent corporation and each of the 10 subsidiary corporations). Under the proposed regulations, each ALE member with full-time employees, rather than the group of entities that comprise the applicable large employer, is the entity responsible for filing and furnishing statements with respect to its full-time employees under section 6056. This is consistent with the manner in which any potential assessable payments under section 4980H will be calculated and administered.

Treasury and the IRS understand that ALE members may benefit from the assistance of a third party in preparing these returns, for example a third-party plan administrator or a related ALE member tasked with preparing the returns for all the members of that applicable large employer. For a discussion of how these third parties may help an ALE member fulfill its reporting obligations, see section XII.C of this preamble.

Whether an employee is a full-time employee is determined under section 4980H(c)(4) and any applicable guidance. See proposed §§ 54.4980H-1(a)(18) and 54.4980H-3. This includes any full-time employees who may perform services for multiple ALE members within the applicable large employer.[5] Under the proposed regulations, only ALE members with full-time employees are subject to the filing and statement furnishing requirements of section 6056 (and only with respect to their full-time employees).

Generally, the ALE member providing the section 6056 reporting is the common law employer. Disregarded entities are treated for section 4980H purposes, and therefore for section 6056 purposes, similarly to the way they are treated for employment tax purposes, so that the reporting requirements under section 6056 are imposed on a disregarded entity that is an applicable large employer, and not on its owner.[6]

IX. *General Method - Content, Manner, and Timing of Information Required to be Reported to the IRS and Furnished to Full-Time Employees*

This section describes the general method for reporting to the IRS and furnishing statements to employees pursuant to section 6056 that is set forth in the proposed regulations. This general method would be available for all employers and with respect to reporting for all employees. Treasury and the IRS are also considering certain simplified reporting methods, such as using codes on Form W-2 to report whether full-time employees, spouses, and their dependents have been offered coverage, which in some cases may be available only with respect to certain groups of employees. In those cases, with respect to those employees for whom the simplified reporting method was not available, the employer would use the general method. In any case, however, the simplified reporting methods under consideration would be optional so that an employer could choose to report for all of its full-time employees using the general method described in these proposed regulations even if a simplified reporting method is available. For a further description of the simplified reporting methods under consideration, see section XI of this preamble.

A. *Information Reporting to the IRS*

In accordance with section 6056, the proposed regulations provide for every ALE member to file a section 6056 return with respect to its full-time employees. Similar to the separate Form W-2, Wage and Tax Statement, filed by an employer for each employee and the Form W-3, Transmittal of Wage and Tax Statements, filed as a transmittal form for the Forms W-2, the proposed regulations provide that a separate return is required for each full-time employee, accompanied by a single transmittal form for all of the returns filed for a given calendar year.

As a general method, the proposed regulations further provide that the section 6056 return may be made by filing Form 1094-C (a transmittal) and Form 1095-C (an employee statement), or other forms the IRS designates. Alternatively, the section 6056 return may be made by filing other form(s) designated by the IRS or a substitute form. Under the proposed regulations, a substitute form must include all of the information required to be reported on Forms 1094-C and 1095-C or other forms the IRS designates and comply with applicable revenue procedures or other published guidance relating to substitute returns. See § 601.601(d)(2). In accordance with usual procedures, these forms will be made available in draft form at a later date.

B. *Information Required to Be Reported and Furnished*

The proposed regulations provide that every ALE member will report on the section 6056 information return the following information: (1) the name, address, and employer identification number of the ALE member, the name and telephone number of the applicable large employer's contact person, and the calendar year for which the information is reported; (2) a certification as to whether the ALE member offered to its full-time employees (and their dependents) the opportunity to enroll in minimum essential coverage under an eligible employer-sponsored plan (as defined in section 5000A(f)(2)), by calendar month; (3) the number of full-time employees for each month during the calendar year; (4) for each full-time employee, the months during the calendar year for which coverage under the plan was available; (5) for each full-time employee, the employee's share of the lowest cost monthly premium (self-only) for coverage providing minimum value offered to that full-time employee under an eligible

---

[5] For example, if an employee performs services for two applicable large employer members within an applicable large employer and the combined hours of service for the two applicable large employer members are sufficient to trigger a reporting obligation under section 6056, each applicable large employer member is required to file and furnish a section 6056 return with respect to services performed by the employee for that applicable large employer member. See proposed § 54.4980H-5(d).

[6] Specifically, the proposed regulations under section 7701 (REG-138006-12 [78 FR 218]) treat the disregarded entity (as defined in § 301.7701-2) as a corporation with respect to the reporting requirements under section 6056. See proposed § 301.7701-2(c)(2)(v)(A)(5). These rules would also apply to a qualified subchapter S subsidiary. See proposed § 1.1361-4(a)(8)(i)(E).

employer-sponsored plan, by calendar month; and (6) the name, address, and taxpayer identification number of each full-time employee during the calendar year and the months, if any, during which the employee was covered under an eligible employer-sponsored plan. In addition, the proposed regulations provide, as with other information reporting, that the section 6056 information return may request such other information as the Secretary may prescribe or as may be required by the form or instructions.

As part of the effort to minimize the cost and administrative steps associated with the reporting requirements, Treasury and the IRS have sought to identify any information that would not be relevant to individual taxpayers or the IRS for purposes of administering the premium tax credit and employer shared responsibility provisions or that is already provided at the same time through other means. Specifically, the proposed regulations do not require the reporting of the following four data elements (a more detailed description of the data elements that Treasury and the IRS anticipate will be included is provided later in this section of the preamble).

First, the proposed regulations do not require the reporting of the length of any waiting period, because the length of the waiting period is not relevant for administration of the premium tax credit or employer shared responsibility provisions or for an individual in preparing his or her tax return. However, Treasury and the IRS anticipate that information will be requested, using an indicator code, regarding whether an employee's coverage was not effective during certain months because of a waiting period since this information is relevant to the administration of the employer shared responsibility provisions.

Second, the proposed regulations do not require reporting of the employer's share of the total allowed costs of benefits provided under the plan because this information also is not relevant to the administration of the premium tax credit and the employer shared responsibility provisions. In contrast, whether the employer-sponsored plan provides minimum value coverage is relevant information; accordingly, Treasury and the IRS anticipate that information will be requested, also using an indicator code.

Third, the proposed regulations do not require the reporting of the monthly premium for the lowest-cost option in each of the enrollment categories (such as self-only coverage or family coverage) under the plan. Rather, because only the lowest-cost option of self-only coverage offered under any of the enrollment categories for which the employee is eligible is relevant to the determination of whether coverage is affordable (and thus to the administration of the premium tax credit and employer shared responsibility provisions), that is the only cost information proposed to be requested.

Fourth, the proposed regulations do not require the reporting of the months, if any, during which any of the employee's dependents were covered under the plan. Instead, the proposed regulations require reporting only regarding whether the employee was covered under a plan. This is because information relating to the months during which any of the employee's dependents were covered under the plan will be reported on the section 6055 information return associated with that employee's coverage.

Under the proposed regulations, each ALE member must file and furnish the section 6056 return and employee statement using its EIN. Any ALE member that does not have an EIN may easily apply for one online, by telephone, fax, or mail. See Publication 1635, Employer Identification Number, for further information at *www.irs.gov*.

Having considered the information required by section 6056 and the information needed to verify employer-sponsored coverage and to administer the employer shared responsibility provisions under section 4980H and the premium tax credit, Treasury and the IRS anticipate that as part of the general method for section 6056 reporting, the IRS will need certain information not specifically set forth under section 6056 but authorized under section 6056(b)(2)(F). Accordingly, the proposed regulations provide, in a manner similar to other information reporting guidance, that additional information may be prescribed by guidance, forms, or instructions. Treasury and the IRS are also considering potential simplified reporting methods that in certain situations may permit an employer to provide less information than all data elements required under the general method for reporting. See section XI of this preamble.

Under the general method of section 6056 reporting, the following information is expected to be requested, through the use of indicator codes for some information, as part of the section 6056 return (as well as an indication of how many individual employee statements are being submitted):

(1) information as to whether the coverage offered to employees and their dependents under an employer-sponsored plan meets minimum value and whether the employee had the opportunity to enroll his or her spouse in the coverage;

(2) the total number of employees, by calendar month;

(3) whether an employee's effective date of coverage was affected by a waiting period;

(4) if the ALE member was not conducting business during any particular month, by month;

(5) if the ALE member expects that it will not be an ALE member the following year;

(6) information regarding whether the ALE member is a person that is a member of an aggregated group, determined under section 414(b), 414(c), 414(m), or 414(o), and, if applicable, the name and EIN of each employer member of the aggregated group constituting the applicable large employer on any day of the calendar year for which the information is reported;

(7) if an appropriately designated entity is reporting on behalf of an ALE member that is a governmental unit or any agency or instrumentality thereof for purposes of section 6056, the name, address, and identification number of the appropriately designated person;

(8) if an ALE member is a contributing employer to a multiemployer plan, whether a full-time employee is treated as eligible to participate in a multiemployer plan due to the employer's contributions to the multiemployer plan; and

(9) if the administrator of a multiemployer plan is reporting on behalf of the ALE member with respect to the ALE member's full-time employees who are eligible for coverage under the multiemployer plan, the name, address, and identification number of the administrator of the multiemployer plan (in addition to the name, address, and EIN of the ALE member already required under the proposed regulations).

C. Use of Indicator Codes to Provide Information With Respect to a Particular Full-Time Employee

In an effort to simplify and streamline the section 6056 reporting process even under the general section 6056 reporting rules, Treasury and the IRS anticipate that certain of the information described above as applied to a particular full-time employee will be reported to the IRS, and furnished to the full-time employee, through the use of a code rather than by providing specific or detailed information. Specifically, it is contemplated that the following information will be reported with respect to each full-time employee for each calendar month using a code:[7]

(1) minimum essential coverage meeting minimum value was offered to:

a. the employee only;

---

[7] Treasury and the IRS have received comments regarding whether transition relief previously provided in the section 4980H proposed regulations (REG-138006-12 [78 FR 218]) with respect to the transition from 2013 to 2014 will be extended to the transition from 2014 to 2015. The issue is currently under consideration and will be addressed in future guidance under section 4980H. If further transition relief is provided under section 4980H, it is expected that additional indicator codes will be available on the section 6056 return to indicate that an employer is using the transition relief.

b. the employee and the employee's dependents only;

c. the employee and the employee's spouse only; or

d. the employee, the employee's spouse and dependents;

(2) coverage was not offered to the employee and:

a. the employee was in a waiting period that complies with the requirements of PHS Act section 2708 and its implementing regulations;

b. the employee was not a full-time employee;

c. the employee was not employed by the ALE member during that month; or

d. no other code or exception applies;

(3) coverage was offered to the employee for the month although the employee was not a full-time employee during that month; and

(4) the ALE member met one of the affordability safe harbors under proposed §54.4980H-5(e)(2) with respect to the employee.

It is anticipated that if multiple codes apply with respect to a full-time employee for a particular calendar month, the reporting format will accommodate the necessary codes.

D. *Section 6056 Statements to Full-time Employees*

Under the general section 6056 reporting rules set forth in the proposed regulations, every ALE member required to file a section 6056 return must furnish a section 6056 employee statement to each of its full-time employees that includes the name, address and EIN of the ALE member and the information required to be shown on the section 6056 return with respect to the full-time employee. The section 6056 employee statement is not required to include a copy of the transmittal form that accompanies the returns. As part of the potential simplified reporting methods Treasury and the IRS are also considering whether, in certain circumstances, other methods of furnishing information to an employee may be sufficient (for example, through the use of a code on the Form W-2). For a detailed description of these potential simplified reporting methods, see section XI of this preamble.

Some employers may wish to have the flexibility to use a substitute type of statement to provide the necessary information to full-time employees. The proposed regulations provide that the section 6056 employee statement may be made by furnishing a copy of the section 6056 return on Form 1095-C (or another form the IRS designates) or a substitute employee statement for that full-time employee. Under the proposed regulations, a substitute statement must include the information required to be shown on the section 6056 return filed with the IRS with respect to that employee and must comply with applicable revenue procedures or other published guidance relating to substitute statements. See §601.601(d)(2). These proposed regulations provide that section 6056 employee statements filed using Form 1095-C or another form the IRS designates will be included in the proposed IRS truncated TIN program. Under this proposed program, an IRS truncated taxpayer identifying number may be used as the identifying number for an individual in lieu of the identifying number appearing on the corresponding information return filed with the IRS. See the proposed regulations on IRS Truncated Taxpayer Identification Numbers (REG-148873-09 [78 FR 913]).

E. *Time for Filing Section 6056 Returns and Furnishing Employee Statements*

The proposed regulations provide that section 6056 returns must be filed with the IRS annually, no later than February 28 (March 31 if filed electronically) of the year immediately following the calendar year to which the return relates. This is the same filing schedule applicable to other information returns with which employers are familiar such as Forms W-2 and 1099. Because Notice 2013-45 provided transition relief for section 6056 reporting for 2014, the first section 6056 returns required to be filed are for the 2015 calendar year and must be filed no later than March 1, 2016 (February 28, 2016, being a Sunday), or March 31, 2016, if filed electronically. In addition, the regulations propose that the section 6056 employee statements be furnished annually to full-time employees on or before January 31 of the year immediately following the calendar year to which the employee statements relate. This means that the first section 6056 employee statements (meaning the statements for 2015) must be furnished no later than February 1, 2016 (January 31, 2016, being a Sunday).

In preparation for the application of the section 4980H provisions beginning in 2015, employers are encouraged to voluntarily comply for 2014 (that is, for section 6056 returns and statements filed and furnished in 2015) with the information reporting provisions (once the information reporting rules have been issued) and to maintain or expand health coverage in 2014. Real-world testing of reporting systems and plan designs through voluntary compliance for 2014 will contribute to a smoother transition to full implementation for 2015.

Some commenters asked for use of an alternate filing date for employers whose health plan is not a calendar year plan. While Treasury and the IRS understand that employers may collect information on a plan year basis, employees generally will need to receive their section 6056 employee statements early in the calendar year in order to have the requisite information to correctly and completely file their income tax returns reflecting any available premium tax credit. For this reason, the proposed regulations do not adopt this suggestion. However, Treasury and the IRS are considering a simplified reporting method, described in section XI of this preamble, that in certain circumstances could permit the employer to report the required information on the Form W-2 which is already being furnished to an employee on the same schedule.

These proposed regulations do not include rules regarding extensions of the time to file section 6056 returns but this topic is addressed elsewhere. Specifically, the notice of proposed rulemaking under section 6055 (REG-132455-11) includes proposed amendments to the regulations under section 6081 relating to general rules on extensions of time to file to include returns under both sections 6055 and 6056. The final section 6056 regulations are expected to cross-reference the amendments to the regulations under section 6081. These proposed regulations reserve a paragraph for this cross-reference.

F. *Manner of Filing of Section 6056 Information Returns and Furnishing of Section 6056 Employee Statements.*

Treasury and the IRS understand that electronic filing is often easier and more efficient for taxpayers, and several commenters requested that employers be permitted to file section 6056 returns electronically. The proposed regulations require electronic filing of section 6056 information returns except for an ALE member filing fewer than 250 returns during the calendar year. Each section 6056 return for a full-time employee is a separate return. Although an ALE member filing fewer than 250 returns during the calendar year may always choose to make the section 6056 returns on the prescribed paper form, that member is permitted (and encouraged) to file section 6056 returns electronically. This proposed requirement for electronic filing is the same as the current requirements for other information returns.

The proposed regulations provide that all returns are aggregated for the purpose of applying the 250-return threshold so that, for example, an ALE member required to file 150 section 6056 returns and 200 Forms W-2 will be required to electronically file section 6056 returns. A reporting entity must submit the prescribed form(s) to request authorization and obtain a Transmitter Control Code from the IRS to be able to file an information return electronically.

In addition to electronic filing, Treasury and the IRS understand that electronic methods are often a simpler and more efficient method to supply employees with the required information, and several commenters requested that employers be permitted to electronically furnish section 6056 employee statements to full-time employees. In response, the proposed regulations permit electronic furnishing of section 6056 employee statements if certain notice, consent, and hardware or software requirements are met. To provide rules for electronic furnishing with which employers are already familiar, the proposed regulations adopt by analogy the process currently in place for the electronic furnishing of employee statements (that is, Forms W-2) pursuant to section 6051 and applicable regulations.

X. Combined Reporting Under Section 6056 and Section 6051 or 6055

In addition to the reporting under section 6056, two other reporting provisions provide for annual reporting with respect to certain individuals and the furnishing of statements to those individuals. Specifically, section 6051 requires employers to provide Forms W-2 reporting wages paid and taxes withheld. Section 6055 requires information reporting by any person that provides minimum essential coverage to an individual. ALE members that provide minimum essential coverage on a self-insured basis are subject to the reporting requirements of all three sections (6051, 6055 and 6056). Notices 2012-32 and 2012-33 requested comments on how to minimize duplication in reporting under these provisions.

Several commenters recommended that the regulations allow combined information reporting under sections 6055 and 6056 for applicable large employers that sponsor self-insured plans and must report under both sections. Other commenters recommended that employers be permitted to use a single information return to report under sections 6051 (Form W-2) and 6055. Some commenters suggested adding section 6055 or section 6056 reporting to Form W-2.

Because not all employers are subject to each of these three reporting requirements, independent reporting methods under each section need to be available; otherwise, employers subject to only one reporting requirement may have to expend additional effort to use a combined reporting method. Optional combined reporting therefore would require development of multiple forms for each reporting requirement (some forms for combined reporting, other forms for separate reporting), which could create administrative complexity and create confusion for employees.

In addition, any consideration of combined reporting must take into account that sections 6051, 6055 and 6056 apply to different types of entities (subject to the various reporting requirements, which differ among the Code provisions), and require reporting of different types of information. Section 6051 requires reporting of certain wage and wage-related information on an annual basis by all employers for all employees (and only employees). Section 6055 requires reporting of certain health coverage information by various entities (issuers, employers sponsoring self-insured group health plans, and governmental units) only for individuals who are actually covered (and not for individuals who are offered coverage but do not enroll), and multiple covered individuals may be included on one return. Section 6056 requires reporting of information by applicable large employers on offers of coverage that have or have not been made only to full-time employees (whether or not the offer has been accepted). Further, unlike Form W-2 reporting under section 6051, which provides annual information, both sections 6055 and 6056 require reporting some information on a monthly basis. Accordingly, the general section 6056 reporting method under the proposed regulations does not assume overall combined reporting under sections 6051, 6055, and 6056.

However, as described more fully below in section XI of this preamble, Treasury and the IRS are considering whether it may be possible to permit a type of combined reporting under sections 6051 and 6056 by providing an option to use a code on the Form W-2 in certain circumstances to provide information needed by both the employee and the IRS rather than through the use of the section 6056 employee statement (with employer-level information being provided separately). In addition, in other limited circumstances involving no-cost or very low-cost coverage provided under a self-insured group health plan, Treasury and the IRS are considering whether the employee and the IRS could rely solely on the information provided by the employer on a section 6055 return and the Form W-2 without any further information reporting under section 6056. For further discussion of these potential approaches, see section XI of this preamble.

In response to comments, Treasury and the IRS also have considered suggestions to use, for section 6055 and 6056 reporting purposes, information that employers communicate to employees about employer-sponsored coverage prior to employees' potential enrollment in Exchange coverage. These comments have observed that, under the Affordable Care Act, employers are required to provide pre-enrollment information to employees by various means, including information in the Notice of Coverage Options provided to employees pursuant to the requirements under section 18B of the Fair Labor Standards Act[8] in the Exchanges and potentially via the Employer Coverage Tool developed by the Department of Health and Human Services (HHS) that supports the application for enrollment in a qualified health plan and insurance affordability programs.[9]

Treasury and the IRS have considered and coordinated with the Departments of HHS and Labor regarding the various reporting provisions with a view to identifying ways to make the entire process as effective and efficient as possible for all parties. That said, the various reports are designed for different purposes, and pre-enrollment reporting regarding anticipated employer coverage in an upcoming coverage year is unlikely to be helpful to individual taxpayers in accurately completing their tax returns more than a year later, after the coverage year. Among other issues, the pre-enrollment information may not be readily available to individuals at the time they are filing their tax returns, could be confused with the more recently received pre-enrollment information that applies to the subsequent year (not the year for which the tax return is being filed), and is in a format that does not facilitate easy transfer to the appropriate location on the Federal income tax return. Notwithstanding these challenges, Treasury and the IRS continue to work with the other Departments and stakeholders to consider approaches that might help minimize cost and administrative complexity and realize efficiencies in the reporting process.

Both sections 6055 and 6056 require employers to furnish to employees information about health care coverage. Solely for the purpose of furnishing information to employees (as opposed to filing with the IRS), Treasury and the IRS are considering whether employers sponsoring self-insured group health plans could fulfill their obligation to furnish an employee statement under both sections 6055 and 6056 through the use of a single substitute statement, within the parameters of the rules provided in revenue procedures or other published guidance relating to substitute returns. See § 601.601(d)(2) of this chapter.

XI. Potential Simplified Methods for Section 6056 Information Reporting

In developing these regulations, Treasury and the IRS have sought to develop simplified reporting methods that will minimize the cost and administrative tasks for employers, consistent with the statutory requirements to file an information return and furnish an employee statement to each full-time employee. Comments have suggested that, at least for some employers, the collection, assembling and processing of the necessary data into an appropriate format for filing may not be necessary if the employer offers sufficient coverage to make it unlikely that the employer will be subject to an assessable payment under section 4980H because the employee will be ineligible for a premium tax credit. Treasury and the IRS have considered these comments in formulating the potential simplified reporting methods described in this section. If Treasury and the IRS adopt one or more of these simplified reporting methods, they would be optional alternatives to the general reporting method set forth in the proposed regulations, which could substantially reduce the data elements reported using the general method. It is anticipated that, if an employer uses one or more of the simplified reporting methods, the employer would indicate on its section 6056 transmittal which simplified reporting method(s) was used and the number of employees for which the particular method was used. Comments are invited on these potential simplified reporting methods and on other possible simplified approaches that would benefit employers while providing sufficient and timely information to individual taxpayers and the IRS.

---

[8] On May 8, 2013, the Department of Labor issued Technical Release 2013-02 providing temporary guidance under Fair Labor Standards Act section 18B, as well as model notices. See Technical Release 2013-02, model notice for employers who offer a health plan to some or all employees, and model notice for employers who do not offer a health

plan, available at http://www.dol.gov/ebsa/healthreform/. Guidance on the Notice to Employees of Coverage

[9] Available at https://www.healthcare.gov/downloads/ECT_Application_508_130615.pdf

The information provided to the IRS and the employee pursuant to section 6056 is important for administering the section 4980H shared employer responsibility provisions and the premium tax credit. However, in looking at the potential flow of information, Treasury and the IRS have determined that in some circumstances only some of the information required under the general method is necessary. Treasury and the IRS have attempted to identify the specific groups of employees for whom simplified reporting would provide sufficient information, and simplified reporting approaches for these groups are outlined below. In many situations, not every full-time employee of an employer would fit into the groups of employees for which simplified reporting would be available. In that case, the employer would continue to use the general reporting method in the proposed regulations for those full-time employees for whom the employers could not use a simplified method. However, it is anticipated that a significant number of employers will have a sufficient number of employees that fit into one or more of the categories described below to make use of the simplified reporting method preferable to the general reporting method.

Subsections A through F of this section XI of the preamble describe, and comments are invited on, possible simplified methods of reporting under section 6056. Each of these possible methods would be optional for the reporting employer, and, except where specifically noted, would not affect any reporting obligations under section 6055.

Subsection A . . . . Eliminating Section 6056 Employee Statements in Favor of Form W-2 Reporting for Certain Groups of Employees Offered Coverage

Subsection B . . . . No Need to Determine Full-Time Employees If Minimum Value Coverage Is Offered to All Potentially Full-Time Employees

Subsection C . . . . Self-Insured Employers Offering Employees, Their Spouses and Dependents Mandatory No-Cost Minimum Value Coverage

Subsection D . . . . Voluntarily Reporting Section 6056 Elements During or Prior to the Year of Coverage

Subsection E . . . . Reporting for Employees Potentially Ineligible for the Premium Tax Credit

Subsection F . . . . Combinations of Simplified Reporting Methods

A. Eliminating Section 6056 Employee Statements in Favor of Form W-2 Reporting for Certain Groups of Employees Offered Coverage

In response to stakeholder comments, Treasury and the IRS are considering allowing employers in certain circumstances to report offers of minimum value coverage on an employee's Form W-2, instead of reporting the offers to the IRS on a section 6056 employee statement or furnishing a section 6056 employee statement to the employee. The reporting is envisioned as using an existing box on the Form W-2 to provide the monthly dollar amount of the required employee contribution for the lowest cost minimum value self-only coverage offered to the employee and using a letter code to describe the offer of coverage. Specifically, Treasury and the IRS anticipate that this approach could be used for any employee employed by the employer for the entire calendar year when the offer, the individuals to whom the offer is made, and the employee contribution for the lowest-cost option for self-only coverage all remained the same for all twelve months of the calendar year. The letter code could be used to indicate that minimum value coverage was offered to: (1) the employee, the employee's spouse and the employee's dependents, (2) the employee and the employee's dependents but not the employee's spouse; (3) the employee and the employee's spouse but not the employee's dependents; (4) the employee, but not the employee's spouse or the employee's dependents; or that the employee was (5) only offered coverage that was not minimum value coverage; or (6) not offered coverage. For this purpose, an employer is treated as offering coverage to the employee's spouse or dependents even if the employee does not have a spouse or dependent, if the employee could elect such coverage if the employee did have a spouse or dependent. If an employee was not offered coverage, it is anticipated that the dollar amount of the employee share of the lowest-cost employee-only coverage option would be shown as zero.

Example: Employer has 100 full-time employees, all of whom are employed for the entire year. Employer offers all of its full-time employees, spouses and dependents the opportunity to enroll in health care coverage that provides minimum value. Under the potential simplified reporting method, it is contemplated that, for all employees, Employer would be permitted to avoid filing or furnishing section 6056 employee statements if it used a letter code on the Form W-2 to report that an offer of coverage had been made to the employee, the employee's spouse (if any), and the employee's dependents (if any), and a dollar amount indicating the required monthly employee contribution to purchase the lowest cost option offered to the employee for self-only coverage.

Treasury and the IRS are also considering whether this or a similar simplified reporting method could be extended to cases in which the required monthly employee contribution is below a specified threshold. For example, if the annual employee cost of self-only coverage is $800 or less, the employer would be permitted to report zero as the employee cost. The $800 amount is less than 9.5 percent of the federal poverty line for a single individual. Thus, regardless of the size of the employee's household or the level of other income or loss of any member of the employee's household, either the employer's coverage will be affordable for purposes of section 36B(c)(2)(C)(i) or the employee's household income will be less than 100 percent of the federal poverty line and the employee will not be an applicable taxpayer under section 36B(c)(2) who is eligible for the credit. In addition, even if other income increases the employee's household income, the employee would not be entitled to the affordability exemption to the shared responsibility payment under section 5000A(e)(1) because the $800 amount would not exceed 8 percent of the employee's household income. Alternatively, if other losses reduce the employee's household income below the income tax filing threshold, the employee will qualify for the exemption under section 5000A(e)(2), and the information otherwise reported under section 6056 would not be required to determine whether the employee satisfied section 5000A. Comments are also requested on the extent to which this approach could reasonably be combined with the other simplified reporting methods described in this section XI of the preamble.

An employer that decides to use this simplified reporting method would not be required to file or furnish a section 6056 employee statement with respect to the employees for whom this method was used. Instead, the employer would simply indicate on a section 6056 transmittal that it had chosen to use this method. If the Form W-2 for an employee used an EIN other than the employer's EIN (for example, a thirdparty payor treated as an employer under section 3401(d)(1) of the Code filed the Form W-2), the employer (that is, the ALE member) may be required as part of the 6056 transmittal to identify those employees for whom a third party reported on Form W-2 without the employer's EIN and to list the employees' social security numbers.

Stakeholders have inquired whether a similar optional Form W-2 reporting method could be used for employees offered coverage under their employer's plan for less than a full calendar year (for example for a new employee hired during the year), but offered no coverage for the remainder of the year. Treasury and the IRS note that this type of reporting would leave gaps in information that would otherwise be used for tax administration purposes. For example, the reporting would not provide any information regarding the particular calendar months during which coverage was offered (or not offered). Even if the employer represented that the coverage was offered during all periods of employment, the reporting would not be able to be reconciled, for example, with another Form W-2 received by the employee from another employer using the same reporting method. That is because while both employers would report the number of months coverage was offered, that information would not be sufficient to determine whether offers of coverage were overlapping (because the employee was employed simultaneously at both employers).

Additionally, for months for which coverage was not offered, information as to whether the employee was employed and also the reason coverage was not offered during certain months of the calendar year would not be captured (for example, the employee was in a waiting period or employed but not as a full-time employee). The specific reason coverage was not offered is relevant to the administration of the employer shared responsibility provisions since the failure to offer coverage for certain reasons does not result in an assessable payment under the employer shared responsibility provisions for a calendar month, even if the full-time employee receives a premium tax credit for that month. Comments are requested on whether this approach to reporting would be useful for employers and, if so, on possible ways to address issues concerning the information gaps that would exist in reporting on employees offered coverage for less than a full calendar year.

B. *No Need to Determine Full-Time Employees If Minimum Value Coverage Is Offered to All Potentially Full-Time Employees*

Treasury and the IRS understand that some employers offer coverage to all or nearly all of their employees, and are able to accurately represent that the only employees not offered coverage are not full-time employees. In that case, the employer will have determined that it would not owe an assessable payment under section 4980H(a) because it would have made an offer of coverage to all of its full-time employees. However, the employer might not have determined whether every employee to whom coverage is offered is or is not a full-time employee. Treasury and the IRS are considering whether these employers may provide section 6056 reporting that does not identify the number of full-time employees and that does not specify whether a particular employee offered coverage is a full-time employee, provided that the employer certifies that all of its employees to whom it did not offer coverage during the calendar year were not full-time employees (or were otherwise ineligible for coverage, for example because they were in the initial permitted waiting period following the date of hire). This method would permit the employer to forgo identifying the full-time status of its employees prior to filing a section 6056 return. However, if an employee who was offered coverage claimed a premium tax credit, the employer could be asked to confirm at a later date (after the filing of the section 6056 return and the relevant Form 1040 return) whether that employee was a full-time employee during that calendar year (in the same manner that an employer reporting only on behalf of full-time employees might later be asked about the status of an employee claiming the premium tax credit if the employee was not listed on that employer's section 6056 return). Treasury and the IRS recognize that this method often would result in over-reporting of certain elements in the sense that reporting would occur with respect to one or more employees who may not be full-time employees during the calendar year. But some employers have indicated that they anticipate relatively few of their employees will claim the premium tax credit, and that determining those few employees' status as full-time employees later would be administratively easier than determining the full-time employee status of all employees at the time of the initial filing.

Example: Employer has 100 employees. Employer makes an offer of minimum value coverage to 90 of the employees. Employer has determined that the ten employees to whom coverage is not offered are not full-time employees for any calendar month during the year. Employer has not determined which of the remaining 90 employees were full-time employees for one or more calendar months during the year. Employer certifies as part of its section 6056 transmittal return that the only employees to whom it did not offer coverage were not full-time employees or were otherwise not required to be offered coverage for all months of employment (for example, a full-time employee was hired in November and, under the terms of the plan, which comply with the Affordable Care Act, would not be initially offered coverage until the following calendar year).

Employer would file a section 6056 return and furnish an employee statement for each of the 90 employees, but would not be required to report either the total number of full-time employees for the year or whether any particular employee was a full-time employee for any calendar month during the year. If one of the employees included as part of the return declined the offer of coverage and properly claimed a premium tax credit with respect to coverage provided through an Exchange, and the employer were contacted by the IRS to determine whether the employer did or did not owe an assessable payment under section 4980H(b), the employer could determine at that point whether the employee was a full-time employee for one or more months during that calendar year and supply that information to the IRS.

C. *Self-Insured Employers Offering Employees, Their Spouses, and Dependents Mandatory No-Cost Minimum Value Coverage*

Some employers may provide mandatory minimum value coverage under a selfinsured group health plan to an employee, an employee's spouse, and an employee's dependents, with no employee contribution. In that case, none of those individuals would be eligible for a premium tax credit for any month during which the coverage was provided, and the employer would indicate on the return required under section 6055 for the employee all months for which that coverage was provided with respect to each individual in the employee's family. Because the section 6055 return would provide the individual taxpayers the necessary information to accurately file the taxpayers' income tax returns, and would provide the IRS the information concerning those employees to administer the premium tax credit and employer shared responsibility provisions, Treasury and the IRS are considering whether for those employees the employer could file and furnish only the return required under section 6055, a code on the Form W-2, the summary information provided in the section 6056 transmittal form, and no further information reporting under section 6056.

D. *Voluntarily Reporting Section 6056 Elements During or Prior to the Year of Coverage*

Some employers have expressed an interest in voluntarily reporting information about the coverage they offer their employees prior to the end of a coverage year, for example at their open enrollment or before the open enrollment at the Exchanges, on the theory that earlier section 6056 reporting to the IRS could lead to greater efficiency in the employer verification system employed by Exchanges to determine eligibility for premium tax credits. Under such an arrangement, they believe that if some employers chose to provide part of their section 6056 reporting to the IRS earlier in the process, the IRS, in turn, would be able to transmit any pertinent data to the Exchanges.

A proposal of this kind would need to address a number of issues. First, the regulations under section 6103 do not authorize the IRS to share taxpayer information in this manner. Even if this information sharing were permitted, information reporting plays a role in enabling individuals to file complete and accurate tax returns. Under the proposal, individuals would not receive the information for their tax return preparation proximate to when they are completing their tax returns. Employees may bear less burden and prepare more accurate tax returns when their employer furnishes a statement at the start of the relevant tax season reflecting all the information the employee needs to file a correct tax return for the prior year. Gaps in complete and timely information increase the need for additional follow-up communication among employers, employees, and the IRS.

Also, offering two sets of reporting alternatives with filing occurring at different time periods would present challenges. Because the reporting options would be voluntary, different reporting protocols and regimes would need to be established and would need to accommodate employer choices to change the method of reporting from year to year. The multiple forms, procedures, and protocols could create complexity and be difficult to administer.

In addition, the information about the offer of coverage made before the year starts may change during the calendar year. For example, during the year, an employee may be hired or may terminate employment, a part-time employee may become full-time and be eligible for different coverage options, or an employee may change positions during the year and no longer be offered coverage. Accordingly, disclosure before the coverage year does not adequately substitute for disclosure to employees and reporting to the IRS after the coverage year.

Employers, employees, and the IRS share the goal of aligning eligibility for advance payments of premium tax credits as closely as possible with eligibility for the premium tax credit on the employee's annual tax return filed after the coverage year. This would reduce confusion and minimize the risk of employees owing advance payments back as liabilities on their tax returns. Regardless of the final rules on section 6056 information reporting, employers are encouraged to make their pre-enrollment disclosures to employees and Exchanges as effective and helpful to individuals as possible.

Comments are invited on whether there could be a way to design such a voluntary partial early reporting arrangement that would reduce complexity and avoid confusion for employers and employees, be administrable for the IRS, and provide timely information to individuals so that they can meet their income tax filing obligation without undue burden or undue risk of inaccuracy.

E. *Reporting for Employees Potentially Ineligible for the Premium Tax Credit*

Some employers have indicated that, because many of their employees are relatively highly paid, they are unlikely to be eligible for a premium tax credit. The assumption is that the employee's household income is likely to exceed 400 percent of the Federal poverty line, and therefore the employee would not benefit from receiving the information otherwise included with a section 6056 employee statement. Further, because the employee is unlikely to qualify for a premium tax credit, employers have stated that the information will not be useful to the IRS in administering the employer shared responsibility provisions because the precondition of a section 4980H(b) assessable payment—that the employee receive a premium tax credit—is unlikely to be satisfied.

Treasury and the IRS have considered this request and welcome comments both on its potential usefulness to employers and its administrability. Employers would still need to report to the IRS the months during which the employee was a full-time employee, at least to the extent the employee being was included in a full-time employee count. Additionally, employers will not be in a position to know the correlation between an employee's Form W-2 wages and household income with sufficient accuracy to determine whether an employee may be eligible for the premium tax credit. The only pertinent information the employer retains is the employee's annual wages, yet the poverty level from which the premium tax credit income threshold is determined varies considerably based on family size (which employers will not necessarily know). In addition, employees for whom an employer may use an affordability safe harbor based on wages for purposes of compliance with the employer shared responsibility provisions under section 4980H might still be eligible for a premium tax credit based on their household income. Employers generally do not know employees' household income, and will not have information as to whether the employee (or another member of the employee's household) has incurred losses or expenses (such as alimony, casualty losses, Schedule C business deductions, and the like) that reduce the employee's household modified adjusted gross income below 400 percent of the Federal poverty line. Accordingly, it is unclear whether Form W-2 wages alone would provide sufficient information to determine eligibility for the premium tax credit because the employee's household income may be well below the employee's Form W-2 wages. Comments are requested as to whether there is a level of Form W-2 wages at which such a determination might be made with sufficient confidence, and whether that level of wages is so high as not to be of practical use to employers.

F. *Combinations of Simplified Reporting Methods*

The potential simplified reporting methods described above would apply to particular groups of employees that in many cases would not overlap. In such cases, two different potential simplified reporting methods could not be applied to the same employee. Treasury and the IRS anticipate that, to the extent any of these potential reporting methods are adopted in final regulations or other administrative guidance, including forms and instructions, an employer would be permitted to use different simplified methods for different employees at the employer's election.

XII. *Person Responsible For Section 6056 Reporting*

Under the proposed regulations, in general, each ALE member must file a section 6056 return with respect to its full-time employees for a calendar year.

A. *Special Rules for Governmental Units: Designation*

In accordance with section 6056(e), the proposed regulations provide that in the case of any ALE member that is a governmental unit or any agency or instrumentality thereof (together referred to in this preamble as a governmental unit), that governmental unit may report under section 6056 on its own behalf or may appropriately designate another person or persons to report on its behalf.[10] For purposes of designation, another person is appropriately designated for purposes of the filing and furnishing requirements of section 6056 if that other person is part of or related to the same governmental unit as the ALE member. For example, a political subdivision of a state may designate the state, another political subdivision of the state, or an agency or instrumentality of the foregoing as the designated person for purposes of section 6056 reporting. The person designated might be the governmental unit that operates the relevant health plan or the governmental unit that does other information reporting on behalf of the designating governmental unit. Further, the governmental unit may designate more than one governmental unit to file and furnish under section 6056 on its behalf, such as, for example, if different categories of employees are offered coverage under different health plans operated by different governmental units. In addition, a governmental unit may designate another person to file and furnish with respect to all or some of its full-time employees. If the designation is accepted by the designee and is made before the filing deadline, the designated governmental unit is the designated entity responsible for section 6056 reporting.

The person (or persons) appropriately designated for this purpose would report under section 6056 on behalf of the ALE member. Accordingly, the person (or persons) appropriately designated is (are) the person(s) responsible for section 6056 reporting on behalf of the ALE member and subject to the penalties for failure to comply with information return requirements under sections 6721 and 6722. However, the ALE member remains subject to the requirements of section 4980H.

Under the proposed regulations, a separate section 6056 return and transmittal must be filed for each ALE member for which the appropriately designated person is reporting. The designated entity must report its name, address, and EIN on the section 6056 return to indicate it is the appropriately designated person.

The proposed regulations further provide that the designation under section 6056(e) must be in writing and must contain certain language. Specifically, under the proposed regulations, the designation must be signed by both the ALE member and the designated person, and must be effective under all applicable laws. The proposed regulations also require that the designation set forth the name and EIN of the designated person, and appoint that person as the person responsible for reporting under section 6056 on behalf of the ALE member. The designation must contain information identifying the category of full-time employees (which may be full-time employees eligible for a specified health plan, or in a particular job category, provided that the specific employees covered by the designation can be identified) for which the designated person is responsible for reporting under section 6056 on behalf of the ALE member. If the designated person is responsible for reporting under section 6056 for all full-time employees of an ALE member, the designation should so indicate.

The designation must also contain language that the designated person agrees that it is the appropriately designated person under section 6056(e), and an acknowledgement that the designated person is responsible for reporting under section 6056 on behalf of the ALE member and subject to the requirements of section 6056, and the information reporting penalty provisions of sections 6721 and 6722. The designation must also set forth the name and EIN of the ALE member, identifying the ALE member as the person subject to the requirements of section 4980H. The proposed regulations provide that an equivalent applicable statutory or regulatory designation containing similar language will be treated as a written designation for purposes of section 6056(e).

---

[10] Until further guidance is issued, government entities, churches, and a convention or association of churches may apply a reasonable, good faith interpretation of section 414(b), (c), (m), and (o) in determining whether a person or group of persons is an applicable large employer.

B. *ALE Members Participating in Multiemployer Plans*

Several commenters suggested that administrators of multiemployer plans may be willing to file section 6056 returns reporting information for coverage offered to full-time employees under the multiemployer plan and recommended in such cases that an ALE member not be required to report coverage information for those employees.

Treasury and the IRS understand that the plan administrator of a multiemployer plan may have better access than a participating employer to certain information on participating employees required to be included as part of section 6056 reporting. For this reason, Treasury and the IRS anticipate that the section 6056 reporting with respect to full-time employees eligible to participate in a multiemployer plan will be permitted to be provided in a bifurcated manner. Under the bifurcated approach, one return would pertain to the full-time employees eligible to participate in the multiemployer plan (or, if the employer participates in more than one multiemployer plan, one return for each relevant multiemployer plan in which full-time employees are eligible to participate), and another return would pertain to the remaining full-time employees (those who are not eligible to participate in a multiemployer plan). As in the case of other third parties, as discussed in section XII.C of this preamble, the administrator (or administrators, in the case of an employer contributing to two or more multiemployer plans) of a multiemployer plan is permitted to report on behalf of an ALE member that is a contributing employer, and is permitted to report with respect to the ALE member's full-time employees who are eligible for coverage under the multiemployer plan (but not with respect to any other full-time employees of the ALE member). The administrator of the multiemployer plan would file a separate section 6056 return for any ALE member that is a contributing employer on behalf of whom it files using the ALE member's EIN. The administrator of the multiemployer plan would also provide its own name, address, and identification number (in addition to the name, address, and EIN of the ALE member already required). The ALE member would remain the responsible person under section 6056 with respect to all of its full-time employees and accordingly would be required to sign the section 6056 return filed on its behalf and be subject to any potential liability for failure to properly file returns or furnish statements. To the extent the plan administrator that prepares returns or statements required under section 6056 is a tax return preparer, it will be subject to the requirements generally applicable to return preparers.

C. *Section 6056 Reporting Facilitated by Third Parties*

Treasury and the IRS understand that third party administrators or other third party service providers are integral to the operation of many employers' health plans, including with respect to compliance with any reporting requirements. As requested by several commenters, ALE members are permitted to contract with and use third parties to facilitate filing returns and furnishing employee statements to comply with section 6056. The proposed regulations make clear, however, that ALE members are responsible for reporting under section 6056, with the exception of certain governmental unit applicable large employers that properly designate under section 6056(e). While the proposed regulations do not provide guidance on contractual or other reporting arrangements between private ALE members and other parties, they do not prohibit these arrangements. Such contractual arrangements would not transfer the potential liability of the ALE member for failure to report and furnish under section 6056 and the regulations, or the ALE member's potential liability under section 4980H.

As one example, an applicable large employer that is a member of an aggregated group of related entities (determined under section 414(b), 414(c), 414(m) or 414(o)), may file returns and furnish employee statements on behalf of one or more of the other ALE members of the aggregated group. Each other ALE member of the group, for example, could have the ALE member that operates the employer-sponsored plan file section 6056 returns and furnish section 6056 employee statements on its behalf. However, a separate section 6056 return must be filed for each ALE member, providing that ALE member's EIN. Each ALE member in the aggregated group would continue to be the responsible person under section 6056, would be required to sign the return filed on its behalf, and would be subject to any potential liability for failure to properly file returns or furnish statements. To the extent the other party that prepares returns or statements required under section 6056 is a tax return preparer, it will be subject to the requirements generally applicable to return preparers.

XIII. *Applicability of Information Return Requirements*

The proposed regulations provide that an ALE member that fails to comply with the section 6056 information return and employee statement requirements may be subject to the general reporting penalty provisions under sections 6721 (failure to file correct information returns), and 6722 (failure to furnish correct payee statement). The proposed regulations also provide, however, that the waiver of penalty and special rules under section 6724 and the applicable regulations, including abatement of information return penalties for reasonable cause, apply. The proposed regulations under section 6055 (REG-132455-11) include proposed amendments to the regulations under sections 6721 and 6722 to include returns under both sections 6055 and 6056 in the definitions of information return and payee statement. Treasury and the IRS anticipate that the final regulations under section 6056 will cross-reference those amendments to the regulations under sections 6721 and 6722.

Proposed Effective/Applicability Dates

These regulations are proposed to be effective the date the final regulations are published in the **Federal Register**. These regulations are proposed to apply for calendar years beginning after December 31, 2014. Consistent with Notice 2013-45, reporting entities will not be subject to penalties for failure to comply with the section 6506 information reporting provisions for 2014 (including the furnishing of employee statements in 2015). Accordingly, a reporting entity will not be subject to penalties if it first reports beginning in 2016 for 2015 (including the furnishing of employee statements). Taxpayers are encouraged, however, to voluntarily comply with section 6056 information reporting for 2014 by using the general reporting method set forth in these regulations once finalized.

Special Analyses

It has been determined that this notice of proposed rulemaking is not a significant regulatory action as defined in Executive Order 12866, as supplemented by Executive Order 13563. Therefore, a regulatory assessment is not required. It has also been determined that section 553(b) of the Administrative Procedure Act (5 U.S.C. chapter 5) does not apply to these regulations.

It is hereby certified that these regulations will not have a significant economic impact on a substantial number of small entities. This certification is based on the fact that the regulations are consistent with the requirements imposed by section 6056. Consistent with the statute, the regulations require applicable large employers, as defined in section 4980H(c)(2), to file a return with the IRS, using either the prescribed form or a substitute form, for each full-time employee reporting certain information regarding the health care coverage offered and provided to the employee for the year. Consistent with the statute, the proposed regulations further require applicable large employers to furnish to each full-time employee a copy of the return, or a substitute statement, required to be filed by the applicable large employer with respect to the employee. Accordingly, these regulations merely prescribe the method of filing and furnishing returns and employee statements as required under section 6056. Moreover, the proposed regulations attempt to minimize the burden associated with this collection of information by requiring that applicable large employers file and furnish only information that the IRS will utilize to administer the shared employer responsibility provisions under section 4980H and administer the premium tax credit under section 36B, and information employees will need in order to complete their tax returns.

Based on these facts, a Regulatory Flexibility Analysis under the Regulatory Flexibility Act (5 U.S.C. chapter 6) is not required.

Pursuant to section 7805(f) of the Code, this notice of proposed rulemaking has been submitted to the Chief Counsel for Advocacy of the Small Business Administration for comment on its impact on small business.

Comments and a Public Hearing

Before these proposed regulations are adopted as final regulations, consideration will be given to any written comments (a signed original and eight (8) copies) or electronic comments that are submitted timely to the IRS as prescribed in this preamble under the "Addresses" heading. Treasury and the IRS specifically request comments on the clarity of the proposed rules and how they can be made easier to understand. All comments will be available for public inspection at www.regulations.gov or upon request. A public hearing has been scheduled for November 18, 2013, in the Auditorium, Internal Revenue Building, 1111 Constitution Avenue, NW, Washington, DC. Due to building security procedures, visitors must enter at the Constitution Avenue entrance. In addition, all visitors must present photo identification to enter the building. Because of access restrictions, visitors will not be admitted beyond the immediate entrance area more than 30 minutes before the hearing starts. For information about having your name placed on the building access list to attend the hearing, see the "FOR FURTHER INFORMATION CONTACT" section of this preamble.

The rules of 26 CFR 601.601(a)(3) apply to the hearing. Persons who wish to present oral comments at the hearing must submit written or electronic comments by November 8, 2013 and an outline of the topics to be discussed and the time to be devoted to each topic (signed original and eight (8) copies) by November 8, 2013.

A period of 10 minutes will be allotted to each person for making comments. An agenda showing the scheduling of the speakers will be prepared after the deadline for receiving outlines has passed. Copies of the agenda will be available free of charge at the hearing.

Drafting Information

The principal author of these proposed regulations is Ligeia M. Donis of the Office of the Division Counsel/Associate Chief Counsel (Tax Exempt and Government Entities). However, other personnel from the IRS and Treasury participated in their development.

[¶ 49,593]   **Proposed Amendments of Regulations (REG-120927-13)**, published in the Federal Register on November 15, 2013.

[Code Sec. 415]

Retirement plans: Indian tribal governments: Exempt income: Safe harbors: Compensation.—Amendments of Reg. §1.415(c)-2, clarifying that amounts paid to an Indian tribe member as remuneration for services performed in a fishing rights-related activity may be treated as compensation for purposes of applying the limits on qualified plan benefits and contributions, are proposed.

AGENCY: Internal Revenue Service (IRS), Treasury

ACTION: Notice of proposed rulemaking.

SUMMARY: This document contains proposed regulations that would clarify that amounts paid to an Indian tribe member as remuneration for services performed in a fishing rights-related activity may be treated as compensation for purposes of applying the limits on qualified plan benefits and contributions. These regulations would affect sponsors of, and participants in, employee benefit plans of Indian tribal governments.

DATES: Comments and requests for a public hearing must be received by February 13, 2014.

ADDRESSES: Send submissions to CC:PA:LPD:PR (REG-120927-13), room 5205, Internal Revenue Service, PO Box 7604, Ben Franklin Station, Washington D.C. 20044. Submissions may be hand-delivered Monday through Friday between the hours of 8 a.m. and 4 p.m. to CC:PA:LPD:PR (REG-120927-13), Courier's Desk, Internal Revenue Service, 1111 Constitution Avenue, N.W., Washington, DC, 20224, or sent electronically via the Federal eRulemaking Portal at *www.regulations.gov* (IRS REG-120927-13).

FOR FURTHER INFORMATION CONTACT: Concerning the proposed regulations, Sarah Bolen or Pamela Kinard at (202) 622-6060 or (202) 317-6700; concerning the submission of comments or to request a public hearing, Oluwafunmilayo Taylor, (202) 622-7180 or (202) 317-6901 (not toll-free numbers).

SUPPLEMENTARY INFORMATION:

Background

Indian tribal governments (ITGs) and individual tribe members conduct fishing activities to generate revenue, protect critical habitats, and preserve tribal customs and traditions. Various treaties, federal statutes, and Presidential executive orders reserve to Indian tribe members the right to fish for subsistence and commercial purposes both on and off reservations. Because many of the treaties, statutes, and executive orders were adopted before passage of the Federal income tax, they often do not expressly address the question of whether income derived by Indians and ITGs from protected fishing activities is exempt from taxation. *See* H.R. Rep. 100-1104, at p. 77 (1988).

Congress added section 7873 to the Internal Revenue Code as part of the Technical and Miscellaneous Revenue Act of 1988 (Public Law 100-647). Section 7873(a)(1) provides that no income tax shall be imposed on income derived from a fishing rights-related activity of an Indian tribe by (A) a member of the tribe directly or through a qualified Indian entity, or (B) a qualified Indian entity. Section 7873(a)(2) provides that no employment tax shall be imposed on remuneration paid for services performed in a fishing rights-related activity of an Indian tribe by a member of such tribe for another member of such tribe or for a qualified Indian entity. Thus, section 7873(a) exempts income derived from a fishing rights-related activity ("fishing rights-related income") from both income and employment taxes.

Section 7873(b)(1) defines fishing rights-related activity with respect to an Indian tribe as any activity directly related to harvesting, processing, or transporting fish harvested in the exercise of a recognized fishing right of the tribe or to selling such fish but only if substantially all of such harvesting was performed by members of such tribe.

Section 415(a)(1) provides that a trust that is part of a pension, profit-sharing, or stock bonus plan shall not constitute a qualified trust under section 401(a) if (A) in the case of a defined benefit plan, the plan provides for the payment of benefits with respect to a participant which exceed the limitation of section 415(b), or (B) in the case of a defined contribution plan, contributions and other additions under the plan with respect to any participant for any taxable year exceed the limitation of section 415(c).

Section 415(b)(1) provides that benefits with respect to a participant exceed the annual limitation for defined benefit plans if, when expressed as an annual benefit (within the meaning of section 415(b)(2)), the participant's annual benefit is greater than the lesser of $160,000 (as adjusted in accordance with section 415(d)(1)) or 100 percent of the participant's average compensation for the participant's high 3 years.

Section 415(b)(3) provides that, for purposes of section 415(b)(1), a participant's high 3 years will be the period of consecutive calendar years (not more than 3) during which the participant had the greatest aggregate compensation from the employer. In the case of an employee within the meaning of section 401(c)(1) (that is, a self-employed individual treated as an employee), the preceding sentence is applied by substituting for "compensation from the employer" the following: "the participant's earned income (within the meaning of section 401(c)(2) but determined without regard to any exclusion under section 911)."

Section 415(c)(1) provides that contributions and other additions with respect to a participant exceed the annual limitation for defined contribution plans if, when expressed as an annual addition (within the meaning of section 415(c)(2)) to the participant's account, the participant's annual addition is greater than the lesser of $40,000 (as adjusted in accordance with section 415(d)(1)) or 100 percent of the participant's compensation. Section 415(c)(3) provides that the term "participant's compensation" means the compensation of the participant from the employer for the year. Section 1.415(c)-2(a) of the Income Tax Regulations generally provides that compensation from the employer within the meaning of section 415(c)(3) includes all items of remuneration described in § 1.415(c)-2(b), but excludes the items of remuneration described in § 1.415(c)-2(c).

Section 1.415(c)-2(b) generally provides that, for purposes of applying the limitations of section 415, the term compensation means remuneration for services. Specifically, under § 1.415(c)-2(b)(1), compensation includes employee wages, salaries, fees for professional services, and other amounts received (without regard to whether or not an amount is paid in cash) for personal services actually rendered in the course of employment with the employer maintaining the plan, to the extent that the amounts are includible in gross income. In addition, § 1.415(c)-2(b)(2) provides that in the case of an employee within the meaning of section 401(c)(1) (a self-employed employee), compensation includes the employee's earned income (as described in section 401(c)(2)) plus amounts deferred at the election of the employee that would be includible in gross income but for the rules of section 402(e)(3), 402(h)(1)(B), 402(k), or 457(b).

Section 1.415(c)-2(c) excludes certain items from the definition of compensation under section 415(c)(3). Specifically, § 1.415(c)-2(c)(1) excludes contributions (other than certain elective contributions) made by the employer to a plan of deferred compensation to the extent that the contributions are not includible in the gross income of the employee for the taxable year in which contributed. Likewise, distributions from plans (whether qualified or not) are generally not considered to be compensation for section 415 purposes. Section 1.415(c)-2(c)(2) excludes from compensation amounts realized from the exercise of nonstatutory options and amounts realized when restricted stock or other property held by an employee becomes freely transferable or is no longer subject to a substantial risk of forfeiture. Section 1.415(c)-2(c)(3) excludes from compensation amounts realized from the sale, exchange, or other disposition of stock acquired under a statutory stock option (as defined in § 1.421-1(b)). Finally, § 1.415(c)-2(c)(4) excludes from compensation other amounts that receive special tax benefits, such as certain premiums for group-term life insurance.

Section 1.415(c)-2(d) provides safe harbor definitions that a plan is permitted to use to define compensation in a manner that satisfies section 415(c)(3). Section 1.415(c)-2(d)(2) provides a safe harbor definition of compensation that includes only those items listed in § 1.415(c)-2(b)(1) or (b)(2) and excludes all the items listed in § 1.415(c)-2(c). Section 415(c)-2(d)(3) provides a separate safe harbor definition of compensation that includes wages within the meaning of section 3401(a), plus amounts that would be included in wages but for an election under section 125(a), 132(f)(4), 402(e)(3), 402(h)(1)(b), 402(k), or 457(b).

Explanation of Provisions

Because fishing rights-related income is not subject to income tax, an issue has been raised as to whether such income is included as compensation for purposes of section 415(c)(3) and § 1.415(c)-2(b). The proposed regulations would clarify that certain fishing rights-related income is included in the definition of compensation. Specifically, these regulations would provide that amounts paid to a member of an Indian tribe as remuneration for services performed in a fishing rights-related activity (as defined in section 7873(b)(1)) do not fail to be treated as compensation under § 1.415(c)-2(b)(1) and (b)(2) (and are not excluded from the definition of compensation pursuant to § 1.415(c)-2(c)(4)) merely because those amounts are not subject to income tax as a result of section 7873(a)(1). Thus, the determination of whether an amount constitutes wages, salaries, or earned income for purposes of § 1.415(c)-2(b)(1) or (b)(2) is made without regard to the exemption from taxation under section 7873(b)(1) and (b)(2). In addition, by permitting fishing rights-related income to be treated as wages, salaries, or earned income under § 1.415(c)-2(b)(1) and (b)(2), plans that accept contributions of fishing rights-related income would not be precluded from utilizing the safe harbor definitions of compensation under § 1.415(c)-2(d)(2) and (d)(3) of the regulations.

Proposed Applicability Date

These regulations are proposed to apply for taxable years ending on or after the date of publication of the Treasury decision adopting these rules as final regulations in the **Federal Register**. Taxpayers, however, may rely on these proposed regulations for periods preceding the effective date, pending the issuance of final regulations. If, and to the extent, the final regulations are more restrictive than the rules in these proposed regulations, those provisions of the final regulations will be applied without retroactive effect.

Special Analyses

It has been determined that this notice of proposed rulemaking is not a significant regulatory action as defined in Executive Order 12866, as supplemented by Executive Order 13563. Therefore, a regulatory assessment is not required. It has also been determined that 5 U.S.C. 533(b) of the Administrative Procedure Act (5 U.S.C. chapter 5) does not apply to these regulations. Because these regulations do not impose a collection of information on small entities, the provisions of the Regulatory Flexibility Act (5 U.S.C. chapter 6) do not apply and a Regulatory Flexibility Analysis is not required. Pursuant to section 7805(f) of the Internal Revenue Code, these regulations have been submitted to the Office of Chief Counsel for Advocacy of the Small Business Administration for comments on its impact on small business.

Comments and Requests for Public Hearing

Before these proposed regulations are adopted as final regulations, consideration will be given to any comments that are submitted timely to the IRS as prescribed in this preamble under the "Addresses" heading. In addition to general comments on the proposed regulations, the IRS and the Treasury Department request comments on the taxation of qualified plan distributions that are attributable to fishing rights-related income, and the application of section 72(f)(2) (which treats certain amounts as basis for purposes of computing employee contributions if those amounts would have not been includible in income had they been paid directly to the employee). All comments are available at *www.regulations.gov* or upon request. A public hearing will be scheduled if requested in writing by any person who timely submits written comments. If a public hearing is scheduled, notice of the date, time, and place of the public hearing will be published in the **Federal Register**.

Consultation and Coordination with Indian Tribal Governments

These proposed regulations take into account comments provided through a number of general consultation sessions held with the Indian tribal community in recent years. Consistent with Executive Order 13175, the Treasury Department and the IRS expect to hold a telephone consultation on a date between November 15, 2013 and February 13, 2014. This telephone consultation session will focus principally on the contribution of section 7873 income to qualified retirement plans and the taxation of qualified plan distributions that are attributable to this income. Information relating to the consultation, including the date, time, registration requirements, and procedures for submitting written and oral comments, will be available on the IRS website relating to Indian tribal governments at: http://www.irs.gov/Government-Entities/Indian-Tribal-Governments.

Drafting Information

The principal author of these regulations is Sarah R. Bolen, Office of Division Counsel/Associate Chief Counsel (Tax Exempt and Government Entities). However, other personnel from the IRS and the Treasury Department participated in the development of these regulations.

[¶ 49,594] Proposed Amendments of Regulations and Withdrawal of Proposed Regulations (REG-130843-13), published in the Federal Register on December 2, 2013 (corrected 2/24/2014).

[Code Sec. 1411]

Patient Protection and Affordable Care Act: Net investment income tax: Net investment income: Computation.—Reg. § 1.1411-7 and amendments of Reg. §§ 1.1411-0, 1.1411-3 and 1.1411-4, providing guidance on the computation of net investment income, are proposed. Reg. § 1.1411-7, proposed on December 5, 2012 (REG-130507-11), is withdrawn.

AGENCY: Internal Revenue Service (IRS), Treasury.

ACTION: Withdrawal of notice of proposed rulemaking and notice of proposed rulemaking.

SUMMARY: This document contains proposed regulations under section 1411 of the Internal Revenue Code (Code). These regulations provide guidance on the computation of net investment income. The regulations affect individuals, estates, and trusts whose incomes meet certain income thresholds.

DATES: The proposed rule published December 5, 2012 (77 FR 72612), is withdrawn as of December 2, 2013. Comments on this proposed rule must be received by March 3, 2014. Comments on the collection of information for this proposed rule should be received by January 31, 2014.

ADDRESSES: Send submissions to: CC:PA:LPD:PR (REG-130843-13), room 5205, Internal Revenue Service, PO Box 7604, Ben Franklin Station, Washington, DC 20044. Submissions may be hand-delivered Monday through Friday between the hours of 8 a.m. and 4 p.m. to CC:PA:LPD:PR (REG-130843-13), Courier's Desk, Internal Revenue Service, 1111 Constitution Avenue, NW., Washington, DC, or sent electronically, via the Federal eRulemaking portal at *www.regulations.gov* (IRS REG-130843-13).

FOR FURTHER INFORMATION CONTACT: Concerning the proposed regulations, David H. Kirk or Adrienne M. Mikolashek at (202) 317-6852; concerning submissions of comments or to request a hearing, Oluwafunmilayo Taylor, (202) 317-6901 (not toll-free numbers).

SUPPLEMENTARY INFORMATION:

Paperwork Reduction Act

The collection of information contained in this notice of proposed rulemaking has been submitted to the Office of Management and Budget for review in accordance with the Paperwork Reduction Act of 1995 (44 U.S.C. 3507(d)) under control number 1545-2227. Comments on the collection of information should be sent to the **Office of Management and Budget**, Attn: Desk Officer for the Department of the Treasury, Office of Information and Regulatory Affairs, Washington, DC 20503, with copies to the **Internal Revenue Service**, Attn: IRS Reports Clearance Officer, SE:W:CAR:MP:T:T:SP, Washington, DC 20224. Comments on the collection of information should be received by January 31, 2014. Comments are specifically requested concerning:

Whether the proposed collection of information is necessary for the proper performance of the functions of the IRS, including whether the information will have practical utility;

The accuracy of the estimated burden associated with the proposed collection of information; and

Estimates of capital or start-up costs and costs of operation, maintenance, and purchase of services to provide information.

The collection of information in these proposed regulations is in § 1.1411-7(g).

The information collected in proposed § 1.1411-7(g) is required by the IRS to verify the taxpayer's reported adjustment under section 1411(c)(4). This information will be used to determine whether the amount of tax has been reported and calculated correctly. The likely respondents are owners of interests in partnerships and S corporations.

The burden for the collection of information contained in these proposed regulations will be reflected in the burden on Form 8960 or another form that the IRS designates, which will request the information in the proposed regulations.

An agency may not conduct or sponsor, and a person is not required to respond to, a collection of information unless it displays a valid control number assigned by the Office of Management and Budget.

Books or records relating to a collection of information must be retained as long as their contents may become material in the administration of any internal revenue law. Generally, tax returns and tax return information are confidential, as required by section 6103.

Background

I. *Statutory Background*

Section 1402(a)(1) of the Health Care and Education Reconciliation Act of 2010 (Public Law 111-152, 124 Stat. 1029) added section 1411 to a new chapter 2A of subtitle A (Income Taxes) of the Code effective for taxable years beginning after December 31, 2012. Section 1411 imposes a 3.8 percent tax on certain individuals, estates, and trusts.

In the case of an individual, section 1411(a)(1) imposes a tax (in addition to any other tax imposed by subtitle A) for each taxable year equal to 3.8 percent of the lesser of: (A) the individual's net investment income for such taxable year, or (B) the excess (if any) of: (i) the individual's modified adjusted gross income for such taxable year, over (ii) the threshold amount. Section 1411(b) provides that the threshold amount is: (1) in the case of a taxpayer making a joint return under section 6013 or a surviving spouse (as defined in section 2(a)), $250,000; (2) in the case of a married taxpayer (as defined in section 7703) filing a separate return, $125,000; and (3) in the case of any other individual, $200,000. Section 1411(d) defines modified adjusted gross income as adjusted gross income increased by the excess of: (1) the amount excluded from gross income under section 911(a)(1), over (2) the amount of any deductions (taken into account in computing adjusted gross income) or exclusions disallowed under section 911(d)(6) with respect to the amount excluded from gross income under section 911(a)(1).

In the case of an estate or trust, section 1411(a)(2) imposes a tax (in addition to any other tax imposed by subtitle A) for each taxable year equal to 3.8 percent of the lesser of: (A) the estate's or trust's undistributed net investment income, or (B) the excess (if any) of (i) the estate's or trust's adjusted gross income (as defined in section 67(e)) for such taxable year, over (ii) the dollar amount at which the highest tax bracket in section 1(e) begins for such taxable year.

Section 1411(c)(1) provides that net investment income means the excess (if any) of: (A) the sum of (i) gross income from interest, dividends, annuities, royalties, and rents, other than such income derived in the ordinary course of a trade or business to which the tax does not apply, (ii) other gross income derived from a trade or business to which the tax applies, and (iii) net gain (to the extent taken into account in computing taxable income) attributable to the disposition of property other than property held in a trade or business to which the tax does not apply; over (B) the deductions allowed by subtitle A that are properly allocable to such gross income or net gain.

II. *Regulatory Background*

This document contains proposed amendments to 26 CFR part 1 under section 1411 of the Code. On December 5, 2012, the Treasury Department and the IRS published a notice of proposed rulemaking in the **Federal Register** (REG-130507-11; 77 FR 72612) relating to the Net Investment Income Tax. On January 31, 2013, corrections to the proposed regulations were published in the **Federal Register** (78 FR 6781) (collectively, the "2012 Proposed Regulations"). Final regulations, issued contemporaneously with these proposed regulations in the Rules and Regulations section of this issue of the **Federal Register**, contain amendments to the Income Tax Regulations (26 CFR Part 1), which finalize the 2012 Proposed Regulations (the "2013 Final Regulations"). However, the Treasury Department and the IRS also are proposing amendments to the 2013 Final Regulations to provide additional clarification and guidance with respect to the application of section 1411 to certain specific types of property. Furthermore, the Treasury Department and the IRS are also interested in receiving comments about other aspects of section 1411 that are not addressed in the 2013 Final Regulations or these proposed regulations. If such comments are received, the Treasury Department and the IRS will consider them for inclusion on future Guidance Priority Lists.

The Treasury Department and the IRS received comments on the 2012 Proposed Regulations requesting that they address the treatment of section 707(c) guaranteed payments for capital, section 736 payments to retiring or deceased partners for section 1411 purposes, and certain capital loss carryovers. After consideration of all comments received, the Treasury Department and the IRS believe that it is appropriate to address the treatment of these items in regulations. Because such guidance had not been proposed in the 2012 Proposed Regulations, it is being issued for notice and comment in these new proposed regulations.

The Treasury Department and the IRS also received comments on the simplified method for applying section 1411 to income recipients of charitable remainder trusts (CRTs) that was proposed in the 2012 Proposed Regulations. The comments recommended that the section 1411 classification incorporate the existing category and class system under section 664. These proposed regulations provide special rules for the application of the section 664 system to CRTs that derive income from controlled foreign corporations (CFCs) or passive foreign investment companies (PFICs) with respect to which an election under § 1.1411-10(g) is not in place. Specifically, these proposed regulations coordinate the application of the rules applicable to shareholders of CFCs and PFICs in § 1.1411-10 with the section 664 category and class system adopted in § 1.1411-3(d)(2) of the 2013 Final Regulations.

Furthermore, these proposed regulations allow CRTs to elect to apply the section 664 system adopted in the 2013 Final Regulations or the simplified method set forth in the 2012 Proposed Regulations. Some comments responding to the 2012 Proposed Regulations requested that we provide an election. The Treasury Department and the IRS request comments with regard to whether or not taxpayers believe this election is preferable to the section 664 system adopted in the 2013 Final Regulations. If it appears that there is no significant interest in having the election, the Treasury Department and the IRS may omit it from the regulations when finalized, and the simplified method contained in the 2012 Proposed Regulations would no longer be an option.

These proposed regulations also address the net investment income tax characterization of income and deductions attributable to common trust funds (CTFs), residual interests in real estate mortgage investment conduits (REMICs), and certain notional principal contracts.

The Treasury Department and the IRS also received comments on the 2012 Proposed Regulations questioning the proposed regulation's methodology for adjusting a transferor's gain or loss on the disposition of its partnership interest or S corporation stock. In view of these comments, the 2013 Final Regulations removed § 1.1411-7 of the 2012 Proposed Regulations and reserved § 1.1411-7 in the 2013 Final Regulations. This notice of proposed rulemaking proposes revised rules regarding the calculation of net gain from the disposition of a partnership interest or S corporation stock (each a "Passthrough Entity") to which section 1411(c)(4) may apply.

Explanation of Provisions

1. *Overview of Proposed Regulations*

These proposed regulations propose additions and modifications to the 2013 Final Regulations, including guidance with respect to certain paragraphs that were reserved in the 2013 Final Regulations.

To coordinate these proposed regulations with the 2013 Final Regulations, the proposed regulations are proposed to have the same effective date as the 2013 Final Regulations. However, any provisions adopted when these proposed regulations are finalized that are more restrictive than these proposed regulations would apply prospectively only. Taxpayers may rely on these proposed regulations for purposes of compliance with section 1411 until the issuance of these regulations as final regulations. See § 1.1411-1(f).

2. *Special Rules for Certain Partnership Payments*

Section 731(a) treats gain from distributions as gain from the sale or exchange of a partnership interest. In general, the section 1411 treatment of gain to a partner under section 731 is governed by the rules of section 1411(c)(1)(A)(iii). Such gain is thus generally treated as net investment income for purposes of section 1411 (other than as determined under section 1411(c)(4)). However, certain partnership payments to partners are treated as not from the sale or exchange of a partnership interest. These payments include section 707(c) guaranteed payments for services or the use of capital and certain section 736 distributions to a partner in liquidation of that partner's partnership interest. Because these payments are not treated as from the sale or exchange of a partnership interest, their treatment under section 1411 may differ from the general rule of section 1411(c)(1)(A)(iii). The proposed regulations therefore provide rules for the section 1411 treatment of these payments.

A. *Section 707(c) payments*

Section 707(c) provides that a partnership payment to a partner is a "guaranteed payment" if the payment is made for services or the use of the capital, and the payment amount does not depend on partnership income. Section 1.707-1(c) provides that guaranteed payments to a partner for services are considered as made to a person who is not a partner, but only for the purposes of section 61(a) (relating to gross income) and, subject to section 263, section 162(a) (relating to trade or business expenses). Section 1.704-1(b)(2)(iv)(o) provides that guaranteed payments are not part of a partner's distributive share for purposes of section 704(b).

The proposed regulations' treatment of section 707(c) guaranteed payments under section 1411 depends on whether the partner receives the payment for services or the use of capital. The proposed regulations exclude all section 707(c) payments received for services from net investment income, regardless of whether these payments are subject to self-employment tax, because payments for services are not included in net investment income.

The Treasury Department and the IRS believe that guaranteed payments for the use of capital share many of the characteristics of substitute interest, and therefore should be included as net investment income. This treatment is consistent with existing guidance under section 707(c) and other sections of the Code in which guaranteed payments for the use of capital are treated as interest. See, for example, §§ 1.263A-9(c)(2)(iii) and 1.469-2(e)(2)(ii).

B. *Treatment of section 736 payments*

i. In General

Section 736 applies to payments made by a partnership to a retiring partner or to a deceased partner's successor in interest in liquidation of the partner's entire interest in the partnership. Section 736 does not apply to distributions made to a continuing partner, distributions made in the course of liquidating a partnership entirely, or to payments received from persons other than the partnership in exchange for the partner's interest. Section 736 categorizes liquidating distributions based on the nature of the payment as in consideration for either the partner's share of partnership property or the partner's share of partnership income. Section 736(b) generally treats a payment in exchange for the retiring partner's share of partnership property as a distribution governed by section 731. Section 736(a) treats payments in exchange for past services or use of capital as either distributive share or a guaranteed payment. Section 736(a) payments also include payments to retiring general partners of service partnerships in exchange for unrealized receivables (other than receivables described in the flush language of section 751(c)) or for goodwill (other than payments for goodwill provided for in the partnership agreement) (collectively, "Section 736(a) Property").

Because the application of section 1411 depends on the underlying nature of the payment received, the section 736 categorization controls whether a liquidating distribution is treated as net investment income for purposes of section 1411. Thus, the treatment of the payment for purposes of section 1411 differs depending on whether the distribution is a section 736(b) distribution in exchange for partnership property or a section 736(a) distribution in exchange for past services, use of capital, or Section 736(a) Property. Among section 736(a) payments, the proposed regulations further differentiate the treatment of payments depending on: (i) whether or not the payment amounts are determined with regard to the income of the partnership and (ii) whether the payment relates to Section 736(a) Property or relates to services or use of capital.

Section 1.469-2(e)(2)(iii) contains rules pertaining to whether section 736 liquidating distributions paid to a partner will be treated as income or loss from a passive activity. Where payments to a retiring partner are made over a period of years, the composition of the assets and the status of the partner as passive or nonpassive may change. Section 1.469-2(e)(2)(iii) contains rules on the extent to which those payments are classified as passive or nonpassive for purposes of section 469. The proposed regulations generally align the section 1411 characterization of section 736 payments with the treatment of the payments as passive or nonpassive under §1.469-2(e)(2)(iii).

ii. Treatment of Section 736(b) Payments

Section 736(b) payments to retiring partners in exchange for partnership property (other than payments to retiring general partners of service partnerships in exchange for Section 736(a) Property) are governed by the rules generally applicable to partnership distributions. Thus, gain or loss recognized on these distributions is treated as gain or loss from the sale or exchange of the distributee partner's partnership interest under section 731(a).

The proposed regulations provide that section 736(b) payments will be taken into account as net investment income for section 1411 purposes under section 1411(c)(1)(A)(iii) as net gain or loss from the disposition of property. If the retiring partner materially participates in a partnership trade or business, then the retiring partner must also apply §1.1411-7 of these proposed regulations to reduce appropriately the net investment income under section 1411(c)(4). Gain or loss relating to section 736(b) payments is included in net investment income under section 1411(c)(1)(A)(iii) regardless of whether the payments are classified as capital gain or ordinary income (for example, by reason of section 751).

In the case of section 736(b) payments that are paid over multiple years, the proposed regulations provide that the characterization of gain or loss as passive or nonpassive is determined for all payments as though all payments were made at the time that the liquidation of the exiting partner's interest commenced and is not retested annually. The proposed regulations thus adopt for section 1411 purposes the section 469 treatment of section 736(b) payments paid over multiple years as set forth in §1.469-2(e)(2)(iii)(A).

iii. Treatment of Section 736(a) Payments

As described in part 2.B.i., section 736 provides for several different categories of liquidating distributions under section 736(a). Payments received under section 736(a) may be an amount determined with regard to the income of the partnership taxable as distributive share under section 736(a)(1) or a fixed amount taxable as a guaranteed payment under section 736(a)(2). The categorization of the payment as distributive share or guaranteed payment will govern the treatment of the payment for purposes of section 1411.

The determination of whether section 736(a) payments received over multiple years are characterized as passive or nonpassive depends on whether the payments are received in exchange for Section 736(a) Property. With respect to section 736(a)(1) payments in exchange for Section 736(a) Property, §1.469-2(e)(2)(iii)(B) provides a special rule that computes a percentage of passive income that would result if the partnership sold the retiring partner's entire share of Section 736(a) Property at the time that the liquidation of the partner's interest commenced. The percentage of passive income is then applied to each payment received. See §1.469-2(e)(2)(iii)(B)(1). These rules apply to section 736(a)(1) and section 736(a)(2) payments for Section 736(a) Property. The proposed regulations adopt this treatment as set forth in section 469 for purposes of section 1411.

a. Section 736(a)(1) payments taxable as distributive share

Section 736(a)(1) provides that if the amount of a liquidating distribution (other than a payment for partnership property described in section 736(b)) is determined with regard to the partnership's income, then the payment is treated as a distributive share of income to the retiring partner. For purposes of section 1411, the items of income, gain, loss, and deduction attributable to the distributive share are taken into account in computing net investment income under section 1411(c)(1) in a manner consistent with the item's chapter 1 character and treatment. For example, if the partner's distributive share includes income from a trade or business not described in section 1411(c)(2), that income will be excluded from net investment income. However, if the distributive share includes, for example, interest income from working capital, then that income is net investment income.

The proposed regulations treat section 736(a)(1) payments unrelated to Section 736(a) Property as characterized annually as passive or nonpassive by applying the general rules of section 469 to each payment in the year received. To the extent that any payment under section 736(a)(1) is characterized as passive income under the principles of section 469, that payment also will be characterized as passive income for purposes of section 1411.

b. Section 736(a)(2) payments taxable as guaranteed payments

Section 736(a)(2) provides that if the amount of a liquidating distribution (other than a payment for partnership property described in section 736(b)) is determined without regard to the partnership's income, then the payment is treated as a guaranteed payment as described in section 707(c). Payments under section 736(a)(2) might be in exchange for services, use of capital, or Section 736(a) Property. The section 1411 treatment of guaranteed payments for services or the use of capital follows the general rules for guaranteed payments set forth in part 2.A of this preamble. Thus, section 736(a)(2) payments for services are not included as net investment income, and section 736(a)(2) payments for the use of capital are included as net investment income.

Section 736(a)(2) payments in exchange for Section 736 Property are treated as gain or loss from the disposition of a partnership interest, which is generally included in net investment income under section 1411(c)(1)(A)(iii). If the retiring partner materially participates in a partnership trade or business, then the retiring partner must also apply § 1.1411-7 of these proposed regulations to reduce appropriately the net investment income under section 1411(c)(4). To the extent that section 736(a)(2) payments exceed the fair market value of Section 736(a) Property, the proposed regulations provide that the excess will be treated as either interest income or as income in exchange for services, in a manner consistent with the treatment under § 1.469-2(e)(2)(iii). iv. Application of Section 1411(c)(4) to Section 736 Payments

The proposed regulations provide that section 1411(c)(4) applies to section 736(a)(2) and section 736(b) payments. Thus, the inclusion of these payments as net investment income may be limited if the retiring partner materially participated in all or a portion of the partnership's trade or business. The extent of any limitation is determined under the rules of § 1.1411-7.

The proposed regulations provide that, when section 736 payments are made over multiple years, the characterization of gain or loss as passive or nonpassive and the values of the partnership assets are computed for all payments as though all payments were made at the time that the liquidation of the exiting partner's interest commenced, similar to the treatment in § 1.469-2(e)(2)(iii)(A).

If a partner's net investment income is reduced pursuant to section 1411(c)(4), then the difference between the amount of gain recognized for chapter 1 and the amount includable in net investment income after the application of section 1411(c)(4) is treated as an addition to basis, in a manner similar to an installment sale for purposes of calculating the partner's net investment income attributable to these payments.

v. Additional Public Comments

Commentators to the 2012 Proposed Regulations requested that the Treasury Department and the IRS issue guidance under section 1411 regarding the treatment of section 736 payments to retiring and deceased partners. Some commentators sought clarification regarding the interaction between section 736 payments and the net investment income exclusions in sections 1411(c)(5) and 1411(c)(6).

Section 1411(c)(5) provides that net investment income shall not include certain items of income attributable to distributions from specifically enumerated qualified plans. One commentator suggested that section 736 payments should be excluded from net investment income under section 1411(c)(5) as analogous to qualified plan distributions. The Treasury Department and the IRS believe that section 1411(c)(5) does not apply to section 736 payments because these payments do not originate from a qualified plan described in section 1411(c)(5). Therefore, section 736 payments are not excluded by reason of section 1411(c)(5).

Section 1411(c)(6) provides that net investment income does not include any item taken into account in determining self-employment income for a taxable year on which a tax is imposed by section 1401(b). In the context of section 1411(c)(6), § 1.1411-9(a) of the 2013 Final Regulations provides that the term "taken into account" for self-employment tax purposes does not include amounts excluded from net earnings from self-employment under sections 1402(a)(1)-(17). Commentators suggested that certain section 736 payments are excluded from net earnings from self-employment by reason of section 1402(a)(10) and § 1.1402(a)-17, and therefore should be excluded from net investment income under section 1411(c)(6) for similar policy reasons. The Treasury Department and the IRS believe that section 1411(c)(6) does not apply to section 736 payments, except to the extent that such payments are taken into account, within the meaning of § 1.1411-9(a), in determining net earnings from self-employment. In such a case, the section 736 payment would be subject to self-employment tax and therefore is not included in net investment income by reason of section 1411(c)(6) and § 1.1411-9(a).

Commentators also recommended special rules for the interaction between section 736 payments and the section 469 material participation rules solely for purposes of section 1411. As discussed in this part of the preamble, the proposed section 1411 rules rely heavily on the chacterization of the section 736 payments under section 469. Therefore, the Treasury Department and the IRS do not believe that special section 469 rules are necessary solely for purposes of section 1411.

3. *Treatment of Certain Capital Loss Carryforwards*

In general, under chapter 1, capital losses that exceed capital gains are allowed as a deduction against ordinary income only to the extent allowed by section 1211(b). In the case of capital losses in excess of the amounts allowed by section 1211(b), section 1212(b)(1) treats these losses as incurred in the following year. Section 1.1411-4(d) adopts these principles when computing net gain under section 1411(c)(1)(A)(iii). Therefore, capital losses incurred in a year prior to the effective date of section 1411 may be taken into account in the computation of section 1411(c)(1)(A)(iii) net gain by reason of the mechanics of section 1212(b)(1). However, certain capital losses may not be taken into account in determining net investment income within the meaning of section 1411(c)(1)(A)(iii) or by reason of the exception in section 1411(c)(4)(B) (generally, an "excluded capital loss"). In the case of section 1411(c)(1)(A)(iii), § 1.1411-4(d)(4)(i) provides that capital losses attributable to the disposition of property used in a trade or business not described in section 1411(c)(2) and § 1.1411-5 are excluded from the computation of net gain. In the case of section 1411(c)(4)(B), some or all of a capital loss resulting from the disposition of certain partnerships or S corporations is excluded from the determination of net gain. Although these capital losses are excluded from the calculation of net gain in the year of recognition by reason of § 1.1411-4(d)(4), such losses may not be fully offset by capital gains for chapter 1 purposes in the same year. In that case, some (or all) of the capital loss carryforward will constitute excluded capital losses in the subsequent year(s) by reason of the mechanics of section 1212(b)(1). Several commentators identified this issue and requested that the Treasury Department and the IRS provide guidance on the identification, tracking, and use of embedded, excluded capital losses within a capital loss carryforward.

In response to these comments, proposed § 1.1411-4(d)(4)(iii) creates an annual adjustment to capital loss carryforwards to prevent capital losses excluded from the net investment income calculation in the year of recognition from becoming deductible losses in future years. The annual adjustment in § 1.1411-4(d)(4)(iii) provides a method of identification and an ordering rule that eliminate the need for taxpayers to maintain a separate set of books and records for this item to comply with section 1411. However, the rule requires that taxpayers perform the calculation annually, regardless of whether they have a section 1411 tax liability in a particular year, to maintain the integrity of the rule's carryforward adjustment amounts for a subsequent year in which they are subject to liability under section 1411.

The rule provides that, for purposes of computing net gain in § 1.1411-4(d) and any properly allocable deduction for excess losses in § 1.1411-4(f)(4) (if any), the taxpayer's capital loss carryforward from the previous year is reduced by the lesser of: (A) the amount of capital loss taken into account in the current year by reason of section 1212(b)(1), or (B) the amount of net capital loss excluded from net investment income in the immediately preceding year. For purposes of (B), the amount of net capital loss excluded from net investment income in the previous year includes amounts excluded by reason of § 1.1411-4(d)(4) (amount of capital losses recognized in the preceding year) plus the amount of the previous year's adjustment required by this rule. Section 1.1411-4(d)(4)(iii) provides a multi-year example to illustrate the application of the rule.

The mechanics of the capital loss adjustment accomplishes several objectives. First, the rule causes all capital losses incurred prior to 2013 to be allowable losses for the computation of net gain under § 1.1411-4(d) and any properly allocable deduction for excess losses in § 1.1411-4(f)(4) (if any). This result is accomplished by the application of part (B) of the rule described in the preceding paragraph. Since the adjustment is based on the lesser of (A) or (B), the amount of excluded capital losses in the year immediately before the effective date of section 1411 is zero, so the loss adjustment in the year following the effective date of section 1411 will also be zero. Second, the rule only requires an adjustment when a taxpayer has excluded losses embedded within a capital loss carryforward. Therefore, taxpayers with no excluded capital losses do not have to make any adjustment. Third, the rule also provides a mechanism for ordering the use of capital losses to offset gains. The rule causes excluded capital gains recognized in the current year to be offset by excluded capital losses that are embedded in the capital loss carryforward from the previous year. This matching is accomplished by the use of the term "net capital loss" in § 1.1411-4(d)(4)(iii)(B). If the excluded gain exceeds the amount of excluded capital loss included in the carryforward amount and any excluded capital loss amounts recognized in the current year, the amount of adjustment will be zero in the subsequent year because there was no "net capital loss" in the preceding year. In this situation, no adjustment is required because the previous year's excluded gains were fully absorbed by the excluded losses. Finally, the rule allows taxpayers to use capital non-excluded losses for purposes of the excess loss deduction in § 1.1411-4(f)(4) before subjecting excluded losses to the limitation.

4. Treatment of Income and Deductions from Common Trust Funds (CTFs)

Section 584(c) provides that each participant in a CTF shall include in its taxable income, whether or not distributed and whether or not distributable, its proportionate share of: (1) short-term capital gain or loss, (2) long-term capital gain or loss, and (3) ordinary taxable income or the ordinary net loss of the CTF. The flush language of section 584(c) further provides that "the proportionate share of each participant in the amount of dividends received by the CTF and to which section 1(h)(11) applies shall be considered for purposes of such paragraph as having been received by such participant."

Section 584(d) provides, in relevant part, that "[t]he taxable income of a common trust fund shall be computed in the same manner and on the same basis as in the case of an individual, except . . . after excluding all items of gain and loss from sales or exchanges of capital assets, there shall be computed (A) an ordinary taxable income which shall consist of the excess of the gross income over deductions; or (B) an ordinary net loss which shall consist of the excess of the deductions over the gross income."

The Treasury Department and the IRS have become aware that taxpayers may be considering the use of CTFs to recharacterize income items that otherwise would be includable in net investment income under section 1411. Because section 584(c)(3) simply requires the participant to include in its income its share of "net ordinary income or loss," taxpayers may attempt to claim that section 584(c)(3) ordinary income or loss inclusions are not explicitly section 1411(c)(1)(A)(i) net investment income, and therefore escape taxation under section 1411.

Using a CTF to recharacterize the underlying character of CTF income for section 1411 purposes is closely analogous to the past use of CTFs to cleanse unrelated business taxable income (UBTI) for tax-exempt participants. In 1984, the Treasury Department and the IRS promulgated § 1.584-2(c)(3), which created a special look-through rule to prevent taxpayers from using CTFs to recharacterize UBTI. Section 1.584-2(c)(3) provides, in relevant part, that "any amount of income or loss of the common trust fund which is included in the computation of a participant's taxable income for the taxable year shall be treated as income or loss from an unrelated trade or business to the extent that such amount would have been income or loss from an unrelated trade or business if such participant had made directly the investments of the common trust fund."

Similarly, proposed § 1.1411-4(e)(3) includes a rule that provides income or loss from a CTF is net investment income or deduction to the extent that such amount would have been net investment income or deduction if the participant had made directly the investments of the CTF.

5. Treatment of Income and Deductions Related to Residual Interests in REMICs

The 2012 Proposed Regulations did not explicitly address income and deductions related to residual interests in REMICs. A REMIC residual interest represents an equity-like interest in a REMIC. A REMIC is not treated as carrying on a trade or business for purposes of section 162, and a REMIC's taxable income or net loss generally is derived from dispositions of qualified mortgages or permitted investments, interest income from the mortgages, and interest expense from the regular interests (treated as debt) issued by the REMIC. Section 860C(a)(1) generally requires the holder of a REMIC residual interest to take into account the daily portion of the REMIC's taxable income or net loss. One commentator suggested that the regulations expressly include income from a REMIC residual interest in determining net investment income. The Treasury Department and the IRS agree with this comment because, if a taxpayer directly held the underlying assets of the REMIC, the items of income, gain, loss, and deductions attributable to those assets would be taken into account in computing net investment income. Therefore, the proposed regulations provide that a holder of a residual interest in a REMIC takes into account the daily portion of taxable income (or net loss) under section 860C in determining net investment income.

6. Treatment of Income and Deductions from Certain Notional Principal Contracts (NPCs)

Under the 2012 Proposed Regulations (and the 2013 Final Regulations), gain on the disposition of an NPC is included in net investment income, and any other gross income from an NPC (including net income attributable to periodic payments on an NPC) is included in net investment income if it is derived from a trade or business described in § 1.1411-5. Several commentators on the 2012 Proposed Regulations suggested that the proper treatment of periodic payments on an NPC should not turn solely upon whether the NPC was entered into as part of a trading business and recommended that NPC periodic payments should be included in net investment income. One commentator indicated that the omission of NPC periodic income seems unusual and inconsistent with the portions of the 2012 Proposed Regulations (and 2013 Final Regulations) that provide for the inclusion in net investment income of substitute interest and substitute dividends.

After consideration of the comments, the Treasury Department and the IRS agree that periodic payments on an NPC should be included in net investment income even if the net income from such payments is not derived in a trade or business described in § 1.1411-5. As a result, the proposed regulations provide that net income (or net deduction) attributable to periodic and nonperiodic payments on an NPC under § 1.446-3(c)(1) is taken into account in determining net investment income. However, the proposed regulations only apply to the net income (or net deduction) on an NPC described in § 1.446-3(c)(1) that is referenced to property (including an index) that produces (or would produce if the property were to produce income) interest, dividends, royalties, or rents if the property were held directly by the taxpayer. The proposed regulations would not affect the treatment of net income attributable to periodic and nonperiodic payments on any NPC derived in a trade or business described in § 1.1411-5, that is net investment income under section 1411(c)(1)(A)(ii).

7. Charitable Remainder Trusts (CRTs) with Income from Controlled Foreign Corporations (CFCs) or Passive Foreign Investment Companies (PFICs)

Section 1.1411-3(d)(2) of the 2013 Final Regulations provides rules on the categorization and distribution of net investment income from a CRT based on the existing section 664 category and class system. In general, § 1.1411-3(d)(2) provides that, if a CRT has both excluded income and accumulated net investment income (ANII) in an income category, such excluded income and ANII constitute separate classes of income for purposes of § 1.664-1(d)(1)(i)(b). Section 1.1411-10 of the 2013 Final Regulations provides rules for calculating net investment income when a taxpayer owns a direct or indirect interest in a CFC or PFIC.

The 2013 Final Regulations reserve paragraph § 1.1411-3(d)(2)(ii) for special rules that the Treasury Department and the IRS believe are necessary to apply the section 664 category and class system contained in § 1.664-1(d), and adopted by § 1.1411-3(d)(2), to CRTs that own interests in certain CFCs or PFICs. The special rules generally apply to taxpayers that: (i) own CFCs or qualified electing funds (QEFs) with respect to which an election under § 1.1411-10(g) is not in place; or (ii) are subject to the rules of section 1291 with respect to a PFIC. These proposed regulations provide those special rules and are proposed to apply to taxable years beginning after December 31, 2013. There are no special rules necessary for a United States person that has elected to mark to market its PFIC stock under section 1296. See § 1.1411-10(c)(2)(ii).

A. CFCs and QEFs

For purposes of chapter 1, a United States shareholder (as defined in section 951(b)) of a CFC is required to include certain amounts in income currently under section 951(a) (section 951 inclusions). Similarly, a U.S. person that owns shares of a PFIC also is required to include amounts in income currently under section 1293(a) (section 1293 inclusions) if the person makes a QEF election under section 1295 with respect to the PFIC.

For purposes of chapter 1, a CRT's section 951 inclusions and section 1293 inclusions are included in the appropriate section 664 category and class for the year in which those amounts are includable in the CRT's income for purposes of chapter 1. The application of the ordering rules in §1.664-1(d)(1) determines the tax character of the annuity or unitrust distributions to the CRT's income beneficiary. These ordering rules are equally applicable for purposes of section 1411 under the 2013 Final Regulations. In the case of a CRT that directly or indirectly owns an interest in a CFC or QEF, some portion of the annual distribution(s) may consist of current or previous years' section 951 inclusions or section 1293 inclusions.

As discussed in the preamble to the 2013 Final Regulations, §1.1411-10 generally provides that distributions of previously taxed earnings and profits attributable to section 951 inclusions and section 1293 inclusions that are not treated as dividends for purposes of chapter 1 under section 959(d) or section 1293(c) are dividends for purposes of section 1411, absent an election under §1.1411-10(g). Without that election, taxpayers generally do not include section 951 inclusions or section 1293 inclusions in net investment income for purposes of section 1411. As a result, the timing of income derived from an investment in a CFC or QEF may be different for purposes of chapter 1 and section 1411. Thus, §1.1411-10(e) provides adjustments to a taxpayer's modified adjusted gross income (MAGI), or to the adjusted gross income (AGI) of an estate or trust, when the taxpayer owns a CFC or QEF with respect to which an election is not in place to coordinate the rules in §1.1411-10 with calculation of the section 1411 tax, the applicability of which is based, in part, on MAGI or AGI.

B. *Section 1291 funds*

The 2013 Final Regulations also provide special rules that apply to a United States shareholder of a PFIC who is subject to the tax and interest charge applicable to excess distributions under section 1291. Accordingly, §1.1411-10(e) also provides adjustments to a taxpayer's MAGI, or to the AGI of an estate or trust, when the taxpayer owns a PFIC and is subject to these special rules. In particular, MAGI (or AGI for an estate or trust) is increased by: (i) the amount of any excess distribution to the extent the distribution is a dividend under section 316(a) and is not otherwise included in income for purposes of chapter 1 under section 1291(a)(1)(B), and (ii) any gain treated as an excess distribution under section 1291(a)(2) to the extent not otherwise included in income for purposes of chapter 1 under section 1291(a)(1)(B).

C. *Rules in proposed regulation §1.1411-3(d)(2)(ii)*

The rules in proposed §1.1411-3(d)(2)(ii) coordinate the rules of §1.1411-10 with the section 664 category and class system. These proposed regulations contain three rules that generally apply when a CRT directly or indirectly owns an interest in a CFC or QEF and a §1.1411-10(g) election is not in effect with respect to the CFC or QEF. First, §1.1411-3(d)(2)(ii)(A) provides that section 951 inclusions and section 1293 inclusions that are included in gross income for purposes of chapter 1 for a calendar year and in one or more categories described in §1.664-1(d)(1) are considered excluded income (within the meaning of §1.1411-1(d)) in the year the amount is included in income for purposes of chapter 1.

Second, proposed §1.1411-3(d)(2)(ii)(B) provides that, when a CRT receives a distribution of previously taxed earnings and profits that is not treated as a dividend for purposes of chapter 1 under sections 953(d) and 1293(c) but that is taken into account as net investment income for purposes of section 1411 (referred to as an *NII Inclusion Amount*), the CRT must allocate such amounts among the categories described in section 664(b)(1)-(3). For this purpose, the NII Inclusion Amount includes net investment income described in §1.1411-10(c)(1)(i) (certain distributions from a CFC or QEF), §1.1411-10(c)(1)(ii) (certain distributions from a section 1291 fund), §1.1411-10(c)(2)(i) (gain derived from the disposition of a section 1291 fund), and §1.1411-10(c)(4) (distributions from an estate or trust attributable to income or gain derived from a CFC or QEF with respect to which an election under §1.1411-10(g) is not in effect). Specifically, proposed §1.1411-3(d)(2)(ii)(B) provides that, to the extent the CRT has amounts of excluded income in the Ordinary Income Category and the Capital Gain Category under §1.664-1(d)(1), the NII Inclusion Amount is allocated to the CRT's classes of excluded income in the Ordinary Income Category, and then to the classes of excluded income in the Capital Gain Category, in turn, until exhaustion of each such class, beginning with the class of excluded income within a category with the highest Federal income tax rate. Any remaining NII Inclusion Amount not so allocated to classes within the Ordinary Income and Capital Gain Categories shall be placed in the category described in section 664(b)(3) (the Other Income Category). To the extent the CRT distributes amounts from this Other Income Category, that distribution shall constitute a distribution described in §1.1411-10(c)(4) and thus §1.1411-10(e)(1) causes the beneficiary to increase its MAGI (or AGI for an estate or trust) by the same amount.

The third rule in proposed §1.1411-3(d)(2)(ii) addresses the differential in gain or loss associated with tax basis disparities between chapter 1 and section 1411 that are caused by the recognition of income under chapter 1 and of the corresponding net investment income in different taxable years. See §1.1411-10(d) for special basis calculation rules for CFCs, QEFs, and partnerships and S corporations that own interests in CFCs or QEFs. The proposed rules for the allocation of such gain or loss within the section 664 categories and classes generally are consistent with the allocation rules for NII Inclusions Amounts, except that the Capital Gain Category is the first category to which the gain or loss is to be allocated, and then the Ordinary Income Category. The order of the categories is changed for gains and losses to more closely match the adjustments to the income that produced the net investment income, and to minimize the need for adjustments to MAGI or AGI.

Proposed §1.1411-3(d)(2)(ii)(C)(*1*) provides rules similar to proposed §1.1411-3(d)(2)(ii)(B) for gains that are higher for section 1411 purposes than they are for chapter 1 purposes. The difference between the rule for gains in proposed §§1.1411-3(d)(2)(ii)(C)(*1*) and 1.1411-3(d)(2)(ii)(B) is that proposed §1.1411-3(d)(2)(ii)(C)(*1*) requires this additional gain to be allocated within the Capital Gain Category before any allocation within the Ordinary Income Category. The Treasury Department and the IRS believe this difference more accurately reflects the nature of the net investment income within the section 664 category and class system because this NII Inclusion Amount is attributable to a transaction that generated capital gain or loss (rather than ordinary income inclusions and dividends attributable to proposed §1.1411-3(d)(2)(ii)(B) items).

Proposed §1.1411-3(d)(2)(ii)(C)(*2*) provides rules similar to proposed §1.1411-3(d)(2)(ii)(C)(*1*) for losses (and gains that are lower for section 1411 purposes than they are for chapter 1), but with a different ordering rule. In these cases, the tax basis is higher for section 1411 (generating a smaller gain or larger loss for 1411 purposes). However, unlike dividends and gains addressed in proposed §§1.1411-3(d)(2)(ii)(B) and 1.1411-3(d)(2)(ii)(C)(*1*), respectively, which can require an increase in MAGI (or AGI for an estate or trust), losses are accompanied by a reduction in MAGI (or AGI for an estate or trust) under §1.1411-10(e). Therefore, proposed §1.1411-3(d)(2)(ii)(C)(*2*) generally follows the ordering rule for gains with one exception. The loss ordering rule in proposed §1.1411-3(d)(2)(ii)(C)(*2*) begins with allocating the decrease to the Other Income Category that was created or increased in the current or previous year, presumably due to an allocation under §1.1411-3(d)(2)(ii)(B). The purpose of the different ordering rule is to eliminate the ANII within Other Income Category first in an effort to reduce the incidence of required MAGI (or AGI for an estate or trust) adjustments by the beneficiary. Once this income is eliminated, the CRT or beneficiary will not have to separately account for a MAGI (or AGI for an estate or trust) increase because the timing differences caused by §1.1411-10 may have been corrected within the 664 class and category system before such income is distributed to the beneficiary.

8. *Simplified Method for Charitable Remainder Trusts*

The 2012 Proposed Regulations provided a method for the CRT to track net investment income received after December 31, 2012, and later distributed to the beneficiary. Section 1.1411-3(c)(2)(i) of the 2012 Proposed Regulations provided that distributions from a CRT to a beneficiary for a taxable year consist of net investment income in an amount equal to the lesser of the total amount of the distributions for that year, or the current and accumulated net investment income of the CRT.

As discussed in part 4.C of the preamble to the 2013 Final Regulations, multiple commentators asked that the final regulations follow the existing rules under section 664 that create subclasses in each category of income as the tax rates on certain types of income are changed from time to time.

However, some of the commentators suggested that the final regulations allow the trustee to elect between the method described in the 2012 Proposed Regulations and the existing rules under section 664.

These proposed regulations provide CRTs with a choice of methods. Section 1.1411-3(d)(2) of the 2013 Final Regulations, along with the proposed additions in these proposed regulations, provide guidance on the application of the section 664 method of tracking net investment income. Proposed §1.1411-3(d)(3) allows the CRT to elect to use the simplified method included in the 2012 Proposed Regulations, with one modification. Proposed §1.1411-3(d)(3)(ii) provides that a CRT that elects to use the simplified method is not limited by the general excess deduction rule in §1.1411-4(f)(1)(ii). Section 1.1411-4(f)(1)(ii) provides that section 1411(c)(1)(B) deductions in excess of gross income and net gain described in section 1411(c)(1)(A) are not taken into account in determining net investment income in any other taxable year, except as allowed under chapter 1. In the case of CRTs, for chapter 1 purposes, the section 664(d) regulations allow for losses within each income class to be carried forward to offset income earned by the CRT within the same class in a future year. Therefore, this provision of the simplified method retains the chapter 1 principle that a CRT's losses are carried forward and offset income in future years. For example, if a CRT has a longterm capital loss of $10,000 in year 1 and a $11,000 long-term capital gain in year 2, the section 664(d) regulations provide that the CRT will have $1,000 of long-term gain available for distribution in year 2. Proposed §1.1411-3(d)(3)(ii) is intended to provide the same result such that the CRT would have $1,000 of accumulated net investment income available for distribution in year 2.

In the case of a CRT established after December 31, 2012, the CRT's election must be made on its income tax return for the taxable year in which the CRT is established. In the case of a CRT established before January 1, 2013, the CRT's election must be made on its income tax return for its first taxable year beginning on or after January 1, 2013. Additionally, the CRT may make the election on an amended return for that year only if neither the taxable year for which the election is made, nor any taxable year that is affected by the election, for both the CRT and its beneficiaries, is closed by the period of limitations on assessments under section 6501. Once made, the election is irrevocable.

If, after consideration of all comments received in response to these proposed regulations, it appears that there is no significant interest among taxpayers in having the option of using the simplified method, the Treasury Department and the IRS may omit this election from the regulations when finalized.

9. Calculation of Gain or Loss Attributable to the Disposition of Certain Interests in Partnerships and S Corporations

Section 1411(c)(4)(A) provides that, in the case of a disposition of an interest in a partnership or of stock in an S corporation (either, a "*Passthrough Entity*"), gain from the disposition shall be taken into account under section 1411(c)(1)(A)(iii) only to the extent of the net gain which would be taken into account by the transferor if the Passthrough Entity sold all of its property for fair market value immediately before the disposition of the interest. Section 1411(c)(4)(B) provides a similar rule for losses from dispositions.

The 2012 Proposed Regulations required that a transferor of a partnership interest or S corporation stock first compute its gain (or loss) from the disposition of the interest in the Passthrough Entity to which section 1411(c)(4) may apply, and then reduce that gain (or loss) by the amount of non-passive gain (or loss) that would have been allocated to the transferor upon a hypothetical sale of all of the Passthrough Entity's assets for fair market value immediately before the transfer. The Treasury Department and the IRS received several comments questioning this approach based on the commentators' reading of section 1411(c)(4) to include gain/loss from the disposition of a partnership interest or S corporation stock *only to the extent of* the transferor's share of gain/loss from the Passthrough Entity's passive assets.

The 2013 Final Regulations do not provide rules regarding the calculation of net gain from the disposition of an interest in a Passthrough Entity to which section 1411(c)(4) may apply. After considering the comments received, the Treasury Department and the IRS have withdrawn the 2012 Proposed Regulations implementing section 1411(c)(4) and are issuing this notice of proposed rulemaking to propose revised rules for the implementation of section 1411(c)(4) adopting the commentators' suggestion. Accordingly, the 2013 Final Regulations reserve on this issue.

Proposed §1.1411-7(b) provides a calculation to determine how much of the gain or loss that is recognized for chapter 1 purposes is attributable to property owned, directly or indirectly, by the Passthrough Entity that, if sold, would give rise to net gain within the meaning of section 1411(c)(1)(A)(iii) ("*Section 1411 Property*"). Section 1411 Property is any property owned by, or held through, the Passthrough Entity that, if sold, would result in net gain or loss allocable to the partner or shareholder that is includable in determining the partner or shareholder's net investment income under §1.1411-4(a)(1)(iii). This definition recognizes that the items of property inside the Passthrough Entity that constitute Section 1411 Property might vary among transferors because a transferor may or may not be "passive" with respect to the property.

Proposed §1.1411-7(c) provides an optional simplified reporting method that qualified transferors may use in lieu of the calculation described in proposed §1.1411-7(b). Proposed §1.1411-7(d) contains additional rules that apply when a transferor disposes of its interest in the Passthrough Entity in a deferred recognition transaction to which section 1411 applies. Proposed §1.1411-7(f) provides rules for adjusting the amount of gain or loss computed under this paragraph for transferors subject to basis adjustments required by §1.1411-10(d). Proposed §1.1411-7(g) provides rules for information disclosures by a Passthrough Entity to transferors and for information reporting by individuals, trusts, and estates.

A. *Applicability of section 1411(c)(4)*

In the case of an individual, trust, or estate, the proposed regulations provide that section 1411(c)(4) applies to "*Section 1411(c)(4) Dispositions.*" A Section 1411(c)(4) Disposition is the disposition of an interest in a Passthrough Entity by an individual, estate, or trust if: (i) the Passthrough Entity is engaged in one or more trades or businesses, or owns an interest (directly or indirectly) in another Passthrough Entity that is engaged in one or more trades or businesses, other than the business of trading in financial instruments or commodities (within the meaning of §1.1411-5(a)(2)); and (ii) one or more of the trades or businesses of the Passthrough Entity is not a passive activity (within the meaning of §1.1411-5(a)(1)) of the transferor. Thus, if the transferor materially participates in one or more of the Passthrough Entity's trades or businesses (other than a trade or business of trading in financial instruments or commodities), then the transferor must use section 1411(c)(4) to calculate how much of the chapter 1 gain or loss from the disposition to include under section 1411(c)(1)(A)(iii). Section 1411(c)(4) only applies to dispositions of equity interests in partnerships and stock in S corporations, and does not apply to gain or loss recognized on, for example, indebtedness owed to the taxpayer by a partnership or S corporation.

Proposed §1.1411-7(a)(3) also addresses dispositions by Passthrough Entities of interests in lower-tier Passthrough Entities (a "*Subsidiary Passthrough Entity*"). Proposed §1.1411-7(a)(3)(ii) provides a "look through rule" that treats a partner or shareholder as owning a proportionate share of any Subsidiary Passthrough Entity, as if the partner or shareholder owned the interest directly. Thus, each partner of the uppertier Passthrough Entity must determine whether the disposition of the Subsidiary Passthrough Entity is a Section 1411(c)(4) Disposition based on whether the disposition would qualify as a Section 1411(c)(4) Disposition if that owner owned its interest in the Subsidiary Passthrough Entity directly.

The Treasury Department and the IRS anticipate that taxpayers who dispose of an interest in a partial recognition transaction or partial disposition transaction will apply the principles of this section by including a pro rata amount of gain or loss from the Passthrough Entity's Section 1411 Property. In addition, the Treasury Department and the IRS believe that the application of section 1411(c)(4) to gain or loss on distributions from a Passthrough Entity is adequately addressed in section 469, which is incorporated into section 1411(c)(4) through the general definition of passive activity contained in section 1411(c)(2)(A). Thus, the proposed regulations do not include special rules on partial recognition, partial disposition, and distribution transactions. However, the Treasury Department and the IRS request comments on whether additional rules on these topics are required.

B. *Definitions and special rules*

Proposed § 1.1411-7(a)(2) contains certain definitions and special rules that are unique to determining gain or loss under section 1411(c)(4) and apply only for purposes of proposed § 1.1411-7.

i. Definitions

Proposed § 1.1411-7 refers to partnerships or S corporations collectively as "Passthrough Entities" and the disposition of an interest in one of these entities is referred to as a "Section 1411(c)(4) Disposition." The purpose of section 1411(c)(4) is to allow gain attributable to non-passive activities to be excluded from the calculation of section 1411 tax upon the disposition of an interest in a Passthrough Entity. To accomplish this, section 1411(c)(4)(A) provides that gain from the disposition of an interest in a Passthrough Entity shall be taken into account in computing net investment income only to the extent of the amount of gain the transferor would have included under section 1411(c)(1)(A)(iii) if the Passthrough Entity sold all of its assets immediately before the Section 1411(c)(4) Disposition. The proposed regulations refer to the property that would generate gain for inclusion in section 1411(c)(1)(A)(iii) as "Section 1411 Property."

ii. Rules for Certain Liquidations

Proposed § 1.1411-7(a)(4)(i) provides that if a fully taxable disposition of the Passthrough Entity's assets is followed by the liquidation of the Passthrough Entity as part of a single plan, then the disposition will be treated as an asset sale for purposes of section 1411. Thus, no additional gain or loss is included in net investment income under § 1.1411-4(a)(1)(iii) on the subsequent liquidation of the Passthrough Entity by any transferor provided that the transferor would have satisfied proposed § 1.1411-7(a)(3) prior to the sale. The proposed regulations also state that, when an S corporation makes a section 336(e) or section 338(h)(10) election on the sale of its stock, the transaction will be treated under section 1411 as a fully taxable asset sale by the Passthrough Entity followed by a liquidation of the entity. Thus, no additional gain or loss is included in net investment income on the subsequent liquidation of the S corporation stock, provided a section 336(e) or section 338(h)(10) election is in effect.

iii. Rules for S Corporation Shareholders

Proposed § 1.1411-7(a)(4) provides two special rules for S corporation shareholders. First, proposed § 1.1411-7(a)(4)(ii) provides that the Passthrough Entity will be considered an S corporation for purposes of section 1411 and proposed § 1.1411-7 even though § 1.1362-3(a) treats the day of the transfer as the first date of the Passthrough Entity's C corporation short year (as defined therein). Second, proposed § 1.1411-7(a)(4)(iii) provides that the calculation under proposed § 1.1411-7(b) does not take into account any adjustment resulting from the hypothetical imposition of tax under section 1374 as a result of the proposed § 1.1411-7(b) deemed sale. This provision was also included in the 2012 Proposed Regulations. See also part 9.H of this preamble for a discussion of the application of section 1411(c)(4) to Qualified Subchapter S Trusts.

C. *Calculation of gain or loss includable in net investment income*

i. Primary Method - Proposed § 1.1411-7(b)

Proposed § 1.1411-7(b) provides the calculation for determining the amount of the transferor's gain or loss under section 1411(c)(1)(A)(iii) from the disposition of an interest in a Passthrough Entity. For dispositions resulting in chapter 1 gain, the transferor's gain equals the lesser of: (i) the amount of gain the transferor recognizes for chapter 1 purposes, or (ii) the transferor's allocable share of net gain from a deemed sale of the Passthrough Entity's Section 1411 Property (in other words, property which, if sold, would give rise to gain or loss that is includable in determining the transferor's net investment income under § 1.1411-4(a)(1)(iii)). The proposed regulations contain a similar rule when a transferor recognizes a loss for chapter 1 purposes.

The 2012 Proposed Regulations required that a transferor of an interest in a Passthrough Entity in which the transferor materially participated value each asset held by the Passthrough Entity to determine the total amount of gain or loss to include under section 1411(c)(4). Commentators indicated that this valuation requirement imposed undue administrative burdens on the transferor. The Treasury Department and the IRS acknowledge that for transferors of certain active interests in Passthrough Entities this property-by-property valuation requirement could be burdensome. Accordingly, these proposed regulations instead direct the transferor to rely on the valuation requirements under § 1.469-2T(e)(3), which the materially participating transferor should already be applying for purposes of chapter 1. These valuation requirements allow the transferor to compute gain or loss activity by activity.

Section 1.469-2T(e)(3) addresses dispositions of partnership interests and S corporation stock in the context of the passive activity loss rules for purposes of chapter 1. Section 1.469-2T(e)(3) provides guidance on allocating disposition gains or losses among the activities of the entity. These rules require the taxpayer to determine the overall gain or loss from each activity (regardless of whether or not the taxpayer materially participates in the activity). For this purpose, § 1.469-2T(e)(3)(ii)(B)(*1*)(*i*) to compute for each activity "the amount of net gain . . . that would have been allocated to the holder of such interest with respect thereto if the passthrough entity had sold its entire interest in such activity for its fair market value on the applicable valuation date." Section 1.469-2T(e)(3)(ii)(B)(*2*)(*i*) contains a corollary rule for dispositions at a loss.

Thus, the proposed regulations require a materially participating transferor to calculate its section 1411(c)(4) gain or loss by reference to the activity gain and loss amounts computed for chapter 1 purposes under § § 1.469-2T(e)(3)(ii)(B)(*1*)(*i*) and (e)(3)(ii)(B)(*2*)(*i*). Specifically for purposes of section 1411, the transferor's allocable share of gain or loss from a deemed sale of the Passthrough Entity's Section 1411 Property equals the sum of the transferor's allocable shares of net gains and net losses (as determined under the section 469 principles described above) from a hypothetical deemed sale of the activities in which the transferor does not materially participate.

Because section 1411(c)(4) applies to all activities in which a transferor in a Section 1411(c)(4) Disposition does not materially participate (whether held at a gain or a loss), certain provisions under section 469 do not apply for purposes of these rules. Proposed § 1.1411-7(b)(1)(i)(B) and (b)(1)(ii)(B) both apply § 1.469-2T(e)(3) without the recharacterization rule of § 1.469-2T(e)(3)(iii) because the recharacterization rule in § 1.469-2T(e)(3)(iii) is intended to recharacterize gains in certain circumstances as not being from a passive activity, and is thus not relevant in the context of section 1411.

The Treasury Department and the IRS request comments on other possible methods that would implement section 1411(c)(4) for dispositions described in proposed § 1.1411-7(a)(3)(i) (individuals, estates, and trusts) and proposed § 1.1411-7(a)(3)(ii) (tiered Passthrough Entity structures) in a manner consistent with the statute while reducing the administrative burden to the transferor and the Passthrough Entity.

ii. Optional Simplified Reporting Method - Proposed § 1.1411-7(c)

The proposed regulations also allow certain transferors to apply an optional simplified method in proposed § 1.1411-7(c) for calculating gain or loss for purposes of § 1.1411-4(a)(1)(iii). The Treasury Department and the IRS believe a simplified method is warranted when the amount of gain associated with passive assets owned by the Passthrough Entity is likely to be relatively small. To use the optional simplified reporting method, the transferor must meet certain qualifications under proposed § 1.1411-7(c)(2) and not be otherwise excluded under proposed § 1.1411-7(c)(3). Use of this simplified method is not mandatory for qualifying transferors. However, as discussed in part 10.G of this preamble, the Passthrough Entity may not be required under proposed § 1.1411-7(g) to provide (but is not precluded from providing) a transferor who qualifies to use the simplified method with information that the transferor would need to report under the primary method described in proposed § 1.1411-7(g).

The simplified reporting method is intended to limit the information sharing burden on Passthrough Entities by allowing transferors to rely on readily available information to calculate the amount of gain or loss included in net investment income under section 1411(c)(4). For this purpose, the optional simplified method relies on historic distributive share amounts received by the transferor from the Passthrough Entity to extrapolate a percentage of the assets within the Passthrough Entity that are passive with respect to the transferor for purposes of section 1411(c)(4). For example, if ten percent of the income reported on the applicable Schedules K-1 is of a type that would be included in net investment income, then the simplified reporting method presumes that ten percent of the chapter 1 gain on the disposition of the transferor's interest relates to Section 1411 Property of the Passthrough Entity for purposes of section 1411(c)(4).

a. Qualifications

To qualify for the optional simplified reporting method, a transferor in a Section 1411(c)(4) Disposition must meet at least one of two requirements. A transferor satisfies the first requirement if: (i) the sum of the transferor's allocable share during the "*Section 1411 Holding Period*" (as defined in the following paragraph, but generally the year of the disposition and the preceding two years) of separately stated items of income, gain, loss, and deduction (with any separately stated loss and deduction items included as positive numbers) of a type that the transferor would take into account in calculating net investment income is five percent or less of the sum of all separately stated items of income, gain, loss, and deduction (with any separately stated loss and deduction items included as positive numbers) allocated to the transferor during the Section 1411 Holding Period, and (ii) the gain recognized under chapter 1 by the transferor from the disposition of the Passthrough Entity is $5 million or less (including gains from multiple dispositions as part of a plan). A transferor satisfies the second alternative requirement if the gain recognized under chapter 1 by the transferor from the disposition of the Passthrough Entity is $250,000 or less (including gains from multiple dispositions as part of a plan). All dispositions of interests in the Passthrough Entity that occur during the transferor's taxable year will be presumed to be part of a plan.

Section 1411 Holding Period is defined to mean the year of disposition and the transferor's two taxable years preceding the disposition or the time period the transferor held the interest, whichever is less. Where the transferor acquires its interest from another Passthrough Entity in a nonrecognition transaction during the year of disposition or the prior two taxable years, the transferor must include in its Section 1411 Holding Period the period that the previous owner or owners held the interest. Also, where the transferor transferred an interest in a Subsidiary Passthrough Entity to a Passthrough Entity in a nonrecognition transaction during the year of the disposition or the prior two taxable years, the transferor must include in its Section 1411 Holding Period that period that it held the interest in the Subsidiary Passthrough Entity.

b. Nonavailability of optional simplified reporting method

Proposed § 1.1411-7(c)(4) provides certain exceptions for situations in which a transferor is ineligible to use the optional simplified reporting method. These exceptions include situations in which the transferor's historical distributive share amounts are less likely to reflect the gain in the Passthrough Entity's Section 1411 Property on the date of the transferor's disposition. The proposed regulations provide five exceptions for this purpose: (i) transferors that have held the interest for less than 12 months, (ii) certain contributions and distributions during the Section 1411 Holding Period, (iii) Passthrough Entities that have significantly modified the composition of their assets, (iv) S corporations that have recently converted from C corporations, and (v) partial dispositions.

The first exception requires that the transferor has held directly the interest in the Passthrough Entity (or held the interest indirectly in the case of a Subsidiary Passthrough Entity) for the twelve-month period preceding the Section 1411(c)(4) Disposition.

The second exception provides that a transferor is ineligible to use the optional simplified reporting method if the transferor transferred Section 1411 Property (other than cash or cash equivalents) to the Passthrough Entity, or received a distribution of property (other than Section 1411 property) from the Passthrough Entity, as part of a plan that includes the transfer of the interest in the Passthrough Entity. A transferor who contributes, directly or indirectly, Section 1411 Property (other than cash or cash equivalents) within 120 days of the disposition of the interest in the Passthrough Entity is presumed to have made the contribution as part of a plan that includes the transfer of the interest in the Passthrough Entity.

The third exception focuses on changes to the composition of the Passthrough Entity's assets during the Section 1411 Holding Period. Under this exception, the transferor is ineligible to use the optional simplified reporting method if the transferor knows or has reason to know that the percentage of the Passthrough Entity's gross assets that consists of Section 1411 Property (other than cash or cash equivalents) has increased or decreased by 25 percentage points or more during the transferor's Section 1411 Holding Period due to contributions, distributions, or asset acquisitions or dispositions in taxable or nonrecognition transactions.

The fourth exception provides that the optional simplified reporting method is not available if the Passthrough Entity was a C corporation during the Section 1411 Holding Period, and elected under section 1361 during that period to be taxed as an S corporation.

The final exception provides that a transferor partner cannot use the optional simplified reporting method if the transferor transfers only a partial interest that does not represent a proportionate share of all of the partner's economic rights in the partnership. For example, a partner who transfers a preferred interest in a partnership while retaining a common interest in that partnership cannot use the optional simplified reporting method.

iii. Request for Comments

The Treasury Department and the IRS request comments on the proposed section 1411(c)(4) calculation and on the optional simplified reporting method, including recommendations for other simplified means of calculating the gain or loss under section 1411(c)(4). The Treasury Department and the IRS also request comments regarding all aspects of the provisions relating to eligibility for the simplified method, including whether the 25 percentage point threshold for changes in the asset composition of a Passthrough Entity is appropriate.

D. *Tiered passthrough dispositions*

The Treasury Department and the IRS have reserved proposed § 1.1411-7(e) to further consider a simplified method for determining the section 1411(c)(4) gain resulting from the disposition by a Passthrough Entity of an interest in a Subsidiary Passthrough Entity as illustrated by the following example: A holds an interest in UTP, a Passthrough Entity that owns a 50-percent interest in LTP, a Subsidiary Passthrough Entity that is a real estate development company. A is a real estate developer and elected to group his real estate activities under § 1.469-9. When UTP sells its interest in LTP, any gain from the sale of that interest allocable to A through UTP may qualify under proposed § 1.1411-7(a)(2). However, A lacks access to the books of LTP that would allow A to compute its section 1411(c)(4) inclusion under the general rule of proposed § 1.1411-7(b). Additionally, A receives insufficient information from UTP to allow A to determine whether A qualifies to apply the Optional Simplified Reporting Method of proposed § 1.1411-7(c) or to undertake that computation. The Treasury Department and the IRS request comments regarding a simplified method for determining the section 1411(c)(4) gain resulting in such cases, including a detailed technical analysis with examples.

E. *Deferred recognition transactions*

To address the application of proposed §1.1411-7 to deferred recognition transactions, such as installment sales and certain private annuities, the proposed regulations provide that the calculations under proposed §§1.1411-7(b)(1), 1.1411-7(c)(2) and 1.1411-7(c)(4) (as applicable) are performed in the year of disposition as though the entire gain was recognized and taken into account in that year. For this purpose, it is assumed that any contingencies potentially affecting consideration to the transferor that are reasonably expected to occur will occur, and in the case of annuities based on the life expectancy of one or more individuals, the present value of the annuity (using existing Federal tax valuation methods) is used to determine the estimated gain. This approach allows the transferor to determine its section 1411 inclusion for each future installment. If under this approach no gain or loss from the disposition would be included in net investment income, then the transferor excludes each payment received from the deferred recognition transaction from net investment income. If under this approach only a portion of the chapter 1 gain on the disposition would be included in net investment income, then the difference between the gain recognized for chapter 1 purposes and the gain recognized for section 1411 purposes is considered an addition to basis, and after taking those basis adjustments into account, gain amounts are included in net investment income under §1.1411-4(a)(1)(iii) as payments are received in accordance with the existing rules for installment sales or private annuities.

F. *Adjustment to gain or loss due to section 1411 basis differences*

In addition to the calculation of gain or loss included in net investment income by reason of section 1411(c)(4) and proposed §1.1411-7, proposed §1.1411-7(f)(2) adjusts the gain or loss to take into account any disparities in the transferor's interest in the Passthrough Entity as a result of §1.1411-10(d) (relating to certain income from controlled foreign corporations and passive foreign investment companies where no §1.1411-10(g) election is made). These adjustments apply after applying the calculations set forth in paragraphs (b) through (e) of proposed §1.1411-7. Because the proposed §1.1411-7(f)(2) adjustments operate independently of the rules in paragraphs (b) through (e) of proposed §1.1411-7, they may result in gain for section 1411 purposes that exceeds chapter 1 gain (or a loss that exceeds the chapter 1 loss), or may result in a section 1411 loss when the transferor recognizes a chapter 1 gain (or vice versa).

G. *Information reporting*

Several commentators to the 2012 Proposed Regulations requested revisions to the proposed information reporting requirements. Other commentators expressed concern that the 2012 Proposed Regulations lacked provisions to compel a Passthrough Entity to provide the transferor with information required to comply with the 2012 Proposed Regulations §1.1411-7. In response, these proposed regulations simplify the information reporting requirements for transferors of interests in Passthrough Entities and impose information reporting requirements on certain Passthrough Entities to ensure that the transferor has sufficient information to comply with the computational requirements of proposed §1.1411-7.

i. Information Reporting by the Passthrough Entity

To compute the amount of gain or loss under proposed §1.1411-7(b), the transferors that compute section 1411(c)(4) gain or loss under the primary computation method of proposed §1.1411-7(b) must generally obtain from the Passthrough Entity the transferor's allocable share of the net gain or loss from the deemed sale of the Passthrough Entity's Section 1411 Property. However, the proposed regulations only require the Passthrough Entity to provide this information to transferors that are ineligible for the optional simplified reporting method in proposed §1.1411-7(c).

If a transferor qualifies to use the optional simplified reporting method in proposed §1.1411-7(c), but prefers to determine net gain or loss under proposed §1.1411-7(b), then the transferor must negotiate with the Passthrough Entity the terms under which the information will be supplied.

ii. Information Reporting by the Seller

Any transferor applying proposed §1.1411-7, including in reliance on the proposed regulations, must attach a statement to the transferor's income tax return for the year of disposition. That statement must include: (1) the taxpayer's name and taxpayer identification number; (2) the name and taxpayer identification number of the Passthrough Entity in which the interest was transferred; (3) the amount of the transferor's gain or loss on the disposition of the interest under chapter 1; and (4) the amount of adjustment to gain or loss by reason of basis differences for chapter 1 and section 1411 purposes. The transferor must also attach a copy of any information provided by the Passthrough Entity to the transferor relating to the transferor's allocable share of gain or loss from the deemed sale of the Passthrough Entity's Section 1411 Property.

H. *Qualified subchapter S trusts (QSSTs)*

The preamble to the 2012 Proposed Regulations requested comments on whether special coordination rules are necessary to address dispositions of stock in an S corporation held by a QSST. Specifically, the request for comments deals with the application of section 1411(c)(4) to the existing QSST stock disposition mechanics in §1.1361-1(j)(8).

In general, if an income beneficiary of a trust that meets the QSST requirements under section 1361(d)(3) makes a QSST election, the income beneficiary is treated as the section 678 owner with respect to the S corporation stock held by the trust. Section 1.1361-1(j)(8), however, provides that the trust, rather than the income beneficiary, is treated as the owner of the S corporation stock in determining the income tax consequences of the disposition of the stock by the QSST. Section 1361(d)(1)(C) and the last sentence of §1.1361-1(j)(8) provide that, solely for purposes of applying sections 465 and 469 to the income beneficiary, a disposition of S corporation stock by a QSST is treated as a disposition by the income beneficiary. However, in this special case, the QSST beneficiary, for chapter 1 purposes, does not have any passive activity gain from the disposition. Therefore, the entire suspended loss (to the extent not allowed by reason of the beneficiary's other passive net income in the disposition year) is a section 469(g)(1) loss, and is considered a loss from a nonpassive activity.

For purposes of section 1411, the inclusion of the operating income or loss of an S corporation in the beneficiary's net investment income is determined in a manner consistent with the treatment of a QSST beneficiary in chapter 1 (as explained in the preceding paragraph), which includes the determination of whether the S corporation is a passive activity of the beneficiary under section 469. However, because gain or loss resulting from the sale of S corporation stock by the QSST will be reported by the QSST and taxed to the trust by reason of §1.1361-1(j)(8), it is not clear whether the beneficiary's section 469 status with respect to the S corporation is attributed to the trust.

One commentator recommended that the disposition of S corporation stock by a QSST should be treated as a disposition of the stock by the income beneficiary for purposes of determining material participation for purposes of section 1411. In addition, the commentator recommended that the final regulations confirm that the special rule stated in the last sentence of §1.1361-1(j)(8) applies for purposes of section 1411 as it does for section 469 and 465.

After consideration of the comments, these proposed regulations provide that, in the case of a QSST, the application of section 1411(c)(4) is made at the trust level. This treatment is consistent with the chapter 1 treatment of the QSST by reason of §1.1361-1(j)(8). However, these proposed regulations do not provide any special computational rules for QSSTs within the context of section 1411(c)(4) for two reasons. First, the treatment of the stock sale as passive or nonpassive income is determined under section 469, which involves the issue of whether there is material participation by the trust. As discussed in part 4.F of the preamble to the 2013 Final Regulations, the Treasury Department and the IRS believe that the issue of material participation by estates and trusts, including QSSTs, is more appropriately addressed under section 469.

Additionally, one commentator noted that the IRS has addressed the treatment of certain asset sales as the functional equivalent of stock sales for purposes of §1.1361-1(j)(8) in a limited number of private letter rulings. In these cases, the private letter rulings held that gain from the sale of assets, which was followed by a liquidation, would be taxed at the trust level under §1.1361-1(j)(8) rather than being taxed at the beneficiary level. The commentator recommended that an asset sale followed by a liquidation, within the context of §1.1361-1(j)(8), should have a similar result under section 1411(c)(4). Similar to the issue of material participation by QSSTs discussed in the preceding paragraph, the Treasury Department and the IRS believe that the issue of whether an asset sale (deemed or actual) is the equivalent of a stock sale for purpose of the QSST rules should be addressed under the §1.1361-1(j) QSST regulations, rather than in §1.1411-7. However, the Treasury Department and the IRS believe that proposed §1.1411-7(a)(4)(i), which provides that asset sales followed by a liquidation is a disposition of S corporation stock for purposes of section 1411(c)(4), address the commentator's QSST issue.

Second, with respect to the section 1411 treatment of the disposition by the beneficiary by reason of section 1361(d)(1)(C) and the last sentence of §1.1361-1(j)(8), the Treasury Department and the IRS believe that the general administrative principles enumerated in §1.1411-1(a), when combined with the general treatment of section 469(g) losses within §1.1411-4, provide an adequate framework for the treatment of QSSTs beneficiaries without the need for a special computational rule within §1.1411-7.

Proposed Applicability Date

These regulations are proposed to apply for taxable years beginning after December 31, 2013, except that §1.1411-3(d)(3) is proposed to apply to taxable years beginning after December 31, 2012.

Special Analyses

It has been determined that this notice of proposed rulemaking is not a significant regulatory action as defined in Executive Order 12866, as supplemented by Executive Order 13563. Therefore, a regulatory assessment is not required. It also has been determined that section 553(b) of the Administrative Procedure Act (5 U.S.C. chapter 5) does not apply to the proposed regulations. Pursuant to the Regulatory Flexibility Act (RFA) (5 U.S.C. chapter 6), it is hereby certified that the proposed regulations will not have a significant economic impact on a substantial number of small entities. The applicability of the proposed regulations are limited to individuals, estates, and trusts, that are not small entities as defined by the RFA (5 U.S.C. 601). Accordingly, the RFA does not apply. Therefore, a regulatory flexibility analysis is not required. Pursuant to section 7805(f) of the Code, the proposed regulations have been submitted to the Chief Counsel for Advocacy of the Small Business Administration for comment on its impact on small business.

Comments and Requests for a Public Hearing

Before these proposed regulations are adopted as final regulations, consideration will be given to any comments that are submitted timely to the IRS as prescribed in this preamble under the "Addresses" heading. The Treasury Department and the IRS specifically request comments on all aspects of the proposed rules. All comments will be available at *www.regulations.gov* or upon request. A public hearing will be scheduled if requested in writing by any person that timely submits written comments. If a public hearing is scheduled, notice of the date, time, and place for the public hearing will be published in the **Federal Register**.

Drafting Information

The principal authors of the proposed regulations are David H. Kirk and Adrienne M. Mikolashek, IRS Office of the Associate Chief Counsel (Passthroughs and Special Industries). However, other personnel from the Treasury Department and the IRS participated in their development.

[¶ 49,595] Proposed Amendments of Regulations (REG-134417-13), published in the Federal Register on November 29, 2013.

[Code Sec. 501]

Tax-exempt organizations: Social welfare organizations: Qualifications: Candidate-related political activity.—Amendments of Reg. §1.501(c)(4)-1, providing guidance to tax-exempt social welfare organizations on political activities related to candidates that will not be considered to promote social welfare, are proposed.

AGENCY: Internal Revenue Service (IRS), Treasury.

ACTION: Notice of proposed rulemaking.

SUMMARY: This document contains proposed regulations that provide guidance to tax-exempt social welfare organizations on political activities related to candidates that will not be considered to promote social welfare. These regulations will affect tax-exempt social welfare organizations and organizations seeking such status. This document requests comments from the public regarding these proposed regulations. This document also requests comments from the public regarding the standard under current regulations that considers a tax-exempt social welfare organization to be operated exclusively for the promotion of social welfare if it is "primarily" engaged in activities that promote the common good and general welfare of the people of the community, including how this standard should be measured and whether this standard should be changed.

DATES: Written or electronic comments and requests for a public hearing must be received by February 27, 2014.

ADDRESSES: Send submissions to: CC:PA:LPD:PR (REG-134417-13), Room 5205, Internal Revenue Service, P.O. Box 7604, Ben Franklin Station, Washington, DC 20044. Submissions may be hand-delivered Monday through Friday between the hours of 8 a.m. and 4 p.m. to CC:PA:LPD:PR (REG-134417-13), Courier's Desk, Internal Revenue Service, 1111 Constitution Avenue NW, Washington, DC, or sent electronically via the Federal eRulemaking Portal at *http://www.regulations.gov* (IRS REG-134417-13).

FOR FURTHER INFORMATION CONTACT: Concerning the proposed regulations, Amy F. Giuliano at (202) 317-5800; concerning submission of comments and requests for a public hearing, Oluwafunmilayo Taylor at (202) 317-6901 (not toll-free numbers).

SUPPLEMENTARY INFORMATION:

Paperwork Reduction Act

The collection of information contained in this notice of proposed rulemaking has been submitted to the Office of Management and Budget for review in accordance with the Paperwork Reduction Act of 1995 (44 U.S.C. 3507(d)). Comments on the collection of information should be sent to the **Office of Management and Budget**, Attn: Desk Officer for the Department of the Treasury, Office of Information and Regulatory Affairs, Washington, DC 20503, with copies to the **Internal Revenue Service**, Attn: IRS Reports Clearance Officer, SE:W:CAR:MP:T:T:SP, Washington, DC 20224. Comments on the collection of information should be received by January 28, 2014.

Comments are specifically requested concerning:

Whether the proposed collection of information is necessary for the proper performance of the functions of the IRS, including whether the information will have practical utility;

The accuracy of the estimated burden associated with the proposed collection of information;

How the quality, utility, and clarity of the information to be collected may be enhanced; and

How the burden of complying with the proposed collection of information may be minimized, including through forms of information technology.

The collection of information in these proposed regulations is in § 1.501(c)(4)-1(a)(2)(iii)(D), which provides a special rule for contributions by an organization described in section 501(c)(4) of the Internal Revenue Code (Code) to an organization described in section 501(c). Generally, a contribution by a section 501(c)(4) organization to a section 501(c) organization that engages in candidate-related political activity will be considered candidate-related political activity by the section 501(c)(4) organization. The special rule in § 1.501(c)(4)-1(a)(2)(iii)(D) provides that a contribution to a section 501(c) organization will not be treated as a contribution to an organization engaged in candidate-related political activity if the contributor organization obtains a written representation from an authorized officer of the recipient organization stating that the recipient organization does not engage in any such activity and the contribution is subject to a written restriction that it not be used for candidate-related political activity. This special provision would not apply if the contributor organization knows or has reason to know that the representation is inaccurate or unreliable. The expected recordkeepers are section 501(c)(4) organizations that choose to contribute to, and to seek a written representation from, a section 501(c) organization.

Estimated number of recordkeepers: 2,000.

Estimated average annual burden hours per recordkeeper: 2 hours.

Estimated total annual recordkeeping burden: 4,000 hours.

A particular section 501(c)(4) organization may require more or less time, depending on the number of contributions for which a representation is sought.

An agency may not conduct or sponsor, and a person is not required to respond to, a collection of information unless it displays a valid control number assigned by the Office of Management and Budget.

Books or records relating to a collection of information must be retained as long as their contents may become material in the administration of any internal revenue law. Generally, tax returns and return information are confidential, as required by section 6103.

Background

Section 501(c)(4) of the Code provides a Federal income tax exemption, in part, for "[c]ivic leagues or organizations not organized for profit but operated exclusively for the promotion of social welfare." This exemption dates back to the enactment of the federal income tax in 1913. See Tariff Act of 1913, 38 Stat. 114 (1913). The statutory provision was largely unchanged until 1996, when section 501(c)(4) was amended to prohibit inurement of an organization's net earnings to private shareholders or individuals.

Prior to 1924, the accompanying Treasury regulations did not elaborate on the meaning of "promotion of social welfare." See Regulations 33 (Rev.), art. 67 (1918). Treasury regulations promulgated in 1924 explained that civic leagues qualifying for exemption under section 231(8) of the Revenue Act of 1924, the predecessor to section 501(c)(4) of the 1986 Code, are "those not organized for profit but operated exclusively for purposes beneficial to the community as a whole," and generally include "organizations engaged in promoting the welfare of mankind, other than organizations comprehended within [section 231(6) of the Revenue Act of 1924, the predecessor to section 501(c)(3) of the 1986 Code]." See Regulations 65, art. 519 (1924). The regulations remained substantially the same until 1959.

The current regulations under section 501(c)(4) were proposed and finalized in 1959. They provide that "[a]n organization is operated exclusively for the promotion of social welfare if it is primarily engaged in promoting in some way the common good and general welfare of the people of the community." Treas. Reg. § 1.501(c)(4)-1(a)(2)(i). An organization "embraced" within section 501(c)(4) is one that is "operated primarily for the purpose of bringing about civic betterments and social improvements." Id. The regulations further provide that "[t]he promotion of social welfare does not include direct or indirect participation or intervention in political campaigns on behalf of or in opposition to any candidate for public office." Treas. Reg. § 1.501(c)(4)-1(a)(2)(ii). This language is similar to language that appears in section 501(c)(3) requiring section 501(c)(3) organizations not to "participate in, or intervene in (including the publishing or distributing of statements), any political campaign on behalf of (or in opposition to) any candidate for public office" ("political campaign intervention"). However, unlike the absolute prohibition that applies to charitable organizations described in section 501(c)(3), an organization that primarily engages in activities that promote social welfare will be considered under the current regulations to be operating exclusively for the promotion of social welfare, and may qualify for taxexempt status under section 501(c)(4), even though it engages in some political campaign intervention.

The section 501(c)(4) regulations have not been amended since 1959, although Congress took steps in the intervening years to address further the relationship of political campaign activities to tax-exempt status. In particular, section 527, which governs the tax treatment of political organizations, was enacted in 1975 and provides generally that amounts received as contributions and other funds raised for political purposes (section 527 exempt function income) are not subject to tax. Section 527(e)(1) defines a "political organization" as "a party, committee, association, fund, or other organization (whether or not incorporated) organized and operated primarily for the purpose of directly or indirectly accepting contributions or making expenditures, or both, for an exempt function." Section 527(f) also imposes a tax on exempt organizations described in section 501(c), including section 501(c)(4) social welfare organizations, that make an expenditure furthering a section 527 exempt function. The tax is imposed on the lesser of the organization's net investment income or section 527 exempt function expenditures. Section 527(e)(2) defines "exempt function" as "the function of influencing or attempting to influence the selection, nomination, election, or appointment of any individual to any federal, state, or local public office or office in a political organization, or the election of Presidential or Vice-Presidential electors" (referred to in this document as "section 527 exempt function").[1]

Unlike the section 501(c)(3) standard of political campaign intervention, and the similar standard currently applied under section 501(c)(4), both of which focus solely on candidates for elective public office, a section 527 exempt function encompasses activities related to a broader range of officials, including those who are appointed or nominated, such as executive branch officials and certain judges. Thus, while there is currently significant overlap in the activities that constitute political campaign intervention under sections 501(c)(3) and 501(c)(4) and those that further a section 527 exempt function, the concepts are not synonymous.

Over the years, the IRS has stated that whether an organization is engaged in political campaign intervention depends upon all of the facts and circumstances of each case. See Rev. Rul. 78-248 (1978-1 CB 154) (illustrating application of the facts and circumstances analysis to voter education activities conducted by section 501(c)(3) organizations); Rev. Rul. 80-282 (1980-2 CB 178) (amplifying Rev. Rul. 78-248 regarding the timing and distribution of voter education materials); Rev. Rul. 86-95 (1986-2 CB 73) (holding a public forum for the purpose of educating and informing the voters, which provides fair and impartial treatment of candidates, and which does not promote or advance one candidate over another; does not constitute political campaign intervention under section 501(c)(3)). More recently, the IRS released Rev. Rul. 2007-41 (2007-1 CB 1421), providing 21

---

[1] In 2000 and 2002, section 527 was amended to require political organizations (with some exceptions) to file a notice with the IRS when first organized and to periodically disclose publicly certain information regarding their expenditures and contributions. See sections 527(i) and 527(j).

examples illustrating facts and circumstances to be considered in determining whether a section 501(c)(3) organization's activities (including voter education, voter registration, and get-out-the-vote drives; individual activity by organization leaders; candidate appearances; business activities; and Web sites) result in political campaign intervention. The IRS generally applies the same facts and circumstances analysis under section 501(c)(4). See Rev. Rul. 81-95 (1981-1 CB 332) (citing revenue rulings under section 501(c)(3) for examples of what constitutes participation or intervention in political campaigns for purposes of section 501(c)(4)).

Similarly, Rev. Rul. 2004-6 (2004-1 CB 328) provides six examples illustrating facts and circumstances to be considered in determining whether a section 501(c) organization (such as a section 501(c)(4) social welfare organization) that engages in public policy advocacy has expended funds for a section 527 exempt function. The analysis reflected in these revenue rulings for determining whether an organization has engaged in political campaign intervention, or has expended funds for a section 527 exempt function, is fact-intensive.

Recently, increased attention has been focused on potential political campaign intervention by section 501(c)(4) organizations. A recent IRS report relating to IRS review of applications for tax-exempt status states that "[o]ne of the significant challenges with the 501(c)(4) [application] review process has been the lack of a clear and concise definition of 'political campaign intervention.'" Internal Revenue Service, "Charting a Path Forward at the IRS: Initial Assessment and Plan of Action" at 20 (June 24, 2013). In addition, "[t]he distinction between campaign intervention and social welfare activity, and the measurement of the organization's social welfare activities relative to its total activities, have created considerable confusion for both the public and the IRS in making appropriate section 501(c)(4) determinations." *Id.* at 28. The Treasury Department and the IRS recognize that both the public and the IRS would benefit from clearer definitions of these concepts.

Explanation of Provisions

1. Overview

The Treasury Department and the IRS recognize that more definitive rules with respect to political activities related to candidates -rather than the existing, fact-intensive analysis - would be helpful in applying the rules regarding qualification for tax-exempt status under section 501(c)(4). Although more definitive rules might fail to capture (or might sweep in) activities that would (or would not) be captured under the IRS' traditional facts and circumstances approach, adopting rules with sharper distinctions in this area would provide greater certainty and reduce the need for detailed factual analysis in determining whether an organization is described in section 501(c)(4). Accordingly, the Treasury Department and the IRS propose to amend Treas. Reg. § 1.501(c)(4)-1(a)(2) to identify specific political activities that would be considered candidate-related political activities that do not promote social welfare.

To distinguish the proposed rules under section 501(c)(4) from the section 501(c)(3) standard and the similar standard currently applied under section 501(c)(4), the proposed regulations would amend Treas. Reg. §1.501(c)(4)-1(a)(2)(ii) to delete the current reference to "direct or indirect participation or intervention in political campaigns on behalf of or in opposition to any candidate for public office," which is similar to language in the section 501(c)(3) statute and regulations. Instead the proposed regulations would revise Treas. Reg. §1.501(c)(4)-1(a)(2)(ii) to state that "[t]he promotion of social welfare does not include direct or indirect candidate-related political activity." As explained in more detail in section 2 of this preamble, the proposed rules draw upon existing definitions of political campaign activity, both in the Code and in federal election law, to define candidate-related political activity that would not be considered to promote social welfare. The proposed rules draw in particular from certain statutory provisions of section 527, which specifically deals with political organizations and taxes section 501(c) organizations, including section 501(c)(4) organizations, on certain types of political campaign activities. Recognizing that it may be beneficial to have a more uniform set of rules relating to political campaign activity for tax-exempt organizations, the Treasury Department and the IRS request comments in subparagraphs a through c of this section of the preamble regarding whether the same or a similar approach should be adopted in addressing political campaign activities of other section 501(c) organizations, as well as whether the regulations under section 527 should be revised to adopt the same or a similar approach in defining section 527 exempt function activity.

a. Interaction with section 501(c)(3)

These proposed regulations do not address the definition of political campaign intervention under section 501(c)(3). The Treasury Department and the IRS recognize that, because such intervention is absolutely prohibited under section 501(c)(3), a more nuanced consideration of the totality of facts and circumstances may be appropriate in that context. The Treasury Department and the IRS request comments on the advisability of adopting an approach to defining political campaign intervention under section 501(c)(3) similar to the approach set forth in these regulations, either in lieu of the facts and circumstances approach reflected in Rev. Rul. 2007-41 or in addition to that approach (for example, by creating a clearly defined presumption or safe harbor). The Treasury Department and the IRS also request comments on whether any modifications or exceptions would be needed in the section 501(c)(3) context and, if so, how to ensure that any such modifications or exceptions are clearly defined and administrable. Any such change would be introduced in the form of proposed regulations to allow an additional opportunity for public comment.

b. Interaction with section 527

As noted in the "Background" section of this preamble, a section 501(c)(4) organization is subject to tax under section 527(f) if it makes expenditures for a section 527 exempt function. Consistent with section 527, the proposed regulations provide that "candidate-related political activity" for purposes of section 501(c)(4) includes activities relating to selection, nomination, election, or appointment of individuals to serve as public officials, officers in a political organization, or Presidential or Vice Presidential electors. These proposed regulations do not, however, address the definition of "exempt function" activity under section 527 or the application of section 527(f). The Treasury Department and the IRS request comments on the advisability of adopting rules that are the same as or similar to these proposed regulations for purposes of defining section 527 exempt function activity in lieu of the facts and circumstances approach reflected in Rev. Rul. 2004-6. Any such change would be introduced in the form of proposed regulations to allow an additional opportunity for public comment.

c. Interaction with sections 501(c)(5) and 501(c)(6)

The proposed regulations define candidate-related political activity for social welfare organizations described in section 501(c)(4). The Treasury Department and the IRS are considering whether to amend the current regulations under sections 501(c)(5) and 501(c)(6) to provide that exempt purposes under those regulations (which include "the betterment of the conditions of those engaged in [labor, agricultural, or horticultural] pursuits" in the case of a section 501(c)(5) organization and promoting a "common business interest" in the case of a section 501(c)(6) organization) do not include candidaterelated political activity as defined in these proposed regulations. The Treasury Department and the IRS request comments on the advisability of adopting this approach in defining activities that do not further exempt purposes under sections 501(c)(5) and 501(c)(6). Any such change would be introduced in the form of proposed regulations to allow an additional opportunity for public comment.

d. Additional guidance on the meaning of "operated exclusively for the promotion of social welfare"

The Treasury Department and the IRS have received requests for guidance on the meaning of "primarily" as used in the current regulations under section 501(c)(4). The current regulations provide, in part, that an organization is operated exclusively for the promotion of social welfare within the meaning of section 501(c)(4) if it is "primarily engaged" in promoting in some way the common good and general welfare of the people of the community. Treas. Reg. §1.501(c)(4)-1(a)(2)(i). As part of the same 1959 Treasury decision promulgating the current section 501(c)(4) regulations, regulations under section 501(c)(3) were adopted containing similar language: "[a]n organization will be regarded as 'operated exclusively' for one or more exempt purposes only if it engages primarily in activities which accomplish one or more of such exempt purposes specified in section 501(c)(3)." Treas. Reg. §1.501(c)(3)-1(c)(1). Unlike the section 501(c)(4) regulations, however, the section 501(c)(3) regulations also provide that "[a]n organization will not be so regarded if more than an insubstantial part of its activities is not in furtherance of an exempt purpose." *Id.*

Some have questioned the use of the "primarily" standard in the section 501(c)(4) regulations and suggested that this standard should be changed. The Treasury Department and the IRS are considering whether the current section 501(c)(4) regulations should be modified in this regard and, if the "primarily" standard is retained, whether the standard should be defined with more precision or revised to mirror the standard under the section 501(c)(3) regulations. Given the potential impact on organizations currently recognized as described in section 501(c)(4) of any change in the "primarily" standard, the Treasury Department and the IRS wish to receive comments from a broad range of organizations before deciding how to proceed. Accordingly, the Treasury Department and the IRS invite comments from the public on what proportion of an organization's activities must promote social welfare for an organization to qualify under section 501(c)(4) and whether additional limits should be imposed on any or all activities that do not further social welfare. The Treasury Department and the IRS also request comments on how to measure the activities of organizations seeking to qualify as section 501(c)(4) social welfare organizations for these purposes.

2. *Definition of Candidate-Related Political Activity*

These proposed regulations provide guidance on which activities will be considered candidate-related political activity for purposes of the regulations under section 501(c)(4). These proposed regulations would replace the language in the existing final regulation under section 501(c)(4) – "participation or intervention in political campaigns on behalf of or in opposition to any candidate for public office" – with a new term – "candidate-related political activity" – to differentiate the proposed section 501(c)(4) rule from the standard employed under section 501(c)(3) (and currently employed under section 501(c)(4)). The proposed rule is intended to help organizations and the IRS more readily identify activities that constitute candidate-related political activity and, therefore, do not promote social welfare within the meaning of section 501(c)(4). These proposed regulations do not otherwise define the promotion of social welfare under section 501(c)(4). The Treasury Department and the IRS note that the fact that an activity is not candidate-related political activity under these proposed regulations does not mean that the activity promotes social welfare. Whether such an activity promotes social welfare is an independent determination.

In defining candidate-related political activity for purposes of section 501(c)(4), these proposed regulations draw key concepts from the federal election campaign laws, with appropriate modifications reflecting the purpose of these regulations to define which organizations may receive the benefits of section 501(c)(4) tax-exempt status and to promote tax compliance (as opposed to campaign finance regulation). In addition, the concepts drawn from the federal election campaign laws have been modified to reflect that section 501(c)(4) organizations may be involved in activities related to local or state elections (in addition to federal elections), as well as the broader scope of the proposed definition of candidate (which is not limited to candidates for federal elective office).

The proposed regulations provide that candidate-related political activity includes activities that the IRS has traditionally considered to be political campaign activity per se, such as contributions to candidates and communications that expressly advocate for the election or defeat of a candidate. The proposed regulations also would treat as candidate-related political activity certain activities that, because they occur close in time to an election or are election-related, have a greater potential to affect the outcome of an election. Currently, such activities are subject to a facts and circumstances analysis before a determination can be made as to whether the activity furthers social welfare within the meaning of section 501(c)(4). Under the approach in these proposed regulations, such activities instead would be subject to a more definitive rule. In addition, consistent with the goal of providing greater clarity, the proposed regulations would identify certain specific activities as candidate-related political activity. The Treasury Department and the IRS acknowledge that the approach taken in these proposed regulations, while clearer, may be both more restrictive and more permissive than the current approach, but believe the proposed approach is justified by the need to provide greater certainty to section 501(c)(4) organizations regarding their activities and reduce the need for fact-intensive determinations.

The Treasury Department and the IRS note that a particular activity may fit within one or more categories of candidate-related political activity described in subsections b through e of this section 2 of the preamble; the categories are not mutually exclusive. For example, the category of express advocacy communications may overlap with the category of certain communications close in time to an election.

a. *Definition of "candidate"*

These proposed regulations provide that, consistent with the scope of section 527, "candidate" means an individual who identifies himself or is proposed by another for selection, nomination, election, or appointment to any public office or office in a political organization, or to be a Presidential or Vice-Presidential elector, whether or not the individual is ultimately selected, nominated, elected, or appointed. In addition, the proposed regulations clarify that for these purposes the term "candidate" also includes any officeholder who is the subject of a recall election. The Treasury Department and the IRS note that defining "candidate-related political activity" in these proposed regulations to include activities related to candidates for a broader range of offices (such as activities relating to the appointment or confirmation of executive branch officials and judicial nominees) is a change from the historical application in the section 501(c)(4) context of the section 501(c)(3) standard of political campaign intervention, which focuses on candidates for elective public office only. See Treas. Reg. §1.501(c)(3)-1(c)(3)(iii). These proposed regulations instead would apply a definition that reflects the broader scope of section 527 and that is already applied to a section 501(c)(4) organization engaged in section 527 exempt function activity through section 527(f).

b. *Express advocacy communications*

These proposed regulations provide that candidate-related political activity includes communications that expressly advocate for or against a candidate. These proposed regulations draw from Federal Election Commission rules in defining "expressly advocate," but expand the concept to include communications expressing a view on the selection, nomination, or appointment of individuals, or on the election or defeat of one or more candidates or of candidates of a political party. These proposed regulations make clear that all communications – including written, printed, electronic (including Internet), video, and oral communications – that express a view, whether for or against, on a clearly identified candidate (or on candidates of a political party) would constitute candidate-related political activity. A candidate can be "clearly identified" in a communication by name, photograph, or reference (such as "the incumbent" or a reference to a particular issue or characteristic distinguishing the candidate from others). The proposed regulations also provide that candidate-related political activity includes any express advocacy communication the expenditures for which an organization reports to the Federal Election Commission under the Federal Election Campaign Act as an independent expenditure.

c. *Public communications close in time to an election*

Under current guidance, the timing of a communication about a candidate that is made shortly before an election is a factor tending to indicate a greater risk of political campaign intervention or section 527 exempt function activity. In the interest of greater clarity, these proposed regulations would move away from the facts and circumstances approach that the IRS has traditionally applied in analyzing certain activities conducted close in time to an election. These proposed regulations draw from provisions of federal election campaign laws that treat certain communications that are close in time to an election and that refer to a clearly identified candidate as electioneering communications, but make certain modifications. The proposed regulations expand the types of candidates and communications that are covered to reflect the types of activities an organization might conduct related to local and state, as well as federal, contests, including any election or ballot measure to recall an individual who holds state or local elective public office. In addition, the expansion of the types of communications covered in the proposed regulations reflects the fact that an organization's tax exempt status is determined based on all of its activities, even low cost and volunteer activities, not just its large expenditures.

Under the proposed definition, any public communication that is made within 60 days before a general election or 30 days before a primary election and that clearly identifies a candidate for public office (or, in the case of a general election, refers to a political party represented in that election) would be considered candidate-related political activity. These timeframes are the same as those appearing in the Federal Election Campaign Act definition of electioneering communications. The definition of "election," including what would be treated as a primary or a general election, is consistent with section 527(j) and the federal election campaign laws.

A communication is "public" if it is made using certain mass media (specifically, by broadcast, in a newspaper, or on the Internet), constitutes paid advertising, or reaches or is intended to reach at least 500 people (including mass mailings or telephone banks). The Treasury Department and the IRS intend that content previously posted by an organization on its Web site that clearly identifies a candidate and remains on the Web site during the specified pre-election period would be treated as candidate-related political activity.

The proposed regulations also provide that candidate-related political activity includes any communication the expenditures for which an organization reports to the Federal Election Commission under the Federal Election Campaign Act, including electioneering communications.

The approach taken in the proposed definition of candidate-related political activity would avoid the need to consider potential mitigating or aggravating circumstances in particular cases (such as whether an issue-oriented communication is "neutral" or "biased" with respect to a candidate). Thus, this definition would apply without regard to whether a public communication is intended to influence the election or some other, non-electoral action (such as a vote on pending legislation) and without regard to whether such communication was part of a series of similar communications. Moreover, a public communication made outside the 60-day or 30-day period would not be candidate-related political activity if it does not fall within the ambit of express advocacy communications or another specific provision of the definition. The Treasury Department and the IRS request comments on whether the length of the period should be longer (or shorter) and whether there are particular communications that (regardless of timing) should be excluded from the definition because they can be presumed to neither influence nor constitute an attempt to influence the outcome of an election. Any comments should specifically address how the proposed exclusion is consistent with the goal of providing clear rules that avoid fact-intensive determinations.

The Treasury Department and the IRS also note that this rule regarding public communications close in time to an election would not apply to public communications identifying a candidate for a state or federal appointive office that are made within a specified number of days before a scheduled appointment, confirmation hearing or vote, or other selection event. The Treasury Department and the IRS request comments on whether a similar rule should apply with respect to communications within a specified period of time before such a scheduled appointment, confirmation hearing or vote, or other selection event.

d. *Contributions to a candidate, political organization, or any section 501(c) entity engaged in candidate-related political activity*

The proposed definition of candidate-related political activity would include contributions of money or anything of value to or the solicitation of contributions on behalf of (1) any person if such contribution is recognized under applicable federal, state, or local campaign finance law as a reportable contribution; (2) any political party, political committee, or other section 527 organization; or (3) any organization described in section 501(c) that engages in candidate-related political activity within the meaning of this proposed rule. This definition of contribution is similar to the definition of contribution that applies for purposes of section 527. The Treasury Department and the IRS intend that the term "anything of value" would include both in-kind donations and other support (for example, volunteer hours and free or discounted rentals of facilities or mailing lists). The Treasury Department and the IRS request comments on whether other transfers, such as indirect contributions described in section 276 to political parties or political candidates, should be treated as candidate-related political activity.

The Treasury Department and the IRS recognize that a section 501(c)(4) organization making a contribution may not know whether a recipient section 501(c) organization engages in candidate-related political activity. The proposed regulations provide that, for purposes of this definition, a recipient organization would not be treated as a section 501(c) organization engaged in candidate-related political activity if the contributor organization obtains a written representation from an authorized officer of the recipient organization stating that the recipient organization does not engage in any such activity and the contribution is subject to a written restriction that it not be used for candidate-related political activity. This special provision would apply only if the contributor organization does not know or have reason to know that the representation is inaccurate or unreliable.

e. *Election-related activities*

The proposed definition of candidate-related political activity would include certain specified election-related activities, including the conduct of voter registration and get-out-the-vote drives, distribution of material prepared by or on behalf of a candidate or section 527 organization, and preparation or distribution of a voter guide and accompanying material that refers to a candidate or a political party. In addition, an organization that hosts an event on its premises or conducts an event off-site within 30 days of a primary election or 60 days of a general election at which one or more candidates in such election appear as part of the program (whether or not such appearance was previously scheduled) would be engaged in candidate-related political activity under the proposed definition.

The Treasury Department and the IRS acknowledge that under the facts and circumstances analysis currently used for section 501(c)(4) organizations as well as for section 501(c)(3) organizations, these election-related activities may not be considered political campaign intervention if conducted in a non-partisan and unbiased manner. However, these determinations are highly fact-intensive. The Treasury Department and the IRS request comments on whether any particular activities conducted by section 501(c)(4) organizations should be excepted from the definition of candidate-related political activity as voter education activity and, if so, a description of how the proposed exception will both ensure that excepted activities are conducted in a non-partisan and unbiased manner and avoid a fact-intensive analysis.

f. *Attribution to a section 501(c)(4) organization of certain activities and communications*

These proposed regulations provide that activities conducted by an organization include, but are not limited to, (1) activities paid for by the organization or conducted by the organization's officers, directors, or employees acting in that capacity, or by volunteers acting under the organization's direction or supervision; (2) communications made (whether or not such communications were previously scheduled) as part of the program at an official function of the organization or in an official publication of the organization; and (3) other communications (such as television advertisements) the creation or distribution of which is paid for by the organization. These proposed regulations also provide that an organization's Web site is an official publication of the organization, so that material posted by the organization on its Web site may constitute candidate-related political activity. The proposed regulations do not specifically address material posted by third parties on an organization's Web site. The Treasury Department and the IRS request comments on whether, and under what circumstances, material posted by a third party on an interactive part of the organization's Web site should be attributed to the organization for purposes of this rule. In addition, the Treasury Department and the IRS have stated in guidance under section 501(c)(3) regarding political campaign intervention that when a charitable organization chooses to establish a link to another Web site, the organization is responsible for the consequences of establishing and maintaining that link, even if it does not have control over the content of the linked site. See Rev. Rul. 2007-41. The Treasury Department and the IRS request comments on whether the consequences of establishing and maintaining a link to another Web site should be the same or different for purposes of the proposed definition of candidate-related political activity.

Proposed Effective/Applicability Date

These regulations are proposed to be effective the date of publication of the Treasury decision adopting these rules as final regulations in the **Federal Register**. For proposed date of applicability, see § 1.501(c)(4)-1(c).

Statement of Availability for IRS Documents

For copies of recently issued Revenue Procedures, Revenue Rulings, Notices, and other guidance published in the Internal Revenue Bulletin or Cumulative Bulletin, please visit the IRS Web site at *http://www.irs.gov* or the Superintendent of Documents, U.S. Government Printing Office, Washington, DC 20402.

Special Analyses

It has been determined that this notice of proposed rulemaking is not a significant regulatory action as defined in Executive Order 12866, as supplemented by Executive Order 13563. Therefore, a regulatory assessment is not required. It also has been determined that section 553(b) of the Administrative Procedure Act (5 U.S.C. chapter 5) does not apply to these regulations. It is hereby certified that this rule will not have a significant economic impact on a substantial number of small entities. This certification is based on the fact that only a minimal burden would be imposed by the rule, if adopted. Under the proposal, if a section 501(c)(4) organization chooses to contribute to a section 501(c) organization and wants assurance that the contribution will not be treated as candidate-related political activity, it may seek a written representation that the recipient does not engage in candidate-related political activity within the meaning of these regulations. Therefore, a regulatory flexibility analysis under the Regulatory Flexibility Act (5 U.S.C. chapter 6) is not required. Pursuant to section 7805(f) of the Code, this notice of proposed rulemaking has been submitted to the Chief Counsel for Advocacy of the Small Business Administration for comment on its impact on small business.

Comments and Requests for Public Hearing

Before these proposed regulations are adopted as final regulations, consideration will be given to any written comments (a signed original and eight (8) copies) or electronic comments that are submitted timely to the IRS. The Treasury Department and the IRS generally request comments on all aspects of the proposed rules. In particular, the Treasury Department and the IRS request comments on whether there are other specific activities that should be included in, or excepted from, the definition of candidate-related political activity for purposes of section 501(c)(4). Such comments should address how the proposed addition or exception is consistent with the goals of providing more definitive rules and reducing the need for fact-intensive analysis of the activity. All comments submitted by the public will be made available for public inspection and copying at *www.regulations.gov* or upon request.

A public hearing will be scheduled if requested in writing by any person who timely submits written comments. If a public hearing is scheduled, notice of the date, time, and place for the public hearing will be published in the **Federal Register**.

Drafting Information

The principal author of these regulations is Amy F. Giuliano, Office of Associate Chief Counsel (Tax Exempt and Government Entities). However, other personnel from the IRS and Treasury Department participated in their development.

[¶ 49,599]   Proposed Amendments of Regulations (REG-159420-04), published in the Federal Register on December 13, 2013.

[Code Sec. 41]

Research credit: Qualified research expenditures: Intra-group gross receipts: Controlled groups of corporations.—Amendments of Reg. §§ 1.41-0 and 1.41-6, relating to the treatment of qualified research expenditures (QREs) and gross receipts resulting from transactions between members of a controlled group of corporations or a group of trades or businesses under common control (intra-group transactions) for purposes of determining the credit under Code Sec. 41 for increasing research activities, are proposed.

AGENCY: Internal Revenue Service (IRS), Treasury.

ACTION: Notice of proposed rulemaking and notice of public hearing.

SUMMARY: This document contains proposed regulations under section 41 of the Internal Revenue Code (Code) relating to the treatment of qualified research expenditures (QREs) and gross receipts resulting from transactions between members of a controlled group of corporations or a group of trades or businesses under common control (intra-group transactions) for purposes of determining the credit under section 41 for increasing research activities (research credit). These proposed regulations will affect controlled groups of corporations or groups of trades or businesses under common control (controlled groups) that are engaged in research activities. This document also provides notice of a public hearing on these proposed regulations.

DATES: Written or electronic comments must be received by March 13, 2014. Outlines of topics to be discussed at the public hearing scheduled for April 23, 2014, at 10:00 a.m. must be received by March 13, 2014.

ADDRESSES: Send submissions to: CC:PA:LPD:PR (REG-159420-04), Room 5205, Internal Revenue Service, PO Box 7604, Ben Franklin Station, Washington, DC 20044. Submissions also may be hand delivered Monday through Friday between the hours of 8 a.m. and 4 p.m. to: CC:PA:LPD:PR (REG-159420-04), Courier's Desk, Internal Revenue Service, 1111 Constitution Avenue, NW, Washington, DC, or sent electronically via the Federal eRulemaking Portal at http://www.regulations.gov (IRS REG-159420-04). The public hearing will be held in the IRS Auditorium, Internal Revenue Building, 1111 Constitution Avenue, NW, Washington, DC.

FOR FURTHER INFORMATION CONTACT: Concerning these proposed regulations, David Selig, (202) 317-4137; concerning submission of comments, the hearing, and/or to be placed on the building access list to attend the hearing, Oluwafunmilayo (Funmi) Taylor, (202) 317-6901 (not toll-free numbers).

SUPPLEMENTARY INFORMATION:

Background

These proposed regulations address how the interaction of section 41(f)(1) (relating to the treatment of controlled groups as a single taxpayer) and section 41(c)(7) (relating to the exclusion from gross receipts of amounts received by a foreign corporation that are not effectively connected to a United States trade or business) affects the computation of gross receipts resulting from intra-group transactions between domestic controlled group members (domestic members) and foreign corporate members of the controlled group (foreign corporate members). These proposed regulations apply to an intra-group transaction that is followed by a transaction between a foreign corporate member and a party outside of the controlled group involving the same or a modified version of tangible or intangible property or services that was the subject of the intra-group transaction, and the transaction with the party outside of the controlled group does not give rise to gross receipts that are effectively connected with a trade or business within the United States, the Commonwealth of Puerto Rico, or any possession of the United States.

Section 41(f)(1) provides that in determining the amount of the research credit, all members of the same controlled group of corporations and all commonly controlled trades or businesses (whether or not incorporated) shall be treated as a single taxpayer. For this purpose, controlled group is defined by reference to section 1563(a), except that "more than 50 percent" is substituted for "at least 80 percent," and the determination is made without regard to subsections (a)(4) (regarding certain insurance companies) and (e)(3)(C) (regarding stock owned by an employees' trust). The statute provides no rules, however, regarding how the single taxpayer treatment is to be implemented. Commentators have noted the ambiguity associated with similar provisions of the Code. See, e.g., Prop. Reg. §1.199-1, 70 FR 67220, 67236 (November 4, 2005) ("the single corporation language in section 199(d)(4)(A) has created confusion among commentators and the proposed regulations clarify the meaning of this language").

The IRS and the Treasury Department believe that the single taxpayer concept should be interpreted consistently with the purpose the statute is intended to advance. The single taxpayer concept as it relates to the computation of the research credit first appeared in 1981 when Congress initially enacted the research credit. As originally enacted, the research credit was determined solely by reference to a taxpayer's QREs. Specifically, to ensure that the research credit was available only for actual increases in research expenditures, former section 44F(f)(1) provided that the QREs of a controlled group of corporations and all commonly controlled trades or businesses (whether or not incorporated) were aggregated and treated as those of a single taxpayer. H. Rept. No. 97-201, 1981-2 CB 364-365 (demonstrating that controlled groups are prevented from increasing research expenditures by shifting these expenditures from an entity that has a high baseline of research expenditures to one that does not).

In 1989, Congress modified the computation of the research credit (now section 41 of the Code) by adding the base amount concept embodied in section 41(a)(1)(B), which included gross receipts in the calculation of the research credit for the first time. See the Omnibus Budget Reconciliation Act of 1989 (Public Law 101-239, §7110) (the "1989 Act"). The legislative history of the 1989 Act explains that gross receipts were included in the computation of the research credit to address concerns with the existing rules and incentivize spending on research activities. In particular, Congress wished to modify the pre-existing incremental credit structure in order to maximize the research credit's efficiency by not allowing (to the extent possible) credits for research that would have been undertaken in any event. Congress believed that businesses often determine their research budgets as a fixed percentage of gross receipts and determined that it was appropriate to compute the research credit, in part, based on the increase in a taxpayer's gross receipts. This approach also had the advantage of effectively indexing the research credit for inflation and preventing taxpayers from being rewarded for increases in research spending that are attributable solely to inflation. See H.R. Rep. No. 101-247, 101st Cong., 1st Sess. 1199-1200 (1989).

The 1989 Act also amended section 41 to provide certain parameters for measuring gross receipts. Specifically, section 41(c)(7) provides that gross receipts are reduced by returns and allowances made during the taxable year. Section 41(c)(7) also provides that in the case of a foreign corporation, only gross receipts effectively connected with the conduct of a trade or business within the United States, the Commonwealth of Puerto Rico, or any possession of the United States are taken into account in the computation of the research credit. See section 41(c)(7), as amended. The legislative history of the 1989 Act does not expressly address the purpose of the gross receipts provision relating to foreign corporations. The enactment of the controlled group aggregation rules in section 41(f)(1) (treating all members of a controlled group as a single taxpayer) preceded the enactment of the foreign corporation gross receipts rule in section 41(c)(7). Congress, however, did not make clear how the two provisions should interact and did not provide any additional indication regarding the consequences of being treated as a single taxpayer, including when the deemed single taxpayer is comprised of both domestic and foreign controlled group members.

Current Regulatory Scheme

Section 1.41-3(c) defines gross receipts generally as the total amount, determined under the taxpayer's method of accounting, derived from all its activities and from all sources. Section 1.41-6(i) interprets the single taxpayer concept of section 41(f)(1) to provide that transfers between members of a controlled group of corporations are generally disregarded for purposes of determining the research credit under section 41 for both gross receipts and QREs. The IRS and the Treasury Department believe that, in most cases, the general rule that disregards intra-group transactions for both gross receipts and QREs furthers the statutory purpose of ensuring that the computation of the research credit is based upon an economic measure of gross receipts relative to QREs and not artificially increased by multiple intra-group transactions.

The IRS and the Treasury Department believe, however, that an interpretation of section 41(f)(1) that completely excludes gross receipts associated with certain transactions is inconsistent with Congressional intent. For example, assume that a domestic corporation incurs research expenditures and sells a product that it produced to a foreign corporate member, and the foreign corporate member then sells the product to a customer in a transaction that does not give rise to gross receipts effectively connected with a trade or business within the United States, the Commonwealth of Puerto Rico, or any possession of the United States. If gross receipts from the sales transactions are excluded because the intra-group transaction is disregarded under §1.41-6 and the foreign corporate member's gross receipts are excluded under section 41(c)(7) for the second transaction, the aggregate amount of gross receipts for purposes of determining the research credit is distorted. The distortion results because the QREs of the domestic member are included, but its gross receipts from the sale to the foreign corporate member are not. Accordingly, the IRS and the Treasury Department propose to revise the regulations to include gross receipts in this situation, including in cases where the property is modified prior to being transferred by the foreign corporate member, the gross receipts are in the form of royalties, interest, or other cash or non-cash remuneration, or the gross receipts relate to services ultimately provided by the foreign corporate member to a third-party customer.

However, the IRS and the Treasury Department believe that multiple inclusions of gross receipts associated with intra-group transactions involving the same or a modified version of tangible or intangible property or services would be inconsistent with Congressional intent. Thus, for example, it would not be appropriate to overstate gross receipts, and thereby reduce the research credit available to a controlled group, by taking into account the transfer of a single piece of property (including a modified form of the same property) more than one time (that is, first as a transfer between controlled group members and then as a transfer with a third party).

Explanation of Provisions

The proposed regulations retain the current rule that generally disregards transactions among members of a controlled group for purposes of computing the research credit, but provide a narrow exception to this rule. Under the exception, gross receipts (within the meaning of §1.41-3(c)) from an intra-group transaction are taken into account if (1) a foreign corporate member engages in a transaction with a party outside of the group (external transaction) involving the same or a modified version of tangible or intangible property or a service that was previously the subject of one or more intra-group transactions (an internal transaction); and (2) the external transaction does not give rise to gross receipts that are effectively connected with a trade or business within the United States, the Commonwealth of Puerto Rico, or any possession of the United States. The exception harmonizes the application of sections 41(f)(1) and 41(c)(7) and is consistent with the purposes of these provisions as well as the broader statutory changes that made gross receipts a central feature of the research credit computation.

For example, if a domestic member transfers property to a foreign corporate member, and the foreign corporate member then transfers the property outside of the controlled group in a transaction that does not give rise to gross receipts that are effectively connected with a trade or business within the United States, the Commonwealth of Puerto Rico, or any possession of the United States, the proposed regulations provide that the domestic member includes in its gross receipts amounts received from the foreign corporate member for that transaction. The amounts are taken into account in computing gross receipts in the taxable year in which the foreign corporate member engages in the external transaction. The fact that the foreign corporate member that ultimately engages in a transaction involving the property outside of the controlled group is not the same foreign corporate member to which the domestic member directly transferred the property (for example, one foreign corporate member re-transfers the property to another foreign corporate member) is not material to the determination of the domestic member's gross receipts.

To prevent multiple inclusions of gross receipts in cases in which transactions involving the same or a modified version of tangible or intangible property or services occur successively between domestic and foreign corporate members, the proposed regulations provide that only the last internal transaction giving rise to gross receipts (within the meaning of section 1.41-3(c)) is taken into account in the research credit computation.

These proposed regulations embody the statutory requirement of consistency in determining a taxpayer's base amount (generally, the product of the fixed-base percentage and 4-year average annual gross receipts preceding the credit year). *See* section 41(c)(6). Accordingly, in computing the research credit for taxable years beginning on or after the date of publication of these proposed regulations as final regulations, QREs and gross receipts taken into account in computing a taxpayer's fixed-base percentage and a taxpayer's base amount must be determined on a basis consistent with the definition of QREs and gross receipts for the credit year, without regard to the law in effect for the earlier taxable years that are taken into account in computing the fixed-base percentage or the base amount. However, the proposed regulations do not specify the manner in which a taxpayer must make the base amount adjustments. The IRS and the Treasury Department recognize that accounting for intra-group transactions in prior years presents a unique burden because taxpayers may not have records for the base years with sufficient information to satisfy the proposed regulations' requirement of consistency. These proposed regulations are intended to capture some measure of intra-group gross receipts for purposes of satisfying the requirement of consistency, but are not intended to preclude research credit claims for taxpayers that do not have adequate information in their books and records for the base years. Accordingly, the IRS and Treasury Department request comments regarding the need for a rule or safe harbor in applying the consistency rule for purposes of determining the base amount in accordance with these proposed regulations.

QREs

These proposed regulations remove the rules in § 1.41-6(i)(4) (relating to the treatment of lease payments as QREs) to reflect changes to section 41 by the Tax Reform Act of 1986, Public Law 99-514.

These proposed regulations generally would not change the rules concerning whether payments between members of a controlled group constitute QREs. The IRS and the Treasury Department request comments concerning whether any revisions are necessary.

Proposed Effective Date

The amendments to § 1.41-6(i) are proposed to apply to taxable years beginning on or after the date that these regulations are published as final regulations in the **Federal Register**.

Special Analysis

It has been determined that this notice of proposed rulemaking is not a significant regulatory action as defined in Executive Order 12866, as supplemented by Executive Order 13563. It also has been determined that section 553(b) of the Administrative Procedures Act (5 U.S.C. chapter 5) does not apply to these regulations, and because these regulations do not impose a collection of information on small entities, the Regulatory Flexibility Act (5 U.S.C. chapter 6) does not apply. Therefore, a Regulatory Flexibility Analysis is not required. Pursuant to section 7805(f) of the Code, this notice of proposed rulemaking has been submitted to the Chief Counsel for Advocacy of the Small Business Administration for comment on its impact on small business.

Comments and Public Hearing

Before these proposed regulations are adopted as final regulations, consideration will be given to any electronic or written comments (a signed original and eight (8) copies) that are submitted timely to the IRS. The IRS and the Treasury Department request comments on all aspects of the proposed rules.

All comments will be available for public inspection and copying.

A public hearing has been scheduled for April 23, 2014, beginning at 10:00 a.m. in the IRS Auditorium, Internal Revenue Building, 1111 Constitution Avenue, N.W., Washington, DC. Due to building security procedures, visitors must enter at the Constitution Avenue entrance. In addition, all visitors must present photo identification to enter the building. Because of access restrictions, visitors will not be admitted beyond the immediate entrance area more than 30 minutes before the hearing starts. For information about having your name placed on the building access list to attend the hearing, see the "FOR FURTHER INFORMATION CONTACT" section of this preamble.

The rules of 26 CFR 601.601(a)(3) apply to the hearing. Persons who wish to present oral comments at the hearing must submit electronic or written comments by March 13, 2014, and submit an outline of the topics to be discussed and the amount of time to be devoted to each topic (a signed original and eight (8) copies) by March 13, 2014. A period of 10 minutes will be allotted to each person for making comments. An agenda showing the scheduling of the speakers will be prepared after the deadline for receiving outlines has passed. Copies of the agenda will be available free of charge at the hearing.

Drafting Information

The principal author of these proposed regulations is David Selig, Office of the Associate Chief Counsel (Passthroughs and Special Industries). However, other personnel from the IRS and the Treasury Department participated in their development.

[¶ 49,600] Proposed Amendments of Regulations (REG-136984-12), published in the Federal Register on December 16, 2013 (corrected 5/23/2014).

[Code Sec. 752]

Partnerships: Partners: Overlapping economic risk of loss: Nonrecourse loan to partnership.—Amendments of Reg. §§ 1.752-0, 1.752-2, 1.752-4 and 1.752-5, relating to recourse liabilities of a partnership and the special rules for related persons, are proposed.

AGENCY: Internal Revenue Service (IRS), Treasury.

ACTION: Notice of proposed rulemaking.

SUMMARY: This document contains proposed regulations under section 752 of the Internal Revenue Code (Code) relating to recourse liabilities of a partnership and the special rules for related persons. The proposed regulations affect partnerships and their partners.

DATES: Written or electronic comments and request for a public hearing must be received by March 17, 2014.

ADDRESSES: Send submissions to: CC:PA:LPD:PR (REG-136984-12), room 5203, Internal Revenue Service, PO Box 7604, Ben Franklin Station, Washington, DC 20044. Submissions may be hand-delivered Monday through Friday between the hours of 8 a.m. and 4 p.m. to CC:PA:LPD:PR (REG-136984-12), Courier's Desk, Internal Revenue Service, 1111 Constitution Avenue, NW, Washington, DC, or sent electronically, via the Federal eRulemaking Portal at *www.regulations.gov* (IRS REG-136984-12).

FOR FURTHER INFORMATION CONTACT: Concerning the proposed regulations, Caroline E. Hay or Deane M. Burke, at (202) 317-5279; concerning the submissions of comments and requests for a public hearing, Oluwafunmilayo (Funmi) Taylor at (202) 317-5179 (not toll-free numbers).

SUPPLEMENTARY INFORMATION:

Background

This document contains proposed amendments to the Income Tax Regulations (26 CFR part 1) under section 752 regarding a partner's share of recourse partnership liabilities.

Section 752(a) provides, in general, that any increase in a partner's share of partnership liabilities (or an increase in a partner's individual liabilities by reason of the assumption by the partner of partnership liabilities) will be considered a contribution of money by such partner to the partnership. Conversely, section 752(b) provides that any decrease in a partner's share of partnership liabilities (or a decrease in a partner's individual liabilities by reason of the assumption by the partnership of such individual liabilities) will be considered a distribution of money to the partner by the partnership.

When determining a partner's share of partnership liabilities, the regulations under section 752 distinguish between two categories of liabilities—recourse and nonrecourse. In general, a partnership liability is recourse to the extent that a partner or related person bears the economic risk of loss as provided in § 1.752-2 and nonrecourse to the extent that no partner or related person bears the economic risk of loss. See § 1.752-1(a)(1) and (2).

These proposed regulations provide guidance as to when and to what extent a partner is treated as bearing the economic risk of loss for a partnership liability when multiple partners bear the economic risk of loss for the same partnership liability (overlapping economic risk of loss). In addition, these proposed regulations provide guidance when a partner has a payment obligation with respect to a liability or makes a nonrecourse loan to the partnership (and no other partner bears the economic risk of loss for that liability) and such partner is related to another partner in the partnership.

Explanation of Provisions

1. Overlapping Risk of Loss

Under § 1.752-2(a), a partner's share of a recourse partnership liability equals the portion of that liability, if any, for which the partner or related person bears the economic risk of loss. Section 1.752-2(b)(1) provides that a partner bears the economic risk of loss for a partnership liability to the extent that, if the partnership constructively liquidated, the partner or related person would be obligated to make a payment on the partnership obligation to any person or a contribution to the partnership (payment obligation) because the liability becomes due and payable and the partner or related person would not be entitled to reimbursement from another partner or a person that is related to another partner. Moreover, under § 1.752-2(c)(1), a partner bears the economic risk of loss for a partnership liability to the extent that the partner or a related person makes (or acquires an interest in) a nonrecourse loan to the partnership and the economic risk of loss for the liability is not borne by another partner. Section 1.752-4(c) provides that the amount of an indebtedness is taken into account only once.

The IRS and the Treasury Department are aware that there is uncertainty as to how partners should share a partnership liability if multiple partners bear the economic risk of loss with respect to the same liability. The temporary regulations under § 1.752-1T(d)(3)(i) that preceded the existing final regulations under section 752 addressed the issue of overlapping economic risk of loss by providing that "if the aggregate amount of the economic risk of loss that all partners are determined to bear with respect to a partnership liability (or portion thereof) . . . exceeds the amount of such liability (or portion thereof), then the economic risk of loss borne by each partner with respect to such liability shall equal the amount determined by multiplying the amount of such liability (or portion thereof) by the fraction obtained by dividing the amount of the economic risk of loss that such partner is determined to bear with respect to that liability (or portion thereof) by the sum of such amounts for all partners." The rule in the temporary regulations, however, was not included in the final regulations in part in response to comments that the proposed regulations addressed too many topics generally and should be simplified to focus on more basic concepts. See 56 FR 36704-02 (1991-2 CB 1125).

The IRS and the Treasury Department have received comments requesting guidance in this area. The IRS and the Treasury Department continue to balance the importance of simplicity in regulations under section 752 against the utility of providing additional guidance on identified issues. In light of comments received, the IRS and the Treasury Department believe that a rule is needed to address overlapping economic risk of loss due to uncertainty under the current regulations and believe that the concepts from the temporary regulations regarding the overlapping risk of loss rule provide a reasonable approach in addressing how a partnership liability should be shared among partners bearing the economic risk of loss for the same liability. Accordingly, these proposed regulations adopt the rule from the temporary regulations.

2. Tiered Partnerships

The rules under section 752 regarding the allocation of liabilities in a tiered partnership structure also may result in overlapping economic risk of loss. Section 1.752-2(i) provides that if a partnership (the "upper-tier partnership") owns (directly or indirectly through one or more partnerships) an interest in another partnership (the "lower-tier partnership"), the liabilities of the lower-tier partnership are allocated to the upper-tier partnership in an amount equal to the sum of the following: (1) the amount of the economic risk of loss that the upper-tier partnership bears with respect to the liabilities; and (2) the amount of any other liabilities with respect to which partners of the upper-tier partnership bear the economic risk of loss. Section 1.752-4(a) further provides that an upper-tier partnership's share of the liabilities of a lower-tier partnership (other than any liability of the lower-tier partnership that is owed to the upper-tier partnership) is treated as a liability of the upper-tier partnership for purposes of applying section 752 and the regulations thereunder to the partners of the upper-tier partnership.

The regulations therefore allocate a recourse liability of a lower-tier partnership to an upper-tier partnership if either that upper-tier partnership, or one of its partners, bears the economic risk of loss for the liability. When a partner of the upper-tier partnership is also a partner in the lower-tier partnership, and that partner bears the economic risk of loss with respect to a liability of the lower-tier partnership, the current regulations do not provide guidance as to how the lower-tier partnership should allocate the liability between the upper-tier partnership and the partner. The IRS and the Treasury Department believe that the lower-tier partnership should allocate the liability directly to the partner. The IRS and the Treasury Department believe that this approach is more administrable and ensures that the additional basis resulting from the liability is only for the benefit of the partner that bears the economic risk of loss for the liability. Thus, the proposed regulations modify the tiered-partnership rule in § 1.752-2(i)(2) to prevent a liability of a lower-tier partnership from being allocated to an upper-tier partnership when a partner of the lower-tier partnership and the upper-tier partnership bears the economic risk of loss for such liability.

3. *Related Party Rules*

A. *Constructive Owner of Stock*

Under § 1.752-4(b)(1), a person is related to a partner if the partner and the person bear a relationship to each other that is specified in sections 267(b) or 707(b)(1), except that 80 percent or more is substituted for 50 percent or more in each of those sections, a person's family is determined by excluding siblings, and sections 267(e)(1) and 267(f)(1)(A) are disregarded.

In determining whether a partner and a person bear a relationship to each other that is specified in section 267(b), the constructive stock ownership rules in section 267(c) are applicable. Specific to partnerships, section 267(c)(1) provides, in part, that stock owned directly or indirectly by or for a partnership is considered as being owned proportionately by or for its partners. Therefore, if a partnership owns all of the stock in a corporation, a partner that owns 80 percent or more of the interests in the partnership is considered to be related to the corporation under § 1.752-4(b)(1). If the corporation has a payment obligation with respect to a liability of its partnership owner, or the corporation lends to the partnership and the economic risk of loss for the liability is not borne by another partner, any partner that is treated as related to the corporation bears the economic risk of loss for the partnership liability under § 1.752-2. The IRS and the Treasury Department believe that partners in a partnership, where that partnership owns stock in a corporation that is a lender to the partnership or has a payment obligation with respect to a liability of its partnership owner, should not be treated as related, through ownership of the partnership, to the corporation. A partner's economic risk of loss that is limited to the partner's equity investment in the partnership should be treated differently than the risk of loss beyond that investment. Thus, for purposes of § 1.752-4(b)(1), the proposed regulations disregard section 267(c)(1) in determining whether a partner in a partnership is considered as owning stock in a corporation to the extent the corporation is a lender or has a payment obligation with respect to a liability of its partnership owner.

B. *Person Related to Multiple Partners*

Section 1.752-4(b)(2)(i) provides that if a person is related to more than one partner in a partnership under § 1.752-4(b)(1), the related party rules in § 1.752-4(b)(1) are applied by treating the person as related only to the partner with whom there is the highest percentage of related ownership (greatest percentage rule). If, however, two or more partners have the same percentage of related ownership and no other partner has a greater percentage, the liability is allocated equally among the partners having the equal percentages of related ownership.

The IRS and the Treasury Department have recently received comments requesting that the greatest percentage rule be removed. The commenter explains that if a person is related to more than one partner under § 1.752-4(b)(1), the ultimate determination of a person's relatedness to a partner should not be based on which partner has the highest percentage of related ownership because differences in ownership percentages within a 20-percent range do not justify treating a person as related to one partner over another. After considering the comments, the IRS and the Treasury Department agree with the comments, especially given the administrative burden associated with determining precise ownership percentages above the 80-percent threshold in § 1.752-4(b)(1)(i). Therefore, the proposed regulations remove the greatest percentage rule and provide that if a person is a lender or has a payment obligation for a partnership liability and is related to more than one partner, those partners share the liability equally.

C. *Related Partner Exception to Related Party Rules*

Section 1.752-4(b)(2)(iii) provides that persons owning interests directly or indirectly in the same partnership are not treated as related persons for purposes of determining the economic risk of loss borne by each of them for the liabilities of the partnership (the related partner exception). The IRS and the Treasury Department are aware that taxpayers are uncertain of the application of the related partner exception following the decision in *IPO II v. Commissioner*, 122 T.C. 295 (2004). *IPO II* involved an individual, Mr. Forsythe, who owned 100 percent of an S corporation, Indeck Overseas, and 70 percent of a second S corporation, Indeck Energy. Mr. Forsythe's children owned the remaining 30 percent of Indeck Energy. Mr. Forsythe and Indeck Overseas formed a partnership, IPO II, which received a loan from a bank. To secure that loan, Mr. Forsythe, Indeck Energy, and Indeck Power (a C corporation of which Mr. Forsythe owned 63 percent) entered into guarantees with the bank. IPO II allocated 99 percent of the increase in basis attributable to this liability to Indeck Overseas. *Id.* at 296-97. The Tax Court held that this allocation was incorrect because Indeck Overseas was not directly or indirectly liable for the debt. The court, while stressing that it interprets "the policy behind the related partner exception as preventing the shifting of basis from a party who bears actual economic risk of loss to one who does not," did not end its analysis by stating that Mr. Forsythe guaranteed the debt, and thus his economic risk of loss could not be shifted to Indeck Overseas which did not guarantee the debt. *Id.* at 303. The court instead examined whether Indeck Overseas indirectly bore the economic risk of loss due to its relationship with a related party, Indeck Energy. The Tax Court held that the relationship between Indeck Overseas and Indeck Energy arose through Mr. Forsythe. Because the related partner exception shuts off the relationship between Mr. Forsythe and Indeck Overseas, it should be turned off for all purposes; therefore, Indeck Energy was not related to Indeck Overseas. *Id.* at 304.

The IRS and Treasury Department believe the related partner exception should only apply where a partner has a payment obligation or is the lender with respect to a partnership liability. *IPO II* may be read to expand the related partner exception to turn off relationships between related partners in a partnership without limitation. Under this broad interpretation, the related partner exception could be improperly applied to turn off attribution of economic risk of loss between related partners even when none of the related partners directly bears the economic risk of loss for a partnership liability. The IRS and the Treasury Department believe that such an interpretation could have unintended results, including causing intercompany debts to be treated as nonrecourse because no partner alone owns 80 percent or more of the lending company and the partners are not treated as related to each other. The proposed regulations provide that the related partner exception only applies when a partner bears the economic risk of loss for a liability of the partnership because the partner is a lender under § 1.752-2(c)(1) or has a payment obligation for the partnership liability. The proposed regulations also clarify that an indirect interest in a partnership is an indirect interest through one or more partnerships.

D. *Special Rule Where Entity Structured To Avoid Related Person Status*

Section 1.752-4(b)(2)(iv) provides special rules for when an entity is structured to avoid related person status. The proposed regulations do not propose any changes to these rules. However, as a result of other changes made to simplify the organization of § 1.752-4, the rules in § 1.752-4(b)(2)(iv) are now in § 1.752-4(b)(4) of the proposed regulations. In addition, the example in § 1.752-4(b)(2)(iv)(C) is now *Example 5* under § 1.752-4(b)(5) of the proposed regulations.

4. *Request for Comments: Liquidating Distributions of Tiered Partnership Interests*

The IRS and the Treasury Department are considering the proper treatment of liabilities when an upper-tier partnership (transferor) bears the economic risk of loss for a lower-tier partnership liability and distributes, in a liquidating distribution, its interest in the lower-tier partnership to one of its partners (transferee) but the partner does not bear the economic risk of loss for the lower-tier partnership's liability. The IRS and the Treasury Department request comments on the timing of the liability reallocation relative to the transaction that causes the liability to change from recourse to nonrecourse.

Proposed Applicability Date

The regulations are proposed to apply to liabilities incurred or assumed by a partnership on or after the date these regulations are published as final regulations in the **Federal Register**, other than liabilities incurred or assumed by a partnership pursuant to a written binding contract in effect prior to that date.

Special Analyses

It has been determined that this notice of proposed rulemaking is not a significant regulatory action as defined in Executive Order 12866, as supplemented by Executive Order 13563. Therefore, a regulatory assessment is not required. It also has been determined that section 553(b) of the Administrative Procedure Act (5 U.S.C. chapter 5) does not apply to these proposed regulations. Because these proposed regulations do not impose a collection of information on small entities, the Regulatory Flexibility Act (5 U.S.C. chapter 6) does not apply. Pursuant to section 7805(f) of the Code, this notice of proposed rulemaking will be submitted to the Chief Counsel for Advocacy of the Small Business Administration for comment on its impact on small business.

Comments and Requests for a Public Hearing

Before these proposed regulations are adopted as final regulations, consideration will be given to any comments that are submitted timely to the IRS as prescribed in this preamble under the "Addresses" heading. The IRS and the Treasury Department request comments on all aspects of the proposed rules. All comments will be available at www.regulations.gov or upon request. A public hearing will be scheduled if requested in writing by any person that timely submits written comments. If a public hearing is scheduled, notice of the date, time, and place for the public hearing will be published in the **Federal Register**.

Drafting Information

The principal authors of these proposed regulations are Caroline E. Hay and Deane M. Burke, Office of the Associate Chief Counsel (Passthroughs and Special Industries). However, other personnel from the IRS and Treasury Department participated in their development.

[¶ 49,604] **Proposed Amendments of Regulations (REG-144468-05)**, published in the Federal Register on January 16, 2014 (corrected 4/15/2014).

[Code Secs. 704, 732, 734, 737, 743, 755 and 1502]

Partnerships: Built-in gains and losses: Partnership allocations.—Amendments of Reg. §§1.704-3, 1.704-4, 1.732-2, 1.734-1, 1.734-2, 1.737-1, 1.743-1, 1.755-1 and 1.1502-13, providing guidance on certain provisions of the American Jobs Creation Act of 2004 and conforming the regulations to statutory changes in the Taxpayer Relief Act of 1997, are proposed.

AGENCY: Internal Revenue Service (IRS), Treasury.

ACTION: Notice of proposed rulemaking and notice of public hearing.

SUMMARY: The proposed regulations provide guidance on certain provisions of the American Jobs Creation Act of 2004 and conform the regulations to statutory changes in the Taxpayer Relief Act of 1997. The proposed regulations also modify the basis allocation rules to prevent certain unintended consequences of the current basis allocation rules for substituted basis transactions. Finally, the proposed regulations provide additional guidance on allocations resulting from revaluations of partnership property. The proposed regulations affect partnerships and their partners. This document also contains a notice of a public hearing on these proposed regulations. DATES: Comments must be received by April 16, 2014. Requests to speak and outlines of the topics to be discussed at the public hearing scheduled for April 30, 2014, at 10 a.m., must be received by April 16, 2014.

ADDRESSES: Send submissions to: CC:PA:LPD:PR (REG-144468-05), room 5203, Internal Revenue Service, P.O. Box 7604, Ben Franklin Station, Washington, DC 20044. Submissions may be hand-delivered Monday through Friday between the hours of 8 a.m. and 4 p.m. to: CC:PA:LPD:PR (REG-144468-05), Courier's Desk, Internal Revenue Service, 1111 Constitution Avenue NW, Washington, DC. Alternatively, taxpayers may submit comments electronically via the Federal eRulemaking Portal at *www.regulations.gov* (IRS REG-144468-05).

FOR FURTHER INFORMATION CONTACT: Concerning the proposed regulations, Wendy Kribell or Benjamin Weaver at (202) 317-6850; concerning submissions of comments, the hearing, and/or to be placed on the building access list to attend the hearing, Oluwafunmilayo (Funmi) Taylor, (202) 317-6901 (not toll-free numbers).

SUPPLEMENTARY INFORMATION:

Paperwork Reduction Act

The collection of information contained in this notice of proposed rulemaking has been submitted to the Office of Management and Budget for review in accordance with the Paperwork Reduction Act of 1995 (44 U.S.C. 3507(d)). Comments on the collection of information should be sent to the **Office of Management and Budget**, Attn: Desk Officer for the Department of the Treasury, Office of Information and Regulatory Affairs, Washington, DC 20503, with copies to the **Internal Revenue Service**, Attn: IRS Reports Clearance Officer, SE:W:CAR:MP:T:T:SP, Washington, DC 20224. Comments on the collection of information should be received by March 17, 2014. Comments are specifically requested concerning:

Whether the proposed collection of information is necessary for the proper performance of the functions of the IRS, including whether the information will have practical utility;

The accuracy of the estimated burden associated with the proposed collection of information; and

Estimates of capital or start-up costs and costs of operation, maintenance, and purchase of services to provide information.

The collections of information in the proposed regulations are in proposed §§1.704-3(f), 1.734-1(d), 1.743-1(k), and 1.743-1(n). This information will be used by the IRS to assure compliance with certain provisions of the American Jobs Creation Act of 2004. The collections of information are either required to obtain a benefit or are mandatory. The likely respondents are individuals and partnerships.

The burden for the collection of information in § 1.704-3(f) is as follows:

Estimated total annual reporting burden: 324,850 hours.

Estimated average annual burden per respondent: 2 hours.

Estimated number of respondents: 162,425.

Estimated annual frequency of responses: On occasion.

The burden for the collection of information in § 1.734-1(d) is as follows:

Estimated total annual reporting burden: 1,650 hours.

Estimated average annual burden per respondent: 3 hours.

Estimated number of respondents: 550.

Estimated annual frequency of responses: On occasion.

The burden for the collection of information in § 1.743-1(k)(1) is as follows:

Estimated total annual reporting burden: 1,650 hours.

Estimated average annual burden per respondent: 3 hours.

Estimated number of respondents: 550.

Estimated annual frequency of responses: On occasion.

The burden for the collection of information in § 1.743-1(k)(2) is as follows:

Estimated total annual reporting burden: 550 hours.

Estimated average annual burden per respondent: 1 hour.

Estimated number of respondents: 550.

Estimated annual frequency of responses: On occasion.

The burden for the collection of information in § 1.743-1(n)(10) is as follows:

Estimated total annual reporting burden: 3,600.

Estimated average annual burden per respondent: 1 hour.

Estimated number of respondents: 3,600 hours.

Estimated annual frequency of responses: Various.

The burden for the collection of information in § 1.743-1(n)(11) is as follows:

Estimated total annual reporting burden: 2,700 hours.

Estimated average annual burden per respondent: 1.5 hours.

Estimated number of respondents: 1,800.

Estimated annual frequency of responses: On occasion

An agency may not conduct or sponsor, and a person is not required to respond to, a collection of information unless it displays a valid control number assigned by the Office of Management and Budget.

Books or records relating to a collection of information must be retained as long as their contents may become material in the administration of any internal revenue law. Generally, tax returns and tax return information are confidential, as required by section 6103.

Background

1. *Contributions of Built-in Loss Property*

Under section 721(a) of the Internal Revenue Code (the Code), if a partner contributes property in exchange for a partnership interest, neither the partners nor the partnership recognize gain or loss. Section 722 provides that when a partner contributes property to a partnership, the basis in the partnership interest received equals the adjusted basis of the contributed property. Similarly, under section 723, the partnership's adjusted basis in the contributed property equals the contributing partner's adjusted basis in the property. Section 704(c)(1)(A) requires the partnership to allocate items of partnership income, gain, loss, and deduction with respect to contributed property among the partners so as to take into account any built-in gain or built-in loss in the contributed property. This rule is intended to prevent the transfer of built-in gain or built-in loss from the contributing partner to other partners. If a partner contributes built-in gain or built-in loss property to a partnership and later transfers the interest in the partnership, § 1.704-3(a)(7) provides that the built-in gain or built-in loss must be allocated to the transferee as it would have been allocated to the transferor.

Section 833(a) of the American Jobs Creation Act of 2004, Public Law 108-357, 118 Stat. 1418 (the AJCA) added section 704(c)(1)(C) to the Code for contributions of built-in loss property to partnerships after October 22, 2004. In general, section 704(c)(1)(C) provides that a partner's built-in loss may only be taken into account in determining the contributing partner's share of partnership items. Prior to the AJCA, a contributing partner could transfer losses to a transferee partner or other partners when the contributing partner was no longer a partner in the partnership. *See* H. R. Rep. 108-548 at 282 (2004) (House Committee Report) and H.R. Rep. 108-755 at 622 (2004) (Conference Report). Thus, Congress enacted section 704(c)(1)(C) to prevent the inappropriate transfer of built-in losses to partners other than the contributing partner. *See* House Committee Report, at 283. More specifically, Congress enacted section 704(c)(1)(C) to prevent a transferee partner from receiving an allocation of the transferor partner's share of losses relating to the transferor's contribution of built-in loss property and to prevent remaining partners from receiving an allocation of a distributee partner's share of losses relating to the distributee's contribution of built-in loss property when the distributee receives a liquidating distribution. *See* House Committee Report, at 282 and Conference Report, at 621-622. To that end, section 704(c)(1)(C) provides that if property contributed to a partnership has a built-in loss, (i) such built-in loss shall be taken into account only in determining the amount of items allocated to the contributing partner; and (ii) except as provided by regulations, in determining the amount of items allocated to other partners, the basis of the contributed property in the hands of the partnership is equal to its fair market value at the time of the contribution. For purposes of section 704(c)(1)(C), the term *built-in loss* means the excess of the adjusted basis of the property (determined without regard to section 704(c)(1)(C)(ii)) over its fair market value at the time of contribution.

2. *Mandatory Basis Adjustment Provisions*

a. *Overview*

The mandatory basis adjustment provisions in section 833(b) and (c) of the AJCA reflect Congress' belief that the "electivity of partnership basis adjustments upon transfers and distributions leads to anomalous tax results, causes inaccurate income measurement, and gives rise to opportunities for tax sheltering." *See* S. Rep. 108-192 at 189 (2003) (Grassley Report). Specifically, Congress was concerned that the optional basis adjustment regime permitted partners to duplicate losses and inappropriately transfer losses among partners. *Id.* According to the legislative history, Congress intended these amendments to prevent the inappropriate transfer of losses among partners, while preserving the simplification aspects of the existing partnership rules for transactions involving smaller amounts (as described in this preamble, a $250,000 threshold). *See* House Committee Report, at 283. Thus, section 743 and section 734 were amended as described in sections 2.b. and 2.c. of the background section of this preamble.

b. *Section 743 substantial built-in loss provisions*

i. *In general*

Before the enactment of the AJCA, under section 743(a), upon the transfer of a partnership interest by sale or exchange or upon the death of a partner, a partnership was not required to adjust the basis of partnership property unless the partnership had a section 754 election in effect. If the partnership had a section 754 election in effect at the time of a transfer, section 743(b) required the partnership to increase or decrease the adjusted basis of the partnership property to take into account the difference between the transferee's proportionate share of the adjusted basis of the partnership property and the transferee's basis in its partnership interest.

As amended by the AJCA, section 743(a) and (b) require a partnership to adjust the basis of partnership property upon a sale or exchange of an interest in the partnership or upon the death of a partner if there is a section 754 election in effect, or, for transfers after October 22, 2004, if the partnership has a substantial built-in loss immediately after the transfer (regardless of whether the partnership has a section 754 election in effect). Section 743(d)(1) provides that, for purposes of section 743, a partnership has a substantial built-in loss if the partnership's adjusted basis in the partnership property exceeds the fair market value of the property by more than $250,000. Section 743(d)(2) provides that the Secretary shall prescribe such regulations as may be appropriate to carry out the purposes of section 743(d)(1), including regulations aggregating related partnerships and disregarding property acquired by the partnership in an attempt to avoid such purposes.

ii. *Electing investment partnerships*

Section 833(b) of the AJCA also added section 743(e) to the Code, which provides alternative rules for electing investment partnerships (EIPs). According to the legislative history, Congress was aware that mandating section 743(b) adjustments would impose administrative difficulties on certain types of investment partnerships that are engaged in investment activities and that typically did not make section 754 elections prior to the AJCA, even when the adjustments to the bases of partnership property would be upward adjustments. *See* House Committee Report, at 283. Accordingly, for partnerships that meet the requirements of an EIP in section 743(e)(6) and that elect to apply the provisions of section 743(e), section 743(e)(1) provides that for purposes of section 743, an EIP shall not be treated as having a substantial built-in loss with respect to any transfer occurring while the EIP election is in effect. Instead, section 743(e)(2) provides that, in the case of a transfer of an interest in an EIP, the transferee's distributive share of losses (without regard to gains) from the sale or exchange of partnership property shall not be allowed except to the extent that it is established that such losses exceed the loss (if any) recognized by the transferor (or any prior transferor to the extent not fully offset by a prior disallowance under section 743(e)(2)) on the transfer of the partnership interest. Section 743(e)(3) further provides that losses disallowed under section 743(e)(2) shall not decrease the transferee's basis in the partnership interest. In the case of partnership property that has a built-in loss at the time of the transfer, the loss disallowance rules in section 743(e)(2) and (e)(3) approximate the effect of a basis adjustment and prevent the transferee from taking into account an allocation of the preexisting built-in loss (and the corresponding basis reduction) without requiring the partnership to adjust the bases of all partnership property. In addition, section 743(e)(5) provides that in the case of a transferee whose basis in distributed partnership property is reduced under section 732(a)(2), the amount of the loss recognized by the transferor on the transfer that is taken into account under section 743(e)(2) shall be reduced by the amount of such basis reduction.

Section 743(e)(6) defines an *electing investment partnership* as any partnership if (A) the partnership makes an election to have section 743(e) apply; (B) the partnership would be an investment company under section 3(a)(1)(A) of the Investment Company Act of 1940 but for an exemption under paragraph (1) or (7) of section 3(c) of the Act; (C) the partnership has never been engaged in a trade or business; (D) substantially all of the assets of the partnership are held for investment; (E) at least 95 percent of the assets contributed to the partnership consist of money; (F) no assets contributed to the partnership had an adjusted basis in excess of fair market value at the time of contribution; (G) all partnership interests are issued pursuant to a private offering before the date that is 24 months after the date of the first capital contribution to the partnership; (H) the partnership agreement has substantive restrictions on each partner's ability to cause a redemption of the partner's interest; and (I) the partnership agreement provides for a term that is not in excess of 15 years. The flush language of section 743(e)(6) provides that the EIP election, once made, shall be irrevocable except with the consent of the Secretary. Section 833(d) of the AJCA provides a transition rule with respect to section 743(e)(6)(H) and (I) for partnerships eligible to make an election to be an EIP that were in existence on June 4, 2004. For those partnerships, section 743(e)(6)(H) does not apply and the term in section 743(e)(6)(I) is 20 years.

According to the legislative history, Congress expected EIPs to include venture capital funds, buyout funds, and funds of funds. *See* Conference Report, at 626. The legislative history further indicates that, with respect to the requirement in section 743(e)(6)(G), Congress intended that "dry" closings in which partnership interests are issued without the contribution of capital not start the running of the 24-month period. *Id.* Furthermore, with respect to the requirement in section 743(e)(6)(H), Congress provided illustrative examples of substantive restrictions: a violation of Federal or State law (such as ERISA or the Bank Holding Company Act) or an imposition of the Federal excise tax on, or a change in the Federal tax-exempt status of, a tax-exempt partner. *Id.*

Section 743(e)(4) also provides that section 743(e) shall be applied without regard to any termination of a partnership under section 708(b)(1)(B). Finally, section 743(e)(7) provides that the Secretary shall prescribe such regulations as may be appropriate to carry out the purposes of section 743(e), including regulations for applying section 743(e) to tiered partnerships.

Section 833(b) of the AJCA prescribed certain reporting requirements for EIPs by adding section 6031(f) to the Code. Section 6031(f) provides that in the case of an EIP, the information required under section 6031(b) (relating to furnishing copies of returns of partnership income to partners) to be furnished to a partner to whom section 743(e)(2) applies shall include information as is necessary to enable the partner to compute the amount of losses disallowed under section 743(e).

On April 1, 2005, the Treasury Department and the IRS issued Notice 2005-32 (2005-1 CB 895), which provides, in part, interim procedures and reporting requirements for EIPs; interim procedures for transferors of EIP interests; and guidance regarding whether a partnership is engaged in a trade or business for purposes of section 743(e)(6)(C). Public comments on Notice 2005-32 are discussed in Parts 2.a.i and 2.a.ii of the Explanation of Provisions section of this preamble. *See* § 601.601(d)(2)(ii)(b).

iii. *Securitization partnerships*

Finally, section 833 of the AJCA added section 743(f) to the Code, which provides an exception from the mandatory basis adjustment provisions in section 743(a) and (b) for securitization partnerships. Section 743(f)(1) states that for purposes of section 743, a securitization partnership shall not be treated as having a substantial built-in loss with respect to any transfer. Section 743(f)(2) provides that the term *securitization partnership* means a partnership the sole business activity of which is to issue securities that provide for a fixed principal (or similar) amount and that are primarily serviced by the cash flows of a discrete pool (either fixed or revolving) of receivables or other financial assets that by their terms convert into cash in a finite period, but only if the sponsor of the pool reasonably believes that the receivables and other financial assets comprising the pool are not acquired so as to be disposed of. For purposes of the "reasonable belief" standard, the legislative history indicates that Congress intended rules similar to the rules in § 1.860G-2(a)(3) (relating to a reasonable belief safe harbor for obligations principally secured by an interest in real property) to apply. *See* Conference Report, at 627. Furthermore, Congress did not intend for the mandatory basis adjustment rules to be avoided by securitization partnerships through dispositions of pool assets. *Id.* Finally, the legislative history states that if a partnership ceases to meet the qualifications of a securitization partnership, the mandatory basis adjustment provisions apply to the first transfer thereafter and to each subsequent transfer. *Id.*

c. *Section 734 substantial basis reduction provisions*

Section 734(b) requires a partnership to increase or decrease the adjusted basis of partnership property to take into account any gain or loss recognized to the distributee and the difference between the partnership's and the distributee's bases in distributed property. Similar to section 743, prior to the AJCA, section 734(a) did not require a partnership to adjust the basis of partnership property upon a distribution of partnership property to a partner unless the partnership had a section 754 election in effect.

Consistent with the amendments to section 743, section 833(c) of the AJCA amended section 734(a) and (b) to require a partnership to adjust the basis of partnership property upon a distribution of partnership property to a partner if there is a section 754 election in effect or, for distributions occurring after October 22, 2004, if there is a substantial basis reduction with respect to the distribution. Section 734(d)(1) provides that for purposes of section 734, there is a substantial basis reduction with respect to a distribution if the sum of the amounts described in section 734(b)(2)(A) and 734(b)(2)(B) exceeds $250,000. The amount described in section 734(b)(2)(A) is the amount of loss recognized to the distributee partner with respect to the distribution under section 731(a)(2). The amount described in section 734(b)(2)(B) is, in the case of distributed property to which section 732(b) applies, the excess of the basis of the distributed property to the distributee, as determined under section 732, over the adjusted basis of the distributed property to the partnership immediately before the distribution (as adjusted by section 732(d)). Section 734(d)(2) provides regulatory authority for the Secretary to carry out the purposes of section 734(d) by crossreference to section 743(d)(2). Section 743(d)(2) is discussed in Part 2.b.i of the Background section of this preamble.

As with section 743(b) adjustments, section 734(e) provides an exception to the mandatory basis adjustment provisions in section 734 for securitization partnerships. A securitization partnership (which is defined by reference to section 743(f)) is not treated as having a substantial basis reduction with respect to any distribution of property to a partner. *See* Part 2.b.iii of the Background section of this preamble for the definition of securitization partnership in section 743(f). Like the rules under section 743, the mandatory basis adjustment provisions under section 734 will apply with respect to the first distribution that occurs after the partnership ceases to meet the definition of a securitization partnership and to each subsequent distribution.

d. *Interim reporting requirements for mandatory basis adjustments*

The Treasury Department and the IRS issued general interim procedures for mandatory basis adjustments under sections 734 and 743. These interim procedures, which are described in Notice 2005-32, state that until further guidance is provided, partnerships required to reduce the bases of partnership properties under the substantial basis reduction provisions in section 734 must comply with §1.734-1(d) as if an election under section 754 were in effect at the time of the relevant distribution. Similarly, partnerships that are required to reduce the bases of partnership properties under the substantial built-in loss provisions in section 743 must comply with §1.743-1(k)(1), (3), (4), and (5) as if an election under section 754 were in effect at the time of the relevant transfer. Furthermore, a transferee of an interest in a partnership that is required to reduce the bases of partnership properties under the substantial built-in loss provisions must comply with §1.743-1(k)(2) as if an election under section 754 were in effect at the time of the relevant transfer.

3. *Section 755 Rules for Allocation of Basis*

a. *Section 755(c)*

If section 734(a) requires a basis adjustment (either because the partnership has a section 754 election in effect or because there is a substantial basis reduction with respect to the distribution), section 734(b) provides that the partnership increases or decreases the basis of partnership property by any gain or loss recognized by the distributee and the difference (if any) between the partnership's and the distributee's adjusted bases in the distributed property. Section 755(a) generally provides that any increase or decrease in the adjusted basis of partnership property under section 734(b) shall be allocated in a manner that: (1) reduces the difference between the fair market value and the adjusted basis of partnership properties, or (2) in any other manner permitted by regulations. Generally, section 755(b) requires a partnership to allocate increases or decreases in the adjusted basis of partnership property arising from the distribution of property to property of a like character to the property distributed (either to (1) capital assets and property described in section 1231(b), or (2) any other property).

According to the Joint Committee on Taxation's (the JCT's) investigative report of Enron Corporation (*See* Joint Committee on Taxation, Report of Investigation of Enron Corporation and Related Entities Regarding Federal Tax and Compensation Issues, and Policy Recommendations, JCS-3-03 (February 2003) (JCT Enron Report)), taxpayers were engaging in transactions to achieve unintended tax results through the interaction of these partnership basis adjustment rules and the rules in section 1032 protecting a corporation from recognizing gain on its stock. Section 1032(a) provides that no gain or loss is recognized to a corporation on the receipt of money or other property in exchange for stock of the corporation. In particular, the JCT Enron Report describes Enron Corporation's Project Condor as structured to take advantage of the interaction between sections 754 and 1032 by increasing the basis of depreciable assets under section 732 while decreasing the basis under section 734(b) of preferred stock of a corporate partner held by the partnership. The step down in the basis of the corporate partner's preferred stock had no ultimate tax effect because the corporate partner could avoid recognizing the gain in the stock through section 1032, which prevents a corporation from recognizing gain on the sale of its stock. The transaction thus duplicated tax deductions at no economic cost. *See* Grassley Report, at 127 and House Committee Report, at 287. The JCT expressed specific concern about the exclusion of gain under section 1032 following a negative basis adjustment under section 734(b) to stock of a corporate partner. JCT Enron Report, at 220-21. Therefore, the JCT recommended that the partnership basis rules preclude an increase in basis to an asset if the offsetting basis reduction would be allocated to stock of a partner (or related party). *Id.* at 221.

In response to these recommendations, section 834(a) of the AJCA enacted section 755(c), which provides that in making an allocation under section 755(a) of any decrease in the adjusted basis of partnership property under section 734(b)—(1) no allocation may be made to stock in a corporation (or any person related (within the meaning of sections 267(b) and 707(b)(1)) to such corporation) that is a partner in the partnership, and (2) any amount not allocable to stock by reason of section 755(c)(1) shall be allocated under section 755(a) to other partnership property. The flush language of section 755(c) further provides that a partnership recognizes gain to the extent that the amount required to be allocated under section 755(c)(2) to other partnership property exceeds the aggregate adjusted basis of such other property immediately before the required allocation.

b. *Basis adjustment allocation rules for substituted basis transactions*

A basis adjustment under section 743(a) is determined in accordance with section 743(b). The partnership must allocate any increase or decrease in the adjusted basis of partnership property required under section 743(b) under the rules of section 755. Section 1.755-1(b)(5) provides additional guidance on how to allocate basis adjustments under section 743(b) that result from substituted basis transactions, which are defined as exchanges in which the transferee's basis in the partnership interest is determined in whole or in part by reference to the transferor's basis in that interest. For exchanges on or after June 9, 2003, §1.755-1(b)(5) also applies to basis adjustments that result from exchanges in which the transferee's basis in the partnership interest is determined by reference to other property held at any time by the transferee.

Generally, §1.755-1(b)(5)(ii) provides that if there is an increase in basis to be allocated to partnership assets, the increase must be allocated to capital gain property or ordinary income property, respectively, only if the total amount of gain or loss (including any remedial allocations under §1.704-3(d)) that would be allocated to the transferee (to the extent attributable to the acquired partnership interest) from the hypothetical sale of all such property would result in a net gain or net income, as the case may be, to the transferee. Similarly, if there is a decrease in basis to be allocated to partnership assets, §1.755-1(b)(5)(ii) generally provides that the decrease must be allocated to capital gain property or ordinary income property, respectively, only if the total amount of gain or loss (including any remedial allocations under §1.704-3(d)) that would be allocated to the transferee (to the extent attributable to the acquired partnership interest) from the hypothetical sale of all such property would result in a net loss to the transferee. Thus, whether or not a basis adjustment resulting from a substituted basis transaction can be allocated to partnership property depends on whether the transferee partner would be allocated a net gain or net income, in the case of a positive basis adjustment, or net loss, in the case of a negative basis adjustment.

Section 1.755-1(b)(5)(iii) provides rules for allocating increases or decreases in basis within the classes of property. Of note, in the case of a decrease, §1.755-1(b)(5)(iii)(B) states that the decrease must be allocated first to properties with unrealized depreciation in proportion to the transferee's shares of the respective amounts of unrealized depreciation before the decrease (but only to the extent of the transferee's share of each property's unrealized depreciation). Any remaining decrease must be allocated among the properties within the class in proportion to the transferee's shares of their adjusted bases (as adjusted under the preceding sentence) (subject to a limitation in decrease of basis in §1.755-1(b)(5)(iii)(C) and a carryover rule in §1.755-1(b)(5)(iii)(D)).

In addition, §1.743-1(f) provides that, when there has been more than one transfer of a partnership interest, a partnership determines a transferee's basis adjustment without regard to any prior transferee's basis adjustment. Accordingly, if a partner acquires its partnership interest in a transaction other than a substituted basis transaction and then subsequently transfers its interest in a substituted basis transaction, the transferee's basis adjustment may shift among partnership assets.

4. Miscellaneous Provisions

a. Section 704(c) allocations

Property contributed to a partnership by a partner is section 704(c) property if, at the time of contribution, the property has a built-in gain or built-in loss ("forward section 704(c) gain or loss"). Section 704(c)(1)(A) requires a partnership to allocate income, gain, loss, and deduction so as to take into account the built-in gain or built-in loss. For this purpose, §1.704-3(a)(3)(ii) provides that a built-in gain or built-in loss is generally the difference between the property's book value and the contributing partner's adjusted tax basis upon contribution (reduced by decreases in the difference between the property's book value and adjusted tax basis). Section 1.704-3(a)(6)(i) provides that the principles of section 704(c) also apply to allocations with respect to property for which differences between book value and adjusted tax basis are created when a partnership revalues property pursuant to §1.704-1(b)(2)(iv)(f) or §1.704-1(b)(2)(iv)(s) ("reverse section 704(c) allocations"). Partnerships are not required to use the same allocation method for forward and reverse section 704(c) allocations, but the allocation method (or combination of methods) must be reasonable. See §§1.704-3(a)(6)(i) and 1.704-3(a)(10)(i). Section 1.704-3(a)(10)(i) provides that an allocation method is not reasonable if the contribution or revaluation event and the corresponding allocation are made with a view to shifting the tax consequences of built-in gain or built-in loss among the partners in a manner that substantially reduces the present value of the partners' aggregate tax liability.

On August 12, 2009, the Treasury Department and the IRS published Notice 2009-70, 2009-2 CB 255, which requested comments on the proper application of the rules relating to the creation and maintenance of forward and multiple reverse section 704(c) allocations (referred to as "section 704(c) layers" in this preamble). Specifically, Notice 2009-70 requested comments on, among other things, whether taxpayers should net reverse section 704(c) allocations against existing section 704(c) layers or maintain separate section 704(c) layers if the section 704(c) layers offset one another; how partnerships should allocate tax depreciation, depletion, amortization, and gain or loss between multiple section 704(c) layers (including any offsetting section 704(c) layers); and whether there are other issues relating to section 704(c) layers. Public comments on Notice 2009-70 are discussed in Part 4.a of the Explanation of Provisions section of this preamble. See §601.601(d)(2)(ii)(b).

b. Extension of time period for taxing precontribution gain

The Taxpayer Relief Act of 1997 (Pub. Law 105-34, 111 Stat. 788) extended the time period in sections 704(c)(1)(B) and 737(b)(1) for taxing precontribution gain for property contributed to a partnership after June 8, 1997, from five years to seven years (the rule does not, however, apply to any property contributed pursuant to a written binding contract in effect on June 8, 1997, and at all times thereafter before such contribution if such contract provides for the contribution of a fixed amount of property). The regulations under sections 704, 737, and 1502 have not been revised to reflect this statutory change.

Explanation of Provisions

1. Contributions of Built-in Loss Property

a. Overview

Section 704(c)(1)(C)(i) provides that if property contributed to a partnership has a built-in loss ("section 704(c)(1)(C) property"), such built-in loss shall be taken into account only in determining the amount of items allocated to the contributing partner ("section 704(c)(1)(C) partner"). Section 704(c)(1)(C)(ii) further provides that, except as provided by regulations, in determining the amount of items allocated to other partners, the basis of the contributed property in the hands of the partnership is equal to its fair market value at the time of the contribution. For purposes of section 704(c)(1)(C), the term *built-in loss* means the excess of the adjusted basis of the section 704(c)(1)(C) property (determined without regard to section 704(c)(1)(C)(ii)) over its fair market value at the time of contribution.

The Treasury Department and the IRS believe additional guidance is needed with respect to the application of section 704(c)(1)(C). Accordingly, the proposed regulations provide rules regarding: (1) the scope of section 704(c)(1)(C); (2) the effect of the built-in loss; (3) distributions by partnerships holding section 704(c)(1)(C) property; (4) transfers of a section 704(c)(1)(C) partner's partnership interest; (5) transfers of section 704(c)(1)(C) property; and (6) reporting requirements.

b. Scope of section 704(c)(1)(C)

The proposed regulations define section 704(c)(1)(C) property as section 704(c) property with a built-in loss at the time of contribution. Thus, in addition to the rules in the proposed regulations, section 704(c)(1)(C) property is subject to the existing rules and regulations applicable to section 704(c) property generally (see, for example, §1.704-3(a)(9), which provides special rules for tiered partnerships), except as provided in the proposed regulations.

The Treasury Department and the IRS considered whether the principles of section 704(c)(1)(C) should apply to reverse section 704(c) allocations (within the meaning of §1.704-3(a)(6)(i)). The Treasury Department and the IRS concluded that applying the proposed regulations to reverse section 704(c) allocations would be difficult for taxpayers to comply with and for the IRS to administer. Therefore, the proposed regulations do not apply to reverse section 704(c) allocations.

The Treasury Department and the IRS also considered whether section 704(c)(1)(C) should apply to §1.752-7 liabilities. Under §1.752-7(b)(3)(i), a §1.752-7 liability is an obligation described in §1.752-1(a)(4)(ii) (generally any fixed or contingent obligation to make payment without regard to whether the obligation is otherwise taken into account for purposes of Code) to the extent that the obligation either is not described in §1.752-1(a)(4)(i) or the amount of the obligation exceeds the amount taken into account under §1.752-1(a)(4)(i). The preamble to the final regulations under §1.752-7, published on May 26, 2005, acknowledges that the rules in section 704(c)(1)(C) and the rules under §1.752-7 are similar. *See* TD 9207, 70 FR 30334. The preamble explains that it is possible to view the contribution of property with an adjusted tax basis equal to the fair market value of the property, determined without regard to any §1.752-7 liabilities, as built-in loss property after the §1.752-7 liability is taken into account (when the §1.752-7 liability is related to the contributed property). However, the preamble further provides that §1.752-7 shall be applied without regard to the amendments made by the AJCA, unless future guidance provides to the contrary. The Treasury Department and the IRS believe the rules regarding §1.752-7 liabilities adequately address the issues posed by §1.752-7 liabilities and, thus, the proposed regulations provide that section 704(c)(1)(C) property does not include a §1.752-7 liability.

c. *Effect of section 704(c)(1)(C) basis adjustment*

The legislative history indicates that Congress intended the built-in loss attributable to section 704(c)(1)(C) property to be for the benefit of the contributing partner only. Conceptually, the built-in loss is similar to a section 743(b) adjustment, which is an adjustment to the basis of partnership property solely with respect to the transferee partner. The current regulations under section 743 provide detailed rules regarding accounting for, maintenance of, recovery of, and transfers of assets with, section 743(b) adjustments. The Treasury Department and the IRS believe it is appropriate that the proposed regulations provide rules similar to those applicable to positive basis adjustments under section 743(b). The Treasury Department and the IRS believe that this approach simplifies the application and administration of section 704(c)(1)(C) and provides a framework of rules familiar to partners, partnerships, and the IRS. Even though the proposed regulations generally adopt the approach taken with respect to section 743(b) adjustments, the Treasury Department and the IRS believe that some of the rules governing section 743(b) adjustments should not apply with respect to a built-in loss and that additional rules are necessary for section 704(c)(1)(C). Thus, the proposed regulations import and specifically apply certain concepts contained in the section 743 regulations to section 704(c)(1)(C), as opposed to simply providing that principles similar to those contained in the regulations under section 743 apply to section 704(c)(1)(C) by cross-reference. The following discussion describes both the substantive rules applied under section 704(c)(1)(C) and, where applicable, how those rules differ from their counterparts under section 743(b).

The proposed regulations create the concept of a section 704(c)(1)(C) basis adjustment. The section 704(c)(1)(C) basis adjustment is initially equal to the built-in loss associated with the section 704(c)(1)(C) property at the contribution and then is adjusted in accordance with the proposed regulations. For example, if A contributes, in a section 721 transaction, property with a fair market value of $6,000 and an adjusted basis of $11,000 to a partnership, the partnership's basis in the property is $6,000, A's basis in its partnership interest is $11,000, and A has a section 704(c)(1)(C) basis adjustment of $5,000. Similar to basis adjustments under section 743(b), a section 704(c)(1)(C) basis adjustment is unique to the section 704(c)(1)(C) partner and does not affect the basis of partnership property or the partnership's computation of any item under section 703. The rules regarding the effect of the section 704(c)(1)(C) basis adjustment are similar to the rules for section 743(b) adjustments in §§1.743-1(j)(1) through (j)(3), including: (1) the effect of the section 704(c)(1)(C) basis adjustment on the basis of partnership property; (2) the computation and allocation of the partnership's items of income, deduction, gain, or loss; (3) adjustments to the partners' capital accounts; (4) adjustments to the section 704(c)(1)(C) partner's distributive share; and (5) the determination of a section 704(c)(1)(C) partner's income, gain, or loss from the sale or exchange of section 704(c)(1)(C) property. The Treasury Department and the IRS believe the rule regarding recovery of the section 704(c)(1)(C) basis adjustment should be consistent with the rule regarding recovery of the adjusted tax basis in the property that is not subject to section 704(c)(1)(C). Thus, for property eligible for cost recovery, the proposed regulations provide that, regarding the effect of the basis adjustment in determining items of deduction, if section 704(c)(1)(C) property is subject to amortization under section 197, depreciation under section 168, or other cost recovery in the hands of the section 704(c)(1)(C) partner, the section 704(c)(1)(C) basis adjustment associated with the property is recovered in accordance with section 197(f)(2), section 168(i)(7), or other applicable Code sections. Similar to section 743, the proposed regulations further provide that the amount of any section 704(c)(1)(C) basis adjustment that is recovered by the section 704(c)(1)(C) partner in any year is added to the section 704(c)(1)(C) partner's distributive share of the partnership's depreciation or amortization deductions for the year. The section 704(c)(1)(C) basis adjustment is adjusted under section 1016(a)(2) to reflect the recovery of the section 704(c)(1)(C) basis adjustment.

d. *Distribution by partnership holding section 704(c)(1)(C) property*

The proposed regulations provide guidance on current distributions of section 704(c)(1)(C) property to the section 704(c)(1)(C) partner; distributions of section 704(c)(1)(C) property to another partner; and liquidating distributions to a section 704(c)(1)(C) partner. The Treasury Department and the IRS believe it is appropriate to apply principles similar to section 743 to simplify the administration of section 704(c)(1)(C) for partners, partnerships, and the IRS. Thus, the proposed regulations generally provide rules similar to those for section 743(b) adjustments.

i. *Current distribution of section 704(c)(1)(C) property to section 704(c)(1)(C) partner*

Under the proposed regulations, the adjusted partnership basis of section 704(c)(1)(C) property distributed to the section 704(c)(1)(C) partner includes the section 704(c)(1)(C) basis adjustment for purposes of determining the amount of any adjustment under section 734. However, the proposed regulations provide that section 704(c)(1)(C) basis adjustments are not taken into account in making allocations under §1.755-1(c).

ii. *Distribution of section 704(c)(1)(C) property to another partner*

Under the proposed regulations, if a partner receives a distribution of property in which another partner has a section 704(c)(1)(C) basis adjustment, the distributee partner does not take the section 704(c)(1)(C) basis adjustment into account under section 732. However, the Treasury Department and the IRS request comments on whether a section 704(c)(1)(C) adjustment to distributed stock should be taken into account for purposes of section 732(f) notwithstanding the general rule that section 704(c)(1)(C) adjustments are not taken into account under section 732.

Upon the distribution of section 704(c)(1)(C) property to another partner, the section 704(c)(1)(C) partner reallocates its section 704(c)(1)(C) basis adjustment relating to the distributed property among the remaining items of partnership property under §1.755-1(c), which is similar to the rule in §1.743-1(g)(2)(ii) for reallocating section 743(b) adjustments. This rule allocates the basis adjustment to partnership property without regard to the section 704(c)(1)(C) partner's allocable share of income, gain, or loss in each partnership asset. The Treasury Department and the IRS request comments on whether the reallocations of section 704(c)(1)(C) basis adjustments and section 743(b) basis adjustments should instead be made under the principles of §1.755-1(b)(5)(iii) to take into account the partner's allocable share of income, gain, or loss from each partnership asset.

The proposed regulations further provide that if section 704(c)(1)(B) applies to treat the section 704(c)(1)(C) partner as recognizing loss on the sale of the distributed property, the section 704(c)(1)(C) basis adjustment is taken into account in determining the amount of loss. Accordingly, when the section 704(c)(1)(C) property is distributed to a partner other than the contributing partner within seven years of its contribution to the partnership, the loss will be taken into account by the contributing partner. The Treasury Department and the IRS considered extending the seven-year period so that the loss will be taken into account by the contributing partner on any distribution of section 704(c)(1)(C) property to a partner other than the contributing partner. The Treasury Department and the IRS do not adopt this approach in the proposed regulations because it would be inconsistent with section 704(c)(1)(B) generally and would be more difficult to administer.

iii. *Distribution in complete liquidation of a section 704(c)(1)(C) partner's interest*

The proposed regulations provide that if a section 704(c)(1)(C) partner receives a distribution of property (whether or not the property is section 704(c)(1)(C) property) in liquidation of its interest in the partnership, the adjusted basis to the partnership of the distributed property immediately before the distribution includes the section 704(c)(1)(C) partner's section 704(c)(1)(C) basis adjustment for the property in which the section 704(c)(1)(C) partner relinquished an interest (if any) by reason of the liquidation. For purposes of determining the redeemed section 704(c)(1)(C) partner's basis in distributed property under section 732, the partnership reallocates any section 704(c)(1)(C) basis adjustment from section 704(c)(1)(C) property retained by the partnership to distributed properties of like character under the principles of §1.755-1(c)(i), after applying sections 704(c)(1)(B) and 737. If section 704(c)(1)(C) property is retained by the partnership, and no property of like character is distributed, then that property's section 704(c)(1)(C) basis adjustment is not reallocated to the distributed property for purposes of applying section 732.

If any section 704(c)(1)(C) basis adjustment is not reallocated to the distributed property in connection with the distribution, then that remaining section 704(c)(1)(C) basis adjustment shall be treated as a positive section 734(b) adjustment. If the distribution also gives rise to a negative section 734(b) adjustment, then the negative section 734(b) adjustment and the section 704(c)(1)(C) basis adjustment reallocation are netted together, and the net amount is allocated under §1.755-1(c). If the partnership does not have a section 754 election in effect at the time of the liquidating distribution, the partnership shall be treated as having made a section 754 election solely for purposes of computing any negative section 734(b) adjustment that would arise from the distribution.

e. *Transfer of section 704(c)(1)(C) partner's partnership interest*

i. *In general*

Under section 722, a section 704(c)(1)(C) partner's basis in its partnership interest fully reflects the built-in loss portion of the basis of the contributed property and the built-in loss generally is taken into account by the section 704(c)(1)(C) partner upon disposition of the partnership interest. Therefore, in accordance with section 704(c)(1)(C)'s overall policy objective of preventing the inappropriate transfer of built-in losses through partnerships, the proposed regulations provide that the transferee of a section 704(c)(1)(C) partner's partnership interest generally does not succeed to the section 704(c)(1)(C) partner's section 704(c)(1)(C) basis adjustment. Instead, the share of the section 704(c)(1)(C) basis adjustment attributable to the interest transferred is eliminated. For example, if a section 704(c)(1)(C) partner sells 20 percent of its interest in a partnership, the partner recognizes its outside loss with respect to that 20 percent but 20 percent of the partner's section 704(c)(1)(C) basis adjustment for each section 704(c)(1)(C) property contributed by the partner is eliminated. The transferor remains a section 704(c)(1)(C) partner with respect to any remaining section 704(c)(1)(C) basis adjustments. The proposed regulations provide exceptions to this general rule for nonrecognition transactions, which are discussed in Part 1.e.ii of the Explanation of Provisions section of this preamble.

ii. *Nonrecognition transactions*

Under the proposed regulations, the general rule that a section 704(c)(1)(C) basis adjustment is not transferred with the related partnership interest does not apply to the extent a section 704(c)(1)(C) partner transfers its partnership interest in a nonrecognition transaction, with certain exceptions. The legislative history notes that Congress intended to treat a corporation succeeding to the attributes of a contributing corporate partner under section 381 in the same manner as the contributing partner. *See* Conference Report, at 623 n. 546. The Treasury Department and the IRS considered whether similar successor rules should apply in other nonrecognition transactions. Some of the considerations included: (1) providing consistent results regardless of the order in which a transaction occurs; (2) ensuring that built-in losses are not duplicated; (3) preventing the shifting of basis to other assets; (4) recognizing that other provisions in subchapter K (for example, section 743(b)) already apply to prevent many of the potential abuses; and (5) providing administrable rules for partners, partnerships, and the IRS. The Treasury Department and the IRS concluded that these considerations and the policy rationale underlying the successor rule for section 381 transactions in the legislative history weigh in favor of applying similar successor rules to other nonrecognition transactions, including section 721 transactions, section 351 transactions, and distributions governed by section 731. Thus, when the partnership interest is transferred in one of these nonrecognition transactions, the transferee generally succeeds to the transferor's section 704(c)(1)(C) basis adjustments attributable to the interest transferred and is treated as the section 704(c)(1)(C) partner with respect to such interest. If the nonrecognition transaction is described in section 168(i)(7)(B), then the rules in section 168(i)(7)(A) apply with respect to the transferor's cost recovery deductions under section 168 with respect to the section 704(c)(1)(C) basis adjustment. The proposed regulations further provide that if gain or loss is recognized in the transaction, appropriate adjustments must be made to the section 704(c)(1)(C) basis adjustment.

The Treasury Department and the IRS believe that a section 743(b) adjustment generally will prevent inappropriate duplication of loss when a partnership has a section 754 election in effect or a substantial built-in loss with respect to the transfer. (*See* Part 2.a.i. of the Explanation of Provisions section of this preamble for rules regarding substantial built-in loss transactions). To the extent that the transferee partner's basis in the transferred partnership interest does not reflect a built-in loss, a section 743(b) adjustment should require the partnership to reduce the basis of its properties to reflect the elimination of the built-in loss. The Treasury Department and the IRS believe that the amount of the section 704(c)(1)(C) adjustment and any negative 743(b) adjustment should be netted for this purpose. The Treasury Department and the IRS believe that similar treatment is appropriate when a partnership does not have a section 754 election in effect at the time of transfer to prevent duplication of the built-in loss. Therefore, regardless of whether a section 754 election is in effect or a substantial builtin loss exists with respect to a transfer, the proposed regulations provide that the transferee partner succeeds to the transferor's section 704(c)(1)(C) basis adjustment, as reduced by the amount of any negative section 743(b) adjustment that would be allocated to the section 704(c)(1)(C) property if the partnership had a section 754 election in effect at the time of the transfer.

The proposed regulations also provide that the general rule regarding nonrecognition transactions does not apply to the transfer of all or a portion of a section 704(c)(1)(C) partner's partnership interest by gift because the gift recipient does not fit within Congress's notion of a successor as described in the legislative history. *See* Conference Report, at 623 n. 546. Thus, the general transfer rule applies instead, and the section 704(c)(1)(C) basis adjustment is eliminated.

f. *Transfers of section 704(c)(1)(C) property*

The proposed regulations also provide guidance on the treatment of the section 704(c)(1)(C) partner and the section 704(c)(1)(C) basis adjustment when the partnership transfers section 704(c)(1)(C) property. Consistent with the rules under section 743, a section 704(c)(1)(C) partner's section 704(c)(1)(C) basis adjustment is generally taken into account in determining the section 704(c)(1)(C) partner's income, gain, loss, or deduction from the sale or exchange of section 704(c)(1)(C) property.

With certain exceptions, if section 704(c)(1)(C) property is transferred in a nonrecognition transaction, the proposed regulations provide that the section 704(c)(1)(C) partner retains the section 704(c)(1)(C) basis adjustment in the replacement property (in the case of a section 1031 transaction), in stock (in the case of a section 351 transaction), in a lower-tier partnership interest (in the case of a section 721 transaction), or in the same property held by a new partnership (in the case of a section 708(b)(1)(B) technical termination). The proposed regulations also provide additional rules for section 721 and section 351 transactions, which are described in the following sections.

i. *Contribution of section 704(c)(1)(C) property under section 721*

The proposed regulations provide rules for when, after a section 704(c)(1)(C) partner contributes section 704(c)(1)(C) property to an upper-tier partnership, the uppertier partnership contributes the property to a lower-tier partnership in a transaction described in section 721(a). The proposed regulations ensure that the section 704(c)(1)(C) adjustment amount is ultimately tracked back to the initial contributing partner, similar to the rules for section 721 contributions of property in which a partner has a section 743(b) adjustment.

In particular, the proposed regulations provide that the interest in the lower-tier partnership received by the upper-tier partnership is treated as the section 704(c)(1)(C) property with the same section 704(c)(1)(C) basis adjustment as the contributed property. The lower-tier partnership determines its basis in the contributed property by excluding the existing section 704(c)(1)(C) basis adjustment. However, the lower-tier partnership also succeeds to the upper-tier partnership's section 704(c)(1)(C) basis adjustment. The portion of the upper-tier partnership's basis in its interest in the lowertier partnership attributable to the section 704(c)(1)(C) basis adjustment must be segregated and allocated solely to the section 704(c)(1)(C) partner for whom the initial section 704(c)(1)(C) basis adjustment was made. Similarly, the section 704(c)(1)(C) basis adjustment to which the lower-tier partnership succeeds must be segregated and allocated solely to the upper-tier partnership, and the section 704(c)(1)(C) partner for whom the initial section 704(c)(1)(C) basis adjustment was made. If gain or loss is recognized on the transaction, appropriate adjustments must be made to the section 704(c)(1)(C) basis adjustment.

The proposed regulations provide that to the extent that any section 704(c)(1)(C) basis adjustment in a tiered partnership is recovered (for example, by sale or depreciation of the property), or is otherwise reduced, upper or lower partnerships in the tiered structure must make conforming reductions to related section 704(c)(1)(C) basis adjustments to prevent duplication of loss.

The proposed regulations recognize that the contribution from the upper-tier partnership to the lower-tier partnership will give rise to an additional section 704(c)(1)(C) basis adjustment if the value of the property has fallen below its common basis to the upper-tier partnership; this additional section 704(c)(1)(C) adjustment will be allocated among the partners of the upper-tier partnership in a manner that reflects their relative shares of that loss.

ii. *Transfer of section 704(c)(1)(C) property in a section 351 transaction*

The transfer of the section 704(c)(1)(C) property by a partnership to a corporation in a section 351 transaction severs the contributing partner's connection with the section 704(c)(1)(C) property at the partnership level. The section 704(c)(1)(C) partner, now an indirect shareholder of the corporation, no longer has a section 704(c)(1)(C) basis adjustment with respect to the property. The proposed regulations provide that if, in an exchange described in section 351, a partnership transfers section 704(c)(1)(C) property to a corporation, the stock the partnership receives in the exchange is treated, solely with respect to the section 704(c)(1)(C) partner, as section 704(c)(1)(C) property that generally has the same section 704(c)(1)(C) basis adjustment as the section 704(c)(1)(C) property transferred to the corporation (reduced by any portion of the section 704(c)(1)(C) basis adjustment that reduced the partner's share of any gain on the transaction). The transferee corporation's adjusted basis in the transferred property is determined under section 362 (including by applying section 362(e)), taking into account any section 704(c)(1)(C) basis adjustments in the transferred property. However, the proposed regulations provide that, if a partnership recognizes gain on the transfer, the partnership's gain is determined without regard to any section 704(c)(1)(C) basis adjustment, but the section 704(c)(1)(C) partner's gain does take into account the section 704(c)(1)(C) basis adjustment. See § 1.362-4(e)(1) for additional rules regarding the application of section 362(e) to transfers by partnerships.

iii. *Partnership technical terminations*

The proposed regulations provide that a partner with a section 704(c)(1)(C) basis adjustment in section 704(c)(1)(C) property held by a partnership that terminates under section 708(b)(1)(B) will continue to have the same section 704(c)(1)(C) basis adjustment with respect to section 704(c)(1)(C) property deemed contributed by the terminated partnership to the new partnership under § 1.708-1(b)(4). In addition, the deemed contribution of property by a terminated partnership to a new partnership is not subject to the proposed regulations and does not create a section 704(c)(1)(C) basis adjustment.

iv. *Miscellaneous provisions*

The proposed regulations also provide additional rules for like-kind exchanges of section 704(c)(1)(C) property, dispositions of section 704(c)(1)(C) property in installment sales, and contributed contracts.

g. *Reporting requirements under section 704(c)(1)(C)*

The proposed regulations prescribe certain reporting requirements for section 704(c)(1)(C) basis adjustments that are similar to the requirements for section 743(b) adjustments. Specifically, the proposed regulations provide that a partnership that owns property for which there is a section 704(c)(1)(C) basis adjustment must attach a statement to the partnership return for the year of the contribution of the section 704(c)(1)(C) property setting forth the name and taxpayer identification number of the section 704(c)(1)(C) partner as well as the section 704(c)(1)(C) basis adjustment and the section 704(c)(1)(C) property to which the adjustment relates.

2. *Mandatory Basis Adjustment Provisions*

a. *Section 743 substantial built-in loss provisions*

i. *General provisions*

The proposed regulations generally restate the statutory language in section 743(a) and (b) regarding substantial built-in losses, but provide additional guidance in several areas. The proposed regulations clarify that, if a partnership has a substantial built-in loss immediately after the transfer of a partnership interest, the partnership is treated as having a section 754 election in effect for the taxable year in which the transfer occurs, but only with respect to that transfer (unless another transaction is also subject to the mandatory basis adjustment provisions of sections 734 or 743).

The proposed regulations also provide that in determining whether there is a substantial built-in loss, section 743(b) adjustments and section 704(c)(1)(C) basis adjustments (except the transferee's section 743(b) adjustments and section 704(c)(1)(C) basis adjustments, if any) are disregarded.

The proposed regulations also provide special rules for determining fair market value in the case of a tiered partnership. The Treasury Department and the IRS are aware that there is some uncertainty as to how to determine the fair market value of a lower-tier partnership interest for purposes of determining whether the partnership has a substantial built-in loss in its assets when the upper-tier partnership is allocated a share of the lower-tier partnership's liabilities under section 752. The Treasury Department and the IRS believe it is appropriate for this purpose to gross up the fair market value of the lower-tier partnership interest by the upper-tier partnership's allocated share of liabilities; otherwise, the regulations could inappropriately treat a lower-tier partnership interest as a loss asset. Thus, under the proposed regulations, the fair market value of a lower-tier partnership interest (solely for purposes of computing the upper-tier partnership's basis adjustment under section 743(b)) is equal to the sum of: (i) the amount of cash that the upper-tier partnership would receive if the lower-tier partnership sold all of its property for cash to an unrelated person for an amount equal to the fair market value of such property, satisfied all of its liabilities, and liquidated; and (ii) the upper-tier partnership's share of the lower-tier partnership's liabilities (as determined under section 752 and the regulations).

In addition, the proposed regulations provide special rules for basis adjustments with respect to tiered partnerships. Under the authority granted by section 743(d)(2), the proposed regulations provide that if a partner transfers an interest in an upper-tier partnership that holds a direct or indirect interest in a lower-tier partnership, and the upper-tier partnership has a substantial built-in loss with respect to the transfer, each lower-tier partnership is treated, solely with respect to the transfer, as if it had made a section 754 election for the taxable year of the transfer. The Treasury Department and the IRS are aware of the practical and administrative difficulties associated with requiring a lower-tier partnership that has not elected under section 754 to adjust the basis of its assets in connection with the transfer of an interest in an upper-tier partnership. Comments are requested on the scope of this rule and on measures to ease administrative burdens while still accomplishing the objective of the statute.

These proposed regulations also provide guidance on the application of section 743(b) adjustments in tiered partnership situations generally. Consistent with Rev. Rul. 87-115, 1987-2 CB 163, the proposed regulations provide that if an interest in an uppertier partnership that holds an interest in a lower-tier partnership is transferred by sale or exchange or upon the death of a partner, and the upper-tier partnership and the lowertier partnership both have elections in effect under section 754, then an interest in the lower-tier partnership will be deemed to have been transferred by sale or exchange or upon the death of a partner, as the case may be. The amount of the interest in the lower-tier partnership deemed to have been transferred is the portion of the upper-tier partnership's interest in the lower-tier partnership that is attributable to the interest in the upper-tier partnership being transferred. Accordingly, to the extent the adjusted basis of the upper-tier partnership's interest in a lower-tier partnership is adjusted, the lower-tier partnership must adjust the basis of its properties.

Section 743(e)(7) provides that the Secretary may prescribe regulations for applying the EIP rules to tiered partnerships, and the legislative history makes clear that Congress did not intend for EIPs to avoid the mandatory basis adjustment provisions through the use of tiered partnerships. *See* Conference Report, at 627. The Treasury Department and the IRS believe that the same concerns exist for tiered EIPs as exist for all other partnerships subject to the mandatory basis adjustment provisions. Accordingly, the proposed regulations do not include specific rules for tiered EIPs beyond the rules governing all tiered partnerships.

The proposed regulations provide anti-abuse rules. The purpose of the amendments to section 743 is to prevent a partner that purchases an interest in a partnership with an existing built-in loss and no election under section 754 in effect from being allocated a share of the loss when the partnership disposes of the property or takes cost recovery deductions with respect to the property. Accordingly, consistent with the purpose of the amendments and the specific grant of regulatory authority in section 743(d)(2), the proposed regulations provide that the provisions of section 743 and the regulations thereunder regarding substantial built-in loss transactions must be applied in a manner consistent with the purpose of such provisions and the substance of the transaction. Thus, if a principal purpose of a transaction is to avoid the application of the substantial built-in loss rules with respect to a transfer, the Commissioner can recast the transaction for Federal income tax purposes as appropriate to achieve tax results that are consistent with the purpose of the provisions. Whether a tax result is inconsistent with the purpose of the substantial built-in loss provisions is determined based on all the facts and circumstances. For example, under the proposed regulations, property held by related partnerships may be aggregated and a contribution of property to a partnership may be disregarded in applying the substantial built-in loss provisions in section 743 and the regulations thereunder if the property was transferred with a principal purpose of avoiding the application of such provisions.

Finally, the proposed regulations clarify that a partnership that has a substantial built-in loss immediately following the transfer of a partnership interest must comply with certain provisions of § 1.743-1(k). In this case, the partnership must attach a statement of adjustments to its partnership return as if an election under section 754 were in effect at the time of the transfer solely with respect to the transfer for which there is a substantial built-in loss.

One commenter on the Notice requested that the Treasury Department and the IRS provide a de minimis exception for the substantial built-in loss provisions for transfers of small interests (subject to an annual limit on aggregate transfers during a taxable year). The substantial built-in loss provisions are intended to prevent the inappropriate shifting of losses among partners, and neither the legislative history nor the statute suggests that Congress intended to limit the scope of the rule to the transfer of large interests. Accordingly, the Treasury Department and the IRS decline to provide an exception to the substantial built-in loss rules based on the size of the interest transferred. The Treasury Department and the IRS will continue to study, and request comments on, whether a rule is warranted that excludes de minimis basis adjustments from the mandatory adjustment provisions.

ii. *EIPs*

The proposed regulations generally adopt the statutory language in section 743(e) and the provisions in the Notice. The Notice requested comments on certain aspects of the interim procedures for EIPs, and the Treasury Department and the IRS received comments in response to that request, which are described in this section.

The Notice detailed reporting requirements for transferors of EIP interests so that transferees could comply with the loss limitation rule in section 743(e)(2). The proposed regulations clarify that the reporting requirements with respect to transferors of an interest in an EIP described in the Notice do not apply if the transferor recognizes gain on the transfer and no prior transferor recognized a loss on any transfer. The Treasury Department and the IRS do not believe reporting is necessary in this limited circumstance because the transferee should not be subject to the loss limitation rule of section 743(e)(2).

In regard to the requirement in section 743(e)(6)(I) that the partnership agreement provide for a term that is not in excess of 15 years, one commenter requested that regulations provide that a partnership may still qualify as an EIP even if the partnership's initial term is greater than 15 years, particularly in cases in which the amount of the partnership's equity investment in the remaining assets is small (for example, 25 percent of the total committed capital). However, Congress considered the circumstances in which it would be appropriate to provide an extension of the term and specifically provided an exception to the 15-year requirement for EIPs in existence on June 4, 2004. Accordingly, the Treasury Department and the IRS decline to adopt this comment in the proposed regulations.

The Notice also provides guidance on whether a partnership has ever been engaged in a trade or business for purposes of section 743(e)(6)(C). The Notice provides that until further guidance is issued, an upper-tier partnership will not be treated as engaged in the trade or business of a lower-tier partnership if, at all times during the period in which the upper-tier partnership owns an interest in the lower-tier partnership, the adjusted basis of its interest in the lower-tier partnership is less than 25 percent of the total capital that is required to be contributed to the upper-tier partnership by its partners during the entire term of the upper-tier partnership (the "25% Rule"). The Notice specifically requests comments on rules that would be appropriate for future guidance in determining whether an upper-tier partnership is treated as engaged in a trade or business that is conducted by a lower-tier partnership. One commenter requested that the Treasury Department and the IRS confirm whether the 25% Rule is a safe harbor or whether a violation of the 25% Rule disqualifies a partnership from being an EIP. This commenter also requested that the Treasury Department and the IRS clarify the 25% Rule in the case of borrowing. The commenter noted that lower-tier partnership interests are often acquired with capital contributions and the proceeds of borrowing. Therefore, the commenter requested that any safe harbor take into account leverage. This commenter further suggested that rules similar to the rules in §1.731-2(e)(3) (providing circumstances in which a partnership would not be treated as engaged in a trade or business for purposes of section 731(c)(3)(C)) should apply for purposes of section 743(e)(6)(C). Finally, the commenter requested that the Treasury Department and the IRS provide additional safe harbors (for example, where the upper-tier partnership is organized for investment services and the partners and managers of the upper-tier partnership do not engage in the day-to-day operations of the lower-tier partnership's trade or business activity, but partners and/or managers are on the board of directors of the lower-tier partnership).

The Treasury Department and the IRS view the 25% Rule as a bright-line rule. Therefore, a failure to meet the 25% Rule will mean that the partnership fails to qualify as an EIP. The Treasury Department and the IRS agree that the rules in §1.731-2(e)(3) should apply for purposes of section 743(e)(6)(C). Therefore, the proposed regulations provide a safe harbor by cross-referencing those rules. Under the proposed regulations, if a partnership would not be treated as engaged in a trade or business under §1.731-2(e)(3) for purposes of section 731(c)(3)(C), the partnership also will not be treated as engaged in a trade or business for purposes of section 743(e)(6)(C). The Treasury Department and the IRS believe the 25% Rule and the cross-reference to §1.731-2(e)(3) provide appropriate guidance under section 743(e)(6)(C) and therefore the proposed regulations do not provide any additional safe harbors. The Treasury Department and the IRS are continuing to study the extent to which borrowing should be taken into account in applying the 25% Rule and therefore request comments on appropriate rules.

A commenter also requested additional guidance regarding section 743(e)(6)(H), which provides that one of the eligibility requirements for an EIP is that the partnership agreement have substantive restrictions on each partner's ability to cause a redemption of the partner's interest. The proposed regulations follow the examples in the legislative history and provide that substantive restrictions for purposes of section 743(e)(7)(H) include cases in which a redemption is permitted under a partnership agreement only if the redemption is necessary to avoid a violation of state, federal, or local laws (such as ERISA or the Bank Holding Company Act) or the imposition of a federal excise tax on, or a change in the federal tax-exempt status of, a tax-exempt partner. *See* Conference Report at 626. The Treasury Department and the IRS request comments on other restrictions that could be considered substantive restrictions on a partner's ability to cause a redemption of the partner's interest for purposes of section 743(e)(6)(H).

The proposed regulations provide that the EIP election must be made on a timely filed original return, including extensions. One commenter requested relief for certain instances in which the partnership fails to make a valid EIP election. The commenter requested relief when: (1) a partnership makes an EIP election, but did not qualify to make the election; (2) the partnership attempts to make an EIP election, but it is defective; or (3) the partnership makes an EIP election, but fails to continue to qualify. In each case, the commenter believes that the Treasury Department and the IRS should treat the partnership as an EIP if: (a) its failure to qualify or the defect was inadvertent; (b) the partners and the partnership consistently treated the partnership as an EIP; (c) steps were taken to cure the defect in a reasonable period of time; and (d) the partners and the EIP agree to make any necessary adjustments. The Treasury Department and the IRS do not adopt this comment in the proposed regulations because there are existing procedures for situations in which a regulatory election is defective.

The Treasury Department and the IRS request comments on appropriate rules for situations in which a partnership that has elected to be an EIP fails to qualify in a particular year, but then qualifies again in a future year. The Treasury Department and the IRS also request comments on the circumstances in which a qualifying partnership that has revoked an EIP election should be permitted to reelect and the rules and procedures that should apply to the reelection.

iii. *Securitization partnerships*

The proposed regulations generally restate the statutory provisions relating to the exception from the substantial built-in loss provisions for securitization partnerships.

b. *Section 734 substantial basis reduction provisions*

i. *General provisions*

The proposed regulations generally follow the statutory provisions regarding substantial basis reductions. Questions have been raised regarding whether the $250,000 threshold in section 734(d)(1) applies to a partnership's aggregate distributions for a taxable year. The Treasury Department and the IRS believe that the better interpretation of section 734(a), (b), and (d) is that the threshold applies separately with respect to each distributee because: (1) both section 734(a) and (b) refer to a distribution of property to "a partner;" and (2) section 734(b)(2)(A) and (B), referenced in section 734(d), refer to the "distributee partner" or the "distributee." These references indicate that the substantial built-in loss provisions apply to each partner-distributee separately, but with respect to the entire distribution made to the distributee. That is, where multiple properties are distributed to a partner-distributee, the $250,000 threshold is determined by reference to all properties distributed to the partner-distributee as part of the same distribution.

The proposed regulations also provide additional guidance in several areas. The proposed regulations provide that if there is a substantial basis reduction, the partnership is treated as having an election under section 754 in effect for the taxable year in which the distribution occurs, but solely for the distribution to which the substantial basis reduction relates (unless another transaction is subject to the mandatory basis adjustment provisions of sections 734 or 743). For example, if a partnership without a section 754 election in effect has a substantial basis reduction with respect to a distribution, and a partner in the partnership in that same year transfers a partnership interest (and the partnership does not have a substantial built-in loss immediately after the transfer), the partnership will be treated as having a section 754 election in effect for the distribution but not the transfer.

The same issues exist in the context of section 734(b) adjustments and tiered partnerships as exist with respect to section 743(b) adjustments and tiered partnerships. Thus, the proposed regulations also provide guidance for substantial basis reductions in tiered partnership arrangements. Under the proposed regulations, if there is a substantial basis reduction with respect to a distribution by an upper-tier partnership that (either directly or indirectly through one or more partnerships) holds an interest in a lower-tier partnership, each lower-tier partnership is treated, solely with respect to the distribution, as if it had made an election under section 754 for the taxable year in which the distribution occurs.

These proposed regulations also provide guidance on the application of section 734(b) adjustments in tiered partnership situations generally. Consistent with Rev. Rul. 92-15, 1992-1 CB 215, if an upper-tier partnership makes an adjustment under section 734(b) to the basis of an interest it holds in a lower-tier partnership that has an election under section 754 in effect, the lower-tier partnership must make adjustments to the upper-tier partnership's share of the lower-tier partnership's assets. The amount of the lower-tier partnership's adjustment is equal to the adjustment made by the upper-tier partnership to the basis of its interest in the lower-tier partnership. The lower-tier partnership's adjustment to the upper-tier partnership's share of its assets is for the upper-tier partnership only and does not affect the basis in the lower-tier partnership's property for the other partners of the lower-tier partnership.

The Treasury Department and the IRS are aware of the practical and administrative difficulties associated with the requirement that a lower-tier partnership adjust the basis of its assets with respect to adjustments under both section 734 and section 743 and request comments on the scope of this rule and measures to ease the administrative burden while still accomplishing the objective of the statute.

The proposed regulations also update §1.734-1(d) to clarify that its reporting requirements apply if there is a substantial basis reduction with respect to a distribution. In this case, the provisions of §1.734-1(d) apply solely with respect to the distribution to which the substantial basis reduction relates as if an election under section 754 were in effect at the time of the transfer.

ii. *Securitization partnerships*

The proposed regulations generally restate the statutory provisions relating to the exception from the substantial basis reduction provisions for securitization partnerships.

3. *Section 755 Basis Allocation Rules*

a. *Section 755(c)*

The proposed regulations generally restate the statutory provisions of section 755(c) and provide rules applicable to an allocation of a downward adjustment in the basis of partnership property under sections 734(b) and 755(a). As discussed in Part 3 of the Background section of this preamble, Congress enacted section 755(c) in response to the JCT's investigation of Enron Corporation. In addressing transactions among related parties, the JCT Enron Report specifically provides that:

> Partnership allocations between members of the same affiliated group (and, in general, related parties) may not have the same economic consequences as allocations between unrelated partners. As a result, related partners can use the partnership allocation rules inappropriately to shift basis among assets . . . The Joint Committee staff recommends that . . . the partnership basis rules should be altered to preclude an increase in basis to an asset if the offsetting basis reduction would be allocated to stock of a partner (or related party).

JCT Enron Report, at 29-30. The proposed regulations provide that in making an allocation under section 755(a) of any decrease in the adjusted basis of partnership property under section 734(b), no allocation may be made to stock in a corporation (or any person related (within the meaning of sections 267(b) or 707(b)(1)) to such corporation) that is a partner in the partnership. Given Congress's intent to prevent taxpayers from shifting tax gain to stock of a corporate partner or corporation related to a corporate partner, the Treasury Department and the IRS believe it is appropriate to interpret section 755(c) to apply broadly to related persons under either section 267(b) or section 707(b)(1). *See* Grassley Report, at 127 and House Committee Report, at 287. If section 755(c) only applied to persons treated as related within the meaning of both section 267(b) and section 707(b)(1), then the provision would apply in very limited circumstances, significantly restricting the scope of section 755(c).

b. *Modification of basis allocation rules for substituted basis transactions*

The Treasury Department and the IRS are aware that the current basis allocation rules for substituted basis transactions can result in unintended consequences, particularly with regard to the "net gain" and "net loss" requirement in §1.755-1(b)(5)(ii). The net gain or net loss requirement in §1.755-1(b)(5)(ii) may, in certain situations, cause a partnership to be unable to properly adjust the basis of partnership property with respect to a transferee partner. For example, when there is an increase in basis to be allocated to partnership assets and the property of the partnership does not have overall unrealized net gain or net income, the basis increase cannot be allocated under §1.755-1(b)(5). Conversely, if there is a decrease in basis to be allocated to partnership assets and the property of the partnership does not have overall unrealized net loss, the basis decrease cannot be allocated under §1.755-1(b)(5). The Treasury Department and the IRS believe this result is inappropriate. Accordingly, the Treasury Department and the IRS propose to amend the current regulations as described in this preamble.

i. *Allocations between classes of property*

The proposed regulations provide that if there is an increase in basis to be allocated to partnership assets under §1.755-1(b)(5), the increase must be allocated between capital gain property and ordinary income property in proportion to, and to the extent of, gross gain or gross income (including any remedial allocations under §1.704-3(d)) that would be allocated to the transferee (to the extent attributable to the acquired partnership interest) from the hypothetical sale of all property in each class. The proposed regulations further provide that any remaining increase must be allocated between the classes in proportion to the fair market value of all property in each class.

If there is a decrease in basis to be allocated to partnership assets under §1.755-1(b)(5), the proposed regulations provide that the decrease must be allocated between capital gain property and ordinary income property in proportion to, and to the extent of, the gross loss (including any remedial allocations under §1.704-3(d)) that would be allocated to the transferee (to the extent attributable to the acquired partnership interest) from the hypothetical sale of all property in each class. Any remaining decrease must be allocated between the classes in proportion to the transferee's shares of the adjusted bases of all property in each class (as adjusted under the preceding sentence). Thus, the proposed regulations remove the requirements that (1) there be an overall net gain or net income in partnership property for an increase in basis to be allocated to a particular class of property; and (2) there be an overall net loss in partnership property for a decrease in basis to be allocated to a particular class of property.

ii. *Allocations within classes of property*

The Treasury Department and the IRS are aware that there is uncertainty regarding whether the transferee's shares of unrealized appreciation and depreciation described in §1.755-1(b)(5)(iii)(A) and (B) include only amounts attributable to the acquired partnership interest. The proposed regulations clarify that the transferee's shares of the items are limited to the amounts attributable to the acquired partnership interest.

In addition, §1.755-1(b)(5)(iii)(C) has a limitation that provides that a transferee's negative basis adjustment is limited to the transferee's share of the partnership's adjusted basis in all depreciated assets in that class. By focusing on the transferee's share of adjusted basis with respect to only depreciated assets in the class, as opposed to all assets in the class, this rule subjects more of the negative basis adjustment to the carryover rules in §1.755-1(b)(5)(iii)(D). The Treasury Department and the IRS believe this result is inappropriate. Accordingly, the proposed regulations provide that if a decrease in basis must be allocated to partnership property and the amount of the decrease otherwise allocable to a particular class exceeds the transferee's share of the adjusted basis to the partnership of all assets in that class, the basis of the property is reduced to zero (but not below zero). Therefore, under the proposed regulations, the negative basis adjustment is no longer limited to the transferee's share of the partnership's adjusted basis in all depreciated assets in a class.

c. *Succeeding to transferor's basis adjustment*

The proposed regulations amend the regulations under section 743 to provide an exception to the rule that a transferee's basis adjustment is determined without regard to any prior transferee's basis adjustment. The Treasury Department and the IRS believe that this rule can lead to inappropriate results when the transferor transfers its partnership interest in a substituted basis transaction (within the meaning of §1.755-1(b)(5)) and the transferor had a basis adjustment under section 743(b) attributable to the transferred interest that was allocated pursuant to §1.755-1(b)(2) through (b)(4). Under the current regulations, the transferee does not succeed to the transferor's section 743(b) adjustment but, rather, is entitled to a new section 743(b) adjustment that is allocated under a different set of rules, which may result in the inappropriate shifting of basis among the partnership's assets. The proposed regulations provide that the transferee in a substituted basis transaction succeeds to that portion of the transferor's basis adjustment attributable to the transferred partnership interest and that the adjustment is taken into account in determining the transferee's share of the adjusted basis to the partnership for purposes of §§1.743-1(b) and 1.755-1(b)(5).

4. *Miscellaneous Provisions*

a. *Special rules for forward and reverse section 704(c) allocations*

One commenter on Notice 2009-70 noted that the definitions of the terms "built-in gain" and "built-in loss" in § 1.704-3(a)(3)(ii) imply that section 704(c) layers with "different signs" should be netted against each other because the regulations provide that built-in gain or built-in loss is reduced by decreases in the difference between the property's adjusted tax basis and book value.

In response to this comment, the proposed regulations provide that built-in gain and built-in loss do not take into account any decreases or increases, as the case may be, to the property's book value pursuant to a revaluation of partnership property under § 1.704-1(b)(2)(iv)(*f*) or § 1.704-1(b)(2)(iv)(*s*). Thus, for example, under the proposed regulations, reverse section 704(c) allocations do not reduce forward section 704(c) gain or loss.

The Treasury Department and the IRS also received several comments regarding the proper treatment of section 704(c) layers, suggesting one of two approaches. Under the layering approach, a partnership would create and maintain multiple section 704(c) layers for the property. Under the netting approach, a partnership would net multiple section 704(c) layers for the property and therefore each section 704(c) property would have one section 704(c) layer. One commenter recommended that the layering approach be the default rule, but that certain partnerships should be permitted to adopt a netting approach depending on the value of the partnership's assets. This commenter believed that the layering approach is more appropriate because the netting approach can result in distortions when partnerships use the traditional method of allocating section 704(c) amounts and the ceiling rule is implicated. The commenter also argued that the layering approach better maintains the economic expectations of the partners and is generally more consistent with the policy underlying section 704(c). However, this commenter also acknowledged that the netting approach is simpler to apply, and that in many cases both approaches will reach the same result. Another commenter suggested that partnerships be given the option of using either the layering approach or the netting approach. According to the commenter, this would allow partnerships to avoid the burden and expense of maintaining section 704(c) layers, particularly when maintaining section 704(c) layers is unnecessary.

The proposed regulations do not permit taxpayers to use a netting approach because a netting approach could lead to distortions. The Treasury Department and the IRS understand, however, that maintaining section 704(c) layers may result in additional administrative burdens and, therefore, request comments on when it is appropriate for partnerships to use a netting approach (for example, small partnerships).

One commenter noted that guidance was necessary with respect to how to allocate tax items among multiple section 704(c) layers. This commenter suggested three methods for allocating tax items: (1) allocate tax items to the oldest layer first; (2) allocate tax items to the newest section 704(c) layers first; and (3) allocate tax items among the section 704(c) layers pro rata based on the amount of each layer. The commenter suggested that the Treasury Department and the IRS provide a default rule that would allocate to the oldest section 704(c) layers first, but permit partnerships to elect any reasonable method (such as the three methods described).

The Treasury Department and the IRS agree that partnerships should be permitted to use any reasonable method in allocating tax items. The Treasury Department and the IRS decline to adopt a default rule for allocating tax items because no single method is more appropriate than other methods. Therefore, the proposed regulations provide that a partnership may use any reasonable method to allocate items of income, gain, loss, and deduction associated with an item of property among the property's forward and reverse section 704(c) layers subject to the anti-abuse rule in § 1.704-3(a)(10). The partnership's choice of method is also subject to § 1.704-3(a)(2), which provides that a partnership may use different methods with respect to different items of contributed property, provided that the partnership and the partners consistently apply a single reasonable method for each item of contributed property and that the overall method or combination of methods is reasonable based on the facts and circumstances and consistent with the purpose of section 704(c). The Treasury Department and the IRS are considering providing examples of reasonable methods in future guidance and therefore request comments on these and other methods for allocating tax items.

b. *Extension of time period for taxing precontribution gain*

The proposed regulations amend various provisions in § § 1.704-4, 1.737-1, and 1.1502-13 to reflect the amendments to sections 704(c)(1)(B) and 737(b)(1) that lengthen the period of time for taxing precontribution gain from five years to seven years. The proposed regulations also clarify how partners determine the seven-year period. Specifically, the proposed regulations provide that the seven-year period begins on, and includes, the date of contribution, and ends on, and includes, the last date that is within seven years of the contribution.

Proposed Effective Date

These regulations are generally proposed to apply to partnership contributions and transactions occurring on or after the date final regulations are published in the **Federal Register**. The proposed regulations under § 1.755-1(b)(5) will apply to transfers of partnership interests occurring on or after January 16, 2014. No inference is intended as to the tax consequences of transactions occurring before the effective date of these regulations.

Special Analyses

It has been determined that this notice of proposed rulemaking is not a significant regulatory action as defined in Executive Order 12866, as supplemented by Executive Order 13563. Therefore, a regulatory assessment is not required. It has also been determined that section 553(b) of the Administrative Procedure Act (5 U.S.C. chapter 5) does not apply to these regulations. It is hereby certified that the collection of information in this notice of proposed rulemaking will not have a significant economic impact on a substantial number of small entities within the meaning of section 601(6) of the Regulatory Flexibility Act (5 U.S.C. chapter 6). The Treasury Department and the IRS believe that the economic impact on small entities as a result of the collection of information in this notice of proposed rulemaking will not be significant. The small entities subject to the collection are business entities formed as partnerships that: (1) receive a contribution of built-in loss property; (2) are required to make a mandatory basis adjustment under section 734 or section 743; and/or (3) are eligible for, and elect to apply, the electing investment partnership provisions in section 743(e). In the case of the contribution of built-in loss property, the partnership is required to provide a statement in the year of contribution setting forth basic information that the partnership will need in order to properly apply the rules. Similarly, in the case of the mandatory basis adjustment provisions, the partnership will already have the information subject to the collection in order to comply with the rules. In the case of EIPs, the collections are either one-time (election) or annual (annual statement). The collection only applies if the partnership elects to be an EIP. Furthermore, the proposed regulations provide the specific language for the annual statement. Finally, the collection regarding the mandatory basis adjustment provisions and the EIP rules have been in effect since 2005, as required by Notice 2005-32, and the Treasury Department and the IRS have not received comments that the collections have a significant economic impact. For these reasons, the Treasury Department and the IRS do not believe that the collection of information in this notice of proposed rulemaking has a significant economic impact. Pursuant to section 7805(f) of the Code, this notice of proposed rulemaking will be submitted to the Chief Counsel for Advocacy of the Small Business Administration for comment on its impact on small business.

Comments and Public Hearing

Before the proposed regulations are adopted as final regulations, consideration will be given to any written (a signed original and eight (8) copies) or electronic comments that are submitted timely to the IRS. The Treasury Department and the IRS request comments on all aspects of the proposed rules. All comments will be available for public inspection and copying.

A public hearing has been scheduled for April 30, 2014 beginning at 10:00 a.m. in the Auditorium, Internal Revenue Building, 1111 Constitution Avenue NW, Washington, DC. Due to building security procedures, visitors must enter at the Constitution Avenue entrance. In addition, all visitors must present photo identification to enter the building. Because of access restrictions, visitors will not be admitted beyond the immediate entrance area more than 30 minutes before the hearing starts. For information about having your name placed on the building access list to attend the hearing, see the "FOR FURTHER INFORMATION CONTACT" section of this preamble.

The rules of 26 CFR 601.601(a)(3) apply to the hearing. Persons who wish to present oral comments at the hearing must submit electronic or written comments by April 16, 2014, and an outline of the topics to be discussed and the time to be devoted to each topic (signed original and eight (8) copies) by April 16, 2014. A period of 10 minutes will be allotted to each person for making comments. An agenda showing the scheduling of the speakers will be prepared after the deadline for receiving outlines has passed. Copies of the agenda will be available free of charge at the hearing.

Drafting Information

The principal authors of these regulations are Wendy L. Kribell and Benjamin H. Weaver, Office of the Associate Chief Counsel (Passthroughs & Special Industries). However, other personnel from the Treasury Department and the IRS participated in their development.

[¶ 49,609]   Proposed Regulations (REG-143874-10) and Withdrawal of Notice of Proposed Rulemaking (EE-96-85), published in the Federal Register on February 6, 2014.

[Code Sec. 512]

Exempt organizations: Unrelated business income: Covered entities.—Reg. § 1.512(a)-5, providing guidance on how certain organizations that provide employee benefits must calculate unrelated business taxable income (UBTI), is proposed. Reg. § 1.512(a)-5 that was proposed on February 4, 1986, is withdrawn.

AGENCY: Internal Revenue Service (IRS), Treasury.

ACTION: Withdrawal of notice of proposed rulemaking and notice of proposed rulemaking.

SUMMARY: This document contains a new proposed regulation providing guidance on how certain organizations that provide employee benefits must calculate unrelated business taxable income (UBTI). This document also withdraws the notice of proposed rulemaking relating to UBTI that was published on February 4, 1986.

DATES: The notice of proposed rulemaking that was published on February 4, 1986, at 51 FR 4391 is withdrawn as of February 6, 2014. Written or electronic comments and request for a public hearing must be received by May 7, 2014.

ADDRESSES: Send Submissions to: CC:PA:LPD:PR (REG-143874-10), room 5203, Internal Revenue Service, P.O. Box 7604, Ben Franklin Station, Washington, DC 20224. Submissions may be hand delivered Monday through Friday between the hours of 8 a.m. and 4 p.m. to CC:PA:LPD:PR (REG-143874-10), Courier's Desk, Internal Revenue Service, 1111 Constitution Avenue NW, Washington, DC, or sent electronically via the Federal eRulemaking Portal at *www.regulations.gov* (IRS REG-143874-10).

FOR FURTHER INFORMATION CONTACT: Concerning the proposed regulation, Dara Alderman or Janet Laufer at (202) 317-5500 (not a toll-free number); concerning submissions of comments and/or to request a hearing, Oluwafunmilayo (Funmi) Taylor at (202) 317-6901 (not a toll-free number).

SUPPLEMENTARY INFORMATION:

Background

This document contains proposed Income Tax Regulations (26 CFR part 1) under section 512(a) of the Code. Organizations that are otherwise exempt from tax under section 501(a) are subject to tax on their unrelated business taxable income (UBTI) under section 511(a). Section 512(a) of the Code generally defines UBTI of exempt organizations and provides special rules for calculating UBTI for organizations described in section 501(c)(7) (social and recreational clubs), voluntary employees' beneficiary associations described in section 501(c)(9) (VEBAs), supplemental unemployment benefit trusts described in section 501(c)(17) (SUBs), and group legal services organizations described in section 501(c)(20) (GLSOs).

Section 512(a)(1) provides a general rule that UBTI is the gross income from any unrelated trade or business regularly carried on by the organization, less certain deductions. Under section 512(a)(3)(A), in the case of social and recreational clubs, VEBAs, SUBs, and GLSOs, UBTI is defined as gross income, less directly connected expenses, but excluding "exempt function income."

Exempt function income is defined in section 512(a)(3)(B) as gross income from two sources. The first type of exempt function income is amounts paid by members as consideration for providing the members or their dependents or guests with goods, facilities, or services in furtherance of the organization's exempt purposes. The second type of exempt function income is all income (other than an amount equal to the gross income derived from any unrelated trade or business regularly carried on by the organization computed as if the organization were subject to section 512(a)(1)) that is set aside: (1) for a charitable purpose specified in section 170(c)(4); (2) in the case of a VEBA, SUB, or GLSO, to provide for the payment of life, sick, accident, or other benefits; or (3) for reasonable costs of administration directly connected with a purpose described in (1) or (2).

Section 512(a)(3)(E) generally limits the amount that a VEBA, SUB, or GLSO may set aside as exempt function income to an amount that does not result in an amount of total assets in the VEBA, SUB, or GLSO at the end of the taxable year that exceeds the section 419A account limit for the taxable year. For this purpose, however, the account limit does not take into account any reserve under section 419A(c)(2)(A) for post-retirement medical benefits.

Section 512(a)(3)(E) was added to the Code under the Tax Reform Act of 1984, Public Law 98-369 (98 Stat. 598 (1984)). Congress enacted section 512(a)(3)(E) to limit the extent to which a VEBA, SUB, or GLSO's income is exempt from tax, noting that "[p]resent law does not specifically limit the amount of income that can be set aside" by a VEBA, SUB, or GLSO on a tax-free basis. H.R. Rep. No. 98-432, pt. 2, at 1275.

To implement section 512(a)(3)(E), § 1.512(a)-5T was published in the **Federal Register** as TD 8073 on February 4, 1986 (51 FR 4312), with an immediate effective date. A cross-referencing Notice of Proposed Rulemaking (the 1986 Proposed Regulation) was issued contemporaneously with the temporary regulation. Written comments were received on the 1986 Proposed Regulation, and a public hearing was held on June 26, 1986. The 1986 Proposed Regulation is hereby withdrawn and replaced by the new proposed regulation that is published in this document. Section 1.512(a)-5T will continue to apply until it is removed by a final rule published in the **Federal Register**. This new proposed regulation contains some changes to improve clarity and respond to comments received on the 1986 Proposed Regulation, but otherwise generally has the same effect as the 1986 Proposed Regulation and § 1.512(a)-5T.

Explanation of Provisions

Covered Entity

This new proposed regulation uses the uniform term "Covered Entity" to describe VEBAs and SUBs subject to the UBTI computation rules of section 512(a)(3).[1] For taxable years beginning after June 30, 1992, GLSOs are no longer exempt as section 501(c)(20) organizations. *See* section 120(e). Therefore, a GLSO is no longer a Covered Entity. Effective July 1, 1992, a GLSO could, if it otherwise qualified, request a ruling or determination modifying the basis for its exemption from section 501(c)(20) to section 501(c)(9).

Limitation on Amounts Set Aside for Exempt Purposes

The 1986 Proposed Regulation and § 1.512(a)-5T provide that under section 512(a)(3)(E)(i), a Covered Entity's UBTI is generally the lesser of two amounts: (1) the investment income of the Covered Entity for the taxable year (excluding member contributions), or (2) the excess of the total amount set aside as of the close of the taxable year (including member contributions and excluding certain long-term assets) over the qualified asset account limit (calculated without regard to the otherwise permitted reserve for post-retirement medical benefits) for the taxable year. In the view of the Treasury Department and the IRS, this means that UBTI is calculated based on the extent to which the assets of a Covered Entity at the end of the year exceed the section 512 limitation, regardless of whether income was allocated to payment of benefits during the course of the year.

In *CNG Transmission Mgmt. VEBA v. U.S.*, 588 F.3d 1376 (Fed. Cir. 2009), *aff'g*, 84 Fed. Cl. 327 (2008), the Federal Circuit Court of Appeals decided in favor of the IRS on this issue. The Court said that the "language of section 512(a)(3)(E) is clear and unambiguous," and that a VEBA "may not avoid the limitation on exempt function income in [section] 512(a)(3)(E)(i) merely by allocating investment income toward the payment of welfare benefits during the course of the tax year." *CNG*, 558 F.3d at 1379, 1377-78; *accord Northrop Corp. Employee Insurance Benefit Plans Master Trust v. U.S.*, 99 Fed. Cl. 1 (2011), *aff'd*, 467 Fed. Appx. 886 (Fed. Cir. April 10, 2012), *cert. denied*, (Dec. 3, 2012).

Notwithstanding the view of the Treasury Department and the IRS and support for that view in the foregoing cases, one court has applied a different interpretation. In *Sherwin-Williams Co. Employee Health Plan Trust v. Comm'r*, 330 F.3d 449 (6th Cir. 2003), *rev'g*, 115 T.C. 440 (2000), the Sixth Circuit Court of Appeals held that investment income that the taxpayer VEBA earmarked and claimed was spent before year-end on reasonable costs of administration was not subject to the section 512(a)(3)(E) limit on exempt function income.[2] The Treasury Department and the IRS believe that the decision in *Sherwin-Williams* is contrary to the statute, the legislative history of section 512(a)(3)(E), § 1.512(a)-5T, and the 1986 Proposed Regulation, and have determined that it is appropriate to issue this proposed regulation clarifying the proper way to make the calculation.[3] If the final regulation follows the approach taken in this proposed regulation, the IRS will no longer recognize the precedential effect of *Sherwin-Williams* in the Sixth Circuit.

This new proposed regulation retains the formula set forth in the 1986 Proposed Regulation and § 1.512(a)-5T but modifies and clarifies the description and adds examples. This new proposed regulation specifically states that any investment income a Covered Entity earns during the taxable year is subject to unrelated business income tax (UBIT) to the extent the Covered Entity's year-end assets exceed the account limit, and clarifies that this rule applies regardless of how that income is used.

To further improve clarity, this new proposed regulation slightly modifies language from the prior version of Q&A-3, separates it into a new Q&A-2 and -3, and adds examples.

This new proposed regulation also reflects the rule under section 512(a)(3)(B) that the UBTI of a Covered Entity includes UBTI derived by the Covered Entity from any unrelated trade or business (as defined in section 513) regularly carried on by it, computed as if the organization were subject to section 512(a)(1).

In addition, this new proposed regulation reflects the special rule under section 512(a)(3)(E)(iii). Accordingly, a Covered Entity is not subject to the limitation under section 512(a)(3)(E) if substantially all of the contributions to the Covered Entity are made by employers who were tax exempt throughout the five-year taxable period ending with the taxable year in which the contributions are made.

Special Rules Relating to Sections 419A(f)(5) and 419A(f)(6)

Some commenters on the 1986 Proposed Regulation requested that the regulations explicitly provide that the special account limits under section 419A(f)(5) for collectively bargained plans be used in determining the set aside limits under section 512. The 1986 Proposed Regulation contained a rule that references § 1.419A-2T for special rules relating to collectively bargained welfare benefit funds. The Treasury Department and the IRS are actively working on regulations under section 419A(f)(5) relating to collectively-bargained welfare benefit funds and believe it is appropriate to address issues related to collectively bargained welfare benefit funds in that project.

A number of commenters suggested that a VEBA that is part of a 10 or more employer plan described in section 419A(f)(6) should be exempted from the UBTI rules under section 512. However, after the 1986 Proposed Regulation and § 1.512(a)-5T were published, the Technical Corrections to the Tax Reform Act of 1984, which was part of the Tax Reform Act of 1986, Public Law 99-514, added language to section 512(a)(3)(E)(i) that specifically subjects 10 or more employer plans to the set aside limit described in that section. *See* section 1851(a)(10)(A) of Public Law 99-514. Consistent with this change in the law, this new proposed regulation provides that a Covered Entity that is part of a 10 or more employer plan is subject to the set aside limit, and that the account limit is determined as if the plan is not subject to the exception under section 419A(f)(6).

Treatment of Existing Reserves

A number of concerns were raised by commenters relating to the rules in the 1986 Proposed Regulation regarding existing reserves. For example, one commentator stated that the requirement that an employer must charge all post-retirement claims paid on or after July 18, 1984 against any existing reserve as of July 18, 1984 (and earnings on existing reserves) is burdensome. However, this treatment of existing reserves is required under section 512(a)(3)(E)(ii)(III). Thus, this new proposed regulation retains the rules regarding existing reserves in the 1986 Proposed Regulation and adds a clarification to the example.

---

[1] While section 501(c)(7) organizations are also subject to the UBTI computation rules of section 512(a)(3), this proposed regulation addresses only computations for VEBAs and SUBs.

[2] As noted by the Federal Circuit in *CNG*, *Sherwin-Williams* can be viewed as distinguishable on its facts because the government there agreed to a stipulation that the investment income at issue had been spent on administrative costs, and in *CNG* there was not an equivalent stipulation. The Treasury Department and the IRS believe that the stipulation in *Sherwin-Williams* is not a distinction that should have affected the outcome. Specifically, the Treasury Department and the IRS believe that regardless of whether investment income is earmarked for (or otherwise traceable to) the payment of program benefits and administrative expenses during the year, the formula set forth in the 1986 Proposed Regulation and § 1.512(a)-5T, as well as the new proposed regulation, operates the same way.

[3] The IRS's interpretation is set forth in its non-acquiescence to the *Sherwin-Williams* decision (AOD 2005-02, 2005 35 I.R.B. 422). In AOD 2005-02, the IRS recognized the precedential effect of the decision to cases appealable to the Sixth Circuit and indicated that it would follow *Sherwin-Williams* with respect to cases within that circuit if the opinion cannot be meaningfully distinguished.

Proposed Effective Date

This regulation is proposed to apply to taxable years ending on or after the date of publication of the final regulation.

Special Analyses

It has been determined that this notice of proposed rulemaking is not a significant regulatory action as defined in Executive Order 12866. Therefore, a regulatory assessment is not required. It has also been determined that section 553(b) of the Administrative Procedure Act (5 U.S.C. chapter 5) does not apply to this regulation, and because the regulation does not impose a collection of information on small entities, the Regulatory Flexibility Act (5 U.S.C. chapter 6) does not apply. Pursuant to section 7805(f) of the Code, this regulation has been submitted to the Chief Counsel for Advocacy of the Small Business Administration for comment on its impact on small business.

Comments and Requests for Public Hearing

Before this proposed regulation is adopted as a final regulation, consideration will be given to any written (a signed original and eight (8) copies) or electronic comments that are timely submitted to the IRS. The Treasury Department and the IRS request comments on all aspects of the proposed rules. All comments will be available for public inspection and copying. A public hearing will be scheduled if requested in writing by any person that timely submits written or electronic comments. If a public hearing is scheduled, notice of the date, time, and place for the hearing will be published in the **Federal Register**.

Drafting Information

The principal authors of this regulation are Dara Alderman and Janet Laufer, Office of Division Counsel/Associate Chief Counsel (Tax Exempt and Government Entities). However, other personnel from the Treasury Department and the IRS participated in the development of this regulation.

[¶ 49,619]   **Proposed Amendments of Regulations (REG-110948-14)**, published in the Federal Register on July 2, 2014.

[Code Secs. 501 and 508]

Tax-exempt status: Application for exemption: Streamlined process.—Amendments of Reg. §§ 1.501(a)-1, 1.501(c)(3)-1 and 1.508-1, providing guidance to organizations that seek recognition of tax-exempt status under Code Sec. 501(c)(3), are proposed.

AGENCY: Internal Revenue Service (IRS), Treasury.

ACTION: Notice of proposed rulemaking by cross-reference to temporary regulations.

SUMMARY: In the Rules and Regulations section of this issue of the **Federal Register**, the IRS is issuing regulations that provide guidance to organizations that seek recognition of tax-exempt status under section 501(c)(3) of the Internal Revenue Code. The final and temporary regulations amend current regulations to allow the Commissioner of Internal Revenue to adopt a streamlined application process that certain organizations may use to apply for recognition of tax-exempt status under section 501(c)(3). The text of those temporary regulations also serves as the text of these proposed regulations.

DATES: Comments and requests for a public hearing must be received by September 30, 2014.

ADDRESSES: Send submissions to: CC:PA:LPD:PR (REG-110948-14), room 5205, Internal Revenue Service, PO Box 7604, Ben Franklin Station, Washington, DC 20044. Submissions may be hand-delivered Monday through Friday between the hours of 8 a.m. and 4 p.m. to CC:PA:LPD:PR (REG-110948-14), Courier's Desk, Internal Revenue Service, 1111 Constitution Avenue NW, Washington, DC, or sent electronically via the Federal eRulemaking Portal at *http://www.regulations.gov* (IRS REG-110948-14).

FOR FURTHER INFORMATION CONTACT: Concerning the proposed regulations, James R. Martin or Robin Ehrenberg at (202) 317-5800; concerning submission of comments and request for hearing, Oluwafunmilayo Taylor at (202) 317-6901 (not toll-free numbers).

SUPPLEMENTARY INFORMATION:

Background and Explanation of Provisions

Temporary regulations in the Rules and Regulations section of this issue of the **Federal Register** amend the existing regulations under sections 501 and 508 to allow for an additional form of application to be used to satisfy the notice requirement under section 508(a). The text of those temporary regulations also serves as the text of these proposed regulations. The preamble to the temporary regulations explains the amendments.

Special Analyses

It has been determined that this notice of proposed rulemaking is not a significant regulatory action as defined in Executive Order 12866, as supplemented by Executive Order 13563. Therefore, a regulatory assessment is not required. It also has been determined that section 553(b) of the Administrative Procedure Act (5 U.S.C. chapter 5) does not apply to these regulations. It is hereby certified that this rule will not have a significant economic impact on a substantial number of small entities. Although this rule may affect a substantial number of small entities that choose to use the new form that streamlines the application process that eligible organizations may use to apply for recognition of tax-exempt status under section 501(c)(3), we intend for this rule to reduce the economic impact on small entities. This rule merely provides guidance about the streamlined form of application available to satisfy the notice requirement under Section 508(a). Therefore, a Regulatory Flexibility Analysis under the Regulatory Flexibility Act (5 U.S.C. Chapter 6) is not required.

Comments and Requests for Public Hearing

Before these proposed regulations are adopted as final regulations, consideration will be given to any comments that are submitted timely to the IRS as prescribed in this preamble under the "Addresses" heading. The Treasury Department and the IRS request comments on all aspects of the proposed rules. All comments will be available at *www.regulations.gov* or upon request.

A public hearing will be scheduled if requested in writing by any person that timely submits written comments. If a public hearing is scheduled, notice of the date, time, and place for the public hearing will be published in the **Federal Register**.

Drafting Information

The principal authors of these regulations are James R. Martin and Robin Ehrenberg, Office of Associate Chief Counsel (Tax Exempt and Government Entities). However, other personnel from the IRS and the Treasury Department participated in their development.

[¶ 49,624]   Proposed Amendments of Regulations (REG-104579-13), published in the Federal Register on July 28, 2014.

[Code Secs. 36B and 162]

Qualified health plan: Affordable insurance exchanges: Premium tax credit: Guidance.—Reg. §1.162(l)-1 and amendments of Reg. §§1.36B-2, 1.36B-3 and 1.36B-4, providing guidance to individuals who enroll in qualified health plans through Affordable Insurance Exchanges and claim the premium tax credit, and Exchanges that make qualified health plans available to individuals and employers, are proposed.

AGENCY: Internal Revenue Service (IRS), Treasury.

ACTION: Notice of proposed rulemaking by cross-reference to temporary regulations.

SUMMARY: In the Rules and Regulations section of this issue of the **Federal Register**, the IRS is issuing final and temporary regulations under section 36B of the Internal Revenue Code (Code) relating to the health insurance premium tax credit. The regulations provide guidance to individuals who enroll in qualified health plans through Affordable Insurance Exchanges (Exchanges) and claim the premium tax credit, and Exchanges that make qualified health plans available to individuals and employers. The text of those temporary regulations also serves as the text of these proposed regulations.

DATES: Comments and requests for a public hearing must be received by October 27, 2014.

ADDRESSES: Send submissions to: CC:PA:LPD:PR (REG-104579-13), Internal Revenue Service, POB 7604, Ben Franklin Station, Washington, DC 20044. Taxpayers also may submit comments electronically via the Federal eRulemaking Portal at *www.regulations.gov* (IRS REG-104579-13).

FOR FURTHER INFORMATION CONTACT: Concerning the proposed regulations, Arvind Ravichandran, (202) 317-4718; concerning submission of comments or to request a hearing, Oluwafunmilayo Taylor, (202) 317-6901 (not toll-free numbers).

SUPPLEMENTARY INFORMATION:

Background and Explanation of Provisions

Final and temporary regulations in the Rules and Regulations section of this issue of the **Federal Register** amend the Income Tax Regulations (26 CFR Part 1) relating to section 36B and section 162(l) of the Code. The final and temporary regulations provide guidance for individuals who enroll in qualified health plans through Affordable Insurance Exchanges (Exchanges) and claim the premium tax credit, and Exchanges that make qualified health plans available to individuals and employers. The text of those temporary regulations also serves as the text of these proposed regulations. The preamble to the final and temporary regulations explains the amendments.

Proposed Effective Date

These regulations are proposed to apply for taxable years ending after December 31, 2013. *See* §1.36B-1(o). Taxpayers must apply the final and temporary regulations until publication of final regulations.

Special Analyses

It has been determined that this notice of proposed rulemaking is not a significant regulatory action as defined in Executive Order 12866. Therefore, a regulatory assessment is not required. It also has been determined that section 553(b) of the Administrative Procedure Act (5 U.S.C. chapter 5) does not apply to these regulations, and because the regulations do not impose a collection of information on small entities, the Regulatory Flexibility Act (5 U.S.C. chapter 6) does not apply. Pursuant to section 7805(f) of the Code, this regulation has been submitted to the Chief Counsel for Advocacy of the Small Business Administration for comment on its impact on small business.

Comments and Requests for a Public Hearing

Before these proposed regulations are adopted as final regulations, consideration will be given to any comments that are submitted timely to the IRS as prescribed in this preamble under "Addresses" heading. The IRS and the Treasury Department request comments on all aspects of the proposed rules. All comments will be available at www.regulations.gov or upon request. A public hearing will be scheduled if requested in writing by any person that timely submits written comments. If a public hearing is scheduled, notice of the date, time, and place for the public hearing will be published in the **Federal Register**.

Drafting Information

The principal authors of these regulations are Arvind Ravichandran, Shareen Pflanz and Steve Toomey of the Office of Associate Chief Counsel (Income Tax & Accounting). However, other personnel from the IRS and the Treasury Department participated in their development.

[¶ 49,625]   Proposed Amendments of Regulations (REG-123286-14), published in the Federal Register on July 28, 2014 (corrected 9/26/2014).

[Code Sec. 275]

Branded prescription drug fee: Prescription drugs: Fee calculation: Dispute resolution: Deadline: Covered entities: Error reports: Refund claims.—Amendments of Reg. §§51.2 and 51.11, relating to the branded prescription drug fee, are proposed.

AGENCY: Internal Revenue Service (IRS), Treasury.

ACTION: Notice of proposed rulemaking by cross-reference to temporary regulations.

SUMMARY: In the Rules and Regulations section of this issue of the **Federal Register**, the IRS is issuing temporary regulations relating to the branded prescription drug fee. This fee was enacted by section 9008 of the Patient Protection and Affordable Care Act, as amended by section 1404 of the Health Care and Education Reconciliation Act of 2010, and the Health Care and Reconciliation Act of 2010 (collectively the ACA). The proposed regulations modify the definition of controlled group for purposes of the branded prescription drug fee. The proposed regulations affect persons engaged in the business of manufacturing or importing certain branded prescription drugs. The text of the temporary regulations also serves as the text of the proposed regulations.

DATES: Comments and requests for a public hearing must be received by October 27, 2014.

ADDRESSES: Send submissions to: CC:PA:LPD:PR (REG-123286-14), room 5205, Internal Revenue Service, PO Box 7604, Ben Franklin Station, Washington, DC 20044. Submissions may be hand-delivered Monday through Friday between the hours of 8 a.m. and 4 p.m. to: CC:PA:LPD:PR (REG-123286-14), Courier's Desk, Internal Revenue Service, 1111 Constitution Avenue, NW, Washington, DC, or sent electronically via the Federal eRulemaking Portal at *www.regulations.gov* (IRS REG-123286-14).

FOR FURTHER INFORMATION CONTACT: Concerning the proposed regulations, Celia Gabrysh, (202) 317-6855; concerning submissions of comments and request for a hearing, Oluwafunmilayo Taylor, (202) 317-6901 (not toll-free calls).

SUPPLEMENTARY INFORMATION:

Background

Temporary regulations in the Rules and Regulations section of this issue of the **Federal Register** amend §§ 51.2(e)(3) and 51.11(c) of the Branded Prescription Drug Fee Regulations, 26 CFR Part 51. The text of those regulations also serves as the text of these proposed regulations. The preamble to the temporary regulations explains the amendment.

Special Analyses

It has been determined that this notice of proposed rulemaking is not a significant regulatory action as defined in Executive Order 12866, as supplemented by Executive Order 13563. Therefore, a regulatory flexibility assessment is not required. It also has been determined that section 553(b) of the Administrative Procedure Act (5 U.S.C. chapter 5) does not apply to these regulations. Because these regulations do not impose a collection of information on small entities, a Regulatory Flexibility Analysis under the Regulatory Flexibility Act (5 U.S.C. chapter 6) is not required. Pursuant to section 7805(f) of the Internal Revenue Code, this notice of proposed rulemaking has been submitted to the Chief Counsel for Advocacy of the Small Business Administration for comment on its impact on small business.

Comments and Requests for a Public Hearing

Before these proposed regulations are adopted as final regulations, consideration will be given to any comments that are submitted timely to the IRS as prescribed in this preamble under the "Addresses" heading. Comments are requested on all aspects of the proposed regulations. All comments will be available at www.regulations.gov or upon request. A public hearing may be scheduled if requested in writing by any person that timely submits written comments. If a public hearing is scheduled, notice of the date, time, and place for the hearing will be published in the **Federal Register**.

Drafting Information

The principal author of these regulations is Celia Gabrysh, Office of Associate Chief Counsel (Passthroughs and Special Industries). However, other personnel from the IRS and the Treasury Department participated in their development.

[¶ 49,633] Proposed Amendments of Regulations (REG-151416-06), published in the Federal Register on November 3, 2014 (corrected 1/26/2015).

[Code Secs. 617, 704, 732, 736, 751, 755, 995, 1231, 1245, 1248, 1250, 1252, 1254 and 6050K]

Partners and partnerships: Inventories, appreciation in value.—Amendments of Reg. §§ 1.617-4, 1.704-1, 1.704-3, 1.732-1, 1.736-1, 1.751-1, 1.755-1, 1.995-4, 1.1231-1, 1.1245-1, 1.1245-2, 1.1245-4, 1.1248-1, 1.1250-1, 1.1252-2, 1.1254-5 and 1.6050K-1, prescribing how a partner should measure its interest in a partnership's unrealized receivables and inventory items and providing guidance regarding the tax consequences of a distribution that causes a reduction in that interest, are proposed.

AGENCY: Internal Revenue Service (IRS), Treasury.

ACTION: Notice of proposed rulemaking.

SUMMARY: This document contains proposed regulations that prescribe how a partner should measure its interest in a partnership's unrealized receivables and inventory items, and that provide guidance regarding the tax consequences of a distribution that causes a reduction in that interest. The proposed regulations take into account statutory changes that have occurred subsequent to the issuance of the existing regulations. The proposed regulations affect partners in partnerships that own unrealized receivables and inventory items and that make a distribution to one or more partners.

DATES: Comments and requests for a public hearing must be received by February 2, 2015.

ADDRESSES: Send submissions to CC:PA:LPD:PR (REG-151416-06), room 5203, Internal Revenue Service, P.O. Box 7604, Ben Franklin Station, Washington, D.C., 20044. Submissions may be hand-delivered Monday through Friday between the hours of 8 a.m. and 4 p.m. to CC:PA:LPD:PR (REG-151416-06), Courier's Desk, Internal Revenue Service, 1111 Constitution Avenue, N.W., Washington, D.C., 20224, or via the Federal eRulemaking Portal at *www.regulations.gov* (IRS REG-151416-06).

FOR FURTHER INFORMATION CONTACT: Concerning the proposed regulations, Allison R. Carmody at (202) 317-5279 or Frank J. Fisher at (202) 317-6850; concerning submissions of comments and requests for hearing, Oluwafunmilayo Taylor at (202) 317-6901 (not toll-free numbers).

SUPPLEMENTARY INFORMATION:

Paperwork Reduction Act

The collection of information contained in this notice of proposed rulemaking has been submitted to the Office of Management and Budget for review in accordance with the Paperwork Reduction Act of 1995 (44 U.S.C. 3507(d)). Comments on the collection of information should be sent to the Office of Management and Budget, Attn: Desk Officer for the Department of the Treasury, Office of Information and Regulatory Affairs, Washington, DC 20503, with copies to the Internal Revenue Service, Attn: IRS Reports Clearance Officer, SE-:CAR:MP:T:T:SP, Washington, DC 20224. Comments on the collection of information should be received by January 2, 2015.

Comments are specifically requested concerning:

Whether the proposed collection of information is necessary for the proper performance of the Internal Revenue Service, including whether the information will have practical utility;

The accuracy of the estimated burden associated with the proposed collection of information;

How the quality, utility, and clarity of the information to be collected may be enhanced;

How the burden of complying with the proposed collection of information may be minimized, including through the application of automated collection techniques or other forms of information technology; and

Estimates of capital or start-up costs and costs of operation, maintenance, and purchase of service to provide information.

The collection of information required by this proposed regulation is in § 1.751-1(b)(3) and (b)(6), and in § 1.755-1(c)(2)(vi). This information is required for a partnership and certain partners to report the information to the IRS necessary to ensure that the partners of the partnership properly report in accordance with the rules of the proposed regulations the correct amount of ordinary income and/or capital gain upon a distribution of property from the partnership to its partners. The collection of information is necessary to ensure tax compliance.

The likely respondents are business or other for-profit institutions.

Estimated total annual reporting burden: 22,500 hours.

Estimated average annual burden hours per respondent vary from 30 minutes to 2 hours, depending on individual circumstances, with an estimated average of 1 hour.

Estimated number of respondents: 22,500.

Estimated annual frequency of responses: annually.

An agency may not conduct or sponsor, and a person is not required to respond to, a collection of information unless it displays a valid control number assigned by the Office of Management and Budget.

Books or records relating to a collection of information must be retained as long as their contents may become material in the administration of any internal revenue law. Generally, tax returns and tax return information are confidential, as required by section 6103.

Background

This document contains proposed amendments to the Income Tax Regulations (26 CFR part 1) under section 751(b) of the Internal Revenue Code (the Code). In 1954, Congress enacted section 751 to prevent the use of a partnership to convert potential ordinary income into capital gain. *See* H.R. Rep. No. 1337 at 70 (1954), reprinted in 1954 U.S.C.C.A.N. 4017, 4097. To that end, section 751(a) provides that the amount of any money, or the fair market value of any property, received by a transferor partner in exchange for all or part of that partner's interest in the partnership's unrealized receivables and inventory items is considered as an amount realized from the sale or exchange of property other than a capital asset. Further, section 751(b) overrides the nonrecognition provisions of section 731 to the extent a partner receives a distribution from the partnership that causes a shift between the partner's interest in the partnership's unrealized receivables or substantially appreciated inventory items (collectively, the partnership's "section 751 property") and the partner's interest in the partnership's other property.

Whether section 751(b) applies depends on the partner's interest in the partnership's section 751 property before and after a distribution. The statute does not define a partner's interest in a partnership's section 751 property, but the legislative history indicates that Congress believed a partner's interest in a partnership's section 751 property equals the partner's rights to income from the partnership's section 751 property:

The provisions relating to unrealized receivables and appreciated inventory items are necessary to prevent the use of the partnership as a device for obtaining capital-gain treatment on fees or other rights to income and on appreciated inventory. Amounts attributable to such rights would be treated as ordinary income if realized in normal course by the partnership. The sale of a partnership interest or distributions to partners should not be permitted to change the character of this income. *The statutory treatment proposed, in general, regards the income rights as severable from the partnership interest and as subject to the same tax consequences which would be accorded an individual entrepreneur.*

S. Rep. No. 1622 at 99 (1954), reprinted in 1954 U.S.C.C.A.N. 4621, 4732. (Emphasis added.)

In 1984, Congress amended section 704(c), making mandatory its application to property contributed to a partnership. While Congress did not specifically address the overlap of section 704(c) and section 751, the Conference Report indicates that the 1984 Congress understood that the section 704(c) amendment would impact other provisions in subchapter K and provides regulatory authority to the Secretary of the Treasury to address those repercussions. *See* H.R. Conf. Rep. No. 861, 98th Cong., 2d Sess., June 23, 1984, reprinted in 1984 U.S.C.C.A.N. 1445, 1545.

The IRS and the Treasury Department first issued regulations implementing section 751 in 1956. Following the changes to section 704(c) making its application mandatory, the IRS and the Treasury Department amended the regulations under section 751(a) to provide generally that a partner's interest in section 751 property is the amount of income or loss from section 751 property that would be allocated to the partner if the partnership had sold all of its property in a fully taxable transaction for cash in an amount equal to the fair market value of such property. (*See* TD 8847, 64 FR 69903, Dec. 15, 1999.) However, the 1956 regulations with respect to section 751(b) remained unchanged.

The examples in the current regulations under section 751(b) determine a partner's interest in section 751 property by reference to the partner's share of the gross value of the partnership's assets (the "gross value" approach), not by reference to the partner's share of the unrealized gain or loss in the property. *See*, for example, § 1.751-1(g), *Example 2*. Because the gross value approach focuses on a partner's share of the asset's value rather than the partner's share of the unrealized gain, the examples in the current regulations may be too narrow in some respects, and too broad in others, to carry out the intended purpose of section 751(b). That is, the gross value approach may allow a distribution that reduces a partner's share of the unrealized gain in the partnership's section 751 property without triggering section 751(b), and, conversely, may trigger section 751(b) even if the partner's share of the unrealized gain in the partnership's section 751 property is not reduced. For example, Rev. Rul. 84-102 (1984-2 CB 119) provides that deemed distributions under section 752 resulting from shifting allocations of indebtedness may result in the partners' shares of asset gross value changing, even though the partners' shares of unrealized gain associated with section 751 property would not necessarily have changed.

If the distribution results in a shift between the partner's interest in the partnership's section 751 property and the partnership's other property, the current regulations require a deemed asset exchange of both section 751 property and other property between the partner and the partnership to determine the tax consequences of the distribution (the "asset exchange" approach). *See*, for example, § 1.751-1(g), *Example 6*, of the current regulations. The asset exchange approach is complex, requiring the partnership and partner to determine the tax consequences of both a deemed distribution of relinquished property and a deemed taxable exchange of that property back to the partnership. The asset exchange approach also often accelerates capital gain unnecessarily by requiring certain partners to recognize capital gain even when their shares of partnership capital gain have not been reduced.

In 2006, the IRS and the Treasury Department published Notice 2006-14 (2006-1 CB 498), which suggested, and requested comments on, alternative approaches to section 751(b) that were intended to better achieve the purpose of the statute while providing greater simplicity. *See* § 601.601(d)(2)(ii)(*b*). Specifically, Notice 2006-14 asked for comments on: (1) replacing the gross value approach with a "hypothetical sale" approach for purposes of determining a partner's interest in the partnership's section 751 property, and (2) replacing the asset exchange approach with a "hot asset sale" approach to determine the tax consequences when section 751(b) applies. The hypothetical sale approach and the hot asset sale approach are described in Parts 1.A and 3, respectively, of the Summary of Comments and Explanation of Provisions section of this preamble. Notice 2006-14 also requested comments on other possible approaches to simplifying compliance with section 751(b).

As described in Notice 2006-14, the hypothetical sale approach for section 751(b) is similar to the approach taken in the 1999 regulations issued under section 751(a), shifting the focus to tax gain and away from gross value. Under the hypothetical sale approach, a partner's interest in section 751 property is determined by reference to the amount of ordinary income that would be allocated to the partner if the partnership disposed of all of its property for fair market value immediately before the distribution. More specifically, the hypothetical sale approach applies section 704(c) principles in comparing: (1) the amount of ordinary income that each partner would recognize if the partnership sold all of its property for fair market value immediately before the distribution, with (2) the amount of ordinary income each partner would recognize if the partnership sold all of its property (and the distributee partners sold the distributed assets) for fair market value immediately after the distribution. If the distribution reduces the amount of ordinary income (or increases the amount of ordinary loss) from section 751 property that would be allocated to, or recognized by, a partner (thus reducing that partner's interest in the partnership's section 751 property), the distribution triggers section 751(b).

Notice 2006-14 indicated that changes to the framework of subchapter K since the promulgation of the existing regulations would work in tandem with the hypothetical sale approach to achieve the statute's objective of ensuring that a partner recognizes its proper share of the partnership's income from section 751 property without unnecessarily accelerating the recognition of that income. For example, regulations under section 704(b) allow a partnership to revalue its assets upon a distribution in consideration of a partnership interest. Any revaluation gain or loss is subject to the rules of section 704(c), which generally preserve each partner's share of the unrealized gain and loss in the partnership's assets.

Notice 2006-14 also requested comments on using the hot asset sale approach, rather than the asset exchange approach, to determine the tax consequences of the distribution that is subject to section 751(b). The hot asset sale approach deems the partnership to distribute the relinquished section 751 property to the partner whose interest in the partnership's section 751 property is reduced, and then deems the partner to sell the relinquished section 751 property back to the partnership immediately before the actual distribution.

Summary of Comments and Explanation of Provisions

The IRS and the Treasury Department received both formal and informal responses to Notice 2006-14. In addition, a number of commentators published articles analyzing the proposals outlined in Notice 2006-14. Commentators' responses to Notice 2006-14 were predominantly favorable.

These proposed regulations adopt many of the principles described in Notice 2006-14. Part 1 of this section describes the rules included in the proposed regulations for determining partners' interests in section 751 property. Part 2 of this section sets forth the proposed regulations' test to determine whether section 751(b) applies to a partnership distribution, including anti-abuse principles that may apply in certain situations in which the test would not otherwise be satisfied. Part 3 of this section explains the tax consequences of a section 751(b) distribution under the proposed regulations. Finally, Part 4 of this section describes certain ancillary issues relating to the proposed regulations, including a clarification to the scope of § 1.751-1(a).

1. *Determination of a Partner's Interest in Section 751 Property*

Section 751(b) applies to a partnership distribution to the extent the distribution reduces a partner's interest in section 751 property. As discussed further in this Part 1, the proposed regulations establish an approach for measuring partners' interests in section 751 property, provide new rules under section 704(c) to help partnerships compute partner gain in section 751 property more precisely, and describe how basis adjustments under sections 734(b) and 743(b) affect the computation of partners' interests in section 751 property.

A. *Adoption of Hypothetical Sale Approach*

The first step in computing the effect of section 751(b) is to measure the partners' interests in section 751 property. Commentators generally agreed that the hypothetical sale approach is a substantial improvement over the gross value approach in the existing regulations. As described in this preamble, the hypothetical sale approach requires a partnership to compare: (1) the amount of ordinary income (or ordinary loss) that each partner would recognize if the partnership sold its property for fair market value immediately before the distribution with (2) the amount of ordinary income (or ordinary loss) each partner would recognize if the partnership sold its property, and the distributee partner sold the distributed assets, for fair market value immediately after the distribution. The commentators agreed that, when compared against the gross value approach, the hypothetical sale approach is more consistent with Congress's intent in enacting section 751(b), is easier to apply, and reduces the likelihood that section 751(b) would unnecessarily accelerate ordinary income. Accordingly, these proposed regulations adopt the hypothetical sale approach as the method by which the partners must measure their respective interests in section 751 property for the purpose of determining whether a distribution reduces a partner's interest in the partnership's section 751 property. (A distribution that reduces a partner's interest in the partnership's section 751 property is referred to as a "section 751(b) distribution.")

B. *Revaluations*

Because the hypothetical sale approach relies on the principles of section 704(c) to preserve a partner's share of the unrealized gain and loss in the partnership's section 751 property, these proposed regulations make several changes to the regulations relating to section 704(c). Specifically, the proposed regulations revise § 1.704-1(b)(2)(iv)(f), regarding revaluations of partnership property, to make its provisions mandatory if a partnership distributes money or other property to a partner as consideration for an interest in the partnership, and the partnership owns section 751 property immediately after the distribution. (A partnership that does not own section 751 property immediately after the distribution may still revalue its property under the existing regulation, but is not required to do so under these proposed regulations.) If a partnership does not maintain capital accounts in accordance with § 1.704-1(b)(2)(iv), the partnership must comply with this requirement by computing each partner's share of gain or loss in each partnership asset prior to a distribution, and making future allocations of partnership items in a manner that takes these amounts into account (making subsequent adjustments for cost recovery and other events that affect the property basis of each such asset).

In addition, the proposed regulations contain a special revaluation rule for distributing partnerships that own an interest in a lower-tier partnership. Because a partnership's section 751 property includes, under section 751(f), the partnership's proportionate share of section 751 property owned by any other partnership in which the distributing partnership is a partner, these proposed regulations also require a partnership in which the distributing partnership owns a controlling interest (which is defined as a greater than 50 percent interest) to revalue its property if the lower-tier partnership owns section 751 property immediately after the distribution. If the distributing partnership owns a non-controlling (that is, less than or equal to 50 percent) interest in a lower-tier partnership, these proposed regulations require the distributing partnership to allocate its distributive share of the lower-tier partnership's items among its partners in a manner that reflects the allocations that would have been made had the lower-tier partnership revalued its partnership property. The IRS and the Treasury Department are aware that in some instances a distributing partnership may be unable to obtain sufficient information to comply with this requirement from a lower-tier partnership in which the distributing partnership holds a non-controlling interest. We request comments on reasonable approaches to address this issue.

Upon the revaluation of partnership property in connection with a partnership distribution, the regulations under section 704(c) permit a partnership to choose any reasonable method to account for the built-in gain or built-in loss that is consistent with the purpose of section 704(c). If property with built-in gain decreases in value (or property with built-in loss increases in value), then the partnership may be unable to allocate tax losses (or gains) to a non-contributing partner in an amount equal to the partner's economic loss (or gain). If the property with built-in gain (or loss) is section 751 property, then the inability to allocate those tax losses (or gains) may cause ordinary income to shift among the partners. The regulations under section 704(c) provide two reasonable methods for a partnership to allocate items to cure or remediate that shift. However, the regulations under section 704(c) also provide a third reasonable method, the traditional method, under which the shift of ordinary income is not cured. The IRS and the Treasury Department are aware that distortions created under the section 704(c) traditional method may cause ordinary income to shift among partners. However, the regulations under section 704(c) contain an anti-abuse rule that provides that a method is not reasonable if, for example, the event that results in a reverse section 704(c) allocation and the corresponding allocation of tax items with respect to the property are made with a view to shifting the tax consequences of built-in gain or built-in loss among the partners in a manner that substantially reduces the present value of the partners' aggregate tax liability. The IRS and the Treasury Department believe that this anti-abuse provision under section 704(c) properly addresses the possibility that taxpayers would use the traditional method to shift ordinary income.

Some commentators suggested changing the regulations under section 704(c) to minimize the situations in which section 751(b) applies. Generally, when a partnership revalues its assets, the partnership allocates a reverse section 704(c) amount with respect to each partnership asset, as opposed to an aggregate section 704(c) amount with respect to all assets (subject to certain exceptions). As a result, any distribution of appreciated section 751 property in which another partner has a share of income would trigger section 751(b) under the hypothetical sale approach. The commentators recommended that the IRS and the Treasury Department narrow the application of section 751(b) by allowing partners (subject to the substantiality requirements of § 1.704-1(b)(2)(iii)) to "exchange" reverse section 704(c) amounts resulting from a section 751 distribution. These proposed regulations do not adopt this comment because it is beyond the scope of these regulations and would impact other provisions of subchapter K. However, the IRS and the Treasury Department believe that the issue merits further study and request comments on how such permissible exchanges of reverse section 704(c) amounts might be addressed in future regulations.

C. *Effect of Basis Adjustments on Section 751(b) Computations*

While section 704(c) revaluations generally preserve partners' interests in section 751 property upon a partnership distribution, certain basis adjustments under sections 732(c) or 734(b) may alter partners' interests in section 751 property following the distribution. Accordingly, these proposed regulations provide rules on the effect of these basis adjustments on the computation of partners' interests in section 751 property.

If a distribution of capital gain property results in a basis adjustment under section 734(b), that basis adjustment is allocated to capital gain property of the partnership under § 1.755-1(c)(1). However, some property that is characterized as capital gain property for purposes of section 755 can also result in ordinary income when sold. For example, section 1231 property is characterized as a capital asset for purposes of section 755, but selling the property can also result in ordinary income from recapture under section 1245(a)(1). The regulations under section 755 do not differentiate between the capital gain aspect of the property and the ordinary income aspect of the property for this purpose. Accordingly, allocating a section 734(b) positive basis adjustment to such property as capital gain property may reduce the amount of ordinary income that would result on a sale of the property. Under these proposed regulations, that reduction in ordinary income would constitute a reduction in the partners' shares of unrealized gain in the partnership's section 751 property, which could trigger section 751(b) in situations in which section 751(b) would not have otherwise applied. A similar reduction in section 751 property could occur if the basis of the distributed property increases under section 732.

One commentator recommended allowing partnerships to avoid this result by eliminating a positive section 734(b) adjustment to the extent the section 734(b) adjustment would reduce the partnership's ordinary income. Another commentator recommended allocating the section 734(b) adjustment to other partnership capital gain property. The same commentator alternatively recommended treating a positive section 734(b) adjustment that reduced the partnership's ordinary income as a separate asset.

Although these proposed regulations do not treat the section 734(b) adjustment as a separate asset, the proposed regulations reach a similar result to this last recommendation. They provide that a basis adjustment under section 732(c) or section 734(b) (as adjusted for recovery of the basis adjustment) that is allocated to capital gain property and that reduces the ordinary income (attributable, for example, to recapture under section 1245(a)(1)) that the partner or partnership would recognize on a taxable disposition of the property is not taken into account in determining (1) the partnership's basis for purposes of sections 617(d)(1), 1245(a)(1), 1250(a)(1), 1252(a)(1), and 1254(a)(1), and (2) the partner or partnership's respective gain or loss for purposes of sections 995(c), 1231(a), and 1248(a). The IRS and the Treasury Department intend for these amendments to apply for purposes of other provisions that cross-reference those sections (for example, the reference in § 1.367(b)-2(c) to section 1248). The IRS and the Treasury Department are aware that these rules may result in additional administrative burden and, therefore, permit a partnership and its partners to elect to recognize ordinary income currently under section 751(b) in lieu of applying these rules.

In addition, one commentator raised questions about the application of section 751(b) upon the distribution to a partner of section 751 property for which another partner has a basis adjustment under section 743(b) (the transferee partner). The commentator questioned whether the distributee partner's share of section 751 property could be increased inappropriately if the special basis adjustment is not taken into account in determining the distributee's basis in the section 751 property under section 732. The IRS and the Treasury Department believe that although the distributee partner does not take the section 743(b) basis adjustment into account in determining its basis in the distributed property, the reallocation of the section 743(b) basis adjustment pursuant to § 1.743-1(g)(2)(ii) should generally reduce the transferee partner's share of section 751 property, triggering an income inclusion to that partner under section 751(b) which is offset by the basis adjustment. The IRS and the Treasury Department acknowledge that, in situations in which the partnership holds no other section 751 property (and the section 743(b) basis adjustment is temporarily suspended under §§ 1.743-1(g)(2)(ii) and 1.755-1(c)(4) until the partnership acquires additional ordinary income property), the application of section 751(b) may be unclear. Accordingly, the proposed regulations require that partners include the effect of carryover basis adjustments when determining their shares of section 751 property, as though those basis adjustments were immediately allocable to ordinary income property. *See Example 4* in § 1.751-1(g) of the proposed regulations.

2. *Distributions to which Section 751(b) Applies*

A. *General Principle*

The purpose of section 751 is to prevent a partner from converting its share of potential ordinary income into capital gain. A distribution of partnership property (including money) is a section 751(b) distribution if the distribution reduces any partner's share of net section 751 unrealized gain or increases any partner's share of net section 751 unrealized loss (as determined under the hypothetical sale approach described in Part 1.A of the Summary of Comments and Explanation of Provisions section of this preamble). For this purpose, a partner's net section 751 unrealized gain or loss immediately before a distribution equals the amount of net gain or loss, as the case may be, from section 751 property that would be allocated to the partner if the partnership disposed of all of the partnership's assets for cash in an amount equal to the fair market value of such property (taking into account section 7701(g)). A partner's net section 751 unrealized gain or loss includes any remedial allocations under § 1.704-3(d).

A partner's net section 751 unrealized gain or loss also takes into account any section 743 basis adjustment pursuant to § 1.743-1(j)(3), including any carryover basis adjustment that results under any of § 1.743-1(g)(2)(ii), § 1.755-1(b)(5)(iii)(D), or § 1.755-1(c)(4) when the partnership must adjust the basis of a specific class of assets, but that adjustment is suspended because the partnership does not own assets in that class. The regulations take such suspended basis adjustments into account as though the basis adjustment is applied to the basis of notional partnership section 751 property with a fair market value of zero. For example, if A and B are partners in the AB partnership, which owns capital assets and a single ordinary income asset that is the subject of a section 743(b) adjustment with respect to B, and that asset is distributed to partner A, B's basis adjustment is suspended because the partnership lacks other ordinary income property. However, the basis adjustment will eventually benefit B when the partnership acquires new ordinary income property. For this reason, the proposed regulations require B to take the suspended adjustment into account when determining whether section 751(b) applies to B with respect to the distribution.

A partner's share of net section 751 unrealized gain or loss from section 751 property immediately following a distribution is computed using the same formula. However, the distributee partner also includes in its post-distribution amount its share of net income or loss from a hypothetical sale of the distributed section 751 property.

If section 751(b) applies to a distribution, each partner must generally recognize or take into account currently ordinary income equal to its "section 751(b) amount." If a partner has net section 751 unrealized gain both before and after the distribution, then the partner's section 751(b) amount equals the partner's net section 751 unrealized gain immediately before the distribution less the partner's net section 751 unrealized gain immediately after the distribution. If a partner has net section 751 unrealized loss both before and after the distribution, then the partner's section

751(b) amount equals the partner's net section 751 unrealized loss immediately after the distribution less the partner's net section 751 unrealized loss immediately before the distribution. If a partner has net section 751 unrealized gain before the distribution and net section 751 unrealized loss after the distribution, then the partner's section 751(b) amount equals the sum of the partner's net section 751 unrealized gain immediately before the distribution and the partner's net section 751 unrealized loss immediately after the distribution.

Commentators requested a de minimis exception to section 751(b). The IRS and the Treasury Department continue to study the issue and request comments describing the parameters of a de minimis rule that would be helpful.

B. *Section 751 Anti-Abuse Rule*

The IRS and the Treasury Department believe that, despite the general principle that section 751(b) should apply only at the time that a partner's share of net section 751 unrealized gain is reduced (or net section 751 loss is increased), the deferral of ordinary income upon the receipt of a distribution is inappropriate in certain circumstances. Specifically, deferral is inappropriate if a partner engages in a transaction that relies on the rules of section 704(c) to defer or eliminate ordinary income while monetizing most of the value of the partnership interest. Accordingly, these proposed regulations provide an anti-abuse rule that requires taxpayers to apply the rules set forth in the proposed regulations in a manner consistent with the purpose of section 751, and that allows the Commissioner to recast transactions for federal tax purposes as appropriate to achieve tax results that are consistent with the purpose of section 751.

The proposed regulations provide a list of situations that are presumed inconsistent with the purpose of section 751. Under this list, a distribution is presumed inconsistent with the purpose of section 751 if section 751(b) would apply but for the application of section 704(c) principles, and one or more of the following conditions exists: (1) a partner's interest in net section 751 unrealized gain is at least four times greater than the partner's capital account immediately after the distribution, (2) a distribution reduces a partner's interest to such an extent that the partner has little or no exposure to partnership losses and does not meaningfully participate in partnership profits aside from a preferred return for the use of capital, (3) the net value of the partner (or its successor) becomes less than its potential tax liability from section 751 property as a result of a transaction, (4) a partner transfers a portion of its partnership interest within five years after the distribution to a tax-indifferent party in a manner that would not trigger ordinary income recognition in the absence of this anti-abuse rule, or (5) a partnership transfers to a corporation in a nonrecognition transaction section 751 property other than pursuant to a transfer of all property used in a trade or business (excluding assets that are not material to a continuation of the trade or business). In addition, the proposed regulations provide that an amendment to the partnership agreement that results in a reduction in a partner's interest in section 751 property is also presumed inconsistent with the purpose of section 751. A partnership or a partner taking a position on its return that section 751 does not apply to a transaction that meets one or more of these situations must disclose its position on Form 8275-R, Regulation Disclosure Statement.

3. *Tax Consequences of a Section 751(b) Distribution*

If section 751(b) applies to a distribution under the principles set forth in Part 2 of the Summary of Comments and Explanation of Provisions section of this preamble, then the partners must determine the consequences of its application to the partnership and its partners. As described in the Background section of this preamble, Notice 2006-14 discussed replacing the asset exchange approach with a hot asset sale approach to determine these consequences. While most commentators agreed that the hot asset sale approach is an improvement over the existing regulations' asset exchange approach, commentators were able to identify situations in which the hot asset sale approach fails to achieve the correct result or causes undesirable results under other Code provisions. Two commentators advocated adopting, in lieu of the hot asset sale approach, an approach similar to that taken in section 704(c)(1)(B) (referred to in this preamble as a "deemed gain" approach), in which a section 751(b) distribution results in: (1) the partnership recognizing ordinary income in the aggregate amount of each partner's reduction in the partner's interest in section 751 property, (2) the partnership allocating ordinary income to the partner or partners whose interest in section 751(b) property was reduced by the distribution, and (3) the partnership making appropriate basis adjustments to its assets to reflect its ordinary income recognition. One variation of the deemed gain approach would require capital gain recognition in certain cases.

The IRS and the Treasury Department determined that a deemed gain approach produces an appropriate outcome in the greatest number of circumstances out of the approaches under consideration, and that the hot asset sale approach also produced an appropriate outcome in most circumstances. However, no one approach produced an appropriate outcome in all circumstances. Therefore, these proposed regulations withdraw the asset exchange approach of the current regulations, but do not require the use of a particular approach for determining the tax consequences of a section 751(b) distribution. Instead, these proposed regulations provide that if, under the hypothetical sale approach, a distribution reduces a partner's interest in the partnership's section 751 property, giving rise to a section 751(b) amount, then the partnership must use a reasonable approach that is consistent with the purpose of section 751(b) to determine the tax consequences of the reduction. Except in limited situations, a partnership must continue to use the same approach, once chosen, including after a termination of the partnership under section 708(b)(1)(B). These proposed regulations include examples in which the approach adopted is generally reasonable based on the facts of the examples, and one example in which it is determined that the adopted approach is not reasonable based on the facts of the example.

Finally, some commentators recommended allowing taxpayers to elect to recognize capital gain in certain situations (for example, in the situation described in *Example 2* in Notice 2006-14 involving distributions of section 751(b) property to a partner that has insufficient basis in its partnership interest to absorb fully the partnership's basis in the distributed property). Recognition of gain may be appropriate where failing to recognize gain would cause an adjustment to the basis of distributed property (under section 732) or to the basis of partnership property (under section 734(b)) if those basis adjustments would change the partners' shares of ordinary income already determined under the principles described in Part 1 of the Summary of Comments and Explanation of Provisions section of this preamble. Such changes in ordinary income amounts could (in the case of certain adjustments under section 734(b)) decrease partners' shares of partnership ordinary income, requiring the recognition of additional income under section 751(b), or could (in the case of certain adjustments under section 732) convert a distributee partner's share of capital gain into ordinary income. Thus, these proposed regulations require that distributee partners recognize capital gain in certain situations, and permit distributee partners to elect to recognize capital gain in certain other situations.

The proposed regulations require a distributee partner to recognize capital gain to the extent necessary to prevent the distribution from triggering a basis adjustment under section 734(b) that would reduce other partners' shares of net unrealized section 751 gain or loss. Capital gain recognition is necessary in this situation because the section 734(b) basis adjustment was not taken into account in determining the partners' net section 751 unrealized gain or loss immediately after the section 751 distribution, and the IRS and the Treasury Department believe that an approach under which a partnership redetermines a partner's net section 751 unrealized gain or loss to account for section 734(b) basis adjustments would be both administratively burdensome and would accelerate ordinary income unnecessarily. *See Examples 5* and *6* in §1.751-1(g) of the proposed regulations. Gain recognized in this event is generally capital; however, if the partnership makes an election under §1.755-1(c)(2)(vi), then the partner must characterize all or a portion of the gain recognized under this rule as ordinary income or a dividend, as appropriate, to preserve the character of the gain in the adjusted asset. *See Example 9* in §1.751-1(g) of the proposed regulations.

These proposed regulations also allow distributee partners to elect to recognize capital gain in certain circumstances to avoid decreases to the basis of distributed section 751 property. Elective capital gain recognition is appropriate to eliminate a negative section 732(a)(2) or (b) basis adjustment to the asset or assets received in distribution if, and to the extent that, the distributee partner's net section 751 unrealized gain would otherwise be greater immediately after the distribution than it was immediately before the distribution (or would cause the distributee partner's net section 751 unrealized loss to be less immediately after the distribution than it was immediately before the distribution). For example, elective capital gain recognition is appropriate if a partner with zero basis in its partnership interest receives a distribution of partnership section 751 property with basis in the hands of the partnership equal to its value, and the distribution otherwise increases the distributee partner's net section 751 unrealized gain.

4. Miscellaneous

A. *Section 751(a)*

As described in Parts 2.A and 2.B of this preamble, these proposed regulations generally defer the recognition of ordinary income upon a distribution when the partner's unrealized gain and loss in the partnership's section 751 property is preserved through the application of the principles of section 704(c). This approach is consistent with the 1984 amendment to section 704(c). By mandating the application of section 704(c) principles, that amendment partially severed the relationship that had generally existed between a partner's distributive share (that is, the right to share in the economic gain or loss) associated with a partnership item and the partner's share of tax gain or loss from the sale of that item. The IRS and the Treasury Department believe that, by mandating the application of section 704(c) principles in 1984, Congress intended that impacted provisions be interpreted consistent with this new emphasis on tax gain or loss. Congress provided a broad delegation of authority to the Treasury Department to address these repercussions of amending section 704(c) on other provisions in subchapter K.

Some commentators interpret section 751(a) as limiting the amount of ordinary income that a transferor partner may recognize upon a transfer of a partnership interest to the amount of any money or property received by the transferor partner, without taking into account the total amount of ordinary income attributable to the partnership interest transferred that relates to section 751 property. However, interpreting section 751(a) as limiting ordinary income in this way would contravene Congress's intent to tax partners on their shares of partnership ordinary income as determined by applying section 704(c) principles. The IRS and the Treasury Department believe that section 751(a) should be interpreted in a manner that accounts for the impact of section 704(c). Thus, these proposed regulations provide that the amount of money or the fair market value of property received for purposes of section 751(a) takes into account the transferor partner's share of income or gain from section 751 property.

The IRS and the Treasury Department alternatively considered addressing this issue by deeming a partner that sells or exchanges its partnership interest to receive a distribution of the partner's share of the section 751 property, followed by a sale of the property back to the partnership for its fair market value, recognizing the deferred ordinary income inherent in the section 751 property. The partner would then be deemed to contribute the cash proceeds to the partnership thereby increasing the partner's basis in the partner's partnership interest. Finally, upon the sale or exchange of the partnership interest, the partner would recognize the appropriate amount of capital loss. This potential multi-step deemed approach would result in additional complexity and would reach the same result that the current regulations under § 1.751-1(a) reach as clarified by these proposed regulations. Therefore, the IRS and the Treasury Department are not proposing this alternative approach.

B. *Previously Contributed Property Exception*

Section 751(b)(2)(A) provides that section 751(b) does not apply to a distribution of property that the distributee contributed to the partnership ("previously contributed property exception"). Unlike other provisions in subchapter K that include similar previously contributed property exceptions, the current regulations under section 751(b) do not contain successor rules for purposes of applying the section 751(b) previously contributed property exception. These proposed regulations add successor rules to section 751(b) similar to the successor rules contained in other previously contributed property exceptions within subchapter K.

C. *Mergers and Divisions*

A commentator requested guidance confirming how the rules of section 751(b) apply in the case of an incorporation, merger, or division of a partnership. The proposed regulations do not adopt this comment because the IRS and the Treasury Department believe such guidance is beyond the scope of these proposed regulations.

D. *Substantial Appreciation Test*

These proposed regulations also make a number of technical corrections to account for changes in the law since the issuance of existing regulations under section 751. For example, these proposed regulations remove the language "substantially appreciated" from the first sentence of § 1.751-1(a)(1), which applies with respect to sales or exchanges of an interest in a partnership. In addition to conforming the language of the regulations to that of the Code, this change is intended to clarify that, upon a sale or exchange of a partnership interest, unrealized receivables and inventory items are treated in the same manner. Thus, a transferor partner may recognize an ordinary loss with respect to inventory items pursuant to section 751(a) to the extent the transferor would be allocated a net ordinary loss pursuant to § 1.751-1(a)(2). These proposed regulations also update the definition of "inventory items which have appreciated substantially in value" with respect to section 751(b) to reflect the 1993 amendment to the statute that eliminated the 10-percent test from the definition of "*substantial appreciation*." *See* Public Law 103-66, Sec. 13206(e)(1). These proposed regulations also clarify that unrealized receivables are not included in the term "inventory items which have appreciated substantially in value."

E. *Other Changes Relating to Revaluations*

Finally, these proposed regulations address some of the comments received in response to Notice 2009-70 (2009-2 CB 255), in which the IRS and the Treasury Department requested comments on, among other things, whether additional events should be added to the list of events permitting a revaluation of partnership property pursuant to § 1.704-1(b)(2)(iv)(*f*) and whether, in a tiered partnership structure, a revaluation at one partnership in the tier should permit another partnership in the tier to revalue that partnership's property. Commentators recommended that partnership recapitalizations (changes to the way partners agree to share partnership profits and losses) be added as a permissible revaluation event. The IRS and the Treasury Department agree that partnership recapitalizations should be added as a permissible event because, absent providing for a special allocation of any unrealized gain or loss in partnership assets that arose prior to the recapitalization, a revaluation is necessary to preserve each partner's share of such unrealized amounts. In addition, commentators recommended that a partnership in a tiered partnership structure be able to revalue its partnership property if another partnership in the tiered structure was permitted to revalue its partnership property. The IRS and the Treasury Department agree and believe that permitting successive revaluations in a tiered partnership structure is necessary to properly allocate items with respect to a reverse section 704(c) allocation to the appropriate partner.

Availability of IRS Documents

IRS notices cited in this preamble are made available by the Superintendent of Documents, U.S. Government Printing Office, Washington, DC 20402.

Effect on Other Documents

The following publication will be obsolete as of the date of publication of a Treasury decision adopting these rules as final regulations in the *Federal Register*:

Rev. Rul. 84-102 (1984-2 CB 119).

Proposed Effective/Applicability Date

The regulations, as proposed, apply to distributions occurring in any taxable period ending on or after the date of publication of a Treasury decision adopting these rules as final regulations in the **Federal Register**. The rules contained in §1.751-1(a)(2) would apply to transfers of partnership interests that occur on or after November 3, 2014. However, the rules contained in §1.751-1(a)(2) are a clarification of existing rules, and no inference is intended from the change to §1.751-1(a)(2) with respect to sales or exchanges of partnership interests prior to the effective date for §1.751-1(a)(2). The rules contained in §1.751-1(a)(3) continue to apply to transfers of partnership interests that occur on or after December 15, 1999. A partnership and its partners would be able to rely on §1.751-1(b)(2) of these proposed regulations for purposes of determining a partner's interest in the partnership's section 751 property on or after November 3, 2014 provided the partnership and its partners apply each of §1.751-1(a)(2), §1.751-1(b)(2), and §1.751-1(b)(4) of these proposed regulations consistently for all partnership distributions and sales or exchanges, including for any distributions and sales or exchanges the partnership makes after a termination of the partnership under section 708(b)(1)(B).

Special Analyses

It has been determined that this notice of proposed rulemaking is not a significant regulatory action as defined in Executive Order 12866, as supplemented by Executive Order 13653. Therefore, a regulatory assessment is not required. It has also been determined that section 553(b) of the Administrative Procedure Act (5 U.S.C. chapter 5) does not apply to these regulations. It is hereby certified that the collection of information in these regulations will not have a significant economic impact on a substantial number of small entities. This certification is based on the fact that the amount of time necessary to prepare the required disclosure is not lengthy and few small businesses are likely to be partners or partnerships required to make the disclosures required by the rule. Accordingly, a Regulatory Flexibility Analysis under the Regulatory Flexibility Act (5 U.S.C. chapter 6) does not apply. Pursuant to section 7805(f) of the Code, this notice of proposed rulemaking has been submitted to the Chief Counsel for Advocacy of the Small Business Administration for comment on its impact on small business.

Comments and Requests for Public Hearing

The IRS and the Treasury Department request comments on all aspects of the proposed rules. In particular, the IRS and the Treasury Department request comments, in addition to those previously requested in this preamble, on: (1) whether and how carryover adjustments to ordinary income property under sections 734(b) and 743(b) should be taken into account under the hypothetical sale approach, (2) whether the final regulations should exclude certain types of transactions from the previously contributed property successor rules provided in these proposed regulations, (3) whether the regulations should specifically describe approaches as generally reasonable approaches for determining the tax consequences of a section 751(b) distribution, and which approaches should be specified as generally reasonable, (4) whether the final regulations should provide rules similar to those proposed in new §1.755-1(c)(2)(iii) through (vi) in §1.755-1(b)(5) with respect to section 743(b) adjustments in substituted basis transactions, and (5) what disclosures the IRS and the Treasury Department should require from partners and partnerships that either recognize gain under section 751(a) or (b), or rely on reverse section 704(c) allocations to defer the gain recognition required by section 751(a) or (b).

The IRS and the Treasury Department also request comments on a topic that, although not specific to section 751, may impact the rules under section 751. The IRS and the Treasury Department are aware that the regulations under §1.1245-1(e)(3) (concerning the interaction of section 1245 and section 743), and §1.1250-1(f), by reference to §1.1245-1(e)(3), are out of date. The intent of the regulations under §1.1245-1(e)(3) is, in part, to ensure that a transferee partner does not recognize ordinary income with respect to section 1245 property to the extent a section 743 adjustment has displaced that ordinary income. For example, if a partner sells in a fully taxable exchange its interest in a partnership that has elected under section 754, and the selling partner recognizes ordinary income under section 751(a) with respect to partnership section 1245 property, then the rules under sections 1245 and 743 are intended to ensure that the transferee partner recognizes no ordinary income on an immediately subsequent disposition of the section 1245 property in a fully taxable transaction. However, the regulations under §1.1245-1(e)(3) have not been amended to take into account changes to subchapter K, including the regulations under section 751, resulting in issues and uncertainties. The IRS and the Treasury Department are studying these issues and request comments in this area.

Finally, the IRS and the Treasury Department request comments as to how section 751(b) should interact with rules for withholding and reporting with respect to nonresident aliens and foreign corporations. For example, the IRS and the Treasury Department are considering whether regulations should provide that for purposes of withholding under chapter 3 of Subtitle A (for example, under section 1446), income recognized as a result of a section 751(b) distribution is treated as recognized by the partnership regardless of the approach chosen to determine the U.S. tax consequences of the section 751(b) distribution. The IRS and the Treasury Department are also considering whether additional guidance with respect to tax or information returns (for example, pursuant to section 6031(b) or section 6050K) is necessary for gain recognized on section 751(b) distributions affecting these taxpayers.

Before these proposed regulations are adopted as final regulations, consideration will be given to any comments that are submitted timely to the IRS as prescribed in this preamble under the "Addresses" heading. All comments will be available at *www.regulations.gov* or upon request. A public hearing will be scheduled if requested in writing by any person who submits timely written or electronic comments. If a public hearing is scheduled, notice of the date, time, and place for the public hearing will be published in the **Federal Register**.

Drafting Information

The principal authors of these regulations are Allison R. Carmody and Frank J. Fisher, Office of the Associate Chief Counsel (Passthroughs and Special Industries). However, other personnel from the IRS and the Treasury Department participated in their development.

[¶ 49,635]   Proposed Regulations (REG-109187-11), published in the Federal Register on December 23, 2014.

[Code Secs. 351, Code Sec. 361, Code Sec. 453B and Code Sec. 721]

Accounting methods: Installment method: Gain or loss on disposition of installment obligations.—Reg. §1.453B-1 and amendments of Reg. §§1.351-1(a)(1), 1.361-1 and 1.721-1(a), relating to the nonrecognition of gain or loss on certain dispositions of an installment obligation, are proposed.

AGENCY: Internal Revenue Service (IRS), Treasury.

ACTION: Notice of proposed rulemaking.

SUMMARY: This document contains proposed regulations relating to the nonrecognition of gain or loss on certain dispositions of an installment obligation. In general, under the proposed regulations a transferor does not recognize gain or loss on certain dispositions of an installment obligation if gain or loss is not recognized on the disposition under another provision of the Internal Revenue Code. The proposed regulations also provide that this general rule does not apply to the satisfaction of an installment obligation. For example, an installment obligation of an issuer, such as a corporation or partnership, is satisfied when the holder transfers the obligation to the issuer for an equity interest in the issuer.

DATES: Comments or a request for a public hearing must be received by March 23, 2015. ADDRESSES: Send submissions to CC:PA:LPD:PR (REG-109187-11), room 5203, Internal Revenue Service, PO Box 7604, Ben Franklin Station, Washington, DC 20044. Submissions may be hand delivered Monday through Friday between the hours of 8 a.m. and 4 p.m. to CC:PA:LPD:PR (REG-109187-11), Courier's Desk, Internal Revenue Service, 1111 Constitution Avenue, NW., Washington, DC, or sent electronically via the Federal eRulemaking Portal at *www.regulations.gov* (IRS REG-109187-11).

FOR FURTHER INFORMATION CONTACT: Concerning the proposed regulations, Arvind Ravichandran, (202) 317-4718; concerning the submission of comments and/or requests for a public hearing, Olawafunmilayo (Funmi) Taylor at (202) 317-6901 (not toll-free numbers).

SUPPLEMENTARY INFORMATION:

Background

This document contains proposed amendments to the regulations in 26 CFR part 1 under section 453B of the Internal Revenue Code (Code) relating to gain or loss on the disposition of installment obligations. Section 453B was added to the Code by the Installment Sales Revision Act of 1980, Public Law 96-471 (94 Stat. 2252 (1980)).

Section 453B replaces and provides generally the same rules as former section 453(d). In general, under section 453B(a) gain or loss is recognized upon the satisfaction of an installment obligation at other than its face value, or upon the distribution, transmission, sale, or other disposition of the installment obligation. Section 1.453-9(c)(2) of the Income Tax Regulations, issued under former section 453(d), provides an exception to the general rule. Under §1.453-9(c)(2), if the Code provides an exception to the recognition of gain or loss for certain dispositions, then gain or loss is not recognized under former section 453(d) on the disposition of an installment obligation within that exception. The exceptions identified in §1.453-9(c)(2) include certain transfers to corporations under sections 351 and 361, contributions to partnerships under section 721, and distributions by partnerships to partners under section 731 (except as provided by section 736 and section 751).

Under Rev. Rul. 73-423, 1973-2 CB 161, the exceptions in §1.453-9(c)(2) to recognition of gain or loss under the installment sale rules do not apply to the transfer of an installment obligation that results in a satisfaction of the obligation. Thus, the revenue ruling holds that the transfer of a corporation's installment obligation to the issuing corporation in exchange for stock of the issuing corporation results in a satisfaction of the obligation. In that case, the transferor must recognize gain or loss on the satisfaction of the obligation to the extent of the difference between the transferor's basis in the obligation and the fair market value of the stock received, even though gain or loss generally is not recognized on section 351 transfers.

Explanation of Provisions

These proposed regulations republish in §1.453B-1(c) the general rule in §1.4539(c)(2) under which gain or loss is not recognized upon certain dispositions. In addition, the proposed regulations incorporate and expand the holding of Rev. Rul. 73-423 to provide that a transferor recognizes gain or loss under section 453B(a) when the transferor disposes of an installment obligation in a transaction that results in the satisfaction of the installment obligation, including, for example, when an installment obligation of a corporation or partnership is contributed to the corporation or partnership in exchange for an equity interest in the corporation or partnership. Finally, the proposed regulations amend the regulations under sections 351, 361, and 721 to include a cross-reference to the regulations under section 453B regarding recognition of any gain or loss upon the satisfaction of an installment obligation. The IRS and the Treasury Department anticipate publishing regulations addressing the general rule under section 453B(a) and the basis of an obligation under section 453B(b) in the future. Therefore, regulations under §1.453B-1(a) and (b) are reserved.

Proposed Effective/Applicability Date

These regulations are proposed to apply to satisfactions, distributions, transmissions, sales, or other dispositions of installment obligations after the date these regulations are published as final regulations in the **Federal Register**.

Special Analyses

This notice of proposed rulemaking is not a significant regulatory action as defined in Executive Order 12866, as supplemented by Executive Order 13563. Therefore, a regulatory assessment is not required. It also has been determined that section 553(b) of the Administrative Procedure Act (5 U.S.C. chapter 5) does not apply to these regulations, and because the regulation does not impose a collection of information on small entities, the Regulatory Flexibility Act (5 U.S.C. chapter 6) does not apply. Pursuant to section 7805(f) of the Code, this notice of proposed rulemaking has been submitted to the Chief Counsel for Advocacy of the Small Business Administration for comment on its impact on small business.

Comments and Requests for a Public Hearing

Before these proposed regulations are adopted as final regulations, consideration will be given to any written comments that are submitted timely to the IRS as prescribed in this preamble under the "Addresses" heading. The Treasury Department and the IRS invite comments on all aspects of the proposed rules. In particular, the Treasury Department and the IRS request comments on how a partnership's distribution of a partner's installment obligation to the obligor partnershould be treated under section 453B, and whether there are circumstances in which such a distribution should not result in gain or loss recognition by the partnership. All comments will be available for public inspection and copying at www.regulations.gov or upon request. A public hearing will be scheduled if requested in writing by any person who timely submits written comments. If a public hearing is scheduled, notice of the date, time and place for the hearing will be published in the **Federal Register**.

Drafting Information

The principal author of these regulations is Arvind Ravichandran, Office of the Associate Chief Counsel (Income Tax and Accounting). However, other personnel from the IRS and the Treasury Department participated in their development.

[¶ 49,640] **Proposed Amendments of Regulations (REG-100400-14)**, published in the Federal Register on March 6, 2015.

[Code Secs. 1361, 1362 and 1502]

Proposed regulations: Consolidated returns: Corporations becoming members: Corporations ceasing to be members: Reporting periods: Short period returns: Change in status: End of the day rule: Next day rule: Previous day rule: S corporation exception: Anti-avoidance rule.—Amendments of Reg. §§1.1361-5, 1.1362-3, 1.1502-13, 1.1502-21, 1.1502-22, 1.1502-28 and 1.1502-76, containing proposed amendments to the consolidated return regulations, are proposed.

AGENCY: Internal Revenue Service (IRS), Treasury.

ACTION: Notice of proposed rulemaking.

SUMMARY: This document contains proposed amendments to the consolidated return regulations. These proposed regulations would revise the rules for reporting certain items of income and deduction that are reportable on the day a corporation joins or leaves a consolidated group. The proposed regulations would affect such corporations and the consolidated groups that they join or leave.

DATES: Written or electronic comments and requests for a public hearing must be received by June 4, 2015.

ADDRESSES: Send submissions to: CC:PA:LPD:PR (REG-100400-14), Room 5203, Internal Revenue Service, P.O. Box 7604, Ben Franklin Station, Washington, DC 20044. Submissions may be hand-delivered Monday through Friday between the hours of 8 a.m. and 4 p.m. to CC:PA:LPD:PR (REG-100400-14), Courier's Desk, Internal Revenue Service, 1111 Constitution Avenue NW., Washington, DC, or sent electronically via the Federal eRulemaking Portal at *http://www.regulations.gov/* (IRS REG-100400-14).

FOR FURTHER INFORMATION CONTACT: Concerning the proposed regulations, Russell G. Jones, (202) 317-6847; concerning the submission of comments or to request a public hearing, Oluwafunmilayo (Funmi) P. Taylor, (202) 317-6901 (not toll-free numbers).

SUPPLEMENTARY INFORMATION:

Background and Explanation of Provisions

1. Introduction

This notice of proposed rulemaking contains proposed regulations that amend 26 CFR part 1 under section 1502 of the Internal Revenue Code (Code). Section 1502 authorizes the Secretary to prescribe regulations for corporations that join in filing a consolidated return, and it expressly provides that those rules may be different from the provisions of chapter 1 of subtitle A of the Code that would apply if those corporations filed separate returns. Terms used in the consolidated return regulations generally are defined in § 1.1502-1.

These proposed regulations provide guidance under § 1.1502-76, which prescribes rules for determining the taxable period in which items of income, gain, deduction, loss, and credit (tax items) of a corporation that joins in filing a consolidated return are included. Section 1.1502-76(b) provides, in part, that if a corporation (S) becomes or ceases to be a member of a consolidated group during a consolidated return year, S must include in the consolidated return its tax items for the period during which it is a member. S also must file a separate return (including a consolidated return of another group) that includes its items for the period during which it is not a member.

2. Prior and Current Regulations

On September 8, 1966, the IRS and the Treasury Department promulgated regulations under § 1.1502-76 in TD 6894, 31 FR 11794 (1966 regulations). Section 1.1502-76(b) of the 1966 regulations was silent regarding the treatment of S's tax items that accrued on the day S became or ceased to be a member of a consolidated group (S's change in status). Thus, whether S's tax items for the day of S's change in status should have been reflected on S's tax return for the short period ending with S's change in status, or whether these tax items should have been reflected instead on S's tax return for the short period beginning after S's change in status, was unclear under the 1966 regulations.

On August 15, 1994, the IRS and the Treasury Department published final regulations (TD 8560; 59 FR 41666) under § 1.1502-76(b) (current regulations) that revised the 1966 regulations to eliminate uncertainty regarding the treatment of tax items recognized by S on the day of S's change in status. Under the general rule of § 1.1502-76(b)(1)(ii)(A)(*1*) of the current regulations (current end of the day rule), S is treated for all federal income tax purposes as becoming or ceasing to be a member of a consolidated group at the end of the day of S's change in status, and S's tax items that are reportable on that day generally are included in the tax return for the taxable year that ends as a result of S's change in status.

The notice of proposed rulemaking that proposed the current end of the day rule (57 FR 53634, Nov. 12, 1992) (1992 NPRM) indicated that the current end of the day rule was intended to provide certainty and prevent inconsistent reporting of S's items between the consolidated and separate returns. Prior to the 1992 NPRM, some taxpayers had inferred (based upon the administrative practice of the IRS) that the inclusion in a particular return of a tax item of S incurred on the day of S's change in status depended on a factual determination of whether the transaction occurred before or after noon on the day of S's change in status (the so-called "lunch rule").

There are two exceptions to the current end of the day rule. The first exception (in § 1.1502-76(b)(1)(ii)(A)(2)) provides that if a corporation is an S corporation (within the meaning of section 1361(a)(1)) immediately before becoming a member of a consolidated group, the corporation becomes a member of the group at the beginning of the day the termination of its S corporation election is effective (termination date), and its taxable year ends for all federal income tax purposes at the end of the preceding day (S corporation exception). The S corporation exception was added by TD 8842 (64 FR 61205; Nov. 10, 1999) to eliminate the need to file a one-day C corporation return for the day an S corporation is acquired by a consolidated group. No additional rule was necessary with respect to a qualified S corporation subsidiary (QSub) of an S corporation that joins a consolidated group. See § 1.1361-5(a)(3).

Added at the same time as the current end of the day rule, the second exception (in § 1.1502-76(b)(1)(ii)(B)) provides that if a transaction occurs on the day of S's change in status that is properly allocable to the portion of S's day after the event resulting in S's change in status, S and certain related persons must treat the transaction as occurring at the beginning of the following day for all federal income tax purposes (current next day rule). The current next day rule was added in response to comments to the 1992 NPRM suggesting that the current end of the day rule created a "seller beware" problem with respect to S's tax items arising on the day of S's change in status but after the event causing S's change in status. Commenters suggested that, for example, if consolidated group A sold the stock of S to consolidated group B, and group B caused S to sell one of its divisions on the same day it was acquired by group B, the gain from the sale of the division would be inappropriately allocable to group A's consolidated return. Commenters recommended that final regulations adopt rules substantially similar to the current next day rule to protect the reasonable expectations of sellers and buyers of S's stock. Commenters suggested that a rule providing this type of protection was most appropriate with respect to extraordinary items, and some commenters suggested that a rule similar to the current next day rule should operate unless the seller and buyer of S agreed otherwise.

3. Proposed Regulations

A. Overview

The IRS and the Treasury Department have determined that changes should be made to the regulations under § 1.1502-76(b) due to uncertainty regarding the appropriate application of the current next day rule. These proposed regulations address this concern as well as additional concerns with the current regulations, as summarized in this section 3.A. and discussed in greater detail in sections 3.B. through 3.K. of this preamble.

To provide certainty, the proposed regulations generally clarify the period in which S must report certain tax items by replacing the current next day rule with a new exception to the end of the day rule (proposed next day rule) that is more narrowly tailored to clearly reflect taxable income and prevent certain post-closing actions from adversely impacting S's tax return for the period ending on the day of S's change in status. The proposed next day rule applies only to "extraordinary items" (as defined in § 1.1502-76(b)(2)(ii)(C) of the proposed regulations) that result from transactions that occur on the day of S's change in status, but after the event causing the change, and that would be taken into account by S on that day. This rule requires those extraordinary items to be allocated to S's tax return for the period beginning the next day. The proposed next day rule is expressly inapplicable to any extraordinary item that arises simultaneously with the event that causes S's change in status.

The proposed regulations further clarify that fees for services rendered in connection with S's change in status constitute a "compensation-related deduction" for purposes of §1.1502-76(b)(2)(ii)(C)(9) (if payment of the fees would give rise to a deduction), and therefore an extraordinary item. The proposed regulations also clarify that the anti-avoidance rule in §1.1502-76(b)(3) may apply to situations in which a person modifies an existing contract or other agreement in anticipation of S's change in status.

The proposed regulations also add a rule (previous day rule, described in section 3.C. of this preamble) to clarify the application of the S corporation exception. In addition, the proposed regulations limit the scope of the end of the day rule, the next day rule, the S corporation exception, and the previous day rule to determining the period in which S must report certain tax items and determining the treatment of an asset or a tax item for purposes of sections 382(h) and 1374 (as opposed to applying for all federal income tax purposes).

Additionally, the proposed regulations provide that short taxable years resulting from intercompany transactions to which section 381(a) applies (intercompany section 381 transactions) are not taken into account in determining the carryover period for a tax item of the distributor or transferor member in the intercompany section 381 transaction or for purposes of section 481(a). Furthermore, the proposed regulations provide that the due date for filing S's separate return for the taxable year that ends as a result of S becoming a member is not accelerated if S ceases to exist in the same consolidated return year.

The proposed regulations make several other conforming and non-substantive changes to the current regulations as well. Finally, the proposed regulations add several examples to illustrate the proposed rules.

The IRS and the Treasury Department note that neither the current regulations nor the proposed regulations are intended to supersede general rules in the Code and regulations concerning whether an item is otherwise includible or deductible.

B. Proposed Next Day Rule

The current next day rule provides that S and certain related persons must treat a transaction as occurring at the beginning of the day following S's change in status if the transaction occurs on the day of S's change in status and is "properly allocable" to the portion of that day following S's change in status. The IRS and the Treasury Department believe, however, that the standards provided in the current next day rule for determining whether a transaction is "properly allocable" to the portion of S's day after the event resulting in S's change in status have been inappropriately interpreted by taxpayers. The current next day rule provides that a determination of whether a transaction is "properly allocable" to the portion of S's day after the event resulting in S's change in status is respected if it is "reasonable and consistently applied by all affected persons." In determining whether an allocation is "reasonable," certain factors enumerated in the current regulations are to be considered, including whether tax items arising from the same transaction are allocated inconsistently. Some taxpayers have interpreted these rules as providing flexibility in reporting tax items that result from transactions occurring on the day of S's change in status so that those items can be allocated by agreement to the day of, or to the day following, S's change in status. The IRS and the Treasury Department view this interpretation of the current next day rule as inappropriate because it effectively would permit taxpayers to elect the income tax return on which these tax items are reported and therefore may not result in an allocation that clearly reflects taxable income. This electivity is inconsistent with the purpose of §1.1502-76(b) to clearly reflect the income of S and the consolidated group. Further, the IRS and the Treasury Department have observed that the current regulations create controversy between taxpayers and the IRS as to whether certain of S's tax items that become reportable on the day of S's change in status are properly allocated to S's tax return for the period ending that day rather than to S's tax return for the period beginning the next day.

The proposed next day rule is intended to eliminate the perceived electivity and the source of these controversies. Under the proposed regulations, the application of the proposed next day rule is mandatory rather than elective—if an extraordinary item results from a transaction that occurs on the day of S's change in status, but after the event resulting in the change, and if the item would be taken into account by S on that day, the transaction resulting in the extraordinary item is treated as occurring at the beginning of the following day for purposes of determining the period in which S must report the item.

The proposed regulations also provide that the proposed next day rule is inapplicable to items that arise simultaneously with the event that causes S's change in status. Under the end of the day rule (as revised by these proposed regulations), those items are reported on S's tax return for the short period ending on the day of S's change in status. The proposed regulations are expected to afford taxpayers and the IRS greater certainty regarding the period to which S's tax items resulting from such a transaction are allocated.

C. Previous Day Rule

As noted in section 2 of this preamble, the special rule for S corporations provides an exception to the end of the day rule if an S corporation joins a consolidated group. To avoid creating a one-day C corporation tax return for the termination date, the S corporation exception provides that S becomes a member of the group at the beginning of the termination date, and that S's taxable year ends for all federal income tax purposes at the end of the preceding day.

Although these proposed regulations retain the S corporation exception, the proposed regulations add a previous day rule that mirrors the principles of the proposed next day rule. Whereas the proposed next day rule requires extraordinary items resulting from transactions that occur on the day of S's change in status (but after the event causing the change) to be allocated to S's tax return for the short period that begins the following day, the previous day rule requires extraordinary items resulting from transactions that occur on the termination date (but before or simultaneously with the event causing S's status as an S corporation to terminate) to be allocated to S's tax return for the short period that ends on the previous day (that is, the day preceding the termination date).

D. Revised Scope of the End of the Day Rule and Related Rules

Under the current end of the day rule, S becomes or ceases to be a member at the end of the day on which its status as a member changes, and its tax year ends "for all federal income tax purposes" at the end of that day. However, applying the end of the day rule for purposes other than the reporting of S's tax items could yield results inconsistent with other consolidated return rules. For example, under §§1.1502-13 and 1.1502-80(d)(1), if a member contributes property subject to a liability in excess of the property's basis to a nonmember in exchange for the nonmember's stock, and if the transferee becomes a member of the transferor's consolidated group as a result of the exchange, the transaction is treated as an intercompany transaction and section 357(c) does not apply. However, if the end of the day rule applies "for all federal income tax purposes," it may be unclear whether the transferee becomes a member "immediately after the transaction," whether the transaction is an intercompany transaction, and whether section 357(c) could apply to the transaction.

To eliminate possible confusion arising from application of the current end of the day rule and related rules, these proposed regulations provide that the end of the day rule, the proposed next day rule, the S corporation exception, and the previous day rule apply for purposes of determining the period in which S must report its tax items, as well as for purposes of sections 382(h) and 1374 (discussed in section 3.I. of this preamble).

E. Extraordinary Items

The proposed next day rule mandatorily applies to extraordinary items that result from a transaction that occurs on the day of S's change in status but after the event that causes the change. In contrast, the previous day rule mandatorily applies to extraordinary items that result from a transaction that occurs on the day of S's change in status but before or simultaneously with the event that causes S's status as an S corporation to terminate.

One category of extraordinary items, set forth in §1.1502-76(b)(2)(ii)(C)(9) of the current regulations, applies to any "compensation-related deduction in connection with S's change in status." The proposed regulations clarify that this category of extraordinary items includes (among other items) a deduction for fees for services rendered in connection with S's change in status. For example, if payment of a fee for the services of a financial adviser is contingent upon a successful acquisition of S's stock, to the extent the fee gives rise to a deduction, the deduction for the accrual of that expense is an extraordinary item, and the deduction is allowable only in S's taxable year that ends at the close of the day of the change.

The IRS and the Treasury Department request comments as to whether the list of extraordinary items set forth in §1.1502-76(b)(2)(ii)(C) should be modified to include any item not currently listed or whether any item currently included should be deleted or modified. Specifically, the IRS and the Treasury Department are considering whether the item in §1.1502-76(b)(2)(ii)(C)(5) ("[a]ny item carried to or from any portion of the original year (e.g., a net operating loss carried under section 172), and any section 481(a) adjustment") should be modified to include "any section 481(a) adjustment or the acceleration thereof," and whether the item in §1.1502-76(b)(2)(ii)(C)(6) ("[t]he effects of any change in accounting method initiated by the filing of the appropriate form after S's change in status") should continue to be included in the list of extraordinary items.

The IRS and the Treasury Department also request comments as to whether any extraordinary item should be excluded, in whole or in part, from application of the next day rule and the previous day rule. In particular, the IRS and the Treasury Department request comments as to whether the extraordinary items set forth in §1.1502-76(b)(2)(ii)(C)(5) and (6) of the current regulations should be excluded, in whole or in part, from application of these rules.

F. Ratable Allocation

Rather than require S to perform a closing of the books on the day of its change in status, the current regulations under §1.1502-76(b)(2)(ii) permit S's tax items, other than the extraordinary items, to be ratably allocated between S's two short taxable years if certain conditions are met. The IRS and the Treasury Department request comments as to whether S no longer should be permitted to elect to ratably allocate its tax items between the periods ending and beginning with S's change in status.

G. Certain Foreign Entities

Solely for purposes of determining the short taxable year of S to which the items of a passthrough entity in which S owns an interest are allocated, §1.1502-76(b)(2)(vi)(A) of the current regulations generally provides that S is treated as selling or exchanging its entire interest in the entity immediately before S's change in status. This rule does not apply to certain foreign corporations the ownership of which may give rise to deemed income inclusions under the Code. In addition, a deemed income inclusion from a foreign corporation and a deferred tax amount from a passive foreign investment company under section 1291 are treated as extraordinary items under §1.1502-76(b)(2)(ii)(C)(11). The IRS and the Treasury Department request comments as to whether such deemed income inclusions or deferred tax amounts should continue to be treated as extraordinary items, whether rules having similar effects to the rule in §1.1502-76(b)(2)(vi)(A) relating to passthrough entities should be adopted for controlled foreign corporations and passive foreign investment companies in which S owns an interest, and whether any other changes should be made to §1.1502-76(b)(2)(vi) of the current regulations.

H. Anti-Avoidance Rule

Under §1.1502-76(b)(3) of the current regulations, if any person acts with a principal purpose contrary to the purposes of §1.1502-76(b) to substantially reduce the federal income tax liability of any person (prohibited purpose), adjustments must be made as necessary to carry out the purposes of §1.1502-76 of the current regulations (anti-avoidance rule). The proposed regulations clarify that the anti-avoidance rule may apply to situations in which a person modifies an existing contract or other agreement in anticipation of S's change in status in order to shift an item between the taxable years that end and begin as a result of S's change in status if such actions are undertaken with a prohibited purpose. The IRS and the Treasury Department request comments regarding this proposed amendment to the anti-avoidance rule.

I. Coordination With Sections 382(h) and 1374

1. Section 382

For purposes of section 382, the term *recognized built-in loss* (RBIL) means any loss recognized during the recognition period on the disposition of any asset held by the loss corporation immediately before the date of the section 382 ownership change (change date), to the extent the loss reflects a built-in loss on the change date. Section 382(h)(2)(B). The term *recognition period* means the five-year period beginning on the change date. Section 382(h)(7)(A).

Section 382(h)(1)(B) generally provides that if a loss corporation has a net unrealized built-in loss (NUBIL), then any RBIL taken into account in a taxable year any portion of which falls in the recognition period (recognition period taxable year) is treated as a deduction subject to the loss corporation's section 382 limitation as if the RBIL were a pre-change loss. The amount of RBILs subject to the section 382 limitation in any recognition period taxable year is limited, however, to the excess of the NUBIL over total RBILs in prior taxable years ending in the recognition period. (The amount of such excess is referred to in this preamble as the outstanding NUBIL balance.) In other words, the amount of the NUBIL limits the amount of RBILs that are treated as pre-change losses, and any built-in loss treated as an RBIL further reduces the outstanding NUBIL balance.

In many cases, the event that causes S's change in status for purposes of §1.1502-76(b)(1)(ii) also causes S to undergo an ownership change for purposes of section 382. Thus, an item of deduction or loss that becomes reportable on the day of S's change in status falls within the recognition period beginning that day, even if the item is allocated to S's short period ending that day under the end of the day rule. As a consequence, an item that should be a pre-change loss is treated as an RBIL that reduces the outstanding NUBIL balance. For example, assume consolidated group A sells all of S's stock to consolidated group B. If on the day of S's change in status (but before the event causing the change), S recognizes a loss on the sale of an asset, under the end of the day rule the loss is reported on group A's consolidated return. However, notwithstanding that the loss may not be claimed by group B, the loss may be treated as an RBIL and reduce the outstanding NUBIL balance.

To prevent such an outcome, these proposed regulations provide that, for purposes of section 382(h), items includible in the short taxable year that ends as a result of S's change in status (including items allocated to that taxable year under the end of the day rule) are not treated as occurring in the recognition period. Rather, only items includible in S's short taxable year that begins as a result of S's change in status (including items allocated to that taxable year under the proposed next day rule) are treated as occurring in the recognition period. Therefore, the beginning of the recognition period for purposes of section 382(h) would correspond with the beginning of S's short taxable year that begins on the day after S's change in status.

2. Section 1374

Section 1374 generally imposes a corporate-level tax (section 1374 tax) on the recognition of gain by an S corporation that formerly was a C corporation (or that acquired assets from a C corporation in a transferred basis transaction) during a recognition period specified in section

1374(d)(7) (section 1374 recognition period), but only to the extent of the corporation's net recognized built-in gain (as defined in section 1374(d)(2)) for a given taxable year. The section 1374 tax also applies to certain tax items attributable to the corporation's C corporation taxable years. In addition, regulations under section 337(d) extend section 1374 treatment to (1) a C corporation's conversion to a real estate investment trust (REIT), regulated investment company (RIC), and certain tax-exempt entities, or (2) certain cases in which a REIT, RIC, or tax-exempt entity acquires assets in a transferred basis transaction from a C corporation.

As with the application of section 382(h), the event that causes S's change in status for purposes of §1.1502-76(b)(1)(ii) may be the event that results in S being a corporation that is subject to the section 1374 tax. Therefore, it is necessary to determine in which return (the group's consolidated return or S's separate return beginning the day after S's change in status) S's tax items for the day of S's change in status are included. Similarly, if the event that causes S's change in status for purposes of §1.1502-76(b)(1)(ii) is the event that results in S ceasing to be a corporation subject to the section 1374 tax, it is necessary to determine in which return (the group's consolidated return or S's separate return for the period ending the day before S's change in status) S's tax items for the day of S's change in status are included. The proposed regulations thus provide that if S ceases to be a corporation subject to the section 1374 tax upon becoming a member, or if S elects to be a corporation that is subject to the section 1374 tax for its first separate return year after ceasing to be a member, S's items of recognized built-in gain or loss for purposes of section 1374 will include only the amounts reported on S's separate return (including items reported on that return under the previous day rule or the next day rule).

J. Intercompany Section 381 Transactions

Under the current consolidated return regulations, if a member distributes or transfers its assets to another corporation that is a member immediately after the distribution or transfer in an intercompany section 381 transaction, and if the distributor or transferor member has a net operating loss carryover or a net capital loss carryover, the distributor or transferor member will not be treated as having a short taxable year for purposes of determining the years to which the loss may be carried. Sections 1.1502-21(b)(3)(iii) and 1.1502-22(b)(4).

These proposed regulations would amend current law by moving these rules to §1.1502-76(b)(2)(i) and making conforming changes to §§1.1502-21(b)(3)(iii) and 1.1502-22(b)(4). In addition, these proposed regulations would expand these rules by providing that a short taxable year of the distributor or transferor member by reason of an intercompany section 381 transaction is not counted as a separate taxable year for purposes of determining either the taxable years to which any tax attribute of the distributor or transferor member may be carried or the taxable years in which an adjustment under section 481(a) is taken into account. No inference should be drawn from the proposed changes to these rules as to whether a short taxable year of a member resulting from an intercompany section 381 transaction is counted under current law for purposes of determining the years to which a tax credit may be carried or in which a section 481 adjustment is taken into account.

K. Due Date for Filing Tax Returns

The proposed regulations also eliminate a provision that could cause taxpayers to inadvertently miss a return filing deadline. Under §1.1502-76(b)(4) of the current regulations, if S joins a consolidated group, the due date for filing S's separate return is the earlier of the due date (with extensions) of the group's return or the due date (with extensions) of S's return if S had not joined the group. If S goes out of existence during the consolidated return year in which S joins a group, its taxable year would end. Under section 6072, the due date for S's short period return would be the 15th day of the third month (ninth month, with extensions) following the date on which S ceases to exist. Accordingly, if S ceases to exist during the same consolidated return year in which it becomes a member, the due date for S's tax return for the short period that ended as a result of S becoming a member could be accelerated. To prevent a taxpayer from inadvertently missing a filing date and being subject to potential penalties for filing a late return, the proposed regulations provide that if S goes out of existence in the same consolidated return year in which it becomes a member, the due date for filing S's separate return is determined without regard to S's ceasing to exist.

L. Non-Substantive Changes

In addition to the changes described in this preamble, the proposed regulations make several non-substantive changes to the current regulations, including moving an example concerning §1.1502-80(d) from the text of §1.1502-76(b)(1)(ii)(B)(2) of the current regulations to §1.1502-13(c)(7)(ii), Example 3(e).

Effective/Applicability Date

The amendments to §§1.1502-21(b)(3)(iii), 1.1502-22(b)(4)(i), 1.1502-76(b)(2)(i), and 1.1502-76(b)(4) will apply to consolidated return years beginning on or after the date these regulations are published as final regulations in the March 5, 2015. The other amendments to §1.1502-76(b) will apply to corporations becoming or ceasing to be members of consolidated groups on or after the date these regulations are published as final regulations in the March 5, 2015.

Special Analyses

It has been determined that this notice of proposed rulemaking is not a significant regulatory action as defined in Executive Order 12866, as supplemented by Executive Order 13563. Therefore, a regulatory assessment is not required. It is hereby certified that these regulations will not have a significant impact on a substantial number of small entities. This certification is based on the fact that the regulations apply only to transactions involving corporations that file consolidated federal income tax returns, and that such corporations tend to be larger businesses. Accordingly, a Regulatory Flexibility Analysis under the Regulatory Flexibility Act (5 U.S.C. chapter 6) is not required. Pursuant to section 7805(f) of the Code, these regulations will be submitted to the Chief Counsel for Advocacy of the Small Business Administration for comment on their impact on small business.

Comments and Public Hearing

Before these proposed regulations are adopted as final regulations, consideration will be given to any comments that are submitted timely to the IRS as prescribed in this preamble under the "Addresses" heading. The IRS and the Treasury Department request comments on all aspects of the proposed rules. All comments will be available for public inspection and copying. A public hearing may be scheduled if requested in writing by any person who timely submits written comments. If a public hearing is scheduled, notice of the date, time, and place of the hearing will be published in the March 5, 2015.

Drafting Information

The principal author of these proposed regulations is Russell G. Jones of the Office of Associate Chief Counsel (Corporate). However, other personnel from the IRS and the Treasury Department participated in their development.

[¶ 49,647] **Proposed Amendments of Regulations and Withdrawal of Notice of Proposed Regulations (REG-102656-15; REG-107548-11)**, published in the Federal Register on May 8, 2015.

[Code Secs. 446 and 956]

Notional principal contracts: Swaps with nonperiodic payments: United States property.—Amendments of Reg. §§1.446-3 and 1.956-2, amending the treatment of nonperiodic payments made or received pursuant to certain notional principal contracts, are proposed. Amendments of Reg. §1.956-2, proposed on May 11, 2012 (REG-107548-11), are withdrawn.

AGENCY: Internal Revenue Service (IRS), Treasury.

ACTION: Withdrawal of notice of proposed rulemaking; notice of proposed rulemaking by cross-reference to temporary regulations.

SUMMARY: In the Rules and Regulations section of this issue of the **Federal Register**, the IRS is issuing final and temporary regulations that amend the treatment of nonperiodic payments made or received pursuant to certain notional principal contracts. These regulations provide that, subject to certain exceptions, a notional principal contract with a nonperiodic payment, regardless of whether it is significant, must be treated as two separate transactions consisting of one or more loans and an on-market, level payment swap. The regulations provide an exception from the definition of United States property. These regulations affect parties making and receiving payments under notional principal contracts, including United States shareholders of controlled foreign corporations and tax-exempt organizations. The text of the temporary regulations also serves as the text of these proposed regulations. This document withdraws the notice of proposed rulemaking (REG-107548-11; RIN 1545-BK10) published in the **Federal Register** on May 11, 2012 (77 FR 27669).

DATES: Comments and requests for a public hearing must be received by August 6, 2015.

ADDRESSES: Send submissions to CC:PA:LPD:PR (REG-102656-15), room 5203, Internal Revenue Service, P.O. Box 7604, Ben Franklin Station, Washington, DC 20044. Submissions may be hand-delivered Monday through Friday between the hours of 8 a.m. and 4 p.m. to CC:PA:LPD:PR (REG-102656-15), Courier's Desk, Internal Revenue Service, 1111 Constitution Avenue NW., Washington, DC 20224, or sent electronically via the Federal eRulemaking Portal at *www.regulations.gov* (IRS REG-102656-15).

FOR FURTHER INFORMATION CONTACT: Concerning the proposed regulations under section 446, Alexa T. Dubert or Anna H. Kim at (202) 317-6895; concerning the proposed regulations under section 956, Kristine A. Crabtree at (202) 317-6934; concerning submissions of comments or to request a public hearing, Oluwafunmilayo Taylor, (202) 317-6901 (not toll-free numbers).

SUPPLEMENTARY INFORMATION:

Background and Explanation of Provisions

On May 11, 2012, the Treasury Department and the IRS published temporary regulations under section 956 (TD 9589) in the **Federal Register** (77 FR 27612). On the same date, a notice of proposed rulemaking (REG-107548-11) by cross-reference to the temporary regulations was published in the **Federal Register** (77 FR 27669). This document withdraws those proposed regulations (REG-107548-11; RIN 1545-BK10) and provides new proposed regulations (REG-102656-15).

Final and temporary regulations in the Rules and Regulations section of this issue of the **Federal Register** amend the Income Tax Regulations (26 CFR Part 1). The final and temporary regulations amend the regulations under section 446 of the Internal Revenue Code (Code) relating to the treatment of nonperiodic payments made or received pursuant to certain notional principal contracts for U.S. federal income tax purposes. The final and temporary regulations also amend the regulations under section 956 of the Code regarding an exception from the definition of United States property. The text of the final and temporary regulations also serves as the text of these proposed regulations. The preamble to the final and temporary regulations explains those regulations and these proposed regulations.

Special Analyses

It has been determined that this notice of proposed rulemaking is not a significant regulatory action as defined in Executive Order 12866, as supplemented by Executive Order 13653. Therefore, a regulatory assessment is not required. It also has been determined that section 553(b) of the Administrative Procedure Act (5 U.S.C. chapter 5) does not apply to these regulations, and because these regulations do not impose a collection of information on small entities, the Regulatory Flexibility Act (5 U.S.C. chapter 6) does not apply. Pursuant to section 7805(f) of the Code, this notice of proposed rulemaking has been submitted to the Chief Counsel for Advocacy of the Small Business Administration for comment on its impact on small entities.

Comments and Requests for Public Hearing

Before these proposed regulations are adopted as final regulations, consideration will be given to any comments that are submitted timely to the IRS as prescribed in this preamble under the "Addresses" heading. The Treasury Department and the IRS request comments on all aspects of the proposed rules. All comments will be available at *www.regulations.gov* or upon request. A public hearing will be scheduled if requested in writing by any person that timely submits written comments. If a public hearing is scheduled, notice of the date, time, and place for the hearing will be published in the **Federal Register**.

Drafting information

The principal authors of these regulations are Alexa T. Dubert and Anna H. Kim of the Office of Associate Chief Counsel (Financial Institutions and Products). However, other personnel from the Treasury Department and the IRS participated in their development.

[¶49,650]   Proposed Amendments of Regulations (REG-101652-10), published in the Federal Register on June 11, 2015.

[Code Secs. 1502 and 6402]

Consolidated returns: Consolidated net operating loss: Disposition of subsidiary's stock: Apportionment of consolidated net operating loss: Absorption of member's losses: Circular basis adjustments.—Amendments of Reg. §§1.1502-11, 1.1502-12, 1.1502-21, 1.1502-21A, 1.1502-22, 1.1502-22A, 1.1502-23A, 1.1502-24 and 301.6402-7, containing proposed amendments to the consolidated return regulations, are proposed.

AGENCY: Internal Revenue Service (IRS), Treasury.

ACTION: Notice of proposed rulemaking.

SUMMARY: This document contains proposed amendments to the consolidated return regulations. These amendments would revise the rules concerning the use of a consolidated group's losses in a consolidated return year in which stock of a subsidiary is disposed of. The regulations would affect corporations filing consolidated returns.

DATES: Written or electronic comments, and a request for a public hearing, must be received by September 9, 2015.

ADDRESSES: Send submissions to: CC:PA:LPD:PR (REG-101652-10), room 5205, Internal Revenue Service, PO Box 7604, Ben Franklin Station, Washington, DC 20044. Submissions may be hand-delivered Monday through Friday between the hours of 8 a.m. and 4 p.m. to CC:PA:LPD:PR

(REG-101652-10), Courier's Desk, Internal Revenue Service, 1111 Constitution Avenue, N.W., Washington, DC, or sent electronically via the Federal eRulemaking Portal at *http://www.regulations.gov* (IRS REG-101652-10). FOR FURTHER INFORMATION CONTACT: Concerning the proposed regulations, Robert M. Rhyne, (202) 317-6848; concerning submissions of comments or to request a public hearing, Oluwafunmilayo (Funmi) Taylor, (202) 317-6901 (not toll-free numbers).

SUPPLEMENTARY INFORMATION:

Background and Explanation of Provisions

1. Introduction

This document contains proposed amendments to 26 CFR part 1 under section 1502 of the Internal Revenue Code (Code). Section 1502 authorizes the Secretary to prescribe regulations for corporations that join in filing consolidated returns to reflect clearly the income tax liability of the group and to prevent avoidance of such tax liability, and provides that these rules may be different from the provisions of chapter 1 of subtitle A of the Code that would apply if the corporations filed separate returns. Terms used in the consolidated return regulations generally are defined in § 1.1502-1.

These proposed regulations would provide guidance regarding the absorption of members' losses in a consolidated return year, and provide guidance to eliminate the "circular basis problem" in a broader class of transactions than under current law.

This document also contains proposed conforming amendments to 26 CFR part 301 under section 6402. Section 6402 authorizes the Secretary to make credits and refunds. The proposed regulations would amend § 301.6402-7(g) (relating to claims for refunds and application for tentative carryback adjustments involving consolidated groups that include financial institutions) by revising the definition of separate net operating loss of a member in light of the proposed amendments to § 1.1502-21 (relating to the determination and treatment of consolidated and separate net operating losses, carrybacks, and carryovers).

2. Allocation and Absorption of Members' Losses

In general, the consolidated taxable income (CTI) or consolidated net operating loss (CNOL) of a consolidated group is the sum of each member's separately computed taxable income or loss (computed pursuant to § 1.1502-12) and certain items of income and deduction that are computed on a consolidated basis pursuant to § 1.1502-11.

Section 1.1502-21(b)(2)(i) (relating to carryovers and carrybacks of CNOLs to separate return years) provides generally that if a group has a CNOL and a portion of the CNOL would be carried to a member's separate return year, the CNOL must be apportioned between the group and the member (or members) with the separate return year(s) in accordance with the amount of the CNOL attributable to those member(s). For this purpose, § 1.1502-21(b)(2)(iv) employs a fraction to determine the percentage amount of the CNOL attributable to a member. The numerator of the fraction is the separate net operating loss of the member for the consolidated return year, and the denominator is the sum of the separate net operating losses of all members for that year. For this purpose, the separate net operating loss of a member is determined by computing the CNOL, taking into account only the member's items of income, gain, deduction, and loss. Although the current consolidated return regulations provide rules for apportioning a CNOL among members when a member's loss may be carried to a separate return year, the regulations do not expressly adopt the fraction-based methodology of § 1.1502-21(b)(2)(iv) for computing the amount of each member's absorbed loss that is used to offset the income of members with positive separate taxable income or net capital gain for the consolidated return year in which the loss is recognized.

Furthermore, although the method provided for apportioning a CNOL under current law generally yields appropriate results, the apportionment may produce anomalies if capital gains are present. For example, assume a stand-alone corporation, P, acquires the stock of corporation S, and P and S file a consolidated return for the first taxable year of P ending after the acquisition. For the consolidated return year, P generates $100 of capital gain and incurs $100 of deductible expenses. S incurs a $100 capital loss. Thus, the group has a $100 CNOL. Under current law, the percentage of the CNOL attributable to each member is determined by its relative separate net operating loss, taking into account only its items. The CNOL that the group would have if only P's items were taken into account is zero ($100 of capital gain offset by $100 of deductible expenses). If only S's items were taken into account the group would have a consolidated net capital loss, but the CNOL would also be zero. Accordingly, because neither P nor S has a separate net operating loss, the allocation of the group's $100 CNOL is not clear.

Both to provide an absorption rule for apportioning ordinary and capital losses incurred in the same consolidated return year, and to address the CNOL apportionment issue, the proposed regulations would amend the current regulations in the following two ways. First, the proposed regulations add a new paragraph (e) to § 1.1502-11 to clarify that the absorption of members' losses to offset income of other members in the consolidated return year is made on a pro rata basis, consistent with the pro rata absorption of losses from taxable years ending on the same date that are carried back or forward under the rules of §§ 1.1502-21(b) and 1.1502-22(b) (relating to net capital loss carrybacks and carryovers). Second, to address apportionment anomalies that may arise if capital gains are present, the proposed regulations would provide that the separate net operating loss of a member, solely for apportionment purposes, is its loss determined without regard to capital gains (or losses) or amounts treated as capital gains. Thus, in the example in the preceding paragraph, P would be allocated the entire $100 CNOL. Excluding capital gains and losses from the computation is consistent with excluding capital gains and losses in determining a member's separate taxable income under § 1.1502-12, and taking capital gains and losses into account on a group, rather than a separate member, basis. A conforming amendment is made to § 301.6402-7(g)(2)(ii) (relating to refunds to certain statutory or court-appointed fiduciaries of an insolvent financial institution), which contains a similar allocation rule.

3. Circular Adjustments to Basis

A. The circular basis problem and current regulations

To prevent the income, gain, deduction, or loss of a subsidiary from being reflected more than once in a consolidated group's income, the consolidated return regulations adjust an owning member's basis in a subsidiary's stock to reflect those items. As a group takes into account a subsidiary's items of income or gain, an owning member's basis in the subsidiary's stock increases. Likewise, as a group absorbs a subsidiary's deductions or losses, an owning member's basis in the subsidiary's stock decreases. These adjustments take place under what is generally referred to as the investment adjustment system. See § 1.1502-32.

If a group absorbs a portion of a subsidiary's loss in the same consolidated return year in which an owning member disposes of that subsidiary's stock, the owning member's basis in the subsidiary's stock is reduced immediately before the disposition. Consequently, the amount of the owning member's gain or loss on the disposition may be affected. Any change in the amount of gain or loss resulting from the disposition may in turn affect the amount of the subsidiary's loss that the group absorbs. Any further absorption of the subsidiary's loss triggers further adjustments to the basis in the subsidiary's stock. These iterative computations, which may completely eliminate the benefit of the disposed of member's losses, are referred to as the circular basis problem.

For example, assume P owns all the stock of S, and the group has a $100 consolidated net capital loss carryover, all of which is attributable to S. On December 31, P sells all of S's stock to a nonmember at a $10 gain. Absent the current rules in § 1.1502-11(b), P's $10 capital gain on the sale of S's stock would be offset by $10 of the consolidated net capital loss carryover (all of which is attributable to S). The use of the loss would cause P's basis in S's stock to be reduced by $10 (immediately before the sale), causing P to recognize $20 of gain on the sale of S's stock. Similarly, that $20 gain would be offset by $20 of S's consolidated net capital loss carryover, and so on, until the entire consolidated net capital loss carryover was depleted. At the end of these iterative calculations, the group would still report $10 of consolidated net capital gain. The current regulations prevent this result.

The Treasury Department and the IRS have considered a variety of approaches to the circular basis problem since the introduction of the investment adjustment system in 1966. The options considered, and either rejected or adopted in regulations to date, appear to have been motivated by differing views concerning the scope and severity of the circular basis problem. The circumstances in which the consolidated return regulations have provided relief to date have been limited to preventing the disposed of subsidiary's loss absorption from affecting the gain or loss recognized on the sale of that subsidiary. This is the case notwithstanding that many commentators have criticized the scope of relief as being too narrow, and have maintained that relief should be extended to, for example, the sales of brother-sister subsidiaries within the same consolidated return year.

Regulations promulgated in 1966 provided no relief from the circular basis problem, even though some relief was initially proposed. Section 1.1502-11(b), published in 1972, provided some relief from the circular basis problem, and those regulations were revised in 1994 into their current form (the circular basis rules).

To resolve the circular basis problem, the circular basis rules require that a tentative computation of CTI be made without taking into account any gain or loss on the disposition of a subsidiary's stock. The amount of the subsidiary's losses that would be absorbed under the tentative computation becomes a limitation on that subsidiary's losses that may be absorbed in the consolidated return year of disposition or as a carryback to a prior year. The limitation is intended to eliminate the circular basis adjustments to the subsidiary's stock and thus prevent iterative computations.

For example, assume a consolidated group consists of P, the common parent, and S, its wholly owned subsidiary, and neither P nor S had income or gain in a prior year. At the beginning of the consolidated return year, P has a $500 basis in S's stock. P sells S's stock for $520 at the end of the year. For the year, P has $30 of ordinary income (determined without taking into account P's gain or loss on the disposition of S's stock) and S has $80 of ordinary loss. To determine the limitation on the amount of S's loss that the group may use during the consolidated return year or as a carryback to a prior year, CTI is tentatively determined without taking into account P's gain or loss on the disposition of S's stock. Accordingly, the use of S's loss in the consolidated return year of disposition is limited to $30. The group is tentatively treated as having a CNOL of $50 (P's $30 of income minus S's $80 loss). The absorption of $30 of S's loss reduces P's basis in S's stock to $470, and results in $50 [$520 − ($500 - $30)] of gain to P on the disposition. Thus, iterative computations are avoided.

Nevertheless, the circular basis rules do not prevent iterative computations in all cases — not even all cases in which the stock of a single subsidiary with a loss is disposed of. For example, if a member other than the disposed of subsidiary also has a loss, and the sum of the losses of the disposed subsidiary and the other member exceeds the income of the group (without regard to gain on the disposed subsidiary's stock) a tentative computation applying a pro rata rule for absorption establishes a limitation on the use of the disposed of subsidiary's loss. That amount will be used to reduce the owning member's basis in the subsidiary's stock and determine the gain or loss on the stock disposition. If the stock disposition results in gain, that gain will be taken into account in an actual computation of CTI. If the sum of the other member's loss and the disposed of subsidiary's limited loss still exceeds the income and gain of other members, the pro rata absorption rule will be applied again. That computation will result in a lower amount for the absorption of the disposed of subsidiary's loss, which will be different than the amount by which the owning member's stock basis was reduced. Accordingly, iterative computations would be required.

To illustrate, assume a consolidated group consists of P, the common parent, and its wholly owned subsidiaries, S1 and S2. At the beginning of the consolidated return year, P has a $500 basis in S1's stock. P sells all of its S1 stock for $500 at the end of the year. For the year, P has a $60 capital gain (determined without taking into account P's gain or loss on the disposition of S1's stock), S1 has a $40 net capital loss and S2 has an $80 net capital loss. To determine the limitation on the amount of S1's capital loss that the group may use during the consolidated return year, CTI is tentatively determined without taking into account gain or loss on the disposition of S1's stock, but with regard to S2's net capital loss. Because S2 has an $80 net capital loss in addition to S1's $40 net capital loss, $40 of S2's loss [$60 × ($80/$120)] and $20 of S1's loss [$60 × ($40/$120)] will be used (assuming pro rata absorption of losses as described in section 2 of the Explanation of Provisions of this preamble). Accordingly, the group's use of S1's loss is limited to $20. Thus, P's basis in S1's stock is reduced by $20 before P disposes of the stock. Therefore, P is assumed to recognize $20 [$500 - ($500 - $20)] of gain on the disposition of its S1 stock, which leaves P with a total capital gain for the year of $80. Again, because S2 has an $80 loss in addition to S1's $20 usable loss, a pro rata portion of each subsidiary's losses will be absorbed in computing the P group's CTI. Assuming pro rata absorption of losses, P's $80 capital gain is offset with $16 of S1's capital loss [$80 × ($20/$100)]. This amount, however, is less than the $20 amount determined in the tentative computation by which P's basis in S1's stock was reduced. Thus, iterative computations would be required.

In considering the circular basis problem, the Treasury Department and the IRS have become aware that taxpayers have taken a broad range of approaches in cases in which the circular basis problem persists. Some taxpayers may undertake many iterative computations while, under similar facts, others will undertake few. Some commentators have suggested using simultaneous equations. That method can produce appropriate results in the simplest fact patterns, but becomes highly complex if both ordinary income and capital gains are present, or if the stock of more than one subsidiary is sold.

One approach that the Treasury Department and IRS considered but did not adopt in these proposed regulations was to disallow the absorption of any losses of a subsidiary in the year of disposition. Such a rule would have an adverse impact on any consolidated group with ordinary income that otherwise would be offset by the subsidiary's losses. Furthermore, a blanket prohibition on the use of a subsidiary's losses would be inappropriately harsh if a subsidiary's stock was sold at a loss and the unified loss rules required a stock basis reduction that was greater than the amount of S's loss. In such a case, the use of S's loss to offset income of other members allowed under current law reduces CTI, but the basis reduction that results from the absorption of the loss has no net effect on the owning member's basis in the subsidiary's stock. Prohibiting the use of the disposed of subsidiary's losses would simply increase the group's CTI.

The Treasury Department and IRS also considered but did not adopt an approach similar to the current rules that would compute a tentative amount of S's losses, and then require a reduction to P's basis in S's stock, regardless of whether S's losses were actually absorbed. This approach could lead to non-economic consequences when another subsidiary's losses are actually absorbed instead of S's according to the general rules of the Code and regulations, but S's losses are nonetheless treated as absorbed for purposes of reducing P's basis in S's stock.

A third approach that the Treasury Department and IRS considered but did not adopt was to turn-off the investment adjustment rules for losses of a subsidiary used in the year of disposition. Such an approach would allow a double deduction and undermine a bedrock principle of consolidated returns as articulated by the Supreme Court in *Charles Ilfeld Co. v. Hernandez*, 292 U.S. 62 (1934).

B. Proposed circular basis rules

i. In general.

The proposed regulations would provide relief and certainty to cases in which the circular basis problem persists, yet adhere to underlying consolidated return concepts without undue complexity. To prevent iterative computations for a consolidated return year in which the stock of one or more subsidiaries is disposed of, these proposed regulations require a group to first determine the amount of each disposed subsidiary's loss that will be absorbed by computing CTI without regard to gain or loss on the disposition of the stock of any subsidiary (the absorbed amount). Once the amount of a subsidiary's absorbed loss is determined under that computation, the absorbed amount for each disposed of subsidiary is not redetermined. Determining each disposed of subsidiary's absorbed amount establishes an immutable number that will also be the amount of reduction to the basis of S's stock taken into account in computing the owning member's gain or loss on the disposition of S's stock. After the absorbed amount is determined, the owning member's basis of the S stock is adjusted under § 1.1502-32 (and § 1.1502-36 as relevant). The actual computation of CTI can then be made, taking into account losses of each disposed of subsidiary equal to that amount. In some cases, however, applying the generally applicable rules of the Code and regulations would result in less than all of a disposed of subsidiary's absorbed amount being used.

For example, assume S has an ordinary loss of $100 and P has capital gain net income of $100 (unrelated to its disposition of S stock), then S's absorbed amount would be determined to be $100. If after taking into account S's $100 absorbed amount P would have a $100 capital loss on a sale of S's stock, P's capital loss on its S stock would offset P's $100 capital gain, and S's ordinary loss would not be used in that year and would become a CNOL carryover (assuming no ability to carry back the loss). If an amount of S's losses equal to its absorbed amount were not used, P's basis in its S stock would not be reduced by the absorbed amount, and the amount of P's loss on S's stock would be changed.

The proposed regulations prevent such a result by providing for an alternative four-step computation of CTI if, applying the general ordering rules of the Code and regulations, less than all of a disposed of subsidiary's absorbed amount would be used. See *Examples 5, 6, 7, 8* and *9* of § 1.1502-11(b)(2)(vi) as proposed herein.

Under the first step, any income, gain, or loss on any share of subsidiary stock is excluded from the computation of CTI and the group uses losses of each disposed of subsidiary equal in both amount and character and from the same taxable years as those used in the computation of its absorbed amount. Thus, by excluding any income, gain, or loss on a stock disposition, and by giving priority to the losses of all disposed of subsidiaries, the proposed regulations would solve the circularity problem.

Under the second step, a disposing member offsets its gain on subsidiary stock with its losses on subsidiary stock (determined after applying § 1.1502-36(b) and (c), and so much of § 1.1502-36(d) as is necessary to give effect to an election actually made under § 1.1502-36(d)(6)). If the disposing member has net income or gain on the subsidiary stock, and if the disposing member also has a loss of the same character (determined without regard to the stock net income or gain), the disposing member's loss is used to offset the net income or gain on the subsidiary stock to the extent of such income or gain. Any remaining net income or gain is added to the group's remaining income or gain as determined under the first step. Giving priority to S's losses ahead of other members' losses and excluding gain or loss on subsidiary stock are departures from the general rules that require a member to net its income and gain with its own losses before those amounts are combined in a consolidated computation. These departures may distort the amount of absorbed losses of a disposing member relative to the absorbed losses of other members. Thus, in order to put losses of a disposing member (unrelated to its loss on a stock disposition) on a par with losses of other members, the proposed regulations allow P's losses to offset the group's income before other members, but only to the extent of the gain (or income) on the disposed of subsidiary's stock.

Under the third step if, after the application of the second step of the alternative computation, the group has remaining income or gain and a disposing member has a net loss on subsidiary stock (determined after applying § 1.1502-36(b) and (c), and so much of § 1.1502-36(d) as is necessary to give effect to an election actually made under § 1.1502-36(d)(6)), that income or gain is then offset by the loss on the disposition of subsidiary stock, subject to generally applicable rules of the Code and regulations. The amount of the offset, however, is limited to the lesser of the total remaining ordinary income or capital gain of the group (determined after the application of the second step) or the amount of the disposing member's ordinary income or capital gain (determined without regard to the stock loss).

Finally, under the fourth step, if the group has remaining income or gain, the unused losses of all members are applied on a pro rata basis.

The Treasury Department and the IRS recognize that the special rules in these proposed regulations may in certain cases alter the general rule under section 1211(a) that allows the deduction of losses from the sale or exchange of capital assets to the extent of capital gains. However, giving priority to the absorption of a disposed subsidiary's losses will prevent the need for iterative computations.

The Treasury Department and the IRS also recognize that the proposed regulations may increase the number of cases in which the general ordering rules for the absorption of members' losses will be altered and may in certain cases result in more gain (or less loss) on the sale of a subsidiary's stock than under current law. However, the Treasury Department and the IRS believe that the benefits derived from the certainty that the proposed rules achieve generally outweigh the potential detriments of these deviations from the general rules. Comments are requested on whether there are alternative approaches that would both eliminate the circular basis problem and preserve the general rule for the absorption of capital and ordinary losses.

ii. Higher-tier subsidiaries.

Under § 1.1502-11(b)(4)(ii) of the current regulations, if S is a higher-tier subsidiary of another subsidiary (T), the use of T's losses is subject to the circular basis rules upon a disposition of S's stock, but only if 100 percent of T's items of income, gain, deduction, and loss would be reflected in the basis of S's stock in the hands of the owning member (100-percent requirement). If another member of S's consolidated group or a nonmember owns any stock of either S or T, the circular basis rules do not apply.

These proposed regulations would remove the 100-percent requirement. Thus, if any stock of a higher-tier subsidiary is disposed of, the absorption of losses of a lower-tier subsidiary is subject to the proposed circular basis rules by treating the lower-tier subsidiary as if its stock had been disposed of. The Treasury Department and the IRS request comments regarding whether, and under what circumstances, the 100-percent requirement should be retained.

C. Other Provisions

Ordinary income and deductions are generally taken into account on a separate company basis before the computation of CTI occurs. A member's separate taxable income under § 1.1502-12 is computed in accordance with the provisions of the Code subject to certain modifications. These modifications generally relate to items that are determined on a consolidated basis (for example, the use of capital losses and the limitation on charitable contribution deductions). Although gain or loss on the disposition of a subsidiary's stock is usually capital, a worthless stock deduction could be ordinary if the conditions of section 165(g)(3) are satisfied. In addition, a gain on the disposition of such stock can be ordinary if the recapture rules of section 1017(d) apply. Under these proposed regulations, gain and loss on the disposition of subsidiary stock are disregarded in determining the subsidiary's absorbed amount, and in an alternative computation of CTI. Consequently, if stock of a subsidiary is disposed of, these proposed regulations may require a departure from the general rules for the computation of an owning member's separate taxable income.

The Treasury Department and the IRS believe that this departure from the general rules is necessary to avoid iterative computations and request comments as to whether an alternative methodology would be preferable.

These proposed regulations clarify the interaction of the Unified Loss Rule of §1.1502-36 with the circular basis rules. Adjustments under §1.1502-36(b), (c), and (d)(6) (if an election is made to reattribute losses or reduce stock basis) will affect the computation of CTI. Therefore, these proposed regulations contain guidance as to the point in the computation that those adjustments are made.

The proposed regulations also contain a rule to prevent iterative computations in determining the amount of deductions that are determined by reference to or are limited by the group's CTI, for example, the consolidated charitable contributions deduction under §1.1502-24 and a member's percentage depletion deduction with respect to oil or gas property for independent producers and royalty owners under §1.1502-44. The amount of those deductions is taken into account in determining the group's CTI and may affect the computation of a disposed of subsidiary's absorbed amount. The absorbed amount will reduce the stock basis and affect the amount of gain or loss on the disposition of the subsidiary's stock, which will change the amount of CTI, and thus the amount of the group's deduction. To prevent these iterative computations, the proposed regulations provide that the amount of those deductions is determined without regard to gain or loss on the disposition of a subsidiary's stock.

As a result of the later addition of §1.1502-11(c), current §1.1502-11(b) does not apply if a member realizes discharge of indebtedness income that is excluded from gross income under section 108(a). The rules applicable in that case, contained in paragraph (c) of §1.1502-11, are generally not addressed by these proposed regulations, but to the extent that paragraph (c) uses the absorbed amount described in §1.1502-11(b)(2) as a starting point, the computation will be affected. Comments are requested regarding appropriate additional changes to §1.1502-11(c).

Finally, the proposed regulations include modifications to §§1.1502-11(a), 1.1502-12, 1.1502-22(a), and 1.1502-24 of the current regulations and removal of §§1.1502-21A, 1.1502-22A and 1.1502-23A. These modifications are not changes to current substantive law; they are intended solely to update the regulations to reflect certain statutory changes and remove cross-references to outdated regulatory provisions.

Proposed Effective Date

These regulations are proposed to be effective for consolidated return years beginning on or after the date these regulations are published as final regulations in the **Federal Register**.

Special Analyses

It has been determined that this notice of proposed rulemaking is not a significant regulatory action as defined in Executive Order 12866, as supplemented by Executive Order 13563. Therefore, a regulatory assessment is not required. These proposed regulations would not impose a collection of information on small entities. Further, under the Regulatory Flexibility Act (5 U.S.C. chapter 6), it is hereby certified that these proposed regulations would not have a significant economic impact on a substantial number of small entities. This certification is based on the fact that these proposed regulations would primarily affect members of consolidated groups that tend to be large corporations. Accordingly, a regulatory flexibility analysis is not required. Pursuant to section 7805(f) of the Code, this notice of proposed rulemaking has been submitted to the Chief Counsel for Advocacy of the Small Business Administration for comment on its impact on small business.

Comments and Requests for a Public Hearing

Before these proposed regulations are adopted as final regulations, consideration will be given to any written (a signed original with eight (8) copies) or electronic comments that are submitted timely to the IRS. The Treasury Department and the IRS request comments on all aspects of the proposed regulations.

All comments will be available for public inspection and copying at *www.regulations.gov* or upon request. A public hearing may be scheduled if requested by any person that timely submits comments. If a public hearing is scheduled, notice of the date, time, and place for the public hearing will be published in the **Federal Register**.

Drafting Information

The principal author of these regulations is Robert M. Rhyne, Office of Associate Chief Counsel (Corporate). However, other personnel from the IRS and the Treasury Department participated in their development.

[¶ 49,654] Proposed Amendments of Regulations (REG-102837-15), published in the Federal Register on June 22, 2015 (corrected 8/7/2015).

[Code Secs. 511, 513, 529A and 6011]

ABLE account: Program requirements: Proposed regulations.—Reg. §§1.529A-0, 1.529A-1, 1.529A-2, 1.529A-3, 1.529A-4, 1.529A-5, 1.529A-6 and 1.529A-7 and amendments of Reg. §§1.511-2, 1.513-1 and 301.6011-2, regarding programs under The Stephen Beck, Jr., Achieving a Better Life Experience Act of 2014, are proposed.

AGENCY: Internal Revenue Service (IRS), Treasury.

ACTION: Notice of proposed rulemaking and notice of public hearing.

SUMMARY: This document contains proposed regulations under section 529A of the Internal Revenue Code that provide guidance regarding programs under The Stephen Beck, Jr., Achieving a Better Life Experience Act of 2014. Section 529A provides rules under which States or State agencies or instrumentalities may establish and maintain a new type of tax-favored savings program through which contributions may be made to the account of an eligible disabled individual to meet qualified disability expenses. These accounts also receive favorable treatment for purposes of certain means-tested Federal programs. In addition, these proposed regulations provide corresponding amendments to regulations under sections 511 and 513, with respect to unrelated business taxable income, sections 2501, 2503, 2511, 2642 and 2652, with respect to gift and generation-skipping transfer taxes, and section 6011, with respect to reporting requirements. This document also provides notice of a public hearing on these proposed regulations.

DATES: Comments must be received by September 21, 2015. Outlines of topics to be discussed at the public hearing scheduled for October 14, 2015, at 10 am, must be received by September 21, 2015.

ADDRESSES: Send submissions to: CC:PA:LPD:PR (REG-102837-15), room 5203, Internal Revenue Service, PO Box 7604, Ben Franklin Station, Washington DC 20044. Submissions may be hand delivered Monday through Friday between the hours of 8 a.m. and 4 p.m. to CC:PA:LPD:PR (REG-102837-15), Courier's Desk, Internal Revenue Service, 1111 Constitution Avenue NW, Washington, DC, or sent electronically via the Federal eRulemaking Portal at *http://www.regulations.gov* (IRS REG-102837-15). The public hearing will be held in the Auditorium, Internal Revenue Building, 1111 Constitution Avenue, NW, Washington, DC.

FOR FURTHER INFORMATION CONTACT: Concerning the proposed regulations under section 529A, Taina Edlund or Terri Harris, (202) 317-4541, or Sean Barnett, (202) 317-5800; concerning the proposed estate and gift tax regulations, Theresa Melchiorre, (202) 317-4643; concerning the reporting provisions under section 529A, Mark Bond, (202) 317-6844; concerning submissions of comments, the hearing, and/or to be placed on the building access list to attend the hearing, call Regina Johnson, (202) 317-6901 (not toll-free numbers).

SUPPLEMENTARY INFORMATION:

Paperwork Reduction Act

The collection of information contained in this notice of proposed rulemaking has been submitted to the Office of Management and Budget for review and approval in accordance with the Paperwork Reduction Act of 1995 (44 U.S.C. 3507(d)). Comments on the collection of information should be sent to the **Office of Management and Budget**, Attn: Desk Officer for the Department of the Treasury, Office of Information and Regulatory Affairs, Washington, DC 20503, with copies to the **Internal Revenue Service**, Attn: IRS Reports Clearance Officer, SE:W:CAR:MP:T:T:SP, Washington, DC 20224. Comments on the collection of information should be received by August 21, 2015.

Comments are specifically requested concerning:

Whether the proposed collection of information is necessary for the proper performance of the functions of the Internal Revenue Service, including whether the information will have practical utility;

The accuracy of the estimated burden associated with the proposed collection of information;

How the quality, utility, and clarity of the information to be collected may be enhanced;

How the burden of complying with the proposed collection of information may be minimized, including through forms of information technology; and

Estimates of capital or start-up costs and costs of operation, maintenance, and purchase of services to provide information.

The collection of information in the proposed regulations is in §§1.529A-2, 1.529A-5, 1.529A-6 and 1.529A-7. The collection of information flows from sections 529A(d)(1), (d)(2), (d)(3), (e)(1) and (e)(2) of the Internal Revenue Code (Code). Section 529A(d)(1) requires qualified ABLE programs to provide reports to the Secretary and to designated beneficiaries with respect to contributions, distributions, the return of excess contributions, and such other matters as the Secretary may require. Section 529A(d)(2) provides that the Secretary shall make available to the public reports containing aggregate information, by diagnosis and other relevant characteristics, on contributions and distributions from the qualified ABLE program. Section 529(d)(3) requires qualified ABLE. Programs to provide notice to the Secretary upon the establishment of an ABLE account, containing the name and State of residence of the designated beneficiary and such other information as the Secretary may require. Section 529A(e)(1) requires that a disability certification with respect to certain individuals be filed with the Secretary. Section 529A(e)(2) provides that the disability certification include a certification to the satisfaction of the Secretary that the individual has a medically determinable physical or mental impairment that occurred before the date on which the individual attained age 26 and also include a copy of a physician's diagnosis. The burden under §§1.529A-5 and 1.529A-6 is reflected in the burden under the new Form 5498-QA, "ABLE Account Contribution Information," and the new Form 1099-QA, "Distributions from ABLE Accounts," respectively.

The expected recordkeepers are programs described in section 529A, established and maintained by a State or a State agency or instrumentality and individuals with ABLE accounts.

Estimated number of recordkeepers: 10,050.

Estimated average annual burden hours per recordkeeper: 1.6 hours.

Estimated total annual recordkeeping burden: 16,080.

An agency may not conduct or sponsor, and a person is not required to respond to, a collection of information unless it displays a valid control number assigned by the Office of Management and Budget.

Books or records relating to a collection of information must be retained as long as their contents may become material in the administration of any internal revenue law. Generally, tax returns and return information are confidential, as required by 26 U.S.C. 6103.

Background

The Stephen Beck, Jr., Achieving a Better Life Experience (ABLE) Act of 2014, enacted on December 19, 2014, as part of The Tax Increase Prevention Act of 2014 (Public Law 113-295), added section 529A to the Internal Revenue Code. Congress recognized the special financial burdens borne by families raising children with disabilities and the fact that increased financial needs generally continue throughout the disabled person's lifetime. Section 101 of the ABLE Act confirms that one of the purposes of the Act is to "provide secure funding for disability-related expenses on behalf of designated beneficiaries with disabilities that will supplement, but not supplant, benefits" otherwise available to those individuals, whether through private sources, employment, public programs, or otherwise. Prior to the enactment of the ABLE Act, various types of tax-advantaged savings arrangements existed, but none adequately served the goal of promoting saving for these financial needs. Section 529A allows the creation of a qualified ABLE program by a State (or agency or instrumentality thereof) under which a separate ABLE account may be established for a disabled individual who is the designated beneficiary and owner of that account. Generally, contributions to that account are subject to both an annual and a cumulative limit, and, when made by a person other than the designated beneficiary, are treated as non-taxable gifts to the designated beneficiary. Distributions made from an ABLE account for qualified disability expenses of the designated beneficiary are not included in the designated beneficiary's gross income. The earnings portion of distributions from the ABLE account in excess of the qualified disability expenses is includible in the gross income of the designated beneficiary. An ABLE account may be used for the long-term benefit and/or short-term needs of the designated beneficiary.

Section 103 of the ABLE Act, while not a tax provision, is critical to achieving the goal of the ABLE Act of providing financial resources for the benefit of disabled individuals. Because so many of the programs that provide essential financial, occupational, and other resources and services to disabled individuals are available only to persons whose resources and income do not exceed relatively low dollar limits, section 103 generally provides that a designated beneficiary's ABLE account (specifically, its account balance, contributions to the account, and distributions from the account) is disregarded for purposes of determining the designated beneficiary's eligibility for and the amount of any assistance or benefit provided under certain means-tested Federal programs. However, in the case of the Supplemental Security Income program under title XVI of the Social Security Act, distributions for certain housing expenses are not disregarded, and the balance (including earnings) in an ABLE account is considered a resource of the designated beneficiary to the extent that balance exceeds $100,000. Section 103 also addresses the impact of an excess balance in an ABLE account on the designated beneficiary's eligibility under the Supplemental Security Income program and Medicaid.

Finally, section 104 of the ABLE Act addresses the treatment of ABLE accounts in bankruptcy proceedings.

Notice 2015-18, 2015-12 IRB 765 (March 23, 2015), provides that the section 529A guidance will confirm that the owner of the ABLE account is the designated beneficiary of the account, and that the person with signature authority over (if not the designated beneficiary of) the account may neither have nor acquire any beneficial interest in the ABLE account and must administer that account for the benefit of the designated beneficiary of that account. The Notice further provides that, in the event that state legislation creating ABLE programs enacted in accordance with section 529A prior to issuance of guidance does not fully comport with the guidance when issued, the Treasury Department and the IRS intend to provide transition relief to provide sufficient time to allow States to implement the changes necessary to avoid the disqualification of the program and of the ABLE accounts already established under the program.

The Treasury Department and the IRS reiterate that States that enact legislation creating an ABLE program in accordance with section 529A, and those individuals establishing ABLE accounts in accordance with such legislation, will not fail to receive the benefits of section 529A merely because the legislation or the account documents do not fully comport with the final regulations when they are issued. The Treasury Department and the IRS intend to provide transition relief to enable those State programs and accounts to be brought into compliance with the requirements in the final regulations, including providing sufficient time after issuance of the final regulations in order for changes to be implemented.

Explanation of Provisions

Qualification as an ABLE program

The proposed regulations provide guidance on the requirements a program must satisfy in order to be a qualified ABLE program described in section 529A. Specifically, in addition to other requirements, the program must: be established and maintained by a State or a State's agency or instrumentality; permit the establishment of an ABLE account only for a designated beneficiary who is a resident of that State, or a State contracting with that State for purposes of the ABLE program; permit the establishment of an ABLE account only for a designated beneficiary who is an eligible individual; limit a designated beneficiary to only one ABLE account, wherever located; permit contributions to an ABLE account established to meet the qualified disability expenses of the account's designated beneficiary; limit the nature and amount of contributions that can be made to an ABLE account; require a separate accounting for the ABLE account of each designated beneficiary with an ABLE account in the program; limit the designated beneficiary to no more than two opportunities in any calendar year to provide investment direction, whether directly or indirectly, for the ABLE account; and prohibit the pledging of an interest in an ABLE account as security for a loan.

Because each qualified ABLE program will have significant administrative obligations beyond what is required for the administration of qualified tuition programs under section 529 (on which section 529A was loosely modeled), and because the frequency of distributions from the ABLE accounts is likely to be far greater than those made from qualified tuition accounts, the proposed regulations expressly allow a qualified ABLE program or any of its contractors to contract with one or more Community Development Financial Institutions (CDFIs) that commonly serve disabled individuals and their families to provide one or more required services. For example, a CDFI could provide screening and verification of disabilities, certification of the qualified purpose of distributions, debit card services to facilitate distributions, and social data collection and reporting. A CDFI also may be able to obtain grants to defray the cost of administering the program. In general, if certified by the Treasury Department, a CDFI may receive a financial assistance award from the CDFI Fund that was established within the Treasury Department in 1994 to promote community development in economically distressed communities through investments in CDFIs across the country.

Established and maintained

The proposed regulations provide that a program is established by a State, or its agency or instrumentality, if the program is initiated by State statute or regulation, or by an act of a State official or agency with the authority to act on behalf of the State. A program is maintained by a State or its agency or instrumentality if: all the terms and conditions of the program are set by the State or its agency or instrumentality, and the State or its agency or instrumentality is actively involved on an ongoing basis in the administration of the program, including supervising all decisions relating to the investment of assets contributed to the program. The proposed regulations set forth factors that are relevant in determining whether a State, or its agency or instrumentality, is actively involved in the administration of the program. Included in the factors is the manner and extent to which it is permissible for the program to contract out for professional and financial services.

Establishment of an ABLE account

The proposed regulations provide that, consistent with the definition of a designated beneficiary in section 529A(e)(3), the designated beneficiary of an ABLE account is the eligible individual who establishes the account or an eligible individual who succeeded the original designated beneficiary. The proposed regulations also provide that the designated beneficiary is the owner of that account.

The Treasury Department and the IRS recognize, however, that certain eligible individuals may be unable to establish an account themselves. Therefore, the proposed regulations clarify that, if the eligible individual cannot establish the account, the eligible individual's agent under a power of attorney or, if none, his or her parent or legal guardian may establish the ABLE account for that eligible individual. For purposes of these proposed regulations, because each of these individuals would be acting on behalf of the designated beneficiary, references to actions of the designated beneficiary, such as opening or managing the ABLE account, are deemed to include the actions of any other such individual with signature authority over the ABLE account. The proposed regulations also provide that, consistent with Notice 2015-18, a person other than the designated beneficiary with signature authority over the account of the designated beneficiary may neither have, nor acquire, any beneficial interest in the account during the designated beneficiary's lifetime and must administer the account for the benefit of the designated beneficiary.

At the time an ABLE account is created for a designated beneficiary, the designated beneficiary must provide evidence that the designated beneficiary is an eligible individual as defined in section 529A(e)(1). Section 529A(e)(1) provides that an individual is an eligible individual for a taxable year if, during that year, either the individual is entitled to benefits based on blindness or disability under title II or XVI of the Social Security Act and the blindness or disability occurred before the date on which the individual attained age 26, or a disability certification meeting specified requirements is filed with the Secretary. If an individual is asserting he or she is entitled to benefits based on blindness or disability under title II or XVI of the Social Security Act and the blindness or disability occurred before the date on which the individual attained age 26, the proposed regulations provide that each qualified ABLE program may determine the evidence required to establish the individual's eligibility. For example, a qualified ABLE program could require the individual to provide a copy of a benefit verification letter from the Social Security Administration and allow the individual to certify, under penalties of perjury, that the blindness or disability occurred before the date on which the individual attained age 26.

Alternatively, the designated beneficiary must submit the disability certification when opening the ABLE account. Consistent with section 529A(e)(2), the proposed regulations provide that a disability certification is a certification by the designated beneficiary that he or she: (1) has a medically determinable physical or mental impairment, which results in marked or severe functional limitations, and which (i) can be expected to result in death or (ii) has lasted or can be expected to last for a continuous period of not less than 12 months; or (2) is blind (within the meaning of section 1614(a)(2) of the Social Security Act) and that such blindness or disability occurred before the date on which the individual attained age 26. The certification must include a copy of the individual's diagnosis relating to the individual's relevant impairment or impairments, signed by a licensed physician (as defined in section 1861(r) of the Social Security Act, 42 U.S.C. 1395x(r)). Consistent with other IRS filing requirements, the proposed regulations also provide that the certification must be signed under penalties of perjury.

While evidence of an individual's eligibility based on entitlement to Social Security benefits should be objectively verifiable, the sufficiency of a disability certification that an individual is an eligible individual for purposes of section 529A might not be as easy to establish. Nevertheless, the Treasury Department and the IRS wish to facilitate an eligible individual's ability to establish an ABLE account without undue delay. Therefore, the proposed regulations provide that an eligible individual must present the disability certification, accompanied by the diagnosis, to the qualified ABLE program to demonstrate eligibility to establish an ABLE account. The proposed regulations further provide that the disability certification will be deemed to be filed with the Secretary once the qualified ABLE program has received the disability certification or a disability certification has been deemed to have been received under the rules of the qualified ABLE program, which information the qualified ABLE program, as discussed further below, will file with the IRS in accordance with the filing requirements under § 1.529A-5(c)(2)(iv).

Disability determination

Consistent with section 529A(g)(4), the Treasury Department and the IRS have consulted with the Commissioner of Social Security regarding disability certifications and determinations of disability. For purposes of the disability certification, the proposed regulations provide that the phrase "marked and severe functional limitations" means the standard of disability in the Social Security Act for children claiming benefits under the Supplemental Security Income for the Aged, Blind, and Disabled (SSI) program based on disability, but without regard to the age of the individual. This phrase refers to a level of severity of an impairment that meets, medically equals, or functionally equals the listings in the Listing of Impairments (the listings) in appendix 1 of subpart P of 20 CFR part 404. (See 20 CFR 416.906, 416.924 and 416.926a). This listing developed and used by the Social Security Administration describes for each of the major body systems impairments that cause marked and severe functional limitations. Most body system sections are in two parts: an introduction, followed by the specific listings. The introduction contains information relevant to the use of the listings with respect to that body system, such as examples of common impairments in the body system and definitions used in the listings for that body system. The introduction may also include specific criteria for establishing a diagnosis, confirming the existence of an impairment, or establishing that an impairment satisfies the criteria of a particular listing with respect to the body system. The specific listings that follow the introduction for each body system specify the objective medical and other findings needed to satisfy the criteria of that listing. Most of the listed impairments are permanent or expected to result in death, although some listings state a specific period of time for which an impairment will meet the listing.

An impairment is medically equivalent to a listing if it is at least equal in severity and duration to the severity and duration of any listing. An impairment that does not meet or medically equal any listing may result in limitations that functionally equal the listings if it results in marked limitations in two domains of functioning or an extreme limitation in one domain of functioning, as explained in 20 CFR 416.926a. In addition, the proposed regulations provide that certain conditions, specifically those listed in the Compassionate Allowances Conditions list maintained by the Social Security Administration, are deemed to meet the requirements of an impairment sufficient for a disability certification without a physician's diagnosis, provided that the condition was present before the date on which the individual attained age 26. The proposed regulations also provide the flexibility from time to time to identify additional impairments that will be deemed to meet these requirements. The Treasury Department and the IRS request comments on what other conditions should be deemed to meet the requirements of section 529A(e)(2)(A)(i).

Change in eligible individual status

The Treasury Department and the IRS recognize that there may be circumstances in which a designated beneficiary ceases to be an eligible individual but subsequently regains that status. Consequently, the Treasury Department and the IRS believe that it is appropriate to permit continuation of the ABLE account (albeit with some changes in the applicable rules) during the period in which a designated beneficiary is not an eligible individual as long as the designated beneficiary was an eligible individual when the account was established. Therefore, if at any time a designated beneficiary no longer meets the definition of an eligible individual, his or her ABLE account remains an ABLE account to which all of the provisions of the ABLE Act continue to apply, and no (taxable) distribution of the account balance is deemed to occur. However, the proposed regulations provide that, beginning on the first day of the taxable year following the taxable year in which the designated beneficiary ceased to be an eligible individual, no contributions to the ABLE account may be accepted. If the designated beneficiary subsequently again becomes an eligible individual, then additional contributions may be accepted subject to the applicable annual and cumulative limits. In this way, the Treasury Department and the IRS intend to prevent a deemed distribution of the ABLE account (and preserve the account's qualification as an ABLE account for all purposes) if, for example, the disease that caused the impairment goes into a temporary remission, and to preserve the ABLE account with its tax-free distributions for qualified disability expenses if the impairment resumes and once again qualifies the designated beneficiary as an eligible individual. Note that expenses will not be qualified disability expenses if they are incurred at a time when a designated beneficiary is neither disabled nor blind within the meaning of § 1.529A-1(b)(9)(A) or § 1.529A-2(e)(1)(i).

The proposed regulations provide flexibility regarding annual recertifications. A qualified ABLE program generally must require annual recertifications that the designated beneficiary continues to satisfy the definition of an eligible individual. However, a qualified ABLE program may deem an annual recertification to have been provided in appropriate circumstances. For example, a qualified ABLE program may permit certification by an individual that he or she has a permanent disability to be considered to meet the annual requirement to present a certification to the qualified ABLE program. In other cases, a program may require all of the same evidence needed for the initial disability certification when the account was established, may require a statement under penalties of perjury that nothing has changed that would change the original disability certification, or may incorporate some other method of ensuring that the designated beneficiary continuously qualifies as an eligible individual. Alternatively, a qualified ABLE program may identify certain impairments or categories of impairments for which recertifications will be deemed to have been made annually to the qualified ABLE program unless and until the qualified ABLE program provides otherwise (for example, if a cure is discovered for a disease that causes an impairment). An initial certification or recertification that meets the requirements of the qualified ABLE program will be deemed to have met the requirement of section 529A(e)(1)(B). The Treasury Department and the IRS request comments regarding how a qualified ABLE program will be able to demonstrate eligibility in subsequent years if it allows deemed recertifications.

Contributions to an ABLE account

The proposed regulations provide that, as a general rule, all contributions to an ABLE account must be made in cash. The proposed regulations provide that a qualified ABLE program may accept cash contributions in the form of cash or a check, money order, credit card payment, or other similar method of payment. In addition, the proposed regulations provide that the total contributions to an ABLE account in the designated beneficiary's taxable year, other than amounts received in rollovers and program-to-program transfers, must not exceed the amount of the annual per-donee gift tax exclusion under section 2503(b) in effect for that calendar year (currently $14,000) in which the designated beneficiary's taxable year begins. Finally, a qualified ABLE program must provide adequate safeguards to ensure that total contributions to an ABLE account (including the proceeds from a preexisting ABLE account) do not exceed that State's limit for aggregate contributions under its qualified tuition program.

To implement these requirements, the proposed regulations provide that a qualified ABLE program must return contributions in excess of the annual gift tax exclusion (excess contributions) to the contributor(s), along with all net income attributable to those excess contributions. Similarly, the proposed regulations also require the return of all contributions, along with all net income attributable to those contributions, that caused an ABLE account to exceed the limit established by the State for its qualified tuition program (excess aggregate contributions). If an excess contribution or excess aggregate contribution is returned to a contributor other than the designated beneficiary, the qualified ABLE program must notify the designated beneficiary of such return at the time of the return. The proposed regulations further provide that such returns of excess contributions and excess aggregate contributions must be received by the contributor(s) on or before the due date (including extensions) of the designated beneficiary's income tax return for the year in which the excess contributions were made or in the year the excess aggregate contributions caused amounts in the ABLE account to exceed the limit in effect under section 529A(b)(6), respectively. The proposed regulations provide rules for determining the net income attributable to a contribution made to an ABLE account, and also provide that these excess contributions and excess aggregate contributions must be returned to contributors on a last-in, first-out basis. In the case of contributions that exceed the annual gift tax exclusion, a failure to return such excess contributions within the time period discussed in this paragraph will result in the imposition on the designated beneficiary of a 6 percent excise tax under section 4973(a)(6) on the amount of excess contributions. As part of a planned revision of IRA regulations, the Treasury Department and the IRS intend to propose regulations under section 4973 to reflect that ABLE accounts are subject to section 4973.

Application of gift tax to contributions to an ABLE account

Gift tax consequences may arise from contributions to an ABLE account even though the aggregate amount of such contributions to an ABLE account from all contributors may not exceed the annual exclusion amount under section 2503(b) applicable to any single contributor. Specifically, if a contributor makes other gifts to a designated beneficiary in addition to the gift to the designated beneficiary's ABLE account, the contributor's total gifts made to the designated beneficiary in that year could give rise to a gift tax liability.

Contributions may be made by any person. The term *person* is defined in section 7701(a)(1) to include an individual, trust, estate, partnership, association, company, or corporation. Therefore, for purposes of section 529A(b)(1)(A), a person would include an individual and each of the entities described in section 7701(a)(1). Under section 2501(a)(1), the gift tax applies only to gifts by individuals, but it also applies to gifts made directly or indirectly. As a result, a gift made by a trust, estate, association, company, corporation, or partnership is treated as having been made by the owner(s) of that entity. For example, a gift from a corporation to a designated beneficiary is treated as a gift from the shareholders of the corporation to the designated beneficiary. *See Example (1)* of §25.2511-1(h). Accordingly, the proposed regulations provide that, for purposes of sections 529A(b)(1)(A) and 529A(c)(1)(C), a contribution by a corporation is treated as a gift by its shareholders and a contribution by a partnership is treated as a gift by its partners. This rule also applies to trusts, estates, associations, and companies. *See* section 2511 and §25.2511-1(c).

The legislative history of section 529A suggests that a "person" described in section 529A(b)(1)(A) includes the designated beneficiary of an ABLE account. *See* 160 CONG. REC. H7051, H8317, H8318, H8321, H8322 (2014). A person may transfer his or her property into an account, such as a bank account or a trust, for his or her benefit and retain dominion and control over the property transferred. Because an individual cannot make a transfer of property to himself or herself and a transfer of property is a fundamental requirement for a completed gift, this type of transfer from a person's own property cannot be treated as a completed gift for tax purposes. *See* §25.2511-2(b) and (c). Therefore, the proposed regulations provide that any contribution by a designated beneficiary to a qualified ABLE program benefitting the designated beneficiary is not treated as a completed gift. Because the designated beneficiary remains the owner of the account for purposes of chapter 12, if the designated beneficiary transfers the funds in the account to another person as permitted under these proposed regulations, the designated beneficiary making the transfer is the donor for purposes of chapter 12 and the transferor for generation-skipping transfer tax purposes of chapter 13.

Distributions

If distributions from an ABLE account do not exceed the designated beneficiary's qualified disability expenses, no amount is includible in the designated beneficiary's gross income. Otherwise, the earnings portion of the distributions from the ABLE account as determined in the manner provided under section 72, reduced by the product of such earnings portion and the ratio of the amount of the distributions for qualified disability expenses to total distributions, is includible in the gross income of the designated beneficiary to the extent not otherwise excluded from gross income. As required by section 529A(c)(1)(D), the proposed regulations provide that, for purposes of applying section 72 to amounts distributed from an ABLE account: (1) all distributions during a taxable year are treated as one distribution; and (2) the value of the contract, income on the contract, and investment in the contract are computed as of the close of the calendar year in which the designated beneficiary's taxable year begins.

The proposed regulations also provide that, in addition to the income tax on the portion of a distribution included in gross income, an additional tax of 10 percent of the amount includible in gross income is imposed. This additional tax does not apply, however, to distributions on or after the designated beneficiary's death or to returns of excess contributions, excess aggregate contributions, or contributions to additional purported ABLE accounts made by the due date (including extensions) of the designated beneficiary's tax return for the year in which the relevant contributions were made.

Section 529A(c)(1)(C) addresses the tax consequences of the rollover of an ABLE account to an ABLE account for the same designated beneficiary maintained under a different State's qualified ABLE program, as well as a change of designated beneficiary. The proposed regulations describe with respect to these two situations the circumstances in which amounts will not be includible in income. The first is any change of designated beneficiary if the new designated beneficiary is both (1) an eligible individual for his or her taxable year in which the change is made and (2) a sibling of the former designated beneficiary. For purposes of these proposed regulations, a sibling also includes step-siblings and half-siblings, whether by blood or by adoption. The proposed regulations provide that a qualified ABLE program must permit a change of designated beneficiary, as long as the change is made prior to the death of the former designated beneficiary and as long as the successor designated beneficiary is an eligible individual. Because the designated beneficiary will be subject to gift and/or generation-skipping transfer tax if the successor designated beneficiary is not a sibling of the designated beneficiary, the Treasury Department and the IRS request comments regarding whether the final regulations should permit States to require that a successor designated beneficiary also must be a sibling of the designated beneficiary.

The second situation in which a distribution is not included in gross income arises if a distribution to the designated beneficiary of the ABLE account is paid, not later than the 60th day after the date of the distribution, to another (or the same) ABLE account for the benefit of the designated beneficiary or for the benefit of an eligible individual who is a sibling of the designated beneficiary. However, the preceding sentence does not apply to such a distribution that occurs within 12 months of a previous rollover to another ABLE account for the same designated beneficiary.

The Treasury Department and the IRS have been asked whether a qualified tuition account under section 529 may be rolled into an ABLE account for the same designated beneficiary free of tax. Because such a distribution to the ABLE account would not constitute a qualified higher education expense under section 529, the Treasury Department and the IRS do not believe they have the authority to allow such a transfer on a tax-free basis.

In addition, the proposed regulations authorize a qualified ABLE program to allow program-to-program transfers to effectuate a change of qualified ABLE program or a change of designated beneficiary to another eligible individual. Such a direct transfer is neither a distribution taxed in accordance with section 72 nor an excess contribution. A program-to-program transfer also could be accomplished, if permitted by the qualified ABLE program, through a check delivered to the designated beneficiary but negotiable only by the qualified State program under which the new ABLE account is being established.

The Treasury Department and the IRS recognize that moving funds by use of a program-to-program transfer may be preferable to moving them by a rollover because a rollover, even if made within the permissible 60-day period, may jeopardize the designated beneficiary's eligibility for certain benefits under various means-tested programs. Moreover, a direct program-to-program transfer could facilitate the efficient transfer of all relevant information regarding the application of contribution limits and the total amount of accumulated earnings that will also apply to the new account. The Treasury Department and the IRS request comments as to whether and to what extent a qualified ABLE program should be permitted to require that funds from another State's ABLE program be accepted only through program-to-program transfers.

Qualified disability expenses

Section 529A(e)(5) defines a *qualified disability expense*. Consistent with that subsection, the proposed regulations provide that qualified disability expenses are expenses that relate to the designated beneficiary's blindness or disability and are for the benefit of that designated beneficiary in maintaining or improving his or her health, independence, or quality of life. Such expenses include, but are not limited to, expenses for education, housing, transportation, employment training and support, assistive technology and personal support services, health, prevention and wellness, financial management and administrative services, legal fees, expenses for oversight and monitoring, funeral and burial expenses, and other expenses that may be identified from time to time in future guidance published in the Internal Revenue Bulletin. As previously stated, expenses incurred at a time when a designated beneficiary is neither disabled nor blind within the meaning of the proposed regulations are not qualified disability expenses.

In order to implement the legislative purpose of assisting eligible individuals in maintaining or improving their health, independence, or quality of life, the Treasury Department and the IRS conclude that the term "qualified disability expenses" should be broadly construed to permit the inclusion of basic living expenses and should not be limited to expenses for items for which there is a medical necessity or which provide no benefits to others in addition to the benefit to the eligible individual. For example, expenses for common items such as smart phones could be considered qualified disability expenses if they are an effective and safe communication or navigation aid for a child with autism. The Treasury Department and the IRS request comments regarding what types of expenses should be considered qualified disability expenses and under what circumstances. The proposed regulations authorize the identification of additional types of qualified disability expenses in guidance published in the Internal Revenue Bulletin. *See* §601.601(d)(2). A qualified ABLE program must establish safeguards to distinguish between distributions used for the payment of qualified disability expenses and other distributions, and to permit the identification of the amounts distributed for housing expenses as that term is defined for purposes of the Supplemental Security Income program of the Social Security Administration.

Limitation on number of ABLE accounts of a designated beneficiary

Section 529A(c)(4) generally provides that, except with respect to certain rollovers, once an ABLE account has been established for a designated beneficiary, no account subsequently established for that same designated beneficiary may qualify as an ABLE account. The proposed regulations provide that, except with respect to rollovers and program-to-program transfers, no designated beneficiary may have more than one ABLE account in existence at the same time, but provides that a prior ABLE account that has been closed does not prohibit the subsequent creation of another ABLE account for the same designated beneficiary. A qualified ABLE program must obtain a verification from the eligible individual, signed under penalties of perjury, that he or she has no other ABLE account (except in the case of a rollover or program-to-program transfer). The proposed regulations provide that, in the event that any additional ABLE account is opened for a designated beneficiary with an ABLE account already in existence, only the first such account created for that designated beneficiary qualifies as an ABLE account, and each other account is treated for all purposes as being an account of the designated beneficiary that is not an ABLE account under a qualified ABLE program. The proposed regulations also provide, however, that a return, in accordance with the rules that apply to returns of excess contributions and excess aggregate contributions under §1.529A-2(g)(4), of the entire balance of a second or other subsequent account received by the contributor(s) on or before the due date (including extensions) for filing the designated beneficiary's income tax return for the year in which the account was opened and contributions to the second or subsequent account were made will not be treated as a gift or distribution to the designated beneficiary for purposes of section 529A.

The prohibition of multiple ABLE accounts, however, does not apply to prevent a timely rollover or program-to-program transfer of the designated beneficiary's account to an ABLE account under a different qualified ABLE program.

Residency requirements

Consistent with section 529A(b)(1)(C), the proposed regulations require that an ABLE account for a designated beneficiary may be established only under the qualified ABLE program of the State in which that designated beneficiary is a resident or with which the State of the designated beneficiary's residence has contracted for the provision of ABLE accounts. If a State does not establish and maintain a qualified ABLE program, it may contract with another State to provide an ABLE program for its residents. The statute is silent as to whether a designated beneficiary must move his or her existing ABLE account when the designated beneficiary changes his or her residence. The Treasury Department and the IRS are concerned about imposing undue administrative burdens and costs on designated beneficiaries who frequently change State residency, such as members of military families. Therefore, the proposed regulations provide that a qualified ABLE program may permit a designated beneficiary to continue to maintain his or her ABLE account that was created in that State, even after the designated beneficiary is no longer a resident of that State. However, in order to enforce the one ABLE account limitation and in accordance with section 529A(g)(1), the proposed regulations provide that, other than in the case of a rollover or a program-to-program transfer of a designated beneficiary's ABLE account, a qualified ABLE program must require the designated beneficiary to verify, under penalties of perjury, when creating an ABLE account that the account being established is the designated beneficiary's only ABLE account. For example, the eligible individual could be required to check a box providing such verification on a form used to establish the account. The Treasury Department and the IRS are concerned that without such safeguards individuals could inadvertently establish two accounts with adverse tax consequences due to the loss of ABLE account status for the second account and expect qualified ABLE programs to establish safeguards to ensure that the required limit of one ABLE account per designated beneficiary is not violated.

Investment direction

Section 529A(b)(4) states that a program shall not be treated as a qualified ABLE program unless it provides that the designated beneficiary may directly or indirectly direct the investment of any contributions to the program or any earnings thereon no more than two times in any calendar year. A program will not violate this requirement merely because it permits a designated beneficiary or a person with signature authority over a designated beneficiary's account to serve as one of the program's board members or employees, or as a board member or employee of a contractor that the program hires to perform administrative services.

Cap on contributions

Section 529A(b)(6) provides that a qualified ABLE program must provide adequate safeguards to prevent aggregate contributions on behalf of a designated beneficiary in excess of the limit established by the State under section 529(b)(6) relating to Qualified State Tuition Programs. The proposed regulations provide a safe harbor that permits a qualified ABLE program to satisfy this requirement regarding total cumulative contributions if the program prohibits any additional contributions to an account as soon as the account balance reaches the specified contribution limit under such State's program established under section 529. Once the account balance falls below the prescribed limit, contributions may resume, subject to the same limitation. The Treasury Department and the IRS believe that recommencement of contributions is appropriate based on the nature and purposes of the ABLE program.

Gift and generation-skipping transfer (GST) taxes

The proposed regulations provide that contributions to an ABLE account by a person other than the designated beneficiary are treated as completed gifts to the designated beneficiary of the account, and that such gifts are neither gifts of a future interest nor a qualified transfer under section 2503(e). Accordingly, no distribution from an ABLE account to the designated beneficiary of that account is treated as a taxable gift. Finally, neither gift nor GST taxes apply to the change of designated beneficiary of an ABLE account, as long as the new designated beneficiary is an eligible individual who is a sibling of the former designated beneficiary.

Distribution on death

The proposed regulations provide that, upon the death of the designated beneficiary, all amounts remaining in the ABLE account are includible in the designated beneficiary's gross estate for purposes of the estate tax. *See* section 2031. Further, the proposed regulations cross-reference section 2053 for purposes of determining the deductibility by the designated beneficiary's estate of amounts payable from the ABLE account to satisfy claims by creditors such as a State and also cross-reference section 2652(a)(1) for treatment of the deceased designated beneficiary as the transferor of any property remaining in the ABLE account that may pass to a beneficiary.

Pursuant to section 529A(f), a qualified ABLE program must provide that, upon the designated beneficiary's death, any State may file a claim (either with the person with signature authority over the ABLE account or the executor of the designated beneficiary's estate as defined in section 2203) for the amount of the total medical assistance paid for the designated beneficiary under the State's Medicaid plan after the establishment of the ABLE account. The amount paid in satisfaction of such a claim is not a taxable distribution from the ABLE account. Further, the amount is to be paid only after the payment of all outstanding payments due for the qualified disability expenses of the designated beneficiary and is to be reduced by the amount of all premiums paid by or on behalf of the designated beneficiary to a Medicaid Buy-In program under that State's Medicaid plan.

Unrelated business taxable income and filing requirements

A qualified ABLE program generally is exempt from income taxation. A qualified ABLE program, however, is subject to the taxes imposed by section 511 relating to the imposition of tax on unrelated business taxable income ("UBTI"). For purposes of this tax, certain administrative and other fees do not constitute unrelated business income to the ABLE program. A qualified ABLE program is not required to file Form 990, "Return of Organization Exempt From Income Tax," but will be required to file Form 990-T, "Exempt Organization Business Income Tax Return," if a filing would be required under the rules of §§ 1.6012-2(e) and 1.6012-3(a)(5) if the ABLE program were an organization described in those sections.

Reporting requirements

The proposed regulations set forth recordkeeping and reporting requirements. A qualified ABLE program must maintain records that enable the program to account to the Secretary with respect to all contributions, distributions, returns of excess contributions or additional accounts, income earned, and account balances for any designated beneficiary's ABLE account. In addition, a qualified ABLE program must report to the Secretary the establishment of each ABLE account, including the name and residence of the designated beneficiary, and other relevant information regarding the account that is included on the new Form 5498-QA, "ABLE Account Contribution Information." It is anticipated that the qualified ABLE program will report if the eligible individual has presented an adequate disability certification, accompanied by a diagnosis, to demonstrate eligibility to establish an account. Information regarding distributions will be reported on the new Form 1099-QA, "Distributions from ABLE Accounts." The proposed regulations contain more detail on how the information must be reported.

In addition, section 529A(b)(3) requires that a qualified ABLE program provide separate accounting for each designated beneficiary. Separate accounting requires that contributions for the benefit of a designated beneficiary, as well as earnings attributable to those contributions, are allocated to that designated beneficiary's account. Whether or not a program ordinarily provides each designated beneficiary an annual account statement showing the income and transactions related to the account, the program must give this information to the designated beneficiary upon request.

Section 529A(d)(4) provides that States are required to submit electronically to the Commissioner of Social Security, on a monthly basis and in the manner specified by the Commissioner of Social Security, statements on relevant distributions and account balances from all ABLE accounts. The report of the Committee on Ways and Means (H.R. Rep. No. 113-614, pt. 1, at 15 (2014)) indicates that States should work with the Commissioner of Social Security to identify data elements for the monthly reports, including the type of qualified disability expenses.

Effective Date/Applicability Date

These regulations are proposed to be effective as of the date of publication of the Treasury decision adopting these rules as final regulations in the **Federal Register**. These rules, when adopted as final regulations, will apply to taxable years beginning after December 31, 2014. The reporting requirements of §§ 1.529A-5 through 1.529A-7 will apply to information returns required to be filed, and payee statements required to be furnished, after December 31, 2015. Until the issuance of final regulations, taxpayers and qualified ABLE programs may rely on these proposed regulations.

Special Analyses

It has been determined that this notice of proposed rulemaking is not a significant regulatory action as defined in Executive Order 12866, as supplemented by Executive Order 13563. It has also been determined that section 553(b) of the Administrative Procedure Act (5 U.S.C. chapter 5) does not apply to this regulation and, because the regulation does not impose a collection of information on small entities, the Regulatory Flexibility Act (5 U.S.C. chapter 6) does not apply. This regulation, if adopted, would primarily affect states and individuals and therefore would not have a significant economic impact on a substantial number of small entities. Therefore, a regulatory flexibility analysis is not required. Pursuant to section 7805(f) of the Internal Revenue Code, this notice of proposed rulemaking will be submitted to the Chief Counsel for Advocacy of the Small Business Administration for comment on its impact on small businesses.

Comments and Public Hearing

Before these proposed regulations are adopted as final regulations, consideration will be given to any comments that are timely submitted to the IRS as prescribed in this preamble under the "Addresses" heading. The Treasury Department and the IRS request comments on all aspects of the proposed rules. All comments will be available at *www.regulations.gov* or upon request. A public hearing will be scheduled if requested in writing by any person that timely submits written or electronic comments. If a public hearing is scheduled, notice of the date, time, and place for the hearing will be published in the **Federal Register**.

A public hearing has been scheduled for **October 14, 2015**, beginning at **10:00 am** in the Auditorium, Internal Revenue Building, 1111 Constitution Avenue, NW, Washington, DC. Due to building security procedures, visitors must enter at the Constitution Avenue entrance. In addition, all visitors must present photo identification to enter the building. Because of access restrictions, visitors will not be admitted beyond the immediate entrance area more than 30 minutes before the hearing starts. For information about having your name placed on the building access list to attend the hearing, see the "FOR FURTHER INFORMATION CONTACT" section of this preamble.

The rules of 26 CFR 601.601(a)(3) apply to the hearing. Persons who wish to present oral comments at the hearing must submit written comments by September 21, 2015, and an outline of the topics to be discussed and the time to be devoted to each topic (signed original and eight (8) copies) by September 21, 2015. Submit a signed paper original and eight (8) copies or an electronic copy. A period of 10 minutes will be allotted to each person for making comments. An agenda showing the scheduling of the speakers will be prepared after the deadline for receiving outlines has passed. Copies of the agenda will be available free of charge at the hearing.

Drafting Information

The principal authors of these regulations are Terri Harris and Sean Barnett, Office of Associate Chief Counsel (Tax Exempt and Government Entities). However, other personnel from the Treasury Department and the IRS participated in the development of these regulations.

[¶ 49,657] **Proposed Amendments of Regulations (REG-115452-14)**, published in the Federal Register on July 23, 2015 (corrected 8/19/2015).

[Code Sec. 707]

Partnerships: Partners: Transactions between partner and partnership: Transfers of property: Disguised payment for services.—Reg. § 1.707-2 and amendments of Reg. § § 1.707-0, 1.707-1, 1.707-9 and 1.736-1, relating to disguised payments for services under section 707(a)(2)(A) of the Internal Revenue Code, are proposed.

AGENCY: Internal Revenue Service (IRS), Treasury

ACTION: Notice of proposed rulemaking.

SUMMARY: This document contains proposed regulations relating to disguised payments for services under section 707(a)(2)(A) of the Internal Revenue Code. The proposed regulations provide guidance to partnerships and their partners regarding when an arrangement will be treated as a disguised payment for services. This document also proposes conforming modifications to the regulations governing guaranteed payments under section 707(c). Additionally, this document provides notice of proposed modifications to Rev. Procs. 93-27 and 2001-43 relating to the issuance of interests in partnership profits to service providers.

DATES: Written and electronic comments and requests for a public hearing must be received by October 21, 2015.

ADDRESSES: Send submissions to CC:PA:LPD:PR (REG-115452-14), room 5203, Internal Revenue Service, PO Box 7604, Ben Franklin Station, Washington, DC 20044. Submissions may be hand-delivered Monday through Friday between the hours of 8 a.m. and 4 p.m. to CC:PA:LPD:PR (REG-115452-14), Courier's Desk, Internal Revenue Service, 1111 Constitution Avenue, N.W., Washington, DC, 20224 or sent electronically, via the Federal eRulemaking Portal at *http://www.regulations.gov* (indicate IRS and REG-115452-14).

FOR FURTHER INFORMATION CONTACT: Concerning submissions of comments, Oluwafunmilayo (Funmi) Taylor (202) 517-6901; concerning the proposed regulations, Jaclyn M. Goldberg (202) 317-6850 (not toll-free numbers).

SUPPLEMENTARY INFORMATION:

Background

Generally, under the statutory framework of Subchapter K of the Code, an allocation or distribution between a partnership and a partner for the provision of services can be treated in one of three ways: (1) a distributive share under section 704(b); (2) a guaranteed payment under section 707(c); or (3) as a transaction in which a partner has rendered services to the partnership in its capacity as other than a partner under section 707(a).

Distributive Share Treatment

Partnership allocations that are determined with regard to partnership income and that are made to a partner for services rendered by the partner in its capacity as a partner are generally treated as distributive shares of partnership income, taxable under the general rules of sections 702, 703, and 704. In some cases, the right to a distributive share may qualify as a profits interest defined in Rev. Proc. 93-27, 1993-2 C.B. 343. Rev. Proc. 93-27, clarified by Rev. Proc. 2001-43, 2001-2 C.B. 191, provides guidance on the treatment of the receipt of a profits interest for services provided to or for the benefit of the partnership.

Arrangements subject to sections 707(c) or 707(a)(1).

In 1954, Congress added section 707 to the Code to clarify transactions between a partner and a partnership. Section 707(a) addresses arrangements in which a partner engages with the partnership other than in its capacity as a partner. The legislative history to section 707(a) provides the general rule that a partner who engages in a transaction with the partnership, other than in its capacity as a partner is treated as though it were not a partner. The provision was intended to apply to the sale of property by the partner to the partnership, the purchase of property by the partner from the partnership, and the rendering of services by the partner to the partnership or by the partnership to the partner. H.R. Rep. No. 1337, 83d Cong., 2d Sess. 227 (1954) (House Report); S. Rep. No. 1622, 83d Cong., 2d Sess. 387 (1954) (Senate Report).

Congress simultaneously added section 707(c) to address payments to partners of the partnership acting in their partner capacity. Section 707(c) provides that to the extent determined without regard to the income of the partnership, payment to a partner for services shall be considered as made to a person who is not a partner, but only for purposes of sections 61(a) and 162(a). The Senate Report and the House Report provide that a fixed salary, payable without regard to partnership income, to a partner who renders services to the partnership is a guaranteed payment. The amount of the payment shall be included in the partner's gross income, and shall not be considered a distributive share of income or gain. A partner who is guaranteed a minimum annual amount for its services shall be treated as receiving a fixed payment in that amount. House Report at 227; Senate Report at 387.

In 1956, the Treasury Department and the IRS issued additional guidance under § 1.707-1 relating to a partner not acting in its capacity as a partner under section 707(a) and to guaranteed payments under section 707(c). See TD 6175. However, it remained unclear when a partner's services to the partnership were rendered in a non-partner capacity under section 707(a) rather than in a partner capacity under section 707(c).

In 1975, the Tax Court distinguished sections 707(a) and 707(c) payments in *Pratt v. Commissioner*, 64 T.C. 204 (1975), *aff'd* in part, *rev'd* in part, 550 F.2d 1023 (5th Cir. 1977). In *Pratt*, the general partners in two limited partnerships formed to purchase, develop, and operate two shopping centers received a fixed percentage of gross rentals in exchange for the performance of managerial services. The Tax Court held that these payments were not guaranteed payments under section 707(c) because they were computed based on a percentage of gross rental income and therefore were not paid without regard to partnership income. The Tax Court further held that section 707(a) did not apply because the general partners performed managerial duties in their partner capacities in accordance with their basic duties under the partnership agreement. On appeal, the Fifth Circuit affirmed the Tax Court's decision. The Fifth Circuit reasoned that Congress enacted section 707(a) to apply to partners who perform services for the partnership that are outside the scope of the partnership's activities. The Court indicated that if the partner performs services that the partnership itself provides, then the compensation to the service provider is merely a rearrangement among the partners of their distributive shares in the partnership income.

In response to the decision in *Pratt*, the Treasury Department and the IRS issued Rev. Rul. 81-300, 1981-2 C.B. 143 and Rev. Rul. 81-301, 1981-2 C.B. 144 to clarify the treatment of transactions under sections 707(a) and 707(c). As in the *Pratt* case, Rev. Rul. 81-300 considers a partnership formed to purchase, develop, and operate a shopping center. The partnership agreement required the general partners to contribute their time, managerial abilities, and best efforts to the partnership. In return for these services, the general partners received a fee equal to five percent of the partnership's gross rental income. The ruling concluded that the taxpayers performed managerial services in their capacities as general partners, and characterized the management fees as guaranteed payments under section 707(c). The ruling provides that, although guaranteed payments under section 707(c) frequently involve a fixed amount, they are not limited to fixed amounts. Thus, the ruling concluded that a payment for services determined by reference to an item of gross income will be a guaranteed payment if, on the basis of all facts and circumstances, the payment is compensation rather than a share of profits.

Rev. Rul. 81-301 describes a limited partnership which has two classes of general partners. The first class of general partner (director general partners) had complete control over the management, conduct, and operation of partnership activities. The second class of general partner (adviser general partner) rendered to the partnership services that were substantially the same as those that the adviser general partner rendered to other persons as an independent contractor. The adviser general partner received 10 percent of daily gross income in exchange for the management services it provided to the partnership. Rev. Rul. 81-301 held that the adviser general partner received its gross income allocation in a non-partner capacity under section 707(a) because the adviser general partner provided similar services to other parties, was subject to removal by the director general partners, was not personally liable to the other partners for any losses, and its management was supervised by the director general partners.

Enactment of Section 707(a)(2)(A)

Congress revisited the scope of section 707(a) in 1984, in part to prevent partners from circumventing the capitalization requirements of sections 263 and 709 by structuring payments for services as allocations of partnership income under section 704. H.R. Rep. No. 432 (Pt. 2), 98th Cong., 2d Sess. 1216-21 (1984) (H.R. Rep.); S. Prt. No. 169 (Vol. 1), 98th Cong., 2d Sess. 223-32 (1984) (S. Prt.). Congress specifically addressed the holdings in Rev. Rul. 81-300 and Rev. Rul. 81-301, affirming Rev. Rul. 81-301 and concluding that the payment in Rev. Rul. 81-300 should be recharacterized as a section 707(a) payment. S. Prt. at 230. Accordingly, the Treasury Department and the IRS are obsoleting Rev. Rul. 81-300 and request comments on whether it should be reissued with modified facts.

Congress also added an anti-abuse rule to section 707(a) relating to payments to partner service providers. Section 707(a)(2)(A) provides that if a partner performs services for a partnership and receives a related direct or indirect allocation and distribution, and the performance of services and allocation and distribution, when viewed together, are properly characterized as a transaction occurring between the partnership and a partner acting other than in its capacity as a partner, the transaction will be treated as occurring between the partnership and one who is not a partner under section 707(a)(1). See section 73 of the Tax Reform Act of 1984 (the 1984 Act). The Treasury Department and the IRS have concluded that section 707(a)(2) applies to arrangements in which distributions to the service provider depend on an allocation of an item of income, and section 707(c) applies to amounts whose payments are unrelated to partnership income.

Section 707(a)(2) grants the Secretary broad regulatory authority to identify transactions involving disguised payments for services under section 707(a)(2)(A). This grant of regulatory authority stems from Congress's concern that partnerships and service providers were inappropriately treating payments as allocations and distributions to a partner even when the service provider acted in a capacity other than as a partner. S. Prt. at 225. Congress determined that allocations and distributions that were, in substance, direct payments for services should be treated as a payment of fees rather than as an arrangement for the allocation and distribution of partnership income. H.R. Rep. at 1218; S. Prt. at 225. Congress differentiated these arrangements from situations in which a partner receives an allocation (or increased allocation) for an extended period to reflect its contribution of property or services to the partnership, such that the partner receives the allocation in its capacity as a partner. In balancing these potentially conflicting concerns, Congress anticipated that the regulations would take five factors into account in determining whether a service provider would receive its putative allocation and distribution in its capacity as a partner. H.R. Rep. at 1219-20; S. Prt. at 227.

Congress identified as its first and most important factor whether the payment is subject to significant entrepreneurial risk as to both the amount and fact of payment. In explaining why entrepreneurial risk is the most important factor, Congress provides that "[p]artners extract the profits of the partnership with reference to the business success of the venture, while third parties generally receive payments which are not subject to this risk." S. Prt. at 227. An arrangement for an allocation and distribution to a service provider which involves limited risk as to amount and payment is treated as a fee under section 707(a)(2)(A). Congress specified examples of allocations that presumptively limit a partner's risk, including (i) capped allocations of income, (ii) allocations for a fixed number of years under which the income that will go to the partner is reasonably certain, (iii) continuing arrangements in which purported allocations and distributions are fixed in amount or reasonably determinable under all facts and circumstances, and (iv) allocations of gross income items.

An arrangement in which an allocation and distribution to a service provider are subject to significant entrepreneurial risk as to amount will generally be recognized as a distributive share, although other factors are also relevant. The legislative history to section 707(a)(2)(A) includes the following examples of factors that could bear on this determination: (i) whether the partner status of the recipient is transitory; (ii) whether the allocation and distribution that are made to the partner are close in time to the partner's performance of services; (iii) whether the facts and circumstances indicate that the recipient became a partner primarily to obtain tax benefits for itself or the partnership that would not otherwise have been available; and (iv) whether the value of the recipient's interest in general and in continuing partnership profits is small in relation to the allocation in question.

Explanation of Provisions

Section 1.707-1 sets forth general rules on the operation of section 707. Section 1.707-2 is titled "Disguised payments for services" and is currently reserved. Sections 1.707-3 through 1.707-7 provide guidance regarding transactions involving disguised sales under section 707(a)(2)(B). These proposed regulations are issued under §1.707-2 and provide guidance regarding transactions involving disguised payments for services under section 707(a)(2)(A). The effective date of the proposed regulations is provided under §1.707-9.

I. General Rules Regarding Disguised Payments for Services

A. Scope

Consistent with the language of section 707(a)(2)(A), §1.707-2(b) of the proposed regulations provides that an arrangement will be treated as a disguised payment for services if (i) a person (service provider), either in a partner capacity or in anticipation of being a partner, performs services (directly or through its delegate) to or for the benefit of the partnership; (ii) there is a related direct or indirect allocation and distribution to the service provider; and (iii) the performance of the services and the allocation and distribution when viewed together, are properly characterized as a transaction occurring between the partnership and a person acting other than in that person's capacity as a partner.

The proposed regulations provide a mechanism for determining whether or not an arrangement is treated as a disguised payment for services under section 707(a)(2)(A). An arrangement that is treated as a disguised payment for services under these proposed regulations will be treated as a payment for services for all purposes of the Code. Thus, the partnership must treat the payments as payments to a non-partner in determining the remaining partners' shares of taxable income or loss. Where appropriate, the partnership must capitalize the payments or otherwise treat them in a manner consistent with the recharacterization.

The consequence of characterizing an arrangement as a payment for services is otherwise beyond the scope of these regulations. For example, the proposed regulations do not address the timing of inclusion by the service provider or the timing of a deduction by the partnership other than to provide that each is taken into account as provided for under applicable law by applying all relevant sections of the Code and all relevant judicial doctrines. Further, if an arrangement is subject to section 707(a), taxpayers should look to relevant authorities to determine the status of the service provider as an independent contractor or employee. See, generally, Rev. Rul. 69-184, 1969-1 C.B. 256. The Treasury Department and the IRS believe that section 707(a)(2)(A) generally should not apply to arrangements that the partnership has reasonably characterized as a guaranteed payment under section 707(c).

Allocations pursuant to an arrangement between a partnership and a service provider to which sections 707(a) and 707(c) do not apply will be treated as a distributive share under section 704(b). Rev. Proc. 93-27 and Rev. Proc. 2001-43 may apply to such an arrangement if the specific requirements of those Revenue Procedures are also satisfied. The Treasury Department and the IRS intend to modify the exceptions set forth in those revenue procedures to include an additional exception for profits interests issued in conjunction with a partner forgoing payment of a substantially fixed amount. This exception is discussed in part IV of the Explanation of Provisions section of this preamble.

B. *Application and Timing*

These proposed regulations apply to a service provider who purports to be a partner even if applying the regulations causes the service provider to be treated as a person who is not a partner. S. Prt. at 227. Further, the proposed regulations may apply even if their application results in a determination that no partnership exists. The regulations also apply to a special allocation and distribution received in exchange for services by a service provider who receives other allocations and distributions in a partner capacity under section 704(b).

The proposed regulations characterize the nature of an arrangement at the time at which the parties enter into or modify the arrangement. Although section 707(a)(2)(A)(ii) requires both an allocation and a distribution to the service provider, the Treasury Department and the IRS believe that a premise of section 704(b) is that an income allocation correlates with an increased distribution right, justifying the assumption that an arrangement that provides for an income allocation should be treated as also providing for an associated distribution for purposes of applying section 707(a)(2)(A). The Treasury Department and the IRS considered that some arrangements provide for distributions in a later year, and that those later distributions may be subject to independent risk. However, the Treasury Department and the IRS believe that recharacterizing an arrangement retroactively is administratively difficult. Thus, the proposed regulations characterize the nature of an arrangement when the arrangement is entered into (or modified) regardless of when income is allocated and when money or property is distributed. The proposed regulations apply to both onetime transactions and continuing arrangements. S. Prt. at 226.

II. *Factors Considered*

Whether an arrangement constitutes a payment for services (in whole or in part) depends on all of the facts and circumstances. The proposed regulations include six non-exclusive factors that may indicate that an arrangement constitutes a disguised payment for services. Of these factors, the first five factors generally track the facts and circumstances identified as relevant in the legislative history for purposes of applying section 707(a)(2)(A). The proposed regulations also add a sixth factor not specifically identified by Congress. The first of these six factors, the existence of significant entrepreneurial risk, is accorded more weight than the other factors, and arrangements that lack significant entrepreneurial risk are treated as disguised payments for services. The weight given to each of the other five factors depends on the particular case, and the absence of a particular factor (other than significant entrepreneurial risk) is not necessarily determinative of whether an arrangement is treated as a payment for services.

A. *Significant Entrepreneurial Risk*

As described in the Background section of this preamble, Congress indicated that the most important factor in determining whether or not an arrangement constitutes a payment for services is that the allocation and distribution is subject to significant entrepreneurial risk. S. Prt. at 227. Congress noted that partners extract the profits of the partnership based on the business success of the venture, while third parties generally receive payments that are not subject to this risk. Id.

The proposed regulations reflect Congress's view that this factor is most important. Under the proposed regulations, an arrangement that lacks significant entrepreneurial risk constitutes a disguised payment for services. An arrangement in which allocations and distributions to the service provider are subject to significant entrepreneurial risk will generally be recognized as a distributive share but the ultimate determination depends on the totality of the facts and circumstances. The Treasury Department and the IRS request comments on whether allocations to service providers that lack significant entrepreneurial risk could be characterized as distributive shares under section 704(b) in any circumstances.

Whether an arrangement lacks significant entrepreneurial risk is based on the service provider's entrepreneurial risk relative to the overall entrepreneurial risk of the partnership. For example, a service provider who receives a percentage of net profits in each of a partnership that invests in high-quality debt instruments and a partnership that invests in volatile or unproven businesses may have significant entrepreneurial risk with respect to both interests.

Section 1.707-2(c)(1)(i) through (v) of the proposed regulations set forth arrangements that presumptively lack significant entrepreneurial risk. These arrangements are presumed to result in an absence of significant entrepreneurial risk (and therefore, a disguised payment for services) unless other facts and circumstances can establish the presence of significant entrepreneurial risk by clear and convincing evidence. These examples generally describe facts and circumstances in which there is a high likelihood that the service provider will receive an allocation regardless of the overall success of the business operation, including (i) capped allocations of partnership income if the cap would reasonably be expected to apply in most years, (ii) allocations for a fixed number of years under which the service provider's distributive share of income is reasonably certain, (iii) allocations of gross income items, (iv) an allocation (under a formula or otherwise) that is predominantly fixed in amount, is reasonably determinable under all the facts and circumstances, or is designed to assure that sufficient net profits are highly likely to be available to make the allocation to the service provider (for example, if the partnership agreement provides for an allocation of net profits from specific transactions or accounting periods and this allocation does not depend on the overall success of the enterprise), and (v) arrangements in which a service provider either waives its right to receive payment for the future performance of services in a manner that is non-binding or fails to timely notify the partnership and its partners of the waiver and its terms.

With respect to the fourth example, the presence of certain facts, when coupled with a priority allocation to the service provider that is measured over any accounting period of the partnership of 12 months or less, may create opportunities that will lead to a higher likelihood that sufficient net profits will be available to make the allocation. One fact is that the value of partnership assets is not easily ascertainable and the partnership agreement allows the service provider or a related party in connection with a revaluation to control the determination of asset values, including by controlling events that may affect those values (such as timing of announcements that affect the value of the assets). (See Example 3(iv).) Another fact is that the service provider or a related party controls the entities in which the partnership invests, including controlling the timing and amount of distributions by those controlled entities. (These two facts by themselves do not, however, necessarily establish the absence of significant entrepreneurial risk.) By contrast, certain priority allocations that are intended to equalize a service provider's return with priority allocations already allocated to investing partners over the life of the partnership (commonly known as "catch-up allocations") typically will not fall within the types of allocations covered by the fourth example and will not lack significant entrepreneurial risk, although all of the facts and circumstances are considered in making that determination.

With respect to the fifth example, the Treasury Department and the IRS request suggestions regarding fee waiver requirements that sufficiently bind the waiving service provider and that are administrable by the partnership and its partners.

Congress's emphasis on entrepreneurial risk requires changes to existing regulations under section 707(c). Specifically, Example 2 of § 1.707-1(c) provides that if a partner is entitled to an allocation of the greater of 30 percent of partnership income or a minimum guaranteed amount, and the income allocation exceeds the minimum guaranteed amount, then the entire income allocation is treated as a distributive share under section 704(b). Example 2 also provides that if the income allocation is less than the guaranteed amount, then the partner is treated as receiving a distributive share to the extent of the income allocation and a guaranteed payment to the extent that the minimum guaranteed payment exceeds the income allocation. The treatment of the arrangements in Example 2 is inconsistent with the concept that an allocation must be subject to significant entrepreneurial risk to be treated as a distributive share under section 704(b). Accordingly, the proposed regulations modify Example 2 to provide that the entire minimum amount is treated as a guaranteed payment under section 707(c) regardless of the amount of the income allocation. Rev. Rul. 66-95, 1966-1 C.B. 169, and Rev. Rul. 69-180, 1969-1 C.B. 183, are also inconsistent with these proposed regulations. The Treasury Department and the IRS intend to obsolete Rev. Rul. 66-95 and Rev. Rul. 69-180, when these regulations are published in final form.

B. *Secondary factors*

Section 1.707-2(c)(2) through (6) describes additional factors of secondary importance in determining whether or not an arrangement that gives the appearance of significant entrepreneurial risk constitutes a payment for services. The weight given to each of the other factors depends on the particular case, and the absence of a particular factor is not necessarily determinative of whether an arrangement is treated as a payment for services. Four of these factors, described by Congress in the legislative history to section 707(a)(2)(A), are (i) that the service provider holds, or is expected to hold, a transitory partnership interest or a partnership interest for only a short duration, (ii) that the service provider receives an allocation and distribution in a time frame comparable to the time frame that a non-partner service provider would typically receive payment, (iii) that the service provider became a partner primarily to obtain tax benefits which would not have been available if the services were rendered to the partnership in a third party capacity, and (iv) that the value of the service provider's interest in general and continuing partnership profits is small in relation to the allocation and distribution.

To these four factors, the proposed regulations add a fifth factor. The fifth factor is present if the arrangement provides for different allocations or distributions with respect to different services received, where the services are provided either by a single person or by persons that are related under sections 707(b) or 267(b), and the terms of the differing allocations or distributions are subject to levels of entrepreneurial risk that vary significantly. For example, assume that a partnership receives services from both its general partner and from a management company that is related to the general partner under section 707(b). Both the general partner and the management company receive a share in future partnership net profits in exchange for their services. The general partner is entitled to an allocation of 20 percent of net profits and undertakes an enforceable obligation to repay any amounts distributed pursuant to its interest (reduced by reasonable allowance for tax payments made on the general partner's allocable shares of partnership income and gain) that exceed 20 percent of the overall net amount of partnership profits computed over the partnership's life and it is reasonable to anticipate that the general partner can and will comply fully with this obligation. The proposed regulations refer to this type of obligation and similar obligations, as a "clawback obligation." In contrast, the management company is entitled to a preferred amount of net income that, once paid, is not subject to a clawback obligation. Because the general partner and the management company are service providers that are related parties under section 707(b), and because the terms of the allocations and distributions to the management company create a significantly lower level of economic risk than the terms for the general partner, the management company's arrangement might properly be treated as a disguised payment for services (depending on all other facts and circumstances, including amount of entrepreneurial risk).

III. *Examples*

Section 1.707-2(d) of the proposed regulations contains a number of examples illustrating the application of the factors described in § 1.707-2(c). The examples illustrate the application of these regulations to arrangements that contain certain facts and circumstances that the Treasury Department and the IRS believe demonstrate the existence or absence of significant entrepreneurial risk.

Several of the examples consider arrangements in which a partner agrees to forgo fees for services and also receives a share of future partnership income and gains. The examples consider the application of section 707(a)(2)(A) based on the manner in which the service provider (i) forgoes its right to receive fees, and (ii) is entitled to share in future partnership income and gains. In Examples 5 and 6, the service provider forgoes the right to receive fees in a manner that supports the existence of significant entrepreneurial risk by forgoing its right to receive fees before the period begins and by executing a waiver that is binding, irrevocable, and clearly communicated to the other partners. Similarly, the service provider's arrangement in these examples include the following facts and circumstances that taken together support the existence of significant entrepreneurial risk: the allocation to the service provider is determined out of net profits and is neither highly likely to be available nor reasonably determinable based on all facts and circumstances available at the time of the arrangement, and the service provider undertakes a clawback obligation and is reasonably expected to be able to comply with that obligation. The presence of each fact described in these examples is not necessarily required to determine that section 707(a)(2)(A) does not apply to an arrangement. However, the absence of certain facts, such as a failure to measure future profits over at least a 12-month period, may suggest that an arrangement constitutes a fee for services.

The proposed regulations also contain examples that consider arrangements to which section 707(a)(2)(A) applies. Example 1 concludes that an arrangement in which a service provider receives a capped amount of partnership allocations and distributions and the cap is likely to apply provides for a disguised payment for services under section 707(a)(2)(A). In Example 3(iii), a service provider is entitled to a share of future partnership net profits, the partnership can allocate net profits from specific transactions or accounting periods, those allocations do not depend on the long-term future success of the enterprise, and a party that is related to the service provider controls the timing of purchases, sales, and distributions. The example concludes that under these facts, the arrangement lacks significant entrepreneurial risk and provides for a disguised payment for services. Example 4 considers similar facts, but assumes that the partnership's assets are publicly traded and are marked-to-market under section 475(f)(1). Under these facts, the example concludes that the arrangement has significant entrepreneurial risk, and thus that section 707(a)(2)(A) does not apply.

IV. *Safe Harbor Revenue Procedures*

Rev. Proc. 93-27 provides that in certain circumstances if a person receives a profits interest for the provision of services to or for the benefit of a partnership in a partner capacity or in anticipation of becoming a partner, the IRS will not treat the receipt of such interest as a taxable event for the partner or the partnership. The revenue procedure does not apply if (1) the profits interest relates to a substantially certain and predictable stream of income from partnership assets, such as income from high-quality debt securities or a high-quality net lease; (2) within two years of receipt, the partner disposes of the profits interest; or (3) the profits interest is a limited partnership interest in a "publicly traded partnership" within the meaning of section 7704(b).

Rev. Proc. 2001-43 provides that, for purposes of Rev. Proc. 93-27, if a partnership grants a substantially nonvested profits interest in the partnership to a service provider, the service provider will be treated as receiving the interest on the date of its grant, provided that: (i) the partnership and the service provider treat the service provider as the owner of the partnership interest from the date of its grant, and the service provider takes into account the distributive share of partnership income, gain, loss, deduction and credit associated with that interest in computing the service provider's income tax liability for the entire period during which the service provider has the interest; (ii) upon the grant of the interest or at the time that the interest becomes substantially vested, neither the partnership nor any of the partners deducts any amount (as wages, compensation, or otherwise) for the fair market value of the interest; and (iii) all other conditions of Rev. Proc. 93-27 are satisfied.

The Treasury Department and the IRS are aware of transactions in which one party provides services and another party receives a seemingly associated allocation and distribution of partnership income or gain. For example, a management company that provides services to a fund in exchange for a fee may waive that fee, while a party related to the management company receives an interest in future partnership profits the value of which approximates the amount of the waived fee. The Treasury Department and the IRS have determined that Rev. Proc. 93-27 does not apply to such transactions because they would not satisfy the requirement that receipt of an interest in partnership profits be for the provision of services to or for the benefit of the partnership in a partner capacity or in anticipation of being a partner, and because the service provider would effectively have disposed of the partnership interest (through a constructive transfer to the related party) within two years of receipt.

Further, the Treasury Department and the IRS plan to issue a revenue procedure providing an additional exception to the safe harbor in Rev. Proc. 93-27 in conjunction with the publication of these regulations in final form. The additional exception will apply to a profits interest issued in conjunction with a partner forgoing payment of an amount that is substantially fixed (including a substantially fixed amount determined by formula, such as a fee based on a percentage of partner capital commitments) for the performance of services, including a guaranteed payment under section 707(c) or a payment in a non-partner capacity under section 707(a).

In conjunction with the issuance of proposed regulations (REG-105346-03; 70 FR 29675-01; 2005-1 C.B. 1244) relating to the tax treatment of certain transfers of partnership equity in connection with the performance of services, the Treasury Department and the IRS issued Notice 2005-43, 2005-24 I.R.B. 1221. Notice 2005-43 includes a proposed revenue procedure regarding partnership interests transferred in connection with the performance of services. In the event that the proposed revenue procedure provided for in Notice 2005-43 is finalized, it will include the additional exception referenced.

Effective Dates

The proposed regulations would be effective on the date the final regulations are published in the **Federal Register** and would apply to any arrangement entered into or modified on or after the date of publication of the final regulations. In the case of any arrangement entered into or modified before the final regulations are published in the **Federal Register**, the determination of whether an arrangement is a disguised payment for services under section 707(a)(2)(A) is made on the basis of the statute and the guidance provided regarding that provision in the legislative history of section 707(a)(2)(A). Pending the publication of final regulations, the position of the Treasury Department and the IRS is that the proposed regulations generally reflect Congressional intent as to which arrangements are appropriately treated as disguised payments for services.

Effect on Other Documents

The following publication is obsolete as of July 23, 2015:

Rev. Rul. 81-300 (1981-2 C.B. 143).

The following publications will be obsolete as of the date of a Treasury decision adopting these rules as final regulations in the **Federal Register**:

Rev. Rul. 66-95 (1966-1 C.B. 169); and

Rev. Rul. 69-180 (1969-1 C.B. 183).

Special Analyses

It has been determined that this notice of proposed rulemaking is not a significant regulatory action as defined in Executive Order 12866, as supplemented by Executive Order 13563. Therefore, a regulatory assessment is not required. It has also been determined that section 553(b) of the Administrative Procedure Act (5 U.S.C. chapter 5) does not apply to these regulations, and because the regulation does not impose a collection of information on small entities, the Regulatory Flexibility Act (5 U.S.C. chapter 6) does not apply. Pursuant to section 7805(f) of the Code, this notice of proposed rulemaking will be submitted to the Chief Counsel for Advocacy of the Small Business Administration for comment on its impact on small business.

Comments and Requests for Public Hearing

The Treasury Department and the IRS invite public comment on these proposed regulations. The legislative history supporting section 707(a)(2)(A) indicates that an arrangement that lacks significant entrepreneurial risk is generally treated as a disguised payment for services. The Treasury Department and the IRS have concluded that the presence of significant entrepreneurial risk in an arrangement is necessary for the arrangement to be treated as occurring between a partnership and a partner acting in a partner capacity. Nonetheless, the Treasury Department and the IRS request comments on, and examples of, whether arrangements could exist that should be treated as a distributive share under section 704(b) despite the absence of significant entrepreneurial risk. In addition, the Treasury Department and the IRS request comments on sufficient notification requirements to effectively render a fee waiver binding upon the service provider and the partnership.

The Treasury Department and the IRS have become aware that some partnerships that assert reliance on §1.704-1(b)(2)(ii)(i) (the economic effect equivalence rule) have expressed uncertainty on the proper treatment of partners who receive an increased right to share in partnership property upon a partnership liquidation without respect to the partnership's net income. These partnerships typically set forth each partner's distribution rights upon a liquidation of the partnership and require the partnership to allocate net income annually in a manner that causes partners' capital accounts to match partnership distribution rights to the extent possible. Such agreements are commonly referred to as "targeted capital account agreements." Some taxpayers have expressed uncertainty whether a partnership with a targeted capital account agreement must allocate income or a guaranteed payment to a partner who has an increased right to partnership assets determined as if the partnership liquidated at the end of the year even in the event that the partnership recognizes no, or insufficient, net income. The Treasury Department and the IRS generally believe that existing rules under §§1.704-1(b)(2)(ii) and 1.707-1(c) address this circumstance by requiring partner capital accounts to reflect the partner's distribution rights as if the partnership liquidated at the end of the taxable year, but request comments on specific issues and examples with respect to which further guidance would be helpful. No inference is intended as to whether and when targeted capital account agreements could satisfy the economic effect equivalence rule.

Before these proposed regulations are adopted as final regulations, consideration will be given to any written (a signed original and eight (8) copies) or electronic comments that are submitted timely to the IRS. The Treasury Department and the IRS request comments on all aspects of the proposed regulations. All comments will be available for public inspection and copying upon request. A public hearing will be scheduled if requested in writing by any person that timely submits written or electronic comments. If a public hearing is scheduled, notice of the date, time, and place for the public hearing will be published in the **Federal Register**.

Drafting Information

The principal author of these proposed regulations is Jaclyn M. Goldberg of the Office Associate Chief Counsel (Passthroughs and Special Industries). However, other personnel from the Internal Revenue Service and the Treasury Department participated in their development.

[¶ 49,658]   Proposed Amendments of Regulations and Partial Withdrawal of Notice of Proposed Regulations (REG-109370-10), published in the Federal Register on August 3, 2015 (corrected 10/29/2015).

[Code Sec. 706]

Tiered partnerships: Partnership income: Distributive share: Allocable cash basis: Partnership's tax year: Partners: Partner's tax year: Change of interest.—Reg. §§ 1.706-2 and 1.706-3 and amendments of 1.706-0, 1.706-2T, 1.706-3 and 1.706-4, during a partnership taxable year in which a partner's interest changes, are proposed. Amendments of Reg. § 1.706-3(a), proposed on May 24, 2005, are withdrawn.

AGENCY: Internal Revenue Service (IRS), Treasury.

ACTION: Partial withdrawal of notice of proposed rulemaking and notice of proposed rulemaking.

SUMMARY: This document contains proposed regulations regarding the determination of a partner's distributive share of certain allocable cash basis items and items attributable to an interest in a lower-tier partnership during a partnership taxable year in which a partner's interest changes. These proposed regulations affect partnerships and their partners.

DATES: Written or electronic comments and requests for a public hearing must be received by November 2, 2015. As of August 3, 2015, the notice of proposed rulemaking that was published in the **Federal Register** on May 24, 2005 (70 FR 29675), is partially withdrawn.

ADDRESSES: Send submissions to: CC:PA:LPD:PR (REG-109370-10), room 5203, Internal Revenue Service, PO Box 7604, Ben Franklin Station, Washington, DC 20044. Submissions may be hand-delivered Monday through Friday between the hours of 8 a.m. and 4 p.m. to: CC:PA:LPD:PR (REG-109370-10), Courier's Desk, Internal Revenue Service, 1111 Constitution Avenue, NW, Washington, DC, or sent electronically, via the Federal eRulemaking Portal at http://www.regulations.gov/(IRS REG-109370-10).

FOR FURTHER INFORMATION CONTACT: Concerning the proposed regulations, Benjamin H. Weaver, (202) 317-6850; concerning submissions of comments and requests for public hearing, Regina Johnson, (202) 317-6901 (not toll free numbers).

SUPPLEMENTARY INFORMATION:

Background

Section 706 of the Internal Revenue Code (the Code) generally provides rules for the taxable years of partners and partnerships. Section 72 of the Deficit Reduction Act of 1984, Public Law 98-369 (98 Stat. 494 (1984)) added section 706(d) to the Code to prevent a partner who acquires an interest in the partnership late in the taxable year from deducting partnership expenses incurred prior to the partner's entry into the partnership (retroactive allocations). Section 706(d)(1) provides that, except as provided in section 706(d)(2) and (d)(3), if during any taxable year of the partnership there is a change in any partner's interest in the partnership, each partner's distributive share of any item of income, gain, loss, deduction, or credit of the partnership for such taxable year shall be determined by the use of any method prescribed by regulations which takes into account the varying interests of the partners in the partnership during such taxable year.

On April 14, 2009, the Treasury Department and the IRS published a notice of proposed rulemaking (REG-144689-04) (the 2009 proposed regulations) in the **Federal Register** to provide guidance under section 706(d)(1) and to conform the Income Tax Regulations for certain provisions of section 1246 of the Taxpayer Relief Act of 1997, Public Law 105-34 (111 Stat. 788 (1997)) and section 72 of the Deficit Reduction Act of 1984, Public Law 98-369 (98 Stat. 494 (1984)). The Treasury Department and the IRS are publishing final regulations under section 706(d)(1) (the final regulations) contemporaneously with these proposed regulations. However, the Treasury Department and the IRS have decided to propose an amendment to the final regulations expanding the list of extraordinary items to include two new items: (1) for publicly traded partnerships, any item of income that is an amount subject to withholding as defined in § 1.1441-2(a) (excluding amounts effectively connected with the conduct of a trade or business within the United States) or a withholdable payment under § 1.1473-1(a) occurring during a taxable year if, for that taxable year, the partners agree to treat all such items as extraordinary items, and (2) for any partnership, deductions for the transfer of partnership equity in connection with the performance of services. In addition, these proposed regulations provide guidance under sections 706(d)(2) and (3).

1. Allocable cash basis items

Section 706(d)(2) provides rules for certain allocable cash basis items. Section 706(d)(2)(A) provides that if during any taxable year of the partnership there is a change in any partner's interest in the partnership, then (except to the extent provided in regulations) each partner's distributive share of any allocable cash basis item shall be determined (i) by assigning the appropriate portion of such item to each day in the period to which it is attributable, and (ii) by allocating the portion assigned to any such day among the partners in proportion to their interests in the partnership at the close of such day. Section 706(d)(2)(B) defines "allocable cash basis item" as any of the following items with respect to which the partnership uses the cash receipts and disbursements method of accounting (cash method): (i) interest, (ii) taxes, (iii) payments for services or for the use of property, or (iv) any other item of a kind specified in regulations prescribed by the Secretary as being an item with respect to which the application of section 706(d)(2) is appropriate to avoid significant misstatements of the income of the partners. Section 706(d)(2)(C) further provides that if any portion of any allocable cash basis item is attributable to (i) any period before the beginning of the taxable year, such portion shall be assigned under section 706(d)(2)(A)(i) to the first day of the taxable year, or (ii) any period after the close of the taxable year, such portion shall be assigned under section 706(d)(2)(A)(i) to the last day of the taxable year. Finally, section 706(d)(2)(D) provides that if any portion of a deductible cash basis item is assigned under section 706(d)(2)(C)(i) to the first day of any taxable year, (i) such portion shall be allocated among persons who are partners in the partnership during the period to which such portion is attributable in accordance with their varying interests in the partnership during such period, and (ii) any amount allocated under section 706(d)(2)(D)(i) to a person who is not a partner in the partnership on such first day shall be capitalized by the partnership and treated in the manner provided for in section 755.

The legislative history explains that section 706(d)(2) was enacted to prevent cash method partnerships from avoiding the retroactive allocation rules:

[P]artnerships may attempt to avoid the retroactive allocation rules by using the cash method of accounting and deferring actual payment of deductible items until near the close of the partnership's taxable year. For example, if a partnership defers the payment of an expense (e.g., interest) until December 31, and the partnership uses the interim closing method of allocations, a partner admitted on December 31 may be allowed a deduction for a full portion of the expense. This may be the case although the expense has economically accrued at an equal rate throughout the taxable year . . . In adding these rules, Congress rejected the argument that the retroactive allocations were proper because the funds invested by the new partners served to reimburse the original partners for their expenditures so that, as an economic matter, the new partners had incurred the costs for which they were claiming deductions.

H.R. Rep. No. 98-432, at 1212-1213 (1984).

On November 30, 1984, the Treasury Department and the IRS issued temporary regulations under section 706(d)(2) (§ 1.706-2T (TD 7991)) to address the interaction of sections 706(d)(2) and 267(a)(2). The temporary regulations provide that a deduction for any expense that is deferred under section 267 constitutes an allocable cash basis item under section 706(d)(2)(B)(iv). Specifically, the temporary regulations provide:

Question 1: For purposes of section 706(d), how is an otherwise deductible amount that is deferred under section 267(a)(2) treated?

Answer 1: In the year the deduction is allowed, the deduction will constitute an allocable cash basis item under section 706(d)(2)(B)(iv).

Neither the 2009 proposed regulations nor the final regulations provide guidance under section 706(d)(2). However, the 2009 proposed regulations specifically requested comments on issues that arise concerning allocable cash basis items, in particular whether the list of items in section 706(d)(2)(B) should be expanded (to include, for example, items such as property insurance), as well as any other issues with regard to allocating cash basis items. The Treasury Department and the IRS received comments relating to allocable cash basis items in response to the 2009 proposed regulations. The comments are discussed in this preamble.

2. *Tiered Partnerships*

Section 706(a) provides that, in computing the taxable income of a partner for a taxable year, the inclusions required by section 702 and section 707(c) with respect to a partnership shall be based on the income, gain, loss, deduction, or credit of the partnership for any taxable year of the partnership ending within or with the taxable year of the partner. Prior to the issuance of Rev. Rul. 77-311, 1977-2 CB 218, in 1977 and the enactment of section 706(d)(3) in 1984, some taxpayers took the position that, in the case of tiered partnerships, the language of section 706(a) means that an upper-tier partnership's distributive share of items from a lower-tier partnership is sustained by the upper-tier partnership on the last day of the lower-tier partnership's taxable year. These taxpayers therefore allocated the upper-tier partnership's share of the lower-tier partnership's items based solely upon the upper-tier partnership's partners' interests as of the last day of the lower-tier partnerships' taxable year. Rev. Rul. 77-311 rejected that position, and explains through an example that an upper-tier partnership's distributive share of any items of income, gain, loss, deduction, or credit from a lower-tier partnership is considered to be realized or sustained by the upper-tier partnership at the same time and in the same manner as such items were realized or sustained by the lower-tier partnership. Therefore, in allocating items from a lower-tier partnership, the upper-tier partnership must take into account variations among its partners' interests throughout the year, rather than merely looking to its partners' interests as of the last day of the lower-tier partnership's taxable year.

Section 706(d)(3) was enacted in 1984 and confirms the analysis of Rev. Rul. 77-311. Section 706(d)(3) provides that if during any taxable year of the partnership there is a change in any partner's interest in the partnership (the "upper-tier partnership"), and such partnership is a partner in another partnership (the "lower-tier partnership"), then (except to the extent provided in regulations) each partner's distributive share of any item of the upper-tier partnership attributable to the lower-tier partnership shall be determined by assigning the appropriate portion (determined by applying principles similar to the principles of section 706(d)(2)(C) and (D)) of each such item to the appropriate days during which the upper-tier partnership is a partner in the lower-tier partnership and by allocating the portion assigned to any such day among the partners in proportion to their interests in the upper-tier partnership at the close of such day.

Neither the 2009 proposed regulations nor the final regulations provide guidance under section 706(d)(3). However, the 2009 proposed regulations specifically requested comments on issues that arise concerning tiered partnerships, and stated that the daily allocation method, used for cash basis items, applies to all items of the lower-tier partnership if there is a change in the partnership interests in the upper-tier partnership. The Treasury Department and the IRS received comments relating to tiered partnerships in response to the 2009 proposed regulations. The comments are discussed in this preamble.

Explanation of Provisions and Summary of Comments

1. *Allocable cash basis items*

With respect to allocable cash basis items, the proposed regulations generally restate the statutory provisions. Commenters requested that regulations clarify whether section 706(d)(2) applies only to items of deduction and loss or whether it also applies to items of income and gain. Generally, under the Code, the word "item" includes items of income, gain, deduction, and loss. Other than the item "taxes," the items listed in section 706(d)(2)(B) can be either items of income (and gain) or deduction (and loss), depending on a taxpayer's particular circumstances. Section 706(d)(2)(B)(iv) also provides broad regulatory authority for the Secretary to add "any other item . . . with respect to which the application of this paragraph is appropriate to avoid significant misstatements of the income of the partners." A significant misstatement of the income of partners can occur equally through an item of deduction or loss or an item of income or gain. Partnerships using the cash method that also use the interim closing method for accounting for partners' varying interests can use this distortion to affect the allocation of income to an incoming or outgoing partner. For these reasons, the proposed regulations provide that the allocable cash basis item rules apply to items of deduction, loss, income, and gain.

The proposed regulations provide that the term "allocable cash basis item" generally includes items of deduction, loss, income, or gain specifically listed in the statute: (i) interest, (ii) taxes, and (iii) payments for services or for the use of property. However, as discussed in part 4 of this preamble, the proposed regulations contain an exception for deductions for the transfer of an interest in the partnership in connection with the performance of services; such deductions generally must be allocated under the rules for extraordinary items in § 1.706-4(d).

Section 706(d)(2)(B)(iv) specifically grants the Secretary regulatory authority to include additional items in the list of allocable cash basis items to avoid significant misstatements of the income of the partners. Pursuant to the regulatory authority granted in section 706(d)(2)(B)(iv), the proposed regulations provide that the term "allocable cash basis item" includes any allowable deduction that had been previously deferred under section 267(a)(2). This provision incorporates the concept of § 1.706-2T and includes within the meaning of "allocable cash basis item" amounts deferred under section 267(a)(2) in the year in which the deduction is allowed. Accordingly, § 1.706-2T is proposed to be withdrawn by final regulations issued under section 706(d)(2).

Finally, pursuant to the regulatory authority granted in section 706(d)(2)(B)(iv), the proposed regulations provide that the term "allocable cash basis item" also includes any item of income, gain, loss, or deduction that accrues over time and that would, if not allocated as an allocable cash basis item, result in the significant misstatement of a partner's income. To provide additional clarification on the scope of the rule in proposed § 1.706-2(a)(2)(v), the Treasury Department and the IRS believe that items such as rebate payments, refund payments, insurance premiums, prepayments, and cash advances are examples of items which, if not allocated in the manner described in section 706(d)(2), could result in the significant misstatement of a partner's income. The Treasury Department and the IRS request comments on the inclusion of these items and other items within the meaning of "allocable cash basis items."

One commenter noted that section 706(d)(2) imposes the same administrative burden on partnerships regardless of the percentage of the partner's total expenses that are allocable cash basis items and therefore recommended that regulations under section 706(d)(2) include a de minimis rule. The Treasury Department and the IRS agree that a de minimis rule is appropriate given the scope of the proposed regulations. Accordingly, the proposed regulations provide that an allocable cash basis item will not be subject to the rules in section 706(d)(2) if, for the partnership's taxable year: (1) the total of the particular class of allocable cash basis items (for example, all interest income) is less than five percent of the partnership's (a) gross income, including tax-exempt income described in section 705(a)(1)(B), in the case of income or gain items, or (b) gross expenses and losses, including section 705(a)(2)(B) expenditures, in the case of losses and expense items; and (2) the total amount of allocable cash basis items from all classes of allocable cash basis items amounting to less than five percent of the partnership's (a) gross income, including tax-exempt income described in section 705(a)(1)(B), in the case of income or gain items, or (b) gross expenses and losses, including section 705(a)(2)(B) expenditures, in the case of losses and expense items, does not exceed $10 million in the taxable year, determined by treating all such allocable cash basis items as positive amounts.

Additionally, the Treasury Department and the IRS request comments on whether the final regulations should provide an exception for certain items of income or deduction arising from payments for services or for the use of property. For example, comments are requested on whether payments for services or for the use of property should be excluded from the rules in section 706(d)(2) if they arise and are, as applicable, paid or received in the ordinary course of the partnership's business (such as the regular payment of wages to employees), and whether deferred compensation or contingency or success-based fees and other payments for services based on performance conditions (which are not calculated based on an hourly rate) should be subject to the rules of section 706(d)(2) (and, if so, on the proper method for assigning the appropriate portion of such item to each day in the period).

The proposed regulations contain two examples illustrating the operation of section 706(d)(2)(D)(ii), which requires certain portions of deductible cash basis items to be capitalized in the manner provided in section 755 in the event that the deduction is otherwise partially allocable to a former partner who is no longer a partner as of the first day of the partnership's taxable year. The Treasury Department and the IRS request comments on the appropriate interaction between the principles and rules of section 755 and section 706(d), including whether the final regulations should provide an exception to the capitalization rules of section 706(d)(2)(D)(ii) in cases where the former partner ceased to be a partner in the partnership as a result of the partner's contribution of its partnership interest to another entity in a non-recognition transaction.

2. Tiered Partnerships

With respect to tiered partnerships, the proposed regulations provide that the daily allocation method used for cash basis items applies to all items of the lower-tier partnership if there is a change in any partner's interest in the upper-tier partnership.

Commenters noted the administrative burden of the daily allocation method on tiered partnerships. Commenters stated that obtaining information from a lower-tier partnership to track changes in the ownership interest in an upper-tier partnership is burdensome, and often impractical, unless the upper-tier partnership owns a controlling interest in the lower-tier partnership. One commenter suggested that the Treasury Department and the IRS issue interim guidance to provide that section 706(d)(3) should not apply to a change in a partner's interest in an upper-tier partnership unless the upper-tier partnership owns an interest in more than 50 percent of the profits and capital of the lower-tier partnership. Another commenter recommended an exception when the upper-tier partnership owns a relatively small portion (such as 10 percent or less) of the lower-tier partnership. The Treasury Department and the IRS acknowledge that a lack of information sharing among tiered partnerships may make it difficult to comply with a daily allocation requirement. Thus, the proposed regulations provide an exception from section 706(d)(3) if the upper-tier partnership directly owns an interest in less than 10 percent of the profits and capital of the lower-tier partnership ("a de minimis upper-tier partnership"), all de minimis upper-tier partnerships in aggregate own an interest in less than 30 percent of the profits and capital of the lower-tier partnership, and if no partnership is created with a purpose of avoiding the application of the tiered partnership rules of section 706(d)(3). The application of this exception is determined at each tier, depending on the interests held by the direct partners at each tier. Thus, in the case of an upper-tier partnership owning an interest in a middle tier partnership, which in turn owns an interest in a lower-tier partnership, it may be the case that the exception applies to the upper-tier partnership's interest in the middle tier partnership, but not to the middle tier partnership's interest in the lower-tier partnership (or vice-versa).

If the de minimis upper-tier partnership exception applies, the upper-tier partnership may, but is not required to, apply the general rules of §1.706-4 in allocating items attributable to the lower-tier partnership. However, as explained in Rev. Rul. 77-311, an upper-tier partnership's distributive share of any items of income, gain, loss, deduction, or credit from a lower-tier partnership is considered to be realized or sustained by the upper-tier partnership at the same time and in the same manner as such items were realized or sustained by the lower-tier partnership. Thus, if the de minimis upper-tier partnership exception applies to an upper-tier partnership using the interim closing method, the upper-tier partnership's allocations of the lower-tier partnership items under the general rules of §1.706-4 will generally reach the same result as applying the rules of section 706(d)(3). On the other hand, if the de minimis upper-tier partnership exception applies to an upper-tier partnership using the proration method, the upper-tier partnership may prorate the items from the lower-tier partnership across the upper-tier partnership's segments (or, if the upper-tier partnership has only one segment for its entire taxable year, it may prorate the items across its entire taxable year). Even if the de minimis upper-tier partnership exception applies, the upper-tier partnership may choose to allocate the items attributable to the lower-tier partnership according to the tiered partnership rules instead. However, the proposed regulations do not impose on lower-tier partnerships an obligation to disclose to upper-tier partnerships the timing of the lower-tier partnership's items. The proposed regulations contain three examples illustrating these principles.

Commenters also requested additional guidance on the application of section 706(d)(3) in certain circumstances. One commenter requested that the final regulations provide guidance on tiered partnerships that would allow an upper-tier partnership to determine the items from the lower-tier partnership that are allocable to the upper-tier partnership segments based on an interim closing method (as of any upper-tier partnership segment end) applied to the lower-tier partnership if the upper-tier partnership: (i) has the same taxable year as its lower-tier partnership; (ii) holds a fixed percentage interest in the lower-tier partnership during a taxable year; and (iii) uses the interim closing method. This commenter also recommended that guidance provide that an upper-tier partnership that has the same taxable year as its lower-tier partnership and holds a fixed percentage interest in that lower-tier partnership during the upper-tier partnership's taxable year may prorate the non-extraordinary items of the lower-tier partnership as of the last day of the upper-tier partnership's taxable year, without regard to whether the upper-tier partnership uses the proration method or the interim closing method.

However, as explained in this preamble, the Treasury Department and the IRS believe that because an upper-tier partnership's distributive share of any items of income, gain, loss, deduction, or credit from a lower-tier partnership is considered to be realized or sustained by the upper-tier partnership at the same time and in the same manner as such items were realized or sustained by the lower-tier partnership, application of the interim closing method will generally reach the same result as applying the rules of section 706(d)(3). The Treasury Department and the IRS also believe that allowing an upper-tier partnership that uses the interim closing method to prorate items from a lower-tier partnership across the upper-tier partnership's entire taxable year would be inconsistent with the principles explained in Rev. Rul. 77-311. Therefore, the proposed regulations do not adopt these comments. However, the Treasury Department and the IRS request comments on safe harbors that might be appropriate in these circumstances as well as comments on the treatment of an upper-tier partnership and a lower-tier partnership that have different taxable years.

One commenter also recommended that guidance provide that the default method for tiered partnerships is the proration method unless the upper-tier partnership agrees to use the interim closing method and receives sufficient information from the lower-tier partnership to use that method. Under section 706(d)(1) as implemented by §1.706-4, the interim closing method is the default method unless the partners agree in writing to use the proration method. Because the recommended rule would be inconsistent with section 706(d)(1) as implemented by §1.706-4, the Treasury Department and the IRS did not adopt this rule in the proposed regulations.

A commenter further recommended that any conventions applicable to the upper-tier partnership should apply to income from the lower-tier partnership. In general, the Treasury Department and the IRS believe that any conventions applicable to the upper-tier partnership should apply to items from the lower-tier partnership, but are continuing to consider this recommendation in the context of section 706(d)(3) and request comments on safe harbors when the upper-tier partnership and the lower-tier partnership use the same method, but different conventions.

Another commenter recommended that the final regulations permit partnerships to voluntarily apply the rules of section 706(d)(3) if the upper-tier partnership and the lower-tier partnership have an advance agreement establishing the allocation method for items derived from the upper-tier partnership's interest in the lower-tier partnership. As described in this preamble, the Treasury Department and the IRS are requesting comments on appropriate safe harbors and will continue to consider this recommendation.

The Treasury Department and the IRS also request comments on appropriate rules, if any, when there is a variance at both the upper-tier partnership and lower-tier partnership.

More generally, the Treasury Department and the IRS request comments on the appropriate coordination between the rules of sections 706(d)(2) and (3) and the rules of §1.706-4. In particular, the Treasury Department and the IRS request comments on whether certain items such as contingency or success-based fees and other payments for services based on performance conditions are more appropriately addressed under the rules of section 706(d)(2) and (3), which require allocation of items across the period to which they are attributable, or under the rules for the allocation of extraordinary items under §1.706-4(e), which requires allocation of items according to the partners' interests at the time of day on which the extraordinary item occurs. Additionally, the Treasury Department and the IRS request comments on whether certain items subject to section 706(d)(2) and (3) may instead be simply allocated under the proration method of §1.706-4(d) without impinging on the Congressional intent behind sections 706(d)(2) and (3) or resulting in a substantial distortion of income.

3. Additional Extraordinary Item for Publicly Traded Partnerships (PTPs)

Section 1.706-4(e) of the final regulations provides rules for the allocation of certain "extraordinary items." In general, extraordinary items must be allocated among the partners in proportion to their interests in the partnership item at the time of day on which the extraordinary item occurs. Section 1.706-4(e)(2) contains a list of extraordinary items. These proposed regulations add two additional extraordinary items to that list.

The first proposed additional extraordinary item responds to comments received on the 2009 proposed regulations regarding the administrative difficulty PTPs face in satisfying withholding obligations under section 1441 if PTPs are not permitted to use a quarterly convention. As explained in Part 1.C.iii of the preamble to the final regulations, the final regulations do not permit PTPs to use a quarterly convention. One commenter on the 2009 proposed regulations suggested other options of addressing this issue if the Treasury Department and the IRS are concerned that allowing a quarterly convention would be too broad. One option suggested was to permit PTPs that have income subject to withholding under section 1441 to treat that income as an extraordinary item allocated to PTP unit holders who are the record holders on the date the distribution is declared. The Treasury Department and the IRS agree that a special rule is desirable to link each partner's distributive share to the related cash distributions, thereby enabling PTPs and their transfer agents to satisfy their withholding obligations under chapter 4 of the Code and sections 1441 through 1443 from distributions. Therefore, these proposed regulations generally adopt this suggested alternative to a quarterly convention.

Specifically, these proposed regulations provide that for PTPs, all items of income that are amounts subject to withholding as defined in §1.1441-2(a) (excluding income effectively connected with the conduct of a trade or business within the United States) or withholdable payments under §1.1473-1(a) occurring during a taxable year may be treated as extraordinary items if the partners agree (within the meaning of §1.706-4(f)) to consistently treat all such items as extraordinary items for that taxable year. If the partners so agree, then for purposes of section 706 such items shall be treated as occurring at the next time as of which the recipients of a distribution by the PTP are determined, or, to the extent such income items arise between the final time during the taxable year as of which the recipients of a distribution are determined and the end of the taxable year, such items shall be treated as occurring at the final time during the taxable year as of which the recipients of a distribution by the PTP are determined. However, this rule does not apply unless the PTP has a regular practice of making at least four distributions (other than de minimis distributions) to its partners each taxable year. The proposed regulations contain an example illustrating this rule.

The final regulations generally require extraordinary items to be allocated without regard to the partnership's method or convention. However, §1.706-4(e)(1) of the final regulations provides that PTPs may, but are not required to, respect the applicable conventions in determining who held their publicly traded units at the time of the occurrence of an extraordinary item. The Treasury Department and the IRS believe that this exception should be turned off for all items subject to the new proposed extraordinary item rule for PTPs to ensure that each partner's distributive share of such items is linked to the related cash distributions. Accordingly, the proposed regulations modify the rule in §1.706-4(e)(1) to provide that PTPs that choose to treat items subject to withholding under section 1441 as extraordinary items must allocate those items among the partners in proportion to their interests in those items at the time as of which the recipients of the relevant distribution are determined, regardless of the method and convention otherwise used by the PTP.

Taxpayers may rely on this proposed additional extraordinary item until final regulations are published. The proposed regulations do not use the phrase "record holders on the date the distribution is declared," because the Treasury Department and the IRS understand that the recipients of a distribution by a PTP may be determined as of a time other than on the date the distribution is declared. The Treasury Department and the IRS request comments on the operation of this special rule, and on the interaction between the rules under section 706 and PTP allocations generally.

4. Coordination with proposed Partnership Equity for Services regulations

On May 24, 2005, the Treasury Department and the IRS published a notice of proposed rulemaking (REG-105346-03, 70 FR 29675) in the **Federal Register,** the proposed Partnership Equity for Services regulations, relating to the tax treatment of certain transfers of partnership interests in connection with the performance of services. The proposed Partnership Equity for Services regulations provide rules for coordinating section 83 with partnership taxation principles. On June 13, 2005, the Treasury Department and the IRS published Notice 2005-43, I.R.B. 2005-24, setting forth a proposed revenue procedure providing additional related guidance. The proposed Partnership Equity for Services regulations and the proposed revenue procedure are not effective until finalized. Notice 2005-43 provides that, until then, taxpayers may continue to rely on Rev. Proc. 93-27, 1993-2 C.B. 343, and Rev. Proc. 2001-43, 2001-2 C.B. 191. The Treasury Department and the IRS continue to consider the interaction of section 83 with partnership taxation principles. No inferences should be drawn from these proposed regulations as to the resolution of the issues addressed in the proposed Partnership Equity for Services regulations or any other related issues.

The proposed Partnership Equity for Services regulations contain two provisions relating to the varying interest rule under section 706. First, proposed §1.706-3(a) of the proposed Partnership Equity for Services regulations is intended to provide an exception to the allocable cash basis item rules of section 706(d)(2) for deductions for the transfer of partnership interests and other property subject to section 83. The preamble to the proposed Partnership Equity for Services regulations indicates that the exception was intended to allow partnerships to allocate such deductions under a closing of the books method. The preamble indicates that the Treasury Department and the IRS had concluded that, absent treatment under the allocable cash basis item rules of section 706(d)(2), the application of section 706(d)(1) would adequately ensure that partnership deductions that are attributable to the portion of the partnership's taxable year prior to a new partner's entry into the partnership are allocated to the historic partners.

The Treasury Department and the IRS have concluded that, in the case of a transfer of a partnership interest in connection with the performance of services, no portion of the partnership's deduction should be allocated to the person who performs the services. However, the Treasury Department and the IRS have also concluded that the scope of the exception to allocable cash basis treatment in proposed §1.706-3(a) may have been too broad because it applies to all transfers of property subject to section 83, for which the Treasury Department and the IRS request comments under these proposed regulations. Therefore, the Treasury Department and the IRS withdraw proposed §1.706-3(a). Instead, these proposed regulations provide an exception to allocable cash basis treatment for deductions for transfers of partnership interests in connection with the performance of services. Additionally, to ensure that such deductions are allocated solely to partners other than the person who performed the services, the proposed regulations add to the list of extraordinary items in §1.706-4(e)(2) any deduction for the transfer of an interest in the partnership in connection with the performance of services, and clarify that such extraordinary item is treated as occurring immediately before the transfer or vesting of the partnership interest that results in compensation income for the person who performs the services.

As explained in the final § 1.706-4 in the Rules and Regulations section of this issue of the Federal Register, extraordinary items generally must be allocated among the partners in proportion to their interests in the partnership item at the time of day on which the extraordinary item occurs. However, there are exceptions to the extraordinary item rules for certain small items in § 1.704-4(e)(3) and for partnerships for which capital is not a material income-producing factor in § 1.706-4(b)(2)). To ensure that partnership deductions attributable to the transfer of interests in the partnership in connection with the performance of services are always allocated solely to the historic partners, the proposed regulations turn off these exceptions to extraordinary item treatment for such deductions. Thus, treatment as an extraordinary item subject to the special timing rule will ensure that, for both accrual and cash-method partnerships, no portion of the deduction for the transfer of a partnership interest in connection with the performance of services will be allocated to the person who performs the services.

Second, proposed § 1.706-3(b) of the proposed Partnership Equity for Services regulations provides that a partnership must make certain forfeiture allocations upon forfeiture of a partnership interest for which a section 83(b) election was made. In particular, proposed § 1.706-3(b) provides that although the person forfeiting the interest may not have been a partner for the entire taxable year, forfeiture allocations may be made out of the partnership's items for the entire taxable year. The Treasury Department and the IRS anticipate that if the rules for forfeiture allocations in proposed § 1.706-3(b) are adopted when the proposed Partnership Equity for Services regulations are finalized, those rules will include in § 1.706-3(b) an additional exception to the general application of the varying interest rule. In the meantime, these proposed regulations move § 1.706-3(b) of the proposed Partnership Equity for Services regulations to new proposed § 1.706-6(a) to accommodate the new proposed regulations in § 1.706-3.

Proposed Effective Date

The regulations are proposed to apply to partnership taxable years beginning on or after the date of publication of the Treasury decision adopting these regulations as final regulations in the **Federal Register**.

Reliance on Proposed Regulations

Taxpayers may rely on §§ 1.706-4(e)(1) and 1.706-4(e)(2)(ix) of the proposed regulations (relating to a publicly traded partnership's treatment of all amounts subject to withholding as defined in § 1.1441-2(a) that are not effectively connected with the conduct of a trade or business within the United States or withholdable payments under § 1.1473-1(a) as extraordinary items) until final regulations are issued.

Special Analyses

It has been determined that this notice of proposed rulemaking is not a significant regulatory action as defined in Executive Order 12866, as supplemented by Executive Order 13563. Therefore, a regulatory assessment is not required. It has also been determined that section 553(b) of the Administrative Procedure Act (5 U.S.C. chapter 5) does not apply to this proposed regulation, and because this proposed regulation does not impose a collection of information on small entities, the Regulatory Flexibility Act (5 U.S.C. chapter 6) does not apply. Pursuant to section 7805(f) of the Code, these regulations have been submitted to the Chief Counsel for Advocacy of the Small Business Administration for comment on its impact on small business.

Comments and Requests for a Public Hearing

Before these proposed regulations are adopted as final regulations, consideration will be given to any written comments (a signed original and eight (8) copies) or electronic comments that are submitted timely to the IRS. The Treasury Department and the IRS specifically request comments on the clarity of the proposed rules and how they can be made easier to understand. All comments will be available for public inspection and copying. A public hearing will be scheduled if requested in writing by any person that timely submits written comments. If a public hearing is scheduled, notice of the date, time, and place for the public hearing will be published in the **Federal Register**.

Drafting Information

The principal author of these proposed regulations is Benjamin H. Weaver, Office of the Associate Chief Counsel (Passthroughs and Special Industries). However, other personnel from the Treasury Department and the IRS participated in their development.

Withdrawal of Notice of Proposed Rulemaking

Accordingly, under the authority of 26 U.S.C. 7805 and 706(d)(2), § 1.706-3(a) of the notice of proposed rulemaking that was published in the **Federal Register** on May 24, 2005 (70 FR 29675), is withdrawn.

[¶ 49,662]   Proposed Amendments of Regulations (REG-109813-11), published in the Federal Register on August 27, 2015.

[Code Sec. 937]

U.S. possessions: Bona fide residence: Presence test.—Amendments of Reg. § 1.937-1, determining whether an individual is a bona fide resident of a U.S. territory, is proposed. The text is at: ¶ 28,396C.

AGENCY: Internal Revenue Service (IRS), Treasury.

ACTION: Notice of proposed rulemaking.

SUMMARY: This document contains proposed amendments to the regulations for determining whether an individual is a bona fide resident of a U.S. territory. These proposed amendments affect individuals establishing bona fide residency in a U.S. territory by allowing additional days of constructive presence in a U.S. territory.

DATES: Written or electronic comments and requests for a public hearing must be received by November 27, 2015.

ADDRESSES: Send submissions to: CC:PA:LPD:PR (REG-109813-11), room 5203, Internal Revenue Service, PO Box 7604, Ben Franklin Station, Washington, DC 20044. Submissions may be hand-delivered Monday through Friday between the hours of 8 a.m. and 4 p.m. to CC:PA:LPD:PR (REG-109813-11), Courier's Desk, Internal Revenue Service, 1111 Constitution Avenue, NW, Washington, DC, or sent electronically, via the Federal eRulemaking Portal at *www.regulations.gov* (IRS REG-109813-11).

FOR FURTHER INFORMATION CONTACT: Concerning the proposed regulations, Stephen Huggs, (202) 317-6941; concerning submission of comments and/or requests for a hearing, Oluwafunmilayo (Funmi) Taylor, (202) 317-6901 (not toll-free numbers). SUPPLEMENTARY INFORMATION:

Background

This document contains proposed amendments to the Income Tax Regulations (26 CFR part 1) under section 937 of the Internal Revenue Code (Code). Section 937 was added to the Code by the American Jobs Creation Act of 2004 (Public Law 108-357, 118 Stat. 1418 (2004)). Section 937(a) provides rules for determining if an individual is a bona fide resident of a U.S. possession (generally referred to in this preamble as a "U.S. territory").

On April 11, 2005, the **Federal Register** published temporary regulations (TD 9194, 70 FR 18920) and proposed regulations (REG-159243-03, 70 FR 18949) under section 937, providing rules to implement section 937 and conforming existing regulations to other legislative changes with respect to the U.S. territories. On January 31, 2006, the **Federal Register** published final regulations (TD 9248, 71 FR 4996) under section 937(a) concerning whether an individual is a bona fide resident of a U.S. territory. Section 1.937-1 was amended on November 14, 2006, and on April 9, 2008, to provide additional guidance concerning bona fide residency in the U.S. territories. See TD 9297 (71 FR 66232) and TD 9391 (73 FR 19350).

Section 937(a) provides that an individual is a bona fide resident of a U.S. territory if the individual meets a presence test, a tax home test, and a closer connection test. In order to satisfy the presence test, an individual must be present in the U.S. territory for at least 183 days during the taxable year (183-day rule), unless otherwise provided in regulations.

Section 1.937-1 provides several alternatives to the 183-day rule. An individual who does not satisfy the 183-day rule nevertheless meets the presence test if the individual satisfies one of four alternative tests: (1) the individual is present in the relevant U.S. territory for at least 549 days during the three-year period consisting of the current taxable year and the two immediately preceding taxable years, provided the individual is present in the U.S. territory for at least 60 days during each taxable year of the period; (2) the individual is present no more than 90 days in the United States during the taxable year; (3) the individual has no more than $3,000 of earned income from U.S. sources and is present for more days in the U.S. territory than in the United States during the taxable year; or (4) the individual has no significant connection to the United States during the taxable year. The term "significant connection" is generally defined as a permanent home, voter registration, spouse, or minor child in the United States. See § 1.937-1(c)(5). Section 1.937-1 also provides that certain days count as days of presence in the relevant U.S. territory for purposes of the presence test, even if the individual is not physically present in the U.S. territory (constructive presence).

Explanation of Provisions

Following the original issuance of § 1.937-1, the Department of the Treasury (Treasury Department) and the Internal Revenue Service (IRS) received comments requesting that the presence test be revisited to make it more flexible. These comments included a proposal to allow days of constructive presence for business or personal travel outside of the relevant U.S. territory. The Treasury Department and the IRS have concluded that it would be appropriate to allow additional days of constructive presence subject to certain limitations. Accordingly, these proposed regulations provide an additional rule for calculating days of presence in the relevant U.S. territory for purposes of the presence test in § 1.937-1(c)(1).

Under the proposed amendment, an individual would be considered to be present in the relevant U.S. territory for up to 30 days during which the individual is outside of both the United States and the relevant U.S. territory. The proposed amendment would not apply, however, if the number of days that the individual is considered to be present in the United States during the taxable year equals or exceeds the number of days that the individual is considered to be present in the relevant U.S. territory during the taxable year, determined without taking into account any days for which the individual would be treated as present in the U.S. territory under this proposed amendment. Furthermore, the 30-day constructive presence rule would not apply for purposes of calculating the minimum 60 days of presence in the relevant U.S. territory that is required for the 549-day test under § 1.937-1(c)(1)(ii). Therefore, an individual invoking § 1.937-1(c)(1)(ii) must otherwise be considered to have been present at least 60 days in the relevant U.S. territory in each of the three years in order to benefit from the 30-day constructive presence rule.

Proposed Effective/Applicability Date

These amendments to the regulations are proposed to apply to taxable years beginning after the date these regulations are published as final regulations in the **Federal Register**.

Reliance on Proposed Regulations

Until these regulations are published as final regulations in the **Federal Register**, taxpayers may rely on these proposed regulations with respect to taxable years beginning on or after the date these proposed regulations are published in the **Federal Register**.

Special Analyses

Certain IRS regulations, including this one, are exempt from the requirements of Executive Order 12866, as supplemented and reaffirmed by Executive Order 13563. Therefore, a regulatory impact assessment is not required. It has also been determined that section 553(b) of the Administrative Procedure Act (5 U.S.C. chapter 5) does not apply to these regulations, and because the regulations do not impose a collection of information on small entities, the Regulatory Flexibility Act (5 U.S.C. chapter 6) does not apply. Pursuant to section 7805(f) of the Code, this regulation has been submitted to the Chief Counsel for Advocacy of the Small Business Administration for comment on its impact on small business.

Comments and Requests for Public Hearing

Before these proposed regulations are adopted as final regulations, consideration will be given to any comments that are submitted timely to the IRS as prescribed in this preamble under the "Addresses" heading. The Treasury Department and the IRS request comments on all aspects of the proposed rules. All comments will be available at *www.regulations.gov* or upon request. A public hearing will be scheduled if requested in writing by any person that timely submits written comments. If a public hearing is scheduled, notice of the date, time, and place for the public hearing will be published in the **Federal Register**.

Drafting Information

The principal author of these proposed regulations is Cleve Lisecki, formerly of the Office of Associate Chief Counsel (International). However, other personnel from the Treasury Department and the IRS participated in their development.

[¶ 49,664]   **Proposed Amendments of Regulations and Partial Withdrawal of Notice of Proposed Regulations (REG-143800-14)**, published in the Federal Register on September 1, 2015.

[Code Sec. 36B]

Health coverage. Employer-sponsored plan: Minimum value. Amendments of Reg. § 1.36B-6, determining whether health coverage under an eligible employer-sponsored plan provides minimum value, are proposed. Previously proposed amendments to Reg. § 1.36B-6(a) and (g) were withdrawn (see ¶ 49,574). Portions of the 2015 proposed amendments to Reg. § 1.36B-6 were adopted by T.D. 9745. The text is at ¶ 4196U.

AGENCY: Internal Revenue Service (IRS), Treasury.

ACTION: Supplemental notice of proposed rulemaking.

SUMMARY: This document withdraws, in part, a notice of proposed rulemaking published on May 3, 2013, relating to the health insurance premium tax credit enacted by the Affordable Care Act (including guidance on determining whether health coverage under an eligible employer-sponsored plan provides minimum value) and replaces the withdrawn portion with new proposed regulations providing guidance on determining whether health coverage under an eligible employer-sponsored plan provides minimum value. The proposed regulations affect participants in eligible employer-sponsored health plans and employers that sponsor these plans.

DATES: Written (including electronic) comments and requests for a public hearing must be received by November 1, 2015.

ADDRESSES: Send submissions to: CC:PA:LPD:PR (REG-143800-14), Room 5203, Internal Revenue Service, PO Box 7604, Ben Franklin Station, Washington, DC 20044. Submissions may be hand-delivered Monday through Friday between the hours of 8 a.m. and 4 p.m. to CC:PA:LPD:PR (REG-143800-14), Courier's Desk, Internal Revenue Service, 1111 Constitution Avenue, NW., Washington, DC, or sent electronically via the Federal eRulemaking Portal at *www.regulations.gov* (IRS REG-143800-14).

FOR FURTHER INFORMATION CONTACT: Concerning the proposed regulations, Andrew S. Braden, (202) 317-4725; concerning the submission of comments and/or requests for a public hearing, Oluwafunmilayo Taylor, (202) 317-5179 (not toll-free calls).

SUPPLEMENTARY INFORMATION:

Background

This document withdraws, in part, a notice of proposed rulemaking (REG-125398-12), which was published in the **Federal Register** on May 3, 2013 (78 FR 25909) and replaces the portion withdrawn with new proposed regulations. The 2013 proposed regulations added § 1.36B-6 of the Income Tax Regulations, providing rules for determining the minimum value of eligible employer-sponsored plans for purposes of the premium tax credit under section 36B of the Internal Revenue Code (Code). Notice 2014-69 (2014-48 IRB 903) advised taxpayers that the Department of Health and Human Service (HHS) and the Treasury Department and the IRS intended to propose regulations providing that plans that fail to provide substantial coverage for inpatient hospitalization or physician services do not provide minimum value. Accordingly, the proposed regulations under § 1.36B-6(a) and (g) are withdrawn.

Beginning in 2014, under the Patient Protection and Affordable Care Act, Public Law 111-148 (124 Stat. 119 (2010)), and the Health Care and Education Reconciliation Act of 2010, Public Law 111-152 (124 Stat. 1029 (2010)) (collectively, the Affordable Care Act), eligible individuals who enroll in, or whose family member enrolls in, coverage under a qualified health plan through an Affordable Insurance Exchange (Exchange), also known as a Health Insurance Marketplace, may receive a premium tax credit under section 36B of the Code.

Premium Tax Credit

Section 36B allows a refundable premium tax credit, which subsidizes the cost of health insurance coverage enrolled in through an Exchange. A taxpayer may claim the premium tax credit on the taxpayer's tax return only if the taxpayer or a member of the taxpayer's tax family (the persons for whom the taxpayer claims a personal exemption deduction on the taxpayer's tax return, generally the taxpayer, spouse, and dependents) has a coverage month. An individual has a coverage month only if the individual enrolls in a qualified health plan through an Exchange, is not eligible for minimum essential coverage other than coverage in the individual market, and premiums for the qualified health plan are paid. Section 36B(b) and (c)(2)(B). Minimum essential coverage includes coverage under an eligible employer-sponsored plan. See section 5000A(f)(1)(B). However, for purposes of the premium tax credit, an individual is not eligible for coverage under an eligible employer-sponsored plan unless the coverage is affordable and provides minimum value or unless the individual enrolls in the plan. Section 36B(c)(2)(C). Final regulations under section 36B (TD 9590) were published on May 23, 2012 (77 FR 30377).

Employer Shared Responsibility Provision

Section 4980H(b) imposes an assessable payment on applicable large employers (as defined in section 4980H(c)(2)) that offer minimum essential coverage under an eligible employer-sponsored plan that is not affordable or does not provide minimum value for one or more full-time employees who receive a premium tax credit subsidy. Final regulations under section 4980H (TD 9655) were published on February 12, 2014 (79 FR 8544).

Minimum Value

Under section 36B(c)(2)(C)(ii), an eligible employer-sponsored plan provides minimum value only if the plan's share of the total allowed costs of benefits provided under the plan is at least 60 percent. Section 1302(d)(2)(C) of the Affordable Care Act provides that, in determining the percentage of the total allowed costs of benefits provided under a group health plan, the regulations promulgated by HHS under section 1302(d)(2), dealing with actuarial value, apply.

HHS published final regulations under section 1302(d)(2) on February 25, 2013 (78 FR 12834). HHS regulations at 45 CFR 156.20, which apply to the actuarial value of plans required to provide coverage of all essential health benefits, define the percentage of the total allowed costs of benefits provided under a group health plan as (1) the anticipated covered medical spending for essential health benefits coverage (as defined in 45 CFR 156.110(a)) paid by a health plan for a standard population, computed in accordance with the plan's cost-sharing, divided by (2) the total anticipated allowed charges for essential health benefit coverage provided to a standard population.

Under section 1302(b) of the Affordable Care Act, only individual market and insured small group market health plans are required to cover the essential health benefits. Minimum value, however, applies to all eligible employer-sponsored plans, including self-insured plans and insured plans in the large group market. Accordingly, HHS regulations at 45 CFR 156.145(b)(2) and (c) apply the actuarial value definition in the context of minimum value by (1) defining the standard population as the population covered by typical self-insured group health plans, and (2) taking into account the benefits a plan provides that are included in any one benchmark plan a state uses to specify the benefits included in essential health benefits.

Notice 2014-69, advising taxpayers of the intent to propose regulations providing that plans that fail to provide substantial coverage for inpatient hospitalization or physician services do not provide minimum value, was released on November 4, 2014. Notice 2014-69 also advised that it was anticipated that, for purposes of section 4980H liability, the final regulations would not apply to certain plans (as described later in this preamble) before the end of a plan year beginning no later than March 1, 2015. However, an offer of coverage under these plans to an employee does not preclude the employee from obtaining a premium tax credit, if otherwise eligible.

As announced by Notice 2014-69, HHS published proposed regulations on November 26, 2014 (79 FR 70674, 70757), and final regulations on February 27, 2015 (80 FR 10872), amending 45 CFR 156.145(a). The HHS regulations provide that an eligible employer-sponsored plan provides minimum value only if, in addition to covering at least 60 percent of the total allowed costs of benefits provided under the plan, the plan benefits include substantial coverage of inpatient hospitalization and physician services. Consistent with Notice 2014-69, the HHS regulations indicate that the changes to the minimum value regulations do not apply before the end of the plan year beginning no later than March 1, 2015 to a plan that fails to provide substantial coverage for inpatient hospitalization services or for physician services (or both), provided that the employer had entered into a binding written commitment to adopt, or had begun enrolling employees in, the plan before November 4, 2014. For this purpose, the plan year is the plan year in effect under the terms of the plan on November 3, 2014. Also for this purpose, a binding written commitment exists when an employer is contractually required to pay for an arrangement, and a plan begins enrolling employees when it begins accepting employee elections to participate in the plan. See 80 FR 10828.

Explanation of Provisions

The preamble to the HHS regulations acknowledges that self-insured and large group market group health plans are not required to cover the essential health benefits, but notes that a health plan that does not provide substantial coverage for inpatient hospitalization and physician services does not meet a universally accepted minimum standard of value expected from and inherent in any arrangement that can reasonably be called a health plan and that is intended to provide the primary health coverage for employees. The preamble concludes that it is evident in the structure of and policy underlying the Affordable Care Act that the minimum value standard may be interpreted to require that employer-sponsored plans cover critical benefits. See 80 FR 10827-10828.

As the preamble notes, allowing plans that fail to provide substantial coverage of inpatient hospital or physician services to be treated as providing minimum value would adversely affect employees (particularly those with significant health risks) who may find this coverage insufficient, by denying them access to a premium tax credit for individual coverage purchased through an Exchange, while at the same time avoiding the employer shared responsibility payment under section 4980H. Plans that omit critical benefits used disproportionately by individuals in poor health would likely enroll far fewer of these individuals, effectively driving down employer costs at the expense of those who, because of their individual health status, are discouraged from enrolling. See 80 FR 10827-10829.

Accordingly, these proposed regulations incorporate the substance of the rule in the HHS regulations. They provide that an eligible employer-sponsored plan provides minimum value only if the plan's share of the total allowed costs of benefits provided to an employee is at least 60 percent and the plan provides substantial coverage of inpatient hospital and physician services. Comments are requested on rules for determining whether a plan provides "substantial coverage" of inpatient hospital and physician services.

Effective/Applicability Date and Transition Relief

These regulations are proposed to apply for plan years beginning after November 3, 2014. However, for purposes of section 4980H(b), the changes to the minimum value regulations (in §1.36B-6(a)(2) of these proposed regulations) do not apply before the end of the plan year beginning no later than March 1, 2015 to a plan that fails to provide substantial coverage for in-patient hospitalization services or for physician services (or both), provided that the employer had entered into a binding written commitment to adopt the noncompliant plan terms, or had begun enrolling employees in the plan with noncompliant plan terms, before November 4, 2014. For this purpose, the plan year is the plan year in effect under the terms of the plan on November 3, 2014. Also for this purpose, a binding written commitment exists when an employer is contractually required to pay for an arrangement, and a plan begins enrolling employees when it begins accepting employee elections to participate in the plan. The relief provided in this section does not apply to an applicable large employer that would have been liable for a payment under section 4980H without regard to §1.36B-6(a)(2) of these proposed regulations.

An offer of coverage under an eligible employer-sponsored plan that does not comply with §1.36B-6(a)(2) of these proposed regulations does not preclude an employee from obtaining a premium tax credit under section 36B, if otherwise eligible.

Special Analyses

Certain IRS regulations, including this one, are exempt from the requirements of Executive Order 12866, as supplemented and reaffirmed by Executive Order 13563. Therefore, a regulatory impact assessment is not required. It has been determined that section 553(b) of the Administrative Procedure Act (5 U.S.C. chapter 5) does not apply to these regulations and, because the regulations do not impose a collection of information on small entities, the Regulatory Flexibility Act (5 U.S.C. chapter 6) does not apply. Pursuant to section 7805(f) of the Code, this notice of proposed rulemaking has been submitted to the Chief Counsel for Advocacy of the Small Business Administration for comment on its impact on small business.

Comments and Requests for Public Hearing

Before these proposed regulations are adopted as final regulations, consideration will be given to any comments that are submitted timely to the IRS as prescribed in this preamble under the "Addresses" heading. The Treasury Department and the IRS request comments on all aspects of the proposed rules. All comments will be available at *www.regulations.gov* or upon request. A public hearing will be scheduled if requested in writing by any person who timely submits written comments. If a public hearing is scheduled, notice of the date, time, and place for the hearing will be published in the **Federal Register**.

Drafting Information

The principal author of these regulations is Andrew Braden of the Office of the Associate Chief Counsel (Income Tax and Accounting). However, other personnel from the Treasury Department and the IRS participated in their development.

[¶ 49,667] Proposed Amendments of Regulations (REG-139483-13), published in the Federal Register on September 16, 2015 (corrected 11/4/2015).

[Code Secs. 367, 482, 884, 1248 and 6038]

Property transfers: U.S. to foreign corporation: Nonrecognition transaction: Foreign goodwill: Going concern value: Transfer pricing .— Reg. §1.482-1, relating to certain transfers of property by United States persons to foreign corporations, are proposed. Reg. §§1.367(a)-0, 1.367(a)-6 and 1.367(d)-1 and amendments of Reg. §§1.367(a)-1, 1.367(a)-2, 1.367(a)-3, 1.367(a)-4, 1.367(a)-5, 1.367(a)-7, 1.367(a)-8, 1.367(e)-2, 1.884-5, 1.1248-8, 1.1248(f)-2 and 1.6038B-1 were adopted by T.D. 9803 on December 14, 2016.

AGENCY: Internal Revenue Service (IRS), Treasury.

ACTION: Notice of proposed rulemaking; notice of proposed rulemaking by cross-reference to temporary regulation.

SUMMARY: This document contains proposed regulations relating to certain transfers of property by United States persons to foreign corporations. The proposed regulations affect United States persons that transfer certain property, including foreign goodwill and going concern value, to foreign corporations in nonrecognition transactions described in section 367 of the Internal Revenue Code (Code). The proposed regulations also combine portions of the existing regulations under section 367(a) into a single regulation. In addition, in the Rules and Regulations section of this issue of the **Federal Register**, temporary regulations are being issued under section 482 to clarify the coordination of the transfer pricing rules with other Code provisions. The text of those temporary regulations serves as the text of a portion of these proposed regulations.

DATES: Written or electronic comments and requests for a public hearing must be received by December 15, 2015.

ADDRESSES: Send submissions to: CC:PA:LPD:PR (REG-139483-13), Internal Revenue Service, Room 5203, P.O. Box 7604, Ben Franklin Station, Washington, DC 20044. Submissions may be hand-delivered Monday through Friday between the hours of 8 a.m. and 4 p.m. to CC:PA:LPD:PR (REG-139483-13), Courier's Desk, Internal Revenue Service, 1111 Constitution Avenue, NW, Washington, DC 20224; or sent electronically via the Federal eRulemaking Portal at http://www.regulations.gov (IRS REG-139483-13).

FOR FURTHER INFORMATION CONTACT: Concerning the proposed regulations, Ryan A. Bowen, (202) 317-6937; concerning submissions of comments or requests for a public hearing, Regina Johnson, (202) 317-6901 (not toll-free numbers). SUPPLEMENTARY INFORMATION:

Paperwork Reduction Act

The collections of information contained in the regulations have been submitted for review and approved by the Office of Management and Budget in accordance with the Paperwork Reduction Act of 1995 (44 U.S.C. 3507 (d)) under control number 1545-0026.

The collections of information are in §1.6038B-1(c)(4) and (d)(1). The collections of information are mandatory. The likely respondents are domestic corporations. Burdens associated with these requirements will be reflected in the burden for Form 926. Estimates for completing the Form 926 can be located in the form instructions.

An agency may not conduct or sponsor, and a person is not required to respond to, a collection of information unless it displays a valid control number.

Books and records relating to a collection of information must be retained as long as their contents might become material in the administration of any internal revenue law. Generally, tax returns and tax return information are confidential, as required by 26 U.S.C. 6103.

Background

I. *Current Law*

A. *Section 367(a)*

Section 367(a)(1) provides that if, in connection with any exchange described in section 332, 351, 354, 356, or 361, a United States person (U.S. transferor) transfers property to a foreign corporation (outbound transfer), the transferee foreign corporation will not, for purposes of determining the extent to which gain shall be recognized on such transfer, be considered to be a corporation. As a result, under section 367(a)(1), the U.S. transferor recognizes any gain (but not loss) on the outbound transfer of the property. Section 367(a)(2) provides an exception to the application of section 367(a)(1) for certain transfers of stock or securities, and section 367(a)(3) provides an exception for transfers of certain property used in a trade or business.

Specifically, section 367(a)(3)(A) provides that, except as provided in regulations prescribed by the Secretary, the general rule of section 367(a)(1) will not apply to any property transferred to a foreign corporation for use by such foreign corporation in the active conduct of a trade or business outside of the United States (ATB exception). Section 367(a)(3)(B) provides that, except as provided in regulations prescribed by the Secretary, certain property is not eligible for the ATB exception. The statute describes five categories of property that are not eligible for the ATB exception: (i) property described in paragraph (1) or (3) of section 1221(a) (relating to inventory and copyrights, etc.); (ii) installment obligations, accounts receivable, or similar property; (iii) foreign currency or other property denominated in foreign currency; (iv) intangible property within the meaning of section 936(h)(3)(B); and (v) property with respect to which the U.S. transferor is a lessor at the time of the transfer, unless the foreign corporation was the lessee.

Section 367(a)(3)(C) provides that, except as provided in regulations prescribed by the Secretary, the ATB exception will not apply to gain realized on an outbound transfer of the assets of a foreign branch to the extent that previously deducted losses of the branch exceed the taxable income earned by the branch after the losses were incurred (branch loss recapture rule). However, any realized gain in the property transferred that exceeds the branch losses that must be recaptured under this rule may qualify for the ATB exception.

Section 367(a)(6) provides that section 367(a)(1) will not apply to an outbound transfer of any property that the Secretary, in order to carry out the purposes of section 367(a), designates by regulation.

Sections 1.367(a)-2 and 1.367(a)-2T provide general rules for determining whether property is transferred for use by a transferee foreign corporation in the active conduct of a trade or business outside of the United States for purposes of the ATB exception.

Sections 1.367(a)-4 and 1.367(a)-4T provide special rules for determining whether certain property satisfies the ATB exception, including rules that apply to (i) property to be leased by the transferee foreign corporation, (ii) oil and gas working interests, (iii) compulsory transfers of property, and (iv) property to be sold by the foreign corporation. Section 1.367(a)-4T also provides special rules requiring the recapture of depreciation upon an outbound transfer of U.S. depreciated property and exempting outbound transfers of property to a FSC (within the meaning of section 922(a)) from the application of paragraphs (a) and (d) of section 367.

Sections 1.367(a)-5 and 1.367(a)-5T address the five categories of property ineligible for the ATB exception that are described in section 367(a)(3)(B) and provide narrow exceptions to certain of those categories. Section 1.367(a)-5T(d) (which addresses foreign currency and other property denominated in a foreign currency) allows certain property denominated in the foreign currency of the country in which the foreign corporation is organized to qualify under the ATB exception if that property was acquired in the ordinary course of the business of the U.S. transferor that will be carried on by the foreign corporation. Section 1.367(a)-5T(e) (which addresses intangible property) contains a deadwood reference to the application of section 367(a)(1) to a transfer of intangible property pursuant to section 332. In this regard, see §1.367(e)-2(a)(2), providing that section 367(a) does not apply to a liquidation described in section 332 of a U.S. subsidiary into a foreign parent corporation. Section 1.367(a)-5T(e) also provides a cross reference to section 367(d) for transfers of intangible property described in section 351 or 361.

Sections 1.367(a)-6 and 1.367(a)-6T provide rules for applying the branch loss recapture rule of section 367(a)(3)(C).

B. *Section 367(d)*

Section 367(d) provides rules for certain outbound transfers of intangible property. Section 367(d)(1) provides that, except as provided in regulations, if a U.S. transferor transfers any intangible property, within the meaning of section 936(h)(3)(B), to a foreign corporation in an exchange described in section 351 or 361, section 367(d) (and not section 367(a)) applies to such transfer.

Section 936(h)(3)(B) defines intangible property broadly to mean any:

(i) patent, invention, formula, process, design, pattern, or know-how;

(ii) copyright, literary, musical, or artistic composition;

(iii) trademark, trade name, or brand name;

(iv) franchise, license, or contract;

(v) method, program, system, procedure, campaign, survey, study, forecast, estimate, customer list, or technical data; or

(vi) any similar item,

which has substantial value independent of the services of any individual (section 936(h)(3)(B) intangible property).

Section 367(d)(2)(A) provides that a U.S. transferor that transfers intangible property subject to section 367(d) is treated as having sold the property in exchange for payments that are contingent upon the productivity, use, or disposition of the property. Specifically, the U.S. transferor is treated as receiving amounts that reasonably reflect the amounts that would have been received annually in the form of such payments over the useful life of such property (section 367(d)(2)(A)(ii)(I)), or in the case of a disposition of the intangible property following such transfer (whether direct or indirect), at the time of the disposition (section 367(d)(2)(A)(ii)(II)). The amounts taken into account under section 367(d)(2)(A)(ii) must be commensurate with the income attributable to the intangible. Section 367(d)(2)(A) (flush language).

Section 1.367(d)-1T(b) generally provides that section 367(d) and § 1.367(d)-1T apply to the transfer of any intangible property, but not to the transfer of foreign goodwill or going concern value, as defined in § 1.367(a)-1T(d)(5)(iii) (foreign goodwill exception). Section 1.367(a)-1T(d)(5)(i) generally defines "intangible property," for purposes of section 367, as knowledge, rights, documents, and any other intangible item within the meaning of section 936(h)(3)(B) that constitutes property for purposes of section 332, 351, 354, 355, 356, or 361, as applicable. The regulation further provides that a working interest in oil and gas property will not be considered to be intangible property for purposes of section 367 and the regulations thereunder.

Section 1.367(a)-1T(d)(5)(iii) defines "foreign goodwill or going concern value" as the residual value of a business operation conducted outside of the United States after all other tangible and intangible assets have been identified and valued. Section 1.367(a)-1T(d)(5)(iii) also provides that, for purposes of section 367 and the regulations thereunder, the value of a right to use a corporate name in a foreign country is treated as foreign goodwill or going concern value.

In addition to providing the foreign goodwill exception, § 1.367(d)-1T(b) also excepts from section 367(d) property that is described in § 1.367(a)-5T(b)(2), which, in general, consists of copyrights and other items described in section 1221(a)(3). Those items, however, are not eligible for the ATB exception by reason of § 1.367(a)-5T.

For purposes of § 1.367(d)-1T, the useful life of intangible property is limited to 20 years under § 1.367(d)-1T(c)(3).

C. Legislative History of Section 367(d)

Congress amended section 367 in 1984 to create objective statutory rules because, among other reasons, the IRS was experiencing challenges administering the prior version of the statute. The prior version provided that certain outbound transfers of property qualified for tax-free treatment only if the U.S. transferor established that the outbound transfer was "not in pursuance of a plan having as one its principal purposes the avoidance of Federal income taxes."

In amending section 367, Congress also noted that "specific and unique problems exist" with respect to outbound transfers of intangible property and enacted section 367(d) in substantially its present form to address these transfers. S. REP. NO. 169, 98th Cong., 2d Sess., at 360 (1984); H.R. REP. NO. 432, 98th Cong., 2d Sess., at 1315 (1984). Congress identified problems as arising when "transferor U.S. companies hope to reduce their U.S. taxable income by deducting substantial research and experimentation expenses associated with the development of the transferred intangible and, by transferring the intangible to a foreign corporation at the point of profitability, to ensure deferral of U.S. tax on the profits generated by the intangible." *Id.*

The favorable treatment of foreign goodwill and going concern value available under existing law is premised on statements in the legislative history of section 367(d). "The committee contemplates that, ordinarily, no gain will be recognized on the transfer of goodwill or going concern value for use in an active trade or business." S. REP. NO. 169, 98th Cong., 2d Sess., at 364; H.R. REP. NO. 432, 98th Cong., 2d Sess., at 1319. The Senate Finance Committee and the House Committee on Ways and Means each noted, without explanation, that it "does not anticipate that the transfer of goodwill or going concern value developed by a foreign branch to a newly organized foreign corporation will result in abuse of the U.S. tax system." S. REP. NO. 169, 98th Cong., 2d Sess., at 362; H.R. REP. NO. 432, 98th Cong., 2d Sess., at 1317. However, neither section 367 nor its legislative history defines goodwill or going concern value of a foreign branch or discusses how goodwill or going concern value is attributed to a foreign branch.

D. Taxpayer Interpretations Regarding Foreign Goodwill and Going Concern Value Under Section 367

In general, taxpayers interpret section 367 and the regulations under section 367(a) and (d) in one of two alternative ways when claiming favorable treatment for foreign goodwill and going concern value.

Under one interpretation, taxpayers take the position that goodwill and going concern value are not section 936(h)(3)(B) intangible property and therefore are not subject to section 367(d) because section 367(d) applies only to section 936(h)(3)(B) intangible property. Under this interpretation, taxpayers assert that the foreign goodwill exception has no application. Furthermore, these taxpayers assert that gain realized with respect to the outbound transfer of goodwill or going concern value is not recognized under the general rule of section 367(a)(1) because the goodwill or going concern value is eligible for, and satisfies, the ATB exception under section 367(a)(3)(A).

Under a second interpretation, taxpayers take the position that, although goodwill and going concern value are section 936(h)(3)(B) intangible property, the foreign goodwill exception applies. These taxpayers also assert that section 367(a)(1) does not apply to foreign goodwill or going concern value, either because of section 367(d)(1)(A) (providing that, except as provided in regulations, section 367(d) and not section 367(a) applies to section 936(h)(3)(B) intangible property) or because of the ATB exception.

II. Reasons for Change

The Treasury Department and the IRS are aware that, in the context of outbound transfers, certain taxpayers attempt to avoid recognizing gain or income attributable to high-value intangible property by asserting that an inappropriately large share (in many cases, the majority) of the value of the property transferred is foreign goodwill or going concern value that is eligible for favorable treatment under section 367.

Specifically, the Treasury Department and the IRS are aware that some taxpayers value the property transferred in a manner contrary to section 482 in order to minimize the value of the property transferred that they identify as section 936(h)(3)(B) intangible property for which a deemed income inclusion is required under section 367(d) and to maximize the value of the property transferred that they identify as exempt from current tax. For example, some taxpayers (i) use valuation methods that value items of intangible property on an item-by-item basis, when valuing the items on an aggregate basis would achieve a more reliable result under the arm's length standard of the section 482 regulations, or (ii) do not properly perform a full factual and functional analysis of the business in which the intangible property is employed.

The Treasury Department and the IRS also are aware that some taxpayers broadly interpret the meaning of foreign goodwill and going concern value for purposes of section 367. Specifically, although the existing regulations under section 367 define foreign goodwill or going concern value by reference to a business operation conducted outside of the United States, some taxpayers have asserted that they have transferred significant foreign goodwill or going concern value when a large share of that value was associated with a business operated primarily by employees in the United States, where the business simply earned income remotely from foreign customers. In addition, some taxpayers take the position that value created through customer-facing activities occurring within the United States is foreign goodwill or going concern value.

The Treasury Department and the IRS have concluded that the taxpayer positions and interpretations described in this section of the preamble raise significant policy concerns and are inconsistent with the expectation, expressed in legislative history, that the transfer of foreign goodwill or going concern value developed by a foreign branch to a foreign corporation was unlikely to result in abuse of the U.S. tax system. *See* S. REP. NO. 169, 98th Cong., 2d Sess., at 362; H.R. REP. NO. 432, 98th Cong., 2d Sess., at 1317. The Treasury Department and the IRS considered whether the favorable treatment for foreign goodwill and going concern value under current law could be preserved while protecting the U.S. tax base through regulations expressly prescribing parameters for the portion of the value of a business that qualifies for the favorable treatment. For example, regulations could require that, to be eligible for the favorable treatment, the value must have been created by activities conducted outside of the United States through an actual foreign branch that had been in operation for a minimum number of years and be attributable to unrelated foreign customers. The Treasury Department and the IRS ultimately determined, however, that such an approach would be impractical to administer. In particular, while the temporary regulations under section 482 that are published in the Rules and Regulations section of this issue of the **Federal Register** clarify the proper application of section 482 in important respects, there will continue to be challenges in administering the transfer pricing rules whenever the transfer of different types of intangible property gives rise to significantly different tax consequences. Given the amounts at stake, as long as foreign goodwill and going concern value are afforded favorable treatment, taxpayers will continue to have strong incentives to take aggressive transfer pricing positions to inappropriately exploit the favorable treatment of foreign goodwill and going concern value, however defined, and thereby erode the U.S. tax base.

For the reasons discussed in this section of the preamble, the Treasury Department and the IRS have determined that allowing intangible property to be transferred outbound in a tax-free manner is inconsistent with the policies of section 367 and sound tax administration and therefore will amend the regulations under section 367 as described in the Explanation of Provisions section of this preamble.

III. *Coordination with Section 482*

The temporary regulations under section 482 published in the Rules and Regulations section of this issue of the **Federal Register** clarify the coordination of the application of the arm's length standard and the best method rule in the regulations under section 482 in conjunction with other Code provisions, including section 367, in determining the proper tax treatment of controlled transactions. The text of the temporary regulations under section 482 also serves as the text of a portion of these proposed regulations. The preamble to the temporary regulations explains the temporary regulations and the corresponding proposed regulations.

Explanation of Provisions

I. *Eliminating the Foreign Goodwill Exception and Limiting the Scope of the ATB Exception*

A. *In General*

The proposed regulations eliminate the foreign goodwill exception under §1.367(d)-1T and limit the scope of property that is eligible for the ATB exception generally to certain tangible property and financial assets. Accordingly, under the proposed regulations, upon an outbound transfer of foreign goodwill or going concern value, a U.S. transferor will be subject to either current gain recognition under section 367(a)(1) or the tax treatment provided under section 367(d).

B. *Modifications to §1.367(d)-1T*

Proposed §1.367(d)-1(b) provides that section 367(d) and §1.367(d)-1 apply to an outbound transfer of intangible property, as defined in proposed §1.367(a)-1(d)(5). Proposed §1.367(d)-1(b) does not provide an exception for any intangible property. Rather, as described in part II. of the Explanation of Provisions section of this preamble, proposed §1.367(a)-1(d)(5) modifies the definition of intangible property that applies for purposes of section 367(a) and (d). The modified definition facilitates both the elimination of the foreign goodwill exception as well as the addition of a rule under which U.S. transferors may apply section 367(d) with respect to certain outbound transfers of property that otherwise would be subject to section 367(a) under the U.S. transferor's interpretation of section 936(h)(3)(B). The proposed regulations make certain coordinating changes to §1.367(d)-1T to take into account the elimination of the foreign goodwill exception and the revised definition of intangible property. The specific provisions of the temporary regulations that will be replaced by the proposed regulations will be removed upon finalization. The proposed regulations also eliminate the definition of foreign goodwill and going concern value under existing §1.367(a)-1T(d)(5)(iii) because it is no longer needed.

In addition, the proposed regulations eliminate the existing rule under §1.367(d)-1T(c)(3) that limits the useful life of intangible property to 20 years. When the useful life of the intangible property transferred exceeds 20 years, the limitation might result in less than all of the income attributable to the property being taken into account by the U.S. transferor. Accordingly, proposed §1.367(d)-1(c)(3) provides that the useful life of intangible property is the entire period during which the exploitation of the intangible property is reasonably anticipated to occur, as of the time of transfer. For this purpose, exploitation includes use of the intangible property in research and development. Consistent with the guidance for cost sharing arrangements in §1.482-7(g)(2)(ii)(A), if the intangible property is reasonably anticipated to contribute to its own further development or to developing other intangibles, then the period includes the period, reasonably anticipated at the time of the transfer, of exploiting (including use in research and development) such further development. Consequently, depending on the facts, the cessation of exploitation activity after a specific period of time may or may not be reasonably anticipated. *See, e.g.,* §1.482-7(g)(4)(viii), *Examples 1* (cessation anticipated after 15 years) and 7 (cessation not anticipated at any determinable date).

C. *Modifications Relating to the ATB Exception*

The rules for determining whether property is eligible for the ATB exception and whether the property satisfies the ATB exception currently are found in numerous regulations, namely §§1.367(a)-2, 1.367(a)-2T, 1.367(a)-4, 1.367(a)-4T, 1.367(a)-5, and 1.367(a)-5T (collectively, the ATB regulations). To make the regulations more accessible, the proposed regulations combine the ATB regulations, other than the depreciation recapture rule, into a single regulation under proposed § 1.367(a)-2. Accordingly, upon finalization of the proposed regulations, current §§ 1.367(a)-2T, 4T, and 5T will be removed. The proposed regulations retain a coordination rule pursuant to which a transfer of stock or securities in an exchange subject to §1.367(a)-3 is not subject to §1.367(a)-2. *See* §1.367(a)-2(a)(1). The proposed regulations make conforming changes to the depreciation recapture rule, which is moved from §1.367(a)-4T to §1.367(a)-4, and the branch loss recapture rule, which remains under §§1.367(a)-6 and 1.367(a)-6T. Although minor wording changes have been made to certain aspects of the ATB regulations as part of consolidating them into a single regulation, the proposed regulations are not intended to be interpreted as making substantive changes to the ATB regulations except as otherwise described in this section of the preamble.

Under existing regulations, all property is eligible for the ATB exception, unless the property is specifically excluded. Under this structure, taxpayers have an incentive to take the position that certain intangible property is not described in section 936(h)(3)(B) and therefore not subject to section 367(d) and is instead subject to section 367(a) but eligible for the ATB exception because the intangible property is not specifically excluded from the ATB exception. The Treasury Department and the IRS have concluded that providing an exclusive list of property eligible for the ATB exception will reduce the incentives for taxpayers to undervalue intangible property subject to section 367(d).

Thus, the proposed regulations provide that only certain types of property (as described in the next paragraph) are eligible for the ATB exception. However, in order for eligible property to satisfy the ATB exception, that property must also be considered transferred for use in the active conduct of a trade or business outside of the United States. Specifically, proposed §1.367(a)-2(a)(2) provides the general rule that an outbound transfer of property satisfies the ATB exception if (i) the property constitutes eligible property, (ii) the property is transferred for use by the foreign corporation in the active conduct of a trade or business outside of the United States, and (iii) certain reporting requirements under section 6038B are satisfied.

Under proposed §1.367(a)-2(b), eligible property is tangible property, working interests in oil and gas property, and certain financial assets, unless the property is also described in one of four categories of ineligible property. Proposed §1.367(a)-2(c) lists four categories of property not eligible for the ATB exception, which, in general, are (i) inventory or similar property; (ii) installment obligations, accounts receivable, or similar property; (iii) foreign currency or certain other property denominated in foreign currency; and (iv) certain leased tangible property. These four categories of property not eligible for the ATB exception include four of the five categories described in existing regulations under §§1.367(a)-5 and 1.367-5T. The category for intangible property is not retained because it is not relevant: Intangible property transferred to a foreign corporation pursuant to section 351 or 361 is not eligible property under proposed §1.367(a)-2(b) without regard to the application of proposed §1.367(a)-2(c).

The proposed regulations also eliminate the exception in existing §1.367(a)-5T(d)(2) that allows certain property denominated in the foreign currency of the country in which the foreign corporation is organized to qualify under the ATB exception if that property was acquired in the ordinary course of the business of the U.S. transferor that will be carried on by the foreign corporation. The Treasury Department and the IRS have determined that removing the exception is consistent with the general policy of section 367(a)(3)(B)(iii) to require gain to be recognized on an outbound transfer of foreign currency denominated property. Removing the exception will preserve the character, source, and amount of gain attributable to section 988 transactions that otherwise could be lost or changed if such gain were not immediately recognized but instead were reflected only in the U.S. transferor's basis in the stock of the foreign corporation.

The general rules for determining whether eligible property is transferred for use in the active conduct of a trade or business outside of the United States are described in proposed §1.367(a)-2(d). Also, paragraphs (e) through (h) of proposed §1.367(a)-2 provide special rules for certain property to be leased after the transfer, a working interest in oil and gas property, property that is re-transferred by the transferee foreign corporation to another person, and certain compulsory transfers of property, respectively. The proposed regulations also combine existing §1.367(a)-2T(c) (relating to property that is re-transferred by the foreign corporation) and a portion of §1.367(a)-4T(d) (relating to property to be sold by the foreign corporation) into proposed §1.367(a)-2(g), because both of these existing provisions relate to subsequent transfers of property by the foreign corporation. See proposed §1.367(a)-2(g)(1) and (2), respectively. Proposed §1.367(a)-2(g)(2) does not retain the portion of existing §1.367(a)-4T(d) that applies to certain transfers of stock or securities. The Treasury Department and the IRS have determined that §§1.367(a)-3 and 1.367(a)-8 (generally requiring U.S. transferors that own five-percent or more of the stock of the foreign corporation to enter into a gain recognition agreement to avoid recognizing gain under section 367(a)(1) upon the outbound transfer of stock or securities) adequately carry out the policy of section 367(a) with respect to the transfer of stock or securities.

The proposed regulations modify the scope of the term U.S. depreciated property for purposes of the depreciation recapture rule to include section 126 property (as defined in section 1255(a)(2)).

The proposed regulations eliminate the special rules for outbound transfers of property to a FSC, because the FSC provisions have been repealed. Tax Increase Prevention and Reconciliation Act of 2005, Pub L. No. 109-222, §513, 120 Stat. 366 (2006); FSC Repeal and Extraterritorial Income Exclusion Act of 2000, Pub. L. No. 106-519, §2, 114 Stat. 2423 (2000).

Finally, the proposed regulations make conforming changes to the reporting requirements under §1.6038B-1(c)(4) to take into account the proposed regulations under §1.367(a)-2. The proposed regulations retain a rule providing relief for certain failures to comply with the reporting requirements of section 6038B and the regulations thereunder for qualification under the ATB exception, but that rule is moved to proposed §1.367(a)-2(j).

II. *Treatment of Certain Property as Subject to Section 367(d)*

Taxpayers take different positions as to whether goodwill and going concern value are section 936(h)(3)(B) intangible property, as discussed in part I.D. of the Background section of this preamble. The proposed regulations do not address this issue. However, the proposed regulations under §1.367(a)-1(b)(5) provide that a U.S. transferor may apply section 367(d) to a transfer of property, other than certain property described below, that otherwise would be subject to section 367(a) under the U.S. transferor's interpretation of section 936(h)(3)(B). Under this rule, a U.S. transferor that takes the position that goodwill and going concern value are not section 936(h)(3)(B) intangible property may nonetheless apply section 367(d) to goodwill and going concern value. This rule furthers sound tax administration by reducing the consequences of uncertainty as to whether value is attributable to property subject to section 367(a) or property subject to section 367(d). The application of section 367(d) in lieu of section 367(a) is available only for property that is not eligible property, as defined in proposed §1.367(a)-2(b) but, for this purpose, determined without regard to §1.367(a)-2(c) (which describes four categories of property explicitly excluded from the ATB exception). A U.S. transferor must disclose whether it is applying section 367(a) or (d) to a transfer of such property. See proposed §§1.6038B-1(c)(4)(vii) and -1(d)(1)(iv).

To implement this new rule under proposed §1.367(a)-1(b)(5) and the removal of the foreign goodwill exception, the proposed regulations revise the definition of "intangible property" that applies for purposes of sections 367(a) and (d). As revised, the term means either property described in section 936(h)(3)(B) or property to which a U.S. transferor applies section 367(d) (in lieu of applying section 367(a)). However, for this purpose and consistent with existing regulations, intangible property does not include property described in section 1221(a)(3) (generally relating to certain copyrights) or a working interest in oil and gas property.

The regulations under §1.367(a)-7 (concerning outbound transfers of property subject to section 367(a) in certain asset reorganizations) use the term "section 367(d) property" to describe property that is not subject to section 367(a) and is therefore not subject to §1.367(a)-7. The proposed regulations modify the definition of section 367(d) property in §1.367(a)-7(f)(11) (which currently defines section 367(d) property as property described in section 936(h)(3)(B)) by reference to the new definition of "intangible property" under the proposed regulations. When the Treasury Department and the IRS issue regulations to implement the guidance described in Notice 2012-39 (IRB 2012-31) (announcing regulations to be issued addressing outbound transfers of intangible property subject to section 367(d) in certain asset reorganizations), the definition of "section 367(d) property" provided in section 4.05(3) of the notice will be similarly modified.

III. *Modifications to §1.367(a)-1T*

Section 1.482-1T(f)(2)(i) of the temporary regulations published elsewhere in the Rules and Regulations section of this issue of the **Federal Register** clarify the coordination of the application of the arm's length standard and the best method rule in the regulations under section 482 in conjunction with other Code provisions, including section 367, in determining the proper tax treatment of controlled transactions. Proposed §1.367(a)-1(b)(3) provides that, in cases where an outbound transfer of property subject to section 367(a) constitutes a controlled transaction, as defined in §1.482-1(i)(8), the value of the property transferred is determined in accordance with section 482 and the regulations thereunder. This rule replaces existing §1.367(a)-1T(b)(3), which includes three rules.

First, §1.367(a)-1T(b)(3)(i) provides that "the gain required to be recognized . . . shall in no event exceed the gain that would have been recognized on a taxable sale of those items of property *if sold individually and without offsetting individual losses against individual gains*" (emphasis added). The Treasury Department and the IRS are concerned that in controlled transactions, taxpayers might have interpreted the wording "if sold individually" as inconsistent with § 1.482-1T(f)(2)(i)(B) (as clarified in temporary regulations published elsewhere in the Rules and Regulations section in this issue of the **Federal Register**), which provides that an aggregate analysis of transactions may provide the most reliable measure of an arm's length result in certain circumstances.

Second, § 1.367(a)-1T(b)(3)(ii) provides that no loss may be recognized by reason of section 367. That rule duplicates a loss disallowance rule in § 1.367(a)-1T(b)(1), which provides that section 367(a)(1) denies nonrecognition only to transfers of items of property on which gain is realized and that losses do not affect the amount of the gain recognized because of section 367(a)(1).

Third, § 1.367(a)-1T(b)(3)(iii) provides a rule to address a scenario in which ordinary income and capital gain could exceed the amount described in § 1.367(a)-1T(b)(3)(i). Because these regulations replace § 1.367(a)-1T(b)(3)(i), § 1.367(a)-1T(b)(3)(iii) is no longer necessary.

IV. Proposed Effective/Applicability Dates

The proposed regulations are proposed to apply to transfers occurring on or after September 14, 2015 and to transfers occurring before September 14, 2015 resulting from entity classification elections made under § 301.7701-3 that are filed on or after September 14, 2015. However, the removal of the exception currently provided in § 1.367(a)-5T(d)(2) will apply to transfers occurring on or after the date that the rules proposed in this section are adopted as final regulations in a Treasury decision published in the **Federal Register** and to transfers occurring before that date resulting from entity classification elections made under § 301.7701-3 that are filed on or after that date. For proposed dates of applicability, see § 1.367(a)-1(g)(5), -2(k), -4(b), -6(k), -7(j)(2), 1.367(d)-1(j), and 1.6038B-1(g)(7). No inference is intended as to the application of the provisions proposed to be amended by these proposed regulations under current law. The IRS may, where appropriate, challenge transactions under applicable provisions or judicial doctrines.

Special Analyses

Certain IRS regulations, including this one, are exempt from the requirements of Executive Order 12866, as supplemented and reaffirmed by Executive Order 13563. Therefore, a regulatory impact assessment is not required. It has been determined that section 553(b) and (d) of the Administrative Procedure Act (5 U.S.C. chapter 5) does not apply to these regulations. It is hereby certified that the collection of information contained in this regulation will not have a significant economic impact on a substantial number of small entities. Accordingly, a regulatory flexibility analysis is not required. This certification is based on the fact that the proposed regulations under section 367(a) and (d) simplify existing regulations, and the regulations under section 6038B make relatively minor changes to existing information reporting requirements. Moreover, these regulations primarily will affect large domestic corporations filing consolidated returns. In addition, the Regulatory Flexibility Act (5 U.S.C. chapter 6) does not apply to the regulations under section 482 that are proposed herein, and published as temporary regulations in the Rules and Regulations section of this issue of the **Federal Register**, because those regulations do not impose a collection of information requirement on small entities. Pursuant to section 7805(f) of the Code, these regulations have been submitted to the Chief Counsel for Advocacy of the Small Business Administration for comment on their impact on small business.

Comments and Requests for Public Hearing

Before these proposed regulations are adopted as final regulations, consideration will be given to any comments that are submitted timely to the IRS as prescribed in this preamble under the "Addresses" heading. The Treasury Department and the IRS request comments on all aspects of the proposed rules. In particular, comments are requested on whether, with respect to the proposed elimination of the foreign goodwill exception and narrowing of the scope of the ATB exception, a limited exception should be provided for certain narrow cases where there is limited potential for abuse. One such case, for example, might be a financial services business that operates in true branch form and for which there is regulatory pressure or compulsion to incorporate the assets of the branch in a foreign corporation. Comments should discuss how the IRS would administer any such exception. With respect to the ATB exception, comments are requested as to whether the definition of "financial asset" under proposed § 1.367(a)-2(b)(3) should be expanded to include other items. With respect to the proposed elimination of the 20-year limitation on the useful life of intangible property under § 1.367(d)-1T(c)(3), comments are requested on ways to simplify the administration of inclusions that section 367(d) requires for property with a very long useful life. All comments will be available at www.regulations.gov or upon request. A public hearing will be scheduled if requested in writing by any person that timely submits written comments. If a public hearing is scheduled, notice of the date, time, and place for the public hearing will be published in the **Federal Register**.

Drafting information

The principal author of these proposed regulations is Ryan Bowen, Office of Associate Chief Counsel (International). However, other personnel from the Treasury Department and the IRS participated in their development.

[¶ **49,674**] **Proposed Amendments of Regulations (REG-134219-08)**, published in the Federal Register on November 20, 2015 (corrected 1/13/2016).

[Code Secs. 66 and 6015]

Equitable relief: Joint and several liability: Innocent spouse relief: Suspension of collection: Statute of limitations: Res judicata: Underpayment, definition: Meaningful participation in prior hearing.—Amendments of Reg. §§ 1.66-1, 1.66-2, 1.66-3, 1.66-4, 1.66-5, 1.6015-0, 1.6015-1, 1.6015-2, 1.6015-3, 1.6015-4, 1.6015-5, 1.6015-6, 1.6015-7, 1.6015-8 and 1.6015-9 relating to relief from joint and several liability under section 6015 of the Internal Revenue Code (Code), are proposed.

AGENCY: Internal Revenue Service (IRS), Treasury.

ACTION: Notice of proposed rulemaking.

SUMMARY: This document contains proposed regulations relating to relief from joint and several liability under section 6015 of the Internal Revenue Code (Code). The regulations reflect changes in the law made by the Tax Relief and Health Care Act of 2006 as well as changes in the law arising from litigation. The regulations provide guidance to married individuals who filed joint returns and later seek relief from joint and several liability.

DATES: Written or electronic comments and requests for a public hearing must be received by February 18, 2016.

ADDRESSES: Send submissions to: CC:PA:LPD:PR (REG-134219-08), room 5203, Internal Revenue Service, PO Box 7604, Ben Franklin Station, Washington, DC 20044. Submissions may be hand-delivered Monday through Friday between the hours of 8 a.m. and 4 p.m. to CC:PA:LPD:PR (REG-134219-08), Courier's Desk, Internal Revenue Service, 1111 Constitution Avenue, N.W., Washington, DC; or sent electronically via the Federal eRulemaking Portal at www.regulations.gov (IRS REG-134219-08).

FOR FURTHER INFORMATION CONTACT: Concerning the proposed regulations, Nancy Rose at (202) 317-6844; concerning submissions of comments contact Oluwafunmilayo Taylor, (202) 317-6901 (not toll-free numbers).

SUPPLEMENTARY INFORMATION:

Background

This document contains proposed amendments to the Income Tax Regulations (26 CFR part 1) for relief from joint and several liability under section 6015 of the Code and relief from the operation of state community property law under section 66.

Section 6013(a) permits a husband and wife to file a joint income tax return. Section 6013(d)(3) provides that spouses filing a joint income tax return are jointly and severally liable for liabilities for tax arising from that return. The term "tax" includes additions to tax, additional amounts, penalties, and interest. See sections 6665(a)(2) and 6601(e)(1). Joint and several liability allows the IRS to collect the entire liability from either spouse who signed the joint return, without regard to whom the items of income, deduction, credit, or basis that gave rise to the liability are attributable. Prior to 1998, section 6013(e) provided limited relief from joint and several liability. In 1998, Congress enacted the Internal Revenue Service Restructuring and Reform Act of 1998, Public Law No. 105-206, 112 Stat. 685 (1998), which repealed section 6013(e) and replaced it with section 6015. Section 6015 applies to liabilities arising after July 22, 1998, and liabilities that arose on or before July 22, 1998, but remained unpaid as of that date.

Section 6015 provides three avenues for relief from joint and several liability-sections 6015(b), (c) and (f). To be eligible for relief from joint and several liability, a spouse must request relief. Under section 6015(b), a requesting spouse may be entitled to relief from joint and several liability for an understatement of tax attributable to erroneous items of the nonrequesting spouse. Section 6015(c) permits a taxpayer who is divorced, separated, widowed, or who had been living apart from the other spouse for 12 months to allocate his or her tax deficiency between the spouses as if separate returns had been filed. Claims for relief under section 6015(b) and (c) must be made within two years of the IRS's first collection activity against the requesting spouse. Finally, section 6015(f) confers discretion upon the Commissioner to grant equitable relief from joint and several liability for understatements and underpayments, based on all the facts and circumstances. Regulations under section 6015 were first prescribed in TD 9003, **Federal Register** (67 FR 47278) on July 18, 2002.

These proposed amendments are necessary to carry out the provisions of section 6015 and to reflect changes in the law since the publication of TD 9003. On December 20, 2006, Congress enacted the Tax Relief and Health Care Act of 2006, Public Law No. 109-432, div. C, title IV, section 408, 120 Stat. 2922, 3061-62 (2006) (the 2006 Act). The 2006 Act amended section 6015 to provide the United States Tax Court with jurisdiction to review the Commissioner's determination to deny equitable relief under section 6015(f) when the Commissioner has not determined a deficiency and to suspend the period of limitation for collection under section 6502 when relief is requested only under section 6015(f). The proposed regulations also provide clarification and additional guidance on procedural and substantive issues related to the three types of relief from joint and several liability under section 6015.

Section 66 provides relief for a spouse who did not file a joint return in a community property state and did not include in gross income an item of community income that would be attributable solely to the nonrequesting spouse but for the operation of state community property law. Regulations under section 66 were first prescribed in TD 9074, **Federal Register** (68 FR 41067) on July 10, 2003. The proposed regulations under section 66 contain only non-substantive changes.

Recently, other amendments to the regulations under section 6015 were proposed in a notice of proposed rulemaking (REG-132251-11) published in the **Federal Register** (78 FR 49242) on August 13, 2013. Those regulations proposed changes to § 1.6015-5 to remove the two-year deadline for taxpayers to file requests for equitable relief under section 6015(f), and other changes related to the time and manner for requesting relief. Additionally, on September 16, 2013, the IRS issued Rev. Proc. 2013-34 (2013-2 CB 397). Rev. Proc. 2013-34 revised the factors used in determining if a requesting spouse is eligible for equitable relief under sections 66(c) and 6015(f).

Explanation of Provisions

These regulations propose to make a number of significant changes to the existing regulations. These changes include providing additional guidance on the judicial doctrine of res judicata and the section 6015(g)(2) exception to res judicata when a requesting spouse did not meaningfully participate in a prior court proceeding. The regulations propose to add a list of acts to be considered in making the determination as to whether the requesting spouse meaningfully participated in a prior proceeding and provide examples of the operation of these rules. The regulations also (1) propose a definition of underpayment or unpaid tax for purposes of section 6015(f); (2) provide detailed rules regarding credits and refunds in innocent spouse cases; (3) expand the rule that penalties and interest are not separate items from which relief can be obtained to cases involving underpayments; (4) incorporate an administratively developed rule that attribution of an erroneous item follows the attribution of the underlying item that caused the increase to adjusted gross income (AGI); (5) update the discussion of the allocation rules under section 6015(c) and (d); and (6) revise the rules regarding prohibition on collection and suspension of the collection statute.

1. Section 1.6015-1

The procedures for requesting relief on Form 8857, "Request for Innocent Spouse Relief," under section 6015 have changed since 2006 because of the amendments to section 6015(e) made by Section 408 of Title IV of Division C of the 2006 Act. The amendments to section 6015(e) conferred jurisdiction on the Tax Court to review the Commissioner's denial of relief under section 6015(f) in cases in which a deficiency had not been asserted. The amendments also provided for a prohibition on collection and a corresponding tolling of the collection statute under section 6502 upon the filing of a request for relief under section 6015(f). The amendments apply to any liability for taxes arising on or after December 20, 2006, and to any liability for taxes arising before December 20, 2006, and remaining unpaid as of that date. As a result of the amendments, any request for relief under section 6015 will toll the collection statute, making it unnecessary for a spouse to elect or request a particular type of relief as required under § 1.6015-1(a)(2) of the current regulations. Accordingly, § 1.6015-1 and all sections referencing an election under §§ 1.6015-2 and 1.6015-3 or a request for relief under § 1.6015-4 are proposed to be revised to reflect that a requesting spouse is no longer required to elect or request relief under a specific provision of section 6015. Thus, beginning with the June 2007 revision to the Form 8857, a requesting spouse makes a single request for relief on Form 8857. Section 1.6015-1 is also being revised to provide that the IRS will consider in all cases whether the requesting spouse is eligible for relief under § 1.6015-2 or § 1.6015-3, and if relief is not available under either of those sections, under § 1.6015-4.

Section 6015(g)(2) provides an exception to the common law doctrine of res judicata except in a case in which relief under section 6015 was at issue in a prior court proceeding or if a requesting spouse meaningfully participated in a prior proceeding in which relief under section 6015 could have been raised. Current § 1.6015-(e) is being revised in these proposed regulations to provide more detailed guidance on how the exception to res judicata and the meaningful participation rule work, and to reflect developments in the case law since 2002 (described below). Proposed § 1.6015-1(e)(1) restates the general rule from the current regulations.

Proposed § 1.6015-1(e)(2) incorporates the holding in *Deihl v. Commissioner*, 134 T.C. 156 (2010) (When a requesting spouse generally raises relief under section 6015 in a proceeding but does not specifically plead relief under any subsection of section 6015, relief under section 6015(c) will not be treated as being at issue in that proceeding if the requesting spouse was not eligible to elect relief under section 6015(c) because the requesting spouse was not divorced, widowed, legally separated, or living apart for 12 months at any time during the prior proceeding.).

Proposed § 1.6015-1(e)(3) provides guidance on the meaningful participation exception to res judicata provided by section 6015(g)(2). A requesting spouse meaningfully participated in the prior proceeding if the requesting spouse was involved in the proceeding so that the requesting spouse could have raised the issue of relief under section 6015 in that proceeding. Meaningful participation is a facts and circumstances determination. A nonexclusive list of acts was added in proposed § 1.6015-1(e)(3) to provide indicators of "meaningful participation" within the context of a bar against relief based on the judicial doctrine of res judicata. Whether a requesting spouse meaningfully participated in a prior proceeding is based on all the facts and circumstances. No one act necessarily determines the outcome. The degree of importance of each act varies depending on the requesting spouse's facts and circumstances. The following acts, derived from case law and experience since 2002, are among the acts the IRS and courts consider in making the determination regarding meaningful participation: whether the requesting spouse participated in the IRS Appeals process while the prior case was docketed; whether the requesting spouse participated in discovery; whether the requesting spouse participated in pretrial meetings, settlement negotiations, or trial; whether the requesting spouse signed court documents; and whether the requesting spouse was represented by counsel in the prior proceedings.

Proposed § 1.6015-1(e)(3)(i) provides a new rule under which the requesting spouse will not be considered to have meaningfully participated in the prior proceeding if the requesting spouse establishes that the requesting spouse performed any of the acts listed in proposed § 1.6015-1(e)(3) because the nonrequesting spouse abused or maintained control over the requesting spouse, and the requesting spouse did not challenge the nonrequesting spouse for fear of the nonrequesting spouse's retaliation. Proposed § 1.6015-1(e)(3)(ii) restates the rule from the current regulations that a requesting spouse did not meaningfully participate in a prior proceeding if, due to the effective date of section 6015, relief under section 6015 was not available in that proceeding.

Proposed § 1.6015-1(e)(3)(iii) provides that in a case petitioned from a statutory notice of deficiency under section 6213, the fact that the requesting spouse did not have the ability to effectively contest the underlying deficiency is irrelevant for purposes of determining whether the requesting spouse meaningfully participated in the prior proceeding. Treasury and the IRS disagree with the holding in *Harbin v. Commissioner*, 137 T.C. 93 (2011), in which the Tax Court concluded that Mr. Harbin did not meaningfully participate in the deficiency case in part because he could not effectively contest the part of the deficiency related to his ex-wife's gambling losses without her. The Tax Court found that Mr. Harbin could not effectively contest this part of the deficiency without his ex-wife because she "was the one with personal knowledge of the winnings and losses from the gambling activities" and was the one "who maintained and provided all of the documentation relating to the gambling activities." The Tax Court concluded that this knowledge and control of the documentation resulted in Mr. Harbin's ex-wife effectively exercising "exclusive control" of the case. *Harbin v. Commissioner*, 137 T.C. at 98.

Treasury and the IRS believe that the Tax Court applied the incorrect standard to determine whether a taxpayer meaningfully participated in a proceeding for purposes of section 6015(g)(2). The purpose of the meaningful participation exception to res judicata is not to ensure that a taxpayer had the opportunity to contest the deficiency but rather to ensure that the taxpayer could have raised relief under section 6015. *Moore v. Commissioner*, T.C. Memo. 2007-156. This is evident because, if section 6015 relief was at issue in the prior case, the taxpayer is not permitted to raise section 6015 relief in a subsequent proceeding regardless of the degree to which the taxpayer participated or whether the taxpayer's ability to contest the deficiency was impaired. *See Deihl v. Commissioner*, 134 T.C. 156, 161 (2010).

Proposed § 1.6015-1(e)(4) provides examples of how the rules in paragraphs (e)(1), (e)(2), and (e)(3) work. Proposed § 1.6015-1(e)(5) restates the collateral estoppel rule from current § 1.6015-1(e) without change.

Proposed § 1.6015-1(h)(1) and (h)(5) are being revised to remove the distinction between electing and requesting relief as discussed earlier in this preamble.

Proposed § 1.6015-1(h)(6) defines "unpaid tax" for purposes of § 1.6015-4. For purposes of § 1.6015-4, the regulations propose that the terms "unpaid tax" and "underpayment" have the same meaning. The unpaid tax or underpayment on a joint return is the balance shown as due on the return reduced by the tax paid with the return or paid on or before the due date for payment (without considering any extension of time to pay). The balance due is determined after applying withholding credits, estimated tax payments, payments with an extension, and other credits applied against the total tax reported on the return. Payments made with the return include payments made by check in the same envelope with the return or remitted at a later date (but before the due date for payment) with Form 1040-V, "Payment Voucher." Payments made with the return also include remittances made by direct debit, credit card, or other commercially acceptable means under section 6311 on or before the due date for payment. The determination of the existence and amount of unpaid tax is made as of the date the joint return is filed, or as of the due date for payment if payments are made after the return is filed but on or before the due date.

If the payments made with the joint return, including any payments made on or before the due date for payment (without considering any extension of time for payment), completely satisfy the balance due shown on the return, then there is no unpaid tax for purposes of § 1.6015-4. A requesting spouse is not entitled to be considered for relief (credit or refund) under § 1.6015-4 for any tax paid with the joint return (including a joint amended return). Payments made after the later of the date the joint return is filed or the due date for payment (without considering any extension of time for payment), including offsets of overpayments from other tax years, do not change the amount of unpaid tax reported on the joint return. Under § 1.6015-4, a requesting spouse can only get relief from the unpaid tax on the return, and if refunds are available, from any payments made on the liability after the later of the date the joint return was filed or the due date for payment (without considering any extension of time for payment).

Proposed § 1.6015-1(h)(7) and (h)(8) define understatement and deficiency, respectively. Section 6015(b)(3) provides that an "understatement" for purposes of section 6015 has the same meaning given to that term by section 6662(d)(2)(A). The definition of understatement is in current § 1.6015-2(b) and therefore only applies to requests under that section. The term "understatement," however, is a term that is relevant to relief under sections 6015(b), (c), and (f). These regulations propose to move the definition of "understatement" to proposed § 1.6015-1(h)(7) to allow a consistent definition to apply throughout the regulations. Likewise, proposed § 1.6015-1(h)(8) adds a definition of deficiency, by reference to section 6211 and the regulations under section 6211, to clarify that the term deficiency has the same meaning throughout the regulations.

Section 6015(g)(1) provides that requesting spouses generally can receive a credit or refund of payments made on the joint liability if the requesting spouse is entitled to relief under section 6015. This general rule is set forth in proposed § 1.6015-1(k)(1). Section 6015(g) also provides some limitations on the availability of credit or refund. New § 1.6015-1(k)(2) through (5) discuss these and other limitations on credit or refund when a requesting spouse is eligible for relief.

Proposed § 1.6015-1(k)(2) sets forth the limitation on refunds from section 6015(g)(3) when a requesting spouse is entitled to relief under § 1.6015-3. Proposed § 1.6015-1(k)(3) sets forth the rule from current § 1.6015-4(b) that relief under § 1.6015-4 is not available when the requesting spouse is entitled to full relief under § 1.6015-3 but is not entitled to a refund because of the limitation in section 6015(g)(3) and proposed § 1.6015-1(k)(2). Proposed § 1.6015-1(k)(4) incorporates, consistent with section 6015(g)(1), the limitations on credit or refund provided by sections 6511 (general limitations on credits or refunds) and 6512(b) (limitations on credits or refunds where the Tax Court determines that a taxpayer made an overpayment). This section also clarifies that, in general, Form 8857 will be treated as the requesting spouse's claim for credit or refund.

Proposed § 1.6015-1(k)(5) sets forth the general rule that a requesting spouse who is entitled to relief is generally not eligible for a credit or refund of joint payments made with the nonrequesting spouse. Under the proposed rule, a requesting spouse, however, may be eligible for a credit or refund of the requesting spouse's portion of the requesting and nonrequesting spouse's joint overpayment from another tax year that was applied to the joint income tax liability to the extent that the requesting spouse can establish his or her contribution to the overpayment. Both spouses have an interest in a joint overpayment relative to each spouse's contribution to the overpayment. See, for example, *Gordon v. United States*, 757 F.2d 1157, 1160 (11th Cir. 1985) ("Where spouses claim a refund under a joint return, the refund is divided between the spouses, with each receiving a percentage of the refund equivalent to his or her proportion of the withheld tax payments."). If the requesting spouse contributed to the joint overpayment through withholding, estimated tax, or other payments, then the requesting spouse may be entitled to a refund of that portion of the overpayment that was applied to the joint liability. Under the proposed rule, a requesting spouse in a state that is not a community property state may establish his or her portion of a joint overpayment using the allocation rules of Rev. Rul. 80-7 (1980-1 CB 296), or successor guidance. A requesting spouse in a community property state may establish his or her portion of a joint overpayment using the allocation rules of Rev. Rul. 2004-71 (2004-2 CB 74), Rev. Rul. 2004-72 (2004-2 CB 77), Rev. Rul. 2004-73 (2004-2 CB 80), or Rev. Rul. 2004-74 (2004-2 CB 84), or successor guidance, whichever is applicable to the state in which the requesting spouse is domiciled. For copies of Revenue Procedures, Revenue Rulings, notices, and other guidance published in the Internal Revenue Bulletin, please visit the IRS website at http://www.irs.gov.

These proposed regulations reflect the elimination of the more restrictive rule regarding credit or refund when relief is granted under § 1.6015-4 in cases involving a deficiency, as provided by Rev. Proc. 2013-34. A credit or refund, subject to the limitations in § 1.6015-1(k), is available to a requesting spouse who is entitled to relief under § 1.6015-4 in both underpayment and deficiency cases.

Current § 1.6015-1(h)(4) provides, in part, that penalties and interest are not separate erroneous items from which a requesting spouse can be relieved separate from the tax. Rather, relief from penalties and interest related to an understatement or deficiency will generally be determined based on the proportion of the total erroneous items from which the requesting spouse is relieved.

Thus, under the existing regulations, a requesting spouse who is determined not to be eligible for relief from the understatement or deficiency stemming from an erroneous item cannot be separately relieved from a penalty, such as the accuracy-related penalty, related to the item under section 6015. If a requesting spouse is entitled to partial relief (such as relief from two of three erroneous items giving rise to the understatement or deficiency), then the requesting spouse will be entitled to relief from the accuracy-related penalty applicable to those two items.

These regulations propose to move the discussion in current § 1.6015-1(h)(4) to proposed § 1.6015-1(m). Proposed § 1.6015-1(m) additionally clarifies, consistent with the statutory interpretation in current § 1.6015-1(h)(4), that penalties and interest on an underpayment also are not separate items from which a requesting spouse may obtain relief under § 1.6015-4. Rather, relief from penalties and interest on the underpayment will be determined based on the amount of relief from the underpayment to which the requesting spouse is entitled. If a requesting spouse remains liable for a portion of the underpayment after application of § 1.6015-4, the requesting spouse is not eligible for relief under section 6015 for the penalties and interest related to that portion of the underpayment. *Cf. Weiler v. Commissioner*, T.C. Memo. 2003-255 (a requesting spouse is not relieved from liabilities for penalties and interest resulting from items attributable to the requesting spouse). This position is consistent with how the IRS currently treats relief from penalties and interest after determining the relief from the underlying tax. See IRM 25.15.3.4.1.1(2) (Revised 03/08/2013).

If an assessed deficiency is paid in full, or the unpaid tax reported on the joint return is later paid in full, but penalties and interest remain unpaid, under the proposed rule, a requesting spouse may be considered for relief from the penalties and interest under section 6015. The determination of relief from the penalties and interest is made by considering whether the requesting spouse would be entitled to relief from the underlying tax and not considering the penalties and interest as if they were separate items. A requesting spouse may be relieved from the penalties and interest even if relief in the form of a refund of the payments made on the underlying tax is barred (for example, § 1.6015-1(k)(2) (no refunds allowed under § 1.6015-3) or § 1.6015-1(k)(4) (refund barred by the limitations of sections 6511 or 6512(b)).

Proposed § 1.6015-1(n) provides attribution rules for a portion of an understatement or deficiency relating to the disallowance of certain items. Specifically, § 1.6015-1(n) addresses items that are otherwise not erroneous items, but are disallowed solely due to the increase of adjusted gross income (or modified adjusted gross income) over a phase-out threshold as a result of an erroneous item attributable to the nonrequesting spouse. One common example of this is when the nonrequesting spouse's omitted income increases adjusted gross income so that the Earned Income Tax Credit (EITC) is phased out and the understatement or deficiency partially represents the recapture of the refunded EITC.

Under proposed § 1.6015-1(n), the understatement or deficiency related to the item disallowed due to the increase to adjusted gross income will be attributable to the spouse whose erroneous item caused the increase to adjusted gross income, unless the evidence shows that a different result is appropriate. If the increase to adjusted gross income is the result of erroneous items of both spouses, the item disallowed due to the increase to adjusted gross income will be attributable to the requesting spouse in the same ratio as the amount of the item or items attributable to the requesting spouse over the total amount of the items that resulted in the increase to adjusted gross income. Corresponding rules are proposed to be added to §§ 1.6015-2(b) and 1.6015-3(c)(2)(i) to provide that a requesting spouse knows or has reason to know of the item disallowed due to the increase in adjusted gross income if the requesting spouse knows or has reason to know of the erroneous item or items that resulted in the increase to adjusted gross income. Likewise, for purposes of proposed § 1.6015-4 and Rev. Proc. 2013-34, a requesting spouse knows or has reason to know of the portion of an understatement or deficiency related to an item attributable to the nonrequesting spouse under § 1.6015-1(n) if the requesting spouse knows or has reason to know of the nonrequesting spouse's erroneous item or items that resulted in the increase to adjusted gross income.

Examples are provided to illustrate how this rule applies in situations involving the EITC, the phase-out of itemized deductions, and the application of the alternative minimum tax. This rule, however, can be implicated in other situations. It should be noted that this proposed rule would not apply if there is another reason for disallowing the item, such as no qualifying child for the EITC, no substantiation for a claimed deduction, or the lack of any basis in law or fact for the deduction. In this situation, the normal attribution rules applicable to §§ 1.6015-2, 1.6015-3, and 1.6015-4 apply.

Proposed § 1.6015-1(o) provides a definition of abuse for purposes of proposed §§ 1.6015-2(b) and 1.6015-3(c)(vi). The definition of abuse is taken directly from Rev. Proc. 2013-34, section 4.03(2)(c)(iv).

2. Section 1.6015-2

Only minor substantive changes are proposed to current § 1.6015-2. The proposed amendments reorganize the section, update references, and provide clarification where needed. Proposed § 1.6015-2(a) changes the language in the existing regulations, "the requesting spouse elects the application of this section," to "the requesting spouse requests relief" consistent with the discussion earlier in this preamble. The definition of "understatement" in current § 1.6015-2(b) is removed as the definition will now be located in proposed § 1.6015-1(h)(7). Current § 1.6015-2(c) is redesignated as proposed § 1.6015-2(b), adds additional facts and circumstances from Rev. Proc. 2013-34 to consider in determining whether a requesting spouse had reason to know, adds a knowledge rule to correspond to proposed § 1.6015-1(n) as discussed earlier in this preamble, and clarifies, consistent with the changes made in Rev. Proc. 2013-34, that abuse or financial control by the nonrequesting spouse will result in the requesting spouse being treated as not having knowledge or reason to know of the items giving rise to the understatement. Current § 1.6015-2(d) is redesignated as proposed § 1.6015-2(c) and provides an updated cross-reference to the most recent revenue procedure providing the criteria to be used in determining equitable relief, Rev. Proc. 2013-34. Current § 1.6015-2(e)(1) is redesignated as proposed § 1.6015-2(d)(1) and the word "only" is removed to clarify the rule. Current § 1.6015-2(e)(2) is redesignated as proposed § 1.6015-2(d)(2) and the example is updated to use more current years and dates, but otherwise no substantive changes were made.

3. Section 1.6015-3

Among other clarifying changes, these regulations propose to clarify the difference between full and partial relief under section 6015(c) and to reflect case law regarding the tax benefit rule of section 6015(d)(3)(B), including new examples.

Proposed § 1.6015-3(a) provides a revised heading and a cross-reference to the definition of deficiency in proposed § 1.6015-1(h)(8).

Section 6015(g)(3) provides that no credit or refund is allowed as a result of an allocation of a deficiency under section 6015(c). Proposed § 1.6015-3(c)(1) clarifies the existing regulations and provides that whether relief is available to a requesting spouse under section 6015(c) is not dependent on the availability of credit or refund. Thus, if a requesting spouse is eligible to allocate the entire deficiency to the nonrequesting spouse, the requesting spouse has received full relief even if the requesting spouse made payments on the deficiency and is not entitled to a refund of those payments because of section 6015(g)(3). Further, the requesting spouse is not eligible to be considered for relief (and a refund) under section 6015(f) for the amount of any paid liability because a prerequisite to relief under section 6015(f) is the unavailability of relief under section 6015(b) or (c) and the spouse received full relief under section 6015(c). A requesting spouse may still be considered for relief (and a refund) under section 6015(b) for the amount of any paid liability. If a requesting spouse only receives partial relief (for example, some part of the deficiency is still allocated to the requesting spouse), then the requesting spouse may be considered for relief under section 6015(f) for the portion of the deficiency allocable to the requesting spouse. A new sentence is added to § 1.6015-3(c)(2)(i) to add a knowledge rule to correspond to proposed § 1.6015-1(n), which, as discussed earlier in this preamble, provides an attribution rule for the portion of a deficiency relating to the disallowance or reduction of an otherwise valid item solely due to the increase in AGI as a result of the disallowance of an erroneous item.

Proposed § 1.6015-3(d)(2)(i) illustrates that, under the tax benefit rule of section 6015(d)(3)(B), the amount of an erroneous item allocated to a requesting spouse may increase or decrease depending upon the tax benefit to the requesting and nonrequesting spouses. Thus, these proposed regulations adopt the holding of *Hopkins v. Commissioner*, 121 T.C. 73 (2003) (a requesting spouse was entitled to relief from her own item under the tax benefit rule of section 6015(d)(3)(B) because the nonrequesting spouse was the only person who reported income on the returns, and therefore, the only one who received any tax benefit from the item). In addition, five new examples have been added to § 1.6015-3(d)(5) to provide additional guidance on the application of the tax benefit rule of § 1.6015-3(d)(2)(i). *Example 7* demonstrates the application of § 1.6015-3(d)(2)(i)(B), which provides that each spouse's hypothetical separate taxable income may need to be determined to properly apply the tax benefit rule. *Example 8* demonstrates the holding in *Hopkins* by showing that a requesting spouse's allocated portion of a deficiency will be decreased when the nonrequesting spouse receives a tax benefit from the item. *Example 9* demonstrates the allocation of a liability when the erroneous item is a loss from a jointly-owned investment. *Example 10* demonstrates how the tax benefit rule works when the erroneous item is a loss from a jointly-owned investment. In addition, *Example 11* is added to demonstrate how the rule in § 1.6015-3(d)(2)(ii) regarding fraud works.

Section 1.6015-3(c)(2)(iv) currently provides that the requesting spouse's joint ownership (with the nonrequesting spouse) of the property that resulted in the erroneous item is a factor that may be relied upon in demonstrating that the requesting spouse had actual knowledge of the item. Under the tax benefit rule of § 1.6015-3(d)(2)(i), as stated earlier in this preamble, a requesting spouse can be relieved of liability for the requesting spouse's own erroneous item if the item is otherwise allocable in full or in part to the nonrequesting spouse under section 6015(d). Therefore, proposed § 1.6015-3(c)(2)(iv) revises the current regulations to clarify that the requesting spouse's separate ownership of the erroneous item is also a factor that may be relied upon in demonstrating that the requesting spouse had actual knowledge of the item. Current § 1.6015-3(c)(2)(v) is redesignated as proposed § 1.6015-3(c)(2)(vi) and the discussion of community property in current § 1.6015-3(c)(iv) is removed and is now located in proposed § 1.6015-3(c)(2)(v). Proposed § 1.6015-3(c)(vi) is revised to clarify, consistent with the changes made in Rev. Proc. 2013-34, that abuse or financial control by the nonrequesting spouse will result in the requesting spouse being treated as not having actual knowledge of the items giving rise to the understatement.

4. Section 1.6015-4

No substantive changes are proposed to current § 1.6015-4. The proposed amendments update references and provide a clarifying change consistent with proposed § 1.6015-3(c)(1), which provides the rule that refunds are not allowed under section 6015(c).

Proposed § 1.6015-4(a) was revised to provide a cross-reference to the definitions of unpaid tax, understatement, and deficiency in proposed §§ 1.6015-1(h)(6), (h)(7), and (h)(8).

Proposed § 1.6015-4(b) was revised to provide a cross-reference to proposed § 1.6015-1(k)(3). The paragraph also clarifies that if only partial relief is available under § 1.6015-3, then relief may be considered under § 1.6015-4 for the portion of the deficiency for which the requesting spouse remains liable.

Proposed § 1.6015-4(c) replaces the citation to Rev. Proc. 2000-15 (2000-1 CB 447) with Rev. Proc. 2013-34, which revised the factors used in determining if the requesting spouse is eligible for equitable relief under section 6015(f).

5. Section 1.6015-5

A notice of proposed rulemaking (REG-132251-11) was published in the **Federal Register** (78 FR 49242) on August 13, 2013. Those regulations proposed changes to § 1.6015-5 to remove the two-year deadline for taxpayers to file requests for equitable relief under section 6015(f), and other changes related to the time and manner for requesting relief. These proposed regulations revise the notice of proposed rulemaking published on August 13, 2013 to add an effective date provision.

6. Section 1.6015-6

The changes in proposed § 1.6015-6 are intended to update the current regulations to reflect existing practice and guidance. Proposed § 1.6015-6(a)(1) replaces the term "election" under § 1.6015-2 or § 1.6015-3 with "request for relief." Proposed § 1.6015-6(a)(2) includes a reference to Rev. Proc. 2003-19 (2003-1 CB 371), which provides guidance on a nonrequesting spouse's right to appeal a preliminary determination to IRS Appeals.

7. Section 1.6015-7

Section 1.6015-7 was revised to reflect the amendments to section 6015(e) in the 2006 Act that, as noted earlier in this preamble, conferred jurisdiction on the United States Tax Court to review the IRS's denial of relief in cases in which taxpayers requested equitable relief under section 6015(f), without regard to whether the IRS has determined a deficiency. Prior to these amendments, the United States Tax Court lacked jurisdiction to review section 6015(f) determinations if no deficiency had been determined. The amendments apply to any liability for tax that arose on or after December 20, 2006, and any liability for tax that arose before December 20, 2006, but remained unpaid as of that date. Proposed § 1.6015-7(c) revises the current regulations to reflect the changes to the restrictions on collection and corresponding tolling of the collection statute under section 6502. On versions of the Form 8857 dated before June 2007 a requesting spouse could request relief under just one subsection of section 6015. For claims for relief that were made under sections 6015(b) and (c) (and the corresponding §§ 1.6015-2 and 1.6015-3), the IRS is prohibited from collecting against the requesting spouse (and the collection statute is tolled) beginning on the date the claim is filed. For requests for relief made solely under section 6015(f) (and the corresponding § 1.6015-4), the IRS is prohibited from collecting against the requesting spouse (and the collection statute is tolled) only for liabilities arising on or after December 20, 2006, or liabilities arising before December 20, 2006, but remaining unpaid as of that date. For requests for relief made solely under § 1.6015-4, the restrictions on collection and tolling of the collection statute do not start until December 20, 2006, for any requests filed before that date, assuming the tax remained unpaid as of that date. The restrictions on collection and tolling of the collection statute start as of the date the request is filed for requests filed on or after December 20, 2006.

8. Section 1.66-4

The only changes to the existing regulations under section 66 are non-substantive changes. Proposed §1.66-4(a)(3) and (b) replace the citation to Rev. Proc. 2000-15 with Rev. Proc. 2013-34, which revised the factors used in determining whether a requesting spouse is eligible for equitable relief under section 66(c).

9. Effective and Applicability Dates

Additionally, the effective and applicability date sections in the regulations under section 66 and section 6015 are reorganized to move the effective and applicability date sections within the specific regulation to which the dates apply. The separate effective date sections under §§1.66-5 and 1.6015-9 are removed.

Special Analyses

Certain IRS regulations, including this one, are exempt from the requirements of Executive Order 12866, as supplemented and reaffirmed by Executive Order 13563. Therefore, a regulatory impact assessment is not required. It has also been determined that section 553(b) of the Administrative Procedure Act (5 U.S.C. chapter 5) does not apply to these regulations. In addition, because the regulations do not impose a collection of information on small entities, the Regulatory Flexibility Act (5 U.S.C. chapter 6) does not apply. Accordingly, a regulatory flexibility analysis is not required under the Regulatory Flexibility Act (5 U.S.C. chapter 6). Pursuant to section 7805(f) of the Code, this notice of proposed rulemaking has been submitted to the Chief Counsel for Advocacy of the Small Business Administration for comment on its impact on small business.

Comments and Requests for Public Hearing

Before these proposed regulations are adopted as final regulations, consideration will be given to any comments that are submitted timely to the IRS as prescribed in the preamble under the "Addresses" heading. Treasury and the IRS request comments on all aspects of the proposed regulations. All comments will be available at www.regulations.gov or upon request. A public hearing will be scheduled if requested in writing by any person that timely submits written comments. If a public hearing is scheduled, notice of the date, time, and place for the public hearing will be published in the **Federal Register**.

Drafting Information

The principal author of these regulations is Nancy Rose of the Office of the Associate Chief Counsel (Procedure and Administration).

[¶49,678]   Proposed Amendments of Regulations (REG-147310-12), published in the Federal Register on January 27, 2016.

[Code Sec. 401]

Retirement defined benefit plans: Governmental plans: Normal Retirement age.—Amendments of Reg. §1.401(a)-1, containing regulations under section 401(a) of the Internal Revenue Code (Code), are proposed. The text is at ¶17,506E.

AGENCY: Internal Revenue Service (IRS), Treasury

ACTION: Notice of proposed rulemaking.

SUMMARY: This document contains proposed regulations under section 401(a) of the Internal Revenue Code (Code). These regulations would provide rules relating to the determination of whether the normal retirement age under a governmental plan (within the meaning of section 414(d) of the Code) that is a pension plan satisfies the requirements of section 401(a) and whether the payment of definitely determinable benefits that commence at the plan's normal retirement age satisfies these requirements. These regulations would affect sponsors and administrators of governmental pension plans, as well as participants in such plans.

DATES: Comments and requests for a public hearing must be received by April 26, 2016.

ADDRESSES: Send submissions to CC:PA:LPD:PR (REG-147310-12), room 5205, Internal Revenue Service, PO Box 7604, Ben Franklin Station, Washington D.C. 20044. Submissions may be hand-delivered Monday through Friday between the hours of 8 a.m. and 4 p.m. to CC:PA:LPD:PR (REG-147310-12), Courier's Desk, Internal Revenue Service, 1111 Constitution Avenue, N.W., Washington, DC, 20224, or sent electronically via the Federal eRulemaking Portal at *www.regulations.gov* (IRS REG-147310-12).

FOR FURTHER INFORMATION CONTACT: Concerning the proposed regulations, Pamela Kinard at (202) 317-4148 or Robert Walsh at (202) 317-4102; concerning the submission of comments or to request a public hearing, Oluwafunmilayo (Funmi) Taylor, (202) 317-7180 or (202) 317-6901 (not toll-free numbers).

SUPPLEMENTARY INFORMATION:

Background

I. *Normal Retirement Age Generally*

This document contains proposed regulations under section 401(a) of the Internal Revenue Code (Code). Section 401(a) sets forth the qualification requirements for a trust forming part of a stock bonus, pension, or profit-sharing plan of an employer. Several of these qualification requirements are based on a plan's normal retirement age, including the regulatory interpretation of the requirement that the plan provide for definitely determinable benefits (generally after retirement). Final regulations defining normal retirement age for the definitely determinable requirement were published in the **Federal Register** as TD 9325 on May 22, 2007 (72 FR 28604) (2007 NRA regulations).

Section 1.401(a)-1(b)(1) of the 2007 NRA regulations generally requires that a pension plan be established and maintained primarily to provide systematically for the payment of definitely determinable benefits over a period of years, usually for life, after retirement. The 2007 NRA regulations include two exceptions to the general rule that payments commence after retirement: (1) payments can commence after attainment of normal retirement age; and (2) in accordance with section 401(a)(36), payments can commence after an employee reaches age 62.

Section 1.401(a)-1(b)(2)(i) of the 2007 NRA regulations provides that, as a general rule, a normal retirement age under a pension plan must be an age that is not earlier than the earliest age that is reasonably representative of the typical retirement age for the industry in which the covered workforce is employed (reasonably representative requirement). Section 1.401(a)-1(b)(2)(ii) of the 2007 NRA regulations provides that a normal retirement age of age 62 or later is deemed to satisfy the reasonably representative requirement. Under section 1.401(a)-1(b)(2)(iii) of the 2007 NRA regulations, whether a normal retirement age that is not earlier than age 55 but is below age 62 satisfies the reasonably representative requirement is based on a facts and circumstances analysis. Section 1.401(a)-1(b)(2)(iv) of the 2007 NRA regulations provides that a normal retirement age that is lower than age 55 is presumed not to satisfy the reasonably representative requirement unless the Commissioner determines otherwise on the basis of facts and circumstances. Under §1.401(a)-1(b)(2)(v) of the 2007 NRA regulations, in the case of a pension plan in which substantially all of the participants are qualified public safety employees (within the meaning of section 72(t)(10)(B)), a normal retirement age of age 50 or later is deemed to satisfy the reasonably representative requirement.

As previously explained, normal retirement age is used by a pension plan in a variety of circumstances relating to plan qualification. Generally, in the case of a pension plan that is not a governmental plan under section 414(d) and is subject to the rules of section 411(a) through (d), normal retirement age is used in applying the rules under section 411(b) that are designed to preclude avoidance of the minimum vesting standards through the backloading of benefits (such as a benefit formula under which the rate of benefit accrual is increased disproportionately for employees with longer service). Normal retirement age is also relevant for such a plan for other purposes, including the application of the rules relating to suspension of benefits under section 411(a)(3)(B), plan offset rules under section 411(b)(1)(H)(iii), and the minimum benefit rules applicable to non-key employee participants in the case of a top-heavy defined benefit plan under section 416. In addition, for such a plan, section 411(a)(8) defines the term *normal retirement age* as the earlier of (a) the time a participant attains normal retirement age under the plan or (b) the later of the time a plan participant attains age 65 or the 5th anniversary of the time a plan participant commenced participation in the plan.[1]

II. *Normal Retirement Age under a Governmental Plan*

A. *Application of section 411 to governmental plans*

Section 414(d) of the Code provides that the term *governmental plan* generally means a plan established and maintained for its employees by the Government of the United States, by the government of any State or political subdivision thereof, or by any agency or instrumentality of any of the foregoing.[2] See sections 3(32) and 4021(b)(2) of ERISA for definitions of the term *governmental plan* for purposes of title I and title IV of ERISA, respectively.

Section 411(e)(1) of the Code provides that the provisions of section 411, other than section 411(e)(2), do not apply to a governmental plan. Under section 411(e)(2), a governmental plan is treated as meeting the requirements of section 411, for purposes of section 401(a), if the plan meets the vesting requirements resulting from the application of sections 401(a)(4) and 401(a)(7) as in effect on September 1, 1974 (pre-ERISA vesting rules). The only requirements under section 411 that apply to a governmental plan are the pre-ERISA vesting rules under section 411(e)(2). Thus, the definition of normal retirement age under section 411(a)(8) does not apply to a governmental plan. In addition, other rules of section 411, including section 411(a)(3)(B) (related to suspension of benefits), section 411(b)(1) (related to backloading of benefits in a defined benefit plan), and section 411(b)(1)(H)(iii) (related to offsets after normal retirement age) do not apply to a governmental plan. Therefore, except for specific circumstances in which in-service benefit payments are permitted under § 1.401(a)-1(b)(1), the definition of normal retirement age need not be used by a governmental plan for the same purposes that apply to a plan subject to section 411(a) through (d).[3]

B. *Pre-ERISA vesting requirements for governmental plans*

Under section 411(e)(2), a normal retirement age under a governmental plan must satisfy the pre-ERISA vesting rules. The pre-ERISA vesting rules applicable to governmental plans contain two basic components: (a) rules relating to vesting and (b) rules relating to the right to commence benefits without reduction for early commencement. Rev. Rul. 66-11, 1966-1 C.B. 71, and Rev. Rul. 68-302, 1968-1 C.B. 163, illustrate the interplay between normal retirement age under the pre-ERISA vesting rules and section 401(a). As described in these rulings, to satisfy the requirements of section 401(a), a plan that is subject to the pre-ERISA vesting rules must provide for full vesting of the contributions made to or benefits payable under the plan for any employee who has attained normal retirement age under the plan and satisfied any reasonable and uniformly applicable requirements as to length of service or participation described in the plan. For more information about these rules, see Part 5(c) of Publication 778, *Guides for Qualification of Pension, Profit-Sharing, and Stock Bonus Plans (Pub. 778)*.

Rev. Rul. 71-24, 1971-1 C.B. 114, illustrates the application of the pre-ERISA vesting rules to benefits provided under a pension plan for employees who continue employment after normal retirement age. Rev. Rul. 71-24 includes an example under which benefits are permitted to commence during employment after normal retirement age.

As described in Rev. Rul. 71-147,[4] 1971-1 C.B. 116, the normal retirement age in a pension or annuity plan under the pre-ERISA vesting rules is generally the lowest age specified in the plan at which the employee has the right to retire without the consent of the employer and receive retirement benefits based on the amount of the employee's service to the date of retirement at the full rate set forth in the plan (that is, without actuarial or similar reduction because of retirement before some later specified age). Rev. Rul. 71-147 does not explicitly require a plan to include a provision defining normal retirement age. Instead, a plan's normal retirement age may be deduced from other plan provisions. As described in Rev. Rul. 71-147, although normal retirement age under a pension or annuity plan is ordinarily age 65, a plan may specify a lower age at which the employee has the right to retire without the consent of the employer and to receive retirement benefits based on the amount of the employee's service at the full rate set forth in the plan if this lower age would be an age at which employees customarily retire in the particular company or industry, and if the provision permitting receipt of unreduced benefits at this age is not a device to accelerate funding. For more information about these rules, see also Part 5(e) of Pub. 778.

III. *Application of the 2007 NRA Regulations to Governmental Plans*

Notice 2007-69, 2007-2 C.B. 468, asked for comments "on whether and how a pension plan with a normal retirement age conditioned on the completion of a stated number of years of service satisfies the requirement in § 1.401(a)-1(b)(1)(i) that a pension plan be maintained primarily to provide for the payment of definitely determinable benefits after retirement or attainment of normal retirement age and how such a plan satisfies the pre-ERISA vesting rules." Comments were received on a variety of issues, including comments that guidance should be issued to (1) clarify that governmental plans are not required to define normal retirement age, (2) provide safe harbor rules that would permit a governmental plan to define normal retirement age that includes a service component, and (3) provide that the age-50 safe harbor rule in § 1.401(a)-1(b)(2)(v) for qualified public safety employees can apply to these employees even if less than substantially all of a plan's participants are qualified public safety employees.

---

[1] Section 411(f) provides a special normal retirement age rule that applies only to certain defined benefit plans that are subject to section 411(a) through (d). Section 411(f) was added to the Code on December 16, 2014 by Section 2 of Division P of the Consolidated and Further Continuing Appropriations Act, 2015, Public Law No. 113-235 (128 Stat. 2130 (2014)), which also made a corresponding change to section 204 of the Employee Retirement Income Security Act of 1974, Public Law 93-406 (88 Stat. 829 (1974)), as amended (ERISA). Under section 101 of Reorganization Plan No. 4 of 1978 (92 Stat. 3790), the Secretary of the Treasury has interpretive jurisdiction over the subject matter addressed in section 411(f) for purposes of ERISA, as well as the Code.

[2] The term *governmental plan* also includes a plan that is established and maintained by an Indian tribal government (as defined in section 7701(a)(40)), a subdivision of an Indian tribal government (determined in accordance with section 7871(d)), or an agency or instrumentality of either, and all the participants of which are employees of such entity substantially all of whose services as such an employee are in the performance of essential governmental functions but not in the performance of commercial activities (whether or not an essential government function). In addition, the term *governmental plan* includes any plan to which the Railroad Retirement Act of 1935 or 1937 (49 Stat. 967, as amended by 50 Stat. 307) applies and which is financed by contributions required under that Act and any plan of an international organization that is exempt from taxation by reason of the International Organizations Immunities Act, Public Law 79-291 (59 Stat. 669).

[3] Normal retirement age may also be relevant to participant eligibility for certain favorable tax treatment, including section 402(l) (providing an income exclusion of up to $3,000 annually for certain distributions for health insurance and long-term care insurance premiums to eligible retired public safety officers who separate from service by reason of disability or attainment of normal retirement age) and the special catch-up provisions of § 1.457-4(c)(3)(v)(A).

[4] Even though Rev. Rul. 71-147 was superseded by Rev. Rul. 80-276, 1980-1 C.B. 131, for plans subject to section 411(a)(8), Rev. Rul. 71-147 remains valid guidance for purposes of the pre-ERISA vesting rules.

The 2007 NRA regulations provided that, in the case of governmental plans, the regulations would be effective for plan years beginning on or after January 1, 2009. Notices 2008-98, 2008-44 I.R.B 1080, and 2009-86, 2009-6 I.R.B. 629, provided that the Department of the Treasury and the IRS intended to amend the 2007 NRA regulations to change the effective date of the 2007 NRA regulations for governmental plans to January 1, 2013.

Notice 2012-29, 2012-18 I.R.B. 872, announced that the Department of the Treasury and the IRS intend to modify provisions of the 2007 NRA regulations as applied to governmental plans in two ways. First, Notice 2012-29 announced the intent to modify the regulations to clarify that a governmental plan that is not subject to section 411(a) through (d) and does not provide for the payment of in-service distributions before age 62 will not fail to satisfy the requirement that the plan provide definitely determinable benefits to employees after retirement or attainment of normal retirement age merely because the pension plan does not have a definition of normal retirement age or does not have a definition of normal retirement age that satisfies the requirements of the 2007 NRA regulations.

Second, Notice 2012-29 announced the intent to modify the 2007 NRA regulations to provide that the rule deeming age 50 or later to be a normal retirement age that satisfies the 2007 NRA regulations will apply to a group of employees substantially all of whom are qualified public safety employees, whether or not the group of qualified public safety employees are covered by a separate plan. Thus, under the intended modification, a governmental plan would be permitted to satisfy the reasonably representative requirement using a normal retirement age as low as 50 for a group substantially all of whom are qualified public safety employees and a later normal retirement age that otherwise satisfies the 2007 NRA requirements for all other participants.

Notice 2012-29 requested comments from governmental stakeholders on the guidance under consideration. Specific comments were requested on whether a new rule should be provided under which retirement after 20 to 30 years of service may be a normal retirement age that is reasonably representative of the typical retirement age for the industry in which qualified public safety employees are employed because these employees tend to have career spans that commence at a young age and continue over a limited number of years. Many commenters wrote that such a rule would be helpful and appropriate. Several commenters requested a rule that would permit a governmental plan to use the completion of 20 or more years of service as a normal retirement age for public safety employees.

Comments were also requested on whether there are other categories of governmental employees who have career spans similar to qualified public safety employees for whom a rule should be provided that is similar to the safe harbor for qualified public safety employees. Many commenters recommended a rule that would permit governmental plans to use the completion of a number of years of service as a normal retirement age for all employees, not just qualified public safety employees.

Notice 2012-29 also requested information on the overall retirement patterns of employees in government service to assist the Department of the Treasury and the IRS in determining the earliest age that is reasonably representative of the typical retirement ages for the industry in which these employees are employed. One commenter provided data on the retirement patterns and median normal retirement ages for participants in a state retirement system.

Notice 2012-29 also provided that the Department of the Treasury and the IRS intend to amend the 2007 NRA regulations to modify the effective date of the 2007 NRA regulations for governmental plans to annuity starting dates that occur in plan years beginning on or after the later of (1) January 1, 2015 or (2) the close of the first regular legislative session of the legislative body with the authority to amend the plan that begins on or after the date that is 3 months after the final regulations are published in the **Federal Register**.

Explanation of Provisions

I. *Overview*

These proposed regulations would provide guidance with respect to the applicability of the 2007 NRA regulations to governmental plans. These proposed regulations, when finalized, would provide guidance relating to the determination of whether the normal retirement age under a governmental plan satisfies the requirements of section 401(a) by amending the 2007 NRA regulations to provide additional rules for governmental plans. In addition, these proposed regulations would also include a minor change to the 2007 NRA regulations to reflect the addition of section 411(f), which provides a special rule for determining a permissible normal retirement age that applies only to certain defined benefit plans that are not governmental plans.

II. *Use of Years of Service as a Component of the Pre-ERISA Vesting Rules*

In response to Notice 2012-29, the Department of the Treasury and the IRS received a range of comments regarding the pre-ERISA vesting rules that apply to a governmental plan's normal retirement age. In particular, the Department of the Treasury and the IRS received many comments requesting rules that would permit governmental plans to define normal retirement age by reference to a period of service. Comments also focused on whether a governmental plan is required to include an explicit definition of normal retirement age.

As previously stated, a normal retirement age under a governmental plan must satisfy the pre-ERISA vesting rules. The Department of the Treasury and the IRS generally agree with those commenters who indicated that the pre-ERISA vesting rules applicable to normal retirement age may be read to permit a governmental plan to use a normal retirement age that reflects a period of service. Under pre-ERISA vesting rules, use of a period of service to determine normal retirement age under a governmental plan would be permissible if the period of service used is reasonable and uniformly applicable and the other pre-ERISA rules related to normal retirement age are satisfied. One of the pre-ERISA rules permits a governmental plan to specify a normal retirement age that is lower than age 65 if that age represents the age at which employees customarily retire in the industry.

Under the pre-ERISA rules related to normal retirement age, the terms of a governmental plan are not required to include an explicit definition of the term normal retirement age in order to satisfy section 401(a). However, in the absence of an explicit definition of normal retirement age, the terms of the plan must specify the earliest age at which a participant has the right to retire without the consent of the employer and to receive retirement benefits based upon the amount of the participant's service on the date of retirement at the full rate set forth in the plan (that is, without actuarial or similar reduction because of retirement before some later specified age). That age (the earliest age described in the preceding sentence) will be considered the plan's normal retirement age for purposes of any statutory or regulatory requirements based on a normal retirement age.

Consistent with Notice 2012-29, the proposed regulations would provide that a governmental plan that does not provide for the payment of in-service distributions before age 62 would not fail to satisfy § 1.401(a)-1(b)(1) under these proposed regulations merely because the pension plan has a normal retirement age that is earlier than otherwise permitted under the requirements of § 1.401(a)-1(b)(2) of the 2007 NRA regulations (as proposed to be amended by these proposed regulations). Instead, because section 411(a) through (d) does not apply, the earlier normal retirement age under such a plan is treated as the age as of which an unreduced early retirement benefit is payable for purposes of these regulations.

III. *Normal Retirement Age Must Satisfy the Reasonably Representative Requirement*

A. *In general*

These proposed regulations would apply the reasonably representative requirement in the 2007 NRA regulations to governmental plans. Thus, the normal retirement age under a governmental plan must be an age that is not earlier than the earliest age that is reasonably representative of the typical retirement age for the industry in which the covered workforce is employed.

B. *General safe harbor*

These proposed regulations would apply to governmental plans the safe harbor in the 2007 NRA regulations that a normal retirement age of at least age 62 is deemed to satisfy the reasonably representative requirement. Thus, a governmental plan satisfies this safe harbor if the normal retirement age under the plan is age 62 or if the normal retirement age is the later of age 62 or another specified date, such as the fifth anniversary of plan participation.

C. *Safe harbors for governmental plans*

To address comments regarding the need for additional safe harbors for governmental plans, including safe harbors that reflect permissible periods of service, these proposed regulations would provide several additional alternative safe harbors that a governmental plan could satisfy. The safe harbors included in these proposed regulations were developed based upon feedback provided in comments received in response to Notices 2007-69 and 2012-29.

1. *Age 60 and 5 years of service*

Under these proposed regulations, a normal retirement age under a governmental plan that is the later of age 60 or the age at which the participant has been credited with at least 5 years of service would be deemed to satisfy the reasonably representative requirement.

2. *Age 55 and 10 years of service*

Similarly, a normal retirement age under a governmental plan that is the later of 55 or the age at which the participant has been credited with at least 10 years of service would be deemed to satisfy the reasonably representative requirement. Thus, for example, a normal retirement age under a governmental plan that is the later of age 55 or the age at which the participant has been credited with 12 years of service would satisfy this safe harbor.

3. *Combined age and years of service of 80 or more*

A normal retirement age under a governmental plan that is the participant's age if the sum of the participant's age plus the number of years of service that have been credited to the participant under the plan equals 80 or more would also be deemed to satisfy the reasonably representative requirement. For example, a participant in a governmental plan who is age 55 and who has been credited with 25 years of service under the plan would satisfy this safe harbor.

4. *Any age with 25 years of service (in combination with a safe harbor that includes an age)*

A governmental plan would also be permitted to combine any of the other safe harbors (except for the qualified public safety employee safe harbors) provided under the proposed regulations with 25 years of service, so that a participant's normal retirement age would be the participant's age when the number of years of service that have been credited to the participant under the plan equals 25 if that age is earlier than what the participant's normal retirement age would be under the other safe harbor(s). For example, a normal retirement age under a governmental plan would satisfy the reasonably representative requirement if the normal retirement age is the earlier of (1) the participant's age when the participant has been credited with 25 years of service under the plan and (2) the later of age 60 or the age when the participant has been credited with 5 years of service under the plan. Use of 25 years of service by a governmental plan for normal retirement age generally would not satisfy the pre-ERISA vesting requirement relating to normal retirement age, unless it is used in conjunction with an alternative normal retirement age that includes an age component and that otherwise satisfies the pre-ERISA rules. This is because the pre-ERISA vesting requirements allow for a service component only if that component does not unreasonably delay full vesting. For example, applying a 25 years of service requirement (without an alternative normal retirement age) to a newly-hired 63-year-old employee would not be reasonable because it would result in a normal retirement age of 88. See generally, Rev. Rul. 66-11.

D. *Qualified public safety employees*

The proposed regulations include three safe harbors specifically for qualified public safety employees. The safe harbors were developed based upon feedback provided in comments received in response to Notices 2007-69 and 2012-29. Consistent with Notice 2012-29 and in response to comments, the proposed regulations would make clear that a governmental plan is permitted to use one or more of the safe harbors for qualified public safety employees to satisfy the reasonably representative requirement for those employees even if a different normal retirement age or ages is used under the plan for one or more other categories of participants who are not qualified public safety employees. The safe harbors for qualified public safety employees are not permitted to be used for these other categories of participants; a different normal retirement age (or ages) must be used for participants in a plan who are not qualified public safety employees.

As under the 2007 NRA regulations, the term *qualified public safety employee* would be defined by reference to section 72(t)(10)(B), under which a qualified public safety employee means any employee of a State or political subdivision of a State who provides police protection, firefighting services, or emergency medical services for any area within the jurisdiction of such State or political subdivision.[5] Defining qualified public safety employee by reference to section 72(t)(10)(B) has been retained because it is closely aligned with the categories of employees described in the Age Discrimination in Employment Act that an employer may refrain from hiring after a certain age.[6] Because qualified public safety employees typically commence plan participation at younger ages, the period of service required for full vesting at normal retirement age under each of the safe harbors for qualified public safety employees should be reasonable.

---

[5] Section 72(t)(10)(B) was amended by section 2(a) of Defending Public Safety Employees' Retirement Act, Public Law 114-26 (129 Stat. 319) (2015)) and section 308 of Protecting Americans From Tax Hikes Act of 2015 (PATH Act), enacted as part of the Consolidated Appropriations Act, 2016, Public Law 114-113 (129 Stat. 2422), to include federal public safety employees as qualified public safety employees for purposes of the rules under section 72(t)(10). Thus, for distributions made after December 31, 2015, the term *qualified public safety employee* means any employee of a State or political subdivision of a State who provides police protection, firefighting services, or emergency medical services for any area within the jurisdiction of such State or political subdivi-

sion, or any Federal law enforcement officer described in section 8331(20) or 8401(17) of title 5, United States Code, any Federal customs and border protection officer described in section 8331(31) or 8401(36) of such title, any Federal firefighter described in section 8331(21) or 8401(14) of such title, or any air traffic controller described in 8331(30) or 8401(35) of such title, any nuclear materials courier described in section 8331(27) or 8401(33) of such title, any member of the United States Capitol Police, any member of the Supreme Court Police, and any diplomatic security special agent of the Department of State.

[6] See section 4(j) of the Age Discrimination in Employment Act, 29 U.S.C. 623(j).

1. *Age 50*

The proposed regulations would modify the safe harbor for qualified public safety employees that was provided in the 2007 NRA regulations under which a normal retirement age of age 50 or later is deemed to satisfy the reasonably representative requirement and would expand on the guidance under consideration described in Notice 2012-29. The proposed regulations would make clear that a governmental plan is permitted to use the safe harbor (alone or together with one or both of the other safe harbors for qualified public safety employees described in this preamble) for one or more qualified public safety employees in a governmental plan without regard to any "substantially all" requirement (that is, without regard to whether substantially all of the participants in the plan or substantially all of the participants within a group of participants are qualified public safety employees).

2. *Combined age and years of service of 70 or more*

The proposed regulations would add a safe harbor under which a normal retirement age for qualified public safety employees under a governmental plan that is the participant's age when the sum of the participant's age plus the number of years of service that have been credited to the participant under the plan equals 70 or more would be deemed to satisfy the reasonably representative requirement.

3. *Any age with 20 years of service*

The proposed regulations would also add a safe harbor under which a normal retirement age for qualified public safety employees under a governmental plan that is the participant's age when the number of years of service that have been credited to the participant under the plan equals 20 or more would be deemed to satisfy the reasonably representative requirement. For example, a normal retirement age for qualified public safety employees under a plan that is 25 years of service would satisfy this safe harbor. The Department of the Treasury and the IRS agree with the comments received in response to Notice 2012-29 that indicated that a safe harbor based solely on a period of service would be appropriate for qualified public safety employees because these employees typically have career spans that commence at a young age and continue over a limited period of years.

E. *Multiple normal retirement ages in a governmental plan*

Commenters on Notice 2012-29 stated that it is a common practice for governmental plans to have a normal retirement age that is a combination of age and years of service. In light of these comments, some of the safe harbors proposed in these regulations contemplate a combination of age and years of service, such as, for example, the use of a normal retirement age that is the earlier of (1) the participant's age when the participant has been credited with 30 years of service under the plan or (2) the later of age 60 or the age when the participant has been credited with 5 years of service under the plan. A normal retirement age under a governmental plan that is consistent with the safe harbors in these proposed regulations would not fail to satisfy the pre-ERISA requirements, including the requirement that any period of service required for vesting at normal retirement age be uniformly applicable to all employees in a plan, merely because the plan uses such a normal retirement age.

Commenters to Notice 2012-29 also stated that governmental plans typically provide multiple normal retirement ages, often based on different benefit structures or classifications of employees in a single plan. These comments expressed concern that certain language in Notice 2012-29[7] could be read to indicate that a governmental plan could only have two normal retirement ages if one of the normal retirement ages covered qualified public safety employees and the other normal retirement age covered all of the other participants in the plan.

Use of one normal retirement age for one classification of employees (such as qualified public safety employees) and one or more other normal retirement ages for one or more different classifications of employees would not be inconsistent with these proposed regulations and generally would not be inconsistent with the applicable pre-ERISA requirements, including the requirement that any period of service required for full vesting at normal retirement age be uniformly applicable. Similarly, the use of one normal retirement age under a governmental plan for employees hired before a certain date and another normal retirement age under the plan for employees hired on or after that date generally would not fail to satisfy the applicable pre-ERISA requirements.

F. *Other normal retirement ages*

The proposed regulations would provide that in the case of a normal retirement age under a governmental plan that fails to satisfy any of the governmental plan safe harbors, whether the normal retirement age satisfies the reasonably representative requirement would be based on all of the relevant facts and circumstances. Similar to the treatment of normal retirement ages between ages 55 and 62 under the 2007 NRA regulations, it is generally expected that a good faith determination of the typical retirement age for the industry in which the covered workforce is employed that is made by the employer will be given deference, assuming that the determination is reasonable under the facts and circumstances and that the normal retirement age is otherwise consistent with the pre-ERISA vesting requirements.

Proposed Effective Date

These regulations are proposed to be effective for employees hired during plan years beginning on or after the later of (1) January 1, 2017 or (2) the close of the first regular legislative session of the legislative body with the authority to amend the plan that begins on or after the date that is 3 months after the final regulations are published in the **Federal Register**. Governmental plan sponsors may rely on these proposed regulations for periods preceding the effective date, pending the issuance of final regulations. If and to the extent the final regulations are more restrictive than the rules in these proposed regulations, those provisions of the final regulations will be applied without retroactive effect.

Statement of Availability for IRS Documents

For copies of recently issued Revenue Procedures, Revenue Rulings, Notices, and other guidance published in the Internal Revenue Bulletin or Cumulative Bulletin, please visit the IRS Web site at http://www.irs.gov or the Superintendent of Documents, U.S. Government Printing Office, Washington, DC 20402.

Special Analyses

Certain IRS regulations, including this one, are exempt from the requirements of Executive Order 12866, as supplemented and reaffirmed by Executive Order 13563. Therefore, a regulatory assessment is not required. It has also been determined that 5 U.S.C. 533(b) of the Administrative Procedure Act (5 U.S.C. chapter 5) does not apply to these regulations. In addition, because no collection of information is imposed on small entities, the provisions of the Regulatory Flexibility Act (5 U.S.C. chapter 6) do not apply and a Regulatory Flexibility Analysis is not required. Pursuant to section 7805(f) of the Internal Revenue Code, these regulations have been submitted to the Office of Chief Counsel for Advocacy of the Small Business Administration for comments on its impact on small business.

---

[7] Notice 2012-29 provided that, under an anticipated amendment to the 2007 NRA regulations, a governmental plan would be permitted to satisfy the reasonably representative requirement using a normal retirement age as low as 50 for a group substantially all of whom are qualified public safety employees and a later normal retirement age that otherwise satisfies the 2007 NRA requirements for all other participants.

Comments and Requests for Public Hearing

Before these proposed regulations are adopted as final regulations, consideration will be given to any comments that are submitted timely to the IRS as prescribed in this preamble under the "Addresses" heading. All comments are available at www.regulations.gov or upon request. A public hearing will be scheduled if requested in writing by any person who timely submits written comments. If a public hearing is scheduled, notice of the date, time, and place of the public hearing will be published in the **Federal Register**.

Drafting Information

The principal authors of these regulations are Sarah R. Bolen and Pamela R. Kinard, Office of Associate Chief Counsel (Tax Exempt and Government Entities). However, other personnel from the Department of the Treasury and the IRS participated in the development of these regulations.

[¶ 49,679] Proposed Amendments of Regulations (REG-125761-14), published in the Federal Register on January 29, 2016.

[Code Sec. 401]

Retirement plans: Nondiscrimination testing: Closed plans.—Amendments of Reg. §§1.401(a)(4)-0, §1.401(a)(4)-2, §1.401(a)(4)-3, §1.401(a)(4)-4, §1.401(a)(4)-8, §1.401(a)(4)-9, §1.401(a)(4)-12 and §1.401(a)(4)-13 following certain changes in the coverage of a defined benefit plan or a defined benefit plan formula, are proposed. The texts are at: ¶17,702B, ¶17,704C, ¶17,705C, ¶17,706D, ¶17,710B, ¶17,711B, ¶17,714C and ¶17,715B.

AGENCY: Internal Revenue Service (IRS), Treasury.

ACTION: Notice of proposed rulemaking and notice of public hearing.

SUMMARY: This document contains proposed regulations that modify the nondiscrimination requirements applicable to certain retirement plans that provide additional benefits to a grandfathered group of employees following certain changes in the coverage of a defined benefit plan or a defined benefit plan formula. The proposed regulations also make certain other changes to the nondiscrimination rules that are not limited to these plans. These regulations would affect participants in, beneficiaries of, employers maintaining, and administrators of tax-qualified retirement plans.

DATES: Written or electronic comments and must be received by April 28, 2016. Outlines of topics to be discussed at the public hearing scheduled for May 19, 2016 at 10 a.m., must be received by April 28, 2016.

ADDRESSES: Send submissions to: CC:PA:LPD:PR (REG-125761-14), room 5203, Internal Revenue Service, PO Box 7604, Ben Franklin Station, Washington D.C. 20044. Submissions may be hand-delivered Monday through Friday between the hours of 8 a.m. and 4 p.m. to: CC:PA:LPD:PR (REG-125761-14), Courier's Desk, Internal Revenue Service, 1111 Constitution Avenue, N.W., Washington, D.C., or sent electronically via the Federal eRulemaking Portal at *http://www.regulations.gov* (IRS REG-125761-14).

FOR FURTHER INFORMATION CONTACT: Concerning the regulations, Kelly C. Scanlon and Linda S. F. Marshall at (202) 317-6700; concerning submissions of comments, the hearing, and/or being placed on the building access list to attend the hearing, Oluwafunmilayo (Funmi) Taylor at (202) 317-6901 (not toll-free numbers).

SUPPLEMENTARY INFORMATION:

Background

Section 401(a)(4) provides generally that a plan is a qualified plan only if the contributions or benefits provided under the plan do not discriminate in favor of highly compensated employees. In 1991, the Treasury Department and the IRS issued comprehensive regulations under section 401(a)(4) (TD 8360, 56 FR 47524) setting forth several alternative methods for testing compliance with this statutory requirement. In 1993, the Treasury Department and the IRS made significant amendments to those regulations (TD 8485, 58 FR 46773).

Under the section 401(a)(4) regulations, a plan is permitted to demonstrate that either the contributions or the benefits provided under the plan are nondiscriminatory in amount, regardless of whether the plan is a defined benefit or defined contribution plan. See § 1.401(a)(4)-1(b)(2). In order to test a defined contribution plan on the basis of benefits, the amounts allocated to employees under the plan must be converted to equivalent benefits. This conversion is done using an interest rate between 7.5% and 8.5%.[1] In addition, for purposes of section 401(a)(4), a defined benefit plan and a defined contribution plan are permitted to be aggregated and treated as a single plan pursuant to § 1.401(a)(4)-9, which refers to such an aggregated plan as a DB/DC plan.

After issuance of the final regulations, a new type of plan design developed. This type of plan is often referred to as a "new comparability" plan and is typically a defined contribution plan that provides higher allocation rates to an older and more highly compensated group of employees. This type of plan nonetheless satisfies the nondiscrimination requirements by testing the contributions on the basis of equivalent benefits because the conversion to equivalent benefits reflects assumed growth to normal retirement age and therefore results in relatively lower equivalent benefits for the highly compensated employees who are closer to normal retirement age. The Treasury Department and the IRS concluded that this type of plan was inconsistent with the intent behind the nondiscrimination regulations. Consequently, the Treasury Department and the IRS amended the section 401(a)(4) regulations in 2001 to require that a new comparability plan provide a higher minimum contribution to nonhighly compensated employees[2] in order for the plan to be eligible to demonstrate compliance with the nondiscrimination requirements of section 401(a)(4) on the basis of equivalent benefits (TD 8954, 66 FR 34535) (the "2001 amendments").

This higher minimum contribution requirement was directed at the new comparability plans. Other defined contribution plans that provide "broadly available allocation rates" or allocation rates that are "based on a gradual age or service schedule" are not subject to the higher minimum contribution requirement even if they demonstrate compliance with the nondiscrimination requirements of section 401(a)(4) on the basis of equivalent benefits.[3] In addition, under the 2001 amendments, defined benefit replacement allocations ("DBRAs") may be disregarded when determining whether a defined contribution plan has broadly available allocation rates. The 2001 amendments also prescribe rules regarding DB/DC plans that provide for benefits in a manner similar to new comparability plans. Under these rules (contained in § 1.401(a)(4)-9(b)(2)(v)), in order for a DB/DC plan to be eligible to demonstrate compliance with the section 401(a)(4) nondiscrimination requirements on the basis of equivalent benefits, it must satisfy a minimum aggregate allocation gateway unless the DB/DC plan either fits within the definition of "primarily defined benefit in character" or consists of "broadly available separate plans." This minimum aggregate allocation gateway requires a minimum allocation rate (or equivalent allocation rate) for each nonhighly compensated employee.

---

[1] See § 1.401(a)(4)-8(c)(2)(ii) and § 1.401(a)(4)-12 (definition of standard interest rate). This standard interest rate is used to determine assumed growth of a defined contribution plan account and to convert the projected account balance to an annuity at normal retirement age.

[2] This higher minimum contribution rate is required under § 1.401(a)(4)-8(b)(1)(i)(B)(3) and (b)(1)(vi)..

[3] See § 1.401(a)(4)-8(b)(1)(i)(B)(1) and (2), (b)(1)(iii), and (b)(1)(iv).

Since 2001, a number of employers have moved away from providing retirement benefits through traditional defined benefit plans. In many of these cases, employers have either significantly changed the type of benefit formula provided under the plan (such as in the case of a conversion to a cash balance plan), or have prohibited new employees from entering the plan entirely. The employers may then have allowed employees who had already begun participation in the defined benefit plan (or who are older or have been credited with longer service under the plan) to continue to earn pension benefits under the defined benefit plan while closing the plan or formula to all other employees. These defined benefit plans are sometimes referred to as "closed plans," and the employees who continue to earn pension benefits under the closed plan are often known as a "grandfathered group of employees." In situations in which new employees continue to earn benefits under the defined benefit plan, but are under a new formula, any formula that continues to apply to a grandfathered group of employees is sometimes referred to as a "closed formula."

Closed plans are required to meet the coverage rules under section 410(b) and the nondiscrimination rules under section 401(a)(4) (including a nondiscrimination requirement regarding the availability of benefits, rights, and features). Many closed plans, however, may eventually find it difficult to meet these requirements because the proportion of the grandfathered group of employees who are highly compensated employees compared to the employer's total workforce increases over time. This occurs because members of the grandfathered group of employees usually continue to receive pay raises (and so may become highly compensated employees), and new employees (who are generally nonhighly compensated employees) are not covered by the closed plan.

When a closed defined benefit plan can no longer meet the nondiscrimination requirements on a stand-alone basis because of the demographic changes previously described, it can demonstrate compliance with section 401(a)(4) by aggregating with the employer's defined contribution plan. In general, it is easier to meet the nondiscrimination requirements if the resulting DB/DC plan demonstrates compliance with section 401(a)(4) based on the benefits or equivalent benefits provided to the employees (rather than based on contributions).

On January 6, 2014, the Treasury Department and the IRS published Notice 2014-5, 2014-2 I.R.B. 276. Notice 2014-5 provided temporary nondiscrimination relief for certain closed plans. Specifically, under Notice 2014-5, if certain criteria are satisfied,[4] a plan sponsor is permitted to test a DB/DC plan that includes a closed plan that was closed before December 13, 2013, on a benefits basis for plan years beginning before January 1, 2016, without complying with the minimum aggregate allocation gateway, even if that would otherwise be required under the current regulations. Notice 2015-28, 2015-14 I.R.B. 848, extended that relief for an additional year by applying it to plan years beginning before 2017 provided that the conditions of Notice 2014-5 are satisfied.

Notice 2014-5 also requested comments on whether the section 401(a)(4) regulations should be amended to provide additional alternatives that would allow a DB/DC plan to satisfy the nondiscrimination in amount requirements on the basis of equivalent benefits, and whether certain other permanent changes should be made to the nondiscrimination regulations, such as modifications to the rules regarding nondiscriminatory benefits, rights, and features.[5] The comments received in response to Notice 2014-5 generally supported these types of changes. In addition, all of the commenters requested permanent changes to the nondiscrimination requirements in order to make it easier for closed plans to continue to satisfy the nondiscrimination requirements.

The Treasury Department and the IRS agree that permanent changes to the nondiscrimination rules should be made in order to help employers and plan sponsors preserve the retirement expectations of certain grandfathered groups of employees. These changes are meant to apply to situations in which the proportion of the grandfathered group of employees who are highly compensated employees compared to the employer's total workforce has increased due to ordinary demographic changes, as previously described in this preamble.

Explanation of Provisions

I. Overview

The proposed regulations modify a number of provisions in the existing regulations under section 401(a)(4) to address situations and plan designs, including closed plans and formulas, that were not contemplated in the development of the regulations and the 2001 amendments. While many of the changes in the proposed regulations provide nondiscrimination relief for certain closed plans and formulas, the proposed regulations also include other changes that are not limited to closed plans and formulas.

II. Rules related to closed plans and similar arrangements

The proposed regulations set forth special rules that allow closed plans and similar arrangements to satisfy the nondiscrimination rules in additional situations. These special rules are based on the existing rules for DBRAs, as modified to respond to concerns raised by stakeholders with respect to those existing rules.

Under the proposed regulations, the eligibility conditions set forth in the modified DBRA rules (described in section II.A of this portion of the preamble) provide a framework for the eligibility conditions for the snapshot rule related to closed plans in a DB/DC plan (described in section II.B of this portion of the preamble). The modified DBRA rules are also used as a basis for the special testing rule for benefits, rights, and features provided to a grandfathered group of employees (described in section II.C of this portion of the preamble). For example, the special testing rule for a benefit, right, or feature provided to a grandfathered group of employees under a defined contribution plan establishes nondiscrimination relief for matching contributions provided to a grandfathered group of employees who formerly participated in a defined benefit plan that is intended to be consistent with the nondiscrimination relief provided by the modified DBRA rules for nonelective contributions provided to such a grandfathered group of employees.

A. Modifications to the DBRA rules under §1.401(a)(4)-8

The proposed regulations modify the rules applicable to DBRAs under §1.401(a)(4)-8, which allow certain defined contribution plan allocations to be disregarded when determining whether a defined contribution plan has broadly available allocation rates. The rules applicable to DBRAs allow employers to provide, in a nondiscriminatory manner, certain allocations to replace defined benefit plan retirement benefits without having to satisfy the minimum aggregate allocation gateway. The modifications in the proposed regulations are intended to allow more allocations to fit within the DBRA rules. For example, under the existing regulations a DBRA must be reasonably designed to replace the benefits that would have been provided under the closed defined benefit plan. The proposed regulations provide greater flexibility in this respect and allow the allocations to be reasonably designed to replace some or all of the benefits that would have been provided under the closed plan, subject to a requirement that the allocations be provided in a consistent manner to all similarly situated employees.

---

[4] Generally, in order to be eligible for the relief provided by Notice 2014-5, each defined benefit plan that is part of an aggregated DB/DC plan must have satisfied the requirements of section 401(a)(4) without using the minimum aggregate allocation gateway under §1.401(a)(4)-9(b)(2)(v)(D). Thus, the defined benefit plan must have either been primarily defined benefit in character (within the meaning of §1.401(a)(4)-9(b)(2)(v)(B)), consisted of broadly available separate plans (within the meaning of §1.401(a)(4)-9(b)(2)(v)(C)), or satisfied the applicable nondiscrimination rules without being aggregated with a DC plan.

[5] Section 1.401(a)(4)-4 provides rules for determining whether the benefits, right, and features provided under a plan are made available in a nondiscriminatory manner. Under these rules, each benefit, right, or feature must satisfy the current availability requirement of §1.401(a)(4)-4(b) (which requires testing of the group to which the benefit, right, or feature is currently available) and the effective availability requirement of §1.401(a)(4)-4(c) (which requires that the group of employees to whom the benefit, right, or feature is effectively available must not substantially favor highly compensated employees).

The proposed regulations incorporate a modified version of the conditions for an allocation to be a DBRA that were reflected in Rev. Rul. 2001-30, 2001-2 C.B. 46. For example, under one of the conditions set forth in Rev. Rul. 2001-30, in order for an allocation to be a DBRA, the defined benefit plan's benefit formula for the group of employees who formerly benefitted under that plan must have generated equivalent normal allocation rates that increased from year to year as employees attained higher ages. The proposed regulations ease this restriction on the types of defined benefit plans with respect to which a DBRA can be provided by allowing a DBRA also to replace the benefit provided under a defined benefit plan with a benefit formula that generated equivalent normal allocation rates that increased from year to year as employees were credited with additional years of service (rather than only as the employees attained higher ages).

The existing regulation also requires that the group of employees who receive a DBRA must be a nondiscriminatory group of employees, and Rev. Rul. 2001-30 interprets this rule as requiring that the group of employees satisfy the minimum coverage requirements of section 410(b) (determined without regard to the average benefit percentage test). The proposed regulations incorporate this interpretation, but limit its application so that the rule only applies for the first 5 years after the closure date. In addition, the proposed regulations incorporate the interpretation in Rev. Rul. 2001-30 regarding whether the defined benefit plan was an established nondiscriminatory defined benefit plan by requiring that the closed plan be in effect for 5 years before the closure date (with one year substituted for 5 years, as provided by Rev. Rul. 2001-30, in the case of a defined benefit plan maintained by a former employer) with no substantial change to the closed plan during that time (except for certain permitted amendments allowed by the proposed regulations).

In addition, the proposed regulations expand the list of permitted amendments to a closed plan that do not prevent allocations under a plan from being DBRAs. For example, the proposed regulations permit an amendment to a closed plan during the 5-year period before it was closed, provided that the amendment does not increase the accrued benefit or future accruals for any employee, does not expand coverage, and does not reduce the ratio-percentage under any applicable nondiscrimination test. In addition, under the proposed regulations, an amendment during this period could extend coverage to an acquired group of employees provided that all similarly situated employees within that group are treated in a consistent manner.

As under the existing regulations, the proposed regulations contain a general restriction on plan amendments relating to a DBRA; however, the proposed regulations expand the list of plan amendments that are excepted from this rule. The proposed regulations retain the exception from this restriction on plan amendments for an amendment that makes *de minimis* changes in the calculation of a DBRA and for an amendment that adds or removes a "greater-of" plan provision (under which a participant receives the greater of the otherwise applicable allocation and the DBRA). In addition, the proposed regulations provide an exception from this restriction for any plan amendment modifying a DBRA that does not reduce the ratio percentage under any applicable nondiscrimination test.

B. Closed plan rule added to the plan aggregation and restructuring rules under §1.401(a)(4)-9

The proposed regulations add a new exception to the requirement that a DB/DC plan must satisfy the minimum aggregate allocation gateway once the other conditions under §1.401(a)(4)-9 are not met (the "closed plan rule"). This closed plan rule, which applies to a DB/DC plan that includes a closed plan, provides an exception to the minimum aggregate allocation gateway that would otherwise apply, but only if the closed plan was in effect for 5 years before the closure date and no significant change was made to the closed plan during or since that time (except for certain permitted amendments).

The DB/DC plan may use this closed plan rule for a plan year that begins on or after the fifth anniversary of the closure date. To be eligible for the closed plan rule, during the 5-year period following the closure date, either the DB/DC plan must satisfy the nondiscrimination in amount requirement of section 401(a)(4) without using the minimum aggregate allocation gateway, or the closed plan must satisfy that requirement without aggregation with any defined contribution plan. This requirement is comparable to the requirement that the group of employees who receive DBRAs must be a group of employees who satisfy the minimum coverage requirements of section 410(b).

Under the proposed regulations, certain amendments to a closed defined benefit plan do not prevent the plan from using the closed plan rule. These plan amendments are intended to allow a plan sponsor of a closed plan to address changed circumstances. For example, under the proposed regulations, a plan amendment during the 5-year period ending on the closure date does not prevent the plan from later using the closed plan rule, provided that the plan amendment does not increase the accrued benefit or future accruals for any employee, does not expand coverage, and does not reduce the ratio percentage under any applicable nondiscrimination test. Similarly, an amendment to the closed plan is permitted after the closure date, provided that the amendment does not reduce the ratio percentage under any applicable nondiscrimination test. Thus, for example, under the proposed regulations, a plan sponsor may add nonhighly compensated employees to a coverage group after it is closed in order to satisfy the nondiscrimination rules. *De minimis* changes to the closed plan's benefit formula are also permitted under the proposed regulations.

C. Special testing rule for the nondiscriminatory availability of a benefit, right, or feature provided to a grandfathered group of employees under §1.401(a)(4)-4

The proposed regulations establish a special nondiscrimination testing rule under §1.401(a)(4)-4 that applies if a benefit, right, or feature is made available only to a grandfathered group of employees with respect to a closed plan. This special rule provides relief in certain circumstances from certain nondiscrimination testing for a benefit, right, or feature provided under the closed plan, or for a rate of matching contributions provided to a grandfathered group under a defined contribution plan.

If the eligibility conditions are satisfied, the special testing rule treats a benefit, right, or feature that is provided only to a grandfathered group of employees as satisfying the current and effective availability tests of §1.401(a)(4)-4(b) and (c). The special testing rule applies to plan years beginning on or after the fifth anniversary of the closure date and applies on a plan-year by plan-year basis. To be eligible for the special testing rule, the benefit, right or feature must be currently available to a group of employees that satisfies the minimum coverage requirements of section 410(b) for the plan years that begin within 5 years after the closure date. Once the special testing rule applies to a benefit, right, or feature, the special testing rule continues to apply for purposes of that benefit, right, or feature indefinitely (unless a later amendment changes the eligibility for the benefit, right, or feature). If a plan amendment changes the eligibility for the benefit, right, or feature after the closure date, then the special testing rule will cease to apply (subject to certain specified exceptions).

If the benefit, right, or feature that is available solely to a grandfathered group of employees is provided under a defined benefit plan, then it must be provided under the closed plan (rather than a different defined benefit plan). This is because the purpose of the special rule is to accommodate a plan amendment under which the benefit formula has been changed, but the prior benefit formula has been preserved for a grandfathered group of employees and the benefit, right, or feature is made available only to the grandfathered group of employees who continue to accrue benefits under the prior benefit formula.[6] Accordingly, the special testing rule is available only if the amendment restricting the availability of the benefit, right, or feature also resulted in a significant change in the type of the defined benefit plan's formula. For example, a conversion to a cash balance plan would be a significant change in the type of benefit formula, so that the special testing rule would apply to facilitate preservation of any subsidized early retirement factors for the employees who continue to benefit under the prior benefit formula. By

---

[6] The existing regulations provide a special rule for current availability testing for a benefit, right, or feature that applies solely to benefits accrued before the amendment date. *See* §1.401(a)(4)-4(d)(2).

contrast, in the case of a benefit formula that determines benefits as a percentage of compensation, a change in that formula to reduce that percentage would not be considered a significant change in the type of benefit formula, even if the reduction is large.

The special testing rule for a benefit, right, or feature provided under the closed plan also requires that the benefit, right, or feature has been in effect without being amended for a 5-year period before the closure date (subject to a limited exception for acquired employees). This rule is designed to ensure that the special treatment is available only for a long-standing provision and cannot be used for a benefit, right, or feature that has not been provided long enough for participants to have established a reasonable expectation that it will continue. In addition, this rule prevents a plan sponsor from obtaining special treatment for a benefit, right, or feature added shortly before and in anticipation of the closure of the plan. The proposed regulations set forth a list of permitted plan amendments that do not result in the loss of this special testing rule that are generally comparable to the list of permitted amendments for other closed plan arrangements.

The special testing rule also applies to a rate of matching contributions under a defined contribution plan that meets certain requirements. In order to be eligible for this testing rule, the rate of matching contributions must be reasonably designed so that the matching contributions will replace some or all of the value of the benefit accruals that each employee in the grandfathered group of employees would have been provided under the closed plan in the absence of a closure amendment. In addition, the rate of matching contributions for the grandfathered group of employees must be provided in a consistent manner to all similarly situated employees.

III. Modification of testing options under §1.401(a)(4)-9 for DB/DC plans, including DB/DC plans that do not include a closed plan

In addition to providing a special rule for closed plans and similar arrangements, the proposed regulations generally ease the rules under which any DB/DC plan can satisfy the nondiscrimination in amount requirement on the basis of benefits. These changes are intended to facilitate the ongoing maintenance of a defined benefit plan that provides coverage to a group of employees that is determined using a reasonable business classification.

The proposed regulations expand the ability to use the average of the equivalent allocation rates under the defined benefit plan for purposes of satisfying the minimum aggregate allocation gateway by permitting the averaging of allocation rates for nonhighly compensated employees under the defined contribution plan for this purpose. This modification is intended to better accommodate plan sponsors that have a defined contribution plan with service-or age-based allocation formulas. The Treasury Department and the IRS have determined that it is appropriate, in this context, to allow shorter-service nonhighly compensated employees to be provided less than the minimum aggregate allocation gateway rate, as long as longer-service nonhighly compensated employees are provided allocation rates that are sufficiently higher than the minimum aggregate allocation gateway rate. The Treasury Department and the IRS are considering whether any restrictions on this rule are appropriate so that the rule serves its intended purpose of facilitating formulas that provide higher allocation rates to longer-service nonhighly compensated employees, and invite comments on ways to permit appropriate flexibility while ensuring the provision is not used to circumvent the purpose of the nondiscrimination rules.

The proposed regulations also include a limitation on the averaging of rates that applies to both defined contribution and defined benefit plans in order to minimize the impact of outliers. In general, this special rule applies a cap under which any equivalent normal allocation rate or allocation rate in excess of 15% is treated as equal to 15%. However, this cap is raised to 25% for any allocation rate or equivalent normal allocation rate that results solely from a plan design providing allocation rates or generating equivalent normal allocation rates that are a function of age or service under which higher rates are provided to older or longer-service employees.

In addition, under the proposed regulations, the average of the matching contributions actually made for nonhighly compensated employees may be used to a limited extent (up to 3 percent of compensation) for purposes of determining whether each nonhighly compensated employee satisfies the minimum aggregate allocation gateway test. Thus, for example, if the minimum aggregate allocation gateway is 7% and the average of the matching contributions actually made for nonhighly compensated employees is 3%, then a non-elective contribution of 4% for each individual would be needed in order to satisfy the minimum aggregate allocation gateway under the proposed regulations. The regulations use the average matching contributions, rather than matching contributions allocated for each employee, in order to avoid diluting the incentive effect of an employer match.

The proposed regulations also provide a new alternative to the minimum aggregate allocation gateway. Under this alternative, a DB/DC plan is not required to satisfy the minimum aggregate allocation gateway if it can satisfy the nondiscrimination in amount requirement on the basis of equivalent benefits using an interest rate of 6%, rather than the current standard interest rate of between 7.5% and 8.5%.

IV. Benefit formulas for individual employees or groups without a reasonable business purpose; modifications to the amounts testing rules under §1.401(a)(4)-2 and §1.401(a)(4)-3

The proposed regulations also include changes to address certain arrangements that take advantage of the flexibility in the existing nondiscrimination rules[7] to provide a special benefit formula for selected employees without extending that formula to a classification of employees that is reasonable and is established under objective business criteria. A plan satisfies the minimum coverage requirements of section 410(b) if the plan's ratio percentage is 70% or higher or the plan satisfies the average benefit test. To satisfy the average benefit test, pursuant to §1.410(b)-4, the group of employees must be determined using a classification that is reasonable and that is established under objective business criteria pursuant to §1.410(b)-4(b) and must have a ratio percentage that is described in §1.410(b)-4(c) (which includes safe harbor and unsafe harbor percentages). A classification of employees that is reasonable and is established under objective business criteria is referred to in this preamble as a "reasonable business classification." To the extent that a plan provides a special benefit formula and can still pass the nondiscrimination requirements, the plan sponsor can use a qualified retirement plan to provide benefits that would otherwise be provided under a nonqualified plan. These arrangements are sometimes referred to as qualified supplemental executive retirement plans (or QSERPs).

Under the general test in the existing regulations, if a plan satisfies the minimum coverage requirements of section 410(b) using the average benefit percentage test, then the rate group for each highly compensated employee is treated as satisfying the minimum coverage requirements if the ratio percentage for the rate group is equal to the midpoint between the safe harbor and the unsafe harbor percentages (or the ratio percentage for the plan as a whole, if less). This rule recognizes that the composition of a rate group may be unpredictable and so the rate group should not be subject to a reasonable business classification standard. However, that same consideration is not relevant if the group of employees to whom the allocation formula under a defined contribution plan (or benefit formula under a defined benefit plan) applies is not a reasonable business classification.

Accordingly, the proposed regulations limit the existing rule under which a rate group with respect to a highly compensated employee is treated as satisfying the average benefit percentage test to those situations in which the allocation formula (or benefit formula) that applies to the highly compensated employee also applies to a reasonable business classification. For example, if a benefit formula applies solely to a highly compensated

---

[7] Under the existing regulations, the nondiscrimination requirements of section 401(a)(4) and the coverage rules of section 410(b) are coordinated. The general test under the section 401(a)(4) regulations is applied by determining whether each rate group under the plan (that is, for each highly compensated employee, the group of employees with a benefit or contribution rate that is greater than or equal to the benefit or contribution rate for the highly compensated employee) satisfies section 410(b) as if it were a plan.

employee who is identified by name, it does not apply to a reasonable business classification. See §1.410(b)-4(b). In such a case, the proposed regulations would require that the rate group with respect to that individual satisfy the ratio percentage test.

Proposed Applicability Date

Except as described below, these regulations are proposed to be applicable to plan years beginning on or after the date of publication of the Treasury decision adopting these rules as final regulations in the **Federal Register**. Taxpayers are permitted to apply the provisions of these proposed regulations except for those described in section III of the Explanation of Provisions portion of the preamble for plan years beginning before this proposed applicability date, but not for plan years earlier than those beginning on or after January 1, 2014. Accordingly, the ability to rely on a provision of these proposed regulations for periods prior to the proposed applicability date for these regulations applies to the disregard of certain defined benefit replacement allocations in cross-testing; the exception from the minimum aggregate allocation gateway with respect to certain closed plans; the special testing rule for benefits, rights, and features with respect to certain closed plans; and the rule applying the ratio percentage test to a rate group in the case of a benefit formula that does not apply to a reasonable business classification. Taxpayers may rely on these provisions (that is, the provisions that the proposed regulations would permit a taxpayer to apply before the proposed applicability date for these regulations) in order to satisfy the nondiscrimination requirements of section 401(a)(4) for plan years beginning on or after January 1, 2014, and until the corresponding final regulations become applicable.

Special Analyses

Certain IRS regulations, including this one, are exempt from the requirements of Executive Order 12866, as supplemented and reaffirmed by Executive Order 13563. Therefore, a regulatory impact assessment is not required. It also has been determined that section 553(b) of the Administrative Procedure Act (5 U.S.C. chapter 5) does not apply to these regulations, and because the regulation does not impose a collection of information on small entities, the Regulatory Flexibility Act (5 U.S.C. chapter 6) does not apply. Pursuant to section 7805(f) of the Internal Revenue Code, these regulations have been submitted to the Chief Counsel for Advocacy of the Small Business Administration for comment on their impact on small business.

Comments and Public Hearing

Before these proposed regulations are adopted as final regulations, consideration will be given to any comments that are submitted timely to the IRS as prescribed in this preamble under the "ADDRESSES" heading. Treasury and the IRS request comments on all aspects of the proposed rules, including the proposed applicability date. Treasury and the IRS also request comments on the following issues:

- Whether guidance needs to be developed for a plan that has more than one closure or closure amendment?

- Whether the rules regarding transition allocations and successor employers are still needed in light of the modifications to the DBRA rules?

All comments will be available for public inspection and copying at www.regulations.gov or upon request.

A public hearing has been scheduled for May 19, 2016, beginning at 10 a.m. in the Auditorium, Internal Revenue Service, 1111 Constitution Avenue, N.W., Washington D.C. Because of building security procedures, visitors must enter at the Constitution Avenue entrance. In addition, all visitors must present photo identification to enter the building. Due to access restrictions, visitors will not be admitted beyond the immediate entrance area more than 30 minutes before the hearing starts. For information about having your name placed on the building access list to attend the hearing, see the "FOR FURTHER INFORMATION CONTACT" section of this preamble.

The rules of 26 CFR 601.601(a)(3) apply to the hearing. Persons who wish to present oral comments at the hearing must submit written or electronic comments by April 28, 2016 and an outline of the topics to be discussed and the time to be devoted to each topic by April 28, 2016. A signed paper or electronic copy of the outline should be submitted as prescribed in this preamble under the "ADDRESSES" heading. A period of 10 minutes will be allotted to each person for making comments. An agenda showing the scheduling of the speakers will be prepared after the deadline for receiving outlines has passed. Copies of the agenda will be available free of charge at the hearing.

Statement of Availability for IRS Documents

For copies of recently issued Revenue Procedures, Revenue Rulings, notices, and other guidance published in the Internal Revenue Bulletin, please visit the IRS website at http://irs.gov.

Drafting Information

The principal authors of these proposed regulations are Kelly C. Scanlon and Linda S. F. Marshall, IRS Office of Associate Chief Counsel (Tax Exempt and Government Entities). However, other personnel from the IRS and the Department of Treasury participated in the development of the proposed regulations.

[¶ 49,682]   **Proposed Amendments of Regulations (REG-118867-10)**, published in the Federal Register on February 19, 2016.

[Code Sec. 509]

Private foundations: Supporting organizations: Integral part test.—Amendments of Reg. §1.509(a)-4, regarding the prohibition on certain contributions to Type I and Type III supporting organizations and the requirements for Type III supporting organizations, are proposed.

AGENCY: Internal Revenue Service (IRS), Treasury.

ACTION: Notice of proposed rulemaking.

SUMMARY: This document contains proposed regulations regarding the prohibition on certain contributions to Type I and Type III supporting organizations and the requirements for Type III supporting organizations. The regulations reflect changes to the law made by the Pension Protection Act of 2006. The regulations will affect Type I and Type III supporting organizations and their supported organizations.

DATES: Written or electronic comments and requests for a public hearing must be received by May 19, 2016.

ADDRESSES: Send submissions to: CC:PA:LPD:PR (REG-118867-10), Room 5203, Internal Revenue Service, P.O. Box 7604, Ben Franklin Station, Washington, DC 20044. Submissions may be hand-delivered Monday through Friday between the hours of 8:00 a.m. and 4 p.m. to CC:PA:LPD:PR (REG-118867-10), Courier's Desk, Internal Revenue Service, 1111 Constitution Avenue, NW, Washington, DC, 20224 or sent electronically via the Federal eRulemaking Portal at http://www.regulations.gov/ (IRS REG-118867-10). FOR FURTHER INFORMATION CONTACT: concerning the proposed regulations, Jonathan Carter at (202) 317-5800 or Mike Repass at (202) 317-4086; concerning submissions of comments and requests for a public hearing, Regina Johnson at (202) 317-6901 (not toll-free numbers).

SUPPLEMENTARY INFORMATION:

Paperwork Reduction Act

The collection of information contained in this notice of proposed rulemaking has been submitted to the Office of Management and Budget for review and approval in accordance with the Paperwork Reduction Act of 1995 (44 U.S.C. 3507(d)). Comments on the collection of information should be sent to the Office of Management and Budget, Attn: Desk Officer for the Department of the Treasury, Office of Information and Regulatory Affairs, Washington, DC 20503, with copies to the Internal Revenue Service, Attn: IRS Reports Clearance Officer, SE:W:CAR:MP:T:T:SP, Washington, DC 20224. Comments on the collection of information should be received by May 19, 2016.

Comments are specifically requested concerning:

- Whether the proposed collection of information is necessary for the proper performance of the functions of the IRS, including whether the information will have practical utility;

- The accuracy of the estimated burden associated with the proposed collection of information;

- How the quality, utility, and clarity of the information to be collected may be enhanced;

- How the burden of complying with the proposed collection of information may be minimized, including through forms of information technology; and

- Estimates of capital or start-up costs and costs of operation, maintenance, and purchase of services to provide information.

The collection of information in these proposed regulations is in § 1.509(a)-4(i)(4)(iv)(D) (written record of close cooperation and coordination by the governmental supported organizations) and § 1.509(a)-4(i)(6)(iii)(B) (written record of contributions received by the supported organization). Requiring the supporting organization to collect written records of its governmental supported organizations' close cooperation and coordination with each other and written records of the contributions its supported organizations directly received in response to solicitations by the supporting organization permits the IRS to determine whether the supporting organization satisfies the requirements to be a functionally integrated or non-functionally integrated Type III supporting organization. The record keepers are Type III supporting organizations.

Estimated number of recordkeepers: 7,872.

Estimated average annual burden hours per recordkeeper: 2 hours.

Estimated total annual recordkeeping burden: 15,744.

Estimated frequency of collection of such information: Annual.

An agency may not conduct or sponsor, and a person is not required to respond to, a collection of information unless it displays a valid control number assigned by the Office of Management and Budget.

Books or records relating to a collection of information must be retained as long as their contents may become material in the administration of any internal revenue law. Generally, tax returns and return information are confidential, as required by 26 U.S.C. 6103.

Background

1. Overview

This document contains proposed amendments to the Income Tax Regulations (26 CFR part 1) regarding organizations described in section 509(a)(3) of the Internal Revenue Code (Code). An organization described in section 501(c)(3) is classified as either a private foundation or a public charity. To be classified as a public charity, an organization must be described in section 509(a)(1), (2), or (3). Organizations described in section 509(a)(3) are known as "supporting organizations." Supporting organizations achieve their public charity status by providing support to one or more organizations described in section 509(a)(1) or (2), which in this context are referred to as "supported organizations."

To be described in section 509(a)(3), an organization must satisfy (1) an organizational test, (2) an operational test, (3) a relationship test, and (4) a disqualified person control test. The organizational and operational tests require that a supporting organization be organized and at all times thereafter operated exclusively for the benefit of, to perform the functions of, or to carry out the purposes of one or more supported organizations. The relationship test requires a supporting organization to establish one of three types of relationships with one or more supported organizations. A supporting organization that is operated, supervised or controlled by one or more supported organizations is known as a "Type I" supporting organization. The relationship of a Type I supporting organization with its supported organization(s) is comparable to that of a corporate parent-subsidiary relationship. A supporting organization that is supervised or controlled in connection with one or more supported organizations is known as a "Type II" supporting organization. The relationship of a Type II supporting organization with its supported organization(s) involves common supervision or control by the persons supervising or controlling both the supporting organization and the supported organization(s). A supporting organization that is operated in connection with one or more supported organizations is known as a "Type III" supporting organization and is discussed further in the remainder of this preamble. Finally, the disqualified person control test requires that a supporting organization not be controlled directly or indirectly by certain disqualified persons.

These proposed regulations focus primarily on the relationship test for Type III supporting organizations. Specifically, the proposed regulations reflect statutory changes enacted by sections 1241 through 1243 of the Pension Protection Act of 2006, Public Law 109-280 (120 Stat. 780) (2006) (PPA)), which made the following five changes to the requirements an organization must satisfy to qualify as a Type III supporting organization:

(1) Removed the ability of a charitable trust to rely on the special rule under § 1.509(a)-4(i)(2)(iii) of the regulations then in effect;

(2) Directed the Secretary of the Treasury to promulgate regulations under section 509 that establish a new distribution requirement for Type III supporting organizations that are not "functionally integrated" (a non-functionally integrated (NFI) Type III supporting organization) to ensure that a "significant amount" is paid to supported organizations (for this purpose the term "functionally integrated" means a Type III supporting organization that is not required under Treasury regulations to make payments to supported organizations, because the supporting organization engages in activities that relate to performing the functions of, or carrying out the purposes of, its supported organization(s));

(3) Required a Type III supporting organization to provide annually to each of its supported organizations the information required by the Treasury Department and the IRS to ensure that the supporting organization is responsive to the needs or demands of its supported organization(s);

(4) Prohibited a Type III supporting organization from supporting any supported organization not organized in the United States; and

(5) Prohibited a Type I or Type III supporting organization from accepting a gift or contribution from a person who, alone or together with certain related persons, directly or indirectly controls the governing body of a supported organization of the Type I or Type III supporting organization.

These proposed regulations set forth additional rules on the requirements for Type III supporting organizations, including additional requirements to meet the responsiveness test for all Type III supporting organizations; additional rules regarding the qualification of an organization as a functionally integrated Type III supporting organization under § 1.509(a)-4(i)(4), including provisions for supporting organizations that support governmental entities; and additional rules regarding the required annual distributions under § 1.509(a)-4(i)(5) by a NFI Type III supporting organization. The proposed regulations also define the term "control" for purposes of section 509(f)(2), which prohibits a Type I supporting organization or a Type III supporting organization from accepting contributions from persons who control the governing body of its supported organization(s).

2. *Prior Rulemaking*

On August 2, 2007, the Treasury Department and the IRS published in the **Federal Register** (72 FR 42335) an advanced notice of proposed rulemaking (ANPRM) (REG-155929-06) in response to the PPA. The ANPRM described proposed rules to implement the changes made by the PPA to the Type III supporting organization requirements and solicited comments regarding those proposed rules.

On September 24, 2009, the Treasury Department and the IRS published in the **Federal Register** (74 FR 48672) a notice of proposed rulemaking (the 2009 NPRM) (REG-155929-06). The 2009 NPRM contained proposed regulations (the 2009 proposed regulations) setting forth the requirements to qualify as a Type III supporting organization under the PPA.

On December 28, 2012, the Treasury Department and the IRS published in the **Federal Register** (77 FR 76382) a Treasury decision (TD 9605) containing final and temporary regulations (the 2012 TD) regarding the requirements to qualify as a Type III supporting organization. Based on the comments received, the 2012 TD made certain changes to the rules proposed in the 2009 NPRM, included in the temporary regulations significant changes to the distribution requirement, and reserved certain topics for further consideration. Also on December 28, 2012, the Treasury Department and the IRS published in the **Federal Register** (77 FR 76426) a notice of proposed rulemaking (the 2012 NPRM) (REG-155929-06) that incorporated the text of the temporary regulations in the 2012 TD by cross-reference. The 2012 TD provided transition relief for Type III supporting organizations in existence on December 28, 2012, that met and continued to meet the test under former § 1.509(a)-4(i)(3)(ii), as in effect prior to December 28, 2012, treating them as functionally integrated until the first day of their second taxable years beginning after December 28, 2012. The preamble to the 2012 TD also identified issues for possible future rulemaking and requested comments. The IRS received three comments on these issues. The comments were considered in developing these proposed regulations and are available for public inspection at *www.regulations.gov* or upon request. No public hearing was requested.

The Treasury Department and the IRS published Notice 2014-4, 2014-2 I.R.B. 274, to provide additional transition relief for any Type III supporting organization that (1) supports at least one governmental supported organization to which the supporting organization is responsive within the meaning of § 1.509(a)-4(i)(3) and (2) engages in activities for or on behalf of the governmental supported organization that perform the functions of, or carry out the purposes of, the governmental supported organization and that, but for the involvement of the supporting organization, would normally be engaged in by the governmental supported organization itself. Notice 2014-4 provides that such an organization will be treated as a functionally integrated Type III supporting organization until the earlier of the date final regulations are published under § 1.509(a)-4(i)(4)(iv) in the **Federal Register** or the first day of the organization's third taxable year beginning after December 31, 2013.

On December 23, 2015, the Treasury Department and the IRS published in the **Federal Register** (80 FR 79684) a Treasury Decision (TD 9746) containing final regulations (the 2015 TD) regarding the distribution requirement for NFI Type III supporting organizations. The preamble of those regulations provided that supporting organizations supporting a governmental supported organization could continue to rely on Notice 2014-4 until the date of publication of the notice of proposed rulemaking prescribing the new proposed regulations under § 1.509(a)-4(i)(4)(iv). The IRS received three comments in response to Notice 2014-4, which the Treasury Department and the IRS considered in developing these proposed regulations.

Explanation of Provisions and Summary of Comments

This section describes the proposed provisions and addresses comments that the Treasury Department and the IRS received in response to the 2012 TD and Notice 2014-4.

1. *Gifts from Controlling Donor - Meaning of Control*

Type I and Type III supporting organizations are prohibited from accepting a gift or contribution from a person who, alone or together with certain related persons, directly or indirectly controls the governing body of a supported organization of the Type I or Type III supporting organization, or from persons related to a person possessing such control. Section 509(f)(2) and § 1.509(a)-4(f)(5). For this purpose, related persons include family members and 35-percent controlled entities within the meaning of section 4958(f). Although the 2012 TD reserved § 1.509(a)-4(f)(5)(ii), "Meaning of control," the preamble to the 2012 TD indicated that the Treasury Department and the IRS intended to issue proposed regulations that would provide such a definition.

These proposed regulations define "control" for this purpose consistently with § 1.509(a)-4(j), which relates to control by disqualified persons for purposes of the disqualified person control test. In general, under the proposed regulations, the governing body of a supported organization is considered "controlled" by a person if that person, alone or by aggregating his or her votes or positions of authority with certain related persons, as described in section 509(f)(2)(B)(ii) and (iii), may require the governing body of the supported organization to perform any act that significantly affects its operations or may prevent the governing body of the supported organization from performing any such act.

2. *Type III Supporting Organization Relationship Test*

Section 1.509(a)-4(i)(1) provides that for each taxable year, a Type III supporting organization must satisfy (i) a notification requirement, (ii) a responsiveness test, and (iii) an integral part test provided in the regulations. These proposed regulations provide additional rules regarding each of these requirements.

A. *Notification Requirement*

Section 509(f)(1)(A) provides that an organization shall not be considered a Type III supporting organization unless the organization provides to each supported organization, for each taxable year, such information as the Secretary may require to ensure that the organization is responsive to the needs or demands of the supported organizations.

To satisfy this notification requirement, § 1.509(a)-4(i)(2) requires a Type III supporting organization to provide to each of its supported organizations for each taxable year: (1) A written notice addressed to a principal officer of the supported organization describing the type and amount of all of the support it provided to the supported organization during the supporting organization's preceding taxable year; (2) a copy of the supporting organization's most recently filed Form 990, "Return of Organization Exempt from Income Tax," or other annual information return required to be filed under section 6033; and (3) a copy of the supporting organization's governing documents, including any amendments (unless previously provided and not subsequently amended). For NFI Type III supporting organizations, the description of support in the written notice includes all of the distributions described in § 1.509(a)-4(i)(6) to the supported organization.

The proposed regulations amend § 1.509(a)-4(i)(2) to clarify that a supporting organization must deliver the required documents to each of its supported organizations by the last day of the fifth month of the taxable year after the taxable year in which the supporting organization provided the support it is reporting. This proposed change is intended to reduce confusion, but does not substantively change the due date or the content of the required notification. Date of delivery is determined applying the general principles of section 7502. B.

B. *Responsiveness Test*

Section 1.509(a)-4(i)(3)(i) provides that a supporting organization meets the responsiveness test if it is "responsive to the needs or demands of a supported organization." To meet this responsiveness test, an organization must satisfy: (1) A relationship test described in § 1.509(a)-4(i)(3)(ii) under which the officers, directors, or trustees of the organization have a specified relationship with the officers, directors, or trustees (and in some cases the members) of the supported organization; and (2) a significant voice test described in § 1.509(a)-4(i)(3)(iii) under which the officers, directors, or trustees of the supported organization, by reason of this relationship, have a significant voice in the investment policies of the supporting organization, the timing of grants, the manner of making grants, and the selection of grant recipients by the supporting organization, and in otherwise directing the use of the income or assets of the supporting organization. The preamble to the 2012 TD stated that, in determining the appropriate distribution amount for NFI Type III supporting organizations, the Treasury Department and the IRS considered the required relationship between a supporting organization and its supported organizations, and that the Treasury Department and the IRS intended to issue proposed regulations in the future that would amend the responsiveness test by requiring a Type III supporting organization to be responsive to all of its supported organizations.

In response to this proposal in the preamble to the 2012 TD, one commenter stated that a supporting organization should not be required to be responsive to all of its supported organizations because the resulting administrative burden would effectively limit the total number of organizations a supporting organization could support. The commenter suggested alternatives under which a supporting organization would be responsive to only a subset of its supported organizations that would vary from year to year.

The Treasury Department and the IRS note that the distinguishing characteristic of Type III supporting organizations, and the basis for their public charity classification, is that they are responsive to and significantly involved in the operations of their publicly supported organizations. *See* § 1.509(a)-4(f)(4). The Treasury Department and the IRS believe that, unless a Type III supporting organization is responsive to each of its supported organizations, the supported organizations cannot exercise the requisite level of oversight of and engagement with the supporting organization. Limiting the responsiveness requirement to fewer than all of the supported organizations may result in the necessary oversight and accountability being present for less than all of a supporting organization's operations. Therefore, the proposed regulations revise § 1.509(a)-4(i)(3)(i) to require a supporting organization to be responsive to the needs and demands of each of its supported organizations in order to meet the responsiveness test.

To illustrate how concerns about potential administrative burdens may be addressed consistent with the responsiveness test, the proposed regulations include a new example. The proposed example is intended to demonstrate one way in which a Type III supporting organization that supports multiple organizations may satisfy the responsiveness test in a manner that can be cost-effective. The example shows that a supporting organization can, with respect to each of its supported organizations, meet a different subset of the required relationships with the supporting organization's officers, directors, or trustees listed in § 1.509(a)-4(i)(3)(ii). It also shows how a supporting organization can organize and hold regular meetings, provide information, and encourage communication to help ensure that the supported organizations have a significant voice in the operations of the supporting organization.

Another commenter requested additional guidance regarding the ability of trusts to satisfy the significant voice requirement of the responsiveness test. The new Example 3 provides further illustration of how Type III supporting organizations, including charitable trusts, might satisfy the significant voice requirement of the responsiveness test. The Treasury Department and the IRS note that although the examples in the regulations relating to the responsiveness test may involve a Type III supporting organization that is organized as either a corporation or a trust, the applicable law and relevant regulatory provisions, as modified by the proposed regulations, are applicable to all Type III supporting organizations in the same manner, whether organized as a corporation or a trust. The Treasury Department and the IRS anticipate that Type III supporting organizations may be able to demonstrate they satisfy the responsiveness test in a variety of ways, and that the determination will be based on all the facts and circumstances.

As a result of the proposed changes to the responsiveness test, the proposed regulations also include conforming changes to examples and other regulatory provisions.

C. *Integral Part Test - Functionally Integrated Type III Supporting Organizations*

Section 1.509(a)-4(i)(1) provides that, for each taxable year, a Type III supporting organization must satisfy the integral part test. The integral part test is satisfied under § 1.509(a)-4(i)(1)(iii) by maintaining significant involvement in the operations of one or more supported organizations and providing support on which the supported organizations are dependent. To satisfy this test, a Type III supporting organization must meet the requirements either for a functionally integrated Type III supporting organization or for an NFI Type III supporting organization, as set forth in § 1.509(a)-4(i)(4) or (5), respectively.

A Type III organization is functionally integrated under § 1.509(a)-4(i)(4) if (1) it engages in activities substantially all of which directly further the exempt purposes of one or more supported organizations and otherwise meets the requirements described in paragraph (i)(4)(ii) of that section, (2) it is the parent of each of its supported organizations as described in paragraph (i)(4)(iii) of that section, or (3) it supports a governmental supported organization and otherwise meets the requirements of paragraph (i)(4)(iv) of that section. The direct furtherance test is not addressed by these regulations.

i. Parent of Each Supported Organization

Under the current regulations, a supporting organization is the parent of a supported organization if the supporting organization exercises a substantial degree of direction over the policies, programs, and activities of the supported organization and a majority of the officers, directors, or trustees of the supported organization is appointed or elected, directly or indirectly, by the governing body, members of the governing body, or officers (acting in their official capacities) of the supporting organization. *See* § 1.509(a)-4(i)(4)(iii). This definition was adopted by the 2012 TD; however, the preamble to the 2012 TD stated that the Treasury Department and the IRS had determined that the definition of parent was insufficiently specific. It further stated that the Treasury Department and the IRS intended to issue proposed regulations that would provide a new definition of parent.

As noted in the preamble to the 2009 NPRM, the classification of a parent organization as functionally integrated was intended to "apply to supporting organizations that oversee or facilitate the operation of an integrated system, such as hospital systems." To more fully accomplish this purpose, the proposed regulations amend § 1.509(a)-4(i)(4)(iii) to clarify that in order for a supporting organization to qualify as the parent of each of its supported organizations, the supporting organization and its supported organizations must be part of an integrated system (such as a hospital system), and the supporting organization must engage in activities typical of the parent of an integrated system. Examples of these activities include (but are not limited to) coordinating the activities of the supported organizations and engaging in overall planning, policy development, budgeting, and resource allocation for the supported organizations. The Treasury Department and the IRS request comments on what activities are typical of the parent of an integrated system, and whether additional activities should be explicitly listed as examples.

The proposed regulations retain the requirement that the governing body, members of the governing body, or officers of the supporting organization must appoint or elect a majority of the officers, directors, or trustees of the supported organization. The Treasury Department and the IRS intend, as stated in the 2009 NPRM, the use of the phrase "appointed or elected, directly or indirectly" to mean the supporting organization could qualify as a parent of a second-tier (or lower) subsidiary. Thus, for example, if the directors of supporting organization A appoint a majority of the directors of supported organization B, which in turn appoints a majority of the directors of supported organization C, the directors of supporting organization A will be treated as appointing the majority of the directors of both supported organization B and supported organization C.

The preamble to the 2012 TD stated that the Treasury Department and the IRS intended that the new definition of parent would specifically address the power to remove and replace officers, directors, or trustees of the supported organization. The Treasury Department and the IRS interpret the existing requirement under § 1.509(a)-4(i)(4)(iii) that the parent organization have the power to appoint or elect a majority of the officers, directors, or trustees of each supported organization to include the requirement that the parent organization also have the power to remove and replace such officers, directors, or trustees, or otherwise have an ongoing power to appoint or elect with reasonable frequency. The Treasury Department and the IRS request comments on whether § 1.509(a)-4(i)(4)(iii) should be amended to provide further clarification on this issue.

ii. Supporting a Governmental Supported Organization

The 2009 NPRM proposed an exception to the general rules for qualifying as a functionally integrated Type III supporting organization if the supporting organization supported only one governmental entity, which was defined as an entity the assets of which are subject to the appropriations process of a federal, state, local, or Indian tribal government. The 2009 NPRM also provided that in order to be considered functionally integrated, a substantial part of the supporting organization's total activities had to directly further the exempt purpose(s) of its supported organization, and that exempt purposes are not directly furthered by fundraising, grantmaking, or investing and managing non-exempt-use assets. The Treasury Department and IRS received multiple comments regarding this proposal. The 2012 TD stated the Treasury Department and the IRS were continuing to consider the public comments on the 2009 NPRM regarding this governmental entity exception and reserved § 1.509(a)-4(i)(4)(iv) for future guidance on how a Type III supporting organization can qualify as functionally integrated by supporting a governmental entity.

These proposed regulations take the prior comments into consideration and provide rules to qualify as functionally integrated both for new and existing Type III supporting organizations that support governmental supported organizations. These proposed rules also define the term "governmental supported organization."

One commenter stated that the definition of a governmental supported organization in the 2009 NPRM was too complicated and difficult to understand and administer. This commenter proposed using the existing definition of a governmental unit in section 170(b)(1)(A)(v) and (c)(1).

The Treasury Department and the IRS agree with the commenter that for simplicity and administrability the term "governmental supported organization" should be defined by using an existing Code definition of a governmental unit. The proposed regulations define a governmental supported organization as a governmental unit described in section 170(c)(1), or an organization described in section 170(c)(2) and (b)(1)(A) (other than in clauses (vii) and (viii)) that is an instrumentality of one or more governmental units described in section 170(c)(1). The Treasury Department and the IRS further note that a governmental unit described in section 170(c)(1) includes all of the agencies, departments, and divisions of the governmental unit, and all such agencies, departments, and divisions will be treated as one governmental supported organization for purposes of § 1.509(a)-4(i)(4)(iv). The Treasury Department and the IRS specifically request comments on the proposed definition of governmental supported organization.

Two commenters said that the 2009 NPRM's limit of only one governmental supported organization was too strict and instead recommended allowing a supporting organization to qualify for this exception if it supports at least one governmental supported organization, as Notice 2014-4 provides. One commenter noted that the 2009 NPRM's limit of only one governmental supported organization would adversely affect existing supporting organizations that support an additional supported organization that is not itself a governmental entity, but that has a substantial operational connection with the governmental supported organization. Another commenter said that the test in Notice 2014-4 was not sufficient because it did not cover activities, such as fundraising and grant making, that the governmental supported organization could not otherwise perform.

In response to these comments, the Treasury Department and the IRS propose a new test for Type III supporting organizations that support only governmental supported organizations to qualify as functionally integrated. The Treasury Department and the IRS agree it would be appropriate to treat a Type III supporting organization that supports two or more governmental supported organizations as functionally integrated, provided that the governmental supported organizations are themselves connected geographically or operationally, which will help ensure that the supported organizations provide sufficient input to and oversight of the supporting organization. Thus, the proposed regulations provide that a supporting organization that supports more than one governmental supported organization may be considered functionally integrated if all of its governmental supported organizations either: (1) Operate within the same geographic region (defined as a city, county, or metropolitan area); or (2) work in close coordination or collaboration with one another to conduct a service, program, or activity that the supporting organization supports. To satisfy the close cooperation or coordination requirement, the proposed regulations require a supporting organization to maintain on file a letter from each of the governmental supported organizations (or a joint letter from all of them) describing their collaborative or cooperative efforts with respect to the particular service, program, or activity. In addition, the proposed regulations incorporate the 2009 NPRM proposed requirement that a substantial part of the supporting organization's total activities must directly further the exempt purposes of its governmental supported organization(s). The Treasury Department and the IRS believe that using a substantial part requirement, instead of the substantially all requirement in § 1.509(a)-4(i)(4)(iv)(A), is appropriate when supporting organizations support only governmental supported organizations operating in the same geographic region or working in close collaboration because the input from and oversight by the governmental supported organizations minimize the potential for abuse.

Two commenters stated that activities such as fundraising, grant-making, and managing non-exempt-use assets should be considered activities that directly further the exempt purposes of a governmental supported organization. The Treasury Department and the IRS note that the integral part test's definition of "directly further" in § 1.509(a)-4(i)(4)(ii)(C) generally excludes fundraising, making grants, and investing and managing non-exempt-use assets. The Treasury Department and the IRS excluded these items because they determined that a Type III supporting organization should qualify as functionally integrated only if the supporting organization itself conducts activities that perform the functions of or carry out the purposes of the supported organization (as distinguished from providing financial support for the activities carried out by the supported organization). The Treasury Department and the IRS do not believe a different definition of "directly further" should apply to supporting organizations that support governmental supported organizations. Accordingly, the proposed regulations do not adopt this comment. However, under the proposed rules, these types of organizations would be considered functionally integrated if a substantial part, but not substantially all, of their total activities directly further the exempt purposes of their governmental supported organization(s). Accordingly, these proposed regulations allow these organizations to conduct more fundraising and other financial activities, if certain requirements are met, than is permitted under the substantially all test of § 1.509(a)-4(i)(4)(ii).

In response to comments, the proposed regulations also provide a special rule for existing Type III supporting organizations, provided that they support no more than one additional supported organization that is not a governmental supported organization. A Type III supporting organization in existence on or before February 19, 2016 is treated as functionally integrated if: (1) It supports one or more governmental supported organizations and no more than one supported organization that is not a governmental supported organization; (2) it designated each of its supported organizations as provided in § 1.509(a)-4(d)(4) on or before February 19, 2016; and (3) a substantial part of its total activities directly furthers the exempt purposes of its governmental supported organization(s).

The proposed regulations also further extend the transition relief provided in Notice 2014-4 and extended by the 2015 TD. Under the proposed regulations, a Type III supporting organization in existence on or before February 19, 2016 that continues to meet the requirements of Notice 2014-4 is treated as functionally integrated until the earlier of the first day of the organization's first taxable year beginning after the date final regulations under § 1.509(a)-4(i)(4)(iv) are published or the first day of the organization's second taxable year beginning after February 19, 2016.

D. *Integral Part Test - Non-Functionally Integrated Type III Supporting Organizations*

Section 1.509(a)-4(i)(5) generally provides that an NFI Type III supporting organization meets the integral part test if it satisfies the distribution requirement of paragraph (i)(5)(ii) of that section and the attentiveness requirement of paragraph (i)(5)(iii) of that section. Section 1.509(a)-4(i)(5)(ii) provides that, with respect to each taxable year, a supporting organization must distribute to or for the use of one or more supported organizations an amount equaling or exceeding its "distributable amount". Section 1.509(a)-4(i)(6) provides the amount of a distribution made to a supported organization is the amount of cash or the fair market value of the property distributed.

For clarity and consistency, the proposed regulations revise § 1.509(a)-4(i)(5)(ii) to state that a supporting organization must make distributions as described in § 1.509(a)-4(i)(6) to satisfy the distribution requirement, and revise section 1.509(a)-4(i)(6) to describe in detail what distributions count towards the distribution requirement.

i. Reduction of Distributable Amount for Taxes Subtitle A Imposes

Section 1.509(a)-4(i)(5)(ii)(B) provides that the distributable amount is equal to the greater of 85 percent of an organization's adjusted net income for the immediately preceding taxable year (as determined by applying the principles of section 4942(f) and § 53.4942(a)-2(d)) or its minimum asset amount for the immediately preceding taxable year, reduced by the amount of taxes imposed on the supporting organization under subtitle A of the Code during the immediately preceding taxable year. *See* § 1.509(a)-4(i)(5)(ii)(B).

The Treasury Department and the IRS believe that, because the taxes under subtitle A of the Code are imposed on a supporting organization's unrelated business taxable income (pursuant to section 511) and the activity that produces the unrelated business taxable income does not further the supported organization's exempt purposes, these taxes should not be treated as an amount distributed to a supported organization. Therefore, the proposed regulations remove the provision in § 1.509(a)-4(i)(5)(ii)(B) that reduces the distributable amount by the amount of taxes subtitle A of the Code imposed on a supporting organization during the immediately preceding taxable year.

ii. Distributions that Count toward Distribution Requirement

As noted above, § 1.509(a)-4(i)(6) provides details on the distributions by a supporting organization that count toward satisfying the distribution requirement imposed in § 1.509(a)-4(i)(5)(ii). The current regulations provide that distributions include but are not limited to: (1) Any amount paid to a supported organization to accomplish the supported organization's exempt purposes; (2) any amount paid by the supporting organization to perform an activity that directly furthers the exempt purposes of the supported organization within the meaning of § 1.509(a)-4(i)(4)(ii), but only to the extent such amount exceeds any income derived by the supporting organization from the activity; (3) any reasonable and necessary administrative expenses paid to accomplish the exempt purposes of the supported organization(s), which do not include expenses incurred in the production of investment income; (4) any amount paid to acquire an exempt-use asset described in § 1.509(a)-4(i)(8)(ii); and (5) any amount set aside for a specific project that accomplishes the exempt purposes of a supported organization to which the supporting organization is responsive.

The preamble to the 2012 TD stated that the list in § 1.509(a)-4(i)(6) is not exhaustive and other distributions may count toward the distribution requirement. The preamble further stated the Treasury Department and the IRS intended to propose regulations that more fully describe the expenditures (including expenditures for administrative and additional charitable activities) that do and do not count toward the distribution requirement.

The Treasury Department and the IRS believe that the non-exclusive list in the current regulations creates uncertainty for supporting organizations and the IRS about what counts toward the distribution requirement. Therefore, the proposed regulations revise and clarify the list in § 1.509(a)-4(i)(6) of what counts toward the distribution requirement and make it an exclusive list.

The 2012 TD clarified that reasonable and necessary administrative expenses paid to accomplish the exempt purposes of supported organizations, and not expenses incurred in the production of investment income, count toward the distribution requirement. For example, if a supporting organization conducts exempt activities that are for the benefit of, perform the functions of, or carry out the purposes of its supported organization(s) and also conducts nonexempt activities (such as investment activities or unrelated business activities), then the supporting organization's administrative expenses (such as salaries, rent, utilities and other overhead expenses) must be allocated between the exempt and nonexempt activities on a reasonable and consistently-applied basis. The administrative expenses attributable to the exempt activities are treated as distributions to its supported organization(s) if such expenses are reasonable and necessary. The administrative expenses and operating costs attributable to the nonexempt activities are not treated as distributions to the supported organization(s). The proposed regulations retain this provision, but also provide additional guidance on fundraising expenses.

The 2012 TD did not specifically address whether fundraising expenses count toward the distribution requirement. The proposed regulations specify that reasonable and necessary administrative expenses paid to accomplish the exempt purposes of a supported organization generally do not include fundraising expenses the supporting organization incurs. However, under the proposed regulations, reasonable and necessary expenses incurred by the supporting organization to solicit contributions that a supported organization receives directly from donors count toward the distribution requirement, but only to the extent that the amount of such expenses does not exceed the amount of contributions actually received by the supported organization as a result of the solicitation activities of the supporting organization. The Treasury Department and the IRS believe this rule would provide greater consistency with the treatment of contributions that supporting organizations receive directly and then distribute to their supported organizations (net of the supporting organizations' solicitation expenses). To ensure that a supporting organization has the information it needs to calculate the allowable expenses, the proposed regulations require the supporting organization to obtain written substantiation from the supported organization of the amount of contributions the supported organization actually received as a result of the supporting organization's solicitations.

One commenter requested that program related investments (PRIs) count toward the distribution requirement. The preamble to the 2012 TD stated the 2012 final and temporary regulations did not specifically address whether or not PRIs may count toward the distribution requirement or are excluded in calculating a supporting organization's distributable amount for a taxable year. The Treasury Department and the IRS recognize that private foundations may use PRIs in a variety of ways to accomplish their exempt purposes and that PRIs thus are treated as qualifying distributions under section 4942. However, because supporting organizations must be operated exclusively for the benefit of, to perform the functions of, or to carry out the purposes of their supported organizations, they differ from private foundations. For purposes of meeting the integral part test, the Treasury Department and the IRS do not believe that PRIs should be treated as distributions to supported organizations. The Treasury Department and the IRS believe that other provisions relating to the distribution requirement, such as the availability of set asides and the potential for carry-forwards of excess distributions, provide significant flexibility for supporting organizations to meet the current and future needs of their supported organizations. For these reasons, the proposed regulations do not adopt this comment.

Effective Date and Reliance

These regulations are proposed to be effective on the date the Treasury decision adopting these rules as final or temporary regulations is published in the **Federal Register**. However, taxpayers may rely on the provisions of the proposed regulations until final or temporary regulations are issued.

Statement of Availability of IRS Documents

The IRS Notice 2014-4 cited in this preamble is published in the Internal Revenue Bulletin and is available from the Superintendent of Documents, U.S. Government Printing Office, Washington, DC 20402, or by visiting the IRS Web site at http://www.irs.gov.

Special Analyses

Certain IRS regulations, including this one, are exempt from the requirements of Executive Order 12866, as supplemented and reaffirmed by Executive Order 13563. Therefore, a regulatory impact assessment is not required. It has also been determined that section 553(b) of the Administrative Procedure Act (5 U.S.C. chapter 5) does not apply to these regulations.

In connection with the requirements of the Regulatory Flexibility Act (5 U.S.C. chapter 6), it is hereby certified that the collection of information contained in the proposed regulations will not have a significant economic impact on a substantial number of small entities. This certification is based on the fact that the proposed regulations will not impact a substantial number of small entities.

Based on IRS Statistics of Income data for 2013, there are 1,052,495 active nonprofit charitable organizations recognized by the IRS under section 501(c)(3), of which only 7,872 organizations self-identified as Type III supporting organizations. The universe of organizations that would be affected by the collection of information under proposed § 1.509(a)-4(i)(4)(iii) and § 1.509(a)-4(i)(6)(iii) is a subset of all Type III supporting organizations. Thus, the number of organizations that would be affected by the collection of information under proposed § 1.509(a)-4(i)(4)(iii) and (i)(6)(iii), which is expected to be significantly less than 7,872, would not be substantial. Moreover, the time to complete the recordkeeping requirements is expected to be no more than 2 hours for each organization, which would not have a significant economic impact. Therefore, the collection of information under proposed § 1.509(a)-4(i)(4)(iii) and (i)(6)(iii) would not have a significant economic impact.

Pursuant to section 7805(f) of the Code, this regulation has been submitted to the Chief Counsel for Advocacy of the Small Business Administration for comment on its impact on small business.

Comments and Requests for a Public Hearing

Before these proposed regulations are adopted as final regulations, consideration will be given to any electronic comments or written comments (a signed original and eight (8) copies) that are submitted timely to the IRS. The Treasury Department and the IRS request comments on all aspects of the proposed rules. All comments that are submitted by the public will be available for public inspection and copying at www.regulations.gov or upon request. A public hearing may be scheduled if requested in writing by any person that timely submits written comments. If a public hearing is scheduled, notice of the date, time, and place for the public hearing will be published in the **Federal Register**.

Drafting Information

The principal authors of these regulations are Jonathan Carter and Mike Repass, Office of Associate Chief Counsel (Tax-Exempt and Government Entities). However, other personnel from the Treasury Department and the IRS participated in their development.

[¶ 49,687] Proposed Amendments of Regulations (REG-150349-12), published in the Federal Register on February 25, 2016.

[Code Sec. 42]

Low-income housing credit: Physical inspection: Certification review.—Amendments of Reg. § 1.42-5, concerning the compliance-monitoring duties of a State or local housing credit agency for purposes of the low-income housing credit, are proposed.

AGENCY: Internal Revenue Service (IRS), Treasury.

ACTION: Notice of proposed rulemaking by cross-reference to temporary regulations.

SUMMARY: In the Rules and Regulations section of this issue of the **Federal Register**, the IRS is issuing final and temporary regulations concerning the compliance-monitoring duties of a State or local housing credit agency (Agency) for purposes of the low-income housing credit. The final and temporary regulations revise and clarify certain rules relating to the requirements to conduct physical inspections and review low-income certifications and other documentation. The text of the temporary regulations also serves as the text of these proposed regulations.

DATES: Comments and requests for a public hearing must be received by May 25, 2016. ADDRESSES: Send submissions to: CC:PA:LPD:PR (REG-150349-12), room 5203, Internal Revenue Service, P.O. Box 7604, Ben Franklin Station, Washington, DC 20044. Submissions may be hand delivered Monday through Friday between the hours of 8 a.m. and 4 p.m. to: CC:PA:LPD:PR (REG-150349-12), Courier's Desk, Internal Revenue Service, 1111 Constitution Avenue, NW., Washington, DC. Submissions may also be sent electronically via the Federal eRulemaking Portal at www.regulations.gov (IRS REG-150349-12).

FOR FURTHER INFORMATION CONTACT: Concerning the regulations, Jian H. Grant, (202) 317-4137, and Martha M. Garcia, (202) 317-6853 (not toll-free numbers); concerning submission of comments, the hearing, and/or to be placed on the building access list to attend the hearing, Oluwafunmilayo Taylor at (202) 317-6901 (not a toll-free number).

SUPPLEMENTARY INFORMATION:

Background

Final and temporary regulations in the Rules and Regulations section of this issue of the **Federal Register** amend the Income Tax Regulations (26 CFR Part 1) relating to section 42 and serve as the text for these proposed regulations.

Special Analyses

Certain IRS regulations, including this one, are exempt from the requirements of Executive Order 12866, as supplemented and reaffirmed by Executive Order 13563. Therefore, a regulatory assessment is not required. It also has been determined that section 553(b) of the Administrative Procedure Act (5 U.S.C. chapter 5) does not apply to these regulations, and because the regulations do not impose a collection of information on small entities, the Regulatory Flexibility Act (5 U.S.C. chapter 6) does not apply. Pursuant to section 7805(f) of the Internal Revenue Code, this notice of proposed rulemaking will be submitted to the Chief Counsel for Advocacy of the Small Business Administration for comment on their impact on small business.

Comments and Requests for Public Hearing

Before these proposed regulations are adopted as final regulations, consideration will be given to any comments that are submitted timely to the IRS as prescribed in this preamble under the "Addresses" heading. The Treasury Department and the IRS request comments on all aspects of the proposed rules. All comments will be available at www.regulations.gov or upon request. A public hearing will be scheduled if requested in writing by any person that timely submits written comments. If a public hearing is scheduled, notice of the date, time, and place for the public hearing will be published in the **Federal Register**.

Drafting Information

The principal authors of these regulations are Jian H. Grant and Martha M. Garcia, Office of the Associate Chief Counsel (Passthroughs and Special Industries). However, other personnel from the IRS and the Treasury Department participated in their development.

[¶ 49,688]   Financial Crimes Enforcement Network Proposed Rule (RIN 1506-AB26), March 2, 2016.

[31 USC 5311-5330]

Treasury Department: Financial Crimes Enforcement Network: Bank Secrecy Act: Reports of Foreign Bank and Financial Accounts (FBAR): Foreign financial accounts: Reporting requirements.—Amendments of Reg. §§1010.306, Reg. §1010.350 and 1010.420, revising the regulations implementing the Bank Secrecy Act ("BSA") regarding Reports of Foreign Bank and Financial Accounts ("FBAR"), are proposed.

AGENCY: Financial Crimes Enforcement Network ("FinCEN"), Treasury.

ACTION: Notice of proposed rulemaking ("NPRM").

SUMMARY: FinCEN, a bureau of the Department of the Treasury ("Treasury"), is proposing to revise the regulations implementing the Bank Secrecy Act ("BSA") regarding Reports of Foreign Bank and Financial Accounts ("FBAR"). The proposed rule would expand and clarify the exemptions for certain U.S. persons with signature or other authority over foreign financial accounts. In addition, the proposed rule would remove the special rules permitting limited account information to be reported when a U.S. person has financial interest in or signature authority over 25 or more foreign financial accounts. The proposed rule would also make several other changes, including a change to the filing date for FBAR reports due in 2017 and a revision to reflect electronic filing of FBARs.

DATES: Written comments on the notice of proposed rulemaking may be submitted on or before May 2, 2016.

ADDRESSES: Comments may be submitted, identified by Regulatory Identification Number ("RIN") 1506-AB26, by any of the following methods:

- *Federal E-rulemaking Portal: http://www.regulations.gov.* Follow the instructions for submitting comments. Include RIN 1506-AB26 in the submission. Refer to Docket Number FINCEN–2014–0006.

- *Mail:* FinCEN, P.O. Box 39, Vienna, VA 22183. Include 1506-AB26 in the body of the text. Please submit comments by one method only. All comments submitted in response to this NPRM will become a matter of public record. Therefore, you should submit only information that you wish to make publicly available.

- *Inspection of comments:* The public dockets for FinCEN can be found at *Regulations.gov. Federal Register* notices published by FinCEN are searchable by docket number, RIN, or document title, among other things, and the docket number, RIN, and title may be found at the beginning of the notice. FinCEN uses the electronic, Internet-accessible dockets at *Regulations.gov* as their complete, official-record docket; all hard copies of materials that should be in the docket, including public comments, are electronically scanned and placed in the docket. In general, FinCEN will make all comments publicly available by posting them on *http://www.regulations.gov.*

FOR FURTHER INFORMATION CONTACT: FinCEN Resource Center at 1-800-767-2825 or 1-703-905-3591 (not a toll free number) and select option 3 for regulatory questions. E-mail inquiries can be sent to FRC@fincen.gov.

SUPPLEMENTARY INFORMATION

I. Introduction

The potential misuse of foreign financial accounts to evade domestic criminal, tax, and regulatory laws has been a long-held congressional concern. The House report on the bill leading to the enactment of the BSA described the use of undisclosed foreign financial accounts for a wide range of abuses.[1] More than four decades after the BSA's enactment, foreign financial accounts can still be used for many of the abuses Congress catalogued when it passed the BSA, and transparency with respect to the foreign accounts of U.S. persons continues to aid law enforcement and deter illicit use.

II. Background

A. Statutory and Regulatory Background

The BSA, Titles I and II of Public Law 91-508, as amended, codified at 12 U.S.C. 1829b, 12 U.S.C. 1951-1959, and 31 U.S.C. 5311-5314 and 5316-5332, authorizes the Secretary of the Treasury ("Secretary"), among other things, to issue regulations requiring persons to keep records and file reports that are determined to have a high degree of usefulness in criminal, tax, regulatory, and counter-terrorism matters. The regulations implementing the BSA appear at 31 CFR Chapter X. The Secretary's authority to administer the BSA has been delegated to the Director of FinCEN.[2]

Under 31 U.S.C. 5314 the Secretary is authorized to require any "resident or citizen of the United States or a person in, and doing business in, the United States, to . . . keep records and file reports, when the resident, citizen, or person makes a transaction or maintains a relation for any person with a foreign financial agency." The term "foreign financial agency" encompasses the activities found in the statutory definition of "financial agency,"[3] which means, in pertinent part, "a person acting for a person as a financial institution, bailee, depository trustee, or agent, or acting in a similar way related to money, credit, securities, gold, or a transaction in money, credit, securities, or gold."[4] The Secretary is also authorized to prescribe exemptions to the reporting requirement and to prescribe other matters the Secretary considers necessary to carry out section 5314.[5]

---

[1] The House report states:

Considerable testimony was received by the Committee from the Justice Department, the United States Attorney for the Southern District of New York, the Treasury Department, the Internal Revenue Service, the Securities and Exchange Commission, the Defense Department and the Agency for International Development about serious and widespread use of foreign financial facilities located in secrecy jurisdictions for the purpose of violating American law. H.R. Rep. No 975 91st Cong. 2d Sess. 12 (1970).

[2] Treasury Order 180-01 (Sept. 26, 2002).

[3] 31 U.S.C. 5312(b)(2).

[4] *See* 31 U.S.C. 5312(a)(1), which exempts from the definition of financial agency a person acting for a country, a monetary or financial authority acting as a monetary or financial authority or an international financial institution of which the United States government is a member.

[5] FinCEN is proposing to replace the term exception, as was previously used in the FBAR regulation text, with the term exemption to reflect the language in 31 U.S.C. 5314 more accurately. For that reason, the preamble will refer to signature authority exemptions, as opposed to signature authority exceptions.

The regulations implementing 31 U.S.C. 5314 appear at 31 CFR 1010.350, 1010.306, and 1010.420. Section 1010.350 generally requires each U.S. person having a financial interest in, or signature or other authority over, a bank, securities, or other financial account in a foreign country to report such relationship to the Commissioner of Internal Revenue for each year in which such relationship exists, and "provide such information as shall be specified in a reporting form prescribed under 31 U.S.C. 5314 to be filed by such persons." Section 1010.306 requires the form to be filed with respect to foreign financial accounts exceeding $10,000 maintained during the previous calendar year. The form must be filed on or before June 30 of each calendar year for accounts maintained during the previous calendar year.[6] The form used to file the report required by section 1010.350 is the Report of Foreign Bank and Financial Accounts – FinCEN Form 114 ("FBAR"), which, since July 1, 2013, must be filed electronically.[7] Section 1010.420 requires records of foreign financial accounts to be maintained for each U.S. person having a financial interest in or signature or other authority over such accounts. The records must be maintained for a period of five years.[8]

The authority to enforce the provisions of 31 U.S.C. 5314 and its implementing regulations has been re-delegated from FinCEN to the Commissioner of Internal Revenue by means of a Memorandum of Agreement between FinCEN and the Internal Revenue Service ("IRS") dated April 2, 2003.[9] With this delegation, FinCEN conferred upon the IRS the authority to enforce the FBAR provisions of the BSA and its implementing regulations, investigate possible violations, and assess and collect civil penalties in connection therewith. The delegation also conferred upon the IRS the authority to: (1) respond to public inquiries and requests for advice, (2) issue administrative rulings, and (3) provide related assistance to the public with respect to compliance with FBAR requirements. Finally, the delegation conferred upon the IRS the authority to revise the FBAR form and instructions, and to propose to FinCEN revisions of the applicable regulations for the purpose of enhancing FBAR compliance and enforcement.[10]

B. Signature Authority Exemptions Provision

Prior to 2011, FinCEN's FBAR regulation text referred filers to the FBAR form instructions for guidance as to the specific information to be reported on the FBAR. The detailed requirements for reporting were included in the FBAR form instructions previously issued by the IRS and FinCEN. A revised FBAR form, which modified several aspects of the instructions to the form, was issued in October 2008. In the ensuing months, a number of questions and comments were received from the public seeking guidance on compliance with the revised instructions. In response to these questions and comments, FinCEN, in consultation with the IRS, issued a Notice of Proposed Rulemaking revising the reporting rules.[11] The proposal was finalized in 2011 (the "2011 FBAR regulations").[12]

As part of the 2011 FBAR regulations, FinCEN included changes to exemptions, which previously appeared only in the instructions to the FBAR form, for certain U.S. persons with signature or other authority over the foreign financial accounts of certain types of federally regulated entities. These changes expanded the exemptions so that they applied to accounts held by more types of federally regulated entities.

As a result, officers and employees of the federally regulated entities ("covered entities") listed below, are currently exempt from FBAR reporting for their signature authority over the entities' foreign financial accounts if the officer or employee has no financial interest in the foreign account:

- a bank examined by a Federal banking agency;

- a financial institution registered with and examined by the Securities and Exchange Commission ("SEC") or the Commodity Futures Trading Commission ("CFTC");

- an Authorized Service Provider with signature authority over a foreign financial account owned or maintained by an investment company registered with the SEC;[13]

- an entity with a class of equity securities listed (or American depository receipts listed) on any U.S. national securities exchange ("listed corporation") or a U.S. subsidiary if the subsidiary is included in the consolidated report the parent filed;[14] or

- an entity that has a class of equity securities registered (or American depository receipts registered) under section 12(g) of the Securities Exchange Act ("section 12(g) corporation").[15]

Subsequent to the publication of the 2011 amendments to the FBAR regulation, FinCEN received several questions from industry with respect to the signature authority exemptions. In particular, many filers asked how the exemptions applied with respect to scenarios involving overlapping signature authority.[16] Many filers were unsure of the breadth of the amended exemptions as they applied to scenarios involving over-lapping signature authority. "Over-lapping" signature authority occurs when an officer or employee of a *parent* entity also has signature authority over the foreign financial accounts of the parent's controlled *subsidiary* entity and vice versa. Under a literal reading of the regulation, the exemption only applies if the individual is actually "an officer or employee of" the particular corporate entity that holds the account, and not to situations in which the individual may have control over accounts held by affiliated corporate or other business entities that do not employ the individual.[17]

Some filers believed that the pre-2011 exemptions, outlined in the FBAR form instructions, were broader than they actually were, with many filers treating the pre-2011 signature authority exemptions as being applicable to all instances of an officer or employee's over-lapping signature authority within a corporate or other business structure.[18] The 2011 FBAR regulations made it clear that the signature authority exemptions did not apply to all instances of over-lapping signature authority. Following the 2011 FBAR regulations, FinCEN received requests from industry to exempt officers or employees of covered entities and their controlled subsidiaries for instances in which the officers or employees have over-lapping signature authority with respect to foreign financial accounts owned by the employer, as well as foreign financial accounts of the employer's parent and subsidiaries.[19]

---

[6] In accordance with section 2006(b)(11) of PL 114-41 the filing due date for the report will be April 15 effective with the 2016 reporting year. Extensions to October 15 of the reporting year are available upon request.

[7] Formerly Form TD-F 90-22.1. FinCEN Form 114 can be completed by accessing FinCEN's BSA E-Filing System website -http://bsaefiling.fincen.treas.gov/main.html.

[8] The penalties addressed in the BSA apply to both the FBAR reporting and record-keeping requirement.

[9] See 31 CFR 1010.810(g).

[10] Beginning in March 2011, with the implementation of mandatory electronic filing, FinCEN has managed and instituted all changes to the FBAR and related line item and electronic instructions. FinCEN and the IRS collaborate on FBAR actions regardless of the nature of these actions.

[11] See 75 FR 8844 (February 26, 2010).

[12] See 76 FR 10234 (February 24, 2011).

[13] "Authorized Service Provider" means an entity that is registered with and examined by the SEC and that provides services to an investment company registered under the Investment Company Act of 1940. See 31 CFR § 1010.350(f)(2)(iii).

[14] A U.S. entity that owns directly or indirectly more than a 50-percent interest in one or more entities required to report is permitted to file a consolidated report on behalf of itself and such other entity. See 31 CFR § 1010.350(g)(3).

[15] Section 12(g) corporations must have more than $10 million in assets and a class of equity security held of record by either 2,000 persons, or 500 persons who are not accredited investors (as defined by the SEC).

[16] FinCEN received letters from six large trade associations and 12 of the largest financial institutions, all raising similar concerns regarding the signature authority exemptions.

[17] As clarified at 31 CFR 1010.350(g)(3), an entity that is a United States person and which owns directly or indirectly more than a 50 percent interest in one or more other entities required to report under this section will be permitted to file a consolidated report on behalf of itself and such other entities. FinCEN considers all entities permitted to be reported together on a consolidated FBAR to be entities within the same corporate or other business structure.

[18] FinCEN was made aware that many large companies may have one "treasury group," which may be either at the parent corporation level or the controlled subsidiary level where employees have signature authority over the foreign financial accounts of both the parent corporation and its controlled subsidiaries, domestic and foreign.

[19] In response to ongoing questions regarding the scope of the signature authority exemptions, and in order for FinCEN to assess the full extent of the impact of the revised signature authority exemptions, FinCEN, in close coordination with the IRS, issued FinCEN Notices 2011-1 and 2011-2 (collectively, the "2011 Notices") on May 31 and June 17, 2011, respectively, to extend to June 30, 2012 the FBAR filing due date for certain

FinCEN believes that the exemptions, in practice, may impose greater obligations on filers than necessary given the nature of the reporting.[20] As a result, FinCEN, in consultation with the IRS, has made a policy decision to provide a simplified and expanded exemption.[21] Additionally, FinCEN proposes to use the term "agent" to incorporate entities and individuals, such as authorized service providers and their employees, within the scope of the proposed exemption.[22] The proposed exemption would eliminate the requirement for officers, employees, and agents of U.S. entities to report on accounts owned by the entity over which the officer, employee, or agent has signature authority solely due to their employment when those accounts are already required to be reported by their employer, or any other U.S. entity within the same corporate or other business structure as their U.S. employer. This proposed exemption is intended to address instances in which employees have over-lapping signature authority with respect to U.S. parent and subsidiary accounts within the same corporate or other business structure. However, the exemption for employees to report their signature authority over the foreign financial accounts of their employer would not extend to U.S. persons in instances in which no entity within their employer's corporate or other business structure has an obligation to report to FinCEN its financial interest in such accounts. For example, in instances in which a U.S. person is employed by a non-U.S. entity with no obligation to report its foreign financial accounts, and the foreign entity is not included as a subsidiary of a U.S. entity that is filing, the U.S. person would have an obligation to report his or her signature authority over the non-U.S. entity's foreign financial accounts.[23] In this regard the scope of the reporting obligation remains unchanged.

In the past, FinCEN saw value in having these individuals report on the same foreign financial accounts as their employers as a check to ensure that the employers themselves had reported their financial interest in these accounts. It should be noted that in accordance with the 2011 FBAR regulations this dual reporting did not absolve either party from filing an FBAR as required under the regulation, except in those instances in which an officer or employee qualified for the signature authority exemptions. However, FinCEN now believes that such a check on a non-filing employer may be of limited practical value because FinCEN was made aware, particularly during the first required FBAR e-filing season, due by June 30, 2014, that employers often file FBARs on behalf of their employees with signature authority because the employers maintain the account information.[24] This is in keeping with the report's instructions prior to the 2011 FBAR regulations with respect to officers and employees of U.S. entities who had signature authority over, but no financial interest in, foreign financial accounts owned by the U.S. employer, which stated that if an employer notified the employee, in writing, that the required FBAR had been filed, the employee was relieved of filing on his or her own behalf.

To maintain transparency with respect to U.S. persons eligible for the exemption for officers, employees, or agents of U.S. entities, employers would be required to maintain information identifying all officers, employees, or agents with signature authority over, but no financial interest in, those same accounts. FinCEN proposes to require that this information be made available to FinCEN upon request and that such records be maintained for a period of 5 years. In instances in which a U.S. parent entity is filing a consolidated FBAR on behalf of itself and its controlled (i.e., greater than 50-percent owned) subsidiaries required to file an FBAR, the U.S. parent entity would be responsible for maintaining information identifying all of its employees and its subsidiaries' employees with signature authority over such foreign financial accounts. In instances in which the U.S. parent entity and its controlled subsidiaries choose to file separate FBARs regarding their respective financial interest in foreign financial accounts, each such entity would be responsible for maintaining information identifying all employees with signature authority over such accounts, regardless of whether the employees are their own employees or are employed by another entity within the same corporate structure.

C. Special Rules Provisions – 25 or More Foreign Financial Accounts

While assessing options to address concerns raised by industry regarding the signature authority exemptions, FinCEN determined that the provisions limiting information reported with respect to situations where a filer has 25 or more foreign financial accounts also should be reevaluated. Under the "special rules" provisions at 31 CFR 1010.350(g)(1)-(2), when a person or entity has a financial interest in, or signature authority over, 25 or more foreign financial accounts, the filer is required to report the number of accounts and the filer's identifying information (name, address, taxpayer identification number, and for individual filers date of birth).[25] However, these filers are exempted from providing detailed account information on each of their foreign financial accounts. For instance, filers submitting FBARs covered by the special rules are not required to provide the account number, the name of the foreign financial institution that holds the account, the address of the foreign financial institution, the maximum value of the account during the calendar year, or the type of account.

(Footnote Continued)

individuals affected by the signature authority exemptions. On February 14, 2012, FinCEN further extended the FBAR due date to June 30, 2013 via FinCEN Notice 2012-1, for filers that met the requirements of the original 2011 Notices. On December 26, 2012, FinCEN again extended the FBAR due date to June 30, 2014 via FinCEN Notice 2012-2, for those same filers. Again on December 20, 2013, FinCEN extended the FBAR due date to June 30, 2015 via FinCEN Notice 2013-1, for those same filers. Once more on December 10, 2014, FinCEN extended the FBAR due date to June 30, 2016 via FinCEN Notice 2014-1, for those same filers. Due to the strong possibility of a regulatory change to the signature authority issue, along with the need to coordinate with the IRS, FinCEN further extended the FBAR due date to April 15, 2017 via FinCEN Notice 2015-1, dated December 8, 2015, for filers that met the requirements of the previous Notices. See FinCEN Notice 2015-1. https://www.fincen.gov/whatsnew/pdf/20151208.pdf. Note that the FBAR is a calendar year report ending December 31 of the reportable year. Beginning with the 2016 tax year, the due date for FBAR reporting is April 15 of the year following the December 31 report ending date as changed by section 2006(b)(11) of PL 114-41. If requested, this change also provided for a six-month extension of time to file the form (for tax years beginning after 2015).

[20] FinCEN has learned that up to 100 employees may have signature authority over one foreign financial account during a calendar year in order to perform their jobs. In such a scenario under the present rule, FinCEN would receive over 100 FBARs regarding the same foreign financial account information.

[21] This proposed amendment is consistent with Executive Order 13563, "Improving Regulation and Regulatory Review," issued by the President on January 18, 2011. Section 6 of Executive Order 13563 emphasizes the importance of retrospective analysis of rules to determine whether any such regulations should be modified, expanded, streamlined, or repealed so as to make the agency's regulatory program more effective or less burdensome in achieving the regulatory objectives.

[22] Note that the exemption would only apply to "agents" who are not owners of record or holders of legal title, as described in 31 CFR 1010.350(e)(1), and that have no financial interest in the foreign financial account over which they have signature authority.

[23] See Item Instructions-Part IV of the BSA Electronic Filing Requirements For Report of Foreign Bank and Financial Accounts (FinCEN Form 114) for certain instances of truncated filing as it relates to signature authority over the foreign financial accounts of a foreign located employer. The instructions specifically note the following: "a United

States person who (1) resides outside of the United States, (2) is an officer or employee of an employer who is physically located outside of the United States, and (3) has signature authority over a foreign financial account that is owned or maintained by the individual's employer should only complete Part I and Items 34-43 of Part IV." Such U.S. persons are excluded from reporting items 15-23 regarding account information, including the account number, the name of the foreign financial institution that holds the account, the address of the foreign financial institution, the maximum value of the account during the calendar year, and the type of account. http://www.fincen.gov/forms/files/FBAR%20Line%20Item%20Filing%20Instructions.pdf.

[24] Due to a number of requests from employers to e-file FBARs on behalf of their employees, on March 28, 2014, FinCEN revised the FBAR E-filing FAQs to clarify the following: **FBAR E-Filing FAQs 6 - Can an employer submit an FBAR via the BSA E-Filing System on behalf of its employee, who has an obligation to file an FBAR due to their signature authority over the employer's account(s)?** Yes. An employer may assist its employees in the preparation of electronic FBAR forms for BSA E-Filing. Consistent with FinCEN's instructions that provide for approved third-party filing of the FBAR, if an employer has been provided documented authority (Form 114a) by the legally obligated filers (employees with signature authority over the employer's foreign financial account(s)) to sign and submit FBARs on their behalf through the BSA E-Filing System, that employer can do so through a single BSA E-Filing institutional account established on the BSA E-File System for the employer. Form 114a (http://www.fincen.gov/forms/files/FBARE-FileAuth114aRecordSP.pdf) should be completed designating the employer as the filer/preparer of the employee's FBAR. A copy of the Form 114a should be retained by the filer/employer and not sent to FinCEN. Employers can establish their institution accounts by accessing the BSA E-Filing System enrollment page (http://bsaefiling.fincen.treas.gov/Enroll.html), selecting the Institution option, and following the steps to enroll. If the employee does not provide its employer with the Form 114a the filings must be signed and submitted by the employee. An employee signing and submitting his or her own FBAR may use the BSA E-Filing System by accessing the No Registration FBAR page (http://bsaefiling.fincen.treas.gov/NoRegFBARFiler.html). If such authority is not provided, the filings must be signed and submitted by the employee. In this case, the employee would be filing as an individual (See FAQ 1 above). http://bsaefiling.fincen.treas.gov/docs/FBAR_EFILING_FAQ.pdf.

[25] U.S. persons reporting signature authority over 25 or more foreign financial accounts are also required to report the name, address, and taxpayer identification number of the account owner.

In 2013, approximately 10,800 FBARs were filed by individuals or entities with financial interest in 25 or more foreign financial accounts. Those individuals or entities had a combined total of approximately 5,366,000 foreign financial accounts, which represents approximately 56% of the total number of all foreign financial accounts reported in 2013.[26] As a result, FinCEN and law enforcement did not have detailed account information on any of these accounts because of the exemption for FBAR filers with 25 or more foreign financial accounts.

The FBAR regulations, originally issued in April 1972, 37 Federal Register 6913, and amended in December 1977, 42 Federal Register 63774, *previously* provided:

Each person subject to the jurisdiction of the United States (except a foreign subsidiary of a U.S. person) having a financial interest in, or signature or other authority over, a bank, securities or other financial account in a foreign country shall report such relationship to the Secretary for each year in which such relationship exists, and shall provide such information as shall be specified in a reporting form prescribed by the Secretary to be filed by such persons. Persons having a financial interest in 25 or more foreign financial accounts need only note that fact on the form. Such persons will be required to provide detailed information concerning each account when so requested by the Secretary or his delegate.

The preamble amending the FBAR regulation in 1977 noted the following:

[P]ersons having a financial interest in 25 or more foreign accounts will be required to provide detailed information concerning each account only when so requested by the Secretary or his delegate. This modification in filing procedure is designed to minimize the practical difficulties of reporting a large number of accounts by taxpayers having extensive international interests.

Since the implementation of this provision of the FBAR regulations over 35 years ago, the ease with which individuals can establish overseas accounts has increased and foreign accounts remain vulnerable to exploitation by those seeking to launder money, finance terrorist acts, or engage in other financial crimes. In addition, the implementation of BSA E-filing has made the technological limitations and practical difficulties of reporting the required information less burdensome to industry and individuals.

The provisions limiting information reported with respect to situations where a filer has 25 or more foreign financial accounts has created a significant gap in FinCEN's and law enforcement's ability to analyze a comprehensive set of data on all otherwise reportable foreign financial accounts. A lack of account numbers limits the applicability and efficacy of link analysis that can be done to expand investigations of potential criminal and civil violations of law. Moreover, the enhancement of FinCEN's analytical tools allows it to analyze larger amounts of data more effectively, therefore making account information reported on FBARs that much more accessible. These are just a few examples resulting from the information gap.

For these reasons, FinCEN is proposing to remove the provisions that limit the information reported with respect to situations when a filer has financial interest in, or signature authority over, 25 or more foreign financial accounts. Instead, all U.S. persons will be required to report detailed account information on all foreign financial accounts for which they have a financial interest or signature authority in those instances in which a signature authority exemption does not apply. This will enable FinCEN and law enforcement to receive detailed account information on *all* foreign financial accounts in which a U.S. person has financial interest for the first time since 1977.

III. Section-by-Section Analysis

In an effort to strike the balance of providing FinCEN and law enforcement with the foreign financial account information useful to their investigations, while taking into consideration the burdens upon industry associated with employee-related signature authority reporting, FinCEN is proposing to:

- Amend the FBAR regulations by eliminating the requirement for officers, employees, and agents of U.S. entities to report signature authority over entity-owned foreign financial accounts for which they have no financial interest, if those accounts are already required to be reported by their employer or any other entity within the same corporate or other business structure as their employer.[27] Instead, entities/employers would be required to maintain information identifying all officers, employees, or agents with signature authority over those same accounts; this information would be maintained for a period of 5 years and made available to FinCEN upon request.

- Remove the provisions that limit the information required to be reported with respect to situations when a filer has 25 or more foreign financial accounts. As a result, U.S. persons with 25 or more foreign financial accounts would be required to provide the detailed account information that is already being provided by those U.S. persons with fewer than 25 foreign financial accounts.

- Make several other changes including a change to the filing date for FBARs to be filed in 2017 and a revision to reflect the electronic filing of FBARs.

A. Signature Authority Exemption Provision

FinCEN proposes to amend 31 CFR 1010.350(f)(2) by removing the current signature authority exemptions and adding a single, broader signature authority exemption. The current signature authority exemptions at 31 CFR 1010.350(f)(2) read as follows:

(i) An officer or employee of a bank that is examined by the Office of the Comptroller of the Currency, the Board of Governors of the Federal Reserve System, the Federal Deposit Insurance Corporation, the Office of Thrift Supervision, or the National Credit Union Administration need not report that he has signature or other authority over a foreign financial account owned or maintained by the bank if the officer or employee has no financial interest in the account.

(ii) An officer or employee of a financial institution that is registered with and examined by the Securities and Exchange Commission or Commodity Futures Trading Commission need not report that he has signature or other authority over a foreign financial account owned or maintained by such financial institution if the officer or employee has no financial interest in the account.

(iii) An officer or employee of an Authorized Service Provider need not report that he has signature or other authority over a foreign financial account owned or maintained by an investment company that is registered with the Securities and Exchange Commission if the officer or employee has no financial interest in the account. "Authorized service provider" means an entity that is registered with and examined by the Securities and Exchange Commission and that provides services to an investment company registered under the Investment Company Act of 1940.

(iv) An officer or employee of an entity with a class of equity securities listed (or American depository receipts listed) on any United States national securities exchange need not report that he has signature or other authority over a foreign financial account of such entity if the officer or employee has no financial interest in the account. An officer or employee of a United States subsidiary of a United States entity with a class of equity securities listed on a United States national securities exchange need not file a report concerning signature or other authority over a foreign financial account of the subsidiary if he has no financial interest in the account and the United States subsidiary is included in a consolidated report of the parent filed under this section.

---

[26] In 2013, approximately 4,167,000 foreign financial accounts were reported by filers with less than 25 foreign financial accounts.

[27] *See supra* note 17.

(v) An officer or employee of an entity that has a class of equity securities registered (or American depository receipts in respect of equity securities registered) under section 12(g) of the Securities Exchange Act need not report that he has signature or other authority over the foreign financial accounts of such entity or if he has no financial interest in the accounts.

The proposed signature authority exemption would read as follows:

(2) *Exemption*— An officer, employee, or agent of an entity need not submit a report to FinCEN regarding signature or other authority over a foreign financial account in which such entity, or a subsidiary, parent entity, or other entity within the same corporate or other business structure of such entity has a financial interest, if the officer, employee, or agent has no financial interest in the account and the account is required to be reported under 31 CFR § 1010.350 by the entity or any other entity within the same corporate or other business structure.[28] An entity will be required to maintain information identifying all officers, employees, and agents with signature or other authority over a foreign financial account in which it has financial interest and to provide this information when so requested by the Financial Crimes Enforcement Network. Such information regarding officers, employees, and agents shall be identified, and maintained by the entity, and shall be deemed to have been filed with FinCEN Form 114. Such records shall be retained for a period of 5 years.

This exemption would be available to all U.S. persons that currently have a reporting obligation solely due to their signature or other authority over the foreign financial accounts of their employers or any other entities within the same corporate or other business structure as their employers, except in those instances in which the entity that has a financial interest in the foreign financial account over which the officer, employee, or agent has signature authority does not have an obligation to report to FinCEN its financial interest in such accounts. This may be the case in instances in which a U.S. person is employed by a foreign entity and has signature authority over the foreign financial accounts of the foreign entity in which case the foreign entity/employer has no obligation to report its financial interest to FinCEN under the FBAR regulations. If the officer, employee, or agent is eligible for this signature authority exemption, the employer that is required to report the account details of the foreign financial account on an FBAR due to its financial interest in the account would be required to maintain information identifying those officers, employees, or agents with signature or other authority over such account, which would be made available to FinCEN upon request. Such records would be required to be retained for a period of 5 years.[29]

B. Special Rules Provisions – 25 or More Foreign Financial Accounts

FinCEN proposes to remove 31 CFR 1010.350(g)(1) and (g)(2):

(g) Special rules—

(1) Financial interest in 25 or more foreign financial accounts. A United States person having a financial interest in 25 or more foreign financial accounts need only provide the number of financial accounts and certain other basic information on the report, but will be required to provide detailed information concerning each account when so requested by the Secretary or his delegate.

(2) Signature or other authority over 25 or more foreign financial accounts. A United States person having signature or other authority over 25 or more foreign financial accounts need only provide the number of financial accounts and certain other basic information on the report, but will be required to provide detailed information concerning each account when so requested by the Secretary or his delegate.

Detailed account information on all foreign financial accounts in which a U.S. person has financial interest would be reported for the first time, due to the removal of the special rules.[30] As noted above, in 2013, approximately 10,800 FBARs were filed by individuals or entities with financial interest in 25 or more foreign financial accounts. Those individuals or entities had a financial interest in a combined total of approximately 5,366,000 foreign financial accounts. U.S. persons are already required to maintain and make available upon request detailed account information on all foreign financial accounts in which they have financial interest or signature authority, which may assist in filing the FBARs that the proposed rule would require of U.S. persons with 25 or more foreign financial accounts.[31]

C. Other Proposed Revisions

The revisions to the signature authority exemption provision and the special rules provisions require certain other revisions to the regulation text for the purpose of consistency and order throughout sections 1010.350, 1010.306, and 1010.420.

Revise section 1010.350(a); section 1010.306(c); and section 1010.420

Paragraph (a) of section 1010.350 is being revised to strike the last sentence of the paragraph that reads as follow:

"*See* paragraphs (g)(1) and (g)(2) of this section for a special rule for persons with a financial interest in 25 or more accounts, or signature or other authority over 25 or more accounts."

Paragraph (a) of section 1010.350 is also being revised to reflect the change in the name of the FBAR form from TD-F 90-22.1 to FinCEN Form 114 and to reflect the reporting, electronically through BSA E-Filing, of the FBAR form to FinCEN as well as the reporting, on a return, to the Commissioner of Internal Revenue. This technical change will also be reflected in section 1010.306(c) and section 1010.420. Section 1010.306(c) is being revised to reflect the new FBAR filing due date of April 15, effective with the 2016 reporting year, in accordance with section 2006(b)(11) of PL 114-41. In addition, section 1010.306(c) is being revised to reflect that extensions to October 15 of the reporting year are available upon request, also in accordance with section 2006(b)(11) of PL 114-41. Section 1010.420 is also being revised to include a few other minor changes.

Re-designate paragraphs (g)(3) though (5) of section 1010.350 as paragraphs (g)(1) through (3)

Because section 1010.350(g) - Special rules (1) and (2) regarding reporting on 25 or more foreign financial accounts are being removed, the remainder of the special rules designated as (g)(3) Consolidated reports; (g)(4) Participants and beneficiaries in certain retirement plans; and (g)(5) Certain trust beneficiaries are being re-designated as paragraphs (g)(1) through (3).

D. Revisions to FinCEN Form 114

If the proposed rule is finalized, consistent with the proposed removal of special rules provisions regarding 25 or more foreign financial accounts, FinCEN would remove FinCEN Form 114 data field 14a (Does the filer have a financial interest in 25 or more financial accounts?); and data field 14b (Does the filer have signature authority over, but no financial interest in, 25 or more foreign financial accounts?). No other FinCEN Form 114 data fields would need to be amended as a result of the proposed revisions to the FBAR regulations. While no other data fields will be changed, several existing data fields in each section will be designated as "critical" requiring completion for the FBAR to be accepted by BSA E-Filing. The

---

[28] *See supra* note 17.

[29] FinCEN understands that, as part of a final rule, it would need to determine the effect of the provisions of this proposed rule on earlier FBAR deferrals pursuant to FinCEN Notices 2011-1; 2011-2; 2012-1; 2012-2; 2013-1; 2014-1; and 2015-1. *See* IV. Questions for Public Comment.

[30] As discussed above, detailed account information includes: the account number, the name of the foreign financial institution that holds the account, the address of the foreign financial institution, the maximum value of the account during the calendar year, and the type of account.

[31] *See* 31 CFR section 1010.420.

batch filing electronic filing specifications will also require updating to the same standard. Upon finalizing the revisions to the FBAR as proposed in this NPRM, FinCEN would also amend the FinCEN Form 114 instructions consistent with the revisions to the FBAR regulations.[32]

IV. Questions for Public Comment

A. FinCEN requests comment on whether expanding the signature authority exemption provision as proposed will reduce burden, and if so, by how much.

B. FinCEN requests comment on whether it should allow entities and individuals to rely upon the provisions of this proposed rule, if finalized, with regard to FBAR filings properly deferred pursuant to FinCEN Notices 2011-1; 2011-2; 2012-1; 2012-2; 2013-1; 2014-1; and 2015-1.

C. FinCEN requests comment on whether removing the special rules provisions regarding reporting on 25 or more foreign financial accounts will increase burden on impacted entities and individuals, and if so, by how much. Specifically, will technological costs be incurred to implement systems to transfer account information to the BSA E-filing system for FBAR reporting?

D. If technological modifications are necessary to report 25 or more foreign financial accounts, FinCEN requests comment on the estimated timeframe to implement those modifications.

E. FinCEN requests comment on whether the amendments in this proposed rule regarding broadening signature authority exemptions combined with the removal of the special rules regarding 25 or more foreign financial accounts will increase or decrease burden on those entities and individuals impacted by both amendments to the FBAR regulation, and if so, by how much.

V. Regulatory Flexibility Act

Pursuant to the Regulatory Flexibility Act (5 U.S.C. 601 et seq.), FinCEN certifies that these proposed regulation revisions will not have a significant economic impact on a substantial number of small entities. The proposed rule applies to U.S. persons, a term which includes entities of all sizes and individuals, if they have reportable accounts under this rule. However, we expect that small entities will be less likely to have reportable foreign financial accounts or to have many such accounts, unlike larger entities, which likely have a broader base of business operations. In addition, we expect a reduction in burden for individuals, because FinCEN is exempting all individuals that currently have a reporting obligation solely due to their signature authority over the foreign financial accounts of their employers or any other entities within the same corporate or other business structure as their employers, except in those instances in which no such entity has an obligation to report to FinCEN its financial interest in such accounts.

With regard to the proposed amendment to remove the provisions that limit the information required to be reported with respect to situations when a filer has 25 or more foreign financial accounts, FinCEN expects that most U.S. persons reporting on 25 or more foreign financial accounts will be large entities. U.S. persons with 25 or more foreign financial accounts reportable on the FBAR will be required to provide the same account information currently required to be provided by U.S. persons with less than 25 foreign financial accounts. The information required to be reported on the FBAR is basic information U.S. persons will have received on account statements from the foreign financial institutions at which the accounts are opened and maintained. Those statements will provide a U.S. person with the information about an account needed to file the FBAR. No special accounting or legal skills would be necessary to transfer the basic information required to be reported, such as the name of the foreign financial institution, the type of account, and the account number, to the FBAR. FinCEN requests comment on the accuracy of the statement that the regulations in this document will not have a significant economic impact on a substantial number of small entities.

VI. Executive Order 13563 and 12866

Executive Orders 13563 and 12866 direct agencies to assess costs and benefits of available regulatory alternatives and, if regulation is necessary, to select regulatory approaches that maximize net benefits (including potential economic, environmental, public health and safety effects, distributive impacts, and equity). Executive Order 13563 emphasizes the importance of quantifying both costs and benefits, of reducing costs, of harmonizing rules, and of promoting flexibility. This rule has been designated a "significant regulatory action" although not economically significant, under section 3(f) of Executive Order 12866. Accordingly, the rule has been reviewed by the Office of Management and Budget.

VII. Paperwork Reduction Act ("PRA") Notices

The reporting requirements contained in this proposed rule (31 CFR 1010.350) are being submitted to the Office of Management and Budget for review in accordance with the Paperwork Reduction Act of 1995 (44 U.S.C. 3507(d)). Comments concerning the estimated burden and other questions should be sent to the Desk Officer for the Department of the Treasury, Office of Information and Regulatory Affairs, Office of Management and Budget, Paperwork Reduction Project (1506), Washington, D.C. 20503 with a copy to FinCEN by mail, or comments may be submitted by e-mail to oira submission@omb.eop.gov. Please submit comments by one method only. Comments are welcome and must be received by May 2, 2016. In accordance with requirements of the Paperwork Reduction Act of 1995, 44 U.S.C. 3506(c)(2)(A), and its implementing regulations, 5 CFR §1320, the following information concerning the collection of information of the *Amendment to the Bank Secrecy Act Regulations - Reports of Foreign Financial Accounts* is presented to assist those persons wishing to comment on the information collection.

Signature authority exemption provision

The proposed rulemaking seeks to expand and clarify the exemption to the signature authority reporting requirement. By making the signature authority exemption broader and clearer there is potential for a reduction in signature authority reporting by individuals with signature authority over, but no financial interest in, foreign financial accounts.

The proposed rulemaking also seeks to clarify that entities/employers would be required to maintain information identifying all officers and employees with signature authority over the foreign financial accounts in which the entities/employers have financial interest; this information would be retained for a period of 5 years and be made available to FinCEN upon request. FinCEN expects there will be little to no effect on burden as a result of this recordkeeping requirement since these entities/employers, in all likelihood, maintain this information in the normal course of business.

Description of Affected Filers: Individuals/agents with signature authority over, but no financial interest in, foreign financial accounts reportable by the individual/agent under 31 CFR 1010.350 solely due to their employment.

Estimate Number of Affected Filing Individuals: 5,660. Approximately 11,600 FBARs were filed by U.S. persons in 2013 solely due to reporting on signature authority, but no financial interest. Of those FBARs, approximately 280 were filed by a U.S. person who was reporting signature authority over the foreign financial account of an account owner with a foreign address. As a result of questions raised by industry, we estimate that at least 50 percent of the remaining FBARs (11, 600 − 280 = 11,320) were filed by individuals with signature authority over, but no financial interest in, a foreign financial account, solely due to their employment.[33]

---

[32] FinCEN Form 114 instructions -*http://www.fincen.gov/forms/files/ FBAR%20Line%20Item%20Filing%20Instructions.pdf.*

[33] FinCEN is excluding FBARs filed by a U.S. person who was reporting signature authority over the foreign financial account of an account owner with a foreign address because such scenarios likely include individuals reporting signature authority solely

Estimate Average Annual Burden Hours Reduction Per Affected Filer: The estimated average burden reduction associated with the reporting requirement in this rule will vary depending on the number of reportable accounts. Based on past filings, we estimate that the average reporting burden will range from approximately twenty minutes to one hour and that the average reporting burden will be approximately 45 minutes. The reporting burden is reflected in the burden listed for completing FinCEN Form 114 (See OMB Control Number 1506-0009). *Estimated Total Annual Burden Reduction:* 4,245 hours.[34]

Removal of special rules provisions – 25 or more foreign financial accounts

The proposed rulemaking also seeks to remove the special rules permitting limited account information to be reported on the FBAR when a person has financial interest in or signature authority over 25 or more foreign financial accounts. There should not be a net increase in the number of FBARs filed, although there will be a net increase in the time it takes to file an FBAR when reporting 25 or more accounts. However, individuals are already required to maintain records regarding account information for such foreign financial accounts under the rule, therefore there will be no impact on the recordkeeping requirement, and these records can be leveraged to obtain the information necessary to report.

Description of Affected Filers: Individuals and entities that maintain 25 or more foreign financial accounts reportable under 31 CFR 1010.350.

Estimate Number of Affected Filing Individuals and Entities: 12,580.[35]

Estimate Average Annual Burden Hours Per Affected Filer: The estimated average burden associated with the reporting requirement (FBAR form completion) will vary depending on the number of reportable accounts. FinCEN estimates that the average increase in the reporting burden will be approximately 2 minutes per foreign financial account reported on the FBAR. In 2013, approximately 10,800 FBARs were filed by individuals or entities with financial interest in 25 or more foreign financial accounts. Those entities had a combined total of approximately 5,366,000 foreign financial accounts. The average number of foreign financial accounts reported per FBAR filed was 497. This translates to approximately 16.6 burden hours per affected filer.[36] The reporting burden is reflected in the burden listed for completing FinCEN Form 114 (See OMB Control Number 1506-0009).

Estimated Total Annual Burden: 208,828 hours (12,580 FBARs X 16.6 hours per FBAR filer).

Summary Total of Estimated Annual Burden: 204,583 hours (208,828 – 4,245)

Questions for comment

FinCEN specifically invites comment on the accuracy of FinCEN's estimate of the burden on respondents and any other aspects of our PRA estimates. Comments are specifically requested concerning: (a) whether the proposed collection of information is necessary for the proper performance of the functions of FinCEN, including whether the information will have practical utility; (b) the accuracy of the estimated burden associated with the proposed collection of information; (c) how the quality, utility, and clarity of the information to be collected may be enhanced; and (d) how the burden of complying with the proposed collection of information may be minimized, including through the application of automated collection techniques or other forms of information technology.

VIII. Unfunded Mandates Act of 1995 Statement

Section 202 of the Unfunded Mandates Reform Act of 1995 ("Unfunded Mandates Act"), Public Law 104-4 (March 22, 1995), requires that an agency prepare a budgetary impact statement before promulgating a rule that may result in expenditure by state, local, and tribal governments, in the aggregate, or by the private sector, of $100 million or more in any one year. If a budgetary impact statement is required, section 202 of the Unfunded Mandates Act also requires an agency to identify and consider a reasonable number of regulatory alternatives before promulgating a rule. FinCEN has determined that it is not required to prepare a written statement under section 202 and has concluded that on balance the proposals in the Notice of Proposed Rulemaking provide the most cost-effective and least burdensome alternative to achieve the objectives of the rule.

[¶ 49,689]   **Proposed Amendments of Regulations (REG-123867-14)**, published in the Federal Register on March 3, 2016.

[Code Sec. 42]

Low-income housing credit: Utility allowance: Submetering rules.—Amendment of Reg. §1.42-10, containing proposed regulations that amend the utility allowance regulations concerning the low-income housing credit, is proposed.

AGENCY: Internal Revenue Service (IRS), Treasury.

ACTION: Notice of proposed rulemaking by cross-reference to temporary regulations.

SUMMARY: This document contains proposed regulations that amend the utility allowance regulations concerning the low-income housing credit. The proposed regulations relate to the circumstances in which utility costs paid by a tenant based on actual consumption in a submetered rent-restricted unit are treated as paid by the tenant directly to the utility company. The proposed regulations extend those rules to situations in which a building owner sells to tenants energy that is produced from a renewable source and that is not delivered by a local utility company. The proposed regulations affect owners of low-income housing projects that claim the credit, the tenants in those low-income housing projects, and the State and local housing credit agencies that administer the credit. In the Rules and Regulations section of this issue of the **Federal Register**, the IRS is issuing temporary regulations concerning utility allowance regulations when the utility is generated from renewable sources and is not delivered by the local utility company. The text of those regulations also serves as the text of these proposed regulations. This document also contains a notice of a public hearing on these proposed regulations.

DATES: Comments and requests for a public hearing must be received by May 2, 2016.

(Footnote Continued)

due to their employment with a foreign parent corporation. In such a scenario, the proposed signature authority exemption would not apply because a foreign parent corporation does not have a requirement to report its financial interest in a foreign financial account on the FBAR.

[34] 5,660 filers multiplied by 45 minutes and converted to hours is 4,245 hours.

[35] This figure represents the actual number of FBARs filed in calendar year 2013 when 25 or more foreign financial accounts were reported. 10,800 FBARs were filed by U.S. persons reporting financial interest in 25 or more foreign financial accounts. 8,900 FBARs were filed by U.S. persons reporting signature authority over 25 or more foreign financial accounts. FinCEN estimates that at least 80 percent of these FBARs were filed by individuals with signature authority over, but no financial interest in, a foreign financial account, solely due to their employment. Based on questions raised by industry

following the issuance of the 2011 FBAR final rule, FinCEN believes that most FBAR reporting on signature authority over 25 or more foreign financial accounts is by individuals who are reporting solely due to their signature authority over their employers' foreign financial accounts. Because FinCEN is proposing to exempt all of those FBAR filers due to such scenarios, so long as those accounts are already required to be reported by their employer or another entity with the same corporate structure as their employer, we have factored that into our estimate of the number of FBARs we expect to be filed by U.S. persons with 25 or more foreign financial accounts due to signature authority. (8,900 FBARs X 0.2 = 1,780). The estimated total FBARs to be reported with 25 or more foreign financial accounts due to financial interest and signature authority is 12,580 (10,800 + 1,780).

[36] 497 accounts multiplied by 2 minutes per account and converted to hours is 16.6 hours.

ADRESSES: Send submissions to: CC:PA:LPD:PR (REG-123867-14), room 5203, Internal Revenue Service, P.O. Box 7604, Ben Franklin Station, Washington, DC 20044. Submissions may be hand-delivered Monday through Friday between the hours of 8 a.m. and 4 p.m. to CC:PA:LPD:PR (REG-123867-14), Courier's Desk, Internal Revenue Service, 1111 Constitution Avenue, NW., Washington, DC, or sent electronically, via the Federal eRulemaking Portal at http://www.regulations.gov/ (IRS REG-123867-14).

FOR FURTHER INFORMATION CONTACT: Concerning the proposed regulations, James Rider at (202) 317-4137; concerning submissions of comments and requests for a public hearing, Oluwafunmilayo Taylor at (202) 317-6901 (not toll-free numbers).

SUPPLEMENTARY INFORMATION:

Background

Temporary regulations in the Rules and Regulations section of this issue of the **Federal Register** amend 26 CFR part 1. The temporary regulations provide a special rule for a renewable-source utility arrangement in which the building owner does not pay a local utility company for the utility consumed by the tenant. The text of those regulations also serves as the text of these regulations. The preamble to the temporary regulations explains the temporary regulations and these proposed regulations.

Special Analyses

Certain IRS regulations, including this one, are exempt from the requirements of Executive Order 12866, as supplemented and reaffirmed by Executive Order 13563. Therefore, a regulatory assessment is not required. It also has been determined that section 553(b) of the Administrative Procedure Act (5 U.S.C. chapter 5) does not apply to this regulation, and because the regulation does not impose a collection of information on small entities, the Regulatory Flexibility Act (5 U.S.C. chapter 6) does not apply. Pursuant to section 7805(f) of the Internal Revenue Code, this notice of proposed rulemaking has been submitted to the Chief Counsel for Advocacy of the Small Business Administration for comment on its impact on small business.

Comments and Requests for Public Hearing

Before these proposed regulations are adopted as final regulations, consideration will be given to any written comments (a signed original and eight (8) copies) or electronic comments that are submitted timely to the IRS as prescribed in this preamble under the "**ADDRESSES**" heading. The IRS and the Treasury Department request comments on all aspects of the proposed regulations. All comments that are submitted by the public will be available for public inspection and copying at www.regulations.gov or upon request. A public hearing will be scheduled if requested in writing by any person that timely submits comments. If a public hearing is scheduled, notice of the date, time, and place for the public hearing will be published in the **Federal Register**.

Drafting Information

The principal author of these regulations is David Selig, Office of the Associate Chief Counsel (Passthroughs and Special Industries), IRS. However, other personnel from the IRS and the Treasury Department participated in their development.

[¶ 49,690] **Proposed Amendments of Regulations (REG-127923-15)**, published in the Federal Register on March 4, 2016.

[Code Secs. 1014, 6035, 6662, 6721 and 6722]

Estates: Estate tax: Property: Basis: Reporting.—Reg. §§1.1014-10, 1.6035-2 and 1.6662-8, and amendments of Reg. §§1.6035-1, 301.6721-1 and 301.6722-1, regarding the requirement that a recipient's basis in certain property acquired from a decedent be consistent with the value of the property as finally determined for Federal estate tax purposes, are proposed.

AGENCY: Internal Revenue Service (IRS), Treasury.

ACTION: Notice of proposed rulemaking, and notice of proposed rulemaking by cross-reference to temporary regulations.

SUMMARY: This document contains proposed regulations that provide guidance regarding the requirement that a recipient's basis in certain property acquired from a decedent be consistent with the value of the property as finally determined for Federal estate tax purposes. In addition, these proposed regulations provide guidance on the reporting requirements for executors or other persons required to file Federal estate tax returns. Temporary regulations in the Rules and Regulations section of this issue of the **Federal Register** provide transition relief to executors and other persons required to file or furnish certain statements. The text of those temporary regulations (TD 9757) published in the Rules and Regulations section of this issue of the **Federal Register** also serves as the text of the proposed regulations regarding the transition relief. These proposed regulations as well as TD 9757 published elsewhere in the Rules and Regulations section of this issue of this **Federal Register** affect executors or other persons who file estate tax returns after July 31, 2015. The proposed regulations also affect beneficiaries who acquire certain property from these estates, and subsequent transferees to whom beneficiaries transfer the property in transactions that do not result in the recognition of gain or loss for Federal income tax purposes.

DATES: Written or electronic comments and requests for a public hearing must be received by June 2, 2016.

ADDRESSES: Send submissions to: CC:PA:LPD:PR (REG-127923-15), Internal Revenue Service, Room 5203, PO Box 7604, Ben Franklin Station, Washington, DC 20044. Submissions may be hand delivered Monday through Friday between the hours of 8 a.m. and 4 p.m. to CC:PA:LPD:PR (REG-127923-15), Courier's Desk, Internal Revenue Service, 1111 Constitution Avenue NW, Washington, DC 20224; or sent electronically via the Federal eRulemaking Portal at *http://www.regulations.gov* (IRS-REG-127923-15).

FOR FURTHER INFORMATION CONTACT: Concerning the proposed regulations, Theresa M. Melchiorre, at (202) 317-6859; concerning submissions of comments or, to request a hearing, Regina Johnson, at (202) 317-6901 (not toll-free numbers). SUPPLEMENTARY INFORMATION:

Paperwork Reduction Act

The collection of information contained in this notice of proposed rulemaking has been submitted to the Office of Management and Budget for review in accordance with the Paperwork Reduction Act of 1995 (44 U.S.C. 3507(d). Comments on the collection of information should be sent to the Office of Management and Budget, Attn: Desk Officer for the Department of the Treasury, Office of Information and Regulatory Affairs, Washington, DC 20503, with copies to the Internal Revenue Service, Attn: IRS Reports Clearance Officer, SE:W:CAR:MP:T:T:SP, Washington, DC 20224. Comments on the collection of information should be received by May 3, 2016.

Comments are specifically requested concerning:

Whether the proposed collection of information is necessary for the proper performance of the functions of the Internal Revenue Service (IRS), including whether the information will have practical utility;

The accuracy of the estimated burden associated with the proposed collection of information;

How the quality, utility, and clarity of the information to be collected may be enhanced;

How the burden of complying with the proposed collection of information may be minimized, including through the application of automated collection techniques or other forms of information technology; and

Estimates of capital or start-up costs and costs of operation, maintenance, and purchase of service to provide information.

The reporting requirements in these proposed regulations are in §1.6035-1(a) and (d) and require executors and other persons required to file a return under section 6018 to furnish a statement to the IRS and to each beneficiary providing information regarding the value of the property the beneficiary acquires from the decedent. The IRS will use this information to determine whether the beneficiary (or transferee) reports a basis for that property that is consistent with the value of that property as finally determined for Federal estate tax purposes when the beneficiary (or transferee) depreciates the property, or sells, exchanges, or otherwise disposes of some or all of that property in transactions that result in the recognition of gain or loss for Federal income tax purposes.

The collection of information may vary depending on the property includible in the gross estate and the number of beneficiaries receiving the property. The following estimates are based on the information that is available to the IRS. A respondent may require more or less time, depending on the circumstances.

Estimated total annual reporting burden. The estimated total annual reporting burden per respondent is 5.31 hours.

Estimated annual number of respondents. The estimated annual number of respondents is 10,000.

An agency may not conduct or sponsor, and a person is not required to respond to, a collection of information unless it displays a valid control number assigned by the Office of Management and Budget.

Books or records relating to a collection of information must be retained as long as their contents may become material in the administration of any internal revenue law. Generally, tax returns and tax return information are confidential, as required by 26 U.S.C. 6103.

Background

1. Overview.

On July 31, 2015, the President of the United States signed into law H.R. 3236, the *Surface Transportation and Veterans Health Care Choice Improvement Act of 2015*, Public Law 114-41, 129 Stat. 443 (Act). Section 2004 of the Act enacted sections 1014(f), 6035, 6662(b)(8), 6662(k), 6724(d)(1)(D), and 6724(d)(2)(II) of the Internal Revenue Code (Code). This document contains proposed regulations that amend 26 CFR parts 1 and 301 under those Code provisions to achieve consistency between a recipient's basis in certain property acquired from a decedent and the value of the property as finally determined for Federal estate tax purposes. This notice of proposed rulemaking also cross-references to temporary regulations (TD 9757) published in the Rules and Regulations section of this issue of the **Federal Register**, which provide transition relief to certain persons required to file or furnish statements under section 6035. This document also proposes to remove from 26 CFR part 1 regulations under former section 6035 as a result of the repeal of that Code provision in 2004.

2. Summary of new statutory framework.

A. Section 1014(f).

Section 1014(f) imposes an obligation of consistency between the basis of certain inherited property and the value of that property for Federal estate tax purposes. Section 1014(f)(1) provides that the basis of property acquired from a decedent cannot exceed that property's final value for purposes of the Federal estate tax imposed on the estate of the decedent, or, if the final value has not been determined, the value reported on a statement required by section 6035(a).

Section 1014(f)(2) provides that section 1014(f)(1) only applies to property the inclusion of which in the decedent's gross estate increased the estate's liability for the Federal estate tax (reduced by credits allowable against the tax).

Section 1014(f)(3) provides that, for purposes of section 1014(f)(1), the basis of property has been determined for Federal estate tax purposes if (A) the value of the property is shown on a return under section 6018 and that value is not contested by the Secretary before the expiration of the time for assessing the estate tax; (B) in a case not described in (A), the value is specified by the Secretary and that value is not timely contested by the executor of the estate; or (C) the value is determined by a court or pursuant to a settlement agreement with the Secretary.

B. Section 6035.

Section 6035 requires the reporting, both to the IRS and the beneficiary, of the value of property included on a required Federal estate tax return.

Section 6035(a)(1) provides that the executor of any estate required to file a return under section 6018(a) must furnish, both to the Secretary and to the person acquiring any interest in property included in the estate, a statement identifying the value of each interest in the property as reported on the return and any other information as the Secretary may prescribe.

Section 6035(a)(2) provides that each person required to file a return under section 6018(b) must furnish to the Secretary and to each other person who holds a legal or beneficial interest in the property to which the return relates a statement identifying the information described in section 6035(a)(1).

Section 6035(a)(3)(A) provides that this statement is due no later than the earlier of (i) 30 days after the due date of the return under section 6018 (including extensions, if any) or (ii) 30 days after the date the return is filed. If there is an adjustment to the information required to be included on this statement, section 6035(a)(3)(B) requires the executor (or other person required to file the statement) to provide a supplemental statement to the Secretary and to each affected beneficiary no later than 30 days after the adjustment is made.

Section 6035(b) authorizes the Secretary to prescribe regulations to carry out section 6035, including regulations relating to (1) the application of this section to property to which no Federal estate tax return is required to be filed, and (2) situations in which the surviving joint tenant or other recipient may have better information than the executor regarding the basis or fair market value of the property.

C. Penalties under sections 6662, 6721, and 6722.

Section 2004(c) of the Act added a new accuracy-related penalty for underpayments attributable to an inconsistent estate basis. See section 6662(b)(8). Section 6662(k) provides that there is an inconsistent estate basis if the basis of property claimed on a return exceeds the basis as determined under section 1014(f).

Section 2004(c) of the Act adds statements under section 6035 to the list of information returns and payee statements subject to the penalties under section 6721 and section 6722, respectively. Specifically, the Act adds new paragraph (D) to section 6724(d)(1) to provide that the term *information return* means any statement required to be filed with the Secretary under section 6035. The Act also adds new paragraph (II) to section

6724(d)(2) to provide that the term *payee statement* means any statement required to be furnished under section 6035 (other than a statement described in section 6724(d)(1)(D)).

3. Notice 2015-57.

On August 21, 2015, the Treasury Department and the IRS issued Notice 2015-57, 2015-36 IRB 294. That notice delayed until February 29, 2016, the due date for any statements required under section 6035(a)(3)(A) to be provided before February 29, 2016. The notice also stated that the Treasury Department and the IRS expect to issue additional guidance to assist taxpayers in complying with sections 1014(f) and 6035 and invited comments. The Treasury Department and the IRS received numerous comments in response to the notice and considered all comments in the drafting of the proposed regulations. The comments are discussed in more detail in this preamble.

4. Notice 2016-19.

On February 11, 2016, the Treasury Department and the IRS issued Notice 2016-19, 2016-09 IRB 362. That notice provides that executors or other persons required to file or furnish a statement under section 6035(a)(1) or (a)(2) before March 31, 2016, need not do so until March 31, 2016.

Summary of Comments on Notice 2015-57 and Explanation of Provisions

1. Section 1014(f)(1) – Consistency of basis with estate tax return.

The general rule of section 1014 is that the basis of property received from a decedent (or as a result of a decedent's death) is that property's fair market value on the decedent's date of death (or the alternate valuation date, if elected). Newly enacted section 1014(f)(1) provides that the basis of certain property acquired from a decedent cannot exceed that property's final value as determined for Federal estate tax purposes. If no final value has been determined when the taxpayer's basis in the property becomes relevant for Federal tax purposes, for example, to calculate depreciation or amortization, or to calculate gain or loss on the sale, exchange or disposition of the property, the taxpayer uses the value reported on the statement required by section 6035(a) (the fair market value reported on the Federal estate tax return) to determine the taxpayer's basis for Federal tax purposes.

Proposed § 1.1014-10(a)(1) provides that a taxpayer's initial basis in certain property acquired from a decedent may not exceed the *final value* of the property as that term is defined in § 1.1014-10(c). This limitation applies to the property whenever the taxpayer reports to the IRS a taxable event with respect to the property (for example, depreciation or amortization) and continues to apply until the property is sold, exchanged, or otherwise disposed of in one or more transactions that result in the recognition of gain or loss for Federal income tax purposes. The property for this purpose includes any other property the basis of which is determined in whole or in part by reference to the basis of the property acquired from the estate or as a result of the death of the decedent (for example as the result of a like-kind exchange or involuntary conversion).

2. Effect of other provisions of the Code that govern basis.

Section 6662(b)(8) imposes an accuracy-related penalty on the portion of any underpayment of tax required to be shown on a return that is attributable to an *inconsistent estate basis*. Under newly enacted section 6662(k), an inconsistent estate basis arises if the basis of property claimed on a return exceeds its final value as determined under section 1014(f).

Commenters have expressed concern that section 1014(f) and section 6662(k) appear to prohibit otherwise permissible adjustments to the basis of property as a result of post-death events. In response, proposed § § 1.1014-10(a)(2) and 1.6662-8(b) clarify that sections 1014(f) and 6662(k) do not prohibit adjustments to the basis of property as a result of post-death events that are allowed under other sections of the Code, and provide that such basis adjustments will not cause a taxpayer to violate the provisions of section 1014(f) or section 6662(k) on the date of sale, exchange, or disposition. The proposed regulations interpret sections 1014(f) and 6662(k) to require only that the beneficiary's initial basis of the inherited property cannot exceed the final value of the property for Federal estate tax purposes. Adjustments to the basis of the inherited property permitted by other sections of the Code as a result of post-death events (for example, depreciation or amortization, or a sale, exchange, or disposition of the property) will not cause the taxpayer's basis in the property on the date of a taxable event with respect to the property to be treated as exceeding the final value of the property. As a result, there cannot be an underpayment attributable to an inconsistent estate basis arising from these basis adjustments, and the accuracy-related penalty under section 6662(b)(8) cannot apply solely as a result of these basis adjustments.

3. Section 1014(f)(2) – Property that increases estate tax liability.

The consistent basis requirement of section 1014(f)(1) applies only to property the inclusion of which in the decedent's gross estate for Federal estate tax purposes increases the Federal estate tax liability payable by the decedent's estate. Proposed § 1.1014-10(b) defines this property as property includible in the gross estate under section 2031, as well as property subject to tax under section 2106, that generates a Federal estate tax liability in excess of allowable credits. The proposed regulations specifically exclude all property reported on a Federal estate tax return required to be filed by section 6018 if no Federal estate tax is imposed upon the estate due to allowable credits (other than a credit for a prepayment of that tax). In cases where Federal estate tax is imposed on the estate, the proposed regulations exclude property that qualifies for a charitable or marital deduction under section 2055, 2056, or 2056A because this property does not increase the Federal estate tax liability. In addition, the proposed regulations exclude any tangible personal property for which an appraisal is not required under § 20.2031-6(b) (relating to the valuation of certain household and personal effects) because of its value. Thus, if any Federal estate tax liability is incurred, all of the property in the gross estate (other than that described in the preceding two sentences) is deemed to increase the Federal estate tax liability and is subject to the consistency requirement of section 1014(f).

4. Section 1014(f)(3) – Final value of property acquired from a decedent.

Section 1014(f)(3) provides that, for purposes of section 1014(f)(1), the *final value* of property has been determined for Federal estate tax purposes if: (A) the value is reported on a Federal estate tax return filed with the IRS and is not contested by the IRS before the period of limitation on assessment expires; (B) the value is specified by the IRS and is not timely contested by the executor of the estate; or (C) the value is determined by a court or pursuant to a settlement agreement with the IRS.

Proposed § 1.1014-10(c)(1) defines the *final value* of property that is reported on a Federal estate tax return filed with the IRS. That value is the value reported on the Federal estate tax return once the period of limitations on assessment for adjusting or contesting that value has expired. The IRS may specify a value for the property by determining a value in the course of carrying out its responsibilities under section 7803(a)(2). If the IRS determines a value different from the value reported, the final value is the value determined by the IRS once that value can no longer be contested by the estate. If the value determined or specified by the IRS is timely contested by the estate, the final value is the value determined in an agreement that is binding on all parties, or the value determined by a court once the court's determination is final.

Proposed § 1.1014-10(c)(2) provides that the recipient of property to which the consistency requirement applies may not claim a basis in excess of the value reported on the statement required to be furnished under section 6035(a) (the value shown on the Federal estate tax return) if the taxpayer's basis in the property is relevant for any purpose under the Internal Revenue Code before the final value of that property has been determined under proposed § 1.1014-10(c)(1). However, under section 1014(f)(1), basis cannot exceed the property's final value. Therefore, proposed § 1.1014-10(c)(2) provides that, if the final value is determined before the period of limitation on assessment expires for any Federal income tax return of the recipient on which the taxpayer's basis is relevant and the final value differs from the initial basis claimed with respect to that return, a deficiency and an underpayment may result.

5. *After-discovered or omitted property.*

Commenters requested that the regulations clarify how the consistent basis requirement applies to property that is discovered after the filing of the Federal estate tax return or is otherwise omitted from that return. If this property would have generated a Federal estate tax liability if it had been reported on the Federal estate tax return that was filed with IRS, proposed § 1.1014-10(c)(3)(i) provides two different results based upon whether the period of limitation on assessment has expired for the Federal estate tax imposed on the estate. Proposed § 1.1014-10(c)(3)(i)(A) provides that, if the executor reports the after-discovered or omitted property on an estate tax return filed before the expiration of the period of limitation on assessment of the estate tax, the final value of the property is determined under proposed § 1.1014-10(c)(1) or (2). Alternatively, proposed § 1.1014-10(c)(3)(i)(B) provides that, if the after-discovered or omitted property is not reported before the period of limitation on assessment expires, the final value of the after-discovered or omitted property is zero.

Finally, to address situations in which no Federal estate tax return was filed, proposed § 1.1014-10(c)(3)(ii) provides that the final value of all property includible in the gross estate subject to the consistent basis requirement is zero until the final value is determined under proposed § 1.1014-10(c)(1) or (2).

6. *Definition of executor for purposes of sections 1014(f) and 6035.*

The proposed regulations adopt the definition of the term *executor* found in section 2203 applicable for Federal estate tax purposes and expand it to include a person required to file a return under section 6018(b).

7. *Requirement to provide Information Return and Statement(s) under section 6035.*

The proposed regulations define the term *Information Return* as the Form 8971, Information Regarding Beneficiaries Acquiring Property from a Decedent, which includes a copy of a Schedule A (Statement) for each person who has received or will receive property from the estate or by reason of the decedent's death.

Proposed § 1.6035-1(a)(1) provides that an executor who is required to file a Federal estate tax return also is required to file an Information Return with the IRS to report the final value of certain property, the recipient of that property, and other information prescribed by the Information Return and the related instructions. The executor also is required to furnish a Statement to each beneficiary who has acquired (or will acquire) property from the decedent or by reason of the death of the decedent to report the property the beneficiary has acquired (or will acquire) and the final value of that property.

8. *Circumstances under which no Information Return or Statement(s) is required under section 6035.*

Commenters expressed concern that the section 6035 filing requirements might extend to a return filed by an estate solely to make the portability election under section 2010(c)(5), or a generation-skipping transfer tax election or exemption allocation. The proposed regulations provide that the filing requirements of section 6035 do not apply to such returns because these returns are not required by section 6018.

9. *Property to be reported on an Information Return and Statement(s).*

Commenters requested that the regulations clarify the types of property to be reported on the Information Return and one or more Statements. In response, proposed § 1.6035-1(b) defines the property to be reported on an Information Return and Statement(s) as all property included in the gross estate for Federal estate tax purposes with four exceptions: cash (other than coins or paper bills with numismatic value); income in respect of a decedent; those items of tangible personal property for which an appraisal is not required under § 20.2031-6(b); and property that is sold or otherwise disposed of by the estate (and therefore not distributed to a beneficiary) in a transaction in which capital gain or loss is recognized.

10. *Beneficiaries.*

Proposed § 1.6035-1(c)(1) provides that each beneficiary (including a beneficiary who is also the executor of the estate) who receives property to be reported on the estate's Information Return must receive a copy of the Statement reporting the property distributable to that beneficiary. Proposed § 1.6035-1(c)(2) provides that, if the beneficiary is a trust, estate, or business entity instead of an individual, the executor is to furnish the entity's Statement to the trustee, executor, or to the business entity itself, and not to the beneficiaries of the trust or estate or to the owners of the business entity.

Commenters requested guidance on how to comply with the section 6035 reporting requirements when the executor cannot determine the exact distribution of the estate's property and thus the beneficiary of each property by the due date of the Information Return and the related Statements. This situation can arise, for example, when tangible personal property defined in § 20.2031-6 is to be distributed among a group of beneficiaries as that group determines, the residuary estate is distributable to multiple beneficiaries, or when multiple residuary trusts are to be funded. In response, proposed § 1.6035-1(c)(3) provides that, if by the due date the executor does not yet know what property will be used to satisfy the interest of each beneficiary, the executor is required to report on the Statement for each beneficiary all of the property that could be used to satisfy that beneficiary's interest. This results in the duplicate reporting of those assets on multiple Statements, but each beneficiary will have been advised of the final value of each property that may be received by that beneficiary and therefore will be able to comply with the basis consistency requirement, if applicable.

Proposed § 1.6035-1(c)(4) provides that, if the executor is unable to locate a beneficiary by the due date of the Information Return, the executor is required to report that on that Information Return and explain the efforts taken to locate the beneficiary. If the executor subsequently locates the beneficiary, the executor is required to furnish the beneficiary with a Statement and file a supplemental Information Return with the IRS within 30 days of locating the beneficiary. If the executor is unable to locate a beneficiary and distributes the property to a different beneficiary who was not identified in the Information Return as the recipient of that property, the executor is required to file a supplemental Information Return with the IRS and furnish the successor beneficiary with a Statement within 30 days after distributing the property.

11. *Due date for Information Return and Statements.*

Proposed § 1.6035-1(d)(1) provides that the executor is required to file the Information Return with the IRS, and is required to furnish each beneficiary with that beneficiary's Statement, on or before the earlier of the date that is 30 days after the due date of the Federal estate tax return (including extensions actually granted, if any), or the date that is 30 days after the date on which that return is filed with the IRS. In response to comments, proposed § 1.6035-1(d)(2) provides a transition rule for any Federal estate tax return that was due on or before July 31, 2015, but that is filed after July 31, 2015. In this case, the due date of the Information Return and all Statements is 30 days after the date on which the return is filed. Otherwise, as commenters noted, the due date for the Information Return and Statement(s) may be prior to the effective date of section 6035.

12. *Supplemental Information Return and Statement(s).*

Proposed § 1.6035-1(e)(1) and (2) generally requires a supplemental Information Return and corresponding supplemental Statement(s) upon a change to the information required to be reported on the Information Return or a Statement that causes the information as reported to be incorrect or incomplete. Such changes include, for example, the discovery of property that should have been, but was not, reported on the Federal estate tax return, a change in the value of property pursuant to an examination or litigation, or (except as provided by proposed § 1.6035-1(e)(3)(B)) a change in the identity of the beneficiary to whom the property is to be distributed (for example, pursuant to a death, disclaimer, bankruptcy, or otherwise). Proposed § 1.6035-1(e)(3) provides that a supplemental Information Return and Statement(s) may be filed, but they are not required, to correct an inconsequential error or omission within the meaning of § 301.6722-1(b) or to specify the actual distribution of assets previously reported as being available to satisfy the interests of multiple beneficiaries in the situation described in proposed § 1.6035-1(c)(3).

Proposed § 1.6035-1(e)(4) provides that the due date for the supplemental Information Return and each supplemental Statement is 30 days after: (i) the final value (within the meaning of proposed § 1.1014-10(c)(1)) of property is determined; (ii) the executor discovers that the information reported on the Information Return or Statement is otherwise incorrect or incomplete; or (iii) a supplemental Federal estate tax return is filed. However, at the suggestion of a commenter, if these events occur prior to the distribution to the beneficiary of probate property or of the property of a revocable trust, a supplemental Information Return or Statement is not due until 30 days after the property is distributed. This is likely to be approximately the same time when the executor would provide the beneficiary with information as to changes, if any, to the basis of the property that have occurred since the decedent's death and prior to the distribution. Because that basis adjustment information is not part of what is required to be reported under section 6035, however, if the executor chooses to provide that basis adjustment information on the Schedule A provided to the beneficiary, the basis adjustment information must be shown separately from the final value required to be reported on the beneficiary's Statement.

13. *Subsequent transfers.*

As discussed earlier in this preamble, section 6035(a)(2) imposes a reporting requirement on the executor of the decedent's estate and on any other person required to file a return under section 6018. The purpose of this reporting is to enable the IRS to monitor whether the basis claimed by an owner of the property is properly based on the final value of that property for estate tax purposes. The Treasury Department and the IRS are concerned, however, that opportunities may exist in some circumstances for the recipient of such reporting to circumvent the purpose of the statute (for example, by making a gift of the property to a complex trust for the benefit of the transferor's family).

Accordingly, pursuant to the regulatory authority granted in section 6035(b)(2), the proposed regulations require additional information reporting by certain subsequent transferors in limited circumstances. Specifically, proposed § 1.6035-1(f) provides that, with regard to property that previously was reported or is required to be reported on a Statement furnished to a recipient, when the recipient distributes or transfers (by gift or otherwise) all or any portion of that property to a related transferee, whether directly or indirectly, in a transaction in which the transferee's basis for Federal income tax purposes is determined in whole or in part with reference to the transferor's basis, the transferor is required to file and furnish with the IRS and the transferee, respectively, a supplemental Statement documenting the new ownership of this property. This proposed reporting requirement is imposed on each such recipient of the property. For purposes of this provision, a related transferee means any member of the transferor's family as defined in section 2704(c)(2), any controlled entity (a corporation or any other entity in which the transferor and members of the transferor's family, whether directly or indirectly, have control within the meaning of section 2701(b)(2)(A) or (B)), and any trust of which the transferor is a deemed owner for income tax purposes.

In the event such transfer occurs before a final value is determined within the meaning of proposed § 1.1014-10(c), the transferor must provide the executor with a copy of the supplemental Statement filed with the IRS and furnished to the transferee reporting the new ownership of the property. When a final value is determined, the executor will then provide a supplemental Statement to the new transferee instead of to the transferor. The supplemental Statements are due no later than 30 days after the transferor distributes or transfers all or a portion of the property to the transferee.

14. *Surviving joint tenants or other recipients under section 6035(b)(2).*

Section 6035(b)(2) authorizes the IRS to prescribe regulations relating to situations in which the surviving joint tenant or other recipient may have better information than the executor regarding the basis or fair market value of the property received by reason of the decedent's death. Section 6018(b) addresses these situations. Section 6018(b) generally requires that, if the executor is unable to make a complete return as to any part of the gross estate of the decedent, the executor must include on the return a description of that part of the gross estate and the name of every person holding a legal or beneficial interest in it. Upon notice from the Secretary, any such person must in like manner make a return as to this part of the gross estate. Section 6035(a)(2) and these proposed regulations require a person required to file a return under section 6018(b) to file an Information Return with the IRS and to furnish the Statement(s) to each beneficiary of that property. Therefore, the Treasury Department and the IRS have determined that no additional regulations applicable only to surviving joint tenants or other recipients are necessary for this purpose.

15. *Removal of regulations under former Section 6035*

The *American Jobs Creation Act of 2004* (Public Law 108-357, 118 Stat. 1418) (Jobs Act) repealed former section 6035, effective for taxable years of foreign corporations beginning after December 31, 2004, and for taxable years of United States shareholders with or within which the tax years of foreign corporations end. Prior to repeal, former section 6035 set forth information reporting requirements for certain United States persons that were officers, directors, or 10-percent shareholders of a foreign personal holding company. Section 1.6035-1 (TD 8573), § 301.6035-1 (TD 6498), § 1.6035-2 (TD 8028), and § 1.6035-3 (TD 8028) (collectively, the FPHC regulations) provide guidance on the information reporting required under former section 6035, as in effect prior to amendment by the *Tax Equity and Fiscal Responsibility Act of 1982* (Public Law 97-248, 96 Stat. 328), and prior to its repeal by the Jobs Act.

This document proposes to withdraw the FPHC regulations. However, the FPHC regulations referenced above contained in 26 CFR parts 1 and 301, revised as of April 1, 2015, continue to apply for taxable years of foreign corporations beginning on or before December 31, 2004, and for taxable years of United States shareholders in which former section 6035 applies with or within which the tax years of foreign corporations end.

16. *Request for new process.*

One commenter requested the creation of a process to allow an estate beneficiary to challenge the value reported by the executor. There is no such process under the Federal law regarding returns described in section 6018. The beneficiary's rights with regard to the estate tax valuation of property are governed by applicable state law. Accordingly, the proposed regulations do not create a new Federal process for challenging the value reported by the executor.

Proposed Effective/Applicability Date

Upon the publication of the Treasury Decision adopting these rules as final in the **Federal Register**, these proposed regulations will apply to property acquired from a decedent or by reason of the death of a decedent whose return required by section 6018 is filed after July 31, 2015. Persons may rely upon these rules before the date of publication of the Treasury Decision adopting these rules as final in the **Federal Register**.

Statement of Availability of IRS Documents

IRS Revenue Procedures, Revenue Rulings notices, notices and other guidance cited in this preamble are published in the Internal Revenue Bulletin (or Cumulative Bulletin) and are available from the Superintendent of Documents, U.S. Government Printing Office, Washington, DC 20402, or by visiting the IRS website at *http://www.irs.gov*.

Special Analyses

Certain IRS regulations, including this one, are exempt from the requirements of Executive Order 12866, as supplemented and reaffirmed by Executive Order 13563. Therefore, a regulatory impact assessment is not required. It is hereby certified that the collection of information in these regulations will not have a significant economic impact on a substantial number of small entities. This certification is based on the fact that this rule primarily affects individuals (or their estates) and trusts, which are not small entities as defined by the Regulatory Flexibility Act (5 U.S.C. 601). Although it is anticipated that there may be an incremental economic impact on executors that are small entities, including entities that provide tax and legal services that assist individuals in preparing tax returns, any impact would not be significant and would not affect a substantial number of small entities. Therefore, a Regulatory Flexibility Analysis under the Regulatory Flexibility Act (5 U.S.C. chapter 6) is not required. Pursuant to section 7805(f) of the Code, the notice of proposed rulemaking will be submitted to the Chief Counsel for Advocacy of the Small Business Administration for comment on its impact on small business.

Comments and Requests for a Public Hearing

Before these proposed regulations are adopted as final regulations, consideration will be given to any written (a signed original and eight (8) copies) or electronic comments that are submitted timely to the IRS. Comments are requested on all aspects of the proposed rules. All comments will be available for public inspection and copying. A public hearing may be scheduled if requested in writing by any person that timely submits written comments. If a public hearing is scheduled, notice of the date, time, and place for the hearing will be published in the **Federal Register.**
Drafting Information

The principal author of these proposed regulations is Theresa M. Melchiorre, Office of Associate Chief Counsel (Passthroughs and Special Industries). Other personnel from the Treasury Department and the IRS participated in their development.

[¶ 49,695] Proposed Amendments of Regulations (REG-133673-15), published in the Federal Register on April 13, 2016 (corrected 7/5/2016).

[Code Secs. 305, 860G, 861, 1441, 1461, 1471, 1473 and 6045B]

Corporations: Stock rights: Deemed distributions.—Amendments of Reg. §§1.305-1, 1.305-3, 1.305-7, 1.860G-3, 1.861-3, 1.1441-2, 1.1441-3, 1.1441-7, 1.1461-2, 1.1471-2, 1.1473-1 and 1.6045B-1, containing proposed regulations regarding deemed distributions of stock and rights to acquire stock, are proposed.

AGENCY: Internal Revenue Service (IRS), Treasury.

ACTION: Notice of proposed rulemaking.

SUMMARY: This document contains proposed regulations regarding deemed distributions of stock and rights to acquire stock. The proposed regulations would resolve ambiguities concerning the amount and timing of deemed distributions that are or result from adjustments to rights to acquire stock. The proposed regulations also would provide additional guidance to withholding agents regarding their current withholding and information reporting obligations under chapters 3 and 4 with respect to these deemed distributions. The proposed regulations would affect corporations issuing rights to acquire stock, their shareholders and holders of these rights, and withholding agents with respect to these deemed distributions.

DATES: Written or electronic comments and requests for a public hearing must be received by July 12, 2016.

ADDRESSES: Send submissions to: CC:PA:LPD:PR (REG-133673-15), Room 5203, Internal Revenue Service, PO Box 7604, Ben Franklin Station, Washington, DC, 20044. Submissions may be hand-delivered Monday through Friday between the hours of 8 a.m. and 4 p.m. to CC:PA:LPD:PR (REG-133673-15), Courier's Desk, Internal Revenue Service, 1111 Constitution Avenue, NW, Washington, DC, 20224 or sent electronically, via the Federal eRulemaking Portal at www.regulations.gov (indicate IRS and REG-133673-15).

FOR FURTHER INFORMATION CONTACT: Concerning the proposed regulations under section 305, Maurice M. LaBrie, (202) 317-5322; concerning the proposed regulations under sections 860G, 861, 1441, 1461, 1471, and 1473, Subin Seth, (202) 317-6942; concerning the proposed regulations under section 6045B, Pamela Lew, (202) 317-7053; concerning submission of comments, contact Regina Johnson, (202) 317-6901 (not toll-free numbers).

SUPPLEMENTARY INFORMATION:

Background and Explanation of Provisions

1. Overview

This document contains proposed regulations that amend 26 CFR part 1 under sections 305, 860G, 861, 1441, 1461, 1471, 1473, and 6045B of the Internal Revenue Code of 1986 (Code) concerning deemed distributions that are or result from adjustments to rights to acquire stock.

Final regulations under section 305 were published in the **Federal Register** on July 12, 1973 (TD 7281, 38 FR 18531), and amendments to those final regulations were published in the **Federal Register** on October 15, 1974 (TD 7329, 39 FR 36860), and in the **Federal Register** on December 21, 1995 (TD 8643, 60 FR 66134).

Final regulations under sections 1441 and 1461 were published in the **Federal Register** on October 14, 1997 (TD 8734, 62 FR 53387), and the following amendments to those final regulations were published in the **Federal Register** on: December 31, 1998 (TD 8804, 63 FR 72187); December 30, 1999 (TD 8856, 64 FR 73412); May 22, 2000 (TD 8881, 65 FR 32186); August 1, 2006 (TD 9272, 71 FR 43366); July 14, 2008 (TD 9415, 73 FR 40172) (corrected on August 6, 2008 (73 FR 45612)); January 23, 2012 (TD 9572, 77 FR 3109); December 5, 2013 (TD 9648, 78 FR 73081); March 6, 2014 (TD 9658, 79 FR 12726) (corrected on July 1, 2014 (79 FR 37175)); and, September 18, 2015 (TD 9734, 80 FR 56866). Final regulations under sections 1471 and 1473 were published in the **Federal Register** on January 28, 2013 (TD 9610, 78 FR 5874) (corrected on September 10, 2013 (78 FR 55202)), and the amendments to those final regulations were published as temporary regulations in the **Federal Register** on March 6, 2014 (TD 9657, 79 FR 12812) (corrected on July 1, 2014 (79 FR 37175)).

Final regulations under section 6045B were published in the **Federal Register** on October 18, 2010 (TD 9504, 75 FR 64072), and amendments to those final regulations were published in the **Federal Register** on April 18, 2013 (TD 9616, 78 FR 23116).

2. Amount and Timing of Deemed Distributions Under Section 305(c)

A. Application of section 305(b) and (c) generally

Section 305 and the regulations thereunder apply to actual and deemed distributions by a corporation of its own stock and rights to acquire its own stock. Section 305(a) provides the general rule that the receipt of these distributions is not included in the gross income of the recipient; however, under section 305(b)(1) through (b)(5) certain actual and deemed distributions of stock and stock rights are treated as distributions of property to which section 301 applies. For example, under section 305(b)(2), if a distribution (or series of distributions) by a corporation has the result of a receipt of property by some shareholders and an increase in the proportionate interests of other shareholders in the assets or earnings and profits of the corporation, all the distributions are treated as distributions of property to which section 301 applies.

Section 305(c) authorizes the Secretary to prescribe regulations to treat changes in the conversion ratio of instruments convertible into stock and other events having similar effects as distributions to shareholders whose proportionate interests in the assets or earnings and profits of the corporation are increased by such events.

Under section 305(d)(1) and current § 1.305-1(d), for purposes of section 305 and the regulations thereunder, the term *stock* includes rights to acquire stock, and under section 305(d)(2), for purposes of section 305(b) and (c) and the regulations thereunder, the term *shareholder* includes a holder of rights to acquire stock. For purposes of this preamble:

The term *actual shareholder* means a holder of stock (not including rights to acquire stock).

The term *deemed shareholder* means a holder of a right to acquire stock.

The term *deemed distribution* means a transaction or event, other than an actual distribution of stock, money, or other property, that is a distribution under section 305(b) and (c).

The term *applicable adjustment* means an adjustment to a right to acquire stock, including an increase or reduction in conversion ratio, conversion price, option price, or number of shares the holder would receive upon conversion or exercise.

The term *right to acquire stock* means any right to acquire stock, whether pursuant to a convertible instrument (such as a debt instrument that is convertible into shares of stock), a warrant, subscription right, or stock right issued by the corporation that issued or will issue the underlying stock, or any other right to acquire stock of the corporation issuing such right (whether settled in stock or in cash).

Under current § 1.305-1(b)(1), when a distribution of stock (including a right to acquire stock) is a distribution of property to which sections 305(b) and 301 apply, the amount of the distribution is the fair market value, on the date of the distribution, of the stock or right to acquire stock that is distributed.

B. Application of section 305(b) and (c) to adjustments to rights to acquire stock

A corporation may issue rights to acquire its stock in a number of forms, including warrants, subscription rights, options, convertible instruments that give the holder a right to convert the instruments into shares of stock in the issuing corporation, and similar instruments. In any of these forms, rights to acquire stock may provide for applicable adjustments that grant deemed shareholders economic benefits that correspond to distributions of stock, cash, or other property made to actual shareholders. Similarly, rights to acquire stock may provide for adjustments to prevent actual shareholders' interests from being diluted as a result of distributions of stock, cash, or other property to deemed shareholders (that is, holders of rights to acquire stock).

An applicable adjustment to a convertible instrument may consist of an increase in the number of shares of stock a holder would receive upon conversion. Similarly, an applicable adjustment to a warrant, subscription right, stock right, option, or similar right to acquire stock may consist of an increase in the number of shares the holder would receive upon exercise. In either situation, the applicable adjustment may have the effect of increasing the deemed shareholders' proportionate interests in the assets or earnings and profits of the corporation. If this increase has a result described in section 305(b), then under section 305(c) the applicable adjustment is a deemed distribution to the deemed shareholder, and section 301 applies to the deemed distribution.

Under current § 1.305-7(b)(1), an applicable adjustment made pursuant to a bona fide, reasonable adjustment formula that has the effect of preventing dilution of a shareholder's interest is not a deemed distribution of stock to which sections 305(b) and 301 apply. However, also under current § 1.305-7(b)(1), an applicable adjustment to compensate for a distribution of cash or property to actual shareholders that is taxable under section 301, 356(a)(2), 871(a)(1)(A), 881(a)(1), 852(b), or 857(b) is not considered as made pursuant to such a bona fide, reasonable adjustment formula, and therefore may be a distribution to which sections 305(b) and 301 apply.

The Treasury Department and the IRS have concluded that, under section 305(b) and (c) and the regulations thereunder, it is clear that an applicable adjustment is a deemed distribution to which section 301 applies, if: (i) the applicable adjustment increases the proportionate interest of an actual shareholder or a deemed shareholder in the corporation's assets or earnings and profits; (ii) such increase in proportionate interest has a result described in section 305(b); and (iii) the anti-dilution exception of § 1.305-7(b)(1) does not apply. For example, it has been the position of the Treasury Department and the IRS for over forty years that, under section 305(b) and (c) and the regulations thereunder, an increase in the conversion ratio of a convertible debt instrument may be treated as a deemed distribution to the deemed shareholder that holds the instrument, and, if so treated, section 301 applies to the deemed distribution. *See* Rev. Rul. 75-513 (1975-2 CB 114) (section 301 applied to deemed distribution where conversion ratio of convertible debentures increased due to payment of cash dividend to common shareholders); and Rev. Rul. 76-186 (1976-1 CB 86) (same; basis of the convertible debentures was increased by the value of the deemed distribution); *cf.* Rev. Rul. 77-37 (1977-1 CB 85) (no deemed distribution because anti-dilution exception of § 1.305-7(b) applied where distribution to actual shareholders was tax-free under section 355).

The current regulations are unclear, however, as to the amount of a deemed distribution to a deemed shareholder. The current regulations may reasonably be interpreted as providing either that such a deemed distribution is treated as a distribution of a right to acquire stock (the amount of which is the fair market value of the right), or that such a distribution is treated as a distribution of the actual stock to which the right relates (the amount of which is the fair market value of the stock). Accordingly, for deemed distributions to deemed shareholders occurring before final regulations are published, the IRS will not challenge either position.

The current regulations are also unclear as to the timing of such a distribution. Under the proposed regulations, such a distribution generally would be deemed to occur at the time the applicable adjustment occurs, in accordance with the instrument setting forth the terms of the right to acquire stock, but in no event later than the date of the distribution of cash or property that results in the deemed distribution (taking into account § 1.305-3(b)).

These proposed regulations would amend the current regulations under section 305(b) and (c) only to clarify the amount and timing of such deemed distributions, not the fact of their occurrence, which is clear under current law.

C. Summary of proposed regulations

i. Amount of deemed distributions

After studying this area, the Treasury Department and the IRS have concluded that a deemed distribution of a right to acquire stock is more accurately viewed as a distribution of additional rights to acquire stock, the amount of which is the fair market value of the right.

Under the terms of a convertible instrument, a distribution of cash or property to actual shareholders may increase the number of shares the holder of the convertible instrument would receive upon conversion. Similarly, a distribution of cash or property to actual shareholders may increase the number of shares the holder of other rights to acquire stock, such as warrants or options, would receive upon exercise. In either case, the increase is an applicable adjustment and a deemed distribution of additional rights to acquire stock to the holders of the rights to acquire stock. Under the proposed regulations, the amount of the deemed distribution would be the excess of (i) the fair market value of the right to acquire stock immediately after the applicable adjustment over (ii) the fair market value of the right to acquire stock without the applicable adjustment. In determining the fair market value of a right to acquire stock, any particular facts pertaining to the deemed shareholder's rights, including the number of actual shares of stock or rights to acquire stock held by such deemed shareholder, would be disregarded.

Also, under the terms of a convertible debt instrument or other right to acquire stock, a payment of cash or property to the holder may cause a reduction in the number of shares the holder would receive upon conversion or exercise. Such a reduction is an applicable adjustment that increases the actual shareholders' proportionate interests in the assets or earnings and profits of the corporation. Thus, the applicable adjustment results in a deemed distribution of stock to the actual shareholders, and section 301 applies to the deemed distribution. Under the proposed regulations, the amount of this deemed distribution would be the fair market value of the stock deemed distributed, determined in accordance with § 1.305-3(e), *Examples 8* and *9* (relating to deemed distributions to shareholders resulting from certain redemptions of stock from other shareholders). *See also* Tax Revenue Act of 1969: Hearings on H.R. 13270 Before the House Ways and Means Comm., 91st Cong. 1st Sess., pt. 14, 5196-98 (1969).

ii. Timing of deemed distributions

When an applicable adjustment is or results in a deemed distribution under proposed § 1.305-7(c)(1) or (2), the deemed distribution occurs at the time such applicable adjustment occurs, in accordance with the instrument setting forth the terms of the right to acquire stock, but in no event later than the date of the distribution of cash or property that results in the deemed distribution (taking into account § 1.305-3(b)). For such an applicable adjustment relating to a right to acquire publicly-traded stock, if the instrument setting forth the terms of such right does not set forth the date and time the applicable adjustment occurs, the deemed distribution would occur immediately prior to the opening of business on the ex-dividend date for the distribution of cash or property that results in the deemed distribution. For such an applicable adjustment relating to a right to acquire non-publicly traded stock, if the instrument setting forth the terms of such right does not set forth the date and time the applicable adjustment occurs, the deemed distribution occurs on the date that a holder is legally entitled to the distribution of cash or property that results in the deemed distribution.

3. Withholding under Chapters 3 and 4 on Deemed Distributions under Section 305(c)

This section provides a discussion of the proposed rules regarding deemed distributions under section 305(c). Section 4 of the preamble provides a discussion of the proposed rules regarding substitute dividend payments that are deemed payments determined with respect to a deemed distribution under section 305(c). The proposed rules that would apply for deemed payments are analogous to the proposed rules that would apply to deemed distributions.

A. Background

Sections 1441 and 1442 (referred to herein as "chapter 3") require all persons having the control, receipt, custody, disposal, or payment of items of income subject to withholding of any nonresident alien, foreign partnership, or foreign corporation to withhold tax at a 30-percent rate unless a reduced rate of withholding applies. Amounts subject to withholding include amounts from sources within the United States that are fixed or determinable annual or periodical income, which generally includes, among other things, interest, dividends, and similar types of investment income. § 1.1441-2(b)(1)(i). Under § 1.1441-2(e)(1), "a payment" is considered made to a person "if that person realizes income whether or not such income results from an actual transfer of cash or other property." For this purpose, a payment is considered made when the amount would be includible in the income of the beneficial owner under the U.S. tax principles governing the cash basis method of accounting. § 1.1441-2(e)(1).

On March 18, 2010, the Hiring Incentives to Restore Employment Act of 2010, Pub. L. 111-147 (H.R. 2847), added chapter 4 to the Code (sections 1471 through 1474, commonly known as "FATCA"). Chapter 4 generally requires a withholding agent to withhold tax at a 30-percent rate on a "withholdable payment" (as defined in § 1.1473-1(a)) made to a foreign financial institution (FFI) unless the FFI has entered into an agreement described in section 1471(b) to obtain status as a participating FFI or the FFI is deemed to have satisfied the requirements of section 1471(b). Chapter 4 also generally requires a withholding agent to withhold tax at a 30-percent rate on a withholdable payment made to a nonfinancial foreign entity (NFFE) unless the NFFE has provided information to the withholding agent with respect to the NFFE's substantial U.S. owners or has certified that it has no such owners. *See* section 1472.

These proposed regulations would provide guidance to withholding agents regarding their obligations to withhold under chapters 3 and 4 on deemed distributions under section 305(c). Withholding agents have commented that ambiguities in the current law have made it difficult for them to satisfy their withholding obligations. In particular, withholding agents have commented that these deemed distributions often occur when there is no cash payment that corresponds to the deemed distribution, which makes it difficult for them to satisfy their withholding obligation on the date of the deemed distribution. In addition, withholding agents commented that they often lack knowledge of the fact that a deemed distribution on a security has been made and are therefore unable to withhold on the date of the deemed distribution.

B. Amendments to Chapter 3

i. Withholding on deemed distributions, and new exception for deemed distributions on specified securities

Proposed § 1.1441-2(d)(4)(i) would clarify that a withholding agent has an obligation to withhold on a deemed distribution (as defined in § 1.305-1(d)(7)) that is made on a security. Proposed § 1.1441-7(a)(4) would clarify that an issuer of a security upon which a deemed distribution is made and any person that holds directly or indirectly (for example, through an account maintained for an intermediary) a security on behalf of the beneficial owner of the security, or a flow-through entity that owns directly or indirectly (through another flow-through entity) a security, is considered to have custody of or control over the deemed distribution made on the security and, therefore, is a withholding agent with respect to the distribution.

Under current § 1.1441-2(d)(1), a withholding agent does not have an obligation to withhold on a payment when it lacks control over, or custody of, money or property of the recipient, or knowledge of the facts giving rise to the payment (the general exception). This general exception does not apply when, in relevant part, the payment is a distribution with respect to stock. The proposed regulations, however, would allow a withholding agent (other than the issuer of the specified security) to benefit from a new exception to withholding in proposed § 1.1441-2(d)(4) for deemed distributions (as defined in §1.305-1(d)(7)) of stock or a right to acquire stock on a specified security (as defined in §1.6045-1(a)(14)). Under this new exception, a withholding agent (other than the issuer of the specified security) would have an obligation to withhold on such a deemed distribution only if, before the due date (not including extensions) for filing Form 1042, Annual Withholding Tax Return for U.S. Source Income of Foreign Persons, with respect to the calendar year in which the deemed distribution occurred, either (i) the issuer meets its reporting requirements under §1.6045B-1 (by furnishing an issuer statement or publicly reporting the information required under that section) or (ii) the withholding agent has actual knowledge that a deemed distribution has occurred, in which case the obligation to withhold would not arise until January 15 of the year following the calendar year of the deemed distribution.

ii. When and how to withhold

Once the requirements of proposed §1.1441-2(d)(4)(i) have been satisfied, a withholding agent would have an obligation to withhold on a deemed distribution. Except as provided in §1.1441-5 regarding the time to withhold for partnerships and trusts, under proposed §1.1441-2(d)(4)(ii), a withholding agent would be required to satisfy its withholding obligation by withholding on the earliest of (i) the date on which a future cash payment is made with respect to the security; (ii) the date on which the security is sold, exchanged, or otherwise disposed of (including a transfer of the security to another account not maintained by the withholding agent or a termination of the account relationship); or (iii) the due date (not including extensions) for filing Form 1042 with respect to the calendar year in which the deemed distribution occurred. Under this approach, a withholding agent that continues to directly or indirectly hold or own the security when the requirements of proposed §1.1441-2(d)(4)(i) are satisfied generally would be able to satisfy its withholding obligation by withholding on future cash payments on the security (for example, an interest payment on a convertible bond). If, however, the security is disposed of before sufficient future cash payments have been made on the security, the withholding agent would be required to withhold at the time of disposition and generally would be expected to do so by, for example, withholding on the proceeds from the disposal, liquidating other property held in custody for the beneficial owner, or obtaining other funds directly or indirectly from the beneficial owner to satisfy the withholding.

If there are not sufficient future cash payments on the security and the security has not been disposed of or transferred before the due date (not including extensions) for filing Form 1042 with respect to the calendar year in which the deemed distribution occurred, then, to avoid having to pay the tax out of the withholding agent's own funds, the withholding agent may apply current §1.1461-2(b) in order to collect the underwithheld amount. Under these rules, the withholding agent can satisfy the tax by withholding on other cash payments made to the same beneficial owner or by liquidating other property held in custody for the beneficial owner or over which it has control. The proposed regulations would amend current §1.1461-2(b) to clarify that a withholding agent may obtain the property from which to withhold under these rules through additional contributions obtained directly or indirectly from the beneficial owner. The proposed regulations also would add a sentence to current §1.1461-2(b) to clarify that a withholding agent that satisfies its obligation to withhold under §1.1461-2(b) will not be subject to any penalties for failure to deposit or failure to pay under sections 6656, 6672, and 7202 when it deposits the amounts obtained in this manner by the due date (not including extensions) for filing Form 1042 with respect to the calendar year in which the deemed distribution occurred. These clarifications reflect the IRS interpretation of current §1.1461-2(b) in applying these penalties, and thus no penalties will be imposed for withholding agents that apply these rules to satisfy their obligations to withhold before the effective date of these regulations.

When the requirements of proposed §1.1441-2(d)(4)(i) are satisfied after a withholding agent has terminated its relationship with the beneficial owner of the security, the withholding agent would remain liable for any underwithheld amount with respect to the deemed distribution. In order to avoid having to pay the tax due out of the withholding agent's own funds, before terminating an account relationship, a withholding agent should make arrangements with the beneficial owner to ensure that the withholding agent can satisfy any tax due, such as by retaining funds or other property of the owner.

iii. Foreign entities assuming withholding responsibilities

Proposed §1.1441-2(d)(4)(iii) would provide that a withholding agent may treat certain foreign entities (qualified intermediaries, withholding foreign partnerships, withholding foreign trusts, and U.S. branches treated as U.S. persons) as assuming primary chapter 3 withholding responsibilities for a deemed distribution on a specified security only if (i) the withholding agent provides the foreign entity with a copy of the issuer statement described in §1.6045B-1(b)(1) within 10 days of the issuer furnishing the statement to the holder of record or its nominee, or (ii) the issuer has met the public reporting requirements under §1.6045B-1(a)(3). The foreign entity would have an obligation to withhold on the deemed distribution only if it receives a copy of the issuer statement or if the issuer has met the public reporting requirements by the due date (not including extensions) for filing Form 1042 with respect to the calendar year in which the deemed distribution occurred. A withholding agent that fails to provide a copy of the issuer statement to a foreign entity (in the absence of public reporting) would not be permitted to treat the foreign entity as having assumed primary withholding responsibilities for the deemed distribution and would therefore have to withhold and report based on the information that it has regarding the recipient of the deemed distribution. The purpose of this proposed rule is to ensure that foreign entities that assume primary withholding responsibilities for deemed distributions will possess the information described in §1.6045B-1 to meet their withholding and information reporting obligations, as these entities (or their nominees) may not be holders of record that otherwise would receive the issuer statement described in §1.6045B-1(b)(1).

iv. Reliance on issuer information reporting

Under proposed §1.1441-3(c)(5), a withholding agent (other than the issuer of the specified security) would be permitted to rely on the information that an issuer provides on an issuer statement described in §1.6045B-1(b)(1) or on a public website described in §1.6045B-1(a)(3) to determine the proper amount of withholding on a deemed distribution on a specified security unless it knows that the information is incorrect or unreliable. Additionally, a foreign entity that has assumed primary withholding responsibilities would be permitted to rely on the copy of the issuer statement described in §1.6045B-1(b)(1) that it receives from another withholding agent under the circumstances described in proposed §1.1441-2(d)(4)(iii) unless it knows that the information is incorrect or unreliable.

v. Other changes to current §1.1441-2(d)(1)

The proposed regulations would add language to §1.1441-2(d)(1) to clarify that a withholding agent does not lack control over money or property if it directs another person to make a payment, and that a withholding agent does not lack knowledge of the facts that give rise to a payment merely because the withholding agent does not know the character or source of the payment for U.S. tax purposes. The proposed regulations also would add an example to §1.1441-2(d)(1) of when a withholding agent lacks knowledge of the facts that give rise to a payment. These clarifications and the example are consistent with similar rules in current §1.1471-2(a)(4)(i) that apply for chapter 4 purposes.

The proposed regulations also would make nonsubstantive changes to reorganize the structure of current §1.1441-2(d)(1).

C. Amendments to Chapter 4

The proposed regulations would modify the regulations under chapter 4 to provide guidance similar to the rules described in proposed §§1.1441-2(d)(1), 1.1441-2(d)(4), 1.1441-3(c)(5), and 1.1441-7(a)(4) for withholding on a deemed distribution (as defined in §1.305-1(d)(7)) that is a withholdable payment under chapter 4. The amendment to proposed §1.1461-2(b) that clarifies that a withholding agent may obtain additional contributions of property directly or indirectly from a beneficial owner and the new sentence added to proposed §1.1461-2(b) regarding penalties also would apply to withholding agents adjusting underwithholding under chapter 4 through cross-reference in § 1.1474-2(b). The proposed regulations also would make nonsubstantive changes to reorganize the structure of current § 1.1471-2(a)(4)(i), which are consistent with the organizational changes proposed for current § 1.1441-2(d)(1).

4. A Substitute Dividend May Include Deemed Payments

Section 1.861-3(a)(6) provides that a substitute dividend payment made to a transferor in a securities lending transaction or sale-repurchase transaction is sourced in the same manner as a dividend on the transferred securities. The regulations define a substitute dividend payment as "a payment, made to the transferor of a security in a securities lending transaction or a sale-repurchase transaction, of an amount equivalent to a dividend distribution which the owner of the transferred security is entitled to receive during the term of the transaction." These proposed regulations would modify § 1.861-3(a)(6) to clarify that a substitute dividend payment includes a deemed payment made in the amount (as determined under § 1.305-7(c)(4)) of a deemed distribution (as defined in § 1.305-1(d)(7)).

These proposed regulations would provide that the general exception to withholding in § 1.1441-2(d)(1)(i) does not apply for deemed payments (as defined in § 1.861-3(a)(6)). However, proposed § 1.1441-2(d)(4) would allow a withholding agent to benefit from the same exception to withholding that would apply to deemed distributions (as defined in § 1.305-1(d)(7)) on a specified security for deemed payments (as defined in § 1.861-3(a)(6)) that are determined with respect to a deemed distribution on a specified security. Thus, a withholding agent would have an obligation to withhold on such a deemed payment only if, before the due date (not including extensions) for filing Form 1042, Annual Withholding Tax Return for U.S. Source Income of Foreign Persons, with respect to the calendar year in which the deemed distribution on a specified security occurred, either (i) the issuer meets its reporting requirements under § 1.6045B-1 (by furnishing an issuer statement or publicly reporting the information required under that section) or (ii) the withholding agent has actual knowledge that a deemed distribution has occurred, in which case the obligation to withhold would not arise until January 15 of the year following the calendar year of the deemed distribution or the deemed payment. If a withholding agent has an obligation to withhold on a deemed payment (as defined in § 1.861-3(a)(6)) under § 1.1441-2(d)(4)(i), it would be required to withhold subject to the rules regarding when and how to withhold in proposed § 1.1441-2(d)(4)(ii) and the rules regarding foreign entities that assume withholding responsibilities in § 1.1441-2(d)(4)(iii). These proposed regulations also would modify the regulations under chapter 4 to provide similar guidance with respect to deemed payments that are withholdable payments.

5. Issuer Reporting Under Section 6045B

To facilitate broker reporting of a security's adjusted basis to the holder of the security under section 6045, section 6045B provides that, according to the forms or regulations prescribed by the Secretary, an issuer of a specified security (for example, stock, a convertible debt instrument, or a warrant) must report certain information relating to an organizational action that affects the basis of the security to both the IRS and the holders of the security. Under section 6045B and current § 1.6045B-1, an issuer must file an issuer return (Form 8937, Report of Organizational Actions Affecting Basis of Securities) with the IRS by the earlier of 45 days after the organizational action or January 15 of the calendar year following the organizational action. In addition, the issuer must send a written statement (for example, a copy of the issuer return) to holders by January 15 of the calendar year following the organizational action. In lieu of filing the issuer return with the IRS and furnishing the written statement to holders, current § 1.6045B-1(a)(3) permits an issuer to post the required information on its public website by the due date for reporting the issuer return to the IRS. Under current § 1.6045B-1, however, an issuer is not required to send a statement to exempt recipients, such as C corporations and foreign persons, nor is an issuer required to file an issuer return if the issuer reasonably determines that all of the holders of the security are exempt recipients. An issuer must comply with current § 1.6045B-1 for an organizational action that occurs on or after the applicability date prescribed in current § 1.6045B-1(j). For example, an issuer of a convertible debt instrument must comply with current § 1.6045B-1 for an organizational action that occurs after December 31, 2015.

An applicable adjustment, including a conversion ratio adjustment, is an organizational action that often will affect the holder's basis in a specified security. For example, the instructions to Form 8937 provide that if a conversion ratio adjustment on a convertible debt instrument occurring after December 31, 2015, results in a distribution under section 305(c) (for example, because it is made in conjunction with a cash distribution to shareholders), the issuer of the debt instrument must file Form 8937.

Brokers and withholding agents have expressed concerns about the difficulty of complying with their reporting and withholding obligations in the absence of information about the fact and amount of a deemed distribution under section 305(c), including a deemed distribution under section 305(c) resulting from an applicable adjustment. Even after December 31, 2015, when issuers are generally required to report an applicable adjustment on a convertible debt instrument, brokers and withholding agents may not have the necessary information to comply with their reporting and withholding obligations because of the exempt recipient exception for providing a written statement (and assuming that the issuer does not choose the public reporting alternative). In response to these concerns, § 1.6045B-1(i)(2) of the proposed regulations would require that an issuer provide an issuer return to the IRS and a written statement to each holder of record of a specified security (or to the holder's nominee) relating to a deemed distribution under section 305(c) on the security, without regard to any of the general exceptions in the current regulations under section 6045B or in the instructions to Form 8937. The proposed regulations, like the current regulations, permit an issuer to not provide an issuer return to the IRS or a written statement to the holders regarding the deemed distribution if the issuer satisfies the public reporting requirements in current § 1.6045B-1(a)(3).

6. Reporting for U.S. Persons

Section 1.6045B-1 generally applies when a deemed distribution affects the basis of a specified security. It is expected that similar principles would apply under section 6042 with respect to reporting of deemed distributions made to U.S. persons on Form 1099-DIV. Comments are requested on the implementation of Form 1099-DIV reporting on these amounts.

Proposed Effective/Applicability Date

The proposed regulations under section 305 would apply to deemed distributions occurring on or after the date of publication of the Treasury decision adopting these rules as final regulations in the **Federal Register**. A taxpayer, however, may rely on these proposed regulations for deemed distributions under section 305(c) that occur prior to such date. For purposes of determining the amount of a deemed distribution to a deemed shareholder occurring prior to the date of publication, a taxpayer may determine the amount of the deemed distribution by treating such distribution either as a distribution of a right to acquire stock or as a distribution of the actual stock to which the right relates.

The proposed regulations under sections 860G, 861, 1441, 1461, 1471, and 1473 would apply to payments made on or after the date of publication. A withholding agent, however, may rely on the proposed regulations under sections 861, 1441, 1471, and 1473 for all deemed distributions under section 305(c) or, to the extent applicable, deemed payments (as defined in § 1.861-3(a)(6)) occurring on or after January 1, 2016 until the date of publication. No inference as to the application of these provisions under current law is intended by permitting reliance on these proposed regulations. A withholding agent also may rely on the proposed regulations under section 1461 for any payments occurring on or after January 1, 2016 until the date of publication, including for any deemed distribution under section 305(c) or deemed payment (as defined in § 1.861-3(a)(6)) for which the withholding agent failed to withhold.

Section 1.6045B-1(i)(2) would apply to a deemed distribution under section 305(c) occurring on or after the date of publication. In addition, an issuer would report the amount and timing of a deemed distribution in accordance with the proposed regulations under section 305 for a deemed distribution occurring on or after the date of publication. For purposes of reporting the amount of a deemed distribution occurring prior to the date of publication, an issuer may determine the amount of the deemed distribution by treating such distribution either as a distribution of a right to acquire stock, or as a distribution of the shares of stock that would be received upon exercise of the right. In addition, an issuer may rely on § 1.305-7(c)(5) of the proposed regulations to determine the date of a deemed distribution occurring prior to the date of publication.

Statement of Availability of IRS Documents

IRS Revenue Rulings cited in this preamble are published in the Internal Revenue Bulletin (or Cumulative Bulletin) and are available from the Superintendent of Documents, U.S. Government Printing Office, Washington, DC 20402, or by visiting the IRS website at *http://www.irs.gov*.

Effect on Other Documents

The IRS will modify, clarify, or obsolete publications as necessary to conform to these proposed regulations as of the date of publication of the Treasury decision adopting these rules as final regulations in the **Federal Register**. *See, e.g.*, Rev. Rul. 75-513 (1975-2 CB 114) and Rev. Rul. 76-186 (1976-1 CB 186). The IRS solicits comments as to whether other publications should be modified, clarified, or obsoleted.

Special Analyses

Certain IRS regulations, including this one, are exempt from the requirements of Executive Order 12866, as supplemented and reaffirmed by Executive Order 13563. Therefore, a regulatory impact assessment is not required. It also has been determined that section 553(b) of the Administrative Procedure Act (5 U.S.C. chapter 5) does not apply to these regulations.

Pursuant to the Regulatory Flexibility Act (5 U.S.C. chapter 6), it is hereby certified that the proposed regulations under section 6045B in this document will not have a significant economic impact on a substantial number of small entities. Any effect on small entities by the rules in the proposed regulations flows directly from section 403 of the Energy Improvement and Extension Act of 2008, Division B of Public Law 110-343 (122 Stat. 3765, 3854 (2008)) (the Act).

Section 403(d) of the Act added section 6045B, which requires an issuer, including an issuer that is a small entity, to report certain information relating to any organizational action by the issuer that affects the basis of a specified security. In general, an issuer reports the information required under section 6045B to the IRS and to holders or nominees on Form 8937. The proposed regulations limit reporting to the information necessary to meet the Act's requirements. In addition, the proposed regulations retain the rule in the current regulations under section 6045B that permits an issuer to report each action publicly on its website instead of filing a return and furnishing each holder or nominee a statement about the action. The proposed regulations therefore do not add to the statutory impact on small entities but instead eases this impact to the extent the statute permits. Moreover, any economic impact on small entities is expected to be minimal.

Therefore, because the proposed regulations in this document will not have a significant economic impact on a substantial number of small entities, a regulatory flexibility analysis is not required.

Pursuant to section 7805(f) of the Code, this notice of proposed rulemaking has been submitted to the Chief Counsel for Advocacy of the Small Business Administration for comment on its impact on small business.

Comments and Requests for Public Hearing

Before the proposed regulations are adopted as final regulations, consideration will be given to any comments that are submitted timely to the IRS as prescribed in this preamble under the "Addresses" heading. The Treasury Department and the IRS request comments on all aspects of the proposed regulations. All comments will be available for public inspection and copying upon request, or at *www.regulations.gov*. A public hearing will be scheduled if requested in writing by any person that timely submits written comments. If a public hearing is scheduled, notice of the date, time, and place for the public hearing will be published in the **Federal Register**.

Drafting Information

The principal authors of these regulations are: with respect to the regulations under section 305, Maurice M. LaBrie of the Office of Associate Chief Counsel (Corporate); with respect to the regulations under sections 860G, 861, 1441, 1461, 1471, and 1473, Subin Seth of the Office of Associate Chief Counsel (International); and with respect to the regulations under section 6045B, Pamela Lew of the Office of Associate Chief Counsel (Financial Institutions and Products), all within the Office of Chief Counsel, IRS. Other personnel from the Treasury Department and the IRS participated in developing the regulations.

[¶ 49,696]   **Proposed Amendments of Regulations (NPRM REG-114307-15)**, published in the Federal Register on May 4, 2016.

[Code Sec. 7701]

Definitions: Disregarded entities: Partnerships: Self-employment tax.—Amendments of Reg. § 301.7701-2, clarifying the employment tax treatment of partners in a partnership that owns a disregarded entity, are proposed.

AGENCY: Internal Revenue Service (IRS), Treasury.

ACTION: Notice of proposed rulemaking by cross-reference to temporary regulations.

SUMMARY: In the Rules and Regulations section of this issue of the **Federal Register**, the IRS is issuing temporary regulations that clarify the employment tax treatment of partners in a partnership that owns a disregarded entity. These regulations affect partners in a partnership that owns a disregarded entity. The text of those temporary regulations serves as the text of these proposed regulations.

DATES: Comments and requests for a public hearing must be received by August 2, 2016.

ADDRESSES: Send submissions to: CC:PA:LPD:PR (REG-114307-15), room 5203, Internal Revenue Service, PO Box 7604, Ben Franklin Station, Washington, DC 20044. Submissions may be hand-delivered Monday through Friday between the hours of 8 a.m. and 4 p.m. to CC:PA:LPD:PR (REG-114307-15), Courier's Desk, Internal Revenue Service, 1111 Constitution Avenue, N.W., Washington, DC, 20224 or sent electronically, via the Federal eRulemaking Portal at http://www.regulations.gov/ (IRS REG-114307-15).

FOR FUTHER INFORMATION CONTACT: Concerning the proposed regulations, Andrew K. Holubeck at (202) 317-4774; concerning submission of comments, or a request for a public hearing please contact Regina Johnson at (202) 317-6901 (not toll-free numbers).

SUPPLEMENTARY INFORMATION

Background and Explanation of Provisions

Temporary regulations in the Rules and Regulations section of this issue of the **Federal Register** amend the Procedure and Administration Regulations (26 CFR part 301) relating to section 7701. The temporary regulations clarify that an entity disregarded as separate from its owner (a disregarded entity), that is treated as a corporation for purposes of employment taxes imposed under subtitle C, is not treated as a corporation for purposes of employing its individual owner (who is treated as a sole proprietor) or for purposes of employing an individual that is a partner in a partnership that owns the disregarded entity. Rather, the entity is disregarded as an entity separate from its owner for this purpose. The partners are subject to the same self-employment tax rules as partners in a partnership that does not own an entity that is disregarded as separate from its owner. The text of those regulations also serves as the text of these proposed regulations. The preamble to the temporary regulations explains the amendments.

Special Analysis

Certain IRS regulations, including this one, are exempt from the requirements of Executive Order 12866, as supplemented and reaffirmed by Executive Order 13563. Therefore, a regulatory impact assessment is not required. It has also been determined that section 553(b) of the Administrative Procedure Act (5 U.S.C. chapter 5) does not apply to these regulations, and because the regulations do not impose a collection of information on small entities, the Regulatory Flexibility Act (5 U.S.C. chapter 6) does not apply. Pursuant to section 7805(f) of the Internal Revenue Code, this notice of proposed rulemaking will be submitted to the Chief Counsel for Advocacy of the Small Business Administration for comment on their impact on small business.

Comments and Requests for Public Hearing

Before these proposed regulations are adopted as final regulations, consideration will be given to any comments that are submitted timely to the IRS as prescribed in this preamble under the "Addresses" heading. The Treasury Department and the IRS request comments on all aspects of the proposed rules. All comments will be available at www.regulations.gov or upon request. A public hearing will be scheduled if requested in writing by any person that timely submits written comments. If a public hearing is scheduled, notice of the date, time, and place for the hearing will be published in the **Federal Register**.

Drafting Information

The principal author of these regulations is Andrew Holubeck of the Office of the Division Counsel/Associate Chief Counsel (Tax Exempt and Government Entities). However, other personnel from the IRS and the Treasury Department participated in their development.

[¶ 49,701]   Proposed Amendments of Regulations (REG-135702-15), published in the Federal Register on June 10, 2016.

[Code Secs. 162, 5000A, 6055, 6056, 9801, 9815, 9831 and 9833]

International tax: Health care coverage: Expatriates: Expatriate health coverage: Expatriate health plan issuers: Expatriate health plans.—Amendments of Reg. §§1.162-31, 1.5000A-2, 1.6055-2, 54.9801-2, 54.9831-1, and 301.6056-2 relating to the rules for expatriate health plans, expatriate health plan issuers, and qualified expatriates under the Expatriate Health Coverage Clarification Act of 2014 (EHCCA), are proposed. Amendments of Reg. §§54.9815-2711 and 54.9833-1 and portions of amendments of Reg. §§54.9801-2 and 54.9831-1 adopted by T.D. 9791 on October 28, 2016.

AGENCIES: Internal Revenue Service, Department of the Treasury; Employee Benefits

Security Administration, Department of Labor; Centers for Medicare & Medicaid Services,

Department of Health and Human Services.

ACTION: Proposed rule.

SUMMARY: This document contains proposed regulations on the rules for expatriate health plans, expatriate health plan issuers, and qualified expatriates under the Expatriate Health Coverage Clarification Act of 2014 (EHCCA). This document also includes proposed conforming amendments to certain regulations to implement the provisions of the EHCCA. Further, this document proposes standards for travel insurance and supplemental health insurance coverage to be considered excepted benefits and revisions to the definition of short-term, limited-duration insurance for purposes of the exclusion from the definition of individual health insurance coverage. These proposed regulations affect expatriates with health coverage under expatriate health plans and sponsors, issuers and administrators of expatriate health plans, individuals with and plan sponsors of travel insurance and supplemental health insurance coverage, and individuals with short-term, limited-duration insurance. In addition, this document proposes to amend a reference in the final regulations relating to prohibitions on lifetime and annual dollar limits and proposes to require that a notice be provided in connection with hospital indemnity and other fixed indemnity insurance in the group health insurance market for it to be considered excepted benefits.

DATES: Comments are due on or before August 9, 2016.

ADDRESSES: Comments, identified by "Expatriate Health Plans and other issues," may be submitted by one of the following methods:

Hand delivery or mail: Written comment submissions may be submitted to CC:PA:LPD:PR (REG-135702-15), Internal Revenue Service, PO Box 7604, Ben Franklin Station, Washington DC 20044. Comment submissions may be hand-delivered Monday through Friday between the hours of 8 a.m. and 4 p.m. to CC:PA:LPD:PR (REG-135702-15).

Federal eRulemaking Portal: http://www.regulations.gov. Follow the instructions for submitting comments.

Comments received will be posted without change to www.regulations.gov and available for public inspection. Any comment that is submitted will be shared with the Department of Labor (DOL) and Department of Health and Human Services (HHS). Warning: Do not include any personally identifiable information (such as name, address, or other contact information) or confidential business information that you do not want publicly disclosed. All comments may be posted on the Internet and can be retrieved by most Internet search engines. No deletions, modifications, or redactions will be made to the comments received, as they are public records. **FOR FURTHER INFORMATION CONTACT:** Concerning the proposed regulations, with respect to the treatment of expatriate health plan coverage as minimum essential coverage under section 5000A of the Internal Revenue Code, John Lovelace, at 202-317-7006; with respect to the provisions relating to the health insurance providers fee imposed by section 9010 of the Affordable Care Act, Rachel Smith, at 202-317-6855; with respect to the definition of expatriate health plans, expatriate health insurance issuers, and qualified expatriates, and the provisions relating to the market reforms (such as excepted benefits, and short-term, limited-duration coverage), R. Lisa Mojiri-Azad of the IRS Office of Chief Counsel, at 202-317-5500, Elizabeth Schumacher or Matthew Litton of the Department of Labor, at 202-693-8335, Jacob Ackerman of the Centers for Medicare & Medicaid Services, Department of Health and Human

Services, at 301-492-4179. Concerning the submission of comments or to request a public hearing, Regina Johnson. (202) 317-6901 (not toll-free numbers).

Customer Service Information: Individuals interested in obtaining information from the Department of Labor concerning employment-based health coverage laws may call the EBSA Toll-Free Hotline, at 1-866-444-EBSA (3272) or visit the Department of Labor's website (http://www.dol.gov/ebsa). In addition, information from HHS on private health insurance for consumers can be found on the Centers for Medicare & Medicaid Services (CMS) website (www.cms.gov/cciio) and information on health reform can be found at www.HealthCare.gov.

SUPPLEMENTARY INFORMATION:

I. Background

This document contains proposed amendments to Department of the Treasury (Treasury Department) regulations at 26 CFR part 1 (Income taxes), 26 CFR part 46 (Excise taxes, Health care, Health insurance, Pensions, Reporting and recordkeeping requirements), 26 CFR part 54 (Pension and excise taxes), 26 CFR part 57 (Health insurance providers fee), and 26 CFR part 301 (relating to procedure and administration) to implement the rules for expatriate health plans, expatriate health plan issuers, and qualified expatriates under the Expatriate Health Coverage Clarification Act of 2014 (EHCCA), which was enacted as Division M of the Consolidated and Further Continuing Appropriations Act, 2015, Public Law 113-235 (128 Stat. 2130). This document also contains proposed amendments to DOL regulations at 29 CFR part 2590 and HHS regulations at 45 CFR part 147, which are substantively identical to the amendments to 26 CFR part 54.

The EHCCA generally provides that the requirements of the Affordable Care Act[1] (ACA) do not apply with respect to expatriate health plans, expatriate health insurance issuers for coverage under expatriate health plans, and employers in their capacity as plan sponsors of expatriate health plans, except that: (1) an expatriate health plan shall be treated as minimum essential coverage under section 5000A(f) of the Internal Revenue Code of 1986, as amended (the Code) and any other section of the Code that incorporates the definition of minimum essential coverage; (2) the employer shared responsibility provisions of section 4980H of the Code continue to apply; (3) the health care reporting provisions of sections 6055 and 6056 of the Code continue to apply but with certain modifications relating to the use of electronic media for required statements to enrollees; (4) the excise tax provisions of section 4980I of the Code continue to apply with respect to coverage of certain qualified expatriates who are assigned (rather than transferred) to work in the United States; and (5) the annual health insurance providers fee imposed by section 9010 of the ACA takes into account expatriate health insurance issuers for certain purposes for calendar years 2014 and 2015 only.

This document also contains proposed amendments to 26 CFR part 54, 29 CFR part 2590, and 45 CFR parts 146 and 148, which would specify conditions for travel insurance, supplemental health insurance coverage, and hospital indemnity and other fixed indemnity insurance to be considered excepted benefits. Excepted benefits are exempt from the requirements that generally apply under title XXVII of the Public Health Service Act (PHS Act), part 7 of the Employee Retirement Income Security Act of 1974, as amended (ERISA), and Chapter 100 of the Code. In addition, this document contains proposed amendments to (1) the definition of "short-term, limited-duration insurance," for purposes of the exclusion from the definition of "individual health insurance coverage" and (2) the definition of "essential health benefits," for purposes of the prohibition on annual and lifetime dollar limits in 26 CFR part 54, 29 CFR 2590, and 45 CFR parts 144 and 147.

This document clarifies an exemption set forth in 45 CFR 153.400(a)(1)(iii) related to the transitional reinsurance program. Section 1341 of the Affordable Care Act provides for the establishment of a transitional reinsurance program in each State to help pay the cost of treating high-cost enrollees in the individual market in the 2014 through 2016 benefit years. Section 1341(b)(3)(B) of the ACA and 45 CFR 153.400(a)(1) require contributing entities to make reinsurance contributions for major medical coverage that is considered to be part of a commercial book of business.

This document also contains proposed conforming amendments to 45 CFR part 158 that address the separate medical loss ratio (MLR) reporting requirements for expatriate policies that are not expatriate health plans under the EHCCA.

General Statutory Background and Enactment of ACA

The Health Insurance Portability and Accountability Act of 1996 (HIPAA), Public Law 104-191 (110 Stat. 1936), added title XXVII of the PHS Act, part 7 of ERISA, and Chapter 100 of the Code, which impose portability and nondiscrimination rules with respect to health coverage. These provisions of the PHS Act, ERISA, and the Code were later augmented by other consumer protection laws, including the Mental Health Parity Act of 1996, the Paul Wellstone and Pete Domenici Mental Health Parity and Addiction Equity Act of 2008, the Newborns' and Mothers' Health Protection Act, the Women's Health and Cancer Rights Act, the Genetic Information Nondiscrimination Act of 2008, the Children's Health Insurance Program Reauthorization Act of 2009, Michelle's Law, and the ACA.

The ACA reorganizes, amends, and adds to the provisions of part A of title XXVII of the PHS Act relating to group health plans and health insurance issuers in the group and individual markets. For this purpose, the term "group health plan" includes both insured and self-insured group health plans.[2] The ACA added section 715(a)(1) of ERISA and section 9815(a)(1) of the Code to incorporate the provisions of part A of title XXVII of the PHS Act (generally, sections 2701 through 2728 of the PHS Act) into ERISA and the Code to make them applicable to group health plans and health insurance issuers providing health insurance coverage in connection with group health plans.

Expatriate Health Plans, Expatriate Health Plan Issuers and Qualified Expatriates

Prior to the enactment of the EHCCA, employers, issuers and covered individuals had expressed concerns about the application of the ACA market reform rules to expatriate health plans and whether coverage under expatriate health plans was minimum essential coverage for purposes of section 5000A of the Code. To address these concerns on an interim basis, on March 8, 2013, the Departments of Labor, HHS, and the Treasury (collectively, the Departments[3]) issued Affordable Care Act Implementation Frequently Asked Questions (FAQs) Part XIII, Q&A-1, providing relief from the ACA market reform requirements for certain expatriate group health insurance coverage.[4] For plan years ending on or before December 31, 2015, the FAQ provides that, with respect to expatriate health plans, the Departments will consider the requirements of subtitles A and C of title I of the ACA to be satisfied if the plan and issuer comply with the pre-ACA version of title XXVII of the PHS Act. For purposes of the relief, an expatriate health plan is an insured group health plan with respect to which enrollment is limited to primary insureds who reside outside of their home country for at least six months of the plan year and any covered dependents, and its associated group health insurance coverage. The FAQ also states that coverage provided under an expatriate group health plan is a form of minimum essential coverage under section 5000A of the Code. On January 9, 2014, the Departments issued Affordable Care Act Implementation FAQs Part XVIII, Q&A-6 and Q&A-7, which extended the relief of Affordable Care Act Implementation FAQs Part XIII, Q&A-1 for insured expatriate health plans to subtitle D of title I of the ACA and also provided that the relief from the requirements of subtitles A, C, and D of title I of the ACA would apply for plan years ending on or before December 31, 2016.[5]

---

[1] The Patient Protection and Affordable Care Act, Pub. L. 111-148, was enacted on March 23, 2010, and the Health Care and Education Reconciliation Act, Pub. L. 111-152, was enacted on March 30, 2010. They are collectively known as the "Affordable Care Act."

[2] The term "group health plan" is used in title XXVII of the PHS Act, part 7 of ERISA, and Chapter 100 of the Code, and is distinct from the term "health plan," as used in other provisions of title I of the ACA. The term "health plan" does not include self-insured group health plans.

[3] Note, however, that in sections under headings listing only two of the three Departments, the term "Departments" generally refers only to the two Departments listed in the heading.

[4] Frequently Asked Questions about Affordable Care Act Implementation (Part XIII), available at http://www.dol.gov/ebsa/pdf/faq-aca13.pdf and http://www.cms.gov/CCIIO/Resources/Fact-Sheets-andFAQs/ACA_implementation_faq13.html.

[5] Frequently Asked Questions about Affordable Care Act Implementation (Part XVIII), available at https://www.dol.gov/ebsa/faqs/faq-aca18.html and https://

Subsequently, the EHCCA was enacted on December 16, 2014. Section 3(a) of the EHCCA provides that the ACA generally does not apply to expatriate health plans, employers with respect to expatriate health plans but solely in their capacity as plan sponsors of these plans, and expatriate health insurance issuers with respect to coverage offered by such issuers under expatriate health plans. Under section 3(b) of the EHCCA, however, the ACA continues to apply to expatriate health plans with respect to the employer shared responsibility provisions of section 4980H of the Code, the reporting requirements of sections 6055 and 6056 of the Code, and the excise tax provisions of section 4980I of the Code. Section 3(b) of the EHCCA further provides that an expatriate health plan offered to primary enrollees described in sections 3(d)(3)(A) and (B) of the EHCCA shall be treated as an eligible employer sponsored plan under section 5000A(f)(2) of the Code, and that an expatriate health plan offered to primary enrollees described in section 3(d)(3)(C) of the EHCCA shall be treated as a plan in the individual market under section 5000A(f)(1)(C) of the Code. Section 3(c) of the EHCCA sets forth rules for expatriate health plans with respect to the annual health insurance providers fee imposed by section 9010 of the ACA.

Sections 4375 and 4376 of the Code impose the Patient-Centered Outcomes Research Trust Fund (PCORTF) fee only with respect to individuals residing in the United States. Final regulations regarding the PCORTF fee exempt any specified health insurance policy or applicable self-insured group health plan designed and issued specifically to cover employees who are working and residing outside the United States from the fee. The exclusion from the ACA for expatriate health plans, employers with respect to expatriate health plans but solely in their capacity as plan sponsors of these plans, and expatriate health insurance issuers with respect to coverage offered by such issuers under expatriate health plans would apply to the PCORTF fee to the extent an expatriate health plan was not already excluded from the fee.

Section 1341 of the ACA establishes a transitional reinsurance program to help stabilize premiums for non-grandfathered health insurance coverage in the individual health insurance market from 2014 through 2016. Section 1341(b)(3)(B) of the ACA and the implementing regulations at 45 CFR 153.400(a)(1) require health insurance issuers and certain self-insured group health plans ("contributing entities") to make reinsurance contributions for major medical coverage that is considered to be part of a commercial book of business. This language has been interpreted to exclude "expatriate health coverage."[6] As such, HHS regulation at 45 CFR 153.400(a)(1)(iii) provides that a contributing entity must make reinsurance contributions for lives covered by its self-insured group health plans and health insurance coverage, except to the extent that such plan or coverage is expatriate health coverage, as defined by the Secretary of HHS, or for the 2015 and 2016 benefit years only, is a self-insured group health plan with respect to which enrollment is limited to participants who reside outside of their home country for at least six months of the plan year and any covered dependents of such participants. As noted in the March 8, 2013 Affordable Care Act Implementation FAQs Part XIII, Q&A-1, the FAQ definition of "expatriate health plan" was extended to the definition of "expatriate health coverage" under 45 CFR 153.400(a)(1)(iii).

Section 3(a) of the EHCCA provides that the ACA generally does not apply to expatriate health plans, employers with respect to expatriate health plans but solely in their capacity as plan sponsors of expatriate health plans, and expatriate health insurance issuers with respect to coverage offered by such issuers under expatriate health plans. Accordingly, under the EHCCA, the transitional reinsurance program contribution obligation under section 1341 of the ACA does not apply to expatriate health plans.

Section 5000A of the Code, as added by section 1501 of the ACA, provides that, for each month, taxpayers must have minimum essential coverage, qualify for a health coverage exemption, or make an individual shared responsibility payment when filing a federal income tax return. Section 5000A(f)(1)(B) of the Code provides that minimum essential coverage includes coverage under an eligible employer-sponsored plan. Section 5000A(f)(2) of the Code and 26 CFR 1.5000A-2(c) provide that an eligible employer-sponsored plan means, with respect to an employee, group health insurance coverage that is a governmental plan or any other plan or coverage offered in the small or large group market within a State, or a self-insured group health plan. Under section 5000A(f)(1)(C) of the Code, minimum essential coverage includes coverage under a health plan offered in the individual market within a State.

Section 3(b)(1)(A) of the EHCCA provides that an expatriate health plan that is offered to primary enrollees who are qualified expatriates described in sections 3(d)(3)(A) and 3(d)(3)(B) of the EHCCA is treated as an eligible employer-sponsored plan within the meaning of section 5000A(f)(2) of the Code. Section 3(b)(1)(B) of the EHCCA provides that, in the case of an expatriate health plan that is offered to primary enrollees who are qualified expatriates described in section 3(d)(3)(C) of the EHCCA, the coverage is treated as a plan in the individual market within the meaning of section 5000A(f)(1)(C) of the Code, for purposes of sections 36B, 5000A and 6055 of the Code.

Under section 6055 of the Code, as added by section 1502 of the ACA, providers of minimum essential coverage must file an information return with the Internal Revenue Service (IRS) and furnish a written statement to covered individuals reporting the months that an individual had minimum essential coverage. Under section 6056 of the Code, as added by section 1514 of the ACA, an applicable large employer (as defined in section 4980H(c)(2) of the Code and 26 CFR 54.4980H-1(a)(4) and 54.4980H-2) must file an information return with the IRS and furnish a written statement to its full-time employees reporting details regarding the minimum essential coverage, if any, offered by the employer. Under both sections 6055 and 6056 of the Code, reporting entities may satisfy the requirement to furnish statements to covered individuals and employees, respectively, by electronic means only if the individual or employee affirmatively consents to receiving the statements electronically.[7]

Under section 4980H of the Code, as added by section 1513 of the ACA, an applicable large employer that does not offer minimum essential coverage to its full-time employees (and their dependents) or offers minimum essential coverage that does not meet the standards for affordability and minimum value will owe an assessable payment if a full-time employee is certified as having enrolled in a qualified health plan on an Exchange with respect to which a premium tax credit is allowed with respect to the employee.

Section 3(b)(2) of the EHCCA provides that the reporting requirements of sections 6055 and 6056 of the Code and the provisions of section 4980H of the Code relating to the employer shared responsibility provisions for applicable large employers continue to apply with respect to expatriate health plans and qualified expatriates. Section 3(b)(2) of the EHCCA provides a special rule for the use of electronic media for statements required under sections 6055 and 6056 of the Code. Specifically, the required statements may be provided to a primary insured for coverage under an expatriate health plan using electronic media unless the primary insured has explicitly refused to consent to receive the statement electronically.

Section 4980I of the Code, as added by section 9001 of the ACA, imposes an excise tax if the aggregate cost of applicable employer-sponsored coverage provided to an employee exceeds a statutory dollar limit. Section 3(b)(2) of the EHCCA provides that section 4980I of the Code continues to apply to applicable employer-sponsored coverage (as defined in section 4980I(d)(1) of the Code) of a qualified expatriate (as described in section 3(d)(3)(A)(i) of the EHCCA) who is assigned (rather than transferred) to work in the United States.

Section 9010 of the ACA imposes a fee on covered entities engaged in the business of providing health insurance for United States health risks. Section 3(c)(1) of the EHCCA excludes expatriate health plans from the health insurance providers fee imposed by section 9010 of the ACA by providing that, for calendar years after 2015, a qualified expatriate (and any spouse, dependent, or any other individual enrolled in the plan)

(Footnote Continued)

[6] See HHS Notice of Benefit and Payment Parameters for 2014 (78 FR 15410) (March 11, 2013) and HHS Notice of Benefit and Payment Parameters for 2016 (80 FR 10750) (February 27, 2015).

[7] See 26 CFR 1.6055-2(a)(2)(i) and 301.6056-2(a)(2)(i).

enrolled in an expatriate health plan is not considered a United States health risk. Section 3(c)(2) of the EHCCA provides a special rule solely for purposes of determining the health insurance providers fee imposed by section 9010 of the ACA for the 2014 and 2015 fee years.

Section 162(m)(6) of the Code, as added by section 9014 of the ACA, in general, limits to $500,000 the allowable deduction for remuneration attributable to services performed by certain individuals for a covered health insurance provider. For taxable years beginning after December 31, 2012, section 162(m)(6)(C)(i) of the Code and 26 CFR 1.162-31(b)(4)(A) provide that a health insurance issuer is a covered health insurance provider if not less than 25 percent of the gross premiums that it receives from providing health insurance coverage during the taxable year are from minimum essential coverage. Section 3(a)(3) of the EHCCA provides that the provisions of the ACA (including section 162(m)(6) of the Code) do not apply to expatriate health insurance issuers with respect to coverage offered by such issuers under expatriate health plans.

Section 3(d)(2) of the EHCCA provides that an expatriate health plan means a group health plan, health insurance coverage offered in connection with a group health plan, or health insurance coverage offered to certain groups of similarly situated individuals, provided that the plan or coverage meets a number of specific requirements. Section 3(d)(2)(A) of the EHCCA provides that substantially all of the primary enrollees of an expatriate health plan must be qualified expatriates. For this purpose, primary enrollees do not include individuals who are not nationals of the United States and reside in the country of their citizenship. Section 3(d)(2)(B) of the EHCCA provides that substantially all of the benefits provided under a plan or coverage must be benefits that are not excepted benefits. Section 3(d)(2)(C) of the EHCCA provides that the plan or coverage must provide coverage for inpatient hospital services, outpatient facility services, physician services, and emergency services that are comparable to the emergency services coverage that was described in or offered under 5 U.S.C. 8903(1) for the 2009 plan year.[8] Also, coverage for these services must be provided in certain countries. For qualified expatriates described in section 3(d)(3)(A) of the EHCCA (category A) and qualified expatriates described in section 3(d)(3)(B) of the EHCCA (category B), coverage for these services must be provided in the country or countries where the individual is working, and such other country or countries as the Secretary of HHS, in consultation with the Secretary of the Treasury and the Secretary of Labor, may designate. For qualified expatriates who are members of a group of similarly situated individuals described in section 3(d)(3)(C) of the EHCCA (category C), the coverage must be provided in the country or countries that the Secretary of HHS, in consultation with the Secretary of the Treasury and the Secretary of Labor, may designate.

Section 3(d)(2)(D) of the EHCCA provides that a plan qualifies as an expatriate health plan under the EHCCA only if the plan sponsor reasonably believes that benefits under the plan satisfy a standard at least actuarially equivalent to the level provided for in section 36B(c)(2)(C)(ii) of the Code (that is, "minimum value"). Section 3(d)(2)(E) of the EHCCA provides that dependent coverage of children, if offered under the expatriate health plan, must continue to be available until the individual attains age 26 (unless the individual is the child of a child receiving dependent coverage). Section 3(d)(2)(G) of the EHCCA provides that an expatriate health plan must satisfy the provisions of title XXVII of the PHS Act, Chapter 100 of the Code, and part 7 of subtitle B of title I of ERISA, that would otherwise apply if the ACA had not been enacted. These provisions are sometimes referred to as the HIPAA portability and nondiscrimination requirements.

Section 3(d)(1) of the EHCCA provides that an expatriate health insurance issuer means a health insurance issuer that issues expatriate health plans. Section 3(d)(2)(F)(i) of the EHCCA provides that an expatriate health plan or coverage must be issued by an expatriate health plan issuer, or administered by an administrator, that together with any person in the issuer's or administrator's controlled group: (1) maintains network provider agreements that provide for direct claims payments (directly or through third-party contracts), with health care providers in eight or more countries; (2) maintains call centers (directly or through third-party contracts) in three or more countries and accepts calls in eight or more languages; (3) processes at least $ 1 million in claims in foreign currency equivalents each year; (4) makes global evacuation/repatriation coverage available; (5) maintains legal and compliance resources in three or more countries; and (6) has licenses to sell insurance in more than two countries. In addition, section 3(d)(2)(F)(ii) of the EHCCA provides that the plan or coverage must offer reimbursement for items or services under such plan or coverage in the local currency in eight or more countries.

Section 3(d)(3) of the EHCCA describes three categories of qualified expatriates. A category A qualified expatriate, under section 3(d)(3)(A) of the EHCCA, is an individual whose skills, qualifications, job duties, or expertise has caused the individual's employer to transfer or assign the individual to the United States for a specific and temporary purpose or assignment tied to the individual's employment and who the plan sponsor has reasonably determined requires access to health insurance and other related services and support in multiple countries, and is offered other multinational benefits on a periodic basis (such as tax equalization, compensation for cross-border moving expenses, or compensation to enable the expatriate to return to the expatriate's home country). A category B qualified expatriate, under section 3(d)(3)(B) of the EHCCA, is a primary insured who is working outside the United States for at least 180 days during a consecutive 12-month period that overlaps with the plan year. A category C qualified expatriate, under section 3(d)(3)(C) of the EHCCA, is an individual who is a member of a group of similarly situated individuals that is formed for the purpose of traveling or relocating internationally in service of one or more of the purposes listed in section 501(c)(3) or (4) of the Code, or similarly situated organizations or groups, provided the group is not formed primarily for the sale of health insurance coverage and the Secretary of HHS, in consultation with the Secretary of the Treasury and the Secretary of Labor, determines the group requires access to health insurance and other related services and support in multiple countries.

Section 3(d)(4) of the EHCCA defines the United States as the 50 States, the District of Columbia, and Puerto Rico.

Section 3(f) of the EHCCA provides that, unless otherwise specified, the requirements of the EHCCA apply to expatriate health plans issued or renewed on or after July 1, 2015.

IRS Notice 2015-43

On July 20, 2015, the Treasury Department and the IRS issued Notice 2015-43 (2015-29 IRB 73) to provide interim guidance on the implementation of the EHCCA and the application of certain provisions of the ACA to expatriate health insurance issuers, expatriate health plans, and employers in their capacity as plan sponsors of expatriate health plans. The Departments of Labor and HHS reviewed and concurred with the interim guidance of Notice 2015-43. Comments were received in response to Notice 2015-43, and these comments have been considered in drafting these proposed regulations. The relevant portions of Notice 2015-43 and the related comments are discussed in the Overview of Proposed Regulations section of this preamble.[9]

IRS Notices 2015-29 and 2016-14

On March 30, 2015, the Treasury Department and the IRS issued Notice 2015-29 (2015-15 IRB 873) to provide guidance implementing the special rule of section 3(c)(2) of the EHCCA for fee years 2014 and 2015 with respect to the health insurance providers fee imposed by section 9010 of the ACA. Notice 2015-29 defines expatriate health plan by reference to the definition of expatriate policies in the MLR final rule issued by HHS[10] (MLR final rule definition) solely for the purpose of applying the special rule for fee years 2014 and 2015. The Treasury Department and the IRS determined that the MLR final rule definition of expatriate policies was sufficiently broad to cover potential expatriate health plans described in section 3(d)(2) of the EHCCA. The MLR final rule defines expatriate policies as predominantly group health insurance policies that provide

---

[8] These are emergency services comparable to emergency services offered under a government-wide comprehensive health plan under the Federal Employees Health Benefits (FEHB) program prior to the enactment of the ACA.

[9] See 26 CFR 601.601(d)(2)(ii)(B).

[10] 45 CFR 158.120(d)(4).

coverage to employees, substantially all of whom are: (1) working outside their country of citizenship; (2) working outside their country of citizenship and outside the employer's country of domicile; or (3) non-U.S. citizens working in their home country.

On January 29, 2016, the Treasury Department and the IRS issued Notice 2016-14 (2016-7 IRB 315) to provide guidance implementing the definition of expatriate health plan for fee year 2016 with respect to the health insurance providers fee imposed by section 9010 of the ACA. Like Notice 2015-29, Notice 2016-14 provides that the definition of expatriate health plan will be the same as provided in the MLR final rule definition, solely for the purpose of the health insurance providers fee imposed by section 9010 of the ACA for fee year 2016.[11]

The Consolidated Appropriations Act, 2016, Public Law 114-113, Division P, Title II, §201, Moratorium on Annual Fee on Health Insurance Providers (the Consolidated Appropriations Act), suspends collection of the health insurance providers fee for the 2017 calendar year. Thus, health insurance issuers are not required to pay the fee for 2017.

Excepted Benefits

Sections 2722 and 2763 of the PHS Act, section 732 of ERISA, and section 9831 of the Code provide that the respective requirements of title XXVII of the PHS Act, part 7 of ERISA, and Chapter 100 of the Code generally do not apply to the provision of certain types of benefits, known as "excepted benefits." These excepted benefits are described in section 2791(c) of the PHS Act, section 733(c) of ERISA, and section 9832(c) of the Code.

There are four statutorily enumerated categories of excepted benefits. One category, under section 2791(c)(1) of the PHS Act, section 733(c)(1) of ERISA, and section 9832(c)(1) of the Code, identifies benefits that are excepted in all circumstances, including automobile insurance, liability insurance, workers compensation, and accidental death and dismemberment coverage. Under section 2791(c)(1)(H) of the PHS Act (and the parallel provisions of ERISA and the Code), this category of excepted benefits also includes "[o]ther similar insurance coverage, specified in regulations, under which benefits for medical care are secondary or incidental to other insurance benefits."

The second category of excepted benefits is limited excepted benefits, which may include limited scope vision or dental benefits, and benefits for long-term care, nursing home care, home health care, or community-based care. Section 2791(c)(2)(C) of the PHS Act, section 733(c)(2)(C) of ERISA, and section 9832(c)(2)(C) of the Code authorize the Secretaries of HHS, Labor, and the Treasury (collectively, the Secretaries) to issue regulations establishing other, similar limited benefits as excepted benefits. The Secretaries exercised this authority previously with respect to certain health flexible spending arrangements.[12] To be an excepted benefit under this second category, the statute provides that these limited benefits must either: (1) be provided under a separate policy, certificate, or contract of insurance; or (2) otherwise not be an integral part of a group health plan, whether insured or self-insured.[13]

The third category of excepted benefits, referred to as "noncoordinated excepted benefits," includes both coverage for only a specified disease or illness (such as cancer-only policies), and hospital indemnity or other fixed indemnity insurance. These benefits are excepted under section 2722(c)(2) of the PHS Act, section 732(c)(2) of ERISA, and section 9831(c)(2) of the Code only if all of the following conditions are met: (1) the benefits are provided under a separate policy, certificate, or contract of insurance; (2) there is no coordination between the provision of such benefits and any exclusion of benefits under any group health plan maintained by the same plan sponsor; and (3) the benefits are paid with respect to any event without regard to whether benefits are provided under any group health plan maintained by the same plan sponsor. In the group market, the regulations further provide that to be hospital indemnity or other fixed indemnity insurance, the insurance must pay a fixed dollar amount per day (or per other time period) of hospitalization or illness (for example, $100/day) regardless of the amount of expenses incurred.[14]

Since the issuance of these regulations, the Departments have released FAQs to address various requests for clarification as to what types of coverage meet the conditions necessary to be hospital indemnity or other fixed indemnity insurance that are excepted benefits. Affordable Care Act Implementation FAQs Part XI, Q&A-7 clarified that group health insurance coverage in which benefits are provided in varying amounts based on the type of procedure or item, such as the type of surgery actually performed or prescription drug provided is not a hospital indemnity or other fixed indemnity insurance excepted benefit because it does not meet the condition that benefits be provided on a per day (or per other time period, such as per week) basis, regardless of the amount of expenses incurred.[15]

The fourth category, under section 2791(c)(4) of the PHS Act, section 733(c)(4) of ERISA, and section 9832(c)(4) of the Code, is supplemental excepted benefits. Benefits are supplemental excepted benefits only if they are provided under a separate policy, certificate, or contract of insurance and are Medicare supplemental health insurance (also known as Medigap), TRICARE supplemental programs, or "similar supplemental coverage provided to coverage under a group health plan." The phrase "similar supplemental coverage provided to coverage under a group health plan" is not defined in the statute or regulations. However, the Departments' regulations clarify that one requirement to be similar supplemental coverage is that the coverage "must be specifically designed to fill gaps in primary coverage, such as coinsurance or deductibles."[16]

In 2007 and 2008, the Departments issued guidance on the circumstances under which supplemental health insurance would be considered excepted benefits under section 2791(c)(4) of the PHS Act (and the parallel provisions of ERISA, and the Code).[17] The guidance identifies several factors the Departments will apply when evaluating whether supplemental health insurance will be considered to be "similar supplemental coverage provided to coverage under a group health plan." Specifically the Departments' guidance provides that supplemental health insurance will be considered an excepted benefit if it is provided through a policy, certificate, or contract of insurance separate from the primary coverage under the plan and meets all of the following requirements: (1) the supplemental policy, certificate, or contract of insurance is issued by an entity that does not provide the primary coverage under the plan; (2) the supplemental policy, certificate, or contract of insurance is specifically designed to fill gaps in primary coverage, such as coinsurance or deductibles, but does not include a policy, certificate, or contract of insurance that becomes secondary or supplemental only under a coordination of benefits provision; (3) the cost of the supplemental coverage is 15 percent or less of the cost of primary coverage (determined in the same manner as the applicable premium is calculated under a COBRA continuation provision); and (4) the supplemental coverage sold in the group health insurance market does not differentiate among individuals in eligibility, benefits, or premiums based upon any health factor of the individual (or any dependents of the individual).

On February 13, 2015, the Departments issued Affordable Care Act Implementation FAQs Part XXIII, providing additional guidance on the circumstances under which health insurance coverage that supplements group health plan coverage may be considered supplemental excepted benefits.[18] The FAQ states that the Departments intend to propose regulations clarifying the circumstances under which supplemental insurance products that do not fill in cost-sharing under the primary plan are considered to be specifically designed to fill gaps in primary coverage.

---

[11] See 26 CFR 601.601(d)(2)(ii)(B).

[12] 26 CFR 54.9831-1(c)(3)(v), 29 CFR 2590.732(c)(3)(v), 45 CFR 146.145(b)(3)(v).

[13] PHS Act section 2722(c)(1), ERISA section 732(c)(1), Code section 9831(c)(1).

[14] 26 CFR 54.9831-1(c)(4)(i), 29 CFR 2590.732(c)(4)(i), 45 CFR 146.145(b)(4)(i).

[15] Frequently Asked Questions about Affordable Care Act Implementation (Part XI), available at http://www.dol.gov/ebsa/faqs/faq-aca11.html and http://www.cms.gov/CCIIO/Resources/Fact-Sheets-and-FAQs/aca_implementation_faqs11.html.

[16] 26 CFR 54.9831-1(c)(5)(i)(C), 29 CFR 2590.732(c)(5)(i)(C), and 45 CFR 146.145(b)(5)(i)(C)

[17] See EBSA Field Assistance Bulletin No. 2007-04 (available at http://www.dol.gov/ebsa/regs/fab2007-4.html); CMS Insurance Standards Bulletin 08-01 (available at http://www.cms.gov/CCIIO/Resources/Files/Downloads/hipaa_08_01_508.pdf); and IRS Notice 2008-23 (available at http://www.irs.gov/irb/2008-07_IRB/ar09.html).

[18] Frequently Asked Questions about Affordable Care Act Implementation (Part XXIII), available at http://www.dol.gov/ebsa/pdf/faq-aca23.pdf and https://www.cms.gov/CCIIO/Resources/Fact-Sheets-and-FAQs/Downloads/Supplmental-FAQ_2-13-15-final.pdf.

Specifically, the FAQ provides that health insurance coverage that supplements group health coverage by providing coverage of additional categories of benefits (as opposed to filling in cost-sharing gaps under the primary plan) would be considered to be designed to "fill in the gaps" of the primary coverage only if the benefits covered by the supplemental insurance product are not essential health benefits (EHB) in the State in which the product is being marketed. The FAQ further states that, until regulations are issued and effective, the Departments will not take enforcement action under certain conditions for failure to comply with the applicable insurance market reforms with respect to group or individual health insurance coverage that provides coverage of additional categories of benefits that are not EHBs in the applicable State. States were encouraged to exercise similar enforcement discretion.

Short-Term, Limited-Duration Insurance Coverage

Short-term limited duration insurance is a type of health insurance coverage that is designed to fill in temporary gaps in coverage when an individual is transitioning from one plan or coverage to another plan or coverage. Although short-term, limited-duration insurance is not an excepted benefit, it is similarly exempt from PHS Act requirements because it is not individual health insurance coverage. Section 2791(b)(5) of the PHS Act provides that the term "individual health insurance coverage" means health insurance coverage offered to individuals in the individual market, but does not include short-term, limited-duration insurance. The PHS Act does not define short-term, limited-duration insurance. Under existing regulations, short-term, limited-duration insurance means "health insurance coverage provided pursuant to a contract with an issuer that has an expiration date specified in the contract (taking into account any extensions that may be elected by the policyholder without the issuer's consent) that is less than 12 months after the original effective date of the contract."[19]

Prohibition on Lifetime and Annual Limits

Section 2711 of the PHS Act, as added by the ACA, generally prohibits group health plans and health insurance issuers offering group or individual health insurance coverage from imposing lifetime and annual dollar limits on EHB, as defined in section 1302(b) of the ACA. These prohibitions apply to both grandfathered and non-grandfathered health plans, except the annual limits prohibition does not apply to grandfathered individual health insurance coverage.

Under the ACA, self-insured group health plans, large group market health plans, and grandfathered health plans are not required to offer EHB, but they generally cannot place lifetime or annual dollar limits on covered services that are considered EHB. The Departments' regulations provide that, for plan years (in the individual market, policy years) beginning on or after January 1, 2017, a plan or issuer that is not required to provide EHB may select from among any of the 51 base-benchmark plans selected by a State or applied by default pursuant to 45 CFR 156.100, or one of the three FEHBP options specified at 45 CFR 156.100(a)(3), for purposes of complying with the lifetime and annual limits prohibition in section 2711 of the PHS Act.[20]

II. Overview of the Proposed Regulations

A. Expatriate Health Plans

In General

Section 3(a) of the EHCCA provides that the ACA generally does not apply to expatriate health plans, employers with respect to expatriate health plans but solely in their capacity as plan sponsors of expatriate health plans, and expatriate health insurance issuers with respect to coverage offered by such issuers under expatriate health plans. Consistent with this provision, the proposed regulations provide that the market reform provisions enacted or amended as part of the ACA, included in sections 2701 through 2728 of the PHS Act and incorporated into section 9815 of the Code and section 715 of ERISA, do not apply to an expatriate health plan, an employer, solely in its capacity as plan sponsor of an expatriate health plan, and an expatriate health insurance issuer with respect to coverage under an expatriate health plan. Similarly, section 162(m)(6) of the Code does not apply to an expatriate health insurance issuer with respect to premiums received for coverage under an expatriate health plan. In addition, under the EHCCA, the PCORTF fee under sections 4375 and 4376 of the Code and the transitional reinsurance program fee under section 1341 of the ACA do not apply to expatriate health plans. The EHCCA excludes expatriate health plans from the health insurance providers fee imposed by section 9010 except that the EHCCA provides a special rule solely for purposes of determining the fee for the 2014 and 2015 fee years. The EHCCA also designates certain coverage by an expatriate health plan as minimum essential coverage under section 5000A(f) of the Code, and provides special rules for the application of the reporting rules under sections 6055 and 6056 of the Code to expatriate health plans.

Definition of Expatriate Health Insurance Issuer

Consistent with sections 3(d)(1) and (d)(2)(F) of the EHCCA, the proposed regulations define "expatriate health insurance issuer" as a health insurance issuer (as defined under 26 CFR 54.9801-2, 29 CFR 2590.701-2 and 45 CFR 144.103) that issues expatriate health plans and satisfies certain requirements.[21] The requirements for the issuer to be an expatriate health insurance issuer include that, in the course of its normal business operations, the issuer: (1) maintains network provider agreements that provide for direct claims payments with health care providers in eight or more countries; (2) maintains call centers in three or more countries, and accepts calls from customers in eight or more languages; (3) processed at least $1 million in claims in foreign currency equivalents during the preceding calendar year; (4) makes global evacuation/repatriation coverage available; (5) maintains legal and compliance resources in three or more countries; and (6) has licenses or other authority to sell insurance in more than two countries, including the United States. For purposes of meeting the $1 million threshold for claims processed in foreign currency equivalents, the proposed regulations provide that the dollar value of claims processed is determined using the Treasury Department's currency exchange rate in effect on the last day of the preceding calendar year.[22] Comments are requested regarding whether use of the calendar year as the basis for measuring the dollar amount of claims processed presents administrative challenges, and how the resulting challenges, if any, may be addressed. The proposed regulations provide that each of the applicable requirements may be satisfied by two or more entities (including one entity that is the health insurance issuer) that are members of the health insurance issuer's controlled group or through contracts between the expatriate health insurance issuer and third parties.

Definition of Expatriate Health Plan

Consistent with section 3(d)(2) of the EHCCA, the proposed regulations define "expatriate health plan" as a plan offered to qualified expatriates and that satisfies certain requirements. With respect to qualified expatriates in categories A or B, the plan must be a group health plan (whether or not insured). In contrast, with respect to qualified expatriates in category C, the plan must be health insurance coverage that is not a group health

---

[19] 26 CFR 54.9801-2, 29 CFR 2590.701-2, 45 CFR 144.103.

[20] 26 CFR 54.9815-2711(c), 29 CFR 2590.715-2711(c), 45 CFR 147.126(c).

[21] Section 3(d)(1) of the EHCCA provides that the term "expatriate health insurance issuer" means a health insurance issuer that issues expatriate health plans; section 3(d)(5)(A) of the EHCCA provides that the term "health insurance issuer" has the meaning given in section 2791 of the PHS Act. The definition of health insurance issuer in section 9832(b)(2) of the Code and section 733(b)(2) of ERISA and underlying

regulations are substantively identical to the definition under section 2791 of the PHS Act and its underlying regulations. As discussed in the section of this preamble entitled "Definition of Expatriate Health Plan" a health insurance issuer as defined in section 2791 of the PHS Act is limited to an entity licensed to engage in the business of insurance in a State and subject to State law that regulates insurance.

[22] The most recent Treasury Department currency exchange rate can be found at https://www.fiscal.treasury.gov/fsreports/rpt/treasRptRateExch/currentRates.htm.

plan. In addition, consistent with section 3(d)(2)(A) of the EHCCA, the proposed regulations require that substantially all primary enrollees in the expatriate health plan must be qualified expatriates. The proposed regulations define a primary enrollee as the individual covered by the plan or policy whose eligibility for coverage is not due to that individual's status as the spouse, dependent, or other beneficiary of another covered individual. However, notwithstanding this definition, an individual is not a primary enrollee if the individual is not a national of the United States and the individual resides in his or her country of citizenship. Further, the proposed regulations provide that, for this purpose, a "national of the United States" has the meaning used in the Immigration and Nationality Act (8 U.S.C. 1101 et. seq.) and 8 CFR parts 301 to 392, including U.S. citizens. Thus, for example, an individual born in American Samoa is a national of the United States at birth for purposes of the EHCCA and the proposed regulations.

Comments in response to Notice 2015-43 requested clarification of the "substantially all" enrollment requirement, with one comment suggesting that 93 percent of the enrollees would be an appropriate threshold. In response to the request for clarification, the proposed regulations provide that a plan satisfies the "substantially all" enrollment requirement if, on the first day of the plan year, less than 5 percent of the primary enrollees (or less than 5 primary enrollees if greater) are not qualified expatriates (effectively a 95 percent threshold). Consistent with section 3(d)(2)(B) of the EHCCA, the proposed regulations further provide that substantially all of the benefits provided under an expatriate health plan must be benefits that are not excepted benefits as described in 26 CFR 54.9831-1(c), 29 CFR 2590.732(c), 45 CFR 146.145(b) and 148.220, as applicable. The Departments intend that the first day of the plan year approach, which has been used in other contexts, will be simple to administer.[23] Moreover, the 95% threshold has been used in certain other circumstances in applying a "substantially all" standard.[24] The Departments solicit comment on this regulatory approach and whether the current regulatory language is sufficient to protect against potential abuses, or whether any further anti-abuse provision is necessary.

Consistent with section 3(d)(2)(C) of the EHCCA, the proposed regulations also require that an expatriate health plan cover certain types of services. Specifically, an expatriate health plan must provide coverage for inpatient hospital services, outpatient facility services, physician services, and emergency services (comparable to emergency services coverage that was described in and offered under section 8903(1) of title 5, United States Code for plan year 2009). Coverage for such services must be available in certain countries depending on the type of qualified expatriates covered by the plan. The statute authorizes the Secretary of HHS, in consultation with the Secretary of the Treasury and Secretary of Labor, to designate other countries where coverage for such services must be made available to the qualified expatriate.

Consistent with section 3(d)(2)(D) of the EHCCA, the proposed regulations provide that in the case of an expatriate health plan, the plan sponsor must reasonably believe that benefits provided by the plan satisfy the minimum value requirements of section 36B(c)(2)(C)(ii) of the Code.[25] For this purpose, the proposed regulations provide that the plan sponsor is permitted to rely on the reasonable representations of the issuer or administrator regarding whether benefits offered by the group health plan or issuer satisfy the minimum value requirements unless the plan sponsor knows or has reason to know that the benefits fail to satisfy the minimum value requirements. Consistent with section 3(d)(2)(D) of the EHCCA, in the case of an expatriate health plan that provides dependent coverage of children, the proposed regulations provide that such coverage must be available until the individual attains age 26, unless the individual is the child of a child receiving dependent coverage. Additionally, consistent with section 3(d)(2)(F)(ii) of the EHCCA, the plan or coverage must offer reimbursements for items or services in the local currency in eight or more countries.

Consistent with section 3(d)(2)(F) of the EHCCA, the proposed regulations also provide that the policy or coverage under an expatriate health plan must be issued by an expatriate health insurance issuer or administered by an expatriate health plan administrator. With respect to qualified expatriates in categories A or B (generally, individuals whose travel or relocation is related to their employment with an employer), the coverage must be under a group health plan (whether insured or self-insured). With respect to qualified expatriates in category C (generally, groups of similarly situated individuals travelling for certain tax-exempt purposes), the coverage must be under a policy issued by an expatriate health insurance issuer.

Finally, consistent with section 3(d)(2)(G) of the EHCCA, the proposed regulations provide that an expatriate health plan must satisfy the provisions of Chapter 100 of the Code, part 7 of subtitle B of title I of ERISA and title XXVII of the PHS Act that would otherwise apply if the ACA had not been enacted. Among other requirements, those provisions limited the ability of a group health plan or group health insurance issuer to impose preexisting condition exclusions (which are now prohibited for grandfathered and non-grandfathered group health plans and health insurance coverage offered in connection with such plans, and non-grandfathered individual health insurance coverage under the ACA), including a requirement that the period of any preexisting condition exclusion be reduced by the length of any period of creditable coverage the individual had without a 63-day break in coverage.

Prior to the enactment of the ACA, HIPAA and underlying regulations also generally required that plans and issuers provide certificates of creditable coverage when an individual ceased to be covered by a plan or policy and upon request. Following the enactment of the ACA, the regulations under these provisions have eliminated the requirement for providing certificates of creditable coverage beginning December 31, 2014, because the requirement is generally no longer relevant to plans and participants as a result of the prohibition on preexisting condition exclusions. The Departments recognize that reimposing the requirement to provide certificates of creditable coverage on expatriate health plans would only be useful in situations in which an individual transferred from one expatriate health plan to another and that reimposing the requirement on all health plans would require certificates that would be unnecessary except in limited cases, such as for an individual who ceased coverage with a health plan or policy and began coverage under an expatriate health plan that imposed a preexisting condition exclusion. Because reimposing the requirement to provide certificates of creditable coverage would be inefficient and overly broad, and relevant in only limited circumstances, the proposed regulations do not require expatriate health plans to provide certificates of creditable coverage. However, expatriate health plans imposing a preexisting condition exclusion must still comply with certain limitations on preexisting condition exclusions that would otherwise apply if the ACA had not been enacted. Therefore, the proposed regulations require expatriate health plans to ensure that individuals who enroll in the expatriate health plan are provided an opportunity to demonstrate creditable coverage to offset any preexisting condition exclusion. For example, an email from the prior issuer (or former plan administrator or plan sponsor) providing information about past coverage could be sufficient confirmation of prior creditable coverage.

Comments in response to Notice 2015-43 requested clarification of the treatment of health coverage provided by a foreign government. Specifically, comments requested that health coverage provided by a foreign government be treated as minimum essential coverage under section 5000A of the Code, and that, for purposes of the employer shared responsibility provision of section 4980H of the Code, an offer of such coverage be treated as an offer of minimum essential coverage for certain foreign employees working in the United States. These issues are generally beyond the scope of these proposed regulations. Under the existing regulations under section 5000A(f)(1)(E) of the Code, there are procedures for health benefits coverage not otherwise designated under section 5000A(f)(1) of the Code as minimum essential coverage to be recognized by the Secretary of HHS, in coordination with the Secretary of the Treasury, as minimum essential coverage. The Secretary of HHS has provided that coverage under a group health plan provided through insurance regulated by a foreign government is minimum essential coverage for expatriates who meet

---

[23] 26 CFR 54.9831-1(b), 29 CFR 2590.732(b), 45 CFR 146.145(b).

[24] See e.g., 26 CFR 1.460-6(d)(4)(i)(D)(1).

[25] For this purpose, generally "minimum value" takes into account the provision of "essential health benefits" as defined in section 1302(b)(1) of the Affordable Care Act.

specified conditions.[26] Furthermore, plan sponsors of health coverage that is not recognized as minimum essential coverage through statute, regulation, or guidance may submit an application to CMS for minimum essential coverage recognition pursuant to 45 CFR 156.604.[27] For a complete list of coverage recognized by CMS as minimum essential coverage under section 5000A(f)(1)(E) of the Code, see https://www.cms.gov/CCIIO/Programs-and-Initiatives/Health-Insurance-Market-Reforms/minimum-essential-coverage.html.

Comments also requested that policies sold by non-United States health insurance issuers be treated as minimum essential coverage under section 5000A of the Code, or as expatriate health plans. Section 3(d)(5)(A) of the EHCCA specifies that the terms "health insurance issuer" and "health insurance coverage" have the meanings given those terms by section 2791 of the PHS Act. Section 2791 of the PHS Act (and parallel provisions in section 9832(b) of the Code and section 733(b) of ERISA) define those terms by reference to an entity licensed to engage in the business of insurance in a State and subject to State law that regulates insurance. Under section 2791 of the PHS Act, the term "State" means each of the several States, the District of Columbia, Puerto Rico, the Virgin Islands, Guam, American Samoa, and the Northern Mariana Islands. Consistent with those provisions, these proposed regulations limit an expatriate health insurance issuer to a health insurance issuer within the meaning of those sections (and that meets the other requirements set forth in the proposed regulations). As such, a non-United States health insurance issuer does not qualify as an expatriate health insurance issuer within the meaning of the EHCCA, and coverage issued by a non-United States issuer that is not otherwise minimum essential coverage is not minimum essential coverage pursuant to the EHCCA.

Definition of Expatriate Health Plan Administrator

The proposed regulations define "expatriate health plan administrator," with respect to self-insured coverage, as an administrator of self-insured coverage that generally satisfies the same requirements as an "expatriate health insurance issuer."

Definition of Qualified Expatriate

Consistent with section 3(d)(3) of the EHCCA, the proposed regulations define "qualified expatriate" as one of three types of individuals. The first type of qualified expatriate, a category A expatriate, is an individual who has the skills, qualifications, job duties, or expertise that has caused the individual's employer to transfer or assign the individual to the United States for a specific and temporary purpose or assignment that is tied to the individual's employment with the employer. A category A expatriate may only be an individual who: (1) the plan sponsor has reasonably determined requires access to health coverage and other related services and support in multiple countries, (2) is offered other multinational benefits on a periodic basis (such as tax equalization, compensation for cross-border moving expenses, or compensation to enable the individual to return to the individual's home country), and (3) is not a national of the United States. The proposed regulations provide that an individual who is not expected to travel outside the United States at least one time per year during the coverage period would not reasonably "require access" to health coverage and other related services and support in multiple countries. Furthermore, under the proposed regulations, the offer of a one-time *de minimis* benefit would not meet the standard for the "periodic" offer of "other multinational benefits."

Section 3(d)(3)(B) of the EHCCA provides that a second type of qualified expatriate, a category B expatriate, is an individual who works outside the United States for a period of at least 180 days in a consecutive 12-month period that overlaps with the plan year. A comment requested that the regulations clarify that the 12-month period could either be within a single plan year, or across two consecutive plan years. Consistent with the statutory language, the proposed regulations provide that a category B expatriate is an individual who is a national of the United States and who works outside the United States for at least 180 days in a consecutive 12-month period that is within a single plan year, or across two consecutive plan years. Section 3(d)(2)(C)(ii) of the EHCCA requires an expatriate health plan provided to category B expatriates to cover certain specified services, such as inpatient and outpatient services, in the country in which the individual is "present in connection" with his employment. The Departments request comments on whether it would be helpful to provide further administrative clarification of this statutory language regarding the country or countries in which the services must be provided, and, if so, whether there are facts or circumstances that will present particular challenges in applying this rule.

Finally, consistent with section 3(d)(3)(C) of the EHCCA, the proposed regulations provide that a third type of qualified expatriate, a category C expatriate, is an individual who is a member of a group of similarly situated individuals that is formed for the purpose of traveling or relocating internationally in service of one or more of the purposes listed in section 501(c)(3) or (4) of the Code, or similarly situated organizations or groups, and meets certain other conditions.[28] A category C expatriate does not include an individual in a group that is formed primarily for the sale or purchase of health insurance coverage. To qualify as this type of qualified expatriate, the Secretary of HHS, in consultation with the Secretary of the Treasury and the Secretary of Labor, must determine that the group requires access to health coverage and other related services and support in multiple countries. The proposed regulations clarify that a category C expatriate does not include an individual whose international travel or relocation is related to employment. Thus, an individual whose travel is employment-related may be a qualified expatriate only in category A or B. The proposed regulations also provide that, in the case of a group organized to travel or relocate outside the United States, the individual must be expected to travel or reside outside the United States for at least 180 days in a consecutive 12-month period that overlaps with the policy year (or in the case of a policy year that is less than 12 months, at least half of the policy year), and in the case of a group organized to travel or relocate within the United States, the individual must be expected to travel or reside in the United States for not more than 12 months. The proposed regulations provide that a group of category C expatriates must also meet the test for having associational ties under section 2791(d)(3)(B) through (F) of the PHS Act (42 U.S.C. 300gg-91(d)(3)(B) through (F)).

For purposes of section 3(d)(3)(C)(iii) of the EHCCA, the proposed regulations provide that the Secretary of HHS, in consultation with the Secretary of the Treasury and the Secretary of Labor, has determined that, in the case of a group of similarly situated individuals that meets all of the criteria in the proposed regulations, the group requires access to health coverage and other related services and support in multiple countries.

Comments in response to Notice 2015-43 requested that category C expatriates not be limited to individuals expected to travel or reside in the United States for 12 or fewer months. While the EHCCA does not include a time limit for category C expatriates, section 3(e) of the EHCCA provides that the Departments "may promulgate regulations necessary to carry out this Act, including such rules as may be necessary to prevent inappropriate expansion of the exclusions under the Act from applicable laws and regulations." In the group market, the EHCCA and the proposed regulations define a category A expatriate with respect to a "specific and temporary purpose or assignment" tied to the individual's employment in the United States. It is the view of HHS, in consultation with the Departments of Labor and the Treasury, that similar safeguards are necessary in the individual market to prevent inappropriate expansion of the exception for category C expatriates.

Comments are requested on all aspects of the proposed definition of a category C expatriate. Comments are also requested on the time limit for category C expatriates being expected to travel or reside in the United States, and what standards, if any, may be adopted in lieu of the 12-month

---

[26] See CMS Insurance Standards Bulletin Series. CCIIO Sub-Regulatory Guidance: Process for Obtaining Recognition as Minimum Essential Coverage (Oct. 31, 2013), available at https://www.cms.gov/CCIIO/Resources/Regulations-and-Guidance/Downloads/mec-guidance-10-31-2013.pdf.

[27] See CMS Insurance Standards Bulletin Series. CCIIO Sub-Regulatory Guidance: Process for Obtaining Recognition as Minimum Essential Coverage (Oct. 31, 2013), available at https://www.cms.gov/CCIIO/Resources/Regulations-and-Guidance/

Downloads/mec-guidance-10-31-2013.pdf. See also CMS Insurance Standards Bulletin Series. CCIIO Sub-Regulatory Guidance: Minimum Essential Coverage

[28] Code section 501(c)(3) describes an organization formed for religious, charitable, scientific, public safety, literary, or educational purposes, or to foster national or international amateur sports competition, or for the prevention of cruelty to children or animals, and not for political candidate campaign or legislative purposes or propaganda. Code section 501(c)(4) describes an organization operated exclusively for the promotion of social welfare.

maximum that would ensure that the definition does not permit inappropriate expansion of the exception. For example, comments are requested on whether a "specific and temporary purpose" standard should be adopted for category C expatriates, consistent with the standard for category A expatriates, or whether category C expatriates should be expected to seek medical care outside the United States at least one time per year in order to be considered to reasonably require access to health coverage and other related services and support in multiple countries. Comments are also requested on the proposed standard with respect to category C expatriates being expected to travel or reside outside the United States for at least 180 days in a consecutive 12-month period that overlaps with the policy year, and whether there are fact patterns in which the 12-month period could either be within a single policy year, or across two consecutive policy years.

Definitions of Group Health Plan and United States

Consistent with section 3(d)(5)(A) of the EHCCA, for purposes of applying the definition of expatriate health plan, "group health plan" means a group health plan as defined under 26 CFR 54.9831-1(a)(1), 29 CFR 2590.732(a)(1) or 45 CFR 146.145(a)(1), as applicable. Consistent with section 3(d)(4) of the EHCCA, the proposed regulations define "United States" to mean the 50 States, the District of Columbia and Puerto Rico.

Section 9010 of the ACA

Section 3(c)(1) of the EHCCA provides that, for purposes of the health insurance providers fee imposed by section 9010 of the ACA, a qualified expatriate enrolled in an expatriate health plan is not a United States health risk for calendar years after 2015. Section 3(c)(2) of the EHCCA provides a special rule applicable to calendar years 2014 and 2015. The Treasury Department and the IRS issued Notices 2015-29 and 2016-14 to address the definition of expatriate health plan for purposes of the health insurance providers fee imposed by section 9010 for the 2014, 2015, and 2016 fee years. No fee is due in the 2017 fee year because the Consolidated Appropriations Act suspends collection of the health insurance providers fee imposed by section 9010 of ACA for 2017.

These proposed regulations provide that, for any fee that is due on or after the date final regulations are published in the Federal Register, a qualified expatriate enrolled in an expatriate health plan as defined in these proposed regulations is not a United States health risk. These proposed regulations also authorize the IRS to specify in guidance in the Internal Revenue Bulletin the manner of determining excluded premiums for qualified expatriates in expatriate health plans. Until the date the final regulations are published in the Federal Register, taxpayers may rely on these proposed regulations with respect to any fee that is due beginning with the 2018 fee year.

Federal Tax Provision: Section 162(m)(6) of the Code

Section 162(m)(6) of the Code, as added by section 9014 of the ACA, in general, limits to $500,000 the allowable deduction for remuneration attributable to services performed by certain individuals for a covered health insurance provider. For taxable years beginning after December 31, 2012, section 162(m)(6)(C)(i) of the Code and 26 CFR 1.162-31(b)(4)(A) provide that a health insurance issuer is a covered health insurance provider if not less than 25 percent of the gross premiums that it receives from providing health insurance coverage during the taxable year are from minimum essential coverage. Section 3(a)(3) of the EHCCA provides that the provisions of the ACA (which include section 162(m)(6) of the Code) do not apply to expatriate health insurance issuers with respect to coverage offered by such issuers under expatriate health plans. Consistent with this rule, the proposed regulations exclude from the definition of the term "premium" for purposes of section 162(m)(6) of the Code amounts received in payment for coverage under an expatriate health plan. As a result, those amounts received are included in neither the numerator nor the denominator for purposes of determining whether the 25 percent standard under section 162(m)(6)(C)(i) of the Code and 26 CFR 1.162-31(b)(4)(A) is met, and they have no impact on whether a particular issuer is a covered health insurance provider.

Federal Tax Provision: Section 4980I of the Code

Section 3(b)(2) of the EHCCA provides that section 4980I of the Code applies to employer-sponsored coverage of a qualified expatriate who is assigned, rather than transferred, to work in the United States. As amended by section 101 of Division P of the Consolidated Appropriations Act, section 4980I of the Code first applies to coverage provided in taxable years beginning after December 31, 2019. Comments in response to Notice 2015-43 requested additional guidance on what it means for an employer to assign rather than transfer an employee. These proposed regulations do not address the interaction of the EHCCA and section 4980I of the Code because the Treasury Department and the IRS anticipate that this issue will be addressed in future guidance promulgated under section 4980I of the Code.

Federal Tax Provision: Section 5000A of the Code and Minimum Essential Coverage

The proposed regulations provide that, beginning January 1, 2017, coverage under an expatriate health plan that provides coverage for a qualified expatriate qualifies as minimum essential coverage for all participants in the plan. If the expatriate health plan provides coverage to category A or category B expatriates, the coverage of any participant in the plan is treated as an eligible employer-sponsored plan under section 5000A(f)(2) of the Code. If the expatriate health plan provides coverage to category C expatriates, the coverage of any enrollee in the plan is treated as a plan in the individual market under section 5000A(f)(1)(C) of the Code.

Federal Tax Provision: Sections 6055 and 6056 of the Code

Section 3(b)(2) of the EHCCA permits the use of electronic media to provide the statements required under sections 6055 and 6056 of the Code to individuals for coverage under an expatriate health plan unless the primary insured has explicitly refused to receive the statement electronically. The proposed regulations provide that, for an expatriate health plan, the recipient is treated as having consented to receive the required statement electronically unless the recipient has explicitly refused to receive the statement in an electronic format. In addition, the proposed regulations provide that the recipient may explicitly refuse either electronically or in a paper document. For a recipient to be treated as having consented under this special rule, the furnisher must provide a notice in compliance with the general disclosure requirements under sections 6055 and 6056 that informs the recipient that the statement will be furnished electronically unless the recipient explicitly refuses to consent to receive the statement in electronic form. The notice must be provided to the recipient at least 30 days prior to the due date for furnishing of the first statement the furnisher intends to furnish electronically to the recipient. Absent receipt of this notice, a recipient will not be treated as having consented to electronic furnishing of statements. Treasury and IRS request comments on further guidance that will assist issuers and plan sponsors in providing this notice in the least burdensome manner while still ensuring that the recipient has sufficient information and opportunity to opt out of the electronic reporting if the recipient desires. For example, Treasury and the IRS specifically request comments on whether the ability to provide this notice as part of the enrollment materials for the coverage would meet these goals.

Federal Tax Provision: PCORTF Fee

The proposed regulations provide that the excise tax under sections 4375 and 4376 of the Code (the PCORTF fee) does not apply to an expatriate health plan as defined at 26 CFR 54.9831-1(f)(3). Section 4375 of the Code limits the application of the fee to policies issued to individuals residing in the United States. Existing regulations under sections 4375, 4376, and 4377 of the Code exclude coverage under a plan from the fee if the plan is designed specifically to cover primarily employees who are working and residing outside the United States. A comment requested clarification about the existing PCORTF fee exemption for plans that primarily cover employees working and residing outside the United States. Consistent with the provisions of the EHCCA, the proposed regulations expand the exclusion from the PCORTF fee to also exclude an expatriate health plan regardless of whether the plan provides coverage for qualified expatriates residing or working in or outside the United States if the plan is an expatriate health plan.

Section 1341 of the ACA: Transitional Reinsurance Program

A comment also requested that the current exclusion under the PCORTF fee regulations for individuals working and residing outside the United States be applied to the transitional reinsurance fee under section 1341 of the ACA. Existing regulations relating to section 1341 of the ACA include an exception for certain expatriate health plans,[29] including expatriate group health coverage as defined by the Secretary of HHS and, for the 2015 and 2016 benefit years, self-insured group health plans with respect to which enrollment is limited to participants who reside outside their home country for at least six months of the plan year, and any covered dependents. HHS solicits comment on whether amendments are needed to 45 CFR 153.400(a)(1)(iii) to clarify the alignment with the EHCCA and exempt all expatriate plans from the requirement to make reinsurance contributions.

Section 2718 of the PHS Act: MLR Program

Section 2718 of the PHS Act, as added by sections 1001 and 10101 of the ACA, generally requires health insurance issuers to provide rebates to consumers if issuers do not achieve specified MLRs, as well as to submit an annual MLR report to HHS. The proposed regulations provide that expatriate policies described in 45 CFR 158.120(d)(4) continue to be subject to the reporting and rebate requirements of 45 CFR Part 158, but update the description of expatriate policies in 45 CFR 158.120(d)(4) to exclude policies that are expatriate health plans under the EHCCA. Given this modification, issuers may find that the number of expatriate policies that remain subject to MLR requirements is low, and that it is administratively burdensome and there is no longer a qualitative justification for continuing separate reporting of such policies. Therefore, comments are requested on whether the treatment of expatriate policies for purposes of the MLR regulations should be amended so that expatriate policies that do not meet the definition of expatriate health plan under the EHCCA would not be required to be reported separately from other health insurance policies.

Section 833(c)(5) of the Code, as added by section 9016 of the ACA, and amended by section 102 of Division N of the Consolidated and Further Continuing Appropriations Act, 2015 (Public Law 113-235, 128 Stat. 2130), provides that section 833(a)(2) and (3) do not apply to any organization unless the organization's MLR for the taxable year was at least 85 percent. In describing the MLR computation under section 833(c)(5), the statute and implementing regulations provide that the elements in the MLR computation are to be "as reported under section 2718 of the Public Service Health Act." Accordingly, the proposed regulations under section 2718 of the PHS Act would effectively apply the EHCCA exemption to section 833(c)(5) of the Code by carving out expatriate health plans under the EHCCA from the section 833(c)(5) requirements as well.

Excepted Benefits

Supplemental Health Insurance Coverage

The proposed regulations incorporate the guidance from the Affordable Care Act Implementation FAQs Part XXIII addressing supplemental health insurance products that provide categories of benefits in addition to those in the primary coverage. Under the proposed regulations, if group or individual supplemental health insurance coverage provides benefits for items and services not covered by the primary coverage (referred to as providing "additional categories of benefits"), the coverage would be considered to be designed "to fill gaps in primary coverage," for purposes of being supplemental excepted benefits if none of the benefits provided by the supplemental policy are an EHB, as defined for purposes of section 1302(b) of the ACA, in the State in which the coverage is issued. Conversely, if any benefit provided by the supplemental policy is an EHB in the State where the coverage is issued, the insurance coverage would not be supplemental excepted benefits under the proposed regulations. This standard is proposed to apply only to the extent that the supplemental health insurance provides coverage of additional categories of benefits. Supplemental health insurance products that both fill in cost sharing in the primary coverage, such as coinsurance or deductibles, and cover additional categories of benefits that are not EHB, also would be considered supplemental excepted benefits under these proposed regulations provided all other criteria are met.

Travel Insurance

The Departments are aware that certain travel insurance products may include limited health benefits. However, these products typically are not designed as major medical coverage. Instead, the risks being insured relate primarily to: (1) the interruption or cancellation of a trip (2) the loss of baggage or personal effects; (3) damages to accommodations or rental vehicles; or (4) sickness, accident, disability, or death occurring during travel, with any health benefits usually incidental to other coverage.

Section 2791(c)(1)(H) of the PHS Act, section 733(c)(1)(H) of ERISA, and section 9832(c)(1)(H) of the Code provide that the Departments may, in regulations, designate as excepted benefits "benefits for medical care that are secondary or incidental to other insurance benefits." Pursuant to this authority, and to clarify which types of travel-related insurance products are excepted benefits under the PHS Act, ERISA, and the Code, the proposed regulations provide that certain travel-related products that provide only incidental health benefits are excepted benefits. The proposed regulations define the term "travel insurance" as insurance coverage for personal risks incident to planned travel, which may include, but is not limited to, interruption or cancellation of a trip or event, loss of baggage or personal effects, damages to accommodations or rental vehicles, and sickness, accident, disability, or death occurring during travel, provided that the health benefits are not offered on a stand-alone basis and are incidental to other coverage. For this purpose, travel insurance does not include major medical plans that provide comprehensive medical protection for travelers with trips lasting 6 months or longer, including, for example, those working overseas as an expatriate or military personnel being deployed. This definition is consistent with the definition of travel insurance under final regulations for the health insurance providers fee imposed by section 9010 of the ACA issued by the Treasury Department and the IRS,[30] which uses a modified version of the National Association of Insurance Commissioners (NAIC) definition of travel insurance.

Hospital Indemnity and Other Fixed Indemnity Insurance

These proposed regulations also include an amendment to the "noncoordinated excepted benefits" category as it relates to hospital indemnity and other fixed indemnity insurance in the group market. Since the issuance of final regulations defining excepted benefits, the Departments have become aware of some hospital indemnity and other fixed indemnity insurance policies that provide comprehensive benefits related to health care costs. In addition, although hospital indemnity and other fixed indemnity insurance under section 2791 of the PHS Act, section 733 of ERISA, and section 9832 of the Code is not intended to be major medical coverage, the Departments are aware that some group health plans that provide coverage through hospital indemnity or other fixed indemnity insurance policies that meet the conditions necessary to be an excepted benefit have made representations to participants that the coverage is minimum essential coverage under section 5000A of the Code. The Departments are concerned that some individuals may incorrectly understand these policies to be comprehensive major medical coverage that would be considered minimum essential coverage.

To avoid confusion among group health plan enrollees and potential enrollees, the proposed regulations revise the conditions necessary for hospital indemnity and other fixed indemnity insurance in the group market to be excepted benefits so that any application or enrollment materials provided to enrollees and potential enrollees at or before the time enrollees and potential enrollees are given the opportunity to enroll in the

---

[29] 45 CFR 153.400(a)(1)(iii).

[30] 26 CFR 57.2(h)(4).

coverage must include a statement that the coverage is a supplement to, rather than a substitute for, major medical coverage and that a lack of minimum essential coverage may result in an additional tax payment. The proposed regulations include specific language that must be used by group health plans and issuers of group health insurance coverage to satisfy this notice requirement, which is consistent with the notice requirement for individual market fixed indemnity coverage under regulations issued by HHS.[31] The Departments request comments on this proposed notice requirement as well as whether any additional requirements should be added to prevent confusion among enrollees and potential enrollees regarding the limited coverage provided by hospital indemnity and other fixed indemnity insurance. The Departments anticipate that conforming changes will be made in the final regulations to ensure the notice language in the individual market is consistent with the notice language in the group market, and solicit comments on this approach.

Additionally, the Departments have become aware of hospital indemnity or other fixed indemnity insurance policies that provide benefits for doctors' visits at a fixed amount per visit, for prescription drugs at a fixed amount per drug, or for certain services at a fixed amount per day but in amounts that vary by the type of service. These types of policies do not meet the condition that benefits be provided on a per day (or per other time period, such as per week) basis. Accordingly, the proposed regulations clarify this standard by stating that the amount of benefits provided must be determined without regard to the type of items or services received. The proposed regulations add two examples demonstrating that group health plans and issuers of group health insurance coverage that provide coverage through hospital indemnity or fixed indemnity insurance policies that provide benefits based on the type of item or services received do not meet the conditions necessary to be an excepted benefit. The first example would incorporate into regulations guidance previously provided by the Departments in Affordable Care Act Implementation FAQs Part XI, which clarified that if a policy provides benefits in varying amounts based on the type of procedure or item received, the policy does not satisfy the condition that benefits be provided on a per day (or per other time period, such as per week) basis. The second example demonstrates that a hospital indemnity or other fixed indemnity insurance policy that provides benefits for certain services at a fixed amount per day, but in varying amounts depending on the type of service, does not meet the condition that benefits be provided on a per day (or per other time period, such as per week) basis. The Departments request comments on these examples specifically, as well as on the requirement that hospital indemnity and other fixed indemnity insurance in the group market that are excepted benefits must provide benefits on a per day (or per other time period, such as per week) basis in an amount that does not vary based on the type of items or services received. The Departments also request comments on whether the conditions for hospital indemnity or other fixed indemnity insurance to be considered excepted benefits should be more substantively aligned between the group and individual markets. For example, the requirements for hospital indemnity or other fixed indemnity insurance in the individual market could be modified to be consistent with the group market provisions of these proposed regulations by limiting payment strictly on a per-period basis and not on a per-service basis.

Specified Disease Coverage

The Departments have been asked whether a policy covering multiple specified diseases or illnesses may be considered to be excepted benefits. The statute provides that the noncoordinated excepted benefits category includes "coverage of a specified disease or illness" if the coverage meets the conditions for being offered as independent, noncoordinated benefits, and the Departments' implementing regulations identify cancer-only policies as one example of specified disease coverage.[32] The Departments are concerned that individuals who purchase a specified disease policy covering multiple diseases or illnesses (including policies that cover one overarching medical condition such as "mental illness" as opposed to a specific condition such as depression) may incorrectly believe they are purchasing comprehensive medical coverage when, in fact, these polices may not include many of the important consumer protections under the PHS Act, ERISA, and the Code. The Departments solicit comments on this issue and on whether, if such policies are permitted to be considered excepted benefits, protections are needed to ensure such policies are not mistaken for comprehensive medical coverage. For example, the Departments solicit comments on whether to limit the number of diseases or illnesses that may be covered in a specified disease policy that is considered to be excepted benefits or whether issuers should be required to disclose that such policies are not minimum essential coverage under section 5000A(f) of the Code.

Short-Term, Limited-Duration Insurance

Under existing regulations, short-term, limited-duration insurance means "health insurance coverage provided pursuant to a contract with an issuer that has an expiration date specified in the contract (taking into account any extensions that may be elected by the policyholder without the issuer's consent) that is less than 12 months after the original effective date of the contract."[33] Before enactment of the ACA, short-term, limited-duration insurance was an important means for individuals to obtain health coverage when transitioning from one job to another (and from one group health plan to another) or in a similar situation. But with the guaranteed availability of coverage and special enrollment period requirements in the individual health insurance market under the ACA, short-term, limited-duration insurance is no longer the only means to obtain transitional coverage.

The Departments recently have become aware that short-term, limited-duration insurance is being sold to address situations other than the situations that the exception was initially intended to address.[34] In some instances individuals are purchasing this coverage as their primary form of health coverage and, contrary to the intent of the 12-month coverage limitation in the current definition of short-term, limited-duration insurance, some issuers are providing renewals of the coverage that extend the duration beyond 12 months. The Departments are concerned that these policies, because they are exempt from market reforms, may have significant limitations, such as lifetime and annual dollar limits on EHBs and pre-existing condition exclusions, and therefore may not provide meaningful health coverage. Further, because these policies can be medically underwritten based on health status, healthier individuals may be targeted for this type of coverage, thus adversely impacting the risk pool for ACA-compliant coverage.

To address the issue of short-term, limited-duration insurance being sold as a type of primary coverage, the proposed regulations revise the definition of short-term, limited-duration insurance so that the coverage must be less than three months in duration, including any period for which the policyholder renews or has an option to renew with or without the issuer's consent. The proposed regulations also provide that a notice must be prominently displayed in the contract and in any application materials provided in connection with enrollment in such coverage with the following language: THIS IS NOT QUALIFYING HEALTH COVERAGE ("MINIMUM ESSENTIAL COVERAGE") THAT SATISFIES THE HEALTH COVERAGE REQUIREMENT OF THE AFFORDABLE CARE ACT. IF YOU DON'T HAVE MINIMUM ESSENTIAL COVERAGE, YOU MAY OWE AN ADDITIONAL PAYMENT WITH YOUR TAXES.

This change would align the definition more closely with the initial intent of the regulation: to refer to coverage intended to fill temporary coverage gaps when an individual transitions between primary coverage. Further, limiting the coverage to less than three months improves coordination with the exemption from the individual shared responsibility provision of section 5000A of the Code for gaps in coverage of less than three months (the short coverage gap exemption), 26 CFR 1.5000A-3. Under current law, individuals who are enrolled in short-term, limited-duration coverage instead of minimum essential coverage for three months or more are generally not eligible for the short coverage gap exemption.

---

[31] 45 CFR 148.220(b)(4)(iv).

[32] 26 CFR 54.9831-1(c)(4), 29 CFR 2590.732(c)(4), 45 CFR 146.145(b)(4) and 148.220(b)(3).

[33] 26 CFR 54.9801-2, 29 CFR 2590.702-2, 45 CFR 144.103.

[34] See e.g., Mathews, Anna W. "Sales of Short-Term Health Policics Surge," *The Wall Street Journal* April 10, 2016, available at http://www.wsj.com/articles/sales-of-short-term-health-policies-surge-1460328539.

The proposed regulations help ensure that individuals who purchase short-term, limited-duration coverage will still be eligible for the short coverage gap exemption (assuming other requirements are met) during the temporary coverage period.

In addition to proposing to reduce the length of short-term, limited-duration insurance to less than three months, the proposed regulations add the words "with or" in front of "without the issuer's consent" to address the Departments' concern that some issuers are taking liberty with the current definition of short-term, limited-duration insurance either by automatically renewing such policies or having a simplified reapplication process with the result being that such coverage lasts much longer than 12 months and serves as an individual's primary coverage but does not contain the important protections of the ACA. As indicated above, this type of coverage should only be sold for the purpose of providing coverage on a short-term basis such as filling in coverage gaps as a result of transitioning from one group health plan to another. The addition of the words "with or" clarifies that short-term, limited-duration insurance must be less than 3 months in total taking into account any option to renew or to reapply for the same or similar coverage.

The Departments seek comment on this proposal, including information and data on the number of short-term, limited-duration insurance policies offered for sale in the market, the types of individuals who typically purchase this coverage, and the reasons for which they purchase it.

Definition of EHB for Purposes of the Prohibition on Lifetime and Annual Limits.

On November 18, 2015, the Departments issued final regulations implementing section 2711 of the PHS Act.[35] The final regulations provide that, for plan years beginning on or after January 1, 2017, a plan or issuer that is not required to provide EHBs must define EHB, for purposes of the prohibition on lifetime and annual dollar limits, in a manner consistent with any of the 51 EHB base-benchmark plans applicable in a State or the District of Columbia, or one of the three FEHBP base-benchmarks, as specified under 45 CFR 156.100.

The final regulations under section 2711 of the PHS Act include a reference to selecting a "base-benchmark" plan, as specified under 45 CFR 156.100, for purposes of determining which benefits cannot be subject to lifetime or annual dollar limits. The base-benchmark plan selected by a State or applied by default under 45 CFR 156.100, however, may not reflect the complete definition of EHB in the applicable State. For that reason, the Departments propose to amend the regulations at 26 CFR 54.9815-2711(c), 29 CFR 2590.715-2711(c), and 45 CFR 147.126(c) to refer to the provisions that capture the complete definition of EHB in a State. Specifically, the Departments propose to replace the phrase "in a manner consistent with one of the three Federal Employees Health Benefit Program (FEHBP) options as defined by 45 CFR 156.100(a)(3) or one of the base-benchmark plans selected by a State or applied by default pursuant to 45 CFR 156.100" in each of the regulations with the following: "in a manner that is consistent with (1) one of the EHB-benchmark plans applicable in a State under 45 CFR 156.110, and includes coverage of any additional required benefits that are considered essential health benefits consistent with 45 CFR 155.170(a)(2); or (2) one of the three Federal Employees Health Benefit Program (FEHBP) options as defined by 45 CFR 156.100(a)(3), supplemented, as necessary, to meet the standards in 45 CFR 156.110." This change reflects the possibility that base-benchmark plans, including the FEHBP plan options, could require supplementation under 45 CFR 156.110, and ensures the inclusion of State-required benefit mandates enacted on or before December 31, 2011 in accordance with 45 CFR 155.170, which when coupled with a State's EHB-benchmark plan, establish the definition of EHB in that State under regulations implementing section 1302(b) of the ACA.[36] The Departments seek comment on the requirement that, when one of the FEHBP plan options is selected as the benchmark, it would be supplemented, as needed, to ensure coverage in all ten statutory EHB categories, and the benchmark plan options that should be available for this purpose.

Proposed Applicability Date and Reliance

Except as otherwise provided herein, these proposed regulations are proposed to be applicable for plan years (or, in the individual market, policy years) beginning on or after January 1, 2017. Issuers, employers, administrators, and individuals are permitted to rely on these proposed regulations pending the applicability date of final regulations in the **Federal Register**. To the extent final regulations or other guidance is more restrictive on issuers, employers, administrators, and individuals than these proposed regulations, the final regulations or other guidance will be applied without retroactive effect and issuers, employers, administrators, and individuals will be provided sufficient time to come into compliance with the final regulations.

III. Economic Impact and Paperwork Burden

A. *Summary — Department of Labor and Department of Health and Human Services*

As stated above, the proposed regulations would provide guidance on the rules for expatriate health plans, expatriate health plan issuers, and qualified expatriates under the EHCCA. The EHCCA generally provides that the requirements of the ACA do not apply with respect to expatriate health plans, expatriate health insurance issuers for coverage under expatriate health plans, and employers in their capacity as plan sponsors of expatriate health plans.

The proposed regulations address how certain requirements relating to minimum essential coverage under section 5000A of the Code, the health care reporting provisions of sections 6055 and 6056 of the Code, and the health insurance providers fee imposed by section 9010 of the ACA continue to apply subject to certain provisions while providing that the excise tax under sections 4375 and 4376 of the Code do not apply to expatriate health plans.

The proposed regulations also propose amendments to the Departments' regulations concerning excepted benefits, which would specify the conditions for supplemental health insurance products that are designed "to fill gaps in primary coverage" by providing additional categories of benefits (as opposed to filling in gaps in cost sharing) to constitute supplemental excepted benefits, and clarify that certain travel-related insurance products that provide only incidental health benefits constitute excepted benefits. The proposed regulations also require that, to be considered hospital indemnity or other fixed indemnity insurance in the group market, any application or enrollment materials provided to participants at or before the time participants are given the opportunity to enroll in the coverage must include a statement that the coverage is a supplement to, rather than a substitute for, major medical coverage and that a lack of minimum essential coverage may result in an additional tax payment. Further, the regulations clarify that hospital indemnity and other fixed indemnity insurance must pay a fixed dollar amount per day (or per other time period, such as per week) regardless of the type of items or services received.

The regulations also propose revisions to the definition of short-term, limited-duration insurance so that the coverage has to be less than 3 months in duration (as opposed to the current definition of less than 12 months in duration), and that a notice must be prominently displayed in the contract and in any application materials provided in connection with the coverage that provides that such coverage is not minimum essential coverage.

---

[35] 80 FR 72192.

[36] In the HHS Notice of Benefit and Payment Parameters for 2016 published February 27, 2015 (80 FR 10750), HHS instructed States to select a new base-benchmark plan to take effect beginning with plan or policy years beginning in 2017. The new final EHB base-benchmark plans selected as a result of this process are publicly available at downloads.cms.gov/cciio/Final%20List%20of%20BMPs_15_10_21.pdf. Additional information about the new base-benchmark plans, including plan documents and summaries of benefits, is available at www.cms.gov/CCIIO/Resources/Data-Resources/ehb.html. The definition of EHB in each of the 50 states and the District of Columbia is based on the base-benchmark plan, and takes into account any additions to the base-benchmark plan, such as supplementation under 45 CFR 156.110, and State-required benefit mandates in accordance with 45 CFR 155.170.

The proposed regulations also include amendments to 45 CFR part 158 to clarify that the MLR reporting requirements do not apply to expatriate health plans under the EHCCA.

Finally, the proposed regulations propose to amend the definition of "essential health benefits" for purposes of the prohibition of annual and lifetime dollar limits for group health plans and health insurance issuers that are not required to provide essential health benefits.

The Departments are publishing these proposed regulations to implement the protections intended by the Congress in the most economically efficient manner possible. The Departments have examined the effects of this rule as required by Executive Order 13563 (76 FR 3821, January 21, 2011), Executive Order 12866 (58 FR 51735, September 1993, Regulatory Planning and Review), the Regulatory Flexibility Act (RFA) (September 19, 1980, Pub. L. 96-354), the Unfunded Mandates Reform Act of 1995 (Pub. L. 104-4), Executive Order 13132 on Federalism, and the Congressional Review Act (5 U.S.C. 804(2)).

B. *Executive Orders 12866 and 13563 — Department of Labor and Department of Health and Human Services*

Executive Order 12866 (58 FR 51735) directs agencies to assess all costs and benefits of available regulatory alternatives and, if regulation is necessary, to select regulatory approaches that maximize net benefits (including potential economic, environmental, public health and safety effects; distributive impacts; and equity). Executive Order 13563 (76 FR 3821, January 21, 2011) is supplemental to and reaffirms the principles, structures, and definitions governing regulatory review as established in Executive Order 12866.

Section 3(f) of Executive Order 12866 defines a "significant regulatory action" as an action that is likely to result in a final rule — (1) having an annual effect on the economy of $100 million or more in any one year, or adversely and materially affecting a sector of the economy, productivity, competition, jobs, the environment, public health or safety, or state, local or tribal governments or communities (also referred to as "economically significant"); (2) creating a serious inconsistency or otherwise interfering with an action taken or planned by another agency; (3) materially altering the budgetary impacts of entitlement grants, user fees, or loan programs or the rights and obligations of recipients thereof; or (4) raising novel legal or policy issues arising out of legal mandates, the President's priorities, or the principles set forth in the Executive Order.

A regulatory impact analysis (RIA) must be prepared for rules with economically significant effects (for example, $100 million or more in any 1 year), and a "significant" regulatory action is subject to review by the OMB. The Departments have determined that this regulatory action is not likely to have economic impacts of $100 million or more in any one year, and therefore is not significant within the meaning of Executive Order 12866. The Departments expect the impact of these proposed regulations to be limited because they do not require any additional action or impose any requirements on issuers, employers and plan sponsors.

1. *Need for Regulatory Action*

Consistent with the EHCCA, enacted as Division M of the Consolidated Clarification Continuing Appropriations Act, 2015 Public Law 113-235 (128 Stat. 2130), these proposed regulations provide that the market reform provisions enacted as part of the ACA generally do not apply to expatriate health plans, any employer solely in its capacity as a plan sponsor of an expatriate health plan, and any expatriate health insurance issuer with respect to coverage under an expatriate health plan. Further, the proposed regulations define the benefit and administrative requirements for expatriate health issuers, expatriate health plans, and qualified expatriates and provide clarification regarding the applicability of certain fee and reporting requirements under the Code.

Consistent with section 2 of the EHCCA, these proposed regulations are necessary to carry out the intent of Congress that (1) American expatriate health insurance issuers should be permitted to compete on a level playing field in the global marketplace; (2) the global competitiveness of American companies should be encouraged; and (3) in implementing the health insurance providers fee imposed by section 9010 of the ACA and other provisions of the ACA, the unique and multinational features of expatriate health plans and the United States companies that operate such plans and the competitive pressures of such plans and companies should continue to be recognized.

In response to feedback the Departments have received from stakeholders, the proposed regulations would also clarify the conditions for supplemental health insurance and travel insurance to be considered excepted benefits. These clarifications will provide health insurance issuers offering supplemental insurance coverage and travel insurance products with a clearer understanding of whether these types of coverage are subject to the market reforms under title XXVII of the PHS Act, part 7 of ERISA, and Chapter 100 of the Code. The proposed regulations also would amend the definition of short-term, limited-duration insurance and impose a new notice requirement in response to recent reports that this type of coverage is being sold for purposes other than for which the exclusion for short-term, limited-duration insurance was initially intended to cover.

2. *Summary of Impacts*

These proposed regulations would implement the rules for expatriate health plans, expatriate health insurance issuers, and qualified expatriates under the EHCCA. The proposed regulations also outline the conditions for travel insurance and supplemental insurance coverage to be considered excepted benefits, and revise the definition of short-term, limited-duration insurance.

Based on the NAIC 2014 Supplemental Health Care Exhibit Report,[37] which generally uses the definition of expatriate coverage in the MLR final rule at 45 CFR 158.120(d)(4),[38] there are an estimated eight issuers (one issuer in the small group market and seven issuers in the large group market) domiciled in the United States that provide expatriate health plans for approximately 270,349 enrollees. While the Departments acknowledge that some expatriate health insurance issuers and employers in their capacity as plan sponsor of an expatriate health plan may incur costs in order to comply with certain provisions of the EHCCA and these proposed regulations, as discussed below, the Departments believe that these costs will be relatively insignificant and limited.

The vast majority of expatriate health plans described in the EHCCA would qualify as expatriate health plans under the transitional relief provided in the Departments' Affordable Care Act Implementation FAQs Part XVIII, Q&A-6 and Q&A-7. The FAQs provide that expatriate health plans with plan years ending on or before December 31, 2016 are exempt from the ACA market reforms and provide that coverage provided under an expatriate group health plan is a form of minimum essential coverage under section 5000A of the Code. The EHCCA permanently exempts expatriate health plans with plan or policy years beginning on or after July 1, 2015 from the ACA market reform requirements and provides that coverage provided under an expatriate health plan is a form of minimum essential coverage under section 5000A of the Code.

Because the Departments believe that most, if not all, expatriate health plans described in the EHCCA would qualify as expatriate health plans under the Departments' previous guidance, and the proposed regulations codify the provisions of the EHCCA by making the temporary relief in the Departments' Affordable Care Act Implementation FAQs Part XVIII, Q&A-6 and Q&A-7 permanent for specified expatriate health plans, the Departments believe that the proposed regulations will result in only marginal, if any, impact on these plans. Furthermore, the Departments believe the proposed regulations outlining the conditions for travel insurance and supplemental insurance coverage to be considered excepted benefits are consistent with prevailing industry practice and will not result in significant cost to health insurance issuers of these products.

---

[37] NAIC, 2014 Supplemental Health Care Exhibit Report, Volume 1 (2015), available at http://www.naic.org/documents/prod_serv_statistical_hce_zb.pdf.

[38] Section 45 CFR 158.120(d)(4) defines expatriate policies as predominantly group health insurance policies that provide coverage to employees, substantially all of whom

are: (1) working outside their country of citizenship; (2) working outside their country of citizenship and outside the employer's country of domicile; or (3) non-U.S. citizens working in their home country.

The Departments believe that any costs incurred by issuers of short-term, limited-duration insurance and hospital indemnity and other fixed indemnity insurance to include the required notice in application or enrollment materials will be negligible since the Departments have provided the exact text for the notice. Further, the Departments note that issuers of hospital indemnity and other fixed indemnity insurance in the individual market already provide a similar notice.

As a result, the Departments have concluded that the impacts of these proposed regulations are not economically significant. The Departments request comments on the assumptions used to evaluate the economic impact of these proposed regulations, including specific data and information on the number of expatriate health plans.

C. *Paperwork Reduction Act*

1. *Department of the Treasury.*

The collection of information in these proposed regulations are in 26 CFR 1.6055-2(a)(8) and 301.6056-2(a)(8). The collection of information in these proposed regulations relates to statements required to be furnished to a responsible individual under section 6055 of the Code and statements required to be furnished to an employee under section 6056 of the Code. The collection of information in these proposed regulations would, in accordance with the EHCCA, permit a furnisher to furnish the required statements electronically unless the recipient has explicitly refused to consent to receive the statement in an electronic format. The collection of information contained in this notice of proposed rulemaking will be taken into account and submitted to the Office of Management and Budget in accordance with the Paperwork Reduction Act of 1995 (44 U.S.C. 3507(d)) in connection with the next review of the collection of information for IRS Form 1095-B (OMB # 1545-2252) and IRS Form 1095-C (OMB # 1545-2251).

Comments on the collection of information should be sent to the Office of Management and Budget, Attn: Desk Officer for the Department of the Treasury, Office of Information and Regulatory Affairs, Washington, DC 20503, with copies to the Internal Revenue Service, Attn: IRS Reports Clearance Officer, SE:CAR:MP:T:T:SP, Washington DC 20224. Comments on the collection of information should be received by August 9, 2016. Comments are sought on whether the proposed collection of information is necessary for the proper performance of the IRS, including whether the information will have practical utility; the accuracy of the estimated burden associated with the proposed collection of information; how the quality, utility, and clarity of the information to be collected may be enhanced; how the burden of complying with the proposed collection of information may be minimized, including through the application of automated collection techniques and other forms of information technology; and estimates of capital or start-up costs and costs of operation, maintenance, and purchase of service to provide information. Comments on the collection of information should be received by August 9, 2016.

An agency may not conduct or sponsor, and a person is not required to respond to, a collection of information unless it displays a valid control number assigned by the Office of Management and Budget.

Books or records relating to a collection of information must be retained as long as their contents may become material in the administration of any internal revenue law. Generally, tax returns and tax return information are confidential, as required by 26 U.S.C. 6103.

2. *Department of the Treasury, Department of Labor, and Department of Health and Human Services.*

The proposed regulations provide that to be considered hospital or other fixed indemnity excepted benefits in the group market for plan years beginning on or after January 1, 2017, a notice must be included in any application or enrollment materials provided to participants at or before the time participants are given the opportunity to enroll in the coverage, indicating that the coverage is a supplement to, rather than a substitute for major medical coverage and that a lack of minimum essential coverage may result in an additional tax payment. The proposed regulations also provide that to be considered short-term, limited-duration insurance for policy years beginning on or after January 1, 2017, a notice must be prominently displayed in the contract and in any application materials, stating that the coverage is not minimum essential coverage and that failure to have minimum essential coverage may result in an additional tax payment. The Departments have provided the exact text for these notice requirements and the language will not need to be customized. The burden associated with these notices is not subject to the Paperwork Reduction Act of 1995 in accordance with 5 CFR 1320.3(c)(2) because they do not contain a "collection of information" as defined in 44 U.S.C. 3502(11).

D. *Regulatory Flexibility Act*

The Regulatory Flexibility Act (5 U.S.C. 601 *et seq.*) (RFA) imposes certain requirements with respect to Federal rules that are subject to the notice and comment requirements of section 553(b) of the Administrative Procedure Act (5 U.S.C. 551 *et seq.*) and that are likely to have a significant economic impact on a substantial number of small entities. Unless an agency certifies that a proposed rule is not likely to have a significant economic impact on a substantial number of small entities, section 603 of RFA requires that the agency present an initial regulatory flexibility analysis at the time of the publication of the notice of proposed rulemaking describing the impact of the rule on small entities and seeking public comment on such impact. Small entities include small businesses, organizations and governmental jurisdictions.

The RFA generally defines a "small entity" as (1) a proprietary firm meeting the size standards of the Small Business Administration (SBA) (13 CFR 121.201); (2) a nonprofit organization that is not dominant in its field; or (3) a small government jurisdiction with a population of less than 50,000. (States and individuals are not included in the definition of "small entity.") The Departments use as their measure of significant economic impact on a substantial number of small entities a change in revenues of more than 3 to 5 percent.

These proposed regulations are not likely to impose additional costs on small entities. According to SBA size standards, entities with average annual receipts of $38.5 million or less would be considered small entities for these North American Industry Classification System codes. The Departments believe that, since the majority of small issuers belong to larger holding groups, many if not all are likely to have non-health lines of business that would result in their revenues exceeding $38.5 million. Therefore, the Departments certify that the proposed regulations will not have a significant impact on a substantial number of small entities. In addition, section 1102(b) of the Social Security Act requires agencies to prepare a regulatory impact analysis if a rule may have a significant economic impact on the operations of a substantial number of small rural hospitals. This analysis must conform to the provisions of section 604 of the RFA. These proposed regulations would not affect small rural hospitals. Therefore, the Departments have determined that these proposed regulations would not have a significant impact on the operations of a substantial number of small rural hospitals.

E. *Special Analysis - Department of the Treasury*

Certain IRS regulations, including this one, are exempt from the requirements of Executive Order 12866, as supplemented and reaffirmed by Executive Order 13563. Therefore, a regulatory impact assessment is not required. It also has been determined that section 553(b) of the Administrative Procedure Act (5 U.S.C. Chapter 5) does not apply to these regulations. For applicability of RFA, see paragraph D of this section III. Pursuant to section 7805(f) of the Code, these regulations have been submitted to the Chief Counsel for Advocacy of the Small Business Administration for comment on their impact on small business.

F. Unfunded Mandates Reform Act

For purposes of the Unfunded Mandates Reform Act of 1995 (2 U.S.C. 1501 *et seq.*), as well as Executive Order 12875, these proposed rules do not include any Federal mandate that may result in expenditures by State, local, or tribal governments, or the private sector, which may impose an annual burden of $146 million adjusted for inflation since 1995.

G. Federalism — Department of Labor and Department of Health and Human Services

Executive Order 13132 outlines fundamental principles of federalism. It requires adherence to specific criteria by Federal agencies in formulating and implementing policies that have "substantial direct effects" on the States, the relationship between the national government and States, or on the distribution of power and responsibilities among the various levels of government. Federal agencies promulgating regulations that have these federalism implications must consult with State and local officials, and describe the extent of their consultation and the nature of the concerns of State and local officials in the preamble to the final regulation.

In the Departments' view, these proposed regulations do not have federalism implications, because they do not have direct effects on the States, the relationship between the national government and States, or on the distribution of power and responsibilities among various levels of government.

H. Congressional Review Act

These proposed regulations are subject to the Congressional Review Act provisions of the Small Business Regulatory Enforcement Fairness Act of 1996 (5 U.S.C. 801 et seq.), and, if finalized, will be transmitted to the Congress and to the **Comptroller General** for review in accordance with such provisions.

I. Statement of Availability of IRS Documents

IRS Revenue Procedures, Revenue Rulings notices, and other guidance cited in this document are published in the Internal Revenue Bulletin (or Cumulative Bulletin) and are available from the Superintendent of Documents, U.S. Government Printing Office, Washington, DC 20402, or by visiting the IRS website at *http://www.irs.gov*.

IV. Statutory Authority

The Department of the Treasury regulations are proposed to be adopted pursuant to the authority contained in sections 7805 and 9833 of the Code.

The Department of Labor regulations are proposed pursuant to the authority contained in 29 U.S.C. 1135,and 1191c; Secretary of Labor's Order 1-2011, 77 FR 1088 (Jan. 9, 2012).

The Department of Health and Human Services regulations are proposed to be adopted pursuant to the authority contained in sections 2701 through 2763, 2791, and 2792 of the PHS Act (42 U.S.C. 300gg through 300gg-63, 300gg-91, and 300gg-92), as amended.

[¶ 49,702]   Proposed Amendments of Regulations (REG-123854-12) Proposed Regulations, NPRM REG-123854-12, published in the Federal Register on June 22, 2016 (corrected 8/4/2016).

[Code Sec. 409A]

Nonqualified deferred compensation plans: Code Sec. 409A: Proposed regulations.—Amendments of Reg. §§1.409A-0, 1.409A-1, 1.409A-2,1.409A-3, 1.409A-4 and 1.409A-6, regarding the calculation of amounts includible in income under section 409A(a)(1), are proposed. The texts are at ¶18,952G,¶18,953B, ¶18,954B, ¶18,955B, ¶18,956J and ¶18,958B.

AGENCY: Internal Revenue Service (IRS), Treasury.

ACTION: Partial withdrawal of notice of proposed rulemaking; notice of proposed rulemaking.

SUMMARY: This document contains proposed regulations that would clarify or modify certain specific provisions of the final regulations under section 409A (TD 9321, 72 FR 19234). This document also withdraws a specific provision of the notice of proposed rulemaking (REG-148326-05) published in the *Federal Register* on December 8, 2008 (73 FR 74380) regarding the calculation of amounts includible in income under section 409A(a)(1) and replaces that provision with revised proposed regulations. These proposed regulations would affect participants, beneficiaries, sponsors, and administrators of nonqualified deferred compensation plans.

DATES: Comments and requests for a public hearing must be received by September 20, 2016.

ADDRESSES: Send submissions to: CC:PA:LPD:PR (REG-123854-12), Room 5203, Internal Revenue Service, PO Box 7604, Ben Franklin Station, Washington DC, 20044. Submissions may be hand delivered Monday through Friday, between the hours of 8 a.m. and 4 p.m. to CC:PA:LPD:PR (REG-123854-12), Courier's Desk, Internal Revenue Service, 1111 Constitution Avenue, NW., Washington, DC, 20224 or sent electronically, via the Federal Rulemaking Portal at www.regulations.gov (IRS REG-123854-12).

FOR FURTHER INFORMATION CONTACT: Concerning these proposed regulations under section 409A, Gregory Burns at (202) 927-9639, concerning submission of comments and/or requests for a hearing, Regina Johnson at (202) 317-6901 (not toll-free numbers).

SUPPLEMENTARY INFORMATION:

Background

Section 885 of the American Jobs Creation Act of 2004, Public Law 108-357 (118 Stat. 1418) (AJCA '04) added section 409A to the Internal Revenue Code (Code). Section 409A(a)(1)(A) generally provides that, if certain requirements are not met at any time during a taxable year, amounts deferred under a nonqualified deferred compensation plan for that year and all previous taxable years are currently includible in gross income to the extent not subject to a substantial risk of forfeiture and not previously included in gross income.

On April 17, 2007 (72 FR 19234), the Treasury Department and the IRS issued final regulations under section 409A (TD 9321), which include §§1.409A-1, 1.409A-2, 1.409A-3, and 1.409A-6 (the final regulations). The final regulations define certain terms used in section 409A and in the final regulations, set forth the requirements for deferral elections and for the time and form of payments under nonqualified deferred compensation plans, and address certain other issues under section 409A.

On December 8, 2008 (73 FR 74380), the Treasury Department and the IRS issued additional proposed regulations under section 409A (REG-148326-05), which include proposed §1.409A-4 (the proposed income inclusion regulations). The proposed income inclusion regulations provide guidance regarding the calculation of amounts includible in income under section 409A(a)(1) and the additional taxes imposed by section

409A with respect to service providers participating in certain nonqualified deferred compensation plans and other arrangements that do not comply with the requirements of section 409A(a).

Explanation of Provisions

I. Overview

The Treasury Department and the IRS have concluded that certain clarifications and modifications to the final regulations and the proposed income inclusion regulations will help taxpayers comply with the requirements of section 409A. These proposed regulations address certain specific provisions of the final regulations and the proposed income inclusion regulations and are not intended to propose a general revision of, or broad changes to, the final regulations or the proposed income inclusion regulations. The narrow and specific purpose of these proposed regulations should be taken into account when submitting comments on these proposed regulations. As provided in the section of this preamble titled "Proposed Effective Dates," taxpayers may rely upon these proposed regulations immediately.

These proposed regulations:

(1) Clarify that the rules under section 409A apply to nonqualified deferred compensation plans separately and in addition to the rules under section 457A.

(2) Modify the short-term deferral rule to permit a delay in payments to avoid violating Federal securities laws or other applicable law.

(3) Clarify that a stock right that does not otherwise provide for a deferral of compensation will not be treated as providing for a deferral of compensation solely because the amount payable under the stock right upon an involuntary separation from service for cause, or the occurrence of a condition within the service provider's control, is based on a measure that is less than fair market value.

(4) Modify the definition of the term "eligible issuer of service recipient stock" to provide that it includes a corporation (or other entity) for which a person is reasonably expected to begin, and actually begins, providing services within 12 months after the grant date of a stock right.

(5) Clarify that certain separation pay plans that do not provide for a deferral of compensation may apply to a service provider who had no compensation from the service recipient during the year preceding the year in which a separation from service occurs.

(6) Provide that a plan under which a service provider has a right to payment or reimbursement of reasonable attorneys' fees and other expenses incurred to pursue a bona fide legal claim against the service recipient with respect to the service relationship does not provide for a deferral of compensation.

(7) Modify the rules regarding recurring part-year compensation.

(8) Clarify that a stock purchase treated as a deemed asset sale under section 338 is not a sale or other disposition of assets for purposes of determining whether a service provider has a separation from service.

(9) Clarify that a service provider who ceases providing services as an employee and begins providing services as an independent contractor is treated as having a separation from service if, at the time of the change in employment status, the level of services reasonably anticipated to be provided after the change would result in a separation from service under the rules applicable to employees.

(10) Provide a rule that is generally applicable to determine when a "payment" has been made for purposes of section 409A.

(11) Modify the rules applicable to amounts payable following death.

(12) Clarify that the rules for transaction-based compensation apply to stock rights that do not provide for a deferral of compensation and statutory stock options.

(13) Provide that the addition of the death, disability, or unforeseeable emergency of a beneficiary who has become entitled to a payment due to a service provider's death as a potentially earlier or intervening payment event will not violate the prohibition on the acceleration of payments.

(14) Modify the conflict of interest exception to the prohibition on the acceleration of payments to permit the payment of all types of deferred compensation (and not only certain types of foreign earned income) to comply with bona fide foreign ethics or conflicts of interest laws.

(15) Clarify the provision permitting payments upon the termination and liquidation of a plan in connection with bankruptcy.

(16) Clarify other rules permitting payments in connection with the termination and liquidation of a plan.

(17) Provide that a plan may accelerate the time of payment to comply with Federal debt collection laws.

(18) Clarify and modify § 1.409A-4(a)(1)(ii)(B) of the proposed income inclusion regulations regarding the treatment of deferred amounts subject to a substantial risk of forfeiture for purposes of calculating the amount includible in income under section 409A(a)(1).

(19) Clarify various provisions of the final regulations to recognize that a service provider can be an entity as well as an individual.

II. Deferral of Compensation

A. Section 457(f) and Section 457A Plans

Section 457(f) generally provides that compensation deferred under a plan of an eligible employer (as that term is defined under section 457) is included in gross income in the first taxable year in which there is no substantial risk of forfeiture of the rights to the compensation. The final regulations provide that a deferred compensation plan subject to section 457(f) may be a nonqualified deferred compensation plan for purposes of section 409A and that the rules of section 409A apply to deferred compensation plans separately and in addition to any requirements applicable to such plans under section 457(f).

Similarly, section 457A, which was enacted more than a year after publication of the final regulations, generally provides that any compensation deferred under a nonqualified deferred compensation plan of a nonqualified entity (as these terms are defined under section 457A) is includible in gross income when there is no substantial risk of forfeiture of the rights to the compensation. These proposed regulations clarify that a nonqualified deferred compensation plan under section 457A, like a deferred compensation plan under section 457(f), may be a nonqualified deferred compensation plan for purposes of section 409A and that the rules of section 409A apply to such a plan separately and in addition to any requirements applicable to the plan under section 457A.

B. Short-term Deferral Rule

The final regulations provide that a deferral of compensation does not occur for purposes of section 409A under a plan with respect to any payment that is not a deferred payment[1] provided that the service provider actually or constructively receives the payment on or before the later of:

---

[1] Under § 1.409A-1(b)(4)(i)(D), a payment is a deferred payment if it is made pursuant to a provision of a plan that provides for the payment to be made or completed on or after any date, or upon the occurrence of any event, that will or may occur later than the end of the applicable 2½ month period.

(1) The 15th day of the third month following the end of the service provider's first taxable year in which the right to the payment is no longer subject to a substantial risk of forfeiture, or (2) the 15th day of the third month following the end of the service recipient's first taxable year in which the right to the payment is no longer subject to a substantial risk of forfeiture (the applicable 2 1/2 month period). A payment that meets these requirements of the short-term deferral rule (described more fully in §1.409A-1(b)(4)) is referred to as a short-term deferral and is generally exempt from the requirements applicable to plans that provide for a deferral of compensation.

The final regulations provide that a payment that otherwise qualifies as a short-term deferral, but is made after the applicable 2 1/2 month period, may continue to qualify as a short-term deferral if the payment is delayed for one of three reasons: (1) The taxpayer establishes that it was administratively impracticable for the service recipient to make the payment by the end of the applicable 2 1/2 month period; (2) making the payment by the end of the applicable 2 1/2 month period would have jeopardized the service recipient's ability to continue as a going concern; or (3) the service recipient reasonably anticipates that a deduction for the payment would not be permitted under section 162(m).

Similar exceptions apply under the general time and form of payment rules of section 409A. Under §1.409A-3(d), a payment is treated as made on the date specified under the plan if the payment is delayed due to administrative impracticability or because making the payment would jeopardize the ability of the service recipient to continue as a going concern. Under §1.409A-2(b)(7), a payment may be delayed to a date after the payment date designated in a plan without failing to meet the requirements of section 409A(a) if the service recipient reasonably anticipates that a deduction for the payment would not be permitted under section 162(m) or if making the payment would violate Federal securities laws or other applicable law. Together, these rules generally permit payments under section 409A to be delayed due to administrative impracticability or because making the payment would jeopardize the ability of the service recipient to continue as a going concern, the payment would not be deductible under section 162(m), or making the payment would violate Federal securities laws or other applicable law.

Some commenters have suggested that the exception for payments that would violate Federal securities laws or other applicable law should also apply to payments that are intended to be short-term deferrals. These commenters have noted that the policy reasons for excusing a timely payment when the payment would violate Federal securities laws or other applicable law apply equally to the general time and form of payment rules under section 409A and the short-term deferral rule. In response to these comments, the Treasury Department and the IRS have determined that it is appropriate to extend this exception to the short-term deferral rule. Accordingly, these proposed regulations provide that a payment that otherwise qualifies as a short-term deferral, but is made after the end of the applicable 2 1/2 month period, may still qualify as a short-term deferral if the service recipient reasonably anticipates that making the payment during the applicable 2 1/2 month period will violate Federal securities laws or other applicable law and the payment is made as soon as reasonably practicable following the first date on which the service recipient anticipates or reasonably should anticipate that making the payment would not cause a violation. For this purpose, making a payment that would cause inclusion in gross income or the application of any penalty provision or other provision of the Code is not treated as a violation of applicable law.

C. Stock rights

1. Service Recipient Stock

The final regulations provide that certain stock options and stock appreciation rights (collectively, stock rights) granted with respect to service recipient stock do not provide for the deferral of compensation. The term "service recipient stock" means a class of stock that, as of the date of grant, is common stock for purposes of section 305 and the regulations thereunder of a corporation that is an eligible issuer of service recipient stock. For this purpose, service recipient stock does not include any stock that is subject to a mandatory repurchase obligation (other than a right of first refusal), or a permanent put or call right, if the stock price under such right or obligation is based on a measure other than the fair market value (disregarding lapse restrictions) of the equity interest in the corporation represented by the stock.

Commenters have noted that employers often want to deter employees from engaging in behavior that could be detrimental to the employer and have customarily reduced the amount that an employee receives under a stock rights arrangement if the employee is dismissed for cause or violates a noncompetition or nondisclosure agreement. These commenters have observed that this type of reduction is generally prohibited under the definition of service recipient stock in the final regulations but have argued that neither the statutory language nor the underlying policies of section 409A should prohibit a reduction under these circumstances. The Treasury Department and the IRS agree with these conclusions. Accordingly, these proposed regulations provide that a stock price will not be treated as based on a measure other than fair market value if the amount payable upon a service provider's involuntary separation from service for cause, or the occurrence of a condition that is within the control of the service provider, such as the violation of a covenant not to compete or a covenant not to disclose certain information, is based on a measure that is less than fair market value.

2. Eligible Issuer of Service Recipient Stock

Under the final regulations, the term "eligible issuer of service recipient stock" means the corporation or other entity for which the service provider provides direct services on the date of grant of the stock right and certain affiliated corporations or entities. Some commenters have asserted that this definition of "eligible issuer of service recipient stock" hinders employment negotiations because it prevents service recipients from granting stock rights to service providers before they are employed by the service recipient. In response to these comments, these proposed regulations provide that, if it is reasonably anticipated that a person will begin providing services to a corporation or other entity within 12 months after the date of grant of a stock right, and the person actually begins providing services to the corporation or other entity within 12 months after the date of grant (or, if services do not begin within that period, the stock right is forfeited), the corporation or other entity will be an eligible issuer of service recipient stock.

D. Separation pay plans

Under the final regulations, separation pay plans that provide for payment only upon an involuntary separation from service or pursuant to a window program do not provide for a deferral of compensation to the extent that they meet certain requirements. One of these requirements is that the separation pay generally not exceed two times the lesser of (1) the service provider's annualized compensation based upon the annual rate of pay for the service provider's taxable year preceding the service provider's taxable year in which the separation from service occurs, or (2) the limit under section 401(a)(17) for the year in which the service provider separates from service.

Some commenters have questioned whether this exception for separation pay plans is available for a service provider whose employment begins and ends during the same taxable year because the service provider was not employed by, and did not receive any compensation from, the service recipient for the taxable year preceding the taxable year in which the separation from service occurs. These proposed regulations clarify that the separation pay plan exception is available for service providers whose employment begins and ends in the same taxable year. In that circumstance, these proposed regulations provide that the service provider's annualized compensation for the taxable year in which the service provider separates from service may be used for purposes of this separation pay plan exception if the service provider had no compensation from the service recipient in the taxable year preceding the year in which the service provider separates from service.

E. Employment-related legal fees and expenses

Under the final regulations, an arrangement does not provide for a deferral of compensation to the extent that it provides for amounts to be paid as settlements or awards resolving *bona fide* legal claims based on wrongful termination, employment discrimination, the Fair Labor Standards Act, or workers' compensation statutes, including claims under applicable Federal, state, local, or foreign laws, or for reimbursements or payments of reasonable attorneys' fees or other reasonable expenses incurred by the service provider related to such *bona fide* legal claims.

Commenters have requested guidance on the application of section 409A(a) to provisions commonly included in employment agreements that provide for the reimbursement of attorneys' fees in connection with employment-related disputes and have asserted that there is no reason to distinguish between arrangements that provide for payment of reasonable attorneys' fees and expenses for the types of legal claims currently specified in the final regulations and any other *bona fide* legal claim with respect to the service relationship between a service provider and a service recipient. In response to these comments, these proposed regulations provide that an arrangement does not provide for a deferral of compensation to the extent that it provides for the payment or reimbursement of a service provider's reasonable attorneys' fees and other expenses incurred to enforce a claim by the service provider against the service recipient with respect to the service relationship.

F. Recurring Part-year Compensation

After publication of the final regulations, commenters have expressed concerns about the application of section 409A to recurring part-year compensation. The final regulations define recurring part-year compensation as compensation paid for services rendered in a position that the service recipient and service provider reasonably anticipate will continue on similar terms and conditions in subsequent years, and will require services to be provided during successive service periods each of which comprises less than 12 months and each of which begins in one taxable year of the service provider and ends in the next taxable year. For example, a teacher providing services during school years comprised of 10 consecutive months would have recurring part-year compensation. See §1.409A-2(a)(14). In general, commenters have asserted that section 409A should not apply to this situation because the amount being deferred from one taxable year to a subsequent taxable year is typically only a small amount and because most service providers who receive recurring part-year compensation (typically teachers and other educational workers) view an election to annualize this compensation as a cash flow decision, rather than a tax-deferral opportunity.

In response, the Treasury Department and the IRS issued Notice 2008-62 (2008-29 IRB 130), which provides that arrangements involving recurring part-year compensation do not provide for a deferral of compensation for purposes of section 409A or section 457(f) if: (1) The arrangement does not defer payment of any of the recurring part-year compensation beyond the last day of the 13th month following the beginning of the service period, and (2) the arrangement does not defer from one taxable year to the next taxable year the payment of more than the applicable dollar amount under section 402(g)(1)(B) in effect for the calendar year in which the service period begins ($18,000 for 2016). Notice 2008-62 also states that a conforming change is intended be made to the final regulations to reflect these rules.

Commenters have expressed concerns that Notice 2008-62 would not adequately address some teaching positions, such as college and university faculty members. They have noted that, depending on several variables (such as the calendar month in which a service provider commences service or the length of the service period), the dollar limitation in the notice may result in adverse tax consequences to service providers with annual compensation as low as $80,000. Commenters have further observed that some of these arrangements are nonelective, and therefore some service providers cannot opt out of a recurring part-year compensation arrangement. In recognition that service recipients in the field of education frequently structure their pay plans to include recurring part-year compensation and that the main purpose of this design is to provide uninterrupted cash flow for service providers who do not work for a portion of the year, these proposed regulations modify the recurring part-year compensation rule. These proposed regulations provide that a plan or arrangement under which a service provider receives recurring part-year compensation that is earned over a period of service does not provide for the deferral of compensation if the plan does not defer payment of any of the recurring part-year compensation to a date beyond the last day of the 13th month following the first day of the service period for which the recurring part-year compensation is paid, and the amount of the service provider's recurring part-year compensation (not merely the amount deferred) does not exceed the annual compensation limit under section 401(a)(17) ($265,000 for 2016) for the calendar year in which the service period commences. A conforming change is being made for purposes of section 457(f) under proposed section 457(f) regulations (REG-147196-07) that are also published in the Proposed Rules section of this issue of the *Federal Register*.

III. Separation from Service Definition

A. Asset Purchase Transactions

The final regulations permit the seller and an unrelated buyer in an asset purchase transaction to specify whether a person who is a service provider of the seller immediately before the transaction is treated as separating from service if the service provider provides services to the buyer after and as a result of the transaction. Commenters have asked whether this rule may be used with respect to a transaction that is treated as a deemed asset sale under section 338.

The provision of the final regulations giving buyers and sellers in asset transactions the discretion to treat employees as separating from service is based on the recognition that, while employees formally terminate employment with the seller and immediately recommence employment with the buyer in a typical asset transaction, the employees often experience no change in the type or level of services they provide. In a deemed asset sale under section 338, however, employees do not experience a termination of employment, formal or otherwise. Accordingly, the Treasury Department and the IRS have determined that it would be inconsistent with section 409A to permit the parties to a deemed asset sale to treat service providers as having separated from service upon the occurrence of the transaction. These proposed regulations affirm and make explicit that a stock purchase transaction that is treated as a deemed asset sale under section 338 is not a sale or other disposition of assets for purposes of this rule under section 409A.

B. Dual Status As Employee and Independent Contractor and Changes in Status from Employee to Independent Contractor (or Vice Versa)

The final regulations provide that an employee separates from service with an employer if the employee dies, retires, or otherwise has a termination of employment with the employer. Under the final regulations, a termination of employment generally occurs if the facts and circumstances indicate that the employer and employee reasonably anticipate that no further services would be performed after a certain date or that the level of *bona fide* services the employee would perform after that date (whether as an employee or as an independent contractor) would permanently decrease to no more than 20 percent of the average level of *bona fide* services performed (whether as an employee or an independent contractor) over the immediately preceding 36-month period (or if the employee has been providing services to the employer for less than 36 months, the full period of services). The final regulations provide that an independent contractor separates from service with a service recipient upon the expiration of the contract (or, if applicable, all contracts) under which services are performed for the service recipient if the expiration is a good-faith and complete termination of the contractual relationship.

The final regulations also provide that if a service provider provides services both as an employee and an independent contractor of a service recipient, the service provider must separate from service both as an employee and as an independent contractor to be treated as having separated from service. The final regulations further provide that "[i]f a service provider ceases providing services as an independent contractor and begins providing services as an employee, or ceases providing services as an employee and begins providing services as an independent contractor, the service provider will not be considered to have a separation from service until the service provider has ceased providing services in both capacities."

Some commenters have observed that the quoted sentence could be read to provide that a service provider who performs services for a service recipient as an employee, but who becomes an independent contractor for the same service recipient and whose anticipated level of services upon becoming an independent contractor are 20 percent or less than the average level of services performed during the immediately preceding 36-month period, would not have a separation from service because a complete termination of the contractual relationship with the service recipient has not occurred and, therefore, there is no separation from service as an independent contractor. Such a reading, however, would be inconsistent with the more specific rule that a service provider who is an employee separates from service if the employer and employee reasonably anticipate that the level of services to be performed after a certain date (whether as an employee or as an independent contractor) would permanently decrease to no more than 20 percent of the average level of services performed (whether as an employee or an independent contractor) over the immediately preceding 36-month period. To avoid potential confusion, these proposed regulations delete the quoted sentence from the regulations.

However, if a service provider, who performs services for a service recipient as an employee, becomes an independent contractor for the same service recipient but does not have a separation from service when he or she becomes an independent contractor (because at that time it is not reasonably anticipated that the level of services that would be provided by the service provider in the future would decrease to no more than 20 percent of the average level of services performed over the immediately preceding 36-month period), the service provider will have a separation from service in the future when the service provider has a separation from service based on the rules that apply to independent contractors.

IV. References to a Payment Being Made

As discussed in section II.B of this preamble entitled "Short-term Deferral Rule," the final regulations provide that a deferral of compensation does not occur under a plan if the service provider actually or constructively receives a payment that is not a deferred payment on or before the last day of the applicable 2½ month period. The final regulations further provide that, for this purpose, a payment is treated as actually or constructively received if the payment is includible in income, including if the payment is includible under the economic benefit doctrine, section 83, section 402(b), or section 457(f). Further, §1.409A-2(b)(2) of the final regulations provides that, for purposes of subsequent changes in the time or form of payment, the term "payment" generally refers to each separately identified amount to which a service provider is entitled to payment under a plan on a determinable date. This section of the final regulations provides that a payment includes the provision of any taxable benefit, including cash or property. It also provides that a payment includes, but is not limited to, the transfer, cancellation, or reduction of an amount of deferred compensation in exchange for benefits under a welfare plan, a fringe benefit excludible from income, or any other benefit excludible from income. The final regulations, however, do not include a rule that is generally applicable for all purposes under section 409A to determine when a payment is made.

These proposed regulations add a generally applicable rule to determine when a payment has been made for all provisions of the regulations under section 409A. Under these proposed regulations, a payment is made, or the payment of an amount occurs, when any taxable benefit is actually or constructively received. Consistent with the final regulations, these proposed regulations provide that a payment includes a transfer of cash, any event that results in the inclusion of an amount in income under the economic benefit doctrine, a transfer of property includible in income under section 83, a contribution to a trust described in section 402(b) at the time includible in income under section 402(b), and the transfer or creation of a beneficial interest in a section 402(b) trust at the time includible in income under section 402(b). In addition, a payment is made upon the transfer, cancellation, or reduction of an amount of deferred compensation in exchange for benefits under a welfare plan, a non-taxable fringe benefit, or any other nontaxable benefit.

The final regulations generally provide that the inclusion of an amount in income under section 457(f)(1)(A) is treated as a payment under section 409A for purposes of the short-term deferral rule under §1.409A-1(b)(4), but is generally not treated as a payment for other purposes under section 409A. Commenters, however, have observed that this treatment of income inclusion under section 457(f)(1)(A) is inconsistent with the rules under section 409A that generally treat the inclusion of any amount in income as a payment for all purposes under section 409A. These commenters have also noted that a primary purpose of section 409A is to limit the ability of a service provider or service recipient to change the time at which deferred compensation is included in income after the time of payment is established and that the failure to treat income inclusion under section 457(f)(1)(A) as a payment would be inconsistent with this purpose. In response to these observations, these proposed regulations provide that the inclusion of an amount in income under section 457(f)(1)(A) is treated a payment for all purposes under section 409A.

Under this rule, if the plan provides for a deferral of compensation under section 409A: (1) Plan terms that specify the conditions to which the payment is subject and thus when a substantial risk of forfeiture lapses for purposes of section 457(f)(1)(A) (and, consequently, determine when an amount is includible in income) would be treated as plan terms providing for the payment of the amount includible in income, and (2) all rules under section 409A applicable to the payment of an amount would apply to the inclusion of an amount under section 457(f)(1)(A). A plan would not be a deferred compensation plan within the meaning of section 409A to the extent that the amounts payable under the plan are short-term deferrals under §1.409A-1(b)(4). However, in certain limited circumstances, amounts includible in income under section 457(f)(1)(A) may not be short-term deferrals under §1.409A-1(b)(4). For example, under the proposed section 457(f) regulations (REG-147196-07), which are also published in the Proposed Rules section of this issue of the *Federal Register*, in certain circumstances conditioning a payment upon compliance with a noncompetition agreement will result in the payment being subject to a substantial risk of forfeiture for purposes of section 457(f)(1)(A), but that payment would not be treated as subject to a substantial risk of forfeiture for purposes of section 409A. In such cases, the amount payable at the end of the term of the noncompetition agreement upon compliance with the noncompete will be includible in income under section 457(f)(1)(A) only at the end of the term of the agreement under the section 457(f) regulations as proposed, but for purposes of section 409A will be deferred compensation (and not a short-term deferral), the payment of which is subject to the rules of section 409A.[2] See proposed §1.457-12(e) (REG-147196-07); see also proposed §1.457-12(a)(4) (REG-147196-07).

The Treasury Department and the IRS request comments on whether rules similar to those applicable to amounts included in income under section 457(f) should be adopted for amounts included in income under section 457A.

These proposed regulations also clarify that a transfer of property that is substantially nonvested (as defined under §1.83-3(b)) to satisfy an obligation under a nonqualified deferred compensation plan is not a payment for purposes of section 409A unless the recipient makes an election under section 83(b) to include in income the fair market value of the property (disregarding lapse restrictions), less any amount paid for the property. These proposed regulations also make conforming clarifications to rules under §1.409A-1(a)(4) regarding nonqualified deferred compensation plans subject to sections 457(f) and 457A, §1.409A-1(b)(4) regarding the short-term deferral rule, and §1.409A-2(b)(2) regarding the separate payment rule.

---

[2] There may also be instances in which a portion of an amount payable under an arrangement that is subject to section 457(f) is a short-term deferral for purposes of both section 409A and section 457(f)(1)(A), while another portion of the amount is a deferral of compensation for purposes of section 409A. For example, assume an arrangement subject to section 457(f) provides for payment of a specified dollar amount plus earnings upon separation from service, with vesting to occur when the service provider has completed three years of service. The specified dollar amount plus earnings to date is includible in income under section 457(f)(1)(A) when the service provider completes three years of service, and that amount will be a short-term deferral under section 409A if the service provider includes it in income at that time. The service provider's right to receive a payment of additional earnings accruing after the vesting date is a deferred compensation plan under section 409A.

V. Permissible Payments

A. *Death*

The final regulations provide that an amount deferred under a nonqualified deferred compensation plan may be paid only at a specified time or upon an event set forth under the regulations. One of the permissible events upon which an amount may be paid is the service provider's death. The final regulations also provide that a payment is treated as made upon a date specified under the plan (including at the time a specified event occurs) if the payment is made on that date or on a later date within the same taxable year of the service provider or, if later, by the 15th day of the third calendar month following the date specified under the plan, provided that the service provider is not permitted, directly or indirectly, to designate the taxable year of the payment.

Some commenters have questioned whether these and other rules in the final regulations applicable to amounts payable upon the death of a service provider also apply in the case of the death of a beneficiary who has become entitled to the payment of an amount due to a service provider's death. These proposed regulations clarify that the rules applicable to amounts payable upon the death of a service provider also apply to amounts payable upon the death of a beneficiary.

Also, some commenters have indicated that the time periods for the payment of amounts following death often are not long enough to resolve certain issues related to the death (for example, confirming the death and completing probate). In view of the practical issues that often arise following a death, these proposed regulations provide that an amount payable following the death of a service provider, or following the death of a beneficiary who has become entitled to payment due to the service provider's death, that is to be paid at any time during the period beginning on the date of death and ending on December 31 of the first calendar year following the calendar year during which the death occurs is treated as timely paid if it is paid at any time during this period. A plan is not required to specify any particular date within this period as the payment date and may rely on this rule if the plan provides that an amount will be paid at some time during this period, including if the plan provides that payment will be made upon death without defining the period for payment following death in any other manner, and including if the plan provides that payment will be made on a date within this period determined in the discretion of the beneficiary. These proposed regulations further provide that a plan providing for the payment of an amount at any time during this specified period may be amended to provide for the payment of that amount (or the payment of that amount may be made without amending the plan) at any other time during this period (including a time determined in the discretion of a beneficiary) without failing to meet the requirements of the deferral election provisions of § 1.409A-2 or the permissible payment provisions of § 1.409A-3, including the prohibition on the acceleration of payments under § 1.409A-3(j). For example, a plan that provides for a payment to be made during the first calendar year beginning after the death of a service provider may be amended to provide for the payment of the amount (or the payment may be made under the plan without such amendment) at any time during the period beginning on the date of death and ending on December 31 of the first calendar year following the calendar year during which the death occurs. For additional rules concerning payments due upon a beneficiary's death, see section VI.A of this preamble.

B. *Certain Transaction-based Compensation*

The final regulations provide special rules for payments of transaction-based compensation. Transaction-based compensation payments are payments related to certain types of changes in control that (1) occur because a service recipient purchases its stock held by a service provider or because the service recipient or a third party purchases a stock right held by a service provider, or (2) are calculated by reference to the value of service recipient stock. Under the final regulations, transaction-based compensation may be treated as paid at a designated date or pursuant to a payment schedule that complies with the requirements of section 409A(a) if it is paid on the same schedule and under the same terms and conditions as apply to payments to shareholders generally with respect to stock of the service recipient pursuant to the change in control. Likewise, transaction-based compensation meeting these requirements will not fail to meet the requirements of the initial or subsequent deferral election rules under section 409A if it is paid not later than five years after the change in control event. These proposed regulations clarify that the special payment rules for transaction-based compensation apply to a statutory stock option or a stock right that did not otherwise provide for deferred compensation before the purchase or agreement to purchase the stock right. Accordingly, the purchase (or agreement to purchase) such a statutory stock option or stock right in a manner consistent with these rules does not result in the statutory stock option or stock right being treated as having provided for the deferral of compensation from the original grant date.

VI. Prohibition on Acceleration of Payments

A. *Payments to Beneficiaries Upon Death, Disability, or Unforeseeable Emergency*

Under the final regulations, a prohibited acceleration of a payment does not result from the addition of death, disability, or unforeseeable emergency as a potentially earlier alternative payment event for an amount previously deferred. However, under the final regulations, this exception applies only with respect to a service provider's death, disability, or unforeseeable emergency and does not apply with respect to the death, disability, or unforeseeable emergency of a beneficiary who has become entitled to a payment due to the service provider's death. These proposed regulations provide that this exception also applies to the payment of deferred amounts upon the death, disability, or unforeseeable emergency of a beneficiary who has become entitled to payment due to a service provider's death. These proposed regulations also clarify that a schedule of payments (including payments treated as a single payment) that has already commenced prior to a service provider's or a beneficiary's death, disability, or unforeseeable emergency may be accelerated upon the death, disability, or unforeseeable emergency.

B. *Compliance With Bona Fide Foreign Ethics Laws or Conflicts of Interest Laws*

Under the final regulations, a plan may provide for acceleration of the time or schedule of a payment, or a payment may be made under a plan, to the extent reasonably necessary to avoid the violation of a Federal, state, local, or foreign ethics or conflicts of interest law. However, with respect to a foreign ethics or conflicts of interest law, this exception applies only to foreign earned income from sources within the foreign country that promulgated the law. Commenters have suggested that this provision should not be limited to foreign earned income because the requirements of foreign ethics or conflicts of interest laws may affect both the payment of foreign and United States earned income. These proposed regulations expand the scope of this provision to permit the acceleration of any nonqualified deferred compensation if the acceleration is reasonably necessary to comply with a *bona fide* foreign ethics or conflicts of interest law.

C. *Plan Terminations and Liquidations*

Under the final regulations, a plan may provide for the acceleration of a payment made pursuant to the termination and liquidation of a plan under certain circumstances. Specifically, a plan may provide for the acceleration of a payment if the plan is terminated and liquidated within 12 months of a corporate dissolution taxed under section 331, or with the approval of a bankruptcy court pursuant to 11 U.S.C. section 503(b)(1)(A) if certain other conditions are satisfied. The citation to 11 U.S.C. section 503(b)(1)(A) is erroneous. These proposed regulations correct this provision by retaining the operative rule but deleting the section reference.

The final regulations also provide that a payment may be accelerated pursuant to a change in control event as described under § 1.409A-3(j)(4)(ix)(B) or in other circumstances provided certain requirements are satisfied, as described under § 1.409A-3(j)(4)(ix)(C). To terminate a plan pursuant to § 1.409A-3(j)(4)(ix)(C), the final regulations provide that the service recipient must terminate and liquidate all plans sponsored by the service recipient that would be aggregated with the terminated plan under the plan aggregation rules under §1.409A-1(c) of the final regulations if the same service provider had deferrals of compensation under all such plans. The final regulations also provide that for three years following the date on which the service recipient took all necessary action to irrevocably terminate and liquidate the plan the service recipient cannot adopt a new plan that would be aggregated with the terminated and liquidated plan if the same service provider participated in both plans. Some commenters have asked whether these rules mean that only the plans of a particular category in which a particular service provider actually participates must be terminated if a plan in which that service provider participates is terminated.

The plan aggregation rules under §1.409A-1(c)(2) of the final regulations identify nine different types of nonqualified deferred compensation plans - account balance plans providing for elective deferrals, account balance plans that do not provide for elective deferrals, nonaccount balance plans, separation pay plans, plans providing for in-kind benefits or reimbursements, split-dollar plans, foreign earned income plans, stock right plans, and plans that are not any of the foregoing. All plans of the same type in which the same service provider participates are treated as a single plan. The rule set forth under §1.409A-3(j)(4)(ix)(C) that requires the termination and liquidation of all plans sponsored by the service recipient that would be aggregated with the terminated plan "if the same service provider had deferrals of compensation" under all of those plans is intended to require the termination of all plans in the same plan category sponsored by the service recipient. The reference to the "same service provider" having deferrals of compensation under all of those plans refers to participation of a hypothetical service provider in all such plans, which would be required to aggregate all of the plans under the section 409A plan aggregation rules.

The Treasury Department and the IRS have concluded that the meaning of the plan termination rule under §1.409A-3(j)(4)(ix)(C) is not ambiguous. However, to address the questions raised by commenters, these proposed regulations further clarify that the acceleration of a payment pursuant to this rule is permitted only if the service recipient terminates and liquidates all plans of the same category that the service recipient sponsors, and not merely all plans of the same category in which a particular service provider actually participates. These proposed regulations also clarify that under this rule, for a period of three years following the termination and liquidation of a plan, the service recipient cannot adopt a new plan of the same category as the terminated and liquidated plan, regardless of which service providers participate in the plan.

D. Offset Provisions

The final regulations provide that the payment of an amount as a substitute for a payment of deferred compensation is generally treated as a payment of the deferred compensation. They also provide that when the payment of an amount results in an actual or potential reduction of, or current or future offset to, an amount of deferred compensation, the payment is a substitute for the deferred compensation. Further, the final regulations provide that if a service provider's right to deferred compensation is made subject to anticipation, alienation, sale, transfer, assignment, pledge, encumbrance, attachment, or garnishment by the service provider's creditors, the deferred compensation is treated as having been paid. Under certain circumstances, these provisions may result in an amount being paid (or treated as paid) before the payment date or event specified in the plan in violation of the prohibition on the acceleration of payments under section 409A. The final regulations, however, include a de minimis exception to these rules pursuant to which a plan may provide for the acceleration of the time or schedule of a payment, or a payment may be made under a plan, in satisfaction of a debt of the service provider if the debt is incurred in the ordinary course of the service relationship, the entire offset in any taxable year does not exceed $5,000, and the offset is taken at the same time and in the same amount as the debt otherwise would have been due from the service provider.

Stakeholders have observed that the prohibition on offsets may conflict with certain laws regarding debt collection by the Federal government (for example, 31 U.S.C. sections 3711, *et. seq.*), and that the exception for small debts is insufficient to permit the enforcement of these laws. Because these laws would effectively prevent certain government entities from providing nonqualified deferred compensation in a manner that complies with the requirements of section 409A(a) and because of the limited applicability of Federal debt collection laws, the Treasury Department and the IRS have determined that it is appropriate to expand the current exception to the prohibition on accelerated payments for certain offsets to permit a plan to provide for the acceleration of the time or schedule of a payment, or to make a payment, to the extent reasonably necessary to comply with Federal laws regarding debt collection.

VII. Amount Includible in Income under Section 409A

The proposed income inclusion regulations provide that the amount includible in income for a taxable year if a nonqualified deferred compensation plan fails to meet the requirements of section 409A(a) at any time during that taxable year equals the excess of (1) the total amount deferred under the plan for that taxable year, including any payments under the plan during that taxable year, over (2) the portion of that amount, if any, that is either subject to a substantial risk of forfeiture or has been previously included in income. The proposed income inclusion regulations, however, include an anti-abuse provision under §1.409A-4(a)(1)(ii)(B), which provides that an amount otherwise subject to a substantial risk of forfeiture for purposes of determining the amount includible in income under a plan will be treated as not subject to a substantial risk of forfeiture for these purposes if the facts and circumstances indicate that a service recipient has a pattern or practice of permitting impermissible changes in the time or form of payment with respect to nonvested deferred amounts under one or more nonqualified deferred compensation plans and either (i) an impermissible change in the time or form of payment applies to the amount or (ii) the facts and circumstances indicate that the amount would be affected by the pattern or practice.

Although these rules permit the correction of certain plan provisions that fail to comply with the requirements of section 409A(a) while amounts are nonvested without including the amounts in income or incurring an additional tax, they were not intended to allow service recipients to change time or form of payment provisions that otherwise meet the requirements of section 409A(a) in a manner that fails to comply with section 409A(a), and they were not intended to permit service recipients to create errors in nonqualified deferred compensation plans with respect to nonvested amounts with the intention of using those errors as a pretext for establishing or changing a time or form of payment in a manner that fails to comply with section 409A(a). Accordingly, these proposed regulations clarify and modify the anti-abuse rule under §1.409A-4(a)(1)(ii)(B) of the proposed income inclusion regulations to preclude changes of this nature.

First, these proposed regulations clarify that a deferred amount that is otherwise subject to a substantial risk of forfeiture is treated as not subject to a substantial risk of forfeiture for a service provider's taxable year during which there is a change in a plan provision (including an initial deferral election provision) that is not otherwise permitted under section 409A and the final regulations and that affects the time or form of payment of the amount if there is no reasonable, good faith basis for concluding that the original provision failed to meet the requirements of section 409A(a) and that the change is necessary to bring the plan into compliance with the requirements of section 409A(a).

Second, these proposed regulations provide examples of the types of facts and circumstances that indicate whether a service recipient has a pattern or practice of permitting impermissible changes in the time or form of payment with respect to nonvested deferred amounts under one or more plans. If the service recipient has such a pattern or practice that would affect a nonvested deferred amount, that amount is treated as not subject to a substantial risk of forfeiture. The facts and circumstances include: Whether a service recipient has taken commercially reasonable measures to identify and correct substantially similar failures promptly upon discovery; whether substantially similar failures have occurred with respect to nonvested deferred amounts to a greater extent than with respect to vested deferred amounts; whether substantially similar failures occur more frequently with respect to newly adopted plans; and whether substantially similar failures appear intentional, are numerous, or repeat common past failures that have since been corrected.

Third, these proposed regulations provide that, to the extent generally applicable guidance regarding the correction of section 409A failures prescribes a particular correction method (or methods) for a type of plan failure, that correction method (or one of the permissible correction methods) must be used if a service recipient chooses to correct that type of a failure with respect to a nonvested deferred amount. In addition, these proposed regulations provide that substantially similar failures affecting nonvested deferred amounts must be corrected in substantially the same manner.

A service recipient correcting a plan failure affecting a nonvested deferred amount is not required, solely with respect to the nonvested deferred amount, to comply with any requirement under generally applicable guidance regarding the correction of section 409A failures that is unrelated to the method for correcting the failure, such as general eligibility requirements, income inclusion, additional taxes, premium interest, or information reporting by the service recipient or service provider. Accordingly, a service recipient may amend a noncompliant plan term in a manner permitted under applicable correction guidance even though the failure may not have been eligible for correction under that guidance (for example, due to applicable timing requirements). In addition, the portion of the nonvested deferred amount that is affected by the correction is not subject to income inclusion, additional taxes, or applicable premium interest under section 409A(a)(1), and neither the service recipient nor the service provider is required to notify the IRS of the correction. For a description of the currently available corrections methods, see Notice 2008-113 (2008-51 IRB 1305), Notice 2010-6 (2010-3 IRB 275), and Notice 2010-80 (2010-51 IRB 853).

VIII. Individual and Entity Service Providers

Under the final regulations, the term service provider includes an individual, corporation, subchapter S corporation, partnership, personal service corporation, noncorporate entity that would be a personal service corporation if it were a corporation, qualified personal service corporation, and noncorporate entity that would be a qualified personal service corporation if it were a corporation. These proposed regulations clarify §§ 1.409A-1(b)(5)(vi)(A), 1.409A-1(b)(5)(vi)(E), 1.409A-1(b)(5)(vi)(F), and 1.409A-3(i)(5)(iii) of the final regulations to reflect that a service provider can be an entity as well as an individual. These proposed regulations also clarify § 1.409A-1(b)(3) of the final regulations to correct an erroneous reference to "service provider" that should be "service recipient."

Proposed Effective Dates

General Applicability Date for Amendments to Final Regulations

The provisions of these proposed regulations amending the final regulations are proposed to be applicable on or after the date on which they are published as final regulations in the *Federal Register*. For periods before this date, the existing final regulations and other applicable guidance apply (without regard to these proposed regulations). The applicability date for the existing final regulations in § 1.409A-6(b) is accordingly amended to reflect extension of certain transition relief through 2008 under Notice 2007-86, 2007-46 IRB 990. Taxpayers may, however, rely on these proposed regulations before they are published as final regulations, and until final regulations are published the IRS will not assert positions that are contrary to the positions set forth in these proposed regulations.

Certain provisions of these proposed amendments to the final regulations are not intended as substantive changes to the current requirements under section 409A. Accordingly, the Treasury Department and the IRS have concluded that the following positions may not properly be taken under the existing final regulations: (1) That the transfer of restricted stock for which no section 83(b) election is made or the transfer of a stock option that does not have a readily ascertainable fair market value would result in a payment under a plan; (2) that a contribution to a section 402(b) trust includible in income under section 402(b) to fund an obligation under a plan would not result in a payment under a plan; (3) that a stock purchase treated as a deemed asset sale under section 338 is a sale or other disposition of assets for purposes of determining when a service provider separates from service as a result of an asset purchase transaction; or (4) that the exception to the prohibition on acceleration of a payment upon a termination and liquidation of a plan pursuant to § 1.409A-3(j)(4)(ix)(C) applies if the service recipient terminates and liquidates only the plans of the same category in which a particular service provider participates, rather than all plans of the same category that the service recipient sponsors.

General Applicability Date for Amendments to Proposed Income Inclusion Regulations

The proposed income inclusion regulations are proposed to be applicable on or after the date on which they are published as final regulations in the *Federal Register*. Notice 2008-115 provides that, until the Treasury Department and the IRS issue further guidance, compliance with the provisions of the proposed income inclusion regulations with respect to the calculation of the amount includible in income under section 409A(a)(1) and the calculation of the additional taxes under section 409A(a)(1) will be treated as compliance with the requirements of section 409A(a), provided that the taxpayer complies with all of the provisions of the proposed regulations. Until the Treasury Department and the IRS issue further guidance, taxpayers may rely on the proposed income inclusion regulations, as modified by the amendment of § 1.409A-4(a)(1)(ii)(B) in these proposed regulations, for purposes of calculating the amount includible in income under section 409A(a)(1) (including the identification and treatment of deferred amounts subject to a substantial risk of forfeiture) and the calculation of the additional taxes under section 409A(a)(1), and the IRS will not assert positions with respect to periods before the date final regulations are published in the *Federal Register* that are contrary to the positions set forth in the proposed income inclusion regulations as amended by these proposed regulations.

Special Applicability Dates for Amendments to Recurring Part-Year Compensation Rules

The rules set forth in these proposed regulations regarding recurring part-year compensation are proposed to be applicable on and after the date on which these proposed regulations are published as final regulations in the *Federal Register*. However, taxpayers may rely on either the rules in these proposed regulations or the rules in Notice 2008-62 relating to recurring part-year compensation for the taxable year in which these proposed regulations are published as final regulations and all prior taxable years.

Effect on Other Documents

These proposed regulations do not affect the applicability of other guidance issued with respect to section 409A, including Notice 2008-115, except that, for the permitted reliance on the proposed income inclusion regulations, these proposed regulations withdraw § 1.409A-4(a)(1)(ii)(B) of the proposed income inclusion regulations and replace it with a new § 1.409A-4(a)(1)(ii)(B).

Statement of Availability of IRS Documents

IRS Revenue Procedures, Revenue Rulings notices, and other guidance cited in this document are published in the Internal Revenue Bulletin (or Cumulative Bulletin) and are available from the Superintendent of Documents, U.S. Government Printing Office, Washington, DC 20402, or by visiting the IRS website at *http://www.irs.gov*. (See § 601.601(d)(2)(ii)(*b*) of this chapter.)

Special Analyses

Certain IRS regulations, including this one, are exempt from the requirements of Executive Order 12866, as supplemented and reaffirmed by Executive Order 13563. Therefore, a regulatory impact assessment is not required. It also has been determined that section 553(b) of the Administrative Procedure Act (5 U.S.C. chapter 5) does not apply to these proposed regulations. It is hereby certified that the collection of information in these proposed regulations would not have a significant impact on a substantial number of small entities. This certification is based on the fact that these proposed regulations only provide guidance on how to satisfy existing collection of information requirements. Accordingly, a Regulatory Flexibility Analysis is not required. Pursuant to section 7805(f) of the Code, these proposed regulations have been submitted to the Chief Counsel for Advocacy of the Small Business Administration for comment on its impact on small business.

Comments and Requests for Public Hearing

Before these proposed regulations are adopted as final regulations, consideration will be given to any comments that are submitted timely to the IRS as prescribed in this preamble under the "ADDRESSES" heading. The Treasury Department and the IRS request comments on all aspects of the rules proposed by these proposed regulations. All comments will be available at www.regulations.gov or upon request. A public hearing may be scheduled if requested by any person who timely submits comments. If a public hearing is scheduled, notice of the date, time and place for the hearing will be published in the *Federal Register*.

Drafting Information

The principal author of these proposed regulations is Gregory Burns, Office of Division Counsel/Associate Chief Counsel (Tax Exempt and Government Entities). However, other personnel from the Treasury Department and the IRS participated in their development.

[¶ 49,703]   **Proposed Amendments of Regulations (REG-147196-07) Proposed Regulations, NPRM REG-147196-07**, published in the Federal Register on June 22, 2016.

[Code Sec. 457]

Deferred compensation plans: Government and Tax-Exempt: Proposed regulations.—Amendments of Reg. §§ 1.457-1, 1.457-2, 1.457-4, 1.457-6, 1.457-7, 1.457-9, 1.457-10, 1.457-11, 1.457-12 and 1.457-13, prescribing rules under section 457 of the Internal Revenue Code for the taxation of compensation deferred under plans established and maintained by State or local governments or other tax exempt organizations, are proposed. The texts are at ¶ 21,532B, ¶ 21,533C, ¶ 21,535D, ¶ 21,535K, ¶ 21,535N, ¶ 21,535S, ¶ 21,535V, ¶ 21,535X, ¶ 21,535ZA and ¶ 21,535ZD.

AGENCY: Internal Revenue Service (IRS), Treasury.

ACTION: Notice of proposed rulemaking and notice of public hearing.

SUMMARY: This document contains proposed regulations prescribing rules under section 457 of the Internal Revenue Code for the taxation of compensation deferred under plans established and maintained by State or local governments or other tax exempt organizations. These proposed regulations include rules for determining when amounts deferred under these plans are includible in income, the amounts that are includible in income, and the types of plans that are not subject to these rules. The proposed regulations would affect participants, beneficiaries, sponsors, and administrators of certain plans sponsored by State or local governments or tax-exempt organizations that provide for a deferral of compensation. This document also provides a notice of a public hearing on the proposed regulations.

DATES: Written or electronic comments on these proposed regulations must be received by September 20, 2016. Outline of topics to be discussed at the public hearing scheduled for October 18, 2016 at 10 a.m. must be received by September 20, 2016.

ADDRESSES: Send submissions to: CC:PA:LPD:PR (REG-147196-07), room 5203, Internal Revenue Service, P.O. Box 7604, Ben Franklin Station, Washington DC, 20044. Submissions may be hand delivered Monday through Friday, between the hours of 8 a.m. and 4 p.m. to CC:PA:LPD:PR (REG-147196-07), Courier's Desk, Internal Revenue Service, 1111 Constitution Avenue, N.W., Washington DC, 20224 or sent electronically, via the Federal eRulemaking Portal at www.regulations.gov (IRS REG-147196-07). The public hearing will be held in the IRS Auditorium, Internal Revenue Building, 1111 Constitution Avenue, N.W., Washington DC, 20224.

FOR FURTHER INFORMATION CONTACT: Concerning the proposed regulations under section 457, Keith Kost at (202) 317-6799 or Cheryl Press at (202) 317-4148, concerning submission of comments, the hearing, and/or to be placed on the building access list to attend the hearing, Regina Johnson at (202) 317-6901 (not toll-free numbers).

SUPPLEMENTARY INFORMATION:

Background

This document contains proposed amendments to the Income Tax Regulations (26 CFR part 1) under section 457(a), (b), and (f) of the Internal Revenue Code (Code), as well as proposed regulations under section 457(e)(11), (e)(12), and (g)(4). Generally, if a deferred compensation plan of a State or local government or tax-exempt entity does not satisfy the requirements of section 457(b), (c), (d), and, in the case of a plan that is maintained by a State or local government, (g), compensation deferred under the plan will be included in income in accordance with section 457(f) unless the plan is not subject to section 457 or is treated as not providing for a deferral of compensation for purposes of section 457. Section 457(e) includes certain definitions and special rules for purposes of section 457 and describes certain plans that either are not subject to section 457 or are treated as not providing for a deferral of compensation under section 457.[1]

Section 457(a)(1) provides that any amount of compensation deferred under an eligible deferred compensation plan as defined in section 457(b) (an eligible plan), and any income attributable to the amounts so deferred, is includible in gross income only for the taxable year in which the compensation or other income is paid to the participant or beneficiary in the case of an eligible employer described in section 457(e)(1)(A) or is paid or otherwise made available to the participant or beneficiary in the case of an eligible employer described in section 457(e)(1)(B). An eligible employer described in section 457(e)(1)(A) means a State, a political subdivision of a State, or any agency or instrumentality of a State or political subdivision of a State (a governmental entity). An eligible employer described in section 457(e)(1)(B) means any organization other than a governmental entity that is exempt from tax under subtitle A (a tax-exempt entity).

Section 457(f)(1)(A) provides that, in the case of a plan of an eligible employer providing for a deferral of compensation, if the plan is not an eligible plan, the compensation is included in gross income when the rights to payment of the compensation are not subject to a substantial risk of forfeiture, as defined in section 457(f)(3)(B).[2] Section 457(f)(1)(B) provides that the tax treatment of any amount made available under the plan will be determined under section 72. Section 457(f)(2) provides that section 457(f)(1) does not apply to a plan that is described in section 401(a) or an annuity plan or contract described in section 403, the portion of any plan that consists of a transfer of property described in section 83, the portion

---

[1] Plans described in certain statutes that are not incorporated into the Code are not subject to section 457. See sections 1107(c)(3)(B), 1107(c)(4), and 1107(c)(5) of the Tax Reform Act of 1986, Public Law 99-514 (100 Stat. 2494 (1986)), as amended, and sections 1101(e)(6), 6064(d)(2), and 6064(d)(3) of the Technical and Miscellaneous Revenue Act of 1988, Public Law 100-647 (102 Stat. 3342 (1988)).

[2] In Notice 2007-62 (2007-2 CB 331 (August 6, 2007)), the Treasury Department and the IRS announced the intent to issue guidance under section 457, including providing

definitions of a bona fide severance pay plan under section 457(e)(11) and substantial risk of forfeiture under section 457(f)(3)(B). In response to comments received in response to a request in Notice 2007-62 (on subjects including but not limited to severance pay, covenants not to compete, and the definition of substantial risk of forfeiture), the rules in these proposed regulations have been modified from the proposals announced in that notice.

of a plan that consists of a trust described in section 402(b), a qualified governmental excess benefit arrangement described in section 415(m), or the portion of any applicable employment retention plan described in section 457(f)(4).

Section 457(e)(11) provides that certain plans are treated as not providing for a deferral of compensation. These plans include any bona fide vacation leave, sick leave, compensatory time, severance pay, disability pay, or death benefit plan, as well as any plan paying solely length of service awards to certain bona fide volunteers (or their beneficiaries) and certain voluntary early retirement incentive plans.[3] Section 457(e)(12) provides that section 457 does not apply to certain nonelective deferred compensation of nonemployees.

On July 11, 2003, the Treasury Department and the IRS issued final regulations under section 457 (TD 9075) (68 FR 41230) (2003 final regulations). The 2003 final regulations provide guidance on deferred compensation plans of eligible employers, including eligible plans under section 457(b). The 2003 final regulations also reflect the changes made to section 457 by the Tax Reform Act of 1986, Public Law 99-514 (100 Stat. 2494), the Small Business Job Protection Act of 1996, Public Law 104-188 (110 Stat. 1755), the Taxpayer Relief Act of 1997, Public Law 105-34 (111 Stat. 788), the Economic Growth and Tax Relief Reconciliation Act of 2001, Public Law 107-16 (115 Stat. 38), and the Job Creation and Worker Assistance Act of 2002, Public Law 107-147 (116 Stat. 21). The proposed amendments to the 2003 final regulations under section 457(a), (b), and (g) contained in this document include amendments to reflect subsequent statutory changes made to section 457. The following sections of this preamble provide a chronological description of the relevant changes made after the 2003 final regulations were issued. (For a summary of the proposed changes to the 2003 final regulations, see the Explanation of Provisions section of this preamble.)

I. *American Jobs Creation Act of 2004*

Section 885 of the American Jobs Creation Act of 2004, Public Law 108-357 (118 Stat. 1418), added section 409A to the Code. Section 409A generally provides that, if at any time during a taxable year a nonqualified deferred compensation plan fails to meet the requirements of section 409A or is not operated in accordance with those requirements, all amounts deferred under the plan for the taxable year and all preceding taxable years are includible in gross income to the extent the amounts are not subject to a substantial risk of forfeiture and were not previously included in gross income.

On April 17, 2007, the Treasury Department and the IRS issued final regulations under section 409A (TD 9312) at 72 FR 19234 (final section 409A regulations). The final section 409A regulations provide guidance on the definition of certain terms and the types of plans covered under section 409A, permissible deferral elections under section 409A, and permissible payments under section 409A. The final section 409A regulations provide that a deferred compensation plan of a governmental entity or a tax-exempt entity that is subject to section 457(f) may constitute a nonqualified deferred compensation plan for purposes of section 409A and that the rules of section 409A apply separately and in addition to any requirements applicable to these plans under section 457(f).

On December 8, 2008, proposed regulations under section 409A were published in the **Federal Register** (73 FR 74380) (proposed section 409A regulations) that provide guidance on the calculation of amounts includible in income under section 409A(a) and the additional taxes imposed by that section with respect to arrangements that do not comply with the requirements of section 409A(a).

In Notice 2008-62 (2008-29 IRB 130 (July 21, 2008)), the Treasury Department and the IRS provided guidance under sections 409A and 457(f) regarding recurring part-year compensation. For this purpose, recurring part-year compensation is compensation paid for services rendered in a position that the employer and employee reasonably anticipate will continue under similar terms and conditions in subsequent years, and under which the employee will be required to provide services during successive service periods each of which comprises less than 12 months (for example, a teacher providing services during a school year comprised of 10 consecutive months) and each of which begins in one taxable year of the employee and ends in the next taxable year. Notice 2008-62 provides that an arrangement under which an employee or independent contractor receives recurring part-year compensation does not provide for the deferral of compensation for purposes of section 409A or for purposes of section 457(f) if (A) the arrangement does not defer payment of any of the recurring part-year compensation beyond the last day of the 13th month following the beginning of the service period, and (B) the arrangement does not defer from one taxable year to the next taxable year the payment of more than the applicable dollar amount under section 402(g)(1)(B) ($18,000 for 2016). The notice provides that taxpayers may rely on this rule beginning in the first taxable year that includes July 1, 2008.

II. *Pension Protection Act of 2006*

The Pension Protection Act of 2006, Public Law 109-280 (120 Stat. 780) (PPA '06), permits a participant's designated beneficiary who is not a surviving spouse to roll over, in a direct trustee-to-trustee transfer, distributions from an eligible plan maintained by a governmental entity (an eligible governmental plan) to an individual retirement account or annuity (IRA). Section 829 of PPA '06 added section 402(c)(11) to the Code, which provides that this type of transfer is treated as an eligible rollover distribution for purposes of section 402(c).

Section 845(b)(3) of PPA '06 added section 457(a)(3) to the Code, which provides an exclusion from gross income for amounts that are distributed from an eligible governmental plan to the extent provided in section 402(l). Section 402(l) provides that distributions from certain governmental retirement plans are excluded from the gross income of an eligible retired public safety officer to the extent the distributions do not exceed the amount paid by the retired officer for qualified health insurance premiums for the year, up to a maximum of $3,000. See Notice 2007-7, part IV (2007-1 CB 395 (January 29, 2007)), as well as Notice 2007-99 (2007-2 CB 1243 (December 26, 2007)), for guidance on the application of section 402(l).

Section 1104(a)(1) of PPA '06 added section 457(e)(11)(D) to the Code, which treats applicable voluntary early retirement incentive plans as bona fide severance pay plans that do not provide for a deferral of compensation under section 457 with respect to payments or supplements that are an early retirement benefit, a retirement-type subsidy, or a social security supplement in coordination with a defined benefit pension plan. This treatment applies only to the extent the payments otherwise could have been provided under the defined benefit plan (determined as if section 411 applied to the defined benefit plan). Under section 457(e)(11)(D)(ii), an applicable voluntary early retirement incentive plan may be maintained only by a local educational agency or a tax-exempt education association.[4]

Section 1104(b)(1) of PPA '06 added section 457(f)(2)(F) to the Code, which provides that section 457(f)(1) does not apply to an applicable employment retention plan. Under section 457(f)(4), an applicable employment retention plan is a plan maintained by a local educational agency or a tax-exempt education association to pay additional compensation upon severance from employment for purposes of employee retention or

---

[3] Announcement 2000-1 (2000-1 CB 294 (January 1, 2000)), provides transitional guidance on the reporting requirements for certain broad-based, nonelective deferred compensation plans maintained by State or local governments. The announcement states that, pending the issuance of further guidance, a State or local government should not report amounts for any year before the year in which a participant or beneficiary is in actual or constructive receipt of those amounts if the amounts are provided under a plan that the State or local government has been treating as a bona fide severance pay plan under section 457(e)(11) for years before calendar year 1999. To be eligible for this transitional relief, the plan must satisfy certain requirements described in the announcement.

[4] A local education agency is defined in section 9101 of the Elementary and Secondary Education Act of 1965, Public Law 89-10 (79 Stat. 27), as a public board of education or other public authority legally constituted within a State for either administrative control or direction of, or to perform a service function for, public elementary schools or secondary schools in a city, county, township, school district, or other political subdivision of a State, or of or for a combination of school districts or counties that is recognized in a State as an administrative agency for its public elementary schools or secondary schools. A tax-exempt education association is an association that principally represents employees of one or more local education agencies and is an entity described in section 501(c)(5) or (6) that is exempt from tax under section 501(a).

rewarding employees to the extent that the benefits payable under the plan do not exceed twice the applicable annual dollar limit on deferrals in section 457(e)(15).[5]

III. *Heroes Earnings Assistance and Relief Tax Act of 2008*

Section 104(c) of the Heroes Earnings Assistance and Relief Tax Act of 2008, Public Law 110-245 (122 Stat. 1624) (HEART Act), amended section 457 to add section 457(g)(4) regarding benefits payable upon death during qualified active military service under the Uniformed Services Employment and Reemployment Rights Act of 1994, Public Law 103-353 (108 Stat. 3149). Section 457(g)(4) provides that an eligible governmental plan must meet the requirements of section 401(a)(37). Under section 401(a)(37), a plan is not treated as a qualified retirement plan unless the plan provides that, in the case of a participant who dies while performing qualified military service, the survivors of the participant are generally entitled to any additional benefits that would have been provided under the plan if the participant had resumed and then terminated employment on account of death. Section 105(b) of the HEART Act added section 414(u)(12) to the Code, which provides rules regarding (A) the treatment of differential wage payments as compensation and (B) the treatment of service in the uniformed services (as described in section 3401(h)(2)(A)) as a severance from employment for purposes of plan distribution requirements, including the distribution requirements of section 457(d)(1)(A)(ii).

IV. *Small Business Jobs Act of 2010 and American Taxpayer Relief Act of 2012*

Section 2111 of the Small Business Jobs Act of 2010, Public Law 111-240 (124 Stat. 2504) (SBJA), amended section 402A of the Code to allow an eligible governmental plan to include a qualified Roth contribution program, effective for taxable years beginning after December 31, 2010. SBJA also amended section 402A to permit taxable in-plan rollovers to qualified Roth accounts under eligible governmental plans. Section 902 of the American Taxpayer Relief Act of 2012, Public Law 112-240 (126 Stat. 2313), expanded the types of amounts eligible for an in-plan Roth rollover. For guidance relating to in-plan rollovers to qualified Roth accounts, see Notice 2013-74 (2013-52 IRB 819 (December 23, 2013)) and Notice 2010-84 (2010-51 IRB 872 (July 19, 2010)).

Explanation of Provisions

I. *Overview*

These proposed regulations make certain changes to the 2003 final regulations under sections 457(a), 457(b), and 457(g) to reflect statutory changes to section 457 since the publication of those regulations. In addition, these proposed regulations provide guidance on certain issues under sections 457(e)(11) and 457(e)(12) that are not addressed in the 2003 final regulations and provide additional guidance under section 457(f). Consistent with the 2003 final regulations, although the rules under section 457 apply to plan participants and beneficiaries without regard to whether the related services are provided by an employee or independent contractor, these proposed regulations often use the terms employee and employer to describe a service provider and a service recipient, respectively, without regard to whether the service provider is an independent contractor.[6]

II. *Regulatory Amendments to Reflect Statutory Changes to Section 457*

A. *Qualified Roth contribution program*

Section 1.457-4 of the 2003 final regulations provides that annual deferrals to an eligible plan that satisfy certain requirements are excluded from the gross income of the participant in the year deferred or contributed and are not includable in gross income until paid to the participant, in the case of an eligible governmental plan, or until paid or otherwise made available to the participant, in the case of an eligible plan of a tax-exempt entity. These proposed regulations amend § 1.457-4(a) and (b) to reflect the change made by SBJA to allow an eligible governmental plan to include a qualified Roth contribution program, as defined in section 402A(c)(1), under which designated Roth contributions are included in income in the year of deferral. Consistent with section 402A(b)(2), these proposed regulations provide that contributions and withdrawals of a participant's designated Roth contributions must be credited and debited to a designated Roth account maintained for the participant, and that the plan must maintain a record of each participant's investment in the contract with respect to the account. In addition, the proposed regulations provide that no forfeitures may be allocated to a designated Roth account and that no contributions other than designated Roth contributions and rollover contributions described in section 402A(c)(3)(A) may be made to the account.

These proposed regulations also amend § 1.457-7(b)(1), which provides guidance regarding the circumstances under which amounts are included in income under an eligible governmental plan, to specify that qualified distributions from a designated Roth account are excluded from gross income.

B. *Certain distributions for qualified accident and health insurance premiums*

The proposed regulations amend the rules for the taxation of eligible governmental plan distributions under § 1.457-7(b) to reflect the change made by PPA '06 with respect to certain amounts distributed to an eligible public safety officer. The proposed regulations provide that distributions from an eligible governmental plan meeting the requirements of section 402(l) are excluded from gross income and are not subject to the general rule providing that amounts deferred under an eligible governmental plan are includable in the gross income of a participant or beneficiary for the taxable year in which they are paid. For this purpose, see section 402(l) for rules regarding the extent to which this income exclusion applies to a distribution (including the dollar limitation on the exclusion) and section 402(l)(4)(C) for the meaning of the term public safety officer.

C. *Rules related to qualified military service*

The proposed regulations amend § 1.457-2(f) to implement the requirements of section 457(g)(4), which was added by the HEART Act and which provides that an eligible governmental plan must meet the requirements of section 401(a)(37) (providing that, in the case of a participant who dies while performing qualified military service, the survivors of the participant generally are entitled to any additional benefits that would have been provided under the plan if the participant had resumed and then terminated employment on account of death). In addition the proposed regulations amend § 1.457-6(b)(1) to provide a cross reference to the rules under section 414(u)(12)(B) (providing that leave for certain military service is treated as a severance from employment for purposes of the plan distribution restrictions that apply to eligible plans).

---

[5] See also section 1104(c) of PPA '06, which amended section 3(2) of the Employee Retirement Income Security Act of 1974, Public Law 93-406 (88 Stat. 829) (ERISA), to provide that applicable voluntary early retirement incentive plans and applicable employment retention plans are treated as welfare plans (and not pension plans) for purposes of ERISA.

[6] Section 457(e)(2) provides that the performance of services for purposes of section 457 includes the performance of services as an independent contractor and that the person (or governmental entity) for whom these services are performed is treated as an employer.

III. *Certain Plans That Are Not Subject to Section 457 or Are Not Treated as Providing for a Deferral of Compensation Under Section 457*

A. *In general*

Section 1.457-2(k) of the 2003 final regulations defines the term plan for purposes of section 457 to include any plan, agreement, method, program, or other arrangement, including an individual employment agreement, of an eligible employer under which the payment of compensation is deferred. Section 1.457-2(k) of the 2003 regulations also identifies certain plans that are not subject to section 457 (pursuant to section 457(e)(12) and (f)(2) and statutes not incorporated into the Code) and certain plans that are treated as not providing for a deferral of compensation for purposes of section 457 (pursuant to section 457(e)(11)). These proposed regulations amend the definition of plan for purposes of section 457 to remove from §1.457-2(k) the provisions identifying plans that are not subject to section 457 and plans that are treated as not providing for a deferral of compensation for purposes of section 457, and move the provisions regarding most of these plans to §1.457-11 of the proposed regulations. In addition, §1.457-11 provides additional guidance on:

- bona fide vacation leave, sick leave, compensatory time, severance pay, disability pay, and death benefit plans, as described in section 457(e)(11)(A)(i), which are treated as not providing for a deferral of compensation for purposes of section 457; and

- plans paying solely length of service awards to bona fide volunteers (or their beneficiaries), as described in section 457(e)(11)(A)(ii), that also are treated as not providing for a deferral of compensation for purposes of section 457.[7]

The proposed regulations also provide guidance in a new §1.457-12 on plans described in section 457(f)(2), to which section 457(f)(1) does not apply.

B. *Bona fide severance pay plans*

1. General Requirements

The proposed regulations provide that a plan must meet certain requirements to be a bona fide severance pay plan that is treated under section 457(e)(11)(A)(i) as not providing for the deferral of compensation (and therefore not subject to section 457). First, the benefits provided under the plan must be payable only upon a participant's involuntary severance from employment or pursuant to a window program or voluntary early retirement incentive plan. Second, the amount payable under the plan with respect to a participant must not exceed two times the participant's annualized compensation based upon the annual rate of pay for services provided to the eligible employer for the calendar year preceding the calendar year in which the participant has a severance from employment (or the current calendar year if the participant had no compensation from the eligible employer in the preceding calendar year), adjusted for any increase in compensation during the year used to measure the rate of pay that was expected to continue indefinitely if the participant had not had a severance from employment. Third, pursuant to the written terms of the plan, the severance benefits must be paid no later than the last day of the second calendar year following the calendar year in which the severance from employment occurs. The rules in these proposed regulations for severance pay plans are similar to the rules for separation pay plans in §1.409A-1(b)(9) of the final section 409A regulations.

2. Involuntary Severance from Employment

a. In general

The proposed regulations require that benefits under a bona fide severance pay plan be payable only upon an involuntary severance from employment or pursuant to a window or voluntary early retirement incentive program. For this purpose, an involuntary severance from employment is a severance from employment due to the eligible employer's independent exercise of its authority to terminate the participant's services, other than due to the participant's implicit or explicit request, if the participant is willing and able to continue to perform services. The determination of whether a severance from employment is involuntary is based on the relevant facts and circumstances. If a severance from employment is designated as an involuntary severance from employment, but the facts and circumstances indicate otherwise, the severance from employment will not be treated as involuntary for purposes of section 457.

b. Severance from employment for good reason

The proposed regulations provide that an employee's voluntary severance from employment may be treated as an involuntary severance from employment for purposes of section 457 if the severance from employment is for good reason. A severance from employment is for good reason if it occurs under certain bona fide conditions that are pre-specified in writing under circumstances in which the avoidance of section 457 is not the primary purpose of the inclusion of these conditions in the plan or of the actions by the employer in connection with the satisfaction of those conditions. Notwithstanding the previous sentence, once the bona fide conditions have been established, the elimination of one or more of the conditions may result in the extension of a substantial risk of forfeiture, the recognition of which would be subject to the rules discussed in section III.E of this preamble.

To be treated as an involuntary severance from employment, a severance from employment for good reason must result from unilateral action taken by the eligible employer resulting in a material adverse change to the working relationship (such as a material reduction in the employee's duties, working conditions, or pay). Other factors that may be taken into account in determining whether a termination for good reason effectively constitutes an involuntary severance from employment include the following:

- whether the payments upon severance from employment for good reason are in the same amount and paid at the same time as payments conditioned upon an employer-initiated severance from employment without cause; and

- whether the employee is required to give notice to the employer of the material adverse change in conditions and provide the employer with an opportunity to remedy the adverse change.

The proposed regulations also provide a safe harbor under which a plan providing for the payment of amounts upon a voluntary severance from employment under certain conditions, that are specified in writing by the time the legally binding right to the payment arises, will be treated as providing for a payment upon a severance from employment for good reason.

c. Window programs

The proposed regulations provide that the involuntary severance from employment requirement does not apply to window programs. The proposed regulations define the term window program to mean a program established by an employer to provide separation pay in connection with an impending severance from employment. To be a window program, the program must be offered for a limited period of time (typically no longer than 12 months), and the eligible employer must make the program available to employees who have a severance from employment during that period or who have a severance from employment during that period under specified circumstances. A program is not offered for a limited period of time (and, therefore, is not a window program) if there is a pattern of repeatedly providing similar programs. Whether the recurrence of

---

[7] See section 457(e)(11)(B) for special rules relating to length of service award plans.

programs constitutes a pattern of repeatedly providing similar programs is based on all of the relevant facts and circumstances, including whether the benefits are on account of a specific reduction in workforce (or other operational conditions), whether there is a relationship between the separation pay and an event or condition, and whether the event or condition is temporary and discrete or is a permanent aspect of the employer's operations.

d. Voluntary early retirement incentive plans

The proposed regulations also provide that the involuntary severance from employment requirement does not apply to an applicable voluntary early retirement incentive plan described in section 457(e)(11)(D)(ii). That section describes an applicable voluntary early retirement incentive plan as a bona fide severance pay plan for purposes of section 457 with respect to payments or supplements that are made as an early retirement benefit, a retirement-type subsidy, or an early retirement benefit that is greater than a normal retirement benefit, as described in section 411(a)(9), and that are paid in coordination with a defined benefit pension plan that is qualified under section 401(a) and maintained by an eligible employer that is a governmental entity or a tax-exempt education association as described in section 457(e)(11)(D)(ii)(II). Section 457(e)(11)(D) provides that these payments or supplements are treated as provided under a bona fide severance pay plan only to the extent that they otherwise could have been provided under the defined benefit plan with which the applicable voluntary early retirement incentive plan is coordinated (determined as if the rules in section 411 applied to the defined benefit plan).

e. Transitional relief in Announcement 2000-1

Announcement 2000-1 provides transitional guidance on certain broad-based nonelective plans of State or local governments that were in existence before December 22, 1999, and were treated as bona fide severance pay plans for years before 1999. Under the announcement, an eligible employer that is a governmental entity is not required to report, including on Form W-2, "Wage and Tax Statement," or Form 1099-R "Distributions From Pensions, Annuities, Retirement or Profit-Sharing Plans, IRAs, Insurance Contracts, etc.," amounts payable under plans that meet certain requirements until the amounts are actually or constructively received. The rules described in these proposed regulations regarding bona fide severance pay plans, as modified when these proposed regulations are finalized and become applicable, will supersede the transitional guidance in Announcement 2000-1. See section V.B of this preamble for special applicability dates for governmental plans.

C. *Bona fide death benefit plan*

The proposed regulations provide that a bona fide death benefit plan, which is treated as not providing for the deferral of compensation pursuant to section 457(e)(11)(A)(i), is a plan providing for death benefits as defined in §31.3121(v)(2)-1(b)(4)(iv)(C) (relating to the application of the Federal Insurance Contributions Act to nonqualified deferred compensation). The proposed regulations further provide that benefits under a bona fide death benefit plan may be provided through insurance and that any lifetime benefits payable under the plan that may be includible in gross income will not be treated as including the value of any term life insurance coverage provided under the plan.

D. *Bona fide disability pay plan*

The proposed regulations provide that a bona fide disability pay plan, which is treated as not providing for the deferral of compensation pursuant to section 457(e)(11)(A)(i), is a plan that pays benefits only in the event of a participant's disability. For this purpose, the value of any taxable disability insurance coverage under the plan that is included in gross income is disregarded. These proposed regulations provide that a participant is disabled for this purpose if the participant meets any of the following three conditions:

- the participant is unable to engage in substantial gainful activity by reason of a medically determinable physical or mental impairment that can be expected to result in death or last for a continuous period of not less than 12 months;

- the participant is, by reason of any medically determinable physical or mental impairment that can be expected to result in death or last for a continuous period of not less than 12 months, receiving income replacement benefits for a continuous period of not less than three months under an accident or health plan covering employees of the eligible employer; or

- the participant is determined to be totally disabled by the Social Security Administration or the Railroad Retirement Board.

E. *Bona fide sick leave and vacation leave plans*

1. General Requirements

Under the proposed regulations, whether a sick or vacation leave plan is a bona fide sick or vacation leave plan, and therefore treated as not providing for the deferral of compensation under section 457(e)(11)(A)(i), is determined based on the facts and circumstances. A sick or vacation leave plan is generally treated as bona fide, and not as a plan providing for the deferral of compensation, if the facts and circumstances demonstrate that the primary purpose of the plan is to provide employees with paid time off from work because of sickness, vacation, or other personal reasons. Factors used in determining whether a plan is a bona fide sick or vacation leave plan include the following:

- whether the amount of leave provided could reasonably be expected to be used by the employee in the normal course (and before the cessation of services);

- limits, if any, on the ability to exchange unused accumulated leave for cash or other benefits and any applicable accrual restrictions (for example, where permissible under applicable law, the use of forfeiture provisions often referred to as use-or-lose rules);

- the amount and frequency of any in-service distributions of cash or other benefits offered in exchange for accumulated and unused leave;

- whether the payment of unused sick or vacation leave is made promptly upon severance from employment (or, instead, is paid over a period of time after severance from employment); and

- whether the sick leave, vacation leave, or combined sick and vacation leave offered under the plan is broadly applicable or is available only to certain employees.

2. Delegation of Authority to Commissioner

The Treasury Department and the IRS recognize that eligible employers sponsor a wide variety of sick and vacation leave plans and that additional rules on more specific arrangements or features of these plans may be beneficial. Accordingly, the proposed regulations provide that the Commissioner may issue additional rules regarding bona fide sick or vacation leave plans in revenue rulings, notices, or other guidance published in the Internal Revenue Bulletin, as the Commissioner determines to be necessary or appropriate.

F. *Constructive receipt*

Bona fide sick or vacation leave plans (and certain other plans) are treated as not providing for the deferral of compensation for purposes of section 457, and the general federal tax principles for determining the timing and amount of income inclusion, including the constructive receipt rules of section 451, apply to these plans. See §§ 1.451-1 and 1.451-2 for rules regarding constructive receipt of income.

IV. *Ineligible Plans Under Section 457(f)*

A. *Tax treatment of amounts deferred under section 457(f)*

Consistent with section 457(f)(1)(A), the proposed regulations provide that if a plan of an eligible employer provides for a deferral of compensation for the benefit of a participant or beneficiary and the plan is not an eligible plan (an ineligible plan), the compensation deferred under the plan is includible in the gross income of the participant or beneficiary under section 457(f)(1)(A) on the date (referred to in this preamble and the proposed regulations as the applicable date) that is the later of the date the participant or beneficiary obtains a legally binding right to the compensation or, if the compensation is subject to a substantial risk of forfeiture at that time, the date the substantial risk of forfeiture lapses. Generally, the amount of the compensation deferred under the plan that is includible in gross income on the applicable date is the present value, as of that date, of the amount of compensation deferred. For this purpose, the amount of compensation deferred under a plan as of an applicable date includes any earnings as of that date on amounts deferred under the plan.

Consistent with section 457(f)(1)(B), the proposed regulations provide that any earnings credited thereafter on compensation that was included in gross income under section 457(f)(1)(A) are includible in the gross income of a participant or beneficiary when paid or made available to the participant or beneficiary and are taxable under section 72. For purposes of section 72, the participant (or beneficiary) is treated as having an investment in the contract equal to the amount actually included in gross income on the applicable date.

Consistent with section 457(f)(2), the proposed regulations provide that section 457(f)(1) does not apply to a qualified plan described in section 401(a), an annuity plan or contract described in section 403, the portion of a plan that consists of a trust to which section 402(b) applies, a qualified governmental excess benefit arrangement described in section 415(m), the portion of a plan that consists of a transfer of property to which section 83 applies, or the portion of an applicable employment retention plan described in section 457(f)(4) with respect to any participant.

B. *Calculation of the present value of compensation deferred under an ineligible plan*

1. Overview

The proposed regulations provide general rules for determining the present value of compensation deferred under an ineligible plan. The proposed regulations also include specific rules for determining the present value of compensation deferred under ineligible plans that are account balance plans. The rules for determining present value in the proposed regulations are similar to the rules for determining present value in the proposed section 409A regulations.[8]

The Treasury Department and the IRS expect that these regulations will be finalized after the proposed section 409A regulations are finalized and that these proposed regulations, when finalized, will adopt many provisions of §1.409A-4 for ease of administration. Accordingly, these proposed regulations include cross references to certain provisions of §1.409A-4 as currently proposed, including rules for determining present value under certain specific types of plans, such as reimbursement and in-kind benefit arrangements[9] and split-dollar life insurance arrangements,[10] and rules regarding the treatment of payment restrictions and alternative times and forms of a future payment. The Treasury Department and the IRS request comments on whether it is appropriate to provide any additional exceptions from the application of the rules currently described in the proposed section 409A regulations to amounts includible in income under section 457(f), to account for the different manners in which the two provisions apply to an amount deferred.

2. Present Value of Compensation Deferred Under an Account Balance Plan

The proposed regulations provide specific rules for calculating the present value of compensation deferred under an ineligible plan that is an account balance plan (as defined in §31.3121(v)(2)-1(c)(1)(ii) and (iii)).[11] Provided that the account balance is determined using a predetermined actual investment or a reasonable rate of interest, the present value of an amount payable under an account balance plan as of an applicable date is generally the amount credited to the account, which includes both the principal and any earnings or losses through the applicable date. If the account balance is not determined using a predetermined actual investment or a reasonable rate of interest, the present value of compensation deferred under the plan as of an applicable date is equal to the amount credited to the participant's account as of that date, plus the present value of the excess (if any) of the earnings to be credited under the plan after the applicable date and through the projected payment date over the earnings that would be credited during that period using a reasonable rate of interest. If the present value of compensation deferred under the plan is not determined and is not taken into account by the taxpayer in this manner, the present value of the compensation deferred under the plan as of the applicable date will be treated as equal to the amount credited to the participant's account as of that date, plus the present value of the excess (if any) of the earnings to be credited under the plan through the projected payment date over the earnings that would be credited using the applicable Federal rate. The proposed regulations also provide that if the amount of earnings or losses credited under an account balance plan is based on the greater of the earnings on two or more investments or interest rates, then the amount included in income on the applicable date is the sum of the amount credited to the participant's account as of the applicable date and the present value (determined as described in section IV.B.3 of this preamble) of the right to future earnings.

3. Present Value of Compensation Deferred Under a Plan That Is Not an Account Balance Plan

a. Reasonable actuarial assumptions

The proposed regulations also set forth rules for calculating the present value of compensation deferred under an ineligible plan that is not an account balance plan. Under the proposed regulations, the present value of an amount deferred under such a plan as of an applicable date is the value, as of that date, of the right to receive payment of the compensation in the future, taking into account the time value of money and the probability that the payment will be made. Any actuarial assumptions used to calculate the present value of the compensation deferred must be reasonable as of the applicable date, determined based on all of the relevant facts and circumstances. For this purpose, taking into account the probability that a participant might die before receiving certain benefits is a reasonable actuarial assumption only if the plan provides that the benefits will be forfeited upon death. Discounts based on the probability that payments will not be made due to the unfunded status of the plan, the risk that the eligible employer or another party may be unwilling or unable to pay, the possibility of future plan amendments or changes in law, and other similar contingencies are not permitted for purposes of determining present value under the proposed regulations.

---

[8] One difference between these proposed regulations and the proposed section 409A regulations is that income inclusion under section 457(f) and §1.457-12(a)(2), and the present value calculation under these proposed regulations, is determined as of the applicable date, whereas income inclusion under section 409A, and the present value calculation under the proposed §1.409A-4, is determined as of the end of the service provider's taxable year.

[9] A reimbursement or in-kind benefit arrangement is an arrangement in which benefits for a participant are provided under a nonqualified deferred compensation arrangement described in §1.409A-1(c)(2)(i)(E).

[10] A split-dollar insurance arrangement is an arrangement in which benefits for a participant are provided under a nonqualified deferred compensation plan described in §1.409A-1(c)(2)(i)(F).

[11] The rules in these regulations, however, do not apply with respect to Federal Insurance Contributions Act and Federal Unemployment Tax Act taxation liability under sections 3121(v)(2) and 3306(r)(2), respectively, and the regulations thereunder.

b. Treatment of severance from employment

If the present value of an amount depends on the time when a severance from employment occurs and the severance from employment has not occurred by the applicable date, then, for purposes of determining the present value of the amount, the severance from employment generally may be treated as occurring on any date on or before the fifth anniversary of the applicable date, unless, as of the applicable date, it would be unreasonable to use such an assumption. For example, if the applicable date occurs in 2017 and the employer knows on the applicable date that the severance from employment will occur in 2018, it would be unreasonable to use a date after the expected severance from employment date to determine the present value of the compensation.

c. Treatment of payments based on formula amounts

Some ineligible plans may provide that all or part of the amount payable under the plan is determined by reference to one or more factors that are indeterminable on the applicable date. For example, an amount payable may be dependent on a participant's final average compensation and total years of service. These proposed regulations refer to such an amount as a formula amount. The proposed regulations provide that the determination of the present value of a formula amount under an ineligible plan must be based on reasonable, good faith assumptions with respect to any contingencies as to the amount of the payment, with the assumptions based on all the facts and circumstances existing on the applicable date. The proposed regulations also provide that, if only a portion of the compensation deferred under the plan consists of a formula amount, the amount payable with respect to that portion is determined under the rules applicable to formula amounts, and the remaining balance is determined under the rules applicable to amounts that are not formula amounts.

d. Unreasonable actuarial assumptions

If the Commissioner determines that the actuarial assumptions used by an employer in determining present value are not reasonable, the proposed regulations provide that the Commissioner will determine the present value of the compensation deferred using actuarial assumptions and methods that the Commissioner determines to be reasonable based on all of the facts and circumstances.

4. Loss Deduction Rules

The proposed regulations contain rules similar to the loss deduction rules in the proposed section 409A regulations. Under the rules in these proposed regulations, if a participant includes an amount of deferred compensation in income under section 457(f)(1)(A), but the compensation that is subsequently paid or made available is less than the amount included in income because the participant has forfeited or lost some or all of the compensation due to death or some other reason (for example, due to investment performance), the participant is entitled to a deduction for the taxable year in which any remaining right to the amount is permanently forfeited under the plan's terms or otherwise permanently lost. The deduction allowed for the taxable year in which the permanent forfeiture or loss occurs is equal to the amount previously included in income under section 457(f)(1)(A), less the total amount of compensation that is actually paid or made available under the plan that constitutes a return of investment in the contract. In the case of an employee, the available deduction generally would be treated as a miscellaneous itemized deduction, subject to the deduction limitations applicable to such expenses under sections 67 and 68.[12]

5. Examples Illustrating the Present Value Rules

The proposed regulations include several examples illustrating the application of the present value rules to the more common types of plans providing for the deferral of compensation under section 457(f). The regulations do not illustrate the application of these valuation rules to plans that are more unusual for employees of governmental and tax-exempt entities, such as compensatory options to acquire stock or other property. The amount includible in income on the applicable date under these less common types of plans would be determined under the general rules for plans that are not account balance plans.

C. Definition of deferral of compensation

1. In General

The proposed regulations define the term deferral of compensation for purposes of determining whether section 457(f) applies to an arrangement because it provides for a deferral of compensation. In general, a plan provides for a deferral of compensation if a participant has a legally binding right during a taxable year to compensation that, pursuant to the terms of the plan, is or may be payable in a later taxable year. However, the proposed regulations generally provide that a participant does not have a legally binding right to compensation to the extent that it may be unilaterally reduced or eliminated by the employer after the services creating the right have been performed.

Whether a plan provides for a deferral of compensation is generally based on the terms of the plan and the relevant facts and circumstances at the time that the participant obtains a legally binding right to the compensation, or, if later, when a plan is amended to convert a right that does not provide for a deferral of compensation into a right that does provide for a deferral of compensation. For example, if a plan providing retiree health care does not initially provide for a deferral of compensation but is later amended to provide the ability to receive future cash payments instead of health benefits, it may become a plan that provides for the deferral of compensation at the time of the amendment.

Under the proposed regulations, an amount of compensation deferred under a plan that provides for the deferral of compensation does not cease to be an amount subject to section 457(f) by reason of any change to the plan that would recharacterize the right to the amount as a right that does not provide for the deferral of compensation. In addition, any change under the plan that results in an exchange of an amount deferred under the plan for some other right or benefit that would otherwise be excluded from the participants' gross income does not affect the characterization of the plan as one that provides for a deferral of compensation. Thus, for example, if a plan that provides for a deferral of compensation is amended to provide health benefits instead of cash, it will retain its character as a plan that provides for a deferral of compensation.

2. Short-term Deferrals

The proposed regulations provide that a deferral of compensation does not occur with respect to any amount that would be a short-term deferral under § 1.409A-1(b)(4), substituting the definition of a substantial risk of forfeiture provided under these proposed regulations for the definition under § 1.409A-1(d). Accordingly, a deferral of compensation does not occur with respect to any payment that is not a deferred payment, provided that the participant actually or constructively receives the payment on or before the last day of the applicable 2 1/2 month period. For this purpose, the applicable 2 1/2 month period is the period ending on the later of the 15th day of the third month following the end of the first calendar year in which the right to the payment is no longer subject to a substantial risk of forfeiture or the 15th day of the third month following the end of the eligible employer's first taxable year in which the right to the payment is no longer subject to a substantial risk of forfeiture.

Because there is considerable overlap between the definition of substantial risk of forfeiture for purposes of section 457(f) and the definition of substantial risk of forfeiture for purposes of section 409A, in many cases amounts that, under this rule, are not deferred compensation subject to

---

[12] Section 1341 would not be applicable to this type of loss because inclusion of an amount in income as a result of section 457(f) would not constitute receipt of an amount

to which it appeared that the taxpayer had an unrestricted right in the taxable year of inclusion.

section 457(f) are also not deferred compensation subject to section 409A. For example, if an arrangement provides for the payment of a bonus on or before March 15 of the year following the calendar year in which the right to the bonus is no longer subject to a substantial risk of forfeiture (within the meaning of both these proposed regulations and § 1.409A-1(d)) and the bonus is paid on or before that March 15, the arrangement would not be a plan providing for a deferral of compensation to which section 457(f) (or section 409A) applies. For circumstances in which a payment under a plan made after that March 15 may still qualify as a short-term deferral for purposes of sections 409A and 457(f) (due to incorporation of the section 409A regulatory provisions into these proposed regulations under section 457(f)), see § 1.409A-1(b)(4)(ii).

3. Recurring Part-Year Compensation

After issuance of the final section 409A regulations, commenters expressed concerns about the application of section 409A to situations involving certain recurring part-year compensation. For this purpose, recurring part-year compensation is compensation paid for services rendered in a position that the employer and employee reasonably anticipate will continue under similar terms and conditions in subsequent years, and under which the employee will be required to provide services during successive service periods each of which comprises less than 12 months (for example, a teacher providing services during a school year comprised of 10 consecutive months) and each of which begins in one taxable year of the employee and ends in the next taxable year. In general, commenters asserted that section 409A should not apply to situations involving recurring part-year compensation because the amount being deferred from one taxable year to the next taxable year is typically small and because most taxpayers view that type of arrangement as a method of managing cash flow, rather than a tax-deferral opportunity.

In response to these comments, Notice 2008-62 provided that an arrangement under which an employee or independent contractor receives recurring part-year compensation does not provide for the deferral of compensation for purposes of section 409A or for purposes of section 457(f) if (i) the arrangement does not defer payment of any of the recurring part-year compensation beyond the last day of the 13th month following the beginning of the service period, and (ii) the arrangement does not defer from one taxable year to the next taxable year the payment of more than the applicable dollar amount under section 402(g)(1)(B) ($18,000 for 2016).

Some commenters, however, subsequently expressed concerns that Notice 2008-62 does not adequately address some teaching positions, such as those of college and university faculty members. They asserted that, depending on several variables (such as the month in which the service period begins), the dollar limitation in the notice could result in adverse tax consequences to teachers with academic year compensation as low as $80,000. Commenters further observed that some of these arrangements are nonelective and, therefore, some employees cannot opt out of a recurring part-year compensation arrangement. Some commenters also contended that the rules set forth in the notice were difficult to apply.

To simplify the rule set forth in Notice 2008-62, and recognizing that educational employers frequently structure their pay plans to include recurring part-year compensation and that the main purpose of this design is to achieve an even cash flow for employees who do not work for a portion of the year, these proposed regulations modify the recurring part-year compensation rule for purposes of section 457(f). The proposed regulations provide that a plan or arrangement under which an employee receives recurring part-year compensation that is earned over a period of service does not provide for the deferral of compensation if the plan or arrangement does not defer payment of any of the recurring part-year compensation to a date beyond the last day of the 13th month following the first day of the service period for which the recurring part-year compensation is paid, and the amount of the recurring part-year compensation (not merely the amount deferred) does not exceed the annual compensation limit under section 401(a)(17) ($265,000 for 2016) for the calendar year in which the service period commences. A conforming change is included in proposed regulations under section 409A that are also published in the Proposed Rules section of this issue of the **Federal Register**.

D. *Interaction of section 457 with section 409A*

The proposed regulations also address the interaction of the rules under section 457(f) and section 409A. Section 409A(c) provides that nothing in section 409A is to be construed to prevent the inclusion of amounts in gross income under any other provision of chapter 1 of subtitle A of the Code (Normal taxes and surtaxes) or any other rule of law earlier than the time provided in section 409A. In addition, it provides that any amount included in gross income under section 409A is not required to be included in gross income under any other provision of chapter 1 of subtitle A or any other rule of law later than the time provided in section 409A. The proposed regulations provide that the rules under section 457(f) apply to plans separately and in addition to the requirements under section 409A.[13] Thus, a deferred compensation plan of an eligible employer that is subject to section 457(f) may also be a nonqualified deferred compensation plan that is subject to section 409A. Section 1.457-12(d)(5)(iii) of the proposed regulations provides an example of the interaction of sections 409A and 457(f), and it is intended that this example will also be included in § 1.409A-4 when those currently proposed regulations are finalized.

E. *Rules relating to substantial risk of forfeiture*

The proposed regulations provide rules regarding the conditions that constitute a substantial risk of forfeiture for purposes of section 457(f). As discussed in section IV.A of this preamble, an amount to which an employee has a legally binding right under an ineligible plan is generally includible in gross income on the later of the date the employee obtains the legally binding right to the compensation or, if the compensation is subject to a substantial risk of forfeiture, the date the substantial risk of forfeiture lapses. The proposed regulations provide that an amount is generally subject to a substantial risk of forfeiture for this purpose only if entitlement to that amount is conditioned on the future performance of substantial services, or upon the occurrence of a condition that is related to a purpose of the compensation if the possibility of forfeiture is substantial. A special rule applies to determine whether initial deferrals of current compensation may be treated as subject to a substantial risk of forfeiture and whether a substantial risk of forfeiture can be extended. For this purpose, current compensation refers to compensation that is payable on a current basis such as salary, commissions, and certain bonuses, and does not include compensation that is deferred compensation.

Whether an amount is conditioned on the future performance of substantial services is based on all of the relevant facts and circumstances, such as whether the hours required to be performed during the relevant period are substantial in relation to the amount of compensation. A condition is related to a purpose of the compensation only if the condition relates to the employee's performance of services for the employer or to the employer's tax exempt or governmental activities, as applicable, or organizational goals. A substantial risk of forfeiture exists based on a condition related to the purpose of the compensation only if the likelihood that the forfeiture event will occur is substantial. Also, an amount is not subject to a substantial risk of forfeiture if the facts and circumstances indicate that the forfeiture condition is unlikely to be enforced. Factors considered for purposes of determining the likelihood that the forfeiture will be enforced include, but are not limited to, the past practices of the employer, the level of control or influence of the employee with respect to the organization and the individual(s) who would be responsible for enforcing the forfeiture, and the enforceability of the provisions under applicable law.

Under these proposed regulations, if a plan provides that entitlement to an amount is conditioned on an involuntary severance from employment without cause, the right is subject to a substantial risk of forfeiture if the possibility of forfeiture is substantial. For this purpose, a voluntary severance from employment that would be treated as an involuntary severance from employment under a bona fide severance pay plan for purposes of section 457(e)(11)(A)(i) (that is, a severance from employment for good reason) is also treated as an involuntary severance from employment without cause. See section III.B.2 of this preamble for a discussion of circumstances under which a severance from employment for good reason may be treated as an involuntary severance from employment for purposes of section 457(e)(11)(A)(i).

---

[13] See also § 1.409A-1(a)(4).

The proposed regulations provide that compensation is not considered to be subject to a substantial risk of forfeiture merely because it would be forfeited if the employee accepts a position with a competing employer unless certain conditions are satisfied. First, the right to the compensation must be expressly conditioned on the employee refraining from the performance of future services pursuant to a written agreement that is enforceable under applicable law. Second, the employer must consistently make reasonable efforts to verify compliance with all of the noncompetition agreements to which it is a party (including the noncompetition agreement at issue). Third, at the time the noncompetition agreement becomes binding, the facts and circumstances must show that the employer has a substantial and bona fide interest in preventing the employee from performing the prohibited services and that the employee has a bona fide interest in engaging, and an ability to engage, in the prohibited services. The proposed regulations identify several factors that are relevant for this purpose.

Additional conditions apply with respect to the ability to treat initial deferrals of current compensation as being subject to a substantial risk of forfeiture. Similarly, an attempt to extend the period covered by a risk of forfeiture, often referred to as a rolling risk of forfeiture, is generally disregarded under the proposed regulations unless certain conditions are met.

Specifically, the proposed regulations permit initial deferrals of current compensation to be subject to a substantial risk of forfeiture and also allow an existing risk of forfeiture to be extended only if all of the following requirements are met. First, the present value of the amount to be paid upon the lapse of the substantial risk of forfeiture (as extended, if applicable) must be materially greater than the amount the employee otherwise would be paid in the absence of the substantial risk of forfeiture (or absence of the extension). The proposed regulations provide that an amount is materially greater for this purpose only if the present value of the amount to be paid upon the lapse of the substantial risk of forfeiture, measured as of the date the amount would have otherwise been paid (or in the case of an extension of the risk of forfeiture, the date that the substantial risk of forfeiture would have lapsed without regard to the extension), is more than 125 percent of the amount the participant otherwise would have received on that date in the absence of the new or extended substantial risk of forfeiture. (No implication is intended that this standard would also apply for purposes of §1.409A-1(d)(1).)

Second, the initial or extended substantial risk of forfeiture must be based upon the future performance of substantial services or adherence to an agreement not to compete. It may not be based solely on the occurrence of a condition related to the purpose of the transfer (for example, a performance goal for the organization), though that type of condition may be combined with a sufficient service condition.

Third, the period for which substantial future services must be performed may not be less than two years (absent an intervening event such as death, disability, or involuntary severance from employment).

Fourth, the agreement subjecting the amount to a substantial risk of forfeiture must be made in writing before the beginning of the calendar year in which any services giving rise to the compensation are performed in the case of initial deferrals of current compensation or at least 90 days before the date on which an existing substantial risk of forfeiture would have lapsed in the absence of an extension. Special rules apply to new employees. The proposed regulations do not extend these special rules for new employees to employees who are newly eligible to participate in a plan. The Treasury Department and the IRS request comments on whether special provisions for newly eligible employees are needed in the context of arrangements subject to section 457(f), and if so whether the rules under §§1.409A-1(c)(2) and 1.409A-2(a)(7) would be a useful basis for similar rules under section 457(f) and how an aggregated single plan (versus multiple plans) should be defined for this purpose to ensure that the rules are not subject to manipulation.

V. Proposed Applicability Dates

A. General applicability date

Generally, these regulations are proposed to apply to compensation deferred under a plan for calendar years beginning after the date of publication of the Treasury decision adopting these rules as final regulations in the **Federal Register**, including deferred amounts to which the legally binding right arose during prior calendar years that were not previously included in income during one or more prior calendar years. No implication is intended regarding application of the law before these proposed regulations become applicable. Taxpayers may rely on these proposed regulations until the applicability date.

B. Special applicability dates

These regulations are proposed to include three special applicability dates for specific provisions. First, in the case of a plan that is maintained pursuant to one or more collective bargaining agreements that have been ratified and are in effect on the date of publication of the Treasury decision adopting these rules as final regulations in the **Federal Register,** these regulations would not apply to compensation deferred under the plan before the earlier of (1) the date on which the last of the collective bargaining agreements terminates (determined without regard to any extension thereof after the date of publication of the Treasury decision adopting these rules as final regulations in the **Federal Register**, or (2) the date that is three years after the date of publication of the Treasury decision adopting these rules as final regulations in the **Federal Register**.

Second, for all plans, with respect to the rules regarding recurring part-year compensation for periods before the applicability date of these regulations, taxpayers may rely on either the rules set forth in these proposed regulations or the rules set forth in Notice 2008-62.

Third, to the extent that legislation is required to amend a governmental plan, the proposed regulations would apply only to compensation deferred under the plan in calendar years beginning on or after the close of the second regular legislative session of the legislative body with the authority to amend the plan that begins after the date of publication of the Treasury decision adopting these rules as final regulations in the **Federal Register**.

Special Analyses

Certain IRS regulations, including this one, are exempt from the requirements of Executive Order 12866, as supplemented and reaffirmed by Executive Order 13563. Therefore, a regulatory impact assessment is not required. It also has been determined that section 553(b) of the Administrative Procedure Act (5 U.S.C. chapter 5) does not apply to these regulations, and because the regulations do not impose a collection of information on small entities, the Regulatory Flexibility Act (5 U.S.C. chapter 6) does not apply. Pursuant to section 7805(f) of the Code, this notice of proposed rulemaking has been submitted to the Chief Counsel for Advocacy of the Small Business Administration for comment on its impact on small business.

Comments and Public Hearing

Before the proposed regulations are adopted as final regulations, consideration will be given to any written (a signed original and eight (8) copies) or electronic comments that are submitted timely to the IRS as prescribed in this preamble under the "ADDRESSES" heading. The Treasury Department and the IRS request comments on all aspects of the proposed rules, including whether special transition rules are needed for plans established before the proposed applicability dates of these regulations (including sick and vacation leave or severance pay plans that may be treated as providing deferred compensation subject to section 457, but that, under the proposed regulations, may be treated as providing deferred compensation subject to section 457(f), whether additional exceptions are appropriate to the general application of the rules currently described in the proposed section 409A regulations to determine the amounts includible in income under section 457(f), and whether special provisions for newly eligible employees are needed in the context of arrangements subject to section 457(f) (and if so whether the rules under §§1.409A-1(c)(2) and 1.409A-2(a)(7) would be a useful basis for similar rules under section 457(f)). All comments submitted by the public will be available at www.regulations.gov or upon request.

A public hearing has been scheduled for October 18, 2016, beginning at 10 a.m. in the Auditorium, Internal Revenue Service, 1111 Constitution Avenue, N.W., Washington, DC. Due to building security procedures, visitors must enter at the Constitution Avenue entrance. In addition, all visitors must present photo identification to enter the building. Because of access restrictions, visitors will not be admitted beyond the immediate entrance area more than 30 minutes before the hearing starts. For information about having your name placed on the building access list to attend the hearing, see the "FOR FURTHER INFORMATION CONTACT" section of this preamble.

The rules of 26 CFR 601.601(a)(3) apply to the hearing. Persons who wish to present oral comments at the hearing must submit written or electronic comments by September 20, 2016 and an outline of the topics to be discussed and the amount of time to be devoted to each topic (a signed original and eight (8) copies) by September 20, 2016. A period of 10 minutes will be allotted to each person for making comments. An agenda showing the scheduling of the speakers will be prepared after the deadline for receiving outlines has passed. Copies of the agenda will be available free of charge at the hearing.

Statement of Availability of IRS Documents

For copies of recently issued revenue procedures, revenue rulings, notices, and other guidance published in the Internal Revenue Bulletin, please visit the IRS website at http://www.irs.gov or contact the Superintendent of Documents, U.S. Government Printing Office, Washington, DC 20402.

Drafting Information

The principal author of the proposed regulations is Keith R. Kost, Office of Associate Chief Counsel (Tax Exempt and Government Entities). However, other personnel from the Treasury Department and the IRS participated in their development.

[¶ 49,704]   **Proposed Amendments of Regulations (REG-109086-15)**, published in the Federal Register on July 8, 2016 (corrected 9/14/2016).

[Code Secs. 36B and 5000A]

Affordable Care Act: Premium tax credit: Individual shared responsibility.—Amendments of Reg. §§1.36B-2 and 1.5000A-3, relating to the health insurance premium tax credit (premium tax credit) and the individual shared responsibility provision, are proposed. Amendments of Reg. SS1.36B-0, 1.36B-1, 1.36B-2, 1.36B-3, 1.36B-5, 1.6011-8 and 301.6011-2 were adopted by T.D. 9804 on December 14, 2016.

AGENCY: Internal Revenue Service (IRS), Treasury.

ACTION: Notice of proposed rulemaking.

SUMMARY: This document contains proposed regulations relating to the health insurance premium tax credit (premium tax credit) and the individual shared responsibility provision. These proposed regulations affect individuals who enroll in qualified health plans through Health Insurance Exchanges (Exchanges, also called Marketplaces) and claim the premium tax credit, and Exchanges that make qualified health plans available to individuals and employers. These proposed regulations also affect individuals who are eligible for employer-sponsored health coverage and individuals who seek to claim an exemption from the individual shared responsibility provision because of unaffordable coverage. Although employers are not directly affected by rules governing the premium tax credit, these proposed regulations may indirectly affect employers through the employer shared responsibility provisions and the related information reporting provisions.

DATES: Written (including electronic) comments and requests for a public hearing must be received by September 6, 2016.

ADDRESSES: Send submissions to: CC:PA:LPD:PR (REG-109086-15), Room 5203, Internal Revenue Service, PO Box 7604, Ben Franklin Station, Washington, DC 20044. Submissions may be hand-delivered Monday through Friday between the hours of 8 a.m. and 4 p.m. to CC:PA:LPD:PR (REG-109086-15), Courier's Desk, Internal Revenue Service, 1111 Constitution Avenue, NW, Washington, DC, or sent electronically via the Federal eRulemaking Portal at *http://www.regulations.gov* (REG-109086-15).

FOR FURTHER INFORMATION CONTACT: Concerning the proposed regulations, Shareen Pflanz, (202) 317-4727; concerning the submission of comments and/or requests for a public hearing, Oluwafunmilayo Taylor, (202) 317-6901 (not toll-free calls).

SUPPLEMENTARY INFORMATION:

Paperwork Reduction Act

The collection of information contained in this notice of proposed rulemaking has been submitted to the Office of Management and Budget in accordance with the Paperwork Reduction Act of 1995 (44 U.S.C. 3507(d)). Comments on the collection of information should be sent to the **Office of Management and Budget**, Attn: Desk Officer for the Department of the Treasury, Office of Information and Regulatory Affairs, Washington, DC 20503, with copies to the **Internal Revenue Service**, Attn: IRS Reports Clearance Officer, SE:W:CAR:MP:T:T:SP, Washington, DC 20224. Comments on the collection of information should be received by September 6, 2016. Comments are specifically requested concerning:

Whether the proposed collection of information is necessary for the proper performance of the functions of the IRS, including whether the information will have practical utility;

How the quality, utility, and clarity of the information to be collected may be enhanced;

How the burden of complying with the proposed collection of information may be minimized, including through the application of automated collection techniques or other forms of information technology; and

Estimates of capital or start-up costs and costs of operation, maintenance, and purchase of services to provide information.

The collection of information in these proposed regulations is in §1.36B-5. The collection of information is necessary to reconcile advance payments of the premium tax credit and determine the allowable premium tax credit. The collection of information is required to comply with the provisions of section 36B of the Internal Revenue Code (Code). The likely respondents are Marketplaces that enroll individuals in qualified health plans.

The burden for the collection of information contained in these proposed regulations will be reflected in the burden on Form 1095-A, *Health Insurance Marketplace Statement*, which is the form that will request the information—Prom the Marketplaces in the proposed regulations.

An agency may not conduct or sponsor, and a person is not required to respond to, a collection of information unless it displays a valid control number assigned by the Office of Management and Budget.

Background

Beginning in 2014, under the Patient Protection and Affordable Care Act, Public Law 111-148 (124 Stat. 119 (2010)), and the Health Care and Education Reconciliation Act of 2010, Public Law 111-152 (124 Stat. 1029 (2010)) (collectively, the Affordable Care Act), eligible individuals who purchase coverage under a qualified health plan through an Exchange may claim a premium tax credit under section 36B of the Code. Section 36B was subsequently amended by the Medicare and Medicaid Extenders Act of 2010, Public Law 111-309 (124 Stat. 3285 (2010)); the Comprehensive 1099 Taxpayer Protection and Repayment of Exchange Subsidy Overpayments Act of 2011, Public Law 112-9 (125 Stat. 36 (2011)); and the Department of Defense and Full-Year Continuing Appropriations Act, 2011, Public Law 112-10 (125 Stat. 38 (2011)).

The Affordable Care Act also added section 5000A to the Code. Section 5000A was subsequently amended by the TRICARE Affirmation Act of 2010, Public Law 111-159 (124 Stat. 1123 (2010)) and Public Law 111-173 (124 Stat. 1215 (2010)). Section 5000A provides that, for months beginning after December 31, 2013, a nonexempt individual must have qualifying healthcare coverage (called minimum essential coverage) or make an individual shared responsibility payment.

Applicable Taxpayers

To be eligible for a premium tax credit, an individual must be an applicable taxpayer. Among other requirements, under section 36B(c)(1) an applicable taxpayer is a taxpayer whose household income for the taxable year is between 100 percent and 400 percent of the Federal poverty line (FPL) for the taxpayer's family size (or is a lawfully present non-citizen who has income below 100 percent of the FPL and is ineligible for Medicaid). A taxpayer's family size is equal to the number of individuals in the taxpayer's family. Under section 36B(d)(1), a taxpayer's family consists of the individuals for whom the taxpayer claims a personal exemption deduction under section 151 for the taxable year. Taxpayers may claim a personal exemption deduction for themselves, a spouse, and each of their dependents.

Under section 1412 of the Affordable Care Act, advance payments of the premium tax credit (advance credit payments) may be made directly to insurers on behalf of eligible individuals. The amount of advance credit payments made on behalf of a taxpayer in a taxable year is determined by a number of factors including projections of the taxpayer's household income and family size for the taxable year. Taxpayers who receive the benefit of advance credit payments are required to file an income tax return to reconcile the amount of advance credit payments made during the year with the amount of the credit allowable for the taxable year.

Under §1.36B-2(b)(6), in general, a taxpayer whose household income for a taxable year is less than 100 percent of the applicable FPL is nonetheless treated as an applicable taxpayer if (1) the taxpayer or a family member enrolls in a qualified health plan, (2) an Exchange estimates at the time of enrollment that the taxpayer's household income for the taxable year will be between 100 and 400 percent of the applicable FPL, (3) advance credit payments are authorized and paid for one or more months during the taxable year, and (4) the taxpayer would be an applicable taxpayer but for the fact that the taxpayer's household income for the taxable year is below 100 percent of the applicable FPL.

Premium Assistance Credit Amount

Under section 36B(a), a taxpayer's premium tax credit is equal to the premium assistance credit amount for the taxable year. Section 36B(b)(1) and §1.36B-3(d) generally provide that the premium assistance credit amount is the sum of the premium assistance amounts for all coverage months in the taxable year for individuals in the taxpayer's family. The premium assistance amount for a coverage month is the lesser of (1) the premiums for the month for one or more qualified health plans that cover a taxpayer or family member (enrollment premium), or (2) the excess of the adjusted monthly premium for the second lowest cost silver plan (as described in section 1302(d)(1)(B) of the Affordable Care Act (42 U.S.C. 18022(d)(1)(B)) offered through the Exchange for the rating area where the taxpayer resides that would provide coverage to the taxpayer's coverage family (the benchmark plan), over 1/12 of the product of the taxpayer's household income and the applicable percentage for the taxable year (the contribution amount). In general, the benchmark plan's adjusted monthly premium is the premium an insurer would charge for the plan adjusted only for the ages of the covered individuals. The applicable percentage is provided in a table that is updated annually and represents the portion of a taxpayer's household income that the taxpayer is expected to pay if the taxpayer's coverage family enrolls in the benchmark plan. See, for example, Rev. Proc. 2014-62, 2014-2 C.B. 948 (providing the applicable percentage table for taxable years beginning in 2016) and Rev. Proc. 2014-37, 2014-2 C.B. 363 (providing the applicable percentage table for taxable years beginning in 2015). A taxpayer's coverage family refers to all members of the taxpayer's family who enroll in a qualified health plan in a month and are not eligible for minimum essential coverage as defined in section 5000A(f) (other than coverage in the individual market) for that month.

Under section 1301(a)(1)(B) of the Affordable Care Act, a qualified health plan must offer the essential health benefits package described in section 1302(a). Under section 1302(b)(1)(J) of the Affordable Care Act, the essential health benefits package includes pediatric services, including oral and vision care. Section 1302(b)(4)(F) of the Affordable Care Act provides that, if an Exchange offers a plan described in section 1311(d)(2)(B)(ii)(I) of the Affordable Care Act (42 U.S.C. 13031(d)(2)(B)(ii)(I)) (a stand-alone dental plan), other health plans offered through the Exchange will not fail to be qualified health plans solely because the plans do not offer pediatric dental benefits.

For purposes of calculating the premium assistance amount for a taxpayer who enrolls in both a qualified health plan and a stand-alone dental plan, section 36B(b)(3)(E) provides that the enrollment premium includes the portion of the premium for the stand-alone dental plan properly allocable to pediatric dental benefits that are included in the essential health benefits required to be provided by a qualified health plan.

Section 36B(b)(3)(B) provides that the benchmark plan with respect to an applicable taxpayer is the second lowest cost silver plan offered by the Marketplace through which the applicable taxpayer (or a family member) enrolled and which provides (1) self-only coverage, in the case of unmarried individuals (other than a surviving spouse or head of household) who do not claim any dependents, or any other individual who enrolls in self-only coverage, and (2) family coverage, in the case of any other applicable taxpayer. Section 1.36B-1(l) provides that self-only coverage means health insurance that covers one individual. Section 1.36B-1(m) provides that family coverage means health insurance that covers more than one individual.

Under §1.36B-3(f)(3), if there are one or more silver-level plans offered through the Exchange for the rating area where the taxpayer resides that do not cover all members of a taxpayer's coverage family under one policy (for example, because of the relationships within the family), the benchmark plan premium is the second lowest-cost option for covering all members of the taxpayer's family, which may be either a single silver-level policy or more than one silver-level policy.

Section 1.36B-3(d)(2) provides that, if a qualified health plan is terminated before the last day of a month or an individual is enrolled in coverage effective on the date of the individual's birth, adoption, or placement for adoption or in foster care, or on the effective date of a court order, the premium assistance amount for the month is the lesser of the enrollment premiums for the month (reduced by any amounts that were refunded) or the excess of the benchmark plan premium for a full month of coverage over the full contribution amount for the month.

Coverage Month

Under section 36B(c)(2)(A) and §1.36B-3(c)(1), a coverage month is generally any month for which the taxpayer or a family member is covered by a qualified health plan enrolled in through an Exchange on the first day of the month and the premium is paid by the taxpayer or through an advance credit payment. However, section 36B(c)(2) provides that a month is not a coverage month for an individual who is eligible for minimum essential coverage other than coverage in the individual market. Under section 36B(c)(2)(B)(ii), minimum essential coverage is defined by reference to section 5000A(f). Minimum essential coverage includes government-sponsored programs such as most Medicaid coverage, Medicare part A, the Children's Health Insurance Program (CHIP), most TRICARE programs, most coverage provided to veterans under title 38 of the United States Code, and the Nonappropriated Fund Health Benefits Program of the Department of Defense. See section 5000A(f)(1) and §1.5000A-2(b). Section 1.36B-2(c)(3)(i) provides that, for purposes of section 36B, the government-sponsored programs described in section 5000A(f)(1)(A) are not considered eligible employer-sponsored plans.

Under §1.36B-2(c)(2)(i), an individual generally is treated as eligible for government-sponsored minimum essential coverage as of the first day of the first full month that the individual meets the criteria for coverage and is eligible to receive benefits under the government program. However, under §1.36B-2(c)(2)(v) an individual is treated as not eligible for Medicaid, CHIP, or a similar program for a period of coverage under a qualified health plan if, when the individual enrolls in the qualified health plan, an Exchange determines or considers (within the meaning of 45 CFR 155.302(b)) the individual to be ineligible for such program. In addition, §1.36B-2(c)(2)(iv) provides that if an individual receiving the benefit of advance credit payments is determined to be eligible for a government-sponsored program, and that eligibility is effective retroactively, then, for purposes of the premium tax credit, the individual is treated as eligible for the program no earlier than the first day of the first calendar month beginning after the approval.

Coverage under an eligible employer-sponsored plan is minimum essential coverage. In general, an eligible employer-sponsored plan is coverage provided by an employer to its employees (and their dependents) under a group health plan maintained by the employer. See section 5000A(f)(2) and §1.5000A-2(c). Under section 5000A(f)(3) and §1.5000A-2(g), minimum essential coverage does not include any coverage that consists solely of excepted benefits described in section 2791(c)(1), (c)(2), (c)(3), or (c)(4) of the Public Health Service Act (PHS Act) (42 U.S.C. 300gg-91(c)), or regulations issued under those provisions (45 CFR 148.220). In general, excepted benefits are benefits that are limited in scope or are conditional.

Under section 36B(c)(2)(C) and §1.36B-2(c)(3)(i), except as provided in the next paragraph of this preamble, an individual is treated as eligible for coverage under an eligible employer-sponsored plan only if the employee's share of the premium is affordable and the coverage provides minimum value. Under section 36B(c)(2)(C), an eligible employer-sponsored plan is treated as affordable for an employee if the amount of the employee's required contribution (within the meaning of section 5000A(e)(1)(B)) for self-only coverage does not exceed a specified percentage of the employee's household income. The affordability of coverage for individuals related to an employee is determined in the same manner. Thus, under section 36B(c)(2)(C)(i) and §1.36B-2(c)(3)(v)(A)(2), an eligible employer-sponsored plan is treated as affordable for an individual eligible for the plan because of a relationship to an employee if the amount of the employee's required contribution for self-only coverage does not exceed a specified percentage of the employee's household income.

Under §1.36B-2(c)(3)(v)(A)(3), an eligible employer-sponsored plan is not considered affordable if, when an individual enrolls in a qualified health plan, the Marketplace determines that the eligible employer-sponsored plan is not affordable. However, that rule does not apply for an individual who, with reckless disregard for the facts, provides incorrect information to a Marketplace concerning the employee's portion of the annual premium for coverage under the eligible employer-sponsored plan. In addition, under section 36B(c)(2)(C)(iii) and §1.36B-2(c)(3)(vii)(A), an individual is treated as eligible for employer-sponsored coverage if the individual actually enrolls in an eligible employer-sponsored plan, even if the coverage is not affordable or does not provide minimum value.

Section 1.36B-2(c)(3)(iii)(A) provides that, subject to the rules described above, an employee or related individual may be considered eligible for coverage under an eligible employer-sponsored plan for a month during a plan year if the employee or related individual could have enrolled in the plan for that month during an open or special enrollment period. Under §1.36B-2(c)(3)(ii), plan year means an eligible employer-sponsored plan's regular 12-month coverage period (or the remainder of a 12-month coverage period for a new employee or an individual who enrolls during a special enrollment period).

Although coverage in the individual market is minimum essential coverage under section 5000A(f)(1)(C), under section 36B(c)(2)(B)(i), an individual who is eligible for or enrolled in coverage in the individual market (whether or not obtained through the Marketplace) nevertheless may have a coverage month for purposes of the premium tax credit.

Required Contribution for Employer-Sponsored Coverage

Under section 36B(c)(2)(C) and §1.36B-2(c)(3)(v)(A)(1) and (2), an eligible employer-sponsored plan is treated as affordable for an employee or a related individual if the amount the employee must pay for self-only coverage whether by salary reduction or otherwise (the employee's required contribution) does not exceed a specified percentage of the employee's household income. Under section 36B(c)(2)(C)(i)(II), an employee's required contribution has the same meaning for purposes of the premium tax credit as in section 5000A(e)(1)(B).

Section 5000A provides that, for each month, taxpayers must have minimum essential coverage, qualify for a health coverage exemption, or make an individual shared responsibility payment when they file a Federal income tax return. Section 5000A(e)(1) and §1.5000A-3(e)(1) provide that an individual is exempt for a month when the individual cannot afford minimum essential coverage. For this purpose, an individual cannot afford coverage if the individual's required contribution (determined on an annual basis) for minimum essential coverage exceeds a specified percentage of the individual's household income. Under section 5000A(e)(1)(B)(i) and §1.5000A-3(e)(3)(ii)(A), for employees eligible for coverage under an eligible employer-sponsored plan, the employee's required contribution is the amount an employee would have to pay for self-only coverage (whether paid through salary reduction or otherwise) under the plan. For individuals eligible to enroll in employer-sponsored coverage because of a relationship to an employee (related individual), under section 5000A(e)(1)(C) and §1.5000A-3(e)(3)(ii)(B), the required contribution is the portion of the annual premium that the employee would pay (whether through salary reduction or otherwise) for the lowest cost family coverage that would cover the employee and all related individuals who are included in the employee's family and are not otherwise exempt under §1.5000A-3.

Notice 2015-87, 2015-52 I.R.B. 889, provides guidance on determining the affordability of an employer's offer of eligible employer-sponsored coverage for purposes of sections 36B, 5000A, and 4980H (and the related information reporting under section 6056).[1] In relevant part, Notice 2015-87 addresses how to determine the affordability of an employer's offer of eligible employer-sponsored coverage if an employer also makes available an opt-out payment, which is a payment that (1) is available only if the employee declines coverage (which includes waiving coverage in which the employee would otherwise be enrolled) under the employer-sponsored plan, and (2) cannot be used to pay for coverage under the employer-sponsored plan. The arrangement under which the opt-out payment is made available is an opt-out arrangement.

---

[1] An assessable payment under section 4980H(b) may arise if at least one full-time employee (as defined in §54.4980H-1(a)(21)) of the applicable large employer (as defined in §54.4980H-1(a)(4)) receives the premium tax credit. A full-time employee generally is ineligible for the premium tax credit if the employee is offered minimum essential coverage under an eligible employer-sponsored plan that is affordable and provides minimum value. The determination of whether an applicable large employer has made an offer of affordable coverage under an eligible employer-sponsored plan for purposes of section 4980H(b) generally is based on the standard set forth in section 36B, which provides that an offer is affordable if the employee's required contribution is at or below 9.5 percent (as indexed) of the employee's household income. However, because an employer generally will not know the taxpayer employee's household income, §54.4980H-5(e)(2) sets forth three safe harbors under which an employer may determine affordability (solely for purposes of section 4980H) based on information that is readily available to the employer (that is, Form W-2 wages, the rate of pay, or the Federal poverty line).

As Notice 2015-87 explains, the Treasury Department and the IRS have determined that it is generally appropriate to treat an opt-out payment that is made available under an unconditional opt-out arrangement in the same manner as a salary reduction contribution for purposes of determining an employee's required contribution under sections 36B and 5000A and any related consequences under sections 4980H(b) and 6056. Accordingly, Notice 2015-87 provides that the Treasury Department and the IRS intend to propose regulations reflecting this rule and to request comments on those regulations. For this purpose, an unconditional opt-out arrangement refers to an arrangement providing payments conditioned solely on an employee declining coverage under employer-sponsored coverage and not on an employee satisfying any other meaningful requirement related to the provision of health care to employees, such as a requirement to provide proof of coverage through a plan of a spouse's employer.

Notice 2015-87 also provides that the Treasury Department and the IRS anticipate requesting comments on the treatment of conditional opt-out arrangements, meaning opt-out arrangements under which payments are conditioned not only on the employee declining employer-sponsored coverage but also on satisfaction of one or more additional meaningful conditions (such as the employee providing proof of enrollment in coverage provided by a spouse's employer or other coverage).

Notice 2015-87 provides that, until the applicability date of any final regulations (and in any event for plan years beginning before 2017), individuals may treat opt-out payments made available under unconditional opt-out arrangements as increasing the employee's required contribution for purposes of sections 36B and 5000A.[2] In addition, for the same period, an individual who can demonstrate that he or she meets the condition(s) (in addition to declining the employer's health coverage) that must be satisfied to receive an opt-out payment (such as demonstrating that the employee has coverage under a spouse's group health plan) may treat the amount of the conditional opt-out payment as increasing the employee's required contribution for purposes of sections 36B and 5000A. See the section of this preamble entitled *"Effective/Applicability Date"* for additional related discussion.

Notice 2015-87 included a request for comments on opt-out arrangements. The Treasury Department and the IRS received a number of comments, and the comments are discussed in section 2.f. of this preamble entitled *"Opt-out arrangements and an employee's required contribution."*

Information Reporting

Section 36B(f)(3) provides that Exchanges must report to the IRS and to taxpayers certain information required to administer the premium tax credit. Section 1.36B-5(c)(1) provides that the information required to be reported annually includes (1) identifying information for each enrollee, (2) identifying information for the coverage, (3) the amount of enrollment premiums and advance credit payments for the coverage, (4) the premium for the benchmark plan used to calculate the amount of the advance credit payments made on behalf of the taxpayer or other enrollee, if advance credit payments were made, and the benchmark plan premium that would apply to all individuals enrolled in the coverage if advance credit payments were not made, and (5) the dates the coverage started and ended. Section 1.36B-5(c)(3)(i) provides that an Exchange must report this information for each family enrolled in the coverage.

Explanation of Provisions

1. Effective/Applicability Date

Except as otherwise provided in this section, these regulations are proposed to apply for taxable years beginning after December 31, 2016. As indicated in this section, taxpayers may rely on certain provisions of the proposed regulations for taxable years ending after December 31, 2013. In addition, several rules are proposed to apply for taxable years beginning after December 31, 2018. See the later section of this preamble entitled *"Effective/Applicability Date"* for information on the applicability date for the regulations on opt-out arrangements.

2. Eligibility

a. Applicable taxpayers

To avoid repayments of advance credit payments for taxpayers who experience an unforeseen decline in income, the existing regulations provide that if an Exchange determines at enrollment that the taxpayer's household income will be at least 100 percent but will not exceed 400 percent of the applicable FPL, the taxpayer will not lose his or her status as an applicable taxpayer solely because household income for the year turns out to be below 100 percent of the applicable FPL. To reduce the likelihood that individuals who recklessly or intentionally provide inaccurate information to an Exchange will benefit from an Exchange determination, the proposed regulations provide that a taxpayer whose household income is below 100 percent of the FPL for the taxpayer's family size is not treated as an applicable taxpayer if, with intentional or reckless disregard for the facts, the taxpayer provided incorrect information to an Exchange for the year of coverage.

b. Exchange determination of ineligibility for Medicaid or CHIP

Similar to the rule for taxpayers who received the benefit of advance credit payments but ended the taxable year with household income below 100 percent of the applicable FPL, the existing regulations do not require a repayment of advance credit payments for taxpayers with household income within the range for eligibility for certain government-sponsored programs if an Exchange determined or considered (within the meaning of 45 CFR 155.302(b)) the taxpayer or a member of the taxpayer's family to be ineligible for the program. To reduce the likelihood that individuals who recklessly or intentionally provide inaccurate information to an Exchange will benefit from an Exchange determination, the proposed regulations provide that an individual who was determined or considered by an Exchange to be ineligible for Medicaid, CHIP, or a similar program (such as a Basic Health Program) may be treated as eligible for coverage under the program if, with intentional or reckless disregard for the facts, the individual (or a person claiming a personal exemption for the individual) provided incorrect information to the Exchange.

c. Nonappropriated Fund Health Benefits Program

The existing regulations under section 36B provide that government-sponsored programs described in section 5000A(f)(1)(A), which include the Nonappropriated Fund Health Benefits Program of the Department of Defense, established under section 349 of the National Defense Authorization Act for Fiscal Year 1995 (Public Law 103-337; 10 U.S.C. 1587 note), are not eligible employer-sponsored plans. However, § 1.5000A-2(c)(2) provides that, because the Nonappropriated Fund Health Benefits Program (Program) is offered by an instrumentality of the Department of Defense to its employees, the Program is an eligible employer-sponsored plan. The proposed regulations conform the section 36B regulations to the section 5000A regulations and provide that the Program is treated as an eligible employer-sponsored plan for purposes of determining if an individual is eligible for minimum essential coverage under section 36B. Thus, if coverage under the Program does not provide minimum value

---

[2] Notice 2015-87 also provides that the Treasury Department and the IRS anticipate that the regulations generally will apply only for periods after the issuance of final regulations and that for the period prior to the applicability date of the final regulations, employers are not required to increase the amount of an employee's required contribution by the amount of an opt-out payment made available under an opt-out arrangement (other than a payment made available under a non-relief-eligible opt-out arrangement) for purposes of section 6056 (Form 1095-C), and an opt-out payment made available under an opt-out arrangement (other than a payment made available under a non-relief-eligible opt-out arrangement) will not be treated as increasing an employee's required contribution for purposes of any potential consequences under section 4980H(b). For a discussion of non-relief-eligible opt-out arrangements see Notice 2015-87, Q&A-9.

(under § 1.36B-2(c)(3)(vi)) or is not affordable (under § 36B-2(c)(3)(v)) for an individual who does not enroll in the coverage, he or she is not treated as eligible for minimum essential coverage under the Program for purposes of premium tax credit eligibility.

d. Eligibility for employer-sponsored coverage for months during a plan year

The existing regulations under section 36B provide that an individual is eligible for minimum essential coverage through an eligible employer-sponsored plan if the individual had the opportunity to enroll in the plan and the plan is affordable and provides minimum value. The Treasury Department and the IRS are aware that in some instances individuals may not be allowed an annual opportunity to decide whether to enroll in eligible employer-sponsored coverage. This lack of an annual opportunity to enroll in employer-sponsored coverage should not limit an individual's annual choice from available coverage options through the Marketplace with the possibility of benefitting from the premium tax credit. Thus, the proposed regulations clarify that if an individual declines to enroll in employer-sponsored coverage for a plan year and does not have the opportunity to enroll in that coverage for one or more succeeding plan years, for purposes of section 36B, the individual is treated as ineligible for that coverage for the succeeding plan year or years for which there is no enrollment opportunity.[3]

e. Excepted benefits

Under section 36B and § 1.36B-2(c)(3)(vii)(A), an individual is treated as eligible for minimum essential coverage through an eligible employer-sponsored plan if the individual actually enrolls in the coverage, even if the coverage is not affordable or does not provide minimum value. Although health coverage that consists solely of excepted benefits may be a group health plan and, therefore, is an eligible employer-sponsored plan under section 5000A(f)(2) and § 1.5000A-2(c)(1), section 5000A(f)(3) provides that health coverage that consists solely of excepted benefits is not minimum essential coverage. Therefore, individuals enrolled in a plan consisting solely of excepted benefits still must obtain minimum essential coverage to satisfy the individual shared responsibility provision. The proposed regulations clarify that for purposes of section 36B an individual is considered eligible for coverage under an eligible employer-sponsored plan only if that plan is minimum essential coverage. Accordingly, an individual enrolled in or offered a plan consisting solely of excepted benefits is not denied the premium tax credit by virtue of that excepted benefits offer or coverage. Taxpayers may rely on this rule for all taxable years beginning after December 31, 2013.

f. Opt-out arrangements and an employee's required contribution

Sections 1.36B-2(c)(3)(v) and 1.5000A-3(e)(3)(ii)(A) provide that, in determining whether employer-sponsored coverage is affordable to an employee, an employee's required contribution for the coverage includes the amount by which the employee's salary would be reduced to enroll in the coverage.[4] If an employer makes an opt-out payment available to an employee, the choice between cash and health coverage presented by the opt-out arrangement is analogous to the cash-or-coverage choice presented by the option to pay for coverage by salary reduction. In both cases, the employee may purchase the employer-sponsored coverage only at the price of forgoing a specified amount of cash compensation that the employee would otherwise receive - salary, in the case of a salary reduction, or an equal amount of other compensation, in the case of an opt-out payment. Therefore, the economic cost to the employee of the employer-sponsored coverage is the same under both arrangements. Accordingly, the employee's required contribution generally should be determined similarly regardless of the type of payment that an employee must forgo.

Notice 2015-87 requested comments on the proposed treatment of opt-out arrangements outlined in Q&A-9 of that notice. Several commenters objected to the proposal that the amount of an available unconditional opt-out payment increases the employee's required contribution on the basis that forgoing opt-out payments as part of enrolling in coverage has not traditionally been viewed by employers or employees as economically equivalent to making a salary reduction election and that such a rule would discourage employers from making opt-out payments available. None of the commenters, however, offered a persuasive economic basis for distinguishing unconditional opt-out payments from other compensation that an employee must forgo to enroll in employer-sponsored coverage, such as a salary reduction. Because forgoing an unconditional opt-out payment is economically equivalent to forgoing salary pursuant to a salary reduction election, and because §§ 1.36B-2(c)(3)(v) and 1.5000A-3(e)(3)(ii)(A) provide that the employee's required contribution includes the amount of any salary reduction, the proposed regulations adopt the approach described in Notice 2015-87 for opt-out payments made available under unconditional opt-out arrangements and provide that the amount of an opt-out payment made available to the employee under an unconditional opt-out arrangement increases the employee's required contribution.[5]

Notice 2015-87 provides that, for periods prior to the applicability date of any final regulations, employers are not required to increase the amount of an employee's required contribution by amounts made available under an opt-out arrangement for purposes of section 4980H(b) or section 6056 (in particular Form 1095-C, *Employer-Provided Health Insurance Offer and Coverage*), except that, for periods after December 16, 2015, the employee's required contribution must include amounts made available under an unconditional opt-out arrangement that is adopted after December 16, 2015. However, Notice 2015-87 provided that, for this purpose, an opt-out arrangement will not be treated as adopted after December 16, 2015, under limited circumstances, including in cases in which a board, committee, or similar body or an authorized officer of the employer specifically adopted the opt-out arrangement before December 16, 2015.

Some commenters requested clarification that an unconditional opt-out arrangement that is required under the terms of a collective bargaining agreement in effect before December 16, 2015, should be treated as having been adopted prior to December 16, 2015, and that amounts made available under such an opt-out arrangement should not be included in an employee's required contribution for purposes of sections 4980H(b) or 6056 through the expiration of the collective bargaining agreement that provides for the opt-out arrangement. The Treasury Department and the IRS now clarify that, under Notice 2015-87, for purposes of sections 4980H(b) and 6056, an unconditional opt-out arrangement that is required under the terms of a collective bargaining agreement in effect before December 16, 2015, will be treated as having been adopted prior to December 16, 2015. In addition, until the later of (1) the beginning of the first plan year that begins following the expiration of the collective bargaining agreement in effect before December 16, 2015 (disregarding any extensions on or after December 16, 2015), or (2) the applicability date of these regulations with respect to sections 4980H and 6056, employers participating in the collective bargaining agreement are not required to increase the amount of an employee's required contribution by amounts made available under such an opt-out arrangement for purposes of sections 4980H(b) or 6056 (Form 1095-C). The Treasury Department and the IRS further adopt these commenters' request that this treatment apply to any successor employer adopting the opt-out arrangement before the expiration of the collective bargaining agreement in effect before December 16, 2015 (disregarding any extensions on or after December 16, 2015). Commenters raised the issue of whether other types of agreements covering employees may need a similar extension of the relief through the end of the agreement's term. The Treasury Department and the IRS request

---

[3] Note that for purposes of section 4980H, in general, an applicable large employer will not be treated as having made an offer of coverage to a full-time employee for a plan year if the employee does not have an effective opportunity to elect to enroll in the coverage at least once with respect to the plan year. For this purpose, a plan year must be twelve consecutive months, unless a short plan year of less than twelve consecutive months is permitted for a valid business purpose. For additional rules on the definition of "offer" and "plan year" under section 4980H, see §§ 54.4980H-1(a)(35), 54.4980H-4(b), and 54.4980H-5(b).

[4] Section 5000A(e)(1)(C) and § 1.5000A-3(e)(3)(ii)(B) provide that, for purposes of the individual shared responsibility provision, the required contribution for individuals eligible to enroll in employer coverage because of a relationship to an employee (related individual) is the portion of the annual premium that the employee would pay (whether

through salary reduction or otherwise) for the lowest cost family coverage that would cover the employee and all related individuals who are included in the employee's family and are not otherwise exempt under § 1.5000A-3.

[5] To distinguish between opt-out payments and employer contributions to a section 125 cafeteria plan (which in some cases could be paid in cash to an employee who declines coverage in the health plan or other available benefits), the proposed regulations further clarify that an amount provided as an employer contribution to a cafeteria plan and that may be used by the employee to purchase minimum essential coverage is not an opt-out payment, whether or not the employee may receive the amount as a taxable benefit. This provision clarifies that the effect on an employee's required contribution of employer contributions to a cafeteria plan is determined under § 1.36B-2(c)(3)(v)(A)(6) rather than § 1.36B-2(c)(3)(v)(A)(7).

comments identifying the types of agreements raising this issue due to their similarity to collective bargaining agreements because, for example, the agreement is similar in scope to a collective bargaining agreement, binding on the parties involved for a multi-year period, and subject to a statutory or regulatory regime.

Several commenters suggested that, notwithstanding the proposal on unconditional opt-out arrangements, the amount of an opt-out payment made available should not increase an employee's required contribution if the opt-out payment is conditioned on the employee having minimum essential coverage through another source, such as a spouse's employer-sponsored plan. These commenters argued that the amount of such a conditional opt-out payment should not affect the affordability of an employer's offer of employer-sponsored coverage for an employee who does not satisfy the applicable condition because that employee is ineligible to receive the opt-out payment. Moreover, commenters argued that an employee who satisfies the condition (that is, who has alternative minimum essential coverage) is ineligible for the premium tax credit and does not need to determine the affordability of the employer's coverage offer. Thus, the commenters asserted, an amount made available under such an arrangement should be excluded from the required contribution.

While it is clear that the availability of an unconditional opt-out payment increases an individual's required contribution, the effect of the availability of a conditional opt-out payment is less obvious. In particular, under an unconditional opt-out arrangement, an individual who enrolls in the employer coverage loses the opt-out payment as a direct result of enrolling in the employer coverage. By contrast, in the case of a conditional opt-out arrangement, the availability of the opt-out payment may depend on information that is not generally available to the employer (who, if it is an applicable large employer, must report the required contribution under section 6056 and whose potential liability under section 4980H may be affected). Because of this difficulty of ascertaining which individuals could have met the condition and, therefore, would actually forgo the opt-out payment when enrolling in employer-sponsored coverage, it generally is not feasible to have a rule under which the required contribution perfectly captures the cost of coverage for each specific individual offered a conditional opt-out payment.

Similarly, another way to view opt-out payments that are conditioned on alternative coverage is that, rather than raising the cost to the employee of the employer's coverage, they reduce the cost to the employee of the alternative coverage. However, because employers generally do not have information about the existence and cost of other options available to the individual, it is not practical to take into account any offer of coverage other than the offer made by the employer in determining the required contribution with respect to the employer coverage (that is, the coverage that the employee must decline to receive the opt-out payment).

While commenters indicated that the required contribution with respect to the employer coverage does not matter for an individual enrolled in any other minimum essential coverage because the individual would be ineligible for the premium tax credit, this statement is not true if the other coverage is individual market coverage. In particular, while enrollment in most types of minimum essential coverage results in an individual being ineligible for a premium tax credit, that is not the case for coverage in the individual market. Moreover, for individual market coverage offered through a Marketplace, the required contribution with respect to the employer coverage frequently will be relevant in determining whether the individual is eligible for a premium tax credit. In such cases, as in the case of an unconditional opt-out payment, the availability of a conditional opt-out payment effectively increases the cost to the individual of enrolling in the employer coverage (at least relative to Marketplace coverage).

Further, an opt-out arrangement that is conditioned on an employee's ability to obtain other coverage (if that coverage can be coverage in the individual market, whether inside or outside the Marketplace) does not generally raise the issues described earlier in this section of the preamble regarding the difficulty of ascertaining which individuals could meet the condition under a conditional opt-out arrangement. This is because generally all individuals are able to obtain coverage in the individual market, pursuant to the guaranteed issue requirements in section 2702 of the PHS Act. Thus, in the sense that all individuals can satisfy the applicable condition, such an opt-out arrangement is similar to an unconditional opt-out arrangement.

In an effort to provide a workable rule that balances these competing concerns, the proposed regulations provide that amounts made available under conditional opt-out arrangements are disregarded in determining the required contribution if the arrangement satisfies certain conditions (an "eligible opt-out arrangement"), but otherwise the amounts are taken into account. The proposed regulations define an "eligible opt-out arrangement" as an arrangement under which the employee's right to receive the opt-out payment is conditioned on (1) the employee declining to enroll in the employer-sponsored coverage and (2) the employee providing reasonable evidence that the employee and all other individuals for whom the employee reasonably expects to claim a personal exemption deduction for the taxable year or years that begin or end in or with the employer's plan year to which the opt-out arrangement applies (employee's expected tax family) have or will have minimum essential coverage (other than coverage in the individual market, whether or not obtained through the Marketplace) during the period of coverage to which the opt-out arrangement applies. For example, if an employee's expected tax family consists of the employee, the employee's spouse, and two children, the employee would meet this requirement by providing reasonable evidence that the employee, the employee's spouse, and the two children, will have coverage under the group health plan of the spouse' s employer for the period to which the opt-out arrangement applies.[6]

The Treasury Department and the IRS invite comments on this proposed rule, including suggestions for other workable rules that result in the required contribution more accurately reflecting the individual's cost of coverage while minimizing undesirable consequences and incentives.

For purposes of the proposed eligible opt-out arrangement rule, reasonable evidence of alternative coverage includes the employee's attestation that the employee and all other members of the employee's expected tax family, if any, have or will have minimum essential coverage (other than coverage in the individual market, whether or not obtained through the Marketplace) or other reasonable evidence. Notwithstanding the evidence of alternative coverage required under the arrangement, to qualify as an eligible opt-out arrangement, the arrangement must also provide that any opt-out payment will not be made (and the payment must not in fact be made) if the employer knows or has reason to know that the employee or any other member of the employee's expected tax family does not have (or will not have) the required alternative coverage. An eligible opt-out arrangement must also require that the evidence of coverage be provided no less frequently than every plan year to which the eligible opt-out arrangement applies, and that the evidence be provided no earlier than a reasonable period before the commencement of the period of coverage to which the eligible opt-out arrangement applies. Obtaining the reasonable evidence (such as an attestation) as part of the regular annual open enrollment period that occurs within a few months before the commencement of the next plan year of employer-sponsored coverage meets this reasonable period requirement. Alternatively, the eligible opt-out arrangement would be permitted to require evidence of alternative coverage to be provided later, such as after the plan year starts, which would enable the employer to require evidence that the employee and other members of the employee's expected tax family have already obtained the alternative coverage.

Commenters on Notice 2015-87 generally stated that typical conditions under an opt-out arrangement include a requirement that the employee have alternative coverage through employer-sponsored coverage of a spouse or another relative, such as a parent. Provided that, as required under the opt-out arrangement, the employee provided reasonable evidence of this alternative coverage for the employee and the other members of the employee's expected tax family, and met the related conditions described in this preamble, these types of opt-out arrangements would be eligible opt-out arrangements, and opt-out payments made available under such arrangements would not increase the employee's required contribution.

---

[6] The Treasury Department and the IRS note that if an opt-out payment is conditioned on an employee obtaining individual market coverage, that opt-out arrangement could act as a reimbursement arrangement for some or all of the employee's premium for that individual market coverage; therefore, the opt-out arrangement could operate as an employer payment plan as discussed in Notice 2015-87, Notice 2015-17, 2015-14 I.R.B. 845, and Notice 2013-54, 2013-40 I.R.B. 287. Nothing in these proposed regulations is intended to affect the prior guidance on employer payment plans.

The Treasury Department and the IRS did not receive comments on opt-out arrangements indicating that the meaningful conditions imposed include any requirement other than one relating to alternative coverage. Therefore, the proposed rules do not address other opt-out conditions and would not treat an opt-out arrangement based on other conditions as an eligible opt-out arrangement. However, the Treasury Department and the IRS invite comments on whether opt-out payments are made subject to additional types of conditions in some cases, whether those types of conditions should be addressed in further guidance, and, if so, how.

One commenter suggested that, if opt-out payments conditioned on alternative coverage are not included in an employee's required contribution, rules will be needed for cases in which an employee receives an opt-out payment and that employee's alternative coverage subsequently terminates. The commenter suggested that, in that case, the termination of the alternative coverage should have no impact on the determination of the employee's required contribution for the employer-sponsored coverage from which the employee opted out. In response, under the proposed regulations, provided that the reasonable evidence requirement is met, the amount of an opt-out payment made available under an eligible opt-out arrangement may continue to be excluded from the employee's required contribution for the remainder of the period of coverage to which the opt-out payment originally applied. The opt-out payment may be excluded for this period even if the alternative coverage subsequently terminates for the employee or any other member of the employee's expected tax family, regardless of whether the opt-out payment is required to be adjusted or terminated due to the loss of alternative coverage, and regardless of whether the employee is required to provide notice of the loss of alternative coverage to the employer.

The Treasury Department and the IRS are aware that the way in which opt-out arrangements affect the calculation of affordability is important not only to an employee and the other members of the employee's expected tax family in determining whether they may be eligible for a premium tax credit or whether an individual may be exempt under the individual shared responsibility provisions, but also to an employer subject to the employer shared responsibility provisions under section 4980H in determining whether the employer may be subject to an assessable payment under section 4980H(b). An employer subject to the employer shared responsibility provisions will be subject to a payment under section 4980H(b) only with respect to a full-time employee who receives a premium tax credit, and an employee will not be eligible for the premium tax credit if the employer's offer of coverage was affordable and provided minimum value.[7] Commenters expressed concern that if the rule adopted for conditional opt-outs required an employee to provide reasonable evidence that the employee has or will have minimum essential coverage, the employer may not know whether the employee is being truthful and has obtained (or will obtain) such coverage, or how long such coverage will continue. Under these proposed regulations, however, the employee's required contribution will not be increased by an opt-out payment made available under an eligible opt-out arrangement, provided that the arrangement provides that the employer makes the payment only if the employee provides reasonable evidence of alternative coverage and the employer does not know or have reason to know that the employee or any other member of the employee's expected tax family fails or will fail to meet the requirement to have alternative coverage (other than individual market coverage, whether or not obtained through the Marketplace).

Some commenters requested exceptions for special circumstances from the general rule that the employee's required contribution is increased by the amount of an opt-out payment made available. These circumstances include (1) conditional opt-out payments that are required under the terms of a collective bargaining agreement and (2) opt-out payments that are below a de minimis amount. Regarding opt-out arrangements contained in collective bargaining agreements, the Treasury Department and the IRS anticipate that the proposed treatment of eligible opt-out arrangements, generally, will address the concerns raised in the comments. Accordingly, the Treasury Department and the IRS do not propose to provide a permanent exception for opt-out arrangements provided under collective bargaining agreements. Earlier in this section of the preamble, however, the Treasury Department and the IRS clarify and expand the transition relief provided under Notice 2015-87 for opt-out arrangements provided under collective bargaining agreements in effect before December 16, 2015. As for an exception for de minimis amounts, the Treasury Department and the IRS decline to adopt such an exception because there is neither a statutory nor an economic basis for establishing a de minimis threshold under which an unconditional opt-out payment would be excluded from the employee's required contribution.

g. Effective date of eligibility for minimum essential coverage when advance credit payments discontinuance is delayed

Section 36B and the regulations under section 36B provide that an individual who may enroll in minimum essential coverage outside the Marketplace (other than individual market coverage) for a month is generally not allowed a premium tax credit for that month. Consequently, individuals enrolled in a qualified health plan with advance credit payments must return to the Exchange to report eligibility for other minimum essential coverage so the Exchange can discontinue the advance credit payments for Marketplace coverage. Similarly, individuals enrolled in a qualified health plan with advance credit payments may be determined eligible for coverage under a government-sponsored program, such as Medicaid. In some cases, individuals may inform the Exchange of their opportunity to enroll in other minimum essential coverage or receive approval for coverage under a government-sponsored program after the time for which the Exchange can discontinue advance credit payments for the next month. Because taxpayers should generally not have to repay the advance credit payments for that next month in these circumstances, the proposed regulations provide a rule for situations in which an Exchange's discontinuance of advance credit payments is delayed. Under the proposed regulations, if an individual who is enrolled in a qualified health plan for which advance credit payments are made informs the Exchange that the individual is or will soon be eligible for other minimum essential coverage and that advance credit payments should be discontinued, but the Exchange does not discontinue advance credit payments for the first calendar month beginning after the month the individual notifies the Exchange, the individual is treated as eligible for the other minimum essential coverage no earlier than the first day of the second calendar month beginning after the first month the individual may enroll in the other minimum essential coverage. Similarly, if a determination is made that an individual is eligible for Medicaid or CHIP but advance credit payments are not discontinued for the first calendar month beginning after the eligibility determination, the individual is treated as eligible for Medicaid or CHIP no earlier than the first day of the second calendar month beginning after the determination. Taxpayers may rely on this rule for all taxable years beginning after December 31, 2013.

3. Premium Assistance Amount

a. Payment of taxpayer's share of premiums for advance credit payments following appeal determinations

Under §1.36B-3(c)(1)(ii), a month in which an individual who is enrolled in a qualified health plan is a coverage month for the individual only if the taxpayer's share of the premium for the individual's coverage for the month is paid by the unextended due date of the taxpayer's income tax return for the year of coverage, or the premium is fully paid by advance credit payments.

One of the functions of an Exchange is to make determinations as to whether an individual who enrolls in a qualified health plan is eligible for advance credit payments for the coverage. If an Exchange determines that the individual is not eligible for advance credit payments, the individual may appeal that decision. An individual who is initially determined ineligible for advance credit payments, does not enroll in a qualified health plan under the contested determination, and is later determined to be eligible for advance credit payments through the appeals process, may elect to be retroactively enrolled in a health plan through the Exchange. In that case, the individual is treated as having been enrolled in the qualified health plan from the date on which the individual would have enrolled had he or she initially been determined eligible for advance credit

---

[7] The affordability rules under section 36B, including rules regarding opt-out payments, may also affect the application of section 4980H(a) because one element that is required for an applicable large employer to be subject to an assessable payment under section 4980H(a) is that at least one full-time employee must receive the premium tax credit.

payments. If retroactively enrolled, the deadline for paying premiums for the retroactive coverage may be after the unextended due date for filing an income tax return for the year of coverage. Consequently, the proposed regulations provide that a taxpayer who is eligible for advance credit payments pursuant to an eligibility appeal for a member of the taxpayer's coverage family who, based on the appeals decision, retroactively enrolls in a qualified health plan, is considered to have met the requirement in § 1.36B-3(c)(1)(ii) for a month if the taxpayer pays the taxpayer's share of the premium for coverage under the plan for the month on or before the 120th day following the date of the appeals decision. Taxpayers may rely on this rule for all taxable years beginning after December 31, 2013.

b. Month that coverage is terminated

Section 1.36B-3(d)(2) provides that if a qualified health plan is terminated before the last day of a month, the premium assistance amount for the month is the lesser of the enrollment premiums for the month (reduced by any amounts that were refunded), or the excess of the benchmark plan premium for a full month of coverage over the full contribution amount for the month. Section 1.36B-3(c)(2) provides that an individual whose enrollment in a qualified health plan is effective on the date of the individual's birth or adoption, or placement for foster care, or upon the effective date of a court order, is treated as enrolled as of the first day of the month and, therefore, the month of enrollment may be a coverage month. The regulations, however, do not expressly address how the premium assistance amount is computed when a covered individual disenrolls before the last day of a month but the plan is not terminated because other individuals remain enrolled. For purposes of the premium tax credit, the premium assistance amount for an individual who is not enrolled for an entire month should be the same regardless of the circumstances causing the partial-month coverage, provided that the individual was enrolled, or is treated as enrolled, as of the first day of the month (that is, so long as the month is a coverage month). Accordingly, to provide consistency for all individuals who have a coverage month that is less than a full calendar month, the proposed regulations provide that the premium assistance amount for a month is the lesser of the enrollment premiums for the month (reduced by any amounts that were refunded), or the excess of the benchmark plan premium over the contribution amount for the month. Taxpayers may rely on this rule for all taxable years beginning after December 31, 2013.

4. Benchmark Plan Premium

a. Effective/applicability date of benchmark plan rules

The rules relating to the benchmark plan in this section are proposed to apply for taxable years beginning after December 31, 2018.

b. Pediatric dental benefits

Under section 1311(d)(2)(B) of the Affordable Care Act, only qualified health plans, including stand-alone dental plans offering pediatric dental benefits, may be offered through a Marketplace. In general, a qualified health plan is required to provide coverage for all ten essential health benefits described in section 1302(b) of the Affordable Care Act, including pediatric dental coverage. However, under section 1302(b)(4)(F), a plan that does not provide pediatric dental benefits may nonetheless be a qualified health plan if it covers each essential health benefit described in section 1302(b) other than pediatric dental benefits and if it is offered through a Marketplace in which a stand-alone dental plan offering pediatric dental benefits is offered as well.

Section 36B(b)(3)(E) and § 1.36B-3(k) provide that if an individual enrolls in both a qualified health plan and a stand-alone dental plan, the portion of the premium for the stand-alone dental plan properly allocable to pediatric dental benefits is treated as a premium payable for the individual's qualified health plan. Thus, in determining a taxpayer's premium assistance amount for a month in which a member of the taxpayer's coverage family is enrolled in a stand-alone dental plan, the taxpayer's enrollment premium includes the portion of the premium for the stand-alone dental plan allocable to pediatric dental benefits. The existing regulations do not provide a similar adjustment for the taxpayer's applicable benchmark plan premium to reflect the cost of pediatric dental benefits in cases where the second-lowest cost silver plan does not provide pediatric dental benefits.

Section 36B(b)(3)(B) provides that the applicable benchmark plan with respect to a taxpayer is the second lowest cost silver plan available through the applicable Marketplace that provides "self-only coverage" or "family coverage," depending generally on whether the coverage family includes one or more individuals. Neither the Code nor the Affordable Care Act defines the terms "self-only coverage" or "family coverage" for this purpose.

Under the existing regulations, the references in section 36B(b)(3)(B) to plans that provide self-only coverage and family coverage are interpreted to refer to all qualified health plans offered through the applicable Marketplace, regardless of whether the coverage offered by those plans includes all ten essential health benefits. Because qualified health plans that do not offer pediatric dental benefits tend to be cheaper than qualified health plans that cover all ten essential health benefits, the second lowest-cost silver plan (and therefore the premium tax credit) for taxpayers purchasing coverage through a Marketplace in which stand-alone dental plans are offered is likely to not account for the cost of obtaining pediatric dental coverage.

The Treasury Department and the IRS believe that the current rule frustrates the statute's goal of making coverage that provides the essential health benefits affordable to individuals eligible for the premium tax credit. Accordingly, the proposed regulations reflect a modification in the interpretation of the terms "self-only coverage" and "family coverage" in section 36B(b)(3)(B) to refer to coverage that provides each of the essential health benefits described in section 1302(b) of the Affordable Care Act. This coverage may be obtained from either a qualified health plan alone or from a qualified health plan in combination with a stand-alone dental plan. In particular, self-only coverage refers to coverage obtained from such plans where the coverage family is a single individual. Similarly, family coverage refers to coverage obtained from such plans where the coverage family includes more than one individual.

Consistent with this interpretation, the proposed regulations provide that for taxable years beginning after December 31, 2018, if an Exchange offers one or more silver-level qualified health plans that do not cover pediatric dental benefits, the applicable benchmark plan is determined by ranking (1) the premiums for the silver-level qualified health plans that include pediatric dental benefits offered by the Exchange and (2) the aggregate of the premiums for the silver-level qualified health plans offered by the Exchange that do not include pediatric dental benefits plus the portion of the premium allocable to pediatric dental benefits for stand-alone dental plans offered by the Exchange. In constructing this ranking, the premium for the lowest-cost silver plan that does not include pediatric dental benefits is added to the lowest-cost portion of the premium for a stand-alone dental plan that is allocable to pediatric dental benefits, and similarly, the premium for the second lowest-cost silver plan that does not include pediatric dental benefits is added to the secondlowest- cost portion of the premium for a stand-alone dental plan that is allocable to pediatric dental benefits. The second lowest-cost amount from this combined ranking is the taxpayer's applicable benchmark plan premium.

c. Coverage family members residing in different locations

Under § 1.36B-3(f), a taxpayer's applicable benchmark plan is the second lowest cost silver plan offered at the time a taxpayer or family member enrolls in a qualified health plan through the Exchange for the rating area where the taxpayer resides. Under § 1.36B-3(f)(4), if members of a taxpayer's family reside in different states and enroll in separate qualified health plans, the premium for the taxpayer's applicable benchmark plan is the sum of the premiums for the applicable benchmark plans for each group of family members living in the same state.

Referring to the residence of the taxpayer to establish the cost for a benchmark health plan is appropriate when the taxpayer and all members of the taxpayer's coverage family live in the same location because it reflects the cost of available coverage for the taxpayer's coverage family. However, because premiums and plan availability may vary based on location, the existing rule for a taxpayer whose family members reside in different locations in the same state may not accurately reflect the cost of available coverage. In addition, the rules for calculating the premium tax credit should operate the same for families residing in multiple locations within a state and families residing in multiple states. Accordingly, § 1.36B-3(f)(4) of the proposed regulations provides that if a taxpayer's coverage family members reside in multiple locations, whether within the same state or in different states, the taxpayer's benchmark plan is determined based on the cost of available coverage in the locations where members of the taxpayer's coverage family reside. In particular, if members of a taxpayer's coverage family reside in different locations, the taxpayer's benchmark plan premium is the sum of the premiums for the applicable benchmark plans for each group of coverage family members residing in different locations, based on the plans offered to the group through the Exchange for the rating area where the group resides. If all members of a taxpayer's coverage family reside in a single location that is different from where the taxpayer resides, the taxpayer's benchmark plan premium is the premium for the applicable benchmark plan for the coverage family, based on the plans offered to the taxpayer's coverage family through the Exchange for the rating area where the coverage family resides.

d. Aggregation of silver-level policies

Section 1.36B-3(f)(3) provides that if one or more silver-level plans offered through an Exchange do not cover all members of a taxpayer's coverage family under one policy (for example, because an issuer will not cover a taxpayer's dependent parent on the same policy the taxpayer enrolls in), the premium for the applicable benchmark plan may be the premium for a single policy or for more than one policy, whichever is the second lowest-cost silver option. This rule does not specify which combinations of policies must be taken into account for this purpose, suggesting that all such combinations must be considered, which is unduly complex for taxpayers, difficult for Exchanges to implement, and difficult for the IRS to administer. Accordingly, to clarify and simplify the benchmark premium determination for situations in which a silver-level plan does not cover all the members of a taxpayer's coverage family under one policy, the proposed regulations delete the existing rule and provide a new rule in its place.

Under the proposed regulations, if a silver-level plan offers coverage to all members of a taxpayer's coverage family who reside in the same location under a single policy, the plan premium taken into account for purposes of determining the applicable benchmark plan is the premium for that policy. In contrast, if a silver-level plan would require multiple policies to cover all members of a taxpayer's coverage family who reside in the same location, the plan premium taken into account for purposes of determining the applicable benchmark plan is the sum of the premiums for self-only policies under the plan for each member of the coverage family who resides in the same location. Under the proposed regulations, similar rules would apply to the portion of premiums for stand-alone dental plans allocable to pediatric dental coverage taken into account for purposes of determining the premium for a taxpayer's applicable benchmark plan.

Comments are requested on the rule contained in the proposed regulations, as well as on an alternative rule under which the plan premium taken into account for purposes of determining a taxpayer's applicable benchmark plan would be equal to the sum of the self-only policies under a plan for each member of the taxpayer's coverage family, regardless of whether all members of the taxpayer's coverage family could be covered under a single policy under the plan.

e. Silver-level plan not available for enrollment

Section 1.36B-3(f)(5) provides that if a qualified health plan is closed to enrollment for a taxpayer or a member of the taxpayer's coverage family, that plan is disregarded in determining the taxpayer's applicable benchmark plan. Similarly, § 1.36B-3(f)(6) provides that a plan that is the applicable benchmark plan for a taxpayer does not cease to be the applicable benchmark plan solely because the plan or a lower cost plan terminates or closes to enrollment during the taxable year. Because standalone dental plans are considered in determining a taxpayer's applicable benchmark plan under the proposed regulations, the proposed regulations provide consistency in the treatment of qualified health plans and stand-alone dental plans that are closed to enrollment or that terminate during the taxable year.

f. Only one silver-level plan offered to the coverage family

In general, § 1.36B-3(f)(1) provides that a taxpayer's applicable benchmark plan is the second lowest-cost silver-level plan available to the taxpayer for self-only or family coverage. However, for taxpayers who reside in certain locations, only one silver-level plan providing such coverage may be available. Section § 1.36B-3(f)(8) of the proposed regulations clarifies that if there is only one silver-level qualified health plan offered through the Exchange that would cover all members of the taxpayer's coverage family (whether under one policy or multiple policies), that silver-level plan is used for purposes of the taxpayer's applicable benchmark plan. Similarly, if there is only one stand-alone dental plan offered through the Exchange that would cover all members of the taxpayer's coverage family (whether under one policy or multiple policies), the portion of the premium of that plan that is allocable to pediatric dental benefits is used for purposes of determining the taxpayer's applicable benchmark plan.

5. Reconciliation of Advance Credit Payments

Section 301.6011-8 provides that a taxpayer who receives the benefit of advance credit payments must file an income tax return for that taxable year on or before the due date for the return (including extensions of time for filing) and reconcile the advance credit payments. In addition, the regulations under section 36B provide that if advance credit payments are made for coverage of an individual for whom no taxpayer claims a personal exemption deduction, the taxpayer who attests to the Exchange to the intention to claim a personal exemption deduction for the individual as part of the determination that the taxpayer is eligible for advance credit payments for coverage of the individual must reconcile the advance credit payments.

Questions have been raised concerning how these two rules apply, and consequently which individual must reconcile advance credit payments, when a taxpayer (a parent, for example) attests that he or she will claim a personal exemption deduction for an individual, the advance payments are made with respect to coverage for the individual, the taxpayer does not claim a personal exemption deduction for the individual, and the individual does not file a tax return for the year. The intent of the existing regulation is that the taxpayer, not the individual for whose coverage advance credit payments were made, must reconcile the advance credit payments in situations in which a taxpayer attests to the intention to claim a personal exemption for the individual and no one claims a personal exemption deduction for the individual. Consequently, the proposed regulations clarify that if advance credit payments are made for coverage of an individual for whom no taxpayer claims a personal exemption deduction, the taxpayer who attests to the Exchange to the intention to claim a personal exemption deduction for the individual, not the individual for whose coverage the advance credit payments were made, must file a tax return and reconcile the advance credit payments.

6. Information Reporting

a. Two or more families enrolled in single qualified health plan

Section 1.36B-3(h) provides that if a qualified health plan covers more than one family under a single policy (for example, a plan covers a taxpayer and the taxpayer's child who is 25 and not a dependent of the taxpayer), the premium tax credit is computed for each applicable taxpayer covered by the plan. In addition, in computing the tax credit for each taxpayer, premiums for the qualified health plan the taxpayers purchase (the enrollment premiums) are allocated to each taxpayer in proportion to the premiums for each taxpayer's applicable benchmark plan.

The existing regulations provide that the Exchange must report the enrollment premiums for each family, but do not specify the manner in which the Exchange must divide the enrollment premiums among the families enrolled in the policy. Consequently, the proposed regulations clarify that when multiple families enroll in a single qualified health plan and advance credit payments are made for the coverage, the enrollment premiums reported by the Exchange for each family is the family's allocable share of the enrollment premiums, which is based on the proportion of each family's applicable benchmark plan premium.

b. Partial months of enrollment

The existing regulations do not specify how the enrollment premiums and benchmark plan premiums are reported in cases in which one or more individuals is enrolled or disenrolled in coverage mid-month. To ensure that this reporting is consistent with the rules for calculating the premium assistance amounts for partial months of coverage, the proposed regulations provide that, if an individual is enrolled in a qualified health plan after the first day of a month, generally no value should be reported for the individual's enrollment premium or benchmark plan premium for that month. However, if an individual's coverage in a qualified health plan is terminated before the last day of a month, or an individual is enrolled in coverage after the first day of a month and the coverage is effective on the date of the individual's birth, adoption, or placement for adoption or in foster care, or on the effective date of a court order, an Exchange must report the premium for the applicable benchmark plan for a full month of coverage (excluding the premium allocated to benefits in excess of essential health benefits). In addition, the proposed regulations provide that the Exchange must report the enrollment premiums for the month (excluding the premium allocated to benefits in excess of essential health benefits), reduced by any amount that was refunded due to the plan's termination.

c. Use of electronic media

Section 301.6011-2(b) provides that if the use of certain forms, including the Form 1095 series, is required by the applicable regulations or revenue procedures for the purpose of making an information return, the information required by the form must be submitted on magnetic media. Form 1095-A should not have been included in § 301.6011-2 because Form 1095-A is not an information return. Consequently, the proposed regulations replace the general reference in § 301.6011-2(b) to the forms in the 1095 series with specific references to Forms 1095-B and 1095-C, but not Form 1095-A.

Effective/Applicability Date

Except as otherwise provided, these regulations are proposed to apply for taxable years beginning after December 31, 2016. In addition, taxpayers may rely on certain provisions of the proposed regulations for taxable years ending after December 31, 2013, as indicated earlier in this preamble. In addition, rules relating to the benchmark plan described in section 4 of this preamble are proposed to apply for taxable years beginning after December 31, 2018.

Notwithstanding the proposed applicability date, nothing in the proposed regulations is intended to limit any relief for opt-out arrangements provided in Notice 2015-87, Q&A 9, or in section 2.f of the preamble to these proposed regulations (regarding opt-out arrangements provided for in collective bargaining agreements). For purposes of sections 36B and 5000A, although under the proposed regulations amounts made available under an eligible opt-out arrangement are not added to an employee's required contribution, for periods before the final regulations are applicable and, if later, through the end of the most recent plan year beginning before January 1, 2017, an individual who can demonstrate that he or she meets the condition for an opt-out payment under an eligible opt-out arrangement is permitted to treat the opt-out payment as increasing the employee's required contribution.[8]

For purposes of the consequences of these regulations under sections 4980H and 6056 (and in particular Form 1095-C), the regulations regarding opt-out arrangements are proposed to be first applicable for plan years beginning on or after January 1, 2017,[9] and for the period prior to this applicability date employers are not required to increase the amount of an employee's required contribution by the amount of an opt-out payment made available under an opt-out arrangement (other than a payment made available under a non-relief-eligible opt-out arrangement[10]). See also section 2.f of this preamble for transition relief provided under Notice 2015-87 as clarified and expanded for opt-out arrangements contained in collective bargaining agreements in effect before December 16, 2015. See § 601.601(d)(2)(ii)(b).

Special Analyses

Certain IRS regulations, including this one, are exempt from the requirements of Executive Order 12866, as supplemented and reaffirmed by Executive Order 13563. Therefore, a regulatory assessment is not required. It has also been determined that section 553(b) of the Administrative Procedure Act (5 U.S.C. chapter 5) does not apply to these regulations.

It is hereby certified that these regulations will not have a significant economic impact on a substantial number of small entities. This certification is based on the fact that the information collection required under these regulations is imposed under section 36B. Consistent with the statute, the proposed regulations require a person that provides minimum essential coverage to an individual to file a return with the IRS reporting certain information and to furnish a statement to the responsible individual who enrolled an individual or family in the coverage. These regulations merely provide the method of filing and furnishing returns and statements under section 36B. Moreover, the proposed regulations attempt to minimize the burden associated with this collection of information by limiting reporting to the information that the IRS requires to verify minimum essential coverage and administer tax credits.

Based on these facts, a Regulatory Flexibility Analysis under the Regulatory Flexibility Act (5 U.S.C. chapter 6) is not required.

Pursuant to section 7805(f) of the Code, this notice of proposed rulemaking has been submitted to the Chief Counsel for Advocacy of the Small Business Administration for comment on its impact on small business.

Comments and Requests for Public Hearing

Before these proposed regulations are adopted as final regulations, consideration will be given to any comments that are submitted timely to the IRS as prescribed in this preamble under the "Addresses" heading. Treasury and the IRS request comments on all aspects of the proposed rules. All comments will be available at *www.regulations.gov* or upon request. A public hearing will be scheduled if requested in writing by any person who timely submits written comments. If a public hearing is scheduled, notice of the date, time, and place for the hearing will be published in the **Federal Register**.

---

[8] For periods prior to the applicability date, an individual who cannot demonstrate that he or she meets the condition for an opt-out payment under an eligible opt-out arrangement is not permitted to treat the opt-out payment as increasing the employee's required contribution.

[9] Notice 2015-87, Q&A 9 provides that the Treasury Department and the IRS anticipate that the regulations on opt-out arrangements generally will apply only for periods after

the issuance of final regulations. The Treasury Department and the IRS anticipate finalizing these regulations prior to the end of 2016.

[10] For a discussion of non-relief-eligible opt-out arrangements see Notice 2015-87, Q&A-9.

Drafting Information

The principal authors of these proposed regulations are Shareen S. Pflanz and Stephen J. Toomey of the Office of Associate Chief Counsel (Income Tax and Accounting). However, other personnel from the IRS and the Treasury Department participated in the development of the regulations.

[¶ 49,706]   Proposed Amendments of Regulations (REG-134016-15), published in the Federal Register on July 15, 2016.

[Code Sec. 355]

Divisive transactions: Code Sec. 355 distributions: Active business requirement: Device and nondevice factors: Per se device test: Five-year active business asset percentage.—Reg. §§ 1.355-8 and 1.355-9 and amendments of Reg. §§ 1.355-0 and 1.355-2, clarifying the application of the device prohibition and the active business requirement of section 355, are proposed.

AGENCY: Internal Revenue Service (IRS), Treasury.

ACTION: Notice of proposed rulemaking.

SUMMARY: This document contains proposed regulations under section 355 of the Internal Revenue Code (Code). The proposed regulations would clarify the application of the device prohibition and the active business requirement of section 355. The proposed regulations would affect corporations that distribute the stock of controlled corporations, their shareholders, and their security holders.

DATES: Written or electronic comments and requests for a public hearing must be received by October 13, 2016.

ADDRESSES: Send submissions to: CC:PA:LPD:PR (REG-134016-15), Room 5203, Internal Revenue Service, P.O. Box 7604, Ben Franklin Station, Washington, DC 20224. Submissions may be hand-delivered Monday through Friday between the hours of 8 a.m. and 4 p.m. to: CC:PA:LPD:PR (REG-134016-15), Courier's Desk, Internal Revenue Service, 1111 Constitution Avenue, NW, Washington, DC 20224. Submissions may also be sent electronically via the Federal eRulemaking Portal at *http://www.regulations.gov* (IRS REG-134016-15).

FOR FURTHER INFORMATION CONTACT: Concerning the proposed regulations, Stephanie D. Floyd or Russell P. Subin at (202) 317-6848; concerning submissions of comments and/or requests for a public hearing, Regina Johnson at (202) 317-6901 (not toll-free numbers).

SUPPLEMENTARY INFORMATION:

Background

A. *Introduction*

This document contains proposed regulations that would amend 26 CFR part 1 under section 355 of the Code. The proposed regulations would provide additional guidance regarding the device prohibition of section 355(a)(1)(B) and provide a minimum threshold for the assets of one or more active trades or businesses, within the meaning of section 355(a)(1)(C) and (b), of the distributing corporation and each controlled corporation (in each case, within the meaning of section 355(a)(1)(A)).

This Background section of the preamble (1) summarizes the requirements of section 355, (2) discusses the development of current law and IRS practice under section 355 and the regulations thereunder, and (3) explains the reasons for the proposed regulations.

B. *Section 355 Requirements*

Generally, if a corporation distributes property with respect to its stock to a shareholder, section 301(b) provides that the amount of the distribution is equal to the amount of money and the fair market value of other property received. Under section 301(c), this amount is treated as (1) the receipt by the shareholder of a dividend to the extent of the corporation's earnings and profits, (2) the recovery of the shareholder's basis in the stock, and/or (3) gain from the sale or exchange of property. The corporation recognizes gain under section 311(b) to the extent the fair market value of the property distributed exceeds the corporation's adjusted basis in the property. However, section 355 provides that, under certain circumstances, a corporation (Distributing) may distribute stock and securities in a corporation it controls within the meaning of section 368(c) (Controlled) to its shareholders and security holders without causing either Distributing or its shareholders or security holders to recognize income, gain, or loss on the distribution.

Section 355 has numerous requirements for a distribution to be tax-free to Distributing and its shareholders. Some of these requirements are intended to prevent a distribution from being used inappropriately to avoid shareholder-level tax on dividend income. As examples, section 355(a)(1)(B) provides that the transaction must not be used principally as a device for the distribution of the earnings and profits of Distributing or Controlled or both (a device), and section 355(a)(1)(C) and (b) require Distributing and Controlled each to be engaged, immediately after the distribution, in the active conduct of a trade or business (an active business). To qualify for this purpose, an active business must have been actively conducted throughout the five-year period ending on the date of the distribution and must not have been acquired, directly or indirectly, within this period in a transaction in which gain or loss was recognized. Section 355(b)(2)(B), (C), and (D).

Distributions of the stock of Controlled generally take three different forms: (1) a pro rata distribution to Distributing's shareholders of the stock of Controlled (a spin-off), (2) a distribution of the stock of Controlled in redemption of Distributing stock (a split-off), or (3) a liquidating distribution in which Distributing distributes the stock of more than one Controlled, either pro rata or non-pro rata (in either case, a split-up).

C. *Development of Current Law and IRS Practice*

1. *Early legislation*

The earliest predecessor of section 355 was section 202(b) of the Revenue Act of 1918, ch. 18 (40 Stat. 1057, 1060), which permitted a tax-free exchange by a shareholder of stock in a corporation for stock in another corporation in connection with a reorganization. This section did not allow tax-free spin-offs. In section 203(c) of the Revenue Act of 1924, ch. 234 (43 Stat. 253, 256), Congress amended this provision to allow tax-free spin-offs pursuant to plans of reorganization.

Taxpayers tried to use this provision to avoid the dividend provisions of the Code by having Distributing contribute surplus cash or liquid assets to a newly formed Controlled and distribute the Controlled stock to its shareholders. *See, e.g., Gregory v. Helvering*, 293 U.S. 465 (1935). Congress reacted to this abuse by eliminating the spin-off provision in the Revenue Act of 1934, ch. 277 (48 Stat. 680). The legislative history states that the provision had provided a method for corporations "to pay what would otherwise be taxable dividends, without any taxes upon their shareholders" and that "this means of avoidance should be ended." H.R. Rep. No. 73-704, at 14 (1934).

In section 317(a) of the Revenue Act of 1951, ch. 521 (65 Stat. 452, 493), Congress re-authorized spin-offs pursuant to plans of reorganization:

. . . unless it appears that (A) any corporation which is a party to such reorganization was not intended to continue the active conduct of a trade or business after such reorganization, or (B) the corporation whose stock is distributed was used principally as a device for the distribution of earnings and profits to the shareholders of any corporation a party to the reorganization.

During debate on this legislation, Senator Hubert Humphrey expressed concerns about spin-offs and argued that these restrictions were necessary. *See, e.g.,* 97 Cong. Rec. 11812 (1951) ("Unless strictly safeguarded, [a spin-off provision] can result in a loophole that will enable a corporation to distribute earnings and profits to stockholders without payment of the usual income taxes."); *Id.* ("Clauses (A) and (B) of section 317 provide very important safeguards against the tax avoidance which would be possible if section 317 were adopted without clauses (A) and (B)."). *See also* 96 Cong. Rec. 13686 (1950) ("It was the viewpoint of the committee that [a spin-off] must be strictly a bona fide transaction, not colorable, not for the purpose of evading the tax.").

Until 1954, a spin-off, split-off, or split-up was eligible for tax-free treatment only if Distributing transferred property to Controlled as part of a reorganization. In 1954, Congress adopted section 355 as part of the 1954 Code. As a significant innovation, section 355 allowed spin-offs, split-offs, and split-ups to be tax-free without a reorganization, and this innovation remains in effect.

2. *Case law*

Courts applying section 355 (or a predecessor provision) have generally placed greater emphasis on the substance of the transaction than on compliance with the technical requirements of the statute. Thus, some courts have determined that a transaction does not qualify under section 355 (or a predecessor provision), notwithstanding strict statutory compliance, on the basis that the substance of the transaction was inconsistent with congressional intent. For example, in *Gregory*, the Supreme Court held that compliance with the letter of the spin-off statute was insufficient if the transaction was otherwise indistinguishable from a dividend. The Supreme Court observed that the transaction in *Gregory* was "an operation having no business or corporate purpose-a mere device which put on the form of a corporate reorganization as a disguise for concealing its real character." *Gregory*, 293 U.S. at 469.

Other courts have found that a transaction does qualify under section 355 despite its failure to comply with all of the statutory requirements. For example, in *Commissioner v. Gordon*, 382 F.2d 499 (2d Cir.1967), *rev'd on other grounds*, 391 U.S. 83 (1968), the court addressed section 355(b)(2)(C). Pursuant to that section, a corporation is treated as engaged in the active conduct of a trade or business only if the trade or business was not acquired in a transaction in which gain or loss was recognized in whole or in part within the five-year period ending on the date of the distribution. The court concluded that, despite the fact that gain was recognized when Distributing transferred a trade or business to Controlled, section 355(b)(2)(C) was not violated because new assets were not brought within the combined corporate shells of Distributing and Controlled. The court stated:

We think that the draftsmen of Section 355 intended these subsections to apply only to the bringing of new assets within the combined corporate shells of the distributing and the controlled corporations. Therefore, it is irrelevant in this case whether gain was recognized on the intercorporate transfer.

Id. at 507.

3. *Device regulations*

a. 1955 Regulations

Regulations under section 355 of the 1954 Code were issued in 1955 (the 1955 regulations). TD 6152 (20 FR 8875). These regulations included § 1.355-2(b)(3), which provided the following:

In determining whether a transaction was used principally as a device for the distribution of the earnings and profits of the distributing corporation or of the controlled corporation or both, consideration will be given to all of the facts and circumstances of the transaction. In particular, consideration will be given to the nature, kind and amount of the assets of both corporations (and corporations controlled by them) immediately after the transaction. The fact that at the time of the transaction substantially all of the assets of each of the corporations involved are and have been used in the active conduct of trades or businesses which meet the requirements of section 355(b) will be considered evidence that the transaction was not used principally as such a device.

b. 1989 Regulations

Additional regulations under section 355 were issued in 1989 (the 1989 regulations). TD 8238 (54 FR 283). These regulations provide substantially more guidance than the 1955 regulations to determine whether a distribution was a device. Section 1.355-2(d)(1) provides that "a tax-free distribution of the stock of a controlled corporation presents a potential for tax avoidance by facilitating the avoidance of the dividend provisions of the Code through the subsequent sale or exchange of stock of one corporation and the retention of the stock of another corporation. A device can include a transaction that effects a recovery of basis."

This provision clarifies that, although the device prohibition primarily targets the conversion of dividend income to capital gain, a device can still exist if there would be a recovery of stock basis in lieu of receipt of dividend income and even if the shareholder's federal income tax rates on dividend income and capital gain are the same.

The 1989 regulations also expand on the statement in the 1955 regulations that the device analysis takes into account all of the facts and circumstances by specifying three factors that are evidence of device and three factors that are evidence of nondevice. One of the device factors, described in § 1.355-2(d)(2)(iv)(B), expands the statement in the 1955 regulations that consideration will be given to the nature, kind, and amount of the assets of Distributing and Controlled immediately after the transaction (the nature and use of assets device factor). First, this provision provides that "[t]he existence of assets that are not used in a trade or business that satisfies the requirements of section 355(b) is evidence of device. For this purpose, assets that are not used in a trade or business that satisfies the requirements of section 355(b) include, but are not limited to, cash and other liquid assets that are not related to the reasonable needs of a business satisfying such section." This provision continues to provide that "[t]he strength of the evidence of device depends on all the facts and circumstances, including, but not limited to, the ratio for each corporation of the value of assets not used in a trade or business that satisfies the requirements of section 355(b) to the value of its business that satisfies such requirements." Finally, the provision provides that "[a] difference in the ratio described in the preceding sentence for the distributing and controlled corporation is ordinarily not evidence of device if the distribution is not pro rata among the shareholders of the distributing corporation and such difference is attributable to a need to equalize the value of the stock distributed and the value of the stock or securities exchanged by the distributees."

Although this provision describes the factor, it provides little guidance relating to the quality or quantity of the relevant assets and no guidance on how the factor relates to other device factors or nondevice factors.

The nondevice factors in § 1.355-2(d)(3) are the presence of a corporate business purpose, the fact that the stock of Distributing is publicly traded and widely held, and the fact that the distribution is made to certain domestic corporate shareholders.

Section 1.355-2(d)(5) specifies certain distributions that ordinarily are not considered a device, notwithstanding the presence of device factors, because they ordinarily do not present the potential for federal income tax avoidance in converting dividend income to capital gain or using stock basis to reduce shareholder-level tax. These transactions include a distribution that, in the absence of section 355, with respect to each distributee, would be a redemption to which sale-or-exchange treatment applies.

4. *Active business requirement regulations*

Section 1.355-3 provides rules for determining whether Distributing and Controlled satisfy the active business requirement. Proposed regulations issued in 2007 would amend § 1.355-3. REG-123365-03 (72 FR 26012). The Treasury Department and the IRS continue to study the active business requirement issues considered in those proposed regulations.

5. *Administration of the active business requirement*

The fact that Distributing's or Controlled's qualifying active business is small in relation to all the assets of Distributing or Controlled is generally recognized as a device factor. A separate issue is whether a relatively small active business satisfies the active business requirement. In Rev. Rul. 73-44 (1973-1 CB 182), Controlled's active business represented a "substantial portion" but less than half of the value of its total assets. The revenue ruling states:

There is no requirement in section 355(b) that a specific percentage of the corporation's assets be devoted to the active conduct of a trade or business. In the instant case, therefore, it is not controlling for purposes of the active business requirement that the active business assets of the controlled corporation, Y, represent less than half of the value of the controlled corporation immediately after the distribution.

The IRS has taken the position, in letter rulings and internal memoranda, that an active business can satisfy the active business requirement regardless of its absolute or relative size. However, no published guidance issued by the Treasury Department or the IRS takes this position.

In 1996, the Treasury Department and the IRS issued Rev. Proc. 96-43 (1996-2 CB 330), which provided that (1) the IRS ordinarily would not issue a letter ruling or determination letter on whether a distribution was described in section 355(a)(1) if the gross assets of the active business would have a fair market value that was less than five percent of the total fair market value of the gross assets of the corporation directly conducting the active business, but (2) a ruling might be issued "if it can be established that, based upon all relevant facts and circumstances, the trades or businesses are not de minimis compared with the other assets or activities of the corporation and its subsidiaries." This no-rule provision was eliminated in Rev. Proc. 2003-48 (2003-2 CB 86). Since that time, until the publication of Rev. Proc. 2015-43 (2015-40 IRB 467) and Notice 2015-59 (2015-40 IRB 459), discussed in Part D.1 of this Background section of the preamble, the IRS maintained its position that the relative size of an active business is a device factor rather than a section 355(b) requirement. The IRS issued numerous letter rulings on section 355 distributions involving active businesses that were de minimis in value compared to the other assets of Distributing or Controlled.

The IRS interpreted section 355(b) in this manner in part as a result of the mechanical difficulties of satisfying the active business requirement. These mechanical difficulties are discussed further in Part D.3.c of this Background section of the preamble.

As an example, until section 355(b) was amended by section 202 of the Tax Increase Prevention and Reconciliation Act of 2005, Public Law 109-222 (120 Stat. 345, 348); Division A, section 410 of the Tax Relief and Health Care Act of 2006, Public Law 109-432 (120 Stat. 2922, 2963); and section 4(b) of the Tax Technical Corrections Act of 2007, Public Law 110-172 (121 Stat. 2473, 2476) (the Separate Affiliated Group, or SAG, Amendments), if, immediately after the distribution, a corporation did not directly engage in an active business, it could satisfy the active business requirement only if substantially all of its assets consisted of stock and securities of corporations it controlled that were engaged in an active business (the holding company rule). *See* section 355(b) prior to the SAG Amendments. Because of the limited application of the holding company rule, corporations often had to undergo burdensome restructurings prior to section 355 distributions merely to satisfy the active business requirement. *See, e.g.*, H.R. Rep. No. 109-304, at 54 (2005).

As another example, until 1992, no guidance provided that Distributing or Controlled could rely on activities conducted by a partnership to satisfy the active business requirement, even if Distributing or Controlled held a substantial interest in the partnership and participated in its management. This situation changed after the Treasury Department and the IRS published revenue rulings permitting this reliance. *See* Rev. Rul. 92-17 (1992-1 CB 142) *amplified by* Rev. Rul. 2002-49 (2002-2 CB 288) *and modified by* Rev. Rul. 2007-42 (2007-2 CB 44).

6. *Administration of the device prohibition*

The device prohibition continues to be important even though the federal income tax rates for dividend income and capital gain may be identical for many taxpayers. In Rev. Proc. 2003-48, the Treasury Department and the IRS announced that the IRS would no longer rule on whether a transaction is a device or has a business purpose. As a result, since the publication of Rev. Proc. 2003-48, the IRS has made only limited inquiries as to device and business purpose issues raised in requests for private letter rulings under section 355.

D. *Reasons for Proposed Regulations*

1. *Rev. Proc. 2015-43 and Notice 2015-59*

As explained in Part C of this Background section of the preamble, section 355 and its predecessors have had a long and contentious history. Despite the safeguards in the Code and regulations, and the courts' interpretations in accordance with congressionally-articulated statutory purposes, taxpayers have attempted to use section 355 distributions in ways that the Treasury Department and the IRS have determined to be inconsistent with the purpose of section 355.

On September 14, 2015, the Treasury Department and the IRS issued Rev. Proc. 2015-43 and Notice 2015-59 in response to concerns relating to distributions involving relatively small active businesses, substantial amounts of investment assets, and regulated investment companies (RICs) or real estate investment trusts (REITs). The notice states that the Treasury Department and the IRS are studying issues under sections 337(d) and 355 relating to these transactions and that these transactions may present evidence of device, lack an adequate business purpose or a qualifying active business, or circumvent the purposes of Code provisions intended to implement repeal of the *General Utilities* doctrine, a doctrine under which a corporation generally could distribute appreciated property to its shareholders without recognizing gain (*General Utilities* repeal). The notice invited comments with respect to these issues and one commenter (the commenter) submitted a comment letter.

The proposed regulations in this notice of proposed rulemaking would address the device prohibition (including the business purpose requirement as it pertains to device) and the active business requirement. Congress has addressed certain other issues discussed in Notice 2015-59. *See* section 311 of the Protecting Americans from Tax Hikes Act of 2015, Public Law 114-113 (129 Stat. 3040, 3090), in which Congress added section 355(h), which generally denies section 355 treatment if either Distributing or Controlled is a REIT unless both are REITs immediately after the distribution, and section 856(c)(8), which generally provides that Distributing or Controlled will not be eligible to make a REIT election within the ten-year period after a section 355 distribution. Separate temporary and proposed regulations address transactions that avoid the application of sections 355(h) and 856(c)(8). *See* REG-126452-15 (Certain Transfers of Property to RICs and REITs) (81 FR 36816), cross-referencing TD 9770 (81 FR 36793). The Treasury Department and the IRS continue to study issues relating to *General Utilities* repeal presented by other transactions involving the separation of nonbusiness assets from business assets, and are considering issuing guidance under section 337(d) to address these issues. *See* Part D.4 of this Background section of the preamble.

2. *Comments regarding device*

The commenter believes that new rules are not needed for transactions that raise the purely shareholder-level concerns that are the subject of the device prohibition. According to the commenter, those transactions likely do not qualify under section 355 under current law and are infrequent. Although largely agreeing with this statement, the Treasury Department and the IRS have determined that certain clarifying changes should be made to the device rules. As discussed in Part C.3.b of this Background section of the preamble, the current regulations relating to device are not specific as to the quality or quantity of assets relevant in the nature and use of assets device factor or the appropriate weighing of the device and nondevice factors. The Treasury Department and the IRS have determined that, in some situations, insufficient weight has been given to the nature and use of assets device factor and that device factors have not been balanced correctly against nondevice factors.

For example, if, after a distribution, Distributing or Controlled holds mostly liquid nonbusiness assets, the shareholders of that corporation can sell their stock at a price that reflects the value of the nonbusiness assets, and such a sale is economically similar to a distribution of the liquid nonbusiness assets to the shareholders that would have been treated as a dividend to the extent of earnings and profits of the corporation. *See, e.g., Gregory.* If Distributing's ratio of nonbusiness assets to total assets differs substantially from Controlled's ratio, the distribution could facilitate a separation of the nonbusiness assets from the business assets by means of the sale of the stock in the corporation with a large percentage of nonbusiness assets. No corporate-level gain, and possibly little or no shareholder-level gain, would be recognized.

Taxpayers have taken the position that nondevice factors in the regulations can outweigh the substantial evidence of device presented in such distributions. For example, certain taxpayers have viewed even a weak business purpose, combined with the fact that the stock of Distributing is publicly traded, as offsetting evidence of device presented by distributions effecting a separation of nonbusiness assets from business assets, even if pressure from public shareholders was a significant motivation for the distribution. The Treasury Department and the IRS do not agree that these types of nondevice factors should outweigh the substantial evidence of device presented by a distribution that separates nonbusiness assets from business assets.

Accordingly, the Treasury Department and the IRS have determined that the regulations should provide clearer, more objective guidance regarding the nature and use of assets device factor and the appropriate weighing of device factors and nondevice factors. The Treasury Department and the IRS also have determined that if a high enough proportion of assets of Distributing or Controlled consists of nonbusiness assets, and if the assets of the other corporation include a much lower proportion of nonbusiness assets, the evidence of device is so strong that nondevice factors generally should not be allowed to overcome the evidence of device.

The commenter also noted that the importance of device, traditionally understood as reflecting shareholder-level policies, has diminished in the context of a unified rate regime for long-term capital gains and qualified dividend income for some taxpayers. However, because of continuing differences in the federal income tax treatment of capital gains and dividends, including the potential for basis recovery (*see* § 1.355-2(d)(1)) and the availability of capital gains to absorb capital losses, the device prohibition continues to be important.

3. *Comments regarding active business*

a. Section 355(b) Requires Minimum Size Active Business

The commenter stated that section 355 is meant to apply to genuine separations of businesses, and that section 355(b) should not function as a formality. Nevertheless, the commenter does not believe that the active business requirement needs to be strengthened through the adoption of a requirement of a minimum amount of active business assets.

After studying this issue, the Treasury Department and the IRS have determined that Distributing or Controlled should not satisfy the active business requirement by holding a relatively de minimis active business. As described in the remainder of this Part D.3, the Treasury Department and the IRS have determined that interpreting section 355(b) as having meaning and substance and therefore requiring an active business that is economically significant is consistent with congressional intent, case law, and the reorganization provisions. In addition, given the developments in the tax law described in Part D.3.c of this Background section of the preamble, the Treasury Department and the IRS have determined that allowing a de minimis active business to satisfy the active business requirement is not necessary to reduce the burden of compliance with the active business requirement. Furthermore, requiring a minimum relative size for an active business is not inconsistent with the facts of Rev. Rul. 73-44 or with its conclusion. *See* Part D.3.d of this Background section of the preamble.

b. Consistent with Congressional Intent, Case Law, and the Reorganization Provisions

Allowing section 355(b) to be satisfied with an active business that is economically insignificant in relation to other assets of Distributing or Controlled is not consistent with the congressional purpose for adopting the active business requirement. It is generally understood that Congress intended section 355 to be used to separate businesses, not to separate inactive assets from a business. *See* S. Rep. No. 83-1622, at 50-51 (section 355 "contemplates that a tax-free separation shall involve only the separation of assets attributable to the carrying on of an active business" and does not permit "the tax free separation of an existing corporation into active and inactive entities"); *see also Coady v. Commissioner*, 33 T.C. 771, 777 (1960), *aff'd*, 289 F.2d 490 (6th Cir. 1961) (stating that a function of section 355(b) is "to prevent the tax-free separation of *active* and *inactive* assets into *active* and *inactive* corporate entities" (emphasis in original); § 1.355-1(b) ("[s]ection 355 provides for the separation . . . of one or more existing businesses"). Additionally, when the active business of Distributing or Controlled is economically insignificant in relation to its other assets, it is unlikely that any non-federal tax purpose for separating that business from other businesses is a significant purpose for the distribution. *See* § 1.355-2(b)(1) ("Section 355 applies to a transaction only if it is carried out for one or more corporate business purposes . . . . The potential for the avoidance of Federal taxes by the distributing or controlled corporations . . . is relevant in determining the extent to which an existing corporate business purpose motivated the distribution.").

Further, as the Supreme Court held in *Gregory*, transactions are to be taxed in accordance with their substance. The reorganization regulations adopt the same principle. For example, § 1.368-1(b) provides that "[b]oth the terms of the specifications [of the reorganization provisions] and their underlying assumptions and purposes must be satisfied in order to entitle the taxpayer to the benefit of the exception from the general rule." Additionally, § 1.368-1(c) provides that "[a] scheme, which involves an abrupt departure from normal reorganization procedure in connection with a transaction on which the imposition of tax is imminent, such as a mere device that puts on the form of a corporate reorganization as a disguise for concealing its real character, and the object and accomplishment of which is the consummation of a preconceived plan having no business or corporate purpose, is not a plan of reorganization."

Accordingly, when a corporation that owns only nonbusiness assets and a relatively de minimis active business is separated from a corporation with another active business, the substance of the transaction is not a separation of businesses as contemplated by section 355.

c. Developments in the Tax Law Reduce the Burden of Complying with Section 355

In the past, the active business requirement was more difficult to satisfy than it is today, in part because of the limited application of the holding company rule, discussed in Part C.5 of this Background section of the preamble. However, several developments in the tax law have occurred that make the active business requirement easier to satisfy and negate the historical need to reduce the administrative burden of complying with section 355(b).

In the SAG Amendments, Congress amended section 355(b) to adopt the separate affiliated group rules of section 355(b)(3). Section 355(b)(3)(A) provides that, for purposes of determining whether a corporation meets the requirements of section 355(b)(2)(A), all members of the corporation's separate affiliated group (SAG) are treated as one corporation. Section 355(b)(3)(B) provides that a corporation's SAG is the affiliated group which would be determined under section 1504(a) if the corporation were the common parent and section 1504(b) did not apply.

Additionally, as discussed in Part C.5 of this Background section of the preamble, section 355(b) now can be satisfied through the ownership of certain interests in a partnership that is engaged in an active business. See Rev. Rul. 2007-42 and Rev. Rul. 92-17. Similarly, § 301.7701-3 now allows an eligible entity to elect to be disregarded as an entity separate from its owner and permits a corporation to satisfy the active business requirement through a tax-free acquisition without having to assume liabilities relating to an active business. Finally, the expansion rules of § 1.355-3(b)(3)(ii) have been developed so that it is easier to acquire the assets of an active business in a taxable transaction while complying with section 355(b). See, e.g., Rev. Rul. 2003-18 (2003-1 CB 467) and Rev. Rul. 2003-38 (2003-1 CB 811) (both describing facts and circumstances to be considered in determining whether one trade or business is in the same line of business as another).

d. Rev. Rul. 73-44

Rev. Rul. 73-44 is sometimes cited in support of the proposition that a de minimis active business satisfies the section 355(b) requirement. However, Rev. Rul. 73-44 states only that there is no requirement in section 355(b) that a specific percentage of a corporation's assets be devoted to the active conduct of a trade or business, not that any size active business can satisfy section 355(b). In fact, the size of the active business in that ruling represented a substantial portion of Controlled's assets, although less than half of Controlled's value. Accordingly, Rev. Rul. 73-44 does not validate a section 355 distribution involving a de minimis active business, and the proposed regulations in this notice of proposed rulemaking addressing the minimum relative size of active businesses would not change the conclusion set forth in that revenue ruling. Nevertheless, the Treasury Department and the IRS intend to modify Rev. Rul. 73-44 with regard to the statement in the revenue ruling that there is no requirement that a specific percentage of a corporation's assets be devoted to the active conduct of a trade or business.

4. *General Utilities repeal*

The Treasury Department and the IRS have observed, as noted in Notice 2015-59, that taxpayers may attempt to use section 355 distributions in ways that are inconsistent with the purpose of *General Utilities* repeal. Specifically, the Treasury Department and the IRS are concerned that certain taxpayers may be interpreting the current regulations under sections 337(d) and 355 in a manner allowing tax-free distributions motivated in whole or substantial part by a purpose of avoiding corporate-level taxation of built-in gain in investment or nonbusiness assets. See § 1.355-1(b) ("Section 355 provides for the separation . . . of one or more existing businesses formerly operated, directly or indirectly, by a single corporation . . . ."). The Treasury Department and the IRS continue to study whether permitting tax-free separations of large amounts of nonbusiness assets from business assets, especially when the gain in the nonbusiness assets is expected to be eliminated, is consistent with *General Utilities* repeal in all circumstances. Comments are welcome on potential additional guidance under section 337(d) addressing such transactions.

Explanation of Provisions

A. *Modification of Device Regulations*

The proposed regulations would modify § 1.355-2(d), which addresses transactions that are or are not a device. The proposed regulations would modify the nature and use of assets device factor in § 1.355-2(d)(2)(iv), modify the corporate business purpose nondevice factor in § 1.355-2(d)(3)(ii), and add a per se device test.

1. *Nature and use of assets*

The Treasury Department and the IRS have determined that device potential generally exists either if Distributing or Controlled owns a large percentage of assets not used in business operations compared to total assets or if Distributing's and Controlled's percentages of these assets differs substantially. A proposed change to the nature and use of assets device factor in § 1.355-2(d)(2)(iv) would focus on assets used in a Business (Business Assets) (each as defined in proposed § 1.355-2(d)(2)(iv)(B)) rather than assets used in an active business meeting the requirements of section 355(b) (a Five-Year-Active Business, as defined in proposed § 1.355-9(a)(2)). In general, Business would have the same meaning as a Five-Year-Active Business, but without regard to whether the business has been operated or owned for at least five years prior to the date of the distribution or whether the collection of income requirement in § 1.355-3(b)(2)(ii) is satisfied. Business Assets would be gross assets used in a Business, including reasonable amounts of cash and cash equivalents held for working capital and assets required to be held to provide for exigencies related to a Business or for regulatory purposes with respect to a Business. The Treasury Department and the IRS have determined that the presence of Business Assets generally does not raise any more device concerns than the presence of assets used in a Five-Year-Active Business (Five-Year-Active-Business Assets). Thus, the proposed regulations would modify § 1.355-2(d)(2)(iv)(B) to take into account Business Assets, not just Five-Year-Active-Business Assets.

Rev. Proc. 2015-43 (now incorporated into Rev. Proc. 2016-3 (2016-1 IRB 126)) and Notice 2015-59 focus on investment assets (using a modified section 355(g) definition) of a corporation as assets that may raise device concerns. However, after further study, the Treasury Department and the IRS have determined that investment assets as defined therein may include certain assets that do not raise device concerns, such as cash needed by a corporation for working capital, and may not include other assets that do raise device concerns, such as real estate not related to the taxpayer's Business. The Treasury Department and the IRS have determined that focusing on Nonbusiness Assets, as defined in the proposed regulations, is a better method of evaluating device or nondevice as compared to using investment assets as described in Rev. Proc. 2016-3 and Notice 2015-59. Thus, the proposed regulations would focus on Nonbusiness Assets rather than investment assets.

The proposed regulations would provide thresholds for determining whether the ownership of Nonbusiness Assets (gross assets that are not Business Assets) and/or differences in the Nonbusiness Asset Percentages (the percentage of a corporation's Total Assets (its Business Assets and Nonbusiness Assets) that are Nonbusiness Assets) for Distributing and Controlled are evidence of device. If neither Distributing nor Controlled has Nonbusiness Assets that comprise 20 percent or more of its Total Assets, the ownership of Nonbusiness Assets ordinarily would not be evidence of device. Additionally, a difference in the Nonbusiness Asset Percentages for Distributing and Controlled ordinarily would not be evidence of device if such difference is less than 10 percentage points or, in the case of a non-pro rata distribution, if the difference is attributable to a need to equalize the value of the Controlled stock and securities distributed and the consideration exchanged therefor by the distributees. Accordingly, the Treasury Department and the IRS propose to treat such circumstances as ordinarily not constituting evidence of device.

2. *Corporate business purpose*

The Treasury Department and the IRS also propose to revise the nondevice factor in § 1.355-2(d)(3)(ii), which relates to corporate business purpose for a transaction as evidence of nondevice. Under the proposed revision, a corporate business purpose that relates to a separation of Nonbusiness Assets from one or more Businesses or from Business Assets would not be evidence of nondevice, unless the business purpose involves an exigency that requires an investment or other use of the Nonbusiness Assets in a Business. The Treasury Department and the IRS have determined that, absent such an exigency, such separations are not consistent with the intent of Congress to prevent section 355 from applying to a distribution that is used principally as a device.

3. *Per se device test*

The Treasury Department and the IRS also propose to add a per se device test to the device determination in proposed §1.355-2(d)(5). Under proposed §1.355-2(d)(5), if designated percentages of Distributing's and/or Controlled's Total Assets are Nonbusiness Assets, the transaction would be considered a device, notwithstanding the presence of any other nondevice factors, for example, a corporate business purpose or stock being publicly traded and widely held. By their nature, these transactions present such clear evidence of device that the Treasury Department and the IRS have determined that the nondevice factors can never overcome the device potential. The only exceptions to this per se device rule would apply if the distribution is also described in §1.355-2(d)(3)(iv) (distributions in which the corporate distributee would be entitled to a dividends received deduction under section 243(a) or 245(b)) or in redesignated §1.355-2(d)(6) (§1.355-2(d)(5) of the current regulations, relating to transactions ordinarily not considered as a device).

The per se device test would have two prongs, both of which must be met for the distribution to be treated as a per se device.

The first prong would be if Distributing or Controlled has a Nonbusiness Asset Percentage of 66 $^2/_3$ percent or more. If 66 $^2/_3$ percent or more of the Total Assets of either corporation consist of Nonbusiness Assets, a strong device potential exists.

The second prong of the test would compare the Nonbusiness Asset Percentage of Distributing with that of Controlled. The comparison would be similar to the comparison, in §1.355-2(d)(2)(iv)(B) of the current regulations, between Distributing's ratio of assets not used in a Five-Year-Active Business to assets used in a Five-Year-Active Business and Controlled's ratio of such assets. However, the Treasury Department and the IRS recognize that valuation of assets may be difficult and that determining whether certain assets are Business Assets also may be difficult. Accordingly, rather than requiring Distributing and Controlled to make exact determinations of their Nonbusiness Asset Percentages, which would then be compared to the other corporation's Nonbusiness Asset Percentage, the second prong of the per se device test would provide for three bands in making this comparison. These bands generally would provide for the comparison of the Nonbusiness Asset Percentages of Distributing and Controlled but require less precision in asset valuation.

In the first band, if one corporation's Nonbusiness Asset Percentage is 66 $^2/_3$ percent or more, but less than 80 percent, the distribution would fall within the band if the other corporation's Nonbusiness Asset Percentage is less than 30 percent. In the second band, if one corporation's Nonbusiness Asset Percentage is 80 percent or more, but less than 90 percent, the distribution would fall within the band if the other corporation's Nonbusiness Asset Percentage is less than 40 percent. In the third band, if one corporation's Nonbusiness Asset Percentage is 90 percent or more, the distribution would fall within the band if the other corporation's Nonbusiness Asset Percentage is less than 50 percent. All of these bands represent cases in which the Nonbusiness Asset Percentages of Distributing and Controlled are significantly different.

If both prongs of the per se device test are met, that is, if the Nonbusiness Asset Percentage for either Distributing or Controlled is 66 $^2/_3$ percent or more and the Nonbusiness Asset Percentages of Distributing and Controlled fall within one of the three bands, the distribution would be a per se device. Otherwise, the general facts-and-circumstances test of §1.355-2(d), as modified by these proposed regulations, would apply to determine if the transaction was a device.

4. *Certain operating rules*

In making the determination of which assets of a corporation are Business Assets and which are Nonbusiness Assets, if Distributing or Controlled owns a partnership interest or stock in another corporation, the proposed regulations would provide four operating rules.

First, all members of a SAG with respect to which Controlled is the common parent (CSAG) and all members of a SAG with respect to which Distributing is the common parent excluding Controlled and its SAG (DSAG) would be treated as a single corporation. Thus, any stock owned by one member of a SAG in another member of the same SAG and any intercompany obligations between the same SAG members would be disregarded.

Second, a partnership interest would generally be considered a Nonbusiness Asset. However, if, by reason of a corporation's ownership interest or its ownership interest and participation in management of the partnership, the corporation is considered to be engaged in the Business conducted by such partnership (based on the criteria that would be used to determine whether such corporation is considered to be engaged in the Five-Year-Active Business of such partnership under Rev. Ruls. 92-17, 2002-49, and 2007-42), the fair market value of the partnership interest would be allocated between Business Assets and Nonbusiness Assets in the same proportion as the proportion of the fair market values of the Business Assets and the Nonbusiness Assets of the partnership.

Third, a rule similar to the partnership interest rule would apply for corporate stock owned by Distributing or Controlled. That is, stock in a corporation, other than a member of the DSAG or the CSAG, would generally be a Nonbusiness Asset. However, there would be an exception for stock in a Member of a 50-Percent-Owned Group. For this purpose, a 50-Percent-Owned Group would have the same meaning as SAG, except substituting "50-percent" for "80-percent," and a Member of a 50-Percent-Owned Group would be a corporation that would be a member of a DSAG or CSAG, with such substitution. If a Member of a 50-Percent-Owned Group with respect to Distributing or Controlled owns stock in another Member of such 50-Percent-Owned Group (other than a member of the DSAG or the CSAG, respectively), the fair market value of such stock would be allocated between Business Assets and Nonbusiness Assets in the same proportion as the proportion of the fair market values of the Business Assets and the Nonbusiness Assets of the issuing corporation.

Fourth, the proposed regulations would provide for adjustments to prevent distortion if Distributing or Controlled owes money to or is owed money by a partnership or Member of a 50-Percent-Owned Group.

The partnership rules and the 50-Percent-Owned Group rules are designed to recognize that ownership of a partnership interest or stock in a Member of a 50-Percent-Owned Group may reflect an investment in Business Assets, Nonbusiness Assets, or both, while minimizing the significance of changes in the form of ownership of Business Assets and Nonbusiness Assets.

5. *Multiple Controlleds*

If a transaction involves distributions by Distributing of the stock of more than one Controlled, proposed §§1.355-2(d)(2)(iv) and 1.355-2(d)(5) would apply to all such Controlleds. To the extent any rule would require a comparison between characteristics of Distributing and Controlled, there would have to be a comparison between Distributing and each Controlled and between each Controlled and each other Controlled. If any comparison under proposed §1.355-2(d)(2)(iv) or §1.355-2(d)(5) would result in a determination that a distribution is a device, then all distributions involved in the transaction would be considered a device.

B. *Minimum Size for Active Business*

Section 355(b) does not literally provide a minimum absolute or relative size requirement for an active business to qualify under section 355(b). Nevertheless, as discussed in Part D.3 of the Background section of the preamble, the Treasury Department and the IRS have determined that Congress intended that section 355(b) would require that distributions have substance and that a distribution involving only a relatively de minimis active business should not qualify under section 355 because such a distribution is not a separation of businesses as contemplated by section 355.

To ensure that congressional intent is satisfied and to reduce uncertainty, the Treasury Department and the IRS propose to add new § 1.355-9. This section would provide that, for the requirements of section 355(a)(1)(C) and (b) to be satisfied with respect to a distribution, the Five-Year-Active-Business Asset Percentage (the percentage determined by dividing the fair market value of a corporation's Five-Year-Active-Business Assets by the fair market value of its Total Assets) of each of Controlled (or the CSAG) and Distributing (or the DSAG excluding Controlled and other CSAG members) must be at least five percent. Similar to the proposed definition of Business Assets, Five-Year-Active-Business Assets would include reasonable amounts of cash and cash equivalents held for working capital and assets required to be held to provide for exigencies related to a Five-Year-Active Business or for regulatory purposes with respect to a Five-Year-Active Business.

In making the determination of the percentage of a corporation's assets that are Five-Year-Active-Business Assets, if a corporation is considered to be engaged in a Five-Year-Active Business of a partnership, the fair market value of the partnership interest would be allocated between Five-Year-Active-Business Assets and Non-Five-Year-Active-Business Assets (assets other than Five-Year-Active-Business Assets) in the same proportion as the proportion of the fair market values of Five-Year-Active-Business Assets and Non-Five-Year-Active-Business Assets of the partnership.

Except in the case of a member of its SAG, neither Distributing nor Controlled would be considered to be engaged in the Five-Year-Active Business of a corporation in which it owns stock. Accordingly, such stock in a corporation would be considered a Non-Five-Year-Active-Business Asset. Although the proposed regulations relating to the device prohibition would provide an allocation rule for assets held by a Member of a 50-Percent-Owned Group, discussed in Part A.4 of this Explanation of Provisions section of the preamble, the Treasury Department and the IRS believe the SAG Amendments, discussed in Parts C.5 and D.3.c of the Background section of the preamble, limit the ability to take into account assets held by subsidiaries for purposes of the active business requirement. Accordingly, proposed § 1.355-9 would not provide a similar allocation rule for stock owned by Distributing or Controlled.

The commenter stated that the regulations should not provide a minimum size requirement for an active business in any distribution and that such a requirement could be especially problematic in intra-group distributions in preparation for a distribution outside of a group. Internal distributions often are necessary to align the proper assets within Distributing and Controlled prior to a distribution of the stock of Controlled outside the group. If a minimum size requirement is imposed on each of these internal distributions, taxpayers may have to undertake movements of active businesses within groups to meet the minimum size requirement for each internal distribution.

In enacting the SAG Amendments, Congress did not provide an exception to the requirements of section 355(b) for internal distributions that are preparatory to external distributions, although Congress permitted Distributing and Controlled to rely on active businesses held by members of their respective SAGs, even if such assets were distributed or sold within the SAG in a taxable transaction. Under the commenter's rationale, the regulations should not only permit an internal distribution with a de minimis active business, but could also permit tax-free treatment for taxable distributions or sales of assets within the SAG if such assets need to be moved in preparation of the external distribution. The Treasury Department and the IRS have determined that each distribution must meet all the requirements of section 355, including the requirement that Distributing and each Controlled conduct an active business immediately after the distribution. Accordingly, the proposed regulations would provide a five-percent minimum Five-Year-Active-Business Asset Percentage requirement for all distributions.

C. *Timing of Asset Identification, Characterization, and Valuation*

For purposes of determining whether a transaction would be considered a device and whether one or more Five-Year-Active Businesses would meet the five-percent minimum Five-Year-Active-Business Asset Percentage requirement of proposed § 1.355-9, the assets held by Distributing and by Controlled must be identified, and their character and fair market value must be determined. The assets under consideration would be the assets held by Distributing and by Controlled immediately after the distribution. Thus, for example, the stock of Controlled that is distributed would not be an asset of Distributing for this purpose. The character of the assets held by Distributing and by Controlled, as Business Assets or Nonbusiness Assets or as Five-Year-Active-Business Assets or Non-Five-Year-Active-Business Assets, also would be the character as determined immediately after the distribution.

The proposed regulations would provide, however, that the fair market value of assets would be determined, at the election of the parties on a consistent basis, either (a) immediately before the distribution, (b) on any date within the 60-day period before the distribution, (c) on the date of an agreement with respect to the distribution that was binding on Distributing on such date and at all times thereafter, or (d) on the date of a public announcement or filing with the Securities and Exchange Commission with respect to the distribution. The parties would be required to make consistent determinations between themselves, and use the same date, for purposes of applying the device rules of proposed § 1.355-2(d) and the five-percent minimum Five-Year-Active-Business Asset Percentage requirement of proposed § 1.355-9. If the parties do not meet these consistency requirements, the valuation would be determined as of immediately before the distribution unless the Commissioner determines that the use of such date is inconsistent with the purposes of section 355 and the regulations thereunder.

D. *Anti-abuse Rules*

The proposed regulations would also provide anti-abuse rules. Under the anti-abuse rules, a transaction or series of transactions (such as a change in the form of ownership of an asset; an issuance, assumption or repayment of indebtedness; or an issuance or redemption of stock) would not be given effect if undertaken with a principal purpose of affecting the Nonbusiness Asset Percentage of any corporation in order to avoid a determination that a distribution was a device or affecting the Five-Year-Active-Business Asset Percentage of any corporation in order to avoid a determination that a distribution does not meet the requirements of § 1.355-9. The transactions covered by the anti-abuse rules generally would not include an acquisition or disposition of assets, other than an acquisition from or disposition to a person the ownership of whose stock would, under section 318(a) (other than paragraph (4) thereof), be attributed to Distributing or Controlled, or a transfer of assets between Distributing and Controlled. However, such transactions would not be given effect if they are transitory, for example, if Distributing contributes cash to Controlled and retains some of the stock of Controlled or Controlled debt instruments, and there is a plan or intention for Controlled to return the cash to Distributing in redemption of the stock or repayment of the debt.

Statement of Availability of IRS Documents

IRS revenue procedures, revenue rulings, notices, and other guidance cited in this document are published in the Internal Revenue Bulletin (or Cumulative Bulletin) and are available from the Superintendent of Documents, U.S. Government Printing Office, Washington, D.C. 20402, or by visiting the IRS website at http://www.irs.gov.

Effect on Other Documents

Section 3 of Notice 2015-59 is obsolete as of July 15, 2016. The IRS will modify Rev. Rul. 73-44, as of the date the Treasury decision adopting these regulations as final regulations is published in the **Federal Register**, as necessary to conform to § 1.355-9 of these proposed regulations. The IRS solicits comments as to whether other publications should be modified, clarified, or obsoleted.

Special Analyses

Certain IRS regulations, including this one, are exempt from the requirements of Executive Order 12866, as supplemented and reaffirmed by Executive Order 13563. Therefore, a regulatory impact assessment is not required. It has also been determined that section 553(b) of the Administrative Procedure Act (5 U.S.C. chapter 5) does not apply to these proposed regulations. Pursuant to the Regulatory Flexibility Act (5 U.S.C. chapter 6), it is hereby certified that this regulation will not have a significant economic impact on a substantial number of small entities. This certification is based on the fact that these regulations primarily affect larger corporations operating more than one business and with a substantial number of shareholders. Thus, these regulations are not expected to affect a substantial number of small entities. Accordingly, a regulatory flexibility analysis is not required. Pursuant to section 7805(f) of the Code, these regulations will be submitted to the Chief Counsel for Advocacy of the Small Business Administration for comment on their impact on small business.

Comments and Requests for Public Hearing

Before these proposed regulations are adopted as final regulations, consideration will be given to any written or electronic comments that are submitted timely to the IRS as prescribed in this preamble under the **ADDRESSES** heading. The Treasury Department and the IRS request comments on all aspects of the proposed regulations, including—

1. Whether there should be any exceptions to the application of proposed §1.355-9.

2. Whether additional exceptions should be incorporated into the per se device rule in proposed §1.355-2(d)(5).

3. The scope of the safe harbors relating to presence of Nonbusiness Assets as evidence of device under proposed §1.355-2(d)(2)(iv)(C)(*1*) and (*2*) and whether additional safe harbors should be added to proposed §1.355-2(d).

4. Whether the definition of Business Assets in proposed §1.355-2(d)(2)(iv)(B)(*2*) should be revised, for example, to include additional categories of assets or to include cash or cash equivalents expected to be used for other categories of expenditures.

5. Whether the operating rules applicable to proposed §1.355-2(d)(2)(iv)(D)(*6*) through (*8*) concerning the allocation of the value of a partnership interest between Business Assets and Nonbusiness Assets to its partners, the allocation of the value of the stock of a Member of a 50-Percent-Owned Group between Business Assets and Nonbusiness Assets to its shareholders, and certain borrowings should be modified, including whether the partnership rule should allocate an allocable share of the partnership's gross assets to its partners, whether different allocation rules should be used for partnership interests with different characteristics(for example, limited liability vs. non-limited liability), and whether the rules relating to borrowing between a partnership and a partner or between a Member of a 50-Percent-Owned Group and a shareholder should be made more specific.

6. Whether the anti-abuse rules in the proposed regulations pertaining to device and the five-percent minimum Five-Year-Active-Business Assets requirement should be revised, for example, to include or exclude additional transactions or to include a reference to acquisitions of assets by Distributing or Controlled on behalf of shareholders.

7. Whether the absence of any device factor, for example, a small difference in Nonbusiness Asset Percentages for Distributing and Controlled, should be considered a nondevice factor.

All comments will be available at www.regulations.gov or upon request.

A public hearing will be scheduled if requested in writing by any person that timely submits written or electronic comments. If a public hearing is scheduled, notice of the date, time, and place for the public hearing will be published in the **Federal Register**.

Drafting Information

The principal authors of these proposed regulations are Stephanie D. Floyd and Russell P. Subin of the Office of Associate Chief Counsel (Corporate). Other personnel from the Treasury Department and the IRS participated in their development.

[¶ 49,708] **Proposed Amendments of Regulations (REG-103058-16)**, published in the Federal Register on August 2, 2016.

[Code Secs. 6055 and 6724]

Affordable Care Act: Information Reporting: Health insurance issuers.—Amendments of Reg. §1.6055-1 and Reg. §301.6724-1, relating to information reporting of minimum essential coverage under section 6055 of the Internal Revenue Code, are proposed.

AGENCY: Internal Revenue Service (IRS), Treasury.

ACTION: Notice of proposed rulemaking.

SUMMARY: This document contains proposed regulations relating to information reporting of minimum essential coverage under section 6055 of the Internal Revenue Code (Code). Health insurance issuers, certain employers, and others that provide minimum essential coverage to individuals must report to the IRS information about the type and period of coverage and furnish related statements to covered individuals. These proposed regulations affect health insurance issuers, employers, governments, and other persons that provide minimum essential coverage to individuals.

DATES: Written or electronic comments and requests for a public hearing must be received by October 1, 2016.

ADDRESSES: Send submissions to: CC:PA:LPD:PR (REG-103058-16), Room 5203, Internal Revenue Service, PO Box 7604, Ben Franklin Station, Washington, DC 20044. Submissions may be hand-delivered Monday through Friday between the hours of 8 a.m. and 4 p.m. to CC:PA:LPD:PR (REG-103058-16), Courier's Desk, Internal Revenue Service, 1111 Constitution Avenue, NW, Washington, DC 20224, or sent electronically via the Federal eRulemaking Portal at *http://www.regulations.gov* (IRS REG-103058-16).

FOR FURTHER INFORMATION CONTACT: Concerning the proposed regulations under section 6055, John B. Lovelace, (202) 317-7006; concerning the proposed regulations under section 6724, Hollie Marx, (202) 317-6844; concerning the submission of comments, Regina Johnson, (202) 317-6901 (not toll-free calls). SUPPLEMENTARY INFORMATION:

Paperwork Reduction Act

The collection of information contained in this notice of proposed rulemaking has been submitted to the Office of Management and Budget in accordance with the Paperwork Reduction Act of 1995 (44 U.S.C. 3507(d)). Comments on the collection of information should be sent to the **Office of Management and Budget**, Attn: Desk Officer for the Department of the Treasury, Office of Information and Regulatory Affairs, Washington, DC 20503, with copies to the **Internal Revenue Service**, Attn: IRS Reports Clearance Officer, SE:W:CAR:MP:T:T:SP, Washington, DC 20224. Comments on the collection of information should be received by October 1, 2016. Comments are specifically requested concerning:

Whether the proposed collection of information is necessary for the proper performance of the functions of the IRS, including whether the information will have practical utility;

How the quality, utility, and clarity of the information to be collected may be enhanced;

How the burden of complying with the proposed collection of information may be minimized, including through the application of automated collection techniques or other forms of information technology; and

Estimates of capital or start-up costs and costs of operation, maintenance, and purchase of services to provide information.

The collection of information in these proposed regulations is in §1.6055-1. The collection of information will be used to determine whether an individual has minimum essential coverage under section 1501(b) of the Patient Protection and Affordable Care Act (26 U.S.C. 5000A(f)). The collection of information is required to comply with the provisions of section 6055. The likely respondents are health insurers, self-insured employers or other sponsors of self-insured health plans, and governments that provide minimum essential coverage.

The burden for the collection of information contained in these proposed regulations will be reflected in the burden on Form 1095-B, Health Coverage, or another form that the IRS designates, which will request the information in the proposed regulation.

An agency may not conduct or sponsor, and a person is not required to respond to, a collection of information unless it displays a valid control number assigned by the Office of Management and Budget.

Background

Under section 5000A, individuals must for each month have minimum essential coverage, qualify for a health coverage exemption, or make an individual shared responsibility payment with their income tax returns. Section 6055 provides that all persons who provide minimum essential coverage to an individual must report certain information to the IRS that identifies covered individuals and the period of coverage, and must furnish a statement to the covered individuals containing the same information. The information reported under section 6055 allows individuals to establish, and the IRS to verify, that the individuals were covered by minimum essential coverage for months during the year.

Information returns under section 6055 generally are filed using Form 1095-B. A separate and distinct health coverage-related reporting requirement under section 6056 requires that certain large employers report information on Form 1095-C, Employer-Provided Health Insurance Offer and Coverage. Self-insured employers required to file Form 1095-C use Part III of that form, rather than Form 1095-B, to report information required under section 6055 for individuals enrolled in the self-insured employer-sponsored coverage. These proposed regulations provide guidance under section 6055 only, which relates to Form 1095-B and Form 1095-C, Part III. These proposed regulations do not affect information reporting under section 6056 on Form 1095-C, Parts I and II.

Under section 5000A(f)(1), various types of health plans and programs are minimum essential coverage, including: (1) specified government-sponsored programs such as Medicare Part A, the Medicaid program under Title XIX of the Social Security Act (42 U.S.C. 1936 and following sections), the Children's Health Insurance Program under Title XXI of the Social Security Act (42 U.S.C. 1397aa and following sections) (CHIP), the TRICARE program under chapter 55 of Title 10, U.S.C., health care programs for veterans and other individuals under chapter 17 or 18 of Title 38 U.S.C., coverage for Peace Corps volunteers under 22 U.S.C. 2504(e), and coverage under the Nonappropriated Fund Health Benefits Program under section 349 of Public Law 103-337, (2) coverage under an eligible employer-sponsored plan, (3) coverage under a plan in the individual market (such as a qualified health plan offered through an Affordable Insurance Exchange (Exchange, also known as a Marketplace)), (4) coverage under a grandfathered health plan, and (5) other coverage recognized as minimum essential coverage by the Secretary of Health and Human Services, in coordination with the Secretary of the Treasury.

Under section 5000A(f)(3) and §1.5000A-2(g) of the Income Tax Regulations, coverage that consists solely of excepted benefits described in section 2791(c)(1), (c)(2), (c)(3), or (c)(4) of the Public Health Service Act (42 U.S.C. 300gg-91(c)), and the regulations under that section, is not minimum essential coverage. Section 1.5000A-2(b)(2) lists government-sponsored programs that provide limited benefits and which are not minimum essential coverage.

Under section 5000A(f)(4), an individual who is a bona fide resident of a United States possession for a month is treated as having minimum essential coverage for that month.

Notice 2015-68, 2015-41 I.R.B. 547, provides guidance on various issues under section 6055. In Notice 2015-68, the Treasury Department and the IRS stated that they intend to propose regulations under section 6055 addressing certain of these issues and requested comments. Comments were requested about the application of the reasonable cause rules under section 6724 to section 6055 reporting, in particular as applied to taxpayer identification number (TIN) solicitation and reporting.

Persons Required To Report

Under §1.6055-1(c)(1)(iii), the executive department or agency of the governmental unit that provides coverage under a government-sponsored program is the reporting entity for government-sponsored minimum essential coverage. Section 1.6055-1(c)(3)(i) specifically provides that the State agency that administers the Medicaid or CHIP program, respectively, must report government-sponsored coverage under section 6055. Notice 2015-68 provides that Medicaid and CHIP agencies in U.S. possessions or territories are not required to report Medicaid and CHIP coverage because an individual eligible for that coverage is generally a bona fide resident of the possession or territory who is deemed to have minimum essential coverage under section 5000A(f)(4) and, therefore, does not require reporting under section 6055 to verify compliance with section 5000A.

In general, under §1.6055-1(c)(1)(ii) the reporting entity for coverage under a self-insured group health plan is the plan sponsor. Section 1.6055-1(c)(2) provides rules for identifying which entity is the plan sponsor of a self-insured group health plan for purposes of section 6055. For this purpose, the employer is the plan sponsor of a self-insured group health plan established by a single employer (determined without aggregating related entities under section 414). If the plan or arrangement is established or maintained by more than one employer (including a Multiple Employer Welfare Arrangement (as defined in section 3(40) of the Employee Retirement Income Security Act of 1974 (ERISA)), and the plan is not a multiemployer plan (as defined in section 3(37) of ERISA), each participating employer is a plan sponsor with respect to that employer's employees. For a self-insured group health plan or arrangement that is a multiemployer plan, the plan sponsor is the association, committee, joint board of trustees, or other similar group of representatives of the parties who establish or maintain the plan. For a self-insured group health plan or arrangement maintained solely by an employee organization, the plan sponsor is the employee organization.

The existing regulations at §1.6055-1(d)(2) provide that no reporting is required for minimum essential coverage that provides benefits in addition or as a supplement to other coverage that is minimum essential coverage if the primary and supplemental coverage have the same plan sponsor or the coverage supplements government-sponsored minimum essential coverage. Notice 2015-68 explained that this rule had proven to be confusing, and, accordingly, the Treasury Department and the IRS intended to propose regulations providing that (1) if an individual is covered by multiple minimum essential coverage plans or programs provided by the same provider, reporting is only required for one of the plans or programs; and (2) reporting generally is not required for an individual's minimum essential coverage to the extent that the individual is eligible for that coverage only if the individual is also covered by other minimum essential coverage for which section 6055 reporting is required.

Information Required To Be Reported

Under section 6055(b) and §1.6055-1(e)(1), providers of minimum essential coverage must report to the IRS (1) the name, address, and employer identification number (EIN) of the reporting entity required to file the return, (2) the name, address, and TIN, or date of birth if a TIN is not available, of the responsible individual (except that a reporting entity may, but is not required to, report the TIN of a responsible individual not enrolled in the coverage); (3) the name and TIN, or date of birth if a TIN is not available, of each individual who is covered under the policy or program; and (4) the months of coverage for each covered individual.[1] Section 1.6055-1(b)(11) provides that the responsible individual includes a primary insured, employee, former employee, uniformed services sponsor, parent, or other related person named on an application who enrolls one or more individuals, including him or herself, in minimum essential coverage.

In addition, under § 1.6055-1(e)(2), for coverage provided by a health insurance issuer through a group health plan, information returns must report (1) the name, address, and EIN of the employer maintaining the plan, and (2) any other information that the Secretary requires for administering the credit under section 45R (relating to the tax credit for employee health insurance expenses of small employers).

A reporting entity that fails to comply with the filing and statement furnishing requirements of section 6055 may be subject to penalties for failure to file timely a correct information return (section 6721) or failure to furnish timely a correct statement (section 6722). See section 6724(d); see also § 1.6055-1(h)(1). These penalties may be waived if the failure is due to reasonable cause and is not due to willful neglect. See section 6724(a). In particular, under § 301.6724-1(a)(2) of the Procedure and Administration Regulations penalties are waived if a reporting entity demonstrates that it acted in a responsible manner and that the failure is due to significant mitigating factors or events beyond the reporting entity's control. For purposes of section 6055 reporting, if the information reported on a return is incomplete or incorrect as a result of a change in circumstances (such as a retroactive change in coverage), a failure to timely file or furnish a corrected document is a failure to file a correct return or furnish a correct statement under sections 6721 and 6722. See § 1.6055-1(h)(2).

In general, under § 301.6724-1(e) a person will be treated as acting in a responsible manner if the person properly solicits a TIN but does not receive it. For this purpose, proper solicitation of a TIN involves an initial solicitation and two subsequent annual solicitations. In general, an initial solicitation is made when the relationship between the reporting entity and the taxpayer is established. If the reporting entity does not receive the TIN, the first annual solicitation is generally required by December 31 of the year in which the relationship with the taxpayer begins (January 31 of the following year if the relationship begins in December). Generally, if the TIN is still not provided, a second annual solicitation is required by December 31 of the following year. Similar rules applying to filers who file or furnish information reports with incorrect TINs are in § 301.6724-1(f).

The preamble to the section 6055 regulations (T.D. 9660, 79 FR 13220) provides short-term relief from reporting penalties for 2015 coverage. Specifically, the IRS will not impose penalties under sections 6721 and 6722 on reporting entities that can show that they have made good faith efforts to comply with the information reporting requirements. This relief applies to incorrect or incomplete information, including TINs or dates of birth, reported on a return or statement.

Explanation of Provisions and Summary of Comments

1. Reporting of Catastrophic Plans

Under § 1.36B-5(a), Exchanges must report to the IRS information relating to qualified health plans in which individuals enroll through the Exchange. Under section 36B(c)(3)(A), the term qualified health plan has the same meaning as defined in section 1301 of the Affordable Care Act except that it does not include a catastrophic plan described in section 1302 of the Affordable Care Act. Thus, Exchanges are not required to report on catastrophic coverage. Section 1.6055-1(d) provides that health insurance issuers need not report on coverage in a qualified health plan in the individual market enrolled in through an Exchange, because that information is generally reported by Exchanges pursuant to § 1.36B-5. Thus, currently neither the Exchanges nor health insurance issuers are responsible for reporting coverage under a catastrophic plan.

Effective administration of section 5000A generally requires reporting of all minimum essential coverage, including catastrophic plans in which individuals enroll through an Exchange. Accordingly, Notice 2015-68 indicated that the Treasury Department and the IRS intended to propose regulations under section 6055 to narrow the relief provided to issuers in § 1.6055-1(d) by requiring issuers of catastrophic plans to report catastrophic plan coverage on Form 1095-B, effective for coverage in 2016 and returns and statements filed and furnished in 2017. Consistent with Notice 2015-68, the proposed regulations include this requirement but, to allow reporting entities sufficient time to implement these reporting requirements, are proposed to be effective for coverage in 2017 and returns and statements filed and furnished in 2018.

Notice 2015-68 indicated that health insurance issuers could voluntarily report on 2015 catastrophic coverage (on returns and statements filed and furnished in 2016) and were encouraged to do so. Notice 2015-68 further provided that an issuer that reports on 2015 catastrophic coverage will not be subject to penalties for these returns. Given the 2017 effective date for reporting of catastrophic coverage provided in these proposed regulations, health insurance issuers similarly may voluntarily report on 2016 catastrophic coverage (on returns and statements filed and furnished in 2017) and are encouraged to do so. An issuer that reports on 2016 catastrophic coverage will not be subject to penalties for these returns.

2. Reporting of Coverage under Basic Health Programs

Section 1331 of the Affordable Care Act allows states to establish a Basic Health Program to provide an additional healthcare coverage option to certain individuals not eligible for Medicaid. See 42 CFR Part 600. The Basic Health Program is designated as minimum essential coverage under 42 CFR 600.5.

Section 5000A(f) does not identify the Basic Health Program as a government-sponsored program, but it closely resembles government-sponsored coverage such as Medicaid and CHIP. Accordingly, Notice 2015-68 indicated that the state agency that administers the Basic Health Program is the entity that must report that coverage under section 6055. Consistent with Notice 2015-68, these proposed regulations provide that the State agency administering coverage under the Basic Health Program is required to report that coverage under section 6055.

3. Truncated TINs

Section 6055(b) and § 1.6055-1(e) require that health insurance issuers and carriers reporting coverage under insured group health plans report information about the employer sponsoring the plan, including the employer's EIN, to the IRS. Section 6055(c) and § 1.6055-1(g) require that health insurance issuers and carriers reporting information to the IRS furnish a statement to a taxpayer providing information about the filer and the covered individuals. Section 301.6109-4(b)(1) provides that the TIN of a person other than the filer, including an EIN, may be truncated on statements furnished to recipients unless, among other reasons, such truncation is otherwise prohibited by statute or regulations. Thus, under § 1.6055-1(g)(3) of the existing regulations, a recipient's TIN may appear in the form of an IRS truncated taxpayer identification number (TTIN) on a statement furnished to the recipient. These proposed regulations amend the existing regulations to clarify that a TTIN is not an alternative identifying number; rather, it is one of the ways that a TIN may appear, subject to the rules in § 301.6109-4(b)(1).

Existing regulations do not address whether health insurance issuers and carriers are permitted to truncate a sponsoring employer's EIN on statements furnished to taxpayers. Notice 2015-68 advised that the Treasury Department and the IRS intended to propose regulations to clarify that

---

[1] The Affordable Care Act also added section 6056, which requires that applicable large employers file and furnish statements containing information related to offers of coverage, if any, made to each full-time employee. To complete these statements properly, employers must have each employee's TIN. In accordance with the requirements of a different Code section (section 3402(f)(2)(A)), employers should have already sought each employee's TIN in advance of the deadline for filing and furnishing statements required under section 6056. Therefore, the TIN solicitation rules in these proposed regulations *only apply* to information reporting under section 6055 (which in the case of an applicable large employer providing coverage under a self-insured plan, includes information reporting on Form 1095-C, Part III).

the EIN of the employer sponsoring the plan may be truncated to appear as an IRS TTIN on statements health insurance issuers and carriers furnish to taxpayers. Consistent with Notice 2015-68, the proposed regulations clarify that the EIN of the employer sponsoring the plan may be truncated to appear as an IRS TTIN on statements health insurance issuers and carriers furnish to taxpayers. Section 301.6109-4(b)(2)(ii) prohibits using TTINs if, among other things, a statute specifically requires the use of an EIN. While section 6055(b)(2)(A) requires that the information return filed with the IRS includes the employer's EIN, and section 6055(c)(1)(B) requires that the statement furnished to a taxpayer includes the information required to be shown on the information return with respect to such individual, the statute does not require that the full EIN appear on the statement furnished to taxpayers and the employer's EIN may be truncated to appear in the form of an IRS TTIN.

4. Plans for Which Reporting is Not Required

Information reporting under section 6055(a) is generally required of every person who provides minimum essential coverage to an individual during the year. In certain instances where the reporting would be duplicative, the existing regulations allow the person who provides supplemental coverage to forgo information reporting. This supplemental coverage rule in § 1.6055–1(d)(2) was intended to eliminate duplicate reporting of an individual's minimum essential coverage under circumstances when there is reasonable certainty that the provider of the "primary" coverage will report. This rule has proven to be confusing.

The Treasury Department and the IRS indicated in Notice 2015-68 that regulations would be proposed to replace the existing rules. Accordingly, the proposed regulations provide that (1) if an individual is covered by more than one minimum essential coverage plan or program provided by the same reporting entity, reporting is required for only one of the plans or programs; and (2) reporting is not required for an individual's minimum essential coverage to the extent that the individual is eligible for that coverage only if the individual is also covered by other minimum essential coverage for which section 6055 reporting is required. As in Notice 2015-68, the proposed regulations provide that the second rule applies to eligible employer-sponsored coverage only if the supplemental coverage is offered by the same employer that offered the eligible employer-sponsored coverage for which section 6055 reporting is required. These rules apply month by month and individual by individual.

Thus, under the proposed regulations, applying the first rule, if for a month an individual is enrolled in a self-insured group health plan provided by an employer and also is enrolled in a self-insured health reimbursement arrangement (HRA) provided by the same employer, the reporting entity (the employer) is required to report only one type of coverage for that individual. If an employee is covered under both self-insured arrangements for some months of the year but retires or otherwise drops coverage under the non-HRA group health plan and is covered only under the HRA for other months, the employer must report coverage under the HRA for the months after the employee retires or drops the non-HRA coverage.

Applying the second rule, reporting is not required for minimum essential coverage for a month if that coverage is offered only to individuals who are also covered by other minimum essential coverage, including Medicare, TRICARE, Medicaid, or certain employer-sponsored coverage, for which reporting is required. In these arrangements, the program for which reporting is required represents the primary coverage while the other minimum essential coverage is supplemental to the primary plan.

Under the application of the second rule to eligible employer-sponsored coverage, if an employer offers both an insured group health plan and an HRA for which an employee is eligible if enrolled in the insured group health plan, and an employee enrolls in both, the employer is not required to report the employee's coverage under the HRA. However, if an employee is enrolled in his or her employer's HRA and in a spouse's non-HRA group health plan, the employee's employer is required to report for the HRA, and the employee's spouse's employer (or the health insurance issuer or carrier, if the plan is insured) is required to report for the non-HRA group health plan coverage. The proposed regulations clarify that, for purposes of this rule, an employer is treated as offering minimum essential coverage that is offered by another employer with whom the employer is treated as a single employer under section 414(b), (c), (m), or (o).

Separately, Notice 2015-68 also stated that, because Medicaid and CHIP coverage provided by the governments of American Samoa, the Commonwealth of the Northern Mariana Islands, Guam, Puerto Rico, and the U.S. Virgin Islands is generally made available only to individuals who are treated as having minimum essential coverage under section 5000A(f)(4) (and, therefore, do not need section 6055 reporting to verify minimum essential coverage), the Medicaid and CHIP agencies in those U.S. possessions or territories are not required to report that coverage under section 6055. Consistent with that rule, the proposed regulations provide that reporting under section 6055 is not required with respect to Medicaid and CHIP agencies in U.S. possessions or territories.

5. TIN Solicitation

Information reporting under section 6055 is subject to the penalty provisions of sections 6721 and 6722 for failure to file timely a correct information return or failure to furnish timely a correct statement to the individual. See § 1.6055-1(h). The penalties may be waived under section 6724(a) if the failure is due to reasonable cause and not due to willful neglect; that is, if a reporting entity demonstrates that it acted in a responsible manner and that the failure is due to significant mitigating factors or events beyond the reporting entity's control. See § 301.6724-1(a)(2). Under § 301.6724-1(e), in cases of a missing TIN, the reporting entity is treated as acting in a responsible manner in soliciting a TIN if the reporting entity makes (1) an initial solicitation when an account is opened or a relationship is established, (2) a first annual solicitation by December 31 of the year the account is opened (or January 31 of the following year if the account is opened in December), and (3) a second annual solicitation by December 31 of the year following the year in which the account is opened. Similar rules apply regarding incorrect TINs under § 301.6724-1(f). The rules in § 301.6724-1(e) and (f) were issued prior to the enactment of section 6055 and apply to most forms of information reporting.

Comments received in response to the first notice of proposed rulemaking (REG-132455-11) under section 6055, published in the **Federal Register** (78 FR 54986) on September 9, 2013, raised concerns about the application of the TIN solicitation rules to section 6055 reporting. Accordingly, Notice 2015-68 provided that, pending the issuance of additional guidance, reporting entities will not be subject to penalties for failure to report a TIN if they comply with the requirements of § 301.6724-1(e) with the following modifications: (1) the initial solicitation is made at an individual's first enrollment or, if already enrolled on September 17, 2015, the next open season, (2) the second solicitation (the first annual solicitation) is made at a reasonable time thereafter, and (3) the third solicitation (the second annual solicitation) is made by December 31 of the year following the initial solicitation. Notice 2015-68 also requested comments on the application of the reasonable cause rules under section 6724 to section 6055 reporting.

In response to the request for comments in Notice 2015-68, one commenter requested that the proposed regulations include detailed rules tailored to TIN solicitation for information returns required by section 6055. This commenter expressed concern that, because the current rules were designed primarily to apply to financial relationships, they are difficult to apply to section 6055 reporting, particularly the rules for demonstrating that the filer acted in a responsible manner as described in § 301.6724-1(e) and (f). The Treasury Department and the IRS agree with the commenter that some modification to the rules in § 301.6724-1(e) is warranted to account for the differences between information reporting under section 6055 and information reporting under other provisions of the Code. Accordingly, the Treasury Department and the IRS propose regulations to provide specific TIN solicitation rules for section 6055 reporting. Until final regulations are released, reporting entities may rely on these proposed rules and Notice 2015-68. The preamble below also includes some additional transition rules that apply to reporting entities in certain situations.

Section 301.6724-1(e)(1)(i) provides that an initial TIN solicitation must occur when an account (which includes accounts, relationships, and other transactions) is opened. Section 301.6724-1(e) does not define the term "opened" for this purpose. Commenters requested clarification as to how the term "opened" should be interpreted for purposes of reporting under section 6055. In the context of financial accounts, an account is generally considered opened on the first day it is available for use by its owner. In most cases, this would be shortly after the application to open that account is received, and this day would be no earlier than the day the application was received. Health coverage does not work in the same way. In some cases, the first effective date of health coverage is before the day the application was received, making it impractical to solicit TINs before the coverage takes effect. In other cases, the effective date of coverage may be months after the day the application was received. To account for this different timing, the proposed regulations provide that, for purposes of section 6055 reporting, an account is considered "opened" on the date the filer receives a substantially complete application for new coverage or to add an individual to existing coverage. Accordingly, health coverage providers may generally satisfy the requirement for the initial solicitation by requesting enrollees' TINs as part of the application for coverage.

To address differences in the way financial accounts and health coverage are opened, the proposed regulations also change the timing of the first annual solicitation (the second solicitation overall) with respect to missing TINs. Under § 301.6724-1(e)(1)(ii), a first annual solicitation must be made by December 31 of the year the account is opened (or by January 31 of the following calendar year if the account is opened in December). The timing of the first annual solicitation is dictated by the need to have accurate reporting of information to taxpayers and the IRS in preparation for the filing of an income tax return. Accounts, relationships, and other transactions may be opened or begun throughout the year, and may remain active indefinitely. It is beneficial to the IRS, filers, and taxpayers in the context of accounts, relationships, and other transactions to have a single deadline for the first annual solicitation at the end of the calendar year (or January if the account is opened in December).

By contrast, health coverage is generally offered on an annual basis. While individuals may, depending on their circumstances, enroll in coverage at any point during the year, many covered individuals enroll in coverage during the open enrollment period, which is in advance of the beginning of the coverage year. The most common coverage year is the calendar year and many individuals enroll late each year for coverage the following year. For such individuals, requiring the first annual solicitation (the second solicitation overall) by December 31 of the year in which the application is received is earlier than is necessary (because reporting is not due until more than a year later) and coincides with the end of a plan year, which is already the busiest time of year for coverage providers. To address these considerations, the proposed regulations require that the first annual solicitation be made no later than seventy-five days after the date on which the account was "opened" (i.e., the day the filer received the substantially complete application for coverage), or, if the coverage is retroactive, no later than the seventy-fifth day after the determination of retroactive coverage is made. The deadline for the second annual solicitation (third solicitation overall) remains December 31 of the year following the year the account is opened as required by § 301.6724-1(e)(1)(iii).

As noted above, taxpayers may rely on these proposed regulations and on Notice 2015-68 until final regulations are published. To provide additional relief and ensure that the requirements for the first annual and second annual solicitations may be satisfied with respect to individuals already enrolled in coverage, an additional rule is provided. Under this rule, if an individual was enrolled in coverage on any day before **July 29, 2016**, the account is considered opened on **July 29, 2016**. Accordingly, reporting entities have satisfied the requirement for the initial solicitation with respect to already enrolled individuals so long as they requested enrollee TINs either as part of the application for coverage or at any other point before **July 29, 2016**. The deadlines for the first and second annual solicitations are set by reference to the date the account is opened. Thus, the rule above that treats all accounts for individuals currently enrolled in coverage for which a TIN has not been provided as opened on **July 29, 2016**, provides additional time for the annual solicitations as well. Specifically, consistent with Notice 2015-68, the first annual solicitation should be made at a reasonable time after **July 29, 2016**. For this purpose, a reporting entity that makes the first annual solicitation within 75 days of the initial solicitation will be treated as having made the second solicitation within a reasonable time. Reporting entities that have not made the initial solicitation before **July 29, 2016** should comply with the first annual solicitation requirement by making a solicitation within a reasonable time of **July 29, 2016**. Notice 2015-68 also provided that a reporting entity is deemed to have satisfied the initial, first annual, and second annual solicitations for an individual whose coverage was terminated prior to September 17, 2015, and taxpayers may continue to rely on this rule as well.

Section 301.6724-1(e)(1)(v) provides that the initial and first annual solicitations relate to failures on returns filed for the year in which the account is opened (meaning that showing reasonable cause with respect to the year the account is opened generally requires making the initial and first annual solicitations in the year the account is opened). Because these proposed regulations provide that an account is considered opened for section 6055 purposes when a substantially complete application for that account is received, an account would, in some cases, be considered open in a year prior to the year for which coverage is actually effective and for which reporting is required. This would occur, for example, when a reporting entity receives an application during open enrollment for coverage effective as of the first day of the next coverage year. To ensure that reporting entities that make the initial solicitation and first annual solicitation are eligible for relief for the first year for which reporting is required, the proposed regulations provide that, for purposes of reporting under section 6055, the initial and first annual solicitations relate to failures on returns required to be filed for the year that includes the day that is the first effective date of coverage for a covered individual. Similarly, § 301.6724-1(e)(1)(v) provides that the second annual solicitation relates to failures on returns filed for the year immediately following the year in which the account is opened and succeeding calendar years (meaning that showing reasonable cause with respect to years after the account is opened generally requires making the second annual solicitation during the year following the year the account is opened). As with the initial and first annual solicitations, the existing rule under § 301.6724-1(e)(1)(v) could provide relief for the wrong year when combined with the proposed definition of account opening under section 6055. Accordingly, the proposed regulations provide that the second annual solicitation relates to failures on returns filed for the year immediately following the year to which the first annual solicitation relates, and succeeding calendar years.

In contrast to missing TINs, the Treasury Department and the IRS do not recognize a similar need to modify the existing first annual solicitation rules for incorrect TINs in § 301.6724-1(f)(1)(ii). As with many other types of information reports, information reports of health coverage are generally filed after the end of the tax year, and thus, it is only after the tax year that a filer would generally receive notice of an incorrect TIN. Because the end of the tax year typically corresponds with the end of the coverage year, there is no reason to distinguish the timing of the correction of incorrect TINs for health coverage from all other types of accounts for which information reporting is required. Consequently, the proposed regulations do not alter the rules for incorrect TINs in § 301.6724-1(f)(1)(ii) and (iii) as applied to information reporting under section 6055. However, as with the rules regarding missing TINs under § 301.6724-1(e)(1)(ii), the rules regarding incorrect TINs in § 301.6724-1(f)(1)(i) make reference to the time an account is "opened." Accordingly, the proposed regulations, which provides that for purposes of section 6055 reporting an account is considered "opened" at the time the filer receives an application for new coverage or to add an individual to existing coverage, also applies for purposes of the initial solicitation for incorrect TINs in § 301.6724-1(f)(1)(i).[2]

a. *Application of the TIN Solicitation Rules to "Responsible Individuals" and "Covered Individuals"*

A commenter requested clarification that the initial and annual solicitations of § 301.6724-1(e)(1)(i) and (ii) need be made only to the responsible individual for all individuals covered under a single policy. The commenter further suggested that TIN solicitations made to a responsible individual be treated as TIN solicitations made to all individuals named on the responsible individual's policy.

Under § 1.6055-1(e)(1)(ii) and (iii), filers must report the TIN of each covered individual (who, under § 301.6721-1(g)(5), are also "payees"), and § 1.6055-1(g)(1) requires that the TIN of each covered individual be shown on statements furnished to the responsible individual. Current § 1.6055-1(g)(1) provides that, for purposes of the penalties under section 6722, the furnishing of a statement to the responsible individual is treated as the furnishing of a statement to a covered individual. This rule is intended to allow reporting entities to satisfy the section 6722 requirements for

---

[2] A filer of the information return required under § 1.6055-1 may receive an error message from the IRS indicating that a TIN and name provided on the return do not match IRS records. An error message is neither a Notice 972CG, Notice of Proposed Civil Penalty, nor a requirement that the filer must solicit a TIN in response to the error message.

all covered individuals by furnishing the required statement only to the responsible individual. The Treasury Department and the IRS also intend for a similar rule to apply to the TIN solicitation rules under the section 6724 regulations. To clarify that this is how these rules apply, the proposed regulations expressly provide that TIN solicitations (both initial and annual) made to the responsible individual for a policy or plan are treated as TIN solicitations of every covered individual on the policy or plan for purposes of § 301.6724-1(e)(1) and (f)(1). The filer does not need to make separate solicitations from the responsible individual for each covered individual nor does it need to separately solicit the TINs of each covered individual by contacting each covered individual directly. However, we decline to adopt the commenter's suggestion that a TIN solicitation made to a responsible individual be treated as a TIN solicitation made to all individuals named on that responsible individual's policy at any time, including those individuals added to a policy after the TIN solicitations. When a new individual is added to a policy, the coverage provider establishes a relationship with that individual. The individual is new to the filer, and it is the filer's responsibility to solicit that individual's TIN. Accordingly, to qualify for the penalty waiver, filers must solicit TINs for each individual added to a policy under the procedures outlined in § 301.6724-1(e)(1)(i) and (f)(1)(i); however, any other individual for whom the filer already has a TIN or already has solicited a TIN the prescribed amount of times need not be solicited again regardless of what changes take place during the filer's coverage of that individual.

b. *Different Forms of TIN Solicitations*

A commenter to Notice 2015-68 requested that the provision of renewal applications to enrollees be permitted to satisfy the annual solicitation requirement for purposes of § 301.6724-1(e)(1)(ii) and (iii) and (f)(1)(ii) and (iii) if those renewal applications request TINs from covered individuals. Under current law, TIN requests may be made in a number of different formats. The provision of a renewal application that requests TINs for all covered individuals satisfies the annual solicitation provisions of § 301.6724-1(e)(1)(ii) and (iii) and (f)(1)(ii) and (iii) if it is sent by the deadline for those annual solicitations. Thus, no changes to the regulations are necessary for renewal applications to satisfy the annual solicitation requirement.

The same commenter requested that the requirement in § 301.6724-1(e)(2)(i)(B) to provide the responsible individual with a Form W-9 should be eliminated. The commenter was concerned that this requirement imposes burdens on responsible individuals that make it less likely that they will respond to a TIN solicitation. Section 301.6724-1(e)(2)(i)(B) requires that an annual solicitation include a "Form W-9 or an acceptable substitute . . . " Thus, the existing regulations do not require that Form W-9 be sent. Filers are allowed to request TINs on an acceptable substitute for Form W-9, which includes a renewal application or other request for a TIN. Thus, this comment is not adopted.

This commenter also requested that the requirement in § 301.6724-1(e)(2)(i)(C) that annual solicitations include a return envelope be eliminated, and, if not eliminated, that clarification be provided as to how this requirement applies to multiple TINs. Existing regulations include this requirement because individuals are more likely to comply with a TIN solicitation if that solicitation includes a return envelope. We see no reason that the requirement to include a return envelope, which exists for other information reporting provisions, should be removed for reporting under section 6055. Thus, the proposed regulations do not adopt this comment. However, filers may request more than one TIN at the same time and do not need to send separate envelopes with each request. For example, on a renewal application requesting the TINs for all covered individuals, filers need only provide one return envelope for that application or request.

c. *Solicitations by Employers*

A commenter requested that employers be permitted to make TIN solicitations on behalf of filers. The commenter offered that employers are frequently in a better position than coverage providers to request TINs from the employers' employees and the employees' dependents, and, for practical reasons, it would make sense to allow employers to step in the shoes of the coverage provider for purposes of making the solicitations under § 301.6724-1(e)(1) and (f)(1).

Under existing regulations, actions taken by employers may satisfy the requirement for making an initial or annual TIN solicitation. Employers may, for example, provide their employees with applications for health coverage. If these applications request that the applicants provide TINs for all individuals to be covered, the coverage provider has made an initial solicitation for these individuals' TINs.

The commenter further requested that a filer that arranges to have an employer take on responsibility for the TIN solicitations be treated as having met the penalty waiver requirements of § 301.6724-1(e)(1) and (f)(1). Under existing regulations, qualifying for a penalty waiver requires that the solicitations actually be made. To avoid creating a less stringent standard in cases where an employer is acting on the filer's behalf, the proposed regulations do not adopt the commenter's proposal.

d. *Electronic TIN Solicitations*

A commenter requested that filers be permitted to make annual TIN solicitations by electronic means if the responsible individual has consented to the receipt of information concerning his or her coverage in the same electronic format in which the annual solicitation is made. IRS Publication 1586, Reasonable Cause Regulations and Requirements for Missing and Incorrect Name/TINs (including instructions for reading CD/DVDs), provides that filers may establish an electronic system for payees (including covered individuals) to receive and respond to TIN solicitations, provided certain listed requirements are met. IRS Publication 1586 can be found at *www.irs.gov/forms-pubs*. Because filers are already able to solicit TINs electronically, it is unnecessary to address the commenter's recommendation for electronic TIN solicitations with these proposed regulations.

Proposed Effective/Applicability Date

These regulations are generally proposed to apply for taxable years ending after December 31, 2015, and may be relied on for calendar years ending after December 31, 2013.

The only exception is the rules in section 1 of this preamble relating to reporting of coverage under catastrophic plans. Those rules are proposed to apply for calendar years beginning after December 31, 2016. Health insurance issuers may voluntarily report on 2015 and 2016 catastrophic coverage (on returns and statements filed and furnished in 2016 and 2017 respectively). An issuer that reports on 2015 and/or 2016 catastrophic coverage will not be subject to penalties for these returns.

In addition, until these the proposed regulations are finalized, taxpayers may continue to rely on the rules provided in Notice 2015-68.

Special Analyses

Certain IRS regulations, including this one, are exempt from the requirements of Executive Order 12866, as supplemented and reaffirmed by Executive Order 13563. Therefore, a regulatory impact assessment is not required.

It has also been determined that section 553(b) of the Administrative Procedure Act (5 U.S.C. chapter 5) does not apply to these regulations.

It is hereby certified that these regulations will not have a significant economic impact on a substantial number of small entities. This certification is based on the fact that the information collection required under these regulations is imposed under section 6055. Consistent with the statute, the proposed regulations require a person that provides minimum essential coverage to an individual to file a return with the IRS reporting certain information and to furnish a statement to the responsible individual who enrolled an individual or family in the coverage. These regulations primarily provide the method of filing and furnishing returns and statements under section 6055. Moreover, the proposed regulations attempt to minimize the burden associated with this collection of information by limiting reporting to the information that the IRS will use to verify minimum essential coverage and administer tax credits.

Based on these facts, a Regulatory Flexibility Analysis under the Regulatory Flexibility Act (5 U.S.C. chapter 6) is not required.

Pursuant to section 7805(f), this notice of proposed rulemaking will be submitted to the Chief Counsel for Advocacy of the Small Business Administration for comment on its impact on small business.

Statement of Availability of IRS Documents

IRS Revenue Procedures, Revenue Rulings notices, notices and other guidance cited in this preamble are published in the Internal Revenue Bulletin (or Cumulative Bulletin) and are available from the Superintendent of Documents, U.S. Government Printing Office, Washington, DC 20402, or by visiting the IRS website at *http://www.irs.gov*.

Comments and Requests for Public Hearing

Before these proposed regulations are adopted as final regulations, consideration will be given to any comments that are submitted timely to the IRS as prescribed in this preamble under the "Addresses" heading. The Treasury Department and the IRS request comments on all aspects of the proposed rules. All comments will be available for public inspection at *www.regulations.gov* or upon request. A public hearing will be scheduled if requested in writing by any person that timely submits written comments. If a public hearing is scheduled, notice of the date, time, and place for the public hearing will be published in the **Federal Register**.

Drafting Information

The principal author of these proposed regulations is John B. Lovelace of the Office of Associate Chief Counsel (Income Tax and Accounting). However, other personnel from the IRS and the Treasury Department participated in the development of the regulations.

[¶ 49,709] Proposed Amendments of Regulations (REG-131418-14), published in the Federal Register on August 2, 2016 (corrected 9/26/2016).

[Code Secs. 25A, 6050S and 6724]

Education tax credits: Qualified tuition expenses: Related expenses: Form 1098-T: Reporting requirements: Protecting Americans from Tax Hikes Act of 2015.—Amendments of Reg. §§1.25A-0, Reg. §1.25A-1, Reg. §1.25A-2, Reg. §1.25A-5, Reg. §1.6050S-0, Reg. §1.6050S-1 and Reg. §301.6724-1, reporting qualified tuition and related expenses under section 6050S on a Form 1098-T, "Tuition Statement," and conforming the regulations to the changes made to section 6050S by the Protecting Americans from Tax Hikes Act of 2015, are proposed.

AGENCY: Internal Revenue Service (IRS), Treasury.

ACTION: Notice of proposed rulemaking and notice of public hearing.

SUMMARY: This document contains proposed regulations that revise the rules for reporting qualified tuition and related expenses under section 6050S on a Form 1098-T, "Tuition Statement," and conforms the regulations to the changes made to section 6050S by the Protecting Americans from Tax Hikes Act of 2015. This document also seeks to amend the regulations on the education tax credits under section 25A generally as well as to conform the regulations to changes made to section 25A by the Trade Preferences Extension Act of 2015 and the Protecting Americans from Tax Hikes Act of 2015. The proposed regulations affect certain higher educational institutions required to file Form 1098-T and taxpayers eligible to claim an education tax credit. This document also provides notice of a public hearing on these proposed regulations. DATES: Written or electronic comments must be received by November 1, 2016. Outlines of topics to be discussed at the public hearing scheduled for November 30, 2016 must be received by November 1, 2016. ADDRESSES: Send submissions to: CC:PA:LPD:PR (REG-131418-14), room 5203, Internal Revenue Service, P.O. Box 7604, Ben Franklin Station, Washington, DC 20044. Submissions may be hand-delivered Monday through Friday between the hours of 8:00 a.m. and 4:00 p.m. to CC:PA:LPD:PR (REG-131418-14), Courier's Desk, Internal Revenue Service, 1111 Constitution Avenue, NW., Washington, DC 20224. Alternatively, taxpayers may submit comments electronically via the Federal eRulemaking Portal at www.regulations.gov (IRS REG-131418-14).

FOR FURTHER INFORMATION CONTACT: Concerning the proposed regulations, Gerald Semasek of the Office of Associate Chief Counsel (Procedure and Administration) for the proposed regulations under sections 6050S and 6724, (202) 317-6845, and Sheldon Iskow of the Office of Associate Chief Counsel (Income Tax and Accounting) for the proposed regulations under section 25A, (202) 317-4718; concerning the submission of comments and requests for a public hearing, Regina Johnson, (202) 317-6901 (not toll-free calls).

SUPPLEMENTARY INFORMATION:

Paperwork Reduction Act

The collection of information contained in this notice of proposed rulemaking has been approved by the Office of Management and Budget through Form 1040 (OMB No. 1545-0074), Form 8863 (OMB No. 1545-0074) and Form 1098-T (OMB No. 1545-1574) in accordance with the Paperwork Reduction Act of 1995 (44 U.S.C. 3507(d)). Notice and an opportunity to comment on the proposed changes to burden hours for the forms related to this proposed rule will be published in a separate notice in the **Federal Register**.

Background

This document contains proposed regulations to amend the Income Tax Regulations (26 CFR part 1) under section 25A of the Internal Revenue Code (Code) and the Procedure and Administration Regulations (26 CFR Part 301) under section 6050S, to reflect the amendments to sections 25A and 6724 under the Trade Preferences Extension Act of 2015 (Public Law 114-27 (129 Stat. 362 (2015)) (TPEA) and the amendments to sections 25A and 6050S under the Protecting Americans from Tax Hikes Act of 2015 (Public Law 114-113 (129 Stat. 2242 (2015)) (PATH). Furthermore, the document contains proposed regulations to amend the Income Tax Regulations under section 25A to update the definition of qualified tuition and related expenses in §1.25A-2(d) to reflect the changes made by the American Recovery and Reinvestment Act of 2009 (Public Law 111-5 (123 Stat. 115) (ARRA)), to clarify the prepayment rule in §1.25A-5(e), and to clarify the rule for refunds in §1.25A-5(f).

1. Section 25A-Education Tax Credits

The Taxpayer Relief Act of 1997 (Public Law 105-34 (111 Stat. 788) (TRA '97)) added section 25A to provide students and their families with two new nonrefundable tax credits to help pay for college (education tax credits). Pursuant to TRA '97, section 25A allowed eligible taxpayers to claim either the Hope Scholarship Credit or the Lifetime Learning Credit (LLC) for qualified tuition and related expenses paid during the taxable year for an academic period beginning during the taxable year. In general, either the student or the parent who claims a dependency exemption for the student may claim a credit for the student's qualified tuition and related expenses. Section 25A(f)(1) defines "qualified tuition and related expenses" as tuition and fees required for enrollment or attendance at an eligible educational institution (institution). Section 25A(f)(2) generally defines an "eligible educational institution" as an institution described in the Higher Education Act of 1965 that is eligible to participate in federal college financial aid programs. Section 25A(g)(4) provides that amounts paid during the taxable year for enrollment during an academic period beginning within the first three months of the following taxable year are treated as amounts paid for an academic period beginning during the taxable year. Section 25A(g)(5) provides that no credit is allowed for any expenses for which a deduction is allowed under another provision of the Code.

Final regulations under section 25A were published in the **Federal Register** (67 FR 78687) on December 26, 2002. Section 1.25A-2(d)(1) of these regulations defines "qualified tuition and related expenses" to mean tuition and fees required for the enrollment or attendance of a student for courses of instruction at an institution. Section 1.25A-2(d)(2)(i) provides that only fees required to be paid to the institution as a condition of the student's enrollment or attendance at the institution are treated as qualified tuition and related expenses for purposes of section 25A. Under this rule, fees for books, supplies, and equipment used in a course of study are required fees only if the fees must be paid to the institution for the enrollment or attendance of the student at the institution. See §1.25A-2(d)(2)(ii). In addition, §1.25A-5(e)(1) provides that an education tax credit is allowed only for payments of qualified tuition and related expenses for an academic period beginning in the same taxable year as the year the payment is made. Section 1.25A-5(e)(2) provides that qualified tuition and related expenses paid during one taxable year for an academic period beginning in the first three months of the taxable year following the taxable year in which the payment is made will be treated as paid for an academic period beginning in the same taxable year as the year the payment is made (prepayment rule).

Section 1.25A-5(f) provides rules for refunds of qualified tuition and related expenses. If qualified tuition and related expenses are paid and a refund of these expenses is received in the same taxable year, qualified tuition and related expenses for the taxable year are reduced by the amount of the refund. Section 1.25A-5(f)(1). If a taxpayer receives a refund of qualified tuition and related expenses in the current taxable year (current year) that were paid in the prior taxable year (prior year) before the taxpayer files his/her federal income tax return for the prior year, the taxpayer reduces the qualified tuition and related expenses for the prior year by the refund amount. Section 1.25A-5(f)(2). However, if the taxpayer receives the refund after filing his/her federal income tax return for the prior year, the taxpayer must increase the tax imposed for the current year by the recapture amount. Section 1.25A-5(f)(3)(i). The recapture amount is calculated in the manner provided in §1.25A-5(f)(3)(ii). Sections 1.25A-5(f)(4) and (f)(5) provide that refunds of loan proceeds and receipt of excludable educational assistance are treated as refunds for purposes of §1.25A-5(f)(1), (2), and (3), as appropriate.

In 2009, ARRA enacted section 25A(i), which expanded the Hope Scholarship Credit with the American Opportunity Tax Credit (AOTC) for taxable years beginning after 2008. The definition of "qualified tuition and related expenses" for purposes of the AOTC is broader than the definition of qualified tuition and related expenses for the Hope Scholarship Credit and the LLC because it includes expenses paid for course materials. See section 25A(i)(3).

2. Section 222-Deduction for Qualified Expenses

Section 431(a) of the Economic Growth and Tax Relief Reconciliation Act of 2001, Public Law 107-16 (115 Stat. 38) added section 222, which generally allows a deduction for qualified tuition and related expenses paid by a taxpayer during the taxable year subject to certain dollar and income limitations. Section 222(b) provides that no deduction is allowed if the taxpayer claims an education tax credit for the student.

3. Section 6050S-Information Reporting for Eligible Educational Institutions

TRA '97 also added section 6050S to require eligible educational institutions to file information returns and to furnish written statements to assist taxpayers and the IRS in determining whether a taxpayer is eligible for an education tax credit under section 25A, as well as other education tax benefits. These returns and statements are made on Form 1098-T, "Tuition Statement." Prior to the enactment of PATH, section 6050S(b)(2)(B)(i) permitted institutions to report either the aggregate amount of payments received or the aggregate amount billed for qualified tuition and related expenses during the calendar year for individuals enrolled for any academic period. Institutions also must report the aggregate amount of scholarships or grants received for an individual's costs of attendance that the institution administered and processed during the calendar year. See section 6050S(b)(2)(B)(ii). Section 6050S(b)(2)(B)(iii) requires that institutions must separately report adjustments (that is, refunds of payments or reductions in charges) made during the calendar year to qualified tuition and related expenses that were reported in a prior calendar year and that institutions also must separately report adjustments (that is, refunds or reductions) made during the calendar year to scholarships that were reported in a prior calendar year. Section 6050S(b)(2)(D) requires that the information return include other information as the Secretary may prescribe.

In addition, sections 6050S(a)(2) and (a)(3) require any person engaged in a trade or business of making payments to any individual under an insurance agreement as reimbursements or refunds of qualified expenses (an insurer) or who receives from any individual $600 or more of interest during the calendar year on qualified education loans to file information returns and to furnish written information statements. Section 6050S(b)(2) provides that these information returns must contain the name, address, and TIN of any individual with respect to whom these payments were made or received, the aggregate amount of reimbursements or refunds (or similar amounts paid to such individuals during the calendar year by an insurer), the aggregate amount of interest received for the calendar year from the individual, and such other information as the Secretary may prescribe.

Section 6050S(d) provides that every person required to make a return under section 6050S(a) must furnish a written statement to each individual whose name is set forth on the return showing the name, address, and phone number of the person required to make the return and the amounts described in section 6050S(b)(2)(B). For taxable years beginning after June 29, 2015, all of the information required by section 6050S(b)(2), not just the amounts, must be included on the written statement. The written statement must be furnished by January 31 of the year following the year for which the return is required to be made.

Final regulations under section 6050S were published in the **Federal Register** (67 FR 77678) in the same Treasury Decision as the final regulations for section 25A on December 19, 2002. The section 6050S regulations provide exceptions to the reporting requirements for educational institutions for students who are nonresident aliens, for noncredit courses, for certain billing arrangements, and in cases where qualified tuition and related expenses are paid entirely with scholarships or grants. These regulations also set forth the specific information that institutions must report to the IRS, as well as information that the institution must include with the statement furnished to the student. These regulations also include requirements regarding the time and manner for soliciting the student's TIN.

4. Sections 6721, 6722 and 6724-Information Reporting Penalties and Penalty Relief

Section 6721 imposes a penalty on an eligible educational institution that fails to timely file correct information returns with the IRS. Section 6722 imposes a penalty on an educational institution that fails to timely furnish correct written statements to the student. Generally, the penalty under section 6721 and section 6722 is $100 per failure, with an annual maximum penalty of $1.5 million. The penalty is increased to $250 per failure and the annual maximum penalty is increased to $3 million for returns required to be filed and statements required to be made after December 31, 2015. However, section 6724(a) provides that the penalty under section 6721 or 6722 may be waived if it is shown that the failure was due to reasonable cause and not due to willful neglect.

Section 301.6724-1(a)(2) provides that the penalty is waived for reasonable cause only if the filer establishes that: (1) either there are significant mitigating factors with respect to the failure or that the failure arose from events beyond the filer's control and (2) the filer acted in a responsible manner both before and after the failure. In the case of a missing or incorrect TIN, §301.6724-1(d)(2) provides that the filer acted in a responsible manner if the filer satisfies the solicitation requirements in §301.6724-1(e) (regarding a missing TIN) or (f) (regarding an incorrect TIN).

Section 1.6050S-1(e)(3) provides that the rules regarding reasonable cause under §301.6724-1 do not apply in the case of failure to include a correct TIN on a Form 1098-T. Instead, §1.6050S-1(e)(3) provides special rules for institutions to establish reasonable cause for a failure to include a correct TIN on Form 1098-T.

Section 1.6050S-1(e)(3)(i) provides that reasonable cause for a failure to include a correct TIN on the Form 1098-T may be established if (1) the failure arose from events beyond the institution's control, such as a failure of the individual to furnish a correct TIN, and (2) the institution acted in a responsible manner before and after the failure. Section 1.6050S-1(e)(3)(ii) provides that if the institution does not have the student's correct TIN in its records, acting in a responsible manner means making a single solicitation for the TIN by December 31 of the calendar year for which the payment is made, the amount is billed, or a reimbursement is made. Section 1.6050S-1(e)(3)(iii) also provides for the manner by which an educational institution should request the individual's TIN. The solicitation must be done in writing and must clearly notify the individual that the law requires the individual to furnish a TIN so that it may be included on an information return filed by the institution. The solicitation may be made on Form W-9S, "Request for Student's or Borrower's Taxpayer Identification Number and Certification," or the institution may develop its own form and incorporate it into other forms customarily used by the institution, such as financial aid forms. In the instance that an institution does not have a student's TIN in its records and the student does not provide the TIN in response to a solicitation described in §1.6050S-1(e), the institution must file and furnish the Form 1098-T, leaving the space for the TIN blank.

5. TPEA Amendments to Sections 25A, 222 and 6724

Section 804(a) of TPEA amended section 25A by adding a new subparagraph (g)(8), which provides that, for taxable years beginning after June 29, 2015, except as provided by the Secretary, a taxpayer may not claim an education tax credit under section 25A unless the taxpayer receives a statement furnished by an eligible educational institution that contains all of the information required in section 6050S(d)(2) (that is, the recipient's copy of the Form 1098-T). Section 804(b) similarly amends section 222(d) to provide that, for taxable years beginning after June 29, 2015, except as provided by the Secretary, a taxpayer may not claim a deduction for qualified tuition and related expenses unless the taxpayer receives the recipient's copy of the Form 1098-T. For purposes of both the education tax credit and the deduction, a taxpayer who claims a student as a dependent will be treated as receiving the statement if the student receives the statement.

Section 805 of TPEA amends section 6724 by adding a new subsection (f), which provides that no penalty will be imposed under section 6721 or 6722 against an eligible educational institution solely by reason of failing to include the individual's TIN on a Form 1098-T or related statement if the institution contemporaneously certifies under penalties of perjury in the form and manner prescribed by the Secretary that it has complied with the standards promulgated by the Secretary for obtaining the individual's TIN. The provision applies to returns required to be made and statements required to be furnished after December 31, 2015.

6. PATH Amendments to Sections 25A, 222 and 6050S

a. AOTC permanent and section 222 extended

Section 102(a) of PATH amends section 25A(i) to make the AOTC permanent. Section 153(a) of PATH amends section 222(e) to retroactively extend the deduction for qualified tuition and related expenses for taxable years beginning after December 31, 2014, and ending on or before December 31, 2016.

b. Amendments to section 25A

Section 206(a)(2) of PATH amends section 25A(i) to provide that the AOTC is not allowed if the student's TIN and the TIN of the taxpayer claiming the credit is issued after the due date for filing the return for the taxable year. Pursuant to section 206(b)(1), this amendment is effective for returns (including an amended return) filed after December 18, 2015. Section 206(b)(2) of PATH provides, however, that this amendment does not apply to any return (other than an amendment to any return) for a taxable year that includes the date of enactment of PATH (December 18, 2015) if the return is filed on or before the due date for such return.

Section 211(a) of PATH amends section 25A(i) to provide that the AOTC is not allowed if the return does not include the employer identification number (EIN) of any institution to which the qualified tuition and related expenses were paid with respect to the student. This amendment is effective for taxable years beginning after December 31, 2015.

c. Amendments to section 6050S

Section 211(b) of PATH amends section 6050S(b)(2) to require eligible educational institutions and insurers to report their EIN on the return and statement. This amendment is effective for expenses paid after December 31, 2015, for education furnished in academic periods beginning after such date.

Section 212 of PATH amends section 6050S(b)(2)(B)(i) to eliminate the option for eligible educational institutions to report aggregate qualified tuition and related expenses billed for the calendar year. Accordingly, for expenses paid after December 31, 2015, for education furnished in academic periods beginning after such date, eligible educational institutions are required to report aggregate payments of qualified tuition and related expenses received during the calendar year.

Explanation of Provisions

1. Changes to Implement TPEA and PATH

a. Changes to section 25A and section 222

Both TPEA and PATH add new requirements for claiming education tax benefits. Under TPEA, the student is required to receive a Form 1098-T in order to claim the LLC or the AOTC or claim the deduction under section 222. Under PATH, the ability to claim the AOTC is further limited. First, the taxpayer can claim the AOTC only if the taxpayer includes, on his/her return for which the credit is claimed, the EIN of any educational institution to which qualified tuition and related expenses are paid. Second, the taxpayer can claim the AOTC only if the TIN of the student and the TIN of the taxpayer, on the return for which the credit is claimed, are issued on or before the due date of the original return.

i. Form 1098-T requirement under TPEA

Form 1098-T assists taxpayers in determining whether they are eligible to claim education tax credits under section 25A or the deduction for qualified tuition and related expenses under section 222. However, before TPEA, there was no requirement that the taxpayer (or the taxpayer's dependent if the taxpayer's dependent is the student) receive a Form 1098-T to claim these tax benefits.

Section 804 of TPEA changes the requirements for a taxpayer to claim education tax benefits under section 25A or section 222. For qualified tuition and related expenses paid during taxable years beginning after June 29, 2015, TPEA provides that, unless the Secretary provides otherwise, a taxpayer must receive a Form 1098-T to claim either a credit under section 25A or a deduction under section 222.

The proposed regulations reflect these changes. Specifically, the proposed regulations add a new paragraph (f) to §1.25A-1 to require that for taxable years beginning after June 29, 2015, unless an exception applies, no education tax credit is allowed unless the taxpayer (or the taxpayer's dependent) receives a Form 1098-T. However, the proposed regulations explain that the amount reported on the Form 1098-T may not reflect the total amount of qualified tuition and related expenses that the taxpayer has paid during the taxable year because certain expenses are not required to be reported on the Form 1098-T. For example, under §1.25A-2(d)(3), expenses for course materials paid to a vendor other than an eligible educational institution are eligible for the AOTC. However, because these expenses are not paid to an eligible educational institution, these expenses are not required to be reported on a Form 1098-T. Accordingly, a taxpayer who meets the requirements in §1.25A-1(f) regarding the Form 1098-T requirement to claim the credit and who can substantiate payment of qualified tuition and related expenses may include these unreported expenses in the computation of the amount of the education tax credit allowable for the taxable year even though the expenses are not reported on a Form 1098-T.

Proposed §1.25A-1(f)(2)(i) provides an exception to the Form 1098-T requirement in §1.25A-1(f)(1) if the student has not received a Form 1098-T by the later of (a) January 31 of the taxable year following the taxable year to which the education credit relates or (b) the date the federal income tax return claiming the education tax credit is filed. This exception only applies if the taxpayer or taxpayer's dependent (i) has requested, in the manner prescribed in publications, forms and instructions, or published guidance, the eligible educational institution to furnish the Form 1098-T after January 31 of the year following the taxable year to which the education tax credit relates but on or before the date the return is filed claiming the education tax credit, and (ii) has cooperated fully with the eligible educational institution's efforts to obtain information necessary to furnish the statement. Proposed §1.25A-1(f)(2)(ii) provides that the receipt of a Form 1098-T is not required if the reporting rules under section 6050S and related regulations provide that the eligible educational institution is exempt from providing a Form 1098-T to the student (for example, non-credit courses). Proposed §1.25A-1(f)(2)(iii) also provides that the IRS may provide additional exceptions in published guidance of general applicability, see §601.601(d)(2). The proposed regulations under §1.25A-1(f) apply to education tax credits claimed for taxable years beginning after June 29, 2015.

Until the proposed regulations under §§1.25A-1(f) and 1.6050S-1(a) are published in the **Federal Register** as final regulations, a taxpayer (or the taxpayer's dependent) (other than a non-resident alien) who does not receive a Form 1098-T because its institution is exempt from furnishing a Form 1098-T under current §1.6050S-1(a)(2) may claim an education tax credit under section 25A(a) if the taxpayer (1) is otherwise qualified, (2) can demonstrate that the taxpayer (or the taxpayer's dependent) was enrolled at an eligible educational institution, and (3) can substantiate the payment of qualified tuition and related expenses. Section 804(b) of TPEA also amends section 222 to require a Form 1098-T to claim a deduction for qualified tuition and related expenses for taxable years beginning after June 29, 2015. Rules similar to those in proposed §1.25A-1(f), including the exceptions, apply for purposes of section 222.

ii. Identification requirements for AOTC under PATH

Section 206(a)(2) of PATH amends section 25A(i) to provide that the AOTC is not allowed if the student's TIN or the TIN of the taxpayer claiming the credit is issued after the due date for filing the return for the taxable year. This amendment is generally effective for any return or amended return filed after December 18, 2015. The proposed regulations reflect this change. Specifically, the proposed regulations add new §1.25A-1(e)(2)(i), which provides that, for any federal income tax return (including an amended return) filed after December 18, 2015, no AOTC is allowed unless the student's TIN and the taxpayer's TIN are issued on or before the due date (including an extension, if timely requested) for filing the return for that taxable year.

Section 211 of PATH amends section 25A(i) to provide that the AOTC is not allowed unless the taxpayer's return includes the EIN of any institution to which the qualified tuition and related expenses were paid with respect to the student. The proposed regulations reflect this change by adding new §1.25A-1(e)(2)(ii).

b. Changes to section 6050S reporting to conform with TPEA 1098-T requirement

i. Exceptions to reporting requirement and clarifying changes

Currently, the regulations under section 6050S include exceptions to reporting. For instance, under §1.6050S-1(a)(2)(i), institutions are not required to file a Form 1098-T with the IRS or provide a Form 1098-T to a nonresident alien, unless the individual requests a Form 1098-T. Under §1.6050S-1(a)(2)(ii), institutions are not required to report information with respect to courses for which no academic credit is awarded. In addition, reporting is not required with respect to individuals whose qualified tuition and related expenses are paid entirely with scholarships under §1.6050S-1(a)(2)(iii) or individuals whose qualified tuition and related expenses are paid under a formal billing arrangement under §1.6050S-1(a)(2)(iv).

The exceptions in §§1.6050S-1(a)(2)(i), (iii), and (iv) to reporting on Form 1098-T are inconsistent with the TPEA, which generally requires a student to receive a Form 1098-T from the educational institution to claim a section 25A education credit. With these exceptions, a significant number of taxpayers claiming the credit will not have a Form 1098-T, which would frustrate the explicit purpose of TPEA. Therefore, the proposed regulations remove these exceptions.

Removal of the exceptions in §§1.6050S-1(a)(2)(i), (iii), and (iv) also assists students. Students to whom these exceptions apply are deprived of important information that they need to determine their eligibility for education tax credits. The Form 1098-T provides students with the amount of tuition paid (or billed for calendar year 2016 only), the amount of scholarships and grants that the institution administered and processed, and an indication of whether the student was enrolled at least a half time for an academic period. Students who do not receive a Form 1098-T cannot use the information that would be provided on the form to assist them in determining the proper amount of education credits they may claim. Further, removal of these exceptions will improve the IRS's ability to use the Form 1098-T to verify whether taxpayers should be allowed the education tax benefits that are claimed. In addition, removal of these exceptions would improve the IRS's ability to determine whether the institutions are complying with their reporting obligations.

The proposed regulations would not remove the exception to reporting under §1.6050S-1(a)(2)(ii) for courses for which no academic credit is awarded. Treasury and the IRS understand that in many cases fees for these courses are charged outside of the financial systems used for students who are taking courses for credit. In addition, given that non-credit courses would not be eligible for the AOTC (or Hope Credit) and would only be eligible for the LLC if the student is taking the course to acquire or improve job skills, reporting expenses paid for non-credit courses could cause confusion and unintended non-compliance.

Treasury and the IRS believe that students benefit from receipt of the Form 1098-T because the information on the form assists the student in determining eligibility for education tax benefits that make higher education more affordable. Reporting that does not provide useful information to students and the IRS, however, unduly burdens institutions and the IRS and could confuse students about whether they are eligible to claim education tax benefits. Therefore, Treasury and the IRS are asking for comments regarding exceptions to the reporting under section 6050S. Specifically, comments are requested regarding the exception to reporting for students who are nonresident aliens, including how an institution determines that a student is a nonresident alien and experience administering the existing exception. Comments are also requested regarding whether the exception for noncredit courses should be retained, and if so, whether there should be any changes to the exception.

The proposed regulations also revise the information that institutions are required to report on the Form 1098-T in an effort to provide more precise information for students to use when determining eligibility for and the amount of an education tax credit and for the IRS to use to verify compliance with the requirements for claiming the education tax credits. For instance, the current regulations under §1.6050S-1(b)(2)(ii)(D) require that the Form 1098-T include an indication of whether amounts reported relate to an academic period that begins in the first three months of the next calendar year pursuant to the prepayment rule in §1.25A-5(e)(2). The proposed regulations revise this section to include a requirement that the amount paid that relates to an academic period that begins in the first three months of the next calendar year be specifically stated on the Form 1098-T. This will assist the IRS in identifying credits claimed in two years for the same qualified tuition and related expenses.

In addition, the proposed regulations add a new paragraph (I) to §1.6050S-1(b)(2)(ii) to require the institution to indicate the number of months that a student was a full-time student during the calendar year. The proposed regulations also add to that paragraph a definition of what constitutes a month. This information will assist the IRS in determining whether a parent properly claimed the student as a dependent and, therefore, properly claimed the credit for the student's qualified tuition and related expenses. See §1.25A-1(f) for rules relating to claiming the credit in the case of a dependent.

The proposed regulations clarify §1.6050S-1(b)(2)(v) regarding the rules for determining the amount of payments received for qualified tuition and related expenses. This clarification is intended to provide a uniform rule for all institutions to determine whether a payment received by an institution should be reported on a Form 1098-T as qualified tuition and related expenses in the current year. Under the proposed rule, payments received during a calendar year are treated first as payments of qualified tuition and related expenses up to the total amount billed by the institution for qualified tuition and related expenses for enrollment during the calendar year and then as payments of expenses other than qualified tuition and related expenses for enrollment during the calendar year. A similar rule applies in the case of payments received during the calendar year with respect to enrollment in an academic period beginning during the first three months of the next calendar year. In that case, the payments received by the institution with respect to the amount billed for enrollment in an academic period beginning during the first three months of the next calendar year are treated as payments of qualified tuition and related expenses for the calendar year in which the payments are received. Examples have been added to §1.6050S-1(b)(2)(vii) to illustrate these rules. Treasury and the IRS request comments regarding these rules, including alternative approaches and recommendations for addressing other issues that should be covered by these rules.

The proposed regulations also revise §1.6050S-1(c)(1)(iii) regarding the instructions accompanying the Form 1098-T that the institution must furnish to students. The proposed regulations add a new paragraph (D) to §1.6050S-1(c)(1)(iii) to require institutions to include a paragraph in the instructions informing students that they may be able to optimize their federal tax benefits by taking a portion of a scholarship or grant into income. This new paragraph will alert students about their ability to optimize their federal education tax benefits by allocating all or a portion of their scholarship or grant to pay the student's actual living expenses (if permitted by the terms of the scholarship or grant) by including such amounts in income on the student's tax return if the student is required to file a return. By including such amounts in income, the scholarship or grant is no longer tax free, and the student is not required to reduce qualified tuition and related expenses by the amount paid with the now taxable scholarship or grant. See section 25A(g)(2) and §1.25A-5(c)(3) for rules regarding allocation of scholarships and grants between qualified tuition and related expenses and other expenses. Minor revisions have also been made to the other paragraphs required to be included in instructions, including addition of the name of the form (Form 1098-T) on which reporting occurs and specific identification of Publication 970, "Tax Benefits for Education," as a resource for taxpayers.

The proposed regulations also provide a definition of "administered and processed" for purposes of determining which scholarships and grants an institution is required to report on the Form 1098-T. The current regulations do not have a definition of this term, and the lack of a definition has resulted in uncertainty and inconsistent reporting. The proposed regulations resolve this by adding a definition of "administered and processed" to §1.6050S-1(e)(1)(i). Under this definition, a scholarship or grant is administered and processed by an institution if the institution receives payment of an amount (whether by cash, check, or other means of payment) that the institution knows or reasonably should know, is a scholarship or grant, regardless of whether the institution is named as the payee or a co-payee of the amount and regardless of whether, in the case of a payment other than in cash, the student endorses the check or other means of payment for the benefit of the institution. Pell Grants are provided as an example of a scholarship or grant that is treated as administered and processed by an institution.

ii. PATH eliminates option to report amount billed

These proposed regulations also implement the amendment to section 6050S(b)(2)(B)(i) under PATH, which eliminates the option for eligible educational institutions to report the aggregate amount billed for qualified tuition and related expenses for expenses paid after December 31, 2015, for education furnished in academic periods beginning after such date. Eligible educational institutions have informed the IRS that they cannot implement the necessary changes in technology to enable reporting of aggregate payments of qualified tuition and expenses for the first year in which the statutory amendment applies, calendar year 2016. Therefore, in Announcement 2016-17, I.R.B. 2016-20, the IRS stated that it will not impose penalties under section 6721 or 6722 against an eligible educational institution required to file 2016 Forms 1098-T solely because the institution reports the aggregate amount billed for qualified tuition and expenses rather than the aggregate payments of qualified tuition and related expenses received. Thus, for calendar year 2016, no penalties will be imposed if an educational institution fails to implement the PATH's amendment to section 6050S(b)(2)(B)(i) and continues to report the amount billed.

The proposed regulations reflect the PATH amendment by eliminating the option to report the amount billed. These regulations are proposed to be effective on publication of final regulations in the **Federal Register**. In the interim, the limited penalty relief in Announcement 2016-17 will apply to allow educational institutions to report the amount billed for calendar year 2016.

iii. No change required to implement EIN reporting requirement

Current regulations under §1.6050S-1(b)(2)(ii)(A) require that the eligible educational institution report its name, address, and TIN on the Form 1098-T. Accordingly, the amendment to section 6050S(b)(2) by section 211(b) of PATH requiring eligible educational institutions and insurers to report their EIN does not require a change to the regulations.

c. Changes to implement new section 6724(f)

Section 1.6050S-1(f)(4) of the proposed regulations reflects the enactment of section 6724(f) by section 805 of TPEA. Under section 6724(f), the IRS may not impose information reporting penalties under section 6721 and section 6722 against an eligible educational institution for failure to include a correct TIN on the Form 1098-T if the institution certifies compliance with IRS standards for soliciting TINs. Relief under section 6724(f) applies only to eligible educational institutions and does not apply to insurers required to file Forms 1098-T under section 6050S(a)(2).

The IRS generally sends penalty notices to taxpayers who fail to file information returns when required or who file incorrect information returns. Filers seeking penalty relief based on reasonable cause must respond to the penalty notice with a statement explaining how the filer qualifies for relief. Under section 6724(f), however, no penalty under section 6721 or 6722 is imposed in the first instance if the educational institution contemporaneously makes a true and accurate certification under penalties of perjury in such form and manner as may be prescribed by the Secretary that it complied with the standards promulgated by the Secretary to obtain the student's TIN. Section 6724(f) is effective for returns required to be filed and statements required to be furnished after December 31, 2015.

Standards for obtaining the student's TIN are set forth in § 1.6050S-1(e)(3)(ii) and (iii) of the existing regulations. These regulations are proposed to be redesignated as § 1.6050S-1(f)(3)(ii) and (iii). Under these standards, the institution does not have to solicit a student's TIN, but may use the TIN that it has in its records. If the institution does not have the student's correct TIN in its records, then it must solicit the TIN in the time and manner described in redesignated § 1.6050S-1(f). To implement section 6724(f), § 1.6050S-1(f)(4) of the proposed regulations has been added to provide that for returns required to be filed and statements required to be furnished after December 31, 2015, the IRS will not impose a penalty against an institution under section 6721 or 6722 for failure to include the student's correct TIN on the return or statement if the institution certifies to the IRS under penalties of perjury in the form and manner prescribed by the Secretary in publications, forms and instructions, or other published guidance at the time of filing of the return that the institution complied with the requirements in § 1.6050S-1(f)(3)(ii) and (iii). However, the proposed regulations make clear that the certification will not protect the institution from penalty if the IRS determines subsequently that the requirements of § 1.6050S-1(f)(3)(ii) and (iii) were not satisfied or if the failure to file correct information returns relates to something other than a failure to provide the correct TIN for the student. In addition, a cross-reference is proposed to be added to the regulations under section 6724 to alert taxpayers that the rules for penalty relief for eligible educational institutions with respect to reporting obligations under section 6050S are contained in § 1.6050S-1(f).

d. Penalty relief under section 6724(f) for calendar year 2015 Forms 1098-T

Section 6724(f) requires the IRS to develop procedures enabling an eligible educational institution to avoid imposition of the section 6721 and section 6722 penalty for failure to include a student's correct TIN on the Form 1098-T by certifying under penalties of perjury at the time of filing or furnishing the form that the institution complied with the IRS standards for obtaining a student's TIN. In Announcement 2016-03, I.R.B. 2016-4, the IRS stated that it will not impose penalties under section 6721 or 6722 against an eligible educational institution required to file Forms 1098-T for calendar year 2015 solely because the student's TIN is missing or incorrect.

2. Other Changes to Regulations Under Section 25A and Section 6050S

The proposed regulations also update and clarify the regulations under section 25A. The proposed regulations update § 1.25A-2(d) to reflect the changes made by ARRA allowing students to claim the AOTC for expenses paid for course materials (such as books, supplies, and equipment) required for enrollment or attendance, whether or not the course materials are purchased from the institution. Prior to ARRA, the term "qualified tuition and related expenses" included tuition and fees, but did not include course materials, such as books, unless the cost of these materials was a fee that was required to be paid to the institution as a condition of attendance or enrollment. See section 25A(f)(1) and § 1.25A-2(d)(2)(ii).

When Congress enacted the AOTC in 2009, it expanded the definition of qualified tuition and related expenses for purposes of the AOTC to include expenses paid for course materials. See H.R. Conf. Rep. 111-16, 111th Cong., 1st Sess. p. 525 (February 29, 2009). Course materials are qualified expenses only for the AOTC and not for the LLC. See Tax Increase Prevention Act of 2014 (Public Law 113-295, 128 Stat. 4010). The proposed regulations update § 1.25A-2(d) to provide that, for purposes of claiming the AOTC for tax years beginning after December 31, 2008, the definition of qualified tuition and related expenses includes not only tuition and fees required for enrollment or attendance at an eligible educational institution, but also expenses paid for course materials needed for enrollment or attendance at an eligible educational institution. Accordingly, after ARRA, for purposes of claiming the Hope Scholarship Credit and LLC, qualified tuition and related expenses continue to exclude the cost of books, supplies, and equipment if they can be purchased from any vendor. However, for purposes of claiming the AOTC, qualified tuition and related expenses includes the cost of course materials such as books, supplies and equipment that is needed for meaningful attendance or enrollment in a course of study, whether or not the materials are purchased from the institution. The proposed regulations provide an example that illustrates that for purposes of the AOTC qualified tuition and related expenses includes the cost of course material, including books, even if a taxpayer purchases these materials from a vendor other than the institution.

In addition, the proposed regulations add a new section under section 6050S to eliminate uncertainty in the reporting requirements that may result from these proposed amendments to § 1.25A-2(d). Under proposed § 1.6050S-1(a)(2)(i), an institution is not required to report the amount paid or billed for books, supplies, and equipment unless the amount is a fee that must be paid to the eligible educational institution as a condition of enrollment or attendance under § 1.25A-2(d)(2)(ii).

The proposed regulations also clarify the example in § 1.25A-5(e)(2)(ii) regarding the prepayment rule. Under § 1.25A-5(e)(2)(i), if qualified tuition and related expenses are paid during one taxable year for an academic period that begins during the first three months of the taxpayer's next taxable year (that is, in January, February, or March of the next taxable year for calendar year taxpayers), an education tax credit is allowed for the qualified tuition and related expenses only in the taxable year in which the taxpayer pays the expenses. The Treasury Department and the IRS are aware that there is some uncertainty regarding the application of the prepayment rule to amounts paid in the prior year and the current year for an academic period beginning during the current year. The proposed regulations clarify the proper treatment in this situation by expanding the Example in § 1.25A-5(e)(2)(ii) to illustrate that a student who pays part of a semester's tuition in Year 1, and the remainder in Year 2, may claim a credit for Year 1, for the portion of the tuition paid in December Year 1 and a separate credit for Year 2 for the portion of the tuition paid in February Year 2.

The proposed regulations also clarify the rules under § 1.25A-5(f) regarding a refund of qualified tuition and related expenses received from an eligible educational institution. The current regulations do not address the situation where the taxpayer receives a refund in the current taxable year of qualified tuition and related expenses for an academic period beginning in the current taxable year for which payments were made during the prior taxable year under the prepayment rule and payments were made during the current taxable year. To address this situation, the proposed regulations provide that the taxpayer may allocate the refund in any proportion to reduce qualified tuition and related expenses paid in either taxable year, except that the amount of the refund allocated to a taxable year may not exceed the qualified tuition and related expenses paid in the taxable year for the academic period to which the refund relates. The sum of the amounts allocated to each taxable year cannot exceed the amount of the refund. The proposed regulations add an example to illustrate this rule.

Proposed Effective and Applicability Dates

These regulations are proposed to take effect when published in the **Federal Register** as final regulations.

Statement of Availability of IRS Documents

IRS published guidance cited in this preamble is published in the Internal Revenue Bulletin and is available from the Superintendent of Documents, U.S. Government Publishing Office, Washington, DC 20402, or by visiting the IRS website at http://www.irs.gov.

Special Analyses

Certain IRS regulations, including this one, are exempt from the requirements of Executive Order 12866, as supplemented and reaffirmed by Executive Order 13563. Therefore, a regulatory impact assessment is not required. It has also been determined that section 553(b) of the Administrative Procedure Act (5 U.S.C. chapter 5) does not apply to these regulations.

It is hereby certified that the collection of information in this notice of proposed rulemaking will not have a significant economic impact on a substantial number of small entities within the meaning of section 601(6) of the Regulatory Flexibility Act (5 U.S.C. chapter 6). The type of small entities to which the regulations may apply are small eligible educational institutions (generally colleges and universities eligible to receive federal financial aid for education under the Higher Education Act of 1965). This certification is based on the fact that few, if any, new eligible educational institutions will be subject to reporting and the changes made by this notice of proposed rulemaking require little, if any, additional time for compliance by institutions currently subject to reporting requirements. The collection of information in this regulation implements the statute and should not require eligible educational institutions to collect information that is not already maintained by the institution. Eligible educational institutions have been subject to information reporting under section 6050S since 1998, and the obligations under the existing final regulations that are the foundation for these proposed regulations are already in place. Any additional information returns required to be filed under this notice of proposed rulemaking should result in few, if any, new eligible educational institutions being subject to reporting that were not already required to file Forms 1098-T. Only eligible educational institutions, not all educational institutions, are subject to these reporting rules. For this purpose, an eligible educational institution means an institution described in section 481 of the Higher Education Act of 1965 (20 U.S.C. 1088) as in effect on the date of enactment (August 5, 1997), and which is eligible to participate in a program under title IV of such act (generally colleges and universities whose students are eligible to receive federal financial aid for higher education). See sections 25A(f)(2) and 6050S(e). Further, this notice of proposed rulemaking contains modifications that should simplify compliance and thereby reduce the time needed to comply with the information reporting obligations under section 6050S. Therefore, a Regulatory Flexibility Analysis under the Regulatory Flexibility Act is not required. Pursuant to section 7805(f) of the Code, this proposed regulation has been submitted to the Chief Counsel for Advocacy of the Small Business Administration for comment on its impact on small businesses. The Internal Revenue Service invites the public to comment on this certification.

Comments and Requests for a Public Hearing

Before these proposed regulations are adopted as final regulations, consideration will be given to any comments that are submitted timely to the IRS as prescribed in this preamble under the "DATES" and "ADDRESSES" headings. The Treasury Department and the IRS request comments on all aspects of the proposed rules. All comments will be available at www.regulations.gov or upon request.

A public hearing has been scheduled for November 30, 2016 at 10:00 a.m. in the IRS Auditorium, Internal Revenue Service Building, 1111 Constitution Avenue, NW, Washington, DC 20224. Due to building security procedures, visitors must enter at the Constitution Avenue entrance. In addition, all visitors must present photo identification to enter the building. Because of access restrictions, visitors will not be admitted beyond the immediate entrance area more than 30 minutes before the hearing starts. For information about having your name placed onto the building access list to attend the hearing, see the "FOR FURTHER INFORMATION CONTACT" section of this preamble.

The rules of 26 CFR 601.601(a)(3) apply to the hearing. Persons who wish to present oral comments at the hearing must submit written or electronic comments by November 1, 2016 and an outline of the topics to be discussed and the time to be devoted to each topic (a signed original and eight (8) copies) by November 1, 2016. A period of 10 minutes will be allotted to each person for making comments. An agenda showing the scheduling of speakers will be prepared after the deadline for receiving outlines has passed. Copies of the agenda will be available free of charge at the hearing.

Drafting Information

The principal author of these proposed regulations is Gerald Semasek of the Office of Associate Chief Counsel (Procedure and Administration) for the proposed regulations under section 6050S and section 6724 and Sheldon Iskow of the Office of Associate Chief Counsel (Income Tax and Accounting) for the proposed regulations under section 25A.

[¶ 49,713]   Proposed Amendments of Regulations (REG-123600-16), published in the Federal Register on September 28, 2016.

[Code Sec. 851]

Regulated investment company: Income test: Asset diversification requirements.—Amendments of Reg. §1.851-2, relating to the income test and the asset diversification requirements that are used to determine whether a corporation may qualify as a regulated investment company (RIC) for federal income tax purposes, is proposed. The text is at ¶ 26,402B.

AGENCY: Internal Revenue Service (IRS), Treasury.

ACTION: Notice of proposed rulemaking.

SUMMARY: This document provides guidance relating to the income test and the asset diversification requirements that are used to determine whether a corporation may qualify as a regulated investment company (RIC) for federal income tax purposes. These proposed regulations provide guidance to corporations that intend to qualify as RICs.

DATES: Written or electronic comments and requests for a public hearing must be received by December 27, 2016.

ADDRESSES: Send submissions to: CC:PA:LPD:PR (REG-123600-16), room 5203, Internal Revenue Service, PO Box 7604, Ben Franklin Station, Washington, DC 20044. Submissions may be hand delivered Monday through Friday between the hours of 8 am and 4 pm to: CC:PA:LPD:PR (REG-123600-16), Courier's Desk, Internal Revenue Service, 1111 Constitution Avenue, NW, Washington, DC 20224, or sent electronically via the Federal eRulemaking Portal at *www.regulations.gov* (IRS REG-123600-16).

FOR FURTHER INFORMATION CONTACT: Concerning the proposed regulations, Matthew Howard of the Office of Associate Chief Counsel (Financial Institutions and Products) at (202) 317-7053; concerning submissions of comments and requests for a public hearing, Regina Johnson (202) 317-6901 (not toll-free numbers).

SUPPLEMENTARY INFORMATION:

Background and Explanation of Provisions

This document contains amendments to the Income Tax Regulations (26 CFR part 1) relating to RICs. Section 851 of the Internal Revenue Code (Code) sets forth requirements for qualifying as a RIC.

Section 851(a) provides that a RIC is any domestic corporation that (1) at all times during the taxable year is registered under the Investment Company Act of 1940, Pub. L. No. 76-768, 54 Stat. 789 (codified as amended at 15 U.S.C. 80a-1 – 80a-64 (2016)) (the 1940 Act), as a management company or unit investment trust or has in effect an election under the 1940 Act to be treated as a business development company; or (2) is a common trust fund or other similar fund excluded by section 3(c)(3) of the 1940 Act from the definition of "investment company" and is not included in the definition of "common trust fund" by section 584(a).

To be treated as a RIC for a taxable year, a corporation must satisfy the income test set forth in section 851(b). The income test under section 851(b)(2) requires that at least 90 percent of the corporation's gross income for the taxable year be derived from:

(A) dividends, interest, payments with respect to securities loans (as defined in section 512(a)(5)), and gains from the sale or other disposition of stock or securities (as defined in section 2(a)(36) of the [1940 Act]) or foreign currencies, or other income (including but not limited to gains from options, futures or forward contracts) derived with respect to its business of investing in such stock, securities, or currencies, and

(B) net income derived from an interest in a qualified publicly traded partnership (as defined in [section 851(h)]).

Section 851(b)(3) provides that to be treated as a RIC a corporation also must satisfy the following asset diversification requirements at the close of each quarter of the corporation's taxable year:

(A) at least 50 percent of the value of its total assets is represented by—

(i) cash and cash items (including receivables), Government securities and securities of other [RICs], and

(ii) other securities for purposes of this calculation limited, except and to the extent provided in [section 851(e)], in respect of any one issuer to an amount not greater in value than 5 percent of the value of the total assets of the taxpayer and to not more than 10 percent of the outstanding voting securities of such issuer, and

(B) not more than 25 percent of the value of its total assets is invested in—

(i) the securities (other than Government securities or the securities of other [RICs]) of any one issuer,

(ii) the securities (other than the securities of other [RICs]) of two or more issuers which the taxpayer controls and which are determined, under regulations prescribed by the Secretary, to be engaged in the same or similar trades or businesses or related trades or businesses, or

(iii) the securities of one or more qualified publicly traded partnerships (as defined in [section 851(h)]).

These proposed regulations relate to the RIC income test and asset diversification requirements. Section A. of this preamble concerns the meaning of security. Section B. of this preamble addresses inclusions under sections 951(a)(1)(A)(i) and 1293(a). These proposed regulations also revise § 1.851-2(b)(1) of the existing final regulations to merely incorporate changes to section 851(b)(2) since the existing final regulations were published in the **Federal Register** on November 26, 1960, in TD 6500 (25 FR 11910).

A. *Defining Securities*

The income test and asset diversification requirements both use the term "securities." For purposes of the income test, a security is defined by reference to section 2(a)(36) of the 1940 Act, while section 851(c) provides rules and definitions that apply for purposes of the asset diversification requirements of section 851(b)(3) but does not specifically define "security." Section 851(c)(6), however, provides that the terms used in section 851(b)(3) and (c) have the same meaning as when used in the 1940 Act. An asset is therefore a security for purposes of the income test and the asset diversification requirements if it is a security under the 1940 Act.

The Treasury Department and the IRS have in the past addressed whether certain instruments or positions are securities for purposes of section 851. In particular, Rev. Rul. 2006-1 (2006-1 CB 261) concludes that a derivative contract with respect to a commodity index is not a security for purposes of section 851(b)(2). The ruling also holds that income from such a contract is not qualifying other income for purposes of section 851(b)(2) because that income is not derived with respect to the RIC's business of investing in stocks, securities, or currencies. Rev. Rul. 2006-1 was modified and clarified by Rev. Rul. 2006-31 (2006-1 CB 1133), which states that Rev. Rul. 2006-1 was not intended to preclude a conclusion that income from certain instruments (such as certain structured notes) that create commodity exposure for the holder is qualifying income under section 851(b)(2).

After the issuance of Rev. Rul. 2006-31, the IRS received a number of private letter ruling requests concerning whether certain instruments that provide RICs with commodity exposure were securities for purposes of the income test and the asset diversification requirements. By 2010, the IRS was devoting substantial resources to these private letter ruling requests. Moreover, it is not clear whether Congress intended to allow RICs to invest in securities that provided commodity exposure. Consequently, in July 2011, the IRS notified taxpayers that the IRS would not issue further private letter rulings addressing specific proposed RIC commodity-related investments while the IRS reviewed the issues and considered guidance of broader applicability.

Finally, determining whether certain investments that provide RICs with commodity exposure are securities for purposes of the income test and the asset diversification requirements requires the IRS implicitly to determine what is a security within the meaning of section 2(a)(36) of the 1940 Act. Section 38 of the 1940 Act, however, grants exclusive rulemaking authority under the 1940 Act to the Securities and Exchange Commission (SEC), including "defining accounting, technical, and trade terms" used in the 1940 Act. Any future guidance regarding whether particular financial instruments, including investments that provide RICs with commodity exposure, are securities for purposes of the 1940 Act is therefore within the jurisdiction of the SEC.

Section 2.01 of Rev. Proc. 2016-3 (2016-1 IRB 126) provides that the IRS may decline to issue a letter ruling or a determination letter when appropriate in the interest of sound tax administration (including due to resource constraints) or on other grounds whenever warranted by the facts or circumstances of a particular case. If the IRS determines that it is not in the interest of sound tax administration to issue a letter ruling or determination letter due to resource constraints, the IRS will adopt a consistent approach with respect to taxpayers that request a ruling on the same issue. The IRS will also consider adding the issue to the no rule list at the first opportunity.

The Treasury Department and the IRS have reviewed the issues, considered the concerns expressed, considered resource constraints, and determined that the IRS should no longer issue letter rulings on questions relating to the treatment of a corporation as a RIC that require a determination of whether a financial instrument or position is a security under the 1940 Act. Contemporaneously with the publication of these proposed regulations, the Treasury Department and the IRS are issuing Rev. Proc. 2016-50 (2016-43 IRB __), which provides that the IRS ordinarily will not issue rulings or determination letters on any issue relating to the treatment of a corporation as a RIC that requires a determination of whether a financial instrument or position is a security under the 1940 Act. Thus, for example, the IRS ordinarily will not issue a ruling on whether income is of a type described in the income test of section 851(b)(2) if that ruling depends on whether an instrument is a security under the 1940 Act.

The Treasury Department and the IRS request comments as to whether Rev. Rul. 2006-1, Rev. Rul. 2006-31, and other previously issued guidance that involves determinations of whether a financial instrument or position held by a RIC is a security under the 1940 Act should be withdrawn effective as of the date of publication in the **Federal Register** of a Treasury decision adopting these proposed regulations as final regulations.

B. *Inclusions Under Section 951(a)(1)(A)(i) or 1293(a)*

In certain circumstances, a U.S. person may be required under section 951(a)(1)(A)(i) or 1293(a) to include in taxable income certain earnings of a foreign corporation in which the U.S. person holds an interest, without regard to whether the foreign corporation makes a corresponding distribution of cash or property to the U.S. person. Section 851(b) was amended by the Tax Reduction Act of 1975, Pub. L. No. 94-12, section 602, 89 Stat. 26, 58 (the "1975 Act") (for inclusions under section 951(a)(1)(A)(i)), and by the Tax Reform Act of 1986, Pub. L. No. 99-514, section 1235, 100 Stat. 2085, 2575 (the "1986 Act") (for inclusions under section 1293(a)), to specify how a RIC treats amounts included in income under section 951(a)(1)(A)(i) or 1293(a) for purposes of the income test of section 851(b)(2). The language added in those amendments provides:

For purposes of [section 851(b)(2)], there shall be treated as dividends amounts included in gross income under section 951(a)(1)(A)(i) or 1293(a) for the taxable year to the extent that, under section 959(a)(1) or 1293(c) (as the case may be), there is a distribution out of the earnings and profits of the taxable year which are attributable to the amounts so included.

The significance of treating an inclusion as a dividend under section 851 is that a dividend is qualifying income under section 851(b)(2). The amendments to section 851(b) made by the 1975 Act and the 1986 Act unambiguously condition dividend treatment of an inclusion under section 951(a)(1)(A)(i) or 1293(a) on a distribution from the foreign corporation's earnings and profits attributable to the amount included. Absent a distribution, there is no support in the Code for treating an inclusion under section 951(a)(1)(A)(i) or 1293(a) as a dividend under section 851.

Notwithstanding the distribution required by section 851(b), in certain circumstances the IRS has previously issued letter rulings under section 851(b)(2) that permit an inclusion under section 951(a)(1)(A)(i) or 1293(a) to qualify as "other income" derived with respect to a RIC's business of investing in currencies or 1940 Act stock or securities even in the absence of a distribution. Reading section 851(b)(2) in this manner ignores the requirement in section 851(b) that amounts be distributed in order to treat these inclusions as dividends. This distribution requirement is a more specific provision than the other income clause. In addition, it cannot be suggested that the distribution requirement was superseded by the other income clause because the other income clause and the distribution requirement for inclusions under section 1293(a) were both added by the 1986 Act. Therefore, these proposed regulations specify that an inclusion under section 951(a)(1)(A)(i) or 1293(a) is treated as a dividend for purposes of section 851(b)(2) only to the extent that the distribution requirement in section 851(b) is met. These proposed regulations further provide that, for purposes of section 851(b)(2), an inclusion under section 951(a)(1) or 1293(a) does not qualify as other income derived with respect to a RIC's business of investing in stock, securities, or currencies.

Proposed Effective/Applicability Date

The rule in §1.851-2(b)(2)(iii) of the proposed regulations applies to taxable years that begin on or after the date that is 90 days after the date of publication in the **Federal Register** of a Treasury decision adopting these proposed regulations as final regulations.

Special Analyses

Certain IRS regulations, including this one, are exempt from the requirements of Executive Order 12866, as supplemented and reaffirmed by Executive Order 13563. Therefore, a regulatory impact assessment is not required. It also has been determined that section 553(b) of the Administrative Procedure Act (5 U.S.C. chapter 5) does not apply to these regulations, and because the regulations do not impose a collection of information on small entities, the Regulatory Flexibility Act (5 U.S.C. chapter 6) does not apply. Pursuant to section 7805(f) of the Internal Revenue Code, this notice of proposed rulemaking will be submitted to the Chief Counsel for Advocacy of the Small Business Administration for comment on its impact on small business.

Comments and Requests for a Public Hearing

Before these proposed regulations are adopted as final regulations, consideration will be given to any comments that are submitted timely to the IRS as prescribed in this preamble under the "Addresses" heading. The Treasury Department and the IRS specifically request comments on the clarity of the proposed regulations and how they can be made easier to understand. All comments will be made available for public inspection at www.regulations.gov or upon request. A public hearing will be scheduled if requested in writing by any person that timely submits written comments. If a public hearing is scheduled, notice of the date, time, and place for the public hearing will be published in the **Federal Register**.

Drafting Information

The principal author of these proposed regulations is Matthew Howard, Office of Associate Chief Council (Financial Institutions and Products). However, other personnel from the Treasury Department and the IRS participated in their development.

Statement of Availability of IRS Documents

The IRS revenue rulings and revenue procedure cited in this preamble are published in the Internal Revenue Bulletin (or Cumulative Bulletin) and are available from the Superintendent of Documents, U.S. Government Publishing Office, Washington, DC 20402, or by visiting the IRS website at www.irs.gov.

[¶ 49,715]   Proposed Amendments of Regulations (REG-108934-16), published in the Federal Register on October 13, 2016.

[Code Sec. 7122]

Offers in compromise: User fee: Fee increase.—Amendments of Reg. §300.3, affecting taxpayers who wish to pay their liabilities through offers in compromise, is adopted.

[¶ 49,716]   Proposed Amendments of Regulations (REG-150992-13), published in the Federal Register on October 14, 2016.

[Code Sec. 165]

Disaster loss: Disaster loss election: Prior year election: Federally declared disaster area.—Amendments of Reg. §1.165-11, relating to the election to take a disaster loss in the preceding year, are proposed.

AGENCY: Internal Revenue Service (IRS), Treasury.

ACTION: Notice of Proposed Rulemaking by cross-reference to temporary regulations.

SUMMARY: In the Rules and Regulations section of this issue of the **Federal Register**, the IRS is issuing temporary regulations under section 165(i) of the Internal Revenue Code (Code) relating to the election to take a disaster loss in the preceding year. The text of those temporary regulations also serves as the text of these proposed regulations. This document also invites comments from the public regarding these proposed regulations.

DATES: Written or electronic comments and requests for a public hearing must be received by January 12, 2017.

ADDRESSES: Send submissions to CC:PA:LPD:PR (REG-150992-13), room 5203, Internal Revenue Service, POB 7604, Ben Franklin Station, Washington, DC 20044. Submissions may be hand-delivered Monday through Friday between the hours of 8 a.m. and 4 p.m. to: CC:PA:LPD:PR (REG-150992-13), Courier's Desk, Internal Revenue Service, 1111 Constitution Avenue, NW, Washington, DC, or sent electronically via the Federal eRulemaking Portal at www.regulations.gov (IRS REG-150992-13).

FOR FURTHER INFORMATION CONTACT: Concerning the proposed regulations, Daniel Cassano at (202) 317-7011; concerning comments or a request for a public hearing, Oluwafunmilayo Taylor (202) 317-6901 (not toll-free numbers).

SUPPLEMENTARY INFORMATION:

Background and Explanation of Provisions

Final and temporary regulations in the Rules and Regulations section of this issue of the **Federal Register** amend the Income Tax Regulations (26 CFR part 1) relating to section 165(i) of the Code. The temporary regulations extend the due date by which a taxpayer may elect to treat an allowable loss occurring in a disaster area and attributable to a Federally declared disaster as sustained in the taxable year immediately prior to the taxable year in which the disaster occurred, as provided in section 165(i). The temporary regulations provide rules governing the time and manner of making a section 165(i) election, as well as the time and manner of revoking a section 165(i) election. The text of those temporary regulations also serves as the text of these proposed regulations. The preamble to the temporary regulations explains the amendments.

Special Analyses

Certain IRS regulations, including these, are exempt from the requirements of Executive Order 12866, as supplemented and reaffirmed by Executive Order 13563. Therefore, a regulatory assessment is not required. It also has been determined that section 553(b) of the Administrative Procedure Act (5 U.S.C. chapter 5) does not apply to these regulations, and because the regulation does not impose a collection of information on small entities, the Regulatory Flexibility Act (5 U.S.C. chapter 6) does not apply. Pursuant to section 7805(f) of the Internal Revenue Code, this notice of proposed rulemaking will be submitted to the Chief Counsel for Advocacy of the Small Business Administration for comment on its impact on small business.

Comments and Requests for a Public Hearing

Before these proposed regulations are adopted as final regulations, consideration will be given to any written comments (a signed original and eight (8) copies) or electronic comments that are submitted timely to the IRS. The Department of the Treasury and the IRS request comments concerning the extension of the due date by which a taxpayer may make a section 165(i) election, as well as the time and manner in which a taxpayer may revoke a section 165(i) election. All comments will be available for public inspection and copying.

A public hearing will be scheduled if requested in writing by any person who timely submits comments. If a public hearing is scheduled, notice of the date, time, and place for the public hearing will be published in the **Federal Register**.

Drafting Information

The principal authors of these regulations are Daniel Cassano and Christopher Wrobel of the Office of the Associate Chief Counsel (Income Tax & Accounting). However, other personnel from the Department of the Treasury and the IRS participated in their development.

[¶ 49,717] Proposed Amendments of Regulations (REG-130314-16), published in the Federal Register on October 21, 2016.

[Code Secs. 385 and 752]

Corporations: Multinational corporations: Related-party transactions: Indebtedness: Equity.—Reg. §1.385-4 and amendments of Reg. §§1.385-3, and 1.752-2 affecting corporations and partnerships that issue purported indebtedness to related corporations or partnerships in the Rules and Regulations section of this issue of the Federal Register, are proposed.

AGENCY: Internal Revenue Service (IRS), Treasury.

ACTION: Notice of proposed rulemaking by cross-reference to temporary regulation.

SUMMARY: The Department of the Treasury (Treasury Department) and the IRS are issuing temporary regulations that affect corporations and partnerships that issue purported indebtedness to related corporations or partnerships in the Rules and Regulations section of this issue of the **Federal Register**. The temporary regulations provide rules addressing the treatment of instruments issued by partnerships, consolidated groups, and certain transactions involving qualified cash-management arrangements. The text of the temporary regulations also serves as the text of these proposed regulations.

DATES: Written or electronic comments and requests for a public hearing must be received by January 19, 2017.

ADDRESSES: Send submissions to: CC:PA:LPD:PR (REG-130314-16), room 5203, Internal Revenue Service, P.O. Box 7604, Ben Franklin Station, Washington, DC 20224. Submissions may be hand-delivered Monday through Friday between the hours of 8 a.m. and 4 p.m. to CC:PA:LPD:PR (REG-130314-16), Courier's Desk, Internal Revenue Service, 1111 Constitution Avenue NW, Washington, DC 20224, or sent electronically via the Federal eRulemaking Portal at *http://www.regulations.gov* (IRS REG-130314-16).

FOR FURTHER INFORMATION CONTACT: Concerning the proposed regulations, Austin M. Diamond-Jones, (202) 317-5363, or Joshua G. Rabon, (202) 317-6937; concerning submissions of comments or requests for a public hearing, Regina Johnson, (202) 317-5177 (not toll-free numbers).

SUPPLEMENTARY INFORMATION:

Background

The temporary regulations in the Rules and Regulations section of this issue of the **Federal Register** contain rules under sections 385 and 752 of the Internal Revenue Code (Code) that establish requirements that ordinarily must be satisfied in order for certain related-party interests in a corporation to be treated as indebtedness for federal tax purposes. The text of the temporary regulations also serves as the text of the proposed regulations herein. The preamble to the temporary regulations explains the temporary regulations and the corresponding proposed regulations.

Special Analyses

I. *Regulatory Planning and Review*

Executive Orders 13563 and 12866 direct agencies to assess costs and benefits of available regulatory alternatives and, if regulation is necessary, to select regulatory approaches that maximize net benefits (including potential economic, environmental, public health and safety effects, distributive impacts, and equity). Executive Order 13563 emphasizes the importance of quantifying both costs and benefits, of reducing costs, of harmonizing rules, and of promoting flexibility. Related rules in the final and temporary regulations under section 385 in TD 9790, published in the Rules and Regulations section of this issue of the **Federal Register**, have been designated a "significant regulatory action" under section 3(f) of Executive Order 12866. For a discussion of the economic impact of those final and temporary regulations, as well as these proposed regulations, please see the Regulatory Assessment accompanying TD 9790, published in the Rules and Regulations section of this issue of the **Federal Register**.

II. *Regulatory Flexibility Act*

Pursuant to the Regulatory Flexibility Act (5 U.S.C. Chapter 6), it is hereby certified that the final and temporary regulations in TD 9790, published in the Rules and Regulations section of this issue of the **Federal Register**, and accordingly, these proposed regulations proposed by cross-reference to the temporary regulations, will not have a significant economic impact on a substantial number of small entities. Accordingly, a regulatory flexibility analysis is not required.

To facilitate the federal tax analysis of an interest in a corporation, taxpayers are required under existing law to substantiate their classification of an interest as stock or indebtedness for federal tax purposes. Section 1.385-3 provides that certain interests in a corporation that are held by a member of the corporation's expanded group and that otherwise would be treated as indebtedness for federal tax purposes are treated as stock. Section 1.385-3T provides that for certain debt instruments issued by a controlled partnership, the holder is deemed to transfer all or a portion of the debt instrument to the partner or partners in the partnership in exchange for stock in the partner or partners. Section 1.385-4T provides rules regarding the application of §§ 1.385-3 and 1.385-3T to members of a consolidated group. Sections 1.385-3 and 1.385-3T include multiple exceptions that limit their application. In particular, the threshold exception provides that the first $50 million of expanded group debt instruments that otherwise would be reclassified as stock or deemed to be transferred to a partner in a controlled partnership under § 1.385-3 or § 1.385-3T will not be reclassified or deemed transferred under § 1.385-3 or § 1.385-3T. Although it is possible that the classification rules in §§ 1.385-3, 1.385-3T, and 1.385-4T could have an effect on small entities, the threshold exception of the first $50 million of debt instruments otherwise subject to recharacterization or deemed transfer under §§ 1.385-3, 1.385-3T, and 1.385-4T makes it unlikely that a substantial number of small entities will be affected by §§ 1.385-3T or 1.385-4T.

Pursuant to section 7805(f) of the Code, the final regulations in TD 9790, published in the Rules and Regulations section of this issue of the **Federal Register**, have been submitted to the Chief Counsel for Advocacy of the Small Business Administration for comment on their impact on small business. Comments were received requesting that the monetary thresholds contained in proposed §§ 1.385-2, 1.385-3, and 1.385-4 be increased in order to mitigate the impact on small businesses. These comments are addressed in Parts IV.B.1.d and V.E.4 of the Summary of Comments and Explanation of Revisions in the preamble of TD 9790, published in the Rules and Regulations section of this issue of the **Federal Register**. No comments were received concerning the economic impact on small entities from the Small Business Administration.

Comments and Requests for Public Hearing

Before these proposed regulations are adopted as final regulations, consideration will be given to any comments that are submitted timely to the IRS as prescribed in this preamble under the "Addresses" heading. Treasury and the IRS request comments on all aspects of the proposed rules. All comments will be available at *www.regulations.gov* or upon request. A public hearing will be scheduled if requested in writing by any person that timely submits electronic or written comments. If a public hearing is scheduled, notice of the date, time, and place for the public hearing will be published in the **Federal Register**.

Drafting Information

The principal authors of these regulations are Austin M. Diamond-Jones of the Office of Associate Chief Counsel (Corporate) and Joshua G. Rabon of the Office of Associate Chief Counsel (International). However, other personnel from the Treasury Department and the IRS participated in their development.

[¶ 49,720] **Proposed Amendments of Regulations (REG-114734-16)**, published in the Federal Register on November 3, 2016 (corrected 12/28/2016).

[Code Sec. 956]

Controlled foreign corporation: U.S. property: CFC property held through partnership: Earnings invested in U.S. property.—Amendments of Reg. § 1.956-4, regarding the determination of the amount of United States property treated as held by a controlled foreign corporation (CFC) through a partnership, are proposed.

AGENCY: Internal Revenue Service (IRS), Treasury.

ACTION: Notice of proposed rulemaking.

SUMMARY: This document contains proposed regulations that provide rules regarding the determination of the amount of United States property treated as held by a controlled foreign corporation (CFC) through a partnership. The proposed regulations affect United States shareholders of CFCs.

DATES: Written or electronic comments and requests for a public hearing must be received by February 1, 2017.

ADDRESSES: Send submissions to: CC:PA:LPD:PR (REG-114734-16), room 5203, Internal Revenue Service, P.O. Box 7604, Ben Franklin Station, Washington, DC 20044. Submissions may be hand-delivered Monday through Friday between the hours of 8 a.m. and 4 p.m. to CC:PA:LPD:PR (REG-114734-16), Courier's Desk, Internal Revenue Service, 1111 Constitution Avenue NW, Washington, DC, or sent electronically via the Federal eRulemaking Portal at *http://www.regulations.gov* (IRS REG-114734-16).

FOR FURTHER INFORMATION CONTACT: Concerning the proposed regulations, Rose E. Jenkins, (202) 317-6934; concerning submissions of comments or requests for a public hearing, Regina Johnson, (202) 317-6901 (not toll-free numbers). SUPPLEMENTARY INFORMATION:

Background

In the Rules and Regulations section of this issue of the **Federal Register**, the Department of Treasury (Treasury Department) and the IRS are issuing final regulations that amend the Income Tax Regulations (26 CFR part 1) relating to sections 954 and 956. Under § 1.956-4(b), a CFC that is a partner in a partnership determines its share of United States property held by the partnership in accordance with the CFC's liquidation value percentage in the partnership, or, when relevant, based on a special allocation of income (or, where appropriate, gain) from the property. This document proposes to amend § 1.956-4(b) so that a CFC that is a partner in a controlled partnership determines its share of United States property held by the partnership under the liquidation value percentage method, regardless of the existence of any special allocation of income or gain from the property.

Explanation of Provisions

Section 956 determines the amount that a United States shareholder (as defined in section 951(b)) of a CFC must include in gross income with respect to the CFC under section 951(a)(1)(B). This amount is determined, in part, based on the average of the amounts of United States property held, directly or indirectly, by the CFC at the close of each quarter during its taxable year. For this purpose, in general, the amount taken into account with respect to any United States property is the adjusted basis of the property, reduced by any liability to which the property is subject. See section 956(a) and § 1.956-1(e). Section 956(e) grants the Secretary authority to prescribe such regulations as may be necessary to carry out the purposes of section 956, including regulations to prevent the avoidance of section 956 through reorganizations or otherwise.

Under § 1.956-4(b), a CFC that is a partner in a partnership generally is treated as holding its share of United States property held by the partnership in accordance with the CFC partner's liquidation value percentage in the partnership. However, if there is a special allocation of income (or, where appropriate, gain) from United States property that is respected for Federal income tax purposes under section 704(b) and the regulations thereunder and does not have a principal purpose of avoiding the purposes of section 956, the partner's attributable share of that property is determined solely by reference to the special allocation. See §1.956-4(b)(2)(ii). The Treasury Department and the IRS have concluded that, in general, these rules provide a reasonable means of determining a partner's interest in property held by a partnership for purposes of section 956 because they generally result in an allocation of specific items of property that corresponds with each partner's economic interest in that property, including any income or gain that may be subject to special allocations.

The Treasury Department and the IRS are concerned, however, that special allocations with respect to a partnership that is controlled by a single multinational group are unlikely to have economic significance for the group as a whole and can facilitate tax planning that is inconsistent with the purposes of section 956. Accordingly, these proposed regulations propose to revise §1.956-4(b) such that a partner's attributable share of each item of property of a partnership controlled by the partner would be determined solely in accordance with the partner's liquidation value percentage, even if income or gain from the property is subject to a special allocation. Specifically, under proposed §1.956-4(b)(2)(iii), the rule in §1.956-4(b)(2)(ii) requiring a partner's attributable share of partnership property to be determined by reference to special allocations with respect to the property would not apply in the case of a partnership controlled by the partner. For this purpose, a partner is treated as controlling a partnership if the partner and the partnership are related within the meaning of section 267(b) or section 707(b), substituting "at least 80 percent" for "more than 50 percent". The examples in §1.956-4(b)(3) are proposed to be modified in accordance with the proposed rule.

These proposed regulations are proposed to be effective for taxable years of CFCs ending on or after the date of publication in the **Federal Register** of the Treasury decision adopting them as final regulations, and taxable years of United States shareholders in which or with which such taxable years end, with respect to property acquired on or after the date of publication in the **Federal Register** of the Treasury decision adopting them as final regulations. The IRS may, where appropriate, challenge transactions under currently applicable Code or regulatory provisions or judicial doctrines.

Special Analyses

Certain IRS regulations, including these regulations, are exempt from the requirements of Executive Order 12866, as supplemented and reaffirmed by Executive Order 13563. Therefore, a regulatory assessment is not required. It has also been determined that section 553(b) of the Administrative Procedure Act (5 U.S.C. Chapter 5) does not apply to these regulations, and because the regulations do not impose a collection of information on small entities, the Regulatory Flexibility Act (5 U.S.C. chapter 6) does not apply. Pursuant to section 7805(f), this notice of proposed rulemaking has been submitted to the Chief Counsel of Advocacy of the Small Business Administration for comment on its impact on small business.

Comments and Requests for Public Hearing

Before these proposed regulations are adopted as final regulations, consideration will be given to any comments that are submitted timely to the IRS as prescribed in this preamble under the "Addresses" heading. The Treasury Department and the IRS request comments on all aspects of the proposed rules. All comments will be available at *www.regulations.gov* or upon request. A public hearing will be scheduled if requested in writing by any person that timely submits electronic or written comments. If a public hearing is scheduled, notice of the date, time, and place for the public hearing will be published in the **Federal Register**.

Drafting Information

The principal author of these proposed regulations is Rose E. Jenkins of the Office of Associate Chief Counsel (International). However, other personnel from the Treasury Department and the IRS participated in their development.

[¶49,721]   **Proposed Amendments of Regulations (REG-136978-12)**, published in the Federal Register on November 23, 2016.

[Code Sec. 514]

Debt financed income, unrelated: Real estate investments: Qualified organizations.—Amendments of Reg. §1.514(c)-2, relating to the application of section 514(c)(9)(E) of the Internal Revenue Code (Code) to partnerships that hold debt-financed real property and have one or more (but not all) qualified tax-exempt organization partners within the meaning of section 514(c)(9)(C), are proposed.

AGENCY: Internal Revenue Service (IRS), Treasury.

ACTION: Notice of proposed rulemaking.

SUMMARY: This document contains proposed regulations relating to the application of section 514(c)(9)(E) of the Internal Revenue Code (Code) to partnerships that hold debt-financed real property and have one or more (but not all) qualified tax-exempt organization partners within the meaning of section 514(c)(9)(C). The proposed regulations amend the current regulations under section 514(c)(9)(E) to allow certain allocations resulting from specified common business practices to comply with the rules under section 514(c)(9)(E). These regulations affect partnerships with qualified tax-exempt organization partners and their partners.

DATES: Written and electronic comments and requests for a public hearing must be received by February 21, 2017.

ADDRESSES: Send submissions to: CC:PA:LPD:PR (REG-136978-12), room 5203, Internal Revenue Service, PO Box 7604, Ben Franklin Station, Washington, DC 20044. Submissions may be hand-delivered Monday through Friday between the hours of 8 a.m. and 4 p.m. to: CC:PA:LPD:PR (REG-136978-12), Courier's Desk, Internal Revenue Service, 1111 Constitution Avenue, N.W., Washington, DC, or sent electronically, via the Federal eRulemaking Portal site at *http://www.regulations.gov* (indicate IRS and REG-136978-12).

FOR FURTHER INFORMATION CONTACT: Concerning the proposed regulations, Caroline E. Hay at (202) 317-5279; concerning the submissions of comments and requests for a public hearing, Regina L. Johnson at (202) 317-6901 (not toll-free numbers).

SUPPLEMENTARY INFORMATION:

Background

This document proposes amendments to the Income Tax Regulations (26 CFR part 1) under section 514(c)(9)(E) regarding the application of the fractions rule (as defined in the Background section of this preamble) to partnerships that hold debt-financed real property and have one or more (but not all) qualified tax-exempt organization partners.

In general, section 511 imposes a tax on the unrelated business taxable income (UBTI) of tax-exempt organizations. Section 514(a) defines UBTI to include a specified percentage of the gross income derived from debt-financed property described in section 514(b). Section 514(c)(9)(A) generally excepts from UBTI income derived from debt-financed real property acquired or improved by certain qualified organizations (QOs) described in section 514(c)(9)(C). Under section 514(c)(9)(C), a QO includes an educational organization described in section 170(b)(1)(A)(ii) and its affiliated support organizations described in section 509(a)(3), any trust which constitutes a qualified trust under section 401, an organization described in section 501(c)(25), and a retirement income account described in section 403(b)(9).

Section 514(c)(9)(B)(vi) provides that the exception from UBTI in section 514(c)(9)(A) does not apply if a QO owns an interest in a partnership that holds debt-financed real property (the partnership limitation), unless the partnership meets one of the following requirements: (1) all of the partners of the partnership are QOs, (2) each allocation to a QO is a qualified allocation (within the meaning of section 168(h)(6)), or (3) each partnership allocation has substantial economic effect under section 704(b)(2) and satisfies section 514(c)(9)(E)(i)(I) (the fractions rule).

A partnership allocation satisfies the fractions rule if the allocation of items to any partner that is a QO does not result in that partner having a share of overall partnership income for any taxable year greater than that partner's fractions rule percentage (the partner's share of overall partnership loss for the taxable year for which the partner's loss share is the smallest). Section 1.514(c)-2(c)(1) describes overall partnership income as the amount by which the aggregate items of partnership income and gain for the taxable year exceed the aggregate items of partnership loss and deduction for the year. Overall partnership loss is the amount by which the aggregate items of partnership loss and deduction for the taxable year exceed the aggregate items of partnership income and gain for the year.

Generally, under §1.514(c)-2(b)(2)(i), a partnership must satisfy the fractions rule both on a prospective basis and on an actual basis for each taxable year of the partnership, beginning with the first taxable year of the partnership in which the partnership holds debt-financed real property and has a QO partner. However, certain allocations are taken into account for purposes of determining overall partnership income or loss only when actually made, and do not create an immediate violation of the fractions rule. See §1.514(c)-2(b)(2)(i). Certain other allocations are disregarded for purposes of making fractions rule calculations. See, for example, §1.514(c)-2(d) (reasonable preferred returns and reasonable guaranteed payments), §1.514(c)-2(e) (certain chargebacks and offsets), §1.514(c)-2(f) (reasonable partner-specific items of deduction and loss), §1.514(c)-2(g) (unlikely losses and deductions), and §1.514(c)-2(k)(3) (certain de minimis allocations of losses and deductions). In addition, §1.514(c)-2(k)(1) provides that changes in partnership allocations that result from transfers or shifts of partnership interests (other than transfers from a QO to another QO) will be closely scrutinized, but generally will be taken into account only in determining whether the partnership satisfies the fractions rule in the taxable year of the change and subsequent taxable years. Section 1.514(c)-2(m) provides special rules for applying the fractions rule to tiered partnerships.

The Treasury Department and the IRS have received comments requesting targeted changes to the existing regulations under section 514(c)(9)(E) to allow certain allocations resulting from specified common business practices to comply with the rules under section 514(c)(9)(E). Section 514(c)(9)(E)(iii) grants the Secretary authority to prescribe regulations as may be necessary to carry out the purposes of section 514(c)(9)(E), including regulations that may provide for the exclusion or segregation of items. In response to comments and under the regulatory authority in section 514(c)(9)(E), these proposed regulations provide guidance in determining a partner's share of overall partnership income or loss for purposes of the fractions rule, including allowing allocations consistent with common arrangements involving preferred returns, partner-specific expenditures, unlikely losses, and chargebacks of partner-specific expenditures and unlikely losses. The proposed regulations also simplify one of the examples involving tiered partnerships and provide rules regarding changes to partnership allocations as a result of capital commitment defaults and later acquisitions of partnership interests. These proposed regulations except from applying the fractions rule certain partnerships in which all partners other than QOs own five percent or less of the capital or profits interests in the partnership. Finally, these proposed regulations increase the threshold for de minimis allocations away from QO partners.

Explanation of Provisions

1. Preferred Returns

Section 1.514(c)-2(d)(1) and (2) of the existing regulations disregard in computing overall partnership income for purposes of the fractions rule items of income (including gross income) and gain that may be allocated to a partner with respect to a current or cumulative reasonable preferred return for capital (including allocations of minimum gain attributable to nonrecourse liability (or partner nonrecourse debt) proceeds distributed to the partner as a reasonable preferred return) if that preferred return is set forth in a binding, written partnership agreement. Section 1.514(c)-2(d)(2) of the existing regulations also provides that if a partnership agreement provides for a reasonable preferred return with an allocation of what would otherwise be overall partnership income, items comprising that allocation are disregarded in computing overall partnership income for purposes of the fractions rule.

Section 1.514(c)-2(d)(6)(i) of the existing regulations limits the amount of income and gain allocated with respect to a preferred return that can be disregarded for purposes of the fractions rule to: (A) the aggregate of the amount that has been distributed to the partner as a reasonable preferred return for the taxable year of the allocation and prior taxable years, on or before the due date (not including extensions) for filing the partnership's return for the taxable year of the allocation; minus (B) the aggregate amount of corresponding income and gain (and what would otherwise be overall partnership income) allocated to the partner in all prior years. Thus, this rule requires a current distribution of preferred returns for the allocations of income with respect to those preferred returns to be disregarded.

The Treasury Department and the IRS have received comments requesting that the current distribution requirement be eliminated from the regulations because it interferes with normal market practice, creates unnecessary complication, and, in some cases, causes economic distortions for partnerships with QO partners. The preamble to the existing final regulations under section 514(c)(9)(E) responded to objections regarding the current distribution requirement by explaining that if the requirement were eliminated, partnerships might attempt to optimize their overall economics by allocating significant amounts of partnership income and gain to QOs in the form of preferred returns. The preamble explained that these allocations "would be a departure from the normal commercial practice followed by partnerships in which the money partners are generally subject to income tax." TD 8539, 59 FR 24924. A recent commenter explained that the vast majority of partnerships holding debt-financed real property (real estate partnerships) with preferred returns to investing partners (either the QO or the taxable partner) make allocations that match the preferred return as it accrues, without regard to whether cash has been distributed with respect to the preferred return. Instead of requiring distributions equal to the full amount of their preferred returns, taxable partners generally negotiate for tax distributions to pay any tax liabilities associated with their partnership interest.

The Treasury Department and the IRS have reconsidered the necessity of the current distribution requirement to prevent abuses of the fractions rule. So long as the preferred return is required to be distributed prior to other distributions (with an exception for certain distributions intended to facilitate the payment of taxes) and any undistributed amount compounds, the likelihood of abuse is minimized. Therefore, the proposed regulations remove the current distribution requirement and instead disregard allocations of items of income and gain with respect to a preferred return for purposes of the fractions rule, but only if the partnership agreement requires that the partnership make distributions first to pay any accrued, cumulative, and compounding unpaid preferred return to the extent such accrued but unpaid preferred return has not otherwise been reversed by an allocation of loss prior to such distribution (preferred return distribution requirement). The preferred return distribution requirement, however, is subject to an exception under the proposed regulations that allows distributions intended to facilitate partner payment of taxes imposed on the partner's allocable share of partnership income or gain, if the distributions are made pursuant to a provision in the partnership agreement, are treated as an advance against distributions to which the distributee partner would otherwise be entitled under the partnership agreement, and do not exceed the distributee partner's allocable share of net partnership income and gain multiplied by the sum of the highest statutory federal, state, and local tax rates applicable to that partner.

2. *Partner-Specific Expenditures and Management Fees*

Section 1.514(c)-2(f) of the existing regulations provides a list of certain partner-specific expenditures that are disregarded in computing overall partnership income or loss for purposes of the fractions rule. These expenditures include expenditures attributable to a partner for additional record-keeping and accounting costs including in connection with the transfer of a partnership interest, additional administrative costs from having a foreign partner, and state and local taxes. The Treasury Department and the IRS are aware that some real estate partnerships allow investing partners to negotiate for management and similar fees paid to the general partner that differ from fees paid with respect to investments by other partners. These fees include the general partner's fees for managing the partnership and may include fees paid in connection with the acquisition, disposition, or refinancing of an investment. Compliance with the fractions rule may preclude a real estate partnership with QO partners from allocating deductions attributable to these management expenses in a manner that follows the economic fee arrangement because the fractions rule limits the ability of the partnership to make disproportionate allocations.

The Treasury Department and the IRS have determined that real estate partnerships with QO partners should be permitted to allocate management and similar fees among partners to reflect the manner in which the partners agreed to bear the expense without causing a fractions rule violation. Accordingly, the proposed regulations add management (and similar) fees to the current list of excluded partner-specific expenditures in §1.514(c)-2(f) of the existing regulations to the extent such fees do not, in the aggregate, exceed two percent of the partner's aggregate committed capital.

It has been suggested to the Treasury Department and the IRS that similar partner-specific expenditure issues may arise under the new partnership audit rules in section 1101 of the Bipartisan Budget Act of 2015, Public Law No. 114-74 (the BBA), which was enacted into law on November 2, 2015. Section 1101 of the BBA repeals the current rules governing partnership audits and replaces them with a new centralized partnership audit regime that, in general, assesses and collects tax at the partnership level as an imputed underpayment. Some have suggested that the manner in which an imputed underpayment is borne by partners potentially could implicate similar concerns as special allocations of partner-specific items. As the Treasury Department and the IRS continue to consider how to implement the BBA, the Treasury Department and the IRS request comments regarding whether an imputed underpayment should be included among the list of partner-specific expenditures.

3. *Unlikely Losses*

Similar to §1.514(c)-2(f), §1.514(c)-2(g) of the existing regulations generally disregards specially allocated unlikely losses or deductions (other than items of nonrecourse deduction) in computing overall partnership income or loss for purposes of the fractions rule. To be disregarded under §1.514(c)-2(g), a loss or deduction must have a low likelihood of occurring, taking into account all relevant facts, circumstances, and information available to the partners (including bona fide financial projections). Section 1.514(c)-2(g) describes types of events that give rise to unlikely losses or deductions.

The Treasury Department and the IRS have received comments suggesting that a "more likely than not" standard is appropriate for determining when a loss or deduction is unlikely to occur. Notice 90-41 (1990-1 CB 350) (see §601.601(d)(2)(ii)(b)), which preceded the initial proposed regulations under section 514(c)(9)(E), outlined this standard. The commenter explained that the "low likelihood of occurring" standard in the existing regulations is vague and gives little comfort to QOs and their taxable partners when drafting allocations to reflect legitimate business arrangements (such as, drafting allocations to account for cost overruns). The Treasury Department and the IRS are considering changing the standard in §1.514(c)-2(g) and request further comments explaining why "more likely than not" is a more appropriate standard than the standard contained in the existing regulations, or whether another standard turning upon a level of risk that is between "more likely than not" and "low likelihood of occurring" might be more appropriate and what such other standard could be.

4. *Chargebacks of Partner-Specific Expenditures and Unlikely Losses*

Because allocations of partner-specific expenditures in §1.514(c)-2(f) and unlikely losses in §1.514(c)-2(g) are disregarded in computing overall partnership income or loss, allocations of items of income or gain or net income to reverse the prior partner-specific expenditure or unlikely loss could cause a violation of the fractions rule. For example, a QO may contribute capital to a partnership to pay a specific expenditure with the understanding that it will receive a special allocation of income to reverse the prior expenditure once the partnership earns certain profits. If the allocation of income is greater than the QO's fractions rule percentage, the allocation will cause a fractions rule violation.

Section 1.514(c)-2(e)(1) of the existing regulations generally disregards certain allocations of income or loss made to chargeback previous allocations of income or loss in computing overall partnership income or loss for purposes of the fractions rule. Specifically, §1.514(c)-2(e)(1)(i) disregards allocations of what would otherwise be overall partnership income that chargeback (that is, reverse) prior disproportionately large allocations of overall partnership loss (or part of the overall partnership loss) to a QO (the chargeback exception). The chargeback exception applies to a chargeback of an allocation of part of the overall partnership income or loss only if that part consists of a pro rata portion of each item of partnership income, gain, loss, and deduction (other than nonrecourse deductions, as well as partner nonrecourse deductions and compensating allocations) that is included in computing overall partnership income or loss.

The Treasury Department and the IRS understand that often a real estate partnership with QO partners may seek to reverse a special allocation of unlikely losses or partner-specific items with net profits of the partnership, which could result in allocations that would violate the fractions rule. Such allocations of net income to reverse special allocations of unlikely losses or partner-specific items that were disregarded in computing overall partnership income or loss for purposes of the fractions rule under §1.514(c)-2(f) or (g), respectively, do not violate the purpose of the fractions rule. Accordingly, the proposed regulations modify the chargeback exception to disregard in computing overall partnership income or loss for purposes of the fractions rule an allocation of what would otherwise have been an allocation of overall partnership income to chargeback (that is, reverse) a special allocation of a partner-specific expenditure under §1.514(c)-2(f) or a special allocation of an unlikely loss under §1.514(c)-2(g). Notwithstanding the rule in the proposed regulations, an allocation of an unlikely loss or a partner-specific expenditure that is disregarded when allocated, but is taken into account for purposes of determining the partners' economic entitlement to a chargeback of such loss or expense may, in certain circumstances, give rise to complexities in determining applicable percentages for purposes of fractions rule compliance. Accordingly, the Treasury Department and the IRS request comments regarding the interaction of disregarded partner-specific expenditures and unlikely losses with chargebacks of such items with overall partnership income.

5. *Acquisition of Partnership Interests after Initial Formation of Partnership*

Section 1.514(c)-2(k)(1) of the existing regulations provides special rules regarding changes in partnership allocations arising from a change in partners' interests. Specifically, §1.514(c)-2(k)(1) provides that changes in partnership allocations that result from transfers or shifts of partnership interests (other than transfers from a QO to another QO) will be closely scrutinized (to determine whether the transfer or shift stems from a prior agreement, understanding, or plan or could otherwise be expected given the structure of the transaction), but generally will be taken into account only in determining whether the partnership satisfies the fractions rule in the taxable year of the change and subsequent taxable years. Section 1.514(c)-2(k)(4) of the existing regulations provides that §1.514(c)-2 may not be applied in a manner inconsistent with the purpose of the fractions rule, which is to prevent tax avoidance by limiting the permanent or temporary transfer of tax benefits from tax-exempt partners to taxable partners.

The Treasury Department and the IRS have received comments requesting guidance in applying the fractions rule when additional partners are admitted to a partnership after the initial formation of the partnership. The commenter explained that many real estate partnerships with QO partners admit new partners in a number of rounds of closings, but treat the partners as having entered at the same time for purposes of sharing in profits and losses (staged closings). A number of commercial arrangements are used to effect staged closings. For example, the initial operations of the partnership may be funded entirely through debt financing, with all partners contributing their committed capital at a later date. Alternatively, later entering partners may contribute capital and an interest factor, some or both of which is then distributed to the earlier admitted partners to compensate them for the time value of their earlier contributions.

Under existing regulations, staged closings could cause violations of the fractions rule in two ways. First, when new partners are admitted to a partnership, shifts of partnership interests occur. Changes in allocations that result from shifts of partnership interests are closely scrutinized under § 1.514(c)-2(k)(1) of the existing regulations if pursuant to a prior agreement and could be determined to violate the fractions rule. Second, after admitting new partners, partnerships may disproportionately allocate income or loss to the partners to adjust the partners' capital accounts as a result of the staged closings. These disproportionate allocations could cause fractions rule violations if one of the partners is a QO.

The Treasury Department and the IRS have determined that changes in allocations and disproportionate allocations resulting from common commercial staged closings should not violate the fractions rule if they are not inconsistent with the purpose of the fractions rule under § 1.514(c)-2(k)(4) and certain conditions are satisfied. The conditions include the following: (A) the new partner acquires the partnership interest no later than 18 months following the formation of the partnership (applicable period); (B) the partnership agreement and other relevant documents anticipate the new partners acquiring the partnership interests during the applicable period, set forth the time frame in which the new partners will acquire the partnership interests, and provide for the amount of capital the partnership intends to raise; (C) the partnership agreement and any other relevant documents specifically set forth the method of determining any applicable interest factor and for allocating income, loss, or deduction to the partners to adjust partners' capital accounts after the new partner acquires the partnership interest; and (D) the interest rate for any applicable interest factor is not greater than 150 percent of the highest applicable Federal rate, at the appropriate compounding period or periods, at the time the partnership was formed.

Under the proposed regulations, if those conditions are satisfied, the IRS will not closely scrutinize changes in allocations resulting from staged closings under § 1.514(c)-2(k)(1) and will disregard in computing overall partnership income or loss for purposes of the fractions rule disproportionate allocations of income, loss, or deduction made to adjust the capital accounts when a new partner acquires its partnership interest after the partnership's formation.

6. Capital Commitment Defaults or Reductions

The Treasury Department and the IRS received comments requesting guidance with respect to calculations of overall partnership income and loss when allocations change as a result of capital commitment defaults or reductions. The commenter indicated that, in the typical real estate partnership, a limited partner generally will not contribute its entire investment upon being admitted as a partner. Rather, that limited partner will commit to contribute a certain dollar amount over a fixed period of time, and the general partner will then "call" on that committed, but uncontributed, capital as needed. These calls will be made in proportion to the partners' commitments to the partnership.

The commenter identified certain remedies that partnership agreements provide if a partner fails to contribute a portion (or all) of its committed capital. These remedies commonly include: (i) allowing the non-defaulting partner(s) to contribute additional capital in return for a preferred return on that additional capital; (ii) causing the defaulting partner to forfeit all or a portion of its interest in the partnership; (iii) forcing the defaulting partner to sell its interest in the partnership, or (iv) excluding the defaulting partner from making future capital contributions. Alternatively, the agreement may allow partners to reduce their commitment amounts, reducing allocations of income and loss as well. The commenter noted that, depending on the facts, any of these partnership agreement provisions could raise fractions rule concerns.

There is little guidance in the existing regulations regarding changes to allocations of a partner's share of income and losses from defaulted capital calls and reductions in capital commitments. Section 1.514(c)-2(k)(1) applies to changes in allocations resulting from a default if there is a "transfer or shift" of partnership interests. The Treasury Department and the IRS have determined that changes in allocations resulting from unanticipated defaults or reductions do not run afoul of the purpose of the fractions rule if such changes are provided for in the partnership agreement. Therefore, the proposed regulations provide that, if the partnership agreement provides for changes to allocations due to an unanticipated partner default on a capital contribution commitment or an unanticipated reduction in a partner's capital contribution commitment, and those changes in allocations are not inconsistent with the purpose of the fractions rule under § 1.514(c)-2(k)(4), then: (A) changes to partnership allocations provided in the agreement will not be closely scrutinized under § 1.514(c)-2(k)(1) and (B) partnership allocations of income, loss, or deduction (including allocations to adjust partners' capital accounts to be consistent with the partners' adjusted capital commitments) to partners to adjust the partners' capital accounts as a result of unanticipated capital contribution defaults or reductions will be disregarded in computing overall partnership income or loss for purposes of the fractions rule.

7. Applying the Fractions Rule to Tiered Partnerships

Section 1.514(c)-2(m)(1) of the existing regulations provides that if a QO holds an indirect interest in real property through one or more tiers of partnerships (a chain), the fractions rule is satisfied if: (i) the avoidance of tax is not a principal purpose for using the tiered-ownership structure; and (ii) the relevant partnerships can demonstrate under "any reasonable method" that the relevant chains satisfy the requirements of § 1.514(c)-2(b)(2) through (k). Section 1.514(c)-2(m)(2) of the existing regulations provides examples that illustrate three different "reasonable methods:" the collapsing approach, the entity-by-entity approach, and the independent chain approach.

The Treasury Department and the IRS have received comments requesting guidance with respect to tiered partnerships and the application of the independent chain approach. Under the independent chain approach in § 1.514(c)-2(m)(2) *Example 3* of the existing regulations, different lower-tiered partnership chains (one or more tiers of partnerships) are examined independently of each other, even if these lower-tiered partnerships are owned by a common upper-tier partnership. The example provides, however, that chains are examined independently only if the upper-tier partnership allocates the items of each lower-tier partnership separately from the items of another lower-tier partnership.

The comment noted that in practice, a real estate partnership generally invests in a significant number of properties, often through joint ventures with other partners. A typical real estate partnership will not make separate allocations to its partners of lower-tier partnership items. Accordingly, the proposed regulations amend § 1.514(c)-2(m)(2) *Example 3* to remove the requirement that a partnership allocate items from lower-tier partnerships separately from one another. Partnership provisions require that partnership items such as items that would give rise to UBTI be separately stated. *See* § 1.702-1(a)(8)(ii). That requirement suffices to separate the tiers of partnerships, and, thus, the proposed regulations do not require the upper-tier partnership to separately allocate partnership items from separate lower-tier partnerships. The proposed regulations also revise § 1.514(c)-2(m)(1)(ii) to remove the discussion of minimum gain chargebacks that refers to language that has been deleted from the example.

8. De Minimis Exceptions from Application of the Fractions Rule

Section 1.514(c)-2(k)(2) of the existing regulations provides that the partnership limitation in section 514(c)(9)(B)(vi) does not apply to a partnership if all QOs hold a de minimis interest in the partnership, defined as no more than five percent in the capital or profits of the partnership, and taxable partners own substantial interests in the partnership through which they participate in the partnership on substantially the same terms as the QO partners. If the partnership limitation in section 514(c)(9)(B)(vi) does not apply to the partnership, the fractions rule does not apply to the partnership. Because the fractions rule does not apply to a partnership if all QOs are de minimis interest holders in the partnership, the Treasury Department and the IRS considered whether the inverse fact pattern, in which all non-QO partners are de minimis partners, implicates the purpose of the fractions rule. *See* §1.514(c)-2(k)(4) (providing that the purpose of the fractions rule is to "prevent tax avoidance by limiting the permanent or temporary transfer of tax benefits from tax-exempt partners to taxable partners, whether by directing income or gain to tax-exempt partners, by directing losses, deductions or credits to taxable partners, or by some similar manner.").

The Treasury Department and the IRS have determined that the purpose of the fractions rule is similarly not violated if all non-QO partners hold a de minimis interest. Therefore, the proposed regulations provide that the fractions rule does not apply to a partnership in which non-QO partners do not hold (directly or indirectly through a partnership), in the aggregate, interests of greater than five percent in the capital or profits of the partnership, so long as the partnership's allocations have substantial economic effect. For purposes of the proposed rule, the determination of whether an allocation has substantial economic effect is made without application of the special rules in §1.704-1(b)(2)(iii)(*c*)(2) (regarding the presumption that there is a reasonable possibility that allocations will affect substantially the dollar amounts to be received by the partners from the partnership if there is a strong likelihood that offsetting allocations will not be made in five years, and the presumption that the adjusted tax basis (or book value) of partnership property is equal to the fair market value of such property).

The existing regulations also provide for a de minimis exception for allocations away from QO partners. Section 1.514(c)-2(k)(3) of the existing regulations provides that a QO's fractions rule percentage of the partnership's items of loss and deduction, other than nonrecourse and partner nonrecourse deductions, that are allocated away from the QO and to other partners in any taxable year, are treated as having been allocated to the QO for purposes of the fractions rule if: (i) the allocation was neither planned nor motivated by tax avoidance; and (ii) the total amount of those items of partnership loss or deduction is less than both one percent of the partnership's aggregate items of gross loss and deduction for the taxable year and $50,000. The preamble to the existing final regulations under section 514(c)(9)(E) explained that the de minimis allocation exception was "to provide relief for what would otherwise be minor inadvertent violations of the fractions rule." TD 8539, 59 FR 24924. The exception was "not intended . . . [to] be used routinely by partnerships to allocate some of the partnership's losses and deductions." *Id.* To that end, the final regulations limited the exception to $50,000. As an example of a de minimis allocation intended to meet this exception, the preamble described a scenario in which a plumber's bill is paid by the partnership but overlooked until after the partner's allocations have been computed and then is allocated entirely to the taxable partner. *Id.*

In current business practices, a $50,000 threshold does not provide sufficient relief for de minimis allocations away from the QO partner. The proposed regulations still require that allocations not exceed one percent of the partnership's aggregate items of gross loss and deduction for the taxable year, but raise the threshold from $50,000 to $1,000,000.

Proposed Applicability Date

The regulations under section 514(c)(9)(E) are proposed to apply to taxable years ending on or after the date these regulations are published as final regulations in the **Federal Register**. However, a partnership and its partners may apply all the rules in these proposed regulations for taxable years ending on or after November 23, 2016.

Special Analyses

Certain IRS regulations, including this one, are exempt from the requirements of Executive Order 12866, as supplemented and reaffirmed by Executive Order 13563. Therefore, a regulatory impact assessment is not required. It also has been determined that section 553(b) of the Administrative Procedure Act (5 U.S.C. chapter 5) does not apply to these regulations. Because these proposed regulations do not impose a collection of information on small entities, the Regulatory Flexibility Act (5 U.S.C. chapter 6) does not apply. Pursuant to section 7805(f) of the Code, this notice of proposed rulemaking has been submitted to the Chief Counsel for Advocacy of the Small Business Administration for comment on its impact on small business.

Comments and Requests for a Public Hearing

Before these proposed regulations are adopted as final regulations, consideration will be given to any comments that are submitted timely to the IRS as prescribed in this preamble under the "Addresses" heading. The Treasury Department and the IRS request comments on all aspects of the proposed rules. All comments will be available at *www.regulations.gov* or upon request. A public hearing will be scheduled if requested in writing by any person that timely submits written comments. If a public hearing is scheduled, notice of the date, time, and place for the public hearing will be published in the **Federal Register**.

Drafting Information

The principal author of these proposed regulations is Caroline E. Hay, Office of the Associate Chief Counsel (Passthroughs and Special Industries). However, other personnel from the Treasury Department and the IRS participated in their development.

[¶49,722] Proposed Amendments of Regulations (REG-107424-12), published in the Federal Register on November 25, 2016.

[Code Sec. 417]

Pension plans: Cash-outs of accrued benefits: Minimum present value requirements.—Amendments of Reg. §1.417(e)-1, relating to the minimum present value requirements applicable to certain defined benefit pension plans, are proposed.

AGENCY: Internal Revenue Service (IRS), Treasury.

ACTION: Notice of proposed rulemaking and notice of public hearing.

SUMMARY: This document contains proposed regulations providing guidance relating to the minimum present value requirements applicable to certain defined benefit pension plans. These proposed regulations would provide guidance on changes made by the Pension Protection Act of 2006 and would provide other modifications to these rules as well. These regulations would affect participants, beneficiaries, sponsors, and administrators of defined benefit pension plans. This document also provides a notice of a public hearing on these proposed regulations.

DATES: Written or electronic comments must be received by February 23, 2017. Outlines of topics to be discussed at the public hearing scheduled for March 7, 2017, must be received by February 23, 2017.

ADDRESSES: Send submissions to: CC:PA:LPD:PR (REG-107424-12), Room 5203, Internal Revenue Service, PO Box 7604, Ben Franklin Station, Washington, DC 20044. Submissions may be hand-delivered Monday through Friday between the hours of 8 a.m. and 4 p.m. to: CC:PA:LPD:PR (REG-107424-12), Courier's Desk, Internal Revenue Service, 1111 Constitution Avenue, NW, Washington, DC, or sent electronically, via the Federal eRulemaking Portal at *http://www.regulations.gov* (IRS REG-107424-12). The public hearing will be held in the IRS Auditorium, Internal Revenue Building, 1111 Constitution Avenue, NW., Washington, DC.

FOR FURTHER INFORMATION CONTACT: Concerning the regulations, Neil S. Sandhu or Linda S. F. Marshall at (202) 317-6700; concerning submissions of comments, the hearing, and/or being placed on the building access list to attend the hearing, Oluwafunmilayo (Funmi) Taylor at (202) 317-6901 (not toll-free numbers).

SUPPLEMENTARY INFORMATION:

Background

Section 401(a)(11) of the Internal Revenue Code (Code) provides that, in order for a defined benefit plan to qualify under section 401(a), except as provided under section 417, in the case of a vested participant who does not die before the annuity starting date, the accrued benefit payable to such participant must be provided in the form of a qualified joint and survivor annuity. In the case of a vested participant who dies before the annuity starting date and who has a surviving spouse, a defined benefit plan must provide a qualified preretirement survivor annuity to the surviving spouse of such participant, except as provided under section 417.

Section 411(d)(6)(B) provides that a plan amendment that has the effect of eliminating or reducing an early retirement benefit or a retirement-type subsidy, or eliminating an optional form of benefit, with respect to benefits attributable to service before the amendment is treated as impermissibly reducing accrued benefits. However, the last sentence of section 411(d)(6)(B) provides that the Secretary may by regulations provide that section 411(d)(6)(B) does not apply to a plan amendment that eliminates an optional form of benefit (other than a plan amendment that has the effect of eliminating or reducing an early retirement benefit or a retirement-type subsidy).

Section 417(e)(1) provides that a plan may provide that the present value of a qualified joint and survivor annuity or a qualified preretirement survivor annuity will be immediately distributed if that present value does not exceed the amount that can be distributed without the participant's consent under section 411(a)(11). Section 417(e)(2) provides that, if the present value of the qualified joint and survivor annuity or the qualified preretirement survivor annuity exceeds the amount that can be distributed without the participant's consent under section 411(a)(11), then a plan may immediately distribute the present value of a qualified joint and survivor annuity or the qualified preretirement survivor annuity only if the participant and the spouse of the participant (or where the participant has died, the surviving spouse) consent in writing to the distribution.

Section 417(e)(3)(A) provides that the present value shall not be less than the present value calculated by using the applicable mortality table and the applicable interest rate.[1]

Section 417(e)(3)(B) of the Code, as amended by section 302 of the Pension Protection Act of 2006 (PPA '06), Public Law 109-280, 120 Stat. 780 (2006), provides that the term "applicable mortality table" means a mortality table, modified as appropriate by the Secretary, based on the mortality table specified for the plan year under section 430(h)(3)(A) (without regard to section 430(h)(3)(C) or (3)(D)).

Section 417(e)(3)(C) of the Code, as amended by section 302 of PPA '06, provides that the term "applicable interest rate" means the adjusted first, second, and third segment rates applied under rules similar to the rules of section 430(h)(2)(C) of the Code for the month before the date of the distribution or such other time as the Secretary may prescribe by regulations. However, for purposes of section 417(e)(3), these rates are to be determined without regard to the segment rate stabilization rules of section 430(h)(2)(C)(iv). In addition, under section 417(e)(3)(D), these rates are to be determined using the average yields for a month, rather than the 24-month average used under section 430(h)(2)(D).

Section 411(a)(13) of the Code, as added by section 701(b) of PPA '06, provides that an "applicable defined benefit plan," as defined by section 411(a)(13)(C), is not treated as failing to meet the requirements of section 417(e) with respect to accrued benefits derived from employer contributions solely because the present value of a participant's accrued benefit (or any portion thereof) may be, under the terms of the plan, equal to the amount expressed as the hypothetical account balance or as an accumulated percentage of such participant's final average compensation.

Section 1107(a)(2) of PPA '06 provides that a pension plan does not fail to meet the requirements of section 411(d)(6) by reason of a plan amendment to which section 1107 applies, except as provided by the Secretary of the Treasury. Section 1107 of PPA '06 applies to plan amendments made pursuant to the provisions of PPA '06 or regulations issued thereunder that are adopted no later than a specified date, generally the last day of the first plan year beginning on or after January 1, 2009.

Final regulations under section 417 relating to the qualified joint and survivor and qualified preretirement survivor annuity requirements have not been amended to reflect PPA '06. The regulations, which were issued on August 22, 1988, were amended on April 3, 1998, to reflect changes enacted by the Uruguay Round Agreements Act, Public Law 103-465 (GATT).

Section 1.417(e)-1(d)(1) provides that a defined benefit plan generally must provide that the present value of any accrued benefit and the amount of any distribution, including a single sum, must not be less than the amount calculated using the specified applicable interest rate and the specified applicable mortality table. The present value of any optional form of benefit cannot be less than the present value of the accrued benefit determined in accordance with the preceding sentence.

Section 1.417(e)-1(d)(6) provides an exception from the minimum present value requirements of section 417(e) and §1.417(e)-1(d). This exception applies to the amount of a distribution paid in the form of an annual benefit that either does not decrease during the life of the participant (or, in the case of a qualified preretirement survivor annuity, the life of the participant's spouse), or that decreases during the life of the participant merely because of the death of the survivor annuitant (but only if the reduction is to a level not below 50 percent of the annual benefit payable before the death of such survivor annuitant) or the cessation or reduction of Social Security supplements or qualified disability benefits.

Notice 2007-81, 2007-2 CB 899 (see 26 CFR 601.601(d)(2)(ii)(*b*)), provides guidance on the applicable interest rate. Rev. Rul. 2007-67, 2007-2 CB 1047 (see 26 CFR 601.601(d)(2)(ii)(*b*)), provides guidance on the applicable mortality table[2] and the timing rules that apply to the determination of the applicable interest rate and the applicable mortality table.

The Worker, Retiree, and Employer Recovery Act of 2008, Public Law 109-280 (120 Stat. 780), amended section 415(b)(2)(E)(v) to provide that the applicable mortality table under section 417(e)(3)(B) applies for purposes of adjusting a benefit or limitation pursuant to section 415(b)(2)(B), (C), or (D).

Sections 205(g), 203(e), and 204(g) of the Employee Retirement Income Security Act of 1974 (ERISA) contain rules that are parallel to Code sections 417(e), 411(a)(11), and 411(d)(6), respectively. Under section 101 of Reorganization Plan No. 4 of 1978 (43 FR 47713), the Secretary of the Treasury has interpretive jurisdiction over the subject matter addressed in these regulations for purposes of ERISA, as well as the Code. Thus, these regulations apply for purposes of the Code and the corresponding provisions of ERISA.

In *West v. AK Steel Corporation Retirement Accumulation Pension Plan*, 484 F.3d 395 (6th Cir. 2007), the court held that a preretirement mortality discount could not be used in the computation of the present value of a participant's single-sum distribution under a cash balance plan if the death benefit under the plan was equal in value to the participant's accrued benefit under the plan. The court found that, if a participant's beneficiary is entitled to the participant's entire accrued benefit upon the participant's death before attainment of normal retirement age, the use of a mortality

---

[1] Under section 411(a)(11)(B), the same applicable mortality table and applicable interest rate are used for purposes of determining whether the present value of a participant's nonforfeitable accrued benefit exceeds the maximum amount that can be immediately distributed without the participant's consent.

[2] Notice 2008-85, 2008-2 CB 905, Notice 2013-49, 2013-32 IRB 127, Notice 2015-53, 2015-33 IRB 190, and Notice 2016-50, 2016-38 IRB 371, set forth the section 417(e)(3) applicable mortality tables for 2009 through 2017.

discount for the period before normal retirement age would result in a partial forfeiture of benefits in violation of the ERISA vesting rules that correspond to the rules of section 411(a). See also *Berger v. Xerox Corporation Retirement Income Guarantee Plan*, 338 F.3d 755 (7th Cir. 2003); *Crosby v. Bowater, Inc. Ret. Plan*, 212 F.R.D. 350 (W.D. Mich. 2002), rev'd on other grounds, 382 F.3d 587 (6th Cir. 2004) (accrued benefits include not only retirement benefits themselves, but also death benefits which are directly related to the value of the retirement benefits). In *Stewart v. AT&T Inc.*, 354 Fed. Appx. 111 (5th Cir. 2009), however, the court held that a preretirement mortality discount was appropriately applied to determine a single-sum distribution under a traditional defined benefit plan. The court distinguished *AK Steel* and *Berger* on the basis that the plans at issue in those cases did not provide for a forfeiture of the accrued benefit on the death of the participant before retirement, whereas the plan at issue in *Stewart* provided for such a forfeiture.

Final regulations (TD 9783) under section 417(e) that permit defined benefit plans to simplify the treatment of certain optional forms of benefit that are paid partly in the form of an annuity and partly in a more accelerated form were published by the Treasury Department and the IRS in the **Federal Register** on September 9, 2016 (81 FR 62359).

Explanation of Provisions

Overview

These proposed regulations would amend the current final regulations under section 417(e) regarding the minimum present value requirements of section 417(e)(3) in several areas. Specifically, the proposed regulations would update the regulations for changes made by PPA '06 and to eliminate certain obsolete provisions. The proposed regulations also contain a few other clarifying changes.

Updates to reflect statutory and regulatory changes

The proposed regulations would update the existing regulatory provisions to reflect the statutory changes made by PPA '06, including the new interest rates and mortality tables set forth in section 417(e)(3) and the exception from the valuation rules for certain applicable defined benefit plans set forth in section 411(a)(13). The proposed regulations clarify that the interest rates that are published by the Commissioner pursuant to the provisions as modified by PPA '06 are to be used without further adjustment. In addition, the proposed regulations would eliminate obsolete provisions of the regulations relating to the transition from pre-1995 law to the interest rates and mortality assumptions provided by GATT. Furthermore, the proposed regulations make conforming changes to reflect the final regulations under section 417(e) that permit defined benefit plans to simplify the treatment of certain optional forms of benefit that are paid partly in the form of an annuity and partly in a more accelerated form.

Other clarifying changes

A. Treatment of preretirement mortality

The proposed regulations would include rules relating to the treatment of preretirement mortality discounts in determining the minimum present value of accrued benefits under the regulations to address the issue raised by *AK Steel* and *Berger* of whether a plan that provides a death benefit equal in value to the accrued benefit may apply a preretirement mortality discount for the probability of death when determining the amount of a single-sum distribution.

Section 411(a) generally prohibits forfeitures of accrued benefits. Under section 411(a)(1), an employee's rights in his accrued benefit derived from employee contributions must be nonforfeitable, and under section 411(a)(2), an employee's rights in his accrued benefit derived from employer contributions must become nonforfeitable in accordance with a vesting schedule that is specified in the statute. Section 411(a)(3)(A) provides that a right to an accrued benefit derived from employer contributions is not treated as forfeitable solely because the plan provides that it is not payable if the participant dies (except in the case of a survivor annuity which is payable as provided in section 401(a)(11)).

Section 411(a)(7)(A)(i) defines a participant's accrued benefit under a defined benefit plan as the employee's accrued benefit determined under the plan and, except as provided in section 411(c)(3), expressed in the form of an annual benefit commencing at normal retirement age. Section 1.411(a)-7(a)(1) defines a participant's accrued benefit under a defined benefit plan as the annual benefit commencing at normal retirement age if the plan provides an accrued benefit in that form. If a defined benefit plan does not provide an accrued benefit in the form of an annual benefit commencing at normal retirement age, § 1.411(a)-7(a)(1)(ii) defines the accrued benefit as an annual benefit commencing at normal retirement age which is the actuarial equivalent of the accrued benefit determined under the plan. The regulation further clarifies that the term "accrued benefits" refers only to pension or retirement benefits. Consequently, accrued benefits do not include ancillary benefits not directly related to retirement benefits, such as incidental death benefits.

Section 411(d)(6)(A) prohibits a plan amendment that decreases a participant's accrued benefit. Section 411(d)(6)(B) provides that a plan amendment that has the effect of eliminating or reducing an early retirement benefit or retirement-type subsidy or eliminating an optional form of benefit with respect to benefits attributable to service before the amendment is treated as reducing accrued benefits for this purpose. Section 1.411(d)-3(g)(2)(v) provides that a death benefit under a defined benefit plan other than a death benefit that is part of an optional form of benefit is an ancillary benefit. Section 1.411(d)-3(g)(6)(ii)(B) describes death benefits payable after the annuity starting date that are considered part of an optional form of benefit. Pursuant to § 1.411(d)-3(g)(14) and (15), section 411(d)(6) protected benefits do not include a death benefit under a defined benefit plan that is an ancillary benefit and not part of an optional form of benefit.

A death benefit under a defined benefit plan that is payable when the participant dies before attaining normal retirement age and before benefits commence is not part of the participant's accrued benefit within the meaning of section 411(a)(7). Accordingly, the anti-forfeiture rules of section 411(a) do not apply to such a death benefit. This is the case even if the amount of the death benefit is the same as the amount the participant would have received had the participant separated from service and elected to receive a distribution immediately before death. Moreover, such a death benefit is an ancillary benefit within the meaning of § 1.411(d)-3(g)(2)(v) — rather than a section 411(d)(6) protected benefit — and therefore can be eliminated by plan amendment (provided that a qualified preretirement survivor annuity for a surviving spouse is preserved, pursuant to section 401(a)(11)).

The minimum present value requirements of section 417(e)(3) do not take into account the value of ancillary benefits that are not part of the participant's accrued benefit under the plan. Consistent with this, § 1.417(e)-1(d)(1)(i) does not require ancillary death benefits to be taken into account in the required minimum present value calculation. Because questions have arisen regarding this rule, the proposed regulations would clarify that the probability of death under the applicable mortality table is generally taken into account for purposes of determining the present value under section 417(e)(3), without regard to the death benefits provided under the plan other than a death benefit that is part of the normal form of benefit or part of another optional form of benefit (as described in § 1.411(d)-3(g)(6)(ii)(B)) for which present value is determined.

However, a different rule applies with respect to whether the probability of death under the applicable mortality table is taken into account for purposes of determining the present value with respect to the accrued benefit derived from contributions made by an employee. This is because an employee's rights in the accrued benefit derived from the employee's own contributions are nonforfeitable under section 411(a)(1), and the exception for death under section 411(a)(3)(A) to the nonforfeitability of accrued benefits does not apply to the accrued benefit derived from employee contributions. As a result, for purposes of determining the present value under section 417(e)(3) with respect to the accrued benefit derived from contributions made by an employee (that is computed in accordance with the requirements of section 411(c)(3)), the probability of death during the assumed deferral period, if any, is not taken into account. For purposes of the preceding sentence, the assumed deferral period is the period between the date of the present value determination and the assumed commencement date for the annuity attributable to contributions made by an employee.

The proposed regulations include an example to illustrate the application of the minimum present value requirements of section 417(e)(3) in the case of a single-sum distribution of a participant's entire accrued benefit that consists both of an accrued benefit derived from employee contributions and an employer-provided accrued benefit. Consistent with the rules in these proposed regulations, the example illustrates that a single-sum distribution of the participant's entire accrued benefit in such a case must equal the sum of the minimum present value of the accrued benefit derived from employee contributions, determined under section 417(e)(3) (applying the special rules set forth in the preceding paragraph), and the minimum present value of the employer-provided accrued benefit, determined under section 417(e)(3). Note that Rev. Rul. 89-60, 1989-1 CB 113 (1989) suggests that it is sufficient for a single-sum distribution in such a case to merely equal the greater of the minimum present value of the accrued benefit derived from employee contributions and the minimum present value of the participant's entire accrued benefit. To the extent the guidance under Rev. Rul. 89-60 is inconsistent with the final regulations that adopt these proposed regulations, the regulations would supersede the guidance in Rev. Rul. 89-60.

B. *Social security level income options*

Questions have arisen regarding whether the minimum present value requirements of section 417(e)(3) apply to a social security level income option. As noted above, §1.417(e)-1(d)(6) provides that the minimum present value requirements of section 417(e)(3) do not apply to the amount of a distribution paid in the form of an annual benefit that does not decrease during the life of the participant, or that decreases during the life of the participant merely because of the death of the survivor annuitant or the cessation or reduction of social security supplements or qualified disability benefits.

A social security supplement is defined in §1.411(a)-7(c)(4) as a benefit for plan participants that commences before and terminates before the age when participants are entitled to old-age insurance benefits, unreduced on account of age, under title II of the Social Security Act, and does not exceed such old-age insurance benefit. A social security supplement (other than a QSUPP as defined in §1.401(a)(4)-12) is an ancillary benefit that is not a section 411(d)(6) protected benefit.

A social security level income option is an optional form of benefit (protected under section 411(d)(6)) under which a participant's accrued benefit is paid in the form of an annuity with larger payments in earlier years, before an assumed social security commencement age, to provide the participant with approximately level retirement income when the assumed social security payments are taken into account. It is appropriate to subject a social security level income option to the rules of section 417(e)(3) because, when a participant's accrued benefit is paid as a social security level income option, a portion of the participant's accrued benefit (which may be substantial) is accelerated and paid over a short period of time until social security retirement age. Because the periodic payments under a social security level income option decrease during the lifetime of the participant and the decrease is not the result of the cessation of an ancillary social security supplement, §1.417(e)-1(d)(6) does not provide an exception from the minimum present value requirements of section 417(e)(3) for such a distribution. These proposed regulations contain an example that illustrates this point.

C. *Application of required assumptions to the accrued benefit*

The proposed regulations would clarify the scope of the rule of §1.417(e)-1(d)(1) under which the present value of any optional form of benefit cannot be less than the present value of the normal retirement benefit (with both values determined using the applicable interest rate and the applicable mortality table). The proposed regulations would require that the present value of any optional form of benefit cannot be less than the present value of the accrued benefit payable at normal retirement age, and would provide an exception for an optional form of benefit payable after normal retirement age to the extent that a suspension of benefits applies pursuant to section 411(a)(3)(B).

Effective/Applicability Dates

The changes under the proposed regulations are proposed to apply to distributions with annuity starting dates in plan years beginning on or after the date regulations that finalize these proposed regulations are published in the **Federal Register**. Prior to this applicability date, taxpayers must continue to apply existing regulations relating to section 417(e), modified to reflect the relevant statutory provisions during the applicable period (and guidance of general applicability relating to those statutory provisions, such as Rev. Rul. 2007-67).

Special Analyses

Certain IRS regulations, including this one, are exempt from the requirements of Executive Order 12866, as supplemented and reaffirmed by Executive Order 13563. Therefore, a regulatory assessment is not required. It also has been determined that section 553(b) of the Administrative Procedure Act (5 U.S.C. chapter 5) does not apply to these regulations, and because the proposed regulation does not impose a collection of information on small entities, the Regulatory Flexibility Act (5 U.S.C. chapter 6) does not apply. Pursuant to section 7805(f) of the Code, this notice of proposed rulemaking has been submitted to the Chief Counsel for Advocacy of the Small Business Administration for comment on its impact on small business.

Comments and Public Hearing

Before these proposed regulations are adopted as final regulations, consideration will be given to any written (a signed original and eight (8) copies) or electronic comments that are submitted timely to the IRS. The Treasury Department and the IRS request comments on all aspects of these proposed regulations. In addition, the Treasury Department and the IRS specifically request comments on whether, in the case of a plan that provides a subsidized annuity payable upon early retirement and determines a single-sum distribution as the present value of the early retirement annuity, the present-value determination should be required to be calculated using the applicable interest rate and the applicable mortality table applied to the early retirement annuity (or whether the requirement to have a minimum present value that is equal to the present value of the annuity payable at normal retirement age determined in accordance with section 417(e)(3) provides the level of protection for the participant that is required by section 417(e)(3)). See *Rybarczyk v. TRW*, 235 F.3d 975 (6th Cir. 2000).

All comments will be available at www.regulations.gov or upon request. A public hearing has been scheduled for March 7, 2017, beginning at 10 a.m. in the Auditorium, Internal Revenue Service, 1111 Constitution Avenue, NW., Washington, DC. Due to building security procedures, visitors must enter at the Constitution Avenue entrance. In addition, all visitors must present photo identification to enter the building. Because of access restrictions, visitors will not be admitted beyond the immediate entrance area more than 30 minutes before the hearing starts. For information about having your name placed on the building access list to attend the hearing, see the **FOR FURTHER INFORMATION CONTACT** section of this preamble.

The rules of 26 CFR 601.601(a)(3) apply to the hearing. Persons who wish to present oral comments at the hearing must submit written or electronic comments by February 23, 2017, and an outline of topics to be discussed and the amount of time to be devoted to each topic (a signed original and eight (8) copies) by February 23, 2017. A period of 10 minutes will be allotted to each person for making comments. An agenda showing the scheduling of the speakers will be prepared after the deadline for receiving outlines has passed. Copies of the agenda will be available free of charge at the hearing.

Drafting Information

The principal authors of these regulations are Neil S. Sandhu and Linda S. F. Marshall, Office of Division Counsel/Associate Chief Counsel (Tax Exempt and Government Entities). However, other personnel from the IRS and the Treasury Department participated in the development of these regulations.

[¶49,723] **Proposed Amendments of Regulations (REG-125946-10)**, published in the Federal Register on November 28, 2016.

[Code Sec. 472]

Tax Accounting: Inventory: Dollar-Value LIFO Method: IPIC Pools.—Amendments of Reg. §1.472-8, relating to the establishment of dollar-value last-in, first-out (LIFO) inventory pools by certain taxpayers that use the inventory price index computation (IPIC) pooling method, are proposed.

AGENCY: Internal Revenue Service (IRS), Treasury.

ACTION: Notice of proposed rulemaking.

SUMMARY: This document contains proposed regulations that relate to the establishment of dollar-value last-in, first-out (LIFO) inventory pools by certain taxpayers that use the inventory price index computation (IPIC) pooling method. The proposed regulations provide rules regarding the proper pooling of manufactured or processed goods and wholesale or retail (resale) goods. The proposed regulations would affect taxpayers who use the IPIC pooling method and whose inventory for a trade or business consists of manufactured or processed goods and resale goods.

DATES: Comments and requests for a public hearing must be received by February 27, 2017.

ADDRESSES: Send submissions to: CC:PA:LPD:PR (REG-125946-10), Room 5205, Internal Revenue Service, PO Box 7604, Ben Franklin Station, Washington, DC 20044. Submissions may be hand delivered Monday through Friday between the hours of 8 a.m. and 4 p.m. to: CC:PA:LPD:PR (REG-125946-10), Courier's Desk, Internal Revenue Service, 1111 Constitution Avenue NW., Washington, DC, or sent electronically via the Federal eRulemaking Portal at *http://www.regulations.gov/* (IRS REG-125946-10).

FOR FURTHER INFORMATION CONTACT: Concerning the proposed regulations, Natasha M. Mulleneaux, (202) 317-7007; concerning submission of comments and requests for a public hearing, Regina Johnson, (202) 317-6901 (not toll-free numbers).

SUPPLEMENTARY INFORMATION:

Background

Section 472 of the Internal Revenue Code permits a taxpayer to account for inventories using the LIFO method of accounting. The LIFO method of accounting for goods treats inventories on hand at the end of the year as consisting first of inventory on hand at the beginning of the year and then of inventories acquired during the year.

Section 1.472-8(a) of the Income Tax Regulations (26 CFR part 1) provides that any taxpayer may elect to determine the cost of its LIFO inventories using the dollar-value method, provided such method is used consistently and clearly reflects income. The dollar-value method of valuing LIFO inventories is a method of determining cost by using "base-year" cost expressed in terms of total dollars rather than the quantity and price of specific goods as the unit of measurement. The "base-year" cost is the aggregate of the cost (determined as of the beginning of the tax year for which the LIFO method is first adopted) of all items in a pool.

Pooling is central to the operation of the dollar-value LIFO method. Pooling requires costs related to different inventory products to be grouped into one or more inventory pools. To determine whether there is an increment or liquidation in a pool for a particular taxable year, the end of the year inventory of the pool expressed in terms of base-year cost is compared with the beginning of the year inventory of the pool expressed in terms of base-year cost. The regulations prescribe rules for determining whether the number and composition of the pools used by the taxpayer are appropriate. The rules vary depending upon whether the taxpayer is engaged in the activity of manufacturing or processing or the activity of wholesaling or retailing.

The general pooling rules applicable to dollar-value LIFO taxpayers are in §1.472-8(b) and (c). These paragraphs provide separate pooling principles for taxpayers engaged in the manufacturing or processing of goods (§1.472-8(b)), and for taxpayers engaged in the wholesaling or retailing of goods purchased from others (§1.472-8(c)).

Section 1.472-8(b)(1) requires a manufacturer or processor to establish one pool for each natural business unit (natural business unit pooling method) unless the manufacturer or processor elects under §1.472-8(b)(3) to establish multiple pools. Further, §1.472-8(b)(2) provides that where a manufacturer or processor is also engaged in the wholesaling or retailing of goods purchased from others, the wholesaling or retailing operations with respect to such purchased goods shall not be considered a part of any manufacturing or processing unit. Additionally, §1.472-8(b)(1) requires that where the manufacturer or processor is also engaged in the wholesaling or retailing of goods purchased from others, any pooling of the LIFO inventory of such purchased goods for wholesaling and retailing operations shall be determined in accordance with §1.472-8(c).

In *Amity Leather Products Co.* v. *Commissioner*, 82 T.C. 726 (1984), the Tax Court considered whether a taxpayer that used the natural business unit pooling method was subject to the separate pooling requirements by virtue of being both a manufacturer and a wholesaler or retailer of merchandise. The court concluded that requiring separate inventory accounting for the two functions was reasonable and held that, where the taxpayer manufactured goods and regularly purchased identical goods from a subsidiary for resale, it was required to maintain separate pools for manufactured and purchased inventory.

A manufacturer or processor using the natural business unit pooling method may elect to use the multiple pooling method described in §1.472-8(b)(3) for inventory items that are not within a natural business unit. Alternatively, a manufacturer or processor that does not use the natural business unit pooling method may elect to use the multiple pooling method. Under the multiple pooling method, generally each pool should consist of a group of inventory items that are substantially similar. Thus, raw materials that are substantially similar should be pooled together. Similarly, finished goods and goods-in-process should be placed in pools classified by major classes or types of goods.

Section 1.472-8(c)(1) requires wholesalers, retailer, jobbers, and distributors to establish inventory pools by major lines, types, or classes of goods. Mirroring §1.472-8(b)(1), §1.472-8(c)(1) requires that where a wholesaler or retailer is also engaged in the manufacturing or processing of goods, the pooling of the LIFO inventory for the manufacturing or processing operations must be determined in accordance with §1.472-8(b).

In general, any taxpayer that elects to use the dollar-value LIFO method to value LIFO inventories may elect to use the IPIC method to compute the base-year cost and determine the LIFO value of a dollar-value pool for a trade or business. A taxpayer that elects to use the IPIC method of determining the value of a dollar-value LIFO pool for a trade or business may also elect to establish dollar-value pools, for those items accounted for using the IPIC method, using the IPIC pooling method provided in §1.472-8(b)(4) and (c)(2). Section 1.472-8(b)(4) governs the application of the IPIC pooling method to manufacturers and processors that elect to use the IPIC method for a trade or business. Section 1.472-8(c)(2) governs the application of the IPIC pooling method to wholesalers, retailers, jobbers, and distributors that elect to use the IPIC method for a trade or business.

For manufacturers and processors using the IPIC pooling method under §1.472-8(b)(4), pools may be established for those items accounted for using the IPIC method based on the 2-digit commodity codes (that is, major commodity groups) in Table 9 (formerly Table 6) of the Producer Price Index Detailed Report (PPI Detailed Report), which is published monthly by the United States Bureau of Labor Statistics (BLS). A taxpayer establishing IPIC pools under §1.472-8(b)(4) may combine IPIC pools that comprise less than 5 percent of the total inventory value of all dollar-value pools to form a single miscellaneous IPIC pool. If the resulting miscellaneous IPIC pool is less than 5 percent of the total inventory value of all dollar-value pools, the taxpayer may combine the miscellaneous IPIC pool with its largest IPIC pool.

For retailers using the IPIC pooling method under §1.472-8(c)(2), pools may be established for those purchased items accounted for using the IPIC method based on either the general expenditure categories (that is, major groups) in Table 3 of the Consumer Price Index Detailed Report (CPI Detailed Report), published monthly by BLS, or the 2-digit commodity codes (that is, major commodity groups) in Table 9 of the PPI Detailed Report. For wholesalers, jobbers, or distributors using the IPIC pooling method under §1.472-8(c)(2), pools may be established for those items accounted for using the IPIC method based on the 2-digit commodity codes in Table 9 of the PPI Detailed Report. A taxpayer establishing IPIC pools under §1.472-8(c)(2) may combine pools that comprise less than 5 percent of the total inventory value of all dollar-value pools to form a single miscellaneous IPIC pool. If the resulting miscellaneous IPIC pool is less than 5 percent of the total inventory value of all dollar-value pools, the taxpayer may combine the miscellaneous IPIC pool with its largest IPIC pool.

Each of the 5-percent rules provided in §1.472-8(b)(4) or (c)(2) is a method of accounting. Thus, a taxpayer may not change to, or cease using either 5-percent rule without obtaining the prior consent of the Commissioner. Whether a specific IPIC pool or the miscellaneous IPIC pool satisfies the applicable 5-percent rule must be determined in the year of adoption or year of change (whichever is applicable) and redetermined every third taxable year. Any change in pooling required or permitted under a 5-percent rule is also a change in method of accounting. A taxpayer must secure the consent of the Commissioner before combining or separating pools. The general procedures under section 446(e) and §1.446-1(e) that a taxpayer must follow to obtain the consent of the Commissioner to change a method of accounting for federal income tax purposes are contained in Rev. Proc. 2015-13, 2015-5 I.R.B. 419 (or its successors), as modified by Rev. Proc. 2015-33, 2015-24 I.R.B. 1067. See §601.601(d)(2)(ii)(b).

The general pooling rules of §1.472-8(b) and (c) provide that where a taxpayer is engaged in both a manufacturing or processing activity and a wholesaling or retailing activity, separate pooling rules apply to the separate activities, and goods purchased for resale may not be included in the same pool as manufactured or purchased goods. On the other hand, the IPIC pooling rules address circumstances where a trade or business consists entirely of a manufacturing, processing, retailing, or wholesaling activity. The Treasury Department and the IRS have become aware of confusion concerning how the IPIC pooling rules apply where a taxpayer is engaged in both a manufacturing or processing activity and a wholesaling or retailing activity. Accordingly, these proposed regulations address this issue.

Explanation of Provisions

Changes to IPIC Pooling Rules

The proposed regulations amend the IPIC pooling rules to clarify that those rules are applied consistently with the general LIFO pooling rule that manufactured or processed goods and resale goods may not be included in the same dollar-value LIFO pool. This general rule is intended to limit cost transference, an inherent problem with pooling. Cost transference may occur, among other circumstances, when inventory items from separate economic activities (for example, manufacturing and resale activities) are placed in the same pool and may cause misallocation of cost or distortion of income.

Accordingly, the proposed regulations clarify that an IPIC-method taxpayer who elects the IPIC pooling method described in §1.472-8(b)(4) or (c)(2) and whose trade or business consists of both manufacturing or processing activity and resale activity may not commingle the manufactured or processed goods and the resale goods within the same IPIC pool.

Specifically, the proposed regulations provide that a manufacturer or processor using the IPIC pooling method under §1.472-8(b)(4) that is also engaged, within the same trade or business, in wholesaling or retailing goods purchased from others may elect to establish dollar-value pools for the manufactured or processed items accounted for using the IPIC method based on the 2-digit commodity codes in Table 9 of the PPI Detailed Report. If the manufacturer or processor makes this election, the manufacturer or processor must also establish pools for its resale goods in accordance with §1.472-8(c)(2) (that is, based on the general expenditure categories in Table 3 of the CPI Detailed Report in the case of a retailer or the 2-digit commodity codes in Table 9 of the PPI Detailed Report in the case of a retailer, wholesaler, jobber, or distributor).

If the manufacturer or processor chooses to use the 5-percent method of pooling, manufactured or processed IPIC pools (IPIC pools consisting of manufactured or processed goods) of less than 5 percent of the total current year cost of all dollar-value pools may be combined to form a single miscellaneous IPIC pool of manufactured or processed goods. The manufacturer or processor may also combine resale IPIC pools (IPIC pools consisting of resale goods) of less than 5 percent of the total value of inventory to form a single miscellaneous IPIC pool of resale goods. If the miscellaneous IPIC pool of manufactured or processed goods is less than 5 percent of the total value of inventory, the manufacturer or processor may combine the miscellaneous IPIC pool of manufactured or processed goods with its largest manufactured or processed IPIC pool. The miscellaneous IPIC pool of resale goods may not be combined with any other IPIC pool.

The proposed regulations also provide that a wholesaler, retailer, jobber, or distributor using the IPIC pooling method under §1.472-8(c)(2) that is also engaged, within the same trade or business, in manufacturing or processing activities may elect to establish dollar-value pools for the resale goods accounted for using the IPIC method in accordance with §1.472-8(c)(2) (that is, based on the general expenditure categories in Table 3 of the CPI Detailed Report in the case of retailer or the 2-digit commodity codes in Table 9 of the PPI Detailed Report in the case of a wholesaler, retailer, jobber, or distributor). If the wholesaler, retailer, jobber, or distributor makes this election, it must also establish pools for its manufactured or processed goods based on the 2-digit commodity codes in Table 9 of the PPI Detailed Report.

If the wholesaler, retailer, jobber, or distributor chooses to use the 5-percent method of pooling, resale IPIC pools of less than 5 percent of the total value of inventory may be combined to form a single miscellaneous IPIC pool of resale goods. The wholesaler, retailer, jobber, or distributor may also combine the IPIC pools of manufactured or processed goods of less than 5 percent of the total value of inventory to form a single miscellaneous IPIC pool of manufactured or processed goods. If the resale miscellaneous IPIC pool is less than 5 percent of the total value of inventory, the wholesaler, retailer, jobber, or distributor may combine the resale miscellaneous IPIC pool with the largest resale IPIC pool. The miscellaneous IPIC pool of manufactured or processed goods may not be combined with any other IPIC pool.

The Treasury Department and the IRS specifically request comments on the requirement that a taxpayer engaged in both manufacturing and resale activities within the same trade or business is required to use IPIC pooling for both activities.

Changes To Conform With Current BLS Publications

These proposed regulations modify §1.472-8(b), (c), and (e)(3) to update references from Table 6 (Producer price indexes and percent changes for commodity groupings and individual items, not seasonally adjusted) to Table 9 (Producer price indexes and percent changes for commodity and service groupings and individual items, not seasonally adjusted) because of BLS changes in the PPI Detailed Report.

These proposed regulations also modify §1.472-8(e)(3)(ii) to remove the exception to the trade or business requirement for taxpayers using the Department Store Inventory Price Indexes because BLS discontinued publishing these indexes after December 2013.

Effective/Applicability Date

These regulations are proposed to apply for taxable years ending on or after the date the regulations are published as final regulations in the **Federal Register**.

Special Analyses

Certain IRS regulations, including these, are exempt from the requirements of Executive Order 12866, as supplemented and reaffirmed by Executive Order 13563. Therefore, a regulatory impact assessment is not required. It also has been determined that section 553(b) of the Administrative Procedure Act (5 U.S.C. chapter 5) does not apply to these regulations, and, because these regulations do not impose a collection of information on small entities, the Regulatory Flexibility Act (5 U.S.C. chapter 6) does not apply. Pursuant to section 7805(f) of the Internal Revenue Code, these proposed regulations will be submitted to the Chief Counsel for Advocacy of the Small Business Administration for comment on their impact on small business.

Comments and Request for a Public Hearing

Before these proposed regulations are adopted as final regulations, consideration will be given to any written (a signed original and eight (8) copies) or electronic comments that are submitted timely to the IRS. The Treasury Department and the IRS request comments on all aspects of the proposed rules. All comments will be available at *www.regulations.gov* or upon request.

A public hearing will be scheduled if requested in writing by any person that timely submits written comments. If a public hearing is scheduled, notice of the date, time, and place for the public hearing will be published in the **Federal Register**.

Drafting Information

The principal author of these regulations is Natasha M. Mulleneaux of the Office of the Associate Chief Counsel (Income Tax & Accounting). However, other personnel from the IRS and the Treasury Department participated in their development.

[¶49,725] **Proposed Amendments of Regulations (REG-129128-14)**, published in the Federal Register on December 7, 2016.

[Code Secs. 704 and 901]

Foreign taxes: Foreign tax credit: Covered asset acquisitions.—Reg. §§1.901(m)-1, 1.901(m)-2, 1.901(m)-3, 1.901(m)-4, 1.901(m)-5, 1.901(m)-6, 1.901(m)-7, 1.901(m)-8 and amendments of Reg. §§1.704-1, respecting to transactions that generally are treated as asset acquisitions for U.S. income tax purposes and either are treated as stock acquisitions or are disregarded for foreign income tax purposes, are adopted.

[¶49,726] **Proposed Amendments of Regulations (REG-128276-12)**, published in the Federal Register on December 8, 2016.

[Code Secs. 987 and 988]

Branch transactions: Qualified business units: Income from U.S. sources: Functional currency: Foreign currency transactions: Character of gain or loss: Exchange gain or loss: Special rules.—Amendments of Reg. §1.987-1, 1.987-3, 1.987-6, 1.987-8, 1.988-1 and 1.988-2, relating to the recognition and deferral of foreign currency gain or loss under section 987 with respect to a qualified business unit (QBU) in connection with certain QBU terminations and certain other transactions involving partnerships, are proposed. Amendments to Reg. §§1.987-2, 1.987-4 and 1.987-12 adopted and amendments to Reg. §1.987-7 are withdrawn by T.D. 9857, May 10, 2019.

AGENCY: Internal Revenue Service (IRS), Treasury.

ACTION: Notice of proposed rulemaking by cross-reference to temporary regulations.

SUMMARY: Published elsewhere in this issue of the **Federal Register**, the Treasury Department and the IRS are issuing temporary regulations under section 987 of the Code relating to the recognition and deferral of foreign currency gain or loss under section 987 with respect to a qualified business unit (QBU) in connection with certain QBU terminations and certain other transactions involving partnerships. The temporary regulations also contain rules providing: an annual deemed termination election for a section 987 QBU; an elective method, available to taxpayers that make the annual deemed termination election, for translating all items of income or loss with respect to a section 987 QBU at the yearly average exchange rate; rules regarding the treatment of section 988 transactions of a section 987 QBU; rules regarding QBUs with the U.S. dollar as their functional currency; rules regarding combinations and separations of section 987 QBUs; rules regarding the translation of income used to pay creditable foreign income taxes; and rules regarding the allocation of assets and liabilities of certain partnerships for purposes of section 987. Finally, the temporary regulations contain rules under section 988 requiring the deferral of certain section 988 loss that arises with respect to related-party loans. The text of the temporary regulations serves as the text of these proposed regulations.

DATES: Written or electronic comments and requests for a public hearing must be received by March 8, 2016.

ADDRESSES: Send submissions to: CC:PA:LPD:PR (REG-128276-12), room 5203, Internal Revenue Service, P.O. Box 7604, Ben Franklin Station, Washington, DC 20044. Submissions may be hand-delivered Monday through Friday between the hours of 8 a.m. and 4 p.m. to CC:PA:LPD:PR (REG-128276-12), Courier's Desk, Internal Revenue Service, 1111 Constitution Avenue NW, Washington, DC, or sent electronically via the Federal eRulemaking Portal at *http://www.regulations.gov* (IRS REG-128276-12).

FOR FURTHER INFORMATION CONTACT: Concerning the proposed regulations, Steven D. Jensen at (202) 317-6938; concerning submissions of comments or requests for a public hearing, Regina Johnson, (202) 317-6901 (not toll-free numbers).

SUPPLEMENTARY INFORMATION:

Paperwork Reduction Act

The collection of information contained in this notice proposed rulemaking has been submitted to the Office of Management and Budget for review in accordance with the Paperwork Reduction Act of 1995 (44 U.S.C. 3507(d)). Comments on the collection of information should be sent to the **Office of Management and Budget**, Attn: Desk Officer for the Department of the Treasury, Office of Information and Regulatory Affairs,

Washington, DC 20503, with copies to the **Internal Revenue Service**, Attn: IRS Reports Clearance Officer, SE:CAR:MP:T:T:SP, Washington, DC 20224. Comments on the collection of information should be received by February 8, 2017. Comments are specifically requested concerning:

Whether the proposed collection of information is necessary for the proper performance of the Internal Revenue Service, including whether the information will have practical utility;

The accuracy of the estimated burden associated with the proposed collection of information (see below);

How the quality, utility, and clarity of the information to be collected may be enhanced;

How the burden of complying with the proposed collection of information may be minimized, including through the application of automated collection techniques or other forms of information technology; and

Estimates of capital or start-up costs and costs of operation, maintenance, and purchase of service to provide information.

The collection of information in this proposed regulation is in: (1) §§ 1.987-1(b)(6)(iii)(A) and 1.987-1(g)(3)(i)(E); (2) §§ 1.987-3(b)(4)(iii)(C) and 1.987-1(g)(3)(i)(F); (3) §§ 1.987-3(d) and 1.987-1(g)(3)(i)(G); and (4) §§ 1.987-8(d) and 1.987-1(g)(3)(i)(H). Sections 1.987-1(b)(6)(iii)(A) and 1.987-1(g)(3)(i)(E) allow a controlled foreign corporation to elect to apply section 987 and the regulations thereunder (with certain exceptions) to a dollar QBU. Sections 1.987-3(b)(4)(iii)(C) and 1.987-1(g)(3)(i)(F) allow a taxpayer to elect to apply a foreign currency mark-to-market method of accounting for qualified short-term section 988 transactions. Sections 1.987-3(d) and 1.987-1(g)(3)(i)(G) allow a taxpayer to elect to translate all items of income, gain, deduction, and loss of the section 987 QBU at the yearly average exchange rate. Sections 1.987-8(d) and 1.987-1(g)(3)(i)(H) allow a taxpayer to elect to deem all of its section 987 QBUs to terminate on the last day of each taxable year. The preceding elections are to be made pursuant to § 1.987-1(g). The collection of information is voluntary to obtain a benefit. The likely respondents are business or other for-profit institutions.

Estimated total annual reporting burden: 1,000 hours.

Estimated average annual burden hours per respondent: 1 hour.

Estimated number of respondents: 1,000.

Estimated annual frequency of responses: on occasion.

An agency may not conduct or sponsor, and a person is not required to respond to, a collection of information unless it displays a valid control number assigned by the Office of Management and Budget.

Books or records relating to a collection of information must be retained as long as their contents may become material in the administration of any internal revenue law. Generally, tax returns and tax return information are confidential, as required by 26 U.S.C. 6103.

Background and Explanation of Provisions

The temporary regulations (published in the Rules and Regulations section of this issue of the **Federal Register)** contain rules relating to the recognition and deferral of section 987 gain or loss with respect to a QBU. The temporary regulations also contain rules regarding an annual deemed termination election, an elective method for translating taxable income or loss with respect to a QBU, section 988 transactions of a section 987 QBU, QBUs with the U.S. dollar as their functional currency, combinations and separations of section 987 QBUs, translation of income used to pay creditable foreign income taxes, the allocation of assets and liabilities of certain partnerships for purposes of section 987, and the deferral of section 988 loss with respect to certain related-party loans. The text of the temporary regulations also serves as the text of these proposed regulations. The preamble to the temporary regulations explains those regulations and these proposed regulations.

Special Analyses

Certain IRS regulations, including these, are exempt from the requirements of Executive Order 12866, as supplemented and reaffirmed by Executive Order 13563. Therefore, a regulatory impact assessment is not required. It is hereby certified that these regulations will not have a significant economic impact on a substantial number of small entities within the meaning of section 601(6) of the Regulatory Flexibility Act (5 U.S.C. chapter 6). Accordingly, a regulatory flexibility analysis is not required. This certification is based on the fact that these regulations will primarily affect U.S. corporations that have foreign operations, which tend to be larger businesses. Pursuant to section 7805(f) of the Code, these regulations have been submitted to the Chief Counsel for Advocacy of the Small Business Administration for comment on their impact on small business.

Comments and Public Hearing

Before these proposed regulations are adopted as final regulations, consideration will be given to any comments that are submitted timely to the IRS as prescribed in this preamble under the "Addresses" heading. The Treasury Department and the IRS request comments on all aspects of the proposed rules. In addition, the Treasury Department and the IRS request comments on the application of section 987 to entities and QBUs described in § 1.987-1(b)(1)(ii) to which the final regulations are not applicable (excluded entities and QBUs). Comments are requested on whether the Treasury Department and the IRS should issue regulations applying the foreign exchange exposure pool methodology described in §§ 1.987-3 and -4 to excluded entities and QBUs. Comments are also requested on the modifications, if any, that should be made to the foreign exchange exposure pool methodology adopted in the final regulations with respect to excluded entities and QBUs. All comments will be available at *www.regulations.gov* or upon request. A public hearing will be scheduled if requested in writing by any person that timely submits written comments. If a public hearing is scheduled, notice of the date, time, and place for the hearing will be published in the **Federal Register**.

Drafting Information

The principal author of these regulations is Mark E. Erwin of the Office of Associate Chief Counsel (International). However, other personnel from the IRS and the Treasury Department participated in their development.

[¶ 49,727] **Proposed Amendments of Regulations (REG-133353-16)**, published in the Federal Register on December 9, 2016.

[Code Sec. 6103]

Return information: Authorized disclosure.—Amendments to Reg. § 301.6103(j)(1)-1, authorizing the disclosure of specified return information to the Bureau of the Census (Bureau) for purposes of structuring the censuses and national economic accounts and conducting related statistical activities authorized by title 13, are proposed.

AGENCY: Internal Revenue Service (IRS), Treasury

ACTION: Notice of proposed rulemaking by cross-reference to temporary regulation. SUMMARY: In the Rules and Regulations section of this issue of the **Federal Register** the IRS is issuing temporary regulations authorizing the disclosure of specified return information to the Bureau of the

Census (Bureau) for purposes of structuring the censuses and national economic accounts and conducting related statistical activities authorized by title 13. The temporary regulations are made pursuant to a request from the Secretary of Commerce. The temporary regulations also provide clarifying language for an item of return information and remove duplicative paragraphs contained in the existing final regulations. These regulations require no action by taxpayers and have no effect on their tax liabilities. Thus, no taxpayers are likely to be affected by the disclosures authorized by this guidance. The text of the temporary regulations published in the Rules and Regulations section of the **Federal Register** serves as the text of these proposed regulations.

DATES: Written and electronic comments and requests for a public hearing must be received by March 9, 2016.

Applicability Date: For dates of applicability, see § 301.6103(j)(1)-1(e). ADDRESSES: Send submissions to CC:PA:LPD:PR (REG-133353-16), room 5203, Internal Revenue Service, Post Office Box 7604, Ben Franklin Station, Washington, DC 20044. Submissions may be hand-delivered Monday through Friday between the hours of 8 a.m. and 4 p.m. to CC:PA:LPD:PR (REG-133353-16), Courier's Desk, Internal Revenue Service, 1111 Constitution Avenue, N.W., Washington, DC 20224, or sent electronically, via the Federal eRulemaking Portal at *www.regulations.gov* (IRS REG-133353-16).

FOR FURTHER INFORMATION CONTACT: Concerning the proposed regulations, William Rowe, (202) 317-6834; concerning submissions of comments, Regina Johnson, (202) 317-5177 (not toll-free numbers).

SUPPLEMENTARY INFORMATION:

Background and Explanation of Provisions

This document contains proposed amendments to 26 CFR part 301 relating to section 6103(j)(1)(A) of the Internal Revenue Code (Code). Section 6103(j)(1)(A) authorizes the Secretary of the Treasury to furnish, upon written request by the Secretary of Commerce, such returns or return information as the Secretary of Treasury may prescribe by regulation to officers and employees of the Bureau for the purpose of, but only to the extent necessary in, the structuring of censuses and national economic accounts and conducting related statistical activities authorized by law. Section 301.6103(j)(1)-1 of the regulations further defines such purposes by reference to 13 U.S.C. chapter 5 and provides an itemized description of the return information authorized to be disclosed for such purposes. This document contains proposed regulations authorizing the disclosure of additional items of return information requested by the Secretary of Commerce. These proposed regulations also provide clarifying language for an item of return information and remove duplicative paragraphs contained in the existing regulations. Temporary regulations in the Rules and Regulations section of this issue of the **Federal Register** amend 26 CFR part 301. The text of those temporary regulations serves as the text of these proposed regulations. The preamble to the temporary regulations explains the temporary regulations and these proposed regulations.

Special Analyses

Certain IRS regulations, including this one, are exempt from the requirements of Executive Order 12866, as supplemented and reaffirmed by Executive Order 13563. Therefore, a regulatory assessment is not required. It is hereby certified that these regulations will not have a significant economic impact on a substantial number of small entities because the regulations do not impose a collection of information on small entities. Accordingly, a regulatory flexibility analysis is not required under the Regulatory Flexibility Act (5 U.S.C. chapter 6). Pursuant to section 7805(f) of the Internal Revenue Code, this regulation has been submitted to the Chief Counsel for Advocacy of the Small Business Administration for comment on its impact on small businesses.

Comments and Requests for Public Hearing

Before these proposed regulations are adopted as final regulations, consideration will be given to any comments that are submitted timely to the IRS as prescribed in this preamble under the "Addresses" heading. The IRS and Treasury Department request comments on all aspects of the proposed regulations. All comments that are submitted will be available for public inspection and copying at *www.regulations.gov* or upon request. A public hearing may be scheduled if requested in writing by any person that timely submits written or electronic comments. If a public hearing is scheduled, notice of the date, time, and place for the public hearing will be published in the **Federal Register**.

Drafting Information

The principal author of these proposed regulations is William Rowe, Office of the Associate Chief Counsel (Procedure & Administration).

[¶ 49,728] Proposed Amendments of Regulations and Withdrawal of Notice of Proposed Regulations (REG-140328-15), published in the Federal Register on December 19, 2016.

[Code Sec. 355]

Corporate divisions: Section 355 distribution: Prohibited stock acquisitions: Predecessor of distributing corporation: Predecessor of controlled corporation: Distributions of stock between affiliated group members.—Amendments of Reg. §§ 1.355-0 and 1.355-8, regarding the distribution by a distributing corporation of stock or securities of a controlled corporation without the recognition of income, gain, or loss, are adopted. Amendments of Reg. § 1.355-8 proposed on November 22, 2004, are withdrawn.

[¶ 49,730] Proposed Amendments of Regulations (REG-112800-16), published in the Federal Register on December 29, 2016.

[Code Sec. 468A]

Deductions: Nuclear Power Plants: Decommissioning Costs.—Amendments of Reg. §§ 1.468A-1 and 1.468A-5, relating to deductions for contributions to trusts maintained for decommissioning nuclear power plants and the use of the amounts in those trusts to decommission nuclear plants, are proposed.

AGENCY: Internal Revenue Service (IRS), Treasury.

ACTION: Notice of proposed rulemaking.

SUMMARY: This document provides proposed changes to the regulations under section 468A of the Internal Revenue Code of 1986 (Code) relating to deductions for contributions to trusts maintained for decommissioning nuclear power plants and the use of the amounts in those trusts to decommission nuclear plants. The proposed regulations revise certain provisions to: address issues that have arisen as more nuclear plants have begun the decommissioning process; and clarify provisions in the current regulations regarding self-dealing and the definition of substantial completion of decommissioning.

DATES: Written or electronic comments and requests for a public hearing must be received by March 29, 2017.

ADDRESSES: Send submissions to: CC:PA:LPD:PR (REG-112800-16), room 5203, Internal Revenue Service, PO Box 7604, Ben Franklin Station, Washington, DC 20044. Submissions may be hand delivered Monday through Friday between the hours of 8 a.m. and 4 p.m. to: CC:PA:LPD:PR (REG-112800-16), Courier's Desk, Internal Revenue Service, 1111 Constitution Avenue N.W., Washington, DC, or sent electronically, via the Federal eRulemaking Portal at http://www.regulations.gov/ (IRS REG-112800-16).

FOR FURTHER INFORMATION CONTACT: Concerning the regulations, Jennifer C. Bernardini, (202) 317-6853; concerning submissions and to request a hearing, Regina Johnson, (202) 317-6901 (not toll-free numbers).

SUPPLEMENTARY INFORMATION:

Paperwork Reduction Act

There is no new collection of information contained in this notice of proposed rulemaking. The collection of information contained in the regulations under section 468A has been reviewed and approved by the Office of Management and Budget in accordance with the Paperwork Reduction Act of 1995 (44 U.S.C. 3507(d)) under control number 1545-2091. Responses to these collections of information are required to obtain a tax benefit.

An agency may not conduct or sponsor, and a person is not required to respond to, a collection of information unless it displays a valid control number assigned by the Office of Management and Budget.

Books or records relating to a collection of information must be retained as long as their contents may become material in the administration of any internal revenue law. Generally, tax returns and tax return information are confidential, as required by section 6103 of the Code.

Background

This proposed rulemaking consists of several amendments to the existing regulations under section 468A. Section 468A was originally enacted by section 91(c)(1) of the Deficit Reduction Act of 1984, Public Law 98-369, (98 Stat 604) and has been amended, most recently by section 1310 of the Energy Policy Act of 2005, Public Law 109-58 (119 Stat 594). Temporary regulations (TD 9374) under section 468A were published in the **Federal Register** for December 31, 2007 (72 FR 74175). Regulations finalizing and removing the temporary regulations (TD 9512) were published in the **Federal Register** on December 23, 2010 (75 FR 80697).

Explanation of Provisions

1. *Definition of Nuclear Decommissioning Costs*

A. *Inclusion of amounts related to the storage of spent fuel within definition of nuclear decommissioning costs*

Section 468A is intended to allow taxpayers to currently deduct amounts set aside in a qualified fund (Fund) for the purpose of decommissioning a nuclear power plant. The taxpayer must include the amount of any actual or deemed distribution from the Fund in gross income in the year of the distribution, as provided in § 1.468A-2(d)(1). Taxpayers may then claim an offsetting deduction for amounts spent on decommissioning costs as determined under section 461(h) and other sections. See § 1.468A-2(e).

Taxpayers that operate nuclear power plants, whether such plants are currently operating or have ceased operations, must safely store spent fuel. Nuclear fuel assemblies are removed from the reactor and those assemblies are stored in a spent fuel pool for cooling. Subsequently, the spent fuel may be inserted into storage casks and the casks transferred to an on-site Independent Spent Fuel Storage Installation (ISFSI). An ISFSI consists of a concrete storage pad on which the storage casks are placed. Although the Nuclear Waste Policy Act of 1982, 42 U.S.C. 10101, et seq, requires the Department of Energy (DOE) to take and dispose of spent nuclear fuel in a permanent geologic repository, no such repository has been established and the government has not yet begun accepting spent fuel. Thus, operators of nuclear power plants must safely store spent fuel in an on-site ISFSI.

Existing § 1.468A-1(b)(6) defines nuclear decommissioning costs as including "all otherwise deductible expenses to be incurred in connection with" the disposal of certain nuclear assets. Section 1.468A-1(b)(6) continues that "such term also includes costs incurred in connection with the construction, operation, and ultimate decommissioning of a facility used solely to store, pending acceptance by the government for permanent storage or disposal, spent nuclear fuel generated by the nuclear power plant or plants located on the same site as the storage facility." The Treasury Department and the IRS have become aware that there are questions regarding whether ISFSI-related costs for the construction or purchase of assets that would not necessarily qualify as "otherwise deductible" expenses under the current regulation are included as nuclear decommissioning costs. The proposed regulations clarify the definition of nuclear decommissioning costs to specifically provide for ISFSI-related costs.

B. *Inclusion of amounts for purchase or construction of a depreciable asset as part of decommissioning process within definition of nuclear decommissioning costs*

Under the existing regulations, questions have arisen as to whether a cost must be currently deductible for that amount to be payable currently from the Fund under the "otherwise deductible" language of § 1.468A-1(b)(6). For example, where a depreciable asset is purchased or constructed as part of the decommissioning process (and the asset is not considered abandoned) questions have arisen regarding whether the "otherwise deductible" language is satisfied solely by the fact that the property is depreciable or whether the expense is treated as a deductible decommissioning expense only to the extent that depreciation is currently allowed. This raises a timing issue regarding whether a fund may pay for the purchase or construction of a depreciable asset to be used in decommissioning that is not considered abandoned when completed. Under the present regulations, because the asset would be fully depreciable but the cost of the asset is not otherwise deductible, a fund may only pay for the portion of the depreciation allowable in the tax year in which such property is placed in service. The intent of section 468A is to allow owners of nuclear power plants to put amounts in a Fund on a tax-free basis and then to use those amounts and the earnings on those amounts to pay for decommissioning. In order to effectuate that intent, the proposed regulations broaden the definition of nuclear decommissioning costs to include the total cost of depreciable assets by adding the words "or recoverable through depreciation" following "otherwise deductible" in § 1.468A-1(b)(6).

2. *Clarification of the Applicability of the Self-Dealing Rules to Transactions Between the Fund and Related Parties*

Section 4951 imposes an excise tax on acts of self-dealing between a "disqualified person" and a trust described in section 501(c)(21). Section 468A(e)(5) provides that, under regulations prescribed by the Secretary, for purposes of section 4951, the Fund shall be treated in the same manner as a trust described in section 501(c)(21). Section 1.468A-5(b)(1) states that the excise taxes imposed by section 4951 apply to each act of self-dealing between the Fund and a disqualified person. Section 1.468A-5(b)(2) defines "self-dealing," for purposes of § 1.468A-5(b), as any act described in section 4951(d), but provides for some exclusions, including a payment by a Fund for the purpose of satisfying, in whole or in part, the liability of the taxpayer who has elected section 468A and established a Fund (electing taxpayer) for decommissioning costs of the nuclear power plant to which the Fund relates. Section 1.468A-5(b)(3), by reference to section 4951(e)(4) and § 53.4951-1(d), provides that the term "disqualified person" includes, with respect to a trust, a contributor to the trust and a trustee of the trust.

The IRS has issued several private letter rulings holding that a reimbursement to an electing taxpayer or an unrelated party by a Fund of decommissioning costs, such as severance payments and pre-dismantlement decommissioning costs, is made for the purpose of satisfying the liability of the electing taxpayer for decommissioning costs of the nuclear power plant to which the Fund relates and therefore is not self-dealing. Thus, under these rulings, the reimbursement by a Fund of these costs represents a permissible use of the Funds. To remove any lingering uncertainty, as well as to avoid the burden on taxpayers of filing additional ruling requests on these issues, the proposed regulations clarify that reimbursements of decommissioning costs by the Fund to related parties (including the electing taxpayer) that paid such costs are not an act of self-dealing. However, no amount beyond what is actually paid by the related party, including amounts such as direct or indirect overhead or a reasonable profit element, may be included in the reimbursement by the Fund.

3. *Definition of "Substantial Completion" in § 1.468A-5(d)(3)(i)*

Existing § 1.468A-5(d)(3)(i) defines the substantial completion date as "the date that the maximum acceptable radioactivity levels mandated by the Nuclear Regulatory Commission [NRC] with respect to a decommissioned nuclear power plant are satisfied." However, § 1.468A-5(d)(3)(ii) provides that, if a significant portion of the total estimated decommissioning costs are not incurred on or before the substantial completion date, the electing taxpayer may request a ruling that designates a date subsequent to the substantial completion date as the termination date; such later date may be no later than the last day of the third taxable year after the taxable year that includes the substantial completion date. Under certain state and local requirements, the plant operator must return the site of the plant to conditions requiring time beyond that needed to reach the maximum radioactivity level mandated by the NRC. To accommodate these situations without requiring that the taxpayer request a ruling, the proposed regulations amend the definition of "substantial completion" to the date on which all Federal, state, local, and contractual decommissioning liabilities are fully satisfied.

Proposed Effective/Applicability Date

The rules contained in these regulations are proposed to apply to taxable years ending on or after the date of publication of the Treasury decision adopting these rules as final regulations in the **Federal Register**. Notwithstanding the prospective effective date, the IRS will not challenge return positions consistent with these proposed regulations for taxable years ending on or after the date these proposed regulations are published.

Special Analyses

Certain IRS regulations, including these, are exempt from the requirements of Executive Order 12866, as supplemented and affirmed by Executive Order 13563. Therefore, a regulatory assessment is not required. It is hereby certified that these regulations will not have a significant economic impact on a substantial number of small entities. This certification is based on (1) the fact that the rules in these proposed regulations primarily affect owners of nuclear power plants which are not small entities as defined by the Regulatory Flexibility Act (5 U.S.C. 601) and (2) the proposed regulations do not impose a collection of information on small entities. Accordingly, a Regulatory Flexibility Analysis under the Regulatory Flexibility Act (5 U.S.C. 601) is not required. We request comment on the accuracy of this certification. Pursuant to section 7805(f) of the Code, these regulations have been submitted to the Chief Counsel for Advocacy of the Small Business Administration for comment on their impact on small business.

Comments and Requests for a Public Hearing

Before these proposed regulations are adopted as final regulations, consideration will be given to any written comments (a signed original and eight (8) copies) or electronically generated comments that are submitted timely to the IRS. The Treasury Department and the IRS generally request comments on the clarity of the proposed rule and how it may be made easier to understand. All comments will be available for public inspection and copying. A public hearing may be scheduled if requested in writing by a person who timely submits comments. If a public hearing is scheduled, notice of the date, time, and place for the hearing will be published in the **Federal Register**.

Drafting Information

The principal author of these regulations is Jennifer C. Bernardini, Office of Associate Chief Counsel (Passthroughs and Special Industries). However, other personnel from the IRS and Treasury Department participated in their development.

[¶ 49,732] Proposed Amendments of Regulations (REG-103477-14), published in the Federal Register on January 6, 2017 (corrected September 15, 2017).

[Code Secs. 1471, 1472 and 1474]

Foreign Account Tax Compliance Act (FATCA): Foreign financial institution (FFI): FFI agreement: Chapter 4 due diligence.—Amendments of Reg. §§ 1.1471-1, 1.1471-3, 1.1471-4 and 1.1474-1, regarding reporting requirements on behalf of certain foreign financial institutions (FFIs) and the chapter 4 due diligence and reporting obligations on behalf of certain nonfinancial foreign entities, are adopted. Proposed amendments to Reg. §§ 1.1471-5 and 1.1472-1 and portions of proposed amendments to Reg. §§ 1.1471-1 and 1.1471-4 adopted by T.D. 9852 on March 21, 2019.

[¶ 49,733] Proposed Amendments of Regulations (REG-134247-16), published in the Federal Register on January 6, 2017 (corrected September 15, 2017).

[Code Sec. 1441]

Foreign Account Tax Compliance Act (FATCA): Foreign financial institution (FFI): FFI agreement: Withholding.—Amendments of Reg. §§ 1.1441-1, 1.1441-2, 1.1441-6 and 1.1441-7, regarding withholding of tax on certain U.S. source income paid to foreign persons and requirements for certain claims for refund or credit of income tax made by foreign persons, are adopted.

[¶ 49,737] Proposed Amendments of Regulation and Withdrawal of Notice of Proposed Rulemaking (REG-137604-07), published in the Federal Register on January 19, 2017.

[Code Secs. 2, 3, 21, 32, 63, 151, 152, 6013 and 6109]

Dependency exemptions: Filing status: Tax tables: Earned income credit: Standard deduction: Taxpayer identification number.—Reg. §§ 1.63-3, 1.152-0, and 1.152-4, and amendments of Reg. §§ 1.2-1, 1.2-2, 1.3-1, 1.21-1, 1.32-2, 1.63-1, 1.63-2, 1.151-1, 1.151-2, 1.151-3, 1.151-4, 1.152-1, 1.152-2, 1.152-3, 1.152-4, 1.152-5, 1.6013-1, and 301.6109-3, relating to the definition of an authorized placement agency for purposes of a dependency exemption for a child placed for adoption that were issued prior to the changes made to the law by the Working Families Tax Relief Act of 2004 (WFTRA), are proposed. Amendments of Reg. § 1.152-2, proposed by REG-107279-00 on November 30, 2000, are withdrawn.

AGENCY: Internal Revenue Service (IRS), Treasury.

ACTION: Withdrawal of notice of proposed rulemaking and notice of proposed rulemaking.

SUMMARY: This document withdraws proposed regulations relating to the definition of an authorized placement agency for purposes of a dependency exemption for a child placed for adoption that were issued prior to the changes made to the law by the Working Families Tax Relief Act of 2004 (WFTRA). This document contains proposed regulations that reflect changes made by WFTRA and by the Fostering Connections to Success and Increasing Adoptions Act of 2008 (FCSIAA) relating to the dependency exemption. This document also contains proposed regulations that, to reflect current law, amend the regulations relating to the surviving spouse and head of household filing statuses, the tax tables for individuals, the child and dependent care credit, the earned income credit, the standard deduction, joint tax returns, and taxpayer identification numbers for children placed for adoption. These proposed regulations change the IRS's position regarding the category of taxpayers permitted to claim the childless earned income credit. In determining a taxpayer's eligibility to claim a dependency exemption, these proposed regulations change the IRS's position regarding the adjusted gross income of a taxpayer filing a joint return for purposes of the tiebreaker rules and the source of support of certain payments that originated as governmental payments. These regulations provide guidance to individuals who may claim certain child-related tax benefits.

DATES: Written or electronic comments and requests for a public hearing must be received by April 19, 2017.

ADDRESSES: Send submissions to: CC:PA:LPD:PR (REG-137604-07), Room 5203, Internal Revenue Service, PO Box 7604, Ben Franklin Station, Washington, DC 20044. Submissions may be hand-delivered Monday through Friday between the hours of 8 a.m. and 4 p.m. to CC:PA:LPD:PR (REG-137604-07), Courier's Desk, Internal Revenue Service, 1111 Constitution Avenue, NW., Washington, DC 20224, or sent electronically via the Federal eRulemaking Portal at *www.regulations.gov* (IRS REG-137604-07). FOR FURTHER INFORMATION CONTACT: Concerning the proposed regulations, Victoria J. Driscoll, (202) 317-4718; concerning the submission of comments and requests for a public hearing, Regina Johnson, (202) 317-6901 (not toll-free calls). SUPPLEMENTARY INFORMATION:

Background

This document withdraws a notice of proposed rulemaking (REG-107279-00) amending § 1.152-2(c)(2) of the Income Tax Regulations that was published in the **Federal Register** (65 FR 71277) on November 30, 2000 (2000 proposed regulations) relating to the definition of an authorized placement agency for purposes of a dependency exemption for a child placed for adoption under prior law. Prior law required that a child be placed with the taxpayer for adoption by an authorized placement agency. Section 152 of the Internal Revenue Code was amended by section 201 of WFTRA (Public Law 108-311, 118 Stat. 1166, 1169) to provide that a qualifying child eligible to be the dependent of a taxpayer may include a child lawfully placed with the taxpayer for adoption. Accordingly, the proposed regulations in § 1.152-2(c)(2) under prior law are withdrawn.

This document also contains proposed amendments to 26 CFR Part 1 under sections 2, 3, 21, 32, 63, 151, 152, 6013, and to Part 301 under section 6109 to reflect the changes made by WFTRA and FCSIAA (Public Law 110-351, 122 Stat. 3949) relating to the dependency exemption, as well as changes to these sections by other acts. WFTRA amended section 152, in part, to provide a uniform definition of a qualifying child; FCSIAA added to the definition of a qualifying child the requirements that the child must be younger than the taxpayer and that the child must not file a joint return (other than as a claim for refund). FCSIAA also amended the rules that apply if two or more taxpayers are eligible to claim an individual as a qualifying child.

1. *Dependency Rules*

Under section 151, a taxpayer may deduct an exemption amount for a dependent as defined in section 152. Prior to WFTRA, section 151 contained many of the rules related to the definition of a dependent. WFTRA moved those rules to section 152. As amended, section 152(a) defines a *dependent* as a qualifying child or a qualifying relative. Taxpayers should note that a taxpayer's treatment of the dependency exemption under section 151 for a particular qualifying child or qualifying relative might have tax consequences under other Code provisions, such as the education tax credits under section 25A, the premium tax credit under section 36B, and the penalty for failure to maintain minimum essential coverage under section 5000A.

a. *Individual not a dependent*

Section 152(b) provides that an individual who is a qualifying child or a qualifying relative of a taxpayer is not a taxpayer's dependent in certain circumstances. Section 152(b)(2) provides that, to be a dependent of a taxpayer, an individual must not have filed a joint return with his or her spouse. However, the WFTRA conference report provides that the "restriction does not apply if the return was filed solely to obtain a refund and no tax liability would exist for either spouse if they filed separate returns." See H.R. Rep. No. 108-696, at 55 n.38 (2004) (Conf. Rep.).

b. *Qualifying child*

WFTRA established under section 152(c) a uniform definition of a qualifying child. The legislative history identifies five child-related benefits to which the uniform definition applies: the filing status of head of household under section 2(b), the child and dependent care credit under section 21, the child tax credit under section 24, the earned income credit under section 32, and the dependency exemption under section 151. See H.R. Rep. No. 108-696, at 55-65.

Section 152(c) defines a qualifying child as an individual who bears a certain relationship to the taxpayer (qualifying child relationship test), has the same principal place of abode as the taxpayer for more than one-half of the taxable year (residency test), is younger than the taxpayer and is under the age of 19 (or age 24 if a full-time student or any age if permanently and totally disabled) (age test), does not provide more than one-half of his or her own support (qualifying child support test), and does not file a joint return with a spouse except to claim a refund of estimated or withheld taxes (joint return test).

c. *Temporary absence*

A child is considered to reside in the same principal place of abode as a taxpayer during a temporary absence. Under the existing section 152 regulations, a nonpermanent failure to occupy a common abode by reason of illness, education, business, vacation, military service, or a custody agreement may be a temporary absence due to special circumstances. The existing regulations under section 2 defining surviving spouse and head of household include a similar rule relating to the effect of a temporary absence on the requirement to maintain a household, but add the requirement that it is reasonable to assume that the absent person will return to the household. Under case law, a factor to consider in determining whether an absence is temporary is whether the individual intends to establish a new principal place of abode. In *Rowe v. Commissioner*, 128 T.C. 13 (2007), the court concluded that it was reasonable to assume that a taxpayer would return to her home after pretrial confinement and that the taxpayer's absence was temporary. See also *Hein v. Commissioner*, 28 T.C. 826 (1957) (*acq.*, 1958-2 CB 6), and Rev. Rul. 66-28 (1966-1 CB 31).

d. *Two or more taxpayers eligible to claim individual as qualifying child*

Section 152(c)(4) provides tiebreaker rules that apply if an individual meets the definition of a qualifying child for two or more taxpayers (eligible taxpayers). In general, the eligible taxpayer who is a parent (eligible parent) of the individual may claim the individual as a qualifying child or, if there is no eligible parent, then the individual may be claimed by the eligible taxpayer with the highest adjusted gross income.

If more than one of the eligible taxpayers is a parent of the individual, more than one eligible parent claims the individual as a qualifying child, and the eligible parents claiming the individual do not file a joint return with each other, the individual is treated as the qualifying child of the eligible parent claiming the individual with whom the individual resided for the longest period of time during the taxable year. If the individual resided with each eligible parent claiming the individual for the same amount of time during the taxable year, the individual is treated as the qualifying child of the eligible parent claiming the individual with the highest adjusted gross income.

If at least one, but not all, of two or more eligible taxpayers is a parent of the individual, but no eligible parent claims the individual as a qualifying child, another eligible taxpayer may claim the individual, but only if the eligible taxpayer's adjusted gross income is higher than the adjusted gross income of each eligible parent. Since 2009, IRS Publication 501, *Exemptions, Standard Deduction, and Filing Information*, has stated that "[i]f a child's parents file a joint return with each other, this rule may be applied by dividing the parents' combined AGI equally between the parents."

Notice 2006-86 (2006-2 CB 680) provides interim guidance on these rules prior to the amendments by FCSIAA. The notice provides that, except to the extent that a noncustodial parent may claim the child as a qualifying child under the special rule for divorced or separated parents in section 152(e), discussed in the next paragraph, if more than one taxpayer claims a child as a qualifying child, the child is treated as the qualifying child of only one taxpayer (as determined under the tiebreaker rules of section 152(c)(4)) for purposes of the five provisions subject to the uniform definition of a qualifying child (the filing status of head of household under section 2(b), the child and dependent care credit under section 21, the child tax credit under section 24, the earned income credit under section 32, and the dependency exemption under section 151, as well as for purposes of the exclusion for dependent care assistance under section 129 (which may apply to the care of a dependent qualifying child under age 13)). Thus, in general, the tiebreaker rules for determining which taxpayer may claim a child as a qualifying child apply to these provisions as a group, rather than on a section-by-section basis.

Notice 2006-86 contains an exception to the rule that only one taxpayer may claim a child as a qualifying child for all purposes. Section 152(e) has a special rule for divorced or separated parents that determines who, as between the custodial and noncustodial parent, may claim a child as a qualifying child or qualifying relative if certain tests (different from the general tests under sections 152(c) and (d)) regarding residency and support are met and the custodial parent releases a claim to exemption for the child. The notice provides that, if this special rule applies, a noncustodial parent may claim a child as a qualifying child for purposes of the dependency exemption and the child tax credit (the only two of the provisions addressed in the notice to which section 152(e) applies in determining who is a qualifying child), and another taxpayer may claim the child for one or more of the other benefits to which section 152(e) does not apply.

Although FCSIAA affects other aspects of section 152(c)(4) and Notice 2006-86, there is nothing in FCSIAA that would compel a change in the rule described in Notice 2006-86 that an individual is treated as the qualifying child of only one taxpayer for the listed child-related tax benefits, except if the special rule in section 152(e) applies.

e. Qualifying relative

Under section 152(d), a qualifying relative is an individual who bears a certain relationship to the taxpayer, including an individual who has the same principal place of abode as the taxpayer and is a member of the taxpayer's household for the taxable year (qualifying relative relationship test), has gross income less than the exemption amount for the taxable year (gross income test), receives more than one-half of his or her support from the taxpayer (qualifying relative support test), and is not a qualifying child of any taxpayer (not a qualifying child test).

Notice 2008-5 (2008-1 CB 256) addresses whether a taxpayer meets the test under section 152(d)(1)(D) to claim an individual as a qualifying relative. That provision requires that the individual not be a qualifying child of either the taxpayer or any other taxpayer during a taxable year beginning in the calendar year in which the taxpayer's taxable year begins. The notice provides that, for purposes of section 152(d)(1)(D), an individual is not a qualifying child of "any other taxpayer" if the individual's parent (or other person for whom the individual is defined as a qualifying child) is not required by section 6012 to file an income tax return and (1) does not file an income tax return, or (2) files an income tax return solely to obtain a refund of withheld income taxes.

f. Support tests

Under section 152(c)(1)(D), to be a taxpayer's qualifying child, an individual must not have provided over one-half of the individual's own support for the calendar year. Under section 152(d)(1)(C), to be a taxpayer's qualifying relative, a taxpayer must have provided over one-half of an individual's support for the calendar year.

Regarding governmental payments to a person with a qualifying need, the WFTRA conference report, H.R. Rep. No. 108-696, at 57, states that "[g]overnmental payments and subsidies (e.g., Temporary Assistance [for] Needy Families, food stamps, and housing) generally are treated as support provided by a third party." The IRS has successfully asserted in litigation that governmental payments provided to a parent to aid a family with dependent children and used by the parent for support of her children was support of the children provided by the government, and not support provided by the parent. See *Lutter v. Commissioner*, 61 T.C. 685 (1974), *affd. per curiam*, 514 F.2d 1095 (7th Cir. 1975).

2. Surviving Spouse and Head of Household, and Conforming Changes

Prior to amendment by section 803(b) of the Tax Reform Act of 1969 (Public Law 91-172, 83 Stat. 487), section 2(a) provided that the return of a surviving spouse is treated as a joint return for purposes of the tax rates, the tax tables for individuals, and the standard deduction. Following the 1969 amendments, section 2(a) defines the term *surviving spouse* for purposes of section 1. The return of a taxpayer filing as a surviving spouse is no longer treated as a joint return under sections 2, 3, or 63. Section 3 provides tax tables for certain individuals in lieu of the tax imposed by section 1. Section 63(c) provides the same basic standard deduction for a taxpayer filing as a surviving spouse as a taxpayer filing a joint return. Accordingly, a taxpayer filing as a surviving spouse is no longer treated as filing a joint return for any tax purpose, but rather, a taxpayer filing as a surviving spouse simply uses the same tax rates under section 1, the same amounts in the tax tables under section 3, and the same standard deduction under section 63 as a taxpayer filing a joint return.

Generally, under section 2(b), to qualify as a head of household, a taxpayer must maintain a household that is the principal place of abode of a qualifying child or other dependent for more than one-half of the taxable year. If the dependent is a parent of the taxpayer and the parent does not share a principal place of abode with the taxpayer, the household maintained by the taxpayer must be the parent's principal place of abode for the entire taxable year.

Prior to WFTRA, section 21 required that a taxpayer maintain a household to claim the credit for dependent care expenses, and regulations on maintaining a household were published under that section. WFTRA removed that requirement from the dependent care credit.

3. Earned Income Credit

Section 32 provides a tax credit to eligible taxpayers who work and have earned income below a certain dollar amount. Before the amendment of section 32 by the Omnibus Reconciliation Act of 1993 (Public Law 103-66, 107 Stat. 312), the earned income credit (EIC) was allowable only to a taxpayer with one or more qualifying children. If an individual met the definition of a qualifying child for more than one taxpayer, a tiebreaker rule in section 32 determined which taxpayer was allowed to claim the individual as a qualifying child for the EIC. For taxable years beginning after 1993, section 32(c)(1)(A)(ii) allows a taxpayer without a qualifying child to claim the EIC (childless EIC) if certain requirements are met. Although there is no regulatory guidance on this issue, since 1995, the IRS has taken the position in IRS Publication 596, *Earned Income Credit*, that if an individual meets the definition of a qualifying child for more than one taxpayer and the individual is not treated as the qualifying child of a taxpayer under the tiebreaker rules, then that taxpayer is precluded from claiming the childless EIC. WFTRA moved the tiebreaker rules from section 32 to section 152(c)(4).

Before repeal in 2010, section 3507 allowed advance payment of the EIC. Section 3507 was repealed by the FAA Air Transportation Modernization and Safety Improvement Act (Public Law 111-226, 124 Stat. 2389).

4. *Additional Standard Deduction for the Aged and Blind*

Before the amendments to sections 63 and 151 made by the Tax Reform Act of 1986 (Public Law 99-514, 100 Stat. 2085), a taxpayer was entitled to an additional personal exemption under section 151 for the taxpayer or the taxpayer's spouse (or both), if either was age 65 or older or was blind at the close of the taxable year. As amended, section 63 provides an additional standard deduction for age or blindness instead of an additional personal exemption under section 151.

Explanation of Provisions

The proposed regulations reflect statutory amendments to sections 2, 3, 21, 32, 63, 151, 152, 6013, and 6109. In addition, the regulations address certain significant issues arising under these sections and modify certain IRS positions, as explained below.

1. *Dependency Exemption*

Consistent with the amendments made to sections 151 and 152 by WFTRA, the proposed regulations move rules related to the definition of a dependent from the regulations under section 151 to the regulations under section 152.

a. *Relationship test*

i. General Rules

Section 152(c)(2) provides that a qualifying child must be a child or a descendant of a child of the taxpayer, or a brother, sister, stepbrother, or stepsister of the taxpayer, or a descendant of any of these relatives. Section 152(d)(2) provides that a qualifying relative must bear a certain relationship to the taxpayer, which includes a child or a descendant of a child, a brother, sister, stepbrother, stepsister, parent or ancestor of a parent, or an aunt or uncle of the taxpayer. An individual (other than the taxpayer's spouse) who is not related to the taxpayer in one of the named relationships nevertheless may satisfy the relationship test for a qualifying relative if the individual has the same principal place of abode as the taxpayer and is a member of the taxpayer's household for the taxpayer's taxable year.

The proposed regulations adopt the rule in Notice 2008-5 regarding whether an individual is a qualifying child of a taxpayer for purposes of determining whether that individual may be a qualifying relative. That is, the proposed regulations provide that an individual is not a qualifying child of a person if that person is not required to file an income tax return under section 6012, and either does not file an income tax return or files an income tax return solely to claim a refund of estimated or withheld taxes.

ii. Adopted Child—Adoption by Individual Other than the Taxpayer

Prior to 2005, for purposes of the relationship test, a person's legally adopted child was treated as that person's child by blood. Specifically, section 152(b)(2) provided that "a legally adopted child of an individual (and a child who is a member of an individual's household, if placed with such individual by an authorized placement agency for legal adoption by such individual), . . . shall be treated as a child of such individual by blood." Therefore, a taxpayer other than the adopting "individual" could be eligible to claim an exemption for an adopted child. For example, the parent of the adopting parent could claim a dependency exemption for the legally adopted child of the taxpayer's son or daughter (just as biological grandparents may claim an exemption for a grandchild) if all other requirements were met.

WFTRA amended section 152 to change the reference from a child placed by an authorized placement agency for adoption to a child who is "lawfully placed" for legal adoption. In making that change, however, WFTRA also changed the reference to the adopting person from "an individual" to "the taxpayer," so that section 152(f)(1)(B) currently provides that a legally adopted individual of the taxpayer is treated as a child by blood of the taxpayer. The use of the word "taxpayer" rather than "individual" arguably limits the recognition of a relationship through adoption only to those situations in which the taxpayer claiming a dependency exemption for the child is the person who adopts the child. This interpretation of the amended statutory language would diverge from the results of a legal adoption under property, inheritance, and other nontax law, and from the prior tax treatment of adoptions - a significant change in the applicable law. However, there is nothing in the legislative history indicating that Congress intended to limit the treatment of an adopted child as a child by blood in this manner or that otherwise suggests this change in language was intended to effect a change in existing law.

To fill this apparent gap in the statute, the proposed regulations provide that any child legally adopted by a "person," or any child who is placed with a "person" for legal adoption by that "person," is treated as a child by blood of that person for purposes of the relationship tests under sections 152(c)(2) and 152(d)(2). Similarly, the proposed regulations provide that an eligible foster child is a child who is placed with a "person" rather than with a taxpayer.

iii. Adopted Child and Foster Child—Child Placement

Although WFTRA removed the reference to an authorized placement agency from the provisions relating to an adopted child in section 152(f)(1)(B), the reference to an authorized placement agency continues to appear in section 152(f)(1)(C), relating to an eligible foster child. Prior to amendment by WFTRA, section 152 treated a child who was a member of an individual's household pending adoption as a child by blood of the individual for purposes of the relationship test only if the child was a foster child living with the individual or if the child was placed with the individual by an authorized placement agency for adoption by the individual. Similarly, § 301.6109-3(a) currently provides that a taxpayer may obtain an adoption taxpayer identification number (ATIN) only for a child who was placed for adoption by an authorized placement agency.

As amended by WFTRA, section 152 treats a child placed for adoption as a child by blood of the taxpayer if the child "is lawfully placed with the taxpayer for legal adoption by the taxpayer." A child may be lawfully placed for legal adoption by an authorized placement agency, the child's parents, or other persons authorized by State law to place children for legal adoption. These proposed regulations reflect the changes made by WFTRA and amend the regulations under section 6109 to provide that the IRS will assign an ATIN to a child who has been lawfully placed with a person for legal adoption.

Under section 152(f)(1)(A)(ii) and § 1.152-1(b)(1)(iii) of these proposed regulations, the term *child* also includes an eligible foster child of the taxpayer as defined in 152(f)(1)(C), that is, a child who is placed with the taxpayer by an authorized placement agency or by the judgment, decree, or other order of a court of competent jurisdiction.

iv. Definition of Authorized Placement Agency

The 2000 proposed regulations under §1.152-2(c)(2) defined an authorized placement agency for purposes of the prior law regarding a child placed for legal adoption. These proposed regulations define an authorized placement agency for purposes of the definition of an eligible foster child and withdraw the 2000 proposed regulations, which defined that term without reference to an Indian Tribal Government (ITG).

These proposed regulations provide that an *authorized placement agency* may be a State, the District of Columbia, a possession of the United States, a foreign country, an agency or organization authorized by, or a political subdivision of, any of these entities to place children in foster care or for adoption. Under the Indian Child Welfare Act of 1978 (25 U.S.C. chapter 21), ITGs and states perform similar functions for foster care and adoption programs. Thus, the proposed regulations provide that an authorized placement agency also may be an ITG (as defined in section 7701(a)(40)), or an agency or organization authorized by, or a political subdivision of, an ITG that places children in foster care or for adoption.

b. *Residency test—principal place of abode*

For purposes of determining whether an individual has the same principal place of abode as the taxpayer in applying the residency test for a qualifying child and the relationship test for a qualifying relative who does not have one of the listed relationships to the taxpayer, the proposed regulations provide that the term *principal place of abode* means a person's main home or dwelling where the person resides. A person's principal place of abode need not be the same physical location throughout the taxable year and may be temporary lodging such as a homeless shelter or relief housing resulting from displacement caused by a natural disaster.

The proposed regulations further provide that a taxpayer and an individual have the same principal place of abode despite a temporary absence by either person. A person is temporarily absent if, based on the facts and circumstances, the person would have resided with the taxpayer but for the temporary absence and it is reasonable to assume the person will return to reside at the place of abode. Thus, the proposed regulations adopt the "reasonable to assume" language from the existing regulations under section 2. The proposed regulations indicate that a nonpermanent failure to occupy the abode by reason of illness, education, business, vacation, military service, institutionalized care for a child who is permanently and totally disabled (as defined in section 22(e)(3)), or incarceration may be treated as a temporary absence due to special circumstances. This definition of temporary absence applies to the residency test for a qualifying child, to the relationship test for a qualifying relative who does not have a listed relationship to the taxpayer, and to the requirements to maintain a household for surviving spouse and head of household.

For purposes of the residency test for a qualifying child, the proposed regulations provide that an individual is treated as having the same principal place of abode as the taxpayer for more than one-half of the taxable year if the individual resides with the taxpayer for at least 183 nights during the taxpayer's taxable year or for at least 184 nights during the taxpayer's taxable year that includes a leap day (residing for more than one-half of the taxable year). The proposed regulations further provide that an individual resides with the taxpayer for a night if the individual sleeps (1) at the taxpayer's residence, or (2) in the company of the taxpayer when the individual does not sleep at the taxpayer's residence (for example, when the parent and the child are on vacation). The regulations provide additional rules for counting nights if a night extends over two taxable years and for taxpayers who work at night.

The proposed regulations provide special rules for determining whether an individual satisfies a residency test if the individual is born or dies during the taxable year, is adopted or placed for adoption, is an eligible foster child, or is a missing child.

c. *Age test*

The age test for a qualifying child requires that an individual be younger than the taxpayer claiming the individual as a qualifying child, and the individual must not have attained the age of 19 (or age 24 if the individual is a student). The age requirement is treated as satisfied if the individual is permanently and totally disabled.

For purposes of this age test, the proposed regulations substantially adopt the existing definition of a student. Accordingly, the proposed regulations provide that the term *student* means an individual who, during some part of each of 5 calendar months during the calendar year in which the taxable year of the taxpayer begins, is a full-time student at an educational organization described in section 170(b)(1)(A)(ii) or is pursuing a full-time course of institutional on-farm training under the supervision of an accredited agent of an educational institution or of a State or political subdivision of a State. An *educational organization*, as defined in section 170(b)(1)(A)(ii), is a school normally maintaining a regular faculty and curriculum and having a regularly enrolled body of students in attendance at the place where its educational activities are regularly carried on.

d. *Support tests*

In determining whether an individual provided more than one-half of the individual's own support (qualifying child support test), or whether a taxpayer provided more than one-half of an individual's support (qualifying relative support test), the proposed regulations compare the amount of support provided by the individual or the taxpayer to the total amount of the individual's support from all sources. In general, the amount of an individual's support from all sources includes support the individual provides and income that is excludable from gross income. The proposed regulations further provide that the amount of an item of support is the amount of expenses paid or incurred to furnish the item of support. If support is furnished in the form of property or a benefit (such as lodging), the amount of that support is the fair market value of the item furnished (Rev. Rul. 58-302 (1958-1 CB 62)).

The proposed regulations provide that the term *support* includes food, shelter, clothing, medical and dental care, education, and similar items for the benefit of the supported individual. Support does not include Federal, State, and local income taxes, or Social Security and Medicare taxes, of an individual paid from the individual's own income (Rev. Rul. 58-67 (1958-1 CB 62)), funeral expenses (Rev. Rul. 65-307 (1965-2 CB 40)), life insurance premiums, or scholarships received by a taxpayer's child who is a student as defined in section 152(f)(2).

The proposed regulations provide that medical insurance premiums are treated as support. These premiums include Part A Basic Medicare premiums, if any, under Title XVIII of the Social Security Act (42 U.S.C. 1395c to 1395i-5), Part B Supplemental Medicare premiums under Title XVIII of the Social Security Act (42 U.S.C. 1395j to 1395w-6), Part C Medicare + Choice Program premiums under Title XVIII of the Social Security Act (42 U.S.C. 1395w-21 to 1395w-29), and Part D Voluntary Prescription Drug Benefit Medicare premiums under Title XVIII of the Social Security Act (42 U.S.C. 1395w-101 to 1395w-154). However, medical insurance proceeds, including benefits received under Medicare Part A, Part B, Part C, and Part D, are not treated as support and are disregarded in determining the amount of the individual's support. Thus, only the premiums paid and the unreimbursed portion of the expenses for the individual's medical care are support. See Rev. Rul. 64-223 (1964-2 CB 50); and Rev. Rul. 70-341 (1970-2 CB 31), revoked in part by Rev. Rul. 79-173 (1979-1 CB 86) to the extent that it held that Part A Medicare benefits are included as a recipient's contribution to support. In addition, services provided to individuals under the medical and dental care provisions of the Armed Forces Act (10 U.S.C. chapter 55) are not treated as support and are disregarded in determining the amount of the individual's support. Finally, payments from a third party (including a third party's insurance company) for the medical care of an injured individual in satisfaction of a legal claim for the personal injury of the individual are not items of support and are disregarded in determining the amount of the individual's support. See Rev. Rul. 64-223.

The proposed regulations provide that, in general, governmental payments and subsidies are treated as support provided by a third party. Consistent with previously issued rulings and case law, these payments and subsidies include, for example, Temporary Assistance for Needy

Families (TANF) (42 U.S.C. 601-619), low-income housing assistance (42 U.S.C. 1437f), benefits under the Supplemental Nutrition Assistance Program (7 U.S.C. chapter 51), Supplemental Security Income payments (42 U.S.C. 1381-1383f), foster care maintenance payments, and adoption assistance payments. See H.R. Rep. No. 108-696, at 57 (2004) (Conf. Rep.); *Gulvin v. Commissioner*, 644 F.2d 2 (5th Cir. 1981); and Rev. Rul. 74-153 (1974-1 CB 20).

However, unlike the subsidies described in the previous paragraph that generally are based solely on need, old age benefits under section 202(b) of Title II of the Social Security Act (SSA) (42 U.S.C. 402) are based on an individual's earnings and contributions into the Social Security system and thus are treated as support provided by the recipient to the extent the recipient uses the payments for support. See Rev. Rul. 58-419 (1958-2 CB 57), as modified by Rev. Rul. 64-222 (1964-2 CB 47). Similarly, Social Security survivor and disability insurance benefit payments made under section 202(d) of the SSA to the child of a deceased or disabled parent are treated as support provided by the child to the extent those payments are used for the child's support. See Rev. Rul. 57-344 (1957-2 CB 112) and Rev. Rul. 74-543 (1974-2 CB 39).

The proposed regulations provide a special rule for governmental payments used by the recipient or other intended beneficiary to support another individual. The proposed regulations draw a distinction between: (1) governmental payments (such as Social Security old age benefits, or survivor and disability insurance benefits for a child) made to a recipient that are intended to benefit a particular named individual (whether the recipient, or another intended beneficiary for whom the recipient merely acts as the payee on behalf of that other intended beneficiary); and (2) governmental payments made to a recipient that are intended to support the recipient and other individuals (such as TANF). Although the governmental payments of the former variety are intended to benefit a particular named individual, because money is fungible, the intended beneficiary might use the governmental payments to support another individual. In this situation, the proposed regulations provide that, if the intended beneficiary (whether the recipient or another individual) uses the governmental payments to support another individual, that amount would constitute support of that other individual provided by the intended beneficiary. Similarly, the proposed regulations provide that the use of governmental payments of the latter variety by the recipient to support another individual would constitute support of that other individual provided by the recipient, whereas any part of such a payment used for the support of the recipient would constitute support of the recipient by a third party. For example, if a mother receives TANF and uses the TANF payments to support her children, the proposed regulations treat the mother as having provided that support. Thus, the IRS will no longer assert the position that it took in *Lutter*, which concerned payments received by a mother under a program that was the predecessor of TANF. The Treasury Department and the IRS are proposing this rule for the administrative convenience of both the IRS and taxpayers to avoid the need to trace the use of such governmental payments, as opposed to the use of other funds of the recipient, for the support of another individual.

The Treasury Department and IRS request comments on whether various payments made pursuant to the Patient Protection And Affordable Care Act (Public Law 111-148, 124 Stat. 119) in the form of a cost-sharing reduction, an advanced payment of the premium tax credit, or as a reimbursement of health insurance premiums in the form of a premium tax credit, when used for the benefit of another individual, are support provided by the recipient of those benefits or support provided by a third party.

e. *Citizenship*

Under section 152(b)(3)(A), an individual who is not a citizen or national of the United States is not a dependent unless the individual is a resident of the United States, Canada, or Mexico. Nevertheless, consistent with the exception for certain adopted children in section 152(b)(3)(B), the proposed regulations provide that an adopted child of a taxpayer who is a U.S. citizen or national may qualify as a dependent if, for the taxpayer's taxable year, the child has the same principal place of abode as the taxpayer and is a member of the taxpayer's household, and otherwise qualifies as the taxpayer's dependent.

f. *Tiebreaker rules*

The proposed regulations change the interpretation in Publication 501 regarding a taxpayer's adjusted gross income on a joint return and provide that, in applying the tiebreaker rules that treat an individual as the qualifying child of the eligible taxpayer with the higher or highest adjusted gross income, the adjusted gross income of a taxpayer who files a joint tax return is the total adjusted gross income shown on the return. The prior interpretation is changed to be consistent with other Code sections that require the filing of a joint return to claim a benefit and therefore calculate income based on the entire amount shown on the joint return. For example, the earned income credit under section 32 calculates the earned income amount based on the entire amount shown on the joint return. This joint return rule also is relevant for determining whether section 152(c)(4)(C) applies. Under that provision, if an eligible parent does not claim an individual as a qualifying child, another eligible taxpayer may claim the individual as a qualifying child only if that taxpayer's adjusted gross income is higher than the adjusted gross income of any eligible parent.

The proposed regulations also expand the tiebreaker rule in section 152(c)(4)(C) to address the situation in which an eligible parent does not claim an individual as a qualifying child and two or more taxpayers, none of whom is a parent, are eligible to claim the individual as a qualifying child and each has adjusted gross income higher than any eligible parent. In this situation, the proposed regulations provide that the individual is treated as the qualifying child of the eligible taxpayer with the highest adjusted gross income.

g. *Child of parents who are divorced, separated, or living apart*

Section 152(e) provides, in general, that a child is treated as the qualifying child or qualifying relative of a noncustodial parent for a calendar year if, among other things, the custodial parent provides to the noncustodial parent a written declaration that the custodial parent will not claim the child as a dependent for any taxable year beginning in that calendar year. Under section 152(e)(2)(B), the noncustodial parent must attach the written declaration to his or her return.

The proposed regulations provide that the noncustodial parent must attach a copy of the written declaration to an original or amended return. A taxpayer may submit a copy of the written declaration to the IRS during an examination of that parent's return. However, to provide certainty for both taxpayers and the IRS, the proposed regulations provide that a copy of a written declaration attached to an amended return or provided during an examination will not meet the requirements of section 152(e) and §1.152-5(e) if the custodial parent signed the written declaration after the custodial parent filed a return claiming a dependency exemption for the child for the year at issue, and the custodial parent has not filed an amended return to remove that claim to a dependency exemption. The proposed regulations provide similar rules for a parent revoking a written declaration.

h. *Filing a return solely to obtain a refund of taxes*

Individuals who file an income tax return solely to obtain a refund of estimated or withheld taxes are subject to special rules under various provisions of section 152. Section 152(c)(1)(E) provides that, for an individual to be a qualifying child of a taxpayer, the individual cannot have filed a joint return "other than only for a claim of refund." Section 152(b)(2) provides that, for an individual to be a dependent of a taxpayer, the individual cannot have filed a joint return with the individual's spouse. However, the WFTRA conference report states that "[t]his restriction does not apply if the return was filed solely to obtain a refund and no tax liability would exist for either spouse if they filed separate returns." Section 152(d)(1)(D) provides that, to be a qualifying relative, an individual may not be the qualifying child of the taxpayer or of any other taxpayer. Notice 2008-5 concludes that an individual is not the qualifying child of "any other taxpayer," within the meaning of section 152(d)(1)(D), if the person who could have claimed the individual as a qualifying child does not have a filing obligation and either does not file a return or files a return solely to obtain a refund of withheld taxes.

The proposed regulations provide a similar exception to the rule in section 152(b)(1) that a taxpayer cannot have a dependent if the taxpayer himself or herself is a dependent of another taxpayer. Specifically, the proposed regulations provide that an individual is not a dependent of a person if that person is not required to file an income tax return under section 6012 and either does not file an income tax return or files an income tax return solely to claim a refund of estimated or withheld taxes.

2. *Surviving Spouse, Head of Household, and Conforming Changes*

The proposed regulations amend the regulations under section 2 regarding the definition of surviving spouse and the definition of head of household to conform to the amendments made by WFTRA. To reflect the amendments made by the Tax Reform Act of 1969, the proposed regulations remove from the regulations under sections 2, 3, and 6013 references to the return of a surviving spouse being treated as a joint return. The proposed regulations also revise and move from the regulations under section 21 to the regulations under section 2 the definition of maintaining a household, in part, to conform to the amendments to section 21 made by WFTRA, which removed the requirement that a taxpayer maintain a household to claim the credit under section 21.

a. *Surviving spouse*

From the time of the 1969 amendment until the enactment of WFTRA, section 2(a)(1)(B) provided that a taxpayer who is a surviving spouse described in section 2(a)(1)(A) may file as a surviving spouse (and thus may use the tax rates of joint filers) only if the taxpayer "maintains as his home a household which constitutes for the taxable year the principal place of abode (as a member of such household) of a dependent (i) who (within the meaning of section 152) is a son, stepson, daughter, or stepdaughter of the taxpayer, and (ii) with respect to whom the taxpayer is entitled to a deduction for the taxable year under section 151." Thus, the member of the taxpayer's household had to be a son or daughter or stepson or stepdaughter for whom the taxpayer was entitled to a dependency deduction.

WFTRA amended section 2(a), as well as certain other sections such as section 42 relating to the low-income housing credit and section 125 relating to cafeteria plans, to provide that the reference to section 152 applies "without regard to subsections (b)(1), (b)(2), and (d)(1)(B)." These three subsections, respectively: (1) deny a dependency exemption to a dependent, (2) deny a dependency exemption for a person filing a joint return with his or her spouse, and (3) require the gross income of a qualifying relative to be less than the amount of the dependency exemption. Thus, the language inserted by the WFTRA technical amendment to section 2(a) was intended to broaden the class of individuals whose members could qualify a taxpayer as a surviving spouse for purposes of section 2. See also Staff of Joint Comm. on Taxation, 108th Cong., *General Explanation of Tax Legislation Enacted in the 108 th Congress* 130 (Comm. Print 2005) ("technical and conforming amendments . . . provide that an individual may qualify as a dependent for certain purposes . . . without regard to whether the individual has gross income . . . or is married and files a joint return.")

However, in amending section 2(a) for this purpose, WFTRA inserted the direction to exclude the three referenced provisions after the reference to section 152 in section 2(a)(1)(B)(i). Thus, this section currently provides, "(i) who (within the meaning of section 152, determined without regard to subsections (b)(1), (b)(2), and (d)(1)(B) thereof) is a son, stepson, daughter, or stepdaughter of the taxpayer." Because section 2(a)(1)(B)(ii) continues to require that the taxpayer be entitled to a deduction under section 151 for the dependent (a requirement that could not be met if any of these three sections applied), read literally, section 2(a)(1)(B)(ii) would override the intent of the statutory change in section 2(a)(1)(B)(i), thus preventing the WFTRA amendment from effecting any change in the statute. Therefore, to give effect to the statutory amendment, the proposed regulations construe the language added by WFTRA instead to modify the section 152 requirements that apply in determining whether the taxpayer is entitled to the dependency exemption under section 151 for purposes of section 2(a)(1)(B)(ii). Accordingly, the proposed regulations provide that an individual is a dependent for purposes of section 2(a) if the taxpayer may claim a deduction under section 151 for the individual without applying sections 152(b)(1), (b)(2), and (d)(1)(B).

b. *Head of household*

The proposed regulations under section 2(b) update and simplify the existing regulations defining head of household. Consistent with the statutory amendments to the definition of a dependent, the proposed regulations provide rules on qualifying as a head of household by maintaining a household that is the principal place of abode of a qualifying child or a dependent. The proposed regulations on head of household apply the rules in the proposed regulations under section 152 for determining principal place of abode, including whether an absence is temporary.

c. *Maintaining a household*

The proposed regulations provide that a taxpayer maintains a household only if the taxpayer pays more than one-half of the cost related to operating the household for the relevant period. Expenses related to operating the household include property taxes, mortgage interest, rent, utility charges, upkeep and repairs, property insurance, and food consumed on the premises. A taxpayer may treat a home's fair market rental value as a cost of maintaining a household (instead of the sum of payments for mortgage interest, property taxes, and insurance). The proposed regulations provide rules that, in certain circumstances, prorate on a monthly basis the annual cost of maintaining a household when a qualifying child or dependent resides in the household for less than the entire taxable year. The proposed regulations also, in certain circumstances, recognize the creation of a new household during a year and treat shared living quarters as separate households.

3. *Tax Tables for Individuals*

The proposed regulations remove from the regulations under section 3 references to the return of a surviving spouse being treated as a joint return to conform to the amendments made by the Tax Reform Act of 1969. The proposed regulations also update the regulations under section 3 to reflect current law.

4. *Earned Income Credit*

The proposed regulations conform the regulations under section 32 to amendments made to section 32 by WFTRA. Consistent with the 2010 repeal of section 3507 by the FAA Air Transportation Modernization and Safety Improvement Act, the proposed regulations delete the paragraphs of the regulations under section 32 discussing advance payment of the earned income credit.

In addition, the proposed regulations reflect a change in the IRS's position on the interaction of sections 152(c)(4) and 32. Specifically, the proposed regulations provide that, if an individual meets the definition of a qualifying child under section 152(c)(1) for more than one taxpayer and the individual is not treated as the qualifying child of one such taxpayer under the tiebreaker rules of section 152(c)(4), then the individual also is not treated as a qualifying child of that taxpayer for purposes of section 32(c)(1)(A). Thus, that taxpayer may be an eligible individual under section 32(c)(1)(A)(ii) and may claim the childless EIC if he or she meets the other requirements of that section. The Treasury Department and the IRS have concluded that this change in position is consistent with the language and purpose of section 32 and will be less confusing to taxpayers and easier for the IRS to administer.

The problems with the current rule may be illustrated by the following example. Two sisters (B and C) live together and each of them is a low-income taxpayer. Neither has a child and each may claim the childless EIC under section 32(c)(1)(A)(ii). Later, B has a child, and B's child meets the definition of a qualifying child under section 152(c)(1) for both B and C. The child is treated as the qualifying child of B under the tiebreaker rules of section 152(c)(4), and B may claim the EIC as an eligible individual with a qualifying child under section 32(c)(1)(A)(i). Under the current rule, C would not be allowed to claim the childless EIC under section 32(c)(1)(A)(ii). The Treasury Department and the IRS have determined that allowing C to continue to claim the childless EIC after the child is born is equitable and consistent with the purpose of section 32 to assist working, low-income taxpayers. Accordingly, the proposed regulations provide that, if an individual is not treated as a qualifying child of a taxpayer after applying the tiebreaker rules of section 152(c)(4), then the individual will not prevent that taxpayer from qualifying for the childless EIC.

5. *Additional Standard Deduction for the Aged and Blind*

The proposed regulations remove the provisions on additional exemptions for age and blindness from the regulations under section 151 and add regulations under section 63 on the additional standard deduction for the aged and the blind to reflect the changes made by the Tax Reform Act of 1986. The proposed regulations amend the regulations under section 63 to remove a cross reference to now-repealed statutory provisions relating to a charitable deduction for taxpayers who do not itemize. To limit impediments to electronic filing, the proposed regulations also delete the requirement that a taxpayer claiming a tax benefit for blindness must attach a certificate or statement to the taxpayer's tax return. Instead, a taxpayer must maintain the certificate or statement in the taxpayer's records.

Applicability Date

These regulations are proposed to apply to taxable years beginning after the date the regulations are published as final regulations in the **Federal Register**. Pending the issuance of the final regulations, taxpayers may choose to apply these proposed regulations in any open taxable years.

Effect on Other Documents

When finalized, the proposed regulations will obsolete Rev. Rul. 57-344, Rev. Rul. 58-67, Rev. Rul. 58-302, Rev. Rul. 64-223, Rev. Rul. 65-307, Rev. Rul. 70-341, Rev. Rul. 74-153, Rev. Rul. 74-543, Rev. Rul. 79-173, Rev. Rul. 84-89, Notice 2006-86, and Notice 2008-5.

Special Analyses

Certain IRS regulations, including these, are exempt from the requirements of Executive Order 12866, as supplemented and reaffirmed by Executive Order 13563. Therefore, a regulatory impact assessment is not required. The regulations affect individuals and do not impose a collection of information on small entities, therefore the Regulatory Flexibility Act (5 U.S.C. chapter 6) does not apply. Pursuant to section 7805(f) of the Code, this notice of proposed rulemaking will be submitted to the Chief Counsel for Advocacy of the Small Business Administration for comment on its impact on small business.

Statement of Availability of IRS Documents

IRS revenue procedures, revenue rulings, notices and other guidance cited in this preamble are published in the Internal Revenue Bulletin (or Cumulative Bulletin) and are available from the Superintendent of Documents, U.S. Government Publishing Office, Washington, DC 20402, or by visiting the IRS website at http://www.irs.gov.

Comments and Requests for a Public Hearing

Before these proposed regulations are adopted as final regulations, consideration will be given to any comments that are submitted timely to the IRS, as prescribed in this preamble under the "Addresses" heading. The IRS and Treasury Department request comments on all aspects of the proposed rules. All comments will be available at www.regulations.gov or upon request. A public hearing will be scheduled if requested in writing by any person that timely submits written comments. If a public hearing is scheduled, notice of the date, time, and place for the hearing will be published in the **Federal Register**.

Drafting Information

The principal authors of these proposed regulations are Christina M. Glendening and Victoria J. Driscoll of the Office of Associate Chief Counsel (Income Tax and Accounting). However, other personnel from the Treasury Department and the IRS participated in the development of the regulations.

[¶ 49,738] **Proposed Amendments of Regulations (REG-127203-15)**, published in the Federal Register on January 19, 2017.

[Code Sec. 197, 704, 721 and 6038B]

International tax: Partnerships: Partnership with foreign partners: Transfers of appreciated property: Related parties.—Reg. §§ 1.721(c)-1, 1.721(c)-2, 1.721(c)-3, 1.721(c)-4, 1.721(c)-5, 1.721(c)-6, 1.721(c)-7 and amendments of Reg. §§ 1.197-2, 1.704-1, 1.704-3 and 1.6038B-2, addressing transfers of appreciated property by U.S. persons to partnerships with foreign partners related to the transferor, are adopted.

[¶ 49,740] **Proposed Amendments of Regulations (NPRM REG-135122-16)**, published in the Federal Register on January 24, 2017.

[Code Sec. 871]

International tax: Nonresident aliens: Financial products: Dividend equivalents: U.S. source dividend payments.—Amendments of Reg. § 1.871-15, relating to certain financial products providing for payments that are contingent upon or determined by reference to U.S. source dividend payments, are proposed.

AGENCY: Internal Revenue Service (IRS), Treasury.

ACTION: Notice of proposed rulemaking by cross-reference to temporary regulations.

SUMMARY: This document contains proposed regulations relating to certain financial products providing for payments that are contingent upon or determined by reference to U.S. source dividend payments.

DATES: Written or electronic comments must be received by April 24, 2017.

ADDRESSES: Send submissions to CC:PA:LPD:PR (REG-135122-16), room 5203, Internal Revenue Service, PO Box 7604, Ben Franklin Station, Washington, DC 20044. Submissions may be hand delivered Monday through Friday between the hours of 8 a.m. and 4 p.m. to CC:PA:LPD:PR (REG-135122-16), Courier's desk, Internal Revenue Service, 1111 Constitution Avenue, NW., Washington, DC 20044, or sent electronically, via the Federal eRulemaking Portal at www.regulations.gov (IRS REG-135122-16). The public hearing will be held in the IRS Auditorium, Internal Revenue Building, 1111 Constitution Avenue, N.W., Washington, DC.

FOR FURTHER INFORMATION CONTACT: Concerning the regulations, D. Peter Merkel or Karen Walny at (202) 317-6938; concerning submissions of comments, the hearing, and/or to be placed on the building access list to attend the hearing Regina Johnson at (202) 317-6901 (not toll-free numbers).

SUPPLEMENTARY INFORMATION:

Background and Explanation of Provisions

Final and temporary regulations in the Rules and Regulations section of this issue of the **Federal Register** contain amendments to the Income Tax Regulations (26 CFR Part 1), which provide rules relating to dividend equivalents for purposes of section 871(m). The temporary regulations provide guidance relating to when the delta of an option that is listed on a foreign regulated exchange may be calculated based on the delta of that option at the close of business on the business day prior to the date of issuance. The temporary regulations also provide guidance identifying which party to a potential section 871(m) transaction is responsible for determining whether a transaction is a section 871(m) transaction when multiple brokers or dealers are involved in the transaction. The text of those temporary regulations also serves as the text of these proposed regulations. The preamble to the final and temporary regulations explains the temporary regulations and these proposed regulations. The regulations affect nonresident alien individuals, foreign corporations, and withholding agents, as well as certain other parties to section 871(m) transactions and their agents.

Special Analyses

Certain IRS regulations, including this one, are exempt from the requirements of Executive Order 12866, as supplemented and reaffirmed by Executive Order 13563. Therefore, a regulatory impact assessment is not required. Because the regulations do not impose a collection of information on small entities, the Regulatory Flexibility Act (5 U.S.C. chapter 6) does not apply. Pursuant to section 7805(f), these regulations have been submitted to the Chief Counsel for Advocacy of the Small Business Administration for comment on its impact on small business.

Comments and Request for Public Hearing

Before these proposed regulations are adopted as final regulations, consideration will be given to any comments that are submitted timely to the IRS as prescribed in this preamble under the "Addresses" heading. The Treasury Department and the IRS request comments on all aspects of the proposed rules. All comments will be available at www.regulations.gov or upon request. A public hearing will be scheduled if requested in writing by any person that timely submits written comments. If a public hearing is scheduled, notice of the date, time, and place for the public hearing will be published in the **Federal Register**.

Drafting Information

The principal authors of these regulations are D. Peter Merkel and Karen Walny of the Office of Chief Counsel (International). However, other personnel from the Treasury Department and the IRS participated in their development.

[¶ 49,743]   Proposed Amendments of Regulations (REG-128483-15), published in the Federal Register on July 20, 2017.

[Code Secs. 1446, 6012, 6031, 6032, 6033, 6041, 6071, 6072 and 6081]

Information returns: Due dates: Extensions of time to file: Income tax returns.—Amendments of Reg. §§1.1446-3, 1.6012-6, 1.6031(a)-1, 1.6032-1, 1.6033-2, 1.6041-2, 1.6041-6, 1.6072-2, 1.6081-1, 1.6081-2, 1.6081-3, 1.6081-5, 1.6081-6, 1.6081-9, 31.6071(a)-1, issuing temporary regulations that update the due dates and extensions of time to file certain tax returns and information returns, are adopted.

[¶ 49,744]   Proposed Amendments of Regulations (REG-125374-16), published in the Federal Register on September 19, 2017(corrected 9/25/2017).

[Code Secs. 63, 103, 163, 165, 860D, 871, 881, 1287, 4701, 6045, 6049]

Registration-required obligations; Registered form: Passthrough certificates.—Reg. §§1.149(a)-1 and amendments of 1.163-5, 1.163-5T, 1.165-12, 1.860D-1, 1.871-14, 1.881-3, 1.1287-1, 1.6045-1, 1.6049-5, 5f.103-1, 5f.163-1 and 46.4701-1, including guidance on the issuance of pass-through certificates and participation interests in registered form, are proposed. Amendments of Reg. §5f.163-1, proposed on January 21, 1993, are withdrawn.

AGENCY: Internal Revenue Service (IRS), Treasury.

ACTION: Partial withdrawal of notice of proposed rulemaking and notice of proposed rulemaking.

SUMMARY: This document contains proposed regulations that provide guidance on the definitions of registration-required obligation and registered form, including guidance on the issuance of pass-through certificates and participation interests in registered form. This document also withdraws a portion of previously proposed regulations regarding the definition of a registration-required obligation. The proposed regulations generally are necessary to address changes in market practices as well as issues raised by the statutory repeal of the foreign-targeted bearer obligation exception to the registered form requirement. The proposed regulations will affect issuers and holders of obligations in registered form as well as issuers and holders of registration-required obligations that are not issued in registered form.

DATES: Comments and requests for a public hearing must be received by December 18, 2017.

ADDRESSES: Send submissions to CC:PA:LPD:PR (REG-125374-16), room 5203, Internal Revenue Service, P.O. Box 7604, Ben Franklin Station, Washington, DC 20044. Submissions may be hand-delivered Monday through Friday between the hours of 8 a.m. and 4 p.m. to CC:PA:LPD:PR (REG-125374-16), Courier's Desk, Internal Revenue Service, 1111 Constitution Avenue NW, Washington, DC 20224, or sent electronically via the Federal eRulemaking Portal at *www.regulations.gov* (IRS REG-125374-16).

FOR FURTHER INFORMATION CONTACT: Concerning the proposed regulations, Spence Hanemann at (202) 317-6980; concerning submissions of comments and requesting a hearing, Regina Johnson at (202) 317-6901 (not toll-free numbers). SUPPLEMENTARY INFORMATION:

Paperwork Reduction Act

The collection of information contained in this notice of proposed rulemaking has been submitted to the Office of Management and Budget for review under control number 1545-0945 in accordance with the Paperwork Reduction Act of 1995 (44 U.S.C. 3507(d)). The collection of information in this proposed regulation is in §1.163-5(b), which permits issuers of registration-required obligations to satisfy the requirement for those obligations to be in registered form by maintaining a book entry system. Sections 163(f) and 149(a) require that certain obligations be in registered form and expressly permit issuers to satisfy that requirement through a book entry system. Accordingly, the proposed regulations permit issuers to satisfy the registration requirement through a book entry system and detail certain arrangements that qualify as book entry systems. The collection of information in proposed § 1.163-5(b) is an increase in the total annual burden under control number 1545-0945. The respondents are businesses and other for-profit organizations, non-profit organizations, and state, local and tribal governments.

Estimated total annual recordkeeping burden: 95,105 hours.

Estimated average annual burden hours per respondent: 0.5 hours.

Estimated number of respondents: 190,210.

Estimated annual frequency of responses: 190,210.

Comments on the collection of information should be sent to the Office of Management and Budget, Attn: Desk Officer for the Department of the Treasury, Office of Information and Regulatory Affairs, Washington, DC 20503, with copies to the Internal Revenue Service, Attn: IRS Reports Clearance Officer, SE:CAR:MP:T:T:SP, Washington DC 20224. Comments on the collection of information should be received by November 18, 2017.

Comments are specifically requested concerning:

Whether the proposed collection of information is necessary for the proper performance of the Internal Revenue Service, including whether the information will have practical utility;

The accuracy of the estimated burden associated with the proposed collection of information;

How the quality, utility, and clarity of the information to be collected may be enhanced;

How the burden of complying with the proposed collection of information may be minimized, including through the application of automated collection techniques or other forms of information technology; and

Estimates of capital or start-up costs and costs of operation, maintenance, and purchase of service to provide information.

An agency may not conduct or sponsor, and a person is not required to respond to, a collection of information unless it displays a valid control number assigned by the Office of Management and Budget.

Books or records relating to a collection of information must be retained as long as their contents may become material in the administration of any internal revenue law. Generally tax returns and tax return information are confidential, as required by section 26 U.S.C. 6103.

Background

This document contains proposed amendments to 26 CFR parts 1, 5f, and 46 under sections 103, 149, 163, 165, 860D, 871, 881, 1287, 4701, 6045, and 6049 of the Internal Revenue Code (Code).

1. In General

The classification of an obligation as in bearer or registered form has significant tax implications because a number of Code provisions impose sanctions on issuers and holders of registration-required obligations that are not issued in registered form. An obligation not issued in registered form is a bearer form obligation. Most of the Code provisions that pertain to registration-required obligations were enacted as part of the Tax Equity and Fiscal Responsibility Act of 1982 (TEFRA), Public Law 97-248, 96 Stat. 324, § 310. Among these provisions, section 163(f) denies an issuer an interest deduction for interest on a registration-required obligation that is not in registered form. Section 4701 imposes an excise tax on the issuer of a registration-required obligation that is not in registered form. The excise tax is equal to 1 percent of the principal amount of the obligation multiplied by the number of calendar years (or portions thereof) between the issue date of the obligation and the date of maturity. Section 149(a) provides that interest on a registration-required bond is not exempt from tax under section 103(a) unless the bond is in registered form. In addition, section 871(h) and section 881(c) exempt from federal income tax portfolio interest from sources within the U.S. received by a nonresident alien or foreign corporation (portfolio interest exception) only if the obligation with respect to which the interest was paid is in registered form. Similar restrictions are found in sections 165(j) (generally denying the holder a deduction for a loss sustained on a registration-required obligation not in registered form), 312(m) (generally providing that the issuer's earnings and profits cannot be decreased by interest paid on a registration-required obligation not in registered form), and 1287 (generally treating the holder's gain on sale of a registration-required obligation not in registered form as ordinary income).

Historically, the Code provisions referenced in the preceding paragraph generally did not apply to obligations that complied with the foreign-targeting rules of prior section 163(f)(2)(B) and § 1.163-5(c) (foreign-targeted bearer obligations). Under the foreign-targeting rules, an issuer could issue foreign-targeted bearer obligations without penalty provided the obligations were issued under arrangements reasonably designed to ensure that the obligations were sold only to non-U.S. persons. The portfolio interest exception also applied to interest paid on foreign-targeted bearer obligations issued under such reasonably designed arrangements.

The Hiring Incentives to Restore Employment Act (the HIRE Act), Public Law 111-147, 124 Stat. 71, section 502, repealed section 163(f)(2)(B) and generally eliminated the special treatment of foreign-targeted bearer obligations. Foreign-targeted bearer obligations issued after March 18, 2012, are subject to the sanctions on bearer form obligations under sections 149(a), 163(f), 165(j), 312(m), and 1287. The HIRE Act also revoked the portfolio interest exception for foreign-targeted bearer obligations, thus requiring that obligations issued after March 18, 2012, be in registered form to qualify for that exception. The HIRE Act did not, however, repeal the foreign-targeted bearer obligation exception to the excise tax under section 4701. See section 4701(b)(1)(B)(i).

2. Registration-Required Obligations

A. In general

Under section 163(f)(2)(A), as amended by the HIRE Act, the term *registration-required obligation* means any obligation other than an obligation that: (1) is issued by a natural person; (2) is not of a type offered to the public; or (3) has a maturity at issue of not more than 1 year. For purposes of sections 165(j), 312(m), and 1287, registration-required obligation has the same meaning as when used in section 163(f). See also section 149(a) (providing a similar definition except for the exclusion for instruments issued by a natural person). For purposes of section 4701, that term also has the same meaning as when used in section 163(f), except that tax-exempt bonds and foreign-targeted bearer obligations are excluded.

Section 5f.163-1(b)(2) provides that the determination as to whether an obligation is of a type offered to the public is based on whether similar obligations are in fact publicly offered or traded. On January 21, 1993, the Department of the Treasury (Treasury) and the IRS published in the **Federal Register** (58 FR 5316) a notice of proposed rulemaking (INTL-0115-90) containing proposed regulations that elaborated upon the meaning of "of a type offered to the public" for purposes of section 163(f)(2)(A) (the 1993 proposed regulations). See Prop. Treas. Reg. § 5f.163-1(b)(2). The preamble to the 1993 proposed regulations cited the report of the Senate Finance Committee on TEFRA for the conclusion that an obligation that represents a "readily negotiable substitute for cash" should be a registration-required obligation. 58 FR 5316 (citing S. Rep. No. 97-494, at 242 (1982)). Treasury and the IRS reasoned in the preamble to the 1993 proposed regulations that, because the standards for determining if an obligation is "readily tradable in an established securities market" under section 453(f)(4)(B) and §15a.453-1(e)(4) address an analogous concern with negotiability, similar standards should apply for determining whether an obligation is "of a type offered to the public" under section 163(f)(2)(A).

B. *Pass-through certificates*

Section 1.163-5T provides rules to address whether pass-through certificates are registration-required obligations. In their most common form, pass-through certificates are issued by an investment entity (typically a trust) that holds a pool of obligations, such as mortgage loans. Each pass-through certificate represents an interest in the investment entity.

To accommodate these securitization transactions, §1.163-5T(d)(1) generally provides that a pass-through certificate evidencing an interest in a pool of mortgage loans that is treated as a trust of which the grantor is the owner is considered to be a registration-required obligation if, standing alone, the pass-through certificate meets the definition of a registration-required obligation. Section 1.163-5T(d)(1) also applies to "similar evidence of interest in a similar pooled fund or pooled trust treated as a grantor trust," although commenters have noted the ambiguity of the reference. Similarly, §1.871-14(d)(1) provides that interest received on a pass-through certificate qualifies for the portfolio interest exception if, standing alone, the pass-through certificate is in registered form.

Commenters have asked that Treasury and the IRS describe the types of arrangements that qualify as pass-through certificates. Specifically, commenters have requested that Treasury and the IRS amend the definition of a pass-through certificate to clarify that the issuer of a pass-through certificate may be either a grantor trust or another type of entity, such as a partnership or a disregarded entity, so long as the obligations in the pool are held through an arrangement that meets the requirements to be in registered form. Commenters have also requested that Treasury and the IRS amend §1.871-14(d)(1) so that the definition of pass-through certificate for purposes of the portfolio interest exception is identical to the definition of pass-through certificate under §1.163-5T(d)(1).

3. *Definition of Registered Form*

A. *In general*

For purposes of determining whether an obligation is in registered form under section 163(f)[1], the principles of section 149(a)(3) apply. See section 163(f)(3). Section 149(a)(3)(A) provides that a bond is treated as being in registered form if the right to the principal of, and stated interest on, the bond may be transferred only through a book entry consistent with regulations prescribed by the Secretary. Section 149(a)(3)(B) authorizes the Secretary to prescribe regulations to carry out the requirement that a bond be issued in registered form when there is one or more nominee. For purposes of section 149(a), the conditions for an obligation to be considered in registered form are described in §5f.103-1(c).[2] The regulations under both section 163(f) and section 871(h), specifically §§5f.163-1(a) and 1.871-14(c), refer to §5f.103-1(c) for a definition of registered form. Obligations that do not meet the conditions described in §5f.103-1(c) are treated as issued in bearer form.

Generally, under §5f.103-1(c), an obligation is in registered form if: (1) the obligation is registered as to both principal and any stated interest with the issuer (or its agent) and any transfer of the obligation may be effected only by surrender of the old obligation and reissuance to the new holder; (2) the right to principal and stated interest with respect to the obligation may be transferred only through a book entry system maintained by the issuer or its agent; or (3) the obligation is registered as to both principal and stated interest with the issuer or its agent and may be transferred both by surrender and reissuance and through a book entry system. An obligation is considered transferable through a book entry system if ownership of an interest in the obligation is required to be reflected in a book entry, whether or not physical securities are issued. An obligation that would otherwise be considered to be in registered form is not considered to be in registered form if the obligation may be converted at any time in the future into an obligation that is not in registered form. See §5f.103-1(e).

B. *Dematerialized book entry systems*

Since the publication of §5f.103-1, market practices have changed with respect to how interests in obligations are recorded and transferred. For example, many obligations trade in fully dematerialized form. An obligation that is fully dematerialized is not represented by a physical (paper) certificate, and a clearing organization that is the registered holder of the obligation operates an electronic book entry system that identifies the clearing organization's member or members holding the obligation (or interests in the obligation). The clearing organization facilitates and records transfers of the obligation (or interests in the obligation) among the clearing organization's members. The members (typically, banks or broker-dealers), in turn, record their clients' ownership of the obligation (or interests in the obligation) in their book entry systems. Alternatively, an obligation may be represented by a physical global certificate that is nominally in bearer form but that is immobilized in a clearing organization, which handles the obligation thereafter exactly as it does an obligation that was fully dematerialized when issued. Commenters have requested additional guidance on how the registered form rules in §5f.103-1 apply to these arrangements.

Treasury and the IRS provided guidance on how to apply the registered form rules to certain of these arrangements in Notice 2006-99, 2006-2 CB 907. Notice 2006-99 addresses an arrangement in which no physical certificates are issued and under which ownership interests in bonds are required to be represented only by book entries in a dematerialized book entry system maintained by a clearing organization. Notice 2006-99 provides that an obligation issued under such an arrangement is treated as in registered form notwithstanding the ability of holders to obtain physical certificates in bearer form upon the termination of the business of the clearing organization without a successor.

The HIRE Act also addressed dematerialized book entry systems. For obligations issued after March 18, 2012, section 163(f)(3), as amended by the HIRE Act, provides that, for purposes of section 163(f), a dematerialized book entry system or other book entry system specified by the Secretary will be treated as a book entry system described in section 149(a)(3). The Joint Committee on Taxation's technical explanation of the HIRE Act further explained that an obligation "that is formally in bearer form is treated, for the purposes of section 163(f), as held in a book entry system as long as the debt obligation may be transferred only through a dematerialized book entry system or other book entry system specified by the Secretary." J. Comm. on Tax'n, *Technical Explanation of the Revenue Provisions Contained in Senate Amendment 3310, the "Hiring Incentives to Restore Employment Act," Under Consideration by the Senate* (JCX-4-10), Feb. 23, 2010, at 53.

C. *Notice 2012-20*

Commenters expressed concern that the explicit reference to a "dematerialized book entry system" in section 163(f)(3), as amended by the HIRE Act, would create uncertainty about obligations issued in a manner not specifically described in Notice 2006-99. In particular, commenters requested guidance to address the treatment of obligations represented by a physical global certificate that is nominally in bearer form, but that is immobilized in a clearing system. In addition, commenters requested guidance regarding whether an obligation will be considered to be in registered form if holders may obtain physical certificates in bearer form under circumstances not described in Notice 2006-99.

---

[1] For purposes of sections 165(j), 312(m), 871(h)(7), 881(c)(7), 1287, and 4701, the term *registered form* has the same meaning as when used in section 163(f).

[2] Section 5f.103-1 was originally published under section 103(j) of the Internal Revenue Code of 1954, which was enacted as part of TEFRA and provided that obligations must be in registered form to be tax-exempt. Section 103(j) was recodified as section 149(a) by section 1301 of the Tax Reform Act of 1986, Public Law 99-514, 100 Stat. 2085.

In response to these comments, Treasury and the IRS published Notice 2012-20, 2012-13 IRB 574, on March 26, 2012. Notice 2012-20 provides additional guidance on the definition of registered form and further states that Treasury and the IRS intend to publish regulations consistent with the guidance described in the notice. Under Notice 2012-20, an obligation is considered to be in registered form if it is issued either through a dematerialized book entry system in which beneficial interests are transferable only through a book entry system maintained by a clearing organization (or by an agent of the clearing organization) or through a clearing system in which the obligation is effectively immobilized. Notice 2012-20 provides that an obligation is considered to be effectively immobilized if: (1) the obligation is represented by one or more global securities in physical form that are issued to and held by a clearing organization (or by a custodian or depository acting as an agent of the clearing organization) for the benefit of purchasers of interests in the obligation under arrangements that prohibit the transfer of the global securities except to a successor clearing organization subject to the same terms; and (2) beneficial interests in the underlying obligation are transferable only through a book entry system maintained by the clearing organization (or an agent of the clearing organization). Notice 2012-20 further states that an interest in an obligation is considered to be transferable only through a book entry system if the interest would be considered transferable through a book entry system under § 5f.103-1(c)(2), except that holders may obtain physical certificates in bearer form in certain limited circumstances stated in the notice. Finally, Notice 2012-20 states that, for purposes of determining when an obligation is a registration-required obligation under section 4701, rules identical to the foreign-targeting rules under section 163(f)(2)(B), prior to its amendment by the HIRE Act, and § 1.163-5(c) will apply to obligations issued after March 18, 2012.

Explanation of Provisions

1. *In General*

Consistent with Notice 2012-20, these proposed regulations amend the definition of registered form to take into account current market practices and changes made by the HIRE Act, including the repeal of the foreign-targeting rules in section 163(f)(2)(B). In addition, these proposed regulations amend the definition of a registration-required obligation in two ways. First, the proposed regulations specify the types of obligations that are treated as "of a type offered to the public" and withdraw the 1993 proposed regulations. Second, the proposed regulations take into account comments requesting clarification on the types of arrangements that qualify as pass-through certificates.

Though the definitions of the terms *registered form* and *registration-required obligation* are generally consistent across the various provisions in which they are used, the rules are set forth in a number of existing regulations, including several promulgated under section 163(f). To the extent possible, these proposed regulations simplify the definitions of registered form and registration-required obligation by centralizing the rules in § 1.163-5. Thus, the applicable rules have been relocated from §§ 5f.103-1 (definition of registered form), 1.163-5T (pass-through certificates and regular interests in REMICs), and 5f.163-1 (definition of registration-required obligation) to paragraphs (a) and (b) of proposed § 1.163-5. Appropriate cross-references to § 1.163-5 are proposed to be added to regulations that rely on one or both definitions, including §§ 1.149(a)-1, 1.165-12, 1.860D-1(b)(5)(i)(A), 1.871-14, 1.1287-1, and 46.4701-1.

2. *Registration-Required Obligations*

A. *Obligation of a type offered to the public*

Consistent with the 1993 proposed regulations, Treasury and the IRS continue to believe that it is appropriate to determine whether an obligation is of a type offered to the public by reference to whether the obligation is "traded on an established market." Although a number of Code and regulation sections refer to and define that phrase (for example, sections 453, 1092, 1273, and 7704, as well as the regulations promulgated under those Code sections), Treasury and the IRS have concluded that the definition provided in § 1.1273-2(f) is most appropriate for purposes of defining a registration-required obligation. Thus, the proposed regulations generally treat an obligation as of a type offered to the public if the obligation is traded on an established market as determined under § 1.1273-2(f). For this purpose, however, the proposed regulations do not take into account the exception for small debt issues in § 1.1273-2(f)(6).

B. *Pass-through certificates and participation interests*

Commenters indicated that an entity that issues pass-through certificates may hold a pool of debt instruments that is either fixed or that changes over time. For example, the issuing entity may have the right to acquire additional assets after formation, or the right to dispose of assets at any time. In those situations, the entity generally will not be classified as a grantor trust for federal tax purposes, but that does not preclude it from issuing pass-through certificates. To address these situations, the proposed regulations amend the definition of a pass-through certificate to provide that a pass-through certificate may be issued by a grantor trust or a similar fund, and specify that a similar fund includes entities that are partnerships or disregarded for federal tax purposes and funds that have the power to vary the assets they hold or the sequence of payments to holders. A similar fund, however, does not include a business entity classified as a corporation.

In addition, Treasury and the IRS have concluded that an arrangement that satisfies the definition of a registration-required obligation and the registered form rules should be treated the same as a pass-through certificate even if the arrangement is with respect to only one underlying obligation or if the arrangement is treated as co-ownership of one or more obligations (rather than, for purposes of TEFRA or otherwise, ownership of an entity that holds the underlying obligations). The proposed regulations eliminate the requirement that the fund hold a pool of loans and replace it with a requirement that the fund primarily hold debt instruments. Thus, a fund can hold one or more debt instruments, so long as the fund primarily holds debt instruments.

In addition, the proposed regulations treat an interest that evidences co-ownership of one or more obligations (including a participation interest) as a registration-required obligation if, standing alone, the interest satisfies the definition of a registration-required obligation. The proposed regulations also propose to amend § 1.871-14(d)(1) to include a cross-reference to the rules for pass-through certificates and participation interests in proposed § 1.163-5(a)(3)(i) and (ii) such that similar rules apply for purposes of the portfolio interest exception.

3. *Definition of Registered Form*

The proposed regulations amend the definition of registered form in a number of ways. First, the proposed regulations provide that an obligation is considered to be in registered form if it is transferable through a book entry system, including a dematerialized book entry system, maintained by the issuer of the obligation, an agent of the issuer, or a clearing organization. A clearing organization includes an entity that holds obligations for its members or maintains a system that reflects the ownership interests of members and transfers of obligations among members' accounts without the necessity of physical delivery of the obligation.

Second, the proposed regulations provide that an obligation represented by a physical certificate in bearer form will be considered to be in registered form if the physical certificate is effectively immobilized. To be effectively immobilized, the physical certificate evidencing an obligation must be issued to and held by a clearing organization for the benefit of purchasers of interests in the obligation under arrangements that prohibit the transfer of the physical certificate except to a successor clearing organization and permit transfers of ownership interests in the underlying obligation only through a book entry system maintained by the clearing organization (or a successor clearing organization). As suggested in comments, the proposed regulations change the requirement in Notice 2012-20 that a successor clearing organization hold the physical certificate subject to the same terms as the predecessor; Treasury and the IRS concluded that it is sufficient if the successor clearing organization has rules that effectively immobilize the physical certificate.

Third, the proposed regulations permit holders of obligations (or interests in obligations) to have a right to obtain physical certificates evidencing the obligation (or interests in the obligation) in bearer form without causing the obligation to be treated as not in registered form in two circumstances: (1) a termination of the clearing organization's business without a successor; or (2) the issuance of physical securities at the issuer's request upon a change in tax law that would be adverse to the issuer but for the issuance of physical securities in bearer form. This exception from bearer form treatment is consistent with the guidance provided in Notice 2012-20, except that the proposed regulations do not permit a holder to have a right to obtain a physical bearer certificate if there is an issuer event of default (default exception). Treasury and the IRS understand that in certain situations holders may be required to obtain physical certificates to pursue claims against the issuer, but in such instances it would be appropriate to expect those physical certificates to be issued in registered form. Taxpayers may rely on the default exception in Notice 2012-20 for obligations issued prior to publication of a Treasury decision adopting these rules as final regulations in the **Federal Register**.

After the occurrence of one of the two events described in the first sentence of the preceding paragraph, an obligation will no longer be in registered form if a holder, or a group of holders acting collectively, has a right to obtain a physical certificate in bearer form, regardless of whether any option to obtain a physical certificate in bearer form has actually been exercised.

4. Section 881

Commenters requested that examples 10 and 19 set forth in §1.881-3(e) be removed or revised to take into account the repeal of the foreign-targeted bearer obligation exception. Consistent with these comments, the proposed regulations propose to remove those examples.

5. Section 4701

Commenters requested clarification on whether the foreign-targeting rules under §1.163-5(c) would apply to obligations issued after March 18, 2012, for purposes of section 4701. Consistent with Notice 2012-20, proposed §46.4701-1 provides that, for purposes of determining whether an obligation is a foreign-targeted bearer obligation, the rules of §1.163-5(c) apply.

6. Applicability Dates

Notice 2012-20 stated that regulations incorporating the guidance described in that notice will be effective for obligations issued after March 18, 2012. Accordingly, the proposed regulations will generally apply to obligations issued after March 18, 2012. However, taxpayers may apply the rules in section 3 of Notice 2012-20, including the default exception, for obligations issued prior to publication of a Treasury decision adopting these rules as final regulations in the **Federal Register**. The rules related to pass-through certificates, participation interests, and regular interests in REMICs and the rules related to obligations not of a type offered to the public are not described in Notice 2012-20 and, therefore, will apply only to obligations issued after the publication of a Treasury decision adopting these rules as final regulations in the **Federal Register**, except as otherwise provided in the next sentence. The existing regulations under §5f.103-1 will continue to apply to tax-exempt bonds issued prior to the date 90 days after publication of a Treasury decision adopting these rules as final regulations in the **Federal Register**.

Special Analyses

Certain IRS regulations, including these, are exempt from the requirements of Executive Order 12866, as supplemented and reaffirmed by Executive Order 13563. Therefore, a regulatory impact assessment is not required. It is hereby certified that these regulations will not have a significant economic impact on a substantial number of small entities. Sections 163(f) and 149(a) require that certain obligations be in registered form which is satisfied if the obligations are transferable only through a book entry system. The existing regulations under these sections therefore permit issuers to satisfy the registration requirement through a book entry system and describe the arrangements that are necessary for a system to qualify as a book entry system. Certain systems that are now common, however, may not qualify as book entry systems under the existing regulations. Because the proposed regulations merely clarify that these systems are book entry systems, the proposed regulations would not impose a significant economic impact. Accordingly, a regulatory flexibility analysis is not required. Pursuant to section 7805(f) of the Code, this notice of proposed rulemaking will be submitted to the Chief Counsel for Advocacy of the Small Business Administration for comment on its impact on small entities.

Comments and Requests for Public Hearing

Before these proposed regulations are adopted as final regulations, consideration will be given to any comments that are submitted timely to the IRS as prescribed in this preamble under the "ADDRESSES" heading. Treasury and the IRS request comments on all aspects of the proposed rules. All comments will be available at *www.regulations.gov* or upon request. A public hearing will be scheduled if requested in writing by any person that timely submits written comments. If a public hearing is scheduled, notice of the date, time, and place for the hearing will be published in the **Federal Register**.

Drafting Information

The principal authors of these regulations are Spence Hanemann and Diana Imholtz, Office of Associate Chief Counsel (Financial Institutions and Products), IRS. However, other personnel from Treasury and the IRS participated in their development.

Availability of IRS Documents

The IRS notices cited in this preamble are published in the Internal Revenue Bulletin (or Cumulative Bulletin) and are available from the Superintendent of Documents, U.S. Government Publishing Office, Washington, DC 20402, or by visiting the IRS website at *www.irs.gov*.

[¶ 49,749] **Proposed Amendments of Regulations (REG-116256-17)**, published in the Federal Register on October 12, 2017.

[Code Sec. 754]

Partnerships and their partners: Partnership property: Basis: Election to adjust basis.—Amendments of Reg. §1.754-1, relating to the requirements for making a valid election under section 754of the Internal Revenue Code of 1986 (Code), as amended, are proposed.

AGENCY: Internal Revenue Service (IRS), Treasury.

ACTION: Notice of proposed rulemaking.

SUMMARY: This document contains proposed amendments to the regulation relating to the requirements for making a valid election under section 754 of the Internal Revenue Code of 1986 (Code), as amended. The proposed regulation affects partnerships and their partners by removing a regulatory burden in making an election to adjust the basis of partnership property.

DATES: Electronic or written comments and requests for a public hearing must be received by November 13, 2017.

ADDRESSES: Send submissions to Internal Revenue Service, CC:PA:LPD:PR (REG-116256-17), Room 5203, PO Box 7604, Ben Franklin Station, Washington, DC 20044. Submissions may be hand-delivered Monday through Friday between the hours of 8 a.m. and 4 p.m. to CC:PA:LPD:PR (REG-116256-17), Courier's Desk, 1111 Constitution Avenue, N.W., Washington, DC, 20224, or sent electronically, via the Federal eRulemaking Portal at www.regulations.gov (indicate IRS and REG-116256-17).

FOR FURTHER INFORMATION CONTACT: Concerning the proposed regulation, Meghan Howard, at (202) 317-5055; concerning submissions of comments and requests for a public hearing, Regina Johnson, at (202) 317-6901 (not toll-free numbers).

SUPPLEMENTARY INFORMATION:

Background and Explanation of Provision

This document contains proposed amendments to 26 CFR part 1 under section 754 of the Code. Specifically, these proposed amendments would remove the signature requirement contained in § 1.754-1(b) (current regulation) in order to eliminate a regulatory burden.

Section 754 provides that if a partnership files an election (section 754 election), in accordance with regulations prescribed by the Secretary, the basis of partnership property shall be adjusted, in the case of a distribution of property, in the manner provided in section 734 and, in the case of a transfer of a partnership interest, in the manner provided in section 743. Such an election applies with respect to all distributions of property by the partnership and to all transfers of interests in the partnership during the taxable year with respect to which such election was filed and all subsequent taxable years. Such election may be revoked by the partnership, subject to such limitations as may be provided by regulations prescribed by the Secretary.

The current regulation provides the method to make the section 754 election and states in relevant part that a section 754 election shall be made in a written statement (section 754 election statement) filed with the partnership return for the taxable year during which the distribution or transfer occurs. For the section 754 election to be valid, the return must be filed not later than the time prescribed for filing the return for such taxable year, including extensions. The current regulation requires that the section 754 election statement (i) set forth the name and address of the partnership making the election, (ii) be signed by any one of the partners, and (iii) contain a declaration that the partnership elects under section 754 to apply the provisions of section 734(b) and section 743(b). Accordingly, under the current regulation, a partnership that files an unsigned section 754 election statement with its partnership return (whether filed electronically or in paper) has not made a valid section 754 election.

Currently the only remedy for failing to make a proper section 754 election is to request "9100 relief" to make a late section 754 election either: (1) through automatic relief, if the error is discovered within 12 months pursuant to § 301.9100-2 of the Procedure and Administration Regulations; or (2) through a private letter ruling request pursuant to § 301.9100-3. The IRS has received numerous requests for 9100 relief with respect to unsigned section 754 election statements, especially where returns have been filed electronically. In order to ease the burden on partnerships seeking to make a valid section 754 election and to eliminate the need to seek 9100 relief, the Treasury Department and the IRS are proposing to amend the current regulation to remove the signature requirement in § 1.754-1(b)(1). The amended regulation will provide that a taxpayer making a section 754 election must file a statement with its return that: (i) sets forth the name and address of the partnership making the section 754 election, and (ii) contains a declaration that the partnership elects under section 754 to apply the provisions of section 734(b) and section 743(b).

Proposed Applicability Date

The amendments to this regulation are proposed to apply to taxable years ending on or after the date of publication of the Treasury decision adopting these rules as a final regulation in the **Federal Register**. Taxpayers, however, may rely on this proposed regulation for periods preceding the proposed applicability date. Accordingly, partnerships that filed a timely partnership return containing an otherwise valid section 754 election statement, but for the missing signature of a partner on the statement, will not need to seek 9100 relief in such cases.

Special Analyses

Certain IRS regulations, including this one, are exempt from the requirements of Executive Order 12866, as supplemented and reaffirmed by Executive Order 13563. Therefore, a regulatory impact assessment is not required. It is hereby certified that this regulation, if adopted, would not have a significant economic impact on a substantial number of small entities under the Regulatory Flexibility Act (5 U.S.C. chapter 6). This certification is based on the fact that this regulation reduces the information currently required to be collected in making an election to adjust the basis of partnership property and thereby reduces burden on small entities. Pursuant to section 7805(f) of the Code, this regulation has been submitted to the Chief Counsel for Advocacy of the Small Business Administration for comment on its impact on small businesses.

Comments and Requests for a Public Hearing

Before this proposed regulation is adopted as a final regulation, consideration will be given to any comments that are submitted timely to the IRS as prescribed in this preamble under the "Addresses" heading. The Treasury Department and the IRS request comments on all aspects of the proposed regulation. All comments will be available at www.regulations.gov or upon request. A public hearing will be scheduled if requested in writing by any person that timely submits written comments. If a public hearing is scheduled, notice of the date, time, and place for the public hearing will be published in the **Federal Register**.

Drafting Information

The principal author of this regulation is Meghan M. Howard of the Office of the Associate Chief Counsel (Passthroughs and Special Industries). However, other personnel from the Treasury Department and the IRS participated in their development.

[¶ 49,753] **Proposed Amendments of Regulations (REG-119514-15)**, published in the Federal Register on December 19, 2017 (corrected 12/27/2016).

[Code Secs. 446, 954 and 988]

Controlled foreign corporation (CFC): Foreign currency gain or loss: Foreign personal holding company income (FPHCI): Mark-to-market method: Exclusions.—Reg. § 1.988-7 and amendments of Reg. § § 1.446-4, 1.954-0 and 1.954-2, providing guidance on the treatment of foreign currency gain or loss of a controlled foreign corporation (CFC) under the business needs exclusion from foreign personal holding company income (FPHCI), are proposed.

AGENCY: Internal Revenue Service (IRS), Treasury.

ACTION: Notice of proposed rulemaking.

SUMMARY: This document contains proposed regulations that provide guidance on the treatment of foreign currency gain or loss of a controlled foreign corporation (CFC) under the business needs exclusion from foreign personal holding company income (FPHCI). The proposed regulations also provide an election for a taxpayer to use a mark-to-market method of accounting for foreign currency gain or loss attributable to section 988 transactions. In addition, the proposed regulations permit the controlling United States shareholders of a CFC to automatically revoke certain elections concerning the treatment of foreign currency gain or loss. The proposed regulations affect taxpayers and United States shareholders of CFCs that engage in transactions giving rise to foreign currency gain or loss under section 988 of the Internal Revenue Code (Code).

DATES: Written or electronic comments and requests for a public hearing must be received by March 19, 2018.

ADDRESSES: Send submissions to CC:PA:LPD:PR (REG-119514-15), room 5203, Internal Revenue Service, P.O. Box 7604, Ben Franklin Station, Washington, DC 20044. Submissions may be hand-delivered Monday through Friday between the hours of 8 a.m. and 4 p.m. to CC:PA:LPD:PR (REG-119514-15), Courier's Desk, Internal Revenue Service, 1111 Constitution Avenue NW, Washington, DC, or sent electronically via the Federal eRulemaking Portal at http://www.regulations.gov (IRS REG-119514-15).

FOR FURTHER INFORMATION CONTACT: Concerning the proposed regulations, Jeffery G. Mitchell, (202) 317-6934; concerning submissions of comments or requests for a public hearing, Regina Johnson, (202) 317-6901 (not toll-free numbers).

SUPPLEMENTARY INFORMATION:

Paperwork Reduction Act

The collections of information contained in this notice of proposed rulemaking have been submitted to the Office of Management and Budget for review in accordance with the Paperwork Reduction Act of 1995 (44 U.S.C. 3507(d)). Comments on the collections of information should be sent to the **Office of Management and Budget**, Attn: Desk Officer for the Department of the Treasury, Office of Information and Regulatory Affairs, Washington, DC 20503, with copies to the **Internal Revenue Service**, Attn: IRS Reports Clearance Officer, SE:W:CAR:MP:T:T:SP, Washington, DC 20224. Comments on the collection of information should be received by February 20, 2018. Comments are specifically requested concerning:

Whether the proposed collection of information is necessary for the proper performance of the duties of the IRS, including whether the information will have practical utility;

The accuracy of the estimated burden associated with the proposed collection of information;

How the quality, utility, and clarity of the information to be collected may be enhanced;

How the burden of complying with the proposed collection of information may be minimized, including through the application of automated collection techniques or other forms of information technology; and

Estimates of capital or start-up costs and costs of operation, maintenance, and purchases of services to provide information.

The collection of information in these proposed regulations is in proposed §§ 1.954-2(g)(3)(iii) and (4)(iii) and 1.988-7. The information is required to be provided by taxpayers and United States shareholders of CFCs that make an election or revoke an election with respect to the treatment of foreign currency gains and losses. The information provided will be used by the IRS for tax compliance purposes.

Estimated total annual reporting burden: 5,000 hours.

Estimated average annual burden hours per respondent: one hour.

Estimated number of respondents: 5,000.

Estimated annual frequency of responses: one.

An agency may not conduct or sponsor, and a person is not required to respond to, a collection of information unless it displays a valid control number assigned by the Office of Management and Budget.

Books or records relating to a collection of information must be retained as long as their contents may become material in the administration of any internal revenue law. Generally, tax returns and tax return information are confidential, as required by 26 U.S.C. 6103.

Background

This document contains proposed amendments to 26 CFR part 1 under sections 446, 954(c)(1)(D), and 988 of the Code. Section 446 requires taxpayers to compute taxable income using accounting methods that clearly reflect income. Section 954(c)(1)(D) provides that FPHCI includes the excess of foreign currency gains over foreign currency losses (as defined in section 988(b)) attributable to section 988 transactions, other than transactions directly related to the business needs of the CFC. Section 988 provides rules for determining the source and character of gain or loss from certain foreign currency transactions.

A. Business Needs Exclusion

1. In general

Section 954 defines foreign base company income (FBCI), which generally is income earned by a CFC that is taken into account in computing the amount that a United States shareholder of the CFC must include in income under section 951(a)(1)(A). Under section 954(a)(1), FBCI includes FPHCI, which is defined in section 954(c). The excess of foreign currency gains over foreign currency losses from section 988 transactions is generally included in FPHCI pursuant to section 954(c)(1)(D).

Section 988 transactions generally include the following: the accrual of any item of income or expense that is to be paid or received in a nonfunctional currency after the date of accrual; lending or borrowing in a nonfunctional currency; entering into or acquiring a forward, future, option, or similar contract denominated in a nonfunctional currency; and the disposition of nonfunctional currency. *See* section 988(c). Thus, accruals in connection with ordinary business transactions, such as purchases and sales of inventory or the provision of services, are section 988 transactions if the receivable or payable is denominated in, or determined by reference to, a currency other than the taxpayer's functional currency, as determined under § 1.985-1.

Notwithstanding the general rule that includes the excess of foreign currency gains over foreign currency losses from section 988 transactions in FPHCI, section 954(c)(1)(D) excludes from FPHCI any foreign currency gain or loss attributable to a transaction directly related to the business needs of the CFC (business needs exclusion). To qualify for the business needs exclusion, a foreign currency gain or loss must, in addition to satisfying other requirements, arise from a transaction entered into, or property used, in the normal course of the CFC's business that does not itself (and could not reasonably be expected to) give rise to subpart F income (as defined in section 952) other than foreign currency gain or loss. *See* § 1.954-2(g)(2)(ii)(B)(*1*).

Foreign currency gain or loss attributable to a bona fide hedging transaction (as defined in § 1.954-2(a)(4)(ii)) with respect to a transaction or property that qualifies for the business needs exclusion also qualifies for the business needs exclusion, provided that any gain or loss with respect to such transaction or property that is attributable to changes in exchange rates is clearly determinable from the records of the CFC as being derived from such property or transaction. *See* § 1.954-2(g)(2)(ii)(B)(*2*). Generally, bona fide hedging transactions are transactions that meet the requirements for a hedging transaction under § 1.1221-2(a) through (d), except that a bona fide hedging transaction also includes a transaction entered into in the normal course of business primarily to manage risk with respect to section 1231 property or a section 988 transaction. Under § 1.1221-2(b), a hedging transaction is defined as a transaction that a taxpayer enters into in the normal course of its trade or business primarily to manage the risk of price changes or currency fluctuations with respect to ordinary property that is held or to be held by the taxpayer, or to manage the risk of interest rate or price changes or currency fluctuations with respect to borrowings made or to be made, or ordinary obligations incurred or to be incurred, by the taxpayer. Transactions that manage risks related to assets that would produce capital gain or loss on disposition (capital assets), or assets owned or liabilities owed by a related party, do not qualify as hedging transactions under §1.1221-2(b). To qualify as a bona fide hedging transaction, the transaction must be clearly identified as a hedging transaction before the end of the day on which the CFC acquired, originated, or entered into the transaction. *See* §§1.1221-2(f) and 1.954-2(a)(4)(ii)(A) and (B).

Section 1.954-2(g)(2)(ii)(C) provides special rules for applying the business needs exclusion to CFCs that are regular dealers as defined in §1.954-2(a)(4)(iv). Transactions in dealer property (as defined in §1.954-2(a)(4)(v)) that are entered into by a CFC that is a regular dealer in such property in its capacity as a dealer are treated as directly related to the business needs of the CFC. *See* §1.954-2(g)(2)(ii)(C)(*1*). In addition, an interest-bearing liability denominated in a nonfunctional currency and incurred by a regular dealer is treated as dealer property if it reduces the CFC's currency risk with respect to dealer property and is identified on the CFC's records as a liability treated as dealer property. *See* §1.954-2(g)(2)(ii)(C)(2). A regular dealer is a CFC that regularly and actively offers to, and in fact does, purchase property from and sell property to unrelated customers in the ordinary course of business, or that regularly and actively offers to, and in fact does, enter into, assume, offset, assign or otherwise terminate positions in property with unrelated customers in the ordinary course of business. *See* §1.954-2(a)(4)(iv).

2. Use of net foreign currency losses

Under section 954(c)(1)(D), although a foreign currency loss that does not qualify for the business needs exclusion reduces the amount of foreign currency gain that is included in FPHCI, an excess of foreign currency losses over foreign currency gains from section 988 transactions generally does not reduce FPHCI. Such a net foreign currency loss does, however, reduce earnings and profits for purposes of the current earnings and profits limitation on subpart F income in section 952(c)(1). Additionally, as described in Part D of this Background section, when an election under §1.954-2(g)(3) or (4) is in effect, a foreign currency loss can reduce FPHCI or, in the case of an election under §1.954-2(g)(3), another category of subpart F income.

3. Inapplicability of business needs exclusion to transactions and property that give rise to both subpart F income and non-subpart F income

In order for the business needs exclusion to apply to exclude foreign currency gain and loss from the computation of FPHCI, the foreign currency gain or loss must arise from a transaction or property that does not itself (and could not reasonably be expected to) give rise to any subpart F income other than foreign currency gain or loss. For example, foreign currency gains and losses related to the purchase and sale of inventory are excluded from the computation of FPHCI if none of the income from the purchase and sale is subpart F income under section 952. However, if the transaction or property gives rise to, or could reasonably be expected to give rise to, any amount of subpart F income (other than foreign currency gain or loss), none of the foreign currency gain or loss attributable to the transaction or property would qualify for the business needs exclusion. Thus, there is a cliff effect: if even a de minimis amount of income or gain from the transaction or property is subpart F income, the entire amount of the foreign currency gain or loss from the transaction or property, or from a bona fide hedging transaction with respect to the transaction or property, is included in the FPHCI computation.

4. Transactions that manage the risk of currency fluctuation in a qualified business unit

A CFC may conduct business through a qualified business unit (as defined in §1.989(a)-1) (QBU) that is not treated as a separate entity for federal income tax purposes, either because it is a branch or division of the CFC or because it is a business entity that is disregarded as separate from its owner. Although the QBU is not treated as a separate entity, it may have a functional currency under §1.985-1 that is different from that of the CFC owner, with consequences for the determination of foreign currency gain and loss under sections 987 and 988. The QBU's transactions in its own functional currency are not section 988 transactions of the CFC, and accordingly the CFC does not realize foreign currency gain or loss on such transactions. The CFC generally must, however, take into account under section 987 foreign currency gain or loss with respect to the QBU upon remittances from the QBU.

For business and financial accounting reasons, a CFC may enter into transactions to manage the exchange rate risk associated with its net investment in its QBU. Under generally accepted accounting principles in the United States (U.S. GAAP), a majority owner of a business entity (parent corporation) must consolidate the accounts of the majority-owned entity, including a foreign entity, with its own accounts for purposes of financial reporting. Under U.S. GAAP, the income, assets, liabilities, and other financial results of foreign operations that are conducted in a functional currency that differs from the consolidated parent's functional currency must be translated into the functional currency of the consolidated parent. Foreign currency gains or losses arising from the translation are recorded in a "cumulative translation adjustment" account and reported as a component of shareholders' equity on the balance sheet. *See generally* Accounting Standards Codification (ASC) 830-30-45. Foreign currency gain or loss from transactions that effectively hedge the risk of currency fluctuations in the net equity investment in foreign operations also are recorded in the cumulative translation adjustment account. *See* ASC 815-35-35. A cumulative translation adjustment is not taken into account in computing the income of the consolidated group until the relevant operations are disposed of or liquidated.

The transactions that a CFC uses to manage its exchange rate risk with respect to its net investment in a QBU are typically section 988 transactions. Thus, foreign currency gains or losses attributable to those transactions are taken into account in computing FPHCI, unless the transactions qualify as bona fide hedging transactions that satisfy the requirements of the business needs exclusion. *See* §1.954-2(g)(2)(ii)(B)(2). Neither the Code nor the section 954 regulations provide specific guidance on whether a transaction entered into to manage exchange rate risk arising from a CFC's net investment in a QBU can qualify as a bona fide hedging transaction eligible for the business needs exclusion. This issue can be consequential because foreign currency gain, but not loss, from a transaction erroneously identified as a bona fide hedging transaction is included in the computation of FPHCI, unless the CFC qualifies for the inadvertent identification exception. *See* §1.954-2(a)(4)(ii)(C) and (g)(2)(ii)(B)(2). Additionally, even if a transaction entered into to manage exchange rate risk arising from a CFC's net investment in a QBU is eligible for treatment as a bona fide hedging transaction, the transaction would not qualify for the business needs exclusion unless the hedged property did not, and could not reasonably be expected to, give rise to any subpart F income.

Also for business and financial accounting reasons, a CFC may enter into transactions to manage the exchange rate risk with respect to its net investment in a subsidiary CFC. A transaction that manages the risk of price or currency fluctuation with respect to a CFC's net investment in a subsidiary CFC is not considered a hedging transaction for federal income tax purposes. In *Hoover Co. v. Commissioner*, 72 T.C. 706 (1979), the Tax Court held that transactions entered into to manage the risk of a decline in value of a taxpayer's net investment in a foreign subsidiary that might occur if the value of the subsidiary's functional currency declined relative to the U.S. dollar were not hedging transactions for federal income tax purposes. *See also* §1.1221-2(b) (providing that a hedging transaction must manage risk with respect to "ordinary property . . . that is held or to be held by the taxpayer"). Thus, foreign currency gains and losses on transactions that manage the risk of currency fluctuation on a CFC's net investment in a subsidiary CFC are taken into account in computing FPHCI. B. Timing of Foreign Currency Gains and Losses

1. Hedge timing rules of §1.446-4

Section 1.446-4 generally requires gain or loss from a hedging transaction, as defined in §1.1221-2(b), to be taken into account at the same time as the gain or loss from the item being hedged. As noted in Part A.1 of this Background section, bona fide hedging transactions under §1.954-2(a)(4)(ii) include both hedging transactions as defined in §1.1221-2(b) and transactions that manage the risk of price or currency fluctuation with respect to section 1231 property and section 988 transactions. Thus, § 1.446-4 does not explicitly apply to all bona fide hedging transactions, which has led to some uncertainty about whether gain or loss from a bona fide hedging transaction that is not described in § 1.1221-2(b) is properly taken into account in the same taxable year as gain or loss on the hedged item. The Department of the Treasury (Treasury Department) and the IRS understand that some taxpayers have applied the hedge timing rules of § 1.446-4 to all bona fide hedging transactions, irrespective of whether those transactions are hedging transactions as defined in § 1.1221-2(b).

2. Treasury center CFCs

It is common for a U.S.-parented multinational group to own one or more CFCs that serve as financing entities for other group members. Such CFCs (treasury center CFCs) may borrow in various currencies from third party lenders or from other members of the group and lend the proceeds to other members of the group. Treasury center CFCs also may be used to centralize the management of currency and other risks of other CFCs within the multinational group. Treasury center CFCs typically qualify as securities dealers under section 475, but if a treasury center CFC transacts primarily or exclusively with related persons, as is often the case, it would not qualify as a regular dealer under § 1.954-2(a)(4)(iv) and thus would not be eligible for the special rules applying the business needs exclusion to certain transactions of regular dealers under § 1.954-2(g)(2)(ii)(C).

When a treasury center CFC borrows nonfunctional currency from related or unrelated parties and makes loans denominated in that nonfunctional currency to a related CFC, the foreign currency gain or loss attributable to the principal amount borrowed by the treasury center CFC will economically offset all or a portion of the foreign currency loss or gain, respectively, attributable to the lending activity. Similarly, the foreign currency gain or loss attributable to the treasury center CFC's accrual of interest income and expense with respect to its lending and borrowing activities, respectively, will offset each other, in whole or in part. Thus, by borrowing and lending in the same nonfunctional currency, a treasury center CFC is said to be "naturally hedged."

Although the borrowing and lending in the same nonfunctional currency are economically offsetting, section 475 creates the potential for a mismatch of gains and losses for a treasury center CFC. If the treasury center CFC qualifies as a dealer under section 475, for example because it regularly purchases debt from related CFCs in the ordinary course of a trade or business, the treasury center CFC generally must use a mark-to-market method of accounting for its securities. See section 475 and § 1.475(c)-1(a)(3)(i). However, § 1.475(c)-2(a)(2) provides that a dealer's own issued debt liabilities are not securities for purposes of section 475. Consequently, a treasury center CFC that marks to market its assets but not its liabilities may recognize any offsetting foreign currency gains and losses in different taxable years. To avoid this mismatch, taxpayers have taken positions that match a treasury center CFC's foreign currency gains and losses under a variety of theories. No inference is intended in these proposed regulations as to whether these positions are permissible in the years prior to the application of these proposed regulations.

C. Foreign Currency Gain or Loss on Interest-Bearing Liabilities and Related Hedging Transactions

As explained in Part A.3 of this Background section, the business needs exclusion does not apply to foreign currency gain or loss with respect to a transaction or property if any subpart F income arises, or could reasonably be expected to arise, from the transaction or property. § 1.954-2(g)(2)(ii)(B)(2). However, § 1.954-2(g)(2)(iii) provides a special rule for foreign currency gain or loss arising from an interest-bearing liability. Under § 1.954-2(g)(2)(iii), such foreign currency gain or loss generally is characterized as subpart F income and non-subpart F income in the same manner that interest expense associated with the liability would be allocated and apportioned between subpart F income and non-subpart F income under §§ 1.861-9T and 1.861-12T. Section 1.954-2(g) does not provide a corresponding rule for a bona fide hedging transaction with respect to an interest-bearing liability. However, § 1.861-9T(b)(2) and (b)(6) provide rules that allocate foreign currency gain or loss on certain hedging transactions in the same manner as interest expense. A foreign currency gain or loss arising from a transaction that hedges an interest-bearing liability and that is not governed by § 1.861-9T is subject to the general rule of § 1.954-2(g)(2)(ii)(B)(2) and its "cliff effect." Consequently, although the foreign currency gain or loss on the hedge of an interest-bearing liability economically offsets the foreign currency loss or gain on that liability, the interaction of the regulations under sections 861 and 954 could result in different allocations of foreign currency gains and losses between subpart F income and non-subpart F income.

D. Elections to Treat Foreign Currency Gain or Loss as a Specific Category of Subpart F Income or FBCI or FPHCI

Section 1.954-2 provides two elections with respect to foreign currency gains or losses. Under the first election, the controlling United States shareholders of a CFC may elect to include foreign currency gain or loss that relates to a specific category of subpart F income or, in the case of FBCI, a specific subcategory of FBCI described in § 1.954-1(c)(1)(iii)(A)(1) or (2), in that category of subpart F income or FBCI, rather than in FPHCI. See § 1.954-2(g)(3). Thus, for example, under this election, foreign currency gain or loss on a transaction that hedges currency risk with respect to transactions that result in foreign base company sales income would be included in the foreign base company sales income category for purposes of determining subpart F income. This election associates foreign currency gain or loss that otherwise would be included in the computation of FPHCI with the categories of subpart F income and foreign base company income to which it relates and allows net foreign currency losses with respect to a category to reduce the income in that category. For this treatment to apply, however, the relationship between the foreign currency gain or loss and the category of income must be clearly determinable from the CFC's records. See § 1.954-2(g)(3)(i)(A).

Under the second election, the controlling United States shareholders of a CFC may elect to include in the computation of FPHCI all foreign currency gain or loss attributable to any section 988 transaction (except a transaction in which gain or loss is treated as capital gain or loss under section 988(a)(1)(B)) and to certain section 1256 contracts. See § 1.954-2(g)(4). When this election is in effect, net foreign currency loss reduces gross income in other categories of FPHCI. Controlling United States shareholders typically make the § 1.954-2(g)(4) election if a CFC has relatively little net foreign currency gain or loss. In those circumstances, the administrative burden of tracing foreign currency gain and loss to specific transactions or property, as is required under the business needs exclusion and the § 1.954-2(g)(3) election, may outweigh the benefit of those provisions. As the CFC's foreign currency gain or loss becomes more significant, the net benefit of the business needs exclusion or the § 1.954-2(g)(3) election may increase and the relative benefit of the § 1.954-2(g)(4) election may decrease.

Explanation of Provisions

A. Business Needs Exclusion

1. Transactions and property that give rise to both subpart F income and non-subpart F income

The Treasury Department and the IRS believe that foreign currency gain or loss arising from a transaction or property, or from a bona hedging transaction with respect to such a transaction or property, should be eligible for the business needs exclusion to the extent the transaction or property generates non-subpart F income. Accordingly, proposed § 1.954-2(g)(2)(ii)(C)(1) provides that foreign currency gain or loss attributable to a transaction or property that gives rise to both subpart F income and non-subpart F income, and that otherwise satisfies the requirements of the business needs exclusion, is allocated between subpart F income and non-subpart F income in the same proportion as the income from the underlying transaction or property. As a result, the amount of foreign currency gain or loss allocable to non-subpart F income qualifies for the business needs exclusion, and the amount allocable to subpart F income is taken into account in computing FPHCI. Under proposed § 1.954-2(g)(2)(ii)(C)(1), the entire foreign currency gain or loss arising from property that does not give rise to income (as defined in § 1.954-2(e)(3)), or from a bona fide hedging transaction with respect to such property, is attributable to subpart F income because any gain upon a disposition of such property would be subpart F income.

2. Hedges of net investment in a QBU

The Treasury Department and the IRS believe that a transaction that manages exchange rate risk with respect to a CFC's net investment in a QBU that is not treated as a separate entity for federal income tax purposes should qualify for the business needs exclusion to the extent the underlying property of the QBU does not give rise to subpart F income. Accordingly, proposed § 1.954-2(g)(2)(ii)(C)(2) provides that the qualifying portion of any foreign currency gain or loss that arises from a "financial statement hedging transaction" with respect to a QBU and that is allocable to non-subpart F income is directly related to the business needs of a CFC. A financial statement hedging transaction is defined as a transaction that is entered into by a CFC for the purpose of managing exchange rate risk with respect to part or all of that CFC's net investment in a QBU that is included in the consolidated financial statements of a United States shareholder of the CFC or a corporation that directly or indirectly owns such United States shareholder. The qualifying portion is defined as the amount of foreign currency gain or loss arising from a financial statement hedging transaction that is properly accounted for under U.S. GAAP as a cumulative foreign currency translation adjustment to shareholders' equity. The qualifying portion of any foreign currency gain or loss arising from a financial statement hedging transaction must be allocated between subpart F income and non-subpart F income using the principles of § 1.987-6(b). The amount of the qualifying portion allocated to non-subpart F income qualifies for the business needs exclusion.

The proposed amendment to § 1.446-4(a), discussed in Part B.1 of this Explanation of Provisions section, provides that a bona fide hedging transaction (as defined in § 1.954-2(a)(4)(ii)) is subject to the hedge timing rules of § 1.446-4. Additionally, as noted earlier, proposed § 1.954-2(g)(2)(ii)(C)(2) provides that part or all of the qualifying portion of any foreign currency gain or loss arising from a financial statement hedging transaction is eligible for the business needs exclusion. However, financial statement hedging transactions are not included in the definition of bona fide hedging transaction under § 1.954-2(a)(4)(ii), as proposed to be amended pursuant to these proposed regulations. Thus, foreign currency gain or loss arising from a financial statement hedging transaction is not subject to the hedge timing rules of § 1.446-4 and is taken into account in accordance with the taxpayer's method of accounting. Generally, a taxpayer's financial statement hedging transaction is a section 988 transaction with respect to the taxpayer. Accordingly, to the extent that the taxpayer elects to use a mark-to-market method of accounting for section 988 gain or loss under proposed § 1.988-7, and also makes the annual deemed termination election described in § 1.987-8T(d), the taxpayer generally would recognize annually foreign currency gain or loss from both the financial statement hedging transaction and the QBU with respect to which exchange rate risk is managed. The Treasury Department and the IRS request comments regarding whether the hedge timing rules of § 1.446-4 should apply to a financial statement hedging transaction (as defined in proposed § 1.954-2(g)(2)(ii)(C)(2)) with respect to section 987 QBUs with respect to which no annual deemed termination election is in effect, and, if so, how the appropriate matching should be achieved.

The Treasury Department and the IRS also request comments regarding whether the business needs exclusion should apply to a transaction that is entered into for the purpose of managing the risk of foreign currency fluctuation with respect to a CFC's net investment in a subsidiary CFC. Comments are requested regarding how the gain or loss on such a transaction could or should be allocated between subpart F and non-subpart F income and whether and how the gain or loss could or should be matched with the foreign currency gain or loss on the "hedged" item.

The Treasury Department and the IRS are aware that a CFC may enter into a transaction that manages exchange rate risk arising from a disregarded loan to a QBU. The Treasury Department and the IRS understand that, for U.S. GAAP purposes, exchange gain or loss with respect to a transaction that manages exchange rate risk with respect to the disregarded loan generally would not be reflected as a cumulative foreign currency translation adjustment. For federal income tax purposes, the loan would be disregarded, and exchange gain or loss on the hedging transaction potentially could be subpart F income. The Treasury Department and the IRS request comments regarding whether, taking into account the amendments in the proposed regulations, additional amendments to the business needs exclusion are appropriate to account for foreign currency gain or loss arising from a transaction that is entered into for the purpose of managing the risk of foreign currency fluctuation with respect to disregarded transactions, including disregarded loans, between a CFC and its QBU. Specifically, comments are requested regarding how the foreign currency gain or loss on such a hedging transaction could or should be allocated between subpart F and non-subpart F income and when such foreign currency gain or should be recognized.

B. *Timing of Foreign Currency Gains and Losses*

1. Extension of § 1.446-4 hedge timing rules to bona fide hedging transactions

The proposed amendment to § 1.446-4(a) extends the hedge timing rules of § 1.446-4 to all bona fide hedging transactions as defined in § 1.954-2(a)(4)(ii). Although this amendment will be particularly useful in connection with foreign currency gains and losses from bona fide hedging transactions of treasury center CFCs, the amendment will eliminate timing mismatches for gains and losses arising from all bona fide hedging transactions and from the hedged property or transaction.

In addition, proposed § 1.954-2(a)(4)(ii) revises the definition of a bona fide hedging transaction to permit the acquisition of a debt instrument by a CFC to be treated as a bona fide hedging transaction with respect to an interest-bearing liability of the CFC, provided that the acquisition of the debt instrument has the effect of managing the CFC's exchange rate risk with respect to the liability within the meaning of § 1.1221-2(c)(4) and (d), determined without regard to § 1.1221-2(d)(5), and otherwise meets the requirements of a bona fide hedging transaction. If a CFC, including a treasury center CFC, identifies a debt instrument that manages exchange rate risk as a hedge of an interest-bearing liability, the foreign currency gain or loss arising from that debt instrument will be taken into account under § 1.446-4 at the same time as the foreign currency gain or loss arising from the hedged interest-bearing liability.

Treating a debt instrument as a hedge of an interest-bearing liability, rather than treating the interest-bearing liability as a hedge of the debt instrument, is consistent with the principles underlying § 1.861-9T(b)(2), which allocates and apportions foreign currency gain or losses on a transaction that hedges an interest-bearing liability in the same manner as interest expense with respect to the liability is allocated and apportioned. See part C of this Explanation of Provisions section for further discussion of the impact of this rule on the allocation of foreign currency gain or loss on a debt instrument between subpart F income and non-subpart F income.

2. Elective mark-to-market method of accounting for foreign currency gain and loss

Proposed § 1.988-7 permits a taxpayer, including a CFC, to elect to use a mark-to-market method of accounting for section 988 gain or loss with respect to section 988 transactions, including becoming an obligor under an interest-bearing liability. This elective mark-to-market method of accounting takes into account only changes in the value of the section 988 transaction attributable to exchange rate fluctuations and does not take into account changes in value due to other factors, such as changes in market interest rates or the creditworthiness of the borrower. The proposed regulations require appropriate adjustments to be made to prevent section 988 gain or loss taken into account under the mark-to-market method of accounting from being taken into account again under section 988 or another provision of the Code.

This election is available to any taxpayer but is expected to be particularly relevant in the case of a treasury center CFC. A treasury center CFC that uses a mark-to-market method for securities under section 475 and that makes the election under proposed § 1.988-7 will be able to match the timing of foreign currency gain or loss with respect to an interest-bearing liability (such as a loan from a related or unrelated party) with economically offsetting foreign currency loss or gain arising from its nonfunctional currency-denominated assets (such as a receivable from a related party). Whether the corresponding foreign currency gains and losses qualify for the business needs exclusion is determined under the rules of § 1.954-2(g)(2), as proposed to be amended pursuant to these proposed regulations. Thus, if the foreign currency gains or losses do not fully offset each other, the difference may increase or decrease the CFC's FPHCI. However, the election under proposed § 1.988-7 does not apply to the following: (1) any securities that are marked to market under any other provision; (2) any securities that, pursuant to an election or an identification made by the taxpayer, are excepted from mark-to-market treatment under any other provision; (3) any transactions of a QBU that is subject to section 987; or (4) any section 988 transactions denominated in, or determined by reference to, a hyperinflationary currency.

The election applies for the year in which the election is made and all subsequent taxable years unless it is revoked by the Commissioner or the taxpayer or, in the case of a CFC, the controlling domestic shareholders of the CFC. Proposed § 1.988-7(d) permits a taxpayer or CFC to revoke the election to use a mark-to-market method of accounting for foreign currency gains or losses on section 988 transactions at any time. A subsequent election cannot be made until the sixth taxable year following the year of revocation and cannot be revoked until the sixth taxable year following the year of such subsequent election.

C. *Hedges of Exchange Rate Risk Arising from an Interest-Bearing Liability*

The Treasury Department and the IRS believe that it is appropriate to require foreign currency gain or loss from transactions that have the effect of managing exchange rate risk arising from an interest-bearing liability to be allocated between subpart F income and non-subpart F income in the same manner as the foreign currency gain or loss on the hedged liability. Accordingly, the proposed amendments to § 1.954-2(g)(2)(iii) require foreign currency gains and losses arising from a transaction or property (including debt instruments) that manages exchange rate risk with respect to an interest-bearing liability to be allocated and apportioned between subpart F income and non-subpart F income in the same manner that foreign currency gain or loss from the interest-bearing liability would be allocated and apportioned. As noted in Part B.1 of this Explanation of Provisions, the proposed amendment to § 1.954-2(a)(4)(ii) revises the definition of a bona fide hedging transaction to permit the acquisition of a debt instrument by a CFC to be treated as a bona fide hedging transaction with respect to an interest-bearing liability of the CFC under certain circumstances. As a result of that proposed amendment and the amendment described in this Part C, if a CFC identifies a debt instrument that manages exchange rate risk as a hedge of an interest-bearing liability, the foreign currency gain or loss arising from that debt instrument will be allocated between subpart F income and non-subpart F income in the same manner as the foreign currency gain or loss arising from the hedged interest-bearing liability. Thus, the proposed amendments to the regulations permit a CFC that timely and properly identifies a debt instrument as a hedge of an interest-bearing liability to alleviate the character mismatch that may occur under the existing regulations, as described in Part C of the Background section of this preamble. The proposed amendments to § 1.954-2(g)(2)(iii) also clarify that the special rules in that paragraph apply to foreign currency gain or loss arising from an interest-bearing liability, or from a bona fide hedging transaction with respect to the liability, in lieu of the general rule of the business needs exclusion in § 1.954-2(g)(2)(ii).

D. *Revocation of Election to Treat Foreign Currency Gain or Loss as a Specific Category of Subpart F Income or as FPHCI*

Proposed § 1.954-2(g)(3)(iii) permits a CFC to revoke its election under § 1.954-2(g)(3) (to characterize foreign currency gain or loss that arises from a specific category of subpart F income as gain or loss in that category) at any time without securing the prior consent of the Commissioner. Similarly, proposed § 1.954-2(g)(4)(iii) permits a CFC to revoke its election under § 1.954-2(g)(4) (to treat all foreign currency gain or loss as FPHCI) at any time without securing the prior consent of the Commissioner. The Treasury Department and the IRS remain concerned about CFCs frequently changing these elections without a substantial business reason but also believe that the ability of a taxpayer to automatically revoke these elections would promote sound tax administration. Therefore, the proposed regulations provide that, if an election has been revoked under proposed § 1.954-2(g)(3)(iii) or proposed § 1.954-2(g)(4)(iii), a subsequent election cannot be made until the sixth taxable year following the year of revocation and any subsequent election cannot be revoked until the sixth year following the year of such subsequent election.

E. *Applicability Dates*

The proposed amendments generally are proposed to apply to taxable years ending on or after the date the proposed regulations are published as final regulations in the *Federal Register*. However, the proposed amendments to §§ 1.446-4(a), 1.954-2(a)(4)(ii)(A), 1.954-2(g)(2)(ii)(C)(1), and 1.954-2(g)(2)(iii) are proposed to apply to bona fide hedging transactions entered into on or after the date the proposed regulations are published as final regulations in the *Federal Register*. A taxpayer may rely on any of the proposed amendments, other than the amendments to §§ 1.446-4(a), 1.954-2(a)(4)(ii)(A), 1.954-2(g)(2)(ii)(C)(1), and 1.954-2(g)(2)(iii), insofar as each applies to a bona fide hedging transaction, for taxable years ending on or after December 19, 2017, provided the taxpayer consistently applies the proposed amendment for all such taxable years that end before the first taxable year ending on or after the date the proposed regulations are published as final regulations in the *Federal Register*. A taxpayer may rely on any of the proposed amendments to §§ 1.446-4(a), 1.954-2(a)(4)(ii)(A), 1.954-2(g)(2)(ii)(C)(1), and 1.954-2(g)(2)(iii) with respect to a bona fide hedging transaction entered into on or after December 19, 2017 and prior to the applicability date, provided the taxpayer consistently applies the proposed amendment to all bona fide hedging transactions entered into on or after December 19, 2017 and prior to the date that these regulations are published as final regulations in the *Federal Register*.

Special Analyses

Certain IRS regulations, including these, are exempt from the requirements of Executive Order 12866, as supplemented and reaffirmed by Executive Order 13563. Therefore, a regulatory impact assessment is not required. It is hereby certified that the collection of information requirement will not have a significant economic impact on a substantial number of small entities. This certification is based on the fact that these regulations primarily will affect domestic corporations that have foreign operations, which tend to be larger businesses, and that the average burden is minimal. Accordingly, the Regulatory Flexibility Act (5 U.S.C. chapter 6) does not apply. Pursuant to section 7805(f), this notice of proposed rulemaking has been submitted to the Chief Counsel for Advocacy of the Small Business Administration for comment on its impact on small business.

Comments and Requests for Public Hearing

Before these proposed regulations are adopted as final regulations, consideration will be given to any comments that are submitted timely to the IRS as prescribed in this preamble under "ADDRESSES." The Treasury Department and the IRS request comments on all aspects of the proposed rules. All comments will be available at *www.regulations.gov* or upon request. A public hearing will be scheduled if requested in writing by any person that timely submits comments. If a public hearing is scheduled, notice of the date, time, and place for the public hearing will be published in the *Federal Register*.

Drafting Information

The principal author of these regulations is Jeffery G. Mitchell of the Office of Associate Chief Counsel (International). However, other personnel from the IRS and the Treasury Department participated in their development.

[¶ 49,758] Proposed Amendments of Regulations (REG-129260-16), published in the Federal Register on March 13, 2018.

[Code Sec. 6103]

Disclosure of information: Seriously delinquent tax debt: State department: Fixing America's Surface Transportation (FAST) Act.— Amendments of Reg. §§ 301.6103(n)-1, authorizing the Department of State to disclose returns and return information to contractors who assist the Department of State in carrying out its responsibilities under section 32101 of the Fixing America's Surface Transportation (FAST) Act, are proposed.

AGENCY: Internal Revenue Service (IRS), Treasury.

ACTION: Notice of proposed rulemaking.

SUMMARY: This document contains proposed regulations under section 6103(n) of the Internal Revenue Code (Code) to authorize the Department of State to disclose returns and return information to its contractors who assist the Department of State in carrying out its responsibilities under section 32101 of the Fixing America's Surface Transportation (FAST) Act. The FAST Act requires the IRS to notify the Department of State of certified seriously delinquent tax debts, and the Department of State procures services from outside contractors in connection with carrying out its responsibilities under the FAST Act.

DATES: Written and electronic comments and requests for a public hearing must be received by April 12, 2018.

ADDRESSES: Send submissions to: CC:PA:LPD:PR (REG-129260-16), Room 5207, Internal Revenue Service, P.O. Box 7604, Ben Franklin Station, Washington, DC 20044. Submissions may be hand delivered Monday through Friday between the hours of 8:00 a.m. and 4:00 p.m. to CC:PA:LPD:PR (REG-129260-16), Courier's Desk, Internal Revenue Service, 1111 Constitution Avenue, NW, Washington, DC 20224. Alternatively, taxpayers may submit comments electronically via the Federal eRulemaking Portal at *www.regulations.gov* (IRS REG-129260-16).

FOR FURTHER INFORMATION CONTACT: Concerning the proposed regulations, Brittany Harrison of the Office of Associate Chief Counsel (Procedure and Administration), (202) 317-6833; concerning the submission of comments and requests for a public hearing, Regina Johnson, (202) 317-6901 (not toll-free numbers).

SUPPLEMENTARY INFORMATION:

Background and Explanation of Provisions

This document contains proposed amendments to the Procedure and Administration Regulations (26 CFR part 301) under section 6103(n) of the Code. On December 4, 2015, the FAST Act, Public Law 114-94, 129 Stat. 1312, was enacted into law. Section 32101 of the FAST Act adds section 7345 to the Internal Revenue Code. Section 7345 requires the IRS to notify the Department of State of tax debts that the IRS certifies as seriously delinquent. Section 7345(b) generally defines a seriously delinquent tax debt as an unpaid, legally enforceable Federal tax liability of an individual that has been assessed, is greater than $50,000 (as indexed for inflation), and with respect to which a notice of lien has been filed pursuant to section 6323 and the administrative rights under section 6320 with respect to such filing have been exhausted or have lapsed, or a levy has been made pursuant to section 6331. Section 32101 of the FAST Act generally requires the Department of State to deny a passport (or the renewal of a passport) in the case of an individual if notified by the IRS that the individual has been certified as having a seriously delinquent tax debt and permits the Department of State to revoke a passport previously issued to such person.

Under section 6103(a) of the Code, returns and return information are confidential unless the Code otherwise authorizes disclosure. The FAST Act added section 6103(k)(11), which provides that, upon certification under section 7345, the IRS is authorized to disclose return information to the Department of State with respect to a taxpayer who has a seriously delinquent tax debt. Specifically, upon certification under section 7345, section 6103(k)(11)(A) authorizes the IRS to disclose to officers and employees of the Department of State (i) the taxpayer identity information with respect to the certified taxpayer and (ii) the amount of such seriously delinquent tax debt. Section 6103(k)(11)(A). Section 6103(k)(11)(B) limits the use of return information disclosed under subparagraph (A) for the purposes of, and to the extent necessary in, carrying out the requirements of section 32101 of the FAST Act.

The Department of State engages contractors to assist in carrying out its responsibilities with respect to passports, including responsibilities related to implementation of section 32101 of the FAST Act. Because such contractors are not "officers and employees" of the Department of State, section 6103(k)(11) of the Code does not authorize the disclosure of return information to such contractors.

Section 6103(n) of the Code authorizes, pursuant to regulations prescribed by the Secretary, the disclosure of returns and return information to any person for purposes of tax administration to the extent necessary in connection with, among other things, a written contract for services. The definition of the term "tax administration" includes "the administration, management, conduct, direction, and supervision of the execution and application of the internal revenue laws or related statutes . . . ." Section 6103(b)(4). Because implementation of the FAST Act relates to the administration, management, conduct, direction, and supervision of the execution and application of the internal revenue laws and related statutes, disclosure of return information for the purpose of carrying out responsibilities under the FAST Act is a tax administration purpose.

The Treasury regulations provide that, pursuant to the provisions of section 6103(n) of the Code and subject to certain conditions, officers and employees of the Treasury Department, a State tax agency, the Social Security Administration, or the Department of Justice are authorized to disclose returns and return information to any person or to an officer or employee of the person, for purposes of tax administration (as defined in section 6103(b)(4)), to the extent necessary in connection with a written contract or an agreement for the acquisition of the providing of services. Section 301.6103(n)-1(a)(1). Any person, or officer or employee of the person, who receives such disclosed returns or return information may further disclose the returns or return information to its own officers or employees whose duties or responsibilities require such information in order to provide the services. Section 301.6103(n)-1(a)(2)(i). When authorized in writing by the IRS, such person, or officer or employee of the person, may further disclose such information to the extent necessary to provide services, including to its agents or subcontractors (or such agents' or subcontractors' officers or employees). Section 301.6103(n)-1(a)(2)(ii). Agents or subcontractors (or their officers or employees) who receive such returns or return information may further disclose the returns or return information to their officers or employees whose duties or responsibilities require the returns or return information for a purpose described in § 301.6103(n)-1(a). Section 301.6103(n)-1(a)(3). The regulations under section 6103(n) of the Code provide a number of rules related to limitations on such disclosures, penalties potentially applicable to recipients of returns and return information, notification requirements applicable to recipients of returns and return information, and safeguards requirements. See section 301.6103(n)-1(b), -1(c), -1(d), -1(e).

These proposed regulations add the Department of State to the list of agencies in current § 301.6103(n)-1(a)(1) whose officers and employees may disclose returns and return information to any person or to an officer or employee of such person for tax administration purposes to the extent necessary in connection with a written contract for the acquisition of property or services. These proposed regulations authorize the Department of State to disclose returns and return information to its contractors providing services in connection with the revocation or denial of passports pursuant to the requirements of section 7345 and the FAST Act.

Special Analyses

Certain IRS regulations, including this one, are exempt from the requirements of Executive Order 12866, as supplemented and reaffirmed by Executive Order 13563. Therefore, a regulatory impact assessment is not required.

The purpose of these regulations is to allow the Department of State to share tax return information with its contractors for tax administration purposes. As a recipient of tax return information, the Department of State is required to comply with the reporting and other requirements under section 6103(p)(4). The Department of State is also responsible for the training and inspection of its contractors and ensuring that all safeguarding standards are met. These proposed regulations do not impose a reporting burden on the Department of State's contractors and will not require the contractors to file information with the IRS. Because the proposed regulations do not impose a collection of information on entities other than the Department of State, they do not impose a collection of information on small entities. Accordingly, it is hereby certified that these regulations will not have a significant economic impact on a substantial number of small entities. Accordingly, a regulatory flexibility analysis is not required under the Regulatory Flexibility Act (5 U.S.C. chapter 6).

Pursuant to section 7805(f) of the Code, these proposed regulations have been submitted to the Chief Counsel for Advocacy of the Small Business Administration for comment on their impact on small business.

Comments and Requests for Public Hearing

Before the regulations proposed herein are adopted as final regulations, consideration will be given to any electronic and written comments that are submitted timely to the IRS as prescribed in this preamble under the **ADDRESSES** heading. The Treasury Department and the IRS request comments on all aspects of the proposed regulations. All comments submitted will be made available at *www.regulations.gov* or upon request. A public hearing may be scheduled if requested in writing by a person that timely submits written comments. If a public hearing is scheduled, notice of the date, time, and place of the hearing will be published in the *Federal Register*.

Drafting Information

The principal author of these proposed regulations is Brittany Harrison of the Office of the Associate Chief Counsel (Procedure and Administration).

[¶ 49,759]   Proposed Amendments of Regulations (REG-132434-17), published in the Federal Register on March 28, 2018.

[Code Sec. 7602]

Nongovernment attorneys: Examinations of books, papers and other data: Summons interview witness: Contractors.—Amendments of Reg. § 301.7602-1, relating to administrative proceedings by generally excluding nongovernment attorneys from receiving summoned books, paper, records, or other data or from participating in the interview of a witness summoned by the IRS to provide testimony under oath, are proposed.

AGENCY: Internal Revenue Service (IRS), Treasury.

ACTION: Notice of proposed rulemaking.

SUMMARY: This document contains proposed regulations to amend regulations under section 7602(a) of the Internal Revenue Code relating to administrative proceedings. Current regulations permit any person authorized to receive returns and return information under section 6103(n) and the regulations thereunder to receive and review summoned books, papers, and other data, and, in the presence and under the guidance of an IRS officer or employee, participate fully in the interview of a witness in a summons interview. These proposed regulations significantly narrow the scope of the current regulations by excluding non-government attorneys from receiving summoned books, papers, records, or other data or from participating in the interview of a witness summoned by the IRS to provide testimony under oath, with a limited exception. These proposed regulations affect taxpayers involved in a federal tax examination and other persons whose books and records or testimony are sought to be examined by the IRS under section 7602(a).

DATES: Written or electronic comments and requests for a public hearing must be received by June 26, 2018.

ADDRESSES: Send submissions to: CC:PA:LPD:PR (REG-132434-17), room 5203, Internal Revenue Service, P.O. Box 7604, Ben Franklin Station, Washington, D.C. 20044. Submissions may be hand-delivered Monday through Friday between the hours of 8 a.m. and 4 p.m. to CC:PA:LPD:PR (REG-132434-17), Courier's Desk, Internal Revenue Service, 1111 Constitution Avenue, NW, Washington D.C., or sent electronically via the Federal eRulemaking Portal at www.regulations.gov (IRS-REG-132434-17).

FOR FURTHER INFORMATION CONTACT: Concerning submission of comments, Regina Johnson, (202) 317-6901; concerning the proposed regulations, William V. Spatz at (202) 317-5461 (not toll-free numbers).

SUPPLEMENTARY INFORMATION:

Background

These proposed regulations amend Procedure and Administration Regulations (26 CFR part 301) under section 7602(a) of the Internal Revenue Code relating to participation by persons described in section 6103(n) and Treas. Reg. § 301.6103(n)-1(a) in receiving and reviewing summoned books, papers, records, or other data and in interviewing a summoned witness under oath. These proposed regulations narrow the scope of the current regulations by providing that certain non-government attorneys hired by the IRS are not authorized to participate in an examination.

On June 18, 2014, temporary regulations (TD 9669) regarding participation in a summons interview of a person described in section 6103(n) were published in the **Federal Register** (79 FR 34625). A notice of proposed rulemaking (REG-121542-14) cross-referencing the temporary regulations was published in the **Federal Register** (79 FR 34668) the same day. No public hearing was requested or held. The Internal Revenue Service received two comments on the proposed regulations. One comment recommended that the regulations be revised to remove the provision permitting a contractor to question a witness under oath or to ask a witness's representative to clarify an objection or assertion of privilege. The other comment recommended that the proposed and temporary regulations be withdrawn. After consideration of these comments, the proposed regulations were adopted in final regulations (TD 9778) published in the **Federal Register** (81 FR 45409) on July 14, 2016 ("Summons Interview Regulations"). The only change from the temporary regulations in the final regulations was to replace the word "examine" with "review" in the phrase describing what contractors may do with books, papers, records, or other data received by the IRS under a summons. The preamble to the final regulations explains that this was intended to clarify that the regulations do not authorize contractors to direct audits of a taxpayer's return. See 81 FR 45410.

Description of Summons Interview Regulations

The United States tax system relies upon taxpayers' self-assessment and reporting of their tax liability. The expansive information-gathering authority that Congress granted to the IRS under the Code includes the IRS's broad examination and summons authority, which allows the IRS to determine the accuracy of that self-assessment. See United States v. Arthur Young & Co., 65 U.S. 805, 816 (1984). Section 7602(a) provides that, for the purpose of ascertaining the correctness of any return, making a return where none has been made, or determining the liability of any person for any internal revenue tax, the IRS is authorized to examine books and records, issue summonses seeking documents and testimony, and take testimony from witnesses under oath. These provisions have been part of the revenue laws since 1864.

Use of outside specialists is appropriate to assist the IRS in determining the correctness of the taxpayer's self-assessed tax liability. The assistance of persons from outside the IRS, such as economists, engineers, appraisers, industry specialists, and actuaries, promotes fair and efficient administration and enforcement of the laws administered by the IRS by providing specialized knowledge, skills, or abilities that the IRS officers or employees assigned to the examination may not possess. Section 6103(n) and Treas. Reg. § 301.6103(n)-1(a) authorize the IRS to disclose returns and return information to these contractors. The regulations under § 301.7602-1(b)(3) were issued to clarify that persons described in section 6103(n) and Treas. Reg. § 301.6103(n)-1(a) may receive and review books, papers, records, or other data summoned by the IRS and, in the presence and under the guidance of an IRS officer or employee, participate fully in the interview of a person who the IRS has summoned as a witness to provide testimony under oath. See 81 FR 45410.

Executive Order 13789, Notice 2017-38, and the Reports to the President

Executive Order 13789, issued on April 21, 2017 (E.O. 13789, 82 FR 19317), instructs the Secretary of the Treasury (the Secretary) to review all significant tax regulations issued on or after January 1, 2016, and to take appropriate action to alleviate the burdens of regulations that (i) impose an undue financial burden on U.S. taxpayers; (ii) add undue complexity to the Federal tax laws; or (iii) exceed the statutory authority of the IRS.

E.O. 13789 further instructs the Secretary to submit to the President within 60 days a report (First Report) that identifies regulations that meet these criteria. Notice 2017-38 (2017-30 I.R.B. 147 (July 24, 2017)) included the Summons Interview Regulations in a list of eight regulations identified by the Secretary in the First Report as meeting at least one of the first two criteria specified in E.O. 13789. E.O. 13789 further instructs the Secretary to submit to the President a second report (Second Report) that recommends specific actions to mitigate the burden imposed by regulations identified in the First Report.

In response to Notice 2017-38, the Treasury Department and the IRS received seven comments from professional and business associations addressing the Summons Interview Regulations. All but one of these comments recommended removal of the regulations based primarily on the commentators' perception that the regulations create longer and less efficient examinations by improperly delegating authority to outside law firms to conduct examinations. The one commenter that did not recommend removal of the regulations in their entirety requested removal of the provisions permitting a contractor to directly question a witness during a summons interview.

As explained in the preamble to the final Summons Interview Regulations, the regulations do not delegate authority to conduct examinations or summons interviews. Rather, the regulations permit contractors authorized under section 6103(n) to review books and records and be present and ask questions during summons interviews, all under the supervision of IRS officers and employees. See 81 FR 45410-45412.

Comments in response to Notice 2017-38 also raised concerns that the regulations permit the IRS to hire law firms to receive and review summoned information and fully participate in a summons interview on behalf of the government.

On October 16, 2017, the Secretary published the Second Report in the **Federal Register** (82 FR 48013) stating that the Treasury Department and the IRS are considering proposing a prospectively effective amendment to the Summons Interview Regulations to narrow their scope to prohibit non-government attorneys from questioning witnesses on behalf of the IRS, reviewing summoned records, or playing a behind-the-scenes role in an examination, such as consulting on IRS legal strategy, with a limited exception.

The Code provides IRS officers and employees with significant and broad powers under its summons authority to question witnesses under oath and to require the production of books and records. The Summons Interview Regulations require the IRS to retain authority over important decisions when section 6103(n) contractors question witnesses, but there is a perceived risk that the IRS may not be able to maintain full control over the actions of a non-government attorney hired by the IRS when such an attorney, with the limited exception described below, questions witnesses. The actions of the non-governmental attorney while questioning witnesses could foreclose IRS officials from independently exercising their judgment. Managing an examination or summons interview is therefore best exercised solely by government employees, including government attorneys, whose only duty is to serve the public interest. These concerns outweigh the countervailing need for the IRS to use non-government attorneys, except in the limited circumstances set forth in proposed paragraph (b)(3)(ii). Treasury and the IRS remain confident that the core functions of questioning witnesses and conducting examinations are well within the expertise and ability of government attorneys and examination agents.

Explanation of Provisions

Proposed § 301.7602-1(b)(3)(i) retains the rule from the Summons Interview Regulations authorizing section 6103(n) contractors to receive and review summoned information and fully participate in the summons interview, including questioning witnesses. However, proposed § 301.7602-1(b)(3)(ii) is added to prohibit contractors who are attorneys, with the limited exception described below, from participating in the administrative process contemplated by section 7602(a). Under this prohibition, a non-government attorney, with the limited exception described below, may not review summoned books, papers, records or other data or question summoned witnesses on behalf of the IRS unless the attorney is hired by the IRS for a permitted purpose.

As a limited exception to that prohibition, proposed § 301.7602-1(b)(3)(ii) permits the IRS to hire a non-government attorney if the attorney is being hired for specialized substantive subject matter expertise in an area other than federal tax law. Specifically, proposed § 301.7602-1(b)(3)(ii) permits the IRS to hire an attorney who has specialized knowledge of foreign, state, or local law, including tax law, or who is a specialist in non-tax substantive law such as patent law, property law, or environmental law. It would not permit IRS to hire an attorney for non-substantive specialized knowledge, such as civil litigation skills. Proposed § 301.7602-1(b)(3)(ii) also permits the IRS to hire a contractor who may happen to be an attorney, but who is hired for knowledge, skills, or abilities other than providing legal services as an attorney. Further, proposed § 301.7602-1(b)(3)(ii) permits the IRS to hire an entity that employs or is owned by attorneys so long as the expertise they are providing is not prohibited by proposed § 301.7602-1(b)(3)(ii).

These changes are proposed to be effective for examinations begun and summonses served by the IRS on or after the date that these proposed regulations are published in the **Federal Register**.

Special Analyses

Certain IRS regulations, including these, are exempt from the requirements of Executive Order 12866, as supplemented and affirmed by Executive Order 13563. Therefore, a regulatory assessment is not required. Because the proposed regulations would not impose a collection of information on small entities, the Regulatory Flexibility Act (5 U.S.C. chapter 6) does not apply. Therefore, a regulatory flexibility analysis is not required. Pursuant to section 7805(f) of the Internal Revenue Code, the IRS will submit the proposed regulations to the Chief Counsel for Advocacy of the Small Business Administration for comments about the regulations' impact on small businesses.

Comments and Request for a Public Hearing

Before these proposed regulations are adopted as final, the IRS will consider any written (signed original and 8 copies) or electronic comments timely submitted. The IRS requests comments on all aspects of these proposed regulations. All comments will be available for public inspection and copying. The IRS will schedule a public meeting if one is requested, in writing, by a person who submits written comments. If the IRS does schedule a public hearing, the IRS will publish notice of the date, time, and place for the public hearing in the **Federal Register**.

Drafting Information

The principal author of these regulations is William V. Spatz of the Office of Associate Chief Counsel (Procedure and Administration).

[¶ 49,760]   Proposed Amendments of Regulations (REG-102951-16), published in the Federal Register on May 31, 2018.

[Code Secs. 6011 and 6721]

Filing requirements: Information returns: Magnetic media.—Amendments of Reg. §§301.6011-2 and 301.6721-1, amending the rules for determining whether information returns must be filed using magnetic media (electronically), are proposed.

AGENCY: Internal Revenue Service (IRS), Treasury.

ACTION: Notice of proposed rulemaking.

SUMMARY: This document contains proposed regulations amending the rules for determining whether information returns must be filed using magnetic media (electronically). The proposed regulations would require that all information returns, regardless of type, be taken into account to determine whether a person meets the 250-return threshold and, therefore, must file the information returns electronically. The proposed regulations also would require any person required to file information returns electronically to file corrected information returns electronically, regardless of the number of corrected information returns being filed. The proposed regulations will affect persons required to file information returns.

DATES: Written or electronic comments and requests for a public hearing must be received by July 30, 2018.

ADDRESSES: Send submissions to: CC:PA:LPD:PR (REG-102951-16), room 5205, Internal Revenue Service, P.O. Box 7604, Ben Franklin Station, Washington, DC 20044. Submissions may be hand-delivered Monday through Friday between the hours of 8:00 a.m. and 4:00 p.m. to CC:PA:LPD:PR (REG-102951-16), Courier's Desk, Internal Revenue Service, 1111 Constitution Avenue, NW., Washington, DC 20224. Alternatively, persons may submit comments electronically via the Federal eRulemaking Portal at *http://www.regulations.gov* (IRS REG-102951-16).

FOR FURTHER INFORMATION CONTACT: Concerning the proposed regulations, Michael Hara, (202) 317-6845; concerning the submission of comments and requests for a public hearing, Regina L. Johnson, (202) 317-5177 (not toll-free calls).

SUPPLEMENTARY INFORMATION:

Background

This document contains proposed amendments to the Regulations on Procedure and Administration (26 CFR part 301) under section 6011(e) relating to the filing of information returns on magnetic media. Section 6011(e) authorizes the Secretary to prescribe regulations regarding the filing of returns on magnetic media. Section 6011(e)(2)(A) prohibits the Secretary from requiring persons to file returns on magnetic media unless the person is required to file at least 250 returns during the calendar year. Section 6011(e)(2)(B) provides that, in prescribing regulations, the Secretary shall consider the taxpayer's ability to comply at reasonable cost with the regulations' requirements. Section 301.6011-2(a)(1) provides that magnetic media includes any magnetic media permitted under the applicable regulations, revenue procedures, or publications, or, in the case of returns filed with the Social Security Administration, any magnetic media permitted under Social Security Administration publications, including electronic filing.

Section 301.6011-2 provides rules for when information returns described in §301.6011-2(b), such as Form 1042-S, "Foreign Person's U.S. Source Income Subject to Withholding;" forms in the 1099 series; and Form W-2, "Wage and Tax Statement," must be filed electronically. Under §301.6011-2(c), a person is not required to file a type of information return covered by §301.6011-2(b) electronically unless the person is required to file 250 or more such returns during the calendar year. Sections 301.6011-2(c)(1)(i) and (iii) and the Examples in §301.6011-2(c)(1)(iv) describe that the 250-return threshold applies separately to each type of information return and each type of corrected information return filed, and, therefore, the forms are not aggregated for purposes of determining whether the 250-return threshold is satisfied. Section 301.6011-2(c)(2) allows the Commissioner to waive the requirement to file electronically if the request for waiver demonstrates hardship and provides that the principal factor in determining hardship will be the extent, if any, to which the cost of electronic filing exceeds the cost of filing on other media.

When the rules for determining the 250-return threshold, including the rule providing that each type of information return is counted separately and not aggregated, were originally published, electronic filing was in the early stages of development and was not as commonly used as it is today. The non-aggregation rule helped to reduce cost and ease burden on taxpayers, given the existing limits on technology and accessibility to such technology. Since then, significant advances in technology have made electronic filing more prevalent and accessible. As a result, electronic filing is less costly and most often easier than paper filing. In fact, most information returns are filed electronically. In tax year 2015, approximately 98 percent of information returns were filed electronically. In tax year 2016, the percentage of information returns filed electronically rose to 98.5 percent. Advances in tax return preparation software, as well as the prevalence of tax return preparers and third-party service providers who offer information return preparation and electronic filing, have also contributed to the increase in electronic filing.

The concerns regarding taxpayer burden and cost associated with electronic filing have been significantly mitigated since the non-aggregation rule in §301.6011-2(c)(1)(i) and (iii) of the regulations was first published. Therefore, determining the 250-return threshold on a form-by-form basis without aggregation is no longer necessary to relieve taxpayer burden and cost. Accordingly, these regulations simplify the rules for determining the 250-return threshold by requiring aggregation of all information returns covered by §301.6011-2(b) for purposes of determining the 250-return threshold. In addition, these regulations provide that corrected information returns must be filed electronically if the original information returns were filed electronically. These rule changes will help facilitate efficient and effective tax administration.

Explanation of Provisions

These proposed regulations remove the non-aggregation rule in §301.6011-2(c)(1)(iii) that counts the number of information returns required to be filed on a form-by-form basis. The proposed regulations add a new paragraph (4) to §301.6011-2(b) to provide that if during a calendar year a person is required to file a total of 250 or more information returns of any type covered by §301.6011-2(b), the person is required to file those information returns electronically. For example, under these proposed regulations, if a person is required to file 200 Forms 1099-INT, "Interest Income," and 200 Forms 1099-DIV, that person must file all Forms 1099-INT and Forms 1099-DIV electronically because that person is required to file, in the aggregate, at least 250 information returns covered by §301.6011-2(b). Corrected information returns are not taken into account in determining whether the 250-return threshold is met under proposed § 301.6011-2(b)(4) for purposes of determining whether information returns covered by § 301.6011-2(b) must be filed electronically. Examples in proposed § 301.6011-2(c)(1)(iv) illustrate this rule.

The proposed regulations also provide that corrected information returns covered by § 301.6011-2(b) must be filed electronically if the information returns originally filed for the calendar year are required to be filed electronically. If fewer than 250 returns covered by § 301.6011-2(b) are required to be filed for the calendar year, the original returns for the calendar year, as well as the corrected returns for the calendar year, are not required to be filed electronically. See proposed § 301.6011-2 (b)(4).

The proposed regulations also amend § 301.6721-1(a)(2)(ii) regarding the penalty for failure to file correct information returns to remove references to the prior rule for determining the number of returns on a form-by-form basis and the prior corrected return rule.

The proposed regulations do not amend the existing regulations allowing persons who are required to file returns electronically to request a waiver of the electronic-filing requirement. See § 301.6011-2(c)(2). This waiver authority will be exercised so as not to unduly burden taxpayers lacking the necessary data-processing capabilities or access to return preparers and third-party service providers at a reasonable cost.

Proposed Effective/Applicability Date

These proposed regulations will be effective on the date of the publication of the Treasury Decision adopting these rules as final in the **Federal Register**. However, to give information-return filers sufficient time to comply with these regulations, these proposed regulations will not apply to information returns required to be filed before January 1, 2019. Accordingly, these proposed regulations provide that § § 301.6011-2(b)(4) and 301.6721-1(a)(2)(ii), as amended, will be effective for information returns required to be filed after December 31, 2018. Section 301.6011-2(b)(5), as amended, will be effective for corrected information returns filed after December 31, 2018.

Special Analyses

This regulation is not subject to review under section 6(b) of Executive Order 12866 pursuant to the Memorandum of Agreement (April 11, 2018) between the Department of the Treasury and the Office of Management and Budget regarding review of tax regulations.

When the Internal Revenue Service issues a proposed rulemaking imposing a collection of information requirement on small entities, the Regulatory Flexibility Act (RFA) requires the agency to "prepare and make available for public comment an initial regulatory flexibility analysis," which will "describe the impact of the proposed rule on small entities." 5 U.S.C. 603(a). Section 605(b) of the RFA allows an agency to certify a rule, in lieu of preparing an analysis, if the proposed rulemaking is not expected to have a significant economic impact on a substantial number of small entities.

This proposed rule directly affects information-return filers that file more than 250 returns of any type covered by § 301.6011-2(b), which includes a substantial number of small entities. However, the IRS has determined that the economic impact on small entities affected by the proposed rule would not be significant. Under sections 6011(e) and § 301.6011-2(c)(1), information-return filers already must file information returns electronically if during a calendar year a person is required to file a total of 250 or more information returns of any type covered by § 301.6011-2(b). The proposed rule merely amends the method of counting those 250 returns to determine if the 250-return threshold is met. Information filers may request a waiver of the electronic-filing requirement if they lack the necessary data-processing capabilities or access to return preparers and third-party service providers at a reasonable cost, and the IRS routinely grants meritorious hardship waiver requests. Accordingly, the burden on the limited number of small entities that are not currently filing electronically will be slight, and small entities that would experience a hardship because of this proposed rule may seek a waiver. The Commissioner of the IRS hereby certifies that this rule will not have a significant economic impact on a substantial number of small entities. The IRS invites comment from members of the public who believe there will be a significant impact on small information return filers. Pursuant to section 7805(f) of the Code, this notice of proposed rulemaking has been submitted to the Chief Counsel for Advocacy of the Small Business Administration for comment on its impact on small business.

Comments and Requests for Public Hearing

Before these proposed regulations are adopted as final regulations, consideration will be given to any electronic and written comments that are submitted timely to the IRS as prescribed in this preamble under the ADDRESSES heading. The Treasury Department and the IRS request comments on all aspects of the proposed rules. All comments will be available at *www.regulations.gov* or upon request. A public hearing will be scheduled if requested in writing by any person that timely submits written comments. If a public hearing is scheduled, then notice of the date, time, and place for the public hearing will be published in the **Federal Register**.

Drafting Information

The principal author of these proposed regulations is Michael Hara of the Office of the Associate Chief Counsel (Procedure and Administration).

[¶ 49,767] **Proposed Amendments of Regulations (REG-136118-15, REG-119337-17, REG-118067-17, REG-120232-17 and REG-120233-17),** published in the Federal Register on August 17, 2018.

[Code Secs. 704, 705, 706, 6221, 6222, 6225, 6226, 6227, 6231, 6232, 6233, 6234, 6235 and 6241]

Centralized partnership audit regime: Technical Corrections Act of 2018 (TTCA): Partnership items: Partnership-related items: Withdrawal of proposed regulations.—Reg. § § 301.6225-4 and 301.6226-4 and amendments of Reg. § § 1.704-1, 1.705-1 and 1.706-4, implementing the centralized partnership audit regime, in order to reflect the changes made by the Technical Corrections Act of 2018, contained in Title II of the Consolidated Appropriations Act of 2018 (TTCA), are reproposed. Amendments of Reg. § § 301.6221(a)-1, 301.6225-1, 301.6226-2, 301.6226-3 and 301.6227-2 proposed on November 30, 2017, Reg. § § 301.6231-1, 301.6232-1, 301.6233(a)-1, 301.6233(b)-1, 301.6234-1 and 301.6235-1 and amendments of Reg. § § 301.6221(a)-1, 301.6225-2, 301.6226-1, 301.6226-2, 301.6226-3 and 301.6227-3 proposed on December 19, 2017, Reg. § § 301.6225-4 and 301.6226-4 and amendments of Reg. § § 1.704-1, 1.705-1, 1.706-4 and 301.6225-3 proposed on February 2, 2018 and Reg. § § 301.6221(a)-1, 301.6222-1, 301.6225-1, 301.6225-2, 301.6225-3, 301.6225-4, 301.6226-1, 301.6226-2, 301.6226-3, 301.6226-4, 301.6227-1, 301.6227-2, 301.6227-3, 301.6241-1, 301.6241-2, 301.6241-3, 301.6241-4 and 301.6241-5 proposed on June 14, 2017, are withdrawn. Reg. § § 301.6221(a)-1, 301.6222-1, 301.6225-1, 301.6225-2, 301.6225-3, 301.6226-1, 301.6226-2, 301.6226-3, 301.6227-1, 301.6227-2, 301.6227-3, 301.6231-1, 301.6232-1, 301.6233(a)-1, 301.6233(b)-1, 301.6234-1, 301.6235-1, 301.6241-1, 301.6241-2, 301.6241-3, 301.6241-4, 301.6241-5 and 301.6241-6 adopted by T.D. 9844.

AGENCY: Internal Revenue Service (IRS), Treasury.

ACTION: Notice of proposed rulemaking; notice of public hearing; withdrawal and partial withdrawal of notices of proposed rulemaking.

SUMMARY: This document contains proposed regulations implementing the centralized partnership audit regime. This document withdraws and reproposes certain portions of proposed regulations implementing the centralized partnership audit regime that have not been finalized to reflect the changes made by the Technical Corrections Act of 2018, contained in Title II of the Consolidated Appropriations Act of 2018 (TTCA). The proposed regulations affect partnerships with respect to partnership taxable years beginning after December 31, 2017, as well as partnerships that make the election under the Bipartisan Budget Act of 2015 (BBA),to apply the centralized partnership audit regime to partnership taxable years beginning on or after November 2, 2015 and before January 1, 2018.

DATES: Written or electronic comments must be received by October 1, 2018. Outlines of topics to be discussed at the public hearing scheduled for October 9, 2018, at 10 A.M. must be received by October 1, 2018.

ADDRESSES: Send submissions to: CC:PA:LPD:PR (REG-136118-15), room 5207, Internal Revenue Service, P.O. Box 7604, Ben Franklin Station, Washington, DC 20044. Submissions may be hand delivered Monday through Friday between the hours of 8 a.m. and 4 p.m. to CC:PA:LPD:PR (REG-136118-15), Courier's Desk, Internal Revenue Service, 1111 Constitution Avenue NW, Washington, DC 20224, or sent electronically via the Federal eRulemaking Portal at *www.regulations.gov* (IRS REG-136118-15).

FOR FURTHER INFORMATION CONTACT: Concerning the proposed regulations under sections 6221, 6226, 6235, and 6241, Jennifer M. Black of the Office of Associate Chief Counsel (Procedure and Administration), (202) 317-6834; concerning the proposed regulations under sections 6225, 6231, and 6234, Joy E. Gerdy-Zogby of the Office of Associate Chief Counsel (Procedure and Administration), (202) 317-6834; concerning the proposed regulations under sections 6222, 6227, 6232, and 6233, Steven L. Karon of the Office of Associate Chief Counsel (Procedure and Administration), (202) 217-6834; concerning the proposed regulations under section 6225 relating to creditable foreign tax expenditures, Larry R. Pounders, Jr. of the Office of Associate Chief Counsel (International), (202) 317-5465; concerning the proposed regulations relating to chapters 3 and 4 of subtitle A of the Internal Revenue Code (other than section 1446), Subin Seth of the Office of Associate Chief Counsel (International), (202) 317-5003; concerning the proposed regulations relating to section 1446, Ronald M. Gootzeit of the Office of Associate Chief Counsel (International), (202) 317-4953; concerning the proposed regulations under sections 704 through 706 and §§301.6225-4 and 301.6226-4, Allison R. Carmody or Meghan M. Howard of the Office of Associate Chief Counsel (Passthroughs and Special Industries), (202) 317-5279; concerning the submission of comments, the hearing, or to be placed on the building access list to attend the hearing, Regina Johnson, (202) 317-6901 (not toll-free numbers).

SUPPLEMENTARY INFORMATION:

Background

This document contains proposed regulations under sections 704 through 706 to amend the Income Tax Regulations (26 CFR Part 1) under Subpart — Partners and Partnerships and proposed regulations under sections 6221 through 6241 to amend the Procedure and Administration Regulations (26 CFR Part 301) under Subpart - Tax Treatment of Partnership Items to implement the centralized partnership audit regime enacted by section 1101 of the BBA, Public Law 114-74 (BBA), as amended by the Protecting Americans from Tax Hikes Act of 2015, Public Law 114-113 (PATH Act) and sections 201 through 207 of the TTCA, Public Law 115-141. This document also withdraws portions of proposed regulations under sections 704 through 706 and 6221 through 6241 that were published in the **Federal Register** on June 14, 2017 (REG-136118-15, 82 FR 27334), November 30, 2017(REG-119337-17, 82 FR 56765), December 19, 2017(REG-120232-17 and REG-120233-17, 82 FR 27071), and February 2, 2018 (REG-118067-17, 83 FR 4868).

Section 1101(a) of the BBA removed subchapter C of chapter 63 of the Internal Revenue Code (Code) effective for partnership taxable years beginning after December 31, 2017. Subchapter C of chapter 63 of the Code (subchapter C of chapter 63) contained the unified partnership audit and litigation rules that were commonly referred to as the TEFRA partnership procedures or simply TEFRA. Section 1101(b) of the BBA also removed subchapter D of chapter 63 of the Code and part IV of subchapter K of chapter 1 of the Code, rules applicable to electing large partnerships, effective for partnership taxable years beginning after December 31, 2017. Section 1101(c) of the BBA replaced the TEFRA partnership procedures and the rules applicable to electing large partnerships with a centralized partnership audit regime that, in general, determines, assesses, and collects tax at the partnership level.

On December 18, 2015, section 1101 of the BBA was amended by the PATH Act. The amendments under the PATH Act are effective as if included in section 1101 of the BBA, and therefore, subject to the effective dates in section 1101(g) of the BBA.

On June 14, 2017, the Treasury Department and the IRS published in the **Federal Register** (82 FR 27334) a notice of proposed rulemaking (REG-136118-15) (June 2017 NPRM) proposing rules under section 6221 regarding the scope and election out of the centralized partnership audit regime, section 6222 regarding consistent treatment by partners, section 6223 regarding the partnership representative, section 6225 regarding partnership adjustments made by the IRS and determination of the amount of the partnership's liability (referred to as the imputed underpayment), section 6226 regarding the election for partners to take partnership adjustments into account, section 6227 regarding administrative adjustment requests (AARs), and section 6241 regarding definitions and special rules. The Treasury Department and the IRS received written public comments in response to the regulations proposed in the June 2017 NPRM, and a public hearing regarding the proposed regulations was held on September 18, 2017.

On November 30, 2017, the Treasury Department and the IRS published in the **Federal Register** (82 FR 56765) a notice of proposed rulemaking (REG-119337-17) (November 2017 NPRM) proposing rules regarding international provisions under the centralized partnership audit regime, including rules relating to the withholding of tax on foreign persons, the withholding of tax to enforce reporting on certain foreign accounts, and the treatment of creditable foreign tax expenditures of a partnership. No written comments were submitted in response to this NPRM, and no hearing was requested or held.

On December 19, 2017, the Treasury Department and the IRS published in the **Federal Register** (82 FR 27071) a notice of proposed rulemaking (REG-120232-17 and REG-120233-17) (December 2017 NPRM) proposing administrative and procedural rules under the centralized partnership audit regime, including rules addressing assessment and collection, penalties and interest, periods of limitations on making partnership adjustments, and judicial review of partnership adjustments. The regulations proposed in the December 2017 NPRM also provided rules addressing how pass-through partners take into account adjustments under the alternative to payment of the imputed underpayment described in section 6226 and under rules similar to section 6226 when a partnership files an AAR under section 6227. Written comments were received in response to the December 2017 NPRM. However, no hearing was requested or held.

On January 2, 2018, the Treasury Department and the IRS published in the **Federal Register** (82 FR 28398) final regulations under section 6221(b) providing rules for electing out of the centralized partnership audit regime.

On February 2, 2018, the Treasury Department and the IRS published in the **Federal Register** (83 FR 4868) a notice of proposed rulemaking (REG-118067-17) (February 2018 NPRM) proposing rules for adjusting tax attributes under the centralized partnership audit regime. Written comments were received in response to the February 2018 NPRM. However, no hearing was requested or held.

On March 23, 2018, Congress enacted the TTCA, which made a number of technical corrections to the rules under the centralized partnership audit regime. The amendments under the TTCA are effective as if included in section 1101 of the BBA, and therefore, subject to the effective dates in section 1101(g) of the BBA.

On August 9, 2018, the Treasury Department and the IRS published in the **Federal Register** (83 FR 39331) final regulations under section 6223 providing rules relating to partnership representatives and final regulations under §301.9100-22 providing rules for electing into the centralized partnership audit regime for taxable years beginning on or after November 2, 2015 and before January 1, 2018. Corresponding temporary regulations under §301.9100-22T were also withdrawn.

In light of the technical corrections made by the TTCA, to the extent regulations have not already been finalized, this document withdraws the regulations proposed in the June 2017 NPRM, the November 2017 NPRM, the December 2017 NPRM, and the February 2018 NPRM (collectively, the prior NPRMs) and proposes regulations reflecting the technical corrections made by the TTCA. The regulations proposed in this document also include clarifications, unrelated to the TTCA as discussed in the Explanation of Provisions section of this preamble. In addition, certain regulations have been reordered and renumbered, typographical errors have been corrected, nonsubstantive editorial changes have been made, and the applicability date provisions in the regulations have been revised to replace references to § 301.9100-22T with references to § 301.9100-22. Finally, the assumed highest rate of tax for corporations in the examples for all applicable periods is now 20 percent to more closely reflect the corporate tax rate in effect under section 11 (as amended by section 13001 of "[a]n Act to provide for the reconciliation pursuant to titles II and V of the concurrent resolution on the budget for fiscal year 2018," Public Law 115-97 (the "Act")).

Although this document withdraws the prior NPRMs, the Explanation of Provisions sections contained in the preambles of the withdrawn NPRMs remain relevant. Therefore, to the extent not inconsistent with the Explanation of Provisions section of this preamble or the preamble to the portions of the proposed regulations that have already been finalized, those Explanation of Provision sections are incorporated by reference in this document. Federal Register citations are provided to assist with locating the relevant section of the preamble in the prior NPRMs. The prior NPRMs are also included in the rulemaking docket for this notice of proposed rulemaking on *www.regulations.gov*.

This document does not address written comments that were submitted in response to the regulations proposed in the prior NPRMs or respond to any statements made during the public hearing held on September 18, 2017. Except to the extent that the written comments relate to the final regulations under section 6221(b) and section 6223, such comments and any comments received in response to this notice of proposed rulemaking will be addressed when the regulations proposed in this document are finalized.

Explanation of Provisions

1. *Scope of the Centralized Partnership Audit Regime and Partnership-Related Item*

Section 6221(a) provides for the determination of certain adjustments at the partnership level under the centralized partnership audit regime. Prior to amendment by the TTCA, section 6221(a) provided that any adjustment to items of income, gain, loss, deduction, or credit of a partnership for a partnership taxable year (and any partner's distributive share thereof) shall be determined, any tax attributable thereto shall be assessed and collected, and the applicability of any penalty, addition to tax, or additional amount which relates to an adjustment to any such item or share shall be determined at the partnership level. Prior to amendment by the TTCA, section 6241(a)(2) provided that the term "partnership adjustment" meant any adjustment in the amount of any item of income, gain, loss, deduction, or credit of a partnership, or any partner's distributive share thereof.

Section 201(c)(2) of the TTCA amended section 6221(a) by replacing the phrase "items of income, gain, loss, deduction, or credit of a partnership for a partnership taxable year (and any partner's distributive share thereof)" with the phrase "a partnership-related item." Section 6221(a) now provides that any adjustment to a partnership-related item and the applicability of any penalty, addition to tax, or additional amount which relates to an adjustment to any partnership-related item shall be determined at the partnership level. Additionally, section 6221(a) provides that any tax attributable to an adjustment to a partnership-related item shall be assessed and collected at the partnership level.

Section 201(a) of the TTCA amended section 6241(2) to provide that the term "partnership adjustment" means any adjustment to a partnership-related item, and the term "partnership-related item" means any item or amount with respect to the partnership (without regard to whether or not such item or amount appears on the partnership's return and including an imputed underpayment and any item or amount relating to any transaction with, basis in, or liability of, the partnership) which is relevant (determined without regard to subchapter C of chapter 63) in determining the tax liability of any person under chapter 1 of the Code (chapter 1) and any partner's distributive share thereof.

By eliminating the reference to items of income, gain, loss, deduction, or credit of a partnership, and instead referring to partnership-related items, which is broadly defined, the amendments by the TTCA clarify that the scope of the centralized partnership audit regime is not narrower than the scope of the partnership audit procedures under TEFRA. Joint Comm. on Taxation, JCX-6-18, *Technical Explanation of the Revenue Provisions of the House Amendment to the Senate Amendment to H.R. 1625 (Rules Committee Print 115-66)*, 37 (2018) (JCX-6-18). Rather, the centralized partnership audit regime is intended to have a scope sufficient to address those items that would have been considered partnership items, affected items, and computational adjustments under TEFRA, including the regulations. *Id.*

A. *Proposed § 301.6221(a)-1*

Proposed rules under § 301.6221(a)-1 were previously published in the **Federal Register** (82 FR 27372-73) in the June 2017 NPRM and the November NPRM (82 FR 56776) (former proposed § 301.6221(a)-1). Former proposed § 301.6221(a)-1(a) provided that the centralized partnership audit regime covers any adjustment to items of income, gain, loss, deduction, or credit of a partnership and any partner's distributive share of those adjusted items. Former proposed § 301.6221(a)-1(b)(1)(i) defined the phrase "items of income, gain, loss, deduction or credit" to mean all items and information required to be shown, or reflected, on a return of the partnership under section 6031, the regulations thereunder, and the forms and instructions prescribed by the IRS for the partnership's taxable year, and any information in the partnership's books and records for the taxable year. In addition, former proposed § 301.6221(a)-1(b)(1)(ii) provided that any factors that needed to be taken into account to determine or allocate the tax treatment of items adjusted under the centralized partnership audit regime were also to be determined at the partnership level. Former proposed § 301.6221(a)-1(b)(2) also addressed items included within the phrase "partner's distributive share." Because the TTCA's amendment of the scope of the centralized partnership audit regime is accomplished by adding a new defined term - "partnership-related item" - the majority of the rules under former proposed § 301.6221(a)-1(b) that addressed the scope of what is adjusted at the partnership level are now incorporated into proposed § 301.6241-6 which defines the term "partnership-related item."

Proposed § 301.6221(a)-1(a) now provides the general rule that, except as otherwise provided under the centralized partnership audit regime, any adjustments to partnership-related items and the applicability of any penalty, addition to tax, or additional amount that relates to an adjustment to any such items are determined at the partnership level. In addition, proposed § 301.6221(a)-1(a) provides that any chapter 1 tax attributable to an adjustment to a partnership-related item is assessed and collected at the partnership level. See section 13 of the preamble for a discussion of special enforcement matters pertaining to partnership-related items that may be adjusted outside of the centralized partnership audit regime.

Proposed § 301.6221(a)-1(a) further provides that any consideration necessary to make a determination at the partnership level under the centralized partnership audit regime is made at the partnership level. This would include the period of limitations on making adjustments under section 6235 as well as any facts necessary to calculate any imputed underpayment under section 6225, except as otherwise provided under the centralized partnership audit regime. These determinations previously constituted factors described under former proposed § 301.6221(a)-1(b)(1)(ii)(F) and (I).

B. *Proposed § 301.6241-6*

Proposed § 301.6241-6 defines the term "partnership-related item." Proposed § 301.6241-6(a) provides the general rule that a partnership-related item is any item or amount with respect to the partnership which is relevant in determining the tax liability of any person under chapter 1 and any partner's distributive share of any such item or amount.

Proposed § 301.6241-6(b) provides that an item or amount is with respect to a partnership without regard to whether or not such item or amount appears on the partnership return. An item or amount is with respect to a partnership if: the item or amount is shown or reflected, or required to be shown, or reflected, on a return of the partnership; the item or amount is in the partnership's books and records; the item or amount is an imputed underpayment; the item or amount relates to any transaction with, basis in, or liability of the partnership; or the item or amount relates to a transaction under section 707(a)(2), 707(b), or 707(c).

Under proposed § 301.6241-6(b)(4) and (7), an item or amount that relates to any transaction with, or liability of, the partnership, is with respect to a partnership only if the item or amount relates to a transaction or liability between the partnership and a partner acting in its capacity as a partner or an indirect partner (as defined in proposed § 301.6241-1(a)(4)) acting in its capacity as an indirect partner. Accordingly, an item or amount that relates to any transaction with or liability of the partnership is not with respect to the partnership if the item or amount is reported (or reportable) solely by a person other than the partnership, a partner not acting in its capacity as a partner, or an indirect partner not acting in its capacity as an indirect partner (except for transactions under section 707). Proposed § 301.6241-6(b)(8) provides that any determination necessary to make an adjustment to an item or amount described in proposed § 301.6241-6(b)(1) through (b)(7) is also an item or amount with respect to the partnership.

Proposed § 301.6241-6(c) provides that the determination of whether an item or amount is relevant in determining the tax liability of any person under chapter 1 is made without regard to the provisions of the centralized partnership audit regime. Proposed § 301.6241-6(c) also clarifies that an item or amount of a partnership is relevant in determining the liability of any person under chapter 1 without regard to whether such item or amount, or adjustment to such item or amount, has an effect on the tax liability of any particular person under chapter 1. Section 6241(2)(B)(i) does not limit whether an item is relevant in determining tax liability under chapter 1 to whether the item is relevant to determining the tax liability of a partner of the partnership under chapter 1. Rather, the statutory language refers to liability under chapter 1 of "any person." An item or amount is a partnership-related item if the item or amount is relevant in determining any person's liability under chapter 1 if the item might have any effect on any person's liability under chapter 1 regardless of whether it actually does have such an effect. Consequently, the IRS is not required to determine if an adjustment would have an actual effect on any person's chapter 1 liability under the Code.

Proposed § 301.6241-6(d) provides a list of examples of partnership-related items. These examples are largely the same as the items described in former proposed § 301.6221(a)-1(b)(1) with a few minor revisions. First, the references to "foreign," "tax," and "§ 1.704-1(b)(4)(viii)(b)" in the example regarding creditable expenditures were removed to clarify that partnership-related item includes any creditable expenditures, not just a creditable foreign tax expenditure. Also, the "including . . ." phrase from each example was removed to be consistent with the broad scope of the centralized partnership audit regime and does not reflect a substantive change. No inference should be drawn from the removal of that language.

Proposed § 301.6241-6(e) provides examples that illustrate the rules under proposed § 301.6241-6.

2. *Partner's Return Must Be Consistent with Partnership Return*

Prior to enactment of the TTCA, section 6222 provided that a partner shall treat on the partner's return "each item of income, gain, loss, deduction, or credit attributable to a partnership" subject to subchapter C of chapter 63 in a manner that is consistent with the treatment of such item on the partnership return. Section 201(c) of the TTCA amended section 6222 to provide that a partner shall treat on the partner's return "any partnership-related item" in a manner which is consistent with the treatment of such item on the partnership return.

A. *Proposed § 301.6222-1*

Proposed rules under § 301.6222-1 were previously published in the **Federal Register** (82 FR 27375-78) in the June 2017 NPRM (former proposed § 301.6222-1). For an explanation of the rules under former proposed 301.6222-1, see 82 FR 27345-46.

Former proposed § 301.6222-1(a) provided that a partner's treatment of each item of income, gain, loss, deduction, or credit attributable to a partnership must be consistent with the treatment of those items on the partnership return, including treatment with respect to the amount, timing, and characterization of those items. The reference in former proposed § 301.6222-1(a) to "each item of income, gain, loss, deduction, or credit attributable to a partnership" has been replaced with a reference to "any partnership-related item" to reflect the statutory change to section 6222(a). In addition, references throughout former proposed § 301.6222-1 to the term "item" have been replaced with references to the term "partnership-related item," as appropriate.

3. *Imputed Underpayment, Modification of Imputed Underpayment, and Adjustments That Do Not Result in an Imputed Underpayment*

Section 6225 provides rules governing the determination of the imputed underpayment, modification of the imputed underpayment, and the treatment of adjustments that do not result in an imputed underpayment. Section 202(c) of the TTCA amended section 6225(a) to reflect the new term "partnership-related item" and to provide that in the case of adjustments to partnership-related items that result in an imputed underpayment the partnership shall pay an amount equal to the imputed underpayment in the adjustment year as provided in section 6232. In the case of adjustments that do not result in an imputed underpayment, such adjustments shall be taken into account by the partnership in the adjustment year.

Section 202(a) of the TTCA amended section 6225(b)(1) to provide that the Secretary shall determine any imputed underpayment with respect to any reviewed year by appropriately netting all partnership adjustments to such reviewed year and applying the highest rate of tax in effect for that year under section 1 or 11. Section 202(a) of the TTCA also amended section 6225(b)(2) to provide that in the case of any adjustment that reallocates the distributive share of any item from one partner to another, such adjustment shall be taken into account by disregarding so much of such adjustment as results in a decrease in the amount of the imputed underpayment.

Section 202(a) of the TTCA also added paragraphs (b)(3) and (b)(4) to section 6225. Section 6225(b)(3) provides that partnership adjustments for any reviewed year shall first be separately determined (and netted as appropriate) within each category of items that are required to be taken into account separately under section 702(a) or other provision of the Code. Section 6225(b)(4) provides if any adjustment would (but for section 6225(b)(4)) result in a decrease in the amount of the imputed underpayment, and could be subject to any additional limitation under the provisions of the Code (or not allowed, in whole or in part, against ordinary income) if such adjustment were taken into account by any person, such adjustment shall not be taken into account when appropriately netting partnership adjustments under section 6225(b)(1)(A) except to the extent otherwise provided by the Secretary.

Section 202(b) of the TTCA amended several provisions relating to modifications of imputed underpayments. Sections 6225(c)(3), (c)(4)(A), and (c)(5)(A)(i), which previously referred to the "portion of the imputed underpayment," were amended to refer to the "portion of the adjustment." This amendment clarifies that modifications under sections 6225(c)(3), (c)(4), and (c)(5) result in disregarding the portion of the partnership adjustment affected by the modification, rather than the portion of the imputed underpayment. Section 202(c) of the TTCA also added section 6225(c)(9), which provides that the Secretary shall establish procedures under which the adjustments described in section 6225(a)(2) - adjustments that do not result in an imputed underpayment - may be modified in such manner as the Secretary determines appropriate.

Section 203 of the TTCA amended section 6225(c)(2) relating to the procedures for partners to take adjustments into account during modification. Section 6225(c)(2)(A) governs the filing of amended returns by partners. Section 6225(c)(2)(B) provides for an alternative procedure to the filing of amended returns. Section 6225(c)(2)(C) provides rules for adjustments that reallocate the distributive share of any item from one partner to another.

Section 6225(c)(2)(D) provides that sections 6501 and 6511 shall not apply in certain situations related to amended returns and the alternative procedure to filing amended returns. Section 6225(c)(2)(E) provides that any adjustments to tax attributes that occur as a result of a modification under section 6225(c)(2) are binding on the partners and the partnership. Section 6225(c)(2)(F) provides rules for tiered structures, including defining the term "relevant partner" to mean any partner in the chain of ownership of any partnerships that are partners in the partnership requesting modification.

A. Proposed §§ 301.6225-1, 301.6225-2, and 301.6225-3

Proposed rules under §§ 301.6225-1, 301.6225-2, and 301.6225-3 were previously published in the **Federal Register** in the June 2017 NPRM (82 FR 27382-91), the November 2017 NPRM (82 FR 56776), and in the December 2017 NPRM (82 FR 60154) (collectively, former proposed §§ 301.6225-1, 301.6225-2, and 301.6225-3). For an explanation of the rules under former proposed §§ 301.6225-1, 301.6225-2, and 301.6225-3, see 82 FR 27350-58, 82 FR 56766-75, and 82 FR 60152-53.

Proposed § 301.6225-1 has been reorganized to clarify the process for determining an imputed underpayment. This reorganization, when compared to former proposed § 301.6225-1 (1) more clearly describes the steps necessary to determine an imputed underpayment and adjustments that do not result in an imputed underpayment; (2) consolidates rules regarding adjustments that do not result in an imputed underpayment; and (3) relocates rules regarding creditable expenditures to more clearly explain how to account for creditable expenditures in the determination of the imputed underpayment.

Proposed § 301.6225-1(b) addresses the calculation of the imputed underpayment. Due to the number of adjustments that could be made based on the definition of partnership-related item, the IRS will need to address circumstances in which multiple partnership-related items are adjusted to address a single issue or transaction in the administrative proceeding. Adjusting multiple partnership-related items that relate to the same issue or transaction could result in an imputed underpayment that double-counts some of the adjustments even though, if the partnership and partners had properly reported the item, one or more adjustments would have been subsumed by another item. To prevent double-counting the individual adjustments as inputs into the imputed underpayment, proposed § 301.6225-1(b)(4) provides that the IRS may treat adjustments that would otherwise be double-counted as zero for purposes of determining the imputed underpayment.

Proposed § 301.6225-1(c) describes the different groupings in which adjustments are placed for purposes of determining an imputed underpayment. These groupings are the reallocation grouping, the credit grouping, the creditable expenditure grouping, and the residual grouping. Proposed § 301.6225-1(c)(1) provides authority for the IRS to alter the manner in which adjustments are grouped to appropriately reflect the facts and circumstances.

Proposed § 301.6225-1(c)(2) defines the term "reallocation adjustment" and provides that in general reallocation adjustments are placed in the reallocation grouping. Under proposed § 301.6225-1(c)(3), however, reallocation adjustments to credits are placed in the credit grouping, and under § 301.6225-1(c)(4), reallocation adjustments to creditable expenditures are placed in the creditable expenditure grouping, similar to the rule under former proposed § 301.6225-1(d)(2)(iv). Proposed § 301.6225-1(c)(2)(ii) provides that each reallocation adjustment results in two separate adjustments - one positive adjustment and one negative adjustment. Proposed § 301.6225-1(c)(6) provides similar rules for recharacterization adjustments.

Proposed § 301.6225-1(c)(5)(ii) provides rules for how to account for adjustments to partnership-related items that are not allocated by the partnership to its partners under section 704(b). Proposed § 301.6225-1(d)(2)(iii)(B) provides that adjustments to such items, solely for purposes of determining an imputed underpayment, are treated as a positive adjustment to income to the extent appropriate. The Treasury Department and the IRS request comments regarding how to treat recharacterization and reallocation adjustments related to items that are not allocated under section 704(b).

To incorporate the additions of sections 6225(b)(3) and (b)(4), proposed § 301.6225-1(d)(1) provides that when the IRS determines a negative adjustment (as defined in proposed § 301.6225-1(d)(2)(ii)), all partnership adjustments are placed into subgroupings based on whether the adjusted items are required to be taken into account separately under section 702 and other provisions of the Code. Proposed § 301.6225-1(d)(1) provides authority for the IRS to alter the manner in which adjustments are subgrouped to appropriately reflect the facts and circumstances.

Proposed § 301.6225-1(d)(2) provides for the treatment of certain partnership adjustments and defines the terms negative adjustment and positive adjustment. A negative adjustment is defined as an adjustment that is a decrease in an item of income, treated as a decrease in an item of income, or that is an increase in an item of credit. A positive adjustment is an adjustment that is not a negative adjustment. Proposed § 301.6225-1(d)(3) requires that positive and negative adjustments resulting from reallocation adjustments and recharacterization adjustments be placed into separate subgroupings.

Proposed § 301.6225-1(e) provides rules for appropriately netting adjustments within each grouping or subgrouping and provides that adjustments are not netted between groupings or subgroupings. The statutory changes referencing section 702(a) and other provisions of the Code and the general inability to net negative adjustments result in restrictions on netting in these proposed rules that are broader than the restrictions described in former proposed § 301.6225-1. The examples in the proposed rules have been revised to reflect these broader restrictions on netting.

Proposed § 301.6225-1(f) provides rules related to determining whether adjustments are adjustments that do not result in an imputed underpayment. If the adjustments do not result in an imputed underpayment, such adjustments are taken into account in accordance with § 301.6225-3.

Proposed § 301.6225-1(g) provides the IRS may create multiple imputed underpayments for a particular tax year. Proposed § 301.6225-1(g)(2)(iii)(B) allows a particular adjustment that does not result in an imputed underpayment to be associated with a particular imputed underpayment. This rule ensures that adjustments that are appropriately associated with the imputed underpayment will be taken into account along with the other adjustments underlying the imputed underpayment if an election under section 6226 is made with respect to that imputed underpayment. For example, a reallocation or recharacterization adjustment generally results in more than one adjustment. In the case of a reallocation adjustment, there are adjustments that affect at least two partners. In a recharacterization adjustment, there is an adjustment to correct the characterization and an adjustment disallowing the incorrect characterization. As a result, if an adjustment that does not result in an imputed underpayment is due to a reallocation or recharacterization adjustment and one side of the adjustment is used to calculate a specific imputed underpayment, the other side of the adjustment, which is an adjustment that does not result in an imputed underpayment, is associated with that specific imputed underpayment.

The IRS may also determine that other adjustments that do not result in an imputed underpayment should be associated with a specific imputed underpayment. An adjustment that does not result in an imputed underpayment and that is not associated with a particular specific imputed underpayment is associated with the general imputed underpayment.

Proposed § 301.6225-2 provides guidance on procedures to modify the imputed underpayment. Former § 301.6225-2(b) provided that the effect of modification was determined by considering how the modification changed the relevant portion of the adjustment. This approach to modification is consistent with the amendments to section 6225(c). Accordingly, proposed § 301.6225-2(b) reflects the rule that modification affects the portion of an adjustment.

Proposed §301.6225-2(b)(3)(iv) provides rules on rate modification in the case of special allocations. Those rules generally mirror the statutory rule under section 6225(c)(4)(B)(ii). The rule in the statute is complex compared with other rate modifications in that they require a valuation analysis. The Treasury Department and the IRS request comments on ways to implement these rules efficiently.

Proposed §301.6225-2(d)(2) provides rules regarding amended returns and the alternative procedure to filing amended returns. Proposed §301.6225-2(d)(2) provides that a partnership may satisfy the requirements of amended return modification by submitting all the information required for amended return modification and the partners paying any amount that would be due if the partners had filed amended returns. The Treasury Department and the IRS request comments on how best to implement the alternative procedure to filing amended returns.

Former proposed §301.6225-2(d)(2)(viii) provided that partners could raise a reasonable cause defense under section 6664(c) (or other partner-level defense as described in former proposed §301.6226-3(i)(3)) with an amended return in modification. Proposed §301.6225-(d)(2)(viii) now provides that such partner-level defenses should be raised through a claim for refund that is submitted outside of the modification process. This rule is similar to the current rule regarding partner-level defenses related to adjustments that are taken into account by partners under section 6226. See proposed §301.6226-3(d)(3).

Section 6225(c)(6) grants the Secretary authority to "by regulations or guidance provide for additional procedures to modify imputed underpayment amounts on the basis of such other factors as the Secretary determines are necessary and appropriate to carry out the purposes of this section." The Treasury Department and the IRS have elected to use this authority in two circumstances that were not included in former proposed §301.6225-2. First, the Treasury Department and the IRS have concluded that the references to the adjustment year in section 6225(c)(5) make the implementation of section 6225(c)(5) unworkable. No partner would qualify as a specified partner until the adjustment year, but at any time during the administrative proceeding that is relevant to modification, the adjustment year does not yet exist. As a result, the only time this type of modification could be used would be in the case of an AAR because in that case, the adjustment year is the year in which the AAR is filed. In order for modification under section 6225(c)(5) to be administrable, proposed §301.6225-2(d)(5)(iv) provides that a "qualified relevant partner" is a person that meets the definition of a specified partner but in a year that can be determined at the time modification is requested. The definition of a specified passive activity loss has also been changed to clarify that the years at issue do not have to be the adjustment year.

Second, the Treasury Department and the IRS are also exercising the authority under section 6225(c)(6) to add a modification for partnerships with partners entitled to benefits under an income tax treaty. Proposed §301.6225-2(d)(9) allows modification if a relevant partner would have qualified for a reduction or exemption from tax with respect to a particular item under an income tax treaty with the United States. The Treasury Department and the IRS request comments on this type of modification.

Proposed §301.6225-2(e) provides rules for modification of certain types of adjustments that do not result in an imputed underpayment (as defined in proposed §301.6225-1(f)). Proposed §301.6225-2(e) limits the ability to modify such adjustments to certain types of modification. The Treasury Department and the IRS request comments on whether the list of allowed modifications under proposed §301.6225-2(e) is sufficient.

Lastly, proposed §301.6225-2 adopts the term "relevant partner" to describe any direct or indirect partner in the partnership seeking modification. See section 6225(c)(2)(F) and proposed §301.6225-2(a).

Proposed §301.6225-3 provides rules regarding adjustments that do not result in in an imputed underpayment. The changes in the TTCA comport with former proposed §301.6225-3, which required that the partnership take the adjustments that do not result in an imputed underpayment into account as separately stated or non-separately stated adjustments as appropriate.

B. *Proposed §301.6225-4*

Proposed rules under §301.6225-4 were previously published in the **Federal Register** (83 FR 4868-82) in the February 2018 NPRM (former proposed §301.6225-4). For an explanation of the rules under former proposed §301.6225-4, see 82 FR 4877.

Proposed §301.6225-4 sets forth rules under which a partnership and its partners must adjust specified tax attributes to take into account partnership adjustments and the partnership's payment of an imputed underpayment. Changes have been made throughout former proposed §301.6225-4 to conform to the changes to the definition of "tax attribute" under proposed §301.6241-1(a)(10). See section 11.A of this preamble regarding the change to the definition of "tax attribute." In addition, the definition of "specified tax attributes" in proposed §301.6225-4(a)(2) now includes earnings and profits under section 312 in response to comments received concerning the effect of partnership adjustments on a corporate partner's earnings and profits.

4. *Election for the Alternative to Payment of the Imputed Underpayment*

Section 6226 provides an alternative to the general rule under section 6225(a)(1) that the partnership must pay an imputed underpayment. Under section 6226, the partnership may elect to have its reviewed year partners take into account adjustments made by the IRS and pay any tax due as a result of those adjustments. If this election is made, the reviewed year partners must pay any chapter 1 tax resulting from taking into account the adjustments, and the partnership is not required to pay the imputed underpayment.

Section 206(d) of TTCA amended section 6226(a) to clarify that if a partnership makes a valid election under section 6226 with respect to an imputed underpayment, no assessment of such imputed underpayment, levy, or proceeding in any court for the collection of such imputed underpayment shall be made against such partnership.

Section 206(e) of the TTCA amended section 6226(b)(1) to provide that when a partner takes into account the adjustments, the partner's chapter 1 tax is adjusted by the aggregate of the "correction amounts" determined under section 6226(b)(2). After amendment by the TTCA, the correction amounts under section 6226(b)(2) are defined as the amounts by which the partner's chapter 1 tax would increase "or decrease" for the partner's first affected year if the partner's share of the adjustments were taken into account for that year. The correction amounts are also the amount by which the partner's chapter 1 tax would increase "or decrease" by reason of the adjustment to tax attributes for any intervening years. See section 6226(b)(2).

Section 204(a) of the TTCA added to the Code section 6226(b)(4), which provides that a partnership or S corporation that receives a statement under section 6226(a)(2) must file a partnership adjustment tracking report with the IRS and furnish statements under rules similar to the rules of section 6226(a)(2). If the partnership or S corporation fails to furnish such statements, the partnership or S corporation must compute and pay an imputed underpayment under rules similar to the rules of section 6225. A partnership that is a partner must file the partnership adjustment tracking report, and furnish statements or pay an imputed underpayment, notwithstanding any election out of the centralized partnership audit regime under section 6221(b) by the partnership for the tax year that includes the end of the reviewed year of the audited partnership. The term "audited partnership" means the partnership in the chain of ownership that originally made the election under section 6226. See section 6226(b)(4)(D).

A. *Proposed §§301.6226-1, 301.6226-2, and 301.6226-3*

Proposed rules under §§301.6226-1, 301.6226-2, and 301.6226-3 were previously published in the **Federal Register** in the June 2017 NPRM (82 FR 27391-97), the November 2017 NPRM (82 FR 56778-79), and the December 2017 NPRM (82 FR 60155-61) (collectively, former proposed

§§ 301.6226-1, 301.6226-2, and 301.6226-3). For an explanation of the rules under former proposed §§ 301.6226-1, 301.6226-2, and 301.6226-3, see 82 FR 27358-66, 82 FR 56769-71, and 82 FR 60148-51.

Former proposed § 301.6226-1(b)(2) provided that if a partnership makes a valid election in accordance with proposed § 301.6226-1, the partnership is not liable for the imputed underpayment to which the election relates. To reflect the statutory change to section 6226(a), language has been added to proposed § 301.6226-1(b)(2) to clarify that if a partnership makes a valid election under section 6226 with respect to an imputed underpayment, the IRS may not assess such imputed underpayment, levy, or bring a proceeding in any court for the collection of that imputed underpayment against such partnership. A similar change has also been made to proposed § 301.6226-1(c)(2) (regarding invalid elections) to clarify that if a final determination is made that a purported election under section 6226 is invalid, the IRS may assess the imputed underpayment with respect to which the election was made against the partnership without regard to the limitations under section 6232(b).

Former proposed § 301.6226-3 provided that a reviewed year partner that is furnished a statement under section 6226(a)(2) is required to pay any additional chapter 1 tax (additional reporting year tax) that results from taking into account the partnership adjustments on that statement. As mentioned above in this section of the preamble, section 206(e) of the TTCA amended section 6226(b) to provide that decreases, as well as increases, in chapter 1 tax that result from taking into account partnership adjustments are used in computing a partner's additional reporting year tax. Section 206(e) of the TTCA also replaced the term "adjustment amount" with "correction amount." Accordingly, proposed § 301.6226-3 now refers to "correction amount" instead of "adjustment amount," as appropriate, and now provides that a reviewed year partner's chapter 1 tax for the reporting year may be increased or decreased by the additional reporting year tax. The additional reporting year tax is the sum of the correction amounts for the first affected year and any correction amounts for the intervening years. Under proposed § 301.6226-3(b)(2) and (3), the correction amounts are the amounts by which the partner's chapter 1 tax for the taxable year would be increased or decreased if the partner's taxable income for that year were recomputed by taking into account, in the case of the first affected year, the partner's share of the partnership adjustments reflected on the statement furnished to the partner or, in the case of any intervening year, any change to tax attributes of the partner resulting from the changes in the first affected year. A correction amount for the first affected year or any intervening year may be less than zero and may be used to offset any correction amounts from any other year in computing the additional reporting year tax. The examples under proposed § 301.6226-3(h) illustrate situations in which a correction amount may be less than zero.

Furthermore, the additional reporting year tax may be less than zero and may offset other taxes owed by the partner on the partner's reporting year return. Accordingly, any references to the additional reporting year tax as a "liability" have been removed from former proposed § 301.6226-3 to account for situations in which the additional reporting year tax is less than zero.

Section 6226(c)(2) provides that interest in the case of a section 6226 election is determined at the partner level, from the due date of the return for the taxable year to which the increase in chapter 1 tax is attributable, and at the underpayment rate under section 6621(a)(2) (substituting 5 percent for 3 percent). As discussed above in this section of the preamble, the TTCA amended section 6226(b) to provide that both increases and decreases in chapter 1 tax are used in computing a partner's additional reporting year tax. However, the TTCA did not similarly amend the reference to "increases" in section 6226(c)(2) with the result that interest only applies to the increases in the chapter 1 tax that would have resulted from taking into account the partnership adjustments under section 6226. No provision under the centralized partnership audit regime provides for interest in the case of a *decrease* in chapter 1 tax that would have resulted in the first affected year or any intervening year if the adjustments were taken into account in those years. Accordingly, proposed § 301.6226-3(c)(1) provides that interest on the correction amounts determined under proposed § 301.6226-3(b) is only calculated for taxable years for which there is a correction amount greater than zero, that is, taxable years for which there would have been an increase in chapter 1 tax if the adjustments were taken into account.

Proposed § 301.6226-3(c)(1) further provides that for purposes of calculating interest on the correction amounts, any correction amount that is less than zero does not offset any correction amount that is greater than zero. Although those amounts may offset when determining the additional reporting year tax (as described in proposed § 301.6226-3(b)), allowing the same offset for purposes of calculating interest is inconsistent with section 6226(c)(2), which provides that interest is determined with respect to any increase determined under section 6226(b)(2).

Proposed § 301.6226-3(d)(3) has also been clarified to provide that if a partner wants to raise a partner-level defense to any penalty, addition to tax, or additional amount, a partner must first pay the penalty, addition to tax, or additional amount and file a claim for refund for the reporting year in order to raise the defense.

As discussed above in this section of the preamble, section 204(a) of the TTCA amended section 6226(b) to provide that partnerships and S corporations that are direct or indirect partners in an audited partnership and that receive statements under 6226(a)(2) must file partnership adjustment tracking reports with the IRS and furnish statements to their owners under rules similar to section 6226. If no statements are furnished, the partnership or S corporation must compute and pay an imputed underpayment.

Former proposed § 301.6226-3(e)(1) provided that a pass-through partner (as defined in proposed § 301.6241-1(a)(5)) that was furnished a statement described in proposed § 301.6226-2 (including a statement as described in former proposed § 301.6226-3(e)(3)) must take into account the adjustments reflected on that statement by either furnishing statements to its partners or by paying an amount calculated like an imputed underpayment. Any statements furnished under those provisions were treated as statements described in proposed § 301.6226-2, and any pass-through partner receiving a statement under former proposed § 301.6226-3(e)(3) was required to also take the adjustments reflected on the statement into account by furnishing statements to its own partners or paying an amount calculated like an imputed underpayment. See former proposed § 301.6226-3(e)(3)(i) and (iv).

Although the rules under former proposed § 301.6226-3(e) were largely consistent with the rules under section 6226(b)(4), some changes were needed to conform the two sets of rules. First, proposed § 301.6226-3(a)(1) now provides that the rules under proposed § 301.6226-3(a)(1) apply to a reviewed year partner except to the extent otherwise provided in proposed § 301.6226-3. Second, proposed § 301.6226-3(e) now includes a requirement that the pass-through partner must file a partnership adjustment tracking report. Third, proposed § 301.6226-3(e) provides a default rule that a pass-through partner must furnish statements to its own partners in accordance with proposed § 301.6226-3(e)(3). If a pass-through partner fails to furnish statements in accordance with proposed § 301.6226-3(e)(3), the pass-through partner must compute and pay an imputed underpayment. Additionally, language referring to a pass-through partner "taking into account" the adjustments under former proposed § 301.6226-3(e) was removed to more closely align with the statutory language in section 6226(b)(4). Fourth, proposed § 301.6226-3(e) defines and refers to the term "audited partnership," which proposed § 301.6226-3(e)(1) defines as the partnership that made the election under § 301.6226-1. See section 6226(b)(4)(D). Lastly, proposed § 301.6226-3(e)(4) provides that the amount a pass-through partner must compute and pay, if it does not furnish statements to its partners, is an "imputed underpayment." See section 6226(b)(4)(A)(ii)(II).

Because under proposed § 301.6226-3(e), pass-through partners compute and pay an "imputed underpayment," rather than calculating correction amounts under proposed § 301.6226-3(b), references in former proposed § 301.6226-3(b) to amended returns filed by indirect partners as part of modification have been deleted. Pass-through partners computing an imputed underpayment under proposed § 301.6226-3(e) may account for modifications submitted by their indirect partners, but non-pass-through partners calculating correction amounts under proposed § 301.6226-3(b) cannot. Accordingly, the references in former proposed § 301.6226-3(b) to amended returns filed by indirect partners were removed.

To reflect the change to the definition of "tax attribute" under proposed § 301.6241-1(a)(10) (see section 11.A. of this preamble), proposed §§ 301.6226-2 and 301.6226-3 now only refer to the tax attributes of the partner. For example, proposed §§ 301.6226-2(e) and 301.6226-3(e)(3)(iii) no longer require that the audited partnership report any changes to *partnership* tax attributes on the statements furnished to its partners under section

6226(a)(2). Therefore, when a partner computes the partner's correction amount for any intervening year, the partner calculates the amount by which the partner's chapter 1 tax for any intervening year would increase or decrease if any tax attribute of that partner (for example, a net operating loss carryover or capital loss carryover) has been adjusted after taking into account the partner's share of the adjustments in the first affected year.

Finally, references to "items" or "items of income, gain, loss, deduction, or credit" throughout former §§ 301.6226-1, 6226-2, and 6226-3 have been replaced with references to "partnership-related items."

B. *Revisions to the regulations under section 6226 unrelated to the TTCA amendments*

In addition to the changes needed to conform to the amendments by the TTCA, some additional changes have been made to former proposed §§ 301.6226-1, 6226-2, and 6226-3. First, proposed § 301.6226-1(b)(2) now provides that only those adjustments that do not result in an imputed underpayment which are associated with an imputed underpayment for which an election under section 6226 is made are included in the reviewed year partner's share of the partnership adjustments reported to the partner. Any adjustments that do not result in an imputed underpayment which are not associated with an imputed underpayment for which an election under section 6226 is made are taken into account under section 6225. This change was necessary to clarify which partnership adjustments are pushed out in the case of multiple imputed underpayments where the push out election is not made with respect to all imputed underpayments. See proposed § 301.6225-1(g) for rules regarding the treatment of adjustments that do not result in an imputed underpayment in the context of specific imputed underpayments.

Second, under proposed § 301.6226-1(c)(1), an election under section 6226 is only valid if all the provisions under proposed § 301.6226-1 (regarding making the election) and § 301.6226-2 (regarding the furnishing of statements) are satisfied, and an election made under section 6226 is valid until the IRS determines that the election is invalid. The rule that an election is valid until the IRS determines it is invalid was moved from former proposed § 301.6226-1(c)(2) to proposed § 301.6226-1(c)(1) to clarify that an election that does not fully satisfy the requirements of proposed §§ 301.6226-1 and 301.6226-2 is valid unless the IRS determines that the purported election is invalid. For example, if a partnership makes an election in accordance with proposed § 301.6226-1 but fails to furnish statements to its partners, that election is valid until the IRS determines otherwise.

In addition, the word "final" was removed from before the word "determination" in proposed § 301.6226-1(c)(2) when referring to a determination made by the IRS that a purported election under section 6226 is invalid. The removal of the word "final" clarifies that the IRS may determine that an election is invalid and assess and collect the imputed underpayment to which the purported election related without first being required to make a proposed or initial determination of invalidity. Although nothing in the regulations precludes the IRS from first notifying the partnership of a potential problem with an election before determining the election is invalid, proposed § 301.6226-1(c)(2) provides that the IRS may determine that an election is invalid even if the partnership has corrected the statements required to be filed and furnished in accordance with proposed § 301.6226-2(d)(3) and also provides that the IRS is not obligated to require the correction of any errors prior to determining an election is invalid.

Third, several changes were made to clarify that the partnership must provide correct information in order to make a valid election under section 6226 and in order for statements to be properly furnished either under proposed § 301.6226-2 or proposed § 301.6226-3(e)(3). Proposed § 301.6226-1(c)(4)(ii) requires the partnership to provide correct information in its election, and proposed § 301.6226-2(e) and proposed § 301.6226-3(e)(3)(iii) require that the statements filed and furnished with the IRS include correct information. Additionally, proposed § 301.6226-2(d)(3) provides that if the IRS cannot determine whether the statements filed and furnished by the partnership are correct because of a failure by the partnership to comply with any requirements (such as filing a partnership adjustment tracking report), the IRS may, but is not obligated to, require the partnership to provide additional information to substantiate the statements. Proposed § 301.6226-2(d)(2) extends the rules governing corrections of errors in statements to statements furnished by pass-through partners under proposed § 301.6226-3(e)(3) and to provide that, if consent of the IRS is required for a correction, that corrected statements may not be furnished until the IRS provides consent.

Fourth, duplicative language regarding the definition of the extended due date for the adjustment year of the audited partnership was removed from former proposed § 301.6226-3(e)(3)(ii) and (e)(4)(ii).

Fifth, in proposed § 301.6226-3(g), the word "grantor" has been added between the words "wholly-owned" and "trusts" to clarify that "wholly-owned trusts" means "wholly-owned grantor trusts."

Sixth, the phrase "an entity described in § 301.7701-2(c)(2)(i)" in former proposed § 301.6226-3(j) was changed to "a wholly-owned entity disregarded as separate from its owner for Federal tax purposes in the reviewed year" to conform to the definition of disregarded entity under proposed § 301.6241-1(a)(4).

Seventh, proposed § 301.6226-3(c)(2) now provides that interest on any penalties, additions to tax, or additional amounts is calculated from each applicable taxable year until the penalty, addition to tax, or additional amount is paid. Former proposed § 301.6226-3(c)(2) provided that interest was calculated from the first affected year. Under proposed § 301.6226-3(d)(2), partners calculate any penalties, additions to tax, or additional amounts that relate to the partnership adjustments at the partner level. Because the adjustments could create tax effects in more than just the first affected year (for example, as a result of changes to tax attributes in an intervening year), a penalty, addition to tax, or additional amount might likewise result in more than just the first affected year. Accordingly, proposed § 301.6226-3(c)(2) provides that interest on penalties, additions to tax, and additional amounts runs from the applicable taxable year (that is, the particular tax year to which the penalty, addition to tax, or additional amount relates).

Finally, certain errors were corrected in the examples under proposed § 301.6226-3(h). Examples 2 through 4 and 6 through 9 under former proposed § 301.6226-3(h) incorrectly listed the last day to file a petition under section 6234 as the date the adjustments became final, and examples 6 through 9 incorrectly referred to former proposed § 301.6226-1(b) as support for this rule. Under proposed § 301.6226-2(b), partnership adjustments become finally determined on the later of the expiration of the time to file a petition under section 6234 or, if a petition is filed under section 6234, the date when the court's decision becomes final. The examples under proposed § 301.6226-3(h) now reflect that the adjustments become final on the day after the last day to file a petition under section 6234 to be consistent with the rule under § 301.6226-2(b), and incorrect references to § 301.6226-1(b) in Examples 6 through 9 under former proposed § 301.6226-3(h) have been replaced with correct references to § 301.6226-2(b).

Proposed § 301.6226-4

Proposed rules under §§ 301.6226-4 were previously published in the **Federal Register** in the February 2018 NPRM (83 FR 4868) (former proposed § 301.6226-4). For an explanation of the rules under former proposed § 301.6226-4, see 83 FR 4874.

Proposed § 301.6226-4 sets forth rules for adjusting reviewed year partners' tax attributes to take into account partnership adjustments when a partnership makes an election under section 6226. To reflect the addition of section 6226(b)(4), proposed § 301.6226-3(e)(4) now provides that a reviewed year partner that is a pass-through partner must pay an imputed underpayment if the pass-through partner does not furnish statements. In addition, changes have been made throughout former proposed § 301.6226-4 to conform to the change to the definition of "tax attribute" under proposed § 301.6241-1(a)(10). See section 11.A of this preamble. These changes reflect that the adjustments to tax attributes taken into account by a partner should be consistent, regardless of whether the partner files an amended return during modification, participates in the alternative procedure to filing an amended return, or receives a statement under section 6226. Accordingly, the proposed regulations under section 6226 have been revised to refer only to the tax attributes of the partner in the intervening years. Additionally, clarifying changes were made in proposed § 301.6226-4(b) to conform to the terminology used in proposed § 301.6226-3. Lastly, an incorrect cross-reference in former proposed § 301.6226-4(c)(4)(iii) has been replaced with the correct cross-reference.

5. *Administrative Adjustment Requests*

Section 6227 provides a mechanism for a partnership to file an AAR to correct errors on a partnership return for a prior year. Prior to amendment by the TTCA, section 6227(a) provided that a partnership may file a request for administrative adjustment in the amount of one or more items of income, gain, loss, deduction, or credit of the partnership or any partnership taxable year. Section 201(c) of the TTCA amended section 6227(a) by striking "items of income, gain, loss, deduction, or credit of the partnership" and inserting "partnership-related items."

Prior to amendment by the TTCA, section 6227(b) provided that any adjustment requested in an AAR is taken into account for the partnership taxable year in which the AAR is made. Section 206(p) of the TTCA amended section 6227(b) by striking "is made" both places it appears and inserting "is filed."

Prior to amendment by the TTCA, section 6227(b)(1) provided that if an adjustment results in an imputed underpayment, the adjustment may be determined and taken into account by the partnership under rules similar to the rules under section 6225 relating to payment of the imputed underpayment by the partnership, except that the provisions under section 6225 pertaining to modification of the imputed underpayment based on amended returns by partners, the time for submitting information to the Secretary for purposes of modification, and approval by the Secretary of any modification do not apply.

Section 206(p) of the TTCA amended section 6227(b)(1) by striking the reference to "paragraphs (2), (6), and (7)" of section 6225(c) (relating to modification) and inserting "paragraphs (2), (7), and (9)" of section 6225(c). As a result, section 6227(b)(1) provides that adjustments requested in an AAR are taken into account by the partnership under rules similar to section 6225 (except for sections 6225(c)(2), (7), and (9)). As amended by TTCA, section 6225(c)(2) provides rules allowing for amended returns and an alternative procedure to filing amended returns for purposes of modification, section 6225(c)(7) provides that information required to be submitted for purposes of modification be submitted within 270 days from the date on which the notice of a proposed partnership adjustment is mailed under section 6231, and section 6225(c)(9) provides for modification with respect to adjustments that do not result in an imputed underpayment.

Lastly, section 206(f) of the TTCA added section 6227(d) to provide that the Secretary shall issue regulations or other guidance which provide for the proper coordination of section 6227 and section 905(c).

A. *Proposed § § 301.6227-1, 301.6227-2, and 301.6227-3*

Proposed rules under § § 301.6227-1, 301.6227-2, and 301.6227-3 were previously published in the **Federal Register** (82 FR 27397-99) in the June 2017 NPRM, November 2017 NPRM (82 FR 56779), and December 2017 NPRM (82 FR 60161) (collectively, former proposed § § 301.6227-1, 301.6227-2, and 301.6227-3). For an explanation of the rules under former proposed § § 301.6227-1, 301.6227-2, and 301.6227-3, see 82 FR 27366-69, 82 FR 56769, and 82 FR 60151.

Former proposed § 301.6227-1(a) provided that a partner may not file an AAR except if the partner is doing so on behalf of the partnership in the partner's capacity as the partnership representative or if the partner is a partnership-partner filing an AAR under former proposed § 301.6227-3(c). Proposed § 301.6227-3(c), however, does not provide for the filing of an AAR by a partnership-partner. Rather, under proposed § 301.6227-3(c), a partnership-partner takes into account adjustments requested in an AAR by the partnership in which it is a partner by following the rules under proposed § 301.6226-3(e) (except to the extent otherwise provided). Proposed § 301.6227-1(a) therefore is changed to remove the reference to partnership-partners, and now only refers to partners filing AARs in their capacity as a partnership representative.

Proposed § 301.6227-2(a)(1) provides the rules for determining whether an imputed underpayment results from adjustments requested in an AAR by referring to the rules under proposed § 301.6225-1. Under proposed § 301.6227-2(a)(2), in the case of an AAR, a partnership may reduce an imputed underpayment as a result of certain modifications permitted under proposed § 301.6225-2. Under former proposed § 301.6227-2(a)(2), these modifications included modifications that relate to tax-exempt partners (proposed § 301.6225-2(d)(3)), rate modification (proposed § 301.6225-2(d)(4)), modification related to certain passive losses of publicly traded partnerships (proposed § 301.6225-2(d)(5)), modification applicable to qualified investment entities described in section 860 (proposed § 301.6225-2(d)(7)), and other modifications to the extent permitted under future IRS guidance (proposed § 301.6225-2(d)(10)). Proposed § 301.6227-2(a)(2) adopts this same list of modifications and adds modifications related to the composition of the groupings that factor into the calculation of the imputed underpayment (proposed § 301.6225-2(d)(6)(ii)) and modifications related to tax treaties (proposed § 301.6225-2(d)(9)).

Proposed § 301.6227-2(a)(2) provides that other types of modification, such as modification under proposed § 301.6225-2(d)(2) with respect to amended returns, including the alternative procedure to filing amended returns, and modification under proposed § 301.6225-2(d)(8) with respect to closing agreements, are not available in the case of an AAR. Modifications with respect to adjustments that do not result in an imputed underpayment also are also not available in the case of an AAR.

Former proposed § 301.6227-2(a)(2)(i) provided that a partnership did not need to seek IRS approval prior to modifying an imputed underpayment that results from adjustments requested in an AAR. Section 6227(b)(1) does not explicitly carve out section 6225(c)(8), which states that any modification to the imputed underpayment made under section 6225(c) shall be made only upon approval of such modification by the Secretary. Section 6227(b)(1) does provide, however, that partnerships take into account adjustments requested in an AAR under rules similar to the rules under section 6225. In proposing rules similar to the rules under section 6225 for the purposes of requesting an AAR and taking into account adjustments, the Treasury Department and the IRS have determined it is more efficient and beneficial for both the IRS and for partnerships to be able to apply modifications when filing an AAR without first securing approval of permitted modifications. Accordingly, although any modifications in connection with an AAR are subject to IRS approval, the rules under proposed § 301.6227-2(a)(2)(i) provide that the partnership is not required to obtain the approval from the IRS before applying modifications when calculating the amount of the imputed underpayment the partnership needs to pay when filing the AAR. Proposed § 301.6227-2(a)(2)(ii) also provides, however, that modifications to an imputed underpayment resulting from adjustments requested in an AAR may not be applied by the partnership if the AAR that is filed does not include notification to the IRS of the modification, a description of the effect of the modification on the imputed underpayment, an explanation of the basis for such modification, and all necessary documentation to support the partnership's entitlement to such modification.

Under proposed § 301.6227-3, a reviewed year partner that receives a statement described in proposed § 301.6227-1(d) must treat that statement as if it were provided under section 6226(a)(2). Former proposed § 301.6227-3(b)(1) also provided that the restriction in former proposed § 301.6226-3(b)(1) - that the correction amount for the first affected year and any intervening year cannot be less than zero - does not apply in the case of taking into account adjustments requested by the partnership in an AAR. Proposed § 301.6227-3(b)(1) no longer needs to address that restriction because the restriction in former proposed § 301.6226-3(b)(1) no longer exists. Therefore, the exception in former proposed § 301.6227-3(b)(1) has been eliminated. Additionally, the provision in former proposed § 301.6227-3(b)(2), stating that when the additional reporting tax results in being less than zero the partner may reduce his chapter 1 tax for the reporting year, is moved to proposed § 301.6227-3(b)(1).

Former proposed § 301.6227-1 included a reserved paragraph regarding notice of change to amounts of creditable foreign tax expenditures. Proposed § 301.6227-1 also reserves this same paragraph and does not contain rules to coordinate sections 6227 and 905(c). The Treasury Department and the IRS seek comments regarding the coordination of sections 6227 and 905(c) for consideration in future guidance.

Lastly, the reference to "items of income, gain, loss, deduction, or credit of the partnership" in former proposed § 301.6227-1(a) has been replaced with a reference to "partnership-related items."

B. *Revisions to the regulations under section 6227 unrelated to the TTCA amendments*

Proposed § 301.6227-1(a) now coordinates the rules regarding the filing of an AAR and the revocation of a designation of the partnership representative under § 301.6223-1. Former proposed § 301.6227-1(a) provided that the partnership may not file an AAR solely for the purpose of allowing the partnership to change the designation of a partnership representative. Proposed § 301.6227-1(a) now adds that when the partnership changes the designation of the partnership representative or the appointment of a designated individual in conjunction with the filing of an AAR, the change in designation or appointment is treated as occurring prior to the filing of the AAR.

Former proposed § 301.6227-1(b) provided that an AAR may not be filed after a notice of administrative proceeding (NAP) has been mailed. To account for situations in which the IRS mails a NAP, but then withdraws it, proposed § 301.6227-1(b) now provides that an AAR may not be filed after a NAP has been mailed, except when the NAP has been withdrawn under proposed § 301.6231-1(f).

Additions were also made in proposed § 301.6227-3(c) to clarify the rules for pass-through partners, unrelated to the changes made by the TTCA. First, proposed § 301.6227-3(c)(1) provides that when a pass-through partner takes into account adjustments requested in an AAR in accordance with proposed § 301.6226-3(e), the pass-through partner must provide the information described in proposed § 301.6227-3(c)(3) as opposed to the information in described in proposed § 301.6226-3(e)(3)(iii) when furnishing statements to its partners. Second, under proposed § 301.6227-3(c)(1), a pass-through partner that computes and pays an imputed underpayment in accordance with proposed § 301.6226-3(e)(4) may not take into account any modifications. Third, proposed § 301.6227-3(c)(4) provides that when a pass-through partner furnishes a statement to an affected partner under proposed § 301.6227-3(c), the affected partner must treat that statement as if it were a statement described in proposed § 301.6227-3(a) that was furnished to such affected partner.

6. *Notices of Proceedings and Adjustments*

Section 6231(a) provides that the Secretary shall mail to the partnership and to the partnership representative a notice of any administrative proceeding initiated at the partnership level, notice of any proposed partnership adjustment resulting from that proceeding (NOPPA), and notice of any final partnership adjustment (FPA). Prior to amendment by the TTCA, section 6231(a) also provided that any FPA shall be mailed no earlier than 270 days after the date on which the NOPPA is mailed. Such notices shall be sufficient if mailed to the last known address of the partnership and the partnership representative, even if the partnership has terminated its existence. See section 6231(a) flush language (prior to amendment by the TTCA).

Prior to amendment by the TTCA, the statute did not limit the period for the IRS to propose adjustments under the centralized partnership audit regime. Section 206(h) of the TTCA amended section 6231 to address this issue. As amended, section 6231(b)(1) provides that any NOPPA shall not be mailed later than the date determined under section 6235(a)(1), which is generally the date that is 3 years after the later of: (1) the date on which the partnership return for the taxable year was filed, (2) the return due date for the taxable year, or (3) the date on which the partnership filed an AAR with respect to the taxable year.

Section 206(h) of the TTCA makes a conforming amendment to section 6231(a) to reflect the addition of the period of limitations to made partnership adjustments. Prior to amendment, section 6231(a) provided that "Such notices shall be sufficient if mailed to the last known address of the partnership representative or the partnership (even if the partnership has terminated its existence)." The amendment replaced the words "Such notices" with "Any notice of final partnership adjustment."

Section 201(c) of the TTCA also makes a conforming amendment to section 6231(a) by striking the phrase "all items of income, gain, loss, deduction, or credit of the partnership" and inserting "all partnership-related items."

A. *Proposed § 301.6231-1*

Proposed rules under § 301.6231-1 were previously published in the **Federal Register** (82 FR 60161-62) in the December 2017 NPRM (former proposed § 301.6231-1). For an explanation of the rules under former proposed § 301.6231-1, see 82 FR 60151-52.

Although not required by statute, former proposed § 301.6231-1(b)(1) provided a period of limitations for making partnership adjustment. That section provided that a NOPPA may not be mailed after the expiration of the period described in section 6235(a)(1), including any extensions of that period and after applying any of the special rules in section 6235(c) (providing additional time for situations where no return is filed, fraud, and other specified reasons).

Former proposed § 301.6231-1(c) provided that NAPs, NOPPAs, and FPAs are sufficient if mailed to the last known address of the partnership and the partnership representative. As discussed above in this section of the preamble, section 6231(a) now provides that any FPA is sufficient if mailed to the last known address of the partnership and the partnership representative. The Treasury Department and the IRS have determined that while the last known address requirement under section 6231(a) only applies to a notice of final partnership adjustment, the IRS will also mail the NAP and the NOPPA to the last known address of the partnership and the partnership representative.

Accordingly, because the rules under former proposed § 301.6231-1(b)(1) and (c) are consistent with the statutory changes to section 6231(a), those rules are unchanged. The only change to former proposed § 301.6231-1 was to replace references to "item of income, gain, loss, deduction, or credit" and to a "partner's distributive share" in former proposed § 301.6231-1(a)(1) with a reference to "partnership-related item".

7. *Assessment, Collection, and Payment of Imputed Underpayments*

Section 6232(a) provides rules for the assessment, collection, and payment of imputed underpayments. Section 206(g) of the TTCA amended section 6232(a) to clarify that the assessment of any imputed underpayment is not subject to the deficiency procedures under subchapter B of chapter 63 of the Code and to clarify that in the case of an AAR, the underpayment may be assessed when the AAR is filed. See JCX-6-18, at 48.

Section 6232(b) provides limitations on the assessment of an imputed underpayment. Section 206(g) of the TTCA amended section 6232(b) to correct a reference to "assessment of a deficiency" to now refer to "assessment of an imputed underpayment." Section 206(p) of the TTCA also amends section 6232(b) to strike the reference to "this chapter" and replace it with "this subtitle (other than subchapter B of this chapter)."

Section 205 of the TTCA added a new subsection (f) to section 6232 to provide a mechanism for collection of tax due in the case of a failure of a partnership or S corporation to pay an imputed underpayment or specified similar amount. Under section 6232(f)(1), if any amount of any imputed underpayment to which section 6225 applies or any specified similar amount as defined in section 6232(f)(2) has not been paid by the date which is 10 days after the date on which the Secretary provides notice and demand for such payment, the Secretary may assess upon each partner of the partnership a tax equal to such partner's proportionate share of such amount.

Under section 6232(f)(2), the term "specified similar amount" means the amount determined under section 6226(b)(4)(ii)(II) and any amount assessed upon a partner under section 6232(f)(1)(B) that is a partnership or an S corporation. Section 206(g)(2)(B) of the TTCA amended section 6232(b) to provide that the limitations on assessment with respect to an imputed underpayment do not apply in the case of a specified similar amount defined in section 6232(f)(2).

The Treasury Department and the IRS are not proposing rules under section 6232(f) at this time. The Treasury Department and the IRS request comments with respect to section 6232(f), including the determination of a partner's proportionate share of the unpaid amount, for consideration with respect to future guidance.

A. *Proposed § 301.6232-1*

Proposed rules under § 301.6232-1 were previously published in the **Federal Register** (82 FR 60162-63) in the December 2017 NPRM (former proposed § 301.6232-1). For an explanation of the rules under former proposed §§ 301.6232-1, see 82 FR 60152.

Former proposed § 301.6232-1(a) provided that because the centralized partnership audit regime under subchapter C of chapter 63 applies to an assessment of an imputed underpayment, the deficiency procedures under subchapter B of chapter 63 do not apply. Former proposed § 301.6232-1(b) provided that the IRS may assess an underpayment reflected on an AAR on the date the AAR is filed. Former proposed § 301.6232-1(c) provided limitations on assessment of the imputed underpayment, except as otherwise provided in § 301.6232-1. Because the rules under former proposed § 301.6232-1(a) and (b) are consistent with the statutory changes to section 6232(a), those rules are unchanged.

Proposed § 301.6232-1(c) is generally the same as former proposed § 301.6232-1(c). However, changes were made to take into account section 206(g)(2)(B) of TTCA, providing that the limitations on assessment do not apply to specified similar amounts, and section 206(p) of TTCA, providing that the limitations on assessments under proposed § 301.6232-1(c) apply except as otherwise provided in subtitle F of the Code (other than deficiency procedures under subchapter B of chapter 63).

With respect to former proposed § 301.6232-1(d), the reference to "items of income, gain, loss, deduction, or credit" in former proposed § 301.6232-1(d)(1)(i) was replaced with a reference to "partnership-related items."

8. *Interest and Penalties Related to Imputed Underpayments*

Section 6233 provides rules related to interest and penalties with respect to imputed underpayments. Section 206(i) of the TTCA amended section 6233 by adding a new subsection (c), which provides a cross-reference to section 6603 for rules allowing deposits to suspend the running of interest on potential underpayments.

A. *Proposed §§ 301.6233(a)-1 and 301.6233(b)-1*

Proposed rules under §§ 301.6233(a)-1 and 301.6233(b)-1 were previously published in the **Federal Register** (82 FR 60163-65) in the December 2017 NPRM (former proposed §§ 301.6233(a)-1 and 301.6233(b)-1). For an explanation of the rules under former proposed §§ 301.6233(a)-1 and 301.6233(b)-1, see 82 FR 60152-53.

Proposed § 301.6233(a)-1 provides rules for determining interest and penalties from the reviewed year, and proposed § 301.6233(b)-1 provides rules for determining interest and penalties from the adjustment year. Neither former proposed § 301.6233(a)-1 nor former proposed § 301.6233(b)-1 provided rules regarding deposits to suspend the running of interest on underpayments. The Treasury Department and the IRS are not proposing rules regarding the interaction of the deposit rules under section 6603 and the interest rules under section 6233. However, the Treasury Department and the IRS request comments for consideration in future guidance regarding the interaction between section 6603 and the interest rules under section 6233.

Former proposed § 301.6233(a)-1(c)(2)(ii)(C) provided a definition of "negative adjustment" and defined that term through reference to "items of income, gain, loss, deduction, or credit." Proposed § 301.6225-1 now uses the term "negative adjustment" and the phrase "items of income, gain, loss, deduction, or credit" has been removed from subchapter C of chapter 63. To reflect these changes, proposed § 301.6233(a)-1(c)(2)(ii)(C) now provides that a "decreasing adjustment" is "an adjustment to a partnership-related item that resulted in a decrease to the imputed underpayment." Example 3 under proposed § 301.6233(a)-1(c)(3) also reflects changes to former proposed §§ 301.6225-1 and 301.6225-2.

Former proposed § 301.6233(a)-1(c)(2)(ii), regarding how to calculate the portion of the imputed underpayment to which a penalty applies, referred to "non-credit partnership adjustments" and "credit adjustments." Under proposed § 301.6225-1(e)(3)(iii) certain adjustments to creditable expenditures are treated as an adjustment to a credit and may impact the calculation of the imputed underpayment. To properly account for such adjustments when determining the portion of an imputed underpayment subject to a penalty, the term "non-credit partnership adjustment" was changed to "a partnership adjustment that is not an adjustment to a credit or treated as an adjustment to a credit," and the term "credit adjustment" changed to "an adjustment to a credit or treated as an adjustment to a credit."

Former proposed § 301.6233(a)-1(c)(2)(iii)(B), regarding the application of the substantial understatement penalty under section 6662(d)(1)(A)(i) to imputed underpayments, provided that taxable income meant the net ordinary business income or loss of the partnership. The reference to "ordinary business" failed to account for other sources of income of the partnership that are appropriate to consider for purposes of the substantial understatement penalty. Therefore, proposed § 301.6233(a)-1(c)(2)(iii)(B) now provides that for purposes of determining the amount of tax required to be shown on the return it is the net income or loss of the partnership that is treated as taxable income. See Page 5 of Form 1065, Return of Partnership Income.

Former proposed § 301.6233(a)-1(c)(2)(v), pertaining to reasonable cause and good faith defenses, provided that partner-level defenses may not be raised in a proceeding of the partnership except as provided under the modification procedures pertaining to amended returns and partner closing agreements. For clarity, this provision has been moved to proposed § 301.6233(a)-1(c)(1). Furthermore, the provision allowing partner-level defenses to penalties to be raised under the modification procedures has been removed. A partner may raise a partner-level defense by filing a claim for refund under procedures existing outside of the centralized partnership audit regime or through an agreement with the IRS regarding an adjustment to a partnership-related item.

9. *Judicial Review of Partnership Adjustments*

Section 6234(a) provides that within 90 days after the date on which an FPA is mailed under section 6231 with respect to any partnership taxable year, the partnership may file a petition for readjustment for such taxable year with the Tax Court, the district court in which the partnership's principal place of business is located, or the Court of Federal Claims. Prior to amendment by the TTCA, section 6234(b)(1) provided that a petition for readjustment under section 6234 may be filed in a district court of the United States or the Court of Federal Claims only if the partnership filing the petition deposits with the Secretary, on or before the date the petition is filed, the amount of the imputed underpayment. Section 206(j) of the TTCA amended section 6234(b)(1) to clarify that the amount of the jurisdictional deposit that the partnership must make in order to file a readjustment petition in a district court or the Court of Federal Claims is the amount of (as of the date of the filing of the petition) the imputed underpayment, penalties, additions to tax, and additional amounts with respect to the imputed underpayment. See JCX-0-18, at 49.

A. *Proposed § 301.6234-1*

Proposed rules under § 301.6234-1 were previously published in the **Federal Register** (82 FR 60165-66) in the December 2017 NPRM (former proposed § 301.6234-1). For a further explanation of the rules under former proposed § 301.6234-1, see 82 FR 60153.

Former proposed § 301.6234-1(b) provided that a partnership may file a petition for a readjustment of any partnership adjustment in a district court or the Court of Federal Claims "only if the partnership filing the petition deposits with the [IRS], on or before the date the petition is filed, the amount of any imputed underpayment resulting from the partnership adjustment."

To reflect the amendment to section 6234(b)(1) made by section 206(j) of the TTCA regarding the amount of the deposit, proposed § 301.6234-1(b) now provides that amount required to be deposited is the amount (as of the date of the filing of the petition) of any imputed underpayment and any penalties, additions to tax, and additional amounts with respect to such imputed underpayment.

To account for the possibility that multiple imputed underpayments may be reflected in an FPA, proposed § 301.6234-1(b) also now provides that the partnership must only deposit the amount of any imputed underpayment to which the petition for readjustment relates and the amount of any penalties, additions to tax, and additional amounts with respect to such imputed underpayment.

10. *Period of Limitations on Making Adjustments*

Section 6235 provides the period of limitations on making adjustments under the centralized partnership audit regime. Under section 6235(a), the general rule is that no adjustment for any partnership taxable year may be made after the later of three specified dates. Section 206(k) of the TTCA amended section 6235(a) by inserting "or section 905(c)" after "Except as otherwise provided in this section." The amendment makes clear that the period of limitations on making adjustments under the centralized partnership audit regime does not limit the period for notification of the Secretary and redetermination of tax under section 905(c) with respect to foreign tax redeterminations.

In addition, section 206(k) of the TTCA amended section 6235 by striking paragraph (d), which provided for a suspension of the period on making adjustments when the Secretary mails an FPA. That provision was similar to a provision that existed under TEFRA, but the provision has no effect on making adjustments under the centralized partnership audit regime. See JCX-6-18, at 49-50.

A. *Proposed § 301.6235-1*

Proposed rules under § 301.6235-1 were previously published in the **Federal Register** (82 FR 60166-67) in the December 2017 NPRM (former proposed § 301.6235-1). For an explanation of the rules under former proposed § 301.6235-1, see 82 FR 60153-54.

Proposed § 301.6235-1(a) now reflects the amendments to section 6235 to provide an exception for section 905(c) and to remove the reference to section 6235(d).

11. *Definitions and Special Rules*

A. *Proposed § 301.6241-1*

Proposed rules under § 301.6241-1 were previously published in the **Federal Register** (82 FR 27399-400) in the June 2017 NPRM (former proposed § 301.6241-1). For an explanation of the rules under former proposed § 301.6241-1, see 82 FR 27369.

Former proposed § 301.6241-1(a)(1) defined the term "adjustment year" to mean the partnership taxable year in which a decision of a court becomes final (if a petition is filed under section 6234), an AAR is made, or, in any other case, when an FPA is mailed (or if the partnership waives its right to an FPA, the year the waiver is executed by the IRS). Section 206(p) of the TTCA amended section 6227 to provide that an AAR is "filed," as opposed to "made." To reflect this amendment, proposed § 301.6241-1(a)(1) now provides that an AAR is "filed" and not "made."

Former proposed § 301.6241-1(a)(3) defined the term "imputed underpayment" as the amount determined under § 301.6225-1. Because an imputed underpayment may also be computed and paid pursuant to proposed § 301.6226-3(e)(4) (relating to pass-through partners) as well as under proposed § 301.6227-2 and § 301.6227-3(c) (relating to AARs), proposed § 301.6241-1(a)(3) now refers to imputed underpayments determined under those provisions. Proposed § 301.6241-1(a)(3) was also clarified to provide that an imputed underpayment calculated under section 6225 is calculated under section 6225 and the regulations thereunder.

Proposed § 301.6241-1(a)(4) now provides that the term "indirect partner" includes a person that holds an interest in the partnership through a wholly owned entity that is disregarded as separate from its owner for Federal income tax purposes, such as a disregarded entity or grantor trust. This change from the language in the former proposed regulations clarifies that a partnership may seek modification under proposed § 301.6225-2 based on indirect partners holding an interest through a disregarded entity or grantor trust.

Proposed § 301.6241-1(a)(6) now provides that the term "partnership adjustment" means any adjustment to a partnership-related item (as defined in proposed § 301.6241-6), and such term includes a portion of a partnership adjustment.

Former proposed § 301.6241-1(a)(10) defined a tax attribute as anything that can affect, with respect to a partnership or partner, the amount or timing of an item of income, gain, loss, deduction, or credit or that can affect the amount of tax due in any taxable year. As discussed in section 4.A. of this preamble, section 203(a) of the TTCA amended section 6225 to provide an alternative procedure to filing amended returns during modification under which a partner agrees to take into account adjustments to the tax attributes "of such partner". Section 6225(c)(2)(B)(ii). To reflect the amendment to section 6225(c)(2)(B) regarding tax attributes of a partner, the phrase "with respect to a partnership or a partner" was removed from the definition of tax attribute under former proposed § 301.6241-1(a)(10). The reference to "items of income, gain, loss, deduction, or credit" in former proposed § 301.6241-1(a)(10) was also replaced with a reference to "partnership-related item."

B. *Proposed § 301.6241-2*

Proposed rules under § 301.6241-2 were previously published in the **Federal Register** (82 FR 27400) in the June 2017 NPRM (former proposed § 301.6241-2). Former proposed § 301.6241-2 provided for coordination between Title 11 of the United States Code, which deals with bankruptcy, and the centralized partnership audit regime. Because the amendments by the TTCA did not affect section 6241(6), the rules under former proposed § 301.6241-2 are unchanged. For an explanation of the rules under former proposed § 301.6241-2, see 82 FR 27369-70.

C. *Proposed § 301.6241-3*

Proposed rules under § 301.6241-3 were previously published in the **Federal Register** (82 FR 27400-02) in the June 2017 NPRM (former proposed § 301.6241-3). For an explanation of the rules under former proposed § 301.6241-3, see 82 FR 27370-71.

Former proposed § 301.6241-3(a)(3) provided that the rules requiring former partners to take into account adjustments of a partnership which the IRS determined had ceased to exist did not apply to the former partners of a partnership that had elected out of the centralized partnership audit regime under section 6221(b). Because under section 6226(b)(4) a partnership-partner that has elected out of the centralized partnership audit regime may be liable for an imputed underpayment in the case of a push out election, proposed § 301.6241-3(a)(3) now provides that the rules under proposed § 301.6241-3 apply to a partnership-partner and its former partners, regardless of whether the partnership-partner has elected out of the centralized partnership audit regime. Accordingly, under proposed §301.6241-3(a)(3), the former partners of any partnership that may be liable for an imputed underpayment, including a partnership-partner that has elected out of the centralized partnership audit regime, will be required to take into account a partnership adjustment if the IRS determines that such partnership ceased to exist before the partnership adjustment had taken effect. Example 2 under proposed §301.6241-3(f) illustrates this rule.

Former proposed §301.6241-3(b)(2)(i) provided that the IRS will not determine that a partnership has ceased to exist solely because: (i) a partnership has technically terminated under section 708(b)(1)(B); (ii) the partnership has made a valid election under section 6226 and the regulations thereunder with respect to any imputed underpayment; or (iii) the partnership has not paid any amount the partnership is liable for under subchapter C of chapter 63. To reflect the amendment to section 708 by the Act to eliminate technical terminations, the reference to section 708(b)(1)(B) was removed from former proposed §301.6241-3(b)(2)(i). In addition, a rule was added to former proposed §301.6241-3(b)(2)(i) to provide that a partnership also does not cease to exist solely because it furnished statements in accordance with proposed §301.6226-3(e)(3). This change clarifies that partnership-partners that properly furnish statements in accordance with proposed §301.6226-3(e)(3) (and therefore are not liable for an imputed underpayment) are treated the same as an audited partnership who made a valid election under section 6226.

Additional clarifications were made to proposed §301.6241-3. First, the phrase "any amounts" in former proposed §301.6241-3(a)(2) was replaced with the phrase "any unpaid amounts." This clarification was made to eliminate the implication that the partnership was not liable for the original amount due and to clarify that if the IRS determines that a partnership has ceased to exist, the partnership is no longer liable for any remaining unpaid amounts due under subchapter C of chapter 63, meaning that if the partnership had made a prior payment, the IRS can retain that payment. Second, former proposed §301.6241-3(b)(2)(iii) provided that the IRS may not determine that a partnership has ceased to exist after the expiration of the period of limitations on collection. Proposed §301.6241-3(b)(2)(iii) now provides that the period relevant to this determination is the period of limitations on collection with respect to the imputed underpayment that was assessed against the partnership that ceased to exist. Finally, prior references to section 708(b)(1)(A) in former proposed §301.6241-3(b)(2), (d)(2), and (f) were changed to refer to section 708(b)(1) to reflect the amendment to section 708 made by the Act.

D. *Proposed §301.6241-4*

Proposed rules under §301.6241-4 were previously published in the **Federal Register** (82 FR 27402) in the June 2017 NPRM (former proposed §301.6241-4). For an explanation of the rules under former proposed §301.6241-4, see 82 FR 27371.

Former proposed §301.6241-4 provided that payments made by a partnership under the centralized partnership audit regime, including payment of any imputed underpayment and any amount under proposed §301.6226-3, were not deductible to the partnership. Because the payment amount for a partnership-partner in the case of a push out election is referred to as an imputed underpayment, reference to any amount under §301.6226-3 in former proposed §301.6241-4 became superfluous and thus was removed.

E. *Proposed §301.6241-5*

Proposed rules under §301.6241-5 were previously published in the **Federal Register** (82 FR 27402) in the June 2017 NPRM (former proposed §301.6241-5). For an explanation of the rules under former proposed §301.6241-5, see 82 FR 27371.

Former proposed §301.6241-5 provided rules for extending the centralized partnership audit regime to entities filing partnership returns. References in former proposed §301.6241-5(a) to "items of income, gain, loss, deduction, or credit" and "partner's distributive share" were replaced with a reference to "partnership-related item." Proposed §301.6241-5(c) now also reflects the fact that certain business arrangements, which may not be classified as entities, can file partnership returns to make an election under section 761(a). Under proposed §301.6241-5(c), the centralized partnership audit regime does not apply in that case notwithstanding the filing of a partnership return.

12. *Coordination with Other Chapters of the Code*

Section 201(b) of the TTCA added section 6241(9) to the Code regarding the coordination of the centralized partnership audit regime with chapters of the Code other than chapter 1. Section 6241(9)(A) provides that the centralized partnership audit regime shall not apply with respect to any tax imposed (including any amount required to be deducted or withheld) under chapter 2, 2A, 3, or 4 of subtitle A of the Code, except that any partnership adjustment determined under the centralized partnership audit regime for purposes of chapter 1 shall be taken into account for purposes of determining any such tax to the extent that such adjustment is relevant to such determination. Section 6241(9)(B) provides that in the case of any tax imposed (including any amount required to be deducted or withheld) under chapters 3 and 4 of the Code, which is determined with respect to a partnership adjustment, such tax shall be so determined with respect to the reviewed year and shall be so imposed (or so required to be deducted or withheld) with respect to the adjustment year.

Section 201(b) also added section 6501(c)(12) to the Code regarding the statute of limitation on assessment of taxes under chapter 2 or 2A which are attributable to any partnership adjustment. Section 6501(c)(12) provides in the case of any partnership adjustment determined under the centralized partnership audit regime, the period for assessment of any tax imposed under chapter 2 or 2A of the Code which is attributable to such adjustment shall not expire before the date that is one year after one of two events. In the case of an adjustment pursuant to the decision of a court in a proceeding brought under section 6234, the period for assessment shall not expire before the date that is one year after the decision becomes final. In any other case, the period for assessment shall not expire before the date that is one year after 90 days after the date on which the FPA is mailed under section 6231.

A. *Proposed §301.6241-7*

Former proposed §301.6221(a)-1(d) provided that nothing in subchapter C of chapter 63 precluded the IRS from making any adjustment to an item of a partnership (as described in the prior version of §301.6221(a)-1(b)) outside of the centralized partnership audit regime for purposes of determining tax imposed by provisions of the Code other than chapter 1. Accordingly, under former proposed §301.6221(a)-1(d), the IRS was not precluded from examining a partnership's compliance with its obligations under chapters 3 and 4 (or any other chapter of the Code other than chapter 1) in a proceeding outside of the centralized partnership audit regime. Former proposed §301.6221(a)-1(f) provided examples to illustrate this concept.

The rules contained in former proposed §301.6221(a)-1(d), and the examples in former proposed §301.6221(a)-1(f), are consistent with section 6241(9)(A). However, given that these concepts are now codified in section 6241, the rules and examples under former proposed §301.6221(a)-1(d) and (f) are now under proposed §301.6241-7(a)(1) and (2). References to "items of income, gain, loss, deduction, or credit" were replaced with references to "partnership-related item" as defined under proposed §301.6241-6. Other editorial changes were made to reflect revisions to former proposed §301.6221(a)-1.

Proposed §301.6241-7(a)(1) provides that the centralized partnership audit regime does not apply with respect to any tax imposed (including any amount required to be deducted or withheld) under any chapter of the Code other than chapter 1, including chapter 2, 2A, 3, or 4 of the Code. Accordingly, for purposes of determining taxes under chapters of the Code other than chapter 1, the IRS may make adjustments to partnership-related items in proceedings not subject to the centralized partnership audit regime. However, to the extent an adjustment to a partnership-related item or a determination made under the centralized partnership audit regime is relevant in determining tax outside of chapter 1, such adjustment or determination must be taken into account in determining that non-chapter 1 tax. Proposed § 301.6241-7(a)(2) provides examples to illustrate these concepts.

Proposed § 301.6241-7(b) provides rules for coordinating the centralized partnership audit regime with chapters 3 and 4 of the Code. Proposed § 301.6241-7(b)(1) restates the rule in section 6241(9)(B) regarding the timing of withholding for tax imposed under chapters 3 and 4 that is determined with respect to a partnership adjustment. Proposed § 301.6241-7(b)(2) defines the terms chapter 3, chapter 4, and amount subject to withholding.

Former proposed § § 301.6225-1(a)(4) and 301.6226-2(h) provided rules to coordinate the collection of tax in the case of partnership adjustments to amounts subject to withholding under chapters 3 and 4, including rules for when the partnership pays an imputed underpayment resulting from such an adjustment and rules for when the partnership makes the election under section 6226 with respect to such an imputed underpayment. These rules now fall within proposed § 301.6241-7(b)(3) and (b)(4). Proposed § 301.6241-7(b)(4) now provides that a partnership required to pay tax under chapter 3 or chapter 4 when it makes an election under section 6226 is required to pay the tax before the due date of the partnership return for the adjustment year (without regard to extension).

13. *Other Amendments by the TTCA to the Centralized Partnership Audit Regime*

Section 206(l) of the TTCA amended section 6241 by adding a new provision, section 6241(11), providing for the treatment of special enforcement matters. Under section 6241(11), in the case of partnership-related items which involve special enforcement matters, the Secretary may prescribe regulations pursuant to which the centralized partnership audit regime (or any portion thereof) does not apply to such items, and that such items are subject to special rules (including rules related to assessment and collection) as the Secretary determines to be necessary for the effective and efficient enforcement of the Code. For purposes of section 6241(11), the term "special enforcement matters" means: (1) failure to comply with the requirements of section 6226(b)(4)(A)(ii) (regarding the requirement for a pass-through partner to furnish statements or compute and pay an imputed underpayment); (2) assessments under section 6851 (relating to termination assessments of income tax) or section 6861 (relating to jeopardy assessments of income, estate, gift, and certain excise taxes); (3) criminal investigations; (4) indirect methods of proof of income; (5) foreign partners or partnerships; and (6) other matters that the Secretary determines by regulation present special enforcement considerations. Rules under this provision may be provided in future guidance. The Treasury Department and the IRS are considering proposing rules under section 6241(11)(B)(vi) (dealing with other matters that present special enforcement considerations) which allow certain partnership-related items reported solely by persons other than the partnership to be adjusted outside the centralized partnership audit regime. The Treasury Department and the IRS request comments on this provision, including whether there are any additional special enforcement considerations that should be addressed through regulations.

Section 206(m) of the TTCA amended section 6241 by adding a new provision, section 6241(12), to clarify that a U.S. shareholder of a controlled foreign corporation (CFC) which is a partner of a partnership shall be treated as a partner of such partnership for purposes of the centralized partnership audit regime. The U.S. shareholder's distributive share of the partnership is the U.S. shareholder's pro rata share of the CFC's Subpart F income determined under rules similar to section 951(a)(2). Similarly, a taxpayer that makes a Qualified Electing Fund (QEF) election with respect to a passive foreign investment company (PFIC) that is a partner in a partnership shall be treated as a partner of such partnership. In this case, a taxpayer's distributive share of the partnership is the taxpayer's pro rata share of the PFIC's ordinary earnings and net capital gain determined under rules similar to section 1293(b). Consequently, in both circumstances, the U.S. shareholder of a CFC and the taxpayer of a PFIC will be treated as the adjustment year partner or reviewed year partner under the centralized partnership audit regime, where applicable. Regulatory authority was also given to issue regulations or other guidance as necessary or appropriate to carry out the purpose of the provision, including regulations which apply the rule in similar circumstances or with respect to similarly situated persons. Consequently, in both circumstances, the U.S. shareholder of a CFC and the taxpayer of a PFIC will be treated as the adjustment year partner or reviewed year partner under proposed § § 301.6241-1(a)(2) and 301.6241-1(a)(9) where applicable.

Special Analyses

This regulation is not subject to review under section 6(b) of Executive Order 12866 pursuant to the Memorandum of Agreement (April 11, 2018) between the Department of the Treasury and the Office of Management and Budget regarding review of tax regulations.

Because the proposed regulations would not impose a collection of information on small entities, the Regulatory Flexibility Act (5 U.S.C. chapter 6) does not apply.

Pursuant to section 7805(f) of the Code, this notice of proposed rulemaking has been submitted to the Chief Counsel for Advocacy of the Small Business Administration for comment on its impact on small business.

Statement of Availability of IRS Documents

IRS Revenue Procedures, Revenue Rulings, Notices, and other guidance cited in this preamble are published in the Internal Revenue Bulletin (or Cumulative Bulletin) and are available from the Superintendent of Documents, U.S. Government Publishing Office, Washington, DC 20402, or by visiting the IRS website at *www.irs.gov*.

Comments and Public Hearing

Before these proposed regulations are adopted as final regulations, consideration will be given to any electronic and written comments that are submitted timely to the IRS as prescribed in this preamble under the ADDRESSES heading. The Treasury Department and the IRS request comments on all aspects of the proposed rules. All comments will be available at *www.regulations.gov* or upon request.

A public hearing has been scheduled for October 9, 2018, beginning at 10 a.m. in the Auditorium of the Internal Revenue Building, 1111 Constitution Avenue, NW., Washington, DC. Due to building security procedures, visitors must enter at the Constitution Avenue entrance. In addition, all visitors must present photo identification to enter the building. Because of access restrictions, visitors will not be admitted beyond the immediate entrance area more than 30 minutes before the hearing starts. For more information about having your name placed on the building access list to attend the hearing, see the FOR FURTHER INFORMATION CONTACT section of this preamble.

The rules of 26 CFR 601.601(a)(3) apply to the hearing. Persons who wish to present oral comments at the hearing must submit an outline of the topics to be discussed and the time to be devoted to each topic by October 1, 2018. Submit a signed paper or electronic copy of the outline as prescribed in this preamble under the ADDRESSES heading. A period of 10 minutes will be allotted to each person for making comments. An agenda showing the scheduling of the speakers will be prepared after the deadline for receiving outlines has passed. Copies of the agenda will be available free of charge at the hearing.

Drafting Information

The principal authors of these proposed regulations are Jennifer M. Black, Joy E. Gerdy-Zogby, Steven L. Karon, and Brittany Harrison of the Associate Chief Counsel (Procedure and Administration). However, other personnel from the Treasury Department and the IRS participated in their development.

[¶ 49,772] Proposed Amendments of Regulations (REG-118826-16), published in the Federal Register on October 17, 2018.

[Code Secs. 6045, 6721, 6722 and 6724]

Safe harbor exceptions: Information returns: Penalties: Payee statements.—Amendments of Reg. §§1.6045-1, 301.6721-0, 301.6721-1, 301.6722-1 and 301.6724-1, relating to penalties for failure to file correct information returns or furnish correct payee statements, are proposed.

AGENCY: Internal Revenue Service (IRS), Treasury.

ACTION: Notice of proposed rulemaking.

SUMMARY: This document contains proposed regulations relating to penalties for failure to file correct information returns or furnish correct payee statements. The proposed regulations contain safe harbor rules that, for penalty purposes, generally treat as correct payee statements or corresponding information returns that contain errors relating to de minimis incorrect dollar amounts. They prescribe the time and manner in which a payee may elect not to have the safe harbor rules apply. They also update penalty amounts and update references to information reporting obligations. Finally, they provide rules relating to the reporting of basis of securities by brokers as this reporting relates to the de minimis error safe harbor rules. The proposed regulations affect persons required to either file information returns or to furnish payee statements (filers), and recipients of payee statements (payees).

DATES: Written or electronic comments and requests for a public hearing must be received by December 14, 2018.

ADDRESSES: Send submissions to: CC:PA:LPD:PR (REG-118826-16), Room 5203, Internal Revenue Service, P.O. Box 7604, Ben Franklin Station, Washington, DC 20044. Submissions may be hand-delivered between the hours of 8 a.m. and 4 p.m. to CC:PA:LPD:PR (REG-118826-16), Courier's Desk, Internal Revenue Service, 1111 Constitution Avenue NW., Washington, DC, or sent via the Federal eRulemaking Portal at *www.regulations.gov* (REG-118826-16).

FOR FURTHER INFORMATION CONTACT: Concerning the proposed regulations Mark A. Bond of the Office of Associate Chief Counsel (Procedure and Administration), (202) 317-6844; concerning the submission of comments and a request for a public hearing, Regina L. Johnson, (202) 317-6901 (not toll-free numbers).

SUPPLEMENTARY INFORMATION:

Paperwork Reduction Act

The collection of information contained in this notice of proposed rulemaking has been submitted to the Office of Management and Budget for review in accordance with the Paperwork Reduction Act of 1995 (44 U.S.C. 3507(d)). Comments on the collection of information should be sent to the Office of Management and Budget, Attn: Desk Officer for the Department of the Treasury, Office of Information and Regulatory Affairs, Washington, DC 20503, with copies to the Internal Revenue Service, Attn: IRS Reports Clearance Officer, SE:CAR:MP:T:T:SP, Washington, DC 20224. Comments on the collection of information should be received by December 14, 2018. Comments are specifically requested concerning:

Whether the proposed collection of information is necessary for the proper performance of the Internal Revenue Service, including whether the information will have practical utility;

The accuracy of the estimated burden associated with the proposed collection of information (see below);

How the quality, utility, and clarity of the information to be collected may be enhanced;

How the burden of complying with the proposed collection of information may be minimized, including through the application of automated collection techniques or other forms of information technology; and

Estimates of capital or start-up costs and costs of operation, maintenance, and purchase of service to provide information.

The collection of information in these proposed regulations is in proposed regulations §§301.6722-1(d)(3)(iii) regarding the payee election, 301.6722-1(d)(3)(v)(B) regarding the filer notification, 301.6722-1(d)(3)(vii) regarding the payee revocation, and 301.6722-1(d)(4) regarding record retention. The information in proposed regulations §§301.6722-1(d)(3)(iii) and 301.6722-1(d)(3)(vii) will be used by payees to make and revoke elections and by filers to determine whether they are required to furnish corrected payee statements to payees and file corrected information returns with the IRS to avoid application of penalties under sections 6721 and 6722. The information under proposed regulation §301.6722-1(d)(3)(v)(B) will be used to give filers and payees flexibility in establishing reasonable alternative manners for elections. And the information in proposed regulation §301.6722-1(d)(4) will be used by the IRS to determine whether filers are subject to penalties under sections 6721 and 6722. The collection of information in proposed regulations §§301.6722-1(d)(3)(iii) regarding the payee election, 301.6722-1(d)(3)(v)(B) regarding the filer notification, and 301.6722-1(d)(3)(vii) regarding the payee revocation is voluntary to obtain a benefit. The collection of information in proposed regulation §301.6722-1(d)(4) regarding record retention is mandatory. The likely respondents are individuals, state or local governments, farms, business or other for-profit institutions, nonprofit institutions, and small businesses or organizations.

Estimated total annual reporting burden: 992,102 hours.

Estimated average annual burden hours per respondent: approximately 0.10 hours.

Estimated number of respondents: 10,057,746.

Estimated annual frequency of responses: 16,123,292.

An agency may not conduct or sponsor, and a person is not required to respond to, a collection of information unless it displays a valid control number assigned by the Office of Management and Budget.

Books or records relating to a collection of information must be retained as long as their contents may become material in the administration of any internal revenue law. Generally, tax returns and tax return information are confidential, as required by 26 U.S.C. 6103.

Background

This document contains proposed amendments to the Income Tax Regulations (26 CFR part 1) under section 6045(g) of the Internal Revenue Code (Code) relating to returns of brokers in the case of securities transactions, as well as proposed amendments to the Procedure and Administration Regulations (26 CFR part 301) under section 6721(c)(3) relating to the safe harbor exception for certain de minimis errors from the penalty for failure to file correct information returns, section 6722(c)(3) relating to the safe harbor exception for certain de minimis errors from the penalty for failure to furnish correct payee statements, and section 6724 relating to the reasonable cause waiver to the section 6721 and section 6722 penalties. It also contains proposed amendments to the regulations under sections 6721, 6722, and 6724 to update penalty amounts and references to specific information reporting obligations.

Section 6045 provides for information reporting by persons doing business as brokers. Section 6045(g) provides for specific rules in the case of reporting of securities transactions, including for the reporting of basis amounts.

Section 6721 imposes a penalty when a person fails to file an information return on or before the prescribed date, fails to include all of the information required to be shown on the information return, or includes incorrect information on the information return. Section 6722 imposes a penalty when a person fails to furnish a payee statement on or before the prescribed date, fails to include all of the information required to be shown on the payee statement, or includes incorrect information on the payee statement. Section 6724 provides definitions, special rules, and a reasonable cause waiver from penalties for a failure relating to an information reporting requirement.

PATH Act Amendments

Section 202(a) of the Protecting Americans from Tax Hikes Act of 2015, Public Law 114-113 (129 Stat. 2242, 3077 (2015)) (PATH Act), added section 6721(c)(3), effective for information returns required to be filed after December 31, 2016. Section 202(b) of the PATH Act added section 6722(c)(3), effective for payee statements required to be furnished after December 31, 2016. Section 202(c) of the PATH Act added section 6045(g)(2)(B)(iii), effective for information returns required to be filed, and payee statements required to be furnished, after December 31, 2016.

Sections 6721(c)(3)(A) and 6722(c)(3)(A) provide that an information return or payee statement that includes one or more de minimis errors in a dollar amount appearing on the information return or payee statement shall be treated as correct for penalty purposes. An error in a dollar amount is de minimis if the difference between any single amount in error and the correct amount does not exceed $100 and, if the difference is with respect to an amount of tax withheld, the difference is not more than $25.

Under section 6722(c)(3)(B), the safe harbor exception does not apply to any payee statement when the person to whom the payee statement is required to be furnished (that is, the payee) makes an election, at the time and in the manner as the Secretary may prescribe, that the safe harbor exception not apply with respect to such statement. Under section 6721(c)(3)(B), an election by the payee with respect to a payee statement operates to make the safe harbor exception for de minimis errors inapplicable to errors on the corresponding information return.

Sections 6721(c)(3)(C) and 6722(c)(3)(C) provide that the Secretary may issue regulations to prevent the abuse of the safe harbor exceptions, including regulations providing that the safe harbor exceptions shall not apply to the extent necessary to prevent abuse.

Section 6045(g)(2)(B)(iii) provides that except as otherwise provided by the Secretary, a customer's adjusted basis for purposes of section 6045 shall be determined by treating any incorrect dollar amount which is not required to be corrected by reason of section 6721(c)(3) or section 6722(c)(3) as the correct amount.

Other Statutory Amendments

Section 1211(b)(2) of the Pension Protection Act of 2006, Public Law 109-280 (120 Stat. 780, 1073 (2006)), added section 6721(e)(2)(D), providing for calculation of the section 6721 penalty for failures due to intentional disregard in the case of a return required to be filed under section 6050V, effective for acquisitions of contracts after August 17, 2006.

Section 2102 of the Creating Small Business Jobs Act of 2010, Public Law 111-240 (124 Stat. 2504, 2561-64 (2010)), increased penalty amounts throughout sections 6721 and 6722 for information returns required to be filed and payee statements required to be furnished on or after January 1, 2011.

Section 208 of the Tax Increase Prevention Act of 2014, Public Law 113-295 (128 Stat. 4010, 4074 (2014)), amended sections 6721(f)(1) and 6722(f)(1) effective for information returns required to be filed and payee statements required to be furnished after December 31, 2014. The amended paragraphs provide for annual inflationary adjustments to the section 6721 and section 6722 penalties.

Section 806 of the Trade Preferences Extension Act of 2015, Public Law 114-27 (129 Stat. 362, 416-18 (2015)), increased the penalty amounts throughout sections 6721 and 6722, effective for returns required to be filed and statements required to be furnished after December 31, 2015.

Section 6724 and the regulations thereunder define the terms "information return" and "payee statement" and provide that the penalties under sections 6721 and 6722 will not be imposed with respect to any failure if it is shown that the failure was due to reasonable cause and not to willful neglect.

Section 2004 of the Surface Transportation and Veterans Health Care Choice Improvement Act of 2015, Public Law 114-41 (129 Stat. 443, 454-55 (2015)), amended section 6724(d)(1) and 6724(d)(2) to add information reporting under section 6035, relating to basis information with respect to property acquired from decedents, to the definitions of information return and payee statement, respectively.

Section 13520(c) of An Act to provide for reconciliation pursuant to titles II and V of the concurrent resolution on the budget for fiscal year 2018, Public Law 115-97 (131 Stat. 2054, 2150 (2017)) (Pub. L. 115-97), amended section 6724(d)(1) and 6724(d)(2) to add information reporting under section 6050Y, regarding returns relating to certain life insurance contract transactions, to the definitions of information return and payee statement, respectively.

Section 206(o) of the Consolidated Appropriations Act of 2018, Public Law 115-141 (132 Stat. 348, 1182 (2018)), amended section 6724(d)(2) to add information reporting under section 6226(a)(2) (regarding statements relating to alternative to payment of imputed underpayment by a partnership) or under any other provision of Title 26 which provides for the application of rules similar to section 6226(a)(2), to the definition of payee statement.

Notice 2017-09, 2017-4 I.R.B. 542, and Comments in Response to the Notice

On January 4, 2017, the Treasury Department and the IRS released Notice 2017-09, 2017-4 I.R.B. 542, "De Minimis Error Safe Harbor to the I.R.C. §§6721 and 6722 Penalties," to provide guidance regarding the de minimis error safe harbor exceptions from information reporting penalties under sections 6721 and 6722. The notice provided requirements for the payee election under section 6722(c)(3)(B), including the time and manner for making the election. The notice clarified that the de minimis error safe harbor exceptions do not apply in the case of an intentional error or if a filer fails to file an information return or furnish a payee statement. The notice required filers to retain certain records. The notice announced the intention of the Treasury Department and the IRS to issue regulations with respect to the de minimis error safe harbor exceptions and the payee election to have the safe harbor exceptions not apply, and stated that to the extent the regulations incorporate the rules contained in the notice, the regulations will be effective for returns required to be filed, and payee statements required to be furnished, after December 31, 2016. The notice solicited comments regarding the rules contained in the notice and regarding any potential abuse of the de minimis error safe harbor exceptions. In response to the notice, the Treasury Department and IRS received 11 comments. The Treasury Department and IRS have considered all of the comments and addressed them in this preamble.

One comment in response to the notice focused on the administrative burden of the election process provided for by Notice 2017-09 and requested that the IRS consider this burden. The comment stated that the framework in Notice 2017-09 misses Congressional intent to reduce the burden of increased penalties as a result of the Trade Preferences Extension Act of 2015 and the costs of correcting information returns for de minimis amounts. Additionally, the comment stated that it could not envision a single reason an individual, financial institution, or the IRS would want a corrected information return issued for a de minimis amount. Congress determined that there was a need for the payee election; therefore, the Treasury Department and the IRS do not propose to deny payees the ability to elect to have a corrected information return filed and payee statement furnished when an error is de minimis, in particular, prior to the issuance of regulations providing the time and manner for how such an election is to be made. The Treasury Department and the IRS have determined that potential administrative burden on filers is one, but not the only, factor that must be considered in implementing these provisions.

The comment requested that the concept of de minimis and the minor dollar amounts subject to the payee election be weighed against the cost and complexity of instituting and monitoring the payee election process described in Notice 2017-09. It stated that a way to ensure reasonability is to integrate the payee election process into existing procedures, systems, and data structures. The Treasury Department and the IRS acknowledge the potential administrative burden on filers inherent to any new rules; however, the Treasury Department and the IRS note that filers are free to integrate the payee election process allowed by the proposed regulations within existing procedures, systems, and data structures. Further, the Treasury Department and the IRS have determined that potential administrative burden on filers is one, but not the only, factor that must be considered in implementing these provisions and that the need to provide an effective framework for payees to make the payee election is an additional factor that must be considered.

The comment further stated that the best framework to satisfy Congressional intent would be one in which a filer could alert a payee at account opening, or on a one-time basis for currently opened accounts, to the fact that the filer will not issue a corrected statement for any errors that fall within the de minimis error limits of $100 and $25. Under the comment's proposal, the notice would specify that the payee could elect to receive corrected payee statements by making an election in a manner prescribed by the filer. The Treasury Department and the IRS note that proposed regulation § 301.6722-1(d)(3)(v) incorporates rules similar to this proposal by providing the option for filers to give notification to every payee to whom the filer furnishes a payee statement of the payee's ability to elect that the safe harbor exception for de minimis errors not apply and by providing the payee reasonable alternative options to make the election, such as by telephone or through a web site. Proposed regulation § 301.6722-1(d)(3)(v)(D)(2) provides that in cases where valid notification has been provided with respect to a particular account, no further notification is required unless the filer wishes to change the reasonable alternative manner. This rule balances the need for payees to have up-to-date information of any reasonable alternative manners proposed by each filer furnishing statements to the payee with the administrative costs to filers who opt to provide notifications.

The comment stated that the payee election should be on an annual basis, applied only to transactions reportable in the year the election is made. Because this suggestion would place considerable burden on payees to make annual elections, either as a precautionary measure or after monitoring payee statements for accuracy, proposed regulation § 301.6722-1(d)(3)(ii) adopts a different rule, providing that the election shall remain in effect until revoked. This rule allows payees to elect to receive corrections whenever they may become necessary, regardless of whether it is the payee or the filer who becomes aware of the de minimis error. In general, the filer will be best positioned to first become aware of any de minimis error. An election with indefinite effect obviates the need for payees to make annual cautionary elections, in case there is an error of which they are not aware.

The comment also stated that an election without the specific account number associated with it should not be valid and that the election should not include the payee's taxpayer identification number (TIN) and address information. The comment raised the issue of fraudulent activity through identity theft, but the comment did not provide details regarding how providing TIN and address information in a payee election raises identify theft concerns. The Treasury Department and the IRS recognize that in some instances the provision of an account number will be expedient for filers, but also recognize that payees, particularly those who may have had accounts for extended periods, may not have ready access to their full account numbers. Further, the provision of a payee's TIN and address information ensures that filers will have at their disposal information reasonably sufficient to identify the payee that is making the payee election. Proposed regulation § 301.6722-1(d)(3)(iii) therefore provides that as a default rule a filer shall treat an election as valid regardless of whether the payee provides an account number, and it requires the payee's TIN and address information.

Proposed regulation § 301.6722-1(d)(3)(v), however, also provides that if the filer provides notification to the payee under proposed regulation § 301.6722-1(d)(3)(v)(B), the filer may specify that an election using a reasonable alternative manner under proposed regulation § 301.6722-1(d)(3)(v) need not include the payee's TIN and address information, and must include the payee's account information. These rules would apply only if the payee decides to make use of the alternative election manner proposed by the filer under proposed regulation § 301.6722-1(d)(3)(v) and not the default election manner under proposed regulation § 301.6722-1(d)(3)(iii). The proposed rules thus generally provide for flexibility for filers who choose to send notifications to payees, while maintaining a simple default election option for payees.

The comment also proposed that an election relating to a specific account should apply to all payee statements or to no payee statements in that account. It focused on the burden to filers of elections applied on a statement-by-statement basis, and the potential that an election might apply to payee statements made in composite form. Additionally, the comment requested that the IRS provide some of the reasons it expects a taxpayer will request corrected returns in the de minimis error context on a statement-by-statement basis. The comment's suggested rule is inconsistent with the statutory framework of sections 6721 through 6724, which applies generally on a per statement basis. Section 6722(c)(3)(A) prescribes the de minimis error safe harbor exception "with respect to any payee statement." Additionally, the comment's proposal would significantly limit payees' options for making elections. Further, the Treasury Department and the IRS note that the Code permits filers to provide corrected statements regardless of the de minimis error safe harbor exceptions or payee election. Thus, filers may provide corrections on an account-wide basis once a payee makes an election with respect to a single type of payee statement associated with that account. For example, if a payee submits an election to a filer with respect to the Form 1099-DIV, "Dividends and Distributions," that the filer is required to furnish to the payee, the filer is required under sections 6721(c)(3) and 6722(c)(3) and these proposed regulations to issue corrections even for de minimis errors. Under the proposed regulations, if the filer is also required to furnish a Form 1099-B, "Proceeds From Broker and Barter Exchange Transactions," to the payee, and the payee specifically made the payee's election with respect to the Form 1099-DIV (and not the Form 1099-B), the election under proposed regulation § 301.6722-1(d)(3)(i) does not apply with respect to the Form 1099-B, and the filer is not required to correct Forms 1099-B for de minimis errors. But the filer may decide that it is more administrable for the filer to correct for de minimis errors for every payee statement the filer sends to the payee, including the Form 1099-B. Thus, the per-statement election provides flexibility to filers. In addition, proposed regulation § 301.6722-1(d)(3)(iv) provides that if a payee does not identify the type of payee statement to which the election relates, the filer shall treat the election as applying to all types of payee statements the filer is required to furnish to the payee. Finally, as described above, filers who choose to provide notification and a reasonable alternative manner for the election may provide that as a condition of using the reasonable alternative manner the payee must provide the filer the payee's account number, and the filer may then provide corrections on an account-wide basis. For these reasons, proposed regulation § 301.6722-1(d)(3)(iii) does not adopt the comment's suggested rule.

The comment noted that section 202 of the PATH Act does not contain explicit language regarding a payee's ability to revoke a prior election under section 6722(c)(3)(B). The comment stated that providing for a revocation is unnecessary to accomplish Congress's specific mandate and may prove to be more costly and burdensome than continuing to issue corrections for de minimis errors. The comment further stated that, if revocations are permitted, they should be permitted only on an annual basis applied to the next year after the year in which the revocation was made. The comment's concern is that the language regarding revocations in section 3.02 of Notice 2017-09 could lead to a revocation being applicable to a portion of a calendar year, with an election applicable to a separate portion of that year. The Treasury Department and the IRS do not agree that this will cause significant burden to filers because a revocation does not mandate changes in behavior on behalf of the filer, but rather provides penalty relief for the filer if an information return contains a de minimis error and is not corrected. As a result, proposed regulation §301.6722-1(d)(3)(vii) provides that a revocation will apply to payee statements that are furnished or are due to be furnished after the revocation is received by the filer.

The Treasury Department and the IRS note that while the revocation may cause the election to apply for only the first part of a calendar year, nothing prevents filers from continuing to issue corrections for the rest of the calendar year (as they had been doing with respect to the portion of the year when the election was in effect). Immediate effect of the revocation provides immediate penalty relief for filers in the case of a de minimis error that is uncorrected and allows filers to stop issuing corrections for de minimis errors as soon after receipt of the revocation as they wish. In the unlikely scenario of an election in a calendar year, followed by a revocation in the same calendar year, followed by another election in the same calendar year, the situation will not be that of various rules for various periods within the calendar year - rather, because the election is effective for the entire calendar year and subsequent years until revoked under proposed regulations §§301.6721-1(e)(3) and 301.6722-1(d)(3)(ii), the last, valid election would apply to the same period it would absent the prior election and prior revocation. Because the Treasury Department and the IRS do not view the potential for multiple filings of elections and revocations within a year as a significant concern, the proposed regulations do not complicate the rules in an effort to further address this issue. Regarding the length of the effectiveness of a revocation, an indefinite revocation, rather than an annual revocation system, should impose less administrative burden both on filers and payees given the decreased frequency of filing.

The comment also stated that brokers should be specifically permitted to ignore the use of the de minimis error safe harbor exceptions and continue to issue corrections for de minimis amounts. The Treasury Department and the IRS agree that brokers, like other filers, may do so without specific permission. Because there is no need for the regulations to provide brokers with specific permission, this comment was not adopted.

The comment also commented on the final and temporary regulations under §§1.6081-8 and 1.6081-8T contained in TD 9730, stating that the automatic extension to file various information returns should, as a general matter, remain in place. This portion of the comment is beyond the scope of these regulations.

In addition the comment asked for clarification of a filer's reporting obligations under the de minimis error safe harbor exceptions where the threshold reporting obligation is not initially met, but upon a subsequent corrective event, the reportable dollar amount exceeds the threshold amount but does not exceed the de minimis error limit. The de minimis error safe harbor exceptions do not apply to this situation, because they do not apply to a failure to file; the safe harbor exceptions apply only to inadvertent errors on a filed information return or furnished payee statement. This rule is reflected in proposed regulation §301.6722-1(d)(1). The comment further asked whether an election applies only to payee statements and information returns required to be furnished or filed in the year of the election, or later, or to any corrections made after the election, regardless of when the reporting to which the correction is related is required. Proposed regulation §301.6722-1(d)(3)(ii) addresses this question by providing that an election under proposed regulation §301.6722-1(d)(3)(i) applies to payee statements required to be furnished and information returns required to be filed during the calendar year of the election, or later; if a payee statement is required to be furnished or an information return is required to be filed before the beginning of the calendar year of the election, the election would not apply, regardless of when the filer realizes a reporting error was made. The comment asked whether the language in Notice 2017-09 reading "within 30 days of the date of the election" should instead reference 30 days from discovery of the error for purposes of the error being treated as due to reasonable cause and not willful neglect. The "within 30 days of the date of the election" language in the notice is now reflected in proposed regulation §301.6724-1(h). The Treasury Department and the IRS determined that the election, rather than the discovery of the error, is the appropriate focus because a special rule is needed only in those situations where a payee election causes the de minimis error safe harbor exceptions to not apply. In cases where a payee has made an election under proposed regulation §301.6722(d)(3)(i) and a filer subsequently discovers an error, whether the error is de minimis or not, the normal reasonable cause rules under section 6724, such as in §301.6724-1(d)(1) relating to responsible manner, apply. Examples 8 and 9 in proposed regulation §301.6724-1(k) illustrate these rules.

The comment also requested clarification regarding the following language in section 3.02 of Notice 2017-09:

Nothing in this notice prevents a payee from requesting that the filer file a corrected information return or furnish a corrected payee statement required to be filed or furnished in a calendar year preceding the calendar year in which the payee makes the election.

The comment asked whether the "or" in the phrase "filed or furnished" should be "and" because, regardless of the payee's request, the filer would both furnish the corrected payee statement and file the corrected information return. The comment also asked whether this language places any obligation upon the filer to oblige the payee's request pursuant to this language. The Treasury Department and the IRS note that the proposed regulations do not include the quoted language, so the comment's inquiries regarding it are not applicable.

Six additional comments concurred with the comments and questions made by the one comment that has been described thus far in this preamble. One of these six additional comments also emphasized the administrative burden needed for financial firms to implement the rules described in Notice 2017-09, and the impact especially on smaller or midsized firms. The comment stated that the increased cost has no tangible benefit or demonstrated revenue-raising impact. The Treasury Department and the IRS note that the statute provides payees with the ability to elect that the de minimis error safe harbor exceptions not apply. The regulations strike a balance between the benefit of the de minimis error safe harbor exceptions for filers and the statutory ability for payees to elect that the de minimis error safe harbor exceptions not apply. The statutory ability for payees to make an election that the de minimis error safe harbor exceptions not apply, rather than any revenue-raising metric, is the benefit to be weighed against administrative burdens to filers.

The comment also stated that the framework set forth in Notice 2017-09 runs contrary to the intent of the notice, existing regulations, and the Trade Preferences Extension Act of 2015, but the comment does not provide details as to how this is the case and we cannot therefore address this portion of the comment.

An additional comment quoted the following language from Notice 2017-09, section 3.01: "This notice does not prohibit a filer from filing corrected information returns and furnishing corrected payee statements if the payee does not make an election." The comment stated that the mitigation of administrative burden of processing corrections under the de minimis error safe harbor exceptions is realized not only by filers but by payees as well, and recommended that guidance discourage corrected statements for de minimis errors. The Treasury Department and the IRS do not agree; accurate reporting is an important goal that should not be discouraged. Thus, the proposed regulations do not adopt the comment's suggestion.

The comment also stated that requiring a filer to provide each payee with written notification of the de minimis error safe harbor exception rules and election out provisions would be unduly burdensome to filers, shifting administrative burden from processing corrected statements to the notification process. The comment recommended that the IRS include a general disclosure regarding the de minimis error safe harbor exceptions in general instructions relating to information returns. The Treasury Department and the IRS decided to not include a notification requirement in the proposed regulations. Rather, the proposed regulations provide only that if filers wish to set up election systems that vary from the default contained in proposed regulation §301.6722-1(d)(3)(iii), a notification is required for that reasonable alternative manner of election under proposed regulation §301.6722-1(d)(3)(v). For this reason, the proposed regulations do not reflect this comment. The Treasury Department and the IRS are considering whether to include references to the de minimis error safe harbor exceptions, the election under §301.6722-1(d)(3)(i), and other information in general instructions or in specific forms or instructions, and note that the current (2018) General Instructions for Certain Information

Returns as well as the current (2018) General Instructions for Forms W-2 and W-3 contain discussions of the de minimis error safe harbor exceptions and related information.

The comment also requested clarification regarding whether the de minimis error safe harbor exception is for the cumulative total of multiple errors, or one particular error. The comment noted that the safe harbor exception would be easier to apply if it is calculated on an error-by-error basis. Proposed regulation § 301.6722-1(d)(2) clarifies that the safe harbor exception is calculated on an error-by-error basis.

The comment further stated that if an error is discovered by the filer, the payee should not be able to elect that the de minimis error safe harbor exceptions not apply and that the filer should make the determination of whether a corrected form is needed, in light of the threshold amounts of $100 and $25. The comment stated that the election process does not lead to a reduction in the administrative burden. Because this suggestion is contrary to section 6722(c)(3)(B), which specifically provides for the payee to make the election under section 6722(c)(3)(B), the proposed regulations do not adopt the suggestion.

The comment also stated, regarding any notification requirement, that errors may be identified by the payee and communicated to the filer and then at that point, if the dollar amount is below the applicable threshold, the filer should inform the payee of the de minimis error safe harbor exceptions and the payee's ability to elect that the safe harbor exceptions not apply. As noted above, the proposed regulations do not contain a notification requirement.

The comment stated that additional consideration should be given to allow the payee election to expire, noting that such a rule could reduce administrative burden for filers, given a resulting decrease in required corrections. Because a rule under which the payee election expires after a set amount of time would increase the complexity of the election and revocation framework both for filers (tracking years in which the election is in effect) and for payees (same, and refiling elections after expiration, if desired), proposed regulation § 301.6722-1(d)(3)(ii) does not adopt such a rule.

The comment also requested examples of what a de minimis error correction would look like. A de minimis error correction would be substantially similar to a correction of an error greater than a de minimis error in the context of corrected information reporting -that is, the filing of a corrected information return, and the furnishing of a corrected payee statement (for example, filing a corrected Form 1099-MISC with the IRS, and furnishing a corrected Form 1099-MISC to the payee).

The comment also requested explanation of what "de minimis" is and is not. Proposed regulation § 301.6722-1(d)(2) provides the definition of de minimis error, and proposed regulation § 301.6722-1(d)(5) illustrates this definition with examples.

The comment requested an opt-out provision for filers that, if selected, would remove any responsibility to collect information and keep records under Notice 2017-09. The Treasury Department and the IRS have considered potential expenses that filers might incur in meeting the record retention requirements in proposed regulation § 301.6722-1(d)(4) and have determined that an opt-out provision, while potentially reducing expenses borne by filers, would render the record retention rules ineffective. The record retention requirements facilitate tax administration by providing proof of compliance and assisting filers to avoid penalties under sections 6721 and 6722. The Treasury Department and the IRS note that the notification under proposed regulation § 301.6722-1(d)(3)(v)(B) is a voluntary collection of information because the notification is optional. Therefore, the proposed regulations do not adopt this comment.

Finally, the comment asked whether any notification requirement will be effective for payees receiving their statements in 2016. The effective/applicability date provisions in proposed regulation § 301.6722-1(g) provide that the rules relating to the optional notification by filers under proposed regulation § 301.6722-1(d)(3)(v) are proposed to apply with respect to information returns and payee statements due on or after January 1 of the calendar year immediately following the date of publication of a Treasury decision adopting these rules as final regulations in the **Federal Register**.

An additional comment requested that the payee election provisions under section 6722(c)(3)(B) and proposed regulation § 301.6722-1(d)(3)(i) not apply to Form 8937, "Report of Organizational Actions Affecting Basis of Securities." The comment noted that under section 6045B(e) and regulation § 1.6045B-1(a)(3) a filer need not file and issue individual Forms 8937, but can opt to post a single Form 8937 on its public web site. The comment noted that the Form 8937 is not specific to an individual payee, but instead describes tax basis adjustments in the abstract for use by brokers in determining the basis reporting for their customers. It noted that the individually-focused nature of the payee election is at odds with the public reporting enabled by section 6045B(e) and regulation § 1.6045B-1(a)(3). And it noted that a single election with respect to a posted Form 8937 could lead to inefficiencies for numbers of brokers (including those who did not make the election) once a correction is issued.

The Treasury Department and the IRS acknowledge these concerns. However, Congress presumably was aware of the public reporting option under section 6045B(e) and regulation § 1.6045B-1(a)(3) (enacted October 3, 2008, and published October 18, 2010, respectively) when it enacted the de minimis error safe harbor exceptions. Congress did not provide for authority to exclude information returns or payee statements from the de minimis error safe harbor, or the payee election, based on administrative inconvenience. The proposed regulations therefore do not adopt this comment's suggested rule.

A final comment requested that the payee election be available only as a one-time election and apply prospectively only. The comment stated that nothing in the notice prevents a payee from requesting that the filer file a corrected information return or furnish a corrected payee statement from years preceding the election, and noted that this presents burdens and potential for abuse by payees. The comment may have misconstrued Notice 2017-09, in part, because nothing in the notice provided for an election for a year preceding the year in which the election was made. In like manner, proposed regulation § 301.6722-1(d)(3)(ii) provides that an election made by October 15 of a calendar year -for example, Calendar Year 1 - can apply retrospectively to a Form 1099-MISC required to be furnished in January of Calendar Year 1, but the election would have no validity with respect to any payee statements required to be furnished in any calendar years preceding Calendar Year 1. Thus, the retrospective application is limited to the current calendar year, along with the potential administrative burden and any potential for abuse. The comment does not adequately establish that "cherry picking" the corrections of de minimis dollar amounts poses a significant threat of abuse. Regarding potential administrative burden to filers, while a one-time prospective election might be less burdensome, this is but one factor that must be considered; flexibility for payees in requesting corrected statements is another. As discussed below, proposed regulation § 301.6722-1(d)(3)(ii) balances these factors.

The comment requested the information required for a payee election be streamlined to simplify elections as a matter of customer service. Proposed regulation § 301.6722-1(d)(3)(v) allows filers to provide a reasonable alternative manner that they view as satisfactory to their customers.

The comment also echoed previous comments in requesting the flexibility to issue corrections, despite generally taking advantage of the de minimis error safe harbor exceptions, for purposes of cost basis adjustments under section 6045. To address this and similar comments, proposed regulation § 1.6045-1(d)(6)(vii) provides that when a broker both files a corrected information return and issues a corrected payee statement showing the correct dollar amount, even though not required by section 6721(c)(3) or section 6722(c)(3), the corrected amount is the adjusted basis for section 6045 purposes.

The comment asked that the recordkeeping requirement in section 3.05 of Notice 2017-09, of ". . . as long as that information may be relevant to the administration of any internal revenue law" be reduced from a potentially open-ended length of time to a range of three years (the general statute of limitations on assessment under section 6501) to seven years (the time period used for various Securities and Exchange Commission and Financial Industry Regulatory Authority recordkeeping requirements), stating that the open-ended retention schedule is unnecessary and burdensome. Proposed regulation § 301.6722-1(d)(4) does not adopt this comment, because the records under this section (such as an election, until revoked) may be relevant to tax administration in years beyond the general statute of limitations on assessment under section 6501 for a particular year. For example, if an election is made in 2019 and not revoked until 2025, that election will be relevant with respect to information returns required to be filed and payee statements required to be furnished in 2024. The rules in proposed regulation § 301.6722-1(d)(4) therefore reflect the general record retention rules in section 6001 and § 1.6001-1(e), providing for record retention as long as the contents of an election, revocation, or notification may be material in the administration of any internal revenue law.

Finally, the comment requested guidance regarding how a payee election that the de minimis error safe harbor exceptions not apply would apply to joint accounts, such as when joint account payees submit contrary elections, or one joint account payee submits an election but another does not. Absent contrary provisions under the Internal Revenue Code or Code of Federal Regulations, the rules that typically govern issues of authority over joint accounts should address these matters, and a special rule for purposes of de minimis error reporting is unnecessary. The Treasury Department and the IRS note that filers have the option to ignore the availability of the de minimis error safe harbor exceptions and issue corrections for de minimis amounts as was required to avoid penalties prior to the enactment of the PATH Act. Filers can therefore issue corrections to all joint account payees even if joint account payees submit contrary elections, or one joint account payee submits an election but another does not.

Explanation of Provisions

1. Safe Harbor Exceptions From Penalties for Certain De Minimis Errors

In accord with sections 6721(c)(3)(A) and 6722(c)(3)(A), proposed regulations §§ 301.6721-1 and 301.6722-1 provide for safe harbor exceptions to the section 6721 and section 6722 penalties. With certain exceptions discussed below, the safe harbor exceptions apply in circumstances when an information return or payee statement is otherwise correct and is timely filed or furnished and includes a de minimis error in a dollar amount reported on the information return or payee statement. When the safe harbor exception applies to an information return or payee statement and the information return or payee statement is otherwise correctly and timely filed or furnished, no correction is required and, for purposes of sections 6721 or 6722, respectively, the information return or payee statement is treated as having been filed or furnished with all of the correct required information.

Pursuant to sections 6721(c)(3)(A) and 6722(c)(3)(A), an error is a de minimis error if the difference between any single amount in error and the correct amount is not more than $100, or, if the difference is with respect to an amount of tax withheld, it is not more than $25. Proposed regulation § 301.6722-1(d)(2) defines tax withheld to include any amount required to be shown on an information return or payee statement (as defined in section 6724(d)(1) and (d)(2), respectively) withheld under section 3402, as well as any such amount that is creditable under sections 27, 31, 33, or 1474. This is not an exclusive definition but is intended to ensure that all amounts giving rise to dollar-for-dollar reductions in tax, including foreign tax credits under section 27, are included as tax withheld.

2. Errors Due to Intentional Disregard of Information Reporting Requirements

In accord with sections 6721(e) and 6722(e), proposed regulations §§ 301.6721-1(e)(1) and 301.6722-1(d)(1) provide that the safe harbor exceptions for certain de minimis errors do not apply in cases of intentional disregard of the requirements to file correct information returns or furnish correct payee statements. In those cases, higher penalty amounts imposed by sections 6721(e) and 6722(e) and proposed regulations §§ 301.6721-1(g) and 301.6722-1(c) apply. For example, a person may not choose to forgo filing information returns or furnishing payee statements that the person is required to file or furnish under the Code and that report amounts less than $100 and tax withheld less than $25. To do so would be an intentional disregard of the filing requirement and result in higher penalties.

3. Payee Election to Receive Corrected Payee Statement

In accord with sections 6721(c)(3)(B) and 6722(c)(3)(B), proposed regulations §§ 301.6721-1(e)(3) and 301.6722-1(d)(3)(i) allow a payee to elect to have the safe harbor exceptions for certain de minimis errors not apply to the information reporting penalties. The proposed regulations provide that a payee may elect that the safe harbor exception to section 6722 penalties not apply to a payee statement, and that the election will also apply to the safe harbor exception to section 6721 penalties with respect to corresponding information returns. Proposed regulation § 301.6722-1(d)(3)(vi) provides that the election is not available with respect to information that may not be altered under specific information reporting rules. For example, § 1.6045-4(i)(5) provides special rules for defining gross proceeds in the context of multiple transfers for information reporting on real estate transactions, and prohibits altering information after the due date for filing the Form 1099-S, "Proceeds From Real Estate Transactions." Allowing an election under proposed regulation § 301.6722-1(d)(3)(i) with respect to the Form 1099-S would suggest that a correction would or should be made. To resolve any ambiguity between these provisions, proposed regulation § 301.6722-1(d)(3)(vi) prohibits an election with respect to information that may not be altered under specific information reporting rules, such as under § 1.6045-4(i)(5).

Proposed regulation § 301.6722-1(d)(3)(ii) provides that a payee must make any election no later than the later of 30 days after the date on which the payee statement is required to be furnished to the payee, or October 15 of the calendar year, to receive a correct payee statement required to be furnished in that calendar year without having the safe harbor exceptions for certain de minimis errors apply. The October 15 date coincides with the fully-extended due date an individual may have to file an income tax return. In arriving at this date, the Treasury Department and the IRS considered both the needs of persons who furnish payee statements and the needs of payees, who will generally have a filing due date no later than October 15 if their taxable year corresponds to the calendar year referenced on the payee statements they receive. Prior to promulgation of these proposed regulations, the IRS advised payees to request corrected payee statements from filers in cases in which information is incorrect, without time limit on making this request. Imposing a deadline to elect before October 15 could limit a taxpayer's ability to correct errors discovered while the payee is preparing his or her return. The allowance of an election after the due date for most payee statements and through October 15 allows payees to inspect payee statements and make elections for purposes of timely filing their income tax returns. On the other hand, the existence of an election cutoff date of October 15 in the case of most payee statements reduces administrative burden on filers by eliminating elections after October 15. The 30-day rule provides a deadline in cases of payee statements required to be furnished later in the calendar year, such as the Schedule K-1 (Form 1065), "Partner's Share of Income, Deductions, Credits, etc.," required to be furnished to payees by fiscal year partnerships.

To reduce the administrative burden of yearly elections on both payees and filers, an election remains in effect for all subsequent years until revoked under proposed regulation § 301.6722-1(d)(3)(vii). The effect of a revocation of a prior election is that the safe harbor exceptions for de minimis errors apply. The revocation will be effective for payee statements furnished or due to be furnished after the revocation is received. Because a revocation makes the safe harbor for certain de minimis errors applicable, potentially reducing the accuracy of information returns and payee statements, payees have no need to be able to make a retroactive revocation after receipt of any payee statements and during the period of preparing individual income tax returns. Likewise, the immediate effect of the revocation is beneficial to the filer, because it immediately applies the de minimis error safe harbor exceptions, eliminating the requirement to issue corrected information returns containing only de minimis errors incurred by an election under proposed regulation § 301.6722-1(d)(3)(i). If issuing corrections is easier for the filer, the filer can always do so. A revocation will remain in effect until the payee makes a valid and timely election under proposed regulation § 301.6722-1(d)(3)(i).

For determining the "date of receipt" by the filer, paragraphs (ii) and (vii) of proposed regulation § 301.6722-1(d)(3), relating to elections and revocations, respectively, provide that for purposes of proposed regulation § 301.6722-1 the provisions of section 7502 relating to timely mailing treated as timely delivery apply in determining the date an election under proposed regulation § 301.6722-1(d)(3)(ii) or revocation under proposed regulation §301.6722-1(d)(3)(vii) is considered to be received by the filer, treating delivery to the filer as if the filer were an agency, officer, or office under section 7502, so that the date of mailing may control the timeliness of an election or revocation. These rules provide for more clarity regarding the date of an election or revocation.

Under proposed regulation §301.6722-1(d)(3)(iii), the default manner for an election by the payee that the de minimis error safe harbor exceptions not apply is by writing on paper, mailed to the address for the filer appearing on the payee statement the payee received from the filer with respect to which the election is being made, or as provided to them by the filer. Proposed regulation §301.6722-1(d)(3)(iii)(A) through (D) provide the requirements for what information must be included in the written election, such as the payee's name, address, and taxpayer identification number (TIN). This information is necessary for the filer to implement the election.

Proposed regulation §301.6722-1(d)(3)(v) provides that the payee may make the election under proposed regulation §301.6722-1(d)(3)(i) in a reasonable alternative manner if the filer provides a valid notification to the payee describing the reasonable alternative manner. The reasonable alternative manner, as described in proposed regulation §301.6722-1(d)(3)(v)(E), may include electronic elections by e-mail or telephonic elections. For a notification under proposed regulation §301.6722-1(d)(3)(v) to be valid, and make available the reasonable alternative manner, the notification must be written (paper or electronic), must be timely under the provisions of proposed regulation §301.6722-1(d)(3)(v)(D), must explain to the payee the payee's ability to make the election under proposed regulation §301.6722-1(d)(3)(i), must provide an address to which the payee may send a written election under proposed regulation §301.6722-1(d)(3)(i) and (iii), and must describe the information required for making the election as described by proposed regulation §301.6722-1(d)(3)(iii)(A) through (D). To be timely under proposed regulation §301.6722-1(d)(3)(v)(D), a notification must be provided to the payee with, or at the time of, the furnishing of the payee statement, or have previously been timely provided (under the with, or at the time of, rule) to the payee with a payee statement associated with the relevant account. Under proposed regulation §301.6722-1(d)(3)(v)(D)(2), if a filer wishes to provide for a different reasonable alternative manner than a previous reasonable alternative manner, the applicable timeliness rule is under proposed regulation §301.6722-1(d)(3)(v)(D)(1) (the with, or at the time of, rule) and the filer must accept payee elections under the previous reasonable alternative manner for a period of at least 60 days after the receipt of the new notification by the payee.

To ease the administrative burden on filers, the notification may provide that certain of the information otherwise required under proposed regulation §301.6722-1(d)(3)(iii)(B) is not required, and that certain of the information (the otherwise optional account number) is required, if the payee decides to use the reasonable alternative manner rather than the default manner.

The combination of the default election under proposed regulation §301.6722-1(d)(3)(iii) and the reasonable alternative manner, including electronic and telephonic elections, pursuant to a valid notification by the filer, provides a straightforward election process for payees who do not have notification provided them, as well as additional flexibility to filers who wish to provide notification to payees of the election and alternative methods for making the election.

Proposed regulation §301.6722-1(d)(3)(vii)(A) through (F) provides requirements for a revocation that are similar to the requirements for an election.

4. Reasonable Cause

When a payee makes an election under §301.6722-1(d)(3)(i) by the later of 30 days after the date on which the payee statement is required to be furnished to the payee, or October 15 of the calendar year, the safe harbor exceptions for de minimis errors no longer apply with respect to the payee statement, and corresponding information return, required to be furnished and filed that year. If the payee statement has already been furnished or the information return already been filed, and they contain de minimis errors, the section 6721 and 6722 penalties will apply absent the applicability of an exception other than the safe harbor exceptions for certain de minimis errors. Proposed regulation §301.6724-1(h) provides special rules to determine whether the exception for reasonable cause applies in this situation. Section 301.6724-1(h) only applies when the safe harbor for certain de minimis errors would have applied, but for an election under §301.6722-1(d)(3)(i).

Under this provision, a filer may establish that a failure caused by the presence of de minimis errors and an election under §301.6722-1(d)(3)(i) is due to reasonable cause and not willful neglect by filing a corrected information return or furnishing a corrected payee statement, or both, as applicable, within 30 days of the date of the election. Where specific rules provide for additional time in which to furnish a corrected payee statement and file a corrected information return, for example with Forms W-2C, the 30-day rule does not apply and the specific rules will apply. In the case of filing or furnishing outside of the 30-day period the determination of reasonable cause will be on a case-by-case basis. Examples 8 and 9 in proposed regulation §301.6724-1(k) illustrate reasonable cause under this provision and when reasonable cause might occur under a separate provision.

5. Cost Basis

To encourage correct reporting, and to facilitate brokers with the accurate maintenance of cost basis systems, proposed regulation §1.6045-1(d)(6)(vii) provides that voluntary corrections by brokers will result in updated adjusted basis under section 6045, even when the incorrect dollar amounts are not "required to be corrected by reason of section 6721(c)(3) or section 6722(c)(3)." See I.R.C. section 6045(g)(2)(B)(iii). This proposed regulation allows brokers who identify a de minimis error in their cost basis systems to fix the mismatch between their systems and the previously-reported (incorrect) dollar amount through voluntary subsequent reporting. The updated adjusted basis under section 6045 has no effect on calculating basis under other basis determination sections, such as section 1012.

6. Record Retention

To facilitate proof of compliance, proposed regulation §301.6722-1(d)(4) provides that filers must retain records of any election, revocation, or notification for as long as the contents of the election, revocation, or notification may be material in the administration of any internal revenue law. Whether an election, revocation, or notification was effectively made under these regulations can affect whether the section 6721 or 6722 penalties apply. Thus, records of any election, revocation, or notification are relevant to determining the tax liability of any person under sections 6721 or 6722. See section 6001 and §1.6001-1(e).

7. Updates and Conforming Amendments

To reflect increased penalty amounts due to section 2102 of the Creating Small Business Jobs Act of 2010 and section 806 of the Trade Preferences Extension Act of 2015, the proposed regulations update dollar amounts throughout. Additionally, to reflect the provision for annual inflationary adjustments in section 208 of the Tax Increase Prevention Act of 2014, proposed regulations §§301.6721-1(i) and 301.6722-1(f) provide for adjustments for inflation.

To reflect the amendments by section 2004 of the Surface Transportation and Veterans Health Care Choice Improvement Act of 2015, section 13520(c) of Public Law 115-97, and section 206(o) of the Consolidated Appropriations Act of 2018 to sections 6724(d)(1) and 6724(d)(2), proposed regulations §§301.6721-1(h)(2)(xii) and (h)(3)(xxvi) and 301.6722-1(e)(2)(xxxv), (xxxvi), and (xxxvii) are added to update the definitions of information return and payee statement.

To reflect the amendments by section 1211(b)(2) of the Pension Protection Act of 2006 to section 6721(e)(2), proposed regulation § 301.6721-1(g)(4)(iv)(D) provides for the calculation of the section 6721 penalty in case of intentional disregard in the case of a return required to be filed under section 6050V.

Proposed regulation § 301.6724-1(m) provides for updated procedures for a taxpayer to use to seek an administrative waiver that a failure is due to reasonable cause and not due to willful neglect, as the prior language referencing the district director was out of date.

The proposed regulations remove outdated references to various taxable years, replacing with updated years where necessary, such as in examples.

The proposed regulations make numerous conforming amendments to reflect the addition and renumbering of paragraphs. Proposed regulation § 301.6721-0 provides an updated table of contents.

Proposed Effective/Applicability Date

The regulations, as proposed, would generally apply with respect to information returns required to be filed and payee statements required to be furnished on or after January 1 of the calendar year immediately following the date of publication of a Treasury decision adopting these rules as final regulations in the **Federal Register**. Proposed regulation § 301.6724-1(h), however, would apply with respect to information returns required to be filed and payee statements required to be furnished on or after January 1, 2017. See I.R.C. section 7805(b)(1)(C) and section 4 of Notice 2017-09, IRB-2017-4 (January 23, 2017).

Effect on Other Documents

Upon the publication of final regulations pursuant to the proposed regulations under sections 6045, 6721, 6722, and 6724 in this notice of proposed rulemaking in the **Federal Register**, Notice 2017-09 will be superseded with respect to information returns required to be filed and payee statements required to be furnished on or after January 1 of the calendar year immediately following the date of publication of a Treasury decision adopting these rules as final regulations in the **Federal Register**.

Special Analyses

These regulations are not subject to review under section 6(b) of Executive Order 12866 pursuant to the Memorandum of Agreement (April 11, 2018) between the Treasury Department and the Office of Management and Budget regarding review of tax regulations.

Pursuant to the Regulatory Flexibility Act (5 U.S.C. chapter 6), it is hereby certified that the collection of information contained in these regulations, if adopted, would not have a significant economic impact on a substantial number of small entities. Accordingly, a regulatory flexibility analysis is not required. As stated in this preamble, the proposed regulations would implement the de minimis error safe harbor exceptions in sections 6721(c)(3) and 6722(c)(3) to the section 6721 and 6722 penalties. Pursuant to section 6722(c)(3)(B), the proposed regulations would also provide for the time and manner for elections by payees that the de minimis error safe harbor exceptions not apply, including optional notifications by filers to provide for an alternative reasonable manner for the election. Finally, the proposed regulations would provide rules for revocations by payees of elections and record retention rules.

Although the proposed regulations may potentially affect a substantial number of small entities, the economic impact on these entities is not expected to be significant. The de minimis error safe harbor exceptions are expected to greatly reduce the burden on filers to file corrected information returns and furnish corrected payee statements because of de minimis errors. In those cases where payees opt to elect that the de minimis error safe harbor exceptions not apply, the expense of making the election will be borne by the payees, which generally will not be small entities.

Filers that are small entities receiving elections may incur costs in processing the elections, including initial costs in implementing systems or modifying existing systems to process elections, and subsequently in time incurred administering these systems. However, because section 6722(c)(3)(B) provides for a payee election, costs flow from the statute regardless of the proposed regulations. Additionally, filers that are small entities generally will have information reporting systems currently in place, and any costs incurred pursuant to the proposed regulations in modifying and implementing these systems are not expected to be significant. The rules in the proposed regulations provide clarity regarding the election process, which is expected to result in a more streamlined process.

Similarly, in those cases where payees opt to revoke a prior election, the expense of making the revocation will be borne by the payees, which generally will not be small entities. Filers that are small entities receiving revocations will benefit from the resulting applicability of the de minimis error safe harbor exceptions, resulting in reduced burden to file corrected information returns and furnish corrected payee statements because of de minimis errors. Filers that are small entities receiving revocations may incur costs in processing the revocations similar to those incurred in processing elections; however, it is expected that systems implementing payee elections can be modified with minimal additional cost to account for revocations in addition to elections. Filers that are small entities opting to provide the optional notification to payees regarding an alternative reasonable manner for making the election may incur costs in providing the notification. However, it is expected that filers will only provide optional notifications when they have determined that any cost in providing the notification is offset by a resulting economic benefit to the filer, such as a more cost-efficient election system. The record retention rules may also increase expenses for filers that are small entities; however, any added expenses are expected to be minimal given existing record retention systems. Pursuant to section 7805(f) of the Code, this notice of proposed rulemaking has been submitted to the Chief Counsel for Advocacy of the Small Business Administration for comment on its impact on small business.

Comments and Requests for Public Hearing

Before these proposed regulations are adopted as final regulations, consideration will be given to any comments that are timely submitted to the IRS as prescribed in the preamble under the **"ADDRESSES"** section. The Treasury Department and the IRS request comments on all aspects of these proposed regulations. All comments submitted will be made available at *www.regulations.gov* or upon request. A public hearing may be scheduled if requested in writing by any person that timely submits written comments. If a public hearing is scheduled, notice of the date, time, and place for the hearing will be published in the **Federal Register**.

Drafting Information

The principal author of these regulations is Mark A. Bond of the Office of the Associate Chief Counsel (Procedure and Administration).

[¶ 49,773] **Proposed Amendments of Regulations (REG-115420-18)**, published in the Federal Register on October 29, 2018 (corrected 12/31/2018).

[Code Sec. 1400Z-2]

Qualified opportunity zones: Qualified opportunity fund: Buildings and land: Original use and substantial improvement requirements.— Reg. §1.1400Z-2(a)-1, Reg. §1.1400Z-2(c)-1, Reg. §1.1400Z-2(d)-1 and Reg. §1.1400Z-2(e)-1, relating to gains that may be deferred as a result of a taxpayer's investment in a qualified opportunity fund (QOF), are adopted.

[¶ 49,780]   **Proposed Amendments of Regulations (REG-106089-18)**, published in the Federal Register on December 28, 2018.

[Code Secs. 163, 263A, 382, 383, 446, 469, 860C, 882, 1502 and 1504]

Trade or business: Interest deduction: Real property.—Reg. §§1.163(j)-0—1.163(j)-11 and amendments of Reg. §§1.263A-9, 1.381(c)(20)-1, 1.382-1, 1.382-2, 1.382-5, 1.382-6, 1.383-0, 1.383-1, 1.446-3, 1.469-9, 1.469-11, 1.860C-2, 1.882-5, 1.1502-13, 1.1502-21, 1.1502-36, 1.1502-79, 1.1502-90, 1.1502-91, 1.1502-95, 1.1502-98, 1.1502-99 and 1.1504-4, regarding the limitation on the deduction for business interest expense after the enactment of recent tax legislation, are proposed. Reg. Reg. §§1.163(j)-0—1.163(j)-10, proposed on June 18, 1991, are withdrawn.

AGENCY: Internal Revenue Service (IRS), Treasury.

ACTION: Notice of proposed rulemaking; notification of public hearing; and withdrawal of notice of proposed rulemaking.

SUMMARY: This notice of proposed rulemaking provides rules regarding the limitation on the deduction for business interest expense after the enactment of recent tax legislation. Specifically, these regulations provide general rules and definitions. The regulations also provide rules for calculating the limitation in consolidated group, partnership, and international contexts. The regulations affect taxpayers that have deductible business interest expense, other than certain small businesses, electing real property trades or businesses, electing farming businesses, and certain utility businesses. This document also withdraws a notice of proposed rulemaking relating to the disallowance of a deduction for certain interest paid or accrued by a corporation. This document also provides notice of a public hearing on the proposed regulations. DATES: Written or electronic comments must be received by February 26, 2019. Outlines of topics to be discussed at the public hearing scheduled for February 27, 2019, at 10 a.m. must be received by February 26, 2019. If there is not sufficient time to discuss all of the topics on February 27, 2019, the hearing will continue the following day at 10 a.m. in the same location.

ADDRESSES: Send submissions to: CC:PA:LPD:PR (REG-106089-18), Room 5203, P.O. Box 7604, Ben Franklin Station, Washington, DC 20044. Submissions may be hand-delivered Monday through Friday between the hours of 8 a.m. and 4 p.m. to CC:PA:LPD:PR (REG-106089-18), Courier's Desk, Internal Revenue Service, 1111 Constitution Avenue, NW, Washington, DC, 20224, or sent electronically, via the Federal Rulemaking Portal at http://www.regulations.gov (indicate IRS and REG-106089-18). The public hearing will be held in the Main IRS Auditorium beginning at 10 a.m. in the Internal Revenue Building, 1111 Constitution Avenue, NW, Washington, DC 20224.

FOR FURTHER INFORMATION CONTACT: Concerning §1.163(j)-1, §1.163(j)-2, §1.163(j)-3, §1.163(j)-9, or §1.263A-9, Zachary King, (202) 317-4875, Charles Gorham, (202) 317-5091, Susie Bird, (202) 317-4860, Jaime Park, (202) 317-4877, or Sophia Wang, (202) 317-4890; concerning §1.163(j)-4, §1.163(j)-5, §1.163(j)-10, §1.163(j)-11, §1.381(c)(20)-1, §1.382-1, §1.382-2, §1.382-5, §1.382-6, §1.383-0, §1.383-1, §1.1502-13, §1.1502-21, §1.1502-36, §1.1502-79, §1.1502-91, §1.1502-95, §1.1502-98, §1.1502-99, or §1.1504-4, Kevin M. Jacobs, (202) 317-5332, Russell Jones, (202) 317-5357, or John Lovelace, (202) 317-5363; concerning §1.163(j)-6 or §1.469-9(b)(2), Meghan Howard, (202) 317-5055, William Kostak, (202) 317-6852, Anthony McQuillen, (202) 317-5027, Adrienne Mikolashek, (202) 317-5050, or James Quinn (202) 317-5054; concerning §1.163(j)-7, §1.163(j)-8, or §1.882-5, Angela Holland, (202) 317-5474, Steve Jensen, (202) 317-6938, or Charles Rioux, (202) 317-6842; concerning §1.446-3, RICs, REITs, REMICs, and the definition of the term "interest", Michael Chin, (202) 317-5846; concerning submissions of comments and outlines of topics for the public hearing, Regina Johnson (202) 317-6901 (not toll-free numbers).

SUPPLEMENTARY INFORMATION:

Background

This document contains proposed amendments to the Income Tax Regulations (26 CFR part 1) under section 163(j) of the Internal Revenue Code (Code). Section 163(j) was amended as part of "An Act to provide for reconciliation pursuant to titles II and V of the concurrent resolution on the budget for fiscal year 2018," Public Law 115-97 (2017) (TCJA). Section 13301(a) of the TCJA amended section 163(j) by removing prior section 163(j)(1) through (9) and adding section 163(j)(1) through (10). The provisions of section 163(j) as amended by section 13301 of the TCJA are effective for tax years beginning after December 31, 2017. Unless otherwise indicated, all references to section 163(j) in this document are references to section 163(j) as amended by the TCJA.

Section 163(j), prior to the amendment by the TCJA (old section 163(j)), disallowed a deduction for "disqualified interest" paid or accrued by a corporation in a taxable year if two threshold tests were satisfied. The first threshold test under old section 163(j) was satisfied if the payor's debt-to-equity ratio exceeded 1.5 to 1.0 (safe harbor ratio). The second threshold test under old section 163(j) was satisfied if the payor's net interest expense exceeded 50 percent of its adjusted taxable income, generally, taxable income computed without regard to deductions for net interest expense, net operating losses, domestic production activities under section 199, depreciation, amortization, and depletion. Disqualified interest for purposes of old section 163(j) included interest paid or accrued to (1) related parties when no Federal income tax was imposed with respect to such interest; (2) unrelated parties in certain instances in which a related party guaranteed the debt; or (3) a real estate investment trust (REIT) by a taxable REIT subsidiary of that REIT. Interest amounts disallowed for any taxable year under old section 163(j) were treated as interest paid or accrued in the succeeding taxable year and could be carried forward indefinitely. In addition, any excess limitation, namely, the excess of 50 percent of the adjusted taxable income of the payor over the payor's net interest expense, could be carried forward three years under old section 163(j)(2)(B). On June 18, 1991, the Department of the Treasury (Treasury Department) and the IRS published in the **Federal Register** (56 FR 27907) a notice of proposed rulemaking (1991-2 C.B. 1040) (Prior Proposed Regulations) to implement the rules under old section 163(j).

In contrast to old section 163(j), for tax years beginning after December 31, 2017, section 163(j) generally limits the amount of business interest expense that can be deducted in the current taxable year (also referred to in this Explanation of Provisions as the current year). Under section 163(j)(1), the amount allowed as a deduction for business interest expense is limited to the sum of (1) the taxpayer's business interest income for the taxable year; (2) 30 percent of the taxpayer's adjusted taxable income (ATI) for the taxable year; and (3) the taxpayer's floor plan financing interest expense for the taxable year. The limitation under section 163(j)(1) applies to all taxpayers, except for certain small businesses that meet the gross receipts test in section 448(c) and certain trades or businesses listed in section 163(j)(7).

Section 163(j)(2) provides that the amount of any business interest not allowed as a deduction for any taxable year as a result of the limitation under section 163(j)(1) is carried forward and treated as business interest paid or accrued in the next taxable year. In contrast to old section 163(j), section 163(j) does not provide for the carryforward of any excess limitation.

Section 163(j)(3) provides that the limitation under section 163(j)(1) does not apply to a taxpayer, other than a tax shelter as defined in section 448(a)(3), with average annual gross receipts of $25 million or less, determined under section 448(c) (including any adjustment for inflation under section 448(c)(4)). For taxpayers other than corporations or partnerships, section 163(j)(3) provides that the gross receipts test is determined for purposes of section 163(j) as if the taxpayer were a corporation or partnership.

Section 163(j)(4) provides special rules for applying section 163(j) in the case of partnerships and S corporations. Section 163(j)(4)(A) requires that the limitation on the deduction for business interest expense be applied at the partnership level, and that a partner's ATI be increased by the partner's share of excess taxable income, as defined in section 163(j)(4)(C), but not by the partner's distributive share of income, gain, deduction, or loss. Section 163(j)(4)(B) provides that the amount of partnership business interest expense limited by section 163(j)(1) is carried forward at the partner-level. Section 163(j)(4)(B)(ii) provides that excess business interest expense allocated to a partner and carried forward is available to be deducted in a subsequent year only if the partnership allocates excess taxable income to the partner. Section 163(j)(4)(B)(iii) provides rules for the adjusted basis in a partnership of a partner that is allocated excess business interest expense. Section 163(j)(4)(D) provides that rules similar to the rules of section 163(j)(4)(A) and (C) apply to S corporations and S corporation shareholders.

Section 163(j)(5) and (6) defines "business interest" and "business interest income," respectively, for purposes of section 163(j). Generally, these terms include interest expense and interest includible in gross income that is properly allocable to a trade or business (as defined in section 163(j)(7)). The legislative history states that "a corporation has neither investment interest nor investment income within the meaning of section 163(d). Thus, interest income and interest expense of a corporation is properly allocable to a trade or business, unless such trade or business is otherwise explicitly excluded from the application of the provision." H. Rept. 115-466, at 386, fn. 688 (2017).

Under section 163(j)(7), the limitation on the deduction for business interest expense in section 163(j)(1) does not apply to certain trades or businesses. The excepted trades or businesses are the trade or business of providing services as an employee, electing real property businesses, electing farming businesses, and certain regulated utility businesses.

Section 163(j)(8) defines ATI as the taxable income of the taxpayer without regard to the following: items not properly allocable to a trade or business; business interest and business interest income; net operating loss deductions; and deductions for qualified business income under section 199A. ATI also generally excludes deductions for depreciation, amortization, and depletion with respect to taxable years beginning before January 1, 2022 and includes other adjustments provided by the Secretary of the Treasury.

Section 163(j)(9) defines "floor plan financing interest" as interest paid or accrued on "floor plan financing indebtedness." These provisions allow taxpayers incurring interest expense for the purpose of securing an inventory of motor vehicles held for sale or lease to deduct the full expense without regard to the limitation under section 163(j)(1).

Section 163(j)(10) provides cross references to provisions requiring that electing farming businesses and electing real property businesses excepted from the limitation under section 163(j)(1) use the alternative depreciation system (ADS), rather than the general depreciation system for certain types of property. The required use of ADS results in the inability of these electing trades or businesses to use the additional first-year depreciation deduction under section 168(k) for those types of property.

The Conference Report states that "[i]n the case of a group of affiliated corporations that file a consolidated return, the limitation applies at the consolidated tax return filing level." H. Rept. 115-466, at 386 (2017). Old section 163(j) treated an affiliated group as one taxpayer, and authorized super-affiliation rules for treating certain other groups as one taxpayer. Both of these provisions were removed by the TCJA, and no equivalent provisions are included in section 163(j).

On April 16, 2018, the Treasury Department and the IRS published Notice 2018-28 (2018-16 I.R.B. 492) to announce an intent to issue proposed regulations that will provide guidance to assist taxpayers in complying with section 163(j). Notice 2018-28 further describes certain rules that those proposed regulations will include to provide taxpayers with interim guidance as more comprehensive guidance is developed. In addition, Notice 2018-28 requested comments from taxpayers about the application of section 163(j). Where relevant to the provisions of these proposed regulations, comments are addressed in the Explanation of Provisions section.

Notice 2018-28 also stated the intent of the Treasury Department and the IRS to withdraw the Prior Proposed Regulations issued under old section 163(j).

Explanation of Provisions

These proposed regulations would withdraw the Prior Proposed Regulations and provide guidance regarding the new limitation on the deduction for business interest expense under section 163(j). These proposed regulations also would add or amend regulations under certain other provisions of the Code where necessary to provide conformity across the Income Tax Regulations. A significant number of the terms used throughout these proposed regulations are defined in proposed § 1.163(j)-1. Some of these terms are discussed in this Explanation of Provisions section as they relate to specific provisions of these proposed regulations.

Consistent with section 163(j)(1), these proposed regulations would limit a taxpayer's deduction for business interest expense to the sum of the taxpayer's current-year business interest income, 30 percent of the taxpayer's ATI, and certain floor plan financing interest expense. These proposed regulations would provide that any amount of business interest expense that cannot be deducted because of the limitation under section 163(j)(1) (section 163(j) limitation) can be carried forward and treated as business interest expense in future years. These proposed regulations also would provide special rules related to the business interest expense carried forward ("disallowed business interest expense carryforwards") by passthrough entities, C corporations, and consolidated groups. Amounts carried forward under old section 163(j) as disallowed disqualified interest are included as disallowed business interest expense carryforwards of a taxpayer to the extent that the amounts otherwise qualify as business interest expense of the taxpayer under these proposed regulations.

These proposed regulations are organized into eleven sections, proposed §§ 1.163(j)-1 through 1.163(j)-11. Proposed § 1.163(j)-1 would provide common definitions used throughout the proposed regulations. Proposed § 1.163(j)-2 would provide general rules relating to the computation of a taxpayer's section 163(j) limitation and proposed § 1.163(j)-3 would provide ordering and other rules regarding the relationship of the section 163(j) limitation and other provisions of the Code affecting interest. Proposed § 1.163(j)-4 would provide rules applicable to C corporations (including REITs, RICs, and consolidated group members) and tax-exempt corporations, whereas proposed § 1.163(j)-5 would provide rules governing the disallowed business interest expense carryforwards of C corporations. Proposed § 1.163(j)-6 would provide special rules for applying the section 163(j) limitation to partnerships and S corporations. Proposed § 1.163(j)-7 would provide rules regarding the application of section 163(j) to foreign corporations and their shareholders, whereas proposed § 1.163(j)-8 would provide rules regarding the application of section 163(j) to foreign persons with effectively connected income. Proposed § 1.163(j)-9 would provide rules regarding elections for excepted trades or businesses as well as a safe harbor for certain REITs. Proposed § 1.163(j)-10 would provide rules to allocate expense and income between non-excepted and excepted trades or businesses. Finally, proposed § 1.163(j)-11 would provide certain transition rules relating to the application of the section 163(j) limitation. The remainder of this Explanation of Provisions section discusses these eleven sections, as well as related conforming and coordinating provisions set forth in these proposed regulations.

1. Proposed § 1.163(j)-1: Definitions

Proposed § 1.163(j)-1 would provide definitions of terms used in these proposed regulations. This part 1 of the Explanation of Provisions section briefly discusses the most significant definitions contained in proposed § 1.163(j)-1.

A. Adjusted Taxable Income

i. Background

The Prior Proposed Regulations under old section 163(j) defined adjusted taxable income to include a number of adjustments in addition to those set forth in the statutory text of old section 163(j). Some of the additional adjustments resulted in an adjusted taxable income value that approximated cash flow. Two commenters to Notice 2018-28 asked if ATI for purposes of section 163(j) would also attempt to approximate cash flow. Comments on the Prior Proposed Regulations raised a number of administrative concerns with the additions and subtractions to ATI that approximated cash flow in those proposed regulations. The Prior Proposed Regulations were not finalized and therefore did not incorporate the suggestions of these comments to abandon this approach. In addition, because the Prior Proposed Regulations were never finalized, the approach of the Prior Proposed Regulations was never formally required or adopted. Finally, nothing in the Conference Report or the text of section 163(j) requires or suggests that adjustments should be made to ATI in order to approximate cash flow. Such a requirement could have been written into the statutory language or the discussion of section 163(j) contained in the Conference Report if Congress intended ATI to be adjusted in such a manner.

As a result, these proposed regulations would not adopt a cash flow approach to ATI. Instead, proposed §1.163(j)-1(b)(1) would follow the statutory framework of section 163(j)(8) and define ATI to include the adjustments specified in section 163(j)(8)(A), as well as additional adjustments under the authority granted in section 163(j)(8)(B) to prevent double counting and other distortions of items such as floor plan financing interest expense and certain deductions for depreciation, amortization, or depletion upon the sale or disposition of property.

ii. General Application of the Definition of ATI

To compute ATI, taxpayers would first compute taxable income, as defined in proposed §1.163(j)-1(b)(37), in accordance with section 63. In computing taxable income for this purpose, taxpayers would treat all business interest expense as deductible without regard to the section 163(j) limitation. Second, taxpayers would add or subtract, as appropriate, the items specified in these proposed regulations as adjustments to taxable income.

iii. Adjustments to ATI Specifically Referenced in Section 163(j)(8)(A)

Proposed §1.163(j)-1(b)(1) includes as adjustments to taxable income items specifically referenced in section 163(j)(8)(A): any item of income, gain, deduction, or loss which is not properly allocable to a trade or business; business interest and business interest income; net operating loss deductions under section 172; deductions for qualified business income under section 199A; and, deductions for depreciation, amortization, and depletion, but only with respect to taxable years beginning before January 1, 2022. *Net* operating losses under section 172 are added to taxable income in determining ATI, including net operating losses arising in taxable years prior to the effective date of these proposed regulations and carried forward. For purposes of computing ATI, it is intended that deductions for depreciation include special allowances under section 168(k). Additionally, to clarify an issue raised by a commenter in response to Notice 2018-28, the Treasury Department and the IRS note that an amount incurred as depreciation, amortization, or depletion, but capitalized to inventory under section 263A and included in cost of goods sold, is not a deduction for depreciation, amortization, or depletion for purposes of section 163(j).

iv. Other Adjustments to ATI Under Section 163(j)(8)(B)

These proposed regulations would include a number of adjustments under the authority granted in section 163(j)(8)(B). For example, these proposed regulations would include special rules that apply in defining the taxable income of: a regulated investment company (RIC) or REIT in proposed §1.163(j)-4(b)(4)(ii); a consolidated group in proposed §1.163(j)-4(d)(2)(iv); a partnership in proposed §1.163(j)-6(d)(1); an S corporation in proposed §1.163(j)-6(l)(3); and certain controlled foreign corporations in proposed §1.163(j)-7(c)(1).

Under the authority granted in section 163(j)(8)(B), proposed §1.163(j)-1(b)(1) also includes additional adjustments to prevent double counting. Thus, in addition to a subtraction for any floor plan financing interest expense, these proposed regulations include adjustments for sales or dispositions of certain property for taxable years beginning before January 1, 2022. Proposed §1.163(j)-1(b)(1)(i)(D), (E), and (F) would provide that in determining the amount of a taxpayer's ATI for a taxable year, deductions for depreciation under section 167 or 168, the amortization of intangibles and other amortized expenditures, and depletion under section 611 are added back to a taxpayer's taxable income. As a result, the taxpayer would have increased their taxable income by these amounts for section 163(j) purposes. However, the Treasury Department and the IRS note that a taxpayer could receive a double benefit associated with the depreciation, amortization, and depletion, for ATI calculation purposes if the taxpayer's ATI is increased in respect of a deduction associated with depreciation, amortization, or depletion and then the taxpayer sells or otherwise disposes of the property that was depreciated, amortized, or depleted. This double benefit would result because the amount of the gain that would otherwise be reflected in the ATI in respect of the sale or other disposition would reflect the decreased basis in such assets as a result of the depreciation, amortization, or depletion. Additionally, similar concerns are present if the property was held by either a partnership or a member of a consolidated group and the partnership interest or the stock of the member is sold or otherwise disposed of, because the adjusted basis in the partnership interest or member stock would have been reduced to reflect the depreciation, amortization, or depletion. As a result, these proposed regulations would eliminate the double benefit associated with these sales or other dispositions of property. See proposed §1.163(j)-1(b)(1)(ii)(C), (D), and (E).

v. Other Rules for Adjusting ATI

Taxpayers can take each adjustment into account only once for purposes of computing ATI; for instance, a deduction for the depreciation of nonbusiness property under section 167 cannot be taken into account as an adjustment to taxable income as both a deduction for depreciation and an item of deduction that is not properly allocable to a trade or business. For purposes of computing ATI, only the adjustments to taxable income that are specified in these proposed regulations may be made. For instance, a deduction under section 243 for dividends received by a C corporation that is neither a RIC nor a REIT reduces the taxable income of the C corporation, and the C corporation cannot add back the amount of such deduction in computing ATI. Proposed §1.163(j)-4(c)(2) would provide special rules that affect deductions under section 243 for RICs and REITs.

If for a taxable year a taxpayer is allowed a deduction under section 250(a)(1), the taxpayer should take into account the deduction when computing taxable income that is used to calculate ATI, but these proposed regulations would provide that the taxable income limitation in section 250(a)(2) does not apply for this purpose. Taxpayers, however, may be required to make adjustments adding back the section 250(a)(1) deduction to the extent that some or all of the deduction is attributable to an inclusion under section 951A. See proposed §1.163(j)-7(d).

A separate set of proposed regulations under development will provide general guidance regarding section 250, including the computation of the section 250 deduction and the application of the taxable income limitation in section 250(a)(2).

vi. Comment Request Related to Ordering of Code Provisions

The Treasury Department and the IRS are also aware that various Code provisions in addition to sections 163(j) and 250 (for example, see section 246(b)), affect the amount of taxable income of a taxpayer and are based on, or are limited in some fashion based upon, the taxable income of the taxpayer. As a result, ordering rules are necessary to coordinate application of all of these provisions of the Code with one another. The Treasury Department and the IRS request comments on this matter, which presents broader issues than the ordering of these provisions relative to the application of section 163(j) and may therefore be addressed in guidance unrelated to these proposed regulations.

vii. Comment Request Related to the Computation of ATI

The Treasury Department and the IRS request comments regarding the methodology for computing ATI for purposes of these proposed section 163(j) regulations, including any items that should be included as additional adjustments to taxable income.

B. Interest

There are no generally applicable regulations or statutory provisions addressing when financial instruments are treated as debt for Federal income tax purposes or when a payment is interest. As a result, the proposed regulations draw upon past guidance and case law that address the meaning of interest in the context of Federal tax law. As a general matter, the factors that distinguish debt from equity are described in Notice 94-47, 1994-1 C.B. 357, and interest is defined as compensation for the use or forbearance of money. *Deputy v. Dupont*, 308 U.S. 488 (1940). Using these well-established principles regarding the meaning of interest, these proposed regulations would define interest to include any amount paid or accrued as compensation for the use or forbearance of money under the terms of an instrument or contractual arrangement, including a series of transactions, that is treated as a debt instrument for purposes of section 1275(a) and §1.1275-1(d) (similar to the definition of interest described in *Deputy v. Dupont*). Thus, these proposed regulations would apply to interest associated with conventional debt instruments, as well as transactions that are indebtedness in substance although not in form. See *Schering-Plough Corp. v. U.S.*, 651 F.Supp. 2d 219 (N.J. Dist. Ct. 2009), aff'd sub nom. *Merck & Co., Inc. v. U.S.*, 652 F.3d 475 (3d Cir. 2011); *Mapco Inc. v. U.S.*, 556 F.2d 1107 (Ct. Cl. 1977). The interest definition in these proposed regulations also would include any amount treated as interest under other provisions of the Code or the regulations thereunder, such as original issue discount, accrued market discount, and amounts with respect to an integrated transaction under §1.1275-6.

For purposes of section 163(j), these proposed regulations also would treat as interest certain amounts that are closely related to interest and that affect the economic yield or cost of funds of a transaction involving interest, but that may not be compensation for the use or forbearance of money on a stand-alone basis. Income, deduction, gain, or loss from a transaction used to hedge an interest bearing asset or liability, a substitute interest payment made on a debt instrument under the terms of a securities lending or a sale-repurchase transaction, certain commitment fees, and certain debt issuance costs are examples of amounts that would be treated as interest under these proposed regulations. In addition, in order to prevent transactions that are essentially financing transactions from avoiding the application of section 163(j), these proposed regulations contain an anti-avoidance rule that treats as interest expense for purposes of section 163(j) an expense or loss predominantly incurred in consideration of the time value of money in a transaction or series of integrated or related transactions in which a taxpayer secures the use of funds for a period of time.

Treating amounts that are closely related to interest as interest income or expense when appropriate to achieve a statutory purpose is not new; most of the rules treating such payments as interest in these proposed regulations were developed in §§1.861-9T and 1.954-2. As a consequence of these rules, however, in some cases certain items could be tested under section 163(j) that are not treated as interest under other provisions that interpret the definition of interest more narrowly. Thus, for example, in certain cases, an amount that was previously deductible under section 162 without limitation could now be tested as business interest expense under section 163(j).

As previously noted, these proposed regulations address the treatment of a commitment fee paid in connection with a lending transaction. This treatment is based on a rule in §1.954-2(h). The Treasury Department and the IRS request comments on whether other types of fees paid in connection with a lending transaction that are not otherwise treated as interest for Federal income tax purposes should be treated as interest for purposes of section 163(j). As also previously noted, these proposed regulations would treat as interest certain amounts that are closely related to interest and that affect the economic yield or cost of funds of transactions involving interest. The Treasury Department and the IRS request comments on whether additional guidance is needed regarding amounts that are covered or not covered by this rule, specific types of amounts that should or should not be covered, how such amounts are linked to related transactions involving interest, and how such amounts are treated for financial reporting or other nontax purposes. More generally, the Treasury Department and the IRS request comments on whether other types of income and expense should be treated as interest income or interest expense for purposes of section 163(j). For example, should income earned by a taxpayer in a transaction in which the taxpayer provides the use of funds be treated as interest income of the taxpayer if such income is earned predominantly in consideration of the time value of money?

Finally, these proposed regulations generally would treat a swap with significant nonperiodic payments as two separate transactions consisting of an on-market, level payment swap and a loan. The loan would be accounted for by the parties to the contract independently of the swap. The time value component associated with the loan, determined in accordance with §1.446-3(f)(2)(iii)(A), would be recognized as interest expense to the payor and interest income to the recipient. This provision in these proposed regulations would apply in the same manner as §1.446-3(g)(4) before it was amended on May 8, 2015, by T.D. 9719 (80 FR 26437, as corrected by 80 FR 61308 (October 13, 2015)), except that this provision would not apply to a collateralized swap that is cleared by a derivatives clearing organization or by a clearing agency. The treatment of such collateralized cleared swaps is reserved, and these proposed regulations would not require testing the assets used for collateralization or condition the exception for collateralized cleared swaps on the extent of collateralization. The Treasury Department and the IRS request comments on the proper treatment of swaps that are cleared by a derivatives clearing organization or by a clearing agency, and any requirements with respect to collateralization that would be necessary or appropriate to identify swaps that could be used to effectively advance funds through the use of nonperiodic payments.

The Treasury Department and the IRS considered three options with respect to the definition of interest. The first option considered was to not provide a definition of interest, and thus rely on general tax principles and case law for purposes of defining interest for purposes of section 163(j). While adopting this option might reduce the compliance burden for some taxpayers, not providing an explicit definition of interest would create its own uncertainty as neither taxpayers nor the IRS might have a clear sense of what types of payments are treated as interest income and interest expense for purposes of section 163(j). Such uncertainty could increase burdens to the IRS and taxpayers including with respect to disputes and litigation about whether particular payments are interest for section 163(j) purposes. Importantly, this option could be distortive as it could result in inappropriate outcomes for taxpayers that earn income that is economically similar to interest income but that has not historically been so treated under general tax principles. For example, in the case of the acquisition of a customer receivable at a discount, existing income tax principles may treat the difference between the acquisition price and the amount ultimately paid on the receivable as ordinary income that is not interest income. In addition, such an approach to the definition of interest would incentivize taxpayers to engage in transactions that provide leverage while generating deductions economically similar to interest but make arguments that such deductions fail to be described by existing principles defining interest expense. If successful, such strategies may greatly limit the application of section 163(j), contrary to the Congressional intent of limiting the deductibility of interest of businesses with the greatest levels of leverage. See House Report, H.R. 115-409 at 248. In addition, such an approach may ignore the statutory language of section 163(j)(1) "[t]he amount allowed as a deduction *under this chapter* for any taxable year for business interest . . . " (emphasis added), which is, on its face, broader than merely deductions under section 163.

The second option considered would have been to adopt a definition of interest but limit the scope of the definition to cover only amounts associated with conventional debt instruments and amounts that are generally treated as interest under the Code or regulations for all purposes prior to the passage of the TCJA. For example, this is similar to the definition of interest proposed in §1.163(j)-1(b)(20)(i). While this would bring clarity to many transactions regarding what would be deemed interest for the section 163(j) limitation, the Treasury Department and the IRS believe that this approach would potentially distort future financing transactions. Some taxpayers would choose to use financial instruments and transactions that provide a similar economic result to using a conventional debt instrument, but would avoid the label of interest expense under such a definition, potentially enabling these taxpayers to avoid the section 163(j) limitation without a substantive change in capital structure. As a result, the transactions discussed in the prior paragraph would continue to be possible and incentivized under this approach.

In addition, there are certain transactions where under a specific provision of the Code and regulations, amounts could be characterized as ordinary income when in substance the amounts are interest income. For example, in the case of the acquisition of a customer receivable at a discount, existing income tax principles may treat the difference between the acquisition price and the amount ultimately paid on the receivable as ordinary income that is not interest income; however, such income would count as interest income under economic principles. As another example, the receipt of substitute interest paid on a securities loan arrangement may, under existing income tax principles, also be treated as ordinary income rather than interest income despite the fact that such income would also be treated as interest income under economic principles. Prior to the enactment of the section 163(j) interest limitation in TCJA, whether such amounts were labeled as ordinary income or interest income was not often material to the overall tax liability of most taxpayers, but now this distinction may have a significant impact on a large number of taxpayers.

The final option considered and the one ultimately adopted in these proposed regulations is to provide a complete definition of interest that addresses all transactions that are commonly understood to produce interest income and expense, including transactions that may otherwise have been entered into to avoid the application of section 163(j). This approach has the advantage of also providing rules that clearly treat amounts as interest in appropriate cases. Although a comprehensive definition of interest requires an unavoidable degree of detail, the benefits of a detailed definition should decidedly outweigh any complexity that results. The proposed regulations also reduce taxpayer burden by adopting definitions of interest that have already been developed and administered in §§ 1.861-9T and 1.954-2, and add several definitions of interest income that were suggested by commenters (such as the rules regarding amounts on contingent payment debt instruments in § 1.163(j)-1(b)(20)(iii)(B)).

The Treasury Department and the IRS invite comments on the definition of interest for purposes of section 163(j) contained in these proposed regulations, whether another definition of interest would be more appropriate in the context of section 163(j), and, generally, what definition of interest would be the most appropriate definition for purposes of section 163(j).

C. Trades or Businesses and Excepted Trades or Businesses

While section 163(j) and the legislative history to section 163(j) provide that certain activities are not treated as trades or businesses, neither section 163(j) nor its legislative history provide a definition of what activities generally constitute a trade or business. The most established and developed definition of trade or business is found under section 162(a), which permits a deduction for ordinary and necessary expenses paid or incurred in carrying on a trade or business. The rules under section 162 for determining the existence of a trade or business are well-established, and there is a large body of case law and administrative guidance interpreting the meaning in section 162 of a trade or business. Therefore, these proposed regulations would define a trade or business as a trade or business within the meaning of section 162, and such definition should aid taxpayers in the proper allocation of interest expense, interest income, and other tax items to a trade or business and an excepted trade or business.

These proposed regulations would also define excepted trades or businesses that are not subject to the limitation of interest expense deduction under section 163(j). These excepted trades or businesses are defined in 163(j)(7)(A), and include (1) the trade or business of providing services as an employee; (2) certain real property businesses that elect to be excepted; (3) certain farming businesses that elect to be excepted; and (4) certain regulated utility businesses. These proposed regulations would provide additional guidance with respect to regulated utility businesses and the allocation of interest expense to such businesses. See proposed §§ 1.163(j)-1(b)(13) and 1.163(j)-10. Proposed regulations under section 469 would provide additional detail with respect to the definition of a real property trade or business. See proposed § 1.469-9(b).

The Treasury Department and the IRS invite comments on whether another definition of trade or business would be preferable or appropriate in the context of section 163(j).

D. Electing Real Property Trade or Business

These proposed regulations would provide that taxpayers can make an election to treat certain trades or businesses as an excepted trade or business if it is a real property trade or business under section 469(c)(7)(C), or certain trades or businesses that are conducted by REITs. Definitions and special rules for REITs would be provided in proposed § 1.163(j)-9.

E. Electing Farming Business

These proposed regulations would provide that taxpayers can make an election to treat a trade or business that is a farming business as defined in section 263A(e)(4) or that is a farming business under § 1.263A-4(a)(4) for capitalization purposes as an excepted farming business for purposes of section 163(j). These proposed regulations would also provide that a trade or business that is a specified agricultural or horticultural cooperative under section 199A(g)(4) and regulations thereunder can elect to be an excepted farming business for purposes of section 163(j). The Treasury Department and the IRS note that section 163(j)(7)(B) cites section 199A(g)(2) for the definition of a specified agricultural or horticultural cooperative. However, after Public Law 115-141 amended section 199A, the correct citation is section 199A(g)(4). Additionally, the Treasury Department and the IRS are developing separate proposed regulations to provide additional guidance under section 199A(g).

F. Regulated Utility Trade or Business

Consistent with section 163(j)(7)(A)(iv), these proposed regulations would provide that an excepted trade or business includes a regulated utility trade or business that furnishes or sells certain regulated items to the extent the rates for such furnishing or sale have been established or approved by a State or political subdivision thereof, by any agency or instrumentality of the United States, by a public service or public utility commission or other similar body of any State or political subdivision thereof, or by the governing or ratemaking body of an electric cooperative. Certain regulated items are electrical energy, water, or sewage disposal services; gas or steam through a local distribution system; or transportation of gas or steam by pipeline.

Section 163(j) does not define the term "electric cooperative" either directly or by reference to other provisions of the Code. The tax treatment of an electric cooperative is generally governed by section 501(c)(12) of the Code, sections 1381 through 1388 in subchapter T of chapter 1 of subtitle A of the Code (subchapter T), or the common law applicable to cooperatives prior to the enactment of subchapter T. For purposes of section 163(j), the tax treatment of an electric cooperative is not relevant because the statutory language of section 163(j)(7)(A) only requires that rates be set by the ratemaking body of an electric cooperative and does not impose a requirement that the electric cooperative have any particular tax treatment. Accordingly, for purposes of section 163(j), the term electric cooperative includes an electric cooperative that is exempt from income tax under section 501(c)(12), an electric cooperative that is taxable under subchapter T, and an electric cooperative furnishing electric energy to persons in rural areas that is taxable under pre-subchapter T law.

A commenter suggested that rules similar to those that have been used to define public utility property under section 168(i)(10) be used to determine the trade or business that qualifies as a regulated public utility and to distinguish between a regulated and a non-regulated trade or business. The statutory language of section 163(j)(7)(A)(iv) is very similar to that provided under section 168(i)(10) for the definition of a public utility property. Under section 168(i)(10), public utility property is defined as property that is predominately used in one of the enumerated trades or business, which includes the furnishing or sale of certain regulated items listed in section 163(j)(7)(A)(iv), and where the rates for such furnishing or sale are established or approved on a cost of service and rate of return basis.

The Treasury Department and the IRS are aware that such furnishing or sale of the regulated items may not have been established or approved on a cost of service and rate of return basis by a governing or ratemaking body. For example, a public utility may sell some of its electrical energy output at market rates. In this situation, the activity related to the sales at market rates would not be treated as activities related to an excepted regulated utility trade or business under these proposed regulations. Thus, these proposed regulations would provide that to the extent a taxpayer is engaged in both excepted and non-excepted regulated utility trades or businesses, the taxpayer must allocate tax items between the trades or businesses if less than 90 percent of the total output is sold on a cost of service and rate of return basis. Some regulated utility trades or businesses with de minimis market rate sales, rather than pursuant to a cost of service and rate of return basis, are treated as entirely excepted trades or businesses. See proposed §1.163(j)-10(c)(3)(iii)(C)(3). Guidance related to the allocation methodology for regulated public utility trades or businesses is also provided in proposed §1.163(j)-10(c)(3)(ii)(C).

G. Floor Plan Financing Interest Expense

These proposed regulations would provide that certain business interest expense paid or accrued on indebtedness used to acquire an inventory of motor vehicles is deductible without regard to the section 163(j) limitation. These proposed regulations would treat all floor plan financing interest expense as business interest expense for purposes of section 163(j), regardless of whether it would otherwise be considered properly allocable to a trade or business that is not excepted under section 163(j).

One commenter to Notice 2018-28 recommended a rule that debt incurred to purchase construction machinery or equipment for sale or lease to farmers should be considered floor plan financing indebtedness for purposes of section 163(j). While H.R. 1, 115th Cong. (as passed by the House of Representatives, November 16, 2017) included construction machinery and equipment in the definition of "motor vehicle" for purposes of floor plan financing indebtedness, the TCJA does not include such machinery and equipment in the statutory definition. The definition of "motor vehicle" for purposes of floor plan financing indebtedness is based on the equipment held for sale or lease, not on the kind of business that the purchaser or lessee is engaged in. Therefore, these proposed regulations do not include the rule suggested by the commenter and merely cross-reference the definition of "motor vehicle" as set forth in section 163(j)(9)(C).

2. Proposed §1.163(j)-2: Deduction for Business Interest Expense Limited

A. General Rules

Consistent with section 163(j)(1), these proposed regulations would provide that the deduction for business interest expense for any taxpayer, other than businesses qualifying for the small business exemption, cannot exceed the sum of current-year business interest income, 30 percent of ATI, and current-year floor plan financing interest expense. See proposed §1.163(j)-2(b).

To the extent that a taxpayer has business interest expense for the taxable year in excess of the section 163(j) limitation, these proposed regulations would allow the taxpayer a disallowed business interest expense carryforward to the next taxable year. See proposed §1.163(j)-2(c). The limitation under section 163(j)(1) applies to the total amount of business interest expense of the taxpayer in a taxable year (including disallowed business interest expense carryforwards from prior taxable years) and does not directly trace to interest expense in respect of any particular debt obligation of the taxpayer. Similarly, the disallowed business interest expense carryforward allowed in a taxable year represents the total amount of disallowed business interest expense that is carried forward to the taxable year and does not directly trace to a particular debt obligation of a taxpayer.

B. Exemption for Certain Small Taxpayers; Aggregation; Inherently Personal Items

Consistent with section 163(j)(3), these proposed regulations would provide that taxpayers that meet the gross receipts test of section 448(c) are not subject to the section 163(j) limitation. Eligible taxpayers are those, other than tax shelters under section 448(a)(3), with average annual gross receipts of $25 million or less, tested for the three taxable years immediately preceding the current taxable year. Such a taxpayer is not permitted to make an election under either section 163(j)(7)(B) or (C) because the taxpayer is already not subject to the section 163(j) limitation.

The gross receipts test of section 448(c) is an annual determination based on the prior three taxable years. Thus, a taxpayer's status as an exempt small business under section 163(j) may change from year to year. Because the exemption applies to the taxpayer, any interest paid or accrued in the taxable year in which the taxpayer meets the gross receipts test under section 448(c) is not subject to the section 163(j) limitation. Accordingly, and consistent with section 163(j)(2), these proposed regulations would provide that if a taxpayer who is subject to the limitation under section 163(j)(1) carries disallowed business interest expense forward to a taxable year in which the taxpayer qualifies for the small business exemption, the amount of the carryforward is not subject to the section 163(j) limitation in that taxable year and would be deductible in that taxable year unless disallowed, deferred, or capitalized under another provision of the Code.

Consistent with the regulations under section 448(c), for organizations that are exempt from tax under section 501(a), these proposed regulations would provide that only gross receipts from the activities of such organization that constitute unrelated trades or businesses are taken into account in determining whether the gross receipts test is satisfied. The Treasury Department and the IRS request comments on whether additional guidance is needed in the case of any other exempt organizations with respect to the application of the gross receipts test for purposes of section 163(j).

These proposed regulations would also provide that each partner in a partnership includes a share of partnership gross receipts in proportion to such partner's distributive share of items of gross income that were taken into account by the partnership under section 703. With respect to shareholders in S corporations, these regulations would provide that such shareholders include a pro rata share of the S corporation's gross receipts. The Treasury Department and the IRS request comments on this approach, and also whether other approaches to determining the gross receipts of partners and S corporation shareholders for purposes of section 163(j) would more accurately measure the gross receipts of such partners and shareholders.

These proposed regulations would provide that a taxpayer who is not subject to section 448 is treated as though it were a partnership or corporation when applying the section 448(c) gross receipts test for purposes of the section 163(j) small business exemption. The aggregation rules of sections 52 and 414 would apply to determine whether entities should be aggregated for purposes of the gross receipts test. For an individual taxpayer, it is intended that gross receipts include all items that a business entity could receive, including, but not limited to, business receipts and investment receipts. The only items that an individual taxpayer may exclude from gross receipts for the purpose of the section 163(j) small business exemption are inherently personal items. Inherently personal items include Social Security benefits, personal injury awards and settlements, disability benefits, and wages received as an employee that are reported on Form W-2. Guaranteed payments are not generally equivalent to salaries and wages. See Rev. Rul. 69-187. The Treasury Department and the IRS request comments regarding the scope of inherently personal items.

3. Proposed §1.163(j)-3: Relationship of Business Interest Deduction Limitation to Other Provisions Affecting Interest

These proposed regulations would provide ordering and operating rules to control the interaction of the section 163(j) limitation with other provisions of the Code. The legislative history to the TCJA shows an intent for section 163(j) to apply after other provisions that defer, capitalize, or disallow interest expense. See H. Rept. 115-466, at 387 (2017). Therefore, these proposed regulations generally would apply to interest expense that could be deducted without regard to the section 163(j) limitation; interest expense that has been disallowed, deferred, or capitalized in the current taxable year, or which has not yet been accrued, would not be taken into account for purposes of section 163(j). However, it is intended that, under these proposed regulations, section 163(j) would apply before the operation of the loss limitation rules in sections 465 and 469 and before the application of section 461(l), consistent with how taxpayers apply old section 163(j)(7). In addition, the Treasury Department and the IRS request comments regarding the interaction between section 163(j) and the rules addressing income from discharge of indebtedness under section 108.

The Treasury Department and the IRS have received comments on the interaction of sections 163(j) and 59A, relating to the tax on the base erosion minimum tax amount. These proposed regulations reserve on the interaction of these provisions. The comments previously received, as well as any additional comments received, will be further considered in conjunction with separate guidance under section 59A.

4. *Proposed § 1.163(j)-4: General Rules Applicable to C Corporations (including REITs, RICs, and Members of Consolidated Groups) and Tax-Exempt Corporations*

Proposed § 1.163(j)-4 would provide certain rules regarding the computation of items of income and expense under section 163(j) for taxpayers that are C corporations (including members of a consolidated group, REITs, and RICs) and tax-exempt corporations. Proposed § 1.163(j)-4(b) would provide rules regarding the characterization of items of income, gain, deduction, or loss. Proposed § 1.163(j)-4(c) would provide rules regarding adjustments to earnings and profits. Proposed § 1.163(j)-4(d) would provide special rules applicable to members of a consolidated group.

A. Proposed § 1.163(j)-4(b): Characterization of Items of Income, Gain, Deduction, or Loss

Like other taxpayers, corporations are subject to the limitations on the deductibility of business interest expense in section 163(j). However, unlike other taxpayers, corporations are not subject to the limitations on the deductibility of investment interest expense in section 163(d). In enacting section 163(j), which excludes from the definition of business interest in section 163(j)(5), investment interest within the meaning of section 163(d), and excludes from the definition of business interest income, investment income within the meaning of section 163(d), Congress commented on the interaction between section 163(d) and (j) and the implications thereof for the application of section 163(j) to corporations. More specifically, the legislative history states that—

[s]ection 163(d) applies in the case of a taxpayer other than a corporation. Thus, a corporation has neither investment interest nor investment income within the meaning of section 163(d). Thus, interest income and interest expense of a corporation is properly allocable to a trade or business, unless such trade or business is otherwise explicitly excluded from the application of the provision.

H. Rept. 115-466, at 386, fn. 688 (2017).

Although the foregoing language could be read to apply to both C corporations and S corporations, it is clear that an S corporation can have investment income and investment expenses within the meaning of section 163(d). These items are separately stated on an S corporation's Schedule K-1, "Partner's Share of Income, Deductions, Credits, etc.," and they are passed through to an S corporation's shareholders. Thus, Congress appears to have made the foregoing statement with C corporations in mind.

Consistent with congressional intent, proposed § 1.163(j)-4(b) would provide that, solely for purposes of section 163(j), and except as otherwise provided in proposed § 1.163(j)-10 (concerning allocations between excepted and non-excepted trades or businesses), all interest paid or accrued by a taxpayer that is a C corporation is treated as business interest expense, and all interest received or accrued by a taxpayer that is a C corporation and that is includible in the taxpayer's gross income is treated as business interest income. Thus, all of a C corporation's interest expense would be subject to limitation under section 163(j), and all of a C corporation's interest income would increase the C corporation's section 163(j) limitation, except to the extent such interest expense or interest income is allocable to an excepted trade or business under proposed § 1.163(j)-10.

To reflect congressional intent, and to achieve consistency with the treatment of interest income and interest expense, proposed § 1.163(j)-4(b) would further provide that, solely for purposes of section 163(j), and except as otherwise provided in proposed § 1.163(j)-10, all other items of income, gain, deduction, or loss of a taxpayer that is a C corporation are properly allocable to a trade or business. As a result, such tax items would be factored into a C corporation's calculation of its ATI (except to the extent such items are allocable to an excepted trade or business).

Although a C corporation cannot have investment interest, investment expenses, or investment income, within the meaning of section 163(d), for purposes of section 163(j), a partnership in which a C corporation is a partner may have such tax items. The partnership will allocate such tax items to its partners, including its C corporation partners, as separately stated items. Thus, the question arises how to treat investment interest, investment expenses, and investment income that is allocated by a partnership to a C corporation partner.

To address this situation, proposed § 1.163(j)-4(b) would recharacterize investment interest expense that a partnership allocates to a C corporation partner as interest expense properly allocable to a trade or business of the C corporation.

Similarly, proposed § 1.163(j)-4(b) would treat investment income and investment expenses that a partnership allocates to a C corporation partner as properly allocable to a trade or business of the C corporation. See the discussion in part 6(G) of this Explanation of Provisions section. However, this rule would not apply to the extent a C corporation partner is allocated a share of a domestic partnership's gross income inclusions under section 951(a) or 951A(a) that are treated as investment income at the partnership level. See § 1.163(j)-7(d)(1)(ii) and the discussion in part 7 of this Explanation of Provisions section.

The recharacterization of investment items at the C corporation partner level under proposed § 1.163(j)-4(b) would not affect the character of these items at the partnership level. It also would not affect the character of the investment interest, investment income, and investment expenses allocated to other (non-C corporation) partners.

Investment interest expense of a partnership that is treated as business interest expense by the C corporation partner would not be treated as excess business interest expense within the meaning of section 163(j)(4)(b)(i) and proposed § 1.163(j)-6. Similarly, investment interest income of a partnership that is treated as business interest income by the C corporation partner would not be treated as excess taxable income within the meaning of section 163(j)(4)(C) and proposed § 1.163(j)-6. This is the case because these items were not treated as business interest expense or factored into the ATI calculation, respectively, at the partnership level. For a discussion of the rules governing excess business interest expense and excess taxable income, see part 6 of this Explanation of Provisions section.

Except as otherwise provided in proposed § 1.163(j)-4(b)(4)(ii) and (iii), the foregoing rules would apply to RICs and REITs. The Treasury Department and the IRS request comments on whether additional special rules are needed for any other entities that are generally taxed as C corporations, including but not limited to cooperatives (as defined in section 1381(a)) and publicly traded partnerships (as defined in section 7704(b)).

These rules also would apply to a corporation that is subject to the unrelated business income tax under section 511, but only with respect to such corporation's items of income, gain, deduction, or loss that are taken into account in computing the corporation's unrelated business taxable income.

B. Proposed § 1.163(j)-4(c): Effect on Earnings and Profits

Distributions by a C corporation to its shareholders out of earnings and profits (E&P) are treated as dividends under section 316(a). Although the Code does not define the term "earnings and profits," the computation of E&P generally is based upon accounting concepts that take into account the economic realities of corporate transactions, in particular, their impact on the corporation's economic ability to pay dividends to its shareholders, and the applicable tax laws.

Proposed § 1.163(j)-4(c) generally would provide that the disallowance and carryforward of a deduction for a C corporation's business interest expense under proposed § 1.163(j)-2 will not affect whether or when such business interest expense reduces the taxpayer's E&P. In other words, C corporations generally should not wait to reduce their E&P for business interest expense until the taxable year in which a deduction for such expense is allowed under section 163(j). This approach, which is the same approach used in the Prior Proposed Regulations under old section 163(j) (see § 1.163(j)-1(e), 56 FR 27907 (June 18, 1991)), reflects the fact that the payment or accrual of business interest expense generally reduces the C corporation's dividend-paying capacity in the year the expense is paid or accrued, without regard to the application of section 163(j). Additionally, disallowed business interest expense carryforwards are somewhat analogous to net operating loss (NOL) carryovers, and taxpayers reduce their E&P in the year the losses that give rise to an NOL are incurred rather than in a subsequent year in which an NOL carryover is absorbed.

However, the section 163(j) regulations would contain several modifications to or clarifications of the general rule regarding E&P. First, if a taxpayer is a RIC or a REIT for the taxable year in which a deduction is disallowed under section 163(j), or in which the RIC or REIT is allocated excess business interest expense from a partnership under section 163(j)(4)(B)(i) and proposed § 1.163(j)-6, then the taxpayer's E&P would not be reduced in the year the expense is paid or accrued without regard to the application of section 163(j). Rather, the taxpayer's E&P would be reduced in the taxable year(s) in which the business interest expense is deductible or, if earlier, in the first taxable year for which the taxpayer no longer is a RIC or a REIT. See proposed § 1.163(j)-4(c)(2) and the discussion of RICs and REITs later in part 4(C) of this Explanation of Provisions section.

Second, a taxpayer would not reduce its E&P in a taxable year beginning after December 31, 2017, to reflect any carryforwards of disallowed disqualified interest (within the meaning of old section 163(j)) to the extent the taxpayer previously reduced its E&P to reflect those interest payments in a prior taxable year. See proposed § 1.163(j)-11(b).

Third, C corporations other than REITs and RICs would make special E&P adjustments with respect to excess business interest expense allocated from a partnership. In general, a C corporation partner must reduce its E&P to reflect expense allocations from the partnership, including allocations of excess business interest expense. However, with respect to excess business interest expense in particular, the C corporation partner also must increase its E&P upon the disposition of the partnership interest to reflect the amount of excess business interest expense that the partner did not take into account while it held the partnership interest.

C. RICs and REITs

RICs and REITs are C corporations and are generally subject to the rules that apply to other C corporations, unless a provision in subchapter M of chapter 1 of the Code makes the rules inapplicable. There are no rules in subchapter M or section 163(j) that make section 163(j) inapplicable to REITs or RICs. Therefore, under these proposed regulations, RICs and REITs would be subject to section 163(j). Some REITs may not have any business interest expense subject to limitation under section 163(j) because they have only electing real property trades or businesses described in section 163(j)(7)(B). Other REITs, however, will have trades or businesses for which the REIT cannot or will not make the election under section 163(j)(7)(B). For example, a mortgage REIT cannot make such an election because real property financing is not an activity described in section 469(c)(7)(C).

RICs and REITs often derive a significant amount (if not all) of their income from property held for investment. However, under these proposed regulations, RICs and REITs would apply the same rules as other C corporations in determining which items are properly allocable to a trade or business. Thus, solely for purposes of 163(j), all of the interest expense and interest income of a RIC or REIT would be treated as business interest expense and business interest income, and all other items of income, gain, deduction, or loss of a RIC or REIT would be treated as properly allocable to a trade or business under proposed § 1.163(j) 4(b), except as otherwise provided in proposed § 1.163(j)-10.

RICs and REITs differ from other taxpayers because the income tax liability of a RIC or REIT is not based directly on its taxable income. Instead, tax is imposed on a RIC's investment company taxable income (ICTI) and a REIT's real estate investment trust taxable income (REITTI), each of which is determined by making certain adjustments to taxable income. These adjustments include the allowance of the deduction for dividends paid and the disallowance of the special corporate deductions in part VIII of subchapter B of chapter 1 of the Code (sections 241 and following) except section 248. The special corporate deductions include the dividends received deduction and the deductions under section 250 in respect of foreign-derived intangible income and global intangible low-taxed income (GILTI).

Under section 163(j)(8), a taxpayer's ATI generally is based on its taxable income, and there is no statutory requirement under which the ATI of a RIC or REIT would be based on ICTI or REITTI. Therefore, unless regulations provide otherwise, the ATI of a RIC or REIT does not reflect the deduction for dividends paid. A RIC or REIT typically pays dividends sufficient to eliminate all or nearly all ICTI or REITTI. As a result, if the ATI of a RIC or REIT took into account the deduction for dividends paid, the ATI of the RIC or REIT typically would be zero, or close to zero. It would be distortive to treat the deduction for dividends paid as reducing ATI because this deduction is merely the mechanism by which RICs and REITs shift the tax liability associated with their income to their shareholders, as intended pursuant to subchapter M of the Code. Therefore, these proposed regulations would not provide a rule that would cause the ATI of a RIC or REIT to take into account the deduction for dividends paid. The deduction for dividends received and the other special corporate deductions previously mentioned, however, are deductions that should reduce the ATI only of taxpayers that benefit from the deductions in determining tax liability. To reduce ATI for such items for taxpayers that cannot in fact utilize these deductions would be distortive. Therefore, under these proposed regulations, the ATI of a RIC or REIT would be increased by the amounts of these special corporate deductions, which decreased the RIC's or REIT's taxable income, because the deductions do not reduce the tax liability of RICs and REITs (or the amounts that RICs or REITs must distribute to eliminate entity-level tax).

RICs and REITs must meet distribution requirements each year in order to be allowed the deduction for dividends paid. If interest expense paid or accrued by a RIC or REIT is disallowed or deferred under section 163(j), or if a RIC or REIT is allocated any excess business interest expense from a partnership, such expense will not reduce the entity's taxable income, the entity's ICTI or REITTI as the case may be, or the amount of dividends that the entity must pay from its earnings and profits. Therefore, the earnings and profits of the RIC or REIT also should not be reduced. Accordingly, these proposed regulations would contain a special rule for RICs and REITs under which their earnings and profits generally would not be reduced by a disallowed business interest expense deduction in the year it is disallowed, or by any excess business interest expense allocated from a partnership.

D. Proposed § 1.163(j)-4(d): Special Rules for Consolidated Groups

Section 1502 provides broad authority for the Secretary of the Treasury to prescribe such regulations as are necessary in order that the tax liability of any affiliated group of corporations filing a consolidated return may be returned, determined, computed, assessed, collected, and adjusted, in order to clearly reflect the income tax liability of the consolidated group and to prevent the avoidance of such tax liability. The legislative history of section 163(j) states that, "[i]n the case of a group of affiliated corporations that file a consolidated return, the limitation applies at the consolidated tax return filing level." H. Rept. 115-466, at 386 (2017). Consistent with legislative intent, proposed § 1.163(j)-4(d) generally would provide that a consolidated group (as defined in §1.1502-1(h)) has a single section 163(j) limitation. In contrast, members of an affiliated group that does not file a consolidated return would not be aggregated for purposes of applying the section 163(j) limitation. Additionally, partnerships that are wholly owned by members of a consolidated group would not be aggregated with the consolidated group for purposes of applying the section 163(j) limitation. The Treasury Department and the IRS have determined that non-consolidated entities should not be aggregated for purposes of applying the section 163(j) limitation because, whereas old section 163(j)(6)(C) expressly provided that "[a]ll members of the same affiliated group (within the meaning of section 1504(a)) shall be treated as 1 taxpayer," section 163(j) no longer contains such language, and nothing in the legislative history of section 163(j) suggests that Congress intended non-consolidated entities to be treated as a single taxpayer for purposes of section 163(j).

Proposed §1.163(j)-4(d) would provide specific rules regarding the calculation of the section 163(j) limitation for a consolidated group. In particular, proposed §1.163(j)-4(d) would provide that the relevant taxable income in computing the group's ATI is the group's consolidated taxable income determined under §1.1502-11 without regard to any carryforwards or disallowances under section 163(j). Additionally, if for a taxable year a member of a consolidated group is allowed a deduction under section 250(a)(1) that is properly allocable to a non-excepted trade or business, then, for purposes of calculating ATI, consolidated taxable income for the taxable year is determined as if the deduction were not subject to the limitation in section 250(a)(2) and the regulations thereunder. For this purpose, the amount of the deduction allowed under section 250(a)(1) is determined without regard to the application of section 163(j) and the section 163(j) regulations. Moreover, for purposes of calculating the group's section 163(j) limitation, the group's current-year business interest expense and business interest income, respectively, would be the sum of the current-year business interest expense and business interest income of all members of the group. For purposes of this Explanation of Provisions and the proposed section 163(j) regulations, the term "current-year business interest expense" means business interest expense that would be deductible in the current taxable year without regard to section 163(j) and that is not a disallowed business interest expense carryforward from a prior taxable year (see proposed §1.163(j)-5(a)(2)(i)). Additionally, intercompany obligations (as defined in §1.1502-13(g)(2)(ii)) would be disregarded for purposes of determining a member's current-year business interest expense and business interest income and for purposes of calculating the consolidated group's ATI, and intercompany items and corresponding items (within the meaning of §1.1502-13(b)(2)(i) and (b)(3)(i), respectively) would be disregarded for purposes of calculating the group's ATI to the extent those items offset in amount.

Proposed §1.163(j)-4(d) also cross-references the rules in §1.1502-32(b), which govern investment adjustments within a consolidated group. Under those rules, if a member has current-year business interest expense for which a deduction is disallowed in the current taxable year under section 163(j), basis in the member's stock would be adjusted in a later taxable year when the expense is absorbed by the group.

Proposed §1.163(j)-4(d) would further clarify that the transfer of a partnership interest in an intercompany transaction that does not result in the termination of the partnership is treated as a disposition for purposes of the basis adjustment rule in section 163(j)(4)(B)(iii)(II), regardless of whether the transfer is one in which gain or loss is recognized. Several examples would be added to §1.1502-13(c)(7)(ii) to illustrate the application of these rules. The Treasury Department and the IRS have determined that intercompany transfers of partnership interests should be treated as dispositions for purposes of section 163(j)(4) because dispositions are broadly defined in section 163(j)(4)(B)(iii)(II), and because ignoring intercompany transfers of partnership interests for purposes of section 163(j)(4) would be inconsistent with the view that an entity whose owners are all members of the same consolidated group can be a partnership. In contrast, a change in status of a member, becoming or ceasing to be a member of a consolidated group, would not be treated as a disposition for these purposes.

The Treasury Department and the IRS request comments as to whether the intercompany transfer of a partnership interest in a nonrecognition transaction should constitute a disposition for purposes of section 163(j)(4)(B)(iii)(II) and, if so, how §1.1502-13(c) should apply to such a transfer if there is excess taxable income in a succeeding taxable year. The Treasury Department and the IRS also request comments as to the treatment of the transfer of a partnership interest in an intercompany transaction that results in the termination of the partnership.

Additionally, proposed §1.163(j)-4(d) would provide that a member's allocation of excess business interest expense from a partnership and the resulting decrease in basis in the partnership interest under section 163(j)(4)(B) is not a noncapital, nondeductible expense for purposes of §1.1502-32(b)(3)(iii). Similarly, an increase in a member's basis in a partnership interest under section 163(j)(4)(B)(iii)(II) to reflect excess business interest expense not deducted by the consolidated group is not tax-exempt income for purposes of §1.1502-32(b)(3)(ii). These special rules are intended to ensure that the allocations and basis adjustments under proposed §1.163(j)-6 do not result in investment adjustments within the consolidated group. This result is appropriate because the application of the proposed §1.163(j)-6 rules does not result in a net reduction in the tax attributes of the member partner; rather, there is an exchange of one type of attribute for another (excess business interest expense allocated from the partnership vs. basis in the partnership interest). The Treasury Department and the IRS request comments as to whether additional rules are needed to prevent loss duplication upon the disposition of stock of a member holding partnership interests.

5. *Proposed §1.163(j)-5: General Rules Governing Disallowed Business Interest Expense Carryforwards for C Corporations*

Proposed §1.163(j)-5 would provide certain rules regarding disallowed business interest expense carryforwards for taxpayers that are C corporations, including members of a consolidated group. Proposed §1.163(j)-5(b) would provide rules regarding the treatment of disallowed business interest expense carryforwards. Proposed §1.163(j)-5(c) would provide cross-references to rules regarding disallowed business interest expense carryforwards in transactions to which section 381(a) applies. Proposed §1.163(j)-5(d) would provide rules regarding limitations on disallowed business interest expense carryforwards from separate return limitation years (SRLYs). Proposed §1.163(j)-5(e) would provide cross-references to rules regarding the application of section 382. Proposed §1.163(j)-5(f) would provide rules regarding the overlap of the SRLY limitation with section 382.

A. Proposed §1.163(j)-5(b): Treatment of Disallowed Business Interest Expense Carryforwards

Proposed §1.163(j)-2 limits the amount of business interest expense for which a deduction is allowed in the taxable year. Proposed §1.163(j)-2 further provides that the amount of any business interest expense not allowed as a deduction for any taxable year as a result of the section 163(j) limitation is carried forward to the succeeding taxable year as a disallowed business interest expense carryforward.

Proposed §1.163(j)-5(b)(2) generally would provide that, for a C corporation taxpayer that is not a member of a consolidated group, current-year business interest expense is deducted in the current taxable year before any disallowed business interest expense carryforwards from a prior taxable year are deducted in that year. Disallowed business interest expense carryforwards are then deducted in the order of the taxable years in which they arose, beginning with the earliest taxable year, subject to certain limitations (for example, the limitation under section 382). S corporations would be subject to similar rules (see proposed §1.163(j)-6(l)(5)).

Proposed §1.163(j)-5(b)(3) would provide similar rules applicable to consolidated groups. In addition, disallowed business interest expense carryforwards from prior separate limitation years (as defined in §1.1502-1(e)) would be subject to the SRLY limitation. See the discussion of the SRLY rules in part 5(C) of this Explanation of Provisions section.

There are several reasons why the Treasury Department and the IRS have determined that current-year business interest expense and disallowed business interest expense carryforwards should be distinguished for taxpayers that are C corporations and S corporations, and why current-year business interest expense should be deducted before carryforwards from prior taxable years.

First, section 163(j) generally reflects an annual accounting approach. The section 163(j) limitation is calculated anew each year based on the taxpayer's taxable income for that year, and no excess limitation from prior taxable years carries forward to succeeding taxable years. By prioritizing the deduction of current-year business interest expense over disallowed business interest expense carryforwards from prior taxable years, this rule conforms to the annual accounting approach of section 163(j).

Second, if taxpayers were required to deduct disallowed business interest expense carryforwards before or simultaneously with current-year business interest expense, they could end up using some or all of their section 382 limitation on disallowed business interest expense carryforwards rather than on NOLs or other tax items subject to the section 382 limitation. For example, assume that X, a stand-alone C corporation, has $40x of disallowed business interest expense carryforwards and $30x of NOL carryovers from Year 1, both subject to a section 382 limitation of $35x. In Year 2, X has $50x of current-year business interest expense and a section 163(j) limitation of $45x. If X were required to use its disallowed business interest expense carryforwards before its current-year business interest expense, such carryforwards would absorb all of X's section 382 limitation for the current taxable year, and X would not be able to use any of its NOL carryovers. In contrast, under the rule in proposed §1.163(j)-5(b), X would use $45x of its current-year business interest expense and none of its disallowed business interest expense carryforwards, thus freeing up its section 382 limitation for its NOL carryovers.

Third, taxpayers that file a consolidated return are required to track their losses by taxable year for purposes of applying the NOL carryover and carryback rules of §1.1502-21(b) and the NOL SRLY limitation rules of §1.1502-21(c). As noted in part 5(C) of this Explanation of Provisions section, similar SRLY rules would apply to disallowed business interest expense carryforwards. Thus, a non-consolidated corporation must track its disallowed business interest expenses by the year in which such expenses are paid or accrued without regard to section 163(j) so that such corporation can comply with the SRLY limitation rules in the event the corporation joins a consolidated group.

Finally, the Treasury Department and the IRS note that, under proposed §1.163(j)-4(c), C corporations must track their disallowed business interest expense carryforwards by the year in which such items arose (and in which an E&P adjustment was made; see the discussion of proposed §1.163(j)-4(c) in part 4 of this Explanation of Provisions section) to ensure that E&P is not further reduced in a subsequent year in which the carryforward is deducted. Thus, the Treasury Department and the IRS have determined that these proposed rules should not create an additional administrative burden for C corporations.

Proposed §1.163(j)-5(b)(3) would further provide rules regarding which member's business interest expense would be deducted by the consolidated group in the current taxable year. If a group's section 163(j) limitation for the taxable year exceeds the aggregate amount of business interest expense, including disallowed business interest expense carryforwards, of all members, then each member's business interest expense, including carryforwards, would be fully deducted in that year, subject to other limitations, such as the section 382 limitation and the SRLY limitation. However, if the aggregate amount of business interest expense, including carryforwards, of all members exceeds the group's section 163(j) limitation for the year, then certain ordering rules would apply:

- *Step 1*: First, the consolidated group would determine whether its section 163(j) limitation for the current year equals or exceeds the members' aggregate current-year business interest expense. If so, then no amount of the consolidated group's current-year business interest expense would be subject to disallowance in the current year under section 163(j), and the consolidated group would skip Steps 2 and 3 of these ordering rules. If not, then the consolidated group must apply Step 2.

- *Step 2*: If the members' aggregate current-year business interest expense exceeds the group's section 163(j) limitation for the current year, each member with current-year business interest expense and either current-year business interest income or floor plan financing interest expense would deduct its current-year business interest expense up to the amount of its business interest income and floor plan financing interest expense for the year.

- *Step 3*: If the consolidated group has any section 163(j) limitation remaining after the application of Step 2 of these ordering rules, each member with remaining current-year business interest expense would deduct its current-year business interest expense pro rata, based on the relative amounts of remaining current-year business interest expense of all members.

- *Step 4*: If the consolidated group has any section 163(j) limitation remaining after the application of Step 1 of these ordering rules, each member's disallowed business interest expense carryforwards from a prior taxable year would be deducted on a pro rata basis, beginning with the earliest year, subject to certain limitations such as the section 382 limitation and the SRLY limitation. For example, assume that P and S are the only members of a consolidated group with a section 163(j) limitation of $200x for the current year (Year 2). Further assume that the amount of current-year business interest expense deducted in Year 2 is $100x, and that P and S, respectively, have $140x and $60x of disallowed business interest expense carryforwards from Year 1 that are not otherwise subject to limitation (for example, under section 382). Under these facts, P would be allowed to deduct $70x of its carryforwards from Year 1 (($140x / ($60x + $140x)) x $100) in Year 2, and S would be allowed to deduct $30x of its carryforwards from Year 1 (($60x / ($60x + $140x)) x $100) in Year 2.

- *Step 5*: Any member with remaining business interest expense after applying Steps 1 through 4 of these ordering rules would carry such expense forward to the succeeding taxable year as a disallowed business interest expense carryforward.

If a corporation ceases to be a member during a consolidated return year, the amount of its business interest expense, including carryforwards from prior taxable years, that is neither deducted by the consolidated group in that year nor reduced under §1.1502-36(d) would be carried forward to the corporation's first separate return year.

The foregoing rules are intended to roughly mirror the rules in §1.1502-21 governing the absorption of a consolidated net operating loss (CNOL). However, the Treasury Department and the IRS considered various other approaches to allocating disallowed business interest expense carryforwards among members of a consolidated group. For example, one alternative approach under consideration was a regime whereby disallowed business interest expense carryforwards would be allocated based upon the actual use of externally borrowed funds by each member. Under such an approach, intercompany obligations would be taken into account in allocating disallowed business interest expense carryforwards.

The Treasury Department and the IRS do not propose to adopt such an approach, for several reasons. First, requiring taxpayers to trace externally borrowed funds to the member that ultimately uses such funds would create an administrative burden for taxpayers. Second, because money is fungible, a tracing regime would place undue importance on the location of intercompany obligations. Thus, this approach would permit significant manipulation through the creation of intercompany obligations for the purpose of shifting disallowed business interest expense carryforwards among members. Third, this approach could result in the non-economic allocation of disallowed business interest expense carryforwards to members with no business interest expense to creditors outside the consolidated group. This approach would result in value transfers among consolidated group members and require complex rules to account for those transfers. These proposed regulations implement the statute consistent with legislative intent while avoiding these complications.

The Treasury Department and the IRS request comments on the rules in proposed §1.163(j)-5(b)(3), including comments on whether these rules should be revised to incorporate additional language or principles from the CNOL allocation rules in §1.1502-21.

B. Proposed §1.163(j)-5(c): Disallowed Business Interest Expense Carryforwards in Transactions to Which Section 381(a) Applies

In the case of certain asset acquisitions, section 381(a) generally requires the acquiring corporation to succeed to and take into account the tax items described in section 381(c) of the distributor or transferor corporation. In the TCJA, Congress added disallowed business interest expense carryforwards to the list of items to which the acquiring corporation succeeds in a transaction to which section 381(a) applies (see section 381(c)(20)).

Sections 1.381(c)(1)-1 and 1.381(c)(1)-2 provide rules that, in part, limit the acquiring corporation's ability to use NOL carryforwards in the acquiring corporation's first taxable year ending after the acquisition date. The Treasury Department and the IRS have determined that similar rules should apply to disallowed business interest expense carryforwards. See proposed §§ 1.163(j)-5(c) and 1.381(c)(20)-1.

The Treasury Department and the IRS request comments as to whether section 381(c)(20) and proposed §§ 1.163(j)-5(c) and 1.381(c)(20)-1 should apply to excess business interest expense allocated to a corporate partner.

C. Proposed § 1.163(j)-5(d): Limitations on Disallowed Business Interest Expense Carryforwards From Separate Return Limitation Years

In general, the taxable income of a consolidated group is determined by aggregating the income and losses of each member. Thus, a consolidated group may offset the income earned by profitable members against the losses incurred by other members. However, an exception to this general rule applies to losses incurred by a member in a taxable year in which the member did not join in filing a consolidated return with the current group. The SRLY limitation in § 1.1502-21(c) generally limits the amount of a member's losses arising in a SRLY that may be included in the consolidated group's CNOL to the amount of net income generated by that member. Similar rules in §§ 1.1502-15 and 1.1502-22(c) apply to built-in losses and net capital losses, respectively. Absent a SRLY limitation and other limitations, notably section 382, the consolidated group could reduce its consolidated taxable income simply by acquiring new members with built-in losses, NOLs, net capital losses, or disallowed business interest expense carryforwards.

The Treasury Department and the IRS have determined that rules similar to those in § 1.1502-21(c) should apply to disallowed business interest expense carryforwards. See proposed § 1.163(j)-5(d). However, the calculation of the SRLY limitation for disallowed business interest expense carryforwards would differ from the calculation of the SRLY limitation for NOL carryovers. The SRLY limitation for NOL carryovers is cumulative—in other words, it is based upon a member's aggregate contribution to consolidated taxable income, determined by reference to only the member's tax items, for all consolidated return years of the consolidated group in which the member was included in the group. As a result, a member may carry forward its unused SRLY limitation from one year to the next. In contrast, the SRLY limitation for disallowed business interest expense carryforwards would be calculated annually based upon a member's section 163(j) limitation, determined by reference to only the member's tax items, for any given taxable year. As a result, a member may not carry forward its unused section 163(j) SRLY limitation from one year to the next. The Treasury Department and the IRS have determined that this result is appropriate because Congress did not retain the excess limitation carryforward provisions from old section 163(j). Thus, allowing members to carry forward their unused section 163(j) SRLY limitation would be inconsistent with congressional intent.

Proposed § 1.163(j)-5(d) would provide several additional limitations on a member's ability to use its disallowed business interest expense carryforwards arising in a SRLY. First, such items only may be taken into account by the consolidated group in a taxable year to the extent the group has any remaining section 163(j) limitation for that year after applying the rules in proposed § 1.163(j)-5(b). Second, such items only may be taken into account to the extent the SRLY member's section 163(j) limitation for that year exceeds the amount of the member's business interest expense already taken into account by the group in that year under the rules in proposed § 1.163(j)-5(b). Third, SRLY-limited disallowed business interest expense carryforwards would be deducted on a pro rata basis with non-SRLY limited disallowed business interest expense carryforwards from taxable years ending on the same date.

The Treasury Department and the IRS request comments on the SRLY rules in proposed § 1.163(j)-5(d), including whether a member's SRLY-limited disallowed business interest expense carryforwards should cease to be subject to a SRLY limitation (to the extent of the member's stand-alone section 163(j) limitation) in taxable years in which the member's stand-alone section 163(j) limitation exceeds the consolidated group's section 163(j) limitation.

D. Proposed § 1.163(j)-5(e): Application of Section 382

Like the SRLY limitation, the section 382 limitation limits a taxpayer's ability to reduce its taxable income simply by acquiring a loss corporation. In general, if a loss corporation experiences an ownership change, section 382 limits the amount of the new loss corporation's taxable income that can be offset by pre-change losses to the product of the old loss corporation's value at the time of the ownership change times the long-term tax-exempt rate. For a discussion of the regulations under sections 163(j), 382, and 383 that govern the applicability of section 382 to business interest expense, see parts 11 and 14 through 16 of this Explanation of Provisions section.

E. Proposed § 1.163(j)-5(f): Overlap of SRLY Limitation with Section 382

As noted in parts 5(C) and 5(D) of this Explanation of Provisions section, both the SRLY limitation and the section 382 limitation are intended to prevent taxpayers from trafficking in loss corporations. Moreover, both of these limitations could apply to the same corporation as a result of the same transaction (for example, if a consolidated group acquires a loss corporation in a transaction that is an ownership change for purposes of section 382) or as a result of several transactions that occur within a short period of time.

Section 1.1502-21(g) provides an overlap rule to prevent both the section 382 limitation and the SRLY limitation from applying to NOL carryovers under certain circumstances. The Treasury Department and the IRS have determined that a similar overlap rule should apply with respect to disallowed business interest expense carryforwards. Thus, proposed § 1.163(j)-5(f) would apply the principles of § 1.1502-21(g) to disallowed business interest expense carryforwards when the application of the SRLY limitation would result in an overlap with the application of section 382.

6. Proposed § 1.163(j)-6: Application of the Business Interest Expense Deduction Limitations to Partnerships and Subchapter S Corporations

A. In General

Proposed § 1.163(j)-6 would provide guidance regarding partnership and S corporation deductions and carryforwards under section 163(j). To the extent a partnership is subject to the limitations imposed by section 163(j), the section 163(j) limitation shall be applied at the partnership level and any deduction for business interest expense not disallowed under section 163(j) is taken into account in determining the nonseparately stated taxable income or loss of the partnership. Similar rules shall apply to an S corporation. See part 6(H) of this Explanation of Provisions section for a discussion of rules specific to S corporations.

The phrase "nonseparately stated taxable income or loss of the partnership" has not previously been defined by statute. However, section 1366(a)(2) provides a definition of "nonseparately computed income or loss" as applied to S corporations. The legislative history of section 163(j) references "ordinary business income or loss" as reflected on Form 1065, "U.S. Return of Partnership Income," and the partner's distributive share as reflected in Box 1 of Schedule K-1. H. Rept. 115-466, at 387, fn. 690 (2017).

One commenter noted that, in general, an item of income or deduction that is included in nonseparately stated income of a partnership, as determined under section 702(a)(8), loses its tax character in the hands of the partner to whom the item is allocated. The Treasury Department and the IRS agree that for purposes of proposed § 1.163(j)-6(a), to the extent a partnership's business interest expense is less than or equal to the partnership's section 163(j) limitation, such business interest expense loses its character as business interest expense at the partner's level for purposes of the partner's section 163(j) calculation (that is, the business interest expense is not subject to further limitations under section 163(j)). See proposed § 1.163(j)-6(c).

For purposes of the Code other than section 163(j), proposed § 1.163(j)-6(c) would provide that business interest expense and, in the case of a partnership, excess business interest expense, retains its character as business interest expense at the partner and S corporation shareholder-level. For purposes of section 469, such interest retains its characterization as either passive or non-passive when allocated to the partner or shareholder. Additionally, for purposes of section 469, business interest expense from a partnership or S corporation and, in the case of a partnership, excess business interest expense, remains interest derived from a trade or business in the hands of a partner or shareholder, even if the partner or shareholder does not materially participate in the partnership or S corporation's trade or business activity. See proposed § 1.163(j)-3 for additional rules regarding the interaction among sections 461(l), 465, 469, and 163(j).

The Treasury Department and the IRS intend to adopt rules for the proper treatment of business interest income and business interest expense with respect to lending transactions between a passthrough entity and an owner of the entity (self-charged lending transactions). Although reserved in these proposed regulations, the Treasury Department and the IRS intend to adopt certain rules to re-characterize, for both the lender and the borrower, the business interest expense and corresponding business interest income arising from a self-charged lending transaction that may be allocable to the owner, to prevent such business interest income and expense from entering or affecting the section 163(j) limitation calculations for both the lender and the borrower in such situations. One possible approach is to adopt rules similar in scope as those contained in § 1.469-7, dealing with the treatment of self-charged lending transactions for purposes of section 469. The Treasury Department and the IRS request comments with respect to any potential rules that may be considered to achieve this result, as well as comments regarding the potential adverse effects that such rules may have with respect to other Code provisions, such as section 163(d), and any methods for mitigating or eliminating those effects.

Guidance on the treatment of excess business interest expense in tiered partnerships has been reserved in these proposed regulations. Section 163(j)(4) requires the section 163(j) limitation to be taken into account at the entity-level and for business interest expense carryforwards to be allocated to partners. The Treasury Department and the IRS request comments regarding whether, in a tiered partnership arrangement, carryforwards should be allocated through upper-tier partnerships. Additionally, comments are requested regarding how and when an upper-tier partner's basis should be adjusted when a lower-tier partnership is subject to a section 163(j) limitation.

Guidance regarding the application of section 163(j) to a partnership merger or division has been also reserved in these proposed regulations. The Treasury Department and the IRS request comments on the effect of partnership mergers and divisions on excess business interest expense, excess taxable income, and excepted trade or business elections in the context of section 163(j).

B. ATI of a Partnership

i. In General

Proposed § 1.163(j)-6(d) would provide guidance on the ATI of a partnership. Subject to the modifications set forth in proposed § 1.163(j)-6(d) and described in this part 6.B of this Explanation of Provisions section, the ATI of a partnership would be calculated in accordance with proposed § 1.163(j)-1(b)(1). The ATI of the partnership would include any items described in section 703(a)(1), including both separately and nonseparately stated items, to the extent such items are otherwise included under proposed § 1.163(j)-1(b)(1).

ii. Section 743(b), Section 704(c)(1)(C), and Remedial Allocations

The Treasury Department and the IRS considered multiple possible approaches to address the treatment of section 743(b) adjustments to the basis of partnership property upon the transfer of a partnership interest, built-in loss amounts with respect to partnership property under section 704(c)(1)(C), and remedial allocations of income, gain, loss or deduction to a partner pursuant to section 704(c) and § 1.704-3(d) (collectively, partner-level adjustments) under section 163(j). One approach would disregard partner-level adjustments when calculating both the partnership's and the partner's ATI for purposes of section 163(j). This approach is consistent with section 743(b) and the accompanying regulations, which mandate that section 743(b) adjustments are not to be taken into account when determining the partnership's income, gain, deduction, or loss under section 703; and that section 743(b) adjustments are not taken into account until after a partner's distributive share of a deduction is determined.

This approach could, however, lead to odd results. For example, if because of positive section 743(b) adjustments, no current partner includes gain in taxable income on the sale of the partnership property, but the partnership still receives the benefit of the taxable income in its ATI, the partners would be allowed to take a larger amount of business interest expense as a current-year deduction than if the partnership's ATI had included the section 743(b) adjustment. Additionally, when the transferor sells its partnership interest, it generally includes in taxable income the gain resulting from the sale and could possibly include the gain in its own ATI calculation for purposes of its own section 163(j) limitation calculation. This situation could result in the double counting of the income in ATI for section 163(j) purposes, first by the transferor partner on the sale of the partnership interest and again by the partnership on a sale of partnership property.

Under a second approach considered, the partnership would increase or decrease its ATI by the amount of the partner-level adjustments allocated to each partner. Essentially, the partnership would be required to aggregate all partner-level adjustments and take them into account at the partnership level for purposes of section 163(j). The Treasury Department and the IRS viewed taking partner-level adjustments into account at the partnership level as being contrary to the intent of section 743(b), section 704(c)(1)(C), and remedial allocations, and have therefore not adopted this approach.

Under a third approach, (i) partner-level adjustments are not taken into account when computing ATI for purposes of the partnership's section 163(j) limitation; and (ii) each partner's partner-level adjustments are taken into account as items derived directly by the partner in determining its own section 163(j) limitation. This approach takes partner-level adjustments into account at the partner, rather than partnership, level when determining the partner's ATI.

This third approach was recommended by a commenter with respect to section 743(b) adjustments. The commenter argued that if a rule was adopted requiring that a partner's section 743(b) adjustment be included in the computation of a partnership's ATI for purposes of applying section 163(j) at the partnership level, then a particular partner's section 743(b) adjustment could impact the deductibility of partnership interest by other partners, which would be inconsistent with the basic approach taken in the section 743(b) regulations. The Treasury Department and the IRS agree that this approach strikes the best balance between the entity-level calculation under section 163(j) and the aggregate nature of section 743(b) adjustments, as well as other partner-level adjustments. Accordingly, partner-level adjustments are not taken into account when the partnership determines its section 163(j) limitation under proposed § 1.163(j)-6(f). Instead, partner-level adjustments are taken into account by the partner in determining the partner's ATI pursuant to proposed § 1.163(j)-6(e). However, in keeping with the entity approach taken under section 163(j)(4), a partnership shall take adjustments made to the basis of its property pursuant to section 734(b) into account for purposes of calculating its ATI pursuant to proposed § 1.163(j)-6(d).

The commenter acknowledged that this approach would create disparities between the situation where a partnership purchases assets in which, until 2022, depreciation will enter into the partnership's ATI; and a transaction structured as a purchase of partnership interests, where depreciation generated by a section 743(b) basis adjustment or section 704(c) remedial allocation will not enter into a partnership's ATI. The Treasury Department and the IRS are aware of these concerns and request additional comments on the impact of partner-level adjustments on a partnership's ATI calculation under section 163(j), particularly as it relates to publicly traded partnerships.

C. ATI and Business Interest Income of Partners

i. In General

Proposed § 1.163(j)-6(e) would provide that the ATI of a partner shall generally be determined in accordance with proposed § 1.163(j)-1(b)(1) without regard to such partner's distributive share of any items of income, gain, deduction or loss of such partnership, and shall be increased by such partner's share of excess taxable income, as defined in proposed § 1.163(j)-1(b)(13) and determined pursuant to proposed § 1.163(j)-6(f). This provision prohibits the double counting of items in ATI by a partner in its own section 163(j) calculation when a partnership has already taken those items into account under section 163(j). To the extent a partnership has excess taxable income, a partner may include its share of the partnership's excess taxable income, as determined in proposed § 1.163(j)-6(f), in the partner's own ATI for purposes of determining the partner's section 163(j) limitation. For guidance regarding the partner's inclusion of partner-level adjustments, see proposed § 1.163(j)-6(e). For guidance regarding the recharacterization of a partnership's investment interest, investment income, and investment expenses at the C corporation partner-level, see proposed § 1.163(j)-4(b)(3).

ii. Sale of Partnership Interests

Proposed § 1.163(j)-6(e)(3) would provide guidance on the inclusion of the proceeds from the sale of a partnership interest in the selling partner's ATI. In the event a partner sells a partnership interest and the partnership in which the interest is being sold owns only non-excepted trade or business assets, as such term is defined in proposed § 1.163(j)-6(b)(6), the gain or loss on the sale of the partnership interest is included in the partner's ATI. If a partner sells a partnership interest and the partnership in which the interest is being sold owns both excepted assets, as such term is defined in proposed § 1.163(j)-6(b)(7), and non-excepted assets, the partner shall generally use the method set forth in proposed § 1.163(j)-10(c) in order to determine the amount properly allocable to a non-excepted trade or business, and therefore, properly includible in the partner's ATI. Proposed § 1.163(j)-6(e)(4) would also apply to tiered partnerships.

The Treasury Department and the IRS also considered adopting a reasonable method standard by which a partnership could determine the amount properly allocable to a non-excepted trade or business, and therefore, properly includible in the partner's ATI. Such provisions would have adopted tracing rules similar to those set forth in § 1.163-8T, as modified by Notice 88-20, 1988-9 I.R.B. 5 (Feb. 9, 1988), Notice 88-37, 1988-15 I.R.B. 8 (Mar. 16, 1988), and Notice 89-35, 1989-13 I.R.B. 4 (Mar. 9, 1989). The Treasury Department and the IRS request comments on what reasonable methods other than the method set forth in proposed § 1.163(j)-10(c), possibly including a tracing method similar to § 1.163-8T, would be appropriate in order to determine the amount properly allocable to a non-excepted trade or business and under what circumstances such methods would be appropriate.

iii. Double Counting of Business Interest Income Prohibited

Notice 2018-28 stated that for purposes of calculating a partner's annual deduction limitation under section 163(j) for business interest expense paid or accrued by the partner, the partner shall only include business interest income from a partnership in its section 163(j)(1)(A) amount to the extent that business interest income exceeds business interest expense determined at the partnership level under section 163(j). Additionally, a partner shall not include its share of the partnership's floor plan financing for purposes of determining the partner's annual deduction limitation for business interest expense under section 163(j)(1)(C). Proposed § 1.163(j)-6(e)(2) would incorporate these limitations into these proposed regulations.

D. Section 163(j) Partnership Calculation

i. Allocation of Deductible Business Interest Expense and Section 163(j) Excess Items - Made in the Same Manner as the Nonseparately Stated Taxable Income or Loss of the Partnership

Section 163(j)(4)(A)(ii)(II) states that a partner's excess taxable income is determined in the same manner as the nonseparately stated taxable income or loss of the partnership. Section 163(j)(4)(B)(i)(II) states that excess business interest expense is allocated to each partner in the same manner as the nonseparately stated taxable income or loss of the partnership. Similarly, excess business interest income is allocated to each partner in the same manner as the nonseparately stated taxable income or loss of the partnership. The phrase "nonseparately stated taxable income or loss of the partnership" is not defined in section 163(j), and as mentioned in part 6(A) of this Explanation of Provisions section, has not previously been defined by statute or regulations. The phrase "in the same manner as" is also undefined.

Under the proposed regulations, the manner for allocating excess taxable income, excess business interest income, and excess business interest expense (hereinafter "section 163(j) excess items") must be consistent with the Treasury Department and the IRS's resolution of the following three descriptive (1 through 3) and two normative (4 through 5) issues: (1) Section 163(j) is applied at the partnership level; (2) a partnership cannot have both excess taxable income (or excess business interest income) and excess business interest expense in the same taxable year; (3) parity must be preserved between a partnership's deductible business interest expense and section 163(j) excess items and the aggregate of each partner's share of deductible business interest expense and section 163(j) excess items from such partnership; (4) if in a given year a partnership has both deductible business interest expense and excess business interest expense, a partnership should not allocate excess business interest expense to a partner to the extent such partner was allocated the items comprising ATI (or business interest income) that supported the partnership's deductible business interest expense; and (5) if in a given year a partnership has excess taxable income (or excess business interest income), only partners allocated more items comprising ATI (or business interest income) than necessary to support their allocation of business interest expense should be allocated a share of excess taxable income (or excess business interest income).

One commenter proposed a manner for allocating section 163(j) excess items that would require a partnership to allocate each section 163(j) excess item (for example, excess business interest expense) in the same proportion as its underlying section 163(j) item (business interest expense). For example, if partnership AB had $30 of business interest income, which it allocated solely to A, and $40 of business interest expense, which it allocated $20 each to A and B, then A and B would each have $15 of deductible business interest expense and $5 of excess business interest expense. In situations where the partnership does not allocate all of its section 163(j) items pro rata, such as this example, this method could require a partnership to allocate its section 163(j) excess items in a manner inconsistent with the Treasury Department and the IRS's resolution of issues four and five. Because this approach could require a partnership to arguably allocate inappropriate amounts of section 163(j) excess items to its partners, it is not adopted in these proposed regulations.

The calculation adopted in proposed § 1.163(j)-6(f)(2) preserves the entity-level calculation requirement set forth in section 163(j)(4), while also preserving the economics of the partnership and respecting any special allocations made by the partnership in accordance with section 704 and the regulations thereunder. Applying the method in these proposed regulations to the previous example, A would have $20 of deductible business interest expense, and B would have $10 of deductible business interest expense and $10 of excess business interest expense. This result is consistent with the Treasury Department and the IRS's interpretation of section 163(j) as previously discussed.

ii. Allocation of Deductible Business Interest Expense and Section 163(j) Excess Items - General Calculation

Proposed § 1.163(j)-6(f)(2) provides that partnerships must allocate any section 163(j) excess items and any deductible business interest expense in the manner described in paragraphs (f)(2)(i) through (xi). In general, each paragraph (i) through (xi) is a step in a set of instructions that, when completed, provide the partnership with the proper allocation of each of its section 163(j) excess items to each of its partners. This resulting array of allocations is consistent with the Treasury Department and the IRS's resolution of the five key issues described in part 6(D)(i) of this Explanation of Provisions section. Stated otherwise, such prescribed allocations recognize the aggregate nature of partnerships under subchapter K of the Code to the greatest extent possible while remaining consistent with section 163(j) applying at the partnership level.

No rule set forth in proposed § 1.163(j)-6(f)(2) of this section prohibits a partnership from making an allocation to a partner of any section 163(j) item that is otherwise permitted under section 704 and the regulations thereunder. Accordingly, any calculations in proposed § 1.163(j)-6(f)(2)(i) through (xi) are solely for the purpose of determining each partner's deductible business interest expense and section 163(j) excess items, and do not otherwise affect any other provision under the Code, such as section 704(b). Proposed § 1.163(j)-6(f)(2) creates numerous defined terms. These defined terms are solely for the purpose of proposed § 1.163(j)-6(f)(2) and are meant to aid the partnership in its application of proposed § 1.163(j)-6(f)(2) by allowing the calculation to be broken into discrete steps.

Proposed § 1.163(j)-6(f)(2)(i) requires the partnership to calculate its section 163(j) deduction pursuant to proposed § 1.163(j)-2(b). This step is the entity-level calculation required by section 163(j)(4)(A), and it provides the partnership with its total amount of deductible business interest expense, excess business interest income, excess taxable income, and excess business interest expense under section 163(j) for a taxable year. The remaining steps in proposed § 1.163(j)-6(f)(2)(ii) through (xi) determine the allocations a partnership must make of its deductible business interest expense and each section 163(j) excess item to its partners. At the conclusion of the eleven steps set forth in proposed § 1.163(j)-6(f)(2), the total amount of deductible business interest expense and section 163(j) excess items allocated to each partner will equal the partnership's total amount of deductible business interest expense and section 163(j) excess items.

Proposed § 1.163(j)-6(f)(2)(ii) begins the partner-level calculations. It should be noted that the calculations under proposed § 1.163(j)-6(f)(2) do not determine a partner's allocation of business interest expense, business interest income or items comprising ATI, as these allocations are determined under section 704(b) and (c) and the regulations thereunder. Rather, the proposed § 1.163(j)-6(f)(2) partner-level calculations determine each partner's amount of deductible business interest expense and amount of any section 163(j) excess items. This determination provides the starting point for the remainder of the steps in proposed § 1.163(j)-6(f)(2). Only items that were taken into account in the partnership's section 163(j) calculation are taken into account for the proposed § 1.163(j)-6(f)(2) partner-level calculation. Section 743(b) adjustments, built-in loss amounts with respect to partnership property under section 704(c)(1)(C), section 704(c) remedial allocations, allocations of investment income and expense, and amounts determined for the partner under § 1.882-5 are therefore not taken into account for purposes of the proposed § 1.163(j)-6(f)(2) partner-level calculation. To clarify that only section 163(j) items of the partnership are relevant for the calculations under proposed § 1.163(j)-6(f)(2), paragraph (f)(2)(ii) defines "allocable ATI" as a partner's allocable share of the partnership's ATI, "allocable business interest income" as a partner's allocable share of the partnership's business interest income, and "allocable business interest expense" as a partner's allocable share of the partnership's business interest expense that is not floor plan financing interest expense.

As noted previously, the primary goal of proposed § 1.163(j)-6(f)(2) is to provide the partnership with an array of allocations that recognizes the aggregate nature of partnerships under subchapter K of the Code to the greatest extent possible while still remaining consistent with section 163(j) applying at the partnership level. Proposed § 1.163(j)-6(f)(2)(iii) through (v) contain the adjustment mechanism necessary to achieve this goal. Section 163(j) permits taxpayers with a sufficient amount of appropriate income (ATI and business interest income) to deduct their business interest expense. However, section 163(j) applies at the entity level with respect to partnerships under section 163(j)(4). Proposed § 1.163(j)-6(f)(2)(iii) recognizes this normative principle of the statute, and then proposed § 1.163(j)-6(f)(2)(iv) and (v) reconcile the proposed § 1.163(j)-6(f)(2)(iii) partner-level calculation with the proposed § 1.163(j)-6(f)(2)(i) partnership-level result.

To illustrate the mechanism at work in proposed § 1.163(j)-6(f)(2)(iii) through (v), consider the example used above. Partnership AB has $30 of business interest income, which it allocates solely to A, and $40 of business interest expense, which it allocates $20 each to A and B. Upon applying proposed § 1.163(j)-6(f)(2)(iii), AB determines that A has been allocated more allocable business interest income than necessary to deduct its allocable business interest expense ($10 of allocable business interest income excess), and B has not been allocated enough allocable business interest income to deduct its allocable business interest expense ($20 of allocable business interest income deficit). Because AB cannot have both excess business interest income and excess business interest expense in the same year, proposed § 1.163(j)-6(f)(2)(iv) and (v) reconcile the proposed § 1.163(j)-6(f)(2)(iii) partner-level calculation with the proposed § 1.163(j)-6(f)(2)(i) partnership-level result. This process of reallocating allocable business interest income excess to partners with allocable business interest income deficits is broken into two steps; proposed § 1.163(j)-6(f)(2)(iv) first proportionately reduces each partner's excess amount, and then proposed § 1.163(j)-6(f)(2)(v) proportionately reduces each partner's deficit amount to reflect the reallocation of the benefit of the excess amounts.

Proposed § 1.163(j)-6(f)(2)(vii), (ix), and (x) contain the same adjustment mechanism as proposed § 1.163(j)-6(f)(2)(iii) through (v), except for ATI instead of business interest income. To illustrate, if in the previous example AB had $100 of ATI which it allocated solely to A instead of $30 of business interest income, AB would perform the calculations in proposed § 1.163(j)-6(f)(2)(vii), (ix), and (x) - which parallel the calculations in proposed § 1.163(j)-6(f)(2)(iii) through (v) - and arrive at the same result. The partnership must make the adjustments regarding business interest income (proposed § 1.163(j)-6(f)(2)(iii) through (v)) before the adjustments regarding ATI (proposed § 1.163(j)-6(f)(2)(vii), (ix), and (x)) due to section 163(j)(4)(C), which requires partnerships to first fully offset business interest expense using business interest income before turning to ATI.

Finally, proposed § 1.163(j)-6(f)(2)(xi) allocates section 163(j) excess items and deductible business interest expense to the partners. Excess business interest income as determined in proposed § 1.163(j)-6(f)(2)(i) is allocated dollar for dollar to the partners with final allocable excess business interest income determined pursuant to proposed § 1.163(j)-6(f)(2)(iv). After grossing up each partner's final ATI capacity excess amount by ten-thirds (10/3) (the multiplicative inverse of the 30 percent ATI limitation), excess taxable income, as determined in proposed § 1.163(j)-6(f)(2)(i), is allocated dollar for dollar to partners with final ATI capacity excess amounts determined pursuant to proposed § 1.163(j)-6(f)(2)(ix). It is necessary to gross up the ATI capacity excess amount by ten thirds in order to account for the reduction in ATI capacity that occurred in proposed § 1.163(j)-6(f)(2)(vii). Excess business interest expense is allocated dollar for dollar to partners with final ATI capacity deficit amounts determined pursuant to proposed § 1.163(j)-6(f)(2)(x). A partner's allocable business interest expense is deductible business interest expense to the extent it exceeds such partner's share of excess business interest expense.

iii. Allocation of Deductible Business Interest Expense and Section 163(j) Excess Items - Steps 6 and 8

In a given year, if a partnership does not have any partners with a negative allocable ATI under proposed § 1.163(j)-6(f)(2)(vi) (that is, an allocable ATI under proposed § 1.163(j)-6(f)(2)(ii) that is comprised of more items of deduction and loss than income and gain), then the partnership would not have any adjustments under proposed § 1.163(j)-6(f)(2)(vi) and (viii). Thus, the only adjustments and reallocations the partnership would have to perform as part of its proposed § 1.163(j)-6(f)(2) calculation are described in part 6(D)(ii) of this Explanation of Provisions section. However, if a partnership does have a total negative allocable ATI that is greater than zero, then the partnership would have adjustments under proposed § 1.163(j)-6(f)(2)(vi), and may have adjustments under proposed § 1.163(j)-6(f)(2)(viii) as well. Proposed § 1.163(j)-6(f)(2)(vi) and (viii) are closely related. In general, proposed § 1.163(j)-6(f)(2)(viii) corrects distortions that would otherwise occur following certain proposed § 1.163(j)-6(f)(2)(vi) adjustments.

The purpose of proposed §1.163(j)-6(f)(2)(vi) is to address the situation in which a partner's allocable ATI under proposed §1.163(j)-6(f)(2)(ii) is comprised of more items of deduction and loss than income and gain - that is, negative allocable ATI. For purposes of the section 163(j) calculation, a partnership that has ATI of less than zero will not be able to deduct business interest expense with respect to ATI under section 163(j)(1). Accordingly, for purposes of the proposed §1.163(j)-6(f)(2) calculation, the partnership must ensure that each partner has a "final allocable ATI" of at least zero before performing the ATI adjustment calculation described in proposed §1.163(j)-6(f)(2)(vii), (ix), and (x). This is accomplished by proportionately reallocating positive allocable ATI from partners with positive allocable ATI to partners with negative allocable ATI in order to gross such partners up to zero. Upon completion of the calculation in proposed §1.163(j)-6(f)(2)(vi), the aggregate of the partners' final allocable ATI amounts will equal the partnership's ATI amount used in calculating its section 163(j) limitation under proposed §1.163(j)-6(f)(2)(i), and no partner will have a final allocable ATI amount less than zero.

A partnership must always apply proposed §1.163(j)-6(f)(2)(vi), even if the partnership does not have any numerical adjustment resulting from it. For example, if a partnership has a total negative allocable ATI of $0 in proposed §1.163(j)-6(f)(2)(vi), then even though the partnership will not reallocate any positive allocable ATI in proposed §1.163(j)-6(f)(2)(vi), the partnership must still apply proposed §1.163(j)-6(f)(2)(vi) to convert each partner's positive allocable ATI to final allocable ATI, which is used in subsequent paragraphs as the successor term of allocable ATI.

The purpose of proposed §1.163(j)-6(f)(2)(viii) is to ensure that any adjustments the partnership was required to make under proposed §1.163(j)-6(f)(2)(vi) do not result in proposed §1.163(j)-6(f)(2) requiring the partnership to allocate deductible business interest expense and section 163(j) excess items in an inequitable manner. To illustrate, consider the following example. Partnership ABC has $100 of ATI, comprised of $200 of items of income and gain and $100 of deduction and loss, and $40 of business interest expense. ABC allocates the income and gain $100 each to A and C, and all $100 of the deduction and loss to B. ABC has $40 of business interest expense, which it allocates $20 each to A and B. Upon applying proposed §1.163(j)-6(f)(2)(i), ABC has $30 of deductible business interest expense and $10 of excess business interest expense.

Given these facts and the Treasury Department and the IRS's interpretation of section 163(j), A is clearly entitled to treat all $20 of its allocable business interest expense as deductible business interest expense in the current year, and B should be allocated the $10 of excess business interest expense. However, in the absence of proposed §1.163(j)-6(f)(2)(viii), proposed §1.163(j)-6(f)(2) would require ABC to make different, less equitable, allocations. The issue stems from proposed §1.163(j)-6(f)(2)(vi). Following the application of proposed §1.163(j)-6(f)(2)(vi) and (vii), A has an ATI capacity deficit of $5, B has an ATI capacity deficit of $20, and C has an ATI capacity excess of $15. The calculations in proposed §1.163(j)-6(f)(2)(ix) and (x) reallocate ATI capacity excess to partners with ATI capacity deficits solely based on each partners ATI capacity deficit relative to the total ATI capacity deficit. Because proposed §1.163(j)-6(f)(2)(ix) and (x) only takes each partner's proportionate share of ATI capacity deficit into account when reallocating ATI capacity excess, proposed §1.163(j)-6(f)(2)(ix) and (x) always treat all of partners as though they are on equal footing regardless of any adjustments that may have happened in proposed §1.163(j)-6(f)(2)(vi). As a result, in the absence of proposed §1.163(j)-6(f)(2)(viii), A would be allocated deductible business interest expense of only $18 (instead of $20), and B would be allocated excess business interest expense of only $8 (instead of $10).

The proposed §1.163(j)-6(f)(2)(viii) adjustment begins by filtering out partnerships that do not need to make the adjustment using the criteria listed in proposed §1.163(j)-6(f)(2)(viii)(A). This treatment is possible due to the predictability and limited universe of situations that require a proposed §1.163(j)-6(f)(2)(viii) adjustment. Specifically, a proposed §1.163(j)-6(f)(2)(viii) adjustment is always triggered when a positive allocable ATI partner that helped gross up a negative allocable ATI partner in proposed §1.163(j)-6(f)(2)(vi) is subsequently forced to compete with such partner for a limited amount of ATI capacity excess.

Next, under proposed §1.163(j)-6(f)(2)(viii)(B), a partnership must determine each partner's priority amount. This priority amount represents what a partner's ATI capacity would have been if such partner had not been required under proposed §1.163(j)-6(f)(2)(vi) to offset another partner's negative allocable ATI. For purposes of determining whether to apply proposed §1.163(j)-6(f)(2)(viii)(C) or (D) and performing the calculations under the applicable paragraph, each partner's usable priority amount must be determined. A partner's usable priority amount is the lesser of its priority amount and ATI capacity deficit.

A partnership must use the amounts it determined under proposed §1.163(j)-6(f)(2)(viii)(B) to determine whether it must perform the calculations in proposed §1.163(j)-6(f)(2)(viii)(C) or (D). If the total ATI capacity excess amount, as determined under proposed §1.163(j)-6(f)(2)(vii), is greater than or equal to the total usable priority amount, then the adjustments in proposed §1.163(j)-6(f)(2)(viii)(C) must occur. If the total usable priority amount is greater than the total ATI capacity excess amount, as determined under proposed §1.163(j)-6(f)(2)(vii), then the adjustments in proposed §1.163(j)-6(f)(2)(viii)(D) must occur. The application of proposed §1.163(j)-6(f)(2)(viii)(C) or (D) may result in adjustments to the partner's ATI capacity excess (and deficit) amounts used in proposed §1.163(j)-6(f)(2)(ix) and (x).

The purpose of these adjustments is to ensure that the partners who had a negative allocable ATI do not improperly benefit under proposed §1.163(j)-6(f)(2)(ix) through (xi) to the detriment of the partners who had a positive allocable ATI. In general, proposed §1.163(j)-6(f)(2)(viii)(C) and (D) correct any artificial distortion of the economics between the partners that may have occurred under proposed §1.163(j)-6(f)(2)(vi) by modifying the outputs of proposed §1.163(j)-6(f)(2)(vii) to restore the partners' true economic arrangement before such outputs are used in proposed §1.163(j)-6(f)(2)(ix) and (x). Stated otherwise, proposed §1.163(j)-6(f)(2)(viii)(C) and (D) compensate for the assumption made by proposed §1.163(j)-6(f)(2)(ix) and (x) that all partners are always on equal footing by modifying the outputs of proposed §1.163(j)-6(f)(2)(vii) to put all partners on equal footing before allowing such outputs to reach proposed §1.163(j)-6(f)(2)(ix) and (x).

Turning back to the foregoing example, in accordance with proposed §1.163(j)-6(f)(2)(viii), ABC would first determine whether it has all three attributes in proposed §1.163(j)-6(f)(2)(viii)(A)(1) through (3). Because ABC (1) has excess business interest expense under proposed §1.163(j)-6(f)(2)(i); (2) has total negative allocable ATI greater than $0 under proposed §1.163(j)-6(f)(2)(vi); and (3) has a total ATI capacity excess amount greater than $0 under proposed §1.163(j)-6(f)(2)(vii), ABC must perform the calculations and make the necessary adjustments described under proposed §1.163(j)-6(f)(2)(viii)(B) and (C) or (D). Given ABC's facts, proposed §1.163(j)-6(f)(2)(viii)(B) would require ABC to perform the calculations in proposed §1.163(j)-6(f)(2)(viii)(C). As a result, A would be allocated deductible business interest expense of $20, and B would be allocated excess business interest expense of $10 and deductible business interest expense of $10. This result is consistent with the Treasury Department and the IRS's resolution of the five key issues described in part 6(D)(i) of this Explanation of Provisions section.

The Treasury Department and the IRS request comments on the approach described in this part 6(D). Specifically, comments are requested regarding other reasonable methods to allocate deductible business interest expense, excess taxable income, and excess business interest expense in a manner that permits partners that bear the taxable income supporting the deductible business interest expense to be allocated a disproportionate share of deductible business interest expense and excess taxable income. Finally, comments are requested regarding the fungibility of publicly traded partnership interests with respect to the foregoing approach.

E. Business Interest Expense Carryforwards

i. In General

Proposed §1.163(j)-6(g) would provide that to the extent a partnership has business interest expense in excess of its section 163(j) limitation, such excess business interest expense shall not be carried forward by the partnership. Instead, such excess business interest expense would be allocated to the partners in accordance with proposed §1.163(j)-6(f).

A commenter requested guidance regarding whether a partner will be permitted to use its share of the partnership's excess business interest income in the current taxable year to absorb the partner's excess business interest expense allocated from such partnership in prior years. The Treasury Department and the IRS believe that it is consistent with section 163(j) to allow excess business interest income allocated to a partner from a partnership to absorb the partner's excess business interest expenses allocated from that same partnership in an earlier taxable year to the extent of the excess business interest income allocated to the partner. This allowance places partners in a similar position to other taxpayers with carryforwards.

Regarding a partner's allocation of excess taxable income, the Treasury Department and the IRS considered three options when drafting guidance on the deductibility of a partner's excess business interest expense carryforward as it relates to a partner's share of excess taxable income. Section 163(j)(4)(B)(ii)(I) provides that the carryforward "shall be treated as business interest expense paid or accrued by the partner in the next succeeding taxable year in which the partner is allocated excess taxable income from such partnership, but only to the extent of such excess taxable income." The first option would apply a plain reading of the statutory language to treat as paid or accrued by the partner the amount of excess business interest expense carryforward from the partnership equal to the excess taxable income the partner is allocated from the partnership, but it would limit the deductibility of the excess business interest expense by a partner to the partner's business interest income and 30 percent of the partner's ATI for the taxable year. Given this interpretation is the most consistent with the plain meaning of the statute, proposed § 1.163(j)-6(g) would provide that to the extent a partner receives an allocation of excess taxable income from a partnership in a taxable year, such partner's excess business interest expense is treated as paid or accrued in that year in an amount equal to the partner's share of the excess taxable income. To the extent the partner's excess business interest expense exceeds its share of the partnership's excess taxable income in a taxable year, it remains excess business interest expense and is carried over to the following taxable year. When the excess business interest expense is treated as paid or accrued, it becomes business interest paid or accrued by the partner and may be deducted by the partner, subject to any partner-level section 163(j) limitation and any other applicable limitations.

The second option considered would entitle a partner to deduct excess business interest expense only to the extent the partner can deduct that excess business interest expense against the excess taxable income received from the partnership (for example, 30 percent of excess taxable income which increases the partner's ATI under section 163(j)(4)(A)(ii)(II)), regardless of any ATI or business interest income that the partner has from sources other than the partnership. This option would produce the same result as if the partnership had paid or accrued all the relevant income and expense in a single year. The legislative history can be read to suggest this result: "The partner may deduct its share of the partnership's excess business interest in any future year, but only against excess taxable income attributed to the partner by the partnership the activities of which gave rise to the excess business interest carryforward." H. Rept. 115-466, at 391 (2017). However, this interpretation does not appear to be consistent with the plain language of the statute, which states that excess business interest expense is treated as paid or accrued to the extent of the partner's excess taxable income.

The third option considered would entitle a partner to fully deduct excess business interest expense to the extent it receives an allocation of excess taxable income from the same partnership (for example, for every dollar of excess taxable income a partner is allocated, the partner is able to deduct one dollar of excess business interest expense). This interpretation would treat all excess business interest expense, to the extent of excess taxable income, as interest deductible under section 163(a). However, this interpretation ignores the possibility that the partner may be subject to its own section 163(j) limitation and ignores the 30 percent limitation on ATI that a partnership would be subject to had the business interest expense been paid or accrued in the current year. Accordingly, this option is not adopted in the proposed regulations.

ii. Ordering Rule

The ordering rule in proposed § 1.163(j)-6(f)(2)(iii) would clarify that to the extent a partner is allocated excess taxable income or excess business interest income from a partnership in the current taxable year and, in a prior year, that partner was allocated excess business interest expense from that same partnership that has not been previously treated as paid or accrued by the partner, the partner must treat that current-year excess taxable income and excess business interest income as causing the excess business interest expense carried forward from the partnership to be treated as paid or accrued in such year to the extent of the excess taxable income and excess business interest income. In the event a partner receives excess taxable income or excess business interest income from a partnership, it cannot choose to keep excess business interest expense as not paid or accrued in the current taxable year.

F. Basis Adjustments

i. Basis and Capital Account Adjustments for Excess Business Interest Expense Allocations

Generally, a partner's adjusted basis in its partnership interest shall be reduced by allocated items of partnership loss or deduction, but not below zero, pursuant to § 1.704-1(d)(2). Deductible business interest expense and excess business interest expense are subject to section 704(d). If a partner is subject to a limitation on loss under section 704(d) and a partner is allocated losses from a partnership in a taxable year, § 1.704-1(d)(2) requires that the limitation on losses under section 704(d) be apportioned amongst these losses based on the character of each loss (each grouping of losses based on character being a "section 704(d) loss class"). If there are multiple section 704(d) loss classes in a given year, § 1.704-1(d)(2) requires the partner to apportion the limitation on losses under section 704(d) to each section 704(d) loss class proportionately. For purposes of applying this proportionate rule, any deductible business interest expense (whether allocated to the partner in the current taxable year or suspended under section 704(d) in a prior taxable year), any excess business interest expense allocated to the partner in the current taxable year, and any excess business interest expense from a prior taxable year that was suspended under section 704(d) ("negative section 163(j) expense") shall comprise the same section 704(d) loss class. Once the partner determines the amount of limitation on losses apportioned to this section 704(d) loss class, any deductible business interest expense is taken into account before any excess business interest expense or negative section 163(j) expense.

The adjusted basis of a partner in a partnership interest is reduced, but not below zero, by the amount of excess business interest expense allocated to the partner pursuant to proposed § 1.163(j)-6(f)(2). Negative section 163(j) expense is not treated as excess business interest expense in any subsequent year until such negative section 163(j) expense is no longer suspended under section 704(d). Consequently, an allocation of excess taxable income or excess business interest income does not result in the negative section 163(j) expense being treated as business interest expense paid or accrued by the partner. Further, unlike excess business interest expense preventing a partner from including excess taxable income in its ATI as described in section 163(j)(4)(B)(ii) flush language, negative section 163(j) expense does not affect, and is not affected by, any allocation of excess taxable income to the partner. Accordingly, any excess taxable income allocated to a partner from a partnership while the partner still has a negative section 163(j) expense will be included in the partner's ATI. However, once the negative section 163(j) expense is no longer suspended under section 704(d), it becomes excess business interest expense, which is subject to the general rules in proposed § 1.163(j)-6(g). Section 163(j) has no effect on the maintenance of capital accounts (for example, a partner's capital account is reduced in the year such partner is allocated excess business interest expense). See § 1.704-1(b)(2)(iv)(b).

The guidance provided in proposed § 1.163(j)-6(h)(2) is intended to address situations in which a partner is subject to a limitation under section 704(d) and is also allocated excess taxable income. Pursuant to proposed § 1.163(j)-6(g), excess business interest expense would otherwise be treated as paid or accrued by the partner in an amount equal to the excess taxable income, but the partner's basis in the partnership does not increase in an amount equal to the allocated excess taxable income and, therefore, remains subject to the loss limitation in section 704(d). The approach taken in proposed § 1.163(j)-6(h)(2) attempts to reconcile the competing deduction limitations imposed by sections 704(d) and 163(j) along with section 163(j) treating excess business interest expense as paid or accrued by the partner when the partner is allocated excess taxable income. The Treasury Department and the IRS request comments on this issue.

ii. Basis Adjustments Upon Disposition of Partnership Interests Pursuant to Section 163(j)(4)(B)(iii)(II)

Proposed § 1.163(j)-6(h)(3) would provide that if a partner disposes of all or substantially all of its partnership interest, the adjusted basis of the partner in the partnership interest shall be increased immediately before the disposition by the amount of excess, if any, of the amount of the basis reduction under proposed § 1.163(j)-6(h)(1) over the portion of any excess business interest expense allocated to the partner under proposed § 1.163(j)-6(f)(2) which has not been previously treated under proposed § 1.163(j)-6(g) as business interest expense paid or accrued by the partner, regardless of whether the disposition was as a result of a taxable or non-taxable transaction. No deduction under section 163(j) shall be allowed to the transferor or transferee under chapter 1 of the Code for any excess business interest expense resulting in a basis increase under section 163(j) and these proposed regulations or for any negative section 163(j) expense.

In the event a partner disposes of less than substantially all of its interest in a partnership, proposed § 1.163(j)-6(h)(2) would provide that a partner shall not increase its basis in its partnership by the amount of any excess business interest expense that has not yet been treated as paid or accrued by the partner in accordance with proposed § 1.163(j)-6(g). Any such excess business interest expense would remain excess business interest expense in the hands of the transferor partner until such time as the transferor partner is allocated an appropriate amount of excess taxable income or excess business interest income from the partnership or added to the basis of its partnership interest when the partner fully disposes of the partnership interest. Additionally, any negative section 163(j) expense shall remain negative section 163(j) expense of the transferor partner until such negative section 163(j) expense is no longer suspended under section 704(d). These rules are similar to the rules found under section 469 and the regulations thereunder relating to suspended passive activity loss deductions.

The Treasury Department and the IRS considered alternate approaches when analyzing the effect of partial dispositions on a partner's basis. One alternate approach would add excess business interest expense to the partner's basis in the partnership interest to the extent the partner's capital account is reduced by the transfer or redemption. A second approach would increase the partner's remaining basis in the partnership interest by the amount of excess business interest expense that is proportionate to the amount of the partner's adjusted basis in the partnership interest that was transferred or redeemed. This method would require a partner to track its basis in the partnership interest in a manner similar to that set forth in Rev. Rul. 84-53, 1984-15 I.R.B. 17, 1984-1 C.B. 159 (Apr. 9, 1984). The Treasury Department and the IRS request comments on this issue.

G. Investment Items

Proposed § 1.163(j)-6(j) would provide guidance on the treatment of investment income and expense items under section 163(d) allocated by a partnership to its partners. Notice 2018-28 stated that the Treasury Department and the IRS intend to issue regulations clarifying that, solely for purposes of section 163(j), in the case of a taxpayer that is a C corporation, all interest paid or accrued by the C corporation on indebtedness of such C corporation will be business interest expense within the meaning of section 163(j)(5), and all interest on indebtedness held by the C corporation that is includible in gross income of such C corporation will be business interest income within the meaning of section 163(j)(6). Additionally, comments were received requesting guidance on the treatment of investment interest expense and investment interest income, as defined in section 163(d), allocated to a C corporation (corporate partner) by a partnership.

The Treasury Department and the IRS considered two approaches to address this issue. Under the first approach, the investment interest expense would be allocated directly from the partnership to the corporate partner without being subject to the section 163(j) limitations of the partnership. This option is most consistent with a plain reading of the statute. The definition of business interest expense under section 163(j)(5) specifically excludes investment interest. Section 163(j)(4) requires the business interest expense deduction to be calculated with respect to the partnership's specific items of income and expense, and the statute does not require any partner-specific considerations to be taken into account when performing the calculation at the partnership level.

The legislative history of section 163(j) indicates that a corporation can never have investment income and expenses, and instead, those items shall be treated as business interest income and expenses: "Section 163(d) applies in the case of a taxpayer other than a corporation. Thus, a corporation has neither investment interest nor investment income within the meaning of section 163(d). Therefore, interest income and interest expense of a corporation is properly allocable to a trade or business, unless such trade or business is otherwise explicitly excluded from the application of the provision." H. Rept. 115-466, at 386, fn. 688 (2017).

This language suggests a legislative intent to transform any interest that would otherwise be classified as investment interest in the hands of the corporate partner into business interest expense, thereby subjecting that interest to the corporate partner's limitations under section 163(j).

The second approach considered would require a partnership to perform a notional calculation under section 163(j) with respect to the investment interest that is allocated to its corporate partners. Based on the text and legislative history, this provision could arguably be interpreted to mean that investment interest expenses should be classified as business interest expenses at the time they are allocated to a corporate partner, and accordingly, the partnership should perform a section 163(j) calculation with respect to those items because section 163(j) requires a partnership to take the business interest expense deduction into account. Because this calculation would be done at the partnership level, any partnership with both corporate and non-corporate partners would need to make two section 163(j) calculations: one for any corporate partners and one for non-corporate partners.

Proposed § 1.163(j)-6(j) would adopt the first approach. Section 163(j)(4) does not require the partnership to look beyond its own tax attributes to that of its partners when making a determination as to whether a section 163(j) calculation is necessary. Accordingly, a plain reading of the statute does not support the partnership treating investment interest as business interest expense prior to allocating the interest to its partners. Instead, the statute appears to require the corporate partner to calculate its section 163(j) limitation while including this investment interest as it would with all other business and investment interest it receives from all sources.

It should be noted that, with respect to passthrough entities, including S corporations, engaged in trades or businesses that are not passive activities and with respect to which certain owners of the passthrough entities do not materially participate for purposes of section 469, as described in section 163(d)(5)(A)(ii) and as illustrated in Rev. Rul. 2008-12, the rules of section 163(j)(4) will apply to business interest expense allocable to such trades or businesses of those passthrough entities if those entities are otherwise subject to section 163(j). To the extent business interest expense of a passthrough entity is not limited under section 163(j), such business interest expense may still be limited by section 163(d) at the passthrough entity owner level in these situations. With respect to partnerships, to the extent that such business interest expense is limited under section 163(j)(4) and becomes a carryover item of partners who do not materially participate with respect to such trades or businesses, those items will be treated as items of investment interest expense in the hands of those owners for purposes of section 163(d) once those carryover items are treated as paid or accrued in a succeeding taxable year. The Treasury Department and the IRS have concluded that this is the result of the statutory rules contained in section 163(d)(4)(B) and (d)(5)(A)(ii) and, therefore, no additional rules are needed in regulations to reach this result.

H. S Corporations

i. In General

Section 163(j)(4)(D) provides that rules similar to those contained in section 163(j)(4)(A), relating to the entity-level treatment of the section 163(j) deduction, and section 163(j)(4)(C), relating to the definition of excess taxable income, apply to S corporations. Accordingly, proposed § 1.163(j)-6(l) would provide that, in the case of any S corporation, (i) the section 163(j) deduction limitation would be applied at the S corporation level, and (ii) any deduction for business interest expense would be taken into account in determining the nonseparately stated taxable income or loss of the S corporation.

An S corporation would determine its amount allowed as a deduction for business interest expense for the taxable year, that is, its section 163(j) deduction limitation, in the same manner as set forth in proposed § 1.163(j)-2(b). Due to the fact that S corporations generally are required to make pro rata distributions of income, allocations of excess taxable income and excess business interest income would be made in accordance with the shareholders' respective interests in the S corporation after the S corporation determines its section 163(j) deduction limitation pursuant to proposed § 1.163(j)-2(b), in accordance with section 1366(a)(1). See section 1361(b)(1)(D); § 1.1361-1(l) (non-pro rata distributions may create a second class of stock). Because partner-level adjustments are not applicable to S corporation shareholders, the ATI of an S corporation generally would be determined in accordance with proposed § 1.163(j)-1(b)(1) without additional modifications.

ii. Dispositions of S Corporation Stock

Proposed §§ 1.163(j)-6(l)(4)(ii) and 1.163(j)-10(b)(4)(ii) would provide guidance regarding the inclusion of the proceeds from the dispositions of S corporation stock in the selling shareholder's ATI. Specifically, proposed § 1.163(j)-6(l)(4)(ii) would provide that, in the event that a shareholder of an S corporation recognizes gain or loss upon the disposition of stock of the S corporation, and the corporation in which the stock is being disposed owns only non-excepted trade or business assets, the gain or loss on the disposition of the stock would be included in the shareholder's ATI. Under proposed § 1.163(j)-10(b)(4)(ii), if a shareholder recognizes gain or loss upon the disposition of stock in an S corporation that owns (1) non-excepted assets and excepted assets, (2) investment assets, or (3) both, the shareholder would determine the proportionate share of the amount properly allocable to a non-excepted trade or business, in accordance with the allocation rules set forth in proposed § 1.163(j)-10(c)(5)(ii)(B)(3), and would include such proportionate share of gain or loss in the shareholder's ATI. Proposed § 1.163(j)-10(b)(4)(ii) would also apply to tiered passthrough entities, as defined in proposed § 1.163(j)-7(f)(13), by looking through each passthrough entity tier (for example, an S corporation that is the partner of the highest-tier partnership would look through each lower-tier partnership), subject to proposed § 1.163(j)-10(c)(5)(ii)(D).

iii Double Counting of Business Interest Income Prohibited

Proposed § 1.163(j)-6(l)(4)(iii) would incorporate the limitations set forth in Notice 2018-28, which the Treasury Department and the IRS issued "to prevent the double counting of business interest income and floor plan financing interest expense for purposes of the deduction afforded by section 163(j)." Notice 2018-28, section 7. Consistent with the Notice's statement regarding the application of such limitations to S corporations and their shareholders, proposed § 1.163(j)-6(l)(4)(iii) would provide that, for purposes of calculating an S corporation shareholder's section 163(j) limitation, the shareholder would not include business interest income from an S corporation that is subject to section 163(j) except to the extent it is allocated excess business interest income from that S corporation pursuant to proposed § 1.163(j)-6(l)(1). In addition, proposed § 1.163(j)-6(l)(4)(iii) would provide that an S corporation shareholder could not include its share of the S corporation's floor plan financing interest expense for purposes of calculating a shareholder's section 163(j) limitation because such floor plan financing interest expense would have already have been taken into account by the S corporation in determining its nonseparately stated taxable income or loss for purposes of section 163(j).

iv. Business Interest Expense Carryforwards

Section 163(j)(4) does not indicate the manner by which disallowed business interest expense carryforwards should be treated by an S corporation and its shareholders. However, by virtue of the fact that section 163(j)(4)(D) references both sections 163(j)(4)(A) and (C), but not (B), an inference could be made that Congress intended that disallowed business interest expense carryforwards that arise from an S corporation should be treated differently than excess business interest expense incurred by a partnership. The legislative history appears to support such inference by indicating that the "special rule for carryforward of disallowed partnership interest" in section 163(j)(4)(B) "does not apply to S corporations and their shareholders." H. Rept. 115-466, at 391 (2017).

In light of the statutory language and the legislative history, proposed § 1.163(j)-6(l)(5) provides that the rules set forth in proposed § 1.163(j)-2(c) govern the treatment of S corporation business interest expense carryforwards. Consequently, if an S corporation has a disallowed business interest expense carryforward in the year the S corporation terminates, such item will be carried forward to the succeeding C corporation taxable year. The Treasury Department and the IRS request comments regarding the treatment of disallowed business interest expense carryforwards as an attribute of the S corporation, subject to section 382 limitations, as opposed to the shareholders, and the timing for any adjustments to shareholder basis and the S corporation's accumulated adjustment account. By deferring adjustments to shareholder basis and the S corporation's accumulated adjustments account until any carryforwards are deductible at the corporate level, these proposed regulations generally would match the economics of these adjustments to the shareholders holding stock at the time the S corporation's carryforwards would become deductible.

The Treasury Department and the IRS, however, have considered an alternative option to the rules set forth in proposed § 1.163(j)-6(l)(5). This alternative option would allocate carryforwards from an S corporation to its shareholders in a manner similar to proposed § 1.163(j)-6(g) for partnerships and their partners. This option would require shareholders to receive excess taxable income or excess business interest income from the S corporation in order to treat the disallowed business interest carryforwards as paid or accrued by the shareholder. The shareholder's basis and the S corporation's accumulated adjustment account would be reduced upon an allocation of excess business interest expense to the shareholders.

This alternative option would set forth a framework that would be consistent with the flow-through nature of S corporations. For example, S corporations, similar to partnerships, allocate items of deduction and expense in the year that they occur, even if such items might be suspended at the shareholder-level under section 1366(d). In addition, S corporation shareholders calculate their respective bases in a manner similar to partners, except that S corporation shareholders do not take into account entity-level debt. Thus, corporate attributes generally are suspended at the shareholder-level under the existing subchapter S framework. The Treasury Department and the IRS request comments on this alternative approach and the authoritative support for adopting it.

v. Applicability of Section 382 to S Corporations Regarding Disallowed Business Interest Expense Carryforwards

Although the Treasury Department and the IRS have determined that sections 381(c)(20) and 382(d)(3) and (k)(1) apply to S corporations with respect to disallowed business interest expense carryforwards, the Treasury Department and the IRS continue to consider the extent to which section 382 should apply to S corporations for purposes other than section 163(j). The application of section 382 to S corporations for purposes of section 163(j) should not be construed as creating any inference regarding the application of section 382 to S corporations for other purposes. The Treasury Department and the IRS seek comments regarding the proper integration of these two Code sections and subchapter S of the Code (for example, comments regarding the interaction between sections 382 and 1362(e)(6)(D)).

I. Partnership or S Corporation Not Subject to Section 163(j)

Proposed §1.163(j)-6(m) would provide guidance regarding partnerships and S corporations not subject to section 163(j). If a partnership or S corporation is not subject to section 163(j) by reason of proposed §1.163(j)-2(d) (exempt entity), the exempt entity would not be required to perform the business interest expense limitation calculations under proposed §§1.163(j)-2(b) and 1.163(j)-6. To the extent a partner or shareholder receives business interest expense from an exempt entity, however, that business interest expense will be subject to the partner or shareholder's own section 163(j) deduction. In the event a partner or shareholder is subject to section 163(j) and the S corporation or partnership is not, the partnership or S corporation shall provide the partner or shareholder with the information necessary to inform the partner or shareholder of the partner or shareholder's share of the partnership or S corporation's business interest expense, business interest income, and items of ATI.

To the extent a partnership or S corporation is not subject to section 163(j) by reason of proposed §1.163(j)-1(b)(38)(ii) because it has an excepted trade or business (excepted entity), the excepted entity would not have to perform the business interest expense limitation calculations under proposed §§1.163(j)-2(b) and 1.163(j)-6 with respect to the business interest expense that is allocated to such electing trade or business. To the extent a partner or shareholder is allocated any section 163(j) item that is allocated to the partnership's excepted trade or business (excepted 163(j) items), such excepted 163(j) items would be excluded from the partner or shareholder's section 163(j) deduction calculation.

In the event a partnership allocates excess business interest expense to one or more of its partners, and in a later taxable year becomes exempt from the requirements of section 163(j)(4), proposed §1.163(j)-6(l) would provide that the excess business interest expense from the prior taxable years is treated as paid or accrued by the partner in such later taxable year.

7. Proposed §1.163(j)-7: Application of Section 163(j) to Foreign Corporations and Their Shareholders

A. Overview

The Treasury Department and the IRS received comments requesting clarification on whether section 163(j) applies to a controlled foreign corporation (as defined in section 957) (CFC) and, if so, the manner in which it applies.

These proposed regulations would provide the general rule that section 163(j) and the section 163(j) regulations apply to determine the deductibility of a CFC's business interest expense in the same manner as those provisions apply to determine the deductibility of a domestic C corporation's business interest expense. See proposed §1.163(j)-7(b)(2). Thus, a CFC with business interest expense would apply section 163(j) to determine the extent to which that expense is deductible for purposes of computing subpart F income as defined under section 952, tested income as defined under section 951A(c)(2)(A), and income which is effectively connected with the conduct of a U.S. trade or business (ECI), as applicable. Additional guidance for a CFC (and other foreign persons) with ECI is provided in proposed §1.163(j)-8 and discussed in part 8 of this Explanation of Provisions section.

Notwithstanding the general applicability of section 163(j) to CFCs under these proposed regulations, the Treasury Department and the IRS have determined that it is appropriate in certain cases to modify its application. As discussed in part 7(B) and part 7(C) of this Explanation of Provisions section, these proposed regulations would, in certain cases, limit the amount of a CFC's business interest expense subject to the section 163(j) limitation and modify the computation of a CFC's ATI, respectively.

The Treasury Department and the IRS continue to study whether it would be appropriate to provide additional modifications to the application of section 163(j) to CFCs and whether there are particular circumstances in which it may be appropriate to exempt a CFC from the application of section 163(j). The Treasury Department and the IRS request comments on this matter.

B. Computation of Amount of Business Interest Expense Subject to Section 163(j)

The Treasury Department and the IRS are aware that if business interest expense is paid by one CFC to a related CFC, the application of section 163(j) could result in an inappropriate mismatch of a deduction and payee income item. Such mismatch could inappropriately impact the calculation of the tax liability of a United States shareholder, as defined in section 951(b), under section 951A or the GILTI provision. Consider an example where a United States person (USP) wholly owns two CFCs (CFC1 and CFC2), and CFC1 has made a loan to CFC2 with respect to which CFC1 annually accrues $100x of business interest income that is included in CFC1's tested income, and CFC2 pays or accrues $100x of business interest expense, which absent section 163(j), would be fully deductible in computing CFC2's tested income or tested loss, as applicable. Thus, the intercompany business interest income and business interest expense would fully offset one another for purposes of computing USP's inclusion under section 951A(a). To the extent section 163(j) were to disallow a deduction for business interest expense to CFC2 while the business interest income would be included in CFC1's tested income, the amounts would not fully offset, and USP's inclusion under section 951A(a) may be increased solely due to the use of intercompany debt between CFC1 and CFC2.

The Treasury Department and the IRS considered the possibility of completely disregarding all business interest income and business interest expense with respect to intercompany debt between related CFCs for purposes of computing the section 163(j) limitation of the lender CFC and borrower CFC (the disregard approach). However, the disregard approach was rejected because it could cause inappropriate results where, for example, one CFC (CFC finco) borrows from a third party and on-lends the debt proceeds to one or more other CFCs within a group (funded CFCs). Assume for purposes of simplicity that a CFC finco charges interest on loans to the funded CFCs at the same rate that it is charged by the third party. If intercompany business interest income received by CFC finco and business interest expense paid or accrued by the funded CFCs were disregarded in determining each CFC's section 163(j) limitation, then CFC finco would have no business interest income, and all of CFC finco's business interest expense paid to the third party would be subject to the section 163(j) limitation. Furthermore, all of the funded CFCs would have no business interest expense subject to the section 163(j) limitation. This would be the case, even though the funded CFCs have borrowed from CFC finco and have the use of the funds originally borrowed from the third party.

The Treasury Department and the IRS have determined that an approach that better reflects the reality of borrowings by related CFCs is one that takes into account the principle that money is fungible within a group of highly related CFCs (such a group, a "CFC group" and a CFC that is a member of the group, a "CFC group member"). Accordingly, these proposed regulations would provide for an election to apply an alternative method that would limit the amount of business interest expense of a CFC group member subject to the section 163(j) limitation to the amount of the CFC group member's allocable share of the CFC group's applicable net business interest expense. See proposed §1.163(j)-7(b)(3). The applicable net business interest expense of a CFC group is the excess, if any, of the sum of the amounts of business interest expense of each CFC group member over the sum of the amounts of business interest income of each CFC group member. See proposed §1.163(j)-7(f)(3). A CFC group member's allocable share is computed by multiplying the applicable net business interest expense of the CFC group by a fraction, the numerator of which is the CFC group member's net business interest expense (computed on a separate company basis), and the denominator of which is the sum of the amounts of the net business interest expense of each CFC group member with net business interest expense (computed on a separate company basis). See proposed §1.163(j)-7(f)(1).

Thus, if an election is made to apply the alternative method and if a CFC group has only intercompany debt within the CFC group, then the amount of the CFC group's applicable net business interest expense is zero, and no business interest expense of any CFC group member would be subject to the section 163(j) limitation. As a result, for example, there would be no increase in an inclusion under section 951A(a) solely by reason of the use of intercompany debt within a CFC group. On the other hand, if a CFC group has applicable net business interest expense, then, consistent with the principle that money is fungible, each CFC group member that has net business interest expense, computed on a separate company basis, will determine its allocable share of the applicable net business interest expense, and such allocable share is the amount of business interest expense of the CFC group member that is subject to the section 163(j) limitation. Using its allocable share of the CFC group's applicable net business interest expense, a CFC group member computes its section 163(j) limitation on a separate company basis. However, as discussed in part 7(C) of this Explanation of Provisions section, under these proposed regulations, for purposes of computing a CFC's ATI, an upper-tier CFC group member takes into account a proportionate share of the "excess" ATI of a lower-tier CFC group member.

In general, for purposes of these proposed regulations, a CFC group means two or more CFCs, if at least 80 percent of the stock by value of each CFC is owned, within the meaning of section 958(a), by a single U.S. shareholder or, in aggregate, by related U.S. shareholders that own stock of each member in the same proportion. See proposed § 1.163(j)-7(f)(6). For purposes of identifying a CFC group, members of a consolidated group are treated as a single person, as are individuals filing a joint return, and stock owned by certain passthrough entities is treated as owned by the owners or beneficiaries of the passthrough entity. The Treasury Department and the IRS determined that the alternative method is appropriately limited to situations in which a payor CFC and payee CFC have substantially identical ownership by United States shareholders because the alternative is based on the principle that money is fungible. The alternative is based on the principle that money is fungible, but fungibility should only apply in cases of close relationship where borrowings essentially support the entire group. Furthermore, the mismatch of a deduction and a payee income item is most significant when the payee and payor CFC have substantially identical ownership by United States shareholders. These proposed regulations narrow the scope of foreign corporations that are CFCs for this purpose to those foreign corporations in which at least one United States shareholder owns stock, within the meaning of section 958. These proposed regulations refer to such a CFC as an "applicable CFC." See proposed § 1.163(j)-7(f)(2).

If one or more CFC group members conduct a financial services business, the alternative method is applied by treating those entities as comprising a separate subgroup (such a subgroup, a "financial services subgroup" and such a member, a "financial services subgroup member"). For this purpose, an entity conducts a financial services business if it is an eligible controlled foreign corporation, as defined in section 954(h)(2)(A), is a qualified insurance company, as defined in section 953(e)(3), or is eligible for the dealer exception in computing foreign personal holding company income as described in section 954(c)(2)(C). The Treasury Department and the IRS determined that it is appropriate to apply the alternative method separately for entities that conduct financial services businesses, because those businesses are typically highly leveraged with significant amounts of business interest income and business interest expense and could reasonably be expected to cause distortion if included in the alternative method with other, non-financial services business CFC group members.

These proposed regulations generally treat a controlled partnership (in general, a partnership in which CFC group members own, in aggregate, at least 80 percent of the interests) as a CFC group member and the interest in the controlled partnership is treated as stock. Thus, for example, if a U.S. person wholly owns two applicable CFCs, which each own a 50-percent interest in a partnership, then, if an election is made to apply the alternative method, the partnership will also apply the alternative method. The Treasury Department and the IRS determined that it is appropriate to extend the relief to partnerships that are substantially owned by CFC group members because the principle that money is fungible is not limited to corporate entities. Furthermore, absent such a rule, a partnership could be used to inappropriately exclude an applicable CFC from the CFC group by having the partnership own the applicable CFC.

These proposed regulations exclude from the definition of a CFC group member an applicable CFC that has ECI. Thus, an applicable CFC with ECI may not compute its section 163(j) limitation under the alternative method, and furthermore, the CFC group, and any financial services subgroup, must exclude such CFC from all group-level computations (for example, in determining the amount of the CFC group's applicable net business interest expense). The Treasury Department and the IRS determined that it is appropriate to exclude an applicable CFC with ECI from application of the alternative method so that section 163(j) applies to a CFC with ECI in the same manner as it does to a domestic C corporation. However, although an applicable CFC with ECI cannot use the alternative method, an applicable CFC with ECI is treated as a CFC group member solely for purposes of determining a CFC group. Thus, for example, if an applicable CFC with ECI is wholly owned by an upper-tier CFC and the applicable CFC with ECI wholly owns a lower-tier CFC, the lower-tier CFC may still qualify as a CFC group member.

If not all CFC group members have the same taxable year, then, if the election is made, these proposed regulations require that all group-level computations be made with respect to a majority U.S. shareholder taxable year. See proposed § 1.163(j)-7(f)(11). Thus, if, for example, USP, a domestic corporation with a calendar taxable year, wholly owns two applicable CFCs, one with a calendar year and one with a November 30 fiscal year, then, with respect to USP's 2019 calendar year, the group-level computations must be determined using amounts for the taxable year ending November 30, 2019, for the one applicable CFC, and amounts for the taxable year ending December 31, 2019, for the other applicable CFC.

Finally, these proposed regulations provide rules concerning the election (referred to as a "CFC group election"), including the requirements for making the CFC group election, the manner for making the CFC group election, and the duration of the CFC group election. See proposed § 1.163(j)-7(b)(5). The Treasury Department and the IRS determined that the alternative method should be elective, rather than required, because for certain situations, the general application of section 163(j) may be preferable to taxpayers.

C. Rules for Computing the ATI of an Applicable CFC

Proposed § 1.163(j)-7(c) would provide rules for computing the ATI of an applicable CFC. The principles of § 1.952-2 for determining the CFC's income and deductions or, for CFCs with ECI, the rules of section 882, apply for purposes of computing the CFC's taxable income. See proposed § 1.163(j)-7(c)(1). The Treasury Department and the IRS request comments on the application of the rules under § 1.952-2 for purposes of determining a CFC's taxable income for purposes of section 163(j). In particular, comments are requested as to whether these rules should allow a CFC a deduction, or require a CFC to take into account income, that is expressly limited to domestic corporations under the Code. For example, questions have arisen as to whether a CFC should be allowed a dividends-received deduction under section 245A, even though section 245A by its terms applies only to dividends received by a domestic corporation.

To mitigate potential double-counting of income in ATI, any dividend received by an applicable CFC from a related person is subtracted from the distributee's taxable income for purposes of computing ATI as the dividend represents income that could be part of the distributing corporation's ATI. See proposed § 1.163(j)-7(c)(2).

If a CFC group election is in effect with respect to a CFC group, then an upper-tier CFC group member takes into account a proportionate share of the "excess" ATI (referred to in these proposed regulations as "CFC excess taxable income") of each lower-tier member in which it directly owns stock for purposes of computing the upper-tier member's ATI. See proposed § 1.163(j)-7(c)(3). The meaning of the term CFC excess taxable income is analogous to the meaning of the term "excess taxable income" in the context of a partnership and S corporation, and, in general, means the amount of a CFC group member's ATI in excess of the amount needed before there would be disallowed business interest expense. See proposed § 1.163(j)-7(f)(5). A CFC group member that is a partnership does not have CFC excess taxable income because under the statute and proposed § 1.163(j)-6, the partnership has excess taxable income and such excess taxable income is allocated to the partners of the partnership. For a discussion of the computation of a partnership's excess taxable income and the treatment of a partner's distributive share of any such excess taxable income, see the discussion in part 6 of this Explanation of Provisions section.

The process of computing and "rolling up" CFC excess taxable income among CFC group members for purposes of computing ATI of each of the CFC group members begins with a lowest-tier member and continues through the chain of ownership to a highest-tier member of the CFC group (referred to in these proposed regulations as a "specified highest-tier member"). Thus, a lowest-tier member computes its section 163(j) limitation, and if the lowest-tier member has CFC excess taxable income, the CFC excess taxable income is taken into account proportionately by one or more higher-tier members that directly own stock of the lower-tier member for purposes of computing ATI; and, if such a higher-tier member has CFC excess taxable income, such CFC excess taxable income is taken into account by a next higher-tier member, and so forth.

A higher-tier member that is a partnership may take into account a pro rata share of the CFC excess taxable income of a lower-tier member, other than a partnership, which does not have CFC excess taxable income, for purposes of computing the higher-tier member partnership's ATI and determining if the higher-tier member partnership has excess taxable income that may be allocated to CFC group members that are partners.

D. Rules for Computing ATI of a United States Shareholder

i. General Rules

In general, a United States shareholder that owns, within the meaning of section 958(a), stock of a CFC is required to include in its gross income each year its pro rata share of the CFC's subpart F income, and investments in U.S. property, as defined in section 956. In addition, a United States shareholder that owns stock of a CFC is required to include in its gross income for each year its GILTI. Thus, these income inclusions are included in the United States shareholder's taxable income, and absent an exercise of regulatory authority, would be included in ATI.

To avoid double counting of the taxable income of a CFC already taken into account to determine the CFC's section 163(j) limitation, proposed §1.163(j)-7(d)(1)(i) would provide the general rule (the double counting rule) that the ATI of a United States shareholder is computed without regard to any amounts included in gross income under sections 78, 951(a), and 951A(a) that are properly allocable to a non-excepted trade or business of the United States shareholder (each amount, a "specified deemed inclusion" and such amounts, collectively "specified deemed inclusions") and any deduction allowable under section 250(a)(1)(B), without regard to the taxable income limitation in section 250(a)(2), by reason of a specified deemed inclusion (such a deduction, a "specified section 250 deduction").

To the extent a United States shareholder includes amounts in gross income under section 78, 951(a), or 951A(a) that are not properly allocable to a non-excepted trade or business, for example, because such amounts are treated as investment income, within the meaning of section 163(d), of the United States shareholder, then such amounts are not included in ATI (see proposed §1.163(j)-1(b)(1)(ii)(F)). Thus, for example, if a United States shareholder that is a domestic partnership includes amounts in gross income under section 951(a) or 951A(a) that are treated as investment income with respect to the domestic partnership and therefore are not properly allocable to a trade or business, then such amounts are not included in the ATI of the domestic partnership. However, absent a special rule, to the extent such income inclusions are taken into account as a distributive share of a C corporation partner, the income inclusions would be included in the ATI of the C corporation partner (see proposed §1.163(j)-4(b)(3)). This result would be contrary to the purpose of the double counting rule. Accordingly, to prevent income inclusions under sections 951(a) and 951A(a) that are treated as investment income with respect to a domestic partnership from being included in the ATI of a corporate partner, these proposed regulations provide that a C corporation partner may not treat such amounts as properly allocable to a trade or business of the C corporation partner. See proposed §1.163(j)-7(d)(1)(ii).

ii. Rules for a United States Shareholder of a CFC group Member with a CFC Group Election in Effect

If a United States shareholder owns directly or indirectly through one or more foreign partnerships stock of a CFC group member that is a specified highest-tier member for which a CFC group election is in effect, and the specified highest-tier member has CFC excess taxable income that is treated as being attributable to taxable income of the CFC group that resulted in the United States shareholder having specified income inclusions, the United States shareholder may add to its taxable income an amount equal to its proportionate share of the "eligible" CFC excess taxable income of the specified highest-tier member and any other highest-tier members (the addback rule). See proposed §1.163(j)-7(d)(2). However, the addition to taxable income under the addback rule is limited to the portion of the specified deemed inclusions, all of which are subtracted from taxable income of any United States shareholder under the double-counting rule, that is with respect to CFC group members, reduced by the portion of any specified section 250 deduction that is allowable by reason of such specified deemed inclusions. These proposed regulations refer to the portion described in the preceding sentence as "CFC group inclusions" (see proposed §1.163(j)-7(d)(2)(iii)). Furthermore, the limitation is computed without regard to amounts included in gross income by reason of section 78 with respect to CFC group members. This result is appropriate because section 78 requires a deemed inclusion only in order to carry out the purposes of the foreign tax credit provisions.

To determine the amount of "eligible" CFC excess taxable income (ETI) of a specified highest-tier member (defined under proposed §1.163(j)-7(d)(2)(ii) as "eligible CFC group ETI"), the CFC excess taxable income is multiplied by the specified ETI ratio. The specified ETI ratio is a fraction (expressed as a percentage) that compares the amounts of taxable income of each specified highest-tier member and each specified lower-tier member of the specified highest-tier member to the portions of such taxable income that gave rise to inclusions under section 951(a) or 951A(a). The specified ETI ratio includes in the numerator and the denominator of the fraction only taxable income amounts with respect to CFC group members that have CFC excess taxable income without regard to the "roll up" of CFC excess taxable income from a lower-tier member. See proposed §1.163(j)-7(f)(14). The purpose of the specified ETI ratio is to address the fact that within the CFC group, income of a lower-tier member CFC that is neither subpart F income nor tested income to the extent of GILTI is included in CFC excess taxable income and may be used by an upper-tier CFC group member. It would be distortive for a United States shareholder to obtain an increase in ATI in respect of such income because this income is not taxed in the United States. The specified ETI ratio is intended to provide an estimate of the portion of CFC excess taxable income attributable to this income. The Treasury Department and the IRS determined that this formulaic approach is superior to a tracing approach, because a tracing approach would increase complexity and therefore also generally increase administrative and compliance burdens.

If a United States shareholder of a CFC group member with a CFC group election in effect is a domestic partnership (a U.S. shareholder partnership), the addback rule does not apply to determine the ATI of the U.S. shareholder partnership. See proposed §1.163(j)-7(d)(3). This is because the Treasury Department and the IRS are of the view that if a U.S. shareholder partnership includes amounts in gross income under section 951(a) or 951A(a) with respect to stock of a CFC group member, then such amounts will, in virtually all fact patterns, be treated as investment income with respect to the partnership, and therefore interest expense of the partnership that is allocable to stock of a CFC group member will be treated as investment interest expense that is not subject to section 163(j) at the partnership-level. In this case, however, if a U.S. shareholder partnership has a domestic C corporation partner (a U.S. corporate partner), the addback rule is applied, with certain modifications, to the U.S. corporate partner for purposes of computing the U.S. corporate partner's ATI. In particular, for purposes of computing the amount of the addition to taxable income of the U.S. corporate partner allowed under the addback rule, the addback rule is modified to provide that the U.S. corporate partner takes into account not only its own specified deemed inclusions with respect to stock of a CFC group member, but for this purpose also its distributive share, if any, of amounts included in gross income under section 951(a) or 951A(a) of the U.S. shareholder partnership with respect to stock of a CFC group member. In addition, the addback rule is modified to provide that for purposes of determining a U.S. corporate partner's pro rata share of eligible CFC excess taxable income of a specified highest-tier member, the U.S. shareholder partnership is treated as if it were a foreign partnership.

E. Effect on Earnings and Profits

Under proposed §1.163(j)-7(e), and consistent with the rules in proposed §1.163(j)-4(c), the disallowance and carryforward of a deduction for a foreign corporation's business interest expense does not affect whether and when such business interest expense reduces the corporation's earnings and profits. For example, in the case of a passive foreign investment company (PFIC), the disallowance and carryforward of a deduction will not impact the amount of inclusions of earnings under section 1293 if the PFIC is treated as a qualified electing fund. Similarly, the disallowance and carryforward of a deduction for an applicable CFC's business interest expense will not affect the limitation of subpart F income to earnings and profits under section 952(c).

8. Proposed §1.163(j)-8: Application of Section 163(j) to Foreign Persons with Effectively Connected Income

In general, unlike U.S. citizens or residents that are subject to U.S. tax on their worldwide income, a nonresident alien individual or foreign corporation is subject to net basis income taxation only with respect to its income that is or is treated as effectively connected with a trade or business (ECI) conducted in the United States as provided under section 872 or 882. Deductions are allowed only to the extent that they are connected with such income. In certain circumstances, the tax liability may be reduced or eliminated by the provisions of an income tax treaty entered into by the United States with a foreign country. While a nonresident alien individual or foreign corporation that is not an applicable CFC (hereafter a non-CFC FC) that has ECI is still subject to section 163(j) and the section 163(j) regulations, the rules need to be modified since these foreign persons are only taxed on their ECI. Accordingly, the definitions for ATI, business interest expense, business interest income, and floor plan financing interest expense in §1.163(j)-1 are modified to limit such amounts to income which is effectively connected income and expenses properly allocable to effectively connected income. See proposed §1.163(j)-8(b).

As discussed in part 6 of this Explanation of Provisions section, section 163(j)(4) provides that in the case of a partnership, section 163(j) is applied at the partnership level. The partner's ATI is increased by the partnership's excess taxable income, and the partnership's excess business interest expense is allocated to the partner as disallowed business interest expense carryforward that can be deducted when the partners are allocated excess taxable income from the partnership, but only to the extent of such excess. Pursuant to section 163(j)(8)(B), which permits adjustments to the computation of ATI, a nonresident alien individual or non-CFC FC that is a partner in a partnership that is engaged in a U.S. trade or business modifies the application of the general allocation rules in §1.163(j)-6 with respect to excess taxable income, excess business interest expense, and excess business interest income of the partnership to take into account the limitation of such foreign person's liability for U.S. tax to its ECI. The excess amounts of the partnership, therefore, can be used by the nonresident alien individual or non-CFC FC only to the extent of the partnership's income that would be effectively connected income with respect to the foreign partner. The amount of excess taxable income and excess business interest expense that can be used by such partner is determined by multiplying the amount of the excess taxable income or the excess business interest allocated under §1.163(j)-6 by a ratio equal to the ATI of the partnership, with the adjustments described previously to limit such amount to only effectively connected income or expense items, over the ATI of the partnership determined under §1.163(j)-6(d). The amount of excess business interest income that can be used by such partner is limited to ECI business interest income over allocable ECI business interest expense. See proposed §1.163(j)-8(c).

Proposed §1.163(j)-8(e) would also include rules coordinating section 163(j) and §1.882-5. Section 1.882-5 provides rules for determining the amount of a foreign corporation's interest expense that is allocable under section 882(c) to ECI. These proposed regulations require that a foreign corporation that has ECI must first determine its business interest expense allocable to ECI under §1.882-5 before applying section 163(j). The foreign corporation then applies section 163(j) to its business interest expense to determine if any of that business interest expense is disallowed business interest expense. If the foreign corporation is also a partner in a partnership that has ECI, the foreign corporation must back out that portion of the business interest expense determined under §1.882-5 which is deemed to have come from the partnership as such business interest expense has already been subject to section 163(j) at the partnership level and the foreign corporation is then left with only the non-partnership business interest expense. If the partnership also had disallowed business interest expense, a portion of the partnership-level interest expense that was backed out of the amount determined under §1.882-5 will also be disallowed business interest expense. Disallowed business interest expense determined at either the partner-level or partnership level, as appropriate, will not be taken into account for the purpose of determining interest expense under §1.882-5 in subsequent tax years, but rather will be subject to the limitations of section 163(j).

As provided in proposed §1.163(j)-8(d), an applicable CFC (as defined in proposed §1.163(j)-8(g)(1)) that has ECI must first apply the general rules of section 163(j) and the section 163(j) regulations, pursuant to §1.163(j)-7(b)(2), to determine how section 163(j) applies to the applicable CFC. If, after applying section 163(j) and the section 163(j) regulations, the applicable CFC has disallowed business interest expense, the applicable CFC then must apportion a part of its disallowed business interest expense to interest expense allocable to effectively connected income as determined under §1.882-5.

These proposed regulations also provide that disallowed business interest expense and disallowed business interest expense carryforwards will not affect the determination of effectively connected earnings and profits or U.S. net equity for purposes of the branch profits tax under section 884. These rules are consistent with the general principles of these proposed regulations with respect to earnings and profits. See proposed §§1.163(j)-4(c) and 1.163(j)-8(f).

9. Proposed §1.163(j)-9: Elections for Excepted Trades or Businesses; Safe Harbor for Certain REITs

A. Election Procedure

Proposed §1.163(j)-9 would provide guidance relating to the election to be treated as an excepted trade or business for real property or farming trades or businesses. These proposed regulations clarify that an election is made for a particular trade or business, not necessarily for a particular entity, and would apply for the taxable year that the election is made and all subsequent years.

Proposed §1.163(j)-9 would provide the time and manner in which to make the election. Taxpayers making the election should attach an election statement to their timely filed original Federal income tax return, including extensions. The statement should include basic information of the taxpayer and the electing trade or business. Where a taxpayer has multiple trades or businesses that may be eligible for the election, an election must be made for each trade or business, and the election statement must specify or describe the different electing trades or businesses. The election statement is necessary in order for taxpayers and for the IRS to identify each electing trade or business. The Treasury Department and the IRS request comments on whether the information required to be included in the statement is sufficient, or whether additional information should be included to reduce any potential audit controversy.

Because the election applies to the particular trade or business, the election generally terminates automatically if the taxpayer ceases to exist, or ceases the operation of the electing trade or business. However, these proposed regulations would also provide that where a taxpayer transfers all of the assets of an electing trade or business to a related party, the election does not terminate for that trade or business, and transfers to the related party. The purpose of this rule is to disregard a transaction that purports to be a termination or cessation of a trade or business, but is merely a change in the form of conducting the trade or business where the taxpayer (through a related party) retains a relationship to such trade or business. For this purpose, a related party means any person who bears a relationship to the taxpayer which is described in section 267(b) or 707(b)(1). Additional guidance may be provided detailing transactions in which an election might terminate.

Additionally, these proposed regulations would contain an anti-abuse rule to prevent a situation where the taxpayer attempts to terminate the election through a transfer of the assets in the trade or business, but with the intent of resuming a trade or business of a similar nature. These proposed regulations would provide that if a taxpayer re-acquires substantially all of the assets used in the trade or business, or substantially similar assets, and resumes conducting such prior trade or business within 60 months of ceasing the trade or business, the election will be revived with the resumed trade or business.

The Treasury Department and the IRS request comments on the method by which certain taxpayers can make the election under section 163(j)(7)(B) or (C), and the types of transactions in which the election should terminate.

B. Safe Harbor for Certain REITs

Proposed § 1.163(j)-9(g) provides a special safe harbor for REITs. For REITs that take advantage of this safe harbor, the rules applicable to REITs are substantially similar to the general rules provided for other taxpayers. However, these proposed regulations provide certain modifications to take into account the existing rules governing REIT taxation.

If a REIT holds real property, interests in partnerships holding real property, or shares in other REITs holding real property, the safe harbor provides that the REIT is eligible to make an election to be an electing real property trade or business for all or part of its assets. For this purpose, the term "real property" is defined consistently with the definition of real property under section 856, rather than the more restrictive definition set forth under the proposed section 469 regulations.

The term "real property trade or business" in section 469(c)(7)(C) does not include real property financing and, for purposes of the section 163(j) regulations, any assets used in a real property financing trade or business are generally allocated to a non-excepted trade or business. Under proposed § 1.163(j)-9(g), REIT real property financing assets include mortgages, guaranteed mortgage pass-thru certificates, real estate mortgage investment conduit (REMIC) regular interests, and debt instruments issued by publicly offered REITs.

If a REIT makes an election to be an electing real property trade or business, and the value of the REIT's real property financing assets is 10 percent or less of the value of the REIT's total assets, then, under the safe harbor, all of the REIT's assets are treated as assets of an excepted trade or business. This determination is based on the same values used for the REIT asset test under section 856(c)(4) as of the close of the REIT's taxable year. If a REIT makes an election to be an electing real property trade or business, and the value of a REIT's real property financing assets is more than 10 percent of the value of the REIT's total assets, then, under the safe harbor, the REIT's business interest income, business interest expense, and other items of expense and gross income are allocated between excepted and non-excepted trades or businesses under the rules set forth in proposed § 1.163(j)-10, as modified by proposed § 1.163(j)-9(g)(4).

For purposes of valuing a REIT's assets, REIT real property financing assets also include partnership assets that a REIT is deemed to hold under § 1.856-3(g) and the portion of a REIT's interest in another REIT attributable to that other REIT's real property financing assets. The Treasury Department and the IRS request comments on whether the list of real property financing assets in these proposed regulations includes all direct and indirect investments that REITs make to finance real property.

Under the safe harbor, the definition of real property under § 1.856-10 applies to determine whether the assets of a REIT are properly allocable to an excepted trade or business. If a REIT holds an interest in a partnership, in applying the partnership look-through rule described in proposed § 1.163(j)-10(c)(5)(ii)(A)(2), the REIT also applies this definition of real property to determine whether the partnership's assets are allocable to an excepted trade or business.

Under section 856(c)(5)(B), shares in other REITs qualify as real estate assets without regard to the portion of the REIT owned. Under the safe harbor, if a REIT (shareholder REIT) owns shares in another REIT and all of the other REIT's assets are treated as assets of an excepted trade or business, then all of shareholder REIT's adjusted basis in the shares of the other REIT is properly allocable to an excepted trade or business of shareholder REIT. If this is not the case, the safe harbor provides that shareholder REIT applies the partnership look-through rule described in proposed § 1.163(j)-10(c)(5)(ii)(A)(2) (as if the other REIT were a partnership) in determining the extent to which shareholder REIT's adjusted basis in the shares of the other REIT is properly allocable to an excepted trade or business of shareholder REIT. If shareholder REIT does not receive the information from the other REIT that is necessary to apply the look-through rule, then shareholder REIT's shares of the other REIT are properly allocable to a non-excepted trade or business of shareholder REIT.

C. Anti-abuse Rule for Certain Real Property Trades or Businesses

The Treasury Department and the IRS have determined that it would be inappropriate to allow an election to be an excepted real property trade or business for a trade or business that leases substantially all of its real property to the owner of the real property trade or business, or to a related party of the owner. To permit such an election would encourage a taxpayer to enter into non-economic structures where the real estate components of non-real estate businesses are separated from the rest of such businesses in order to artificially reduce the application of section 163(j) by leasing the real property to the taxpayer or a related party of the taxpayer and electing for this "business" to be an excepted real property trade or business. As a result, these proposed regulations would also contain an anti-abuse rule. If at least 80 percent of the business's real property, determined by fair market value, is leased to a trade or business under common control with the real property trade or business, the trade or business will not be eligible for the election. Common control in this case means that 50 percent of the direct and indirect ownership interests in both businesses are held by related parties within the meaning of sections 267(b) and 707(b). REITs that lease qualified lodging facilities, as defined in section 856(d)(9)(D), and qualified healthcare properties, as defined in section 856(e)(6)(D), are generally permitted pursuant to section 856(d)(8)(B) to lease these properties to a taxable REIT subsidiary; thus, this anti-abuse rule does not apply to these types of REITs. The Treasury Department and the IRS request comments on whether other exceptions to the anti-abuse rule (such as, for example, an exception for certain fact patterns where real property that is leased from a related party is ultimately sub-leased to a third party) would be appropriate.

10. Proposed § 1.163(j)-10: Allocation of Expense and Income to an Excepted Trade or Business

As provided in section 163(j)(7) and proposed § 1.163(j)-2, certain trades or businesses are excepted from the application of section 163(j), including electing real property trades or businesses, electing farming businesses, regulated utility trades or businesses, and the trade or business of performing services as an employee. Section 1.163(j)-10 would provide rules for determining the amount of a taxpayer's interest expense, interest income, and other tax items that is properly allocable to excepted and non-excepted trades or businesses for purposes of section 163(j). It is not necessary for a taxpayer to undertake any allocations under proposed § 1.163(j)-10 if all of the taxpayer's items are properly allocable to non-excepted trades or businesses, or if all of the taxpayer's items are properly allocable to excepted trades or businesses.

Proposed § 1.163(j)-10(a) would provide an overview of the section and certain general rules, including rules regarding the application of the allocation rules to members of a consolidated group. Proposed § 1.163(j)-10(b) would provide rules regarding the allocation of tax items other than interest expense and interest income between excepted and non-excepted trades or businesses. Proposed § 1.163(j)-10(c) would provide the general method of allocating interest expense and interest income between excepted and non-excepted trades or businesses using asset basis, as well as various special rules that would apply under this general method. Proposed § 1.163(j)-10(d) would describe several limited situations in which tracing rather than asset-based allocation is required.

Organizations subject to tax under section 511 are required to compute their unrelated business taxable income separately with respect to each trade or business, resulting in a more granular allocation than is required for purposes of the section 163(j) regulations. Accordingly, proposed § 1.163(j)-10(a)(5) would provide that such organizations would apply the allocation rules under section 512 and the regulations thereunder in determining whether items of income or expense are allocable to an excepted trade or business. The Treasury Department and the IRS request comments as to whether additional guidance is needed regarding the allocation of income and expenses of an organization subject to tax under section 511 to an excepted trade or business for purposes of section 163(j).

A. Proposed § 1.163(j)-10(a): Overview

Before applying the allocation rules in proposed § 1.163(j)-10, a taxpayer first must determine whether any interest paid or accrued is properly allocable to a trade or business. If so, and if the taxpayer does not qualify for the small business exemption under section 163(j)(3) and proposed § 1.163(j)-2, the taxpayer must apply the allocation rules of proposed § 1.163(j)-10 if the taxpayer has tax items from both excepted and non-excepted trades or businesses. The taxpayer must do so in order to determine the amount of interest expense that is business interest expense subject to limitation under section 163(j) and to determine which items are included or excluded in computing its section 163(j) limitation.

For purposes of the allocation rules in proposed § 1.163(j)-10, a taxpayer's activities are not treated as a trade or business if those activities do not involve the provision of services or products to a person other than the taxpayer. For example, if a taxpayer engaged in a manufacturing trade or business has in-house legal personnel that provide legal services solely to the taxpayer, the taxpayer is not treated as also engaged in the trade or business of providing legal services.

Additionally, for purposes of the allocation rules in proposed § 1.163(j)-10, a consolidated group would be treated as a single corporation. Thus, stock of a member that is owned by another member of the same group would not be treated as an asset for purposes of proposed § 1.163(j)-10, and the transfer of member stock to a nonmember would be treated by the group as the transfer of the member's assets. Additionally, the group, rather than a particular member, would be treated as engaged in excepted or non-excepted trades or businesses. Intercompany obligations issued by a member borrower would not be considered an asset of the creditor member for purposes of allocating asset basis between excepted and non-excepted trades or businesses. Moreover, intercompany transactions would be disregarded for purposes of proposed § 1.163(j)-10, along with the resulting offsetting items.

The Treasury Department and the IRS have determined that this approach to consolidated groups is necessary for purposes of proposed § 1.163(j)-10 because a particular trade or business may be conducted by multiple group members that also are engaged in other trades or businesses. Under these proposed regulations, the distinction between excepted and non-excepted trades or businesses applies at the level of the trade or business, not at the level of the group member; thus, the allocation rules in this section apply without regard to which member conducts a trade or business or possesses assets used in a trade or business.

The Treasury Department and the IRS considered an approach to the allocation rules in proposed § 1.163(j)-10 that would have taken into account intercompany transactions between consolidated group members engaged in excepted trades or businesses and members engaged in non-excepted trades or businesses. However, this approach would have resulted in different treatment for consolidated groups in which each member conducts a single trade or business and consolidated groups in which a single member engages in multiple trades or businesses. Moreover, if intercompany transactions were taken into account for purposes of proposed § 1.163(j)-10, then taxpayers potentially could increase the amount of interest allocable to an excepted trade or business or increase their section 163(j) limitation by engaging in intercompany transactions. Thus, the Treasury Department and the IRS have determined that intercompany transactions should be disregarded for purposes of proposed § 1.163(j)-10.

After a consolidated group has determined the percentage of the group's interest expense that is allocable to an excepted trade or business and thus is not subject to limitation under section 163(j), this exempt percentage would be applied proportionally to each member that has paid or accrued interest to a person other than a group member during the taxable year. Thus, in general, each member with interest paid or accrued to a lender that is not a group member will have the same percentage of interest allocable to excepted trades or businesses, regardless of whether any particular member actually engaged in an excepted trade or business. For rules regarding the deduction of interest expense paid or accrued by group members, see the discussion of proposed § 1.163(j)-5(b) in part 5 of this Explanation of Provisions section.

B. Proposed § 1.163(j)-10(b): Allocating Tax Items Other Than Interest Income and Interest Expense

In general, gross income other than dividends and interest income would be allocated to the trade or business that generated such gross income. The Treasury Department and the IRS request comments regarding this method of allocating items of income other than dividends and interest, including comments as to how this rule should be expanded or clarified.

With regard to dividend income, the Treasury Department and the IRS have determined that, if a taxpayer's ownership interest in a corporation equals or exceeds a certain threshold, the taxpayer generally should look through to the business activities of the corporation that paid the dividend. More specifically, if a taxpayer owns at least 80 percent of the stock of a domestic C corporation or a CFC (by vote and value; see section 1504(a)(2)) that is not eligible for the small business exemption under section 163(j)(3) and proposed § 1.163(j)-2(d)(1), then the taxpayer's dividend income would be treated as allocable to excepted or non-excepted trades or businesses based upon the relative amounts of the payor corporation's adjusted basis in the assets used in such trades or businesses. Additionally, if at least 90 percent of the payor corporation's adjusted basis in its assets is allocable to either excepted trades or businesses or non-excepted trades or businesses, then all of the taxpayer's dividend income from such corporation for the taxable year would be treated as allocable to either excepted or non-excepted trades or businesses, respectively.

If a shareholder in an S corporation looks through to the S corporation's basis in its assets for purposes of the basis allocation rules in proposed § 1.163(j)-10(c), the shareholder also would be required to look through to the S corporation's basis in its assets for purposes of characterizing any dividends received from the S corporation.

If a taxpayer receives a dividend that is not investment income, and if the dividend look-through rule is inapplicable to the taxpayer, then the taxpayer would treat the dividend income as allocable to a non-excepted trade or business. The Treasury Department and the IRS request comments on this proposed rule, including whether taxpayers that are C corporations or tax-exempt corporations should treat dividend income as allocable to a non-excepted trade or business if they fail to meet the minimum ownership threshold for dividends from domestic C corporations and CFCs.

With regard to dispositions of stock in a corporation or interests in a partnership, if a taxpayer recognizes gain or loss upon the disposition of stock in a non-consolidated C corporation that is not property held for investment, within the meaning of section 163(d)(5), and if the taxpayer looks through to the corporation's basis in its assets for purposes of the basis allocation rules in proposed § 1.163(j)-10(c), then the taxpayer would allocate the gain or loss to excepted or non-excepted trades or businesses based upon the relative amounts of the corporation's adjusted basis in the assets used in its trades or businesses, determined pursuant to proposed § 1.163(j)-10(c). If the taxpayer does not look through to the corporation's basis in its assets, the taxpayer would treat the gain or loss as allocable to a non-excepted trade or business. If a taxpayer recognizes gain or loss upon the disposition of interests in a partnership or stock in an S corporation that owns (1) non-excepted assets and excepted assets, (2) investment assets, or (3) both, the taxpayer would determine the proportionate share of the amount of basis properly allocable to a non-excepted trade or business in accordance with the allocation rules set forth in proposed § 1.163(j)-10(c)(5)(ii)(A) or proposed § 1.163(j)-10(c)(5)(ii)(B)(3), as appropriate, and include such proportionate amount of gain or loss in the taxpayer's ATI.

With regard to expenses, losses, and deductions other than interest, any such items that are definitely related to a trade or business, within the meaning of § 1.861-8(b), would be allocable to that trade or business. All other expenses would be ratably apportioned to gross income. The Treasury Department and the IRS request comments on this proposed method of allocating expenses other than interest expense, including whether this proposed rule should incorporate any of the special allocation rules in § 1.861-8(e).

C. Proposed § 1.163(j)-10(c): Allocating Interest Expense and Interest Income

Proposed § 1.163(j)-10(c) would set forth the general rule for allocating interest expense and interest income between excepted and non-excepted trades or businesses. Under this general rule, interest expense and interest income would be allocated between excepted and non-excepted trades or businesses based upon the relative amounts of the taxpayer's adjusted basis in the assets used in its excepted and non-excepted trades or businesses. This general method of allocation reflects the fact that money is fungible and the view that interest expense is attributable to all activities and property, regardless of any specific purpose for incurring an obligation on which interest is paid.

Under proposed § 1.163(j)-10(c), a taxpayer would determine the adjusted basis in its assets on a quarterly basis (each such quarterly period, a "determination period") and average those amounts to determine the relative amounts of asset basis for its excepted and non-excepted trades or businesses for a taxable year. The Treasury Department and the IRS request comments on the frequency of asset basis determinations required under proposed § 1.163(j)-10(c).

Proposed § 1.163(j)-10(c)(1) contains a general de minimis rule. Under this rule, if at least 90 percent of a taxpayer's basis in its assets for the taxable year is allocable to either excepted or non-excepted trades or businesses, determined under proposed § 1.163(j)-10(c), then all of the taxpayer's interest expense and interest income for that year that is properly allocable to a trade or business would be treated as allocable to excepted or non-excepted trades or businesses, respectively. The Treasury Department and the IRS request comments as to whether the application of this de minimis rule should be elective.

If an asset is used in more than one trade or business during a determination period, the taxpayer's basis in such asset would be allocated to each trade or business using the permissible methodology (see the following paragraph) that most reasonably reflects the use of the asset in each trade or business during the determination period. An allocation methodology most reasonably reflects the use of the asset in each trade or business if the methodology most properly reflects the proportionate benefit derived from the use of the asset in each trade or business.

Proposed § 1.163(j)-10(c) would provide several permissible methodologies for allocating basis in an asset used in more than one trade or business during a determination period, including the following: the relative amounts of gross income that an asset generates, has generated, or may reasonably be expected to generate with respect to the trades or businesses; the relative amounts of physical space used by each trade or business if the asset is land or an inherently permanent structure; and the relative amounts of output of each trade or business if each trade or business generates the same unit of output. The choice of method would be subject to de minimis exceptions, and taxpayers generally would not be permitted to vary their allocation methodology across determination periods within a taxable year or from one year to the next. Additionally, if none of the permissible methodologies reasonably reflects the use of an asset in each trade or business, the taxpayer's basis in the asset would not be taken into account for purposes of proposed § 1.163(j)-10(c). The Treasury Department and the IRS request comments on these proposed methods of allocating basis in an asset used in more than one trade or business.

Proposed § 1.163(j)-10(c)(3)(iii) would provide that for utility trades or businesses, the only permissible method for allocating asset basis between excepted and non-excepted utility activities is the relative amounts of output of the trades or businesses. For example, if an asset is used to furnish or sell electric energy, and a portion of the energy is sold to wholesale customers where rates are not set on a cost of service and rate of return basis while the remaining portion is sold at a rate established by a ratemaking body described in proposed § 1.163(j)-1(b)(13), the taxpayer must allocate the basis in the asset between the taxpayer's excepted and non-excepted trades or businesses. The Treasury Department and the IRS believe that other methods listed in proposed § 1.163(j)-10(c) that do not take into account the relative amounts of regulated and unregulated utility activities do not properly reflect the proportionate benefit derived from the use of the asset in each trade or business. The Treasury Department and the IRS request comments on this allocation methodology, including whether another methodology would more accurately reflect the extent to which a trade or business is an excepted utility business for this purpose.

These proposed regulations also would provide a de minimis rule for utility trades or businesses. Under the proposed de minimis rule, if more than 90 percent of the output of a trade or business is sold at rates described in the exception for regulated utility trades or businesses, the taxpayer would treat the entire trade or business as an excepted trade or business. The Treasury Department and the IRS request comments with respect to the de minimis rule for assets used in a utility trade or business, including whether another percentage threshold with respect to the de minimis rule would be more appropriate.

The allocation of asset basis between excepted and non-excepted trades or businesses under proposed § 1.163(j)-10(c) would be subject to numerous additional special rules. First, a taxpayer's adjusted basis in tangible depreciable property other than inherently permanent structures for which a deduction is allowable under section 167 would be determined using the alternative depreciation system under section 168(g). Additional first year depreciation, for example under section 168(k), would not be taken into account for purposes of the basis allocation rule in proposed § 1.163(j)-10(c) due to the distortive effects that such depreciation would have upon the relative adjusted basis of assets. Further, a taxpayer's adjusted basis in tangible depreciable property other than inherently permanent structures for which a deduction is allowable under section 168 of the 1954 Code (former section 168) would be determined using the taxpayer's method of computing depreciation for the property under former section 168. Additionally, a taxpayer's adjusted basis in any intangible asset with respect to which a deduction is allowable under section 167 or section 197 would be determined in accordance with section 167 or section 197, as applicable. Self-created intangibles would not be taken into account for purposes of the allocation rules in proposed § 1.163(j)-10(c). The Treasury Department and the IRS request comments on these proposed rules regarding asset basis in depreciable property, including whether taxpayers should be permitted to use other methods of depreciation, such as the general depreciation system under section 168(a), for purposes of proposed § 1.163(j)-10(c).

Second, the adjusted basis of any asset that is land, including nondepreciable improvements to land, or an inherently permanent structure used in a trade or business generally would be its unadjusted basis rather than its adjusted basis. This special rule, which would not apply to land or inherently permanent structures that fall within the special rule described in the following paragraph, is intended to provide taxpayers with a readily ascertainable figure that better reflects the relative underlying value of this limited class of assets—which, in some cases, are held for many years—than adjusted basis. The Treasury Department and the IRS request comments regarding this approach to allocating basis to land and inherently permanent structures, including whether this rule should be elective, and whether taxpayers should be able to use fair market value rather than acquisition basis for land or inherently permanent structures used in a trade or business.

Third, assets that have been acquired or that are under development but that are not yet used in a trade or business would not be taken into account for purposes of proposed § 1.163(j)-10(c). Such assets would include (but would not be limited to) construction works in progress, such as buildings, airplanes, or ships, prior to their completion, and land that was acquired by a taxpayer for construction of a building by the taxpayer to be used in a trade or business if the building is not yet placed in service. This rule would not apply to stock in a corporation or interests in a partnership. The Treasury Department and the IRS request comments on this special rule, including whether and to what extent exceptions are needed (for example, with respect to start-up businesses).

Fourth, trusts required by law to fund specific liabilities (for example, pension trusts and plant decommissioning trusts) would not be taken into account for purposes of proposed § 1.163(j)-10(c).

Fifth, taxpayers generally would be permitted to look through their interests in partnerships or S corporations, and taxpayers that satisfy a minimum ownership threshold in non-consolidated domestic C corporations and CFCs would be required to look through their interests in such corporations, in determining the extent to which their basis in a partnership interest or corporate stock is allocable to excepted or non-excepted trades or businesses. For domestic C corporations and CFCs, the minimum ownership threshold would be 80 percent by vote and value (see section 1504(a)(2)). Partners that own 80 percent or more of the capital or profits interests in a partnership, and shareholders that own 80 percent or more of S corporation stock by vote and value, generally would be required, rather than merely permitted, to look through their interests in the partnership or S corporation for this purpose.

These look-through rules would not apply to a taxpayer with an interest in a partnership or non-consolidated subsidiary that is eligible for the small business exemption under section 163(j)(3) and proposed §1.163(j)-2(d)(1). The Treasury Department and the IRS have determined that the look-through rules should not be available in these cases because of the administrative burden that would be imposed on small businesses from collecting and providing information to their shareholders or partners regarding inside asset basis when those small businesses are themselves exempt from the application of section 163(j). The Treasury Department and the IRS also have determined that small businesses that are exempt under section 163(j)(3) and proposed §1.163(j)-2(d)(1) may not make an election under proposed §1.163(j)-9.

If a taxpayer does not look through a C corporation for purposes of the allocation rules in §1.163(j)-10(c), and if the taxpayer is not a C corporation or tax-exempt corporation, the taxpayer generally would treat its basis in the stock as an asset held for investment; if the taxpayer is a C corporation or tax-exempt corporation, the taxpayer would treat its entire basis in the C corporation stock as allocable to a non-excepted trade or business. If a taxpayer does not look through a partnership or S corporation, and if the taxpayer is not a C corporation or tax-exempt corporation, the taxpayer would generally treat its basis in a partnership interest or S corporation stock as either an investment asset or a non-excepted trade or business asset. If the taxpayer does not look through a partnership or S corporation, and if the taxpayer is a C corporation or a tax-exempt corporation, the taxpayer would treat its entire basis in the partnership interest or S corporation stock as allocable to a non-excepted trade or business.

The Treasury Department and the IRS request comments on these proposed look-through rules, including whether any further adjustments should be made to the taxpayer's basis in its partnership interest or corporate stock (for example, under §1.861-12(c)(2)) and whether the minimum ownership threshold for nonconsolidated domestic C corporations and CFCs should be modified.

Sixth, a taxpayer's basis in its customer receivables and cash and cash equivalents would be disregarded for purposes of proposed §1.163(j)-10(c). This rule is intended to discourage taxpayers from moving cash to excepted trades or businesses to increase the amount of asset basis therein. For these purposes, the term "cash and cash equivalents" would include cash, foreign currency, commercial paper, interests in certain investment companies, government obligations, derivatives that are substantially secured by an obligation of a government, and similar assets. The Treasury Department and the IRS request comments on this special rule, including the list of assets to which it would apply, and whether any exceptions should apply, such as for working capital.

Seventh, solely for purposes of determining the amount of basis allocable to excepted and non-excepted trades or businesses under proposed §1.163(j)-10(c), an election under section 336, 338, or 754, as applicable, would be deemed to have been made for any acquisition of corporate stock or partnership interests with respect to which the taxpayer demonstrates to the satisfaction of the Commissioner of the Internal Revenue Service (the Commissioner) that the taxpayer was eligible to make such an election but was actually or effectively precluded from doing so by a regulatory agency with respect to a regulated utility trade or business. The Treasury Department and the IRS have determined that such a rule is necessary to place taxpayers that are actually or effectively precluded from making an election under section 336, 338, or 754 on the same footing for purposes of the basis allocation rules in proposed §1.163(j)-10(c) as taxpayers that are not subject to such limitations. The Treasury Department and the IRS request comments on this special rule.

Eighth, taxpayers would be required to comply with certain reporting requirements regarding their asset basis allocation under proposed §1.163(j)-10(c). Additionally, taxpayers would be required to keep books of account and other records and data as necessary to substantiate the taxpayer's use of an asset in an excepted trade or business (see §1.6001-1). If the taxpayer fails to provide the required information, proposed §1.163(j)-10(c) would permit the Commissioner to treat all of the taxpayer's interest expense as properly allocable to a non-excepted trade or business, unless the taxpayer shows that there was reasonable cause for failing to comply with, and the taxpayer acted in good faith with respect to, these reporting requirements. The Treasury Department and the IRS request comments on these proposed reporting requirements and the consequences of failing to satisfy these requirements.

Finally, proposed §1.163(j)-10(c) would provide that a taxpayer's adjusted basis in an asset will not be taken into account for purposes of this section if one of the principal purposes for the acquisition, disposition, or change in use of that asset is to increase artificially the amount of basis allocable to excepted or non-excepted trades or businesses.

The foregoing basis allocation rules would not apply to disallowed business interest expense carryforwards, with the exception of disallowed disqualified interest. Disallowed business interest expense carryforwards other than disallowed disqualified interest would have been allocated during the year in which they were first disallowed under section 163(j). On becoming carryforwards, these disallowed expenses would retain their allocation from prior taxable years and would not be reallocated in a subsequent taxable year. The Treasury Department and the IRS request comments as to how the allocation rules in proposed §1.163(j)-10 should apply to disallowed disqualified interest.

These basis allocation rules also would not apply to floor plan financing interest expense. As provided in section 163(j)(1)(C) and proposed §1.163(j)-2, taxpayers are entitled to deduct their business interest expense to the full extent of their floor plan financing interest expense.

The Treasury Department and the IRS considered various alternatives to asset basis in determining how interest expense should be allocated between excepted and non-excepted trades or businesses. One such alternative was a tracing regime whereby taxpayers would be required to trace disbursements of debt proceeds to specific expenditures. However, tracing would impose a significant administrative burden upon taxpayers. Further, it is not clear how taxpayers would retroactively apply a tracing regime to existing debt. In particular, because C corporations would have had no reason to trace the proceeds of any existing indebtedness, imposing a tracing regime on existing indebtedness would require corporations to reconstruct the use of funds within their treasury operations at the time such indebtedness was issued, even if the issuance occurred many years ago, and even if the funds were used for a myriad of purposes across a large number of entities. Such an approach would involve a great deal of administrative cost and may be impractical or even impossible for indebtedness issued years ago.

Moreover, because money is fungible, the Treasury Department and the IRS have determined that a tracing regime would be distortive and subject to manipulation, and thus would not be appropriate. Although taxpayers are impacted from both a commercial and tax perspective by the amount of capital raised through the issuance of equity and indebtedness, any trade or business conducted by a taxpayer is generally indifferent to the source of funds. As a result, if taxpayers were allowed to use a tracing regime to allocate indebtedness to excepted trades or businesses, there would be an incentive to treat excepted trades or businesses as funded largely from indebtedness, and to treat non-excepted trades or businesses as funded largely from other types of funding, such as equity funding, despite the fact that, as an economic matter, all of a taxpayer's trades or businesses are funded based on the taxpayer's overall capital structure.

The assumption that a trade or business is indifferent to its source of funds may not be appropriate in cases in which certain indebtedness is secured by the assets of the trade or business and cash flow from those assets is expected to support the payments required on the indebtedness. These proposed regulations would provide for a limited tracing rule in those cases. See the discussion of qualified non-recourse indebtedness in proposed §1.163(j)-10(d) in part 10(D) of this Explanation of Provisions section.

The Treasury Department and the IRS also considered allocating interest expense based upon the relative fair market value of the assets used in excepted and non-excepted trades or businesses. However, determinations of fair market value frequently are burdensome for taxpayers, which may have numerous assets without a readily established market price, and for the IRS. For this reason, disputes between taxpayers and the IRS over the fair market value of an asset are a common and costly occurrence. In the TCJA, Congress repealed the use of fair market value in the apportionment of interest expense under section 864 of the Code (see section 14502(a) of the TCJA). Thus, the Treasury Department and the IRS have determined that allocating interest expense based upon the relative fair market value of assets is a less viable approach than a regime based upon relative amounts of asset basis.

The Treasury Department and the IRS also considered allocating interest expense to excepted and non-excepted trades or businesses based on the relative amounts of gross income generated by such trades or businesses. However, gross income is more variable and volatile than asset basis, in part because it is based on an annual measurement. Methods could be developed to look at multiple years of gross income through an averaging or other smoothing methodology, but any such approach would necessarily create a number of difficult technical questions because the income of different trades or businesses may be subject to differing business cycles and the timing of income items may be within taxpayers' control. In the TCJA, Congress also repealed the use of gross income in the apportionment of interest expense under section 864 of the Code (see section 14502(a) of the TCJA).

Thus, although allocating interest expense between excepted and non-excepted trades or businesses using asset basis is not without its shortcomings, the Treasury Department and the IRS have determined that this approach represents the most viable option. The Treasury Department and the IRS also note that various commenters recommended using this approach to allocate interest expense between excepted and non-excepted trades or businesses.

The Treasury Department and the IRS have determined that the same approach should be used to allocate interest income, for several reasons. Such an approach is simpler to administer than applying a separate regime to interest income. Additionally, using the same regime for both interest expense and interest income reduces the likelihood that the IRS or taxpayers will be whipsawed. Under this rule, the greater the amount of basis in assets used in excepted trades or businesses, the greater the amount of both interest expense that is not subject to the section 163(j) limitation and interest income that is not properly allocable to a trade or business and that, as a result, is not factored into the taxpayer's calculation of ATI, which reduces the amount of interest expense that may be deducted.

The Treasury Department and the IRS request comments on the use of asset basis to allocate interest expense and interest income between excepted and non-excepted trades or businesses, including whether other measures, such as gross income, should be used in addition to, or instead of, asset basis. The Treasury Department and the IRS also request comments on the special rules contained in proposed § 1.163(j)-10(c), including whether additional special rules are needed (for example, for financial instruments that are marked to market within the meaning of section 475, or additional rules contained in § 1.861-12T).

D. Proposed § 1.163(j)-10(d): Direct Allocations

The basis allocation rules in proposed § 1.163(j)-10(c) would not apply to interest expense and interest income in several circumstances. First, a taxpayer with qualified nonrecourse indebtedness would be required to directly allocate interest expense from such indebtedness to the taxpayer's assets, as provided in § 1.861-10T(b). Second, a taxpayer that is engaged in the trade or business of banking, insurance, financing, or a similar business would be required to directly allocate interest expense and interest income from such business to the taxpayer's assets used in that business. The special rule for cash and cash equivalents under proposed § 1.163(j)-10(c) would not apply to such taxpayers.

A taxpayer to which both proposed § 1.163(j)-10(c) and (d) apply would be required to reduce its asset basis for purposes of proposed § 1.163(j)-10(c) to reflect assets to which interest expense is directly allocated under proposed § 1.163(j)-10(d).

The Treasury Department and the IRS request comments as to whether direct allocation should be required in any other circumstances, including but not limited to circumstances in which a taxpayer with both excepted and non-excepted trades or businesses is subject to significant limitations on transferring borrowed funds outside the excepted trade or business. The Treasury Department and the IRS also request comments on whether a taxpayer should be permitted to elect to treat all of its interest expense and interest income as properly allocable to non-excepted trades or businesses for purposes of section 163(j), in lieu of applying the allocation rules in proposed § 1.163(j)-10(c) and (d).

11. *Proposed § 1.163(j)-11: Transition Rules*

Proposed § 1.163(j)-11 would provide certain transition rules. Proposed § 1.163(j)-11(a) would provide rules that apply if a corporation (S) that is subject to the section 163(j) limitation joins a consolidated group whose taxable year began before January 1, 2018, and thus is not currently subject to the section 163(j) limitation. For example, assume that S is a calendar-year, stand-alone C corporation, and that S is acquired by Acquiring Group (with a November 30 fiscal year) on May 31, 2018. Acquiring Group is not subject to the section 163(j) limitation during its taxable year beginning December 1, 2017, but S is subject to the section 163(j) limitation for its short taxable year beginning January 1, 2018. Is S subject to the section 163(j) limitation for the taxable period beginning June 1, 2018? What happens to any disallowed business interest expense carryforwards from S's short taxable year ending May 31, 2018?

Proposed § 1.163(j)-11(a) would provide that, in those situations to which proposed § 1.163(j)-11(a) applies, the status of the acquiring group will control the application of section 163(j) to a target during the period that the target is included in the group. Therefore, if S is subject to the section 163(j) limitation at the time of its acquisition by a consolidated group with a taxable year beginning before January 1, 2018, then S will not be subject to the section 163(j) limitation for the portion of the acquiring group's taxable year in which S is a member. Additionally, any disallowed business interest expense carryforwards from S's taxable year that ended on the date of S's change in status will be carried forward to the acquiring group's first taxable year beginning after December 31, 2017.

Proposed § 1.163(j)-11(b) of this section would provide special rules for taxpayers with carryforwards under old section 163(j). Old section 163(j)(1)(A) disallowed a deduction to a corporation for disqualified interest (within the meaning of old section 163(j)(3)) paid or accrued by the corporation during the taxable year if old section 163(j) applied to such year. Old section 163(j)(1)(B) provided that any amount disallowed under old section 163(j)(1)(A) for any taxable year would be treated as disqualified interest paid or accrued in the succeeding taxable year.

Proposed § 1.163(j)-11(b) would provide that a taxpayer's interest expense for which a deduction was disallowed under old section 163(j) is carried forward to the taxpayer's first taxable year beginning after December 31, 2017, and is subject to disallowance under section 163(j) and proposed § 1.163(j)-2, except to the extent such interest is allocable to an excepted trade or business under proposed § 1.163(j)-10.

As noted in part 4(D) of this Explanation of Provisions section, old section 163(j) treated all members of the same affiliated group as a single taxpayer regardless of whether such members filed a consolidated return, but the section 163(j) regulations would treat members of the same affiliated group as one taxpayer only if such members file a consolidated return. Proposed § 1.163(j)-11(b) would provide rules based upon the rules in § 1.163(j)-5(c)(2) of the Prior Proposed Regulations for allocating disallowed disqualified interest carryforwards among members of an affiliated group that was treated as a single taxpayer under old section 163(j).

Proposed § 1.163(j)-11(b) also would clarify the application of section 382 to disallowed disqualified interest carryforwards. For example, disallowed disqualified interest would not be treated as a pre-change loss subject to a section 382 limitation under section 382(d)(3) with regard to an ownership change on a change date occurring before the date the Treasury decision adopting these regulations as final regulations is published in the **Federal Register**, unless the disallowed disqualified interest is carried forward under section 163(j)(2). But see section 382(h)(6)(B) regarding built-in deduction items.

Similarly, for purposes of section 382(k)(1), regarding determination of status as a loss corporation, disallowed disqualified interest would not be treated as a carryforward of disallowed interest described in section 381(c)(20) with regard to an ownership change on a change date occurring before the date the Treasury decision adopting these regulations as final regulations is published in the **Federal Register**, unless the disallowed disqualified interest is carried forward under section 163(j)(2). But see section 382(h)(6) regarding built-in deductions. For a description of changes to regulations under section 382, see the discussion of proposed §§ 1.382-2 and 1.382-6 in parts 14 and 15 of this Explanation of Provisions section.

Finally, whereas old section 163(j)(2)(B)(ii) permitted taxpayers with excess limitation, within the meaning of old section 163(j)(2)(B)(iii), to carry such limitation forward, section 163(j) contains no such language. Thus, the Treasury Department and the IRS have determined that no amount of excess limitation under old section 163(j)(2)(B) may be carried forward to taxable years beginning after December 31, 2017.

12. Proposed § 1.263A-9

Because of the amendments to section 163(j), a conforming amendment to § 1.263A-9(g) is required. Proposed § 1.263A-9 would update references to section 163(j) to reflect current law.

13. Proposed § 1.381(c)(20)-1

As noted in part 5 of this Explanation of Provisions section, Congress added disallowed business interest expense carryforwards to the list of items to which the acquiring corporation succeeds in a transaction to which section 381(a) applies. See section 381(c)(20). Sections 1.381(c)(1)-1 and 1.381(c)(1)-2 provide rules that, in part, limit the acquiring corporation's ability to use NOL carryforwards in the acquiring corporation's first taxable year ending after the acquisition date. The Treasury Department and the IRS have determined that similar rules should apply to disallowed business interest expense carryforwards.

Proposed § 1.381(c)(20)-1 also would provide that, for purposes of section 381(c)(20), the term "carryover of disallowed business interest described in section 163(j)(2)" includes disallowed disqualified interest.

14. Proposed § 1.382-2

In the TCJA, Congress added section 382(d)(3) and a new sentence to section 382(k)(1) for taxable years beginning after December 31, 2017. Section 1.382-2 contains certain definitions for purposes of sections 382 and 383 and the regulations thereunder, including definitions of the terms "pre-change loss" and "loss corporation."

Section 382(d)(3) provides that, for purposes of section 382, the term "pre-change loss" includes carryovers of disallowed interest described in section 163(j)(2) "under rules similar to the rules" in section 382(d)(1). Section 163(j)(2) provides that interest expense paid or accrued in a taxable year that is not allowed as a deduction pursuant to section 163(j)(1) is carried forward to the succeeding taxable year. Section 382(d)(1) treats as a "pre-change loss" both (i) net operating loss carryforwards to the taxable year in which the change date occurs (change year), and (ii) the net operating loss carryforward for the change year, to the extent such loss is allocable to the pre-change period. Proposed § 1.382-2 would clarify the equivalent treatment of items under section 382(d)(1) and (3) by providing that a "pre-change loss" includes the portion of any disallowed business interest expense of the old loss corporation paid or accrued in the taxable year of the testing date that is attributable to the pre-change period.

For purposes of determining the portion of disallowed business interest expense that is attributable to the pre-change period, proposed § 1.382-2 would require that disallowed business interest expense be ratably allocated to each day in the year, regardless of whether the loss corporation makes a closing-of-the-books election under § 1.382-6(b)(2) with regard to allocating its other taxable items to the pre-change period and the post-change period within the change year. This ratable allocation of disallowed business interest expense is consistent with the allocation of the loss corporation's deduction for business interest expense in the taxable year of the ownership change (see proposed § 1.382-6). Ratable allocation also is consistent with the general application of the section 163(j) regulations, which apply without regard to any particular debt instrument or particular date of payment or accrual of interest. See the discussion in part 2(A) of this Explanation of Provisions section.

The TCJA also modified section 382(k)(1) to provide that the term "loss corporation" includes a corporation entitled to use a disallowed business interest expense carryforward. These proposed regulations would revise § 1.382-2 to reflect the changes to the definitions of the terms "pre-change loss" and "loss corporation." These provisions would be applicable with regard to ownership changes occurring on or after the date on which the Treasury decision adopting these regulations as final regulations is published in the **Federal Register**.

15. Proposed § 1.382-6

When a loss corporation experiences an ownership change, § 1.382-6(a) provides that, in general, the loss corporation must allocate its NOL or taxable income and its net capital loss or modified capital gain net income for the change year between the pre-change period and the post-change period by ratably allocating an equal portion to each day in the year. However, instead of using ratable allocation, a loss corporation may elect to use the closing-of-the-books method in § 1.382-6(b). A closing-of-the-books election applies only for purposes of certain allocations, such as NOL or taxable income allocations, and does not terminate the loss corporation's taxable year as of the change date.

Proposed § 1.382-6 would clarify that, for purposes of section 163(j), a loss corporation's current-year business interest expense may not be allocated under the closing-of-the-books method. Thus, even if a taxpayer generally has a closing-of-the-books election in effect for the change year, the taxpayer would be required to ratably allocate its current-year business interest expense for which a deduction is allowable under section 163(j) in that year between the pre-change period and the post-change period. For example, if X, a calendar-year loss corporation, experiences an ownership change on May 26, 2019, and if X has $100x of current-year business interest expense for which a deduction is allowable under section 163(j) for that year, $40x of X's business interest expense deduction would be allocated to the pre-change period, and $60x of X's business interest expense deduction would be allocated to the post-change period, regardless of which of the two general allocation methods - ratable allocation or closing-of-the-books - X uses. Under this approach, taxpayers would not need to compute ATI separately for the pre-change and post-change periods.

The Treasury Department and the IRS are considering publishing a separate notice of proposed rulemaking to address, among other issues, the treatment of a corporate partner's excess business interest expense (including negative section 163(j) expense) under section 382.

16. Proposed § 1.383-1

Section 1.383-1(d) provides ordering rules for the utilization of pre-change losses and pre-change credits and for the absorption of the section 382 limitation and the section 383 credit limitation. Generally, pre-change capital losses are absorbed first for these purposes, followed by NOLs and recognized built-in losses, other pre-change losses and, finally, pre-change credits.

The Treasury Department and the IRS have determined that disallowed business interest expense carryforwards should be absorbed after pre-change capital losses and all recognized built-in losses, but before NOLs. Disallowed business interest expense carryforwards should be absorbed before NOLs because taxpayers must calculate their current-year income or loss in order to determine whether and to what extent they can use an NOL in that year, and deductions for business interest expense, including carryforwards from prior taxable years, factor into the calculation of current-year income or loss.

Proposed § 1.383-1 would reflect the addition of disallowed business interest expense to the ordering rules, would make conforming changes to other provisions, and would update other provisions to reflect additional changes effectuated by the TCJA. The ordering rules in proposed § 1.383-1 include alternative rules that reflect the fact that certain regulations pertaining to the interaction between sections 163(j) and 382 may not be applicable to all ownership changes.

17. Proposed § 1.469-9(b)

These proposed regulations would also propose amendments to § 1.469-9(b) to provide rules relating to the definition of real property trade or business under section 469(c)(7)(C). Specifically, these proposed regulations would provide guidance on the meaning of real property and on the types of trades or businesses that qualify as "real property trades or businesses" for purposes of section 469(c)(7).

Section 469(a) of the Code disallows passive activity losses or credits. In general, a passive activity loss is the excess of the aggregate losses over the aggregate income from all passive activities in a taxable year. A passive activity is defined as any trade or business activity in which the taxpayer does not materially participate, and any rental activity subject to the exception for rental real estate under section 469(c)(7). Generally, under section 469(c)(2), a rental activity is treated as a per se passive activity regardless of whether the taxpayer materially participates in the activity.

The Omnibus Budget Reconciliation Act of 1993, Public Law 103-66, sec. 13143(a), added section 469(c)(7) to the Code effective for tax years beginning after December 31, 1993. In doing so, Congress expressed the belief that applying the "per se" passive rule to all rental real estate activities disadvantaged taxpayers who were otherwise actively engaged in real estate businesses and who also owned rental real estate. According to H. Rept. 103-111, 103rd Cong., 1st sess. (May 25, 1993), "[t]he committee considers it unfair that a person who performs personal services in a real estate trade or business in which he materially participates may not offset losses from rental real estate activities against income from nonrental real estate activities or against other types of income such as portfolio investment income." Section 469(c)(7) was added to alleviate this unfair treatment.

Section 469(c)(7) provides that the rental real estate activities of qualifying taxpayers who are actively engaged in real property trades or businesses are not subject to the "per se" passive rule in section 469(c)(2). Instead, under section 469(c)(7), a rental real estate activity of a qualifying taxpayer will not be a passive activity if the taxpayer materially participates in the rental real estate activity.

In section 469(c)(7)(C), Congress defined "real property trade or business" as "any real property development, redevelopment, construction, reconstruction, acquisition, conversion, rental, operation, management, leasing, or brokerage trade or business." However, neither section 469 nor the legislative history defines any of the terms contained in section 469(c)(7)(C).

These proposed regulations would amend the regulations under section 469 to provide a definition of the term "real property" along with certain other terms contained in section 469(c)(7)(C). Consistent with ordinary usage, these proposed regulations would define "real property" to include land, buildings, and other inherently permanent structures that are permanently affixed to land, and exclude from the definition certain other items, such as machines and equipment that serve an active function, which may be permanently affixed to real property.

Given Congress's focus in enacting section 469(c)(7) to provide relief to entrepreneurs in real property trades or businesses with some nexus to or involvement with rental real estate, these proposed regulations would not include trades or businesses that generally do not play a significant or substantial role in the creation, acquisition, or management of rental real estate in the definition of real property trade or business under section 469(c)(7)(C). Therefore, taxpayers engaged in trades or businesses that are not directly or substantially involved in the creation, acquisition, or management of rental real estate, or that provide personal services which are merely ancillary to a real property trade or business, will generally not be treated as engaged in real property trades or businesses for this purpose. In addition, machinery, equipment, and other assets or items that are not generally viewed as items of real property until after their installation or permanent affixation to real property (for example, HVAC systems, elevators, escalators, solar panels, glass fixtures, doors, windows, tiling, etc.) will not be treated as real property for these purposes and, accordingly, taxpayers engaged in trades or businesses of manufacturing, installing, operating, maintaining, or repairing such items generally will not be treated as engaged in real property trades or businesses within the meaning of section 469(c)(7)(C).

As the Treasury Department and the IRS have previously recognized (see Notice of Proposed Rulemaking, "Definition of Real Estate Investment Trust Real Property," published in the **Federal Register** (79 FR 27508, 27510) on May 14, 2014), the term "real property" appears in numerous Code provisions, which could ordinarily imply that, absent specific statutory modifications, the term "real property" should have the same meaning throughout the Code. However, the context and legislative purpose underlying a specific Code provision may necessitate a broader or narrower definition of the term "real property" than may be applied for other Code provisions. These proposed regulations under section 469 provide a definition of real property that is, for example, narrower than the one provided in the REIT context. The definition provided in these proposed regulations would apply solely for purposes of section 469(c)(7), and these regulations should not be construed in any way as applying to, or changing, the definitions in other Code provisions.

These proposed regulations would also define "real property operation" to mean the work done on a day-to-day basis by a direct, or indirect, owner of the real property, in a trade or business relating to the maintenance and occupancy of the real property to make the property available to be used, or held out for use, by customers. Similarly, these proposed regulations would define "real property management" to mean work performed by third party managers on behalf of owners in a trade or business relating to the day-to-day maintenance and occupancy of the real property to make it available to be used, or held out for use, by customers. In both instances, the principal purpose of the trade or business must be the provision of the use of the real property (or physical space accorded by or within the real property) to one or more customers, and not the provision of other significant or extraordinary services to customers in conjunction with the customers' incidental use of the real property or physical space accorded by or within the real property.

These proposed regulations would reserve on the remaining terms in section 469(c)(7)(C). Comments are requested as to whether further definitions are needed.

18. Proposed § 1.860C-2

Because REMICs are not treated as carrying on a trade or business for purposes of section 162 and are not C corporations, the Treasury Department and the IRS have determined that section 163(j) should not apply to REMICs, and these proposed regulations would amend § 1.860C-2 to provide that a REMIC is allowed a deduction, determined without regard to section 163(j), for any interest expense accrued during the taxable year. Section 1.860C-2(b)(2)(ii) of these proposed regulations would apply for taxable years beginning after December 31, 2017. However, taxpayers may rely on proposed § 1.860C-2(b)(2)(ii) prior to the date final regulations are published in the **Federal Register**.

19. *Proposed § 1.1502-36*

Section 1.1502-36 contains the unified loss rule, which limits the ability of a consolidated group to recognize non-economic or duplicated losses on subsidiary stock. The rule applies when a consolidated group member transfers subsidiary (S) stock that has a loss. If § 1.1502-36(d) applies to the transfer of a loss share, the attributes of S and its lower-tier subsidiaries are reduced as needed to prevent the duplication of any loss recognized on the transferred stock. Such attributes include capital loss carryovers, NOL carryovers, deferred deductions, and basis of assets other than cash and general deposit accounts. See § 1.1502-36(d)(4).

The Treasury Department and the IRS have determined that, for purposes of § 1.1502-36(d), disallowed business interest expenses should be treated as deferred deductions. Section 1.1502-36 would be modified accordingly.

20. *Proposed § § 1.1502-91 through 1.1502-99*

As discussed in parts 11 and 14 through 16 of this Explanation of Provisions section, the section 163(j) regulations and § § 1.382-2, 1.382-6, and 1.383-1 of these proposed regulations would address the application of section 382 to business interest expense, including disallowed business interest expense carryforwards. Sections 1.1502-90 through 1.1502-99 contain rules applying section 382 to a consolidated group. These proposed regulations would add a new coordination rule in § 1.1502-98(b) pursuant to which the rules in § § 1.1502-91 through 1.1502-96 would apply to business interest expense, including disallowed business interest expense carryforwards, of members of a consolidated group (or corporations that join or leave a consolidated group), with appropriate adjustments.

The Treasury Department and the IRS request comments on the new coordination rule in § 1.1502-98(b), including whether additional examples should be added to clarify the application of this rule.

21. *Areas Where the Proposed Regulations Have Reserved on Issues*

The proposed regulations reserve on a number of issues, either where the reserved issue is expected to be addressed in other guidance, where comments would be helpful in determining the best manner of addressing an issue, or where the Treasury Department and the IRS are unsure whether additional guidance would be helpful.

A. Reservations Made Because Other Guidance May Address the Reserved Issue

The proposed regulations reserve on the interaction of sections 163(j) and 59A because separate guidance under section 59A is expected to address these issues.

The proposed regulations under sections 382 and 383 also reserve on a number of paragraphs related to the treatment of a corporate partner's excess business interest expense (including negative section 163(j) expense) under section 382. The Treasury Department and the IRS are considering publishing a separate notice of proposed rulemaking to address these and other issues related to section 382.

B. Reservations Made Where Comments Would Be Helpful in Determining the Best Manner of Addressing an Issue

The proposed regulations reserve on the treatment of collateralized cleared swaps and the types of fees that should be treated as interest for purposes of the interest definition because comments would be helpful in determining the best manner of addressing these issues. The proposed regulations also reserve on the coordination with certain other statutory provisions based on or limited by the income of taxpayers because determining the best approach for ordering such provisions would benefit from comments.

For similar reasons, the proposed regulations also reserve on the proper treatment of business interest income and business interest expense with respect to lending transactions between a passthrough entity and an owner of the entity (self-charged lending transactions), the treatment of excess business interest expense in tiered partnerships has been reserved in these proposed regulations, and the application of section 163(j) to a partnership merger or division.

C. *Reservations Made Where the Treasury Department and the IRS are Unsure Whether Additional Guidance Would Be Helpful*

The proposed regulations reserve on nine of the eleven terms listed in section 469(c)(7)(C). Comments are requested as to whether further definitions are needed. However, in the absence of comments requesting additional guidance with respect to these terms, it is unclear whether such additional guidance would be helpful.

Finally, the proposed regulations also reserve on additional guidance in the case of certain exempt organizations with respect to the application of the gross receipts test for purposes of section 163(j) because in the absence of comments it is unclear whether any such rules are necessary.

Statement of Availability of IRS Documents

The IRS Notices and Revenue Procedures cited in this document are published in the Internal Revenue Bulletin (or Cumulative Bulletin) and are available from the Superintendent of Documents, U.S. Government Printing Office, Washington, DC 20402, or by visiting the IRS website at *http://www.irs.gov*.

Proposed Applicability/Effective Dates

Except as otherwise provided in this section, the regulations are proposed to be effective for taxable years ending after the date the Treasury decision adopting these regulations as final is published in the **Federal Register**. However, taxpayers and their related parties, within the meaning of sections 267(b) and 707(b)(1), may apply the rules of these regulations to a taxable year beginning after December 31, 2017, so long as the taxpayers and their related parties consistently apply the rules of § § 1.163(j)-1, 1.163(j)-2, 1.163(j)-3, 1.163(j)-4, 1.163(j)-5, 1.163(j)-6, 1.163(j)-7, 1.163(j)-8, 1.163(j)-9, 1.163(j)-10, and 1.163(j)-11, and if applicable, § § 1.263A-9, 1.381(c)(20)-1, 1.382-6, 1.383-1, 1.469-9, 1.882-5, 1.1502-13, 1.1502-21, 1.1502-36, 1.1502-79, 1.1502-91 through 1.1502-99 (to the extent they effectuate the rules of § § 1.382-6 and 1.383-1), and 1.1504-4 to those taxable years.

With respect to proposed § § 1.382-2, 1.382-5, and 1.1502-91 through 1.1502-99 (to the extent they effectuate the rules of § § 1.382-2 and 1.382-5), if applicable, the regulations are proposed to be effective for ownership changes occurring on or after the date the Treasury decision adopting these regulations as final regulations is published in the **Federal Register**. However, taxpayers and their related parties, within the meaning of sections 267(b) and 707(b)(1), may apply the rules of § § 1.382-2 and 1.382-5, and 1.1502-91 through 1.1502-99 (to the extent they effectuate the rules of § § 1.382-2 and 1.382-5), if applicable, to an ownership change that occurs in a taxable year beginning after December 31, 2017, so long as the taxpayers and their related parties consistently apply the rules of § § 1.163(j)-1, 1.163(j)-2, 1.163(j)-3, 1.163(j)-4, 1.163(j)-5, 1.163(j)-6, 1.163(j)-7, 1.163(j)-8, 1.163(j)-9, 1.163(j)-10, and 1.163(j)-11, and if applicable, § § 1.263A-9, 1.381(c)(20)-1, 1.382-6, 1.383-1, 1.469-9, 1.882-5, 1.1502-13, 1.1502-21, 1.1502-36, 1.1502-79, and 1.1504-4 to taxable years beginning after Decembers 31, 2017.

Special Analyses

I. *Regulatory Planning and Review - Economic Analysis*

Executive Orders 13771, 13563 and 12866 direct agencies to assess costs and benefits of available regulatory alternatives and, if regulation is necessary, to select regulatory approaches that maximize net benefits (including potential economic, environmental, public health and safety effects, distributive impacts, and equity). Executive Order 13563 emphasizes the importance of quantifying both costs and benefits, of reducing costs, of harmonizing rules, and of promoting flexibility.

These proposed regulations have been designated by the Office of Information and Regulatory Affairs (OIRA) as Economically Significant under section 1(c) of the Memorandum of Agreement (April 11, 2018) between the Treasury Department and the Office of Management and Budget (OMB) regarding review of tax regulations and thereby subject to review under Executive Order 12866. Accordingly, these proposed regulations have been reviewed by OIRA. In addition, the Treasury Department and the IRS expect the proposed regulations, when final, to be an Executive Order 13771 regulatory action and request comment on this designation. For more detail on the economic analysis, please refer to the following analysis.

A. Background and Overview

The TCJA substantially modified the statutory rules of section 163(j) to limit the amount of net business interest expense that can be deducted in the current taxable year of any taxpayer with only limited exceptions. As previously described in this preamble, section 163(j) prior to TCJA generally applied to domestic corporations with interest paid or accrued to related persons that were not subject to Federal income tax. As described in the Explanation of Provisions section, the amount allowed under section 163(j)(1) as a deduction for business interest expense is limited to the sum of (1) the taxpayer's business interest income for the taxable year; (2) 30 percent of the taxpayer's ATI for the taxable year; and (3) the taxpayer's floor plan financing interest expense for the taxable year. The section 163(j) limitation applies to all taxpayers, except for certain small businesses with average annual gross receipts of $25 million or less and certain trades or businesses. Any amount of business interest not allowed as a deduction for any taxable year as a result of the limitation under section 163(j)(1) is carried forward and treated as business interest paid or accrued in the next taxable year under section 163(j)(2).

Congress modified section 163(j) under TCJA, in part, out of concern that prior law treated debt-financed investment more favorably than equity-financed investment. This debt bias generally encouraged taxpayers to utilize more leverage than would occur in the absence of the Code. Limiting the deduction of business interest is meant to reduce the relative favorability of debt and hence encourage a more efficient capital structure for firms. Congress also believed it necessary to apply the limit broadly across different types of taxpayers so as not to distort the choice of entity (see H. Rept. 115-409, at 247 (2017)).

B. Need for the Proposed Regulations

Because the section 163(j) limitation has been substantially modified, a large number of the relevant terms and necessary calculations that taxpayers are currently required to apply under the statute can benefit from greater specificity. Among other benefits, the clarity provided by the proposed regulations generally helps ensure that all taxpayers calculate the business interest expense limitation in a similar manner.

For example, there is no universal definition for the term "interest" under the Code. In general, because section 163(j) applies to limit certain deductions for interest under chapter A of the Code, the proposed regulations' definition of the term "interest" is relatively broad to create a balanced application of section 163(j). This definition limits tax-avoidance incentives for taxpayers to, in form, label payments as something other than interest that, in substance, are economically interest. At the same time, this definition allows taxpayers to treat certain amounts of income as business interest income for purposes of calculating the section 163(j) limitation that they may be required to, for non-tax reasons, label as something other than interest, so that taxpayers with such income are not unduly impacted by the section 163(j) limitation.

Pursuant to section 163(j)(8)(B), the proposed regulations prescribe adjustments to the calculation of ATI to prevent double counting of deductions and to provide relief for particular types of taxpayers or taxpayers in particular circumstances to ensure that such taxpayers are treated similarly to other taxpayers when calculating ATI.

The statute applies broadly to different types of entities, including passthrough entities such as partnerships and S corporations. The statute specifies that the section 163(j) limitation applies at the entity level for a partnership but that items such as excess business interest expense and excess taxable income must be allocated to partners for a variety of reasons including to compute their own 163(j) limitation. The statute further specifies that the items should be allocated in the same manner as "nonseparately stated taxable income or loss of the partnership"; however, this concept has not previously been defined by statute or regulations. Without the specified method of allocating these excess items provided by the proposed regulations, partnerships would likely have both significant flexibility but also uncertainty in determining which partners receive excess items. This flexibility could potentially lead partnerships to specially allocate items of income or expense such that they are separately stated to change the partner's allocation of excess interest expense or excess taxable income.

There are a number of potential uncertainties in how taxpayers should apply the section 163(j) limitation to CFCs in a manner consistent with other provisions of the Code. For example, interest deductions of individual CFCs may be limited by section 163(j) but might not be if the interest deductions of CFCs were computed on a group basis. The proposed regulations provide an election for treating related CFCs similarly to a consolidated group for the purpose of calculating the amount of business interest expense for purposes of the section 163(j) limitation. This election also provides clarity that in performing a CFC group calculation, finance and non-finance businesses are largely treated as separate groups (because of the dual role of interest payments as a cost of goods or services sold as well as a payment for debt finance and because of possible distortions in the case of conglomerate companies with financial and nonfinancial businesses in their CFCs, due to financial businesses' outsize amounts of interest expense and income). The proposed regulations also provide clarity by permitting the bottom-up transfer within chains of CFCs of excess taxable income for electing groups of CFCs.

Other areas where clarity is provided under the proposed regulations for CFCs include adjustments for partnerships held by CFCs, the treatment of CFCs with effectively connected income (ECI), the treatment of intergroup dividends (to avoid double counting of ATI), the effect of deemed inclusions (from branch income, Subpart F income, and GILTI) (also to avoid double counting of ATI), and the effect foreign derived intangible income (FDII) on ATI.

For purposes of section 163(j), the statute states in section 163(j)(7) that the term "trade or business" does not include certain regulated utilities, or an electing real property trade or business or an electing farming business. While the statute does reference other places in the Code where a farming business and a real property trade or business are described or defined, regulations have not previously been issued under section 469(c)(7)(C), the rule that section 163(j) refers to in order to define a real property trade or business. The proposed regulations provide such a definition, which clarifies whether a trade or business could elect as a real property trade or business to be excepted from section 163(j). In addition, the proposed regulations describe procedures for allocating income and business interest income and expense between excepted and non-excepted trades or businesses of the taxpayer. The proposed regulations provide a uniform method for allocating income and business interest income and expense which should lower administrative and compliance costs relative to no guidance being provided.

C. Economic Analysis

1. Baseline

The analysis in this section compares the proposed regulations to a no-action baseline reflecting anticipated Federal income tax-related and other economic behavior in the absence of these proposed regulations.

2. Anticipated Benefits

a. In General

The Treasury Department and the IRS expect that the definitions and guidance provided in the proposed regulations will enhance U.S. economic performance relative to the baseline. An economically efficient tax system generally aims to treat income and expense derived from similar economic decisions similarly in order to reduce incentives to make choices based on tax rather than market incentives. In this context, an important benefit of this part of the proposed regulations is to reduce taxpayer uncertainty regarding the calculation of the section 163(j) limitation relative to an alternative scenario in which no such regulations were issued and thus to help ensure that all taxpayers interpret the statutory rules of section 163(j) in a similar manner, a tenet of economic efficiency.

b. Proposed §§1.163(j)-1 through 1.163(j)-5

The proposed regulations make several adjustments to the calculation of ATI. One of these adjustments prevents the double counting of depreciation deductions when a depreciable asset is sold (only relevant for taxable years beginning before January 1, 2022). Other adjustments apply to particular types of taxpayers, such as RICs, REITs, or consolidated groups. These adjustments ensure that the section 163(j) limitation is applied evenly across different types of taxpayers in a manner consistent with the Code. Without such adjustments, certain taxpayers may be disadvantaged relative to otherwise similar taxpayers. For example, if RICs and REITs included the dividends paid deduction when calculating ATI, then these taxpayers would almost always have ATI of zero or close to zero, which would limit the ability of such taxpayers to ever deduct business interest expense for Federal income tax purposes.

In addition, the proposed regulations define the term "interest." There are several places in the Code and regulations where interest expense or interest income is defined, such as in the regulations that allocate and apportion interest expense (§1.861-9T) and in the subpart F regulations (§1.954-2). However, these rules only apply to particular taxpayers in particular situations. As described in the Explanation of Provisions section, there are no generally applicable statutory provisions or regulations addressing when financial instruments are treated as debt for Federal income tax purposes or when a payment is interest. The approach taken to defining interest for the section 163(j) limitation in these proposed regulations is to (1) include amounts associated with conventional debt instruments and amounts already treated as interest for all purposes under existing statutory provisions or regulations; (2) add some additional amounts that are functionally similar to interest, such as the rules regarding amounts on contingent payment debt instruments in §1.163(j)-1(b)(20)(iii)(B), which was drafted in response to comments, or amounts treated as interest for certain purposes, such as amounts described in §§1.861-9T and 1.954-2; and (3) provide an anti-avoidance rule based on the economic principle that any expense or loss predominantly incurred in consideration of the time value of money is treated as an interest expense for section 163(j). Thus, the proposed regulations would apply to interest associated with conventional debt instruments, as well as transactions that are indebtedness in substance even if not in form.

Other options for defining interest were considered by the Treasury Department and the IRS but were determined to be less beneficial and not chosen. The first option considered would be to not provide a definition of interest in the proposed regulations, and thus rely on general tax principles and case law for purposes of defining interest for purposes of section 163(j). While adopting this option might reduce the compliance burden for some taxpayers, not providing an explicit definition of interest would create its own uncertainty (as neither taxpayers nor the IRS might have a clear sense of what types of payments are treated as interest income and interest expense for purposes of section 163(j)). Such uncertainty could increase burdens to the IRS and taxpayers including with respect to disputes and litigation about whether particular payments are interest for section 163(j) purposes.

In addition, such an approach to the definition of interest could encourage taxpayers to engage in transactions that provide financing while generating deductions economically similar to interest but make arguments that such deductions fail to be described by existing principles defining interest expense. There are several reasons why curbing such taxpayer behavior would be beneficial. First, taxpayer use of such transactions is likely to be uneven and dependent in part on the subjective understanding of taxpayers regarding whether such transactions would be allowable under the statute. Second, the ability of taxpayers to engage in such transactions would likely be correlated with size of the trade or business, with large businesses more likely to benefit from such avoidance strategies than small businesses. Third, when the deciding factor for using such transactions is the tax benefit of avoiding a section 163(j) limitation, then such transactions would impose more cost or risk on the taxpayer than using a traditional debt instrument. Engaging in such transactions is an inefficient use of resources. Fourth, such avoidance strategies may also discourage taxpayers from shifting to a less leveraged capital structure, and thus would counteract the intention of the statute to reduce the prevalence of highly-leveraged firms and the probability of systemic financial distress. Fifth, greater use of financing outside of conventional debt instruments may make it more difficult for financial institutions to determine the overall level of leverage and credit risk of firms seeking financing, which may distort the allocation of capital across businesses away from firms and investments with less credit risk.

The second option considered would have been to adopt a definition of interest but limit it to amounts associated with conventional debt instruments and amounts that were already treated as interest under the Code or regulations for all purposes prior to the passage of the TCJA. For example, this is similar to the definition of interest proposed in §1.163(j)-1(b)(20)(i). While this would bring clarity to many transactions regarding what would be deemed interest for the section 163(j) limitation, it would potentially distort future financing transactions. Some taxpayers would choose to use financial instruments and transactions that provide a similar economic result of using a conventional debt instrument, but would avoid the label of business interest expense, potentially enabling these taxpayers to avoid the section 163(j) limitation without a substantive change in capital structure. The arguments discussed above regarding the costs of this situation would continue to apply.

In addition, there are certain transactions where under a specific provision of the Code and regulations, amounts could be deemed ordinary income when in substance the amounts are interest income. For example, the receipt of substitute interest paid on a securities loan arrangement may, under existing income tax principles, be treated as ordinary income rather than interest income despite the fact that such income is economically equivalent to interest income. Prior to the enactment of the 163(j) interest limitation, whether the amount was labeled as ordinary income or interest was not material to the overall tax liability of the taxpayer, but now this distinction matters.

Because of the tax-motivated financing distortions that would arise from a less comprehensive definition of interest, the Treasury Department and the IRS consider the best approach to the definition of interest is to expand the definition beyond §1.163(j)-1(b)(20)(i). Under §1.163(j)-1(b)(20)(ii) and (iii), the Treasury Department and the IRS identified existing financial transactions that have the economic substance of debt and interest, but under the existing Code and regulations may have been deemed ordinary income or gain or may have been treated as interest for limited purposes, and clarifies that such amounts would be considered interest income or expense for the purpose of the new section 163(j) limitation.

In addition, it is difficult for the Treasury Department and the IRS to specifically identify every type of transaction already in practice or to anticipate future innovations in financial transactions, therefore, proposed § 1.163(j)-1(b)(20)(iv) provides an anti-avoidance rule that any expense or loss predominately incurred in consideration of the time value of money is treated as an interest expense for purposes of section 163(j). This should help limit the ability of taxpayers to structure transactions in such a way that would allow deductible expenses that are economically similar to interest and frustrate the application of the statute.

In summary, the definition of interest in these proposed regulations provides clarity to taxpayers and the IRS regarding which specific transactions and types of transactions generate interest subject to the section 163(j) limitation, which should lower compliance and administrative costs relative to providing no definition or a more limited definition of interest. Also, the proposed definition should encourage a more efficient allocation of capital and use of financing across taxpayers.

c. Proposed § 1.163(j)-6

The proposed regulations § 1.163(j)-6 provide guidance on how to allocate partnership excess business interest expense, excess business interest income, and excess taxable income to partners. The statute specifies that the limitation applies at the partnership level but that these items must be allocated to partners for their own 163(j) limitation and because carryforwards of these items occurs at the partner level. Without a specified method of allocating these excess items, partnerships would likely have significant freedom to determine which partners receive excess items. While the statute specifies that the items should be allocated in the same manner as "nonseparately stated taxable income or loss of the partnership", this concept has not previously been defined by statute or regulations. Partnerships have significant control over what items are separately and nonseparately stated for each partner and could potentially reclassify income to be separately stated to favorably change the partner's allocation of excess interest expense or excess taxable income.

The allocation method detailed in the proposed regulations follows a number of principles. First, it ensures that the sum of the excess items at the partner level is equal to the partnership level. Second, it ensures that the partnership does not allocate excess business interest expense to a partner that was allocated items comprising ATI and business interest income that supported the partnership's deductible business interest expense (unless the partner was allocated more interest expense than its share of deductible business interest expense). Finally, it ensures that the partnership allocates any excess taxable income or excess business interest income to partners that are allocated more items comprising ATI or business interest income than necessary to support their allocation of business interest expense. The proposed regulations provide a method to ensure that all partnerships allocate these items consistently and in a way that matches income and interest expense, thus promoting economically efficient investment decisions. Equivalently, they address tax motivated allocations of excess items to avoid the section 163(j) limitation.

The proposed regulations also ensure that, for owners of partnerships and S corporations, business interest income is used only once, at the entity level, in offsetting business interest expenses. This eliminates the incentive to create tiered partnerships purely to double-count interest income in order to avoid the Section 163(j) limitation. It also avoids exacerbating the incentive to seek out interest income relative to other forms of income in order to avoid the Section 163(j) limitation. By avoiding these incentives, the proposed regulations would reduce economically inefficient uses of resources.

d. Proposed §§ 1.163(j)-7 through 1.163(j)-8

The Treasury Department and the IRS expect that proposed §§ 1.163(j)-7 through 1.163(j)-8 will implement the section 163(j) limitation consistent with preserving the integrity of the international tax system reflected in the Code after TCJA. As described in the Explanation of Provisions section, business interest deductions of individual CFCs may be limited by section 163(j) even when, if calculated on a group basis, business interest deductions would not be limited. The application of section 163(j) to CFCs on an individual basis can result in inappropriate results in certain cases. In particular, to the extent section 163(j) were to disallow a deduction for business interest expense to a CFC that has borrowed from a related CFC, the interest paid to the lender CFC would be included in the income of the lender CFC, the amounts would not fully offset, and the United States shareholder's inclusion under subpart F and GILTI may be increased solely due to the use of intercompany debt between these CFCs. Taxpayers could restructure or "self-help" to reduce this problem, but that option involves economically wasteful restructuring costs to the taxpayer. Another option is to ignore within-group interest payments (the "disregard approach"), but that could lead to inappropriate results, for example, a CFC group member borrowing from a third party and using the loan proceeds to lend to related CFCs (borrowing CFCs) would not be able to have interest income from the loans to the borrowing CFCs offset the interest expense to the third party lender for purposes of the section 163(j) limitation while the borrowing CFCs would not have any interest expense subject to the section 163(j) limitation, even though they are benefiting from the capital provided by the third party loan. The Treasury Department and the IRS consider a preferable option within the authority of the Treasury Department and the IRS to be to allow an election to treat related CFCs and their U.S. shareholders as a group for purposes of calculating the amount of business interest expense subject to the section 163(j) limitation (the "alternative method").

e. Proposed §§ 1.163(j)-9 through 1.163(j)-11

Proposed § 1.163(j)-9 provides (1) guidance in applying the rules for farming and real property trade or business elections and (2) guidance in use of a safe harbor for REITs. For electing real property trade or business and electing farming business, the statue specifies that "any such election shall be made at such time and in such manner as the Secretary shall prescribe, and once made, shall be irrevocable." Therefore proposed § 1.163(j)-9 provides taxpayers with the time and manner for electing real property trades or businesses and electing farming businesses. In addition, proposed § 1.163(j)-9 defines the conditions under which an election terminates. Without these conditions specified, taxpayers may engage in behavior which counteracts the intention of the statute and would not otherwise be taken except to game the irrevocable nature of the election the statute specified. The conditions specified increase the likelihood that all similarly situated taxpayers interpret the 'irrevocable' designation similarly and will not engage in tax-motivated behavior to appear to cease operations in an effort to change an irrevocable designation.

Proposed § 1.163(j)-9(g) provides a safe harbor for certain REITs to elect to be electing real property trades or businesses. In addition, a special rule applies to REITs for which 10 percent or less of the value of the REIT's assets are real property financing assets. Under this rule, all of the assets of the REIT are treated as real property trade or business assets. The benefit of the safe harbor is to provide REITs the same tax treatment and apply the same general rules as apply to other taxpayers, an economically efficient approach. The special rule threshold of 10 percent for real property financing assets has the benefit of maintaining consistency with section 856(c)(4), which uses the same values for the REIT asset test at the close of the REIT's taxable year. Taxpayers will benefit in reduced time and cost applying new rules if they are familiar and consistent with other rules that they must comply with under the Code.

Proposed § 1.163(j)-9 provides a rule that stipulates that if at least 80 percent of a trade or business's real property (by fair market value) is leased to a trade or business under common control with the real property trade or business, the trade or business cannot make an election to be an electing real trade or business. In the absence of such a rule, taxpayers could restructure their business such that real estate components of non-real estate businesses are separated from the rest of their business to artificially reduce the application of section 163(j) by leasing the real property to the taxpayer and electing this "business" to be an excepted real property trade or business. Therefore, the prime benefit of this rule is to preserve the intent of the statute of allowing elections in the real property sector without incentivizing other sectors of the economy to restructure their business for the sole intent of avoiding the section 163(j) limitation. This guidance ensures that taxpayers face more uniform incentives when making economic decisions, a tenet of economic efficiency. Rules that maintain consistent structuring activity across taxpayers also increases IRS's ability to consistently enforce the tax rules, thus decreasing opportunities for tax evasion.

Proposed § 1.163(j)-10 provides rules for allocations of ATI and interest expense and interest income between excepted and non-excepted trades or businesses. The proposed regulations allocate interest expense and interest income between the related excepted and non-excepted trades or businesses based upon the relative amounts of the taxpayer's adjusted tax basis in the assets used in its excepted and non-excepted trades or businesses. As discussed in the Explanation of Provisions section, this general method of allocation reflects the fact that money is fungible and the view that interest expense is attributable to all activities and property, regardless of any specific purpose for incurring an obligation on which interest is paid. Since any allocation method will require an increase in compliance costs for taxpayers, an allocation is only required when the share of the asset tax basis in the excepted or non-excepted business exceeds 10 percent. Finally, this asset basis approach provides consistency with the regulations under section 861. By providing taxpayer guidance that is already familiar to them and consistent with other parts of the Code, taxpayers benefit in reduced time and cost spent learning and applying new rules.

The Treasury Department and the IRS considered several alternatives to this asset basis approach for allocating interest income and expense. First, a tracing approach was considered whereby taxpayers would be required to trace disbursements of debt proceeds to specific expenditures. However, tracing would impose a significant administrative burden upon taxpayers due to the complexity of matching interest income and expense among related companies. Further, it is not clear how taxpayers would retroactively apply a tracing regime to existing debt. In particular, because C corporations would have had no reason to trace the proceeds of any existing indebtedness, imposing a tracing regime on existing indebtedness would require corporations to reconstruct the use of funds within their treasury operations at the time such indebtedness was issued, even if the issuance occurred many years ago, and even if the funds were used for a myriad of purposes across a large number of entities. Such an approach would involve a great deal of administrative cost and may be impractical or even impossible for indebtedness issued years ago.

Moreover, because money is fungible, a tracing regime would be distortive and subject to manipulation. Although taxpayers are impacted from both a commercial and tax perspective by the amount of capital raised through the issuance of equity and indebtedness, any trade or business conducted by a taxpayer is generally indifferent to the source of funds. As a result, if taxpayers were allowed to use a tracing regime to allocate indebtedness to excepted trades or businesses, there would be an incentive to treat excepted trades or businesses as funded largely from indebtedness, and to treat non-excepted trades or businesses as funded largely from other types of funding, such as equity funding, despite the fact that, as an economic matter, all of a taxpayer's trades or businesses are funded based on the taxpayer's overall capital structure.

The Treasury Department and the IRS rejected a tracing approach because the complexity of such an approach could be more difficult for taxpayers and the IRS to administer and would create too great an incentive to structure financing with the sole purpose of avoiding the application of the statute. The assumption that a trade or business is indifferent to its source of funds may not be appropriate in cases in which certain indebtedness is secured by the assets of the trade or business and cash flow from those assets is expected to support the payments required on the indebtedness. These proposed regulations would provide for a limited tracing rule in those cases. See the discussion of qualified non-recourse indebtedness in proposed § 1.163(j)-10(d) in part 10(D) of the Explanation of Provisions section.

Second, the Treasury Department and the IRS also considered allocating interest expense based upon the relative fair market value of the assets used in excepted and non-excepted trades or businesses. However, determinations of fair market value frequently are burdensome for taxpayers, which may have numerous assets without a readily established market price, and for the IRS. For this reason, disputes between taxpayers and the IRS over the fair market value of an asset are a common and costly occurrence. In the TCJA, Congress repealed the use of fair market value in the apportionment of interest expense under section 864 of the Code (see section 14502(a) of the TCJA). Thus, the Treasury Department and the IRS have determined that allocating interest expense based upon the relative fair market value of assets is a less viable approach than a regime based upon relative amounts of asset basis.

Third, the Treasury Department and the IRS also considered allocating interest expense to excepted and non-excepted trades or businesses based on the relative amounts of gross income generated by such trades or businesses. However, gross income is more variable and volatile than asset basis, in part because it is based on an annual measurement. Methods could be developed to look at multiple years of gross income through an averaging or other smoothing methodology, but any such approach would necessarily create a number of difficult technical questions because the income of different trades or businesses may be subject to differing business cycles and the timing of income items may be within taxpayers' control. In the TCJA, Congress also repealed the use of gross income in the apportionment of interest expense under section 864 of the Code (see section 14502(a) of the TCJA). The Treasury Department and the IRS request comment on the approaches and decisions discussed in this section.

3. Anticipated Impacts on Administrative and Compliance Costs

The proposed regulations include requirements about how excess interest income, interest expense, and taxable income should be allocated to partners. This allocation method will require some partnerships to do a number of calculations to figure out the appropriate allocations.

The proposed regulations as applied to CFCs involve additional tax calculations, such as aggregating CFC income, separating finance from non-finance businesses, and eliminating intra-group dividends, but these calculations are relatively simple and involve data that are already collected. Hence, the increase in compliance costs should not be substantial. Furthermore, because the alternative method is elective, the associated compliance costs would be avoided if the election is not made.

As the compliance costs in both of these cases would be part of the cost of filing tax Form 8990, "Limitation on Business Interest Expense," the estimate of the cost of these calculations will be included as part of the overall reporting burden of Form 8990, as is further discussed in the next section.

D. Paperwork Reduction Act

The collection of information contained in this notice of proposed rulemaking has been submitted to the Office of Management and Budget for review in accordance with the Paperwork Reduction Act of 1995 (44 U.S.C. 3507(d)). An agency may not conduct or sponsor, and a person is not required to respond to, a collection of information unless it displays a valid control number assigned by the Office of Management and Budget.

Books or records relating to a collection of information must be retained as long as their contents may become material in the administration of any internal revenue law. Generally, tax returns and return information are confidential, as required by section 6103.

1. Collections of Information

The collection of information in these proposed regulations is in §§ 1.163(j)-9 and 1.163(j)-10. The collection of information in proposed § 1.163(j)-9 is required for taxpayers to make a one-time election to treat their real property or farming trade or business as an electing real property trade or business or an electing farming trade or business under section 163(j)(7)(B) and (C). The collection of information in proposed § 1.163(j)-10 is required for taxpayers to demonstrate how they allocated their interest expense, interest income, and other items of income and deduction between excepted and non-excepted trades or businesses. It is necessary to report this information to the IRS to ensure that taxpayers properly report the amount of interest that is potentially subject to the limitation.

The collection of information is necessary to ensure tax compliance but is not expected to be available as a finalized IRS form by the end of the calendar year. When available, draft revised versions of the affected IRS forms will be posted for comment at *https://apps.irs.gov/app/picklist/list/draftTaxForms.html*. All of the information collections mentioned in §§ 1.163(j)-9 and 1.163(j)-10 may eventually be reported on a form. The specific forms that are expected to change as a result of these proposed regulations are described in more detail in the next section.

2. Future Expected Modifications to Forms to Collect Information

In order to collect necessary information, we are modifying four forms (Forms 1120, 1120S, 1065, and 1120-REIT) and creating one new form (Form 8990). We are modifying Forms 1120, 1120S, 1065, and 1120-REIT to ask filers about the applicability of section 163(j) and the need to file the new Form 8990, as well as the related one-time election statement. When the changes to the IRS forms are finalized, every taxpayer who deducts business interest beginning in tax year 2018 generally will be required to file a new tax Form 8990, "Limitation on Business Interest Expense IRC 163(j)," except for taxpayers with average annual gross receipts of $25 million or less for the three prior tax years (as determined under section 448(c) principles, and as adjusted for inflation starting in 2019). For purposes of the Paperwork Reduction Act of 1995 (44 U.S.C. 3507(d)), the reporting burden of tax form 8990 is associated with OMB control number 1545-0123. Tax form 8990 is estimated to be required by fewer than 92,500 taxpayers in 2018.

The draft forms are available on the IRS website at:

Draft Form	IRS Website Link
Form 1120	https://www.irs.gov/pub/irs-dft/f1120—dft.pdf (Draft instructions: https://www.irs.gov/pub/irs-dft/i1120—dft.pdf)
Form 1120S	https://www.irs.gov/pub/irs-dft/f1120s—dft.pdf (Draft instructions: https://www.irs.gov/pub/irs-dft/i1120s—dft.pdf)
Form 1065	https://www.irs.gov/pub/irs-dft/f1065—dft.pdf (Draft instructions: https://www.irs.gov/pub/irs-dft/i1065—dft.pdf)
Form 1120-REIT	https://www.irs.gov/pub/irs-dft/f1120rei—dft.pdf (Draft instructions: https://www.irs.gov/pub/irs-dft/i1120rei—dft.pdf)
Form 8990	https://www.irs.gov/pub/irs-dft/f8990—dft.pdf

A draft of the Form 8990 instructions is not available at the time of the proposed rule-making. When available, a draft of the IRS Form 8990 instructions will be posted for comment at https://www.irs.gov/pub/irs-dft/f8990—dft.pdf.

3. Burden Estimates

The following estimates are based on the information that is available to the IRS. The most recently available 2015 Statistics of Income (SOI) tax data indicates that 80,702 firms would have contemplated a one-time election to opt out of the section 163(j) limitation as an electing real property trade or business or as an electing farming business were the statute then in effect. The Treasury Department and the IRS anticipate that these proposed regulations will apply to a similar proportion of taxpayers going forward. This estimate is based on a count of filers of Forms 1120, 1120S, 1065, and 1120-REIT in the real estate and farming industries that had over $25 million in gross receipts in taxable year 2015. Each of these forms for taxable years after 2017 will ask filers about the applicability of 163(j) and the need to file Form 8890 as well as the related one-time election. Similarly, using the 2015 SOI tax data, we estimate that 82,755 firms would have allocated interest income and expenses among multiple trades or businesses, some of which are excepted from the section 163(j) limitation and some that are not. This estimate is a count of all tax Forms 1120, 1120S, and 1065 in real estate, farming, and public utilities industries that had over $25 million in gross receipts. While the number of affected taxpayers will increase with growth in the economy, the Treasury Department and the IRS expect that the portion of affected taxpayers will remain approximately the same over the foreseeable future.

The time and dollar compliance burden are derived from the Business Taxpayers Burden model provided by the IRS's Office of Research, Applied Analytics, and Statistics (RAAS). This model relates the time and out-of-pocket costs of business tax preparation, derived from survey data, to assets and receipts of affected taxpayers along with other relevant variables. See Tax Compliance Burden (John Guyton et al, July 2018) at https://www.irs.gov/pub/irs-soi/d13315.pdf. A respondent may require more or less time than the estimated burden, depending on the circumstances.

The burden estimates listed in the below table attempt to capture only those discretionary changes made in these proposed regulations, and may not include burden estimates for forms associated with the statute. Changes made by the Act or through new information collections are captured separately in forthcoming published Supporting Statements for each of these forms and will be aggregated with the estimates provided below to summarize the total burden estimates for each information collection listed below. Those total burden estimates will be available for review and public comment at https://www.reginfo.gov/public/Forward?SearchTarget=PRA&textfield. The Treasury Department and the IRS request comment on these estimates.

	Likely Respondents	Estimated number of respondents (2015 levels)	Estimated average annual burden hours per respondent	Estimated total annual reporting burden (hours) (2015 levels)	Estimated monetized burden @ $95/hour ($2017 millions)	Estimated frequency of responses
§ 1.163(j)-9 (one-time election statement)	Individuals, corporations, and partnerships with real property or farming trades or businesses with gross receipts exceeding the statutory threshold of $25 million	80,702 business respondents (including Forms 1120, 1120-REIT, 1120-S, and 1065 filers)	0 to 30 minutes (estimated average:15 minutes)	20,176	$1.9	One-time
§ 1.163(j)-10 (annual allocation statement)	Individuals, corporations, and partnerships (1) with more than one trade or business (at least one of which is a real property or farming trade or business), and (2) public utilities, with gross receipts exceeding the statutory threshold of $25 million	82,755 business respondents (including Forms 1120, 1120-S, and 1065 filers)	15 minutes to 2 hours (estimated average: 1 hour)	82,755	$7.9	Annually

	Likely Respondents	Estimated number of respondents (2015 levels)	Estimated average annual burden hours per respondent	Estimated total annual reporting burden (hours) (2015 levels)	Estimated monetized burden @ $95/hour ($2017 millions)	Estimated frequency of responses
§ 1.163(j)-10 (one-time start-up cost to develop procedures for filing an annual allocation statement)	Same as above	82,755	4 hours (start-up burden)	331,020	$31.4	One-time
Three year monetized burden estimate					$19.0	Three year annual average

The three-year annual average of the monetized burden for the information collection and resulting from discretionary requirements contained in this rulemaking is estimated to be19.0 million ($2017) ([($1.9 million+ $31.4 million) + ($7.9 million x 3)]/3). To ensure more accuracy and consistency across its information collections, the IRS is currently in the process of revising the methodology it uses to estimate burden and costs. Once this methodology is complete, the IRS will provide this information to reflect a more precise estimate of burdens and costs.

The Treasury Department and the IRS request comment on the assumptions, methodology, and burden estimates related to this information collection. Comments on the collection of information should be sent to the Office of Management and Budget, Attn: Desk Officer for the Department of the Treasury, Office of Information and Regulatory Affairs, Washington, DC 20503, with copies to the Internal Revenue Service, Attn: IRS Reports Clearance Officer, SE:W:CAR:MP:T:T:SP, Washington, DC 20224. Comments on the collection of information should be received by February 26, 2019.

Comments are specifically requested concerning—

Whether the proposed collection of information is necessary for the proper performance of the functions of the IRS, including whether the information will have practical utility;

The accuracy of the estimated burden associated with the proposed collection of information;

How the quality, utility, and clarity of the information to be collected may be enhanced;

How the burden of complying with the proposed collection of information may be minimized, including through the application of automated collection techniques or other forms of information technology; and

Estimates of capital or start-up costs and costs of operation, maintenance, and purchase of services to provide information.

II. *Regulatory Flexibility Act*

It is hereby certified that these proposed regulations, if adopted as final, will not have a significant economic impact on a substantial number of small entities. Although the Treasury Department and the IRS believe that the proposed regulations may impact small entities, the number of small entities impacted is low.

Section 163(j) provides exceptions for which many small entities will qualify. First, under section 163(j)(3), the limitation does not apply to any taxpayer, other than a tax shelter under section 448(a)(3), which meets the gross receipts test under section 448(c) for any taxable year. A taxpayer meets the gross receipts test under section 448(c) if the taxpayer has average annual gross receipts for the 3-taxable year period ending with the taxable year that precedes the current taxable year that do not exceed $25,000,000. Second, section 163(j) provides that certain trades or businesses are not subject to the limitation, including the trade or business of performing services as an employee, electing real property trades or businesses, electing farming businesses, and certain utilities as defined in section 163(j)(7)(A)(iv). Lastly, certain REITs, as described in proposed § 1.163(j)-9(g), are eligible to make the election out of the limitation as a real property trades or businesses.

Any economic impact on any small entities as a result of the requirements in this notice of proposed rulemaking are not expected to be significant. The small entities potentially subject to the provision in proposed § 1.163(j)-9 are individuals, corporations, including S corporations, and partnerships that (1) have average annual gross receipts for the 3-taxable year period ending with the taxable year that precedes the current taxable year exceeding $25,000,000, and (2) want to make the election out of the limitation as an electing real property trade or business under section 163(j)(7)(B) or electing farming business under section 163(j)(7)(C). Proposed § 1.163(j)-9 requires such taxpayers to attach a one-time statement to their return providing the taxpayer's name, address, social security number (SSN) or employer identification number (EIN), a description of the taxpayer's electing trade or business, including the principal business activity code, a statement that the taxpayer acknowledges the election is irrevocable, and a statement that the taxpayer is making an election under section 163(j)(7)(B) or (C), as applicable.

The small entities potentially subject to the requirements in proposed § 1.163(j)-10 are individuals, corporations (including S corporations), and partnerships that (1) have average annual gross receipts for the 3-taxable year period ending with the taxable year that precedes the current taxable year exceeding $25,000,000, and (2) have multiple trades or businesses, some of which are excepted from the limitation and some of which are not excepted from the limitation, for which the taxpayer must properly allocate business interest expense. Proposed § 1.163(j)-10 requires such taxpayers to attach an annual statement to their return demonstrating the following: (1) The taxpayer's adjusted basis in the aggregated assets used in its excepted and non-excepted businesses, (2) the determination dates on which asset basis was measured during the taxable year, (3) the names and TINs of all entities for which basis information is being provided, (4) asset basis information for corporations or partnerships if the taxpayer looks through to the corporation's or partnership's basis in the corporation's or partnership's assets under proposed § 1.163(j)-10(c)(5)(ii), and (5) a summary of the method or methods used to determine asset basis in property used in both excepted and non-excepted businesses.

As discussed elsewhere in this preamble, the reporting burden for the one-time election statement is estimated at 0 to 30 minutes, depending on individual circumstances, with an estimated average of 15 minutes for all affected entities, regardless of size. The reporting burden for the annual allocation statement is estimated at 15 minutes to 2 hours, depending on individual circumstances, with an estimated average of 1 hour. The estimated monetized burden for compliance is $95 per hour.

For these reasons, the Treasury Department and the IRS have determined that the collections of information in this notice of proposed rulemaking will not have a significant economic impact. Accordingly, a regulatory flexibility analysis under the Regulatory Flexibility Act (5 U.S.C. chapter 6) is not required. Notwithstanding this certification, the Treasury Department and the IRS invite comments from interested members of the public on both the number of entities affected and the economic impact on small entities.

It is hereby certified that proposed §§ 1.163(j)-4, 1.163(j)-5, and 1.163(j)-6 will not have a significant economic impact on a substantial number of small entities. Although the Treasury Department and the IRS believe that the proposed regulations may affect small entities, the economic impact on small entities as a result of the notice of proposed rulemaking is not expected to be significant. In particular, only firms with more than $25 million in gross receipts are required to file a tax Form 8990. Accordingly, a regulatory flexibility analysis under the Regulatory Flexibility Act (5

U.S.C. chapter 6) is not required. Notwithstanding this certification, the Treasury Department and the IRS invite comments from interested members of the public on both the number of entities affected and the economic impact on small entities.

Pursuant to section 7805(f) of the Code, this notice of proposed rulemaking has been submitted to the Chief Counsel for Advocacy of the Small Business Administration for comment on its impact on small business.

Comments and Public Hearing

Before these proposed regulations are adopted as final regulations, consideration will be given to any comments that are submitted timely to the IRS in the preamble under the **ADDRESSES** section. The Treasury Department and the IRS request comments on all aspects of the proposed rules.

All comments submitted will be made available at *http://www.regulations.gov* for public inspection and copying. A public hearing has been scheduled for February 27, 2019, beginning at 10 a.m. in the Auditorium of the Internal Revenue Building, 1111 Constitution Avenue NW, Washington, DC 20224. If there is not sufficient time to discuss all of the topics on February 27, 2019, the hearing will continue the following day at 10 a.m. in the same location. Due to building security procedures, visitors must enter at the Constitution Avenue entrance. In addition, all visitors must present photo identification to enter the building. Because of access restrictions, visitors will not be admitted beyond the immediate entrance area more than 30 minutes before the hearing starts. For more information about having your name placed on the building access list to attend the hearing, see the **FOR FURTHER INFORMATION CONTACT** section of this preamble.

The rules of 26 CFR 601.601(a)(3) apply to the hearing. Persons who wish to present oral comments at the hearing must submit an outline of the topics to be discussed and the time to be devoted to each topic by February 26, 2019. Submit a signed paper or electronic copy of the outline as prescribed in this preamble under the **ADDRESSES** heading. An agenda showing the scheduling of the speakers will be prepared after the deadline for receiving outlines has passed. Copies of the agenda will be available free of charge at the hearing.

Drafting Information

The principal authors of these regulations are Susie Bird, Charles Gorham, Zachary King, Jaime Park, Kathy Reed, and Sophia Wang, Office of the Associate Chief Counsel (Income Tax and Accounting); Kevin M. Jacobs, Russell Jones, and John Lovelace, Office of the Associate Chief Counsel (Corporate); Meghan Howard, William Kostak, Anthony McQuillen, Adrienne Mikolashek, and James Quinn, Office of the Associate Chief Counsel (Passthroughs and Special Industries); Angela Holland, Steve Jensen, and Charles Rioux, Office of the Associate Chief Counsel (International); William E. Blanchard, Michael Chin, Steven Harrison, Andrea Hoffenson, and Diana Imholtz, Office of the Associate Chief Counsel (Financial Institutions and Products). Other personnel from the Treasury Department and the IRS participated in their development.

List of Subjects in 26 CFR Part 1

Income taxes, Reporting and recordkeeping requirements.

Withdrawal of Proposed Regulations

Under the authority of 26 U.S.C. 7805, the notice of proposed rulemaking that was published in the **Federal Register** on Tuesday, June 18, 1991, (56 FR 27907, as corrected by 56 FR 40285 (August 14, 1991)) is withdrawn.

[¶ 49,781] Proposed Amendments of Regulations (REG-105600-18), published in the Federal Register on December 7, 2018 (corrected 3/6/2019).

[Code Secs. 78, 861, 901, 904, 952, 954, 960, 965]

Foreign Tax Credit: Dividends: Foreign subsidiaries.—Reg. §§ 1.861-13, 1.901(j)-1, 1.904(b)-3 and amendments of 1.861-8, 1.861-9, 1.861-10, 1.861-11, 1.861-12, 1.861-14, 1.861-17, 1.904-1, 1.904-2, 1.904-3, 1.904-4, 1.904-5, 1.904-6, 1.904(f)-12, 1.952-1, 1.954-1, 1.960-1, 1.960-2, 1.960-3, 1.960-4, 1.960-5, 1.960-6, 1.960-7, 1.965-5, relating to the determination of the foreign tax credit under the Internal Revenue Code (the "Code"), are adopted. Amendments of Reg. §§ Reg. §§ 1.78-1, 1.965-7 and portions of Reg. § 1.861-12 were adopted by T.D. 9866 on 6/14/2019.

[¶ 49,782] Proposed Amendments of Regulations (REG-132881-17), published in the Federal Register on December 18, 2018.

[Code Secs. 1441, 1461, 1471, 1473 and 1474]

Withholding: Nonresident aliens: Foreign financial institutions (FFIs): Non-financial foreign entities (NFFEs): Foreign Account Tax Compliance Act (FATCA): Foreign passthru payments.—Amendments of 1.1461-1, 1.1461-2, 1.1471-2—1.1471-5, 1.1473-1, 1.1474-1 and 1.1474-2, eliminating withholding on payments of gross proceeds, deferring withholding on foreign passthru payments, eliminating withholding on certain insurance premiums, and clarifying the definition of investment entity, are proposed. Reg. §§ 1.1441-1, 1.1441-6 and 1.1471-1 were adopted by T.D. 9890 on December 27, 2019.

AGENCY: Internal Revenue Service (IRS), Treasury.

ACTION: Notice of proposed rulemaking.

SUMMARY: This document contains proposed regulations eliminating withholding on payments of gross proceeds, deferring withholding on foreign passthru payments, eliminating withholding on certain insurance premiums, and clarifying the definition of investment entity. This notice of proposed rulemaking also includes guidance concerning certain due diligence requirements of withholding agents and guidance on refunds and credits of amounts withheld.

DATES: Written or electronic comments and requests for a public hearing must be received by February 16, 2019.

ADDRESSES: Send submissions to: CC:PA:LPD:PR (REG-132881-17), Internal Revenue Service, Room 5203, PO Box 7604, Ben Franklin Station, Washington, DC 20044. Submissions may also be hand-delivered Monday through Friday between the hours of 8 a.m. and 4 p.m. to CC:PA:LPD:PR (REG-132881-17), Courier's Desk, Internal Revenue Service, 1111 Constitution Avenue, NW, Washington, DC 20224; or sent electronically via the Federal eRulemaking Portal at *http://www.regulations.gov* (IRS REG-132881-17).

FOR FURTHER INFORMATION CONTACT: Concerning the proposed regulations, John Sweeney, Nancy Lee, or Subin Seth, (202) 317-6942; concerning submissions of comments and/or requests for a public hearing, Regina Johnson, (202) 317-6901 (not toll free numbers).

SUPPLEMENTARY INFORMATION:

Background

This document contains amendments to the Income Tax Regulations (26 CFR part 1) under chapter 4 (sections 1471 through 1474) commonly known as the Foreign Account Tax Compliance Act (FATCA). This document also contains amendments to the Income Tax Regulations (26 CFR part 1) under sections 1441 and 1461.

On January 28, 2013, the Department of the Treasury (Treasury Department) and the IRS published final regulations under chapter 4 in the **Federal Register** (TD 9610, 78 FR 5873), and on September 10, 2013, corrections to the final regulations were published in the **Federal Register** (78 FR 55202). The regulations in TD 9610 and the corrections thereto are collectively referred to in this preamble as the 2013 final chapter 4 regulations. On March 6, 2014, the Treasury Department and the IRS published temporary regulations under chapter 4 (TD 9657, 79 FR 12812) that clarify and modify certain provisions of the 2013 final chapter 4 regulations, and corrections to the temporary regulations were published in the **Federal Register** on July 1, 2014, and November 18, 2014 (79 FR 37175 and 78 FR 68619, respectively). The regulations in TD 9657 and the corrections thereto are referred to in this preamble as the 2014 temporary chapter 4 regulations. A notice of proposed rulemaking cross-referencing the 2014 temporary chapter 4 regulations was published in the **Federal Register** on March 6, 2014 (79 FR 12868).

On March 6, 2014, the Treasury Department and the IRS published temporary regulations under chapters 3 and 61 in the **Federal Register** (TD 9658, 79 FR 12726) to coordinate with the regulations under chapter 4, and corrections to those temporary regulations were published in the **Federal Register** (79 FR 37181) on July 1, 2014. Collectively, the regulations in TD 9657 and the corrections thereto are referred to in this preamble as the 2014 temporary coordination regulations. A notice of proposed rulemaking cross-referencing the 2014 temporary coordination regulations was published in the **Federal Register** on March 6, 2014 (79 FR 12880).

On January 6, 2017, the Treasury Department and the IRS published final and temporary regulations under chapter 4 in the **Federal Register** (TD 9809, 82 FR 2124), and corrections to those final regulations were published on June 30, 2017 in the **Federal Register** (82 FR 27928). Collectively, the regulations in TD 9809 and the corrections thereto are referred to in this preamble as the 2017 chapter 4 regulations. A notice of proposed rulemaking cross-referencing the temporary regulations in TD 9809 and proposing regulations under chapter 4 relating to verification requirements for certain entities was published in the **Federal Register** on January 6, 2017 (82 FR 1629). Also on January 6, 2017, the Treasury Department and the IRS published final and temporary regulations under chapters 3 and 61 in the **Federal Register** (TD 9808, 82 FR 2046), and corrections to those final regulations were published on June 30, 2017 in the **Federal Register** (82 FR 29719). Collectively, the regulations in TD 9808 and the corrections thereto are referred to in this preamble as the 2017 coordination regulations. A notice of proposed rulemaking cross-referencing the temporary regulations in TD 9808 was published in the **Federal Register** on January 6, 2017 (82 FR 1645).

Pursuant to Executive Order 13777, Presidential Executive Order on Enforcing the Regulatory Reform Agenda (82 FR 9339), the Treasury Department is responsible for conducting a broad review of existing regulations. In a Request for Information published on June 14, 2017 (82 FR 27217), the Treasury Department invited public comment concerning regulations that should be modified or eliminated in order to reduce unnecessary burdens. In addition, in Notice 2017-28 (2017-19 I.R.B. 1235), the Treasury Department and the IRS invited public comment on recommendations for the 2017–2018 Priority Guidance Plan for tax guidance, including recommendations relating to Executive Order 13777. In response to the invitations for comments in the Request for Information and Notice 2017-28, the Treasury Department and the IRS received comments suggesting modifications to the regulations under chapters 3 and 4. See also Executive Order 13789, Identifying and Reducing Tax Regulatory Burdens, issued on April 21, 2017 (82 FR 19317) and the second report issued in response (82 FR 48013) (stating that the Treasury Department continues to analyze all recently issued significant regulations and is considering possible reforms of recent regulations, which include regulations under chapter 4).

Based on public input, and taking into account the burden-reducing policies described in Executive Orders 13777 and 13789, these regulations propose certain amendments to the regulations under chapters 3 and 4, including certain refund related issues for which comments were received. The Explanation of Provisions section of this preamble describes these proposed amendments and addresses public comments received in response to the Request for Information and Notice 2017-28, other than comments that would require a statutory change or were addressed in prior Treasury decisions. The Explanation of Provisions section of this preamble also discusses comments to the 2017 chapter 4 regulations and 2017 coordination regulations to the extent the comments relate to amendments that are included in these proposed regulations. The Treasury Department and the IRS continue to study other public comments.

Explanation of Provisions

I. *Elimination of Withholding on Payments of Gross Proceeds from the Sale or Other Disposition of Any Property of a Type Which Can Produce Interest or Dividends from Sources Within the United States*

Under sections 1471(a) and 1472, withholdable payments made to certain foreign financial institutions (FFIs) and certain non-financial foreign entities (NFFEs) are subject to withholding under chapter 4. Section 1473(1) states that, except as otherwise provided by the Secretary, the term "withholdable payment" means: (i) Any payment of interest (including any original issue discount), dividends, rents, salaries, wages, premiums, annuities, compensations, remunerations, emoluments, and other fixed or determinable annual or periodical gains, profits, and income, if such payment is from sources within the United States; and (ii) any gross proceeds from the sale or other disposition of any property of a type which can produce interest or dividends from sources within the United States.

Since the enactment of chapter 4, the Treasury Department and the IRS have received comments from withholding agents on the burden of implementing a requirement to withhold on gross proceeds. The comments have noted in particular the lead time required to implement such a requirement and the potential complexity of a sufficient regulatory framework. The comments assert that withholding on gross proceeds would require significant efforts by withholding agents, including executing brokers that do not obtain tax documentation. The comments assert that adding this withholding requirement is of limited incremental benefit in supporting the objectives of chapter 4 with respect to foreign entities investing in U.S. securities. In response to these comments, the Treasury Department and the IRS have repeatedly issued guidance deferring the date when withholding on gross proceeds would begin. The 2017 chapter 4 regulations provide that such withholding will begin on January 1, 2019.

Many U.S. and foreign financial institutions, foreign governments, the Treasury Department, the IRS, and other stakeholders have devoted substantial resources to implementing FATCA withholding on withholdable payments. At the same time, 87 jurisdictions have an IGA in force or in effect and 26 jurisdictions are treated as having an IGA in effect because they have an IGA signed or agreed in substance, which allows for international cooperation to facilitate FATCA implementation. The Treasury Department and the IRS have determined that the current withholding requirements under chapter 4 on U.S. investments already serve as a significant incentive for FFIs investing in U.S. securities to avoid status as nonparticipating FFIs, and that withholding on gross proceeds is no longer necessary in light of the current compliance with FATCA. For these reasons, under the authority provided under section 1473(1) these proposed regulations would eliminate withholding on gross proceeds by removing gross proceeds from the definition of the term "withholdable payment" in §1.1473-1(a)(1) and by removing certain other provisions in the chapter 4 regulations that relate to withholding on gross proceeds. As a result of these proposed changes to the chapter 4 regulations, only payments of U.S. source FDAP that are withholdable payments under §1.1473-1(a) and that are not otherwise excepted from withholding under §1.1471-2(a) or (b) would be subject to withholding under sections 1471(a) and 1472.

II. *Deferral of Withholding on Foreign Passthru Payments*

An FFI that has an agreement described in section 1471(b) in effect with the IRS is required to withhold on any passthru payments made to its recalcitrant account holders and to FFIs that are not compliant with chapter 4 (nonparticipating FFIs). Section 1471(d)(7) defines a "passthru payment" as any withholdable payment or other payment to the extent attributable to a withholdable payment.

In Notice 2010-60 (2010-37 I.R.B. 329), the Treasury Department and the IRS requested comments on methods a participating FFI could use to determine whether payments it makes are attributable to withholdable payments. In Notice 2011-34 (2011-19 I.R.B. 765), the Treasury Department and the IRS set forth a proposed framework for participating FFIs to withhold on such payments based on a methodology for determining a "passthru payment percentage" to be applied to certain payments made by FFIs. After the publication of Notice 2011-34, stakeholders noted the burdens and complexities in implementing a system for withholding on these payments along the lines of that described in the notice. In light of those comments, the framework outlined in Notice 2011-34 was not incorporated into the 2013 final chapter 4 regulations. In addition, the Treasury Department and the IRS have repeatedly issued guidance deferring the date when withholding on these payments would begin (referred to in guidance as "foreign passthru payments"). The 2017 chapter 4 regulations provide that such withholding will not begin until the later of January 1, 2019, or the date of publication in the **Federal Register** of final regulations defining the term "foreign passthru payment."

The Treasury Department and the IRS have received comments noting that withholding on foreign passthru payments may not be needed given the number of IGAs in effect. One comment also recommended that if the Treasury Department and the IRS determine, based on an evaluation of the data received from FFIs on payments to nonparticipating FFIs in 2015 and 2016, that withholding on foreign passthru payments is necessary, the Treasury Department and the IRS should develop a more targeted solution.

Both in recognition of the time necessary to implement a system for withholding on foreign passthru payments and in recognition of the successful engagement of Treasury and partner jurisdictions to conclude intergovernmental agreements to implement FATCA, these proposed regulations further extend the time for withholding on foreign passthru payments. Accordingly, under proposed regulation § 1.1471-4(b)(4), a participating FFI will not be required to withhold tax on a foreign passthru payment made to a recalcitrant account holder or nonparticipating FFI before the date that is two years after the date of publication in the **Federal Register** of final regulations defining the term "foreign passthru payment." The proposed regulations also make conforming changes to other provisions in the chapter 4 regulations that relate to foreign passthru payment withholding.

Notwithstanding these proposed amendments, the Treasury Department and the IRS remain concerned about the long-term omission of withholding on foreign passthru payments. The Treasury Department and the IRS acknowledge the progress made in implementing FATCA. Nevertheless, concerns remain regarding account holders of participating FFIs that remain recalcitrant account holders or nonparticipating FFIs and regarding payments made to nonparticipating FFIs. Withholding on foreign passthru payments serves important purposes. First, it provides one way for an FFI that has entered into an FFI agreement to continue to remain in compliance with its agreement, even if some of its account holders have failed to provide the FFI with the information necessary for the FFI to properly determine whether the accounts are U.S. accounts and perform the required reporting, or, in the case of account holders that are FFIs, have failed to enter into an FFI agreement. Second, withholding on foreign passthru payments prevents nonparticipating FFIs from avoiding FATCA by investing in the United States through a participating FFI "blocker." For example, a participating FFI that is an investment entity could receive U.S. source FDAP income free of withholding under chapter 4 and then effectively pay the amount over to a nonparticipating FFI as a corporate distribution. Despite being attributable to the U.S. source payment, the payment made to the nonparticipating FFI may be treated as foreign source income and therefore not a withholdable payment subject to chapter 4 withholding.

Accordingly, the Treasury Department and the IRS continue to consider the feasibility of a system for implementing withholding on foreign passthru payments. The Treasury Department and the IRS request additional comments from stakeholders on alternative approaches that would serve the same compliance objectives as would foreign passthru payment withholding and that could be more efficiently implemented by FFIs.

III. *Elimination of Withholding on Non-Cash Value Insurance Premiums Under Chapter 4*

Under § 1.1473-1(a)(1), a withholdable payment generally includes any payment of U.S. source FDAP income, subject to certain exclusions, such as for "excluded nonfinancial payments." Excluded nonfinancial payments do not include premiums for insurance contracts. The 2013 final chapter 4 regulations included, however, a transitional rule that deferred withholding on payments with respect to offshore obligations until January 1, 2017, which was extended in the 2014 chapter 4 regulations to include premiums paid by persons acting as insurance brokers with respect to offshore obligations. Additionally, in response to comments noting the burden of providing to withholding agents withholding certificates and withholding statements for payments of insurance premiums, the chapter 4 regulations provide a rule generally allowing a withholding agent to treat as a U.S. payee a U.S. broker receiving a payment of an insurance premium in its capacity as an intermediary or an agent of a foreign insurer. The IRS also generally permits non-U.S. insurance brokers that are NFFEs to become qualified intermediaries in order to alleviate burden on the foreign brokers and U.S. withholding agents.

Notwithstanding these allowances, the Treasury Department and the IRS continued to receive comments requesting elimination of withholding under chapter 4 on premiums for insurance contracts that do not have cash value (non-cash value insurance premiums). The comments cited the burden on insurance brokers of documenting insurance carriers, intermediaries, and syndicates of insurers for chapter 4 purposes, noting examples to demonstrate the volume and complexity of placements with insurers of the insurance policies typically arranged by the brokers for their clients. The comments argued that withholding on non-cash value insurance premiums is not necessary to further the purposes of chapter 4.

At the same time, certain foreign entities that conducted a relatively small amount of insurance business had taken the position that they were not passive foreign investment companies (PFICs) under section 1297(a). Section 1297(a) generally defines a PFIC as a foreign corporation if 75 percent or more of the corporation's gross income for the taxable year is passive income or 50 percent or more of its assets produce, or are held for the production of, passive income. Section 1297(b)(2)(B), prior to a recent change in law (described below), provided an exception from the U.S. owner reporting and anti-deferral rules applicable to PFICs for corporations "predominantly engaged" in an insurance business. Withholding under chapter 4 on non-cash value insurance premiums strengthened the IRS's enforcement efforts, with respect to the use of the exception in section 1297(b)(2)(B) by U.S. owners of foreign corporations for tax avoidance and evasion, by facilitating reporting of the U.S. owners to avoid withholding on premiums received by the entity.

The preamble to the 2017 chapter 4 regulations noted that future changes to the PFIC rules may create an opportunity to revise the treatment of foreign insurance companies under chapter 4. 82 FR 2140. On December 22, 2017, the Tax Cuts and Jobs Act, Pub.L. No. 115-97 (2017) amended section 1297(b)(2)(B) to provide a more limited exception to PFIC status by replacing the exception for corporations predominantly engaged in an insurance business with a more stringent test based generally on a comparison of the corporation's insurance liabilities and its total assets. This amendment is expected to mitigate the need for reporting on the U.S. owners of these companies under chapter 4 because the Treasury Department and the IRS anticipate that these entities will either amend their business models on account of the change in law or will otherwise comply with the PFIC reporting requirements.

In light of the aforementioned change in law and in furtherance of the burden-reducing policies in Executive Orders 13777 and 13789, these proposed regulations provide that premiums for insurance contracts that do not have cash value (as defined in § 1.1471-5(b)(3)(vii)(B)) are excluded nonfinancial payments and, therefore, not withholdable payments.

IV. *Clarification of Definition of Investment Entity*

Under § 1.1471-5(e)(4)(i)(B), an entity is an investment entity (and therefore a financial institution) if the entity's gross income is primarily attributable to investing, reinvesting, or trading in financial assets and the entity is "managed by" another entity that is a depository institution, custodial institution, insurance company, or an investment entity described in § 1.1471-5(e)(4)(i)(A). Section 1.1471-5(e)(4)(v), *Example 2*, illustrates this rule with an example in which a fund is an investment entity because another financial institution (an investment advisor) provides investment advice to the fund and has discretionary management of the assets held by a fund and the fund meets the gross income test. In *Example 6* of § 1.1471-5(e)(4)(v), a trust is an investment entity because the trustee (an FFI) manages and administers the assets of the trust in accordance with the terms of the trust instrument and the trust meets the gross income test. Section 1.1471-5(e)(4)(v), *Example 8*, provides an example in which an entity is an investment entity because an introducing broker (that is, a broker using another broker to clear and settle its trades) has discretionary authority to manage the entity's assets and provides services as an investment advisor and manager to the entity and the entity meets the gross income test.

The Treasury Department and the IRS received a comment requesting that "discretionary authority" be more narrowly construed for purposes of treating an entity as an investment entity described in § 1.1471-5(e)(4)(i)(B). The comment suggested that an entity should not be treated as an investment entity solely because the entity invests in a mutual fund or similar vehicle because the investments made by the mutual fund are not tailored to the entity that invests in it. The comment requested the same result for a variety of other types of investment products and solutions with varying degrees of investor involvement and standardization, including an investment in a "discretionary mandate." According to the comment, a "discretionary mandate" is an investment product or solution offered by a financial institution to certain clients where the financial institution manages and invests the client's funds directly (rather than the client investing in a separate entity) in accordance with the client's investment goals. The comment noted that some discretionary mandate clients claim to be passive NFFEs rather than FFIs.

As described in the examples, the "managed by" category of investment entities generally covers entities that receive specific professional management advice from an advisor that is tailored to the investment needs of the entity. A financial institution does not have discretionary authority over an entity merely because it sells the entity shares in a widely-held fund that employs a predetermined investment strategy. These proposed regulations clarify that an entity is not "managed by" another entity for purposes of § 1.1471-5(e)(4)(i)(B) solely because the first-mentioned entity invests all or a portion of its assets in such other entity, and such other entity is a mutual fund, an exchange traded fund, or a collective investment entity that is widely held and is subject to investor-protection regulation. In contrast, an investor in a discretionary mandate described above is "managed by" the financial institution under § 1.1471-5(e)(4)(i)(B).

The clarification in these proposed regulations is similar to the guidance published by the OECD interpreting the definition of a "managed by" investment entity under the Common Reporting Standard.

V. *Modifications to Due Diligence Requirements of Withholding Agents Under Chapters 3 and 4*

A. *Treaty statements provided with documentary evidence for chapter 3*

Under chapter 3, a withholding agent must generally obtain either a withholding certificate or documentary evidence and a treaty statement in order to apply a reduced rate of withholding based on a payee's claim for benefits under a tax treaty. The 2017 coordination regulations added a requirement that when a treaty statement is provided with documentary evidence by an entity beneficial owner to claim treaty benefits, the statement must identify the specific limitation on benefits (LOB) provision relied upon in the treaty. In addition, the 2017 coordination regulations added a three-year validity period applicable to treaty statements provided with documentary evidence and a transition period that expires January 1, 2019, for withholding agents to obtain new treaty statements that comply with the new LOB requirement for accounts that were documented with documentary evidence before January 6, 2017 (preexisting accounts). The QI agreement in Revenue Procedure 2017-15, 2017-3 I.R.B. 437 (2017 QI agreement) cross-references the 2017 coordination regulations for the three-year validity period for treaty statements provided with documentary evidence and provides a two-year transition rule for accounts documented before January 1, 2017. Similar provisions are included in the WP and WT agreements in Revenue Procedure 2017-21, 2017-6 I.R.B. 791 (2017 WP and WT agreements).

Comments have noted the burden of complying with the new treaty statement requirements, including difficulties in obtaining new treaty statements for preexisting accounts within the transitional period given the large number of account holders impacted by this requirement. The comments requested an additional one-year period for withholding agents to obtain new treaty statements for preexisting accounts, and the removal of the three-year validity period for a treaty statement that meets the LOB requirement. A comment also noted that a three-year validity period for a treaty statement is not needed for certain categories of entities whose treaty status is unlikely to change, such as publicly traded corporations and government entities.

In response to these comments, these proposed regulations include several changes to the rules on treaty statements provided with documentary evidence. First, these proposed regulations extend the time for withholding agents to obtain treaty statements with the specific LOB provision identified for preexisting accounts until January 1, 2020 (rather than January 1, 2019). Second, these proposed regulations add exceptions to the three-year validity period for treaty statements provided by tax exempt organizations (other than tax-exempt pension trusts or pension funds), governments, and publicly traded corporations, entities whose qualification under an applicable treaty is unlikely to change. See proposed § 1.1441-1(e)(4)(ii)(A)(2). In addition, these proposed regulations correct an inadvertent omission of the actual knowledge standard for a withholding agent's reliance on the beneficial owner's identification of an LOB provision on a treaty statement provided with documentary evidence, the same as the standard that applies to a withholding certificate used to make a treaty claim. See proposed § 1.1441-6(c)(5)(i). The proposed amendments described in this section V.A. will also be incorporated into the 2017 QI agreement and 2017 WP and WT agreements, and a QI, WP, or WT may rely upon these proposed modifications until such time.

B. *Permanent residence address subject to hold mail instruction for chapters 3 and 4*

In response to comments received on the 2014 temporary coordination regulations and the 2014 QI agreement regarding the definition of a "permanent residence address," the 2017 coordination regulations (and the 2017 chapter 4 regulations by cross-reference) allow an address to be treated as a permanent residence address despite being subject to a hold mail instruction when a person provides documentary evidence establishing residence in the country in which the person claims to be a resident for tax purposes. Comments noted that the allowance to obtain documentary evidence establishing residence in a particular country is unnecessarily strict when the person is not claiming treaty benefits, and that it is unclear what documentary evidence may be used to establish residence for purposes of this allowance.

These proposed regulations provide that the documentary evidence required in order to treat an address that is provided subject to a hold mail instruction as a permanent residence address is documentary evidence that supports the person's claim of foreign status or, for a person claiming treaty benefits, documentary evidence that supports the person's residence in the country where the person claims treaty benefits. Regardless of whether the person claims treaty benefits, the documentary evidence on which a withholding agent may rely is the documentary evidence described in § 1.1471-3(c)(5)(i), without regard to the requirement that the documentation contain a permanent residence address.

A comment also requested the removal of any limitation on reliance on a permanent residence address subject to a hold mail instruction because many account holders prefer to receive electronic correspondence rather than paper mail. In response to this comment, proposed § 1.1471-1(b)(62) adds a definition of a hold mail instruction to clarify that a hold mail instruction does not include a request to receive all correspondence (including account statements) electronically.

These proposed regulations apply for purposes of chapters 3 and 4. A QI, WP, or WT may rely upon these proposed modifications until they are incorporated into the 2017 QI agreement and 2017 WP and WT agreements.

VI. *Revisions Related to Credits and Refunds of Overwithheld Tax*

A. *Withholding and reporting in a subsequent year*

Under § 1.1441-5(b)(2)(i)(A), a U.S. partnership is required to withhold on an amount subject to chapter 3 withholding (as defined in § 1.1441-2(a)) that is includible in the gross income of a partner that is a foreign person. A U.S. partnership satisfies this requirement by withholding on distributions to the foreign partner that include an amount subject to chapter 3 withholding. To the extent a foreign partner's distributive share of income subject to chapter 3 withholding is not actually distributed to the partner, the U.S. partnership must withhold on the partner's distributive share of the income on the earlier of the date that the statement required under section 6031(b) (Schedule K-1, Partner's Share of Income, Deductions, Credits, etc.) is mailed or otherwise provided to the partner or the due date for furnishing the statement. Under section 6031(b), a partnership that files its return for a calendar year (calendar-year partnership) must generally furnish to each partner a Schedule K-1 on or before March 15 following the close of the taxable year, a due date that may be extended up to six months. See § § 1.6031(b)-1T(b) and 1.6081-2T(a). Similar requirements apply to a foreign partnership that has entered into an agreement with the IRS to act as a WP. See the 2017 WP agreement. A foreign partnership other than a WP generally satisfies its withholding requirement in the same manner for amounts received from a withholding agent that failed to withhold to the extent required. See § 1.1441-5(c)(2) and (c)(3)(v). For purposes of chapter 4, similar withholding rules apply to a partnership that receives a withholdable payment allocable to a foreign partner. See § 1.1473-1(a)(5)(ii) and (vi).

Under § 1.1461-1(c)(1) and (2), a partnership is required to report on Form 1042-S, Foreign Person's U.S. Source Income Subject to Withholding, any amount subject to withholding that is allocable to a foreign partner for a calendar year. The partnership must file Form 1042-S (and furnish a copy to the partner) by March 15 of the calendar year following the year in which it receives the amount subject to withholding. The due date for filing a Form 1042-S may be automatically extended by 30 days (and an additional 30 days at the discretion of the IRS). See § 1.6081-8T(a). Amounts that are reportable on Forms 1042-S are also required to be reported on a withholding agent's income tax return, Form 1042, Annual Withholding Tax Return for U.S. Source Income of Foreign Persons. The due date for Form 1042 is March 15, which may be automatically extended for six months. See § 1.6081-10. Similar reporting rules apply to a partnership that receives a withholdable payment and withholds under chapter 4. See § 1.1474-1(c) and (d)(1).

Because the extended due date for filing a Form 1042-S generally occurs before the extended due date for furnishing a Schedule K-1 to a foreign partner, a partnership may be required to report an amount subject to withholding on a Form 1042-S before it performs all of the withholding required on such amount under § 1.1441-5(b)(2)(i)(A) or § 1.1473-1(a)(5)(ii) and (vi). To address this case, the Instructions for Form 1042 require a domestic partnership to report any withholding that occurs with respect to an amount that a partnership received but did not distribute to a partner in a calendar year (preceding year) on the partnership's Form 1042 for the following calendar year (subsequent year) (referred to as the "lag method" of reporting). In this case, the partnership would deposit the amount in the subsequent year and designate the deposit as made for that year for reporting on Form 1042. To correspond to the timing of the reporting on Form 1042, the partnership must also report this withholding on Forms 1042-S filed and issued for the subsequent year. For example, a calendar year domestic partnership that receives U.S. source dividends in 2017 (but does not make a distribution to its foreign partners), must withhold on the foreign partners' share of the dividend income by the time the partnership issues Schedules K-1 to the foreign partners, which could be as late as September 15, 2018. The lag method of reporting requires the partnership to report the withholding on the Forms 1042-S and 1042 for the 2018 year (which are issued and filed in 2019). The WP agreement includes a similar requirement to that described in this paragraph when a WP withholds after the due date for Form 1042-S (including extensions). The Instructions for Form 1042 provide a similar reporting rule for a domestic trust that withholds in a subsequent year on income of the trust that it is required to distribute but has not actually distributed to a foreign beneficiary. See § 1.1441-5(b)(2)(ii) and (iii). The WT agreement includes a similar requirement for a WT.

Apart from the cases described in the preceding paragraph, in certain other cases, a withholding agent is permitted to withhold an amount in a subsequent year that relates to the preceding year. For example, a withholding agent adjusting underwithholding under § 1.1461-2(b) or § 1.1474-2(b) may withhold the additional amount by the due date (without extensions) of Form 1042. In these cases, the Instructions for Form 1042 provide that, in contrast to the reporting required by partnerships and certain trusts described in the preceding paragraph, a withholding agent withholding in a subsequent year must designate the deposit and report the tax for the preceding year.

Comments have noted issues that arise under the lag method when a partner files an income tax return to report the partnership income allocated to the partner and to claim credit under section 33 (or a refund) based on the partnership's withholding. When a partnership applies the lag method, it issues a Form 1042-S for the subsequent year (and the related withholding) that generally reflects the income received by the partnership in the preceding year. However, the income is reported to the partner on Schedule K-1 for the preceding year, thus resulting in a mismatch between the income allocated to the partner and the withholding on that income. Because a partner must attach to its income tax return a Form 1042-S that it receives from a partnership to claim a credit or refund of overwithholding under § 301.6402-3(e), the partner cannot support the claim with the Form 1042-S until after the year in which the partner is required to report the income shown on the Schedule K-1.

These proposed regulations generally require a withholding agent (including a partnership or trust) that withholds in a subsequent year to designate the deposit as attributable to the preceding year and report the amount on Forms 1042 and 1042-S for the preceding year. This proposed rule incorporates the existing rule for withholding agents (other than partnerships and trusts) from the form instructions, and extends the rule to partnerships and trusts. An exception to this requirement for a partnership that is not a calendar-year partnership (a fiscal-year partnership) provides that such partnership may designate a deposit as made for the subsequent year and report the amount on Forms 1042 and 1042-S for the subsequent year. This exception allows a fiscal-year partnership flexibility to determine the year for reporting that will result in the best matching of the income and the related withholding.

These proposed regulations also provide a revised due date for a partnership to file and furnish Form 1042-S when it withholds the tax after March 15 of the subsequent year that it designates as deposited for the preceding year. Under this new rule, the due date for a partnership to file and furnish a Form 1042-S in such a case will be September 15 of the subsequent year. This revised due date corresponds to the due date for a partnership to file Form 1042 with an extension and the due date for a calendar-year partnership to furnish a Schedule K-1 to a partner with an extension so that the partnership has sufficient time to determine the amount of withholding due and to coordinate with the extended due date for furnishing the Schedule K-1.

Based on the revisions included in these proposed regulations, the IRS intends to amend the Instructions for the 2019 Form 1042 to remove the requirement that a partnership or trust apply the lag method and to incorporate these proposed regulations. The IRS also intends to amend the Instructions to the 2019 Form 1042-S to require that in a case when a partnership is filing Form 1042-S after March 15 for a partner's distributive share of an amount received by the partnership in the preceding year, the partnership must file and issue a separate Form 1042-S for such amount for the preceding year (in addition to any Forms 1042-S filed and issued to the partner for amounts that are withheld when distributed to the partner before March 15 and reported for the preceding year).

The Treasury Department and the IRS intend to amend the WP and WT agreements to the extent necessary to incorporate the proposed regulations, and until such time a WP or WT may rely on these proposed modifications for purposes of its filing and deposit requirements.

B. *Adjustments to overwithholding under the reimbursement and set-off procedures*

Under §1.1461-2(a), a withholding agent that has overwithheld and deposited the tax may adjust the overwithheld amount under either the reimbursement procedure or the set-off procedure. Under the reimbursement procedure, a withholding agent may repay the beneficial owner or payee the amount of tax overwithheld and then reimburse itself by reducing, by the amount of such repayment, any deposit of withholding tax otherwise required to be made before the end of the calendar year following the year of overwithholding. The withholding agent must make any repayment to the beneficial owner or payee before the earlier of the due date for filing Form 1042-S (without extensions) for the calendar year of overwithholding or the date on which the Form 1042-S is actually filed with the IRS, and must state on a timely filed Form 1042 (without extensions) for the calendar year of overwithholding that the filing constitutes a claim for credit in accordance with §1.6414-1.

Under the set-off procedure, a withholding agent may apply the overwithheld amount against any amount which would otherwise be subject to withholding that is paid to the beneficial owner or payee before the earlier of the due date for filing Form 1042-S (without extensions) for the calendar year of overwithholding or the date that the Form 1042-S is actually filed with the IRS. Similar rules for adjusting overwithholding apply for purposes of chapter 4. See §1.1474-2(a)(3) and (4).

If a withholding agent cannot apply the reimbursement or set-off procedure, a beneficial owner or payee must file a claim for credit or refund with the IRS in order to recover the overwithheld tax. Informal comments have requested to expand the cases in which a withholding agent may apply the reimbursement and set-off procedures in order to limit the need for a beneficial owner or payee to claim a credit or refund. These proposed regulations respond to these comments by modifying the reimbursement procedure to allow a withholding agent to use the extended due date for filing Forms 1042 and 1042-S to make a repayment and claim a credit. These proposed regulations also include revisions to conform the requirements for the set-off procedures to those that apply to the reimbursement procedures. In addition, these proposed regulations remove the requirement that a withholding agent include with its Form 1042 a statement that the filing constitutes a claim for credit when it applies reimbursement in the year following the year of the overwithholding. This statement is no longer necessary because Form 1042 was revised in 2016 to provide separate fields for adjustments to overwithholding and underwithholding.

These proposed regulations also provide that a withholding agent may not apply the reimbursement and set-off procedures after the date on which Form 1042-S has been furnished to the beneficial owner or payee (in addition to, under the current regulations, after the date a Form 1042-S has been filed). Because of the liberalizing amendments described in the preceding paragraph, this change is needed to ensure that a Form 1042-S furnished to a beneficial owner or payee reflects any repayments made pursuant to these adjustment procedures and is consistent with the associated Form 1042-S that is filed with the IRS. A QI, WP, or WT may rely upon the proposed modifications described in this section VI.B until they are incorporated into the 2017 QI agreement and 2017 WP and WT agreements.

C. *Reporting of withholding by nonqualified intermediaries*

A withholding agent that makes a payment subject to chapter 3 withholding to a nonqualified intermediary (as defined in §1.1441-1(c)(14)) can reliably associate the payment with documentation when it obtains a valid intermediary withholding certificate (that is, Form W-8IMY, Certificate of Foreign Intermediary, Foreign Flow-Through Entity, or Certain U.S. Branches for United States Tax Withholding) from the nonqualified intermediary and a withholding statement that allocates the payment among the payees and includes the documentation for each payee as described in §1441-1(b)(2)(vii)(B) and (e)(3)(iii). For purposes of chapter 4, a withholding agent making a withholdable payment to a nonqualified intermediary that is a participating FFI or a registered deemed-compliant FFI may rely on a withholding statement that includes an allocation of the payment to a chapter 4 withholding rate pool of payees, and must obtain payee-specific documentation for payees that are not includible in a chapter 4 withholding rate pool to permit any reduced rate of withholding. See §1.1471-3(c)(3)(iii)(B).

To the extent that a withholding agent cannot reliably associate a withholdable payment made to a nonqualified intermediary with valid documentation under §1.1471-3(c), the withholding agent must presume that the payment is made to a nonparticipating FFI and withhold 30 percent of the payment. See §1.1471-3(f)(5). In such a case, the withholding agent is required to report the payment as a chapter 4 reportable amount made to an unknown recipient on a Form 1042-S that reports the nonqualified intermediary as an intermediary and the amount withheld as chapter 4 withholding. See the Instructions for Form 1042-S. If the amount withheld upon under chapter 4 is an amount subject to withholding under chapter 3, the withholding agent is relieved from its obligation to also withhold under chapter 3 on the payment. §1.1441-3(a)(2). To the extent that a nonqualified intermediary is required to report the same payments to its account holders on Forms 1042 and 1042-S under the chapter 3 or 4 regulations, the nonqualified intermediary need not withhold when chapter 3 or 4 withholding has already been applied by its withholding agent, and it substantiates the withholding by attaching to its Form 1042 a copy of the Form 1042-S furnished by the withholding agent.

Comments have noted that some U.S. withholding agents charge fees for the administrative burden associated with reviewing underlying documentation that is included with a withholding statement provided by a nonqualified intermediary. In other cases, nonqualified intermediaries may not be able to obtain such documentation from account holders. For these reasons, some nonqualified intermediaries provide withholding agents with valid Forms W-8IMY to establish their chapter 4 statuses but do not provide any underlying payee documentation or withholding rate pool information to substantiate the allocations to payees shown on a withholding statement. Comments have stated that the requirement for withholding agents to report the withholding applied to withholdable payments as chapter 4 withholding in these cases (because the payees are presumed to be nonparticipating FFIs) has made it difficult for account holders to claim foreign tax credits from foreign jurisdictions that do not view the chapter 4 withholding tax as a creditable income tax. These comments recommended various proposals to allow a nonqualified intermediary to report the withholding as chapter 3 withholding applied to its account holders.

In response to the comments described in the preceding paragraph, these proposed regulations modify the rules for reporting by a nonqualified intermediary under §§1.1461-1(c)(4)(iv) and 1.1474-1(d)(2)(ii) to address a case in which a nonqualified intermediary receives a payment for which a withholding agent has withheld at the 30-percent rate under chapter 4 and reported the payment on Form 1042-S as made to an unknown recipient. In such a case, these proposed regulations permit a nonqualified intermediary that is a participating FFI or registered deemed-compliant FFI to report the withholding applied to the nonqualified intermediary on a Form 1042-S as chapter 3 withholding to the extent that the nonqualified intermediary determines that the payment is not an amount for which withholding is required under chapter 4 based on the payee's chapter 4 status. Under the existing reporting requirements, the nonqualified intermediary would be required to file a Form 1042 and would need to be furnished a copy of the Form 1042-S filed by the withholding agent to substantiate the credit against its withholding tax liability for the withholding applied by its withholding agent. Under the modified requirement, the nonqualified intermediary would be permitted to substantiate the credit even though the Form 1042-S furnished to it reports chapter 4 withholding and the corresponding Forms 1042-S that the nonqualified intermediary issues reports chapter 3 withholding. This change should assist account holders using Form 1042-S to claim foreign tax credits in their jurisdictions of residence in these cases. The Treasury Department and the IRS are of the view that this determination should be limited to a nonqualified intermediary that is a participating FFI or registered deemed-compliant FFI given the role of these FFIs in documenting their account holders for chapter 4 purposes and their compliance requirements under the chapter 4 regulations or an applicable IGA jurisdiction.

Reliance on Proposed Regulations

Under section 7805(b)(1)(C), taxpayers may rely on the proposed regulations until final regulations are issued, except as otherwise provided in this paragraph. With respect to the elimination of withholding on non-cash value insurance premiums under proposed § 1.1473-1(a)(3)(iii), the clarification of the definition of a "managed by" investment entity under proposed § 1.1471-5(e)(4)(i)(B), and the revised allowance for a permanent residence address subject to a hold mail instruction under proposed § § 1.1441-1(c)(38) and 1.1471-1(b)(99), taxpayers may apply the modifications in these proposed regulations for all open tax years until final regulations are issued. For the revisions included in these proposed regulations that relate to credits and refunds of withheld tax, taxpayers may not rely on these proposed regulations until Form 1042 and Form 1042-S are updated for the 2019 calendar year.

Special Analyses

The Administrator of the Office of Information and Regulatory Affairs (OIRA), Office of Management and Budget (OMB), has waived review of this proposed rule in accordance with section 6(a)(3)(A) of Executive Order 12866. OIRA will subsequently make a significance determination of the final rule, pursuant to section 3(f) of Executive Order 12866 and the April 11, 2018, Memorandum of Agreement between the Treasury Department and the OMB.

The Treasury Department and the IRS expect the proposed regulation, when final, to be an Executive Order 13771 deregulatory action and request comment on this designation.

Paperwork Reduction Act

The collection of information contained in these proposed regulations is in a number of provisions, including § § 1.1441-1, 1.1461-1, 1.1461-2, 1.1474-1, and 1.1474-2. The IRS intends that the information collection requirements of these regulations will be implemented through the use of Forms 1042 and 1042-S. As a result, for purposes of the Paperwork Reduction Act (44 U.S.C. 3507), the reporting burden associated with the collection of information in these regulations will be reflected in the information burden and OMB control number of the appropriate IRS form.

An agency may not conduct or sponsor, and a person is not required to respond to, a collection of information unless the collection of information displays a valid control number.

The proposed regulations will not increase the number of taxpayers required to file a return. Current filers may have to modify slightly how they report, but the burden of reporting should not increase.

As described in section VI.A of the Explanations of Provisions, the proposed regulations allow a partnership that withholds in a subsequent year to designate the deposit as attributable to the preceding year and report the withholding on Forms 1042 and 1042-S for the preceding year (rather than the subsequent year). In addition, the proposed regulations allow a partnership that withholds after March 15 of the subsequent year to file Form 1042-S on or before September 15 of such year. The IRS intends to modify Form 1042-S to add a check box to the form so that a partnership filer can indicate that it qualifies for the September 15 due date for filing the form. A partnership that relies on the September 15 due date may need to file an additional Form 1042-S if it is filing to report a partner's distributive share of an amount received by the partnership in the preceding year and it has already filed a Form 1042-S for such partner for the same year. Information on the number of partnerships that withhold in a year subsequent to the year in which the amount was received is not available. However, as an upper bound, table 1 shows the estimated number of partnerships that file Form 1042.

As explained in section IV.B of the Explanation of Provisions, the proposed regulations provide additional time for withholding agents to apply the reimbursement or set-off procedure to adjust overwithholding. The proposed revision may increase the amounts reported by filers of Forms 1042 and 1042-S, but should not affect the number of filers. It is unknown how many withholding agents will use the reimbursement and set-off procedures as a result of the modifications to those procedures in the proposed regulations. However, as an upper bound, table 1 shows the estimated number of withholding agents that report non-zero amounts as adjustments to overwithholding.

Finally, as described in section IV.C of the Explanation of Provisions, the proposed regulations permit certain nonqualified intermediaries to report on certain payments on Form 1042-S using the code for chapter 3 withholding rather than the code for chapter 4 withholding in certain cases in which chapter 4 withholding is applied on payments made to the nonqualified intermediaries. This modification in the proposed regulations should not affect the number of filers or increase any burdens, but rather change how nonqualified intermediaries report to certain recipients. It is not possible to estimate the number of nonqualified intermediaries that may change the code from chapter 4 to chapter 3, so as an upper bound, table 1 shows the estimated number of withholding agents that are nonqualified intermediaries that file Form 1042-S.

Table 1: Related Tax Form Counts

	Number of respondents (estimated)
Total number of Form 1042 filers	45,000 - 50,000
Partnership filers of Form 1042	2,000 – 3,000
Form 1042 filers reporting adjustments to overwithholding	4,000 – 5,000
Nonqualified intermediaries filers of Form 1042-S	500

Tax Form 1042 data are from administrative tax files while the Form 1042-S information is from a 2016 data file on foreign tax withholding.

Books and records relating to a collection of information must be retained as long as their contents may be material in the administration of any internal revenue law. Generally, tax returns and tax return information are confidential, as required by 26 U.S.C. 6103.

Regulatory Flexibility Act

It is hereby certified that the collection of information requirements in this notice of proposed rulemaking will not have a significant economic impact on a substantial number of small business entities within the meaning of section 601(6) of the Regulatory Flexibility Act (5 U.S.C. chapter 6). This notice of proposed rulemaking reduces the information required to be reported under chapters 3 and 4 as required by TDs 9610, 9657, 9658, 9808, and 9809, information collections that were certified by the Treasury Department and the IRS as not resulting in a significant economic impact on a substantial number of small business entities. The burden-reducing information collections of this notice of proposed rulemaking provide benefits for small business entities consistent with the Regulatory Flexibility Act's objective that information collections achieve statutory objectives while minimizing any significant impact on small business entities. Therefore, a Regulatory Flexibility Analysis is not required.

Pursuant to section 7805(f), this regulation has been submitted to the Chief Counsel for Advocacy of the Small Business Administration for comment on its impact on small businesses.

Statement of Availability of IRS Documents

IRS Revenue Procedures, Revenue Rulings, Notices, and other guidance cited in this preamble are published in the Internal Revenue Bulletin (or Cumulative Bulletin) and are available from the Superintendent of Documents, U.S. Government Publishing Office, Washington, DC 20402, or by visiting the IRS website at *www.irs.gov*.

Comments and Requests for Public Hearing

Before these proposed regulations are adopted as final regulations, consideration will be given to any comments that are submitted timely to the IRS as prescribed in this preamble under the "Addresses" heading. The Treasury Department and the IRS request comments on all aspects of the proposed rules but specifically on foreign passthru payment withholding and the definition of investment entity, as discussed in section II of the Explanation of Provisions. All comments will be available for public inspection and copying. A public hearing will be scheduled if requested in writing by any person that timely submits written comments. If a public hearing is scheduled, notice of the date, time, and place for the public hearing will be published in the **Federal Register**.

Drafting Information

The principal authors of these proposed regulations are John Sweeney, Nancy Lee, and Subin Seth, Office of Associate Chief Counsel (International). However, other personnel from the IRS and the Treasury Department participated in their development.

[¶ 49,783] Proposed Amendments of Regulations (REG-104259-18), published in the Federal Register on December 21, 2018.

[Code Secs. 59A, 383, 1502, 6038A and 6655]

Tax Cuts and Jobs Act (TCJA): Base erosion: Anti-abuse tax.—Reg. §§1.59A-1—1.59A-10, 1.1502.59A and amendments of Reg. §§1.383-1, 1.1502-2, 1.1502-4, 1.1502-43, 1.1502-47, 1.1502-100, 1.6038A-1, 1.6038A-2, 1.6038A-4 and 1.6655-5 regarding the tax on base erosion payments of taxpayers with substantial gross receipts and reporting requirements thereunder, are proposed. Proposed Reg. §1.1502-2 proposed on December 30, 1992, is withdrawn.

AGENCY: Internal Revenue Service (IRS), Treasury.

ACTION: Notice of proposed rulemaking.

SUMMARY: This document contains proposed regulations that provide guidance regarding the tax on base erosion payments of taxpayers with substantial gross receipts and reporting requirements thereunder. The proposed regulations would affect corporations with substantial gross receipts that make payments to foreign related parties. The proposed regulations under section 6038A would affect any reporting corporations within the meaning of section 6038A or 6038C.

DATES: Written or electronic comments and requests for a public hearing must be received by February 9, 2019.

ADDRESSES: Send submissions to CC:PA:LPD:PR (REG-104259-18), room 5203, Internal Revenue Service, PO Box 7604, Ben Franklin Station, Washington, DC 20044. Submissions may be hand delivered Monday through Friday between the hours of 8 a.m. and 4 p.m. to CC:PA:LPD:PR (REG-104259-18), Courier's desk, Internal Revenue Service, 1111 Constitution Avenue, NW., Washington, DC 20224, or sent electronically, via the Federal eRulemaking Portal at www.regulations.gov (IRS REG-104259-18).

FOR FURTHER INFORMATION CONTACT: Concerning §§1.59A-1 through -10 of the proposed regulations, Sheila Ramaswamy or Karen Walny at (202) 317-6938; concerning the services cost method exception, L. Ulysses Chatman at (202) 317-6939; concerning §§1.383-1, 1.1502-2, 1.1502-4, 1.1502-43, 1.1502-47, 1.1502-59A, 1.1502-100, and 1.6655-5 of the proposed regulations, Julie Wang at (202) 317-6975 or John P. Stemwedel at (202) 317-5024; concerning §§1.6038A-1, 1.6038A-2, and 1.6038A-4 of the proposed regulations, Brad McCormack or Anand Desai at (202) 317-6939; concerning submissions of comments and requests for a public hearing, Regina Johnson at (202) 317-6901 (not toll-free numbers).

SUPPLEMENTARY INFORMATION:

Background

This document contains proposed amendments to 26 CFR part 1 under sections 59A, 383, 1502, 6038A, 6038C, and 6655 of the Internal Revenue Code (the "Code"). The Tax Cuts and Jobs Act, Pub. L. 115-97 (2017) (the "Act"), which was enacted on December 22, 2017, added section 59A to the Code. Section 59A imposes on each applicable taxpayer a tax equal to the base erosion minimum tax amount for the taxable year (the "base erosion and anti-abuse tax" or "BEAT").

The Act also added reporting obligations regarding this tax for 25-percent foreign-owned corporations subject to section 6038A and foreign corporations subject to section 6038C and addressed other issues for which information reporting under those sections is important to tax administration.

Explanation of Provisions

I. *Overview*

These proposed regulations provide guidance under section 59A regarding the determination of the tax on base erosion payments for certain taxpayers with substantial gross receipts. In general, the proposed regulations provide rules for determining whether a taxpayer is an applicable taxpayer on which the BEAT may be imposed and rules for computing the taxpayer's BEAT liability.

Part II of this Explanation of Provisions section describes the rules in proposed §1.59A-2 for determining whether a taxpayer is an applicable taxpayer on which the BEAT may be imposed. Part III of this Explanation of Provisions section describes the rules in proposed §1.59A-3(b) for determining the amount of base erosion payments. Part IV of this Explanation of Provisions section describes the rules in proposed §1.59A-3(c) for determining base erosion tax benefits arising from base erosion payments. Part V of this Explanation of Provisions section describes the rules in proposed §1.59A-4 for determining the amount of modified taxable income, which is computed in part by reference to a taxpayer's base erosion tax benefits and base erosion percentage of any net operating loss deduction. Part VI of this Explanation of Provisions section describes the rules in proposed §1.59A-5 for computing the base erosion minimum tax amount, which is computed by reference to modified taxable income. Part VII of this Explanation of Provisions section describes general rules in proposed §1.59A-7 for applying the proposed regulations to partnerships. Part VIII of this Explanation of Provisions section describes certain rules in the proposed regulations that are specific to banks and registered securities dealers. Part IX of this Explanation of Provisions section describes certain rules in the proposed regulations that are specific to insurance companies. Part X of this Explanation of Provisions section describes the anti-abuse rules in proposed §1.59A-9.

Parts XI-XIII of this Explanation of Provisions section address rules in proposed §1.1502-59A regarding the general application of the BEAT to consolidated groups. Part XIV of this Explanation of Provisions section addresses proposed amendments to §1.383-1 to address limitations on a loss corporation's items under section 382 and 383 in the context of the BEAT. Part XV of this Explanation of Provisions section describes reporting and record keeping requirements.

II. *Applicable Taxpayer*

The BEAT applies only to a taxpayer that is an applicable taxpayer. Proposed §1.59A-2 provides rules for determining if a taxpayer is an applicable taxpayer.

Generally, an applicable taxpayer is a corporation (other than (1) a regulated investment company ("RIC"), (2) a real estate investment trust ("REIT"), or (3) an S corporation) that satisfies the gross receipts test and the base erosion percentage test. Section 59A and the proposed regulations provide that the taxpayer and certain other corporations that are related to the taxpayer are treated as one person for purposes of determining whether a taxpayer satisfies these tests.

Part II.A of this Explanation of Provisions section describes the proposed rules for determining the aggregate group for applying the gross receipts test and the base erosion percentage test. Part II.B of this Explanation of Provisions section describes the proposed rules for applying the gross receipts test. Part II.C of this Explanation of Provisions section describes the proposed rules for applying the base erosion percentage test. Part II.D of this Explanation of Provisions section describes the proposed rules for applying these tests on an aggregate group basis when members of the aggregate group have different taxable years. Part II.E of this Explanation of Provisions section describes proposed rules for computing the base erosion percentage for a taxpayer with deductions taken into account under a mark-to-market method of accounting.

A. *Determining the Aggregate Group for Purposes of Applying the Gross Receipts Test and the Base Erosion Percentage Test*

Section 59A(e)(3) aggregates corporations ("aggregate group") on the basis of persons treated as a single employer under section 52(a), which treats members of the "same controlled group of corporations" (as defined in section 1563(a) with certain modifications) as one person. Although a section 1563(a) controlled group can include both foreign and domestic corporations, the proposed regulations treat foreign corporations as outside of the controlled group for purposes of applying the aggregation rules, except to the extent that the foreign corporation has effectively connected income. This limitation on the extent to which foreign corporations are included in the aggregate group ensures that payments made by a domestic corporation, or a foreign corporation with respect to its effectively connected income, to a foreign related corporation are not inappropriately excluded from the base erosion percentage test. Accordingly, the proposed regulations provide that a taxpayer must apply the gross receipts test and the base erosion percentage test using the aggregate group consisting of members of the same controlled group of corporations for purposes of section 52(a) that are (i) domestic corporations and (ii) foreign corporations, but only with regard to gross receipts taken into account in determining income which is effectively connected with the conduct of a trade or business in the United States and subject to tax under section 882(a). The proposed regulations limit the aggregate group to corporations that benefit from deductions, and accordingly may have base erosion tax benefits, while excluding foreign corporations that are not subject to U.S. income tax (except on a gross basis under section 881, with respect to income that is not effectively connected with a trade or business in the United States) and do not benefit from deductions. In the case of a foreign corporation that determines its net taxable income under an applicable income tax treaty of the United States, the foreign corporation is a member of the aggregate group with regard to gross receipts taken into account in determining its net taxable income.

The proposed regulations generally provide that payments between members of the aggregate group are not included in the gross receipts of the aggregate group, consistent with the single entity concept in section 59A(e)(3). Similarly, the proposed regulations generally provide that payments between members of the aggregate group are also not taken into account for purposes of the numerator or the denominator in the base erosion percentage calculation.

Payments between the aggregate group and any foreign corporation that is not within the aggregate group with respect to the payment are taken into account in applying both the gross receipts test and the base erosion percentage test. However, because a foreign corporation is considered within the aggregate group to the extent it is subject to net income tax in the United States, payments to a foreign corporation from within the aggregate group that are subject to net income tax in the United States are eliminated and not taken into account in applying the gross receipts test and the base erosion percentage test. Thus, it may be the case that a payment by a domestic corporation to a foreign corporation is not taken into account in determining applicable taxpayer status because the payee is subject to net income tax in the United States on that payment, while another payment by the same domestic corporation to the same foreign corporation is taken into account in determining applicable taxpayer status because the payee is not subject to net income tax in the United States on that payment. The Treasury Department and the IRS welcome comments on the proposed regulations addressing the aggregate group for purposes of the gross receipts test and the base erosion percentage test.

B. *Gross Receipts Test*

A taxpayer satisfies the gross receipts test if the taxpayer, or the aggregate group of which the taxpayer is a member, has $500 million or more of average annual gross receipts during the three prior taxable years. In the case of a foreign corporation, the gross receipts test only takes into account gross receipts that are taken into account in determining income that is subject to net income tax as income effectively connected with the conduct of a trade or business within the United States, or taken into account in determining net taxable income under an applicable U.S. income tax treaty.

In the case of an aggregate group, the proposed regulations measure gross receipts of a taxpayer by reference to the taxpayer's aggregate group determined as of the end of the taxpayer's taxable year for which BEAT liability is being computed, and takes into account gross receipts of those aggregate group members during the three-year period preceding that taxable year.

The proposed regulations further clarify how a taxpayer computes gross receipts, including providing rules for corporations that have been in existence for fewer than three years or have short years. These proposed rules are generally consistent with rules set forth in section 448(c). See section 59A(e)(2)(B) (providing that rules similar to the rules of section 448(c)(3)(B) through (D) apply in determining gross receipts for purposes of section 59A). The proposed regulations also clarify how gross receipts are determined if members of the aggregate group have different taxable years, as discussed in Part II.D of this Explanation of Provisions section.

In addition, the proposed regulations clarify how gross receipts are determined for corporations subject to tax under subchapter L (including a foreign corporation subject to tax under section 842(a)).

If a member of an aggregate group owns an interest in a partnership, the proposed regulations provide that the group includes its share of the gross receipts of the partnership in its gross receipts computation. The aggregate group's share of the gross receipts of the partnership is proportionate to its distributive share of items of gross income from the partnership. See Part VII of this Explanation of Provisions section for a more detailed description of the application of section 59A to partnerships.

C. *Base Erosion Percentage Test*

The base erosion percentage test is satisfied with respect to a taxpayer if the taxpayer (or if the taxpayer is a member of an aggregate group, the aggregate group of which the taxpayer is a member) has a base erosion percentage of three percent or more. Generally, a lower threshold of two percent applies if the taxpayer, or a member of the taxpayer's aggregate group, is a member of an affiliated group (as defined in section 1504(a)(1)) that included a domestic bank or registered securities dealer. The proposed regulations provide that the lower two percent threshold does not apply, however, in the case of an aggregate group or consolidated group that has de minimis bank or registered securities dealer activities. See Part VIII of this Explanation of Provisions section for a more detailed description of these rules.

The proposed regulations provide that the base erosion percentage for a taxable year is computed by dividing (1) the aggregate amount of base erosion tax benefits (the "numerator") by (2) the sum of the aggregate amount of deductions plus certain other base erosion tax benefits (the "denominator"). As described in Part II.A of this Explanation of Provisions section, in the case of a taxpayer that is a member of an aggregate group, the base erosion percentage is measured by reference to the deductions or certain reductions in gross income of the taxpayer and members of the taxpayer's aggregate group as of the end of the taxpayer's taxable year. Base erosion tax benefits are generally the deductions or reductions in gross income that result from base erosion payments. Part III of this Explanation of Provisions section describes the proposed rules for determining the amount of base erosion payments, and Part IV of this Explanation of Provisions section describes the proposed rules for determining the base erosion payments that give rise to base erosion tax benefits.

The numerator of the base erosion percentage excludes deductions for (i) amounts paid or accrued to foreign related parties for services qualifying for the exception in proposed §1.59A-3(b)(3)(i) (the "services cost method ("SCM") exception"), (ii) payments covered by the qualified derivatives payments ("QDP") exception in proposed §1.59A-3(b)(3)(ii), and (iii) amounts excluded pursuant to the total loss-absorbing capacity ("TLAC") exception in proposed §1.59A-3(b)(3)(v). See Parts III.B.1, III.B.2, and III.B.5 of this Explanation of Provisions section, for discussions of the SCM exception, QDP exception, and TLAC exception, respectively. Generally, these deductions are also excluded from the denominator of the base erosion percentage.

An applicable taxpayer may make a payment to a foreign related party that is not a member of the aggregate group, if, for example, the recipient of the payment is a 25-percent owner as described in proposed §1.59A-1(b)(17) who does not own more than 50 percent of the applicable taxpayer, and that payment may qualify for the ECI exception described in proposed §1.59A-3(b)(3)(iii). If so, and if that payment also qualifies for either the SCM exception described in proposed §1.59A-3(b)(3)(i), the QDP exception described in proposed §1.59A-3(b)(3)(ii), or the TLAC exception described in proposed §1.59A-3(b)(3)(v), the payment will be included in the denominator for purposes of the base erosion percentage. For example, if an applicable taxpayer makes a deductible payment to a foreign related person who is a 25-percent owner and that payment is both a QDP and subject to federal income taxation as income that is, or is treated as, effectively connected with the conduct of a trade or business in the United States under an applicable provision of the Internal Revenue Code or regulations, that deductible payment is included in the denominator of the base erosion percentage. However, if the applicable taxpayer makes a deductible payment to a foreign related person and that payment is a QDP, but not otherwise subject to federal income taxation, that deductible payment is excluded from the denominator of the base erosion percentage.

The proposed regulations also exclude any section 988 losses from the numerator and the denominator in determining the base erosion percentage. See Part III.B.4 of this Explanation of Provisions section, describing the exception for section 988 losses from the definition of base erosion payments.

The numerator of the base erosion percentage only takes into account base erosion tax benefits, which generally are base erosion payments for which a deduction is allowed under the Code for a taxable year. See Part IV of this Explanation of Provisions section. Similarly, the proposed regulations ensure that the denominator of the base erosion percentage only takes into account deductions allowed under the Code by providing that the denominator of the base erosion percentage does not include deductions that are not allowed in determining taxable income for the taxable year.

Finally, because a deduction allowed under section 965(c) to a United States shareholder of a deferred foreign income corporation is not one of the categories of deductions specifically excluded from the denominator under section 59A(c)(4)(B), that deduction is included in the denominator.

In general, as discussed in more detail in Part IV.A of this Explanation of Provisions section, if tax is imposed by section 871 or 881 and that tax has been deducted and withheld under section 1441 or 1442 on a base erosion payment, the base erosion payment is not treated as a base erosion tax benefit for purposes of calculating a taxpayer's modified taxable income. If an income tax treaty reduces the amount of withholding imposed on the base erosion payment, the base erosion payment is treated as a base erosion tax benefit to the extent of the reduction in withholding under rules similar to those in section 163(j)(5)(B) as in effect before the Act.

The proposed regulations apply the same rule concerning withholding taxes for purposes of the base erosion percentage computation. Accordingly, a base erosion tax benefit is not included in the numerator when the payment was subject to tax under section 871 or 881 and that tax has been deducted and withheld under section 1441 or 1442. In addition, the proposed regulations provide that for any base erosion payment subject to a reduced rate of withholding tax under an income tax treaty, the associated amount of base erosion tax benefits eliminated from the numerator of the base erosion percentage calculation is determined using rules similar to those in section 163(j)(5)(B) as in effect before the Act.

The base erosion percentage also takes into account the two categories of base erosion tax benefits that result from reductions in gross income rather than deductions allowed under the Code (that is, (1) certain premium or other consideration paid to a foreign related party for reinsurance, and (2) amounts paid or accrued by the taxpayer to certain surrogate foreign corporations that result in a reduction in gross receipts to the taxpayer). Section 59A(c)(4)(A)(ii)(II) provides that those base erosion tax benefits that result from reductions in gross income are included in the both the numerator and the denominator in the same amount. Other payments that reduce gross income but that are not base erosion payments are not included in the denominator of the base erosion percentage.

D. *Taxpayers in an Aggregate Group with Different Taxable Years*

Section 59A determines the status of a corporation as an applicable taxpayer on the basis of the aggregate group rules by taking into account the gross receipts and base erosion payments of each member of the aggregate group. However, each member must compute the aggregate group amount of gross receipts and base erosion payments based on its own taxable year and based on those corporations that are members of the aggregate group at the end of such taxable year. Therefore, members with different taxable years may have different base erosion percentages.

However, each corporation that is an applicable taxpayer computes its modified taxable income and base erosion minimum tax amount on a separate taxpayer basis. In the case of a group of affiliated corporations filing a consolidated tax return, the consolidated group is treated as a single taxpayer for purposes of section 59A, and its modified taxable income and base erosion minimum tax amount are determined on a consolidated group basis.

The proposed regulations provide rules for determining whether the gross receipts test and base erosion percentage test are satisfied with respect to a specific taxpayer when other members of its aggregate group have different taxable years. See proposed §1.59A-2(e)(3)(vii). In general, the proposed regulations provide that each taxpayer determines its gross receipts and base erosion percentage by reference to its own taxable year, taking into account the results of other members of its aggregate group during that taxable year. In other words, for purposes of determining the gross receipts, base erosion tax benefits, and deductions of the aggregate group, the taxpayer must include those amounts that occur during the course of the taxpayer's own taxable year, not another member of the aggregate group's taxable year, if different. The proposed regulations adopt this approach to provide certainty for taxpayers and avoid the complexity of a rule that identifies a single taxable year for an aggregate group for purposes of section 59A that may differ from a particular member of the aggregate group's taxable year. As a result of this rule, two related taxpayers with different taxable years will compute their applicable gross receipts and base erosion percentage by reference to different periods, even though in each case the calculations are done on an aggregate group basis that takes into account other members of the controlled group. Taxpayers may use a reasonable method to determine the gross receipts and base erosion percentage information for the time period of the member of the aggregate group with a different taxable year. For an illustration of this rule, see proposed § 1.59A-2(f)(2) (*Example 2*).

The proposed regulations also provide that when determining the base erosion percentage for a taxpayer that is a member of an aggregate group with other members that have a different taxable year, the effective date in section 14401(e) of the Act, as it applies to the taxpayer making the return, controls whether that taxpayer takes into account transactions of other members of its aggregate group. (Section 14401(e) of the Act provides that section 59A applies only to base erosion payments paid or accrued in taxable years beginning after December 31, 2017.)

Thus, if one corporation (US1) that has a calendar year is a member of an aggregate group with another corporation (US2) that has a taxable year ending November 30, when US1 computes its base erosion percentage for its calendar year ending December 31, 2018, the base erosion payments made by US2 during the period from January 1, 2018, through December 31, 2018, are taken into account with respect to US1 for its computations even though US2's base erosion payments in its taxable year ending November 30, 2018, are not base erosion payments with respect to US2 because of section 14401(e) of the Act. Correspondingly, US2's taxable year beginning December 1, 2017, and ending November 30, 2018, is not subject to section 59A because US2's base erosion payments occur in a year beginning before January 1, 2018, and base erosion payments made by US1 during the period from December 1, 2017 through November 30, 2018, do not change that result. For a general discussion of the Act's effective date for section 59A, see Part III.C of this Explanation of Provisions section.

E. *Mark-to-Market Deductions*

As discussed in Part II.C of this Explanation of Provisions section, the taxpayer (or in the case of a taxpayer that is a member of an aggregate group, the aggregate group) must determine the amount of base erosion tax benefits in the numerator and the total amount of certain deductions, including base erosion tax benefits, in the denominator to determine the base erosion percentage for the year. The proposed regulations provide rules for determining the amount of base erosion tax benefits in the case of transactions that are marked to market. These proposed rules also apply for determining the total amount of the deductions that are included in the denominator of the base erosion percentage computation.

Specifically, to ensure that only a single deduction is claimed with respect to each transaction, the proposed regulations combine all income, deduction, gain, or loss on each transaction for the year to determine the amount of the deduction that is used for purposes of the base erosion percentage test. This rule does not modify the net amount allowed as a deduction pursuant to the Code and regulations. This rule is intended to prevent distortions in deductions from being included in the denominator of the base erosion percentage, including as a result of the use of an accounting method that values a position more frequently than annually.

III. *Base Erosion Payments*

The proposed regulations define a base erosion payment as a payment or accrual by the taxpayer to a foreign related party (as defined in § 1.59A-1(b)(12)) that is described in one of four categories: (1) a payment with respect to which a deduction is allowable; (2) a payment made in connection with the acquisition of depreciable or amortizable property; (3) premiums or other consideration paid or accrued for reinsurance that is taken into account under section 803(a)(1)(B) or 832(b)(4)(A); or (4) a payment resulting in a reduction of the gross receipts of the taxpayer that is with respect to certain surrogate foreign corporations or related foreign persons.

A payment or accrual that is not within one of the categories may be a base erosion payment described in one of the other categories. For example, a deductible payment related to reinsurance that does not meet the requirements for the third category of base erosion payments may still be a base erosion payment under the first category because the payment is deductible. Nonetheless, to the extent all or a portion of a payment or accrual is described in more than one of these categories, the amount is only taken into account once as a base erosion payment.

Except as otherwise provided in the proposed regulations, the determination of whether a payment or accrual by the taxpayer to a foreign related party is described in one of these four categories is made under general U.S. federal income tax law. For example, the proposed regulations do not explicitly address whether a royalty payment is classified as deductible under section 162 or as a cost includible in inventory under sections 471 and 263A resulting in a reduction in gross income under section 61.

In general, the treatment of a payment as deductible, or as other than deductible, such as an amount that reduces gross income or is excluded from gross income because it is beneficially owned by another person, generally will have federal income tax consequences that will affect the application of section 59A and will also have consequences for other provisions of the Code. In light of existing tax law dealing with identifying who is the beneficial owner of income, who owns an asset, and the related tax consequences (including under principal-agent principles, reimbursement doctrine, case law conduit principles, assignment of income or other principles of generally applicable tax law), the proposed regulations do not establish any specific rules for purposes of section 59A for determining whether a payment is treated as a deductible payment or, when viewed as part of a series of transactions, should be characterized in a different manner.

Part III.A of this Explanation of Provisions section discusses the operating rules for certain specific types of base erosion payments and Part III.B of this Explanation of Provisions section describes certain exceptions to the definition of base erosion payments.

A. *Certain Specific Types of Base Erosion Payments*

This Part III.A of this Explanation of Provisions describes proposed operating rules for determining whether there is a payment or accrual that can give rise to a base erosion payment. This part also discusses proposed rules coordinating the definition of base erosion payment with rules that allocate deductions for purposes of determining a foreign corporation's effectively connected income.

1. Payments or Accruals That Consist of Non-Cash Consideration

The proposed regulations clarify that a payment or accrual by a taxpayer to a foreign related party may be a base erosion payment regardless of whether the payment is in cash or in any form of non-cash consideration. See proposed § 1.59A-3(b)(2)(i). There may be situations where a taxpayer incurs a non-cash payment or accrual to a foreign related party in a transaction that meets one of the definitions of a base erosion payment, and that transaction may also qualify under certain nonrecognition provisions of the Code. Examples of these transactions include a domestic corporation's acquisition of depreciable assets from a foreign related party in an exchange described in section 351, a liquidation described in section 332, and a reorganization described in section 368.

The proposed regulations do not include any specific exceptions for these types of transactions even though (a) the transferor of the assets acquired by the domestic corporation may not recognize gain or loss, (b) the acquiring domestic corporation may take a carryover basis in the depreciable or amortizable assets, and (c) the importation of depreciable or amortizable assets into the United States in these transactions may increase the regular income tax base as compared to the non-importation of those assets. The Treasury Department and the IRS have determined that neither the nonrecognition of gain or loss to the transferor nor the absence of a step-up in basis to the transferee establishes a basis to create a separate exclusion from the definition of a base erosion payment. The statutory definition of this type of base erosion payment that results from the acquisition of depreciable or amortizable assets in exchange for a payment or accrual to a foreign related party is based on the amount of imported basis in the asset. That amount of basis is imported regardless of whether the transaction is a recognition transaction or a transaction subject to rules in subchapter C or elsewhere in the Code.

In contrast, for transactions in which a taxpayer that owns stock in a foreign related party receives depreciable property from the foreign related party as an in-kind distribution subject to section 301, there is no base erosion payment because there is no consideration provided by the taxpayer to the foreign related party in exchange for the property. Thus, there is no payment or accrual.

In addition, because section 59A(d)(1) defines the first category of base erosion payment as "any amount paid or accrued by the taxpayer to a foreign person which is a related party of the taxpayer and with respect to which a deduction is allowable under this chapter," a base erosion payment also includes a payment to a foreign related party resulting in a recognized loss; for example, a loss recognized on the transfer of property to a foreign related party. The Treasury Department and the IRS welcome comments about the treatment of payments or accruals that consist of non-cash consideration. See Part III.B.4 of this Explanation of Provisions section for a specific exception from the base erosion payment definition for exchange loss from a section 988 transaction.

2. Interest Expense Allocable to a Foreign Corporation's Effectively Connected Income

Section 59A applies to foreign corporations that have income that is subject to net income taxation as effectively connected with the conduct of a trade or business in the United States, taking into account any applicable income tax treaty of the United States. These proposed regulations generally provide that a foreign corporation that has interest expense allocable under section 882(c) to income that is effectively connected with the conduct of a trade or business within the United States will have a base erosion payment to the extent the interest expense results from a payment or accrual to a foreign related party. The amount of interest that will be treated as a base erosion payment depends on the method used under § 1.882-5.

If a foreign corporation uses the method described in § 1.882-5(b) through (d), interest on direct allocations and on U.S.-booked liabilities that is paid or accrued to a foreign related party will be a base erosion payment. If U.S.-booked liabilities exceed U.S.-connected liabilities, a foreign corporation computing its interest expense under this method must apply the scaling ratio to all of its interest expense on a pro-rata basis to determine the amount that is a base erosion payment. Interest on excess U.S.-connected liabilities also may be a base erosion payment if the foreign corporation has liabilities with a foreign related party.

If a foreign corporation determines its interest expense under the separate currency pools method described in § 1.882-5(e), the amount of interest expense that is a base erosion payment is equal to the sum of (1) the interest expense on direct allocations paid or accrued to a foreign related party and (2) the interest expense in each currency pool multiplied by the ratio of average foreign related party liabilities over average total liabilities for that pool. The base erosion payment exceptions discussed in Part III.B of this Explanation of Provisions section may apply and may lower the amount of interest expense that is a base erosion payment.

The Treasury Department and the IRS recognize that § 1.882-5 provides certain simplifying elections for determining the interest deduction of a foreign corporation. In particular, § 1.882-5(c) generally provides that the amount of U.S.-connected liabilities equals the total value of U.S. assets multiplied by the taxpayer's worldwide leverage ratio. However, § 1.882-5(c)(4) allows a taxpayer to elect to use a fixed ratio instead of its actual worldwide leverage ratio. Similarly, § 1.882-5(d)(5)(ii)(A) provides a general rule that the deduction for interest on excess U.S.-connected liabilities is determined by reference to the average rate of interest on U.S.-dollar liabilities that are not U.S.-booked liabilities. However, § 1.882-5(d)(5)(ii)(B) allows certain taxpayers to elect to determine the deduction by reference to the 30-day London Interbank Offering Rate. The Treasury Department and the IRS request comments about similar simplifying elections for determining the portion of U.S.-connected liabilities that are paid to a foreign related party.

3. Other Deductions Allowed with Respect to Effectively Connected Income

Like excess interest expense, the proposed regulations provide that the amount of a foreign corporation's other deductions properly allocated and apportioned to effectively connected gross income under § 1.882-4 are base erosion payments to the extent that those deductions are paid or accrued to a foreign related party. Section 1.882-4(a)(1) generally provides that a foreign corporation engaged in a trade or business within the United States is allowed the deductions which are properly allocated and apportioned to the foreign corporation's gross income which is effectively connected its conduct of a trade or business within the United States. The proposed regulations follow the approach under § 1.882-4. Accordingly, the regulations identify base erosion payments by tracing each item of deduction, and determining whether the deduction arises from a payment to a foreign related party.

If a foreign corporation engaged in a trade or business within the United States acquires property of a character subject to the allowance for depreciation (or amortization in lieu of depreciation) from a foreign related party, the amount paid or accrued by the taxpayer to the foreign related party is a base erosion payment to the extent the property is used, or held for use, in the conduct of a trade or business within the United States.

4. Income Tax Treaties

Certain U.S. income tax treaties provide alternative approaches for the allocation or attribution of business profits of an enterprise of one contracting state to its permanent establishment in the other contracting state on the basis of assets used, risks assumed, and functions performed by the permanent establishment. The use of a treaty-based expense allocation or attribution method does not, in and of itself, create legal obligations between the U.S. permanent establishment and the rest of the enterprise. These proposed regulations recognize that as a result of a treaty-based expense allocation or attribution method, amounts equivalent to deductible payments may be allowed in computing the business profits of an enterprise with respect to transactions between the permanent establishment and the home office or other branches of the foreign corporation ("internal dealings"). The deductions from internal dealings would not be allowed under the Code and regulations, which generally allow deductions only for allocable and apportioned costs incurred by the enterprise as a whole. The proposed regulations require that these deductions from internal dealings allowed in computing the business profits of the permanent establishment be treated in a manner consistent with their treatment under the treaty-based position and be included as base erosion payments.

The proposed regulations include rules to recognize the distinction between the allocations of expenses that are addressed in Parts III.A.2 and 3 of this Explanation of Provisions section, and internal dealings. In the first instance, the allocation and apportionment of expenses of the enterprise to the branch or permanent establishment is not itself a base erosion payment because the allocation represents a division of the expenses of the enterprise, rather than a payment between the branch or permanent establishment and the rest of the enterprise. In the second instance, internal dealings are not mere divisions of enterprise expenses, but rather are priced on the basis of assets used, risks assumed, and functions performed by the permanent establishment in a manner consistent with the arm's length principle. The approach in the proposed regulations creates parity between deductions for actual regarded payments between two separate corporations (which are subject to section 482), and internal dealings (which are generally priced in a manner consistent with the applicable treaty and, if applicable, the OECD Transfer Pricing Guidelines). The rules in the proposed regulations applicable to foreign corporations using this approach apply only to deductions attributable to internal dealings, and not to payments to entities outside of the enterprise, which are subject to the general base erosion payment rules as provided in proposed § 1.59A-3(b)(4)(v)(A).

5. Certain Payments to Domestic Passthrough Entities with Foreign Owners or to Another Aggregate Group Member

The proposed regulations also provide rules for certain payments to a domestic trust, REIT or RIC, and for certain payments to a related domestic corporation that is not part of a consolidated group. Proposed § 1.59A-3(b)(2)(v) provides a rule that applies when a domestic trust, REIT or RIC receives a payment that otherwise would be a base erosion payment. Proposed §1.59A-3(b)(2)(vi) applies when a taxpayer transfers certain property to a member of an aggregate group that includes the taxpayer, to ensure that any deduction for depreciation (or amortization in lieu of depreciation) by the transferee taxpayer remains a base erosion tax benefit to the same extent as the amount that would have been a base erosion tax benefit in the hands of the transferor.

B. *Exceptions from the Base Erosion Payment Definition*

1. Exception for Certain Amounts with Respect to Services

The SCM exception described in section 59A(d)(5) provides that section 59A(d)(1) (which sets forth the general definition of a base erosion payment) does not apply to any amount paid or accrued by a taxpayer for services if (A) the services are eligible for the services cost method under section 482 (determined without regard to the requirement that the services not contribute significantly to fundamental risks of business success or failure) and (B) the amount constitutes the total services cost with no markup component. The Treasury Department and the IRS interpret "services cost method" to refer to the services cost method described in §1.482-9(b), interpret the requirement regarding "fundamental risks of business success or failure" to refer to the test in §1.482-9(b)(5) commonly called the business judgment rule, and interpret "total services cost" to refer to the definition of "total services costs" in §1.482-9(j).

Section 59A(d)(5) is ambiguous as to whether the SCM exception applies when an amount paid or accrued for services exceeds the total services cost, but the payment otherwise meets the other requirements for the SCM exception set forth in section 59A(d)(5). Under one interpretation of section 59A(d)(5), the SCM exception does not apply to any portion of a payment that includes any mark-up component. Under another interpretation of section 59A(d)(5), the SCM exception is available if there is a markup, but only to the extent of the total services costs. Under the former interpretation, any amount of markup would disqualify a payment, in some cases resulting in dramatically different tax effects based on a small difference in charged costs. In addition, if any markup were required, for example because of a foreign tax law or non-tax reason, a payment would not qualify for the SCM exception. Under the latter approach, the services cost would continue to qualify for the SCM exception provided the other requirements of the SCM exception are met. The latter approach to the SCM exception is more expansive because it does not limit qualification to payments made exactly at cost.

The proposed regulations provide that the SCM exception is available if there is a markup (and if other requirements are satisfied), but that the portion of any payment that exceeds the total cost of services is not eligible for the SCM exception and is a base erosion payment. The Treasury Department and the IRS have determined that this interpretation is more consistent with the text of section 59A(d)(5). Rather than require an all-or-nothing approach to service payments, section 59A(d)(5) provides an exception for "any amount" that meets the specified test. This language suggests that a service payment may be disaggregated into its component amounts, just as the general definition of base erosion payment applies to the deductible amount of a foreign related party payment even if the entire payment is not deductible. See section 59A(d)(1). The most logical interpretation is that a payment for a service that satisfies subparagraph (A) is excepted up to the qualifying amount under subparagraph (B), but amounts that do not qualify (i.e., the markup component) are not excepted. This interpretation is reinforced by the fact that section 59A(d)(5)(A) makes the SCM exception available to taxpayers that cannot apply the services cost method described in §1.482-9(b) (which permits pricing a services transaction at cost for section 482 purposes) because the taxpayer cannot satisfy the business judgment rule in §1.482-9(b)(5). Because a taxpayer in that situation cannot ordinarily charge cost, without a mark-up, for transfer pricing purposes, failing to adopt this approach would render the parenthetical reference in section 59A(d)(5)(A) a nullity. The interpretation the proposed regulations adopt gives effect to the reference to the business judgment rule in section 59A(d)(5). The Treasury Department and the IRS welcome comments on whether the regulations should instead adopt the interpretation of section 59A(d)(5) whereby the SCM exception is unavailable to a payment that includes any mark-up component.

To be eligible for the SCM exception, the proposed regulations require that all of the requirements of §1.482-9(b) must be satisfied, except as modified by the proposed regulations. Therefore, a taxpayer's determination that a service qualifies for the SCM exception is subject to review under the requirements of §1.482-9(b)(3) and (b)(4), and its determination of the amount of total services cost and allocation and apportionment of costs to a particular service is subject to review under the rules of §1.482-9(j) and §1.482-9(k), respectively.

Although the proposed regulations do not require a taxpayer to maintain separate accounts to bifurcate the cost and markup components of its services charges to qualify for the SCM exception, the proposed regulations do require that taxpayers maintain books and records adequate to permit verification of, among other things, the amount paid for services, the total services cost incurred by the renderer, and the allocation and apportionment of costs to services in accordance with §1.482-9(k). Because payments for certain services that are not eligible for the SCM due to the business judgment rule or for which taxpayers select another transfer pricing method may still be eligible for the SCM exception to the extent of total services cost, the record-keeping requirements in the proposed regulations differ from the requirements in §1.482-9(b)(6). See §1.59A-3(b)(3)(i)(B)(2). Unlike §1.482-9(b)(6), the proposed regulations do not require that taxpayers "include a statement evidencing [their] intention to apply the services cost method to evaluate the arm's length charge for such services," but the proposed regulations do require that taxpayers include a calculation of the amount of profit mark-up (if any) paid for the services. For purposes of qualifying for the SCM exception under section 59A(d)(5), taxpayers are required to comply with the books and records requirements under these proposed regulations but not §1.482-9(b)(6).

The proposed regulations also clarify that the parenthetical reference in section 59A(d)(5) to the business judgment rule prerequisite for applicability of the services cost method — "(determined without regard to the requirement that the services not contribute significantly to fundamental risks of business success or failure)" — disregards the entire requirement set forth in §1.482-9(b)(5) solely for purposes of section 59A(d)(5).

2. Qualified Derivative Payments

Section 59A(h) provides that a qualified derivative payment (QDP) is not a base erosion payment. Proposed §1.59A-6 defines a QDP as any payment made by a taxpayer to a foreign related party pursuant to a derivative for which the taxpayer recognizes gain or loss on the derivative on a mark-to-market basis (treats the derivative as sold on the last business day of the taxable year), the gain or loss is ordinary, and any gain, loss, income or deduction on a payment made pursuant to the derivative is also treated as ordinary.

The QDP exception applies only if the taxpayer satisfies reporting requirements in proposed §1.6038A-2(b)(7)(ix). If a taxpayer satisfies the reporting requirements for some QDPs, but not all, then only the payments for which the taxpayer fails to satisfy the reporting requirements will be ineligible for the QDP exception. Section 1.6038A-2(b)(7)(ix) will first apply to taxable years beginning after final regulations are published, which provides taxpayers additional time to meet those reporting requirements. The proposed regulations provide that before final regulations are published, taxpayers satisfy the reporting requirements for QDPs by reporting the aggregate amount of QDPs for the taxable year on Form 8991, *Tax on Base Erosion Payments of Taxpayers With Substantial Gross Receipts.*

Section 59A(h)(3) provides two exceptions to the QDP exception. Specifically, the QDP exception does not apply (1) to a payment that would be treated as a base erosion payment if it were not made pursuant to a derivative or (2) with respect to a contract that has derivative and nonderivative components, to a payment that is properly allocable to the nonderivative component. The proposed regulations do not specifically address or modify these statutory provisions. For the avoidance of doubt, the Treasury Department and the IRS observe that these rules in section 59A(h)(3) are self-executing; thus, taxpayers must apply these two rules to determine whether any of their payments pursuant to derivatives fail to qualify for the QDP exception. The Treasury Department and the IRS request comments on whether regulations should further clarify the statutory provisions in section 59A(h)(3).

Proposed § 1.59A-6(d) defines a derivative as any contract, the value of which, or any payment with respect to which, is determined by reference to any stock, evidence of indebtedness, actively traded commodity, currency, or any rate, price, amount, index, formula or algorithm. However, direct ownership of any of these items is not ownership of a derivative. The proposed regulations clarify that for purposes of section 59A(h)(4), a derivative does not include an insurance contract, a securities lending transaction, a sale-repurchase transaction, or any substantially similar transaction.

For federal tax purposes, a sale-repurchase transaction satisfying certain conditions is treated as a secured loan. Sections 59A(h)(3) and 59A(h)(4) explicitly exclude from qualified derivatives payment status any payment that would be treated as a base erosion payment if it were not made pursuant to a derivative, such as a payment of interest on a debt instrument. Accordingly, for purposes of section 59A(h), the proposed regulations provide that sale-repurchase transactions are not treated as derivatives. Because sale-repurchase transactions and securities lending transactions are economically similar to each other, the Treasury Department and the IRS have determined that these transactions should be treated similarly for purposes of section 59A(h)(4), and therefore payments on those transactions are not treated as QDPs. The Treasury Department and the IRS request comments on whether securities lending transactions and sale-repurchase transactions have been properly excluded from the definition of a derivative, including whether certain transactions lack a significant financing component such that those transactions should be treated as derivatives for purposes of section 59A(h). The Treasury Department and the IRS also request comments regarding whether any additional transactions or financial instruments should be explicitly excluded from the definition of a derivative.

3. Exception to Base Erosion Payment Status for Payments the Recipient of which is Subject to U.S. Tax

In general, for a payment or accrual to be treated as a base erosion payment, the recipient must be a foreign person (within the meaning of section 6038A(c)(3)) that is a related party with respect to the taxpayer, and a deduction must be allowable with respect to the payment or accrual. See section 59A(f). Section 6038A(c)(3) defines "foreign person" as any person that is not a United States person within the meaning of section 7701(a)(30), but for this purpose the term "United States person" does not include any individual who is a citizen of any U.S. territory (but not otherwise a citizen of the United States) and who is not a resident of the United States. See proposed § 1.59A-1(b)(10). The Treasury Department and the IRS have determined that it is appropriate in defining a base erosion payment to consider the U.S. tax treatment of the foreign recipient. In particular, the Treasury Department and the IRS have determined that a payment to a foreign person should not be taxed as a base erosion payment to the extent that payments to the foreign related party are effectively connected income. Those amounts are subject to tax under sections 871(b) and 882(a) on a net basis in substantially the same manner as amounts paid to a United States citizen or resident or a domestic corporation. Accordingly, the proposed regulations include an exception from the definition of base erosion payment for amounts that are subject to tax as income effectively connected with the conduct of a U.S. trade or business. In the case of a foreign recipient that determines its net taxable income under an applicable income tax treaty, the exception from the definition of base erosion payment applies to payments taken into account in determining net taxable income under the treaty.

4. Exchange Loss from a Section 988 Transaction

Proposed § 1.59A-3(b)(3)(iv) provides that exchange losses from section 988 transactions described in § 1.988-1(a)(1) are not base erosion payments. The Treasury Department and the IRS have determined that these losses do not present the same base erosion concerns as other types of losses that arise in connection with payments to a foreign related party. Accordingly, under these proposed regulations, section 988 losses are excluded from the numerator.

The proposed regulations also provide that section 988 losses are excluded from the denominator of the base erosion percentage. Specifically, proposed § 1.59A-2(e)(3)(ii)(D) provides that an exchange loss from a section 988 transaction (including with respect to persons other than foreign related parties) is not included in the denominator when calculating the base erosion percentage. Exchange gain from a section 988 transaction, however, is included as a gross receipt for purposes of the gross receipts test under proposed § 1.59A-2(d).

The Treasury Department and the IRS request comments on the treatment of section 988 losses in the context of section 59A, including whether the rule relating to section 988 losses in the denominator of the base erosion percentage calculation should be limited to transactions with a foreign related party.

5. Exception for Interest on Certain Instruments Issued by Globally Systemically Important Banking Organizations.

The Federal Reserve requires that certain global systemically important banking organizations (GSIBs) issue TLAC securities as part of a global framework for bank capital that has sought to minimize the risk of insolvency. In particular, the Board of Governors of the Federal Reserve (the Board) has issued regulations that prescribe the amount and form of external TLAC securities that domestic GSIBs must issue and internal TLAC securities that certain foreign GSIBs must issue. In the case of internal TLAC securities, the Board regulations require the domestic intermediate holding company of a foreign GSIB to issue a specified minimum amount of TLAC to its foreign parent. Section 59A(i) provides that the Secretary shall prescribe such regulations or other guidance as may be necessary or appropriate to carry out the provisions of section 59A, including regulations addressing specifically enumerated situations. The Treasury Department and the IRS have determined that because of the special status of TLAC as part of a global system to address bank solvency and the precise limits that Board regulations place on the terms of TLAC securities and structure of intragroup TLAC funding, it is necessary and appropriate to include an exception to base erosion payment status for interest paid or accrued on TLAC securities required by the Federal Reserve.

Specifically, the proposed regulations include a TLAC exception that applies only to the extent of the amount of TLAC securities required by the Federal Reserve under subpart P of part 252 of 12 C.F.R. As a result, the exception is scaled back if the adjusted issue price of the average amount of TLAC securities issued and outstanding exceeds the average amount of TLAC long-term debt required by the Federal Reserve for the taxable year. The TLAC exception applies only to securities required by the Federal Reserve, and as a result generally does not apply to securities issued by a foreign corporation engaged in a U.S. trade or business because the applicable Federal Reserve requirement applies only to domestic institutions. However, the Treasury Department and the IRS acknowledge that foreign regulators may impose similar requirements on the financial institutions they regulate. The Treasury Department and the IRS request comments regarding a similar exception for foreign corporations that are required by law to issue a similar type of loss-absorbing instrument, including the appropriate scope of an exception that would provide parity between the treatment of domestic corporations and foreign corporations engaged in a U.S. trade or business.

C. Base Erosion Payments Occurring Before the Effective Date and Pre-2018 Disallowed Business Interest

Section 14401(e) of the Act provides that section 59A applies only to base erosion payments paid or accrued in taxable years beginning after December 31, 2017. The statutory definition of a base erosion tax benefit is based upon the definition of a base erosion payment. Accordingly, the proposed regulations confirm the exclusion of a deduction described in section 59A(c)(2)(A)(i) (deduction allowed under Chapter 1 for the taxable year with respect to any base erosion payment) or section 59A(c)(2)(A)(ii) (deduction allowed under Chapter 1 for the taxable year for depreciation or amortization with respect to any property acquired with such payment) that is allowed in a taxable year beginning after December 31, 2017, if it relates to a base erosion payment that occurred in a taxable year beginning before January 1, 2018.

For example, if in 2015, a calendar year taxpayer makes a payment or accrual to a foreign related party to acquire depreciable property, the 2015 payment is excluded from the definition of a base erosion payment because of section 14401(e) of the Act. As a result, the taxpayer's depreciation deduction allowed in 2018 with respect to this property is not a base erosion tax benefit.

Similarly, if in 2016, a taxpayer with a calendar year had paid or accrued interest on an obligation to a foreign related party, but the interest was not deductible in 2016 due to the application of section 267(a), the 2016 accrual of the interest amount is excluded from the definition of a base erosion payment because of section 14401(e) of the Act. As a result, if the interest amount becomes deductible in 2018, the taxpayer's deduction allowed in 2018 with respect to this item is not a base erosion tax benefit.

In the case of business interest expense that is not allowed as a deduction under section 163(j)(1), the proposed regulations provide a rule that clarifies that the effective date rules apply in a similar manner as with other base erosion payments that initially arose before the effective date in section 14401(e) of the Act. Section 163(j), as modified by the Act, provides that the deduction for business interest expense is limited to the sum of business interest income, 30 percent of adjusted taxable income ("ATI"), and the amount of any floor plan financing interest. Section 163(j)(2) further provides that any disallowed business interest is carried forward to the succeeding year, and that the carryforward amount is treated as "paid or accrued" in the succeeding taxable year.

In Notice 2018-28, 2018-16 I.R.B. 492, Section 3, the Treasury Department and the IRS stated that business interest carried forward from a taxable year beginning before January 1, 2018, will be treated in the same manner as interest paid or accrued in a taxable year beginning after December 31, 2017, for purposes of section 59A. Under this approach, business interest expense that was initially paid or accrued in a taxable year beginning before January 1, 2018, could nonetheless be a base erosion payment in a taxable year beginning after December 31, 2017, because section 163(j)(2) deems a recurring "payment or accrual" for such item in each carryforward year. Comments requested that the Treasury Department and the IRS reconsider the position taken in Notice 2018-28, on the basis that the determination of whether a payment is a base erosion payment should be made as of the date of the actual payment of interest rather than the date that a deduction is allowed under section 163(j).

The Treasury Department and the IRS agree and have determined that the approach described in Notice 2018-28 is not consistent with the general effective date provision in Section 14401(e) of the Act because the language in section 163(j)(2) deeming a recurring "payment or accrual" is primarily to implement the carryforward mechanism in section 163(j), rather than to treat interest that is carried forward to a subsequent taxable year as paid or accrued for all tax purposes in that subsequent taxable year. Accordingly, the proposed regulations do not follow the approach described in Notice 2018-28. Instead, the proposed regulations provide that any disallowed disqualified interest under section 163(j) that resulted from a payment or accrual to a foreign related party and that is carried forward from a taxable year beginning before January 1, 2018, is not a base erosion payment. The proposed regulations also clarify that any disallowed business interest carryforward under section 163(j) that resulted from a payment or accrual to a foreign related party is treated as a base erosion payment in the year that the interest was paid or accrued even though the interest may be deemed to be paid or accrued again in the year in which it is actually deducted. The rule in the proposed regulations generally is consistent with excluding interest paid or accrued before January 1, 2018 (generally under financing arranged prior to the Act) from treatment as a base erosion payment. The Treasury Department and the IRS welcome comments with respect to the treatment of disallowed disqualified interest under section 163(j) from a taxable year beginning before January 1, 2018. See Part IV.B of this Explanation of Provisions section for proposed rules determining the amount of business interest expense for which a deduction is allowed when section 163(j) applies to limit interest deductions.

IV. *Base Erosion Tax Benefits*

The amount of base erosion tax benefits is an input in (i) the computation of the base erosion percentage test (discussed in Part II.C of this Explanation of Provisions section) and (ii) the determination of modified taxable income (discussed in Part V of this Explanation of Provisions section). Generally, a base erosion tax benefit is the amount of any deduction relating to a base erosion payment that is allowed under the Code for the taxable year. Base erosion tax benefits are defined in proposed § 1.59A-3(c).

A. *Withholding Tax on Payments*

As discussed in Part II.C of this Explanation of Provisions section, if tax is imposed by section 871 or 881 and the tax is deducted and withheld under section 1441 or 1442 without reduction by an applicable income tax treaty on a base erosion payment, the base erosion payment is treated as having a base erosion tax benefit of zero for purposes of calculating a taxpayer's modified taxable income. If an income tax treaty reduces the amount of withholding imposed on the base erosion payment, the base erosion payment is treated as a base erosion tax benefit to the extent of the reduction in withholding under rules similar to those in section 163(j)(5)(B) as in effect before the Act.

B. *Rules for Classifying Interest for which a Deduction is Allowed when Section 163(j) Limits Deductions*

Section 59A(c)(3) provides a stacking rule in cases in which section 163(j) applies to a taxpayer, under which the reduction in the amount of deductible interest is treated as allocable first to interest paid or accrued to persons who are not related parties with respect to the taxpayer and then to related parties. The statute does not provide a rule for determining which portion of the interest treated as paid to related parties (and thus potentially treated as a base erosion payment) is treated as paid to a foreign related person as opposed to a domestic related person. Proposed § 1.59A-3(c)(4) provides rules coordinating section 163(j) with the determination of the amount of base erosion tax benefits. This rule provides, consistent with section 59A(c)(3), that where section 163(j) applies to limit the amount of a taxpayer's business interest expense that is deductible in the taxable year, a taxpayer is required to treat all disallowed business interest first as interest paid or accrued to persons who are not related parties, and then as interest paid or accrued to related parties for purposes of section 59A. More specifically, the proposed regulations provide that when a corporation has business interest expense paid or accrued to both unrelated parties and related parties, the amount of allowed business interest expense is treated first as the business interest expense paid to related parties, proportionately between foreign and domestic related parties, and then as business interest expense paid to unrelated parties. Conversely, the amount of a disallowed business interest expense carryforward is treated first as business interest expense paid to unrelated parties, and then as business interest expense paid to related parties, proportionately between foreign and domestic related party business interest expense.

Because section 163(j) and the proposed regulations thereunder provide an ordering rule that allocates business interest expense deductions first to business interest expense incurred in the current year and then to business interest expense carryforwards from prior years (starting with the earliest year) in order to separately track the attributes on a year-by-year layered approach for subchapter C purposes, these proposed regulations follow that convention. Accordingly, the proposed regulations also follow a year-by-year convention in the allocation of business interest expense and carryovers among the related and unrelated party classifications. See also the discussion of singular tax attributes in Part V.A of this Explanation of Provisions section. The proposed regulations adopt a similar approach for business interest expense and excess business interest of a partnership that is allocated to a corporate partner by separately tracking and ordering items allocated from a partnership.

V. *Modified Taxable Income*

For any taxable year, section 59A imposes a tax on each applicable taxpayer equal to the base erosion minimum tax amount for that year. Section 59A(b)(1) provides that the base erosion minimum tax amount is determined based on an applicable taxpayer's modified taxable income for the taxable year. Part V.A of this Explanation of Provisions section discusses how an applicable taxpayer computes its modified taxable income. Part V.B of this Explanation of Provisions section describes how modified taxable income is calculated if an applicable taxpayer has an overall taxable loss for a taxable year. Finally, Part V.C of this Explanation of Provisions section describes the base erosion percentage that is used when the base erosion percentage of a net operating loss deduction ("NOL deduction") is added back to taxable income for purposes of the modified taxable income calculation.

A. *Method of Computation*

Section 59A(c)(1) provides that the term modified taxable income means the taxable income of the taxpayer computed under Chapter 1 for the taxable year, determined without regard to base erosion tax benefits and the base erosion percentage of any NOL deduction under section 172 for the taxable year. The proposed regulations clarify that the computation of modified taxable income and the computation of the base erosion minimum tax amount (which is discussed in Part VI of this Explanation of Provisions section) are made on a taxpayer-by-taxpayer basis. That is, under the proposed regulations, the aggregate group concept is used solely for determining whether a taxpayer is an applicable taxpayer and the base erosion percentage of any NOL deduction. This approach is consistent with section 59A(a)'s imposition of a tax equal to the base erosion minimum tax amount, which is in addition to the regular tax liability of a taxpayer.

The proposed regulations also provide that the computation of modified taxable income is done on an add-back basis. The computation starts with taxable income (or taxable loss) of the taxpayer as computed for regular tax purposes, and adds to that amount (a) the gross amount of base erosion tax benefits for the taxable year and (b) the base erosion percentage of any NOL deduction under section 172 for the taxable year.

The proposed regulations do not provide for the recomputation of income under an approach similar to the alternative minimum tax, which the Act repealed for corporations. See section 12001(a) of the Act. Under a recomputation approach, attributes that are limited based on taxable income would be subject to different annual limitations, and those attributes would have to be re-computed for purposes of section 59A. Applying this approach in a manner that reflects the results of the BEAT-basis recomputation to subsequent years would lead to parallel attributes that are maintained separately in a manner similar to the pre-Act corporate alternative minimum tax. For example, the amount of the net operating loss used to reduce modified taxable income would differ from the amount used in computing regular tax liability, and the carryforward of unused net operating loss that is used to compute regular tax liability would not reflect the net operating loss amount used to reduce modified taxable income (absent a separate BEAT-basis carryover). The annual limitation under section 163(j)(1), which generally limits a corporation's annual deduction for business interest expense, would present similar issues under a recomputation approach. Consequently, the add-back approach also provides simplification relative to the recomputation approach because the add-back approach eliminates the need to engage in the more complex tracking of separate attributes on a BEAT basis in a manner similar to the repealed corporate AMT. The Treasury Department and the IRS welcome comments on the add-back approach provided in the proposed regulations, and the practical effects of an alternative recomputation-based approach.

B. *Conventions for Computing Modified Taxable Income - Current Year Losses and Excess Net Operating Loss Carryovers*

If a taxpayer has an excess of deductions allowed by Chapter 1 over gross income, computed without regard to the NOL deduction, the taxpayer has negative taxable income for the taxable year. Generally, the proposed regulations provide that a negative amount is the starting point for computing modified taxable income when there is no NOL deduction from net operating loss carryovers and carrybacks.

The proposed regulations further provide a rule applicable to situations in which there is a NOL deduction from a net operating loss carryover or carryback to the taxable year and that NOL deduction exceeds the amount of positive taxable income before that deduction (because, for example, the loss arose in a year beginning before January 1, 2018). The proposed regulations provide that the excess amount of NOL deduction does not reduce taxable income below zero for determining the starting point for computing modified taxable income. The Treasury Department and the IRS have determined that this rule is necessary because section 172(a) could be read to provide that, for example, if a taxpayer has a net operating loss of $100x that arose in a taxable year beginning before January 1, 2018, that is carried forward, and in a subsequent year the taxpayer has taxable income of $5x before taking into account the $100x net operating loss carryover deduction, the taxpayer may nonetheless have a $100x NOL deduction in that year or a $95x taxable loss (even though $95x of the net operating loss would remain as a carryforward to future years, as well). Because the proposed regulations recognize the notion of a taxable loss when deductions other than the NOL deduction exceed gross income (as discussed earlier in this Part V), this rule clarifies that the taxpayer's starting point for computing modified taxable income in this situation is zero, rather than negative $95x.

The proposed regulations further clarify that the NOL deduction taken into account for purposes of adding the base erosion percentage of the NOL deduction to taxable income under section 59A(c)(1)(B) is determined in the same manner. Accordingly, in the example above, the base erosion percentage of the NOL deduction added to taxable income is computed based on the $5x NOL deduction that reduces regular taxable income to zero, rather than the entire $100x of net operating loss carryforward, $95x of which is not absorbed in the current taxable year.

Finally, the proposed regulations provide that an applicable taxpayer's taxable income is determined according to section 63(a) without regard to the rule in section 860E(a)(1). That rule generally provides that a holder of a residual interest in a real estate mortgage investment conduit ("REMIC") may not have taxable income less than its excess inclusion amount. As a result of section 860E(a)(1), a holder of a REMIC residual interest may have taxable income for purposes of computing its regular tax liability even though it has a current year loss. The proposed regulations provide that the limitation in section 860E(a)(1) is disregarded for purposes of calculating modified taxable income under section 59A. The rule described in this paragraph is relevant, for example, in situations when the taxpayer would have negative taxable income attributable to a current year loss, as described in this Part V.B, or no taxable income as a result of a net operating loss. Because section 860E(a)(1) ensures that the excess inclusion is subject to tax under section 11, the Treasury Department and the IRS have determined that it is not appropriate to apply the rule in section 860E(a)(1) for the purpose of calculating modified taxable income under section 59A.

C. *Conventions for Computing Modified Taxable Income - Determining the Base Erosion Percentage of NOL Deductions*

Section 59A(c)(1)(B) provides that modified taxable income includes the base erosion percentage of any NOL deduction allowed under section 172 for the taxable year. In this context, the relevant base erosion percentage could be either the base erosion percentage in the year that the net operating loss arose, or alternatively, the base erosion percentage in the year in which the taxpayer takes the NOL deduction. Proposed § 1.59A-4(b)(2)(ii) applies the base erosion percentage of the year in which the loss arose, or vintage year, because the base erosion percentage of the vintage year reflects the portion of base eroding payments that are reflected in the net operating loss carryover. In addition, because the vintage-year base erosion percentage is a fixed percentage, taxpayers will have greater certainty as to the amount of the future add-back to modified taxable income (as compared to using the utilization-year base erosion percentage).

Based on this approach, the proposed regulations also provide that in the case of net operating losses that arose in taxable years beginning before January 1, 2018, and that are deducted as carryovers in taxable years beginning after December 31, 2017, the base erosion percentage is zero because section 59A applies only to base erosion payments that are paid or accrued in taxable years beginning after December 31, 2017. See section 14401(e) of the Act. As a result, there is no add-back to modified taxable income for the use of those net operating loss carryovers. The Treasury Department and the IRS welcome comments on the vintage-year approach as well as the alternative utilization-year approach.

The proposed regulations also clarify that in computing the add-back for NOL deductions for purposes of the modified taxable income calculation, the relevant base erosion percentage is the base erosion percentage for the aggregate group that is used to determine whether the taxpayer is an applicable taxpayer, rather than a separate computation of base erosion percentage computed solely by reference to the single taxpayer.

VI. *Base Erosion Minimum Tax Amount*

An applicable taxpayer computes its base erosion minimum tax amount ("BEMTA") for the taxable year to determine its liability under section 59A(a). Proposed § 1.59A-5 describes the calculation of the BEMTA. Generally, the taxpayer's BEMTA equals the excess of (1) the applicable tax rate for the taxable year ("BEAT rate") multiplied by the taxpayer's modified taxable income for the taxable year over (2) the taxpayer's adjusted regular tax liability for that year. See Part VIII of this Explanation of Provisions section for a discussion of the higher BEAT rate for certain banks and registered securities dealers.

In determining the taxpayer's adjusted regular tax liability for the taxable year, credits (including the foreign tax credit) are generally subtracted from the regular tax liability amount. To prevent an inappropriate understatement of a taxpayer's adjusted regular tax liability, the proposed regulations provide that credits for overpayment of taxes and for taxes withheld at source are not subtracted from the taxpayer's regular tax liability because these credits relate to federal income tax paid for the current or previous year.

For taxable years beginning before January 1, 2026, under section 59A(b)(1)(B), the credits allowed against regular tax liability (which reduce the amount of regular tax liability for purposes of calculating BEMTA) are not reduced by the research credit determined under section 41(a) or by a portion of applicable section 38 credits. For taxable years beginning after December 31, 2025, this special treatment of the research credit and applicable section 38 credits no longer applies. As a result, an applicable taxpayer may have a greater BEMTA than would be the case in taxable years beginning before January 1, 2026. In general, foreign tax credits are taken into account in computing a taxpayer's regular tax liability before other credits. See section 26(a). As a result, a taxpayer with foreign tax credits that reduce its regular tax liability to, or close to, zero may not use its section 41(a) credits or its applicable section 38 credits in computing its regular tax liability. In these situations, those credits will not be taken into account in computing the taxpayer's BEMTA even in a pre-2026 year. Instead, those credits will reduce (or, put differently, will prevent an increase in) the BEMTA in the year when those credits are used for regular tax purposes (provided that the taxable year begins before January 1, 2026).

VII. *Application of Section 59A to Partnerships*

A partnership is not an "applicable taxpayer" as defined in Section 59A; only corporations can be applicable taxpayers. In general, however, a partnership also is not subject to the income tax imposed by Chapter 1 of Subtitle A of the Code. Instead, partners are liable for income tax only in their separate capacities. Each taxpayer that is a partner in a partnership takes into account separately the partner's distributive share of the partner's income or loss in determining its taxable income. Accordingly, an item of income is subject to federal income taxation based on the status of the partners, and not the partnership as an entity. Similarly, a partnership does not itself benefit from a deduction. Instead, the tax benefit from a deduction is taken by the taxpayer that is allocated the deduction under section 704. Section 702(b) provides that the character of any item be taken into account as if such item were realized directly from the source from which realized by the partnership, or incurred in the same manner as incurred by the partnership. Section 702(b) acknowledges that differences in partner tax characteristics (for example, whether the partner is a corporation or an individual, or domestic or foreign) may result in differences in the tax consequences of items the partnership allocates to its partners.

The proposed regulations generally apply an aggregate approach in conjunction with the gross receipts test for evaluating whether a corporation is an applicable taxpayer and in addressing the treatment of payments made by a partnership or received by a partnership for purposes of section 59A. The proposed regulations generally provide that partnerships are treated as an aggregate of the partners in determining whether payments to or payments from a partnership are base erosion payments consistent with the approach described in subchapter K as well as the authority provided in section 59A(i)(1) to prescribe such regulations that are necessary or appropriate to carry out the provisions of section 59A, including through the use of intermediaries or by characterizing payments otherwise subject to section 59A as payments not subject to 59A. Thus, when determining whether a corporate partner that is an applicable taxpayer has made a base erosion payment, amounts paid or accrued by a partnership are treated as paid by each partner to the extent an item of expense is allocated to the partner under section 704. Similarly, any amounts received by or accrued to a partnership are treated as received by each partner to the extent the item of income or gain is allocated to each partner under section 704. The rules and exceptions for base erosion payments and base erosion tax benefits then apply accordingly on an aggregate basis.

The Treasury Department and the IRS have determined that a rule that applies the aggregate principle consistently is necessary to align the treatment of economically similar transactions. The proposed rule prevents an applicable taxpayer from (a) paying a domestic partnership that is owned by foreign related parties, rather than paying those foreign partners directly, to circumvent the BEAT and (b) causing a partnership in which an applicable taxpayer is a partner to make a payment to a foreign related party, rather than paying that foreign related party directly. The rule applies consistently when a payment is to a foreign partnership that is owned, for example, by domestic corporations. This rule also addresses situations in which a partnership with an applicable taxpayer partner makes a payment to a foreign related party. Partners with certain small ownership interests are excluded from this aggregate approach for purposes of determining base erosion tax benefits from the partnership. This small ownership interests exclusion generally applies to partnership interests that represent less than ten percent of the capital and profits of the partnership and less than ten percent of each item of income, gain, loss, deduction, and credit; and that have a fair market value of less than $25 million. See proposed § 1.59A-7(b)(4). The Treasury Department and the IRS determined that a threshold of ten percent appropriately balanced the administrative burdens of determining whether deductions allocated to a partner with a small ownership interest in a partnership are base erosion payments with the Treasury Department and IRS's interest in maintaining a consistent aggregate approach to partnerships in applying to the BEAT. In determining the appropriate threshold for a small ownership interest, the Treasury Department and the IRS considered the treatment of small ownership interests in partnerships in analogous situations in other Treasury regulations. The Treasury Department and the IRS welcome comments on the aggregate approach to partnerships as well as the exception for small ownership interests, including the specific thresholds for the exception.

The proposed regulations do not provide for special treatment of base erosion tax benefits attributable to a partnership or to partnership nonrecognition transactions. Instead, the aggregate principle generally applies to these situations. For example, if a partnership acquires property from a foreign related party of a taxpayer that is a partner in the partnership, deductions for depreciation of the property allocated to the taxpayer generally are base erosion tax benefits. Similarly, if a foreign related party and a taxpayer form a partnership, and the foreign related party contributes depreciable property, deductions for depreciation of the property generally are base erosion tax benefits, in part, because the partnership is treated as acquiring the property in exchange for an interest in the partnership under section 721. This approach is consistent with the approach taken with respect to subchapter C transactions, as described in Part III.A.1 of this Explanation of Provisions section.

The proposed regulations provide that with respect to any person that owns an interest in a partnership, the related party determination under section 59A(g) applies at the partner level.

VIII. Rules Relating to Banks and Dealers for Purposes of Computing the Base Erosion Percentage and Determining the BEAT Rate for Computing BEMTA

Section 59A modifies two general rules in the case of certain banks or registered securities dealers. First, section 59A(e)(1)(C) lowers the base erosion percentage threshold for certain banks and registered securities dealers from three percent or more to two percent or more. See Part II.C of this Explanation of Provisions section for additional discussion of this rule. Second, section 59A(b)(3) provides that the BEAT rate is one percentage point higher for those banks or registered securities dealers.

The proposed regulations do not modify the statutory definition of the term "bank" for these purposes from its reference to section 581, which defines a bank by reference to a bank or trust company incorporated and doing business under the laws of United States (including laws related to the District of Columbia) or of any state. Thus, a foreign corporation licensed to conduct a banking business in the United States and subject to taxation with respect to income that is, or is treated as, effectively connected with the conduct of a trade or business in the United States is not included in this definition.

The proposed regulations clarify that the term "registered securities dealer" is limited to a dealer as defined in section 3(a)(5) of the Securities Exchange Act of 1934 that is registered, or required to be registered, under section 15 of the Securities Exchange Act of 1934.

The proposed regulations also confirm that the operative rules that lower the base erosion percentage threshold and that increase the BEAT rate apply only to a taxpayer that is a member of an affiliated group as defined in section 1504(a)(1), and thus do not apply, for example, if the taxpayer is not affiliated with another includible corporation (within the meaning of section 1504(b)(1)), or if the taxpayer is not itself an includible corporation (for example, a foreign corporation that is an applicable taxpayer).

For purposes of applying the lower base erosion percentage threshold to banks and registered securities dealers, the proposed regulations clarify that because the base erosion percentage is determined on an aggregate group basis, the lower threshold applies if any member of the aggregate group is a member of an affiliated group that includes a bank or registered securities dealer. The proposed regulations provide a limited exception for members of an affiliated group that includes a bank or registered securities dealer where the bank or registered securities dealer activities are de minimis. This de minimis rule provides that a consolidated group, or a member of the aggregate group of which the taxpayer is a member, is not subject to the lower base erosion percentage threshold if its gross receipts attributable to the bank or the registered securities dealer are less than two percent of the aggregate group's total gross revenue. This de minimis rule uses the same threshold measurement for exclusion from the special rule for banks and registered securities dealers (two percent) that is used as the base erosion percentage threshold for banks or registered securities dealers to determine whether such taxpayers are applicable taxpayers that are subject to the BEAT, with the latter test functioning in a manner similar to a de minimis threshold for the application of the BEAT. See Part II.C of this Explanation of Provisions section. The Treasury Department and the IRS welcome comments on the scope of the de minimis rule for banks and registered securities dealers. See also Part III.B.5 of this Explanation of Provisions section for a discussion of an exception to base erosion payment status for interest on TLAC securities.

IX. Rules Relating to Insurance Companies

The definition of a base erosion payment in section 59A(d) includes any premiums or other consideration paid or accrued by a taxpayer to a foreign related party for any reinsurance payments taken into account under section 803(a)(1)(B) or 832(b)(4)(A). Generally, section 803(a)(1) defines gross income for a life insurance company to include the gross amount of premiums and other consideration on insurance and annuity contracts less return premiums and premiums and other consideration arising out of indemnity reinsurance. For an insurance company other than a life insurance company, under section 832(b), gross income generally includes underwriting income, which is comprised of premiums earned during the taxable year less losses incurred and expenses incurred. Section 832(b)(4)(A) provides that the amount of premiums earned on insurance contracts is the amount of gross premiums written on insurance contracts during the taxable year less return premiums and premiums paid for reinsurance.

The Treasury Department and the IRS are aware that certain reinsurance agreements provide that amounts paid to and from a reinsurer are settled on a net basis or netted under the terms of the agreement. The Treasury Department and the IRS are also aware that other commercial agreements with reciprocal payments may be settled on a net basis or netted under the terms of those agreements. The proposed regulations do not provide a rule permitting netting in any of these circumstances because the BEAT statutory framework is based on including the gross amount of deductible and certain other payments (base erosion payments) in the BEAT's expanded modified taxable income base without regard to reciprocal obligations or payments that are taken into account in the regular income tax base, but not the BEAT's modified taxable income base. Generally, the amounts of income and deduction are determined on a gross basis under the Code; however, as discussed in Part III of this Explanation of Provisions section, if there are situations where an application of otherwise generally applicable tax law would provide that a deduction is computed on a net basis (because an item received reduces the item of deduction rather than increasing gross income), the proposed regulations do not change that result. The Treasury Department and the IRS request comments addressing whether a distinction should be made between reinsurance contracts entered into by an applicable taxpayer and a foreign related party that provide for settlement of amounts owed on a net basis and other commercial contracts entered into by an applicable taxpayer and a foreign related party that provide for netting of items payable by one party against items payable by the other party in determining that net amount to be paid between the parties.

The proposed regulations also do not provide any specific rules for payments by a domestic reinsurance company to a foreign related insurance company. In the case of a domestic reinsurance company, claims payments for losses incurred and other payments are deductible and are thus potentially within the scope of section 59A(d)(1). See sections 803(c) and 832(c). In the case of an insurance company other than a life insurance company (non-life insurance company) that reinsures foreign risk, certain of these payments may also be treated as reductions in gross income under section 832(b)(3), which are not deductions and also not the type of reductions in gross income described in sections 59A(d)(3). The Treasury Department and the IRS request comments on the appropriate treatment of these items under subchapter L. The Treasury Department and the IRS also recognize that to the extent that the items are not treated as deductions for non-life insurance companies this may lead to asymmetric treatment for life insurance companies that reinsure foreign risk because part I of subchapter L (the rules for life insurance companies) refers to these costs only as deductions (that is, does not also refer to the costs as reductions in gross income in a manner similar to section 832(b)(3)). The Treasury Department and the IRS request comments on whether the regulations should provide that a life insurance company that reinsures foreign risk is treated in the same manner as a non-life insurance company that reinsures foreign risk.

The proposed regulations do not address a foreign insurance company that has in effect an election to be treated as a domestic corporation for purposes of the Code. Amounts paid or accrued to such a company are not base erosion payments because the corporation is treated as a domestic corporation for purposes of the Code.

X. Anti-Abuse and Recharacterization Rules

Proposed § 1.59A-9(b) provides that certain transactions that have a principal purpose of avoiding section 59A will be disregarded or deemed to result in a base erosion payment. This proposed anti-abuse rule addresses the following types of transactions: (a) transactions involving intermediaries acting as a conduit to avoid a base erosion payment; (b) transactions entered into to increase the deductions taken into account in the denominator of the base erosion percentage; and (c) transactions among related parties entered into to avoid the application of rules applicable to banks and registered securities dealers (for example, causing a bank or registered securities dealer to disaffiliate from an affiliated group so as to avoid the requirement that it be a member of such a group).

XI. *Consolidated Groups as Taxpayers*

Affiliated groups of domestic corporations that elect to file a consolidated income tax return generally compute their income tax liability on a "single-entity" basis. Because the regular tax liability is computed on a single entity basis, the additional tax imposed by section 59A must also be imposed on the same basis (because it is an addition to that regular tax liability). Accordingly, the proposed regulations provide that for affiliated corporations electing to file a consolidated income tax return, the tax under section 59A is determined at the consolidated group level, rather than determined separately for each member of the group. The BEAT is an addition to the regular corporate income tax under section 11, and the regular corporate income tax is applied to a consolidated group on a consolidated basis. Further, application of the BEAT on a group level eliminates the differences in the aggregate amount of taxation to a consolidated group that would otherwise occur, based on the location of deductions, including, for example, the location of related party interest payments within the group. Accordingly, the BEAT is also applied on a consolidated basis. This single taxpayer treatment for members of a consolidated group applies separately from the aggregate group concept in proposed § 1.59A-2(c), which also treats all members of the aggregate group as a single entity, but in that case, only for purposes of applying the gross receipts test and base erosion percentage test for determining whether a particular taxpayer is an applicable taxpayer. See generally, Part II of this Explanation of Provisions section.

To properly reflect the taxable income of the group, consolidated return regulations generally determine the tax treatment of items resulting from intercompany transactions (as defined in §1.1502-13(b)(1)(ii)) by treating members of the consolidated group as divisions of a single corporation (single entity treatment). In general, the existence of an intercompany transaction should not change the consolidated taxable income or consolidated tax liability of a consolidated group. Consistent with single entity treatment, items from intercompany transactions are not taken into account for purposes of making the computations under section 59A. For example, any increase in depreciation deductions resulting from intercompany sales of property are disregarded for purposes of determining the taxpayer's base erosion percentage. Similarly, interest payments on intercompany obligations (as defined in § 1.1502-13(g)(2)(ii)) are not taken into account in making the computations under section 59A.

XII. *Coordinating Consolidated Group Rules for Sections 59A(c)(3) and 163(j)*

Section 59A(c)(3) and proposed §1.59A-3(c)(4) coordinate the application of section 163(j) with the determination of the amount of base erosion tax benefits when a taxpayer has business interest expense paid to both unrelated parties and related parties. Those rules provide that, where section 163(j) applies to limit the amount of a taxpayer's business interest that is deductible in a taxable year, the taxpayer is required to treat all disallowed business interest as allocable first to interest paid or accrued to persons who are not related parties, and then to related parties. See Part IV.B of this Explanation of Provisions section.

Proposed § 1.1502-59A provides rules regarding application of section 59A(c)(3) to consolidated groups. These rules are required for the allocation of the BEMTA among members of the group under section 1552. In addition, apportionment of the domestic related party status and foreign related party status (defined later in this Part XII) of section 163(j) carryforwards among members of the group is necessary when a member deconsolidates from the group.

The proposed regulations implement the classification approach of proposed §1.59A-3(c)(4) on a consolidated basis (the "classification rule"), to identify which interest deductions are allocable to domestic related party payments, foreign related party payments, and unrelated party payments. Slightly different rules apply to the deduction of current year business interest expense than to the deduction of section 163(j) carryforwards. A consolidated group applies these rules to the amount of business interest expense (either from current year business interest expense or from carryforward amounts) that is actually deducted pursuant to section 163(j) and proposed §§1.163(j)-4(d) and 1.163(j)-5(b)(3). If the group deducts business interest expense paid or accrued in different taxable years (for example, both current year business interest expense and section 163(j) carryforwards), the classification rule applies separately to business interest expense incurred in each taxable year. For purposes of the proposed regulations, a member's current year business interest expense is the member's business interest expense that would be deductible in the current taxable year without regard to section 163(j) and that is not a disallowed business interest expense carryforward from a prior taxable year.

The classification rule applies on a single-entity basis to deductions of current year business interest expense. The consolidated group classifies its aggregate business interest deduction from current year business interest expense based on the aggregate current year business interest expense of all types (related or unrelated) paid by members of the group to nonmembers. Business interest deductions are treated as from payments or accruals to related parties first, and then from payments or accruals to unrelated parties. If there are payments to both foreign related parties and domestic related parties, the deductions are classified as to the related parties on a pro-rata basis.

Recognizing the flexibility of related-party financing, these proposed regulations provide that, if the group has aggregate business interest deductions classified as payments or accruals to a domestic related party (domestic related party status) or foreign related party (foreign related party status), the status of such payments or accruals is spread among members of the group (the allocation rule). Specifically, the domestic related party status and foreign related party status of the deduction is allocated among members of the group in proportion to the amount of each member's deduction of its current year business interest expense. Similarly, if any part of a section 163(j) carryforward is from a payment or accrual to a domestic related party or a foreign related party, the related party status of the section 163(j) carryforwards for the year will be allocated among members of the group. The allocation is in proportion to the relative amount of each member's section 163(j) carryforward from that year. Members' additional section 163(j) carryforward amounts are treated as payments or accruals to unrelated parties. The allocation rule applies separately to each carryforward year.

With regard to the deduction of any member's section 163(j) carryforward, the classification rule applies on an entity-by-entity basis. As discussed, before a member's section 163(j) carryforward moves forward into subsequent years, it is allocated a domestic related party status, foreign related party status, or unrelated party status. This allocation ensures that business interest deductions drawn from any carryforward originating in the same consolidated return year bear the same ratio of domestic related, foreign related, and unrelated statuses. When a member deducts any portion of its section 163(j) carryforward, the member applies section 59A(c)(3) and proposed § 1.59A-3(c)(4) to determine the status of the deducted carryforward, based on the status previously allocated to the member's section 163(j) carryforward for the relevant tax year. The tax liability imposed under section 59A on the consolidated group is allocated among the members of the consolidated group pursuant to the consolidated group's tax allocation method, taking into account these allocations. See section 1552.

If a member that is allocated a foreign related party status or domestic related party status to its section 163(j) carryforward deconsolidates from the group, the departing member's carryforward retains the allocated status. The departing member (and not the original consolidated group) takes into account the status of that carryforward for purposes of computing the BEAT in future years.

XIII. *Consolidated Tax Liability*

In §1.1502-2, a reference is added to the base erosion anti-abuse tax as a tax included in the computation of consolidated tax liability. Additionally, the proposed regulations make the following changes: (1) remove paragraph (j) of this regulation section because section 1333, relating to war loss recoveries, was repealed by section 1901(a)(145)(A) of the Tax Reform Act of 1976, Pub. L. 94-455, (2) remove paragraph (h) of this regulation section because section 1201, relating to the alternative tax for corporations, was repealed by section 13001(b)(2)(A) of the Act, and (3) update the cross reference to life insurance taxable income to section 801, following the revision of subchapter L of chapter 1 of the code in section 211 of the Deficit Reduction Act of 1984, Pub. L. 98-369.

In addition, the proposed regulations also make nonsubstantive changes to reorganize the structure of current § 1.1502-2. Specifically, the proposed regulations reorganize the current § 1.1502-2 to properly designate the unnumbered paragraphs. The proposed regulations also update other regulation sections that reference § 1.1502-2.

Finally, the proposed regulations correct an error in § 1.6655-5(e) *Example 10*. The proposed regulations replace the reference to "§ 1.1502-2(h)" with a reference to "1.1502-1(h)" because the context of *Example 10* demonstrates that the intended reference was to the definition of a consolidated group.

XIV. *Sections 382 and 383*

Section 1.383-1 provides that only otherwise currently allowable pre-change losses and pre-change credits will result in the absorption of the section 382 limitation and the section 383 credit limitation. The limitations under sections 382 and 383 are applied after the application of all other limitations contained in subtitle A of the Code. If the pre-change losses or pre-change credits cannot be deducted or otherwise used, they are carried forward to the next taxable year. The BEAT is not a modification to the normal computation of income tax under Subtitle A of the Code but an addition to that income tax. Therefore, these proposed regulations clarify that additions to tax under section 59A do not affect whether a loss, deduction, or credit is absorbed under section 382 or section 383.

XV. *Reporting and Recordkeeping Requirements Pursuant to Section 6038A*

Section 6038A imposes reporting and recordkeeping requirements on domestic corporations that are 25-percent foreign-owned. Section 6038C imposes the same reporting and recordkeeping requirements on certain foreign corporations engaged in a U.S. trade or business. These corporations are collectively known as "reporting corporations."

Reporting corporations are required to file an annual return on Form 5472, *Information Return of a 25% Foreign-Owned U.S. Corporation or a Foreign Corporation Engaged in a U.S. Trade or Business (Under Sections 6038A and 6038C of the Internal Revenue Code)*, with respect to each related party with which the reporting corporation has had any "reportable transactions." See § 1.6038A-2. Reporting corporations are also subject to specific requirements under sections 6038A and 6038C to maintain and make available the permanent books of account or records as required by section 6001 that are sufficient to establish the accuracy of the federal income tax return of the corporation, including information, documents, or records to the extent they may be relevant to determine the correct U.S. tax treatment of transactions with related parties. See § 1.6038A-3.

The Act amended section 6038A by adding paragraph (b)(2), which authorizes regulations requiring information from a reporting corporation that is also a section 59A "applicable taxpayer" for purposes of administering section 59A. Section 6038A(b)(2) applies to taxable years beginning after December 31, 2017. These proposed regulations identify certain types of information that will be required to be reported on Form 5472 and Form 8991, *Tax on Base Erosion Payments of Taxpayers With Substantial Gross Receipts*, and also provide the time and manner for reporting. While an applicable taxpayer that is not a reporting corporation would not be subject to monetary penalties and collateral provisions specific to sections 6038A and 6038C, the taxpayer remains subject to BEAT-related reporting obligations, including Form 8991, and applicable consequences for noncompliance.

Under section 59A(d)(4), the status of a foreign shareholder as a surrogate foreign corporation as defined in section 7874(a)(2)(B) or as a member of the same expanded affiliated group, as defined in section 7874(c)(1), as the surrogate foreign corporation can affect the treatment of payments from a taxpayer to that corporation under section 59A(d). If the reporting corporation is an expatriated entity as defined in section 7874(a)(2), the taxation of certain transactions between it and its foreign related persons as defined in section 7874(d)(3) may be affected. Consequently, the proposed regulations require all reporting corporations to state whether a foreign shareholder required to be listed on Form 5472 is a surrogate foreign corporation. The form may provide for reporting of whether the shareholder is a member of an expanded affiliated group including the surrogate foreign corporation.

In addition, to facilitate screening for important tax compliance concerns under section 59A as well as other provisions at the return filing stage, these proposed regulations clarify that the IRS may require by form or by form instructions the following information: (1) reporting of particular details of the reporting corporation's relationships with related parties in regard to which it is required to file a Form 5472, (2) reporting of transactions within certain categories on a more detailed basis, (3) reporting of the manner (such as type of transfer pricing method used) in which the reporting corporation determined the amount of particular reportable transactions and items, and (4) summarization of a reporting corporation's reportable transactions and items with all foreign related parties on a schedule to its annual Form 5472 filing.

XVI. *Partial withdrawal of proposed regulations*

The proposed regulations also withdraw, in part, a notice of proposed rulemaking. Because of statutory changes in section 12001 of the Act, the proposed regulations would not incorporate the substance of § 1.1502-2, relating to the computation of a consolidated group's alternative minimum tax, of the notice of proposed rulemaking (IA-57-89) published in the **Federal Register** on December 30, 1992 (57 FR 62251). Accordingly, the Partial Withdrawal of Proposed Regulations section in this document withdraws that section of the notice of proposed rulemaking.

Proposed Applicability Date

Under section 7805(b)(2), and consistent with the applicability date of section 59A, these regulations (other than the proposed reporting requirements for QDPs in proposed § 1.6038A-2(b)(7)) are proposed to apply to taxable years beginning after December 31, 2017. Until finalization, a taxpayer may rely on these proposed regulations for taxable years beginning after December 31, 2017, provided the taxpayer and all related parties of the taxpayer (as defined in proposed § 1.59A-1(b)(17)) consistently apply the proposed regulations for all those taxable years that end before the finalization date.

With respect to the reporting requirements for QDPs, proposed § 1.6038A-2(b)(7)(ix) applies to taxable years beginning one year after final regulations are published in the **Federal Register**, although simplified QDP reporting requirements provided in § 1.6038A-2(g) are also proposed to apply to taxable years beginning after December 31, 2017.

If any provision is finalized after June 22, 2019, the Treasury Department and the IRS generally expect that such provision will apply only to taxable years ending on or after December 17, 2018. *See* section 7805(b)(1)(B).

Special Analyses

Regulatory Planning and Review - Economic Analysis

Executive Orders 13563 and 12866 direct agencies to assess costs and benefits of available regulatory alternatives and, if regulation is necessary, to select regulatory approaches that maximize net benefits (including potential economic, environmental, public health and safety effects, distributive impacts, and equity). Executive Order 13563 emphasizes the importance of quantifying both costs and benefits, of reducing costs, of harmonizing rules, and of promoting flexibility. The preliminary Executive Order 13771 designation for this proposed rule is regulatory.

The proposed regulations have been designated by the Office of Management and Budget's ("OMB") Office of Information and Regulatory Affairs ("OIRA") as subject to review under Executive Order 12866 pursuant to the Memorandum of Agreement (April 11, 2018) between the

Treasury Department and OMB regarding review of tax regulations. OIRA has determined that the proposed rulemaking is economically significant under section 1(c) of the Memorandum of Agreement and thereby subject to review. Accordingly, the proposed regulations have been reviewed by OMB.

A. Overview

The proposed regulations provide guidance under section 59A regarding the determination of the tax on base erosion payments for certain taxpayers with substantial gross receipts. They provide guidance for applicable taxpayers to determine the amount of BEAT liability and how to compute the components of the tax calculation. Among other benefits, this clarity helps ensure that all taxpayers apply section 59A in a similar manner, which promotes efficiency and equity with respect to the provisions of the overall Code.

The proposed regulations under sections 59A (proposed §§ 1.59A-1 through 1.59A-10) provide details for taxpayers regarding whether a taxpayer is an applicable taxpayer and the computation of certain components of the base erosion minimum tax, including the amount of base erosion payments, the amount of base erosion tax benefits arising from base erosion payments, and modified taxable income. The proposed regulations also provide guidance for banks, registered securities dealers, and insurance companies and provide guidance attributing partnership income and deductions involving partnerships to the owners of the partnerships (amounts paid by and to partnerships). These proposed regulations also establish anti-abuse rules to prevent taxpayers from taking measures to inappropriately avoid section 59A.

The proposed regulations under sections 383, 1502 and 6038A (proposed §§ 1.383-1, 1.502-2, 1.502-59A, 1.6038A-1, 1.6038A-2, and 1.6038-4) provide rules for the application of section 59A with respect to limitations on certain capital losses and excess credits, consolidated groups and their members, and reporting requirements, which include submitting, in certain cases, new Form 8991, Tax on Base Erosion Payments of Taxpayers With Substantial Gross Receipts. This economic analysis describes the economic benefits and costs of the proposed regulations. The Treasury Department and the IRS anticipate that any final rule will contain the analysis prescribed by the Memorandum of Agreement (April 11, 2018) between the Treasury Department and OMB.

B. Economic Analysis of the Proposed Regulations

1. Background

Congress was concerned, in part, that foreign-owned U.S. subsidiaries are able to reduce their U.S. tax liability by making deductible payments to a foreign parent or foreign affiliates, eroding the U.S tax base if the payments are subject to little or no U.S. withholding tax. This result may favor foreign-headquartered companies over U.S. headquartered companies, creating a tax-driven incentive for foreign takeovers of U.S. firms and enhancing the pressure for U.S headquartered companies to re-domicile abroad and shift income to low-tax jurisdictions. Senate Committee on Finance, Explanation of the Bill, S. Rpt. 115-20, at 391. Section 59A was introduced, in part, as a minimum tax to prevent excessive reduction in corporate tax liability using deductible and certain other payments to foreign related parties.

The Treasury Department views section 59A as largely self-executing, which means that it is binding on taxpayers and the IRS without any regulatory action. The Treasury Department and the IRS recognize, however, that section 59A, while self-executing, provides interpretive latitude for taxpayers and the IRS that could, without further implementation guidance, prompt a variety of responses. Consequently, many of the details behind the relevant terms and necessary calculations required for the computation of an applicable taxpayer's BEAT liability would benefit from greater specificity. As is expected after the passage of major tax reform legislation, the proposed regulations answer unresolved questions and provide detail and specificity for the definitions and concepts described in section 59A, so that taxpayers can readily and accurately determine if they are applicable taxpayers and, if so, compute their BEMTA. For example, the proposed regulations define the scope of crucial terms such as applicable taxpayer, base erosion payments, base erosion tax benefits, de minimis exemptions, and modified taxable income. Specific examples of where these proposed regulations provide clarification of the statute are discussed in this Part B of the Special Analyses section.

As explained in Part VI of the Explanation of Provisions section, an applicable taxpayer computes its BEMTA for the taxable year to determine its liability under section 59A(a). In general, the taxpayer's BEMTA is equal to the excess of (1) the applicable tax rate for the year at issue multiplied by the taxpayer's modified taxable income over (2) the taxpayer's adjusted regular tax liability for that year. Modified taxable income is a taxpayer's taxable income for the year calculated without regard to any base erosion tax benefit or the base erosion percentage of any allowable net operating loss deductions.

In general, the proposed regulations interpret the statute by answering two important questions: (1) to which taxpayers does the BEAT apply, and (2) how do the rules apply to those taxpayers?

a. Applicable Taxpayer

In order for the BEAT to apply, a taxpayer must be an applicable taxpayer, as described in Part II of the Explanation of Provisions section. In general, an applicable taxpayer is a corporation, other than a RIC, REIT, or an S corporation, that satisfies the gross receipts test and the base erosion percentage test. For purposes of these tests, members of a group of corporations related by stock ownership are aggregated. Section 59A(e)(3) refers to aggregation on the basis of persons treated as a single taxpayer under section 52(a) (controlled group of corporations), which includes both domestic and foreign persons. As discussed in Part II.A of the Explanation of Provisions section, the Treasury Department and the IRS determined that to implement the provisions of section 59A, it was necessary to treat foreign corporations as outside of the controlled group for purposes of applying the aggregation rules, except to the extent that the foreign corporation is subject to net income tax under section 882(a) (tax on income of foreign corporations connected with U.S. business). Upon aggregation of domestic and foreign controlled groups of corporations, intra-aggregate group transactions are eliminated. If aggregation were defined to include both domestic and all foreign persons (i.e., a "single employer" under section 52(a)), this elimination would include most base erosion payments, which are defined by section 59A(d)(1) as "any amount paid or accrued by the taxpayer to a foreign person which is a related party of the taxpayer and with respect to which a deduction is allowed under this chapter." Without these base erosion payments, virtually no taxpayer or aggregated group would satisfy the base erosion percentage test; thus substantially all taxpayers (or the aggregate group of which the taxpayer was a member) would be excluded from the requirement to pay a tax equal to the BEMTA.

A taxpayer, or the aggregate group of which the taxpayer is a member, satisfies the gross receipts test if it has average annual gross receipts of at least $500 million for the three taxable years ending with the preceding taxable year.

The base erosion percentage test is satisfied if the taxpayer (or aggregated group) has a base erosion percentage of three percent or more. A lower two percent base erosion percentage applies for banks and registered securities dealers. As explained in proposed § 1.52A-2(e), the base erosion percentage is computed by dividing (1) the aggregate amount of base erosion tax benefits by (2) the sum of the aggregate amount of deductions plus certain other base erosion tax benefits.

The statute is ambiguous or silent on certain details for determining whether a taxpayer is an applicable taxpayer, including the aggregation rule described in Part II.A. of the Explanation of Provisions section. Absent these proposed regulations, there would be uncertainty among taxpayers as to whether the tax equal to the BEMTA would apply to them. Without guidance, different taxpayers would likely take different positions regarding the determination of their status as an applicable taxpayer, which would result in inefficient decision-making and inconsistent application of the statute as taxpayers engage in corporate restructurings, or adjust investment and spending policies based on tax planning strategies to manage

BEAT liability (as discussed in this Part B.2.b. of the Special Analyses section). The proposed regulations provide clarity by (1) defining the aggregate group to which the gross receipts and base erosion percentage tests apply, and (2) providing guidance on the definitions and computations necessary to apply those tests.

b. *BEAT Calculation*

Part III of the Explanation of Provisions section discusses the rules regarding the types of payments that are base erosion payments (as defined in proposed § 1.52A-3(b)). Section 59A(d)(5) provides an exception from the definition of a base erosion payment for an amount paid or accrued by a taxpayer for services if the services are eligible for the services cost method under section 482 (without regard to certain requirements under the section 482 regulations) and the amount constitutes the total services cost with no markup component. The statute is ambiguous as to whether the SCM exception (1) does not apply to a payment or accrual that includes a markup component, or (2) does apply to such a payment or accrual that includes a markup component, but only to the extent of the total services costs. The proposed regulations follow the latter approach as discussed in Part B.2.b. of this Special Analyses section.

As discussed in Part III.B.3 of the Explanation of Provisions section, the proposed regulations provide an exception from the definition of base erosion payment for payments to the U.S. branch of a foreign person to the extent that payments to the foreign related party are treated as effectively connected income. In general, whether a payment is a base erosion payment is determined based on whether the recipient is a foreign person (as defined in section 6038A(c)(3)) and a related party, and whether the payment is deductible to the payor. See section 59A(f). A foreign person means any person who is not a United States person. However, as discussed in Part III.B.3. of the Explanation of Provisions section, the Treasury Department and the IRS determined that establishing whether a payment is a base erosion payment based solely on the status of the recipient as a foreign person is inconsistent with the statute's intent of eliminating base erosion. Deductible payments to a foreign person that are treated as effectively connected income are subject to tax under section 871(b) and 882(a) in substantially the same manner as payments to a U.S. citizen or resident, or a domestic corporation, and, thus, such payments do not result in base erosion. Proposed § 1.52A-3(b)(3)(iii) adopts an exception for such amounts.

As described in this Part B.1. of the Special Analyses section, modified taxable income is a taxpayer's taxable income for the year calculated without regard to any base erosion tax benefit or the base erosion percentage of any allowable net operating loss deductions under section 172 (net operating loss deduction). As discussed in Part V.A. of the Explanation of Provisions section, modified taxable income is not calculated by recomputing the tax base without base erosion tax benefits under an approach similar to the alternative minimum tax, which the Act repealed for corporations. To do so would require taxpayers to maintain records for separate carryforward balances for attributes, such as net operating loss deductions and business interest expense carryovers. These items are limited based on taxable income, so under the recomputation or alternative minimum tax-approach, there would most likely be different annual limitations and other computational differences for regular tax purposes and section 59A purposes.

As discussed in Part VII of the Explanation of Provisions section, the proposed regulations apply the aggregate approach to base erosion payments involving partnerships because partnerships are pass-through entities that are not themselves subject to U.S. income tax, but rather the income of the partnership is taxed to the partners in the partnership. Accordingly, the proposed regulations provide that payments by a corporation to a partnership, and payments by a partnership to a corporation, are treated in the first instance as payments to the partners in the partnership and in second instance as payments by the partners in the partnership. For example, in the absence of this aggregate approach rule, a payment by an applicable taxpayer (corporation) to a related foreign partnership could be a base erosion payment even if all of the partners in the partnership are domestic persons. Under this rule, which applies an aggregate approach to partnerships, the payment by the applicable taxpayer (corporation) to a related foreign partnership is only treated as a base erosion payment to the extent that the partners in the foreign partnership are themselves foreign related parties. Conversely, also in the absence of this aggregate approach rule, a payment by an applicable taxpayer (corporation) to a related domestic partnership could not be a base erosion payment even if some or all of the partners in the partnership are foreign related parties. Under the aggregate approach, the payment by an applicable taxpayer (corporation) to a related domestic partnership is treated as a base erosion payment to the extent that the partners in the domestic partnership are foreign related parties. This approach is thus neutral in both preventing potential abuse and preventing potential over breadth. The regulations thus eliminate a distortion that would otherwise be present if the status of base erosion payments is made by reference to the partnership, rather than by reference to the partners. For example, in the absence of the proposed regulations, taxpayers might be incentivized to route payments through a domestic partnership that is formed by foreign persons as an intermediary to avoid the BEAT. Conversely, in the absence of the proposed regulations, taxpayers would be incentivized to restructure to avoid making any payments to a foreign partnership that has partners that are solely domestic because such payment could be inappropriately classified as a base erosion payment. The Treasury Department requests comments on the approach to partnerships in the proposed regulations.

c. *Anti-abuse and Reporting Requirements*

Section 59A(i) provides the Secretary authority to issue regulations and other guidance to prevent the avoidance of the purposes of section 59A. As such, proposed § 1.59A-9 provides rules recharacterizing certain specified transactions as necessary to prevent the avoidance of section 59A, and provides examples.

The proposed regulations also provide reporting requirements necessary to properly administer and enforce section 59A. In particular, the Treasury Department and the IRS have identified certain types of information from taxpayers who are applicable taxpayers for purposes of section 59A that will be required to be reported on Form 5472, Information Return of a 25% Foreign-Owned U.S. Corporation or a Foreign Corporation Engaged in a U.S. Trade or Business (Under Sections 6038A and 6038C of the Internal Revenue Code), and a new Form 8991, Tax on Base Erosion Payments of Taxpayers With Substantial Gross Receipts. Further detail regarding anticipated paperwork burdens can be found in Part C (Paperwork Reduction Act) of this Special Analyses section, which includes a link to draft forms and guidance for providing comment on the proposed forms.

2. *Anticipated Benefits and Costs of the Proposed Regulations*

a. *Baseline*

The Treasury Department and the IRS have assessed the impacts, benefits, and costs of the proposed regulations against a "no action" baseline that reflects projected tax-related and other behavior in the absence of the proposed regulations.

The Treasury Department projects that the proposed regulations will have a non-revenue effect on the economy of at least $100 million per year ($2018) measured against this baseline. The Treasury Department requests comments on this conclusion.

b. *Anticipated Benefits*

The Treasury Department and IRS expect that the certainty and clarity provided by these proposed regulations, relative to the baseline, will enhance U.S. economic performance under the statute. Because a tax has not previously been imposed on base-eroding payments in this manner and the statute is silent on certain aspects of definitions and calculations, taxpayers can particularly benefit from enhanced specificity regarding the relevant terms and necessary calculations they are required to apply under the statute. In the absence of this enhanced specificity, similarly situated taxpayers might interpret the statutory rules of section 59A differently. For example, different taxpayers might pursue intercompany investment and payment policies based on different assumptions about whether such investments and payments are base eroding payments subject to section 59A, and some taxpayers may forego specific investments and payments that other taxpayers deem worthwhile based on different interpretations of the tax consequences alone. The guidance provided in these proposed regulations helps to ensure that taxpayers face more uniform incentives when making economic decisions, a tenet of economic efficiency. Consistent reporting across taxpayers also increases the IRS's ability to consistently enforce the tax rules, thus increasing equity and decreasing opportunities for tax evasion.

For example, as described in Part III.B.3 of the Explanation of Provisions section, the proposed regulations exclude from base erosion payments those payments made to a foreign related party that are treated as effectively connected income of the foreign payee. Such payments are treated as income to the recipient and subject to U.S. tax, substantially similar to any payment between related U.S. corporations. The payments are not base eroding because their receipt is taxable by the United States. Further, treatment of effectively connected income payments to a foreign related party would produce different tax results for two similarly situated U.S. taxpayers. That is, if the taxpayer were to make a payment to a related U.S. corporation, the payment generally would not be subject to the BEAT, but if a taxpayer were to make a payment to a foreign person with respect to its effectively connected income, it would give rise to BEAT liability, despite the fact that in both cases the recipients include the payment in U.S. taxable income.

The Treasury Department and the IRS also considered the benefits and costs of providing the specific proposed terms, calculations, and other details regarding the BEAT. In developing these proposed regulations, the Treasury Department and the IRS have generally aimed to apply the principle that an economically efficient tax system would treat income derived from similar economic decisions similarly, to the extent consistent with the statute and considerations of administrability of the tax system. For example, as noted in Part B.1.b. of this Special Analyses section, section 59A(d)(5) provides an exception to the definition of a base erosion payment for certain payments made to foreign related parties for services that meet the eligibility requirements for use of the SCM (under section 482). The proposed regulations adopt an approach that allows an SCM exception for the total cost of services even if there is a profit markup so long as a transaction meets certain other requirements for using the SCM (under section 482). The proposed regulations provide that the portion of any payment that exceeds the total cost of services is not eligible for the SCM exception and is a base eroding payment.

Alternatives would have been to disallow the SCM exception for the entire amount of any payment that includes a markup component, or to not provide any guidance at all regarding the SCM exception. The Treasury Department and the IRS rejected the former approach. The section 482 regulations mandate intercompany pricing under an "arm's length standard." Under specific circumstances, the section 482 regulations provide that intercompany payments for services can be set by a taxpayer at the cost of providing the service with no profit markup. However, the section 482 regulations prohibit use of this cost-only SCM approach for services "that contribute significantly to fundamental risks of business success or failure" (the "business judgment rule"). See § 1.482-9(b)(5). At arm's length, such services would generally be priced to include a profit element to satisfy the market's demand for, and supply of, services among recipients and providers. Section 59A(d)(5)(A) explicitly allows an exception from the BEAT for services that would be eligible for the SCM, "determined without regard to [the business judgment rule]." By allowing an exception from the BEAT for intercompany service payments that do not include a profit markup (i.e., under the SCM transfer pricing method), but also for intercompany service payments that must apply a different transfer pricing method, and therefore generally would include a profit markup at arm's length (i.e., those subject to the business judgment rule), the statute creates ambiguity about the SCM exception's application with respect to the portion of intercompany prices paid for services reflecting the cost of providing the services when there is also a mark-up component.

To promote the consistent application by taxpayers of a SCM exception to the BEAT, and to provide greater clarity, the proposed regulations provide that the SCM exception is available if there is a profit markup (provided that other requirements are satisfied), but the portion of any payment exceeding cost is not eligible for the SCM exception. The Treasury Department and the IRS also rejected the option of not providing any guidance at all regarding the SCM exception because if taxpayers relied on statutory language alone, taxpayers would adopt different approaches due to ambiguity in the statute, leaving it open to differing statutory interpretations and an inconsistent application of the statute. The Treasury Department and IRS expect that approximately one-half of taxpayers filing Form 8891 would avail themselves of the SCM exception. The Treasury Department and the IRS request comments about application of the SCM exception.

As discussed in Part V.A of the Explanation of Provisions section, the Treasury Department and the IRS also considered alternatives regarding the method by which modified taxable income could be calculated for purposes of the BEAT. The proposed regulations could have followed an add-back approach or an approach more similar to that used for the alternative minimum tax. As noted in Part B.1.b. of this Special Analyses section, the proposed regulations adopt the former approach, which is expected to be less costly for taxpayers to apply since taxpayers will not have to recompute their entire tax return on a different basis, or maintain separate sets of records to track annual limitations on attributes such as net operating loss carryforwards or business interest expense carryforwards.

In addition, the proposed regulations clarify that the computations of modified taxable income and BEMTA are done on a taxpayer-by-taxpayer basis. That is, the aggregate group concept is used solely for determining whether a taxpayer is an applicable taxpayer, and does not apply to the computations of modified taxable income and the BEMTA. In the absence of these clarifying definitions, taxpayers could calculate the BEMTA differently depending on their differing views of the base on which the BEAT should be calculated (i.e., aggregated group, consolidated group, individual company), leading to inequitable results across otherwise similar taxpayers. Under the proposed regulations' approach for the calculation of modified taxable income and BEMTA, it is also expected to be less costly for taxpayers to calculate BEMTA since the statutory framework of section 59A applies in addition to the regular tax liability of a taxpayer. Calculation of BEAT liability at an aggregate level, for example, would require taxpayers to first aggregate regular taxable liabilities of the different taxpayers, calculate the BEMTA on an aggregated basis, and then reallocate any BEAT liability among the separate taxpayers. The approach of the proposed regulations, which clarify that the tax should be calculated on a separate taxpayer basis, simplifies these calculations.

The proposed regulations also include de minimis thresholds for partnerships and for registered securities dealers. In general, such thresholds reduce compliance costs for the large number of small taxpayers that would fall below such threshold without substantially affecting the BEAT base. For the de minimis exception for banks and registered securities dealers, in the absence of an exception, affiliated groups that are not principally engaged in banking or securities dealing would be incentivized to alter their business structure to eliminate minimal banks or registered securities dealers from their aggregate groups. These changes would give rise to tax-motivated, inefficient restructuring costs. A de minimis threshold reduces this potential inefficiency again without substantially affecting the BEAT base. In both cases, the thresholds were chosen to balance these competing concerns and to adhere to generally similar standards elsewhere in the Code. The Treasury Department and IRS request comment on the impact of this approach.

3. Anticipated impacts on administrative and compliance costs

Because the statute requires payment of tax regardless of the issuance of regulations or instructions, the new forms, revisions to existing forms, and other proposed regulations can lower the burden on taxpayers of determining their tax liability. The Treasury Department and the IRS expect that the proposed regulations will reduce the costs for taxpayers to comply with the Act, on balance, relative to the baseline of no promulgated regulations.

Certain record-keeping requirements added by the proposed regulations derive directly from statutory changes that require information from a reporting corporation that is also a section 59A applicable taxpayer. Proposed § 1.6038A-2 increases record-keeping requirements for taxpayers because additional information is to be reported on Form 5472 and Form 8991.

Proposed § 1.59A-3(b)(3) also increases record-keeping requirements for taxpayers because additional information is required for taxpayers to satisfy a regulatory requirement of the SCM exception. The requirement added by these proposed regulations is consistent with the requirements for eligibility for the services cost method under section 482, including the existing requirements of § 1.482-9(b).

C. *Paperwork Reduction Act*

1. *Collections of Information - Forms 8891, 5471, 5472, and 8858*

The collections of information in these proposed regulations with respect to section 59A are in proposed §§ 1.59-3(b)(3) and 1.6038A-2. The information collection requirements pursuant to proposed § 1.59A-3(b)(3)(i)(C) are discussed further below. The IRS intends that the collections of information pursuant to section 59A, except with respect to information collected under proposed § 1.59A-3(b)(3), will be conducted by way of the following:

- Form 8991, Tax on Base Erosion Payments of Taxpayers With Substantial Gross Receipts;

- Schedule G to the Form 5471, Information Return of U.S. Persons With Respect to Certain Foreign Corporations;

- Part VIII of the updated Form 5472, Information Return of a 25% Foreign-Owned U.S. Corporation or a Foreign Corporation Engaged in a U.S. Trade or Business;

- Revised Form 8858, Information Return of U.S. Persons With Respect to Foreign Disregarded Entities.

For purposes of the Paperwork Reduction Act, the reporting burden associated with the collections of information with respect to section 59A, other than with respect to proposed § 1.59A-3(b)(3), will be reflected in the IRS Forms 14029 Paperwork Reduction Act Submission, associated with Forms 5471 (OMB control numbers 1545-0123, and 1545-0074), 5472 (OMB control number 1545-0123), 8858 (OMB control numbers 1545-0123, 1545-0074, and 1545-1910), and 8991 (OMB control number 1545-0123).

The current status of the Paperwork Reduction Act submissions related to BEAT is provided in the following table. The BEAT provisions are included in aggregated burden estimates for the OMB control numbers listed below which, in the case of 1545-0123, represents a total estimated burden time, including all other related forms and schedules for corporations, of 3.157 billion hours and total estimated monetized costs of $58.148 billion ($2017) and, in the case of 1545-0074, a total estimated burden time, including all other related forms and schedules for individuals, of 1.784 billion hours and total estimated monetized costs of $31.764 billion ($2017). The burden estimates provided in the OMB control numbers below are aggregate amounts that relate to the entire package of forms associated with the OMB control number, and will in the future include but not isolate the estimated burden of only the BEAT requirements. These numbers are therefore unrelated to the future calculations needed to assess the burden imposed by the proposed regulations. The Treasury Department and IRS urge readers to recognize that these numbers are duplicates and to guard against overcounting the burden that international tax provisions imposed prior to TCJA. No burden estimates specific to the proposed regulations are currently available. The Treasury Department has not estimated the burden, including that of any new information collections, related to the requirements under the proposed regulations. Those estimates would capture both changes made by the Act and those that arise out of discretionary authority exercised in the proposed regulations. The Treasury Department and the IRS request comment on all aspects of information collection burdens related to the proposed regulations. In addition, when available, drafts of IRS forms are posted for comment at *https:// apps.irs.gov/app/picklist/list/draftTaxForms.htm.*

Form	Type of Filer	OMB Number(s)	Status
Form 5471 (including Schedule G)	Business (NEW Model)	1545-0123	Published in the FRN on 10/8/18. Public Comment period closes on 12/10/18.
	Link: https://www.federalregister.gov/documents/2018/10/09/2018-21846/proposed-collection-comment-request-for-forms-1065-1065-b-1066-1120-1120-c-1120-f-1120-h-1120-nd		
	Individual (NEW Model)	1545-0074	Limited Scope submission (1040 only) on 10/11/18 at OIRA for review. Full ICR submission for all forms in 3/2019. 60 Day FRN not published yet for full collection.
	Link: https://www.reginfo.gov/public/do/PRAViewICR?ref_nbr=201808-1545-031		
Form 5472 (including Part VIII)	Business (NEW Model)	1545-0123	Published in the FRN on 10/11/18. Public Comment period closes on 12/10/18.
	Link: https://www.federalregister.gov/documents/2018/10/09/2018-21846/proposed-collection-comment-request-for-forms-1065-1065-b-1066-1120-1120-c-1120-f-1120-h-1120-nd		
Form 8858	All other Filers (mainly trusts and estates) (Legacy system)	1545-1910	Published in the FRN on 10/30/18. Public Comment period closes on 11/30/18. ICR in process by the Treasury Department as of 9/6/18.
	Link: https://www.federalregister.gov/documents/2018/10/30/2018-23644/agency-information-collection-activities-submission-for-omb-review-comment-request-multiple-irs		
	Business (NEW Model)	1545-0123	Published in the FRN on 10/8/18. Public Comment period closes on 12/10/18.
	Link: https://www.federalregister.gov/documents/2018/10/09/2018-21846/proposed-collection-comment-request-for-forms-1065-1065-b-1066-1120-1120-c-1120-f-1120-h-1120-nd		
	Individual (NEW Model)	1545-0074	Limited Scope submission (1040 only) on 10/11/18 at OIRA for review. Full ICR submission for all forms in 3-2019. 60 Day FRN not published yet for full collection.
	Link: https://www.reginfo.gov/public/do/PRAViewICR?ref_nbr=201808-1545-031		
Form 8991	Business (NEW Model)	1545-0123	Published in the FRN on 10/11/18. Public Comment period closes on 12/10/18.

Form	Type of Filer	OMB Number(s)	Status
		Link: *https://www.federalregister.gov/documents/2018/10/09/2018-21846/proposed-collection-comment-request-for-forms-1065-1065-b-1066-1120-1120-c-1120-f-1120-h-1120-nd*		

Related New or Revised Tax Forms

	New	Revision of existing form	Number of respondents (2018, estimated)
Form 8991	✓		3,500 - 4,500
Form 5471, Schedule G		✓	15,000 - 25,000
Form 5472, Part VIII	✓		80,000 - 100,000
Form 8858		✓	15,000 - 25,000

The numbers of respondents in the Related New or Revised Tax Forms table were estimated by Treasury's Office of Tax Analysis based on data from IRS Compliance Planning and Analytics using tax return data for tax years 2015 and 2016. Data for Form 8991 represent preliminary estimates of the total number of taxpayers which may be required to file the new Form 8991. Only certain large corporate taxpayers with gross receipts of at least $500 million are expected to file this form. Data for each of the Forms 5471, 5472, and 8858 represent preliminary estimates of the total number of taxpayers that are expected to file these information returns regardless of whether that taxpayer must also file Form 8991.

2. Collection of Information - Proposed § 1.59A-3(b)(3)

In contrast to the collections of information pursuant to other provisions of section 59A (as discussed above), the IRS intends that the information collection requirements pursuant to proposed § 1.59A-3(b)(3)(i)(C) will be satisfied by the taxpayer maintaining permanent books and records that are adequate to verify the amount charged for the services and the total services costs incurred by the renderer, including a description of the services in question, identification of the renderer and the recipient of the services, calculation of the amount of profit mark-up (if any) paid for the services, and sufficient documentation to allow verification of the methods used to allocate and apportion the costs to the services.

The collection of information contained in proposed § 1.59A-3(b)(3) has been submitted to the Office of Management and Budget for review in accordance with the Paperwork Reduction Act of 1994 (44 U.S.C. 3507(d)). Comments on the collection of information should be sent to the Office of Management and Budget, Attn: Desk Officer for the Department of the Treasury, Office of Information and Regulatory Affairs, Washington, DC 20503, with copies to the Internal Revenue Service, Attn: IRS Reports Clearance Officer, SE:W:CAR:MP:T:T:SP, Washington, DC 20224. Comments on the collection of information should be received by February 9, 2019.

Comments are specifically requested concerning:

Whether the proposed collection of information is necessary for the proper performance of the duties of the IRS, including whether the information will have practical utility;

The accuracy of the estimated burden associated with the proposed collection of information (including underlying assumptions and methodology);

How the quality, utility, and clarity of the information to be collected may be enhanced;

How the burden of complying with the proposed collection of information may be minimized, including through the application of automated collection techniques or other forms of information technology; and

Estimates of capital or start-up costs and costs of operation, maintenance, and purchases of services to provide information.

The collection of information in proposed § 1.59A-3(b)(3) is mandatory for taxpayers seeking to exclude certain amounts paid or accrued to a foreign related party for services from treatment as base erosion payments for purposes of section 59A (the "SCM exception to the BEAT", as discussed this Part B.2.b. of the Special Analyses section). Taxpayers seeking to rely on the SCM exception to the BEAT are aggregate groups of corporations with average annual gross receipts of at least $500 million and that make payments to foreign related parties. The information required to be maintained will be used by the IRS for tax compliance purposes.

Estimated total annual reporting burden: 5,000 hours.

Estimated average annual burden hours per respondent: 2.5 hours.

Estimated average cost per respondent ($2017): $238.00.

Estimated number of respondents: 2,000. This estimate is based on the assumption that only a portion of taxpayers will qualify for the SCM exception, multiplied by the number of respondents shown above.

Estimated annual frequency of responses: Once.

Based on these estimates, the annual three-year reporting burden for those electing the SCM exemption is $0.16 mn/yr ($2017) ($238 x 2000/3, converted to millions).

An agency may not conduct or sponsor, and a person is not required to respond to, a collection of information unless it displays a valid control number assigned by the Office of Management and Budget.

Books or records relating to a collection of information must be retained as long as their contents may become material in the administration of any internal revenue law. Generally, tax returns and tax return information are confidential, as required by 26 U.S.C. 6103.

D. *Regulatory Flexibility Act*

It is hereby certified that these regulations will not have a significant economic impact on a substantial number of small entities within the meaning of section 601(6) of the Regulatory Flexibility Act (5 U.S.C. chapter 6). Accordingly, a regulatory flexibility analysis is not required. This certification is based on the fact that these regulations will primarily affect aggregate groups of corporations with average annual gross receipts of at least $500 million and that make payments to foreign related parties. Generally only large businesses both have substantial gross receipts and make payments to foreign related parties.

Notwithstanding this certification, the Treasury Department and the IRS invite comments from the public about the impact of this proposed rule on small entities.

Pursuant to section 7805(f), these regulations will be submitted to the Chief Counsel for Advocacy of the Small Business Administration for comment on their impact on small business.

E. *Unfunded Mandates Reform Act*

Section 202 of the Unfunded Mandates Reform Act of 1995 (UMRA) requires that agencies assess anticipated costs and benefits and take certain other actions before issuing a final rule that includes any Federal mandate that may result in expenditures in any one year by a state, local, or tribal government, in the aggregate, or by the private sector, of $100 million in 1995 dollars, updated annually for inflation. In 2018, that threshold is approximately $150 million. This rule does not include any Federal mandate that may result in expenditures by state, local, or tribal governments, or by the private sector in excess of that threshold.

F. *Executive Order 13132: Federalism*

Executive Order 13132 (entitled "Federalism") prohibits an agency from publishing any rule that has federalism implications if the rule either imposes substantial, direct compliance costs on state and local governments, and is not required by statute, or preempts state law, unless the agency meets the consultation and funding requirements of section 6 of the Executive Order. This proposed rule does not have federalism implications and does not impose substantial direct compliance costs on state and local governments or preempt state law within the meaning of the Executive Order.

Comments and Request for Public Hearing

Before these proposed regulations are adopted as final regulations, consideration will be given to any comments that are submitted timely to the IRS as prescribed in this preamble under the "Addresses" heading. The Treasury Department and the IRS request comments on all aspects of the proposed rules.

All comments will be available at *www.regulations.gov* or upon request. A public hearing will be scheduled if requested in writing by any person that timely submits written comments. If a public hearing is scheduled, notice of the date, time, and place for the public hearing will be published in the **Federal Register**.

Statement of Availability of IRS Documents

IRS revenue procedures, revenue rulings, notices, and other guidance cited in this preamble are published in the Internal Revenue Bulletin and are available from the Superintendent of Documents, U.S. Government Publishing Office, Washington, DC 20402, or by visiting the IRS website at *http://www.irs.gov*.

Drafting Information

The principal authors of the proposed regulations are Sheila Ramaswamy and Karen Walny of the Office of Associate Chief Counsel (International) and Julie Wang and John P. Stemwedel of the Office of Associate Chief Counsel (Corporate). However, other personnel from the Treasury Department and the IRS participated in their development.

Partial Withdrawal of Proposed Regulations

Accordingly, under the authority of 26 U.S.C. 7805 and 26 U.S.C. 1502, § 1.1502-2 of the notice of proposed rulemaking (IA-57-89) published in the **Federal Register** on December 30, 1992 (57 FR 62251) is withdrawn.

[¶ 49,784] Proposed Amendments of Regulations (REG-113604-18), published in the Federal Register on December 27, 2018.

[Code Secs. 864 and 897]

Source of income: Foreign income: Nonresident aliens: Foreign corporations: US real property.Reg. §§ 1.864(c)(8)-1 and 1.897-7 and amendments of Reg. § 1.897-7T, implementing section 864(c)(8) of the Internal Revenue Code, are proposed.

AGENCY: Internal Revenue Service (IRS), Treasury.

ACTION: Notice of proposed rulemaking.

SUMMARY: This document contains proposed regulations implementing section 864(c)(8) of the Internal Revenue Code. The proposed regulations affect certain foreign persons that recognize gain or loss from the sale or exchange of an interest in a partnership that is engaged in a trade or business within the United States. The proposed regulations also affect partnerships that, directly or indirectly, have foreign persons as partners.

DATES: Written or electronic comments and requests for a public hearing must be received by February 25, 2019.

ADDRESSES: Send submissions to: CC:PA:LPD:PR (REG-113604-18), Internal Revenue Service, Room 5203, P.O. Box 7604, Ben Franklin Station, Washington, DC 20044. Submissions may be hand-delivered Monday through Friday between the hours of 8 a.m. and 4 p.m. to CC:PA:LPD:PR (REG-113604-18), Courier's Desk, Internal Revenue Service, 1111 Constitution Avenue, NW., Washington, DC 20224, or sent electronically via the Federal eRulemaking Portal at *http://www.regulations.gov* (IRS REG-113604-18).

FOR FURTHER INFORMATION CONTACT: Concerning the proposed regulations, Ronald M. Gootzeit or Chadwick Rowland, (202) 317-6937; concerning submissions of comments or requests for a public hearing, Regina L. Johnson, (202) 317-6901 (not toll-free numbers).

SUPPLEMENTARY INFORMATION:

Background

A foreign partner in a partnership that is engaged in the conduct of a trade or business within the United States is itself considered to be so engaged. *See* section 875. Under a 1991 revenue ruling, in determining the tax consequences of the sale or exchange of a foreign partner's interest in a partnership engaged in the conduct of a trade or business within the United States, the IRS held that the partnership's property located in the United States that is used or held for use in the partnership's trade or business within the United States is used to determine the extent to which income derived from the sale or exchange of the partnership interest is effectively connected with the conduct of the partner's trade or business within the United States. Rev. Rul. 91-32, 1991-1 C.B. 107. Under the ruling, if there is unrealized gain or loss in partnership assets that would be treated as effectively connected with the conduct of the partnership's trade or business within the United States if those assets were sold by the partnership, some or all of the foreign person's gain or loss from the sale or exchange of a partnership interest may be treated as effectively connected with the partner's conduct of a trade or business within the United States. However, a 2017 Tax Court case held instead that, generally, gain or loss on the sale or exchange by a foreign person of an interest in such a partnership is foreign source gain or loss based on the residence of the selling partner because gain on the sale of the partnership interest is not attributable to the partnership's assets and activities. As a result, such gain or loss generally would not be treated as effectively connected with the conduct of a trade or business. *Grecian Magnesite Mining v. Commissioner*, 149 T.C. No. 3 (2017), *appeal argued*, No. 17-1268 (D.C. Cir. Oct. 9, 2018).

Section 864(c)(8), which was added to the Internal Revenue Code (the "Code") by section 13501 of the Tax Cuts and Jobs Act, Public Law 115-97 (2017) (the "Act"), generally overturns the result of *Grecian Magnesite Mining v. Commissioner* by providing that gain or loss of a nonresident alien individual or foreign corporation (a "foreign transferor") from the sale, exchange, or other disposition ("transfer") of a partnership interest is treated as effectively connected with the conduct of a trade or business within the United States ("effectively connected gain" or "effectively connected loss") to the extent that the transferor would have had effectively connected gain or loss if the partnership had sold all of its assets at fair market value as of the date of the sale or exchange ("deemed sale").

Section 864(c)(8)(E) generally provides that the Secretary shall prescribe such regulations or other guidance as the Secretary determines appropriate for the application of section 864(c)(8). Section 864(c)(8) is effective for sales, exchanges, and dispositions on or after November 27, 2017.

New section 1446(f) was also added to the Code by section 13501 of the Act. Section 1446(f)(1) requires that the transferee of a partnership interest withhold 10 percent of the amount realized on the transferor's disposition of the partnership interest (if any portion of the gain would be treated as effectively connected gain) unless the transferor certifies that the transferor is not a foreign person. Section 1446(f) is effective for sales, exchanges, and dispositions after December 31, 2017.

On December 29, 2017, the Department of the Treasury (the "Treasury Department") and the IRS released Notice 2018-08, 2018-7 I.R.B. 352 (the "PTP Notice"). The PTP Notice temporarily suspends the requirement to withhold on amounts realized in connection with the sale, exchange, or disposition of certain interests in publicly traded partnerships ("PTPs") in response to stakeholder concerns that applying section 1446(f) to dispositions of interests in PTPs without guidance presented significant practical problems. On April 2, 2018, the Treasury Department and the IRS released Notice 2018-29, 2018-16 I.R.B. 495, which announced an intent to issue proposed regulations under section 1446(f) that apply in the case of a disposition of a partnership interest that is not publicly traded and provided temporary guidance.

Explanation of Provisions

I. Gain or Loss on the Transfer of a Partnership Interest

Section 864(c)(8)(A) provides that gain or loss of a foreign transferor from the transfer of an interest, owned directly or indirectly, in a partnership that is engaged in any trade or business within the United States is treated as effectively connected gain or loss to the extent such gain or loss does not exceed the amount determined under section 864(c)(8)(B). In general, section 864(c)(8)(B) limits the amount of effectively connected gain or loss to the portion of the foreign transferor's distributive share of gain or loss that would have been effectively connected gain or loss if the partnership had sold all of its assets at fair market value. The proposed regulations set forth rules for determining gain or loss described in section 864(c)(8)(A) and the limitation described in section 864(c)(8)(B), each of which is discussed in this section I of this Explanation of Provisions.

A. Determination of Gain or Loss Described in Section 864(c)(8)(A)

To determine the amount of gain or loss described in section 864(c)(8)(A), generally, the proposed regulations require that a foreign transferor first determine its gain or loss on the transfer of a partnership interest ("outside gain" and "outside loss"). For this purpose, the proposed regulations provide that outside gain or loss is determined under all relevant provisions of the Code and the regulations thereunder. As described in section I.A.1 of this Explanation of Provisions, a foreign transferor may recognize capital gain or loss ("outside capital gain" or "outside capital loss") and ordinary gain or loss ("outside ordinary gain" or "outside ordinary loss") on the transfer of its partnership interest and must separately apply section 864(c)(8) with respect to its capital gain or loss and its ordinary gain or loss.

1. Interaction with Sections 741 and 751

Section 864(c)(8) provides rules regarding the treatment of gain or loss on the transfer of a partnership interest as effectively connected gain or loss, but it does not address the computation of the amount of gain or loss to a partner upon the transfer. Rather, applicable tax law, including subchapter K, determines the amount and character of outside gain or loss on the transfer of a partnership interest. For example, the reduction in a transferor's share of partnership liabilities is treated as an amount realized on the transfer of the partnership interest under section 1001 and the regulations thereunder. See section 752(d) and § 1.752-1(h).

Section 741 provides that on a sale or exchange of an interest in a partnership, gain or loss is recognized by the transferor, and shall be considered capital gain or loss except as otherwise provided in section 751. Section 751 provides that an amount received by a transferor of a partnership interest that is attributable to unrealized receivables or inventory items of the partnership ("section 751 property") is considered ordinary income or loss. As a result of sections 741 and 751 and the regulations thereunder, gain or loss on a sale or exchange of a partnership interest can comprise capital gain, capital loss, ordinary income, or ordinary loss (or a combination thereof). See § § 1.741-1(a) and 1.751-1(a).

In general, the proposed regulations provide that a foreign transferor must determine the portion of its capital gain or loss, and the portion of its ordinary income or loss from section 751 property, that must each be characterized as effectively connected gain or loss under section 864(c)(8). See proposed § 1.864(c)(8)-1(b). As provided in section 864(c)(8)(A) and further described in section I.B of this Explanation of Provisions, the proposed regulations provide that a foreign partner's effectively connected gain or loss will not exceed its outside gain or loss on the sale of the interest as determined under sections 741 and 751 and the regulations thereunder. Thus, the amount of gain or loss determined under section 741 (before application of section 751) is not a limitation on the amount of gain or loss characterized as effectively connected with the conduct of a trade or business within the United States under the proposed regulations.

2. Nonrecognition Transactions

The proposed regulations provide that the gain or loss on the transfer of a partnership interest that is subject to tax as effectively connected gain or loss is limited to gain or loss otherwise recognized under the Code. See proposed § 1.864(c)(8)-1(b)(2)(ii). When a nonrecognition provision results in a foreign transferor recognizing only a portion of its gain or loss on the transfer of an interest in a partnership, section 864(c)(8) may apply with respect to the portion of the gain or loss recognized.

Although section 864(c)(8)(E) authorizes regulations or other guidance with respect to the application of section 864(c)(8) to nonrecognition transactions, the proposed regulations do not contain special rules applicable to nonrecognition transactions. The Treasury Department and the IRS recognize, however, that certain nonrecognition transactions may have the effect of reducing gain or loss that would be taken into account for U.S. federal income tax purposes. For example, if a partnership that conducts a trade or business within the United States owns property not subject to tax under section 871(b) or 882(a) in the hands of a foreign partner, the partnership may distribute that property to the foreign partner rather than a U.S. partner. The Treasury Department and the IRS continue to consider, and comments are requested regarding, whether other Code provisions adequately address transactions that rely on section 731 distributions to reduce the scope of assets subject to U.S. federal income taxation, and may propose rules addressing these types of transactions.

B. Determination of Deemed Sale Gain or Loss

1. In General

After outside gain and loss are determined under proposed § 1.864(c)(8)-1(b), the proposed regulations set forth three amounts that a foreign transferor must determine to derive the limitation in section 864(c)(8)(B) against which the outside gain or loss is computed. (1) With respect to each asset held by the partnership, the amount of gain or loss that the partnership would recognize in connection with a deemed sale to an unrelated party in a fully taxable transaction for cash equal to the asset's fair market value immediately before the partner's transfer of its partnership interest; (2) the amount of that gain or loss that would be treated as effectively connected gain or loss ("deemed sale EC gain" and "deemed sale EC loss"); and (3) the foreign transferor's distributive share of the ordinary and capital components of any deemed sale EC gain and deemed sale EC loss. The proposed regulations refer to the separate sums of the foreign transferor's distributive shares of the ordinary and capital components of deemed sale EC gain and deemed sale EC loss items for all assets, determined at the level of the foreign transferor, as "aggregate deemed sale EC capital gain," "aggregate deemed sale EC capital loss," "aggregate deemed sale EC ordinary gain," and "aggregate deemed sale EC ordinary loss."

After each of these aggregate amounts is determined, the proposed regulations implement the limitation described in section 864(c)(8)(B), generally, by comparing the foreign transferor's outside gain or loss amounts with the relevant aggregate deemed sale EC gain or loss. This determination is made separately with respect to capital gain or capital loss and gain or loss treated as ordinary income or ordinary loss. Thus, for example, a foreign transferor would compare its outside capital gain to its aggregate deemed sale EC capital gain, treating the former as effectively connected gain only to the extent it does not exceed the latter. See proposed § 1.864(c)(8)-1(b)(3).

2. Treatment of Deemed Sale Gain or Loss as Effectively Connected Gain or Loss

As described in Part I.B.1 of this Explanation of Provisions, the proposed regulations require a foreign transferor to determine the amount of gain or loss that would arise in a deemed asset sale that would be treated as effectively connected gain or loss. In general, gain or loss on the sale of personal property is effectively connected with the conduct of a trade or business within the United States if the gain is from sources within the United States and it satisfies the requirements of section 864(c) and the regulations thereunder. Accordingly, the proposed regulations provide that section 864 and the regulations thereunder apply for purposes of determining whether gain or loss that would arise in a deemed asset sale would be treated as effectively connected gain or loss. See proposed § 1.864(c)(8)-1(c)(2)(i).

The determination as to whether gain or loss from a deemed asset sale by the partnership would be from sources within or without the United States, and whether that income would be treated as effectively connected gain or loss, is based on certain factual determinations, including whether the gain or loss results from a sale that is attributable to an office or other fixed place of business in the United States. The proposed regulations provide that, for purposes of determining whether gain or loss recognized in connection with a deemed asset sale by the partnership would be from sources within or without the United States, and thus whether that income would be treated as effectively connected gain or loss, the deemed asset sale is treated as attributable to an office or fixed place of business in the United States maintained by the partnership. As a result, deemed sale gain or loss generally would be treated as from sources within the United States. To prevent this rule from potentially converting gain or loss from assets with no connection to the partnership's trade or business within the United States into effectively connected gain or loss, the proposed regulations provide that gain or loss from the deemed sale of a partnership asset is not treated as effectively connected gain or loss if (1) no income or gain previously produced by the asset was taxable as effectively connected with the conduct of a trade or business within the United States by the partnership (or a predecessor of the partnership) during the ten-year period ending on the date of the transfer, and (2) the asset was not used, or held for use, in the conduct of a trade or business within the United States by the partnership (or a predecessor of the partnership) during the ten-year period ending on the date of transfer. See proposed § 1.864(c)(8)-1(c)(2)(ii). Comments are requested as to whether additional guidance is needed regarding the source of gain or loss resulting from a deemed sale by the partnership, including rules coordinating this rule with section 865(e)(2)(B).

3. Determining Distributive Share of Deemed Sale EC Gain and Deemed Sale EC Loss

The flush language of section 864(c)(8)(B) provides that a transferor partner's distributive share of gain or loss on the deemed sale is determined in the same manner as the transferor partner's distributive share of the non-separately stated taxable income or loss of the partnership. The term "non-separately stated taxable income or loss of the partnership" is not defined in the Code or regulations. The proposed regulations provide that a partner's distributive share of gain or loss from the deemed sale is determined under all applicable Code sections (including section 704), taking into account allocations of tax items applying the principles of section 704(c), including any remedial allocations under § 1.704-3(d), and any section 743 basis adjustment pursuant to § 1.743-1(j)(3). The Treasury Department and IRS propose this approach because applying section 704 more closely ties the results of the deemed sale with regard to the selling foreign partner to the economic results of an actual sale, as compared (for example) to an approach that did not consider special allocations or considered only a partner's share of ordinary business income, which would distort the economic agreement among the partners. See proposed § 1.864(c)(8)-1(c)(3)(i).

The Treasury Department and the IRS are considering whether section 704 and the regulations thereunder adequately prevent the avoidance of the purposes of section 864(c)(8) through allocations of effectively connected gain or loss to specific partners. For example, immediately before a foreign transferor sells its interest in a partnership, adjustments could be made to partnership allocations that would result in the foreign transferor recognizing less effectively connected gain from the deemed sale by the partnership. While statutory and regulatory provisions, as well as judicial doctrines, may limit the extent to which inappropriate results may be obtained in that transaction or similar transactions, the Treasury Department and the IRS are considering whether additional guidance is necessary to prevent abuse. Comments are requested as to whether there are specific situations in which the purposes of section 864(c)(8) may be avoided and specific suggestions for additional guidance to address those situations.

C. Source

Neither section 864(c)(8) nor the proposed regulations address the source of gain or loss from the transfer of a partnership interest. Section 864(c)(4) provides that, except as enumerated in section 864(c)(4)(B) and (C), no income, gain, or loss from sources without the United States is treated as effectively connected gain or loss. Section 864(c)(8)(A) and the proposed regulations, however, apply "[n]otwithstanding any other provision of [subtitle A of the Code]," such that gain or loss recognized on the transfer of an interest in a partnership that is engaged in a trade or business within the United States may be treated as effectively connected gain or loss even if it is from sources without the United States. Comments are requested as to whether, and what, additional guidance is necessary regarding the source of gain or loss subject to section 864(c)(8).

D. Provision is Non-Exclusive

The proposed regulations clarify that they do not apply to prevent any portion of gain or loss recognized on the transfer of a partnership interest from being treated as effectively connected gain or loss under other provisions of the Code (subject to a special rule coordinating the application of section 864(c)(8) and section 897). Thus, if a foreign transferor maintains an office or fixed place of business in the United States, and sells a partnership interest in a transaction that generates gain or loss attributable to that office, gain or loss recognized in connection with that transfer may be United States source income under section 865(e)(2), and may be treated as effectively connected income under section 864(c)(2). If the amount of gain or loss recognized that would be treated as effectively connected gain or loss under section 864(c)(2) exceeds the amount of gain that would be treated as effectively connected gain under section 864(c)(8), then the larger amount would be treated as effectively connected gain. See proposed § 1.864(c)(8)-1(b)(1).

II. Coordination with Section 897

Section 897(g) generally provides that, under regulations prescribed by the Secretary, the amount realized by a nonresident alien individual or foreign corporation in exchange for all or part of its interest in a partnership is, to the extent attributable to United States real property interests (as defined in section 897(c)), considered as an amount received from the sale or exchange in the United States of such property. Accordingly, section 897(g) generally provides the same result for United States real property interests as Revenue Ruling 91-32 provides for property used, or held for use, in a trade or business in the United States. In general, section 864(c)(8)(C) provides that if a partnership described in section 864(c)(8)(A) holds any United States real property interest at the time of the transfer of the partnership interest, then the gain or loss treated as effectively connected gain or loss under section 864(c)(8)(A) is reduced by the amount treated as effectively connected gain or loss with respect to that United States real property interest under section 897. The effect of section 864(c)(8)(C) is to prevent gain or loss from a United States real property interest that is taxed under section 897 from being taken into account a second time under section 864(c)(8).

In the proposed regulations, the limitation on effectively connected gain or loss in section 864(c)(8)(B) is based on a deemed sale by the partnership of all of its assets, including all United States real property interests held by the partnership, which are treated as effectively connected assets under section 897. See proposed § 1.864(c)(8)-1(c)(2)(i). To coordinate the taxation of United States real property interests under sections 897(g) and 864(c)(8), the proposed regulations provide that when a partnership holds United States real property interests and is also subject to section 864(c)(8) because it is engaged in the conduct of a trade or business within the United States without regard to section 897, the amount of the foreign transferor's effectively connected gain or loss will be determined under section 864(c)(8) and not under section 897(g). Therefore, the reduction called for by section 864(c)(8)(C) is not necessary. See proposed § 1.864(c)(8)-1(d).

The regulations include a proposed rule in regulations under section 897, which serves as a cross-reference to this coordination rule. See section V of this Explanation of Provisions for a discussion of a proposed anti-stuffing rule that also applies in the context of section 897. Further, comments are requested as to the interaction of this rule with other rules in the regulations under section 897, including the special rule for publicly traded partnerships in § 1.897-1(c)(2)(iv).

III. *Tiered Partnerships*

Section 864(c)(8) applies to a foreign nonresident alien individual or foreign corporation that owns an interest in a partnership directly or indirectly. Consistent with section 12 of Notice 2018-29, the proposed regulations provide that if a foreign transferor transfers an interest in an upper-tier partnership that owns, directly or indirectly, an interest in one or more lower-tier partnerships that are engaged in the conduct of a trade or business within the United States, then the deemed sale gain or loss must be computed with respect to each lower-tier partnership, the amount of effectively connected gain or loss that would be allocated to the upper-tier partnership must be determined, and the amount of gain or loss recognized by a foreign transferor that is treated as effectively connected gain or loss under proposed § 1.864(c)(8)-1(c) must be determined by reference to the transferor's distributive share of effectively connected gain or loss arising from each lower-tier partnership. See proposed § 1.864(c)(8)-1(e)(1).

The proposed regulations also clarify that when a foreign transferor is a partner in an upper-tier partnership and the upper-tier partnership transfers an interest in a lower-tier partnership that is engaged in the conduct of a trade or business within the United States, the upper-tier partnership must determine its effectively connected gain or loss by applying the principles of the proposed regulations, including the tiered partnership rules described in proposed § 1.864(c)(8)-1(e)(1).

IV. *Treaties*

The business profits articles of many U.S. income tax treaties limit the taxation of income that is otherwise treated as effectively connected with the conduct of a trade or business within the United States under the Code to income and gain attributable to a permanent establishment in the United States. The applicable gains articles of many U.S. income tax treaties allow the country in which a permanent establishment is located to tax gains from the alienation of movable property forming part of the business property of a permanent establishment, including gains from the alienation of a permanent establishment, alone or with the whole enterprise of which it is a part. In general, the permanent establishment of a partnership in the United States is considered a permanent establishment of the partners of the partnership. See *Donroy, Ltd. v. United States*, 196 F.Supp. 54 (N.D. Cal. 1961), *aff'd* 301 F.2d 200 (9th Cir. 1962), and *Unger v. Comm'r*, T.C. Memo. 1990-15, 58 TCM 1157, *aff'd* 936 F.2d 1316 (D.C. Cir. 1991).

The proposed regulations provide that the disposition of a foreign partner's interest in a partnership, in whole or in part, is a disposition of all or part of a partner's permanent establishment. Thus, to the extent the partnership's assets form part of a foreign partner's permanent establishment in the United States, the permanent establishment paragraph of the gains article would generally preserve the United States' taxing jurisdiction over the gain on the transfer of a partnership interest that is subject to tax under section 864(c)(8). In addition, if an income tax treaty has a gains article that permits the United States to apply its domestic laws to tax gains or does not have a gains article, the treaty does not prevent the application of section 864(c)(8).

Gains articles of treaties also frequently have special provisions covering certain assets, regardless of whether the assets form part of a permanent establishment, such as gains from dispositions of United States real property interests and ships and aircraft used in international traffic. If a gains article of an income tax treaty prohibits taxation of the gain from the disposition of any asset, such as ships or aircraft used in international traffic, the gains and losses from those assets will not be considered assets that form part of the permanent establishment, nor will they be taken into account in determining deemed sale EC gain or deemed sale EC loss, for purposes of computing the section 864(c)(8)(B) limitation. If the gains article of an applicable income tax treaty allows the taxation of gain from the disposition of a United States real property interest, the transfer of an interest in a partnership that holds a United States real property interest remains subject to section 897(g) even if the transfer is not subject to section 864(c)(8) (because the partnership's assets are not treated as forming part of a permanent establishment in the United States). See proposed § 1.864(c)(8)-1(d).

V. *Anti-Stuffing Rule*

The proposed regulations include an anti-stuffing rule applicable to both these regulations and section 897. This rule is included to prevent inappropriate reductions in amounts characterized as effectively connected with the conduct of a trade or business within the United States under section 864(c)(8) or section 897. A cross-reference to this rule is also included in the proposed regulation under section 897.

VI. *Section 1446(f) Guidance*

The proposed regulations do not provide guidance under section 1446(f). The Treasury Department and the IRS intend to issue guidance under section 1446(f) expeditiously.

Applicability Dates

The proposed regulations apply to transfers occurring on or after November 27, 2017, the effective date of section 864(c)(8). See section 7805(b)(2). If any provision is finalized after June 22, 2019, the Treasury Department and the IRS expect that such provision will apply only to transfers occurring on or after December 26, 2018. *See* section 7805(b)(1)(B).

Special Analyses

Executive Orders 13771, 13563, and 12866 direct agencies to assess costs and benefits of available regulatory alternatives and, if regulation is necessary, to select regulatory approaches that maximize net benefits, including potential economic, environmental, public health and safety effects, distributive impacts, and equity. Executive Order 13563 emphasizes the importance of quantifying both costs and benefits, reducing costs, harmonizing rules, and promoting flexibility.

These proposed regulations have been designated by the Office of Management and Budget's Office of Information and Regulatory Affairs (OIRA) as subject to review under Executive Order 12866 pursuant to the Memorandum of Agreement (April 11, 2018) between the Treasury Department and the Office of Management and Budget regarding review of tax regulations. OIRA has determined that the proposed rulemaking is significant and subject to review under EO 12866 and section 1(b) of the Memorandum of Agreement. Accordingly, the proposed regulations have been reviewed by the Office of Management and Budget.

The Treasury Department and the IRS have assessed the benefits and costs of the proposed regulations relative to a no-action baseline reflecting anticipated tax-related behavior and other economic behavior in the absence of these proposed regulations. Because the proposed regulations generally provide taxpayers with additional certainty on the amount and character of gain or loss treated as effectively connected income as a result of section 864(c)(8) and concurrently coordinate section 864(c)(8) with other provisions in the Code, the Treasury Department and the IRS anticipate only minimal economic or revenue effects from the proposed regulations. The Treasury Department and the IRS estimate that between 5,000 and 10,000 taxpayers are potentially affected by section 864(c)(8), with only a fraction of these taxpayers having gain or loss from disposition of a partnership in any one year. The Treasury Department and the IRS estimate that the affected taxpayers would see a minimal difference in treatment between these proposed regulations and Revenue Ruling 91-32. Comments are requested regarding these assessments. The Treasury Department and the IRS have assessed that the proposed regulations do not establish a new collection of information nor modify an existing collection that requires the approval of the Office of Management and Budget under the Paperwork Reduction Act (44 U.S.C. chapter 35). The Treasury Department and the IRS seek comments on this assessment.

Section 864(c)(8) and the proposed regulations generally apply to nonresident alien individuals and foreign corporations on the transfer of an interest in a partnership that is engaged in a trade or business within the United States, and not directly to the trade or business the partnership conducts in the United States. Under section 605 of the Regulatory Flexibility Act (5 U.S.C. chapter 6), the Treasury Department and the IRS certify that the proposed regulations will not have a significant economic impact on a substantial number of small entities. The reason is that the proposed regulations generally apply to nonresident alien individuals and foreign corporations on the transfer of an interest in a partnership and not directly to a domestic small business. Pursuant to section 7805(f), this notice of proposed rulemaking has been submitted to the Chief Counsel for Advocacy of the Small Business Administration for comment on their impact on small business.

Comments and Requests for Public Hearing

Before the proposed regulations are adopted as final regulations, consideration will be given to any comments that are submitted timely to the IRS as prescribed in this preamble under the "**ADDRESSES**" heading. The Treasury Department and the IRS request comments on all aspects of the proposed regulations, and specifically on the issues identified in sections I.A.2, I.B, and I.C of the Explanations of Provisions. All comments will be available at *www.regulations.gov* or upon request. A public hearing will be scheduled if requested in writing by any person that timely submits written comments. If a public hearing is scheduled, then notice of the date, time, and place for the public hearing will be published in the **Federal Register**.

Drafting Information

The principal authors of the proposed regulations are Ronald M. Gootzeit and Chadwick Rowland, Office of Associate Chief Counsel (International). However, other personnel from the Treasury Department and the IRS participated in their development.

Statement of Availability of IRS Documents

IRS Revenue Procedures, Revenue Rulings, notices, and other guidance cited in this document are published in the Internal Revenue Bulletin (or Cumulative Bulletin) and are available from the Superintendent of Documents, U.S. Government Printing Office, Washington, DC 20402, or by visiting the IRS website at *http://www.irs.gov*.

[¶ 49,785]   **Proposed Amendments of Regulations (REG-104352-18)**, published in the Federal Register on December 28, 2018.

[Code Secs. 245A, 267A, 1503, 6038, 6038A and 7701]

Foreign corporations: Transactions between related taxpayers: Consolidated returns: Computation of tax.Reg. §§1.245A(e)-1, 1.267A-1—1.267A-7 and amendments of Reg. §§1.1503(d)-1, 1.1503(d)-3, 1.1503(d)-6, 1.1503(d)-7, 1.1503(d)-8, 1.6038-2, 1.6038-3, 1.6038A-2 and 301.7701-3 implementing sections 245A(e) and 267A of the Internal Revenue Code ("Code") regarding hybrid dividends and certain amounts paid or accrued in hybrid transactions or with hybrid entities, are adopted.

[¶ 49,786]   **Proposed Amendments of Regulations (REG-141739-08)**, published in the Federal Register on December 28, 2018.

[Code Secs. 150 and 1001]

Closing agreement programs: Tax-exempt bonds: Reissuance of bonds: State and local bonds: Computation of gain and loss.—Reg. §1.150-3 and amendments of Reg. §1.1001-3, addressing when tax-exempt bonds are treated as retired for purposes of section 103 and sections 141 through Code Sec. 150 of the Internal Revenue Code (Code), are proposed.

AGENCY: Internal Revenue Service (IRS), Treasury.

ACTION: Notice of proposed rulemaking.

SUMMARY: This document contains proposed regulations that address when tax-exempt bonds are treated as retired for purposes of section 103 and sections 141 through 150 of the Internal Revenue Code (Code). The proposed regulations are necessary to unify and to clarify existing guidance on this subject. The proposed regulations affect State and local governments that issue tax-exempt bonds.

DATES: Comments and requests for a public hearing must be received by March 1, 2019.

ADDRESSES: Send submissions to: CC:PA:LPD:PR (REG-141739-08), Room 5203, Internal Revenue Service, P.O. Box 7604, Ben Franklin Station, Washington, DC 20044. Submissions may be hand-delivered Monday through Friday between the hours of 8 a.m. and 4 p.m. to CC:PA:LPD:PR (REG-141739-08), Courier's Desk, Internal Revenue Service, 1111 Constitution Avenue, NW., Washington, DC 20224, or sent electronically via the Federal eRulemaking Portal at *www.regulations.gov* (REG-141739-08).

FOR FURTHER INFORMATION CONTACT: Concerning the proposed regulations, Spence Hanemann, (202) 317-6980; concerning submissions of comments and requesting a hearing, Regina Johnson, (202) 317-6901 (not toll-free numbers). SUPPLEMENTARY INFORMATION:

Background

This document contains proposed amendments to 26 CFR part 1 under sections 150 and 1001 of the Code (Proposed Regulations).

1. In general

In general, under section 103, interest received by the holders of certain bonds issued by State and local governments is exempt from Federal income tax. To qualify for the tax exemption, a bond issued by a State or local government must satisfy various eligibility requirements under sections 141 through 150 at the time of issuance of the bond. If the issuer and holder agree after issuance to modify the terms of a tax-exempt bond significantly, the original bond may be treated as having been retired and exchanged for a newly issued, modified bond. Similarly, if the issuer or its agent acquires and resells the bond, the bond may be treated as having been retired upon acquisition and replaced upon resale with a newly issued bond.

The term "reissuance" commonly refers to the effect of a transaction in which a new debt instrument replaces an old debt instrument as a result of retirement of the old debt instrument pursuant to such an exchange or extinguishment. In the case of a reissuance, the reissued bond must be retested for qualification under sections 103 and 141 through 150. The reissuance of an issue of tax-exempt bonds may result in various negative consequences to the issuer, such as changes in yield for purposes of the arbitrage investment yield restrictions under section 148(a), acceleration of arbitrage rebate payment obligations under section 148(f), and change-in-law risk.

2. Tender Option Bonds

Tender option bonds and variable rate demand bonds (collectively, tender option bonds) have special features that present reissuance questions. Specifically, tender option bonds have original terms that provide for a tender option interest rate mode, as described in this paragraph. Issuers of tax-exempt bonds often preauthorize several different interest rate modes in the bond documents and retain an option to switch interest rate modes under parameters set forth in the bond documents. During a tender option mode, tender option bonds have short-term interest rates that are reset periodically at various short-term intervals (typically, every seven days) based on the current market rate necessary to remarket the bonds at par. In connection with each resetting of the interest rate, the holder of a tender option bond has a right or requirement to tender the bond back to the issuer or its agent for purchase at par. Tender option bonds also may have interest rate mode conversion options that permit the issuer or conduit borrower to change the interest rate mode on the bonds from a tender option mode to another short-term interest rate mode or to a fixed interest rate to maturity. At the time of a conversion to another interest rate mode, the holder of a tender option bond typically has the right or requirement to tender the bond for purchase at par.

Tender option bonds generally have third-party liquidity facilities from banks or other liquidity providers to ensure that there is sufficient cash to repurchase the bonds upon a holder's tender, and they also commonly have credit enhancement from bond insurers or other third-party guarantors. Upon a holder's exercise of its tender rights in connection with either a resetting of the interest rate during a tender option mode or a conversion to another interest rate mode, a remarketing agent or a liquidity provider typically will acquire the bonds subject to the tender and resell the bonds either to the same bondholders or to others willing to purchase such bonds.

3. Existing Guidance

To address reissuance questions related to tax-exempt bonds, on December 27, 1988, the IRS published Notice 88-130, 1988-2 CB 543, which provides rules for determining when a tax-exempt bond is retired for purposes of sections 103 and 141 through 150. Notice 88-130 provides in part that a tax-exempt bond is retired when there is a change to the terms of the bond that results in a disposition of the bond for purposes of section 1001. In addition, Notice 88-130 provides special rules for retirement of certain tender option bonds that meet a definition of the term "qualified tender bond."

On June 26, 1996, the Department of the Treasury (Treasury Department) and the IRS published final regulations under § 1.1001-3 (1996 Final Regulations) in the **Federal Register** (61 FR 32926). These regulations provide rules for determining whether a modification of the terms of a debt instrument, including a tax-exempt bond, results in an exchange for purposes of section 1001. In recognition of a need to coordinate the interaction of the prior guidance in Notice 88-130 with the subsequent final regulations under § 1.1001-3 for particular tax-exempt bond purposes, the Treasury Department and the IRS stated their intention to issue regulations under section 150 on this subject in the **Federal Register** (61 FR 32930).

On April 14, 2008, the IRS published Notice 2008-41, 2008-1 CB 742. Like Notice 88-130, Notice 2008-41 provides rules for determining when a tax-exempt bond is retired for purposes of sections 103 and 141 through 150 and includes special rules for qualified tender bonds. While the retirement standards provided in these two notices are similar, Notice 2008-41 was intended to coordinate the retirement standards for tax-exempt bond purposes with the 1996 Final Regulations on modifications of debt instruments under § 1.1001-3 and to be more administrable than Notice 88-130. In order to preserve flexibility and to limit potential unintended consequences during the 2008 financial crisis, Notice 2008-41 permitted issuers to apply either notice. Generally, under Notice 2008-41, a tax-exempt bond is retired when a significant modification to the terms of the bond occurs under § 1.1001-3, the bond is acquired by or on behalf of its issuer, or the bond is otherwise redeemed or retired. The notice clarifies that, for purposes of these retirement standards, the purchase of a tax-exempt bond by a third-party guarantor or third-party liquidity facility provider pursuant to the terms of the guarantee or liquidity facility is not treated as a purchase or other acquisition by or on behalf of a governmental issuer. Although these general rules apply to a qualified tender bond, Notice 2008-41 also provides that certain features of qualified tender bonds will not result in a retirement. In Notice 2008-41, the Treasury Department and the IRS reiterated their intention to provide guidance on the retirement of tax-exempt bonds in regulations under section 150.

The Proposed Regulations provide rules for determining when tax-exempt bonds are treated as retired for purposes of sections 103 and 141 through 150. The Proposed Regulations also amend § 1.1001-3(a)(2) to conform that section to the special rules in the Proposed Regulations for retirement of qualified tender bonds.

Explanation of provisions

1. Section 1.150-3: Retirement of Tax-Exempt Bonds

A. General Rules for Retirement of a Tax-Exempt Bond

The Proposed Regulations generally provide retirement standards that apply to tax-exempt bonds for purposes of sections 103 and 141 through 150. These retirement standards follow the guidance in Notice 2008-41 with technical refinements. The Proposed Regulations provide that a tax-exempt bond is retired if a significant modification to the terms of the bond occurs under § 1.1001-3, if the issuer or an agent acting on its behalf acquires the bond in a manner that liquidates or extinguishes the bondholder's investment in the bond, or if the bond is otherwise redeemed (for example, redeemed at maturity).

For this purpose, the Proposed Regulations define the term "issuer" to mean the State or local governmental unit that actually issues the bonds and any related party (as defined in § 1.150-1(b)) to that actual issuer. In the case of a governmental unit, the applicable related party definition under § 1.150-1(b) applies a controlled group test under § 1.150-1(e) to determine related party status, based generally on all of the facts and circumstances. This controlled group test includes special rules which specifically treat control over the governing board of a governmental unit and control over use of funds or assets of a governmental unit as giving rise to controlled group status.

By focusing on the actual issuer rather than on a conduit borrower, this definition of issuer maintains and respects the essential legal construct necessary for issuance of many tax-exempt bonds, such as qualified private activity bonds under section 141(e), that the actual issuer be treated as the obligor in conduit financings. Thus, under the Proposed Regulations, the acquisition of a tax-exempt bond by a conduit borrower that is not a related party to the actual issuer does not result in the retirement of that bond.

The Proposed Regulations also prescribe certain consequences for a bond that is retired pursuant to a deemed exchange under § 1.1001-3 or following the acquisition of the bond by the issuer or the issuer's agent. In the former case, the bond is treated as a new bond issued at the time of the modification as determined under § 1.1001-3. In the latter case, if the issuer resells the bond, the bond is treated as a new bond issued at the time of resale. If the issuer does not resell the acquired bond, the acquired bond is simply retired. In either case in which a retired bond is treated as a newly issued bond, the issuer must consider whether the new bond refunds the retired bond. For this purpose, the rules regarding the definition of a refunding issue under § 1.150-1(d) apply. For example, if the issuer of the bond retired pursuant to § 1.1001-3 is the same as the issuer (or a related party to the issuer) of the newly issued bond, the newly issued bond will be part of a current refunding issue that refunds the retired bond.

B. Exceptions to Retirement of a Tax-Exempt Bond

The Proposed Regulations provide three exceptions that limit retirements resulting from the operation of the general rules. Two of these exceptions are intended to prevent the special features of tender option bonds from resulting in a retirement. A third exception applies to all tax-exempt bonds.

The first two exceptions in the Proposed Regulations apply to qualified tender bonds, a defined term that is essentially a tender option bond meeting certain requirements. Specifically, a qualified tender bond is a tax-exempt bond that, pursuant to the terms of its governing contract, bears interest during each interest rate mode at a fixed rate, a qualified floating rate under § 1.1275-5, or an objective rate that is permitted for a tax-exempt bond under § 1.1275-5(c)(5). Furthermore, interest on a qualified tender bond must be unconditionally payable at periodic intervals of no more than a year. Finally, a qualified tender bond may not have a stated maturity date later than 40 years after its issue date and must include a qualified tender right. This definition is similar to the definition of qualified tender bond provided in Notice 2008-41.

The Proposed Regulations define a qualified tender right required for a qualified tender bond in terms of the mechanics by which the tender right operates. The Proposed Regulations define a qualified tender right to include either a tender right that arises periodically during a tender option mode or a tender right that arises upon the exercise of the issuer's option under the original terms of the bond to change the interest rate mode.

A qualified tender bond has two features that otherwise could result in retirement of the bond under the general rules for retirement in the Proposed Regulations. First, when accompanied by a qualified tender right, an exercise of the issuer's option to change the interest rate mode might, in some circumstances, qualify as a modification under the rule in § 1.1001-3(c)(2)(iii) for alterations that result from the exercise of an option. Thus, absent the exception in the Proposed Regulations, a qualified tender right might result in a modification that, if significant, would cause the qualified tender bond to be retired. To address this circumstance, the Proposed Regulations provide an exception that avoids retirement by disregarding a qualified tender right for purposes of determining whether a significant modification of a qualified tender bond under § 1.1001-3 results in retirement of the bond. Consequently, the issuer's option to change the interest rate mode typically would qualify as a unilateral option and the change of interest rate mode resulting from exercise of that option would not be a modification of the qualified tender bond.

The second feature of a qualified tender bond that could result in retirement of the bond under the general rules for retirement in the Proposed Regulations is the financing structure feature that may require the issuer or its agent to acquire the bond upon exercise of the qualified tender right. To address this circumstance, the Proposed Regulations provide another exception under which an acquisition of a qualified tender bond pursuant to the exercise of a qualified tender right will not result in retirement, provided that neither the issuer nor its agent holds the bond for longer than 90 days. This 90-day period is intended to provide the issuer or its remarketing agent with sufficient time to resell a tendered bond to a new holder.

The Proposed Regulations also provide an exception to the general rules of retirement for all tax-exempt bonds. This exception, carried forward from Notice 2008-41, provides that acquisition of a tax-exempt bond by a guarantor or liquidity facility provider acting as the issuer's agent does not result in retirement of the bond if the acquisition is pursuant to the terms of the guarantee or liquidity facility and the guarantor or liquidity facility provider is not a related party (as defined in § 1.150-1(b)) to the issuer.

2. Applicability Dates

The rules in § 1.150-3 of the Proposed Regulations are proposed to apply to events and actions taken with respect to bonds that occur on or after the date that is 90 days after the date of publication of the Treasury decision adopting these rules as final regulations in the **Federal Register**. Issuers may apply these regulations to events and actions taken with respect to bonds that occur before that date. The Treasury Department and the IRS expect that the final regulations will obsolete Notice 88-130 and Notice 2008-41.

Special Analyses

This regulation is not subject to review under section 6(b) of Executive Order 12866 pursuant to the Memorandum of Agreement (April 11, 2018) between the Department of the Treasury and the Office of Management and Budget regarding review of tax regulations. Because these regulations do not impose a collection of information on small entities, the Regulatory Flexibility Act (5 U.S.C. chapter 6) does not apply. Pursuant to section 7805(f) of the Code, this notice of proposed rulemaking will be submitted to the Chief Counsel for Advocacy of the Small Business Administration for comment on its impact on small entities.

Comments and Requests for Public Hearing

Before the Proposed Regulations are adopted as final regulations, consideration will be given to any comments that are submitted timely to the IRS as prescribed in this preamble under the ADDRESSES heading. The Treasury Department and the IRS request comments on all aspects of the proposed rules. All comments will be available at *www.regulations.gov* or upon request. A public hearing will be scheduled if requested in writing by any person that timely submits written comments. If a public hearing is scheduled, notice of the date, time, and place for the hearing will be published in the **Federal Register**.

Drafting Information

The principal authors of these regulations are Spence Hanemann of the Office of Associate Chief Counsel (Financial Institutions and Products) and Vicky Tsilas, formerly of the Office of Associate Chief Counsel (Financial Institutions and Products). However, other personnel from the Treasury Department and the IRS participated in their development.

Availability of IRS Documents

The IRS notices cited in this preamble are published in the Internal Revenue Bulletin (or Cumulative Bulletin) and are available from the Superintendent of Documents, U.S. Government Publishing Office, Washington, DC 20402, or by visiting the IRS website at www.irs.gov.

[¶ 49,787] Proposed Amendments of Regulations (REG-134652-18), published in the Federal Register on February 8, 2019.

[Code Sec. 199A]

Qualified business income: Deduction.—Regs. §§ 1.199A-0, 1.199A-3 and 1.199A-6 concerning the deduction for qualified business income under section 199A of the Internal Revenue Code (Code), are proposed.

AGENCY: Internal Revenue Service (IRS), Treasury.

ACTION: Notice of proposed rulemaking.

SUMMARY: This document contains proposed regulations concerning the deduction for qualified business income under section 199A of the Internal Revenue Code (Code). The proposed regulations will affect certain individuals, partnerships, S corporations, trusts, and estates. The proposed regulations provide guidance on the treatment of previously suspended losses that constitute qualified business income. The proposed regulations also provide guidance on the determination of the section 199A deduction for taxpayers that hold interests in regulated investment companies, charitable remainder trusts, and split-interest trusts.

DATES: Written or electronic comments and requests for a public hearing must be received by April 9, 2019.

ADDRESSES: Submit electronic submissions to the Federal eRulemaking Portal at *www.regulations.gov* (indicate IRS and REG-134652-18) by following the online instructions for submitting comments. Once submitted to the Federal eRulemaking Portal, comments cannot be edited or withdrawn. The Department of the Treasury (Treasury Department) and the IRS will publish for public availability any comment received to its public docket, whether submitted electronically or in hard copy. Send hard copy submissions to CC:PA:LPD:PR (REG-134652-18), Room 5203, Internal Revenue Service, P.O. Box 7604, Ben Franklin Station, Washington, D.C., 20044. Submissions may be hand-delivered Monday through Friday between the hours of 8 a.m. and 4 p.m. to CC:PA:LPD:PR (REG-134652-18), Courier's Desk, Internal Revenue Service, 1111 Constitution Avenue, N.W., Washington, D.C., 20224.

FOR FURTHER INFORMATION CONTACT: Concerning § 1.199A-3(d), Michael Y. Chin or Steven Harrison at (202) 317-6842; concerning §§ 1.199A-3(b) and 1.199A-6, Vishal R. Amin or Frank J. Fisher at (202) 317-6850 or Robert D. Alinsky or Margaret Burow at 202-317-5279; concerning submissions of comments or requests for a public hearing, Regina Johnson at (202) 317-6901 (not toll-free numbers).

SUPPLEMENTARY INFORMATION:

Background

This document contains proposed amendments to the Income Tax Regulations (26 CFR part 1) under section 199A of the Code.

Section 199A was enacted on December 22, 2017, by section 11011 of "An Act to provide for reconciliation pursuant to titles II and V of the concurrent resolution on the budget for fiscal year 2018," Pub.L. 115-97 (TCJA), and was amended on March 23, 2018, retroactively to January 1, 2018, by section 101 of Division T of the Consolidated Appropriations Act, 2018, Pub.L. 115-141, (2018 Act). Section 199A applies to taxable years beginning after 2017 and before 2026.

Section 199A provides a deduction of up to 20 percent of qualified business income from a U.S. trade or business operated as a sole proprietorship or through a partnership, S corporation, trust, or estate (section 199A deduction). The section 199A deduction may be taken by individuals and by some estates and trusts. A section 199A deduction is not available for wage income or for income earned by a C corporation. For taxpayers whose taxable income exceeds a statutorily-defined amount (threshold amount), section 199A may limit the taxpayer's section 199A deduction based on (i) the type of trade or business engaged in by the taxpayer, (ii) the amount of W-2 wages paid with respect to the trade or business (W-2 wages), and/or (iii) the unadjusted basis immediately after acquisition (UBIA) of qualified property held for use in the trade or business (UBIA of qualified property). These statutory limitations are subject to phase-in rules based upon taxable income above the threshold amount.

Section 199A also allows individuals and some trusts and estates (but not corporations) a deduction of up to 20 percent of their combined qualified real estate investment trust (REIT) dividends and qualified publicly traded partnership (PTP) income, including qualified REIT dividends and qualified PTP income earned through passthrough entities. This component of the section 199A deduction is not limited by W-2 wages or UBIA of qualified property.

The section 199A deduction is the lesser of (1) the sum of the combined amounts described in the prior two paragraphs or (2) an amount equal to 20 percent of the excess (if any) of taxable income of the taxpayer for the taxable year over the net capital gain of the taxpayer for the taxable year.

Additionally, section 199A(g) provides that specified agricultural or horticultural cooperatives may claim a special entity-level deduction that is substantially similar to the domestic production activities deduction under former section 199.

The statute expressly grants the Secretary authority to prescribe such regulations as are necessary to carry out the purposes of section 199A (section 199A(f)(4)), and also provides specific grants of authority with respect to certain issues: the treatment of acquisitions, dispositions, and short-tax years (section 199A(b)(5)); certain payments to partners for services rendered in a non-partner capacity (section 199A(c)(4)(C)); the allocation of W-2 wages and UBIA of qualified property (section 199A(f)(1)(A)(iii)); restricting the allocation of items and wages under section 199A and such reporting requirements as the Secretary determines appropriate (section 199A(f)(4)(A)); the application of section 199A in the case of tiered entities (section 199A(f)(4)(B); preventing the manipulation of the depreciable period of qualified property using transactions between related parties (section 199A(h)(1)); and determining the UBIA of qualified property acquired in like-kind exchanges or involuntary conversions (section 199A(h)(2)).

The Treasury Department and the Internal Revenue Service published proposed regulations interpreting section 199A on August 16, 2018 (the August Proposed Regulations) (83 FR 40884). The August Proposed Regulations contain six substantive sections, §§ 1.199A-1 through 1.199A-6, each of which provides rules relevant to the calculation of the section 199A deduction. The August Proposed Regulations, with modifications in response to comments and testimony received, were adopted as final regulations in TD 9847, issued concurrently with this notice of proposed rulemaking and published elsewhere in this issue of the Federal Register.

Explanation of Provisions

These proposed regulations propose rules addressing issues not addressed in the August Proposed Regulations that are necessary to provide taxpayers with computational, definitional, and anti-avoidance guidance regarding the application of section 199A. Specifically, these proposed regulations contain amendments to two substantive sections of the August Proposed Regulations, §§ 1.199A-3 and 1.199A-6, each of which provides rules relevant to the calculation of the section 199A deduction. These additional proposed rules respond to comments received on the August Proposed Regulations as well as address certain issues identified after additional study. This Explanation of Provisions describes each of the proposed rules contained in this document in turn. The Treasury Department and the IRS request comments on all aspects of these proposed regulations.

I. *Treatment of Previously Suspended Losses That Constitute QBI.*

Section 1.199A-3(b)(1)(iv) of the final regulations provides that previously disallowed losses or deductions (including under sections 465, 469, 704(d), and 1366(d)) allowed in the taxable year are generally taken into account for purposes of computing QBI except to the extent the losses or deductions were disallowed, suspended, limited, or carried over from taxable years ending before January 1, 2018. The final regulations also provide a first-in-first-out ordering rule. One commenter on the August Proposed Regulations suggested that a special rule should be provided to identify the section 469 trade or business losses that are used to offset income if the taxpayer's section 469 groupings differ from the taxpayer's section 199A aggregations. The commenter recommended that any section 469 loss carryforward that is later used should be allocated across the taxpayer's section 199A aggregations based on income with respect to such aggregations in the year the loss was generated.

The Treasury Department and the IRS believe that that previously disallowed losses should be treated as losses from a separate trade or business for both the reasons stated by the commenter and because the losses may relate to a trade or business that is no longer in existence. Accordingly, these proposed regulations amend § 1.199A-3(b)(1)(iv) to provide that such losses are treated as loss from a separate trade or business. To the extent that losses relate to a PTP, they must be treated as losses from a separate PTP. Section 1.199A-3(b)(1)(iv)(B) provides that attributes of the disallowed loss are determined in the year the loss is incurred.

II. *Regulated Investment Companies with Interests in REITs and PTPs*

A. *REITs*

Section 1.199A-3 restates the definitions in section 199A(c) and provides additional guidance on the determination of QBI, qualified REIT dividends, and qualified PTP income. For simplicity, the regulations use the term *individual* when referring to an individual, trust, estate, or other person eligible to claim the section 199A deduction. *See* § 1.199A-1(a)(2). The term *relevant passthrough entity (RPE)* is used to describe passthrough entities that directly operate the trade or business or pass through the trade or business' items of income, gain, loss, or deduction from lower-tier RPEs to the individual. *See* § 1.199A-1(b)(10).

A number of commenters on the August Proposed Regulations requested guidance that would allow a shareholder in a regulated investment company within the meaning of section 851(a) (RIC) to take a section 199A deduction with respect to certain income of, or distributions from, the RIC. Because a RIC is a subchapter C corporation, a shareholder in a RIC generally does not take into account a share of the RIC's items of income, deduction, gain, or loss. Part 1 of subchapter M, however, has features that allow the tax consequences of investing in a RIC to approximate those of a direct investment in the assets of the RIC. The principal feature is the allowance of the deduction for dividends paid under section 852(b)(2)(D). If a corporation qualifies as a RIC under section 851 and meets the distribution requirements and other requirements in section 852(a), the RIC's income tax is computed on its investment company taxable income (ICTI), which is its taxable income with certain adjustments, including the allowance of the deduction for dividends paid. *See* section 852(b)(2). ICTI also excludes the amount of the RIC's net capital gain, but tax is separately imposed on that amount to the extent it exceeds the deduction for dividends paid, taking into account only capital gain dividends. *See* section 852(b)(3)(A). The deduction for dividends paid allows RICs to eliminate all or most of their corporate income tax liability.

If a RIC has certain items of income or gain, subchapter M also provides rules under which a RIC may pay dividends that a shareholder in the RIC may treat in the same manner (or a similar manner) as the shareholder would treat the underlying item of income or gain if the shareholder realized it directly. Although this treatment differs fundamentally from the pass-through treatment of partners or trust beneficiaries, this preamble refers to is as "conduit treatment." For example, under section 852(b)(3), a RIC that has net capital gain for a taxable year generally may pay capital gain dividends, and shareholders receiving the capital gain dividends treat them as gain from the sale or exchange of a capital asset held for more than one year. Section 852(b)(3) provides necessary limits and procedures that apply to capital gain dividends. There are similar statutory provisions for exempt-interest dividends under section 852(b)(5), interest-related dividends under section 871(k)(1), short-term capital gain dividends under section 871(k)(2), dividends eligible for the dividends received deduction under section 854(b)(1)(A), and qualified dividend income under section 854(b)(1)(B). Rules for paying dividends corresponding to different types of long-term capital gain have been provided in guidance under regulatory authority granted in section 1(h). *See* Notice 2015-41, 2015-24 I.R.B. 1058, modifying Notice 2004-39, 2004-1 C.B. 982 and Notice 97-64, 1997-2 C.B. 323.

Investing in RICs enables small investors to gain benefits, such as professional management and broad diversification, that otherwise would be available only to investors with more resources. The House Report for the enactment of the Internal Revenue Code of 1954 explained that the RIC regime "permits investors to pool their funds through the use of a corporation in order to obtain skilled, diversified investment in corporate securities without having to pay an additional layer of corporate tax." H.R. Rep. No. 83-1337, p. 73 (1954). The ability to elect to be taxed as a RIC is available typically only to domestic corporations that, at all times during the taxable year, are registered under the Investment Company Act of 1940, as amended (15 U.S.C. 80a-1 to 80b–2). *See* section 851(a)(1)(A).

Section 199A(f)(4) directs the Secretary to prescribe such regulations as are necessary to carry out the purposes of section 199A, including regulations for its application in the case of tiered entities. The Treasury Department and the IRS have determined that it is consistent with the grant of authority under section 199A and the purposes of part 1 of subchapter M of chapter 1 of the Code to provide for conduit treatment of qualified REIT dividends. The Treasury Department and the IRS continue to consider whether it is appropriate to provide for conduit treatment of qualified PTP income.

These proposed regulations provide rules under which a RIC that receives qualified REIT dividends may pay section 199A dividends. Non-corporate shareholders receiving section 199A dividends would treat them as qualified REIT dividends under section 199A(e)(3), provided the shareholder meets the holding period requirements for its shares in the RIC.

The rules under which a RIC would compute and report section 199A dividends are based on the rules for capital gain dividends in section 852(b)(3) and exempt-interest dividends in section 852(b)(5). The amount of a RIC's section 199A dividends for a taxable year would be limited to the excess of the RIC's qualified REIT dividends for the taxable year over allocable expenses. Section 199A dividends generally are also subject to the principles that apply to other RIC dividends. *See, e.g.,* Rev. Rul. 2005-31, 2005-1 C.B. 1084; Rev. Rul. 89-81, 1989-1 C.B. 226.

B. *PTPs*

One of the commenters recommending that the regulations permit conduit treatment for qualified REIT dividends received by a RIC also recommended that the regulations permit conduit treatment for qualified PTP income received by a RIC. In response to this comment, the Treasury Department and the IRS have given significant consideration to including in this notice of proposed rulemaking regulations that would provide conduit treatment for qualified PTP income. However, unlike conduit treatment for qualified REIT dividends received by a RIC, conduit treatment of qualified PTP income received by a RIC presents several novel issues. The commenter recommending this conduit treatment did not address these issues or make any suggestions as to how they should be resolved. The need to resolve these issues in a way that would afford RIC shareholders treatment that is similar to the treatment they would receive if they held the PTP interests directly while preserving the relative simplicity of the tax treatment of RIC investors has prevented the Treasury Department and the IRS from crafting and including appropriate rules in these proposed regulations. As noted later in this part of the Explanation of Provisions, the Treasury Department and the IRS continue to consider permitting conduit treatment for qualified PTP income received by a RIC to further the purposes of section 199A(b)(1)(B) and seek public comment to assist in resolving these novel issues with a view to developing regulations permitting conduit treatment for qualified PTP income.

These issues arise in part from the fact that income attributable to a specified service trade or business within the meaning of section 199A(d)(2) (SSTB) of a PTP may be qualified PTP income for taxpayers with taxable income below the threshold amount, but not for taxpayers with taxable income above the top of the phase-out range. For taxpayers with taxable income in the phase-out range, a portion of PTP income attributable to an SSTB is qualified PTP income. There is no precedent for providing conduit treatment for a RIC (or any other C corporation) with respect to income of a PTP or other partnership taxed in this manner, and the complexity and potential confusion such treatment might create for RIC investors is arguably inconsistent with the relative simplicity that the tax system has historically provided for RIC investors. This is particularly true given the limitation on the portion of a RIC's assets that can be invested in qualified PTPs as defined in section 851(h) (the type of PTP likely to be engaged in a trade or business) and the limited portion of the RIC's dividends that would likely be attributable to income from such PTPs.

Another novel issue is presented by the rules relating to the treatment of losses for purposes of section 199A. First, a PTP may not net losses from an SSTB against income from a non-SSTB, and vice versa, in determining the amounts that it reports to its partners. Thus, PTPs are required to separately calculate income and deductions from SSTBs and non-SSTBs and report that information to their partners. Second, if a taxpayer has a net loss from an SSTB or a non-SSTB that is allowed in determining taxable income for a taxable year, that loss may be required to be carried over to the subsequent year for section 199A attribute purposes. In the case of a RIC, it is not clear to what extent these requirements can be implemented by permitting RIC dividends to reflect attributes of the RIC's investment experiences in PTPs. For example, it is difficult to conceive how losses of a RIC can be passed through to shareholders upon the payment of a dividend, which would be inconsistent with the status of a RIC as a C corporation. *See* section 311(a). In addition, RICs and RIC shareholders would experience complexity inconsistent with the longstanding tax policy of providing simplified reporting for RIC investors.

Consistent with RICs' status as C corporations, RICs could instead offset losses from PTPs against qualified REIT dividends received, with any excess PTP losses carried forward as negative qualified PTP income for section 199A attribute purposes at the RIC level. To the extent RICs would be required to carry forward PTP losses, it would appear that RICs would need to track separate loss carryforwards for SSTB PTP losses and non-SSTB PTP losses. While netting qualified non-SSTB losses from PTPs against larger amounts of qualified REIT dividends would support RIC dividends that could be treated as eligible for the section 199A deduction by the RICs' shareholders regardless of income level, SSTB losses from PTPs would complicate the offset of qualified PTP losses against qualified REIT dividends by RICs because SSTB losses from a PTP do not offset qualified REIT dividends for taxpayers with taxable income above the phase-out range. Such losses do, however, offset qualified REIT dividends for taxpayers with income below the threshold amount. For taxpayers with income in the phase-out range, these losses partially offset qualified REIT dividends to a greater or lesser extent depending on where the taxpayer's income falls in the phase-out range. It is not clear how a conduit regime for qualified PTP income could work in terms of treating RIC shareholders in the phase-out range in a manner that is consistent with the treatment they would receive if they received the qualified REIT dividend and the qualified PTP loss from an SSTB directly rather than through a RIC.

Providing conduit treatment for qualified PTP income would also raise potentially significant issues with respect to the treatment of RIC shareholders that are non-U.S. persons, tax-exempt organizations, and trusts underlying individual retirement accounts (IRAs) and qualified retirement plans. In order to be qualified PTP income, section 199A(c)(3)(A)(i) requires that the income must be effectively connected with a U.S. trade or business. If conduit treatment is afforded to RIC dividends attributable to such PTP income for section 199A purposes, it is not clear that a RIC dividend attributable to such income could be disregarded for purposes of calculating effectively connected income of a non-U.S. shareholder or unrelated business taxable income of a tax-exempt organization or trust underlying an IRA or qualified retirement plan. Given that such investors typically do not hold directly interests in PTPs intentionally, but do so through corporate "blockers," allowing conduit treatment for qualified PTP income through RICs could cause unwelcome results for non-U.S. shareholders, tax-exempt organizations, and trusts underlying IRAs and qualified retirement plans holding RIC stock.

The Treasury Department and the IRS continue to evaluate whether it is appropriate to provide conduit treatment for qualified PTP income through RICs, and request detailed comments on these novel issues. In particular, comments are requested concerning: (1) Whether RICs have sufficient qualified items of PTP income, gain, deduction, or loss to warrant a conduit regime that would permit RICs to pay qualified PTP dividends to shareholders; (2) How to provide conduit treatment for qualified PTP income for taxpayers with income below the threshold amount or within the phase-out range, particularly where a RIC has qualified REIT dividends and a qualified PTP loss from an SSTB; (3) How to treat losses of PTPs arising from SSTBs and non-SSTBs; (4) Whether conduit treatment for qualified PTP income can be disregarded for purposes of determining the effectively connected income or unrelated business taxable income of certain RIC shareholders; (5) Whether SSTB items are sufficiently rare or incidental for PTPs that a conduit regime for PTP dividends should exclude all SSTB items; and (6) How to implement conduit treatment for qualified PTP income in a way that is consistent with the policy goal of preserving the overall relative simplicity of the tax treatment of investors in RICs while still achieving the policy goals of section 199A and section 199A(b)(1)(B) in particular.

III. *Special Rules for Trusts and Estates*

Section 1.199A-6 provides guidance that certain specified entities (for example, trusts and estates) may need to follow to enable the computation of the section 199A deduction of the entity and each of its owners. Section 1.199A-6(d) contains special rules for applying section 199A to trusts and decedents' estates. The August Proposed Regulations expressly requested comments, and comments were submitted, on whether and how certain trusts and other entities would be able to take a deduction under section 199A. These proposed regulations take those suggestions into consideration in proposing rules applicable to those particular situations identified by commenters.

In the case of a section 199A deduction claimed by a non-grantor trust or estate, section 199A(f)(1)(B) applies rules similar to the rules under former section 199(d)(1)(B)(i) for the apportionment of W–2 wages and the apportionment of UBIA of qualified property. In the case of a non-grantor trust or estate, the QBI and expenses properly allocable to the business, including the W-2 wages relevant to the computation of the wage limitation, and relevant UBIA of depreciable property must be allocated among the trust or estate and its various beneficiaries. Specifically, §1.199A-6(d)(3)(ii) provides that each beneficiary's share of the trust's or estate's QBI and W-2 wages is determined based on the proportion of the trust's or estate's DNI that is deemed to be distributed to that beneficiary for that taxable year. Similarly, the proportion of the entity's DNI that is not deemed distributed by the trust or estate will determine the entity's share of the QBI and W-2 wages. In addition, if the trust or estate has no DNI in a particular taxable year, any QBI and W-2 wages are allocated to the trust or estate, and not to any beneficiary.

In addition, §1.199A-6(d)(3)(ii) provides that, to the extent the trust's or estate's UBIA of qualified property is relevant to a trust or estate and any beneficiary, the trust's or estate's UBIA of qualified property will be allocated among the trust or estate and its beneficiaries in the same proportions as is the DNI of the trust or estate. This is the case regardless of how any depreciation or depletion deductions resulting from the same property may be allocated under section 643(c) among the trust or estate and its beneficiaries for purposes other than section 199A.

Under §1.199A-6(d)(3)(iv), the threshold amount is determined at the trust level after taking into account any distribution deductions. Commenters have noted that taxpayers could circumvent the threshold amount by dividing assets among multiple trusts, each of which would claim its own threshold amount. This result is inappropriate and inconsistent with the purpose of section 199A. Therefore, §1.199A-6(d)(3)(vii) provides that a trust formed or funded with a principal purpose of receiving a deduction under section 199A will not be respected for purposes of determining the threshold amount under section 199A.

In the August Proposed Regulations, the Treasury Department and the IRS requested comments with respect to whether taxable recipients of annuity and unitrust interests in charitable remainder trusts and taxable beneficiaries of other split-interest trusts may be eligible for the section 199A deduction to the extent that the amounts received by such recipients include amounts that may give rise to the deduction. The request for such comments indicated that such comments should include explanations of how amounts that may give rise to the section 199A deduction would be identified and reported in the various classes of income of the trusts received by such recipients and how the excise tax rules in section 664(c) would apply to such amounts.

A. *Charitable remainder trust beneficiary's eligibility for the deduction*

A few commenters suggested that a charitable remainder trust under section 664 should be allowed to calculate the deduction at the trust level and that the charitable remainder trust should be treated as a single taxpayer for purposes of the thresholds for taxable income, W-2 wages, and UBIA of qualified property.

Several commenters recommended that, if unrelated business taxable income (UBTI) is qualified business income, the section 199A deduction should be allowed before the UBTI excise tax is imposed. However, other commenters disagreed. Another commenter stated that the section 199A deduction should not be allowed when calculating UBTI because it is not a deduction directly connected with carrying on the trade or business and is allowable only for purposes of chapter 1, while the excise tax on UBTI is imposed under chapter 42 (that is, it is not an income tax). Another commenter said the UBTI excise tax under section 664(c) should not affect QBI because that tax is charged to principal.

One commenter recommended that QBI should be allocated to the ordinary income tier. Another recommended that QBI should be the bottom of the first tier (last to be distributed) and section 199A items should be reported on the Schedule K-1 when QBI is deemed distributed. Another commenter stated that a charitable remainder trust has no taxable income and no DNI, so the allocation of QBI, W-2 wages, and UBIA of qualified property should be allocated to beneficiaries based on the percentage of distributions from the ordinary income tier, with QBI allocated to the charitable remainder trust remaining a tier one item. Another commenter stated that QBI cannot be a separate tier because it is a deduction, rather than a rate difference.

The Treasury Department and the IRS believe that, because a charitable remainder trust described in section 664 is not subject to income tax, and because the excise tax imposed by section 664(c) is treated as imposed under chapter 42, the trust does not either have or calculate a section 199A deduction and the threshold amount described in section 199A(e)(2) does not apply to the trust. Furthermore, application of section 199A to effectively reduce the 100 percent rate of tax imposed by section 664(c) on any UBTI would be inconsistent with the intent of section 664(c) to deter trusts from making investments that generate significant UBTI. However, any taxable recipient of a unitrust or annuity amount from the trust must determine and apply the recipient's own threshold amount for purposes of section 199A, taking into account any annuity or unitrust amounts received from the trust. Therefore, a taxable recipient of a unitrust or annuity amount from a charitable remainder trust may take into account QBI, qualified REIT dividends, and qualified PTP income for purposes of determining the recipient's section 199A deduction for the taxable year to the extent that the unitrust or annuity amount distributed to such recipient consists of such section 199A items under §1.664-1(d).

In order to determine the order of distribution of the various classes of income of the trust for purposes of applying §1.664-1(d), QBI, qualified REIT dividends, and qualified PTP income of a charitable remainder trust will be allocated to the classes of income within the category of income described in §1.664-1(d)(1)(i)(a)(1) based on the rate of tax that normally would apply to that type of income, not taking into account the characterization of that income as QBI, qualified REIT dividends, or qualified PTP income for purposes of section 199A. Accordingly, any QBI, qualified REIT dividends, and qualified PTP income will be treated as distributed from the trust to a unitrust or annuity recipient only when all other classes of income within the ordinary income category subject to a higher rate of tax (not taking into account section 199A) have been exhausted. The unitrust or annuity recipient will be treated as receiving a proportionate amount of any QBI, qualified REIT dividends, and qualified PTP income that is distributed along with other income in the same class within the ordinary income category. To the extent that a trust is treated as distributing QBI, qualified REIT dividends, or qualified PTP income to more than one unitrust or annuity recipient in the taxable year, the distribution of such income will be treated as made to the recipients proportionately, based on their respective shares of the total of QBI, qualified REIT dividends, and qualified PTP income distributed for that year. The amount of any W-2 wages or UBIA of qualified property of the charitable remainder trust in a taxable year will be allocable to unitrust or annuity recipients based on each recipient's share of the trust's total QBI (whether or not distributed) for that taxable year.

Any QBI, qualified REIT dividends, or qualified PTP income of the trust that is unrelated business taxable income is subject to excise tax and §1.664-1(c) requires that tax to be allocated to the corpus of the trust. Certain other rules relating to charitable remainder trusts are provided.

B. *Split-interest trusts*

The August Proposed Regulations requested comments on whether any special rules were necessary with respect to split-interest trusts. One commenter suggested that additional rules may be necessary for split-interest trusts other than charitable reminder trusts. After considering the comment and studying other split-interest trusts in more depth after the publication of the August Proposed Regulations, the Treasury Department and the IRS have determined that special rules for other split-interest trusts, such as non-grantor charitable lead trusts or pooled income funds, are not necessary because such trusts are taxable under part I, subchapter J, chapter 1 of the Code, except subpart E. Such split-interest trusts would apply the rules for non-grantor trusts and estates set forth in §1.199A-6(d)(3) to determine any applicable section 199A deduction for the trust or its taxable beneficiaries.

C. *Separate shares*

Although no comments were received with respect the application of the threshold amount to separate shares, the Treasury Department and the IRS believe that clarification with respect to this issue may be necessary. These proposed regulations provide that, in the case of a trust described in section 663(c) with substantially separate and independent shares for multiple beneficiaries, such separate shares will not be treated as separate trusts for purposes of applying the threshold amount. Instead, the trust will be treated as a single trust for purposes of determining whether the taxable income of the trust exceeds the threshold amount. The purpose of the separate share rule in section 663(c) is to treat distributions of trust DNI to trust beneficiaries as independent taxable events solely for purposes of applying sections 661 and 662 with respect to each beneficiary's separate share. The rule determines each beneficiary's share of DNI based on the amount of DNI from that beneficiary's separate share, rather than as a percentage of the trust's DNI.

Nevertheless, under the separate share rule, if a trust retains any portion of DNI, the trust will be subject to tax as a single trust with respect to the retained DNI. Only trusts with retained DNI will be eligible for the section 199A deduction, because a trust will be allocated QBI, qualified REIT dividends, and qualified PTP income only in proportion to the amount of DNI retained by the trust for the taxable year. For this reason, a trust, regardless of the number of separate shares it has for its beneficiaries under the separate share rule of section 663(c), will be treated as a single trust for purposes of applying the threshold amount under section 199A. To the extent that a taxable beneficiary of a trust receives a distribution of DNI from the beneficiary's separate share of the trust which includes section 199A items, the beneficiary would apply its own threshold amount to those section 199A items in computing its section 199A deduction in accordance with the rules of § 1.199A-6(d).

Availability of IRS Documents

IRS notices cited in this preamble are made available by the Superintendent of Documents, U.S. Government Printing Office, Washington, DC 20402.

Proposed Effective/Applicability Date

Section 7805(b)(1)(A) and (B) of the Code generally provide that no temporary, proposed, or final regulation relating to the internal revenue laws may apply to any taxable period ending before the earliest of (A) the date on which such regulation is filed with the **Federal Register**, or (B) in the case of a final regulation, the date on which a proposed or temporary regulation to which the final regulation relates was filed with the **Federal Register**.

The amendments to §§ 1.199A-3 and 1.199A-6 set forth in this notice of proposed rulemaking generally are proposed to apply to taxable years ending after the date of publication of a Treasury decision adopting these rules as final regulations in the **Federal Register**. However, taxpayers may rely on the rules in the amendments to §§ 1.199A-3 and 1.199A-6 set forth in this notice of proposed rulemaking, in their entirety, until the date a Treasury decision adopting these regulations as final regulations is published in the **Federal Register**.

Special Analyses

I. *Regulatory Planning and Review - Economic Analysis*

Executive Orders 13563 and 12866 direct agencies to assess costs and benefits of available regulatory alternatives and, if regulation is necessary, to select regulatory approaches that maximize net benefits (including potential economic, environmental, public health and safety effects, distributive impacts, and equity). Executive Order 13563 emphasizes the importance of quantifying both costs and benefits, of reducing costs, of harmonizing rules, and of promoting flexibility.

The proposed regulations have been designated by the Office of Management and Budget's ("OMB") Office of Information and Regulatory Affairs ("OIRA") as subject to review under Executive Order 12866 pursuant to the Memorandum of Agreement (April 11, 2018) between the Treasury Department and OMB regarding review of tax regulations. It has been determined that the proposed rulemaking is economically significant under section 1(c) of the Memorandum of Agreement and thereby subject to review. Accordingly, the proposed regulations have been reviewed by OMB.

A. *Overview*

Congress enacted section 199A to provide taxpayers other than corporations a deduction of up to 20 percent of QBI from domestic businesses plus up to 20 percent of their combined qualified REIT dividends and qualified PTP income. As stated in the Explanation of Provisions, these regulations are necessary to provide taxpayers with computational, definitional, and anti-avoidance guidance regarding the application of section 199A. These proposed regulations contain amendments to § 1.199A-3, providing further guidance to taxpayers for purposes of calculating the section 199A deduction. They provide clarity for taxpayers in determining their eligibility for the deduction and the amount of the allowed deduction. Among other benefits, this clarity helps ensure that taxpayers all calculate the deduction in a similar manner, which encourages decision-making that is economically efficient contingent on the provisions of the overall Code.

B. *Baseline*

The analysis in this section compares the proposed regulation to a no-action baseline reflecting anticipated Federal income tax-related behavior in the absence of these regulations.

C. *Economic Analysis of the Proposed Amendments to § 1.199A-3*

1. *Background*

Because the section 199A deduction has not previously been available, §§ 1.199A-1 through 1.199A-6 provide greater specificity for a large number of the relevant terms and necessary calculations taxpayers are currently required to apply under the statute. However, one subject not covered by the August 2018 Proposed Regulations is the treatment of REIT dividends received by RICs. Because RICs are taxed as C corporations, they are ineligible for the section 199A deduction under the statute, which generally does not apply to C corporations. However, the statute also directs the Secretary to prescribe such regulations as are necessary to carry out the purposes of section 199A, including regulations for its application in the case of tiered entities. Thus these proposed regulations establish rules under which a RIC that earns qualified REIT dividends may pay section 199A dividends to its shareholders.

An alternative approach the Treasury Department and the IRS could have taken would be to remain silent on this issue. For reasons given below, the Treasury Department and the IRS concluded such an approach would likely give rise to less economically efficient decisions than the approach taken in these proposed regulations.

2. *Anticipated benefits of the Proposed Amendments to § 1.199A-3*

The Treasury Department and the IRS expect that the definitions and guidance provided in the proposed amendments to § 1.199A-3 will implement the section 199A deduction in an economically efficient manner. An economically efficient tax system generally aims to treat income derived from similar economic decisions similarly in order to reduce incentives to make choices based on tax rather than market incentives. In absence of these proposed regulations, the section 199A statute would not accomplish this in the case of REIT dividends. Under the statute and the section 199A final regulations, individuals who directly hold ownership interests in a REIT would generally qualify for the section 199A deduction on their qualified REIT dividends. However, individuals who are shareholders of a RIC that has an ownership interest in a REIT would not receive any benefit from section 199A on REIT dividends received by the RIC, even if the RIC pays dividends to the individual. Thus, in the absence of these supplemental proposed regulations, a market distortion is introduced by section 199A whereby direct ownership of REITs is tax-advantaged relative to indirect ownership of REITs through RICs.

These proposed regulations remove this distortion. The proposed amendments to § 1.199A-3 establish rules under which a RIC that earns qualified REIT dividends may pay section 199A dividends to its shareholders, such that the effective tax treatment of qualified REIT dividends is similar under the proposed regulations regardless of whether a taxpayer invests in a REIT directly or through a RIC.

3. *Anticipated costs of the Proposed Amendments to § 1.199A-3*

The Treasury Department and the IRS do not anticipate any meaningful economic distortions to be induced by the proposed amendments to § 1.199A-3 because the proposed amendments seek to continue to provide similar tax treatment to REIT income regardless of whether it is held directly or through a RIC. Prior to TCJA, the tax treatment was similar, but TCJA made REIT dividends eligible for the section 199A deduction, and the section 199A final regulations did not address this uncertainty. This proposed amendment ensures that REIT income earned through a RIC is also eligible for the same deduction. RICs are financial intermediaries, and, as a general rule, economic distortion is minimized to the extent that the tax consequences of investment through an intermediary correspond to the tax consequences of direct investment. The Treasury Department and the IRS request comments regarding any anticipated economic costs. Changes to the collective paperwork burden arising from this and other sections of these regulations are discussed in section D, *Anticipated impacts on administrative and compliance costs*, of this analysis.

D. *Anticipated impacts on administrative and compliance costs*

The proposed regulations add to the compliance costs of RICs and intermediaries such as brokerage firms that hold RIC shares. In order for a RIC's shareholders to benefit from the section 199A deduction on qualified REIT dividends earned by the RIC, the proposed regulations require the RIC to compute and report section 199A dividends to its shareholders. Though many RICs keep detailed records of their investment portfolios, this action nonetheless creates non-trivial administrative costs for any RICs and intermediaries that wish to provide section 199A dividends to their shareholders. These costs and the associated impacted tax forms are described in the Paperwork Reduction Act section of this proposed amendment.

E. *Executive Order 13771.*

These regulations have been designated as regulatory under E.O. 13771.

II. **Paperwork Reduction Act**

The collection of information required by this proposed regulation is in proposed §1.199A-3. The collection of information in proposed §1.199A-3 is required for RICs that choose to report information regarding qualified REIT dividends to their shareholders. It is necessary to report the information to the IRS and relevant taxpayers in order to ensure that taxpayers properly report in accordance with the rules of the proposed regulations the correct amount of deduction under section 199A. The collection of information in proposed §1.199A-3 is satisfied by providing information about section 199A dividends as Form 1099-DIV and its instructions may prescribe.

For purpose of the PRA, the reporting burden associated with §1.199A-3 will be reflected in the IRS Form 14029, Paperwork Reduction Act Submission, associated with Form 1099-DIV (OMB control number 1545-0110). The burden associated with the information collection in the proposed regulations represents 1.567 million hours and $149 million ($2018) annually to comply with the information collection requirement in the proposed regulations. The burden hours estimate was derived from IRS's legacy burden model and is discussed in further detail on 1545-0110. The hourly rate is derived from RAAS's Business Taxpayer Burden model that relates time and out-of-pocket costs of business tax preparation, derived from survey data, to assets and receipts of affected taxpayers along with other relevant variables, and converted by the Treasury Department to $2017. The Treasury Department and the IRS request comments on all aspects of information collection burdens related to the proposed regulations. In addition, when available, drafts of the applicable IRS forms are posted for comment at https://www.irs.gov/pub/irs-pdf/f1099div.pdf.

III. *Regulatory Flexibility Act*

It is hereby certified that the collections of information in proposed §1.199A-3 will not have a significant economic impact on a substantial number of small entities.

The collection in proposed §1.199A-3 applies only to RICs that pay section 199A dividends. As described above, Congress created RICs to give small investors access to the professional management and asset diversification that are available only with very large investment portfolios. To insure appropriate non-tax regulation of these substantial investment portfolios, subchapter M of chapter 1 of subtitle A the Code requires that such RICs must be eligible for registration, and must actually be registered, with the Securities and Exchange Commission under the Investment Company Act of 1940. There are some small businesses that are publicly traded, but most publicly traded businesses are not small entities as defined by the Regulatory Flexibility Act. Thus, the Treasury Department and IRS expect that most RICs are not small entities for purposes of the Regulatory Flexibility Act. Accordingly, the Treasury Department and the IRS have determined that the collection of information in this notice of proposed rulemaking will not have a significant economic impact. Accordingly, a regulatory flexibility analysis under the Regulatory Flexibility Act (5 U.S.C. chapter 6) is not required. Notwithstanding this certification, the Treasury Department and the IRS invite comments from interested members of the public on both the number of entities affected and the economic impact on small entities.

Pursuant to section 7805(f) of the Code, this notice of proposed rulemaking has been submitted to the Chief Counsel for Advocacy of the Small Business Administration for comment on its impact on small business.

Pursuant to section 7805(f) of the Code, this notice of proposed rulemaking has been submitted to the Chief Counsel for Advocacy of the Small Business Administration for comment on its impact on small business.

Comments and Requests for Public Hearing

The Treasury Department and the IRS request comments on all aspects of the proposed rules.

Before these proposed regulations are adopted as final regulations, consideration will be given to any comments that are submitted timely to the IRS as prescribed in this preamble under the "Addresses" heading. All comments will be available at *www.regulations.gov* or upon request. A public hearing will be scheduled if requested in writing by any person that timely submits written comments. If a public hearing is scheduled, then notice of the date, time, and place for the public hearing will be published in the **Federal Register**.

Drafting Information

The principal authors of these regulations are Michael Y. Chin and Steven Harrison, Office of the Associate Chief Counsel (Financial Institutions and Products) and Robert Alinsky, Vishal R. Amin, Margaret Burow, and Frank J. Fisher, Office of the Associate Chief Counsel (Passthroughs and Special Industries). However, other personnel from the Treasury Department and the IRS participated in their development.

[¶ 49,788]   Proposed Amendments of Regulations (REG-104464-18), published in the Federal Register on March 6, 2019 (corrected 4/11/2019 and 4/12/2019).

[Code Secs. 250, 962, 1502, 6038, 6038A]

Deductions: Foreign-derived intangible income: Global intangible low-taxed income.—Reg. §§1.250-0, 1.250-1, 1.250(a)-1, 1.250(b)-1— 1.250(b)-6 and 1.1502-50 and amendments of Reg. §§1.962-1, 1.1502-12, 1.1502-13, 1.6038-2, 1.6038-3 and 1.6038A-2, providing guidance to determine the amount of the deduction for foreign-derived intangible income and global intangible low-taxed income.

AGENCY: Internal Revenue Service (IRS), Treasury.

ACTION: Notice of proposed rulemaking.

SUMMARY: This document contains proposed regulations that provide guidance to determine the amount of the deduction for foreign-derived intangible income and global intangible low-taxed income. This document also contains proposed regulations coordinating the deduction for foreign-derived intangible income and global intangible low-taxed income with other provisions in the Internal Revenue Code.

DATES: Written or electronic comments and requests for a public hearing must be received by May 6, 2019.

ADDRESSES: Send submissions to: CC:PA:LPD:PR (REG-104464-18), Room 5203, Internal Revenue Service, P.O. Box 7604, Ben Franklin Station, Washington, DC 20044. Submissions may be hand-delivered Monday through Friday between the hours of 8 a.m. and 4 p.m. to: CC:PA:LPD:PR (REG-104464-18), Courier's Desk, Internal Revenue Service, 1111 Constitution Avenue NW, Washington, DC 20224. Alternatively, taxpayers may submit comments electronically via the Federal eRulemaking Portal at *http://www.regulations.gov* (REG-104464-18).

FOR FURTHER INFORMATION CONTACT: Concerning proposed §§ 1.250(a)-1 through 1.250(b)-6, 1.962-1, 1.6038-2, 1.6038-3, and 1.6038A-2, Kenneth Jeruchim at (202) 317-6939; concerning proposed §§ 1.1502-12, 1.1502-13 and 1.1502-50, Michelle A. Monroy at (202) 317-5363 or Austin Diamond-Jones at (202) 317-6847; concerning submissions of comments and requests for a public hearing, Regina L. Johnson, (202) 317-6901 (not toll free numbers).

SUPPLEMENTARY INFORMATION:

Background

This document contains proposed amendments to 26 CFR part 1 under sections 250, 962, 1502, 6038, and 6038A ("proposed regulations"). Section 14202(a) of the Tax Cuts and Jobs Act, Public Law 115-97 (2017) (the "Act"), added section 250 to the Internal Revenue Code (the "Code").[1] The new section provides a domestic corporation with a deduction ("section 250 deduction") for its foreign-derived intangible income ("FDII") and its global intangible low-taxed income ("GILTI") and the amount treated as a dividend under section 78 which is attributable to its GILTI. Section 14202(c) of the Act provides that section 250 and the conforming amendments in section 14202(b) apply to taxable years beginning after December 31, 2017.

Section 14201(a) of the Act (codified in section 951A) requires a United States shareholder ("U.S. shareholder") of any controlled foreign corporation ("CFC") for any taxable year to include in gross income the shareholder's GILTI for the year. The Department of the Treasury ("Treasury Department") and the IRS published a separate notice of proposed rulemaking that provides guidance to U.S. shareholders on how to determine the amount of GILTI to include in gross income. See 83 FR 51072 (Oct. 10, 2018).

Section 14302(a) of the Act also added a new foreign tax credit category for foreign branch income (defined in section 904(d)(2)(J)), which is cross-referenced in section 250(b)(3)(A)(i)(VI). The Treasury Department and the IRS published a separate notice of proposed rulemaking that provides rules for determining a corporation's foreign branch income for purposes of section 904. See 83 FR 63200 (Dec. 7, 2018).

Explanation of Provisions

I. *Overview of Proposed Regulations*

In general, income earned directly by a U.S. person on foreign business income is subject to U.S. tax on a current basis. Before the Act, foreign business income earned indirectly by a U.S. person through a foreign corporation was not generally subject to U.S. tax until such income was distributed as a dividend to the U.S. person. Certain anti-deferral regimes could cause the U.S. owner to be taxed on a current basis in the United States regardless of whether the income had been distributed as a dividend to the U.S. owner. Sections 951 through 965 of the Code (generally referred to as the "subpart F" provisions), applicable to certain passive and mobile categories of income earned by CFCs, is the main anti-deferral regime of relevance to U.S.-based corporate groups. However, because subpart F does not generally apply to active foreign business income of a CFC (as defined in section 957(a)), U.S. shareholders before the Act could indefinitely defer U.S. taxation with respect to their foreign business income — in particular, mobile income arising from the exploitation of intangible property — by allocating such income to its CFCs operating in low- or zero-tax jurisdictions. This system of deferral, in turn, resulted in a "lock-out effect," whereby U.S. shareholders that had allocated income to CFCs formed in low- or zero-tax jurisdictions could not repatriate such income to the United States without incurring significant U.S. tax.

In order to facilitate the efficient redeployment of foreign earnings in the United States, the Act established a participation exemption system under which certain earnings of a foreign corporation can be repatriated to a corporate U.S. shareholder without U.S. tax. See section 14101(a) of the Act and section 245A. However, Congress recognized that, without any base protection measures, the participation exemption system could further incentivize taxpayers to allocate intangible income to CFCs formed in low- or zero-tax jurisdictions because the earnings related to such intangible income could now be repatriated to the United States without incurring any U.S. tax. See Senate Committee on the Budget, 115th Cong., "Reconciliation Recommendations Pursuant to H. Con. Res. 71," at 370 (Comm. Print 2017) ("Senate Explanation"). Therefore, Congress enacted section 951A, which subjects a U.S. shareholder's "global intangible low-taxed income" or "GILTI" (a new term created by the Act) derived through its CFCs to U.S. tax on a current basis, similar to the taxation of such CFCs' subpart F income under section 951(a)(1)(A).

Most member countries of the Organisation for Economic Co-operation and Development ("OECD") provide a full or partial (e.g., 95 percent) participation exemption with respect to income of foreign subsidiaries distributed to domestic shareholders. See OECD (2018), *Tax Policy Reforms 2018: OECD and Selected Partner Economies*, at 73, OECD Publishing, Paris (Sept. 2018). While some countries also have CFC inclusion regimes similar to subpart F that subject certain narrow classes of income of foreign subsidiaries to current tax in the home country, many countries do not subject active foreign business income of foreign subsidiaries to current tax. Congress recognized that taxing such income at the full U.S. corporate tax rate could hurt the competitive position of U.S. corporations relative to their foreign peers, and therefore determined that GILTI earned by such corporations should be subject to a reduced effective U.S. tax rate. See Senate Explanation, at 370. Accordingly, Congress enacted section 250, which provides corporate U.S. shareholders a deduction of 50 percent for taxable years beginning after December 31, 2017, and before January 1, 2026, with respect to their GILTI, and the amount treated as a dividend under section 78 which is attributable to their GILTI ("section 78 gross-up"). In contrast, a domestic corporation's inclusion of its CFCs' subpart F income is not eligible for the section 250 deduction, and is therefore generally subject to U.S. tax at the full corporate rate.

After the Act, income earned directly by a domestic corporation is subject to a 21 percent rate. Absent a deduction with respect to intangible income attributable to foreign market activity earned directly by a domestic corporation, the lower effective tax rate applicable to GILTI by reason of the section 250 deduction would perpetuate the pre-Act incentive for domestic corporations to allocate intangible income to CFCs formed in low- or zero-tax jurisdictions. Therefore, to neutralize the effect of providing a lower U.S. effective tax rate with respect to the active earnings of a CFC of a domestic corporation through a deduction for GILTI, section 250 provides a lower effective U.S. tax rate with respect to "foreign-derived intangible income" or "FDII" (a new term created by the Act) earned directly by the domestic corporation through a deduction of 37.5 percent for taxable years beginning after December 31, 2017, and before January 1, 2026. The result of the section 250 deduction for both GILTI and FDII is to

---

[1] Except as otherwise stated, all section references in this preamble are to the Internal Revenue Code.

help neutralize the role that tax considerations play when a domestic corporation chooses the location of intangible income attributable to foreign-market activity, that is, whether to earn such income through its U.S.-based operations or through its CFCs.

The proposed regulations provide guidance for determining the amount of the section 250 deduction allowed to a domestic corporation for its FDII and GILTI. Proposed §1.250(a)-1 provides rules for determining the amount of the deduction, including rules for applying the taxable income limitation of section 250(a)(2). Proposed §1.250(b)-1 provides general rules for computing a domestic corporation's FDII. Proposed §1.250(b)-2 provides rules for determining a domestic corporation's qualified business asset investment ("QBAI"), which is a component of the computation of FDII. Proposed §1.250(b)-3 provides general rules for determining gross income included in gross foreign-derived deduction eligible income ("gross FDDEI"), which is a component of the computation of FDII. Proposed §1.250(b)-4 provides rules for determining gross FDDEI from sales of property. Proposed §1.250(b)-5 provides rules for determining gross FDDEI from the provision of a service. Proposed §1.250(b)-6 provides rules relating to the sale of property or the provision of a service to a related party.

II. *Amount of Deduction Allowed Under Section 250(a)*

Proposed §1.250(a)-1 provides general rules to determine the amount of a domestic corporation's section 250 deduction and associated definitions that apply for purposes of the proposed regulations. The section 250 deduction is available only to domestic corporations. See section 250(a)(1) and proposed §1.250(a)-1(b)(1). For this purpose, the term "domestic corporation" has the meaning set forth in section 7701(a) — an association, joint-stock company, or insurance company created or organized in the United States or under the law of the United States or of any State — but does not include a regulated investment company (as defined in section 851), a real estate investment trust (as defined in section 856), or an S corporation (as defined in section 1361). See proposed §1.250(a)-1(c)(1). The section 250 deduction is not available to individuals except in certain cases where an individual makes an election under section 962. See part IV of this Explanation of Provisions section for more information about that provision.

As discussed in part I of this Explanation of Provisions section, the deduction under section 250 is generally intended to reduce the effective rate of U.S. income tax on FDII and GILTI in order to help neutralize the role that tax considerations play when a domestic corporation chooses the location of intangible income attributable to foreign-market activity. There is no indication that Congress intended the section 250 deduction to reduce the effective rate of tax imposed by non-income tax provisions outside of chapter 1 of the Internal Revenue Code. Accordingly, for purposes of the excise tax imposed by section 4940(a), the proposed regulations provide that a section 250 deduction is not treated as an ordinary and necessary expense paid or incurred for the production or collection of gross investment income within the meaning of section 4940(c)(3)(A). See proposed §1.250(a)-1(b)(4).

The section 250 deduction is subject to a taxable income limitation. If, for any taxable year, the sum of a domestic corporation's FDII and GILTI exceeds its taxable income, the excess is allocated pro rata to reduce the corporation's FDII and GILTI solely for purposes of computing the amount of the section 250 deduction. See section 250(a)(2) and proposed §1.250(a)-1(b)(2). For this purpose, a domestic corporation's taxable income is determined without regard to the section 250 deduction. See section 250(a)(2)(A)(ii) and proposed §1.250(a)-1(c)(4). The Code does not otherwise define "taxable income" for purposes of applying the taxable income limitation of section 250(a)(2).

In general, a taxpayer's taxable income is based, in part, upon the availability, and proper calculation, of deductions. However, multiple Code provisions simultaneously limit the availability of a deduction based, directly or indirectly, upon a taxpayer's taxable income, including sections 163(j)(1) (limiting a deduction for business interest) and 172(a)(2) (limiting a net operating loss deduction). Sections 163(j)(2) and 172(b) also provide that any deduction not allowed to a taxpayer for a taxable year by reason of the limitation in section 163(j)(1) or 172(a)(2), respectively, may be allowed to the taxpayer, subject to the same limitation, in its succeeding taxable year. A taxpayer's net operating loss for a taxable year is determined without regard to the section 250 deduction (see section 172(d)(9)), and a taxpayer's adjusted taxable income is determined without regard to section 172. See section 163(j)(8)(A)(iii). However, neither section 163(j) nor section 250 prescribes an ordering rule with respect to the other provision.

The Treasury Department and the IRS considered proposing computations requiring the use of simultaneous equations in lieu of an ordering rule but determined that an approach that requires such computations would result in undue administrative and compliance burdens. Therefore, the proposed regulations provide an ordering rule for applying sections 163(j) and 172 in conjunction with section 250 that the Treasury Department and the IRS have determined is consistent with the statutory language for each provision. Specifically, the proposed regulations provide that a domestic corporation's taxable income for purposes of applying the taxable income limitation of section 250(a)(2) is determined after all of the corporation's other deductions are taken into account. See proposed §1.250(a)-1(c)(4). Accordingly, a domestic corporation's taxable income for purposes of section 250(a)(2) is its taxable income determined without regard to section 250, but taking into account the application of sections 163(j) and 172(a), including amounts permitted to be carried forward to such taxable year by reason of sections 163(j)(2) and 172(b).

Proposed regulations issued under section 163(j) provide guidance on the interaction of sections 163(j) and 250 that the Treasury Department and the IRS consider to be consistent with these proposed regulations under section 250. See 83 FR 67490 (Dec. 28, 2018). Specifically, the proposed regulations under section 163(j) provide that, for purposes of determining the limitation under section 163(j), a deduction under section 250(a)(1) that is properly allocable to a non-excepted trade or business is taken into account in determining a taxpayer's taxable income and thus its adjusted taxable income. See proposed §1.163(j)-1(b)(37)(ii). However, for this purpose, the taxpayer's deduction under section 250(a)(1) is determined without regard to the limitations under sections 250(a)(2) and 163(j). See id.

As a result of these proposed regulations under section 250 and the proposed regulations under section 163(j), a domestic corporation's allowable business interest under section 163(j), its net operating loss deduction under section 172(a), and its section 250 deduction are determined in the following manner: First, a domestic corporation computes the tentative amount of its FDII and the tentative amount of its section 250 deduction ("tentative section 250 deduction") taking into account all deductions, but without regard to any carryforwards or disallowances under section 163(j), the amount of any net operating loss deduction under section 172(a), or the taxable income limitation of section 250(a)(2) and proposed §1.250(a)-1(b)(2). Second, the corporation computes the amount of its business interest allowed after the application of section 163(j), for this purpose taking into account the amount of its tentative section 250 deduction but without regard to the amount of any net operating loss deduction under section 172(a). See section 163(j)(8)(A)(iii) and proposed §1.163(j)-1(b)(1)(i)(B) and (b)(37)(ii). Third, the corporation computes the amount of its net operating loss deduction under section 172(a), for this purpose taking into account the amount of its business interest allowed after application of section 163(j) and the taxable income limitation of section 172(a)(2), but without regard to the amount of its section 250 deduction (including its tentative section 250 deduction). See section 172(d)(9). Fourth, the corporation computes the amount of its FDII, for this purpose taking into account the amount of its business interest allowed after application of section 163(j) and the amount of its net operating loss deduction under section 172(a) (determined in steps two and three, respectively). See part III(A)(2) of this Explanation of Provisions section for a discussion on the allocation of deductions to gross DEI and gross FDDEI. Fifth, the corporation computes the amount of its section 250 deduction after the application of the taxable income limitation of section 250(a)(2) and proposed §1.250(a)-1(b)(2), for this purpose taking into account the amount of its business interest allowed after application of section 163(j) and the amount of its net operating loss deduction under section 172(a). See proposed §1.250(a)-1(f)(2) (*Example 2*), which illustrates the interaction of sections 163(j), 172, and 250.

The Treasury Department and the IRS request comments on the proposed ordering rule, as well as how the section 250 deduction should be accounted for in determining adjusted taxable income at the partnership level under section 163(j)(4)(A).

III. *Determination of FDII*

A. General Computational Rules

1. In General

A domestic corporation's FDII is the corporation's deemed intangible income ("DII") multiplied by the corporation's foreign-derived ratio. Proposed § 1.250(b)-1(b). A domestic corporation's DII is the excess (if any) of the corporation's deduction eligible income ("DEI") over its deemed tangible income return ("DTIR"). Proposed § 1.250(b)-1(c)(3). A domestic corporation's DTIR is 10 percent of the corporation's QBAI. Proposed § 1.250(b)-1(c)(4). The foreign-derived ratio is the domestic corporation's ratio of foreign-derived deduction eligible income ("FDDEI") to DEI. Proposed § 1.250(b)-1(c)(13).

2. Determination of DEI and FDDEI

A domestic corporation's DEI is the excess of its gross income without regard to certain excluded items ("gross DEI") over the deductions properly allocable to gross DEI. See proposed § 1.250(b)-1(c)(2). Gross DEI excludes six categories of gross income: any amount included in gross income under section 951(a), GILTI, financial services income, dividends from CFCs, domestic oil and gas extraction income, and foreign branch income. See proposed § 1.250(b)-1(c)(14). The proposed regulations clarify that, for this purpose, a dividend includes any amount treated as a dividend under any other provision of subtitle A of the Internal Revenue Code, including the section 78 gross-up attributable to inclusions under sections 951(a) and 951A(a). See proposed § 1.250(b)-1(c)(5). In addition, the proposed regulations define foreign branch income by reference to proposed § 1.904-4(f), except that it also includes the sale, directly or indirectly, of any asset (other than stock) that produces gross income attributable to a foreign branch, including by reason of the sale of a disregarded entity or partnership interest. See proposed § 1.250(b)-1(c)(11). The result is that income from the sale of any such asset is not included in gross DEI. Finally, the proposed regulations define financial services income by reference to section 904(d)(2)(D) and proposed § 1.904-4(e)(1)(ii).

For purposes of calculating the foreign-derived ratio, FDDEI is the excess of gross FDDEI over deductions properly allocable to gross FDDEI. See proposed § 1.250(b)-1(c)(12). The proposed regulations define gross FDDEI as the portion of a corporation's gross DEI that is derived from all of its "FDDEI sales" and "FDDEI services" (collectively, "FDDEI transactions"). See proposed § 1.250(b)-1(c)(8), (9), (10), and (15). The determination of whether a sale of property or a provision of a service is a FDDEI sale or a FDDEI service, respectively, is made under the provisions of proposed §§ 1.250(b)-3 through 1.250(b)-6. See part III(B) through (F) of this Explanation of Provisions section. The portion of a corporation's gross DEI that is not gross FDDEI is referred to as gross non-FDDEI. See proposed § 1.250(b)-1(c)(16). Therefore, all income included in gross DEI is included in either gross FDDEI or gross non-FDDEI, and all income included in either gross FDDEI or gross non-FDDEI is included in gross DEI.

In the case of property produced or acquired for resale, gross income is generally determined by subtracting cost of goods sold from gross sales receipts. In determining the amount of gross income included in gross DEI or gross FDDEI, cost of goods sold is attributed to gross receipts with respect to gross DEI and gross FDDEI using any reasonable method. See proposed § 1.250(b)-1(d)(1). The proposed regulations clarify that cost of goods sold that is associated with activities undertaken in an earlier taxable year cannot be segregated into component costs and attributed disproportionately to amounts excluded from gross FDDEI or to amounts excluded from gross DEI. See id. This is similar to the clarification in proposed § 1.199-4(b)(2)(iii)(A) and is intended to preclude a method that attributes cost of goods sold of an inventory item to gross receipts other than gross receipts included in the computation of gross DEI or gross FDDEI if the gross receipts from the sale of that item are included in the computation of amounts included in the computation of gross DEI or gross FDDEI, respectively. See 80 FR 51978, 51990 (Aug. 27, 2015). The Treasury Department and the IRS request comments on whether there are alternative approaches for dealing with timing issues, and whether additional rules should be provided for attributing cost of goods sold in determining gross DEI and gross FDDEI. Cf. § 1.199-4(b)(2) through (6).

Section 250(b)(3)(A) defines DEI as the excess of a domestic corporation's gross income (excluding certain items) over "the deductions (including taxes) properly allocable to such gross income." FDDEI is defined as "any deduction eligible income" of the taxpayer generated through foreign-market sales and services. See section 250(b)(4). Therefore, a taxpayer's deductions that are "properly allocable" to gross DEI and gross FDDEI must be determined for purposes of calculating its DEI and FDDEI. The statute does not specify how deductions should be allocated for purposes of determining DEI and FDDEI. However, the rules set forth in §§ 1.861-8 through 1.861-14T and 1.861-17 apply for purposes of several other provisions in the Code which require the determination of taxable income from specific sources or activities, for example, for purposes of determining the foreign tax credit limitation under section 904 or qualified production activities income under former section 199. See generally §§ 1.199-4 and 1.861-8(f)(1). Accordingly, the proposed regulations provide that the rules set forth in §§ 1.861-8 through 1.861-14T and 1.861-17 apply for purposes of determining DEI and FDDEI. See proposed § 1.250(b)-1(d)(2)(i). In order to avoid circularity, in applying those rules for purposes of determining DEI and FDDEI, the section 250 deduction is not treated as giving rise to exempt income or assets. See proposed § 1.861-8(d)(2)(ii)(C)(4). Comments are requested on whether alternative approaches should be considered or additional rules are needed for purposes of allocating and apportioning a net operating loss deduction to gross DEI and gross FDDEI.

In certain circumstances, as a result of expense apportionment or attribution of cost of goods sold, a domestic corporation's FDDEI could exceed its DEI. For example, a domestic corporation could have $80x of DEI and $100x of FDDEI, with losses attributable to domestic market sales accounting for the $20x difference between DEI and FDDEI. However, it would be inconsistent with the statutory language to treat a domestic corporation as having a foreign-derived ratio in excess of one, and therefore FDII in excess of DII. In particular, section 250(b)(4) defines FDDEI as a subset of DEI, that is, "any deduction eligible income of such taxpayer which is derived in connection with" certain transactions. Therefore, the proposed regulations clarify that the foreign-derived ratio cannot exceed one. See proposed § 1.250(b)-1(c)(13).

3. Treatment of Partnerships

Section 250(a)(1) allows a deduction to a domestic corporation, but does not provide any rules for domestic corporations that are partners in a partnership. However, the conference report accompanying the Act ("Conference Report") suggests that Congress intended that a domestic corporate partner of a partnership receive the benefit of a section 250 deduction for its FDII and GILTI. See H. Rept. 115-466, at 623, fn. 1517 (2017) (Conf. Rep.) ("The Committee intends that the deduction allowed by new Code section 250 be treated as exempting the deducted income from tax. Thus, for example, the deduction for global intangible low-taxed income could give rise to an increase in a domestic corporate partner's basis in a domestic partnership under section 705(a)(1)(B).").

The proposed regulations give effect to this legislative intent by adopting an aggregate approach to partnerships for determining a domestic corporate partner's FDII attributable to the income and assets of a partnership. Specifically, the proposed regulations provide that a domestic corporate partner of a partnership takes into account its distributive share of a partnership's gross DEI, gross FDDEI, and deductions in order to calculate the partner's FDII. See proposed § 1.250(b)-1(e)(1). In addition, for purposes of determining a domestic corporate partner's DTIR, a domestic corporation's QBAI is increased by its share of the partnership's adjusted basis in partnership specified tangible property. See proposed § 1.250(b)-2(g).

Under the proposed regulations, the section 250 deduction is computed and allowed solely at the level of a domestic corporate partner. The Conference Report in footnote 1517 suggests that the section 250 deduction could give rise to an increase in a domestic corporate partner's basis in a domestic partnership under section 705(a)(1)(B) because some of the partnership's income may be treated as exempt income by reason of section

250. However, regardless of whether the deduction gives rise to exempt income in other contexts, because the section 250 deduction is computed and allowed solely at the level of a domestic corporate partner, the section 250 deduction does not exempt the deducted income from tax for purposes of applying section 705(a)(1)(B). As a result, a basis adjustment to a domestic corporate partner's interest in a domestic partnership is not appropriate to account for a section 250 deduction.

4. Treatment of Tax-Exempt Corporations

A domestic corporation that is subject to the unrelated business income tax under section 511 may claim a section 250 deduction. However, the proposed regulations clarify that such corporation's FDII for this purpose is determined only with respect to the corporation's items of income, gain, deduction, or loss, and adjusted bases in property, that are taken into account in computing its unrelated business taxable income. See proposed § 1.250(b)-1(g). The proposed regulations also clarify how a tax-exempt corporation subject to the unrelated business income tax under section 511 computes the dual use ratio with respect to property used in the production of gross DEI and income that is not gross DEI for purposes of determining its QBAI. See id.

5. Determination of QBAI

Section 250(b)(2)(B) provides that QBAI for purposes of section 250 is defined under section 951A(d), and is determined by substituting "deduction eligible income" for "tested income" and without regard to whether the corporation is a CFC. Accordingly, the determination of QBAI for purposes of FDII is similar to the determination of QBAI for purposes of GILTI. Compare proposed § 1.951A-3 with proposed § 1.250(b)-2. A domestic corporation's QBAI for FDII is equal to its aggregate average adjusted bases in specified tangible property, which is defined as tangible property used in the production of gross DEI. See proposed § 1.250(b)-2(b) and (c). The proposed regulations also provide rules for dual use property, calculating QBAI in a short taxable year, and calculating a domestic corporate partner's share of partnership QBAI. See proposed § 1.250(b)-2(d), (f), and (g).

In order to prevent the avoidance of the purposes of QBAI, the proposed regulations disregard certain transfers of specified tangible property by a domestic corporation to a related party where the corporation continues to use the property in production of gross DEI. See sections 250(c) and 951A(d)(4). Specifically, for purposes of calculating a domestic corporation's QBAI, the proposed regulations disregard a transfer of specified tangible property by the domestic corporation to a related party (whose QBAI would not be taken into account in calculating the corporation's DTIR) if, within a two-year period beginning one year before the transfer, the domestic corporation (or a related party whose QBAI would be taken into account in calculating the corporation's DTIR) leases the same or substantially similar property from a related party and such transfer and lease occur pursuant to a principal purpose of reducing the domestic corporation's DTIR. See proposed § 1.250(b)-2(h)(1) and (h)(4)(i) through (iv). A transfer and lease described in the preceding sentence is treated per se as occurring pursuant to a principal purpose of reducing a domestic corporation's DTIR if both the transfer and the lease occur within the same six-month period. See proposed § 1.250(b)-2(h)(3). If the anti-avoidance rule applies, the domestic corporation that transferred the property is treated as owning such property from the later of the beginning of the term of the lease or date of the transfer until the earlier of the end of the term of the lease or the end of the recovery period of the transferred property. See proposed § 1.250(b)-2(h)(1).

The anti-avoidance rule does not apply to a transfer to and lease from an unrelated party, unless the transfer to and lease from the unrelated party is pursuant to a structured arrangement. See proposed § 1.250(b)-2(h)(2). A structured arrangement exists only if either a reduction in the domestic corporation's DTIR is a material factor in the pricing of the arrangement with the transferee or, based on all the facts and circumstances, the reduction in the domestic corporation's DTIR is a principal purpose of the arrangement. See id. The proposed regulations provide a non-inclusive list of facts and circumstances indicating that a principal purpose of an arrangement is the reduction of DTIR. See proposed § 1.250(b)-2(h)(2)(ii)(A) through (D). The Treasury Department and the IRS welcome comments on alternative approaches to identifying a structured arrangement involving unrelated parties.

No inference is intended regarding the application of any other Code section or judicial doctrine that may apply to affect the determination of FDII and its components.

B. General Rules for FDDEI Transactions

1. Definitions of Sale, Foreign Person, and United States

Proposed § 1.250(b)-3 provides rules relevant to determining whether a sale of property is a FDDEI sale and whether a provision of a service is a FDDEI service.

Section 250(b)(5)(E) provides that for purposes of section 250(b), the term "sale" includes any lease, license, exchange, or other disposition. Accordingly, for purposes of determining whether a sale of property is a FDDEI sale, the proposed regulations define "sale" to include a lease, license, exchange, or other disposition of property, including a transfer of property resulting in gain or an income inclusion under section 367. See proposed § 1.250(b)-3(b)(7).

The proposed regulations define a foreign person as a person that is not a United States person, which includes a foreign government or international organization for purposes of the proposed regulations. See proposed § 1.250(b)-3(b)(2). A United States person ("U.S. person") has the same meaning as under section 7701(a)(30), except that an individual that is a bona fide resident of a U.S. territory within the meaning of section 937(a) is excluded. See proposed § 1.250(b)-3(b)(10). While corporations formed in U.S. territories are generally treated as foreign corporations, under section 7701(a)(30), U.S. persons include all U.S. citizens or residents, regardless of whether they reside in a U.S. territory. However, a bona fide resident of a U.S. territory is generally exempt from U.S. tax on income sourced in that territory. See sections 931(a), 932(c)(4), 933(1), and 935. Therefore, to prevent the disparate treatment of sales to entities in a U.S. territory (potentially qualifying as a FDDEI sale) and sales to individuals in a U.S. territory (not qualifying as a FDDEI sale), the proposed regulations exclude bona fide residents of a U.S. territory from the definition of U.S. person.

A partnership is generally a "person" for purposes of the Code. See section 7701(a)(1). Accordingly, in determining whether a sale of property to or by a partnership qualifies as a FDDEI sale, or the provision of a service to or by a partnership qualifies as a FDDEI service, the proposed regulations treat a partnership as a person. See proposed § 1.250(b)-3(g). Therefore, for example, a sale of property to a foreign partnership for a foreign use may constitute a FDDEI sale because such sale is to a foreign person, whereas a sale of property to a domestic partnership, even if for a foreign use, will not constitute a FDDEI sale because such sale is to a domestic person. The Treasury Department and the IRS request comments on whether there are circumstances where it would be appropriate to treat a partnership as an aggregate of its partners for purposes of determining whether a sale of property or a provision of a service to a partnership is a sale or service to a foreign person.

The proposed regulations provide that the term "United States" generally has the meaning described in section 7701(a)(9). See proposed § 1.250(b)-3(b)(9). However, with respect to mines, oil and gas wells, and other natural deposits, the term United States includes certain seabed and subsoil of submarine areas adjacent to the territorial waters of the United States, as described in section 638(1). See id.

2. Foreign Military Sales

The Treasury Department and the IRS recognize that the statute is unclear as to whether a sale of property or the provision of a service to the U.S. government for resale or on-service to a foreign government under the Arms Export Control Act of 1976, as amended (22 U.S.C. 2751 et seq.), may qualify for the section 250 deduction. In general, the Arms Export Control Act governs the export of certain sales and services to foreign governments. Under the Arms Export Control Act, a seller or service provider provides sales or services to the U.S. government that are for the ultimate benefit of a foreign government. The concern is that such sale or service to the U.S. government governed by the Arms Export Control Act is not a sale to a "person who is not a United States person" within the meaning of section 250(b)(4)(A) or a service to a "person not located within the United States" within the meaning of section 250(b)(4)(B), notwithstanding that such a sale or service is ultimately provided to the foreign government.

The proposed regulations provide that, for purposes of section 250, a sale of property or the provision of a service to the U.S. government under the Arms Export Control Act of 1976 is treated as a sale of property or provision of a service to a foreign government. See proposed § 1.250(b)-3(c). See part I(D)(3) of the Special Analyses section for additional discussion regarding the analysis for the adoption of this rule. As discussed in part III(B)(1) of this Explanation of Provisions section, a foreign government or international organization is a foreign person for purposes of section 250 and the proposed regulations. See proposed § 1.250(b)-3(b)(2). Therefore, a sale of property or provision of a service to the U.S. government under the Arms Export Control Act may qualify as a FDDEI transaction if the other requirements under proposed §§ 1.250(b)-3 through 1.250(b)-6 are satisfied. To the extent other requirements under proposed §§ 1.250(b)-3 through 1.250(b)-6 are not satisfied, a sale or service will not qualify as a FDDEI transaction regardless of whether such sale or service is pursuant to the Arms Export Control Act.

The Treasury Department and the IRS have not currently identified readily available documentation sufficient to demonstrate that a particular sale or service was made pursuant to the Arms Export Control Act. Comments are requested on whether final regulations should provide guidance on how taxpayers can demonstrate that a sale or service has been made pursuant to the Arms Export Control Act.

3. Knowledge and Reason to Know

As discussed in part III(C) of this Explanation of Provisions section, the proposed regulations provide that a sale of property qualifies as a FDDEI sale only if the seller or renderer does not know or have reason to know that the recipient is not a foreign person or that the property will not be for a foreign use. See proposed § 1.250(b)-4(c), (d), and (e). In addition, as discussed in part III(D) of this Explanation of Provisions section, the proposed regulations provide that the provision of a general service (as defined in proposed § 1.250(b)-5(c)(4)) qualifies as a FDDEI service only if the renderer of the service does not know or have reason to know that the recipient is located within the United States. See proposed § 1.250(b)-5(d)(1) and (e)(1). The terms "know" and "reason to know" are used throughout the Code and Treasury regulations. The Treasury Department and the IRS request comments regarding whether definitions of "know" and "reason to know" are necessary for purposes of the section 250 regulations.

4. Reliability of Documentation

In order for a transaction to constitute a FDDEI transaction, the proposed regulations prescribe different types of documentation that are required to be obtained for each type of transaction. For example, in the case of a sale of property, the seller must obtain documentation that establishes the recipient's status as a foreign person. See proposed § 1.250(b)-4(c)(2). See parts III(C) and III(D) of this Explanation of Provisions section for an explanation of the documentation requirements in these proposed regulations; see also part II of the Special Analyses section for a discussion of the Paperwork Reduction Act.

The proposed regulations provide that, for any documentation described in the proposed regulations to be relied upon, the seller or renderer must obtain the documentation by the FDII filing date, the documentation must be obtained no earlier than one year before the sale or service, and the seller or renderer must not know or have reason to know that the documentation is incorrect or unreliable. See proposed § 1.250(b)-3(d); see also proposed § 1.250(b)-3(b)(1) (defining the term "FDII filing date"). For this purpose, a seller or renderer has reason to know that documentation is unreliable or incorrect if its knowledge of all the relevant facts or statements contained in the documentation is such that a reasonably prudent person in the position of the seller or renderer would question the accuracy of the documentation. See proposed § 1.250(b)-3(d)(1).

The Treasury Department and the IRS welcome comments on the documentation requirements in the proposed regulations.

5. Transactions Consisting of Both Sales and Services

Under section 250(b)(4) and (5) and these proposed regulations, the criteria for establishing that a transaction is foreign-derived is different for sales and services. For example, a transaction with a U.S. person that is located outside of the United States may qualify as a FDDEI service, but cannot qualify as a FDDEI sale. Because a transaction might include elements of both a sale and a service, the proposed regulations clarify that a transaction is classified according to the overall predominant character of the transaction. See proposed § 1.250(b)-3(e). For example, a sale of equipment that includes incidental support services from the seller at no additional cost would be classified as a sale, and therefore the provisions of proposed § 1.250(b)-4 would apply to determine whether gross income from the transaction is included in gross FDDEI.

6. Special Rule for Certain Loss Transactions

A domestic corporation's FDDEI includes all gross income included in gross DEI that is derived from FDDEI sales and FDDEI services in a taxable year, reduced by the amount of deductions properly allocable to such income. See proposed § 1.250(b)-1(c)(12) and part III(A)(2) of this Explanation of Provisions section. In most cases, a FDDEI sale or FDDEI service will increase a domestic corporation's section 250 deduction, because the income from such sale or service will increase the corporation's FDDEI and thus its foreign-derived ratio. However, in some cases, a FDDEI sale or a FDDEI service could have the effect of reducing FDDEI and thus a domestic corporation's section 250 deduction for the year. This could happen where, for instance, the domestic corporation's cost of goods sold attributed to property sold in a FDDEI sale exceeds its gross receipts from the sale, or the expenses allocated to the gross income from a FDDEI sale or FDDEI service exceed the gross income arising from the sale or service. In such a case, absent a rule to the contrary, a domestic corporation could intentionally fail to satisfy the documentation requirements with respect to a transaction that would otherwise qualify as a FDDEI sale or FDDEI service in order to prevent the transaction from reducing its FDDEI and thereby its section 250 deduction.

Section 250(b) does not contemplate a transaction-by-transaction determination of FDII, but rather an aggregate calculation based on all gross income "which is derived in connection with" sales and services described in section 250(b)(4). Therefore, it would be inappropriate to permit taxpayers to elect to exclude losses related to sales to foreign persons for a foreign use and services to persons located outside the United States by merely failing the documentation requirements. Accordingly, the proposed regulations provide that if a seller or renderer knows or has reason to know that property is sold to a foreign person for a foreign use or a general service is provided to a person located outside the United States, but the seller or renderer does not satisfy the documentation requirements applicable to such sale or service, the sale of property or provision of a service is nonetheless deemed a FDDEI transaction if treating the sale or service as a FDDEI transaction would reduce a domestic corporation's FDDEI. See proposed § 1.250(b)-3(f).

The special loss transaction rule in proposed § 1.250(b)-3(f) does not apply to proximate services, property services, and transportation services, each of which is defined and discussed in part III(D)(3) through (5) of this Explanation of Provisions section, because the proposed regulations do not require documentation with respect to such services. Therefore, a proximate service, property service, or transportation service is a FDDEI service if it meets the applicable substantive requirements for a FDDEI service described in § 1.250(b)-5(f), (g), and (h), respectively.

C. FDDEI Sales

1. In General

Section 250(b)(4)(A) provides that FDDEI includes income from property the taxpayer sells to any person who is not a U.S. person, and which the taxpayer establishes to the satisfaction of the Secretary is for a foreign use. Accordingly, the proposed regulations define a FDDEI sale as a sale of property to a foreign person for a foreign use. See proposed § 1.250(b)-4(b).

2. Foreign Person

The proposed regulations provide that a recipient is treated as a foreign person only if the seller obtains documentation of the recipient's foreign status and does not know or have reason to know that the recipient is not a foreign person. See proposed § 1.250(b)-4(c)(1). The proposed regulations provide several types of permissible documentation for this purpose, such as a written statement by the recipient indicating that the recipient is a foreign person. See proposed § 1.250(b)-4(c)(2)(i). To alleviate the burden of documentation on small businesses and small transactions, the proposed regulations allow a seller that has less than $10,000,000 of gross receipts in the prior taxable year, or less than $5,000 in gross receipts from a single recipient during the current taxable year, to treat a recipient as a foreign person if the seller has a shipping address for the recipient that is outside the United States. See proposed § 1.250(b)-4(c)(2)(ii). The $10,000,000 and $5,000 thresholds were chosen based on the experience of the Treasury Department and the IRS and not based on any specific quantitative analysis. The Treasury Department and the IRS request comments regarding whether the $10,000,000 and $5,000 thresholds are appropriate and especially solicit comments that provide data, other evidence, and models that can enhance the rigor of the process by which such thresholds are determined.

3. Foreign Use

Under the proposed regulations, the rules applicable to the determination of whether a sale of property is for a foreign use depends on whether the property sold is "general property" or "intangible property." See proposed § 1.250(b)-4(d) and (e). The proposed regulations define general property as property other than intangible property, a security (as defined in section 475(c)(2)), or a commodity (as defined in section 475(e)(2)(B) through (D)). See proposed § 1.250(b)-3(b)(3). The proposed regulations define intangible property by cross-reference to section 367(d)(4). See proposed § 1.250(b)-3(b)(4).

The proposed regulations provide that a sale of a security (as defined in section 475(c)(2)) or a commodity (as defined in section 475(e)(2)(B) through (D)) is not a FDDEI sale because such financial instruments are not subject to "any use, consumption, or disposition" outside the United States within the meaning of section 250(b)(5)(A). See proposed § 1.250(b)-4(f).

The proposed regulations provide that a sale of property (whether general property or intangible property) is treated as for a foreign use only if the seller obtains documentation that the property is for a foreign use and does not know or have reason to know, as of the FDII filing date, that the property is not for a foreign use (or, in the case of intangible property, that the portion of the sale of the intangible property for which the seller establishes foreign use is not for a foreign use). See proposed § 1.250(b)-4(d)(1) and (e)(1). Accordingly, if, as of the FDII filing date, the seller does not know or have reason to know that either the documentation obtained with respect to the sale is not reliable or that the property is not for a foreign use within the meaning of § 1.250(b)-4(d)(2) or (e)(2), then the sale of the property is treated as for a foreign use under § 1.250(b)-4(d)(1) or (e)(1) even if, in fact, the sale of such property is not for a foreign use within the meaning of § 1.250(b)-4(d)(2) or (e)(2).

a. Foreign Use for General Property

The sale of general property is for a foreign use if either the property is not subject to domestic use within three years of delivery of the property or the property is subject to manufacture, assembly, or other processing outside the United States before any domestic use of the property. See proposed § 1.250(b)-4(d)(2)(i) and Conf. Rep. at 625, fn. 1522 ("If property is sold by a taxpayer to a person who is not a U.S. person, and after such sale the property is subject to manufacture, assembly, or other processing (including the incorporation of such property, as a component, into a second product by means of production, manufacture, or assembly) outside the United States by such person, then the property is for a foreign use."). Domestic use is defined as the use, consumption, or disposition of property within the United States, including manufacture, assembly, or other processing within the United States. See proposed § 1.250(b)-4(d)(2)(ii). Comments are requested on the supply chain implications of these rules.

General property is subject to manufacturing, assembly, or other processing only if it meets either of the following two tests: (1) there is a physical and material change to the property, or (2) the property is incorporated as a component into a second product. See proposed § 1.250(b)-4(d)(2)(iii)(A). The proposed regulations clarify that a physical and material change does not include "minor assembly, packaging, or labeling." See proposed § 1.250(b)-4(d)(2)(iii)(B). However, whether property has undergone a physical and material change (as opposed to minor assembly, packaging, or labeling) is determined based on all the relevant facts and circumstances. The Treasury Department and the IRS request comments regarding whether additional guidance should be provided for determining whether property has undergone a physical and material change.

General property is incorporated as a component into a second product only if the fair market value of the property when it is delivered to the recipient constitutes no more than 20 percent of the fair market value of the second product, determined when the second product is completed. See proposed § 1.250(b)-4(d)(2)(iii)(C). If the seller sells multiple items of property that are incorporated into the second product, an aggregation rule treats all of the property sold by the seller that is incorporated into the second product as a single item of property for purposes of determining whether the property constitutes more than 20 percent of the fair market value of the second product. See id.

In order to establish that general property is for a foreign use, the seller must generally obtain documentation with respect to the sale. See proposed § 1.250(b)-4(d)(3). Such documentation could include, for example, proof of shipment of the property to a foreign address. See proposed § 1.250(b)-4(d)(3)(i). However, in the case of certain small businesses and small transactions, the seller may rely on a foreign shipping address for the recipient instead of obtaining documentation. See proposed § 1.250(b)-4(d)(3)(ii).

In lieu of the general documentation requirements for determining foreign use for sales of general property, in the case of a sale of multiple items of general property, which because of their fungible nature cannot reasonably be specifically traced to the location of use ("fungible mass"), a seller may establish that some, but not all, of the property is for a foreign use through market research, including statistical sampling, economic modeling, and other similar methods. See proposed § 1.250(b)-4(d)(3)(iii). A de minimis rule applies to treat the entire fungible mass as for a foreign use if a seller obtains documentation establishing that 90 percent or more of the fungible mass is for a foreign use. See id. Conversely, no portion of the fungible mass is treated as for a foreign use if the seller does not obtain documentation establishing that 10 percent or more of the fungible mass is for a foreign use. Id.

A special rule applies for purposes of determining whether the sale of certain transportation property is for a foreign use, which takes into account the special nature of property used for international transportation. Specifically, the sale of aircraft, railroad rolling stock, vessel, motor vehicle, or similar property that provides a mode of transportation and is capable of traveling internationally is for a foreign use only if, during the three-year period from the date of delivery of the property, the property is located outside the United States more than 50 percent of the time and more than 50 percent of the miles traversed in the use of such property will be traversed outside the United States. See proposed § 1.250(b)-4(d)(2)(iv). The seller can establish that a sale of general property used for international transportation is for a foreign use through, for example, a written statement from the recipient that the property is anticipated to satisfy the test described in the preceding sentence. See proposed § 1.250(b)-4(d)(3)(i)(A).

b. Foreign Use for Intangible Property

As discussed in part III(B) of this Explanation of Provisions section, a sale includes a license and any transfer of property in which gain or income is recognized under section 367, including a transfer of intangible property subject to section 367(d). See proposed § 1.250(b)-3(b)(7). The proposed regulations provide that a sale of intangible property is for a foreign use to the extent revenue is earned from exploiting the intangible property outside the United States, the documentation requirements are satisfied, and the seller does not know or have reason to know that the portion of the sale of the intangible property for which the seller establishes foreign use is not for a foreign use. See proposed § 1.250(b)-4(e)(1). Unlike a sale of general property (other than a sale of a fungible mass), a seller may establish foreign use for a portion of the income from the sale of intangible property. For purposes of determining whether a sale of intangible property is for a foreign use, the location where revenue is earned is generally determined based on the location of end-user customers licensing the intangible property or purchasing products for which the intangible property was used in development, manufacture, sale, or distribution. See proposed § 1.250(b)-4(e)(2). This determination is generally made on an annual basis based on the actual revenue earned by the recipient. Id.

Special rules apply to lump sum sales because, in these cases, it may be difficult or impossible to know the location where revenue will be generated when the sale occurs. The determination of foreign use in these cases is made based on the net present value of revenue the seller would have reasonably expected to earn from the exploitation of the intangible property. See proposed § 1.250(b)-4(e)(2)(iii). For sales of rights to intangible property for use both within and outside the United States, the seller must establish the proportionate amount of revenue earned within and outside the United States from use of the intangible property to establish foreign use. The proposed regulations describe documentation that can be used to establish where revenue is earned from use of the intangible property. See proposed § 1.250(b)-4(e)(3)(i). For example, if a domestic corporation licenses to a foreign person the worldwide rights to market and sell an item protected by a copyright, the domestic corporation would need to obtain documentation, as provided in the proposed regulations, establishing where revenue is earned from sales of the copyright-protected item.

A seller may establish the extent to which a sale of intangible property for a lump sum is for a foreign use through documentation containing reasonable projections of the amount and location of revenue that the seller would have reasonably expected to earn from the use of intangible property. See proposed § 1.250(b)-4(e)(3)(iii). To be considered reasonable, the net present value must be consistent with the financial data and projections used by the seller to determine the sales price to the foreign person. See id. The same rule for documentation applies to a sale to a foreign person (other than a related party of the seller) for annual payments that are not contingent on revenue or profit unless the seller has access to reliable information to determine the actual revenue earned by the foreign unrelated party from the exploitation of the intangible property. See proposed § 1.250(b)-4(e)(3)(ii).

As discussed in part III(C)(3)(a) of this Explanation of Provisions section, a sale of general property is treated as for a foreign use if the property is subject to manufacturing, assembly, or other processing outside the United States. See proposed § 1.250(b)-4(d)(2)(i)(B). This rule is based on footnote 1522 of the Conference Report, which provides that "[i]f property is sold by a taxpayer to a person who is not a U.S. person, and after such sale the property is subject to manufacture, assembly, or other processing (including the incorporation of such property, as a component, into a second product by means of production, manufacture, or assembly) outside the United States by such person, then the property is for a foreign use." Intangible property is not "subject to" manufacture, assembly, or processing, and there is no other discussion in the Conference Report that indicates an intent to provide an analogous rule for intangible property otherwise used in the manufacturing process. However, comments are requested on whether a rule for intangible property similar to proposed § 1.250(b)-4(d)(2)(i)(B) is appropriate. Comments are also requested on what additional rules may be needed for determining the location of revenue generation from end-users and what types of documentation should be accepted to document the location of revenue generation with respect to intangible property.

D. FDDEI Services

1. In General

Section 250(b)(4)(B) provides that FDDEI includes income from services provided by a domestic corporation to any person, or with respect to property, not located within the United States. Section 250 does not prescribe rules for determining whether a person or property is "not located within the United States." Proposed § 1.250(b)-5 provides rules for determining whether a service is provided to a person, or with respect to property, located outside the United States.

Under the proposed regulations, whether a service is provided to a person, or with respect to property, located outside the United States, depends on the type of service provided and, in the case of a general service (defined below), the type of recipient of the service. The proposed regulations distinguish between services where the service provider (the "renderer") and the recipient are in physical proximity when the service is performed ("proximate services"), services with respect to tangible property ("property services"), services to transport people or property ("transportation services"), and all other services ("general services"). See proposed § 1.250(b)-5(b) and (c)(4) through (7). For purposes of determining whether a service constitutes a FDDEI service, the proposed regulations look to the location of the performance of the service for proximate services, the location of the property for property services, the origin and destination of transportation services, and the location of the recipient for general services. See proposed § 1.250(b)-5(d) through (h).

Each category of service described in § 1.250(b)-5 is mutually exclusive of each other category, and every possible service is described in a single category. Therefore, whether a service is a FDDEI service is determined under the rules relevant to one, and only one, category of service described in § 1.250(b)-5. For example, a general service that is provided to a recipient located within the United States is not a FDDEI service, even if the service is performed outside the United States, whereas a property service that is performed outside the United States is a FDDEI service, even if the recipient of the service is located within the United States. See parts III(D)(2) and (4) of this Explanation of Provisions section.

2. General Services to Persons Located Outside the United States

A general service is a service other than a proximate service, a property service, or a transportation service. See proposed § 1.250(b)-5(c)(4). General services is the residual category of services. Accordingly, a service that is not a property service, a transportation service, or a proximate service is analyzed as a general service.

For general services, the proposed regulations distinguish between services provided to "consumers" and services provided to "business recipients." A consumer is defined as an individual that purchases a service for personal consumption. See proposed § 1.250(b)-5(c)(3). A business recipient is defined as any recipient other than a consumer. See proposed § 1.250(b)-5(c)(2). In both cases, general services are treated as provided to a person located outside the United States if the renderer does not know or have reason to know that the consumer or business recipient is located within the United States and obtains appropriate documentation. See proposed § 1.250(b)-5(d)(1) and (e)(1).

a. General Services to Consumers

The provision of a general service to a consumer located outside the United States is a FDDEI service. See proposed §1.250(b)-5(b)(1). The proposed regulations provide that the consumer is located where a consumer resides when the service is provided. See proposed §1.250(b)-5(d)(2).

The proposed regulations require a domestic corporation to document the location of the consumer. See proposed §1.250(b)-5(d)(1) and (3). The proposed regulations provide several types of permissible documentation for this purpose, including a written statement by the consumer indicating the residence of the consumer when the service is provided. See proposed §1.250(b)-5(d)(3)(i). However, in the case of certain small businesses and small transactions, the renderer may rely on a foreign billing address for the consumer instead of obtaining documentation. See proposed §1.250(b)-5(d)(3)(ii).

b. General Services to Business Recipients

The provision of a general service to a business recipient located outside the United States is a FDDEI service. See proposed §1.250(b)-5(b)(2). Under the proposed regulations, all general services that are not provided to consumers are treated as services provided to business recipients, regardless of whether the recipient is engaged in a trade or business. See proposed §1.250(b)-5(c)(2).

The proposed regulations determine the location of a business recipient based on the location of the business recipient's operations, and the operations of any related party of the recipient, that receive a benefit (as defined in §1.482-9(l)(3)) from such service. See proposed §1.250(b)-5(e)(2) and (4). For purposes of this determination, the location of residence, incorporation, or formation of a business recipient is not relevant. For example, a general service that confers a benefit only on the U.S. operations of a foreign person will generally not qualify as a FDDEI service, whereas a service that confers a benefit only on the foreign operations of a U.S. person will generally qualify as a FDDEI service. For purposes of this rule, a business recipient is treated as having operations in any location where it maintains an office or other fixed place of business. See proposed §1.250(b)-5(e)(2)(ii).

The proposed regulations provide that a service is generally provided to a business recipient located outside the United States to the extent that the renderer's gross income from providing the service is allocated to the business recipient's operations outside the United States. See proposed §1.250(b)-5(e)(2)(i). To make this allocation, the renderer must first determine which of the business recipient's operations receive a benefit from the service. See proposed §1.250(b)-5(e)(2)(i)(A). Where the service confers a benefit on the operations of the business recipient in specific locations, gross income of the renderer is allocated based on the location of the operations in specific locations that receive the benefit. See id. Where a service confers a benefit on the recipient's business as a whole, or where reliable information about the particular portion of the operations that specifically receive a benefit from the service is unavailable, the proposed regulations provide that the service is deemed to confer a benefit on all of the business recipient's operations. See id. The renderer then must allocate its gross income from providing the service between the operations that receive a benefit from the service that are located within and outside the United States. See proposed §1.250(b)-5(e)(2)(i)(B). For this purpose, any reasonable method may be used, and the principles of §1.482-9(k) apply to determine whether a method is reasonable. See id. A reasonable method may include, for example, an allocation based on the renderer's time spent working with different offices of the business recipient or publicly available information about the business recipient's revenue from different markets. See id. The Treasury Department and the IRS request comments on this approach for determining the location of a business recipient that operates both within and outside of the United States.

The proposed regulations also require a domestic corporation to obtain documentation sufficient to establish the location of a business recipient's operations that benefit from the service. See proposed §1.250(b)-5(e)(1) and (3). A domestic corporation may obtain a statement from the recipient specifying the location of the operations that will benefit from the service or include a similar statement in a binding contract. See proposed §1.250(b)-5(e)(3)(i)(A) and (B). A domestic corporation may also establish the location of the business recipient using information provided in the ordinary course of the provision of a service or publicly available information. See proposed §1.250(b)-5(e)(3)(i)(C) and (D). However, in the case of certain small businesses and small transactions, the renderer may rely on a foreign billing address for the business recipient instead of obtaining documentation. See proposed §1.250(b)-5(e)(3)(ii).

3. Proximate Services

The provision of a proximate service to a recipient located outside the United States is a FDDEI service. See proposed §1.250(b)-5(b)(3). A proximate service is defined as a service, other than a property service or a transportation service, substantially all of which is performed in the physical presence of the recipient or, in the case of a business recipient, its employees. See proposed §1.250(b)-5(c)(6). For example, a training, consulting, or auditing service that is performed on-site would generally constitute a proximate service. Substantially all of a service is performed in the physical presence of the recipient or its employees if the renderer spends more than 80 percent of the time providing the service in the physical presence of the recipient or its employees. See proposed §1.250(b)-5(c)(6). The recipient of a proximate service is treated as located where the service is performed. See proposed §1.250(b)-5(f). If a proximate service is performed partly within and partly outside the United States, a proportionate amount of the service is treated as rendered to a person located outside the United States corresponding to the portion of time spent providing the proximate service outside the United States. See id.

4. Property Services

The provision of a property service with respect to tangible property located outside the United States is a FDDEI service. See proposed §1.250(b)-5(b)(4). A property service is defined as a service, other than a transportation service, provided with respect to tangible property, but only if substantially all of the service is performed at the location of the property and results in physical manipulation of the property such as through assembly, maintenance, or repair. See proposed §1.250(b)-5(c)(5). The proposed regulations provide that substantially all of a service is performed at the location of property if the renderer spends more than 80 percent of the time providing the service at or near the location of the property. See id. A property service is a FDDEI service only if the tangible property with respect to which the service is performed is located outside the United States for the duration of the period of performance. See proposed §1.250(b)-5(g). The Treasury Department and the IRS request comments on whether to consider an exception for property that is located in the United States temporarily solely for purposes of the performance of certain services, such as maintenance or repairs. As discussed in part III(E) of this Explanation of Provisions section, a property service may qualify as a FDDEI service even if it is performed for a person located within the United States.

Other services that relate to property but may not necessarily be provided in close proximity to tangible property or do not result in the physical manipulation of such property such as through assembly, maintenance, or repair may be subject to the rules for proximate services, transportation services, or general services. For example, an architectural or engineering service that is not performed in physical proximity to the property or the recipient will be evaluated as a general service even if the service relates to property located outside the United States, and thus whether such a service is a FDDEI service will be determined based on the location of the recipient rather than the location of the property.

5. Transportation Services

The provision of a transportation service to a recipient, or with respect to property, located outside the United States is a FDDEI service. See proposed §1.250(b)-5(b)(5). A transportation service is defined as a service to transport a person or property using any mode of transportation (such as an airplane). See proposed §1.250(b)-5(c)(7).

Basing the location of a transportation service on the residence of the recipient of the transportation service could provide inconsistent results with respect to similar services. Similarly, providing different rules for the transportation of a person or property could provide inconsistent results with respect to similar services. Therefore, the proposed regulations provide that whether a "transportation service" is provided to a recipient, or with respect to property, located outside the United States is determined based on the origin and destination of the service. See proposed § 1.250(b)-5(h). If both the origin and destination of a transportation service are outside of the United States, then the service is a FDDEI service. See id. If either the origin or the destination of the transportation service is outside of the United States, but not both, then 50 percent of the service is a FDDEI service and thus 50 percent of the gross income from the provision of the service is included in the renderer's gross FDDEI. See id.

E. Domestic Intermediary Rules

Section 250(b)(5)(B) describes special rules for "domestic intermediaries" (the "domestic intermediary rules"). Section 250(b)(5)(B)(i) provides that if a seller sells property to another person (other than a related party) for further manufacture or other modification within the United States, the property is not treated as sold for a foreign use even if such other person subsequently uses such property for a foreign use. Section 250(b)(5)(B)(ii) provides that services provided to a person (other than a related party) located within the United States are not treated as services described in section 250(b)(4)(B) even if such other person uses such services in providing services that are described in section 250(b)(4)(B).

The proposed regulations do not contain specific rules corresponding to the domestic intermediary rules because those rules are encompassed within the general rules relating to FDDEI sales and FDDEI services in the proposed regulations. With respect to sales of property, the proposed regulations provide that general property is not for a foreign use if, before being subject to manufacture, assembly, or other processing outside the United States, the property is subject to a domestic use. See proposed § 1.250(b)-4(d)(2)(i). For this purpose, domestic use includes manufacture, assembly, or other processing within the United States. See proposed § 1.250(b)-4(d)(2)(ii)(B). In addition, a sale of property to a U.S. person cannot qualify as a FDDEI sale under any circumstance. See section 250(b)(4)(A) and proposed § 1.250(b)-4(b). Therefore, a sale of property to a foreign person for further manufacture in the United States or to a U.S. person does not qualify for a FDDEI sale, regardless of the ultimate use of the property by the recipient.

With respect to the provision of services, the proposed regulations provide that a service is a FDDEI service only if the recipient of the service, or the property to which the service relates, is located outside the United States. See proposed § 1.250(b)-5(b)(1) through (5). Therefore, a service provided to a person, or with respect to property, located within the United States is not a FDDEI service, regardless of the ultimate use of the service by the recipient.

Section 250(b)(5)(B)(ii) could be read literally to provide that a FDDEI service includes only services provided to a person not located within the United States, in which case a service provided "with respect to property located outside the United States" would not qualify as a FDDEI service if the recipient of such service was located within the United States. As discussed in part III(D) of this Explanation of Provisions section, consistent with the general rule of section 250(b)(4)(B), the proposed regulations clarify that a service qualifies as a FDDEI service if it is provided either to a person located outside the United States or with respect to property located outside the United States. The Treasury Department and the IRS have determined that an interpretation of section 250(b)(5)(B)(ii) that effectively eliminates the disjunctive test of section 250(b)(4)(B) would not be reasonable. Therefore, under the proposed regulations, whether a service that is treated as with respect to property — a property service or a transportation service — is a FDDEI service is determined solely by reference to the location of the property, and not the location of the recipient. See proposed § 1.250(b)-5(g) and (h).

Finally, the parenthetical references to related parties in the domestic intermediary rules could be read to imply the existence of an exception for further manufacture or modification in the United States by a related party or a service provided to a related party located within the United States. However, the general rules of section 250(b)(4)(A) and (B) do not authorize such exceptions, and the domestic intermediary rules do not purport to expand these general rules, but rather to limit the transactions that qualify under them. Therefore, with respect to related party domestic intermediaries, the proposed regulations do not provide an exception to the general rule that property must be sold to a foreign person to qualify as a FDDEI sale or that a service must be provided to a person located outside the United States to qualify as a FDDEI service. Cf. part V of this Explanation of Provisions section regarding the applicability of the attribute redetermination rule of § 1.1502-13(c)(1)(i) to the determination of FDDEI of a member of a consolidated group.

F. Related Party Transactions

A sale of property or a provision of a service may qualify as a FDDEI transaction, regardless of whether the recipient of such service is a related party of the seller or renderer. However, in the case of a sale of general property or a provision of a general service to a related party, section 250(b)(5)(C) and proposed § 1.250(b)-6 provide additional requirements that must be satisfied for the transaction to qualify as a FDDEI sale or FDDEI service. These requirements must be satisfied in addition to the general requirements that apply to such sales and services as provided in proposed §§ 1.250(b)-3 through 1.250(b)-5.

The proposed regulations define a related party with respect to any person as any member of a modified affiliated group that includes such person. Proposed § 1.250(b)-1(c)(19). A modified affiliated group is defined as an affiliated group as provided in section 1504(a) by substituting "more than 50 percent" for "at least 80 percent" each place it appears, and without regard to section 1504(b)(2) and (3). Proposed § 1.250(b)-1(c)(17)(i). A modified affiliated group also includes any person other than a corporation that is controlled by one or more members of a modified affiliated group or that controls such a member. Proposed § 1.250(b)-1(c)(17)(ii). For this purpose, "control" is defined as provided in section 954(d)(3), meaning direct, indirect, or constructive ownership under section 958 of more than 50 percent of the value of the beneficial interests in such person. Proposed § 1.250(b)-1(c)(17)(iii).

1. Related Party Sales

Section 250(b)(5)(C)(i) provides that property sold to a related party that is not a U.S. person "shall not be treated as for a foreign use unless (I) such property is ultimately sold by a related party, or used by a related party in connection with property which is sold or the provision of services, to another person who is an unrelated party who is not a United States person, and (II) the taxpayer establishes to the satisfaction of the Secretary that such property is for a foreign use." Accordingly, the proposed regulations provide that a sale of general property to a foreign related party (a "related party sale") qualifies as a FDDEI sale only if certain additional requirements described in § 1.250(b)-6(c)(1)(i) or (ii) are satisfied. See proposed § 1.250(b)-6(c)(1).

If a foreign related party resells the purchased property (such as where the foreign related party is a distributor or a manufacturer of a product that incorporates the purchased property as a component), the sale to the foreign related party qualifies as a FDDEI sale only if an unrelated party transaction with respect to such sale occurs and the unrelated party transaction is a FDDEI sale. An unrelated party transaction is generally a transaction between the foreign related party and an unrelated foreign person in which the property purchased by the foreign related party is sold or used. See proposed § 1.250(b)-6(b)(5). For purposes of this rule, whether property is a component of another property that is subsequently sold in an unrelated party transaction is determined without regard to the rule defining a "component" for purposes of determining whether general property is subject to manufacturing, assembly, or other processing, as described in part III(C)(3)(a) of this Explanation of Provisions section. The unrelated party sale generally must occur on or before the FDII filing date; otherwise the gross income from the related party sale is included in the domestic corporation's gross DEI for the taxable year of the related party sale, but is not included in its gross FDDEI. See proposed

§1.250(b)-6(c)(1)(i). However, if an unrelated party transaction occurs after the FDII filing date but within the period of limitations provided by section 6511, the proposed regulations provide that the domestic corporation may file an amended return for the taxable year in which the related party sale occurred claiming the related party sale as a FDDEI sale for purposes of determining the taxpayer's foreign-derived intangible income for that taxable year, provided that the sale otherwise meets the requirements in proposed §1.250(b)-6(c)(1)(i). See id. The Treasury Department and the IRS welcome comments on whether alternatives should be considered in lieu of requiring the filing of an amended return.

For transactions other than the resale of purchased property, such as where the foreign related party uses the purchased property to produce other property that is sold in unrelated party transactions, or where the foreign related party uses the property in the provision of a service in an unrelated party transaction, the sale of property does not qualify as a FDDEI sale unless, as of the FDII filing date, the seller reasonably expects that more than 80 percent of the revenue earned by the foreign related party from the use of the property in all transactions will be earned from unrelated party transactions that are FDDEI transactions (determined without regard to the documentation requirements in §1.250(b)-4 or §1.250(b)-5). See proposed §1.250(b)-6(c)(1)(ii).

The rules applicable to related party sales apply only to determine whether sales of general property qualify as a FDDEI sale. See proposed §1.250(b)-6(c)(1). Sales of intangible property, whether to a related or an unrelated party, are for a foreign use only to the extent that the intangible property generated revenue from exploitation outside the United States. See proposed §1.250(b)-4(e)(2) and part III(C)(3)(b) of this Explanation of Provisions section. Thus, additional rules with respect to related party sales of intangible property are unnecessary to ensure that such sales are ultimately for a foreign use.

2. Related Party Services

Section 250(b)(5)(C)(ii) provides that a service provided to a related party not located in the United States "shall not be treated [as a FDDEI service] unless the taxpayer establishe[s] to the satisfaction of the Secretary that such service is not substantially similar to services provided by such related party to persons located within the United States." Accordingly, the proposed regulations generally provide that a provision of a general service to a business recipient that is a related party qualifies as a FDDEI service only if the service is not substantially similar to a service provided by the related party to persons located within the United States. See proposed §1.250(b)-6(d)(1).

Absent section 250(b)(5)(C)(ii) and proposed §1.250(b)-6(d)(1) (the "related party services rule"), a domestic corporation could generate gross FDDEI from the provision of services that primarily benefit persons within the United States by using a related party located outside the United States as a conduit. The related party services rule prevents taxpayers from claiming gross FDDEI derived from such "round tripping" arrangements. In contrast, proximate services, property services, and transportation services by their nature present minimal risk for "round tripping," because the location of the recipient or property, as applicable, for purposes of such services is generally determined based on the place of performance. See proposed §1.250(b)-5(f), (g), and (h), and parts III(D)(3), (4), and (5) of this Explanation of Provisions section. Further, a general service provided to a consumer that is a related party cannot be substantially similar to a service provided by a consumer to a person located within the United States, because a consumer, by definition, is an individual that purchases the service for personal use. See proposed §1.250(b)-5(c)(3). Accordingly, the proposed regulations provide that the related party services rule applies only to determine whether a general service provided to a business recipient that is a related party is a FDDEI service. See proposed §1.250(b)-6(d)(1).

A service provided by a renderer to a related party is "substantially similar" to a service provided by the related party to a person located within the United States if the renderer's service (or "related party service") is used by the related party to provide a service to a person located within the United States and either the "benefit test" of proposed §1.250(b)-6(d)(2)(i) or the "price test" of proposed §1.250(b)-6(d)(2)(ii) is satisfied. The rules to determine the location of a recipient of a service provided by a related party are generally the same as the rules for determining the location of a recipient of a service provided by the renderer.

The benefit test is satisfied if 60 percent or more of the benefits conferred by the related party service are to persons located within the United States. See proposed §1.250(b)-6(d)(2)(i). For this purpose, the term "benefit" has the meaning provided in §1.482-9(l)(3). See proposed §1.250(b)-5(c)(1). Therefore, a related party service provides a benefit to a customer of the related party if it provides "a reasonably identifiable increment of economic or commercial value" to the customer, rather than an indirect or remote benefit. See §1.482-9(l)(3)(i) and (ii). Because the benefit test compares the benefits from the service provided to persons located in the United States to the total benefits from the service provided by the renderer (rather than to the total benefits of the service provided by the related party), a service provided to a related party is "substantially similar" to a service provided by the related party to persons located within the United States if 60 percent or more of the benefits of the service are conferred on persons located within the United States, even if the related party adds significant value to the service through, for instance, bundling the related party service with other high value services.

Under the price test, a service provided by a renderer to a related party is "substantially similar" to a service provided by the related party to a person located within the United States if the renderer's service is used by the related party to provide a service to a person located within the United States and 60 percent or more of the price that persons located within the United States pay for the service provided by the related party is attributable to the renderer's service. See proposed §1.250(b)-6(d)(2)(ii). Therefore, the price test compares the value of the service that is provided by the renderer to the related party to the value of the service that is provided by the related party to its customers. Consequently, a related party service that is not treated as substantially similar to a service provided by the related party to persons located in the United States under the benefit test, because more than 40 percent of the benefits from the service are conferred to persons located outside the United States, is nonetheless treated as "substantially similar" under the price test if the related party service accounts for 60 percent or more of the total price that is charged to customers located within the United States.

If a related party service is treated as substantially similar to a service provided by the related party to a person located within the United States solely by reason of the price test, the general rule that wholly disqualifies the related party service as a FDDEI service does not apply. Rather, in such case, a portion of the gross income from the related party service will be treated as a FDDEI service corresponding to the ratio of benefits conferred by the related party service to persons not located within the United States to the sum of all benefits conferred by the related party service. See proposed §1.250(b)-6(d)(1).

IV. *Section 250 Deduction for Individuals Making a Section 962 Election*

As discussed in part II of this Explanation of Provisions section, the section 250 deduction for FDII and GILTI is available only to domestic corporations. However, section 962(a)(1) provides that an individual that is a U.S. shareholder may generally elect to be taxed on amounts included in the individual's gross income under section 951(a) in "an amount equal to the tax that would be imposed under section 11 if such amounts were received by a domestic corporation." GILTI is treated as an amount included under section 951(a) for purposes of section 962. See section 951A(f)(1)(A) and proposed §1.951A-6(b)(1). A section 962 election can be made by an individual U.S. shareholder who is considered, by reason of section 958(b), to own stock of a foreign corporation owned (within the meaning of section 958(a)) by a domestic pass-through entity, including a partnership or an S corporation. See §1.962-2(a).

Congress enacted section 962 to ensure that individuals' tax burdens with respect to undistributed foreign earnings of their CFCs "will be no heavier than they would have been had they invested in an American corporation doing business abroad." S. Rept. 1881, 1962-3 C.B. 784, at 798. Existing §1.962-1(b)(1)(i) provides that a deduction of a U.S. shareholder does not reduce the amount included in gross income under section 951(a) for purposes of computing the amount of tax that would be imposed under section 11. However, allowing a section 250 deduction with respect to

GILTI of an individual (including an individual that is a shareholder of an S corporation or a partner in a partnership) that makes an election under section 962 is consistent with the purpose of that provision of ensuring that such individual's tax burden with respect to its CFC's undistributed foreign earnings is no greater than if the individual owned such CFC through a domestic corporation. Accordingly, the proposed regulations provide that, for purposes of section 962, "taxable income" as used in section 11 of an electing individual is reduced by the portion of the section 250 deduction that would be allowed to a domestic corporation with respect to the individual's GILTI and the section 78 gross-up attributable to the shareholder's GILTI. See proposed § 1.962-1(b)(1)(i)(B)(3).

V. *Application of Section 250 to Consolidated Groups*

As discussed in the Background section of this preamble, section 250 provides a domestic corporation a deduction for its FDII, GILTI, and the section 78 gross-up attributable to its GILTI. The section 250 deduction is available to a member of a consolidated group ("member") in the same manner as the deduction is available to any domestic corporation. However, a computation of a member's section 250 deduction based solely on its items of income and QBAI may not result in a clear reflection of the consolidated group's income tax liability. For example, a consolidated group could segregate all of its QBAI in one member, thereby decreasing the DTIR of other members relative to the consolidated group's DTIR if determined at a group level. Alternatively, a strict, separate-entity application of section 250 could inappropriately decrease a consolidated group's aggregate amount of deduction for its FDII, for instance, because one member's DII (which is the excess of DEI over DTIR) would not be taken into account in calculating the FDII of another member that has FDDEI in excess of its DEI.

Based on the foregoing, the proposed regulations provide that a member's section 250 deduction is determined by reference to the relevant items of all members of the same consolidated group. Consistent with the authority provided by section 1502, the proposed regulations ensure that the aggregate amount of section 250 deductions allowed to members appropriately reflects the income, expenses, gains, losses, and property of all members. Definitions in proposed § 1.1502-50(f) result in the aggregation of the DEI, FDDEI, DTIR, and GILTI of all members. These aggregate numbers and the consolidated group's consolidated taxable income are then used to calculate an overall deduction amount for the group. Proposed § 1.1502-50(b) then allocates this overall deduction amount among the members on the basis of their respective contributions to the consolidated group's aggregate amount of FDDEI and the consolidated group's aggregate amount of GILTI.

The proposed regulations also address two issues relating to intercompany transactions. First, the proposed regulations add an example to § 1.1502-13 demonstrating the applicability of the attribute redetermination rule of § 1.1502-13(c)(1)(i) to the determination of FDDEI. This example applies the intercompany transaction rules to clearly reflect consolidated taxable income. It does not indicate a change in the law. In this example, the attribute redetermination rule applies to gross DEI and gross FDDEI, which are attributes of an intercompany or corresponding item. The Treasury Department and the IRS were concerned that applying § 1.1502-13(c) to DEI and FDDEI directly could result in circular computations due to the apportionment of certain expenses on a gross income basis. In addition, the example illustrates the applicability of the attribute redetermination rule in the context of an intercompany loss. In such circumstances, the application of the allocation and apportionment rules of § § 1.861-8 through 1.861-14T and 1.861-17 may be modified in order to achieve the same overall result within the consolidated group that would occur if the members were divisions of a single corporation.

Second, the proposed regulations provide that, for purposes of determining a member's QBAI, the basis of specified tangible property will not be affected by an intercompany transaction. See proposed § 1.1502-50(c)(1). Accordingly, an intercompany transaction cannot result in the increase or decrease of a consolidated group's aggregate amount of DTIR or, in turn, aggregate amount of deduction.

VI. *Reporting Requirements*

To claim a deduction under section 250 by reason of having FDII, a taxpayer must calculate its deemed intangible income, deduction eligible income, and foreign-derived deduction eligible income. None of these terms are used in other provisions of the Code, and thus pre-existing forms do not collect data relevant to determining these amounts. In addition, when calculating its deduction under section 250, a taxpayer must determine the application of the taxable income limitation of section 250(a)(2). In order to effectively administer and enforce section 250, the proposed regulations require the collection of relevant information on new or existing forms.

A domestic corporation or an individual making an election under section 962 that claims a deduction under section 250 for a taxable year must make an annual return on Form 8993, "Section 250 Deduction for Foreign-Derived Intangible Income (FDII) and Global Intangible Low-Taxed Income (GILTI)" (or any successor form) for such year, providing the information required by the form. See proposed § 1.250(a)-1(d).

Certain related party transactions are reported on various information returns under sections 6038 and 6038A. Under section 6038(a)(1), U.S. persons that control foreign business entities ("controlling U.S. persons") must report certain information with respect to those entities, which includes information listed in section 6038(a)(1)(A) through (E), as well as information that "the Secretary determines to be appropriate to carry out the provisions of this title." This information is reported on Form 5471, "Information Return of U.S. Persons With Respect To Certain Foreign Corporations," or Form 8865, "Return of U.S. Persons With Respect to Certain Foreign Partnerships," as applicable. Section 6038A requires 25-percent foreign-owned domestic corporations ("reporting corporations") to file certain information returns with respect to those corporations, including information related to transactions between the reporting corporation and each foreign person which is a related party to the reporting corporation. This information is reported on Form 5472, "Information Return of a 25% Foreign-Owned U.S. Corporation or a Foreign Corporation Engaged in a U.S. Trade or Business." In order to effectively administer and enforce section 250, the proposed regulations provide that controlling U.S. persons or reporting corporations, as described above, that claim a deduction under section 250 determined by reference to FDII with respect to amounts reported on Form 5471, 5472, or 8865 must report certain information relating to transactions with foreign business entities or related parties in accordance with sections 6038 and 6038A. See proposed § § 1.6038-2(f)(15), 1.6038-3(g)(4), and 1.6038A-2(b)(5)(iv).

Certain partnerships and their partners also have reporting requirements under sections 6031 and 6038 with respect to partnership income. A domestic partnership is generally required to file an annual information return (Form 1065, "U.S. Return of Partnership Income") and provide information to its partners on Schedule K-1 (Form 1065), "Partner's Share of Income, Deductions, Credits, etc.," with respect to each partner's distributive share of partnership items and other information. See section 6031 and § 1.6031(b)-1T. The proposed regulations provide that a partnership that has one or more direct or indirect partners that are domestic corporations and that is required to file a return under section 6031 must furnish on Schedule K-1 (Form 1065) the partner's share of the partnership's gross DEI, gross FDDEI, deductions that are definitely related to the partnership's gross DEI and gross FDDEI, and partnership QBAI for each taxable year in which the partnership has gross DEI, gross FDDEI, or partnership specified tangible property. See proposed § 1.250(b)-1(e)(2). Although a foreign partnership that does not have income effectively connected with a trade or business within the United States or U.S. source income is not required to file Form 1065, a U.S. person who owns a ten-percent interest or a fifty-percent interest of a foreign partnership controlled by U.S. persons is required to report certain information under section 6038. Similar to the requirements for partnership reporting on Form 1065, the proposed regulations require controlling ten-percent partners and controlling fifty-percent partners (as defined in § 1.6038-3(a)(1) and (2)) of certain foreign partnerships controlled by U.S. persons to report on Schedule K-1 (Form 8865), "Partner's Share of Income, Deductions, Credits, etc.," the partner's share of the partnership's gross DEI, gross FDDEI, deductions that are definitely related to the partnership's gross DEI and gross FDDEI, and partnership QBAI. See proposed § 1.6038-3(g)(4).

VII. *Applicability Dates*

Proposed §§ 1.250(a)-1 through 1.250(b)-6 are proposed to apply to taxable years ending on or after March 4, 2019. See section 7805(b)(1)(B). However, the Treasury Department and the IRS recognize that these rules may apply to transactions that have occurred before the filing of these proposed regulations and that taxpayers may not be able to obtain the documentation required for transactions that have already been completed. Accordingly, for taxable years beginning on or before March 4, 2019, taxpayers may use any reasonable documentation maintained in the ordinary course of the taxpayer's business that establishes that a recipient is a foreign person, property is for a foreign use (within the meaning of proposed § 1.250(b)-4(d) and (e)), or a recipient of a general service is located outside the United States (within the meaning of proposed § 1.250(b)-5(d)(2) and (e)(2)), as applicable, in lieu of the documentation required in proposed §§ 1.250(b)-4(c)(2), (d)(3), and (e)(3) and 1.250(b)-5(d)(3) and (e)(3), provided that such documentation meets the reliability requirements described in proposed § 1.250(b)-3(d). Reasonable documentation includes, but is not limited to, documents described in or similar to the documents described in proposed §§ 1.250(b)-4(c)(2), (d)(3), and (e)(3) and 1.250(b)-5(d)(3) and (e)(3). For this purpose, reasonable documentation also includes the documentation described in the special rules for small businesses and small transactions in proposed §§ 1.250(b)-4(c)(2)(ii) and (d)(3)(ii) and 1.250(b)-5(d)(3)(ii) and (e)(3)(ii), even if the taxpayer would not otherwise qualify for the special rules. The Treasury Department and the IRS welcome comments on this special applicability date rule.

Proposed § 1.962-1(b)(1)(i)(B)(3), which allows individuals making an election under section 962 to take into account the section 250 deduction, is proposed to apply to taxable years of a foreign corporation ending on or after March 4, 2019, and with respect to a U.S. person, for the taxable year in which or with which such taxable year of the foreign corporations ends. See id. Taxpayers may rely on proposed §§ 1.250(a)-1 through 1.250(b)-6 and § 1.962-1(b)(1)(i)(B)(3) for taxable years ending before March 4, 2019.

Proposed § 1.1502-50 is proposed to apply to consolidated return years ending on or after the date of publication of the Treasury decision adopting these rules as final regulations in the **Federal Register**. See sections 1503(a) and 7805(b)(1)(A). Taxpayers may rely on proposed § 1.1502-50 for taxable years ending before the date of publication of the Treasury decision adopting these rules as final regulations in the **Federal Register**.

Proposed §§ 1.6038-2(f)(15) and 1.6038A-2(b)(5)(iv) are proposed to apply with respect to information for annual accounting periods beginning on or after March 4, 2019. See sections 6038(a)(3) and 7805(b)(1)(B). Proposed § 1.6038-3(g)(4) is proposed to apply to taxable years of a foreign partnership beginning on or after March 4, 2019. See section 7805(b)(1)(B).

Special Analyses

I. *Regulatory Planning and Review — Economic Analysis*

Executive Orders 13563 and 12866 direct agencies to assess costs and benefits of available regulatory alternatives and, if regulation is necessary, to select regulatory approaches that maximize net benefits (including potential economic, environmental, public health and safety effects, distributive impacts, and equity). Executive Order 13563 emphasizes the importance of quantifying both costs and benefits, of reducing costs, of harmonizing rules, and of promoting flexibility.

These proposed regulations have been designated as economically significant by the Office of Management and Budget's Office of Information and Regulatory Affairs (OIRA) and subject to review under Executive Order 12866 pursuant to the Memorandum of Agreement (April 11, 2018) between the Treasury Department and the Office of Management and Budget regarding review of tax regulations.

A. Background

As described in part I of the Explanation of Provisions section, the section 250 deduction is an important component of the changes to the U.S. international tax system included in the Act. The purpose of the section 250 deduction is to minimize the role that U.S. tax considerations play in a domestic corporation's decision whether to service foreign markets directly or through a controlled foreign corporation ("CFC"). See Senate Explanation, at 370 ("[O]ffering similar, preferential rates for intangible income derived from serving foreign markets, whether through U.S.-based operations or through CFCs, reduces or eliminates the tax incentive to locate or move intangible income abroad, thereby limiting one margin where the Code distorts business investment decisions."). Further, the section 250 deduction protects the U.S. tax base against base erosion incentives created by the new participation exemption system established under section 245A, discussed in part I of the Explanation of Provisions section. At the most basic level, the section 250 deduction is allowed to a domestic corporation with respect to its intangible income derived from foreign markets, resulting in a lower effective rate of U.S. tax on its global intangible low-taxed income ("GILTI") and foreign-derived intangible income ("FDII").

The Act defines a corporation's FDII as the portion of its return in excess of a return on tangible assets that is derived from serving foreign markets, while it defines a corporation's GILTI as the portion of its return in excess of a return on tangible assets that is derived through its foreign affiliates. FDII and GILTI are calculated through formulas set out in sections 250 and 951A, respectively. For taxable years between 2018 and 2026, section 250 generally allows a deduction equal to the sum of 37.5 percent of the corporation's FDII plus 50 percent of its GILTI (thereafter, these deductions are reduced to 21.875 percent and 37.5 percent, respectively). These deduction rates produce comparable tax rates on income earned from serving foreign markets, regardless of where such income is earned. Different percentages are required by the Act to achieve approximate parity, given that the 80 percent limitation on foreign tax credits in section 960(d) results in additional U.S. tax.[2] More specifically, the Act defines a domestic corporation's FDII as its deemed intangible income ("DII") multiplied by the percentage of its deduction eligible income ("DEI") that is foreign-derived deduction eligible income ("FDDEI"). The Act defines DEI as the excess of the corporation's gross income (with certain exclusions[3]) over deductions (including taxes) properly allocable to the income. The Act defines DII as the excess (if any) of its DEI over 10 percent of its qualified business asset investment ("QBAI"), or tangible asset base. The Act defines FDDEI as DEI derived from sales of property to foreign persons for foreign use and from the provision of services to persons, or with respect to property, located outside the United States. Finally, if the sum of a corporation's FDII and GILTI exceeds its taxable income (determined without regard to section 250), then the Act requires that the amount of FDII and GILTI for which a deduction is allowed is reduced pro rata by the excess. While the Act provides the framework for determining a domestic corporation's FDII, it grants discretion to the Secretary to establish how certain requirements, such as whether sales are for a foreign use, are satisfied. See sections 250(b)(4)(A) and (B), (b)(5)(C)(i)(II), and (b)(5)(C)(ii). In addition, the Act does not address all of the details necessary to calculate FDII, such as the allocation of expenses. Further, the Act is unclear regarding whether the section 250 deduction for FDII is available for certain foreign military sales or services and whether a section 250 deduction for GILTI is available for an individual taxpayer making a section 962 election. The following analysis describes the need for the proposed regulations and discusses the costs and benefits relative to the baseline, as well as the important alternative regulatory choices that were considered.

---

[2] At the most basic level, abstracting from various complexities of the GILTI regime, the 21 percent U.S. statutory rate with a 50 percent deduction for GILTI implies that at foreign effective rates in excess of 10.5 percent (assuming no U.S. expenses), foreign tax credits are sufficient to fully offset U.S. tax on GILTI income. However, the GILTI regime limits foreign tax credits to 80 percent of their total value, so a "baseline" GILTI scenario, with zero expense allocations, implies that foreign tax credits can fully offset U.S. tax on GILTI at foreign effective tax rates in excess of 13.125 percent (i.e., 10.5 / 0.8). The section

250 deduction for FDII is also intended to have a "baseline rate" of 13.125 percent (i.e., 0.21 x (1 - 0.375)); typically foreign tax credits are not relevant for FDII, and there is no 80 percent limitation applied to foreign tax credits with respect to FDII.

[3] The exclusions are: (1) subpart F inclusions (section 951); (2) GILTI; (3) financial services income (as defined in section 904(d)(2)(D)); (4) dividends received from the corporation's CFCs; (5) domestic oil and gas extraction income; and (6) foreign branch income (as defined in section 904(d)(2)(J)).

B. The Need for Proposed Regulations

The purpose of the proposed regulations is to provide guidance to taxpayers in determining the amount of their deduction under section 250. Section 250(c) states that "[t]he Secretary shall prescribe such regulations or other guidance as may be necessary or appropriate to carry out the provisions of [section 250]." Therefore, the proposed regulations seek to provide the detail, structure, and language required to implement section 250.

The proposed regulations seek to assist taxpayers in calculating the allowable section 250 deduction, for example, by providing details on how to compute FDII, and the components of FDII such as QBAI, DEI, and FDDEI. In particular, with respect to FDDEI, the proposed regulations provide guidance on which sales of property and which provisions of services generate gross income included in FDDEI, and on how to allocate expenses to such gross income to determine FDDEI.

In addition, the proposed regulations provide an ordering rule to coordinate the computation of the section 250 taxable income limitation with the taxable income limitations across other provisions of the Code.

The proposed regulations also seek to clarify that the section 250 deduction for FDII is available for certain foreign military sales and services. In addition, the proposed regulations allow a section 250 deduction to individual taxpayers with respect to GILTI if they make an election under section 962.

Finally and importantly, the proposed regulations also seek to provide clarity and guidance regarding the types of documentation required to substantiate that, in fact, sales of property are to foreign persons for a foreign use and provisions of services are to persons, or with respect to property, located outside the United States. In developing the proposed regulations, the Treasury Department and the IRS sought to balance the need for rigorous documentation to ensure compliance with the desire to minimize administrative burden and costs to taxpayers.

C. Baseline

The economic analysis that follows compares the proposed regulations to a no-action baseline reflecting anticipated Federal income tax-related behavior in the absence of the proposed regulations. A no-action baseline reflects the current environment including the existing international tax regulations, prior to any amendment by the proposed regulations.

D. Cost and Benefits of the Proposed Regulations and Potential Alternatives

The proposed regulations provide certainty, clarity, and consistency in the application of the section 250 deduction by unambiguously defining terms, calculations, and acceptable forms of documentation, and also by making clear the conditions under which military sales are eligible to claim the deduction. In the absence of such guidance, the chance that different taxpayers would interpret the statute differently would be exacerbated. Similarly situated taxpayers might interpret the statutory rules pertaining to particular sales or services differently, with one taxpayer pursuing a sale that another taxpayer might decline to make, because of different interpretations of how the income would be treated under section 250. If this second taxpayer's activity were more profitable, an economic loss arises. Such situations are more likely to arise in the absence of guidance. While no guidance can curtail all differential or inaccurate interpretations of the statute, the proposed regulations will significantly mitigate the chance for such interpretations and thereby increase economic efficiency.

In general, the Treasury Department and the IRS expect that in the absence of this guidance, taxpayers would undertake fewer eligible sales and services. Thus, the proposed regulation will generally enhance U.S. sales and services across all eligible activities. The Treasury Department and the IRS have not made quantitative estimates of these effects.

The benefits and costs of major, specific provisions of these proposed regulations relative to the no-action baseline and alternatives to these proposed rules considered by the Treasury Department and the IRS are discussed in further detail below.

1. Documentation Requirements

The proposed regulations set forth what forms of documentation can be used to substantiate that receipts qualify as "foreign-derived" for purposes of FDII and the section 250 deduction. In general, the Treasury Department and the IRS weighed the compliance burden imposed on taxpayers from documentation requirements against the need for documentation to be sufficiently rigorous in establishing foreign use or the location of a person that receives a service. Because the statute provides different requirements for sales or services to qualify for a section 250 deduction and the proposed regulations provide different requirements depending on the type of sale or the type of service, and because documentation needs to be tailored to the applicable requirement, the proposed regulations specify different types of acceptable documentation for different types of transactions. In particular, documentation requirements vary with respect to the determination of whether a sale of property is to a foreign person, whether a sale of general property is for a foreign use, whether a sale of intangible property is for a foreign use, whether an individual consumer of a general service is located outside the United States, and whether a business recipient of a general service is located outside the United States.

In each case, the proposed regulations provide that the list of acceptable documentation constitutes reasonable proof that a transaction is a FDDEI transaction. In general, the types of documentation listed are readily accessible to most taxpayers. For example, with respect to demonstrating foreign use for general property, taxpayers can show evidence of shipment to a location outside the United States (presuming that the seller has no knowledge or reason to know that that information is unreliable or incorrect).

To further reduce compliance burdens, the proposed regulations allow additional flexibility for particular types of taxpayers or transactions. For example, throughout the proposed regulations, small businesses (defined in the proposed regulations as taxpayers with less than $10 million of gross receipts annually) are subject to less stringent documentation requirements because their smaller scale makes compliance more burdensome for them and makes the sophisticated tax minimization planning that can sometimes characterize abuse unlikely. Small transactions (defined in the proposed regulations as less than $5,000 of gross receipts from a single recipient) are also subject to less stringent documentation requirements, because the fixed costs of compliance likely account for a larger fraction of the profit on small transactions, and large scale abuse is less likely. The Treasury Department and the IRS request comments on whether the thresholds in the proposed regulations for small businesses and small transactions are appropriate and especially solicit comments that provide data, other evidence, and models that can enhance the rigor of the process by which such thresholds are determined. Further, the proposed regulations allow a more flexible approach for the documentation of sales of fungible general property because it is burdensome and unnecessary to track each sale of a fungible item as long as the taxpayer can establish by documentation that a certain percentage of the fungible property is for a foreign use.

In determining appropriate documentation requirements, the Treasury Department and the IRS balanced the rigor and reliability of the proof that transactions are foreign-derived with the cost to taxpayers of obtaining such documentation. The Treasury Department and the IRS considered a spectrum of trade-offs between the rigor of proof of foreign use and the burden such proof would impose on taxpayers. One option considered was allowing only the most stringent form of documentation in each case (for example, a written statement of foreign use made under penalties of perjury, plus evidence of such use) without any flexibility, but this was deemed overly burdensome for taxpayers and foreign buyers. Overly burdensome documentation requirements might shift transactions to sellers that do not need or cannot use the FDII deduction, or it may discourage foreign persons from transacting with a U.S. seller or renderer. The Treasury Department and the IRS aimed to propose rules that would not alter economic decisions because of these concerns. In addition, highly burdensome rules may lead to abuse. For example, a foreign buyer that falsifies documentation provided to a domestic corporation to allow the corporation to obtain a deduction would not be subject to penalties by the IRS. Because the incentives for compliance by foreign buyers are limited (for example, contractual liability between the parties), the burden should also be limited. In comparison, chapters 3 and 4 of subtitle A of the Code require U.S. financial institutions to withhold on certain payments to foreign persons if they do not provide documentation. Because of the enforcement mechanism built into the statutes in chapters 3 and 4 (i.e., withholding), the IRS can require stricter documentation (for example, most foreign persons have to provide to the financial institution a specific IRS form, completed and signed under penalties of perjury, and in some cases must attach additional documentation on underlying payees).

The Treasury Department and the IRS also considered a system in which taxpayers submitted documentation in advance of a potential FDDEI transaction for the IRS to review and determine whether the documentation is sufficient. This option was rejected because the time involved would delay normal business transactions.

A third option that the Treasury Department and the IRS considered was to allow a taxpayer to use its discretion to determine what type of documentation is appropriate, but this would not provide sufficient clarity and assurance to taxpayers and is potentially open to abuse. For each type of transaction, the Treasury Department and the IRS chose to allow a menu of acceptable documentation options that vary according to the type of transaction, and selected documentation options that would be readily available to the taxpayer whenever possible. By allowing taxpayers to, in some cases, rely on documents already obtained in the normal course of business, the proposed regulations impose essentially zero documentation cost in such cases. The Treasury Department and the IRS request comments on the approaches and decisions relating to documentation requirements discussed in this part I(D)(1) of this Special Analyses section. See part II of this Special Analyses section regarding the Paperwork Reduction Act for additional discussion on the expected paperwork burden of these documentation requirements.

2. Computation of the Ratio of FDDEI to DEI

The proposed regulations provide guidance on the computation of the foreign-derived ratio. As noted in part I(A) of this Special Analyses section, the Act defines a corporation's FDII as its DII multiplied by the corporation's foreign-derived ratio, which is the ratio of its DEI to its FDDEI. The proposed regulations specify that, for purposes of determining the numerator of the foreign-derived ratio, the domestic corporation must allocate expenses to its gross FDDEI. The Treasury Department and the IRS deemed this approach the most consistent with the statute by providing what the Treasury Department and the IRS have determined to be the most accurate measure of the corporation's income that is "foreign-derived," through matching of expenses to gross income.

The Treasury Department and the IRS considered two other approaches; one, in which the foreign-derived ratio would be computed as the ratio of foreign versus U.S. gross receipts and another in which the ratio would be computed as foreign versus U.S. gross income. The Treasury Department and the IRS have determined that both of these approaches would result in a less accurate measure of foreign-derived net income. The Treasury Department and the IRS have determined that these alternative approaches could also reward low margin (or even loss-leading) sales or services to foreign markets by allowing a section 250 deduction due to positive gross receipts or income from foreign sources, even if the net income from foreign sources after allocated expenses is zero or negative. The Treasury Department and the IRS have determined that the chosen alternative generally provides the most accurate computation of FDII but solicit comments on whether an alternative method would be more appropriate.

3. Military Sales

Section 250 requires sales to be made to a foreign person and services to be provided to a person located outside the United States but does not include specific rules applicable to foreign military sales or services. For example, many sales of military equipment and services by a U.S. defense contractor to a foreign government are structured, pursuant to the Arms Export Control Act, as sales and services provided to the U.S. government for resale or on-service to the foreign government. See part III(B)(2) of the Explanation of Provisions section for additional discussion of the Arms Export Control Act. In effect, the contractor is selling goods and services to a foreign person, but the sale is technically made to the U.S. government. The Treasury Department and the IRS recognize that the statute is unclear as to whether certain foreign military sales and services can qualify for the section 250 deduction, due to the concern that a foreign military sale or service pursuant to the Arms Export Control Act would not qualify as a sale or service to a foreign person since the sale is actually made to the U.S. government and not to a foreign person or a person located outside the United States.

The Treasury Department and the IRS considered several options for addressing this issue. One option was not addressing this issue in the proposed regulations. This option was rejected because the Treasury Department and the IRS determined that it would perpetuate uncertainty about the application of section 250 to foreign military sales and services and could result in economic inequities if some taxpayers took the position that foreign military sales and services qualify for a section 250 deduction but other similarly-situated taxpayers took the position that such sales and services do not qualify. A second option the Treasury Department and the IRS considered was to clarify that a foreign military sale or service through the U.S. government can never qualify for a section 250 deduction. However, this option was rejected because the Treasury Department and the IRS determined that it would treat taxpayers in the defense industry inequitably relative to other industries by denying them a section 250 deduction with respect to a significant amount of their foreign market sales or services. A third option the Treasury Department and the IRS considered was to allow any sale or service to a U.S. person that acts as an intermediary and does not take on the benefits and burdens of ownership to potentially qualify for a section 250 deduction if there is an ultimate foreign recipient. This option was rejected because the Treasury Department and the IRS determined that such a broad exception would allow multiple deductions in instances where both the seller and the intermediary buyer are U.S. taxpayers, because both the seller and the intermediary could potentially qualify for a section 250 deduction. In contrast, the U.S. government is not a taxpayer eligible for a section 250 deduction so only the seller would benefit from a special rule for military exports. Furthermore, determining whether a party is an "intermediary" for this purpose would require a complex facts and circumstances analysis of whether the party had the benefits and burdens of ownership, which could create uncertainty in the application of section 250 with respect to any transaction in which property or services are sold for resale or on-service.

The proposed regulations provide uniform tax treatment across the economy by generally allowing all sectors to claim the section 250 deduction, subject to other applicable rules. Otherwise, certain sales and services by the defense industry that are clearly intended for a foreign use, and that satisfy all other requirements under section 250, would be denied the benefit solely as a result of such sales or services being first made to the U.S. government under the Arms Export Control Act, whereas other industries that are not subject to the Arms Export Control Act would not have this concern. Therefore, the proposed regulations provide that foreign military sales or services to the U.S. government under the Arms Export Control Act would be treated as a sale of property or provision of a service to a foreign person. This rule seeks to provide uniform tax treatment between the defense sector and other sectors of the U.S. economy with respect to sales and services that are clearly meant for a foreign use.

4. Section 962

The section 250 deduction for FDII and GILTI is available only to domestic corporations. However, Congress enacted section 962 in Public Law 89-834 (1962) to ensure that individuals' tax burdens with respect to undistributed foreign earnings of their CFCs are comparable with their tax burdens if they had held their CFCs through a domestic corporation. See S. Rept. 1881, 87th Cong., 2d Sess. 92 (1962). Allowing a section 250 deduction with respect to GILTI of an individual (including an individual that is a shareholder of an S corporation or a partner in a partnership) that makes an election under section 962 provides comparable treatment for this income.

The Treasury Department and the IRS considered two options with respect to extending the section 250 deduction to individuals (which include, for this purpose, individual partners in partnerships and individual shareholders in S corporations) that make an election under section 962. The first option considered was to not allow the deduction for individuals. Not allowing the section 250 deduction would require that individuals that own their CFCs directly (or indirectly through a partnership or S corporation) transfer the stock of their CFCs to new U.S. corporations in order to obtain the benefit of the section 250 deduction. The Treasury Department and the IRS determined that such reorganization would be economically costly, both in terms of legal fees and substantive economic costs related to organizing and operating new corporate entities. The second option considered was to give individuals the section 250 deduction with respect to their GILTI if they make the section 962 election. The Treasury Department and the IRS determined that allowing individuals the section 250 deduction would improve economic efficiency by preventing the need for costly restructuring solely for the purpose of tax savings. This is the option adopted by the Treasury Department and the IRS in the proposed regulations. The Treasury Department and the IRS welcome comments on whether an alternative approach would be more appropriate.

II. *Paperwork Reduction Act*

The proposed regulations provide the authority for the IRS to require taxpayers to file certain forms (identified and discussed in further detail below) with the IRS to obtain the benefit of the section 250 deduction. In order to provide advance notice and solicit public comment, the IRS released drafts of the relevant forms in 2018 based on the statutory language and requested comments. The IRS received no comments on the forms during the comment period. The 2018 versions of the forms that were released in 2018 are available at *https://www.irs.gov/forms-instructions*. The Treasury Department and the IRS are not proposing to make any changes to those forms through these regulations. The Treasury Department and the IRS are also soliciting public comment on the forms and paperwork requirements in general discussed in the proposed regulations. The Treasury Department and the IRS specifically request comments on whether there are (1) ways to reduce the burdens associated with the forms, (2) opportunities to clarify the forms or associated instructions, or (3) ways to improve the quality of the collections in general.

The proposed regulations require all taxpayers with a section 250 deduction to file one new form (Form 8993). The proposed regulations also authorize the IRS to request additional information on several existing forms (Forms 1065 (Schedule K-1), 5471, 5472, and 8865) if the filer of the form has a deduction under section 250. With respect to Forms 5471, 5472, and 8993, the proposed regulations do not specify the information that will be required from taxpayers that have a section 250 deduction, but instead provide that this information will be prescribed by the forms and instructions. With respect to Forms 1065 (Schedule K-1) and 8865, the proposed regulations specify the additional information that must be provided. For additional explanation of the reporting requirements contained in these proposed regulations, see part VI of the Explanation of Provisions section. The rest of this part II of the Special Analyses section provides additional details on forms and information about the paperwork burden.

The information collection burdens under the Paperwork Reduction Act, 44 U.S.C. 3501 et seq. ("PRA") from the proposed regulations are in proposed §§ 1.250(a)-1(d), 1.250(b)-1(e)(2), 1.6038-2(f)(15), 1.6038-3(g)(4), and 1.6038A-2(b)(5)(iv).

The collection of information in proposed § 1.250(a)-1(d) would be mandatory for each domestic corporation claiming a deduction under section 250 as well as for any individual making an election under section 962 that claims a deduction under section 250 attributable to the individual's GILTI. The collection of information in proposed § 1.250(a)-1(d) is pursuant to sections 6001 and 6011 and would be satisfied by submitting a new reporting form, Form 8993, "Section 250 Deduction for Foreign-Derived Intangible Income (FDII) and Global Intangible Low-Taxed Income (GILTI)," with an income tax return. For purposes of the PRA, the reporting burden associated with proposed § 1.250(a)-1(d) will be reflected in the PRA submission for new Form 8993 (OMB control numbers 1545-0123 in the case of business taxpayers, and 1545-0074 in the case of individual taxpayers).

The collection of information in proposed § 1.250(b)-1(e)(2) would require each partnership to provide to each of its partners the partner's distributive share of gross DEI, gross FDDEI, deductions that are definitely related to the partnership's gross DEI and gross FDDEI, and partnership QBAI. For purposes of the PRA, the reporting burden associated with proposed § 1.250(b)-1(e)(2) would be reflected in the PRA submission for Form 1065 (OMB control number 1545-0123).

The collection of information in proposed § 1.6038-2(f)(15) would require every U.S. person that controls a foreign corporation during an annual accounting period and files Form 5471, "Information Return of U.S. Persons With Respect to Certain Foreign Corporations," for that period. The collection of information in proposed § 1.6038-2(f)(15) would be satisfied by providing information about the section 250 deduction for the corporation's accounting period as Form 5471 and its instructions may prescribe. For purposes of the PRA, the reporting burden on the applicable business taxpayers associated with proposed § 1.6038-2(f)(15) will be reflected in the PRA submission for Form 5471 (OMB control number 1545-0123).

The collection of information in proposed § 1.6038-3(g)(4) would be mandatory for every U.S. person that controls a foreign partnership during the partnership tax year and files Form 8865, "Return of U.S. Persons With Respect to Certain Foreign Partnerships," for that period. The collection of information in proposed § 1.6038-3(g)(4) would require a controlling ten-percent partner or controlling fifty-percent partner to provide to the IRS on Form 8865 its share of the partnership's gross DEI, gross FDDEI, deductions that are definitely related to the partnership's gross DEI and gross FDDEI, and partnership QBAI. For purposes of the PRA, the reporting burden associated with proposed § 1.6038-3(g)(4) will be reflected in the PRA submission for Form 8865 (OMB control number 1545-1668).

The collection of information in proposed § 1.6038A-2(b)(5)(iv) would be mandatory for every reporting corporation that files Form 5472, "Information Return of a 25% Foreign-Owned U.S. Corporation or a Foreign Corporation Engaged in a U.S. Trade or Business," for the tax year. The collection of information in proposed § 1.6038A-2(b)(5)(iv) would be satisfied by providing information about the section 250 deduction for the tax year as Form 5472 and its instructions may prescribe. For purposes of the PRA, the reporting burden associated with proposed § 1.6038A-2(b)(5)(iv) will be reflected in the PRA submission for Form 5472 (OMB control number 1545-0123).

The tax forms that will be created or revised as a result of the information collections in the proposed regulations, as well as the estimated number of respondents, are as follows:

	Related New or Revised Tax Forms		
	New	Revision of existing form	Number of respondents (estimated)
Form 8993	✓		75,000 – 350,000
Form 1065, Schedule K-1 (for corporate partners only, revision starting TY2020)		✓	15,000 – 45,000
Form 5471		✓	10,000 – 20,000
Form 8865		✓	<10,000
Form 5472		✓	50,000 – 80,000

Source: RAAS:CDW and ITA

The numbers of respondents in the Related New or Revised Tax Forms table were estimated by the Research, Applied Analytics and Statistics Division ("RAAS") of the IRS from the Compliance Data Warehouse ("CDW"), using tax years 2014 through 2016; as well as based on export data from the International Trade Administration ("ITA") for 2015 and 2016. Tax data for 2017 are not yet available due to extended filing dates. Data for Form 8993 represent preliminary estimates of the total number of taxpayers that may be required to file the new Form 8993. The upper bound estimate reflects the total number of exporting companies reported in the ITA data, as well as the CDW-based counts of individuals reporting related party transactions. The lower bound estimate reflects the CDW-based counts of individual and corporate taxpayers reporting related party transactions. Data for each of the Forms 1065, 5471, 5472, and 8865 represent preliminary estimates of the total number of taxpayers that are expected to file these revised forms regardless of whether that taxpayer must also file Form 8993.

The current status of the Paperwork Reduction Act submissions related to the tax forms that will be revised as a result of the information collections in the proposed regulations is provided in the accompanying table. As described above, the reporting burdens associated with the information collections in the proposed regulations are included in the aggregated burden estimates for OMB control numbers 1545-0123 (which represents a total estimated burden time for all forms and schedules for corporations of 3.157 billion hours and total estimated monetized costs of $58.148 billion ($2017)), 1545-0074 (which represents a total estimated burden time, including all other related forms and schedules for individuals, of 1.784 billion hours and total estimated monetized costs of $31.764 billion ($2017)), and 1545-1668 (which represents a total estimated burden time for all related forms and schedules for other filers, in particular trusts and estates, of 281,974 hours and total estimated monetized costs of $25.107 million ($2017)). The overall burden estimates provided for the OMB control numbers below are aggregate amounts that relate to the entire package of forms associated with the applicable OMB control number and will in the future include, but not isolate, the estimated burden of the tax forms that will be created or revised as a result of the information collections in the proposed regulations. These numbers are therefore unrelated to the future calculations needed to assess the burden imposed by the proposed regulations. These burdens have been reported for other regulations related to the taxation of cross-border income and the Treasury Department and the IRS urge readers to recognize that these numbers are duplicates and to guard against overcounting the burden that international tax provisions imposed prior to the Act. No burden estimates specific to the forms affected by the proposed regulations are currently available. The Treasury Department and the IRS have not estimated the burden, including that of any new information collections, related to the requirements under the proposed regulations. The Treasury Department and the IRS request comments on all aspects of information collection burdens related to the proposed regulations, including estimates for how much time it would take to comply with the paperwork burdens described above for each relevant form and ways for the IRS to minimize the paperwork burden.

Form	Type of Filer	OMB Number(s)	Status
Form 8993 (NEW)	Business (NEW Model)	1545-0123	Published in the **Federal Register** Notice (FRN) on 10/11/18. Public Comment period closed on 12/10/18.
	Link: https://www.federalregister.gov/documents/2018/10/09/2018-21846/proposed-collection-comment-request-for-forms-1065-1065-b-1066-1120-1120-c-1120-f-1120-h-1120-nd		
	Individual (NEW Model)	1545-0074	Limited Scope submission (1040 only). Full ICR submission for 2019 for all forms in 3/2019. 60 Day FRN not published yet for full collection for 2019.
	Link: https://www.reginfo.gov/public/do/PRAViewICR?ref_nbr=201808-1545-031		
Form 1065, Schedule K-1	Business (NEW Model)	1545-0123	Published in the FRN on 10/11/18. Public Comment period closed on 12/10/18.
	Link: https://www.federalregister.gov/documents/2018/10/09/2018-21846/proposed-collection-comment-request-for-forms-1065-1065-b-1066-1120-1120-c-1120-f-1120-h-1120-nd		
Form 5471	Business (NEW Model)	1545-0123	Published in the FRN on 10/11/18. Public Comment period closed on 12/10/18.
	Link: https://www.federalregister.gov/documents/2018/10/09/2018-21846/proposed-collection-comment-request-for-forms-1065-1065-b-1066-1120-1120-c-1120-f-1120-h-1120-nd		
Form 8865	All other filers (mainly trusts and estates) (Legacy system)	1545-1668	Published in the FRN on 10/01/18. Public Comment period closed on 11/30/18.
	Link: *https://www.federalregister.gov/documents/2018/10/01/2018-21288/proposed-collection-comment-request-for-regulation-project*		
Form 5472	Business (NEW Model)	1545-0123	Published in the FRN on 10/11/18. Public Comment period closed on 12/10/18.
	Link: https://www.federalregister.gov/documents/2018/10/09/2018-21846/proposed-collection-comment-request-for-forms-1065-1065-b-1066-1120-1120-c-1120-f-1120-h-1120-nd		

III. *Regulatory Flexibility Act*

It is hereby certified that this notice of proposed rulemaking will not have a significant economic impact on a substantial number of small entities within the meaning of section 601(6) of the Regulatory Flexibility Act (5 U.S.C. chapter 6). Although the Treasury Department and the IRS project that the proposed regulations may affect a substantial number of small entities, the economic impact on small entities as a result of this notice of proposed rulemaking is not expected to be significant.

The small business entities that are subject to section 250 and this notice of proposed rulemaking are small domestic corporations claiming a deduction under section 250 based on their FDII and GILTI. Pursuant to proposed § 1.250(a)-1(d), taxpayers are required to file new Form 8993 to compute the amount of the eligible deduction for FDII and GILTI under section 250. The Treasury Department and the IRS estimate that there are between 75,000 and 350,000 respondents of all sizes that are likely to file Form 8993. The lower end estimate comes from IRS-collected data on related party transactions that are indicative of exports to related parties. These data provide a lower bound for the number of taxpayers that export since related party exports are only a part of total exports. The IRS does not collect information on exports to third parties; therefore, International Trade Administration ("ITA") statistics of the number of companies engaged in export activities are used.[4] The ITA data provide the upper bound of the estimate of affected taxpayers. The Treasury Department and the IRS welcome comments on the analysis of number of entities affected, particularly on how such analysis should take into account different industries. Additionally, under proposed § 1.250(b)-1(e), a partnership that has one or more direct or indirect partners that are domestic corporations and that is required to file a return under section 6031 must furnish on

---

[4] ITA data was accessed at *http://tse.export.gov/EDB/SelectReports.aspx?DATA=ExporterDB* in December, 2018.

Schedule K-1 (Form 1065) certain information that would allow the partner to accurately calculate its FDII. The Treasury Department and the IRS estimate the number of domestic corporations that are direct or indirect partners in a partnership affected by proposed § 1.250(a)-1(e) is between 15,000 and 45,000.

In order to substantiate the amount of the section 250 deduction on Form 8993 related to the calculation of FDII for the sale of property or the provision of a service, the proposed regulations in § § 1.250(b)-3 through 1.250(b)-5 prescribe different types of documentation that should be obtained for each transaction. As discussed in the Explanation of Provisions section of the preamble, the proposed regulations provide several types of permissible documentation for the purpose of determining the amount of a domestic corporation's income that is considered foreign-derived. For example, in the case of a sale of general property, the seller must (1) obtain documentation that establishes the recipient's status as a foreign person, such as a written statement by the recipient indicating that the recipient is a foreign person; and (2) obtain documentation that the property is for foreign use, such as proof of shipment of the property to a foreign address.

To alleviate the burden of documentation on many small businesses and small transactions, the proposed regulations allow a seller that has less than $10,000,000 of gross receipts in the prior taxable year, or less than $5,000 in gross receipts from a single recipient during the current taxable year, to treat a recipient as a foreign person if the seller has a shipping address for the recipient that is outside the United States. The small business and small transaction exceptions to establish foreign person status are applicable to sales of both general property and intangible property. Furthermore, to establish that general property is for a foreign use, certain small businesses and businesses with small transactions may rely on the existence of a foreign shipping address for the recipient instead of obtaining documentation. The proposed regulations also contain small business and small transaction exceptions related to general services provided to consumers and business recipients. The Treasury Department and the IRS anticipate that a substantial share of small entities claiming a section 250 deduction will qualify for the small business and small transactions exceptions described above, thereby significantly reducing the overall burden of the proposed regulations on small entities. The Treasury Department and the IRS solicit comments on this issue.

The reporting burden for completing Form 8993 is estimated to average 24 hours for all affected entities, regardless of size. The reporting burden on small entities (those with receipts below $10 million in RAAS calculations) is estimated to average 15 hours. Based on the monetized hourly burden reported below, the annual per-entity reporting burden will be $1,067. The Treasury Department and the IRS project that compliance with the documentation requirements in the proposed regulations will have a de minimis or limited impact on all affected entities, regardless of size, as the majority of taxpayers will be able to use records that are maintained in the normal course of business. Small business entities that have less than $10 million of gross receipts in the prior taxable year, or less than $5,000 in gross receipts from a single recipient during the current taxable year, are expected to experience 0 to 5 minutes, with an average of 2.5 minutes, of recordkeeping per transaction recipient. Taxpayers ineligible to qualify for either exception are expected to experience 0 to 30 minutes, with an average of 15 minutes, of recordkeeping per transaction recipient. These hourly estimates were derived by RAAS based the existence of exceptions available to small businesses, as well as based on the previously noted overlap between acceptable documentation and records kept in the normal course of business, suggesting limited impact. The hourly estimates include all associated activities: recordkeeping, tax planning, learning about the law, gathering tax materials, form completion and submissions, and time with a tax preparer or use of tax software. The estimated monetized burden for compliance is $71.14 per hour, a figure computed from the IRS Business Taxpayer Burden model which assigns each firm in the micro data a monetization rate based on total revenue and assets reported on their tax return. See Tax Compliance Burden (John Guyton et al., July 2018) at *https://www.irs.gov/pub/irs-soi/d13315.pdf*. The assigned monetization rates include, in addition to wages, employer non-wage costs such as employment taxes, benefits, and overhead. For these reasons, the Treasury Department and the IRS have determined that the requirements in proposed § § 1.250(a)-1 and 1.250(b)-3 through 1.250(b)-6 will not have a significant economic impact on a substantial number of small entities. Therefore, a Regulatory Flexibility Analysis under the Regulatory Flexibility Act is not required with respect to proposed § § 1.250(a)-1 and 1.250(b)-3 through 1.250(b)-6.

The small business entities that are subject to proposed § 1.6038-2(f)(15) are domestic small business entities that are controlling U.S. shareholders of a foreign corporation and that claim a deduction under section 250 by reason of having FDII. For these purposes, a domestic small business entity controls a foreign corporation by owning more than 50 percent of that foreign corporation's stock, measured either by value or voting power. The data to assess the number of small entities potentially affected by § 1.6038-2(f)(15) are not readily available. However, businesses that are controlling U.S. shareholders of a foreign corporation are generally not small businesses because the ownership of sufficient stock in a foreign corporation in order to be a controlling U.S. shareholder generally entails significant resources and investment. Therefore, the Treasury Department and the IRS project that a substantial number of domestic small business entities will not be subject to proposed § 1.6038-2(f)(15). Consequently, the Treasury Department and the IRS have determined that proposed § 1.6038-2(f)(15) will not have a significant economic impact on a substantial number of small entities. Therefore, a Regulatory Flexibility Analysis under the Regulatory Flexibility Act is not required with respect to the collection of information requirements of proposed § 1.6038-2(f)(15).

The small business entities that are subject to proposed § 1.6038-3(g)(4) are domestic small entities that are controlling fifty-percent partners or controlling ten-percent partners of a foreign partnership and that claim a deduction under section 250 by reason of having FDII. A controlling fifty-percent partner is a U.S. person that owns more than a fifty-percent interest in a foreign partnership. A controlling ten-percent partner is a U.S. person that owns a ten-percent or greater interest in a foreign partnership that is controlled by U.S. persons owning at least a ten-percent interest. For these purposes, a fifty percent interest or ten percent interest in a partnership is an interest equal to fifty percent or ten percent of the capital or profits interest in a partnership, or an interest to which fifty percent or ten percent of the deductions or losses of the partnership are allocated, respectively. The data to assess the number of small entities potentially affected by proposed § 1.6038-3(g)(4) are not readily available. However, businesses that are controlling fifty-percent partners or controlling ten-percent partners of a foreign partnership are generally not small businesses because the ownership of a sufficient interest in a foreign partnership in order to be a controlling fifty-percent partner or a controlling ten-percent partner generally entails significant resources and investment. Therefore, the Treasury Department and the IRS have determined that proposed § 1.6038-3(g)(4) will not affect a substantial number of domestic small business entities. Moreover, any increase in costs imposed by the rule is likely to be small, relative to total costs, for any entity. Consequently, the Treasury Department and the IRS have determined that proposed § 1.6038-3(g)(4) will not have a significant economic impact on a substantial number of small entities. Therefore, a Regulatory Flexibility Analysis under the Regulatory Flexibility Act is not required with respect to the collection of information requirements of proposed § 1.6038-3(g)(4).

The small business entities that are subject to proposed § 1.6038A-2(b)(5)(iv) are domestic small entities that are at least 25-percent foreign-owned, by vote or value, that claim a deduction under section 250 by reason of having FDII. The data to assess the number of small entities potentially affected by proposed § 1.6038A-2(b)(5)(iv) is not readily available. However, domestic corporations that are at least 25-percent foreign-owned are generally not small businesses because a foreign person's ownership of at least 25 percent of a domestic corporation, whether by vote or value, generally entails significant resources and investment, and a foreign person is unlikely to expend such resources to invest in a small domestic entity. Therefore, the Treasury Department and the IRS project that a substantial number of domestic small business entities will not be subject to proposed § 1.6038A-2(b)(5)(iv). Consequently, the Treasury Department and the IRS have determined that that proposed § 1.6038A-2(b)(5)(iv) will not have a significant economic impact on a substantial number of small entities. Therefore, a Regulatory Flexibility Analysis under the Regulatory Flexibility Act is not required with respect to the collection of information requirements of proposed § 1.6038A-2(b)(5)(iv).

Notwithstanding this certification, the Treasury Department and the IRS invite comments from the public on both the number of entities affected and the economic impact of this proposed rule on small entities.

Pursuant to section 7805(f) of the Code, this notice of proposed rulemaking has been submitted to the Chief Counsel for Advocacy of the Small Business Administration for comment on its impact on small businesses.

IV. *Unfunded Mandates Reform Act*

Section 202 of the Unfunded Mandates Reform Act of 1995 requires that agencies assess anticipated costs and benefits and take certain other actions before issuing a final rule that includes any Federal mandate that may result in expenditures in any one year by a state, local, or tribal government, in the aggregate, or by the private sector, of $100 million in 1995 dollars, updated annually for inflation. In 2018, that threshold is approximately $150 million. This rule does not include any Federal mandate that may result in expenditures by state, local, or tribal governments, or by the private sector in excess of that threshold.

V. *Executive Order 13132: Federalism*

Executive Order 13132 (entitled "Federalism") prohibits an agency from publishing any rule that has federalism implications if the rule either imposes substantial, direct compliance costs on state and local governments, and is not required by statute, or preempts state law, unless the agency meets the consultation and funding requirements of section 6 of the Executive Order. This proposed rule does not have federalism implications, does not impose substantial direct compliance costs on state and local governments, and does not preempt state law within the meaning of the Executive Order.

Comments and Requests for Public Hearing

Before these proposed regulations are adopted as final regulations, consideration will be given to any written or electronic comments that are submitted timely to the IRS as prescribed in this preamble under the **ADDRESSES** section. Comments are requested on all aspects of the proposed regulations. In addition, the Treasury Department and the IRS solicit comments regarding the appropriateness of the numerical thresholds in the following provisions, along with data, other evidence, and models that can enhance the rigor of the process by which such thresholds are determined: proposed § 1.250(b)-4(c)(2)(ii), (d)(2)(iii)(C), (d)(2)(iv), (d)(3)(ii) and (iii); proposed § 1.250(b)-5(c)(5), (c)(6), (d)(3)(ii), (e)(3)(ii), and (h); and proposed § 1.250(b)-6(c)(1)(ii) and (d)(2).

All comments will be available at *http://www.regulations.gov* or upon request. A public hearing will be scheduled if requested in writing by any person that timely submits written comments. If a public hearing is scheduled, notice of the date, time, and place for the public hearing will be published in the **Federal Register**.

Drafting Information

The principal authors of these proposed regulations are Kenneth Jeruchim of the Office of the Associate Chief Counsel (International) and Michelle A. Monroy and Austin Diamond-Jones of the Office of Associate Chief Counsel (Corporate). However, other personnel from the Treasury Department and the IRS participated in their development.

Statement of Availability of IRS Documents

IRS Revenue Procedures, Revenue Rulings, Notices, and other guidance cited in this document are published in the Internal Revenue Bulletin and are available from the Superintendent of Documents, U.S. Government Printing Office, Washington, DC 20402, or by visiting the IRS website at *http://www.irs.gov*.

[¶ 49,790] **Proposed Amendments of Regulations (REG-135671-17)** , published in the Federal Register on March 25, 2019.

[Code Sec. 337]

Corporate partner: Corporate-level gain: Equity interests.—Amendments of Reg. § 1.337(d)-3, amending final regulations that prevent a corporate partner from avoiding corporate-level gain through transactions with a partnership involving equity interests of the partner or certain related entities, are proposed.

AGENCY: Internal Revenue Service (IRS), Treasury.

ACTION: Notice of proposed rulemaking.

SUMMARY: This document contains proposed regulations to amend final regulations that prevent a corporate partner from avoiding corporate-level gain through transactions with a partnership involving equity interests of the partner or certain related entities. These regulations affect partnerships and their partners.

DATES: Comments and requests for a public hearing must be received by June 24, 2019. ADDRESSES: Send submissions to: CC:PA:LPD:PR (REG-135671-17), Room 5203, Internal Revenue Service, P.O. Box 7604, Ben Franklin Station, Washington, DC 20044. Submissions may be hand-delivered Monday through Friday between the hours of 8 a.m. and 4 p.m. to CC:PA:LPD:PR (REG-135671-17), Courier's Desk, Internal Revenue Service, 1111 Constitution Avenue, NW, Washington, DC 20224, or sent electronically, via the Federal eRulemaking Portal at *http://www.regulations.gov* (IRS REG-135671-17).

FOR FURTHER INFORMATION CONTACT: Concerning the proposed regulations, Kevin I. Babitz, (202) 317-6852, or Mary Brewer, (202) 317-6975; concerning submission of comments or to request a public hearing, Regina L. Johnson at (202) 317-6901.

SUPPLEMENTARY INFORMATION:

Background and Explanation of Provisions

This notice of proposed rulemaking contains amendments to the Income Tax Regulations (26 CFR part 1) under section 337(d) of the Internal Revenue Code (Code) set forth in § 1.337(d)-3 (final regulations) that prevent a corporate partner from using a partnership to avoid recognition of corporate-level gain. The final regulations largely adopted proposed regulations (REG-149518-03) published in the **Federal Register** (80 FR 33451) on June 12, 2015 (2015 regulations) with minor, nonsubstantive clarifying changes in response to requests for further certainty in the single comment letter received on the proposed regulations. See the Explanation of Provisions section of the preamble to TD 9833 (83 FR 26580 (June 8, 2018)) for a detailed discussion of each of the specific points raised in the comment letter received on the 2015 regulations.

The rules set forth in this notice of proposed rulemaking contain substantive modifications to the final regulations relating to the definition of Stock of the Corporate Partner. Accordingly, the Treasury Department and the IRS determined it appropriate to publish these modifications in the form of new proposed regulations to afford the public the opportunity to submit additional comments.

1. Stock of the Corporate Partner: Attribution

The final regulations apply to certain partnerships that hold stock of a Corporate Partner. For this purpose, a *Corporate Partner* is defined as a person that holds or acquires an interest in a partnership and that is classified as a corporation for federal income tax purposes. The final regulations define *Stock of the Corporate Partner* expansively to include stock and other equity interests, including warrants, other options, and similar interests, either in the Corporate Partner or in a corporation (referred to in this Background and Explanation of Provisions section as a Controlling Corporation) that controls the Corporate Partner within the meaning of section 304(c), except that section 318(a)(1) and (3) would not apply. Stock of the Corporate Partner also includes an interest in any entity to the extent that the value of the interest is attributable to Stock of the Corporate Partner.

The final regulations adopted a definition of Stock of the Corporate Partner that was modified as compared to the definition in the regulations that the Treasury Department and the IRS proposed on December 15, 1992 (PS-91-90, REG-208989-90, 1993-1 CB 919) (1992 proposed regulations). The final regulations broadened the definition of Stock of the Corporate Partner with respect to the relationship needed for a Controlling Corporation to be treated as controlling the Corporate Partner (using a modified section 304(c) standard instead of section 1504(a)) but also narrowed the definition, generally excluding sister corporations and subsidiary corporations of the Corporate Partner from being treated as Controlling Corporations.

More specifically, the final regulations define Stock of a Corporate Partner by including stock and other equity interests of any corporation that controls the Corporate Partner within the meaning of section 304(c), except that section 318(a)(1) and (3) shall not apply (section 304(c) control). In contrast, the 1992 proposed regulation's definition was limited to stock or other equity interests issued by the Corporate Partner and its "section 337(d) affiliates" – that is any corporation that is a member of an affiliated group as defined in section 1504(a) of the Code without regard to section 1504(b).

Section 304(c) control generally exists when there is ownership of stock of a corporation possessing at least 50 percent of the total combined voting power of all classes of the corporation's stock entitled to vote or at least 50 percent of the value of the shares of all classes of stock of the corporation, while control of a corporation under section 1504(a)(2) requires ownership of stock of the corporation possessing at least 80 percent of the total voting power of the stock of the corporation and at least 80 percent of the total value of the stock of the corporation. The Treasury Department and the IRS adopted this lower ownership threshold for determining control in the final regulations as a more appropriate standard for this purpose because General Utilities repeal could more easily be avoided by acquiring stock of a corporation that owns less than 80 percent of the vote and value of the Corporate Partner's stock. See *General Utilities & Operating Co. v. Helvering*, 296 U.S. 200 (1935).

While section 304(c) incorporates the constructive ownership rules of section 318(a) with some modifications, the 2015 regulations excluded the application of section 318(a)(1) and (3) from their definition of control.

The commenter that submitted the only comment on the 2015 regulations demonstrated that families could use the exclusion of section 318(a)(1) attribution from the determination of section 304(c) control to structure transactions using partnerships to eliminate gain on appreciated assets or contravene the purposes of section 337(d) in other ways. For example—

Husband owns 90 percent of corporation A, which owns 49 percent of Corporate Partner (CP). Wife owns 90 percent of corporation B, which also owns 49 percent of CP. CP owns an interest in partnership PRS. Under these facts, because the 2015 regulations determined section 304(c) control without applying the section 318(a)(1) family attribution rule, neither A nor B control CP. Accordingly, other partners in Partnership could contribute stock of A and B to PRS in exchange for an interest in PRS without triggering gain to A or B.

The Treasury Department and the IRS agree with the commenter that excluding section 318(a)(1) attribution from the determination of section 304(c) control could produce unintended results. In addition, the Treasury Department and the IRS have determined that taxpayers can structure transactions to take advantage of the exclusion of section 318(a)(3) attribution from the determination of section 304(c) control. For example, in the preceding fact pattern, if the interests held by Husband and Wife were instead held by a single corporation, X, neither A nor B would control CP without the application of section 318(a)(3) attribution.

As a result, the Treasury Department and the IRS propose to modify the definition of Stock of the Corporate Partner to eliminate the exclusion of section 318(a)(1) and (3) attribution from the determination of section 304(c) control. However, as explained below, the Treasury Department and the IRS propose to limit this expanded definition of Stock of the Corporate Partner to entities that own a direct or indirect interest in the Corporate Partner.

The exclusion of attribution under sections 318(a)(1) and 318(a)(3) in the 2015 regulations and the final regulations was intended to limit section 304(c) control to entities that own a direct or indirect interest in the Corporate Partner, while excluding entities that do not own a direct or indirect interest in the Corporate Partner. To implement this intent more precisely, the Treasury Department and the IRS propose to limit the proposed scope of section 304(c) control to ownership, direct or indirect, of an interest in the Corporate Partner. For the purpose of testing direct or indirect ownership of an interest in the Corporate Partner, ownership of Stock of the Corporate Partner would be attributed to an entity under section 318(a)(2) (except that the 50-percent ownership limitation in section 318(a)(2)(C) would not apply) and under section 318(a)(4), but otherwise without regard to section 318. Thus, sections 318(a)(1), 318(a)(3), and 318(a)(5) would not apply for determining whether an entity directly or indirectly owns an interest in Stock of the Corporate Partner, but once an entity is found to directly or indirectly own an interest in such stock, then the section 304(c) control definition would apply in its entirety to determine whether the tested entity is a Controlling Corporation. The Treasury Department and the IRS continue to study the appropriate scope of the definition of Stock of the Corporate Partner, and request comments regarding these provisions.

2. Definition of Stock of the Corporate Partner: Affiliated Groups

These proposed regulations, if finalized, would make a second change to the definition of Stock of the Corporate Partner. The final regulations provide that the term Stock of the Corporate Partner does not include any stock or other equity interests held or acquired by a partnership if all interests in the partnership's capital and profits are held by members of an affiliated group as defined in section 1504(a) that includes the Corporate Partner (Affiliated Group Exception). The 1992 proposed regulations included affiliate stock within its definition of the Stock of a Corporate Partner, but the 2015 proposed regulations instead set forth this Affiliated Group Exception, which the final regulations adopted. Thus, the final regulations do not apply if a domestic corporation and its wholly owned domestic subsidiaries (each of which is an includible corporation under section 1504(b)) are the only partners in a partnership and any of these corporations contributes stock of another affiliate to a partnership. The preamble to T.D. 9722 (80 FR 33402 (June 12, 2015)), which contained temporary regulations that accompanied the 2015 regulations, stated that the Treasury Department and the IRS had determined that the Affiliated Group Exception is appropriate because "the purpose of these regulations is not implicated if a partnership is owned entirely by affiliated corporations."

After further study, the Treasury Department and the IRS have determined that the Affiliated Group Exception may result in abuse and therefore is not appropriate. Specifically, the Treasury Department and the IRS believe that a partnership held entirely by members of an affiliated group could enter into transactions that permanently eliminate the built-in gain on an appreciated asset that one partner contributes to the partnership. For example—

Assume that P, a corporation, owns all of the stock of S1, and S1 owns all of the stock of CP. P, S1, and CP are members of an affiliated group. P and CP form a 50-50 partnership; CP contributes an appreciated asset to the partnership; and P contributes S1 stock with basis equal to fair market value. After seven years, the partnership liquidates and distributes the S1 stock to CP and the appreciated asset to P. At that time, the asset may be sold outside of the group with an artificially increased basis. The built-in gain that was in the asset is now preserved in the S1 stock held by CP. The group may permanently eliminate the gain without tax by liquidating CP under section 332. CP would receive nonrecognition treatment on distribution of the S1 stock to S1 under section 332, and S1 would receive nonrecognition treatment on the receipt of its own stock under section 1032. Thus, the liquidation of CP permanently eliminates the built-in gain on the appreciated asset that attached to the hook stock CP held in S1 after the liquidation of the partnership.

This ability to increase the basis of an appreciated asset artificially and to eliminate the built-in gain permanently contravenes the purposes of section 337(d) and these regulations. The Treasury Department and the IRS are also aware that practitioners have observed that the Affiliated Group Exception runs counter to the general rule that related-party transactions are subject to greater scrutiny. In light of these concerns, these proposed regulations would remove the Affiliated Group Exception contained in the final regulations.

However, because there may be specific circumstances under which the elimination of the Affiliated Group Exception could adversely impact ordinary business transactions between affiliated group members and group-owned partnerships, the Treasury Department and the IRS request comments describing situations in which a more tailored version of the Affiliated Group Exception would be warranted.

3. Definition of Stock of the Corporate Partner: Value of an interest attributable to Stock of the Corporate Partner

These proposed regulations would modify the scope of the rule in the final regulations that Stock of the Corporate Partner includes interests in any entity to the extent that the value of the interest is attributable to Stock of the Corporate Partner (Value Rule). Under the final regulations, the Value Rule applies to all interests in an entity regardless of whether the entity is controlled by the Corporate Partner. The sole commenter responding to the 2015 regulations agreed that the scope of the Value Rule was appropriate if the entity was controlled by the Corporate Partner. However, for entities that are not controlled by the Corporate Partner, the commenter asked that the scope of the Value Rule be narrowed to apply only if 20 percent or more of the assets of an entity were Stock of the Corporate Partner.

The Treasury Department and the IRS agree that the Value Rule in the 2015 regulations and the final regulations could be overbroad in certain circumstances. For example—

Assume X, a publicly traded corporation, owns a portfolio investment in P, a publicly traded corporation. P controls CP, a Corporate Partner under the final regulations, within the meaning of section 304(c); thus, P's stock is Stock of the Corporate Partner under the final regulations. Under the Value Rule, X's stock would be Stock of the Corporate Partner to the extent that the value of X is attributable to Stock of the Corporate Partner. If CP contributed appreciated property to a partnership, and another party contributed X stock to the partnership, CP would be unable to determine whether it had engaged in a Section 337(d) Transaction (within the meaning of § 1.337(d)-3(c)(3)) or otherwise apply the rules of the final regulations because CP (through P) might have no way to determine that the X stock used in the transaction could be Stock of the Corporate Partner. Alternatively, if CP were aware that X owned a portfolio investment in P, it would have no ability to determine the amount of X stock that is Stock of the Corporate Partner under the Value Rule. This is because, absent actual or constructive knowledge (for example through required disclosures such as filings with the Securities and Exchange Commission), a widely held corporation might not know or have the ability to know who owns its stock.

For this reason, the Treasury Department and the IRS have determined that narrowing the scope of the Value Rule is appropriate. However, the Treasury Department and the IRS decline to adopt the commenter's specific suggestion that interests in an entity not be subject to the Value Rule unless 20 percent or more of the assets of the entity consisted of Stock of the Corporate Partner. Such a rule would cause the Value Rule to be overly narrow and could permit taxpayers to structure transactions that would contravene the purpose of section 337(d) and these regulations. Instead, the Treasury Department and the IRS propose to narrow the scope of the Value Rule through an alternate measure. Under the proposed regulations, if an entity is not controlled by the Corporate Partner and is not a Controlling Corporation, the Value Rule would apply to treat interests in the entity as Stock of the Corporate Partner only if the entity owns, directly or indirectly, 5 percent or more of the stock, by vote or value, of the Corporate Partner. For this purpose, direct or indirect ownership would mean ownership of stock that would be attributed to a person under section 318(a)(2) (except that the 50-percent ownership limitation in section 318(a)(2)(C) would not apply) and under section 318(a)(4), but otherwise without regard to section 318. The Treasury Department and the IRS believe that using a 5-percent ownership threshold is appropriate because entities have the ability to determine whether they have 5-percent or greater owners, and corporations may track their 5-percent shareholders for other reasons (such as for section 382 purposes). Further, the Treasury Department and the IRS propose to apply this 5-percent threshold to direct or indirect stock ownership, rather than all equity interests, in the Corporate Partner in order to make the Value Rule more readily administrable.

The proposed regulations also would clarify how taxpayers should apply the Value Rule to determine the extent to which the value of an equity interest is attributable to Stock of the Corporate Partner. The proposed regulations would provide that taxpayers would multiply the value of the equity interest in an entity by a ratio, the numerator of which is the fair market value of the Stock of the Corporate Partner owned directly or indirectly by the entity and the denominator of which is the fair market value of all of the equity interests in the entity. For this purpose, direct or indirect ownership would mean ownership of stock that would be attributed to a person under section 318(a)(2) (except that the 50-percent ownership limitation in section 318(a)(2)(C) would not apply) and under section 318(a)(4), but otherwise without regard to section 318. The proposed regulations would also provide that the ratio may not exceed one. The Treasury Department and the IRS determined that the fair market value of all of the equity interests in the entity is the most appropriate measure to determine the value of the entity because the Value Rule seeks to determine what portion of the value of an equity interest in an entity reflects the value of Stock of the Corporate Partner owned by that entity.

Additionally, the proposed regulations would clarify that, if an equity interest is Stock of the Corporate Partner because it is an interest in the Corporate Partner or in an entity with a direct or indirect ownership interest that controls the Corporate Partner within the meaning of section 304(c), then the Value Rule will not apply. The Treasury Department and the IRS request comments on all aspects of the proposed changes to the scope of the Value Rule, including the appropriate measure of the value of the entity.

4. Exception for Certain Dispositions of Stock

Finally, these proposed regulations would make a modification to the exception for certain dispositions of stock in § 1.337(d)-3(f)(2) to make its language consistent with the modified definition of Stock of the Corporate Partner. Under this exception, the final regulations do not apply to Stock of the Corporate Partner that (i) is disposed of (by sale or distribution) by the partnership before the due date (including extensions) of its federal income tax return for the taxable year of the relevant transaction; and (ii) is not distributed to the Corporate Partner or a corporation that controls the Corporate Partner. With respect to the second requirement, the final regulations refer to a corporation that controls the Corporate Partner within the meaning of section 304(c), except that section 318(a)(1) and (3) shall not apply. For the same reasons that these proposed regulations modify the definition of Stock of the Corporate Partner, these proposed regulations also modify the second requirement of this exception to refer to a corporation that controls the Corporate Partner within the meaning of section 304(c), but only if the controlling corporation owns directly or indirectly stock or another equity interest in the Corporate Partner, in order to conform the second requirement with the modified definition of Stock of the Corporate Partner.

Proposed Effective Date

These regulations are proposed to be effective as of the date of their publication as final regulations in the **Federal Register**. Taxpayers may rely on these proposed regulations for transactions occurring on or after June 12, 2015 and prior to the date that these regulations are published as final regulations in the **Federal Register**, provided that the taxpayer consistently applies all of the proposed regulations to such transactions.

Special Analyses

These proposed regulations are not subject to review under section 6(b) of Executive Order 12866 pursuant to the Memorandum of Agreement (April 11, 2018) between the Treasury Department and the Office of Management and Budget regarding review of tax regulations.

These proposed regulations do not impose a collection of information on small entities. Further, pursuant to the Regulatory Flexibility Act (5 U.S.C. chapter 6), it is hereby certified that these proposed regulations would not have a significant economic impact on a substantial number of small entities. This certification is based on the fact that these proposed regulations would primarily affect sophisticated ownership structures with interlocking ownership of corporations, partnerships and corporate stock. Accordingly, a regulatory flexibility analysis is not required. Pursuant to section 7805(f) of the Internal Revenue Code, these regulations have been submitted to the Chief Counsel for Advocacy of the Small Business Administration for comment on its impact on small business.

Comments and Requests for a Public Hearing

Before these proposed regulations are adopted as final regulations, consideration will be given to comments that are submitted timely to the IRS as prescribed in this preamble under the **ADDRESSES** heading. The Treasury Department and the IRS request comments on all aspects of the proposed rules. All comments will be available at *http://www.regulations.gov* or upon request. A public hearing will be scheduled if requested in writing by any person that timely submits written or electronic comments. If a public hearing is scheduled, notice of the date, time, and place for the public hearing will be published in the **Federal Register. Drafting Information**

The principal authors of these regulations are Kevin I. Babitz, Office of the Associate Chief Counsel (Passthroughs and Special Industries) and Mary Brewer, Office of the Associate Chief Counsel (Corporate). However, other personnel from the Treasury Department and the IRS participated in their development.

[¶ 49,792] Proposed Amendments of Regulations (REG-121694-16), published in the Federal Register on March 26, 2019 (corrected 4/23/2019).

[Code Secs. 301, 356, 368 and 902]

Distribution: Stock ownership: Shareholder.—Amendments of Reg. §§1.301-1, 1.356-1, 1.368-2, 1.902-1 and 1.902-3, containing proposed regulations under section 301 of the Internal Revenue Code of 1986 (Code), are proposed.

AGENCY: Internal Revenue Service (IRS), Treasury.

ACTION: Notice of proposed rulemaking.

SUMMARY: This document contains proposed regulations under section 301 of the Internal Revenue Code of 1986 (Code). The proposed regulations would update existing regulations under section 301 to reflect statutory changes made by the Technical and Miscellaneous Revenue Act of 1988, which changes provide that the amount of a distribution of property made by a corporation to its shareholder is the fair market value of the distributed property. The proposed regulations would affect any shareholder who receives a distribution of property from a corporation.

DATES: Written or electronic comments and requests for a public hearing must be received by June 24, 2019.

ADDRESSES: Send submissions to: CC:PA:LPD:PR (REG-121694-16), Room 5203, Internal Revenue Service, PO Box 7604, Ben Franklin Station, Washington, DC 20044. Submissions may be hand-delivered Monday through Friday between the hours of 8 a.m. and 4 p.m. to CC:PA:LPD:PR (REG-121694-16), Courier's Desk, Internal Revenue Service, 1111 Constitution Avenue, NW, Washington, DC 20224, or sent electronically, via the Federal eRulemaking Portal at www.regulations.gov (indicate IRS and REG-121694-16).

FOR FURTHER INFORMATION CONTACT: Concerning the proposed regulations, Grid R. Glyer, (202) 317-6847; concerning submission of comments, Regina Johnson, (202) 317-6901 (not toll-free numbers).

SUPPLEMENTARY INFORMATION:

Background

Section 301 of the Code originally was enacted as part of the Internal Revenue Code of 1954. Section 301 provides rules for the treatment of a distribution of property, including money, made by a corporation to its shareholder with respect to that shareholder's stock ownership in that corporation (distribution).

Section 301(b)(1) provides general rules for determining the amount of a distribution. As enacted in 1954, section 301(b)(1) provided rules for determining the amount of a distribution that differed depending on whether the shareholder receiving the distribution (distributee) was a corporation. Pre-1986 amendments to section 301(b)(1) added special rules to determine the amount of distributions received from foreign distributing corporations and by foreign corporate distributees. Similarly, section 301(d), as enacted in 1954, provided rules for determining the basis of property received in a distribution that differed depending on whether the distributee was a corporation. As with section 301(b)(1), pre-1986 amendments to section 301(d) added special rules to determine the basis of property received from foreign distributing corporations and by foreign corporate distributees.

Section 1006(e)(10) of the Technical and Miscellaneous Revenue Act of 1988, Pub. L. No. 100-647, 102 Stat. 3342 (1988) (the Act), amended section 301(b)(1) to eliminate the distinction between corporate and noncorporate distributees as well as the special rules relating to foreign corporations. Similarly, section 1006(e)(11) of the Act amended section 301(d) to eliminate the distinction between corporate and noncorporate distributees. (These amendments to section 301(b)(1) and (d) are referred to as the 1988 Amendments.) Section 1019(a) of the Act provided that, in general, the 1988 Amendments were effective as if included in the Tax Reform Act of 1986, Pub. L. No. 99-514, 100 Stat. 2085 (1986).

As a result of the 1988 Amendments, effective for taxable years beginning after December 31, 1986, section 301(b)(1) provides that, for purposes of section 301, the amount of any distribution shall be the amount of money received plus the fair market value of the other property received. Section 301(d), as amended by the 1988 Amendments and effective for taxable years beginning after December 31, 1986, provides that the basis of property received in a distribution to which section 301(a) applies shall be the fair market value of such property.

The current regulations issued under section 301 reflect the rules of sections 301(b)(1) and 301(d) as they existed prior to the 1988 Amendments. Accordingly, to the extent preempted by statute, the current regulations have no application.

Explanation of Provisions.

The proposed regulations update § 1.301-1 to reflect the statutory changes made to section 301(b)(1) and (d) by the 1988 Amendments. The scope of the changes to the current regulations issued under section 301 made by these proposed regulations is limited to (1) deleting regulatory provisions made obsolete by statutory changes, (2) making minor additions and revisions to regulatory provisions to reflect current statutory text, and (3) making certain non-substantive changes for purposes of clarity and readability, including reordering and redesignating paragraphs of the current regulations. The proposed regulations also update cross-references in §§ 1.356-1(f), 1.368-2(m)(3)(iii), 1.902-1(a)(12), and 1.902-3(a)(7) to reflect the proposed reordering and redesignating of paragraphs in § 1.301-1.

Specifically, some of the provisions of current § 1.301-1(b) are now found in proposed § 1.301-1(c). Thus, the definition of the amount of a distribution subject to section 301 and the determination of the fair market value of a distribution remain in § 1.301-1(b), while the determination of when to include a distribution in gross income, and its fair market value, is now found in proposed § 1.301-1(c).

In addition, current § 1.301-1(g) is redesignated as proposed § 1.301-1(f) and is revised to clarify the application of the principles of section 357(d) to the limitation on the amount of a distribution provided by section 301(b)(2). Section 357(d) was added to the Code by section 3001(b)(1) of the Miscellaneous Trade and Technical Corrections Act of 1999, Pub.L. No. 106-36, 113 Stat. 127. On January 4, 2001, the Treasury Department and the IRS published a temporary regulation (T.D. 8924) in the **Federal Register** (66 FR 723) to address this interaction. Current § 1.301-1(g), published in the **Federal Register** (66 FR 49278) on September 27, 2001 as T.D. 8964, provides that no reduction shall be made for the amount of any liability, unless the liability is assumed by the shareholder within the meaning of section 357(d). Proposed § 1.301-1(f) would clarify the language of current § 1.301-1(g) by providing that no reduction in the amount of a distribution is made for the amount of any liability except to the extent the liability is assumed by the shareholder within the meaning of section 357(d).

The specific changes to § 1.301-1 are shown in the following table:

Paragraph Designation in § 1.301-1	Change
(a)	Updated to reflect current law
(b)	Updated to reflect current law, with the definition of the amount of a distribution subject to section 301 and the determination of the fair market value of a distribution remaining in paragraph (b) and the determination of when to include a distribution in gross income, and its fair market value, redesignated as paragraph (c)
(c)	Redesignated as paragraph (d)
(d)	Deleted as obsolete
(e)	Deleted as obsolete
(f)	Updated to reflect current law and redesignated as paragraph (e)
(g)	Redesignated as paragraph (f) and revised to clarify that no reduction in the amount of a distribution is made for the amount of any liability except to the extent the liability is assumed by the shareholder within the meaning of section 357(d).
(h)	Updated to reflect current law and redesignated as paragraph (g)
(i)	No change
(j)	Updated to reflect current law and redesignated as paragraph (h)
(k)	Deleted as obsolete
(l)	Redesignated as paragraph (j)
(m)	Redesignated as paragraph (k)
(n)	Deleted as obsolete
(o)	Deleted as obsolete
(p)	Redesignated as paragraph (l)
(q)	Redesignated as paragraph (m)
(n)	New effective date paragraph

Proposed Effective/Applicability Date

The proposed regulations would apply to distributions made after the date of publication of the Treasury decision adopting these rules as final regulations in the **Federal Register**. However, these proposed regulations would update current regulations under section 301 to reflect statutory changes made by the 1988 Amendments, which statutory changes apply to distributions made in taxable years beginning after December 31, 1986.

Special Analyses

This regulation is not subject to review under section 6(b) of Executive Order 12866 pursuant to the Memorandum of Agreement (April 11, 2018) between the Department of the Treasury and the Office of Management and Budget regarding review of tax regulations. Because these regulations do not impose a collection of information on small entities, the Regulatory Flexibility Act (5 U.S.C. chapter 6) does not apply.

Pursuant to section 7805(f), this notice of proposed rulemaking has been submitted to the Chief Counsel for Advocacy of the Small Business Administration for comment on its impact on small business.

Comments and Requests for Public Hearing

Before these proposed regulations are adopted as final regulations, consideration will be given to any comments that are submitted timely to the IRS as prescribed in this preamble under the "Addresses" heading. The Treasury Department and the IRS request comments on all aspects of the proposed rules. All comments will be available at *www.regulations.gov* or upon request. A public hearing will be scheduled if requested in writing by any person that timely submits written comments. If a public hearing is scheduled, notice of the date, time, and place for the public hearing will be published in the **Federal Register**.

Drafting Information

The principal author of these regulations is Grid R. Glyer of the Office of Associate Chief Counsel (Corporate). Other personnel from the Treasury Department and the IRS participated in developing these regulations.

[¶ 49,795] Proposed Amendments of Regulations (REG-120186-18) and partial withdrawal of **Notice of Proposed Regulations, NPRM REG-120186-18**, published in the Federal Register on May 1, 2019.

[Code Sec. 1400Z-2]

Qualified opportunity fund: Capital gains: Opportunity zones.—Reg. §§ 1.1400Z-2(b)(1), 1.1400Z-2(f)(1) and 1.1400Z-2(g)(1) and amendments of Reg. §§ 1.1400Z-2(a)(1), 1.1400Z-2(c)(1) and 1.1400Z-2(d)(1), relating to gains that may be deferred as a result of a taxpayer's investment in a qualified opportunity fund (QOF), as well as special rules for an investment in a QOF held by a taxpayer for at least 10 years, are adopted. Reg. § 1.1400Z-2(d)-1(c)(4)(i), (c)(5), (c)(6), (c)(7), (d)(2)(i)(A), (d)(2)(ii), (d)(2)(iii), (d)(5)(i), and (d)(5)(ii)(B), proposed on October 29, 2018, are withdrawn.

[¶ 49,797] Proposed Amendments of Regulations (REG-105476-18) , published in the Federal Register on May 13, 2019.

[Code Secs. 864, 1445, 1446, 1461, 1463, 1464 and 6050K]

Reporting, withholding and paying tax: Foreign partner: Dispositions of partnership interest: Notice requirements.—Reg. §§ 1.864(c)(8)-2, 1.1446(f)-1—1.1446(f)-5 and amendments of Reg. §§ 1.1445-2, 1.1445-5, 1.1445-8, 1.1446-3, 1.1446-4, 1.1446-7, 1.1461-1—1.1461-3, 1.1463-1, 1.1464-1 and 1.6050K-1, implementing certain sections of the Internal Revenue Code, including sections added to the Internal Revenue Code by the Tax Cuts and Jobs Act, that relate to the withholding of tax and information reporting with respect to certain dispositions of interests in partnerships engaged in the conduct of a trade or business within the United States, are proposed.

AGENCY: Internal Revenue Service (IRS), Treasury.

ACTION: Notice of proposed rulemaking.

SUMMARY: This document contains proposed regulations implementing certain sections of the Internal Revenue Code, including sections added to the Internal Revenue Code by the Tax Cuts and Jobs Act, that relate to the withholding of tax and information reporting with respect to certain dispositions of interests in partnerships engaged in the conduct of a trade or business within the United States. The proposed regulations affect certain foreign persons that recognize gain or loss from the sale or exchange of an interest in a partnership that is engaged in the conduct of a trade or business within the United States, and persons that acquire those interests. The proposed regulations also affect partnerships that, directly or indirectly, have foreign persons as partners.

DATES: Written or electronic comments and requests for a public hearing must be received by July 12, 2019.

ADDRESSES: Send submissions to: CC:PA:LPD:PR (REG-105476-18), Internal Revenue Service, Room 5203, P.O. Box 7604, Ben Franklin Station, Washington, DC 20044. Submissions may be hand-delivered Monday through Friday between the hours of 8 a.m. and 4 p.m. to CC:PA:LPD:PR (REG-105476-18), Courier's Desk, Internal Revenue Service, 1111 Constitution Avenue NW., Washington, DC 20224, or sent electronically via the Federal eRulemaking Portal at *http://www.regulations.gov* (IRS REG-105476-18).

FOR FURTHER INFORMATION CONTACT: Concerning the proposed regulations, Chadwick Rowland, 202-317-6937; concerning submissions of comments or requests for a public hearing, Regina L. Johnson (202) 317-6901 (not toll-free numbers).

SUPPLEMENTARY INFORMATION:

Background

I. *Section 1446(f)*

Section 1446(f), which was added to the Internal Revenue Code (the "Code") by section 13501 of the Tax Cuts and Jobs Act, Public Law 115-97 (2017) (the "Act"), provides rules for withholding on the transfer of a partnership interest described in section 864(c)(8). Section 1446(f)(1) provides that, except as otherwise provided in section 1446(f), if a portion of the gain (if any) on any disposition of an interest in a partnership would be treated under section 864(c)(8) as effectively connected with the conduct of a trade or business within the United States, the transferee is required to deduct and withhold a tax equal to 10 percent of the amount realized on the disposition.

Section 1446(f)(2)(A) provides an exception to the general withholding requirement described in section 1446(f)(1) if the transferor furnishes an affidavit to the transferee stating, under penalties of perjury, the transferor's United States taxpayer identification number and that the transferor is not a foreign person. Section 1446(f)(2)(B)(i) provides that the exception to withholding described in section 1446(f)(2)(A) will not apply if the transferee has actual knowledge that the affidavit furnished is false, or if the transferee receives a notice from a transferor's agent or transferee's agent that the affidavit is false.

Section 1446(f)(3) provides that, at the request of the transferor or transferee, the Secretary may prescribe a reduced amount to be withheld under this section if the Secretary determines that reducing the amount to be withheld will not jeopardize the collection of tax on gain treated under section 864(c)(8) as effectively connected with the conduct of a trade or business within the United States.

Section 1446(f)(4) provides that if a transferee fails to withhold any amount required to be withheld under section 1446(f)(1) then the partnership must deduct and withhold from distributions to the transferee a tax in an amount equal to the amount the transferee failed to withhold, plus interest.

Section 1446(f)(6) generally provides that the Secretary shall prescribe such regulations as may be necessary to carry out the purposes of section 1446(f), including regulations providing for exceptions from the provisions of section 1446(f). Section 1446(f) is effective for sales, exchanges, and other dispositions after December 31, 2017.

On December 29, 2017, the Department of the Treasury (the "Treasury Department") and the Internal Revenue Service (the "IRS") released Notice 2018-08, 2018-7 I.R.B. 352, which temporarily suspends the requirement to withhold on amounts realized in connection with the sale, exchange, or disposition of certain interests in a publicly traded partnership not treated as a corporation under section 7704 and the regulations thereunder. On April 2, 2018, the Treasury Department and the IRS released Notice 2018-29, 2018-16 I.R.B. 495, which provides temporary guidance and announces an intent to issue proposed regulations under section 1446(f) with respect to the sale, exchange, or disposition of certain interests in non-publicly traded partnerships. Notice 2018-29, and section 1446(f)(1) generally, rely on the principles contained within the section 1445 withholding regime. Under section 1445, if a foreign person disposes of a United States real property interest ("U.S. real property interest"), as defined in section 897(c), a withholding obligation is imposed on the transferee of the interest.

On December 27, 2018, the Treasury Department and the IRS published in the **Federal Register** a notice of proposed rulemaking at 83 FR 66647 (REG-113604-18) under section 864(c)(8) (the "proposed section 864(c)(8) regulations"). The proposed section 864(c)(8) regulations provide rules for determining the amount of gain or loss treated as effectively connected with the conduct of a trade or business within the United States ("effectively connected gain" or "effectively connected loss") described in section 864(c)(8), including rules coordinating section 864(c)(8) with sections 741 and 751 (relating to the character of gain or loss realized in connection with the sale or exchange of an interest in a partnership). They also provide rules for coordination of section 864(c)(8) with section 897 (relating to amounts treated as effectively connected gain or loss with respect to U.S. real property interests), tiered partnerships, and U.S. income tax treaties.

II. *Rules for Withholding under Section 1446(a) on Distributions by Publicly Traded Partnerships*

Generally, withholding under section 1446(a) is required by a partnership when effectively connected taxable income ("ECTI") is allocable to a foreign person. *See* §§1.1446-2 and 1.1446-3. However, withholding on ECTI earned by a publicly traded partnership is required when the ECTI is distributed to the foreign person. *See* §1.1446-4. Often, an interest in the publicly traded partnership is held by a nominee, such as a domestic financial institution that holds the publicly traded partnership interest as a custodian for a foreign partner. Section 1.1446-4 provides rules for applying the withholding tax under section 1446(a) to distributions by publicly traded partnerships. Under those rules, when a publicly traded partnership provides a qualified notice (within the meaning of §1.1446-4(b)(4)), a nominee, which must be a domestic person, may be treated as a withholding agent with respect to a distribution. *See* §1.1446-4(b)(4) and 1.1446-4(d). The qualified notice must be given in accordance with notice requirements with respect to dividends under regulations under the Securities Exchange Act of 1934. Section 1.1445-8(f) provides similar qualified notice rules that apply to certain distributions subject to withholding when attributable to the disposition of a U.S. real property interest.

Section 1.1446-4(f)(3) provides an ordering rule for situations in which the distribution is attributable to multiple types of income (such as amounts attributable to income described in section 1441 or 1442 or amounts subject to withholding under section 1446). However, no rule is provided for situations in which a qualified notice does not provide information regarding the types of income being distributed.

Explanation of Provisions

The proposed regulations provide rules for withholding, reporting, and paying tax under section 1446(f) upon the sale, exchange, or other disposition of an interest in a partnership described in section 864(c)(8) and proposed §1.864(c)(8)-1.[1] The proposed regulations would, when finalized, adopt many of the rules that were described in Notice 2018-29, with certain modifications provided, in part, in response to comments. In addition, the proposed regulations provide reporting rules relating to section 864(c)(8) and rules implementing withholding under section 1446(f)(4). They also contain rules clarifying the reporting rules applicable to transfers of partnership interests subject to section 6050K. Further, the proposed regulations provide rules implementing withholding by brokers on transfers of certain interests in publicly traded partnerships subject to section 1446(f)(1), and make related changes to the reporting rules and procedures for adjusting withholding under sections 1461, 1463, and 1464. They also make changes to the rules regarding withholding on distributions by publicly traded partnerships under §1.1446-4, including the rules that apply to qualified notices and nominees. Finally, the proposed regulations provide rules coordinating withholding under section 1446(f) with other withholding regimes to prevent overwithholding of tax.

I. *Reporting Requirements for Foreign Transferors and Partnerships with Foreign Transferors*

A partnership that is engaged in the conduct of a trade or business within the United States is required to file an annual information return, Form 1065, *U.S. Return of Partnership Income*, and also provide information to its partners on Schedule K-1 (Form 1065), *Partner's Share of Income, Deductions, Credits, etc.*, with respect to each partner's distributive share of partnership items and other information. *See* section 6031 and §§1.6031(a)-1 and 1.6031(b)-1T. Domestic partners generally report the information from the Schedule K-1 (Form 1065) on their income tax return, typically Form 1040, *U.S. Individual Income Tax Return*, for an individual, or Form 1120, *U.S. Corporation Income Tax Return*, for a corporation. A foreign partner with a U.S. income tax return filing obligation generally files Form 1040NR, *U.S. Nonresident Alien Income Tax Return*, or Form 1120-F, *U.S. Income Tax Return of a Foreign Corporation*.

A partner (foreign or domestic) that transfers an interest in a partnership in an exchange described in section 751(a) (relating to an exchange of an interest in a partnership that holds unrealized receivables or inventory) generally has an obligation both to inform the partnership of the transfer and to include a statement with respect to the exchange on the partner's income tax return under §1.751-1(a)(3). *See* section 6050K(c) and §1.6050K-1(d). A partnership also has an obligation to provide information with respect to the exchange to the transferee and transferor under section 6050K(c) and §1.6050K-1(c). *See also* Form 8308, *Report of a Sale or Exchange of Certain Partnership Interests*.

Because section 864(c)(8) requires a deemed sale at the partnership level to determine a foreign partner's effectively connected gain or loss, a foreign person that transfers its partnership interest generally will not be able to compute its income tax liability under section 864(c)(8) unless the partnership provides certain information to the foreign partner. The proposed regulations therefore provide rules that facilitate the transfer of information between a foreign partner and the partnership for purposes of section 864(c)(8).

The proposed regulations generally provide that a notifying transferor (generally, any foreign person and certain domestic partnerships that have a foreign person as a direct or indirect partner) that transfers (within the meaning of proposed §1.864(c)(8)-1(g)(5)) an interest in a partnership (other than certain interests in a publicly traded partnership) in a transaction described in section 864(c)(8) must notify the partnership within 30 days of the transfer by providing a statement that includes information relevant to the partnership for making calculations under section 864(c)(8), including the date on which the notifying transferor transferred its interest, and other identifying information regarding the transferor and transferee. *See* proposed §1.864(c)(8)-2(a). This rule generally parallels §1.6050K-1, including the content of the information and when it must be provided.

Proposed §1.864(c)(8)-2(b) requires a specified partnership (generally, a partnership that is engaged in the conduct of a trade or business within the United States or a partnership that owns, directly or indirectly, an interest in a partnership so engaged) to furnish to a notifying transferor the information necessary for the transferor to comply with section 864(c)(8) by the due date of the Schedule K-1 (Form 1065) for the tax year of the partnership in which the transfer occurred. Proposed §1.864(c)(8)-2(b) applies if a specified partnership receives the notification described in proposed §1.864(c)(8)-2(a), or otherwise knows that a relevant transfer has occurred, and the notifying transferor would have had a distributive share of deemed sale EC gain or deemed sale EC loss (within the meaning of proposed §1.864(c)(8)-1(c)) at the time of the transfer. For these purposes, a notifying transferor that is a partnership is treated as a nonresident alien. Proposed §1.864(c)(8)-2(b) provides that, for purposes of the reporting requirements described in proposed §1.864(c)(8)-2, a partnership that makes a distribution to a transferor that qualifies as a transfer under section 864(c)(8) and proposed §1.864(c)(8)-1(b) will be treated as having actual knowledge that a transfer occurred, thereby triggering the reporting requirement of proposed §1.864(c)(8)-2(b) to the extent that the transferee would have had a distributive share of deemed sale EC gain or deemed sale EC loss within the meaning of proposed §1.864(c)(8)-1(c).

Relatedly, the proposed regulations clarify that the information a partnership must provide under section 6050K upon being notified of a transfer includes the information necessary for a transferor to make the transferor's required statement under §1.751-1(a)(3). *See* proposed §1.6050K-1(c)(2).

---

[1] §1.864(c)(8)-1 was proposed to be added on December 27, 2018; 83 FR 66647, 66651.

II. *Definitions and General Rules of Applicability*

A. *Definitions*

For purposes of the proposed regulations under section 1446(f), the term "transfer" means a sale, exchange, or other disposition, and includes a distribution from a partnership to a partner. *See* proposed § 1.1446(f)-1(b)(9). A "transferee" is any person, foreign or domestic, that acquires a partnership interest through a transfer. *See* proposed § 1.1446(f)-1(b)(10). The term "transferor" generally means any person, foreign or domestic, that transfers a partnership interest, and therefore refers to the person that directly owns the interest in the partnership. For a trust, to the extent all or a portion of the trust is treated as owned by the grantor or another person under sections 671 through 679 (such trust, "a grantor trust"), the term "transferor" means the grantor or other person. *See* proposed § 1.1446(f)-1(b)(11). *See also* Rev. Rul. 85-13, 1985-1 C.B. 184.

B. *Certifications and Books and Records*

Similar to the approach described in Notice 2018-29, the proposed regulations provide various exceptions to withholding and procedures for determining the amount to withhold. Under these rules, the person required to withhold may generally rely on information provided in certifications that it receives or that is contained in its own books and records. The general rules of applicability provide the requirements for providing a valid certification and for retaining certifications or information in books and records. *See* proposed § 1.1446(f)-1(c)(2). A certification includes any documents associated with the certification, such as statements from the partnership, IRS forms, withholding certificates, withholding statements, certifications, or other documentation. *Id.*

C. *Determination Dates*

Notice 2018-29 required determinations to be made as of the date of transfer when applying many of its rules and exceptions. Because it may be difficult to make these determinations on the precise date of transfer, the proposed regulations generally allow the choice of one of several dates solely for purposes of making determinations under section 1446(f)(1) with regard to a transfer. This date is referred to as the determination date. It is chosen on a transfer-by-transfer basis and must be used for a transfer for all purposes of section 1446(f). The determination date must be one of the following: the date of the transfer, any date no more than 60 days before the transfer, or, with respect to a transferor that is not a controlling partner, the later of either the first day of the partnership's taxable year in which the transfer occurs or the date before the transfer of the most recent revaluation described in § 1.704-1(b)(2)(iv)(*f*)(*5*) or 1.704-1(b)(2)(iv)(*s*)(*1*). *See* proposed § 1.1446(f)-1(c)(4). As the determination date applies only for purposes of determining the withholding obligation under section 1446(f), the calculation of tax resulting from the application of section 864(c)(8) and the reporting requirements under proposed § 1.864(c)(8)-2 are determined based on the date of the transfer.

D. *IRS Forms and Instructions*

Proposed § 1.1446(f)-1(c)(5) provides that any reference in the proposed regulations to an IRS form includes its successor form and that any form must be filed in the manner provided in the instructions to the forms or in other guidance. The IRS intends to modify publications, instructions and forms (including forms discussed in this Explanation of Provisions) as appropriate to take into account sections 864(c)(8) and 1446(f).

E. *Coordination with Other Withholding Rules*

Proposed § 1.1446(f)-1(d) provides a rule coordinating section 1446(f)(1) with section 1445. Specifically, the rule provides that if a transferee is required to withhold under section 1445(e)(5) or § 1.1445-11T(d)(1) and section 1446(f)(1), then the transferee will be subject to the payment and reporting requirements of section 1445 only. This rule clarifies that even though proposed § 1.864(c)(8)-1(d) provides that section 897(g) does not apply to a transfer that is also subject to section 864(c)(8), the withholding regime provided in section 1445 and the regulations thereunder applies under these circumstances, rather than the rules described in section 1446(f)(1). Thus, if a foreign transferor disposes of an interest in a partnership that is engaged in the conduct of a trade or business within the United States (not taking into account the application of section 897(a)) and in which fifty percent or more of the value of the gross assets consist of U.S. real property interests, and ninety percent or more of the value of the gross assets consist of U.S. real property interests plus any cash or cash equivalents, a transferee must generally withhold under section 1445(a) (at 15 percent of the amount realized) and not section 1446(f). However, this rule applies only if the transferor has not applied for a withholding certificate under § 1.1445-11T(d)(1). *See* proposed § 1.1446(f)-1(d). If the transferor has applied for a withholding certificate, then the transferee must withhold the greater of the amounts required under section 1445(e)(5) or section 1446(f)(1).

Because gain that an upper-tier partnership recognizes on the transfer of an interest in a lower-tier partnership engaged in the conduct of a trade or business within the United States is included when calculating the upper-tier partnership's ECTI, the proposed regulations also provide a coordination rule that allows a partnership that is withheld upon under section 1446(f)(1) (in its capacity as a transferor) to claim a credit for the amount withheld against its withholding tax liability under section 1446(a) (if any). *See* proposed § 1.1446-3(c)(4). *See also* § 1.1446-3(d)(2) for rules on how the partnership or its partners may claim a credit or refund for tax paid under section 1446.

III. *Withholding on the Transfer of a Non-Publicly Traded Partnership Interest by a Foreign Person*

A. *In General*

Under section 1446(f)(1), a transferee of a partnership interest must withhold a tax equal to 10 percent of the amount realized on any disposition when the disposition results in gain that is treated as effectively connected with the conduct of a trade or business within the United States under section 864(c)(8). Proposed § 1.1446(f)-2(a) implements this rule by requiring any transferee to withhold a tax equal to 10 percent of the amount realized on any transfer of a partnership interest (other than certain publicly traded partnership interests) under section 1446(f)(1), unless an exception to withholding applies under proposed § 1.1446(f)-2(b). If an exception does not apply and withholding is required, proposed § 1.1446(f)-2(c) provides rules for determining and adjusting the amount required to be withheld under section 1446(f)(1). The exceptions and determination procedures in the proposed regulations apply solely for purposes of section 1446(f)(1) and do not affect a foreign person's filing obligation under the Code or a foreign person's tax liability resulting from the application of section 864(c)(8).

B. *Exceptions to Withholding*

1. In General

The proposed regulations provide six exceptions to withholding by a transferee under section 1446(f)(1). These exceptions generally allow the transferee to rely on certain certifications that it receives from the transferor or partnership unless it has actual knowledge that the certifications are incorrect or unreliable. *See* proposed § 1.1446(f)-2(b)(1). When the partnership is a transferee because it makes a distribution, it may instead rely on its books and records unless it knows, or has reason to know, that the information is incorrect or unreliable. *Id.*

2. Certification of Non-Foreign Status by Transferor

Consistent with section 6.01 of Notice 2018-29, proposed § 1.1446(f)-2(b)(2) provides the requirements for a certification of non-foreign status (including the requirement that it include the transferor's TIN), and clarifies that a valid Form W-9, *Request for Taxpayer Identification Number and Certification*, may be used for this purpose, including a Form W-9 for the transferor that is already in the transferee's possession. The proposed regulations also clarify that a Form W-9 may be used to establish non-foreign status of a transferor for purposes of section 1445. *See* proposed §§ 1.1445-2(b)(2)(v) and 1.1445-5(b)(3)(iv).

3. No Realized Gain by Transferor

Section 1446(f)(1) applies only when there is gain described in section 864(c)(8) on the transfer of a partnership interest. Consistent with section 6.02 of Notice 2018-29, the proposed regulations provide that a transferee is not required to withhold if the transferor provides the transferee with a certification stating that the transferor would not realize any gain on the transfer of the partnership interest determined as if the transfer occurred on the determination date. Proposed § 1.1446(f)-2(b)(3)(i) provides that this certification of no realized gain must take into account any ordinary income arising from application of section 751(a) and the regulations thereunder. Therefore, a transferor may not provide the certification if section 751(a) and the regulations thereunder require the transferor to realize ordinary income, even if the transferor would realize an overall loss on the transfer.

A similar rule in proposed § 1.1446(f)-2(b)(3)(ii) applies to partnership distributions. Section 731 generally provides that if a distribution of money to a partner exceeds the partner's adjusted basis in its interest in the partnership, then gain will be recognized to the extent of the difference between the money distributed and the partner's basis. That gain or loss is considered as gain or loss from the sale or exchange of the partnership interest of the distributee partner. *See* section 731(a). Consistent with section 9 of Notice 2018-29, proposed § 1.1446(f)-2(b)(3)(ii) provides that for purposes of determining whether withholding is required on a distribution, a partnership is permitted to rely on its books and records or on a certification provided by the transferor (the distributee partner) to determine if there is realized gain to the distributee partner.

4. Effectively Connected Gain upon a Partnership's Deemed Sale

To make the determination of whether there is a transfer to which withholding applies more administrable for transferors and transferees, proposed § 1.1446(f)-2(b)(4) provides that no withholding is required if the transferee receives a certification from the partnership stating that if the partnership sold all of its assets at fair market value, the amount of net effectively connected gain resulting from the deemed sale would be less than 10 percent of the total net gain. Section 6.04 of Notice 2018-29 provided a similar rule, but at a threshold of 25 percent. Proposed § 1.1446(f)-2(b)(4) lowers the percentage threshold in accordance with section 2 of Notice 2018-29, which stated that the Treasury Department and the IRS intend to provide future guidance reducing the percentage threshold provided in section 6.04 of Notice 2018-29. The proposed regulations also allow a partnership that is a transferee because it makes a distribution to use this exception when it determines that the 10-percent test is satisfied from its books and records.

To make it easier for the partnership to calculate its effectively connected gain from the deemed sale, the proposed regulations allow this amount to be determined as of the determination date. Further, the proposed regulations allow a partnership to make this determination when no gain on the deemed sale would have been effectively connected with the conduct of a trade or business within the United States (for example, when the deemed sale would result in a loss that would have been effectively connected with the conduct of a trade or business within the United States). *See* proposed § 1.1446(f)-2(b)(4)(i)(B).

5. Allocable Share of ECTI

Section 6.03 of Notice 2018-29 provided an exception to withholding under section 1446(f)(1) for situations in which a transferor's distributive share of ECTI during the previous three taxable years was less than 25 percent of the transferor's total distributive share of income in each year (the "three-year ECTI exception"). Section 2 of Notice 2018-29 provided that the Treasury Department and the IRS intended to lower the three-year ECTI exception's 25 percent threshold in proposed regulations, and that other limitations for this rule were under consideration. *See also* section III.B.4 of this Explanation of Provisions (describing modifications to the threshold set forth in section 6.04 of Notice 2018-29).

The three-year ECTI exception was intended to relieve potentially significant overwithholding that could arise when a partner transfers an interest in a partnership, recognizes relatively little effectively connected gain under section 864(c)(8), but cannot obtain information from the partnership at the time of the transfer necessary to qualify for the deemed sale exception described in section III.B.4 of this Explanation of Provisions. The three-year ECTI exception uses a transferor's allocable share of ECTI as a proxy for distributive share of effectively connected gain recognized in connection with a deemed sale as described in section 864(c)(8)(B). The Treasury Department and the IRS are aware that the amount of a partner's recent allocable share of ECTI may not accurately indicate whether, and to what extent, the partner would recognize gain taxable under section 864(c)(8) and proposed § 1.864(c)(8)-1. For example, a partnership may recognize relatively little effectively connected income for several years while nonetheless holding assets with significant built-in gain that would be taxable as effectively connected gain. The three-year ECTI exception may in certain cases increase compliance and collection risks if foreign partners with limited connections to the United States and significant tax liability under section 864(c)(8) are not withheld on under section 1446(f)(1).

In the interest of striking the appropriate balance between the risk of noncompliance and the potential for overwithholding, the proposed regulations adopt the three-year ECTI exception from Notice 2018-29 with the modifications described in this section III.B.5 of this Explanation of Provisions. The Treasury Department and the IRS continue to study whether the three-year ECTI exception is appropriate in light of the risk of noncompliance, and request comments on the utility of the rule and modifications to the rule that would reduce that risk.

Accordingly, proposed § 1.1446(f)-2(b)(5)(i) provides that no withholding is required if a transferee receives a certification from a transferor stating that the transferor was at all times a partner in the partnership for the immediately prior taxable year and the two taxable years that precede it and that the transferor's allocable share of ECTI for each of those taxable years was less than 10 percent of the transferor's total distributive share of the partnership's net income for that year. *See* proposed § 1.1446(f)-2(b)(5)(i)(A) and (C). In addition, a transferor must certify that, in the immediately prior taxable year and the two that preceded it, the transferor's allocable share of ECTI was less than $1 million (including ECTI allocated to certain persons related to the transferor). *See* proposed § 1.1446(f)-2(b)(5)(i)(B). A transferor must also certify that its distributive share of income or gain that is effectively connected with the conduct of a trade or business within the United States or deductions or losses properly allocated and apportioned to that income in each of the taxable years described in proposed § 1.1446(f)-2(b)(5)(i)(A) has been reported on a Federal income tax return (filed on or before the due date (including extensions) for filing the return (and all amounts due with respect to the return are timely paid)) for each of the three preceding taxable years, if required to be filed, before the date on which the transferor furnishes the certification. *See* proposed § 1.1446(f)-2(b)(5)(i)(D). For this purpose, if the transferor is a nonresident alien individual or foreign corporation, the Federal income tax return is the transferor's Form 1040NR or Form 1120-F; if the transferor is a partnership, the Federal income tax returns are the Forms 1040NR or 1120-F of the direct or indirect partners of the transferor.

For purposes of this rule, the immediately prior taxable year is the transferor's most recent taxable year with or within which a taxable year of the partnership ended and for which a Schedule K-1 (Form 1065) was due or furnished (if earlier) before the date of the transfer. *See* proposed § 1.1446(f)-2(b)(5)(ii). Consistent with the three-year ECTI exception described in Notice 2018-29, a transferor does not satisfy this requirement if for any of the relevant years it did not receive Form 8805, *Foreign Partner's Information Statement of Section 1446 Withholding Tax*, unless the transferor was allocated an item of deduction or loss that is effectively connected with the conduct of a trade or business within the United States, in which case it is treated as having an allocable share of ECTI for that year of zero. *See* proposed § 1.1446(f)-2(b)(5)(iii).

When a transferor has had neither ECTI nor a net distributive share of income allocated to it in the previous three taxable years, the composition of the income the partnership allocates to the transferor does not provide any indication of the amount of effectively connected gain realized by the transferor in connection with the transfer. Accordingly, the proposed regulations also provide that a transferor does not qualify for the exception provided in proposed § 1.1446(f)-2(b)(5) if the transferor did not have a net distributive share of income allocated to it in any of its previous three taxable years. *See* proposed § 1.1446(f)-2(b)(5)(iv).

Section 6.03 of Notice 2018-29 provided that the three-year ECTI exception does not apply when a partnership is a transferee by reason of making a distribution. Comments noted that, particularly in tiered partnership structures, a distributing partnership may not be able to obtain the information necessary to use the deemed sale exception described in section 6.04 of Notice 2018-29, such that the partnership would be required to withhold under section 1446(f)(1) in cases in which there was relatively limited effectively connected income earned by the partnership. In response to the comments, the proposed regulations allow a distributing partnership to use this exception when it determines that the three-year ECTI exception is applicable based on its books and records, provided that it receives a representation from the transferor stating that income tax returns have been filed, and tax has been paid, for each of the relevant years for which the transferor was allocated effectively connected income (or loss). *See* proposed § 1.1446(f)-2(b)(5)(v).

Finally, proposed § 1.1446(f)-2(b)(5)(vi) provides that a transferor may not make the certification if it has actual knowledge that the information relevant to the certification that is reported by the partnership on any Form 8805 or Schedule K-1 (Form 1065) is incorrect.

6. Nonrecognition by Transferor

Section 864(c)(8) and proposed § 1.864(c)(8)-1 provide that gain from the transfer of a partnership interest that is treated as effectively connected with the conduct of a trade or business within the United States is limited to gain otherwise recognized under the Code. If a nonrecognition provision of the Code applies to all of the gain realized on a transfer, withholding under section 1446(f)(1) does not apply. Accordingly, section 6.05 of Notice 2018-29 provided an exception to withholding for certain nonrecognition transactions if the transferee receives a notice from the transferor describing the application of a nonrecognition provision. This exception was based on the rules in § 1.1445-2(d)(2).

Consistent with the rule provided in Notice 2018-29, the proposed regulations generally permit a transferee to rely on a certification of nonrecognition from the transferor. *See* proposed § 1.1446(f)-2(b)(6). The certification provided by the transferor must include a brief description of the transfer and the relevant law and facts relating to the application of the nonrecognition provision.

If only a portion of the gain realized on the transfer is subject to a nonrecognition provision, an adjustment to the amount required to be withheld may be permitted under proposed § 1.1446(f)-2(c)(4), discussed in section III.C.4 of this Explanation of Provisions (describing the rules in proposed § 1.1446(f)-2(c)(4)(vi) for the certification of maximum tax liability that may be relied upon in these situations).

7. Claim of Treaty Benefits

Notice 2018-29 did not contain specific rules addressing the application of income tax treaties, instead including them in section 6.05 by adopting a modified version of § 1.1445-2(d) (providing an exception from withholding under section 1445 when the transferor certifies that it is not required to recognize gain either under a provision of the Code or under a treaty). The proposed regulations provide an exception to withholding under section 1446(f)(1) when a transferor certifies that it is not subject to tax on any gain from the transfer pursuant to an income tax treaty in effect between the United States and a foreign country. *See* proposed § 1.1446(f)-2(b)(7)(i). This exception applies only when a transferor (as opposed to owners of an interest in the transferor, including partners in a partnership that is a transferor) qualifies for the benefits of an income tax treaty in order to reduce the burden on a transferee of reviewing documentation from multiple persons. The certification to the transferee must include a valid Form W-8BEN, *Certificate of Foreign Status of Beneficial Owner for United States Tax Withholding and Reporting (Individuals)*, or W-8BEN-E, *Certificate of Status of Beneficial Owner for United States Tax Withholding and Reporting (Entities)* (as applicable), that contains the information necessary to support the claim for treaty benefits, and the transferee must mail a copy of the certification to the IRS by the 30th day after the date of the transfer in order to rely upon it. *Id. See also* Form 8833, *Treaty-Based Return Position Disclosure Under Section 6114 or 7701(b)*, and the instructions to the form regarding the requirement for the transferor to disclose a claim for treaty benefits with a return.

To ensure that these procedures are followed for claims involving treaty benefits, this exception is the sole method by which a transferor may claim an exception to withholding by reason of a claim of treaty benefits. *See* proposed § 1.1446(f)-2(b)(7)(iii). For claims involving transfers with respect to which treaty benefits apply to only a portion of the gain from the transfer, see section III.C.4 of this Explanation of Provisions (describing the rules in proposed § 1.1446(f)-2(c)(4)(vi) for the certification of maximum tax liability that that may be relied upon in these situations).

C. *Determining the Amount to Withhold*

1. In General

The proposed regulations provide certain procedures for determining the amount to withhold under section 1446(f)(1). The rules are intended to provide administrable procedures for transferees to determine the amount to withhold, and in some cases, provide procedures intended to better reflect the amount of the transferor's actual tax liability under section 864(c)(8). When applicable, these procedures generally allow the transferee to rely on certifications that it receives from the transferor (or, in certain cases, from the partnership) to determine the amount to withhold unless it has actual knowledge that the certification is incorrect or unreliable. *See* proposed § 1.1446(f)-2(c)(1). In cases in which a partnership is the transferee because it makes a distribution, it may instead rely on its books and records unless it knows, or has reason to know, that the information is incorrect or unreliable. *Id.*

2. Amount Realized

i. In General

The amount required to be withheld under section 1446(f)(1) is determined by reference to the transferor's amount realized on the transfer. *See* section 1446(f)(1). The proposed regulations provide that the amount realized for purposes of proposed § 1.1446(f)-2 is determined under section 1001 and the regulations thereunder and section 752 and the regulations thereunder. *See* proposed § 1.1446(f)-2(c)(2)(i); *see also* §§ 1.752-1(h) and 1.1001-2.

The proposed regulations also clarify that in the case of a distribution, the amount realized is the sum of the amount of cash distributed (or to be distributed), the fair market value of property distributed (or to be distributed), and the reduction in the transferor's share of partnership liabilities. *Id.*

ii. Procedures to Determine Share of Partnership Liabilities

Comments stated that the allocation of liabilities to a partner under section 752 is not information that normally would be available to a transferee and may be difficult for a transferor to determine as of the date of transfer. To address these issues, section 7.02 of Notice 2018-29 provided that a transferee may in certain cases rely on a certification from the transferor as to the amount of the transferor's share of partnership liabilities reported on the transferor's most recently received Schedule K-1 (Form 1065), provided that the form was for a partnership taxable year that closed no more than 10 months before the date of transfer and the transferor is not a controlling partner. Section 7.03 of Notice 2018-29 allowed a transferee to rely on a certification from the partnership that provided the transferor's share of partnership liabilities as reflected on the most recently prepared Schedule K-1 (Form 1065).

The proposed regulations provide procedures similar to sections 7.02 and 7.03 of Notice 2018-29 that allow a transferee to rely on a certification from the transferor or the partnership. Proposed § 1.1446(f)-2(c)(2)(ii)(B) provides that a transferee may generally rely on a certification from a transferor that provides the amount of the transferor's share of partnership liabilities reported on the most recent Schedule K-1 (Form 1065) issued by the partnership. In response to comments stating that a transferor may not possess a Schedule K-1 (Form 1065) that satisfies the 10 month requirement in Notice 2018-29 because of the timing of the extended due date for Schedule K-1 (Form 1065), the proposed regulations provide that a transferee may generally rely on a certification if the last day of the partnership taxable year for which the Schedule K-1 (Form 1065) was provided was no more than 22 months before the date of the transfer. *See* proposed § 1.1446(f)-2(c)(2)(ii)(B). Consistent with Notice 2018-29, a transferor that is a controlling partner may not provide this certification because it will generally be able to require the partnership to provide a partnership-level certification as to the controlling partner's share of partnership liabilities. *Id.*

Proposed § 1.1446(f)-2(c)(2)(ii)(C) allows a transferee to rely on a certification from the partnership that provides the amount of the transferor's share of partnership liabilities. However, unlike the rule in Notice 2018-29, the partnership is required to make this determination as of the determination date rather than relying on its most recently prepared Schedule K-1 (Form 1065). *Id.* The proposed regulations also provide a new procedure that allows a partnership that is a transferee because it makes a distribution to rely on its books and records to determine the transferor's share of partnership liabilities as of the determination date. *See* proposed § 1.1446(f)-2(c)(2)(iii).

If a transferee does not use one of these determination procedures, the reduction in the transferor's share of partnership liabilities must be determined as of the date of the transfer for purposes of computing the amount realized.

iii. Modified Amount Realized for Foreign Partnerships

As discussed in section III.B of this Explanation of Provisions, section 1446(f)(2) and proposed § 1.1446(f)-2(b)(2) provide an exception to withholding when the transferor is not a foreign person. A transferor that is a foreign partnership may not rely on this exception even though it may have U.S. persons (which are not subject to tax under section 864(c)(8)) as its partners. To avoid overwithholding when a foreign partnership transfers its interest in a partnership, proposed § 1.1446(f)-2(c)(2)(iv) provides a procedure to limit the amount realized for withholding purposes to the portion of the amount realized that is attributable to foreign persons. For this purpose, the portion of the amount realized attributable to a direct or indirect partner is determined based on the percentage of gain allocable to that partner. Any partner that does not provide a valid certification of non-foreign status (including a Form W-9) is treated as a foreign person for this purpose.

To make the certification for a modified amount realized, the transferor must provide to the transferee a Form W-8IMY, *Certificate of Foreign Intermediary, Foreign Flow-Through Entity, or Certain U.S. Branches for United States Tax Withholding and Reporting*, that includes a certification of non-foreign status for each partner that is treated as a U.S. person. It must also include a withholding statement that provides the percentage of gain allocable to each direct or indirect partner and that indicates whether that person is a U.S. person or is treated as a foreign person.

3. Lack of Money or Property or Lack of Knowledge Regarding Liabilities

As described in section 8 of Notice 2018-29, in some cases, a reduction in the transferor's share of partnership liabilities may cause the amount otherwise required to be withheld to exceed the cash or other property that the transferee actually pays to the transferor. In other cases, a transferee may have not received, or cannot rely upon, a certification regarding the transferor's share of partnership liabilities, and may not otherwise know the transferor's share of partnership liabilities. In these situations, the proposed regulations generally provide that the amount required to be withheld is equal to the amount realized determined without regard to the decrease in the transferor's share of partnership liabilities. *See* proposed § 1.1446(f)-2(c)(3).

4. Certification of Maximum Tax Liability

To more closely align the amount to withhold with the transferor's tax liability under section 864(c)(8), the proposed regulations provide a procedure to determine the amount to withhold that is intended to estimate the amount of tax the transferor is required to pay under section 864(c)(8). *See* proposed § 1.1446(f)-2(c)(4).

For this procedure to apply, a transferee must receive a certification from the transferor containing certain information relating to the transferor and the transfer. *See* proposed § 1.1446(f)-2(c)(4)(iii). One of the requirements for this certification is for the transferor to identify the amount of outside capital gain and outside ordinary gain that would be treated as effectively connected gain on the determination date. *See* proposed § 1.1446(f)-2(c)(4)(iii)(E). Further, to provide this certification, the transferor must represent that it has obtained a statement from the partnership that includes, among other things, information relating to the transferor's distributive share of effectively connected gain in connection with a deemed sale described in section 864(c)(8)(B) as of the determination date. *See* proposed § 1.1446(f)-2(c)(4)(iii)(G).

When a transferor provides a transferee this information, proposed § 1.1446(f)-2(c)(4)(i) allows the transferee to withhold based on the transferor's maximum tax liability on the transfer. The transferor's maximum tax liability is the amount of the transferor's effectively connected gain multiplied by the applicable percentage. *See* section 1446(b) and § 1.1446-3(a)(2). The applicable percentage applies the highest rate of tax for each particular type of income or gain allocable to a foreign person. *Id.*

Special rules apply for a transfer in which only a portion of the gain is subject to tax under section 864(c)(8) because a nonrecognition provision of the Code or an income tax treaty in effect between the United States and a foreign country applies (for example, when the partnership carries on one trade or business through a U.S. permanent establishment, and another trade or business that is not carried on through a U.S. permanent establishment). *See* proposed § 1.1446(f)-2(c)(4)(v) and (vi). These rules provide that the transferor must, in addition to providing the maximum tax liability certification, comply with the procedural requirements that would otherwise apply when claiming a full exception to withholding based on a nonrecognition provision or treaty benefits.

D. *Reporting and Paying Withheld Amounts*

1. In General

A transferee required to withhold must report and pay any tax withheld by the 20th day after the date of the transfer. *See* proposed § 1.1446(f)-2(d)(1). To report and pay the amount withheld, the proposed regulations direct the transferee to use Forms 8288, *U.S. Withholding Tax Return for Dispositions by Foreign Persons of U.S. Real Property Interests*, and 8288-A, *Statement of Withholding on Dispositions by Foreign Persons of U.S. Real Property Interests*. The IRS will stamp a valid Form 8288-A to show receipt and mail a copy to the transferor.

2. Transferee's Obligation to Certify the Amount Withheld to the Partnership

As discussed in section IV of this Explanation of Provisions, a partnership must withhold on distributions to a transferee under section 1446(f)(4) to the extent the transferee fails to properly withhold under section 1446(f)(1) and proposed § 1.1446(f)-2(a). *See* proposed § 1.1446(f)-3. In order for the partnership to determine whether it must withhold under these rules, proposed § 1.1446(f)-2(d)(2) requires a transferee to timely furnish certain information regarding its compliance with section 1446(f)(1) to the partnership.

Specifically, proposed § 1.1446(f)-2(d)(2) requires a transferee (other than a partnership that is a transferee because it makes a distribution) to furnish, no later than 10 days after the transfer, a certification to the partnership that either includes a copy of the Form 8288-A that it files with the IRS, or states the amount realized on the transfer and any amount withheld by the transferee. The certification must also include any underlying certifications that the transferee has relied upon that claim an exception or adjustment to withholding. As discussed in section IV.B of this Explanation of Provisions, the partnership must conduct its own review of the certification provided by the transferee, including any underlying certifications. Therefore, a transferee that has relied on a certification claiming an exception or adjustment to withholding may want to ensure that the partnership has determined the certification to be correct and reliable before the due date for payment of any withheld amounts to the IRS.

E. *Effect of Withholding on Transferor*

Proposed § 1.1446(f)-2(e) states that a foreign person must file a U.S. tax return and pay any tax due with respect to a transfer that is subject to section 864(c)(8) regardless of whether there is withholding under section 1446(f)(1) and proposed § 1.1446(f)-2. To claim a credit under section 33, a transferor that is an individual or corporation must attach to its return the stamped copy of Form 8288-A, as referenced in section III.D of this Explanation of Provisions. *See* proposed § 1.1446(f)-2(e)(2)(i). If a stamped copy of Form 8288-A has not been provided to the transferor by the IRS, proposed § 1.1446(f)-2(e)(3) provides that a transferor may establish the amount of tax withheld by furnishing substantial evidence of the amount. For a discussion of the rule regarding a transferor that is a foreign partnership claiming a credit for withholding under section 1446(f)(1), see section II.E of this Explanation of Provisions.

IV. *Partnership's Requirement to Withhold under Section 1446(f)(4) on Distributions to Transferee*

A. *In General*

Proposed § 1.1446(f)-3 provides rules under section 1446(f)(4) that would implement the partnership's requirement to withhold on distributions to a transferee on any amount that the transferee failed to properly withhold under section 1446(f)(1), plus any interest on this amount. The rules, when made applicable as final rules, would end the suspension of section 1446(f)(4) withholding provided in section 11 of Notice 2018-29.

B. *Requirement to Withhold*

The proposed regulations provide that, if a transferee fails to withhold any amount required to be withheld under proposed § 1.1446(f)-2 in connection with the transfer of a partnership interest, the partnership must withhold from any distributions made to the transferee in accordance with the rules in proposed § 1.1446(f)-3. Under the general rule, a partnership determines whether a transferee has withheld the amount required to be withheld under proposed § 1.1446(f)-2 by relying on the certification described in proposed § 1.1446(f)-2(d)(2) that it receives from the transferee. *See* proposed § 1.1446(f)-3(a)(1). The partnership may rely on this certification unless it knows, or has reason to know, that the certification is incorrect or unreliable. *Id.* Therefore, the partnership must review the certification received from the transferee, which includes any underlying certifications that the transferee relied on to reduce or eliminate withholding. Because the partnership may have information that may not be available to the transferee (for example, information in its books and records), a partnership may know, or have reason to know, that an underlying certification is incorrect or unreliable even though the transferee properly relied on the certification. In this case, the partnership would be required to withhold on the transferee under section 1446(f)(4) to the extent required in proposed § 1.1446(f)-3.

If the partnership timely receives (within 10 days from the transfer), and may rely on, a certification from the transferee stating that an exception to withholding applies or establishing that the transferee has withheld the amount required to be withheld under proposed § 1.1446(f)-2, then the partnership is not required to withhold under the general rule in proposed § 1.1446(f)-3(a)(1). *See* proposed § 1.1446(f)-3(b)(1). For this purpose, the amount required to be withheld may take into account any adjustment procedures under § 1.1446(f)-2(c) (for which any documents, including underlying certifications, are attached to the certification provided by the transferee). The proposed regulations thus reduce the burden imposed by section 1446(f)(4) by allowing transferees and partnerships to rely on the information produced under the regulations implementing section 1446(f)(1).

The proposed regulations provide an additional rule that allows the IRS, in limited circumstances, to require a partnership to withhold under section 1446(f)(4) when the IRS notifies the partnership that it has determined that the transferee has provided incorrect information on the certification described in proposed § 1.1446(f)-2(d)(2) regarding the amount realized or the amount withheld, or that the transferee failed to pay the amounts reported as withheld to the IRS. *See* proposed § 1.1446(f)-3(a)(2). This rule is meant to induce the transferee to properly determine the amount realized on transfer (in accordance with the rules in proposed § 1.1446(f)-2(c)(2)), and to correctly report to the partnership the amount of tax withheld and paid to the IRS.

Under the proposed regulations, withholding under section 1446(f)(4) does not apply when a partnership is a transferee because it makes a distribution. *See* proposed § 1.1446(f)-3(b)(3). Section 1446(f)(4) imposes a withholding obligation on a secondary party, the partnership, when the transferee fails to withhold under section 1446(f)(1). When the partnership is the transferee because it made a distribution and failed to withhold under section 1446(f)(1) and proposed § 1.1446(f)-2, imposing a section 1446(f)(4) withholding obligation on it does not provide an additional party to ensure the 1446(f) liability is paid. Furthermore, the partnership remains liable for its failure to withhold in its capacity as a transferee. *See* section VI.A of this Explanation of Provisions.

A publicly traded partnership generally is also not required to withhold on distributions made to a transferee under section 1446(f)(4). *See* proposed § 1.1446(f)-3(b)(2)(i). As described in section V of this Explanation of Provisions, it would be administratively difficult for a publicly traded partnership to determine when a transfer of its interest has occurred, and whether the correct amount has been withheld under section 1446(f)(1). However, the proposed regulations do require a publicly traded partnership to withhold under section 1446(f)(4) in certain limited instances. Specifically, a publicly traded partnership may publish a qualified notice that states that withholding under section 1446(f)(1) does not apply with respect to a distribution. *See* section V.B.2 and 3 of this Explanation of Provisions. To ensure that publicly traded partnerships exercise due diligence when publishing these qualified notices, proposed § 1.1446(f)-3(b)(2)(ii) provides that the exception from section 1446(f)(4) withholding applicable to publicly traded partnerships does not apply if a publicly traded partnership determines (including by reason of having received notification from the IRS) that it has published a qualified notice that falsely states that an exemption applied. When a publicly traded partnership makes this determination, it must withhold on distributions to the transferees an amount equal to the amount that any brokers failed to withhold under proposed § 1.1446(f)-4 due to reliance on the qualified notice, plus interest.

C. *Withholding Rules*

A partnership that does not receive, or cannot rely on, a timely certification from a transferee stating that an exception to withholding applies or that the proper amount has been withheld must begin to withhold under the general rule on distributions made to the transferee on the later of the date that is 30 days after the transfer or the date that is 15 days after the partnership acquires actual knowledge of the transfer. *See* proposed § 1.1446(f)-3(c)(1)(i).

The partnership must withhold on the entire amount of each distribution made to the transferee until it may rely on a certification from the transferee that states that an exception to withholding applies or that provides the information necessary to determine the amount required to be withheld. *See* proposed § 1.1446(f)-3(c)(1)(ii). The partnership may rely on this certification to determine its withholding obligation regardless of whether it is provided within the time prescribed in proposed § 1.1446(f)-2(d)(2). If the partnership has not already satisfied the amount required to be withheld, as determined from the certification from the transferee, it must continue to withhold on distributions to the transferee until it has done so. *Id*. However, the partnership may stop withholding if the transferee disposes of all of its interest in the partnership, unless the partnership has actual knowledge that any successor to the transferee is related to the transferee or the transferor from which the transferee acquired the interest. *Id*.

The amount required to be withheld under proposed § 1.1446(f)-3(a)(1), as determined from the certification provided by the transferee, is a tax equal to 10 percent of the amount realized on the transfer, reduced by any amount already withheld by the transferee, plus any computed interest. *See* proposed § 1.1446(f)-3(c)(2)(i). The proposed regulations provide that a partnership that is required to withhold under proposed § 1.1446(f)-3(a)(1) may not take into account any adjustment procedures that would otherwise affect the amount required to be withheld under proposed § 1.1446(f)-2(c)(2)(i). *See* proposed § 1.1446(f)-3(c)(2)(i)(A). Thus, for example, a partnership may not reduce the amount that it is required to withhold under the procedures described in proposed § 1.1446(f)-2(c)(4) (adjusting the amount subject to withholding based on a transferor's maximum tax liability). The Treasury Department and the IRS have determined that it would be inappropriate to permit adjustments that may reduce the amount required to be withheld under section 1446(f)(4). Withholding on distributions to transferees under section 1446(f)(4) applies only after the transferee has either failed to properly withhold under section 1446(f)(1) or has not complied with the applicable procedural requirements in the proposed regulations. Accordingly, permitting adjustments to the amount a partnership is required to withhold under section 1446(f)(4) would reduce transferees' incentive to comply with their obligations under section 1446(f)(1) while potentially increasing the partnership's administrative burden associated with that withholding.

Proposed § 1.1446(f)-3(c)(2)(ii) provides rules for the partnership to compute interest on the amount that the transferee failed to withhold. Proposed § 1.1446(f)-3(c)(3) provides that any amount required to be withheld on a distribution under any other withholding provision in the Code is not required to be withheld under section 1446(f)(4). For example, if a partnership is required to withhold $30 under section 1441 on a $100 distribution, the maximum amount required to be withheld on that distribution under section 1446(f)(4) is $70.

Proposed § 1.1446(f)-3(d) provides that a partnership required to withhold under section 1446(f)(4) must report and pay the tax withheld using Forms 8288, *U.S. Withholding Tax Return for Dispositions by Foreign Persons of U.S. Real Property Interests*, and 8288-C, *Statement of Withholding Under Section 1446(f)(4) for Withholding on Dispositions by Foreign Persons of Partnership Interests*, as provided in forms, instructions, or other guidance.

D. *Effect of Withholding on the Transferor and Transferee*

The withholding of tax under section 1446(f)(4) does not relieve a nonresident alien individual or foreign corporation subject to tax under section 864(c)(8) from filing a U.S. income tax return with respect to the transfer and paying any tax due with the return. *See* proposed § 1.1446(f)-3(e)(1). Because this tax is withheld from the transferee rather than from the transferor, the transferor is not allowed a credit under section 33. *Id*. However, the proposed regulations clarify that tax will not be collected from the transferor to the extent it has already been collected from another person under these rules. *See* section VI.A of this Explanation of Provisions. Therefore, the transferor will not be required to pay tax to the extent the tax (but not any portion treated as interest) has been paid through withholding on the transferee.

A transferee remains liable under section 1446(f)(1) even when the partnership is required to withhold under section 1446(f)(4). However, the transferee is treated as satisfying this withholding tax liability under section 1446(f)(1) to the extent that it is withheld upon under section 1446(f)(4). *See* proposed § 1.1446(f)-3(e)(2). Any amount withheld that is treated as interest is not treated as satisfying the transferee's liability under section 1446(f)(1), but that amount will instead be treated as interest paid by the transferee with respect to its section 1446(f)(1) liability. *Id*. Under the proposed regulations, if the amount of tax withheld from the transferee exceeds its liability under section 1446(f)(1), only the partnership may claim a refund on behalf of the transferee for the excess amount. *Id*. This rule is meant to make the refund process more administrable by having the partnership act on behalf of each of its transferees for purposes of claiming any excess amounts withheld under section 1446(f)(4). The Treasury Department and the IRS anticipate that partnerships and transferees will make arrangements by contract so that the transferees may be reimbursed for amounts refunded to the partnership. The Treasury Department and the IRS request comments on this issue.

V. *Withholding on the Transfer of a Publicly Traded Partnership Interest by a Foreign Person*

The proposed regulations provide rules for withholding and reporting on the transfer of an interest in a publicly traded partnership if the interest is publicly traded on an established securities market or is readily tradable on a secondary market or the substantial equivalent thereof (such interests, "PTP interests"). The rules, when made applicable as final rules, would end the suspension of section 1446(f)(1) withholding on the disposition of PTP interests provided in Notice 2018-08.

A. *In General*

A transfer of a PTP interest raises unique issues for withholding under section 1446(f). For example, when a transfer of a PTP interest is effected through one or more brokers, the transferee will generally not know the identity of the transferor. Accordingly, the Conference Report for the Act acknowledged that transfers involving PTP interests could require withholding rules different from those that apply to transfers involving non-PTP interests. *See* Conference Report on H.R. 1, Tax Cuts and Jobs Act, H.Rep. No. 115-466, at 511 ("[T]he Secretary may provide guidance permitting a broker, as agent of the transferee, to deduct and withhold the tax . . . such guidance may provide that if an interest in a publicly traded partnership is sold by a foreign partner through a broker, the broker may deduct and withhold the 10-percent tax on behalf of the transferee.").

Consistent with the Conference Report, proposed § 1.1446(f)-4(a)(1) provides that if a transfer of a PTP interest is effected through one or more brokers, the transferee is not required to withhold, and the withholding obligation is instead imposed on certain brokers involved with the transfer. Generally, the proposed regulations define a broker to include any person, foreign or domestic, that in the ordinary course of a trade or business during the calendar year stands ready to effect sales made by others, and that, in connection with a transfer of a PTP interest, receives all or a portion of the amount realized on behalf of the transferor. *See* proposed § 1.1446(f)-1(b)(1). For example, when a transfer of a PTP interest occurs through a cash on delivery account, a delivery versus payment account, or other similar account or transaction, this definition would include a broker that receives an amount realized from the sale against delivery of the PTP interest and any other broker that receives an amount realized from that broker. Therefore, the withholding obligation under proposed § 1.1446(f)-4 is generally limited to brokers that receive proceeds from the sale and act on behalf of the transferor. The definition of broker also includes any clearing organization that effects a transfer of a PTP interest on behalf of the transferor. While comments have stated that clearing organizations may not have the capability to complete the withholding required under section 1446(f), the Treasury Department and the IRS anticipate that clearing organizations will make arrangements to ensure that, when effecting the transfer of a PTP interest on behalf of foreign brokers, they act on behalf of brokers that assume withholding responsibility when clearing sales of PTP interests (such as a qualified intermediary ("QI")).

If a transfer of a PTP interest is effected through multiple brokers, proposed § 1.1446(f)-4(a)(2) provides rules that specify which broker or brokers have a withholding obligation. Under proposed § 1.1446(f)-4(a)(2)(i), a broker that pays the amount realized to a foreign broker is required to withhold unless the foreign broker is either a U.S branch treated as a U.S. person or a QI that assumes primary withholding responsibility for the payment. Consistent with this rule, the Treasury Department and the IRS intend to modify the QI agreement provided in Revenue Procedure 2017-15, 2017-3 I.R.B. 437, to allow QIs to assume primary withholding responsibility on the amount realized. Proposed § 1.1446(f)-4(a)(2)(ii) provides an additional rule requiring the broker that effects a transfer for the transferor as its customer to satisfy the withholding obligation. This rule ensures that withholding will be completed on payment of the amount realized to the transferor when another broker has not already satisfied the withholding.

To avoid withholding by multiple brokers, proposed § 1.1446(f)-4(a)(2)(iii) provides the general rule that a broker is not required to withhold when it knows that the withholding obligation has been satisfied by another broker. Proposed § 1.1446(f)-4(a)(2)(iv) provides that a broker must treat another broker as a foreign person unless it obtains documentation (including a certification of non-foreign status) establishing that the other broker is a U.S. person.

If the transfer of a PTP interest is not effected through one or more brokers, then proposed § 1.1446(f)-4 does not apply, and the general rules of section 1446(f)(1) and proposed § 1.1446(f)-2 apply. A transfer that is effected through a broker includes a distribution with respect to a PTP interest held through an account with a broker.

B. *Exceptions to Withholding*

The proposed regulations provide five exceptions to withholding that apply to the transfer of a PTP interest. The exceptions are intended to both reduce the compliance burden placed on brokers and provide rules that are administrable.

1. Certification of Non-Foreign Status

As mentioned in section III.B.2 of this Explanation of Provisions, withholding under section 1446(f)(1) is limited to transfers by foreign partners. Accordingly, a broker is not required to withhold to the extent that it relies on a certification of non-foreign status that it receives from the transferor that claims an exception to withholding. *See* proposed § 1.1446(f)-4(b)(2). For purposes of proposed § 1.1446(f)-4, a certification of non-foreign status means a Form W-9, or valid substitute form, that meets the requirements of § 1.1441-1(d)(2). A broker may rely on a valid Form W-9 that it already possesses, and in certain cases, may instead rely on a certification that it receives from another broker that states the TIN and status of the transferor when that other broker acts as an agent for the transferor and possesses the Form W-9 (for example, from an introducing broker). A broker will not qualify for the exception provided in proposed § 1.1446(f)-4(b)(2) if it has actual knowledge that the certification is incorrect or unreliable.

2. 10-Percent Exception

The proposed regulations include an exception to withholding that may apply if, on a deemed sale of the assets of the publicly traded partnership the interest in which is transferred, the amount of effectively connected gain would be less than 10 percent of the total gain. Specifically, proposed § 1.1446(f)-4(b)(3) provides that a broker is not required to withhold under proposed § 1.1446(f)-4 if it properly relies on a qualified notice stating that the 10-percent exception applies.

The 10-percent exception applies if a hypothetical sale by the publicly traded partnership of all of its assets at fair market value on a specified date would result in an amount of gain effectively connected with the conduct of a trade or business within the United States that is less than 10 percent of the total gain. The specified date must be a date designated by the publicly traded partnership that is within the 92-day period ending on the date that it posts a qualified notice. Unlike the similar exception described in section III.B.4 of this Explanation of Provisions that applies to transfers of non-PTP interests, this rule requires a publicly traded partnership to designate a date for this purpose that generally occurs within the most recent calendar quarter. *Cf.* proposed § 1.1446(f)-2(b)(4) (permitting the deemed sale computation to occur on a determination date, which would allow the deemed sale date to be determined as of the first day of a partnership's taxable year in which the transfer occurred in certain cases). The Treasury Department and the IRS have determined that it is appropriate to limit the availability of this exception to cases in which a publicly traded partnership has designated a deemed sale date occurring within the most recent calendar quarter because publicly traded partnerships are in a better position to determine the value of their assets, and in some cases determine the basis of their assets, on a quarterly basis. The proposed regulations limit reliance on a qualified notice depending on its date of posting. *See* proposed § 1.1446(f)-4(b)(3)(iii).

For a discussion of rules regarding when a publicly traded partnership may be liable under section 1446(f)(4) because it falsely states on a qualified notice that this exception applies, see section IV.B of this Explanation of Provisions. For a discussion of the proposed changes to existing qualified notice rules, see section VII of this Explanation of Provisions.

3. Qualified Current Income Distributions

As discussed in section III.B.3 of this Explanation of Provisions, the proposed regulations allow a transferor of a non-PTP interest to provide a certification stating that the transferor would not realize any gain on the transfer. Because it would be administratively difficult for a broker to timely obtain this type of certification from the transferor of a PTP interest, and difficult for the transferor to determine its basis in the PTP interest, the proposed regulations do not provide a similar exception for transfers of PTP interests.

The Treasury Department and the IRS have determined, however, that it would be appropriate to eliminate withholding under section 1446(f)(1) on distributions (the full amount of which is generally treated as an amount realized under the proposed regulations) by a publicly traded partnership when it is likely that the transferor would realize no gain. In general, under section 705(a)(1), a partner's basis in its interest is increased by its distributive share of income for the taxable year, such that a distribution by the partnership not in excess of that income generally does not result in the recognition of gain under section 731(a)(1). Accordingly, the proposed regulations provide that when a qualified notice posted by a publicly traded partnership indicates that the distribution does not exceed the net income the partnership earned since the record date of the partnership's last distribution, no withholding is required with respect to the distribution. *See* proposed § 1.1446(f)-4(b)(4).

4. Proceeds Subject to Withholding under Section 3406

A broker may also be required to withhold on gross proceeds from the transfer of a PTP interest under section 3406 when a payment is treated as being made to a nonexempt U.S. recipient. To prevent withholding twice on the same payment, proposed § 1.1446(f)-4(b)(5) provides an exception to withholding under section 1446(f)(1) if the amount realized is subject to withholding under section 3406.

5. Claim of Treaty Benefits

The proposed regulations provide an exception similar to the one described in section III.B.6 of this Explanation of Provisions when a transferor states that it is not subject to tax on any gain from the transfer pursuant to an income tax treaty in effect between the United States and a foreign country. *See* proposed § 1.1446(f)-4(b)(6). The exception also requires the transferor to furnish a valid Form W-8 with the information necessary to support the claim. *Id.* Unlike the exception for non-PTP interests, a broker is not required to mail the certification to the IRS because under the proposed regulations brokers are required to file a Form 1042-S, *Foreign Person's U.S. Source Income Subject to Withholding,* to report a transfer of a PTP interest that includes information about the claim of treaty benefits. *See* section V.D of this Explanation of Provisions for reporting requirements with respect to transfers of PTP interests.

C. *Determining the Amount to Withhold*

1. Amount Realized

i. In General

A broker that is required to withhold under proposed § 1.1446(f)-4(a) must withhold 10 percent of the amount realized on the transfer of a PTP interest. As explained in section III.C.2 of this Explanation of Provisions, a reduction in a partner's share of partnership liabilities is treated as an amount realized under proposed § 1.1446(f)-2(c). However, because of the difficulties involved with requiring a broker to timely determine a transferor's share of partnership liabilities, proposed § 1.1446(f)-4(c)(2)(i) provides a special rule that treats the amount realized on the transfer of a PTP interest as the amount of gross proceeds (as defined in § 1.6045-1(d)(5)) paid or credited to the customer or another broker (as applicable). If a publicly traded partnership makes a distribution to a partner, the amount realized is the amount of cash distributed (or to be distributed) and the fair market value of property distributed (or to be distributed).

ii. Modified Amount Realized for Foreign Partnerships

Consistent with the rule described in section III.C.2.iii of this Explanation of Provisions that applies to transfers of non-PTP interests, the proposed regulations include a rule that allows brokers to rely on a certification from a foreign partnership to modify the amount realized based on the extent to which the amount realized is attributable to persons who are (or are presumed to be) foreign persons. *See* proposed § 1.1446(f)-4(c)(2)(ii).

D. *Reporting and Paying Withheld Amounts*

A broker required to withhold under § 1.1446(f)-4 must pay the withheld tax pursuant to the deposit rules in § 1.6302-2, and report the withholding on Forms 1042, *Annual Withholding Tax Return for U.S. Source Income of Foreign Persons,* and 1042-S pursuant to the procedures in § 1.1461-1(b) and (c). The proposed regulations treat as a recipient for Form 1042-S reporting purposes a partner that receives an amount realized from a transfer of a PTP interest subject to § 1.1446(f)-4. *See* proposed § 1.1461-1(c)(1)(ii)(A)(8). This rule also clarifies that a foreign partnership is treated as a recipient for this purpose to ensure that the foreign partnership receives a Form 1042-S that it may use to claim credit for any withholding under proposed § 1.1446(f)-4 against its tax liability under section 1446(a). *See* section II.E of this Explanation of Provisions for discussion of the general coordination rule.

To implement the reporting requirements, the proposed regulations add to the list of amounts subject to reporting on Form 1042-S an amount realized on the transfer of a PTP interest subject to § 1.1446(f)-4 (with limited exceptions). *See* proposed § 1.1461-1(c)(2). The proposed regulations also add to this list any distributions of effectively connected income by a publicly traded partnership subject to § 1.1446-4 to clarify that these amounts are reportable on Form 1042-S. *Id.*

E. *Effect of Withholding on Transferor*

As mentioned in section III.E of this Explanation of Provisions, the proposed regulations neither relieve a transferor of its substantive tax liability under section 864(c)(8), nor relieve a transferor subject to section 864(c)(8) from its filing obligation. *See* proposed § 1.1446(f)-4(e)(1). However, a transferor is allowed a credit under section 33 for the amount withheld under section 1446(f)(1) and proposed § 1.1446(f)-4. *Id.* To claim the credit, the transferor must attach to its return a copy of the Form 1042-S that includes the transferor's TIN. *Id.* For a discussion of the rules regarding a transferor that is a foreign partnership claiming a credit for withholding under section 1446(f)(1), see section II.E of this Explanation of Provisions.

F. *Procedures to Adjust Overwithholding*

Section 1.1461-2(a) allows a withholding agent that overwithheld under chapter 3 of the Code, and made a deposit of tax as provided in § 1.6302-2(a), to adjust the overwithheld amount using either a reimbursement or a set-off procedure. Because these rules are meant to allow withholding agents to adjust overwithholding for any deposited amounts that are reportable on Forms 1042 and 1042-S, the proposed regulations modify § 1.1461-2(a) to allow use of the adjustment procedures for amounts withheld by a broker pursuant to proposed § 1.1446(f)-4 (which are reported on Forms 1042 and 1042-S, as noted in section V.D. of this Explanation of Provisions).

G. *Procedures to Adjust Underwithholding*

In general, § 1.1461-2(b) allows a withholding agent that underwithheld on a beneficial owner under chapter 3 of the Code to withhold from future payments made to the beneficial owner, or satisfy the tax from property or additional contributions of the beneficial owner, before the earlier of the due date for filing Form 1042 or the date on which the form is actually filed. The proposed regulations amend this provision to allow the use of this procedure by brokers that underwithheld under proposed § 1.1446(f)-4 on the transfer of a PTP interest.

H. *Refunds and Credits*

Section 1.1464-1 generally provides that if an overpayment of tax has actually been withheld from the beneficial owner of the income, any refund or credit will be made to that beneficial owner. If, however, the tax was not withheld at source, but was instead paid by the withholding agent, the refund or credit will be made to the withholding agent. The proposed regulations clarify that these rules apply for purposes of section 1446(f). *See* proposed § 1.1464-1(a).

VI. *Liability for Failure to Withhold*

A. *In General*

Proposed § 1.1446(f)-5(a) provides that every person required to deduct and withhold tax under section 1446(f), including under proposed §§ 1.1446(f)-2 through 1.1446(f)-4, but that fails to do so is liable under section 1461. If the tax required to be withheld is paid by another person required to withhold, or by the nonresident alien individual or foreign corporation subject to tax under section 864(c)(8), section 1463 and the proposed regulations clarify that the tax will only be collected once. However, the satisfaction of this liability does not relieve a person that failed to withhold under section 1446(f) from any interest, penalties, or additions to tax that would otherwise apply. The proposed regulations also provide that a partnership that fails to withhold under proposed § 1.1446(f)-3 is liable under section 1461 only for the amount of tax that it failed to withhold, and not any interest computed under § 1.1446(f)-3(c)(2)(ii). This rule ensures that interest will be computed and assessed only once with respect to the same underlying tax liability.

B. *Liability of Agents*

Proposed § 1.1446(f)-5(b) provides rules for the liability of agents, which generally require an agent of a transferor or transferee to notify the transferee (or other person required to withhold) if it has knowledge that a certification furnished to that person is false. A person that receives notice from an agent may not rely on the certification to apply an exception to withholding or for determining the amount to withhold. Proposed § 1.1446(f)-5(b)(2) provides procedural rules regarding the timing and content of the notice, and requires the agent to furnish a copy of the notice to the IRS. An agent that fails to provide the required notice is liable for the tax that the person that should have received the notice would have been required to withhold under section 1446(f). However, under proposed § 1.1446(f)-5(b)(4), this liability is limited to the amount of compensation that the agent derives from the transaction (and any civil or criminal penalties that may apply). The proposed regulations clarify that brokers required to withhold under § 1.1446(f)-4 are not treated as agents for purposes of this rule, and are instead liable for any failure to withhold under the rules described in section V of this Explanation of Provisions.

VII. Amendments to Existing Section 1446 Regulations Relating to Distributions by Publicly Traded Partnerships

In response to comments received outside the context of section 1446(f), the proposed regulations also contain changes to the existing qualified notice rules that apply to distributions that publicly traded partnerships make to foreign partners. The Treasury Department and the IRS are aware that in certain cases nominees receive notices of distribution from publicly traded partnerships that do not provide detailed information regarding the amounts of income comprising the distribution as specified in § 1.1446-4(f)(3) (such as amounts described in section 1441 or section 1442 or subject to withholding under section 1446). The term "qualified notice" under § 1.1446-4(b)(4) is currently defined by reference to the reporting requirements of 17 CFR 240.10b-17(b)(1) or (3), which do not include a requirement to report information regarding the types of income comprising the distribution. Unless a notice provides that information, however, a nominee will not have the information necessary to apply the ordering rule of § 1.1446-4(f)(3) to the distribution for purposes of determining the amount required to be withheld.

The proposed regulations make two changes to resolve this issue. First, proposed § 1.1446-4(b)(4) revises the method for a publicly traded partnership to provide a nominee a qualified notice by requiring that the notice be posted in a readily accessible format in an area of the primary public Web site of the publicly traded partnership that is dedicated to this purpose. Second, proposed § 1.1446-4(d) creates a default withholding rule subjecting gross distributions to the higher of the withholding percentage required under sections 1441 and 1442 or the applicable percentage under section 1446(b)(2), unless a qualified notice provides the nominee sufficient detail to determine the types of income distributed and the appropriate withholding rates to apply. Thus, if a publicly traded partnership is unable to determine the makeup of a distribution when it is made, the nominee must withhold at the highest applicable rate.

The proposed regulations also expand the definition of a nominee for withholding under § 1.1446-4 to include certain foreign persons that agree to assume primary withholding responsibility. Therefore, a QI or a U.S. branch treated as a U.S. person that assumes primary withholding responsibility for a distribution by a publicly traded partnership under proposed § 1.1446-4(b)(3) can act as a nominee with respect to the distribution. The Treasury Department and the IRS intend to modify the QI agreement provided in Revenue Procedure 2017-15 to allow QIs to assume primary withholding responsibility for distributions by publicly traded partnerships under section 1446(a).

The proposed regulations also make changes to the qualified notice rules applicable to publicly traded partnerships, publicly traded trusts, and real estate investment trusts ("REITs") under section 1445 that conform to proposed § 1.1446-4(b)(4) so that those rules also provide more readily available information for nominees. *See* proposed § 1.1445-8(f).

As discussed in sections V.F and V.G of this Explanation of Provisions, the proposed regulations modify § 1.1461-2(a) and (b) to allow use of procedures to adjust overwithholding and underwithholding for amounts withheld by a broker pursuant to proposed § 1.1446(f)-4. The proposed regulations also amend § 1.1461-2(a) to allow the use of reimbursement and set-off procedures with respect to amounts withheld under section 1446(a) on distributions of ECTI by publicly traded partnerships (which are reported on Forms 1042 and 1042-S, as opposed to Forms 8804, *Annual Return for Partnership Withholding Tax (Section 1446)*, and 8805 used by non-publicly traded partnerships to report withholding on ECTI allocable to foreign partners). They also amend § 1.1461-2(b) to clarify that the existing reference to "distributions of effectively connected income under section 1446" is meant to apply only to those distributions that are made by publicly traded partnerships.

Applicability Dates

Proposed § 1.864(c)(8)-2(a) and proposed § 1.6050K-1(d)(3) apply to transfers that occur on or after the date that these regulations are published as final regulations in the **Federal Register** (the "finalization date"). Proposed § 1.864(c)(8)-2(b) and (c) and proposed § 1.6050K-1(c)(2) and (c)(3) apply to returns filed on or after the finalization date. Proposed § 1.864(c)(8)-2(d) applies beginning on the finalization date.

Proposed §§ 1.1445-2(b)(2)(v) and 1.1445-5(b)(3)(iv) apply to certifications provided on or after July 7, 2019, except that a taxpayer may apply those provisions with respect to certifications provided before that date. A taxpayer may rely on the proposed amendments to §§ 1.1445-2 and 1.1445-5 with respect to any period before the finalization date. Proposed § 1.1445-8(f)(1) applies to distributions made on or after the date that is 60 days after the finalization date.

Proposed § 1.1446-3(c)(4) applies to partnership taxable years that include transfers that occur on or after the date that is 60 days after the finalization date. Proposed § 1.1446-4(b)(2), (b)(3), (c), (d), and (f) apply to distributions made on or after the date that is 60 days after the finalization date.

Proposed §§ 1.1446(f)-1 through 1.1446(f)-5 apply to transfers that occur on or after the date that is 60 days after the finalization date. For transfers that occur before the date that is 60 days after the finalization date, taxpayers may apply the rules described in Notice 2018-08 and Notice 2018-29. Alternatively, instead of applying the rules described in Notice 2018-29, taxpayers and other affected persons may choose to apply §§ 1.1446(f)-1, 1.1446(f)-2, and 1.1446(f)-5 of the proposed regulations in their entirety to all transfers as if they were final regulations.

The proposed amendments to § 1.1461-1(a)(1), (c)(1)(i), (c)(1)(ii), (c)(2)(i) and (c)(4) apply with respect to returns for transfers occurring on or after the date that is 60 days after the finalization date. The proposed amendments to § 1.1461-2(a)(1) and (b) apply to transfers occurring on or after the date that is 60 days after the finalization date. The proposed amendments to § 1.1461-3 apply to returns for transfers occurring on or after the date that is 60 days after the finalization date.

The proposed amendments to § 1.1463-1(a) apply to transfers that occur on or after the date that is 60 days after the finalization date.

The proposed amendments to § 1.1464-1(a) apply to transfers that occur on or after the date that is 60 days after the finalization date.

The Treasury Department and the IRS intend to obsolete Notice 2018-08 and Notice 2018-29 effective on the date that is 60 days after the finalization date.

Special Analyses

I. *Regulatory Planning and Review*

This regulation is not subject to review under section 6(b) of Executive Order 12866 pursuant to the Memorandum of Agreement (April 11, 2018) between the Treasury Department and the Office of Management and Budget regarding review of tax regulations.

II. *Paperwork Reduction Act*

The collection of information in these proposed regulations is in proposed § 1.864(c)(8)-2 regarding reporting for transactions described in section 864(c)(8) and proposed § 1.864(c)(8)-1, and proposed §§ 1.1446(f)-1, 1.1446(f)-2, 1.1446(f)-3, and 1.1446(f)-4 regarding the withholding, reporting, and paying of tax under section 1446(f) following the transfer of an interest described in section 864(c)(8) and proposed § 1.864(c)(8)-1. Section II.1 of this

Special Analyses discusses the collections of information that will be conducted using IRS forms. The information collections that will not be conducted through IRS forms are discussed in section II.2 of this Special Analyses.

A. Collections of Information - Forms 1042, 1042-S, 8288, 8288-A, 8288-C, W-8IMY, W-8BEN, and W-8BEN-E

Under proposed §§1.1446(f)-2(b)(2) and 1.1446(f)-4(b)(2), a transferor qualifies for an exception from withholding if it provides to the transferee or broker (as applicable) a certification of non-foreign status, which includes a valid Form W-9 (at the transferor's option). The IRS has determined that Form W-9 is not a collection of information under 5 CFR 1320.3(h)(1) and is exempt from the Paperwork Reduction Act of 1995 (44 U.S.C. 3507(d)) ("PRA").

The collection of information in proposed §1.1446(f)-2(b)(7) is provided by the transferor by submitting a certification and Form W-8BEN or W-8BEN-E to the transferee and is optional. The information will be used by the transferor to determine whether an exception to withholding applies based on an income tax treaty.

The information in proposed §1.1446(f)-2(c)(2)(iv)(C) by the transferor to the transferee is provided on Form W-8IMY and is optional. This information will be used by the transferee to determine the modified amount realized.

The collection of information in proposed §1.1446(f)-2(d)(1) will be provided on Forms 8288 and 8288-A by the transferee to the IRS and is mandatory if the transferee withholds tax under section 1446(f)(1). These forms will be used by the transferee to report and pay any tax under section 1446(f)(1) and proposed §1.1446(f)-2.

The information provided in proposed §1.1446(f)-3(d) by the partnership to the IRS will be used by the partnership to report and pay any tax under section 1446(f)(4) and proposed §1.1446(f)-3 and will be provided on new Form 8288-C. The IRS anticipates that the burden associated with this collection of information will be reflected in OMB control number 1545-0902.

The collection of information provided in proposed §1.1446(f)-4(a)(2)(i) from certain U.S. branches of foreign persons and qualified intermediaries to the broker that effected the transfer of an interest described in section 864(c)(8) and proposed §1.1446(f)-4 will be provided on Form W-8IMY. This information will be used by the broker to determine its withholding obligation under section 1446(f)(1) and proposed §1.1446(f)-4.

The collection of information in proposed §1.1446(f)-4(b)(6) is provided by the transferor by submitting a certification and Form W-8BEN or W-8BEN-E to the broker and is optional. The information will be used by the broker to determine whether an exception to withholding applies based on an income tax treaty.

The information in proposed §1.1446(f)-4(c)(2)(ii)(C) by the transferor to the broker is provided on Form W-8IMY and is optional. This information will be used by the broker to determine the modified amount realized.

The information in proposed §1.1446(f)-4(d) will be provided on Forms 1042 and 1042-S submitted by the broker to the IRS and is mandatory if the broker withholds tax under section 1446(f)(1) or if it applies the exception described in proposed §1.1446(f)-4(b)(6). These forms will be used to report and pay any tax under section 1446(f)(1) and proposed §1.1446(f)-4.

The information in proposed §1.1446(f)-4(e)(2) provided by the transferor to the IRS will be used to claim a credit for an amount withheld under section 1446(f)(1) and proposed §1.1446(f)-4, and will be satisfied by submitting Form 1042-S with an income tax return (Form 1040NR or 1120-F) to the IRS.

The Treasury Department and the IRS intend that the information collection requirements described in this section II.1 will be set forth in the forms and instructions identified in the Revision of Existing Forms and New Forms table. As a result, for purposes of the PRA, the reporting burdens associated with the collections of information in those forms will be reflected in the PRA submissions associated with those forms.

Revision of Existing Forms and New Forms

	New	Revision of existing form	Number of additional respondents (estimated, rounded to nearest 1,000)
Form 1042-S		Y	< 6,000
Form 8288		Y	< 70,000
Form 8288-A		Y	< 70,000
Form 8288-C	Y		<70,000
Form W-8BEN		Y	< 70,000
Form W-8BEN-E		Y	< 70,000
Form W-8IMY		Y	< 70,000

Source: RAAS:CDW and SOI

The numbers of respondents in the Revision of Existing Forms and New Forms table were estimated by the Research, Applied Analytics and Statistics Division of the IRS from the Compliance Data Warehouse and Statistics of Income, using tax years 2013 through 2015. Data for each of the Forms 1042, 1042-S, 8288, 8288-A, W-8BEN, W-8BEN-E, and W-8IMY represent preliminary estimates of the total number of additional taxpayers that are expected to file these forms. The tax data for 2016 and 2017 are not yet available. Data for Forms 8288, 8288-A, W-8BEN, W-8BEN-E, and W-8IMY represent preliminary estimates of the total number of interests in partnerships, other than publicly traded partnership interests, engaged in the conduct of a trade or business in the United States that will be transferred by foreign persons. Data for Form 8288-C represent preliminary estimates of the total number of transferees on whom partnerships must withhold tax under section 1446(f)(4) if the transferees do not fully withhold tax under section 1446(f)(1). Data for Form 1042-S represent preliminary estimates of the total number of interests in publicly traded partnership engaged in the conduct of a trade or business in the United States that will be transferred by foreign persons.

The current status of the PRA submissions related to the tax forms that will be used to conduct the information collections in the proposed regulations is provided in the Current Status of PRA Submissions table. The overall burden estimates provided for the OMB control numbers below are aggregate amounts that relate to the entire package of forms associated with the applicable OMB control number and will in the future include, but not isolate, the estimated burden of the tax forms that will be created or revised as a result of the information collections in the proposed regulations. These numbers are therefore unrelated to the future calculations needed to assess the burden imposed by the proposed regulations. No burden estimates specific to the forms affected by the proposed regulations are currently available. The Treasury Department and the IRS have not estimated the burden, including that of any new information collections, related to the requirements under the proposed regulations. The Treasury Department and the IRS request comments on all aspects of information collection burdens related to the proposed regulations, including estimates for how much time it would take to comply with the paperwork burdens described above for each relevant form and ways for the IRS to minimize the paperwork burden.

Current Status of PRA Submissions

	Type of Filer	OMB Number(s)	Status
Form 1042, Form 1042-S	All filers (Legacy Model)	1545-0096	Approved 12/27/2016 until 12/31/2019.
	Link: https://www.reginfo.gov/public/do/PRAViewICR?ref_nbr=201606-1545-025		
Form 8288, Form 8288-A	All filers (Legacy system)	1545-0902	Approved 1/2/2017 until 1/31/2020.
	Link: https://www.reginfo.gov/public/do/PRAViewICR?ref_nbr=201608-1545-015		
Form W-8BEN, Form W-8BEN-E, Form W-8IMY	Business (NEW Model)	1545-0123	Approved 12/21/2018 until 12/31/2019.
	Link: *https://www.reginfo.gov/public/do/PRAViewICR?ref_nbr=201805-1545-019*		
	All other filers (Legacy system)	1545-1621	Approved 12/19/18 until 12/31/2021.
	Link: https://www.reginfo.gov/public/do/PRAViewICR?ref_nbr=201708-1545-002		

B. *Collections of Information - Proposed §§ 1.864(c)(8)-2(a) and (b), 1.1446(f)-1(c)(3), 1.1446(f)-2(b)(2) through (7), (c)(2), and (c)(4), 1.1446(f)-4(b)(2) and (6), 1.1446(f)-4(b)(3) and (4), and 1.1446(f)-2(d)(2)*

These proposed regulations contain collections of information that are not on existing or new IRS forms. These collections of information include:

(a) Notification by a transferor to a partnership that a transfer has occurred (proposed § 1.864(c)(8)-2(a));

(b) Statement provided by a partnership to a transferor necessary for the transferor to calculate its tax liability (proposed § 1.864(c)(8)-2(b));

(c) Retention of information by partnership in its books and records (proposed § 1.1446(f)-1(c)(3));

(d) Certifications from a transferor (or partnership) to a transferee for an exception from withholding or adjustment to amount realized (proposed § 1.1446(f)-2(b)(2) through (7), (c)(2), and (c)(4));

(e) Certification from a transferee to partnership regarding the transferee's withholding (proposed § 1.1446(f)-2(d)(2)).

(f) Certifications from a transferor to a broker to apply an exception from withholding (proposed § 1.1446(f)-4(b)(2) and (6)); and

(g) Information provided by a publicly traded partnership to a broker (proposed § 1.1446(f)-4(b)(3) and (4)).

The collections of information contained in this notice of proposed rulemaking has been submitted to the Office of Management and Budget for review in accordance with the PRA. Comments on the collection of information should be sent to the Office of Management and Budget, Attn: Desk Officer for the Department of the Treasury, Office of Information and Regulatory Affairs, Washington, DC 20503, with copies to the Internal Revenue Service, Attn: IRS Reports Clearance Officer, SE:W:CAR:MP:T:T:SP, Washington, DC 20224. Comments on the collection of information should be received by July 12, 2019. Comments are specifically requested concerning:

Whether the proposed collection of information is necessary for the proper performance of the IRS, including whether the information will have practical utility;

The accuracy of the estimated burden associated with the proposed collection of information (including underlying assumptions and methodology);

How the quality, utility, and clarity of the information to be collected may be enhanced;

How the burden of complying with the proposed collections of information may be minimized, including through the application of automated collection techniques or other forms of information technology; and

Estimates of capital or start-up costs and costs of operation, maintenance, and purchase of service to provide information.

The collections of information provided in proposed § 1.864(c)(8)-2 will be used by both the partnership engaged in the conduct of a trade or business in the United States and the foreign partner that transfers an interest in the partnership and are mandatory. The notification provided to the partnership by the foreign transferor in proposed § 1.864(c)(8)-2(a) will serve as notice to the partnership that a transfer described in section 864(c)(8) and proposed § 1.864(c)(8)-1 occurred. The statement provided to the foreign transferor by the partnership in proposed § 1.864(c)(8)-2(b) is necessary for the foreign transferor to determine its effectively connected gain or loss as described in proposed § 1.864(c)(8)-1(b) and (c).

The collection of information provided in proposed § 1.1446(f)-1(c)(3) requires a partnership to retain certain identified information in its books and records regarding its obligation to withhold under section 1446(f). The identified information will be used by a partnership to determine the application, and the extent, of withholding under section 1446(f).

The collections of information provided in proposed § 1.1446(f)-2(b)(2) through (7), (c)(2), and (c)(4) from the transferor of an interest described in section 1446(f), or from the partnership whose interest is transferred, to the transferee of the interest will be used by the transferee to determine whether an exception applies or to determine the amount realized. These collections of information are optional. The certification in proposed § 1.1446(f)-2(b)(7) includes the submission of Form W-8BEN or W-8BEN-E and is also discussed in section II.1 of this Special Analyses.

The information provided in proposed § 1.1446(f)-2(d)(2) by the transferee to the partnership will be used by the partnership to determine whether it has a withholding obligation under section 1446(f)(4) and proposed § 1.1446(f)-3.

The collection of information provided in proposed § 1.1446(f)-4(b)(6) by the transferor to the broker will be used by the broker to determine if an exception applies that relieves the broker from its withholding obligation under section 1446(f)(1) and proposed § 1.1446(f)-4. The certification in proposed § 1.1446(f)-4(b)(6) includes the submission of Form W-8BEN or W-8BEN-E and is also discussed in section II.1 of this Special Analyses.

Estimated total annual reporting burden: 50,920 hours.

Estimated average annual burden hours per respondent: Approximately 0.67 hours (40 minutes).

Estimated cost per respondent ($2016): $26.00.

Estimated total annual monetized cost ($2016): $1,827,938.00.

Estimated number of respondents: 76,000.

Estimated annual frequency of responses: 0.4 (as the collections of information do not occur on an annual basis).

An agency may not conduct or sponsor, and a person is not required to respond to, a collection of information unless it displays a valid control number assigned by the Office of Management and Budget.

Books or records relating to a collection of information must be retained as long as their contents may become material in the administration of any internal revenue law. Generally, tax returns and tax return information are confidential, as required by 26 U.S.C. 6103.

III. *Regulatory Flexibility Act*

It is hereby certified that this notice of proposed rulemaking will not have a significant economic impact on a substantial number of small entities within the meaning of section 601(6) of the Regulatory Flexibility Act (5 U.S.C. chapter 6).

The proposed regulations affect (i) foreign persons that recognize gain or loss from the sale or exchange of an interest in a partnership that is engaged in the conduct of a trade or business within the United States, and who are not subject to the Regulatory Flexibility Act, (ii) U.S. persons that are transferors providing Forms W-9 to transferees to certify that they are not foreign persons, (iii) persons who acquire those interests, (iv) partnerships that, directly or indirectly, have foreign persons as partners, and (v) brokers that effect transfers of interests in publicly traded partnerships.

The Treasury Department and the IRS do not have data readily available to assess the number of small entities potentially affected by the proposed regulations. However, entities potentially affected by these proposed regulations are generally not small entities, because of the resources and investment necessary to acquire a partnership interest from a foreign person or to directly, or indirectly, have foreign persons as partners. Therefore, the Treasury Department and the IRS do not believe that a substantial number of domestic small entities will be subject to the proposed regulation's information collections. Consequently, the Treasury Department and the IRS certify that the proposed regulations will not have a significant economic impact on a substantial number of small entities. The IRS invites the public to comment on the impact of these regulations on small entities.

Pursuant to section 7805(f) of the Code, these regulations will be submitted to the Chief Counsel for Advocacy of the Small Business Administration for comment on their impact on small businesses.

Comments and Requests for Public Hearing

Before the proposed regulations are adopted as final regulations, consideration will be given to any comments that are submitted timely to the IRS as prescribed in this preamble under the **"ADDRESSES"** heading. The Treasury Department and the IRS request comments on all aspects of the proposed rules. All comments will be available at www.regulations.gov or upon request. A public hearing will be scheduled if requested in writing by any person that timely submits written comments. If a public hearing is scheduled, notice of the date, time, and place for the public hearing will be published in the **Federal Register**.

Drafting Information

The principal authors of the proposed regulations are Subin Seth, Ronald M. Gootzeit, and Chadwick Rowland, Office of Associate Chief Counsel (International). However, other personnel from the Treasury Department and the IRS participated in their development.

Statement of Availability of IRS Documents

IRS Revenue Procedures, Revenue Rulings, notices, and other guidance cited in this document are published in the Internal Revenue Bulletin and are available from the Superintendent of Documents, U.S. Government Printing Office, Washington, DC 20402, or by visiting the IRS website at *http://www.irs.gov.*

[¶ 49,798] Proposed Amendments of Regulations (REG-125135-15), published in the Federal Register on May 20, 2019.

[Code Secs. 954 and 958]

Controlled foreign corporation (CFC): Related person: Income rules: Foreign base company sales.—Amendments of Reg. §§1.954-0, 1.954-1, 1.954-2 and 1.958-2, regarding the attribution of ownership of stock or other interests for purposes of determining whether a person is a related person with respect to a controlled foreign corporation (CFC) under section 954(d)(3), are adopted.

[¶ 49,799] Proposed Amendments of Regulations (REG-132240-15), published in the Federal Register on May 31, 2019.

[Code Sec. 3405]

Proposed regulation: Withholding on pensions, annuities and deferred income: Distributions delivered outside U.S..—Reg. §31.3405(e)-1, regarding withholding on certain periodic and nonperiodic distributions under Code Sec. 3405, other than eligible rollover distributions, is proposed.

AGENCY: Internal Revenue Service (IRS), Treasury.

ACTION: Notice of proposed rulemaking.

SUMMARY: This document contains a proposed regulation regarding withholding on certain periodic and nonperiodic distributions under section 3405, other than eligible rollover distributions. This regulation would affect payors and payees of these distributions.

DATES: Written or electronic comments and must be received by August 29, 2019. ADDRESSES: Send submissions to CC:PA:LPD:PR (REG-132240-15), room 5203, Internal Revenue Service, P.O. Box 7604, Ben Franklin Station, Washington DC 20044. Submissions may be hand-delivered Monday through Friday between the hours of 8 a.m. and 4 p.m. to CC:PA:LPD:PR (REG-132240-15), Courier's Desk, Internal Revenue Service, 1111 Constitution Avenue, N.W., Washington, DC 20224, or sent electronically via the Federal eRulemaking Portal at *http://www.regulations.gov* (indicate IRS REG-132240-15).

FOR FURTHER INFORMATION CONTACT: Concerning the proposed regulation, Jeremy D. Lamb at (202) 317-6799; concerning submissions of comments, Regina Johnson at (202) 317-6901 (not toll-free numbers).

SUPPLEMENTARY INFORMATION:

Background

Section 3405(a)(1) requires the payor of any periodic payment to withhold income tax from the payment. Under section 3405(a)(2), an individual generally may elect not to have section 3405(a)(1) apply with respect to periodic payments made to the individual. Section 3405(b)(1) requires the payor of any nonperiodic distribution to withhold income tax from the distribution. Under section 3405(b)(2), an individual generally may elect not to have section 3405(b)(1) apply with respect to any nonperiodic distribution.

Section 3405(e)(2) defines a periodic payment as a designated distribution that is an annuity or similar periodic payment. Section 3405(e)(3) defines a nonperiodic distribution as any designated distribution that is not a periodic payment. A designated distribution generally is defined in section 3405(e)(1) as any distribution or payment from or under an employer deferred compensation plan, an individual retirement plan (as defined in section 7701(a)(37)), or a commercial annuity. For this purpose, an employer deferred compensation plan is defined in section 3405(e)(5) as any pension, annuity, profit sharing, or stock bonus plan or other plan deferring the receipt of compensation, and a commercial annuity is defined in section 3405(e)(6) as an annuity, endowment, or life insurance contract issued by an insurance company licensed to do business under the laws of any State.

Section 3405(e)(1)(B) identifies certain amounts or payments that are not a "designated distribution" for purposes of section 3405 withholding. Under section 3405(e)(1)(B)(iii), any amount that is subject to withholding under subchapter A of chapter 3 (relating to withholding of tax on nonresident aliens and foreign corporations) by the person paying such amount or which would be so subject but for a tax treaty is not a designated distribution.

Section 3405(e)(13)(A) provides generally that, in the case of any periodic payment or nonperiodic distribution that is "to be delivered outside of the United States and any possession of the United States," no election may be made under section 3405(a)(2) or (b)(2) with respect to such payment, with the result that withholding may not be waived. Section 3405(e)(13)(B) provides that section 3405(e)(13)(A) does not apply if the recipient certifies to the payor, in such manner as the Secretary of the Treasury may prescribe, that the recipient is not (i) a United States citizen or a resident alien of the United States, or (ii) an individual to whom section 877 applies. Section 877(h) provides that section 877 applies to certain nonresident alien individuals whose expatriation date, as defined in section 877A(g)(3), is before June 17, 2008.

Notice 87-7 (1987-1 C.B. 420), see § 601.601(d)(2)(ii)(*b*), provides guidance under section 3405(e)(13)(A) to payors of designated distributions with respect to their duty to withhold income tax from such distributions. The notice addresses designated distributions to the following categories of payees: (1) payees who have provided the payors with a residence address outside of the United States;[1] (2) payees who have provided the payors with a residence address within the United States; and (3) payees who have not provided the payors with a residence address.

Notice 87-7 specifies that, if a payee has provided the payor with a residence address outside of the United States, the payor is required to withhold income tax from designated distributions to the payee. If a payee has provided the payor with a residence address within the United States, the payor is required to withhold income tax from these distributions to the payee unless the payee has elected no withholding in accordance with the applicable provisions of section 3405. If a payee has not provided the payor with a residence address, the payor is required to withhold income tax from designated distributions; included within this category is a payee who has provided the payor with an address for the payee's nominee, trustee, or agent without also providing the payee's residence address.

Explanation of Provisions

The Department of the Treasury and the IRS have concluded that Notice 87-7 generally provides an administrable standard with respect to withholding under section 3405 that is consistent with the purposes of the statute. Thus, the proposed regulation is based on the guidance provided in Notice 87-7. However, stakeholders have requested clarification regarding the application of Notice 87-7 and section 3405(e)(13)(A) in the following situations:

- The payee provides the payor with an Army Post Office (APO), Fleet Post Office (FPO), or Diplomatic Post Office (DPO) address.[2]

- The payee provides the payor with a residence address located within the United States but provides payment instructions that request delivery of the designated distribution to a financial institution or other person located outside of the United States.

The proposed regulation includes rules that would address these situations, and the regulation when finalized would supersede the guidance in Notice 87-7 for payors of designated distributions with respect to their duty to withhold under sections 3405(a)(1) or (b)(1).

A. Payees with a Military or Diplomatic Post Office Address

For purposes of section 3405(e)(13)(A), the proposed regulation treats an APO, FPO, or DPO address as an address located within the United States. In 1986, section 3405(e) was amended to add section 3405(e)(13) as one of several provisions intended to increase compliance with the internal revenue laws by United States persons resident abroad and green card holders. The legislative history indicates that Congress was concerned, based on data gathered by the General Accounting Office (GAO),[3] that the percentage of taxpayers who fail to file returns is substantially higher among Americans living abroad than it is among those resident in the United States and that it is often difficult for the IRS to enforce compliance by these taxpayers. S. Rep. No. 99-313, pt. 4, at 390 (1986).

The GAO data referred to in the legislative history does not include United States military personnel and their families as taxpayers who are living abroad. Johnny C. Finch, *United States Citizens Living in Foreign Countries and Not Filing Federal Income Tax Returns*, United States General Accounting Office, May 8, 1985. In addition, enforcement of compliance by individuals receiving mail at an APO, FPO, or DPO address generally does not involve the same challenges as enforcing compliance by other taxpayers living abroad. Because APO, FPO, and DPO delivery destinations are generally United States military or diplomatic facilities, taxpayers with an APO, FPO, or DPO address commonly maintain a current or former employment or contractor relationship with the United States federal government. Moreover, these addresses are generally treated as "domestic" by the United States Postal Service. *United States Domestic Mail Manual, 608.2.2.* Accordingly, the Department of the Treasury and the IRS have concluded that designated distributions to United States military and diplomatic personnel or their families should not be treated as delivered outside of the United States solely because those payments or distributions are to be delivered to a United States military or diplomatic post office address. For these reasons, the Department of the Treasury and the IRS have determined that treating an APO, FPO, or DPO address as located within the United States for purposes of section 3405(e)(13)(A) is consistent with the tax avoidance concerns underlying the enactment of section 3405(e)(13).

B. Payees with a Residence Address Located Within the United States

The proposed regulation would impose new withholding requirements on payors regarding certain payees who have provided the payor with a residence address located within the United States. Under Notice 87-7, payors are not required to withhold if a payee provides a residence address located within the United States and the payee elects no withholding. Notice 87-7 does not specifically address whether payors are required to withhold when a payee provides a residence address located within the United States but also provides payment instructions indicating that the funds are to be delivered outside of the United States. As explained above, section 3405(e)(13)(A) was enacted because Congress was concerned about noncompliance. Section 3405(e)(13)(A) refers to "any periodic payment or nonperiodic distribution which is to be delivered outside of the United States." Consistent with the text of section 3405(e)(13)(A) and its purpose, the proposed regulation requires payors to withhold in certain

---

[1] For purposes of this preamble, references to the "United States" include any possession of the United States.

[2] Army Post Office (APO) is associated with Army or Air Force installations. Fleet Post Office (FPO) is associated with Navy installations and ships. APO/FPO addresses are utilized by Department of Defense personnel, their family members, and other

authorized users. Diplomatic Post Office (DPO) provides global mail service to authorized personnel assigned to designated posts abroad.

[3] Effective July 7, 2004, the GAO's legal name was changed from the General Accounting Office to the Government Accountability Office.

circumstances when a payee provides a residence address located within the United States but also provides payment instructions indicating that the funds are to be delivered outside of the United States.

C. Payees with a Residence Address Located Outside of the United States and Payees Who Have not Provided a Residence Address

Unless section 3405(e)(13)(B) applies, if the payee's residence address that is provided to the payor is located outside of the United States, the payor is required to withhold income tax under section 3405 from any designated distribution, without regard to the delivery instructions and without regard to any attempt to elect no withholding. Thus, for example, withholding under section 3405 would be required even if a payee with a foreign residence address has requested that the distribution be deposited with a financial institution located within the United States. Given the ease with which the funds deposited with a financial institution in the United States can be withdrawn by a person located outside the United States, the Department of the Treasury and the IRS have concluded that the payee's residence address is more likely to be indicative of the place the distribution is ultimately to be delivered than the location of the financial institution. As proposed, the same requirement to withhold income tax under section 3405 would apply if a payor has not provided a residence address to the payee. Furthermore, a payee who has provided the payor with an address for the payee's nominee, trustee, or agent without also providing the payee's residence address has not provided a residence address for purposes of this regulation.

These rules are consistent with the approach in Notice 87-7, which uses the residence address of the payee in order to determine whether a taxpayer is permitted to make an election not to have withholding apply under section 3405(a)(2) or (b)(2). The Department of the Treasury and the IRS have determined that this interpretation articulated in Notice 87-7 should be retained because it provides an administrable standard that has been relied upon for many years, is consistent with the legislative history, and appropriately addresses tax avoidance concerns underlying section 3405(e)(13)(A).[4]

D. Payments Subject to Withholding under Subchapter A of Chapter 3

In accordance with section 3405(e)(1)(B)(iii), the proposed regulation clarifies that a designated distribution does not include a distribution that is subject to withholding under subchapter A of chapter 3 or that would be so subject but for a tax treaty and, therefore, the withholding rules under section 3405(a) and (b) do not apply to such distributions. For example, section 3405(a) or (b) withholding would not apply to a United States-source distribution to a nonresident alien individual from a trust described in section 401(a). In such a case, the withholding rules of section 1441 (within subchapter A of chapter 3) would apply to such distributions. See § 1.1441-1(b)(1).

Proposed Applicability Date

This regulation is proposed to apply with respect to distributions on or after the applicability date of the final regulation. Taxpayers may continue to rely upon Notice 87-7 until this regulation is finalized. Upon publication of a final regulation, Notice 87-7 will be superseded. Notwithstanding the previous sentence, taxpayers may rely upon § 31.3405(e)-1(b)(1) and (2) of the proposed regulation until the applicability date of the final regulation.

Special Analyses

This regulation is not subject to review under section 6(b) of Executive Order 12866 pursuant to the Memorandum of Agreement (April 11, 2018) between the Department of the Treasury and the Office of Management and Budget regarding review of tax regulations. Because this regulation does not impose a collection of information on small entities, the Regulatory Flexibility Act (5 U.S.C. chapter 6) does not apply. Pursuant to section 7805(f) of the Internal Revenue Code, this regulation has been submitted to the Chief Counsel for Advocacy of the Small Business Administration for comment on its impact on small business.

Comments and Requests for Public Hearing

Before this proposed regulation is adopted as a final regulation, consideration will be given to any comments that are submitted timely to the IRS as prescribed in this preamble under the "Addresses" heading. The Department of the Treasury and the IRS request comments on all aspects of the proposed rules, including any administrative concerns and how they should be addressed. All comments will be available at www.regulations.gov or upon request. A public hearing will be scheduled if requested in writing by any person who timely submits written comments. If a public hearing is scheduled, notice of the date, time, and place of the public hearing will be published in the **Federal Register**.

Statement of Availability of IRS Documents

IRS revenue procedures, revenue rulings, notices and other guidance cited in this preamble are published in the Internal Revenue Bulletin (or Cumulative Bulletin) and are available from the Superintendent of Documents, U.S. Government Publishing Office, Washington, DC 20402, or by visiting the IRS website at *http://www.irs.gov*.

Drafting Information

The principal author of this proposed regulation is Jeremy D. Lamb, IRS Office of Associate Chief Counsel (Employee Benefits, Exempt Organizations, and Employment Taxes). However, other personnel from the Department of the Treasury and the IRS participated in the development of the proposed regulation.

[¶ 49,800]   Proposed Amendments of Regulations (REG-109826-17), published in the Federal Register on June 7, 2019.

Code Secs. 897, 1441, 1445 and 1446]

Taxation of foreigners on dispositions of U.S. real property interests: Exception for foreign pension funds: Withholding tax: Payments to foreign partners.—Reg. § 1.897(l)-1 and amendments of Reg. §§ 1.1441-3, 1.1445-2, 1.1445-4, 1.1445-5, 1.1445-8, 1.1446-1, 1.1446-2 and 1.1446-7, regarding the exception from taxation with respect to gain or loss of a qualified foreign pension fund attributable to certain interests in United States real property, are proposed.

AGENCY: Internal Revenue Service (IRS), Treasury.

ACTION: Notice of proposed rulemaking.

SUMMARY: This document contains proposed regulations regarding the exception from taxation with respect to gain or loss of a qualified foreign pension fund attributable to certain interests in United States real property. The proposed regulations also include rules for certifying that a qualified foreign pension fund is not subject to withholding on certain dispositions of, and distributions with respect to, certain interests in United

---

[4] The committee report states that "it will be appropriate to require withholding with respect to pension payments to persons with foreign addresses absent a showing that withholding is not required." S. Rep. No. 99-313, pt. 4, at 391 (1986).

States real property. The proposed regulations affect certain holders of certain interests in United States real property and withholding agents that are required to withhold tax on certain dispositions of, and distributions with respect to, such property.

DATES: Written or electronic comments and requests for a public hearing must be received by September 4, 2019.

ADDRESSES: Send submissions to: CC:PA:LPD:PR (REG-109826-17), Internal Revenue Service, Room 5203, P.O. Box 7604, Ben Franklin Station, Washington, DC 20044. Submissions may be hand-delivered Monday through Friday between the hours of 8 a.m. and 4 p.m. to CC:PA:LPD:PR (REG-109826-17), Courier's Desk, Internal Revenue Service, 1111 Constitution Avenue, NW, Washington, DC 20224, or sent electronically via the Federal eRulemaking Portal at *http://www.regulations.gov* (IRS REG-109826-17).

FOR FURTHER INFORMATION CONTACT: Concerning the proposed regulations, Milton Cahn or Logan M. Kincheloe, (202) 317-6937; concerning submissions of comments or requests for a public hearing, Regina Johnson, (202) 317-6901 (not toll-free numbers).

SUPPLEMENTARY INFORMATION:

Background

I. *In General*

This document contains proposed amendments to 26 CFR part 1 under sections 897, 1445, and 1446 (the "proposed regulations"). Section 323(a) of the Protecting Americans from Tax Hikes Act of 2015, Pub. L. 114-113, div. Q (the "PATH Act"), added section 897(l) to the Code, and Section 101(q) of the Tax Technical Corrections Act of 2018, Pub. L. 115-141, div. U (the "Technical Corrections Act") amended certain aspects of section 897(l). Section 897(l) provides an exemption to the application of section 897(a) on gain or loss on certain dispositions of, and distributions with respect to, United States real property interests ("USRPIs") for certain foreign pension funds and their subsidiaries. The proposed regulations contain rules relating to the qualification for the exemption under section 897(l), as well as rules relating to withholding requirements under sections 1445 and 1446 for dispositions of USRPIs by foreign pension funds and their subsidiaries.

II. *Taxation of Foreign Persons under Section 897*

Section 897(a)(1) provides that gain or loss of a nonresident alien individual or foreign corporation from the disposition of a USRPI is taken into account under section 871(b)(1) or 882(a)(1), as applicable, as if the nonresident alien individual or foreign corporation were engaged in a trade or business within the United States during the taxable year and such gain or loss were effectively connected with that trade or business.

Section 897(c)(1)(A) defines a USRPI as an interest in real property (including an interest in a mine, well, or other natural deposit) located in the United States or the Virgin Islands, and any interest (other than solely as a creditor) in any domestic corporation unless the taxpayer establishes that such corporation was at no time a United States real property holding corporation ("USRPHC") during the applicable testing period (generally, the five-year period ending on the date of the disposition of the interest). Under section 897(c)(2), a USRPHC means any corporation if the fair market value of its USRPIs equals or exceeds 50 percent of the total fair market value of its USRPIs, its interests in real property located outside the United States, plus any other assets that are used or held for use in a trade or business. However, section 897(c)(1)(B) generally provides that an interest in a corporation is not a USRPI if the corporation does not hold any USRPIs as of the date its stock is sold and the corporation disposed of all of the USRPIs that it held during the applicable testing period in transactions in which the full amount of gain, if any, was recognized.

Section 897(h)(1) provides that any distribution by a qualified investment entity (QIE) to a nonresident alien individual, a foreign corporation, or other QIE is, to the extent attributable to gain from sales or exchanges by the QIE of USRPIs, treated as gain recognized by such nonresident alien individual, foreign corporation, or other QIE from the sale or exchange of a USRPI, subject to certain exceptions. Under section 897(h)(4)(A), a QIE includes any real estate investment trust (REIT) and certain regulated investment companies.

III. *Exception for Qualified Foreign Pension Funds under Section 897(l)*

Section 897(l)(1) provides that a qualified pension fund is not treated as a nonresident alien individual or foreign corporation for purposes of section 897. Cf. section 897(a) (subjecting nonresident alien individuals and foreign corporations to tax on gain or loss from the disposition of a USRPI). For this purpose, an entity all the interests of which are held by a qualified foreign pension fund (referred to in this Preamble and the proposed regulations as a "qualified controlled entity") is also treated as a qualified foreign pension fund.

Under section 897(l)(2), a qualified foreign pension fund is defined as any trust, corporation, or other organization or arrangement (any one of which is referred to in this Preamble and the proposed regulations as an "eligible fund") that satisfies five separate requirements. Specifically, a qualified foreign pension fund is an eligible fund (A) that is created or organized under the law of a country other than the United States, (B) that is established (i) by such country (or one or more political subdivisions thereof) to provide retirement or pension benefits to participants or beneficiaries that are current or former employees (including self-employed individuals) or persons designated by such employees, as a result of services rendered by such employees to their employers, or (ii) by one or more employers to provide retirement or pension benefits to participants or beneficiaries that are current or former employees (including self-employed individuals) or persons designated by such employees in consideration for services rendered by such employees to such employers, (C) that does not have a single participant or beneficiary with a right to more than five percent of its assets or income, (D) that is subject to government regulation and with respect to which annual information about its beneficiaries is provided, or is otherwise available, to the relevant tax authorities in the country in which it is established or operates, and (E) with respect to which, under the laws of the country in which it is established or operates (i) contributions to such eligible fund that would otherwise be subject to tax under such laws are deductible or excluded from the gross income of such entity or arrangement or taxed at a reduced rate, or (ii) taxation of any investment income of such eligible fund is deferred or such income is excluded from gross income of such entity or arrangement or is taxed at a reduced rate.

Section 897(l)(3) provides that the Secretary of the Treasury (Secretary) shall prescribe such regulations as may be necessary or appropriate to carry out the purposes of section 897(l).

IV. *Applicable Withholding Rules*

A. *Section 1445 withholding*

Section 1445(a) generally imposes a withholding tax obligation on the transferee when a foreign person disposes of a USRPI. Section 1445(e)(6) provides that, if any portion of a distribution from a QIE to a nonresident alien individual or a foreign corporation is treated under section 897(h)(1) as gain realized by such individual or corporation from the sale or exchange of a USRPI, the QIE must deduct and withhold tax under section 1445(a) on the amount so treated.

A transferee of a USRPI is not required to withhold under section 1445(a) if the transferor furnishes to the transferee a certification that, among other things, states that the transferor is not a foreign person. §1.1445-2(b)(2)(i). Generally, upon a distribution and other transactions subject to withholding, certain entities may treat a holder of an interest in the entity as a U.S. person if that interest holder furnishes to the entity or fiduciary a certification stating that the interest holder is not a foreign person. §1.1445-5(b)(3)(ii)(A). Upon the distribution of any amount attributable to the disposition of a USRPI, a QIE may rely on the same certification, a Form W-9, Request for Taxpayer Identification Number and Certification, or a form that is substantially similar to the Form W-9 to determine whether an interest holder is a U.S. person. § 1.1445-8(e).

Section 323(b) of the PATH Act amended section 1445(f)(3) to provide that, for purposes of section 1445, the term "foreign person" means any person other than (A) a United States person, and (B) except as otherwise provided by the Secretary, an entity with respect to which section 897 does not apply by reason of section 897(l). On February 19, 2016, the Department of the Treasury (the "Treasury Department") and the IRS published final regulations under section 1445 of the Code ("updated section 1445 regulations") in the **Federal Register** (81 FR 8398-01) to reflect the PATH Act's amendments to section 1445(f)(3). A correcting amendment to the updated section 1445 regulations was published on April 26, 2016 in the **Federal Register** (81 FR 24484-01). As corrected, the updated section 1445 regulations provide that neither a qualified foreign pension fund nor an entity all of the interests of which are held by a qualified foreign pension fund is treated as a foreign person, and thus may provide a certification to a transferee. *See* §§ 1.1445-2(b)(2)(i) (flush language) and 1.1445-5(b)(3)(ii)(A).

B. *Section 1446 withholding*

A partnership generally must pay a withholding tax under section 1446 on effectively connected taxable income ("ECTI") allocable under section 704 to a foreign partner. Section 1446(c) provides that ECTI includes the taxable income of a partnership that is effectively connected (or treated as effectively connected) with the conduct of a trade or business in the United States, subject to certain adjustments. For this purpose, ECTI includes any partnership income treated as effectively connected with the conduct of a trade or business in the United States pursuant to section 897. § 1.1446-2(b)(2)(ii).

A foreign partner's allocable share of partnership ECTI does not include income or gain exempt from U.S. tax by reason of a provision of the Code or by operation of any U.S. income tax treaty or reciprocal agreement. § 1.1446-2(b)(2)(iii). In the case of income excluded by reason of a treaty provision, such income must be derived by a resident of an applicable treaty jurisdiction, the resident must be the beneficial owner of the item, and all other requirements for benefits under the treaty must be satisfied. To exclude income or gain from ECTI, the partnership must receive from the partner a valid withholding certificate (that is, Form W-8BEN-E, Certificate of Foreign Status of Beneficial Owner for United States Tax Withholding and Reporting (Entities)) containing the information necessary to support the claim for treaty benefits required in the forms and instructions. *Id*.

A domestic partnership required to withhold under both sections 1445 and 1446 with respect to income treated as ECTI pursuant to section 897 is deemed to satisfy the withholding requirements of section 1445 if it complies with the requirements of section 1446. § 1.1446-3(c)(2)(i).

V. *Prior Request for Comments*

In the Preamble to the updated section 1445 regulations that were published on February 19, 2016, the Treasury Department and the IRS requested comments regarding what regulations, if any, should be issued pursuant to section 897(l)(3). Twenty-one comments were received, requesting, in particular, guidance on issues related to qualification as a "qualified foreign pension fund" under section 897(l)(2). The comments will be included in the administrative record for this notice of proposed rulemaking. The Treasury Department and the IRS considered all of the comments, and in response to the comments have issued the proposed regulations to provide clarification on the application of section 897(l). Each significant comment, other than any comment rendered moot by the Technical Corrections Act, is discussed in the relevant part of the Explanation of Provisions section of this preamble.

Explanation of Provisions

The proposed regulations provide guidance regarding the scope of the exception described in section 897(l)(1), the application of the requirements described in section 897(l)(2) that an eligible fund must satisfy to be treated as a qualified foreign pension fund, and rules regarding exemptions from withholding under section 1445 or section 1446.

I. *Scope of the Exception*

A. *General rule*

As described in the Background section of this Preamble, section 897(a) applies to gain or loss of a nonresident alien individual or a foreign corporation from the disposition of a USRPI. Similarly, section 897(h) generally treats any distribution from a QIE to a nonresident alien individual, a foreign corporation, or other QIE, to the extent attributable to gain from sales or exchanges by the QIE of USRPIs, as gain recognized by such nonresident alien individual, foreign corporation, or other QIE from the sale or exchange of a USRPI for purposes of section 897(a). Section 897(l)(1) provides that, for purposes of section 897, a qualified foreign pension fund is not treated as a nonresident alien individual or a foreign corporation. For this purpose, a qualified controlled entity is treated as a qualified foreign pension fund. Accordingly, section 897(l) excepts from section 897(a) gain or loss of a qualified foreign pension fund or a qualified controlled entity from the disposition of a USRPI, including gain from a distribution described in section 897(h).

Consistent with section 897(l), the proposed regulations provide that gain or loss of a qualified foreign pension fund or a qualified controlled entity (under the proposed regulations, each a "qualified holder") from the disposition of a USRPI, including gain from a distribution described in section 897(h), is not subject to section 897(a). This exception from section 897(a) applies solely with respect to gain or loss recognized by a qualified holder that is attributable to one or more qualified segregated accounts maintained by the qualified holder. The proposed regulations define a qualified segregated account as an identifiable pool of assets maintained for the sole purpose of funding qualified benefits (generally, retirement, pension, and certain ancillary benefits) to qualified recipients (generally, plan participants and beneficiaries). See Section II.B of this Explanation of Provisions for a detailed discussion of qualified benefits and qualified recipients.

The proposed regulations provide separate standards for determining whether an identifiable pool of assets constitutes a qualified segregated account depending on whether the pool of assets is maintained by an eligible fund (including an eligible fund that satisfies the requirements to be treated as a qualified foreign pension fund) or a qualified controlled entity. An identifiable pool of assets of an eligible fund is a qualified segregated account if the assets in the pool and the income earned with respect to those assets are subject to legal or contractual requirements requiring that all such income and assets are used exclusively to fund the provision of qualified benefits to qualified recipients or to satisfy necessary reasonable expenses of the eligible fund. A qualified controlled entity is treated as maintaining a qualified segregated account if all of the net earnings of the qualified controlled entity are credited to its own account or to the qualified segregated account of a qualified foreign pension fund or another qualified controlled entity, and all of the assets of the qualified controlled entity, after satisfaction of liabilities to persons having interests in the entity solely as creditors, vest in the qualified segregated account of a qualified foreign pension fund or another qualified controlled entity upon dissolution. In either case, a pool of assets will not be treated as a qualified segregated account if the assets or income associated with such assets may inure to the benefit of a person other than a qualified recipient. For this purpose, the fact that assets or income may inure to the benefit of a governmental unit by operation of escheat or similar laws is ignored.

B. *Qualified controlled entities*

Several comments submitted in response to the updated section 1445 regulations requested clarification concerning the exception under section 897(l) for an entity all the interests of which are held by a qualified foreign pension fund. The proposed regulations define a qualified controlled entity as a trust or corporation organized under the laws of a foreign country all of the interests of which are held directly by one or more qualified foreign pension funds or indirectly through one or more qualified controlled entities or partnerships. The Treasury Department and the IRS have determined that it is unnecessary to treat partnerships as qualified controlled entities because the proposed regulations' exemption from section 897(a) applies to gain or loss earned indirectly through one or more partnerships. Accordingly, the proposed regulations provide that only corporations and trusts may be treated as qualified controlled entities.

1. Indirectly Held Entities

Comments requested that the proposed regulations provide that an entity held indirectly through one or more corporations or partnerships by a qualified foreign pension fund may be treated as a qualified controlled entity. Thus, for example, if a qualified foreign pension fund owned all of the interests of Entity A, and Entity A owned all of the interests of Entity B, the comments indicated that Entity B should be eligible to be treated as a qualified controlled entity. The Treasury Department and the IRS agree that there is no policy reason to distinguish between direct and indirect ownership for purposes of determining whether an entity is a qualified controlled entity. Accordingly, the proposed regulations provide that a qualified controlled entity may be owned directly or indirectly through one or more qualified controlled entities.

2. Multiple Qualified Foreign Pension Fund Owners

Comments requested that the proposed regulations provide that an entity may qualify as a qualified controlled entity when all of its interests are owned by multiple qualified foreign pension funds. Comments noted that qualified foreign pension funds frequently pool their investments, such that permitting qualified controlled entities to be held by multiple qualified foreign pension funds would be consistent with current investment practices. Further, comments argued that there is no policy rationale for providing the exception of section 897(l) to an investment that benefited one qualified foreign pension fund but not to an investment that benefited multiple qualified foreign pension funds. The Treasury Department and the IRS agree with these comments. Accordingly, the proposed regulations provide that the interests in a qualified controlled entity may be held by one or more qualified foreign pension funds directly or indirectly through one or more qualified controlled entities.

3. Creditor Interests

One comment recommended that, for purposes of determining whether an entity is a qualified controlled entity, only equity interests should be taken into account. *Cf.* section 897(c)(1)(A) (defining a USRPI as including any interest (other than solely as a creditor) in any domestic corporation unless the taxpayer establishes that such corporation was at no time a USRPHC during the applicable testing period). The comment noted that requiring a qualified foreign pension fund to hold all of the creditor's interests issued by a qualified controlled entity would prevent the use of external leverage by a qualified controlled entity, even though there is no such restriction on direct leveraged investments by a qualified foreign pension fund. The Treasury Department and the IRS agree that a creditor's interest in an entity should not be an interest taken into account for purposes of determining whether the entity is treated as a qualified controlled entity if the interest does not share in the earnings or growth of the entity. Section 1.897-1(d)(5) provides that, unless otherwise stated, the term "interest" as used with regard to an entity in the regulations under sections 897, 1445, and 6039C, means an interest other than an interest solely as a creditor. Given the absence of an express provision to the contrary in the proposed regulations, the application of § 1.897-1(d)(5) results in an interest in an entity solely as a creditor not being taken into account for purposes of determining whether the entity is a qualified controlled entity.

4. Interaction with Section 892

Comments requested clarification that an entity may constitute a qualified controlled entity whether or not the entity constitutes a controlled entity as defined in § 1.892-2T(a)(3). The Treasury Department and the IRS have determined that the definition of "qualified controlled entity" in the proposed regulations plainly does not limit qualified controlled entity status to only those entities that would qualify as a "controlled entity" within the meaning of § 1.892-2T(a)(3). It is, therefore, unnecessary for these proposed regulations to provide an express rule.

5. De Minimis Ownership

A comment requested that the proposed regulations provide that *de minimis* ownership of a qualified controlled entity be disregarded under certain circumstances. For instance, the comment indicated that de minimis ownership, including by managers or directors, may be required by corporate law in certain jurisdictions. The Treasury Department and the IRS have determined that permitting a person other than a qualified foreign pension fund to own an interest in a qualified controlled entity would impermissibly expand the scope of the exception in section 897(l) by allowing taxpayers other than qualified foreign pension funds to avoid tax under section 897. Accordingly, the proposed regulations do not permit ownership of a qualified controlled entity by a person other than a qualified foreign pension fund or another qualified controlled entity. 6. Avoidance of Section 897

One comment recommended that the Treasury Department and the IRS consider rules to prevent a qualified foreign pension fund from indirectly acquiring a USRPI held by a foreign corporation, which would permit the acquired corporation to avoid tax on gain that would otherwise be subject to tax under section 897. For example, assume that FP, a foreign corporation that is not a qualified holder, owns 100 percent of the stock of FS, a foreign corporation, and that FS owns a USRPI with a basis of $80x and a fair market value of $200x. Assume that FP sells the stock of FS to a qualified foreign pension fund. If FS were treated as a qualified controlled entity and FS later sold the USRPI for $200x, neither FP nor FS would be subject to tax under section 897 on the $120x gain attributable to its investment in the USRPI, even though the gain accrued while FS was owned by FP. Similar issues could arise with entities treated as part of an organization or arrangement that is a qualified foreign pension fund.

To address the inappropriate avoidance of section 897, the proposed regulations provide that a qualified holder does not include any entity or governmental unit that, at any time during the testing period, determined without regard to this limitation, was not a qualified foreign pension fund, a part of a qualified foreign pension fund, or a qualified controlled entity. For this purpose, the testing period generally means the shortest of (i) the period beginning on the date that section 897(l) became effective (December 18, 2015), and ending on the date of a disposition described in section 897(a) or a distribution described in section 897(h), (ii) the ten-year period ending on the date of the disposition or the distribution, or (iii) the period during which the entity (or its predecessor) was in existence. This limitation does not apply to an entity or governmental unit that did not own a USRPI as of the date it became a qualified controlled entity, a qualified foreign pension fund, or part of a qualified foreign pension fund.

C. *Organizations or arrangements*

Section 897(l)(2) provides that a qualified foreign pension fund may include any "trust, corporation, or other organization or arrangement" that satisfies certain requirements. Congress intended the term "arrangement" to be a flexible term that accommodates a broad range of structures. *See* STAFF OF THE JOINT COMM. ON TAX'N, General Explanation of Tax Legislation Enacted in 2015 (JCS-1-16) (General Explanation) 283, n. 967 (2016) ("Foreign pension funds may be structured in a variety of ways, and may comprise one or more separate entities. The word 'arrangement' encompasses such alternative structures.").

Several comments submitted in response to the updated section 1445 regulations described the multiple ways that foreign retirement and pension systems - particularly those that are administered entirely or in part by a foreign government - could be organized. The comments described structures involving multiple entities, one or more accounts on government balance sheets, foreign legal structures, and a combination of the foregoing. Although such pension and retirement plans are often not organized as a single trust or corporation, the organizations or arrangements, when viewed as a whole, may satisfy the requirements set forth in section 897(l)(2). Based on the General Explanation's indication that foreign pension funds may be structured in a variety of ways, and may be comprised of separate entities, the comments recommended that the proposed regulations permit a broad range of alternative structures to be treated as a qualified foreign pension fund.

The Treasury Department and the IRS have determined that the purpose of section 897(l) is best served by permitting a broad range of structures to be eligible to be treated as a qualified foreign pension fund. Accordingly, the proposed regulations provide that, for purposes of section 897(l), the term "organization or arrangement" means one or more trusts, corporations, governmental units, or employers. The proposed regulations provide that the term "governmental unit" means any foreign government or part thereof, including any person, body, group of persons, organization, agency, bureau, fund, instrumentality, however designated, of a foreign government. The proposed regulations include several examples illustrating the application of the requirements of section 897(l) and the proposed regulations to different types of organizations and arrangements, including organizations and arrangements that include governmental units.

The proposed regulations permit an employer to be part of an organization or arrangement to address cases in which an employer is organized as an entity other than a trust or corporation but operates as part of an organization or arrangement to provide pension or retirement benefits.

II. *Requirements Applicable to a Qualified Foreign Pension Fund*

A. *Created or organized*

Section 897(l)(2)(A) and the proposed regulations require that a qualified foreign pension fund must be created or organized under the law of a country other than the United States. Comments indicated that many foreign pension funds are created or organized under the laws of states or political subdivisions of a foreign country and requested that the proposed regulations clarify that those pension funds would satisfy section 897(l)(2)(A). The Treasury Department and the IRS agree that it is appropriate to allow such foreign pension funds to be considered qualified foreign pension funds. Accordingly, the proposed regulations provide that references to a foreign country include references to a state, province, or political subdivision of a foreign country, subject to an exception described in part II.E.4 of this Explanation of Provisions.

B. *Established to provide retirement or pension benefits*

Section 897(l)(2)(B) requires that an eligible fund be established either (i) by the country in which it is created or organized (or one or more political subdivisions thereof) to provide retirement or pension benefits to participants or beneficiaries that are current or former employees (including self-employed individuals), or persons designated by such employees, as a result of services rendered by such employees to their employers; or (ii) by one or more employers to provide retirement or pension benefits to participants or beneficiaries that are current or former employees (including self-employed individuals) or persons designated by such employees in consideration for services rendered by such employees to such employers.

1. Pension Funds Eligible for Section 897(l)(2)(B)

Several comments requested that the regulations clarify that multi-employer pension funds and government-sponsored public pension funds that provide pension and pension-related benefits may satisfy section 897(l)(2)(B). These comments are consistent with the General Explanation, which noted that "[m]ulti-employer and government-sponsored public pension funds that provide pension and pension-related benefits may still satisfy [section 897(l)(2)(B)]. For example, such pension funds may be established for one or more companies or professions, or for the general working public of a foreign country." General Explanation at 283, n. 968.

The Treasury Department and the IRS agree that it is appropriate to allow such multi-employer pension funds and government-sponsored public pension funds to be considered qualified foreign pension funds. Accordingly, the proposed regulations provide that an eligible fund must be established by either (i) the foreign country in which it is created or organized to provide retirement or pension benefits to participants or beneficiaries that are current or former employees or persons designated by such employees as a result of services rendered by such employees to their employers, or (ii) one or more employers to provide retirement or pension benefits to participants or beneficiaries that are current or former employees or persons designated by such employees in consideration for services rendered by such employees to such employers.

Under the proposed regulations, qualified recipients generally include persons eligible to participate in the retirement or pension plan. Therefore, with respect to an eligible fund established by one or more employers, the term "qualified recipient" includes a current or former employee or any person designated by such current or former employee to receive qualified benefits. With respect to an eligible fund established by a foreign country to provide qualified benefits to qualified recipients as a result of services rendered by such qualified recipients to their employers, the term includes any person eligible to be treated as a participant or beneficiary of such eligible fund and any person designated by such person to receive qualified benefits. In response to comments, the proposed regulations provide that a person is treated as designating another person to receive qualified benefits if such other person is entitled to receive benefits under the contractual terms applicable to the eligible fund or under the laws of the foreign country in which the eligible fund is created or organized, whether or not the first person expressly designated such person as a beneficiary.

In response to comments, the proposed regulations clarify that a retirement or pension fund that is organized by a trade union, professional association, or similar group may be treated as a qualified foreign pension fund by providing that an eligible fund is treated as established by any employer that funds, in whole or in part, the eligible fund. In addition, the proposed regulations clarify that, for purposes of the requirement in section 897(l)(2)(B), a self-employed individual is treated as both an employer and an employee.

2. Benefits Other than Retirement or Pension Benefits

Comments noted that many foreign pension funds provide a limited amount of other benefits, including death, disability, survivor, medical, unemployment, and similar benefits, to participants and beneficiaries. Comments requested guidance on whether a qualified foreign pension fund could provide certain benefits other than retirement and pension benefits, and whether there is any limitation on the amount of those benefits that a qualified foreign pension fund may provide to participants and beneficiaries. Some comments recommended that the proposed regulations set forth a specific limitation on the percentage of benefits other than retirement or pension benefits that a qualified foreign pension fund may provide, while other comments recommended a facts and circumstances test or another subjective standard.

The Treasury Department and the IRS have determined that section 897(l) was not intended to exclude common foreign pension arrangements that provide a relatively small amount of ancillary benefits to participants and beneficiaries. The Treasury Department and the IRS have also determined that a specific limit on the percentage of ancillary benefits that a qualified foreign pension fund may provide to its participants and beneficiaries is more administrable and provides more certainty to taxpayers than a subjective standard. Accordingly, the proposed regulations require that all of the benefits that an eligible fund provides are qualified benefits to qualified recipients, and that at least 85 percent of the present value of the qualified benefits that the eligible fund reasonably expects to provide in the future are retirement or pension benefits. For this purpose, qualified benefits include retirement, pension, or ancillary benefits. The proposed regulations define ancillary benefits as benefits payable upon the diagnosis of a terminal illness, death benefits, disability benefits, medical benefits, unemployment benefits, or similar benefits. The Treasury Department and the IRS request comments on whether the regulations should also define retirement or pension benefits (for example, with reference to whether there are penalties for early withdrawals).

3. Insuring Qualified Benefits and Similar Activities

One comment requested that the proposed regulations provide that an eligible fund may be treated as a qualified foreign pension fund if it is established by a foreign government to provide qualified benefits to qualified recipients (directly or indirectly) in the event that one or more qualified foreign pension funds that are created or organized in the same foreign country are unable to satisfy their liabilities with respect to the provision of qualified benefits to their own qualified recipients. Although the proposed regulations do not expressly address such plans, the proposed regulations do not differentiate between plans that are primarily responsible for the provision of qualified benefits to qualified recipients, on the one hand, and plans that are secondarily responsible for the provision of qualified benefits to qualified recipients, on the other hand. Therefore, whether a plan is established to provide qualified benefits to qualified recipients is determined without regard to whether such plan has primary responsibility to provide qualified benefits to qualified recipients or rather is established to provide the qualified benefits to qualified recipients only in the event of the default of one or more other plans.

C. *Five percent limitation*

Consistent with section 897(l)(2)(C), the proposed regulations provide that a qualified foreign pension fund may not have a single participant or beneficiary with a right to more than five percent of its assets or income (the five-percent limitation). Comments submitted in response to the updated section 1445 regulations indicated that it would be appropriate for the proposed regulations to include attribution rules to prevent a single individual from using related parties to circumvent the five-percent limitation. The Treasury Department and the IRS agree with the comments. Accordingly, the proposed regulations provide that, for purposes of applying the five percent limitation, an individual is considered to have a right to the assets and income of an eligible fund to which any person who bears a relationship to the individual described in section 267(b) or section 707(b) has a right.

One comment requested guidance on calculating a participant or beneficiary's entitlement to the assets and income of a qualified foreign pension fund for purposes of applying the five-percent limitation. In light of the complexity that any such rule would entail and the relatively few cases in which it would be expected to apply, the proposed regulations do not provide specific rules regarding the computation of the five-percent limitation. Instead, this determination should be made based on the underlying facts and circumstances of each case.

D. *Regulation and information reporting*

Section 897(l)(2)(D) and the proposed regulations set forth two requirements for a qualified foreign pension fund. First, a qualified foreign pension fund must be subject to government regulation ("regulation requirement"). Second, a qualified foreign pension fund must provide annual information about its beneficiaries to the relevant tax authorities in the country in which it is established or operates, or such information must otherwise be available to those authorities ("information requirement"). Several comments requested that the proposed regulations set forth the specific information that must be provided or otherwise made available pursuant to the information requirement in section 897(l)(2)(D). The proposed regulations adopt the recommendation included in several comments by providing that an eligible fund is treated as satisfying the information requirement only if the eligible fund annually provides to the relevant tax authorities in the foreign country in which it is established or operates the amount of qualified benefits provided to each qualified recipient by the eligible fund (if any), or such information is otherwise available to those authorities. An eligible fund is not treated as failing to satisfy the information requirement if the eligible fund is not required to provide information to the relevant tax authorities in a year in which no qualified benefits are provided to qualified recipients. The Treasury Department and the IRS request comments as to whether the final regulations should permit other types of information to satisfy the information requirement.

Several comments indicated that foreign government-sponsored retirement and pension plans frequently are not subject to substantial information reporting and regulation compared with private foreign pension or retirement plans, in part because the government administers the pension or retirement program itself. The comments recommended that the proposed regulations treat a government-sponsored retirement or pension plan as automatically satisfying both the regulation and information requirements of section 897(l)(2)(D). The Treasury Department and the IRS agree that, when a government administers a pension or retirement plan itself, the requirements of section 897(l)(2)(D) are effectively satisfied because the government has control over the program and access to the information about the program's beneficiaries. Accordingly, the proposed regulations generally provide that an eligible fund that is administered by one or more governmental units, other than in its capacity as an employer, is deemed to satisfy the requirements of section 897(l)(2)(D).

Comments noted that many foreign pension funds must provide information to one or more governmental bodies in the country in which the foreign retirement or pension fund is organized, including agencies that are specifically responsible for regulating pensions. In many cases, those governmental bodies may be distinct from the tax authority in that foreign country. In light of the wide range of foreign information reporting regimes that may apply to an eligible fund, the Treasury Department and the IRS agree that a flexible rule is necessary and appropriate to carry out the purposes of section 897(l). Accordingly, the proposed regulations provide that an eligible fund is treated as satisfying the information requirement of section 897(l)(2)(D) if the eligible fund is required, pursuant to the laws of the foreign country in which it is established or operates, to provide the required information to one or more governmental units of the foreign country in which the eligible fund is created or organized, or if such information is otherwise available to one or more governmental units of the foreign country in which the eligible fund is created or organized.

E. *Foreign tax treatment*

Section 897(l)(2)(E) and the proposed regulations provide that, to be a qualified foreign pension fund, the laws of the foreign country in which the eligible fund is established or operates must provide that either (i) contributions to the eligible fund that would otherwise be subject to tax under such laws are deductible or excluded from the gross income of the eligible fund or taxed at a reduced rate, or (ii) taxation of any investment income of the eligible fund is deferred or such income is excluded from the gross income of the eligible fund or is taxed at a reduced rate.

1. Countries with No Income Tax

Comments requested clarification that an eligible fund may qualify for the exemption in section 897(l) if it is created or organized in a country that does not have an income tax. The Treasury Department and the IRS have determined that the purposes of section 897(l) would not be served by limiting the availability of the exemption to eligible funds organized in jurisdictions with an income tax. Accordingly, the proposed regulations provide that an eligible fund is treated as satisfying the requirement of section 897(l)(2)(E) if the eligible fund is established and operates in a foreign country that has no income tax.

2. Degree of Reduction

Comments noted that an eligible fund that otherwise satisfies section 897(l)(2)(E) may be subject to current income tax at ordinary rates with respect to a relatively small portion of its income or gain. The comments requested guidance on the percentage of income or contributions that must be eligible for preferential tax treatment in order for an eligible fund to satisfy section 897(l)(2)(E). Other comments requested guidance on the extent to which ordinary income tax rates must be reduced under section 897(l)(2)(E). To address these comments, the proposed regulations provide that an eligible fund is treated as satisfying the requirement of section 897(l)(2)(E) in a taxable year if, under the income tax laws of the foreign country in which the eligible fund is established or operates, at least 85 percent of the contributions to the eligible fund are deductible or excluded from the gross income or taxed at a reduced rate, or tax on at least 85 percent of the investment income of the eligible fund is deferred or taxed at a reduced rate (including by excluding such investment income from gross income). The 85 percent threshold was chosen based on the best judgment of the Treasury Department and the IRS, and is consistent with suggestions from commenters for an appropriate threshold in an analogous context in the proposed regulations (namely, for the percentage of benefits provided by an eligible fund that must be retirement or pension benefits as opposed to ancillary benefits), but is not based on any specific quantitative analysis. The Treasury Department and the IRS request additional comments regarding whether the 85 percent threshold is appropriate and especially solicit comments that provide data, other evidence, and models that can enhance the rigor of the process by which such threshold is determined.

3. Other Preferential Regimes

Comments requested that the proposed regulations provide that the requirement of section 897(l)(2)(E) may be satisfied if, under the income tax law of the country in which an eligible fund is established or operates, an eligible fund is subject to a preferential tax regime that is, in substance, equivalent to the type of deductions or exclusions specifically described in section 897(l)(2)(E). For example, one comment described a preferential regime in which certain eligible funds taxable as insurance companies are entitled to reserve deductions designed to effectively exclude from gross income investment income earned by the eligible funds. The Treasury Department and the IRS agree that the purposes of section 897(l) are best served by accommodating a broad range of preferential tax regimes applicable to retirement or pension funds. Therefore, the proposed regulations provide that an eligible fund that is not specifically subject to the tax treatment described in section 897(l)(2)(E) is nonetheless treated as satisfying the requirement of section 897(l)(2)(E) if the eligible fund establishes that it is subject to a preferential tax regime due to its status as a retirement or pension fund, and that the preferential tax regime has a substantially similar effect as the specific tax treatment described in section 897(l)(2)(E).

4. Subnational Tax Exemptions

One comment requested that the proposed regulations provide that preferential treatment with respect to a tax levied by a state, province, or political subdivision (sub-national tax) be sufficient to satisfy the requirement of section 897(l)(2)(E). The Treasury Department and the IRS have determined that the exemption in section 897(l) was not intended to benefit foreign persons that fail to benefit from an exemption from an otherwise applicable national income tax. Sub-national taxes generally constitute a minor component of an entity's overall tax burden in a foreign jurisdiction and therefore it would not be appropriate to allow preferential treatment with respect to sub-national taxes to satisfy the requirement of section 897(l)(2)(E) when such preference had only a minimal impact on reducing the fund's overall tax burden. Accordingly, the proposed regulations do not adopt this recommendation, and, to the contrary, provide that for purposes of section 897(l)(2)(E), references to a foreign country do not include references to a state, province, or political subdivision of a foreign country.

F. *Application to organizations and arrangements*

The proposed regulations provide rules on the application of the requirements described in section 897(l)(2) to an eligible fund that is an organization or arrangement.

1. Single Entity Treatment

The proposed regulations provide that an eligible fund that is an organization or arrangement is treated as a single entity to determine whether the requirements of section 897(l)(2) are satisfied. Notwithstanding the foregoing, the proposed regulations provide that each person or governmental unit that is part of an organization or arrangement must independently satisfy the requirement of section 897(l)(2)(A), such that each component of the organization or arrangement must be created or organized under the law of a country other than the United States.

2. Relevant Income and Assets

As noted in several comments, an eligible fund may be organized in various ways. For example, an eligible fund may be comprised of multiple entities and governmental bodies, one or more of which may conduct activities that are unrelated to the provision of retirement or pension benefits. Applying certain requirements of section 897(l)(2) to an eligible fund requires identifying the specific assets and income of an organization or arrangement that must be tested under the proposed regulations. For instance, under the proposed regulations, an organization or arrangement may include a pension system in which a private employer provides pension benefits to its employees that are funded by the investments of a separate entity, such as a pension trust organized by a foreign government. Assets and income of the private employer that do not fund the provision of pension benefits would generally not be relevant to determining whether the organization or arrangement satisfies the requirements of section 897(l)(2) and the proposed regulations. For instance, income of the employer generally would not be subject to preferential tax treatment, and the assets of the employer not used to fund the provision of pension benefits would not be relevant for purposes of applying the five percent limitation in section 897(l)(2)(C).

Accordingly, the proposed regulations generally provide that the determination as to whether an eligible fund satisfies the requirements of section 897(l)(2) is made solely with respect to income and assets held by the eligible fund in one or more qualified segregated accounts, the qualified benefits funded by the qualified segregated accounts, the information reporting and regulation related to the qualified segregated accounts, and the qualified recipients whose benefits are funded by the qualified segregated accounts. For this purpose, all qualified segregated accounts maintained by an eligible fund are treated as a single qualified segregated account.

G. *Coordination with definition of a pension fund under U.S. income tax treaties*

Comments requested that the proposed regulations provide that an entity that qualifies as a pension fund or scheme under a U.S. income tax treaty or as an exempt beneficial owner under an intergovernmental agreement (IGA) is treated as a qualified foreign pension fund under section 897(l). The statute is clear that an exemption from section 897(a) is allowed only for entities meeting the definition of a "qualified foreign pension fund." There is no indication in the legislative history that Congress intended the Treasury Department and the IRS to expand the exemption to entities that met the definition of a pension fund under a U.S. income tax treaty or IGA. Furthermore, the definitions of pension fund under a U.S. income tax treaty or IGA were designed with policy goals that are unrelated to section 897, and therefore pension funds as defined in those agreements are not necessarily the types of entities for which an exemption from section 897(a) is appropriate. Thus, a foreign pension fund that qualifies for other benefits under an income tax treaty or IGA must make a separate determination as to whether it is a qualified foreign pension fund under section 897(l)(2).

III. *Withholding Rules*

Comments requested clarification regarding the documentation a qualified foreign pension fund should provide to a transferee or partnership to claim an exemption under section 897(l) and requested a form for this purpose. Comments suggested modifying existing forms, such as Form W-8EXP, Certificate of Foreign Government or Other Foreign Organization for United States Tax Withholding and Reporting, for this purpose. Comments also requested clarification regarding the reporting and withholding responsibilities of transferees and partnerships that receive documentation from a qualified foreign pension fund.

In response to comments, the IRS intends to revise Form W-8EXP to permit qualified holders to certify their status under section 897(l). Prior to the release of revised Form W-8EXP, a certificate of non foreign status described in §1.1445-5(b)(3) may be used for purposes of both section 1445 and section 1446. In addition to permitting withholding agents and partnerships to rely on revised Form W-8EXP, the proposed regulations also integrate the new exception for qualified holders into existing reporting regimes as described below.

A. *Withholding under section 1445*

1. Withholding on Dispositions of USRPIs Under Section 1445(a)

Section 1445(a) requires a transferee to withhold 15 percent of the amount realized on any disposition of a USRPI by a foreign person. Section 1445(b)(2) provides that no withholding is required if the transferor furnishes to the transferee a certificate of non-foreign status. Section 1445(f)(3)(B) provides that for purposes of section 1445, the term "foreign person" generally does not include an entity described in section 897(l)(1). The proposed regulations revise the updated section 1445 regulations to utilize the definitions in proposed § 1.897(l)-1(d) and permit a qualified holder to certify that it is exempt from withholding under section 1445 by providing a certificate of non-foreign status to a withholding agent. The proposed regulations provide that a qualified holder may provide a Form W-8EXP for this purpose, but the transferee, at its option, may request a certification of non-foreign status or Form W-8EXP. Consistent with the approach of current § 1.1445-2(b)(1) (permitting a transferee to request documentation satisfactory to the transferee), the transferee may withhold under section 1445 if the requested certification is not provided and will be considered to have been required to withhold for purposes of sections 1461 through 1463.

A transferee must report transactions subject to section 1445(a) using Form 8288, U.S. Withholding Tax Return for Dispositions by Foreign Persons of U.S. Real Property Interests, and Form 8288-A, Statement of Withholding on Dispositions by Foreign Persons of U.S. Real Property Interests. § 1.1445-1(c). However, because a transferee may treat a qualified holder as not foreign, the transferee is not required to file Form 8288 or Form 8288-A but is subject to the retention and reliance rules generally applicable to certificates of non-foreign status. *See* § 1.1445-2(b)(3).

2. Withholding on Certain Distributions Under Section 1445(e)

Certain distributions and other transactions involving domestic or foreign corporations, partnerships, trusts, and estates can give rise to a withholding requirement under section 1445(e). However, an entity or fiduciary is not required to withhold under section 1445(e) with respect to a distribution or transfer to an interest holder that is not a foreign person. Consistent with the changes to the documentation requirements under section 1445(a), the proposed regulations provide that a qualified holder may provide a certificate of non-foreign status or a revised Form W-8EXP to certify its status as a qualified holder. Although providing such documentation will relieve the entity or fiduciary from withholding obligations under section 1445(e), any otherwise applicable reporting requirements (for example, reporting required on Form 1042-S, Foreign Person's U.S. Source Income Subject to Withholding) remain applicable.

B. *Withholding under section 1446*

A partnership determines whether it must withhold tax under section 1446 by first determining whether it has any foreign partners, and, if it does have foreign partners, by determining whether it has ECTI allocable under section 704 to any of its foreign partners. § 1.1446-1(b). A partner that is treated as a U.S. person only for certain specified purposes is considered a foreign partner for purposes of section 1446. § 1.1446-1(c)(1). Accordingly, a qualified holder is treated as a foreign partner for purposes of section 1446. However, the proposed regulations generally provide that any gain from the disposition of a USRPI, or distribution received from a QIE, that is not otherwise treated as effectively connected with a trade or business in the United States will not be treated as ECTI subject to section 1446 withholding to the extent allocable to a qualified holder.

A partnership may rely on a valid Form W-8 submitted for purposes of section 1441 or section 1442 to establish a partner's foreign status. § 1.1446-1(c)(2)(ii). The proposed regulations update the description of withholding certificates applicable to each type of partner by permitting a partnership to rely on Form W-8EXP both to determine a partner's foreign status and, as appropriate, to exclude any gain from the disposition of a USRPI, including any distribution treated as gain from the disposition of a USRPI under section 897(h), from the determination of such partner's allocable share of ECTI. A partnership may also rely on a certificate of non-foreign status to treat a partner as a qualified holder.

The proposed regulations do not modify general reporting requirements applicable to partnerships. For example, a partnership required to file a partnership return for a taxable year "shall furnish to every person who was a partner" a statement of the partner's distributive share of income, gain, loss, deduction, or credit. § 1.6031(b)-1T. The requirement applies regardless of whether the partner is domestic or foreign. As a result, a partnership that is required to file Form 1065, U.S. Return of Partnership Income, and accompanying schedules must report income allocable to a qualified holder on Schedule K-1, Partner's Share of Income, Deductions, Credit, etc., notwithstanding that such income is exempt from section 897.

C. *Coordination with sections 1441 and 1442*

Sections 1441 and 1442 require withholding agents to deduct and withhold a 30 percent tax on payments of U.S. source fixed or determinable, annual or periodical income to foreign persons, including a U.S. source corporate distribution described in section 301(c)(1). A corporate distribution described in section 301(c)(2) or (c)(3) that is not subject to withholding under section 1441 or section 1442 (for example, because the distributing corporation made the election described in § 1.1441-3(c)(1)) may nonetheless be subject to withholding under section 1445 if the distributing corporation is a USRPHC or QIE. Section 1.1441-3(c)(4)(i)(A) and a similar rule in § 1.1441-3(c)(4)(i)(C) coordinate withholding under sections 1441 and 1445 with respect to distributions from USRPHCs and QIEs. Because a qualified holder is treated as foreign for purposes of section 1441 but not for purposes of section 1445, distributions that would otherwise be subject to the coordination rule should be subject exclusively to section 1441 if made to a qualified holder. Accordingly, the proposed regulations provide that distributions made by a USRPHC or QIE to a qualified holder are not subject to the coordination rules under § 1.1441-3(c)(4) and instead are subject only to the requirements of section 1441.

IV. *Applicability Dates*

The proposed regulations are generally proposed to apply with respect to dispositions of USRPIs and distributions described in section 897(h) occurring on or after the date of publication of the Treasury decision adopting these rules as final regulations in the **Federal Register**. However, proposed §§ 1.897(l)-1(b)(1), 1.897(l)-1(d)(5), 1.897(l)-1(d)(7), 1.897(l)-1(d)(9), 1.897(l)-1(d)(11), and 1.897(l)-1(d)(14) are proposed to apply with respect to dispositions of USRPIs and distributions described in section 897(h) occurring on or after June 6, 2019. See section 7805(b)(1)(B). These provisions contain definitions that prevent a person that would otherwise be a qualified holder from claiming the exemption under section 897(l) in situations where the exemption may inure, in whole or in part, to the benefit of a person other than a qualified recipient. See Section I.B.6 of this Explanation of Provisions. The Treasury Department and the IRS have determined that an immediate applicability date under section 7805(b)(1)(B) is appropriate for these provisions in order to address transactions that are inconsistent with the purposes of section 897(l) that may occur before these rules are adopted as final regulations.

A taxpayer may rely on the proposed regulations with respect to dispositions or distributions occurring on or after December 18, 2015, and prior to the applicability date of the final regulations, if the taxpayer consistently and accurately complies with the rules in the proposed regulations.

Special Analyses

I. Regulatory Planning and Review — Economic Analysis

Executive Orders 13563 and 12866 direct agencies to assess costs and benefits of available regulatory alternatives and, if regulation is necessary, to select regulatory approaches that maximize net benefits, including potential economic, environmental, public health and safety effects, distributive impacts, and equity. Executive Order 13563 emphasizes the importance of quantifying both costs and benefits, of reducing costs, of harmonizing rules, and of promoting flexibility.

These proposed regulations have been designated as a significant regulatory action by the Office of Management and Budget's Office of Information and Regulatory Affairs ("OIRA") and subject to review under Executive Order 12866 pursuant to the Memorandum of Agreement (April 11, 2018) between the Treasury Department and the Office of Management and Budget regarding review of tax regulations.

A. Background

Section 897, more commonly known as the Foreign Investment in Real Property Tax Act ("FIRPTA"), was enacted in 1980 due to concerns that the Code provided foreign persons an advantage in investing in U.S. real property interests (USRPI) over U.S. taxpayers because, unlike U.S. taxpayers, foreigners were not subject to U.S. capital gains tax on dispositions of USRPI. Under FIRPTA, when a foreign person sells USRPI, any gain on the sale generally is subject to U.S. income tax.

Section 897(l), enacted in 2015 in the Protecting Americans from Tax Hikes Act ("PATH Act"), exempts qualified foreign pension funds ("QFPFs") from tax under FIRPTA on gain from the sale of USRPI, the so-called "foreign pension fund exemption." Such an exemption has the effect of encouraging foreign pension fund investment in the United States (through investment in real property) and, in general, provides consistent tax treatment between foreign pension funds and U.S. pension funds, which normally are not taxed at the entity level. This exemption is the subject of the proposed regulations.

The foreign pension fund exemption also affects a related withholding tax levied under section 1445 on the sale of USRPI to help enforce payment of the tax owed by reason of section 897. The rate for this withholding is 15 percent of gross sales. In cases where the gross withholding tax would exceed the tax owed on the net capital gains, foreigners typically request and receive approval for reduced rates of gross withholding tax. If withholding is excessive or insufficient relative to tax owed on the net capital gains, the difference is made up on the foreigner's U.S. tax return. Thus, guidance that governs the foreign pension fund exemption additionally necessitates guidance over the withholding tax.

IRS tax data for 2015 and 2016 show an average of approximately 160 foreign pension funds earning income from U.S. real property. Only a fraction of these funds are likely to sell or transfer USRPI in any given year.

B. The need for proposed regulations

Comments received indicate that some foreign pension funds have refrained from investment in U.S. real property, including infrastructure projects, due to ambiguities over their qualification for the foreign pension fund exemption. Affected parties have provided a number of comments requesting clarifications of the statutes. The Treasury Department and the IRS have determined that such comments warrant the issuance of further guidance. The proposed regulations do not specifically aim to increase or decrease foreign pension fund investment in the U.S. Instead, they aim to provide guidance such that investment can be made on an efficient basis consistent with the intents and purposes of the statute.

C. Summary of proposed regulations

The regulations clarify and modify the conditions under which foreign pension funds are exempt from taxation under section 897. In plain language, the proposed regulations provide further clarity over (a) the entities and organizational structures that are eligible for the foreign pension fund exemption; (b) the nature of the benefits, beneficiaries, and foreign taxation of eligible funds; and (c) the documentation rules that apply to exemptions from withholding taxes otherwise required by sections 1445 (these exemptions from withholding taxes flow from the foreign pension fund exemption from tax under section 897). In addition, the proposed regulations provide rules to prevent the inappropriate avoidance of FIRPTA by imposing conditions on the sale of certain investment vehicles wholly owned by a foreign pension fund.

D. Economic analysis

1. Baseline

The Treasury Department and the IRS have assessed the benefits and costs of the proposed regulations relative to a no-action baseline reflecting anticipated Federal income tax-related behavior in the absence of these proposed regulations.

2. Summary of Economic Effects

In general, a tax system that prioritizes minimization of distortions aims to treat income earned by similar economic activities similarly, subject to considerations of compliance burden and tax administrability and to the intents and purposes of Congress. The proposed guidance adheres to this principle. In plain language, section 897(l) exempts certain foreign pension funds from tax under FIRPTA, and the proposed guidance qualifies the terms of this exemption by further defining the permissible activities, ownership patterns, and other economic decisions undertaken by foreign pension funds. Such guidance helps ensure that the tax system does not favor or disfavor particular QFPF activities over economically similar QFPF activities, a requirement for an economically efficient tax system conditional on the underlying Code.

As a result of the added clarity and reduced compliance burdens relative to the baseline, the proposed regulations have the effect of providing more efficient investment incentives, relative to the baseline and in light of the intents and purposes of the statute. The Treasury Department and the IRS have not estimated the effects of the proposed regulations on the U.S. economy.

3. Economic Analysis of Specific Provisions

The Treasury Department and the IRS identified four provisions in the proposed regulations for which economic analysis might play a meaningful role in selecting the form of the regulations. This part I.D.2 of this Special Analyses describes this analysis. The Treasury Department and the IRS solicit comments on the economics of each of the items discussed subsequently and of any other items of the proposed regulations not discussed in this section. The Treasury Department and the IRS particularly solicit comments that provide data, other evidence, or models that could enhance the rigor of the process by which provisions might be developed for the final regulations.

a. Investing in USRPI directly and using pooled investment vehicles

Foreign pension funds often hold USRPI indirectly through intermediate entities, including entities with multiple foreign pension fund owners. While the statute contains language stating that an entity wholly owned by a QFPF is itself a QFPF, section 897(l) is silent on whether the entity must be wholly owned by a single QFPF (or, alternatively, may be wholly owned by multiple QFPFs).

Because the economic incentives faced by foreign pension funds under these various ownership structures regarding investment in USRPI are similar to the incentives faced by QFPFs with simpler structures, the Treasury Department and the IRS have determined that it would be consistent with the intents and purposes of the statute and minimize the potential for distortionary choices for them to be eligible for the foreign pension fund exemption. Thus, the proposed regulations explicitly allow indirect investments and pooled investments to qualify for the exemption. The Treasury Department and the IRS considered alternative guidance that was more restrictive than the proposed regulations but, under that alternative, foreign pension funds could avail themselves of an exemption only on a more restricted set of U.S. investment options and would be denied the exemption on economically similar investments, a situation that would generally lead to an economically inferior outcome.

b. Avoidance through use of foreign subsidiary

A foreign person that is not a qualified foreign pension fund ("non-QFPF") that holds USRPI directly would be taxed under FIRPTA if the non-QFPF sells the USRPI. If the non-QFPF instead holds USRPI indirectly through a foreign subsidiary, the non-QFPF can sell the foreign subsidiary without taxation under section 897, but, in that case, the unrealized gain in the USRPI would remain potentially subject to tax under FIRPTA on disposition of the USRPI. Absent a provision to the contrary in the proposed regulations, if the non-QFPF instead sells the foreign subsidiary to a QFPF, the QFPF could cause the foreign subsidiary to sell the USRPI immediately (or in the future) without incurring tax under section 897, thus eliminating the taxation (or potential for future taxation) of gain in the USRPI. As a result, subject to other provisions and judicial doctrines (for example, the step transaction doctrine and the economic substance doctrine), a QFPF could be used as a conduit for a non-QFPF to sell a USRPI to a purchaser without incurring (or preserving) tax under section 897 on the unrealized gain of the seller. The Treasury Department and the IRS project that such activity would reduce U.S. tax revenue and would not result in an accompanying economic benefit to the U.S. economy.

To curtail this tax avoidance, the proposed regulations provide a transitory restriction on exemption when a foreign subsidiary that owns USRPI is purchased by a QFPF or qualified controlled entity ("QCE") of a QFPF from a non-QFPF or a foreign person that is not a QCE. This transitory restriction, referred to as a testing period, is described in full in part I.B.6 of the Explanation of Provisions of the Preamble. Among other criteria, under the proposed regulations the foreign pension fund exemption generally is not available for gain recognized by an entity from the disposition of a USRPI if such entity was not a QFPF or QCE at any time during the 10-year period prior to the recognition of that gain.

The Treasury Department and the IRS considered as an alternative requiring the controlled entity acquired by the foreign pension fund to account for the gain at the time the entity was acquired by the foreign pension fund (known as mark-to-market) or requiring tracking of the unrealized gain at the time of sale to a QFPF or QCE for later recognition and also considered, under the testing period approach, different lengths for that component of the testing period. The mark-to-market or tracking approaches impose greater compliance and administrative costs relative to the testing period approach without providing any accompanying general economic benefit.

The Treasury Department and the IRS aim, through this testing period approach and accompanying requirements, to minimize tax avoidance while facilitating efficient foreign pension fund investment in USRPI, consistent with the intents and purposes of the statute. The Treasury Department and IRS solicit comments on this proposal, particularly comments that provide data, other evidence, or models that could enhance the rigor of the process by which anti-abuse provisions might be developed for the final regulations.

c. Ancillary benefits

Section 897(l) specifies, along with other qualifications, that the exemption is available to foreign entities that are "established" to provide retirement or pension benefits. However, many foreign pension funds provide ancillary benefits such as death, terminal health, disability, medical, unemployment, and survivor benefits in addition to retirement and pension benefits. These funds may be reluctant to invest in USRPI due to uncertainty over whether the fund meets this particular statutory criterion.

The Treasury Department and the IRS considered an option to deny the exemption to foreign pension funds that provide any benefits other than retirement and pension benefits. This option runs the risk of effectively eliminating foreign pension fund investment in USRPI because it would deny the exemption to foreign pension funds no matter how close to 100 percent of their benefits were retirement or pension related, or would require funds that wanted to invest in the U.S. under competitive conditions to undergo costly restructuring to eliminate or segregate those benefits, if such options were even feasible under the foreign country's laws and institutions. Both of these outcomes are economically inefficient relative to the proposed policies and the baseline because relative to these options, they incentivize socially costly tax avoidance choices and/or overly restrict incrementally improving market-driven choices.

The proposed regulations provide a bright-line test limiting the amount of ancillary benefits to 15 percent or lower. Such threshold was chosen in part based on suggestions from comments. The Treasury Department and the IRS aim, through the bright-line approach and this specific percentage test, to facilitate foreign pension fund investment in the U.S. consistent with the intents and purposes of the statute. The Treasury Department and the IRS solicit comments on this proposed standard, and particularly solicit comments that provide data, other evidence, or models that could enhance the rigor of the process by which the percentage limitation might be developed for the final regulations.

The Treasury Department and the IRS recognize that the threshold approach may result in a small number of foreign pension funds oscillating between qualifying and not qualifying on a year-to-year basis and that such approach requires measurement of ancillary benefits relative to retirement and pension benefits. Thus, the Treasury Department and the IRS further solicit comments on alternatives to the threshold approach and particularly solicit comments that provide data, other evidence, or models that could enhance the rigor of the process by which the tax treatment of foreign pension funds that provide ancillary benefits might be developed for the final regulations.

d. Determination of foreign tax preference

Under the statute, to qualify for exemption a foreign pension fund must be subject to tax laws in the country in which the fund is established or operates such that contributions to the fund are deductible or excluded from the gross income of the fund or taxed at a reduced rate, or tax on investment income of the fund is deferred or that income is taxed a reduced rate.

To provide further specificity over what qualifies as a preferential tax rate on contributions to or income from the fund, the Treasury Department and the IRS considered providing a substantive, analytical test for determining whether a foreign pension fund benefits from a preferential tax rate. This option would prove difficult to administer and require complex rules to determine whether a pension fund benefits from a preferential tax regime in the country in which it is established.

To reduce compliance burden and enhance administrability, the proposed regulations expand the scope of the potential preferential tax regimes and provide a bright-line test for determining preferential treatment by setting a threshold (85 percent) for the percentage of fund contributions/ income that is subject to a preferential regime. The 85 percent threshold was chosen in part based on suggestions from comments. The Treasury Department and the IRS aim, through this bright-line approach and this specific percentage test, to facilitate foreign pension fund investment in USRPI consistent with the intents and purposes of the statute while minimizing the costs of tax administrability.

The Treasury Department and the IRS solicit comments on this proposal, and in particular comments that provide data, other evidence, or models that could enhance the rigor of the process by which the 897(l)(2)(E) requirements might be developed for the final regulations.

II. *Paperwork Reduction Act*

In accordance with the Paperwork Reduction Act, 44 U.S.C. 3501 *et seq.* ("PRA"), information collection requirements contained in these proposed regulations are in §§1.1441-3(c)(4)(iii), 1.1445-2, 1.1445-4, 1.1445-5, 1.1445-8, and 1.1446-1.

In 2018, the IRS released and took comment on drafts of three forms in order to give members of the public the opportunity to benefit from certain specific revisions made to the Code. The forms were Form 1042-S, "Foreign Person's U.S. Source Income Subject to Withholding," Form 1042, "Annual Withholding Tax Return for U.S. Source Income of Foreign Persons" and Form W-8EXP, "Certificate of Foreign Government or Other Foreign Organization for United States Tax Withholding or Reporting." The IRS received no comments on the forms during the comment period. Consequently, the IRS made the forms available for use by the public on November 30, 2018 (in the case of Form 1042-S), November 21, 2018 (in the case of Form 1042), and July 20, 2017 (in the case of Form W-8EXP). The IRS is contemplating making additional changes to those three forms in connection with these regulations.

The Treasury Department and the IRS request comments on all aspects of information collection burdens related to the proposed regulations, including estimates for how much time it would take to comply with the paperwork burdens described below for each relevant form and ways for the IRS to minimize the paperwork burden. Proposed revisions to these forms that reflect the information collections contained in these proposed regulations will be made available for public comment at www.irs.gov/draftforms *and will not be finalized until after these regulations take effect and have been approved by OMB under the PRA.* The Treasury Department and the IRS have not estimated the burden, including that of any new information collections, related to the requirements under the proposed regulations.

A. *Information collections contained in §1.1441-3(c)(4)(iii)*

The proposed regulations provide that distributions made by a USRPHC or QIE to a qualified holder are subject only to the requirements of section 1441 and not the coordination rule under §1.1441-3(c)(4). Proposed §1.1441-3(c)(4)(iii). As a result, a USRPHC or QIE making a distribution to a qualified holder would be required to report the distribution on Form 1042-S, "Foreign Person's U.S. Source Income Subject to Withholding," and file Form 1042, "Annual Withholding Tax Return for U.S. Source Income of Foreign Persons." For purposes of this reporting, the IRS is planning to revise Form 1042-S to include an income code designating payments made to Qualified Foreign Pension Plans. No revisions are being made to Form 1042 in connection with payments made to Qualified Foreign Pension Plans.

For purposes of the PRA, the reporting burden associated with proposed §1.1441-3(c)(4)(iii) will be reflected in the PRA submissions for Form 1042 (OMB control numbers 1545-0123 for business filers and 1545-0096 for all other Form 1042 filers) and Form 1042-S (OMB control number 1545-0096). The PRA submissions for Form 1042 reflect IRS's transition to an updated statistical model that calculates burden based on the taxpayer filing experience as a whole. As such, Form 1042 is in a transition state, as the burden incurred by business filers is captured in OMB control number 1545-0123 (under the updated burden model) and the burden represented incurred by all other filers is represented in 1545-0096 (legacy model).

B. *Information collections in §§1.1445-2, 1.1445-4, 1.1445-5, 1.1445-8, and 1.1446-1*

Proposed §§1.1445-2, 1.1445-4, 1.1445-5, 1.1445-8, and 1.1446-1 would require a qualified foreign pension fund wishing to claim an exemption under section 897(l) to provide a withholding agent with either a Form W-8EXP, "Certificate of Foreign Government or Other Foreign Organization for United States Tax Withholding or Reporting," or, at a withholding agent's request and in lieu of Form W-8EXP, a certificate of non-foreign status containing the same information as Form W-8EXP. The IRS plans to revise Form W-8EXP for use by qualified foreign pension funds. For purposes of the PRA, the reporting burden associated with proposed §§1.1445-2, 1.1445-4, 1.1445-5, 1.1445-8, and 1.1446-1, will be reflected in the PRA submission for Form W-8EXP (OMB control number 1545-1621).

The reporting burdens associated with the information collections in the proposed regulations are included in the aggregate burden estimates for OMB control numbers 1545-0096 (which represents a total estimated burden time for all forms and schedules of 2.70 million hours) and 1545-1621 (which represents a total estimated burden time, including all other related forms and schedules for other filers, of 25.13 million hours and total estimated monetized costs of $2.39 billion). The overall burden estimates for the OMB control numbers are aggregate amounts that relate to the entire package of forms associated with the applicable OMB control number and will in the future include, but not isolate, the estimated burden of the tax forms that will be or have been revised as a result of the information collections in the proposed regulations. These numbers are therefore unrelated to the future calculations needed to assess the burden imposed by the proposed regulations. These burdens have been reported for other regulations related to the taxation of cross-border income and the Treasury Department and the IRS urge readers to recognize that these numbers are duplicates and to guard against overcounting the burden that international tax provisions imposed prior to the PATH Act.

III. *Regulatory Flexibility Act*

Pursuant to the Regulatory Flexibility Act (5 U.S.C. chapter 6), it is hereby certified that the proposed rule will not have a significant economic impact on a substantial number of small entities within the meaning of section 601(6) of the Regulatory Flexibility Act. This certification is based on the fact that foreign entities are not considered small entities. These regulations will affect foreign pension funds and not U.S. pension funds. In addition, based on comments received, the foreign pension funds that are affected are sovereign funds, which are not small entities. Accordingly, a regulatory flexibility analysis under the Regulatory Flexibility Act is not required. Pursuant to section 7805(f), this notice of proposed rulemaking has been submitted to the Chief Counsel for Advocacy of the Small Business Administration for comment on its impact on small business.

IV. *Unfunded Mandates Reform Act*

Section 202 of the Unfunded Mandates Reform Act of 1995 requires that agencies assess anticipated costs and benefits and take certain other actions before issuing a final rule that includes any Federal mandate that may result in expenditures in any one year by a state, local, or tribal government, in the aggregate, or by the private sector, of $100 million in 1995 dollars, updated annually for inflation. In 2018, that threshold is approximately $150 million. This rule does not include any Federal mandate that may result in expenditures by state, local, or tribal governments, or by the private sector in excess of that threshold.

V. *Executive Order 13132: Federalism*

Executive Order 13132 (entitled "Federalism") prohibits an agency from publishing any rule that has federalism implications if the rule either imposes substantial, direct compliance costs on state and local governments, and is not required by statute, or preempts state law, unless the agency meets the consultation and funding requirements of section 6 of the Executive Order. This proposed rule does not have federalism implications, does not impose substantial direct compliance costs on state and local governments, and does not preempt state law within the meaning of the Executive Order.

Comments and Requests for Public Hearing

Before these proposed regulations are adopted as final regulations, consideration will be given to any comments that are submitted timely to the IRS as prescribed in this Preamble under the "Addresses" heading. The Treasury Department and the IRS request comments on all aspects of the proposed rules. All comments will be available at *www.regulations.gov* or upon request. A public hearing will be scheduled if requested in writing by any person that timely submits written comments. If a public hearing is scheduled, notice of the date, time, and place for the public hearing will be published in the **Federal Register**.

Drafting Information

The principal authors of these proposed regulations are Joshua Rabon, formerly with the Office of Associate Chief Counsel (International), and Milton Cahn, Office of Associate Chief Counsel (International). However, other personnel from the Treasury Department and the IRS participated in their development.

[¶ 49,801]   Proposed Amendments of Regulations (REG-101828-19), published in the Federal Register on June 21, 2019 (corrected 8/2/2019).

[Code Secs. 951, 951A, 954, 956, 958 and 1502]

Domestic partnership: Foreign corporation: Gross income.—Amendments of Reg. §§1.951-1, 1.951A-0, 1.951A-2, 1.951A-7, 1.954-1, 1.954-1, 1.956-1, 1.958-1 and 1.1502-51, regarding the treatment of domestic partnerships for purposes of determining amounts included in the gross income of their partners with respect to foreign corporations, are proposed.

AGENCY: Internal Revenue Service (IRS), Treasury.

ACTION: Notice of proposed rulemaking.

SUMMARY: This document contains proposed regulations regarding the treatment of domestic partnerships for purposes of determining amounts included in the gross income of their partners with respect to foreign corporations. In addition, this document contains proposed regulations under the global intangible low-taxed income provisions regarding gross income that is subject to a high rate of foreign tax. The proposed regulations would affect United States persons that own stock of foreign corporations through domestic partnerships and United States shareholders of foreign corporations. DATES: Written or electronic comments and requests for a public hearing must be received by September 19, 2019

ADDRESSES: Send submissions to: Internal Revenue Service, CC:PA:LPD:PR (REG-101828-19), Room 5203, Post Office Box 7604, Ben Franklin Station, Washington, DC 20044. Submissions may be hand-delivered Monday through Friday between the hours of 8 a.m. and 4 p.m. to CC:PA:LPD:PR (REG-101828-19), Courier's Desk, Internal Revenue Service, 1111 Constitution Avenue, N.W., Washington, DC 20024, or sent electronically, via the Federal eRulemaking Portal at *www.regulations.gov* (indicate IRS and REG-101828-19).

FOR FURTHER INFORMATION CONTACT: Concerning the proposed regulations under §§1.951-1, 1.956-1, and 1.958-1, Joshua P. Roffenbender at (202) 317-6934; concerning the proposed regulations under §§1.951A-0, 1.951A-2, 1.951A-7, and 1.954-1, Jorge M. Oben at (202) 317-6934; concerning the proposed regulations under §1.1502-51, Katherine H. Zhang at (202) 317-6848 or Kevin M. Jacobs at (202) 317-5332; concerning submissions of comments or requests for a public hearing, Regina Johnson at (202) 317-6901 (not toll free numbers).

SUPPLEMENTARY INFORMATION:

Background

I. *Subpart F Before Enactment of Section 951A*

The Revenue Act of 1962 (the "1962 Act"), Pub. L. 87-834, sec. 12, 76 Stat. at 1006, enacted subpart F of part III, subchapter N, chapter 1 of the 1954 Internal Revenue Code ("subpart F"), as amended. See sections 951 through 965 of the Internal Revenue Code ("Code").[1] Congress created the subpart F regime to limit the use of corporations organized in low-tax jurisdictions for the purposes of obtaining indefinite deferral of U.S. tax on certain earnings – generally earnings that are passive or highly mobile – that would otherwise be subject to Federal income tax. H.R. Rep. No. 1447 at 57-58 (1962); S. Rep. No. 1881 at 78-80 (1962). Subpart F generally requires a United States shareholder (as defined in section 951(b)) ("U.S. shareholder") to include in its gross income ("subpart F inclusion") its pro rata share of subpart F income (as defined in section 952) earned by a controlled foreign corporation ("CFC") (as defined in section 957(a)) and its pro rata share of earnings and profits ("E&P") invested in certain United States property by the CFC. See section 951(a)(1)(A) and (B) and section 956(a). For purposes of both section 951(a)(1)(A) and (B), the determination of a U.S. shareholder's pro rata share of any amount with respect to a CFC is determined by reference to the stock of the CFC that the shareholder owns (within the meaning of section 958(a)). See sections 951(a)(1) and (2) and 956(a).

Section 957(a) defines a CFC as any foreign corporation if U.S. shareholders own (within the meaning of section 958(a)), or are considered as owning by applying the ownership rules of section 958(b), more than 50 percent of the total combined voting power or value of stock of such corporation on any day during the taxable year of such foreign corporation. Section 951(b) defines a U.S. shareholder of a foreign corporation as a United States person ("U.S. person") that owns (within the meaning of section 958(a)), or is considered as owning by applying the ownership rules of section 958(b), at least 10 percent of the total combined voting power or value of stock of the foreign corporation. Section 957(c) generally defines a U.S. person by reference to section 7701(a)(30), which defines a U.S. person as a citizen or resident of the United States, a domestic partnership, a domestic corporation, and certain estates and trusts.

Stock owned within the meaning of section 958(a) is stock owned directly and stock owned indirectly under section 958(a)(2). Section 958(a)(2) provides that stock owned, directly or indirectly, by or for a foreign corporation, foreign partnership, foreign trust, or foreign estate is considered to be owned proportionately by its shareholders, partners, or beneficiaries. Section 958(a)(2) does not provide rules addressing stock owned by domestic entities, including domestic partnerships.

Section 958(b) provides in relevant part that the constructive ownership rules of section 318(a) apply, with certain modifications, for purposes of determining whether any U.S. person is a U.S. shareholder or any foreign corporation is a CFC. These rules apply to treat a person as owning the stock owned, directly or indirectly, by another person, generally without regard to whether the person to or from which stock is attributed is domestic or foreign. In particular, section 318(a)(2)(A) provides in relevant part that stock owned, directly or indirectly, by or for a partnership is considered as owned proportionately by its partners, and section 318(a)(3)(A) provides that stock owned, directly or indirectly, by or for a partner is considered as owned by the partnership. Further, in determining stock treated as owned by partners of a partnership under section 318(a)(2)(A), section 958(b)(2) provides in relevant part that a partnership that owns, directly or indirectly, more than 50 percent of the voting power of a corporation is considered as owning all the stock entitled to vote. However, a U.S. person that is a U.S. shareholder of a CFC by reason of constructive ownership under section 958(b), but that does not own stock in the CFC within the meaning of section 958(a), does not have a subpart F inclusion with respect to the CFC.

II. *Treatment of Domestic Partnerships as Entities or Aggregates of their Partners, in* General

For purposes of applying a particular provision of the Code, a partnership may be treated as either an entity separate from its partners or as an aggregate of its partners. Under an aggregate approach, the partners of a partnership, and not the partnership, are treated as owning the

---

[1] Except as otherwise stated, all section references in this preamble are to the Internal Revenue Code.

partnership's assets and conducting the partnership's operations. Under an entity approach, the partnership is respected as separate and distinct from its partners, and therefore the partnership, and not the partners, is treated as owning the partnership's assets and conducting the partnership's operations. Based upon the authority of subchapter K and the policies underlying a particular provision of the Code, a partnership is treated as an aggregate of its partners or as an entity separate from its partners, depending on which characterization is more appropriate to carry out the scope and purpose of the Code provision. See H.R. Rep. No. 83-2543, at 59 (1954) (Conf. Rep.) ("Both the House provisions and the Senate amendment provide for the use of the 'entity' approach in the treatment of transactions between a partner and a partnership . . . . No inference is intended, however, that a partnership is to be considered as a separate entity for the purpose of applying other provisions of the internal revenue laws if the concept of the partnership as a collection of individuals is more appropriate for such provisions."). See also *Casel v. Commissioner*, 79 T.C. 424, 433 (1982) ("When the 1954 Code was adopted by Congress, the conference report . . . clearly stated that whether an aggregate or entity theory of partnerships should be applied to a particular Code section depends upon which theory is more appropriate to such section."); *Holiday Village Shopping Center v. United States*, 5 Cl. Ct. 566, 570 (1984), aff'd 773 F.2d 276 (Fed. Cir. 1985) ("[T]he proper inquiry is not whether a partnership is an entity or an aggregate for purposes of applying the internal revenue laws generally, but rather which is the more appropriate and more consistent with Congressional intent with respect to the operation of the particular provision of the Internal Revenue Code at issue."); § 1.701-2(e)(1) ("The Commissioner can treat a partnership as an aggregate of its partners in whole or in part as appropriate to carry out the purpose of any provision of the Internal Revenue Code . . . .").

Consistent with this authority under subchapter K, the Treasury Department and the IRS have adopted an aggregate approach to partnerships to carry out the purpose of various provisions, including international provisions, of the Code. For example, regulations under section 871 treat domestic and foreign partnerships as aggregates of their partners in applying the 10 percent shareholder test of section 871(h)(3) to determine whether interest paid to a partnership would be considered portfolio interest under section 871(h)(2). See § 1.871-14(g)(3)(i). An aggregate approach to partnerships was also adopted in regulations issued under section 367(a) to address the transfer of property by a domestic or foreign partnership to a foreign corporation in an exchange described in section 367(a)(1). See § 1.367(a)-1T(c)(3)(i)(A). Similarly, the Treasury Department and the IRS adopted an aggregate approach to foreign partnerships for purposes of applying the regulations under section 367(b). See § 1.367(b)-2(k); see also § § 1.367(e)-1(b)(2) (treating stock and securities of a distributing corporation owned by or for a partnership (domestic or foreign) as owned proportionately by its partners) and 1.861-9(e)(2) (requiring certain corporate partners to apportion interest expense, including the partner's distributive share of partnership interest expense, by reference to the partner's assets).

III. *Treatment of Domestic Partnerships as Entities or Aggregates for Purposes of Subpart F Before the Tax Cuts and Jobs Act*

Since the enactment of subpart F, domestic partnerships have generally been treated as entities, rather than as aggregates of their partners, for purposes of determining whether U.S. shareholders own more than 50 percent of the stock (by voting power or value) of a foreign corporation and thus whether a foreign corporation is a CFC. See § 1.701-2(f), *Example 3* (concluding that a foreign corporation wholly owned by a domestic partnership is a CFC for purposes of applying the look-through rules of section 904(d)(3)). In addition, domestic partnerships have generally been treated as entities for purposes of treating a domestic partnership as the U.S. shareholder that has the subpart F inclusion with respect to such foreign corporation. But cf. § § 1.951-1(h) and 1.965-1(e) (treating certain domestic partnerships owned by CFCs as foreign partnerships for purposes of determining the U.S. shareholder that has the subpart F inclusion with respect to CFCs owned by such domestic partnerships). If a domestic partnership is treated as the U.S. shareholder with the subpart F inclusion, then each partner of the partnership has a distributive share of the partnership's subpart F inclusion, regardless of whether the partner itself is a U.S. shareholder. See section 702.

This entity treatment is consistent with the inclusion of a domestic partnership in the definition of a U.S. person in section 7701(a)(30), which term is used in the definition of U.S. shareholder by reference to section 957(c). It is also consistent with the legislative history to section 951, which describes domestic partnerships as being included within the definition of a U.S. person and, therefore, a U.S. shareholder. See, for example, S. Rep. No. 1881 at 80 n.1 (1962) ("U.S. shareholders are defined in the bill as 'U.S. persons' with 10-percent stockholding. U.S. persons, in general, are U.S. citizens and residents and domestic corporations, partnerships and estates or trusts."). Furthermore, entity treatment is consistent with sections 958(b) and 318(a)(3)(A), which treat a partnership (including a domestic partnership) as owning the stock owned by its partners for purposes of determining whether the foreign corporation is owned more than 50 percent by U.S. shareholders.

In contrast to the historical treatment of domestic partnerships as entities for purposes of subpart F, foreign partnerships are generally treated as aggregates of their partners for purposes of determining stock ownership under section 958(a). See section 958(a)(2). Accordingly, whether a foreign corporation owned by a foreign partnership is a CFC is determined based on the proportionate amount of stock owned by domestic partners of the partnership and, if the foreign corporation is a CFC, partners that are U.S. shareholders have the subpart F inclusion with respect to the CFC.

IV. *Section 951A*

A. *In general*

The Tax Cuts and Jobs Act, Pub. L. 115-97 (the "Act") established a participation exemption system for the taxation of certain foreign income by allowing a domestic corporation a 100 percent dividends received deduction for the foreign-source portion of a dividend received from a specified 10 percent-owned foreign corporation. See section 14101(a) of the Act and section 245A. The Act's legislative history expresses concern that the new participation exemption could heighten the incentive to shift profits to low-tax foreign jurisdictions or tax havens absent base erosion protections. See S. Comm. on the Budget, Reconciliation Recommendations Pursuant to H. Con. Res. 71, S. Print No. 115-20, at 370 (2017) ("Senate Explanation"). For example, without appropriate limits, domestic corporations might be incentivized to shift income to low-taxed foreign affiliates, and the income could potentially be distributed back to domestic corporate shareholders without the imposition of any U.S. tax. See id. To prevent base erosion, the Act retained the subpart F regime and enacted section 951A, which applies to taxable years of foreign corporations beginning after December 31, 2017, and to taxable years of U.S. shareholders in which or with which such taxable years of foreign corporations end.

Section 951A requires a U.S. shareholder of any CFC for any taxable year to include in gross income the shareholder's global intangible low-taxed income ("GILTI inclusion") for such taxable year in a manner similar to a subpart F inclusion for many purposes of the Code. See sections 951A(a) and (f)(1)(A); H.R. Rep. No. 115-466, at 641 (2017) (Conf. Rep.) ("[A] U.S. shareholder of any CFC must include in gross income for a taxable year its [GILTI] in a manner generally similar to inclusions of subpart F income."). Similar to a subpart F inclusion, the determination of a U.S. shareholder's GILTI inclusion begins with the calculation of relevant items – such as tested income, tested loss, and qualified business asset investment – of each CFC owned by the shareholder ("tested items"). See section 951A(c)(2) and (d) and § § 1.951A-2 through-4. A U.S. shareholder then determines its pro rata share of each of these CFC-level tested items in a manner similar to a U.S. shareholder's pro rata share of subpart F income under section 951(a)(2). See section 951A(e)(1) and § 1.951A-1(d).

In contrast to a subpart F inclusion, however, a U.S. shareholder's pro rata shares of the tested items of a CFC are not amounts included in gross income, but rather are amounts taken into account by the U.S. shareholder in determining the amount of its GILTI inclusion for the taxable year. Section 951A(b) and § 1.951A-1(c). Thus, a U.S. shareholder does not compute a separate GILTI inclusion amount under section 951A(a) with respect to each CFC for a taxable year, but rather computes a single GILTI inclusion amount by reference to all of its CFCs.

Section 951A itself does not contain specific rules regarding the treatment of domestic partnerships and their partners for purposes of GILTI. However, proposed regulations under section 951A that were published in the **Federal Register** on October 10, 2018, (REG-104390-18, 83 FR 51072)

("GILTI proposed regulations") reflect a hybrid approach that treats a domestic partnership that is a U.S. shareholder with respect to a CFC ("U.S. shareholder partnership") as an entity with respect to some partners but as an aggregate of its partners with respect to others. Under the hybrid approach, with respect to partners that are not U.S. shareholders of a CFC owned by a domestic partnership, a U.S. shareholder partnership calculates a GILTI inclusion amount and its partners have a distributive share of such amount (if any). See proposed § 1.951A-5(b)(1). However, with respect to partners that are themselves U.S. shareholders of a CFC owned by a domestic partnership ("U.S. shareholder partners"), the partnership is treated in the same manner as a foreign partnership, with the result that the U.S. shareholder partners are treated as proportionately owning, within the meaning of section 958(a), stock owned by the domestic partnership for purposes of determining their own GILTI inclusion amounts. See proposed § 1.951A-5(c). In the preamble to the GILTI proposed regulations, the Treasury Department and the IRS rejected a pure entity approach to section 951A, because treating a domestic partnership as the section 958(a) owner of stock in all cases would frustrate the GILTI framework by creating unintended planning opportunities for well advised taxpayers and traps for the unwary. However, the Treasury Department and the IRS also did not adopt a pure aggregate approach to domestic partnerships for GILTI because such an approach would be inconsistent with the existing treatment of domestic partnerships as entities for purposes of subpart F.

The Treasury Department and the IRS received many comments in response to the hybrid approach of the GILTI proposed regulations. The comments generally advised against adopting the hybrid approach due primarily to concerns with complexity and administrability arising from the treatment of a partnership as an entity with respect to some partners but as an aggregate with respect to other partners. The comments also generally advised against adopting a pure entity approach because such an approach would result in different treatment for similarly situated taxpayers depending on whether a U.S. shareholder owned stock of a foreign corporation through a domestic partnership or a foreign partnership, which is treated as an aggregate of its partners for purposes of determining CFC status and section 958(a) ownership. The majority of comments on this issue recommended at least some form of aggregate approach for domestic partnerships for purposes of the GILTI regime; some of these comments suggested that an aggregate approach is supported by analogy to other situations where regulations apply an aggregate approach to partnerships. See, for example, §§ 1.954-1(g)(1) and 1.871-14(g)(3)(i).

In response to these comments, the Treasury Department and the IRS are issuing final regulations under section 951A in the Rules and Regulations section of this issue of the **Federal Register** ("GILTI final regulations") that treat stock owned by a domestic partnership as owned within the meaning of section 958(a) by its partners for purposes of determining a partner's GILTI inclusion amount under section 951A. The Treasury Department and the IRS concluded that applying an aggregate approach for purposes of determining a partner's GILTI inclusion amount under section 951A is necessary to ensure that, consistent with the purpose and operation of section 951A, a single GILTI inclusion amount is determined for each taxpayer based on its economic interests in all of its CFCs. The GILTI final regulations apply to taxable years of foreign corporations beginning after December 31, 2017, and to taxable years of U.S. shareholders in which or with which such taxable years of foreign corporations end.

Some comments also recommended adopting an aggregate approach for purposes of section 951, especially if the GILTI final regulations adopt an aggregate approach. These comments generally asserted that there is insufficient policy justification for treating domestic partnerships differently than foreign partnerships for purposes of U.S. shareholder and CFC determinations because the choice of law under which a partnership is organized should be irrelevant. In this regard, these comments criticized entity treatment of domestic partnerships because it results in each partner including in income its distributive share of a domestic partnership's subpart F inclusion with respect to a CFC, even if that partner is not a U.S. shareholder itself and thus would not have had a subpart F inclusion with respect to such CFC if the domestic partnership were instead foreign.

B. *High-tax gross-tested income*

Section 951A(c)(2)(A)(i) provides that the gross tested income of a CFC for a taxable year is all the gross income of the CFC for the year, determined without regard to certain items. See also § 1.951A-2(c)(1). In particular, section 951A(c)(2)(A)(i)(III) excludes from gross tested income any gross income excluded from foreign base company income (as defined in section 954) ("FBCI") or insurance income (as defined in section 953) of a CFC by reason of the exception under section 954(b)(4) (the "GILTI high tax exclusion").

The GILTI proposed regulations clarified that the GILTI high tax exclusion applies only to income that is excluded from FBCI and insurance income solely by reason of an election made to exclude the income under the high tax exception of section 954(b)(4) and § 1.954-1(d)(5). See proposed § 1.951A-2(c)(1)(iii).

Numerous comments requested that the scope of the GILTI high tax exclusion be expanded in the final regulations. These comments asserted that the legislative history to section 951A indicates that Congress intended that income of a CFC should be taxed as GILTI only if it is subject to a low rate of foreign tax, regardless of whether the income is active or passive. Comments also suggested that the GILTI high tax exclusion does not require that income be excluded "solely" by reason of section 954(b)(4). The comments argued that the GILTI high tax exclusion could be interpreted to exclude any item of income that would be FBCI or insurance income, but for another exception to FBCI (for instance, the active financing exception under section 954(h) and the active insurance exception under section 954(i)). Of the comments recommending an expansion of the GILTI high tax exclusion, some recommended that the GILTI high tax exclusion apply to income taxed at a rate above 13.125 percent, while others recommended that the GILTI high tax exclusion apply to income taxed at a rate above 90 percent of the maximum rate of tax specified in section 11, or 18.9 percent. The comments recommended that the GILTI high tax exclusion be applied either on a CFC-by-CFC basis or an item-by-item basis.

Alternatively, comments recommended that the scope of the GILTI high tax exclusion be expanded under section 951A(f) by treating, on an elective basis, a GILTI inclusion as a subpart F inclusion that is potentially excludible from FBCI or insurance income under section 954(b)(4), or by modifying the GILTI high tax exclusion to exclude any item of income subject to a sufficiently high effective foreign tax rate such that it would be excludible under section 954(b)(4) if it were FBCI or insurance income. Other comments recommended the creation of a rebuttable presumption that all income of a CFC is subpart F income, regardless of whether such income is of a character included in FBCI or insurance income, and therefore, if the taxpayer chose not to rebut the presumption, the income would be excluded from gross tested income either because it is included in subpart F income (and thus excluded from gross tested income by reason of the subpart F exclusion under section 951A(c)(2)(A)(i)(II)) or because the income is excluded from subpart F income by reason of section 954(b)(4) (and thus excluded from gross tested income by reason of the GILTI high tax exclusion).

The GILTI final regulations adopt the GILTI high tax exclusion of the proposed regulations without change.

Explanation of Provisions

I. *Partnerships*

A. *Adoption of aggregate treatment for purposes of section 951*

After considering the alternatives, the Treasury Department and the IRS have concluded that, to be consistent with the treatment of domestic partnerships under section 951A, a domestic partnership should also generally be treated as an aggregate of its partners in determining stock owned under section 958(a) for purposes of section 951. Therefore, the proposed regulations provide that, for purposes of sections 951 and 951A, and for purposes of any provision that applies by reference to sections 951 and 951A (for example, sections 959, 960, and 961), a domestic partnership is not treated as owning stock of a foreign corporation within the meaning of section 958(a). See proposed §1.958-1(d)(1). Furthermore, the proposed regulations provide that, for purposes of determining the stock owned under section 958(a) by a partner of a domestic partnership, a domestic partnership is treated in the same manner as a foreign partnership. See id. This rule does not apply, however, for purposes of determining whether any U.S. person is a U.S. shareholder, whether a U.S. shareholder is a controlling domestic shareholder (as defined in §1.964-1(c)(5)), or whether a foreign corporation is a CFC. See proposed §1.958-1(d)(2). Accordingly, under the proposed regulations, a domestic partnership that owns a foreign corporation is treated as an entity for purposes of determining whether the partnership and its partners are U.S. shareholders, whether the partnership is a controlling domestic shareholder, and whether the foreign corporation is a CFC, but the partnership is treated as an aggregate of its partners for purposes of determining whether, and to what extent, its partners have inclusions under sections 951 and 951A and for purposes of any other provision that applies by reference to sections 951 and 951A.

For purposes of subpart F, a foreign partnership is explicitly treated as an aggregate of its partners, and rules regarding this aggregate treatment are relatively well-developed and understood. Therefore, rather than developing a new standard for the treatment of a domestic partnership as an aggregate of its partners, the Treasury Department and the IRS have determined that it would be simpler and more administrable to adopt, by reference, the rules related to foreign partnerships for this limited purpose. The GILTI final regulations adopt the same approach for purposes of section 951A. See §1.951A-1(e). As a result, under the proposed regulations, stock owned directly or indirectly by or for a domestic partnership will generally be treated as owned proportionately by its partners for purposes of sections 951(a) and 951A and any provision that applies by reference to sections 951 and 951A.

The Treasury Department and the IRS have determined that, as a result of the enactment of the GILTI regime, it is no longer appropriate to treat domestic partnerships as entities that are separate from their owners for purposes of determining whether, and to what extent, a partner has an inclusion under section 951. Congress intended for the subpart F and GILTI regimes to work in tandem by providing that both regimes apply to U.S. shareholders of CFCs, that GILTI is included in a U.S. shareholder's gross income in a manner similar to a subpart F inclusion for many purposes of the Code, and that gross income taken into account in determining the subpart F income of a CFC is not taken into account in determining the tested income of such CFC (and, therefore, in determining the GILTI inclusion amount of a U.S. shareholder of such CFC). See section 951A(c)(2)(i)(II) and 951A(f); see also Senate Explanation at 373 ("Although GILTI inclusions do not constitute subpart F income, GILTI inclusions are generally treated similarly to subpart F inclusions."). As a result, treating domestic partnerships inconsistently for subpart F and GILTI purposes would be inconsistent with legislative intent.

Furthermore, inconsistent approaches to the treatment of domestic partnerships for purposes of subpart F and GILTI would introduce substantial complexity and uncertainty, particularly with respect to foreign tax credits, previously taxed earnings and profits ("PTEP") and related basis rules, or any other provision the application of which turns on the owner of stock under section 958(a) and, thus, the U.S. person that has the relevant inclusion. For example, if a domestic partnership were treated as an aggregate of its partners for purposes of GILTI but as an entity for purposes of subpart F, regulations would need to address separately the maintenance of PTEP accounts at the domestic partnership level for subpart F and the maintenance of PTEP accounts at the partner level for GILTI. Similarly, regulations would need to provide separate rules for basis adjustments under section 961 with respect to a domestic partnership and its CFCs depending on whether an amount was included under section 951 or section 951A. The increased complexity of regulations resulting from treating domestic partnerships differently for purposes of subpart F and GILTI would, in turn, increase the burden on taxpayers to comply with, and on the IRS to administer, such regulations. Conversely, aggregate treatment of domestic partnerships in determining section 958(a) stock ownership for purposes of determining a partner's inclusion under both the GILTI and subpart F regimes will result in substantial simplification, as compared to disparate treatment, and will harmonize the two regimes.

The Treasury Department and the IRS also considered extending aggregate treatment for all purposes of subpart F, including for purposes of determining whether a foreign corporation is a CFC under section 957(a). However, the Treasury Department and the IRS determined that an approach that treats a domestic partnership as an aggregate for purposes of determining CFC status is inconsistent with relevant statutory provisions. As discussed in part III of the Background section of this preamble, the Code clearly contemplates that a domestic partnership can be a U.S. shareholder under section 951(b), including by attribution from its partners. See sections 7701(a)(30), 957(c), 951(b), 958(b), 318(a)(2)(A), and 318(a)(3)(A). An approach that treats a domestic partnership as an aggregate for purposes of determining CFC status would not give effect to the statutory treatment of a domestic partnership as a U.S. shareholder.

By contrast, neither section 958(a) nor any other provision of the Code specifies whether and to what extent a domestic partnership should be treated as an entity or an aggregate for purposes of determining stock ownership under section 958(a) for purposes of sections 951 and 951A. According to the legislative history to the 1962 Act, section 958(a) is a "limited rule of stock ownership for determining the amount taxable to a United States person," whereas section 958(b) is "a broader set of constructive rules of ownership for determining whether the requisite ownership by United States persons exists so as to make a corporation a controlled foreign corporation or a United States person has the requisite ownership to be liable for tax under section 951(a)." S. Rep. No. 1881 at 254 (1962). In light of the changes adopted in the Act (including the introduction of the GILTI regime), it is consistent with the intent of the Act to provide that domestic partnerships are treated in the same manner as foreign partnerships under section 958(a)(2) for purposes of sections 951(a) and 951A and any provision that applies by reference to sections 951 and 951A. As discussed in parts II and IV.A. of the Background section of this preamble, a domestic partnership may be treated as an aggregate of its partners or as an entity separate from its partners for purposes of a provision, depending on which characterization is more appropriate to carry out the purpose of the provision. In this regard, the Treasury Department and the IRS have determined that treating a domestic partnership as an aggregate for purposes of sections 951 and 951A is appropriate because the partners of the partnership generally are the ultimate taxable owners of the CFC and thus their inclusions under sections 951 and 951A are properly computed at the partner level regardless of whether the partnership is foreign or domestic.

Based on the foregoing, the Treasury Department and the IRS have determined that a domestic partnership should be treated consistently as an aggregate of its partners in determining the ownership of stock within the meaning of section 958(a) for purposes of sections 951 and 951A, and any provision that applies by reference to section 951 or section 951A, except for purposes of determining whether a U.S. person is a U.S. shareholder, whether a U.S. shareholder is a controlling domestic shareholder (as defined in §1.964-1(c)(5)), and whether a foreign corporation is a CFC. See proposed §1.958-1(d). This aggregate treatment does not apply for any other purposes of the Code, including for purposes of section 1248. However, the Treasury Department and the IRS request comments on other provisions in the Code that apply by reference to ownership within the meaning of section 958(a) for which aggregate treatment for domestic partnerships would be appropriate. The Treasury Department and the IRS also request comments on whether, and for which purposes, the aggregate treatment for domestic partnerships should be extended to the determination of the controlling domestic shareholders (as defined in §1.964-1(c)(5)) of a CFC, such that some or all of the partners who are U.S. shareholders of the CFC, rather than the partnership, make any elections applicable to the CFC for purposes of sections 951 and 951A.

B. *Applicability date and comment request with respect to transition*

The proposed regulations are proposed to apply to taxable years of foreign corporations beginning on or after the date of publication of the Treasury decision adopting these rules as final regulations in the **Federal Register** (the "finalization date"), and to taxable years of a U.S. person in which or with which such taxable years of foreign corporations end. See proposed §1.958-1(d)(4). With respect to taxable years of foreign corporations beginning before the finalization date, the proposed regulations provide that a domestic partnership may apply §1.958-1(d), as included in the final regulations, for taxable years of a foreign corporation beginning after December 31, 2017, and for taxable years of a domestic partnership in which or with which such taxable years of the foreign corporation end (the "applicable years"), provided that the partnership, domestic partnerships that are related (within the meaning of section 267 or 707) to the partnership, and certain partners consistently apply § 1.958-1(d) with respect to all foreign corporations whose stock they own within the meaning of section 958(a) (generally determined without regard to § 1.958-1(d)). See proposed § 1.958-1(d)(4). A domestic partnership may rely on proposed § 1.958-1(d) with respect to taxable years beginning after December 31, 2017, and beginning before the date that these regulations are published as final regulations in the **Federal Register**, provided that the partnership, domestic partnerships that are related (within the meaning of section 267 or 707) to the partnership, and certain partners consistently apply proposed § 1.958-1(d) with respect to all foreign corporations whose stock they own within the meaning of section 958(a) (generally determined without regard to proposed § 1.958-1(d)). See id.

Once proposed § 1.958-1(d) applies as a final regulation, § 1.951A-1(e) and § 1.951-1(h) (providing an aggregate treatment of domestic partnerships, but only for purposes of section 951A and limited subpart F purposes, respectively) would be unnecessary because the scope of those regulations would effectively be subsumed by § 1.958-1(d). Therefore, the proposed regulations would revise the applicability dates of § 1.951A-1(e) and § 1.951-1(h), so that those provisions do not apply once the final regulations under section 958 apply.

Historically, domestic partnerships have been treated as owning stock within the meaning of section 958(a) for purposes of determining their subpart F inclusions, and thus PTEP accounts were maintained, and related basis adjustments were made, at the partnership level. Upon the finalization of the proposed regulations, domestic partnerships will cease to be treated as owning stock of foreign corporations under section 958(a) for purposes of determining a subpart F inclusion, and instead their partners will be treated as owning stock under section 958(a). The Treasury Department and the IRS request comments on appropriate rules for the transition to the aggregate approach to domestic partnerships described in the proposed regulations. Comments are specifically requested as to necessary adjustments to PTEP and related basis amounts and capital accounts after finalization. In addition, comments are requested as to whether aggregate treatment of domestic partnerships should be extended to other "pass-through" entities, such as certain trusts or estates.

Comments are also requested with respect to the application of the PFIC regime after finalization, and whether elections (including elections under sections 1295 and 1296) and income inclusions under the PFIC rules are more appropriately made at the level of the domestic partnership or at the level of the partners. Specifically, the Treasury Department and the IRS are considering the operation of the PFIC regime where U.S. persons are partners of a domestic partnership that owns stock of a foreign corporation that is a PFIC, some of those partners might themselves be U.S. shareholders of the foreign corporation, and the foreign corporation might not be treated as a PFIC with respect to such U.S. shareholders under section 1297(d) if the foreign corporation is also a CFC. Comments should consider how any recommended approach would interact with the determinations of a partner's basis in its interest and capital accounts determined and maintained in accordance with § 1.704-1(b)(2).

II. *GILTI High Tax Exclusion*

A. *Expansion to exclude other high-taxed income*

In response to comments, the Treasury Department and the IRS have determined that the GILTI high tax exclusion should be expanded (on an elective basis) to include certain high-taxed income even if that income would not otherwise be FBCI or insurance income. In particular, the Treasury Department and the IRS have determined that taxpayers should be permitted to elect to apply the exception under section 954(b)(4) with respect to certain classes of income that are subject to high foreign taxes within the meaning of that provision. Before the Act, such an election would have had no effect with respect to items of income that were excluded from FBCI or insurance income for other reasons. Nevertheless, section 954(b)(4) is not explicitly restricted in its application to an item of income that first qualifies as FBCI or insurance income; rather, the provision applies to "any item of income received by a controlled foreign corporation." Therefore, any item of gross income, including an item that would otherwise be gross tested income, could be excluded from FBCI or insurance income "by reason of" section 954(b)(4) if the provision is one of the reasons for such exclusion, even if the exception under section 954(b)(4) is not the sole reason. Any item thus excluded from FBCI or insurance income by reason of section 954(b)(4) would then also be excluded from gross tested income under the GILTI high tax exclusion, as modified in these proposed regulations.

The legislative history evidences an intent to exclude high-taxed income from gross tested income. See Senate Explanation at 371 ("The Committee believes that certain items of income earned by CFCs should be excluded from the GILTI, either because they should be exempt from U.S. tax—as they are generally not the type of income that is the source of base erosion concerns—or are already taxed currently by the United States. Items of income excluded from GILTI because they are exempt from U.S. tax under the bill include foreign oil and gas extraction income (which is generally immobile) and income subject to high levels of foreign tax."). The proposed regulations, which permit taxpayers to electively exclude a CFC's high-taxed income from gross tested income, are consistent, therefore, with this legislative history. Furthermore, an election to exclude a CFC's high-taxed income from gross tested income allows a U.S. shareholder to ensure that its high-taxed non-subpart F income is eligible for the same treatment as its high-taxed FBCI and insurance income, and thus eliminates an incentive for taxpayers to restructure their CFC operations in order to convert gross tested income into FBCI for the sole purpose of availing themselves of section 954(b)(4) and, thus, the GILTI high tax exclusion.

For the foregoing reasons, the proposed regulations provide that an election may be made for a CFC to exclude under section 954(b)(4), and thus to exclude from gross tested income, gross income subject to foreign income tax at an effective rate that is greater than 90 percent of the rate that would apply if the income were subject to the maximum rate of tax specified in section 11 (18.9 percent based on the current rate of 21 percent). See proposed § 1.951A-2(c)(6)(i). The election is made by the CFC's controlling domestic shareholders with respect to the CFC for a CFC inclusion year by attaching a statement to an amended or filed return in accordance with forms, instructions, or administrative pronouncements. See proposed § 1.951A-2(c)(6)(v)(A). If an election is made with respect to a CFC, the election applies to exclude from gross tested income all the CFC's items of income for the taxable year that meet the effective rate test in proposed § 1.951A-2(c)(6)(iii) and is binding on all the U.S. shareholders of the CFC. See proposed § 1.951A-2(c)(6)(v)(B). The election is effective for a CFC for the CFC inclusion year for which it is made and all subsequent CFC inclusion years of the CFC unless revoked by the controlling domestic shareholders of the CFC. See proposed § 1.951A-2(c)(6)(v)(C).

An election may generally be revoked by the controlling domestic shareholders of the CFC for any CFC inclusion year. See proposed § 1.951A-2(c)(6)(v)(D)(1). However, upon revocation for a CFC inclusion year, a new election generally cannot be made for any CFC inclusion year of the CFC that begins within sixty months after the close of the CFC inclusion year for which the election was revoked, and that subsequent election cannot be revoked for a CFC inclusion year that begins within sixty months after the close of the CFC inclusion year for which the subsequent election was made. See proposed § 1.951A-2(c)(6)(v)(D)(2)(i). An exception to this 60-month limitation may be permitted by the Commissioner with respect to a CFC if the CFC undergoes a change of control. See proposed § 1.951A-2(c)(6)(v)(D)(2)(ii).

Finally, if a CFC is a member of a controlling domestic shareholder group, the election applies with respect to each member of the controlling domestic shareholder group. See proposed § 1.951A-2(c)(6)(v)(E)(1). A "controlling domestic shareholder group" is defined as two or more CFCs if more than 50 percent of the stock (by voting power) of each CFC is owned (within the meaning of section 958(a)) by the same controlling domestic shareholder (or persons related to such controlling domestic shareholder) or, if no single controlling domestic shareholder owns (within the meaning of section 958(a)) more than 50 percent of the stock (by voting power) of each corporation, more than 50 percent of the stock (by voting power) of each corporation is owned (within the meaning of section 958(a)) in the aggregate by the same controlling domestic shareholders and each controlling domestic shareholder owns (within the meaning of section 958(a)) the same percentage of stock in each CFC. See proposed

§1.951A-2(c)(6)(v)(E)(2). Accordingly, an election made under proposed §1.951A-2(c)(6)(v) applies with respect to each item of income of each CFC in a group of commonly controlled CFCs that meets the effective rate test in proposed §1.951A-2(c)(6)(iii). The Treasury Department and the IRS request comments on the manner and terms of the election for the exception from gross tested income, including whether the limitations with respect to revocations and the consistency requirements should be modified, such as by allowing the election to be made on an item-by-item or a CFC-by-CFC basis.

In general, the relevant items of income for purposes of the election under section 954(b)(4) pursuant to proposed §1.951A-2(c)(6) are all items of gross tested income attributable to a qualified business unit ("QBU"). See proposed §1.951A-2(c)(6)(ii)(A)(1). For example, a CFC that owns a disregarded entity that qualifies as a QBU may have one item of income with respect to the CFC itself (which is a per se QBU) and another item of income with respect to the disregarded entity. The proposed regulations provide that the gross income attributable to a QBU is determined by reference to the items of gross income reflected on the books and records of the QBU, determined under Federal income tax principles, except that income attributable to a QBU must be adjusted to account for certain disregarded payments. See proposed §1.951A-2(c)(6)(ii)(A)(2). The proposed regulations provide an example to illustrate the application of this rule. See proposed §1.951A-2(c)(6)(vi).

Comments are requested on whether additional rules are needed to properly account for other instances in which the income base upon which foreign tax is imposed does not match the items of income reflected on the books and records of the QBU determined under Federal income tax principles. For example, comments are requested on whether special rules are needed for associating taxes with income with respect to partnerships (including hybrid partnerships), disregarded entities, or reverse hybrid entities, and how to address circumstances in which QBUs are permitted to share losses or determine tax liability based on combined income for foreign tax purposes. Comments are also requested as to whether all of a CFC's QBUs located within a single foreign country or possession should be combined for purposes of performing the effective rate test in proposed §1.951A-2(c)(6)(iii) and whether the definition of QBU should be modified for purposes of the GILTI high tax exclusion in respect of the requirement to have a trade or business, maintain books and records, or other rules relating to QBUs.

Under §1.954-1(d)(3), the determination of taxes paid or accrued with respect to an item of income for purposes of the exception under section 954(b)(4) is determined for each U.S. shareholder based on the amount of foreign income taxes that would be deemed paid under section 960 if the item of income were included by the U.S. shareholder under section 951(a)(1)(A). Calculating the effective tax rate for purposes of the election under section 954(b)(4) with respect to gross tested income by reference to section 960(d) would not be consistent with the aggregate nature of the computation under section 960(d). Furthermore, the Treasury Department and the IRS have determined that the Act's change to section 960(a) from a pooling based approach to an annual attribution of taxes to income requires revising §1.954-1(d)(3). Therefore, the proposed regulations provide that for purposes of both the exception under section 954(b)(4) and the GILTI high tax exclusion, the effective rate of foreign tax imposed on an item of income is determined solely at the CFC level by allocating and apportioning the foreign income taxes paid or accrued by the CFC in the current year to the CFC's gross income in that year based on the rules described in the regulations under section 960 for determining foreign income taxes "properly attributable" to income. See §1.960-1(d), as proposed to be amended in 83 FR 63257 (December 7, 2018).

To the extent foreign income taxes are allocated and apportioned to items of income that are excluded from gross tested income by the GILTI high tax exclusion, none of those foreign income taxes are properly attributable to tested income and thus none are allowed as a deemed paid credit under section 960. See §1.960-1(e), as proposed to be amended in 83 FR 63259 (December 7, 2018). In addition, if an item of income is excluded from gross tested income by reason of the GILTI high tax exclusion, the property used to produce that income, because not used in the production of gross tested income, does not qualify as specified tangible property, in whole or in part, and therefore the adjusted basis in the property is not taken into account in determining qualified business asset investment. See §1.951A-3(b) and (c)(1).

The proposed regulations also clarify the scope of each item of income under §1.954-1(c)(1)(iii), consistent with the rules under §1.960-1(d)(2)(ii)(B), as proposed to be amended in 83 FR 63257 (December 7, 2018).

B. *Applicability date*

The changes related to the election to exclude a CFC's gross income subject to high foreign income taxes under section 954(b)(4) are proposed to apply to taxable years of foreign corporations beginning on or after the date that final regulations are published in the **Federal Register**, and to taxable years of U.S. shareholders in which or with which such taxable years of foreign corporations end.

Special Analyses

I. *Regulatory Planning and Review – Economic Analysis*

Executive Orders 13771, 13563, and 12866 direct agencies to assess costs and benefits of available regulatory alternatives and, if regulation is necessary, to select regulatory approaches that maximize net benefits, including potential economic, environmental, public health and safety effects, distributive impacts, and equity. Executive Order 13563 emphasizes the importance of quantifying both costs and benefits, reducing costs, harmonizing rules, and promoting flexibility. The Executive Order 13771 designation for any final rule resulting from the proposed regulation will be informed by comments received. The preliminary Executive Order 13771 designation for this proposed rule is regulatory.

The proposed regulation has been designated by the Office of Information and Regulatory Affairs (OIRA) as subject to review under Executive Order 12866 pursuant to the Memorandum of Agreement (MOA, April 11, 2018) between the Treasury Department and the Office of Management and Budget regarding review of tax regulations. OIRA has designated this proposed regulation as economically significant under section 1(c) of the MOA. Accordingly, these proposed regulations have been reviewed by the Office of Management and Budget. For more detail on the economic analysis, please refer to the following analysis.

A. *Need for the proposed regulations*

The proposed regulations are required to provide a mechanism by which taxpayers can elect the high tax exception of section 954(b)(4) in order to exclude certain high-taxed income from taxation under section 951A and to conform the treatment of domestic partnerships for purposes of the subpart F regime with the treatment of domestic partnerships for purposes of section 951A.

B. *Background*

The Tax Cuts and Jobs Act (the "Act") established a system under which certain earnings of a foreign corporation can be repatriated to a corporate U.S. shareholder without U.S. tax. See section 14101(a) of the Act and section 245A. However, Congress recognized that, without any base protection measures, this system, known as a participation exemption system, could incentivize taxpayers to allocate income – in particular, mobile income from intangible property that would otherwise be subject to the full U.S. corporate tax rate – to controlled foreign corporations ("CFCs") operating in low-or zero-tax jurisdictions. See Senate Explanation at 365. Therefore, Congress enacted section 951A in order to subject intangible income earned by a CFC to U.S. tax on a current basis, similar to the treatment of a CFC's subpart F income under section 951(a)(1)(A). However, in order to not harm the competitive position of U.S. corporations relative to their foreign peers, the global intangible low tax income ("GILTI") of a corporate U.S. shareholder is effectively taxed at a reduced rate by reason of the deduction under section 250 (with the resulting U.S. tax further reduced by a portion of foreign tax credits under section 960(d)). Id.

The GILTI final regulations generally provide structure and clarity for the implementation of section 951A. However, the Treasury Department and the IRS determined that there remained two outstanding issues pertinent to the implementation of GILTI. The first of these issues pertains to the GILTI high tax exclusion under section 951A(c)(2)(A)(i)(III), which excludes from gross tested income any gross income excluded from foreign base company income ("FBCI") (as defined in section 954) and insurance income (as defined in section 953) by reason of section 954(b)(4). The GILTI proposed regulations limited the application of the exclusion to income that would be included in FBCI or insurance income but for the high tax exception of section 954(b)(4). See proposed § 1.951A-2(c)(1)(iii). However, comments to the GILTI proposed regulations recommended that the statute be interpreted so that the GILTI high tax exclusion applies on an elective basis to a broader category of income, that is, any income that is subject to a high rate of foreign tax. Other comments suggested that because taxpayers have the ability to structure transactions so that they would qualify as FBCI or insurance income, the regulations should allow a taxpayer to elect to treat all income, or all high-taxed income, as FBCI or insurance income, with the result that such income would then be excluded from gross tested income under the GILTI high tax exclusion. Comments noted that, under the narrower application of the exclusion under the GILTI proposed regulations, taxpayers would be incentivized to affirmatively plan into subpart F income to permit such taxpayers to elect the high tax exception under section 954(b)(4) with respect to such income or to allow taxpayers to carry foreign tax credits attributable to such income to another taxable year under section 904(c). However, restructuring activities to convert gross tested income into subpart F income may cost significant time and money and is economically inefficient. The GILTI final regulations adopt this narrower application. See proposed § 1.951A-2(c)(1)(iii). However, the preamble to the GILTI final regulations indicated that proposed regulations would be issued to propose a framework under which taxpayers would be permitted to make an election to apply the high tax exception of section 954(b)(4) with respect to income that would otherwise be gross tested income in order to exclude that income from gross tested income by reason of the GILTI high tax exclusion.

The second of these issues pertains to the treatment of domestic partnerships for purposes of the subpart F regime. A U.S. shareholder of a CFC is required to include in gross income its pro rata share of the CFC's subpart F income under section 951(a)(1)(A), the amount determined under section 956, under section 951(a)(1)(B), and its GILTI inclusion amount under section 951A(a). Since the enactment of subpart F, domestic partnerships have generally been treated as entities separate from their partners, rather than as aggregates of their partners, for purposes of the subpart F regime, including for purposes of treating a domestic partnership as the U.S. shareholder that has the subpart F inclusion with respect to a CFC owned by the partnership. However, the GILTI final regulations generally adopt an aggregate approach to domestic partnerships for purposes of section 951A and the section 951A regulations. See § 1.951A-1(e)(1). Because the GILTI final regulations apply only for purposes of section 951A, absent the proposed regulations, a domestic partnership would still be treated as an entity for purposes of the subpart F regime. This inconsistency in the treatment of a domestic partnership for the purposes of section 951A and for purposes of the subpart F regime is problematic because it necessitates complicated coordination rules which could greatly increase compliance and administrative burden. Therefore, the proposed regulations conform the treatment of domestic partnerships for purposes of the subpart F regime with the treatment of domestic partnerships for purposes of section 951A.

C. *Economic analysis*

1. Baseline

The Treasury Department and the IRS have assessed the benefits and costs of the proposed regulations relative to a no-action baseline reflecting anticipated Federal income tax-related behavior in the absence of these proposed regulations.

2. Summary of Economic Effects

To assess the economic effects of the proposed regulations, the Treasury Department and the IRS considered economic effects arising from two provisions of the proposed regulations. These are (i) effects arising from the provision that provides substance and clarity regarding the application of the GILTI high tax exclusion in 951A(c)(2)(A)(i)(III) and (ii) simplification and coordination effects arising from conforming the treatment of domestic partnerships for purposes of subpart F with their treatment for purposes of section 951A.

The Treasury Department and the IRS have not undertaken quantitative estimates of these effects because any such quantitative estimates would be highly uncertain. For example, the proposed regulations include provisions that permit controlling domestic shareholders of CFCs to elect to apply the high tax exception of section 954(b)(4) to items of gross income that are subject to a foreign tax rate that is greater than 18.9 percent (based on the current U.S. corporate tax rate of 21 percent) for purposes of excluding such income from gross tested income under the GILTI high tax exclusion. Whether controlling domestic shareholders will choose to make the election will depend on their specific facts and circumstances, such as their U.S. expenses allocated to section 951A category income, their foreign tax credit position, and the distribution of their foreign activity between high-and low-tax jurisdictions.[2] Because GILTI is new, the Treasury Department and the IRS do not have readily available data to project these items in this context. Furthermore, the election would be made with respect to qualified business units (QBUs) rather than with respect to CFCs or specific items of income, and the Treasury Department and the IRS do not have readily available data on activities at the QBU level. In addition, due to the taxpayer-specific nature of the factors influencing a decision to utilize the GILTI high-tax exclusion, the Treasury Department and the IRS do not have readily available data or models to predict the marginal effective tax rates that would prevail under these provisions for the varied forms of foreign investments that taxpayers might consider and thus cannot predict with reasonable precision the difference in economic activity, relative to the baseline, that might be undertaken by taxpayers based on this election.

The proposed regulations also contain provisions to conform the treatment of domestic partnerships for purposes of subpart F with their treatment for purposes of section 951A. Under the proposed regulations, the tax treatment of domestic partners that are U.S. shareholders of a CFC owned by the domestic partnership differs from the tax treatment of domestic partners that are not U.S. shareholders of such CFC. The Treasury Department and the IRS do not have readily available data to identify these types of partners. The Treasury Department and the IRS further do not have readily available data or models to predict with reasonable precision the set of marginal effective tax rates that taxpayers might face under these provisions nor the effects of those marginal effective tax rates on economic activity relative to the baseline.

With these considerations in mind, parts I.C.3.a.ii and iii of this Special Analyses section explain the rationale behind the proposed regulations' approach to the GILTI high tax exclusion and qualitatively evaluate the alternatives considered. Part I.C.3.b of this Special Analyses section explains the rationale for the coordination in the treatment of domestic partnerships and qualitatively evaluates the alternatives considered. 3. Economic Effects of Specific Provisions

---

[2] Specifically, the U.S. tax system reduces double taxation on a U.S. shareholder's GILTI inclusion amount by crediting a portion of certain foreign taxes paid by CFCs against the U.S. tax on the U.S. shareholder's GILTI inclusion amount. However, the U.S. foreign tax credit regime requires taxpayers to allocate U.S. deductible expenses, including interest, research and experimentation, and general and administrative expenses, to their foreign source income in the categories described in section 904(d) when determining the allowable foreign tax credits. The allocated expenses reduce net foreign source income within the section 904(d) categories, which can reduce allowable foreign tax credits. This may result in a smaller foreign tax credit than would be allowed if the limitation on foreign tax credits was determined based only on the local country tax

assessed on the tested income taken into account in determining GILTI. The election to apply the high tax exception of section 954(b)(4) with respect to any high-taxed income allows taxpayers to eliminate the need to use foreign tax credits to reduce GILTI tax liability on such income by removing such income from gross tested income; however, taxpayers choosing the election will not be able to use the foreign tax credits associated with that income against other section 951A category income, and they will not be able to use the tangible assets owned by high tax QBUs in their QBAI computation. Therefore, taxpayers will have to evaluate their individual facts and circumstances to determine whether they should make the election.

The Treasury Department and IRS solicit comments on each of the items discussed in this Special Analyses section and on any other items of the proposed regulations not discussed in this section. The Treasury Department and the IRS particularly solicit comments that provide data, other evidence, or models that could enhance the rigor of the process by which the final regulations might be developed. a. Exclusion of Income Subject to High Rate of Foreign Tax

i. Description

The proposed regulations permit U.S. shareholders of CFCs to make an election under section 954(b)(4) with respect to high-taxed income in order to exclude such income from gross tested income under the GILTI high tax exclusion. Under section 954(b)(4), high-taxed income is defined as income subject to a foreign effective tax rate greater than 90 percent of the maximum U.S. corporate tax rate (18.9 percent based on the current U.S. corporate tax rate of 21 percent). Under the proposed regulations, the determination as to whether income is high-taxed is made at the QBU level. However, an election made with respect to a CFC applies with respect to each high-taxed QBU of the CFC (including potentially the CFC itself), and a U.S. shareholder that makes the election with respect to a CFC generally must make the same election with respect to each of its CFCs. In general, the election may be made or revoked at any time, except that, if a U.S. shareholder revokes an election with respect to a CFC, the U.S. shareholder cannot make the election again within five years after the revocation, and then if subsequently made, the election cannot be revoked again within five years of the subsequent election.

ii. Alternatives Considered for Determining the Scope of the GILTI High Tax Exclusion

The Treasury Department and the IRS considered a number of options to address the types of income excluded from gross tested income by the GILTI high tax exclusion. The options were (i) to exclude from gross tested income only income that would be subpart F income but for the high tax exception of section 954(b)(4); (ii) in addition to excluding the aforementioned income, to exclude from gross tested income on an elective basis an item of gross income that is excluded by reason of another exception to subpart F, if such income is subject to a foreign effective tax rate greater than 18.9 percent; and (iii) to exclude from gross tested income on an elective basis any item of gross income subject to a foreign effective tax rate greater than 18.9 percent. The Treasury Department and the IRS considered the other recommended options discussed in part IV.B of the Background section, but determined that those other options are not authorized by the relevant statutory provisions.

The first option considered was to exclude from gross tested income only income that would be FBCI or insurance income but for the high tax exception of section 954(b)(4), which is the interpretation of the GILTI high tax exclusion in the GILTI proposed regulations. This narrow approach is consistent with a reasonable interpretation of the statutory text, which excludes from gross tested income only income that is excluded from subpart F income "by reason of section 954(b)(4)." Moreover, this approach is consistent with current regulations under section 954, which permit an election under section 954(b)(4) only with respect to income that is not otherwise excluded from subpart F income by reason of another exception (for example, section 954(c)(6) or 954(h)). However, under this approach, taxpayers with high-taxed gross tested income would have incentives to restructure their foreign operations in order to convert their gross tested income into subpart F income. For instance, a taxpayer could restructure its operations to have a CFC purchase personal property from, or sell personal property to, a related person without substantially contributing to the manufacture of the property in its country of incorporation, with the result that the CFC's income from the disposition of the property is foreign base company sales income within the meaning of section 954(d). Any such restructuring may be unduly costly and only available to certain taxpayers. Further, such reorganization to realize a specific income treatment suggests that tax instead of business considerations are determining business structures. This can lead to higher compliance costs and inefficient investment. Therefore, the Treasury Department and the IRS rejected this option.

The second option considered was to broaden the application of the GILTI high tax exclusion to allow taxpayers to elect under the high tax exception of section 954(b)(4) to exclude from gross tested income an item of gross income that is subject to a foreign effective tax rate greater than 18.9 percent, if such income was also excluded from FBCI or insurance income by reason of another exception to subpart F. Under this interpretation, income such as active financing income that is excluded from subpart F income under section 954(h), active rents or royalties that are excluded from subpart F income under 954(c)(2)(A), and related party payments that are excluded from subpart F income under section 954(c)(6) could also be excluded from gross tested income under the GILTI high tax exclusion if such items of income are high taxed within the meaning of section 954(b)(4). This broader approach represents a plausible interpretation of the GILTI high tax exclusion; that is, that an item of income could be excluded both "by reason of section 954(b)(4)" and by reason of another exception. However, this approach would provide taxpayers the ability to exclude their CFCs' high-taxed income that would be subpart F income but for an exception (for example, active financing income), while denying taxpayers the same ability with respect to their CFCs' high-taxed income that is not subpart F income in the first instance (for example, active business income), without any general economic benefit from such differential treatment. Furthermore, taxpayers with items of high-taxed income that are not subpart F income would still be incentivized to restructure their foreign operations in order to convert their high-taxed gross tested income into subpart F income, which poses the same compliance costs and inefficiencies as the first option. Therefore, the Treasury Department and the IRS rejected this option.

The third option, which is adopted in the proposed regulations, is to provide an election to broaden the scope of the high tax exception under section 954(b)(4) for purposes of the GILTI high tax exclusion to apply to any item of income that is subject to a foreign effective tax rate greater than 18.9 percent. The proposed regulations permit controlling domestic shareholders of CFCs to elect to apply the high tax exception under section 954(b)(4) to items of gross income that would not otherwise be FBCI or insurance income. If this high tax exception is elected, the GILTI high tax exclusion will exclude the item of gross income from gross tested income. Under the election, an item of gross income is subject to a high rate of foreign tax if, after taking into account properly allocable expenses, the net item of income is subject to a foreign effective tax rate greater than 90 percent of the maximum U.S. corporate tax rate (18.9 percent based on the current U.S. corporate tax rate of 21 percent). This option therefore establishes a framework for applying the high tax exception under section 954(b)(4), including rules to determine the scope of an item of income that would otherwise be gross tested income to which the election applies and to determine the rate of foreign tax on such item.

The approach chosen by the proposed regulations is consistent with the legislative history to section 951A, which evidences an intent to tax low-taxed income of CFCs that presents base erosion concerns. The approach is also supported by a reasonable interpretation of the high tax exception of section 954(b)(4), which applies to "any item of income" of a CFC, not just income that would otherwise be FBCI or insurance income. Furthermore, contrary to the first two options, this approach permits all similarly situated taxpayers with CFCs subject to a high rate of foreign tax to make the election with respect to such income to exclude it from gross tested income, and reduces the incentive for taxpayers to restructure their operations to convert their high-taxed gross tested income into subpart F income for U.S. tax purposes.

For taxpayers that make the election, this approach reduces the taxpayers' cost of capital on foreign investment by reducing U.S. tax on such taxpayers' GILTI relative to the baseline. At the margin, the lower cost of capital may increase foreign investment by U.S.-parented firms. Further, removing high-taxed tested income from the GILTI tax base could change the incentives for the location of tangible assets. The magnitude of these effects is highly uncertain because of the uncertainty surrounding the number and attributes of the taxpayers that will find it advantageous to make the election and because the relationship between the marginal effective tax rate at the QBU level and foreign investment by U.S. taxpayers is not well known. In addition, the impact of tax considerations on taxpayer investment decisions depends on a number of international tax provisions, many of which interact in complex ways.

iii. Alternatives Considered for Determining High-Taxed Income

The Treasury Department and the IRS next considered options for determining whether an item of income is subject to the foreign effective tax rate described in section 954(b)(4). The options considered were (i) apply the determination on an item-by-item basis; (ii) apply the determination on a CFC-by-CFC basis; or (iii) apply the determination on a QBU-by-QBU basis.

The first option was to determine whether income is high-taxed income within the meaning of section 954(b)(4) on an item-by-item basis. This approach would be consistent with the language of section 954(b)(4), which applies to an "item of income" of a CFC that is sufficiently high tax. However, this approach would be complex and difficult to administer because it would require analyzing each item of income to determine whether, under Federal tax principles, such item is subject to a sufficiently high foreign effective tax rate. In fact, for this reason, the current regulations that implement the high tax exception of section 954(b)(4) for purposes of subpart F income do not require an item-by-item determination and aggregate all items of income into separate categories of income for purposes of determining whether each such category is high tax. See § 1.954-1(d)(2). Therefore, the Treasury Department and the IRS rejected this option.

The second option was to apply the determination based on all the items of income of the CFC. On the one hand, this approach would minimize complexity and would be relatively easy to administer. On the other hand, this approach could permit inappropriate tax planning, such as combining operations subject to different rates of tax into a single CFC. This would have the effect of "blending" the rates of foreign tax imposed on the income, which could result in low- or non-taxed income being excluded as high-taxed income by being blended with much higher-taxed income. The low-taxed income in this scenario is precisely the sort of base erosion-type income that the legislative history describes section 951A as intending to tax, and such tax motivated planning behavior is economically inefficient.

The third option, which is adopted in the proposed regulations, is to apply the high tax exception based on the items of gross income of a QBU of the CFC. Under this approach, the net income that is taxed by the foreign jurisdiction in each QBU must be determined. For example, if a CFC earned $100x of tested income through a QBU in Country A and was taxed at a 30 percent rate and earned $100x of tested income through another QBU in Country B and was taxed at 0 percent, the blended rate of tax on all of the CFC's tested income is 15 percent ($30x tax / $200x tested income). However, if the high tax exception applies to each of a CFC's QBUs based on the income earned by that QBU then the blending of different rates would be minimized. Although applying the high tax exception on the basis of a QBU, rather than the CFC as a whole, may be more complex and administratively burdensome under certain circumstances, it more accurately pinpoints income subject to a high rate of foreign tax and therefore continues to subject to tax the low-taxed base erosion-type income that the legislative history describes section 951A as intending to tax. Accordingly, the proposed regulations apply the high tax exception of section 954(b)(4) based on the items of net income of each QBU of the CFC.

iv. Affected Taxpayers

The proposed regulations potentially affect those taxpayers that have at least one CFC with at least one QBU (including, potentially, the CFC itself) that has high-taxed income. A taxpayer with CFCs that have a mix of high-taxed and low-taxed income (determined on a QBU-by-QBU basis) will need to evaluate the benefit of eliminating any tax under section 951A with respect to high-taxed income with the costs of forgoing the use of such taxes against other section 951A category income and the use of tangible assets in the computation of QBAI. Taxpayers with CFCs that have only low-taxed income are not eligible to elect the high tax exception and hence are unaffected by this provision.

The Treasury Department and the IRS estimate that there are approximately 4,000 business entities (corporations, S corporations, and partnerships) with at least one CFC that pays a foreign effective tax rate above 18.9 percent. The Treasury Department and the IRS further estimate that, for the partnerships with at least one CFC that pays a foreign effective tax rate greater than 18.9 percent, there are approximately 1,500 partners that have a large enough share to potentially qualify as a 10 percent U.S. shareholder of the CFC.[3] The 4,000 business entities and the 1,500 partners provide an approximate estimate of the number of taxpayers that could potentially be affected by an election into the high tax exception. The figure is approximate since there is an imperfect correspondence between high-taxed CFCs and high-taxed QBUs, and, furthermore, not all taxpayers that are eligible for the election would choose to make the election. The Treasury Department and the IRS do not have readily available data to determine how many of these taxpayers would benefit from the election.

Tabulations from the IRS Statistics of Income 2014 Form 5471 file[4] further indicate that approximately 85 percent of earnings and profits before taxes of CFCs are subject to an average foreign effective tax rate that is less than or equal to 18.9 percent, accounting for approximately 30 percent of CFCs. The data indicate several examples of jurisdictions with effective tax rates above 18.9 percent, such as France, Italy, and Japan. However, information is not readily available to determine how many QBUs are part of the same CFC and what the effective foreign tax rates are with respect to such QBUs. Furthermore, the determination of whether or not to elect the high tax exception will be made at the shareholder (not CFC) level, after having evaluated the full impact of doing so across all of the shareholder's CFCs. Taxpayers potentially more likely to elect the high tax exception are those taxpayers with CFCs that only operate in high-tax jurisdictions.

b. Domestic Partnership Treatment for Subpart F

i. Description

Under the statute, a U.S. shareholder of a CFC is required to include in gross income its pro rata share of the CFC's subpart F income under section 951(a)(1)(A), the amount determined under section 956, under section 951(a)(1)(B), and its GILTI inclusion amount under section 951A. The Code does not explicitly prescribe the treatment of domestic partnerships and their partners for purposes of subpart F. However, domestic partnerships have generally been treated as entities separate from their partners, rather than as aggregates of their partners, for purposes of subpart F, including for purposes of determining the amount included in the gross income of the domestic partnership (and the distributive share of such amount of its domestic partners) under section 951(a). The GILTI final regulations adopt an aggregate approach to domestic partnerships, but this aggregate treatment applies only for purposes of section 951A.

ii. Alternatives Considered

The Treasury Department and the IRS considered two options for the treatment of domestic partnerships for purposes of subpart F. The first option was to retain the entity approach to domestic partnerships for purposes of subpart F. While this approach would be consistent with the longstanding entity approach to domestic partnerships for purposes of subpart F inclusions, it would result in domestic partnerships being treated inconsistently for purposes of subpart F and section 951A, despite both regimes applying to U.S. shareholders and their CFCs. This inconsistent treatment of domestic partnerships could result in a domestic partnership including subpart F income in gross income under section 951(a) and its partners including GILTI in their gross income under section 951A(a), which would introduce substantial complexity and uncertainty in the

---

[3] Data are from IRS's Research, Applied Analytics, and Statistics division based on E-file data available in the Compliance Data Warehouse, for tax years 2015 and 2016. The counts include Category 4 and Category 5 IRS Form 5471 filers. Category 4 filers are U.S. persons who had control of a foreign corporation during the annual accounting period of the foreign corporation. Category 5 filers are U.S. shareholders who own stock in a foreign corporation that is a CFC and who owned that stock on the last day in the tax year of the foreign corporation in that year in which it was a CFC. For full definitions, see https://www.irs.gov/pub/irs-pdf/i5471.pdf.

[4] The IRS Statistics of Income Tax Stats report on Controlled Foreign Corporations can be accessed here: https://www.irs.gov/statistics/soi-tax-stats-controlled-foreign-corporations.

application of provisions that require basis and E&P adjustments with respect to CFCs and their U.S. shareholders for amounts included in income under sections 951(a) and 951A(a). This option would also continue the inconsistent treatment of domestic partnerships and foreign partnerships (which generally are treated as aggregates) for purposes of the subpart F rules, despite the lack of a substantial policy justification for treating domestic partners of a partnership differently based upon the law under which the partnership is created or organized. In this regard, this option would require "small" partners of a domestic partnership (that is, partners that are not themselves U.S. shareholders of CFCs owned by the domestic partnership) to include in income their distributive share of the domestic partnership's subpart F inclusion with respect to CFCs of which the small partners are not themselves U.S. shareholders. In contrast, if the domestic partnership were instead a foreign partnership, the small partners would not include any amount in gross income under section 951(a) (or a distributive share of such amount) with respect to CFCs of which such partners were not U.S. shareholders.

The second option would adopt an aggregate approach to domestic partnerships by treating stock owned by a domestic partnership as being owned proportionately by its partners for purposes of determining the U.S. shareholder that has the subpart F inclusion. This approach is consistent with the approach adopted for section 951A in the GILTI final regulations. Under this approach, a domestic partnership would not be the U.S. shareholder of a foreign corporation that includes subpart F income in its gross income under section 951(a). Instead, only the partners of the domestic partnership that are U.S. shareholders of a CFC owned through the domestic partnership would include subpart F income of the CFC in their gross income.

This approach is supported by public comments requesting harmonization of the treatment of domestic partnerships for purposes of the GILTI and subpart F regimes. The harmonization of the treatment of domestic partnerships for purposes of the GILTI and subpart F regimes is expected to result in substantial simplification of related rules (for example, previously taxed earnings and profits and related basis rules), consistency in the treatment of domestic partnerships and foreign partnerships, and the reduction of burden (both administrative burden and tax liability) on taxpayers that are small partners. This third option is effectuated in the proposed regulations by using the existing framework for foreign partnerships, which is well-developed and more administrable than a new framework.

iii. Affected Taxpayers

The Treasury Department and the IRS estimate that there were approximately 7,000 U.S. partnerships with CFCs that e-filed at least one Form 5471 as Category 4 or 5 filers in 2015 and 2016.[5] The identified partnerships had approximately 2 million partners, as indicated by the number of Schedules K-1 filed by the partnerships. This number includes both domestic and foreign partners, so it substantially overstates the number of partners that would be affected by the proposed regulations, which potentially affect only domestic partners.[6] The proposed regulations affect domestic partners that are U.S. shareholders of a CFC owned by the domestic partnership because such partners will determine their subpart F inclusion amount by reference to their pro rata shares of subpart F income of CFCs owned by the partnership. Domestic partners that are not U.S. shareholders of a CFC owned by the domestic partnership will neither determine their own subpart F inclusion amount by reference to their pro rata shares of subpart F income of CFCs owned by the partnership nor include in their income a distributive share of the partnership's subpart F inclusion amount. This latter group is likely to be a substantial portion of domestic partners given the high number of partners per partnership, and they will have lower compliance costs as a result of the proposed regulations. Because it is not possible to precisely identify these types of partners based on available data, this number is an upper bound of partners who would have been affected by this rule had this rule been in effect in 2015 or 2016.

II. *Paperwork Reduction Act*

The collection of information in these proposed regulations is in proposed §1.951A-2(c)(6)(v). The collection of information in proposed §1.951A-2(c)(6)(v) is an election that a controlling domestic shareholder of a CFC may make to apply the high tax exception of section 954(b)(4) to gross income of a CFC. The election is made by attaching a statement to an original or amended income tax return in order to elect to apply the high tax exception of section 954(b)(4) to gross income of a CFC. For purposes of the Paperwork Reduction Act of 1995 (44 U.S.C. 3507(d)) ("PRA"), the reporting burden associated with proposed §1.951A-2(c)(6)(v) will be reflected in the PRA submission associated with income tax returns in the Form 990 series, Form 1120 series, Form 1040 series, Form 1041 series, and Form 1065 series (see chart at the end of this part II for the current status of the PRA submissions for these forms). In 2018, the IRS released and invited comments on drafts of the above five forms in order to give members of the public advance notice and an opportunity to submit comments. The IRS received no comments on the portions of the forms that relate to section 951A during the comment period. Consequently, the IRS made the forms available in late 2018 and early 2019 for use by the public. The IRS is contemplating making additional changes to forms to take into account these proposed regulations.

The IRS estimates the number of affected filers to be the following:

Collection of information	Tax Forms Impacted	
	Number of respondents (estimated)	Forms to which the information may be attached
§1.951A-2(c)(6)(v) Election to apply the high tax exception of section 954(b)(4) to gross income of a CFC	25,000 – 35,000	Form 990 series, Form 1120 series, Form 1040 series, Form 1041 series, and Form 1065 series

Source: MeF, DCS, and IRS's Compliance Data Warehouse

This estimate is based on filers of income tax returns with a Form 5471, "Information Return of U.S. Persons With Respect to Certain Foreign Corporations," attached because only filers that are U.S. shareholders of CFCs would be subject to the information collection requirements.

The current status of the PRA submissions related to the tax forms that will be revised as a result of the information collection in proposed §1.951A-2(c)(6)(v) is provided in the accompanying table. The reporting burdens associated with the information collection in the proposed regulations are included in the aggregated burden estimates for OMB control numbers 1545-0123 (which represents a total estimated burden time for all forms and schedules for corporations of 3.157 billion hours and total estimated monetized costs of $58.148 billion ($2017)), 1545-0074 (which represents a total estimated burden time, including all other related forms and schedules for individuals, of 1.784 billion hours and total estimated monetized costs of $31.764 billion ($2017)), 1545-0092 (which represents a total estimated burden time, including all other related forms and schedules for trusts and estates, of 307,844,800 hours and total estimated monetized costs of $9.950 billion ($2016)), and 1545-0047 (which represents a total estimated burden time, including all other related forms and schedules for tax-exempt organizations, of 50.450 million hours and total estimated monetized costs of $1,297,300,000 ($2017)). The overall burden estimates provided for these OMB control numbers are aggregate amounts

---

[5] Data are from IRS's Research, Applied Analytics, and Statistics division based on data available in the Compliance Data Warehouse. Category 4 filer includes a U.S. person who had control of a foreign corporation during the annual accounting period of the foreign corporation. Category 5 includes a U.S. shareholder who owns stock in a foreign corporation that is a CFC and who owned that stock on the last day in the tax year of the foreign corporation in that year in which it was a CFC. For full definitions, see https://www.irs.gov/pub/irs-pdf/i5471.pdf.

[6] This analysis is based on the tax data readily available to the Treasury Department at this time. Some variables may be available on tax forms that are not available for statistical purposes. Moreover, with new tax provisions, such as section 951A, relevant data may not be available for a number of years for statistical purposes.

that relate to the entire package of forms associated with the applicable OMB control number and will in the future include, but not isolate, the estimated burden of the tax forms that will be revised as a result of the information collection in the proposed regulations. These numbers are therefore unrelated to the future calculations needed to assess the burden imposed by the proposed regulations. These burdens have been reported for other regulations related to the taxation of cross-border income and the Treasury Department and the IRS urge readers to recognize that these numbers are duplicates and to guard against overcounting the burden that international tax provisions imposed prior to the Act. No burden estimates specific to the forms affected by the proposed regulations are currently available. The Treasury Department and the IRS have not estimated the burden, including that of any new information collections, related to the requirements under the proposed regulations. The Treasury Department and the IRS estimate PRA burdens on a taxpayer-type basis rather than a provision-specific basis. Those estimates would capture both changes made by the Act and those that arise out of discretionary authority exercised in the final regulations.

The Treasury Department and the IRS request comments on all aspects of information collection burdens related to the proposed regulations, including estimates for how much time it would take to comply with the paperwork burdens described above for each relevant form and ways for the IRS to minimize the paperwork burden. Proposed revisions (if any) to these forms that reflect the information collections contained in these proposed regulations will be made available for public comment at *https://apps.irs.gov/app/picklist/list/draftTaxForms.htm* and will not be finalized until after these forms have been approved by OMB under the PRA.

Form	Type of Filer	OMB Number(s)	Status
Forms 990	Tax exempt entities (NEW Model)	1545-0047	Approved by OIRA 12/21/2018 until 12/31/2019. The form will be updated with OMB number 1545-0047 and the corresponding PRA Notice on the next revision.
	Link: https://www.reginfo.gov/public/do/PRAViewICR?ref_nbr=201811-1545-003		
Form 1040	Individual (NEW Model)	1545-0074	Limited Scope submission (1040 only) approved on 12/7/2018 until 12/31/2019. Full ICR submission for all forms in 6/2019. 60 Day FRN not published yet for full collection.
	Link: https://www.reginfo.gov/public/do/PRAViewICR?ref_nbr=201808-1545-031		
Form 1041	Trusts and estates	1545-0092	Submitted to OIRA for review on 9/27/2018.
	Link: https://www.reginfo.gov/public/do/PRAViewICR?ref_nbr=201806-1545-014		
Form 1065 and 1120	Business (NEW Model)	1545-0123	Approved by OIRA 12/21/2018 until 12/31/2019.
	Link: https://www.reginfo.gov/public/do/PRAViewICR?ref_nbr=201805-1545-019		

III. *Regulatory Flexibility Act*

It is hereby certified that these proposed regulations will not have a significant economic impact on a substantial number of small entities within the meaning of section 601(6) of the Regulatory Flexibility Act (5 U.S.C. chapter 6).

Section 951A generally affects U.S. shareholders of CFCs. The reporting burden in proposed §1.951A-2(c)(6)(v) affects controlling domestic shareholders of a CFC that elect to apply the high tax exception of section 954(b)(4) to gross income of a CFC. Controlling domestic shareholders are generally U.S. shareholders who, in the aggregate, own more than 50 percent of the total combined voting power of all classes of stock of the foreign corporation entitled to vote. As an initial matter, foreign corporations are not considered small entities. Nor are U.S. taxpayers considered small entities to the extent the taxpayers are natural persons or entities other than small entities. Thus, proposed §1.951A-2(c)(6)(v) generally only affects small entities if a U.S. taxpayer that is a U.S. shareholder of a CFC is a small entity.

Examining the gross receipts of the e-filed Forms 5471 that is the basis of the 25,000 – 35,000 respondent estimates, the Treasury Department and the IRS have determined that the tax revenue from section 951A estimated by the Joint Committee on Taxation for businesses of all sizes is less than 0.3 percent of gross receipts as shown in the table below. Based on data for 2015 and 2016, total gross receipts for all businesses with gross receipts under $25 million is $60 billion while those over $25 million is $49.1 trillion. Given that tax on GILTI inclusion amounts is correlated with gross receipts, this results in businesses with less than $25 million in gross receipts accounting for approximately 0.01 percent of the tax revenue. Data are not readily available to determine the sectoral breakdown of these entities. Based on this analysis, smaller businesses are not significantly impacted by these proposed regulations.

	2017	2018	2019	2020	2021	2022	2023	2024	2025	2026
JCT tax revenue	7.7 billion	12.5 billion	9.6 billion	9.5 billion	9.3 billion	9.0 billion	9.2 billion	9.3 billion	15.1 billion	21.2 billion
Total gross receipts	30727 billion	53870 billion	566676 billion	59644 billion	62684 billion	65865 billion	69201 billion	72710 billion	76348 billion	80094 billion
Percent	0.03	0.02	0.02	0.02	0.01	0.01	0.01	0.01	0.02	0.03

Source: Research, Applied Analytics and Statistics division (IRS), Compliance Data Warehouse (IRS) (E-filed Form 5471, category 4 or 5, C and S corporations and partnerships); Conference Report, at 689.

The data to assess the number of small entities potentially affected by proposed §1.951A-2(c)(6)(v) are not readily available. However, businesses that are U.S. shareholders of CFCs are generally not small businesses because the ownership of sufficient stock in a CFC in order to be a U.S. shareholder generally entails significant resources and investment. The Treasury Department and the IRS welcome comments on whether the proposed regulations would affect a substantial number of small entities in any particular industry.

Regardless of the number of small entities potentially affected by proposed §1.951A-2(c)(6)(v), the Treasury Department and the IRS have concluded that there is no significant economic impact on such entities as a result of proposed §1.951A-2(c)(6)(v). As discussed above, smaller businesses are not significantly impacted by the proposed regulations. Furthermore, the requirements in proposed §1.951A-2(c)(6)(v) apply only if a taxpayer chooses to make an election to apply a favorable rule. Consequently, the Treasury Department and the IRS have determined that proposed §1.951A-2(c)(6)(v) will not have a significant economic impact on a substantial number of small entities. Accordingly, it is hereby certified that the collection of information requirements of proposed §1.951A-2(c)(6)(v) would not have a significant economic impact on a substantial number of small entities. Notwithstanding this certification, the Treasury Department and the IRS invite comments from the public on the impact of proposed §1.951A-2(c)(6)(v) on small entities.

The treatment of domestic partnerships as an aggregate of their partners in these proposed regulations for purposes of subpart F would reduce the burden on partners that are not U.S. shareholders of a CFC owned by the partnership because these partners will no longer be required to include in income a distributive share of subpart F income. The proposed regulations would also reduce burden on domestic partnerships that hold CFCs because these partnerships would no longer be required to calculate their partners' distributive share of subpart F income, resulting in compliance cost savings for the affected partnerships. As described in section II of this Special Analyses section, the Treasury Department and the IRS estimate that there are approximately 7,000 U.S. partnerships with CFCs that e-filed at least one Form 5471 as Category 4 or 5 filers in 2015 and 2016.[7] The identified partnerships had approximately 2 million domestic and foreign partners. However, this figure overstates the number of partners that would be affected by the proposed regulations, because the proposed regulations would not affect foreign partners of the affected U.S. partnerships. Of affected U.S. partnerships, business entities are a minority of the affected domestic partners. Because data to identify the size of domestic partners that are business entities are not readily available, this number is a high upper bound and is magnitudes greater than the number of affected domestic partners that are small businesses. Consequently, the Treasury Department and the IRS have determined that the proposed regulations will not have a significant economic impact on a substantial number of small entities. Accordingly, it is hereby certified that the proposed regulations would not have a significant economic impact on a substantial number of small entities.

Pursuant to section 7805(f) of the Code, this notice of proposed rulemaking has been submitted to the Chief Counsel for Advocacy of the Small Business Administration for comment on its impact on small businesses.

IV. *Unfunded Mandates Reform Act*

Section 202 of the Unfunded Mandates Reform Act of 1995 requires that agencies assess anticipated costs and benefits and take certain other actions before issuing a final rule that includes any Federal mandate that may result in expenditures in any one year by a state, local, or tribal government, in the aggregate, or by the private sector, of $100 million in 1995 dollars, updated annually for inflation. In 2019, that threshold is approximately $154 million. These proposed regulations do not include any Federal mandate that may result in expenditures by state, local, or tribal governments, or by the private sector in excess of that threshold.

V. *Executive Order 13132: Federalism*

Executive Order 13132 (entitled "Federalism") prohibits an agency from publishing any rule that has federalism implications if the rule either imposes substantial, direct compliance costs on state and local governments, and is not required by statute, or preempts state law, unless the agency meets the consultation and funding requirements of section 6 of the Executive Order. These proposed regulations do not have federalism implications and do not impose substantial direct compliance costs on state and local governments or preempt state law within the meaning of the Executive Order.

Comments and Requests for Public Hearing

Before the proposed regulations are adopted as final regulations, consideration will be given to any comments that are submitted timely to the IRS as prescribed in this preamble under the "ADDRESSES" heading. The Treasury Department and the IRS request comments on all aspects of the proposed regulations and on changes to forms related to the proposed regulations. See also parts I.B and II.A of the Explanation of Provisions section (requesting specific comments related to the aggregate approach to domestic partnerships and GILTI high tax exclusion, respectively).

All comments will be available at *www.regulations.gov* or upon request. A public hearing will be scheduled if requested in writing by any person that timely submits written comments. If a public hearing is scheduled, then notice of the date, time, and place for the public hearing will be published in the **Federal Register**.

Drafting Information

The principal authors of these regulations are Joshua P. Roffenbender and Jorge M. Oben of the Office of Associate Chief Counsel (International). However, other personnel from the Treasury Department and the IRS participated in their development.

[¶ 49,802] Proposed Amendments of Regulations (REG-106282-18), published in the Federal Register on June 18, 2019 (corrected 8/8/2019).

[Code Secs. 245A, 954 and 6038]

Foreign corporations: Deductions: Dividends.—Reg. §1.245A-1—1.245A-5, 1.954(c)(6)-1 and amendments of Reg. §1.6038-2, limiting the dividends received deduction available for certain dividends received from current or former controlled foreign corporations, are proposed.

AGENCY: Internal Revenue Service (IRS), Treasury.

ACTION: Notice of proposed rulemaking by cross-reference to temporary regulations.

SUMMARY: The Rules and Regulations section of this issue of the **Federal Register** contains temporary regulations under the Internal Revenue Code (the "Code") that limit the dividends received deduction available for certain dividends received from current or former controlled foreign corporations. The temporary regulations also contain rules that limit the applicability of the exception to foreign personal holding company income for certain dividends received by upper-tier controlled foreign corporations from lower-tier controlled foreign corporations and temporary regulations to facilitate administration of certain rules in the temporary regulations. The temporary regulations affect certain U.S. persons that are domestic corporations that receive certain dividends from current or former controlled foreign corporations or are United States shareholders of upper-tier controlled foreign corporations that receive certain dividends from lower-tier controlled foreign corporations.

DATES: Written or electronic comments and requests for a public hearing must be received by September 16, 2019.

ADDRESSES: Send submissions to: CC:PA:LPD:PR (REG-106282-18), Room 5203, Internal Revenue Service, PO Box 7604, Ben Franklin Station, Washington, DC 20044. Submissions may be hand-delivered Monday through Friday between the hours of 8 a.m. and 4 p.m. to CC:PA:LPD:PR (REG-106282-18), Courier's Desk, Internal Revenue Service, 1111 Constitution Avenue, N.W., Washington, DC 20224. Alternatively, taxpayers may submit comments electronically, via the Federal eRulemaking Portal at http://www.regulations.gov (IRS REG-106282-18).

FOR FURTHER INFORMATION CONTACT: Concerning the proposed regulations, Logan M. Kincheloe, (202) 317-6937; concerning submission of comments and/or requests for a hearing Regina Johnson at (202) 317-6901 (not toll-free numbers).

SUPPLEMENTARY INFORMATION:

---

[7] Data are from IRS's Research, Applied Analytics, and Statistics division based on data available in the Compliance Data Warehouse. Category 4 filer includes a U.S. person who had control of a foreign corporation during the annual accounting period of the foreign corporation. Category 5 includes a U.S. shareholder who owns stock in a foreign corporation that is a CFC and who owned that stock on the last day in the tax year of the foreign corporation in that year in which it was a CFC. For full definitions, see https://www.irs.gov/pub/irs-pdf/i5471.pdf.

Background and Explanation of Provisions

Temporary regulations in the Rules and Regulations section of this issue of the **Federal Register** amend 26 CFR 1. The temporary regulations limit the section 245A dividends received deduction for certain dividends from current or former controlled foreign corporations as well as the section 954(c)(6) exception to foreign personal holding company income for certain dividends received by an upper-tier controlled foreign corporation from a lower-tier controlled foreign corporation. The text of those regulations also serves as the text of these regulations. The preamble to the temporary regulations explains the temporary regulations and these proposed regulations.

Special Analyses

I. Paperwork Reduction Act

The collections of information contained in these proposed regulations are explained in the temporary regulations under sections 245A, 954(c)(6), and 6038 published elsewhere in this issue of the **Federal Register**.

II. Regulatory Flexibility Act

It is hereby certified that this rulemaking will not have a significant economic impact on a substantial number of small entities within the meaning of section 601(6) of the Regulatory Flexibility Act (5 U.S.C. chapter 6).

The small entities that are subject to proposed § 1.245A-5 are small entities that are U.S. shareholders of certain foreign corporations that are otherwise eligible for the section 245A deduction on distributions from the foreign corporation. Additionally, to be subject to the proposed regulations, the foreign corporation that is owned by the small entity must have engaged in certain related party transactions described in Part II.B of the Explanation of Provisions section of the preamble to the temporary regulations, or the U.S. shareholder must have transferred certain stock in the foreign corporation during the taxable year.

Based on 2014 Statistics of Income tax data, the Department of the Treasury ("Treasury Department") and the IRS estimate that there are approximately 15,000 U.S. corporations with controlled foreign corporations ("CFCs") of which approximately half (6,000-9,000) have less than $25 million in gross receipts. Not all of these corporations will be affected by the proposed regulations. In particular, only small U.S. taxpayers with fiscal year CFCs that transfer assets in related party transactions during the gap period, or U.S. taxpayers that transfer more than 10 percent of their stock of a CFC in a taxable year or U.S. taxpayers that reduce their ownership of stock of a CFC by more than 10 percent, have the potential to be affected by these regulations.

The Treasury Department and the IRS have concluded that there is no significant economic impact on such entities as a result of these proposed regulations. To make this determination, the Treasury Department calculated the ratio of estimated global intangible lowed-taxed income ("GILTI") and subpart F revenue attributable to these businesses to aggregate total sales data (Data on total sales of all U.S. parented companies are drawn from the Bureau of Economic Analysis Interactive Data accessed at this web address in December, 2018: *https://apps.bea.gov/iTable/iTable.cfm?ReqID=2&step=1*) adjusted to reflect the total sales of these businesses. Projected net tax proceeds from GILTI and subpart F are estimated to be below one percent of the sales of U.S. parented multinational enterprises for 2018 through 2027. The tax thus amounts to less than 3 to 5 percent of receipts (as defined in 13 CFR 121.104), an economic impact that the Treasury Department and IRS regard as the threshold for significant under the Regulatory Flexibility Act. This calculated percentage is furthermore an upper bound on the true expected effect of the proposed regulations because not all the GILTI and subpart F revenue estimated to be attributable to small entities will be captured by the proposed regulations. Consequently, the Treasury Department and the IRS have determined that proposed § 1.245A-5 will not have a significant economic impact on a substantial number of small entities.

Accordingly, it is hereby certified that the proposed rule would not have a significant economic impact on a substantial number of small entities. Notwithstanding this certification, the Treasury Department and the IRS invite comments from the public on both the number of entities affected (including whether specific industries are affected) and the economic impact of this proposed rule on small entities.

Pursuant to section 7805(f) of the Code, these regulations have been submitted to the Chief Counsel for Advocacy of the Small Business Administration for comment on the impact on small businesses.

III. Unfunded Mandates Reform Act

The assessment of costs and benefits under the Unfunded Mandated Reform Act of these proposed regulations are explained in the temporary regulations under 245A, 954(c)(6), and 6038 published in 84 FR 28398 (June 18, 2019).

IV. Executive Order 13132: Federalism

The assessment of the federalism implications as required under Executive Order 13132 of these proposed regulations is explained in the temporary regulations under sections 245A, 954(c)(6), and 6038 published in 84 FR 28398 (June 18, 2019).

Comments and Requests for Public Hearing

Before these proposed regulations are adopted as final regulations, consideration will be given to any written or electronic comments that are submitted timely to the IRS as prescribed in this preamble under the "ADDRESSES" heading. Comments are requested on all aspects of the proposed regulations, and specifically on the issues identified in Part II.B and Part III.A of the Explanation of Provisions section and the Parts I and II of the Special Analysis section of the preamble to the temporary regulations. All comments will be available at www.regulations.gov or upon request. A public hearing will be scheduled if requested in writing by any person that timely submits written comments. If a public hearing is scheduled, then notice of the date, time, and place for the public hearing will be published in the **Federal Register**.

Drafting Information

The principal author of the proposed regulations is Logan M. Kincheloe, Office of Associate Chief Counsel (International). However, other personnel from the Treasury Department and the IRS participated in their development.

[¶ 49,803]   Proposed Amendments of Regulations (REG-118425-18), published in the Federal Register on June 19, 2019 (corrected 8/6/2019).

[Code Sec. 199, 199A and 1388]

Qualified business income: Deduction: Specified cooperatives: Patronage: Domestic production activities.—Reg. §§1.199A-7—1.199A-12 and amendments of Reg. §§1.199-0—1.199-9 and 1.1388-1, regarding the deduction for qualified business income (QBI) under section 199A(a) of the Code as well as guidance to specified agricultural or horticultural cooperatives (Specified Cooperatives) and their patrons regarding the deduction for domestic production activities under section 199A(g) of the Code, are proposed. Amendments of Reg. §§1.199-0—1.199-4, 1.199-6 and 1.199-8 proposed on August 27, 2015, are withdrawn.

AGENCY: Internal Revenue Service (IRS), Treasury.

ACTION: Notice of proposed rulemaking; withdrawal of notice of proposed rulemaking.

SUMMARY: These proposed regulations provide guidance to cooperatives to which sections 1381 through 1388 of the Internal Revenue Code (Code) apply (Cooperatives) and their patrons regarding the deduction for qualified business income (QBI) under section 199A(a) of the Code as well as guidance to specified agricultural or horticultural cooperatives (Specified Cooperatives) and their patrons regarding the deduction for domestic production activities under section 199A(g) of the Code. These proposed regulations also provide guidance on section 199A(b)(7), the rule requiring patrons of Specified Cooperatives to reduce their deduction for QBI under section 199A(a). In addition, these proposed regulations include a single definition of *patronage and nonpatronage* under section 1388 of the Code. Finally, these proposed regulations propose to remove the final regulations, and withdraw the proposed regulations that have not been finalized, under former section 199. These proposed regulations affect Cooperatives as well as patrons that are individuals, partnerships, S corporations, trusts, and estates engaged in domestic trades or businesses.

DATES: Written (including electronic) comments and requests for a public hearing must be received by August 18, 2019. As of June 19, 2019, the proposed rule published on August 27, 2015 (80 FR 51978), is withdrawn.

ADDRESSES: Submit electronic submissions via the Federal eRulemaking Portal at *www.regulations.gov* (indicate IRS and REG-118425-18) by following the online instructions for submitting comments. Once submitted to the Federal eRulemaking Portal, comments cannot be edited or withdrawn. The Department of the Treasury (Treasury Department) and the IRS will publish for public availability any comment received to its public docket, whether submitted electronically or in hard copy. Send hard copy submissions to: CC:PA:LPD:PR (REG-118425-18), Room 5203, Internal Revenue Service, P.O. Box 7604, Ben Franklin Station, Washington, D.C., 20044. Submissions may be hand-delivered Monday through Friday between the hours of 8 a.m. and 4 p.m. to CC:PA:LPD:PR (REG-118425-18), Courier's Desk, Internal Revenue Service, 1111 Constitution Avenue, N.W., Washington, D.C., 20224.

FOR FURTHER INFORMATION CONTACT: Concerning the proposed regulations, James Holmes at (202) 317-4137; concerning submissions of comments and requests for hearing, Regina L. Johnson at (202) 317-6901 (not toll-free numbers).

SUPPLEMENTARY INFORMATION:

Background

This document contains proposed amendments to the Income Tax Regulations (26 CFR part 1) under sections 199A and 1388 of the Code.

Section 199A was enacted on December 22, 2017, by section 11011 of "An Act to provide for reconciliation pursuant to titles II and V of the concurrent resolution on the budget for fiscal year 2018," Public Law 115-97, 131 Stat. 2054, 2063 (TCJA). Parts of section 199A were amended on March 23, 2018, as if included in TCJA, by section 101 of Division T of the Consolidated Appropriations Act, 2018, Public Law 115-141, 132 Stat. 348, 1151 (2018 Act). Section 199A applies to taxable years beginning after 2017 and before 2026. Unless otherwise indicated, all references to section 199A are to section 199A as amended by the 2018 Act.

In addition, section 13305 of the TCJA repealed section 199 (former section 199), which provided a deduction for income attributable to domestic production activities (section 199 deduction). Public Law 115-97, 131 Stat. 2054, 2126. The repeal of former section 199 is effective for all taxable years beginning after 2017. This notice of proposed rulemaking therefore proposes to remove the final regulations under former section 199, and withdraws proposed regulations under former section 199.

Section 199A(a) provides taxpayers a deduction of up to 20 percent of QBI from a domestic business operated as a sole proprietorship or through a partnership, S corporation, trust, or estate, and up to 20 percent of qualified real estate investment trust (REIT) dividends and publicly traded partnership (PTP) income (section 199A(a) deduction). Section 199A(b)(7) requires patrons of Specified Cooperatives to reduce their section 199A(a) deduction if those patrons receive certain payments from such cooperatives. Section 199A(g) provides a deduction for Specified Cooperatives and their patrons (section 199A(g) deduction) that is based on the former section 199 deduction. Before the amendments of the 2018 Act, section 199A(g) provided a modified version of the section 199A(a) deduction for Specified Cooperatives.

The Treasury Department and the IRS published proposed regulations (REG-107892-18) providing guidance on the section 199A(a) deduction in the *Federal Register* (83 FR 40884) on August 16, 2018 (August 2018 NPRM). The final regulations were published in the *Federal Register* (84 FR 2952) on February 8, 2019 (TD 9847).

TD 9847 did not address patrons' treatment of payments received from Cooperatives for purposes of section 199A(a) or the section 199A(g) deduction for Specified Cooperatives, though it did restate the reduction required under section 199A(b)(7). See § 1.199A-1(e)(7). The August 2018 NPRM preamble stated that the Treasury Department and the IRS would continue to study the area and intended to issue separate proposed regulations describing rules for applying section 199A to Specified Cooperatives and their patrons. This notice of proposed rulemaking sets forth those proposed regulations and provides additional guidance to patrons calculating their 199A(a) deduction.

Explanation of Provisions

The purpose of these proposed regulations is to provide guidance regarding the application of sections 199A(a), 199A(b)(7), and 199A(g) to Cooperatives and their patrons as well as to Specified Cooperatives and their patrons. Whereas section 199A(a) is generally available to patrons of all Cooperatives, sections 199A(b)(7) and 199A(g) apply only to Specified Cooperatives and their patrons.

These proposed regulations are organized into six sections: proposed §§ 1.199A-7 through 1.199A-12. Proposed § 1.199A-7 describes rules for patrons of Cooperatives to calculate their section 199A(a) deduction and rules for patrons of Specified Cooperatives to calculate the reduction to their section 199A(a) deduction as required by section 199A(b)(7). Unless otherwise provided in these proposed regulations, all of the rules set forth in TD 9847 relating to the section 199A(a) deduction apply to Cooperatives and their patrons. Specified Cooperatives are a subset of Cooperatives; therefore, the requirements of proposed § 1.199A-7 also apply to Specified Cooperatives.

Proposed § 1.199A-8 sets out the criteria that Specified Cooperatives must satisfy to qualify for the section 199A(g) deduction, and sets forth four steps necessary to calculate this deduction. These proposed regulations provide that the section 199A(g) deduction available to Specified Cooperatives and their patrons is generally computed only with respect to patronage gross receipts and related deductions. Exempt Specified Cooperatives (those that qualify under section 521) may compute their section 199A(g) deductions with respect to both patronage and nonpatronage gross receipts and related deductions.

Proposed §§ 1.199A-9 through 1.199A-11 provide additional guidance, based on the regulations under former section 199, regarding the four steps set forth in proposed § 1.199A-8. Proposed § 1.199A-9 provides additional rules for determining a Specified Cooperative's domestic production gross receipts (DPGR). Proposed § 1.199A-10 provides additional rules for calculating costs (including cost of goods sold (COGS) and other expenses, losses, and deductions) allocable to a Specified Cooperative's DPGR. Proposed § 1.199A-11 provides additional rules for determining the W-2 wage limitation in section 199A(g)(1)(B). Proposed § 1.199A-12 details rules for applying section 199A(g) in the context of an expanded affiliated group (EAG) and other special rules contained in section 199A(g)(5) that are not otherwise addressed in these proposed regulations.

These proposed regulations also include, under section 1388, a single definition of *patronage and nonpatronage* in proposed §1.1388-1(f), which is intended to reflect the current case law under section 1388. This Explanation of Provisions describes each section of the proposed regulations in more detail.

I. *Proposed §1.199A-7, Rules for Patrons of Cooperatives*

A. *In General*

As noted in the Background, section 199A(a) may allow a taxpayer a deduction of up to 20 percent of QBI from a domestic business operated as a sole proprietorship or through a partnership, S corporation, trust, or estate, and up to 20 percent of qualified REIT dividends and PTP income. A section 199A(a) deduction is not available for wage income or for business income earned through a C corporation.

C corporations are not eligible for the section 199A(a) deduction. Cooperatives are C corporations for Federal income tax purposes and, therefore, are not eligible for the section 199A(a) deduction. Similarly, patrons that are C corporations are also not eligible for the section 199A(a) deduction. However, patrons that are individuals are eligible for the section 199A(a) deduction. Section 1.199A-1(a)(2) provides that, for purposes of applying the rules of §§1.199A-1 through 1.199A-6, a reference to an individual includes a reference to a trust (other than a grantor trust) or an estate to the extent that the section 199A(a) deduction is determined by the trust or estate under the rules of §1.199A-6. These proposed regulations apply this same usage of the term *individual*.

The benefits of section 199A(a) are limited to individuals with income from a trade or business as defined in section 199A(d)(1) and §1.199A-1(b)(14) (trade or business) with QBI. To the extent a patron operating a trade or business has income directly from that business (as opposed to receiving a patronage dividend from a Cooperative), the patron must follow the rules of §§1.199A-1 through 1.199A-6 to calculate the section 199A deduction. However, to the extent a patron receives patronage dividends or similar payments from a Cooperative, the patron must follow the additional special rules and clarification in proposed §1.199A-7 to calculate the section 199A deduction.

For these purposes, patronage dividends or similar payments include money, property, qualified written notices of allocations, and qualified per-unit retain certificates for which an exempt or nonexempt Cooperative receives a deduction under section 1382(b), and nonpatronage distributions paid in money, property, qualified written notices of allocation as well as money or property paid in redemption of a nonqualified written notice of allocation for which an exempt Cooperative receives a deduction under section 1382(c)(2) (hereinafter collectively referred to as patronage dividends or similar payments).

Section 1.199A-7(c) and (d) of these proposed regulations provide that these patronage dividends or similar payments may be included in the patron's QBI: (i) To the extent that these payments are related to the patron's trade or business, (ii) are qualified items of income, gain, deduction, or loss at the Cooperative's trade or business level, (iii) are not income from a specified service trade or business (SSTB), as defined in section 199A(d)(2), at the Cooperative's trade or business level (except as permitted by the threshold rules, *see* §1.199A-5(a)(2)), and (iv) provided the patron receives certain information from the Cooperative about these payments (see proposed §1.199A-7(c)(3) and (d)(3)). Proposed §1.199A-7(e) provides that in situations in which a patron conducts a trade or business that receives patronage dividends or similar payments from a Cooperative, the W-2 wages and unadjusted basis immediately after acquisition (UBIA) of qualified property considered are those of the patron's trade or business and not of the Cooperative that directly conducts the trade or business from which the payments arise. All of these proposed rules are discussed further in this section.

B. *QBI of Patrons*

Although Cooperatives are C corporations for Federal income tax purposes, section 1382(b) and (c) allow Cooperatives to determine taxable income after deducting distributions of patronage dividends or similar payments to patrons. The effect of these deductions is to remove the distributions from income taxed at the Cooperative level leaving it subject to income tax only at the patron level. Exempt and nonexempt Cooperatives are both permitted to deduct patronage distributions if they satisfy the requirements described in section 1382(b). Only exempt Cooperatives are permitted to also deduct nonpatronage distributions if the requirements under section 1382(c) are met. Cooperatives are subject to Federal income tax on income for which no deduction may be taken under section 1382(b) or (c), in the same manner as any C corporation.

Section 1.199A-3(b) contains the general rules regarding QBI. QBI is the net amount of qualified items of income, gain, deduction, and loss with respect to any trade or business as determined under those rules. While income from the ownership of a C corporation is generally not QBI, section 199A provides a special rule for patrons receiving patronage dividends from a Cooperative.

Section 199A(c)(3)(B)(ii) provides that any amount described in section 1385(a)(1), which concerns patronage dividends, is not treated as an exclusion to a patron's QBI. The Joint Committee on Taxation Report (JCX-6-18, released March 22, 2018) (Joint Committee Report) states that QBI includes any patronage dividend (as defined in section 1388(a)), per-unit retain allocation (as defined in section 1388(f)), qualified written notice of allocation (as defined in section 1388(c)), or any other similar amount received from a Cooperative, provided such amount is otherwise a qualified item of income, gain, deduction, or loss (that is, such amount is (i) effectively connected with the conduct of a trade or business within the United States, and (ii) included or allowed in determining taxable income for the taxable year). Joint Committee Report, pages 24-25. As a result, the rules of proposed §1.199A-7(c) provide that patronage dividends or similar payments (as previously discussed) are included in calculating QBI for purposes of the patrons' section 199A(a) deduction provided the amounts are otherwise qualified items. To be otherwise qualified, these amounts must be qualified items of income, gain, deduction, and loss under section 199A(c)(3).

Unlike nonexempt Cooperatives, exempt Cooperatives are permitted to deduct nonpatronage distributions under section 1382(c). As a result, this income is subject to taxation only at the patron level. The rules of proposed §1.199A-7(c) provide that a patron's QBI can include payments to patrons for which the exempt Cooperative receives a deduction under section 1382(c)(2) in addition to payments for which the exempt Cooperative receives a deduction under section 1382(b). That is, amounts paid under section 1382(c)(2) are treated by a patron as equivalent to patronage dividends under section 1382(b) for purposes of QBI. Amounts paid under section 1382(c)(1) (dividends on capital stock), however, are dividends from ownership of C corporations, which are not included in QBI.

TD 9847 generally provides that income is tested at the trade or business level where it is directly generated. Accordingly, these proposed regulations provide that patronage dividends or similar payments are considered to be generated from the trade or business the Cooperative conducts on behalf of or with the patron, and are tested by the Cooperative at its trade or business level.

A patron must determine QBI for each trade or business it directly conducts. However, in situations where the patron receives a distribution from a Cooperative that is a patronage dividend or similar payment, the Cooperative determines whether that distribution contains qualified items of income, as defined under §1.199A-3(b), and reports that information to the patron. The patron needs this information to determine its section 199A(a) deduction, and the Cooperative directly conducting the trade or business from which the distribution is derived is in the best position to know whether the patronage dividend or similar payment contains qualified items. The Cooperative must report this information regardless of whether the patron's taxable income does not exceed the threshold amount ($315,000 in the case of joint returns and $157,500 for all other taxpayers for any taxable year beginning before 2019). For taxable years beginning after 2018, *see* Rev. Proc. 2018-57, 2018-49 IRB 827, or its successor (relating to inflation adjustments).

A patron must use that information when determining the patron's section 199A(a) deduction. For example, if the Cooperative determines an entire distribution does not contain any qualified item of income, gain, deduction, and loss because it is not effectively connected with the conduct of the Cooperative's trade or business within the United States, the Cooperative does not include such amount when reporting qualified items to the patron, and the patron does not include the distribution in the patron's QBI. In addition, to the extent the distribution includes interest income that is not properly allocable to the Cooperative's trade or business on behalf of, or with, its patrons, the distribution is not a qualified item of income, gain, deduction, and loss. As a result, the Cooperative does not include such amount when reporting qualified items to the patron, and the patron does not include the income in the patron's QBI.

Proposed § 1.199A-7(c)(3) provides that the Cooperative must report the amount of qualified items of income, gain, deduction, or loss in the distributions made to the patron on an attachment to or on the Form 1099-PATR, Taxable Distributions Received From Cooperatives (Form 1099-PATR) (or any successor form), issued by the Cooperative to the patron, unless otherwise provided by the instructions to the Form. The Cooperative does not include any items from an SSTB in reporting the amount of qualified items of income, gain, deduction, and loss and must instead follow the rules in proposed § 1.199A-7(d) for income from an SSTB. If a patron does not receive such information from the Cooperative on or before the due date of the Form 1099-PATR, the amount of distributions from the Cooperative that may be included in the patron's QBI is presumed to be zero. This presumption does not apply to amounts of qualified items of income, gain, deduction, and loss to the extent that they were not reported on the Form 1099-PATR or attachment thereto before the publication of these proposed regulations in the *Federal Register*. These rules apply to both exempt and nonexempt Cooperatives as well as patronage and nonpatronage distributions. The Treasury Department and the IRS request comments on these reporting requirements and whether any additional information from Cooperatives that make distributions to their patrons is needed for their patrons to determine their section 199A(a) deduction.

C. *Specified Service Trade or Business*

Section 199A(c)(1) provides that only items attributable to a qualified trade or business are taken into account in determining the section 199A(a) deduction for QBI. Under section 199A(d)(1) a "qualified trade or business" excludes (A) an SSTB or (B) the trade or business of performing services as an employee. TD 9847 provides that, unless an exception applies, if a trade or business is an SSTB, none of its items are to be taken into account for purposes of determining a taxpayer's QBI.

Under section 199A(d)(3), individuals with taxable income not exceeding the threshold amount ($315,000 in the case of joint returns and $157,500 for all other taxpayers for any taxable year beginning before 2019), are not subject to a restriction with respect to SSTBs. For taxable years beginning after 2018, *see* Rev. Proc. 2018-57, 2018-49 IRB 827, or its successor. Therefore, if an individual has taxable income not exceeding the threshold amount, the individual is eligible for the section 199A(a) deduction with respect to qualified items of income, gain, deduction, and loss from the SSTB notwithstanding that the trade or business is an SSTB. The inapplicability of the SSTB rules, W-2 wage limitation, and UBIA of qualified property limitation in computing the section 199A(a) deduction is subject to a phase-in for individuals with taxable income within the phase-in range. *See* the rules in § 1.199A-5 for the rules relating to SSTBs.

The rules in proposed § 1.199A-7(d) clarify that a patron (whether the patron is a relevant passthrough entity (RPE) or an individual) must determine whether the trades or businesses it directly conducts are SSTBs. These proposed rules also provide that in the case of a patron's trade or business that receives patronage dividends or similar payments distributed from a Cooperative, the Cooperative must determine whether the distributions from the Cooperative include items of income, gain, deduction, and loss from an SSTB directly conducted by the Cooperative, and whether such items are qualified items with respect to such SSTB. The Cooperative must report to the patron the amount of qualified items of income, gain, deduction, and loss from an SSTB directly conducted by the Cooperative. The patron then determines if the distribution may be included in the patron's QBI depending on the patron's taxable income and the statutory phase-in and threshold amounts. Because the Cooperative may not know whether the patron's taxable income exceeds the threshold amount, the Cooperative must report this information to all patrons. Without this information, a patron with taxable income within the phase-in range or below the threshold amount would not have the information necessary to take into account the amount of qualified items of income, gain, deduction, and loss from an SSTB in determining the patron's section 199A(a) deduction for QBI. The rules in § 1.199A-5 are applied by the Cooperative to determine if the trade or business is an SSTB. For example, the Cooperative will apply the gross receipts de minimis rules in § 1.199A-5(c)(1) to determine if the trade or business is an SSTB.

Proposed § 1.199A-7(d)(3) provides that the Cooperative must report to the patron the amount of SSTB income, gain, deduction, and loss in distributions that is qualified with respect to any SSTB directly conducted by the Cooperative on an attachment to or on the Form 1099-PATR (or any successor form) issued by the Cooperative to the patron, unless otherwise provided by the instructions to the Form. If the Cooperative does not report the amount on or before the due date of the Form 1099-PATR, then only the amount that a Cooperative reports as qualified items of income, gain, deduction, and loss under § 1.199A-7(c)(3) may be included in the patron's QBI, and the remaining amount of distributions from the Cooperative that may be included in the patron's QBI is presumed to be zero. This presumption does not apply to amounts of qualified items of income, gain, deduction, and loss to the extent that they were not reported on the Form 1099-PATR or attachment thereto before the publication of these proposed regulations in the *Federal Register*. These rules apply to both exempt and nonexempt Cooperatives as well as to patronage and nonpatronage distributions. The Treasury Department and the IRS request comments on these reporting requirements and whether any additional information from Cooperatives that make distributions to their patrons is needed for their patrons to determine their section 199A(a) deduction.

D. *Determination of W-2 Wages and UBIA of Qualified Property*

Section 1.199A-1(d) addresses the calculation of the section 199A(a) deduction for individuals with taxable income exceeding the threshold amount and provides guidance on the application of these limitations. All of the rules relating to the REIT dividends and qualified PTP income component of the section 199A(a) deduction applicable to individuals with taxable income not exceeding the threshold amount also apply to individuals with taxable income exceeding the threshold amount. The QBI component of the section 199A(a) deduction, however, is subject to limitations for individuals with taxable income exceeding the threshold amount. These include the limitations based on the W-2 wages of the trade or business or a combination of the W-2 wages and the UBIA of qualified property.

Under § 1.199A-2, W-2 wages and UBIA of qualified property are determined by the individual or RPE that directly conducts the trade or business. Section 199A(f)(1)(A)(2)(iii) requires that S corporations and partnerships allocate W-2 wages and UBIA of qualified property to their owners in accordance with each owner's applicable share, and § 1.199A-6 contains additional information regarding these reporting requirements. Section 199A does not provide a similar rule for Cooperatives.

Section 199A(c)(3)(B)(ii) provides that patronage dividends or similar payments may be treated as qualified items of income. Only the Cooperative knows the origin and character of the patronage dividends or similar payments. As a result, the Cooperative must determine if these payments meet the statutory requirements in section 199A(c)(3), and must provide information to the patron for it to compute its section 199A(a) deduction. In contrast, section 199A contains special rules for W-2 wages and UBIA of qualified property. To provide that Cooperatives allocate their W-2 wages and UBIA of qualified property to their patrons would be to treat the Cooperatives as RPEs when they are C corporations. Therefore, the rules in proposed § 1.199A-7(e) provide that patrons directly conducting trades or businesses that receive patronage dividends or similar payments from a Cooperative calculate the W-2 wage and UBIA of qualified property limitations at the patron level based on the patrons' trades or businesses, without any regard to the Cooperative's W-2 wages or UBIA of qualified property.

In summary, a Cooperative must report to patrons: (i) Whether the patronage dividends or similar payments include qualified items of income, gain, deduction, and loss from a non-SSTB and (ii) whether the distributions from the Cooperative include qualified items of income, gain, deduction, and loss from an SSTB directly conducted by the Cooperative, but a Cooperative does not report any W-2 wages or UBIA of qualified property to patrons. The Treasury Department and the IRS request comments on these proposed rules regarding W-2 wages and UBIA of qualified property and whether it would be appropriate for Cooperatives to be required to report such amounts to patrons to determine their section 199A(a) deduction.

E. *Special Rules for Patrons of Specified Cooperatives*

Section 199A provides special rules for patrons of Specified Cooperatives. Because patrons of Specified Cooperatives may be eligible to take both a section 199A(a) and section 199A(g) deduction, section 199A(b)(7) provides that if a trade or business of a patron of a Specified Cooperative receives qualified payments (as defined in section 199A(g)(2)(e) and proposed § 1.199A-8(d)(2)(ii)) from such Specified Cooperative that are included in the patron's QBI, the patron must reduce its section 199A(a) deduction by the lesser of (i) 9 percent of so much of the QBI with respect to such trade or business that is properly allocable to qualified payments from the Specified Cooperative, or (ii) 50 percent of so much of the patrons' W-2 wages (determined under section 199A(b)(4)) with respect to such trade or business as are so allocable. This reduction is required by section 199A(b)(7) whether the Specified Cooperative passes through all, some, or none of the Specified Cooperative's section 199A(g) deduction to the patron in that taxable year.

Section 1.199A-3(b)(5) provides an allocation method for items of QBI attributable to more than one trade or business. That allocation method also applies to patrons with multiple trades or businesses. The rules in proposed § 1.199A-7(f)(2) provide an additional similar allocation method in situations where a patron receives qualified payments and income that is not a qualified payment in a trade or business. The patron must allocate those items using a reasonable method based on all the facts and circumstances. Different reasonable methods may be used for different items of income, gain, deduction, and loss. The chosen reasonable method for each item must be consistently applied from one taxable year to another and must clearly reflect the income and expenses of each trade or business. The overall combination of methods must also be reasonably based on all the facts and circumstances. The books and records maintained for a trade or business must be consistent with any allocations. The Treasury Department and the IRS are open to considering whether a permissible "reasonable method" should be specified in regulations or permitted to include methods based on direct tracing, allocations based on gross income, or other methods, within appropriate parameters. The Treasury Department and the IRS request comments on possible reasonable methods for the allocation of items not clearly attributable to a single trade or business, and whether any safe harbors may be appropriate.

Because the section 199A(b)(7) reduction applies to the portion of a patron's QBI that relates to qualified payments from a Specified Cooperative, these proposed rules provide a safe harbor allocation method for patrons with taxable income not exceeding the threshold amounts set forth in section 199A(e)(2) to determine how to calculate the section 199A(b)(7) reduction. The safe harbor allocation method is intended to provide a straightforward method for patrons if their trade or business receives qualified payments from a Specified Cooperative in addition to other income. To calculate the required section 199A(b)(7) reduction, the patron must allocate the aggregate business expenses and W-2 wages between qualified payments and other gross receipts. The safe harbor allocation method allows patrons to allocate by ratably apportioning business expenses and W-2 wages based on the proportion that the amount of qualified payments bears to the total gross receipts used to determine QBI. The Treasury Department and the IRS request comments on this safe harbor rule and whether there are additional or alternative safe harbors that may be appropriate.

Further, to make the calculation required by section 199A(b)(7), the patron will need to know the qualified payments allocable to the patron that were used in calculating a Specified Cooperative's section 199A(g) deduction. In order to enable the patron to make this calculation, proposed § 1.199A-7(f)(3) requires the Specified Cooperative to report the amount of such qualified payments on an attachment to or on the Form 1099-PATR, (or any successor form) issued by the Cooperative to the patron, unless otherwise provided by the instructions to the Form.

F. *Transition Rule*

Congress provided a special transition rule relating to qualified payments under former section 199 made by Specified Cooperatives in section 101 of the 2018 Act. Under this transition rule, the repeal of former section 199 for taxable years beginning after December 31, 2017, does not apply to former section 199 qualified payments received by a patron from Specified Cooperatives in a taxable year beginning after December 31, 2017, to the extent such qualified payments are attributable to qualified production activities income (QPAI) with respect to which a deduction is allowable to the Specified Cooperatives under former section 199 for a taxable year of the Specified Cooperatives beginning before January 1, 2018. Such qualified payments remain subject to former section 199, and any deduction under former section 199 allocated by the Specified Cooperatives to their patrons related to such qualified payments may be deducted by such patrons in accordance with former section 199. In addition, no deduction is allowed under section 199A(a) and (g) with respect to such qualified payments. *See* Pub. L. 115-97, title I, § 13305(c), Dec. 22, 2017, 131 Stat. 2054, 2126 (codified as amended at I.R.C. § 74 Note), as amended by Pub. L. 115-141, div. T, § 101(c), Mar. 23, 2018, 132 Stat. 348, 1151, providing a transitional rule for qualified payments of patrons of Cooperatives.

Proposed § 1.199A-7(h)(3) and § 1.199A-8(h)(3) provide that the Cooperative must identify in a written notice to its patrons that a section 199A(a) deduction cannot be claimed for qualified payments that otherwise would constitute QBI in the patron's trade or business in a taxable year in which the qualified payments remain subject to former section 199. The Cooperative must report this information on an attachment to or on the Form 1099-PATR (or any successor form) issued by the Cooperative to the patron, unless otherwise provided by the instructions to the Form.

II. *Proposed § 1.199A-8, Deduction for Income Attributable to Domestic Production Activities of Specified Cooperatives*

A. *In General*

Section 199A(g) provides a deduction for Specified Cooperatives and their patrons that is similar in many respects to the deduction under former section 199. Proposed § 1.199A-8 provides definitions relating to the section 199A(g) deduction, establishes the criteria that a Specified Cooperative must satisfy to be eligible to claim the section 199A(g) deduction, and sets forth the necessary steps for a Specified Cooperative to calculate the section 199A(g) deduction.

B. *Definitions*

Proposed § 1.199A-8 defines the terms *patron*, *Specified Cooperative*, and *agricultural or horticultural products*. In defining *patron*, the Treasury Department and the IRS sought consistency with the rules under subchapter T of chapter 1 of subtitle A of the Code. Thus, the rules in proposed § 1.199A-8 cross-reference the definition of patron found in § 1.1388-1(e).

The definition of *Specified Cooperative* is consistent with the definition set forth in section 199A(g)(4). This definition is different from the definition of *Specified Cooperative* as originally provided by section 11011(a) of the TCJA (former section 199A(g)(3)), as it no longer includes a Cooperative solely engaged in the provision of supplies, equipment, or services to farmers or other Specified Cooperatives (former section 199A(g)(3)(C)).

Proposed §1.199A-8(a)(4) defines *agricultural or horticultural products* as agricultural, horticultural, viticultural, and dairy products, livestock and the products thereof; the products of poultry and bee raising, the edible products of forestry, and any and all products raised or produced on farms and processed or manufactured products thereof within the meaning of the Cooperative Marketing Act of 1926, 44 Stat. 802 (1926). Agricultural or horticultural products also include aquatic products that are farmed whether by exempt or nonexempt Specified Cooperatives. *See* Rev. Rul. 64-246, 1964-2 C.B. 154. In addition, agricultural or horticultural products include fertilizer, diesel fuel, and other supplies used in agricultural or horticultural production that are manufactured, produced, grown, or extracted (MPGE) by the Specified Cooperative. *See* Joint Committee Report, at 23, footnote 120.

Agricultural or horticultural products do not include intangible property. For example, an agricultural or horticultural product includes a seed that is grown, but does not include an intangible property right to reproduce a seed for sale. This exclusion of intangible property does not apply to intangible characteristics of any particular agricultural or horticultural product. For example, gross receipts from the sale of different varieties of oranges would all qualify as DPGR from the disposition of agricultural or horticultural products (assuming all other requirements of section 199A(g) are met). However, gross receipts from the license of the right to produce and sell a certain variety of oranges would be considered separate from the tangible oranges themselves and therefore not gross receipts from an agricultural or horticultural product. This exclusion is consistent with former section 199, which excluded intangible property other than computer software, any property described in section 168(f)(4) (sound recordings), and qualified film products.

The Treasury Department and the IRS considered a similar but alternative definition of *agricultural or horticultural* products as agricultural, horticultural, viticultural, and dairy products, livestock and poultry, bees, forest products, fish and shellfish, and any products thereof, including processed and manufactured products, and any and all products raised or produced on farms and any processed or manufactured product thereof within the meaning of the Agricultural Marketing Act of 1946, 60 Stat. 1091 (1946). While very similar to the definition set forth in these proposed rules, the Treasury Department and the IRS proposed using the definition based on the Cooperative Marketing Act of 1926, which specifically concerns cooperatives, unlike the Agricultural Marketing Act of 1946, which concerns the marketing and distribution of agricultural products.

The Treasury Department and the IRS also considered an alternative definition of *agricultural or horticultural products* based on general regulations under the Commodity Exchange Act. The Commodity Futures Trading Commission defines *agricultural commodities* as wheat, cotton, rice, corn, oats, barley, rye, flaxseed, grain sorghums, mill feeds, butter, eggs, Solanum tuberosum (Irish potatoes), wool, wool tops, fats and oils (including lard, tallow, cottonseed oil, peanut oil, soybean oil and all other fats and oils), cottonseed meal, cottonseed, peanuts, soybeans, soybean meal, livestock, livestock products, and frozen concentrated orange juice, but not onions; other commodities that are, or once were, or are derived from, living organisms, including plant, animal and aquatic life, which are generally fungible, within their respective classes, and are used primarily for human food, shelter, animal feed or natural fiber; tobacco, products of horticulture, and such other commodities used or consumed by animals or humans. 17 CFR 1.3. The Treasury Department and the IRS concluded that this definition was too narrow, because it is limited to products that can be commodities.

The Treasury Department and the IRS are considering alternative definitions of *agricultural or horticultural products* to address concerns that the definition could be interpreted inconsistently with the ordinary meaning of agricultural or horticultural products. A clarification of the definition that is under consideration is the limitation of agricultural or horticultural products to products acquired from original producers, such as farmers, planters, ranchers, dairy farmers, or nut or fruit growers, and products thereof that are MPGE by Specified Cooperatives. The Treasury Department and the IRS request comments on whether the original producer approach being considered would be appropriate, as well as other approaches to defining agricultural or horticultural products. The Treasury Department and the IRS also request comments on the impact, if any, of the proposed definition on which products are MPGE by Specified Cooperatives.

A Specified Cooperative's gross receipts from the disposition of agricultural or horticultural products qualify as DPGR if the products were MPGE by the Specified Cooperative in whole or significant part within the United States. The proposed regulations define *in whole or significant part* for these purposes in proposed §1.199A-9(h) and provide a 20 percent safe harbor for such determination in proposed §1.199A-9(h)(3).

The definition of gross receipts in proposed §1.199A-8(b)(2)(iii) is essentially the same as in §1.199-3(c) issued under former section 199, except that this definition has been modified by removing references to section 1031 (exchange of real property held for productive use or investment) and tax-exempt interest within the meaning of section 103 (interest on State and local bonds). The reference to section 1031 is removed because that provision now applies only to real property. The section 199A(g) deduction is based on gross receipts derived from the disposition of agricultural or horticultural products and section 199A(g)(3)(D)(i) expressly excludes gross receipts derived from the disposition of land from DPGR. The reference to tax-exempt interest under section 103 is removed because it is appropriate for the definition of gross receipts to include only gross receipts that are taken into account in computing gross income under the Cooperative's methods of accounting used for Federal income tax purposes for the taxable year.

The Treasury Department and the IRS welcome comments regarding all aspects of these proposed definitions, including whether there is an alternative or more appropriate definition of *Specified Cooperative* or *agricultural or horticultural products*, and clarification of when MPGE is performed in whole or significant part in the United States that would provide greater certainty for taxpayers in complying with, and the IRS in administering, the requirements for claiming the section 199A(g) deduction. The Treasury Department and the IRS also welcome comments on the appropriateness of the 20 percent safe harbor in proposed §1.199A-9(h)(3).

C. Steps for Calculating Section 199A(g) Deduction

Proposed §1.199A-8 sets forth four required steps to determine the amount of a nonexempt Specified Cooperative's section 199A(g) deduction and provides rules to determine the amount of an exempt Specified Cooperative's section 199A(g) deduction.

i. Patronage/nonpatronage Split

The first step under the rules of proposed §1.199A-8 for calculating the section 199A(g) deduction requires nonexempt Specified Cooperatives to identify the gross receipts and related deductions (other than a deduction under section 199A(g)) that are from patronage sources and from nonpatronage sources. Specified Cooperatives must separate their patronage and nonpatronage gross receipts and related deductions when determining taxable income and allocating expenses between patronage and nonpatronage income to claim the tax deductions under section 1382(b) and (c). Cooperatives that have gross receipts only from patronage sources will be unaffected. Accordingly, the proposed regulations' requirement to divide patronage/nonpatronage gross receipts and related deductions should not significantly impact the existing allocation requirements applicable to Specified Cooperatives.

This step is expressly included in these proposed rules because proposed §1.199A-8 provides that for all purposes of the section 199A(g) deduction, nonexempt Specified Cooperatives may use only patronage gross receipts and related deductions to calculate DPGR, QPAI (including oil-related QPAI), taxable income, and the W-2 wage limitation.

Separating a nonexempt Specified Cooperative's patronage items from its nonpatronage items is consistent with the structure and intent of section 199A. Section 199A in its entirety is structured to give businesses that are not operating as C corporations a deduction that corresponds to the TCJA's reduction of the top corporate rate of tax under section 11. C corporations are expressly prohibited under section 199A(a) from claiming a section 199A(a) deduction, and under section 199A(g)(2)(D)(i) from claiming a section 199A(g) deduction. Although section 199A(g) provides a deduction for Specified Cooperatives, the statutory prohibitions preventing C corporations from benefiting under section 199A(g) (which were absent from the statutory text of former section 199) are in conflict with permitting a section 199A(g) deduction for the nonpatronage business of a nonexempt Specified Cooperative. Instead, nonpatronage source income of a nonexempt Specified Cooperative receives an alternate benefit shared by other C corporations: the TCJA's reduction of the top rate of tax under section 11 from 35 percent to 21 percent.

Moreover, the 2018 Act amended section 199A to address concerns that the TCJA created an unintended incentive for farmers and other producers to sell their agricultural or horticultural products to Cooperatives over independent buyers. The amendment to section 199A was intended to ensure a level playing field between Cooperatives and independent buyers. Without the split between patronage and nonpatronage businesses, Specified Cooperatives that may benefit from both a section 199A(g) deduction (from which taxpayers other than Specified Cooperatives cannot benefit) and the reduced corporate tax rate on nonpatronage business would be significantly advantaged over independent buyers who could benefit only from the reduced corporate tax rate under section 11.

Accordingly, the Treasury Department and the IRS have determined that it is appropriate to limit the source of the gross receipts and related deductions taken into account for purposes of the section 199A(g) deduction for nonexempt Specified Cooperatives to items properly allocated to a nonexempt Specified Cooperative's patronage business. The Treasury Department and the IRS request comments regarding these proposed rules, including comments explaining any policy rationale that would justify treating the nonpatronage business of a nonexempt Specified Cooperative differently from the business operations of any other C corporation subject to the tax imposed under section 11.

ii. *Identifying Patronage DPGR*

The second step set forth in proposed §1.199A-8 is for nonexempt Specified Cooperatives to identify patronage gross receipts that qualify as DPGR. The rules in proposed §1.199A-8 point nonexempt Specified Cooperatives to proposed §1.199A-9 for additional information on DPGR. The rules in proposed §1.199A-9 do not refer to gross receipts from patronage or nonpatronage business because the rules only provide additional information supplementing the determination of DPGR from dispositions of agricultural or horticultural products. When applying §1.199A-9, which occurs after step 1 in §1.199A-8, the only gross receipts of a nonexempt Specified Cooperative considered would be those derived from patronage sources. Proposed §1.199A-9 is essentially the same as §§1.199-1 and 1.199-3 issued under former section 199, adjusted to apply to Specified Cooperatives.

iii. *Calculating Patronage QPAI*

The third step set forth in proposed §1.199A-8 is for nonexempt Specified Cooperatives to calculate QPAI (including oil-related QPAI) from only their patronage DPGR. To do this, nonexempt Specified Cooperatives must determine COGS and other expenses, losses, or deductions that are allocable to patronage DPGR. Nonexempt Specified Cooperatives are directed to consult proposed §1.199A-10 for additional information on making these allocations. Proposed §1.199A-10 does not refer to patronage or nonpatronage QPAI or DPGR because it only provides additional information supplementing the QPAI calculation. Proposed §1.199A-10 is essentially the same as §1.199-4 issued under former section 199, adjusted to apply to Specified Cooperatives.

iv. *Calculating Patronage Section 199A(g) Deduction*

The fourth and final step set forth in proposed §1.199A-8 is for nonexempt Specified Cooperatives to calculate their section 199A(g) deduction, which is equal to 9 percent of the lesser of QPAI or taxable income, and subject to the W-2 wage limitation. Nonexempt Specified Cooperatives are directed to consult proposed §1.199A-11 for additional information on the W-2 wage limitation. Proposed §1.199A-11 does not refer to patronage or nonpatronage QPAI, taxable income, or W-2 wages because it only provides additional information supplementing the W-2 wage limitation. Proposed §1.199A-11 is essentially the same as §1.199-2 issued under former section 199, adjusted to apply to Specified Cooperatives.

v. *Exempt Specified Cooperatives*

Proposed §1.199A-8(c) provides that exempt Specified Cooperatives calculate two separate section 199A(g) deductions, one based on gross receipts and related deductions from patronage sources, and one based on gross receipts and related deductions from nonpatronage sources. Like a nonexempt Specified Cooperative, an exempt Specified Cooperative earns patronage income that is not taxed to the extent of any section 1382(b) deduction for patronage distributions made to patrons. Exempt Specified Cooperatives are also not taxed on any nonpatronage income to the extent of any section 1382(c) deduction for nonpatronage distributions. Unlike the usual taxation of C corporations, the section 1382 deductions allow an exempt Specified Cooperative to be treated more like a passthrough entity by reducing the exempt Specified Cooperative's patronage and nonpatronage income. It is therefore appropriate that the exempt Specified Cooperatives may take a section 199A(g) deduction on both patronage and nonpatronage income that could be deducted under section 1382(b) and (c)(2).

As described earlier, calculating two section 199A(g) deductions is consistent with the administration of former section 199. To calculate the two section 199A(g) deductions, an exempt Specified Cooperative is required under proposed §1.199A-8 to perform steps two through four twice, first using only its patronage gross receipts and related deductions and second using only its nonpatronage gross receipts and related deductions. An exempt Specified Cooperative cannot combine, merge, or net patronage and nonpatronage items at any step in determining its patronage section 199A(g) deduction and its nonpatronage section 199A(g) deduction.

D. *Special Rule for Oil-Related QPAI*

Section 199A(g)(5)(E) contains a special rule for Specified Cooperatives with oil-related QPAI, which requires a reduction by 3 percent of the least of oil-related QPAI, QPAI, or taxable income of the Specified Cooperative for the taxable year. The language of this rule is the same as the language used in former section 199(d)(9). Former section 199(d)(9), which applied to taxable years beginning after December 31, 2008, was added by section 401(a), Division B of the Energy Extension Act of 2008, Public Law 110-343, 122 Stat. 3765 (2008). These proposed rules include rules for oil-related QPAI that are similar to those contained in proposed regulations (REG-136459-09) relating to the section 199 deduction published in the *Federal Register* (80 FR 51978) on August 27, 2015 (2015 Proposed Regulations).

The 2015 Proposed Regulations included rules related to a taxpayer's determination of oil-related QPAI (with respect to which no comments were received). Although not finalized, the 2015 Proposed Regulations are the only existing guidance concerning a taxpayer's determination of oil-related QPAI. The preamble to the 2015 Proposed Regulations includes an explanation of the reasons supporting the proposed provisions, and these reasons continue to apply. These reasons include the determination that gross receipts from transportation and distribution of oil are not included in the calculation of oil-related QPAI, unless the gross receipts are considered DPGR under the de minimis rule or an exception for embedded services now contained in proposed §1.199A-9. Gross receipts from transportation and distribution are not included in QPAI and DPGR (unless an exception applies), and therefore it is appropriate to exclude such gross receipts when calculating oil-related QPAI.

E. *Rules for Passing Section 199A(g) Deduction to Patrons*

Once a Specified Cooperative calculates the section 199A(g) deduction, it may pass on the section 199A(g) deduction to patrons who are eligible taxpayers as defined in section 199A(g)(2)(D), that is, (i) a patron that is other than a C corporation or (ii) a patron that is a Specified Cooperative. Section 199A(g)(2)(A) requires the Specified Cooperative to identify the amount of the section 199A(g) deduction being passed to a patron in a notice (required by proposed § 1.199A-8(d)(3)) mailed to the eligible patron during the payment period described in section 1382(d). The amount of the section 199A(g) deduction that a Specified Cooperative can pass through to an eligible taxpayer is limited to the portion of the section 199A(g) deduction that is allowed with respect to the QPAI to which the qualified payments made to the eligible taxpayer are attributable. Section 199A(g)(2)(E) defines qualified payments as those that are included in the eligible taxpayer's income under section 1385(a)(1) and (3) (referencing patronage dividends and per-unit retain allocations). Proposed § 1.199A-8 further provides that a Specified Cooperative that receives a section 199A(g) deduction as an eligible taxpayer can take the deduction only against patronage gross income and related deductions, or pass on the deduction to its patrons that are eligible taxpayers. The proposed rules do not allow an exempt Specified Cooperative to pass through any of the section 199A(g) deduction attributable to nonpatronage activities because no QPAI is attributable to any qualified payments. The rules of proposed § 1.199A-8 are essentially the same as the rules of § 1.199-6, adjusted to include other provisions of the section 199 final regulations as well as proposed rules set forth in the 2015 Proposed Regulations.

F. *Cooperative as a Partner in a Partnership*

Proposed § 1.199A-8(f) provides guidance regarding circumstances in which a Specified Cooperative is a partner in a partnership as described under section 199A(g)(5)(B). The proposed rules provide that the partnership must separately identify and report on the Schedule K-1 to the Form 1065, U.S. Return of Partnership Income, (or any successor form) issued to its partner, unless otherwise provided by the instructions to the Form, the Specified Cooperative's allocable share of gross receipts and related deductions. This allows the Specified Cooperative partner to apply the four steps in proposed § 1.199A-8 required to calculate its patronage section 199A(g) deduction (or patronage and nonpatronage section 199A(g) deductions in the case of an exempt Specified Cooperative).

III. *Proposed § 1.199A-9, Domestic Production Gross Receipts*

A. *In General*

Section 199A(g)(3)(D) defines the term *domestic production gross receipts* to mean gross receipts of a Specified Cooperative derived from any lease, rental, license, sale, exchange, or other disposition (collectively, a "disposition") of any agricultural or horticultural product which was MPGE (determined after application of section 199A(g)(4)(B)) by the Specified Cooperative in whole or significant part within the United States. Such term does not include gross receipts of the Specified Cooperative derived from a disposition of land or from services. These proposed regulations are based on § 1.199-3 issued under former section 199, but remove provisions that would not apply to the disposition of agricultural or horticultural products.

DPGR includes the gross receipts that a Specified Cooperative derives from marketing agricultural or horticultural products for patrons. Section 199A(g)(4)(B) treats marketing Specified Cooperatives as having MPGE any agricultural or horticultural product in whole or significant part within the United States if their patrons have done so. The Treasury Department and the IRS considered whether this rule should apply between Specified Cooperatives and patrons taxed as C corporations. These proposed regulations allow attribution to apply as provided in section 199A(g)(4)(B) because the statute does not distinguish between types of patrons. However, these proposed regulations do not allow a Specified Cooperative to pass through to a C corporation any of the section 199A(g) deduction of the Specified Cooperative attributable to the disposition of such agricultural or horticultural products. This is because, under section 199A(g)(2)(D), taxpayers taxed as C corporations are not eligible to claim a section 199A(g) deduction from the Specified Cooperative. These proposed regulations incorporate the rules from § 1.199-1(d)(1) through (3) and (e), issued under former section 199, as applicable. These rules relate to the allocation of gross receipts between DPGR and non-DPGR, and the determination of whether an allocation method is reasonable. Further, the rules include provisions permitting Specified Cooperatives to treat de minimis gross receipts as DPGR or non-DPGR without allocating such gross receipts, and a provision permitting the use of historical data to allocate gross receipts for certain multiple-year transactions. The Treasury Department and the IRS welcome comments regarding all aspects of these proposed rules. When incorporating these concepts from the former section 199 regulations, the Treasury Department and the IRS determined that the appropriate section of these proposed regulations in which to include such guidance was proposed § 1.199A-9. This is not a substantive change, but rather a reorganization to improve clarity.

B. *Definition of Manufactured, Produced, Grown, Extracted*

The definition of the term *MPGE* is included in proposed § 1.199A-9 and is generally consistent with the definition in § 1.199-3(e)(1). However, these proposed regulations revise the rule in § 1.199-3(e)(2) by removing the concept of minor assembly. In the 2015 Proposed Regulations, the Treasury Department and the IRS requested comments on defining the term *minor assembly* because of the difficulty in identifying a widely applicable objective test. Based on the comments received and the restriction on the section 199A(g) deduction to agricultural or horticultural products, proposed § 1.199A-9 does not include the term *minor assembly* included in § 1.199-3(e)(2). This exclusion does not impact a taxpayer's obligation to meet all of the other requirements to qualify for the section 199A(g) deduction. The Treasury Department and the IRS request comments on whether the concept of minor assembly should be retained and, if so, how this term should be defined.

C. *By the Taxpayer*

With respect to the phrase "by the taxpayer" as used in section 199A(g)(3)(D)(i), these proposed regulations adopt the rule from § 1.199-3(f)(1) as applicable, rather than the rule in the 2015 Proposed Regulations. In a contract manufacturing arrangement, this means that a Specified Cooperative must have the benefits and burdens of ownership of the agricultural or horticultural product during the period in which the MPGE activity occurs in order for the Specified Cooperative to be treated as engaging in such MPGE activity. The 2015 Proposed Regulations provided a different rule for contract manufacturing arrangements. The 2015 Proposed Regulations provided that if a qualifying activity is performed under a contract, then the party that performs the qualifying activity is the taxpayer for purposes of section 199(c)(4)(A)(i). Under the rule in the 2015 Proposed Regulations, a Specified Cooperative that contracts with another party for the MPGE of an agricultural or horticultural product would never qualify as "the taxpayer" for purposes of the section 199A(g) deduction. This result fails to provide any incentive for Specified Cooperatives to retain the benefits and burdens of ownership and to ensure that production occurs within the United States. Therefore, to maintain such an incentive, the proposed regulations maintain the rule from § 1.199-3(f)(1). The Treasury Department and the IRS request comments on the continued use of the rule from § 1.199-3(f)(1).

D. *Other Provisions in Proposed § 1.199A-9*

The remainder of the rules in proposed § 1.199A-9 are based on the existing regulations in § 1.199-3. These rules should be interpreted in a manner consistent with the interpretation under former section 199. The Treasury Department and the IRS request comments on any conception or definition that in application would be over or under-inclusive under the proposed regulations, or any instances where they should interpret the rules differently from the interpretation under former section 199.

IV. *Proposed § 1.199A-10, Costs Allocable to DPGR*

Proposed § 1.199A-10 provides guidance on the allocation of costs to DPGR. This section provides rules for allocating a taxpayer's COGS, as well as other expenses, losses, and deductions properly allocable to DPGR. These proposed regulations are based on and follow the section 199 regulations in § 1.199-4.

V. Proposed § 1.199A-11, Wage Limitation

Proposed § 1.199A-11 provides guidance regarding the W-2 wage limitation on the section 199A(g) deduction. A notice of proposed revenue procedure, Notice 2019-27, 2019-31 IRB, which proposes a draft revenue procedure providing three proposed methods that Specified Cooperatives may use for calculating W-2 wages, is being issued concurrently with this notice of proposed rulemaking. The guidance contained in the notice of proposed revenue procedure is necessary because changes may be made to the underlying Form W-2, Wage and Tax Statement, on a more frequent basis than updates to the regulations under section 199A(g), for regulatory and statutory reasons independent of section 199A. The three proposed methods for calculating W-2 wages in the notice are substantially similar to the methods provided in Rev. Proc. 2006-47, 2006-2 C.B. 869 (relating to the section 199 deduction), and Rev. Proc. 2019-11, 2019-09 IRB 742 (relating to the section 199A(a) deduction). The Treasury Department and the IRS propose these methods in a notice of proposed revenue procedure rather than in the notice of proposed rulemaking to maintain consistency with the rules under former section 199 and the rules under section 199A. The notice of proposed revenue procedure invites comments from the public.

Under the proposed regulations, W-2 wages for the purpose of the wage limitation in section 199A(g) are generally determined in a manner that is similar to the manner in which W-2 wages are determined for the purpose of the deduction under section 199A(a) (that is, using the definition of W-2 wages under section 199A(b)(4)), with three significant differences. First, section 199A(g)(1)(B)(ii) provides that W-2 wages are determined without regard to section 199A(b)(4)(B), which excludes from the definition amounts not properly allocable to QBI for purposes of section 199A(c)(1). Second, W-2 wages under section 199A(g) do not include any amount that is not properly allocable to DPGR. Finally, W-2 wages under section 199A(g) do not generally include any remuneration paid for services in the commonwealth of Puerto Rico and other United States territories. Specifically, section 199A(g)(1)(B)(ii) provides that W-2 wages are determined in the same manner as under section 199A(b)(4), and section 199A(b)(4)(A) defines wages as amounts described in section 6051(a)(3) and (8). The amounts described in section 6051(a)(3) are "wages as defined in section 3401(a)." Section 3401(a)(8) generally excludes from the definition of wages in section 3401(a) wages paid with respect to employment in the commonwealth of Puerto Rico and other United States territories. Therefore, wages paid with respect to employment in the commonwealth of Puerto Rico and other United States territories are generally not W-2 wages within the meaning of section 199A(b)(4)(A). This contrasts with the section 199A(a) deduction for which section 199A(f)(1)(C)(ii) allows certain taxpayers with QBI from sources within the commonwealth of Puerto Rico (section 199A(f)(1)(C)(ii) applies only to Puerto Rico and not to other United States territories) to compute section 199A(b)(4) W-2 wages without regard to section 3401(a)(8). Since the section 199A(g) deduction is determined based on QPAI, not QBI, section 199A(f)(1)(C)(ii) does not apply to the deduction under section 199A(g). Given the distinction between QBI and QPAI on which the section 199A(a) and section 199A(g) deductions are respectively provided, and the absence of a provision similar to 199A(f)(1)(C)(ii) with respect to QPAI, the Treasury Department and the IRS have determined that remuneration paid with respect to employment in the commonwealth of Puerto Rico cannot be used in determining W-2 wages for purposes of section 199A(g). The Treasury Department and the IRS request comments with respect to this determination.

VI. Proposed § 1.199A-12, EAG Rules

Proposed § 1.199A-12 provides guidance on the application of section 199A(g) to an EAG under section 199A(g)(5)(A)(iii) that includes a Specified Cooperative. Unlike the section 199 deduction, the section 199A(g) deduction is limited to Specified Cooperatives. These proposed regulations address how the rules separating patronage and nonpatronage income and deductions apply in the context of an EAG. Proposed § 1.199A-12 provides that in the case of nonexempt Specified Cooperatives, attribution between the members of an EAG is allowed provided the DPGR and related deductions are patronage. In the case of exempt Specified Cooperatives, attribution is allowed in all events because exempt Specified Cooperatives are allowed to take a separate 199A(g) deduction on both their patronage and nonpatronage income.

Proposed § 1.199A-12 also provides certain rules for partnerships owned by an EAG as described in section 199A(g)(5)(A)(ii).

VII. Proposed § 1.1388-1(f)

Proposed § 1.1388-1(f) sets forth a definition of *patronage and nonpatronage* that is consistent with the current case law under section 1388. Specifically, the proposed definition adopts the directly related test, which is a fact specific test for determining whether income and deductions of a Cooperative are patronage or nonpatronage. The Treasury Department and the IRS request comments with respect to this definition.

VIII. Proposed Removal of Section 199 Regulations and Withdrawal of 2015 Proposed Regulations

In light of the TCJA, the Treasury Department and the IRS propose to remove the section 199 regulations (§§ 1.199-0 through 1.199-9) and withdraw the 2015 Proposed Regulations because the regulations interpret a provision of the Code that has been repealed for taxable years beginning after December 31, 2017.

The proposed removal of these regulations is unrelated to the substance of the rules in the regulations, and no negative inference regarding the stated rules should be made. Such regulations are proposed to be removed from the Code of Federal Regulations (CFR) solely because they have no future applicability. Removal of these regulations is not intended to alter any non-regulatory guidance that cites to or relies upon these regulations. These regulations as contained in 26 CFR part 1, revised April 1, 2019, remain applicable to determining eligibility for the section 199 deduction for any taxable year that began before January 1, 2018. The beginning date of the taxable year of a partnership, S corporation, or a non-grantor trust or estate, rather than the taxable year of a partner, shareholder, or beneficiary is used to determine items that are taken into account for purposes of calculating a section 199 deduction. This is consistent with the initial application of section 199 in 2005. Items arising from a passthrough entity that had a fiscal year beginning before 2005 were not taken into account by calendar-year partners for purposes of the section 199 deduction. Public Law 109-135, section 102(a) (Gulf Opportunity Zone Act of 2005). Further, when section 199 was amended to narrow the definition of W-2 wages, the amendment was effective for taxable years beginning after May 17, 2006. *See* Public Law 109-222, section 514(a) (Tax Increase Prevention and Reconciliation Act of 2005). Under the transition rule in § 1.199-5(b)(4), partners and partnerships used the taxable year of the partnerships to determine the applicable definition of W-2 wages, and there are similar rules in § 1.199-5(c)(4) for S corporations and § 1.199-5(e)(3) for non-grantor trusts and estates.

Proposed Effective/Applicability Date

Section 7805(b)(1)(A) and (B) of the Code generally provide that no temporary, proposed, or final regulation relating to the internal revenue laws may apply to any taxable period ending before the earliest of (A) the date on which such regulation is filed with the *Federal Register*, or (B) in the case of a final regulation, the date on which a proposed or temporary regulation to which the final regulation relates was filed with the *Federal Register*.

Consistent with authority provided by section 7805(b)(1)(A), the proposed regulations are proposed to apply to taxable years beginning after the date of publication of a Treasury decision adopting these rules as final regulations in the *Federal Register*. Taxpayers may rely upon these proposed regulations, in their entirety, before the date of publication of the Treasury Decision adopting these rules as final regulations in the *Federal Register*.

Special Analyses

I. *Regulatory Planning and Review - Economic Analysis*

Executive Orders 13563 and 12866 direct agencies to assess costs and benefits of available regulatory alternatives and, if regulation is necessary, to select regulatory approaches that maximize net benefits (including potential economic, environmental, public health and safety effects, distributive impacts, and equity). Executive Order 13563 emphasizes the importance of quantifying both costs and benefits, of reducing costs, of harmonizing rules, and of promoting flexibility.

These proposed regulations have been designated by the Office of Management and Budget's Office of Information and Regulatory Affairs (OIRA) as subject to review under Executive Order 12866 pursuant to the Memorandum of Agreement (April 11, 2018) between the Treasury Department and the Office of Management and Budget regarding review of tax regulations. OIRA has determined that the proposed rulemaking is significant and subject to review under Executive Order 12866 and section 1(b) of the Memorandum of Agreement. Accordingly, the proposed regulations have been reviewed by the Office of Management and Budget.

In addition, the Treasury Department and the IRS expect the proposed regulations, when final, to be an Executive Order 13771 regulatory action and request comment on this designation.

A. *Background and Overview*

The TCJA repealed section 199, which provided a deduction for income attributable to domestic production activities. In its place it created section 199A, which provides a deduction for qualified business income derived from passthrough businesses - such as sole proprietorships, partnerships, and S corporations - engaged in domestic trades or businesses. While the repealed section 199 deduction was generally available to all taxpayers, the section 199A deduction is available only to taxpayers other than C corporations. On March 23, 2018, the 2018 Act modified section 199A(g) to provide deductions for Specified Cooperatives and their patrons that are substantially similar to those under the repealed section 199 deduction. Accordingly, these regulations generally formalize prior and current practices based on the rules under former section 199. The 2018 Act also added section 199A(b)(7), which requires patrons of Specified Cooperatives to reduce their section 199A(a) deduction if those patrons receive qualified payments from Specified Cooperatives.

The estimated number of Cooperatives affected by the 2018 Act and these proposed regulations is 9,000, including approximately 2,000 Specified Cooperatives, based on 2017 tax filings.

B. *Need for the Proposed Regulations*

The proposed regulations provide guidance regarding the application of sections 199A(a), 199A(b)(7), and 199A(g) to Cooperatives, Specified Cooperatives, and their patrons. The proposed regulations are needed because the 2018 Act introduced a number of terms and calculations. Patrons, Cooperatives, and Specified Cooperatives would benefit from greater specificity regarding these and other items.

C. *Economic Analysis*

1. Baseline

The Treasury Department and the IRS have assessed the benefits and costs of the proposed regulations relative to a no-action baseline reflecting anticipated Federal income tax-related behavior in the absence of these proposed regulations.

2. Economic Rationale for Issuing Guidance for the 2018 Act

The Treasury Department and the IRS anticipate that the issuance of guidance pertaining to sections 199A(a), 199A(b)(7), and 199A(g) of the 2018 Act to Cooperatives, Specified Cooperatives, and their patrons will provide a net economic benefit to the overall U.S. economy.

The proposed regulations clarify a number of concepts related to the section 199A(a) deduction for patrons of Cooperatives, provide guidance to patrons of Specified Cooperatives who may be required to reduce their section 199A(a) deduction under section 199A(b)(7), and provide guidance to Specified Cooperatives on the section 199A(g) deduction on income attributable to their domestic production activities. In the absence of guidance, affected taxpayers would have to calculate their tax liability without the definitions and clarifications provided by the proposed regulations, a situation that is generally considered more burdensome and could lead to greater conflicts with tax administrators. Thus, the Treasury Department and the IRS project that the proposed regulations will reduce taxpayer compliance burden and the costs of tax administration relative to not issuing any such guidance.

This guidance also ensures that section 199A deductions are calculated similarly across taxpayers, avoiding situations where one taxpayer receives preferential treatment over another for fundamentally similar economic activity. For example, in the absence of these proposed regulations, a Specified Cooperative may have uncertainty over what type of income is eligible for the section 199A(g) deduction. If a Specified Cooperative claimed the section 199A(g) deduction on income that already benefits from a lower corporate tax rate, this would confer an unintended economic benefit to the Specified Cooperative over other C corporations performing identical activities that only benefit from a lower corporate tax rate. As discussed further below, this guidance prevents the introduction of distortions of economic decisions in the agricultural or horticultural sector.

In the absence of these proposed regulations, uncertainty over statutory interpretation could lead to economic losses to the extent that taxpayers interpret the statute in ways that are inconsistent with the statute's intents and purposes. For example, a Specified Cooperative may pursue a project involving a certain product that is only profitable if that product is deemed "agricultural or horticultural" and thus eligible for the section 199A(g) deduction. If, in fact, this product is ineligible for the deduction based on the intents and purposes of the statute, then the project should not have been pursued and this results in an economic loss. Alternatively, without a definition of "agricultural or horticultural," a Specified Cooperative may incorrectly assume that a project is not eligible for the deduction and not pursue the project, which could also result in an economic loss. In such cases, guidance provides value by bringing economic decisions closer in line with Congress' intent or, when such intent is broad, with decisions that are economically efficient contingent on the overall Code. While no guidance can fully curtail all inaccurate interpretations of the statute, the proposed regulations significantly mitigate the chance for such interpretations and thereby increase economic efficiency. Due to the lack of readily available data, the Treasury Department and the IRS have not estimated the increase in United States economic activity that would arise from the proposed guidance.

The Treasury Department further projects that the issuance of guidance will reduce taxpayer compliance burden and the costs of tax administration relative to a no-action baseline. Due to the lack of readily available data, the Treasury Department has not estimated the decrease in taxpayer compliance burden nor tax administration costs arising from the issuance of guidance. The Treasury Department and the IRS request comments and information that can allow estimation of economic impacts and any changes in taxpayer compliance burden resulting from the proposed guidance.

3. Economic Analysis of Specific Provisions

The proposed regulations embody certain regulatory decisions that reflect necessary regulatory discretion. These decisions specify more fully how the 2018 Act is to be implemented.

The Treasury Department and the IRS solicit comments on the economic impacts of each of the items discussed in this section and of any other items of the proposed regulations not discussed in this section. The Treasury Department and the IRS particularly solicit comments that provide data, other evidence, or models that could enhance the rigor of the process by which provisions might be developed for the final regulations.

i. Determining Section 199A(g) Deduction

Specified Cooperatives are taxed differently depending on whether they are exempt (qualified as a cooperative under section 521) or nonexempt (qualified under rules elsewhere in the Code) and also whether their income is from patronage (generally related to the cooperative's marketing, purchasing, or services activities) or nonpatronage sources. In the case of exempt Specified Cooperatives patronage and nonpatronage source income is subject to a single level of tax at the patron level. Whereas, for nonexempt Specified Cooperatives only patronage source income is subject to a single level of tax at the patron level; nonpatronage source income is subject to a double level of tax, similar to other C corporations. Because the Code does not define *patronage and nonpatronage* source income, proposed § 1.1388-1(f) sets forth a definition of *patronage and nonpatronage* that is consistent with the current state of federal case law. Specifically, the proposed definition adopts the directly related test, which is a fact specific test for determining whether income and deductions of a Cooperative are patronage or nonpatronage. Specifying a definition that is consistent with current case law will help to minimize the economic impacts of these proposed regulations. The Treasury Department and the IRS request comments with respect to this definition.

The TCJA reduced the corporate tax rate for C corporations under section 11 and provided the section 199A deduction for domestic businesses operated as sole proprietorships or through partnerships, S corporations, trusts, or estates. The TCJA also repealed section 199, which did not preclude deductions on income earned by C corporations. The 2018 Act amended section 199A to address concerns that the TCJA created an unintended incentive for farmers to sell their agricultural or horticultural products to Specified Cooperatives over independent buyers. Specifically, the 2018 Act amended section 199A(g) to allow Specified Cooperatives and their patrons a deduction similar to the former section 199 deduction. Because the section 199A(g) deduction is not intended to benefit C corporations and their shareholders in general, the proposed regulations specify that the section 199A(g) deduction can be claimed on income that can be subject to tax only at the patron level. Under the proposed regulations, non-exempt Specified Cooperatives may not claim the section 199A(g) deductions on income that cannot be paid to patrons and deducted under section 1382(b) and exempt Specified Cooperatives may not claim section 199A(g) deductions on income that cannot be paid to patrons and deducted under sections 1382(b) or 1382(c)(2).

In the absence of these proposed regulations, a Specified Cooperative may have uncertainty as to whether non-patronage source income, which would be taxed in the same manner as a C corporation, could receive both the lower corporate tax rate and be further offset by a section 199A(g) deduction. Other C corporations performing identical activities would only benefit from the lower corporate tax rate.

The Treasury Department and the IRS have determined that this potential uncertainty as to tax treatment could distort economic decisions in the agricultural or horticultural sector. The proposed regulations avoid this outcome, promoting a more efficient allocation of resources by providing more uniform incentives across taxpayers.

ii. Definition of *Agricultural or Horticultural Products*

Proposed § 1.199A-8(a)(4) defines *agricultural or horticultural products* as agricultural, horticultural, viticultural, and dairy products, livestock and the products thereof, the products of poultry and bee raising, the edible products of forestry, and any and all products raised or produced on farms and processed or manufactured products thereof within the meaning of the Cooperative Marketing Act of 1926. Agricultural or horticultural products also include aquatic products that are farmed as well as fertilizer, diesel fuel, and other supplies used in agricultural or horticultural production that are MPGE by the Specified Cooperative. Agricultural or horticultural products, however, do not include intangible property, since agricultural or horticultural products were considered a subset of tangible property under former section 199. Intangible property (defined in § 1.199-3(j)(2)(iii)) was a separate category of property and gross receipts from intangible property did not qualify as DPGR.

The Treasury Department and the IRS considered other definitions of agricultural or horticultural products but determined that taxpayer burden and tax administration costs would be lowest under a definition that was consistent with extant law.

For example, the Treasury Department and the IRS considered a similar but alternative definition of *agricultural or horticultural* products as agricultural, horticultural, viticultural, and dairy products, livestock and poultry, bees, forest products, fish and shellfish, and any products thereof, including processed and manufactured products, and any and all products raised or produced on farms and any processed or manufactured product thereof within the meaning of the Agricultural Marketing Act of 1946. While very similar to the definition in these proposed rules, the Treasury Department and the IRS proposed using the definition based on the Cooperative Marketing Act of 1926, which specifically concerns cooperatives and with which Specified Cooperatives are familiar, unlike the Agricultural Marketing Act of 1946, which concerns the marketing and distribution of agricultural products without reference to Cooperatives. The Treasury Department and the IRS looked to the United States Department of Agriculture (USDA) for definitions because there is no definition of *agricultural or horticultural products* in the Internal Revenue Code or Income Tax Regulations and because the USDA has expertise concerning Specified Cooperatives and because Specified Cooperatives are likely familiar with USDA law.

The Treasury Department and the IRS also considered an alternative definition of *agricultural or horticultural products* based on the definition of agricultural commodities within the meaning of general regulations under the Commodity Exchange Act. The Treasury Department and the IRS concluded that this definition was too narrow, because it is limited to products that can be commodities. The use of this narrow definition would have restricted the range of products for which the section 199A(g) deduction would be otherwise be available.

The Treasury Department and the IRS request comments on other approaches to defining agricultural or horticultural products. The Treasury Department and the IRS did not attempt to provide quantitative estimates of the revenue effects or economic consequences of different designations of agricultural or horticultural products because suitable data are not readily available at this level of detail. The Treasury Department and the IRS request comments that can inform such estimation.

iii. De Minimis Threshold

In general, proposed § 1.199A-9 requires that Specified Cooperatives allocate gross receipts between domestic production gross receipts (DPGR) and non-DPGR. However, proposed § 1.199A-9(c)(3) includes a de minimis provision that allows Specified Cooperatives to allocate total gross receipts to DPGR if less than 5 percent of total gross receipts are non-DPGR or to allocate total gross receipts to non-DPGR if less than 5 percent of total gross receipts are DPGR. The Treasury Department and the IRS chose to include a de minimis rule to reduce compliance costs and simplify tax filing relative to an alternative of no de minimis rule. The de minimis threshold modestly reduces compliance costs for businesses with relatively small amounts of non-DPGR or DPGR by allowing them to avoid allocating receipts between DPGR and non-DPGR activities. The de minimis threshold is unlikely to create any substantial effects on market activity because any change in the ratio of DPGR to non-DPGR will be localized around the threshold, meaning that the movement will be a small fraction of receipts to get below the de minimis threshold.

The thresholds provided in the proposed regulations are based on the thresholds set forth in §1.199-1(d)(3). The Treasury Department and the IRS maintained the de minimis rule from the final regulations under former section 199 because the 2018 Act directed that regulations concerning the section 199A(g) deduction be based on the regulations applicable to Cooperatives and their patrons under former section 199. The Treasury Department and the IRS considered changes in the de minimis provisions but determined that changing these from provisions that were previously available would lead to taxpayer confusion. Because the de minimis provision exempts taxpayers from having to perform certain allocations, the Treasury Department and the IRS do not have sufficient information on taxpayers' use of this exemption under former section 199 to perform a quantitative analysis of the impacts of the de minimis provision.

The Treasury Department and the IRS solicit comments on the de minimis thresholds and particularly request comments that provide data, other evidence, and models that can enhance the rigor of the process by which such thresholds might be determined for the final regulations while maintaining consistency with the statute's directive that the thresholds be based on regulations issued under former section 199.

iv. Reporting Requirements

Proposed §1.199A-7(c) and (d) provide that, when a patron conducts a trade or business that receives distributions from a Cooperative, the Cooperative is required to provide the patron with qualified items of income, gain, deduction, and loss and specified service trade or business (SSTB) determinations with respect to those distributions. This increases the compliance burden on such Cooperatives. However, in the absence of these proposed regulations, the burden for determination of the amount of distributions from a Cooperative that constitute qualified items of income, gain, deduction, and loss from a non-SSTB and an SSTB would lie with the patron. Because patrons are less well positioned to acquire the relevant information to determine whether distributions from a Cooperative are qualified items of income, gain, deduction, and loss and whether items that would otherwise qualify are from an SSTB, the Treasury Department and the IRS expect that these proposed regulations will reduce overall compliance costs relative to an alternative approach of not introducing a reporting requirement.

v. Allocation Safe Harbor

If a patron receives both qualified payments and payments that are not qualified payments in a qualified trade or business, the patron must allocate those items and related deductions using a reasonable method based on all of the facts and circumstances. The proposed regulations provide a safe harbor that allows patrons who receive qualified payments in addition to other income to use a simpler method to allocate business expenses and W-2 wages between qualified payments and other gross receipts to calculate the section 199A(b)(7) reduction to the section 199A(a) deduction. The safe harbor allocation method allows patrons to allocate by ratably apportioning business expenses and W-2 wages based on the proportion that the amount of qualified payments bears to the total gross receipts used to determine QBI. This safe harbor is available to patrons with taxable incomes below the threshold amounts set forth in section 199A(e)(2).

The Treasury Department and the IRS considered an alternative of not allowing a safe harbor but determined that a safe harbor could reduce compliance costs and simplify tax filing. The threshold was set at amounts set forth in section 199A(e)(2) to avoid a proliferation of thresholds applicable to taxpayers claiming a section 199A(a) deduction. Because the threshold amounts are relatively low, the Treasury Department and the IRS expect that the safe harbor would not distort business decisions or reduce revenue to any meaningful extent.

II. *Paperwork Reduction Act*

The collections of information in these proposed regulations are in proposed §1.199A-7(c)(3), (d)(3), (f)(3), and (h)(3), as well as proposed §1.199A-8(d)(3), (f), and (h)(3). The collections of information in proposed §1.199A-7(c)(3), (d)(3), (f)(3), and (h)(3), as well as proposed §1.199A-8(d)(3) and (h)(3) will be conducted through Form 1099-PATR, while the collection of information in proposed §1.199A-8(f) will be conducted through Schedule K-1 to Form 1065. In 2018, the IRS released and invited comments on the draft of Form 1065, Schedule K-1. The IRS received no comments on the form during the comment period. Consequently, the IRS made the form available December 6, 2018 for use by the public. On February 26, 2019, the IRS invited comments on Form 1099-PATR and the comment period closed on April 29, 2019. The IRS plans to issue in the near term an additional notice with a thirty-day comment period on Form 1099-PATR. The IRS is contemplating making additional changes to those two forms as discussed below in these proposed regulations.

A. *Collections of information conducted through Form 1099-PATR*

The collection of information in proposed §1.199A-7(c)(3) requires the Cooperative to inform its patron of the amount of any distribution to the patron that constitutes qualified items of income, gain, deduction, and loss from a non-SSTB conducted directly by the Cooperative. Not all distributions to patrons are qualified items of income, gain, deduction, and loss because the source of the distribution may not be effectively connected with the conduct of a trade or business within the United States or may include interest income that is not properly allocable to the patron's trade or business. The Cooperative directly conducting the trade or business from which the distribution to the patron originates is in the best position to know how much of the distribution is qualified items of income, gain, deduction, and loss. The Cooperative is also in the best position to know if it is generating income from an SSTB. Accordingly, the collection of information is necessary for the patron to calculate correctly the patron's section 199A(a) deduction for the patron's trade or business.

The collection of information in proposed §1.199A-7(d)(3) requires the Cooperative to inform its patron of the amount of any distributions to the patron that constitutes qualified items of income, gain, deduction, and loss from an SSTB conducted directly by the Cooperative. Accordingly, the collection of information is necessary for the patron to correctly calculate the patron's section 199A(a) deduction for the patron's qualified trade or business.

The collection of information in proposed §1.199A-7(f)(3) is essential for the eligible taxpayer's calculation of the reduction in the eligible taxpayer's section 199A(a) deduction for the eligible taxpayer's trade or business that is required by section 199A(b)(7). Section 199A(g)(2)(A) requires the Specified Cooperative to identify the amount of qualified payments being distributed to an eligible taxpayer and identify the portion of the deduction allowed in a notice mailed to the eligible taxpayer during the payment period described in section 1382(d). Section 199A(b)(7) provides that an eligible taxpayer who receives qualified payments from a Specified Cooperative must reduce the eligible taxpayer's section 199A(a) deduction by an amount set forth in this section. Without the notice described in proposed §1.199A-7(f)(3), the eligible taxpayer cannot calculate the reduction required by section 199A(b)(7).

The collection of information in proposed §1.199A-8(d)(3) is necessitated by section 199A(g)(2)(A). Section 199A(g)(2)(A) permits a Specified Cooperative to pass through an amount of its section 199A(g) deduction to an eligible taxpayer. The amount of the section 199A(g) deduction that the Specified Cooperative is permitted to pass through is an amount that is allocable to the QPAI generated from qualified payments distributed to the eligible taxpayer and identified by such cooperative in a written notice mailed to such taxpayer during the payment period described in section 1382(d). Without the notice required in proposed §1.199A-8(d)(3) the eligible taxpayer would not know that the Specified Cooperative is passing a portion of its section 199A(g) deduction to the eligible taxpayer.

The collections of information in proposed §§1.199A-7(h)(3) and 1.199A-8(h)(3) are necessitated by a special transition rule in section 101 of the 2018 Act. Under this transition rule, the repeal of former section 199 for taxable years beginning after December 31, 2017, does not apply to a qualified payment received by a patron from a Specified Cooperative in a taxable year beginning after December 31, 2017, to the extent such qualified payment is attributable to QPAI with respect to which a deduction is allowable to the Specified Cooperative under former section 199 for a taxable year of the Specified Cooperative beginning before January 1, 2018. Such qualified payment remains subject to former section 199 and no deduction is allowed under section 199A(a) or (g) with respect to such qualified payment. Without these collections of information by the Specified Cooperative, the patron has no way of knowing that the patron is barred by the transition rule from using a qualified payment received that is QBI for the patron's trade or business to claim a section 199A(a) deduction for the patron's trade or business.

The collections of information in proposed §1.199A-7(c)(3), (d)(3), (f)(3), and (h)(3) as well as proposed §1.199A-8(d)(3) and (h)(3) are satisfied by providing information about qualified items of income, SSTB determinations, qualified payments, the section 199A(g) deduction, and the use of qualified payments tied to the former section 199 deduction, as applicable, on an attachment to or on the Form 1099-PATR (or any successor form) issued by the Cooperative to the patron, unless otherwise provided by the instructions to the Form.

For purposes of the Paperwork Reduction Act of 1995, (44 U.S.C. 3507(d)) (PRA), the reporting burden associated with proposed §1.199A-7(c)(3), (d)(3), (f)(3), and (h)(3) as well as proposed §1.199A-8(d)(3) and (h)(3) will be reflected in the PRA Submission associated with Form 1099-PATR (OMB control number 1545-0118). As further discussed in this section, the estimated number of respondents for the reporting burden associated with these information collections is 9,000 based on 2017 tax filings.

B. Collections of information conducted through Schedule K-1, Form 1065

The collection of information in proposed §1.199A-8(f) is required by section 199A(g)(5)(B). This section allows a Specified Cooperative that is a partner in a partnership to use its allocable share of gross receipts and related deductions to calculate its section 199A(g) deduction. The proposed rules provide that the partnership must separately identify and report the allocable share of gross receipts and related deductions on or attached to the Schedule K-1 to the Form 1065 (or any successor form) issued to a Specified Cooperative partner, unless otherwise provided by the instructions to the Form. Without this reporting, the Specified Cooperative partner would not have the information necessary to calculate its section 199A(g) deduction from its activities with the partnership.

The Schedule K-1 to the Form 1065 will be modified to include a mechanism to report the Specified Cooperative partner's allocable share of gross receipts and related deductions. The collection of information in proposed §1.199A-8(f) is satisfied when the partnership provides the required information to its Specified Cooperative partners on or attached to the Schedule K-1 of Form 1065 (or any successor form), unless otherwise provided by the instructions to the Form. For purposes of the PRA, the reporting burden associated with proposed §1.199A-8(f) will be reflected in the PRA Submission associated with Form 1065 (OMB control number 1545-0123). As provided in this section, the estimated number of respondents for the reporting burden associated with these information collections is 407 based on 2017 tax filings.

C. Revised tax forms

The revised tax forms are as follows:

	New	Revision of existing form	Number of respondents
Form 1099-PATR		✓	9,000
Schedule K-1 (Form 1065)		✓	407

The current status of the PRA submissions related to the tax forms that will be revised as a result of the information collections in the proposed regulations is provided in the accompanying table. As described previously, the burdens associated with proposed §1.199A-7(c)(3), (d)(3), (f)(3), and (h)(3) as well as proposed §§1.199A-8(d)(3) and (h)(3) will be included in the aggregated burden estimates for OMB control number 1545-0118, which represents a total estimated burden time of 509,895 hours and total estimated monetized costs of $44.733 million ($2018). The burdens associated with the information collection in proposed §1.199A-8(f) will be included in the aggregated burden estimates for OMB control number 1545-0123, which represents a total estimated burden time for all forms and schedules of 3.157 billion hours and total estimated monetized costs of $58.148 billion ($2017). The overall burden estimates provided for 1545-0118 and 1545-0123 are aggregate amounts that relate to all information collections associated with the applicable OMB control number.

No burden estimates specific to the forms affected by the proposed regulations are currently available. The Treasury Department and the IRS have not estimated the burden, including that of any new information collections, related to the requirements under the proposed regulations. Those estimates would need to capture both changes made by the 2018 Act and those that arise out of discretionary authority exercised in the proposed regulations. The Treasury Department and the IRS request comments on all aspects of information collection burdens related to the proposed regulations, including estimates for how much time it would take to comply with the paperwork burdens described above for each relevant form and ways for the IRS to minimize the paperwork burden. Proposed revisions to these forms that reflect the information collections contained in these proposed regulations will be made available for public comment at *https://apps.irs.gov/app/picklist/list/draftTaxForms.htm* and will not be finalized until after these forms have been approved by OMB under the PRA.

Form	Type of Filer	OMB Number(s)	Status
Form 1099-PATR	[Business (Legacy Model)]	1545-0118	Existing collection of information approved by OIRA on 6/3/2016. Public comments will be sought on a revised collection of information that will be submitted for OIRA review before 6/30/2019.
	Link: https://www.reginfo.gov/public/do/PRAViewICR?ref_nbr=201602-1545-024		
Form 1065, Schedule K-1	Business (NEW Model)	1545-0123	Published in the *Federal Register* on 10/11/18. Public Comment period closed on 12/10/18. Approved by OIRA on 12/21/18.
	Link: https://www.federalregister.gov/documents/2018/10/09/2018-21846/proposed-collection-comment-request-for-forms-1065-1065-b-1066-1120-1120-c-1120-f-1120-h-1120-nd		

III. *Regulatory Flexibility Act*

As described in more detail in this section, pursuant to the Regulatory Flexibility Act (RFA), 5 U.S.C. chapter 6, the Treasury Department and the IRS hereby certify that these proposed regulations will not have a significant economic impact on a substantial number of small entities. Notwithstanding this certification, the Treasury Department and the IRS invite comments on any impact this rule would have on small entities.

A. *Proposed § 1.199A-7(c)(3) and (d)(3)*

Although proposed § 1.199A-7(c)(3) and (d)(3) will have an impact on a substantial number of small entities, the economic impact will not be significant. The IRS creates the Business Master File which contains data from Form 1120-C, U.S. Income Tax Return for Cooperative Associations. According to the Business Master File data, in 2017, the IRS received approximately 9,000 Forms 1120-C from Cooperatives. Under the North American Industry Classification System (NAICS), a Cooperative is considered a small entity if it has less than $750,000 in annual gross receipts. Approximately 4,050 (45 percent) of the 9,000 filers of Forms 1120-C reported annual gross receipts of less than $750,000. Therefore, a substantial number of small entities are affected by the requirements in proposed § 1.199A-7(c)(3) and (d)(3).

Proposed § 1.199A-7 provides rules similar to those provided in § 1.199A-6. In § 1.199A-6, relevant passthrough entities (RPEs) are not permitted to take the section 199A deduction but are required to determine and report the information necessary for their direct and indirect owners to determine their individual section 199A(a) deductions. Section 1.199A-6 requires RPEs to determine and report on or attach to the RPEs' Schedule K-1s to the Form 1065 for each trade or business in which the RPE was directly engaged four items: (1) The amount of QBI, (2) W-2 wages, (3) UBIA of qualified property, and (4) SSTBs.

Although Cooperatives are not RPEs, Cooperatives make distributions to patrons that such patrons are permitted to include in calculating their individual section 199A(a) deductions. Proposed § 1.199A-7(c) and (d) require the Cooperatives to determine and report to their patrons whether the distributions for which the Cooperatives take deductions under section 1382(b) and/or (c)(2), as applicable, constitute qualified items of income, gain, deduction, and loss and whether they are from an SSTB in which the Cooperative was directly engaged.

In TD 9847 the Treasury Department and the IRS determined that the reporting burden in § 1.199A-6 was estimated at 30 minutes to 20 hours, depending on individual circumstances, with an estimated average of 2.5 hours for all affected entities, regardless of size. The burden on entities with business receipts below $10 million was expected to be at the lower end of the range (30 minutes to 2.5 hours). The estimated compliance burden for passthrough entities that issue Schedules K-1 is $53 per hour. This estimate was derived from the Business Taxpayer Burden model developed by the IRS's Office of Research, Applied Analytics, and Statistics (RAAS), which relates time and out-of-pocket costs of business tax preparation, derived from survey data, to assets and receipts of affected taxpayers along with other relevant variables. *See* Tax Compliance Burden (John Guyton et al., July 2018) at https://www.irs.gov/pub/irs-soi/d13315.pdf. Thus, the annual aggregate burden on businesses with gross receipts below $10 million was estimated to be between $19.50 and $132.50 per business. The Treasury Department and the IRS determined in TD 9847 that the requirements in § 1.199A-6 imposed no significant economic impact on affected entities.

The reporting requirements under proposed § 1.199A-7(c)(3) and (d)(3) require Specified Cooperatives to report only two of the four pieces of information RPEs are required to report under proposed § 1.199A-6: the amount of qualified items of income, gain, deduction, and loss and whether the distributions are from an SSTB in which the Cooperative was directly engaged.

The burden imposed by proposed § 1.199A-7(c)(3) and (d)(3) only occurs when a Cooperative has net income that it may distribute to its patrons such that the income will qualify for the income tax deductions under section 1382(b) and/or (c), as applicable. With respect to this net income, Cooperatives already know the source of their income and deductions without which information they would not be able to determine the correct distributions to their patrons and to claim the income tax deduction for these distributions under section 1382(b) and/or (c)(2), as applicable. Finally, assuming that the approximately 4,050 filers of Forms 1120-C that reported annual gross receipts of less than $750,000 in 2017 and that each business incurred half of the higher figure of $132.50 ($66.25) determined for the § 1.199A-6 regulations to satisfy the reporting requirements under proposed § 1.199A-7(c)(3) and (d)(3), the annual burden imposed by the reporting requirements would not exceed $66.25 per business. Accordingly, the Treasury Department and the IRS conclude that the requirements in proposed § 1.199A-7(c)(3) and (d)(3) will not impose a significant economic impact on small entities.

B. *Proposed §§ 1.199A-7(h)(3) and 1.199A-8(h)(3)*

Although proposed §§ 1.199A-7(h)(3) and 1.199A-8(h)(3) will have an impact on a substantial number of small entities, this economic impact will not be significant. As previously noted, in 2017, approximately 45 percent of Cooperatives reported on Forms 1120-C gross receipts of less than $750,000. Therefore, a substantial number of small entities are affected by proposed §§ 1.199A-7(h)(3) and 1.199A-8(h)(3).

Proposed §§ 1.199A-7(h)(3) and 1.199A-8(h)(3) requires Cooperatives to notify patrons if, pursuant to the transition rule in section 101 of the 2018 Act, the patron is barred from using certain qualified payments from a Cooperative to claim a section 199A(a) deduction in a taxable year because these qualified payments are attributable to QPAI with respect to which a deduction is allowable to the Cooperative under former section 199 in a taxable year beginning before January 1, 2018. The Cooperative knows which patrons are impacted since, in order to claim its deduction under former section 199, the Cooperative must identify which qualified payments to use. The Treasury Department and the IRS estimate that the annual burden imposed by the requirement in proposed §§ 1.199A-7(h)(3) and 1.199A-8(h)(3) will be far less than the $66.25 per business estimated for the requirements in proposed §§ 1.199A-7(c)(3) and 1.199A-8(c)(3) discussed above, since the Cooperatives know which patrons are impacted and the reporting is limited to informing these patrons that they cannot use such qualified payments to calculate their section 199A(a) deduction.

In addition, absent notice from the Cooperatives, patrons would have no way of determining whether they were barred from claiming the section 199A(a) deduction using such qualified payments. Finally, Cooperatives are not able to claim a deduction under former section 199 for taxable years beginning after December 31, 2017. Therefore, the reporting required by proposed §§ 1.199A-7(h)(3) and 1.199A-8(h)(3) will be for a short duration and have a limited impact on Cooperatives. Accordingly, for all these reasons, the requirements in proposed §§ 1.199A-7(h)(3) and 1.199A-8(h)(3) will not impose a significant economic impact on small entities.

C. *Proposed §§ 1.199A-7(f)(3) and 1.199A-8(d)(3)*

Sections 1.199A-7(f)(3) and 1.199A-8(d)(3) will not have a significant economic impact on a substantial number of small entities. This claim is based on the fact that this rulemaking will impact a population of Specified Cooperatives, only a small percentage of which are considered small entities. According to the Business Master File filing data from the transcribed fields from the Forms 1120-C for 2017, of the approximately 9,000 Forms 1120-C filed by Cooperatives, approximately 2,000 filers identified their Cooperatives as involving agriculture or horticulture using the NAICS. As noted previously, a Cooperative is considered small if it reports less than $750,000 in annual gross receipts. Of the 2,000 filers of Forms 1120-C identifying as Specified Cooperatives, only 175 filers (less than 1 percent) reported annual gross receipts of less than $750,000. Accordingly, proposed §§ 1.199A-7(f)(3) and 1.199A-8(d)(3) will not impose a significant economic impact on a substantial number of small entities.

D. *Proposed § 1.199A-8(f)*

Although proposed § 1.199A-8(f) will have an impact on a substantial number of small entities, this impact will not be economically significant. According to the Business Master File filing data from the transcribed fields from the Forms 1065 for 2017, the IRS estimates that there were 3,954,000 partnerships reporting their partners' share of partnership items on Schedules K-1 (Form 1065). The IRS also identified approximately 407 different partnerships that issued a Schedule K-1 to 680 different Cooperatives in 2017. The IRS does not have information as to whether the 680 Cooperatives all qualified as Specified Cooperatives.

Of the 407 different partnerships, the IRS determined that 344 of the partnerships conducted activities in 2017 that would have required the partnerships to file under proposed § 1.199A-8(f). The IRS does not have sufficient data to determine the type of business activities of the remaining

63 partnerships. To be as comprehensive and transparent as possible in analyzing the potential impact of the proposed regulations, it is assumed that all 63 of these partnerships would be required to file under proposed § 1.199A-8(f) and would be considered small entities.

Of the 344 partnerships identified as having both issued a Schedule K-1 to a Cooperative and conducting eligible activities in 2017, the IRS determined that 158 of these partnerships conducted activities for which the Small Business Administration (SBA) uses the number of employees to determine if an entity is a small entity using the NAICS. The IRS determined that 153 of these 158 partnerships would be small entities, while five would not be small entities based on the reported number of Forms W-2 filed in connection with the Forms 1065 the partnerships filed in 2017.

The SBA uses income to determine if an entity is a small entity for the reported business activities of the remaining 186 partnerships using the NAICS. Based upon the reported income for 2017, 140 of the remaining 186 partnerships are small entities, while 46 partnerships are not small entities. Therefore, a substantial number of small entities are affected by requirements in proposed § 1.199A-8(f).

The economic impact of proposed § 1.199A-8(f), however, will not be significant because the information required to be reported is gross receipts and related deductions. This information is readily available to each partnership and already known for the purpose of determining tax obligations. Because the information required to be reported is already available and familiar to each partnership, the reporting required by proposed § 1.199A-8(f) will not impose a significant economic impact on small entities.

Accordingly, the Treasury Department and the IRS hereby certify that the proposed regulations will not have a significant economic impact on a substantial number of small entities. We invite public comments with respect to this conclusion.

Pursuant to section 7805(f) of the Code, this notice of proposed rulemaking has been submitted to the Chief Counsel for Advocacy of the Small Business Administration for comment on its impact on small business.

IV. *Unfunded Mandates Reform Act*

Section 202 of the Unfunded Mandates Reform Act of 1995 (UMRA) requires that agencies assess anticipated costs and benefits and take certain other actions before issuing a final rule that includes any Federal mandate that may result in expenditures in any one year by a state, local, or tribal government, in the aggregate, or by the private sector, of $100 million in 1995 dollars, updated annually for inflation. In 2018, that threshold is approximately $150 million. This rule does not include any Federal mandate that may result in expenditures by state, local, or tribal governments, or by the private sector in excess of that threshold.

V. *Executive Order 13132: Federalism*

Executive Order 13132 (titled *Federalism*) prohibits an agency from publishing any rule that has federalism implications if the rule either imposes substantial, direct compliance costs on state and local governments, and is not required by statute, or preempts state law, unless the agency meets the consultation and funding requirements of section 6 of the Executive Order. This proposed rule does not have federalism implications, and does not impose substantial direct compliance costs on state and local governments or preempt state law, within the meaning of the Executive Order.

Comments and Requests for a Public Hearing

The Treasury Department and the IRS request comments on all aspects of the proposed rules. Before these proposed regulations are adopted as final regulations, consideration will be given to any written or electronic comments that are submitted timely to the IRS. All comments will be available for public inspection and copying. A public hearing may be scheduled if requested in writing by any person who timely submits written comments. If a public hearing is scheduled, notice of the date, time, and place for the hearing will be published in the *Federal Register*.

Statement of Availability of IRS Documents

IRS Revenue Procedures, Revenue Rulings, Notices and other guidance cited in this document are published in the Internal Revenue Bulletin and are available from the Superintendent of Documents, U.S. Government Publishing Office, Washington, DC 20402, or by visiting the IRS website at http://www.irs.gov.

Drafting Information

The principal author of these proposed regulations is Theresa Melchiorre, Office of Associate Chief Counsel (Passthroughs and Special Industries). Other personnel from the Treasury Department and the IRS participated in their development.

List of Subjects in 26 CFR Part 1

Income taxes, Reporting and recordkeeping requirements.

Withdrawal of Notice of Proposed Rulemaking

Accordingly, under the authority of 26 U.S.C. 7805, the notice of proposed rulemaking (REG-136459-09) published in the *Federal Register* (80 FR 51978) on August 27, 2015, is withdrawn.

[¶ 49,804]   Proposed Regulations (REG-106877-18), published in the Federal Register on July 3, 2019.

[Code Sec. 4968]

Excise tax: Tax Cuts and Jobs Act: Net investment income: Private colleges and universities.—Reg. § 53.4968-1, containing proposed regulations for determining the excise tax applicable to the net investment income of certain private colleges and universities, as provided by the Tax Cuts and Jobs Act, is proposed.

AGENCY: Internal Revenue Service (IRS), Treasury.

ACTION: Notice of proposed rulemaking.

SUMMARY: This document contains proposed regulations for determining the excise tax applicable to the net investment income of certain private colleges and universities, as provided by the Tax Cuts and Jobs Act. These regulations affect applicable educational institutions and their related organizations.

DATES: Written or electronic comments and requests for a public hearing must be received by Ocotber 1, 2019.

ADDRESSES: Submit electronic submissions via the Federal eRulemaking Portal at *http://www.regulations.gov* (indicate IRS and REG-106877-18) by following the online instructions for submitting comments. Once submitted to the Federal eRulemaking Portal, comments cannot be edited or withdrawn. The Department of the Treasury (Treasury Department) and the IRS will publish for public availability any comment received to its public docket, whether submitted electronically or in hard copy. Send hard copy submissions to: CC:PA:LPD:PR (REG-106877-18), Room 5203, Internal Revenue Service, P.O. Box 7604, Ben Franklin Station, Washington, DC 20044. Submissions may be hand-delivered Monday through Friday

between the hours of 8 a.m. and 4 p.m. to CC:PA:LPD:PR (REG-106877-18), Courier's Desk, Internal Revenue Service, 1111 Constitution Avenue NW, Washington, DC 20224.

FOR FURTHER INFORMATION CONTACT: Concerning the proposed regulations, Melinda Williams at (202) 317-6172 or Amber L. MacKenzie at (202) 317-4086; concerning submission of comments and request for hearing, Regina L. Johnson at (202) 317-6901 (not toll-free numbers).

SUPPLEMENTARY INFORMATION:

Background

This document contains proposed regulations under section 4968 of the Internal Revenue Code (Code) to amend part 53 of the Excise Tax Regulations (26 CFR part 53). Section 4968 of the Code, added by section 13701 of the Tax Cuts and Jobs Act, Public Law 115-97, 131 Stat. 2054, 2167-68, (2017) (TCJA), imposes on each applicable educational institution, as defined in section 4968(b)(1), an excise tax equal to 1.4 percent of the institution's net investment income, and, as described in section 4968(d), a portion of certain net investment income of certain related organizations, for the taxable year.

Section 4968(b)(1) defines the term "applicable educational institution" as an eligible educational institution (as defined in section 25A(f)(2)) which during the preceding taxable year had at least 500 tuition-paying students, more than 50 percent of whom were located in the United States, is not a state college or university as described in the first sentence of section 511(a)(2)(B), and had assets (other than those assets used directly in carrying out the institution's exempt purpose) the aggregate fair market value of which was at least $500,000 per student of the institution.

Section 4968(b)(2) provides that, for purposes of section 4968(b)(1), the number of students of an institution (including for purposes of determining the number of students at a particular location) shall be based on the daily average number of full-time students attending such institution (with part-time students taken into account on a full-time student equivalent basis).

Section 4968(c) provides that, for purposes of section 4968, "net investment income" shall be determined under rules similar to the rules of section 4940(c).

Section 4968(d)(1) provides that, for purposes of determining aggregate fair market value of an educational institution's assets not used directly in carrying out its exempt purpose[1] and for purposes of determining an institution's net investment income, the assets and net investment income of any related organization with respect to the institution shall be treated as assets and net investment income, respectively, of the educational institution, with two exceptions. First, no such amount shall be taken into account with respect to more than one educational institution. Second, unless such organization is controlled by such institution or is described in section 509(a)(3) (relating to supporting organizations) with respect to such institution for the taxable year, assets and net investment income which are not intended or available for the use or benefit of the educational institution shall not be taken into account.

Section 4968(d)(2) provides that the term "related organization," with respect to an educational institution, means (1) any organization which controls, or is controlled by, such institution; (2) is controlled by one or more persons that also control such institution; or (3) is a supported organization (as defined in section 509(f)(3)), or a supporting organization (as described in section 509(a)(3)), during the taxable year with respect to the educational institution.

The Conference Report for the TCJA, H. Rept. 115-466, 115th Cong., 1st sess., December 15, 2017 (Conference Report), at 555, states that Congress intended that the Secretary of the Treasury promulgate regulations to carry out the intent of section 4968, including regulations that describe: (1) Assets that are used directly in carrying out an educational institution's exempt purpose; (2) the computation of net investment income; and (3) assets that are intended or available for the use or benefit of an educational institution.

In June 2018, the Treasury Department and the IRS issued Notice 2018-55 (2018-26 I.R.B. 773) (Notice) to provide interim guidance on certain issues related to the application of the tax imposed by section 4968. Specifically, Notice 2018-55 states that, in the case of property held on December 31, 2017, and continuously thereafter to the date of its disposition, the Treasury Department and the IRS intend to propose regulations stating that basis for purposes of determining gain (but not loss) shall be deemed to be not less than the fair market value of such property on December 31, 2017, plus or minus all adjustments after December 31, 2017, and before the date of disposition consistent with the regulations under section 4940(c). The Notice provides that, if the disposition of an asset would result in a capital loss, basis rules that are consistent with the regulations under section 4940(c) will apply. Accordingly, if the value of the asset declines after December 31, 2017, the taxpayer will recognize no gain; however, the taxpayer will recognize a loss only if the proceeds from the sale of the asset are less than the basis of the property as calculated without the special rule in the Notice to increase the basis to fair market value on December 31, 2017. The Notice additionally states that the Treasury Department and the IRS expect the proposed regulations to provide that losses from sales or other dispositions of property generally shall be allowed only to the extent of gains, with no capital loss carryovers or carrybacks, and that losses from sales or other dispositions of property by related organizations will be allowed to offset overall net gains from other related organizations or the applicable educational institution. The Notice provides that applicable educational institutions may rely on the Notice before the issuance of the proposed regulations. Finally, the Notice requests comments on any of the issues addressed in the Notice and on any additional guidance that is needed and whether, and what type of, transitional relief may be necessary.

The Treasury Department and the IRS received two comments in response to Notice 2018-55, which were considered in drafting these proposed regulations. The comments are available at *http://www.regulations.gov* or upon request.

Explanation of Provisions

1. Institutions Subject to the Tax

Section 4968(a) imposes a 1.4 percent excise tax on the net investment income of each applicable educational institution. Section 4968(b) provides that an applicable educational institution is an "eligible educational institution" (as defined in section 25A(f)(2)) if: (i) it had at least 500 tuition-paying students during the preceding taxable year; (ii) more than 50 percent of its tuition-paying students are located in the United States; (iii) it is not a state college or university as described in the first sentence of section 511(a)(2)(B); and (iv) the aggregate fair market value of its assets (other than those assets used directly in carrying out the institution's exempt purpose) was at least $500,000 per student of the institution at the end of the preceding taxable year. Section 53.4968-1(a) of these proposed regulations sets forth definitions to determine whether an entity is an applicable educational institution that is subject to the tax.

Although, pursuant to section 4968(a), the tax on net investment income for each taxable year is based on the net investment income of an applicable educational institution for such taxable year, for purposes of determining whether an institution is an "applicable educational institution" subject to the tax, section 4968(b) provides that the number of an institution's tuition-paying students and the aggregate fair market value of the institution's assets (and the assets of any related organization) are based on the preceding taxable year's number and value.

---

[1] Section 4968(d)(1) erroneously cross references section 4968(b)(1)(C). The correct cross reference should be to section 4968(b)(1)(D). See Joint Committee on Taxation, "General Explanation of Public Law No. 115-97" (JCS-1-18), December 2018, at 290, n. 1357.

A. Eligible Educational Institution Defined in Section 25A(f)(2)

Section 4968(b)(1) defines "applicable educational institution," in part, as an eligible educational institution defined in section 25A(f)(2). In accordance with section 4968(b), the proposed regulations provide that an applicable educational institution must be described in section 25A(f)(2) and the regulations thereunder. Section 25A(f)(2) provides that, for purposes of the allowance of American Opportunity and Lifetime Learning credits, the term "eligible educational institution" means an institution (1) which is described in section 481 of the Higher Education Act of 1965 (20 U.S.C. 1088) (HEA), as in effect on the enactment of section 25A (1997), and (2) which is eligible to participate in a program under title IV of the HEA (relating to the United States federal student financial aid programs). The Treasury Department and the IRS anticipate that colleges and universities already know whether they are described in section 25A, but request comments on whether further guidance is needed for purposes of applying section 4968.

B. Student

i. In General

Section 4968(b)(1) defines "applicable educational institution," in part, by reference to the number of its students and the amount of its assets per student. Section 4968 does not define the term "student." However, section 4968(b)(2) does provide that the number of students of an institution shall be based on the daily average number of full-time students attending an institution, with part-time students taken into account on a full-time student equivalent basis. As described in part 1(A) of this Explanation of Provisions section, the definition of the term "applicable educational institution" in section 4968(b), which references students in some of its definitional criteria, relies on the definition of "eligible educational institution" as defined in section 25A(f)(2).

For purposes of section 25A, the term "eligible student" is defined in section 25A(b)(3) to mean a student who (1) meets the requirements of section 484(a)(1) of the HEA (20 U.S.C. 1091(a)(1)), and (2) is carrying at least half the normal full-time work load for the course of study the student is pursuing. Section 484(a)(1) of the HEA (20 U.S.C. 1091(a)(1)) provides that, in order to receive any grant, loan, or work assistance under the general provisions relating to student assistance programs under the HEA, a student must be enrolled or accepted for enrollment in a degree, certification, or other program (including a program of study abroad approved for credit by the eligible institution at which such student is enrolled) leading to a recognized educational credential at an institution of higher education that is an eligible institution in accordance with the provisions of section 1094 of title 20 of the U.S. Code, except as provided in section 1091(b)(3) and (4) of the HEA,[2] and not enrolled in an elementary or secondary school.

The Treasury Department and the IRS consider the definition of eligible student under section 25A to be an appropriate basis for the definition of student for purposes of section 4968; however, the requirement found in section 25A(b)(3)(B) that a student must carry at least half the normal full-time work load for the course of study the student is pursuing is not relevant for purposes of section 4968. Section 4968(b)(2) does not contain a requirement that a student must carry at least half the normal full-time work load to be considered a student for purposes of the asset measurement requirement; instead, it states that part-time students are taken into account on a full-time student equivalent basis.

Furthermore, section 4968(b)(2) contains a requirement that the number of students of an institution be based on the daily average number of students attending the institution. Therefore, the Treasury Department and the IRS do not view the portion of the rule found in Section 484(a)(1) of the HEA that is incorporated into the definition of "student" in section 25A(b)(3)(B) and includes an individual merely "accepted for enrollment" as appropriate to the application of section 4968 since such an individual may not yet be attending the institution.

Accordingly, the proposed regulations generally follow the standard in section 484(a)(1) of the HEA referenced by section 25A(b)(3)(A) to provide that the term "student" for section 4968 purposes means a person enrolled in a degree, certification, or other program (including a program of study abroad approved for credit by the eligible institution at which such student is enrolled) leading to a recognized educational credential at an eligible educational institution, and not enrolled in an elementary or secondary school. See proposed § 53.4968-1(a)(3)(i). However, the proposed definition of student does not include individuals merely accepted for enrollment, nor does it contain a requirement that the student have at least half the normal full-time work load. Furthermore, the time limitations in section 25A(b)(2) (such as that the American Opportunity Tax Credit is allowed only for 4 taxable years) are not part of the definition of "eligible student" and thus are not incorporated into the definition of student for section 4968 purposes.

Putting together the section 4968(b)(2) requirement that a student be "attending" an institution and the proposed definition that a student is an individual enrolled in a degree, certification, or other program leading to a recognized educational credential at an eligible educational institution, in applying the requirements under section 4968(b)(1), the proposed regulations require that a student be both enrolled at and attending the institution. The Treasury Department and the IRS request comments on whether further guidance is needed on the definitions of "student," "enrolled," or "attending."

Consistent with section 4968(b)(1)(D), the proposed regulations provide that an educational institution determines the fair market value of assets per student based upon the total number of all students, as defined in proposed § 53.4968-1(a)(3)(i), attending an eligible educational institution, not just the number of tuition-paying students.

ii. Tuition-paying

Section 4968(b)(1) defines "applicable educational institution," in part, with respect to how many tuition-paying students attend the institution. Specifically, under section 4968(b)(1)(A) an institution must have had at least 500 tuition-paying students during the preceding taxable year, and under 4968(b)(1)(B), more than 50 percent of its tuition-paying students must have been located in the United States. Section 4968 does not define the term "tuition-paying."

As described in part 1(A) of this Explanation of Provisions section, section 25A provides certain education credits relating to qualified tuition and related expenses paid by certain eligible students. Section 25A(f)(1) and § 1.25A-2(d) provide, in relevant part, that the term "qualified tuition and related expenses" means tuition and fees required for the enrollment or attendance at an eligible educational institution for courses of instruction at such institution. Such term does not include expenses with respect to any course or other education involving sports, games, or hobbies, unless such course or other education is part of the individual's degree program.

The Treasury Department and the IRS propose to base the definition of "tuition-paying" for purposes of section 4968 on the definition of qualified tuition and related expenses that is provided in section 25A(f)(1) and the regulations thereunder, without regard to section 25A(f)(1)(D). Thus, the proposed regulations provide that tuition-paying means the payment of tuition and fees required for the enrollment or attendance of a student for courses of instruction at an eligible educational institution but does not include any separate payment for supplies or equipment required during a specific course once a student is enrolled in and attending the course (for example, art supplies). Tuition-paying also does not

---

[2] Subsections (b)(3) and (4) of 20 U.S.C. 1091 provide exceptions to section 484(a)(1) of the HEA that allows students to be eligible for certain grant programs even if the student does not qualify under section 484(a)(1). Under the exceptions, the student must be carrying at least one half the normal full time work load for the course of study that the student is pursuing, as determined by an eligible institution, and be enrolled in a course of study necessary for enrollment in a program leading to a degree, certificate, professional credential or certification from a State that is required for employment as a teacher in an elementary or secondary school in that State.

include payment of room and board or other personal living expenses, and if a student is required to pay a fee (such as a comprehensive fee or a bundled fee) to an eligible educational institution that combines charges for tuition with charges for personal expenses such as room and board, then the student is a tuition-paying student. The Treasury Department and the IRS note that, notwithstanding the reference to "enrollment" for purposes of identifying tuition and fees, the tuition-paying student must also be attending the educational institution for purposes of determining if there are at least 500 tuition-paying students.

For purposes of section 4968, the proposed regulations also provide that whether a student is "tuition-paying" is determined after taking into account any scholarships provided directly by the educational institution and any work study programs operated directly by the educational institution. However, scholarship payments provided by third parties, even if administered by the institution, are considered payments of tuition on behalf of the student. Accordingly, a student will be considered a tuition-paying student for purposes of section 4968 if payment of any tuition or a fee is required for the enrollment or attendance of the student for courses of instruction after the application of any scholarships offered directly by the institution or work study program operated directly by the institution.

iii. Located in the United States

Section 4968(b)(1)(B) provides, in part, that at least 50 percent of an applicable educational institution's tuition-paying students attending the institution must have been located in the United States. The statute clearly refers to the location of the students, not the location of the educational institution or an instructor. Accordingly, the proposed regulations provide that a student is considered to have been located in the United States if the student resided in the United States for at least a portion of the time the student attended the educational institution. Like the other requirements of section 4968(b), this measurement is based on the applicable educational institution's preceding taxable year.

For example, a student that attended an educational institution in the preceding taxable year who is citizen of a foreign country is considered to have been a student located in the United States if the student resided in the United States for at least a portion of the time the student attended the educational institution. Furthermore, a student attending the educational institution in the preceding taxable year who was studying abroad in a foreign country is considered to have been a student located in the United States if the student resided in the United States for at least a portion of the time the student attended the educational institution. However, if a student did not reside in the United States for any portion of the time the student attended the education institution during the preceding taxable year, then that student would not be considered to have been located in the United States for purposes of section 4968(b)(1)(B) (although he or she may still be considered a student for purposes of section 4968(b)(1)(D)). The Treasury Department and the IRS request comments on whether further guidance is needed relating to whether a student is considered to have been located in the United States in a preceding taxable year.

iv. Full-time Students and Part-time Equivalents

Section 4968(b)(2) provides, in part, that the number of students of an applicable educational institution (including for purposes of determining the number of students at a particular location) is based on the daily average number of full-time students attending such institution, with part-time students taken into account on a full-time student equivalent basis. Section 4968 does not define the terms "full-time" and "part-time" for purposes of the full-time equivalent rule in section 4968(b)(2), nor does it provide how to determine a full-time student equivalent or a daily average. Section 1.25A-3(d)(1)(ii) of the Income Tax Regulations provides for section 25A purposes that the standard for what is half the normal full-time work load is determined by each eligible educational institution; however, the standard for half-time may not be lower than the applicable standard for half-time established by the HEA.

Unlike section 25A, section 4968 does not require that a student be carrying at least half the normal full-time work load for the course of study the student is pursuing in order to be considered a student. However, the Treasury Department and the IRS otherwise view the standard provided in §1.25A-3(d)(1)(ii) as a helpful model in applying the full-time equivalent requirement in section 4968(b)(2) and propose to follow a similar approach.

Accordingly, these proposed regulations provide that, for purposes of section 4968(b)(2), the determinations of full-time students, part-time students, full-time student equivalents, and daily average of students attending the institution are made by each applicable educational institution as long as the determinations are consistent with the institution's practices in determining full-time and part time status for other purposes. For example, it may be reasonable for an institution to determine that two students, each carrying half a full-time load, are equivalent to one full-time student. However, the standards an institution uses may not be lower than the applicable standards established by the Department of Education under the HEA.

The Treasury Department and the IRS seek comments on whether more specific guidance is required concerning the determination of full-time student, part-time student, full-time equivalent, or daily average number of full-time students attending the institution.

C. Assets Used Directly in Carrying out an Institution's Exempt Purpose

i. In General

To be included within the definition of applicable educational institution under section 4968(b)(1), an institution must have assets (other than those assets which are used directly in carrying out the institution's exempt purpose) the aggregate fair market value of which is at least $500,000 per student. The phrase "assets which are used directly in carrying out the institution's exempt purpose" is not defined in section 4968, but a similar phrase is used in section 4942.

For purposes of section 4942, a private foundation must determine its minimum investment return as part of its calculation of its distributable amount for any taxable year. Minimum investment return is defined in section 4942(e) as 5 percent of the excess of the aggregate fair market value of all assets of the foundation "other than those which are used (or held for use) directly in carrying out the foundation's exempt purpose," over the acquisition indebtedness with respect to such assets.

Since section 4968 contains a phrase similar to the language used in section 4942 (other than the omission of the parenthetical "or held for use"), the Treasury Department and the IRS propose generally to follow §53.4942(a)-2(c) for purposes of determining whether an educational institution's assets are used directly in carrying out the institution's exempt purpose, without regard to provisions relating to private foundation assets "held for use." The Treasury Department and the IRS seek comments on whether the use of the principles of the section 4942 regulations for this purpose creates any concerns.

Consistent with section 4942, the proposed regulations provide in §53.4968-1(a)(4)(i) that an asset is used directly in carrying out an institution's exempt purpose only if the asset is actually used by the institution in carrying out its exempt purpose. Administrative assets, real estate, and physical property used by the institution directly in its exempt activities are all examples of such exempt purpose assets. In addition, a reasonable cash balance necessary to cover current administrative expenses and other normal and current disbursements directly connected with the educational institution's exempt activities is considered to be used directly in carrying out the institution's exempt purpose. For section 4942 purposes, a reasonable cash balance is defined as 1.5 percent of the fair market value of the private foundation's non-charitable use assets (i.e., assets not actually used by an institution in carrying out its exempt purpose), determined without regard to the reduction for the reasonable cash balance. For consistency with the 4942 rules, the Treasury Department and the IRS propose that a cash balance of 1.5 percent of the fair market value of the educational institution's non-charitable use assets, determined without regard to the deduction for the reasonable cash balance, will be deemed to be a reasonable cash balance for purposes of section 4968. However, the Treasury Department and the IRS note that the 1.5 percent standard in the section 4942 context is an average monthly amount over the entire taxable year and thus has to take into account fluctuations in cash needs. Thus, in light of the differences in the exempt activities of an educational institution and the section 4968 requirement to measure the assets only at the end of the taxable year, the Treasury Department and the IRS request comments on whether another percentage or other measurement should be deemed to be a reasonable cash balance at the end of the taxable year. The Treasury Department and the IRS specifically request comments supporting why any such other amount would be reasonable, and how utilizing a different amount would be administrable.

The proposed regulations do not address whether a functionally-related business would be considered an exempt use asset for the purposes of this test. Although functionally-related businesses are included as an illustration of an exempt use asset in the section 4942 regulations, it is not clear how the concept of a functionally-related business would apply to an educational institution. The Treasury Department and the IRS request comments on whether and how educational institutions use functionally related businesses in conducting their operations and whether functionally-related businesses should be explicitly included or excluded as examples of exempt use assets in the final regulations.

Whether an asset is used directly by an educational institution to carry out its exempt purpose is determined based on the facts and circumstances. In addition, where property is used both for charitable, educational, or other similar exempt purposes and for other purposes, if the exempt use represents 95 percent or more of the total use, the property is considered to be used exclusively for a charitable, educational, or other similar exempt purpose. If the exempt use represents less than 95 percent of the total use, the institution must make a reasonable allocation between the exempt and nonexempt use.

ii. Exceptions

Similar to the rules under section 4942, the proposed regulations deem certain assets to not be used directly in carrying out an institution's exempt purpose, including assets that are held for the production of income or for investment (for example, stocks, bonds, interest-bearing notes, endowment funds, or, generally, leased real estate), even if the income from such assets is used to carry out the exempt purpose. Similarly, nonexempt use assets include property used for managing endowment funds of the institution.

iii. Valuation of Assets not Used Directly in Carrying out an Institution's Exempt Purpose

For purposes of section 4968(b)(1)(D), the value of an institution's non-exempt use assets must be determined as of the last day of each taxable year for which a valuation must be made. In contrast, section 4942(e)(2)(A) provides generally that a foundation's securities for which market quotations are readily available shall be determined on a monthly basis, and that the values of other assets shall be determined at such times and in such manner as the Secretary shall by regulations prescribe.

Section 53.4942(a)-2(c)(4) provides that a private foundation may use any reasonable method to determine the fair market value on a monthly basis of securities for which market quotations are readily available, as long as such method is consistently used, and provides additional valuation guidelines for assets that are not market securities.

Consistent with the proposed rules for determining whether an asset is used directly in carrying out an institution's exempt purpose, the Treasury Department and the IRS propose that, for purposes of valuing the institution's non-exempt use assets, institutions use rules similar to the rules of section 4942(e) and §53.4942(a)-2(c)(4), with two modifications. First, the phrase "applicable educational institution" is substituted for "private foundation" or "foundation" every place they appear. Second, an institution will have to make such adjustments as are reasonable and necessary to obtain the fair market value of non-exempt use assets as of the last day of the valuation taxable year, rather than any other frequency provided by the section 4942 regulations.

The Treasury Department and the IRS request comments on valuing exempt use assets using the principles of section 4942, as modified by this special timing rule.

2. Determination of Net Investment Income and Basis of Property

A. In General

Section 4968(a) imposes on each applicable educational institution a tax equal to 1.4 percent of its net investment income for the taxable year. Section 4968(c) provides that net investment income is determined under rules similar to the rules of section 4940(c). Accordingly, the proposed regulations provide in §53.4968-1(b) that an institution must calculate its net investment income under the rules of section 4940(c) and §53.4940-1(c) through (f), with certain modifications explained in part 2(B) of this Explanation of Provisions section.

Section 4940(c)(1) defines net investment income as the amount by which the sum of the gross investment income and the capital gain net income exceeds certain specified allowable deductions. Section 4940(c)(1) also states that, except to the extent inconsistent with the provisions of section 4940, net investment income is determined under the principles of subtitle A of the Code.

Section 4940(c)(2) provides that, for purposes of section 4940(c)(1), gross investment income means the gross amount of income from interest, dividends, rents, payments with respect to securities loans (as defined in section 512(a)(5)), and royalties, but not including any such income to the extent included in computing the unrelated business income tax imposed by section 511. The term gross investment income also includes income from sources similar to those specifically listed in the preceding sentence.

Section 4940(c)(3) provides that, for purposes of section 4940(c)(1), there is allowed as a deduction all the ordinary and necessary expenses paid or incurred for the production or collection of gross investment income or for the management, conservation, or maintenance of property held for the production of such income, determined with the following modifications: (1) the deduction provided by section 167 is allowed, but only on the basis of the straight line method of depreciation; and (2) the deduction for depletion provided by section 611 is allowed, but is determined without regard to section 613 (relating to percentage depletion).

Section 4940(c)(4) provides that, for purposes of determining capital gain net income under section 4940(c)(1), (1) no gain or loss from the sale or other disposition of property is taken into account to the extent that any such gain or loss is taken into account for purposes of computing the tax imposed by section 511 on unrelated business taxable income; (2) in the case of property held by a private foundation on December 31, 1969, and continuously thereafter to the date of its disposition, the basis for determining gain is deemed to be not less than the fair market value of such property on December 31, 1969; (3) losses from sales or other dispositions of property are allowed only to the extent of gains from such sales or other dispositions, without capital loss carryovers or carrybacks; and (4) except to the extent provided by regulation, under rules similar to the rules of section 1031 (including the exception under subsection (a)(2) thereof relating to exchanges of real property held primarily for sale), no gain or loss is taken into account with respect to any portion of property used for a period of not less than 1 year for a purpose or function constituting the basis of the private foundation's exemption if the entire property is exchanged immediately following such period solely for property of like kind which is to be used primarily for a purpose or function constituting the basis for such foundation's exemption.

Section 4940(c)(5) provides that, for purposes of section 4940, net investment income is determined by applying section 103 (relating to State and local bonds) and section 265 (relating to expenses and interest relating to tax-exempt income).

Section 4968 does not expressly provide that the tax on net investment income is limited to net investment income derived from assets that are not used directly in carrying out an applicable educational institution's exempt purpose. This lack of a limitation is in contrast to the specific language in section 4968(b)(1)(D) that excludes assets used directly in carrying out an institution's exempt purpose in determining whether the educational institution is an applicable educational institution. Instead, section 4968(c) provides that net investment income shall be determined under rules similar to the rules of section 4940(c). Accordingly, these proposed regulations adopt the rules provided in section 4940(c) and the regulations thereunder, including § 53.4940-1(d)(1), which specifies that "gross investment income" means the gross amounts of income from interest, dividends, rents, royalties (including overriding royalties), and capital gain net income received by a private foundation from all sources, but does not include such income to the extent included in computing the tax imposed by section 511. Under this definition, consistent with specific language in § 53.4940-1(d), interest, dividends, rents, and royalties derived from assets devoted to charitable activities are includible in gross investment income. Therefore, for example, interest received on a student loan would be includible.

The Treasury Department and the IRS request comments on whether specific types of income should be excluded from gross investment income under section 4968 because taxing those types of income would not achieve the congressional intent in enacting section 4968. In explaining why each such type of income should be excluded, please state specifically how the proposed exclusion is still "similar to" the rules of section 4940(c) and the specific characteristics of each type of such income that would warrant deviating from the rules provided in section 4940 and the regulations thereunder.

For example, the rules of section 4940(c) specifically include student loan interest as net investment income. However, the Treasury Department and the IRS recognize that student loans provided directly by an applicable educational institution to its students can be seen as helping the applicable educational institution fulfill its mission of educating its students. Unlike private foundations, colleges and universities educate students and charge tuition as part of their primary exempt activities. Student loans provided by an applicable educational institution to its students arguably can be viewed as a form of deferred tuition which will be paid when the student enters the workforce. Under this rationale, the interest on the student loan may arguably be distinguished from investment income, depending on the interest rate. If the interest is at a market (or higher) rate, it would be difficult to distinguish the interest on the student loan and interest on assets acquired for investment purposes. However, if the interest rate is set at a substantially below-market rate, the difference between the market interest rate and the interest rate on the student loan might be viewed as similar to a scholarship from the school to the student. Under these circumstances, the remaining, below-market rate interest income might be considered distinguishable from income derived from assets acquired primarily for investment purposes.

Any exception for student loan interest that is premised on the utilization of an interest rate that is substantially lower than a market rate would potentially present tax administrative challenges for both the IRS and taxpayers in determining the relevant market-rate and an acceptable lower rate, and in adjusting to rate changes during the course of the loan. Comments advocating an exception for the interest received on student loans should explain how these concerns could be addressed. It would be helpful if such comments also provide information regarding the number of student loans applicable educational institutions make each year, how they set the interest rates on those loans, and whether the rates are set below market, or at market rates.

Allowing an exception from net investment income for certain categories of student loan interest would raise the question of why only those categories of exempt function income are excluded from net investment income. Many other categories of income derived from exempt functions also help an applicable educational institution fulfill its exempt purposes. Private foundations might also argue that many of their types of income help them fulfill their exempt purposes. The Treasury Department and the IRS request comments on why interest income on student loans provided by an applicable educational institution to its students is a logical place to draw the line at the type of income that should be excluded from the net investment income tax, especially given the reference to student loan income in § 1.4940-1(d).

Similarly, under section 4940(c), net investment income includes rents. The Treasury Department and the IRS recognize that colleges and universities offer various types of housing (such as dormitories or apartments) for use by students, non-students (for example, during the summer), and faculty. The Treasury Department and the IRS request comments on the differences, if any, among the housing arrangements, whether any of the arrangements include the signing of leases, the various amounts charged by a college or university related to provision of housing and meals, and particular factors that distinguish room and board payments from students living in a dormitory from rental income that institutions receive.

Consistent with the requirement in section 4968(c) to calculate net investment income under rules similar to the rules under section 4940(c), these proposed regulations generally follow the rules for determining gain upon the sale or other disposition of property that have been used for section 4940(c) purposes since 1969. Section 4940(c)(1) provides that, except to the extent inconsistent with the provisions of section 4940, net investment income is determined under the principles of subtitle A. Subtitle A encompasses all of the income tax provisions (sections 1 through 1564) of the Code, including the basis rules in section 1015 (basis of property acquired by gift is generally the same as the donor's basis). Accordingly, under the proposed regulations, an applicable education institution computes gain on the sale or disposition of donated property using the donor's basis. The Treasury Department and the IRS request comments on whether a special rule excluding any appreciation in a gift of donated property that occurred before the date of receipt by the applicable educational institution should be included in the final regulations and how such a special rule would be consistent with the statutory language of section 4968.

B. Special Rules

The proposed regulations provide in § 53.4968-1(b)(3) that an institution should substitute "applicable educational institution" for "private foundation" or "foundation" every place it appears in § 53.4940-1(c) through (f). In addition, the proposed regulations provide that the rule in § 53.4940-1(d)(3) does not apply because it is narrowly focused on section 302 stock redemptions by corporations that are disqualified persons when the redemptions are part of a transaction designed to reduce section 4943 excess business holdings. Colleges and universities are not subject to section 4943, so they cannot have excess business holdings that could be the subject of a section 302 stock redemption by a disqualified person corporation.

As provided by section 3 of Notice 2018-55 (2018-26 I.R.B. 773), in following the rule in section 4940(c)(4), the proposed regulations substitute "December 31, 2017" for "December 31, 1969" every place it occurs. In addition, in response to a comment requesting clarification of the basis rules for assets held in a partnership on December 31, 2017, these proposed regulations also provide that if an applicable educational institution held an interest in a partnership (including through one or more tiers of partnerships) on December 31, 2017, and continuously thereafter, and the partnership held assets on December 31, 2017, and continuously thereafter to the date of disposition, the partnership's basis in its assets with respect to the applicable educational institution for purposes of determining the applicable educational institution's share of gain upon sale or disposition of the assets shall be not less than the fair market value of such asset on December 31, 2017, plus or minus all adjustments after December 31, 2017, and before the date of disposition. For purposes of applying this special partnership basis rule, an institution must obtain documentation from the partnership to substantiate the claim.

Finally, consistent with section 4 of Notice 2018-55 and section 4940(c)(4)(C), the proposed regulations provide that in applying § 53.4940-1(f), overall net losses from sales or other dispositions of property by one related organization (or by the applicable educational institution) shall reduce (but not below zero) overall net gains from such sales or other dispositions by other related organizations (or by the applicable educational institution).

3. Related Organizations

Section 4968(d)(1) provides, in part, that for purposes of determining the aggregate fair market value of the assets and net investment income of an educational institution, the assets and net investment income of any related organization with respect to the educational institution shall be treated as assets and net investment income, respectively, of the educational institution.

For this purpose, the statute provides two special rules: (1) no such amount shall be taken into account with respect to more than 1 educational institution, and (2) unless such organization is controlled by such institution or is described in section 509(a)(3) (relating to supporting organizations) with respect to such institution for the taxable year, assets and net investment income which are not intended or available for the use or benefit of the educational institution shall not be taken into account. Section 53.4968-1(c) of these proposed regulations provides definitions and special rules relating to related organizations.

A. Definition of Related Organization

Section 4968(d)(2) provides that the term "related organization" means, with respect to an applicable educational institution, any organization which (1) controls, or is controlled by, such institution; (2) is controlled by 1 or more persons which also control such institution; or (3) is a supported organization (as defined in section 509(f)(3)) or a supporting organization (as described in section 509(a)(3)) during the taxable year with respect to such institution.

Section 4968(d)(2) does not define the term "control." The concept of controlled entities is found in numerous other areas of the Code, including section 4960, which was enacted at the same time as section 4968. Consistent with the position taken in Notice 2019-09, "Interim Guidance Under Section 4960" (2019-04 I.R.B. 403), for purposes of defining "control" within the meaning of section 4968(d), these proposed regulations provide rules based on the definition of control under section 512(b)(13)(D) and the regulations thereunder, which includes the constructive ownership rules of section 318, and that generally align with the definition of related organization for purposes of the annual reporting requirements on Form 990. The Treasury Department and the IRS request comments on whether there are any circumstances in which this definition of control should be modified in the context of section 4968.

Thus, the proposed regulations provide in § 53.4968-1(c)(1) that the term "control" means (1) in the case of a corporation, ownership (by vote or value) of more than 50 percent of the stock of the corporation; (2) in the case of a partnership, ownership of more than 50 percent of the profits interests or capital interests in such partnership; (3) in the case of a trust with beneficial interests, ownership of more than 50 percent of the beneficial interests in the trust; or (4) in the case of a nonprofit organization or other organization without owners or persons having beneficial interests (nonstock organization), including a governmental entity, that more than 50 percent of the directors or trustees of the applicable educational institution or nonstock organization are either representatives of, or are directly or indirectly controlled by, the other entity or that more than 50 percent of the directors or trustees of the nonstock organization are either representatives of, or are directly or indirectly controlled by, one or more persons that control the applicable educational institution. For purposes of this paragraph, a "representative" means a trustee, director, agent, or employee, and control includes the power to remove a trustee or director and designate a new trustee or director. Finally, section 318, which contains rules for determining constructive ownership of stock, applies for purposes of determining ownership of stock in a corporation, and similar principles apply for purposes of determining ownership of an interest in any other entity. The Treasury Department and the IRS do not propose to adopt the test for control under section 414(b) and (c), which generally uses the same test for control of a nonprofit organization as section 512(b)(13)(D) except that it replaces the 50-percent threshold with an 80-percent threshold. Instead, the proposed regulations adopt the control test under section 512(b)(13)(D) to align more closely with other exempt organization control tests and to ensure consideration of available assets consistent with congressional intent that would not occur under the higher 80 percent control threshold that was established for qualified plans.

Since the net investment that a taxable entity provides to an applicable educational institution has already been taxed under section 1, the Treasury Department and the IRS do not consider it consistent with congressional intent to tax the income again under section 4968. Furthermore, with regard to the assets of a taxable entity that is a related organization defined in section 4968(d)(2)(A) or (B), the institution likely already has included the value of the stock in its non-exempt use assets; however, the stock value may differ from the value of the taxable entity's underlying assets. The Treasury Department and the IRS request comments on how to account for this difference without double-counting the assets, as well as comments on the treatment of taxable entities that are related organizations for purposes of section 4968.

B. Assets and Net Income Treated as Assets and Net Income of Only One Educational Institution

As noted above, section 4968(d)(1)(A) provides, in part, that for purposes of determining the aggregate fair market value of an institution's assets and its net investment income, the assets and net investment income of any related organization with respect to the educational institution shall be treated as assets and net investment income, respectively, of the educational institution. However section 4968(d)(1)(A) provides an exception under which no such amount shall be taken into account with respect to more than 1 educational institution.

In order to effectuate section 4968(d)(1)(A), the proposed regulations provide in § 53.4968-1(c)(2)(ii)(A) that, in any case in which an organization is a related organization with respect to more than 1 educational institution, the assets and net investment income of the related organization must be allocated between the educational institutions being supported by the related organization. The proposed regulations provide that such allocation must be made in a reasonable manner, taking into account all facts and circumstances, and must be consistently applied across all related organizations. The Treasury Department and the IRS request comments on whether more specific guidance is required concerning the allocation of a related organization's assets and net investment income between multiple educational institutions being supported by the same related organization, and if so, what such additional guidance should provide.

C. Assets and Net Investment income "Not Intended or Available for the Use or Benefit of" an Educational Institution

For purposes of attributing assets and net investment income of related organizations to applicable educational institutions, section 4968(d)(1)(B) provides that, unless a related organization is controlled by the educational institution or is described in section 509(a)(3) with respect to such institution for the taxable year, assets and net investment income of the related organization that are not intended or available for the use or benefit of the educational institution shall not be taken into account. Put another way, if a related organization controls the educational institution or is controlled by 1 or more persons which also control such institution but is not described in section 509(a)(3) with respect to the educational institution for the taxable year, then the assets and net investment income of the related organization are taken into account as assets and net investment income of the educational institution only if the assets and net investment income are intended or available for the use and benefit of the educational institution. However, if a related organization is either controlled by the educational institution or is described in section 509(a)(3) with respect to such institution for the taxable year, then all the assets and net investment income of the related organization are considered assets and net investment income of the educational institution, except as provided below.

The Conference Report description of section 4968 repeats section 4968(d)(1)(B) and adds, "[f]or example, assets of a related organization that are earmarked or restricted for (or fairly attributable to) the educational institution would be treated as assets of the educational institution, whereas assets of a related organization that are held for unrelated purposes (and are not fairly attributable to the educational institution) would be disregarded." H. Rept. 115-466, 115th Cong., 1st sess., at 555 (December 15, 2017).

Thus, the proposed regulations provide in §53.4968-1(c)(2)(ii)(B) that when a related organization controls an educational institution or is controlled by 1 or more persons which also control such institution and is not described in section 509(a)(3) with respect to the educational institution, the assets and net investment income of a related organization must be allocated between those intended or available for the use and benefit of an educational institution and those not intended or not available for the use and benefit of that educational institution. Such allocation must be made in a reasonable manner, taking into account all facts and circumstances, and must be consistently applied across all related organizations.

The proposed regulations further explain that assets and net investment income of such a related organization are intended or available for the use and benefit of an educational institution if such assets and net investment income are specifically earmarked or restricted for the benefit of, or are otherwise fairly attributable to, the educational institution. Conversely, assets and net investment income of a related organization are not intended or available for the use and benefit of an educational institution if such assets and net investment income are specifically earmarked or restricted for another entity or for unrelated purposes or are otherwise not fairly attributable to the educational institution. For purposes of this required allocation, the Treasury Department and the IRS request comments on situations in which an organization's assets or net investment income is not specifically earmarked or restricted for the benefit of any particular organization but is otherwise fairly attributable to the educational institution or to another organization. For example, absent any earmarking or restriction, should total distributions from a related organization to an applicable educational institution in one taxable year establish a presumption for section 4968 purposes that at least an equal amount is fairly attributable to the applicable educational institution for the following taxable year, absent demonstrated facts and circumstances supporting attribution of a lesser amount?

Because section 4968(d)(1)(B) carves out organizations that are controlled by an institution or are described in section 509(a)(3) with respect to such institution for the taxable year from this special rule, the proposed regulations provide that if the related organization is controlled by the educational institution or is described in section 509(a)(3) with respect to the educational institution, the assets and net investment income of the related organization must be taken into account as assets and net investment income of the educational institution, regardless of whether the assets and net investment income are earmarked or restricted for the benefit of, or otherwise fairly attributable to, the educational institution and even if they are specifically earmarked or restricted for another entity or for unrelated purposes or are otherwise not fairly attributable to the educational institution. However, the special rule in section 4968(d)(1)(A) continues to apply, such that the assets and net investment income of the related organization are not taken into account by more than one educational institution. See part 3(B) of the Explanation of Provisions section.

In recognition that section 509(a)(3) Type III supporting organizations, unlike section 509(a)(3) Type I and Type II supporting organizations, are not controlled by their supported organizations,[3] and because applicable educational institutions may not be able to get information from their Type III supporting organizations, the proposed regulations provide a special rule in §53.4968-1(c)(2)(ii)(B)(3)(ii) for related organizations of an educational institution that were Type III supporting organizations with respect to the applicable educational institution on December 31, 2017. The proposed regulations provide that an applicable educational institution with a related organization that was a Type III supporting organization with respect to the applicable educational institution on December 31, 2017, may take into account only the assets and net investment income of the related Type III supporting organization that are intended or available for the use and benefit of the applicable educational institution, as described in this part 3(C) of the Explanation of Provisions section. An applicable educational institution can determine whether the assets and net investment income of such a Type III supporting organization are intended or available for the use and benefit of the applicable educational institution using any reasonable method. A method using all the distributions received from the Type III supporting organization subject to this special rule as net investment income of the applicable educational institution each year will be deemed to be reasonable. Similarly, a method using the distributions received from the Type III supporting organization to calculate the percentage of the Type III supporting organization's total net income that was distributed to the applicable educational institution, and using the same percentage to calculate the value of the underlying assets of the Type III supporting organization that are intended or available for the use and benefit of the applicable educational institution each year, will be deemed to be reasonable. The Treasury Department and the IRS request comments on whether additional guidance pertaining to Type III supporting organizations is needed.

Special Analyses

Executive Orders 12866 and 13563 direct agencies to assess costs and benefits of available regulatory alternatives and, if regulation is necessary, to select regulatory approaches that maximize net benefits (including potential economic, environmental, public health and safety effects, distributive impacts, and equity). Executive Order 13563 emphasizes the importance of quantifying both costs and benefits, of reducing costs, of harmonizing rules, and of promoting flexibility.

The proposed regulations have been designated by the Office of Management and Budget's (OMB) Office of Information and Regulatory Affairs (OIRA) as subject to review under Executive Order 12866 pursuant to the Memorandum of Agreement (April 11, 2018) between the Treasury Department and OMB regarding review of tax regulations. OIRA has determined that the proposed rulemaking is significant and subject to review under Executive Order 12866 and section 1(b) of the Memorandum of Agreement. Accordingly, the proposed regulations have been reviewed by OMB.

I. *Need for Regulation*

The Conference Report, at 555, states that Congress intended that the Secretary promulgate regulations to carry out the intent of section 4968. These proposed regulations are in response to this congressional intent. The proposed regulations provide guidance for determining the excise tax applicable to the net investment income of certain private colleges and universities, as provided by the TCJA. The regulations are intended to clarify which educational institutions are subject to the excise tax under section 4968 (excise tax) and how net investment income is calculated for purposes of this excise tax.

Prior to these proposed regulations, the Treasury Department and the IRS have not issued formal guidance on the definitions of these terms or on the rules under which net investment income for purposes of the excise tax in section 4968 were determined.[4] As a result, there was a degree of taxpayer uncertainty as to the definitions of the various terms and whether net investment income would be determined under rules identical to or similar to the rules of section 4940(c), and if the latter, what the deviations from the rules of section 4940(c) would be.

Pursuant to section 6(a)(3)(B) of Executive Order 12866, the following qualitative analysis provides further details regarding the anticipated impacts of the proposed regulations. After describing briefly the statute and the proposed regulations in Part II, the baseline used for the analysis is

---

[3] Organizations described in section 509(a)(3) are known as "supporting organizations." Supporting organizations achieve their public charity status by providing support to one or more organizations described in section 509(a)(1) or (2), which, in this context, are referred to as "supported organizations." To be described in section 509(a)(3), an organization must satisfy several tests, including having one of three "relationships" with one or more supported organizations. A supporting organization that is operated, supervised or controlled by one or more supported organizations is known as a "Type I" supporting organization. A supporting organization that is supervised or controlled in connection with one or more supported organizations is known as

a "Type II" supporting organization. A supporting organization that is operated in connection with one or more supported organizations is known as a "Type III" supporting organization. The relationship of a Type III supporting organization with its supported organization(s) is much more attenuated than the other two types.

[4] In June 2018, the Treasury Department and the IRS issued Notice 2018-55 (2018-26 I.R.B. 773) to provide clarification regarding the calculation of net investment income for purposes of section 4968(c). The Notice stated that the Treasury Department and the IRS intended to issue proposed regulations relating to those and other issues.

described in Part III of this Special Analyses section. Part IV of this Special Analyses section describes the types of entities affected by the proposed regulations. Part V of this Special Analyses section provides a qualitative assessment of the potential economic effects, including the benefits and costs, of the proposed regulations compared to the baseline.

II. The Statute and the Proposed Regulations

Section 4968 imposes a 1.4 percent excise tax on the net investment income of applicable educational institutions. Under the statute, an "applicable educational institution" is an eligible educational institution (which is described in section 481 of the Higher Education Act of 1968) that has at least 500 tuition-paying students during the preceding taxable year, more than 50 percent of the tuition-paying students of which are located in the United States, is not a state college or university, and the fair market value of the assets of which (other than those assets which are used directly in carrying out the institution's exempt purpose) is at least $500,000 per student at the end of the preceding taxable year. Under section 4968, net investment income is determined under rules "similar to" the rules of section 4940(c) (the rules for calculation of the net investment income of private foundations). In addition, the assets and net investment income of related organizations are generally treated as the assets and net investment income of the educational institution.

Section 4968 does not define the terms "student," "tuition-paying student," or "assets used directly in carrying out the institution's exempt purpose." Section 4968(c) states that, for the purposes of the excise tax in section 4968, net investment income shall be determined under rules "similar to" the rules of section 4940(c), but does not define what is meant by "similar to." Section 4968 does not define the term "control" as it relates to a "related organization with respect to an educational institution." The proposed regulations provide general definitional guidance with respect to these and other terms and rules relevant to the statute. A brief discussion of this guidance follows.

The proposed regulations define "student" to mean, in general, "a person enrolled in a degree, certification, or other program (including a program of study abroad approved for credit by the eligible institution at which such student is enrolled) leading to a recognized educational credential at an institution, and who is not enrolled in an elementary or secondary school." The proposed regulations define "tuition-paying" to mean, in general, "the payment of any tuition or fees required for the enrollment or attendance of a student for a course of instruction at an educational institution." These definitions follow similar definitions in section 25A of the Code. The proposed regulations also provide guidance for determining whether a student is located in the U.S. and for counting full-time and full-time equivalent students.

The proposed regulations define "assets used directly in carrying out an institution's exempt purpose" to mean, in general, assets "actually used by the institution in carrying out its exempt purpose." Whether an asset qualifies "must be determined based on all the facts and circumstances." If the property's "exempt use represents 95 percent or more of the total use, the property is considered to be used exclusively for an exempt purpose. If the exempt use of such property represents less than 95 percent of the total use, the institution must make a reasonable allocation between such exempt and nonexempt uses."

The proposed regulations state that the valuation of assets not used directly in carrying out an institution's exempt purpose is determined under the rules of section 4942 and its regulations, with two modifications. First, "educational institution" is substituted for "private foundation" or "foundation" each place they appear. Second, the educational institution must obtain the fair market value of assets on the last day of the preceding taxable year rather than at other times provided by the regulations under section 4942.

Consistent with 4968(c), the proposed regulations state that net investment income will be determined under the rules of section 4940(c) and its regulations, with five modifications. First, "applicable educational institution" is substituted for "private foundation" or "foundation" each place they appear. Second, the regulations relating to the treatment of certain distributions in redemption of stock do not apply to applicable educational institutions. Third, December 31, 2017, replaces December 31, 1969 (the date used for the excise tax on net investment income of private foundations under section 4940(c)), to determine the basis of assets held on December 31, 2017, for purposes of calculating the excise tax. Fourth, if an applicable educational institution held an interest in a partnership on December 31, 2017, and continuously thereafter, and the partnership held assets on December 31, 2017, and continuously thereafter to the date of disposition, generally the basis of those assets for determining the applicable educational institution's share of gain upon sale or disposition of the assets is not less than the fair market value of such assets on December 31, 2017, plus or minus adjustments provided under the regulations for section 4940 after December 31, 2017, and before the date of disposition. Fifth, overall net losses from sales or other dispositions of property by one related organization or by the applicable educational institution may reduce (but not below zero) overall net gains from such sales or other dispositions by other related organizations or by the applicable educational institution.

Following the rules for section 4960, the proposed regulations define the term "control," as it relates to a "related organization with respect to an educational institution," generally to mean ownership of more than 50 percent of (a) the stock of a corporation, (b) the profits interests or capital interests in a partnership, or (c) the beneficial interests of a trust. For a nonstock corporation, control means (a) more than 50 percent of the directors or trustees of the applicable educational institution or nonstock organization are either representatives of, or are directly or indirectly controlled by, the other entity, or (b) more than 50 percent of the directors or trustees are representatives of, or are directly or indirectly controlled by, one or more persons that control the applicable educational institution. The proposed regulations apply the principles of section 318 for purposes of determining ownership of stock in a corporation and apply similar principles for purposes of determining ownership of an interest in any other entity.

The proposed regulations also provide an allocation rule to effectuate section 4968(d)(1)(A) (providing that income be taken into account by no more than one institution) and 4968(d)(1)(B) (providing that only assets available for use by the institution be taken into account in determining the aggregate amount of assets), in the case of related organizations.

III. *Baseline*

The Treasury Department and the IRS have assessed the benefits and costs of the proposed regulations relative to a no-action baseline reflecting anticipated Federal income tax-related behavior in the absence of these proposed regulations.

IV. *Affected Entities*

One researcher used data from the Integrated Post-Secondary Education Data System (IPEDS) on endowment values at the end of the 2015-2016 academic year and enrollment data to estimate the number of institutions at risk of having liability under this excise tax.[5] Under the assumption that none of the assets in the endowment are for exempt purposes, he estimates that 23 institutions are likely to be currently subject to tax. Using the same IPEDS data, another researcher estimated that in 2016, among four-year public and not-for-profit private institutions located in the United States with at least 500 full-time equivalent students, and excluding endowments held at the university system level, there were 27 endowments worth at least $500,000 per student.[6] These estimates do not take into account all of the provisions of the statute and regulations. For example, limiting this set of institutions to the not-for-profit private institutions subject to tax and excluding assets that are used for the institutions' exempt

[5] Levine, Phillip. "The University Endowment Income Tax: Who Will Pay it and Why Was it Implemented?", Econofact, January 25, 2018, available at https://econofact.org/the-university-endowment-tax-who-will-pay-it-and-why-was-it-implemented, accessed April 29, 2019.

[6] Hinrichs, Peter. "College Endowments." Economic Commentary 2018-04 (May 17, 2018), Federal Reserve Bank of Cleveland, Table 1.

purpose would reduce the number of affected institutions. On the other hand, as both authors note, because the $500,000 per student threshold for the aggregate fair market value of assets (other than those assets which are used directly in carrying out the institution's exempt purpose) that in part determines whether the excise tax in section 4968 applies to an educational institution is not indexed for inflation, the number of institutions to which the excise tax in section 4968 applies is expected to increase over time. In addition, these studies did not consider assets held by related organizations; including such assets could increase the number of affected schools.

V. *Economic Effects of the Proposed Regulations*

The proposed regulations clarify a number of definitions related to the excise tax in section 4968. In the absence of guidance, affected taxpayers would have to calculate their tax liability without the definitions and clarifications provided by the proposed regulations, a situation that is generally considered more burdensome and could lead to greater conflicts with tax administrators. The proposed regulations make use of a number of existing statutory and regulatory provisions in defining students, tuition, exempt purpose, fair market value, net investment income and related organizations. Many taxpayers will already be familiar with these definitions. Thus, although the Treasury Department and the IRS project that the proposed regulations will reduce taxpayer compliance burden, including determining whether the excise tax applies to the institution and the time needed to file the return, and the costs of tax administration, including monitoring the compliance of taxpayers with the excise tax, relative to the no-action baseline, it is possible that the proposed regulations will have other economic effects.

The guidance provided in the proposed regulations also ensures that the excise tax liability is calculated similarly across taxpayers, avoiding situations where one taxpayer receives preferential treatment over another taxpayer for fundamentally similar economic activity. For example, in the absence of these proposed regulations, an applicable educational institution may have uncertainty over whether it is subject to the excise tax under section 4968 and what assets are used in determining the net investment income for purposes of the excise tax under section 4968. As a result, in the absence of guidance, similar institutions might take different positions and pay different amounts of tax, introducing economic inefficiency and inequity.

Based on this analysis, the Treasury Department and the IRS anticipate the net economic contribution of the proposed regulations will be modest, and will be positive relative to not issuing any such guidance and conditional on the relevant statutes. However, as stated earlier in the preamble, the Treasury Department and the IRS request comments on a number of aspects of the proposed regulations, which could include comments on the economic effects, any behavioral changes caused, or the unintended costs and benefits of the proposed regulations.

These proposed regulations provide further clarity on the Treasury Department and IRS policy choices regarding the treatment of investment income under section 4968, including the relationship to section 4940(c). Treasury Department and IRS requests comment on the proposed definitions and treatment of investment income in these regulations.

Paperwork Reduction Act

The collection of information in these proposed regulations is in §§ 53.4968-1(a)(2), (3), and (4), and 53.4968-1(b) and (c)(1) and (2). This information is required to determine whether an educational institution is an applicable educational institution, as defined in section 4968(b); to calculate net investment income as defined in section 4968(c); and to determine the assets and net investment income of related organizations that are treated as assets and net investment income of applicable educational institutions, as defined in section 4968(d). In 2016, the IRS released and invited comments on drafts of an earlier version of Form 4720 in order to give members of the public the opportunity to benefit from certain specific amendments made to the Code. The IRS received no comments on Form 4720 during the comment period. Consequently, the IRS made Form 4720 available on December 9, 2016 for use by the public. The IRS is contemplating making additional changes to Form 4720 based on these regulations. The IRS intends that the burden of the collections of information will be reflected in the burden associated with Form 4720, OMB approval number 1545-0052.

The burden associated with Form 4720 is included in the aggregated burden estimates for OMB control number 1545-0052 (listing a total estimated burden time for all Form 4720 filers of 88,839 hours and total estimated monetized costs of $8.441 million ($2017)). The burden estimates provided for Form 4720 are aggregate amounts that relate to all filers associated with the form, and will in the future include, but not isolate, the estimated burden of only those information collections associated with these proposed regulations. These numbers are therefore unrelated to the future calculations needed to assess the burden imposed by these regulations, specific burden estimates for which are not currently available. The Treasury Department and the IRS have not estimated the burden, including that of any new information collections, related to the requirements under the proposed regulations.

The expected burden for private colleges and universities that are applicable to this rule as described in section 4968(b) is listed below:

Estimated number of respondents: 40

Estimated average annual burden hours per response: 32 hours, 27 minutes

Estimated total annual burden: $123,336 (2017)

Estimated frequency of collection: Annual

The Treasury Department and the IRS request comments on all aspects of information collection burdens related to the proposed regulations, including estimates for how much time it would take to comply with the paperwork burdens described above for each relevant form and ways for the IRS to minimize the paperwork burden. Proposed revisions (if any) to these forms that reflect the information collections contained in these final regulations will be made available for public comment at *https://apps.irs.gov/app/picklist/list/draftTaxForms.html* and will not be finalized until after these forms have been approved by OMB under the PRA. Comments on these forms can be submitted at *https://www.irs.gov/forms-pubs/comment-on-tax-forms-and-publications*.

An agency may not conduct or sponsor, and a person is not required to respond to, a collection of information unless it displays a valid control number assigned by the Office of Management and Budget.

Books or records relating to a collection of information must be retained as long as their contents may become material in the administration of any internal revenue law. Generally, tax returns and return information are confidential, as required by 26 U.S.C. 6103.

Regulatory Flexibility Act

Pursuant to the Regulatory Flexibility Act (5 U.S.C. chapter 6), it is hereby certified that these proposed regulations would not have a significant economic impact on a substantial number of small entities. As discussed elsewhere in this preamble, this rule merely provides definitions regarding the applicability of the section 4968 excise tax to certain private colleges and universities. The requirements in this regulation fall only on educational institutions the aggregate fair market values of the non-charitable use assets of which are at least $500,000 per student of the institution and that have at least 500 tuition-paying students (for a minimum investment asset value of $250,000,000).

This proposed rule would not affect a substantial number of small entities. Only about 1 percent of four-year colleges and universities (less than 30 out of over 2,400 institutions in the National Center for Education Statistics' Integrated Post-Secondary Education System Data for 2016) are expected to be affected by the tax. In addition, they are likely to have income from all sources exceeding $27.5 million, the threshold established by the Small Business Administration for an educational institution to be considered a small entity. This is because at a modest 4 percent rate of return, the minimum endowment alone would generate income of $10 million. To generate another $17.5 million in income would require receipts of $35,000 per student if the school had only the minimum number of students, compared to average tuition and fees at a four-year private school, which was $39,529[7] in 2015-16. Therefore, this rule is not likely to affect a substantial number of small entities.

Notwithstanding this certification, the Treasury Department and the IRS invite comments on the impact this rule may have on small entities.

Pursuant to section 7805(f) of the Code, this proposed rule has been submitted to the Chief Counsel for Advocacy of the Small Business Administration for comment on its impact on small entities.

Comments and Requests for Public Hearing

Before these proposed regulations are adopted as final regulations, consideration will be given to any comments that are timely submitted to the IRS as prescribed in the preamble under the **ADDRESSES** section. All comments submitted will be made available at *https://www.regulations.gov* or upon request.

A public hearing may be scheduled if requested in writing by any person that timely submits written comments. If a public hearing is scheduled, notice of the date, time, and place for the hearing will be published in the **Federal Register**.

Drafting Information

The principal authors of these regulations are Melinda Williams and Amber L. MacKenzie, Office of Associate Chief Counsel (Employee Benefits, Exempt Organizations, and Employment Tax). However, other personnel from the Treasury Department and the IRS participated in their development.

Statement of Availability of IRS Documents

IRS Revenue Procedures, Revenue Rulings, Notices, and other guidance cited in this document are published in the Internal Revenue Bulletin (or Cumulative Bulletin) and are available from the Superintendent of Documents, U.S. Government Publishing Office, Washington, DC 20402, or by visiting the IRS website at http://www.irs.gov.

[¶ 49,805] Proposed Amendments of Regulations (REG-121508-18) , published in the Federal Register on July 3, 2019 (corrected 8/21/2019).

[Code Sec. 413]

Multiple employer plans: Unified plan rule: Proposed exception.—Amendments of Reg. § 1.413-2, relating to the tax qualification of plans maintained by more than one employer, are proposed.

AGENCY: Internal Revenue Service (IRS), Treasury.

ACTION: Notice of proposed rulemaking.

SUMMARY: This document sets forth proposed regulations relating to the tax qualification of plans maintained by more than one employer. These plans, maintained pursuant to section 413(c) of the Internal Revenue Code (Code), are often referred to as multiple employer plans or MEPs. The proposed regulations would provide an exception, if certain requirements are met, to the application of the "unified plan rule" for a defined contribution MEP in the event of a failure by an employer participating in the plan to satisfy a qualification requirement or to provide information needed to determine compliance with a qualification requirement. These proposed regulations would affect MEPs, participants in MEPs (and their beneficiaries), employers participating in MEPs, and MEP plan administrators.

DATES: Comments and requests for a public hearing must be received by October 1, 2019.

ADDRESSES: Submit electronic submissions via the Federal eRulemaking Portal at www.regulations.gov (indicate IRS and REG-121508-18) by following the online instructions for submitting comments. Once submitted to the Federal eRulemaking Portal, comments cannot be edited or withdrawn. The Department of the Treasury (Treasury Department) and the IRS will publish for public availability any comment received to its public docket, whether submitted electronically or in hard copy. Send hard copy submissions to: CC:PA:LPD:PR (REG-121508-18), Room 5203, Internal Revenue Service, P.O. Box 7604, Ben Franklin Station, Washington, DC 20044. Submissions may be hand-delivered Monday through Friday between the hours of 8 a.m. and 4 p.m. to CC:PA:LPD:PR (REG-121508-18), Courier's Desk, Internal Revenue Service, 1111 Constitution Avenue NW, Washington, DC 20224.

FOR FURTHER INFORMATION CONTACT: Concerning the regulations, Pamela Kinard at (202) 317-6000 or Jamie Dvoretzky at (202) 317-4102; concerning submission of comments or to request a public hearing, email or call Regina Johnson at notice.comments@irscounsel.treas.gov, (202) 317-5190, or (202) 317-6901 (not toll-free numbers).

SUPPLEMENTARY INFORMATION:

Background

This document sets forth proposed amendments to the Income Tax Regulations (26 CFR part 1) under section 413(c) of the Internal Revenue Code (Code). Section 413(c) provides rules for the qualification of a plan maintained by more than one employer.[1] A section 413(c) plan is often referred to as a multiple employer plan (MEP).

Final regulations under section 413 were published in the **Federal Register** on November 9, 1979, 44 FR 65061 (the final section 413 regulations). The final section 413 regulations apply to multiple employer plans described in section 413(c) and to collectively bargained plans described in section 413(b) (plans that are maintained pursuant to certain collective-bargaining agreements between employee representatives and one or more employers).

Pursuant to section 413(c) and the final section 413 regulations, all of the employers maintaining a MEP (participating employers) are treated as a single employer for purposes of certain section 401(a) qualification requirements. For example:

- Under section 413(c)(1) and § 1.413-2(b), the rules for participation under section 410(a) and the regulations thereunder are applied as if all employees of each of the employers who maintain the plan are employed by a single employer;

---

[7] U.S. Department of Education, National Center for Education Statistics (2018). Digest of Education Statistics, 2016 (NCES 2017-094).

[1] Section 210 of the Employee Retirement Income Security Act of 1974, Public Law 93-406 (88 Stat. 829 (1974)), as amended (ERISA), also provides rules relating to plans maintained by more than one employer. Similar to section 413(c) of the Code, section

210(a) of ERISA states that the minimum participation standards, minimum vesting standards, and benefit accrual requirements under sections 202, 203, and 204 of ERISA, respectively, shall be applied as if all employees of each of the employers were employed by a single employer. Under section 101 of Reorganization Plan No. 4 of 1978 (43 FR 47713), the Secretary of the Treasury has interpretive jurisdiction over section 413 of the Code, as well as ERISA section 210.

- Under section 413(c)(2) and §1.413-2(c), in determining whether a MEP is, with respect to each participating employer, for the exclusive benefit of its employees (and their beneficiaries), all of the employees participating in the plan are treated as employees of each such employer; and

- Under section 413(c)(3) and §1.413-2(d), the minimum vesting standards under section 411 are applied as if all employers who maintain the plan constitute a single employer.

Other rules are applied separately to each participating employer.[2] For example, under §1.413-2(a)(3)(ii), the minimum coverage requirements of section 410(b) generally are applied to a MEP on an employer-by-employer basis.

A plan is not described in section 413(c) unless it is maintained by more than one employer[3] and is a single plan under section 414(l).[4] See §§1.413-2(a)(2)(i) and 1.413-1(a)(2). Under §1.414(l)-1(b), a plan is a single plan if and only if, on an ongoing basis, all of the plan assets are available to pay benefits to employees who are covered by the plan and their beneficiaries.

Under §1.413-2(a)(3)(iv) (sometimes referred to as the "unified plan rule"), the qualification of a MEP is determined with respect to all employers maintaining the MEP. Consequently, §1.413-2(a)(3)(iv) provides that "the failure by one employer maintaining the plan (or by the plan itself) to satisfy an applicable qualification requirement will result in the disqualification of the MEP for all employers maintaining the plan." Section 1.416-1, Q&A G-2, includes a similar rule relating to the qualification of a MEP, providing that a failure by a MEP to satisfy section 416 with respect to employees of one participating employer means that all participating employers in the MEP are maintaining a plan that is not a qualified plan.[5]

Section 1101(a) of the Pension Protection Act of 2006 (PPA '06), Public Law 109-280 (120 Stat. 780 (2006)), provides that the Secretary has full authority to establish and implement EPCRS[6] (or any successor program) and any other employee plans correction policies, including the authority to waive income, excise, or other taxes to ensure that any tax, penalty, or sanction is not excessive and bears a reasonable relationship to the nature, extent, and severity of the failure. Section 1101(b) of PPA '06 provides that the Secretary shall continue to update and improve EPCRS (or any successor program), giving special attention to a number of items, including special concerns and circumstances that small employers face with respect to compliance and correction of compliance failures. EPCRS has been updated and expanded several times, most recently in Rev. Proc. 2019-19, 2019-19 I.R.B. 1086. In addition, as provided for in Section 1101 of PPA '06, the Treasury Department and the IRS are authorized to establish and implement other employee plans correction policies, outside of EPCRS.

On August 31, 2018, President Trump issued Executive Order 13847 (83 FR 45321 (Sept. 6, 2018)), titled "Strengthening Retirement Security in America" (Executive Order). The Executive Order states that it shall be the policy of the Federal Government to expand access to workplace retirement plans for American workers and that enhancing workplace retirement plan coverage is critical to ensuring that American workers will be financially prepared to retire. The Executive Order also states that, "[e]xpanding access to [MEPs], under which employees of different private-sector employers may participate in a single retirement plan, is an efficient way to reduce administrative costs of retirement plan establishment and maintenance and would encourage more plan formation and broader availability of workplace retirement plans, especially among small employers."[7]

The Executive Order directs the Secretary of the Treasury to "consider proposing amendments to regulations or other guidance, consistent with applicable law and the policy set forth in . . . this order, regarding the circumstances under which a MEP may satisfy the tax qualification requirements . . . , including the consequences if one or more employers that sponsored or adopted the plan fails to take one or more actions necessary to meet those requirements."[8] The Executive Order further directs the Secretary of the Treasury to consult with the Secretary of Labor in advance of issuing any such proposed guidance, and the Secretary of Labor to take steps to facilitate the implementation of any guidance, as appropriate and consistent with applicable law.

Stakeholders have expressed concerns about the risk that the actions of one or more participating employers might disqualify a MEP[9] and that some employers are reluctant to join MEPs without an exception to the unified plan rule. In particular, they have said that the cooperation of participating employers is needed for compliance and when a participating employer refuses to take the steps needed to maintain qualification, the entire plan is at risk of being disqualified. Stakeholders assert that without an exception to the unified plan rule, many employers perceive that the benefits of joining a MEP are outweighed by the risk of plan disqualification based on the actions of an uncooperative participating employer.

---

[2] Proposed rules at §1.413-2(e) and (f) (47 FR 54093) were issued in 1982. Proposed §1.413-2(e) would have provided that the minimum funding standard for a MEP is determined as if all participants in the plan were employed by a single employer, and proposed §1.413-2(f) would have provided rules relating to liability for the excise tax on a failure to meet the minimum funding standards. Because these rules were proposed in 1982, they do not reflect 1988 changes to section 413(c)(4) that were made by section 6058(a) of the Technical and Miscellaneous Revenue Act of 1988, Public Law 100-647 (102 Stat. 3342) (TAMRA). As amended by TAMRA, section 413(c)(4) generally provides that in the case of a plan established after December 31, 1988, and in the case of a plan established before that date for which an election was made, each employer is treated as maintaining a separate plan for purposes of the minimum funding standards. The proposed rules at §1.413-2(e) and (f) are outside the scope of these proposed regulations. Therefore, paragraphs (e) and (f) are "Reserved" for future rulemaking. The Treasury Department and the IRS note that taxpayers must take into account the statutory changes made after the issuance of the proposed regulations as of the effective dates of the relevant legislation.

[3] Section 1.413-2(a)(2), issued in 1979, provides that for purposes of determining the number of employers maintaining a plan, any employers described in section 414(b) that are members of a controlled group of corporations or any employers described in section 414(c) that are trades or businesses under common control, whichever is applicable, are treated as if those employers are a single employer. Because §1.413-2(a)(2) was issued in 1979, it does not address section 414(m), which was added in 1980 by section 201(a) of the Miscellaneous Revenue Act of 1980, Public Law 96-605 (94 Stat. 3521). Section 414(m) provides that all employers in an affiliated service group shall be treated as a single employer. Although amendments to §1.413-2(a)(2) are outside the scope of these proposed regulations, the Treasury Department and the IRS note that taxpayers must take into account the statutory changes made after the issuance of the proposed regulations as of the effective dates of the relevant legislation.

[4] On October 23, 2018 proposed Department of Labor regulations were published in the **Federal Register** (83 FR 53534) clarifying the circumstances in which employer groups or associations and professional employer organizations can constitute "employers" within the meaning of section 3(5) of ERISA for purposes of establishing or maintaining an individual account "employee pension benefit plan" within the meaning

of ERISA section 3(2). Those proposed regulations state that an "employee pension benefit plan" under section 3(2) of ERISA must be established by an "employer," defined in section 3(5) of ERISA to include an "entity acting indirectly in the interest of an employer in relation to an employee benefit plan." The proposed Department of Labor regulations define the terms "bona fide group or association of employers" and "bona fide professional employer organization" and state that, with respect to a "multiple employer defined contribution pension plan," these entities "shall be deemed to be able to act in the interest of an employer" provided that certain conditions are met. See proposed rules at 29 CFR 2510.3-55(a). The proposed Department of Labor regulations solicit comments on, but do not address, other types of entities that may be an employer under ERISA section 3(5).

[5] This rule is based on the unified plan rule in §1.413-2(a)(3)(iv). Therefore, if a defined contribution MEP has an unresponsive employer that fails to satisfy section 416 and the defined contribution MEP meets the conditions for the exception to the unified plan rule in these proposed regulations, the defined contribution MEP will not be disqualified for the section 416 failure. For further information, see the discussion in part II of the Explanation of Provisions section entitled *Conditions for Application of Exception to the Unified Plan Rule.* The rules in §1.416-1 are outside the scope of these proposed regulations, but the Treasury Department and the IRS intend to address the topic in a broader guidance project updating the regulations under section 416.

[6] The Employee Plans Compliance Resolution System (EPCRS) is a comprehensive system of correction programs for sponsors of certain retirement plans, including plans that are intended to satisfy the qualification requirements of section 401(a). EPCRS provides procedures for an employer to correct a plan's failure to satisfy an applicable qualification requirement so that the failure does not result in disqualification of the plan.

[7] *Id.* at 45321.

[8] *Id.* at 45322.

[9] *See also,* U.S. Gov't Accountability Office, GAO-12-665, "Federal Agencies Should Collect Data and Coordinate Oversight of Multiple Employer Plans" (September 2012) (*https://www.gao.gov/assets/650/648285.pdf*) (identifying the unified plan rule as a potential problem for MEPs).

Explanation of Provisions

I. *Overview*

In accordance with the Executive Order and the policy of expanding workplace retirement plan coverage, these proposed regulations, which were developed in consultation with the Secretary of Labor, would provide an exception to the unified plan rule for certain defined contribution MEPs. Under the proposed regulations, a defined contribution MEP would be eligible for the exception to the unified plan rule on account of certain qualification failures due to actions or inaction by a participating employer, if the conditions set forth in the proposed regulations are satisfied. The exception generally would be available if the participating employer in a MEP is responsible for a qualification failure that the employer is unable or unwilling to correct. It would also be available if the participating employer fails to comply with the section 413(c) plan administrator's request for information about a qualification failure that the section 413(c) plan administrator reasonably believes might exist. For the exception to the unified plan rule to apply, certain actions are required to be taken, including, in certain circumstances, a spinoff of the assets and account balances attributable to participants who are employees of such an employer to a separate plan and a termination of that plan.

For purposes of applying the exception to the unified plan rule, under the proposed regulations: (1) a section 413(c) plan administrator is defined as the plan administrator of a MEP, determined under the rules of section 414(g); (2) a participating employer is defined as one of the employers maintaining a MEP; (3) an unresponsive participating employer is defined as a participating employer in a MEP that fails to comply with reasonable and timely requests from the section 413(c) plan administrator for information necessary to determine compliance with a qualification requirement or fails to comply with reasonable and timely requests from the section 413(c) plan administrator to take actions that are needed to correct a failure to satisfy a qualification requirement as it relates to the participating employer; and (4) an employee is defined as a current or former employee of a participating employer.

The exception to the unified plan rule would apply only in the case of certain types of failures to satisfy the qualification requirements, referred to in the proposed regulations as participating employer failures. A participating employer failure is defined as either a known qualification failure or a potential qualification failure. A known qualification failure is defined as a failure to satisfy a qualification requirement with respect to a MEP that is identified by the section 413(c) plan administrator and is attributable solely to an unresponsive participating employer. A potential qualification failure is a failure to satisfy a qualification requirement with respect to a MEP that the section 413(c) plan administrator reasonably believes might exist, but the section 413(c) plan administrator is unable to determine whether the qualification requirement is satisfied solely due to an unresponsive participating employer's failure to provide data, documents, or any other information necessary to determine whether the MEP is in compliance with the qualification requirement as it relates to the participating employer. For purposes of the definitions of known qualification failure and potential qualification failure, an unresponsive participating employer includes any employer that is treated as a single employer with that unresponsive participating employer under section 414(b), (c), (m), or (o).

II. *Conditions for Application of Exception to Unified Plan Rule*

Under the exception to the unified plan rule in the proposed regulations, a defined contribution MEP would not be disqualified on account of a participating employer failure, provided that the following conditions are satisfied: (1) the MEP satisfies certain eligibility requirements (such as a requirement to have established practices and procedures to promote compliance and a requirement to adopt relevant plan language); (2) the section 413(c) plan administrator provides notice and an opportunity for the unresponsive participating employer to take remedial action with respect to the participating employer failure; (3) if the unresponsive participating employer fails to take appropriate remedial action with respect to the participating employer failure, the section 413(c) plan administrator implements a spinoff; and (4) the section 413(c) plan administrator complies with any information request that the IRS or a representative of the spun-off plan makes in connection with an IRS examination of the spun-off plan, including any information request related to the participation of the unresponsive participating employer in the MEP for years prior to the spinoff. A spinoff may either be a spinoff that is initiated by the unresponsive participating employer and implemented by the section 413(c) plan administrator, or a spinoff-termination implemented by the section 413(c) plan administrator pursuant to plan terms.

A. *MEP's Eligibility for Exception to the Unified Plan Rule*

Under the proposed regulations, a threshold condition for the exception to the unified plan rule is that the MEP meet certain eligibility requirements. Specifically, the proposed regulations would require the section 413(c) plan administrator to have established practices and procedures (formal or informal) that are reasonably designed to promote and facilitate overall compliance with applicable Code requirements, including procedures for obtaining information from participating employers. In addition, the plan document would need to include language describing the procedures that would be followed to address participating employer failures, including the procedures that the section 413(c) plan administrator would follow if, after receiving notice from the section 413(c) plan administrator, an unresponsive participating employer fails to take appropriate remedial action or to initiate a spinoff from the MEP pursuant to the regulations.[10] Finally, a MEP is not eligible for the exception to the unified plan rule if, as of the date that the first notice is provided to an unresponsive participating employer, the MEP is under examination. For a description of the first notice, see part II.B. of this Explanation of Provisions section, entitled *Notice Requirements*.

For purposes of the proposed regulations, a plan is under examination if: (1) the plan is under an Employee Plans examination (that is, an examination of a Form 5500 series, "Annual Return/Report of Employee Benefit Plan," or other examination by the Employee Plans Office of the Tax Exempt and Government Entities Division of the IRS (Employee Plans) (or any successor IRS office that has jurisdiction over qualified retirement plans)); (2) the plan is under investigation by the Criminal Investigation Division of the IRS (or its successor); or (3) the plan is treated as under an Employee Plans examination under special rules. Under these special rules, for example, a plan is under an Employee Plans examination if the section 413(c) plan administrator, or an authorized representative, has received verbal or written notification of an impending Employee Plans examination, or of an impending referral for an Employee Plans examination, or if a plan has been under an Employee Plans examination and the plan has an appeal pending with the IRS Office of Appeals (or its successor), or is in litigation with the IRS, regarding issues raised in the Employee Plans examination.

This definition of the term under examination is similar to the definition in EPCRS. *See* Rev. Proc. 2019-19, section 5.08. However, unlike in EPCRS, a plan is not under examination for purposes of these proposed regulations merely because it is maintained by an employer that is under an Exempt Organizations examination (that is, an examination of a Form 990 series or other examination by the Exempt Organizations Office of the Tax Exempt and Government Entities Division of the IRS).

B. *Notice Requirements*

The proposed regulations would require the section 413(c) plan administrator to provide up to three notices regarding a participating employer failure to the unresponsive participating employer; with the third notice, if applicable, also being provided to participants and beneficiaries and the Department of Labor.[11]

---

[10] Once final regulations are issued, the Treasury Department and the IRS intend to publish guidance in the Internal Revenue Bulletin setting forth model language that may be used for this purpose.

[11] If the notices relate to a potential qualification failure, and the potential qualification failure becomes a known qualification failure, then a new series of notices may be required.

The first notice must describe the participating employer failure (or failures), as well as the remedial actions the unresponsive participating employer would need to take to remedy the failure and the employer's option to initiate a spinoff. The first notice must also explain the consequences under plan terms if the unresponsive participating employer neither takes appropriate remedial action with respect to the participating employer failure nor initiates a spinoff, including the possibility that a spinoff of the plan assets and account balances attributable to the employees of that employer into a separate single-employer plan would occur, followed by a termination of that plan (as discussed in this preamble under the heading *Spinoff-Termination*).

If, by the end of the 90-day period following the date the first notice is provided, the unresponsive participating employer neither takes appropriate remedial action nor initiates a spinoff, then no later than 30 days after the expiration of that 90-day period, the section 413(c) plan administrator must provide a second notice to that employer. The second notice must include the information required to be included in the first notice, and must also inform the employer that if it fails either to take appropriate remedial action or to initiate a spinoff within 90 days after the second notice then a notice describing the participating employer failure and the consequences of not correcting that failure will be provided to participants who are employees of the unresponsive participating employer (and their beneficiaries) and to the Department of Labor.

If, by the end of the 90-day period following the date the second notice is provided, the unresponsive participating employer neither takes appropriate remedial action nor initiates a spinoff, then no later than 30 days after the expiration of that 90-day period, the section 413(c) plan administrator must provide a third notice to the unresponsive participating employer, to participants who are employees of that employer (and their beneficiaries), and to the Department of Labor.[12] The third notice must include the information required to be included in the first notice, the deadline for employer action, and an explanation of any adverse consequences to participants in the event that a spinoff-termination occurs, and state that the notice is being provided to participants who are employees of the unresponsive participating employer (and their beneficiaries) and to the Department of Labor.

C. Actions by Unresponsive Participating Employer

The proposed regulations provide that after the unresponsive participating employer has received notice of the participating employer failure, the employer has the opportunity to either take appropriate remedial action or initiate a spinoff. The final deadline for an unresponsive participating employer to take one of these actions is 90 days after the third notice is provided. The consequences of the employer's failure to meet this deadline are described in this Explanation of Provisions section under part II.E., entitled *Spinoff-Termination*.

The proposed regulations provide that an unresponsive participating employer takes appropriate remedial action with respect to a potential qualification failure if the employer provides data, documents, or any other information necessary for the section 413(c) plan administrator to determine whether a qualification failure exists. If (1) the unresponsive participating employer provides this information, (2) the section 413(c) plan administrator determines that, based on this information, a qualification failure exists that is attributable solely to that employer, and (3) the participating employer fails to comply with reasonable and timely requests from the section 413(c) plan administrator to take actions that are needed to correct that qualification failure, then the qualification failure becomes a known qualification failure. In that case, the MEP would be eligible for the exception to the unified plan rule with respect to the known qualification failure by satisfying the conditions with respect to that known qualification failure, taking into account the rules described in this Explanation of Provisions section under part II.D., entitled *Actions by Section 413(c) Plan Administrator Relating to Remedial Action or Employer-Initiated Spinoff*. An unresponsive participating employer takes appropriate remedial action with respect to a known qualification failure if the employer takes action, such as making corrective contributions, that corrects, or enables the section 413(c) plan administrator to correct, the known qualification failure.

As an alternative to taking appropriate remedial action with respect to a potential or a known qualification failure, an unresponsive participating employer may, after receiving notice of the participating employer failure, initiate a spinoff by directing the section 413(c) plan administrator to spin off plan assets and account balances held on behalf of employees of that employer to a separate single-employer plan established and maintained by that employer in a manner consistent with plan terms. In that case, the section 413(c) plan administrator must implement that spinoff, as described in this Explanation of Provisions section under part II.D., entitled *Actions by Section 413(c) Plan Administrator Relating to Remedial Action or Employer-Initiated Spinoff*.

D. Actions by Section 413(c) Plan Administrator Relating to Remedial Action or Employer-Initiated Spinoff

For purposes of applying the conditions of the exception to the unified plan rule to a potential qualification failure that becomes a known qualification failure, actions taken (including notices provided) when the failure was a potential qualification failure are not taken into account. For example, a notice that the section 413(c) plan administrator provided in connection with the potential qualification failure would not satisfy the notice requirements for the known qualification failure. However, in determining whether the MEP is under examination as of the date of the first notice describing the known qualification failure, the section 413(c) plan administrator will be treated as providing that notice on the date the first notice was provided with respect to the related potential qualification failure, but only if the following conditions are satisfied: (1) after determining that a qualification failure exists, the section 413(c) plan administrator makes a reasonable and timely request to the participating employer to take actions that are needed to correct the failure, and (2) as soon as reasonably practicable after the participating employer fails to respond to that request, the section 413(c) plan administrator provides the first notice with respect to the known qualification failure.

The Treasury Department and the IRS anticipate revising EPCRS to provide that, if a section 413(c) plan administrator provides the first notice with respect to a participating employer failure under a MEP at a time that the plan is not under examination, then the MEP will not be considered to be under examination for purposes of determining whether the participating employer failure is eligible to be corrected under the Self Correction Program or Voluntary Correction Program components of EPCRS. It is anticipated that this application of the term under examination under EPCRS will be conditioned on the section 413(c) plan administrator complying with applicable conditions for the exception to the unified plan rule and, for a known qualification failure with respect to which the unresponsive participating employer takes appropriate remedial action, taking any remaining action necessary to correct the qualification failure as soon as reasonably practicable.

If an unresponsive participating employer takes appropriate remedial action with respect to a known qualification failure, then the section 413(c) plan administrator must take any remaining action necessary to correct the qualification failure. If the section 413(c) plan administrator fails to take any remaining action necessary to correct the known qualification failure, the exception to the unified plan rule will not apply and the section 413(c) plan may be disqualified on account of that failure.

If, instead of taking appropriate remedial action (as described in part II.C. of this Explanation of Provisions, entitled *Actions by Unresponsive Participating Employer*), an unresponsive participating employer initiates a spinoff of plan assets and account balances held on behalf of employees of that employer to a separate single-employer plan established and maintained by that employer, the section 413(c) plan administrator must implement and complete a spinoff of the plan assets and account balances held on behalf of the employees of the employer that are attributable to employment by the employer within 180 days of the date on which it was initiated. The section 413(c) plan administrator must also report the spinoff to the IRS (in the manner prescribed by the IRS in forms, instructions, and other guidance).

---

[12] The notice to the Department of Labor should be mailed to the Employee Benefits Security Administration's Office of Enforcement (or its successor office). The Office of Enforcement is currently located at 200 Constitution Ave., NW, Suite 600, Washington, DC 20210.

E. *Spinoff-Termination*

If, after the first notice of a participating employer failure is provided, the unresponsive participating employer neither takes appropriate remedial action nor initiates a spinoff by the date that is 90 days after the third notice is provided, then, for the exception to the unified plan rule to apply, there must be a spinoff of the plan assets and account balances held on behalf of employees of the unresponsive participating employer that are attributable to their employment with that employer to a separate plan, followed by a termination of that plan. The spinoff-termination must be pursuant to plan terms and in accordance with the proposed regulations. The MEP will satisfy this condition, if, as soon as reasonably practicable after the deadline for action by the unresponsive participating employer, the section 413(c) plan administrator: (1) provides notice of the spinoff-termination to participants who are employees of the unresponsive participating employer (and their beneficiaries); (2) stops accepting contributions from the unresponsive participating employer; (3) implements a spinoff, in accordance with the transfer requirements of section 414(l) and the anti-cutback requirements of section 411(d)(6), of the plan assets and account balances held on behalf of employees of the unresponsive participating employer that are attributable to their employment by that employer to a separate single-employer plan and trust that has the same plan administrator, trustee, and substantive plan terms as the MEP; and (4) terminates the spun-off plan and distributes assets of the spun-off plan to plan participants and beneficiaries as soon as reasonably practicable after the plan termination date.[13]

In terminating the spun-off plan, the section 413(c) plan administrator must:

- Reasonably determine whether, and to what extent, the survivor annuity requirements of sections 401(a)(11) and 417 apply to any benefit payable under the plan and take reasonable steps to comply with those requirements (if applicable);

- Provide each participant and beneficiary with a nonforfeitable right to his or her accrued benefits as of the date of plan termination, subject to income, expenses, gains, and losses between that date and the date of distribution; and

- Notify the participants and beneficiaries of their rights under section 402(f).

In providing notice of the spinoff-termination to participants (and their beneficiaries), the section 413(c) plan administrator must provide information relating to the spinoff-termination to participants who are employees of the unresponsive participating employer (and their beneficiaries), including the following: (1) identification of the MEP and contact information for the section 413(c) plan administrator; (2) the effective date of the spinoff-termination; (3) a statement that no more contributions will be made to the MEP; (4) a statement that as soon as practicable after the spinoff-termination, participants and beneficiaries will receive a distribution from the spun-off plan; and (5) a statement that before the distribution occurs, participants and beneficiaries will receive additional information about their options with respect to that distribution.

The section 413(c) plan administrator must report the spinoff-termination to the IRS (in the manner prescribed by the IRS in forms, instructions, and other guidance).

III. *Other Rules*

A. *Form of Notices*

Any notices required to be provided under the proposed regulations may be provided in writing or in electronic form. For notices provided to participants and beneficiaries, see generally § 1.401(a)-21 for rules permitting the use of electronic media to provide applicable notices to recipients with respect to retirement plans.

B. *Qualification of Spun-Off Plan*

In the case of any plan that is spun off in accordance with the proposed regulations, any participating employer failure that would have affected the qualification of a MEP, but for the application of the exception to the unified plan rule, will be a qualification failure with respect to the spun-off plan. In the case of an employer-initiated spinoff, see EPCRS (or its successors) for rules relating to correcting qualification failures.

Under the authority provided by section 1101 of PPA '06, the proposed regulations provide that distributions made from a spun-off plan that is terminated in accordance with these regulations would not, solely because of the participating employer failure, fail to be eligible for favorable tax treatment accorded to distributions from qualified plans (including that the distributions will be treated as eligible rollover distributions under section 402(c)(4)), except as provided in the next paragraph. Under section 1101 of PPA '06, Congress gave the Secretary broad authority to establish employee plans correction policies. In developing a correction policy for MEPs, it is appropriate to treat distributions to rank-and-file participants following a spinoff-termination as eligible for tax-favored treatment in order to ensure that the tax or sanction is not excessive and bears a reasonable relationship to the nature of the failure.[14]

The regulations also provide that, notwithstanding the general rule regarding favorable tax treatment for distributions from a plan following spinoff-termination, the IRS reserves the right to pursue appropriate remedies under the Code against any party (such as the owner of the participating employer) who is responsible for the participating employer failure resulting in the spinoff-termination. The IRS may pursue appropriate remedies against a responsible party even in the party's capacity as a participant or beneficiary under the plan that is spun off and terminated (such as by not treating a plan distribution made to the responsible party as an eligible rollover distribution). This is similar to the approach adopted in EPCRS with respect to terminating orphan plans. *See* Rev. Proc. 2019-19, section 6.02(2)(e)(i).

The proposed regulations also provide that the Commissioner may provide additional guidance, such as in revenue rulings, notices, or other guidance published in the Internal Revenue Bulletin, or in forms and instructions, that the Commissioner determines to be necessary or appropriate with respect to the requirements of the regulations.

Proposed Applicability Date

These regulations generally are proposed to apply on or after the date of publication of the Treasury decision adopting these rules as final regulations in the **Federal Register**. Until regulations finalizing these proposed regulations are issued, taxpayers may not rely on the rules set forth in these proposed regulations.

Availability of IRS Documents

For copies of recently issued revenue procedures, revenue rulings, notices and other guidance published in the Internal Revenue Bulletin, please visit the IRS Web site at *www.irs.gov* or contact the Superintendent of Documents, U.S. Government Printing Office, Washington, DC 20402.

---

[13] The Pension Benefit Guaranty Corporation's Missing Participants Program provides a mechanism for distributing assets to plan participants in a terminating plan. *See* 29 CFR 4050.201 through 4050.207. Use of the Pension Benefit Guaranty Corporation's Missing Participants Program is optional for defined contribution plans. Under the program, the Pension Benefit Guaranty Corporation locates participants and beneficiaries who were missing when their plans terminated. When found, depending on arrangements made by the plan, the Pension Benefit Guaranty Corporation either provides the benefit or information about where the participant's account is being held.

[14] In addition, a participating employer failure could either be a known qualification failure or a potential qualification failure. Treating distributions from a spun-off and terminated plan relating to a potential qualification failure as ineligible for tax-favored treatment does not bear a reasonable relationship to the nature of the failure.

Special Analyses

I. *Regulatory Impact Analysis*

Executive Orders 13771, 13563, and 12866 direct agencies to assess costs and benefits of available regulatory alternatives and, if regulation is necessary, to select regulatory approaches that maximize net benefits, including potential economic, environmental, public health and safety effects, distributive impacts, and equity. Executive Order 13563 emphasizes the importance of quantifying both costs and benefits, reducing costs, harmonizing rules, and promoting flexibility. The Executive Order 13771 designation for any final rule resulting from the proposed regulation will be informed by comments received. The preliminary Executive Order 13771 designation for this proposed rule is deregulatory.

The proposed regulation has been designated by the Office of Information and Regulatory Affairs (OIRA) as significant under Executive Order 12866 pursuant to the Memorandum of Agreement (MOA, April 11, 2018) between the Treasury Department and the Office of Management and Budget regarding review of tax regulations.

1. *Introduction and Need for Regulation*

The U.S. retirement system is comprised of three main pillars of savings: Social Security, workplace pension plans, and individual savings. Yet, roughly 30% of American workers lack access to an employer-sponsored savings vehicle (See Table 1 in Section 7 of this Regulatory Impact Analysis, entitled *Tables*). This is particularly true for employees at small firms, who are roughly half as likely to have access to a retirement plan compared to employees at large firms. This would lead to larger firms enjoying a competitive advantage in labor markets. One factor that may prevent small firms from offering a plan includes the high administrative costs associated with compliance. In order to receive preferential tax treatment, a plan must meet certain criteria specified in the Code and ensuring that those requirements are met can be costly. Furthermore, the costs associated with managing funds in retirement plans tends to be higher for a smaller pool of assets (See Table 3 in Section 7, later), which is more likely to be the case for smaller firms with fewer employees.

One solution that has developed for reducing these administrative and asset management costs is the MEP, through which different employers can form a single plan to take advantage of economies of scale. Under the current regulations under section 413(c), however, the unified plan rule creates a situation whereby should one employer fail to comply with the qualification requirements, then the preferential tax status for a qualified plan is lost for the entire MEP. The proposed regulation provides an exception to the unified plan rule for certain defined contribution MEPs, permitting compliant participating employers to continue to maintain a qualified plan if certain conditions are satisfied. Reducing the perceived risk that a MEP will be disqualified could lead to more small employers adopting these plans.

2. *Affected Entities*

Based on the latest available data, as shown in Table 2, there are about 4,630 defined contribution MEPs with approximately 4.4 million total participants, 3.7 million of whom are active participants. Defined contribution MEPs hold about $181 billion in assets. Fifty-six percent of defined contribution MEP participants are in MEPs with 10,000 or more participants, and 98% are in MEPs with 100 or more participants. As noted earlier, about 30% of employees do not have access to a retirement savings plan through their employer. The proposed regulation, which is limited to defined contribution MEPs, may encourage both the creation of new defined contribution MEPs and the expansion of existing defined contribution MEPs. As a result of the proposed regulation, the cost of providing some existing employer-sponsored retirement plans could fall, and some employees would gain access to employer-sponsored retirement plans.

3. *Baseline*

The analysis in this section compares the proposed regulation to a no-action baseline reflecting anticipated Federal income tax-related behavior in the absence of these proposed regulations.

4. *Benefits*

a. *Expanded Access to Coverage*

Generally, employees rarely choose to save for retirement outside of the workplace, despite having options to save in tax-favored savings vehicles on their own; only about 10% of households without access to an employer-sponsored plan made contributions to traditional or Roth IRAs for 2014.[15] Thus, the availability of workplace retirement plans is a significant factor affecting whether individuals save for their retirement. Yet, despite the advantages of workplace retirements plans, access to such plans for employees of small businesses is relatively low.

The MEP structure may address significant concerns from employers about the costs to set up and administer retirement benefit plans. In order to participate in a MEP, employers would simply execute a participation agreement or similar instrument setting forth the rights and obligations of the MEP and participating employers. Each participating employer would then be participating in a single plan, rather than sponsoring its own separate plan. The individual employers would not be directly responsible for the MEP's overall compliance with reporting and disclosure obligations. Accordingly, the MEP structure may address small employers' concerns regarding the cost associated with fiduciary liability of sponsoring a retirement plan by effectively transferring much of the legal risks and responsibilities to professional fiduciaries who would be responsible for managing plan assets and selecting investment menu options, among other things. Participating employers' continuing involvement in the day-to-day operations and administration of their MEP generally would be limited to enrolling employees and forwarding employee and employer contributions to the plan. Thus, participating employers would keep more of their day-to-day focus on managing their businesses, rather than their retirement plans.

The proposed regulation would reduce the risk to small businesses participating in a MEP. Currently, if one participating employer fails to meet the qualification requirements in the Code for preferential tax treatment, then the entire plan may be disqualified, and employers participating in a MEP and their employees would lose the tax benefits of participating in a qualified retirement plan (deduction for contributions, exclusion of investment returns, deferred income recognition for employees). As a result, the current rule imposes an undue burden on employers who satisfied their requirements but happened to have a bad actor among their plan's other employers. The proposed regulation minimizes this burden by allowing noncompliant or unresponsive participating employers to be dealt with separately while the other participating employers maintain a qualified plan. Thus, the risk taken on by any one participating employer when joining a MEP is reduced as the employer no longer needs to consider the actions of other participating employers over which the employer exerts no control. The proposed regulation may therefore encourage formation of additional MEPs, as well as expanded participation in existing MEPs.

Because more plan formation and broader availability of such plans is likely to occur due to the proposed regulations, especially among small employers, the Treasury Department has determined that the proposed regulation would increase access to retirement plans for many American workers. However, the Treasury Department does not have sufficient data to determine precisely the likely extent of increased participation by small employers under the proposed regulation.

---

[15] Based on tabulations from the Office of Tax Analysis' microsimulation model

b. *Reduced Fees and Administration Savings*

Most MEPs could be expected to benefit from scale advantages that small businesses do not currently enjoy and to pass on some of the savings to participating employers and employees. Grouping small employers together into a MEP may facilitate savings through administrative efficiencies (economies of scale) and potentially through price negotiation (market power).

As scale increases, MEPs would spread fixed costs over a larger pool of participating employers and employee participants. Scale efficiencies can be very large with respect to asset management and may be smaller, but still meaningful, with respect to recordkeeping. Also, as scale increases, so does the negotiating power of MEPs. Negotiating power matters when competition among financial services providers is less than perfect, and they can command greater profits than in an environment with perfect competition. Very large plans may exercise their own market power to negotiate lower prices, translating into savings for member employers and employee participants.

Sometimes, scale efficiencies would not translate into savings for small employer members and their employee participants because regulatory requirements applicable to large MEPs may be more stringent than those applicable to most separate small plans. For example, some small plans are exempt from annual reporting requirements, and many others are subject to more streamlined reporting requirements than larger plans. But in most cases, the savings from the scale efficiency of MEPs would be greater than the savings from scale efficiencies that other providers of bundled financial services may offer to small employers.

First, the legal status of MEPs as a single large plan may streamline certain regulatory burdens under the Code and title I of ERISA. For example, a MEP can file a single annual return/report and obtain a single bond in lieu of the multiple reports and bonds necessary when other providers of bundled financial services administer many separate plans.

Second, relative to separate small employer plans, a MEP operating as a large single plan would likely secure substantially lower prices from financial services companies. Asset managers commonly offer proportionally lower prices, relative to assets invested, to larger investors, under so-called tiered pricing practices. For example, investment companies often offer lower-priced mutual fund share classes to customers whose investments in a fund surpass specified break points. These lower prices may reflect scale economies in any or all aspects of administering larger accounts, such as marketing, distribution, asset management, recordkeeping, and transaction processing. MEPs that are larger would likely qualify for lower pricing compared with separate plans of small employers. MEP participants that benefit from lower asset-based fees would enjoy superior investment returns net of fees.

The availability and magnitude of scale efficiencies may be different with respect to different retirement plan services. For example, asset management generally enjoys very large-scale efficiencies. Investors of all kinds generally benefit by investing in large co-mingled pools. Even within large pools, however, small investors often pay higher fees than larger ones. Investors with more assets to invest may pay lower costs when using mutual funds as investment vehicles.

As with asset management, scale efficiencies often are available with respect to other plan services. For example, the marginal costs of services such as marketing and distribution, account administration, and transaction processing often decrease as customer size increases. Similarly, small pension plans sometimes incur high distribution costs, reflecting commissions paid to agents and brokers who sell investment products to plans. MEPs, as large customers, may enjoy scale efficiencies in the acquisition of such services. It is also possible, however, that the cost to MEPs of servicing many small employer-members may diminish or even offset such efficiencies. Stated differently, MEPs' scale efficiencies may not always exceed the scale efficiencies from other providers of bundled financial services used by small employers that sponsor separate plans. In addition, even if MEPs are able to enjoy scale efficiencies greater than the scale efficiencies available from other providers of bundled financial services, the scale efficiencies of MEPs catering to small businesses would still likely be smaller than the scale efficiencies enjoyed by very large single-employer plans.

By reducing the risk to employers of participating in a MEP, the proposed regulation would allow more MEPs to be established and to pursue scale advantages. It would also extend scale advantages to some existing MEPs that otherwise might have been too small to achieve them and to small employers that absent the proposed regulation would have offered separate plans (or no plans), but that under this proposed regulation may participate in a MEP.

While MEP's scale advantages may be smaller than the scale advantages enjoyed by very large single-employer plans, it nonetheless is illuminating to consider the savings historically enjoyed by the latter. For an illustration of how much investment fees vary based on the amount of assets in a 401(k) plan, see Table 3 in Section 7 of this Regulatory Impact Analysis entitled *Tables*. The table focuses on mutual funds, which are the most common investment vehicle in 401(k) plans, and shows that the average expense ratio is inversely related to plan size. There are some important caveats to interpreting Table 3. The first is that it does not include data for most of the smallest plans since plans with fewer than 100 participants generally are not required to submit audited financial statements with their Form 5500. The second is that there is variation across plans in whether and to what degree the cost of recordkeeping is included in the expense ratios.

Another method for comparing plan size advantages is a broader measure called "total plan cost" calculated by BrightScope that includes fees reported on the audited Form 5500. As Table 4 shows, total plan cost yields generally similar results about the cost differences facing small and large plans. Deloitte Consulting LLP, for the Investment Company Institute, conducted a survey of 361 defined contributions plans.[16] The study calculates the "all-in" fee that is comparable across plans, and includes both administrative and investment fees paid by the plan and participants. Generally, small plans with 10 or fewer participants are paying approximately 50 basis points more than plans with more than 1,000 participants. Generally, small plans with 10 or fewer participants are paying about 90 basis points more than large plans with more than 50,000 participants.

The research studies described under this heading, *Reduced Fees and Administrative Costs*, show that small plans and their participants generally pay higher fees than large plans and their participants. Because this rule would give many small employers the incentive to join a MEP, some of which may become very large plans, many of these employers would likely incur lower fees. Many employers that are not currently offering any retirement plan may join a MEP, leading their employees to save for retirement. Many employers already sponsoring a retirement plan might decide to join a MEP instead. If there are lower fees in the MEPs than in their previous plans, those lower fees would translate into higher savings.

c. *Reduced Reporting and Audit Costs*

The potential for MEPs to enjoy reporting cost savings merits separate attention because this potential is shaped not only by economic forces, but also the reporting requirements applicable to different plans. On the one hand, a MEP, as a single ERISA plan, can file a single report and conduct a single audit, while separate plans may be required to file separate reports and conduct separate audits. On the other hand, a MEP, as a large plan generally is subject to more stringent reporting and audit requirements than a small plan, which likely files no or streamlined reports and undergoes no audits. With respect to reporting and audits, MEPs may offer more savings to medium-sized employers (with 100 or more retirement plan participants) that are already subject to more stringent reporting and audit requirements than to small employers. Small employers that otherwise would have fallen outside of reporting and audit requirements sometimes would incur slightly higher costs by joining MEPs. This cost

---

[16] Deloitte Consulting and Investment Company Institute, "Inside the Structure of Defined Contribution/401(k) Plan Fees, 2013: A Study Assessing the Mechanics of the 'All-in' Fee" (Aug. 2014) (available at *https://www2.deloitte.com/content/dam/Deloitte/us/Documents/human-capital/us-cons-401k-fee-study-2013-082014.pdf*).

increase may still be offset by benefits described in other sections. From a broader point of view, if auditing becomes more prevalent because small employers join MEPs, that would lead to more and better quality data that would improve security for employers, participants and beneficiaries.

Sponsors of ERISA-covered retirement plans generally must file a Form 5500 annually, with all required schedules and attachments. The cost burden incurred to satisfy the Form 5500 related reporting requirements varies by plan type, size and complexity. Analyzing the 2016 Form 5500 filings, the Department of Labor estimates that the average cost to file the Form 5500 is as follows: $276 per filer for small (generally less than 100 plan participants) single-employer defined contribution plans eligible for Form 5500-SF; $437 per filer for small single-employer defined contribution plans not eligible to file Form 5500-SF; and $1,686 per filer for larger (generally 100 participants or more) single-employer defined contribution plans, plus the cost of an audit.

Additional schedules and reporting may be required for large and complex plans. For example, large retirement plans are required to attach auditors' reports to their Form 5500. Most small plans are not required to obtain or attach such reports. Hiring an auditor and obtaining an audit report can be costly for plans, and audit fees may increase as plans get larger or if plans are more complex. A recent report states that the fee to audit a 401(k) plan ranges between $6,500 and $13,000.[17]

If an employer joins a MEP, it may save some costs associated with filing Form 5500 and fulfilling audit requirements to the extent the MEP is considered a single plan under ERISA. Thus, one Form 5500 and audit report would satisfy the reporting requirements, and each participating employer would not need to file its own, separate Form 5500 and, for large plans or those few small plans that do not meet the small plan audit waiver, an audit report. Assuming reporting costs are shared by participating employers within a MEP, an employer joining a MEP can save virtually all the reporting costs discussed above. Large plans may enjoy even higher cost savings if audit costs are taken into account.

It is less clear whether the self-employed would experience similar reporting cost savings by joining a MEP. The Department of Labor estimated these potential cost savings by comparing the reporting costs of an employer that participates in a MEP rather than sponsoring its own plan. However, several retirement savings options are already available for self-employed persons, and most have minimal or no reporting requirements. For example, both SEP IRA and SIMPLE IRA plans are available for small employers and the self-employed and neither option requires Form 5500 filings. Solo 401(k) plans are also available for self-employed persons, and they may be exempt from the Form 5500-EZ reporting requirement if plan assets are less than $250,000. Thus, if self-employed individuals join a MEP, they would be unlikely to realize reporting cost savings. In fact, it is possible that their reporting costs may slightly increase, because the self-employed would share reporting costs with other MEP participating employers that they would otherwise not incur.[18]

d. Reduced Bonding Costs

The potential for bonding cost savings in MEPs merits separate attention. As noted above, ERISA section 412 and related regulations generally require every fiduciary of an employee benefit plan and every person who handles funds or other property of such a plan to be bonded. ERISA's bonding requirements are intended to protect employee benefit plans from risk of loss due to fraud or dishonesty on the part of persons who handle plan funds or other property, generally referred to as plan officials. A plan official must be bonded for at least 10 percent of the amount of funds he or she handles, subject to a minimum bond amount of $1,000 per plan with respect to which the plan official has handling functions. In most instances, the maximum bond amount that can be required under ERISA with respect to any one plan official is $500,000 per plan; however, the maximum required bond amount is $1,000,000 for plan officials of plans that hold employer securities.[19]

Under the proposed regulation, MEPs generally might enjoy lower bonding costs than would an otherwise equivalent collection of small, separate plans, for two reasons. First, it might be less expensive to buy one bond covering a large number of individuals who handle plan funds than a large number of bonds covering the same individuals separately or in small, more numerous groups. Second, the number of people handling plan funds and therefore subject to ERISA's bonding requirement in the context of a MEP may be smaller than in the context of an otherwise equivalent collection of smaller, separate plans.

e. Increased Retirement Savings

The various effects of this rule, if finalized, may lead in aggregate to increased retirement savings. As discussed above, many employees would likely go from not having any access to a retirement plan to having access through a MEP. This has the potential to result in an increase in retirement savings, on average, for this group of employees. While some employees may choose not to participate, surveys indicate that a large number would participate. For a defined contribution pension plan, about 73 percent of all employees with access participate in the plan.[20] Among employees whose salary tends to be in the lowest 10 percent of the salary range, this figure is about 40 percent.[21] One reason that these take-up rates are relatively high is that many plans use automatic enrollment to enroll newly hired employees, as well as, sometimes existing employees. Automatic enrollment is particularly prevalent among large plans; in 2017 about 74 percent of plans with 1,000-4,999 participants used automatic enrollment, while only about 27 percent of plans with 1-49 participants did.[22] Some workers may be saving in an IRA, either in an employer-sponsored IRA, payroll deduction IRA, or on their own. If they begin participating in a MEP 401(k), they would have the opportunity to take advantage of higher contribution limits, and some individuals may begin receiving employer contributions when participating in a MEP when they did not previously.

In general, MEPs may offer participants a way to save for retirement with lower overall costs. In particular, the fees are likely to be lower than in most small plans and in retail IRAs. The savings in fees would result in higher investment returns and thus higher retirement savings.

f. Increased Labor Market Efficiency

The increased prevalence of MEPs would allow small employers the opportunity to offer retirement benefits that are comparable to what large employers provide. Since employees value retirement benefits, this development would tend to shift talented employees toward small businesses. Moreover, certain groups such as secondary earners in high income families who have high marginal tax rates, and therefore larger benefits from tax-preferred savings, might now be more inclined to work for small businesses as those businesses might now offer a retirement plan. Such shifts would make small businesses more competitive. The ensuing reallocation of talent across different sectors of the economy would increase efficiency.

---

[17] See https://www.thayerpartnersllc.com/blog/the-hidden-costs-of-a-401k-audit. However, in a comment letter received by the Department of Labor in response to its October 23, 2018 (83 FR 53534), proposed rule clarifying the circumstances under which an employer group or association or PEO may sponsor a MEP, an association reported that the cost of its MEP audit was $24,000. See comment letter #6 Employers Association of New Jersey, EANJ at https://www.dol.gov/sites/default/files/ebsa/laws-and-regulations/rules-and-regulations/public-comments/1210-AB88/00006.pdf.

[18] However, self-employed participants, like all participants in small plans, would benefit from these enhanced audit and reporting requirements

[19] See DOL Field Assistance Bulletin 2008-04, https://www.dol.gov/agencies/ebsa/employers-and-advisers/guidance/field-assistance-bulletins/2008-04.

[20] U.S. Bureau of Labor Statistics, National Compensation Survey, Employee Benefits in the U.S. (March 2018).

[21] Id.

[22] Plan Sponsor Council of America, "61st Annual Survey of Profit Sharing and 401(k) Plans, Reflecting 2017 Plan Experience" (2018), Table 111.

5. *Costs*

While the proposed regulation effectively lowers the cost of participation in a MEP among employers, the rule may also lead to increased levels of noncompliance. For example, the section 413(c) plan administrator may become less diligent about ensuring that participating employers within a MEP are responsible employers. By potentially increasing noncompliance, the proposed regulation would impose new costs on section 413(c) plan administrators who are ultimately responsible for managing unresponsive employers. In particular, for a plan to maintain its tax-favored status, the section 413(c) plan administrator is required to send notice to an unresponsive employer giving it 90 days to remedy the situation. If the unresponsive employer fails to comply, the plan administrator must send a second notice and then a final notice if the unresponsive employer still fails to comply after specified time periods. In the event of the initiation of the spinoff process, in which assets associated with an unresponsive employer are separated into a new plan that is then terminated, additional costs from the resulting compliance measures will be incurred by the section 413(c) plan administrator, who among other things is tasked with notifying all impacted participants and beneficiaries. These additional costs may be directly passed on to unresponsive employers. However, it's possible that section 413(c) plan administrators may spread these costs across all participating employers that would either absorb or pass those costs on to their employees.

The proposed regulation may also indirectly lead to an increase in investment fees by increasing uncertainty in the size of a MEP's asset pool. For example, a plan may shrink considerably when assets of an unresponsive participating employer are spun off depending on that employer's share of the total asset pool. Since the cost savings in investment fees is derived from economies of scale, introducing uncertainty in plan size might induce management companies to increase prices to account for that risk. This cost would likely be spread across all employers participating in the MEP that might then pass those costs on to their employees.

More general concerns pertaining to MEPs include their potential for abuse, such as fraud, mishandling of plan assets, or charging excessive fees.[23] Relative to single-employer plans, MEPs may be more susceptible to abuse since coordination across participating employers may lead to confusion regarding each individual firm's fiduciary responsibilities. On the other hand, the enhanced disclosure and audit requirements applicable to large plans, together with the increased number of employers participating in a plan, might call attention to abuses that would have otherwise gone unnoticed had a small employer established its own plan.

6. *Regulatory Alternatives*

The Treasury Department and the IRS considered alternatives to the proposed regulation. One alternative would have been to extend the proposed regulations to include defined benefit MEPs. However, this alternative was rejected because defined benefit plans raise additional issues, including issues arising from the minimum funding requirements and spinoff rules, such as the treatment in such a spinoff of any plan underfunding or overfunding. Commenters are asked, in the Comments and Requests for Public Hearing section of the preamble, to address those issues, as well as the circumstances in which the exception to the unified plan rule should be available to defined benefit plans.

The Treasury Department and the IRS also considered whether the proposed regulation should include a more streamlined process for a section 413(c) plan administrator to satisfy the requirements for the exception to the unified plan rule. However, the notice requirements are intended to ensure that the affected participating employers and their employees are aware of the adverse consequences if the unresponsive participating employer neither takes appropriate remedial action nor initiates a spinoff, and the timing requirements are intended to give the unresponsive participating employer an adequate opportunity to take that remedial action or initiate a spinoff. These procedural requirements strike a balance between providing protection for unresponsive participating employers and their employees and not unduly burdening defined contribution MEPs. In the Comments and Requests for Public Hearing section of the preamble, commenters are asked to address whether the regulations should add mechanisms to avoid the potential for repetitive notices, as well as whether additional procedures should be added to facilitate the resolution of disputes between a section 413(c) plan administrator and an unresponsive participating employer.

7. *Tables*

TABLE 1—RETIREMENT PLAN COVERAGE BY EMPLOYER SIZE

Establishment size: Number of workers	Workers:		Establishments:
	Share with access to a retirement plan (%)	*Share participating in a retirement plan (%)*	*Share offering a retirement plan (%)*
1-49	49	34	45
50-99	65	46	75
100-499	79	58	88
500+	89	76	94
All	66	50	48

Source: These statistics apply to private industry. U.S. Bureau of Labor Statistics, National Compensation Survey, Employee Benefits in the U.S. (March 2018).

TABLE 2—CURRENT STATISTICS ON MEPS

	Number of MEPs	Total Participants	Active Participants	Total Assets
MEP Defined Contribution Plans.	4,630	4.4 million	3.7 million	$181 billion.
As a share of all ERISA Defined Contribution Plans	0.7%	4.4%.	4.6%.	3.2%.
MEP Defined Contribution Plans	4,630	4.4 million	3.7 million	$181 billion.
401(k) Plans	4,391	4.1 million	3.4 million	$166 billion.
Other Defined Contribution Plans	239	0.4 million	0.3 million	$15 billion.

Source: The Department of Labor performed these calculations using the 2016 Research File of Form 5500 filings. The estimates are weighted and rounded, which means they may not sum precisely. These estimates were derived by classifying a plan as a MEP if it indicated "multiple employer plan" status on the Form 5500 Part 1 Line A and if it did not report collective bargaining.

23 (00 ГП 50534) (October 22, 2019).

TABLE 3—AVERAGE EXPENSE RATIOS OF MUTUAL FUNDS IN 401(K) PLANS IN BASIS POINTS, 2015

Plan Assets	Domestic equity mutual funds	International equity mutual funds	Domestic bond mutual funds	International bond mutual funds	Target date mutual funds	Balanced mutual funds (non-target date)
$1M-$10M	81	101	72	85	79	80
$10M-$50M	68	85	59	77	68	64
$50M-$100M	55	72	44	66	54	50
$100M-$250M	52	68	40	64	55	45
$250M-$500M	49	63	36	67	50	42
$500M-$1B	45	60	33	65	50	39
More than $1B	36	52	26	65	48	32

Source: Average expense ratios are expressed in basis points and asset-weighted. The sample includes plans with audited 401(k) filings in the BrightScope database for 2015 and comprises 15,110 plans with $1.4 trillion in mutual fund assets. Plans were included if they had at least $1million in assets and between 4 and 100 investment options. BrightScope/ICI, "The BrightScope/ICI Defined Contribution Plan Profile: A Close Look at 401(k) Plans, 2015" (March 2018).

TABLE 4—LARGER PLANS TEND TO HAVE LOWER FEES OVERALL

Plan Assets	Total Plan Cost (in basis points)		
Plan Assets	10th Percentile	Median	90th Percentile
$1M-$10M	75	111	162
$10M-$50M	61	91	129
$50M-$100M	37	65	93
$100M-$250M	22	54	74
$250M-$500M	21	48	66
$500M-$1B	21	43	59
More than $1B	14	27	51

Source: Data is plan-weighted. The sample is plans with audited 401(k) filings in the BrightScope database for 2015, which comprises 18,853 plans with $3.2 trillion in assets. Plans were included if they had at least $1 million in assets and between 4 and 100 investment options. BrightScope/ICI, "The BrightScope/ICI Defined Contribution Plan Profile: A Close Look at 401(k) Plans, 2015" (March 2018).

II. Paperwork Reduction Act

The collection of information in these proposed regulations is in: § 1.413-2(g)(3)(i)(B) (requirement to adopt plan language); § 1.413-2(g)(4) (requirement to provide notice with respect to a participating employer failure); § 1.413-2(g)(7)(i)(C) (requirement that spun-off plan have the same substantive terms as MEP); and § 1.413-2(g)(7)(i)(A) (requirement to provide notice of a spinoff-termination). The collection of information contained in proposed § 1.413-2(g) will be carried out by plan administrators of defined contribution MEPs seeking to satisfy the conditions for the exception to the unified plan rule. The collection of information in this notice of proposed rulemaking has been submitted to the Office of Management and Budget for review in accordance with the Paperwork Reduction Act of 1995 (44 U.S.C. 3507(d)).

1. *Plan Amendment Adoption Requirement, § 1.413-2(g)(3)(i)(B)*

Section 1.413-2(g)(3)(i)(B) states that as a condition of the exception to the unified plan rule, a defined contribution MEP must be amended to include plan language that describes the procedures that would be followed to address participating employer failures, including the applicable procedures that apply if an unresponsive participating employer does not respond to the section 413(c) plan administrator's requests to remedy the failures.

A defined contribution MEP will not be eligible for the exception to the unified plan rule if it does not satisfy this plan-language requirement. Without it, the defined contribution MEP will not be able to avail itself of the exception to the unified plan rule, and will continue to be at risk of disqualification due to the actions or inactions of a single unresponsive participating employer. Since only one amendment is required, this is a one-time paperwork burden for each defined contribution MEP. In addition, after final regulations are issued, the IRS intends to publish a model plan amendment, which will help to minimize the burden.

We estimate that the burden for this requirement under the Paperwork Reduction Act of 1995 will be three hours per defined contribution MEP. Given the size of the burden and the potential benefits of satisfying the exception to the unified plan rule, we estimate that approximately 80 percent of defined contribution MEPs (3,704 MEPs[24]) will amend their plans to satisfy this condition. Therefore, the total burden of this requirement is estimated to be 11,112 hours (3,704 defined contribution MEPs times three hours). However, because each defined contribution MEP that adopts an amendment will do so on a one-time basis, to determine an annual estimate, the total time is divided by three, or 3,704 hours annually (3,704 defined contribution MEPs times one hour).

2. *Notice Requirements, § 1.413-2(g)(4)*

Notice is another condition of the exception to the unified plan rule. The proposed regulations would require a section 413(c) plan administrator to send up to three notices informing the unresponsive participating employer of the participating employer failure and the consequences if the employer fails to take remedial action or initiate a spinoff from the defined contribution MEP. After each notice is provided, the employer has 90 days to take appropriate remedial action or initiate a spinoff from the defined contribution MEP. If the employer takes those actions after the first or second notice is provided, subsequent notices are not required. Thus, it is possible that a section 413(c) plan administrator will send fewer than three notices to an employer. However, because the notice requirements only apply if an employer has already been unresponsive to the section 413(c) plan administrator's requests, we have estimated that in most cases, all three notices will be provided.

We estimate that the burden of preparing the three notices will be three hours. Most of this burden relates to the first notice, which must describe the qualification failure and the potential consequences if the employer fails to take action to address it. The burdens of preparing the second and third notices are expected to be relatively insignificant, given that these notices must generally repeat the information that was included in the first notice. We estimate that approximately 33.3 percent of all defined contribution MEPs (1,542 defined contribution MEPs) have or will have an unresponsive participating employer, necessitating the sending of these notices on an annual basis. Therefore, we estimate a burden of 4,626 hours

---

[24] This calculation uses data from the 2016 Form 5500, "Annual Return/Report of Employee Benefit Plan." As noted earlier, these filings indicate that there are approximately 4,630 defined contribution MEPs.

(1,542 defined contribution MEPs times three hours). We expect to be able to adjust these estimates based on experience after the regulations are finalized.

Section 1.413-2(g)(4) also includes the burden of notice distribution. All three notices must be sent to the unresponsive participating employer. The third notice will also be provided to plan participants who are employees of the unresponsive participating employer (and their beneficiaries) and to the Department of Labor. We estimate that, on average, a section 413(c) plan administrator will send the third notice to approximately 50 recipients (employees of the unresponsive participating employer, the employer, and the Department of Labor). We expect that the burden of distributing these notices will be two hours per defined contribution MEP, for a total burden of 3,084 hours (1,542 defined contribution MEPs times two hours).

3. Terms of Spun-off Plan, § 1.413-2(g)(7)(i)(C)

After the third notice is provided, § 1.413-2(g)(7)(i)(C) requires a section 413(c) plan administrator to implement a spinoff of the plan assets attributable to employees of an unresponsive participating employer. The assets must be spun-off into a separate plan that has the same substantive plan terms as the defined contribution MEP. We estimate that in a given year, a spinoff-termination for an unresponsive participating employer will be made with respect to 20 percent of all defined contribution MEPs (926 defined contribution MEPs therefore will be subject to this requirement). We also estimate that the burden associated with the requirement to create a spinoff plan will be 10 hours. Therefore, the total burden is estimated to be 9,260 hours (926 defined contribution MEPs times 10).

4. Notice of Spinoff-Termination, § 1.413-2(g)(7)(i)(A)

A section 413(c) plan administrator implementing a spinoff-termination pursuant to § 1.413-2(g)(7) must provide notification of the spinoff-termination to participants who are employees of the unresponsive employer. This notice requirement is in § 1.413-2(g)(7)(i)(A). We estimate that in a given year, 20 percent of all defined contribution MEPs (926 defined contribution MEPs) will implement a spinoff-termination of an unresponsive participating employer, and notice to participants will need to be provided with respect to those spinoff-terminations.

Using the same numbers as the estimates for notice requirements under § 1.413-2(g)(4), we estimate that for a defined contribution MEP that uses the exception to the unified plan rule, approximately 50 notices of a spinoff-termination will need to be sent to participants who are employees of the unresponsive participating employer (and their beneficiaries). We also estimate that the total burden for this requirement is five hours. Based on this number, we estimate that the burden of preparing and distributing the notices will be 4,630 hours (926 defined contribution MEPs times five hours).

5. Reporting Spinoff or Spinoff-Termination to IRS, §§ 1.413-2(g)(6)(ii) and (g)(7)(iv)

Any spinoff or spinoff-termination from a defined contribution MEP under the proposed regulations must be reported to the IRS (in accordance with forms, instructions, and other guidance). Because the IRS anticipates issuing a new form or revising an existing form for this purpose, the estimated reporting burden associated with proposed §§ 1.413-2(g)(6)(ii) and (g)(7)(iv) will be reflected in the reporting burden associated with those forms, and therefore is not included here.

Comments on the collection of information should be sent to the **Office of Management and Budget**, Attn: Desk Officer for the Department of the Treasury, Office of Information and Regulatory Affairs, Washington, DC 20503, with copies to the Internal Revenue Service, Attn: IRS Reports Clearance Officer, SE:W:CAR:MP:T:T:SP; Washington, DC 20224. Comments on the collection of information should be received by September 3, 2019. Comments are specifically requested concerning:

Whether the proposed collection of information is necessary for the proper performance of the functions of the IRS, including whether the information will have practical utility;

The accuracy of the estimated burden associated with the proposed collection of information;

How the quality, utility, and clarity of the information to be collected may be enhanced;

How the burden of complying with the proposed collections of information may be minimized, including through the application of automated collection techniques or other forms of information technology; and

Estimates of capital or start-up costs and costs of operation, maintenance, and purchase of service to provide information.

Estimated total average annual recordkeeping burden: 25,304 hours.

Estimated average annual burden per response: Between 7 and 27 hours.

Estimated number of recordkeepers: 926 to 3,704.

An agency may not conduct or sponsor, and a person is not required to respond to, a collection of information unless it displays a valid control number assigned by the Office of Management and Budget.

Books or records relating to a collection of information must be retained as long as their contents may become material in the administration of any internal revenue law. Generally, tax returns and tax return information are confidential, as required by 26 U.S.C. 6103.

III. Regulatory Flexibility Act

The Regulatory Flexibility Act (5 U.S.C. 601 *et seq.*) (RFA) imposes certain requirements with respect to federal rules that are subject to the notice and comment requirements of section 553(b) of the Administrative Procedure Act (5 U.S.C. 551 *et seq.*) and that are likely to have a significant economic impact on a substantial number of small entities. Unless an agency determines that a proposal is not likely to have a significant economic impact on a substantial number of small entities, section 603 of the RFA requires the agency to present an initial regulatory flexibility analysis (IRFA) of the proposed rule. The Treasury Department and the IRS have not determined whether the proposed rule, when finalized, will likely have a significant economic impact on a substantial number of small entities. The determination of whether creating an exception to the unified plan rule for defined contribution MEPs will have a significant economic impact requires further study. However, because there is a possibility of significant economic impact on a substantial number of small entities, an IRFA is provided in these proposed regulations. The Treasury Department and the IRS invite comments on both the number of entities affected and the economic impact on small entities.

Pursuant to section 7805(f) of the Code, this notice of proposed rulemaking has been submitted to the Chief Counsel of Advocacy of the Small Business Administration for comment on its impact on small business.

1. Need for and Objectives of the Rule

As discussed earlier in this preamble, under the unified plan rule, the failure of one employer participating in a MEP to satisfy a qualification requirement or to provide information needed to determine compliance with a qualification requirement puts the tax-favored status of the entire MEP at risk. By creating an exception to the unified plan rule, the proposed rule would ensure that, in certain circumstances, compliant participating employers will continue to maintain a qualified plan. Offering a workplace retirement plan is a valuable tool for small businesses in recruiting and retaining employees. By retaining tax-favored status in a defined contribution MEP, participating employers will continue to be able to offer a workplace retirement plan for their employees.

The proposed rule is expected to encourage the establishment of new defined contribution MEPs, as well as increase the participation of employers in existing defined contribution MEPs, in accordance with Executive Order 13847 and the policy of expanding workplace retirement plan coverage. MEPs are an efficient way to reduce costs and complexity associated with establishing and maintaining defined contribution plans, which could encourage more plan formation and broader availability of more affordable workplace retirement savings plans, especially among small employers and certain working owners. Thus, the Treasury Department and the IRS intend and expect that the proposed rule would deliver benefits primarily to the employees of many small businesses and their families, as well as, many small businesses themselves.

2. Affected Small Entities

The Small Business Administration estimates in its 2018 Small Business Profile that 99.9 percent of United States businesses meet its definition of a small business.[25] The applicability of these proposed regulations does not depend on the size of the business, as defined by the Small Business Administration. The Treasury Department and the IRS expect that the smallest businesses, those with less than 50 employees, are most likely to benefit from the savings derived from retaining tax-favored status in a defined contribution MEP, as well as increasing participation in defined contribution MEPs, which are expected to occur as a result of the proposed rule. In Section 7 of the Regulatory Impact Analysis, see Table 1, which provides statistics on retirement plan coverage by the size of the employer. These same types of employers, which are disproportionately small businesses, are more likely to participate in a workplace retirement plan after the proposed rule is finalized. The proposed rule will also affect small entities that participate in MEPs at the time the rule is finalized.

3. Impact of the Rule

Under the existing unified plan rule, a MEP may be disqualified due to the actions of one unresponsive participating employer. Upon disqualification, employers participating in a MEP and their employees would lose the tax benefits of participating in a qualified retirement plan (deduction for contributions, exclusion of investment returns, and deferred income recognition for employees). By creating an exception to the unified plan rule, the proposed regulation would allow a defined contribution MEP to remain qualified and thereby retain tax-favored benefits for participating employers and their employees. For example, if a defined contribution MEP that would have otherwise been disqualified satisfies the conditions for the exception to the unified plan rule, small entities that participate in the MEP will be able to continue to make contributions to the defined contribution MEP that are deductible under section 404(a)(3).

In addition, as previously stated in the Special Analysis section of this preamble, this proposed rule could potentially result in an expansion of defined contribution MEPs, which could create a more affordable option for retirement savings coverage for many small businesses, thereby potentially yielding economic benefits for participating employers and their employees. Some advantages of a workplace retirement plan (including 401(k) plans, SEP-IRAs, and SIMPLE IRAs) over IRA-based savings options outside the workplace include: (1) higher contribution limits; (2) potentially lower investment management fees, especially in larger plans; (3) a well-established uniform regulatory structure with important consumer protections, including qualification requirements relating to protected benefits, vesting, disclosures, and spousal protections; (4) automatic enrollment; and (5) stronger protections from creditors. At the same time, workplace retirement plans provide employers with choice among plan features and the flexibility to tailor retirement plans that meet their business and employment needs.

The ERISA recordkeeping and reporting requirements could decrease for some small employers that would have maintained a single-employer defined contribution plan but instead join a defined contribution MEP. This includes costs associated with filing Form 5500 and fulfilling audit requirements to the extent a MEP is considered a single plan under ERISA. Thus, one Form 5500 and audit report would satisfy the reporting requirements, and each participating employer would not need to file its own, separate Form 5500 and, for large plans or those few small plans that do not meet the small plan audit waiver, an audit report.

The cost savings of an employer participating in a defined contribution MEP may be partially offset by the costs of complying with the conditions for the exception to the unified plan rule, including new recordkeeping and reporting requirements. Additional costs from these actions will be incurred by the section 413(c) plan administrator, who among other things is tasked with adopting plan language (§ 1.413-2(g)(3)(i)(B)), providing notice concerning a participating employer failure to unresponsive participating employers, participants, beneficiaries, and the Department of Labor (§ 1.413-2(g)(4)), notifying participants and beneficiaries of a spinoff-termination (§ 1.413-2(g)(7)(ii)), and implementing a spinoff of the MEP assets related to an unresponsive participating employer and creating a spun-off plan document (§ 1.413-2(g)(7)(i)). Although the Treasury Department and the IRS do not have sufficient data to determine precisely the likely extent of the increased costs of compliance, the estimated burden of complying with the recordkeeping and reporting requirements are described in the *Paperwork Reduction Act* section of the preamble. While the burdens associated with the recordkeeping and reporting requirements are imposed on the defined contribution MEP and not the participating employers, those additional costs may be directly passed on to participating employers.

Another partial offset to the cost savings is the potential for an unresponsive participating employer to have its participation in a MEP terminated as a result of the MEP's compliance with these proposed regulations. The proposed regulations state that if an unresponsive participating employer fails to take appropriate remedial action to correct a qualification failure, one of the following actions must occur in order for the MEP to meet the conditions for the exception to the unified plan rule: (a) a spinoff initiated by the unresponsive participating employer and implemented by the section 413(c) plan administrator or (b) a spinoff-termination pursuant to plan terms. The Treasury Department and the IRS anticipate that compared to the number of small entities that will benefit from these proposed rules, relatively few employers will have their plans spun-off or spun-off and terminated.

As previously stated in the Regulatory Impact Analysis of this preamble, the Treasury Department and the IRS considered alternatives to the proposed regulations. One of the conditions that a defined contribution MEP must satisfy in order to be eligible for the exception to the unified plan rule is that the section 413(c) plan administrator provides notice and an opportunity for the unresponsive participating employer to take action with respect to the participating employer failure. The proposed regulations would require that the section 413(c) plan administrator provide up to three notices to the unresponsive participating employer, informing the employer (and in some cases, participants and the Department of Labor) of the participating employer failure and the consequences for failing to take remedial action or initiate a spinoff from the defined contribution MEP. After each notice is provided, the unresponsive participating employer has 90 days to take appropriate remedial action or initiate a spinoff from the defined contribution MEP. For more information about the notice requirements, see Section II.B of the Explanation of Provisions in this preamble.

In addition to the alternatives discussed in the Regulatory Impact Analysis of this preamble, the Treasury Department and the IRS considered whether the proposed regulations should reduce the number of notices or the timing between providing notices in order for a section 413(c) plan administrator to satisfy this condition for the exception to the unified plan rule. The notice and accompanying timing requirements were provided for because the notice procedures are intended to ensure that an unresponsive participating employer and its employees are aware of the adverse consequences if the employer neither takes appropriate remedial action nor initiates a spinoff, and the timing requirements are intended to give the unresponsive participating employer sufficient time to take that remedial action or initiate a spinoff. The Treasury Department and the IRS believe

---

[25] The Small Business Administration, Office of Advocacy, 2018 Small Business Profile. *https://www.sba.gov/sites/default/files/advocacy/2018-Small-Business-Profiles-US.pdf*. Last accessed 03/28/2019. For purposes of the 2018 Small Business Profile, small businesses are defined as firms employing fewer than 500 employees.

that, given the adverse consequences of a spinoff-termination to plan participants, the notice and accompanying timing requirements strike a balance between providing protection for unresponsive participating employers and their employees and not unduly burdening the section 413(c) plan administrators in defined contribution MEPs. In the Comments and Requests for Public Hearing section of the preamble, commenters are asked to address whether the regulations should add mechanisms to avoid the potential for repetitive notices, as well as whether additional procedures should be added to facilitate the resolution of disputes between a section 413(c) plan administrator and an unresponsive participating employer.

4. Duplicate, Overlapping, or Relevant Federal Rules

The proposed rule would not conflict with any relevant federal rules. As discussed above, the proposed rule would merely create an exception to the unified plan rule for defined contribution MEPs.

Comments and Requests for Public Hearing

Before these proposed regulations are adopted as final regulations, consideration will be given to any comments that are submitted timely to the Treasury Department and the IRS as prescribed in this preamble under the **"ADDRESSES"** heading. The Treasury Department and the IRS request comments on all aspects of the proposed rules. Comments specifically are requested on the following topics:

- The circumstances, if any, in which the exception to the unified plan rule should be available to defined benefit plans (taking into account issues arising from the minimum funding requirements and spinoff rules for defined benefit plans, including the treatment in such a spinoff of any plan underfunding or overfunding).

- Whether the regulations should include additional requirements for MEPs to be eligible for the exception to the unified plan rule, including additional procedures to facilitate the resolution of disputes between a section 413(c) plan administrator and an unresponsive participating employer.

- Whether the regulations should add appropriate mechanisms to avoid the potential for repetitive notices or to shorten the notice period for a potential qualification failure that becomes a known qualification failure. Those mechanisms might include, for example, treating the first notice that the section 413(c) plan administrator provided in connection with the potential qualification failure as satisfying the requirement to provide the first notice in connection with the known qualification failure, with appropriate modification of the second and third notices.

- For purposes of a spinoff, how to treat participants who have a single account with assets attributable to service with the unresponsive participating employer and one or more other participating employers, or who have a separate rollover account that is not attributable to service with the unresponsive participating employer.

- What additional guidance should be provided on terminating a plan in the case of a spinoff-termination. This might include, for example, rules that are similar to the relief provided in section 4, Q&A-1, of Rev. Proc. 2003-86, 2003-2 C.B. 1211, that any other plan maintained by an unresponsive participating employer will not be treated as an alternative plan under § 1.401(k)-1(d)(4)(i) for purposes of the ability to make distributions upon termination of the spun-off plan. It might also address the § 1.411(a)-11(e)(1) rules for distributions upon plan termination

- Whether there are any studies that would help to quantify the impact of the proposed regulations.

Also, consistent with the Executive Order, comments are specifically requested on any steps that the Secretary of Labor should take to facilitate the implementation of these proposed regulations. The Department of Labor has informed the Treasury Department and the IRS that a section 413(c) plan administrator implementing a spinoff-termination may have concerns about its fiduciary responsibility both to the MEP and to the spun-off plan, as well as potential prohibited transaction issues. Commenters are encouraged to provide feedback on these issues and address the need for additional interpretive guidance or prohibited transaction exemptions from the Department of Labor to facilitate the implementation of these regulations.[26] Copies of comments on these topics will be forwarded to the Department of Labor.

All comments will be available for public inspection and copying at *www.regulations.gov* or upon request. A public hearing will be scheduled if requested in writing by any person who timely submits written comments. If a public hearing is scheduled, notice of the date, time, and place of the public hearing will be published in the **Federal Register**.

Drafting Information

The principal authors of these regulations are Jamie Dvoretzky and Pamela Kinard, Office of Associate Chief Counsel (Employee Benefits, Exempt Organizations, and Employment Taxes (EEE)). However, other personnel from the IRS and the Treasury Department participated in the development of these regulations.

[¶ 49,806] Proposed Amendments of Regulations (REG-105474-18), published in the Federal Register on July 11, 2019.

[Code Secs. 1291, 1297 and 1298]

Assets: Foreign corporation: Passive foreign investment company (PFIC): Ownership in PFIC.—Reg. §§1.1297-1, 1.1297-2, 1.1297-4, 1.1297-5, 1.1298-2, 1.1298-4 and amendments of Reg. §§1.1291-0, 1.1291-1, 1.1297-0 and 1.1298-0, **regarding the determination of ownership in a passive foreign investment company within the meaning of section 1297(a) ("PFIC") and the treatment of certain income received or accrued by a foreign corporation and assets held by a foreign corporation for purposes of section 1297, are proposed. Reg. §1.1297-4, proposed on April 24, 2015, is withdrawn.**

AGENCY: Internal Revenue Service (IRS), Treasury.

ACTION: Withdrawal of notice of proposed rulemaking; notice of proposed rulemaking. SUMMARY: This document contains proposed regulations under sections 1291, 1297, and 1298 of the Internal Revenue Code ("Code") regarding the determination of ownership in a passive foreign investment company within the meaning of section 1297(a) ("PFIC") and the treatment of certain income received or accrued by a foreign corporation and assets held by a foreign corporation for purposes of section 1297. The regulations provide guidance regarding when a foreign corporation is a qualifying insurance corporation ("QIC") under section 1297(f) of the Code and the amounts of income and assets that a QIC excludes from passive income and assets pursuant to section 1297(b)(2)(B) ("PFIC insurance exception") for purposes of section 1297(a). The regulations also clarify the application and scope of certain rules that determine whether a United States person that directly or indirectly holds stock in a PFIC is treated as a shareholder of the PFIC, and whether a foreign corporation is a PFIC. The regulations affect United States persons with direct or indirect ownership interests in certain foreign corporations.

DATES: Written or electronic comments and requests for a public hearing must be received by September 9, 2019.

---

[26] For an example of this type of interpretative guidance and a related prohibited transaction exemption in the context of a terminating abandoned plan, *see* 29 CFR 2578.1 (establishing procedures for qualified termination administrators to terminate aban- doned plans and distribute benefits with limited liability under title I of ERISA) and Prohibited Transaction Exemption 2006-06 (71 FR 20856, Apr. 21, 2006).

ADDRESSES: Send submissions to: CC:PA:LPD:PR (REG-105474-18), room 5203, Internal Revenue Service, P.O. Box 7604, Ben Franklin Station, Washington, DC 20044. Submissions may be hand-delivered Monday through Friday between the hours of 8 a.m. and 4 p.m. to CC:PA:LPD:PR (REG-105474-18), Courier's Desk, Internal Revenue Service, 1111 Constitution Avenue, NW, Washington, DC 20224, or sent electronically via the Federal eRulemaking Portal at www.regulations.gov (IRS REG-105474-18).

FOR FURTHER INFORMATION CONTACT: Concerning the proposed regulations, Josephine Firehock at (202) 317-4932 (for the PFIC Insurance Exception) or Jorge M. Oben at (202) 317-6934 (for general rules, including indirect ownership and look-through rules); concerning submissions and requests for a public hearing, Regina L. Johnson at (202) 317-6901 (not toll-free numbers).

SUPPLEMENTARY INFORMATION:

Background

I. *In General*

This document contains proposed amendments to 26 CFR part 1 under sections 1291, 1297, and 1298. Sections 1291 through 1298 set forth tax regimes for shareholders that own stock of a PFIC. Under section 1297(a), a foreign corporation ("Tested Foreign Corporation") qualifies as a PFIC if it satisfies either of the following tests: (i) 75 percent or more of the Tested Foreign Corporation's gross income for a taxable year is passive ("Income Test"); or (ii) the average percentage of assets held by the Tested Foreign Corporation during a taxable year that produce (or that are held for the production of) passive income is at least 50 percent ("Asset Test"). Section 1297(b)(1) generally defines passive income as any income of a kind that would constitute foreign personal holding company income ("FPHCI") under section 954(c), and section 1297(b)(2) provides exceptions to this general definition. Income of a kind not described in section 954(c)(1) (for example, premiums on insurance and annuity contracts) is excluded from passive income.

In addition, section 1297(c) provides a look-through rule that applies when determining the PFIC status of a Tested Foreign Corporation that directly or indirectly owns at least 25 percent of the stock (determined by value) of another corporation.

Section 1298(b)(3) provides an exception from PFIC status for certain Tested Foreign Corporations that change from one active business to another active business. Section 1298(b)(7) provides that certain stock ("qualified stock") in a domestic C corporation owned by a Tested Foreign Corporation through a 25-percent-owned domestic corporation is treated as an asset generating non-passive income for purposes of section 1297(a), provided that the Tested Foreign Corporation is subject to the accumulated earnings tax or waives any treaty protections against the imposition of the accumulated earnings tax.

Section 1298(a) sets forth special rules applicable to shareholders of PFICs, including attribution rules that treat a United States person as the owner of PFIC stock that is owned by another person (other than an individual). For instance, section 1298(a)(2) sets forth the attribution rules for ownership through a corporation, and section 1298(a)(3) sets forth the attribution rules for ownership through a partnership, estate, or trust. In addition, section 1298(a)(1)(B) provides that, except to the extent provided in regulations, section 1298(a) will not apply to treat stock owned (or treated as owned) by a United States person as owned by another United States person.

The Department of the Treasury ("Treasury Department") and the IRS announced their intention to issue regulations that address the operation of the Income Test and Asset Test in Notice 88-22, 1988-1 C.B. 489 ("Notice 88-22").

II. *PFIC Insurance Exception*

Before its amendment by section 14501 of the Tax Cuts and Jobs Act, Pub. L. 115-97, 131 Stat. 2234 (2017) (the "Act"), former section 1297(b)(2)(B) provided that passive income generally did not include investment income derived in the active conduct of an insurance business by a corporation that is predominantly engaged in an insurance business and that would be subject to tax under subchapter L if it were a domestic corporation. Congress was concerned about a lack of clarity and precision in the PFIC insurance exception, and in particular about the lack of precision regarding how much insurance or reinsurance business a company must do to qualify under the exception, which made the exception difficult to enforce. H.R. Report 115-409 at 409-410. To address these concerns, the Act modified the PFIC insurance exception to provide that passive income does not include investment income derived in the active conduct of an insurance business by a QIC. Thus, for taxable years beginning after December 31, 2017, the PFIC insurance exception provides that a foreign corporation's income attributable to an insurance business will not be passive income if three requirements are met. First, the foreign corporation must be a QIC as defined in section 1297(f). Second, the foreign corporation must be engaged in an "insurance business." Third, the income must be derived from the "active conduct" of that insurance business.

On April 24, 2015, the **Federal Register** published a notice of proposed rulemaking at 80 FR 22954 (the "2015 proposed regulations") under former sections 1297(b)(2)(B) and 1298(g). The 2015 proposed regulations addressed the PFIC insurance exception and provided guidance regarding the extent to which a foreign corporation's investment income and the assets producing that income are excluded from passive income and passive assets for purposes of the passive income and passive asset tests in section 1297(a). Comments were received on the previously proposed regulations. A public hearing was requested and was held on September 18, 2015.

This document withdraws the 2015 proposed regulations and proposes new regulations with respect to the insurance exception as amended by the Act. Accordingly, this preamble does not address the comments received regarding the 2015 proposed regulations unless the comment relates to these new proposed regulations.

Explanation of Provisions

I. *General Rules*

A. *Overview*

These regulations provide guidance with respect to a number of issues that are not specifically addressed in the current regulations and resolve some of the complexities that arise in the determination of the ownership of a PFIC and in the application of the Income Test and Asset Test in cases in which the look-through rule of section 1297(c) applies to a Tested Foreign Corporation.

Specifically, these regulations provide guidance on the application of the corporate attribution rules when a partnership indirectly holds a Tested Foreign Corporation through a corporation that is not a PFIC. These regulations also clarify the scope of the section 1297(b)(1) cross-reference to section 954(c) for purposes of defining passive income, and they set forth rules that address certain computational and characterization issues that arise in applying the Asset Test. In addition, these regulations provide rules concerning the treatment of income and assets of a 25-percent-owned subsidiary under section 1297(c). These regulations provide guidance on the application of the section 1298(b)(3) change of business exception and also propose a new rule analogous to the section 1298(b)(3) change of business exception that takes into consideration the assets of the Tested Foreign Corporation. Finally, these regulations provide guidance on the application of the section 1298(b)(7) qualified stock exception and provide a rule for waiving treaty benefits that would exempt a Tested Foreign Corporation from the accumulated earnings tax.

B. *Determination of ownership and attribution through partnerships*

Section 1298(a) provides attribution rules that apply to the extent that the effect is to treat stock of a PFIC as owned by a United States person. Except as provided in regulations, the attribution rules do not apply to treat stock owned or treated as owned by a United States person as owned by any other person.

Section 1298(a)(2)(A) provides that if 50 percent or more in value of the stock of a corporation is owned, directly or indirectly, by or for any person, that person is considered to own the stock owned directly or indirectly by or for the corporation in proportion to the person's ownership of the corporation. However, under section 1298(a)(2)(B), the 50 percent ownership threshold does not apply in the case of stock held through a PFIC or a corporation that would be a PFIC if it were not a controlled foreign corporation within the meaning of section 957(a) ("CFC"). Section 1298(a)(3) provides that stock owned, directly or indirectly, by a partnership, estate, or trust is considered owned proportionately by its partners or beneficiaries. The current rules in §1.1291-1(b)(8) are consistent with these statutory provisions.

Comments have inquired whether the attribution rules are intended to be applied to a tiered ownership structure on a "top-down" basis, by starting with a United States person and determining what stock is considered owned at each successive lower tier on a proportionate basis. Alternatively, the comments have posited, the rules could be applied on a "bottom-up" basis, by starting with a PFIC and attributing ownership of its stock upwards to each successive upper tier until the United States person whose ownership in the PFIC is being tested is reached.

The two approaches can have different ownership consequences when a partnership indirectly owns stock of a Tested Foreign Corporation through a corporation that is not a PFIC. A United States person not treated as a shareholder of PFIC stock indirectly held by a partnership through a non-PFIC corporation under a "top-down" approach may be treated as a shareholder under a "bottom-up" approach as a result of the application of section 1298(a)(3) and §1.1291-1(b)(8)(iii), which provide that holders of interests in a pass-through entity are considered to proportionately own stock owned directly or indirectly by the pass-through entity. Consider, for example, the following fact pattern. A, a United States citizen, owns 50 percent of the interests in Foreign Partnership, a foreign partnership, the remainder of which is owned by an unrelated foreign person. Foreign Partnership owns 100 percent of the stock of FC1 and 50 percent of the stock of FC2, the remainder of which is owned by an unrelated foreign person. Both FC1 and FC2 are foreign corporations that are not PFICs (determined without applying section 1297(d)). FC1 and FC2 each own 50 percent of the stock of FC3, a foreign corporation that is a PFIC. Under a "bottom-up" approach, Foreign Partnership could be treated as owning 75 percent of the stock of FC3 indirectly through FC1 and FC2, and accordingly, A could be treated as owning 37.5 percent of the stock of FC3. Under a "top-down" approach, however, A would be treated as owning 50 percent of the stock of FC1 and 25 percent of the stock of FC2, and the only stock of FC3 that would be attributed to A would be the 25 percent of the FC3 stock treated as indirectly owned by A through FC1. Comments have noted that a "top-down" approach produces the same result as if the partnership were disregarded and partners were treated as if they directly or indirectly owned a partnership's direct and indirect interests in a non-PFIC foreign corporation; it could thus be viewed as consistent with an aggregate theory of partnerships.

Under the proposed regulations, the attribution rules apply consistently whether a United States person owns stock of a non-PFIC foreign corporation through a partnership or directly, as they would under the "top-down" approach. This ensures that ownership of a foreign corporation that is a PFIC through a partnership will not change the amount of the stock of the PFIC that the United States person is treated as owning. Accordingly, under the proposed regulations, for purposes of determining whether a partner, S corporation shareholder, or beneficiary in a partnership, S corporation, estate, or nongrantor trust is considered under §1.1291-1(b)(8)(ii)(A) to own a portion of stock of a PFIC owned indirectly by the partnership, S corporation, estate, or trust through a non-PFIC foreign corporation, the partner, shareholder, or beneficiary will be considered to own 50 percent or more in value of the stock of the non-PFIC foreign corporation through the partnership, estate, or trust only if the partner, shareholder, or beneficiary directly or indirectly owns 50 percent or more of the ownership interests in the partnership, estate, or trust. *See* proposed §1.1291-1(b)(8)(iii).

If, in the previously posited example, Foreign Partnership were replaced with another foreign corporation, FC4, the proposed regulations would not apply. It may seem less appropriate for the amount of FC3 stock that is treated as owned by A to be limited to the 25 percent of FC3 indirectly owned by A through FC4 and FC1. Instead, FC4 could be treated as owning 25 percent of the stock of FC3 indirectly through FC2, and thus A could be treated as owning 12.5 percent of the stock of FC3 indirectly through FC4 and FC2 in addition to the 25 percent owned indirectly through FC4 and FC1. The Treasury Department and the IRS request comments as to whether a "top-down" attribution analysis or some alternative analysis should apply under section 1298(a) in a purely corporate structure such as this one, such that A would not be treated as owning any stock of FC3 indirectly through FC4 and FC2.

C. *Income test*

1. In General

In the Technical and Miscellaneous Revenue Act of 1988 (Pub. L. 100-647, 102 Stat. 3342), Congress amended section 1297(b)(1) to define the term passive income generally as any income of a kind that would constitute FPHCI under section 954(c). FPHCI, and thus passive income, includes interest income that would be tax-exempt under section 103. *See* §§1.954-2(b)(3), 1.952-2(c)(1). Neither the rules under subtitle A, chapter 1, subchapter N, part III, subpart F of the Code ("subpart F") nor rules under section 1297, however, address the treatment for purposes of FPHCI or the Income Test of other types of income that are otherwise excluded from gross income, such as intercompany dividends that are excluded from the income of a recipient under the consolidated return regulations. *See* §1.1502-13(f)(2)(ii). As discussed in more detail in Part I.F of this Explanation of Provisions, a Tested Foreign Corporation may be treated under section 1297(c) as receiving directly income received by a 25-percent-owned subsidiary, including a domestic corporation. As discussed in more detail in Part I.H of this Explanation of Provisions, a Tested Foreign Corporation could own a second domestic corporation through a 25-percent-owned domestic corporate subsidiary and could thus be treated under sections 1297(c) and 1298(b)(7) as receiving intercompany dividends from the lower-tier domestic corporation that would be excluded from the income of the upper-tier domestic corporation under the consolidated return regulations. Accordingly, the operation of the statutory rules under sections 1297 and 1298 indicate that the Income Test is intended to take into account all income of a Tested Foreign Corporation, without regard to reductions or exclusions that might apply for purposes of determining the U.S. Federal income tax imposed on such income. Consistent with those rules, the Treasury Department and the IRS have concluded that intercompany dividends received by a corporation from a member of its consolidated group and treated as received under section 1297(c) by a Tested Foreign Corporation that directly or indirectly owns stock in the corporation should be taken into account for purposes of the Income Test. Thus, the proposed regulations indicate that income for purposes of the Income Test includes all dividend income, including dividends that are excluded from gross income under section 1502 and §1.1502-13. *See* proposed §1.1297-1(b). The Treasury Department and the IRS welcome comments on this approach. However, see Part I.F.3 of this Explanation of Provisions for a discussion of rules that could eliminate such dividends.

2. Exceptions from Passive Income

Furthermore, there are a number of exceptions to the definition of FPHCI in section 954(c), as well as in section 954(h) and (i), and special rules and definitions in section 954(c) that affect the determination of FPHCI. Specifically, in addition to the exceptions contained within the general definition of FPHCI in section 954(c)(1), section 954(c)(2) provides three exceptions: (i) an active rents and royalties exception; (ii) an export financing exception; and (iii) a dealer exception. Section 954(c)(3) provides two additional exceptions: (i) a related person, same country dividend and interest exception; and (ii) a related person, same country rents and royalty exception. In addition, for taxable years of foreign corporations beginning after December 31, 2005, and before January 1, 2020, section 954(c)(6) excludes from FPHCI certain dividends, interest, rents, and royalties received or accrued from a related corporation that is a CFC. Moreover, section 954(h) provides rules that apply for purposes of section 954(c)(1) pursuant to which income derived in an active banking or financing business is excluded from FPHCI. Additionally, under section 954(i), income from an active insurance business is excluded from FPHCI for purposes of section 954(c)(1). Finally, section 954(c)(4) contains a look-through rule that applies in the case of a sale of certain partnership interests, and section 954(c)(5) contains definitions and special rules applicable to commodity transactions.

Separately, section 1297(b)(2) provides explicit exclusions to the general definition of passive income set forth in section 1297(b)(1). Specifically, section 1297(b)(2) provides four exceptions: (i) an active banking exception; (ii) an active insurance business exception; (iii) a related person interest, dividends, rents, and royalties exception; and (iv) an export trade financing exception.

Questions have been raised regarding the scope of the cross-reference to section 954(c) in section 1297(b)(1) for purposes of defining passive income for PFIC purposes. Comments have inquired whether the section 954(c) reference in section 1297(b) incorporates all of the exceptions to FPHCI that are in section 954(c). In addition, by their terms, certain exceptions to FPHCI apply only to a foreign corporation that is a CFC. If these exceptions apply for PFIC purposes, the comments also question whether a Tested Foreign Corporation must also be a CFC in order to benefit from the exceptions.

The Treasury Department and the IRS understand that Congress did not intend for all of the exceptions in section 954(c) to apply for purposes of determining passive income under the PFIC provisions. In particular, the exceptions in section 954(c)(3) (relating to certain income received from related persons) and 954(c)(6) (relating to certain income received from related CFCs) were not meant to be taken into account for PFIC purposes. The legislative history indicates that Congress intended for the section 1297(c) look-through rules or the section 1297(b)(2)(C) exception to apply to income items that otherwise would be entitled to the section 954(c)(3) exception. It indicates:

The bill conforms the PFIC definition of passive income to the definition of passive income under subpart F (sec. 954(c)). This change, in conjunction with the look-through rule for certain 25-percent-owned corporations and the lookthrough rules added by the bill (described below), makes it explicit that earnings of certain related foreign corporations organized in the same country as its shareholder that, if distributed to the shareholder would be excluded from foreign personal holding company income under the same-country exception of subpart F (sec. 954(c)(3)), are subject to either the section [1297(c)] look-through treatment or the look-through treatment for amounts paid by related parties that are not 25 percent owned (described below).

H.R. Rep. No. 100-795, at 271-272 (1988); S. Rep. No. 100-445, at 285-286 (1988).

Thus, the proposed regulations do not incorporate the section 954(c)(3) exception for purposes of determining passive income for PFIC purposes. Similarly, under the proposed regulations, the section 954(c)(6) exception also does not apply for determining PFIC status because the section 1297(b)(2)(C) related-person exception is intended to be the sole related-person exception applicable for determining passive income under the PFIC rules.

Additional questions are raised with respect to the FPHCI exceptions for active banking, financing, and insurance income because section 1297(b) does not specifically cross-reference section 954(h) and (i). As with section 1297(b)(2)(C), it is possible that sections 1297(b)(2)(A) and (B) were intended to be the sole exceptions for active banking, financing, and insurance income applicable for determining passive income under the PFIC rules because section 1297(b) has specific exceptions for active banking, financing, and insurance income. Alternatively, the section 1297(b) cross-reference to section 954(c) could be read to include the exceptions provided in section 954(h) and (i), which apply for purposes of section 954(c) by their terms. It may be appropriate for income that satisfies the requirements in section 954(h) and (i) to be excluded from passive income because Congress generally defined passive income by reference to FPHCI, and when section 954(h) and (i) were enacted, each with a cross-reference to section 954(c), Congress did not provide that section 954(h) or (i) should not apply for PFIC purposes. Moreover, the fact that the PFIC provisions are more generally not intended to apply to foreign corporations engaged in active businesses supports the application of rules excluding active banking, financing, and insurance income from the definition of passive income.

However, with respect to section 954(i), Congress recently amended the exclusion for income derived in the active conduct of an insurance business in section 1297(b)(2)(B) to require that income be earned by a QIC, as discussed in Part II of the Background section of this preamble. Given this statutory change and the tests contained in the definition of QIC in section 1297(f), the Treasury Department and the IRS have determined that the exception for insurance income in section 954(i) should not apply in addition to the newly modified exception in section 1297(b)(2)(B). Accordingly, the proposed regulations provide that the section 954(i) exception to FPHCI does not apply in addition to the PFIC exception. *See* proposed § 1.1297-1(c)(1)(i)(B). By contrast, given that no final regulations under the PFIC regime provide rules concerning an exclusion of active banking and financing income, these proposed regulations provide that the FPHCI exception for banking and financing income under section 954(h) applies for purposes of determining PFIC status. *See* proposed § 1.1297-1(c)(1)(i)(A). The application of section 954(h) is in addition to the PFIC exception. The Treasury Department and the IRS request comments about whether, when regulations are in force under section 1297(b)(2)(A), the corollary FPHCI exclusion should also continue to apply.

Comments have noted that the application of section 954(c) for PFIC purposes can be uncertain when a Tested Foreign Corporation is not also a CFC. For instance, the application of section 954(h) for PFIC purposes could be interpreted to apply only to amounts received by a Tested Foreign Corporation that also is a CFC. Passive income for PFIC purposes is defined by cross-reference to section 954(c) because the income items that comprise FPHCI are generally passive in nature. The CFC status of the recipient of an item of FPHCI does not affect the passive nature of the item, and thus is not relevant for purposes of determining whether an item is passive under the PFIC rules. Therefore, it is appropriate for income derived by any Tested Foreign Corporation, and not just Tested Foreign Corporations that also are CFCs, to be eligible for the exceptions to FPHCI, including the section 954(h) exception.

For the reasons discussed in this Part I.C.2, the proposed regulations provide that for purposes of section 1297(b)(1), passive income is determined by reference to the items of income listed in section 954(c)(1), subject only to the exceptions found in section 954(c)(1), section 954(c)(2)(A) (relating to active rents and royalties), section 954(c)(2)(B) (relating to certain export financing interest), section 954(c)(2)(C) (relating to dealers), and section 954(h) (relating to entities engaged in the active conduct of a banking, financing, or similar business). *See* proposed § 1.1297-1(c)(1)(i) and (c)(1)(i)(A). In addition, the rules in section 954(c)(4) (relating to sales of certain partnership interests) and 954(c)(5) (relating to certain commodity hedging transactions) apply for PFIC purposes. *See* proposed § 1.1297-1(c)(1)(i)(C). However, for the reasons stated in this Part I.C.2, the exceptions in section 954(c)(3) (relating to certain income received from related persons), section 954(c)(6) (relating to certain amounts received from related controlled foreign corporations), and section 954(i) (relating to entities engaged in the active conduct of an insurance business) are not taken into account for purposes of section 1297(b)(1). *See* proposed § 1.1297-1(c)(1)(i)(B). The proposed regulations also provide that an entity is treated as a CFC for purposes of applying an exception to FPHCI and for purposes of determining whether a person is a related person with respect to the entity. *See* proposed § 1.1297-1(c)(1)(i)(D). Comments are requested as to whether regulations should provide any additional special rules concerning the definition of a related person under section 954(d)(3) for purposes of applying an FPHCI exception to a Tested Foreign Corporation that is not a CFC.

3. Income and Gains from Certain Transactions

The Income Test is computed based on a Tested Foreign Corporation's gross income. However, pursuant to section 954(c), certain categories of income are FPHCI only to the extent that gains exceed losses with respect to the category. For instance, under section 954(c)(1)(B) only "the excess of gains over losses from the sale or exchange" of certain property is treated as FPHCI. Similar rules apply to income from commodities transactions under section 954(c)(1)(C), foreign currency gains under section 954(c)(1)(D), and income from notional principal contracts under section 954(c)(1)(F). The proposed regulations provide that for purposes of the Income Test, items of income under section 954(c) that are determined by netting gains against losses are taken into account by a corporation on that net basis, so that only net gains in a particular category of FPHCI are taken into account. See proposed § 1.1297-1(c)(1)(ii). However, the net amount of income in each category of FPHCI is determined separately for each relevant corporation, such that net gains or losses of a corporation, at least 25 percent of the value of stock of which is owned, directly or indirectly, by a Tested Foreign Corporation ("Look-Through Subsidiary") may not be netted against net losses or gains of another Look-Through Subsidiary or of a Tested Foreign Corporation.

4. Income Earned Through Partnerships

The proposed regulations provide guidance on the treatment of a corporation's distributive share of partnership income for purposes of the Income Test. The Treasury Department and the IRS have determined that income earned by a Tested Foreign Corporation through a partnership should be treated similarly to income earned through a corporate subsidiary. As discussed in more detail in Part I.F of this Explanation of Provisions, if a Tested Foreign Corporation owns a Look-Through Subsidiary, the Tested Foreign Corporation is treated as if it directly received its proportionate share of the income of the Look-Through Subsidiary, and certain items of income received from the Look-Through Subsidiary are proportionately eliminated. If a corporation is not a Look-Through Subsidiary, income received from the corporation is characterized in accordance with the general rules described in Part I.C.2 of this Explanation of Provisions, under which dividends generally will be passive. Accordingly, the proposed regulations provide that a Tested Foreign Corporation's distributive share of any item of income of a partnership is treated as income received directly by the Tested Foreign Corporation, provided the Tested Foreign Corporation owns, directly or indirectly, at least 25 percent of the value of the partnership, in which case the partnership is referred to as a "Look-Through Partnership," and income elimination rules similar to those for Look-Through Subsidiaries apply. See proposed § 1.1297-1(c)(2)(i). If the Tested Foreign Corporation owns less than 25 percent of the value of a partnership, the corporation's distributive share of any item of income of the partnership is passive income. See proposed § 1.1297-1(c)(2)(ii).

As a result of these rules, in cases in which the Tested Foreign Corporation owns at least 25 percent of the value of the partnership, the exceptions to passive income contained in section 1297(b)(2) and the relevant exceptions to foreign personal holding company income in section 954(c) and (h) that are based on whether income is derived in the active conduct of a business generally apply if, and only if, the partnership engages in the relevant business activities. The focus on partnership activities is consistent with the principles applicable to partnership interests under the regulations under subpart F. See § 1.954-2(a)(5)(ii)(A); § 1.954-3(a)(6). However, as described in Part I.F.5 of this Explanation of Provisions, these proposed regulations also include rules that, in certain circumstances, allow the character of income to be determined at the level of the Tested Foreign Corporation, taking into account activities performed by the Tested Foreign Corporation and certain subsidiaries of the Tested Foreign Corporation, whether such subsidiaries are in corporate or partnership form.

Although the subpart F regulations provide rules concerning the classification of a CFC's distributive share of partnership income that, absent these proposed regulations, would generally be applicable by virtue of section 1297's adoption of FPHCI as the basis for passive income, the Treasury Department and the IRS have determined that the differing policies of the subpart F and PFIC regimes warrant different rules for partnerships. Specifically, the Treasury Department and the IRS have concluded that it is appropriate to generally characterize a corporation's distributive share of partnership income as passive when the corporation owns less than 25 percent of the value of the partnership, consistent with the treatment of Look-Through Subsidiary income, notwithstanding the fact that under the subpart F regulations, such income could have been excluded from FPHCI by virtue of the partnership's activities regardless of the corporation's level of ownership. The different treatment is warranted because of the flexibility that entities have in their characterization for U.S. Federal income tax purposes under § 301.7701-3 and because of the fact that treating a subsidiary as a partnership may not have U.S. income tax consequences for a Tested Foreign Corporation, as it could for a CFC. However, the Treasury Department and the IRS request comments as to whether a 25 percent threshold for the Tested Foreign Corporation's percentage ownership in the partnership is the appropriate threshold for distinguishing between a distributive share of partnership income that is automatically treated as passive and a distributive share that is characterized in accordance with the activities undertaken by the partnership (or, as applicable under the rules described in Part I.F.5 of this Explanation of Provisions, the Tested Foreign Corporation and certain subsidiaries of the Tested Foreign Corporation), or whether an alternative threshold should be considered. Furthermore, the Treasury Department and the IRS request comments as to whether different rules should apply with respect to partners in general partnerships than with respect to partners in limited partnerships, or with respect to partners that materially participate in the activities of the partnership.

5. Income from a Related Person

The proposed regulations provide additional guidance on the application of the section 1297(b)(2)(C) related-person exception to dividends, interest, rents, and royalties. The proposed regulations provide that the determination of whether the payor of an item of income is a related person should be made on the date of receipt or accrual, as applicable based on the recipient's method of accounting, of the item of income. See proposed § 1.1297-1(c)(3)(iv).

Under § 1.904-5(c)(2)(ii)(C) (the "cream-skimming rule"), interest paid to a related person is treated as passive income to the payee to the extent that the payor has passive income. Under this rule, if a foreign corporation had $200 of passive gross income and $200 of non-passive gross income, and that foreign corporation made an interest payment of $100 to a related foreign corporation, for purposes of determining the nature of the interest income in the hands of the payee foreign corporation, the entire $100 of interest would be treated as passive income rather than as ratably allocable between passive and non-passive income. Although the Treasury Department and the IRS considered applying a cream-skimming rule for purposes of section 1297(b)(2)(C), the Treasury Department and the IRS have concluded that the PFIC regime does not raise the policy concerns addressed by the cream-skimming rule in the foreign tax credit and subpart F contexts. In those contexts, because interest expense can reduce a foreign corporation's subpart F income or otherwise affect the calculation of foreign tax credits, an interest payment could otherwise be used to try to reduce the passive income of the payor and convert it into non-passive income of the payee. However, because the Income Test is applied on the basis of gross income, an interest payment cannot be used in the same fashion for purposes of the Income Test. Accordingly, under the proposed regulations, for purposes of the section 1297(b)(2)(C) exception, interest is properly allocable to income of the related person that is not passive income based on the relative portion of the related person's income for its taxable year that ends in or with the taxable year of the recipient that is not passive income. See proposed § 1.1297-1(c)(3)(i). Dividends are treated as properly allocable to income of the related person that is not passive income based on the portion of the related payor's current-year earnings and profits for the taxable year that ends in or with the taxable year of the recipient that are attributable to non-passive income. See proposed § 1.1297-1(c)(3)(ii). Comments are specifically requested concerning alternative methods of determining the portion of dividends treated as properly allocable to income of a related person (including if the payor has no current earnings and profits), including by reference to accumulated earnings and profits, and if so, how to address concerns about the availability of information. The proposed regulations further provide that rents and royalties are allocable to income of the related person which is not passive income to the extent the related person's deduction for the rent or royalty is allocated to non-passive income under the principles of §§ 1.861-8 through 1.861-14T. See proposed § 1.1297-1(c)(3)(iii). Comments are specifically requested regarding any concerns about the availability of information and alternative methods of determining the portion of rents and royalties treated as properly allocable to income of a related person that would address any such concerns.

D. *Asset test*

1. Methodology of Application of Asset Test

Section 1297(a)(2) provides that a Tested Foreign Corporation is a PFIC if the average percentage of assets held by the corporation during a taxable year that produce passive income or are held for the production of passive income is at least 50 percent. Notice 88-22 provides that the average percentage of assets of a Tested Foreign Corporation is calculated by averaging the value of the assets of the corporation, determined as of the end of each quarterly period of the corporation's taxable year.

These regulations clarify that the average percentage of a Tested Foreign Corporation's assets is determined using the average of the gross values (or adjusted bases) at the end of each quarter of the foreign corporation's taxable year. *See* proposed § 1.1297-1(d)(1)(i) and (d)(1)(ii)(A). Alternatively, the assets of a Tested Foreign Corporation can be measured for purposes of the Asset Test more frequently than quarterly (for example, weekly or monthly). The quarter or shorter interval used by a Tested Foreign Corporation is referred to as its "measuring period." Applying the Asset Test based on a period that recurs more frequently than a quarter provides a more precise measurement of "average," but the more frequently recurring basis is not required because of the potential administrative burden that it could impose on a shareholder of a Tested Foreign Corporation. The same measuring period must be used for the Tested Foreign Corporation for the initial year (including a short year) that for which the shareholder elects to use the alternative measuring period and any and all subsequent years unless the election to use the more frequently recurring measuring period is revoked. *See* proposed § 1.1297-1(d)(1)(ii)(B).

If a Tested Foreign Corporation has a short taxable year, the quarterly measuring dates for purposes of the Asset Test are the same as they would be for a full taxable year, except that the final quarterly measuring date will be the final day of the short taxable year. *See* proposed § 1.1297-1(d)(1)(ii)(C). Thus, for instance, if a Tested Foreign Corporation for which the election for a shorter period has not been made has a short year of eight months, the corporation would have two quarters ending on the foreign corporation's normal quarterly measuring dates and a third quarter ending on the final day of the short taxable year. The asset amounts for those three quarterly measuring dates would be averaged to determine the average percentage of a Tested Foreign Corporation's assets that are passive for the year. The Treasury Department and the IRS have determined that applying the Asset Test based on the taxable year quarters that ended during the short year properly accounts for the administrative difficulties of calculating quarterly measurements with respect to a short year.

Under section 1297(e), the assets of a Tested Foreign Corporation are required to be measured based on (i) value, pursuant to section 1297(e)(1), if it is a publicly traded corporation for the taxable year, or if section 1297(e)(2) does not apply to it for the taxable year; or (ii) adjusted basis, pursuant to section 1297(e)(2), if it is a CFC, or elects the application of section 1297(e)(2). The statute does not specify whether a corporation that is publicly traded during only part of the taxable year is publicly traded "for the taxable year," and thus whether such a corporation's assets should be measured for the taxable year based on value or on adjusted basis or whether, if the corporation is a CFC for the remainder of the year, a combination of the two should be used. For instance, a Tested Foreign Corporation that is a CFC at the beginning of its taxable year and became publicly traded during the last month of its taxable year could be required under section 1297(e) to have its assets measured based on either adjusted basis or value for all four quarterly measuring periods or based on adjusted basis for its first three quarterly measuring periods and value for its fourth quarterly measuring period. The proposed regulations provide that the Asset Test should apply on the basis of value for the entire year if the corporation was publicly traded on the majority of days during the year or section 1297(e)(2) did not apply to the corporation on the majority of days of the year. Otherwise, the Asset Test should apply on the basis of adjusted basis for the entire year. *See* proposed § 1.1297-1(d)(1)(v). The Treasury Department and the IRS have determined that allowing a shareholder the option of choosing either method with respect to a Tested Foreign Corporation could facilitate the avoidance of the PFIC rules, and that the rule in the proposed regulation imposes the least administrative burden. The Treasury Department and the IRS welcome comments on these rules.

Under the proposed regulations, the rules described in this Part I.D.1 for making or revoking an election for an alternative measuring period also apply for purposes of the election provided in section 1297(e)(2)(B) to use adjusted bases of assets for purposes of the Asset Test. *See* proposed § 1.1297-1(d)(1)(iii)(B) and (d)(1)(iv). Both elections may be made by a United States person that is eligible under § 1.1295-1(d) with respect to the Tested Foreign Corporation or that would be eligible if the Tested Foreign Corporation were a PFIC. *See* proposed § 1.1297-1(d)(1)(iv)(A). Thus, in the case of a Tested Foreign Corporation owned by a domestic partnership in which U.S. individuals are partners, only the domestic partnership and not its partners may make the elections, ensuring that the Tested Foreign Corporation is treated consistently for all of the partners, which would facilitate reporting by the partnership if the Tested Foreign Corporation were a PFIC. However, the Treasury Department and the IRS request comments as to whether either election should be available to any United States person that is a shareholder (within the meaning of § 1.1291-1(b)(7) or (8)) of the Tested Foreign Corporation or that would be a shareholder of the Tested Foreign Corporation if it were a PFIC.

If the person is required to file the Form 8621 (or successor form) with respect to the Tested Foreign Corporation, the elections may be made in the manner provided in the instructions to the Form 8621; until such instructions are provided, the elections may be made by attaching a written statement to the Form 8621 providing for the election to a return for the year for which the election is made. If the person is not required to file the Form 8621 with respect to the Tested Foreign Corporation (for example, because the Tested Foreign Corporation is not a PFIC), the person may make the elections by attaching a written statement providing for the election to a return for the year for which the election is made. *Id.* The elections are revoked in a similar manner. *See* proposed § 1.1297-1(d)(1)(iv)(B). A new election for an alternative measuring period or under section 1297(e)(2)(B) may not be made until the sixth taxable year following the year for which the previous such election was revoked, and such subsequent election may not be revoked until the sixth taxable year following the year for which the subsequent election was made. *See id.*

2. Characterization of Dual-Character Assets

Pursuant to section 1297(a), an asset is considered passive for purposes of the Asset Test if it produces passive income or is held for the production of passive income. Notice 88-22 states that an asset that produces both passive income and non-passive income during a Tested Foreign Corporation's taxable year is treated partly as a passive asset and partly as a non-passive asset in proportion to the relative amounts of income generated by the asset during the year. Proposed § 1.1297-1(d)(2) generally adopts the rule set forth in Notice 88-22, and provides that an asset that produces both passive income and non-passive income during a taxable year is treated as two assets, one of which is passive and one of which is non-passive. Consistent with the rule in Notice 88-22, for purposes of applying the Asset Test, the value (or adjusted basis) of the asset is allocated between the passive assets and non-passive assets based on the ratio of passive income produced by the asset during the taxable year to non-passive income.

The proposed regulation also provides a specific rule for stock of a related person with respect to which no dividends are received or accrued, as applicable based on the recipient's method of accounting, during a taxable year but that previously generated dividends that were characterized as non-passive income, in whole or in part, under section 1297(b)(2)(C). *See* proposed § 1.1297-1(d)(2)(iii). The stock is characterized based on the dividends received or accrued, as applicable based on the recipient's method of accounting, with respect thereto for the prior two years. *Id.*

The Treasury Department and the IRS have determined that it may also be appropriate to bifurcate an asset that in part produces income and in part does not produce income between a passive and a non-passive asset for purposes of the Asset Test in order to provide a more accurate measure of the Tested Foreign Corporation's passive assets. For example, if a Tested Foreign Corporation uses a portion of a building, which is depreciable real property, in its trade or business that generates non-passive income, while renting a portion of the building in exchange for rents that are treated as passive, it would be appropriate for the portions of the building to be considered separately as non-passive and passive assets, respectively. Accordingly, the proposed regulations provide that for purposes of applying the Asset Test, if an asset in part produces income and in part does not produce any income, the asset must be bifurcated pursuant to the method that most reasonably reflects the uses of the property. *See* proposed §1.1297-1(d)(2)(ii). A similar approach applies to characterize gain for subpart F purposes. *See* §1.954-2(e)(1)(iv).

The Treasury Department and the IRS welcome comments on these rules, including suggestions for how to minimize the burden associated with determining how to bifurcate the relevant assets.

3. Characterization of Partnership Interests

The proposed regulations provide guidance on the characterization of a partnership interest for purposes of the Asset Test. As discussed in Part I.C.4 of this Explanation of Provisions, the Treasury Department and the IRS have determined that it is appropriate to treat a partnership in a manner similar to a corporate subsidiary for purposes of determining whether a Tested Foreign Corporation is a PFIC. Accordingly, the proposed regulations provide that for purposes of the Asset Test, a Tested Foreign Corporation that directly or indirectly owns an interest in a partnership is treated as if it held its proportionate share of the assets of a partnership, provided the Tested Foreign Corporation owns, directly or indirectly, at least 25 percent, by value, of the interests in the partnership. *See* proposed §1.1297-1(d)(3)(i). A corporation's proportionate share of a partnership asset is treated as producing passive income, or being held to produce passive income, to the extent the asset produced, or was held to produce, passive income in the partnership's hands, taking into account only the partnership's activities, unless the rules described in Part I.F.5 of this Explanation of Provisions apply to allow the character of the income to be determined at the level of the Tested Foreign Corporation, taking into account activities performed by certain subsidiaries of the Tested Foreign Corporation. If a Tested Foreign corporation owns less than 25 percent of the value of the partnership, its interest in the partnership is treated as a passive asset. *See* proposed §1.1297-1(d)(3)(ii).

4. Characterization of Dealer Property

For purposes of the Asset Test, an asset is considered passive if it produces passive income or is held for the production of passive income. Under the dealer exception in section 954(c)(2)(C), gain from the disposition of certain dealer property is treated as non-passive income for purposes of the Income Test. However, certain other income derived with respect to the dealer property (such as dividends and interest) is treated as passive income. The exception from passive income for dealer property in section 954(c)(2)(C) is predicated on the fact that a dealer holds the property as part of its trade or business and not for the production of passive income. Accordingly, the Treasury Department and the IRS have determined that, given that the PFIC regime is concerned with whether the asset is part of an active business, it is appropriate to characterize dealer property for purposes of the Asset Test based solely on the character of the gain derived from the disposition of the property. Accordingly, the proposed regulations provide that property that is subject to the dealer exception is characterized as a non-passive asset for purposes of the Asset Test, notwithstanding the dual-character asset rules discussed in Part I.D.2 of this Explanation of Provisions. *See* proposed §1.1297-1(d)(4).

E. *Treatment of stapled entities*

The Treasury Department and the IRS understand that, in certain situations, equity interests in two or more foreign entities must be sold together as stapled interests within the meaning of section 269B(c)(3). Stapled entities (as defined in section 269B(c)(2)) may be structured in such a way that income and the assets generating the income are in one entity, while the activities generating the income are engaged in by the other entity. For example, two stapled entities might jointly carry on a real estate business, with one stapled entity owning real property that is leased to third parties to generate rental income, while the other stapled entity provides management services with respect to the real property that, if engaged in by the first stapled entity, would allow the rental income received by it to be characterized as non-passive income pursuant to section 954(c)(2)(A) and these proposed regulations. However, if the PFIC status of the stapled entity receiving the rental income were determined on a standalone basis, the income might be treated as passive income. Given that stapled interests represent a single economic interest to their shareholders, the Treasury Department and the IRS have determined that it is appropriate, for purposes of determining whether a stapled entity is a PFIC, to treat them as such. This is consistent with the treatment of stapled entities in section 269B(a)(3) for purposes of determining whether a stapled entity is a regulated investment company ("RIC") or a real estate investment trust ("REIT"). Accordingly, the proposed regulations provide that for purposes of determining whether any stapled entity is a PFIC, all entities that are stapled entities with respect to each other are treated as one entity. *See* proposed §1.1297-1(e). Comments are requested as to whether similar treatment should be provided for purposes of the subpart F rules.

F. *Look-through rule for 25-percent-owned subsidiaries*

As noted in Part I.C.4 of this Explanation of Provisions, in determining PFIC status, section 1297(c) applies when a Tested Foreign Corporation owns, directly or indirectly, at least 25 percent of the value of the stock of another corporation, a Look-Through Subsidiary. In such instance, the Tested Foreign Corporation is treated as if it directly held its proportionate share of the assets and directly received its proportionate share of the income of the Look-Through Subsidiary. Section 1297(c) was enacted to prevent "foreign corporations owning the stock of subsidiaries engaged in active businesses [from being] classified as PFICs." H.R. Rep. No. 99-841, at II-644 (1986) (Conf. Rep.).

1. Determining a Tested Foreign Corporation's Ownership of a Look-Through Subsidiary and Proportionate Share of a Look-Through Subsidiary's Assets and Income

Neither the statute nor the regulations provide guidance on how to calculate a Tested Foreign Corporation's indirect ownership in another corporation for purposes of determining whether the corporation is a Look-Through Subsidiary under section 1297(c). In addition, the statute and regulations do not provide a methodology for determining a Tested Foreign Corporation's proportionate share of a Look-Through Subsidiary's income and assets for purposes of section 1297(c).

Under section 1297(c), the determination of whether a Tested Foreign Corporation owns, directly or indirectly, at least 25 percent of the stock of another corporation is based on value. The proposed regulations provide that indirect stock ownership for purposes of section 1297(c) is determined under the principles of section 958(a) applicable for determining ownership by value. *See* proposed §1.1297-2(b)(1). The section 958(a) principles apply without regard to whether entities are domestic or foreign, and thus indirect ownership includes corporate ownership through intermediate corporations, partnerships, trusts, and estates, regardless of whether such intermediate entities are foreign or domestic. *Id*. In addition, stock considered owned by reason of applying the section 958(a) indirect ownership rules is generally considered actually owned for purposes of reapplying the indirect ownership rules. *See* §1.958-2(f)(1).

Section 1297(c) provides that a Tested Foreign Corporation is treated as holding its proportionate share of the assets of the Look-Through Subsidiary, and receiving its proportionate share of the income of the Look-Through Subsidiary. The proposed regulations provide guidance on the meaning of "proportionate share" for purposes of section 1297(c). Specifically, proposed §1.1297-2(b)(2) provides that a Tested Foreign Corporation is treated as owning a share of each asset, and receiving a proportionate share of each item of income, of a Look-Through Subsidiary proportionate to the Tested Foreign Corporation's percentage ownership (by value) of the Look-Through Subsidiary. Comments are requested concerning alternative methods that might better determine a Tested Foreign Corporation's proportionate share of income of a Look-Through Subsidiary that has multiple classes of stock outstanding.

Changes in stock ownership may cause fluctuations in a Tested Foreign Corporation's ownership in a Look-Through Subsidiary during a taxable year. For purposes of the Asset Test, ownership of a Look-Through Subsidiary is determined on each measuring date. *See* proposed §1.1297-2(b)(2)(i). If the requisite 25-percent ownership is not met with respect to a corporation on the last day of a measuring period, as defined in Part I.D.1 of this Explanation of Provisions, the stock of the corporation would be a passive asset for purposes of that measuring period, absent the application of a special rule, such as the new rule for dealer property in proposed §1.1297-1(d)(4), described in Part I.D.4 of this Explanation of Provisions. For purposes of the Income Test, a subsidiary is considered a Look-Through Subsidiary if the Tested Foreign Corporation owns an average of 25 percent of the value of the subsidiary for the year, taking into account its ownership on the last day of each measuring period of the Tested Foreign Corporation's taxable year. *See* proposed §1.1297-2(b)(2)(ii)(A). If the Tested Foreign Corporation does not maintain, on average, at least 25-percent ownership of the subsidiary for the taxable year, the Tested Foreign Corporation is not, under the general rule in the proposed regulations, treated as receiving its proportionate share of the income of the subsidiary for that year under section 1297(c). However, the Tested Foreign Corporation may be treated as receiving directly its proportionate share of the income of the subsidiary for each measuring period in a taxable year for which the 25-percent ownership requirement is met on the relevant measuring date, provided the taxpayer can establish gross income for each of those measuring periods. *See* proposed §1.1297-2(b)(2)(ii)(B). Comments are requested concerning appropriate methods for a taxpayer to establish gross income for a measuring period.

2. Overlap Between Section 1297(c) and Section 1298(b)(7)

Section 1298(b)(7) provides a special characterization rule that applies when a Tested Foreign Corporation owns at least 25 percent of the value of the stock of a domestic corporation and is subject to the accumulated earnings tax under section 531 (or waives any benefit under a treaty that would otherwise prevent imposition of such tax). In such instance, section 1298(b)(7) treats the qualified stock held by the domestic corporation as a non-passive asset, and the related income as non-passive income. By its terms, the section 1297(c) look-through rule also could apply to the qualified stock, which is stock in a domestic C corporation that is not a RIC or REIT, and look through to the assets of the corporation that issued the qualified stock for purposes of the Income Test and Asset Test. For example, assume a Tested Foreign Corporation owns 50 percent of the value of the stock in a domestic corporation, US1, which, in turn, owns 50 percent of the stock of a lower tier domestic corporation, US2 (which is not a RIC or a REIT). US2 wholly owns the stock of a foreign corporation, FC. The section 1297(c) look-through rule applies to treat the Tested Foreign Corporation as if it held its proportionate share of the assets, and received a proportionate share of the income, of US1. Both the section 1297(c) look-through rule and the section 1298(b)(7) characterization rule, by their terms, would apply to the stock of US2. The section 1297(c) rule would look through to the assets of US2 and FC. The section 1298(b)(7) characterization rule would treat the stock of US2 as a non-passive asset, and the income derived from the stock as income as non-passive income.

The Treasury Department and the IRS have determined that the special characterization rule of section 1298(b)(7) should generally take precedence over the section 1297(c) look-through rule when both rules would apply simultaneously because the characterization rule of section 1298(b)(7) is the more specific rule where the Tested Foreign Corporation owns a domestic corporation. Thus, the proposed regulations provide that the look-through rule of section 1297(c) does not apply to a domestic corporation, and any subsidiaries of the domestic corporation, if the stock of the domestic corporation is characterized, under section 1298(b)(7), as a non-passive asset producing non-passive income. *See* proposed §1.1297-2(b)(2)(iii). However, these proposed regulations provide certain limitations on the application of section 1298(b)(7), including a new anti-abuse rule, in which case section 1297(c) would apply. The limitations and anti-abuse rule are described in Part I.H of this Explanation of Provisions. The Treasury Department and the IRS welcome comments on these rules.

3. Elimination of Certain Assets and Income for Purposes of Applying Section 1297(a)

Section 1297(c) aggregates the income and assets of a Tested Foreign Corporation and a Look-Through Subsidiary for purposes of testing the PFIC status of the Tested Foreign Corporation. However, there are no statutory or regulatory rules that prevent the double counting of income and assets arising from contracts and other transactions among a Tested Foreign Corporation and one or more Look-Through Subsidiaries. Intercompany items that are not eliminated for purposes of determining a Tested Foreign Corporation's PFIC status may result in a duplication of passive income or passive assets attributed to the Tested Foreign Corporation. For instance, if a wholly-owned Look-Through Subsidiary earned $100x of passive income during a taxable year, and distributed the $100x as a dividend to a Tested Foreign Corporation, the Tested Foreign Corporation would have a total of $200x of passive income ($100x of passive income under section 1297(c) and a $100x dividend) for purposes of the Income Test, even though only $100 of passive income was earned economically. Any double-counting of intercompany income and assets distorts the effect of section 1297(c) on the Income Test and Asset Test.

The legislative history to the PFIC rules provides an approach that would eliminate certain assets and income in order to prevent double-counting. *See* H.R. Rep. No. 100-795, at 268 (1988) ("Under this look-through rule, a foreign corporation that owns at least 25 percent of the stock of another corporation is treated as owning a proportionate part of the other corporation's assets and income. Thus, amounts such as interest and dividends received from foreign or domestic subsidiaries are eliminated from the shareholder's income in applying the income test and the stock or debt investment is eliminated from the shareholder's assets in applying the asset test."); Staff, Joint Committee on Taxation, General Explanation of the Tax Reform Act of 1986, JCS-10-87, at 1026 (1987). The Treasury Department and the IRS have determined that it is appropriate to follow that approach. Thus, the proposed regulations provide that intercompany payments of dividends and interest between a Look-Through Subsidiary and the Tested Foreign Corporation and stock and debt receivables are eliminated in applying the Income Test and the Asset Test. *See* proposed §1.1297-2(c)(1) and (2). In the case of dividends, in order to qualify for elimination, the payment must be attributable to income of a Look-Through Subsidiary that was included in gross income by the Tested Foreign Corporation for purposes of determining its PFIC status. *See* proposed §1.1297-2(c)(2). Thus, dividends attributable to income of the Look-Through Subsidiary earned in a year before the Tested Foreign Corporation owned, on average, at least 25% by value of the Look-Through Subsidiary would generally not qualify for elimination. As a result of the elimination rule, for example, interest and dividends received by a Tested Foreign Corporation from a wholly owned Look-Through Subsidiary are eliminated from the Tested Foreign Corporation's gross income for purposes of applying section 1297(a)(1), except to the extent that dividend amounts are attributable to income that has not been treated as received directly by the Tested Foreign Corporation under the section 1297(c) look-through rule. Additionally, the proposed regulations extend this treatment to intercompany payments between two Look-Through Subsidiaries of a Tested Foreign Corporation and the associated stock and debt receivables. Similarly, stock and debt investments in a lower-tier Look-Through Subsidiary are eliminated for purposes of applying the Income Test and Asset Test to the Tested Foreign Corporation. In the case of a Tested Foreign Corporation that owns less than 100 percent of a Look-Through Subsidiary, the proposed regulations provide that while stock and dividends are eliminated in their entirety, eliminations of debt receivables and interest are made in proportion to the shareholder's direct and indirect ownership (by value) in the Look-Through Subsidiary. The proposed regulations also provide for eliminations under these principles for ownership interests in a Look-Through Partnership, as well as intercompany debt receivables and interest paid or accrued thereon between a Tested Foreign Corporation and a Look-Through Partnership. *See* proposed §1.1297-2(c)(3). Comments are requested on the application of the elimination rule if the Tested Foreign Corporation owns less than 100 percent of the Look-Through Subsidiary or Partnership. Comments are also requested as to whether the Treasury Department and the IRS should consider the elimination of rents, royalties, or any other types of intercompany income, and any related assets, and if so, how to effectuate the elimination.

4. Section 1297(b)(2)(C) Related Person Determination with Respect to Interest, Dividends, Rents, and Royalties Received by Look-Through Subsidiaries and Certain Partnerships

Section 1297(c) provides that a Tested Foreign Corporation is treated as receiving directly its proportionate share of the income of a Look-Through Subsidiary for purposes of applying the Income Test to the Tested Foreign Corporation. Section 1297(b)(2)(C) provides that, for purposes of the Income Test, passive income does not include interest, dividends, rents or royalties received or accrued from a related person (within the meaning of section 954(d)(3)) to the extent such amount is properly allocable to income of the related person that is not passive income. The statute and current regulations do not address the level at which the "related person" determination is made if a Look-Through Subsidiary receives or accrues an item of income that is treated as directly received by a Tested Foreign Corporation pursuant to section 1297(c). Thus, the interaction and application of the two rules is unclear in cases in which the payor of an item of income is a "related person" with respect to either the Look-Through Subsidiary or the Tested Foreign Corporation, but not with respect to both.

The Treasury Department and the IRS have determined that, because section 1297(c) generally applies by classifying an item at the level of Look-Through Subsidiary and then carrying that classification up to the Tested Foreign Corporation, it is appropriate to determine whether the section 1297(b)(2)(C) exception applies (and, thus, determine the passive or non-passive character of an item of income) at the Look-Through Subsidiary level, and then flow up the passive or non-passive character of the item to the Tested Foreign Corporation for purposes of applying the Income Test. Accordingly, proposed §1.1297-2(d)(1) provides that, in applying section 1297(b)(2)(C), "related person" status is tested with respect to the payor of the item of income and the Look-Through Subsidiary. The same rule applies for items of income received by a partnership and treated as received directly by a Tested Foreign Corporation pursuant to proposed §1.1297-1(c)(2). The Treasury Department and the IRS welcome comments on these rules.

5. Attribution of Activities of a Look-Through Subsidiary and Certain Partnerships

The interaction of section 1297(c) and certain exceptions from passive income also raises issues that require a threshold determination of whether an exception should apply at a Look-Through Subsidiary level or a Tested Foreign Corporation level. For instance, under proposed §1.1296-4 in the notice of proposed rulemaking (INTL-0065-93) published in the **Federal Register** (60 FR 20922) on April 28, 1995, the banking exception in section 1297(b)(2)(A) applies only if a number of requirements are satisfied, including a deposit taking requirement, a lending requirement, and a license requirement. *See* proposed §1.1296-4. In a bank holding company structure, in which a Tested Foreign Corporation wholly owns a Look-Through Subsidiary that separately satisfies the section 1297(b)(2)(A) requirements, the banking exception would apply to the income derived by the Look-Through Subsidiary in its banking business if an approach that applied the exception at the Look-Through Subsidiary level were adopted, but would not apply if an approach that applied the exception at the Tested Foreign Corporation level were adopted because the Tested Foreign Corporation would not literally meet all of the banking exception requirements. Similarly, the character of assets held by a Look-Through Subsidiary that is a dealer in property in the ordinary course of its trade or business as a dealer would depend on whether an approach that applied the exception in section 954(c)(2)(C) at the Look-Through Subsidiary level were adopted, or whether an approach were applied that determined the character at the level of a Tested Foreign Corporation that was not itself a dealer.

A corollary issue arises with respect to the application of other exceptions to passive income under section 954(c). For instance, under §1.954-2(c)(1)(ii), the active rental income exception in section 954(c)(2)(A) applies if certain activities are performed with respect to real property by the lessor's own employees. In a structure in which a Tested Foreign Corporation holds real estate assets directly and employees of its Look-Through Subsidiary conduct the activities related to the Tested Foreign Corporation's real estate business necessary to satisfy the exception, the exception would apply if the character of the income were determined at the level of the Tested Foreign Corporation and the activities of the managers and employees of the Look-Through Subsidiary were attributed to the Tested Foreign Corporation. However, the exception would not apply if the activities were not attributed to the Tested Foreign Corporation, because in such case the relevant activities are not performed by employees of the Tested Foreign Corporation, as literally required in the regulation. Additional complexities arise when the Tested Foreign Corporation owns less than 100 percent of the Look-Through Subsidiary.

Under current law, the character of income or assets is determined at the level of the entity that directly earns the income or holds the assets based on the activities of that entity. However, the Treasury Department and the IRS understand that active businesses in foreign jurisdictions generating rent and royalty income are often organized with assets and income, on the one hand, and activities, on the other hand, contained in separate entities for various business reasons. The Treasury Department and the IRS have determined that if assets are held and activities undertaken in separate entities within a group of wholly-owned Look-Through Subsidiaries headed by a Tested Foreign Corporation, the activities of the Look-Through Subsidiaries should be taken into account for purposes of determining whether an item of rent or royalty income of the Tested Foreign Corporation is passive income, as they would if the Look-Through Subsidiaries were disregarded as separate from the Tested Foreign Corporation for U.S. Federal income tax purposes.

Accordingly, the proposed regulations provide that an item of rent or royalty income received or accrued by a Tested Foreign Corporation (or treated as received or accrued by the Tested Foreign Corporation pursuant to section 1297(c)) that would otherwise be passive income under the general rule is not passive income for purposes of section 1297 if the item would be excluded from passive income, determined by taking into account the activities performed by the officers and employees of the Tested Foreign Corporation as well as activities performed by the officers and employees of certain Look-Through Subsidiaries and certain partnerships in which the Tested Foreign Corporation or one of the Look-Through Subsidiaries is a partner. *See* proposed §1.1297-2(e)(1). In some cases, a Look-Through Subsidiary or Look-Through Partnership may have more than one unrelated owner owning at least 25 percent of the entity's value. Activities, unlike income or expense, are qualitative in nature and cannot be easily allocated between owners based on their percentage ownership. If activities are attributed to any owner of 25 percent or more of the Look-Through Subsidiary or partnership, then up to four owners could potentially be able to take into account the same activities. Because it may be difficult to allocate activities among multiple entities but inappropriate to allow double-counting of the activities by attributing the activities of a Look-Through Subsidiary or a partnership to multiple unrelated entities, the proposed regulations provide that a Tested Foreign Corporation may take into account the activities performed only by those Look-Through Subsidiaries or partnerships with respect to which the Tested Foreign Corporation owns (directly or indirectly) more than 50 percent of the value, because at this level of ownership the activities of the Look-Through Subsidiary or Look-Through Partnership could be attributed to only another foreign corporation within the same chain of ownership as the Tested Foreign Corporation and not an unrelated entity.

The Treasury Department and the IRS request comments on the application of the activity attribution rules to Look-Through Subsidiaries that are not wholly owned by a Tested Foreign Corporation, including whether it is appropriate for a Tested Foreign Corporation to take into account all activities of a Look-Through Subsidiary in which the Tested Foreign Corporation owns more than 50 percent of the value of the stock, and whether a different ownership threshold for attribution of activities would be appropriate.

The Treasury Department and the IRS also request comments on whether the ability to apply an exception to passive income at the Tested Foreign Corporation level taking into account the activities of certain subsidiaries should apply for purposes of other exceptions, such as for purposes of the exception in section 1297(b)(2)(A). Comments should consider the interaction of the rules for elimination of intercompany assets and income described in Part I.F.3 of this Explanation of Provisions with the rules for taking into account the activities of certain Look-Through Subsidiaries and Look-Through Partnerships.

6. Gain on the Disposition of Stock of a Look-Through Subsidiary

Section 1297(c) does not address the treatment of a Tested Foreign Corporation's gain from the disposition of stock of a Look-Through Subsidiary for purposes of the Income Test. Questions have been raised as to whether such a disposition should be treated as a disposition of stock or a deemed disposition of the assets of the Look-Through Subsidiary, and how gain on the disposition should be characterized for purposes of the Income Test.

The proposed regulations provide that, for purposes of the Income Test, the disposition of a Look-Through Subsidiary is treated as the disposition of stock, and gain is computed accordingly. However, the proposed regulations limit the amount of the gain taken into account for purposes of the Income Test in order to avoid double-counting any income that the Tested Foreign Corporation takes into account under section 1297(c) in determining the PFIC status of the Tested Foreign Corporation during the year of the disposition or took into account for such purpose in a prior year that has not been distributed as a dividend to the Tested Foreign Corporation. Thus, the amount of gain taken into account for purposes of the Income Test ("Residual Gain") is equal to the total gain recognized by the Tested Foreign Corporation on the disposition, reduced (but not below zero) by the amount (if any) by which (A) the aggregate income (if any) of the Look-Through Subsidiary (and any other Look-Through Subsidiary, to the extent stock in such other Look-Through Subsidiary is owned indirectly through the Look-Through Subsidiary) taken into account by the Tested Foreign Corporation under section 1297(c)(2) with respect to the disposed Look-Through Subsidiary stock exceeds (B) the aggregate dividends (if any) received by the Tested Foreign Corporation from the Look-Through Subsidiary with respect to the disposed stock (including dividends attributable to stock of any other Look-Through Subsidiary owned indirectly through the Look-Through Subsidiary). The Residual Gain is computed on a share-by-share basis with respect to income of a Look-Through Subsidiary that was taken into account by the Tested Foreign Corporation and dividends received from a Look-Through Subsidiary. *See* proposed § 1.1297-2(f)(1). Comments are requested on the calculation of Residual Gain for purposes of section 1297(a).

Gain from the disposition of stock generally is treated as FPHCI under section 954(c)(1)(B)(i). However, section 954(c) does not contain a look-through rule comparable to section 1297(c). In order to comport with the policy underlying section 1297(c), the Treasury Department and the IRS have determined that the character of the gain from the disposition of a Look-Through Subsidiary should correspond to the character of the underlying assets of the Look-Through Subsidiary. Accordingly, proposed § 1.1297-2(f)(2) provides that the Residual Gain taken into account by the Tested Foreign Corporation will be characterized as passive income or non-passive income in proportion to the passive assets and non-passive assets of the disposed-of Look-Through Subsidiary (and any other Look-Through Subsidiary, to the extent owned indirectly through the Look-Through Subsidiary) treated as held by the Tested Foreign Corporation pursuant to section 1297(c) on the date of the disposition, measured using the method (value or adjusted bases) that is used to measure the assets of the Tested Foreign Corporation for purposes of the Asset Test.

Pursuant to proposed § 1.1297-1(c)(1)(i)(C), section 954(c)(4) applies with respect to the disposition of interests in a Look-Through Partnership. Comments are requested concerning whether any additional guidance is needed concerning the disposition of interests in a Look-Through Partnership.

G. *Change-of-business exception (including dispositions of stock of a Look-Through Subsidiary)*

Section 1298(b)(3) provides an exception from PFIC status (the "Change-of-Business Exception") for a Tested Foreign Corporation that is "in transition from one active business to another active business." H.R. Rep. No. 99-841, at II-644 (1986) (Conf. Rep.). Under section 1298(b)(3), the Change-of-Business Exception applies for a taxable year of the Tested Foreign Corporation if (i) neither the Tested Foreign Corporation nor a predecessor of the Tested Foreign Corporation was a PFIC in a prior taxable year; (ii) it is established to the satisfaction of the Secretary that (A) substantially all of the passive income of the Tested Foreign Corporation for the taxable year is attributable to proceeds from the disposition of one or more active trades or businesses, and (B) the Tested Foreign Corporation will not be a PFIC for either of the two taxable years following such taxable year; and (iii) the Tested Foreign Corporation is not, in fact, a PFIC for either of such two taxable years. Thus, notwithstanding the legislative history and the title of section 1298(b)(3), a Tested Foreign Corporation may qualify for the Change-of-Business Exception even if it does not engage in an active business after a disposition.

The proposed regulations provide general guidance with respect to the Change-of-Business Exception. First, the proposed regulations provide that for purposes of section 1298(b)(3)(B), the existence of an active trade or business and the determination of whether assets are used in an active trade or business is determined by reference to Treas. Reg. § 1.367(a)-2(d)(2), (3), and (5), except that officers and employees do not include the officers and employees of related entities as provided in § 1.367(a)-2(d)(3). *See* proposed § 1.1298-2(c)(3). If, however, the activity attribution rules described in Part I.F.5 of this Explanation of Provisions or section 954(h)(3)(E) would apply to cause the activities of another entity to be taken into account, they are taken into account for purposes of determining the applicability of the Change-of-Business Exception. *Id.* In addition, the proposed regulations provide that income attributable to proceeds from the disposition of an active trade or business means income earned on investment of such proceeds but does not include the proceeds themselves. *See* proposed § 1.1298-2(c)(1). The regulations also provide that section 1298(b)(3) may apply to either a taxable year of the disposition of the active trade or business or the immediately succeeding taxable year, but in any event may apply to only one year with respect to a disposition. *See* proposed § 1.1298-2(e). Thus, a Tested Foreign Corporation that receives proceeds from a disposition in more than one taxable year may apply the Change-of-Business Exception to only one year. A Tested Foreign Corporation can choose which year it applies the Change-of-Business Exception if the exception can apply in more than one year.

Several comments have inquired regarding the application of the Change-of-Business Exception to the sale or exchange of stock of a Look-Through Subsidiary that conducts an active trade or business. Specifically, these comments have questioned whether, by reason of section 1297(c), the Tested Foreign Corporation should be treated as disposing of an active trade or business conducted by a Look-Through Subsidiary for purposes of the Change-of-Business Exception. The Treasury Department and the IRS have determined that, given that section 1297(c) applies "for purposes of determining whether [a] foreign corporation is a [PFIC]," the Change-of-Business Exception should, in appropriate circumstances, apply to a Tested Foreign Corporation's disposition of its interest in a Look-Through Subsidiary that is engaged in an active trade or business. Thus, the proposed regulations provide that, for purposes of the Change-of-Business Exception, a disposition of stock of a Look-Through Subsidiary is treated as a disposition of a proportionate share of the assets held by the Look-Through Subsidiary on the date of the disposition. *See* proposed § 1.1298-2(d). Therefore, the portion of the proceeds attributable to assets used by a Look-Through Subsidiary in an active trade or business is considered for purposes of the Change-of-Business Exception to be proceeds from the disposition of an active trade or business.

The Treasury Department and the IRS also understand that Tested Foreign Corporations may not be able to satisfy the requirements of the Change-of-Business Exception provided in section 1298(b)(3) in certain situations in which proceeds from the disposition of an active trade or business cause the Tested Foreign Corporation to qualify as a PFIC pursuant to the Asset Test. The Treasury Department and the IRS have determined that if a Tested Foreign Corporation has historically engaged in an active trade or business and proceeds from the disposition of such business cause it to qualify as a PFIC, it may be appropriate in certain circumstances to which section 1298(b)(3) does not apply to treat the Tested Foreign Corporation as not a PFIC. Accordingly, the proposed regulations expand the Change-of-Business Exception in section 1298(b)(3) to apply if, on the measuring dates that occur during the taxable year to which the Change-of-Business Exception is proposed to apply and after the disposition, on average, substantially all of the passive assets of a corporation are attributable to proceeds from the disposition of one or more active trades or businesses. *See* proposed § 1.1298-2(b)(2)(ii).

Furthermore, the Treasury Department and the IRS understand that in certain circumstances, the Change-of-Business Exception could apply to the liquidation of a Tested Foreign Corporation if it were not for the fact that foreign law restrictions make it difficult to complete the liquidation within the year for which the exception applies. The Treasury Department and the IRS have determined that it is appropriate to allow the Change-of-Business Exception to be relied upon when such a liquidation is completed within a reasonable period of time after the disposition. Accordingly, in the case of a corporation, substantially all of the passive assets of which are attributable to proceeds from the disposition of one or more active trades or businesses, proposed § 1.1298-2(c)(4) provides that a Tested Foreign Corporation will be deemed to satisfy the requirement that the Tested Foreign Corporation not be a PFIC for the two years following the year for which it relies on the Change-of-Business Exception if it completely liquidates by the end of the year following the year for which it relies on the Change-of-Business Exception. U.S. Federal income tax principles apply to determine whether a Tested Foreign Corporation has completely liquidated. See Rev. Rul. 54-518, 1954-2 C.B. 142 (concluding that if a corporation ceases business operations, has retained no assets, and has no income, the mere retention of a charter does not prevent it from being treated as completely liquidated).

The Treasury Department and the IRS request comments concerning whether any other guidance is necessary concerning the application of section 1298(b)(3), including concerning the conditions under which the requirements of section 1298(b)(3)(C) will be considered satisfied.

H. Domestic subsidiary stock rule

As discussed in Part I.F.2 of this Explanation of Provisions, section 1298(b)(7) provides a special characterization rule that applies if a Tested Foreign Corporation owns at least 25 percent of the value of the stock of a domestic corporation and is subject to the accumulated earnings tax under section 531 (or waives any benefit under a treaty that would otherwise prevent imposition of such tax). The proposed regulations clarify that stock of the 25-percent-owned domestic corporation and the qualified stock generally must be owned by the Tested Foreign Corporation and the 25-percent-owned domestic corporation, respectively, either directly or indirectly through one or more partnerships. See proposed § 1.1298-4(b)(1) and (c).

The Treasury Department and the IRS have determined that the accumulated earnings tax need not actually be imposed on a foreign corporation in a taxable year in order for it to qualify for section 1298(b)(7). Furthermore, a Tested Foreign Corporation's ability to rely on section 1298(b)(7) in a given year should not depend on whether it has U.S. source income in that year, as it would if § 1.532-1(c) applied to determine whether the Tested Foreign Corporation was subject to tax under section 531. Accordingly, the regulations provide that a Tested Foreign Corporation is considered subject to the tax imposed by section 531 for purposes of section 1298(b)(7) regardless of whether the tax actually is imposed on the corporation and regardless of whether the requirements of § 1.532-1(c) are met. See proposed § 1.1298-4(d)(1). Additionally, comments have raised questions concerning the waiver of treaty benefits that would prevent imposition of the accumulated earnings tax. The proposed regulations provide that a Tested Foreign Corporation must waive any benefit under a treaty by attaching to its U.S. Federal income tax return for the taxable year for which it applies section 1298(b)(7) a statement that it irrevocably waives treaty protection against the imposition of the accumulated earnings tax, effective for all prior, current, and future taxable years. See proposed § 1.1298-4(d)(2)(i). If a Tested Foreign Corporation is not otherwise required to file a U.S. Federal income tax return, the waiver can be made in a resolution (or other governance document) to be kept in the entity's records or, in the case of a publicly traded corporation, in a statement in the corporation's public filings. See proposed § 1.1298-4(d)(2)(ii).

The Treasury Department and the IRS understand that foreign corporations may be relying on section 1298(b)(7) to avoid being treated as PFICs notwithstanding their direct and indirect ownership of predominantly passive assets by ensuring that a sufficient amount of such assets are held indirectly through two tiers of domestic subsidiaries. For example, a Tested Foreign Corporation might hold stock of another foreign corporation that is PFIC, but rely on a two-tiered domestic chain holding passive assets to avoid being treated as a PFIC; as a result, a United States person holding stock of the Tested Foreign Corporation would generally not be treated as a shareholder of the PFIC stock owned by the Tested Foreign Corporation. Accordingly, the proposed regulations provide that, notwithstanding the general coordination rule between section 1297(c) and section 1298(b)(7) in proposed § 1.1297-2(b)(2)(iii), section 1298(b)(7) does not apply for purposes of determining if a foreign corporation is a PFIC for purposes of the ownership attribution rules in section 1298(a)(2) and Treas. Reg. § 1.1291-1(b)(8)(ii). See proposed § 1.1298-4(e). Thus, if a Tested Foreign Corporation would qualify as a PFIC if section 1298(b)(7) did not apply, either because section 1297(c) applied to treat the Tested Foreign Corporation as owning directly the assets of a domestic corporation in which it indirectly held qualified stock, or because the qualified stock was treated as a passive asset, then persons that held stock of a PFIC through the Tested Foreign Corporation would be considered under section 1298(a)(2)(B) and Treas. Reg. § 1.1291-1(b)(8)(ii)(B) to own a proportionate amount (by value) of the stock of the PFIC regardless of the level of their ownership interest in the Tested Foreign Corporation.

To address the possibility of passive assets - particularly non-stock assets that could not themselves be eligible for the special treatment of section 1298(b)(7) - being held through a two-tiered chain of domestic subsidiaries in order to avoid the PFIC rules, the proposed regulations further provide anti-abuse rules under the authority of section 1298(g), one of which provides that section 1298(b)(7) will not apply if the Tested Foreign Corporation would be a PFIC if the qualified stock or any income received or accrued with respect thereto were disregarded. See proposed § 1.1298-4(f)(1). Furthermore, under a second anti-abuse rule, section 1298(b)(7) will not apply if a principal purpose for the Tested Foreign Corporation's formation or acquisition of the 25-percent-owned domestic corporation is to avoid classification of the Tested Foreign Corporation as a PFIC. A principal purpose will be deemed to exist if the 25-percent-owned domestic corporation is not engaged in an active trade or business in the United States. See proposed § 1.1298-4(f)(2). No inference is intended as to the application of section 1298(b)(7) under prior law. The IRS may, where appropriate, challenge transactions under the Code, regulatory provisions under prior law, or judicial doctrines. The Treasury Department and the IRS welcome comments on these rules.

II. PFIC Insurance Exception Rules

The proposed regulations provide guidance regarding whether the income of a foreign corporation is excluded from passive income pursuant to section 1297(b)(2)(B) because the income is derived in the active conduct of an insurance business by a QIC. Part II.A of this Explanation of Provisions describes the rules in proposed § 1.1297-4 for determining whether a foreign corporation is a QIC. Part II.B of this Explanation of Provisions describes the rules in proposed § 1.1297-5(c)(2) defining the term insurance business. Part II.C of this Explanation of Provisions describes the rules in proposed § 1.1297-5(c) regarding the active conduct of an insurance business. Part II.D of this Explanation of Provisions describes the rules in proposed § 1.1297-5(f) regarding the application of the section 1297(b)(2)(B) exception to items of income treated as received or accrued or assets treated as held by a QIC pursuant to section 1297(c). Part II.E of this Explanation of Provisions describes the rules in proposed § 1.1297-5(d) regarding the treatment of income and assets of certain domestic insurance corporations owned by a QIC as active for purposes of 1297(a). Part II.F of this Explanation of Provisions describes the rule in proposed § 1.1297-5(g) prohibiting the double counting of any item for purposes of proposed §§ 1.1297-4 and 1.1297-5.

A. QIC status requirement

Generally, section 1297(f) provides that a QIC is a foreign corporation that (1) would be subject to tax under subchapter L if it were a domestic corporation and (2) has applicable insurance liabilities that constitute more than 25 percent of its total assets. Proposed § 1.1297-4 provides guidance regarding the requirements under section 1297(f)(1) that a foreign corporation must satisfy to qualify as a QIC.

1. Insurance Company Requirement

Proposed § 1.1297-4(b)(1) provides guidance regarding when a foreign corporation would be the type of corporation that would be taxable under subchapter L (that is, an insurance company) if the corporation were a domestic corporation. See section 1297(f)(1)(A). It provides that a foreign corporation would be subject to tax under subchapter L if it were a domestic corporation if it is an insurance company as defined in section 816(a) (generally requiring more than half of the corporation's business during the taxable year to be the issuing of insurance or annuity contracts, or the reinsuring of risks underwritten by insurance companies).

2. 25 Percent Test

In addition to the insurance company requirement, generally a foreign corporation's "applicable insurance liabilities" (defined in section 1297(f)(3)(A) and proposed §1.1297-4(f)(2)) must exceed 25 percent of its "total assets" (defined in proposed §1.1297-4(f)(7)) to be a QIC. Section 1297(f)(1)(B); *see also* proposed §1.1297-4(c). This determination is made on the basis of the foreign corporation's liabilities and assets as reported on the corporation's applicable financial statement for the last year ending with or within the taxable year. This test hereinafter is referred to as the "25 percent test." Proposed §1.1297-4(c) provides guidance regarding the application of the 25 percent test.

3. Alternative Facts and Circumstance Test

If a foreign corporation fails the 25 percent test, section 1297(f)(2) permits a United States person to elect to treat stock in the corporation as stock of a QIC under certain circumstances. Specifically, to make the election, the foreign corporation must be predominantly engaged in an insurance business, and its applicable insurance liabilities must constitute 10 percent or more of its total assets, hereinafter the "10 percent test." A United States person may only make this election if the foreign corporation fails the 25 percent test solely due to runoff-related or rating-related circumstances involving its insurance business, as further described in Part II.A.3.b of this Explanation of Provisions.

a. Predominantly engaged in an insurance business

Proposed §1.1297-4(d)(2) provides guidance regarding the circumstances under which a foreign corporation is predominantly engaged in an insurance business. In the case of a foreign corporation that fails the 25-percent test, Congress included the predominantly engaged requirement as part of the alternative facts and circumstances test to ascertain whether a foreign corporation is truly engaged in an insurance business despite the low ratio of applicable insurance liabilities to assets. *See* H.R. Rep. No. 115-466, at 671 (2017) (Conf. Rep.) ("Facts and circumstances that tend to show the firm may not be predominantly engaged in an insurance business include a small number of insured risks with low likelihood but large potential costs; workers focused to a greater degree on investment activities than underwriting activities; and low loss exposure. Additional relevant facts for determining whether the foreign corporation is predominantly engaged in an insurance business include: claims payment patterns for the current year and prior years; the foreign corporation's loss exposure as calculated for a regulator or for a rating agency, or if those are not calculated, for internal pricing purposes; the percentage of gross receipts constituting premiums for the current and prior years; and the number and size of insurance contracts issued or taken on through reinsurance by the foreign corporation. The fact that a foreign corporation has been holding itself out as an insurer for a long period is not determinative either way."). The proposed regulations clarify that each of these factors is intended to be tested based on whether the particular facts and circumstances of the foreign corporation are comparable to commercial insurance arrangements providing similar lines of coverage to unrelated parties in arm's length transactions.

As noted in Part II.A.1 of this Explanation of Provisions, to qualify as an insurance company, more than one half of a corporation's business must be the issuing of insurance or annuity contracts or the reinsuring of risks underwritten by insurance companies. *See* sections 816(a) and 831(c). Although such a corporation might otherwise be considered to be "predominantly engaged" in an insurance business (where predominantly means "for the most part"), the predominantly engaged requirement of the alternative facts and circumstances test in section 1297(f) is separate from, and in addition to, the requirement that a corporation would be subject to tax under subchapter L if the foreign corporation were a domestic corporation. Therefore, in order to give effect to this predominantly engaged requirement, proposed §1.1297-4(d)(2) incorporates the specific factors enumerated in the legislative history as a part of a foreign corporation's analysis of whether it is predominantly engaged in an insurance business under the alternative facts and circumstances test, while retaining the requirement that "more than half" of the business be of a certain type, because the foreign corporation must separately satisfy that threshold with respect to the character of its insurance business under section 1297(f)(1)(A).

The Treasury Department and the IRS request comments regarding whether this proposed test appropriately determines whether a foreign corporation is predominantly engaged in an insurance business and invite comments on whether the proposed test would have material effects upon the way in which entities engaged in the provision of insurance are structured.

b. Runoff-related or rating-related circumstances

To qualify for the alternative facts and circumstances test, proposed §1.1297-4(d)(3) and (4) clarify the circumstances under which a foreign corporation fails to satisfy the 25 percent test solely due to runoff-related or rating-related circumstances involving its insurance business.

Proposed §1.1297-4(d)(3) provides that runoff-related circumstances occur when a corporation has adopted a plan of liquidation or termination of operations under the supervision of its applicable insurance regulatory body. Additionally, the corporation may not issue or enter into any new insurance, annuity, or reinsurance contracts during the taxable year (other than contractually obligated renewals of existing insurance contracts or reinsurance contracts pursuant to and consistent with the corporation's plan of liquidation or termination of operations) and must make payments during the annual reporting period covered by the applicable financial statement to satisfy the claims under insurance, annuity, or reinsurance contracts issued or entered into before the corporation ceased entering into new business.

Proposed §1.1297-4(d)(4) provides that rating-related circumstances occur when a generally recognized credit rating agency requires a foreign corporation to maintain a surplus of capital to receive or maintain a minimum credit rating for the foreign corporation to be classified as secure to write new insurance business for the current year. The Treasury Department and the IRS understand that it is possible that the minimum credit rating required to be classified as secure to write new insurance business may be higher for some lines of insurance business than for other lines of insurance business. For this purpose, the proposed rule is intended to apply to the highest minimum credit rating required to be classified as secure to write new insurance business for any line of insurance business.

The Treasury Department and the IRS understand that there may be certain lines of insurance business, such as financial guaranty insurance, where market realities require a credit rating in excess of the minimum credit rating for a foreign corporation to be classified as secure to write new insurance business in the relevant business line for the current year. The Treasury Department and the IRS request comments regarding this fact pattern and how best to address these lines of business in the context of the rating-related circumstances test.

c. Election to apply the alternative facts and circumstances test

Proposed §1.1297-4(d)(5)(i) generally requires that the foreign corporation with respect to which the election is made directly provide the United States person a statement or make a publicly available statement (such as in a public filing, disclosure statement, or other notice provided to United States persons that are shareholders of the foreign corporation) that it satisfied the requirements of section 1297(f)(2) and §1.1297-4(d)(1) during the foreign corporation's taxable year and certain information relevant to that statement. A United States person, however, may not rely upon any statement by the foreign corporation to make the election under section 1297(f)(2) if the shareholder knows or has reason to know that the statement made by the foreign corporation was incorrect. Because the foreign corporation possesses the information necessary to make an election under the alternative facts and circumstances test, the Treasury Department and the IRS have determined that it is appropriate to require a United

States person to obtain that information from the foreign corporation in order to make the election. Comments are requested regarding the form and content of the statement provided by the foreign corporation to United States persons as set forth in proposed § 1.1297-4(d)(5)(i)-(ii), and whether there are alternative ways of satisfying the requirements of 1297(f)(2).

Proposed § 1.1297-4(d)(5)(iii) describes the time and manner for making the election. To make the election before final regulations are published, a United States person that owns stock of a foreign corporation electing to treat that stock as stock of a QIC under the alternative facts and circumstances test must file a limited-information Form 8621 (or successor form). For this purpose, a United States person must file a Form 8621 with the box checked regarding the QIC election and must provide the identifying information of the shareholder and the foreign corporation. The United States person is not required to complete any other part of Form 8621 if that person is only filing the Form 8621 to make the QIC election under the alternative facts and circumstances test.

The Treasury Department and the IRS request comments on ways to reduce burden on small shareholders with respect to the alternative facts and circumstances test.

4. Limitations on the amount of applicable insurance liabilities

When applying the 25 percent test to a foreign corporation, section 1297(f)(3)(B) provides that the amount of the foreign corporation's applicable insurance liabilities cannot exceed the lesser of (i) the amount that the foreign corporation reported to its "applicable insurance regulatory body" (defined in section 1297(f)(4)(B) and proposed § 1.1297-4(f)(3)), (ii) the amount required by applicable law or regulation, or (iii) the amount determined under regulations prescribed by the Treasury Department and the IRS.

Proposed § 1.1297-4(e) provides additional guidance regarding the limitation on the amount of applicable insurance liabilities for purposes of the 25 percent test and the 10 percent test. Specifically, the proposed regulations provide that the amount of applicable insurance liabilities may not exceed the lesser of (1) the amount shown on the most recent applicable financial statement; (2) the minimum amount required by applicable law or regulation of the jurisdiction of the applicable insurance regulatory body; and (3) the amount shown on the most recent financial statement made on the basis of U.S. generally accepted accounting principles ("US GAAP") or international financial reporting standards ("IFRS") if such financial statement was not prepared for financial reporting purposes. The Treasury Department and the IRS have determined that the additional limitations are necessary to clarify which financial statements are used to apply the 25 percent test and the 10 percent test, and that it is appropriate to limit the amount of applicable insurance liabilities to the minimum amount of liabilities required to be reported by an insurance regulator, even if the foreign corporation's regulator would accept a higher liability amount for regulatory purposes. In addition, under section 1297(f)(4), an applicable financial statement only includes financial statements made on the basis of US GAAP or IFRS if such a statement has been prepared for financial reporting purposes. If a foreign corporation prepares a financial statement on the basis of US GAAP or IFRS for a purpose other than financial reporting, the Treasury Department and the IRS have determined that the amount of applicable insurance liabilities under this financial statement, if lower than the amount on the applicable financial statement, is an appropriate limit on the amount of applicable insurance liabilities. This limitation is appropriate because Congress has expressed a preference for widely used standards of financial accounting through its references to such standards in section 1297(f)(4)(A).

Under the proposed regulations, a special rule applies with respect to applicable financial statements that are neither prepared under US GAAP nor IFRS. To the extent that such an applicable financial statement does not discount losses on an economically reasonable basis, the foreign corporation must reduce its applicable insurance liabilities to reflect discounting that would apply under either US GAAP or IFRS. The Treasury Department and the IRS have determined that a method of determining insurance liabilities that fails to provide for a reasonable discounting rate does not take into account a factor that is necessary to appropriately and accurately report the amount of applicable insurance liabilities. For this purpose, the question of whether losses are discounted on an economically reasonable basis is determined under the relevant facts and circumstances. However, in order for losses to be discounted on an economically reasonable basis, discounting must be based on loss and claim payment patterns for either the foreign corporation or insurance companies in similar lines of insurance business. In addition, a discount rate based on these loss and claim payment patterns of at least the risk free rate in U.S. dollars or in a foreign currency in which the foreign corporation conducts some or all of its insurance business must be used. A loss discounting methodology consistent with that used for US GAAP or IFRS purposes is considered reasonable for this purpose.

Finally, a special rule applies for certain foreign corporations that change their method of preparing their applicable financial statement by ceasing to prepare this statement under either US GAAP or IFRS and have no non-Federal tax business purpose for preparing a statement that is not consistent with US GAAP or IFRS. Under the proposed regulations, absent a non-Federal Tax business purpose, a foreign corporation must continue to prepare its applicable financial statement under either US GAAP or IFRS. If the foreign corporation fails to do so, the foreign corporation will be treated as having no applicable insurance liabilities for purposes of the QIC test. Absent this proposed rule, the Treasury Department and the IRS are concerned that a foreign corporation may change its method for preparing its financial statement to benefit from certain elements of a local regulatory accounting regime, such as a more expansive definition of insurance liability or a method of calculating a larger amount of insurance liabilities, solely for purposes of qualifying as a QIC. Comments are requested on this proposed rule.

B. *Insurance business*

For purposes of the PFIC insurance exception, proposed § 1.1297-5(c)(2) defines an insurance business as the business of issuing insurance and annuity contracts or reinsuring risks underwritten by other insurance companies (or both). Under the proposed regulations, an insurance business also includes the investment activities and administrative services required to support (or that are substantially related to) those insurance, annuity, or reinsurance contracts issued or entered into by the QIC. Proposed § 1.1297-5(h)(2) provides that investment activities are any activities that generate income from assets that a QIC holds to meet its obligations under insurance and annuity contracts issued or reinsured by the QIC.

C. *Active conduct*

To give effect to the active conduct requirement, the 2015 proposed regulations differentiated between activities performed by a corporation through its officers and employees and activities performed by other persons (for example, employees of other entities or independent contractors) for the corporation. The 2015 proposed regulations accomplished this separation by defining the term "active conduct" in section 1297(b)(2)(B) to have the same meaning as in § 1.367(a)-2T(b)(3) (now § 1.367(a)-2(d)(3)), except that officers and employees would not have included the officers and employees of related entities. Hence, under the 2015 proposed regulations, only insurance investment business activities performed by a corporation's officers and employees would be included in the corporation's active conduct of its insurance business. Accordingly, under the 2015 proposed regulations, investment income would have qualified for the PFIC insurance exception only if the corporation's own officers and employees performed the insurance business activities that produce the income.

Proposed § 1.1297-5(c)(3)(i) provides that the term active conduct is based on all of the facts and circumstances and that, in general, a QIC actively conducts an insurance business only if the officers and employees of the QIC carry out substantial managerial and operational activities. For this purpose, active conduct is intended to be interpreted consistently with the active conduct standard in § 1.367(a)-2(d)(5). The proposed regulation further provides that a QIC's officers and employees are considered to include the officers and employees of another corporation if the QIC satisfies the control test set forth in proposed § 1.1297-5(c)(3)(ii). Generally, to satisfy the control test, (i) the QIC must either own, directly or indirectly more than 50 percent of the vote and value (for a corporation) or capital and profits interest (for a partnership) of the entity whose officers or employees are performing services for the QIC or (ii) a common parent must own, directly or indirectly, more than 80 percent of the vote and value or capital and profits interest of both the QIC and the entity performing services for the QIC. In addition, the QIC must exercise regular oversight and supervision over the services performed by the other entity's officers and employees for the QIC. The QIC must also either (i) pay directly all the compensation of the other entity's officers and employees attributable to services performed for the QIC for the production or acquisition of premiums and investment income on assets held to meet obligations under insurance, annuity, or reinsurance contracts issued or entered into by the QIC; (ii) reimburse the other entity for the portion of its expenses, including compensation and related expenses (determined in accordance with section 482, taking into account all expenses that would be included in the total services costs under §1.482-9(j) and §1.482-9(k)(2)) and add a profit markup, as appropriate, for these services performed for the QIC by the other entity's officers and employees; or (iii) otherwise pay arm's length compensation in accordance with section 482 on a fee-related basis to the other entity for the services provided to the QIC. For example, it is common to charge for investment advisory or management services via a fee calculated as a percentage of the underlying assets under management (AUM), and a fee calculated on this basis may be arm's length under section 482 principles.

Under proposed §1.1297-5(c)(4), a QIC determines the annual amount of its income that is derived in the active conduct of an insurance business (the active conduct test) and excluded from passive income under section 1297(b)(2)(B) for purposes of section 1297(a). To make this determination, the QIC must determine its active conduct percentage.

If the QIC's active conduct percentage is greater than or equal to 50 percent, then all of the QIC's passive income (as defined in §1.1297-1, taking into account the exceptions in section 1297(b)(2) other than section 1297(b)(2)(B) and §1.1297-5) is excluded from passive income pursuant to the exception in section 1297(b)(2)(B) for the active conduct of an insurance business. If the QIC's active conduct percentage is less than 50 percent, then none of its income is excluded from passive income pursuant to the exception in section 1297(b)(2)(B) for the active conduct of an insurance business. In response to comments made to the 2015 proposed regulations, the active conduct percentage is based on the QIC's expenses to provide a bright-line test for measuring the QIC's active conduct. The Treasury Department and the IRS determined that the amount of expenses for insurance activities performed by the QIC (or by a related party) as compared to the total expenses of the QIC indicates the extent to which the QIC conducts the business itself and therefore, actively engages in an insurance business.

The Treasury Department and the IRS request comments on the following topics:

1. Whether the relative amount of expenses for insurance activities performed by the QIC accurately assesses whether a QIC is engaged in the active conduct of an insurance business.

2. The contours of the control test, which allow for a QIC to benefit from a higher active conduct percentage based on activities (paid for by the QIC) of an entity in which a common parent, but not the QIC itself, owns more than 80 percent of the interests. The Treasury Department and IRS propose this standard based on an understanding of common ownership structures in the insurance industry, and note that the attribution of activities described in Part I.F.5 of this Explanation of Provisions (regarding the active rent or royalty exception) is more limited as it provides that a Tested Foreign Corporation may take into account the activities performed only by those Look-Through Subsidiaries or partnerships with respect to which the Tested Foreign Corporation owns (directly or indirectly) more than 50 percent of the value.

3. The active conduct percentage calculation in general, including whether this test should be the only test for determining whether income is derived in the active conduct of an insurance business or whether such a percentage would better serve as an objective safe harbor alongside a facts and circumstances test.

D. *Treatment of income and assets of certain Look-Through Subsidiaries and Look-Through Partnerships held by a QIC*

Proposed §1.1297-5(f) provides that certain items of income and assets that are passive in the hands of a look-through subsidiary or look-through partnership may be treated as active by a QIC. Under this provision, a Tested Foreign Corporation is treated as if it directly holds its proportionate share of the assets and as if it directly receives its proportionate share of the income of the Look-Through Subsidiary or Look-Through Partnership. Generally, if the income or assets are passive in the hands of the Look-Through Subsidiary or Look-Through Partnership, the income or assets are treated as passive income and passive assets of the Tested Foreign Corporation. However, if the Tested Foreign Corporation is a QIC, the income and assets are tested under section §1.1297-5(c) and (e) to determine if they qualify for the section 1297(b)(2)(B) insurance exception to passive income. However, for this rule to apply, the Look-Through Subsidiary or Look-Through Partnership, as the case may be, must have its assets and liabilities included in the applicable financial statement of the foreign corporation for purposes of the 25 percent test and the 10 percent test. This rule does not change the character of the items of income or assets as passive income or passive assets to the Look-Through Subsidiary or Look-Through Partnership.

E. *Qualifying domestic insurance corporations*

Proposed §1.1297-5(d) provides that income of a qualifying domestic insurance corporation is not treated as passive income. Similarly, proposed §1.1297-5(e)(2) provides that assets of a qualifying domestic insurance corporation are not treated as passive assets. A qualifying domestic insurance corporation is a domestic corporation that is subject to tax as an insurance company under subchapter L of chapter 1 of subtitle A of the Code and is subject to Federal income tax on its net income. This rule is intended to address situations where a Tested Foreign Corporation owns a domestic insurance corporation through a structure to which section 1298(b)(7) does not apply.

F. *No double counting rule*

Proposed §1.1297-5(g) provides that nothing in proposed §1.1297-4 or §1.1297-5 permits any item to be counted more than once (for example, for determining a reserve or an applicable insurance liability for purposes of the 25 percent test and the 10 percent test). Including this general principle is consistent with subchapter L provisions that do not allow double counting. For example, section 811(c)(2) provides that the same item may not be counted more than once for reserve purposes, section 811(c)(3) provides that no item may be deducted (either directly or as an increase in reserves) more than once, and section 832(d) prohibits the same item from being deducted more than once.

Applicability Dates

These regulations are proposed to apply to taxable years of United States persons that are shareholders in certain foreign corporations beginning on or after the date of publication of the Treasury decision adopting these rules as final regulations in the **Federal Register**. However, until these regulations are finalized, taxpayers may choose to apply these proposed regulations (other than the proposed regulations under §§1.1297-4 and 1.1297-5) in their entirety to all open tax years as if they were final regulations provided that taxpayers consistently apply the rules of these proposed regulations. Until finalization, United States persons that are shareholders in certain foreign corporations may apply the rules of §§1.1297-4 and 1.1297-5 for taxable years beginning after December 31, 2017, provided those United States persons consistently apply the rules of §§1.1297-4 and 1.1297-5 as if they were final regulations. In addition, taxpayers may continue to rely on Notice 88-22 until these regulations are finalized.

Special Analyses

I. *Regulatory Planning and Review - Economic Analysis*

Executive Orders 13771, 13563, and 12866 direct agencies to assess costs and benefits of available regulatory alternatives and, if regulation is necessary, to select regulatory approaches that maximize net benefits, including potential economic, environmental, public health and safety effects, distributive impacts, and equity. Executive Order 13563 emphasizes the importance of quantifying both costs and benefits, reducing costs, harmonizing rules, and promoting flexibility. The Executive Order 13771 designation for any final rule resulting from the proposed regulation will be informed by comments received. The preliminary Executive Order 13771 designation for this proposed rule is regulatory.

The proposed regulation has been designated by the Office of Information and Regulatory Affairs (OIRA) as significant under Executive Order 12866 pursuant to the Memorandum of Agreement (MOA, April 11, 2018) between the Treasury Department and the Office of Management and Budget regarding review of tax regulations.

A. *Background*

Various provisions of the tax code allow tax on certain sources of income to be deferred, which means that the income is not taxed when it is earned but at some later date, based on specific events or conditions. Tax deferral is advantageous to taxpayers because the taxpayer can in the meantime earn a return on the amount that would otherwise have been paid as tax. Prior to the Act, income earned abroad generally was not taxed until it was repatriated to the United States. After the Act, income earned abroad by a CFC is generally taxed immediately to the United States shareholders of the CFC, but income earned by foreign corporations that are not CFCs, particularly where the owners of the foreign corporations are individuals or other entities not eligible for the dividends received deduction under section 245A, may still be eligible for deferral. However, deferral is not available with respect to income of foreign corporations that earn primarily certain kinds of passive income, which in general includes dividends, interest, royalties, rents, and certain gains on the exchange of property, commodities, or foreign currency. Limiting deferral of foreign source income discourages U.S. taxpayers from holding mobile, passive investments, such as stock, in a foreign corporation in order to defer U.S. tax.

A particular set of rules limiting deferral applies to U.S. persons who own interests in passive foreign investment companies ("PFICs"). In general, a PFIC is a foreign corporation that, in a given year, has income that is 75 percent or more passive income or that owns, on average, assets that are 50 percent or more passive-income-producing. Taxpayers subject to another set of rules limiting deferral, the subpart F rules, are not subject to the PFIC rules.

Long-standing sections 1291 through 1298 provide rules regarding the tax treatment of income from PFICs. The PFIC itself is not subject to U.S. tax under the PFIC regime; rather, only the U.S. owner of the PFIC is required to determine whether he or she has invested in a PFIC, and if so, what tax is due as a result. The U.S. owner is responsible for getting the appropriate information from the foreign corporation to determine if the corporation is a PFIC.

Before its amendment by the Act, the PFIC provisions provided an exception from passive income for any income (including investment income) earned in the active conduct of an insurance business by a foreign corporation that (i) was predominantly engaged in an insurance business and (ii) would be taxed as an insurance company if it were a domestic corporation. Congress determined that this exception enabled U.S. owners of some foreign insurance companies to escape the PFIC regime. This exception, (the "PFIC insurance exception"), was established because insurance companies must hold significant amounts of investment assets (which generate income that would otherwise be classified as passive under the PFIC rules) in the normal course of business to fund obligations under the insurance contracts they issue. Staff, Joint Committee on Taxation, General Explanation of the Tax Reform Act of 1986, JCS-10-87, at 1025 (1987); IRS, Corporate Income Tax Returns Complete Report, 2013, Table 1).

The Act modified and narrowed the PFIC insurance exception by requiring that the excepted income be derived in the active conduct of an insurance business by a "qualifying insurance corporation" ("QIC"). To be a QIC, a foreign insurance corporation must be an entity that would be taxed as an insurance company if it were a domestic corporation (consistent with prior-law requirements) and, in addition, be able to show that its "applicable insurance liabilities" constitute more than 25 percent of its total assets. The Act specifically defines applicable insurance liabilities for this purpose as including a set of enumerated types of insurance-related loss and expense items. Failing this test, the Code provides that U.S. owners of the foreign corporation may elect to treat their stock in the corporation as stock of a QIC, provided the corporation can satisfy an "alternative facts and circumstances test." However, once a corporation has been identified as a QIC, only income that is derived in the active conduct of an insurance business qualifies as income eligible for the PFIC insurance exception.

Congress modified section 1297 under the Act out of concern that the active insurance company exception to the PFIC rules lacked clarity and precision. This lack of clarity with respect to how much insurance business the company must do to qualify under the exception raised concerns that certain companies with U.S. shareholders were structuring themselves to take advantage of the exception but conducting a token insurance business while focusing primarily on investment activities. Such strategies erode the U.S. tax base, and reflect inefficient investment incentives for U.S. taxpayers. As a result, the Act adopted a more formulaic rule that is easier to enforce and apply, while still allowing a facts and circumstances approach for showing insurance activity. *See* Senate Budget Explanation of the Bill (2017-11-20) at p. 397.

B. *Need for the proposed regulations*

The Treasury Department and the IRS view the Act modifications regarding PFIC determination as generally self-executing (although regulatory guidance is needed in order for U.S. owners to elect QIC status under the facts and circumstances test), which means that the statute is binding on taxpayers and the IRS without further regulatory action. The Treasury Department and the IRS recognize, however, that the statute provides interpretive latitude for taxpayers and the IRS that could, without further guidance, prompt inefficient investment patterns due to divergent interpretations. Consequently, many of the details behind the relevant terms and necessary calculations required for the determination of PFIC status would benefit from greater specificity. The proposed regulations provide details and specifics for the definitions and concepts described in sections 1291, 1297, and 1298 so that taxpayers can readily and accurately determine if their investment is in a PFIC, given the significant consequences of owning a PFIC, which may continue to be treated as such even after the foreign corporation ceases to satisfy the Income Test or Asset Test. *See* section 1298(b)(1). The regulations further resolve ambiguities in determining ownership of a PFIC and in the application of the Income Test and Asset Test under the statutory provisions that existed prior to the Act.

The Treasury Department and the IRS have also identified actions that foreign companies might take to qualify for QIC designation even though the nature of their active insurance business would not merit QIC designation under the intents and purposes of the statute. The proposed regulations are needed to avoid the inefficient economic decisions that would arise from those tax avoidance actions. For example, in the absence of the proposed regulations, taxpayers may be incentivized to adopt accounting methods that inappropriately inflate applicable insurance liabilities or exaggerate the degree to which income of a QIC is derived in the active conduct of an insurance business.

C. *Overview of the proposed regulations*

The proposed regulations can be divided into two parts. The rules described in Part I of the Explanation of Provisions section of this preamble provide general guidance regarding PFICs (the "General Rules"). *See* Part I.D.2 of this Special Analyses section. The rules described in Part II of the Explanation of Provisions section of this preamble relate specifically to the implementation of the PFIC insurance exception (the "PFIC Insurance

Exception Rules"). *See* Part I.D.3 of this Special Analyses section. Among other things, the General Rules (1) describe and clarify how assets are measured for the asset test; and (2) clarify attribution rules for determining some forms of active income. The PFIC Insurance Exception Rules provide guidance regarding qualification for the PFIC insurance exception, define statutory terms relevant to QIC status, and provide instructions on electing QIC status under the alternative facts and circumstances test.

D. *Economic analysis*

1. Baseline

The Treasury Department and the IRS have assessed the benefits and costs of the proposed regulations relative to a no-action baseline reflecting anticipated Federal income tax-related behavior in the absence of these proposed regulations.

2. Summary of Economic Effects

The proposed regulations provide certainty and consistency in the application of sections 1291, 1297, and 1298 with respect to PFICs and QICs by providing definitions and clarifications regarding the statute's terms and rules. In the absence of such guidance, the chances that different U.S. owners (or potential owners) of foreign companies would interpret the statute differently, either from each other or from the intents and purposes of the statute, would be exacerbated. This divergence in interpretation could cause U.S. investors to choose investment vehicles based on different interpretations of, for example, whether particular income would avoid qualifying as passive income and thus avoid the less favorable tax treatment applied by the PFIC regime. If economic investment is not guided by uniform incentives across otherwise similar investors and across otherwise similar investments, the resulting pattern of investment is generally inefficient, conditional on the Code's provisions governing passive income.[1] In the context of U.S. investment in foreign insurance corporations, the proposed regulations help to ensure that similar economic activities, representing similar passive and non-passive attributes, are taxed similarly. Thus, the Treasury Department and the IRS expect that the definitions and guidance provided in the proposed regulation will lead to an improved allocation of investment among taxpayers contingent on the overall Code.

The Treasury Department and the IRS have not quantified the expected economic benefits or the costs to the U.S. economy, or the scope of taxpayers benefitting from or burdened by the proposed regulations. The Treasury Department and the IRS request comment on these issues and particularly solicit comments that provide data, evidence, or models that would enhance the rigor by which the non-revenue economic effects might be determined and quantified for the final regulations.

The following sections describe the economic effects of specific major provisions of these proposed regulations relative to possible alternative provisions. The Treasury Department and IRS solicit comments on each of the items discussed subsequently and on any other provisions of the proposed regulations not discussed in this section. The Treasury Department and the IRS particularly solicit comments that provide data, other evidence, or models that could enhance the rigor of the process by which these or further provisions might be developed for the final regulations.

3. Economic Analysis of Specific Provisions of the General Rules

a. Averaging period for the Asset Test

A foreign corporation is considered a PFIC if it satisfies either of the following tests: (i) 75 percent or more of the corporation's gross income for a taxable year is passive ("Income Test"); or (ii) the average percentage of assets held by the corporation during the year producing passive income is at least 50 percent ("Asset Test"). If a foreign corporation is a PFIC, the U.S. owner of the PFIC is subject to tax under the PFIC regime. Regarding the Asset Test, section 1297(e) provides rules for how to determine the value of assets using either the fair market value or the adjusted basis, but does not indicate what period should be used to determine the "average percentage." Notice 88-22, which was issued following the enactment of the PFIC regime to provide guidance on a number of issues related to the Income and Asset Tests pending regulations, required taxpayers to determine value at the end of each quarter and average those numbers on an annual basis for the test. *See* Part I.D.1 of the Explanation of Provisions section of this preamble. Notice 88-22 announced the intention of the Treasury Department and IRS to issue regulations addressing this and other issues under the PFIC regime; however, no regulations addressing the Asset Test were issued until the proposed regulations.

To remedy this omission and specify the period over which the average percentage would be calculated, the Treasury Department and the IRS considered three alternatives: (i) semi-annual measurement, (ii) quarterly measurement, and (iii) daily measurement.[2] The Treasury Department and the IRS also considered, once a default measuring period was set, offering flexibility to shareholders to determine their own measurement period as long as the period was shorter than the default period. In each respective case, the Asset test would be based on the annual average of the semi-annual, quarterly, or daily asset values.

The first option, to require taxpayers to determine the average value of assets that produce passive income on a semi-annual basis, has lower costs than the other suggested approaches since calculations have to be done just twice a year and these costs (or cost-savings) are borne directly or indirectly by the owners of the corporation. The benefit of these lower costs to U.S. taxpayers must be balanced against the projected accuracy of semi-annual measurement. Because the period examined is long, semi-annual amounts are relatively easy for the corporation to manipulate so as to avoid having 50 percent or more passive-income producing assets as measured by value over the averaging period discussed here (the Asset Test) and therefore avoid PFIC treatment, even in cases where the company held significant amounts of passive-income-producing assets during the year.

The third option, to require taxpayers to average daily asset values for the asset test, provides a more exact measure of the assets of the company but the costs for the company to provide such information to their owners can be significant and some companies might choose not to provide such calculations to their small U.S. owners.[3] On the other hand, daily measurement would make it costly for the entity to avoid PFIC determination by "removing" assets generating passive income at measurement times.

The proposed regulations, consistent with the second option, require at least quarterly measurement and further allow taxpayers to elect to use a shorter period, such as monthly or daily measurement of asset values. Shorter period alternatives (relative to a semi-annual period) curtail the ability of foreign corporations to avoid PFIC designation through asset management strategies that would be tax-driven rather than market-driven. The Treasury Department and the IRS project that the increase in compliance costs of quarterly measurement over semi-annual measurement would be minor, because quarterly measurement aligns with general accounting practices, and because many taxpayers were likely already relying on the provision in Notice 88-22 that provided for quarterly measurement. The election to choose monthly or daily measurement allows U.S. persons who own interests in foreign corporations to use even more precise measurement of asset holdings if, based on business-specific

---

[1] General economic principles do not clearly prescribe the efficient relative tax treatment of passive income versus non-passive income and therefore do not indicate whether a shift in investment from passive-income-producing activities to non-passive-income-producing activities is economically beneficial. This economic analysis draws conclusions about the efficient tax treatment of different investments by evaluating incentives in light of the intents and purposes of the underlying statutes.

[2] Other units could have been considered, such as months or weeks, but these three options span the reasonable possibilities.

[3] It would further generally be difficult for a U.S. owner to calculate, on his or her own, the value of PFIC assets on a daily basis, especially if the owner were a minority shareholder.

accounting practices and the availability of that information to the U.S. person, the U.S. person deems that any higher compliance costs they might incur are warranted.

The Treasury Department and IRS solicit comments on this proposal, particularly comments that provide data, other evidence, or models that could enhance the rigor of the process by which the average percentage period might be developed for the final regulations.

b. Attribution of activities

For purposes of determining whether a corporation is a PFIC, section 1297(c) treats a foreign corporation (FC1) that owns 25 percent or more of another foreign corporation (FC2) as owning and earning the proportional amount of FC2's income and assets under the so called Look-Through Subsidiary rules.[4] However, the statute is silent on whether the activities of FC2 can be attributed to FC1 for purposes of determining whether the income of FC1 qualifies as being treated as non-passive income. Under current practice, some businesses structure their organization for legal or commercial reasons to have all employees for a business in one corporation, say FC2, while the rents and royalties are received by FC1. Without attribution of activities, FC1 could not qualify for an exception that treats these rents and royalties as active, as opposed to passive, income. This could result in FC1 being treated as a PFIC even though, on the whole, its income and economic activities were related to active business operations and not comparable to the passive income generating activities generally undertaken by PFICs.

To address the attribution of activities in foreign businesses in structures similar to those described, the Treasury Department and the IRS considered three alternatives: (1) do not allow any attribution of activities; (2) allow attribution of activities to multiple U.S. owners; or (3) allow attribution only if there is greater than a 50 percent ownership percentage; that is, if the foreign corporation owns more than 50 percent of the other foreign corporation.

Under the first alternative (no attribution), a foreign corporation that separated activities and income could satisfy the passive income exception only if it reorganized such that the entity being tested as a PFIC received both the active rents and royalties as well as had the employees that performed the related activities. This is potentially costly or even infeasible, depending on local requirements. The Treasury Department and the IRS determined that this alternative would potentially lead to costly reorganization, a cost that would either be passed on to U.S. investors or that, in the absence of such reorganization, would inhibit U.S. investment in a foreign corporation that was otherwise similar to corporations that were not PFICs. These are economically undesirable outcomes in light of the intents and purposes of the statute, relative to the proposed regulations.

Under the second alternative, activities could be attributed similarly to how the Look-Through Rule attributes income and assets. In general, because the Look-Through Rule requires ownership of only 25 percent of a foreign corporation in order to apply, the income and assets of a foreign corporation may be attributed to multiple owners. The statute specifies that this be done on a pro rata basis — for example, if a U.S. person owns 100 percent of foreign corporation (FC1) that owns 60 percent of FC2, 60 percent of the income and assets of FC2 could be attributed to FC1 for purposes of applying the Income and Asset tests, and 40 percent of the income and assets could be allocated to another shareholder of FC2. This alternative generates significant difficulties, however, in the context of attribution of activities. While income and assets can be allocated between owners based on percentage ownership, activities are not measured by a numerical amount and thus are not easily separated between two owners. Additionally, allowing multiple shareholders to use the activities of a single corporation to treat income as non-passive could result in double counting of activities (i.e., attributing the same activity to multiple parent companies). The Treasury Department and the IRS determined that potential double counting of activities could result in less tax revenue being raised than intended by Congress.

Under the third alternative, the activities of a foreign corporation could only be attributed to one shareholder. The proposed regulations adopt this third alternative, specifically by allowing attribution if there is an ownership percentage greater than 50 percent. Thus, where FC1 owns 60 percent of FC2 and another shareholder owns the remaining 40 percent, only FC1 could get credit for the activities of FC2 for purposes of applying the active rents and royalties test. No other shareholder of FC2 would qualify for attribution. The Treasury Department and the IRS project that this proposed regulation would allow entities to satisfy the passive income exception under conditions consistent with the intents and purposes of the statute without requiring potentially substantial reorganization costs.

The Treasury Department and the IRS solicit comments on this proposal and in particular solicit data, evidence, or models that could enhance the rigor of the process by which the ownership percentage might be developed for the final regulations.

c. Look-Through Partnerships

As discussed in Part I.D.3.b of this Special Analyses, for purposes of determining whether a corporation is a PFIC, section 1297(c) treats a foreign corporation (FC1) that owns 25 percent or more of another foreign corporation (FC2) as owning and earning the proportional amount of FC2's income and assets under the so called Look-Through Subsidiary rules. Absent this rule, any distributions from FC2 to FC1 would generally be treated as passive income to FC1 for purposes of the Income Test, and the stock of FC2 would generally be treated as a passive income-producing asset for purposes of the Asset Test. The statute does not provide any specific rule for the treatment of a partnership interest owned by a foreign corporation for purposes of determining whether the foreign corporation is a PFIC.

In order to provide guidance on the treatment of partnership interests owned by foreign corporations for purposes of the Income and Asset Tests, the Treasury Department and the IRS considered three principal alternative thresholds regarding when to treat the income and assets of a partnership as earned or held directly by the foreign corporation. These thresholds are: (1) apply no threshold; (2) apply a 10 percent threshold; or (3) apply the same 25 percent ownership threshold to partnership interests as is applied to interests in corporations.

Under the first alternative, a proportionate share (based on the foreign corporation's capital or profits interest in the partnership) of the income and assets of the partnership would be considered as earned or held directly by the foreign corporation for purposes of determining whether the foreign corporation is a PFIC, no matter how much of the partnership was owned by the foreign corporation. A similar rule to this applies for purposes of the subpart F regime, and thus there could be benefits in applying consistent rules across the two regimes. However, the purpose of the Income and Asset Tests is to determine whether the foreign corporation has a primarily active or passive business. An ownership interest of less than 10 percent is unlikely to give the foreign corporation significant control over the partnership activities such that it represents an active business interest. Additionally, providing a lower threshold for partnership interests, by contrast to the threshold applicable to corporate interests, creates incentives for foreign corporations to hold minority interests in partnerships rather than corporations, and in some cases, because of the U.S. entity classification rules, the classification of the entity as a partnership may be solely for U.S. tax purposes. This means that the same investment that Congress determined could only be active if it accounted for 25 percent of the value of the entity would now qualify as active even though the nature of the investment has not substantially changed. This latter case is economically undesirable since it can result in differential tax treatment of corporations and partnerships. Moreover, this outcome is less consistent with the intents and purposes of the statute, than the approach taken in the proposed regulations. Under the second alternative, a proportionate amount of the income and assets of the partnership would be considered as earned or held directly by the foreign corporation only if the foreign corporation owned 10 percent or more of the partnership. Existing rules under section 904, which relates to the foreign tax credit limitation, utilize a 10 percent threshold for purposes of determining whether to

---

[4] For purposes of the rest of this discussion, FC1 can be considered the parent corporation with U.S. owners that is tested as to whether it is a PFIC or not. FC2 is a subsidiary of FC1.

characterize income and assets of a partnership as passive category income and assets. There could be benefits in applying an existing threshold from the foreign tax credit regime to PFICs since taxpayers would be familiar with this regime. However, similar to the no threshold option, because section 1297(c)(2) requires a 25 percent ownership for corporations to apply for the Look-Through Subsidiary rules, this alternative would still lead to differing treatment of minority interests in subsidiary corporations as opposed to partnerships. Again, this could lead to similarly situated entities being treated differently and resultant economic distortions.

Under the third alternative, the same 25 percent ownership threshold is applied to partnership interests as is applied to interests in corporations. The Treasury Department and IRS project this will maintain parity between the treatment of minority interests in corporations and partnership interest for purposes of the Income and Asset test, and it gives effect to the 25 percent limitation in section 1297(c)(2). The Treasury Department and the IRS project that this proposed regulation would achieve consistent treatment across entity types as well as the appropriate treatment of minority interests in corporations and partnerships under conditions consistent with the intents and purposes of the statute.

The Treasury Department and the IRS solicit comments on this proposal and in particular solicit data, evidence, or models that could enhance the rigor of the process by which the treatment of partnership interests might be developed for the final regulations.

4. Economic Analysis of PFIC Insurance Exception Rules

Under the statute, the income of a qualifying insurance corporation (QIC) derived in the active conduct of its insurance business is not treated as passive income for purposes of deciding whether the corporation is a PFIC. The test for a QIC under section 1297(f) is based on the ratio of the foreign insurance company's "applicable insurance liabilities" to its total assets. The statute limits the applicable insurance liabilities to the smallest of: (1) the insurance liabilities shown on the company's most recent applicable financial statement ("AFS"); (2) the amount of such liabilities required by applicable local law or regulation, and (3) as provided under Treasury regulations.

Under the statute, the AFS is the financial statement used by the foreign corporation for financial reporting purposes that is: (i) made on the basis of U.S. generally accepted accounting principles ("US GAAP"); (ii) made on the basis of international financial reporting standards ("IFRS"), if there is no statement that is made on the basis of US GAAP; or (iii) the annual financial statement required to be filed with the applicable insurance regulatory body ("local accounting"), if the company does not prepare a statement for financial reporting purposes based on US GAAP or IFRS. Thus, the statute has a preference for financial statements prepared on the basis of US GAAP or IFRS, which are rigorous and widely-respected accounting standards, but will permit a foreign corporation to use a local accounting AFS if it does not do financial reporting based on US GAAP or IFRS.

The statute creates an incentive for foreign insurance companies (FCos) to inflate applicable insurance liabilities in order to qualify as QICs and avoid PFIC status. This strategy (inflating applicable insurance liabilities to qualify as a QIC) could make the FCo more attractive to U.S. investors relative to investing in a domestic company or a company that is a PFIC, which could potentially lead to investment patterns that are inefficient. Although the statutory caps on applicable insurance liabilities provide a check on this behavior, FCos (and thus their U.S. owners) might look for options under their financial reporting rules to increase the amount of insurance liabilities reported on their AFS, or even shift to a different financial reporting standard with more favorable rules. The proposed regulations address this issue in a number of ways.

a. Change in accounting rules used for an AFS

The statute may, in some circumstances, introduce an incentive for an FCo to change its method of preparing its AFS to benefit from certain elements of a local accounting regime, such as a more expansive definition of insurance liability or a method of calculating a larger amount of insurance liabilities, solely for purposes of increasing its applicable insurance liabilities in order to qualify as a QIC. This strategy, by allowing a company to avoid being characterized as a PFIC and thus providing an incentive for U.S. investors to route their investment dollars through foreign corporations that otherwise would fail the QIC test, yields a potential tax advantage to U.S. investors relative to other investments they might make, an outcome that is economically inefficient in light of the intents and purposes of the statute.

To address this issue, the proposed regulations provide a special rule for FCos that change their method of preparing their AFS by ceasing to prepare this statement under either US GAAP or IFRS without a non-Federal tax business purpose for the change. Under the proposed regulations, an FCo must continue to prepare its AFS under either US GAAP or IFRS and if it fails to do so, it will be treated as having no applicable insurance liabilities for purposes of the QIC test.

The Treasury Department and the IRS considered as an alternative not providing regulations to address a change in the method of preparing an AFS. The Treasury Department and the IRS do not have readily available data to allow estimation of the tax advantage or volume of investment that might be drawn to such companies (and away from others) in the absence of regulations to address a change in the method of preparing an AFS. The Treasury Department and the IRS further have not estimated the benefit that arises from the improved integrity of the tax system under the proposed regulations relative to not providing regulations to govern changes in the FCo's AFS method. The Treasury Department and the IRS solicit comments on all aspects of these proposed regulations, including comments on (1) the determination of a "non-Federal tax business purpose," and (2) how an FCo that changes its AFS method should be treated. The Treasury Department and the IRS particularly solicit comments that would provide data, other evidence, or models that would enhance the rigor of evaluating FCos that change their AFS method, for purposes of developing the final regulations.

b. Cap on applicable insurance liabilities

Under the statute, a foreign corporation that does not prepare an AFS using US GAAP or IFRS may use an AFS prepared under local accounting rules to determine the amount of its applicable insurance liabilities. However, it is possible that local accounting rules in some foreign jurisdictions may permit reporting of insurance liabilities in a way that is economically unreasonable and inconsistent with the intent of the QIC rules. For example, US GAAP and IFRS both require discounting of insurance liabilities to determine the present value of an insurance company's liabilities. However, the Treasury Department and the IRS understand that local accounting rules in some foreign jurisdictions might not require discounting or might not adequately discount reserves (or other applicable insurance liabilities). This would make it easier for a foreign corporation that uses local accounting to qualify as a QIC. This could provide an incentive for U.S. investors to route their investment dollars through foreign corporations that otherwise would fail the QIC test, yielding a potential tax advantage to U.S. investors relative to other investments they might make, an outcome that is economically inefficient.

To address this issue, the proposed regulations provide that, if a foreign insurance company prepares its AFS under a local accounting standard that does not require discounting of unpaid losses and other loss reserves on an economically reasonable basis, for purposes of the QIC test, the company's AFS insurance liabilities must be reduced using US GAAP or IFRS discounting principles. Local accounting rules will otherwise continue to apply for determining amounts relevant to the QIC test. Applicable insurance liabilities may not exceed the discounted amount. As a point of reference, the discounting of unpaid losses is required by all domestic insurance companies that are taxed on their underwriting income or that file US GAAP-based financial statements.

The question of whether losses are discounted on an economically reasonable basis is determined under the relevant facts and circumstances. However, in order for losses to be discounted on an economically reasonable basis, discounting must be based on loss and claim payment patterns for either the foreign corporation or insurance companies in similar lines of insurance business. In addition, a discount rate based on these loss and claim payment patterns of at least the risk free rate in U.S. dollars or in a foreign currency in which the foreign corporation conducts some or all of its insurance business must be used. A loss discounting methodology consistent with that used for US GAAP or IFRS purposes will be considered reasonable for this purpose.

The Treasury Department and the IRS considered as alternatives (i) issuing no regulations to govern discounting of insurance losses for purposes of determining whether applicable insurance liabilities exceed the statutory cap, and (ii) capping the amount of applicable insurance liabilities at the amount that would be permitted to an insurance company subject to the insurance reserve calculation rules under Subchapter L of the Code.

Under the first approach, U.S. investors would have an incentive to seek out those corporations that do not file US GAAP or IFRS statements, an outcome that would provide an economically inefficient tax advantage to U.S. investors in those companies.

The second approach would be considerably more burdensome to a foreign corporation because, as a practical matter, it would require foreign corporations to apply complex U.S. tax rules with which they are likely not familiar. An excessive compliance burden on foreign corporations not subject to U.S. taxation would make it less likely that they would do the work necessary to enable their minority U.S. owners to determine if the corporation is a PFIC. Thus, this alternative was rejected because it could unduly inhibit U.S. investors from placing their funds in profitable foreign corporations that are legitimate active insurance companies, an economically desirable activity in light of the intents and purposes of the statute, relative to the proposed regulations.

The Treasury Department and the IRS do not have data available and models sensitive enough to estimate the additional volume of U.S. investment that might be drawn under this alternative approach to QICs that did not discount insurance losses in an economically reasonable manner, relative to the proposed regulations. The Treasury Department and the IRS also do not have data available and models sensitive enough to estimate the benefit that arises from the improved integrity of the tax system arising from the proposed regulations relative to not issuing such regulations. Further, the Treasury Department and the IRS do not have data available to estimate the additional accounting burden that would fall on FCos under the proposed regulations, relative to not issuing such regulations, a cost that would potentially be passed on to U.S. investors.

The Treasury Department and the IRS also do not have data available to estimate the increased loss to minority U.S. shareholders if the second alternative approach (capping liabilities to the amount that would be permitted under Subchapter L) were adopted.

The Treasury Department and the IRS solicit comments on all aspects of these proposed regulations and particularly solicit comments that would provide data, other evidence, or models that would enhance the rigor by which conditions on the cap on applicable insurance liabilities will be developed for the final regulations.

II. Paperwork Reduction Act

The collections of information in these proposed regulations are in proposed § 1.1297-1(d)(1)(ii)(B), (d)(1)(iii)(B), and (d)(1)(iv), proposed § 1.1297-4(d)(5)(i) and (iii), and proposed § 1.1298-4(d)(2). The information in all of the collections of information provided will be used by the IRS for tax compliance purposes.

A. Collections of information under existing tax forms

The collections of information in proposed § 1.1297-1(d)(1)(ii)(B), (d)(1)(iii)(B), and (d)(1)(iv) are required to be provided by taxpayers that make an election or revoke an election to use an alternative measuring period or adjusted bases to measure assets for purposes of the Asset Test with respect to a foreign corporation. These collections of information are satisfied by filing Form 8621 or attachments thereto. For purposes of the Paperwork Reduction Act, 44 U.S.C. 3501 et seq. ("PRA"), the reporting burden associated with the collection of information in the Form 8621 will be reflected in the Paperwork Reduction Act Submission associated with that form (OMB control number 1545-1002). If a Form 8621 is not required to be filed, the collections of information under proposed § 1.1297-1(d)(1)(ii)(B), (d)(1)(iii)(B), and (d)(1)(iv) are satisfied by attaching a statement to the taxpayer's return. For purposes of the Paperwork Reduction Act, the reporting burden associated with these collections of information will be reflected in the Paperwork Reduction Act Submissions associated with Forms 990-PF and 990-T (OMB control number 1545-0047); Form 1040 (OMB control number 1545-0074); Form 1041 (OMB control number 1545-0092); Form 1065 (OMB control number 1545-0123); and Forms 1120, 1120-C, 1120-F, 1120-L, 1120-PC, 1120-REIT, 1120-RIC, and 1120-S (OMB control number 1545-0123).

The collection of information in proposed § 1.1297-4(d)(5)(iii) is required to be provided by taxpayers that make an election under section 1297(f)(2). This collection of information is satisfied by filing Form 8621. For purposes of the Paperwork Reduction Act, the reporting burden associated with the collection of information in the Form 8621 will be reflected in the Paperwork Reduction Act Submission associated with Form 8621 (OMB control number 1545-1002).

The following table displays the number of respondents estimated to be required to report on Form 8621 or, in the case of individual filers, on attachments to Form 1040, as applicable, with respect to the collections of information in these regulations. Due to the absence of available tax data, estimates of respondents required to attach a statement to other types of tax returns, as applicable, are not available.

	Number of Respondents (Estimated)
Form 1040	35,000-45,000
Form 8621	50,000-55,000

Source: RAAS:CDW

The numbers of respondents in the table were estimated by the Research, Applied Analytics and Statistics Division ("RAAS") of the IRS from the Compliance Data Warehouse ("CDW").

Data for Form 1040 represents estimates of the total number of taxpayers that may attach a statement to their Form 1040 to make or revoke the elections in proposed § 1.1297-1(d)(1)(ii)(B), (d)(1)(iii)(B), and (d)(1)(iv). The lower bound estimate reflects the CDW-based estimate of unique individual taxpayers filing Form 8621 between 2014 and 2017. The upper bound estimate reflects the CDW-based estimate of unique individual taxpayers that filed Form 8938 between 2016 and 2017 indicating that they owned an interest in a foreign partnership or corporation.[5] Accordingly, the difference between the lower bound and upper bound estimates reflects an estimate of the possible change in the number of respondents as a result of the changes made by the Act and the proposed regulations.

Data for Form 8621 represent estimates of the total number of taxpayers that may be required to file Form 8621. The lower bound estimate reflects the CDW-based estimate of unique taxpayers filing Form 8621 between 2014 and 2017. The upper bound estimate reflects an estimated 10 percent increase in the amount of taxpayers that may file to make or revoke the elections in proposed § 1.1297-1(d)(1)(ii)(B), (d)(1)(iii)(B), and (d)(1)(iv) and proposed § 1.1297-4(d)(5)(iii). Accordingly, the difference between the lower bound and upper bound estimates reflect an estimate of the possible change in the number of respondents as a result of the changes made by the Act and the proposed regulations.

---

[5] While PFICs are corporations, partnerships are included in our count given taxpayers may own an interest in a foreign corporation through a foreign partnership. More robust reporting on Form 8938 started in 2016 so we do not include prior years in our estimate.

The current status of the PRA submissions related to the tax forms on which reporting under these regulations will be required is summarized in the following table. The burdens associated with the information collections in the forms are included in aggregated burden estimates for the OMB control numbers 1545-0047 (which represents a total estimated burden time for all forms and schedules for tax-exempt entities of 50.5 million hours and total estimated monetized costs of $3.59 billion ($2018)), 1545-0074 (which represents a total estimated burden time for all forms and schedules for individuals of 1.784 billion hours and total estimated monetized costs of $31.764 billion ($2017)), 1545-0092 (which represents a total estimated burden time for all forms and schedules for trusts and estates of 307.8 million hours and total estimated monetized costs of $9.95 billion ($2016)), and 1545-0123 (which represents a total estimated burden time for all forms and schedules for corporations of 3.157 billion hours and total estimated monetized costs of $58.148 billion ($2017)). The burden estimates provided in the OMB control numbers in the following table are aggregate amounts that relate to the entire package of forms associated with the OMB control number, and will in the future include, but not isolate, the estimated burden of only those information collections associated with these proposed regulations. These numbers are therefore unrelated to the future calculations needed to assess the burden imposed by these regulations. To guard against over-counting the burden that international tax provisions imposed prior to the Act, the Treasury Department and the IRS urge readers to recognize that these burden estimates have also been cited by regulations (such as the foreign tax credit regulations, 83 FR 63200) that rely on the applicable OMB control numbers in order to collect information from the applicable types of filers.

In 2018, the IRS released and invited comment on drafts of Forms 990-PF (Return of Private Foundation or Section 4947(a)(1) Trust Treated as Private Foundation), 990-T (Exempt Organization Business Income Tax Return), 1040 (U.S. Individual Income Tax Return), (U.S. Income Tax Return for Estates and Trusts), 1065 (U.S. Return of Partnership Income), 1120 (U.S. Corporation Income Tax Return), and 8621 (Return by a Shareholder of a Passive Foreign Investment Co. or Qualified Electing Fund). The IRS received comments only regarding Forms 1040, 1065, and 1120 during the comment period. After reviewing all such comments, the IRS made the forms available on December 21, 2018 for use by the public.

No burden estimates specific to the forms affected by the proposed regulations are currently available. The Treasury Department and the IRS have not estimated the burden, including that of any new information collections, related to the requirements under the proposed regulations. The Treasury Department and the IRS request comments on all aspects of information collection burdens related to the proposed regulations, including estimates for how much time it would take to comply with the paperwork burdens described above for each relevant form and ways for the IRS to minimize the paperwork burden. In addition, drafts of IRS forms are posted for public review at https://apps.irs.gov/app/picklist/list/draftTaxForms.htm. Comments on these forms can be submitted at https://www.irs.gov/forms-pubs/comment-on-tax-forms-and-publications. These forms will not be finalized until after they have been approved by OMB under the PRA.

Form	Type of Filer	OMB Number(s)	Status
Forms 990-PF, 990-T	Tax exempt entities (NEW Model)	1545-0047	Published 60-day Federal Register notice on 8/22/18.
	Link: https://www.federalregister.gov/documents/2018/08/22/2018-18135/proposed-collection-comment-request-for-forms-990-990-ez-sch-b-br-br-990-ez-sch-l-lp-990-ez-990-pf		
Form 1040	Individual (NEW Model)	1545-0074	Limited Scope submission (1040 only) approved on 12/7/18. Full ICR submission for all forms in 3/2019. 60 Day Federal Register notice not published yet for full collection.
	Link: https://www.reginfo.gov/public/do/PRAViewICR?ref_nbr=201808-1545-031		
Form 1041	Trusts and estates	1545-0092	Submitted to OMB for review on 9/27/18.
	Link: https://www.reginfo.gov/public/do/PRAViewICR?ref_nbr=201806-1545-014		
Form 1065	Business (NEW Model)	1545-0123	Published in the Federal Register on 10/11/18. Public Comment period closed on 12/10/18.
	Link: https://www.federalregister.gov/documents/2018/10/09/2018-21846/proposed-collection-comment-request-for-forms-1065-1065-b-1066-1120-1120-c-1120-f-1120-h-1120-nd		
Forms 1120, 1120-C, 1120-F, 1120-L, 1120-PC, 1120-REIT, 1120-RIC, 1120-S	Business (NEW Model)	1545-0123	Published in the Federal Register on 10/11/18. Public Comment period closed on 12/10/18.
	Link: https://www.federalregister.gov/documents/2018/10/09/2018-21846/proposed-collection-comment-request-for-forms-1065-1065-b-1066-1120-1120-c-1120-f-1120-h-1120-nd		
Form 8621	Share-holders	1545-1001	Approved by OMB on 12/19/2018.
	Link: https://www.reginfo.gov/public/do/PRAViewICR?ref_nbr=201805-1545-007		

B. *Collections of information generally not included on existing forms*

The collection of information in proposed § 1.1298-4(d)(2) is required for a foreign corporation that relies on the rule in section 1298(b)(7) and proposed § 1.1298-4(b)(1). This collection of information is satisfied by filing a statement attached to the foreign corporation's return. For purposes of the Paperwork Reduction Act, the reporting burden associated with this collection of information will be reflected in the Paperwork Reduction Act Submissions associated with Form 1120-F (OMB control number 1545-0123). The number of affected filers, burden estimates, and Paperwork Reduction Act status for this OMB control number are discussed in connection with the Form 1120 in Part II.A of the Special Analyses.

Alternatively, if a foreign corporation is not required to file a return, the collection of information in proposed § 1.1298-4(d)(2) is satisfied by the foreign corporation's maintaining a statement in its records or including it in its public filings.

The collection of information in proposed § 1.1297-4(d)(5)(i) is required for a foreign corporation for which a taxpayer makes an election under section 1297(f)(2). This collection of information is satisfied by a foreign corporation providing a statement to a shareholder.

The collection of information contained in proposed § 1.1298-4(d)(2) (for foreign corporations that are not required to file Form 1120-F) and proposed § 1.1297-4(d)(5)(i) will be submitted to the Office of Management and Budget in accordance with the Paperwork Reduction Act. Comments on the collections of information should be sent to the **Office of Management and Budget**, Attn: Desk Officer for the Department of the Treasury, Office of Information and Regulatory Affairs, Washington, DC 20503, with copies to the **Internal Revenue Service**, Attn: IRS Reports Clearance Officer, SE:W:CAR:MP:T:T:SP, Washington, DC 20224. Comments on the collection of information should be received by September 9, 2019.

Comments are specifically requested concerning:

Whether the proposed collection of information is necessary for the proper performance of the duties of the IRS, including whether the information will have practical utility;

The accuracy of the estimated burden associated with the proposed collection of information;

How the quality, utility, and clarity of the information to be collected may be enhanced;

How the burden of complying with the proposed collection of information may be minimized, including through the application of automated collection techniques or other forms of information technology; and

Estimates of capital or start-up costs and costs of operation, maintenance, and purchases of services to provide information for the collections discussed in Part II.B of this Special Analyses.

Estimated total annual reporting burden: 200 hours.

Estimated total annual monetized cost burden: $19,000.

Estimated average annual burden hours per respondent: one hour.

Estimated number of respondents: 200.

Estimated annual frequency of responses: once.

An agency may not conduct or sponsor, and a person is not required to respond to, a collection of information unless it displays a valid control number assigned by the Office of Management and Budget.

Books or records relating to a collection of information must be retained as long as their contents may become material in the administration of any internal revenue law. Generally, tax returns and tax return information are confidential, as required by 26 U.S.C. 6103.

III. *Regulatory Flexibility Act*

Pursuant to the Regulatory Flexibility Act (5 U.S.C. chapter 6), it is hereby certified that the proposed regulations will not have a significant economic impact on a substantial number of small entities within the meaning of section 601(6) of the Regulatory Flexibility Act ("small entities").

The statutory provisions in sections 1291 through 1298 (the "PFIC regime") generally affect U.S. taxpayers that have ownership interests in foreign corporations that are not controlled foreign corporations ("CFCs"). The reporting burdens in proposed § 1.1297-1(d)(1)(ii)(B), (d)(1)(iii)(B), and (d)(1)(iv) and proposed § 1.1297-4(d)(5)(iii) generally affect the described U.S. taxpayers that elect to make or revoke certain elections related to the PFIC regime. The reporting burdens in proposed § 1.1297-4(d)(5)(ii) and proposed § 1.1298-4(d)(2) affect only foreign corporations. In general, foreign corporations are not considered small entities. Nor are U.S. taxpayers considered small entities to the extent the taxpayers are natural persons or entities other than small entities. Data estimating the number of filers for the PRA section indicate that individuals (Form 1040 filers) make up approximately 70 percent of those who report PFIC income while U.S. businesses of all sizes make up approximately 20 percent of Form 8621 filers. Most of these U.S. businesses are partnerships that do not pay entity level taxes. Accordingly, only small entities that have ownership interests in foreign corporations that are not CFCs and that wish to make or revoke an election pursuant to proposed § 1.1297-1(d)(1)(ii)(B), (d)(1)(iii)(B), and (d)(1)(iv) and proposed § 1.1297-4(d)(5)(iii) are affected by the proposed regulations.

The data to assess the number of small entities potentially affected by proposed § 1.1297-1(d)(1)(ii)(B), (d)(1)(iii)(B), and (d)(1)(iv) and proposed § 1.1297-4(d)(5)(iii) are not readily available.

Regardless of the number of small entities potentially affected by the proposed regulations, the Treasury Department and the IRS have concluded that there is no significant economic impact on such entities as a result of the proposed regulations.

Data on U.S. businesses that invest in a PFIC is limited. To get a sense of the magnitude of the taxes currently collected by businesses that invest in PFICs, the ratio of PFIC regime tax to (gross) total income was calculated for 2012 through 2017 for C corporations that filed the Form 8621. Total income was determined by matching each C corporation filing the Form 8621 to its Form 1120. Ordinary QEF income was assumed to be taxed at 37 percent while QEF capital gains and mark-to-market income was assumed to be taxed at the lower 20 percent capital gains rate. The section 1291 tax and interest charge tax were included as reported. Only those corporations where a match was found and that had positive total income were included in the analysis.[6] While the number was small, approximately 150 to 250 C corporations per year, the ratio of the tax to total income was less than 0.01 percent even when $100 million of the additional tax estimated by the Joint Committee on Taxation was included each year. Looking only at the approximately 50 to 150 C corporations per year with $25 million or less of total income resulted in the tax to total income percentage increasing to at most 1.39 percent in 2017.

	2012	2013	2014	2015	2016	2017
			($ millions)			
All C corporations						
Tax	99	108	118	126	110	121
Total Income	6,487,867	4,205,127	14,154,789	19,935,845	16,443,073	16,888,107
Tax to Total Income	0.002%	0.003%	0.001%	0.001%	0.001%	0.001%
C corporations with total income of $25 million or less						
Tax	*	*	*	3	3	5
Total Income	302	463	563	627	562	348
Tax to Total Income	0.039%	0.068%	0.008%	0.516%	0.524%	1.390%

Source: RAAS, CDW. * indicates less than $1 million.

Thus, even if the economic impact of the proposed regulations is interpreted broadly to include the tax liability due under the PFIC regime, which small entities would be required to pay even if the proposed regulations were not issued, the economic impact should not be regarded as significant under the Regulatory Flexibility Act.

Additionally, the economic impact of the proposed regulations when considered alone should be minimal. Any economic impact of the final regulations stems from the collection of information requirements imposed by proposed § 1.1297-1(d)(1)(ii)(B), (d)(1)(iii)(B), and (d)(1)(iv) and proposed § 1.1297-4(d)(5)(iii). The Treasury Department and the IRS have determined that the average burden is 1 hour per response. The IRS's Research, Applied Analytics, and Statistics division estimates that the appropriate wage rate for this set of taxpayers is $95 per hour. Thus, the

---

[6] To be conservative, C corporations reporting more than $6 billion of total income are excluded since we suspect these amounts are improperly reported.

annual burden per taxpayer from the collection of information requirement is $95. Furthermore, these requirements apply only if a taxpayer chooses to make an election or rely on a favorable rule.

Accordingly, it is hereby certified that the proposed rule would not have a significant economic impact on a substantial number of small entities. Notwithstanding this certification, the Treasury Department and the IRS invite comments from the public on both the number of entities affected (including whether specific industries are affected) and the economic impact of this proposed rule on small entities.

Pursuant to section 7805(f) of the Code, this notice of proposed rulemaking has been submitted to the Chief Counsel for Advocacy of the Small Business Administration for comment on its impact on small businesses.

IV. *Unfunded Mandates Reform Act*

Section 202 of the Unfunded Mandates Reform Act of 1995 (UMRA) requires that agencies assess anticipated costs and benefits and take certain other actions before issuing a final rule that includes any Federal mandate that may result in expenditures in any one year by a state, local, or tribal government, in the aggregate, or by the private sector, of $100 million in 1995 dollars, updated annually for inflation. In 2018, that threshold is approximately $150 million. This rule does not include any Federal mandate that may result in expenditures by state, local, or tribal governments, or by the private sector in excess of that threshold.

V. *Executive Order 13132: Federalism*

Executive Order 13132 (entitled "Federalism") prohibits an agency from publishing any rule that has federalism implications if the rule either imposes substantial, direct compliance costs on state and local governments, and is not required by statute, or preempts state law, unless the agency meets the consultation and funding requirements of section 6 of the Executive Order. This proposed rule does not have federalism implications and does not impose substantial direct compliance costs on state and local governments or preempt state law within the meaning of the Executive Order.

Comments and Requests for a Public Hearing

Before these proposed regulations are adopted as final regulations, consideration will be given to any comments that are timely submitted to the IRS as prescribed in this preamble under the "Addresses" heading. The Treasury Department and the IRS specifically request comments on all aspects of the proposed rules. All comments will be available for public inspection and copying at *www.regulations.gov* or upon request. A public hearing will be scheduled if requested in writing by any person that timely submits written comments. If a public hearing is scheduled, notice of the date, time and place for the public hearing will be published in the **Federal Register**.

Statement of Availability of IRS Documents

IRS Revenue Procedures, Revenue Rulings, notices, and other guidance cited in this document are published in the Internal Revenue Bulletin (or Cumulative Bulletin) and are available from the Superintendent of Documents, U.S. Government Printing Office, Washington, DC 20402, or by visiting the IRS website at *www.irs.gov*.

Drafting Information

The principal drafters of these regulations are Josephine Firehock, Rose E. Jenkins, and Jorge M. Oben of the Office of Associate Chief Counsel (International). Other personnel from the Treasury Department and the IRS also participated in the development of these regulations.

[¶ 49,807] **Proposed Amendments of Regulations (REG-130700-14)**, published in the Federal Register on August 14, 2019 (corrected 10/2/2019).

[Code Secs. 861 and 937]

Foreign income: Cloud transactions: Classification.—Reg. § 1.861-19 and amendments of Reg. § § 1.861-7, 1.861-18 and 1.937-3, regarding the classification of cloud transactions for purposes of the international provisions of the Internal Revenue Code, are proposed.

AGENCY: Internal Revenue Service (IRS), Treasury.

ACTION: Notice of proposed rulemaking.

SUMMARY: This document contains proposed regulations regarding the classification of cloud transactions for purposes of the international provisions of the Internal Revenue Code. These proposed regulations also modify the rules for classifying transactions involving computer programs, including by applying the rules to transfers of digital content.

DATES: Comments and requests for a public hearing must be received by November 12, 2019.

ADDRESSES: Send submissions to: CC:PA:LPD:PR (REG-130700-14), room 5203, Internal Revenue Service, P.O. Box 7604, Ben Franklin Station, Washington, DC 20044. Submissions may be hand-delivered Monday through Friday between the hours of 8 a.m. and 4 p.m. to: CC:PA:LPD:PR (REG-130700-14), Courier's Desk, Internal Revenue Service, 1111 Constitution Avenue NW., Washington, DC. Alternatively, taxpayers may submit comments electronically via the Federal eRulemaking Portal at *www.regulations.gov* (REG-130700-14).

FOR FURTHER INFORMATION CONTACT: Concerning the proposed regulations Robert Z. Kelley, (202) 317-6939; concerning submissions of comments and requests for a public hearing, Regina L. Johnson, (202) 317-6901 (not toll free numbers). SUPPLEMENTARY INFORMATION:

Background

These regulations (the proposed regulations) clarify the treatment under certain provisions of the Internal Revenue Code (Code) of income from transactions involving on-demand network access to computing and other similar resources. The proposed regulations also extend the classification rules in existing § 1.861-18 to transfers of digital content other than computer programs and clarify the source of income for certain transactions governed by existing § 1.861-18.

Existing § 1.861-18 provides rules for classifying transactions involving computer programs. For this purpose, § 1.861-18(a)(3) defines a computer program as "a set of statements or instructions to be used directly or indirectly in a computer in order to bring about a certain result" and includes "any media, user manuals, documentation, data base or similar item if the media, user manuals, documentation, data base or similar item is incidental to the operation of the computer program." Under § 1.861-18(b)(1), a transaction to which the section applies is categorized as (i) a transfer of a copyright right in a computer program; (ii) a transfer of a copy of a computer program (a "copyrighted article"); (iii) the provision of services for the development or modification of a computer program; or (iv) the provision of know-how relating to computer programming techniques. Section 1.861-18(c) provides that a transfer of a computer program is classified as the transfer of a copyright right if there is a non-de minimis grant of any of the following four rights: (i) The right to make copies of the computer program for purposes of distribution to the public by sale or other transfer of ownership, or by rental, lease, or lending; (ii) the right to prepare derivative computer programs based upon the copyrighted computer program; (iii) the right to make a public performance of the computer program; or (iv) the right to publicly display the computer program. Section 1.861-18(f) further categorizes a transfer of a copyright right as either the sale or license of the copyright right and a transfer of a copyrighted article as either the sale or lease of the copyrighted article.

Section 1.861-18 generally does not provide a comprehensive basis for categorizing many common transactions involving what is commonly referred to as "cloud computing," which typically is characterized by on-demand network access to computing resources, such as networks, servers, storage, and software. *See, e.g.*, National Institute of Standards and Technology, Special Publication 500-322 (February 2018) ("NIST Report"). Cloud computing transactions typically are described for non-tax purposes as following one or more of the following three models: Software as a Service ("SaaS"); Platform as a Service ("PaaS"); and Infrastructure as a Service ("IaaS"). SaaS allows customers to access applications on a provider's cloud infrastructure through an interface such as a web browser. NIST Report, p. 9-10. PaaS allows customers to deploy applications created by the customer onto a provider's cloud infrastructure using programming languages, libraries, services, and tools supported by the provider. NIST Report, pp. 10-11. IaaS allows customers to access processing, storage, networks, and other infrastructure resources on a provider's cloud infrastructure. NIST Report, p. 11. A cloud computing transaction typically does not involve any transfer of a computer program classified under § 1.861-18 as a transfer of a copyright right or copyrighted article or any provision of development services or know-how relating to computer programs or programming. Although certain cloud computing transactions may provide similar functionality with respect to computer programs as transactions subject to § 1.861-18 (for example, the transfer of a computer program via download may provide similar functionality as the same program accessed via a web browser), § 1.861-18 does not address the provision of online access to use the computer program. Accordingly, § 1.861-18 would not apply to classify such a transaction.

In addition to the cloud computing models described above, other transactions exist that are not solely related to computing but still involve on-demand network access to technological resources (these transactions and cloud computing transactions are collectively referred to herein as "cloud transactions"). These transactions have increased in frequency over time and share similarities with the three cloud computing models described above. Examples include streaming music and video, transactions involving mobile device applications ("apps"), and access to data through remotely hosted software. These transactions may not involve, in whole or in part, a transfer under § 1.861-18 of a copyright right or copyrighted article, or a provision of development services or know-how relating to computer programs or programming. In general, a cloud transaction involves access to property or use of property, instead of the sale, exchange, or license of property, and therefore typically would be classified as either a lease of property or a provision of services. Section 7701(e) and case law provide factors that are relevant for classifying a transaction as either a lease of property or a provision of services. In particular, section 7701(e)(1) provides that a contract that purports to be a service contract will be treated instead as a lease of property if the contract is properly treated as a lease taking into account all relevant factors, including whether (1) the service recipient is in physical possession of the property, (2) the service recipient controls the property, (3) the service recipient has a significant economic or possessory interest in the property, (4) the service provider does not bear any risk of substantially diminished receipts or substantially increased expenditures if there is nonperformance under the contract, (5) the service provider does not use the property concurrently to provide significant services to entities unrelated to the service recipient, and (6) the total contract price does not substantially exceed the rental value of the property for the contract period. Section 7701(e)(2) provides that the factors in section 7701(e)(1) apply to determine whether any arrangement, not just contracts which purport to be service contracts, is properly treated as a lease. Consistent with the inclusive statutory language, the legislative history indicates that this list of factors is meant to be non-exclusive and constitutes a balancing test, such that the presence or absence of a single factor may not be dispositive in every case. S. Prt. No. 169 (Vol. I), 98th Cong., 2d Sess., at 138 (1984); Joint Committee on Taxation Staff, *General Explanation of the Revenue Provisions of the Deficit Reduction Act of 1984*, 98th Cong., at 60 (Comm. Print 1984).

In addition, courts have also considered other factors in determining whether transactions are leases of property or the provision of services, including whether the service provider had the right to replace the relevant property with comparable property, whether the property was a component of an integrated operation in which the service provider had other responsibilities, whether the service provider operated the equipment, and whether the service provider's fee was based on a measure of work performed rather than the mere passage of time. *See, e.g., Musco Sports Lighting, Inc. v. Comm'r*, T.C. Memo 1990-331, *aff'd*, 943 F.2d 906 (8th Cir. 1991); *Xerox Corp v. U.S.*, 656 F.2d 659 (Ct. Cl. 1981); and *Smith v. Comm'r*, T.C. Memo 1989-318.

Explanation of Provisions

I. Proposed § 1.861-19

Proposed § 1.861-19 provides rules for classifying a cloud transaction as either a provision of services or a lease of property. Proposed § 1.861-19(a) specifies that the rules apply for purposes of sections 59A, 245A, 250, 267A, 367, 404A, 482, 679, and 1059A; subchapter N of chapter 1; chapters 3 and 4; and sections 842 and 845 (to the extent involving a foreign person), as well as with respect to transfers to foreign trusts not covered by section 679.

In order to make other sections consistent with proposed § 1.861-19, *Example 5* in § 1.937-3(e) is proposed to be removed from the rules for determining whether income is derived from sources within a U.S. possession or territory.

A. Definition of "Cloud Transaction"

Proposed § 1.861-19(b) defines a cloud transaction as a transaction through which a person obtains non-de minimis on-demand network access to computer hardware, digital content (as defined in proposed § 1.861-18(a)(3)), or other similar resources. This definition is not limited to computer hardware and software, or to the IaaS, PaaS, and SaaS models described above, because it is intended also to apply to other transactions that share characteristics of on-demand network access to technological resources, including access to streaming digital content and access to information in certain databases. Although this definition is broad, it does not encompass every transaction executed or completed through the Internet. For example, proposed § 1.861-19 clarifies that the mere download or other electronic transfer of digital content for storage and use on a person's computer hardware or other electronic device does not constitute on-demand network access to the digital content and so would not be considered a cloud transaction for purposes of proposed § 1.861-19.

B. Classification of Cloud Transactions

1. Single Classification

Proposed § 1.861-19(c) provides that a cloud transaction is classified solely as either a lease of property or the provision of services. Certain cloud transactions may have characteristics of both a lease of property and the provision of services. Such transactions are generally classified in their entirety as either a lease or a service, and not bifurcated into a lease transaction and a separate service transaction. For example, section 7701(e)(1) classifies a purported service contract as either a lease or a service contract and does not contemplate mixed classifications of a single, integrated transaction. In *Tidewater v. U.S.*, 565 F.3d 299 (5th Cir. 2009), *action on dec.*, 2010-01 (June 1, 2010) (*Tidewater*), the Fifth Circuit applied the factors in section 7701(e)(1) to determine a single character for a time charter with respect to an ocean-going vessel, rather than following the taxpayer's allocation of consideration from the transaction into separate service and lease components.

In some cases, the facts and circumstances may support the conclusion that an arrangement involves multiple cloud transactions to which proposed § 1.861-19 applies. In such cases, proposed § 1.861-19 requires a separate classification of each cloud transaction except any transaction that is de minimis.

2. Determination Based on All Relevant Factors

Proposed § 1.861-19(c)(1) provides that all relevant factors must be taken into account in determining whether a cloud transaction is classified as a lease of property (specifically, computer hardware, digital content (as defined in proposed § 1.861-18(a)(3)), or other similar resources) or the provision of services. The relevance of any factor varies depending on the factual situation, and any particular factor may not be relevant in a given instance.

Proposed § 1.861-19(c)(2) contains a non-exhaustive list of factors for determining whether a cloud transaction is classified as the provision of services or a lease of property. In general, application of the relevant factors to a cloud transaction will result in the transaction being treated as the provision of services rather than a lease of property. In addition to the statutory factors described in section 7701(e)(1), the proposed regulations set forth several factors applied by courts that the Treasury Department and the IRS have determined are relevant in demonstrating that a cloud transaction is classified as the provision of services: whether the provider has the right to determine the specific property used in the cloud transaction and replace such property with comparable property; whether the property is a component of an integrated operation in which the provider has other responsibilities, including ensuring the property is maintained and updated; and whether the provider's fee is primarily based on a measure of work performed or the level of the customer's use rather than the mere passage of time. The proposed regulations include several examples applying the factors in proposed § 1.861-19(c)(2) to different types of cloud transactions.

Certain factors that are relevant under proposed § 1.861-19(c) may be the same as or similar to those used to determine whether transactions other than cloud transactions are classified as leases or services under other authorities. However, cloud transactions, which involve on-demand network access to property such as computer hardware and digital content, may have significant differences from other lease and service transactions that involve direct physical access to property. Accordingly, the interpretation of factors and their application to cloud transactions require an analysis that is sensitive to the inherent differences between transactions involving physical access to property and transactions involving on-demand network access.

C. Classification of Cloud Transactions Related to Other Transactions

Certain arrangements may involve multiple transactions, where one or more transactions would be classified as a cloud transaction under proposed § 1.861-19(b) and one or more transactions do not qualify as a cloud transaction and would be classified under other sections of the Code and regulations, or under general tax law principles. For example, an arrangement might involve both a cloud transaction and a transaction that would be classified under the rules of § 1.861-18 as a lease of a copyrighted article. Proposed § 1.861-19(c)(3) provides that, in such cases, the classification rules apply only to classify the cloud transaction, and any non-cloud transaction will be classified separately under such other section of the Code or regulations, or under general tax law principles. However, for purposes of administrability, proposed § 1.861-19(c)(3) provides that no transaction will be classified separately if it is de minimis. This rule is illustrated by examples contained in proposed § 1.861-19(d).

II. Modifications of § 1.861-18

A. Scope of Application

The preamble to the final regulations under § 1.861-18 governing the classification of transactions involving computer programs (T.D. 8785, 63 FR 52971 (October 2, 1998)) indicated that § 1.861-18 would apply only to such transactions because the need for guidance with respect to transactions involving computer programs was most pressing. The preamble noted, however, that the Treasury Department and the IRS may consider as part of a separate guidance project whether to apply the principles of those regulations to other transactions. Since § 1.861-18 was adopted as a final regulation in 1998, content in digital format and subject to copyright law, including music, video, and books, has become a common basis for commercial transactions. Consumption of such digital content has grown in part because of new computer hardware, including laptops, tablets, e-readers, and smartphones, that allows users to more easily obtain and use digital content.

The Treasury Department and the IRS have determined that the rules and principles underlying existing § 1.861-18 have provided useful guidance with respect to computer programs and that these rules and principles should apply to certain other digital content. Accordingly, proposed § 1.861-18 broadens the scope of existing § 1.861-18 to apply to all transfers of "digital content," defined in proposed § 1.861-18(a)(3) as any content in digital format and that is either protected by copyright law or is no longer protected by copyright law solely due to the passage of time. Digital content includes, for example, books, movies, and music in digital format in addition to computer programs.

Certain terms have been changed in proposed § 1.861-18, including references to computer programs being replaced with references to digital content. The application of proposed § 1.861-18 to digital content other than computer programs is illustrated by proposed § 1.861-18(h)(19) through (21) (Examples 19 through 21).

B. Rights to Advertise Copyrighted Articles

Comments received on the proposed regulations (REG-251520-96; 61 FR 58152; November 13, 1996) (the "1996 proposed regulations") that were finalized in 1998 as existing § 1.861-18 recommended that the transfer of a right to publicly perform or display a computer program should not be considered the transfer of a copyright right if the right is limited to the advertisement of a copyrighted article and the public performance or display of the entire copyrighted article is not permitted. The recommendation of these comments was not incorporated into existing § 1.861-18, but the Treasury Department and the IRS acknowledged in the preamble to existing § 1.861-18 that it may be appropriate to revisit the issue in the future and observed that the transfer of such rights to advertise a copyrighted article in many cases would be de minimis under existing § 1.861-18(c)(1)(ii).

In light of experience in administering existing § 1.861-18, the Treasury Department and the IRS have determined that the transfer of the right to publicly perform or display digital content for the purpose of advertising the sale of the digital content should not constitute the transfer of a copyright right for purposes of those portions of the Code enumerated in § 1.861-18(a)(1). For example, rights provided to a video game retailer allowing the retailer to display screenshots of a video game on television commercials promoting sales of the game generally would not, on their own, constitute a transfer of copyright rights that is significant in context. Accordingly, proposed § 1.861-18 modifies existing § 1.861-18(c)(2)(iii) and (iv) to provide that a transfer of the mere right to public performance or display of digital content for purposes of advertising the digital content does not by itself constitute a transfer of a copyright right.

C. Source of Income for Sales of Copyrighted Articles in Electronic Medium

Comments received on the 1996 proposed regulations addressed the sourcing of income from the sale of computer programs through electronic downloads and noted uncertainty regarding the application of the title passage rule of § 1.861-7(c) to these sales of copyrighted articles. Although the preamble indicated that the parties in many cases can agree where title passes for inventory property, the final regulations under § 1.861-18 included only a general reference to the relevant source rules and did not specifically address the application of the title passage rule for sales of copyrighted articles. Based on experience in administering existing § 1.861-18 since 1998, the Treasury Department and the IRS have become more aware of the uncertainty associated with determining the source of sales of copyrighted articles by application of § 1.861-7(c), in particular in the context of electronically downloaded software. In many sales of copyrighted articles, the location where rights, title, and interest are transferred is not specified. In some cases, due to intellectual property law concerns, there may be no passage of legal title when the copyrighted article is sold. Moreover, the Treasury Department and the IRS have determined that contractual specification of a location — other than the customer's location — as the location of transfer could be easily manipulated and would bear little connection to economic reality in the case of a transfer by electronic medium of digital content, given that a sale and transfer of digital content by electronic medium generally would not be considered commercially complete until the customer has successfully downloaded the copy.

In light of these considerations, proposed § 1.861-18(f)(2)(ii) provides that when copyrighted articles are sold and transferred through an electronic medium, the sale is deemed to occur at the location of download or installation onto the end-user's device used to access the digital content for purposes of § 1.861-7(c). It is expected that vendors generally will be able to identify the location of such download or installation. Comments are requested as to the availability, reliability and cost of this information. In the absence of information about the location of download or installation onto the end-user's device used to access the digital content, the sale is deemed to have occurred at the location of the customer based on the taxpayer's recorded sales data for business or financial reporting purposes. Consistent with existing § 1.861-18, proposed § 1.861-18(f)(2)(ii) provides that income from sales or exchanges of copyrighted articles is sourced under sections 861(a)(6), 862(a)(6), 863, or 865(a), (b), (c), or (e), as appropriate. The Treasury Department and the IRS do not expect proposed § 1.861-18(f)(2)(ii) to impact the application of income tax treaties to which the United States is a party given that the taxation of gains under those treaties is generally determined by reference to the residence country of the seller and not the source of income from the sale. Income from leases of copyrighted articles is sourced under section 861(a)(4) or 862(a)(4), as appropriate.

In order to make other sections consistent with proposed § 1.861-18(f)(2)(ii), a cross-reference has been added in the rules for sales of inventory property in § 1.861-7(c), and Example 4 in § 1.937-3(e) has been removed from the rules for determining whether income is derived from sources within a U.S. possession or territory.

III. Change in Method of Accounting

The application of these new rules for purposes of the affected Code sections may require certain taxpayers to change their methods of accounting under section 446(e) for affected transactions. Any change in method of accounting that a taxpayer makes in order to comply with these regulations would be a change initiated by the taxpayer. Accordingly, the change in method of accounting must be implemented under the rules of § 1.446-1(e) and the applicable administrative procedures that govern voluntary changes in method of accounting under section 446(e).

IV. Request for Comments

Comments are requested on all aspects of these proposed regulations, including the following topics:

(1) Whether the definition of digital content should be defined more broadly than content protected by copyright law and content that is no longer protected by copyright law solely due to the passage of time;

(2) whether any special considerations should be taken into account in applying the rules in existing § 1.861-18 to transfers of digital content other than computer programs;

(3) whether any other aspects of existing § 1.861-18 need to be modified if that section is amended as proposed;

(4) whether the classification of cloud transactions as either a service or a lease is correct, or whether cloud transactions are more properly classified in another category (for example, a license or a sale);

(5) realistic examples of cloud transactions that would be treated as leases under proposed § 1.861-19;

(6) the existence of arrangements involving both a transaction that would qualify as a cloud transaction and another non-de minimis transaction that would be classified under another provision of the Code or Regulations, or under general tax law principles;

(7) potential bases for allocating consideration in arrangements involving both a transaction that would qualify as a cloud transaction and another non-de minimis transaction that would be classified under another provision of the Code or Regulations, or under general tax law principles;

(8) administrable rules for sourcing income from cloud transactions in a manner consistent with sections 861 through 865; and

(9) application of proposed § 1.861-19 to an arrangement that involves non-de minimis rights both to access digital content on-demand over a network and to download such digital content onto a user's electronic device for offline use.

Proposed Effective Date

The regulations are proposed to apply to taxable years beginning on or after the date of publication of the Treasury decision adopting these regulations as final regulations in the **Federal Register**. No inference should be drawn from the proposed effective date concerning the treatment of transactions involving digital content or cloud transactions entered into before the regulations are applicable. For transactions involving transfers of computer programs occurring pursuant to contracts entered into before publication of the final regulations, the rules in former § 1.861-18, T.D. 8785 and T.D. 9870, will apply. For proposed dates of applicability, see §§ 1.861-18(i) and 1.861-19(e).

Special Analyses

Regulatory Planning and Review

Executive Orders 13563 and 12866 direct agencies to assess costs and benefits of available regulatory alternatives and, if regulation is necessary, to select regulatory approaches that maximize net benefits (including potential economic, environmental, public health and safety effects, distributive impacts, and equity). Executive Order 13563 emphasizes the importance of quantifying both costs and benefits, of reducing costs, of harmonizing rules, and of promoting flexibility.

These proposed rules have been designated by the Office of Management and Budget's Office of Information and Regulatory Affairs as subject to review under Executive Order 12866 pursuant to the Memorandum of Agreement (MOA)(April 11, 2018) between the Treasury Department and the Office of Management and Budget regarding review of tax regulations. The Treasury Department and the IRS project that these rules are not economically significant because current industry practice is generally consistent with the principles underlying the proposed regulations. Comments are requested as to whether this characterization of industry practice is inaccurate.

A. Background

When assessing tax on income arising from international transactions, the "source" of income is important in determining a taxpayer's tax liability. U.S. sourcing rules, generally contained in code sections 861 to 865, determine whether income earned is considered domestic or foreign source. For U.S. resident taxpayers, the U.S. generally taxes both domestic and foreign source income and, for the latter, provides credits for foreign taxes up to the level of U.S. tax. Taxpayers with significant foreign tax credits (FTCs) typically prefer that income be considered foreign rather than U.S. source in order to maximize their use of FTCs and minimize their U.S. taxes.

Proper assessment of the source of a particular item of income depends on the nature and type (or character) of that income (for example, interest, dividend, compensation for services, royalties paid under a license, gains recorded in a sale). Source rules differ for different types of income, so it is first necessary for income tax purposes to classify the character of an item of income. In the case of transactions involving digital content and cloud transactions, the types of income most relevant are sales, licenses, leases, and services, but there are currently no regulations specifically applicable to the classification of transactions involving digital content other than computer programs or the classification of transactions involving remote access to digital content through the cloud. These proposed regulations provide that guidance.

The character of income also affects the U.S. taxation of income earned by U.S. taxpayers through their foreign subsidiary corporations. Certain U.S. shareholders of controlled foreign corporations (as defined in section 957) must include their share of a controlled foreign corporation's subpart F income in the U.S. shareholder's gross income on a current basis. Section 951(a)(1)(A). The characterization of income can impact whether it is considered subpart F income (as defined in section 952).

B. *Need for Proposed Regulations*

Transactions involving digital content and cloud computing have become common due to the growth of electronic commerce. Such transactions must be classified in terms of character in order to apply various provisions of the Code, such as sourcing rules and subpart F. Existing Reg. §1.861-18, finalized in 1998, provides rules for classifying transactions involving computer programs as, for example, a license of a computer program, a rental of a computer program, or a sale of a computer program. These existing regulations, however, do not explicitly cover transactions involving other digital content, such as digital music and video, or to cloud computing transactions, and thus taxpayers must determine how these transactions should be classified for tax purposes without clear guidance. The proposed regulations are needed to reduce this uncertainty. The proposed regulations also reduce the opportunities for taxpayers to take positions on source and character that inappropriately minimize their taxes.

C. *Overview of Proposed Regulations*

The proposed regulations provide updated guidance with respect to the classification of transactions involving digital content (proposed §1.861-18) and new guidance with respect to cloud transactions (proposed §1.861-19).

Existing rules, particularly final regulations under §1.861-18, which were adopted in 1998, govern the classification of transactions involving computer programs. The Treasury Department and the IRS have determined that the rules and principles underlying existing §1.861-18 provide useful guidance for transactions involving digital content. Proposed §1.861-18 broadens the scope of its application to include digital content, which is defined in proposed §1.861-18(a)(3) as any content in digital format that is either protected by copyright law or is no longer protected solely due to the passage of time (e.g., books, movies, and music in digital format, in addition to computer programs).

Cloud computing transactions, which are typically characterized by on-demand network access to computing resources, would not generally be subject to classification under existing §1.861-18 since such transactions typically do not include the transfer of a computer program, nor would such transactions be subject to proposed §1.861-18 since such transactions typically do not include the transfer of a copyright right or copyrighted article, or provision of development services related to computer programming. Consequently, proposed §1.861-19 provides rules for classifying a cloud transaction as either a provision of service or a lease of property.

D. *Economic analysis*

1. Baseline

The Treasury Department and the IRS have assessed the benefits and costs of the proposed regulation compared to a no-action baseline that reflects anticipated Federal income tax-related behavior in the absence of these proposed regulations.

2. Summary of Economic Effects

The proposed regulations provide certainty and clarity with respect to the characterization of income from digital transactions and cloud computing. In the absence of such guidance, the chances that different U.S. taxpayers would interpret the Code differentially, either from each other or from the intents and purposes of the underlying statutes, would be exacerbated. This divergence in interpretation could cause U.S. businesses to make economic decisions based on different interpretations of, for example, whether income from making digital music available to a user would be characterized as derived from a service or a lease transaction for purposes of applying sourcing rules and thus whether such income is considered domestic or foreign. If economic decisions are not guided by uniform incentives across otherwise similar investors and across otherwise similar investments, the resulting pattern of economic activity is generally inefficient. Thus, the Treasury Department and the IRS expect that the definitions and guidance provided in the proposed regulation will help support an efficient allocation of economic activity among taxpayers, relative to the baseline.

The characterization of income from digital transactions and cloud computing, for example, may impact taxpayer incentives under section 59A (the tax on certain base erosion payments) and section 250 (foreign derived intangible income and global intangible low-taxed income). For example, under section 59A, the characterization of a cloud transaction as a service, as opposed to a lease, may implicate the services cost method exception under section 59A(d)(5). Such characterization may also impact the documentation requirements or eligibility for treatment as foreign-derived intangible income under section 250(b). However, because current industry practice is generally consistent with the principles underlying the proposed regulations, the Treasury Department and the IRS expect these regulations to have only a small effect on economic activity or compliance costs relative to the baseline.

The Treasury Department and IRS solicit comments on the economic effects of the proposed regulations.

3. Economic Effects of Specific Provisions

a. Transactions involving copyright-protected digital content

Existing §1.861-18 provides rules for classifying transfers of computer programs as, for example, a license of a computer program, a lease of a computer program, or a sale of a computer program. Proposed §1.861-18 broadens the scope of existing §1.861-18 to apply to all transfers of digital content. In addition, as discussed in Part II.B of the Explanation of Provisions section, proposed §1.861-18 clarifies that a transfer of the mere right to public performance or display of digital content for advertising purposes does not by itself constitute a transfer of a copyright right. Further, as explained in Part II.C of the Explanation of Provisions section, proposed §1.861-18 provides clarity around the title passage rule of §1.861-7(c) by providing that when copyrighted articles are sold, the sale is deemed to occur at the location of the download or installation onto the end-user's device, or in the absence of that information then at the location of the customer. Proposed 1.861-7(c) provides that a sale of personal property is consummated at the place where the rights, title, and interest of the seller in the property are transferred to the buyer, or, when bare legal title is retained by the seller, where beneficial ownership passes.

In considering how the place of sale should be determined for digital content, the Treasury Department and the IRS considered, as an alternative, not issuing specific rules and instead retaining the existing rules without further clarification for copyrighted articles. The Treasury Department and the IRS elected to provided further clarity about the sourcing of income from the sale of copyrighted articles because (1) in the context of electronically downloaded software, the location in which rights, title, and interest are transferred is often difficult to determine or not specified, and (2) the location of transfer could be easily manipulated (for example, the server location from which a copyrighted article is downloaded). Consequently, for administrative and clarification purposes, proposed §1.861-18(f)(2)(ii) provides that when a copyrighted article is sold through an electronic medium, the sale is deemed to occur at the location of download or installation onto the end-user's device. The Treasury Department and the IRS are proposing this location definition because that is where the sale is completed, since until the download is complete, the content is not entirely transferred.

The Treasury Department and the IRS solicit comments on these proposed regulations and particularly solicit comments that provide data, other evidence, or models that would enhance the rigor with which the final regulations governing digital content might be developed.

b. Cloud transactions

Proposed §1.861-19 provides rules for classifying a cloud transaction as either a lease of property (i.e., computer hardware, digital content, or other similar resources) or a provision of services. These rules contain a non-exhaustive list of factors which include statutory factors described in section 7701(e)(1) and factors applied by courts, as explained in Part I.B.2. of the Explanation of Provisions section.

As an alternative, the Treasury Department and the IRS considered not providing further specific guidance regarding how cloud computing transactions should be classified (for sourcing and other purposes). The Treasury Department and the IRS have developed the proposed regulations (proposed §1.861-18 and proposed §1.861-19) because they will provide clarity to taxpayers and the IRS when determining the character of income arising from transactions involving digital content and cloud computing. This increased clarity, relative to the baseline, will reduce the potential for tax planning strategies that exploit uncertainty resulting from the lack of explicit guidance for characterizing common transactions involving digital content and cloud computing. Consistent reporting across taxpayers also increases the IRS's ability to consistently enforce the tax rules, thus increasing equity and decreasing opportunities for tax evasion.

The Treasury Department and the IRS solicit comments on these proposed regulations and particularly solicit comments that provide data, other evidence, or models that would enhance the rigor with which the final regulations governing cloud transactions might be developed.

E. *Regulatory Flexibility Act*

The Regulatory Flexibility Act requires consideration of the regulatory impact on small businesses. It is hereby certified that these proposed regulations will not have a significant economic impact on a substantial number of small entities within the meaning of section 601(6) of the Regulatory Flexibility Act (5 U.S.C. chapter 6).

As discussed elsewhere in the Special Analyses, transactions involving digital content and cloud computing have become common due to the growth of electronic commerce. Such transactions must be classified in terms of character in order to apply various provisions of the Code, such as sourcing rules and subpart F. Existing Reg. §1.861-18, finalized in 1998, provides rules for classifying transactions involving computer programs as, for example, a license of a computer program, a rental of a computer program, or a sale of a computer program. These existing regulations, however, do not explicitly cover transactions involving other digital content, such as digital music and video, or to cloud computing transactions and thus taxpayers must determine how these transactions should be classified for tax purposes without clear guidance. The proposed regulations provide certainty and clarity to these affected taxpayers.

Although data are not readily available to estimate the number of small entities that would be affected by this proposed rule, the Treasury Department and the IRS project that any economic impact of the regulations would be minimal for businesses regardless of size. These proposed regulations generally provide clarification of definitions regarding how transactions are classified, they are not expected to have an impact on burden for large or small businesses. The Treasury Department and the IRS project that any economic impact would be small because current industry practice is generally consistent with the principles underlying the proposed regulations.

Notwithstanding this certification that the proposed rule will not have a significant economic impact on a substantial number of small entities, the Treasury Department and the IRS invite comments on the impact this proposed rule would have on small entities.

Comments and Requests for a Public Hearing

Before these proposed regulations are adopted as final regulations, consideration will be given to any comments that are submitted timely to the IRS as prescribed in this preamble under the "ADDRESSES" section. All comments will be available at www.regulations.gov or upon request. A public hearing will be scheduled if requested in writing by any person that timely submits comments. If a public hearing is scheduled, notice of the date, time, and place for the public hearing will be published in the **Federal Register**.

Drafting Information

The principal author of these proposed regulations is Robert Z. Kelley of the Office of the Associate Chief Counsel (International). However, other personnel from the Treasury Department and the IRS participated in their development.

[¶ 49,808]   Proposed Amendments of Regulations (REG-101378-19), published in the Federal Register on August 23, 2019.

[Code Sec. 61]

Valuation rule: Employer-provided vehicle: Personal use.—Amendments of Reg. §1.61-21, regarding special valuation rules for employers and employees to use in determining the amount to include in an employee's gross income for personal use of an employer-provided vehicle, are adopted.

[¶ 49,809]   Proposed Amendments of Regulations (REG-104554-18), published in the Federal Register on September 9, 2019.

[Code Sec. 451]

Advance payments: Method of accounting: Tax Cuts and Jobs Act (TCJA).—Reg. §1.451-8, regarding the timing of income inclusion under section 451 of the Internal Revenue Code (Code) of advance payments for goods, services, and certain other items, are proposed.

AGENCY: Internal Revenue Service (IRS), Treasury.

ACTION: Notice of proposed rulemaking.

SUMMARY: This document contains proposed regulations regarding the timing of income inclusion under section 451 of the Internal Revenue Code (Code) of advance payments for goods, services, and certain other items. The proposed regulations reflect changes made by the Tax Cuts and Jobs Act. These proposed regulations affect taxpayers that use an accrual method of accounting and receive advance payments. **DATES**: Written or electronic comments or a request for a public hearing must be received by November 8, 2019.

ADDRESSES: Submit electronic submissions via the Federal eRulemaking Portal at *www.regulations.gov* (indicate IRS and REG-104554-18) by following the online instructions for submitting comments. Once submitted to the Federal eRulemaking Portal, comments cannot be edited or withdrawn. The Department of the Treasury (Treasury Department) and the IRS will publish for public availability any comment received to its public docket, whether submitted electronically or in hard copy. Send hard copy submissions to Internal Revenue Service, CC:PA:LPD:PR (REG-104554-18), Room 5205, P.O. Box 7604, Ben Franklin Station, Washington, DC 20044. Submissions may be hand delivered Monday through Friday between the hours of 8 a.m. and 4 p.m. to Courier's Desk, Internal Revenue Service, CC:PA:LPD:PR (REG-104554-18), 1111 Constitution Avenue, NW, Washington, DC 20224.

FOR FURTHER INFORMATION CONTACT: Concerning this proposed regulation, Peter E. Ford, (202) 317-7003; concerning submission of comments or a request for a public hearing, Regina L. Johnson, (202) 317-6901 (not toll-free numbers).

SUPPLEMENTARY INFORMATION:

Background

This document contains proposed amendments to 26 CFR part 1 under section 451(c). On December 22, 2017, section 451(c) was amended by section 13221 of the Tax Cuts and Jobs Act, Public Law No. 115-97 (131 Stat. 2054) (the Act), to provide that a taxpayer using an accrual method of accounting (accrual method taxpayer) with an applicable financial statement (AFS) may use the deferral method of accounting provided in section 451(c) for advance payments. These proposed regulations also provide a deferral method of accounting for taxpayers that do not have an AFS. Unless otherwise indicated, all references to section 451(c) in this preamble are to section 451(c), as amended by the Act.

In general, section 451 provides that the amount of any item of gross income is included in gross income for the taxable year in which it is received by the taxpayer, unless, under the method of accounting used in computing taxable income, the amount is to be properly accounted for as of a different period. Under § 1.451-1, accrual method taxpayers generally include items of income in gross income in the taxable year when all the events occur that fix the right to receive the income and the amount of the income can be determined with reasonable accuracy (the all events test). All the events that fix the right to receive income occur when (1) the required performance takes place, (2) payment is due, or (3) payment is made, whichever happens first. See Revenue Ruling 2003-10 (2003-1 CB 288); Revenue Ruling 84-31 (1984-1 CB 127); Revenue Ruling 80-308 (1980-2 CB 162). Section 451(c) requires an accrual method taxpayer who receives an advance payment to include the amount thereof in income in the taxable year of receipt. Section 451(c) also generally codifies the current deferral method of accounting for certain advance payments for goods, services, and other specified items provided by the IRS under Revenue Procedure 2004-34 (2004-22 IRB 991) by allowing accrual method taxpayers to elect to defer the inclusion of income associated with certain advance payments to the taxable year following the taxable year of receipt if such income also is deferred for AFS purposes.

On April 12, 2018, the Treasury Department and the IRS issued Notice 2018-35 (2018-18 IRB 520) requesting, in part, comments on future guidance under section 451(c). The record of public comments received in response to Notice 2018-35 may be requested by sending an email to *Notice.comments@irscounsel.treas.gov*. This document provides guidance on the application of section 451(c), taking into account comments that were received regarding section 451(c). The application of section 451(c) is addressed in separate guidance published in the same issue of the **Federal Register** as these proposed regulations.

Explanation of Provisions

These proposed regulations describe and clarify the statutory requirements of section 451(c) by providing new § 1.451-8.

1. Deferral Methods under § 1.451-8

A. AFS Deferral Method

Consistent with section 451(c)(1)(A), these proposed regulations provide that an accrual method taxpayer with an AFS includes an advance payment in gross income in the taxable year of receipt unless the taxpayer uses the deferral method in section 451(c)(1)(B) and proposed § 1.451-8(c) (AFS deferral method). A taxpayer using the AFS deferral method must have an AFS, as described in section 451(b)(1)(A)(i) or (ii). These proposed regulations define the term AFS by reference to the definition of that term in proposed § 1.451-3(c)(1) (REG-104870-18). Under the AFS deferral method, a taxpayer with an AFS that receives an advance payment must include: (i) the advance payment in income in the taxable year of receipt, to the extent that it is included in revenue in its AFS, and (ii) the remaining amount of the advance payment in income in the next taxable year. The AFS deferral method provided in these proposed regulations closely follows the deferral method of Revenue Procedure 2004-34, as modified by Revenue Procedure 2011-14 (2011-4 IRB 330), and as modified and clarified by Revenue Procedure 2011-18 (2011-5 IRB 443), and Revenue Procedure 2013-29 (2013-33 IRB 141) (Revenue Procedure deferral method). Because new section 451(c)(1)(B) was intended to generally codify the Revenue Procedure deferral method, the Treasury Department and the IRS believe that rules similar to the Revenue Procedure deferral method are necessary and appropriate for the proper application of section 451(c). *See* H.R. Rep. No. 115-466, at 429 (2017) (Conf. Rep.).

B. Non-AFS Deferral Method

Section 451(c)(4)(A) generally defines an advance payment as any payment the full inclusion of which in gross income of the taxpayer for the year of receipt is a permissible method of accounting, any portion of which is included in revenue by the taxpayer in an AFS, and which is for goods, services, or other items identified by the Secretary. One commenter noted that the financial statement requirement within the definition of an advance payment means that the rule in Revenue Procedure 2004-34 that depended on determining when the advance payment was earned was not within the statutory text of section 451(c). The Treasury Department and the IRS have concluded that section 451(c) does not prohibit a deferral method that is otherwise permissible under Revenue Procedure 2004-34. *See* H.R. Rep. No. 115-466, at 429 (2017) (Conf. Rep.). See also, Joint Committee on Taxation, General Explanation of Public Law 115-97 (JCS-1-18) at 170-171 (Dec. 20, 2018). Revenue Procedure 2004-34 permitted non-AFS taxpayers to use the Revenue Procedure deferral method based on when the income is earned (earned standard). *See* section 5.02(3)(b) of Revenue Procedure 2004-34. The Revenue Procedure deferral method using the earned standard is a permissible method of accounting for non-AFS taxpayers and, therefore, these proposed regulations also provide a similar deferral method for non-AFS taxpayers in proposed § 1.451-8(d) (non-AFS deferral method). Under the non-AFS deferral method, an accrual method taxpayer without an AFS that receives an advance payment must include: (i) the advance payment in income in the taxable year of receipt, to the extent that it is earned, and (ii) the remaining amount of the advance payment in income in the next taxable year.

2. *Definition of Advance Payment*

A. In general

Section 451(c)(4)(A) generally defines advance payment as any payment (i) the full inclusion of which in gross income of the taxpayer for the taxable year of receipt is a permissible method of accounting, (ii) any portion of which is included in revenue by the taxpayer in an AFS (or such other financial statement as the Secretary may specify) for a subsequent taxable year, and (iii) which is for goods, services, or such other items as may be identified by the Secretary.

Proposed § 1.451-8(b)(1)(i) clarifies that the definition of advance payment under the AFS and non-AFS deferral methods is consistent with the definition of advance payment in Revenue Procedure 2004-34, which section 451(c) was meant to codify. See H.R. Rep. No. 115-466, at 429 (2017) (Conf. Rep.). The Treasury Department and the IRS believe this definition of advance payment: (1) is consistent with section 451(c), (2) minimizes additional tax compliance burden and cost, (3) provides clarity to taxpayers, and (4) uses rules which are familiar to both taxpayers and the IRS.

Two commenters suggested that airline miles be explicitly included in the list of items for which an advance payment may be received. The commenters suggested that airline miles are a unique type of item, generally redeemed for air travel and non-travel rewards. The Treasury Department and the IRS decline to specifically include airline miles in the definition of advance payment because the use of the deferral method under these proposed regulations, to the extent airline miles are redeemable for goods or services, is already permissible. Therefore, these proposed regulations include examples to illustrate that, to the extent certain reward points are treated as separate performance obligations, they may be eligible for the deferral methods provided under these proposed regulations.

Another commenter suggested that progress payments with respect to the sale of an interest in real property should be included in the definition of an advance payment. Revenue Procedure 2004-34 was intended to provide a simplified and consistent deferral period for the sale of goods, services, and other items. However, the definition of advance payment in Revenue Procedure 2004-34 does not include prepayments for interests in real property. These proposed regulations generally provide the same types of items in the definition of advance payment to those items provided in Revenue Procedure 2004-34. However, the Treasury Department and IRS will consider any comments received in determining whether it is appropriate to include additional types of items in the definition of advance payment.

B. Items Excluded from the Definition of an Advance Payment

Section 451(c)(4)(B) provides that certain items, except as otherwise provided by the Secretary, are to be excluded from the definition of an advance payment. Pursuant to section 451(c)(4)(B), the term advance payment does not include rent; insurance premiums governed by subchapter L; payments with respect to financial instruments; payments with respect to certain warranty or guaranty contracts; payments subject to section 871(a), 881, 1441, or 1442; payments in property to which section 83 applies; and other payments identified by the Secretary.

Several commenters requested that certain payments for certain types of goods be excluded from the definition of an advance payment under section 451(c)(4)(B). A commenter requested that certain pre-delivery payments for the sale of high-value customer-configured equipment that will be delivered to customers at reasonably certain times not be included in the definition of advance payment. Another commenter requested that an exclusion be provided for goods for which (i) a taxpayer receives a payment in a taxable year with respect to a contract for the sale of goods not properly includible in such taxpayer's finished goods inventory, and (ii) on the last day of such taxable year the taxpayer does not have on hand (or available to it in such year through its normal source of supply) goods of a substantially similar kind and in a sufficient quantity to satisfy the contract during such contract year. This commenter suggested a narrowing of this exclusion could be done according to whether a good is commercially significant or of high-value. A commercially significant good has a useful life equal to or in excess of 10 years and it is developed, marketed, and sold to customers in the aerospace industry. Generally these goods require a significant amount of capital to produce and may require considerable time from development to delivery. Generally, for financial statement purposes, such manufacturers recognize revenue related to these goods when the product is completed and delivered to the customer and title and risk of loss have transferred to the customer.

Proposed § 1.451-8(b)(1)(ii) provides a list of items excluded from the definition of advance payment that is similar to Revenue Procedure 2004-34. An additional exclusion is provided for payments received in a taxable year earlier than the taxable year immediately preceding the taxable year of the contractual delivery date for a specified good, as defined in § 1.451-8(b)(9). In response to the comments received, the Treasury Department and IRS have determined that an exclusion is appropriate for certain goods for which a taxpayer requires a customer to make an upfront payment under the contract if (i) the contracted delivery month and year of the good occurs at least two taxable years after an upfront payment, (ii) the taxpayer does not have the good or a substantially similar good on hand at the end of the year the upfront payment is received, and (iii) the taxpayer recognizes all of the revenue from the sale of the good in its AFS in the year of delivery.

The Treasury Department and the IRS have employed the authority granted to the Secretary in section 451(c)(4)(B)(vii) to exclude certain payments, in a limited manner, that would otherwise constitute advance payments within the meaning of section 451(c)(4)(A), in response to the proposals described in comments already received. In order to fully consider other such potential exclusions, detailed comments that specifically address the following issues are requested:

1. Does the authority granted to the Secretary by section 451(c)(4)(B)(vii) to exclude certain payments from the definition of an advance payment under section 451(c) also permit an exception for those payments from the rules regarding the all events test under section 451(b)?

2. What significance, if any, should the time it takes to manufacture or create an item of property, or such item of property's useful life, be given in determining whether a pre-delivery payment for such item of property should be included in income as an advance payment?

3. Does the authority granted to the Secretary by section 451(c)(4)(B)(vii) authorize rules that change the timing of deductions or provide a safe harbor allowing specified categories of taxpayers to use methods of accounting for recognizing income other than an accrual method under section 451? Is there any particular authority under the Code that would allow changing the timing of deductions in this context under section 451 or another section of Subchapter E?

4. Does the authority granted to the Secretary by section 451(c)(4)(B)(vii) to exclude certain payments from the definition of an advance payment also authorize the imposition of conditions unrelated to an accrual method of accounting with respect to any such exclusions? For example, could the Secretary require that a taxpayer use an alternative method of accounting as a condition for excluding a type of payment from the definition of advance payment?

5. Does the authority granted to the Secretary by section 451(c)(4)(B)(vii) to exclude certain payments from the definition of advance payment also authorize the imposition of a time limit on such exclusion? For example, could an exclusion under section 451(c)(4)(B)(vii) be limited to a specified number of years after which all remaining amounts would have to be recognized in income? If so, what would be an appropriate time limit?

6. Does the authority granted to the Secretary by section 451(c)(4)(B)(vii) allow deferral of income in an amount equal to the estimated future performance costs while requiring current recognition of estimated profits not in excess of the amounts of advance payments? If so, does the authority granted to the Secretary by section 451(c)(4)(B)(vii) permit rules to account for the time value of money for any variances in estimated costs or profits?

7. Would it be inappropriate to reduce the amount a C corporation would be permitted to defer for a given taxable year under a potential exclusion under section 451(c)(4)(B)(vii) by an amount equal to the excess of (i) distributions the C corporation made to its shareholders with respect to its stock, over (ii) the C corporation's taxable income for that taxable year?.

3. *Advance Payment Acceleration Provisions*

Section 451(c)(3) provides that the deferral method does not apply to an advance payment received by the taxpayer during a taxable year if such taxpayer ceases to exist during (or with the close of) the taxable year. In contrast, Revenue Procedure 2004-34 provides more detailed acceleration rules.

The Treasury Department and the IRS have determined that rules similar to the acceleration rules provided in Revenue Procedure 2004-34 are appropriate for the proper application of the AFS and non-AFS deferral methods. The continued use of the deferral method for an advance payment is not appropriate and should be limited in certain situations, such as when the taxpayer ceases to exist, or when their obligation regarding the advance payment is satisfied or otherwise ends. Accordingly, proposed § 1.451-8(c)(2) and (d)(6) provide rules to ensure the acceleration of an advance payment when a taxpayer either dies or ceases to exist, or when a taxpayer's obligation regarding an advance payment is satisfied or otherwise ends, except in certain circumstances. Consistent with Revenue Procedure 2004-34, the acceleration rules do not apply to a taxpayer that engages in a transaction to which section 381 applies or certain transactions in which section 351 applies in the taxable year in which an advance payment is received.

Section 451(c) does not specifically address whether the deferral method may be used when an amount is earned in the taxable year, but deferred for AFS purposes. The deferral method under section 451(c) is an exception to the requirement to include an amount in income when it is received but is not an exception to the requirement to include an amount in income when it is earned under the all events test. Accordingly, consistent with Revenue Procedure 2004-34, these proposed regulations permit deferral of advance payments received to the extent, in the year of receipt, the amount is not included in revenue in the taxpayer's AFS, and is not otherwise earned in the taxable year of receipt. The amounts not included in gross income in the year of receipt must be included in gross income in the next taxable year.

4. *Advance Payments and Financial Statement Adjustments*

Section 451(c) does not address the treatment of financial statement adjustments that cause amounts to not be included in income.

Proposed § 1.451-8(c)(3) and (d)(7) provide that a taxpayer that defers inclusion of all or a portion of an advance payment must include the remainder of the advance payment in gross income in the subsequent year, notwithstanding any write-down or adjustment for financial accounting purposes. This provision is consistent with a plain reading of section 451(c)(1)(B) and the rule in proposed § 1.451-3(j), which require that an item of income treated as deferred revenue in a taxpayer's AFS in one year and charged, in whole or part, to a capital account in a subsequent year, is included in revenue in the subsequent year.

A financial accounting adjustment may occur after certain equity acquisitions. For example, after certain equity acquisitions, the acquiring entity may write-down or adjust the target's deferred revenue in the subsequent year under purchase accounting rules. Some taxpayers have asserted that a write-down or adjustment for financial accounting purposes results in a permanent exclusion of income for federal income tax purposes. Proposed § 1.451-8(c)(3) and (d)(7) provide clarification for instances in which a taxpayer defers inclusion of an advance payment and is subsequently acquired in certain equity acquisitions. The Treasury Department and the IRS believe that financial statement write-downs or adjustments to deferred revenue should not be taken into account for federal income tax purposes when determining the proper amount to be included in income under the deferral method. This clarification ensures that a financial statement write-down or adjustment to deferred revenue does not result in a permanent exclusion of income for federal income tax purposes.

5. *Short Taxable Years and the 92-Day Rule*

Section 451(c) does not provide rules relating to the treatment of short taxable years. Proposed § 1.451-8(c)(4) and (d)(8) use the short taxable year rules of Revenue Procedure 2004-34 for the AFS and non-AFS deferral methods because a rule for short taxable years is necessary to properly implement the deferral method provided in section 451(c)(1)(B).

6. *Performance Obligations for AFS and Non-AFS Taxpayers*

Sections 451(b) and (c)(4)(D) require that taxpayers with contracts that contain multiple performance obligations must allocate transaction price, and therefore defer (or accelerate) income inclusion, consistent with the transaction price allocation used for AFS purposes. Proposed § 1.451-3(c)(3) (REG-104870-18) defines the term performance obligation to mean a promise in a contract with a customer to transfer to the customer either a good or service (or a bundle of goods or services) that is distinct, or a series of distinct goods or services that are substantially the same and that have the same pattern of transfer to the customer. Proposed § 1.451-8(b)(4) defines the term performance obligation by cross-reference to proposed § 1.451-3(c)(3) for purposes of the allocation rule provided in section 451(c)(4)(D).

Proposed § 1.451-8(b)(7) defines the term transaction price by cross-reference to proposed § 1.451-3(c)(6). Proposed § 1.451-3(c)(6) defines the term transaction price to mean the gross amount of consideration to which a taxpayer expects to be entitled for AFS purposes in exchange for transferring promised goods, services, or other property, including amounts referred to in proposed § 1.451-3(i). However, the term transaction price does not include certain items, such as amounts collected on behalf of third parties that are not otherwise income to the taxpayer, increases for consideration to which a taxpayer's entitlement is contingent on the occurrence or nonoccurrence of a future event, and reductions for amounts subject to section 461. Proposed § 1.451-3(c)(6)(ii) presumes that an amount included in the transaction price for AFS purposes is not contingent unless, upon examination of all of the facts and circumstances existing at the end of the taxable year, it can be established to the satisfaction of the Commissioner that the amount is contingent on the occurrence or nonoccurrence of a future event. Proposed § 1.451-3(c)(6)(ii) also provides that certain amounts included in transaction price for AFS purposes, however, will not be treated as contingent on the occurrence or nonoccurrence of a future event.

Comments are requested on allocation of the transaction price (i) to performance obligations that are not contractually based, (ii) for arrangements that include both income subject to section 451 and long-term contracts subject to section 460, and (iii) when the income realization event for federal income tax purposes differs from the income realization event for AFS purposes.

For non-AFS taxpayers, there is a continued need to provide an allocation method consistent with the objective criteria standard in Revenue Procedure 2004-34 because such taxpayers do not have an AFS and cannot use the transaction price allocation used for AFS purposes, as provided in section 451(b)(4). Therefore, proposed § 1.451-8(d)(5) permits a non-AFS taxpayer to allocate the revenue of multiple obligations in a single contract based on how such obligations are separately priced or on any method that may be provided in guidance published in the IRB.

7. *Accelerated Cost Offset*

Several commenters discussed the need for a regulatory exception to the existing statutory and regulatory timing rules that apply to liabilities (for example, deductions and offsets for rebates, refunds, and cost of goods sold (COGS) prior to when the liability for such items is incurred under section 461) when advance payments are required to be included in income under section 451(c) prior to the completion of the sale of goods or provision of services (accelerated cost offset). The commenters argued that not providing an accelerated cost offset in the regulations would cause a mismatch of income and expenses and result in the taxation of gross receipts.

An allowance to account for future cost of goods sold, for future estimated costs, or other cost offset is inconsistent with sections 461(h) and, 471, 263A, and the accompanying regulations. Moreover, section 13221 does not change the timing rules provided in sections 461, 471, 263A and elsewhere that apply to liabilities. Section 13221 changes the timing of income for advance payments for goods and generally codifies Revenue Procedure 2004-34. *See* H.R. Rep. No. 115-466, at 429 (2017) (Conf. Rep.). Revenue Procedure 2004-34 does not include an accelerated cost offset when amounts are included in income prior to the sale of goods or provision of services.

The Conference Report also indicates that section 13221 of the Act is "intended to override any deferral method provided by Treasury Regulation § 1.451-5 for advance payments received for goods." H.R. Rep. No. 115-466, at 429 n 880 (2017) (Conf. Rep.). Section 1.451-5 includes a deferral method that allows an accelerated cost offset when certain amounts are included in income prior to the sale of goods. *See* § 1.451-5(c). Section 451(c) does not provide a cost offset, and the Conference Report does not provide any indication that Congress intended to preserve the cost offset rules permitted under § 1.451-5. See also, Joint Committee on Taxation, General Explanation of Public Law 115-97 (JCS-1-18) at 156-157 and 164-165 (December 20, 2018). Final regulations were published in the **Federal Register** (84 FR 33691) on July 15, 2019, that withdraw § 1.451-5, consistent with the Act.

The Treasury Department and the IRS believe that Congress intentionally simplified the rules for advance payments by limiting the deferral of advance payments for taxpayers with an AFS to a prescribed statutory method that: (1) does not include an accelerated cost offset, (2) is consistent with Revenue Procedure 2004-34, and (3) overrides § 1.451-5. See H.R. Rep. No. 115-466, at 429 (2017) (Conf. Rep.). Accordingly, the Treasury Department and the IRS decline to provide an accelerated cost offset in these proposed regulations. The Treasury Department and the IRS do not agree with the contention that changes to the timing of income under section 451 without an accelerated cost offset cause a taxation of gross receipts. Section 451(c) and these proposed regulations merely change the timing of income recognition, do not preclude any associated reduction or deduction for properly incurred liabilities, and are consistent with existing statutory and regulatory timing requirements that apply to liabilities.

Several commenters proposed a cost offset mechanism for manufacturers of certain property and taxpayers with inventoriable goods in order to ensure matching of income and the associated expenses. Commenters made the following suggestions to alleviate the potential mismatch of the acceleration of income recognition with different timing rules for associated costs: (i) permitting a taxpayer that uses a percentage of completion method for AFS purposes (book PCM), but not subject to section 460, to elect to use their AFS method for tax purposes; (ii) permitting a taxpayer that uses book PCM, but not subject to section 460, to elect to apply section 460 for federal income tax purposes; (iii) expanding the recurring item exception in section 461(h)(3) to permit a taxpayer to offset the portion of the advance payment included in income for the taxable year by the cost of goods sold related to this payment if the goods are completed and shipped to the customer within 8 1/2 months of the end of the taxable year that the advance payment is included in income; or (iv) providing a cost offset for taxpayers that can demonstrate at the time of the purchase agreement that a net operating loss will remain unused for the 5-year period after the taxable year the advance payment is received.

The Treasury Department and the IRS continue to consider whether any such exceptions are an appropriate use of the Secretary's authority under section 461(h) or 460. To facilitate further consideration of such potential exceptions, detailed comments that specifically address the following issues are requested:

1. Under what authority would it be appropriate for the Secretary to permit a taxpayer to use book PCM as its tax method? When inventory is involved, what limitations could be instituted to ensure that book PCM could not be used to recover costs related to inventoriable goods prior to the time when such costs could be recovered under sections 471 and 263A? Under what specific authority would it be appropriate to permit a book PCM method to be used to recover costs related to inventoriable goods?

2. Would elective use of book PCM for tax purposes provide an appropriate cost offset? Would such a method be characterized as one that reports contract revenue according to a taxpayer's book method, while accounting for costs, including nondeductible costs, as deductions under the Code? If not, how would such a method account for costs for federal income tax purposes?

3. Rather than make book PCM elective, would it be appropriate for the definition of "unique item" for purposes of section 460 to be expanded?

4. Section 460 requires use of the look-back method to compensate for improper acceleration or deferral of income under PCM. It also requires that all contract income be reported no later than the year following contract completion. Would elective use of a PCM under section 460 without these provisions invite abuse? If so, how could such abuse be prevented?

8. Section 451(c) is a Method of Accounting

Section 451(c)(2) provides that a taxpayer may elect deferral treatment of an advance payment governed by section 451(c), and such election shall be made at such time and manner and with respect to such categories of advance payments as specified by the Secretary. Section 451(c)(2)(B) provides that the deferral method is treated as a method of accounting and the election is effective for taxable years with respect to which it is first made and for all subsequent taxable years, unless the taxpayer secures the consent of the Secretary to change to a different method of accounting.

The use of the AFS or non-AFS deferral method is the adoption of, or a change in, a method of accounting under section 446. A taxpayer may change its method of accounting to use the deferral methods only with the consent of the Commissioner as required under section 446(e) and the corresponding regulations. The Treasury Department and the IRS intend to issue future guidance that will provide the procedures by which a taxpayer may change its method of accounting to use one of the deferral methods described in these proposed regulations. However, until further guidance for the treatment of advance payments is applicable, a taxpayer may continue to rely on Revenue Procedure 2004-34, as described in Notice 2018-35.

Proposed Applicability Date

Section 7805(b)(1)(A) and (B) of the Code generally provides that no temporary, proposed, or final regulation relating to the internal revenue laws may apply to any taxable period ending before the earliest of (A) the date on which such regulation is filed with the **Federal Register**, or (B) in the case of a final regulation, the date on which a proposed or temporary regulation to which the final regulation relates was filed with the **Federal Register**.

These regulations are proposed to apply to taxable years beginning on or after the date the final regulations are published in the **Federal Register**. Until the date the Treasury decision adopting these regulations as final regulations is published in the **Federal Register**, a taxpayer may rely on these proposed regulations for taxable years beginning after December 31, 2017, provided that the taxpayer: (1) applies all the applicable rules contained in these proposed regulations, and (2) consistently applies these proposed regulations to all advance payments. See section 7805(b)(7).

Statement of Availability of IRS Documents

The IRS notice, revenue ruling, and revenue procedures cited in this preamble are published in the Internal Revenue Bulletin (or Cumulative Bulletin) and are available from the Superintendent of Documents, U.S. Government Publishing Office, Washington, DC 20402, or by visiting the IRS website at http://www.irs.gov.

Special Analysis

I. *Regulatory Planning and Review*

Executive Orders 13771, 13563, and 12866 direct agencies to assess costs and benefits of available regulatory alternatives and, if regulation is necessary, to select regulatory approaches that maximize net benefits, including potential economic, environmental, public health and safety effects, distributive impacts, and equity. Executive Order 13563 emphasizes the importance of quantifying both costs and benefits, reducing costs, harmonizing rules, and promoting flexibility. The Executive Order 13771 designation for any final rule resulting from these proposed regulations will be informed by comments received. The preliminary Executive Order 13771 designation for this proposed rule is regulatory.

The proposed regulations have been designated by the Office of Information and Regulatory Affairs (OIRA) as subject to review under Executive Order 12866 pursuant to the Memorandum of Agreement (MOA, April 11, 2018) between the Treasury Department and the Office of Management and Budget regarding review of tax regulations. The Office of Information and Regulatory Affairs has designated these proposed regulations as significant under section 1(b) of the MOA. Accordingly, OMB has reviewed these proposed regulations.

1. Background

Under section 451(a) of the Internal Revenue Code, income is "recognized" (that is, included in gross income for tax purposes) in the year in which it is received by the taxpayer, unless it is properly accounted for in a different period under the taxpayer's method of accounting. Because of this latter condition, the tax treatment of certain forms of income depends on the method of accounting a taxpayer is using. For taxpayers using the accrual method of accounting, income is generally recognized in the year in which all events have occurred that fix the right to receive that income and when the amount of income can be determined with reasonable accuracy (the "all events test"). Receipt of payment by the business satisfies the all events test. However, recognition of certain payments for goods or services not yet provided may be deferred to the year following receipt of payment, to the extent that recognition is also deferred for on the taxpayer's Applicable Financial Statement (AFS). Such payments are referred to as "advance payments."

Prior to the December 22, 2017, enactment of, "An Act to provide for reconciliation pursuant to titles II and V of the concurrent resolution on the budget for fiscal year 2018," Public Law 115-97, 131 Stat. 2054 (2017), commonly referred to as the Tax Cuts and Jobs Act (TCJA), taxpayers were generally permitted to defer the tax on these advance payments; in other words, advance payments could be recognized in a later taxable year. Section 451(c), added by the TCJA, allows accrual-method taxpayers to elect to recognize as income only a portion of such an advance payment in the taxable year in which it is received, and then recognize the remainder in the following taxable year. Section 451(c) essentially codifies the deferral method of accounting for advance payments that was permitted in Revenue Procedure 2004-34. (Joint Committee on Taxation, *General Explanation of Public Law 115-97*, (Washington, U.S. Government Publishing Office, December 2018), at 167.) New section 451(c), the subject of the proposed regulations, deals with issues around how these advance payments are defined and the timing in which they need to be recognized in the business's income tax.

2. *Need for the Proposed Regulations*

These proposed regulations provide certainty and clarity to taxpayers affected by statutory changes introduced in section 451(c). The Treasury Department and IRS have received questions and comments regarding the meaning of various provisions in section 451(c) and issues not explicitly addressed in the statute. The Treasury Department and the IRS have determined that such comments warrant the issuance of further guidance.

3. *Overview of the proposed regulations*

The proposed regulations provide guidance regarding the new section 451(c). The subsequent economic analysis covers proposed regulations to: (1) describe and clarify the deferral rules for advance payments for taxpayers without an Applicable Financial Statement (AFS); (2) provide acceleration rules for taxpayers that cease to exist; (3) clarify the treatment of financial statement adjustments for taxpayers that have deferred advance payments; (4) provide rules relating to the treatment of short taxable years for taxpayers deferring advance payments; and (5) define and clarify the treatment of performance obligations.

4. *Economic analysis*

A. Baseline

The Treasury Department and the IRS have assessed the benefits and costs of the proposed regulations relative to a no-action baseline reflecting anticipated Federal income tax-related behavior in the absence of these proposed regulations. The following largely qualitative analysis describes the anticipated economic effects of the proposed regulation relative to this baseline.

B. Summary of Economic Effects

The proposed regulations provide certainty and consistency in the application of section 451(c) by providing definitions and clarifications regarding the statute's terms and rules. An economically efficient tax system generally aims to treat income and expense derived from similar economic decisions consistently across taxpayers and across activities in order to reduce incentives for businesses to make choices based on tax rather than market incentives. In the absence of the guidance provided in these proposed regulations, the chances that different taxpayers might interpret the statute differently is exacerbated. For example, two similarly situated taxpayers might interpret the statutory provisions pertaining to the definition of advanced payments differently, with one taxpayer pursuing a project that another comparable taxpayer might decline because of a different interpretation of how the income may be treated under section 451(c). If this second taxpayer's activity is more profitable, an economic loss arises. An economic loss might also arise if all taxpayers have identical interpretations under the baseline of the tax treatment of particular income streams but are more conservative (or less conservative) regarding the interpretation than Congress intended for these income streams. In this case, guidance provides value by bringing economic decisions closer in line with the intents and purposes of the statute.

Because the proposed regulations clarify the tax treatment of certain income streams, there is the possibility that investments or other business decisions may change as a result of these regulations. The Treasury Department and the IRS have not made projections of the change in investment patterns that might arise due to the discretionary aspects of the proposed regulations. The Treasury Department and the IRS have also not made projections of any change in compliance costs arising from the proposed regulations, relative to the baseline. The Treasury Department project that changes in investment patterns and compliance costs relative to the baseline may generally be small because the proposed regulations affect a relatively small number of entities and because they largely mirror the rules of Rev. Proc. 2004-34.

The economic consequences of these proposed regulations depend in part on their interaction with other sections of the Code, including section 460, which governs when costs can be recovered under the percentage of completion method, and section 461(h), which governs when costs incurred by a taxpayer satisfy the all events test, including a requirement for economic performance, and are thereby allowed as deductions for Federal income tax purposes. The economic analysis of the final regulations under section 451(c) may address the economic effects of regulatory guidance, if any, under sections 460 and 461(h) or other sections of the Code that interact with section 451(c), that is issued between the proposed and final regulations.

The Treasury Department and the IRS project that approximately 15,000 business entities may be affected by these regulations.

The Treasury Department and the IRS solicit comments on this conclusion and particularly solicit comments that provide data, evidence, or models that would enhance the rigor by which the non-revenue economic effects might be estimated for the final regulations.

C. Economic Analysis of Specific Provisions

The Treasury Department and the IRS solicit comments on the economics of each of the items discussed subsequently and of any other items of the proposed regulations not discussed in this section. The Treasury Department and the IRS particularly solicit comments that provide data, other evidence, or models that could enhance the rigor of the process by which provisions might be developed for the final regulations.

i. Deferral Methods under section 451(c)

The statute prescribes a particular deferral method for accrual-method taxpayers that have an AFS (AFS taxpayers) but does not explicitly describe a deferral method to be used by taxpayers that do not have an AFS (non-AFS taxpayers). To remedy this gap, the proposed regulations describe and clarify that a method similar to the deferral method available to non-AFS taxpayers under Revenue Procedure 2004-34 will be available to non-AFS taxpayers.

The Treasury Department and the IRS considered and rejected a narrow interpretation of section 451(c) that would have precluded non-AFS taxpayers from using a deferral method similar to that provided in Revenue Procedure 2004-34. Section 451(c) does not explicitly prohibit the use of such a method by non-AFS taxpayers, and the Treasury Department and IRS continue to have authority under the Code to prescribe a deferral method for such taxpayers. Precluding non-AFS taxpayers from using a deferral method similar to that of AFS taxpayers would treat AFS and non-AFS taxpayers quite differently regarding business decisions they might make that are otherwise similar. Such treatment would result in a less economically efficient tax system, which generally treats similar economic decisions similarly.

The Treasury Department and the IRS solicit comments on this decision on the treatment of deferral by non-AFS taxpayers and particularly solicit comments that provide data, other evidence, or models that could enhance the rigor by which the final regulations over non-AFS deferral might be developed.

ii. Advance Payment Acceleration Provisions

If a taxpayer ceases to exist by the close of a taxable year in which an advance payment has been received and deferred, then issues may arise as to when or whether the remaining amount of the payment will be recognized as taxable income because there may not be a succeeding taxable year in which such income can be recognized.

Under the statute, if the taxpayer dies or ceases to exist by the close of the taxable year in which the advance payment was received, any remaining untaxed amounts of advance payments must be included in income in the year they were received. The proposed regulations extend this payment "acceleration" rule to situations in which a performance obligation is satisfied or otherwise ends in the taxable year of receipt or in a succeeding short taxable year, a treatment that is consistent with a similar rule in Revenue Procedure 2004-34.

The Treasury Department and the IRS considered not modifying or expanding the acceleration rule contained in section 451(c), but rejected this alternative because of the remaining amount of the remaining amount may never be picked up into income risking a permanent exclusion of the amount from taxable income. The possibility of a permanent exclusion of income provides incentives for taxpayers to structure payments in ways that avoid tax liability, thus reducing Federal tax revenue without providing an accompanying general economic benefit. The proposed regulations treat the expanded set of accelerated transactions consistently with similar types of transactions based on the timing and structure of the payments involved.

The Treasury Department and the IRS solicit comments on the proposed regulation's treatment of acceleration and particularly solicit comments that provide data, other evidence, or models that would enhance the rigor by which the treatment of acceleration might be developed for the final regulations.

iii. Advance Payments and Financial Statement Adjustments

Under the statute, if a taxpayer counts an advance payment as an item of deferred revenue, under certain conditions (for example, certain acquisitions of one corporation by another), the taxpayer may be required by its system of accounting to adjust that item on the balance sheet in a subsequent year. The item would then not be included in current earnings or AFS revenues. In this case, taxpayers might argue that they can exclude the amount deferred from taxable income because it is never "earned" nor included in revenue under their AFS. If this argument is upheld, taxpayers could convert an income "deferral" amount into an income "exemption" amount. To address this issue and avoid this possibility, the proposed regulations specify that such financial statement adjustments are to be treated as "revenue."

The Treasury Department and the IRS considered not providing clarity on the treatment of financial statement write-downs, but rejected that approach, because it would have risked an inappropriate permanent exclusion of income. The possibility of a permanent exclusion of income provides incentives for taxpayers to structure payments in ways that avoid tax liability, thus reducing Federal tax revenue without providing an accompanying general economic benefit.

The Treasury Department and the IRS solicit comments on these proposed regulations and particularly solicits comments that provide data, other evidence, and models that would enhance the rigor by which the final regulations dealing with financial statement adjustments might be developed.

iv. Short Taxable Years and the 92-Day Rule

Section 451(c) does not provide a rule relating to the treatment of short taxable years. In the absence of such a rule, it will be unclear to taxpayers how they should implement the deferral method provided in section 451(c) in the case of a short taxable year. To address this issue, the proposed regulations provide rules relating to the treatment of short taxable years for advance payments that are generally consistent with Revenue Procedure 2004-34. The Treasury Department and the IRS considered and rejected not providing short taxable year rules because such a decision would have created significant confusion among taxpayers, increased administrative costs for the IRS, and increased compliance costs for taxpayers.

The Treasury Department and the IRS solicit comments on these proposed regulations and particularly solicit comments that would provide data, other evidence, and models that would enhance the rigor by the treatment of short taxable years might be developed for the final regulations.

v. Performance Obligations for Non-AFS Taxpayers

A performance obligation is a contractual arrangement with a customer to provide a good, service or a series of goods or services that are basically the same and have a routine pattern of transfer. The statute requires that taxpayers with contracts that include multiple performance obligations to allocate the transaction price to each performance obligation in the same manner that revenue is allocated in the taxpayer's AFS. The statute does not, however, specify the allocation rules to be used by non-AFS taxpayers.

To address this issue, the proposed regulations provide allocation rules for non-AFS taxpayers consistent with a similar rule in Revenue Procedure 2004-34. That rule specifies that the transaction price be allocated in a manner that is based on payments the taxpayer regularly receives for an item or items it regularly sells or provides separately. The Treasury Department and the IRS considered not providing allocation rules for non-AFS taxpayers but rejected such an approach because it would have treated similarly situated taxpayers quite differently, and would have led to increased administrative costs for the IRS and increased compliance costs for taxpayers. While the allocation rules for AFS taxpayers and non-AFS taxpayers under the proposed regulations do differ, the chosen solution provides a rule upon which non-AFS taxpayers can rely, while minimizing the differences between AFS and non-AFS taxpayers in this regard within the constraints imposed by the statute.

The Treasury Department and the IRS solicit comments on these proposed regulations and particularly solicit comments that would provide data, other evidence, and models that would enhance the rigor by which final regulations affecting the treatment of performance obligations taxable for non-AFS taxpayers might be developed for the final regulations.

II. *Paperwork Reduction Act*

These proposed regulations do not impose any additional information collection requirements in the form of reporting, recordkeeping requirements or third-party disclosure requirements related to tax compliance. However, because the deferral methods described in proposed §§ 1.451-8(c) and (d) are methods of accounting, a portion of affected taxpayers would be required to request the consent of the Commissioner for a change in their method of accounting under section 446(e) and the accompanying regulations. The IRS expects that these taxpayers will request this consent by filing Form 3115, *Application for Change in Accounting Method (Parts I, II, IV and Schedule B)*. Filing of Form 3115 and statements attached thereto (for taxpayers who are required to do so or who elect to do so as a result of the proposed regulations) is the sole collection of information requirement imposed by the statute and the proposed regulations. See subsequent paragraphs for a description of taxpayers who would be required to change the method of accounting under the statute and the proposed regulations.

For purposes of the Paperwork Reduction Act, the reporting burden associated with the collection of information with respect to section 451(c) will be reflected in the Paperwork Reduction Act submissions for IRS Form 3115 (OMB control numbers 1545-0074 for individual filers, 1545-0123 for business filers, and 1545-2070 for all other types of filers). The IRS may provide streamlined method change procedures which could permit the filing of a statement in lieu of filing a Form 3115, or, in certain cases, no notification (see, for example, the revenue procedure accompanying these proposed regulations).

The Treasury Department and the IRS anticipate that these proposed regulations would require an accrual method taxpayer that receives an advance payment and chooses to make an election to use the deferral method described in proposed § 1.451-8(c) or (d) to file a Form 3115 to change the method of accounting to comply with these proposed regulations. See proposed § 1.451-8(e). The Treasury Department and IRS estimate that 20,000-40,000 taxpayers will be required to file a Form 3115 in order to change to the deferral method described in proposed § 1.451-8(c).[a] The Treasury Department and the IRS anticipate a certain number of accrual method taxpayers without an AFS that receive advance payments may choose to use the non-AFS deferral method described in proposed § 1.451-8(d). The Treasury Department and IRS plan to provide streamlined procedures for taxpayers to change to the methods of accounting described in proposed § 1.451-8(c) and (d). See the revenue procedure accompanying these proposed regulations.

[a] This estimate is based on data from the Compliance Data Warehouse of accrual-method taxpayers (includes C corporations, S corporations, partnerships, and sole proprietorships) with an AFS that E-filed schedule M-3 during 2012-2016. Schedule M-3 is used to report a net income (loss) reconciliation but not all taxpayers who should file an M-3 do so. The rules for filing the M-3 differ based on taxpayer status. For example, for C corporations, in general only those with assets of $10 million or more file an M-3 schedule with their Form 1120.

For a taxpayer with an AFS that uses the deferral method in proposed § 1.451-8(c), a change in the taxpayer's revenue recognition policies for financial accounting purposes requires the taxpayer to seek the consent of the Commissioner under section 446(e) to use the method for federal income tax purposes. See proposed § 1.451-8(e). It is anticipated that the reporting burden associated with the collection of information for a statement in lieu of the Form 3115 would be reflected in the Paperwork Reduction Act Submission associated with Revenue Procedure 2018-31, 2018-22 IRB 637 (or successor) (OMB control number 1545-1551). See the revenue procedure accompanying these proposed regulations.

In 2018, the IRS released and invited comment on a draft of Form 3115 in order to give members of the public the opportunity to benefit from certain specific provisions made to the Code. The IRS received no comments on the forms during the comment period. Consequently, the IRS made the forms available in January 2019 for use by the public. The IRS notes that Form 3115 applies to changes of accounting methods generally and is therefore broader than section 451(c).

The current status of the Paperwork Reduction Act submissions related to the information collections in the proposed regulations is provided in the accompanying table. The overall burden estimates provided for the OMB control numbers below are aggregate amounts that relate to the entire package of forms associated with the applicable OMB control number and will in the future include, but not isolate, the estimated burden of the tax forms that will be created or revised as a result of the information collections in the proposed regulations. These numbers are therefore unrelated to the future calculations needed to assess the burden imposed by the proposed regulations. These burdens have been reported for other regulations that rely on the same OMB control numbers to conduct information collections under the Paperwork Reduction Act, and the Treasury Department and the IRS urge readers to recognize that these numbers are duplicates and to guard against overcounting the burden that the regulations that cite these OMB control numbers impose. No burden estimates specific to the forms affected by the proposed regulations are currently available. The Treasury Department and the IRS have not estimated the burden, including that of any new information collections, related to the requirements under the proposed regulations. For the OMB control numbers discussed above, the Treasury Department and the IRS estimate PRA burdens on a taxpayer-type basis rather than a provision-specific basis. Those estimates capture both changes made by the Act and those that arise out of discretionary authority exercised in the proposed regulations (when final) and other regulations that affect the compliance burden for that form.

The Treasury Department and the IRS request comments on all aspects of information collection burdens related to the proposed regulations, including estimates for how much time it would take to comply with the paperwork burdens described above for each relevant form and ways for the IRS to minimize the paperwork burden. In addition, when available, drafts of IRS forms are posted for comment at *https://apps.irs.gov/app/picklist/list/draftTaxForms.htm*. IRS forms are available at *https://www.irs.gov/forms-instructions*. Forms will not be finalized until after they have been approved by OMB under the PRA.

Form	Type of Filer	OMB Number(s)	Status
Form 3115	All other Filers (mainly trusts and estates) (Legacy system)	1545-2070	Published in the Federal Register on 2/15/17 by IRS. Public Comment period closed on 4/17/17.

Link: https://www.federalregister.gov/documents/2017/02/15/2017-02985/proposed-information-collection-comment-request

Business (NEW Model)	1545-0123	Published in the Federal Register on 10/8/18. Public Comment period closed on 12/10/18.	
Link: https://www.federalregister.gov/documents/2018/10/09/2018-21846/proposed-collection-comment-request-for-forms-1065-1065-b-1066-1120-1120-c-1120-f-1120-h-1120-nd			
Individual (NEW Model)	1545-0074	Limited Scope submission (1040 only) on 10/11/18 at OIRA for review. Full ICR submission for all forms in 3-2019. 60-Day Federal Register notice not published yet for full collection.	
Link: https://www.reginfo.gov/public/do/PRAViewICR?ref_nbr=201808-1545-031			
Revenue Procedure 2018-31	IRS Research estimates	1545-1551	Published in the Federal Register on 8-31-16. Public Comment period closed on 9/30/16.
Link: https://www.federalregister.gov/documents/2016/08/31/2016-20993/submission-for-omb-review-comment-request			

III. Regulatory Flexibility Act

It is hereby certified that these proposed regulations will not have a significant economic impact on a substantial number of small entities within the meaning of section 601(6) of the Regulatory Flexibility Act (5 U.S.C. chapter 6).

The Treasury Department and the IRS have estimated the number of business entities that may be affected by the statute and these proposed regulations. The statute and proposed regulations affect only those business entities that use an accrual method of accounting.

Regarding the accrual method of accounting, the Treasury Department and the IRS estimate that approximately 9 percent of business entities with gross receipts of $25 million or less used an accrual method of accounting in taxable year 2016. Furthermore, section 13102 of TCJA modified section 448 to expand the number of taxpayers eligible to use the cash method. In general, C corporations and partnerships with a C corporation partner are now permitted to use the cash receipts and disbursements method of accounting if average annual gross receipts are $25 million or less (up from $5 million or less in 2016). The Treasury Department and the IRS project that in future years, the number of entities with gross receipts not greater than $25 million that will be using the accrual method will be less than 9 percent of all entities with gross receipts not greater than $25 million.

Entity	Number of Returns (Taxable Year 2016) (Thousands)		
	All Returns	Method of Accounting	
		Accrual	Cash
C Corporations			
Gross Receipts > $25 mil.	30	28	2
Gross Receipts <= $25 mil.	1,567	700	867
Total	1,597	728	869
S Corporations			
Gross Receipts > $25 mil.	41	34	7
Gross Receipts <= $25 mil.	4,551	1,140	3,411
Total	4,592	1,174	3,418
Partnerships			
Gross Receipts > $25 mil.	20	17	3
Gross Receipts <= $25 mil.	3,743	860	2,883
Total	3,763	877	2,886
Sole Proprietors and LLCs			
Gross Receipts > $25 mil.	1	1	0
Gross Receipts <= $25 mil.	25,524	358	25,166
Total	25,525	359	25,166
All Entities			
Gross Receipts > $25 mil.	92	80	12
Gross Receipts <= $25 mil.	35,385	3,058	32,327
Total	35,477	3,138	32,339

Source: Statistics of Income data. Cash accounting includes cash, other, and unknown.

Regarding the applicable financial statement, the Treasury Department and the IRS estimate that 235,000 – 250,000 entities with gross receipts of $25 million or less had an audited income statement in taxable year 2016. This is an upper bound estimate of entities that may be affected by these proposed regulations because small entities are less likely to have a financial statement that falls within the definition of AFS in proposed §1.451-3(c)(1) (which generally refers to certified audited financial statements in accordance with GAAP or IFRS). An AFS is generally a financial statement that is certified as being prepared in accordance with GAAP or IFRS that is issued for credit purposes, reporting to shareholders, or other non-tax purpose. The smaller the entity, the less likely that it will engage a CPA firm to audit their financial statements. An AFS does not include financial statements that have only been compiled or reviewed by a CPA firm, which are more affordable for small entities, as these types of statements are not certified as prepared in accordance with GAAP or IFRS.

Affected taxpayers would be required to file Form 3115. As an indicator of whether a taxpayer is likely to have to file a Form 3115, the Treasury Department and the IRS estimated the number of businesses that used the accrual method of accounting, had a financial statement, and indicated they had unearned or deferred income. Approximately 15,000 businesses with gross receipts of $25 million or less fit this category. This is an upper bound estimate of the number of taxpayers relying of Revenue Procedure 2004-34 that will need to file a Form 3115 since some reporting of unearned or deferred income may just have deferral for financial reporting and not tax reporting reasons.

These proposed rules will not have a significant economic impact on small entities affected because the costs to comply with these proposed regulations are not significant. An entity is required to file a Form 3115 (Parts I, II, IV and Schedule B) to change its method of accounting in order to use the deferral method described in proposed §1.451-8(c) or (d). The Treasury Department and IRS plan to provide streamlined procedures for taxpayers to change to the methods of accounting described in proposed §1.451-8(c)1 and (d). See the revenue procedure accompanying these proposed regulations. As noted in this revenue procedure, the estimated cumulative annual reporting and/or recordkeeping burden for the statutory method changes described under OMB control number 1545-1551, before publication of the revenue procedure, is 27,336 respondents, and a total annual reporting and/or recordkeeping burden of 30,580 hours. The estimated annual burden per respondent/recordkeeper under OMB control number 1545-1551 before publication of this revenue procedure varies from 1/6 hour to 8^1/2 hours, depending on individual circumstances, with an estimated average of 1^1/4 hours. The estimated cumulative annual reporting and/or recordkeeping burden for the method changes described under OMB control number 1545-1551 after that revenue procedure is accounted for is 27,346 respondents, and a total annual reporting and/or recordkeeping burden is 31,479 hours, leaving the average reporting and recordkeeping burden essentially unchanged. These burdens are essentially unaffected by these proposed regulations.

Notwithstanding this certification that the proposed rule would not have a significant economic impact on a substantial number of small entities, the Treasury Department and the IRS invite comments from the public about the impact of this proposed rule on small entities.

Pursuant to section 7805(f), these regulations will be submitted to the Chief Counsel for Advocacy of the Small Business Administration for comment on their impact on small business.

IV. *Unfunded Mandates Reform Act*

Section 202 of the Unfunded Mandates Reform Act of 1995 requires that agencies assess anticipated costs and benefits and take certain other actions before issuing a final rule that includes any Federal mandate that may result in expenditures in any one year by a state, local, or tribal government, in the aggregate, or by the private sector, of $100 million in 1995 dollars, updated annually for inflation. In 2018, that threshold is approximately $150 million. This rule does not include any Federal mandate that may result in expenditures by state, local, or tribal governments, or by the private sector in excess of that threshold.

V. *Executive Order 13132: Federalism*

Executive Order 13132 (entitled "Federalism") prohibits an agency from publishing any rule that has federalism implications if the rule either imposes substantial, direct compliance costs on state and local governments, and is not required by statute, or preempts state law, unless the agency meets the consultation and funding requirements of section 6 of the Executive Order. This rule does not have federalism implications and does not impose substantial direct compliance costs on state and local governments or preempt state law within the meaning of the Executive Order.

Comments and Requests for a Public Hearing

Before these proposed regulations are adopted as final regulations, consideration will be given to any comments that are submitted timely to the IRS as prescribed in this preamble under the "**ADDRESSES**" heading. The Treasury Department and the IRS request comments on all aspects of the proposed regulations. All comments will be available at *http://www.regulations.gov* or upon request. A public hearing will be scheduled if requested in writing by any person that timely submits written comments. If a public hearing is scheduled, notice of the date, time, and place for the public hearing will be published in the **Federal Register**.

Effect on Other Documents

When finalized, these proposed regulations will obsolete Revenue Procedure 2004-34, Revenue Procedure 2011-18, Revenue Procedure 2013-29 and Notice 2018-35.

Drafting Information

The principal author of these proposed regulations is Peter E. Ford, IRS Office of the Associate Chief Counsel (Income Tax and Accounting). However, other personnel from the Treasury Department and the IRS participated in their development.

[¶ 49,810] **Proposed Amendments of Regulations (REG-104870-18)**, published in the Federal Register on September 9, 2019 (corrected 10/9/2019).

[Code Secs. 446, 451 and 1275]

Accrual method of accounting: Income inclusion: All events test: Applicable financial statement.—Reg. §1.451-3 and amendments of Reg. §§1.446-1, 1.446-2, 1.451-1 and 1.1275-2, regarding the timing of income inclusion under section 451 of the Internal Revenue Code (Code), are proposed.

AGENCY: Internal Revenue Service (IRS), Treasury.

ACTION: Notice of proposed rulemaking.

SUMMARY: This document contains proposed regulations regarding the timing of income inclusion under section 451 of the Internal Revenue Code (Code). The proposed regulations reflect changes made by the Tax Cuts and Jobs Act. These proposed regulations affect taxpayers that use an accrual method of accounting and have an applicable financial statement.

DATES: Written or electronic comments and requests for a public hearing must be received by November 8, 2019.

ADDRESSES: Send submissions to Internal Revenue Service, CC:PA:LPD:PR (REG-104870-18), Room 5205, P.O. Box 7604, Ben Franklin Station, Washington, DC 20044. Submissions may be hand delivered Monday through Friday between the hours of 8 a.m. and 4 p.m. to Courier's Desk, Internal Revenue Service, CC:PA:LPD:PR (REG-104870-18), 1111 Constitution Avenue, NW, Washington, DC 20224. Alternatively, persons may submit comments electronically via the Federal eRulemaking Portal at http://www.regulations.gov (IRS REG-104870-18). FOR FURTHER INFORMATION CONTACT: Concerning §§1.446-2, 1.451-3(d), 1.451-3(i), 1.1275-2(l), and any other provisions within the jurisdiction of the Associate Chief Counsel (Financial Institutions and Products), Charles Culmer, (202) 317-4528; concerning the rest of the proposed regulations, Charles Gorham, (202) 317-5091; concerning submissions of comments and requests for a public hearing, Regina L. Johnson, (202) 317-6091 (not toll-free numbers).

SUPPLEMENTARY INFORMATION:

Background

This document contains proposed amendments to 26 CFR part 1 under section 451(b). On December 22, 2017, section 451(b) was amended by section 13221 of the Tax Cuts and Jobs Act, Public Law No. 115-97 (131 Stat. 2054) (the Act) to provide that, for a taxpayer using an accrual method of accounting, the all events test with respect to any item of gross income (or portion thereof) is not treated as met any later than when the item (or portion thereof) is included in revenue for financial accounting purposes on an applicable financial statement (AFS) or other financial statement specified by the Secretary. The amendments made to section 451(b) do not change the time at which income subject to the all events test is taken into income for accrual method taxpayers without an AFS or other specified financial statement. Unless otherwise indicated, all references to section 451(b) hereinafter are references to section 451(b), as amended by the Act.

In general, section 451 provides that the amount of any item of gross income is included in gross income for the taxable year in which it is received by the taxpayer, unless, under the method of accounting used in computing taxable income, the amount is to be properly accounted for as of a different period. Under §1.451-1, accrual method taxpayers generally include items of income in gross income in the taxable year when all the events occur that fix the right to receive the income and the amount of the income can be determined with reasonable accuracy (the all events test). All the events that fix the right to receive income occur when (1) the required performance takes place, (2) payment is due, or (3) payment is made, whichever happens first. Revenue Ruling 2003-10 (2003-1 CB 288); Revenue Ruling 84-31 (1984-1 CB 127); Revenue Ruling 80-308 (1980-2 CB 162).

On April 12, 2018, the Treasury Department and the IRS issued Notice 2018-35 (2018-18 IRB 520) requesting, in part, comments on future guidance under section 451(b). The record of public comments received in response to Notice 2018-35 may be requested by sending an email to Notice.comments@irscounsel.treas.gov. This document provides guidance on the application of section 451(b) taking into account comments that were received regarding section 451(b). The application of section 451(c) is addressed in separate guidance published in the same issue of the **Federal Register** as these proposed regulations.

Explanation of Provisions

The proposed regulations describe and clarify the statutory requirements of section 451(b) by providing new §1.451-3.

1. *Applicability of Section 451(b)(1)*

Section 451(b)(1) generally provides that, for an accrual method taxpayer with an AFS or other specified financial statement, the all events test with respect to any item of gross income, or portion thereof, is not treated as met any later than when such item, or portion thereof, has been taken into account as revenue in an AFS or other specified financial statement (the AFS income inclusion rule). The AFS income inclusion rule generally increases financial accounting and tax accounting conformity. On May 28, 2014, the Financial Accounting Standards Board (FASB) and the International Accounting Standards Board (IASB) jointly announced new financial accounting standards for revenue recognition, titled "Revenue from Contracts with Customers (Topic 606)." See ASC Topic 606 and IASB International Financial Reporting Standard (IFRS) 15 (New Standards). Under the New Standards, items of income may be included as revenue in an AFS earlier than they would have been included in income under the all events test prior to the Act.

A. Taxpayers Subject to the AFS Income Inclusion Rule

The proposed regulations clarify how the AFS income inclusion rule applies to accrual method taxpayers with an AFS. Some taxpayers use an accrual method of accounting for all applicable items of income (overall accrual method taxpayers) and others use an accrual method of accounting for only some items of income. Both types of taxpayers (collectively, accrual method taxpayers) compute taxable income, at least in part, under an accrual method. Accordingly, proposed §1.451-3(b) provides that the AFS income inclusion rule generally applies to accrual method taxpayers with an AFS when the timing of income inclusion for one or more items of income is determined using the all events test.

The proposed regulations do not include special rules regarding the applicability of the AFS income inclusion rule to foreign persons. The Treasury Department and the IRS are aware that applying the AFS income inclusion rule to a controlled foreign corporation (CFC) may create mismatches between the CFC's taxable income for U.S. Federal and foreign tax purposes. As a result, certain taxpayers may lose the ability to credit foreign taxes imposed on a CFC's income, particularly where such taxes relate to amounts includible in gross income under section 951A and are therefore ineligible to be carried back or forward under section 904(c). Comments are requested regarding whether special rules are needed to address the applicability of the AFS income inclusion rule to foreign persons, including whether and how the rules for determining the taxable income of a CFC can be adjusted to better align the U.S. Federal and foreign income tax bases.

B. Exceptions to the AFS Income Inclusion Rule

Proposed §1.451-3(d) clarifies that the AFS income inclusion rule applies only to taxpayers that have one or more AFS covering the entire taxable year. This approach is consistent with the exception in section 451(b)(1)(B)(i), which provides that the AFS income inclusion rule does not apply to taxpayers without an AFS for a taxable year. In addition, some accrual method taxpayers may have an AFS in one taxable year and no AFS in another taxable year. To address this situation, the proposed regulations provide that the AFS income inclusion rule applies on a year-by-year basis and, therefore, an accrual method taxpayer with an AFS in one taxable year that does not have an AFS in another taxable year must apply the AFS income inclusion rule in the taxable year that it has an AFS, and does not apply the rule in the taxable year in which it does not have an AFS.

Consistent with section 451(b)(1)(B)(ii), proposed §1.451-3(d) also provides that the AFS income inclusion rule does not apply to items of income in connection with a mortgage servicing contract. A letter addressed to the Treasury Department indicated that it is unclear whether this exclusion can be applied to income relating to interest rate lock commitments (IRLCs) entered into by mortgage lenders. The proposed regulations do not address this issue because section 475 generally would require mortgage lenders to include income relating to IRLCs in taxable income in accordance with the mark-to-market method of accounting. As a result, a mortgage lender generally would not apply section 451(b) to determine when income relating to IRLCs is includible in income.

C. Transactions Treated Differently for Federal Income Tax and AFS Purposes

Except as provided in proposed §1.451-3(e), proposed §1.451-3(e) clarifies that the AFS income inclusion rule does not change the treatment of a transaction for Federal income tax purposes. The treatment of a transaction or event in a taxable year may be different for Federal income tax and AFS purposes. For example, a rental agreement that is treated as a lease for Federal income tax purposes may be treated as a sale or financing for AFS purposes, or vice versa. Similarly, a transaction that is deemed to occur (for example, under a mark-to-market method) for AFS purposes may not be deemed to occur for Federal income tax purposes. The AFS income inclusion rule generally was not intended to require taxpayers to recharacterize a transaction for Federal income tax purposes to conform to the characterization of the transaction in the taxpayer's AFS. As stated in the Conference Report, "The provision does not revise the rules associated with when an item is realized for Federal income tax purposes and, accordingly, does not require the recognition of income in situations where the Federal income tax realization event has not yet occurred." H.R. Rep. No. 115-466, at 428 fn. 872 (2017) (Conf. Rep.).

However, as also stated in the Conference Report, the AFS income inclusion rule was intended to include unbilled receivables for partially performed services:

"Under the provision, an accrual method taxpayer with an applicable financial statement will include an item in income under section 451 upon the earlier of when the all events test is met or when the taxpayer includes such item in revenue in an applicable financial statement. For example, under the provision, any unbilled receivables for partially performed services must be recognized to the extent the amounts are taken into income for financial statement purposes."

H.R. Rep. No. 115-466, at 428 fn. 874 (2017) (Conf. Rep.). Commenters suggested that the intent to include unbilled receivables conflicts with the intent to not change the treatment of a transaction to match the taxpayer's AFS treatment. The Treasury Department and the IRS do not agree. In applying the AFS income inclusion rule to unbilled receivables, a taxpayer is not changing the treatment of the transaction when it includes in income amounts included in its AFS. Moreover, these proposed regulations also apply to unbilled receivables for the sale of goods because there is no distinction in section 451(b) between unbilled receivables for services and unbilled receivables for the sale of goods, and service providers and sellers of goods that are including unbilled receivables in revenue for AFS purposes should be treated similarly for Federal income tax purposes under section 451(b). Accordingly, the proposed regulations provide that the AFS inclusion rule applies to unbilled receivables included in revenue for AFS purposes related to both services and goods.

Commenters raised concerns about the interaction between sections 61 and 461 with the AFS income inclusion rule. For AFS purposes, taxpayers may be required to include variable consideration when determining the transaction price of a contract. Under the New Standards, variable consideration includes items such as discounts, rebates, refunds, credits, price concessions, incentives, performance bonuses, penalties, and other similar items. Variable consideration may also include promised consideration that taxpayers are not yet entitled to under the contract because it is contingent on the occurrence or nonoccurrence of a future event. For Federal income tax purposes, these items of variable consideration may be contingent future income under section 61 or liabilities subject to section 461. Section 451(b) could be read to accelerate the timing of contingent future income and liabilities to match their inclusion in revenue for AFS purposes. However, section 451(b) was intended to change only the timing of income to ensure that those items of income are not included later than when they are included for AFS purposes. See H.R. Rep. No. 115-466, at 428 fn. 874 (2017) (Conf. Rep.) and Joint Committee on Taxation, General Explanation of Public Law 115-97 (JCS-1-18) at 166 (Dec. 20, 2018). Accordingly, proposed § 1.451-3(c)(6) provides that the transaction price that is used to determine whether an amount has been included in revenue does not include items to which a taxpayer's entitlement is contingent on the occurrence or nonoccurrence of a future event, reductions for amounts subject to section 461 (including allowances, adjustments, rebates, chargebacks, refunds, rewards, and amounts included in the cost of goods sold), and amounts collected for third parties. However, in order to reduce compliance burden and prevent abuse and undue administrative burden, proposed § 1.451-3(c)(6) presumes that an amount included in the transaction price for AFS purposes is not contingent future income unless, upon examination of all of the facts and circumstances existing at the end of the taxable year, it can be established to the satisfaction of the Commissioner that the amount is contingent on the occurrence or nonoccurrence of a future event.

In addition, section 451(b) was intended to accelerate income inclusion when (i) the taxpayer's customer controls the asset that is created or enhanced, or (ii) the taxpayer has a right to partial payment, even when a contract requires delivery, acceptance, and title transfer before a taxpayer can bill its customer. See Examples 2 and 4 of the Joint Committee on Taxation, General Explanation of Public Law 115-97 (JCS-1-18) at 162-163 (Dec. 20, 2018). Accordingly, proposed § 1.451-3(c)(6)(ii) provides that an amount included in the transaction price for AFS purposes may not be treated as contingent on the occurrence or nonoccurrence of a future event if the taxpayer has been paid or has an equitable, contractual, or other right to partial payment for performance completed to date. Additionally, proposed § 1.451-3(c)(6)(iii) provides that transaction price may not be reduced for amounts subject to section 461, including, in the case of credit card transactions, reward amounts.

Comments are requested on the interaction among sections 61, 461, and 451(b), and specific situations in which future contingent income and liabilities might be included in revenue for AFS purposes. Comments are requested, for example, on the applicability of the proposed rules to escalating rental agreements not subject to section 467, where amounts included in revenue in an AFS as rent for one year of a multi-year rental agreement exceed actual rent received for that year. Specifically, does the excess of the amount included in revenue as rent over the amount of actual rent in a particular year represent a contingency or merely an allocation of the overall transaction price? Comments are requested on the extent to which certain contract terms might affect the result. Comments also are requested on the proposed presumption that the AFS income inclusion rule should apply when an item is included in revenue in an AFS and what a taxpayer should be required to demonstrate in order to successfully rebut the presumption. Finally, comments are requested on how reassessments of variable consideration after the taxable year of the commencement of the contract should be treated for Federal income tax purposes.

D. Interaction with Exclusion Provisions and Effect on Non-Recognition Transactions

Commenters noted that the AFS income inclusion rule may appear to overturn numerous exclusion provisions and adversely affect the treatment of non-recognition transactions in the Code. For example, the AFS income inclusion rule could be read to apply to a transaction that is treated as a sale of property with profit or loss for AFS purposes but that is treated as a reorganization under section 368 for Federal income tax purposes. The proposed regulations clarify that the AFS income inclusion rule does not change the applicability of any exclusion provision, or the treatment of nonrecognition transactions, in the Code, the Income Tax Regulations, or other guidance published in the Internal Revenue Bulletin, consistent with Congressional intent that the provision does not revise the rules associated with the time at which an item is realized for Federal income tax purposes. H.R. Rep. No. 115-466, at 428 fn. 872 (2017) (Conf. Rep.) and Joint Committee on Taxation, General Explanation of Public Law 115-97 (JCS-1-18) at 166 (Dec. 20, 2018).

E. Special Methods of Accounting

Section 451(b)(2) provides that the AFS income inclusion rule does not apply to any item of gross income for which the taxpayer uses a special method of accounting provided under any provision of Chapter 1, other than any provision of part V of subchapter P. Commenters raised questions about the interaction between the AFS income inclusion rule and special methods of accounting. In response, proposed § 1.451-3(b) amplifies the meaning of the term "special method of accounting" and, except as provided in proposed § 1.451-3(b), provides that the AFS income inclusion rule does not apply to any item of income, or portion of an item of income, when the timing of income inclusion is determined under a required or permitted special method of accounting used for Federal income tax purposes. The proposed regulations also clarify that when a taxpayer uses a special method of accounting, the special method of accounting determines the timing of the income inclusion. The proposed regulations provide a non-exclusive list of examples of special methods of accounting. In addition, the proposed regulations make clear that because the AFS income inclusion rule affects the time at which the all events test is met, the rule applies only to items of income that are subject to the all events test. For a discussion of special methods of accounting under the provisions of part V of subchapter P (relating to income from certain debt instruments), see section 7 of this preamble.

2. Application of the AFS Income Inclusion Rule to Multi-year Contracts

Section 451(b) does not address how to apply the AFS income inclusion rule and all events test to a multi-year contract. Proposed § 1.451-3(k) provides that a taxpayer with a multi-year contract applies the all events test by applying a cumulative approach reflecting amounts previously included under section 451 rather than an annualized approach.

An annualized approach would look at payments received in each taxable year in isolation and compare the amounts included in the taxpayer's AFS and under the all events test to determine whether an amount should be included for Federal income tax purposes. This approach would generally result in an overall acceleration of income relative to income included in revenue for AFS purposes, could cause amounts to be included for Federal income tax purposes earlier than under a contract's terms, and could result in double counting of income. Section 451(b)(1) does not require this treatment.

A cumulative approach better reflects the economic reality of a multi-year transaction. Accordingly, the proposed regulations require taxpayers to take into account the cumulative amounts previously included in prior taxable years in determining a given contract year's income inclusions under section 451(b)(1). Comments are requested regarding the treatment of multi-year contracts under the AFS income inclusion rule.

3. *Applicable Financial Statement (AFS)*

The proposed regulations describe and clarify the definition of AFS under section 451(b)(3). Section 451(b)(3) generally defines AFS to mean financial statements prepared according to generally accepted accounting principles (GAAP financial statements), certain financial statements prepared according to international financial reporting standards (IFRS financial statements), and financial statements filed with certain regulatory or government bodies. Section 451(b)(1)(A)(ii) provides the Secretary with authority to specify other financial statements for purposes of section 451(b)(1).

The list of financial statements qualifying as an AFS under section 451(b)(3) is similar, but not identical, to the list of financial statements in Revenue Procedure 2004-34 (2004-1 CB 991). The general priority for identifying the AFS in section 451(b)(3)(A) through (C) is similar to the priority provided in Revenue Procedure 2004-34. Certain financial statements that have traditionally been treated as AFS under Revenue Procedure 2004-34, such as IFRS financial statements used for (1) credit purposes, (2) reporting to shareholders, partners, or other proprietors or to beneficiaries, and (3) any other substantial nontax purposes, are not expressly included in section 451(b)(3). However, the legislative history indicates that Congress intended for Revenue Procedure 2004-34 to be followed. See H.R. Rep. No. 115-466, at 429 (2017) (Conf. Rep.). Accordingly, proposed § 1.451-3(c)(1) is generally consistent with the list of AFS from Revenue Procedure 2004-34.

The proposed regulations also clarify the financial statements filed with certain regulatory or government bodies that qualify as an AFS under section 451(b)(3)(C), which is similar to section 4.06(3) of Revenue Procedure 2004-34. The proposed regulations clarify that financial statements that are filed with a state government or state agency, or a self-regulatory organization, also qualify as an AFS under section 451(b)(3)(C). For example, the Financial Industry Regulatory Authority and state agencies that regulate insurance companies or public utilities are agencies requiring reports that qualify as an AFS.

Proposed § 1.451-3(h) addresses various issues relating to how financial results are reported for certain taxpayers. These proposed regulations propose rules consistent with the rules provided in § 1.56-1 because Congress indicated a desire for rules similar to those found in Revenue Procedure 2004-34 and the rules in Revenue Procedure 2004-34 follow certain rules in § 1.56-1. See IRS Announcement 2004-48 (2004-22 IRB 998).

Section 451(b)(5) and proposed § 1.451-3(h)(1), (2), and (3) provide that, for purposes of the general rule in section 451(b)(1), if the financial results of a taxpayer are reported on the AFS, as defined in section 451(b)(3), for a group of entities, such statement shall be treated as the AFS of the taxpayer. When a consolidated or combined AFS or other financial statement lists items separately for each member taxpayer, the amount of revenue attributable to a particular taxpayer is determined based on its respective separately stated item. If the amounts are aggregated, however, the taxpayer must rely on the source documents that were used to create the group's AFS to determine its percentage of each aggregated item reported on the consolidated or combined AFS. The source documents should be used to determine the taxpayer's respective share of revenue on the AFS, so as to properly reflect the correct amount of gross income under section 451(b).

Proposed § 1.451-3(h)(4) provides guidance for taxpayers with a financial reporting period that is different than the taxpayer's taxable year. The proposed regulations provide that the taxpayer must use one of three permissible methods in order to determine whether an item of income has been included in revenue on an AFS. Under one method a taxpayer uses the accounting principles used to create its AFS to determine the items of income to be reported in revenue as if its financial reporting period coincided with its taxable year. Under the second method a taxpayer makes a reasonable estimate of revenue for the pro rata portion of the taxable year for which the financial statement year and taxable year do not align. Under the third method, if a taxpayer's financial accounting year ends five or more months after the end of its taxable year, the taxpayer computes revenue based on the revenue reported on the AFS for the financial accounting year ending within its taxable year.

Proposed § 1.451-3(h)(5) provides guidance on a restatement of a taxpayer's financial statements. The rules generally provide that the taxpayer must determine the reason for the restatement of the AFS. For example, if a taxpayer restates revenue on an AFS and such restatement changes the time at which an item of income or a portion thereof is taken into account as revenue on the AFS, the change constitutes a change in method of accounting under section 446. This rule is consistent with current practice regarding the determination of a change in method of accounting.

The regulations under section 6001 require a taxpayer to keep books and records sufficient to establish the amount of gross income, deductions, credits, or other matters required to be shown in an income tax return, which includes the identification of items includible in gross income under section 451. This requirement includes any books and records sufficient to establish a taxpayer's calculation of income when its financial results are included in an AFS of a group of entities.

4. *Revenue in an AFS*

Proposed § 1.451-3(c)(4) defines the term revenue for purposes of section 451(b)(1) broadly to include all items of income under section 61 (gains, profits, and income for Federal income tax purposes). This definition is consistent with the current application of the all events test under § 1.451-1(a) and ensures greater financial accounting and tax accounting conformity.

One commenter discussed the effect of the New Standards on sections 451(b) and (c). The commenter noted that, under the New Standards, certain revenue may be included earlier than under section 451 prior to amendment by the Act. The commenter also noted that an amount booked to retained earnings should be treated as revenue for purposes of section 451(b) even though that amount may not be shown as book revenue for financial accounting purposes. A narrow reading of the term revenue could result in items of income that are taken into account on an AFS and that otherwise would be required to be included in gross income escaping section 451(b) altogether. For example, taxpayers may include items, or portions of items, in other comprehensive income on an AFS that are excluded from the revenue line(s) on the AFS. Accordingly, a broad reading of revenue ensures that the correct amount of income that is taken into account in an AFS is subject to section 451(b).

Multiple commenters proposed allowing a cost offset when income is included under the AFS income inclusion rule. For example, one commenter suggested that, in determining the amount of income to include under section 451(b), taxpayers selling goods should reduce AFS revenue by the cost of goods sold associated with a sale that does not presently reduce AFS revenue. The commenter acknowledged that costs are not taken into account for Federal income tax purposes until the all events test is satisfied, which includes the economic performance rules under section 461. Because of the resulting inconsistency with sections 461 and 471, these regulations do not follow the commenter's suggestion that a cost offset or cost of goods sold reduction should apply without regard to the economic performance rules of section 461 and inventory accounting rules of section 471.

Congress has addressed various cost recovery mechanisms in the past. In 1955, Congress repealed the reserve method for estimated expenses under section 462 of the Code. See An Act to Repeal Sections 452 and 462 of the Internal Revenue Code of 1954, Public Law No. 84-74, section 1(b) (1955). Section 462 of the Code was a companion to section 452, which allowed taxpayers to report certain types of prepaid income over time. In the Senate Report discussing the repeal of sections 452 and 462, Congress noted that "the problem presented by section 462 is that of the timing of deductions when a taxpayer changes accounting methods." S. Rep. 84-372, at 4 (1955). The Senate noted that taxpayers would be entitled to the deductions even without section 462. In addition, section 462 increased the possibility of distortions of income because expenses were being deducted when the amount had not yet been incurred.

Thirty years later, Congress repealed the use of the reserve method for determining losses from bad debts under section 166 in the Tax Reform Act of 1986. In repealing the reserve method, Congress noted that this method was inconsistent with the rules for other deductions under the all events test and could result in deductions being allowed for Federal income tax purposes for losses that may never occur. S. Rep. No. 99-313, at 155 (1986). Moreover, "if a deduction is allowed prior to the taxable year in which the loss occurs, the value of the deduction to the taxpayer will be overstated." S. Rep. No. 99-313, at 155 (1986).

These proposed regulations do not allow a cost offset provision because similar potential distortions of income could result. An allowance to account for future cost of goods sold, for future estimated costs, or other cost offsets also is inconsistent with sections 461 (in particular section 461(h)), 263A, and 471, and the regulations under those sections. In addition, these proposed regulations do not allow a cost offset provision because there is nothing in the statute or legislative history that indicates that in amending section 451 Congress intended to change sections 461, 263A or 471, and the regulations under those sections. See also, General Explanation of Public Law 115-97 (JCS-1-18) at 150-151, and 164-165 (Dec. 20, 2018).

Nevertheless, the Treasury Department and the IRS continue to consider whether any exceptions are an appropriate use of the Secretary's authority under section 461(h) or 460. To facilitate further consideration of any potential exceptions, detailed comments that specifically address the following issues are requested:

1. Under what authority would it be appropriate for the Secretary to permit a taxpayer to use a book percentage-of-completion method (PCM) as its tax method? When inventory is involved, what limitations could be instituted to ensure that book PCM could not be used to recover costs related to inventoriable goods prior to the time when such costs could be recovered under sections 471 and 263A? Under what specific authority would it be appropriate to permit a book PCM method to be used to recover costs related to inventoriable goods?

2. Would elective use of book PCM for tax purposes provide an appropriate cost offset? Would such a method be characterized as one that reports contract revenue according to a taxpayer's book method, while accounting for costs, including nondeductible costs, as deductions under the Code? If not, how would such a method account for costs for Federal income tax purposes?

3. Rather than make book PCM elective, would it be appropriate for the definition of "unique item" for purposes of section 460 to be expanded?

4. Section 460 requires use of the look-back method to compensate for improper acceleration or deferral of income under PCM. It also requires that all contract income be reported no later than the year following contract completion. Would elective use of a PCM under section 460 without these provisions invite abuse? If so, how could such abuse be prevented?

5. *Allocation of Transaction Price*

The proposed regulations describe and clarify the allocation of transaction price under section 451(b)(4). Section 451(b)(4) provides that, in the case of a contract with multiple performance obligations, the allocation of the transaction price to each performance obligation shall be equal to the amount allocated to each performance obligation for purposes of including such item in revenue in the AFS of the taxpayer. Consistent with the definition of performance obligation found in the New Standards, proposed § 1.451-3(c)(3) defines "performance obligation" to mean a promise in a contract with a customer to transfer to the customer either a good or service (or a bundle of goods or services) that is distinct, or a series of distinct goods or services that are substantially the same and that have the same pattern of transfer to the customer. See ASC Topic 606 and IFRS 15.

Comments are requested on allocation of the transaction price (i) to performance obligations that are not contractually based, (ii) for arrangements that include both income subject to section 451 and long-term contracts subject to section 460, and (iii) when the income realization event for Federal income tax purposes differs from the income realization event for AFS purposes.

6. *Taxpayers Including Income Over Time for AFS Purposes*

Commenters proposed allowing taxpayers that include items of income as revenue in an AFS over a period of time under the New Standards (AFS over-time method) to follow that method for Federal income tax purposes. Allowing taxpayers to follow their AFS over-time method for Federal income tax purposes would potentially defer income beyond what is permitted under section 451(b), section 451(c), and the all events test. The AFS income inclusion rule operates only to accelerate income inclusion; the AFS income inclusion rule can never cause income inclusion to occur later than when the all events test is satisfied. Allowing taxpayers to follow their AFS over-time method for Federal income tax purposes may also affect the treatment of costs in a manner that is inconsistent with sections 461 and 471. However, the Treasury Department and the IRS continue to study the commenters' proposal and request additional comments on this issue. Specifically, additional comments are requested regarding: the size of taxpayers likely to be affected; the industries likely to be affected; the number of taxpayers likely to be affected; the compliance burden and administrative complexity likely to be avoided; and the degree to which an over-time method under the New Standards accelerates or defers income relative to the all events test and the AFS income inclusion rule.

7. *Rules for Certain Debt Instruments*

A. Credit Card Fees and Other Fees

The Treasury Department and the IRS have treated certain credit card fees associated with pools of credit card receivables as creating or increasing original issue discount (OID) on those pools. See Revenue Procedure 2004-33 (2004-1 CB 989) (the IRS will not challenge the treatment of late fees as creating or increasing OID); Revenue Procedure 2005-47 (2005-2 CB 269) (the IRS will not challenge the treatment of cash advance fees as creating or increasing OID); Revenue Procedure 2013-26 (2013-22 IRB 1160) (safe harbor method of accounting for OID on a pool of credit card receivables for purposes of section 1272(a)(6)); and Chief Counsel Notice CC-2010-018 (Sept. 27, 2010) (as a result of the Tax Court's decision in *Capital One Financial Corp. and Subsidiaries v. Commissioner*, 133 T.C. 136 (2009), the IRS will no longer challenge or litigate the issue of whether interchange fee income creates or increases OID).

With the enactment of section 451(b), however, Congress expressed its intention to overturn the tax treatment of those credit card fees as OID, including the use of the OID timing rules, and subject them to the all events test. The Conference Report to the Act states, "[section 451(b)] directs accrual method taxpayers with an applicable financial statement to apply the income recognition rules under section 451 before applying the special rules under part V of subchapter P . . . " (which includes the OID rules). H.R. Rep. No. 115-466, at 428 (2017) (Conf. Rep.). In particular, the legislative history describes the treatment of credit card late fees, credit card cash advance fees, and interchange fees as creating or increasing OID for Federal tax purposes and lists these fees as examples of amounts to which section 451(b), as amended, would apply. Id. at 427, 429. These three credit card fees are not generally treated as discount for AFS purposes.

Congress clearly expressed its intention to overturn the tax treatment of credit card late fees, cash advance fees, and interchange fees (specified credit card fees) and to subject these fees to the all events test as modified by section 451(b). Id. at 429. The legislative history quoted in the preceding paragraph further suggests that Congress intended that other fees associated with a lending transaction that might otherwise be accounted for in calculating OID are to be subjected to the AFS income inclusion rule before the application of the OID rules. Based on the legislative history, however, taxpayers have stated that section 451(b) was not intended to affect the application of the general OID timing rules to OID other than with respect to items not treated as discount for financial reporting purposes, such as the specified credit card fees. Id. at 427-429. Moreover, taxpayers have stated that the application of section 451(b) to OID other than items not treated as discount for financial reporting purposes would result in significant administrative burden and very little additional tax revenue. The Treasury Department and the IRS agree with commenters on this issue. Therefore, in the absence of a clear indication in the legislative history that Congress intended for section 451(b) to override the general timing rules for OID, and in order to reduce administrative burden, the proposed section 451(b) regulations would not apply to determine the time at which OID generally is includible in income. See § 1.451-3(c)(5)(ix) of the proposed regulations.

The proposed regulations contain two provisions that implement Congressional intent regarding the treatment of fees, including the specified credit card fees. First, under proposed § 1.451-3(i), if a fee is not treated by a taxpayer as discount or as an adjustment to the yield of a debt instrument over the life of the instrument (such as points) in its AFS and the fee otherwise would be treated as creating or increasing OID for Federal income tax purposes (specified fee), then the rules in the proposed regulations under section 451(b) apply before the rules in sections 1271 through 1275 and the regulations thereunder. For example, proposed § 1.451-3(i) applies to the specified credit card fees. Second, proposed § 1.1275-2(l) includes a proposed amendment to the final regulations under section 1275 to clarify that an item of income that is subject to the timing rules in the proposed regulations under section 451(b) (such as the specified credit card fees) is not taken into account in determining the amount of OID (if any) on the debt instrument. Removing specified fees and specified credit card fees from the calculation of OID will permit taxpayers to apply only the rules of section 451(b) to these fees, without also having to apply the rules relevant to OID. In addition, the Treasury Department and the IRS propose to obsolete Revenue Procedure 2004-33, Revenue Procedure 2005-47, Revenue Procedure 2013-26, and Chief Counsel Notice CC-2010-018. The Treasury Department and the IRS request comments on the proposed obsolescence of these documents.

B. Market Discount

Taxpayers requested guidance as to whether market discount is includible in income under section 451(b). The Treasury Department and the IRS previously announced that proposed regulations would provide that accrued market discount is not includible in income under section 451(b). Notice 2018-80 (2018 42 IRB 609), issued September 27, 2018.

A bond is generally treated as having market discount when the principal amount of the bond exceeds the holder's basis immediately after it was acquired by the holder. Under section 1276(a), market discount is includible in income only upon disposition of a market discount bond at a gain or the receipt of a partial principal payment, unless the holder of the bond elects otherwise. In each case, the market discount inclusion is limited to accrued market discount as defined in section 1276(b). In general, the timing rules for income inclusion in section 1276 are a codification of the pre-1984 timing rules for market discount and confirm that the all events test generally does not determine when accrued market discount is includible in income. The proposed regulations therefore include the market discount rules on the list of special methods of accounting to which section 451(b) does not apply.

Statement of Availability of IRS Documents

The IRS notices, revenue rulings, and revenue procedures cited in this preamble are published in the Internal Revenue Bulletin (or Cumulative Bulletin) and are available from the Superintendent of Documents, U.S. Government Publishing Office, Washington, DC 20402, or by visiting the IRS website at http://www.irs.gov.

Proposed Applicability Date

These regulations are proposed generally to apply to taxable years beginning on or after the date the final regulations are published in the **Federal Register**. However, in the case of a specified fee other than a specified credit card fee, proposed § 1.451-3(i)(2) is proposed to apply for a taxpayer's first taxable year beginning one year after the date the Treasury decision adopting these regulations as final is published in the **Federal Register**. In general, this delayed effective date for specified fees is provided because the treatment of these fees is unclear for tax purposes (and in some cases for financial reporting purposes). This additional time will allow the Treasury Department and the IRS to determine the types of fees that should be subject to section 451(b), which will provide taxpayers with more certainty in complying with section 451(b) and will help to minimize controversies with the IRS with respect to fees.

Until the date the Treasury decision adopting these regulations as final regulations is published in the **Federal Register**, a taxpayer may rely on these proposed regulations (other than the proposed regulations relating to specified fees) for taxable years beginning after December 31, 2017, provided that the taxpayer: (1) applies all the applicable rules contained in these proposed regulations (other than those applicable to specified fees), and (2) consistently applies these proposed regulations to all items of income during the taxable year (other than specified fees). Until the date the Treasury decision adopting these regulations as final regulations is published in the **Federal Register**, in the case of specified credit card fees, a taxpayer may rely on these proposed regulations for taxable years beginning after December 31, 2018, provided that the taxpayer: (1) applies all the applicable rules contained in these proposed regulations for specified credit card fees, and (2) consistently applies these proposed regulations to all items of income during the taxable year (other than specified fees).

Special Analyses

I. *Regulatory Planning and Review*

Executive Orders 13771, 13563, and 12866 direct agencies to assess costs and benefits of available regulatory alternatives and, if regulation is necessary, to select regulatory approaches that maximize net benefits, including potential economic, environmental, public health and safety effects, distributive impacts, and equity. Executive Order 13563 emphasizes the importance of quantifying both costs and benefits, reducing costs, harmonizing rules, and promoting flexibility. The Executive Order 13771 designation for any final rule resulting from the proposed regulation will be informed by comments received. The preliminary Executive Order 13771 designation for this proposed rule is regulatory.

The proposed regulation has been designated by the Office of Information and Regulatory Affairs (OIRA) as subject to review under Executive Order 12866 pursuant to the Memorandum of Agreement (MOA, April 11, 2018) between the Treasury Department and the Office of Management and Budget regarding review of tax regulations. The Office of Information and Regulatory Affairs has designated these proposed regulations as significant under section 1(b) of the MOA. Accordingly, these proposed regulations have been reviewed by OIRA.

1. Background

In plain language, section 451 of the Internal Revenue Code (the "Code") and the proposed regulations deal with differences between when income is recognized for Federal tax purposes and when it is recognized on businesses' financial accounting statements. The recently enacted section 451(b) more closely aligns the timing rules of the tax system with general financial accounting standards.

Under section 451(a) of the Code, any item of gross income is required to be included as income by the taxpayer ("recognized") when it is received by the taxpayer unless, under the taxpayer's method of accounting, the income is properly accounted for in a different period. For this purpose, businesses and individuals are generally required to use the accounting method that is used regularly to keep their financial records. This may be a cash receipts and disbursements accounting method, under which income is recognized when payment is actually or constructively received, or it may be an accounting system based on income and expense accrual principles. Certain corporations and some partnerships are required to use an accrual method, and generally taxpayers employing inventories in their trade or business must use an accrual method with regard to purchases and sales of inventory.

Current regulations require taxpayers using an accrual accounting method to report income in the taxable year in which all events that fix the right to receive such income have occurred, provided the amount can be determined with reasonable accuracy. Under IRS guidance, this "all events test" is met upon the earliest of when (i) payment is earned through performance by the taxpayer (e.g., provision of the contracted goods or services), (ii) payment is due to the taxpayer, or (iii) payment is received by the taxpayer.

In contrast, U.S. generally accepted accounting principles ("GAAP") and international financial reporting standards ("IFRS"), having different purposes from tax law, may often dictate alternative rules as regards the timing of revenue recognition. Differences between these financial accounting standards and the Code in the timing of revenue recognition may arise for a number of reasons. For example, under certain circumstances, financial accounting rules may require revenue to be recognized when the costs of providing goods or services pursuant to a contract are incurred, while the all events test may not be satisfied until the contract obligation is fulfilled. If meeting the taxpayer's performance obligation occurs over more than a single accounting period, then this timing pattern can result in a disparity between the year in which the associated revenue is booked for financial accounting purposes and the year in which the associated taxable gross income is recognized.

Congress enacted new section 451(b) in part because conformity in the timing of income recognition between the accrual system of accounting and the tax system ("book-tax conformity") will generally "promote simplification and reduced compliance costs." See Senate Budget Explanation of the Bill (2017-11-20) at p. 161.

Section 451(b) applies only to taxpayers that use the accrual method and have an Applicable Financial Statement ("AFS"). In plain language, an AFS is a financial statement certified as having been prepared under GAAP or IFRS. All publicly traded U.S. corporations possess an AFS, as do many privately held corporations and partnerships, which may have such certified accounting statements for credit purposes or for shareholder or partner reporting purposes. The income recognition rules for accrual-method taxpayers without an AFS and cash-method taxpayers are not altered by the enactment of section 451(b) or by the proposed regulations. The Treasury Department and the IRS project that there were approximately 3.1 million tax-reporting entities in taxable year 2016 that used an accrual method of accounting. They further project that fewer than 10 percent of these, or approximately 296,000 entities had an AFS, and thus could have been affected by section 451(b) and the proposed regulations had these been in effect in taxable year 2016.

For these taxpayers, Section 451(b) modifies the all-events test by stating that the test is not met for any item of income any later than when it is taken into account as revenue in an AFS or other designated financial statement (the "AFS income inclusion rule"). Thus, this new rule requires taxpayers to recognize income upon the earlier of when the all-events test is met or when the taxpayer includes the amount in revenue (broadly defined) in its AFS ("AFS income inclusion rule"). The AFS income inclusion rule operates only in one direction — to accelerate in time the recognition of gross income for tax purposes. This acceleration occurs in situations where income has been recognized for financial accounting purposes before the all events test has been satisfied.

2. Need for the proposed regulations

The proposed regulations deliver certainty and clarity to taxpayers affected by the Act's introduction of the new section 451(b) and allow them to comply with the new statutory provision with a higher level of confidence.

The Treasury Department and IRS published a Notice in April 2018, requesting public comments regarding the application of the AFS income inclusion rule, the meaning of various concepts and terms used in section 451(b), and other implementation issues not explicitly addressed in the statute. As explained earlier in this Preamble, the proposed regulations address the comments and questions subsequently raised by the public.

3. Overview of the proposed regulations

The proposed regulations include applicability and definitional guidance regarding section 451(b). Specifically, the proposed regulations: (1) clarify how the AFS inclusion rule applies to multi-year contracts; (2) describe and clarify the definition of an AFS for a group of entities; (3) define the meaning of the term revenue in an AFS; (4) define a transaction price and clarify how that price is to be allocated to separate performance obligations in a contract with multiple obligations; and (5) describe and clarify rules for transactions involving certain debt instruments.

4. Economic analysis

A. Baseline

The Treasury Department and the IRS have assessed the benefits and costs of the proposed regulations relative to a no-action baseline reflecting anticipated Federal income tax-related behavior in the absence of these proposed regulations.

B. Summary of Economic Effects

The proposed regulations provide increased certainty, clarity, and consistency in the application of section 451(b) by providing definitions and clarifications regarding the statute's terms and rules. In the absence of such guidance, the chances that different taxpayers would interpret the statute differently would be exacerbated. Similarly situated taxpayers might interpret the statutory provisions pertaining to the recognition of income differently, with one taxpayer pursuing a project that another comparable taxpayer might decline to make because of different interpretations of how the income would be treated under section 451(b). If this second taxpayer's activity were more profitable, an economic loss arises. Even in situations where taxpayers would generally adopt similar interpretations of the Code under the baseline, the lack of guidance increases opportunities for that interpretation to differ from what Congress intended. In this case, guidance provides value by bringing economic decisions closer in line with Congressional intent. In the context of economic activity by businesses that are subject to section 451(b) or that interact with such businesses, the proposed regulations thus help to ensure that similar economic activities, representing similar timing of income, are taxed similarly, thereby improving U.S. economic performance.

The Treasury Department and the IRS have not undertaken quantitative estimates of these possible efficiency gains because any such quantitative estimates would be highly uncertain. For example, the proposed regulations include provisions to clarify how income should be included from multi-year contracts. The Treasury Department and the IRS do not have readily available data or models to determine how businesses might apply the AFS inclusion rule to multi-year contracts in the absence of the proposed regulations or under alternative regulatory approaches. Furthermore, even in the event that most businesses could be presumed to adopt a particular treatment under the baseline, the Treasury Department and the IRS further do not have readily available data or models of the volume or pattern of their multi-year contract payments and they thus cannot project with any degree of precision the differences in tax treatment taxpayers would experience between the proposed regulations and the baseline or alternative regulatory approaches. Such differences are a key component of the marginal effective tax rate that these contracts would experience, which in turn would determine how economic activity would be affected by the proposed regulations relative to the baseline or alternative regulatory approaches.

The Treasury Department and the IRS further project that issuance of the proposed regulations will reduce compliance and enforcement costs relative to the baseline because the enhanced certainty and clarity they provide should make it easier for businesses to calculate their tax liability relative to the baseline. Greater efficiencies should also result from the promulgation of the proposed regulations, relative to the baseline, by reducing taxpayer disputes with the IRS that otherwise would have to be dealt with through sub-regulatory guidance or resolved through increased litigation. By providing greater certainty of how the law will be applied, the Treasury Department and the IRS project that the proposed regulations will reduce these implementation costs. The Treasury Department and the IRS have not made a quantitative estimate of the reduction in compliance and enforcement costs resulting from the proposed regulations. They have not made such an estimate in part because models of compliance cost are not currently available to provide a reasonably precise estimate of compliance costs in the absence of the proposed regulations.

With these limitations in mind, part II.4.C of this Special Analyses section explains the rationale behind the approaches taken by the proposed regulations and qualitatively evaluates the alternatives considered.

The Treasury Department and the IRS solicit comments on the economic effects of the proposed regulations.

C. Economic Effects of Specific Provisions

The proposed regulations embody certain regulatory decisions that reflect the regulatory discretion of the Treasury Department and the IRS. These decisions specify more fully how the AFS income inclusion rule is to be implemented.

The Treasury Department and IRS solicit comments on the economics of each of the items discussed below and of any other items of the proposed regulations not discussed in this section. The Treasury Department and the IRS particularly solicit comments that provide data, other evidence, or models that could enhance the rigor of the process by which the final regulations might be developed.

i. Application of the AFS Income Inclusion Rule to Multi-year Contracts

The proposed regulations clarify how section 451(b) applies to multi-year contracts. The Treasury Department and the IRS considered two alternative approaches for such contracts: (i) an annualized approach and (ii) a cumulative approach. Under an annualized approach, for each year under the contract a taxpayer would compare the income included as revenue in its AFS for that year and the gross income recognized under the all events test for that same year to determine its gross income inclusion, with the proviso that the total amount of gross income recognized under the contract is not to exceed the total contract price. In contrast, under a cumulative approach, in each year a taxpayer would compare the cumulative amount of revenue included in its AFS up to and including that year with the cumulative amount of gross income recognized under the all events test up to and including that year.

Example 4 of the proposed regulations, the summary table of which is reproduced in the first three rows of the following table, shows the treatment of gross income under a cumulative approach. The fourth row in this table shows the treatment of gross income under the annualized approach.

	2018	2019	2020	2021	Total
Payments	$25x	$25x	$25x	$25x	$100x
AFS Revenue	$50x	$0x	$20x	$30x	$100x
Gross Income (cumulative)	$50x	$0x	$25x	$25x	$100x
Gross Income (annualized)	$50x	$25x	$25x	$0x	$100x

An annualized approach could accelerate the recognition of taxable income to a greater degree than what is reflected in revenue for AFS purposes. In this example, such an approach would ignore in 2019 the fact that cumulative AFS revenue of $50x had been recognized as taxable gross income in 2018. Accordingly, the annualized approach would require that an additional $25x of income be recognized in 2019, since a payment of that amount was received in that year. In effect, an annualized approach would accelerate the recognition of $25x from 2021 to 2019 relative to gross income recognition under the cumulative AFS income inclusion rule.

The Treasury Department and IRS concluded that the extent of acceleration of income that may occur when using an annualized approach would be excessive relative to the cumulative approach when considered against the intents and purposes of the statute. The proposed regulations therefore adopt the cumulative approach.

ii. Applicable Financial Statement covering a group of entities

The proposed regulations provide rules for taxpayers whose financial results are included on an AFS covering a group of entities. These rules specify that, if a taxpayer's financial results are reported on the AFS for a group of entities, the taxpayer's AFS is the group's AFS. However, if the taxpayer also reports financial results on a separate AFS that is of equal or higher priority, then the separate AFS is the taxpayer's AFS. The rules also specify how a taxpayer using a group AFS is to determine the amount of revenue allocated to the taxpayer. The Treasury Department and the IRS considered as an alternative not providing substantive rules on how taxpayers should apply the AFS income inclusion rule when their financial results are included in an AFS for a group of entities. This alternative was rejected because it would have increased compliance burdens and potentially led to similarly situated taxpayers applying the AFS income inclusion rule differently.

The Code does not specify how the AFS income inclusion rule is to function whenever the AFS accounting period and the taxable year do not coincide. The proposed regulations do not adopt a single, one-size-fits-all approach, but rather provide taxpayers three separate options for addressing this situation. A change from one option to another, however, would be considered a change in method of accounting requiring the permission of the IRS. By providing taxpayers with several options, the proposed regulations will minimize taxpayer compliance costs when dealing with non-congruent tax and financial accounting periods relative to an alternative approach of specifying a single option, with no significant revenue implications or effects on economic decisions.

iii. Revenue in an AFS

The proposed regulations describe and clarify the definition of revenue to broadly include all items of income under section 61. Because this definition of revenue is based on tax principles, there may be items of revenue included in this definition that adjust retained earnings on financial statements but are not reflected in the revenue line on such financial statements. The Treasury Department and the IRS considered and rejected a narrower definition of revenue or a definition that was tied to the AFS definition of revenue. The definition of revenue advanced in the proposed regulations is consistent with the current application of the all events test under § 1.451-1(a) and ensures that all financial statement items are taken into account for tax purposes. In contrast, a narrow definition of revenue would allow, or even encourage, taxpayers to avoid the AFS income inclusion rule by not classifying an item as revenue on their financial statement.

iv. Allocation of Transaction Price

Section 451(b)(4) specifies that, in the case of a contract which contains multiple performance obligations, the allocation of the transaction price to each obligation is determined using the allocation used in the AFS. The Code, however, does not define either transaction price or performance obligation, thus the proposed regulation defines those terms. The proposed regulations clarify that a transaction price does not include amounts collected on behalf of third parties. Transaction price also does not include amounts that are contingent on the occurrence or non-occurrence of a future event. Without these exclusions, section 451(b) could be used to override other provisions of the Code concerning the definition of what constitutes gross income. This result would be at odds with the purpose of section 451, which is not to determine the existence or the amount of gross income, but rather to determine the timing of its recognition. Consequently, alternatives to these rules were not considered here.

Amounts included in the transaction price for an AFS are presumed to be not contingent, unless the taxpayer demonstrates otherwise. The Treasury Department and the IRS project that this rule will lead to reduced compliance burden for taxpayers, and reduced administrative costs for taxpayers and IRS and should lead to fewer taxpayer disputes on this issue relative to an alternative presumption regarding possible contingent amounts.

v. Rules for certain debt instruments

Section 451(b)(2) states that the AFS inclusion rule does not apply to items of gross income for which a taxpayer uses a special method of accounting provided under the Code. However, the Code does not apply this exception to special accounting rules that apply to original issue discount ("OID"), market discount, and certain other items with respect to debt instruments under part V of Subchapter P of the Code. The proposed regulations implement this provision regarding special methods of accounting, and clarify the effect of section 451(b) on the excepted Subchapter P rules.

The proposed regulations implement this provision by providing a non-exhaustive list of special methods of accounting, and by clarifying how section 451(b) applies to certain credit card receivables. The proposed regulations specifically except from section 451(b) the timing rules for accrued market discount on bonds and the general OID timing rules, as well as the timing rules for OID determined with respect to special debt instruments (contingent payment and variable rate debt instruments, certain hedged debt instruments, and inflation-indexed debt instruments). Nevertheless, following the legislative history of the Act (see Conference Report, p. 276), the proposed regulations provide that credit card late fees, credit card cash advance fees, and interchange fees are subject to the AFS income inclusion rule. The proposed regulations further specify that if these credit card fees are subject to a taxpayer's AFS, they are not to be taken into account in determining whether a debt instrument associated with them has OID. Existing rules continue to apply to these items for taxpayers not possessing an AFS. The Treasury Department and the IRS expect that this treatment will provide a straightforward application of section 451(b) consistent with Congressional intent without unnecessarily complicating OID calculations and adding to taxpayer compliance burdens.

The Treasury Department and the IRS considered and rejected a broader application of the AFS income inclusion rule to include all amounts determined under the OID and market discount accounting methods, even in cases where the items are treated as discount or as an adjustment to the yield of a debt instrument over the life of the instrument in its AFS for financial reporting purposes. The proposed regulations do not subject these amounts to the AFS income inclusion rule because these special accounting methods do not generally rely on the all events test to determine the timing of income inclusion and these current special accounting methods provide workable income-recognition timing rules that appropriately measure income. The Treasury Department and the IRS expect that subjecting these items to the AFS income inclusion rule of section 451(b) would disrupt and complicate current tax accounting practices with no general economic benefit.

II. *Paperwork Reduction Act*

These proposed regulations do not impose any additional information collection requirements in the form of reporting, recordkeeping requirements or third-party disclosure requirements. However, because section 451(b) and the proposed regulations provide methods of accounting affecting the timing of income inclusion, the consent of the Commissioner under section 446(e) is required before using such method. The IRS expects that these taxpayers will request this consent by filing Form 3115, *Application for Change in Accounting Method*. Filing of Form 3115 (for taxpayers who are required to do so or who elect certain methods of accounting described in the proposed regulations) is the sole collection of information requirement imposed by the statute and the proposed regulations. See subsequent paragraphs for a description of taxpayers who would be required to change the method of accounting under the statute and the proposed regulations.

For purposes of the Paperwork Reduction Act, the reporting burden associated with these collections of information will be reflected in the IRS Form 3115 Paperwork Reduction Act Submissions (OMB control number 1545-0074 for individual income tax returns; OMB control number 1545-0123 for business taxpayers). On December 17, 2018, the Treasury Department and the IRS published Revenue Procedure 2018-60, 2018-51 IRB 1045, which provides procedures for taxpayers to make a change in method of accounting to comply with section 451(b)(1)(A) and/or (b)(4). Taxpayers are able to request these section 451 changes using reduced filing requirements, such as by filing a short Form 3115, or for certain taxpayers, by using a streamlined method change procedure that involves not filing a Form 3115. See also the revenue procedure accompanying these regulations for similar simplified method change procedures to make a change in method of accounting to comply with these proposed regulations.

In 2018, the IRS released and invited comment on a draft of Form 3115 in order to give members of the public the opportunity to benefit from certain specific provisions made to the Code. The IRS received no comments on the forms during the comment period. Consequently, the IRS made the forms available in January 2019 for use by the public. The IRS notes that Form 3115 applies to changes of accounting methods generally and is therefore broader than section 451(b).

Additionally, proposed §1.451-3(h) provides additional methods of accounting that require a taxpayer to request consent of the Commissioner under section 446(e) before using such method. Under proposed §1.451-3(h)(4)(iii), for a taxpayer with a financial accounting year that is different from its tax accounting year, a change in the method by which the taxpayer computes its revenue is a change in method of accounting. Under proposed §1.451-3(h)(5), a restatement of an AFS that changes the timing of which an item of income, or portion thereof, is taken into account in revenue on the AFS is also a change in method of accounting. The Treasury Department and the IRS expect that taxpayers will request this consent by filing Form 3115.

For a taxpayer with an AFS required to comply with section 451(b) and/or proposed §1.451-3, a change in the taxpayer's revenue recognition policies for financial accounting purposes requires the taxpayer to seek the consent of the Commissioner under section 446(e) to use the method for Federal income tax purposes. See proposed §1.451-3(l). The reporting burden associated with the collection of information for a statement in lieu of the Form 3115 will be reflected in the Paperwork Reduction Act Submission associated with Revenue Procedure 2018-31, 2018-22 IRB 637 (or successor) (OMB control number 1545-1551). See the revenue procedure accompanying these proposed regulations.

The current status of the Paperwork Reduction Act submissions that will be revised as a result of the information collections in the proposed regulations is provided in the accompanying table. As described above, the reporting burdens associated with the information collections in the proposed regulations are included in the aggregated burden estimates for OMB control numbers 1545-0074 (in the case of individual filers of Form 3115), 1545-0123 (in the case of business filers of Form 3115), and 1545-1551 (in the case of filers subject to Revenue Procedure 2018-31). The overall burden estimates associated with the OMB control numbers below are aggregate amounts that relate to the entire package of forms associated with the applicable OMB control number and will in the future include, but not isolate, the estimated burden of the tax forms that will be created or revised as a result of the information collections in the proposed regulations. These numbers are therefore unrelated to the future calculations needed to assess the burden imposed by the proposed regulations. These burdens have been reported for other income tax regulations that rely on the same information collections and the Treasury Department and the IRS urge readers to recognize that these numbers are duplicates and to guard against overcounting the burdens imposed by tax provisions prior to the Act. No burden estimates specific to the forms affected by the proposed regulations are currently available. The Treasury Department and the IRS have not estimated the burden, including that of any new information collections, related to the requirements under the proposed regulations. For the OMB control numbers discussed in the preceding paragraphs, the Treasury Department and the IRS estimate PRA burdens on a taxpayer-type basis rather than a provision-specific basis. Those estimates capture both changes made by the Act and those that arise out of discretionary authority exercised in the proposed regulations (when final) and other regulations that affect the compliance burden for that form.

The Treasury Department and IRS request comment on all aspects of information collection burdens related to the proposed regulations, including estimates for how much time it would take to comply with the paperwork burdens described above for each relevant form and ways for the IRS to minimize the paperwork burden. In addition, when available, drafts of IRS forms are posted for comment at https://apps.irs.gov/app/picklist/list/draftTaxForms.htm. IRS forms are available at https://www.irs.gov/forms-instructions. Forms will not be finalized until after they have been approved by OMB under the PRA.

Form/Revenue Procedure	Type of Filer	OMB Number(s)	Status
	All other Filers (mainly trusts and estates) (Legacy system)	1545-2070	Published in the Federal Register on 2/15/17. Public comment period closed on 4/17/17.
	Link: https://www.federalregister.gov/documents/2017/02/15/2017-02985/proposed-information-collection-comment-request		
Form 3115	Business (NEW Model)	1545-0123	Published in the Federal Register on 10/8/18. Public comment period closed on 12/10/18.
	Link: https://www.federalregister.gov/documents/2018/10/09/2018-21846/proposed-collection-comment-request-for-forms-1065-1065-b-1066-1120-1120-c-1120-f-1120-h-1120-nd		
	Individual (NEW Model)	1545-0074	Limited scope submission (1040 only) on 10/11/18 at OIRA for review. Full ICR submission for all forms in 2019.
	Link: https://www.reginfo.gov/public/do/PRAViewICR?ref_nbr=201808-1545-031		
Revenue Procedure 2018-31	IRS Research estimates	1545-1551	Published in the Federal Register on 8/31/16. Public Comment period closed on 9/30/16.
	Link: https://www.federalregister.gov/documents/2016/08/31/2016-20993/submission-for-omb-review-comment-request		

D. Regulatory Flexibility Act

It is hereby certified that these regulations will not have a significant economic impact on a substantial number of small entities within the meaning of section 601(6) of the Regulatory Flexibility Act (5 U.S.C. chapter 6).

New section 451(b) of the Act requires that an item of income be included in gross income for tax purposes no later than when the item is counted as revenue in an applicable financial statement. This typically moves the recognition of income forward by a year or two compared to previous law. These proposed regulations provide general guidance on the rule, including the scope of the rule, exceptions to the rule, definitions of key terms, and examples demonstrating applicability of the rule.

The Treasury Department and the IRS have estimated the number of small business entities that may be affected by the statute and these proposed regulations. The statute and proposed regulations affect only those business entities that (i) use an accrual method of accounting, and (ii) have an applicable financial statement.

Regarding an accrual method of accounting, many small business entities use the cash receipts and disbursements method of accounting (cash method), as opposed to an accrual method, and thus are not subject to this provision. The percent of returns that use an accrual method of accounting, by entity types and for entities with gross receipts not greater than $25 million, are shown in the accompanying table.

Total returns and returns using accrual method of accounting (Taxable year 2016)

	Entities with gross receipts not greater than $25 million		
Entity	Total returns (thousands)	Returns using an accrual method of accounting (thousands)	Percent of returns using accrual method of accounting
C corporations	1,567	700	45
S corporations	4,551	1,140	25
Partnerships	3,743	860	23
Sole proprietors and LLCs	25,524	358	1
All entities	35,385	3,058	9

Source: Internal Revenue Service, Statistics of Income.

The Treasury Department and the IRS next examined the second condition, that only entities with an Applicable Financial Statement ("AFS") are affected by the statute and the proposed regulations. The Treasury Department and the IRS do not have readily available data to measure the prevalence of entities with an AFS. However, Schedule M-3, which is used to reconcile an entity's net income or loss for tax purposes with its book income or loss, reports whether an entity has a certified audited income statement. Unfortunately for the current exercise, the Schedule M-3 is required to be filed only by entities possessing at least $10 million of assets. Nevertheless, it is this population that is far more likely to possess an AFS. Furthermore, data are currently available only for electronic filers.

For taxable year 2016, approximately 87 percent of accrual-method entities filing Forms 1120, 1120-S, and 1065 with gross receipts of $25 million or less were filers of electronic tax forms. About 11 percent, or 265,000 of these returns, included a Schedule M-3. About 40 percent of the returns with Schedule M-3, or 106,000, indicated they had a certified audited income statement.[1] Based on the assumption that filers of paper tax forms have the same incidence as electronic filers and that entities that do not file a Schedule M-3 generally do not have an AFS, then the Treasury Department and the IRS estimate that roughly 122,000 (=106,000/0.87) entities with gross receipts of $25 million or less are accrual-method entities that have an AFS. If 5 percent of entities that do not file a Schedule M-3 also have an AFS then approximately 247,000 entities with gross receipts of $25 million or less are potentially affected by the proposed regulations. These estimates of affected filing entities are reproduced in the following table.

Corporation and Partnership Returns Using An Accrual Method of Accounting Taxable year 2016 (Thousands of returns)			
Entities with gross receipts not greater than $25 million			
	E-Filed Returns	Paper-Filed Returns	Total Returns
Returns	2,441	361	2,802
Returns with a Schedule M-3	265	39*	374*
Returns with a Schedule M-3 and an audited income statement	106	16*	122*
Returns without a Schedule M-3	2,176	322*	2,498*
Returns without a Schedule M-3, but with an audited income statement	109**	16**	125**
Returns with an audited income statement	215**	32**	247**

* Estimates are obtained by assuming paper-filed returns are similar to e-filed returns as regards the incidence of a filing entity having a Schedule M-3 and an audited income statement.
** Estimates are obtained by assuming that 5% of returns without a Schedule M-3 have an audited income statement. This compares with approximately 40% of returns with a Schedule M-3 having such a statement.
Source: Non-italic entries are estimates taken from the IRS's Research, Applied Analytics and Statistics Division using data from the Compliance Data Warehouse. The total number of accrual method returns of corporations and partnerships (2,802,000) differs slightly from that reported in the earlier table (2,700,000) due to the use of different data sources for the two estimates. Italicized entries are additional estimates obtained in the manner indicated in the table notes.

This rule would not have a significant economic impact on small entities affected. The costs to comply with these proposed regulations are not significant. Taxpayers needing to make method changes pursuant to section 451(b) or the proposed regulations will be required to file a Form 3115. The Treasury Department and the IRS have provided streamlined procedures for certain taxpayers to change their method of accounting to comply with section 451(b), and plan to provide streamlined procedures for taxpayers to change to the methods of accounting described in these proposed regulations. See Revenue Procedure 2018-60, and the revenue procedure accompanying these regulations. Under the streamlined procedures, certain taxpayers would either complete only a portion of the Form 3115 or would not complete the Form 3115 at all to comply with section 451(b). The streamlined method change procedures are available to taxpayers (other than a tax shelter) who satisfy the gross receipts test under section 448(c) and for taxpayers making such a method change which results in a zero section 481(a) adjustment. (For tax years beginning in 2018, an entity satisfied the gross receipts test if its average annual gross receipts was $25 million or less. For tax years beginning in 2019, this threshold increased to $26 million or less.) In addition, the Treasury Department and the IRS plan to issue a streamlined procedure, using a short Form 3115, for taxpayers using a section 451(b) method who have a change in their AFS for revenue recognition that requires a method change for tax purposes. See the revenue procedure accompanying these regulations.

As noted in the revenue procedure accompanying these regulations, the estimated cumulative annual reporting and/or recordkeeping burden for the statutory method changes described under OMB control number 1545-1551, before publication of the revenue procedure, is 27,336 respondents, and a total annual reporting and/or recordkeeping burden of 30,580 hours. The estimated annual burden per respondent/recordkeeper under OMB control number 1545-1551 before publication of this revenue procedure varies from $1/6$ hour to $8^1/2$ hours, depending on individual circumstances, with an estimated average of $1^1/4$ hours. The estimated cumulative annual reporting and/or recordkeeping burden for the method changes described under OMB control number 1545-1551 after that revenue procedure is accounted for is 27,346 respondents, and a total annual reporting and/or recordkeeping burden is 31,479 hours, leaving the average reporting and recordkeeping burden essentially unchanged. These burdens are essentially unaffected by these proposed regulations.

Notwithstanding this certification, the Treasury Department and the IRS invite comments from the public about the impact of this proposed rule on small entities.

Pursuant to section 7805(f), these regulations will be submitted to the Chief Counsel for Advocacy of the Small Business Administration for comment on their impact on small business.

IV. *Unfunded Mandates Reform Act*

Section 202 of the Unfunded Mandates Reform Act of 1995 requires that agencies assess anticipated costs and benefits and take certain other actions before issuing a final rule that includes any Federal mandate that may result in expenditures in any one year by a state, local, or tribal government, in the aggregate, or by the private sector, of $100 million in 1995 dollars, updated annually for inflation. In 2018, that threshold is approximately $150 million. This rule does not include any Federal mandate that may result in expenditures by state, local, or tribal governments, or by the private sector in excess of that threshold.

V. *Executive Order 13132: Federalism*

Executive Order 13132 (entitled "Federalism") prohibits an agency from publishing any rule that has federalism implications if the rule either imposes substantial, direct compliance costs on state and local governments, and is not required by statute, or preempts state law, unless the agency meets the consultation and funding requirements of section 6 of the Executive Order. This rule does not have federalism implications and does not impose substantial direct compliance costs on state and local governments or preempt state law within the meaning of the Executive Order.

---

[1] Data are based on estimates from the IRS's Research, Applied Analytics and Statistics Division using data from the Compliance Data Warehouse.

Comments and Requests for a Public Hearing

Before these proposed regulations are adopted as final regulations, consideration will be given to any comments that are submitted timely to the IRS as prescribed in this preamble under the "**ADDRESSES**" heading. The Treasury Department and the IRS request comments on all aspects of the proposed rules. All comments will be available at *http://www.regulations.gov* or upon request. A public hearing will be scheduled if requested in writing by any person that timely submits written comments. If a public hearing is scheduled, notice of the date, time, and place for the public hearing will be published in the **Federal Register**.

Drafting Information

The principal author of these proposed regulations is Charles Gorham, IRS Office of the Associate Chief Counsel (Income Tax and Accounting). However, other personnel from the Treasury Department and the IRS participated in their development.

[¶ 49,811] Proposed Amendments of Regulations (REG-102508-16), published in the Federal Register on September 10, 2019.

[Code Sec. 6033]

Reporting requirements: Tax-exempt organizations: Private foundations: Political organization.—Amendments of Reg. §1.6033-2, reporting regulations under section 6033 that are generally applicable to organizations exempt from tax under section 501(a) to reflect statutory amendments and certain grants of reporting relief announced through subregulatory guidance that have been made since the current regulations were adopted, particularly with respect to tax-exempt organizations required to file an annual Form 990 or 990-EZ information return, are proposed.

AGENCY: Internal Revenue Service (IRS), Treasury.

ACTION: Notice of proposed rulemaking.

SUMMARY: This document contains proposed regulations that would update information reporting regulations under section 6033 that are generally applicable to organizations exempt from tax under section 501(a) to reflect statutory amendments and certain grants of reporting relief announced through subregulatory guidance that have been made since the current regulations were adopted, particularly with respect to tax-exempt organizations required to file an annual Form 990 or 990-EZ information return.

DATES: Written or electronic comments and requests for a public hearing must be received by November 9, 2019.

ADDRESSES: Submit electronic submissions via the Federal eRulemaking Portal at http://www.regulations.gov/ (indicate IRS REG-102508-16) by following the online instructions for submitting comments. Once submitted to the Federal eRulemaking Portal, comments cannot be edited or withdrawn. The Department of the Treasury (Treasury Department) and the IRS will publish for public availability any comment submitted to its public docket, whether submitted electronically or in hard copy. Send hard copy submissions to: CC:PA:LPD:PR (REG-102508-16), Room 5203, Internal Revenue Service, P.O. Box 7604, Ben Franklin Station, Washington, DC 20044. Submissions may be hand-delivered Monday through Friday between the hours of 8 a.m. and 4 p.m. to CC:PA:LPD:PR (REG-102508-16), Courier's Desk, Internal Revenue Service, 1111 Constitution Avenue, NW, Washington, DC, 20224.

FOR FURTHER INFORMATION CONTACT: Concerning the proposed regulations, Office of the Associate Chief Counsel (Employee Benefits, Exempt Organizations, and Employment Taxes) at (202) 317-3150; concerning submissions of comments and requests for a public hearing, Regina Johnson at (202) 317-6901 (not toll-free numbers), fdms.database@irscounsel.treas.gov.

SUPPLEMENTARY INFORMATION:

Background

The paragraphs of section 6033 of the Internal Revenue Code (Code) outline various requirements for an annual information return to be filed by organizations that are exempt from tax under section 501(a) or described in section 527, including exceptions to the filing requirement. Section 6033(a)(1) requires certain organizations that are exempt from tax under section 501(a) ("tax-exempt organizations") to file annual information returns that include gross income, receipts and disbursements, and "such other information for the purpose of carrying out the internal revenue laws as the Secretary may by forms or regulations prescribe." The annual information returns required under section 6033 are Forms 990, "Return of Organization Exempt From Income Tax;" 990-EZ, "Short Form Return of Organization Exempt From Income Tax;" 990-PF, "Return of Private Foundation;" and 990-BL, "Information and Initial Excise Tax Return for Black Lung Benefit Trusts and Certain Related Persons." Annual returns filed by tax-exempt organizations, tax-exempt political organizations described in section 527(e) ("section 527 organizations"), and nonexempt private foundations described in section 6033(d) and section 4947(a)(1) trusts (which are both treated as section 501(c)(3) organizations for this purpose) are information returns intended to help ensure that the filing organizations comply with applicable federal tax laws. Additionally, most information on these annual returns under section 6104 of the Code is available for public inspection.

Section 6033(a)(3) provides a list of organizations that are excepted from the filing requirements imposed under section 6033(a)(1). Specifically, section 6033(a)(3)(A)(ii) provides that section 6033(a)(1) shall not apply to any organization (other than a private foundation) that is described in section 6033(a)(3)(C) whose gross receipts are not normally more than $5,000 annually. The list of organizations provided in section 6033(a)(3)(C) includes certain fraternal beneficiary societies, orders or associations described in section 501(c)(8); certain organizations described in section 501(c)(3) (such as religious organizations and educational organizations described in section 170(b)(1)(A)(ii)); and organizations described in section 501(c)(1) that are corporations wholly owned by the United States or any agency or instrumentality thereof or wholly-owned subsidiaries of such corporations.

Section 6033(a)(3)(B) provides discretionary authority to the Secretary to relieve any organization required to file under section 6033(a)(1) (other than supporting organizations described in section 509(a)(3)) from filing an information return where he determines that such filing is "not necessary to the efficient administration of the internal revenue laws."

Section 6033(b) provides a list of items that are required to be furnished annually by organizations described in section 501(c)(3), "at such time and in such manner as the Secretary may by forms or regulations prescribe." The statutory list of items required to be furnished annually has been amended by Congress from time to time to account for additional requirements of organizations described in section 501(c)(3). Section 6033(b) was updated by the Taxpayer Bill of Rights 2, Public Law 104-168, in 1996 to include items in sections 6033(b)(10) (relating to taxes imposed on certain lobbying and political expenditures by organizations described in sections 501(c)(3)) and 6033(b)(11) (relating to taxes imposed with respect to an organization, an organization manager, or any disqualified person under section 4958).

Section 6033(g)(2) provides that a political organization (as defined by section 527(e)(1)) that has gross receipts of $25,000 or more for a taxable year[1] shall file an annual return containing the information required by section 6033(a)(1) for organizations exempt from taxation under section 501(a). The statute authorizes the Secretary to modify the information required to be reported to require only information that is necessary for purposes of carrying out section 527 and such other information as the Secretary deems necessary to carry out the provisions of section 6033(g).

Section 6033(h) provides additional reporting requirements for controlling organizations, within the meaning of section 512(b)(13). Section 6033(h) requires controlling organizations to include on their returns any (1) interest, annuities, royalties, or rents received from each controlled entity (within the meaning of section 512(b)(13)), (2) any loans made to each such controlled entity, and (3) any transfers of funds between such controlling organization and each such controlled entity.

Section 6033(k) provides additional reporting requirements for sponsoring organizations described in section 4966(d)(1). Section 6033(k) requires each such organization to report on its annual return (1) the total number of donor advised funds (as defined in section 4966(d)(2)) it owns at the end of such taxable year, (2) the aggregate value of assets held in such funds at the end of such taxable year, and (3) the aggregate contributions to and grants made from such funds during such taxable year.

Section 6033(l) provides additional reporting requirements for supporting organizations described in section 509(a)(3). Section 6033(l) requires each supporting organization to report on its annual return (1) the supported organizations (as defined in section 509(f)(3)) with respect to which such organization provides support; (2) whether the organization meets the requirements of clause (i), (ii), or (iii) of section 509(a)(3)(B); and (3) a certification that the organization meets the requirements of section 509(a)(3)(C).

The general rule of confidentiality of returns is found in section 6103, which states that returns and return information shall be confidential, and, except as authorized by this title, no person having access to this information shall disclose any return or return information obtained by him in any manner.

One of the exceptions to the general rule of confidentiality can be found in section 6104. In general, under section 6104(b), the Secretary must make the annual returns filed under section 6033 available to the public. However, the Secretary is not authorized to disclose to the public the name or address of any contributor to any tax-exempt organization other than a private foundation (as defined in section 509(a), including trusts described in section 4947(a)(1) that are treated as private foundations) or a section 527 organization. Section 301.6104(b)-1(b)(2) provides that although the names and addresses are not to be disclosed, the amounts of contributions to an organization shall be made available for public inspection unless the disclosure of such information can reasonably be expected to identify any contributor.

In addition to the required disclosure by the Secretary, section 6104(d) and § 301.6104(d)-1 require certain tax-exempt organizations to provide their annual information returns upon request by a member of the public. Similar to the restrictions on disclosing contributor information placed on the Secretary by section 6104(b), an organization, other than a private foundation or a section 527 organization, is not required to disclose the names and addresses of its contributors under section 6104(d)(3)(A).

The current Treasury Regulations ("final regulations") reflect many of the statutory requirements of section 6033. Consistent with section 6033(a)(1), § 1.6033-2(a)(1) of the final regulations states that "except as provided in section 6033(a)(3) and paragraph (g) [of § 1.6033-2], every organization exempt from taxation under section 501(a) shall file an annual information return specifically setting forth its items of gross income, gross receipts and disbursements, and such other information as may be prescribed in the instructions, issued with respect to the return."

Although the information to be reported for any particular year is set forth in the form and instructions, the final regulations under section 6033 provide a list of "information generally required to be furnished by an organization exempt under section 501(a)" on the annual return. The list provided in § 1.6033-2(a)(2)(ii) of the final regulations generally tracks the list set forth for section 501(c)(3) organizations in section 6033(b), though not all items in section 6033(b) are currently included in the regulations because the statute has been amended following the original issuance of the regulations, and not all statutory changes were subsequently reflected in the regulations. The list in the regulations includes, but is not limited to, gross income for the year; dues and assessments from members and affiliates for the year; expenses incurred within the year attributable to gross income; disbursements (including prior years' accumulations) made within the year for the purposes for which it is exempt; a balance sheet showing its assets, liabilities, and net worth as of the beginning and end of such year; the total of the contributions, gifts, grants and similar amounts received by it during the taxable year; the names and addresses of all officers, directors, or trustees (or any person having responsibilities or powers similar to those of officers, directors or trustees) of the organization; and certain compensation and payment information.

As relevant here, § 1.6033-2(a)(2)(ii)(f) provides that organizations required to file an annual information return generally must provide the names and addresses of persons who contribute $5,000 or more during the taxable year. This provision is more expansive than section 6033(b)(5), which applies specifically to organizations described in section 501(c)(3). In addition, § 1.6033-2(a)(2)(iii)(d) provides that organizations described in section 501(c)(7) (social clubs), section 501(c)(8) (fraternal beneficiary societies), or section 501(c)(10) (domestic fraternal societies) generally must report the name of each person who contributes more than $1,000 to be used exclusively for religious, charitable, scientific, literary, or educational purposes, or for the prevention of cruelty to children or animals.

Incorporating section 6033(a)(3), § 1.6033-2(g)(1) provides a list of organizations that are not required to file an annual return under section 6033(a)(1). Within that list, § 1.6033-2(g)(1)(iii) provides that organizations described in section 6033(a)(3)(C) whose gross receipts are generally not more than $5,000 annually are not required to file the return required under section 6033(a)(1). Further, § 1.6033-2(g)(6) provides that the Commissioner may relieve any organization or class of organizations (other than a supporting organization described in section 509(a)(3)) from filing, in whole or in part, the annual return required under section 6033 where the Commissioner "determines that such returns are not necessary for the efficient administration of the internal revenue laws."

Accordingly, other than with regard to supporting organizations, section 6033 and the final regulations in this part issued under section 6033 provide the Commissioner with broad discretionary authority to determine what information is reported and to grant relief, in whole or in part, from the annual filing requirements of tax-exempt organizations if it is determined that the information is not necessary for the efficient administration of the internal revenue laws.

For decades, the Commissioner has exercised the discretion under section 6033(a)(3)(B) and § 1.6033-2(g)(6) to relieve organizations of filing requirements in section 6033 through subregulatory guidance such as revenue procedures and annual information return instructions (for example, Rev. Proc. 95-48, 1995-2 C.B. 418, and Rev. Proc. 96-10, 1996-1 C.B. 577). Revenue Procedure 83-23, 1983-1 C.B. 687, represents one such exercise of this discretion. In that revenue procedure, the Commissioner increased to $25,000 the minimum amount of gross receipts normally required to be received in a year by an organization exempt under section 501(a) to trigger a filing requirement under section 6033(a). That revenue procedure also expanded the group of tax-exempt organizations not required to file an annual information return due to a gross receipts threshold beyond those listed in section 6033(a)(3)(C). Revenue Procedure 2011-15, 2011-3 I.R.B. 322, further increased this gross receipts threshold amount to $50,000 for most organizations exempt under section 501(a).[2] Revenue Procedure 2011-15 also relieved most foreign organizations and organizations formed in a United States possession from a filing requirement under section 6033(a) if their gross receipts from sources within the United States do not

---

[1] In the case of a qualified State or local political organization described in section 527(e)(5), $25,000 is replaced by $100,000.

[2] An organization that is not required to file an annual return by virtue of Rev. Proc. 2011-15 must submit a Form 990-N e-Postcard annually in electronic format as described in section 6033(i)(1). Rev. Proc. 2011-15, section 3.03.

exceed the $50,000 threshold and if they have no significant activity (including lobbying and political activity and the operation of a trade or business, but excluding investment activity) in the United States.

Similarly, consistent with past exercises of authority under section 6033 and the implementing regulations, the Treasury Department and the IRS issued Rev. Proc. 2018-38, 2018-31 I.R.B. 280, granting tax-exempt organizations required to file the Form 990 or Form 990–EZ, other than those described in section 501(c)(3), relief from reporting the names and addresses of contributors on Schedules B, "Schedule of Contributors," filed with Form 990 or 990-EZ (or completing the similar portions of Part IV of the Form 990–BL). Revenue Procedure 2018-38 also provides that organizations described in sections 501(c)(7), (8), or (10) need not provide, on their annual information returns required under section 6033, the names and addresses of persons who contributed more than $1,000 during the taxable year to be used for exclusively charitable purposes. Revenue Procedure 2018-38 does not affect the information required to be reported on Forms 990, 990-EZ, or 990-PF by organizations described in section 501(c)(3) (which for purposes of section 6033 include nonexempt charitable trusts described in section 4947(a)(1) and nonexempt private foundations described in section 6033(d)) or section 527 organizations.

On July 30, 2019, the United States District Court for the District of Montana released its decision in the case of *Bullock, et al. v. IRS*, No. 4:18-cv-00103-BMM (D. Mont. Jul. 30, 2019). The court noted that "the substance of [the Commissioner's] ultimate decision [on reporting the names and addresses of contributors] remains subject to the Commissioner's discretion," but set aside Rev. Proc. 2018-38 and held that the IRS should have followed the notice and comment procedures of the APA in providing the reporting relief set forth in Rev. Proc. 2018-38.

Explanation of Provisions

The proposed regulations contained in this notice of proposed rulemaking modify the final regulations under section 6033 to align them with certain statutory amendments to section 6033 that have not previously been reflected in the regulations and to update the regulations to encompass certain instances in which the Commissioner has previously exercised discretion under the statute and regulations to relieve organizations, in whole or in part, from the filing requirements set forth in section 6033 or the regulations in this part issued under section 6033. The Code provides discretion to the Secretary, and his or her delegate,[3] to determine what information is necessary for the efficient administration of the federal tax laws involving tax-exempt organizations. The Secretary has previously exercised that discretion through various forms or guidance. These proposed regulations would incorporate certain past exercises of discretion into a single location for ease of use. These proposed changes are also intended to update the regulations so that they more fully present the current reporting requirements for most tax-exempt organizations.

Specifically, as further discussed later in this preamble, these changes include the following: (1) adding items listed in section 6033(b)(10) and (11), as applicable, to the list of items generally required to be reported; (2) adding other statutory reporting requirements for controlling organizations, sponsoring organizations, and supporting organizations; (3) amending the gross receipts threshold (with an additional requirement for foreign organizations and United States possession organizations) that triggers a filing requirement under section 6033 for organizations exempt under section 501(a) (other than private foundations and supporting organizations); (4) clarifying that section 527 organizations with gross receipts greater than $25,000 generally are subject to the reporting requirements under section 6033(a)(1) as if they were exempt from taxes under section 501(a); and (5) specifying that only organizations described in section 501(c)(3) and section 527 organizations generally would continue to be required to provide names and addresses of contributors on their Forms 990, Forms 990-EZ, and Forms 990-PF.

The Treasury Department and the IRS request comments on any other grants of section 6033 related reporting relief announced pursuant to past exercises of the Commissioner's discretion that should be incorporated into the regulations or any other clarifications to reflect statutory changes. For example, these proposed regulations do not incorporate Rev. Proc. 96-10, 1996-1 C.B. 138, which relieves from a filing requirement under section 6033(a) certain organizations that are operated, controlled, or supervised by one or more churches, integrated auxiliaries, or conventions or associations of churches because it is unclear whether Rev. Proc. 96-10 currently has practical application. The relevant language provided indicates that these types of organizations are likely supporting organizations under section 509(a)(3). Section 509(a)(3) provides public charity status to organizations, known as supporting organizations, that are operated, supervised, or controlled by, or in connection with, one or more specified organizations described in section 509(a)(1) or (2), which includes churches, conventions or associations of churches, and some integrated auxiliaries of churches.

The Pension Protection Act of 2006, Public Law 109-280, modified the Secretary's general discretion under section 6033(a)(3)(B) so that the Secretary is no longer permitted to relieve a supporting organization of its filing requirements. The Treasury Department and the IRS expect that few, if any, organizations meeting the requirements of Rev. Proc. 96-10 may still rely on this revenue procedure given the 2006 statutory change; thus, incorporating the provisions of Rev. Proc. 96-10 into regulations is unnecessary. However, the Treasury Department and the IRS request comments on the continued usefulness of Rev. Proc. 96-10.

In addition, Rev. Proc. 95-48 grants reporting relief for governmental units and affiliates of governmental units. The Treasury Department and the IRS are considering whether the reporting relief in this revenue procedure should be updated and whether such relief should be incorporated into the regulations under section 6033 and request comments on the relief provided in this revenue procedure, as well as whether any other reporting relief should be specified or added.

ITEMS REQUIRED IN ANNUAL INFORMATION RETURNS

Section 6033(a)(1) provides that the Secretary, or his or her delegate, may by forms or regulations prescribe "other information for the purpose of carrying out the internal revenue laws" to be reported on an annual return required under section 6033. This authority is reflected in § 1.6033-2(a)(1). Consistent with these grants of discretion, § 1.6033-2(a)(2)(ii) provides a general list of items that a tax-exempt organization may expect to provide on its annual information return required by section 6033.

As previously stated in this preamble, the Treasury Department and the IRS have determined that the regulations should be updated to reflect certain additional items listed in section 6033(b) for organizations described in section 501(c)(3).

Therefore, these proposed regulations would amend § 1.6033-2(a)(2)(ii) by adding two new provisions to reflect items that have been added to section 6033(b) but that have not yet been added to the list in the regulations of items generally required to be reported on an organization's annual information return. These items are those found in section 6033(b)(10) (relating to taxes imposed on certain lobbying and political expenditures by organizations described in section 501(c)(3)) and 6033(b)(11) (relating to taxes imposed with respect to an organization, an organization manager, or any disqualified person on any excess benefit transaction under section 4958). In addition, a cross-reference to § 1.6033-2(a)(1) has been added to the introductory sentence of § 1.6033-2(a)(2)(ii).

In an effort to further increase the ability of a taxpayer generally to find its reporting requirements in one place, the Treasury Department and the IRS are also incorporating into the regulations the statutory reporting requirements found in section 6033(h) for controlling organizations (as defined in section 512(b)(13)), section 6033(k) for sponsoring organizations (as defined in section 4966(d)(1)), and section 6033(l) for supporting organizations (as defined in section 509(a)(3)).

---

[3] Section 7701(a)(11)(B) provides that the term "Secretary" means the Secretary of the Treasury or his delegate, which may include the Commissioner.

While these amendments to the regulations are part of an effort to further increase the ability of a taxpayer generally to find its reporting requirements in one place, tax-exempt organizations will continue to find their current annual return reporting requirements in the forms and instructions found at irs.gov. The Treasury Department and the IRS request comments on any other requirements in section 6033 that should be incorporated into § 1.6033-2.

GROSS RECEIPTS FILING THRESHOLD

Section 6033(a)(1)(B) grants the Secretary, or his or her delegate, discretion to relieve any organization (except an organization described in section 509(a)(3)) from the requirement to file a return if the Secretary determines that the filing is not necessary to the efficient administration of the internal revenue laws and § 1.6033-2(g)(6) specifies that this relief from filing may be granted in whole or in part.

The Treasury Department and the IRS have previously determined that the efficient administration of the tax laws does not require the filing of returns by organizations that are exempt under section 501(a) (other than private foundations and supporting organizations) that normally have less than $50,000 in gross receipts annually, except for foreign organizations and organizations formed in a United States possession that have significant activity (including lobbying and political activity and the operation of a trade or business, but excluding investment activity) in the United States. Rev. Proc. 2011-15. This threshold seeks to balance the efficient use of resources for both tax-exempt organizations and the IRS with ensuring compliance with the tax laws by tax-exempt organizations, particularly since such organizations must continue to file Form 990-N under section 6033(i). This notice of proposed rulemaking proposes to amend § 1.6033-2(g)(1)(iii) to reflect the $50,000 gross receipts filing threshold currently in effect, rather than the $5,000 gross receipts threshold found in section 6033(a)(3)(A)(ii), and the application of the $50,000 threshold to organizations other than those listed in section 6033(a)(3)(C). Thus, the proposed regulations would provide that the gross receipts threshold for all organizations (other than private foundations and supporting organizations) formed in the United States would be $50,000. The notice of proposed rulemaking also proposes simply to incorporate the previously granted relief from the filing requirement under section 6033(a) for foreign organizations and organizations formed in a United States possession (other than private foundations and supporting organizations) that is currently found in Rev. Proc. 2011-15.

The proposed regulations will also specify that the Commissioner retains discretion to provide possible further increases in this amount pursuant to § 1.6033-2(g)(6). Therefore, the Treasury Department and the IRS also propose amending § 1.6033-2(g)(6) to clarify that the Commissioner has authority to further provide relief through forms, instructions to forms, or guidance published in the Internal Revenue Bulletin.

CLARIFYING THE TREATMENT OF SECTION 527 ORGANIZATIONS

Section 6033(g)(2) provides that section 527 organizations shall file an annual return containing the information required by section 6033(a)(1) for tax-exempt organizations. As noted previously in this preamble, the Treasury Department and the IRS have determined that the regulations should more fully reflect the requirements of section 6033 for tax-exempt organizations. The Treasury Department and the IRS propose to add § 1.6033-2(a)(5) to state the current requirement that section 527 organizations, subject to the filing exceptions provided by section 6033(g)(3) or as permitted under section 6033(g)(4), follow the reporting requirements under section 6033(a)(1) in the same manner as tax-exempt organizations, except when the Commissioner revises those requirements as appropriate to carry out the purposes of section 527. The proposed § 1.6033-2(a)(5) would also state the current requirement that section 527 organizations, like organizations described in section 501(c)(3), must continue to report the names and addresses of contributors on the section 527 organizations' annual Forms 990 or Forms 990-EZ. The addition of § 1.6033-2(a)(5) does not affect the current reporting requirements of section 527 organizations.

The Treasury Department and the IRS request comments on the proposed clarification of the treatment of section 527 organizations found in § 1.6033-2(a)(5).

REPORTING OF NAMES AND ADDRESSES OF CONTRIBUTORS

Section 6033 does not specify that the names and addresses of contributors to tax-exempt organizations, other than those described in section 501(c)(3), be reported on annual information returns. Consistent with the Secretary's broad discretion under section 6033(a) to set forth information reporting requirements "for the purpose of carrying out the internal revenue laws . . . by forms or regulations," § 1.6033-2(a)(2)(ii) of the final regulations provides a list of items that are generally required to be included in the annual filings of organizations exempt under section 501(a). The proposed regulations would amend the final regulations to clarify that the need to provide the names and addresses of substantial contributors will generally apply only to tax-exempt organizations described in section 501(c)(3). This clarification is consistent with the limited application of the requirement in section 6033(b)(5). As discussed in the prior section of this preamble, section 527 organizations must also continue to report the names and addresses of substantial contributors.

In exercising this discretion, the Treasury Department and the IRS seek to balance the IRS's need for the information against the costs and risks associated with reporting of the information. The IRS does not need the names and addresses of substantial contributors to tax-exempt organizations not described in section 501(c)(3) to be reported annually on Schedule B of Form 990 or Form 990-EZ in order to carry out the internal revenue laws, including provisions dealing with transfer taxes. A requirement to annually report such information—rather than providing it to the IRS as required upon examination—increases compliance costs for affected tax-exempt organizations and consumes IRS resources in connection with the redaction of such information as required in section 6104(b). Some have expressed concern regarding the potential use of the names and addresses of substantial contributors when evaluating possible private benefit or inurement. Tax-exempt organizations continue to be required to file Schedule L of Form 990 or Form 990-EZ identifying transactions between the exempt organization and interested persons (including substantial contributors), which may indicate possible risks of private benefit or inurement. The primary utility of the names and addresses of substantial contributors, however, arises during examination of a tax-exempt organization, at which point such information may be collected from the relevant tax-exempt organization. Under the proposed rule, tax-exempt organizations are still required to report the amounts of contributions from each substantial contributor as required by the Schedule B of the Form 990 and 990-EZ as well as maintain the names and addresses of substantial contributors should the IRS need this information on a case-by-case basis, which the Treasury Department and the IRS have concluded is sufficient for the efficient administration of the Code.

The Treasury Department and the IRS are also concerned that the requirement to report the names and addresses of substantial contributors poses a risk of inadvertent disclosure of information that is not open to public inspection because this information on Schedule B generally must be redacted from an otherwise disclosable information return. The IRS has experienced incidents of inadvertent disclosure and has taken other steps to reduce future occurrences of such disclosures. By reducing the number of organizations providing the names and addresses of contributors on Schedule B, the potential for inadvertent disclosure of names and addresses can be decreased further.

Finally, the Treasury Department and the IRS note that the change in annual reporting to the IRS of the names and addresses of substantial contributors will have no effect on information currently available to the public. Sections 6103 and 6104 prohibit the IRS from publicly disclosing the names and addresses of contributors to tax-exempt organizations (other than private foundations). With respect to such tax-exempt organizations, any names and addresses of substantial contributors on Schedule B are not made public and disclosure restrictions prohibit making such information available for use by other agencies for enforcement purposes, unless a specific exception applies.[4] The Treasury Department and the IRS are aware of concerns raised regarding campaign finance laws; however, Congress has not tasked the IRS with the enforcement of campaign finance laws. Furthermore, the Code generally prohibits the IRS from disclosing any names and addresses of such organizations' substantial contributors to federal agencies for non-tax investigations, including campaign finance matters, except in narrowly prescribed circumstances.[5]

Accordingly, the Treasury Department and the IRS are proposing to modify the regulations to no longer specify that tax-exempt organizations (other than organizations described in section 501(c)(3)) are generally required to report the names and addresses of their substantial contributors on their annual information returns. However, as noted previously in this preamble, tax-exempt organizations must continue to report the amounts of contributions from each substantial contributor as well as maintain the names and addresses of their substantial contributors in their books and records in accordance with section 6001 and § 1.6001-1(a) and (c) in order to permit the IRS to efficiently administer the internal revenue laws through examinations of specific taxpayers. The records retained will enable organizations to substantiate upon examination the number of certain contributors and the amounts of their contributions and to facilitate the reporting of information on certain financial transactions between organizations and certain contributors. The Treasury Department and the IRS request comments on concerns regarding the efficient administration of the Code without the annual reporting of the names and addresses of substantial contributors for tax-exempt organizations other than those described in section 501(c)(3) and section 527 organizations.

The Treasury Department and the IRS propose to revise § 1.6033-2(a)(2)(ii)(f) to provide that organizations described in section 501(c)(3) generally would be required to continue to provide names and addresses of contributors of more than $5,000 on their Forms 990, 990-EZ, and 990-PF. Similarly, § 1.6033-2(a)(2)(iii)(d) would be revised to remove reference to the provision of names of contributors who contribute over $1,000 for a specific charitable purpose to organizations described in sections 501(c)(7), (8), and (10).

Proposed Effective/Applicability Date

These regulations are proposed to be effective as of the date of publication of the Treasury decision adopting these rules as final regulations in the **Federal Register**. While these regulations are not effective until these rules are adopted as final in the **Federal Register**, under section 7805(b)(7), a tax-exempt organization may choose to apply the final regulations to returns filed after September 6, 2019. After issuing the final regulations, the Treasury Department and the IRS will withdraw any revenue procedures superseded by the final regulations.

Special Analyses

This regulation is not subject to review under section 6(b) of Executive Order 12866 pursuant to the Memorandum of Agreement (April 11, 2018) between the Department of the Treasury and the Office of Management and Budget regarding review of tax regulations.

PAPERWORK REDUCTION ACT

The collection of information contained in this notice is reflected in the collection of information for Forms 990 and 990-EZ that have been reviewed and approved by the Office of Management and Budget in accordance with the Paperwork Reduction Act (44 U.S.C. 3507(c)) under control numbers 1545-0047 and 1545-1150, respectively. To the extent there is a decrease in burden as a result of this change, the decrease in burden will be reflected in the updated burden estimates for the Forms 990 and 990-EZ. The requirement to maintain records to substantiate information on the Form 990 or 990-EZ is already contained in the burden associated with the control numbers for those forms and remains unchanged.

An agency may not conduct or sponsor, and a person is not required to respond to, a collection of information unless the collection of information displays a valid OMB control number.

Books or records relating to a collection of information must be retained as long as their contents may become material in the administration of any internal revenue law. Generally, tax returns and return information are confidential, as required by 26 U.S.C. 6103.

REGULATORY FLEXIBILITY ACT

It is hereby certified that these final regulations will not have a significant economic impact on a substantial number of small entities. This certification is based on the fact that these regulations reflect statutory requirements and reporting relief previously announced through forms, instructions to forms, or guidance published in the Internal Revenue Bulletin. The collection of information contained in these proposed regulations instead maintains a current recordkeeping obligation while removing a filing burden. Accordingly, a Regulatory Flexibility Analysis under the Regulatory Flexibility Act (5 U.S.C. chapter 6) is not required. Pursuant to section 7805(f), this regulation has been submitted to the Chief Counsel for Advocacy of the Small Business Administration for comment on its impact on small business.

Comments and Requests for a Public Hearing

Before these proposed regulations are adopted as final regulations, consideration will be given to any comments that are submitted timely to the IRS as prescribed in this preamble under the **Addresses** heading. The Treasury Department and the IRS request comments on all aspects of the proposed regulations. All comments will be available for public inspection and copying. A public hearing may be scheduled if requested in writing by any person that timely submits written comments. If a public hearing is scheduled, notice of the date, time, and place for the hearing will be published in the **Federal Register**.

Drafting Information

The principal authors of these regulations are personnel from the Office of the Associate Chief Counsel (Employee Benefits, Exempt Organizations, and Employment Taxes). However, other personnel from the Treasury Department and the IRS participated in their development.

Statement of Availability of IRS Documents

IRS Revenue Procedures, Revenue Rulings, Notices, and other guidance cited in this document are published in the Internal Revenue Bulletin (or Cumulative Bulletin) and are available from the Superintendent of Documents, U.S. Government Publishing Office, Washington, DC 20402, or by visiting the IRS website at *http://www.irs.gov*.

---

[4] The confidentiality and disclosure of tax returns and return information in both tax and non-tax investigations is governed by section 6103. Section 6103 contains several provisions authorizing the disclosure of returns and return information to Federal law enforcement agencies under prescribed circumstances after meeting specified procedural requirements. For example, these include disclosures to the Department of Justice (DOJ) for the investigation and prosecution of non-tax Federal crimes via an ex parte court order or via a request from the highest ranking official of a Federal agency or the highest officials within DOJ and in the course of an investigation after referral to and approval by DOJ as a Grand Jury Tax Investigation.

In the context of states, sections 6103 and 6104 authorize disclosure of certain returns and return information to the states for specified purposes. Generally, section 6103(d) authorizes disclosure to state tax agencies for state tax administration, while section 6104(c) permits disclosure of return information, in the case of organizations other than those described in section 501(c)(1) or (3), to an appropriate state officer to the extent necessary in administering state laws relating to the solicitation or administration of charitable funds or charitable assets of such organizations. Some states may also independently obtain donor information from the organizations.

[5] See note 4.

[¶ 49,812] Proposed Amendments of Regulations (REG-125710-18), published in the Federal Register on September 10, 2019.

[Code Sec. 382]

Loss limitation: Section 382 limitation: Built-in gains: Built-in losses.—Amendments of Reg. §§ 1.382-1, 1.382-2 and 1.382-7, regarding the items of income and deduction which are included in the calculation of built-in gains and losses under section 382 of the Internal Revenue Code (Code), and reflecting numerous changes made to the Code by the enactment of recent tax legislation, are proposed.

AGENCY: Internal Revenue Service (IRS), Treasury.

ACTION: Notice of proposed rulemaking.

SUMMARY: This document contains proposed regulations regarding the items of income and deduction which are included in the calculation of built-in gains and losses under section 382 of the Internal Revenue Code (Code), and reflecting numerous changes made to the Code by the enactment of recent tax legislation. These proposed regulations would affect corporations that experience an ownership change for purposes of section 382. This document also proposes to withdraw the following IRS notices and incorporate their subject matter, as appropriate, into these proposed regulations under section 382: Notice 87-79, Notice 90-27, Notice 2003-65, and Notice 2018-30.

DATES: Written or electronic comments must be received by November 12, 2019. Written or electronic requests for a public hearing and outlines of topics to be discussed at the public hearing must be received by November 12, 2019.

ADDRESSES: Submit electronic submissions via the Federal eRulemaking Portal at *www.regulations.gov* (indicate IRS and REG-125710-18) by following the online instructions for submitting comments. Once submitted to the Federal eRulemaking Portal, comments cannot be edited or withdrawn. The Department of the Treasury (Treasury Department) and the IRS will publish for public availability any comment received to its public docket, whether submitted electronically or in hard copy. Send hard copy submissions to: Internal Revenue Service, CC:PA:LPD:PR (REG-125710-18), Room 5203, Post Office Box 7604, Ben Franklin Station, Washington, DC 20044. Submissions may be hand-delivered Monday through Friday between the hours of 8 a.m. and 4 p.m. to CC:PA:LPD:PR (indicate REG-125710-18), Courier's Desk, Internal Revenue Service, 1111 Constitution Avenue, NW., Washington, DC 20224.

FOR FURTHER INFORMATION CONTACT: Concerning proposed regulations, Kevin M. Jacobs at (202) 317-5332 or Marie C. Milnes-Vasquez at (202) 317-7700; concerning submissions of comments or requests for a public hearing, Regina L. Johnson at (202) 317-6901 (not toll free numbers).

SUPPLEMENTARY INFORMATION:

Background

I. *Overview*

This document contains proposed amendments to the Income Tax Regulations (26 CFR part 1) under section 382 of the Code.

A. *Section 382 Generally*

Section 382 imposes a value-based limitation (section 382 limitation) on the ability of a "loss corporation" to offset its taxable income in periods subsequent to an "ownership change" with losses attributable to periods prior to that ownership change. A *loss corporation* is defined under section 382 as a corporation that has one or more of the following tax items: (i) certain carryovers (including net operating loss (NOL), capital loss, disallowed business interest under section 163(j), and certain credit carryovers), (ii) certain attributes (including an NOL, net capital loss, and certain credits) for the taxable year during which an ownership change occurs, or (iii) a net unrealized built-in loss (NUBIL) as of the ownership change. (Any recognized built-in loss (RBIL) associated with a NUBIL, as well as each of the items in (i) and (ii) is referred to herein as a *pre-change loss*.) For purposes of section 382, an *ownership change* occurs if the percentage of the loss corporation's stock owned by any "5-percent shareholders" (that is, a shareholder that owns at least five percent of the loss corporation's stock) increases by more than 50 percentage points during a specified testing period. The section 382 limitation imposed on a loss corporation's use of pre-change losses for each year subsequent to an ownership change generally equals the fair market value of the loss corporation immediately before the ownership change, multiplied by the applicable long-term tax-exempt rate as defined in section 382(f).

Section 382(m) requires the Secretary to prescribe such regulations as may be necessary or appropriate to carry out the purposes of section 382 (as well as section 383, which limits the use of certain credits after an ownership change).

The existing regulations under section 382, which have developed over the past three decades, provide detailed guidance on numerous (but not all) aspects of the relatively detailed statutory rules set forth in section 382. However, in some cases, the Treasury Department and the IRS have found it appropriate to provide guidance to the public through the issuance of notices or other sub-regulatory guidance.

B. *Built-in Gains and Losses Generally*

Section 382(h) provides rules relating to the determination of a loss corporation's built-in gains and losses as of the date of the ownership change (change date). In general, built-in gains recognized during the five-year period beginning on the change date (recognition period) allow a loss corporation to increase its section 382 limitation, whereas built-in losses recognized during the recognition period are subject to the loss corporation's section 382 limitation. These rules exist to implement the "neutrality principle" underlying the statute, which is discussed in more detail in part II.B.2. of the Explanation of Provisions. Under this principle, the built-in gains and losses of a loss corporation, if recognized during the recognition period, generally are to be treated in the same manner as if they had been recognized before the ownership change.

Specifically, section 382(h)(1)(A) provides that, if a loss corporation has a net unrealized built-in gain (NUBIG), the section 382 limitation for any taxable year ending during the recognition period is increased by the recognized built-in gain (RBIG) for the taxable year, with cumulative increases limited to the amount of the NUBIG. Section 382(h)(3)(A) defines NUBIG with respect to a loss corporation as the amount by which the fair market value of its assets immediately before an ownership change exceeds the aggregate adjusted basis of such assets at such time. Section 382(h)(2)(A) defines RBIG as any gain recognized during the recognition period on the disposition of any asset of the loss corporation, to the extent the loss corporation establishes that (i) the loss corporation held the asset on the change date, and (ii) such gain does not exceed the asset's built-in gain on the change date. Section 382(h)(6)(A) also treats as RBIG "[a]ny item of income which is properly taken into account during the recognition period . . . but which is attributable to periods before the change date." Because RBIG can increase the section 382 limitation only up to the amount of NUBIG, section 382(h)(6)(C) provides that NUBIG is increased to reflect amounts that would be treated as RBIG under section 382(h)(6)(A) if such amounts were taken into account during the recognition period. This adjustment can cause (i) an increase in NUBIG, (ii) a decrease in NUBIL, or even (iii) a change from NUBIL to NUBIG status.

Section 382(h)(1)(B) provides that, if a loss corporation has a NUBIL, the use of any RBIL recognized during the recognition period is subject to the section 382 limitation. Section 382(h)(3)(A) defines NUBIL with respect to a loss corporation as the amount by which the aggregate adjusted basis of the loss corporation's assets immediately before an ownership change exceeds the fair market value of such assets at such time. Section 382(h)(2)(B) defines RBIL as any loss recognized during the recognition period on the disposition of any asset of the loss corporation, except to the extent the loss corporation establishes that (i) the loss corporation did not hold the asset on the change date, or (ii) such loss exceeds the asset's built-in loss on the change date. Section 382(h)(6)(B) also treats as RBIL "[a]ny amount which is allowable as a deduction during the recognition period (determined without regard to any carryover) but which is attributable to periods before the change date." In addition, section 382(h)(6)(C) provides that a loss corporation's NUBIL is properly adjusted for amounts which would be treated as RBIL under section 382(h)(6)(B) if such amounts were properly allowable as a deduction during the recognition period.

Finally, section 382(h)(3)(B) provides that if a loss corporation's NUBIG or NUBIL is not greater than the lesser of (i) 15 percent of the fair market value of the loss corporation's assets immediately before the ownership change, or (ii) $10,000,000, then the loss corporation's NUBIG or NUBIL is zero.

II. *Notice 2003-65*

The rules for identifying RBIG and RBIL under sections 382(h)(6)(A) and 382(h)(6)(B) are sufficient for determinations regarding dispositions of assets. Section 382(h)(6)(A) and (B) provide that income and deduction items that constitute RBIG and RBIL are those tax items that are "attributable to periods before the change date", but are not taken into account for tax purposes until a later time. However, taxpayers historically have expressed uncertainty regarding how to integrate into their RBIG/RBIL and corresponding NUBIG/NUBIL calculations the effects of (i) discharge of indebtedness income, (ii) contingent liabilities, (iii) bad debt deductions, and (iv) cost-recovery deductions. In many instances, the fact-specific characteristics of those items have presented significant complications for such taxpayers in determining whether those items were attributable to periods before the change date. The Treasury Department and the IRS agree with taxpayers that sections 382(h)(6)(A) and 382(h)(6)(B) do not provide sufficient guidance regarding identification of other items of RBIG and RBIL.

To provide interim guidance regarding the identification of those built-in gains and losses under section 382(h), the IRS published Notice 2003-65 (2003-2 C.B. 747). This notice permits taxpayers to rely on safe harbor approaches for applying section 382(h) to an ownership change "prior to the effective date of temporary or final regulations under section 382(h)." Notice 2003-65, section V. In addition, the IRS announced its intent in the notice to publish proposed regulations to "provid[e] a single set of rules for identifying built-in items for purposes of section 382(h)." *Id.*, section VII. In particular, the notice requested comments regarding "whether one of the two approaches described in th[e] notice should be adopted and to what extent, if any, the approaches should be combined or modified to produce a set of rules that is both reflective of statutory intent and administrable." *Id.*

Notice 2003-65 provides, among other things, a single safe harbor for computing the NUBIG or NUBIL of a loss corporation, which (i) is based on principles underlying the calculation of net recognized built-in gain under section 1374 for purposes of the tax imposed on C corporations that elect to be S corporations, and (ii) analyzes a hypothetical sale or exchange of all assets of the loss corporation to a third party who assumed all of the loss corporation's liabilities. In addition, Notice 2003-65 provides two safe harbors for the computation of a loss corporation's RBIG or RBIL: the 1374 approach and the 338 approach. These safe harbors specifically inform the identification of built-in income and deduction items under section 382(h)(6)(A) and (B), and the adjustments to NUBIG or NUBIL that would result under section 382(h)(6)(C).

The 1374 approach identifies RBIG and RBIL at the time of the disposition of a loss corporation's assets during the recognition period. Generally, this approach relies on accrual method of accounting principles to identify built-in income and deduction items at the time of the ownership change, with certain exceptions. In contrast, the 338 approach identifies items of RBIG and RBIL generally by comparing the loss corporation's actual items of income, gain, deduction, and loss recognized during the recognition period with those that would have been recognized if an election under section 338 (section 338 election) had been made with respect to a hypothetical purchase of all of the outstanding stock of the loss corporation on the change date. Section V. of Notice 2003-65 provides that taxpayers may rely on either the 338 approach or the 1374 approach until the Treasury Department and the IRS issue temporary or final regulations under section 382(h).

Prior to the issuance of Notice 2003-65, the Treasury Department and the IRS issued Notice 87-79 (1987-2 C.B. 387) and Notice 90-29 (1990-1 C.B. 336), which provided much more limited guidance regarding the determination of built-in gains and losses. Notice 87-79, which Notice 2003-65 modified, discussed anticipated regulations regarding the interplay of section 382(h) and discharge of indebtedness income. Notice 90-29 set forth an approach that Notice 2003-65 adopted as part of its section 1374 safe harbor, and similarly discussed anticipated regulations (regarding the application of section 382(h) to gains reported using the installment method under section 453). As discussed in more detail in part I.B.2 of this Explanation of Provisions, the Treasury Department and the IRS published Notice 2018-30 (2018-21 I.R.B. 610) following "An Act to provide for reconciliation pursuant to titles II and V of the concurrent resolution on the budget for fiscal year 2018," Public Law 115-97, 131 Stat. 2054 (2017), commonly referred to as the Tax Cuts and Jobs Act (TCJA). Specifically, Notice 2018-30 makes the section 338 safe harbor of Notice 2003-65 unavailable when computing items arising from bonus depreciation under section 168(k).

III. *Response to Notice 2003-65*

Over the past fifteen years, the Treasury Department and the IRS have received thoughtful formal and informal commentary highlighting numerous shortcomings of the interim guidance set forth in Notice 2003-65. Examples of these shortcomings include: (i) the overstatement of NUBIG (or understatement of NUBIL) that occurs when a loss corporation has excluded discharge or cancellation of indebtedness income (COD income), (ii) the asymmetry that occurs if certain amounts are included in the NUBIG/NUBIL computation when those amounts cannot be treated as RBIG or RBIL (such as contingent liabilities under the 1374 approach), which appears to contravene section 382(h)(6)(C), and (iii) taxpayer uncertainty and tax administration challenges that arise from a lack of definitive guidance under section 382(h). Commenters and commentators (collectively, commentators) generally have emphasized the simplicity, objectivity, and administrability of the accrual-based 1374 approach, as well as that approach's close adherence to a plain reading of the statutory text of section 382(h) and section 382(h)'s legislative history. With regard to the 338 approach, commentators generally have appreciated that approach's attempt to quantify and capture items that were economically built-in at the time of the ownership change, rather than simply accrued under tax accounting principles. Commentators have also noted that the 338 approach will reduce the impact of the recognition period's limited duration, by not requiring taxpayers to dispose of certain assets within such period to be treated as RBIG. In sum, commentators have acknowledged merits, as well as weaknesses, unique to each of the 1374 and 338 approaches but have not reached consensus favoring a universal application of either approach during the 15 years since the IRS published Notice 2003-65.

IV. *Enactment of the TCJA*

On December 22, 2017, Congress enacted the TCJA, which introduced substantial changes to the Code. These changes have generated significant, additional uncertainty regarding the application of section 382 in general, and Notice 2003-65 in particular. As described in greater detail in part II. of the Explanation of Provisions, the changes to various provisions of the Code made by the TCJA have exacerbated longstanding, unresolved issues regarding the application of section 382(h) and created new areas of complexity and ambiguity for taxpayers and the IRS. In particular, the Treasury Department and the IRS have identified numerous issues that would arise from the interaction of the 338 approach with various provisions of the Code following the TCJA's enactment. *See* Explanation of Provisions, part I.B.2.

Consequently, the Treasury Department and the IRS are issuing these proposed regulations to provide clearer and more comprehensive guidance for taxpayers in applying section 382(h) than that currently provided by notice. The Treasury Department and the IRS have determined that the proposed regulations would (i) simplify the application of section 382, (ii) provide more certainty to taxpayers in determining built-in gains and losses for section 382(h) purposes, and (iii) ensure that difficult questions regarding the application of the TCJA do not further complicate the application of section 382(h). The Treasury Department and the IRS note that, as provided in Section V. of Notice 2003-65, taxpayers may rely on the approaches set forth in Notice 2003-65 for purposes of applying section 382(h) to an ownership change that occurred prior to the issuance of Notice 2003-65 or on or after the issuance of the notice and prior to the effective date of temporary or final regulations under section 382(h). After consideration of all comments regarding the proposed regulations set forth in this notice of proposed rulemaking, the Treasury Department and the IRS expect to issue final regulations to adopt the proposed regulations, which may include modifications in response to those comments. It is further expected that the Treasury decision adopting these proposed regulations as final regulations will withdraw and obsolete Notice 2003-65 and other administrative guidance associated with section 382(h) set forth in the Effect on Other Documents section of this notice of proposed rulemaking.

Explanation of Provisions

I. *Proposed Adoption of NUBIG/NUBIL Safe Harbor and 1374 Approach*

A. *Overview*

With regard to the computation of NUBIG and NUBIL, these proposed regulations would adopt as mandatory the safe harbor computation provided in Notice 2003-65 based on the principles of section 1374, with modifications described in part II.B. of this Explanation of Provisions. Regarding the identification of RBIG and RBIL, based on study and taxpayer input, and as discussed further in part I.A. and part I.B. of this Explanation of Provisions, the Treasury Department and the IRS have concluded that the 1374 approach is more consistent with the text and the purpose of section 382 than the 338 approach and would simplify tax administration. Accordingly, these proposed regulations would adopt as mandatory the 1374 approach with certain modifications also described in part II.C. of this Explanation of Provisions.

As previously highlighted, the Treasury Department and the IRS, along with numerous commentators, view favorably the simplicity, objectivity, and administrability of the 1374 approach. The accrual-based 1374 approach to be used in determining RBIG and RBIL is simpler to apply than the 338 approach because, among other reasons, corporate taxpayers and their advisors are familiar with the accrual method of accounting. Indeed, a sizable volume of case law, Code provisions, and regulations govern the accrual method (for example, *Schlude v. Commissioner*, 372 U.S. 128 (1963), *Brown v. Helvering*, 291 U.S. 193 (1934), and *United States v. Anderson*, 269 U.S. 422 (1926); sections 446, 451, and 461; and the regulations under those Code provisions). In addition, the accrual-based 1374 approach avoids many facts-and-circumstance inquiries by avoiding tracing, valuation uncertainties, and presumptions regarding whether items of income are realized for Federal income tax purposes.

The Treasury Department and the IRS have determined that the certainty provided by the 1374 approach would streamline (i) the calculation of built-in gains and losses for taxpayers, as well as (ii) the administration of this area for the IRS. The 1374 approach turns on an accrual analysis of the loss corporation's actual transactions and circumstances, and consequently minimizes the importation of new issues arising from changes made by the TCJA, particularly those issues described in detail later in part I.B.2. of this Explanation of Provisions. The Treasury Department and the IRS welcome public comment on the proposed adoption of a modified 1374 approach for determining RBIG and RBIL.

B. *Consideration and Proposed Elimination of the 338 Approach*

After study, and based on taxpayer input, the Treasury Department and the IRS have decided not to incorporate the 338 approach into these proposed regulations. As described in part I.B.1. of this Explanation of Provisions, the Treasury Department and the IRS have concluded that the 338 approach lacks sufficient grounding in the statutory text of section 382(h). Further, the Treasury Department and the IRS have determined that the mechanics underlying the 338 approach (i) are inherently more complex than the accrual-based 1374 approach, (ii) can result in overstatements of RBIG and RBIL, and (iii) as a result of the TCJA, would require substantial modifications to eliminate increased uncertainty and ensure appropriate results. By eliminating the 338 approach, the Treasury Department and the IRS have determined that these proposed regulations would significantly reduce current and future complexity of section 382(h) computations for taxpayers and the IRS alike. The Treasury Department and the IRS welcome public comment on this proposed elimination of the 338 approach for determining RBIG and RBIL.

1. *Historical Weaknesses of the 338 Approach*

The 338 approach originated in subregulatory guidance set forth in Notice 2003-65, and possesses significantly less grounding in the statutory text of section 382(h) than the 1374 approach. The comparatively tenuous connection between the 338 approach and the plain meaning of the statutory text of section 382(h) is exemplified by the method by which the 338 approach identifies RBIG. Under the 338 approach, depreciation deductions on certain built-in gain assets give rise to RBIG, even though no actual recognition of gain or income has occurred. However, sections 382(h)(2)(A) and 382(h)(6)(A) do not authorize RBIG treatment in the absence of actual gain or income recognized by the loss corporation.

Further, commentators have noted that difficult questions arise regarding deemed tiered section 338 elections when the 338 approach is applied to a loss corporation that is the parent of other corporations. For example, there are often significant differences between the basis of stock held by a loss corporation in subsidiaries and the basis of the assets held by the subsidiaries, and those differences create disparate outcomes. Tiered section 338 elections, including with respect to controlled foreign corporations, could have significant impacts on the outcomes produced under this approach.

2. *Additional Complications of the 338 Approach Following the TCJA*

The Treasury Department and the IRS introduced the 338 approach in 2003 after substantial review of the manner in which then-applicable Code provisions would apply to a section 338 election. In the pre-TCJA environment, provisions of the Code largely would have applied to the taxpayer in the same manner under a hypothetical sale resulting from a section 338 election as those provisions would have applied to the taxpayer without that hypothetical-sale treatment. However, certain important changes under the TCJA have caused the treatment of newly purchased assets to diverge from the treatment of historic assets, thus potentially compromising the mechanics of the 338 approach.

For example, the Treasury Department and the IRS have observed that TCJA amendments to section 168(k) invalidate the key assumption underlying application of the 338 approach to depreciable ("wasting") assets, which is to reflect an estimate of income or expense generated by an asset during a particular period. Consequently, to prevent unintended collateral consequences of the additional first-year depreciation available under amended section 168(k), the Treasury Department and the IRS published Notice 2018-30 (2018-21 I.R.B. 610). Without the additional guidance set forth in Notice 2018-30, the Treasury Department and the IRS concluded that the 338 approach's hypothetical cost recovery deduction resulting from a hypothetical application of additional first-year depreciation under section 168(k) would fail to provide a reasonable estimate of the income or expense produced by a built-in gain or loss asset during the recognition period.

Moreover, the Treasury Department and the IRS have identified additional issues that would arise from the interaction of the 338 approach with other provisions of the TCJA, each of which would require extensive study and potentially the issuance of additional guidance. For example, the limitation on a loss corporation's interest deduction under amended section 163(j) and the modifications to the NOL deduction rules under amended section 172 are each based on variants of taxable income. However, a hypothetical sale of a loss corporation's assets under section 338 upon an ownership change would result in different taxable income computations than before the TCJA. Unanswered questions related to sections 163(j) and 172 would further complicate application of the 338 approach. Further, income inclusions under section 951A may increase existing concerns (including as a result of potential changes in hypothetical QBAI basis from deemed tiered section 338 elections) arising under the 338 approach. Taken as a whole, the Treasury Department and the IRS have determined that the continued application of the 338 approach likely would not be tenable after the changes to the Code enacted by the TCJA. The Treasury Department and the IRS request public comment on the proposed elimination of the 338 approach for determining RBIG and RBIL, including detailed comments with regard to whether it would be appropriate within the limits of the statute to consider special rules for insolvent or bankrupt loss corporations, and whether a redefinition of the date on which the recognition period begins would increase simplification.

II. *Description of Proposed NUBIG/NUBIL Safe Harbor and Proposed 1374 Approach*

A. *Overview*

The proposed approach described in this part II incorporates certain modifications to the NUBIG/NUBIL safe harbor and the 1374 approach to ensure greater consistency between (i) amounts that are included in the NUBIG/NUBIL computation and (ii) items that could become RBIG or RBIL during the recognition period. These modifications would better implement the requirements of section 382(h)(6)(C). As described in this part II, the RBIG and RBIL rules remain closely based upon the 1374 approach set forth in Notice 2003-65. However, these proposed regulations would make the modifications described in this part II to improve accuracy, particularly with regard to COD income and deductions for the payment of contingent liabilities.

B. *Proposed Rules for Computation of NUBIG or NUBIL*

1. *In General*

The proposed rules regarding the computation of NUBIG/NUBIL set forth in these proposed regulations would capture a range of items that closely tracks the NUBIG/NUBIL safe harbor computation under Notice 2003-65. However, the proposed regulations would enhance the transparency and clarity of that computation by making its component steps more explicit. Specifically, the proposed NUBIG/NUBIL computation first takes into account the aggregate amount that would be realized in a hypothetical disposition of all of the loss corporation's assets in two steps treated as taking place immediately before the ownership change. In the first step, the loss corporation is treated as satisfying any inadequately secured nonrecourse liability by surrendering to each creditor the assets securing such debt. In the second step, the loss corporation is treated as selling all remaining assets pertinent to the NUBIG/NUBIL computation in a sale to an unrelated third party, with the hypothetical buyer assuming no amount of the seller's liabilities. That total hypothetical amount realized by the loss corporation pursuant to steps one and two is then decreased by the sum of the loss corporation's deductible liabilities (both fixed and contingent), and also decreased by the loss corporation's basis in its assets. Finally, the decreased hypothetical total is then increased or decreased, as applicable, by the following: (1) the net amount of the total RBIG and RBIL income and deduction items that could be recognized during the recognition period (excluding COD income); and (2) the net amount of positive and negative section 481 adjustments that would be required to be included on the previously-described hypothetical disposal of all of the loss corporation's assets.

The Treasury Department and the IRS welcome public comment on all aspects of these proposed rules regarding the computation of NUBIG and NUBIL.

2. *Proposed Adjustments to Account for Built-In COD Income*

Section 61(a)(12) of the Code provides that gross income includes COD income, except as provided by law. Section 108(a) provides, in part, that gross income of a C corporation does not include COD income of the taxpayer if the discharge occurs in a title 11 case, or the discharge occurs when the taxpayer is insolvent, but only to the extent of the insolvency (excluded COD income).

If a taxpayer has excluded COD income, section 108(b)(1) requires the taxpayer to reduce its tax attributes by the amount excluded. In general, pursuant to section 108(b)(2), tax attributes are reduced in the following order: NOLs and NOL carryovers, general business credits under section 38, minimum tax credits under section 53(b), net capital losses and capital loss carryovers, asset basis, passive activity loss and credit carryovers under section 469(b), and foreign tax credits and foreign tax credit carryovers. Any amount of debt discharge that remains after attribute reduction is not includible in income. See H.R. Rep. No. 96-833 at 11 (1980); S. Rep. No. 96-1035 at 13 (1980).

These provisions are designed to "preserve the debtor's 'fresh start' after bankruptcy." H.R. Rep. No. 96-833 at 9 (1980); see S. Rep. No. 96-1035 at 10 (1980). In addition, they are intended to "carry out the Congressional intent of deferring, but eventually collecting within a reasonable period, tax on ordinary income realized from debt discharge." H.R. Rep. No. 96-833 at 9 (1980); see S. Rep. No. 96-1035 at 10 (1980). By making attributes unavailable to offset income in later years, the provisions offer the debtor a temporary, rather than a permanent, deferral of tax.

As discussed in part II of the Background section, significant uncertainty has existed with regard to administering the built-in gain and loss framework of section 382(h). However, in administering this area, the Treasury Department and the IRS have always sought to implement a guiding principle discussed in the section 382 legislative history, which is commonly referred to as the "neutrality principle." Under this principle, the built-in gains and losses of a loss corporation, once recognized after an ownership change, generally are to be treated in the same manner as if they had been recognized before the ownership change. For example, it is the neutrality principle that causes RBIL to be limited in the same manner as a pre-change NOL carryforward or net capital loss carryforward. Similarly, in the built-in gain context, the neutrality principle dictates that section 382-limited losses be freely usable against RBIG because, had the gain been taken into account before the ownership change, use of the loss would not have been subject to (that is, limited by) section 382. Under section 382(h), RBIG results in a dollar-for-dollar increase in the loss corporation's section 382 limit in order to replicate this pre-ownership change treatment. See S. Rept. 99-313 at 235; H.R. Rept. 99-426 at 261.

In Notice 2003-65, the Treasury Department and the IRS attempted to provide guidance integrating into the NUBIG/NUBIL computation the amount of insolvency of the loss corporation (the amount by which its liabilities exceed the value of its assets) and, therefore, the maximum possible amount of "built-in" COD income, as of the change date. However, Notice 2003-65 does not distinguish between the eventual excluded or included nature of COD income actually recognized by the loss corporation during the recognition period. After administrative experience under Notice 2003-65 and as highlighted by commentators, the Treasury Department and the IRS have determined that this failure to distinguish between includable and excludable COD income results in the overstatement of RBIG (or understatement of RBIL) in contravention of section 382(h)(6)(C). This failure also effectively provides for a duplicated benefit under the section 382(h) RBIG rules in certain cases. The Treasury Department and the IRS interpret section 382(h)(6)(C) as requiring inclusion in the NUBIG/NUBIL computation only the amounts that would be treated as RBIG or RBIL if those amounts were properly taken into account during the recognition period.

Further, the Treasury Department and the IRS have determined that the treatment of COD income under Notice 2003-65 violates the neutrality principle previously discussed. The Treasury Department and the IRS have determined that RBIG treatment (as well as the ancillary increase in NUBIG or decrease in NUBIL) should be available only to the extent that the neutrality principle requires an increase in the loss corporation's section 382 limitation.

The application of the attribute reduction rules of section 108(b) to excluded COD income complicates the RBIG and NUBIG calculation. The Treasury Department and the IRS understand that most excluded COD income is offset under section 108(b) by reducing tax attributes of the loss corporation that are treated as pre-change losses under section 382. To the extent that pre-change losses have already been used to offset this pre-change income, the neutrality principle prohibits an increase in the section 382 limitation. Indeed, such an increase could make excluded COD income more attractive than included COD income (or any other built-in gain item) for purposes of section 382. For this reason, the Treasury Department and the IRS have determined that the recognition of such excluded COD income should not generate RBIG. Because NUBIG functions as a ceiling on the amount of RBIG that may be claimed (and the corresponding amount of increase in the section 382 limitation), there does not appear to be a policy need nor a statutory basis for adjusting the NUBIG/NUBIL computation if there is no need to increase the section 382 limitation.

Inclusion of excludable COD income in the calculation of NUBIG/NUBIL would be particularly distortive if a loss corporation deconsolidates from a group as a result of its ownership change, and recognizes excludable COD income on the change date. Under the consolidated return regulations, any excludable COD income recognized on the date of deconsolidation is treated as attributable to the taxable year of the transferor group (rather than post-change, in the loss corporation's separate taxable year). Therefore, such excludable COD income should not be treated as RBIG (pre-change income recognized in the post-change period).

Accordingly, these proposed regulations generally would not allow COD income to be included in the calculation of NUBIG/NUBIL, but would provide certain exceptions. Includable COD by its nature is not complicated by the interaction of section 108(b). Therefore, to satisfy the neutrality principle, all includable COD income of the loss corporation that is recognized on recourse debt during the 12-month period following the change date would be eligible for inclusion in the NUBIG/NUBIL computation, subject to limitations discussed in part II.C.2 of this Explanation of Provisions. However, these proposed regulations would permit excluded COD income items to be treated as RBIG (and thus affect NUBIG/NUBIL calculation) only to the extent described in part II.C of this Explanation of Provisions. The Treasury Department and the IRS welcome public comment on the proposed regulations' approach regarding excludible and includible COD income in calculating NUBIG and NUBIL, including comments with regard to whether it would be appropriate within the limits of the statute to consider special rules for insolvent or bankrupt loss corporations. Comments are also invited with regard to the possibility of redefining the recognition period to begin on the date after the ownership change, and any issues that might be eliminated or created by such a redefinition.

C. *Proposed Rules for Identification of RBIG and RBIL Income and Deduction Items*

1. *In General*

These proposed regulations would apply a methodology for identifying RBIG or RBIL that closely tracks the 1374 approach described in Notice 2003-65. This approach is generally accrual based, with specific exceptions. Many of the special rules incorporated in these proposed regulations originate in regulations underlying section 1374. However, these proposed regulations would make minor changes to improve the computational accuracy of the 1374 approach. For example, in response to comments on Notice 2003-65, these proposed regulations would provide an improved methodology for computing the amount of depreciation deductions treated as RBIL during the recognition period.

In addition, these proposed regulations would significantly modify the 1374 approach set forth in Notice 2003-65 to include as RBIL the amount of any deductible contingent liabilities paid or accrued during the recognition period, to the extent of the estimated value of those liabilities on the change date. Commentators noted that Notice 2003-65 appeared to include this estimated amount in its NUBIG/NUBIL computation, but did not treat deductible liability payments or accruals as RBIL. That incongruity contravenes section 382(h)(6)(C), which requires that items be included in the NUBIG/NUBIL computation if they would be treated as RBIG or RBIL if properly taken into account during the recognition period.

Further, these proposed regulations would add a rule clarifying that certain items do not constitute RBIG. For example, the proposed regulations provide that dividends paid on stock during the recognition period are not RBIG, even if the loss corporation has a NUBIG and there is gain built into the pertinent stock immediately before the ownership change. On the other hand, gain recognized on the disposition of stock generally would be treated as giving rise to RBIG. However, gain taxable as a dividend under section 1248 would generally give rise to a deduction under section 245A, with no net income being generated. Because no losses would be required to offset this item of income, the Treasury Department and the IRS have determined that this income item should not give rise to RBIG.

The Treasury Department and the IRS welcome public comment on the proposed regulations' identification of RBIG and RBIL. In particular, the Treasury Department and the IRS request comments regarding whether dividends paid on built-in gain stock should constitute RBIG, and whether final regulations should clarify the eligibility of other, similar income items for RBIG treatment.

2. *Proposed Treatment of COD Income as RBIG*

These proposed regulations would provide limitations on the extent to which excluded COD income is treated as RBIG, and thus would impact the calculation of NUBIG/NUBIL. As discussed in part II.B.2 of this Explanation of Provisions, RBIG effectuates the neutrality principle in the post-change period and therefore COD income must be able to be taken into account during the post-change period in order to qualify for RBIG status. Thus, COD income that is taken into account during the pre-change period (for example, excluded COD income recognized by a consolidated group member on an ownership change that causes the member to deconsolidate) should not qualify as RBIG. The proposed regulations also provide that COD income recognized during the post-change period generally would not be treated as RBIG. However, these proposed regulations would provide taxpayers with the option to treat certain COD income recognized during the first 12 months of the recognition period as RBIG (and consequently to make corresponding adjustments to the taxpayer's NUBIG/NUBIL computation). For example, the proposed regulations provide that COD income on recourse debt that is included in a loss corporation's taxable income under section 61(a)(12) during the first 12 months of the post-change period would be treated as RBIG as described in part II.B.2. of this Explanation of Provisions. Therefore, the loss corporation's section 382 limitation would be increased by the amount of such COD income, and pre-change losses may be deducted in the amount of the COD income. The 12-month limitation on RBIG treatment is adopted from the 1374 approach under Notice 2003-65.

Under the proposed regulations, excluded COD income recognized during the post-change period generally would not be treated as RBIG, in order to prevent the duplication of section 382 benefits. For example, if excluded COD income recognized during the post-change period (but not included in a loss corporation's income) is offset by pre-change losses, the loss corporation would receive the same benefit as a loss corporation that recognized included COD income: the ability to offset the COD income with pre-change losses. Therefore, the Treasury Department and the IRS have determined that extending the additional benefit of RBIG treatment (and the resulting increase in NUBIG or decrease in NUBIL) to post-change period excluded COD income generally would result in a duplication of section 382 benefits to the loss corporation.

However, these proposed regulations would provide two exceptions to this general rule to address cases in which excluded COD income recognized by a loss corporation during the first 12 months of its post-change period is offset by post-change tax attributes under section 108(b) or by basis reduction in assets held as of the change date under section 1017. To the extent that excluded COD income is offset by post-change tax attributes, the loss corporation would not yet have used pre-change loss equal to the amount of that excluded COD income. Therefore, the excluded COD income would be treated as RBIG, and the loss corporation's NUBIG/NUBIL would be adjusted accordingly. Similarly, to the extent that excluded COD income is offset by reduction in the tax basis of assets held immediately before the ownership change, the loss corporation would not have used pre-change loss equal to that excluded COD income. Under these proposed regulations (as under Notice 2003-65), that basis reduction would be treated as occurring immediately before the ownership change. As a result of that basis reduction, the corresponding amount of excluded COD income would be included in the NUBIG/NUBIL computation, and no further adjustment would be necessary. Accordingly, the excluded COD income would not be treated as RBIG, to avoid double-counting. Any additional gain on the disposition of assets during the recognition period resulting from the basis adjustment would be treated as RBIG, to the extent of the NUBIG limitation.

Different treatment is required, to the extent that excluded COD is offset by reduction in the tax basis of assets that were acquired after the ownership change. The basis adjustments to those assets would not result in an adjustment to NUBIG/NUBIL, nor could any RBIG be produced from those assets because assets not held at the time of the ownership change are not included in the NUBIG/NUBIL computation. Similarly, RBIG cannot be generated on the sale of assets that were not held at the time of the ownership change. Therefore, the excluded COD income would be treated as RBIG and the NUBIG/NUBIL would be adjusted accordingly.

The Treasury Department and the IRS welcome public comment on the proposed regulations' approach regarding the treatment of excludible and includible COD income as RBIG. Further, the Treasury Department and the IRS request comments regarding what rules should govern the treatment of COD that is excluded under section 108(a)(1)(C) and (D) (qualified farm indebtedness and qualified real estate business indebtedness).

3. *Overall limitations on amount of RBIL for COD on Recourse Debt*

These proposed regulations set forth two different RBIG ceilings with regard to COD on recourse debt. The first ceiling applies to taxpayers that are in bankruptcy at the time of the ownership change, and have COD income pursuant to that bankruptcy action during the first twelve months of the recognition period. The maximum RBIG for those taxpayers related to excluded COD income would be the amount of indebtedness discharged in that bankruptcy action. The second ceiling applies to all other taxpayers who recognize COD income during the first twelve months of the recognition period. The maximum RBIG for those taxpayers is the excess of liabilities over asset value immediately before the change date, with certain adjustments. Adjustments must be made to avoid double counting amounts of excluded COD that are offset by reductions in asset basis under sections 108(b) and 1017. The Treasury Department and the IRS welcome public comment on these two RBIG ceilings with regard to COD income on recourse debt.

4. *Special Rules for Nonrecourse Debt*

RBIG status for COD income on nonrecourse debt recognized in the first 12 months of the recognition period is subject to rules similar to those previously described. However, such COD income is treated as built-in gain only to the extent that the nonrecourse debt was under-secured immediately before the ownership change. Because a nonrecourse creditor has a claim only on the assets securing the indebtedness, the amount of the impairment at the time of the ownership change is the appropriate measure of built-in COD in the nonrecourse debt. Further, RBIG recognized on nonrecourse debt during the recognition period does not result in an adjustment to NUBIG/NUBIL, because the amount of the impairment to the nonrecourse debt is already built into the initial NUBIG/NUBIL computation with regard to the deemed disposition of assets. The Treasury Department and the IRS welcome public comment on the treatment of COD income on non-recourse debt, including comments on the treatment of accrued but unpaid interest.

D. *Interactions between sections 163(j) and 382*

The addition of new section 163(j) under the TCJA has created numerous issues concerning the interaction of those interest deduction limitations with section 382. These proposed regulations attempt to eliminate the possibility of duplication of RBIL items, as well as to clarify the treatment under section 382 of certain items that are allocated from a partnership.

1. *Elimination of Possible Duplicative Recognized Built-in Loss*

Proposed § 1.382-7 addresses the possible duplicative application of section 382 to certain disallowed business interest expense carryforwards, including the portion of any disallowed business interest expense of the old loss corporation that is (i) paid or accrued in the taxable year of the testing date (as defined in § 1.382-2(b)(4)), (ii) attributable to the pre-change period, and (iii) carried forward into later years (collectively, a section 382 disallowed business interest carryforward). Section 382 disallowed business interest carryforwards are subject to section 382 by virtue of section 382(d)(3), which treats any section 163(j)(2) carryover from a pre-change period as a pre-change loss. Additionally, such carryforwards are potentially subject to the section 382 limitation under section 382(h)(6) as RBIL. Section 382(h)(6)(B) provides that any amount allowable as a deduction during the recognition period (within the meaning of section 382(h)(7)), determined without regard to any carryover, that is attributable to periods before the change date is treated as a RBIL for the taxable year for which it is allowable as a deduction. Further, section 382(h)(6)(C) provides that the amount of NUBIG or NUBIL must be properly adjusted for amounts that would be treated as RBIG or RBIL under section 382(h)(6) if such amounts were properly taken into account or allowable as a deduction during the recognition period.

Section 382 disallowed business interest carryforwards should not be counted twice for purposes of the application of section 382. Subjecting the same section 382 disallowed business interest carryforward to the section 382 regime in two different ways could result in a double reduction of the annual section 382 limitation. Moreover, because disallowed business interest expense carryforwards would be absorbed before NOL carryovers under proposed § 1.383-1(d), subjecting the same disallowed business interest expense carryforward to the section 382 regime twice could preclude taxpayers from utilizing their NOL carryovers or other attributes. In addition, treatment of disallowed business interest carryforwards as potential RBIL would result in an unwarranted increase in NUBIL (or decrease in NUBIG).

Accordingly, proposed § 1.382-7(d)(5) would provide that section 382 disallowed business interest carryforwards would not be treated as RBIL under section 382(h)(6)(B) if such amounts were allowable as a deduction during the recognition period.

2. *Treatment of Excess Business Interest Expense of a Partnership*

Proposed § 1.382-7 addresses the application of section 382(h) to excess business interest expense of a partnership to the extent that the item was not suspended under section 704(d) and is allocable to an old loss corporation (as partner) with regard to a period prior to an ownership change (section 382 excess business interest expense). Section 382(h)(3)(A)(i) provides that the amount of the old loss corporation's NUBIG or NUBIL includes the amount by which the aggregate fair market value of certain assets is more or less than the aggregate adjusted basis of such assets. As provided in section 163(j)(4)(B)(iii) and proposed § 1.163-6(h)(3)(i), if a partner disposes of all or substantially all of its partnership interest, the adjusted basis of the partner in the partnership interest would be increased immediately before the disposition to reflect the partner's section 382 excess business interest expense from the partnership, if any. Therefore, proposed § 1.382-7(c)(3)(iii)(E) would provide that, for purposes of determining RBIL under section 382(h)(2)(B)(ii), as well as for computing NUBIG or NUBIL under section 382(h)(3)(A), a loss corporation's adjusted basis in a partnership interest is adjusted as if the loss corporation disposed of all or substantially all of its partnership interests immediately before the ownership change.

During the recognition period, a deduction or loss equal to the section 382 excess business interest expense could be recognized either when the loss corporation is able to deduct the section 382 excess business interest expense, or when it sells all or substantially all of its partnership interest. In either case, such amount is properly characterized as RBIL. However, in either case, no adjustment to the loss corporation's NUBIG or NUBIL computation would be necessary, because the positive adjustment to the basis of the partnership interest ensures that an amount equal to the section 382 excess business interest expense is included in the computation.

A partner also can be allocated section 382 excess business interest expense that is characterized as negative section 163(j) expense. See § 1.163-6(h)(1) as proposed in REG-106089-18 (83 FR 67490, 67556 (Dec. 28, 2018)). Negative section 163(j) expense does not reduce the partner's basis in the partnership and therefore would not be taken into account if the partner sold all or substantially all of its partnership interest. However, if the loss corporation were able to deduct the negative section 163(j) expense during the recognition period, then such expense presumably could be treated as RBIL pursuant to section 382(h)(6)(B). These proposed regulations do not address whether deductions resulting from negative section 163(j) allocations are RBIL.

The Treasury Department and the IRS request comments as to whether a corporate partner's section 382 excess business interest expense and negative section 163(j) expense should be treated as a built-in item under section 382(h)(6) or as a section 382 disallowed business interest carryforward, and therefore be treated as a pre-change loss.

Applicability Dates

Section 7805(b)(1)(A) and (B) of the Code generally provides that no temporary, proposed, or final regulation relating to the internal revenue laws may apply to any taxable period ending before the earliest of (A) the date on which such regulation is filed with the *Federal Register*, or (B) in the case of a final regulation, the date on which a proposed or temporary regulation to which the final regulation relates was filed with the *Federal Register*.

Except as otherwise provided in the following sentence, these regulations are proposed to be effective for ownership changes occurring after the date the Treasury decision adopting these proposed regulations as final regulations is published in the *Federal Register*. However, taxpayers and their related parties, within the meaning of sections 267(b) and 707(b)(1), may apply these proposed regulations to any ownership change occurring during a taxable year with respect to which the period described in section 6511(a) has not expired, so long as the taxpayers and all of their related parties consistently apply the rules of these proposed regulations to such ownership change and all subsequent ownership changes that occur before the applicability date of final regulations.

Effect on Other Documents

The following publications are proposed to be withdrawn and obsoleted effective the day after the date the Treasury decision adopting these proposed regulations as final regulations is published in the *Federal Register* :

Notice 87-79 (1987-2 C.B. 387)

Notice 90-27 (1990-1 C.B. 336)

Notice 2003-65 (2003-2 C.B. 747)

Notice 2018-30 (2018-21 I.R.B. 610)

Special Analyses

I. *Regulatory Planning and Review - Economic Analysis*

Executive Orders 12866 and 13563 direct agencies to assess costs and benefits of available regulatory alternatives and, if regulation is necessary, to select regulatory approaches that maximize net benefits (including (i) potential economic, environmental, and public health and safety effects, (ii) potential distributive impacts, and (iii) equity). Executive Order 13563 emphasizes the importance of quantifying both costs and benefits, reducing costs, harmonizing rules, and promoting flexibility.

These proposed regulations have been designated as subject to review under Executive Order 12866 pursuant to the Memorandum of Agreement (April 11, 2018) (MOA) between the Treasury Department and the Office of Management and Budget (OMB) regarding review of tax regulations. The Office of Information and Regulatory Affairs has designated these proposed regulations as significant under section 1(b) of the MOA. Accordingly, the OMB has reviewed these proposed regulations.

A. *Background*

In general, section 382 limits the usage of a corporation's tax attributes after that corporation experiences an ownership change. Limited tax attributes include, among other items, NOLs and built-in losses. The limit equals the product obtained by multiplying a prescribed interest rate by the value of the stock of the corporation (referred to as the "old loss corporation") on the change date. This product represents a proxy for the amount of income created by the assets held by the corporation prior to the ownership change. The section 382 limit reflects Congress's intent that, generally, NOLs should not be more valuable to an acquirer than to the going concern that created them. In the conference report to the Tax Reform Act of 1986, Congress expressed that the previously described formula "is necessary to ensure that the value of NOL carryforwards to the buying corporation is not more than their value to the loss corporation." H.R. Rep. No. 99-841, at II-185 (1986).

Section 382(h) specifies the treatment of gains and losses accrued by a corporation prior to a change in ownership. As explained in the legislative history, the rules are intended to treat built-in gains and losses that are recognized after the ownership change the same as if they had been recognized before the ownership change. As described by Congress, "[i]f built-in losses were not subject to limitations, taxpayers could reduce or eliminate the impact of the general rules by causing a loss corporation (following an ownership change) to recognize its built-in losses free of the special limitations (and then invest the proceeds in assets similar to the assets sold)." Joint Committee on Tax'n, General Explanation of the Tax Reform Act of 1986 (Pub. L. 99-514) (May 4, 1987), JCS-10-87, at p. 298. The neutral treatment of gains and losses recognized before and after a change in ownership is accomplished by allowing the recognition of built in gain to increase the section 382 limitation whereas the recognition of built in loss is subject to the section 382 limitation.

The following example (Example 1) illustrates this principle. Assume that a loss corporation (LossCorp), as of the change date, has $500 in NOL carryforwards and holds only one asset (Asset A) with a fair market value of $100 and a basis of $120. If LossCorp disposed of Asset A immediately prior to the ownership change, a $20 loss would be recognized. Additionally, assuming the taxpayer made a closing-of-the-books election under § 1.382-6(b), the amount of the NOL carryforwards would be $520. If instead, Asset A was disposed of after the change date, then sections 382(h)(1) and 382(h)(2) recognize that the $20 loss is attributable to the period prior to the ownership change and therefore subject it to a section 382 limitation in the same manner as if it was an NOL carryforward (disregarding a de minimis threshold rule set forth in section 382(h)(3)(B)). In the language of section 382, the $20 loss would be RBIL (that is, recognized built-in loss). These rules operate to eliminate the significance of the disposition's timing and preserve neutrality.

Alternatively, assume in this example (Example 2) that Asset A's fair market value on the change date were $150, and thus LossCorp had a built-in gain on the asset. If LossCorp disposed of Asset A prior to the change date, assuming the taxpayer made a closing-of-the-books election under § 1.382-6(b), then the $30 in income would reduce its NOL carryforward to $470. If instead Asset A were disposed of after the change date, then sections 382(h)(1) and 382(h)(2) recognize that the $30 gain is attributable to the period prior to the ownership change and therefore increases LossCorp's section 382 limitation for the year (disregarding the de minimis threshold rule set forth in section 382(h)(3)(B)), thereby allowing LossCorp to freely use the pre-change NOLs to offset the $30 in income. In the language of section 382, the $30 in income would be RBIG (that is, recognized built-in gain). In this fact pattern, the rules under section 382 would eliminate the significance of the disposition's timing and preserve neutrality by allowing the NOLs to be applied following the ownership change with respect to gain that was "built-in" prior to the ownership change.

Under section 382(h), the total amount of RBIL must not exceed NUBIL (that is, net unrealized built-in loss) and the total amount of RBIG must not exceed NUBIG (that is, net unrealized built-in gain). More precisely, at the change date, a loss corporation must compute the difference between the aggregate fair market value and aggregate basis of all of its assets. In general, (i) to the extent that this difference is positive, a NUBIG results; and (ii) to the extent that the difference is negative, a NUBIL results. Both NUBIG and NUBIL are adjusted by section 382(h)(6)(C), as discussed below. NUBIG and NUBIL act as limitations to the aggregate amount of RBIG and RBIL recognized during the recognition period. For illustration, if Example 2 were modified so that LossCorp owned additional assets such that it had NUBIL, the disposition of Asset A would not create RBIG.

These proposed regulations would primarily address the subcomponents of RBIL, RBIG, NUBIL, and NUBIG that are provided for by section 382(h)(6). Specifically, section 382(h)(6)(A) provides that income items that are "properly taken into account during the recognition period," but which are "attributable to periods before the change date," are treated as RBIG. Section 382(h)(6)(B) provides a similar rule for deductions to be treated as RBIL. Section 382(h)(6)(C) provides that the amount of potential income items under section 382(h)(6)(A) increases NUBIG (or reduces NUBIL), whether or not the income items were actually taken into account during the recognition period. Analogously, section 382(h)(6)(C) provides that the amount of potential deduction items under section 382(h)(6)(B) increases NUBIL (or reduces NUBIG), whether or not the deduction items were actually allowable as a deduction during the recognition period. The proposed regulations clarify the definition and calculation of these components.

As is the case for section 382(h) generally, the rules under section 382(h)(6) are again intended to preserve neutrality between pre- and post-change date transactions. Income items recognized prior to the change date may have been freely offset with pre-change NOLs; thus, if those same income items were recognized after the change date, the neutrality principle requires that pre-change NOLs be allowed to freely offset it. RBIG treatment accomplishes this effect. Similar logic applies with respect to deduction items.

In response to substantial uncertainty regarding which income and deduction items qualify under section 382(h)(6), the IRS issued Notice 2003-65. Generally, Notice 2003-65 provides two safe harbors for computing these items. The first safe harbor, referred to as the "1374 approach" (named after section 1374, which addresses tax consequences regarding built-in gains of C corporations that become S corporations), relies generally on accrual method of accounting principles. The second safe harbor, referred to as the "338 approach," compares actual amounts of income and deductions to the amounts that would have been realized had a section 338 election been made with respect to a hypothetical stock purchase on the change date. Notice 2018-30 amended Notice 2003-65 by reversing an unintended change to both safe harbors that resulted from TCJA amendments to section 168(k).

Broadly, for reasons discussed below, these proposed regulations would make mandatory the 1374 approach with certain adjustments. These adjustments include technical fixes to calculations involving COD income (that is, cancellation of indebtedness income), deductions for contingent liabilities, and cost recovery deductions. Additionally, these proposed regulations clarify that carryovers of section 163(j) disallowed business interest are counted only once for the purpose of section 382.

B. No-action Baseline

The Treasury Department and the IRS have assessed the benefits and costs of the proposed regulations relative to a no-action baseline reflecting anticipated Federal income tax-related behavior in the absence of these proposed regulations.

C. Economic Analysis of Proposed Regulations

1. Framework

In evaluating the economic efficiency of these proposed regulations, this analysis considers two main factors. The first factor regards compliance and administration costs. Mergers and acquisitions can be very complicated transactions; thus, compliance with certain aspects of Federal income tax law can be onerous for taxpayers, and examination can be difficult for the IRS. As discussed further below the Treasury Department projects that the proposed regulations will reduce compliance and enforcement costs relative to the baseline primarily by eliminating duplicative and potentially complicated calculations required to apply the 338 approach. Greater efficiencies will also be gained under the proposed regulations by reducing taxpayer disputes with the IRS regarding the application of the 1374 approach.

The second factor considered is whether changes in mergers and acquisitions potentially induced by the proposed regulations are likely to be efficiency-enhancing or efficiency-reducing. If a merger increases value only because of increased potential NOL usage, then that merger would be economically inefficient (even ignoring antitrust concerns). Section 382 attempts to ensure that the NOLs of the loss corporation can be used to the same extent whether or not the loss corporation is acquired by another corporation, which implies that no transaction would take place solely to increase NOL use. However, currently issued guidance regarding section 382 may not strike that balance perfectly. It is the determination of the Treasury Department and the IRS that, for the reasons discussed below, the currently issued guidance on section 382(h) allows too much NOL usage relative to the neutral baseline. These proposed regulations would modestly restrict NOL usage by reducing the amount that would qualify as RBIG, reducing the incentive to engage in inefficient, tax-motivated mergers and acquisitions.

The Treasury Department and the IRS have not quantified the expected gains to the U.S. economy arising from the discretionary aspects of the proposed regulations but expect them to be less than $100 million per year ($2019), a threshold established by the MOA and Executive Order 12866. For reasons discussed further in section C.2. of the analysis, the Treasury Department and IRS project that the effect of the proposed regulations on the number of mergers and acquisitions will be small. The Treasury Department and the IRS additionally project that the change (that is, reduction) in compliance costs will also be modest. The Treasury Department and the IRS solicit comments on this conclusion and particularly solicit comments that provide data, evidence, or models that would enhance the rigor by which the non-revenue economic effects might be determined for the final regulations.

2. Making the 1374 approach mandatory

The Treasury Department and the IRS have determined that the 1374 approach would be simpler for taxpayers to comply with, and simpler for the IRS to administer. Under Notice 2003-65, as modified by Notice 2018-30, taxpayers subject to section 382 would typically compute estimates of NUBIG/NUBIL and RBIG/RBIL under both the 1374 and 338 approaches to determine which approach would provide the more favorable result. Such duplicative compliance costs are inherently economically wasteful, even if they may have been privately optimal (in other words, they generated expected tax savings for the corporation in excess of compliance costs). Under these proposed regulations, taxpayers would make computations under only one approach, thereby reducing inefficient compliance burdens.

In addition, the 1374 approach has lower compliance costs than the 338 approach. Under the 1374 approach, taxpayers need only record items of income and deductions that they already account for under well-known accrual method of accounting principles. Furthermore, the IRS can easily verify such amounts during an examination. Under the 338 approach, taxpayers must consider a hypothetical transaction involving deemed asset sales. With respect to tiered corporate structures, an ownership change of the corporate parent would require the analysis of deemed asset sales not only at the corporate-parent level, but also an analysis of deemed asset sales at every lower corporate level. The 338 approach would pose significant, iterative complexity for corporate structures with several tiers of subsidiaries.

The Treasury Department and the IRS have determined that between 7,000 and 15,000 firms per year will be affected by these proposed regulations, based on the checkbox on Line 16 of Form 1120, Schedule K and other tax attributes. These firms will see a reduction in compliance costs under the 1374 approach, if they were using the 338 approach or performing calculations under both approaches under the baseline. The Treasury Department and the IRS request public comment on any anticipated changes in compliance costs due to the proposed elimination of the 338 approach.

The Treasury Department and the IRS project that the adoption of the 1374 approach as the sole approach under section 382(h) will not have a large effect on the number of mergers and acquisitions that take place. Such adoption of the 1374 approach will make certain mergers and acquisitions somewhat less attractive. However, the Treasury Department and the IRS have determined that, historically, most acquiring corporations behave as if section 382 will limit the ability to utilize substantially all pre-change NOLs. This heuristic behavior implies that firms will not be highly responsive to the changes set forth by these proposed regulations.

It is important to note that any merger or acquisition dissuaded by these proposed regulations would tend to have been economically inefficient not have been undertaken except for the purpose of reducing tax liability. Recall from Part C.1 of this section that the goal of section 382 is to ensure that NOL usage is approximately unaffected when a loss corporation is acquired by a profitable corporation. The Treasury Department and the IRS have determined that the ability to toggle between the 338 approach and the 1374 approach allows more NOL usage in the case of an acquisition than would be the case if the loss corporation continued independently. By eliminating the 338 approach, these proposed regulations move closer to a neutral, economically efficient position.

In particular, the most notable feature of the 338 approach is that assets with built-in gains can generate RBIG even without a realization event. This is generally advantageous for taxpayers. This treatment follows from the logic that such built-in gain assets would have generated income in subsequent years; in the absence of an acquisition, such income could have been offset freely by the old loss corporation's NOLs. The 338 approach prescribes a proxy for that excess income amount: the extent to which cost recovery deductions (disregarding bonus depreciation under section 168(k), per Notice 2018-30) under a hypothetical purchase of each asset at its current fair market value exceed actual allowable cost recovery deductions.

The Treasury Department and the IRS have determined that this treatment of built-in gain assets under the 338 approach is problematic for two reasons. First, the schedules for cost recovery deductions were never intended to match the production of income from each asset; rather, they were intended to accelerate cost recovery to stimulate investment. Thus, this proxy is likely to, on average, overstate income created by those assets, further increasing NOL usage beyond the neutral baseline. Second, such an adjustment for income created by built-in gain assets is unnecessary, as it is already taken into account by section 382. Section 382 provides that the NOLs of the old loss corporation can be used by the new loss corporation up to the annual limit. This annual limit is equal to a prescribed interest rate multiplied by the value of the stock of the old loss corporation, and serves as a proxy for the income created by the assets of the old loss corporation. Thus, to the extent that the appreciated value of a built-in gain asset is reflected in the value of the stock, the general rule of section 382 allows for the NOLs of the old loss corporation to offset the flow of income created by that asset. Therefore, the treatment created by the 338 approach creates a double benefit. By eliminating this treatment, the proposed regulations reduce the attractiveness of inefficient, tax-motivated acquisitions, which enhances economic efficiency.

3. Modification to treatment of COD income

The proposed regulations also modify the treatment of COD income under the 1374 approach. The baseline rules provide that COD income enters into the NUBIG/NUBIL calculations without regard to whether that income was ultimately included in, or excluded from, income by the new loss corporation under the rules of section 108. This issue is especially relevant under the consolidated return regulations regarding the application of section 108. Such regulations provide that, generally, when a member leaves its consolidated group, excluded COD income will be taken into account by the consolidated group and not the new loss corporation. Therefore, inclusion of the COD amount in the NUBIG/NUBIL calculations does not reflect the economic reality of the taxpayer and may inappropriately influence a taxpayer's decision of whether to voluntarily enter into bankruptcy. The proposed regulations address this issue by ensuring that COD income enters into the RBIG and NUBIG/NUBIL calculations only to the extent actually taken into account by the new loss corporation. The Treasury Department and the IRS have determined that this revision will treat different types of transactions more neutrally. Such treatment will increase economic efficiency by causing taxpayers to choose transactions that are optimal for non-tax reasons rather than for tax reasons.

4. Modification to treatment of contingent liabilities

These proposed regulations would revise the 1374 approach with respect to the treatment of contingent liabilities. Under Notice 2003-65, the estimated value of contingent liabilities (as of the change date) was included in the NUBIG/NUBIL calculation. However, the ultimate payment of such liability did not give rise to RBIL. This asymmetry violates the principle of neutrality between pre-change and post-change deductions. If the old loss corporation were able to pay a third party to assume the liability prior to the ownership change, it would generate a deduction that increases the pre-change NOLs, which would be limited after the ownership change. If the liability were not treated as RBIL, the post-change realization of that liability could freely offset other sources of income. This non-neutrality may distort decision-making and reduce economic efficiency.

These proposed regulations would address this issue by providing that payments of contingent liabilities represent RBIL to the extent of the estimated value of the contingent liability as of the change date.

5. Modification to treatment of cost recovery deductions

Section 382(h)(6)(B) provides that cost recovery deductions during the recognition period are treated as RBIL, except to the extent that the new loss corporation can establish that the deduction is not attributable to a built-in loss. Intuitively, RBIL includes cost recovery deductions taken against assets whose depreciation deductions are too large relative to the value of the asset. Under the baseline rules of Notice 2003-65, the suggested approach is to compare (1) actual depreciation deductions on a given asset to (2) the depreciation deductions that would be allowable (disregarding bonus depreciation under section 168(k), per Notice 2018-30) if the asset were hypothetically purchased at the change date from a third party at its fair market value. The excess of (1) over (2) is treated as RBIL. Because depreciation deductions under section 168 tend to be larger closer to the beginning of an asset's life, this approach can lead to absurd results. In particular, it is possible to create RBIL even when the fair market value is equal to the adjusted basis.

These proposed regulations would abandon that approach. Instead, the hypothetical cost recovery deduction would be computed by applying the same depreciation schedule actually used by the corporation to the fair market value of the asset. This will generally narrow the role of such RBIL treatment to taxpayers with an asset with a fair market value that is less than adjusted basis. Given the front-loading of depreciation schedules (including under section 168(k)), the Treasury Department and the IRS project that the new rule will cause RBIL to be calculated for far fewer taxpayers and thus the change will reduce compliance burden. Additionally, the new rule will generally cause an increase in allowable NOLs by reducing RBIL, contrary to the other rule changes in these proposed regulations. However, the Treasury Department and IRS project that the effect of this change (in terms of generated RBIL/RBIG) will be quantitatively less significant than other modifications, such as the elimination of the section 338 approach.

6. *Clarification of treatment of disallowed business interest expense*

Section 382(d)(3) provides that carryovers of disallowed interest under section 163(j) (as amended by the TCJA) are to be treated analogously to NOLs, meaning that their use would be limited after an ownership change. Additionally, the general rules of section 382(h)(6) could be interpreted to cause such disallowed interest to be RBIL if recognized during the recognition period, as they may be "allowable as a deduction during the recognition period" but "attributable to periods before the change date." Such treatment would cause section 163(j) carryovers to be counted twice for the purpose of section 382.

These proposed regulations would preclude this possibility by clarifying that the use of section 163(j) carryovers during the recognition period would not give rise to RBIL. This proposed clarification would provide certainty to taxpayers that section 382 will operate as intended in this regard.

II. *Paperwork Reduction Act*

Pursuant to § 1.382-11, a loss corporation must include a statement on or with its tax return for each taxable year that it is a loss corporation in which an owner shift, equity structure shift, or other transaction described in § 1.382-2T(a)(2)(i) occurs. The statement must include, among other things, attributes described in § 1.382-2(a)(1)(i) that caused the corporation to be a loss corporation. One of the attributes described in § 1.382-2(a)(1)(i) is a loss corporation's NUBIL (that is, net unrealized built-in loss), if any. The existing collection of information under § 1.382-11 has been reviewed and approved by the OMB in accordance with the Paperwork Reduction Act of 1995 (44 U.S.C. 3507(d)) (PRA) under OMB control number 1545-2019. The collection of information is necessary to enable the IRS to verify the amount of any attributes that are subject to section 382.

These proposed regulations provide guidance regarding the calculation of built-in gains and losses under section 382, including whether a corporation has a NUBIL. Therefore, these proposed regulations could cause a corporation to have a NUBIL when they would not have had one in the absence of these proposed regulations. As a result, a corporation would have to file a statement under § 1.382-11, or include an item on its statement under § 1.382-11, when the corporation would not have had to do so in the absence of these proposed regulations. The § 1.382-11 statement is a one-time paperwork burden that is required to be filed in the taxable year during which an owner shift, equity structure shift, or other transaction described in § 1.382-2T(a)(2)(i) occurs. On the other hand, these proposed regulations, if finalized, also could cause some firms to no longer have a NUBIL, thereby eliminating their requirement to file a statement under § 1.382-11. Furthermore, by eliminating the 338 approach, the Treasury Department and the IRS project that compliance burdens will fall for most existing filers of the § 1.382-11 statement. The Treasury Department and the IRS have based this projection on their observations that (i) taxpayers currently incur costs to compute their NUBIG/NUBIL under each of the two methods in order to be able to choose the more beneficial method, and (ii) the 338 approach requires taxpayers to determine hypothetical amounts (for example, what depreciation would have been available in the case of a deemed asset sale under section 338). As a result, removing the hypothetical computations, as well as the optionality, will reduce compliance burden.

For purposes of the PRA, the reporting burden associated with these proposed regulations will be reflected in the collection of information under § 1.382-11 (OMB control number 1545-2019). The aggregate estimates for all collection of information conducted under OMB control number 1545-2019, including the § 1.382-11 statement and other statements, are that 225,000 respondents will require 1 hour and 40 minutes per response for a total annual reporting burden of 375,000 hours and total annual monetized costs of $15,930,000 (2016 dollars). The Treasury Department and the IRS have not estimated the burden, including that of any new information collections, related to the requirements under these proposed regulations.

Based on the checkbox on Line 16 of Form 1120, Schedule K and other tax attributes, the Treasury Department and the IRS estimate that between 7,000 and 15,000 firms per year will be affected by these proposed regulations. The Treasury Department and the IRS estimate that these proposed regulations will, if anything, cause a slight reduction in the total amount of paperwork burden for most affected taxpayers. This reduction in burden is driven by the elimination of the 338 approach. As a result of such elimination, taxpayers may perform fewer calculations when complying with section 382. The Treasury Department and the IRS, however, have not estimated the burden, including that of any new information collections, related to the requirements under the proposed regulations.

An agency may not conduct or sponsor, and a person is not required to respond to, a collection of information unless the collection of information displays a valid OMB control number.

Books or records relating to a collection of information must be retained as long as their contents may become material in the administration of any internal revenue law. The IRS has posted information for taxpayers on their recordkeeping requirements at https://www.irs.gov/taxtopics/tc305. Generally, tax returns and tax return information are confidential, as required by 26 U.S.C. 6103.

The Treasury Department and the IRS request comments on all aspects of information collection burdens relating to these proposed regulations, including (i) estimates for how much time it would take to comply with the paperwork burdens described earlier for each relevant form and (ii) ways for the IRS to minimize the paperwork burden. Proposed revisions to the information collections contained in these proposed regulations will not be finalized until after these regulations take effect and have been approved by OMB under the PRA. The Treasury Department and the IRS have not estimated the burden, including that of any new information collections, related to the requirements under the proposed regulations. The Treasury Department and the IRS estimate PRA burdens on a taxpayer-type basis rather than a provision-specific basis. Those estimates would capture both changes made by the TJCA and those that arise out of discretionary authority exercised in the proposed regulations.

III. *Regulatory Flexibility Act*

As described in more detail in this section, pursuant to the Regulatory Flexibility Act (RFA), 5 U.S.C. chapter 6, the Treasury Department and the IRS hereby certify that these proposed regulations will not have a significant economic impact on a substantial number of small entities. Notwithstanding this certification, the Treasury Department and the IRS invite comments on any impact that these regulations would have on small entities.

These proposed regulations, if finalized, would amend the calculation of certain items under section 382, which pertains to the tax attributes of certain acquired corporations (known as "loss corporations") in the hands of the acquiring corporation after an ownership change. Broadly, the proposed regulations, if finalized, would (i) eliminate one safe harbor under which firms were formerly entitled to calculate items of income and deduction under section 382(h)(6), and (ii) make a number of other conforming changes. In particular, these regulations could change the amount of net unrealized built-in gain or loss (NUBIG and NUBIL, respectively) computed by the loss corporation. Importantly, section 382(h)(3)(B) provides a de minimis rule for which it is expected that substantially all small entities will qualify. Specifically, if a loss corporation's NUBIG or NUBIL is not greater than the lesser of (i) 15 percent of the fair market value of the loss corporation's non-cash corporate assets on the ownership change or (ii) $10 million, then the loss corporation's NUBIG or NUBIL is deemed to be zero. Furthermore, these proposed regulations would not change this de minimis rule. Therefore, to the extent that small firms understood that they historically qualified for the de minimis rule, substantially all of them could determine, with little burden, that they will qualify as well under these proposed regulations (if finalized). The Treasury Department and the IRS invite comments on the impact of these proposed rules on small entities.

Comments and Requests for Public Hearing

Before the proposed regulations are adopted as final regulations, consideration will be given to any comments that are submitted timely to the IRS as prescribed in this preamble under the "**ADDRESSES**" heading. The Treasury Department and the IRS request comments on all aspects of the proposed regulations. All comments will be available at *www.regulations.gov* for public inspection and copying. A public hearing will be scheduled if requested in writing by any person that timely submits written comments. If a public hearing is scheduled, then notice of the date, time, and place for the public hearing will be published in the *Federal Register*.

Drafting Information

The principal authors of this notice of proposed rulemaking are Kevin M. Jacobs and Marie C. Milnes-Vasquez of the Office of Associate Chief Counsel (Corporate). However, other personnel from the Treasury Department and the IRS participated in their development.

Statement of Availability of IRS Documents

IRS Revenue Procedures, Revenue Rulings, notices, and other guidance cited in this document are published in the Internal Revenue Bulletin (or Cumulative Bulletin) and are available from the Superintendent of Documents, U.S. Government Printing Office, Washington, DC 20402, or by visiting the IRS website at *http://www.irs.gov*.

[¶ 49,813] Proposed Amendments of Regulations (REG-106808-19), published in the Federal Register on September 24, 2019.

[Code Sec. 168(k)]

Depreciation deduction: Qualifying property: Self-constructed property.—Amendments of Reg. §§ 1.168(k)-0 and 1.168(k)-2, regarding the additional first year depreciation deduction under section 168(k) of the Internal Revenue Code (Code), are proposed. Reg. § 1.168(k)-2(b)(3)(iii)(B)(3)(i) through 1.168(k)-2(b)(3)(iii)(B)(3)(iii), Reg. §§ 1.168(k)-2(b)(3)(iii)(C), and 1.168(k)-2(b)(3)(vi) Examples 18 through 22, proposed on August 8, 2018, are withdrawn.

AGENCY: Internal Revenue Service (IRS), Treasury.

ACTION: Notice of proposed rulemaking; partial withdrawal of a notice of proposed rulemaking.

SUMMARY: This document contains proposed regulations that provide guidance regarding the additional first year depreciation deduction under section 168(k) of the Internal Revenue Code (Code). These proposed regulations reflect and clarify the increase of the benefit and expansion of the universe of qualifying property, particularly to certain classes of used property, made by the Tax Cuts and Jobs Act. These proposed regulations generally affect taxpayers who deduct depreciation for qualified property acquired and placed in service after September 27, 2017. This document also provides notice of a public hearing on these proposed regulations. Finally, this document withdraws a portion of the proposed regulations published on August 8, 2018. DATES: Written or electronic comments must be received by November 23, 2019. Outlines of topics to be discussed at the public hearing scheduled for Wednesday, November 13, 2019, at 10 a.m. must be received by October 23, 2019. If no outlines of topics are received by October 23, 2019, the public hearing will be cancelled.

ADDRESSES: Submit electronic submissions via the Federal eRulemaking Portal at *https://www.regulations.gov* (indicate IRS and REG-106808-19) by following the online instructions for submitting comments. Once submitted to the Federal eRulemaking Portal, comments cannot be edited or withdrawn. The Department of the Treasury (Treasury Department) and the IRS will publish for public availability any comment received to its public docket, whether submitted electronically or in hard copy. Send hard copy submissions to: CC:PA:LPD:PR (REG-106808-19), Room 5203, Internal Revenue Service, P.O. Box 7604, Ben Franklin Station, Washington, DC 20044. Submissions may be hand-delivered Monday through Friday between the hours of 8 a.m. and 4 p.m. to CC:PA:LPD:PR (REG-106808-19), Courier's Desk, Internal Revenue Service, 1111 Constitution Avenue, NW, Washington, DC 20224.

FOR FURTHER INFORMATION CONTACT: Concerning the proposed regulations, Elizabeth R. Binder or Kathleen Reed, (202) 317-7005; concerning submissions of comments and outlines of topics, the hearing, or to be placed on the building access list to attend the hearing, Regina L. Johnson, (202) 317-6901 (not toll-free numbers).

SUPPLEMENTARY INFORMATION:

Background

This document contains proposed amendments to the Income Tax Regulations (26 CFR part 1) under section 168(k) of the Code. Section 168(k) was added to the Code by section 101 of the Job Creation and Worker Assistance Act of 2002, Public Law 107-147 (116 Stat. 21). Section 168(k) allows an additional first year depreciation deduction in the placed-in-service year of qualified property. Subsequent amendments to section 168(k) increased the percentage of the additional first year depreciation deduction from 30 percent to 50 percent (to 100 percent for property acquired and placed in service after September 8, 2010, and generally before January 1, 2012), extended the placed-in-service date generally through December 31, 2019, and made other changes.

On December 22, 2017, section 168(k) and related provisions were amended by sections 12001(b)(13), 13201, and 13204 of the Tax Cuts and Jobs Act, Public Law 115-97 (131 Stat. 2054) (the "Act") to provide further changes to the additional first year depreciation deduction. Unless otherwise indicated, all references to section 168(k) hereinafter are references to section 168(k) as amended by the Act.

The Treasury Department and the IRS published proposed regulations interpreting section 168(k) on August 8, 2018 (the August Proposed Regulations) (83 FR 39292). This notice of proposed rulemaking withdraws § 1.168(k)-2(b)(3)(iii)(B)(3)(*i*) through (*iii*) and *Examples 19* through *22* in § 1.168(k)-2(b)(3)(vi) of the August Proposed Regulations, and proposes in their place § 1.168(k)-2(b)(3)(v)(A) through (E) and *Examples 26* through *30* in § 1.168(k)-2(b)(3)(vii)(Z) through (DD), respectively. This notice of proposed rulemaking also withdraws § 1.168(k)-2(b)(3)(iii)(C) and *Example 18* in § 1.168(k)-2(b)(3)(vi) of the August Proposed Regulations, and proposes in their place § 1.168(k)-2(b)(3)(iii)(C) and *Examples 31* through *34* in § 1.168(k)-2(b)(3)(vii)(EE) through (HH), respectively. The August Proposed Regulations, with modifications in response to comments and testimony received, were adopted as final regulations, issued concurrently with these proposed regulations and published elsewhere in this issue of the **Federal Register** (the Final Regulations).

Explanation of Provisions

These proposed regulations propose amendments to the Final Regulations to provide taxpayers with guidance that is not addressed in the Final Regulations regarding the application of section 168(k). Specifically, these proposed regulations contain amendments to § 1.168(k)-2(b)(2), (3), and (5) of the Final Regulations, each of which provides rules relevant to the definition of qualified property for purposes of the additional first year depreciation deduction under section 168(k). These proposed regulations also amend § 1.168(k)-2(b)(3)(v) by adding special rules for consolidated groups. Additionally, these proposed regulations amend § 1.168(k)-2(c) by adding rules regarding components acquired or self-constructed after September 27, 2017, for larger self-constructed property for which manufacture, construction, or production began before September 28, 2017. Further, these proposed regulations amend § 1.168(k)-2(g)(11) by adding rules regarding the application of the mid-quarter convention, as determined under section 168(d). These additional proposed rules respond to comments received on the August Proposed Regulations as well as address certain issues identified after additional study. This Explanation of Provisions section describes each of the proposed rules contained in this document.

1. *Property Excluded from the Additional First Year Depreciation Deduction by Section 168(k)(9)*

Section 1.168(k)-2(b)(2)(ii)(F) of the Final Regulations provides that qualified property does not include any property that is primarily used in a trade or business described in section 163(j)(7)(A)(iv). Section 1.168(k)-2(b)(2)(ii)(G) of the Final Regulations provides that qualified property does not include any property used in a trade or business that has had floor plan financing indebtedness, as defined in section 163(j)(9), if the floor plan financing interest, as defined in section 163(j)(9), related to such indebtedness is taken into account under section 163(j)(1)(C) for the taxable year. Sections 1.168(k)-2(b)(2)(ii)(F) and (G) of the Final Regulations apply to property placed in service by the taxpayer in a taxable year beginning after December 31, 2017.

A. Lessor Leasing Property to a Trade or Business Described in Section 168(k)(9)

Several commenters to the August Proposed Regulations requested guidance on whether a taxpayer that leases property to a trade or business described in section 168(k)(9) is eligible to claim the additional first year depreciation for the property, and they recommend allowing the additional first year depreciation deduction (assuming all other requirements are met). The Treasury Department and the IRS agree with the commenters' recommendation, provided the lessor is not described in section 168(k)(9)(A) or (B). Accordingly, these proposed regulations amend § 1.168(k)-2(b)(2)(ii)(F) and (G) to provide that such exclusion from the additional first year depreciation deduction does not apply to lessors of property to a trade or business described in section 168(k)(9) so long as the lessor is not described in such Code section.

B. Property Described in Section 168(k)(9)(A)

The Treasury Department and the IRS are aware that taxpayers and practitioners have questioned how to determine whether property is primarily used in a trade or business described in section 168(k)(9)(A). For depreciation purposes, § 1.167(a)-11(b)(4)(iii)(*b*) and (e)(3)(iii) classify property according to its primary use. The Treasury Department and the IRS believe that the same standard should apply for purposes of section 168(k)(9)(A). Accordingly, these proposed regulations amend § 1.168(k)-2(b)(2)(ii)(F) to provide that for purposes of section 168(k)(9)(A) and § 1.168(k)-2(b)(2)(ii)(F), the term *primarily used* has the same meaning as that term is used in § 1.167(a)-11(b)(4)(iii)(*b*) and (e)(3)(iii) for classifying property.

C. Property Described in Section 168(k)(9)(B)

A commenter to the August Proposed Regulations requested guidance on when floor plan financing is "taken into account" for purposes of section 168(k)(9)(B). The commenter believed that section 168(k)(9)(B) does not apply when a taxpayer does not deduct interest in excess of the sum of the amounts calculated under section 163(j)(1)(A) and (B). The Treasury Department and the IRS do not believe that section 163(j) is optional. However, the Treasury Department and the IRS agree that, for purposes of section 168(k)(9)(B), floor plan financing interest is not taken into account by a trade or business that has had floor plan financing indebtedness if the sum of the amounts calculated under section 163(j)(1)(A) and (B) for the trade or business for the taxable year equals or exceeds the business interest, as defined in section 163(j)(5) (including carryforwards of disallowed business interest under section 163(j)(2)), which includes floor plan financing interest of the trade or business, for the taxable year. Accordingly, these proposed regulations amend § 1.168(k)-2(b)(2)(ii)(G) to provide that solely for purposes of section 168(k)(9)(B) and § 1.168(k)-2(b)(2)(ii)(G), floor plan financing interest is not taken into account for the taxable year by a trade or business that has had floor plan financing indebtedness if the sum of the amounts calculated under section 163(j)(1)(A) and (B) for the trade or business for the taxable year equals or exceeds the business interest, as defined in section 163(j)(5), for the taxable year.

If floor plan financing interest is taken into account for a taxable year by a trade or business that has had floor plan financing indebtedness, the Treasury Department and the IRS are aware that taxpayers and practitioners have questioned whether the additional first year depreciation deduction is not allowed for property placed in service by that trade or business in any subsequent taxable year. In such a case, the additional first year depreciation deduction for subsequent taxable years would not be allowed, even if the amount of the floor plan financing interest taken into account for the current taxable year is de minimis. For this reason, the Treasury Department and the IRS have decided that, for purposes of section 168(k)(9)(B), the determination of whether a trade or business that has had floor plan financing indebtedness has taken into account floor plan financing interest is made annually. Accordingly, these proposed regulations amend § 1.168(k)-2(b)(2)(ii)(G) to provide that if the trade or business has taken floor plan financing interest into account pursuant to § 1.168(k)-2(b)(2)(ii)(G) for a taxable year, § 1.168(k)-2(b)(2)(ii)(G) applies to any property placed in service by that trade or business in that taxable year.

2. *Used Property*

A. Depreciable Interest

As a result of comments received on the August Proposed Regulations regarding sale-leaseback transactions, the Treasury Department and the IRS have determined that it is appropriate to provide an exception to the depreciable interest rule in the Final Regulations when the taxpayer disposes of property within a short period of time after the taxpayer placed such property in service. Accordingly, these proposed regulations amend § 1.168(k)-2 by adding paragraph (b)(3)(iii)(B)(*4*) to provide that if (a) a taxpayer acquires and places in service property, (b) the taxpayer or a predecessor did not previously have a depreciable interest in the property, (c) the taxpayer disposes of the property to an unrelated party within 90 calendar days after the date the property was originally placed in service by the taxpayer (without taking into account the applicable convention), and (d) the taxpayer reacquires and again places in service the property, the taxpayer's depreciable interest in the property during that 90-day period is not taken into account for determining whether the property was used by the taxpayer or a predecessor at any time prior to its reacquisition by the taxpayer. The 90-day period is consistent with the period of time specified in section 168(k)(2)(E)(iii). To prevent the churning of assets, this proposed rule does not apply if the taxpayer reacquires and again places in service the property during the same taxable year the taxpayer disposed of the property. The proposed regulations also define an *unrelated party* as meaning a person not described in section 179(d)(2)(A) or (B), and § 1.179-4(c)(1)(ii) or (iii), or (c)(2).

B. Application to Partnerships

One commenter to the August Proposed Regulations asked for clarification regarding a partner's depreciable interest in property held by a partnership. The Treasury Department and the IRS clarify in these proposed regulations the extent to which a person is treated as having a depreciable interest in property by virtue of being a partner in a partnership that holds the property.

Under the August Proposed Regulations, each partner is treated as having owned and used the partner's proportionate share of partnership property for purposes of determining whether a section 743(b) basis adjustment meets the used property acquisition requirements of section 168(k)(2)(E)(ii). Consistent with this approach, a person should be considered as having a depreciable interest in a portion of property if the person is a partner in the partnership while the partnership owns the property. The same rule should apply whether a current partner purchases property directly from the partnership or a person acquires property that the partnership previously owned while the person was a partner.

These proposed regulations amend § 1.168(k)-2 by adding paragraph (b)(3)(iii)(B)(5) to provide that a partner is considered to have a depreciable interest in a portion of property equal to the partner's total share of depreciation deductions with respect to the property as a percentage of the total depreciation deductions allocated to all partners with respect to that property during the current calendar year and five calendar years immediately prior to the partnership's current placed-in-service year of the property. For this purpose, only the portion of the current calendar year and previous 5-year period during which the partnership owned the property and the person was a partner is taken into account. The Treasury Department and the IRS believe that this provides an accurate reflection of the partner's prior depreciable interest in the property.

C. Series of Related Transactions

Section 1.168(k)-2(b)(3)(iii)(C) of the August Proposed Regulations provides that, in the case of a series of related transactions, property is treated as directly transferred from the original transferor to the ultimate transferee, and the relationship between the original transferor and the ultimate transferee is tested immediately after the last transaction in the series (related transactions rule).

A commenter requested clarification on whether the related transactions rule applies only to test relatedness under section 179(d)(2)(A) or whether this rule applies more broadly for purposes of all of the rules under section 168(k)(2)(E)(ii). For example, if, in a series of related transactions, A transfers property to B in exchange for cash and B transfers property to C in a nonrecognition transaction in exchange for stock or other property, the commenter states that it is not clear whether the related transactions rule is intended to test only the relatedness between A and C under section 179(d)(2)(A). If this rule is intended to apply more broadly, the commenter states that it is not clear whether the rule also determines the basis of the property or whether B's prior use of the property is relevant.

The commenter also requested clarification on whether the related transactions rule applies to transactions described in § 1.168(k)-2(f)(1)(iii) of the August Proposed Regulations (qualified property that is transferred in a transaction described in section 168(i)(7) in the same taxable year that the qualified property is placed in service by the transferor). For example, if a person purchased qualified property and contributed it to a partnership in a transaction described in section 721 in the same taxable year, the commenter questioned whether the related transactions rule would treat the transfer as occurring directly between the original seller and the partnership, assuming that the initial acquisition of the property by the person and the person's transfer of such property to the partnership are part of a series of related transactions.

The Treasury Department and the IRS intended to apply the related transactions rule only for purposes of testing the relatedness of the parties under section 179(d)(2)(A) or (B) in a series of related transactions. The related transactions rule was not intended to test relatedness between the parties involved in a transaction described in section 168(i)(7).

These proposed regulations amend § 1.168(k)-2 by revising paragraph (b)(3)(iii)(C) to provide rules for a series of related transactions (proposed related transactions rule). The proposed related transactions rule generally provides that the relationship between the parties under section 179(d)(2)(A) or (B) in a series of related transactions is tested immediately after each step in the series, and between the original transferor and the ultimate transferee immediately after the last transaction in the series.

The Treasury Department and the IRS believe that the relationship between the parties in a series of related transactions should not be tested in certain cases. Accordingly, the proposed related transactions rule provides that a party in the series that is neither the original transferor nor the ultimate transferee is disregarded in applying the relatedness test if the party placed in service and disposed of the property in the party's same taxable year or did not place the property in service. The proposed related transactions rule also provides that any step in a series of related transactions that is neither the original step nor the ultimate step is disregarded for purposes of testing relatedness if the step is a transaction described in § 1.168(k)-2(g)(1)(iii) (that is, a transfer of property in a transaction described in section 168(i)(7) in the same taxable year that the property is placed in service by the transferor) (§ 1.168(k)-2(f)(1)(iii) of the August Proposed Regulations). Finally, these proposed regulations provide that the proposed related transactions rule does not apply when all transactions in the series are described in § 1.168(k)-2(g)(1)(iii) or to a syndication transaction described in § 1.168(k)-2(b)(3)(vi).

The commenter also requested clarification on the application of the related transactions rule in transactions involving sections 179(d)(2)(B) and 1563. For example, if there is a series of related transactions involving a sale of qualified property between two corporations that also become members of the same controlled group, section 179(d)(2)(B) would require testing whether the two corporations are component members of the same controlled group for purposes of section 1563. Under section 1563 and the regulations issued thereunder, a corporation is generally a component member of a controlled group if it is a member of the controlled group for at least one half of the days in the relevant taxable year. See § 1.1563-1(b). If corporations both become members of the controlled group pursuant to a series of related transactions ending in the first half of the taxable year, the corporations should be component members for purposes of section 179(d)(2)(B). However, if the series of related transactions ends in the second half of the taxable year, the commenter questioned whether the related transactions rule applies to treat the two corporations as nonmembers prior to the end of the series of related transactions, in which case the purchaser of the qualified property may be eligible for immediate expensing (setting aside the potential application of section 179(d)(2)(A)).

The Treasury Department and the IRS also received comments concerning the application of section 179(d)(2)(B) to *Example 21* of § 1.168(k)-2(b)(3)(vi) in the August Proposed Regulations. In response, the Treasury Department and the IRS have proposed new rules covering the application of section 179(d)(2)(B) to acquisitions of depreciable property between members of the same consolidated group, as explained in the following section of this Explanation of Provisions.

D. Application to Members of a Consolidated Group

i. Overview of Used Property Acquisition Requirements

Section 1.168(k)-2(b)(3)(iii)(A) of the August Proposed Regulations and the Final Regulations lists the following three requirements that must be satisfied in order for acquisitions of used property to qualify for the additional first year depreciation deduction (used property acquisition requirements). First, the property must not have been used by the taxpayer or a predecessor at any time prior to the acquisition (No Prior Use Requirement). Second, the acquisition of the property must satisfy § 1.168(k)-2(b)(3)(iii)(A)(2) of the August Proposed Regulations and the Final Regulations, which requires that (a) the property was not acquired from a related person (within the meaning of section 179(d)(2)(A) and § 1.179-4(c)(1)(ii)) (Related Party Requirement), (b) the property was not acquired by one component member of a controlled group from another component member of the same controlled group (Component Member Requirement), and (c) the basis of the property in the hands of the acquirer is not determined, in whole or in part, by reference to the adjusted basis in the hands of the transferor. Third, the acquisition of the property must meet the requirements of section 179(d)(3) and § 1.179-4(d) (concerning like-kind exchanges and involuntary conversions).

ii. Application of the Used Property Acquisition Requirements to Consolidated Groups

Section 1.168(k)-2(b)(3)(iii)(B)(3) of the August Proposed Regulations provides special rules applying the No Prior Use Requirement to consolidated groups. Section 1.168(k)-2(b)(3)(iii)(B)(3)(*i*) of the August Proposed Regulations treats a member that acquires depreciable property as having a prior depreciable interest in such property if the consolidated group had a depreciable interest at any time prior to the member's acquisition of the property (Group Prior Use Rule). For these purposes, a consolidated group is treated as having a depreciable interest in property during the period in which any current or previous member of the consolidated group had a depreciable interest in the property while a member of the consolidated group. Section 1.168(k)-2(b)(3)(iii)(B)(3)(*ii*) of the August Proposed Regulations provides that, for purposes of applying the No

Prior Use Requirement, a member is treated as having a depreciable interest in property prior to the time of its acquisition if, as part of a series of related transactions, the property is acquired by a member of a consolidated group and a corporation that had a depreciable interest in the property becomes a member of that consolidated group (Stock and Asset Acquisition Rule). For purposes of applying these two rules, §1.168(k)-2(b)(3)(iii)(B)(3)(*iii*) of the August Proposed Regulations provides that, if the acquisition of property is part of a series of related transactions that also includes one or more transactions in which the transferee of the property ceases to be a member of a consolidated group, then whether the taxpayer is a member of a consolidated group is tested immediately after the last transaction in the series.

Commenters have asked for clarification regarding the application of the Group Prior Use Rule to situations in which a consolidated group terminates as a result of all of its members joining another consolidated group, including as a result of a reverse acquisition as defined in §1.1502-75(d)(3). By its terms, the Group Prior Use Rule applies only to the acquisition of property by a member of a consolidated group. Thus, the Treasury Department and the IRS have determined that this rule should apply only as long as the consolidated group remains in existence, as determined under §1.1502-75(d) and other applicable law.

Several commenters also have requested confirmation that a member of a consolidated group that is treated as having a depreciable interest in property solely as a result of the application of the Group Prior Use Rule does not continue to be treated under that rule as having a depreciable interest in the property after the member leaves the consolidated group (that is, deconsolidates). Commenters have noted that, if a former member continues to be treated as having a depreciable interest in the property after deconsolidation, the Stock and Asset Acquisition Rule could apply whenever one consolidated group acquires from another consolidated group both qualified property and the stock of a member of that second consolidated group (the target member), even if the target member had no actual depreciable interest in the qualified property (as opposed to a depreciable interest arising solely from the application of the Group Prior Use Rule).

The Treasury Department and the IRS did not intend the Group Prior Use Rule to continue to apply to a member of a consolidated group after the member leaves that consolidated group. By its terms, the Group Prior Use Rule applies only as long as a corporation remains a member of a consolidated group. Therefore, when a member deconsolidates, it does not continue to be treated under that rule as having a depreciable interest in the property. Accordingly, a departing member does not continue to have a depreciable interest in the property unless it actually owned such property.

Further, the Treasury Department and the IRS intended the Stock and Asset Acquisition Rule to apply only when the member whose stock is acquired had an actual depreciable interest in the qualified property that also is acquired as part of the same series of related transactions. Accordingly, these proposed regulations clarify that the phrase "a corporation that had a depreciable interest in the property" in the Stock and Asset Acquisition Rule refers only to a corporation that has such an interest without regard to the application of the Group Prior Use Rule.

iii. Sales of Property Between Members of the Same Consolidated Group (*Example 21* in §1.168(k)-2(b)(3)(vi) of the August Proposed Regulations)

The Treasury Department and the IRS have received comments regarding the interaction of the August Proposed Regulations for consolidated groups with the statutorily prescribed Related Party Requirement and Component Member Requirement, as illustrated by *Example 21* in §1.168(k)-2(b)(3)(vi) of the August Proposed Regulations (Former *Example 21*). Generally, a corporation qualifies as a component member of a controlled group if the corporation was a member of such controlled group during the majority of the corporation's taxable year. See section 1563(b). In addition, the taxable year of a member of a consolidated group ends for all Federal income tax purposes at the end of the day on which its status as a member changes. See §1.1502-76(b). Therefore, commenters have questioned how the August Proposed Regulations for consolidated groups could apply to treat the Component Member Requirement as satisfied if a member acquires depreciable property from another member of the same consolidated group (selling group) and, as part of an integrated plan that includes the acquisition, the acquiring member deconsolidates from the selling group.

In Former *Example 21*, Parent is the common parent of a consolidated group that includes F Corporation (F) and G Corporation (G). G has a depreciable interest in certain equipment (Equipment #3). As part of a series of related transactions, (1) G sells Equipment #3 to F, and then (2) Parent sells all of its F stock to X Corporation (X), the common parent of an unrelated consolidated group. Based on those facts, Former *Example 21* concludes that the Group Prior Use Rule does not apply to treat F as previously having a depreciable interest in Equipment #3 because F's status as a member of the Parent consolidated group is tested immediately after the last transaction in the related series, at which point F has ceased to be a member of the Parent consolidated group. Former *Example 21* relies on the same analysis to conclude that the Related Party Requirement and Component Member Requirement are also satisfied, and that, assuming all other relevant requirements are satisfied, F would be eligible to claim the additional first year depreciation deduction for Equipment #3.

Commenters also have requested guidance concerning the amount, location, and timing of the additional first year depreciation deduction in transactions similar to the transaction described in Former *Example 21*. In particular, commenters have asked whether the deduction should be reported on the consolidated return of the Parent consolidated group (that is, the selling group) or on the consolidated return of the X consolidated group (that is, the acquiring group), and whether the deduction would be limited by section 168(i)(7). Commenters have noted that, if F were treated as placing Equipment #3 in service while a member of the Parent consolidated group, the deduction might be reported on the consolidated return of the Parent group. In addition, because the transaction between F and G is an intercompany transaction, section 168(i)(7)(B)(ii) might apply to limit the amount of the deduction to an amount equaling G's gain from the transaction. One commenter further noted that, even if section 168(i)(7)(B)(ii) did not apply to the transaction, any amount of the deduction in excess of G's gain nevertheless might be disallowed under §1.1502-13 as a noncapital, nondeductible amount.

Commenters have asserted that these potential results regarding the location (the Parent consolidated group) and the amount (an amount not in excess of G's gain) of the deduction would be improper based on the legislative history of section 168(k), which indicates that Congress intended to stimulate economic activity and promote capital investment. See H. Rept. 115-409, at 232 (2017) ("The Committee believes that providing full expensing for certain business assets lowers the cost of capital for tangible property used in a trade or business. With lower costs of capital, the Committee believes that businesses will be encouraged to purchase equipment and other assets, which will promote capital investment and provide economic growth."); H. Rept. 107-251, at 20 (2001) ("The Committee believes that allowing additional first-year depreciation will accelerate purchases of equipment, promote capital investment, modernization, and growth, and will help to spur an economic recovery.").

The Treasury Department and the IRS agree with commenters that, in situations similar to Former *Example 21*, the additional first year depreciation deduction should be reported on the consolidated return of the acquiring group rather than the selling group. With respect to Former *Example 21*, the Treasury Department and the IRS note that F made the economic outlay for Equipment #3, which was included in the amount paid by X for F's stock. Additionally, F's acquisition of Equipment #3 and Parent's sale of the F stock to X occur as part of the same series of related transactions; thus, at the time of F's acquisition of Equipment #3, the parties expected F to deconsolidate from the Parent consolidated group, and the substance of the transaction is the same as if F first became a member of the X consolidated group and then acquired Equipment #3. Furthermore, F's purchase of Equipment #3 is the type of activity that section 168(k) was intended to encourage—if F had become a member of the X consolidated group before purchasing Equipment #3, it is clear that F, as a member of the X consolidated group, would be allowed the deduction in its full amount.

Moreover, in circumstances similar to Former *Example 21*, the statute and regulations disregard a transitory acquisition of depreciable property when the property is acquired and disposed of within 90 calendar days. See section 168(k)(2)(E)(iii) and §1.168(k)-2(b)(3)(vi) and (b)(4)(iv) (concerning syndication transactions) of the Final Regulations; see also §1.168(k)-2(b)(3)(iii)(B)(4) of these proposed regulations (concerning de minimis uses of property).

To ensure that the additional first year depreciation deduction is reported on the acquiring group's consolidated return in circumstances like those described in Former *Example 21*, §1.168(k)-2(b)(3)(v)(C) of these proposed regulations (Proposed Consolidated Acquisition Rule) provides that, if a member of a consolidated group acquires depreciable property from another member of the same consolidated group (that is, the selling group) in a taxable transaction, and if the transferee member ceases to be a member of the selling group in a series of related transactions that includes the property acquisition within 90 calendar days of the date of the property acquisition, then (1) the disposition and acquisition of the property are treated as occurring one day after the date on which the transferee member ceases to be a member of the selling group (Deconsolidation Date) for all Federal income tax purposes, and (2) the transferee member is treated as placing the depreciable property in service not earlier than one day after the Deconsolidation Date for purposes of claiming depreciation or the investment credit.

The Proposed Consolidated Acquisition Rule would ensure that the used property acquisition requirements, including the No Prior Use Requirement and the Related Party Requirement, are satisfied in cases similar to Former *Example 21*. With respect to the No Prior Use Requirement, because the proposed rule treats the transferee member as acquiring the property after it ceases to be a member of the selling group, the transferee member is not attributed the selling group's usage of the property under the Group Prior Use Rule. The Related Party Requirement and Component Member Requirements would be tested using the same analysis.

The Proposed Consolidated Acquisition Rule applies the same treatment for purposes of determining whether the transaction is covered by section 168(i)(7)(B)(ii). Therefore, because the acquisition is not treated as occurring between members of the same consolidated group, if the transferee member is eligible to claim the additional first year depreciation deduction, then section 168(i)(7)(B)(ii) will not apply to limit the amount of the deduction.

In order to allow the deduction to the appropriate party, the Proposed Consolidated Acquisition Rule also provides that the transferee member is treated as placing the property in service not earlier than one day after the Deconsolidation Date for purposes of sections 167 and 168 and §§1.46-3(d) and 1.167(a)-11(e)(1). In so providing, the Treasury Department and the IRS intend to prohibit the transferee member from claiming the additional first year depreciation deduction on the selling group's consolidated return. The rule also prevents the transferee member from claiming regular depreciation or the investment credit with respect to the acquired property during the period after the transferee member acquires the property but before it leaves the selling group. *Example 28* (that is, revised Former *Example 21*) in proposed §1.168(k)-2(b)(3)(vii)(BB) illustrates the application of the Proposed Consolidated Acquisition Rule to the acquisition of depreciable property by one member of a consolidated group from another member of the same consolidated group. iv. Deemed Acquisitions of Depreciable Property Between Members of the Same Consolidated Group

Commenters have noted that issues similar to those in Former *Example 21* also arise in the context of deemed acquisitions of property within a consolidated group resulting from an election under either section 338(h)(10) or section 336(e). The Treasury Department and the IRS have determined that deemed acquisitions of property should be treated the same as actual acquisitions of property. Thus, §1.168(k)-2(b)(3)(v)(D) of these proposed regulations provides a rule (Proposed Consolidated Deemed Acquisition Rule) that applies if (1) the transferee member acquires the stock of another member of the same group that holds depreciable property (target) in a qualified stock purchase or a qualified stock disposition for which a section 338 election or a section 336(e) election for a disposition described in §1.336-2(b)(1), respectively, is made, and (2) the transferee member and target cease to be members of the consolidated group within 90 calendar days of the acquisition date (within the meaning of §1.338-2(c)(1)) or disposition date (within the meaning of §1.336-1(b)(8)) as part of the same series of related transactions that includes the acquisition. The Proposed Consolidated Deemed Acquisition Rule does not apply to qualified stock dispositions described in section 355(d)(2) or (e)(2) because the rules applicable to such dispositions do not treat a new target corporation as acquiring assets from an unrelated person. See §1.336-2(b)(2).

If the Proposed Consolidated Deemed Acquisition Rule applies, then (a) the acquisition date or disposition date, as applicable, is treated as the date that is one day after the date on which the transferee member and target cease to be members of the consolidated group (Deconsolidation Date) for all Federal income tax purposes, and (b) new target is treated as placing the depreciable property in service not earlier than one day after the Deconsolidation Date for purposes of sections 167 and 168 and §§1.46-3(d) and 1.167(a)-11(e)(1).

Without the proposed rule, new target might be treated as having a depreciable interest in the assets new target is deemed to acquire by virtue of the Group Prior Use Rule because old target, a member of the same consolidated group, had a depreciable interest in those assets. If applicable, the proposed rule prevents new target from being treated as having a depreciable interest in the assets by moving the acquisition date or disposition date to the day after the Deconsolidation Date. New target is therefore a member of the acquiring group at the time it is deemed to acquire the assets. Similar to the Proposed Consolidated Acquisition Rule, this deemed acquisition rule also provides that the transferee member is treated as placing the property in service not earlier than one day after the Deconsolidation Date for purposes of sections 167 and 168 and §§1.46-3(d) and 1.167(a)-11(e)(1). *Example 29* in proposed §1.168(k)-2(b)(3)(vii)(CC) illustrates the application of the rule to the deemed acquisition of depreciable property by one member of a consolidated group from another member of the same consolidated group pursuant to a section 338(h)(10) election.

Neither the Proposed Consolidated Acquisition Rule nor the Proposed Consolidated Deemed Acquisition Rule applies if the property that is acquired (or deemed acquired) is subsequently disposed of by the transferee member (or new target, respectively, in a transaction that is part of the same series of related transactions as the actual or deemed acquisition of the property. For special rules governing the transfer of property in a series of related transactions, see §1.168(k)-2(b)(3)(iii)(C) of these proposed regulations. For special rules governing property placed in service and disposed of in the same taxable year, see §1.168(k)-2(g)(1).

3. *Acquisition of Property*

A. Definition of Binding Contract for Acquisition of Entity

The Treasury Department and the IRS are aware that taxpayers and practitioners are having difficulty applying the binding contract rules in the August Proposed Regulations to transactions involving the acquisition of an entity. Because those rules were written to apply to the purchase of an asset instead of an entity, the Treasury Department and the IRS recognize that a binding contract rule for an acquisition of a trade or business, or an entity, is needed. Accordingly, these proposed regulations amend §1.168(k)-2 by adding paragraph (b)(5)(iii)(G) to provide that a contract to acquire all or substantially all of the assets of a trade or business or to acquire an entity (for example, a corporation, a partnership, or a limited liability company) is binding if it is enforceable under State law against the parties to the contract. The presence of a condition outside the control of the parties, including, for example, regulatory agency approval, will not prevent the contract from being a binding contract. Further, the fact that insubstantial terms remain to be negotiated by the parties to the contract, or that customary conditions remain to be satisfied, does not prevent the contract from being a binding contract. This proposed rule also applies to a contract for the sale of the stock of a corporation that is treated as an asset sale as a result of an election under section 338.

B. Property Not Acquired Pursuant to a Written Binding Contract

The Treasury Department and the IRS also are aware that, in some cases, a taxpayer may acquire property that was not pursuant to a written binding contract. If such property is not self-constructed property, a qualified film, television, or live theatrical production, or a specified plant, these proposed regulations amend § 1.168(k)-2 by adding paragraph (b)(5)(v) to provide that the acquisition date of property acquired pursuant to a contract that is not a written binding contract is the date on which the taxpayer paid or incurred more than 10 percent of the total cost of the property, excluding the cost of any land and preliminary activities such as planning and designing, securing financing, exploring, or researching. This 10-percent proposed rule is the same as the safe harbor provided in § 1.168(k)-2(b)(5)(iv)(B)(2) of the Final Regulations for determining the acquisition date of self-constructed property. This proposed rule does not apply to the acquisition of a trade or business, or an entity. The Treasury Department and the IRS request comments on this proposed rule.

4. *Components*

Multiple commenters to the August Proposed Regulations requested an election similar to the one provided in section 3.02(2)(b) of Rev. Proc. 2011-26 (2011-16 I.R.B. 664 (April 18, 2011)) for components acquired or self-constructed after September 27, 2017, of larger self-constructed property for which the manufacture, construction, or production of the larger self-constructed property begins before September 28, 2017.

The Treasury Department and the IRS have determined that it is appropriate to allow a taxpayer to elect to treat one or more components acquired or self-constructed after September 27, 2017, of certain larger self-constructed property as being eligible for the additional first year depreciation deduction under section 168(k). The larger self-constructed property must be qualified property under section 168(k)(2), as in effect before the enactment of the Act, for which the manufacture, construction, or production began before September 28, 2017. However, the election is not available for components of larger self-constructed property when such property is not eligible for any additional first year depreciation deduction under section 168(k) (for example, property described in section 168(k)(9) and placed in service by the taxpayer in any taxable year beginning after December 31, 2017, or qualified improvement property placed in service by the taxpayer after December 31, 2017). These proposed regulations amend § 1.168(k)-2 by adding paragraph (c) to provide for this election. These proposed regulations also provide rules regarding installation costs and the determination of the basis attributable to the manufacture, construction, or production before January 1, 2020, for longer production period property or certain aircraft property described in section 168(k)(2)(B) or (C). Additionally, these proposed regulations provide the time and manner of making the election, and examples to illustrate the proposed rules.

These proposed regulations also amend § 1.168(k)-2(e)(1)(iii) to provide rules regarding the determination of the basis attributable to the manufacture, construction, or production before January 1, 2027, for longer production period property or certain aircraft property described in section 168(k)(2)(B) or (C).

Commenters to the August Proposed Regulations requested guidance on whether property acquired before September 28, 2017, by a trade or business described in section 168(k)(9)(A) is eligible for the additional first year depreciation deduction provided by section 168(k) as in effect before the enactment of the Act. Another commenter requested clarification on whether any of the costs of property acquired before September 28, 2017, pursuant to a written binding contract, and placed in service after 2017 are eligible for the additional first year depreciation deduction under section 168(k). Property acquired before September 28, 2017, is eligible for the additional first year depreciation deduction provided by section 168(k) as in effect before the enactment of the Act provided such property is qualified property under section 168(k) as in effect before the enactment of the Act. However, if the taxpayer makes the election in proposed § 1.168(k)-2(c), as described above, for components acquired or self-constructed after September 27, 2017, those components are eligible for the additional first year depreciation deduction under section 168(k). Such election, however, does not apply to, among other things, property described in section 168(k)(9) and placed in service in a taxable year beginning after December 31, 2017.

5. *Special Rules: Mid-quarter Convention*

The Treasury Department and the IRS are aware that taxpayers and practitioners have questioned whether the unadjusted depreciable basis of qualified property for which the additional first year depreciation deduction is claimed is taken into account in determining whether the mid-quarter convention under section 168(d) and § 1.168(d)-1 applies for the taxable year. The Treasury Department and the IRS agree that a rule is necessary and that it should be consistent with the definition of depreciable basis in § 1.168(d)-1(b)(4). Accordingly, the proposed regulations amend § 1.168(k)-2 by adding paragraph (g)(11) to provide that in determining whether the mid-quarter convention applies for a taxable year under section 168(d)(3) and § 1.168(d)-1, the depreciable basis, as defined in § 1.168(d)-1(b)(4), for the taxable year the qualified property is placed in service by the taxpayer, is not reduced by the allowed or allowable additional first year depreciation deduction for that taxable year.

Proposed Applicability Date

These regulations are proposed to apply to qualified property placed in service or planted or grafted, as applicable, by the taxpayer during or after the taxpayer's taxable year that includes the date of publication of a Treasury decision adopting these rules as final regulations in the **Federal Register**. These regulations also are proposed to apply to components acquired or self-constructed after September 27, 2017, of larger self-constructed property for which the manufacture, construction, or production begins before September 28, 2017, and that is qualified property under section 168(k)(2) as in effect before the enactment of the Act and placed in service by the taxpayer during or after the taxpayer's taxable year that includes the date of publication of a Treasury decision adopting these rules as final regulations in the **Federal Register**. Pending the issuance of final regulations, a taxpayer may choose to rely on these proposed regulations, in their entirety, to qualified property acquired and placed in service or planted or grafted, as applicable, after September 27, 2017, by the taxpayer during taxable years ending on or after September 28, 2017. Pending the issuance of final regulations, a taxpayer also may choose to rely on these proposed regulations, in their entirety, to components acquired or self-constructed after September 27, 2017, of larger self-constructed property for which the manufacture, construction, or production begins before September 28, 2017, and that is qualified property under section 168(k)(2) as in effect before the enactment of the Act and placed in service by the taxpayer during taxable years ending on or after September 28, 2017. If a taxpayer chooses to rely on these proposed regulations, the taxpayer must consistently apply all rules of these proposed regulations.

Special Analyses

I. *Regulatory Planning and Review - Economic Analysis*

Executive Orders 12866 and 13563 direct agencies to assess costs and benefits of available regulatory alternatives and, if regulation is necessary, to select regulatory approaches that maximize net benefits (including (i) potential economic, environmental, and public health and safety effects, (ii) potential distributive impacts, and (iii) equity). Executive Order 13563 emphasizes the importance of quantifying both costs and benefits, reducing costs, harmonizing rules, and promoting flexibility.

These proposed regulations have been designated as subject to review under Executive Order 12866 pursuant to the Memorandum of Agreement (April 11, 2018) (MOA) between the Treasury Department and the Office of Management and Budget (OMB) regarding review of tax regulations. The Office of Information and Regulatory Affairs has designated these proposed regulations as significant under section 1(b) of the MOA. Accordingly, the OMB has reviewed these proposed regulations.

A. Background

i. Bonus Depreciation Generally

In general, section 168(k) allows taxpayers to immediately deduct some portion of investment in certain types of physical capital, what is colloquially known as bonus depreciation. The Act changed section 168(k) in several ways. Arguably most substantially, the Act increased the bonus percentage as it applies to property generally acquired after September 27, 2017, which accelerates depreciation deductions. The Act also removed the "original use" requirement, meaning that taxpayers could claim bonus depreciation on "used" property. The Act made several other modest changes to the operation of section 168(k). First, it excluded from the definition of qualified property any property used by rate-regulated utilities and firms (primarily automobile dealerships) with "floor plan financing indebtedness" as defined under section 163(j). Furthermore, section 168(k)(2)(a)(ii)(IV) and (V) allowed qualified film, television, and live theatrical productions (as defined under Section 181) to qualify for bonus depreciation.

The regulations under § 1.168(k)-2 generally provide structure and clarity for the implementation of section 168(k). However, Treasury and the IRS determined that there remained several outstanding issues requiring clarification that should be subject to notice and comment. First, these proposed regulations address some ambiguities related to the operation of section 168(k)(9), which describes some property that is ineligible for bonus depreciation. Second, these proposed regulations create a de minimis rule which provides that a taxpayer will not be deemed to have had a prior depreciable interest in a property - and thus that property will be eligible for bonus depreciation in that taxpayer's hands - if the taxpayer previously disposed of that property within 90 days of the date on which that property was placed in service. Third, these proposed regulations clarify the interpretation of an example in the August Proposed Regulations regarding an asset acquisition as part of a sale of a member of a controlled group from one group to another. Fourth, these proposed regulations modify the treatment of series of related transactions. Finally, these proposed regulations provide that certain components of larger self-constructed property can be eligible for the increased bonus depreciation percentage even if the construction of such larger self-constructed property began before September 28, 2017.

B. No-action Baseline

The Treasury Department and the IRS have assessed the benefits and costs of the proposed regulations relative to a no-action baseline reflecting anticipated Federal income tax-related behavior in the absence of these proposed regulations.

C. Economic Analysis of NPRM

This section describes the main provisions of these proposed regulations and provides a qualitative economic analysis of each one.

i. Property Excluded from Bonus Depreciation by Section 168(k)(9)

As discussed above, section 168(k)(9) provides that property used by certain businesses is not eligible for bonus depreciation. These businesses include certain rate-regulated utilities and motor vehicle dealerships with floor plan financing indebtedness.

These proposed regulations first clarify that those taxpayers that lease property to such businesses described by section 168(k)(9) may claim bonus depreciation, so long as other requirements of section 168(k) are met. This approach broadly follows the existing normalization rules (which provide generally for the reconciliation of tax income and book income for regulatory purposes for utilities), which provides that lessors to public utilities are not bound by such rules so long as they themselves are not a public utility. The Treasury Department and the IRS project that this guidance will be easy for taxpayers to interpret and comply with. Additionally, this decision allows businesses to receive some share of the economic benefit of section 168(k). To the extent that lessors can claim bonus depreciation, it is plausible that the market-clearing lease price for such assets will fall, potentially enabling some expansions of output and contributing to economic growth.

These proposed regulations next clarify which businesses fall under the umbrella of section 168(k)(9)(A) (utilities) and section 168(k)(9)(B) (dealerships with floor plan financing indebtedness). For utilities, these proposed regulations clarify that the "primary use" of an item described in the Code is consistent with how primary use is determined in existing regulations under section 167. This application should be familiar to taxpayers, and thus relatively easy to comply with.

The statutory language of section 168(k)(9)(B) is somewhat more ambiguous, and thus more substantive clarifications were necessary. First, section 168(k)(9)(B) provides that dealerships with floor plan financing indebtedness are ineligible for bonus depreciation "if the floor plan financing interest was taken into account under [section 163(j)(1)(C)]." These proposed regulations clarify that such interest is in fact "taken into account" only if the firm in fact received a benefit from section 163(j)(1)(C) - i.e., if total business interest expense (including floor plan financing interest) exceeds business interest income plus 30 percent of adjusted taxable income. This decision allows more firms to claim bonus depreciation than if the Treasury Department and the IRS had made the opposite interpretation (deeming all dealerships with floor plan financing interest to be ineligible for bonus depreciation, regardless of whether the firm received a benefit from section 163(j)(1)(C)).

The Treasury Department and the IRS have undertaken an analysis of the investment effects of this provision, under the assumption that 10 to 50 percent of affected taxpayers would have come to the opposite interpretation in the absence of the proposed regulations. Using tax return data and parameters from the literature on the effect of bonus depreciation on investment, this analysis has found that this provision would increase investment by an annual maximum of $20 to $90 million, although this range would likely decrease over time as uncertainty over the interpretation of the statute is resolved. Additionally, these proposed regulations will resolve a substantial compliance uncertainty facing these taxpayers.

An additional ambiguity in section 168(k)(9)(B) pertains to the length of time that the section applies to a given firm. The section refers to a "trade or business that has had floor plan financing indebtedness . . . if the floor plan financing interest related to such indebtedness was taken into account under [section 163(j)(1)(C)]". Consider a firm (*Example A*) that received a benefit from section 163(j)(C)(1) in tax year 2018 (meaning that its interest deduction would have been smaller if not for section 163(j)(C)(1)) but not in tax year 2019 or any other later year. One interpretation of the statute would deem that firm forever ineligible for bonus depreciation, in 2019 and later. The Treasury Department and the IRS came to the opposite conclusion and deemed that section 168(k)(9)(B) is determined on an annual basis: for example, the firm in *Example A* of this part of the Special Analysis section would not be eligible for bonus depreciation in 2018, but so long as the other requirements were met, it would be eligible for bonus depreciation in 2019. As with the interpretation of "taken into account," this interpretation enables more firms to be eligible for bonus depreciation in more years, potentially increasing investment by such firms. The Treasury Department and the IRS expect that some taxpayers would have come to a different conclusion regarding the interpretation of this timing in the absence of these proposed regulations. Therefore, this provision could also have some economic effects. The Treasury Department and the IRS engaged in an analysis on these effects based on historical tax data, parameter values from the economic literature for the effect of bonus depreciation on investment, and assumptions regarding taxpayer interpretations in the absence of these proposed regulations. The result of this analysis projects that this provision will cause investment to increase in this industry by no greater than $55 million in any year, and approximately $25 million per year on average over the period from 2019 to 2028. The Treasury Department and the IRS additionally project that some share of this increased investment will reduce investment in other industries through crowd-out effects.

Importantly, the estimated effect of this provision interacts substantially with the rule that floor plan financing is "taken into account" only if the firm in fact received a benefit from section 163(j)(1)(C). In the absence of the proposed regulations, the Treasury Department and the IRS project that some share of taxpayers in this industry would have interpreted section 168(k)(9)(B) as rendering them ineligible for bonus depreciation in substantially all circumstances. Therefore, the effect of both provisions together is less than the sum of each of the provisions considered independently. In total, the Treasury Department and the IRS have determined that the effect of both rules related to section 168(k)(9)(B), when considered together, would have a maximum annual effect on investment in the range of $65 million to $90 million and declining over time as uncertainty over the interpretation of the statute is resolved.

ii. Prior Depreciable Interest

In general, to be eligible for bonus depreciation, a given property may not have been owned by the same firm in the past. This requirement was instituted by Congress in order to prevent "churning" of assets, whereby a firm could sell and soon thereafter repurchase the same asset in order to claim the 100 percent deduction. The August Proposed Regulations defined "ownership" for this purpose as having a prior depreciable interest. Section 1.168(k)-2 finalizes this interpretation. These proposed regulations introduce an exception, providing that a taxpayer does not have a depreciable interest in a given property if the taxpayer disposed of the property within 90 days of the initial date when the property was placed in service (so long as the asset is not repurchased and placed in service again within the same taxable year). The Treasury Department and the IRS primarily instituted this rule in order to coordinate with the syndication transaction rules of section 168(k)(E)(2)(iii). The Treasury Department and the IRS do not anticipate substantial economic effects of this provision. Nevertheless, it will generally have the effect of causing more property to be eligible for bonus depreciation (increasing incentives to invest), while minimizing incentives for wasteful churning of assets.

Furthermore, these proposed regulations clarify that partners in a partnership hold a depreciable interest in the property held by that partnership, and that the share of the property to which this applies equals the partner's share of the depreciation deductions of the partnership over a certain period. The Treasury Department and the IRS have determined that this provides an accurate reflection of the partner's prior depreciable interest in the property, and therefore aligns tax consequences and economic consequences, which is generally favorable for economic efficiency. However, as is the case with the "prior use" rules generally, the Treasury Department and the IRS do not project this provision to substantially affect behavior.

iii. Group Prior Use Rule

These proposed regulations clarify several aspects of the "Group Prior Use Rule." Under that rule, all members of a consolidated group are treated as having had a depreciable interest in a property if any member of the consolidated group had such a depreciable interest. First, these proposed regulations clarify that the rule ceases to be in effect once the consolidated group terminates as a result of joining another consolidated group. Second, these proposed regulations clarify that the Group Prior Use Rule does not apply to a corporation after it deconsolidates from the consolidated group, so long as that corporation did not in fact own that property. As is the case with the prior use rules generally, the Treasury Department and the IRS do not anticipate large economic effects as a result of this section of these proposed regulations.

iv. Purchases of Assets as Part of Acquisition of Entire Business

Additionally, these proposed regulations clarify the proper procedure for certain purchases of assets by a given corporation from a related party that are a part of an integrated plan involving the selling of that corporation from one group to another. Specifically, these proposed regulations provide that the deduction for bonus depreciation is allowed in such circumstances, and should be claimed by the acquiring group. These proposed regulations provide for a similar treatment in the case of deemed acquisitions in the case of an election under section 338(h)(10) or section 336(e). These rules cause the tax treatment to reflect the economic reality, in which the acquiring group is bearing the economic outlay of the asset purchase, and that acquiring group had no economic prior depreciable interest. By aligning the tax consequences with the economic allocations, this treatment minimizes potential distortions caused by the anti-churning rules.

v. Component Rule Election

In 2010, Congress increased the bonus percentage from 50 percent to 100 percent for property placed in service between September 9, 2010 and December 31, 2011. In 2011, the IRS issued Revenue Procedure 2011-26 to allow taxpayers to elect to have the 100 percent bonus rate apply to components of larger self-constructed property whose construction began before September 9, 2010, so long as (1) the components were acquired (or self-constructed) after than that date and (2) the larger self-constructed property itself qualifies for bonus depreciation generally. These proposed regulations provide an analogous rule, replacing September 9, 2010 with September 27, 2017. This provision will allow more property to qualify for 100 percent bonus depreciation. Furthermore, this provision provides neutrality between taxpayers who acquire distinct, smaller pieces of depreciable property and those taxpayers that invest a similar amount in fewer, larger pieces of depreciable property whose construction takes place over a longer period of time. By treating similar taxpayers (and similar choices) similarly, this rule enhances economic efficiency by minimizing tax-related distortions. However, the Treasury Department and the IRS project these rules to have only a modest effect on future economic decisions. These rules affect only taxpayers (1) that acquire (or self-construct) components after the date of enactment of these proposed regulations and (2) for whom the construction of the larger self-constructed property began prior to September 28, 2017 (approximately 21 months ago). The Treasury Department and the IRS expect relatively few taxpayers to be affected by this provision going forward.

vi. Series of Related Transactions

The August Proposed Regulations provided that, in a series of related transactions, the relationship between the transferor and transferee of an asset was determined only after the final transaction in the series (the "Series of Related Transaction Rule"). Commenters had expressed confusion regarding whether this applies to testing whether parties are related under section 179(d)(2), or whether it applies more broadly (e.g., in determining whether the taxpayer had a prior depreciable interest). These proposed regulations clarify that this Series of Related Transaction Rule is intended only to test the relatedness of two parties.

These proposed regulations further revise the Series of Related Transaction Rule to address its application in various situations. Under these proposed regulations, the relatedness is tested after each step of the series of related transactions, with the substantial exception that any intermediary (i.e., a taxpayer other than the original transferor or ultimate transferee) is disregarded so long as that intermediary (1) never places the property in service or (2) disposes of the property in the same taxable year in which it was placed in service. This would tend to eliminate the benefit of the Series of Related Transaction Rule in cases where intermediate transferees maintained use of the property for a non-trivial length of time. The Treasury Department and the IRS project that this interpretation will prevent abuse. The Treasury Department and the IRS do not predict substantial economic effects of this provision.

vii. Miscellaneous

Lastly, these proposed regulations put forward rules to the extent existing regulations apply in slightly new contexts. In particular, these proposed regulations clarify when a binding contract is in force to acquire all or substantially all the assets of a trade or business. Additionally, consistent with the rules of §1.168(d)-1(b)(4), these proposed regulations provide that, for the purpose of determining whether the mid-quarter convention applies, depreciable basis is not reduced by the amount of bonus depreciation. The Treasury Department and the IRS do not anticipate large economic effects of these clarifications, though the additional clarity of these regulations will likely reduce compliance burdens.

II. *Paperwork Reduction Act*

The collection of information in these proposed regulations are in proposed §1.168(k)-2(c). The collection of information in proposed §1.168(k)-2(c) is an election that a taxpayer may make to treat one or more components acquired or self-constructed after September 27, 2017, of certain larger self-constructed property as being eligible for the 100-percent additional first year depreciation deduction under section 168(k). The larger self-constructed property must be qualified property under section 168(k)(2) as in effect before the enactment of the Act and for which the manufacture, construction, or production began before September 28, 2017. The election is made by attaching a statement to a Federal income tax return indicating that the taxpayer is making the election under proposed §1.168(k)-2(c) and whether the taxpayer is making the election for all or some of the components described in proposed §1.168(k)-2(c).

For purposes of the Paperwork Reduction Act of 1995 (44 U.S.C. 3507(d)) (PRA), the reporting burden associated with proposed §1.168(k)-2(c) will be reflected in the PRA submission associated with income tax returns in the Form 1120 series, Form 1040 series, Form 1041 series, and Form 1065 series (for OMB control numbers, see chart at the end of this part II of this Special Analysis section). The estimate for the number of impacted filers with respect to the collection of information described in this part is 0 to 137,000 respondents. Historical data was not available to directly estimate the number of impacted filers. This estimate assumes that no more than 10 percent of income tax return filers with a nonzero entry on Form 4562 Line 14 (additional first year depreciation deduction) will make this election (5 percent in the case of filers of Form 1040 series). The IRS estimates the number of affected filers to be the following:

Tax Forms Impacted

Collection of information	Number of respondents (estimated)	Forms to which the information may be attached
Section 1.168(k)-2(c) Election for components of larger self-constructed property for which the manufacture, construction, or production begins before September 28, 2017	0-137,000	Form 1120 series, Form 1040 series, Form 1041 series, and Form 1065 series

Source: IRS:RAAS:KDA (CDW 6-1-19)

The current status of the PRA submissions related to the tax forms that will be revised as a result of the information collections in the section 168(k) regulations is provided in the accompanying table. As described above, the reporting burdens associated with the information collections in the regulations are included in the aggregated burden estimates for OMB control numbers 1545-0123 (which represents a total estimated burden time for all forms and schedules for corporations of 3.157 billion hours and total estimated monetized costs of $58.148 billion ($2017)), 1545-0074 (which represents a total estimated burden time, including all other related forms and schedules for individuals, of 1.784 billion hours and total estimated monetized costs of $31.764 billion ($2017)), and 1545-0092 (which represents a total estimated burden time, including all other related forms and schedules for trusts and estates, of 307,844,800 hours and total estimated monetized costs of $9.950 billion ($2016)). The overall burden estimates provided for the OMB control numbers below are aggregate amounts that relate to the entire package of forms associated with the applicable OMB control number and will in the future include, but not isolate, the estimated burden of the tax forms that will be created or revised as a result of the information collections in the regulations. These numbers are therefore unrelated to the future calculations needed to assess the burden imposed by the regulations. These burdens have been reported for other regulations that rely on the same OMB control numbers to conduct information collections under the PRA, and the Treasury Department and the IRS urge readers to recognize that these numbers are duplicates and to guard against over counting the burden that the regulations that cite these OMB control numbers imposed prior to the Act. No burden estimates specific to the forms affected by the regulations are currently available. The Treasury Department and the IRS have not estimated the burden, including that of any new information collections, related to the requirements under the regulations. For the OMB control numbers discussed in above, the Treasury Department and the IRS estimate PRA burdens on a taxpayer-type basis rather than a provision-specific basis. Those estimates would capture changes made by the Act, the final regulations under section 168(k), and those that arise out of discretionary authority exercised in these proposed regulations and other regulations that affect the compliance burden for those forms.

The Treasury Department and the IRS request comments on all aspects of information collection burdens related to the proposed regulations, including estimates for how much time it would take to comply with the paperwork burdens described above for each relevant form and ways for the IRS to minimize the paperwork burden. In addition, when available, drafts of IRS forms are posted for comment at https://apps.irs.gov/app/picklist/list/draftTaxForms.htm. IRS forms are available at https://www.irs.gov/forms-instructions. Forms will not be finalized until after they have been approved by OMB under the PRA.

Form	Type of Filer	OMB Number(s)	Status
Form 1040	Individual (NEW Model)	1545-0074	Published in the **Federal Register** on 7/20/18. Public Comment period closed on 9/18/18.
	Link: *https://www.federalregister.gov/documents/2018/07/20/2018-15627/proposed-collection-comment-request-for-regulation-project*		
Form 1041	Trusts and estates	1545-0092	Published in the **Federal Register** on 4/4/18. Public Comment period closed on 6/4/18.
	Link: *https://www.federalregister.gov/documents/2018/04/04/2018-06892/proposed-collection-comment-request-for-form-1041*		
Forms 1065 and 1120	Business (NEW Model)	1545-0123	Published in the **Federal Register** on 10/8/18. Public Comment period closed on 12/10/18.
	Link: *https://www.federalregister.gov/documents/2018/10/09/2018-21846/proposed-collection-comment-request-for-forms-1065-1065-b-1066-1120-1120-c-1120-f-1120-h-1120-nd*		

III. *Regulatory Flexibility Act*

It is hereby certified that these proposed regulations will not have a significant economic impact on a substantial number of small entities within the meaning of section 601(6) of the Regulatory Flexibility Act (5 U.S.C. chapter 6).

Section 168(k) generally affects taxpayers that own and use depreciable property in their trades or businesses or for their production of income. The reporting burden in proposed §1.168(k)-2(c) generally affects taxpayers that elect to have the 100 percent additional first year depreciation deduction apply to components that are acquired or self-constructed after September 27, 2017, of depreciable property for which the manufacture, construction, or production began before September 28, 2017, and was completed generally before January 1, 2020. The election is made by attaching a statement to a Federal income tax return indicating that the taxpayer is making the election under proposed §1.168(k)-2(c) and whether the taxpayer is making this election for all or some of the components described in §1.168(k)-2(c).

For purposes of the PRA, the Treasury Department and the IRS estimate that there are 0 to 181,500 respondents of all sizes that are likely to be impacted by this collection of information. Only a small proportion of these filers are likely to be small entities (business entities with gross receipts of $25 million or less pursuant to section 448(c)(1)). The Treasury Department and the IRS estimate the number of filers affected by proposed §1.168(k)-2(c) to be the following:

Form	Gross receipts of $25 million or less	Gross receipts over $25 million
Form 1040	0-12,000 Respondents (estimated)	0-32,500 Respondents (estimated)
Form 1065	0-1,250 Respondents (estimated)	0-35,000 Respondents (estimated)
Form 1120	0-1,750 Respondents (estimated)	0-11,000 Respondents (estimated)
Form 1120S	0-2,500 Respondents (estimated)	0-41,000 Respondents (estimated)
TOTAL	0-29,500 Respondents (estimated)	0-152,000 Respondents (estimated)

Source: IRS:RAAS:KDA (CDW 6-1-19)

Regardless of the number of small entities potentially affected by these proposed regulations, the Treasury Department and the IRS have concluded that proposed §1.168(k)-2(c) will not have a significant economic impact on a substantial number of small entities. As a result of all changes in these proposed regulations, the Treasury Department and the IRS estimate that individual taxpayers who have gross receipts of $25 million or less and experience an increase in burden will incur an average increase of 0 to 3 hours, and business taxpayers that have gross receipts of $25 million or less and experience an increase in burden will incur an average increase of 0 to 2 hours (Source: IRS:RAAS (8-28-2019)). Because the election in proposed §1.168(k)-2(c) is one of several changes in these proposed regulations, the Treasury Department and the IRS expect the average increase in burden to be less for the collection of information in proposed §1.168(k)-2(c) than the average increase in burden in the preceding sentence. The Treasury Department and the IRS also note that many taxpayers with gross receipts of $25 million or less may experience a reduction in burden as a result of all changes in these proposed regulations.

Additionally: (1) Many small businesses are not required to capitalize under section 263(a) the amount paid or incurred for the acquisition of depreciable tangible property that costs $5,000 or less if the business has an applicable financial statement or costs $500 or less if the business does not have an applicable financial statement, pursuant to §1.263(a)-1(f)(1); (2) many small businesses are no longer required to capitalize under section 263A the costs to construct, build, manufacture, install, improve, raise, or grow depreciable property if their average annual gross receipts are $25,000,000 or less; and (3) a small business that capitalizes costs of depreciable tangible property may deduct under section 179 up to $1,020,000 (2019 inflation adjusted amount) of the cost of such property placed in service during the taxable year if the total cost of depreciable tangible property placed in service during the taxable year does not exceed $2,550,000 (2019 inflation adjusted amount). Therefore, the Treasury Department and the IRS have determined that a substantial number of small entities will not be subject to these proposed regulations. Finally, proposed §1.168(k)-2(c) applies only if the taxpayer chooses to make an election to a more favorable rule. Consequently, the Treasury Department and the IRS hereby certify that these proposed regulations will not have a significant economic impact on a substantial number of small entities.

Pursuant to section 7805(f) of the Code, this notice of proposed rulemaking will be submitted to the Chief Counsel for Advocacy of the Small Business Administration for comment on its impact on small business.

IV. *Unfunded Mandates Reform Act*

Section 202 of the Unfunded Mandates Reform Act of 1995 requires that agencies assess anticipated costs and benefits and take certain other actions before issuing a final rule that includes any Federal mandate that may result in expenditures in any one year by a state, local, or tribal government, in the aggregate, or by the private sector, of $100 million in 1995 dollars, updated annually for inflation. In 2019, that threshold is approximately $154 million. These proposed regulations do not include any Federal mandate that may result in expenditures by state, local, or tribal governments, or by the private sector in excess of that threshold.

V. *Executive Order 13132: Federalism*

Executive Order 13132 (entitled "Federalism") prohibits an agency from publishing any rule that has federalism implications if the rule either imposes substantial, direct compliance costs on state and local governments, and is not required by statute, or preempts state law, unless the agency meets the consultation and funding requirements of section 6 of the Executive Order. These proposed regulations do not have federalism implications and do not impose substantial direct compliance costs on state and local governments or preempt state law within the meaning of the Executive Order.

Comments and Public Hearing

Before these proposed regulations are adopted as final regulations, consideration will be given to any comments that are submitted timely to the IRS as prescribed in this preamble under the **ADDRESSES** heading. The Treasury Department and the IRS request comments on all aspects of the proposed rules. All comments will be available at *https://www.regulations.gov* or upon request.

A public hearing is scheduled on November 13, 2019, beginning at 10 a.m. in the Auditorium of the Internal Revenue Building, 1111 Constitution Avenue, NW, Washington, DC 20224. Due to building security procedures, visitors must enter at the Constitution Avenue entrance. In addition, all visitors must present photo identification to enter the building. Because of access restrictions, visitors will not be admitted beyond the immediate entrance area more than 30 minutes before the hearing starts. For more information about having your name placed on the building access list to attend the hearing, see the **FOR FURTHER INFORMATION CONTACT** section of this preamble.

The rules of 26 CFR 601.601(a)(3) apply to the hearing. Persons who wish to present oral comments at the hearing must submit an outline of the topics to be discussed and the time to be devoted to each topic by October 23, 2019. Submit a signed paper or electronic copy of the outline as prescribed in this preamble under the **ADDRESSES** heading. A period of 10 minutes will be allotted to each person making comments. An agenda showing the scheduling of the speakers will be prepared after the deadline for receiving outlines has passed. Copies of the agenda will be available free of charge at the hearing.

If no outline of the topics to be discussed at the hearing is received by October 23, 2019, the public hearing will be cancelled. If the public hearing is cancelled, a notice of cancellation of the public hearing will be published in the **Federal Register**.

Drafting Information

The principal authors of these proposed regulations are Kathleen Reed and Elizabeth R. Binder of the Office of Associate Chief Counsel (Income Tax and Accounting). However, other personnel from the Treasury Department and the IRS participated in their development.

Partial Withdrawal of Proposed Regulations

Under the authority of 26 U.S.C. 7805 and 26 U.S.C. 1502, §1.168(k)-2(b)(3)(iii)(B)(3)(*i*) through (*iii*), §1.168(k)-2(b)(3)(iii)(C), and §1.168(k)-2(b)(3)(vi) *Examples 18* through 22 of the notice of proposed rulemaking (REG-104397-18) published in the **Federal Register** on August 8, 2018 (83 FR 39292) are withdrawn.

Statement of Availability

IRS Revenue Procedures and Notices cited in this preamble are published in the Internal Revenue Bulletin (or Cumulative Bulletin) and are available from the Superintendent of Documents, U.S. Government Publishing Office, Washington, DC 20402, or by visiting the IRS website at *http://www.irs.gov*.

[¶ 49,814]   Proposed Amendments of Regulations (REG-136401-18), published in the Federal Register on September 30, 2019.

[Code Secs. 105 and 4980H]

Qualified health plan: Refundable credit: Health coverage: Employer contributions: Shared responsibility: Pension plan.—Amendments of Reg. §§1.105-11, 54.4980H-4 and 54.4980H-5, clarifying the application of the employer shared responsibility provisions and certain nondiscrimination rules under the Internal Revenue Code (Code) to health reimbursement arrangements (HRAs) and other account-based group health plans integrated with individual health insurance coverage or Medicare (individual coverage HRAs), and to provide certain safe harbors with respect to the application of those provisions to individual coverage HRAs, are proposed.

AGENCY: Internal Revenue Service (IRS), Treasury.

ACTION: Notice of proposed rulemaking.

SUMMARY: This document sets forth proposed regulations to clarify the application of the employer shared responsibility provisions and certain nondiscrimination rules under the Internal Revenue Code (Code) to health reimbursement arrangements (HRAs) and other account-based group health plans integrated with individual health insurance coverage or Medicare (individual coverage HRAs), and to provide certain safe harbors with respect to the application of those provisions to individual coverage HRAs. The proposed regulations are intended to facilitate the adoption of individual coverage HRAs by employers, and taxpayers generally are permitted to rely on the proposed regulations. The proposed regulations would affect employers, employees and their family members, and plan sponsors.

DATES: Written or electronic comments and requests for a public hearing must be received by December 30, 2019.

ADDRESSES: Submit electronic submissions via the Federal eRulemaking Portal at *https://www.regulations.gov* (indicate IRS and REG-136401-18) by following the online instructions for submitting comments. Once submitted to the Federal eRulemaking Portal, comments cannot be edited or withdrawn. The Department of the Treasury (Treasury Department) and the IRS will publish for public availability any comment received to its public docket, whether submitted electronically or in hard copy. Send hard copy submissions to: CC:PA:LPD:PR (REG-136401-18), Room 5203, Internal Revenue Service, P.O. Box 7604, Ben Franklin Station, Washington, DC 20044. Submissions may be hand-delivered Monday through Friday between the hours of 8 a.m. and 4 p.m. to CC:PA:LPD:PR (REG-136401-18), Courier's Desk, Internal Revenue Service, 1111 Constitution Avenue NW, Washington, DC 20224.

FOR FURTHER INFORMATION CONTACT: Concerning the proposed regulations, Jennifer Solomon, (202) 317-5500; concerning submissions of comments and requests for a public hearing, Regina Johnson, (202) 317-6901 (not toll-free numbers).

SUPPLEMENTARY INFORMATION:

I. Background

A. Individual Coverage HRAs and Related Guidance

On October 12, 2017, President Trump issued Executive Order 13813, "Promoting Healthcare Choice and Competition Across the United States."[1] The Executive Order directed the Secretaries of the Treasury, Labor, and Health and Human Services to "consider proposing regulations or revising guidance, to the extent permitted by law and supported by sound policy, to increase the usability of HRAs, to expand employers' ability to offer HRAs to their employees, and to allow HRAs to be used in conjunction with nongroup coverage."[2]

In response to the Executive Order, on October 23, 2018, the Departments of the Treasury, Labor, and Health and Human Services (the Departments) issued proposed regulations[3] under Public Health Service Act (PHS Act) section 2711 and the health nondiscrimination provisions[4] of the Health Insurance Portability and Accountability Act of 1996 (HIPAA)[5] and the Patient Protection and Affordable Care Act,[6] as amended by the Health Care Education and Reconciliation Act[7] (collectively, PPACA) (proposed integration regulations). The proposed integration regulations included a proposal to expand the potential use of HRAs and other account-based group health plans[8] (collectively referred to in this preamble as HRAs) by allowing the integration of HRAs with individual health insurance coverage, subject to certain conditions.

On June 14, 2019, the Departments finalized the proposed integration regulations, generally as proposed but with a number of revisions in response to comments (the final integration regulations).[9] The final integration regulations apply for plan years beginning on or after January 1, 2020.

---

[1] 82 FR 48385 (Oct. 17, 2017).

[2] Id.

[3] See 83 FR 54420 (Oct. 29, 2018).

[4] See Code sections 9802 and 9815, Employee Retirement Income Security Act (ERISA) sections 702 and 715, and PHS Act section 2705. Although Code section 9802 and ERISA section 702 were not amended by PPACA, the requirements of PHS Act section 2705 were also incorporated by reference into Code section 9815 and ERISA section 715. PPACA section 1201 moved the PHS Act nondiscrimination provisions from section 2702 to section 2705, with some modifications.

[5] Public Law 104-191.

[6] Public Law 111-148.

[7] Public Law 111-152.

[8] See §54.9815-2711(d)(6)(i) for the definition of an account-based group health plan. This term does not include qualified small employer health reimbursement arrangements (QSEHRAs) (as defined under section 9831(d)), medical savings accounts (see section 220), or health savings accounts (see section 223). In addition, for purposes of the integration regulations (both proposed and final), the definition does not include an employer arrangement that reimburses the cost of individual health insurance coverage in a cafeteria plan under section 125.

[9] See 84 FR 28888 (June 20, 2019). In addition to the final integration regulations: (1) The Departments issued final regulations setting forth conditions under which certain HRAs will be recognized as limited excepted benefits; (2) the Department of Health and Human Services (HHS) issued final regulations to provide a special enrollment period in the individual market for individuals who newly gain access to an individual coverage HRA or who are newly provided a QSEHRA; (3) the Department of Labor (DOL) finalized a safe harbor to provide assurance that the individual health insurance cover-

B. Premium Tax Credit (Section 36B)

Section 36B allows the premium tax credit (PTC) to certain taxpayers to help with the cost of individual health insurance coverage enrolled in through an Exchange.[10] Under section 36B(a) and (b)(1), and §1.36B-3(d), a taxpayer's PTC is the sum of the premium assistance amounts for all coverage months during the taxable year for individuals in the taxpayer's family.

An individual is eligible for the PTC for a month if the individual satisfies various requirements for the month (a coverage month). Among other requirements, under section 36B(c)(2), a month is not a coverage month for an individual if either: (1) the individual is eligible for coverage under an eligible employer-sponsored plan and that coverage is affordable and provides minimum value (MV); or (2) the individual enrolls in an eligible employer-sponsored plan, even if the coverage is not affordable or does not provide MV.[11]

In general, an eligible employer-sponsored plan is affordable for an employee if the amount the employee must pay for self-only coverage whether by salary reduction or otherwise (the employee's required contribution) for a plan does not exceed a percentage (the required contribution percentage[12]) of the employee's household income.[13] In addition, in general, an eligible employer-sponsored plan provides MV if the plan's share of the total allowed costs of benefits provided under the plan is at least 60 percent of the costs and if the plan provides substantial coverage of inpatient hospitalization and physician services.[14]

An eligible employer-sponsored plan includes coverage under a self-insured group health plan[15] and is minimum essential coverage (MEC) unless it consists solely of excepted benefits.[16] An HRA is a self-insured group health plan and, therefore, is an eligible employer-sponsored plan.[17] Accordingly, an individual is ineligible for the PTC for a month if the individual is (1) covered by an HRA, or (2) eligible for an HRA that is affordable and provides MV for the month (provided the HRA does not consist solely of excepted benefits).

On October 23, 2018, in connection with the proposed integration regulations, the Treasury Department and the IRS proposed regulations under section 36B to provide guidance regarding the circumstances in which an individual coverage HRA would be considered to be affordable and to provide MV. On June 14, 2019, in connection with the final integration regulations, the Treasury Department and the IRS finalized the rules under section 36B, substantially as proposed but with some clarifications in response to comments (the final PTC regulations).[18]

Under the final PTC regulations, an individual coverage HRA is considered to be affordable for a month if the employee's required HRA contribution for the month does not exceed 1/12 of the product of the employee's household income for the taxable year and the required contribution percentage. The required HRA contribution is the excess of: (1) the monthly premium for the lowest cost silver plan for self-only coverage of the employee offered in the Exchange for the rating area in which the employee resides (the PTC affordability plan[19]), over (2) in general, the self-only amount the employer makes newly available to the employee under the individual coverage HRA for the month (the monthly HRA amount).[20] Under the final PTC regulations, an individual coverage HRA that is affordable is treated as providing MV. The final PTC regulations apply for taxable years beginning on or after January 1, 2020.

C. Employer Shared Responsibility Provisions (Section 4980H)

1. In General

The employer shared responsibility provisions under section 4980H apply to an employer that is an applicable large employer (ALE). In general, an employer is an ALE for a calendar year if it had an average of 50 or more full-time employees (including full-time equivalent employees) during the preceding calendar year.[21]

For any month, an ALE may be liable for an employer shared responsibility payment under either section 4980H(a) or 4980H(b), or neither, but an ALE may not be liable for a payment under both sections 4980H(a) and 4980H(b).[22] An ALE generally is liable for a payment under section 4980H(a) for a month if it fails to offer coverage under an eligible employer-sponsored plan to at least 95 percent of its full-time employees (and their dependents) and at least one full-time employee is allowed the PTC for purchasing individual health insurance coverage through an Exchange. An ALE is liable for a payment under section 4980H(b) for a month if it offers coverage under an eligible employer-sponsored plan to at least 95 percent[23] of its full-time employees (and their dependents), but at least one full-time employee is allowed the PTC for purchasing individual health insurance coverage through an Exchange, which may occur because the ALE did not offer coverage to that particular full-time employee or because the coverage the employer offered was unaffordable or did not provide MV.[24]

2. Section 4980H Affordability Safe Harbors Regarding Household Income

Whether an employee may claim the PTC depends on the rules under section 36B, including the rules for whether an offer of coverage by the employer is affordable and provides MV.[25] However, the regulations under section 4980H provide certain safe harbors for determining whether an ALE is treated as making an offer of coverage that is affordable for purposes of section 4980H. More specifically, as noted earlier in this preamble, whether an offer of an eligible employer-sponsored plan is affordable, both for purposes of section 36B and section 4980H, depends in part on the employee's household income. Because an employer generally does not know an employee's household income, §54.4980H-5(e) provides that, for purposes of section 4980H(b), an employer may substitute for an employee's household income an amount based on the employee's wages from

---

(Footnote Continued)

age for which premiums are reimbursed by an HRA or a QSEHRA does not become part of an ERISA plan, provided certain conditions are satisfied (and the Departments provided a related clarification of the definition of the term "group health insurance coverage"); and (4) the Treasury Department and the IRS finalized regulations regarding premium tax credit eligibility for individuals offered an individual coverage HRA, as explained in this preamble. In this document, this package of regulations is referred to collectively as the "final regulations."

[10] Exchanges are entities established under PPACA section 1311 or 1321, through which qualified individuals and qualified employers can purchase health coverage.

[11] See section 36B(c)(2)(C)(iii) and §§1.36B-2(c)(3) and 1.36B-3(c).

[12] See §1.36B-2(c)(3)(v)(C). The required contribution percentage for 2020 is 9.78 percent (see Rev. Proc. 2019-29).

[13] See section 36B(c)(2)(C) and §1.36B-2(c)(3)(v)(A)(1) and (2). See §1.36B-2(c)(3)(v)(A)(3) for a safe harbor that, in certain circumstances, allows an employee to claim the PTC even if the offer of coverage ultimately is affordable.

[14] See section 36B(c)(2)(C)(ii); see also 80 FR 52678 (Sept. 1, 2015).

[15] See §1.5000A-2(c).

[16] See section 5000A(f)(3) and §1.5000A-2(g).

[17] See Notice 2013-54, 2013-40 IRB 287, Q&A 10.

[18] See 84 FR 28888 (June 20, 2019).

[19] The term "affordability plan" is also used in this preamble and refers to the lowest cost silver plan used to determine affordability of an individual coverage HRA, which

for purposes of section 36B means the PTC affordability plan and for section 4980H means either the PTC affordability plan or the lowest cost silver plan determined under the safe harbors provided in the proposed regulations, if applicable.

[20] See §1.36B-2(c)(5)(ii) for more information on how the required HRA contribution is determined, including in cases in which the employer makes the same amount available for all employees regardless of the number of individuals covered.

[21] See section 4980H(c)(2) and §54.4980H-2. See also §54.4980H-1(a) for definitions of the terms used in this preamble.

[22] For simplicity, this preamble refers to ALEs and employers, but to the extent the preamble is addressing the potential for liability under section 4980H, those terms refer to an ALE member. An ALE member is a person that, together with one or more other persons, is treated as a single employer that is an ALE, if applicable. Liability under section 4980H applies separately to each ALE member. See §54.4980H-1(a)(5). Further, the reporting obligations under section 6056 also apply to ALE members and references to employers or ALEs with respect to reporting under section 6056 should be read to refer to ALE members.

[23] If an ALE offers coverage to all but five of its full-time employees (and their dependents), and five is greater than five percent of the employer's full-time employees, the employer will not be liable for an employer shared responsibility payment under section 4980H(a). See §54.4980H-4.

[24] See §54.4980H-5.

[25] See section 4980H(c)(3). See also §§54.4980H-1(a)(28) and 54.4980H-5(e)(1).

the Form W-2, "Wage and Tax Statement," the employee's rate of pay, or the federal poverty line, using the household income safe harbors (the HHI safe harbors).[26]

The HHI safe harbors are optional and apply only for purposes of section 4980H(b). An ALE may choose to use one or more of the HHI safe harbors for all of its employees or for any reasonable category of employees, provided it does so on a uniform and consistent basis for all employees in a category. In addition, an ALE may use an HHI safe harbor only if the ALE offers its full-time employees and their dependents eligible employer-sponsored coverage that provides MV with respect to the self-only coverage offered to the employee. If, in applying one of the HHI safe harbors the offer of coverage is considered affordable, then the employer will not be subject to an employer shared responsibility payment under section 4980H(b) with respect to that employee, even if the employee is allowed the PTC.

3. Application of Section 4980H to Individual Coverage HRAs

In implementing the objectives of Executive Order 13813, the Treasury Department and the IRS considered the application of section 4980H to an ALE that offers an individual coverage HRA. Accordingly, on November 19, 2018, the Treasury Department and the IRS issued Notice 2018-88,[27] which described a number of potential approaches related to the interaction of the proposed integration regulations and section 4980H.

For clarity, the notice confirmed that an individual coverage HRA is an eligible employer-sponsored plan, and, therefore, an offer of an individual coverage HRA constitutes an offer of an eligible employer-sponsored plan for purposes of section 4980H(a). Consequently, if an ALE offers an individual coverage HRA to at least 95 percent of its full-time employees (and their dependents), the ALE will not be liable for an employer shared responsibility payment under section 4980H(a) for the month, regardless of whether any full-time employee is allowed the PTC.

The notice also explained how section 4980H(b) (including the HHI safe harbors) would apply to an ALE that offers an individual coverage HRA, described potential additional affordability safe harbors related to offers of individual coverage HRAs, requested comments, and provided examples. The Treasury Department and the IRS received a number of comments in response to Notice 2018-88, all of which were considered and are addressed in this preamble. See part II of this preamble for a more detailed discussion of the approaches described in Notice 2018-88 and the extent to which those potential approaches are included in the proposed regulations.

D. Section 105

In general, section 105(b) excludes from gross income amounts received by an employee through employer-provided accident or health insurance if those amounts are paid to reimburse expenses for medical care (as defined in section 213(d)) incurred by the employee (for medical care of the employee, the employee's spouse, or the employee's dependents, as well as children of the employee who are not dependents but have not attained age 27 by the end of the taxable year) for personal injuries and sickness.

Section 105(h) provides, however, that excess reimbursements (as defined in section 105(h)(7)) paid to a highly compensated individual (as defined in section 105(h)(5) and §1.105-11(d)) (an HCI)[28] under a self-insured medical reimbursement plan are includible in the gross income of the HCI if either (1) the plan discriminates in favor of HCIs as to eligibility to participate in the plan, or (2) the benefits provided under the plan discriminate in favor of HCIs (nondiscriminatory benefits rule).[29] Section 105(h)(4) provides that a self-insured medical reimbursement plan does not satisfy the nondiscriminatory benefits rule unless all benefits provided to HCIs are also provided to all other participants.[30] However, a plan that reimburses employees solely for premiums paid under an insured plan is treated as an insured plan and is not subject to these rules.[31]

The regulations under section 105(h) provide that, in order to satisfy the nondiscriminatory benefits rule under section 105(h)(4), all benefits made available under a self-insured medical reimbursement plan to an HCI (and the HCI's dependents) must also be made available to all other participants (and their dependents).[32] In addition, the regulations provide that "any maximum limit attributable to employer contributions must be uniform for all participants and for all dependents of employees who are participants and may not be modified by reason of a participant's age or years of service."[33] The consequence of a plan failing to satisfy this nondiscriminatory benefits requirement is that any excess reimbursements paid under the plan to an HCI are includible in the gross income and wages of the HCI.

HRAs generally are subject to the rules under section 105(h) and its related regulations because they are self-insured medical reimbursement plans.[34] However, HRAs that make available reimbursements to employees only for premiums paid to purchase health insurance policies, including individual health insurance policies, but not other expenses, are not subject to the rules under section 105(h) and its related regulations.[35] Notice 2018-88 addressed the interaction of individual coverage HRAs and section 105(h) and explained potential future guidance. The Treasury Department and the IRS received comments in response to the section 105(h) safe harbor in Notice 2018-88, all of which were considered and are addressed in this preamble. See later in this preamble for a more detailed discussion of the approaches described in Notice 2018-88 and the extent to which those approaches are included in the proposed regulations.

II. *Explanation of Provisions and Summary of Comments*

Taking into account the comments received in response to Notice 2018-88, as well as comments received in response to the proposed integration regulations and proposed PTC regulations, the Treasury Department and the IRS propose the following regulations under sections 4980H and 105 to clarify the application of those sections to individual coverage HRAs and to provide related safe harbors to ease the administrative burdens of avoiding liability under section 4980H and avoiding income inclusion under section 105(h). These proposed regulations do not include any changes to the final integration regulations or the final PTC regulations.

A. Section 4980H Proposed Regulations

The Treasury Department and the IRS note that section 4980H relates only to offers of coverage by an ALE to its full-time employees (and their dependents). As a result, to the extent an employer is not an ALE, or is an ALE but offers an individual coverage HRA to employees who are not full-time employees, the employer need not consider the application of section 4980H in determining those offers, and, therefore, it need not identify an affordability plan for those employees.

---

[26] Whether or not an employee has been offered affordable coverage for purposes of eligibility for the PTC is determined under section 36B(c)(2)(C)(i) and the regulations thereunder (as opposed to the section 4980H safe harbors).

[27] See Notice 2018-88, 2018-49 IRB 817.

[28] Generally, section 105(h)(5) and §1.105-11(d) define an HCI to include any employee that is among the highest paid 25 percent of all employees (including the five highest paid officers, but not including employees excludible under §1.105-11(c)(2)(iii) who are not participants in any self-insured medical reimbursement plan of the employer).

[29] See section 105(h)(1) and (2).

[30] See §1.105-11(c)(3)(i).

[31] See §1.105-11(b)(2).

[32] See §1.105-11(c)(3)(i).

[33] Id.

[34] See §1.105-11(b)(1); see also Notice 2002-45, 2002-28 CB 93.

[35] See §1.105-11(b)(2). HRAs that provide for the reimbursement of premiums to purchase health insurance policies in addition to other medical care expenses are subject to the rules under section 105(h) and the regulations thereunder because the HRA amounts may be used to reimburse medical care expenses other than premiums for health insurance policies. PHS Act section 2716, as incorporated into the Code by section 9815, applies nondiscrimination rules similar to section 105(h) to insured coverage and may apply to HRAs that only provide for the reimbursement of premiums. However, under Notice 2011-1, 2011-2 IRB 259, the Departments determined that compliance with PHS Act section 2716 should not be required (and, thus, any sanctions for failure to comply would not apply) until after regulations or other administrative guidance of general applicability has been issued under PHS Act section 2716.

1. Location-Related Issues

a. Location Safe Harbor - In General

As noted earlier in part I(B) of this preamble, under the final PTC regulations, whether an offer of an individual coverage HRA is affordable for an employee depends, in part, on the monthly premium for the PTC affordability plan for that employee (that is, the lowest cost silver plan for self-only coverage of the employee offered through the Exchange for the rating area in which the employee resides). In Notice 2018-88, the Treasury Department and the IRS expressed concerns about the burden on employers that could result from requiring affordability to be determined based on each employee's place of residence, noting that employees' places of residence might change over time and employers may have difficulty keeping their records up to date. Accordingly, Notice 2018-88 described a potential safe harbor under which, for purposes of determining affordability under section 4980H(b), an ALE would be allowed to use the lowest cost silver plan for the employee for self-only coverage offered through the Exchange in the rating area in which the employee's primary site of employment is located, instead of the lowest cost silver plan for the employee in the rating area in which the employee resides (the location safe harbor). The Treasury Department and the IRS requested comments on the location safe harbor and whether an alternative safe harbor would be preferable and, if so, why.

One commenter was not supportive of the need for a location safe harbor, asserting that employers will likely want to determine affordability based on the cost of the lowest cost silver plan where the employee resides and disagreeing with the premise that it is difficult for employers to track employees' current addresses. However, a number of commenters indicated that a location safe harbor is needed, but that the anticipated safe harbor is too narrow because it would require employers with worksites located in multiple rating areas, including national employers, to calculate affordability for section 4980H(b) purposes separately for numerous rating areas. One commenter suggested that larger employers may be unwilling to offer individual coverage HRAs if employers are required to track and align HRAs on a rating-area basis, noting that for traditional employer-sponsored coverage, employers generally need only look to the cost of a single plan to determine affordability.

Some commenters suggested that one lowest cost silver plan be used to determine affordability employer-wide, such as the lowest cost silver plan in the rating area in which the employer's headquarters is located. Some commenters suggested employers be allowed to use one lowest cost silver plan to determine affordability for all employees with a worksite in a particular state or metropolitan statistical area, which, at least one suggested, the Centers for Medicare & Medicaid Services (CMS) could determine and make available to the public. Some commenters suggested a nationwide affordability plan should be provided for purposes of section 4980H, which could apply for all employers, and could be calculated based on the national average cost of lowest cost silver plans, perhaps averaged over multiple years. One commenter noted that although a nationwide plan may have a relatively high cost, it would provide simplicity. Some commenters opposed broadening the location safe harbor, including providing a nationwide safe harbor, due to concerns about evasion of section 4980H and enabling lower contributions to individual coverage HRAs, relative to amounts determined based on an employee's actual residence.

As a general matter, the Treasury Department and the IRS acknowledge that in determining the affordability of traditional employer-sponsored coverage, employers generally use the cost of one plan (that is, the lowest cost plan providing MV that the employer offers to the employees) and that the cost of that plan does not vary by employee (or, in general, varies by broad categories of employees). In contrast, the affordability test for individual coverage HRAs is based on the cost of the applicable lowest cost silver plan for each employee, which will vary by employee, by virtue of the fact that the cost of individual health insurance coverage varies on an individual basis, including based on an individual's residence and age. The Treasury Department and the IRS recognize that this difference may impose additional complexity with respect to the application of section 4980H to individual coverage HRAs, as compared to traditional employer-sponsored coverage. However, for purposes of section 36B, whether coverage is affordable is an employee-by-employee determination and for an individual coverage HRA, where there is no traditional employer-sponsored coverage on which to base an employee contribution, the employee's required contribution must be based on the cost of an individual health insurance plan, as employees generally are required to have individual health insurance coverage in order to enroll in the individual coverage HRA. The Treasury Department and the IRS have considered ways in which, consistent with the law, application of the affordability test under the final PTC regulations can and should be modified in applying section 4980H. However, by virtue of the ways in which individual coverage HRAs differ from traditional employer-sponsored coverage, the determination of affordability under section 36B (and, accordingly, under section 4980H) differs for these two types of coverage, and the Treasury Department and the IRS expect that employers will take those differences into account in determining whether, and to whom, to offer an individual coverage HRA.

The Treasury Department and the IRS continue to be concerned about the burden imposed on employers in determining each full-time employee's place of residence, due to the fact that employees' places of residence might change with some frequency, and it could be difficult for employers to keep their records up to date. The Treasury Department and the IRS also recognize the administrative simplicity for employers with workers in different locations of being able to use the cost of a single plan to determine affordability for all workers. However, none of the suggested expansions of the location safe harbor would be based on a reasonable proxy for the cost that would determine whether the employee would be allowed the PTC (which is the basis for the employer shared responsibility payment under section 4980H(b)), and none would provide a substitute for a cost that the employer would otherwise be unable to identify in advance of the plan year. As a result, adoption of any of the suggested expansions of the location safe harbor could lead to a significant number of cases in which one or more of an ALE's full-time employees are allowed the PTC while the ALE is treated as providing those full-time employees affordable coverage, with the result that the ALE is not liable for an employer shared responsibility payment.

These concerns are particularly acute because of significant differences in individual health insurance plan premiums that exist in different geographic locations, including from rating area to rating area, not only across the country, but also within many states. Accordingly, an affordability plan based on a nationwide average cost or, in many cases, a statewide average cost, would allow an ALE with full-time employees in locations with above-average lowest cost silver plan premiums to offer an individual coverage HRA, the amount of which is based on an affordability calculation using the average cost. The ALE could then ensure that employees were informed of the ability to enroll in an Exchange plan subsidized by a potentially larger PTC, if they declined the individual coverage HRA. In that case, the ALE would not only avoid an employer shared responsibility payment, but also would avoid the cost of funding the employees' individual coverage HRAs (or any other healthcare benefits). Meanwhile, those employers with employees in below-average cost locations generally could use the actual cost in those lower-cost locations to determine affordability for those employees.[36] This result would run counter to the language and intent of section 4980H, which directly ties liability for an employer shared responsibility payment to one or more full-time employees being allowed the PTC.

The Treasury Department and the IRS recognize that a safe harbor based on the employee's primary site of employment could raise similar issues of avoidance of the employer shared responsibility payment, but it would be on a much more limited scale. It is possible that the premium for the lowest cost silver plan based on an employee's worksite will be more expensive or less expensive than the premium for the lowest cost silver plan based on the employee's residence, in cases in which the employee resides in a location that has a different lowest cost silver plan than the location in which the worksite is located. However, the Treasury Department and the IRS expect that many employees live in relatively close proximity to where they work, in which case it is likely that the location used to determine the affordability plan for purposes of sections 4980H and 36B would be the same. Further, the Treasury Department and the IRS also expect that even if an employee does not live and work in the same location for

---

[36] The Treasury Department and the IRS note that, in addition to considering section 4980H, employers will also need to take into account other applicable guidance in determining amounts to make available in individual coverage HRAs, including the same terms requirement (§ 54.9802-4(c)(3)) under the final integration regulations.

purposes of determination of the lowest cost silver plan, the employee is likely to live and work in locations that are relatively close, in which case the variation between the cost of the lowest cost silver plan where the employee lives versus the cost of the lowest cost silver plan where the employee works is likely to be less significant than the variation that would be introduced by a statewide or national average plan cost.

Thus, the Treasury Department and the IRS have concluded that the cost of the affordability plan at an employee's primary site of employment is a reasonable proxy for the cost of the affordability plan at the employee's residence for purposes of section 4980H, while avoiding the burdens that may arise for some employers in keeping records of their employees' current residences. Therefore, the proposed regulations provide that for purposes of section 4980H(b), an employer may use the lowest cost silver plan for the employee for self-only coverage offered through the Exchange where the employee's primary site of employment is located for determining whether an offer of an individual coverage HRA to a full-time employee is affordable. Further, the proposed regulations provide that the location safe harbor may be used in combination with the other safe harbors provided in the proposed regulations.

In response to comments asking for a single affordability plan for purposes of section 4980H, the Treasury Department and the IRS note that an ALE that wants to contribute one set amount to individual coverage HRAs that would protect the ALE from liability under section 4980H(b) could set the amount by determining affordability based on the lowest cost silver plan that has the highest cost premium for self-only coverage for any of its full-time employees (that is, nationally or based on multiple rating areas or states). This would result, however, in employees who live in locations with lower premiums receiving a benefit beyond the minimum required to protect against liability under section 4980H (and, thus, a higher cost to the employer than necessary solely to protect against that liability), and permit those same employees to purchase more generous plans than employees living in the higher-premium locations.

Nonetheless, in view of the many differences in premiums geographically, and in view of the comments requesting a broader location safe harbor, the Treasury Department and the IRS recognize the simplicity that one or more such safe harbors could provide and the value to employers of being able to design uniform health coverage for all employees, without needing to tie the uniform amount to the highest cost affordability plan. Consequently, the Treasury Department and the IRS request comments regarding other methods of determining affordability under section 4980H that would not result in significant discrepancies between full-time employees being allowed the PTC and ALEs avoiding liability under section 4980H, or otherwise allow ALEs to avoid the costs of providing healthcare benefits by shifting those costs to the Federal government through access to the PTC. To the extent any method relies on data such as cost variances across geographic locations, variations of employee populations across geographic locations, or other similar data, considerations should include the availability of the data, including availability of that data at times sufficiently in advance to be usable by employers for determining plan designs for a subsequent year, how the data would be used both by employers and the IRS in determining the affordability plan for purposes of section 4980H, and how changes in the data over time would be integrated into the suggested methodology.

b. Identifying the Primary Site of Employment under the Location Safe Harbor

With respect to the location safe harbor, commenters raised a number of questions as to how and when to determine an employee's primary site of employment. More specifically, commenters noted that determining the primary worksite for employees who work in multiple locations and do not have a set worksite could be challenging and asked that rules allow employers flexibility in making this determination. Commenters also asked for clarification on how the primary site of employment is determined for employees who telework, which commenters noted is increasing the geographic distribution of workers. In addition, commenters also asked for clarification about when in relation to the plan year an employee's worksite is determined, with one suggesting it be determined based on the worksite six months prior to the plan year or as of the date of hire. Commenters further requested that the proposed regulations address mid-year changes in worksite locations and that employers be able to use the initial affordability plan for the plan year regardless of later worksite changes.

In response to these comments, for purposes of the location safe harbor, the proposed regulations provide that an employee's primary site of employment generally is the location at which the employer reasonably expects the employee to perform services on the first day of the plan year (or on the first day the individual coverage HRA may take effect, for an employee who is not eligible for the individual coverage HRA on the first day of the plan year), except that the employee's primary site of employment is treated as changing if the location at which the employee performs services changes and the employer expects the change to be permanent or indefinite.[37] In that case, in general, the employee's primary site of employment is treated as changing no later than the first day of the second calendar month after the employee has begun performing services at the new location. This rule is intended to strike the appropriate balance between requiring that employee-specific, up-to-date information be used to determine affordability under section 4980H and allowing employers time to address the administrative aspects of accounting for an employee's change in primary worksite.

The proposed regulations also include a special rule for determining primary worksite for the first plan year that an employer offers an individual coverage HRA (or first offers an individual coverage HRA to a particular class of employees). Specifically, if an employer is first offering an individual coverage HRA to a class of employees, and the change in worksite occurs prior to the individual coverage HRA's initial plan year, the employee's primary site of employment is treated as changing no later than the later of the first day of the plan year or the first day of the second calendar month after the employee has begun performing services at the new location. This is to provide certainty to employers first offering individual coverage HRAs to account for changes in circumstances that may occur in the months leading up to the plan year, including in close proximity to the first day of the plan year. For subsequent plan years, the general rule should take into account, for instance, changes in residence after an open enrollment period but before the beginning of the plan year.

In the case of an employee who regularly works from home or at another worksite that is not on the employer's premises but who may be required by his or her employer to work at, or report to, a particular worksite, such as a teleworker with an assigned office space, the worksite to which the employee would report to provide services if requested is the applicable primary site of employment. The proposed regulations provide that in the case of an employee who works remotely from home or at another worksite that is not on the employer's premises and who otherwise does not have a particular assigned office space or a worksite to which to report, the employee's residence is the primary site of employment.

The Treasury Department and the IRS recognize that the manner in which employees report to work varies widely across employers and industries. Therefore, the Treasury Department and the IRS request comments on whether any further clarification is needed regarding determination of the primary site of employment for purposes of the section 4980H location safe harbor.

c. Employee Residence

Notwithstanding the location safe harbor, one commenter expressed an interest in using each employee's residence to determine affordability for purposes of section 4980H. The use of the location safe harbor under the proposed regulations is optional for an employer, and if an employer opts not to use the location safe harbor, then the PTC affordability plan (that is, the lowest cost silver plan for the employee based on the employee's

---

[37] The final integration regulations allow individual coverage HRAs to be offered based on different classes of employees. One class of employees, as set forth in §54.9802-4(d)(2)(v), is employees whose primary site of employment is in the same rating area (with rating area defined in 45 CFR 147.102(b)). The final integration regulations do not provide a specific definition for primary site of employment, and the definition provided in the proposed regulations applies only for purposes of section 4980H.

residence) would be used to determine the affordability of the offer of the individual coverage HRA.[38] However, the Treasury Department and the IRS expect that most employers will choose to use the location safe harbor, in part because under the final integration regulations, an employer may offer and vary individual coverage HRAs for a class of employees whose primary site of employment is in the same rating area, but the final integration regulations do not provide a class of employees based on an employee's residence.[39] Thus, because the final integration regulations do not provide for a class of employees based on the location of employees' residences, an employer basing affordability on the residences of employees would need to use the lowest cost silver plan with the highest cost premium for self-only coverage at the residence of any employees in the class.

This commenter also requested clarification regarding when an employer may determine an employee's residence during the calendar year to identify the appropriate plan to be used to determine affordability, and included specific suggestions including a snapshot date six months prior to the plan year or date of hire for those not employed at that time. The proposed regulations do not provide any rules addressing the ability of an employer to identify the residence of the employee in the case of an employer who chooses to determine the affordability of the individual coverage HRA based on the residence of each employee instead of using the location safe harbor. However, the Treasury Department and the IRS request comments on whether, in the case of an individual coverage HRA and for purposes of determining the location of the employee's residence, rules allowing the use of a snapshot date in a specified period prior to the beginning of the plan year, rules allowing a short delay in the application of any change in residence, or a rule similar to one of those alternatives would be helpful to employers, or whether the availability of the location safe harbor, in conjunction with the final integration regulations, generally eliminates the need for such rules. Similar to the location safe harbor, any residence safe harbor would need to include rules providing when a change in an employee's residence must be taken into account.

d. Multiple Affordability Plans in One Rating Area

Although the final PTC regulations refer to the lowest cost silver plan offered through an Exchange for an employee in a rating area, there is not necessarily one lowest cost silver plan per rating area. Rather, CMS has advised the Treasury Department and the IRS that, in some rating areas, there are different lowest cost silver plans in different parts of the rating area because some issuers only offer coverage in parts of rating areas (specifically, by county or zip code). For purposes of the PTC, whether an offer of an individual coverage HRA to an employee is affordable depends, in part, on the premium for the lowest cost silver plan available to that employee, which may differ from the lowest cost silver plan available to another employee located in another part of the same rating area.

For the sake of clarity, the proposed regulations, therefore, provide that the lowest cost silver plan for an employee for a month, for purposes of the safe harbors in the proposed regulations, is the lowest cost silver plan in the part of the rating area that includes the employee's applicable location. For purposes of this preamble and the proposed regulations, an employee's applicable location is either the employee's primary worksite, if the employer uses the location safe harbor, or the employee's residence, if the employer chooses not to use the location safe harbor.

ALEs should be aware of how this rule interacts with the final integration regulations. Specifically, for an ALE using the location safe harbor with multiple worksites within a rating area, it may be the case that for some employees one lowest cost silver plan applies and for other employees, with a worksite in another part of the same rating area, a different lowest cost silver plan applies, perhaps with substantially different premiums. In that sense, the amount the employer needs to make available under the individual coverage HRA, for purposes of avoiding potential liability for an employer shared responsibility payment under section 4980H(b), may vary by zip code or county, rather than by rating area. However, under the final integration regulations, employers may not create classes of employees based on a geographic area smaller than a rating area.[40] Accordingly, to the extent an ALE has multiple worksites in one rating area, the ALE will need to take these different rules into account in determining the amounts to be made available under an individual coverage HRA, and, in order to avoid potential liability for an employer shared responsibility payment under section 4980H(b), may need to base amounts made available in the HRA in a rating area on the most expensive lowest cost silver plan in any part of the rating area in which at least one employee has a primary worksite.

2. Age-Related Issues

a. Consideration of Age Safe Harbor

Under the final PTC regulations, for any given employee, the premium for the PTC affordability plan is based on the particular employee's relevant circumstances, including the particular employee's age. Consequently, even for employees residing in the same location (or working at the same location if the location safe harbor is applied), the cost of the applicable affordability plan is determined on an employee-by-employee basis.[41] In Notice 2018-88, the Treasury Department and the IRS acknowledged that determining the premium for the affordability plan for each employee based on his or her age might be burdensome for some employers, and requested comments on the administrative issues and burdens the age-based determination may raise and on safe harbors that would ease this burden and be consistent with the purpose and policies underlying section 4980H.

One commenter supported an employee-by-employee age-based affordability determination and, therefore, opposed an age-based safe harbor, asserting that employers will want to make HRA contributions based on employee ages. Therefore, the commenter did not see the need for an age-based safe harbor. However, several commenters stated that requiring the determination of affordability on an employee-by-employee basis, based on age, would be very burdensome for employers. These commenters requested an age-based safe harbor and indicated that the lack of such a safe harbor could discourage some larger employers from offering individual coverage HRAs, in particular for employers that want to provide a flat amount in the individual coverage HRA regardless of age.

Commenters provided various suggestions for how an age-based safe harbor could be designed. One commenter suggested that the safe harbor might provide that affordability may be determined based on a composite premium for an employer's employees, at a minimum, at a particular worksite, and preferably at a combination of regional or national worksites. The commenter also suggested a composite premium based on the lowest cost silver plan at a specified age (for example, the lowest cost silver plan for a 40-year-old person in the rating area of the worksite), which an employer could use to determine the cost of the affordability plan for all of its employees at the particular worksite. Another commenter suggested employers should be allowed to use the average age of all employees in each class of employees on the first day of the plan year to determine the premium for the section 4980H affordability calculation for all employees in that class of employees. One commenter suggested an age safe harbor could be based on age bands adopted in a state, while another commented that the use of age bands to develop a safe harbor would introduce too much complexity and variation.

---

[38] Note that, as discussed in part II(A)(4) of this preamble, although the safe harbors in the proposed regulations are optional, if an ALE chooses to use them, it must do so based on the classes of employees set forth in the final integration regulations. Also note that, later in this preamble, the Treasury Department and the IRS explain the extent to which the other safe harbors provided under the proposed regulations may apply to the PTC affordability plan, for purposes of section 4980H.

[39] Section 54.9802-4(d)(2)(v).

[40] Section 54.9802-4(d)(2)(v).

[41] Also note that, under the final integration regulations, a plan sponsor of an individual coverage HRA may increase amounts made available under the HRA based on increases in the ages of participants in a class of employees subject to certain conditions. See §54.9804-2(c)(3). Nothing in the proposed regulations affects the rules allowing plan sponsors of individual coverage HRAs to vary amounts made available based on participants' ages. However, ALEs that offer individual coverage HRAs will need to take into account both the final integration regulations and section 4980H in designing an individual coverage HRA offered to full-time employees.

The Treasury Department and the IRS acknowledge that determining the premium for the affordability plan for purposes of section 4980H for each full-time employee, based on age, may be burdensome for some employers. However, section 4980H incorporates section 36B for purposes of determining whether an ALE is subject to an employer shared responsibility payment under section 4980H(b), and the authority of the Treasury Department and the IRS to provide safe harbors under section 4980H that deviate significantly from the section 36B rules is limited. More specifically, as noted earlier in this preamble, the Treasury Department and the IRS have provided other section 4980H safe harbors, namely the HHI safe harbors, which have been designed to offer a reasonable proxy for information that the employer may not know or would bear significant burdens in determining. By contrast, an employer typically knows the ages of its employees for a variety of unrelated purposes; consequently, it is not the case that employers do not know, or would bear a significant burden in determining, an employee's age. In addition, the average age of a group of employees generally will not be a reasonable proxy for a particular employee's age because, depending on the group, the average age may differ markedly from the ages of the older and younger members of the group. Accordingly, any age-based safe harbor would likely result in a number of employees (those with an age greater than the safe harbor age) receiving the PTC while the employer would not be subject to an employer shared responsibility payment under section 4980H(b), including in some cases by employer design.

For these reasons, the proposed regulations do not provide a safe harbor for the age used to determine the premium of an employee's affordability plan. Rather, under the proposed regulations as under section 36B, affordability of the offer of an individual coverage HRA for purposes of section 4980H is determined, in part, based on each employee's age.

The Treasury Department and the IRS also note that as a practical matter, if an employer wants to make a single amount available under an individual coverage HRA to a class of employees and ensure it avoids an employer shared responsibility payment under section 4980H(b), in general, the employer can use the age of the oldest employee in the class of employees to determine the amount to make available under the HRA to that class of employees. However, if the employer does not make available the full amount of the cost of the affordability plan under the HRA, the employer will also need to compare each full-time employee's required contribution to the applicable amount under an HHI safe harbor to ensure the offer is affordable for all full-time employees. Further, the employer would need to take into account any geographic variation in the cost of the affordability plan (that is, the employer would need to ensure that it is basing affordability on the most expensive lowest cost silver plan available to any employee in the class, which may not be the lowest cost silver plan for the oldest employee in the class depending on whether the lowest cost silver plan of a younger employee in the class in a different geographic location has a higher cost).

b. Age Used to Determine Premium for Affordability Plan for an Employee

One commenter requested information regarding when employers may determine the employee's age for purposes of determining the premium of the affordability plan, for purposes of section 4980H. To align with the rules issued under 45 CFR 147.102(a)(1)(iii) concerning the ability of issuers in the individual and small group markets to vary health insurance premiums based on age, the commenter requested that the Treasury Department and the IRS provide that an employee's age may be determined at the time of the policy issuance or renewal or, if an individual is added after the policy issuance or renewal date, the date the individual is added or enrolled in coverage.[42]

In response to this comment, and to provide clarity to employers, the proposed regulations specify the date as of which an employee's age is to be determined for a plan year for purposes of determining affordability under the section 4980H safe harbors.[43] Specifically, the proposed regulations provide that for an employee who is or will be eligible for an individual coverage HRA on the first day of the plan year, the employee's age for the plan year is the employee's age on the first day of the plan year, and for an employee who becomes eligible for an individual coverage HRA during the plan year, the employee's age for the remainder of the plan year is the employee's age on the date the HRA can first become effective for the employee. This rule is based on, but not an exact incorporation of, the age determination rule that applies for purposes of rate setting in the individual and small group markets, which is tied to the individual market policy issuance or renewal date. The proposed regulations include a rule based on the HRA plan year and HRA effective date instead, to provide more certainty and simplicity for employers.

c. Age Band Used to Identify Affordability Plan for All Employees

The Treasury Department and the IRS understand that, in almost all cases, the plan that is the lowest cost silver plan at one age in a particular location will be the lowest cost silver plan for individuals of all ages in that location. However, CMS has advised the Treasury Department and the IRS that it is theoretically possible that, in some cases, one plan might be the lowest cost silver plan at one age and another plan might be the lowest cost silver plan at another age, in the same location. If that were to occur, however, the differences in premium amounts of the different plans at the same age would be extremely small (less than two dollars).

Therefore, in order to avoid the need for employers to determine different lowest cost silver plans in one location for employees of different ages, and to simplify the information that the Exchanges will make available to employers, the proposed regulations provide that for purposes of the proposed safe harbors, the lowest cost silver plan for an employee for a month is the lowest cost silver plan for the lowest age band in the individual market for the employee's applicable location.

3. Look-back Month Safe Harbor

a. In General

Under the final PTC regulations, the affordability of an individual coverage HRA for a month is determined, in part, based on the cost of the PTC affordability plan for that month. For example, an employee's required contribution for January 2020 for an individual coverage HRA would be based on the cost of the PTC affordability plan for January 2020. Further, Exchange plan premium information for a calendar year generally is not available until shortly before the beginning of the open enrollment period for that calendar year, which generally begins on November 1 of the prior calendar year.[44] In Notice 2018-88, the Treasury Department and the IRS noted that while this time frame is sufficient for individuals and Exchanges to determine potential PTC eligibility for the upcoming calendar year, the Treasury Department and the IRS are aware that employers generally determine the health benefits they will offer for an upcoming plan year (including the employees' required contributions) well in advance of the start of the plan year. Therefore, for an individual coverage HRA with a calendar-year plan year, employers generally would determine the benefits to offer, including the amount to make available in an HRA for the plan year, well before mid-to-late fall of the prior calendar year. Further, the Treasury Department and the IRS noted that under section 4980H, ALEs are intended to be able to decide whether to offer coverage sufficient to avoid an employer shared responsibility payment. ALEs are only able to make that choice if they have timely access to the necessary information.

---

[42] Under 45 CFR 147.102(a)(1)(iii), issuers are required to use the enrollee's age as of the date of policy issuance or renewal.

[43] The age identification rule in the proposed regulations does not apply for purposes of the final integration regulations, under which, in determining age with respect to variation in amounts made available to participants based on age in an individual coverage HRA, plan sponsors may determine the age of the participant using any reasonable method for a plan year, so long as the plan sponsor determines each participant's age using the same method for all participants in the class of employees for the plan year and the method is determined prior to the plan year. See § 54.9802-4(c)(3)(iii)(B). However, to the extent an ALE is offering an individual coverage HRA, the ALE will need to take into account both the final integration regulations and any rules under section 4980H; therefore, the Treasury Department and the IRS have provided a proposed rule under section 4980H that allows compliance with both sets of rules.

[44] See 45 CFR 155.410(e)(3).

To address this issue, Notice 2018-88 provided that the Treasury Department and the IRS anticipated issuing guidance that would allow an ALE sponsoring an individual coverage HRA with a calendar-year plan year to determine affordability for a year using the cost of the affordability plan for the employee's applicable location for the prior calendar year.[45]

A number of commenters supported this safe harbor, asserting that it would be problematic for employers to be required to wait until the fall to determine individual coverage HRA amounts for the upcoming year. However, one commenter opposed the safe harbor, based on concerns that, according to the commenter, the significant volatility in premiums in the individual market from year to year could impose additional costs on employees because individual coverage HRA amounts would be based on prior year individual market premiums and would not reflect current year individual market premiums.

The Treasury Department and the IRS acknowledge that premiums in the individual market may vary from year to year and that a safe harbor based on prior premium information would allow ALEs to determine affordability based on premiums that likely will differ from the actual current year premiums. However, under section 4980H, ALEs are intended to be able to decide whether to offer coverage sufficient to avoid an employer shared responsibility payment, and they may only do so if they have timely access to the relevant information. Therefore, the proposed regulations include a safe harbor that allows employers to use prior premium information to determine affordability for purposes of section 4980H (the look-back month safe harbor), but with some modifications as compared to the anticipated safe harbor in Notice 2018-88, as described in the remainder of this section of the preamble.

As anticipated in Notice 2018-88, under the proposed regulations, an employer offering an individual coverage HRA with a calendar-year plan year may use the look-back month safe harbor. However, the proposed regulations provide additional specificity, to take into account that even within a calendar year, from calendar month to calendar month, the lowest cost silver plan in an employee's applicable location may change due to plan termination or because the plan that was the lowest cost silver plan closes to enrollment (sometimes referred to as plan suppression). Therefore, the proposed regulations provide that in determining an employee's required contribution for any calendar month, for purposes of section 4980H(b), an employer offering an individual coverage HRA with a calendar-year plan year may use the monthly premium for the lowest cost silver plan for January of the prior calendar year.

In addition, the proposed regulations provide that employers offering individual coverage HRAs with non-calendar year plan years (non-calendar year individual coverage HRAs) may also use the look-back month safe harbor, although in that case the look-back month is different. In this respect, the proposed regulations differ from Notice 2018-88, which provided that the Treasury Department and the IRS did not anticipate allowing employers offering non-calendar year individual coverage HRAs to use this safe harbor. However, the rule anticipated in Notice 2018-88 was based on the assumption that employers offering non-calendar year individual coverage HRAs would have the relevant premium information by November of the prior calendar year. The Treasury Department and the IRS now understand that this would not necessarily be the case as the affordability plan may change from month to month during the calendar year; thus, which plan is the affordability plan for a month generally will not be known until shortly before the relevant month.

Further, in Notice 2018-88, the Treasury Department and the IRS requested comments on whether this safe harbor should be allowed to be used by employers that offer non-calendar year individual coverage HRAs and, if so, the range of plan year start dates to which the safe harbor should apply. Some commenters requested that the safe harbor extend to non-calendar year individual coverage HRAs. One commenter recommended allowing, as a general rule, all employers with an individual coverage HRA to use the premiums for the affordability plan in effect six months prior to the first day of the plan year. Another commenter recommended allowing, as a general rule, all employers with individual coverage HRAs to use the premiums for the affordability plan in effect or published no longer than 12 months prior to the start of the plan year.

Based on these comments and that the affordability plan may change from month to month during the year and, therefore, may not be known by November of the prior year, the proposed regulations allow employers offering non-calendar year individual coverage HRAs to use the look-back month safe harbor, in order to provide those employers timely access to the information they need to determine the coverage sufficient to avoid an employer shared responsibility payment, as contemplated by section 4980H(b). More specifically, for an employer offering a non-calendar year individual coverage HRA, the proposed regulations provide that in determining an employee's required contribution for a calendar month, for purposes of section 4980H(b), an employer may use the monthly premium for the affordability plan for January of the current calendar year. The proposed regulations provide a different look-back month for employers offering non-calendar year individual coverage HRAs (that is, January of the current year) than those offering individual coverage HRAs with a calendar-year plan year (that is, January of the prior year) in order to strike the appropriate balance between providing employers with access to information sufficiently in advance of the plan year and avoiding the use of premium information that could be significantly out of date. The Treasury Department and the IRS note that the relevant premium information for non-calendar year individual coverage HRAs (that is, the premium for January of the current year) will be available by November 1 of the prior year, and, therefore, generally ALEs sponsoring non-calendar year individual coverage HRAs should have access to the necessary premium information sufficiently in advance of the start of the plan year. The Treasury Department and the IRS request comments on whether the proposed look-back month for non-calendar year individual coverage HRAs will be sufficient for individual coverage HRAs with plan years that begin relatively early in the calendar year and whether ALEs intend to offer individual coverage HRAs on a non-calendar year basis, including with plan years that begin early in the calendar year.

The proposed regulations provide that an ALE may use the look-back month safe harbor in addition to the other safe harbors included in the proposed regulations, and that an ALE may apply the look-back month safe harbor even if the ALE decides not to use the location safe harbor and, instead, bases the affordability plan on employee residence.

The proposed regulations also clarify that, although the look-back month safe harbor allows the employer to use premium information from the applicable look-back month to determine the cost of the affordability plan for each month of the current plan year, in determining the applicable premium, the employer must use the employee's applicable age for the current plan year and the employee's applicable location for the current month. In general, this means that the ALE may use the same premium (that is, the premium based on the applicable look-back month, applying current employee information) for each month of the plan year. However, to the extent the employee's applicable location changes during the plan year, although the ALE may continue to determine the monthly premium for the applicable lowest cost silver plan based on the applicable look-back month, the ALE must use the employee's new applicable location to determine that monthly premium. See parts II(A)(1)(b) and II(A)(2)(b) of this preamble for a discussion of the date as of which an employee's age is determined for purposes of the section 4980H safe harbors and the date as of which an employee's worksite is considered to have changed, for purposes of the location safe harbor.

Relatedly, Notice 2018-88 also included an anticipated safe harbor which allowed ALEs offering individual coverage HRAs to assume that the cost of the affordability plan for the first month of the plan year is the cost of the affordability plan for all months of the plan year (the non-calendar year safe harbor). This safe harbor was primarily intended to provide certainty to non-calendar year individual coverage HRAs, for which the cost of the affordability plan would change mid-plan year (that is, upon the changing of the calendar year). Commenters supported the non-calendar year safe harbor, and the Treasury Department and the IRS continue to be of the view that ALEs need predictability with respect to the affordability plan that will apply for each month of the plan year. However, the proposed regulations do not include the non-calendar year safe harbor because it is generally subsumed by the look-back month safe harbor under the proposed regulations. Specifically, under the proposed regulations, the

---

[45] This safe harbor was referred to in Notice 2018-88 as the calendar year safe harbor.

look-back month safe harbor applies to non-calendar year individual coverage HRAs and provides a look-back month to determine the cost of the affordability plan for each month of the plan year. As a result, the look-back month safe harbor addresses the issue underlying the non-calendar year safe harbor, and the Treasury Department and the IRS determined that a separate non-calendar year safe harbor would be largely duplicative and confusing. However, the Treasury Department and the IRS request comments on whether any employers do not intend to use the look-back month safe harbor and would, therefore, need a separate safe harbor allowing the use of the premium for the first month of the current plan year to determine affordability for all months of the plan year.

b. Adjustment to Look-back Month Premium Amounts

Notice 2018-88 noted that the Treasury Department and the IRS considered whether to apply an adjustment to the cost of the affordability plan under the look-back month safe harbor, but did not anticipate proposing such an adjustment, to avoid complexity and due to uncertainty regarding how to determine an appropriate adjustment in all circumstances and for all years. The Treasury Department and the IRS requested comments on whether such an adjustment should be included in future guidance and, if so, how the adjustment should be calculated.

A number of commenters opposed applying an adjustment, asserting that, because of volatility in healthcare costs, it would be difficult to develop a benchmark that is representative of the market, and an adjustment could contribute to increasing healthcare costs, further complicate an already complicated rule, and cause confusion for employers. In contrast, a number of commenters supported an adjustment, suggesting that without an adjustment an employee with an individual coverage HRA may be priced out of the market and employer contributions required to satisfy section 4980H would be systematically undervalued.

Regarding the method for calculating an adjustment, commenters suggested basing the adjustment on the average of the three prior years' premium increases in the relevant individual market or PPACA's premium adjustment percentage. Commenters requested that the Treasury Department and the IRS work with HHS to compute these amounts and make them available to plan sponsors in a timely manner.

The Treasury Department and the IRS have considered these comments and continue to be concerned about the complexity and burdens that would be imposed by the application of an adjustment to the prior premiums under the look-back month safe harbor, and agree with commenters regarding the difficulty of producing an accurate adjustment. The Treasury Department and the IRS are concerned about the ability to produce a sufficiently accurate adjustment due to geographic variation in premiums (including geographic variations in the relative annual increases or decreases in premiums) and that the timing of access to information would hamper the ability to apply an adjustment based on up-to-date information. The Treasury Department and the IRS also considered applying more general adjustments (such as the Consumer Price Index overall medical care component or PPACA's premium adjustment percentage[46]) but are concerned that those adjustments would add complexity to the safe harbor while not reflecting premium changes in a way that is sufficiently specific to the employer's employees, including their geographic location. Therefore, under the proposed regulations, the look-back month safe harbor does not include an adjustment to the prior premium information. However, the Treasury Department and the IRS request comments on this issue and will continue to consider whether an adjustment is warranted, and how any such adjustment would be calculated, including in the event that the Treasury Department and the IRS observe that use of the look-back month safe harbor results in significant discrepancies in the affordability determinations as separately applied for purposes of sections 36B and 4980H.

4. Consistency Requirement and Conditions for the Safe Harbors

Notice 2018-88 provided that ALEs would not be required to use any of the anticipated section 4980H safe harbors for individual coverage HRAs, but that the Treasury Department and the IRS anticipated that some level of consistency would be required in the application of the anticipated safe harbors by an employer to its employees. The notice requested comments on the scope of such a requirement, including whether employers should be allowed to choose to apply the safe harbors to reasonable categories of employees, such as some or all of the categories identified in §54.4980H-5(e)(2)(i), which apply for purposes of the HHI safe harbors.[47] One commenter supported the use of consistency requirements based on the current categories of employees used under §54.4980H-5(e)(2)(i).

Under the proposed regulations, use of any of the safe harbors is optional for an ALE. However, rather than providing that a consistency requirement applies based on reasonable categories of employees as set forth in §54.4980H-5(e)(2)(i), the proposed regulations provide that an ALE may choose to apply the safe harbors for any class of employees as defined in the final integration regulations,[48] provided the ALE does so on a uniform and consistent basis for all employees in the class. The proposed regulations base the consistency requirement for the safe harbors in the proposed regulations on the classes of employees in the final integration regulations for the sake of consistency with those rules and to reduce complexity for employers in complying with both sets of rules.

In addition, the proposed regulations clarify the conditions for using the proposed safe harbors, including the HHI safe harbors as applied to offers of individual coverage HRAs. Current regulations under section 4980H provide that an ALE may only use an HHI safe harbor if the ALE offers its full-time employees (and their dependents) eligible employer-sponsored coverage that provides MV with respect to the self-only coverage offered to the employee. Because an individual coverage HRA is deemed to provide MV by virtue of being affordable (and is not an independent determination as it is for other types of employer-sponsored coverage), the proposed regulations do not separately impose this MV requirement on the use of the safe harbors in the proposed regulations.

5. Application of Current HHI Safe Harbors to Individual Coverage HRAs

As described earlier in this preamble, under section 36B, whether an offer of coverage under an eligible employer-sponsored plan is affordable is based on whether the employee's required contribution exceeds the required contribution percentage of the employee's household income. Because an ALE generally will not know an employee's household income, the current section 4980H regulations set forth three HHI safe harbors under which an employer may compare the employee's required contribution to information that is readily available to the employer, rather than to actual household income.[49]

Notice 2018-88 provided that the Treasury Department and the IRS anticipate providing guidance clarifying that an ALE that offers an individual coverage HRA would be permitted to use the HHI safe harbors, subject to the applicable requirements, for purposes of section 4980H(b). Several commenters supported the intent to allow the use of the HHI safe harbors to determine the affordability of individual coverage HRAs.

As with other types of employer-sponsored coverage, employers that offer individual coverage HRAs will not know employees' household incomes. Therefore, the proposed regulations provide that an employer offering an individual coverage HRA to a class of employees may use the HHI safe harbors in determining whether the offer of the HRA is affordable for purposes of section 4980H(b).

The proposed regulations clarify how the HHI safe harbors apply to an offer of an individual coverage HRA. Specifically, the current HHI safe harbors assume that the employee's required contribution will be based on the lowest-cost self-only coverage that provides MV that the employer

---

[46] See PPACA section 1302(c)(4).

[47] Under §54.4980H-5(e)(2)(i), reasonable categories generally include specified job categories, the nature of compensation (hourly or salary), geographic location, and similar bona fide business criteria.

[48] Section 54.9802-4(d)(2). The proposed regulations refer to the definition of classes of employees in the final integration regulations but do not incorporate other related rules, such as the minimum class size requirement set forth in §54.9802-4(d)(3).

[49] See §54.4980H-5(e)(2).

offers to the employee. The proposed regulations clarify that, in applying the HHI safe harbors to an offer of an individual coverage HRA, the employee's required HRA contribution is to be used, taking into account any other applicable safe harbors under the proposed regulations.

Further, the proposed regulations include technical updates to the current HHI safe harbors to reflect that the percentage used to determine affordability is the required contribution percentage (rather than a static 9.5 percent), which is adjusted in accordance with section 36B(c)(2)(C)(iv) and the regulations thereunder. The Treasury Department and the IRS clarified this issue in Notice 2015-87 and now have the opportunity to reflect that clarification in the regulation text.[50] The proposed regulations do not make substantive changes to the current HHI safe harbors as applied to employer-sponsored coverage that is not an individual coverage HRA.[51]

6. Minimum Value

As described earlier in this preamble, in general, under section 36B, an eligible employer-sponsored plan provides MV if the plan's share of the total allowed costs of benefits provided under the plan is at least 60 percent of the costs and if the plan provides substantial coverage of inpatient hospitalization and physician services.[52] Because of the differences between individual coverage HRAs and traditional group health plans, the final PTC regulations provide that an individual coverage HRA that is affordable is treated as providing MV.[53]

Notice 2018-88 explained that the MV definition under the proposed PTC regulations would apply for purposes of determining whether an ALE that offers an individual coverage HRA has made an offer that provides MV for purposes of section 4980H. Therefore, an individual coverage HRA that is affordable (taking into account any affordability safe harbors) would be treated as providing MV for purposes of section 4980H.

One commenter supported the MV rules for individual coverage HRAs, and one commenter opposed the rules, suggesting that any metal level plan should be allowed to be used to determine if an offer provides MV (rather than looking to the lowest cost silver plan). Some commenters suggested the use of a different metal level plan in determining affordability and MV for individual coverage HRAs more generally. The Treasury Department and the IRS considered these issues in connection with the final PTC regulations and addressed comments on these topics in the preamble to the final PTC regulations.[54] Further, section 4908H applies the MV standard by reference to section 36B, and no basis has been provided for applying a different standard under section 4980H. Therefore, under the proposed regulations, an individual coverage HRA that is affordable (as determined under the applicable section 36B rules, in combination with any applicable section 4980H safe harbors), is deemed to provide MV.

7. Reporting under Sections 6055 and 6056

a. Section 6056

Section 6056 requires ALEs to file with the IRS and furnish to full-time employees information about whether the employer offers coverage to full-time employees and, if so, information about the coverage offered. An ALE that offers an individual coverage HRA to its full-time employees, just like all ALEs, is required to satisfy the section 6056 reporting requirements. ALEs use Form 1094-C, "Transmittal of Employer-Provided Health Insurance Offer and Coverage Information Returns," and Form 1095-C, "Employer-Provided Health Insurance Offer and Coverage," to satisfy the section 6056 reporting requirements.

Section 6056 and Form 1095-C require ALEs to report each full-time employee's required contribution.[55] Notice 2018-88 provided that the Treasury Department and the IRS anticipated that an ALE would not be required to report the employee's required contribution that is calculated under the proposed PTC regulations. An ALE would, instead, be required to report the employee's required contribution determined under the applicable safe harbors that were anticipated to be provided with respect to the calculation of an employee's required contribution for an individual coverage HRA under section 4980H. Notice 2018-88 also stated that the Treasury Department and the IRS were continuing to consider the application of section 6056 to an ALE that offers an individual coverage HRA and were anticipating providing additional guidance on these issues.

One commenter requested new reporting guidance as soon as possible. Another commenter requested that any new reporting guidance be provided at least 12 months prior to the effective date of any changes in reporting and asked the Treasury Department and the IRS to consider whether good faith reporting relief would be warranted. Some commenters urged the Treasury Department and the IRS to simplify and minimize section 6056 reporting generally and with respect to individual coverage HRAs.

The proposed regulations do not propose to amend the regulations under section 6056. It is anticipated that guidance regarding reporting in connection with individual coverage HRAs will be provided in other administrative guidance, including forms and instructions. It is also anticipated that the guidance would permit the reporting of the employee's required contribution based on the section 4980H safe harbor(s) used by the ALE, rather than the employee's required contribution determined under the final PTC regulations without application of the relevant safe harbors. The Treasury Department and the IRS continue to consider whether and how to revise the codes used in Form 1095-C reporting to account for the new individual coverage HRA safe harbors. The Treasury Department and the IRS recognize the need for timely guidance in this area to assist taxpayers, plan administrators, and software developers to prepare for the reporting associated with individual coverage HRAs.

b. Section 6055

Section 6055 provides that all persons who provide MEC to an individual must report certain information to the IRS that identifies covered individuals and the period of coverage, and must furnish a statement to the covered individuals including the same information. Information returns under section 6055 generally are filed using Form 1095-B, "Health Coverage." However, self-insured ALEs are required to file Form 1095-C and use Part III of that form, rather than Form 1095-B, to report information required under section 6055.

Individual coverage HRAs are group health plans and, therefore, are eligible employer-sponsored plans that are MEC. Accordingly, reporting under section 6055 is required for individual coverage HRAs. In general, the employer is the entity responsible for this reporting.[56]

The Treasury Department and the IRS note that there are regulations under §1.6055-1(d) that provide exceptions for certain plans from the section 6055 reporting requirements.[57] These regulations include exceptions for certain duplicative coverage or supplemental coverage providing MEC. More specifically, the regulations provide that: (1) if an individual is covered by more than one MEC plan or program provided by the same reporting entity, reporting is required for only one of the plans or programs; and (2) reporting is not required for an individual's MEC to the extent that the individual is eligible for that coverage only if the individual is also covered by other MEC for which section 6055 reporting is required, but for eligible employer-sponsored coverage this exception only applies if the supplemental coverage is offered by the same employer that offers the

---

[50] See Notice 2015-87, 2015-52 IRB 889, Q&A 12. In Notice 2015-87, the Treasury Department and the IRS clarified a number of issues related to section 4980H. The proposed regulations do not affect the guidance provided in that notice, which remains in effect. See also 81 FR 91755, 91758 (Dec. 19, 2016).

[51] The proposed regulations also provide technical updates to §54.4980H-4(b), regarding mandatory offers of coverage, where the use of 9.5 percent needed to be updated to refer instead to the required contribution percentage. The updates incorporate the clarification provided in Notice 2015-87, Q&A 12 and are not substantive changes.

[52] See section 36B(c)(2)(C)(ii); see also 80 FR 52678 (Sept. 1, 2015).

[53] See §1.36B-2(c)(3)(i)(B).

[54] See 84 FR 28888 (June 20, 2019), 28943-28946.

[55] See also §301.6056-1(d)(1)(vi).

[56] Section 1.6055-1(c)(2).

[57] See §1.6055-1(d)(2). See also Prop. Reg. §1.6055-1(d)(2) and (3), in 81 FR 50671 (Aug. 2, 2016) (these regulations may be relied upon for calendar years ending after December 31, 2013) and Notice 2015-68, 2015-41 IRB 547.

eligible employer-sponsored coverage for which section 6055 reporting is required.[58] Although an individual enrolled in an individual coverage HRA is required to be enrolled in individual health insurance coverage, Medicare Part A and B, or Medicare Part C, the employer providing the individual coverage HRA generally is not the same entity that provides the individual health insurance coverage. Accordingly, these section 6055 exceptions generally do not apply to individual coverage HRAs.

The proposed regulations do not propose to amend the regulations under section 6055. However, the Treasury Department and the IRS note that because the individual shared responsibility payment under section 5000A was reduced to zero for months beginning after December 31, 2018, the Treasury Department and the IRS are studying whether and how the reporting requirements under section 6055 should change, if at all, for future years.

8. Application of Tobacco Surcharge and Wellness Incentives to Affordability Determination

One commenter noted that whether an individual is a tobacco user can have an impact on premiums for individual health insurance coverage. This commenter requested that the Treasury Department and the IRS permit employers to use the non-tobacco rate in determining affordability for purposes of the PTC and section 4980H.

In response, and consistent with current related guidance,[59] the final PTC regulations provide that for purposes of determining the premium for the lowest cost silver plan used to determine the employee's required HRA contribution: (1) if the premium differs for tobacco users and non-tobacco users, the premium taken into account is the premium that applies to non-tobacco users; and (2) the premium is determined without regard to any wellness program incentive that affects premiums unless the wellness program incentive relates exclusively to tobacco use, in which case the incentive is treated as earned.[60] The proposed regulations incorporate these rules by reference for purposes of determining the affordability plan and the associated premium.

9. Implementation of Section 4980H Safe Harbors and Reliance on Exchange Information

A number of commenters requested that the Treasury Department and the IRS ensure that employers have access to the information needed to apply section 4980H to individual coverage HRAs. Some commenters asked for an online affordability calculator and for lowest cost silver plan data to be made available by zip code, for each month, and to be retained historically, for use by employers and the IRS.

The Treasury Department and the IRS recognize that access to location-specific lowest cost silver plan premium data, on a month-by-month basis, which is preserved and includes prior year information, is necessary for employers to use the safe harbors included in the proposed regulations. As noted in the preamble to the final integration regulations, lowest cost silver plan data will be made available by HHS for employers in all states that use the Federal HealthCare.gov platform to determine whether the individual coverage HRA offer is affordable for purposes of section 4980H, and the Treasury Department and the IRS are working with HHS to ensure that the necessary information is made available. With regard to states that do not use the Federal *HealthCare.gov* platform (State Exchanges), HHS has begun discussing the information it plans to make available in order to help the State Exchanges prepare to make this information available, and the Treasury Department and the IRS also intend to work with State Exchanges on this aspect of implementation.

Further, the Treasury Department and the IRS recognize that employers are not in a position to verify whether the lowest cost silver plan premium information posted by an Exchange for this purpose has been properly computed and identified, and, therefore, employers will need to be able to rely on the premium information that Exchanges make available. Accordingly, the proposed regulations provide that ALEs may rely on the lowest cost silver plan premium information made available by an Exchange for purposes of determining affordability under section 4980H. Employers are encouraged to retain relevant records.[61]

10. Other Comments Related to Section 4980H

One commenter requested clarification that the offer of an individual coverage HRA is an offer of coverage for purposes of section 4980H, even if the individual offered the individual coverage HRA does not take the HRA or enroll in individual health insurance coverage. To avoid an employer shared responsibility payment, section 4980H requires an ALE to offer its full-time employees (and their dependents) an opportunity to enroll in an eligible employer-sponsored plan. Section 4980H does not require that the full-time employees (or their dependents) actually enroll, in order for the employer to avoid an employer shared responsibility payment. Moreover, as group health plans, individual coverage HRAs are eligible employer-sponsored plans. Therefore, the Treasury Department and the IRS confirm, for the sake of clarity, that the offer of an individual coverage HRA is an offer of an eligible employer-sponsored plan for purposes of section 4980H, without regard to whether the employee accepts the offer. The proposed regulations do not affect existing guidance with respect to this issue.

One commenter requested clarification that, for purposes of section 4980H, an employer that offers an individual coverage HRA will be treated as offering the HRA to Medicare-enrolled and Medicare-eligible employees, even if those employees are unable to obtain individual health insurance coverage on account of their Medicare status. Under section 4980H and the regulations thereunder, in general, an employer is considered to offer coverage to an employee if the employee has an effective opportunity to elect to enroll in coverage at least once with respect to the plan year.[62] Whether an employee has an effective opportunity to enroll is determined based on all the relevant facts and circumstances. Further, under the final integration regulations, an individual coverage HRA may be integrated with Medicare Part A and B or Medicare Part C; therefore, an employee enrolled in Medicare may enroll in the HRA, even though the employee may not be able to obtain individual health insurance coverage due to his or her status as a Medicare enrollee.[63] Thus, if a particular individual coverage HRA may be integrated with Medicare, the offer of the HRA to an employee who is enrolled in Medicare provides the employee an effective opportunity to enroll in the HRA and constitutes an offer of coverage to the employee for purposes of section 4980H. As a result, the offer is taken into account in determining if the ALE offered coverage to a sufficient number of full-time employees (and their dependents) for purposes of avoiding an employer shared responsibility payment under section 4980H(a). In addition, because an individual enrolled in Medicare is not eligible for the PTC[64] and an ALE will only be liable for an employer shared responsibility payment for a month with respect to a full-time employee under section 4980H(b) if the full-time employee is allowed the PTC for that month, an ALE will not be liable for an employer shared responsibility payment under section 4980H(b) for a month with respect to a full-time employee enrolled in Medicare for that month.[65]

Some commenters inquired about the interaction between section 4980H and an offer of an excepted benefit HRA,[66] including the consequences to an ALE if the excepted benefit HRA is used to purchase short-term, limited-duration insurance (STLDI). Among other requirements, in order for

---

[58] Prop. Reg. § 1.6055-1(d)(2) and (3). Id.

[59] See §§ 1.36B-2(c)(3)(v)(A)(4) and 1.36B-3(e).

[60] Section 1.36B-2(c)(5)(iii)(A). See 84 FR 28888 (June 20, 2019), 28496-28497.

[61] The regulations under section 4980H do not include specific recordkeeping requirements; the otherwise generally applicable substantiation and recordkeeping requirements in section 6001 apply.

[62] See § 54.4980H-4(b)(1). The regulations also provide guidance on the circumstances in which an employer is considered to have made an offer of coverage even if the employee does not have an effective opportunity to decline to enroll in the coverage.

[63] See 84 FR 28888 (June 20, 2019), 28928-28931.

[64] See section 36B(c)(2)(B) and § 1.36B-2(a)(2).

[65] The rules under section 4980H for employees eligible for, but not enrolled in, Medicare apply as they do for non-Medicare-eligible employees. However, note that an individual eligible for Medicare generally is ineligible for the PTC. See id.

[66] See § 54.9831-1(c)(3)(viii).

an ALE to avoid an employer shared responsibility payment, it must offer an eligible employer-sponsored plan that is MEC to its full-time employees (and their dependents). Although group health plans generally are eligible employer-sponsored plans that are MEC, excepted benefits are not MEC.[67] Consequently, the offer of an excepted benefit HRA is not treated as an offer of an eligible employer-sponsored plan that is MEC for purposes of section 4980H, regardless of whether the excepted benefit HRA is, or may be, used to purchase STLDI.

However, in order for an HRA to be an excepted benefit HRA, the employer must offer the employees who are offered the excepted benefit HRA other group health plan coverage that is not limited to excepted benefits and that is not an HRA or other account-based group health plan.[68] Because the other group health plan may not be limited to excepted benefits, that offer of coverage is an offer of an eligible employer-sponsored plan that is MEC for purposes of section 4980H. Whether the offer of coverage under the other group health plan in connection with the excepted benefit HRA is an affordable, MV offer depends on the particular characteristics of the group health plan and the coverage offered under that plan. The proposed regulations do not affect existing guidance with respect to this issue.

B. Proposed Regulations under Section 105(h)

Under the final integration regulations, employers may limit the offer of an individual coverage HRA to certain classes of employees and may vary the amounts, terms, and conditions of individual coverage HRAs between the different classes of employees.[69] Further, within any class of employees offered an individual coverage HRA, the employer must offer the HRA on the same terms and conditions to all employees in the class, subject to certain exceptions (the same terms requirement).[70] One of the exceptions to the same terms requirement is that the employer may increase the maximum dollar amounts made available under an individual coverage HRA as the age of the participant increases provided that (1) the same maximum dollar amount attributable to the increase in age is made available to all participants in a class of employees who are the same age, and (2) the maximum dollar amount made available to the oldest participant(s) is not more than three times the maximum dollar amount made available to the youngest participant(s).[71] Other exceptions to the same terms requirement include rules allowing the employer to prorate amounts made available for employees and dependents who enroll in the HRA after the beginning of the HRA plan year, to make available carryover amounts, and for employees with amounts remaining in other HRAs, to make available those remaining amounts in the current individual coverage HRA, each subject to the conditions set forth in the final integration regulations.[72]

As explained earlier in this preamble, HRAs, including individual coverage HRAs, generally are subject to section 105(h) and the regulations thereunder.[73] Further, the regulations under section 105(h) provide that "any maximum limit attributable to employer contributions must be uniform for all participants and for all dependents of employees who are participants and may not be modified by reason of a participant's age or years of service."[74] In Notice 2018-88, the Treasury Department and the IRS explained that varying the maximum amounts made available under an individual coverage HRA for different classes of employees would conflict with the requirement in § 1.105-11(c)(3)(i) that any maximum limit attributable to employer contributions must be uniform for all participants and that, without further guidance, certain amounts paid to an HCI under an individual coverage HRA that implements an age-based increase would be includible in the income of the HCI because the HRA would fail to satisfy the requirement in § 1.105-11(c)(3)(i) that prohibits the maximum limit attributable to employer contributions to the HRA from being modified by reason of a participant's age.

To facilitate the offering of individual coverage HRAs, Notice 2018-88 described a potential safe harbor under which an individual coverage HRA would be treated as not failing to satisfy the nondiscrimination requirement in § 1.105-11(c)(3)(i) that prohibits the maximum limit attributable to employer contributions from being modified by reason of a participant's age. Specifically, Notice 2018-88 described a potential safe harbor under which the HRA would be treated as not failing to satisfy this requirement if it provided that the maximum dollar amount made available to employees who are members of a particular class of employees increases in accordance with the increases in the price of an individual health insurance coverage policy in the relevant individual insurance market based on the ages of the employees who are members of that class of employees, and further provided that the same maximum dollar amount attributable to the increase in age would be made available to all employees who are members of that class of employees who are the same age. Notice 2018-88 also stated that the Treasury Department and the IRS anticipated that future guidance would provide that an individual coverage HRA would be treated as not failing to satisfy the more general requirement in § 1.105-11(c)(3)(i) that any maximum limit attributable to employer contributions must be uniform for all participants, if the HRA provides the same maximum dollar amount to all employees who are members of a particular class of employees, limited to the classes specified in the proposed integration regulations, and subject to the exceptions allowed under the same terms requirement.

Commenters generally supported the potential section 105(h) safe harbors, but some commenters requested clarification as to how the potential section 105(h) safe harbors would function in practice, and commenters requested examples.[75]

In light of the final integration regulations, and for the reasons described in Notice 2018-88 and earlier in this section of the preamble, it continues to be the case that safe harbors are needed under the section 105(h) regulations to facilitate the offering of individual coverage HRAs. However, with respect to age variance, instead of proposing the anticipated safe harbor set forth in Notice 2018-88, to minimize the complexity and employer burden in complying with multiple regulatory requirements, the proposed regulations provide that an individual coverage HRA that satisfies the age variation exception under the same terms requirement at § 54.9802-4(c)(3)(iii)(B) will not be treated as failing to satisfy the requirements to provide nondiscriminatory benefits under § 1.105-11(c)(3)(i) solely due to the variation based on age. More generally, and as anticipated in Notice 2018-88, the proposed regulations also provide that if the maximum dollar amount made available varies for participants within a class of employees, or varies between classes of employees, then with respect to that variance, the individual coverage HRA does not violate the requirement in § 1.105-11(c)(3)(i) that any maximum limit attributable to employer contributions must be uniform for all participants, if within each class of employees, the maximum dollar amount only varies in accordance with the same terms requirement and, with respect to differences in the maximum dollar amount made available for different classes of employees, the classes of employees are classes of employees set forth in § 54.9802-4(d).

Nonetheless, the Treasury Department and the IRS note that satisfying the terms of the safe harbors under the proposed regulations does not automatically satisfy the prohibition on nondiscriminatory operation under § 1.105-11(c)(3)(ii). Thus, among other situations, if a disproportionate number of HCIs qualify for and utilize the maximum HRA amount allowed under the same terms requirement based on age in comparison to the

---

[67] See section 5000A(f)(3).

[68] See § 54.9831-1(c)(3)(viii)(A).

[69] See § 54.9802-4(d).

[70] See § 54.9802-4(c)(3).

[71] Section 54.9802-4(c)(3)(iii)(B). The proposed integration regulations included the same terms requirement, including the exception for age variation, but did not include the limit on the extent to which amounts made available may be increased based on age, which was added to the final integration regulations in response to comments. See 84 FR 28888 (June 20, 2019), 28904-28907.

[72] Section 54.9802-4(c)(3)(ii) and (v).

[73] As noted earlier in this preamble, an HRA that, by its terms, only reimburses premiums for individual health insurance coverage is not subject to section 105(h) (see § 1.105-11(b)(2)). Further, section 105(h) and the regulations thereunder, including these proposed regulations, are only relevant to an individual coverage HRA offered to one or more HCIs and are not relevant for an individual coverage HRA that is not offered to any HCI.

[74] See § 1.105-11(c)(3)(i).

[75] Some commenters addressed the ability to vary individual coverage HRA amounts by age for purposes of integration of HRAs with individual health insurance coverage, and a full response to those comments is included in the preamble to the final integration regulations. See 84 FR 28888 (June 20, 2019), 28904-28907.

number of non-HCIs who qualify for and use lower HRA amounts based on age, the individual coverage HRA may be found to be discriminatory, with the result that excess reimbursements of the HCIs will be included in their income.[76]

C. Application of Section 125 Cafeteria Plan Rules to Arrangements Involving Individual Coverage HRAs

The preamble to the proposed and final HRA integration regulations noted that some employers may want to allow employees to pay the portion of the premium for individual health insurance coverage that is not covered by an individual coverage HRA, if any, through a salary reduction arrangement under a section 125 cafeteria plan. Pursuant to section 125(f)(3), an employer generally may not provide a qualified health plan purchased through an Exchange as a benefit under its cafeteria plan. Therefore, an employer may not permit employees to make salary reduction contributions to a cafeteria plan to purchase a qualified health plan (including individual health insurance coverage) offered through an Exchange. However, section 125(f)(3) does not apply to individual health insurance coverage that is not offered through an Exchange (referred to as "off Exchange"). Therefore, for an employee who purchases off-Exchange individual health insurance coverage, the employer may permit the employee to pay the balance of the premium for the coverage through its cafeteria plan. The Treasury Department and the IRS appreciate the comments received on this topic in response to the proposed integration regulations and request additional comments regarding any specific issues raised by the application of the section 125 cafeteria plan rules to arrangements involving individual coverage HRAs for which clarification is needed or for which a modification of the applicable rules may decrease burdens.

Some commenters in response to the proposed integration regulations requested that individuals be allowed to use a cafeteria plan to pay premiums for qualified health plans offered through an Exchange with salary reduction. As discussed in the preceding paragraph, section 125(f)(3) prohibits using a cafeteria plan to allow employees to pay premiums for a qualified health plan offered through an Exchange.

Proposed Applicability Date

The proposed regulations under section 4980H are proposed to apply for periods beginning after December 31, 2019, and the proposed regulations under section 105(h) are proposed to apply for plan years beginning after December 31, 2019. The Treasury Department and the IRS recognize that employers may want to offer individual coverage HRAs beginning on January 1, 2020, and, therefore, may need applicable guidance with respect to sections 4980H and/or 105(h) to design and implement programs involving individual coverage HRAs prior to the issuance of any final regulations and in advance of the plan year for which the individual coverage HRAs will be offered. Accordingly, taxpayers may rely on the proposed regulations under section 4980H for periods during any plan year of individual coverage HRAs beginning before the date that is six months following the publication of any final regulations, and taxpayers may rely on the proposed regulations under section 105(h) for plan years of individual coverage HRAs beginning before the date that is six months following the publication of any final regulations.

Statutory Authority

The regulations are proposed to be adopted pursuant to the authority contained in sections 7805 and 9833.

Special Analyses

This regulation is not subject to review under section 6(b) of Executive Order 12866 pursuant to the Memorandum of Agreement (April 11, 2018) between the Department of the Treasury and the Office of Management and Budget regarding review of tax regulations. Because this regulation does not impose a collection of information on small entities, the Regulatory Flexibility Act (5 U.S.C. chapter 6) does not apply. Pursuant to section 7805(f) of the Internal Revenue Code, this regulation has been submitted to the Chief Counsel for Advocacy of the Small Business Administration for comment on its impact on small business.

Comments and Requests for Public Hearing

The Treasury Department and the IRS request comments on all aspects of the proposed regulations. Before the proposed regulations are adopted as final regulations, consideration will be given to any comments that are submitted timely to the IRS as prescribed in this preamble under the **ADDRESSES** heading. All comments will be available at *https://www.regulations.gov*. A public hearing will be scheduled if requested in writing by any person that timely submits written comments. If a public hearing is scheduled, then notice of the date, time, and place for the public hearing will be published in the Federal Register.

Drafting Information

The principal author of the proposed regulations is Jennifer Solomon of the Office of Associate Chief Counsel (Employee Benefits, Exempt Organizations, and Employment Taxes). However, other personnel from the Treasury Department and the IRS participated in the development of the proposed regulations.

Statement of Availability of IRS Documents

The Notices cited in this document are published in the Internal Revenue Bulletin (or Cumulative Bulletin) and are available from the Superintendent of Documents, U.S. Government Publishing Office, Washington, DC 20402, or by visiting the IRS website at *http://www.irs.gov*.

[¶ 49,815] Proposed Amendments of Regulations (REG-104223-18), published in the Federal Register on October 2, 2019.

[Code Secs. 267, 332, 367, 672, 706, 863, 904, 958, 1297 and 6049]

Controlled foreign corporations: Taxed earnings: Shareholder: Stock ownership: Related person: Gain: Loss: Liquidation: Gain recognition agreement: Grantor trust rules: Partnership.—Reg. §1.332-8 and amendments of Reg. §§1.267(a)-3, 1.367(a)-8, 1.672(f)-2, 1.706-1, 1.863-8, 1.863-9, 1.904-5, 1.958-2, 1.1297-1 and 1.6049-5, relating to the modification of Code Sec. 958(b) of the Internal Revenue Code ("Code") by the Tax Cuts and Jobs Act, which was enacted on December 22, 2017, are proposed.

AGENCY: Internal Revenue Service (IRS), Treasury.

ACTION: Notice of proposed rulemaking.

SUMMARY: This document contains proposed regulations relating to the modification of section 958(b) of the Internal Revenue Code ("Code") by the Tax Cuts and Jobs Act, which was enacted on December 22, 2017. The proposed regulations affect United States persons that have ownership interests in or that make or receive payments to or from certain foreign corporations.

DATES: Written or electronic comments and requests for a public hearing must be received by December 1, 2019.

ADDRESSES: Send electronic submissions via the Federal eRulemaking Portal at www.regulations.gov (indicate IRS and REG-104223-18) by following the online instructions for submitting comments. Once submitted to the Federal eRulemaking Portal, comments cannot be edited or

---

[76] See §1.105-11(c)(3).

withdrawn. The Department of the Treasury (the "Treasury Department") and the IRS will publish for public availability any comment received to its public docket, whether submitted electronically or in hard copy. Send hard copy submissions to: CC:PA:LPD:PR (REG-104223-18), Room 5203, Internal Revenue Service, PO Box 7604, Ben Franklin Station, Washington, DC 20044. Submissions may be hand delivered Monday through Friday between the hours of 8 a.m. and 4 p.m. to CC:PA:LPD:PR (REG-104223-18), Courier's Desk, Internal Revenue Service, 1111 Constitution Avenue, NW., Washington, DC 20224.

FOR FURTHER INFORMATION CONTACT: Concerning the proposed regulations, Jorge M. Oben, (202) 317-6934; concerning submissions of comments and requests for a public hearing, Regina Johnson at (202) 317-6901 (not toll-free numbers).

SUPPLEMENTARY INFORMATION:

Background

Section 958 provides rules for determining direct, indirect, and constructive stock ownership. Under section 958(a)(1), stock is considered owned by a person if it is owned directly or is owned indirectly through certain foreign entities under section 958(a)(2). Under section 958(b), section 318 applies, with certain modifications, to the extent that the effect is to treat any United States person as a United States shareholder within the meaning of section 951(b) ("U.S. shareholder") of a foreign corporation, to treat a person as a related person within the meaning of section 954(d)(3), to treat the stock of a domestic corporation as owned by a U.S. shareholder of a controlled foreign corporation ("CFC") for purposes of section 956(c)(2), or to treat a foreign corporation as a CFC under section 957.

Section 318 provides rules that attribute the ownership of stock to certain family members, between certain entities and their owners, and to holders of options to acquire stock. Section 318(a)(1) provides rules attributing stock ownership among members of a family. Section 318(a)(2) provides rules attributing stock ownership from partnerships, estates, trusts, and corporations to partners, beneficiaries, owners, and shareholders (so-called "upward attribution"). Section 318(a)(3) generally attributes stock owned by a person to a partnership, estate, trust, or corporation in which the person has an interest (so-called "downward attribution"). In particular, section 318(a)(3)(A) provides that stock owned, directly or indirectly, by or for a partner or a beneficiary of an estate is considered as owned by the partnership or estate. This provision applies to all partners and beneficiaries without regard to the size of their interest in the partnership or estate. Section 318(a)(3)(B) similarly provides, subject to certain exceptions, that stock owned, directly or indirectly, by or for a beneficiary of a trust (or a person who is considered an owner of a trust) is considered owned by the trust. Section 318(a)(3)(C) provides that stock in one corporation owned, directly or indirectly, by or for a shareholder in a second corporation is considered owned by the second corporation if 50 percent or more in value of the stock in the second corporation is owned, directly or indirectly, by such shareholder.

As in effect before repeal, section 958(b)(4) provided that subparagraphs (A), (B), and (C) of section 318(a)(3) (providing for downward attribution) were not to be applied so as to consider a United States person as owning stock owned by a person who is not a United States person (a "foreign person"). Effective for the last taxable year of foreign corporations beginning before January 1, 2018, and each subsequent year of the foreign corporations, and for the taxable years of U.S. shareholders in which or with which such taxable years of the foreign corporations end, section 958(b)(4) was repealed by section 14213 of the Tax Cuts and Jobs Act, Pub. L. 115-97 (2017) (the "Act"). As a result of this repeal, stock of a foreign corporation owned by a foreign person can be attributed to a United States person under section 318(a)(3) for purposes of determining whether a United States person is a U.S. shareholder of the foreign corporation and, therefore, whether the foreign corporation is a CFC. In other words, as a result of the repeal of section 958(b)(4), section 958(b) now provides for downward attribution from a foreign person to a United States person in circumstances in which section 958(b), before the Act, did not so provide. As a result, United States persons that were not previously treated as U.S. shareholders may be treated as U.S. shareholders, and foreign corporations that were not previously treated as CFCs may be treated as CFCs.

The legislative history to the Act indicates that the repeal of section 958(b)(4) was intended "to render ineffective certain transactions that are used to [sic] as a means of avoiding the subpart F provisions." *See* H.R. Rep. No. 115-466, at 633 (2017) (Conf. Rep.). It further provides:

> One such transaction involves effectuating "de-control" of a foreign subsidiary, by taking advantage of the section 958(b)(4) rule that effectively turns off the constructive stock ownership rules of 318(a)(3) when to do otherwise would result in a U.S. person being treated as owning stock owned by a foreign person. Such a transaction converts former CFCs to non-CFCs, despite continuous ownership by U.S. shareholders.

Id. at 633-34.

Explanation of Provisions

I. *Changes in Connection with Repeal of Section 958(b)(4)*

This notice of proposed rulemaking proposes changes that are generally intended to ensure that the operation of certain rules is consistent with their application before the Act's repeal of section 958(b)(4), as further explained in this Part I. Other guidance that provides relief concerning the effect of the repeal of section 958(b)(4) on the application of subpart F more generally is provided separately.

A. *Section 267: Deduction for certain payments to foreign related persons*

Section 267(a)(2) provides a matching rule that governs the time at which an otherwise deductible amount owed to a related person may be deducted. Specifically, section 267(a)(2) provides that, in the case of certain interest and expenses paid by the taxpayer to a related person, if an amount is not includible in the payee's gross income until it is paid, the amount generally is not allowable as a deduction to the taxpayer until the amount is includible in the gross income of the payee.

Section 267(a)(3)(A) provides that the Secretary shall by regulations apply the matching principle in section 267(a)(2) in cases in which the payee is a foreign person. Section 1.267(a)-3(b) generally requires a taxpayer to use the cash method of accounting for deductions of amounts owed to a related foreign person. An exemption is provided in §1.267(a)-3(c)(2) for any amount, other than interest, that is income of a related foreign person with respect to which the related foreign person is exempt from U.S. tax on the amount owed pursuant to a treaty obligation of the United States.

Section 841(b) of Pub. L. 108-357 (2004) added section 267(a)(3)(B) to the Code, effective for payments accrued on or after October 22, 2004. Section 267(a)(3)(B)(i) provides that, notwithstanding section 267(a)(3)(A), in the case of any item payable to a CFC, a deduction is allowable to the payor with respect to the amount for any taxable year before the year in which paid only to the extent that an amount attributable to the item is includible during such prior taxable year in the gross income of a United States person who owns (within the meaning of section 958(a)) stock in such corporation. Section 267(a)(3)(B)(ii) grants the Secretary the authority to issue regulations exempting transactions from section 267(a)(3)(B)(i).

For amounts accrued on or after October 22, 2004, a taxpayer that owes an amount to a CFC cannot rely on the exemption in §1.267(a)-3(c)(2) to generally deduct the amount when accrued, and instead can deduct the amount prior to the year the amount is paid only to the extent that an amount attributable to the item is includible in gross income of a U.S. shareholder that owns (within the meaning of section 958(a)) stock in the CFC. After the repeal of section 958(b)(4), a CFC may not have any U.S. shareholders that own stock within the meaning of section 958(a) ("section 958(a) U.S. shareholders"). Because the repeal of section 958(b)(4) is effective for the last taxable year of foreign corporations beginning before January 1, 2018, and each subsequent taxable year of the foreign corporations, and for the taxable year of U.S. shareholders in which or with which such taxable year of the foreign corporations end, a taxpayer may have, in 2017, deducted an amount accrued in 2017 that, due to the repeal of section 958(b)(4), would no longer be allowable in 2017.

The purpose of the matching principle in section 267(a)(2) is to align the timing of a deduction with the inclusion of the item in income. If an amount is owed to a CFC that has no section 958(a) U.S. shareholders that would include an amount attributable to the item in income, and the CFC is exempt from U.S. tax on the amount owed due to a treaty, it is unnecessary to not allow a taxpayer to take the deduction when the amount is accrued. Accordingly, the proposed regulations provide that an amount (other than interest) that is income of a related foreign person with respect to which the related foreign person is exempt from U.S. taxation on the amount owed pursuant to a treaty obligation of the United States is exempt from the application of section 267(a)(3)(B)(i) if the related foreign person is a CFC that does not have any section 958(a) U.S. shareholders. Proposed § 1.267(a)-3(c)(4).

These proposed regulations also amend § 1.267(a)-3(c)(2) and remove the rules currently in § 1.267(a)-3(c)(4), in order to reflect the changes to section 267 in Pub. L. 108-357. The Treasury Department and the IRS intend to update other provisions in § 1.267(a)-3 to take into account the changes made to section 267(a)(3) by Pub. L. 108-357 in future guidance.

B. *Section 332: Liquidation of applicable holding company*

Section 332(a) provides a general rule that no gain or loss is recognized on the receipt by a corporation of property distributed in complete liquidation of another corporation. Section 332(d) was enacted to disallow the nonrecognition of gain to a foreign corporation through the complete liquidation of certain domestic holding companies, which could avoid the imposition of withholding tax that would otherwise apply to a section 301 distribution from these holding companies. See H.R. Rep. No. 108-755, at 761-62 (2004) (Conf. Rep.). Section 332(d)(1) provides an exception to sections 332(a) and 331 for certain distributions by domestic corporations to foreign corporations. Section 332(d)(1) results in the recognition by a foreign corporation of income from the liquidation of certain domestic holding companies by treating the liquidating distribution as a distribution under section 301. Specifically, section 332(d)(1) provides that section 301, and not section 332(a) nor 331, applies to a distribution to a foreign corporation in complete liquidation of an applicable holding company (as defined in section 332(d)(2)). Section 332(d)(3) provides that, notwithstanding section 332(d)(1), exchange treatment under section 331 applies if the distributee of a distribution in complete liquidation of an applicable holding company is a CFC. In such a case, the gain on the distribution could be foreign personal holding company income ("FPHCI") under section 954(c)(1)(B), and before the Act, CFCs generally had U.S. shareholders that would be subject to tax on their pro rata share of such gain under section 951(a).

Section 332(d)(4) grants the Secretary the authority to issue regulations as appropriate to prevent the abuse of section 332(d). The repeal of section 958(b)(4) broadened the application of section 332(d)(3) to foreign corporations that are CFCs because of downward attribution from a foreign person. This result could lead to inappropriate results because any gain recognized on an exchange of stock of an applicable holding company under section 331 by a foreign corporation that is a CFC due to downward attribution from a foreign person could avoid U.S. tax if the CFC does not have U.S. shareholders that have current income inclusions under section 951(a). Therefore, in accordance with the regulatory authority provided in section 332(d)(4), the proposed regulations modify the definition of a CFC (so as to use the definition of a CFC in effect immediately before the repeal of section 958(b)(4)) for purposes of applying section 332(d)(3). See proposed § 1.332-8(a). The Treasury Department and the IRS request comments on these proposed changes to the definition of a CFC for the purposes of applying section 332(d)(3).

C. *Section 367(a): Triggering events exception for other dispositions or events under § 1.367(a)-8(k)(14)*

Section 367(a)(1) provides that if, in connection with an exchange described in section 332, 351, 354, 356, or 361, a United States person transfers property to a foreign corporation, the foreign corporation is not treated as a corporation for purposes of determining the extent to which gain is recognized on the transfer. Section 367(a)(1) does not apply, however, to certain transfers of stock or securities of a foreign corporation (including an indirect stock transfer) by a United States person ("U.S. transferor") if the U.S. transferor enters into a gain recognition agreement ("GRA") with respect to the transferred stock or securities. See § 1.367(a)-3(b)(1). In general, a U.S. transferor subject to a GRA must recognize gain if a triggering event (as defined in § 1.367(a)-8(j)) occurs during the term of a GRA. See § 1.367(a)-8(j). Section 1.367(a)-8(k) provides several exceptions for certain dispositions that constitute nonrecognition transactions if, immediately after the disposition, the U.S. transferor meets certain requirements. In particular, § 1.367(a)-8(k)(14) generally provides that a disposition or other event is not a triggering event if the disposition or other event qualifies as a nonrecognition transaction, and, immediately after the disposition or other event, the U.S. transferor retains a direct or indirect interest in the transferred stock or securities or, as applicable, in substantially all of the assets of the transferred corporation. The rule further provides that if a foreign corporation acquires the transferred stock or securities or, as applicable, substantially all the assets of the transferred corporation, the exception applies only if the U.S. transferor owns at least five percent (applying the attribution rules of section 318, as modified by section 958(b)) of the total voting power and the total value of the outstanding stock of such foreign corporation. This five-percent ownership condition is intended to limit the application of the general exception to transactions in which the U.S. transferor retains at least a minimal interest in the transferred stock or securities (or substantially all the assets of the transferred corporation). See TD 9446, 74 FR 6952, 6953 (February 11, 2009).

The exception described in the preceding paragraph was added when section 958(b)(4) did not allow for downward attribution from foreign persons. A U.S. transferor that would not have been eligible for the exception because it held a less than five percent interest in the transferred stock or securities (or substantially all the assets of the transferred corporation) could now be eligible for the exception if the U.S. transferor holds at least five percent due to downward attribution of stock owned by a foreign person. A U.S. transferor's constructive ownership interest should not include an interest that is treated as owned as a result of downward attribution from a foreign person as it would inappropriately treat the U.S. transferor as owning an interest it would not have owned under the rules in effect when § 1.367(a)-8(k)(14) was added. Therefore, in accordance with the regulatory authority provided in section 367(a), the proposed regulations revise § 1.367(a)-8(k)(14) to apply section 958(b) without regard to the repeal of section 958(b)(4). See proposed § 1.367(a)-8(k)(14)(ii). The Treasury Department and the IRS request comments on these proposed revisions to § 1.367(a)-8(k)(14).

D. *Section 672: CFC's ownership of a trust*

Section 672(f)(1) generally provides that the grantor trust rules in sections 671 through 679 apply only to the extent they result in income being currently taken into account (either directly or through one or more entities) by a citizen or resident of the United States or a domestic corporation. To the extent that a trust or a portion thereof is not taxed as a grantor trust, the trust and its beneficiaries are taxable in accordance with the rules of sections 641 through 669. In the case of a foreign nongrantor trust, accumulation distributions are not only taxable to U.S. beneficiaries, but also subject to the "throwback rules" of sections 665 through 668.

Section 672(f)(3)(A) provides special rules, however, for a trust that is treated as owned by a CFC. Except as otherwise provided by regulations, CFCs are treated as domestic corporations for purposes of section 672(f)(1). Section 672(f)(3)(A). Before the repeal of section 958(b)(4), the portion of a trust's income that was treated as owned by a CFC would generally have been taxable currently to the U.S. shareholders to the extent the trust's income constituted subpart F income of the CFC.

After the repeal of section 958(b)(4), however, a CFC may have no U.S. shareholders that would be subject to tax on their pro rata share of its subpart F income under section 951(a). A CFC could be formed to facilitate tax-free accumulation of income in a trust for the benefit of United States persons and result in tax-free distributions from the trust to the U.S. beneficiaries. In such a case, none of the income or gain of the grantor trust would be taken into account by U.S. shareholders, despite constituting subpart F income, while distributions of income from the trust to its U.S. beneficiaries would not be subject to tax, and the throwback rules would be avoided entirely.

Therefore, the proposed regulations, in accordance with the regulatory authority provided in section 672(f)(3), provide that the only CFCs taken into account for purposes of section 672(f) are those that are CFCs without regard to downward attribution from foreign persons. *See* proposed § 1.672(f)-2(a). A reference to foreign personal holding companies in § 1.672(f)-2(a) is also deleted, consistent with the repeal of the foreign personal holding company regime by section 413(a) of the American Jobs Creation Act of 2004, Pub. L. 108-357. *Id.* The Treasury Department and the IRS request comments on these proposed revisions to § 1.672(f)-2(a).

E. *Section 706: Taxable year of partnership*

Section 706 provides rules for determining the taxable year of a partnership and its partners. Section 1.706-1(b)(6)(i) provides that in determining the taxable year of a partnership under section 706(b) and the regulations thereunder, any interest held by a disregarded foreign partner is not taken into account. A foreign partner is a disregarded foreign partner unless the foreign partner is allocated any gross income of the partnership that was effectively connected (or treated as effectively connected) with the conduct of a trade or business within the United States ("effectively connected income") during the partnership's taxable year immediately preceding the current taxable year (or, if such partner was not a partner during the partnership's immediately preceding taxable year, the partnership reasonably believes that the partner will be allocated any such income during the current taxable year) and taxation of that income is not otherwise precluded under any U.S. income tax treaty. For purposes of these rules, § 1.706-1(b)(6)(ii) defines a foreign partner as a partner that is not a United States person (as defined in section 7701(a)(30)), but provides that CFCs are not treated as foreign partners. When § 1.706-1(b)(6)(ii) was added, CFCs were not treated as foreign partners for purposes of determining a partnership's taxable year under section 706 because the U.S. owners of such entities were subject to U.S. federal income taxation on a current basis with respect to certain income earned by these entities. *See* 66 FR 3920, 3921 (January 17, 2001). As a result of the repeal of section 958(b)(4), a foreign corporation that is a CFC solely by reason of downward attribution from a foreign person may now be taken into account for purposes of determining the taxable year of such partnership. This would include a foreign corporation that is a CFC even if the CFC does not have a U.S. shareholder who owns stock of the foreign corporation within the meaning of section 958(a) and is required to include amounts in income under section 951(a). Accordingly, the proposed regulations exclude from the definition of foreign partner only CFCs with respect to which a U.S. shareholder owns stock within the meaning of section 958(a) for purposes of determining a partnership taxable year. *See* proposed § 1.706-1(b)(6)(ii). As in proposed § 1.672(f)-2(a), discussed in Part I.D of this Explanation of Provisions, the reference to foreign personal holding companies is also deleted. *See id.* The Treasury Department and the IRS request comments on these proposed revisions to § 1.706-1(b)(6)(ii).

F. *Section 863: Space and ocean income and international communications income of a CFC*

Section 863 and the regulations thereunder provide rules for determining the source of certain items of gross income, including gross income from space and ocean activities and international communications income. Section 863(d)(1) provides that, except as provided in regulations, any income derived from a space or ocean activity ("space and ocean income") by a United States person is sourced in the United States ("U.S. source income") and that any space and ocean income derived by a foreign person is sourced outside the United States ("foreign source income"). Regulations under section 863(d) include an exception from the statutory provision regarding space and ocean income derived by a foreign person if the foreign person is a CFC. Specifically, space and ocean income derived by a CFC is treated as U.S. source income, except to the extent that the income, based on all the facts and circumstances, is attributable to functions performed, resources employed, or risks assumed in a foreign country. *See* § 1.863-8(b)(2)(ii).

In the case of any United States person, 50 percent of any international communications income (as defined in section 863(e)(2)) is treated as U.S. source income and 50 percent of such income is treated as foreign source income. Section 863(e)(1)(A). Subject to certain exceptions, including exceptions set forth in regulations, international communications income derived by a foreign person is treated as foreign source income. Section 863(e)(1)(B)(i). Regulations under section 863(e) provide that international communications income derived by a CFC is treated as one-half U.S. source income and one-half foreign source income. *See* § 1.863-9(b)(2)(ii).

The status of the recipient of space and ocean income and international communications income as a CFC solely by reason of the repeal of section 958(b)(4) should not cause all or part of such income to be U.S. source income if it would not have been treated as such otherwise. Accordingly, in accordance with the regulatory authority provided in section 863(d)(1) and (e)(1)(B)(i), and consistent with the temporary relief announced in section 5.01 of Notice 2018-13, 2018-6 I.R.B. 341, these proposed regulations provide that whether a foreign corporation is a CFC for purposes of the rules under sections 863(d) and (e) treating space and ocean income and international communications income as U.S. source income in whole or in part is determined without regard to downward attribution from a foreign person. *See* proposed §§ 1.863-8(b)(2)(ii) and 1.863-9(b)(2)(ii).

G. *Section 904: Look-through rules and active rents and royalties exception to categorization as passive category income*

In general, section 904(a) limits the amount of foreign income taxes that a taxpayer, including a U.S. shareholder, may claim as a credit against its U.S. income tax based on the taxpayer's foreign source income. Section 904(d) further limits the credit by category of foreign source income, with general category and passive category being two common categories of income. Passive category income includes passive income, which means income that would be FPHCI if the recipient were a CFC. This generally includes dividends, interest, rents, and royalties. *See* section 904(d)(2)(B)(i) and 954(c)(1)(A). However, if such amounts are received or accrued by a U.S. shareholder of a CFC from the CFC, the amounts are treated as passive category income only to the extent they are allocable to passive category income of the CFC (the "CFC look-through rule"). *See* section 904(d)(3). Application of the CFC look-through rule requires determining the category of income of the CFC to which the dividends, interest, rents, or royalties paid to the U.S. shareholder (or other related look-through entity) are allocable.

Rents and royalties received by a CFC are generally passive category income unless the income is derived in the active conduct of a trade or business (the "section 904 active rents and royalties exception"), taking into account activities of affiliated group members. *See* § 1.904-4(b)(2)(iii). The section 904 active rents and royalties exception applies both for determining the category to which a U.S. shareholder's inclusion under section 951(a) attributable to the receipt of rents and royalties by a CFC is assigned under section 904(d)(3)(B), and for purposes of applying the CFC look-through rule to determine the category to which dividends, interest, rents, and royalties paid or accrued by the CFC are allocable under section 904(d)(3)(C) and (D).

Financial services income received by certain CFCs or a domestic corporation is treated as general category income (the "financial services income rule"). *See* section 904(d)(2)(C)(i). In determining whether income is financial services income for purposes of section 904, the activities of affiliated group members, including CFCs, are taken into account to determine whether such entities are financial services entities (the "financial services entity requirement"). *See* section 904(d)(2)(C)(ii) and § 1.904-4(e)(3)(ii).

The formulation of the CFC look-through rule and the affiliated group rules in both the section 904 active rents and royalties exception and the financial services income rules was premised on the assumption that income of CFCs (including affiliated group members meeting the active conduct requirement or the financial services entity requirement) would be subject to U.S. tax under section 951(a) or on a distribution of earnings and profits generated by such income, and that foreign corporations to which the rules applied would be directly or indirectly controlled by United States persons able to obtain information concerning their activities, income, and expenses. *See* H.R. Rep. No. 99-841, Volume II, at 566 and 573-574 (1986) (Conf. Rep.); *see also* T.D. 8412, 57 FR 20639, 20640 (May 14, 1992); *id.* at 20641; and 66 FR 319, 321 (January 3, 2001). Treating foreign corporations as CFCs or United States persons as U.S. shareholders by reason of downward attribution from foreign persons for purposes of the CFC look-through rule and the affiliated group rules would be inconsistent with the intended scope of the rules. Before the repeal of section 958(b)(4), a U.S. shareholder of a foreign corporation in which U.S. shareholders held directly or indirectly at least 10 percent, but not more than 50 percent, of the voting stock or value, would be eligible to treat dividends, but not interest, rents, and royalties, as other than passive category income. *See* section 904(d)(4). Similarly, under the affiliated group rules, neither the active conduct requirement in the section 904 active rents and royalties exception nor the financial services entity requirement in the financial services income rule could be satisfied by a foreign corporation that would be a CFC only by reason of downward attribution from a foreign person.

Accordingly, in accordance with the regulatory authority provided in section 904(d)(7), the regulations under section 904 are revised to limit the application of the affiliated group rules in the section 904 active rents and royalties exception and the financial services income rule, as well as the CFC look-through rule, to foreign corporations that are CFCs without regard to downward attribution from foreign persons. Further, the CFC look-through rule, as proposed to be revised at 83 FR 63200 (December 7, 2018), is further revised to apply only to U.S. shareholders that are U.S. shareholders without regard to downward attribution from foreign persons. *See* proposed § 1.904-5(a)(4)(i) and (vi) (providing definitions that apply for purposes of § § 1.904-4 and 1.904-5, pursuant to § § 1.904-4(a) and 1.904-5(a)(4) as proposed to be revised at 83 FR 63200 (December 7, 2018)). The Treasury Department and the IRS request comments on these proposed revisions to the regulations under section 904.

H. *Section 958: Rules for determining stock ownership*

To ensure that the regulations under section 958 are consistent with the amended statute, this notice of proposed rulemaking removes the rule in § 1.958-2(d)(2) that corresponds to section 958(b)(4). It also revises *Example 4* in § 1.958-2(g) to illustrate the application of the ownership attribution rules in section 958 in the absence of section 958(b)(4).

I. *Section 1297: PFIC asset test*

Section 1297(e) provides the rules used to measure a foreign corporation's assets for purposes of determining whether it meets the asset test in section 1297(a)(2) and is a passive foreign investment company ("PFIC"). If the foreign corporation is a CFC and is not a publicly traded corporation, when determining whether the average percentage of assets of the corporation that produce passive income is at least 50 percent, adjusted basis (rather than value) of the assets must be used. Section 1297(e)(2). Accordingly, shareholders of a foreign corporation that became a CFC as a result of the repeal of section 958(b)(4) will have to determine whether the average percentage of assets that produce passive income is at least 50 percent using adjusted basis.

The legislative history to section 1297(e) indicates that the adjusted basis requirement for CFCs exists because "measurement by adjusted basis is well established in the case of controlled foreign corporations' investments of earnings in U.S. property, and is highly appropriate to the task of measuring the earnings of a controlled foreign corporation that are invested in excess passive assets." H.R. Rep. No. 103-111, at 692 (1993). However, the rule imposes a burden on taxpayers that own stock in foreign corporations that became CFCs solely by reason of the repeal of section 958(b)(4), which may not otherwise be required to account for the basis in assets under U.S. federal income tax rules. Section 1298(g) grants the Secretary the authority to issue regulations that are necessary and appropriate to carry out the purposes of sections 1291 through 1298. In accordance with this authority, the proposed regulations modify the definition of a CFC for purposes of section 1297(e) to disregard downward attribution from foreign persons. *See* proposed § 1.1297-1(d)(1)(iii)(A).

J. *Section 6049: Chapter 61 reporting provisions*

Generally, under chapter 61 of subtitle F of the Code, a payor must report to the IRS (using the appropriate Form 1099) certain payments or transactions with respect to United States persons that are not exempt recipients. The regulations under chapter 61 generally provide that the scope of payments or transactions subject to reporting under chapter 61 depends, in part, on whether or not the payor is a U.S. payor (as defined in § 1.6049-5(c)(5)), which generally includes United States persons and their foreign branches, as well as CFCs.

Foreign corporations that became CFCs solely as a result of the repeal of section 958(b)(4) could be subject to an increased burden from the reporting requirements under chapter 61 (and the backup withholding rules under section 3406). To mitigate the increased Form 1099 reporting by foreign corporations that may have no direct or indirect owners that are United States persons, in accordance with the regulatory authority provided in section 6049(a), proposed § 1.6049-5(c)(5)(i)(C) provides that a U.S. payor includes only a CFC that is a CFC without regard to downward attribution from a foreign person.

II. *Applicability Dates*

These regulations are generally proposed to apply on or after October 1, 2019. *See* section 7805(b)(1)(B). For taxable years before taxable years covered by the regulations, a taxpayer may generally apply the rules set forth in the final regulations to the last taxable year of a foreign corporation beginning before January 1, 2018, and each subsequent taxable year of the foreign corporation, and to taxable years of U.S. shareholders in which or with which such taxable years of the foreign corporation end, provided that the taxpayer and United States persons that are related (within the meaning of section 267 or 707) to the taxpayer consistently apply the relevant rule with respect to all foreign corporations. *See* section 7805(b)(7). Moreover, although proposed § 1.958-2 is proposed to apply to taxable years of foreign corporations ending on or after October 1, 2019, and taxable years of U.S. shareholders in which or with which such taxable years of foreign corporations end, the same result as the proposed revisions applies before such date due to the effective date of the repeal of section 958(b)(4).

A taxpayer may rely on the proposed regulations with respect to any period before the date that these regulations are published as final regulations in the **Federal Register**.

Statement of Availability of IRS Documents

IRS Revenue Procedures, Revenue Rulings, notices, and other guidance cited in this document are published in the Internal Revenue Bulletin and are available from the Superintendent of Documents, U.S. Government Printing Office, Washington, DC 20402, or by visiting the IRS website at http://www.irs.gov.

Special Analyses

I. *Regulatory Planning and Review – Economic Analysis*

Executive Orders 13563 and 12866 direct agencies to assess costs and benefits of available regulatory alternatives and, if regulation is necessary, to select regulatory approaches that maximize net benefits (including potential economic, environmental, public health and safety effects, distributive impacts, and equity). Executive Order 13563 emphasizes the importance of quantifying both costs and benefits, of reducing costs, of harmonizing rules, and of promoting flexibility. The Treasury Department requests comment and any potential data regarding the expected impacts of this proposed regulation.

This regulation is subject to review under section 6(b) of Executive Order 12866 pursuant to the April 11, 2018, Memorandum of Agreement ("April 11, 2018 MOA") between the Treasury Department and the Office of Management and Budget ("OMB") regarding review of tax regulations.

The Acting Administrator of the Office of Information and Regulatory Affairs ("OIRA"), OMB, has waived review of this proposed rule in accordance with section 6(a)(3)(A) of Executive Order 12866. OIRA will subsequently make a significance determination of the final rule under the terms of item 1 of the April 11, 2018 MOA between the Treasury Department and OMB regarding review of tax regulations.

A. *Background*

Section 14213 of the Act repealed section 958(b)(4), effective beginning with the last taxable year of a foreign corporation that begins before January 1, 2018 (and taxable years of U.S. shareholders in which or with which such taxable years of foreign corporations end). The repeal of section 958(b)(4) by the Act modified the constructive ownership rules that determine whether a foreign corporation is a CFC and whether a U.S. person is a U.S. shareholder of a CFC. Under section 318(a)(3), stock owned by a person is attributed downward to (that is, considered to be owned by) a partnership, estate, trust, or corporation in which the person owns an interest. Prior to repeal, section 958(b)(4) limited the application of section 318(a)(3) for purposes of determining whether a foreign corporation is a CFC and whether a U.S. person is a U.S. shareholder by providing that downward attribution under section 318(a)(3) was not applied so as to consider a U.S. person as owning the stock owned by a foreign person. After the repeal of section 958(b)(4), such stock owned by a foreign person can be attributed downward to a U.S. person, for example, to a U.S. subsidiary of a foreign parent. As a result, additional foreign corporations are now CFCs, and U.S. persons are now U.S. shareholders of CFCs, even in cases where the foreign corporation has no or little U.S ownership.

B. *The need for proposed regulations*

The legislative history to the Act states that the repeal of section 958(b)(4) was intended "to render ineffective certain transactions that are used to [sic] as a means of avoiding the subpart F provisions." *See* H.R. 115-466, at 633 (2017). As a consequence of this repeal, many foreign entities that are part of multinational groups with U.S. subsidiaries are now considered CFCs even in cases where there is no avoidance of tax under subpart F.

The treatment of a foreign corporation as a CFC, or a U.S. person as a U.S. shareholder, has consequences outside of subpart F because many statutes and regulations outside of subpart F have rules that turn on the status of a foreign corporation as a CFC or the status of a U.S. person as a U.S. shareholder.

These proposed regulations propose changes that are generally intended to ensure that, in appropriate circumstances, the operation of certain rules is consistent with their application before the repeal of section 958(b)(4). This creates continuity and gives taxpayers tax certainty, which allows them to make economically efficient decisions. By restoring the pre-Act rule for certain provisions, the proposed regulations both alleviate certain burdens of CFC status resulting from the section 958(b)(4) repeal unrelated to the aforementioned intended purposes of the repeal and neutralize possible incentives to unfairly exploit the section 958(b)(4) repeal.

C. *Baseline*

The economic analysis that follows compares the proposed regulations to a no-action baseline reflecting anticipated Federal income tax-related behavior in the absence of the proposed regulations. A no-action baseline reflects the current environment including the existing international tax regulations, prior to any amendment by the proposed regulations.

D. *Cost and benefits of the proposed regulations and potential alternatives*

As described in Part I.A of this Special Analyses, the repeal of section 958(b)(4) causes stock owned by a foreign parent to be attributed to its U.S. subsidiaries, which can cause a foreign subsidiary of a foreign parent to be designated as a CFC, even in instances where there is little or no U.S. ownership in the foreign multinational group. The Treasury Department and the IRS estimate the number of U.S. subsidiaries owned 50 percent or more by a foreign corporation to be roughly 75,000 based on 2016 Treasury tax files data. To the extent that these foreign corporations have foreign subsidiaries, they are potentially affected by the proposed regulations. Unfortunately, however, data do not exist regarding the number of such foreign subsidiaries. The costs and benefits of these proposed regulations are discussed further in this Part I.D.

1. Benefits

Restoring continuity with pre-repeal rules in appropriate cases is beneficial in two primary ways. First, it reinstates expected reporting burdens and tax costs for businesses that would otherwise experience unintended and unanticipated increases in these costs due to the unexpected switch to CFC designation described in Part I.A of this Special Analyses. Unanticipated increases in costs can be detrimental to normal business operations and can put affected groups at a disadvantage relative to competitors who did not experience such changes. Regulations designed to maintain continuity of normal business operations are appropriate and will promote a positive business environment relative to the no action baseline.

One of the provisions in these proposed regulations that alleviates burden is the provision under section 863 on income from space and ocean activities and international communications income. In this case (as well as in all other aspects of these proposed regulations), the proposed regulations prevent unintended disruption in business activity by determining CFC status as if section 958(b)(4) had not been repealed. In the absence of these proposed regulations, foreign-parented multinational groups in the space, ocean, and international communications industries that have U.S. subsidiaries could potentially have their foreign subsidiaries designated as CFCs. The designation of the foreign subsidiaries of the foreign-parented multinational groups as CFCs would result in all (in the case of space and ocean income) or half (in the case of international communications income) of the foreign subsidiary's space and ocean income or international communications income being treated as U.S. source income where the CFCs are controlled directly or indirectly by foreign persons. Comments received suggested that such treatment would render companies' business models untenable. Accordingly, the proposed regulations provide that for purposes of the treatment of space and ocean income and international communications income as U.S. source income, the determination of whether a foreign corporation is a CFC is made without regard to downward attribution from a foreign person. See Part I.F of the Explanation of Provisions for further explanation of this provision.

Another example of reduced burden under this rule relates to the timing of certain transactions. As explained in Part I.A of the Explanation of Provisions, section 267(a)(2) provides a rule for determining the time at which an otherwise deductible amount owed to a related person may be deducted. In general, if a payee is on the cash method of accounting, the payor is not allowed a deduction until the amount is actually paid, even if the payor uses the accrual method of accounting. The current regulations include an exemption that allows an accrual-based payor to deduct certain treaty-exempt amounts before they are actually paid to a related foreign person. However, this exemption is not allowed if the related foreign person is a CFC. Instead, with respect to an amount owed to a CFC, the payor may only take a deduction in an earlier year to the extent that an amount attributable to the item is includible during such prior taxable year in the gross income of a U.S. person who owns stock in the CFC. However, after the repeal of section 958(b)(4), a CFC may not have any U.S. shareholders that would have an income inclusion under subpart F. In this situation, the payor would be unable to deduct the amount until it is actually paid.

Because of the effective date of the repeal of section 958(b)(4), a foreign corporation that was not a CFC under prior law could now become a CFC beginning as early as January 1, 2017 (even though the Act was not enacted until December 22, 2017). Accordingly, a taxpayer may have deducted an amount accrued in 2017 that, due to the repeal of section 958(b)(4), would no longer be allowable in 2017. Furthermore, due to the reduction of the corporate tax rate in the Act, a deduction allowed on a company's 2017 tax return at the then statutory rate of 35 percent would be valued at 21 percent if the taxpayer were forced to move the deduction to 2018 or 2019. The repeal of section 958(b)(4) in this situation may result in an inadvertent deferral of certain deductions with permanent tax effect and correspondingly create unnecessary required adjustments to the income tax provisions in companies' financial accounting statements. The proposed guidance removes inconsistent annual treatment of deductions for certain treaty-exempt payments in the year the amounts are accrued when the amounts are owed to related foreign corporations that do not have any direct or indirect U.S. shareholders.

The second benefit of restoring pre-Act treatment is that doing so can neutralize unanticipated incentives for tax minimization resulting from the repeal. That is, CFC status can both increase burdens and offer benefits, but the unintended increase in CFC designations and the ease with which taxpayers can create a CFC could incentivize taxpayers to take advantage of potential benefits arising from CFC status. For example, Part I.B of the Explanation of Provisions describes a proposed revision that is intended to prevent taxpayers from using the special rule for CFCs in section 332(d)(3) to inappropriately avoid U.S. tax on a liquidating distribution. In addition, Part I.D of the Explanation of Provisions describes a proposed revision that is intended to prevent taxpayers from using a CFC that has no direct or indirect U.S. shareholders to take advantage of the special rule relating to CFCs that are grantors of a trust, facilitating tax-free distributions from the trust to U.S. beneficiaries despite no income inclusion by the shareholders of the CFC. Because these benefits were not intended for CFCs without direct or indirect U.S. shareholders, the anti-abuse aspects of these proposed regulations are designed to remove such incentives for taxpayers with those CFCs. Such regulations are beneficial because they promote an environment in which business operations are undertaken based on sound economic principles rather than for tax-motivated reasons.

2. Costs

The proposed regulations restore pre-section 958(b)(4) repeal CFC designation by determining CFC designation in limited situations as if section 958(b)(4) had not been repealed, essentially restoring the pre-repeal "status quo" in these situations. The proposed regulations do not impose any new systems, methods, structures, reporting, or other potentially burdensome rules that could increase compliance costs. In fact, as described above, they reduce costs or burdens that would ensue in the absence of the proposed regulations. Hence, in restoring the status quo in appropriate circumstances, the proposed regulations are not expected to impose new costs.

II. *Regulatory Flexibility Act*

It is hereby certified that these proposed regulations will not have a significant economic impact on a substantial number of small entities within the meaning of section 601(6) of the Regulatory Flexibility Act (5 U.S.C. chapter 6). The proposed regulations generally affect CFCs and U.S. shareholders of CFCs. As an initial matter, CFCs, as foreign corporations, are not considered small entities. Nor are U.S. taxpayers considered small entities to the extent the taxpayers are natural persons or entities other than small entities. Thus, the proposed regulations generally only affect small entities if a U.S. taxpayer that is a U.S. shareholder of a CFC is a small entity.

Businesses that are U.S. shareholders of CFCs are generally not small businesses because the ownership of sufficient stock of a CFC in order to be a U.S. shareholder generally entails significant resources and investment. Therefore, the Treasury Department and the IRS have determined that the proposed regulations would not affect a substantial number of domestic small business entities. Moreover, the proposed regulations do not impose any new costs on taxpayers. Consequently, the Treasury Department and the IRS have determined that the proposed regulations will not have a significant economic impact on a substantial number of small entities. Therefore, a Regulatory Flexibility Analysis under the Regulatory Flexibility Act is not required.

Pursuant to section 7805(f), this notice of proposed rulemaking has been submitted to the Chief Counsel for Advocacy of the Small Business Administration for comment on its impact on small business. The Treasury Department and the IRS request comments on the impact of these proposed regulations on small business entities.

Comments and Requests for a Public Hearing

Before the proposed regulations are adopted as final regulations, consideration will be given to any comments that are submitted timely to the IRS as prescribed in this preamble under the "ADDRESSES" heading. The Treasury Department and the IRS request comments on all aspects of the proposed regulations. The Treasury Department and the IRS also request comments on whether any other rules should be modified in light of the repeal of section 958(b)(4).

All comments will be available at *www.regulations.gov* or upon request. A public hearing will be scheduled if requested in writing by any person that timely submits written comments. If a public hearing is scheduled, notice of the date, time, and place for the public hearing will be published in the **Federal Register**.

Drafting Information

The principal authors of the proposed regulations are Karen J. Cate and Jorge M. Oben of the Office of Associate Chief Counsel (International). However, other personnel from the Treasury Department and the IRS participated in the development of the proposed regulations.

[¶ 49,816] **Proposed Amendments of Regulations (REG-118784-18)**, published in the Federal Register on October 9, 2019.

[Code Secs. 860A, 860G, 882, 1001, 1271 and 1275]

Interbank offered rates (IBOR): Debt instrument: London interbank offered rate (LIBOR): Financial Stability Board (FSB): Interest rate.—Reg. § 1.1001-6 and amendments of Reg. § § 1.860A-0, 1.860G-1, 1.882-5, 1.1271-0 and 1.1275-2, providing guidance on the tax consequences of the transition to the use of reference rates other than interbank offered rates (IBORs) in debt instruments and non-debt contracts, are proposed.

AGENCY: Internal Revenue Service (IRS), Treasury.

ACTION: Notice of proposed rulemaking.

SUMMARY: This document contains proposed regulations that provide guidance on the tax consequences of the transition to the use of reference rates other than interbank offered rates (IBORs) in debt instruments and non-debt contracts. The proposed regulations are necessary to address the possibility that an alteration of the terms of a debt instrument or a modification of the terms of other types of contracts to replace an IBOR to which the terms of the debt instrument or other contract refers with a new reference rate could result in the realization of income, deduction, gain, or loss for Federal income tax purposes or could result in other tax consequences. The proposed regulations will affect parties to debt instruments and other contracts that reference an IBOR.

DATES: Written or electronic comments and requests for a public hearing must be received by November 25, 2019.

ADDRESSES: Submit electronic submissions via the Federal eRulemaking Portal at https://*www.regulations.gov* (indicate IRS and REG-118784-18) by following the online instructions for submitting comments. Once submitted to the Federal eRulemaking Portal, comments cannot be edited or withdrawn. The Department of the Treasury (Treasury Department) and the IRS will publish for public availability any comment received to its public docket, whether submitted electronically or in hard copy. Send hard copy submissions to: CC:PA:LPD:PR (REG-118784-18), Room 5203, Internal Revenue Service, P.O. Box 7604, Ben Franklin Station, Washington, DC 20044. Submissions may be hand-delivered Monday through Friday

between the hours of 8 a.m. and 4 p.m. to CC:PA:LPD:PR (REG-118784-18), Courier's Desk, Internal Revenue Service, 1111 Constitution Avenue NW, Washington, DC 20224.

FOR FURTHER INFORMATION CONTACT: Concerning the proposed regulations, Caitlin Holzem at (202) 317-4391; concerning submissions of comments and requesting a hearing, Regina L. Johnson at (202) 317-6901 (not toll-free numbers).

SUPPLEMENTARY INFORMATION:

Background

This document contains proposed amendments to the Income Tax Regulations (26 CFR part 1) under sections 860G, 882, 1001, and 1275 of the Internal Revenue Code (Code).

1. *Elimination of IBORs*

On July 27, 2017, the U.K. Financial Conduct Authority, the U.K. regulator tasked with overseeing the London interbank offered rate (LIBOR), announced that all currency and term variants of LIBOR, including U.S.-dollar LIBOR (USD LIBOR), may be phased out after the end of 2021. The Financial Stability Board (FSB) and the Financial Stability Oversight Council (FSOC) have publicly acknowledged that in light of the prevalence of USD LIBOR as the reference rate in a broad range of financial instruments, the probable elimination of USD LIBOR has created risks that pose a potential threat to the safety and soundness of not only individual financial institutions, but also to financial stability generally. In its 2014 report "Reforming Major Interest Rate Benchmarks," the FSB discussed the problems associated with key IBORs and made recommendations to address these problems, including the development and adoption of nearly risk-free reference rates to replace IBORs. The FSB and FSOC have recognized that a sudden cessation of a widely used reference rate could cause considerable disruptions in the marketplace and might adversely affect the normal functioning of a variety of markets in the United States, including business and consumer lending and the derivatives markets.

The Alternative Reference Rates Committee (ARRC), whose ex-officio members include the Board of Governors of the Federal Reserve System, the Treasury Department, the Commodity Futures Trading Commission, and the Office of Financial Research, was convened by the Board of Governors of the Federal Reserve System and the Federal Reserve Bank of New York to identify alternative reference rates that would be both more robust than USD LIBOR and that would comply with standards such as the International Organization of Securities Commissions' "Principles for Financial Benchmarks." The ARRC was also responsible for developing a plan to facilitate the voluntary acceptance of the alternative reference rate or rates that were chosen. On March 5, 2018, the ARRC published a report that summarizes the work done earlier to select the Secured Overnight Financing Rate (SOFR) as the replacement for USD LIBOR. The Federal Reserve Bank of New York began publishing SOFR daily as of April 3, 2018, in cooperation with the Office of Financial Research. In addition, the Chicago Mercantile Exchange and other entities have launched trading in SOFR futures and have begun clearing for over-the-counter SOFR swaps. Although SOFR is calculated from overnight transactions, it is possible that one or more term rates based on SOFR derivatives may be added in the future.

Other jurisdictions have also been working toward replacing the LIBOR associated with their respective currencies. The Working Group on Sterling Risk-Free Reference Rates in the United Kingdom chose the Sterling Overnight Index Average (SONIA) to replace British pound sterling LIBOR; the Study Group on Risk-Free Reference Rates in Japan chose the Tokyo Overnight Average Rate (TONAR) to replace yen LIBOR and to serve as an alternative to the Tokyo Interbank Offered Rate (TIBOR); and the National Working Group in Switzerland selected the Swiss Average Rate Overnight (SARON) to replace Swiss franc LIBOR. Alternatives for the relevant IBOR rate have also been selected for Australia, Canada, Hong Kong, and the Eurozone. Other countries are at various stages of selecting a reference rate to replace their respective versions of IBOR.

2. *Letters on the Tax Implications of the Elimination of IBORs on Debt Instruments and Non-Debt Contracts*

On April 8, 2019, and June 5, 2019, the ARRC submitted to the Treasury Department and the IRS documents that identify various potential tax issues associated with the elimination of IBORs and request tax guidance to address those issues and to facilitate an orderly transition (ARRC letters). The ARRC stated that existing debt instruments and derivatives providing for IBOR-based payments must be amended to address the coming elimination of IBORs. The ARRC indicated that these amendments will likely take one of two forms. First, the parties may alter the instruments to replace the IBOR-referencing rate with another rate, such as one based on SOFR. Second, the parties may alter the instruments to replace an IBOR-referencing fallback rate with another fallback rate upon the discontinuance of the IBOR or at some other appropriate time. The ARRC describes fallback provisions as the provisions specifying what is to occur if an IBOR is permanently discontinued or is judged to have deteriorated to an extent that its relevance as a reliable benchmark has been significantly impaired. The ARRC notes that, regardless of which of these two forms the amendment takes, the rate that replaces the IBOR-referencing rate may include "(i) appropriate adjustments to the spread above the base reference rate in order to account for the expected differences between the two base reference rates (generally representing term premium and credit risk) and/or (ii) a one time, lump-sum payment in lieu of a spread adjustment." The ARRC also stated that newer debt instruments and derivatives may already include fallback provisions that anticipate the elimination of an IBOR and provide a methodology for changing the rate when the relevant IBOR becomes unreliable or ceases to exist.

The ARRC letters urged broad and flexible tax guidance in this area. The ARRC letters requested guidance on specific tax issues that arise as a result of these efforts to transition from IBORs to alternative rates. The ARRC first asked that a debt instrument, derivative, or other contract not be treated as exchanged under section 1001 when the terms of the instrument are amended either to replace an IBOR-referencing rate or to include a fallback rate in anticipation of the elimination of the relevant IBOR. The ARRC noted that these same amendments could cause a taxpayer with a synthetic debt instrument under § 1.1275-6 to be treated as legging out of the integrated transaction, and it also sought clarification on the source and character of a one-time payment in lieu of a spread adjustment on a derivative. The ARRC recommended treating SOFR, similar replacement rates for IBOR-referencing rates in other currencies, and potentially any qualified floating rate under § 1.1275-5 as permitted alternative reference rates to IBOR-referencing rates. The ARRC further requested that alteration of a regular interest in a real estate mortgage investment conduit (REMIC) to replace an IBOR-referencing rate or to change fallback provisions not prevent the regular interest from having fixed terms on the startup day, and that the existence and exercise of a fallback provision not prevent a variable interest rate on a regular interest in a REMIC from being a permitted variable rate under § 1.860G-1. Additionally, the ARRC suggested that, for the purpose of determining the amount and timing of original issue discount (OID) on a debt instrument, an IBOR-referencing qualified floating rate and the fallback rate that replaces the IBOR-referencing rate should be treated as a single qualified floating rate. Finally, the ARRC requested that the reference to 30-day LIBOR in § 1.882-5(d)(5)(ii)(B) be amended so that taxpayers may continue to use the simplified method of computing excess interest permitted under that section. The Treasury Department and the IRS received letters from the Structured Finance Industry Group and the Real Estate Roundtable articulating concerns similar to those set forth in the ARRC letters. The comment letters also raised certain issues that are beyond the scope of this regulation.

3. *Tax Implications of the Elimination of IBORs on Debt Instruments and Non-Debt Contracts*

The following subsections discuss the primary tax issues raised by changes to the terms of debt instruments and non-debt contracts in anticipation of the elimination of IBORs.

A. Section 1001

Section 1001 provides rules for determining the amount and recognition of gain or loss from the sale or other disposition of property. The regulations under section 1001 generally provide that gain or loss is realized upon the exchange of property for other property differing materially either in kind or in extent. See §1.1001-1(a). In the case of a debt instrument, §1.1001-3(b) provides that a significant modification of the debt instrument results in an exchange of the original debt instrument for a modified debt instrument that differs materially either in kind or in extent for purposes of §1.1001-1(a). Under §1.1001-3(c), a modification is generally any alteration, including any deletion or addition, in whole or in part, of a legal right or obligation of the issuer or a holder of a debt instrument. However, a modification generally does not include an alteration of a legal right or obligation that occurs by operation of the terms of a debt instrument. Section 1.1001-3(a)(1) provides that the rules of §1.1001-3 apply to any modification of a debt instrument, regardless of whether the modification takes the form of an amendment to the terms of the debt instrument or an exchange of a new debt instrument for an existing debt instrument. An alteration of a legal right or obligation that is treated as a modification must be tested for significance under §1.1001-3(e). Consequently, changing the interest rate index referenced in a U.S. dollar-denominated debt instrument from USD LIBOR to SOFR if no provision has been made in the terms of the debt instrument for such a change is an alteration of the terms of the debt instrument that could be treated as a significant modification and result in a tax realization event, even when USD LIBOR no longer exists.

Other than §1.1001-4, which generally prescribes the tax consequences to the nonassigning counterparty when there is a transfer or assignment of a derivative contract by a dealer or a clearinghouse, and §1.1001-5, which addresses the conversion of legacy currencies to the euro, there are no regulations that specifically address when a modification of a derivative or other non-debt contract creates a realization event. This absence of regulations has led to concern that modifying a non-debt contract to reflect the elimination of an IBOR, such as changing the floating rate index referenced in an interest rate swap contract from USD LIBOR to SOFR, could cause a deemed termination of the non-debt contract for tax purposes.

Moreover, a modification of the fallback provisions of a debt instrument or non-debt contract to address the possibility of an IBOR being eliminated might require the parties to recognize income, deduction, gain, or loss. For example, if the terms of a derivative provide for payments at an IBOR-referencing rate but contain no fallback provision, a modification to the terms of the derivative to add a fallback to the IBOR-referencing rate could cause a deemed termination of the derivative. Likewise, if the terms of a debt instrument provide for an IBOR-referencing fallback rate, an alteration of the terms of the debt instrument to replace the IBOR-referencing fallback rate with another fallback rate could cause a deemed exchange of the debt instrument. B. Integrated Transactions and Hedges

A debt instrument and one or more hedges may be treated in certain circumstances as a single, integrated instrument for certain specified purposes. For example, §1.1275-6 describes the circumstances under which a debt instrument may be integrated with a hedge for the purpose of determining the amount and timing of the taxpayer's income, deduction, gain, or loss. Sections 1.988-5(a) (regarding foreign currency transactions) and 1.148-4(h) (regarding arbitrage investment restrictions on tax-exempt bonds issued by State and local governments) similarly provide rules by which a debt instrument may be integrated with a hedge for a specific purpose. In each of these cases, amending an IBOR-referencing debt instrument or hedge to address the elimination of the IBOR may cause a deemed termination or legging out of the integrated hedge that in effect dissolves the integrated instrument into its component parts, which may yield undesirable tax consequences or recognition events for the parties to those instruments.

Similarly, §1.446-4 provides rules by which taxpayers determine the timing of income, deduction, gain, or loss attributable to a hedging transaction. These rules generally state that the method of accounting used by a taxpayer for a hedging transaction must reasonably match the timing of income, deduction, gain, or loss from the hedging transaction with the timing of the income, deduction, gain, or loss from the item or items being hedged. If a taxpayer hedges an item and later terminates the item but keeps the hedge, the taxpayer must match the built-in gain or loss on the hedge to the gain or loss on the terminated item. Accordingly, amending the terms of a debt instrument or hedge to address the elimination of an IBOR could affect the timing of gain or loss under §1.446-4 if the amendment results in an exchange under section 1001.

C. Source and Character of a One-Time Payment

The ARRC letters pointed out that, when parties alter the terms of a debt instrument or modify the terms of a non-debt contract to replace a rate referencing an IBOR, the alteration or modification may consist not only of the replacement of the IBOR with a new reference rate such as SOFR but also of an adjustment to the existing spread to account for the differences between the IBOR and the new reference rate. Alternatively, in lieu of (or in addition to) an adjustment to the spread, the parties may agree to a one-time payment as compensation for any reduction in payments attributable to the differences between the IBOR and the new reference rate. In the latter case, questions arise about the source and character of this one-time payment for various purposes of the Internal Revenue Code, such as the withholding rules in sections 1441 and 1442.

D. Grandfathered Debt Instruments and Non-Debt Contracts

The requirements of certain statutes and regulations do not apply to debt instruments and non-debt contracts issued before a specific date. For example, an obligation issued on or before March 18, 2012, is not a registration-required obligation under section 163(f) if the obligation was issued under certain arrangements reasonably designed to ensure that the obligation was sold only to non-U.S. persons. If such an obligation is modified after March 18, 2012, in a manner that results in an exchange for purposes of §1.1001-1(a), the modified obligation is treated as reissued and will be a registration-required obligation unless otherwise excepted under section 163(f)(2)(A). Likewise, payments made on certain debt instruments and non-debt contracts outstanding on July 1, 2014, (grandfathered obligations) are exempt from withholding requirements that may otherwise apply under chapter 4 of the Code, subject to any material modification of a grandfathered obligation that results in the obligation not being treated as outstanding on July 1, 2014. Accordingly, if a debt instrument is altered or a non-debt contract is modified to replace an IBOR-referencing rate in anticipation of the elimination of the IBOR, the debt instrument or non-debt contract may be treated as reissued as a consequence of the alteration or modification and therefore subject to the statute or regulation from which it was previously exempt.

E. OID and Qualified Floating Rate

Section 1.1275-5 defines a variable rate debt instrument (VRDI) and provides rules for determining the amount and accrual of qualified stated interest and OID on a VRDI. Under §1.1275-5(b), a VRDI may provide for stated interest at one or more qualified floating rates. A variable rate is generally a qualified floating rate if variations in the value of the rate can reasonably be expected to measure contemporaneous variations in the cost of newly borrowed funds. The rate may measure contemporaneous variations in borrowing costs for the issuer of the debt instrument or for issuers in general. However, a multiple of a qualified floating rate is not a qualified floating rate, except as permitted within limited parameters. If a debt instrument provides for two or more qualified floating rates that can reasonably be expected to have approximately the same values throughout the term of the instrument, the qualified floating rates together constitute a single qualified floating rate. Under §1.1275-5(e)(2), if a VRDI provides for stated interest at a single qualified floating rate and certain other requirements are satisfied, the amount of any OID that accrues during an accrual period is determined under the rules applicable to fixed rate debt instruments by assuming that the qualified floating rate is a fixed rate equal to the value, as of the issue date, of the qualified floating rate.

Section 1.1275-2(h) describes the treatment under sections 1271 through 1275 and the regulations under those sections of a debt instrument with respect to which one or more payments are subject to a remote contingency. Section 1.1275-2(h)(2) provides that a contingency is remote if there is a remote likelihood that the contingency will occur and that, in such a case, it is assumed that the contingency will not occur. In the event that a remote contingency actually occurs, § 1.1275-2(h)(6) generally provides that the debt instrument, including a VRDI, that undergoes this "change in circumstances" is treated as retired and then reissued for purposes of sections 1272 and 1273.

In general, if a debt instrument provides for a floating rate of interest and the debt instrument does not qualify as a VRDI, the debt instrument is a contingent payment debt instrument (CPDI) that is subject to more complex and less favorable rules under § 1.1275-4. For example, under § 1.1275-4, all of the stated interest is OID and the holder and issuer recognize interest income or deductions at times other than when cash payments are made. In addition, if a debt instrument that provides for a floating rate of interest is subject to a contingency that is not a remote contingency, the instrument may be a CPDI. Even if the contingency is remote, if the contingency occurs, the debt instrument is treated as retired and reissued for purposes of the OID rules. In both cases, the treatment of the contingency affects whether the debt instrument has OID and, if so, the amount of the OID and the accruals of the OID over the term of the debt instrument.

The transition to alternative rates, such as SOFR, in connection with the phaseout of IBORs has raised questions under the OID rules. For example, it is not clear whether certain debt instruments that reference IBOR qualify as VRDIs or whether they are subject to non-remote contingencies that must be taken into account.

F. REMICs

Section 860G(a)(1) provides in part that a regular interest in a REMIC must be issued on the startup day with fixed terms. Section 1.860G-1(a)(4) clarifies that a regular interest has fixed terms on the startup day if, on the startup day, the REMIC's organizational documents irrevocably specify, among other things, the interest rate or rates used to compute any interest payments on the regular interest. Accordingly, an alteration of the terms of the regular interest to change the rate or fallback provisions in anticipation of the cessation of an IBOR could preclude the interest from being a regular interest.

Section 860G(a)(1) also provides in part that interest payments on a regular interest in a REMIC may be payable at a variable rate only to the extent provided in regulations and that a regular interest must unconditionally entitle the holder to receive a specified principal amount. Section 1.860G-1(a)(3) describes the variable rates permitted for this purpose, and § 1.860G-1(a)(5) confirms that the principal amount of a regular interest generally may not be contingent. Notwithstanding these limitations on the payment of principal and interest on a regular interest in a REMIC, § 1.860G-1(b)(3) lists certain contingencies affecting the payment of principal and interest that do not prevent an interest in a REMIC from being a regular interest. The list of excepted contingencies does not, however, include a fallback rate that is triggered by an event, such as the elimination of IBOR, that is likely to occur. Nor does the list expressly include the contingent reduction of principal or interest payments to offset costs incurred by amending a regular interest to replace a rate that refers to an IBOR or by adding a fallback rate in anticipation of the elimination of the relevant IBOR.

Subject to certain exceptions, section 860G(d) imposes a tax equal to 100 percent of amounts contributed to a REMIC after the startup day. If a party other than the REMIC pays costs incurred by the REMIC after the startup day, that payment could be treated as a contribution to the REMIC subject to the tax under section 860G(d).

G. Interest Expense of a Foreign Corporation

A foreign corporation applies § 1.882-5 to determine its interest expense allocable under section 882(c) to income that is effectively connected with the conduct of a trade or business within the United States. If a foreign corporation uses the method described in § 1.882-5(b) through (d), that foreign corporation could have U.S.-connected liabilities that exceed U.S.-booked liabilities (excess U.S.-connected liabilities). When a foreign corporation has excess U.S.-connected liabilities, § 1.882-5(d)(5)(ii)(A) generally provides that the interest rate that applies to the excess U.S.-connected liabilities is the foreign corporation's average U.S.-dollar borrowing cost on all U.S.-dollar liabilities other than its U.S.-booked liabilities. Alternatively, § 1.882-5(d)(5)(ii)(B) provides that a foreign corporation that is a bank, may elect to use a published average 30-day LIBOR for the year instead of determining its average U.S.-dollar borrowing cost. Because the election provided in § 1.882-5(d)(5)(ii)(B) only permits a foreign corporation that is a bank to elect a rate that references 30-day LIBOR, the current election will not be available when LIBOR is phased out.

Explanation of Provisions

1. *Proposed Substantive Amendments to the Regulations*

The Treasury Department and the IRS have determined that it is appropriate to provide guidance on the tax issues discussed earlier in this preamble in order to minimize potential market disruption and to facilitate an orderly transition in connection with the phase-out of IBORs and the attendant need for changes in debt instruments and other non-debt contracts to implement this transition. The Treasury Department and the IRS expect that this guidance will reduce Federal income tax uncertainties and minimize taxpayer burden associated with this transition.

A. Section 1001

The proposed regulations under § 1.1001-6(a) generally provide that, if the terms of a debt instrument are altered or the terms of a non-debt contract, such as a derivative, are modified to replace, or to provide a fallback to, an IBOR-referencing rate and the alteration or modification does not change the fair market value of the debt instrument or non-debt contract or the currency of the reference rate, the alteration or modification does not result in the realization of income, deduction, gain, or loss for purposes of section 1001. The Treasury Department and the IRS intend that the proposed rules in § 1.1001-6(a), as with other regulations under section 1001, apply to both the issuer and holder of a debt instrument and to each party to a non-debt contract. The proposed rules in § 1.1001-6(a) also apply regardless of whether the alteration or modification occurs by an amendment to the terms of the debt instrument or non-debt contract or by an exchange of a new debt instrument or non-debt contract for the existing one.

Section 1.1001-6(a)(1) of the proposed regulations provides that altering the terms of a debt instrument to replace a rate referencing an IBOR with a qualified rate (qualified rates are discussed in detail later in this preamble) is not treated as a modification and therefore does not result in a deemed exchange of the debt instrument for purposes of § 1.1001-3. This same rule applies to "associated alterations," which are alterations that are both associated with the replacement of the IBOR-referencing rate and reasonably necessary to adopt or implement that replacement. One example of an associated alteration is the addition of an obligation for one party to make a one-time payment in connection with the replacement of the IBOR-referencing rate with a qualified rate to offset the change in value of the debt instrument that results from that replacement.

Section 1.1001-6(a)(2) of the proposed regulations provides that modifying a non-debt contract to replace a rate referencing an IBOR with a qualified rate is not treated as a deemed exchange of property for other property differing materially in kind or extent for purposes of § 1.1001-1(a). The rule also applies to "associated modifications," which differ from associated alterations only in that they relate to non-debt contracts. The principal example of a non-debt contract for purposes of the proposed regulations is a derivative contract, but the category is also intended to include any other type of contract (such as a lease) that may refer to an IBOR and that is not debt. Thus, for example, if an interest rate swap is modified to change the floating rate leg of the swap from Overnight USD LIBOR plus 25 basis points to an alternative rate referencing SOFR that meets the requirements for a qualified rate under the proposed regulations (including the requirement that the fair market value of the swap contract after the modification is substantially equivalent to the fair market value of the swap contract before the modification), that modification would not be treated as an exchange of property for other property differing materially in kind or extent and would therefore not be an event that results in the realization of income, deduction, gain or loss under § 1.1001-1(a).

Section 1.1001-6(a)(3) of the proposed regulations provides that an alteration to the terms of a debt instrument to include a qualified rate as a fallback to an IBOR-referencing rate and any associated alteration are not treated as modifications and therefore do not result in an exchange of the debt instrument for purposes of § 1.1001-3. In addition, an alteration to the terms of a debt instrument by which an IBOR-based fallback rate is replaced with a different fallback rate that is a qualified rate and any associated alteration are also not treated as modifications. Similar rules provide that these same changes to a non-debt contract do not result in the exchange of property for other property differing materially in kind or extent for purposes of § 1.1001-1(a).

A coordination rule in § 1.1001-6(a)(4) of the proposed regulations makes clear that any alteration to the terms of a debt instrument that is not given special treatment under either § 1.1001-6(a)(1) or (3) is subject to the ordinary operation of § 1.1001-3. The proposed regulations provide a similar rule for non-debt contracts. These proposed rules contemplate that when an alteration or modification not described in § 1.1001-6(a)(1), (2), or (3) occurs at the same time as the alteration or modification described in those paragraphs, the alteration or modification described in § 1.1001-6(a)(1), (2), or (3) is treated as part of the existing terms of the debt instrument or non-debt contract and, consequently, becomes part of the baseline against which the alteration or modification not described in § 1.1001-6(a)(1), (2), or (3) is tested.

Section 1.1001-6(b) of the proposed regulations sets forth the rules for determining whether a rate is a qualified rate. Section 1.1001-6(b)(1) lists the rates that may be qualified rates for purposes of § 1.1001-6, provided that they satisfy the requirements set forth in § 1.1001-6(b)(2) and (3). The list of potential qualified rates in § 1.1001-6(b)(1) includes a qualified floating rate as defined in § 1.1275-5(b), except that for this purpose a multiple of a qualified floating rate is considered a qualified floating rate. This list also includes any rate selected, endorsed or recommended by the central bank, reserve bank, monetary authority or similar institution (including a committee or working group thereof) as a replacement for an IBOR or its local currency equivalent in that jurisdiction. To avoid any uncertainty on the question of whether the rates identified in § 1.1001-6(b)(1)(i) through (viii) may be qualified rates, those rates are individually enumerated even though each is a qualified floating rate, as defined in § 1.1275-5(b), and each has been selected by a central bank, reserve bank, monetary authority or similar institution as a replacement for an IBOR or its local currency equivalent in that jurisdiction. The proposed regulations further provide that a rate that is determined by reference to one of the rates listed in § 1.1001-6(b)(1) may also be a qualified rate. For example, a rate equal to the compound average of SOFR over the past 30 days may be a qualified rate because that rate is determined by reference to SOFR, which is listed in § 1.1001-6(b)(1). To retain the flexibility to respond to future developments, proposed § 1.1001-6(b)(1)(xii) provides authority to add a rate to this list by identifying the new rate in guidance published in the Internal Revenue Bulletin.

A rate described in § 1.1001-6(b)(1) of the proposed regulations is not a qualified rate if it fails to satisfy the requirement of § 1.1001-6(b)(2)(i). Section 1.1001-6(b)(2)(i) of the proposed regulations generally requires that the fair market value of the debt instrument or non-debt contract after the relevant alteration or modification must be substantially equivalent to the fair market value before that alteration or modification. The purpose of this requirement is to ensure that the alterations or modifications described in § 1.1001-6(a)(1) through (3) are generally no broader than is necessary to replace the IBOR in the terms of the debt instrument or non-debt contract with a new reference rate. However, the Treasury Department and the IRS recognize that the fair market value of a debt instrument or non-debt contract may be difficult to determine precisely and intend that the proposed regulations broadly facilitate the transition away from IBORs. Accordingly, the proposed regulations provide that the fair market value of a debt instrument or derivative may be determined by any reasonable valuation method, as long as that reasonable valuation method is applied consistently and takes into account any one-time payment made in lieu of a spread adjustment.

To further ease compliance with the value equivalence requirement in § 1.1001-6(b)(2)(i), the proposed regulations provide two safe harbors and reserve the authority to provide additional safe harbors in guidance published in the Internal Revenue Bulletin. Under the first safe harbor, the value equivalence requirement is satisfied if at the time of the alteration the historic average of the IBOR-referencing rate is within 25 basis points of the historic average of the rate that replaces it. The parties may use any reasonable method to compute an historic average, subject to two limitations. First, the lookback period from which the historic data are drawn must begin no earlier than 10 years before the alteration or modification and end no earlier than three months before the alteration or modification. Second, once a lookback period is established, the historic average must take into account every instance of the relevant rate published during that period. For example, if the lookback period is comprised of the calendar years 2016 through 2020 and the relevant rate is 30-day USD LIBOR, the historic average of that rate must take into account each of the 60 published instances of 30-day USD LIBOR over the five-year lookback period. Alternatively, the parties may compute the historic average of a rate in accordance with an industry-wide standard, such as a standard for determining an historic average set forth by the International Swaps and Derivatives Association or the ARRC for this or a similar purpose. In any application of this safe harbor, the parties must use the same methodology and lookback period to compute the historic average for each of the rates to be compared.

Under the second safe harbor, the value equivalence requirement of § 1.1001-6(b)(2)(i) is satisfied if the parties to the debt instrument or non-debt contract are not related and, through bona fide, arm's length negotiations over the alteration or modification, determine that the fair market value of the altered debt instrument or modified non-debt contract is substantially equivalent to the fair market value of the debt instrument or non-debt contract before the alteration or modification. In determining the fair market value of an altered debt instrument or modified non-debt contract, the parties must take into account the value of any one-time payment made in lieu of a spread adjustment.

A rate described in § 1.1001-6(b)(1) of the proposed regulations is also not a qualified rate if it fails to satisfy the requirement in § 1.1001-6(b)(3). This paragraph generally requires that any interest rate benchmark included in the replacement rate and the IBOR referenced in the replaced rate are based on transactions conducted in the same currency or are otherwise reasonably expected to measure contemporaneous variations in the cost of newly borrowed funds in the same currency. As is the case with the value equivalence requirement under § 1.1001-6(b)(2)(i), this requirement is intended to ensure that the alterations or modifications described in § 1.1001-6(a)(1) through (3) are no broader than necessary to address the elimination of the relevant IBOR.

B. Integrated Transactions and Hedges

Section 1.1001-6(c) of the proposed regulations confirms that a taxpayer is permitted to alter the terms of a debt instrument or modify one or more of the other components of an integrated or hedged transaction to replace a rate referencing an IBOR with a qualified rate without affecting the tax treatment of either the underlying transaction or the hedge, provided that the integrated or hedged transaction as modified continues to qualify for integration. For example, a taxpayer that has issued a floating rate debt instrument that pays interest at a rate referencing USD LIBOR and has entered into an interest rate swap contract that permits that taxpayer to create a synthetic fixed rate debt instrument under the integration rules of § 1.1275-6 is not treated as legging out of the integrated transaction if the terms of the debt instrument are altered and the swap is modified to replace the USD LIBOR-referencing interest rate with a SOFR-referencing interest rate, provided that in the transaction as modified the § 1.1275-6 hedge continues to meet the requirements for a § 1.1275-6 hedge. The proposed regulations provide similar rules for a foreign currency hedge integrated with a debt instrument under § 1.988-5(a) and for an interest rate hedge integrated with an issue of tax-exempt bonds under § 1.148-4(h). The proposed regulations also provide that, in the case of a transaction subject to the hedge accounting rules under § 1.446-4, altering the terms of a debt instrument or modifying the terms of a derivative to replace an IBOR-referencing rate with a qualified rate on one or more legs of the transaction is not a disposition or termination of either leg under § 1.446-4(e)(6).

C. Source and Character of a One-Time Payment

Section 1.1001-6(d) of the proposed regulations provides that, for all purposes of the Internal Revenue Code, the source and character of a one-time payment that is made by a payor in connection with an alteration or modification described in proposed §1.1001-6(a)(1), (2), or (3) will be the same as the source and character that would otherwise apply to a payment made by the payor with respect to the debt instrument or non-debt contract that is altered or modified. For example, a one-time payment made by a counterparty to an interest rate swap is treated as a payment with respect to the leg of the swap on which the counterparty making the one-time payment is obligated to perform. Accordingly, under §1.863-7(b), the source of that one-time payment would likely be determined by reference to the residence of the recipient of the payment. With respect to a lease of real property, a one-time payment made by the lessee to the lessor is treated as a payment of rent and, under sections 861(a)(4) and 862(a)(4), the source of that one-time payment would be the location of the leased real property.

The Treasury Department and the IRS expect that parties to debt instruments and non-debt contracts will generally replace the IBOR with an overnight, nearly risk-free rate, such as SOFR. Because of differences in term and credit risk, an overnight, nearly risk-free rate will generally be lower than the IBOR it replaces. Accordingly, the Treasury Department and the IRS expect that, for example, one-time payments with respect to a debt instrument will generally not be paid by the lender to the borrower. However, in the event that it is determined that guidance in respect of such payments is needed, the Treasury Department and the IRS request comments on the source and character of a one-time payment on a debt instrument or non-debt contract received by a party (such as the borrower on a debt instrument or the lessee on a lease) that does not ordinarily receive payments during the term of the debt instrument or non-debt contract.

D. Grandfathered Debt Instruments and Non-Debt Contracts

The rules in §1.1001-6(a) of the proposed regulations generally prevent debt instruments and non-debt contracts from being treated as reissued following a deemed exchange under section 1001. Thus, for example, a debt instrument grandfathered under section 163(f), 871(m), or 1471 or a regulation under one of those sections would not lose its grandfathered status as a result of any alterations made in connection with the elimination of an IBOR and described in §1.1001-6(a)(1) or (3) of the proposed regulations. To provide certainty in treating a non-debt contract as a grandfathered obligation for chapter 4 purposes in the case of the modification of the contract to replace an IBOR-referencing rate, §1.1001-6(e) of the proposed regulations provides that any modification of a non-debt contract to which §1.1001-6(a)(2) or (3) applies is not a material modification for purposes of §1.1471-2(b)(2)(iv).

E. OID and Qualified Floating Rate

Section 1.1275-2(m) of the proposed regulations sets forth three special rules for determining the amount and accrual of OID in the case of a VRDI that provides both for interest at an IBOR-referencing qualified floating rate and for a fallback rate that is triggered when the IBOR becomes unavailable or unreliable. Under §1.1275-2(m)(2), the IBOR-referencing qualified floating rate and the fallback rate are treated as a single qualified floating rate for purposes of §1.1275-5. Under §1.1275-2(m)(3), the possibility that the relevant IBOR will become unavailable or unreliable is treated as a remote contingency under §1.1275-2(h). Under §1.1275-2(m)(4), the occurrence of the event that triggers activation of the fallback rate is not treated as a change in circumstances. Thus, for example, the VRDI is not treated as retired and reissued under §1.1275-2(h)(6) when the relevant IBOR becomes unavailable or unreliable and the rate changes to the fallback rate, even if the IBOR becoming unavailable or unreliable was a remote contingency at the time the VRDI was issued. With the exception of these three rules in §1.1275-2(m) of the proposed regulations, the OID regulations apply to an IBOR-referencing VRDI as they would to any other debt instrument.

F. REMICs

Section 1.860G-1(e) of the proposed regulations permits an interest in a REMIC to retain its status as a regular interest despite certain alterations and contingencies. Specifically, if the parties to a regular interest alter the terms after the startup day to replace an IBOR-referencing rate with a qualified rate, to include a qualified rate as a fallback to an IBOR-referencing rate, or to make any other alteration described in §1.1001-6(a)(1) or (3) of the proposed regulations, §1.860G-1(e)(2) provides that those alterations are disregarded for the purpose of determining whether the regular interest has fixed terms on the startup day.

Supplementing the list of disregarded contingencies in §1.860G-1(b)(3), §1.860G-1(e)(3) and (4) of the proposed regulations describe certain contingencies affecting the payment of principal and interest that do not prevent an interest in a REMIC from being a regular interest. Under §1.860G-1(e)(3), an interest in a REMIC does not fail to be a regular interest solely because the terms of the interest permit the rate to change from an IBOR-referencing rate to a fallback rate in anticipation of the relevant IBOR becoming unavailable or unreliable. Although this proposed rule permits taxpayers to disregard the contingency in determining whether the rate is a variable rate permitted under §1.860G-1(a)(3), both the IBOR-referencing rate and the fallback rate considered individually must be rates permitted under section 860G. Under §1.860G-1(e)(4) of the proposed regulations, an interest in a REMIC does not fail to be a regular interest solely because the amount of payments of principal or interest may be reduced by reasonable costs of replacing an IBOR-referencing rate with a qualified rate, of amending fallback provisions to address the elimination of an IBOR, or of modifying a non-debt contract that is associated with the interest in the REMIC, such as a credit enhancement. Section 1.860G-1(e)(4) further provides that, if a party other than the REMIC pays those reasonable costs after the startup day, that payment is not subject to the tax imposed under section 860G(d).

G. Interest Expense of a Foreign Corporation

Because the election provided in §1.882-5(d)(5)(ii)(B) only permits a foreign corporation that is a bank to elect a rate that references 30-day LIBOR, the current election will not be available when LIBOR is phased out. To address this change in facts, the proposed regulations amend the election in §1.882-5(d)(5)(ii)(B) to allow a foreign corporation that is a bank to compute interest expense attributable to excess U.S.-connected liabilities using a yearly average SOFR. The Treasury Department and the IRS have determined that SOFR is an appropriate rate to use in §1.882-5(d)(5)(ii)(B) to replace LIBOR. Since SOFR is an overnight rate that does not reflect credit risk, the use of SOFR is likely to result in a lower rate than the 30-day LIBOR calculation previously allowed under §1.882-5(d)(5)(ii)(B). Because of these differences between SOFR and 30-day LIBOR, the Treasury Department and the IRS request comments on whether another nearly risk-free rate might be more appropriate in computing interest expense on excess U.S.-connected liabilities for purposes of §1.882-5(d)(5)(ii)(B).

2. *Proposed Applicability Dates and Reliance on the Proposed Regulations*

A. Proposed Applicability Dates of the Final Regulations

This part 2(A) of the Explanation of Provisions section describes the various applicability dates proposed to apply to the final regulations. Under the proposed applicability date in §1.1001-6(g), §1.1001-6 of the final regulations would apply to an alteration of the terms of a debt instrument or a modification to the terms of a non-debt contract that occurs on or after the date of publication of a Treasury decision adopting those rules as final regulations in the **Federal Register**. However, under proposed §1.1001-6(g), a taxpayer may choose to apply §1.1001-6 of the final regulations to alterations and modifications that occur before that date, provided that the taxpayer and its related parties consistently apply the rules before that date. See section 7805(b)(7).

Under the proposed applicability date in § 1.1275-2(m)(5), the OID rules in § 1.1275-2(m) of the final regulations would apply to debt instruments issued on or after the date of publication of a Treasury decision adopting those rules as final regulations in the **Federal Register**. However, under proposed § 1.1275-2(m)(5), a taxpayer may choose to apply § 1.1275-2(m) of the final regulations to debt instruments issued before that date. See section 7805(b)(7).

Under the proposed applicability date in § 1.860G-1(e)(5)(i), the REMIC rules in § 1.860G-1(e)(2) and (4) of the final regulations would apply with respect to an alteration or modification that occurs on or after the date of publication of a Treasury decision adopting those rules as final regulations in the **Federal Register**. However, a taxpayer may choose to apply § 1.860G-1(e)(2) and (4) of the final regulations with respect to an alteration or modification that occurs before that date. See section 7805(b)(7). Under the proposed applicability date in § 1.860G-1(e)(5)(ii), § 1.860G-1(e)(3) of the final regulations would apply to a regular interest in a REMIC issued on or after the date of publication of a Treasury decision adopting that rule as a final regulation in the **Federal Register**. However, a taxpayer may choose to apply § 1.860G-1(e)(3) of the final regulations to a regular interest in a REMIC issued before that date. See section 7805(b)(7).

Under the proposed applicability date in § 1.882-5(f)(3), § 1.882-5(d)(5)(ii)(B) of the final regulations would apply to taxable years ending after the date of publication of a Treasury decision adopting that rule as a final regulation is published in the **Federal Register**.

B. Reliance on the Proposed Regulations

A taxpayer may rely on the proposed regulations to the extent provided in this part 2(B) of the Explanation of Provisions section. A taxpayer may rely on § 1.1001-6 of the proposed regulations for any alteration of the terms of a debt instrument or modification of the terms of a non-debt contract that occurs before the date of publication of a Treasury decision adopting those rules as final regulations in the **Federal Register**, provided that the taxpayer and its related parties consistently apply the rules of § 1.1001-6 of the proposed regulations before that date. A taxpayer may rely on § 1.1275-2(m) or § 1.860G-1(e)(3) of the proposed regulations for any debt instrument or regular interest in a REMIC issued before the date of publication of a Treasury decision adopting those rules as final regulations in the **Federal Register**. A taxpayer may rely on § 1.860G-1(e)(2) and (4) of the proposed regulations with respect to any alteration or modification that occurs before the date of publication of a Treasury decision adopting that rule as a final regulation in the **Federal Register**. A taxpayer may rely on § 1.882-5(d)(5)(ii)(B) of the proposed regulations for any taxable year ending after October 9, 2019 but before the date of publication of a Treasury decision adopting these rules as final regulations in the **Federal Register**.

Special Analyses

I. *Regulatory Planning and Review - Economic Analysis*

Executive Orders 12866 and 13563 direct agencies to assess costs and benefits of available regulatory alternatives and, if regulation is necessary, to select regulatory approaches that maximize net benefits (including (i) potential economic, environmental, and public health and safety effects, (ii) potential distributive impacts, and (iii) equity). Executive Order 13563 emphasizes the importance of quantifying both costs and benefits, reducing costs, harmonizing rules, and promoting flexibility.

These proposed regulations have been designated as subject to review under Executive Order 12866 pursuant to the Memorandum of Agreement (April 11, 2018) (MOA) between the Treasury Department and the Office of Management and Budget (OMB) regarding review of tax regulations. The Office of Information and Regulatory Affairs has designated these proposed regulations as economically significant under section 1(c) of the MOA.

A. Background, Need for the Proposed Regulations, and Economic Analysis of Proposed Regulations

A very large volume of U.S. financial products and contracts include terms or conditions that reference LIBOR or, more generally, IBORs. Concern about manipulation and a decline in the volume of the funding from which the LIBOR is calculated led to recommendations for the development of alternatives to the LIBOR, ones that would be based on transactions in a more robust underlying market. In addition, on July 27, 2017, the U.K. Financial Conduct Authority, the U.K. regulator tasked with overseeing LIBOR, announced that all currency and term variants of LIBOR, including USD LIBOR, may be phased out after 2021 and not be published after that timeframe. The ARRC, a group of stakeholders affected by the cessation of the publication of USD LIBOR, was convened to identify an alternative rate and to facilitate its voluntary adoption. The ARRC recommended the SOFR as a potential replacement for USD LIBOR. Essentially all financial products and contracts that currently contain conditions or legal provisions that rely on LIBOR and IBORs are expected to transition to the SOFR or similar alternatives in the next few years. This transition will involve changes in debt, derivatives, and other financial contracts to adopt the SOFR or other alternative reference rates.

The ARRC has estimated that the total exposure to USD LIBOR was close to $200 trillion in 2016, of which approximately 95 percent were in over-the-counter derivatives.[1] ARRC further notes that USD LIBOR is also referenced in several trillion dollars of corporate loans, floating-rate mortgages, and similar financial products.

In the absence of further tax guidance, the vast majority of expected changes in such contracts could lead to the recognition of gains (or losses) in these contracts for U.S. income tax purposes and to correspondingly potentially large tax liabilities for their holders. To address this issue, the proposed regulations provide that changes in debt instruments, derivative contracts, and other affected contracts to replace reference rates based on IBORs with qualified rates (as defined in the proposed regulations) will not result in tax realization events under section 1001 and relevant regulations thereunder. The proposed regulations require that qualified rates be substantially equivalent in fair market value to the replaced rates based on any reasonable, consistently applied method of valuation. The proposed regulations further provide certain safe harbors for this comparability standard, based on historic average rates and bona fide fair market value negotiations between unrelated parties. The proposed regulations also provide corresponding guidance on hedging transactions and derivatives to the effect that taxpayers may modify the components of hedged or integrated transactions to replace IBORs with qualified rates without affecting the tax treatment of the hedges or underlying transactions.

In the absence of these proposed regulations, parties to contracts affected by the cessation of the publication of LIBOR would either suffer tax consequences to the extent that a change to the contract results in a tax realization event under section 1001 or attempt to find alternative contracts that avoid such a tax realization event, which may be difficult as a commercial matter. Both such options would be both costly and highly disruptive to U.S. financial markets. A large number of contracts may end up being breached, leading to bankruptcies or other legal proceedings. The types of actions that contract holders might take in the absence of these proposed regulations are difficult to predict because such an event is outside recent experience in U.S. financial markets. This financial disruption would be particularly unproductive because the economic characteristics of the financial products and contracts under the new rates would be essentially unchanged. Thus, there is no underlying economic rationale for a tax realization event.

---

[1] See Second Report, The Alternative Reference Rates Committee, March 2018, Table 1 and related discussion, available at *https://www.newyorkfed.org/medialibrary/Microsites/ arrc/files/2018/ARRC-Second-report*.

The Treasury Department and the IRS project that these proposed regulations would avoid this costly and unproductive disruption. The Treasury Department and the IRS further project that these proposed regulations, by implementing the regulatory provisions requested by ARRC and taxpayers, will help facilitate the economy's adaptation to the cessation of the LIBOR in a least-cost manner.

The Treasury Department and the IRS request comments on these proposed regulations.

II. *Regulatory Planning and Review and Regulatory Flexibility Act*

Under the Regulatory Flexibility Act (5 U.S.C. chapter 6), it is hereby certified that these proposed regulations will not have a significant economic impact on a substantial number of small entities that are directly affected by the proposed regulations. These proposed regulations provide rules to minimize the economic impact of the elimination of IBORs on all taxpayers. Parties to IBOR-referencing financial instruments are generally expected to alter or to modify those instruments in response to the elimination of the relevant IBOR and, in the absence of rules such as those proposed, those alterations and modifications may trigger significant tax consequences for the parties to those instruments. In addition, these proposed regulations do not impose a collection of information on any taxpayers, including small entities. Accordingly, this rule will not have a significant economic impact on a substantial number of small entities.

Pursuant to section 7805(f) of the Code, this notice of proposed rulemaking will be submitted to the Chief Counsel for Advocacy of the Small Business Administration for comment on its impact on small business.

III. *Unfunded Mandates Reform Act*

Section 202 of the Unfunded Mandates Reform Act of 1995 (UMRA) requires that agencies assess anticipated costs and benefits and take certain other actions before issuing a final rule that includes any Federal mandate that may result in expenditures in any one year by a State, local, or tribal government, in the aggregate, or by the private sector, of $100 million in 1995 dollars, updated annually for inflation. In 2019, that threshold is approximately $150 million. This rule does not include any Federal mandate that may result in expenditures by state, local, or tribal governments, or by the private sector in excess of that threshold.

IV. *Executive Order 13132: Federalism*

Executive Order 13132 (titled "Federalism") prohibits an agency from publishing any rule that has federalism implications if the rule either imposes substantial, direct compliance costs on state and local governments, and is not required by statute, or preempts state law, unless the agency meets the consultation and funding requirements of section 6 of the Executive Order. This proposed rule does not have federalism implications and does not impose substantial direct compliance costs on state and local governments or preempt state law within the meaning of the Executive Order.

Comments and Requests for Public Hearing

Before these proposed regulations are adopted as final regulations, consideration will be given to any comments that are submitted timely to the IRS as prescribed in this preamble under the **ADDRESSES** heading. The Treasury Department and the IRS specifically seek comment on any complications under any section of the Code or existing regulations that may arise from the replacement of an IBOR with a qualified rate and that are not resolved in these proposed regulations. All comments will be available at *http://www.regulations.gov* or upon request. A public hearing will be scheduled if requested in writing by any person that timely submits written comments. If a public hearing is scheduled, notice of the date, time, and place for the hearing will be published in the **Federal Register**.

Drafting Information

The principal authors of these regulations are Caitlin Holzem and Spence Hanemann of the Office of Associate Chief Counsel (Financial Institutions and Products). However, other personnel from the Treasury Department and the IRS participated in their development.

[¶ 49,817]   Proposed Amendments of Regulations (REG-128246-18), published in the Federal Register on October 10, 2019.

[Code Sec. 529A]

ABLE account: Disability expenses: Qualified higher education expenses (QHEEs): Designated beneficiary.—Reg. §1.529A-8 and amendments of Reg. §§1.529A-0 and 1.529A-1, containing proposed regulations related to the Internal Revenue Code (Code), which allows a State (or its agency or instrumentality) to establish and maintain a tax-advantaged savings program under which contributions may be made to an ABLE account for the purpose of paying for the qualified disability expenses of the designated beneficiary of the account, are proposed.

AGENCY: Internal Revenue Service (IRS), Treasury.

ACTION: Notice of proposed rulemaking.

SUMMARY: This document contains proposed regulations related to the Internal Revenue Code (Code), which allows a State (or its agency or instrumentality) to establish and maintain a tax-advantaged savings program under which contributions may be made to an ABLE account for the purpose of paying for the qualified disability expenses of the designated beneficiary of the account. The affected Code section was amended by the Tax Cuts and Jobs Act, signed into law on December 22, 2017. The Tax Cuts and Jobs Act allows certain designated beneficiaries to contribute a limited amount of compensation income to their own ABLE accounts.

DATES: Comments must be received by January 8, 2020.

ADDRESSES: Submit electronic submissions via the Federal eRulemaking Portal at www.regulations.gov (indicate IRS and REG-128246-18) by following the online instructions for submitting comments. Once submitted to the Federal eRulemaking Portal at www.regulations.gov comments cannot be edited or withdrawn. The Department of the Treasury (Treasury Department) and the IRS will publish for public availability any comment received to its public docket, whether submitted electronically or in hard copy. Send hard copy submissions to: CC:PA:LPD:PR (REG-128246-18), Room 5203, Internal Revenue Service, P.O. Box 7604, Ben Franklin Station, Washington, DC 20044. Submissions may be hand-delivered Monday through Friday between the hours of 8 a.m. and 4 p.m. to CC:PA:LPD:PR (REG-128246-18), Courier's Desk, Internal Revenue Service, 1111 Constitution Avenue NW, Washington, DC 20224.

FOR FURTHER INFORMATION CONTACT: Concerning these proposed regulations, Julia Parnell, (202) 317-4086; concerning submissions of comments and requests for a public hearing, Regina Johnson at email address fdms.database@irscounsel.treas.gov and (202) 317-6901 (not toll-free numbers).

SUPPLEMENTARY INFORMATION: This document contains proposed regulations related to section 529A of the Internal Revenue Code (Code), which allows a State (or its agency or instrumentality) to establish and maintain a tax-advantaged savings program under which contributions may be made to an ABLE account for the purpose of paying for the qualified disability expenses of the designated beneficiary of the account. Section

529A was amended by the Tax Cuts and Jobs Act, Public Law 115-97, 131 Stat. 2054, (2017) (2017 Act), signed into law on December 22, 2017. The 2017 Act allows certain designated beneficiaries to contribute a limited amount of compensation income to their own ABLE accounts.

Background

1. The ABLE Act

The Stephen Beck, Jr., Achieving a Better Life Experience Act of 2014 (the "ABLE Act") was enacted on December 19, 2014, as part of the Tax Increase Prevention Act of 2014, Public Law 113-295, 128 Stat. 4010, (2014). The ABLE Act added section 529A to the Code. Section 529A allows a State (or its agency or instrumentality) to establish and maintain a tax-advantaged savings program under which contributions may be made to an ABLE account for the purpose of paying for the qualified disability expenses of the designated beneficiary of the account. Section 529A was amended by the 2017 Act.

Prior to its amendment by the 2017 Act, section 529A(b)(2) stated that a program shall not be treated as a qualified ABLE program unless it provides that no contribution will be accepted unless it is in cash, or if the contribution (other than a rollover contribution described in section 529A(c)(1)(C)) would result in aggregate contributions from all contributors in excess of the amount of the section 2503(b) gift tax exclusion for the calendar year in which the designated beneficiary's taxable year begins. Under section 529A(b)(2), rules similar to the rules of section 408(d)(4) apply to permit the return of excess contributions (with any attributable net income) on or before the due date (including extensions) of the designated beneficiary's income tax return. In addition, under section 529A(b)(6), a qualified ABLE program must provide adequate safeguards to ensure that total contributions do not exceed the State's limit for aggregate contributions under its qualified tuition program as described in section 529(b)(6). A qualified tuition program under section 529 is a program established by a State (or its agency or instrumentality) that permits a person to prepay or contribute to a tax-favored savings account for a designated beneficiary's qualified higher education expenses (QHEEs) or a program established by an eligible educational institution that permits a person to prepay a designated beneficiary's QHEEs.

2. Prior Rulemaking and Statutory Change

On June 22, 2015, the Treasury Department and the IRS published a Notice of Proposed Rulemaking (REG-102837-15) in the **Federal Register** (80 FR 35602) (the 2015 Proposed Regulations). More than 200 written comments were received in response to the 2015 Proposed Regulations and a public hearing was held on October 14, 2015.[1] In addition to these comments, several commenters asked the Treasury Department and the IRS to issue interim guidance to address three particular issues so that these programs could be established before the issuance of final regulations. In order to prevent a delay in the creation of ABLE programs, the Treasury Department and the IRS issued Notice 2015-81, 2015-49 I.R.B. 784 (Dec. 7, 2015), which describes how the Treasury Department and the IRS intend to revise three particular provisions of the proposed regulations under section 529A when those regulations are finalized.

Since the issuance of the 2015 Proposed Regulations and the Notice, two statutes have been enacted that amended one or more provisions of section 529A. On December 18, 2015, section 303 of the Protecting Americans from Tax Hikes Act of 2015 (the PATH Act), was enacted as part of the Consolidated Appropriations Act, Public Law 114-113, 129 Stat. 2242, (2016). The PATH Act amended section 529A(b)(1), effective for taxable years beginning after December 31, 2014, by removing the requirement that a State's qualified ABLE program allow the establishment of an ABLE account only for a designated beneficiary who is a resident of that State or of a contracting State. Due to this amendment, the Treasury Department and the IRS intend to remove references to the residency requirement in the proposed regulations under section 529A when those regulations are finalized. The other statutory change was made in the 2017 Act as described in these proposed regulations.

3. The 2017 Act

The 2017 Act amended section 529A(b)(2)(B) to allow an employed designated beneficiary described in new section 529A(b)(7) to contribute, prior to January 1, 2026, an additional amount in excess of the limit in section 529A(b)(2)(B)(i) (the annual gift tax exclusion amount in section 2503(b), formerly set forth in section 529A(b)(2)(B)). This additional permissible contribution is subject to its own limit as described in section 529A(b)(2)(B)(ii). Specifically, this additional contributed amount may not exceed the lesser of (i) the designated beneficiary's compensation as defined by section 219(f)(1) for the taxable year, or (ii) an amount equal to the poverty line for a one-person household for the calendar year preceding the calendar year in which the taxable year begins. The 2017 Act also amended the section 529A(b)(2) flush language to require the designated beneficiary, or a person acting on behalf of the designated beneficiary, to maintain adequate records to ensure, and to be responsible for ensuring, that the requirements of section 529A(b)(2)(B)(ii) are met.

New section 529A(b)(7)(A) identifies a designated beneficiary eligible to make this additional contribution as one who is an employee (including a self-employed individual) with respect to whom there has been no contribution made for the taxable year to: a defined contribution plan meeting the requirements of sections 401(a) or 403(a); an annuity contract described in section 403(b); or an eligible deferred contribution plan under section 457(b). Section 529A(b)(7)(B) defines the term "poverty line" as having the meaning provided in section 673 of the Community Services Block Grant Act (42 U.S.C. 9902).

The 2017 Act also amended section 529 to allow, before January 1, 2026, a limited amount to be rolled over to an ABLE account from the designated beneficiary's own section 529 qualified tuition program (QTP) account or from the QTP account of certain family members. The 2017 Act added section 529(c)(3)(C)(i)(III), which provides that a distribution from a QTP made after December 22, 2017, and before January 1, 2026, is not subject to income tax if, within 60 days of the distribution, it is transferred to an ABLE account of the designated beneficiary or a member of the family of the designated beneficiary. Under section 529(c)(3)(C)(i), the amount of any rollover to an ABLE account is limited to the amount that, when added to all other contributions made to the ABLE account for the taxable year, does not exceed the contribution limit for the ABLE account under section 529A(b)(2)(B)(i), that is, the annual gift tax exclusion amount under section 2503(b). This limited rollover is described in more detail in Notice 2018-58, 2018-33 I.R.B. 305 (Aug. 13, 2018).

4. Notice 2018-62

To address the 2017 Act modifications to section 529A, the Treasury Department and the IRS published Notice 2018-62, 2018-34 I.R.B. 316 (Aug. 20, 2018), which announces the intent of the Treasury Department and the IRS to issue proposed regulations to implement these changes, and describes the anticipated rules to implement the statutory changes. No comments were received in response to the Notice. These proposed regulations incorporate, without substantive change, the anticipated rules described in that Notice.

---

[1] Comments related to the 2015 Proposed Regulations will be considered prior to finalizing them, which the Treasury Department and the IRS expect to occur in conjunction with the finalization of these proposed regulations.

Explanation of Provisions

1. Additional Contributions

The 2017 Act amended section 529A(b)(2)(B) to permit an employed or self-employed designated beneficiary described in section 529A(b)(7) to contribute to his or her ABLE account the lesser of the designated beneficiary's compensation for the taxable year or an amount equal to the poverty line for a one-person household for the calendar year preceding the calendar year in which the designated beneficiary's taxable year begins. These proposed regulations confirm that the employed designated beneficiary, or the person acting on his or her behalf, is solely responsible for ensuring that the requirements in section 529A(b)(2)(B)(ii) are met and for maintaining adequate records for that purpose. In addition, to minimize burdens for the designated beneficiary and the qualified ABLE program, these proposed regulations provide that ABLE programs may allow a designated beneficiary or the person acting on his or her behalf to certify, under penalties of perjury, that he or she is a designated beneficiary described in section 529A(b)(7) and that his or her contributions of compensation do not exceed the limit set forth in section 529A(b)(2)(B)(ii).

2. Poverty Line

Section 529A(b)(7)(B) provides that the term poverty line referred to in section 529A(b)(2)(B)(ii) has the same meaning given to that term by section 673 of the Community Services Block Grant Act (42 U.S.C. 9902). These proposed regulations clarify that the poverty line in section 529A(b)(7)(B) is to be determined by using the poverty guidelines updated periodically in the **Federal Register** by the U.S. Department of Health and Human Services under the authority of 42 U.S.C. 9902(2). Those guidelines vary based on locality. Specifically, there are separate guidelines for (1) the contiguous 48 states and the District of Columbia, (2) Alaska, and (3) Hawaii. Because the Treasury Department and the IRS have concluded that the poverty guideline that most closely reflects the employed designated beneficiary's cost of living is the most relevant for determining the contribution limit, these proposed regulations provide that a designated beneficiary's contribution limit is to be determined using the poverty guideline applicable in the state of the designated beneficiary's residence.

3. Return of Excess Contributions

Because section 529A(b)(2) provides that rules similar to those set forth in section 408(d)(4) regarding the return of excess contributions to an individual retirement account or annuity apply to ABLE accounts, these proposed regulations provide that a qualified ABLE program must return any contributions of the designated beneficiary's compensation in excess of the limit in section 529A(b)(2)(B)(ii) to the designated beneficiary.

Consistent with section 529A(b)(2), these proposed regulations provide that it will be the sole responsibility of the designated beneficiary (or the person acting on the designated beneficiary's behalf) to identify and request the return of any excess contribution of such compensation income. Such returns of excess compensation contributions must be received by the employed designated beneficiary on or before the due date (including extensions) of the designated beneficiary's income tax return for the year in which the excess compensation contributions were made. A failure to return excess contributions within this time period will result in the imposition on the designated beneficiary of a 6 percent excise tax under section 4973(a)(6) on the amount of excess compensation contributions.

Additionally, in order to minimize administrative burdens for the designated beneficiary and the qualified ABLE program, for purposes of ensuring that the limit on contributions made under section 529A(b)(2)(B)(ii) is not exceeded, the qualified ABLE program may rely on self-certifications, made under penalties of perjury, of the designated beneficiary or the person acting on the designated beneficiary's behalf.

Proposed Effective/Applicability Date

These regulations are proposed to apply to taxable years beginning after the date of publication of the Treasury decision adopting these rules as final regulations in the **Federal Register**. Until the issuance of final regulations, taxpayers and qualified ABLE programs may rely on these proposed regulations.

Special Analyses

This regulation is not subject to review under section 6(b) of Executive Order 12866 pursuant to the Memorandum of Agreement (April 11, 2018) between the Department of the Treasury and the Office of Management and Budget regarding review of tax regulations.

Regulatory Flexibility Act

Pursuant to the Regulatory Flexibility Act (5 U.S.C. chapter 6), it is hereby certified that the collection of information in these regulations will not have a significant economic impact on a substantial number of small entities. This certification is based on the fact that these proposed regulations will not impact a substantial number of small entities. These regulations primarily affect states and individuals and therefore will not have a significant economic impact on a substantial number of small entities. Pursuant to section 7805(f) of the Code, these proposed regulations will be submitted to the Chief Counsel for Advocacy of the Small Business Administration for comment on their impact on small business.

Comments and Requests for Public Hearing

Before these proposed regulations are adopted as final regulations, consideration will be given to any comments that are timely submitted to the IRS as prescribed in this preamble under the **"ADDRESSES"** heading. The Treasury Department and the IRS request comments on all aspects of these proposed rules. All comments will be available at www.regulations.gov or upon request. A public hearing will be scheduled if requested in writing by any person that timely submits written or electronic comments. If a public hearing is scheduled, notice of the date, time, and place for the hearing will be published in the **Federal Register**.

Statement of Availability of IRS Documents

Notices 2015-81, 2018-58 and 2018-62 are published in the Internal Revenue Bulletin and are available from the Superintendent of Documents, U.S. Government Publishing Office, Washington, D.C. 20402, or by visiting the IRS website at *http://www.irs.gov*.

Drafting Information

The principal author of these regulations is Julia Parnell, Office of Associate Chief Counsel (Employee Benefits, Exempt Organizations, and Employment Taxes). However, other personnel from the IRS and the Treasury Department participated in their development.

[¶ 49,818]   **Proposed Amendments of Regulations (REG-131071-18)**, published in the Federal Register on November 7, 2019.

[Code Secs. 316, 481, 1371 and 1377]

Eligible terminated S corporation (ETSC): Post-termination transition period (PTTP): Earnings and profits: Shareholder. Distributions.— Reg. §§1.481-5, 1.1371-1 and 1.1371-2, and amendments of Reg. §§1.316-2, 1.481-5, 1.481-6, 1.1377-2 and 1.1377-3, regarding the definition of an eligible terminated S corporation (ETSC), are proposed.

AGENCY: Internal Revenue Service (IRS), Treasury.

ACTION: Notice of proposed rulemaking.

SUMMARY: This notice of proposed rulemaking provides rules regarding the definition of an eligible terminated S corporation (ETSC). In addition, these proposed regulations provide rules relating to distributions of money by an ETSC after the post-termination transition period (PTTP). Finally, these proposed regulations revise current regulations to extend the treatment of distributions of money during the PTTP to all shareholders of the corporation and to update and clarify the allocation of current earnings and profits to distributions of money and other property. These proposed regulations would affect certain C corporations and the shareholders of such corporations.

DATES: Comments and requests for a public hearing must be received by December 22, 2019. ADDRESSES: Submit electronic submissions via the Federal Rulemaking Portal at https://*www.regulations.gov* (indicate IRS and REG-131071-18) by following the online instructions for submitting comments. The Department of the Treasury (Treasury Department) and the IRS will publish for public availability any comment received to its public docket, whether submitted electronically or in hard copy. Send hard copy submissions to: CC:PA:LPD:PR (REG-131071-18), Room 5203, Internal Revenue Service, P.O. Box 7604, Ben Franklin Station, Washington, DC 20044. Submissions may be hand-delivered Monday through Friday between the hours of 8 a.m. and 4 p.m. to CC:PA:LPD:PR (REG-131071-18), Courier's Desk, Internal Revenue Building, 1111 Constitution Avenue NW, Washington, DC, 20224.

FOR FURTHER INFORMATION CONTACT: Concerning proposed regulations §§ 1.481-5, 1.481-6, 1.1377-2, and 1.1377-3, Margaret Burow or Michael Gould at (202) 317-5279; concerning proposed regulations §§ 1.1371-1 and 1.1371-2, Aglaia Ovtchinnikova at (202) 317-6975, Kevin M. Jacobs at (202) 317-5332, or Margaret Burow or Michael Gould at (202) 317-5279; concerning proposed regulation § 1.316-2, Aglaia Ovtchinnikova at (202) 317-6975 or Kevin M. Jacobs at (202) 317-5332; concerning submissions and the hearing, Regina Johnson at (202) 317-6901 (not toll-free numbers).

SUPPLEMENTARY INFORMATION:

Background

I. *Overview*

This document contains proposed amendments to the Income Tax Regulations (26 CFR part 1) under sections 481 and 1377 of the Internal Revenue Code (Code) and proposed regulations under section 1371 of the Code. Section 13543(a) and (b) of the Tax Cuts and Jobs Act, Public Law 115-97, 131 Stat. 2054, 2155 (2017) (TCJA), amended the Code to add subsection (d) to section 481, and subsection (f) to section 1371. Both section 481(d) and section 1371(f) are effective as of December 22, 2017.

II. *Summary of PTTP and ETSC Period*

Generally, a distribution by a C corporation to its shareholders with respect to their stock ownership is treated as a taxable dividend to the extent of the corporation's earnings and profits. See sections 301(c) and 316(a). However, following the termination of an S corporation's election made under section 1362 (S election), section 1371(e) allows shareholders of the resulting C corporation to benefit from the corporation's former status as an S corporation with respect to distributions of money during the corporation's PTTP, which is generally the one-year period after the S election terminates. Specifically, during the PTTP, a distribution of money by the C corporation is characterized as a distribution from the corporation's accumulated adjustments account (AAA), as defined in § 1.1368-2(a)(1). The receipt of such a distribution is tax-free to the extent of the recipient's basis in its stock with respect to which it received the distribution, and is taxed as gain from the sale of property to the extent the distribution exceeds the recipient's basis in that stock. If the corporation exhausts its AAA during the PTTP, then subsequent distributions are subject to treatment under section 301. Without section 1371(e), shareholders of the former S corporation would be precluded from receiving distributions allocable to AAA.

Section 1371(f) extends the period during which the shareholders of a C corporation can benefit from AAA generated during such corporation's former status as an S corporation (ETSC period) by allowing a C corporation's distribution of money to which section 301 would otherwise apply (qualified distribution) to be sourced, in whole or in part, from AAA. Specifically, section 1371(f) provides that (i) the distributing ETSC's AAA is allocated to a qualified distribution, and (ii) the qualified distribution is chargeable to accumulated earnings and profits (AE&P), in the same ratio as the amount of such AAA bears to the amount of such AE&P (clauses (i) and (ii), collectively, ETSC proration). In enacting section 1371(f), Congress determined that "it is important to provide rules to ease the transition from S corporation to C corporation for the affected taxpayers" because, based on TCJA revisions to the Code, "taxpayers that previously elected to be taxed as S corporations may prefer instead to be taxed as C corporations." H. Rept. 115-409, at 245 115th Cong. 1st Sess., (Nov. 14, 2017) (House Report).

Explanation of Provisions

I. *Requirements to Qualify for Section 1371(f) Treatment*

If a C corporation satisfies the ETSC qualification requirements, section 1371(f) provides special treatment for qualified distributions made by an ETSC during the ETSC period, which begins with the expiration of the PTTP and ends when the corporation exhausts its AAA.

A. ETSC Qualification Requirements

1. In General

In order for section 1371(f) to apply, the distributing corporation must be an ETSC. In conjunction with the enactment of section 1371(f), Congress enacted section 481(d), which includes the definition of an ETSC. Specifically, a C corporation qualifies as an ETSC if the following three requirements are satisfied. First, the corporation was an S corporation on December 21, 2017. Second, during the two-year period beginning on December 22, 2017, the S corporation revoked its S election (revocation requirement). Third, the owners of the stock of the corporation are the same owners (and in identical proportions) on December 22, 2017, and the date that the corporation made a revocation of its S election (shareholder identity requirement).

2. Revocation Requirement

In contrast to the PTTP, which applies regardless of how an S corporation's election terminates, section 1371(f) applies only if the S election is revoked (section 1362(d)(1)), which, under section 1362(d)(1)(B), requires the consent of shareholders holding more than 50 percent of the corporation's shares in the aggregate. Section 1362(d)(1) and its underlying regulations provide the sole means for an S corporation to revoke its S election. Pursuant to § 1.1362-6(a)(3), a valid revocation requires an S corporation to submit a written statement that the corporation revokes its S election. That revocation statement must set forth the number of shares of stock (including nonvoting stock) issued and outstanding at the time of the revocation and must be accompanied by a separate written statement of shareholder consent. See § 1.1362-6(a)(3)(i), (b).

Generally, a revocation made on or before the 15th day of the third month of a taxable year is effective on the first day of that year, and an election made after that date is effective on the first day of the following taxable year. See section 1362(d)(1)(C) and § 1.1362-2(a)(2)(i). However, if the revocation specifies a date for revocation that is on or after the day on which the revocation is made, the revocation becomes effective on that specified date. See section 1362(d)(1)(D) and §1.1362-2(a)(2)(ii). Therefore, under the proposed regulations, the revocation requirement would be satisfied if the revocation of an S election is validly made during the two-year period beginning on December 22, 2017, even if the effective date for the revocation occurs after the conclusion of that two-period.

3. Shareholder Identity Requirement

For a former S corporation to qualify as an ETSC, the owners of its stock must be the same owners (and in identical proportions) on the following two dates: (1) December 22, 2017, and (2) the date on which the S corporation made a revocation of its S election. However, certain events should not affect the shareholder identity requirement because such events would not change in substance the identity of the subject shareholder. Specifically, these proposed regulations identify five categories of stock transfers that do not result in an ownership change for purposes of section 481(d)(2)(B): (1) transfers of stock between a shareholder and that shareholder's trust treated as wholly owned by that shareholder under subpart E of subchapter J of chapter 1; (2) transfers of stock between a shareholder and an entity owned by the shareholder that is disregarded as separate from its owner under §301.7701-2(c)(2)(i) of the Procedure and Administration Regulations; (3) an election by a shareholder trust to be treated as part of a decedent's estate under section 645 or the termination of an election under that section; (4) a change in the status of a shareholder trust from one type of eligible S corporation shareholder trust described in section 1361(c)(2)(A) to another type of eligible S corporation shareholder trust; and (5) a transaction that includes more than one of the events described in (1) through (4).

While specifying transaction categories provides certainty to taxpayers, the Treasury Department and the IRS request comments regarding whether a principle-based rule would be more effective, as well as suggestions as to the rule's proposed operative language.

B. Requirement for Corporation to Have AAA

Section 1371(f) provides that AAA is allocated to a qualified distribution based on the ratio of AAA to AE&P. Thus, if an ETSC has no AAA, section 1371(f) has no application. In addition, as evidenced by the fact that Congress enacted section 1371(f) to ease the transition from S corporation status to C corporation status, the ETSC period is intended to be transitory in nature. Consequently, the Treasury Department and the IRS have determined that such a transition would naturally conclude once the C corporation's AAA balance reaches zero. In other words, an ETSC has an ETSC period only if the ETSC has a AAA balance greater than zero at the end of its PTTP, and the ETSC period ends immediately after the qualified distribution that causes the C corporation's AAA balance to reach zero.

C. Conclusion of PTTP; Multiple PTTPs

Section 1377(b)(1) provides that a PTTP occurs in the following three circumstances. First, a PTTP may occur during the period starting on the day after the last day of the corporation's last taxable year as an S corporation and ending on the later of (i) the day that is one year later or (ii) the due date for filing the return for such last year as an S corporation (including extensions). Second, a PTTP may occur during the 120-day period beginning on the date of any determination pursuant to an audit of a taxpayer that follows the termination of the corporation's election and adjusts a subchapter S item that arose during the S period (intervening audit PTTP). Third, a PTTP may occur during the 120-day period beginning on the date of a determination that the corporation's election under section 1362(a) had terminated for a previous taxable year.

Section 1371(f) applies to certain distributions "after the post-termination transition period." The Treasury Department and the IRS received a comment regarding intervening audit PTTPs and, accordingly, considered whether the ETSC period continues following an intervening audit PTTP that occurs during the ETSC period. Based on the overall purpose of these proposed regulations to ease the transition from S corporation status to C corporation status, the Treasury Department and the IRS have determined that the ETSC period should resume immediately following the conclusion of an intervening audit PTTP, if the ETSC continues to have a AAA balance greater than zero.

II. *Mechanics of Section 1371(f)*

A. Shareholders Eligible to Receive Qualified Distributions

By its terms, section 1371(f) does not require the recipients of qualified distributions to have been shareholders of the S corporation at the time of revocation, and no part of the House Report indicates a Congressional intent to impose such a limitation (no-newcomer rule) on such distributions. The Treasury Department and the IRS received a comment requesting guidance to clarify which shareholders are eligible to receive distributions from a corporation's AAA during the ETSC period. A no-newcomer rule would be inconsistent with Congressional intent to ease the transition of former S corporations to full C corporation status because such a no-newcomer rule would impede an ETSC's ability to exhaust its AAA. A no-newcomer rule also would impose an administrative burden on ETSCs and create complexity by requiring ETSCs to report distributions disparately depending on the recipient. See House Report at 245. Additionally, a rule allowing newcomers would be more consistent with treating the AAA as a corporate-level account.

In the absence of a no-newcomer rule, shareholders that were shareholders on the date that the corporation's S election revocation was made would continue to receive qualified distributions, whether or not there are new shareholders or changes in the historical S corporation shareholders' proportionate interests on or after such date. Moreover, new shareholders, whether eligible S corporation shareholders or not, that acquire stock of an ETSC on or after the date that the revocation was made may receive qualified distributions, all or a portion of which may be sourced from AAA. Such outcomes would best implement the plain language of section 1371(f) and the policy objective of easing the transition of affected taxpayers from S corporation status to C corporation status. Accordingly, these proposed regulations do not impose a no-newcomer rule with respect to the ETSC period.

B. Implementation of ETSC Proration

As discussed in Part II of the Background, section 1371(f) provides that (i) the distributing ETSC's AAA is allocated to a qualified distribution, and (ii) such qualified distribution is chargeable to the ETSC's AE&P, based on the ETSC proration. These proposed regulations would implement this provision in a manner designed to facilitate the ETSC's prompt distribution of AAA and full transition to C corporation status, and thereby "ease the transition from S corporation to C corporation for the affected taxpayers." House Report at 245. Grounded in that policy, these proposed regulations (i) specify the time at which amounts of AAA and AE&P are determined for purposes of the ETSC proration, (ii) clarify the AAA and AE&P ratios used to implement the ETSC proration, and (iii) describe in detail the method of characterizing qualified distributions.

1. When to Determine the Amounts of AAA and AE&P for Purposes of ETSC Proration

The Treasury Department and the IRS considered when to measure the AAA and AE&P for purposes of the ETSC proration. The Treasury Department and the IRS considered a "Snapshot Approach," under which the amounts of AAA and AE&P would be determined on a specified date (historical AAA and historical AE&P, respectively), resulting in the same ETSC proration being applied to all qualified distributions. The Treasury Department and the IRS also considered a "Dynamic Approach," under which the amounts of AAA and AE&P would be recalculated before each qualified distribution.

These proposed regulations adopt the Snapshot Approach, with a special additional rule to facilitate distributions of AAA when the ETSC's historical AE&P has been exhausted and the ETSC still has AAA. See Part II.C.1 of this Explanation of Provisions. The Snapshot Approach would provide affected taxpayers with an easier transition to full subchapter C status. Under this approach, ETSCs generally would be required to calculate AAA and AE&P for purposes of the ETSC proration only once, as opposed to numerous times under the Dynamic Approach. Also, the Dynamic Approach could significantly delay shareholder access to the ETSC's AAA. While the amount of an ETSC's AAA could never increase during the ETSC period (other than by reason of a redetermination of AAA), such ETSC's AE&P would increase as the amount of any undistributed current earnings and profits is carried forward to the next taxable year.

For the Snapshot Approach, the Treasury Department and the IRS considered two possible determination dates: (1) the beginning of the day for which the revocation of an election under section 1362(a) is effective pursuant to section 1362(d)(1), and (2) immediately after the end of the PTTP. Under these proposed regulations, the determination date would be the beginning of the day on which the revocation of an election under section 1362(a) is effective. Determining the amount of AAA on this date, which can be readily achieved by referencing the ETSC's final Form 1120S, would avoid the complexity of determining the proper amount of historical AAA in the event of an intervening audit PTTP for distributions made after the initial PTTP and before the intervening audit PTTP. In addition, the ETSC and its shareholders would have greater certainty during the PTTP as to the tax characterization of distributions to be made during the ETSC period under this approach. Reference to this determination date also would facilitate the receipt of AAA by the ETSC's shareholders as quickly as possible by maximizing the amount of AAA factored into the ETSC proration. Since S corporations with no subchapter C history will have no AE&P as of the beginning of the effective date of the revocation, using this determination date also would minimize the AE&P that is factored into the ETSC proration, as compared to determining AE&P immediately after the end of the PTTP. As a result, the use of this determination date would facilitate the corporation's transition to full subchapter C status.

The Treasury Department and the IRS request comments regarding the proposed regulations' adoption of the Snapshot Approach, in particular with respect to the timing of determining an ETSC's historical AAA and historical AE&P amounts, and whether such amounts should be adjusted by certain transactions, as well as any potential alternative approaches for computing the ETSC proration. For example, the Treasury Department and the IRS acknowledge that not all ETSCs may favor the approach with respect to timing that these proposed regulations adopt. In particular, an ETSC that makes no distributions of AAA and operates at a loss during its PTTP may prefer to determine its AAA and AE&P ratios immediately after the end of the PTTP. Determining the ratios on this later date would result in a lower historical AE&P amount, and therefore the percentage of the qualified distribution that could be characterized as a distribution of AAA would be greater when compared to the approach adopted by these proposed regulations.

2. ETSC Proration Based on Ratios Composed of Historical AAA and Historical AE&P

Section 1371(f) provides that AAA is allocated to a qualified distribution, and such distribution is chargeable to AE&P, in the same ratio as the amount of such AAA bears to the amount of such AE&P. Therefore, section 1371(f) requires an allocation of two distinct pools of an ETSC's historical earnings with respect to a qualified distribution (that is, AAA and AE&P). In order to clarify the calculation of AAA and AE&P allocated to qualified distributions, these proposed regulations provide two ratios for purposes of characterizing the portion of a qualified distribution that is sourced from AAA (AAA ratio) and from AE&P (AE&P ratio).

The numerator and denominator of the AAA ratio and the AE&P ratio are comprised of two factors: the ETSC's historical AAA and its historical AE&P. An ETSC's AAA ratio would be the fraction of which the numerator is its historical AAA, and the denominator is the sum of its historical AAA and its historical AE&P. An ETSC's AE&P ratio would be the fraction of which the numerator is its historical AE&P, and the denominator is the sum of its historical AAA and its historical AE&P. Generally, the amount of a qualified distribution sourced from AAA would be determined by multiplying the amount of the qualified distribution by the ETSC's AAA ratio. A parallel computation would be undertaken to determine the amount that is sourced from AE&P. Part II.C of this Explanation of Provisions describes the rules relating to the application of the ETSC proration to qualified distributions in greater detail.

3. Coordinating ETSC Proration with Sections 301 and 316

In constructing the mechanics of the ETSC proration, the Treasury Department and the IRS sought to harmonize the rules set forth in section 1371(f) with the general section 301(c) characterization and section 316 allocation rules that govern distributions by a C corporation with respect to its stock. Generally, a distribution by a C corporation with respect to its stock is characterized as a dividend (as defined in section 316), then as a return of stock basis, and finally any remaining amount as gain from the sale or exchange of property. See sections 301(a) and (c). In defining a dividend, section 316 provides that "every distribution is made out of earnings and profits to the extent thereof, and from the most recently accumulated earnings and profits." Section 316(a)(2) (flush language). Section 1.316-2(a) provides that "[i]n determining the source of a distribution, consideration should be given first[] to the earnings and profits of the taxable year . . . ." Section 1.316-2(b) further provides that, if distributions during the taxable year consist only of money and exceed the amount of the C corporation's current earnings and profits (CE&P) for the taxable year, CE&P is allocated proportionately to such distributions, while AE&P is allocated on a "first-come-first-served" basis.

Section 1371(f), however, provides special rules with respect to qualified distributions that depart from the general section 301(c) characterization and section 316 allocation rules. From the perspective of sections 301 and 316, 1371(f) is thus an exception to those provisions. See section 301(a) (providing an exception for provisions contained in chapter 1 of subtitle A of title 26 of the Code); section 316(a) (providing an exception for provisions contained in subtitle A of title 26 of the Code). Specifically, section 1371(f) provides that, instead of characterizing a qualified distribution as a dividend as defined in section 316, first AAA "shall be allocated to such [qualified] distribution, and the [qualified] distribution shall be chargeable to [AE&P], in the same ratio as the amount of such [AAA] bears to the amount of such [AE&P]." The allocation of AAA ahead of CE&P, and the allocation of AE&P to a distribution ahead of CE&P, depart from the general characterization rules of section 301 and the general section 316 allocation rules

The Treasury Department and the IRS are aware that this special AE&P allocation rule could impact the normal allocation of AE&P, as well as CE&P, to non-qualified distributions by an ETSC, if an ETSC makes non-qualified and qualified distributions during the same taxable year. For example, the following could result when an ETSC makes a non-qualified distribution followed by a qualified distribution during its taxable year. First, the non-qualified distribution could be allocated an amount of AE&P less than the amount that otherwise would be required under the general section 316 allocation rules, because section 1371(f) would require that a portion of the ETSC's AE&P be allocated instead to the "later-in-time" qualified distribution. Second, because section 1371(f) would cause the "earlier-in-time" non-qualified distribution to be allocated a reduced amount of AE&P, the non-qualified distribution could be characterized differently than it otherwise would have been characterized absent section 1371(f) (that is, a characterization described in section 301(c)(2) or section 301(c)(3), rather than section 301(c)(1)).

With regard to the predictable impacts on the treatment and characterization of non-qualified distributions that result from Congress' specific inclusion of AE&P in section 1371(f)'s AAA allocation methodology, the Treasury Department and the IRS have determined that the exceptions set forth in sections 301(a) and 316(a) naturally extend to such consequences as well. Based on the language of these Code sections, as well as Congress' objective to ease affected taxpayers' transition from S corporation status to C corporation status, the proposed regulations provide a special sourcing rule (Section 1371(f) Priority Rule) for qualified distributions, as described in detail in Part II.C of this Explanation of Provisions.

C. Character and Effect of Distributions during the ETSC Period

The Section 1371(f) Priority Rule essentially provides that, during the ETSC period, the rules of the ETSC proration under section 1371(f) apply before the rules of section 301 and 316. Thus, under the Section 1371(f) Priority rule, the ETSC proration first applies to qualified distributions during the taxable year. Then, the rules of section 301 and 316, as incorporated into the Section 1371(f) Priority Rule, apply to any non-qualified distributions as well as to any qualified distributions or portions thereof that are not fully accounted for by the ETSC proration (i.e., because the corporation's AAA or AE&P are exhausted during the year).

The Treasury Department and the IRS acknowledge that the application of the Section 1371(f) Priority Rule, as set forth in these proposed regulations, departs from the allocation and characterization rules under sections 301 and 316 with which taxpayers and practitioners are familiar. The departure is greatest when an ETSC has both historical AAA and historical AE&P and makes both qualified and non-qualified distributions during the same taxable year. For ETSCs with historical AAA but no historical AE&P, which the Treasury Department and the IRS believe will be the most common situation, the departure is less significant and is the same as the departure that section 1371(e) requires for distributions of AAA during the PTTP. Immediately following the end of the taxable year in which the ETSC period ends, which occurs when the ETSC's AAA balance is reduced to zero, the normal rules of section 301 and section 316 apply as usual to all distributions. These proposed regulations are expected to generally reduce the length of the ETSC period and thus reduce the time during which the departure from the normal rules of sections 301 and 316 occurs.

The following summary provides a reference to taxpayers and practitioners for applying the Section 1371(f) Priority Rule to qualified and non-qualified distributions made during the taxable years of the ETSC period, including the taxable year in which the ETSC period ends.

1. Determination of the AAA Ratio and the AE&P Ratio

The Section 1371(f) Priority Rule applies the ETSC proration to each qualified distribution. To determine the ETSC proration, the AAA ratio and the AE&P ratio must first be calculated. An ETSC's AAA ratio is the fraction of which the numerator is its historical AAA and the denominator is the sum of its historical AAA and historical AE&P. Likewise, an ETSC's AE&P ratio is the fraction of which the numerator is its historical AE&P, and the denominator is the sum of its historical AAA and historical AE&P.

In general, the AAA ratio and the AE&P ratio do not change over the course of the ETSC period. However, if the application of the AE&P ratio to a qualified distribution reduces the ETSC's AE&P to zero, and the ETSC's historical AAA has not been exhausted, then the AAA ratio is one and the AE&P ratio is zero for the remainder of the year and all subsequent taxable years of the ETSC period. Additionally, if the ETSC's AE&P (which includes its historical AE&P) is less than or equal to zero as of the beginning of a taxable year (for example, due to non-qualified distributions or losses incurred during the prior taxable year) and the ETSC's historical AAA has not been exhausted, then the AAA ratio is one and the AE&P ratio is zero for the year and all subsequent taxable years of the ETSC period. These mechanics are responsive to the exhaustion of the ETSC's historical AE&P, and therefore accelerate the distribution of AAA by permitting the entirety of all subsequent qualified distributions to be sourced from the ETSC's AAA.

2. *Identification of Qualified and Non-Qualified Distributions during Taxable Year*

Application of the Section 1371(f) Priority Rule depends, in part, upon whether a distribution by an ETSC is a qualified or non-qualified distribution. As a result, for each taxable year of an ETSC, each distribution must be characterized as a qualified distribution or a non-qualified distribution before determining the characterization of such distribution under the Section 1371(f) Priority Rule.

3. Characterization and Consequences of Qualified Distributions

For each taxable year of the ETSC period, including the taxable year in which the ETSC period ends, the characterization of each qualified distribution must be determined prior to the characterization of each non-qualified distribution. The portion of a qualified distribution that is sourced from AAA is equal to the lesser of (i) the product of the qualified distribution and the AAA ratio, and (ii) the ETSC's AAA immediately before the qualified distribution. Such AAA-sourced portion of the qualified distribution reduces both the ETSC's AAA and the shareholder's adjusted stock basis, applying the principles of section 301(c)(2). If the amount of that AAA-sourced portion exceeds the shareholder's stock basis, the excess is treated as gain from the sale or exchange of property, regardless of whether the corporation has CE&P or AE&P available. If the amount sourced from AAA equals the balance of the ETSC's AAA before the qualified distribution, all subsequent distributions by the ETSC are treated in the manner provided in section 301(c). If the amount sourced from AAA is less than that balance, then any remaining AAA is available to be allocated to later qualified distributions during the taxable year. If any AAA remains after all qualified distributions for the taxable year have been accounted for, it is carried forward to the next taxable year of the ETSC.

The portion of a qualified distribution that is charged to AE&P is equal to the lesser of (i) the product of the qualified distribution and the AE&P ratio, and (ii) the ETSC's AE&P immediately before the qualified distribution. The ETSC's AE&P is reduced by the charged amount in accordance with section 312(a)(1). The ETSC's AE&P is reduced by the portion of the qualified distribution chargeable to AE&P prior to the application of the rules of sections 301 and 316, as incorporated into the Section 1371(f) Priority Rule, to any non-qualified distribution, regardless of whether the non-qualified distribution occurred prior to the qualified distribution. The amount of the qualified distribution that is charged to the ETSC's AE&P is included in the gross income of the shareholder as a dividend under section 301(c)(1).

4. Application of ETSC proration to excess qualified distributions

Any portion of a qualified distribution that is not initially accounted for by the ETSC proration is referred to as an "excess qualified distribution." An excess qualified distribution arises when the ETSC no longer has AAA, AE&P, or both after initially applying the ETSC proration. If the initial application of the ETSC proration to a qualified distribution does not fully account for the amount of the distribution and the ETSC continues to have AAA, the Section 1371(f) Priority Rule requires that the ETSC proration be reapplied to the excess qualified distribution as if the excess qualified distribution were a separate qualified distribution using a AAA ratio of one and an AE&P ratio of zero. See Part II.C.1 of this Explanation of Provisions.

5. Characterization and Consequences of Non-Qualified Distributions and Excess Qualified Distributions

The Section 1371(f) Priority Rule requires non-qualified distributions and excess qualified distributions (to the extent not characterized as a distribution of AAA) to be treated in the manner described in section 301(c). The Section 1371(f) Priority Rule requires that such treatment take into account the treatment of each non-qualified distribution and each excess qualified distribution made by the ETSC during the same taxable year.

6. Requests for Comments

The Treasury Department and the IRS evaluated several other approaches to implementing section 1371(f) and the rules that would be needed to coordinate those approaches with the rules of sections 301 and 316 before settling on the approach adopted in the Section 1371(f) Priority Rule. The Treasury Department and the IRS request comments regarding the advantages and disadvantages of the Section 1371(f) Priority Rule as well as other proposals that would help ease the transition of S corporation status to C corporation status. The Treasury Department and the IRS also request comments regarding the effect of section 381(a) transactions in which an ETSC is either the transferor or the acquiring corporation (including certain triangular acquisitions) as well as the effect of an ETSC electing to file a consolidated return or joining a consolidated group. The Treasury Department and the IRS further request comments on the effect of subchapter C transactions (including section 302(a) redemptions, section 355 transactions, and section 368 reorganizations) and the effect of a deemed distribution (including forgiveness of shareholder debt) on the ETSC's AAA balance.

III. *Amendment of § 1.316-2 to Clarify Allocation of CE&P to Non-Cash Distributions*

Section 316(a) provides that a dividend is a distribution of property made by a corporation to its shareholders out of its CE&P or AE&P, or both. Pursuant to § 1.316-2(a), in determining the source of a distribution under section 316(a), a corporation must first source the distribution from its CE&P before sourcing such distribution from AE&P. If the corporation's CE&P is sufficient to cover "all the distributions" made during the taxable year, then the entirety of each distribution is taxable as a dividend pursuant to the first sentence of § 1.316-2(b). If a corporation's distributions during the taxable year consist "only of money" and exceed CE&P, each distribution is allocated its ratable share of CE&P pursuant to the second sentence of § 1.316-2(b).

The reference to distributions that "consist only of money" has been in the second sentence of § 1.316-2(b) since that regulation was adopted in 1955. Section 1.316-2 was adopted shortly after the enactment of the Internal Revenue Code of 1954 (1954 Code), which contained several provisions relating to distributions of noncash property. A number of these provisions have since changed. In particular, section 311 of the 1954 Code provided that a distributing corporation generally did not recognize any gain or loss on the distribution of noncash property, and section 312 of the 1954 Code provided that the distributing corporation generally reduced its earnings and profits by the adjusted basis of the property distributed. At the same time, section 301(b) of the 1954 Code provided that the amount of a distribution of noncash property to a shareholder depended on the type of shareholder. Individual shareholders were treated as receiving a distribution equal to the fair market value of the property, while corporate shareholders were generally treated as receiving a distribution equal to the lesser of the property's fair market value or the distributing corporation's adjusted basis in the asset distributed. In light of these provisions, the 1955 promulgation of § 1.316-2 illustrated the consequences of the allocation of CE&P in the simplest fact pattern — when the distributions consist only of money.

Under current law, however, a distributing corporation recognizes gain on a section 301 distribution of appreciated noncash property. See section 311. The amount of a distribution of noncash property for purposes of shareholder taxation equals the property's fair market value, irrespective of whether the shareholder is an individual or a corporation. Additionally, section 316(a)(2) makes no distinction between distributions in cash and distributions of other property under section 301. Section 317(a), which section 301 cross-references for purposes of defining property, includes money, securities, and any other property, except a distributing corporation's own stock. Accordingly, the Treasury Department and the IRS do not believe that the language in the second sentence of § 1.316-2(b) should be interpreted as implying that under current law the application of the pro rata allocation rule for CE&P is limited to distributions made only in money. Cf. GCM 36138 (Jan. 15, 1975) (noting that "[section] 316(a)(2) makes no qualitative distinction between distributions in cash and other distributions of property under [section] 301," and "[t]hus, there is no basis under [section] 316(a)(2) for limiting the application of the rules under [§]1.316-2(b) to distributions made solely in money"). Therefore, in order to clarify that the pro rata allocation of CE&P applies to all section 301 distributions made during the taxable year, whether in cash or in kind, the proposed regulations would remove the words "consist only of money and" from the second sentence of paragraph (b).

IV. *Amendment of § 1.1377-2 to Allow for New Shareholders during the PTTP*

The last sentence of § 1.1377-2(b) limits the special treatment provided under section 1371(e)(1) (that is, the PTTP) solely to those shareholders who were shareholders of the S corporation at the time of termination or revocation of its S election. Because the rules pertaining to the PTTP and to the ETSC period serve the similar objective of easing the transition from S corporation status to C corporation status, the Treasury Department and the IRS have determined that these rules regarding newcomers should be consistent. Therefore, based on the rationale for rejecting a no-newcomer rule for the ETSC period, as set forth in Part II.A of this Explanation of Provisions, the Treasury Department and the IRS have determined that a no-newcomer rule should also not apply to the PTTP. The Treasury Department and the IRS request comments regarding this determination.

Proposed Applicability Dates

The regulations are proposed to apply to taxable years beginning after the date of publication of the Treasury decision adopting these regulations as final regulations in the **Federal Register**. However, the proposed regulations provide corporations with the option to apply the final rules in §§ 1.316-2, 1.481-5, 1.1371-1, 1.1371-2, and 1.1377-2 in their entirety, to the extent applicable, to taxable years that began on or before the date of publication of a Treasury decision adopting these rules as final regulations in the **Federal Register** and with respect to which the period described in section 6511(a) has not expired. If the corporation makes the choice described in the previous sentence, all shareholders of the corporation must report consistently.

Special Analyses

This regulation is not subject to review under section 6(b) of Executive Order 12866 pursuant to the Memorandum of Agreement (April 11, 2018) between the Treasury Department and the Office of Management and Budget regarding review of tax regulations.

I. *Regulatory Flexibility Act*

Pursuant to the Regulatory Flexibility Act (5 U.S.C. chapter 6), it is hereby certified that these proposed regulations under sections 481(d), 1371(f), and 1377 of the Code will not have a significant economic impact on a substantial number of small entities within the meaning of section 601(6) of the Regulatory Flexibility Act. Notwithstanding this certification, the Treasury Department and the IRS invite comments on the impact that these proposed regulations would have on small entities.

These proposed regulations generally affect corporations, and their shareholders, that convert from being taxed as an S corporation to being taxed as a C corporation. The Treasury Department and the IRS acknowledge that there is a substantial number of small entities that are S corporations that could convert to being taxed as a C corporation. According to the 2013 Corporate Income Tax Returns Complete Report (https://www.irs.gov/pub/irs-soi/13coccr.pdf), approximately 83 percent of S corporations had gross receipts under $1,000,000. However, the proposed regulations under section 1371(f) are limited to corporations that:

  (i) Revoke their S elections;

 (ii) Make their revocations during a specified two-year period beginning on December 22, 2017;

(iii) Have positive AAA at the conclusion of their PTTP; and

(iv) Have the same shareholders (and in identical proportions) on December 22, 2017, and the date the S election revocation is made (shareholder identity requirement).

Because these proposed regulations apply only to those S corporations that satisfy the criteria above, only a small subset of S corporations will be affected.

The U.S. Department of Treasury, Internal Revenue Service, Data Book 2018 (Data Book) (https://www.irs.gov/pub/irs-soi/18databk.pdf) reports that the IRS received approximately 5.1 million S corporation income tax returns in 2018. According to the Compliance Data Warehouse (CDW), between January 1, 2018, and December 31, 2018, 4,850 S corporations terminated their S elections. Of the 4,850 terminated S corporations:

(i) 286 corporations had more than $35 million in gross receipts;

(ii) 81 corporations had between $25-$35 million in gross receipts;

(iii) 161 corporations had between $15-$25 million in gross receipts; and

(iv) 3,011 corporations had less than $15 million, but at least $1 in gross receipts.

In addition, of those 4,850 terminated S corporations:

(i) 694 corporations reported no gross receipts; and

(ii) The remaining 617 did not file a final return after terminating their S election.

A revocation is one of the three methods by which a corporation may terminate its S election under section 1362(d). Proposed §§ 1.481-5, 1.1371-1, and 1.1371-2 apply only to those corporations that revoke their S election. The CDW does not identify how many of the 4,850 terminations were revocations. In the unlikely scenario that all 4,850 terminations were revocations, approximately 0.0951 percent of the 5.1 million S corporations in existence in 2018 may be affected by these proposed regulations. Extrapolating from the first-year data (January 1, 2018, to December 31, 2018) to the second half of the two-year period (January 1, 2019, to December 21, 2019) during which these proposed regulations are effective, it is possible another 4,850 former S corporations could be affected by these proposed regulations. Thus, these proposed regulations might only affect a total of 9,700 corporations. Assuming that the IRS again receives 5.1 million S corporation income tax returns for the 2019 tax year, these proposed regulations may affect approximately 0.1902 percent of all S corporations in existence in 2018 and 2019. The exact number may be lower because not all terminations are revocations, and a revocation only satisfies one of several criteria that cause these proposed regulations to be applicable. For these proposed regulations to be applicable, the corporation must also have a positive AAA balance at the conclusion of its PTTP and satisfy the shareholder identity requirement. Therefore, the number of affected corporations is likely to be lower.

The other proposed regulation in this notice of proposed rulemaking, proposed § 1.1377-2(b), generally applies to a corporation that terminates its S election with a positive AAA balance, regardless of when or how the termination occurs (see section 1362(d)). As a result, the change made by proposed regulation § 1.1377-2(b) to allow newcomer shareholders will affect a greater number of terminating S corporations than proposed regulation §§ 1.481-5, 1.1371-1, and 1.1371-2. Nevertheless, the number of corporations that terminate their S election remains minimal. According to the CDW, there were 2,798 S corporation terminations in 2015; 2,960 in 2016; 3,125 in 2017; and 4,850 in 2018. When comparing the number of terminating S corporations to the number of S corporation income tax returns filed each year, only a small fraction of S corporations will be affected.

In addition, based on published information from the Conference Report accompanying the Act, H.R. Rep. No. 115-446, at 688 (2017), and Bureau of Economic Analysis aggregate data, which were adjusted to reflect the tax burden of small businesses, the projected net tax proceeds from sections 481(d), 1371(f), and 1377 are estimated to affect only a small fraction of the total number of S corporations.

The Treasury Department and the IRS have determined that no additional burden will be associated with these proposed regulations. In particular, the collection of information necessary to comply with these proposed regulations is already required to be collected by previously existing statutory and regulatory requirements. Additionally, these proposed regulations apply only if an S corporation revokes its S election between December 22, 2017 and December 21, 2019, fulfills the shareholder identity requirement, and has a positive AAA balance at the conclusion of its PTTP. The proposed removal of § 1.1377-2(b)'s last sentence would reduce a taxpayer's compliance burden by eliminating the need to track shareholders during the PTTP.

For the reasons explained above, the Treasury Department and the IRS have determined that the final regulations will not have a significant economic impact on a substantial number of small entities. Pursuant to section 7805(f), the notice of proposed rulemaking will be submitted to the Chief Counsel for Advocacy of the Small Business Administration for comment on its impact on small business.

II. Paperwork Reduction Act

These proposed regulations do not require collection of any new or additional information pursuant to the Paperwork Reduction Act (PRA) (44 U.S.C. 3501 et seq.).

The Treasury Department and the IRS intend that the information necessary to apply these proposed regulations will be collected with the following forms that have been previously reviewed and approved by the Office of Management and Budget (OMB) under the PRA:

(i) Form 1120-S, U.S. Income Tax Return for an S Corporation (OMB Control Number 1545-0123);

(ii) Schedule K-1 (Form 1120-S), Shareholder's Share of Income, Deductions, Credits, etc. (OMB Control Number 1545-0123);

(iii) Form 1120, U.S. Corporation Income Tax Return (OMB Control Number 1545-0123);

(iv) Form 5452, Corporate Report of Nondividend Distributions (OMB Control Number 1545-0123); and

(v) Form 1099-DIV, Dividends and Distributions (OMB Control Number 1545-0110).

Section 1362(e) requires a corporation that revoked or terminated its S election to file a return for its last taxable year as an S corporation on Form 1120-S. This filing requirement includes an eligible terminated S corporation (ETSC). Section 6037(b) and the regulations thereunder require every S corporation to maintain certain information, such as its shareholders' names, addresses, and other identifying information throughout the taxable year, in order to furnish its shareholders with the information necessary to complete their return (in other words, Schedule K-1). Because sections 1366(a) and 1377(a)(1) allocate an S corporation's items of income and loss to shareholders on a per-share, per-day basis, every S corporation effectively tracks its shareholders, and their respective ownership percentages, on a daily basis. The information that every S corporation currently collects to comply with the existing requirements of sections 1366(a), 1377(a)(1), and 6037(b) will be used to determine whether a corporation satisfies the shareholder identity requirement of proposed § 1.481-5(b)(3).

Any corporation that qualifies as an ETSC will refer to Schedule M-2 of its last filed Form 1120-S to calculate each of its AAA and AE&P ratios, within the meaning of proposed § 1.1371-1(a)(2)(vii), to determine its historical AAA and historical AE&P amounts. If an ETSC enters a closing agreement pursuant to a subsequent audit, it will adjust its historical AAA and historical AE&P amounts accordingly.

At the beginning of a corporation's ETSC period, an ETSC will also refer to Schedule M-2 of its last filed Form 1120-S to determine the balance of its accumulated adjustments account (AAA) at the end of its last tax year as an S corporation. If an ETSC makes no cash distributions during its post-termination transition period (PTTP), within the meaning of section 1377(b)(1)(A), then it will start its ETSC period with a AAA balance equal to the amount reported as the AAA balance at the end of the tax year on Schedule M-2 of its last filed Form 1120-S. If an ETSC makes cash distributions during its PTTP, then it will start its ETSC period with a AAA balance equal to the difference between the amount reported as the AAA balance at the end of the tax year on Schedule M-2 of its last filed Form 1120-S and the amount of cash distributions that the ETSC made during its PTTP.

Every domestic C corporation must file an income tax return on Form 1120, and attach Form 5452 if it makes a nondividend distribution to its shareholders. In particular, the instructions for Form 5452 require any corporation that makes a distribution under section 1371(f) to file a Form

5452. In any tax year in which an ETSC makes a qualified distribution, it is required to attach Form 5452 and report its AAA balance, the amount of AE&P at the beginning of the tax year, the amount of CE&P for the current tax year, and the amounts paid during the calendar year from earnings and profits and from "other than earnings and profits." The information collected through Form 5452 is sufficient for an ETSC to apply these proposed regulations. In particular, the information collected through Form 5452 is sufficient for an ETSC to determine its AAA balance both before and after each qualified distribution, as well as determine the impact that each qualified distribution has on its CE&P and AE&P.

With respect to shareholders of ETSC stock, an ETSC is required (like any C corporation that makes a distribution to its shareholders) to provide a statement to its non-corporate recipient shareholders that reports the amounts characterized as a dividend and nondividend distribution on Form 1099-DIV. Form 1099-DIV will inform an ETSC's shareholders of the amount that constitutes a dividend subject to section 301(c)(1) and the amount that constitutes a nondividend distribution. Distributions allocable to AAA will be reported to recipient shareholders as a nondividend distribution. The Treasury Department and the IRS do not anticipate modifying the scope of the information gathered on the aforementioned forms.

Modest burden estimate revisions are anticipated for proposed regulations under § 1.1377-2. Specifically, the proposed removal of § 1.1377-2(b)'s last sentence would reduce a taxpayer's collection burden by eliminating the need to track shareholders during the PTTP. Changes to these burden estimates will be made in accordance with the PRA in the annual review procedure for information collections under OMB Control Number 1545-0123.

These proposed regulations are estimated to affect a total of 9,700 corporations, or 0.1902% of all S corporations in existence in 2018 and 2019. Regarding proposed regulations §§ 1.481-5, 1.481-6, 1.1371-2, and 1.1371-3, the exact number might be lower because the 9,700 is extrapolated from data and projections of S corporation terminations, not the subset revocations, and to qualify as an ETSC the corporation must also have a positive AAA balance at the conclusion of its PTTP and satisfy the shareholder identity requirement.

An agency may not conduct or sponsor, and a person is not required to respond to, a collection of information unless it displays a valid control number assigned by the OMB.

III. *Unfunded Mandates Reform Act*

Section 202 of the Unfunded Mandates Reform Act of 1995 requires that agencies assess anticipated costs and benefits and take certain other actions before issuing a final rule that includes any Federal mandate that may result in expenditures in any one year by a state, local, or tribal government, in the aggregate, or by the private sector, of $100 million in 1995 dollars, updated annually for inflation. In 2019, that threshold is approximately $164 million. This rule does not include any mandate that may result in expenditures by state, local, or tribal governments, or by the private sector in excess of that threshold.

IV. *Executive Order 13132: Federalism*

Executive Order 13132 (entitled "Federalism") prohibits an agency from publishing any rule that has federalism implications if the rule either imposes substantial, direct compliance costs on state and local governments, and is not required by statute, or preempts state law, unless the agency meets the consultation and funding requirements of section 6 of the Executive Order. This rule does not have federalism implications and does not impose substantial, direct compliance costs on state and local governments or preempt state law within the meaning of the Executive Order.

Comments and Public Hearing

Before these proposed regulations are adopted as final regulations, consideration will be given to any comments that are submitted timely to the IRS as prescribed in this preamble under the **ADDRESSES** section. The Treasury Department and the IRS request comments on all aspects of the proposed rules, and specifically on the issues identified in Part I.A.3; in Parts II.B.1 and II.C.6; and in Part IV of this Explanations of Provisions section. All comments will be made available at http://www.regulations.gov or upon request. A public hearing will be scheduled if requested in writing by any person that timely submits written comments. If a public hearing is scheduled, then notice of the date, time, and place for the public hearing will be published in the **Federal Register**.

Drafting Information

The principal authors of these proposed regulations are Margaret Burow and Michael Gould of the Office of Associate Chief Counsel (Passthroughs and Special Industries), and Aglaia Ovtchinnikova and Kevin M. Jacobs of the Office of Associate Chief Counsel (Corporate). However, other personnel from the IRS and the Treasury Department participated in the development of the proposed regulations.

[¶ 49,819] Proposed Amendments of Regulations (REG-132210-18), published in the Federal Register on November 8, 2019.

[Code Sec. 401]

Life expectancy: Distribution period tables: Retirement plans: Individual retirement account (IRA): Distributions.—Amendments of Reg. §§ 1.401(a)(9)-5, 1.401(a)(9)-6, 1.401(a)(9)-8 and 1.401(a)(9)-9, relating to the life expectancy and distribution period tables that are used to calculate required minimum distributions from qualified retirement plans, individual retirement accounts and annuities, and certain other tax-favored employer-provided retirement arrangements, are proposed.

AGENCY: Internal Revenue Service (IRS), Treasury.

ACTION: Notice of proposed rulemaking; notice of public hearing.

SUMMARY: This document sets forth proposed regulations providing guidance relating to the life expectancy and distribution period tables that are used to calculate required minimum distributions from qualified retirement plans, individual retirement accounts and annuities, and certain other tax-favored employer-provided retirement arrangements. These regulations affect participants, beneficiaries, and plan administrators of these qualified retirement plans and other tax-favored employer-provided retirement arrangements, as well as owners, beneficiaries, trustees and custodians of individual retirement accounts and annuities. This document also provides a notice of a public hearing on these proposed regulations.

DATES: Written or electronic comments must be received by January 7, 2020. Outlines of topics to be discussed at the public hearing scheduled for January 23, 2020, must be received by January 7, 2020.

ADDRESSES: Submit electronic submissions via the Federal eRulemaking Portal at www.regulations.gov (indicate IRS and REG-132210-18) by following the online instructions for submitting comments. Once submitted to the Federal eRulemaking Portal, comments cannot be edited or withdrawn. The Department of the Treasury (Treasury Department) and the IRS will publish for public availability any comment received to its public docket, whether submitted electronically or in hard copy. Send hard copy submissions to: CC:PA:LPD:PR (REG-132210-18), Room 5203, Internal Revenue Service, P.O. Box 7604, Ben Franklin Station, Washington, DC 20044. Submissions may be hand-delivered Monday through Friday

between the hours of 8 a.m. and 4 p.m. to CC:PA:LPD:PR (REG-132210-18), Courier's Desk, Internal Revenue Service, 1111 Constitution Avenue NW, Washington, DC 20224.

FOR FURTHER INFORMATION CONTACT: Concerning the proposed regulations, Arslan Malik or Linda S. F. Marshall, (202) 317-6700; concerning submissions of comments and requests to speak at the public hearing, Regina Johnson, (202) 317-6901 (not toll-free numbers).

SUPPLEMENTARY INFORMATION

Background

This document includes proposed amendments to the Income Tax Regulations (26 CFR part 1) under section 401(a)(9) of the Internal Revenue Code (Code) regarding the requirement to take required minimum distributions from qualified trusts. These proposed regulations also apply with respect to the corresponding requirements for individual retirement accounts and annuities described in section 408(a) and (b), and eligible deferred compensation plans under section 457, as well as section 403(a) and 403(b) annuity contracts, custodial accounts, and retirement income accounts.

Section 401(a)(9) provides rules regarding minimum required distributions from qualified retirement plans. The purpose of section 401(a)(9) is to ensure that the favorable tax treatment afforded a qualified plan is used primarily to provide retirement income to a participant and a designated beneficiary, rather than to increase the estate of a participant. Accordingly, section 401(a)(9) provides that a qualified plan must commence benefits to an employee no later than a specified age (or within a specified number of years after the employee's death) and, under the regulations, once benefits commence, the pattern of payment must meet certain standards to ensure that distributions are not unduly deferred.

Section 401(a)(9)(A) provides rules for distributions during the life of the employee. Section 401(a)(9)(A)(ii) provides that the entire interest of an employee in a qualified plan must be distributed, beginning not later than the employee's required beginning date, in accordance with regulations, over the life of the employee or over the lives of the employee and a designated beneficiary (or over a period not extending beyond the life expectancy of the employee and a designated beneficiary).

Section 401(a)(9)(B) provides rules for distributions that are made after the death of the employee. Section 401(a)(9)(B)(i) provides that, if the employee dies after distributions have begun, the employee's interest must be distributed at least as rapidly as under the method used by the employee. Section 401(a)(9)(B)(ii) and (iii) provide that, if the employee dies before distributions have begun, the employee's interest must be either (1) Distributed (in accordance with regulations) over the life or life expectancy of the designated beneficiary with the distributions beginning no later than 1 year after the date of the employee's death, or (2) distributed within 5 years after the death of the employee. However, under section 401(a)(9)(B)(iv), a surviving spouse may wait until the date the employee would have attained age 70¹/₂ to begin receiving required minimum distributions.

Section 401(a)(9)(C) defines the term *required beginning date* for employees (other than 5-percent owners and IRA owners) as April 1 of the calendar year following the later of the calendar year in which the employee attains age 70¹/₂ or the calendar year in which the employee retires. For 5-percent owners and IRA owners, the required beginning date is April 1 of the calendar year following the calendar year in which the employee attains age 70¹/₂, even if the employee has not retired.

Section 401(a)(9)(D) provides that, except in the case of a life annuity, the life expectancy of an employee and the employee's spouse that is used to determine the period over which payments must be made may be re-determined, but not more frequently than annually.

Section 401(a)(9)(E) provides that the term *designated beneficiary* means any individual designated as a beneficiary by the employee.

Section 401(a)(9)(G) provides that any distribution required to satisfy the incidental death benefit requirement of section 401(a)[1] is a required minimum distribution.

Under sections 403(b)(10), 408(a)(6),[2] and 457(d)(2), requirements similar to the requirements of section 401(a)(9) apply to a number of types of retirement arrangements other than qualified plans. Pursuant to sections 403(a)(1) and 404(a)(2), qualified annuity plans must also comply with the requirements of section 401(a)(9).

Comprehensive rules regarding the application of section 401(a)(9) are set forth in §§ 1.401(a)(9)-1 through 8. In the case of a defined contribution plan, § 1.401(a)(9)-5 provides generally that an individual's required minimum distribution for a distribution calendar year is determined by dividing the individual's account balance determined under § 1.401(a)(9)-5, Q&A-3, by the applicable distribution period. Under § 1.401(a)(9)-5, Q&A-1(b), a distribution calendar year is a calendar year for which a minimum distribution is required. For example, if a 5-percent owner participating in a qualified plan attained age 70¹/₂ during August of 2018 (so that the required beginning date was April 1, 2019), then the first distribution calendar year was 2018, and the required minimum distribution for that year was based on the applicable distribution period for a 70-year-old individual for 2018 (even though it could have been paid at any time from January 1, 2018 through April 1, 2019).

Pursuant to § 1.401(a)(9)-5, Q&A-4(a), for required minimum distributions during the employee's lifetime (including the year in which the employee dies), the applicable distribution period for an employee is the distribution period for the employee's age under the Uniform Lifetime Table (which is equal to the joint and last survivor life expectancy for the employee and a hypothetical beneficiary 10 years younger). However, pursuant to § 1.401(a)(9)-5, Q&A-4(b), if an employee's sole beneficiary is the employee's surviving spouse and the spouse is more than 10 years younger than the employee, then the applicable distribution period is the joint and last survivor life expectancy of the employee and spouse under the Joint and Last Survivor Table (which is longer than the distribution period that would apply for the employee under the Uniform Lifetime Table).

Pursuant to § 1.401(a)(9)-5, Q&A-5, for distribution calendar years after the calendar year of the employee's death, the applicable distribution period generally is the remaining life expectancy of the designated beneficiary, subject to certain exceptions. Two of these exceptions, which apply if the employee dies after the required beginning date, substitute the employee's remaining life expectancy for the beneficiary's remaining life expectancy. These two exceptions apply to an employee who does not have a designated beneficiary or is younger than the designated beneficiary.[3] Section 1.401(a)(9)-5, Q&A-5(c)(1) provides that the remaining life expectancy of the designated beneficiary is calculated as the life expectancy under the Single Life Table for the designated beneficiary's age in the calendar year following the calendar year of the employee's death, reduced by 1 for each subsequent year. However, if one of the two exceptions applies (so that the relevant life expectancy is the remaining life expectancy of the employee), then, pursuant to § 1.401(a)(9)-5, Q&A-5(c)(3), the remaining life expectancy of the employee is calculated as the life expectancy under the Single Life Table for the employee's age in the calendar year of the employee's death, reduced by 1 for each subsequent year.

---

[1] The incidental death benefit requirement, which is set forth in § 1.401-1(b)(1), provides that although a qualified pension or profit-sharing plan may provide for incidental death (or life insurance) benefits, such a plan must be established and maintained primarily for the purpose of providing retirement benefits or deferred compensation.

[2] However, pursuant to section 408A(a) and (c)(5), the minimum required distribution rules of section 401(a)(9) apply to a Roth IRA only after the death of the IRA owner.

[3] Another exception applies if the employee dies before the required beginning date and has no designated beneficiary. In that case, the employee's entire interest must be distributed by the end of the calendar year that includes the fifth anniversary of the date of the employee's death.

A special rule applies to determine the designated beneficiary's remaining life expectancy if the employee's surviving spouse is the employee's sole beneficiary. In that case, pursuant to §1.401(a)(9)-5, Q&A-5(c)(2), the designated beneficiary's remaining life expectancy is recalculated each calendar year as the life expectancy under the Single Life Table for the designated beneficiary's age in that year. For calendar years after the year of the spouse's death, the distribution period that applies for the spouse's beneficiary is the spouse's remaining life expectancy from the Single Life Table for the spouse's age for the calendar year of the spouse's death, reduced by 1 for each subsequent year.

Consistent with the policy of section 401(a)(9) to limit deferral of retirement income, §1.401(a)(9)-6, Q&A-1(a) provides that, except as otherwise provided in §1.401(a)(9)-6, payments from a defined benefit plan must be non-increasing in order to satisfy section 401(a)(9).[4] Section 1.401(a)(9)-6, Q&A-14(c) provides that, in the case of annuity payments paid from an annuity contract purchased from an insurance company, certain types of increasing payments will not cause an annuity payment stream to fail to satisfy this non-increasing payment requirement. These exceptions apply only if the total future expected payments under the annuity contract (determined in accordance with §1.401(a)(9)-6, Q&A-14(e)(3)) exceed the total value being annuitized (determined in accordance with §1.401(a)(9)-6, Q&A-14(e)(1)).

Section 1.401(a)(9)-9 provides life expectancy and distribution period tables that are used to apply the rules of §1.401(a)(9)-5 and to make the calculations in §1.401(a)(9)-6, Q&A-14. Section 1.401(a)(9)-9 was issued in 2002 (67 FR 18988), and the tables in that section were developed using mortality rates for 2003. These mortality rates were derived by applying mortality improvement through 2003 to the mortality rates from the Annuity 2000 Basic Table (which was the most recent individual annuity mortality table available in 2002).[5] The rates of mortality improvement used for this purpose were the ones that were used in developing that mortality table. The resulting separate mortality rates for males and females were blended using a fixed 50 percent male/50 percent female blend.

Section 72(t) imposes an additional income tax on early distributions from qualified retirement plans (including plans qualified under section 401(a) or section 403(a), annuity contracts and other arrangements described in section 403(b), and individual retirement arrangements described in section 408(a) or section 408(b)). However, section 72(t)(2)(A)(iv) provides an exception for a series of substantially equal periodic payments made for the life (or life expectancy) of the employee or the joint lives (or joint life expectancies) of the employee and the designated beneficiary. Revenue Ruling 2002-62, 2002-2 C.B. 710, provides that the life expectancy tables set forth in §1.401(a)(9)-9 may be used for purposes of determining payments that satisfy the exception under section 72(t)(2)(A)(iv). Rev. Rul. 2002-62 also provides a fixed annuitization method of determining payments that satisfy this exception. Under the fixed annuitization method, the annual payment for each year (which is determined only for the first year and not reset for subsequent years) is determined by dividing the account balance by an annuity factor that is the present value of an annuity of $1 per year beginning at the taxpayer's age and continuing for the life of the taxpayer (or the joint lives of the taxpayer and his or her beneficiary). The annuity factor is derived using the mortality table used to develop the life expectancy tables set forth in §1.401(a)(9)-9.

Executive Order 13847, 83 FR 45321, which was signed on August 31, 2018, directs the Secretary of the Treasury to examine the life expectancy and distribution period tables in the regulations on required minimum distributions from retirement plans and determine whether they should be updated to reflect current mortality data and whether such updates should be made annually or on another periodic basis. The purpose of any such updates would be to increase the effectiveness of tax-favored retirement programs by allowing retirees to retain sufficient retirement savings in these programs for their later years.

Explanation of Provisions

I. Overview

In accordance with Executive Order 13847, the Department of the Treasury (Treasury Department) and the IRS have examined the life expectancy and distribution period tables in §1.401(a)(9)-9, and have reviewed currently available mortality data. As a result of this review, the Treasury Department and the IRS have determined that those tables should be updated to reflect current life expectancies. Accordingly, these proposed regulations would update those tables.

The life expectancy tables and applicable distribution period tables in the proposed regulations reflect longer life expectancies than the tables in the existing regulations. For example, a 70-year old IRA owner who uses the Uniform Lifetime Table to calculate required minimum distributions must use a life expectancy of 27.4 years under the existing regulations. Using the Uniform Lifetime Table set forth in the proposed regulations, this IRA owner would use a life expectancy of 29.1 years to calculate required minimum distributions. As another example, under the existing regulations, a 75-year old surviving spouse who is the employee's sole beneficiary and uses the Single Life Table to compute required minimum distributions must use a life expectancy of 13.4 years. Under the proposed regulations, the spouse would use a life expectancy of 14.8 years. The effect of these changes is to reduce required minimum distributions, which will allow participants to retain larger amounts in their retirement plans to account for the possibility they may live longer.

II. Updated Life Expectancy and Distribution Period Tables

The life expectancy and distribution period tables in the proposed regulations have been developed based on mortality rates for 2021. These mortality rates were derived by applying mortality improvement through 2021 to the mortality rates from the experience tables used to develop the 2012 Individual Annuity Mortality tables (which are the most recent individual annuity mortality tables).[6] The separate mortality rates for males and females in these experience tables, which were based on the Payout Annuity Mortality Experience Study (which covered the period 2000 to 2004), have been projected from the central year of 2002 using the respective mortality improvement rates from the Mortality Improvement Scale MP-2018 for males and females.[7] The mortality table in the proposed regulations was developed by blending the resulting separate mortality rates for males and females using a fixed 50 percent male/50 percent female blend.

The Single Life Table in the proposed regulations sets forth life expectancies for each age, with the life expectancy for an age calculated as the sum of the probabilities of an individual at that age surviving to each future year. The resulting life expectancy is then increased by 11/24[8] to approximate the effect of monthly payments, and is subject to a floor of 1.0.

The Uniform Lifetime Table in the proposed regulations sets forth joint and last survivor life expectancies for each age beginning with age 70, based on a hypothetical beneficiary. Pursuant to §1.401(a)(9)-5, Q&A-4(a), the Uniform Lifetime Table is used for determining the distribution period for lifetime distributions to an employee in situations in which the employee's surviving spouse either is not the sole designated beneficiary or is the sole designated beneficiary but is not more than 10 years younger than the employee. As under the existing regulations, the joint and last survivor life expectancy of an employee is taken from the Joint and Last Survivor Table using a hypothetical beneficiary who is assumed to be 10 years younger than the employee.

---

[4] Pursuant to §1.401(a)(9)-8, Q&A-2(a)(3), the rules of §1.401(a)(9)-6 also apply to an annuity contract purchased under a defined contribution plan.

[5] The Annuity 2000 Basic Table was developed by projecting mortality rates from the 1983 Individual Annuity Mortality Basic Table.

[6] The experience tables and the 2012 Individual Annuity Mortality tables can be found at https://www.actuary.org/sites/default/files/files/publications/Payout_Annuity_Report_09-28-11.pdf.

[7] The Mortality Improvement Scale MP-2018 can be found at https://www.soa.org/experience-studies/2018/mortality-improvement-scale-mp-2018/.

[8] Assuming an equal distribution of deaths throughout the year, if a retiree is scheduled to receive monthly payments on the last day of each month then, in the year of death, on average, the retiree would receive 11/24th of a full year's worth of payments.

The Joint and Last Survivor Table sets forth joint and last survivor life expectancies of an employee and the employee's beneficiary for each combination of ages of those individuals. The joint and last survivor life expectancy for an employee and a beneficiary at a combination of ages is calculated as the sum of the probabilities of the employee surviving to each future year, plus the sum of the probabilities of the beneficiary surviving to each future year, minus the sum of the probabilities of both the employee and beneficiary surviving to each future year. The resulting joint and last survivor life expectancy is then increased by 11/24 to approximate the effect of monthly payments, and is subject to a floor of 1.0.

The life expectancy tables in the current regulations are used in several examples in §1.401(a)(9)-6, Q&A-14(f) that illustrate the availability of the exception described in §1.401(a)(9)-6, Q&A-14(c) (regarding certain increasing payments under insurance company annuity contracts). These proposed regulations do not include revisions to these examples to reflect the life expectancy tables in the proposed regulations.

III. *Effective/Applicability Date*

The life expectancy tables and Uniform Lifetime Table under these proposed regulations would apply for distribution calendar years beginning on or after January 1, 2021. Thus, for example, for an individual who attains age 70^1/$_2$ during 2020 (so that the minimum required distribution for the distribution calendar year 2020 is due April 1, 2021), the final regulations would not apply to the minimum required distribution for the individual's 2020 distribution calendar year (which is due April 1, 2021), but would apply to the minimum required distribution for the individual's 2021 distribution calendar year (which is due December 31, 2021).

These proposed regulations include a transition rule that applies if an employee died before January 1, 2021, and, under the rules of §1.401(a)(9)-5, Q&A-5, the distribution period that applies for calendar years following the calendar year of the employee's death is equal to a single life expectancy calculated as of the calendar year of the employee's death (or if applicable, the year after the employee's death), reduced by 1 for each subsequent year. Under this transition rule, the initial life expectancy used to determine the distribution period is reset by using the new Single Life Table for the age of the relevant individual in the calendar year for which life expectancy was set under §1.401(a)(9)-5, Q&A 5(c). For distribution calendar years beginning on or after January 1, 2021, the distribution period is determined by reducing that initial life expectancy by 1 for each year subsequent to the year for which it was initially set.

This transition rule applies in three situations: (1) The employee died before the required beginning date with a non-spousal designated beneficiary (so that the applicable distribution period is determined based on the remaining life expectancy of the designated beneficiary for the calendar year following the calendar year of the employee's death); (2) the employee died after the required beginning date without a designated beneficiary (so that the applicable distribution period is determined based on the remaining life expectancy of the employee for the year of the employee's death); and (3) the employee, who is younger than the designated beneficiary, died after the required beginning date (so that the applicable distribution period is determined based on the remaining life expectancy of the employee for the year of the employee's death).

The proposed regulations illustrate the application of this transition rule with an example involving an employee who died at age 80 in 2018 with a designated beneficiary (who was not the employee's spouse) who was age 75 in the year of the employee's death. For 2019, the distribution period that applies for the beneficiary is 12.7 years (the period applicable for a 76 year old under the Single Life Table in current §1.401(a)(9)-9), and for 2020, it is 11.7 years (the original distribution period, reduced by 1 year). For 2021, taking into account the life expectancy tables under the proposed regulations and applying the transition rule, the applicable distribution period would be 12.0 years (the 14.0 year life expectancy for a 76 year old under the Single Life Table in the proposed regulations, reduced by 2 years).

A similar transition rule applies if an employee's sole beneficiary is the employee's surviving spouse and the spouse died before January 1, 2021. Under the rules of §1.401(a)(9)-5, Q&A-5(c)(2), the distribution period that applies for the spouse's beneficiary is equal to the single life expectancy for the spouse calculated for the calendar year of the spouse's death, reduced by 1 for each subsequent year. Under the transition rule, the initial life expectancy used to determine the distribution period is reset by using the new Single Life Table for the age of the spouse in the calendar year of the spouse's death. For distribution calendar years beginning on or after January 1, 2021, the distribution period is determined by reducing that initial life expectancy by 1 for each year subsequent to the year for which it was initially set.

These transition rules, under which there is a one-time reset for the relevant life expectancy using the Single Life Table under the proposed regulations, are designed to recognize that the general population has longer life expectancies than the life expectancies set forth in the 2002 regulations. However, because the reset life expectancy is based on the age for which life expectancy was originally determined (rather than the relevant individual's current age), it is consistent with Congressional intent to limit recalculation of life expectancy to the employee and the employee's spouse.

IV. *Applicability to Revenue Ruling 2002-62*

After final regulations that provide updated life expectancy and distribution period tables under section 401(a)(9) are issued, if a taxpayer commenced receiving substantially equal periodic payments before January 1, 2021, using the required minimum distribution method described in section 2.01(a) of Rev. Rul. 2002-62, then the application of the final regulations will not be treated as a modification to a series of substantially equal periodic payments as described in section 72(t)(4)(A)(ii). In addition, if a taxpayer commences receiving substantially equal periodic payments on or after January 1, 2021, and uses either the fixed amortization method described in section 2.01(b) of Rev. Rul. 2002-62 or the fixed annuitization method described in section 2.01(c) of Rev. Rul. 2002-62, then the method should be applied by applying the corresponding life expectancy, distribution period, and mortality tables in the final regulations in lieu of the tables in formerly applicable §1.401(a)(9)-9 that are referenced in Rev. Rul. 2002-62.

Special Analyses

I. *Regulatory Impact Analysis*

Executive Orders 13771, 13563, and 12866 direct agencies to assess costs and benefits of available regulatory alternatives and, if regulation is necessary, to select regulatory approaches that maximize net benefits, including potential economic, environmental, public health and safety effects, distributive impacts, and equity. Executive Order 13563 emphasizes the importance of quantifying both costs and benefits, reducing costs, harmonizing rules, and promoting flexibility. The Executive Order 13771 designation for any final rule resulting from the proposed regulation will be informed by comments received. The preliminary Executive Order 13771 designation for this proposed rule is deregulatory.

The proposed regulations have been designated by the Office of Management and Budget's (OMB's) Office of Information and Regulatory Affairs (OIRA) as subject to review under Executive Order 12866 pursuant to the Memorandum of Agreement (MOA, April 11, 2018) between the Treasury Department and the Office of Management and Budget regarding review of tax regulations. OIRA has determined that the proposed rulemaking is significant and subject to review under Executive Order 12866 and section 1(b) of the Memorandum of Agreement. Accordingly, the proposed regulations have been reviewed by OMB.

1. *Introduction and Need for Regulation*

As stated earlier in the preamble to the proposed regulations, in accordance with Executive Order 13847, the Treasury Department and the IRS have examined the life expectancy and distribution period tables in §1.401(a)(9)-9 and have reviewed currently available mortality data. As a result of this review, the Treasury Department and the IRS determined that those tables should be updated to reflect current life expectancies.

The life expectancy tables and applicable distribution period tables in the proposed regulations reflect longer life expectancies than the tables in the existing regulations. The effect of these changes is to reduce annual required minimum distributions (RMDs) from qualified defined contribution plans, IRAs, and certain other tax-favored retirement plans (referred to as affected retirement plans). The purpose of such updates is to increase the effectiveness of these tax-favored retirement programs by allowing retirees to retain more retirement savings in these programs for their later years.

Pursuant to section 6(a)(3)(B) of Executive Order 12866, the following qualitative analysis provides further details regarding the anticipated impacts of the proposed regulations. After briefly describing the proposed regulations in Part 2, the baseline used for the analysis is described in Part 3. Part 4 describes the entities and individuals affected by the proposed regulations. Part 5 provides a qualitative assessment of the potential economic effects, including benefits and costs, of the proposed regulations compared to the baseline.

2. The Proposed Regulations

The RMD rules require an individual to withdraw assets from an affected retirement plan as generally taxable distributions over the life expectancy of the individual (or the individual and spouse).[9] Balances remaining at the death of the individual that are paid to a spouse as designated beneficiary must generally be withdrawn over the life expectancy of the spouse.[10] The purpose of the RMD rules is to ensure that the favorable tax treatment afforded a qualified plan is used primarily to provide retirement income to a participant and designated beneficiary, while mitigating the cost to the government of deferred taxation on savings in qualified retirement plans.

The life expectancy tables and applicable distribution period tables in the proposed regulations reflect longer life expectancies than the tables in the existing regulations that are generally between one and two years longer than under the existing regulations. This will give individuals with affected retirement plans the option to withdraw slightly smaller amounts from their plans each year, giving individuals and beneficiaries the option to leave amounts in tax-favored retirement accounts for a slightly longer period of time, to account for the possibility that they may live longer.

3. Baseline

The Treasury Department and the IRS have assessed the benefits and costs of these proposed regulations relative to a no-action baseline reflecting anticipated Federal income tax-related behavior in the absence of these proposed regulations.

4. Affected Entities and Individuals

The proposed regulations affect individuals who withdraw exactly the RMD amount from their affected retirement plan but who would prefer to withdraw less in the absence of the minimum distribution requirements. Individuals who withdraw more than the current RMD are not bound by the current rules and therefore are not expected to reduce withdrawals as a result of the proposed regulations. Using confidential tax return data, the Treasury Department estimates roughly 4.6 million individuals, or 20.5% of all individuals required to take RMDs from an affected retirement plan, will make withdrawals at the minimum required level in 2021, and might reduce withdrawals as a result of the rule.

In addition, Individual Retirement Account (IRA) providers would have to change the administration of their IRAs to reflect the new life expectancy tables. The Treasury Department does not have an estimate of the number of such entities. Additionally, employer plans that do not require benefits to be paid out as a lump sum would have to change the administration of their plans to reflect the new life expectancy tables. The Treasury Department expects that this would include most large plans, which typically do not require benefits to be paid out in a lump sum and thus would be affected by the proposed regulations. The latest available data, the Private Pension Bulletin produced by the Department of Labor, indicate there were 81,469 large qualified pension plans (defined as plans with more than 100 participants) in 2016.[11]

5. Economic Effects

a. Labor Supply Effect

The proposed rule produces a positive wealth effect, as lower levels of RMDs lead to larger amounts of assets earning tax-deferred returns. While this might plausibly lead to a reduction in labor supply, this effect is likely to be small for the following reasons.

First, the proposed regulations would lead to a small decrease in the portion of assets in affected retirement plans that must be withdrawn as an RMD for a 70-year old retiree. Under the current regulations, if a 70-year old retiree had $250,000 in his or her affected retirement plan, the individual is required at age 70 to withdraw $9,124, equal to 3.65% of plan assets. Under the proposed regulations, the individual would be required to withdraw $8,591, equal to 3.44% of plan assets, a decrease of $533 or 0.21% of plan assets. Under the current regulations, a 90-year old retiree with $250,000 in his or her affected retirement plan would be required at age 90 to withdraw $21,930, equal to 8.77% of plan assets. Under the proposed regulations, the individual would be required to withdraw $20,661, equal to 8.26% of plan assets, a decrease of $1,269 or 0.51% of plan assets.

Second, the proposed regulations are expected to affect the labor supply decisions only of individuals who are making withdrawals at or very close to the RMD level. Individuals making withdrawals from affected retirement plans exceeding the current RMD are not bound by the current minimum and are therefore not affected by relaxing the minimum by a small amount. Hence, their labor supply decisions are unlikely to change based on the proposed regulations. Thus, the proposed regulations would likely affect only a very small portion of high income individuals working into their late 60s and early 70s.

The small impact of the proposed regulations is illustrated by an example. Assume the following facts. The individual is unmarried and has $250,000 in his or her IRA and $0 in a taxable account. The individual turns age 70 on January 1 and because the individual turns 70½ in the year must begin taking RMDs. The RMD amount is determined as of January 1, but is withdrawn on December 31 of the year in question. Tax is paid immediately upon the withdrawal of the RMD. Because the individual who is bound by the RMD rules has revealed a preference to continue to save the funds rather than consume them, the amount remaining after the tax has been paid on the distribution is placed into a taxable investment account on January 1 of the following year (the day after the RMD is made). Assets held in the IRA and the taxable account earn a 3% rate of return once the individual turns age 70. The RMDs and the returns in the taxable account are taxed at a marginal rate of 22%.

Under the mortality rates in the proposed regulations, an individual who is 70 is expected to live until approximately age 90. We examine the total assets, i.e., the sum of the assets in the IRA and in the taxable account, that the taxpayer would have at age 90 if the individual only takes RMDs each year. Under the current regulations, the individual's total assets at age 90 would be $371,004. Under the proposed regulations, the individual's total assets at age 90 would be $374,461. This $3,457 (less than 1%) increase in total assets at age 90 is unlikely to allow or incentivize the individual to retire earlier than he or she otherwise would.

---

[9] This requirement to take distributions during the individual's lifetime does not apply to a Roth IRA described in section 408A.

[10] Balances payable to other designated beneficiaries must generally be withdrawn according to the beneficiary's life expectancy (fixed as of the year of death). Different rules apply if the individual dies prior to the required beginning date for RMDs.

[11] https://www.dol.gov/sites/default/files/ebsa/researchers/statistics/retirement-bulletins/private-pension-plan-bulletin-historical-tables-and-graphs.pdf

The proposed regulations could in theory lead to an increase in labor supply. The argument is that because the value of contributing to a retirement fund has increased, the return to working longer has increased. Another example illustrates that the additional return to working is small and very unlikely to induce an increase in labor supply.

Assume the following facts. The individual is unmarried and is age 69. The individual chooses whether to work an additional year or to retire. If the individual works an additional year, the individual's income is sufficiently large so that the individual would choose to contribute the maximum amount to an IRA ($7,000 in 2019). If the individual retires, the individual does not contribute to an IRA. That is, if the individual retires at age 69, the individual will have $250,000 of assets in his or her IRA and $0 in a taxable account on January 1 in the year the individual turns age 70. If the individual retires at age 70, the individual will have $257,000 of assets in his or her IRA and $0 in a taxable account on January 1 in the year the individual turns age 70.

As in the previous example, the individual has RMDs beginning at age 70^1/$_2$. The RMD amount is determined on January 1 but is withdrawn on December 31 of the year in question. Tax is paid immediately upon the withdrawal of the RMD amount. The amount remaining after the tax has been paid on the distribution is placed on January 1 of the following year, i.e., the day after the RMD was made, into a taxable investment account. Assets held in the IRA and the taxable account earn a 3% rate of return once the individual turns age 70. The RMDs and the returns in the taxable account are taxed at a marginal tax rate of 22%.

We again examine the total assets, i.e., the sum of the assets in the IRA and in the taxable account that the individual would have at age 90. If the individual waits to retire at age 70, under the current RMD rules, the individual's total assets at age 90 would be $10,388 more than if the taxpayer retired at age 69. Under the proposed rulemaking, if the individual waits to retire at age 70, the individual's total assets at age 90 would be $10,485 more than if the individual retired at age 69.

The proposed rulemaking, therefore, increases the difference in total assets at age 90 by $97. Even if the individual contributed the $25,000 maximum to a 401(k) plan - $19,000 plus $6,000 in catch-up contributions in 2019 - the proposed rulemaking would increase the difference in total assets at age 90 by only $346. These amounts are likely much too small to affect the individual's decision about whether to retire at age 69 or wait to retire at age 70.

Under the standard assumption that leisure is a normal good, i.e., time spent not working increases as income and wealth increase, the increase in potential retirement income generated by the proposed rulemaking could lead some individuals to work less. However, given the magnitude of the change as suggested in the preceding example, this behavior is unlikely.

b. Increased Fees

Under the proposed regulations, more assets will be left in affected retirement plans. Using confidential tax data, the Treasury Department estimates that in 2021, the proposed regulations would lead to an $8.1 billion reduction in distributions from affected retirement plans. A joint study by Brightscope and the Investment Company Institute indicates that "all-in" fees for large plans, which are the ones most likely not to require distributions to be taken as a lump sum, are typically below 1%.[12] Thus, reduced withdrawals could lead to an increase in fees of about $81 million earned by providers of services to affected retirement plans in 2021. However, in the absence of the proposed regulations, individuals who prefer to make smaller withdrawals would likely transfer these funds into taxable investment accounts, which carry their own fees. As a result, the net additional fees earned by the investment industry as a result of the proposed regulations are expected to be much less than $81 million.

c. Administrative Costs

Under the proposed regulations, all IRA providers and administrators of employer-sponsored retirement plans that allow non-lump sum distributions will need to update their life expectancy and distribution period tables and communicate the changes in their RMDs to their plan participants. However, most employers use purchased software of third-party service providers that provide plan administrative services for many employers. This creates economies of scale and reduces the total cost of the required update. The total cost will then be spread over many employers, such that the cost to each employer is expected to be very low. The Treasury Department and the IRS do not have sufficient data to determine the increased administrative costs of the proposed regulations for an individual IRA provider, plan administrator who uses in-house software, plan service provider or software developer, and invite comments on the cost of implementing the life expectancy and distribution period table in the proposed regulations for these entities. The Treasury Department and the IRS also invite comments on the number of such entities who would have to implement changes to software in order to implement the life expectancy and distribution period table in the proposed regulations.

II. Regulatory Flexibility Act

It is hereby certified pursuant to the Regulatory Flexibility Act *5 U.S.C., chapter 6) that these proposed regulations will not have a significant economic impact on a substantial number of small entities. These proposed regulations will apply to all employers that sponsor defined contribution plans regardless of size. Although data are not available to estimate the number of small entitles affected, the proposed rule may affect a substantial number. As stated above, this rule updates life expectancies that are required to be used by statute.

Although the proposed rule may affect a substantial number of small entities, the economic impact of the proposed regulations is not likely to be significant. Small businesses generally comply with the minimum required distribution rules using either third-party administrators or software, creating economies of scale that mitigate the cost of updating life expectancy tables. Such software is updated periodically irrespective of a change in life expectancies used to determine minimum required distributions. The portion of the cost of a periodic update that is attributable to the implementation of the life expectancy and distribution period tables in the proposed regulations will be spread over the client base of a service provider that uses software developed in-house, and over the group of purchasers of generally-available plan administration software. Because, in either case, the cost of changing software to implement the updated life expectancies is spread over a large group of businesses that maintain retirement plans, it is estimated that the incremental cost for each affected small businesses as a result of the use of updated life expectancies is not significant.

Notwithstanding this certification, Treasury and the IRS invite comments about the impact that the proposed rule would have on small entities. Pursuant to section 7805(f) of the Code, this notice of proposed rulemaking will be submitted to the Chief Counsel for Advocacy of the Small Business Administration for comment on its impact on small entities.

---

[12] See "The Brightscope/ICI Defined Contribution Plan Profile: A Close Look at 401(k) Plans" (December 2014) at https://www.ici.org/pdf/ppr_14_dcplan_profile_401k.pdf. This study points to page 7 of "Inside the Structure of Defined Contribution/401(k) Plan Fees, 2013: A study assessing the mechanics of the 'all-in' fee" (August 2014) at https://www.ici.org/pdf/rpt_14_dc_401k_fee_study.pdf, for a definition of the 'all-in fee.' This definition of 'all-in fee' ". . . includes all administrative or recordkeeping fees as well as investment fees (i.e., the investment option's total expense ratio) whether they are assessed at the plan, employer or participant level. The 'all-in' fee excludes those recordkeeping and administrative activity fees that only apply to particular participants who engage in the activity (e.g., self-directed brokerage, managed accounts, loans, QDROs and distributions)."

Comments and Public Hearing

Before these proposed regulations are adopted as final regulations, consideration will be given to any comments that are submitted timely to the Treasury Department and the IRS as prescribed in this preamble in the **"ADDRESSES"** section. The Treasury Department and the IRS request comments on all aspects of these proposed regulations, including:

- How often the life expectancy and distribution period tables in these regulations should be updated.

- The extent of the administrative burden involved in implementing any such updates.

- Whether guidance is needed so that a participant whose plan administrator or trustee fails to implement the final regulations in a timely fashion may take required minimum distributions (or roll over distributions in excess of the required minimum distribution) in a manner that takes into account the final regulations.

All comments will be available for public inspection and copying at www.regulations.gov or upon request.

A public hearing on these proposed regulations has been scheduled for January 23, 2020, beginning at 10 a.m. in the IRS Auditorium, Internal Revenue Service, 1111 Constitution Avenue, NW, Washington, DC 20224. Due to building security procedures, visitors must enter at the Constitution Avenue entrance. In addition, all visitors must present photo identification to enter the building. Because of access restrictions, visitors will not be admitted beyond the immediate entrance area more than 30 minutes before the hearing starts. For information about having your name placed on the building access list to attend the hearing, see the **"FOR FURTHER INFORMATION CONTACT"** section of this preamble.

The rules of 26 CFR 601.601(a)(3) apply to the hearing. Persons who wish to present oral comments at the hearing must submit written or electronic comments by January 7, 2020, and an outline of topics to be discussed and the amount of time to be devoted to each topic by January 7, 2020. A period of 10 minutes will be allotted to each person for making comments. An agenda showing the scheduling of the speakers will be prepared after the deadline for receiving outlines has passed. Copies of the agenda will be available free of charge at the hearing.

Drafting Information

The principal authors of these proposed regulations are Arslan Malik and Linda S. F. Marshall, of the Office of the Associate Chief Counsel (Employee Benefits, Exempt Organizations, and Employment Taxes). However, other personnel from the Treasury Department and the IRS participated in the development of the proposed regulations.

[¶ 49,820]   Proposed Amendments of Regulations (REG-118378-19), published in the Federal Register on November 27, 2019.

[Code Sec. 9815]

Health insurance: Group health plans: Disclosure.—Reg. §54.9815-2715A, setting forth requirements for group health plans and health insurance issuers in the individual and group markets to disclose cost-sharing information upon request, to a participant, beneficiary, or enrollee (or his or her authorized representative), including an estimate of such individual's cost-sharing liability for covered items or services furnished by a particular provider, is proposed.

AGENCIES: Internal Revenue Service, Department of the Treasury; Employee Benefits Security Administration, Department of Labor; Centers for Medicare & Medicaid Services, Department of Health and Human Services.

ACTION: Proposed rule.

SUMMARY: These proposed rules set forth proposed requirements for group health plans and health insurance issuers in the individual and group markets to disclose cost-sharing information upon request, to a participant, beneficiary, or enrollee (or his or her authorized representative), including an estimate of such individual's cost-sharing liability for covered items or services furnished by a particular provider. Under these proposed rules, plans and issuers would be required to make such information available on an internet website and, if requested, through non-internet means, thereby allowing a participant, beneficiary, or enrollee (or his or her authorized representative) to obtain an estimate and understanding of the individual's out-of-pocket expenses and effectively shop for items and services. These proposed rules also include proposals to require plans and issuers to disclose in-network provider negotiated rates, and historical out-of-network allowed amounts through two machine-readable files posted on an internet website, thereby allowing the public to have access to health insurance coverage information that can be used to understand health care pricing and potentially dampen the rise in health care spending. The Department of Health and Human Services (HHS) also proposes amendments to its medical loss ratio program rules to allow issuers offering group or individual health insurance coverage to receive credit in their medical loss ratio calculations for savings they share with enrollees that result from the enrollee's shopping for, and receiving care from, lower-cost, higher-value providers.

DATES: To be assured consideration, comments must be received at one of the addresses provided below, no later than 5 p.m. on January 14, 2020.

ADDRESSES: Written comments may be submitted to the addresses specified below. Any comment that is submitted will be shared with the Department of the Treasury (Treasury Department), Internal Revenue Service (IRS) and the Department of Labor (DOL). Please do not submit duplicates.

All comments will be made available to the public. Warning: Do not include any personally identifiable information (such as name, address, or other contact information) or confidential business information that you do not want publicly disclosed. All comments are posted on the internet exactly as received, and can be retrieved by most internet search engines. No deletions, modifications, or redactions will be made to the comments received, as they are public records. Comments may be submitted anonymously.

In commenting, please refer to file code CMS-9915-P. Because of staff and resource limitations, the Departments of Labor, HHS, and the Treasury (the Departments) cannot accept comments by facsimile (FAX) transmission.

Comments must be submitted in one of the following three ways (please choose only one of the ways listed):

1. *Electronically*. You may submit electronic comments on this regulation to **http://www.regulations.gov**. Follow the "Submit a comment" instructions.

2. *By regular mail*. You may mail written comments to the following address ONLY:

Centers for Medicare & Medicaid Services,

Department of Health and Human Services,

Attention: CMS-9915-P,

P.O. Box 8010,

Baltimore, MD 21244-8010.

Please allow sufficient time for mailed comments to be received before the close of the comment period.

3. *By express or overnight mail.* You may send written comments to the following address ONLY:

Centers for Medicare & Medicaid Services,

Department of Health and Human Services,

Attention: CMS-9915-P,

Mail Stop C4-26-05,

7500 Security Boulevard,

Baltimore, MD 21244-1850.

Inspection of Public Comments: All comments received before the close of the comment period are available for viewing by the public, including any personally identifiable or confidential business information that is included in a comment. The comments are posted on the following website as soon as possible after they have been received *http://www.regulations.gov*. Follow the search instructions on that website to view public comments.

FOR FURTHER INFORMATION CONTACT: Deborah Bryant, Centers for Medicare and Medicaid Services, (301) 492-4293.

Christopher Dellana, Internal Revenue Service, (202) 317-5500.

Matthew Litton or David Sydlik, Employee Benefits Security Administration, (202) 693-8335. *Customer Service Information:* Individuals interested in obtaining information from the DOL concerning employment-based health coverage laws may call the Employee Benefits Security Administration (EBSA) Toll-Free Hotline at 1–866–444–EBSA (3272) or visit DOL's website (http://www.dol.gov/ebsa). In addition, information from HHS on private health insurance for consumers can be found on the Centers for Medicare & Medicaid Services (CMS) website (www.cms.gov/cciio) and information on health reform can be found at http://www.healthcare.gov.

SUPPLEMENTARY INFORMATION:

I. Background

A. *Executive Order*

On June 24, 2019, President Trump issued Executive Order 13877, "Executive Order on Improving Price and Quality Transparency in American Healthcare to Put Patients First."[1] Section 3(b) of Executive Order 13877 directs the Secretaries of the Departments of Labor, Health and Human Services (HHS), and the Treasury (the Departments) to issue an advance notice of proposed rulemaking (ANPRM), consistent with applicable law, soliciting comment on a proposal to require health care providers, health insurance issuers, and self-insured group health plans to provide or facilitate access to information about expected out-of-pocket costs for items or services to patients before they receive care. The Departments have considered the issue, including by consulting with stakeholders, and have determined that a notice of proposed rulemaking (NPRM), rather than an ANPRM, would allow for more specific and useful feedback from commenters, who would be able to respond to specific proposals. Additionally, increases in health care costs and out-of-pocket liability without transparent, meaningful information about health care pricing have left consumers with little ability to make cost-conscious decisions when purchasing health care items and services. An NPRM, rather than an ANPRM, would enable the Departments to more quickly address this pressing issue.

B. *Benefits of Transparency in Health Coverage and Past Efforts to Promote Transparency*

As explained earlier in this preamble, these proposed rules will fulfill the Departments' responsibility under Executive Order 13877. These proposed rules also would implement legislative mandates under sections 1311(e)(3) of the Patient Protection and Affordable Care Act (PPACA) and section 2715A of the Public Health Service (PHS) Act. The overarching goal of these proposed rules is to support a market-driven health care system by giving consumers the information they need to make informed decisions about their health care and health care purchases. Specifically, the purposes of these proposed rules are to provide consumers with price and benefit information that will enable them to evaluate health care options and to make cost-conscious decisions; reduce surprises in relation to consumers' out-of-pocket costs for health care services; create a competitive dynamic that will begin to narrow price differences for the same services in the same health care markets; foster innovation by providing industry the information necessary to support informed, price-conscious consumers in the health care market; and, over time, potentially lower overall health care costs. The Departments are of the view that this price transparency effort will equip consumers with information to actively and effectively participate in the health care system, the prices for which should be driven and controlled by market forces. For these reasons and those explained in more detail later in this preamble, these price transparency efforts are crucial to providing consumers with information about health care costs and to stabilizing health care spending.

As explained in the report "Reforming America's Healthcare System through Choice and Competition,"[2] consumers have an important role to play in controlling costs, but consumers must have meaningful information in order to create the market forces necessary to achieve lower health care costs. Most health care consumers rely on third-party payers, including the government and private health insurance, to reimburse health care providers for a large portion of their health care costs. Third-party payers negotiate prices with health care providers and reimburse the providers on the consumer's behalf, which conceals from consumers the true market price of their care. When consumers seek care, they do not typically know whether they could have received the same service from another provider offering lower prices. Because a large portion of insured consumers' out-of-pocket financial liability has historically, for many consumers, not been dependent on the provider's negotiated rate with the third-party payer, there has been little or no incentive for some consumers to consider price and seek out lower-cost care.[3] However, as health care spending continues to rise, consumers are shouldering a greater portion of their health care costs.[4]

In the private health insurance market, consumers are responsible for a greater share of their health care costs through higher deductibles and shifts from copayments to coinsurance.[5] A deductible is the amount a consumer pays for covered health services before his or her health plan starts to pay.[6] Generally, the amount the consumer pays for a specific item or service furnished by a network provider before the deductible is met is the rate the group health plan or health insurance issuer has negotiated with the provider, also referred to as the negotiated rate. A study of large

[1] 84 FR 30849 (June 27, 2019). The Executive Order was issued on June 24, 2019 and was published in the **Federal Register** on June 27, 2019.

[2] Azar, A.M., Mnuchin, S.T., and Acosta, A. "Reforming America's Healthcare System Through Choice and Competition." December 3, 2018. Available at: https://www.hhs.gov/sites/default/files/Reforming-Americas-Healthcare-System-Through-Choice-and-Competition.pdf.

[3] *Id.*

[4] Claxton, G., Levitt, L., Long M. "Payments for cost sharing increasing rapidly over time." Peterson-Kaiser Health System Tracker. April 2016. Available at: *https://www.healthsystemtracker.org/brief/payments-for-cost-sharing-increasing-rapidly-over-time/*.

[5] Ray, M., Copeland, R., Cox, C. "Tracking the rise in premium contributions and cost-sharing for families with large employer coverage," Peterson-Kaiser Health System Tracker. August 14, 2019. Available at: https://www.healthsystemtracker.org/brief/tracking-the-rise-in-premium-contributions-and-cost-sharing-for-families-with-large-employer-coverage/

[6] https://www.healthcare.gov/glossary/deductible/

employer health plans found that the portion of payments paid by consumers for deductibles increased from 20 percent to 51 percent between 2003 and 2017.[7] Furthermore, enrollment in health plans with high deductibles is also increasing. In 2018, the Centers for Disease Control and Prevention estimated that 47 percent of persons under age 65 with private health insurance were enrolled in health plans with high deductibles, up from 25.3 percent in 2010.[8]

Coinsurance is the percentage of costs a participant, beneficiary, or enrollee pays for a covered item or service after he or she has paid his or her deductible.[9] Copayments (sometimes called "copays") are a fixed amount ($20, for example) that a consumer pays for a covered item or service, usually when he or she receives the service. Copays can vary for different items or services within the same plan, like prescription drugs, laboratory tests, and visits to specialists.[10] Copayments are both more predictable for consumers, because the copayment amount is set in advance, and often less expensive for consumers than coinsurance amounts. For instance, assuming an individual has met his or her deductible, if a plan or issuer has negotiated the cost of a procedure with a particular provider to be $1000, and the plan or issuer has a 20 percent coinsurance requirement, the individual would be responsible for paying a $200 coinsurance amount toward the cost of the procedure.

In the health care market, where consumers generally are responsible for paying higher deductibles and have more cost sharing in the form of coinsurance, out-of-pocket liability is often directly contingent upon the reimbursement rate a health plan has negotiated with a provider. The fact that more consumers are bearing greater financial responsibility for the cost of their health care provides the opportunity to establish a consumer-driven health care market. If consumers have better pricing information and can shop for health care items and services more efficiently, they can increase competition and demand for lower prices.[11] Currently, however, consumers have little insight into negotiated rates until after services are rendered. As a result, it can be difficult for consumers to estimate potential out-of-pocket costs because of the wide variability in health care prices for the same service.[12]

Without transparency in pricing, there are little to no market forces to drive competition, as demonstrated by significant variations in prices for procedures,[13] even within a local region. For example, a study of price variation in the San Francisco area showed that, even for a relatively commoditized service such as a lower-back MRI, prices ranged from $500 to $10,246.[14] A study on reference pricing in the California Public Employees' Retirement System found a range of $12,000 to $75,000 for the same joint replacement surgery, $1,000 to $6,500 for cataract removal, and $1,250 to $15,500 for arthroscopy of the knee.[15] Variability in pricing, such as in these examples, suggests that there is substantial opportunity for increased transparency to save money by shifting patients from high to lower-cost providers.[16]

Many empirical studies have investigated the impact of price transparency on markets, with most research showing that price transparency leads to lower and more uniform prices, consistent with predictions of standard economic theory. One study notes special characteristics of the health market, including that: (1) diseases and treatments affect each patient differently, making health care difficult to standardize and making price dispersion difficult to monitor; (2) patients cannot always know what they want or need, and physicians must serve as their agents; and (3) patients are in a poor position to choose a hospital because they do not have a lot of information about hospital quality and costs.[17] This study suggests that these special characteristics of the health care market, among other relevant factors, make it difficult to draw conclusions based on empirical evidence gathered from other markets. Nevertheless, the same study concluded that despite these complications, greater price transparency, such as access to posted prices, might lead to more efficient outcomes and lower prices.

In Kentucky, public employees are provided with a price transparency tool that allows them to shop for health care services and share in any cost-savings realized by seeking lower-cost care. Over a 3-year period, 42 percent of eligible employees used the program to look up information about prices and rewards and 57 percent of those chose at least one more cost-effective provider, saving state taxpayers $13.2 million and resulting in $1.9 million in cash benefits paid to public employees for seeking lower cost care.[18] In 2007, New Hampshire launched a website that allows consumers with private health insurance to compare health care costs and quality.[19] In a recent study of the New Hampshire price transparency tool, researchers found that health care price transparency can shift care to lower-cost providers and save consumers and payers money.[20] The study specifically focused on X-rays, CT scans, and MRI scans; determined that the transparency tool reduced the costs of medical imaging procedures by 5 percent for patients and 4 percent for issuers; and estimated savings of $7.9 million for patients and $36 million for issuers over a 5-year period. At the end of the 5-year period, out-of-pocket costs for these services in New Hampshire were 11 percent lower than for medical imaging services not included in the transparency tool. Individuals who had not yet satisfied their deductible saw almost double the savings, and prices for services listed in the tool became less dispersed over time.[21] The Departments are of the view that health care markets could work more efficiently and provide consumers with lower cost health care if individuals could see an estimate of their out-of-pocket liability prior to making their health care purchases.

A study of enrollees in plans with high deductibles found that respondents wanted additional health care pricing information so they could make more informed decisions about where to seek care based on price.[22] Another study found that 71 percent of respondents said that out-of-pocket spending was either important or very important to them when choosing a doctor.[23]

Currently, the information that consumers need to make informed decisions based on the prices of health care services is not readily available. The 2011 Government Accountability Office (GAO) report, "Health Care Price Transparency: Meaningful Price Information is Difficult for

---

[7] Claxton, G., Levitt, L., Long, M. "Payments for cost sharing increasing rapidly over time." Peterson-Kaiser Health System Tracker. April 2016. Available at: *https://www.healthsystemtracker.org/brief/payments-for-cost-sharing-increasing-rapidly-over-time/*.

[8] Cohen, R., Martinez, M., Zammitti, E. "Health insurance Coverage: Early Release of Estimates from the National Health Interview Survey, January-March 2018." August 2018. Available at: https://www.cdc.gov/nchs/data/nhis/earlyrelease/Insur201808.pdf.

[9] *https://www.healthcare.gov/glossary/co-insurance/*.

[10] *https://www.cms.gov/CCIIO/Resources/Files/Downloads/uniform-glossary-final.pdf*

[11] Azar, A.M., Mnuchin, S.T., and Acosta, A. "Reforming America's Healthcare System Through Choice and Competition." December 3, 2018. Available at: https://www.hhs.gov/sites/default/files/Reforming-Americas-Healthcare-System-Through-Choice-and-Competition.pdf.

[12] Cooper, Z., Craig, S., Gaynor, M., Reenen J. "The Price Ain't Right? Hospital Prices and Health Spending on the Privately Insured." 134. Q. J. of Econ 51. September 4, 2018. Available at: https://academic.oup.com/qje/article/134/1/51/5090426?searchresult=1.

[13] *Id.*

[14] Pinder, J. "Why do MRI prices vary so much? And a note about our data." Clear Health Costs. July 17, 2014. Available at: https://clearhealthcosts.com/blog/2014/07/prices-vary-much-mini-case-study-mri/.

[15] Boynton, A., Robinson, J. "Appropriate Use of Reference Pricing Can Increase Value." Health Affairs Blog. July 7, 2015. Available at: https://www.healthaffairs.org/do/10.1377/hblog20150707.049155/full/.

[16] Sinaiko, A., Rosenthal, M. "Examining a Health Care Price Transparency Tool: Who Uses it, and How They Shop for Care." 35 Health Affairs 662. April 2016. Available at: https://www.healthaffairs.org/doi/full/10.1377/hlthaff.2015.0746.

[17] Congressional Research Service Report to Congress: Does Price Transparency Improve Market Efficiency? Implications of Empirical Evidence in Other Markets for the Healthcare Sector, July 24, 2007. Available at: https://fas.org/sgp/crs/secrecy/RL34101.pdf.

[18] Rhoads, J. "Right to Shop for Public Employees: How Health Care Incentives are Saving Money in Kentucky." Dartmouth Inst. for Health Pol'y and Clinical Prac. March 8, 2019. Available at: https://thefga.org/wp-content/uploads/2019/03/RTS-Kentucky-HealthCareIncentivesSavingMoney-DRAFT8.pdf.

[19] "Compare Health Costs & Quality of Care in New Hampshire." NH HealthCost. *https://nhhealthcost.nh.gov/*

[20] Brown, Z. "Equilibrium Effects of Health Care Price Information." 100 Rev. of Econ. and Stat. 1. July 16, 2018. Available at: http://www-personal.umich.edu/~zachb/zbrown_eqm_effects_price_transparency.pdf)

[21] *Id.*

[22] Sinaiko, A., Mehrotra, A., Sood, N. "Cost-Sharing Obligations, High-Deductible Health Plan Growth, and Shopping for Health Care: Enrollees with Skin in the Game." 176 JAMA Intern. Med. 395. March 2016. Available at: https://jamanetwork.com/journals/jamainternalmedicine/fullarticle/2482348.

[23] Ateev, M., Dean, K., Sinaiko, A., Neeraj, S. "Americans Support Price Shopping For Health Care, But Few Actually Seek Out Price Information." 36 Health Affairs. 1392. August 2017. Available at: https://www.healthaffairs.org/doi/full/10.1377/hlthaff.2016.1471.

Consumers to Obtain Prior to Receiving Care," found that the lack of transparency in health care prices, coupled with the wide pricing disparities for particular procedures within the same market, can make it difficult for consumers to understand health care prices and to effectively shop for value.[24] The report references a number of barriers that make it difficult for consumers to obtain price estimates in advance for health care services. Such barriers include, for example, the difficulty of predicting health care service needs in advance, a complex billing structure resulting in bills from multiple providers, the variety of insurance benefit structures, and the lack of public disclosure of rates negotiated between providers and third-party payers.

The GAO report also explored various price transparency initiatives, including tools that consumers could use to generate price estimates before receiving a health care service. The report notes that pricing information displayed by tools varies across initiatives, in large part due to limits reported by the initiatives in their access or authority to collect certain necessary price data. According to the GAO report, transparency initiatives that provided consumers with a reasonable estimate of their complete costs integrated pricing data from both providers and plans and issuers. The GAO report, therefore, recommended that HHS determine the feasibility, and the next steps, of making estimates of out-of-pocket costs[25] for health care services available to consumers.[26]

States have been at the forefront of transparency initiatives and some have required disclosure of pricing information for years. More than half of the states have passed legislation establishing price transparency websites or mandating that health plans, hospitals, or physicians make pricing information available to patients.[27] As of early 2012, there were 62 consumer-oriented, state-based health care price comparison websites. Half of these websites were launched after 2006, and most were hosted by a state government agency (46.8 percent) or hospital association (38.7 percent). Most websites reported prices of inpatient care for medical conditions (72.6 percent) or surgeries (71.0 percent). Information about prices of outpatient services such as diagnostic or screening procedures (37.1 percent), radiology studies (22.6 percent), prescription drugs (14.5 percent), or laboratory tests (9.7 percent) were reported less often.[28] However, it is important to note that the state efforts directed at plans are not applicable to self-insured group health plans. As a result, the data collected does not include data from self-insured group health plans and a significant portion of consumers would not have access to information on their plans.

States have adopted a variety of approaches to improve price transparency.[29] In 2012, Massachusetts began requiring issuers to provide, upon request, the estimated amount insured patients would be responsible to pay for proposed admissions, procedures, or services based upon the information available to the issuer at the time, and also began requiring providers to disclose the charge for the admission, procedure, or service upon request by the patient within 2 working days.[30] Sixteen states have implemented all-payer claims databases that include health care prices and quality information; and of these 16 states, 8 states make both price and quality information available to the public through state-based websites.[31]

Health insurance issuers and self-insured group health plans also have moved in the direction of increased price transparency. For example, some group health plans are using price transparency tools to incentivize employees to make cost conscious decisions when purchasing health care services. Most large issuers have embedded cost estimator tools into their enrollee websites, and some provide their enrollees with comparative cost information, which includes rates that the issuers and plans have negotiated with in-network providers and suppliers.

In the HHS 2020 Notice of Benefit and Payment Parameters (2020 Payment Notice) proposed rule,[32] HHS sought input on ways to provide consumers with greater transparency with regard to their own health care data, Qualified Health Plan (QHP) offerings on the Federally-facilitated Exchanges (FFEs),[33] and the cost of health care services. Additionally, HHS sought comment on ways to further implement section 1311(e)(3) of PPACA, as implemented by 45 CFR 156.220(d), under which, upon the request of an enrollee, a QHP issuer must make available in a timely manner the amount of enrollee cost sharing under the enrollee's coverage for a specific service furnished by an in-network provider. HHS was particularly interested in what types of data would be most useful to improving consumers' abilities to make informed health care decisions, including decisions related to their coverage specifications and ways to improve consumer access to information about health care costs.

Commenters on the 2020 Payment Notice overwhelmingly supported the idea of increased price transparency. Many commenters provided suggestions for defining the scope of price transparency requirements, such as providing costs for both in-network and out-of-network health care, and providing health care cost estimates that include an accounting for consumer-specific benefit information, like progress toward meeting deductibles and out-of-pocket limits, as well as remaining visits under visit limits. Commenters expressed support for implementing price transparency requirements across all private markets and for price transparency efforts to be a part of a larger payment reform effort and a provider empowerment and patient engagement strategy. Some commenters advised HHS to carefully consider how such policies should be implemented, warning against federal duplication of state efforts and requirements that would result in group health plans and health insurance issuers passing along increased administrative costs to consumers, and cautioning that the proprietary and competitive nature of payment data should be protected.

In the summer and fall of 2018, HHS hosted listening sessions related to the goal of empowering consumers by ensuring the availability of useable pricing information. Participants included a wide representation of stakeholders from providers, issuers, researchers, and consumer and patient advocacy groups. Participants noted that currently available pricing tools are underutilized, in part because consumers are often unaware that they exist, and even when used, the tools sometimes convey inconsistent and inaccurate information.

Participants also commented that tool development can be expensive, especially for smaller health plans, which tend to invest less in technology because of the limited return on investment. Participants also commented that most tools developed to date do not allow for comparison shopping. Participants stated that existing tools usually use historical claims data, which results in broad, sometimes regional estimates, rather than accurate and individualized prices. In addition, participants noted pricing tools are rarely available when and where consumers are likely to make health care decisions, for example, during interactions with providers. This means that patients are not able to consider relevant cost issues when discussing referral options or the tradeoffs of various treatment options with referring providers. In a national study, there was alignment between patients, employers, and providers in wanting to know and discuss the cost of care at the point of service.[34] With access to patient-specific cost estimates for services furnished by particular providers, referring providers and their patients could take pricing information into account when considering treatment options.

---

[24] https://www.gao.gov/products/GAO-11-791

[25] GAO defines an estimate of a consumer's complete health care cost as pricing information on a service that identifies a consumer's out-of-pocket cost, including any negotiated discounts, and all costs associated with a service or services.

[26] https://www.gao.gov/products/GAO-11-791

[27] Frakt, A., Mehrotra, A. "What Type of Price Transparency Do We Need in Health Care?" 170 Ann. Intern. Med. 561. April 16, 2019. Available at: https://mfprac.com/web2019/07literature/literature/Misc/HealthTransparency_Frankt.pdf.

[28] Kullgren, J., Duey, K, Werner, R. "A Census of State Health Care Price Transparency Websites." 309 JAMA 2437. June 19, 2013. Available at: https://jamanetwork.com/journals/jama/fullarticle/1697957.

[29] "2017 Price Transparency & Physician Quality Report Card." Catalyst for Payment Reform. Available at: https://www.catalyze.org/product/2017-price-transparency-physician-quality-report-card/.

[30] Jenkins, K. "CMS Price Transparency Push Trails State Initiatives." Nat'l L. Rev. February 8, 2019. Available at: https://www.natlawreview.com/article/cms-price-transparency-push-trails-state-initiatives.

[31] "The State Of State Legislation Addressing Health Care Costs And Quality," Health Affairs Blog. August 22, 2019. Available at: https://www.healthaffairs.org/do/10.1377/hblog20190820.483741/full/.

[32] 84 FR 227 (Jan. 24, 2019).

[33] The term "Exchanges" means American Health Benefit Exchanges established under section 1311 of PPACA. See section 2791(d)(21) of the PHS Act.

[34] "Let's Talk About Money," University of Utah. https://uofuhealth.utah.edu/value/lets-talk-about-money.php.

In response to this feedback, CMS has pursued initiatives in addition to these proposed rules to improve access to the information necessary to empower consumers to make more informed decisions about their health care costs. These initiatives have included a multi-step effort to implement section 2718(e) of the PHS Act, which was added by section 1001 of PPACA (Pub. L. 111-148), as amended by section 10101 of the Health Care and Education Reconciliation Act of 2010 (Pub. L. 111-152). Section 2718(e) of the PHS Act requires each hospital operating within the United States to, for each year, establish (and update) and make public (in accordance with guidelines developed by the Secretary) a list of the hospital's standard charges for items and services provided by the hospital, including for diagnosis-related groups established under section 1886(d)(4) of the Social Security Act (SSA). In the Fiscal Year (FY) 2015 Hospital Inpatient Prospective Payment Systems and Long Term Care Hospital Prospective Payment Systems (IPPS/LTCH PPS) final rule,[35] CMS reminded hospitals of their obligation to comply with the provisions of section 2718(e) of the PHS Act and provided guidelines for its implementation. At that time, CMS required hospitals to either make public a list of their standard charges or their policies for allowing the public to view a list of those charges in response to an inquiry. In addition, CMS stated that it expected hospitals to update the information at least annually, or more often as appropriate, to reflect current charges, and encouraged hospitals to undertake efforts to engage in consumer-friendly communication of their charges to enable consumers to compare charges for similar services across hospitals and to help them understand what their potential financial liability might be for items and services they obtain at the hospital.

In the FY 2019 IPPS/LTCH PPS final rule,[36] CMS again reminded hospitals of their obligation to comply with section 2718(e) of the PHS Act and announced an update to its guidelines. The updated guidelines, which have been effective since January 1, 2019, require hospitals to make available a list of their current standard charges (whether in the form of a "chargemaster" or another form of the hospital's choice) via the internet in a machine-readable format and to update this information at least annually, or more often as appropriate. The intent of the guidelines is to improve consumer access to important information regarding the cost of their health care through hospital websites. Price transparency and the ability to compare standard charges across hospitals can empower consumers to be more informed and exercise greater control over their purchasing decisions.

In response to stakeholder feedback and Executive Order 13877, CMS took another important step toward improving health care value and increasing competition in the Calendar Year 2020 Hospital Outpatient Policy Payment System (OPPS) Policy Changes and Payment Rates and Ambulatory Surgical Center Payment System Policy Changes and Payment Rates: Price Transparency Requirements for Hospitals to Make Standard Charges Public (CMS-1717-F2) final rule (OPPS Price Transparency final rule) by codifying requirements under section 2718(e) of the PHS Act as well as a regulatory scheme under section 2718(b)(3) of the PHS Act that enables CMS to enforce those requirements.[37] To further improve public access to meaningful hospital charge information, CMS is requiring hospitals to make publicly available their gross charges (as found in the hospital's chargemaster), their payer-specific negotiated charges, their discounted cash prices, and their de-identified minimum and maximum negotiated charges for all items and services they provide through a single online machine-readable file that is updated at least once annually. Additionally, the final rule requires hospitals to display online in a consumer-friendly format the payer-specific negotiated charges, discounted cash prices and de-identified minimum and maximum negotiated charges for as many of the 70 shoppable services selected by CMS that the hospital provides and as many additional hospital-selected shoppable services as are necessary for a combined total of at least 300 shoppable services (or if the hospital provides less than 300 shoppable services, then as many as the hospital provides). CMS defines shoppable services as a service that can be scheduled by a health care consumer in advance, and has further explained that shoppable services are typically those that are routinely provided in non-urgent situations that do not require immediate action or attention to the patient, thus allowing patients to price shop and schedule such services at times that are convenient for them.

The Departments have concluded that the final rules under section 2718(e) of the PHS Act would not result in consumers receiving complete price estimates for health care items and services because, as the GAO concluded, complete price estimates require pricing information from both providers and health insurance issuers.[38] In addition, because section 2718(e) of the PHS Act applies only to items and services provided by hospitals, the final requirements under that section would not improve the price transparency of items and services provided by other health care entities. Accordingly, the Departments have concluded that additional price transparency efforts are necessary to empower a more price-conscious and responsible health care consumer, promote competition in the health care industry, and lower the overall rate of growth in health care spending.

Despite these price transparency efforts, there continues to be a lack of easily accessible pricing information for consumers to use when shopping for health care services. While there are several efforts across states, many still do not require private market plans and issuers to provide real-time, out-of-pocket cost estimates to participants, beneficiaries, and enrollees.[39] Furthermore, states do not have authority to require such disclosures to participants and beneficiaries of self-insured group health plans, which compose a significant portion of the private market.[40] These proposed rules are meant, in part, to address this lack of easily accessible pricing information, and represent a critical part of the Departments' overall strategy for reforming health care markets by promoting transparency, competition, and choice across the health care industry.

The Departments, therefore, believe that additional rulemaking is necessary and appropriate to ensure consumers can exercise meaningful control over their health care and health care spending. The disclosures that the Departments are proposing to require would ensure consumers have ready access to the information they need to estimate their potential out-of-pocket costs for health care items and services before a service is delivered. These proposed rules would also empower consumers by incentivizing market innovators to help consumers understand how their plan or coverage pays for health care and to shop for health care based on price, which is a fundamental factor in any purchasing decision.

C. Statutory Background and Enactment of PPACA

The Patient Protection and Affordable Care Act was enacted on March 23, 2010 and the Health Care and Education Reconciliation Act of 2010 was enacted on March 30, 2010 (collectively, PPACA). As relevant here, PPACA reorganized, amended, and added to the provisions of part A of title XXVII of the PHS Act relating to health coverage requirements for group health plans and health insurance issuers in the group and individual markets. The term "group health plan" includes both insured and self-insured group health plans.

PPACA also added section 715 to the Employee Retirement Income Security Act of 1974 (ERISA) and section 9815 to the Internal Revenue Code (Code) to incorporate the provisions of part A of title XXVII of the PHS Act, PHS Act sections 2701 through 2728 into ERISA and the Code, making them applicable to plans and issuers providing health insurance coverage in connection with group health plans.

1. Transparency in Coverage

Section 2715A of the PHS Act provides that group health plans and health insurance issuers offering group or individual health insurance coverage shall comply with section 1311(e)(3) of PPACA, except that a plan or coverage that is not offered through an Exchange shall only be required to submit the information required to the Secretary and the state's insurance commissioner, and make such information available to the

---

[35] 79 FR 49854, 50146, (Aug. 22, 2014).

[36] 83 FR 41144, 41686 (Aug. 17, 2018).

[37] Published elsewhere in this issue of the Federal Register.

[38] https://www.gao.gov/products/GAO-11-791.

[39] "2017 Price Transparency & Physician Quality Report Card." Catalyst for Payment Reform. Available at: https://www.catalyze.org/product/2017-price-transparency-physician-quality-report-card/.

[40] Self-Insured Health Benefit Plans 2019: Based on Filings through Statistical Year 2016. January 7, 2019. Available at: https://www.dol.gov/sites/dolgov/files/EBSA/researchers/statistics/retirement-bulletins/annual-report-on-self-insured-group-health-plans-2019-appendix-b.pdf.

public. Section 1311(e)(3) of PPACA addresses transparency in health care coverage and imposes certain reporting and disclosure requirements for health plans that are seeking certification as QHPs that may be offered on an Exchange.

Paragraph (A) of section 1311(e)(3) of PPACA requires plans seeking certification as a QHP to submit the following information to state insurance regulators, the Secretary of HHS, and the Exchange and to make that information available to the public:

- Claims payment policies and practices,
- Periodic financial disclosures,
- Data on enrollment,
- Data on disenrollment,
- Data on the number of claims that are denied,
- Data on rating practices,
- Information on cost sharing and payments with respect to any out-of-network coverage, and
- Information on enrollee and participant rights under this title.

Paragraph (A) also requires plans seeking certification as a QHP to submit any "[o]ther information as determined appropriate by the Secretary."

Paragraph (C) requires those plans, as a requirement of certification as a QHP, to permit individuals to learn the amount of cost sharing (including deductibles, copayments, and coinsurance) under the individual's coverage that the individual would be responsible for paying with respect to the furnishing of a specific item or service by an in-network provider in a timely manner upon the request of the individual. Paragraph (C) specifies that, at a minimum, such information shall be made available to such individual through an internet website and such other means for individuals without access to the internet.

On March 27, 2012, HHS issued the Exchange Establishment final rule[41] that implemented sections 1311(e)(3)(A) through (C) of PPACA at 45 CFR 155.1040(a) through (c) and 156.220. The Exchange Establishment final rule created standards for QHP issuers to submit specific information related to transparency in coverage. QHPs are required to post and make data related to transparency in coverage available to the public in plain language and submit this same data to HHS, the Exchange, and the state insurance commissioner. In the preamble to the Exchange Establishment final rule, HHS noted that "health plan standards set forth under this final rule are, for the most part, strictly related to QHPs certified to be offered through the Exchange and not the entire individual and small group market. Such policies for the entire individual and small and large group markets have been, and will continue to be, addressed in separate rulemaking issued by HHS, and the Departments of Labor and the Treasury."

2. Medical Loss Ratio (MLR)

Section 2718(a) and (b) of the PHS Act, as added by PPACA, generally requires health insurance issuers to submit an annual MLR report to HHS, and provide rebates to enrollees if the issuers do not achieve specified MLR thresholds. HHS proposes to amend its MLR program rules under section 2718(c) of the PHS Act, under which the methodologies for calculating measures of the activities reported under section 2718(a) of the PHS Act shall be designed to take into account the special circumstances of smaller plans, different types of plans, and newer plans. Specifically, HHS proposes to recognize the special circumstances of a different and newer type of plan for purposes of MLR reporting and calculations when that plan shares savings with consumers who choose lower-cost, higher-value providers. HHS proposes to revise 45 CFR 158.221 to add a new paragraph (b)(9) to allow such shared savings, when offered by an issuer, to be factored into an issuer's MLR numerator calculation beginning with the 2020 MLR reporting year.

II. Overview of the Proposed Rules Regarding Transparency – the Departments of the Treasury, Labor, and Health and Human Services

The Departments propose the price transparency requirements set forth in these proposed rules in new 26 CFR 54.9815-2715A, 29 CFR 2590.715-2715A, and 45 CFR 147.210. Paragraph (a) of the proposed rules sets forth the scope and relevant definitions. Paragraph (b) of the proposed rules includes: (1) a requirement that group health plans and health insurance issuers in the individual and group markets disclose to participants, beneficiaries, or enrollees (or their authorized representatives) upon their request, through a self-service tool made available by the plan or issuer on an internet website, cost-sharing information for a covered item or service from a particular provider or providers, and (2) a requirement that plans and issuers make such information available in paper form. Paragraph (c) of the proposed rules would require that plans and issuers disclose to the public, through two machine-readable files, the negotiated rates for in-network providers, and unique amounts a plan or issuer allowed for items or services furnished by out-of-network providers during a specified time period.

The Departments request comments on all aspects of these proposed rules. In the preamble discussion that follows, the Departments also solicit comments on a number of specific issues related to the proposed rules where stakeholder feedback would be particularly useful in evaluating whether and how to issue final rules.

Sections III and IV of this preamble include requests for information on topics closely related to this rulemaking. Due to the design and capability differences among the information technology systems of plans and issuers, as well as difficulties consumers experience in deciphering information relevant to health care and health insurance, the Departments seek comment on additional price transparency requirements that could supplement the proposed requirements of paragraphs (b) and (c) of these proposed rules. For example, in section III, the Departments seek comment on whether the Departments should require plans and issuers to disclose information necessary to calculate a participant's, beneficiary's, or enrollee's cost-sharing liability through a publicly-available, standards-based application programming interface (API).

Section IV of this preamble requests comment on how existing quality data on health care provider items and services can be leveraged to complement the proposals in these proposed rules. Although these proposed rules do not include any health care quality disclosure requirements, the Departments appreciate the importance of health care quality information in providing consumers the information necessary to make value-based health care decisions.[42]

A. *Proposed Requirements for Disclosing Cost-Sharing Information to Participants, Beneficiaries, or Enrollees*

As described earlier in this preamble, the Departments' intention regarding these proposed rules is to enable participants, beneficiaries, and enrollees to obtain an estimate of their potential cost-sharing liability for covered items and services they might receive from a particular health care provider, consistent with the requirements of section 2715A of the PHS Act and section 1311(e)(3)(C) of PPACA. Accordingly, paragraph (b) of these proposed rules would require group health plans and health insurance issuers to disclose certain information relevant to a determination of a consumer's out-of-pocket costs for a particular health care item or service in accordance with specific method and format requirements, upon the request of a participant, beneficiary, or enrollee (or his or her authorized representative).

---

[41] *https://www.govinfo.gov/content/pkg/FR-2012-03-27/pdf/2012-6125.pdf.*

[42] "2017 Price Transparency & Physician Quality Report Card." Catalyst for Payment Reform. Available at: *https://www.catalyze.org/product/2017-price-transparency-physician-quality-report-card/.*

1. Information Required to be Disclosed to Participants, Beneficiaries, or Enrollees

Based on significant research and stakeholder input, the Departments conclude that requiring group health plans and health insurance issuers to disclose to participants, beneficiaries, or enrollees cost-sharing information in the manner most familiar to them is the best means to empower individuals to understand their potential cost-sharing liability for covered items and services that might be furnished by particular providers. The Departments, therefore, modeled these proposed price transparency requirements on existing notices that plans and issuers generally provide to participants, beneficiaries, or enrollees after health care items and services have been furnished.

Specifically, section 2719 of the PHS Act requires non-grandfathered plans and issuers to provide a notice of adverse benefit determination[43] (commonly referred to as an explanation of benefits (EOB)) to participants, beneficiaries, or enrollees after health care items or services are furnished and claims for benefits are adjudicated. EOBs typically include the amount billed by a provider for items and services, negotiated rates with in-network providers or allowed amounts for out-of-network providers, the amount the plan paid to the provider, and the individual's obligation for deductibles, copayments, coinsurance, and any other balance under the provider's bill. Consumers are accustomed to seeing cost-sharing information as it is presented in an EOB. This proposal similarly would require plans and issuers to provide the specific price and benefit information on which an individual's cost-sharing liability is based.

The Departments have concluded that proposing to require plans and issuers to disclose to participants, beneficiaries, or enrollees price and benefit information that is analogous to the information that generally appears on an EOB would be the most effective and reasonable way to present cost-sharing information prior to the receipt of care, in a manner that can be understood by these individuals. Providing individuals with access to information generally included in EOBs before they receive covered items and services would enable individuals to understand their cost-sharing liability for the item or service and consider price when choosing a provider from whom to receive the item or service. Cost-sharing liability estimates would be required to be built upon accurate information, including actual negotiated rates, out-of-network allowed amounts, and individual-specific accumulated amounts. This does not mean the Departments would require that the estimate reflect the amount that is ultimately charged to a participant, beneficiary, or enrollee. Instead, the estimate would reflect the amount a participant, beneficiary, or enrollee would be expected to pay for the covered item or service for which cost-sharing information is sought. Thus, these proposed rules would not require the cost-sharing liability estimate to include costs for unanticipated items or services the individual could incur due to the severity of the his or her illness or injury, provider treatment decisions, or other unforeseen events.

In designing this price transparency proposal, the Departments also considered stakeholder input regarding the importance of protecting proprietary information. As explained earlier in this preamble, all of the information that would be required to be disclosed under these proposed rules is currently disclosed in EOBs that plans and issuers provide to individuals as a matter of course after services have been furnished and payment has been adjudicated. Therefore, the Departments are of the view that the proposed requirement that plans and issuers disclose this same information, to the same parties, before services are rendered does not pose any greater risk to plan or issuer proprietary information.

Consistent with how the information for an item or service would typically be presented on an EOB, the Departments propose to allow plans and issuers to provide participants, beneficiaries, and enrollees with cost-sharing information for either a discrete item or service or for items or services for a treatment or procedure for which the plan bundles payment, according to how the plan or issuer structures payment for the item or service. Accordingly, these proposed rules set forth seven content elements that a plan or issuer must disclose, upon request, to a participant, beneficiary, or enrollee (or his or her authorized representative) for a covered item or service, to the extent relevant to the individual's cost-sharing liability for the item or service. These seven content elements generally reflect the same information that is included in an EOB after health care services are provided. The Departments have determined that each of the content elements is necessary and appropriate to implement the mandates of section 2715A of the PHS Act and section 1311(e)(3)(C) of PPACA by permitting individuals under a plan or coverage to learn the amount of their cost-sharing liability for specific items or services under a plan or coverage from a particular provider. The Departments propose that plans and issuers must satisfy these elements through disclosure of actual data relevant to an individual's cost-sharing liability that is accurate at the time the request is made. The Departments acknowledge that plans and issuers may not have processed all of an individual's outstanding claims when the individual requests the information; therefore, plans and issuers would not be required to account for outstanding claims that have not yet been processed.

Furthermore, under these proposals, the cost-sharing information would need to be disclosed to the participant, beneficiary, or enrollee in plain language. The proposed rules define "plain language" to mean written and presented in a manner calculated to be understood by the average participant, beneficiary, or enrollee. Determining whether this standard has been satisfied requires an exercise of considered judgment and discretion, taking into account such factors as the level of comprehension and education of typical participants, beneficiaries, or enrollees in the plan or coverage and the complexity of the terms of the plan. Accounting for these factors would likely require limiting or eliminating the use of technical jargon and long, complex sentences, so that the information provided will not have the effect of misleading, misinforming, or failing to inform participants, beneficiaries, or enrollees.

a. First Content Element: Estimated cost-sharing liability

The first content element that plans and issuers would be required to disclose under these proposed rules would be an estimate of the cost-sharing liability for the furnishing of a covered item or service by a particular provider or providers. The calculation of the cost-sharing liability estimate would be required to be computed based on the other relevant cost-sharing information that plans and issuers would be required to disclose, as described later in this section of the preamble.

The proposed rules define "cost-sharing liability" to mean the amount a participant, beneficiary, or enrollee is responsible for paying for a covered item or service under the terms of the plan or coverage. Cost-sharing liability calculations must consider all applicable forms of cost sharing, including deductibles, coinsurance requirements, and copayments. The term cost-sharing liability does not include premiums, balance billing amounts for out-of-network providers, or the cost of non-covered items or services. For QHPs offered through Exchanges, an estimate of cost-sharing liability for a requested covered item or service provided must reflect any cost-sharing reductions the individual would receive under the coverage.

The proposed rules define "items or services" to mean all encounters, procedures, medical tests, supplies, drugs, durable medical equipment, and fees (including facility fees), for which a provider charges a patient in connection with the provision of health care. This proposed definition of items or services is intended to be flexible enough to allow plans and issuers to disclose cost-sharing information for either discrete items or services for which an individual is seeking cost-sharing information, or, if the issuer bundles payment for items or services associated with a treatment or procedure, for a set of items or services included in the bundle. These proposed rules further define "covered items or services" to mean items or services for which the costs are payable, in whole or in part, under the terms of a plan or coverage. The Departments solicit comment on whether other types of information are necessary to provide an estimate of cost-sharing liability prior to an individual's receipt of items or services from a provider or providers. The Departments also solicit comment on these definitions.

---

[43] An adverse benefit determination means an adverse benefit determination as defined in 29 CFR 2560.503-1, as well as any rescission of coverage, as described in 29 CFR 2590.715-2712(a)(2) (whether or not, in connection with the rescission, there is an adverse effect on any particular benefit at that time). *See* 26 CFR 54.9815-2719, 29 CFR 2590.715-2719 and 45 CFR 147.136. Plans subject to the requirements of ERISA (including grandfathered health plans) are also subject to a requirement to provide an adverse benefit determination under 29 CFR 2560.503-1.

b. Second Content Element: Accumulated amounts

The second content element would be a participant's, beneficiary's, or enrollee's accumulated amounts. These proposed rules define "accumulated amounts" to mean the amount of financial responsibility that a participant, beneficiary, or enrollee has incurred at the time the request for cost-sharing information is made, either with respect to a deductible or an out-of-pocket limit (such as the annual limitation on cost sharing provided in section 2707(b) of the PHS Act, as incorporated into ERISA and the Code, or a maximum out-of-pocket amount the plan or issuer establishes that is lower than the requirement under the PHS Act). In the case where an individual is enrolled in a family plan or coverage (or other-than-self-only coverage), these accumulated amounts would include the financial responsibility a participant, beneficiary, or enrollee has incurred toward meeting his or her individual deductible and/or out-of-pocket limit as well as the amount of financial responsibility that the individuals enrolled under the plan or coverage have incurred toward meeting the other-than-self-only coverage deductible and/or out-of-pocket limit, as applicable.[44] For this purpose, accumulated amounts would include any expense that counts toward the deductible or out-of-pocket limit (such as copayments and coinsurance), but would exclude expenses that would not count toward a deductible or out-of-pocket limit (such as premium payments, out-of-pocket expenses for out-of-network services, or amounts for items or services not covered under a plan or coverage).

Furthermore, to the extent a plan or issuer imposes a cumulative treatment limitation on a particular covered item or service (such as a limit on the number of items, days, units, visits, or hours covered in a defined time period) independent of individual medical necessity determinations, the accumulated amounts would also include the amount that has accrued toward the limit on the item or service (such as the number of items, days, units, visits, or hours the participant, beneficiary, or enrollee has used).

The Departments understand that certain cumulative treatment limitations may vary by individual based on a determination of medical necessity and that it may not be reasonable for a plan or issuer to account for this variance as part of the accumulated amounts. Therefore, plans and issuers would be required to provide cost-sharing information with respect to an accumulated amount for a cumulative treatment limitation that reflects the status of the individual's progress toward meeting the limitation, and would not include any individual determination of medical necessity that may affect coverage for the item or service. For example, if the terms of an individual's plan or coverage limit coverage of physical therapy visits to 10 per plan or policy year, subject to a medical necessity determination, and at the time the request for cost-sharing information is made the individual has had claims paid for three physical therapy visits, the plan or coverage would make cost-sharing information disclosures based on the fact that the individual could be covered for seven more physical therapy visits in that plan or policy year, regardless of whether or not a determination of medical necessity has been made at that time.

c. Third Content Element: Negotiated rate

The third content element under these proposed rules would be the negotiated rate, reflected as a dollar amount, for an in-network provider or providers for a requested covered item or service, to the extent necessary to determine the participant's, beneficiary's, or enrollee's cost-sharing liability. These proposed rules define "negotiated rate" to mean the amount a plan or issuer, or a third party (such as a third-party administrator (TPA)) on behalf of a plan or issuer, has contractually agreed to pay an in-network provider for a covered item or service pursuant to the terms of an agreement between the provider and the plan, issuer, or third party on behalf of a plan or issuer. The Departments understand that some provider contracts express negotiated rates as a formula (for example, 150 percent of the Medicare rate), but disclosure of formulas is not likely to be helpful or understandable for many participants, beneficiaries, and enrollees viewing this information. For this reason, these proposed rules would require disclosure of the rate that results from using such a formula, which would be required to be expressed as a dollar amount.

Negotiated rates generally are an essential input for the calculation of a participant's, beneficiary's, or enrollee's cost-sharing liability. For example, cost-sharing liability for a covered service with a 30 percent coinsurance requirement cannot be determined without knowing the negotiated rate of which an individual must pay 30 percent. Additionally, if an individual has not met an applicable deductible and the cost for a covered item or service from an in-network provider is less than the remaining deductible, then the cost-sharing liability will in fact be the negotiated rate. The Departments acknowledge, however, that if the negotiated rate does not impact an individual's cost-sharing liability under a plan or coverage for a covered item or service (for example, the copayment for the item or service is a flat dollar amount or zero dollars and the individual has met a deductible, or a deductible does not apply to that particular item or service), disclosure of the negotiated rate may be unnecessary to calculate cost-sharing liability for that item or service. Therefore, the Departments propose that disclosure of a negotiated rate would not be required under these proposed rules if it is not relevant for calculating an individual's cost-sharing liability for a particular item or service. The Departments seek comment on whether there are any reasons disclosure of negotiated rates should nonetheless be required under these circumstances.

Under these proposed rules, plans and issuers would be required to disclose to participants, beneficiaries, or enrollees an estimate of cost-sharing liability for items and services, including prescription drugs. This would allow individuals to request cost-sharing information for a specific billing code (as described later in this preamble) associated with a prescription drug or by descriptive term (such as the name of the prescription drug), which will permit individuals to learn the estimated cost of a prescription drug obtained directly through a provider, such as a pharmacy or mail order service. In addition to allowing individuals to obtain cost-sharing information by using a billing code or descriptive term, the rules would also permit individuals to learn the cost of a set of items or services that include a prescription drug or drugs that is subject to a bundled payment arrangement for a treatment or procedure. The proposed rules define the term "bundled payment" to mean a payment model under which a provider is paid a single payment for all covered items or services provided to a patient for a specific treatment or procedure. However, the Departments acknowledge that outside of a bundled payment arrangement, plans and issuers often base cost-sharing liability for prescription drugs on the undiscounted list price, such as the average wholesale price or wholesale acquisition cost, which frequently differs from the price the plan or issuer has negotiated for the prescription drug.[45] In these instances, providing the individual with a rate that has been negotiated between the issuer or plan and its pharmacy benefit manager could be misleading, as this rate would reflect rebates and other discounts, and could be lower than what the individual would pay—particularly if the individual has not met his or her deductible. However, arguably, requiring the issuer to disclose only the rate upon which the individual's cost-sharing liability estimate is based would perpetuate the lack of transparency around drug pricing.

The Departments seek comment regarding whether a rate other than the negotiated rate, such as the undiscounted price, should be required to be disclosed for prescription drugs, and whether and how to account for any and all rebates, discounts, and dispensing fees to ensure individuals have access to meaningful cost-sharing liability estimates for prescription drugs. The Departments also solicit comment as to whether there are certain scenarios in which drug pricing information should not be included in an individual's estimated cost-sharing liability. For example, would the cost to an individual for a drug outside of a bundled payment arrangement be so impacted by factors beyond the negotiated rate for the drug,

---

[44] The Departments read section 2707(b) as requiring non-grandfathered group health plans to comply with the maximum annual limitation on cost sharing promulgated under section 1302(c)(1) of PPACA, including the HHS clarification that the self-only maximum annual limitation on cost sharing applies to each individual, regardless of whether the individual is enrolled in self-only coverage or in other-than-self-only coverage. Accordingly, the self-only maximum annual limitation on cost sharing applies to an individual who is enrolled in family coverage or other coverage that is not self-only coverage under a group health plan. See 80 FR 10749, 10824–10825 (Feb. 27, 2015),

see also FAQs About Affordable Care Act Implementation (Part XXVII), Q1, available at https://www.cms.gov/CCIIO/Resources/Fact-Sheets-and-FAQs/Downloads/ACA-FAQs-Part-XXVII-MOOP-2706-FINAL.pdf and https://www.dol.gov/sites/dolgov/files/EBSA/about-ebsa/our-activities/resource-center/faqs/aca-part-xxvii.pdf.

[45] "Follow the Dollar: How the pharmaceutical distribution and payment system shapes the prices of brand medicines." PhRMA. November 2017. Available at https://www.phrma.org/report/follow-the-dollar-report

and not reasonably knowable by the plan or issuer, that the cost-sharing liability estimate for that drug would not be meaningful for the individual and should not be provided outside of a cost-sharing liability estimate for a bundled payment? Alternatively, should drug costs be required to be included in a cost-sharing liability estimate in all scenarios, including when the consumer searches for cost-sharing information for a particular drug by billing code or descriptive term in connection with items and services for which the plan or issuer does not bundle payment? The Departments also seek comment on whether the relationship between plans or issuers and pharmacy benefit managers[46] allows plans and issuers to disclose rate information for drugs, or if contracts between plans and issuers and pharmacy benefit managers would need to be amended to allow plans and issuers to provide a sufficient level of transparency. If those contracts would need to be amended, the Departments seek comment on the time that would be needed to make those changes.

d. Fourth Content Element: Out-of-network allowed amount

The fourth content element would be the out-of-network allowed amount for the requested covered item or service. This element would only be relevant when a participant, beneficiary, or enrollee requests cost-sharing information for a covered item or service furnished by an out-of-network provider. These proposed rules define "out-of-network allowed amount" to mean the maximum amount a plan or issuer would pay for a covered item or service furnished by an out-of-network provider. Under these proposed rules, plans and issuers would be required to disclose an estimate of cost-sharing liability for a participant, beneficiary, or enrollee. Therefore, when disclosing an estimate of cost-sharing liability for an out-of-network item or service, the plan or issuer would disclose the out-of-network allowed amount and any cost-sharing liability the participant, beneficiary, or enrollee would be responsible for paying. For instance, if a plan has established an out-of-network allowed amount of $100 for an item or service from a particular out-of-network provider and the participant, beneficiary, or enrollee is responsible for paying 30 percent of the out-of-network allowed amount ($30), the plan would disclose both the allowed amount ($100) and the individual's cost-sharing liability ($30), indicating that the individual is responsible for 30 percent of the out-of-network allowed amount.

Because the proposed definition of cost-sharing liability does not include amounts charged by out-of-network providers that exceed the out-of-network allowed amount, which participants, beneficiaries, or enrollees must pay (sometimes referred to as balance bills), it may be difficult for participants, beneficiaries, or enrollees to determine their likely out-of-pocket costs for covered items and services furnished by an out-of-network provider. Nonetheless, under section 1311(e)(3)(A)(vii) of PPACA and section 2715A of the PHS Act, Congress intended that participants, beneficiaries, enrollees, and other members of the public have access to accurate and timely information on cost sharing and payments with respect to any out-of-network coverage. In the Departments' view, requiring plans and issuers to disclose out-of-network allowed amounts and a participant's, beneficiary's, or enrollee's cost-sharing obligation for covered items and services is necessary and appropriate to fulfill this statutory mandate, and would give individuals information necessary to estimate their out-of-pocket costs if they request additional information from an out-of-network provider about how much the provider would charge for a particular item or service.

e. Fifth Content Element: Items and services content list

The fifth content element would be a list of those covered items and services for which cost-sharing information is disclosed. This requirement would be relevant only when a participant, beneficiary, or enrollee requests cost-sharing information for an item or service that is subject to a bundled payment arrangement that includes multiple items or services, rather than one discrete item or service. This requirement would not apply when an individual requests cost-sharing information for an item or service not subject to a bundled payment arrangement. In cases in which an individual requests a cost-sharing liability estimate for a covered item or service that is subject to a bundled payment arrangement, plans and issuers would be required to disclose a list of each covered item and service included in the bundled payment arrangement and the individual's cost-sharing liability for those covered items and services as a bundle, but not a cost-sharing liability estimate separately associated with each covered item or service included in the bundle. In the Departments' view, in order to support consumers' ability to shop for services, consumers need to know precisely what items and services are included in the cost-sharing information provided.

f. Sixth Content Element: Notice of prerequisites to coverage

The sixth content element would be a notice, whenever applicable, informing the individual that a specific covered item or service for which the individual requests cost-sharing information may be subject to a prerequisite for coverage. The proposed rules define the term "prerequisite" to mean certain requirements relating to medical management techniques for covered items and services that must be satisfied before a plan or issuer will cover the item or service. Specifically, prerequisites include concurrent review, prior authorization, and step-therapy or fail-first protocols. The definition of prerequisite in these proposed rules is intended to capture medical management techniques that apply to an item or service that require action by the participant, beneficiary, or enrollee before the plan or issuer will cover the item or service. Accordingly, the proposed definition of prerequisite does not include medical necessity determinations generally, or other forms of medical management techniques that do not require action by the participant, beneficiary, or enrollee. The Departments solicit comment on whether there are any additional medical management techniques that should be explicitly included as prerequisites in the final rules.

g. Seventh Content Element: Disclosure notice

The seventh and final content element would be a notice that communicates certain information in plain language and includes several specific disclosures. First, this notice would include a statement that out-of-network providers may bill participants, beneficiaries, or enrollees for the difference between providers' billed charges and the sum of the amount collected from the plan or issuer and the amount collected from the patient in the form of cost sharing (the difference often referred to as balance billing) and that these estimates do not account for those potential additional amounts. The Departments understand that there are numerous state laws that address balance-billing practices such that the notice described in this proposed content element regarding balance bills may be misleading or inaccurate for beneficiaries, participants, or enrollees enrolled in a plan or coverage in certain states. The Departments request comment on whether any modifications to this content element would be appropriate to allow plans and issuers to accurately advise participants, beneficiaries, or enrollees of their potential exposure to or protection from any balance bills.

Second, the notice would be required to convey that actual charges for the participant's, beneficiary's, or enrollee's covered items and services may be different from those described in a cost-sharing liability estimate, depending on the actual items and services received at the point of care.

Third, the notice would be required to include a statement that the estimated cost-sharing liability for a covered item or service is not a guarantee that coverage will be provided for those items and services.

Finally, under these proposed rules, plans and issuers would be permitted to include any additional information, including other disclaimers that the plan or issuer determines appropriate, as long as the additional information does not conflict with the information required to be provided. Plans and issuers would be permitted to include additional language so long as the language could not reasonably be read to disclaim the plan's or issuer's responsibility for providing a participant, beneficiary, or enrollee with accurate cost-sharing information. For example, plans and issuers may choose to provide a disclaimer that informs consumers who are seeking estimates of cost-sharing liability for out-of-network allowed amounts

---

[46] Pharmacy benefit managers are third-party companies that manage prescription drug benefits on behalf of health insurers, Medicare Part D drug plans, self-insured group health plans, and other payers.

that they may have to obtain a price estimate from the out-of-network provider in order to fully understand their out-of-pocket cost liability. Plans and issuers may also provide a disclaimer indicating how long the price estimate will be valid, based on the last date of the contract term for the negotiated rate or rates if multiple providers with different contract terms are involved. The Departments are of the view that this type of disclaimer could provide participants, beneficiaries, and enrollees with a better understanding of how their cost estimate may change over time, and seek comment on whether a disclaimer indicating the expiration of the cost estimate should be required. Furthermore, plans and issuers may also include disclaimer information regarding prescription drug cost estimates and whether rebates, discounts, and dispensing fees may impact the actual cost to the consumer.

The Departments have developed model language that plans and issuers could use, but would not be required to use, to satisfy the disclosure notice requirements described above. This model language is being proposed contemporaneously with, but separate from, these proposed rules. The Departments seek comment on the proposed model language and any additional information that stakeholders believe should be included in the proposed model notice or any information that should be omitted from the proposed model notice. As noted later in the preamble, to obtain copies of the proposed model notice, please visit CMS's Website at www.cms.hhs.gov/PaperworkReductionActof1995, or call the Reports Clearance Office at 410–786–1326. If you wish to comment, please submit your comments electronically as specified in the ADDRESSES section of these proposed rules and identify the rule (CMS–9915–P), the ICR's CFR citation, CMS ID number, and OMB control number.

The Departments further clarify that this proposed disclosure notice would be in addition to the information that QHP issuers are currently required to publish on their websites pursuant to 45 CFR 156.220(a)(7) regarding cost sharing and payments with respect to out-of-network coverage. In addition, some portions of this disclosure may overlap with network adequacy disclosure standards under 45 CFR 156.230(e). That section requires QHP issuers to, notwithstanding 45 CFR 156.130(c), count the cost sharing paid by an enrollee for an out-of-network essential health benefit (EHB) provided by an out-of-network ancillary provider in an in-network setting toward the enrollee's annual limitation on cost sharing or provide a notice to the enrollee that additional costs may be incurred for an EHB, including balance billing charges.

The Departments request comment on the proposed notice disclaimers and whether any additional disclaimers would be necessary or beneficial to consumers' learning about their potential cost-sharing liability for covered items and services. For example, should the Departments require a notice that explains that the cost-sharing information provided may not account for claims an individual has submitted that the plan or issuer has not yet processed? The Departments are also considering whether to require plans and issuers to provide a participant, beneficiary, or enrollee information regarding non-covered items or services for which the individual requests cost-sharing information. For example, there could be a requirement that a plan or issuer provide a statement, as applicable, indicating that the item or service for which the individual has requested cost-sharing information is not a covered benefit under the terms of the plan or coverage, and expenses charged for that item or service will not be reimbursed by the plan or coverage.

2. Required Methods for Disclosing Information to Participants, Beneficiaries, or Enrollees

Section 1311(e)(3)(C) of PPACA requires that cost-sharing information be made available through an internet website and other means for individuals without access to the internet. Therefore, these proposed rules would require that group health plans and health insurance issuers disclose to participants, beneficiaries, or enrollees (or their authorized representatives) the cost-sharing information described earlier in this preamble in two ways: (1) through a self-service tool that meets certain standards and is available on an internet website, and (2) in paper form.

a. First Delivery Method: Internet-based self-service tool

Under these proposed rules, plans and issuers would be required to make available a self-service tool on an internet website for their participants, beneficiaries, or enrollees to use, without a subscription or other fee, to search for cost-sharing information for covered items and services. The tool would be required to allow users to search for cost-sharing information for a covered item or service provided by a specific in-network provider, or by all in-network providers. The tool also would be required to allow users to search for the out-of-network allowed amount for a covered item or service provided by out-of-network providers. The tool would be required to provide users real-time responses that are based on cost-sharing information that is accurate at the time of the request.

In order for plans and issuers to provide accurate cost-sharing information, the Departments understand that the participant, beneficiary, or enrollee will have to input certain data elements into the tool. Therefore, plans and issuers would be required to make available a tool that allows users to search for cost-sharing information: (1) by billing code (for example, CPT Code 87804) or, (2) by a descriptive term (for example, "rapid flu test"), at the option of the user. The tool also would be required to allow users to input the name of a specific in-network provider in conjunction with a billing code or descriptive term, to produce cost-sharing information and a cost-sharing liability estimate for a covered item or service provided by that in-network provider. With respect to a request for cost-sharing information for all in-network providers, if a plan or issuer utilizes a multi-tiered network, the tool would be required to produce the relevant cost-sharing information for the covered item or service for each tier. To the extent that cost-sharing information for a covered item or service under a plan or coverage varies based on factors other than the provider, the tool would also be required to allow users to input sufficient information for the plan or issuer to disclose meaningful cost-sharing information. For example, if the cost-sharing liability estimate for a prescription drug depends on the quantity and dosage of the drug, the tool would be required to allow the user to input a quantity and dosage for the drug for which he or she is seeking cost-sharing information. Similarly, to the extent that the cost-sharing liability estimate varies based on the facility at which an in-network provider furnishes a service (for example, at an outpatient facility versus in a hospital setting), the tool would be required to either permit a user to select a facility, or display in the results cost-sharing liability information for every in-network facility at which the in-network provider furnishes the specified item or service. The Departments request comment on whether there are any scenarios under which plans and issuers may not be able to ascertain the in-network facilities at which an in-network provider furnishes services.

As stated previously, the Departments acknowledge that plans and issuers may not have sufficient information on providers outside of their network to provide the participant, beneficiary, or enrollee a complete estimate of out-of-pocket expenses, since the plan or issuer may not know what the out-of-network provider will bill for an item or service. However, if the plan or issuer provides coverage for out-of-network items or services, the plan or issuer generally will have established an out-of-network allowed amount that the participant, beneficiary, or enrollee could use, in conjunction with information he or she may request from the out-of-network provider about what the total bill for services may be, to compute an estimate of his or her out-of-pocket expenses. It is the Departments' understanding that a plan or issuer may require certain information, in addition to the identification of a covered item or service, before it can provide an out-of-network allowed amount for a covered item or service, and that plans and issuers may have different ways of establishing an out-of-network provider's allowed amount for a covered item or service (such as by zip code or state). Therefore, plans and issuers would be required to allow users to search for the out-of-network allowed amount for a covered item or service provided by out-of-network providers by inputting a billing code or descriptive term and the information that is necessary for the plan or issuer to produce the out-of-network allowed amount (such as the zip code for the location of the out-of-network provider).

To the extent a user's search returns multiple results, the tool would be required to have functionalities that would allow users to refine and reorder results (also referred to as sort and filter functionalities) by geographic proximity and the amount of estimated cost-sharing liability to the beneficiary, participant, or enrollee. The Departments solicit comment on whether the tool should be required to have additional refining and reordering functionality, including whether it would be helpful or feasible to refine and reorder by provider subspecialty (such as providers who specialize in pediatric psychiatry), or by the quality rating of the provider, if the plan or issuer has available data on provider quality.

It is the Departments' intention that these proposed rules would require plans and issuers to create a user-friendly internet-based self-service tool, but these proposed rules do not include a definition for "user-friendly" since there are a variety of ways a tool can be designed to be user-friendly. The Departments want to preserve plan and issuer flexibility to create tools that are best for their participants, beneficiaries, or enrollees, by soliciting user feedback and consumer-testing in the development of their tools. However, it is the Departments' view that a user-friendly tool would mean a tool that allows intended users to search for the cost-sharing information outlined in paragraph (b)(1) of these proposed rules efficiently and effectively, without unnecessary effort. The Departments are of the view that plans and issuers can look to federal plain language guidelines,[47] the requirements for a Summary Plan Description's method of presentation at 29 CFR 2520.102-2(a), and general industry standards for guidance when designing and developing their consumer tools. The Departments solicit comment on whether there is different or additional guidance that should be consulted.

These proposed rules require that the self-service tool be made available on an internet website to provide consistency with section 1311(e)(3)(C) of PPACA, which uses the term "internet website." However, the Departments seek feedback on whether this term should be interpreted to include other comparable methods of accessing internet-based content. The statute was enacted in 2010 when the primary mode of accessing internet-based content was through a personal computer. Since that time, ownership of mobile devices with internet access and use of internet-based mobile applications has become much more common. The Departments acknowledge that there may be technical differences between a website and other methods of viewing internet-based content, such as mobile applications. However, the Departments also understand that technology evolves over time, and it is the Departments' view that Congress did not intend to limit the ability to access information via alternative methods of viewing internet-based content that may be available now or in the future.

Mobile applications also may provide additional benefits beyond those of traditional websites. Due to the portability of mobile devices, a self-service tool that is similar to the kind required for an internet website under these proposed rules that is made available through a mobile application might provide participants, beneficiaries, enrollees, and their health care providers greater opportunities to use the tool together at the point of care to evaluate treatment options based on price. The Departments further understand that mobile applications may, in certain cases, offer greater privacy and security protections than an internet website for the information protected by applicable privacy and security requirements, such as the Health Insurance Portability and Accountability Act of 1996 (HIPAA) Privacy Rules (45 CFR parts 160 and 164) (HIPAA Rules) that would be accessible through the proposed tool. Accordingly, the Departments seek comment on whether the final rules should permit the proposed disclosure requirements to be satisfied with a self-service tool that is made available through a website or comparable means of accessing the internet, such as a mobile application, or whether multiple means, such as websites and mobile applications, should be required. The Departments also seek comment on the relative resources required for building an internet website versus an internet-based mobile application.

b. Second Delivery Method: Paper form

With respect to a delivery method that would not require a participant, beneficiary, or enrollee (or his or her authorized representative) to have access to the internet, plans and issuers would have to furnish, at the request of the of the participant, beneficiary, or enrollee (or his or her authorized representative), without a fee, all of the information required to be disclosed under paragraph (b)(1) of these proposed rules, as outlined earlier in this preamble, in paper form. A plan or issuer would be required to provide the information in accordance with the requirements under paragraph (b)(2)(i) of these proposed rules and as described earlier in this preamble. That is, the plan or issuer would be required to allow an individual to request cost-sharing information for a discrete covered item or service by billing code or descriptive term, according to the participant's, beneficiary's, or enrollee's request. Further, the plan or issuer would be required to provide cost-sharing information for a covered item or service in connection with an in-network provider or providers, or an out-of-network allowed amount for a covered item or service provided by an out-of-network provider, according to the participant's, beneficiary's, or enrollee's request, permitting the individual to specify the information necessary for the plan or issuer to provide meaningful cost-sharing liability information (such as dosage for a prescription drug or zip code for an out-of-network allowed amount). To the extent the information the individual requests returns more than one result, the individual would also be permitted to request that the plan or issuer refine and reorder the information disclosed by geographic proximity and the amount of the cost-sharing liability estimates.

This information would be required to be mailed to a participant, beneficiary, or enrollee no later than 2 business days after a participant's, beneficiary's, or enrollee's request is received. This would mean that cost-sharing information must be mailed via the U.S. Postal Service or some other delivery system within 2 business days of receipt of an individual's request. Nothing in these proposed rules prohibits a plan or issuer from providing individuals with the option to request disclosure of the information required under paragraph (b)(1) of these proposed rules through other methods (such as, over the phone, through face-to-face encounters, by facsimile, or by email).

The Departments request comment on these proposed disclosure methods, including whether additional methods of providing information should be required, rather than permitted. The Departments are particularly interested in feedback on whether plans and issuers should be required to provide the information over the phone, or by email, at the request of a participant, beneficiary, or enrollee.

The Departments also are considering requiring all plans and issuers to allow individuals to seek cost-sharing information by inputting a description of a treatment or procedure (such as knee replacement) that often involves the provision of multiple items and services. The Departments are interested in feedback on whether it would be feasible for plans and issuers to allow individuals to request cost-sharing information by such a treatment or procedure if the plan or issuer makes payments based on a discrete billing code for each item and service associated with a treatment or procedure, and not as a bundled payment for all items and services associated with the treatment or procedure. For instance, if an individual requests cost-sharing information for a knee replacement, and the plan or issuer does not bundle payment for multiple items and services provided in connection with a knee replacement, would it be unduly burdensome for a plan or issuer to disclose meaningful cost-sharing information for items and services typically provided in connection with a knee replacement?

3. Special Rule to Prevent Unnecessary Duplication

These proposed rules include a special rule to streamline the provision of the required disclosures and avoid unnecessary duplication of the disclosures with respect to group health coverage. The proposed special rule is similar to the one that applied with respect to the requirement for group health plans and health insurance issuers to provide certificates of creditable coverage before that requirement was generally superseded by PPACA.[48]

The special rule provides that to the extent coverage under a plan consists of group health insurance coverage, the plan would satisfy the requirements of these proposed rules if the issuer offering the coverage is required to provide the information pursuant to a written agreement

---

[47] https://www.plainlanguage.gov/guidelines

[48] As of December 31, 2014, group health plans are generally no longer required to provide HIPAA certificates of creditable coverage. See 26 CFR 9801-5 and 29 CFR 2590.701-5. An exception to this general rule is expatriate health plans, which must satisfy the provisions of title XXVII of the PHS Act, Chapter 100 of the Code, and part 7 of subtitle B of title I of ERISA that would otherwise apply if PPACA had not been enacted. See section 3(d)(2)(G) of the Expatriate Health Coverage Clarification Act (EHCCA), enacted as Division M of the Consolidated and Further Continuing Appropriations Act of 2015.

between the plan and issuer. Accordingly, for example, if there were a plan and an issuer that enter into a written agreement under which the issuer agrees to provide the information required under these proposed rules, and the issuer failed to provide full or timely information, then the issuer, but not the plan, would violate the transparency disclosure requirements.[49]

4. Privacy, Security, and Accessibility

These proposed requirements for group health plans and health insurance issuers to provide cost-sharing liability estimates and related cost-sharing information would operate in tandem with existing state and federal laws governing the privacy, security, and accessibility of the information that would be disclosed under these proposed disclosure requirements. For example, the Departments are aware that the content proposed to be disclosed by plans and issuers may be subject to the privacy, security, and breach notification rules under HIPAA or similar state laws in the hands of a HIPAA covered entity or business associate. Nothing in these proposed rules is intended to alter or otherwise affect plans' and issuers' data privacy and security responsibilities under HIPAA Rules or other applicable state or federal laws.

The Departments also expect that plans and issuers will follow existing applicable state and federal laws regarding persons who must be allowed to access and receive the information that would be disclosed under these proposed rules. These proposed rules refer to such persons as "authorized representatives" and do not establish any new class of persons or entities who are authorized to access the information that would be provided through the proposed internet-based, self-service tool. Accordingly, the Departments expect plans and issuers to follow existing laws with regard to persons who may or must be allowed to access the cost-sharing information that would be required to be disclosed under these proposed rules.

B. Proposed Requirements for Public Disclosure of Negotiated Rates and Historical Allowed Amount Data for Covered Items and Services from Out-of-Network Providers

The Departments take the position that health care spending cannot be curbed without more competition in the market, and competition cannot be achieved without greater price transparency. As explained earlier in this preamble, section 2715A of the PHS Act and section 1311(e)(3)(A) of PPACA require group health plans and health insurance issuers to make public certain specified information, as well as other information the Secretary of HHS determines to be appropriate to provide transparency in health coverage. Thus, these provisions evidence Congress' intent that members of the public play a role in using health coverage transparency information to promote consumer interests. Consistent with this authority, the Departments have determined that it would be appropriate to require plans and issuers to make public negotiated rates with in-network providers and data outlining the different amounts a plan or issuer has allowed for covered items or services furnished by out-of-network providers.

The Departments have concluded that public availability of such information would create price transparency for persons who are uninsured, as well as insured persons who are considering coverage alternatives. The proposal would also support meaningful comparisons between plan coverage options and issuer options for all consumers, comparisons that would not be supported through the internet-based consumer tool proposed earlier in this rule. In proposing requirements for public disclosure of negotiated rates and historical out-of-network allowed amounts, the Departments are exercising specific authority under section 1311(e)(3)(A)(vii) and (ix) of PPACA (as applied to plans and issuers in the individual and group markets through section 2715A of the PHS Act), which requires plans and issuers to disclose other information the Secretary of HHS determines to be appropriate to create transparency in health coverage.

As explained later in this preamble, the proposed disclosure requirements would provide consumers, including third-party software developers and health care researchers, information about health care prices that is necessary to make informed health care purchasing decisions. These requirements would also help to expose price differences so that consumers can judge the reasonableness of provider prices and shop for care at the best price. Accordingly, it is the Departments' view that public availability of negotiated rates and historical out-of-network allowed amounts is appropriate and necessary to empower consumers to make informed decisions about their health care, spur competition in health care markets, and to slow or potentially reverse the rising cost of health care items and services.

1. Public disclosure of negotiated rates and historical out-of-network allowed amounts is necessary to create price transparency for all consumers and payers of health care items and services, as well as of benefit to state and federal regulators

First, public availability of negotiated rates and historical out-of-network allowed amounts would empower the nation's 28.5 million uninsured consumers[50] to make more informed health care decisions. Uninsured consumers often must pay full cost for health care items and services, such that pricing information is critical to their ability to evaluate their service options and control their health care spending. Uninsured consumers could use publicly-available pricing information to find affordable service providers or providers who offer the lowest price, depending on the consumer's personal needs and priorities. Provider lists of standard charges often do not reflect the true cost of particular items and services.[51] Although a provider's negotiated rates with group health plans and health insurance issuers do not necessarily reflect the prices providers charge to uninsured patients, uninsured consumers could use this information to gain an understanding of the payment amounts a particular provider accepts for a service, which could inform their own negotiations with that provider for the same item or service.

Second, information on negotiated rates and historical out-of-network allowed amounts is critical for any consumer, insured or uninsured, who wishes to evaluate available options for group or individual market coverage. The proposed requirements that plans and issuers disclose negotiated rates and out-of-network allowed amounts to their participants, beneficiaries, or enrollees (or their authorized representatives) through an internet self-service tool or in paper form will make critical pricing information available to consumers with health insurance coverage. However, the Departments are of the view that both insured and uninsured consumers need access to data on negotiated rates and out-of-network allowed amounts across plans and issuers to be able to shop most effectively for their health care coverage.

Public disclosure of plan and issuer negotiated rates and out-of-network allowed amounts would create and promote price transparency in the health care market for all consumers and payers, including insured consumers, uninsured consumers, sponsors of self-insured and fully-insured group health plans, as well as government sponsors and regulators of local, state, and federal health care programs. For any consumer, insured or uninsured, who wishes to evaluate available options for group or individual market coverage, pricing information is also essential.

Specifically, for those uninsured consumers who wish to purchase coverage and become insured, pricing information for different plans or coverage and their in-network providers would be key to consumers' ability to effectively shop for coverage that best meets their needs at prices they can afford. The same is true for insured or uninsured consumers who wish to evaluate coverage options under their employer's plan or shop for coverage in the individual market. Publicly-available negotiated rate data will assist all consumers in choosing the coverage that best meets

---

[49] Under section 4980D(d)(1) of the Code, the excise tax for group health plans failing to satisfy these proposed rules is not imposed on a small employer (generally fewer than 50 employees) which provides health insurance coverage solely through a contract with an issuer on any failure which is solely because of the health insurance coverage offered by the issuer.

[50] Keith, K. "Two New Federal Surveys Show Stable Uninsured Rate." Health Affairs Blog. September 13, 2018. Available at: https://www.healthaffairs.org/do/10.1377/hblog20180913.896261/full/

[51] Arora, V., Moriates, C., Shah, N. "The Challenge of Understanding Health Care Costs and Charges." 17 AMA J. Ethics. 1046. November 2015. Available at: https://journalofethics.ama-assn.org/article/challenge-understanding-health-care-costs-and-charges/2015-11.

their needs in terms of deductible requirements, coinsurance requirements, and maximum out-of-pocket limits - all factors directly determined by a plan's or issuer's negotiated rates or out-of-network allowed amounts. Publicly-available historical allowed amount data for covered items and services provided by out-of-network providers would enable consumers who require specialized services to find the best coverage for their circumstances. For instance, the Departments understand that plans and issuers often place limitations on benefits for specialized services. This causes many specialists to reject insurance, making it difficult, if not impossible, for consumers to find in-network providers in their area who are accepting new patients or who have sufficient availability or expertise to meet their needs. The Departments understand, for example, that many speech therapists and pathologists do not accept insurance because of the limitations plans and issuers place on coverage for their services. Such limitations may include exclusions from coverage for speech issues that are developmental in nature, and are not due to a specific illness or injury.[52] Moreover, many plans and issuers that do provide coverage for developmental speech issues place annual visit limits on speech therapy services. Accordingly, consumers who have a need for such specialized services often base their coverage choices primarily, if not solely, on a plan's or issuer's out-of-network benefits. Historical data outlining different amounts paid to out-of-network providers will enable consumers who rely on out-of-network providers to compare out-of-network benefits among different plans and issuers.

Third, public disclosure of pricing information is necessary to enable consumers to use and understand price transparency data in a manner that will increase competition, reduce disparities in health care prices, and potentially lower health care costs. The Departments are of the view that true downward pressure on health care pricing cannot be fully achieved without public disclosure of pricing. General economic theory holds that markets work best when there is price competition.[53] When consumers can shop for services and items based on price, providers and suppliers compete to lower price and improve quality.[54]

One of the recognized impediments to increased competition through health care consumerism is widespread knowledge gaps most consumers have when it comes to evaluating health care options. Making this information public would facilitate and incentivize the design, development, and offering of consumer tools and support services that are necessary to address the general inability of consumers to use or otherwise make sense of health care pricing information. The Departments' proposal to make this information publicly available would allow health care software application developers and other innovators to compile, consolidate, and present this information to consumers in a manner that supports meaningful comparisons between different coverage options and providers, and that assists consumers in making informed health care and coverage decisions.[55] One of the primary purposes of these proposals to make price information publicly available is to put price information in the hands of those best equipped to use it in a manner that will support greater consumerism in the health care market (for example, information technology developers who build tools to help consumers make informed health care decisions).

In developing these proposed rules, the Departments considered that, due to the complexity of our health care system and the data that drives plan and issuer payments for health care services, such data is unlikely to be usable by the average consumer. Put plainly, consumers would not (or could not) effectively use pricing information they do not understand or cannot decipher. The Departments understand many consumers do not fully comprehend the basics of health coverage, much less the more complex facets of our health care system that can affect an individual's out-of-pocket cost for items and services, including its specialized billing codes and payment processes; the various specialized terms used in plan and coverage contracts and related documents (such as copayment and coinsurance); and the various billing and payment structures plans and issuers use to compensate providers and assign cost-sharing liability to individuals (bundled payment arrangements, for example).[56] As a result, the Departments have determined that the proposal to make public negotiated rates with in-network providers and historical payment data outlining out-of-network allowed amounts is appropriate because it would encourage innovation that could help consumers understand and effectively use price transparency information. The more consumers use transparent price data effectively to find quality services they need at the best available prices, the greater the rise in consumerism and competition, as well as downward pressure on the costs of health care items and services.

The Departments assume that market actors will be incentivized to innovate in the price transparency and health care consumerism space, once access to pricing information that allows for meaningful evaluation of different options for delivering health care items or services, coverage options, and provider options becomes available. The Departments further assume that technology developers will be incentivized to design and make available web tools and mobile applications that can guide consumers in accessing available price information, increasing the likelihood that consumers will use the information to make informed health care purchasing decisions. Ultimately, improved access and usability of this information has the potential to increase health insurance literacy, consumerism, and competition, resulting in more reasonable, controlled costs for health care items and services. Additionally, the information would provide industry researchers and experts with baseline data to assist them with identifying, designing, and testing new or existing health care delivery and coverage models.

Fourth, along with consumers, sponsors of self-insured and fully-insured group health plans are also disadvantaged by the lack of price transparency. Group health plans bear the increasing cost of their participants' and beneficiaries' health care. Without information related to what other plans or issuers are actually paying for particular items and services, plans currently lack the pricing information necessary to shop or effectively negotiate for the best coverage for their participants and beneficiaries. Public availability of pricing information is appropriate to empower plans to make meaningful comparisons between offers from issuers and evaluate the prices offered by providers who wish to be included in their pool of in-network providers. The pricing information will also assist plans that contract with TPAs or issuers to provide a network of physicians. That information would provide valuable data a plan could use to assess the reasonableness of network access prices offered by TPAs and issuers by evaluating the specific prices members of a TPA's or issuer's network are accepting for their services. Given that, as of 2017, more than 55 percent of the nation's population received coverage from their employers,[57] the ability of group health plans to effectively negotiate pricing for coverage and services would be a boon to competition in the health care market.

Fifth, public disclosure of price transparency information is also appropriate because it would assist health care regulators in carrying out their duties to oversee health insurance issuers in their states, as well as in designing and maintaining sustainable health care programs. Public disclosure of pricing information would enable state regulators to monitor actual trends in prices for health care items and services. States would be able to assess whether the trend rates issuers use in their rate filings are reasonable in order to assess whether the rates should be approved. Local, state, and federal agencies responsible for implementing health care programs that rely on issuers to provide access to care would be privy to actual pricing information that would inform their price negotiations with issuers. The Departments understand, however, that some government agencies may already have access to the information proposed to be made public. The Departments, thus, are specifically interested in comments from government stakeholders regarding whether and how the price transparency proposed to be created under these proposed rules would benefit government regulators and health care programs.

---

[52] https://www.asha.org/practice/reimbursement/private-plans/PrivatePlansCoverageSLP/.

[53] https://www.consumer.ftc.gov/sites/default/files/games/off-site/youarehere/pages/pdf/FTC-Competition_How-Comp-Works.pdf

[54] Kessler, D., McClellan, M. "Is Hospital Competition Socially Wasteful?" 115 Q. J. of Econ. 577. May 2, 2000. Available at: https://www.nber.org/papers/w7266.

[55] The Departments recognize that implementation of the API discussed in Section III, Request for Information, could go further toward the goal of empowering application developers and other innovators to support price transparency in the health care market.

[56] See https://www.benefitspro.com/2016/09/30/survey-most-workers-dont-understand-health-insuran/?slreturn=20190803010341 (a UnitedHealthcare Consumer Senti-

ment Survey found that even though 32 percent of respondents were using websites and mobile apps to comparison shop for health care, only 7 percent had a full understanding of all four basic insurance concepts: plan premium, deductible, coinsurance, and out-of-pocket maximum; although 60 percent of respondents were able to successfully define plan premium and deductible, respondents were not as successful in defining out-of-pocket maximum (36 percent) and coinsurance (32 percent)).

[57] As of 2017, employer-based coverage was the most common, covering 56.0 percent of the population for some or all of the calendar year. Berchick, E., Hood, E. Barnett, J. "Health Insurance Coverage in the United States: 2017." U.S. Government Printing Office. September 2018. Available at: https://www.census.gov/content/dam/Census/library/publications/2018/demo/p60-264.pdf.

For these reasons, the Departments propose, in paragraph (c), to require plans and issuers to make available two machine-readable files (as defined later in this preamble) that include information regarding negotiated rates with in-network providers, allowed amounts for covered items or services furnished by particular out-of-network providers, and other relevant information as defined in accordance with specific method and format requirements. These proposed rules would also require plans and issuers to update this information on a monthly basis to ensure it remains accurate.

2. Information Required to be Disclosed to the Public

The Departments are of the view that minimum requirements for standardized data elements would be necessary to ensure users would have access to accurate and useful pricing information. Without such baseline requirements, the negotiated rate and allowed amount data for out-of-network services made available by each group health plan and health insurance issuer could vary dramatically, creating a disincentive to health care innovators developing tools and resources to enable consumers to accurately and meaningfully use, understand, and compare pricing information for covered items and services across providers, plans, and issuers. Accordingly, under these proposed rules a plan or issuer would be required to publish two machine-readable files. The first file would include information regarding rates negotiated with in-network providers. The second file would include historical data showing allowed amounts for covered items and services furnished by out-of-network providers. For convenience, these are respectively referred to as the Negotiated Rate File and the Allowed Amount File in this preamble. The files would include the following content elements.

a. First Content Element: Name or identifier for each plan option or coverage

The first content element that plans and issuers would be required to include in both the Negotiated Rate File and the Allowed Amount File would be the name and identifier for each plan option or coverage offered by a plan or issuer. For the identifier, the Departments propose that plans and issuers use their Employer Identification Number (EIN) or Health Insurance Oversight System (HIOS) IDs, as applicable. The Departments seek comment on whether EINs and HIOS IDs are the appropriate identifiers for this purpose. The Departments also seek comment on whether there are other plan or issuer identifiers that should be considered and adopted.

b. Second Content Element: Billing codes

The second content element that plans and issuers would be required to include in both files would be any billing or other code used by the plan or issuer to identify items or services for purposes of claims adjudication, or accounting or billing for the item or service, including but not limited to, the Current Procedural Terminology (CPT) code, the Healthcare Common Procedure Coding System (HCPCS) code, the Diagnosis Related Group (DRG), the National Drug Code (NDC), or other common payer identifier used by a plan or issuer, such as hospital revenue codes, as applicable.

The Departments propose to require that plans and issuers associate each negotiated rate or out-of-network allowed amount with a CPT or HCPCS code, DRG, NDC, or other common payer identifier, as applicable, because plans, issuers, and providers uniformly understand them and commonly use them for billing and paying claims (including for both individual items and services and service packages). The Departments also propose that plans and issuers must include plain language descriptions for each billing code. In the case of items and services that are associated with common billing codes (such as the HCPCS codes), the plan or issuer could use the codes' associated short text description.

c. Third Content Element: Negotiated rates or out-of-network allowed amounts

Negotiated Rate File

The third content element that plans and issuers would be required to include in the Negotiated Rate File would be negotiated rates under a plan or coverage with respect to each covered item or service furnished by in-network providers. To the extent a plan or issuer reimburses providers for an item or service based on a formula or reference based-pricing (such as a percentage of a Medicare reimbursement rate), the plan or issuer would be required to provide the calculated dollar amount of the negotiated rate for each provider. Negotiated rates would have to be associated with the provider's National Provider Identifier (NPI), which is accessible by providers, plans, and issuers.

The Departments understand that some plans and issuers do not vary negotiated rates across in-network providers. For instance, some plans and issuers have a negotiated rate that applies to every provider in a certain network tier. In such a case, the plan or issuer must provide the negotiated rate for a covered item or service separately for every provider that participates in that tier of the network. If the plan or issuer reimburses for certain items and services (for example, maternity care and childbirth) through a bundled payment arrangement, the plan must identify the bundle of items and services by the relevant code.

Plans and issuers would also be required to include in the Negotiated Rate File the last date of the contract term for each provider-specific negotiated rate that applies to each item or service (including rates for both individual and bundled items and services).

Allowed Amount File

The third content element plans and issuers would be required to include in the Allowed Amount File would be historical out-of-network allowed amounts for covered items and services. These proposed rules would require plans and issuers to include in the Allowed Amount File each unique out-of-network allowed amount in connection with covered items or services furnished by a particular out-of-network provider during the 90-day time period that begins 180 days prior to the publication date of the Allowed Amount File. As with the Negotiated Rate File, where a plan or issuer reimburses providers for an item or service based on a formula or reference based-pricing (such as a percentage of a Medicare reimbursement rate), the plan or issuer would be required to provide the calculated dollar amount of the allowed amount for each provider. Allowed amounts would have to be associated with the provider's NPI, which is accessible by providers, plans, and issuers.

When disclosing an out-of-network allowed amount under this requirement, the plan or issuer would disclose the aggregate of the actual amount the plan or issuer paid to the out-of-network provider, plus the participant's, beneficiary's, or enrollee's share of the cost. For instance, if the out-of-network allowed amount for a covered service is $100, and the plan or issuer paid 80 percent of the out-of-network allowed amount ($80) per the terms of the plan or coverage, the participant, beneficiary, or enrollee was responsible for paying twenty percent of the out-of-network allowed amount ($20), the plan or issuer would report an out-of-network allowed amount of $100. This unique payment amount would be associated with the particular covered item or service (identified by billing code) and the particular out-of-network provider who furnished the item or service (identified by NPI).

As an example, assume Group Health Plan A intends to publish a machine-readable file on July 1 reporting the out-of-network historical allowed amount data the Departments propose to require. Under these proposed requirements, Group Health Plan A's Allowed Amount File must detail each discrete out-of-network allowed amount the plan calculated in connection with a covered item or service furnished by an out-of-network provider between January 1 and April 1. During this 90-day time period, Group Health Plan A paid 23 claims from Provider Z seeking compensation for rapid flu tests (CPT Code 87804), a service covered under the group health plan. Group Health Plan A calculated out-of-network allowed amounts of $100 for three claims, $150 for 10 claims, and $200 for the remaining 10 claims. Under these proposed rules, Group Health Plan A would report in the file published on June 30, that it calculated three different out-of-network allowed amounts of $100, $150, and $200 for rapid flu tests (CPT Code 87804) in connection with covered services furnished by Provider Z from January 1 to April 1. On July 30, Group Health Plan A would update the file to show the unique out-of-network allowed amounts for CPT Code 87804 for Provider Z's services rendered from February through April. On August 30, Group Health Plan A would update the file to show such payments for services rendered from March through May, and so on.

The Departments specifically seek comment on whether the required disclosures of historical out-of-network allowed amounts will provide useful information that can assist consumers in locating services at an affordable cost, or whether there is additional information that is both useful to anticipated users and practical for plans and issuers to disclose for this purpose. For instance, the Departments considered requiring plans and issuers to disclose in the Allowed Amount File amounts out-of-network providers charged participants, beneficiaries, and enrollees for covered services. We understand that such charge amounts would be included in any claim for out-of-network benefits and could be helpful to consumers shopping for services based on price. We seek comment on this data element and other information that would support the transparency goals of these proposed rules.

The Departments designed this reporting requirement to elicit payment data that reflects recent out-of-network allowed amounts in connection with claims for out-of-network covered services. The Departments assume these amounts will provide payment data that is useful to consumers because it is reflective of current reimbursements. Specifically, the Departments propose to require reporting based on dates of service within 180 days of the Allowed Amount File publication date to ensure that data is composed of recent claims (rather than older claims from multiple time periods) and to avoid the reporting of payments from different periods of time. Payment data from defined periods of time will enable users to make meaningful comparisons across plans and coverage options.

The 90-day reporting period ensures that the public has access to reasonable volumes of payment data from which users can make useful and accurate inferences about how much a service would cost if furnished by a particular provider. The Departments are concerned, however, that out-of-network providers may not provide services to participants, beneficiaries, or enrollees on a sufficiently frequent basis during a 90-day period to yield a useful amount of payment data. The Departments seek comment generally on these issues and on whether the Departments should require that reporting of out-of-network allowed amounts cover a longer period of time, such as 120 days, 180 days, or more.

Similarly, the Departments propose to require plans and issuers to report out-of-network allowed amounts for services furnished at least 90 days in the past to help ensure the availability of reasonable volumes of out-of-network allowed amount data in the machine-readable file. The Departments are of the view that a 90-day lag between the end of a reporting period and the publication of required out-of-network allowed amount data will allow plans and issuers sufficient time to adjudicate and pay claims from out-of-network providers for the relevant reporting period. The Departments also understand, however, that claims processing times may vary between plans and issuers, and that external factors may increase processing timelines. For example, the Departments understand that many out-of-network providers do not send claims directly to plans and issuers, but require patients to file out-of-network claims. This could mean that an out-of-network claim may not reach a plan or issuer for 6 to 12 months after a service is rendered. Such delays could negatively affect the volume of out-of-network allowed amount data and the ultimate usefulness of this data. For this reason, the Departments seek comment on whether requiring plans and issuers to report out-of-network allowed amounts for items and services furnished at least 90 days in the past is sufficient to ensure the proposed disclosures will yield sufficient volumes of historical data to be useful to consumers who wish to shop for services based on price. For instance, the Departments seek comment on whether the Departments should require that more time elapses between the end of the reporting period and publication of the data, such as 120 days, 180 days, or more, to increase the likelihood that out-of-network claims from the relevant reporting period have been adjudicated and paid by the time they must be published.

The Departments are aware that providing this information could raise health privacy concerns. For example, there may be instances (such as in a small group health plan or with respect to an item or service for a rare chronic condition) where, through deduction, disclosing the required payment information may enable users to identify the patient who received the service. There may also be instances when this public disclosure requirement would be inconsistent with federal or state laws governing health information that are more stringent than HIPAA Rules with regard to the use, disclosure, and security of health data that was produced pursuant to a legal requirement, such that plans and issuers would be required to further de-identify data to the extent a patient could be identified through deduction. For example, some of the claims for payment from an out-of-network provider could relate to services provided for substance use disorder, which could implicate disclosure limitations under 42 CFR part 2 governing the confidentiality of substance use disorder patient records. Thus, some of the out-of-network allowed amounts that the Departments propose to make public could be subject to disclosure rules and limitations under 42 CFR part 2.

To address privacy concerns, the Departments propose that plans and issuers would not be required to provide out-of-network allowed amount data in relation to a particular provider and a particular item or service when compliance would require a plan or issuer to report out-of-network allowed amounts to a particular provider in connection with fewer than 10 different claims for payment. Furthermore, the Departments note that disclosure of such information would not be required if compliance would violate applicable health information privacy laws. The Departments are committed to protecting sensitive patient health information. For this reason, in addition to proposing this exemption, the Departments propose under paragraph (c)(1)(ii) to require only unique out-of-network allowed amounts to mask the total episodes of care for a particular provider and item or service. The Departments believe these mitigation strategies, in addition to flexibilities proposed to allow the aggregation of reported data (as described later in this preamble), are sufficient to protect patients from identification based on information in the Allowed Amount File. The Departments solicit comment on whether additional privacy protections are required.

The Departments specifically solicit comment on whether a higher minimum claims threshold, such as a threshold of 20 claims, would better mitigate privacy concerns and minimize complexity in complying with federal or state privacy laws without compromising the integrity of the compiled information. The Departments also seek comment on additional approaches that could decrease the potential for aggregated health information that would be disclosed under these proposed rules to be identified, especially with respect to smaller group health plans.

3. Required Method and Format for Disclosing Information to the Public

The Negotiated Rate and Allowed Amounts Files would be required to be disclosed as machine-readable files. These proposed rules define "machine-readable file" to mean a digital representation of data or information in a file that can be imported or read by a computer system for further processing without human intervention, while ensuring no semantic meaning is lost. This means that the machine-readable file can be imported or read by a computer system without those processes resulting in alterations to the ways the data and the commands are presented in the machine-readable file. These proposed rules would require each machine-readable file to use a non-proprietary, open format to be identified by the Departments in technical implementation guidance (for example, JSON, XML, CSV). A PDF file, for example, would not meet this definition due to its proprietary nature.

The Departments considered proposing that group health plans and health insurance issuers post negotiated rates and historical out-of-network allowed amount data for all covered items and services using a single standardized, non-proprietary file format, specifically JSON. The Departments understand that this format generally is easily downloadable, and it could simplify the ability of price transparency tool developers to access the data. The Departments seek comment on whether the final rule should require group health plans and health insurance issuers to make the Negotiated Rate and Allowed Amounts Files available as JSON files.

These machine-readable files would also be required to comply with technical, non-substantive implementation guidance to be published following the finalization of these proposed rules. The guidance will provide technical direction that identifies the specific open, nonproprietary file format in which plans and issuers should produce the machine-readable files. It will, among other things, provide the schema for the file, which is a description of the manner in which the data should be organized and arranged. The guidance would ensure consistent implementation of the machine-readable file requirements across all plans and issuers, and would ensure stability, predictability, and reliability for users of the proposed machine-readable file.

The Departments believe that providing such specific technical direction in separate guidance, rather than in this rule, would better enable the Departments to update these specific requirements to keep pace with and respond to technological developments. The Departments will publish a PRA package that will further describe the specific data elements that would be disclosed in the proposed machine-readable files.

The Departments propose to require plans and issuers to publish their negotiated rates and historical allowed amount data in two machine-readable files, one reporting required negotiated rate data with in-network providers, and a second reporting required out-of-network allowed amount data. The Departments considered allowing plans and issuers to have flexibility to publish this information in either one or two machine-readable files. The Departments solicit comment on whether building and updating one file could be less burdensome for plans and issuers than maintaining multiple files, and whether having the data in a single file could facilitate use by market innovators.

The Departments are specifically interested in comments regarding whether a single file for disclosure of all the required information would likely be extremely large, making it less than optimal for anticipated users, such as software application developers and health care researchers. The Departments propose to require plans and issuers to publish data on negotiated in-network rates and data on historical out-of-network allowed amounts in separate machine-readable files to account for the dissimilarity between the static rates paid to in-network providers under contract and the more variable amounts paid to out-of-network providers. The Departments seek comment on the benefits and challenges to providing all the required data in two separate files, as proposed.

4. Required Accessibility Standards for Disclosure of Information to the Public

These proposed rules include provisions intended to address potential barriers that could inhibit the public's ability to access and use the information should it become available. For example, some plans and issuers require consumers to set up a username and password, or require consumers to submit various types of other information, including their email address, in order to access data offered by plans and issuers. The Departments are concerned that these requirements might deter the public from accessing negotiated rate and allowed amount information. Accordingly, these proposed rules would require a plan or issuer to make available on an internet website the information described earlier in this preamble in two machine-readable files that must be accessible free of charge, without having to establish a user account, password, or other credentials, and without having to submit any personal identifying information such as a name or email address.

The Departments also considered requiring plans and issuers to submit the internet addresses for the machine-readable files to CMS, and having CMS make the information available to the public. A central location could allow the public to access negotiated rate information and historical data for out-of-network allowed amounts in one centralized location, reducing confusion and increasing accessibility. However, the Departments opted to propose flexible rules allowing plans and issuers to publish the files in the location plans and issuers determine will be most easily accessible by the intended users. The Departments also considered that requiring plans and issuers to notify CMS of the internet address for their machine-readable files would increase burden on plans and issuers. The Departments request comment on whether the proposed requirement to allow issuers to display the flat files in the location of their choice is superior to requiring plans and issuers to report the web addresses of their machine-readable files to CMS for public display. The Departments are specifically interested in whether the burden associated with reporting file locations to CMS is outweighed by the risk that members of the public will be unable to easily locate plans' and issuers' machine-readable files.

5. Required Timing of Updates of Information to be Disclosed to the Public

These proposed rules would require a group health plan or health insurance issuer to update monthly the information required to be included in each machine-readable file. The Departments recognize, however, that information in Negotiated Rate Files may change frequently and are considering whether to require plans and issuers to update their Negotiated Rate Files more often than proposed to ensure that consumers have access to the most up-to-date negotiated rate information. Accordingly, the Departments also seek comment on whether the final rules should require plans' and issuers' Negotiated Rate Files to be updated more frequently. For instance, the Departments considered requiring plans and issuers to update negotiated rate information within 10 calendar days after the effective date of new rates with any in-network provider, including rates for in-network providers newly added to a plan's provider network and updates made necessary by a provider leaving the plan's or issuer's network. The Departments seek comment on this alternate proposal and on whether the update timelines for negotiated rate information and historical out-of-network payment data should be the same.

The proposed rules would also require plans and issuers to clearly indicate the date of the last update made to the Negotiated Rate and Allow Amount Files in accordance with guidance issued by the Departments. The Departments seek comment on this proposal.

6. Special Rules to Prevent Unnecessary Duplication and Allow for Aggregation

Similar to the proposed cost-sharing information disclosure requirements for participants, beneficiaries, and enrollees, the Departments propose a special rule to streamline the provision of the required disclosures that would be included in the proposed machine-readable files. This special rule has three components - one for insured group health plans where a health insurance issuer offering coverage in connection with the plan has agreed to provide the required information, another for plans and issuers that contract with third parties to provide the information on their behalf, and a special rule allowing aggregation of out-of-network allowed amount data.

a. Insured group health plans

The Departments propose that, to the extent coverage under a group health plan consists of group health insurance coverage, the plan would satisfy the proposed file requirement if the health insurance issuer offering the coverage is required to provide the information pursuant to a written agreement between the plan and issuer. Accordingly, if a plan sponsor and an issuer enter into a written agreement under which the issuer agrees to provide the information required under these proposed rules, and the issuer fails to provide full or timely information, then the issuer, but not the plan, would violate the transparency disclosure requirements and be subject to enforcement mechanisms applicable to group health plans under the PHS Act.[58]

b. Use of Third Parties to Satisfy Public Disclosure Requirements

Plans and issuers may wish to engage other entities to assist them in complying with the disclosure requirements under these proposed rules. In particular, it is the Departments' understanding that most health care insurance and coverage claims in the U.S. are processed through health care claims clearinghouses[59] and that these entities maintain and standardize health care information, including information on negotiated rates and

---

[58] Section 2723 of the PHS Act.

[59] The Departments propose to adopt the definition of health care clearinghouse in 45 CFR 160.103 for purposes of these proposed rules. Under that definition, health

out-of-network allowed amounts. As a result, plans and issuers may reduce the burden associated with making negotiated rates and out-of-network allowed amounts available in machine-readable files by entering a business associate agreement and contracting with a health care claims clearinghouse or other HIPAA-compliant entity to disclose these data on their behalf.[60] Accordingly, these proposed rules would permit a plan or issuer to satisfy the public disclosure requirement of paragraph (c) of the proposed rules by entering into a written agreement under which another party (such as a TPA or health care claims clearinghouse) will make public the required information in compliance with this section. However, if a plan or issuer chooses to enter into such an agreement and the party with which it contracts fails to provide full or timely information, the plan or issuer would violate the transparency disclosure requirements.

c. Aggregation permitted for Allowed Amount Files

In order to further mitigate privacy concerns and to eliminate unnecessary duplication, the Departments propose to permit plans and issuers to satisfy the requirement of paragraph (c)(1)(ii) of these proposed rules by making available out-of-network allowed amount data that has been aggregated to include information from more than one plan or policy. As previously discussed, a plan or issuer may satisfy the disclosure requirement by disclosing out-of-network allowed amounts made available by, or otherwise obtained from, an issuer, a service provider, or other party with which the plan or issuer has entered into a written agreement to provide the information. Accordingly, under such circumstances, these proposed rules would permit issuers, service providers, or other parties with which the plan or issuer has contracted to aggregate out-of-network allowed amounts for more than one plan or insurance policy or contract. To the extent a plan or issuer is providing out-of-network allowed amount information in the aggregate, the Departments propose to apply the 10 minimum claims threshold to the aggregated claims data set, and not at the plan or issuer level.

7. Additional Comment Solicitation on the Negotiated Rate and Allowed Amount Files

As discussed earlier in this preamble, the Departments assume that some group health plans and health insurance issuers may store data in different systems, including dated legacy systems, which could make it difficult to accurately and efficiently populate a file as required by these proposed rules. The Departments understand that clearinghouses may provide a solution to plans and issuers in this situation, as many clearinghouses already possess the data that would be required to be disclosed in these proposed rules. The Departments seek feedback on the ways plans and issuers may be able to use a health care claims clearinghouse to fulfill the requirements of this rule and the impact this may have in reducing the burden of satisfying these proposed requirements. The Departments further seek comment on whether plans and issuers similarly could use TPAs to reduce the costs and burden of complying with these proposed requirements.

Although the Departments propose in these rules to require plans and issuers to make price and payment information public through machine-readable files, the Departments considered proposing to require plans and issuers to provide rate information through a publicly accessible API that would comply with standards defined by the Departments. The Departments note that there is currently no standard HIPAA transaction applicable to data that will be made available to members of the public who are not covered entities.[61] The Departments also understand that issuer and plan systems could be designed in a manner that providing API access to information that would be disclosed under these proposed rules could be more efficient and less burdensome than maintaining the information in machine-readable files. The Departments are concerned, however, that many plans and issuers could face significant technical issues in complying with such a requirement. The Departments, therefore, seek comment on whether plans and issuers should have the flexibility to provide access to negotiated rates and out-of-network allowed amounts through a publicly accessible API that conforms to defined standards.

Finally, the Departments recognize that the precise impact of making pricing information public cannot be predicted. As discussed in section VII of the preamble to these proposed rules, the Departments are aware that price transparency could have negative unintended consequences in markets where pricing will become very transparent, including narrowing of prices and increases in average costs. The Departments also recognize that information disclosures allowing competitors to know the rates plans and issuers are charging may dampen incentives for competitors to offer lower prices, potentially resulting in higher prices. Some stakeholders also have expressed concern that without additional legislative or regulatory efforts public availability of negotiated rates may have the unintended consequence of increasing costs for services in highly concentrated markets or result in anticompetitive behaviors. Notwithstanding these concerns, the Departments remain confident that the release of the data will help reduce pricing disparities and potentially drive down health care costs, as discussed earlier in this preamble. The Departments seek comment on these potential concerns and what additional rules would help to mitigate risk of these potential consequences.

Interaction of Proposed Requirements with 45 CFR 156.220

The Departments recognize that group and individual market health insurance issuers that offer QHPs through an Exchange are already subject to reporting requirements under 45 CFR 156.220 that implement the transparency in coverage requirements of section 1311(e)(3) of PPACA. Pursuant to 45 CFR 156.220, issuers of QHPs offered through an individual market Exchange or a Small Business Health Options (SHOP) Exchange, including stand-alone dental plans, must submit specific information about their plans' coverage to the appropriate Exchange, HHS, and the state insurance commissioner, as well as make the information available to the public in plain language.

The Departments acknowledge the similar purposes served by 45 CFR 156.220 and these proposed rules. The Departments, however, do not intend for these proposed rules, if finalized, to alter requirements under section 45 CFR 156.220. Accordingly, if these proposed rules are finalized as proposed, QHP issuers would need to comply with requirements under both rules. If necessary and to the extent appropriate, HHS may issue future guidance to address QHP issuers' compliance with both section 45 CFR 156.220 and these proposed rules once they are finalized.

III. Request for Information: Disclosure of Pricing Information through a Standards-based API

The Departments are considering further expanding access to pricing information – both individuals' access to estimates about their own cost-sharing liability, and information about negotiated in-network rates and data for out-of-network allowed amounts in future rulemaking. Specifically, the Departments are considering whether to require, through future rulemaking, that group health plans and health insurance issuers make available as discrete data elements through a standards-based API the cost-sharing information that would be disclosed through the proposed internet-based self-service tool, as well as the in-network negotiated rates and out-of-network allowed amounts that this rule proposes to be publicly disclosed through machine-readable files. Standards-based APIs are also sometimes referred to as "open" APIs to convey that certain technical information for the API is openly published to facilitate uniform use and data sharing in a secure, standardized way.

The availability of patient cost-sharing information prior to the ordering and delivery of services can enable both patients and clinicians to make more informed decisions about the course of treatment and the cost to the patient. Requiring such access through a standards-based API could have

---

(Footnote Continued)

care clearinghouse means a public or private entity, including billing services, repricing companies, community health management information systems or community health information systems, and "value-added" networks and switches, that does either of the following functions: (1) Processes or facilitates the processing of health information received from another entity in a nonstandard format or containing nonstandard data content into standard data elements or a standard transaction. (2) Receives a standard transaction from another entity and processes or facilitates the processing of health information into nonstandard format or nonstandard data content for the receiving entity.

[60] *See* 45 CFR 164.502(a)(3) and 164.504(e)(2).

[61] *See generally* 45 CFR part 162, subparts K-S (describing standard HIPAA transactions).

a number of benefits for patients, providers, and the public at large. It would help promote the Departments' goal of allowing technology innovators to compile, consolidate and present pricing data in a usable format for consumers, thereby helping to make that data more relevant for consumers. For example, providing real-time access to the pricing information as discrete data elements through this mechanism would enable this information to be incorporated into third-party applications used by health care consumers or into electronic medical records for point-of-care decision-making and referral opportunities by clinicians. Additionally, being able to access these data elements through standards-based APIs would allow health care consumers to use a third-party application of their choice to obtain personalized, actionable health care service price estimates, rather than being required to use a specific application or online tool developed or identified by their plan or issuer. Widespread adoption of published, common, technical, content, and vocabulary standards are an important factor in fostering an environment in which third-party vendors can tailor products and services to better serve consumers through making health information accessible and actionable, including information that can support better financial decisions about their health care.

APIs are messengers or translators that work behind the scenes to ensure that software programs can talk to one another.[62] An API can be thought of as a set of commands, functions, protocols, or tools published by one software developer ("A") that enable other software developers to create programs (applications or "apps") that can interact with A's software without the other software developer needing to know the internal workings of A's software, all while maintaining consumer data privacy standards. This is how API technology enables the seamless user experiences associated with applications familiar from other aspects of many consumers' daily lives, such as travel and personal finance. Standardized, transparent, and procompetitive API technology can similarly benefit consumers of health care services. A standards-based, transparent API's technical requirements are consistent with other system APIs that have been developed to the same standards and are openly published, supporting interoperability. Technical consistency is fundamental to scale API-enabled interoperability and reduce the level of custom development and costs necessary to access, exchange, and use health information. Publishing specific technical and business information, such as how to demonstrate authorization to access specific data, necessary for applications to interact successfully with an API in production, is commonplace in many other industries and has fueled innovation, growth, and competition. In addition, a standards-based API does not allow any and all applications or application developers unfettered access to sensitive information within a database or data system. Instead, a standards-based API can enable an application to securely access a specific set of data based on established technical specifications and authentication and access controls. These controls can be implemented consistent with the organization's identity authentication or access authorization verification processes that comply with all applicable privacy and security laws and regulations.

On March 4, 2019, HHS Office of the National Coordinator for Health Information Technology (ONC) published a proposed rule, "21st Century Cures Act: Interoperability, Information Blocking, and the ONC Health IT Certification Program" (ONC 21st Century Cures Act proposed rule), which proposed updates to the standards, implementation specifications and certification criteria as well as Condition and Maintenance of Certification requirements for health information technology (health IT) under the ONC Health IT Certification Program. The ONC 21st Century Cures Act proposed rule specifically describes the requirements health IT developers must meet to comply with the API Condition of Certification as established by the 21st Century Cures Act and to be certified as meeting API-focused certification criteria under the ONC Health IT Certification Program. In the proposed rule, ONC proposed a set of technical API standards including the HL7 Fast Healthcare Interoperability Resources (FHIR) standard and complementary security and app registration protocols, OAuth 2.0 and OpenID Connect Core, for adoption by HHS at 45 CFR 170.215. ONC also proposed the adoption of a standard called the "United States Core Data for Interoperability (USCDI)" at 45 CFR 170.213 (84 FR 7424), which would establish a set of data classes and constituent data elements to support nationwide interoperability. The USCDI standard also references content and vocabulary standards relevant to included data that are adopted under 45 CFR part 170.

On March 4, 2019, CMS also published a proposed rule, "Medicare and Medicaid Programs; Patient Protection and Affordable Care Act; Interoperability and Patient Access for Medicare Advantage Organization and Medicaid Managed Care Plans, State Medicaid Agencies, CHIP Agencies and Chip Managed Care Entities, Issuers of Qualified Health Plans in the Federally-Facilitated Exchanges and Health Care Providers" (CMS Interoperability & Patient Access proposed rule).[63] This rule would require Medicare Advantage organizations, Medicaid and CHIP Fee-for-Service programs, Medicaid managed care plans, CHIP managed care entities, and QHP issuers in the FFEs to provide enrollees with access to select data, including claims data, through a standards-based API that conforms to the technical standards proposed for adoption in the ONC 21st Century Cures Act proposed rule at 45 CFR 170.215. If the CMS Interoperability & Patient Access proposed rule is finalized, certain entities, such as FFE QHP issuers and companies that participate in both Medicare (by offering a Medicare Advantage plan) and the individual or group market, would be required to provide certain data through a standards-based API, while also being subject to future rulemaking under section 2715A of the PHS Act.

Sections 13111 and 13112 of the Health Information Technology for Economic and Clinical Health Act (HITECH Act) require that federal agencies utilize, where available, health information technology systems and products that meet standards and implementation specifications adopted under section 3004 of the PHS Act. Consistent with section 3004 of the PHS Act and sections 13111 and 13112 of the HITECH Act, and to limit additional burden, the Departments would align, to the extent possible, any standards adopted in future rulemaking under section 2715A of the PHS Act that rely on standards-based APIs with the standards adopted by HHS under section 3004 of the PHS Act. This would include the technical standards for APIs proposed in the ONC 21st Century Cures Act proposed rule for HHS adoption at 45 CFR 170.215, which are also referenced in the CMS Interoperability & Patient Access proposed rule, though the Departments recognize that the content and vocabulary standards in the CMS Interoperability & Patient Access proposed rule relating to claims and clinical data are not applicable to pricing data.

The API standards proposed for HHS adoption in the ONC 21st Century Cures Act proposed rule are published standards. Notably, the FHIR standard is a consensus technical standard that holds great potential for supporting interoperability and enabling new entrants and competition throughout the health care industry. FHIR leverages modern computing techniques to enable users to access health care information over the internet via a standardized RESTful API. Specifically, FHIR includes both technical specifications for API transport (RESTful + JSON) and also specifications for API content known as "resources," which are a type of software architecture that provides interoperability between the internet and computer systems. Developers can create tools that interact with FHIR APIs to provide actionable data to their stakeholders. In the short time since FHIR was first created, the health care industry has rapidly embraced the standard through substantial investments in industry pilots, specification development, and the deployment of FHIR APIs supporting a variety of business needs.

The Departments request comment on whether API technical standards, based on the FHIR standard, as aligned with the ONC 21st Century Cures Act proposed rule and the CMS Interoperability & Patient Access proposed rule, should be required in the future across group health plans and health insurance coverage in the group and individual markets.[64] Specifically, the Departments are seeking comment on whether the Departments should propose an approach under which plans and issuers would be required to develop and implement procedures to make data available through APIs using the HL7® FHIR® IG: PSS for Patient Cost Transparency.[65] Recognizing that this IG is currently under development, the Departments could propose a staged approach to the implementation of this API requirement: (1) starting prior to when the IG is final (for example, starting January 1, 2022), payers could be required to make data available through an API; and (2) starting on or after the final IG

[62] For more information on APIs, see https://www.healthit.gov/api-education-module/story_html5.html.

[63] 84 FR 7610 (March 04, 2019).

[64] The Departments note that there is currently no standard HIPAA transaction applicable to data that will be made available to members of the public who are not covered entities. See generally 45 CFR 162.923.

[65] https://www.hl7.org/special/Committees/projman/searchableProjectIndex.cfm?action=edit&ProjectNumber=1514

publication date (anticipated to be October 1, 2023), plans and issuers could be required to make data available through APIs using the HL7® FHIR® IG: PSS for Patient Cost Transparency. The Departments are considering an approach under which initially plans and issuers would not be required to utilize the FHIR standard for this API, but the Departments would strongly encourage such use. While the IG for Patient Cost Transparency would not yet be finalized during this period, prior iteration(s) of the standard for trial use would be publicly available and could provide a development roadmap for payers wishing to deploy a FHIR-based API. The Departments are soliciting comment on the appropriateness of this proposed approach, the challenges it may present, and whether these suggested timeframes are appropriate.

The Departments request comment on what pricing information should be disclosed through an API, including whether all data elements required to be provided through the internet-based self-service tool and the negotiated in-network rate and allowed amount data for out-of-network providers machine-readable files should be required, whether a more limited set of data elements should be required in future rulemaking, and whether there are additional data elements that should be required.

The Departments recognize that requiring plans and issuers to disclose information related to cost-sharing liability, negotiated rates, and allowed-amounts for items and services furnished by out-of-network providers through a standards-based API would place additional burdens on issuers. The Departments seek comment on the possible scope of this burden. The Departments request comment on the potential operational impact on plans and issuers of using an API standard that aligns with the CMS Interoperability & Patient Access proposed rule to make pricing information more accessible. With adequate time for implementation, the Departments believe an API solution would not only greatly benefit patients, but may prove less burdensome for issuers and plans than requiring that the disclosures be made via machine-readable files. The Departments seek comment on plans' and issuers' readiness to disclose such data elements through an API, and the amount of time plans and issuers would need to implement such standards.

While the Departments expect that such a requirement would be justified by the increase in access to pricing information for consumers and the public, the Departments welcome comment on the utility of providing access via a standards-based API in the future, if a plan or issuer based tool and negotiated in-network rate and historical payments to out-of-network providers files are already available, as proposed elsewhere in this rule. The Departments are of the view that requiring plans and issuers to make pricing data available through a standards-based API would spur competition and reduce the burden on application developers to innovate around providing more user-friendly and effective applications for consumers. The ability to develop an application that can effectively interconnect with multiple APIs based on a single standard rather than having to build for separate proprietary APIs (or machine-readable files) allows application developers to focus development on meeting consumer needs. These applications would then allow consumers to realize the potential associated with greater access to these data. The Departments anticipate that a future rule that would propose the use of a standards-based API consistent with the API technical standards proposed for HHS adoption in the ONC 21st Century Cures Act proposed rule, to the extent such proposals are finalized, would encourage innovation and ensure that the pricing data are standardized in ways that promote interoperability and the use of electronic technological and third-party innovation. Access to pricing data through standards-based APIs would encourage application developers to try out different application features in order to determine what features are most engaging and user friendly for consumers. The Departments are also interested in comments from application developers about potential uses for these data.[66]

If the Departments move forward with a proposal in future rulemaking to require plans and issuers to make pricing information available through an API, the Departments have determined that the specific business and technical documentation necessary to interact with the proposed APIs would need to be made freely and publicly accessible. The Departments understand transparency about API technology is critical to ensuring that any interested application developer could easily obtain information needed to develop applications technically compatible with a plan's or issuer's API. Transparency would also be needed so that application developers would understand how to successfully interact with a plan's or issuer's API, including by satisfying any requirements the organization may establish for verification of developers' identity and their applications' authenticity, consistent with its security risk analysis and related organizational policies and procedures to ensure it maintains an appropriate level of privacy and security protection for data required to be disclosed. The Departments would likely propose to use the documentation requirements for standards-based APIs as defined in the ONC 21st Century Cures Act proposed rule and the CMS Interoperability & Patient Access proposed rule, to the extent those standards are finalized (see 84 FR 7634 through 7635). The Departments request comment on the future applicability of the documentation requirements for standards-based APIs as defined in the ONC 21st Century Cures Act proposed rule and the CMS Interoperability & Patient Access proposed rule, for the purposes of this use case specific to price transparency, and on what other documentation requirements are necessary to ensure transparency and consistency of pricing information.

The CMS Interoperability & Patient Access proposed rule proposed requirements for routine testing and monitoring of standards-based APIs (see 84 FR 7635). The Departments seek comment on whether there are reasons why different testing and monitoring requirements should apply to plans and issuers in the group and individual markets, for use specifically regarding price transparency and, if so, what requirements should apply. The Departments are also interested in comments regarding whether requiring the same testing and monitoring requirements would produce efficiencies for entities subject to both the CMS Interoperability & Patient Access proposed rule and section 2715A of the PHS Act.

The Departments recognize that while a specific standard for the standards-based API would need to be codified in regulation, the need for continually evolving standards development has historically outpaced the Departments' ability to amend regulatory text. In order to address how standards development can outpace agencies' rulemaking schedule, the Departments are considering proposing the approach for permitting stakeholders to utilize updated standards required for the API, as proposed in the CMS Interoperability & Patient Access proposed rule, to the extent it is finalized as proposed (see 84 FR 7630-7631), which references the Standards Version Advancement Process discussed in the ONC 21st Century Cures Act proposed rule (84 FR 7497-7498). However, the Departments are interested in comments regarding the impact on plans and issuers of updating APIs, and the frequency with which such updates should occur for this test case. The Departments also welcome comments on the circumstances in which voluntary use of updated versions of adopted standards set forth in future rulemaking should be allowed, and if the Departments should maintain alignment with the approach described in the CMS Interoperability and Patient Access proposed rule.[67]

The Departments are also interested in comments regarding potential privacy and security risks associated with a requirement that plans and issuers make pricing information available through a standards-based API. In the hands of a HIPAA-covered entity, such as a health care provider or health plan, or its business associate, individually identifiable pricing information about one's health care is PHI as defined at 45 CFR 160.103. As explained in the ONC 21st Century Cures Act proposed rule[68] direct-to-consumer health information technology products and services are a growing sector of the health IT market, but are often not regulated by the HIPAA Rules. Rather, the privacy and security practices of consumer-facing health IT products and services are typically regulated by the Federal Trade Commission Act (FTC Act). However, the FTC Act applies to acts and practices that are unfair and deceptive (15 U.S.C. 45(a)(1)), and does not prescribe privacy requirements to be adopted or followed that can be leveraged for the purpose of recognizing reasonable and necessary privacy-protective practices in these proposed rules.[69]

Although nothing would prevent an enrollee from requesting information through the API that is unrelated to the individual's actual health status or needs, the Departments anticipate that individuals typically would be seeking information related to their own potential health conditions

---

[66] *See* 84 FR 7628-7639.

[67] The Departments direct readers to the ONC 21st Century Cures Act proposed rule for further discussion on the voluntary advancement to updated versions of standards adopted for HHS use: https://www.federalregister.gov/d/2019-02224/p-1003.

[68] 84 FR 7424 (March 4, 2019).

[69] *See* HHS, Examining Oversight of the Privacy & Security of Health Data Collected by Entities Not Regulated by HIPAA, available at: https://www.healthit.gov/sites/default/files/non-covered_entities_report_june_17_2016.pdf.

and needs. For example, an individual is more likely to request cost-sharing information with in-network obstetricians if she is pregnant than if she is not. Revealing what information has been requested by individual enrollees could, thus, reveal sensitive information about their health status. Ensuring the privacy and security of these data if they are transmitted through the API would be of critical importance. To the extent that information that could be requested via the API would be considered PHI, covered entities and business associates would be able to disclose that information only to the extent permitted or required by the HIPAA Rules, and other federal and state laws. The Departments request comment on privacy and security standards that would be sufficient to protect the sensitive health data the Departments could propose in future rulemaking to be transmitted via an API, or whether additional privacy and security standards should be required.

If an enrollee directs a covered entity to send his PHI to a third-party application chosen by the individual, and that third-party application developer is neither a covered entity nor business associate under HIPAA Rules, (such as an application developer retained by the covered entity to transmit the PHI to the individual), the PHI to be transmitted through the API would not be protected under HIPAA Rules after being transmitted through the standards-based API and received by the third party, and covered entities would not be responsible for the security of that PHI once it has been received by the third-party application.[70] The Departments recognize that this could present a risk to sensitive information about enrollees' health status if the third party subsequently misuses the data or has a security breach. Nevertheless, the Departments are of the view that consumers should have access to this information to empower them to make informed health care decisions. To this end, the Departments believe consumers should be able to share such data with third-party applications of their choosing, but that they should understand that they are accepting the potential privacy and security risks that come from using a third-party application that is not required to comply with the HIPAA Rules.

The Departments are committed to maximizing enrollees' access to and control over their health information, including information designed to enable them to be more adept consumers of health care. The use of third-party applications to access pricing information is likely to introduce privacy risks of which consumers may be unaware, particularly if they do not understand that third-party application developers that are not providing an application on behalf of a covered entity are not business associates, and are not bound by the HIPAA Rules. The Departments seek comment regarding what information plans, issuers and third-party application developers should make available to individuals to better help them understand essential information about the privacy and security of their information, and what to do if they believe they have been misled or deceived about an application's terms of use or privacy policy. The Departments also seek comment regarding the manner and timing under which such information should be provided.

The Departments are considering requirements that would specify that consistent with the HIPAA Privacy Rule, plans and issuers generally may not deny access to a third party when an enrollee requests that the information be made accessible as proposed in this rule. As noted in guidance from HHS Office for Civil Rights, disagreement with the individual about the worthiness of the third party as a recipient of PHI, or even concerns about what the third party might do with the PHI, are not grounds for denying an access request.[71] However, a HIPAA covered entity is not expected to tolerate unacceptable levels of risk to the PHI in its systems, as determined by its own risk analysis.[72] Accordingly, it may be appropriate for a plan or issuer to deny or terminate specific applications' connection to its API under certain circumstances in which the application poses an unacceptable risk to the PHI on its systems or otherwise violates the terms of use of the API technology. In the CMS Interoperability & Patient Access proposed rule, CMS proposed that applicable entities could, in accordance with the HIPAA Security Rule, deny access to the API if the entity reasonably determines, based on objective, verifiable criteria that are applied fairly and consistently, that allowing that application to connect or remain connected to the API would present an unacceptable level of risk to the security of PHI on the entity's systems. The Departments are considering proposing a similar standard in future rulemaking for this specific use case. The Departments seek comment on this, as well as whether there are other specific circumstances under which plans and issuers should be permitted to decline to establish or permitted to terminate a third-party application's connection to the entity's API while remaining in compliance with a requirement to offer patients access through standards-based APIs for purposes of this specific use case.

In addition, and to address the concerns related to the risk to PHI within a system, the Departments further note that there are extant best practices and technical specifications for security related to authorization and access to data through APIs, which can be applied to health care use cases. In the ONC 21st Century Cures Act proposed rule, the ONC proposed technical standards for an API including complementary security and app registration protocols – OAuth 2.0 and OpenID Connect Core. Specifically, ONC proposed to adopt the "OpenID Connect Core 1.0 incorporating errata set 1" standard in 45 CFR 170.215(b), which complements the SMART Application Launch Framework Implementation Guide Release 1.0.0 [87] (SMART Guide). The OpenID standard is typically paired with OAuth 2.0 implementations and focuses on user authentication. ONC proposed to adopt the SMART Guide in 45 CFR 170.215(a)(5) as an additional implementation specification associated with the FHIR standard. This guide is referenced by the US FHIR Core IG and is generally being implemented by the health IT community as a security layer with which FHIR deployment is being combined (from both a FHIR server and FHIR application perspective). The use of these technical standards creates the ability for plans and issuers to use industry best practices to control authorization and access to the API and establish appropriate technical requirements for the security of third-party application access.

Further, the implementation of OpenID Connect paired with OAuth 2.0 allows organizations to securely deploy and manage APIs consistent with their organizational practices to comply with existing privacy and security laws and regulations. The organization publishing the API retains control over how patients authenticate when interacting with the API. For example, a patient may be required to use the same credentials they created and use to access their health information through the internet-based self-service tool as they do when authorizing an app to access their data. Since patients complete the authentication process directly with the organization, the app would not have access to their credentials. The Departments are of the view that implementing these security controls and safeguards would help to protect health information technology from nefarious actors.

IV. Request for Information: Provider Quality Measurement and Reporting in the Private Health Insurance Market

Quality, in addition to price, is essential for making value-based purchasing decisions.[73] Thus, the Departments are of the view that information relating to the quality of prospective health care services is critical to achieving the objective of increasing the value of health care. The Departments understand that for this reason, many existing cost estimator tools display provider quality information along with cost-sharing information.[74]

---

[70] HHS Office for Civil Rights, *FAQ on Access, Health Apps and APIs*, https://www.hhs.gov/hipaa/for-professionals/privacy/guidance/access-right-health-apps-apis/index.html ("Once health information is received from a covered entity, at the individual's direction, by an app that is neither a covered entity nor a business associate under HIPAA, the information is no longer subject to the protections of the HIPAA Rules. If the individual's app - chosen by an individual to receive the individual's requested ePHI - was not provided by or on behalf of the covered entity (and, thus, does not create, receive, transmit, or maintain ePHI on its behalf), the covered entity would not be liable under the HIPAA Rules for any subsequent use or disclosure of the requested ePHI received by the app."). See also, 45 CFR 164.524(a)(1), (c)(2)(ii), and (c)(3)(ii).

[71] *See* https://www.hhs.gov/hipaa/for-professionals/faq/2037/are-there-any-limits-or-exceptions-to-the-individuals-right/index.html. See also, 45 CFR 164.524(a)(2), (3) and (4).

[72] *See* 45 CFR 164.524(c)(2) and (3) and 164.308(a)(1), OCR HIPAA Guidance/FAQ-2036: https://www.hhs.gov/hipaa/for-professionals/faq/2036/can-an-individual-through-the-hipaa-right/index.html, and OCR HIPAA Guidance/FAQ-2037: https://www.hhs.gov/hipaa/for-professionals/faq/2037/are-there-any-limits-or-exceptions-to-the-individuals-right/index.html.

[73] Damberg, C., Sorbero, M., Lovejoy, S., Martsolf, G., Raaen, L., Mandel, D. "Measuring Success in Health Care Value-Based Purchasing Programs." 4 RAND Health, 2014; 4(3); Q. 9. 2014. Available at: https://www.rand.org/pubs/periodicals/health-quarterly/issues/v4/n3/09.html.

[74] http://www.truthinhealthcare.org/consumer-resources/cost-comparison-tools/.

Many of the cost estimator tools use existing provider-level CMS quality measures and data. For instance, in Colorado, pricing information for health care items and services is displayed along with five-star ratings from the CMS Hospital Consumer Assessment of Healthcare Providers and Systems (HCAHPS) survey results.[75] In Maine, consumers are able to compare median provider payments alongside patient experience HCAHPS survey results and other clinical quality measures, such as measures from CMS' Hospital Compare about how well the provider prevents health care associated infections.[76]

Over the years, CMS has made much progress in improving health care quality measurement and making such quality information publicly available through various mechanisms, including public use files on the CMS website.[77] In addition, CMS makes quality of health care information publicly available at *https://data.Medicare.gov* for a number of different health care providers and suppliers, including hospitals, nursing homes, and physicians. As exemplified in both Colorado and Maine, such data are available for the public and could be used by providers and suppliers of health care and pricing tool developers and integrated into cost-estimator tools.

The Departments also understand that many group health plans and health insurance issuers use other provider-level quality metrics as part of their provider directories and cost-estimator tools and are of the view that quality metrics play a large role in helping their participants, beneficiaries, and enrollees utilize these tools. From stakeholder engagement, the Departments know that the quality information included in these tools varies from issuer to issuer. Similar to states discussed earlier, some issuers have also used HCAHPS to provide meaningful information for consumers on patients' overall satisfaction with hospitals. In addition to CMS measures and data, plans and issuers have also used quality metrics information from the National Committee for Quality Assurance's (NCQA) Healthcare Effectiveness Data and Information Set (HEDIS); Bridges to Excellence, Center for Improvement in Healthcare (CIHQ), DNV GL - Healthcare Accreditations and Certifications, Castle Connelly Top Doctors, the Joint Commission on Accreditation of Healthcare Organizations ("the Joint Commission"), the Core Quality Measures Collaborative, and quality based recognition programs (such as from associations like the American Board of Medical Specialties). In addition, some plans and issuers have also relied on including validated consumer reviews, since consumers often select providers through word of mouth or referral from a provider or friend, relative, or neighbor. In general, the Departments understand that plans and issuers have also found it beneficial to include information on providers' accreditation, certification status, education, and professional achievements in their provider directory tools. This may include information from sources such as Leapfrog Hospital Safety Grade, board certification information on providers, health facilities accreditation program, and the Joint Commission.

The Departments are also aware that there are state and private sector efforts to develop and report on provider quality. In Minnesota, MN Community Measurement develops measures that are used in both the public and private sectors to report on provider quality.[78] Nationally recognized accrediting entities, such as NCQA, URAC, The Joint Commission, and National Quality Forum (NQF) have also been at the forefront of providing health care quality measures for both health plan and provider-level reporting.

The Departments are of the view that these public and private sector quality initiatives can be leveraged to complement the price transparency proposals discussed elsewhere in this proposed rule. The Departments are interested in how these public and private sector quality measures might be used to compliment cost-sharing information for plans and issuers in the private health insurance market.

To enhance the Departments' efforts in promoting competition in the health care market that is based on value, the Departments are interested in stakeholder input on a number of quality reporting related issues, including the following:

1. Whether, in addition to the price transparency requirements the Departments propose in these rules, the Departments should also impose requirements for the disclosure of quality information for providers of health care items and services.

2. Whether health care provider quality reporting and disclosure should be standardized across plans and issuers or if plans and issuers should have the flexibility to include provider quality information that is based on metrics of their choosing, or state-mandated measures.

3. What type of existing quality of health care information would be most beneficial to beneficiaries, participants, and enrollees in the individual and group markets? How can plans and issuers best enable individuals to use health care quality information in conjunction with cost-sharing information in their decision making before or at the time a service is sought?

4. Would it be feasible to use health care quality information from existing CMS quality reporting programs, such as the Medicare Quality Payment Program (QPP)[79] or the Quality Measures Inventory (QMI)[80] for in-network providers in the individual and group markets?

5. Could quality of health care information from state-mandated quality reporting initiatives or quality reporting initiatives by nationally recognized accrediting entities, such as NCQA, URAC, The Joint Commission, and NQF, be used to help participants, beneficiaries and enrollees meaningfully assess health care provider options?

6. What gaps are there in current measures and reporting as it relates to health care services and items in the individual and group markets?

7. The Departments are also interested in understanding any limitations plans and issuers might have in reporting on in-network provider quality in the individual and group markets.

8. The Departments seek more information about how and if quality data is currently used within plans' and issuers' provider directories and cost-estimator tools. The Departments also seek information on the data sources for quality information, and whether plans and issuers are using internal claims data or publicly-available data.

The OPPS Price Transparency final rule, discussed elsewhere in this preamble, also included a request for comment on quality measurement relating to price transparency. The Departments intend to review and consider the public input related to quality in response to that rule for future rulemaking.

V. Overview of the Proposed Rule Regarding Issuer Use of Premium Revenue under the Medical Loss Ratio Program: Reporting and Rebate Requirements – The Department of Health and Human Services

Consumers with health insurance often lack incentives to seek care from lower-cost providers, for example when consumers' out-of-pocket costs are limited to a set copayment amount regardless of the costs incurred by the issuer. Innovative benefit designs can be used to increase consumer engagement in health care purchasing decisions. HHS proposes to allow issuers that empower and incentivize consumers through the introduction of new or different plans that include provisions encouraging consumers to shop for services from lower-cost, higher-value providers, and that share the resulting savings with consumers, to take credit for such "shared savings" payments in their medical loss ratio (MLR) calculations. HHS

---

[75] Center for Improving Value in Health Care. 2019 Public Facility and Quality Reporting. Available here: https://www.civhc.org/wp-content/uploads/2018/12/Prometheus-and-Imaging-Methodology_FAQs_for-Preview.pdf.

[76] https://www.comparemaine.org/?page=methodology

[77] *https://www.cms.gov/CCIIO/Resources/Data-Resources/marketplace-puf.html*

[78] *https://mncm.org/*

[79] https://qpp.cms.gov/

[80] https://www.cms.gov/Medicare/Quality-Initiatives-Patient-Assessment-Instruments/MMS/Quality-Measures-Inventory.html#targetText=Quality%20Measures%20Inventory,quality%2C%20reporting%20and%20payment%20programs.&targetText=It%20is%20important%20to%20note,or%20CMS%20Program%2FMeasure%20Leads.

believes this proposal would preserve the statutorily-required value consumers receive for coverage under the MLR program, while encouraging issuers to offer new or different plan designs that support competition and consumer engagement in health care.

Formula for Calculating an Issuer's Medical Loss Ratio (45 CFR 158.221)

Section 2718(b) of the PHS Act requires a health insurance issuer offering group or individual health insurance coverage (including grandfathered health insurance coverage) to provide rebates to enrollees if the issuer's MLR falls below specified thresholds (generally, 80 percent in the individual and small group markets and 85 percent in the large group market). Section 2718(b) of the PHS Act generally defines MLR as the percentage of premium revenue (after certain adjustments) an issuer expended on reimbursement for clinical services provided to enrollees and on activities that improve health care quality. Consistent with section 2718(c) of the PHS Act, the standardized methodologies for calculating an issuer's MLR must be designed to take into account the special circumstances of smaller plans, different types of plans, and newer plans.

Several states have recently considered or adopted legislation[81] to promote health care cost transparency and encourage issuers to design and make available plans that "share" savings with enrollees who shop for health care services and choose to obtain care from lower-cost, higher-value providers. In addition, at least two states and a number of self-insured group health plans[82] have incorporated such shared savings provisions into their health plans. Under some plan designs, the savings are calculated as a percentage of the difference between the rate charged by the provider chosen by the consumer for a medical procedure and the average negotiated rate for that procedure across all providers in the issuer's network. Under other plan designs, the shared savings are provided as a flat dollar amount according to a schedule that places providers in one or more tiers based on the rate charged by each provider for a specified medical procedure. Under various plan designs, the shared savings may be provided in form of a gift card, a reduction in cost sharing, or a premium credit. HHS is of the view that such unique plan designs would motivate consumers to make more informed choices by providing consumers with tangible incentives to shop for care at the best price. As explained elsewhere in this preamble, there is ample evidence that increased transparency in health care costs would lead to increased competition among providers.[83] HHS is of the view that allowing flexibility for issuers to include savings they share with enrollees in the numerator of the MLR would increase issuers' willingness to undertake the investment necessary to develop and administer plan features that may have the effect of increasing health care cost transparency which in turn would lead to reduced health care costs.

HHS has in the past exercised its authority under section 2718(c) of the PHS Act to take into account the special circumstances of different types of plans by providing adjustments to increase the MLR numerator for "mini-med" and "expatriate" plans,[84] student health insurance plans,[85] as well as for QHPs that incurred Exchange implementation costs[86] and certain non-grandfathered plans (that is, "grandmothered" plans).[87] This authority has also been exercised to recognize the special circumstances of new plans[88] and smaller plans.[89] Consistent with this approach, HHS is proposing to exercise its authority to account for the special circumstances of new and different types of plans that provide "shared savings" to consumers who choose lower-cost, higher-value providers by adding a new paragraph 45 CFR 158.221(b)(9) to allow such shared savings payments to be included in the MLR numerator. HHS makes this proposal to ensure, should the proposal be finalized as proposed, that issuers would not be required to pay MLR rebates based on a plan design that would provide a benefit to consumers that is not currently captured in any existing MLR revenue or expense category. HHS proposes that the amendment to 45 CFR 158.221 become effective beginning with the 2020 MLR reporting year (for reports filed by July 31, 2021). HHS invites comments on this proposal.

VI. Applicability

A. In General

The Departments propose to require group health plans and health insurance issuers of individual market and group market health insurance coverage, including self-insured group health plans, to disclose pricing information as discussed in these proposed rules, with certain exceptions as discussed in more detail in this section of the preamble. The Departments are of the view that consumers across the private health insurance market will benefit from the availability of pricing information that is sufficient to support informed health care decisions on an element as basic as price. Although the Departments considered making the proposed requirements applicable to a more limited part of the private health insurance market, the Departments are of the view that consumers across the market should come to expect and receive the same access to standardized, meaningful pricing information and estimates. This broader applicability also has the greatest potential to reform health care markets.

The Departments also considered limiting applicability to individual market plans and insured group health plans; but concluded that limiting applicability would be inconsistent with section 2715A of the PHS Act. The Departments are concerned that a more limited approach might encourage plans and issuers to simply shift costs to sectors of the market where these proposed requirements would not apply and where consumers have less access to pricing information. The Departments are of the view that consumers in all private market health plans should be able to enjoy the benefits of greater price transparency and that a broader approach will have the greatest impact toward the goal of controlling the cost of health care industry-wide.

The Departments anticipate that pricing information related to items and services that are subject to capitation arrangements under a specific plan or contract could meet transparency standards by disclosing only the consumer's anticipated liability. For example, some providers participate in accountable care organizations (ACOs) and may be reimbursed based on a capitation payment. ACOs are groups of doctors, hospitals, and other health care providers that come together to provide coordinated care for their patients. The goal of ACOs is to ensure that patients get the right care at the right time, while avoiding unnecessary duplication of services and preventing medical errors. When an ACO succeeds both in delivering high-quality care and spending health care dollars more wisely, the ACO will share in the savings it achieves. Under such arrangements, the group health plan or health insurance issuer may reimburse the providers a set dollar payment per patient per unit of time to cover a specified set of services and administrative costs without regard to the actual number of services provided. The Departments also understand that there may be certain plan benefit structures where full disclosure of these data is not aligned with the goals of these proposed rules, such as a staff model health maintenance organization (HMO). The Departments seek comment on whether there are certain reimbursement or payment models that should be partially or fully exempt from these requirements, or should otherwise be treated differently. Further, the Departments seek comment on how consumers may be more informed about their cost-sharing requirements under these reimbursement or payment models.

---

[81] *See, for example,* 24-A Maine Rev. Stat. Ann. sec. 4318-A (adopted June 19, 2017); Neb. Rev. Stat. sec. 44-1401 et seq. (adopted Apr. 23, 2018); Utah Code Ann. sec. 31A-22-647 (adopted March 19, 2018); AZ SB 1471 (2018); N.H. HB 1784-FN (2018); MA H2184 (2017).

[82] *See, for example,* the State of New Hampshire employee medical benefit, the Site of Service and Vitals SmartShopper Programs, https://das.nh.gov/riskmanagement/active/medical-benefits/cost-savings-programs.aspx#vitals-smartshopper; Utah Public Employees Health Program Cost Comparison Tool, https://www.pehp.org/general/how-to-use-cost-saving-tools.

[83] Congressional Research Service Report to Congress: Does Price Transparency Improve Market Efficiency? Implications of Empirical Evidence in Other Markets for the Healthcare Sector, July 24, 2007.

[84] *See* 45 CFR 158.221(b)(3) for "mini-med" plans and 45 CFR 158.221(b)(4) for "expatriate" plans. *Also see* the Health Insurance Issuers Implementing Medical Loss Ratio (MLR) Requirements Under the Patient Protections and Affordable Care Act; Interim Final Rule; 75 FR 74863 at 74872 (December 1, 2010).

[85] *See* 45 CFR 158.221(b)(5). *Also see* the Student Health Insurance Coverage; Final Rule, 77 FR 16453 at 16458-16459 (March 21, 2012).

[86] *See* 45 CFR 158.221(b)(7). *Also see* the Exchange and Insurance Market Standards for 2015 and Beyond; Final Rule; 79 FR 30240 at 30320 (May 27, 2014).

[87] *See* 45 CFR 158.221(b)(6). *Also see* 79 FR at 30320 (May 27, 2014).

[88] See 45 CFR 158.121. *Also see* 75 FR at 74872-74873 (Dec. 01, 2010) and the HHS Notice of Benefit and Payment Parameters for 2018 Final Rule; 81 FR 94058 at 94153-94154 (Dec. 22, 2016).

[89] See 45 CFR 158.230 and 158.232. *Also see* 75 FR at 74880 (Dec. 01, 2010).

By statute, certain plans and coverage are not subject to the transparency provisions under section 2715A of the PHS Act and, therefore, would not be subject to these proposed rules. This includes grandfathered health plans, excepted benefits, and short-term, limited-duration insurance, as discussed later in this section of the preamble.

Grandfathered health plans are health plans that were in existence as of March 23, 2010, the date of enactment of PPACA, and that are only subject to certain provisions of PPACA, as long as they maintain status as grandfathered health plans under the applicable rules.[90] Under section 1251 of PPACA, section 2715A of the PHS Act does not apply to grandfathered health plans. These proposed rules would not apply to grandfathered health plans (as defined in 26 CFR 54.9815-1251, 29 CFR 2590.715-1251, 45 CFR 147.140).

In accordance with sections 2722 and 2763 of the PHS Act, section 732 of ERISA, and section 9831 of the Code, the requirements of title XXVII of the PHS Act, part 7 of ERISA, and chapter 100 of the Code do not apply to any group health plan (or group health insurance coverage offered in connection with a group health plan) or individual health insurance coverage in relation to its provision of excepted benefits, if certain conditions are satisfied. Excepted benefits are described in section 2791 of the PHS Act, section 733 of ERISA, and section 9832 of the Code. Section 2715A of the PHS Act is contained in title XXVII of the PHS Act, and, therefore, these proposed rules would not apply to a plan or coverage consisting solely of excepted benefits.

The Departments propose that the proposed rules would not apply to health reimbursement arrangements, or other account-based group health plans, as defined in 26 CFR 54.9815-2711(d)(6)(i), 29 CFR 2590.715-2711(d)(6)(i), and 45 CFR 147.126(d)(6)(i), that simply make certain dollar amounts available, with the result that cost-sharing concepts are not applicable to those arrangements.

These proposed rules also would not apply to short-term, limited-duration insurance. Under section 2791(b)(5) of the PHS Act, short-term, limited-duration insurance is excluded from the definition of individual health insurance coverage and generally is therefore, exempt from requirements of title XXVII of the PHS Act that apply in the individual market, including section 2715A of the PHS Act.[91]

These proposed rules would apply to "grandmothered" plans. Grandmothered plans refer to certain non-grandfathered health insurance coverage in the individual and small group markets with respect to which CMS has announced it will not take enforcement action even though the coverage is out of compliance with certain specified market requirements. Under current guidance, such coverage may be renewed through policy years beginning on or before October 1, 2020, provided that all such coverage comes into compliance with the specified requirements by January 1, 2021.[92] While grandmothered plans are not treated as being out of compliance with certain specified market reforms, section 2715A of the PHS Act is not among those specified reforms. Therefore, the Departments propose these rules would apply to "grandmothered" plans. The Departments seek comment on whether grandmothered plans may face special challenges in complying with these transparency reporting provisions and whether the proposed rules should or should not apply to grandmothered plans.

Except as otherwise provided for the proposed MLR requirements, the Departments also propose that the requirements discussed in these proposed rules would become effective for plan years (or in the individual market policy years) beginning on or after 1 year after the finalization of this rule. The Departments request feedback about this proposed timing. In particular, the Departments are interested in information and request comment from group health plans, health insurance issuers, and TPAs on the timing necessary to develop cost estimation tools and machine-readable files.

B. Good Faith Special Applicability

These proposed rules include a special applicability provision to address circumstances in which a group health plan or health insurance issuer, acting in good faith, makes an error or omission in its disclosures under these proposed rules. Specifically, a plan or issuer will not fail to comply with this section solely because it, acting in good faith and with reasonable diligence, makes an error or omission in a disclosure, provided that the plan or issuer corrects the information as soon as practicable. Additionally, to the extent such error or omission is due to good faith reliance on information from another entity, these proposed rules include a special applicability provision that holds the plan or issuer harmless, unless the plan or issuer knows, or reasonably should have known, that the information is incomplete or inaccurate. Under these proposed rules, if a plan or issuer has knowledge that such information is incomplete or inaccurate, the plan or issuer must correct the information as soon as practicable in accordance with paragraph (d)(4) of these proposed rules.

Furthermore, these proposed rules also include a special applicability provision to account for circumstances in which a plan or issuer fails to make the required disclosures available due to its internet website being temporarily inaccessible. Accordingly, these proposed rules provide that a plan or issuer will not fail to comply with this section solely because, despite acting in good faith and with reasonable diligence, its internet website is temporarily inaccessible, provided that the plan or issuer makes the information available as soon as practicable. The Departments solicit comments on whether, in addition to these special applicability provisions, additional measures should be taken to ensure that plans and issuers that have taken reasonable steps to ensure the accuracy of required cost-information disclosures are not exposed to liability by virtue of providing such information as required under these proposed rules.

VII. Economic Impact Analysis and Paperwork Burden

A. *Summary/Statement of Need*

This regulatory action is taken, in part, in light of Executive Order 13877 directing the Departments to issue an ANPRM, soliciting comments consistent with applicable law, requiring health care providers, health insurance issuers, and self-insured group health plans to provide or facilitate access to information about expected out-of-pocket costs for items or services to patients before they receive care. As discussed elsewhere in the preamble, the Departments have considered the issue, including consulting with stakeholders, and have determined that an NPRM would allow for greater specificity from commenters, who would be able to respond to specific proposals. In addition, despite the growing number of initiatives and the growing consumer demand for, and awareness of the need for pricing information, there continues to be a gap in easily accessible pricing information for consumers to use for health care shopping purposes. An NPRM enables the Departments to more quickly address this pressing issue. The proposed new requirements added to 26 CFR part 54, 29 CFR part 2590, and 45 CFR part 147 are aimed at addressing this gap, and are a critical part of the Administration's overall strategy for reforming health care markets by promoting transparency and competition, creating choice in the health care industry, and enabling consumers to make informed choices about their health care. By requiring group health plans and health insurance issuers to disclose to participants, beneficiaries, or enrollees (or their authorized representatives) such individual's cost-sharing information for covered items or services furnished by a particular provider, it provides them sufficient information to determine their potential out-of-pocket costs related to needed care and encourage them to consider price when making decisions about their health care.

---

[90] 26 CFR 54.9815-1251, 29 CFR 2590.715-1251, and 45 CFR 147.140.

[91] *See* 26 CFR 54.9801-2, 29 CFR 2590.701-2, and 45 CFR 144.103.

[92] CMS Insurance Standards Bulletin Series - INFORMATION - Extension of Limited Non-Enforcement Policy through 2020. March 25, 2019. Available at: https://www.cms.gov/CCIIO/Resources/Regulations-and-Guidance/Downloads/Limited-Non-Enforcement-Policy-Extension-Through-CY2020.pdf.

B. *Overall Impact*

The Departments have examined the impacts of this rule as required by Executive Order 12866 on Regulatory Planning and Review (September 30, 1993), Executive Order 13563 on Improving Regulation and Regulatory Review (January 18, 2011), the Regulatory Flexibility Act (RFA) (September 19, 1980, Pub. L. 96-354), section 202 of the Unfunded Mandates Reform Act of 1995 (March 22, 1995, Pub. L. 104-4), Executive Order 13132 on Federalism (August 4, 1999), the Congressional Review Act (5 U.S.C. 804(2)), and Executive Order 13771 on Reducing Regulation and Controlling Regulatory Costs (January 30, 2017).

Executive Orders 12866 and 13563 direct agencies to assess all costs and benefits of available regulatory alternatives and, if regulation is necessary, to select regulatory approaches that maximize net benefits (including potential economic, environmental, public health and safety effects, distributive impacts, and equity). Executive Order 13563 emphasizes the importance of quantifying both costs and benefits, reducing costs, harmonizing rules, and promoting flexibility. A regulatory impact analysis (RIA) must be prepared for rules with economically significant effects ($100 million or more in any 1 year).

Section 3(f) of Executive Order 12866 defines a "significant regulatory action" as an action that is likely to result in a rule: (1) having an annual effect on the economy of $100 million or more in any 1 year, or adversely and materially affecting a sector of the economy, productivity, competition, jobs, the environment, public health or safety, or state, local or tribal governments or communities (also referred to as "economically significant"); (2) creating a serious inconsistency or otherwise interfering with an action taken or planned by another agency; (3) materially altering the budgetary impacts of entitlement grants, user fees, or loan programs or the rights and obligations of recipients thereof; or (4) raising novel legal or policy issues arising out of legal mandates, the President's priorities, or the principles set forth in the Executive Order. A RIA must be prepared for major rules with economically significant effects ($100 million or more in any 1 year), and a "significant" regulatory action is subject to review by the Office of Management and Budget (OMB). The Departments have concluded that this rule is likely to have economic impacts of $100 million or more in at least 1 year, and, therefore, meets the definition of "significant rule" under Executive Order 12866. Therefore, the Departments have provided an assessment of the potential costs, benefits, and transfers associated with this rule. In accordance with the provisions of Executive Order 12866, this regulation was reviewed by OMB.

These proposed rules aim to enable participants, beneficiaries, or enrollees to obtain information about their potential cost-sharing liability for covered items and services that they might receive from a particular health care provider or providers by requiring plans and issuers to disclose cost-sharing information as described at 26 CFR 54.9815-2715A, 29 CFR 2590.715-2715A, and 45 CFR 147.210. As discussed previously in these proposed rules, there has been a shift in the health care market from copayments to coinsurance, coupled with increases in plans with high deductibles which generally require sizeable out-of-pocket expenditures prior to receiving coverage under the terms of the plan or policy; therefore, participants, beneficiaries, or enrollees are now beginning to shoulder a greater portion of their health care costs. With access to accurate and actionable pricing information, participants, beneficiaries, and enrollees would be able to consider the costs of an item or service when making decisions related to their health care. The Departments are of the view that disclosure of pricing information is crucial for participants, beneficiaries, and enrollees to engage in informed health care decision-making.

In addition, these proposals would require plans and issuers to make public negotiated rates of in-network providers and historical allowed amounts paid to out-of-network providers for all covered items and services. The Departments are of the view that these requirements would ensure that all consumers have the pricing information they need in a readily accessible format, which could inform their choices and have an impact on the disparities in health care costs. Public availability of information on in-network provider negotiated rates and allowed amounts for out-of-network services would allow consumers who wish to shop between plans to better understand what the cost of their care from a particular provider would be under each plan or policy. Furthermore, the Departments are of the view that the availability of price information to the public would empower the 28.5 million uninsured consumers[93] to make more informed health care decisions. Public availability of this information would also allow third-party developers to provide consumers more accurate information on provider, plan and issuer value and ensure that such information is available to consumers where and when it is needed (for example, via integration into electronic health records, price transparency tools, and consumer mobile applications).

1. Impact Estimates of the Transparency in Coverage Provisions and Accounting Table

This NPRM sets forth proposed requirements for group health plans and health insurance issuers to disclose to a participant, beneficiary, or enrollee, his or her cost-sharing information for covered items or services from a particular provider or providers. This NPRM also includes proposals to require plans and issuers to disclose in-network provider-negotiated rates and historical allowed amounts for out-of-network items and services provided by out-of-network providers through machine-readable files posted on a public internet website. In accordance with OMB Circular A-4, Table 1 depicts an accounting statement summarizing the Departments' assessment of the benefits, costs, and transfers associated with this regulatory action.

The Departments are unable to quantify all benefits and costs of these proposed rules. The effects in Table 1 reflect non-quantified impacts and estimated direct monetary costs and transfers resulting from the provisions of these proposed rules for plans, issuers, beneficiaries, participants, and enrollees.

TABLE 1: Accounting Table

Benefits
Non-Quantified:
• Provides consumers with a tool to determine their estimated out-of-pocket costs, potentially becoming more informed on the cost of their health care which could result in lower overall costs if consumers choose lower-cost providers or health care services.
• Potential increase in timely payments by consumers of medical bills as a result of knowing their expected overall costs prior to receiving services and having the ability to budget for expected health care needs.
• Potential profit gains by third-party mobile application developers and potential benefits to consumers through the development of mobile applications that may be more user-friendly and improve consumer access to cost information, potentially resulting in reductions in out-of-pocket costs.
• Potentially enable consumers shopping for coverage to understand the negotiated rates for providers in different group and individual health plans available to them and choose a plan that could minimize their out-of-pocket costs.
• States could potentially use the negotiated rate file to determine if premium rates are set appropriately.
• Potential reduction in cross-subsidization, which could result in lower prices as prices become more transparent.
• Public posting of negotiated rates could facilitate the review of anti-trust violations.

[93] This is based on 2017 uninsured data from Keith, K. "Two New Federal Surveys Show Stable Uninsured Rate." Health Affairs Blog. September 13, 2018. Available at: https://www.healthaffairs.org/do/10.1377/hblog20180913.896261/full/.

Costs:	Low Estimate	High Estimate	Year Dollar	Discount Rate	Period Covered
	$231.8 million	$298.4 million	2019	7 percent	2020-2024
Annualized Monetized ($/year)	$224.5 million	$286.5 million	2019	3 percent	2020-2024

Quantitative:
- Cost to plans and issuers to plan, develop, and build the proposed internet self-service tool and to provide negotiated in-network rates and out-of-network allowed amounts in machine-readable files, maintain appropriate security standards and update the machine-readable files per the proposed rules.
- Increase operating costs to plans and issuers as a result of training staff to use the internet self-service tool, responding to consumer inquiries, and delivering consumer's cost-sharing information and required notices.
- Cost to plans and issuers to review all the requirements in this proposal.

Non-Quantified:
- Potential cost incurred by plans and issuers that wish to develop a mobile accessible version of their internet-based self-service tool. Potential increase in cyber security costs by plans and issuers to prevent data breaches and potential loss of personally identifiable information.
- Potential increase in out-of-pocket costs for consumers if providers increase prices or issuers shift those costs to consumers in the form of increased cost sharing other than increased deductibles.
- Potential costs to states to review and enforce provisions of the proposed rules.
- Potential increase in consumer costs if reductions in cross-subsidization are for uncompensated care, as this could require providers finding a new way to pay for those uncompensated care costs.
- Potential increase in health care costs if consumers confuse cost with quality and value of service.
- Potential costs to inform and educate consumers on the availability and functionality of internet self-service tool.
- Potential exposure of consumers to identity theft as a result of breaches and theft of personally identifiable information.
- Potential consumer confusion related to low health care literacy and the potential complexity of internet self-service tools
- Potential cost to plans and issuers to a conduct quality control review of the information in the negotiated rate and out-of-network allowed amounts machine-readable files.

Transfers:	Estimate	Year Dollar	Discount Rate	Period Covered
Federal Annualized Monetized ($/year)	$9.3 million	2019	7 percent	2020-2024
	$9.5 million	2019	3 percent	2020-2024
Other Annualized Monetized ($/year)	$150.6 million	2019	7 percent	2020-2024
	$153.7 million	2019	3 percent	2020-2024

Quantitative:
- Transfers from the federal government to consumers in the form of increased premium tax credits by approximately $12 million per year beginning in 2021 as a result of estimated premium increases by issuers in the individual market to comply with these proposed rules.
- Transfer from consumers to issuers in the form of reduced MLR rebate payments in the individual and group markets by approximately $67 million per year by allowing issuers to take credit for "shared savings" payments in issuers' MLR calculations.
- Transfers from providers to consumers and issuers of approximately $128 million per year as a result of lower medical costs for issuers and consumers by allowing issuers to share with consumers the savings that result from consumers shopping for care from lower-cost providers.

Non-Quantified:
- Potential transfer from providers to consumers facing collections to reduce the overall amounts owed to providers if they are able to use competitor pricing as a negotiating tool.
- Potential transfer from providers to consumers if there is an overall decrease in health care costs due to providers reducing prices to compete for customers.
- Potential transfer from consumers to providers if there is an increase in health care costs if providers and services increase their negotiated rates to match those of competitors.
- Potential transfer from issuers to consumers if premiums go down and potential transfer from consumers to issuers if premiums increase.
- Potential transfer from issuers to consumers and the federal government in the form of decreased premiums and premium tax credits as a result of issuers adopting provisions encouraging consumers to shop for services from lower-cost providers and sharing the resulting savings with consumers.

Table 1 provided the anticipated benefits and costs (quantitative and non-quantified) to plans and issuers to disclose cost-sharing information as described at 26 CFR 54.9815-2715A, 29 CFR 2590.715-2715A, and 45 CFR 147.210 and make public negotiated rates of in-network providers and out-of-network allowed amounts paid for covered items and services. The following information describes benefits and costs - qualitative and non-quantified - to plans and issuers separately for these two requirements.

2. Proposed Requirements for Disclosing Cost-Sharing Information to Participant, Beneficiaries, or Enrollees under 26 CFR 54.9815-2715A(b), 29 CFR 2590.715-2715A(b), and 45 CFR 147.210(b)

Costs

In paragraph (b) of the proposed rules, the Departments are proposing to require group health plans and health insurance issuers to disclose certain relevant information in accordance with a prescribed method and format requirements, upon the request of a participant, beneficiary or enrollee (or an authorized representative on behalf of such individual). Under this requirement, the Departments are proposing seven content elements, which are described in paragraph (b)(1) of the proposed rules and discussed earlier in this preamble. The quantitative cost associated with meeting these requirements are detailed in the corresponding information collection requirement (ICR) that is discussed later in this preamble.

In addition to the costs described in the corresponding ICR, the Departments recognize there may be other costs associated with this requirement that are difficult to quantify given the lack of information and data. For example, while the Departments are of the view that the overall effect of this proposal would lower health care costs, the Departments recognize that price transparency may have the opposite effect because in some markets where pricing is very transparent, pricing can narrow and average costs can increase.[94] Additionally, states may incur additional costs to review and enforce the requirements proposed in this rule.

As described in the corresponding ICR section, the Departments assume most self-insured group health plans would work with a TPA to meet the requirements of these proposed rules. The Departments estimated cost assumes in the high-range estimate that all health insurance issuers and TPAs (on behalf of self-insured group health plans) would need to develop and build their internet-based self-service tools from scratch. However, the Departments also provide a low-range estimate assuming that most plans, issuers, and TPAs would modify an existing web-based tool. The Departments recognize that some plans, issuers, and TPAs may also voluntarily elect to develop a mobile application, which would result in additional costs. Additionally, TPAs generally work with multiple self-insured group health plans, and as a result, the costs for each TPA and self-insured group health plan may be lower to the extent they are able to leverage any resulting economies of scale.

Moreover, health care data breach statistics clearly show there has been an upward trend in data breaches over the past 9 years, with 2018 having more reported data breaches than any other year since records first started being published. Between 2009 and 2018, there have been 2,546 health care data breaches resulting in the theft and exposure of 189,945,874 health care records, equating to more than 59 percent of the United States population. Health care data breaches are now being reported at a rate of more than one per day.[95] Based on this information, the Departments recognize the requirements of these proposed rules provide additional opportunities for health care data breaches. Plans and issuers may incur additional expenses to ensure a consumer's PHI and personally identifiable information (PII) is secure and protected. Additionally, as consumers accessing the internet-based self-service tool may be required to input personal data to access the consumer-specific pricing information, consumers may be exposed to increased risk and experience identity theft as a result of breaches and theft of PII.

Benefits

Informed Consumer. A consumer armed with pricing information could potentially have greater control over their own health care spending, which could foster competition among providers resulting in less disparity in health care prices or a reduction in health care prices. Consumers who use this tool would be able to access their cost sharing paid to date, their progress toward meeting their accumulators such as deductibles and out-of-pocket limits, their estimated cost-sharing liability for an identified item or service, the negotiated rates with in-network providers for covered items and services, and the out-of-network allowed amounts for covered items and services. Additionally, consumers might gain some peace of mind in knowing where they stand financially with regard to their current health care needs and have the ability to plan ahead for any items and services they could require in the near future. The Departments are of the view that access to this information is essential to enable consumers to make informed decisions regarding specific services or treatments, budget appropriately to pay any out-of-pocket expenses, and determine what impact any change in providers or items or services would have on the cost of a particular service or treatment.

Consumers may become more cost conscious. The Departments are of the view that consumers may begin to focus on costs of services because under this proposal, plans and issuers would be required to disclose cost-sharing information that puts consumers' cost-sharing liability in the context necessary for truly cost-conscious decision-making. Consumers may know they have a coinsurance of 20 percent for an item or service, but many are unaware of what dollar amount of which they will be responsible for paying 20 percent. Knowing that dollar amount could motivate consumers to seek lower-cost providers and services. As discussed earlier in the preamble, there has been recent evidence in New Hampshire and Kentucky that supports the Departments' assumption that having access to pricing information, along with currently available information on provider quality and incentives to shop for lower prices, can result in consumers choosing providers with lower costs for items and services, thus lowering overall health care costs. The Departments acknowledge that this may only hold true if cost sharing varies between providers. Cost sharing in HMOs and Exclusive Provider Organizations (EPOs) generally is through fixed copayment amounts regardless of the provider who furnishes a covered item or service and, therefore, the proposed rules would provide little incentive for consumers to choose less costly providers in this context.

Timely Payment of Medical Bills. The Departments anticipate that consumers with access to the information provided in response to the proposed rules would be more likely to pay their bills on time. A recent Transunion survey found that 79 percent of respondents said they would be more likely to pay their bills in a timely manner if they had price estimates before getting care.[96] In addition, a non-profit hospital network, found that the more information they shared with patients, the better prepared those patients are for meeting their responsibilities. They further note that they find it valuable to explain to patients what their benefits are, provide an estimate of what the patient might owe for a service, and discuss any pre-payment requirements so that the patient understands what to expect during the billing process and what their options are. The hospital network reports that providing price estimates to patients has resulted in increased point of service cash collections from $3 million in 2010 to $6 million in 2011.[97]

Increased Competition Among Providers. The Departments are of the view that the requirements of these proposed rules would lead to competition among providers as consumers would be aware of and compare the out-of-pocket cost of a covered item or service prior to receiving that item or service, which might force higher-cost providers to lower their prices in order to compete for the price sensitive consumer.

3. Proposed Requirements for Public Disclosure of In-network Negotiated Rates and Historical Payments of Out-of-network Allowed Amounts Through Machine-readable Files under 26 CFR 54.9815-2715A(c), 29 CFR 2590.715-2715A(c), and 45 CFR 147.210(c)

Costs

In paragraph (c) of these proposed rules, the Departments are proposing to require that group health plans and health insurance issuers make available to the public on an internet website two digital files in a machine-readable format. The first file (the Negotiated Rate File) would include information regarding rates negotiated with in-network providers. The second file (the Allowed Amount File) would publish data showing allowed amounts for covered items and services furnished by out-of-network providers over a 90-day period. Plans and issuers would be required to make the required information available in accordance with certain method and format requirements described at paragraph (c)(2) of the proposed rules and update the files monthly. The quantitative cost associated with meeting the proposed requirements are detailed in the associated ICR section.

Non-Quantified Costs for Public Disclosure of In-network Negotiated Rates: In addition to the costs described in the associated ICR, the Departments recognize there may be other costs associated with the requirement to make in-network negotiated rates available publicly that are difficult to quantify given the current lack of information and data. While the Departments are of the view that the overall effect of this proposal would lower health care prices, there are instances in very transparent markets, where pricing can narrow and average costs can increase.[98] The Departments

---

[94] Kutscher, B. "Report: Consumers demand price transparency, but at what cost?" Modern Healthcare. June 2015. Available at: https://www.modernhealthcare.com/article/20150623/NEWS/150629957/consumers-demand-price-transparency-but-at-what-cost.

[95] *See* Report on Healthcare Data Breach Statistics, available at: *https://www.hipaajournal.com/healthcare-data-breach-statistics/*.

[96] Kutscher, B. "Report: Consumers demand price transparency, but at what cost?" Modern Healthcare. June 2015. https://www.modernhealthcare.com/article/20150623/NEWS/150629957/consumers-demand-price-transparency-but-at-what-cost.

[97] HFMA Executive Roundtable: Reimagining Patient Access. December 2015. Available at: https://api.hfma.org/Content.aspx?id=43731.

[98] Kutscher, B. "Report: Consumers demand price transparency, but at what cost?" Modern Healthcare. June 2015. Available at: https://www.modernhealthcare.com/article/20150623/NEWS/150629957/consumers-demand-price-transparency-but-at-what-cost.

also recognize that plans and issuers may experience additional costs (for example, quality control reviews) to ensure they comply with the requirements of these proposed rules. In addition, the Departments are aware that information disclosures allowing competitors to determine the rates their competitors are charging may dampen each competitor's incentive to offer a low price[99] or result in a higher price equilibrium. While health insurance issuers with the highest negotiated rates may see a decrease in their negotiated rates, as their providers respond to consumer and smaller health insurance issuers' concerns of paying more for the same item and service, issuers with the lowest negotiated rates may see their lower cost providers adjust their rates upward to become equal across the board. However, most research suggests that when better price information is available, prices for goods sold to consumers fall. For example, in an advertising-related study, researchers found that the act of advertising the price of a good or service is associated with lower prices.[100]

A potential additional non-quantified cost could be the cost to remove "gag clauses" from contracts between health insurance issuers and providers. Contracts between issuers and providers often include a gag clause, which prevents issuers from disclosing negotiated rates. The Departments recognize that issuers and providers may incur a one-time expense for their attorneys to review and update their provider contracts to remove any relevant gag clause.

Another potential cost is the impact on a plan's or issuer's ability or incentive to establish a robust network of providers. A health insurance provider network is a group of health care providers that have contracted with a group health plan or health insurance issuer to provide care at a specified price the provider must accept as payment in full. Many times, plans and issuers want consumers to use the providers in their network because these providers have met the health plan's quality standards and agreed to accept a negotiated rate for their services in exchange for the patient volume they will receive by being part of the plan's network.[101] Some plans and issuers offer a narrow network. Narrow networks operate with a smaller provider network, meaning a consumer will have few choices when it comes to in-network health care providers but often lower monthly premiums and out-of-pocket costs.[102] The Departments recognize that making negotiated rates public may create a disincentive for plans and issuers to establish a contractual relationship with a provider (including in narrow networks) because providers may be unwilling to give a discount to issuers and plans when that discount will be made public. The requirements of this proposal could also result in a reduction in revenue for those smaller health insurance issuers that are unable to pay higher rates to providers and may require them to narrow their provider networks, which could affect access to care for some consumers. Due to a smaller issuer's potential inability to pay providers with higher rates, smaller issuers may further narrow their networks to include only providers with lower rates, possibly making it more difficult for smaller issuers to fully comply with network adequacy standards described at 45 CFR 156.230 or applicable state network adequacy requirements.

Non-Quantified Cost for Public Disclosure of out-of-network allowed amounts: In addition to the costs described in the associated ICR and the previous analysis related to the public disclosure of negotiated rates, the Departments recognize that there may be other costs associated with the requirement to make historical payments of out-of-network allowed amounts publicly available that are difficult to quantify, given the current lack of information and data. For example, as a result of balance billing by providers, plans and issuers may be forced to increase their allowed amounts (such as the usual and customary and reasonable amount) to meet the demands of the price sensitive consumer.

Furthermore, while plans and issuers must de-identify data (such as claim payment information for a single provider) and ensure certain sensitive data are adequately protected, unauthorized disclosures of PHI and PII may increase as a result of manual preparation and manipulation of the required data.

Benefits

The Departments are of the view that requiring plans and issuers to make available information regarding negotiated in-network provider rates and 90-days of historical allowed amount data for out-of-network allowed amounts for covered items and services to the public would benefit plans and issuers, regulatory authorities, consumers, and the overall health care market.

Group Health Plans and Health Insurance Issuers: Plans and issuers may benefit from these proposals because under these proposed rules a plan or issuer would know the negotiated rates of their competitors. This may allow plans and issuers that are paying higher rates for the same items or services to negotiate with certain providers to lower their rates, thereby lowering provider reimbursement rates. The Departments acknowledge, however, as noted in the costs section earlier in this preamble, that knowledge of other providers' negotiated rates could also drive up rates if a provider discovers it is currently being paid less than other providers by a plan or issuer and, thereby, negotiates higher rates.

In addition, these proposed rules may result in more plans and issuers using a reference pricing structure. Under this structure, participants, beneficiaries, or enrollees who select a provider charging above the reference price (or contribution limit) must pay the entire difference and these differences do not typically count toward that individual's deductible or the annual out-of-pocket limit. Plans and issuers may want to use a reference pricing structure to pass on any potential additional costs associated with what they can identify as higher cost providers to the participant, beneficiary, or enrollee. The Departments recognize that reference pricing might not impact every consumer. For example, CalPERS provides exceptions from reference pricing when a member lives more than 50 miles from a facility that offers the service below the price limit. It also exempts the patient if the patient's physician gives a clinical justification for using a high-priced facility or hospital setting. Another example is a business with a self-insured group health plan that exempts laboratory tests for patients with a diagnosis of cancer from its reference pricing program. However, reference pricing has generally been shown to result in price reductions, not merely slowdowns in the rate of price growth. For example, in the first 2 years after implementation, reference pricing saved CalPERS $2.8 million for joint replacement surgery, $1.3 million for cataract surgery, $7.0 million for colonoscopy, and $2.3 million for arthroscopy.[103]

Regulatory Authorities: In many states, health insurance issuers must obtain prior approval for rate changes from the state's Department of Insurance. Regulatory authorities such as state Departments of Insurance might benefit from this proposal because knowledge of provider negotiated rates and historical out-of-network allowed amounts paid to out-of-network providers could support determinations of whether premium rates, including requests for premium rate increases, are reasonable and justifiable.

Consumers: Access to the negotiated rates between plans and issuers and in-network providers and the amount plans and issuers paid out-of-network providers for covered items and services would allow consumers to understand the impact of their choices for health care coverage options and providers on the cost of a particular service or treatment. Introducing this information into the consumer's health care decision-making process would give the consumer a greater degree of control over their own health care costs. Furthermore, having access to publicly available out-of-network allowed amounts would provide consumers who are shopping for coverage the ability to compare the different plan or issuer payments for items and services, including items and services from providers that might be out-of-network. While the Departments are of the view that

---

[99] Koslov, T., Jex, E. "Price transparency or TMI?" Available at: https://www.ftc.gov/news-events/blogs/competition-matters/2015/07/price-transparency-or-tmi.

[100] Austin, D., Gravelle, J. "Report: Does Price Transparency Improve Market Efficiency? Implications of Empirical Evidence in Other Markets for the Health Sector." CRS Report for Congress. June 2007. Available at: https://fas.org/sgp/crs/secrecy/RL34101.pdf.

[101] See Davis, E. "Health Insurance Provider Network Overview" Verywell Health, August 2019. Available at: https://www.verywellhealth.com/health-insurance-provider-network-1738750

[102] Anderman, T "What to Know About Narrow Network Health Insurance Plans", Consumer Reports, November 2018. Available at: https://www.consumerreports.org/health-insurance/what-to-know-about-narrow-network-health-insurance-plans/

[103] Boynton, A., Robinson, J. "Appropriate Use of Reference Pricing Can Increase Value." Health Affairs Blog. June 2015. Available at: https://www.healthaffairs.org/do/10.1377/hblog20150707.049155/full/.

consumers would benefit from the requirements of this proposal, the Departments recognize that utilizing the required information would not be appropriate or reasonable in an emergency situation.

Overall Health Insurance Market: This proposal may induce an uninsured person to obtain health insurance, depending on premium rates, after learning the actual dollar difference between the usual and customary rates that they pay for items and services as an uninsured consumer and the negotiated rates and out-of-network allowed amounts under the terms of a group health plan or health insurance issuer's policy. In addition, this proposal might force providers to lower their rates for certain items and services in order to compete for the price sensitive consumer or plan; although the immediate payment impact would be categorized as a transfer, any accompanying health and longevity improvements would be considered as benefits (and any accompanying increases in utilization would, thus, be considered costs). And, as discussed elsewhere in this preamble, New Hampshire's HealthCost website was found to reduce the cost of medical imaging procedures by 5 percent. The study further found that patients saved approximately $7.5 million dollars on X-Ray, CT, and MRI scans over the 5 year period studied (dollars are stated in 2010 dollars).[104]

4. Medical Loss Ratio (45 CFR 158.221)

In these proposed rules, HHS proposes to amend §158.221 to allow health insurance issuers that share with consumers savings that result from consumers shopping for lower-cost, higher-value services, to take credit for such "shared savings" payments in issuers' MLR calculations. For this impact estimate, HHS assumed that only relatively larger issuers (with at least 28,000 enrollees) that have consistently reported investment costs in health information technology on the MLR annual reporting form (of at least $6.77 per enrollee, which represents issuers with 70 percent of total reported commercial market health information technology investment) or issuers that operate in states that currently (three states in 2019) or may soon support "shared savings" plan designs would initially choose to offer plan designs with a "shared savings" component, that such issuers would share, on average, 50 percent of the savings with consumers (which would increase the MLR numerator under the proposed rule), and that issuers whose MLRs were previously below the applicable MLR standards would use their retained portion of the savings to lower consumers' premiums in future years (which would reduce the MLR denominator). Based on 2014-2017 MLR and other data, HHS estimates that this proposal could reduce MLR rebate payments from issuers to consumers by approximately $67 million per year, while facilitating savings that would result from lower medical costs of approximately $128 million per year for issuers and consumers (some of which would be retained by issuers, shared directly with consumers, or used by issuers to reduce future premium rates).

5. Summary of Estimated Transfers

The Departments assume that because 2020 premium rates are nearly finalized, that issuers will not be able to charge for the expenses incurred due to these proposed rules in the 2020 rates. Because issuers will not have had an opportunity to reflect the 2020 development costs in the 2020 premium rates, some issuers may apply margin to the assumed ongoing expenses as they develop premium rates for 2021 and after. The Departments estimate premiums for the fully-insured markets would be $450 billion for 2021, which includes the individual, small group, and large group markets.[105] The Departments estimate that the ongoing expense represents approximately 0.03 percent of premiums for the fully-insured market. Assuming this level of premium increase in the individual market, premium tax credit outlays are estimated to increase by about $12 million per year beginning in 2021. Given that 2021

premium tax credit outlays are expected to be $43 billion, the Departments expect the estimated increase of $12 million to have minimal impacts on anticipated enrollment. The Departments note that any impact of these proposed rules on provider prices has not been estimated, as limited evidence has generally shown not much of an effect on health care prices. As a result, the Departments are assuming that the overall impact will be minimal. However, there is a large degree of uncertainty regarding the effect on prices so actual experience could differ.

C. *Regulatory Review Costs*

Affected entities will need to understand the requirements of these proposed rules, if finalized, before they can comply. Group health plans and health insurance issuers are responsible for ensuring compliance with these proposed rules. However, as assumed elsewhere, it is expected that issuers and TPAs, and only the largest self-insured plans will likely incur this burden. The issuers and TPAs will then provide plans with rule compliant services. Therefore, the burden for the regulatory review is estimated to be incurred by the 1,959 issuers and TPAs.

If regulations impose administrative costs on private entities, such as the time needed to read and interpret these proposed rules, if finalized, the Departments should estimate the cost associated with regulatory review. Due to the uncertainty involved with accurately quantifying the number of entities that will review and interpret these proposed rules, the Departments assume that the total number of health insurance issuers and TPAs that would be required to comply with these rules would be a fair estimate of the number of entities affected.

The Departments acknowledge that this assumption may understate or overstate the costs of reviewing these proposed rules. It is possible that not all affected entities will review these rules, if finalized, in detail, and may seek the assistance of outside counsel to read and interpret them. For these reasons, the Departments are of the view that the number of health insurance issuers and TPAs would be a fair estimate of the number of reviewers of these proposed rules. The Departments welcome any comments on the approach in estimating the number of affected entities that will review and interpret these proposed rules, if finalized.

Using the wage information from the BLS for a Computer and Information Systems Manager (Code 11-3021) and a Lawyer (Code 23-1011) the Departments estimate that the cost of reviewing this rule is $285.66 per hour, including overhead and fringe benefits.[106] Assuming an average reading speed, the Departments estimate that it would take approximately 4 hours for the staff to review and interpret these proposed rules (2 hours each for a lawyer and an Information Systems Manager), if finalized; therefore, the Departments estimate that the cost of reviewing and interpreting these proposed rules, if finalized, for each health insurance issuer and TPA is approximately $1,142.64. Thus, the Departments estimate that the overall cost for the estimated 1,959 health insurance issuers and TPAs is $2,238,431.76 ($1,142.64 x 1,959 total number of estimated health insurance issuers and TPAs).

D. *Regulatory Alternatives Considered*

In developing the policies contained in these proposed rules, the Departments considered alternatives to the presented proposals. In the following paragraphs, the Departments discuss the key regulatory alternatives that the Departments considered.

1. Limiting Cost-sharing Disclosures to Certain Covered Items and Services and Certain Types of Group Health Plans and Health Insurance Issuers

These proposed rules require plans and issuers to disclose cost-sharing information for any requested covered item or service. The Departments considered limiting the number of items or services for which plans and issuers would be required to provide cost-sharing information to lessen the burden on these entities. However, limiting disclosures to a specified set of items and services reduces breadth and availability of useful cost

---

[104] Brown. Z. "Equilibrium Effects of Health Care Price Information." 100 Rev. of Econ. and Stat. 1. July 16, 2018. Available at: http://www-personal.umich.edu/~zachb/zbrown_eqm_effects_price_transparency.pdf)

[105] 2017 earned premium data was taken from amounts reported for MLR, and trended forward using overall Private Health Insurance trend rates from the NHE projections.

[106] Wage information is available at https://www.bls.gov/oes/current/oes_nat.htm.

estimates to determine anticipated cost-sharing liability, limiting the impact of price transparency efforts by reducing the incentives to lower prices and provide higher-quality care. The Departments assume that plans (or TPAs on their behalf) and issuers, whether for a limited set of covered items and services or all covered items and services, would be deriving these data from the same data source. Because the data source would be the same, the Departments assume that any additional burden to produce the information required for all covered items and services, as opposed to a limited set of covered items and services, would be minimal. The Departments are of the view that this minimal additional burden is outweighed by the potentially large, albeit unquantifiable, benefit to consumers of having access to the required pricing information for the full breadth of items and services covered by their plan or issuer. For these reasons, in order to achieve lower health care costs and reduce spending through increased price transparency, the Departments propose to require cost-sharing information be disclosed for all covered items and services.

The Departments also considered implementing a more limited approach by imposing requirements only on individual market plans and fully-insured group coverage. However, the Departments are concerned that this limited approach might encourage plans to simply shift costs to sectors of the market where these proposed requirements would not apply and where consumers have less access to pricing information. The Departments are of the view that consumers should be able to enjoy the benefits of greater price transparency and that a broader approach will have the greatest likelihood of controlling the cost of health care industry-wide. Indeed, if the requirements of these proposed rules were limited to only individual market plans, the Departments estimate only 13,700,000 participants, beneficiaries, and enrollees would receive the intended benefits of these rules. In contrast, under these proposed rules, a total of 193,500,000 participants, beneficiaries, and enrollees would receive the intended benefits. The Departments acknowledge that limiting applicability of the requirements of these proposed rules to the individual market would likely reduce the overall cost and hour burden estimates identified in the corresponding ICRs section, but the overall cost and burden estimates per covered life would increase. Further, there is a great deal of overlap in health insurance issuers that offer coverage in both the individual and the group markets. Issuers offering coverage in both markets would be required to comply with the requirements of these proposed rules even if the Department limited the applicability to only the individual market. Because TPAs provide administrative functionality for self-insured group health care coverage, those non-issuer TPA entities would not incur any hourly burden or associated costs because they do not have any overlap between the individual and group markets. The Departments are of the view that the benefits of providing consumer pricing information to an estimated total 193,500,000 participants, beneficiaries, and enrollees outweigh the increased costs and burden hours that a subset of plans and issuers (and TPAs on behalf of self-insured group health plans) that are not active participants in the individual market would incur. The Departments have determined the benefits of expanding the applicability of these proposed rules would not only expand access to health care pricing information to a greater number of individuals, but that any developed economies of scale would have a much greater likelihood of achieving the goal of controlling the cost of health care industry-wide.

2. Requirement to Post Machine-readable Files of Negotiated Rates and Historical Data for Out-of-network Allowed Amount Payments Made to Out-of-network Providers to a Public Website

In proposing the requirement that group health plans and health insurance issuers post their negotiated rates and historical data for out-of-network allowed amount payments made to out-of-network providers on a publicly accessible website, the Departments considered requiring payers to submit the internet addresses for the machine-readable files to CMS, and CMS would make the information available to the public. A central location could allow the public to access negotiated rate information and historical data for out-of-network allowed amounts in one centralized location, reducing confusion and increasing accessibility. Posting negotiated rates and historical data for out-of-network allowed amounts in a central location may also make it easier to post available quality information alongside price information. However, to provide flexibility and reduce burden, the Departments are of the view that plans and issuers should determine where to post negotiated rate and out-of-network allowed amount information rather than prescribing the location the information is to be disclosed. Further, requiring payers to submit internet addresses for their machine-readable files to CMS would result in additional burden to the extent plans and issuers already post this information in a different centralized location.

3. Frequency of Updates to Machine-Readable Files

In proposing paragraph (c) of these proposed rules, the Departments considered requiring more frequent updates (within 10 calendar days of new rate finalization) to the negotiated rates and out-of-network allowed amounts. More frequent updates would provide a number of benefits for the patients, providers, and the public at large. Specifically, such a process could ensure the public has access to the most up-to-date rate information so that consumers can make the most meaningful, informed decisions about their health care utilization. Requiring group health plans and health insurance issuers to update the machine-readable files more frequently would result in increased burdens and costs for those affected entities. With respect to the Negotiated Rate File, the Departments estimate that requiring updates within 10 calendar days of rate finalization would result in each plan, issuer, or TPA (on behalf of a self-insured group health plan) incurring an annual hour burden of 1,110 hours with an associated equivalent cost of $110,290. Based on recent data the Departments estimate a total 1,959 entities - 1,754 issuers[107] and 205 TPAs[108] - will be responsible for implementing the proposals of these rules. For all 1,754 health insurance issuers and 205 TPAs, the total hour burden would be 2,174,490 hours with and associated equivalent annual cost of $216,057,326. As discussed in the corresponding ICR, requiring a less frequent 30 calendar day update would reduce the annual hour burden for each entity to 360 hours with an associated equivalent cost of $35,770. For all 1,754 health insurance issuers and 205 TPAs, the total hour burden is reduced to 705,240 hours with and associated equivalent annual cost of $70,072,646. With respect to the Allowed Amount File, the Departments estimate that requiring updates within 10 calendar days of rate finalization would result in each plan, issuer, or, TPA (on behalf of a self-insured group health plan) incurring an annual hour burden of 481 hours with an associated equivalent cost of $44,952. For all 1,754 health insurance issuers and 205 TPAs, the total hour burden would be 942,279 hours with and associated equivalent annual cost of $88,061,046. As discussed in the corresponding ICR, requiring a less frequent update would reduce the annual hour burden for each plan, issuer, and TPA to 156 hours with an associated equivalent cost of $14,579 per file. For all 1,754 health insurance issuers and 205 TPAs, the total hour burden is reduced to 305,604 hours with an associated equivalent annual cost of $28,560,339. By proposing monthly updates to the machine-readable files, rather than updates every 10 calendar days, the Departments have chosen to strike a balance between placing an undue burden on plans and health insurance issuers and assuring the availability of accurate information.

4. Proposed File Format Requirements

In 26 CFR 54.9815-2715A(c)(2), 29 CFR 2590.715-2715A(c)(2), and 45 CFR 147.210(c)(2), these proposed rules require payers to post information in two machine-readable files. A machine-readable file is defined as a digital representation of data or information in a file that can be imported or read into a computer system for further processing without human intervention, while no semantic meaning is lost. These proposed rules would require each machine-readable file to use a non-proprietary, open format. The Departments considered requiring payers to post negotiated rates and plan-specific historical charges paid for out-of-network services for all items and services using a specific file format, namely JSON. However, the Departments are of the view that being overly prescriptive in the file type would impose an unnecessary burden on payers despite the advantages of JSON, namely being downloadable and readable for many health care consumers, and the potential to simplify the ability of price transparency tool developers to access the data. Therefore, the Departments have proposed that group health plans and health insurance issuers

---

[107] 2018 MLR Data Trends.

[108] Non-issuer TPAs based on data derived from the 2016 Benefit Year reinsurance program contributions.

post the negotiated rate and out-of-network allowed amount information in two distinct machine-readable files using a non-proprietary, open format to be identified by the Departments in future guidance.

In addition, the Departments considered proposing that plans and issuers provide the specific out-of-network allowed amount methodology needed for consumers to determine out-of-pocket liability for services by providers not considered to be in-network by the group health plan or health insurance issuer, rather than historical data on paid out-of-network claims. However, the Departments understand providing a formula or methodology for calculating a provider's out-of-network allowed amount does not provide the data users need in an easy-to-use machine-readable format. The Departments determined that providing monthly data files on amounts paid by plans and issuers over a 90-day period (by date of service with a 90-day lag) for items and services provided by out-of-network providers would enable users to more readily determine what costs a plan or issuer may pay toward items or services obtained out-of-network. Because a plan or issuer does not have a contract with an out-of-network provider that establishes negotiated rates, the plan or issuer cannot anticipate what that provider's charges will be for any given item or service; therefore, the plan or issuer cannot provide an estimate of out-of-pocket costs to the consumer.

Providing data on the costs covered by a plan or issuer for specific items and services allows a consumer to anticipate what their plan or issuer would likely contribute to the costs of items or services obtained from out-of-network providers and allows the consumer to estimate his or her out-of-pocket costs by subtracting that amount from the cost of the out-of-network services. Historical out-of-network allowed amount data will provide increased price transparency for consumers, and the burdens and costs related to producing these data are not considered to be significantly higher than that associated with producing the methodology for determining allowed amounts for payments to out-of-network providers. Given these circumstances, the Departments have proposed that payers provide historical allowed amount data for out-of-network covered items or services furnished by a particular out-of-network provider during the 90-day time period that begins 180 days prior to the publication date of the Allowed Amount File, rather than requiring plans and issuers to report their methodology or formula for calculating the allowed amounts for out-of-network items and services.

5. Proposal to Require Both Disclosure of Cost-sharing Information to Participants, Beneficiaries, and Enrollees and Publicly-posted Machine-readable Files with Negotiated Rates and Out-of-network Allowed Amounts

The Departments considered whether proposing that group health plans and health insurance issuers be required to disclose cost-sharing information through a self-service tool or in paper form to participants, beneficiaries, or enrollees (or their authorized representatives) so that they may obtain an estimate of their cost-sharing liability for covered items and services and publicly-posted machine-readable files containing data on in-network negotiated rates and historical out-of-network allowed amounts would be duplicative. The requirement to disclose cost-sharing information to participants, beneficiaries, or enrollees proposed in these rules would require plans and issuers to provide consumer-specific information on potential cost-sharing liability to enrolled consumers, complete with information about their deductibles, copays, and coinsurance. However, cost-sharing information for these plans and coverage would not be available or applicable to consumers who are uninsured or shopping for plans pre-enrollment. Data disclosed to participants, beneficiaries, and enrollees would also not be available to third parties who are interested in creating consumer tools to assist both uninsured and insured consumers with shopping for the most affordable items or services. Limiting access to data to a subset of consumers would not promote the transparency goals of these proposed rules, and would reduce the potential for these proposed rules to drive down health care costs by increasing competition.

As discussed in more detail in the corresponding ICR sections of this preamble, the Departments estimate that the high-end average 3-year hour burden and cost to develop only the internet-based self-service tool, including the initial tool build and maintenance, customer service training, and customer assistance burdens and costs. The Departments estimate the total hour burden per group health plan, health insurance issuer, or TPA (on behalf of a self-insured group health plan) would be approximately 956 hours, with an associated equivalent average annual cost of approximately $168,804. For all 1,754 health insurance issuers and 205 TPAs, the Departments estimate the total average annual hour burden, over a 3-year period, to be 1,872,564 hours with an associated equivalent total average annual cost of approximately $161,355,868.

In contrast, and as further discussed in the corresponding ICR sections earlier in this preamble, for implementation of the currently proposed internet-based self-service tool in conjunction with the out-of-network allowed amount and in-network negotiated rate machine-readable files, the Departments estimate that the average annual high-end burden and cost, over a 3-year period, for each group health plan and health insurance issuer or TPA would be approximately 2,127 hours, with an associated equivalent cost of approximately $190,356. For all 1,754 health insurance issuers and 205 TPAs, the Departments estimate the total average high-end annual hour burden and cost, over a 3-year period, to be 4,165,900 hours with an associated equivalent total average annual cost of approximately $372,906,502.

Additionally, as discussed in more detail in the corresponding ICR sections, the Departments estimate that that the low-end average 3-year burden and cost to develop and maintain only the internet-based self-service tool, including the initial tool build and maintenance, customer service training, and customer assistance burdens and costs. The Departments estimate the total hour burden per plan and or TPA would be approximately 392 hours, with an associated equivalent average annual cost of approximately $33,194. For all 1,754 health insurance issuers and 205 TPAs, the Departments estimate the total average annual hour burden, over a 3-year period, to be 767,100 hours with an associated equivalent total average annual cost of approximately $65,027,268.

In contrast, and as further discussed in the corresponding ICR sections earlier in this preamble, for implementation of the currently proposed internet-based self-service tool in conjunction with the out-of-network allowed amount and in-network negotiated rate machine-readable files, the Departments estimate that the average annual low-end hour burden and cost, over a 3-year period, for group health plan and health insurance issuer or TPA would be approximately 1,562 hours, with an associated equivalent average annual cost of approximately $141,183. For all 1,754 health insurance issuers and 205 TPAs the Departments estimate the total average annual low-end hour burden and cost, over a 3-year period, to be 3,060,436 hours with an associated equivalent total average annual cost of approximately $276,577,902.

While the Departments recognize that requiring disclosures through both mechanisms increases the cost and hour burdens for plans and issuers required to comply with the requirements of these proposed rules, the Departments are of the view that the these additional costs are outweighed by the benefits accrued to the broader group of consumers (such as the uninsured and individuals shopping for coverage) and other individuals who would benefit directly from the additional information provided through the machine-readable files. Furthermore, as noted earlier in this preamble, researchers and third-party developers would also be able to use the data included in the machine-readable files in a way that could accrue even more benefits to individuals, including those individuals not currently enrolled in a particular plan or coverage. For these reasons, the Departments concluded that, in addition to proposing to require plans and issuers to be required to disclosure cost-sharing information to participants, beneficiaries, or enrollees through an internet-based self-service tool or in paper form, proposing to require plans and issuers to disclose information on negotiated rates and out-of-network allowed amounts would further the goals of price transparency and accrue more benefit to all potentially affected stakeholders.

6. Proposal to Require Machine-readable Files in Lieu of an API

The Departments considered whether to propose a requirement for group health plans and health insurance issuers to make the information required in these proposed rules to be disclosed through a standards-based API, instead of through the proposed internet-based self-service tool and machine-readable files. Access to pricing information through an API could have a number of benefits for consumers, providers, and the public at large. The Departments believe this information could ensure the public has access to the most up-to-date rate information. Providing real-time access to pricing information through a standards-based API could allow third-party innovators to incorporate the information into applications used by consumers or combined with electronic medical records for point-of-care decision-making and referral opportunities by clinicians and their patients. Additionally, being able to access these data through a standards-based APIs would allow consumers to use the application of their choice to obtain personalized, actionable health care item or service price estimates, rather than being required to use one developed by their plan or issuer, although those consumers may be required to pay for access to those applications.

While there are many benefits to a standards-based API, it is the Departments' current view that the burden and costs associated with building and maintaining a standards-based API would result in plans, issuers, and applicable TPAs potentially incurring higher burden and costs than estimated for the internet-based self-service tool and machine-readable files proposed in these rules and discussed in the applicable ICR sections. This view is based on the Departments' preliminary estimate that for all 1,754 health insurance issuers and 205 TPAs, the total cost could range from $500 million to $1.5 billion for the first year. Looking at the average burden and cost over a 3-year period for the API for all 1,754 health insurance issuers and 205 TPAs, the Departments estimate an average annual cost that would significantly exceed the estimated annual cost of publishing the proposed internet-based self-service tool and machine-readable files. The Departments recognize that the development of the API may be streamlined through other development activities related to this proposed rule or by leveraging existing APIs currently used by plans, issuers, or TPAs for their own applications, potentially resulting in significantly lower burden and costs. Although not estimated here, the Departments expect any associated maintenance costs would also decline in succeeding years as group health plans, health insurance issuers or TPAs may gain additional efficiencies or may already undertake similar procedures to maintain any currently used internal APIs. Nonetheless, weighing the burden of group health plans, health insurance issuers and TPAs providing this information using machine-readable files against the potential burden of using a standards-based API, and given the timeframe that group health plans, health insurance issuers and TPAs have to meet the requirements of these proposals, the Departments are of the view that in the short-term, requiring machine-readable files is the more sensible approach.

Even though the Departments are of the view that a machine-readable file is appropriate in the short-term, as discussed earlier in this preamble, the Departments recognize that a standards-based API format in the long-term may be more beneficial to consumers because the public would have access to the most up-to-date rate information and would allow health care consumers to use the application of their choice to obtain personalized, actionable health care service price estimates, and third-party developers could utilize the collected data to develop consumer tools. Therefore, the Departments are considering future rulemaking to further expand access to pricing information through standards-based APIs, including individuals' access to estimates about their own cost-sharing liability and information about negotiated in-network rates and historical payment data for out-of-network allowed amounts.

VIII. Collection of Information Requirements.

Under the Paperwork Reduction Act of 1995, the Departments are required to provide 60-days' notice in the **Federal Register** and solicit public comment before a collection of information requirement is submitted to the Office of Management and Budget (OMB) for review and approval. These proposed rules contain information collection requirements (ICRs) that are subject to review by OMB. A description of these provisions is given in the following paragraphs with an estimate of the annual burden, summarized in Table 16.

To fairly evaluate whether an information collection should be approved by OMB, section 3506(c)(2)(A) of the Paperwork Reduction Act of 1995 (PRA) requires that the Departments solicit comment on the following issues:

• The need for the information collection and its usefulness in carrying out the proper functions of each of the Departments.

• The accuracy of the Departments' estimate of the information collection burden.

• The quality, utility, and clarity of the information to be collected.

• Recommendations to minimize the information collection burden on the affected public, including automated collection techniques.

The Departments solicit public comment on each of these issues in the following sections of this document in relation to the information collection requirements in these proposed rules.

A. *Wage Estimates*

To derive wage estimates, the Departments generally used data from the Bureau of Labor Statistics to derive average labor costs (including a 100 percent increase for fringe benefits and overhead) for estimating the burden associated with the ICRs.[109] Table 2 in these proposed rules presents the mean hourly wage, the cost of fringe benefits and overhead, and the adjusted hourly wage.

As indicated, employee hourly wage estimates have been adjusted by a factor of 100 percent. This is necessarily a rough adjustment, both because fringe benefits and overhead costs vary significantly across employers, and because methods of estimating these costs vary widely across studies. The Departments are of the view that doubling the hourly wage to estimate total cost is a reasonably acceptable estimation method.

TABLE 2: Adjusted Hourly Wages Used in Burden Estimates

Occupation Title	Occupational Code	Mean Hourly Wage ($/hour)	Fringe Benefits and Overhead ($/hour)	Adjusted Hourly Wage ($/hour)
General and Operations Manager	11-1021	$59.56	$59.56	$119.12
Computer and Information Systems Manager	11-3021	$73.49	$73.49	$146.98
Computer Programmer	15-1131	$43.07	$43.07	$86.14
Computer System Analyst	15-1121	$45.01	$45.01	$90.02
Web Developer	15-1134	$36.34	$36.34	$72.68
Business Operations Specialist	13-1199	$37.00	$37.00	$74.00
Other Office and Administrative Support Workers	43-9000	$17.28	$17.28	$34.56
Lawyer	23-1011	$69.34	$69.34	$138.68
Chief Executive Officer	11-1011	$96.22	$96.22	$192.44
Information Security Analysts	15-1122	$49.26	$49.26	$98.52
Customer Service Representatives	43-4051	$17.53	$17.53	$35.06

---

[109] *See* May 2018 Bureau of Labor Statistics, Occupational Employment Statistics, National Occupational Employment and Wage Estimates. Available at: https://www.bls.gov/oes/current/oes_stru.htm.

1. ICR Regarding Requirements for Disclosures to Participants, Beneficiaries, or Enrollees (26 CFR 54.9815-2715A(b), 29 CFR 2590.715-2715A(b), and 45 CFR 147.210(b))

The Departments propose to add 26 CFR 54.9815-2715A(b), 29 CFR 2590.715-2715A(b), and 45 CFR 147.210(b), to require group health plans and health insurance issuers in the group and individual markets to disclose, upon request, to a participant, beneficiary, or enrollee (or his or her authorized representative), such individual's cost-sharing information for covered items and services furnished by a particular provider or providers, as well as allowed amounts for covered items and services from out-of-network providers. As discussed previously in this preamble, the Departments propose in paragraphs (b)(1)(i) through (vii) to require plans and issuers to make this information available through a self-service tool on an internet website and, if requested, in paper form.

The Departments propose to require plans and issuers to disclose, upon request, certain information relevant to a determination of a consumer's cost-sharing liability for a particular health care item or service from a particular provider, to the extent relevant to the individual's cost-sharing liability for the item or service, in accordance with seven content elements: the consumer-specific estimated cost-sharing liability, the consumer-specific accumulated amounts, the negotiated rate, the out-of-network allowed amount for a covered item or service, if applicable, the items and services content list when the information is for items and services subject to a bundled payment arrangement, a notice of prerequisites to coverage (such as prior authorization), and a disclosure notice. The Departments propose to require the disclosure notice to include several statements, written in plain-language, which include disclaimers relevant to the limitations of the cost-sharing information disclosed, including: a statement that out-of-network providers may balance bill participants beneficiaries, or enrollees, a statement that the actual charges may differ from those for which a cost-sharing liability estimate is given, and a statement that the estimated cost-sharing liability for a covered item is not a guarantee that coverage will be provided for those items and services. In addition, plans and issuers would also be permitted to add other disclaimers they determine appropriate so long as such information is not in conflict with the disclosure requirements of these proposed rules. The Departments have developed model language that plans and issuers would be able to use to satisfy the requirement to provide the notice statements described earlier in this preamble.

As discussed earlier in this preamble, the Departments propose that plans and issuers would be required to make available the information described in paragraph (b)(1) of these proposed rules through an internet-based self-service tool as described in paragraph (b)(2)(i) of these proposed rules. The information would be required to be provided in plain-language through real-time responses. Plans and issuers would be required to allow participants, beneficiaries, or enrollees (or their authorized representatives) to search for cost-sharing information for covered items and services by billing code, or by descriptive term, per the user's request, in connection with a specific in-network provider, or for all in-network providers. In addition, the internet-based self-service tool would allow users to input information necessary to determine the out-of-network allowed amount for a covered item or service provided by an out-of-network provider (such as zip code). The tool would be required to have the capability to refine and reorder results by geographic proximity, and the amount of cost-sharing liability to the beneficiary, participant, or enrollee.

Under paragraph (b)(2)(ii) of these proposed rules, the Departments would require plans and issuers to furnish upon request, in paper form, the information required to be disclosed under paragraph (b)(1) of these proposed rules to a participant, beneficiary, or enrollee. As discussed in this preamble, under paragraphs (b)(2)(ii)(A) and (B) of these proposed rules, a paper disclosure would be required to be furnished according to the consumer's filtering and sorting preferences and mailed to the participant, beneficiary, or enrollee (or his or her authorized representative) within 2 business days of receiving the request. As noted in these proposed rules, plans or issuers may, upon request, provide the required information through other methods, such as over the phone, through face-to-face encounters, by facsimile, or by email.

The Departments assume fully-insured group health plans would rely on health insurance issuers to develop and maintain the internet-based self-service tool and disclosure in paper form. While the Departments recognize that some self-insured plans might independently develop and maintain the internet-based self-service tool, at this time the Departments assume that self-insured plans would rely on TPAs (including issuers providing administrative services only and non-issuer TPAs) to develop the required internet-based self-service tool. The Departments make this assumption because the Departments understand that most self-insured group health plans rely on TPAs for performing most administrative duties, such as enrollment and claims processing. For those self-insured plans that choose to develop their own internet-based self-service tools, the Departments assume that they will incur a similar hour burden and cost as estimated for health insurance issuers and TPAs, as discussed later in this preamble. In addition, paragraphs (b)(3) and (c)(4) of these proposed rules provide for a special rule to prevent unnecessary duplication of the disclosures with respect to health coverage, which provides that a plan may satisfy the disclosure requirements if the issuer offering the coverage is required to provide the information pursuant to a written agreement between the plan and issuer. Thus, the Departments use health insurance issuers and TPAs as the unit of analysis for the purposes of estimating required changes to IT infrastructure and administrative hourly burden and costs. The Departments estimate approximately 1,754 issuers and 205 TPAs will be affected by this information collection.

The Departments acknowledge that the costs described in these ICRs may vary depending on the number of lives covered, the number of providers and items and services for which cost-sharing information must be disclosed, and the fact that some plans and issuers already have tools that meet most (if not all) of these requirements or can be easily adapted to meet the requirements of these proposed rules. In addition, plans and issuers may be able to license existing cost estimator tools offered by third-party vendors, obviating the need to establish and maintain their own internet-based, self-service tool. The Departments assume that any related vendor licensing fees would be dependent upon complexity, volume, and frequency of use, but assume that such fees would be lower than an overall initial build and associated maintenance costs. Nonetheless, for purposes of the estimates in these ICRs, the Departments assume all 1,959 health insurance issuers and TPAs would be affected by these proposed rules. The Departments also developed the following estimates based on the mean average size, by covered lives, of issuers or TPAs. As noted later in this section of the preamble, the Departments seek comment on the inputs and assumptions that have been made to develop these burden and cost estimates, particularly with regard to existing efficiencies that would reduce these burden and cost estimates.

The Departments estimate that health insurance issuers and TPAs would incur a one-time cost and hour burden to complete the technical build to implement the requirements of paragraph (b) of these proposed rules to establish the internet-based, self-service tool through which disclosure of cost-sharing information (including required notice statements) in connection with a covered item or service under the terms of the plan or coverage must be made. The Departments estimate an administrative burden on health insurance issuers and TPAs to make appropriate changes to information technology (IT) systems and processes to design, develop, implement, and operate the internet-based, self-service tool and to make this information available in paper form, transmitted through the mail. The Departments estimate that the onetime cost and burden each issuer or TPA would incur to complete the one-time technical build would include activities such as planning, assessment, budgeting, contracting, building and systems testing, incorporating any necessary security measures, incorporating disclaimer and model notice language, or development of the proposed model and disclaimer notice materials for those that choose to make alterations. The Departments assume that this one-time cost and burden would be incurred in 2020. As mentioned earlier in this preamble, the Departments acknowledge that a number of health insurance issuers and TPAs have previously developed some level of price estimator tool similar to, and containing some functionality related to, the requirements in these proposed rules. The Departments, thus, seek to estimate an hourly burden and cost range (high-end and low-end) associated with these proposed rules for those health insurance issuers and TPAs. In order to develop the high-end hourly burden and cost estimates, the Departments assume that all health insurance issuers and TPAs would need to develop and build their internet-based self-service tool project from start-up to operational functionality. The Departments estimate that for each issuer or TPA, on average, it would take business operations specialists 150 hours (at $74 per hour), computer system analysts 1,000 hours (at $90.02 per hour), web developers 40 hours (at $72.68 per hour), computer programmers

1,250 hours (at $86.14 per hour), computer and information systems managers 40 hours (at $146.98 per hour), operations managers 25 hours (at $119.12 per hour), a lawyer 2 hours (at $138.68 per hour), and a chief executive officer 1 hour (at $192.44 per hour) to complete this task. The Departments estimate the total hour burden per issuer or TPA would be approximately 2,508 hours, with an equivalent cost of approximately $221,029. For all 1,754 health insurance issuers and 205 TPAs, the total one-time total hour burden is estimated to be 4,913,172 hours with an equivalent total cost of approximately $432,996,203.

TABLE 3A: Total High- End Estimated One-time Cost and Hour Burden for Internet-based Self-service Tool for Each Health Insurance Issuer or TPA

Occupation	Burden Hours per Respondent	Labor Cost per Hour	Total Cost per Respondent
General and Operations Manager	25	$119.12	$2,978
Computer and Information Systems Manager	40	$146.98	$5,879
Computer Programmer	1,250	$86.14	$107,675
Computer System Analyst	1,000	$90.02	$90,020
Web Developer	40	$72.68	$2,907
Business Operations Specialist	150	$74.00	$11,100
Lawyer	2	$138.68	$277
Chief Executive Officer	1	$192.44	$192
Total per respondent	2,508		$221,029

TABLE 3B: Total High- End Estimated One-time Cost and Hour Burden for Internet-based Self-service Tool for All Health Insurance Issuers and TPAs

Number of Respondents	Number of Responses	Burden Hours Per Respondent	Total Burden Hours	Total Cost
1,959	1,959	2,508	4,913,172	$432,996,203

The Departments recognize that a significant number of health insurance issuers may already have some form of price estimator tool that allows for comparison shopping and a large number of issuers may currently provide the ability for consumers to obtain their estimated out-of-pocket costs.[110] For those health insurance issuers and TPAs, that currently have some level of functional cost estimator tool that would meet some of the requirements of these proposed rules, the Departments recognize that these entities would incur a lower hour burden and cost. Thus, the Departments have estimated a low-end hour burden and cost to comply with these proposed rules. Assuming that 90 percent of health insurance issuers and TPAs currently provide a cost estimator tool and would only be required to make changes to their current system in order to meet the requirements in these proposed rules, the Departments estimate that 175 health insurance issuers and 21 TPAs would be required to develop an internet-based self-service tool from start-up to operational functionality. The Departments estimate that each issuer or TPA would incur a one-time cost and hour burden of approximately 2,508 hours, with an equivalent cost of approximately $221,029 (as discussed previously in this ICR). For the 196 health insurance issuers and TPAs, the total one-time hour burden is estimated to be 491,317 hours with an equivalent total cost of approximately $43,299,620.

Table 4A: Low-Range One-time Cost and Hour Burden for Web-based Consumer Price Tool for Health Insurance Issuers and TPAs Requiring a Complete Build from the Start-Up to operational Functionality.

Number of Respondents	Number of Responses	Burden Hours Per Respondent	Total Burden Hours	Total Cost
196	196	2,508	491,317	$43,299,620

The Departments estimate that those health insurance issuers and TPAs that would only be required to make changes to their existing systems would already have operational capabilities that meet approximately 75 percent of the requirements in these proposed rules and would only incur a cost and hour burden related to changes needed to fully meet the requirements of these proposed rules. Based on this assumption, the Departments estimate that 1,579 health insurance issuers and 184 TPAs would incur a one-time hour burden of 627 hours and an associated cost of $55,257 to fully satisfy the requirements of these proposed rules. For all 1,763 health insurance issuers and TPAs, the total one-time hour burden would be 1,105,464 hours with an equivalent total cost of approximately $97,424,146.

Table 4B: Low-End One-time Cost and Hour Burden for Web-based Consumer Price Tool for Health Insurance Issuers and TPAs Requiring Only a Partial Build.

Number of Respondents	Number of Responses	Burden Hours Per Respondent	Total Burden Hours	Total Cost
1,763	11,763	627	1,105,464	$97,424,146

Table 4C: Total Low-End One-time Cost and Hour Burden for Web-based Consumer Price Tool for Health Insurance Issuers and TPAs.

Number of Respondents	Number of Responses	Burden Hours Per Respondent	Total Burden Hours	Total Cost
1,959	1,959	815	1,596,781	$140,723,766

In addition to the range of one-time costs and hour burdens estimated in Tables 4B and 4C, health insurance issuers and TPAs would incur ongoing annual costs such as those related to ensuring cost estimation accuracy, providing quality assurance, conducting website maintenance and making updates, and enhancing or updating any needed security measures. The Departments estimate that for each issuer and TPA, on average, it would take business operations specialists 15 hours (at $74.00 per hour), computer systems analysts 50 hours (at $90.02 per hour), web developers

---

[110] *See* AHIP release dated August 2, 2019 - AHIP Issues Statement on Proposed Rule Requiring Disclosure of Negotiated Prices. Available at: https://www.ahip.org/ahip-issues-statement-on-proposed-rule-requiring-disclosure-of-negotiated-prices/. *See also* Higgins, A., Brainard, N., Veselovskiy, G. "Characterizing Health Plan Price Estimator Tools: Findings From a National Survey." 22 Am. J. Managed Care 126. 2016. Available at: https://ajmc.s3.amazonaws.com/_media/_pdf/AJMC_02_2016_Higgins%20(final).pdf.

10 hours (at $72.68 per hour), computer programmers 55 hours (at $86.14 per hour), computer and information systems managers 10 hours (at $146.98), and operations managers 5 hours (at $119.12 per hour) each year to perform these tasks. The total annual hour burden for each issuer or TPA would be 145 hours, with an equivalent cost of approximately $13,141. For all 1,754 health insurance issuers and 205 TPAs, the total annual hour burden is estimated to be 284,055 hours with an equivalent total annual cost of approximately $25,743,023. The Departments consider this to be an upper-bound estimate and expect maintenance costs to decline in succeeding years as health insurance issuers and TPAs gain efficiencies and experience in updating and managing their internet-based self-service tool.

TABLE 5A: Estimated Annual Cost and Burden for Maintenance of Internet-based Self-Service Tool for Each Health Insurance Issuer or TPA

Occupation	Burden Hours per Respondent	Labor Cost per Hour	Total Cost per Respondent
General and Operations Manager	5	$119.12	$596
Computer and Information Systems Manager	10	$146.98	$1,470
Business Operations Specialist	15	$74.00	$1,110
Computer System Analyst	50	$90.02	$4,501
Web Developer	10	$72.68	$727
Computer Programmer	55	$86.14	$4,738
Total per Respondent	145		$13,141

Table 5B: Estimated Annual Hour Burden for Maintenance of Internet-based Self-Service Tool for All Health Insurance Issuers and TPAs from 2021 Onwards

Number of Respondents	Number of Responses	Burden Hours Per Respondent	Total Burden Hours	Total Cost
1,959	1,959	145	284,055	$25,743,023

The Departments estimate the high-end average annual total hour burden, for all health insurance issuers and TPAs to develop, build, and maintain an internet-based consumer self-service tool, over three years would be 1,827,094 hours annually with an average annual total equivalent cost of $161,494,083. The Departments acknowledge that the costs described earlier in this section of the preamble may vary depending on the number of lives covered, and the number of providers and items and services incorporated into the internet-based self-service tool. In recognizing that many health insurance issuers and TPAs currently have some form of cost estimator tool in operation that meet most (if not all) of the requirements in these proposed rules, the Departments estimate the low-end average annual total hour burden, for all health insurance issuers and TPAs to develop, build, and maintain an internet-based self-service tool, over a 3-year period would be 721,630 hours annually with an average annual total equivalent cost of $64,069,937. The Departments recognize that group health plans, issuers, and TPAs may be able to license existing online cost estimator tools offered by vendors, obviating the need to establish, upgrade, and maintain their own internet-based self-service tools and that vendor licensing fees, dependent upon complexity, volume and frequency of use, could be lower than the hour burden and costs estimated here.

TABLE 6: Estimated High-End Three Year Average Annual Hour Burden and Costs for All Health Insurance Issuers and TPAs to Develop and Maintain the Internet-based Self-Service Tool

Year	Estimated Number of Health Insurance Issuers and TPAs	Responses	Burden per Respondent (hours)	Total Annual Burden (hours)	Total Estimated Labor Cost
2020	1,959	1,959	2,508	4,913,172	$432,996,203
2021	1,959	1,959	145	284,055	$25,743,023
2022	1,959	1,959	145	284,055	$25,743,023
3 year Average	1,959	1,959	933	1,827,094	$161,494,083

TABLE 7: Estimated Low-End Three Year Average Annual Hour Burden and Costs for All Health Insurance Issuers and TPAs to Develop and Maintain the Internet-based Self-service Tool

Year	Estimated Number of Health Insurance Issuers and TPAs	Responses	Burden per Respondent (hours)	Total Annual Burden (hours)	Total Estimated Labor Cost
2020	1,959	1,959	815	1,596,781	$140,723,766
2021	1,959	1,959	145	284,055	$25,743,023
2022	1,959	1,959	145	284,055	$25,743,023
3 year Average	1,959	1,959	368	721,630	$64,069,937

In addition to the one-time and annual maintenance costs estimated in Table 7, health insurance issuers and TPAs would also incur an annual burden and costs associated with customer service representative training, consumer assistance, and administrative and distribution costs related to the disclosures required under paragraph (b)(2)(ii) of these proposed rules. The Departments estimate that, to understand and navigate the internet-based self-service tool and be able to provide the appropriate assistance to consumers, each customer service representative would require approximately 2 hours (at $35.06 per hour) of annual consumer assistance training at an associated cost of $70 per hour. The Departments estimate that each issuer and TPA would train, on average, 10 customer service representatives annually, resulting in a total annual hour burden of 20 hours and associated total costs of $701 per issuer or TPA. For all 1,754 health insurance issuers and 205 TPAs, the total annual hour burden is estimated to be 39,180 hours with an equivalent total annual cost of approximately $1,373,651.

TABLE 8A: Estimated Annual Cost and Hour Burden per Health Insurance Issuer or TPA to Train Customer Service Representatives to Provide Assistance to Consumers Related to the Internet-based Self-Service Tool

Occupation	Burden Hours per Respondent	Labor Cost per Hour	Total Cost per Respondent
Customer Service Representatives	2	$35.06	$70
Total per Respondent	2		$70

TABLE 8B: Estimated Annual Cost and Hour Burden for All Health Insurance Issuers and TPAs from 2021 onwards to Train Customer Service Representatives to Provide Assistance to Consumers Related to the Internet-based Self-Service Tool

Number of Respondents	Number of Responses	Burden Hours Per Respondent	Total Burden Hours	Total Cost
1,959	19,590	20	39,180	$1,373,651

The Departments assume that the greatest proportion of beneficiaries, participants, and enrollees who would request disclosure of cost-sharing information in paper form would do so because they do not have access to the internet. However, the Departments acknowledge that some consumers with access to the internet would also contact a plan or issuer for assistance and may request to receive cost-sharing information in paper form.

Recent studies have found that approximately 20 million households do not have an internet subscription[111] and that approximately 19 million Americans (6 percent of the population) lack access to fixed broadband services that meet threshold levels.[112] Additionally, a recent Pew Research Center analysis found that 10 percent of U.S. adults do not use the internet, citing the following major factors: difficulty of use, age, cost of internet services, and lack of computer ownership.[113] Additional research indicates that an increasing number, 17 percent, of individuals and households are now considered "smartphone only" and that 37 percent of U.S. adults mostly use smartphones to access the internet and that many adults are forgoing the use of traditional broadband services.[114] Further research indicates that younger individuals and households, including approximately 93 percent of households with householders aged 15 to 34, are more likely to have smartphones compared to those aged over 65.[115] The Departments are of the view that the population most likely to use the internet-based self-service tool would generally consist of higher-income and younger individuals, who are more likely to have internet access via broadband or smartphone technologies.

The Departments estimate there are 193.5 million[116] beneficiaries, participants, or enrollees enrolled in group health plans or with health insurance issuers required to comply with the requirements under paragraph (b) of these proposed rules. On average, it is estimated that each issuer or TPA would annually administer the benefits for 98,775 beneficiaries, participants, or enrollees.

Assuming that 6 percent of covered individuals lack access to fixed broadband service and, taking into account that a recent study noted that only 1 to 12 percent of consumers that have been offered internet-based or mobile application-based price transparency tools use them,[117] the Departments estimate that on average 6 percent of participants, beneficiaries, or enrollees would seek customer support (a mid-range percentage of individuals that currently use available cost estimator tools) and that an estimated 1 percent of those participants, beneficiaries, or enrollees would request any pertinent information be disclosed to them in paper form. The Departments estimate that each health insurance issuer or TPA, on average, would require a customer service representative to interact with a beneficiary, participant, or enrollee approximately 59 times per year on matters related to cost-sharing information disclosures required by these proposed rules. The Departments estimate that each customer service representative would spend, on average, 15 minutes (at $35.06 per hour) for each interaction, resulting in a cost of approximately $9 per interaction. The Departments estimate that each issuer or TPA would incur an annual hour burden of 15 hours with an associated equivalent cost of approximately $519 for each issuer or TPA, resulting in a total annual hour burden of 29,025 hours with an associated cost of approximately $1,017,617 for all issuers or TPAs.

The Departments assume that all beneficiaries, participants, or enrollees that contact a customer service representative representing their plan or issuer would request non-internet disclosure of the internet-based self-service tool information. Of these, the Departments estimate that 54 percent of the requested information would be transmitted via email or facsimile at negligible cost to the issuer or TPA and that 46 percent would request the information be provided via mail. The Departments estimate that, on average, each issuer or TPA would send approximately 27 disclosures via mail annually. Based on these assumptions, the Departments estimate that the total number of annual disclosures sent by mail for all health insurance issuers and TPAs would be 53,406.

The Departments assume the average length of the printed disclosure would be approximately nine single-sided pages in length, assuming two pages of information (similar to that provided in an EOB) for three providers (for a total of six pages) and an additional three pages related to the required notice statements, with a printing cost of $0.05 per page. Therefore, including postage costs of $0.55 per mailing, the Departments estimate that each health

insurance issuer or TPA would incur a material and printing costs of $1.00 ($0.45 printing plus $0.55 postage costs) per mailed request. Based on these assumptions, the Departments estimate that each issuer or TPA would incur an annual printing and mailing cost of approximately $27, resulting in a total annual printing and mailing cost of approximately $53,406 for all health insurance issuers and TPAs.

TABLE 9A: Estimated Annual Cost and Hour Burden per Response per Health Insurance Issuer or TPA to Accept and Fulfill Requests for a Mailed Disclosure

Occupation	Burden Hours per Respondent	Labor Cost per Hour	Total Cost per Respondent
Customer Service Representatives	0.25	$35.06	$9
Total per Respondent	0.25		$9

[111] See 2017 U.S. Census Bureau, 2017 American Community Survey 1-Year Estimates. Available at: https://factfinder.census.gov/faces/tableservices/jsf/pages/productview.xhtml?pid=ACS_17_1YR_S2801&prodType= table.

[112] See Eight Broadband Progress Report. Federal Communications Commission. December 14, 2018. Available at: https://www.fcc.gov/reports-research/reports/broadband-progress-reports/eighth-broadband-progress-report. In addition to the estimated 19 million Americans that lack access, they further estimate that in areas where broadband is available approximately 100 million Americans do not subscribe.

[113] See Anderson, M., Perrin, A., Jiang, J., Kumar, M. "10% of Americans don't use the internet. Who are they?" ((Pew Research Center. April 22, 2019. Available at: https://www.pewresearch.org/fact-tank/2019/04/22/some-americans-dont-use-the-internet-who-are-they/.

[114] See Anderson, M. "Mobile Technology and Home Broadband 2019." Pew Research Center. June 13, 2019. Available at https://www.pewinternet.org/2019/06/13/mobile-technology-and-home-broadband-2019/ (finding that overall 17 percent of Americans are now "smartphone only" internet users, up from 8 percent in 2013. They study also

shows that 45 percent of non-broadband users cite their smartphones as a reason for not subscribing to highspeed internet).

[115] See Ryan, C. "Computer and Internet Use in the United States: 2016." American Community Survey Reports: United States Census Bureau. August 2016 Available at: https://www.census.gov/content/dam/Census/library/publications/2018/acs/ACS-39.pdf.

[116] EBSA estimates that in 2016 there were 135.7 million covered individuals with private sector and 44.1 million with public sector employer sponsored coverage (see https://www.dol.gov/sites/dolgov/files/EBSA/researchers/data/health-and-welfare/health-insurance-coverage-bulletin-2016.pdf). Kaiser Family Foundation reports 13.7 million enrollees in the individual market for the first quarter of 2019 (see: https://www.kff.org/private-insurance/issue-brief/data-note-changes-in-enrollment-in-the-individual-health-insurance-market-through-early-2019/).

[117] See Mehrotra, A., Chernew, M., Sinaiko, A. "Health Policy Report: Promises and Reality of Price Transparency." April 5, 2018. 14 N. Eng. J. Med. 378. Available at: https://www.nejm.org/doi/full/10.1056/NEJMhpr1715229.

TABLE 9B: Estimated Annual Cost and Hour Burden for All Health Insurance Issuers and TPAs from 2021 onwards to Accept and Fulfill Requests for Mailed Disclosures

Number of Respond ents	Number of Respon ses	Burden Hours Per Respond ent	Total Burden Hours	Total Labor Cost of Reporting	Printing and Materials Cost	Total Cost
1,959	116,100	15	29,025	$1,017,617	$53,406	$1,071,023

The Departments solicit comment for this collection of information request related to the overall estimated costs and hour burdens. The Departments also seek comment related to the technical and labor requirements or costs that may be required to meet the requirements of these proposed rules; for example, what costs may be associated with any potential consolidation of information needed for the internet-based self-service tool functionality. The Departments seek comment on the estimated number of health insurance issuers and TPAs currently in the group and individual markets and the number of self-insured group health plans that might seek to independently develop an internet-based self-service tool, the percentage of consumers who might use the internet-based self-service tool, and the percentage of consumers who might contact their plan, issuer, or TPA requesting information via a non-internet disclosure method. The Departments seek comment on any other existing efficiencies that could be leveraged to minimize the burden on group health plans, issuers, and TPAs, as well as how many or what percentage of plans, issuers, and TPAs might leverage such efficiencies. The Departments seek comment on the proposed model notice and any additional information that stakeholders feel should be included, removed, or expanded upon and its overall adaptability.

In conjunction with these proposed rules, CMS is seeking an OMB control number and approval for the proposed information collection (OMB control number: 0938-NEW (Transparency in Coverage (CMS-10715)). CMS is proposing to require the following information collections to include the following burden. DOL and Treasury will submit their burden estimates upon approval.

2. ICRs Regarding Requirements for Public Disclosure of Negotiated Rates and Historical Allowed Amount Data for Covered Items and Services from Out-of-Network Providers under 26 CFR 54.9815-2715A(c), 29 CFR 2590.715-2715A(c), and 45 CFR 147.210(c)

The Departments propose to add paragraph (c) of these proposed rules to require group health plans and health insurance issuers to make public negotiated rates with in-network providers and data outlining the different amounts a plan or issuer has paid to particular out-of-network providers for covered items or services. Plans and issuers would be required to disclose for each covered service or item, the negotiated rates for services and items furnished by particular in-network providers and out-of-network allowed amount data for each covered service or item furnished by particular out-of-network provider through two machine-readable files that must conform to guidance issued by the Departments. The list of required data elements that must be included for each file for each covered item or service are discussed previously and enumerated under paragraph (c)(1)(i) for the Negotiated Rate File and paragraph (c)(1)(ii) for the Allowed Amount File of these proposed rules. Under paragraphs (c)(2) and (3) of these proposed rules, the files must be posted on a public internet site with unrestricted access and must be updated monthly.

For the Allowed Amount File required under proposed paragraph (c)(1)(ii), the proposed rules would require plans and issuers to make available a machine-readable file showing the unique amounts a plan or issuer's coverage allowed for items or services furnished by particular out-of-network providers during the 90-day time period that begins 180 days before the publication date of the file. As discussed previously in these proposed rules, to the extent that a plan or issuer has allowed multiple amounts for an item or service to a particular provider at the same rate, the proposed rules would only require a plan or issuer to list the allowed amount once. Additionally, if the plan or issuer would only display allowed amounts in connection with 10 or fewer claims for a covered item or service for payment to a provider during any relevant 90-day period, the plan or issuer would not be required to report those unique allowed amounts.

As discussed in the previous collection of information, the Departments assume fully-insured group health plans would rely on health insurance issuers and most self-insured group health plans would rely on issuers or TPAs to develop and update the proposed machine-readable files. The Departments recognize that there may be some self-insured plans that wish to individually comply with these proposed rules and would incur a similar hour burden and costs as described in the following paragraphs.

The Departments estimate a one-time hour burden and cost to health insurance issuers and TPAs to make appropriate changes to IT systems and processes, to develop, implement and operate the Negotiated Rate File in order to meet the proposed requirements under paragraph (c)(1)(i). The Departments estimate that for each health insurance issuer or TPA, on average, would require business operations specialists 20 hours (at $74 per hour), computer system analysts 500 hours (at $90.02 per hour), computer programmers 600 hours (at $86.14 per hour), computer and information systems managers 50 hours (at $146.98 per hour) and operations managers 20 hours (at $119.12 per hour) to complete this task. The total burden for each issuer or TPA would be approximately 1,190 hours on average, with an equivalent associated cost of approximately $107,905. For all 1,754 health insurance issuers and 205 TPAs, the Departments estimate the total one-time hour burden would be 2,331,210 hours with an associated cost of approximately $211,386,679. The Departments emphasize that these are upper bound estimates that are meant to be sufficient to cover substantial, complex activities that may be necessary for some plans and issuers to comply with these proposed rules due to the manner in which their current systems are designed. Such activities may include such significant activity as the design and implementation of databases that will support the production of the Negotiated Rate Files. The Departments request comment on these estimates and whether they substantially overestimate expected burden.

TABLE 10A: Estimated One-Time Cost and Hour Burden per Health Insurance Issuer or TPA for the Negotiated Rates for In-Network Providers Negotiated Rate File

Occupation	Burden Hours per Respondent	Labor Cost per Hour	Total Cost per Respondent
General and Operations Manager	20	$119.12	$2,382
Computer and Information Systems Manager	50	$146.98	$7,349
Business Operations Specialist	20	$74.00	$1,480
Computer System Analyst	500	$90.02	$45,010
Computer Programmer	600	$86.14	$51,684
Total per Respondent	1,190		$107,905

TABLE 10B: Estimated One-Time Cost and Hour Burden for All Health Insurance Issuers and TPAs for the Negotiated Rates for In-Network Negotiated Rate File

Number of Respondents	Number of Responses	Burden Hours Per Respondent	Total Burden Hours	Total Cost
1,959	1,959	1,190	2,331,210	$211,386,679

In addition to the one-time costs estimated Tables 10A and 10B, health insurance issuers and TPAs would incur ongoing annual burdens and costs to update the proposed Negotiated Rate File monthly as proposed under paragraph (c)(3). The Departments estimate that for each issuer or TPA, on average, it would require a general and operations manager 3 hours (at $119.12 per hour), computer systems analysts 10 hours (at $90.02 per hour), computer programmers 10 hours (at $86.14 per hour), a computer and information systems manager 5 hours (at $146.98), and a business operations specialist 2 hours (at a rate of $74.00) to make the required updates to the Negotiated Rate File. The Departments estimate that each issuer or TPA would incur a burden of 30 hours with an associated cost of approximately $3,002 to update the Negotiated Rate File. Assuming health insurance issuers and TPAs make changes that would require the file to be updated monthly per the requirements proposed in these rules, an issuer or TPA would need to update the Negotiated Rate File 12 times during a given year, resulting in an ongoing annual hour burden of 360 hours for each issuer or TPA with an associated equivalent cost of approximately $36,022. The Departments estimate the total annual hour burden for all 1,959 health insurance issuers and TPAs would be 705,240 hours, with an associated equivalent cost of approximately $70,567,725. The Departments consider this estimate to be an upper-bound estimate and expect ongoing update costs to decline in succeeding years as health insurance issuers and TPAs gain efficiencies and experience in updating and managing the machine-readable files.

The Departments seek comment on the accuracy of the burden estimates under these proposed rules, as well as any ways to further refine the burden estimates.

TABLE 11A: Estimated Annual Ongoing Cost and Burden per Health Insurance Issuer or TPA for the Negotiated Rates for In-Network Providers Negotiated Rate File

Occupation	Burden Hours per Respondent	Labor Cost per Hour	Total Cost per Respondent
General and Operations Manager	3	$119.12	$357
Computer and Information Systems Manager	5	$146.98	$735
Business Operations Specialist	2	$74.00	$148
Computer System Analyst	10	$90.02	$900
Computer Programmer	10	$86.14	$861
Total per Respondent	30		$3,002

TABLE 11B: Estimated Annual Ongoing Cost and Burden for All Health Insurance Issuers and TPAs from 2021 Onwards for the In-Network Providers Negotiated Rate File

Number of Respondents	Number of Responses	Burden Hours Per Respondent	Total Burden Hours	Total Cost
1,959	23,508	360	705,240	$70,567,725

The Departments estimate the total one-time hour burden for all health insurance issuers and TPAs of 2,331,210 hours and an associated equivalent cost of approximately $211,386,679 to develop and build the Negotiated Rate File in a machine-readable format. In subsequent years, the Departments estimate the total annual hour burden of 705,240 hours to maintain and update the Negotiated Rate File with an annual associated equivalent cost of approximately $70,567,725. The Departments estimate the average annual total hour burden, for all health insurance issuers and TPAs, over three years, would be 1,247,230 hours with an average annual associated equivalent total cost of $117,507,376.

TABLE 12: Estimated Three Year Average Annual Hour Burden and Costs for All Issuers and TPAs to Develop and Maintain the In-Network Providers Negotiated Rate File

Year	Estimated Number of Health Insurance Issuers and TPAs	Responses	Burden per Respondent (hours)	Total Annual Burden (hours)	Total Estimated Labor Cost
2020	1,959	1,959	1,190	2,331,210	$211,386,679
2021	1,959	23,508	360	705,240	$70,567,725
2022	1,959	23,508	360	705,240	$70,567,725
3 year Average	1,959	16,325	637	1,247,230	$117,507,376

The Departments estimate a one-time hour burden and cost to health insurance issuers and TPAs to make appropriate changes to IT systems and processes, to develop, implement, and operate the Allowed Amount File in order to meet the proposed requirements under paragraph (c)(1)(ii) of the proposed rules related to making available a file of certain historical claims paid to out-of-network providers. The Departments estimate that each issuer or TPA, on average, would require business operations specialists 20 hours (at $74 per hour), computer system analysts 500 hours (at $90.02 per hour), computer programmers 600 hours (at $86.14 per hour), computer and information systems managers 50 hours (at $146.98 per hour), information security analysts 100 hours (at $98.52 per hour), and operations managers 20 hours (at $119.12 per hour) to complete this task. The total burden per issuer or TPA would be approximately 1,290 hours on average, with an equivalent associated cost of approximately $117,757. For all 1,754 health insurance issuers and 205 TPAs, the Departments estimate the total one-time hour burden would be 2,527,110 hours with an equivalent associated cost of approximately $230,686,747.

TABLE 13A: Estimated One-Time Cost and Hour Burden per Health Insurance Issuer or TPA for the Out-of-Network Allowed Amount File

Occupation	Burden Hours per Respondent	Labor Cost per Hour	Total Cost per Respondent
General and Operations Manager	20	$119.12	$2,382
Computer and Information Systems Manager	50	$146.98	$7,349
Business Operations Specialist	20	$74.00	$1,480
Computer System Analyst	500	$90.02	$45,010

Occupation	Burden Hours per Respondent	Labor Cost per Hour	Total Cost per Respondent
Information Security Analysts	100	$98.52	$9,852
Computer Programmer	600	$86.14	$51,684
Total per Respondent	1,290		$117,757

TABLE 13B: Estimated One-Time Cost and Hour Burden for All Health Insurance Issuers and TPAs for the Out-of-Network Allowed Amount File

Number of Respondents	Number of Responses	Burden Hours Per Respondent	Total Burden Hours	Total Cost
1,959	1,959	1,290	2,527,110	$230,686,747

In addition to the one-time costs estimated in Tables 13A and 13B, health insurance issuers and TPAs would incur ongoing annual burdens and costs to update the proposed Allowed Amount File monthly. The Departments estimate that for each issuer or TPA, on average, it would require a computer systems analysts 5 hours (at $90.02 per hour), computer programmers 5 hours (at $86.14 per hour), a computer and information systems manager 1 hour (at $146.98), and an information security analyst 2 hours (at $98.52 per hour) to make the required Allowed Amount File updates. The Departments estimate that each issuer or TPA would incur a monthly burden of 13 hours with an equivalent associated cost of approximately $1,225 to update the Allowed Amount File. Assuming health insurance issuers and TPAs make changes that would require the file to be updated monthly per the requirements in these proposed rules an issuer or TPA would need to update Allowed Amount File 12 times during a given year, resulting in an ongoing annual burden of approximately 156 hours for each issuer or TPA with an equivalent associated cost of approximately $14,698. The Departments estimate the total annual hour burden for all 1,959 health insurance issuers and TPAs would be 305,604 hours with an equivalent associated cost of approximately $28,793,069. The Departments consider this estimate to be an upper-bound estimate and expect ongoing Allowed Amount File update costs to decline in succeeding years as health insurance issuers and TPAs gain efficiencies and experience in updating and managing the Allowed Amount File.

TABLE 14A: Estimated Annual Ongoing Cost and Burden per Health Insurance Issuer or TPA for the Out-of-Network Allowed Amount File

Occupation	Burden Hours per Respondent	Labor Cost per Hour	Total Cost per Respondent
Computer and Information Systems Manager	1	$146.98	$147
Computer System Analyst	5	$90.02	$450
Computer Programmer	5	$86.14	$431
Information Security Analysts	2	$98.52	$197
Total per Respondent	13		$1,225

TABLE 14B: Estimated Annual Ongoing Cost and Burden for All Health Insurance Issuers and TPAs from 2021 onwards for the Out-of-Network Allowed Amount File

Number of Respondents	Number of Responses	Burden Hours Per Respondent	Total Burden Hours	Total Cost
1,959	23,508	156	305,604	$28,793,069

The Departments estimate the total one-time hour burden for all health insurance issuers and TPAs of 2,527,110 hours and an equivalent associated cost of approximately $230,686,747 to develop and build the Allowed Amount File to meet the requirements of these proposed rules. In subsequent years, the Departments estimate the total annual hour burden of 305,604 hours to maintain and update the Allowed Amount File with an annual equivalent associated cost of approximately $28,793,069. The Departments estimate the average annual total hour burden, for all health insurance issuers and TPAs, over three years, would be 1,046,106 hours with an average annual total equivalent associated cost of $96,090,961.

TABLE 15: Estimated Three Year Average Annual Hour Burden and Costs for All Health Insurance Issuers and TPAs to Develop and Maintain the Out-of-Network Allowed Amount File

Year	Estimated Number of Health Insurance Issuers and TPAs	Responses	Burden per Respondent (hours)	Total Annual Burden (hours)	Total Estimated Labor Cost
2020	1,959	1,959	1,290	2,527,110	$230,686,747
2021	1,959	23,508	156	305,604	$28,793,069
2022	1,959	23,508	156	305,604	$28,793,069
3 year Average	1,959	16,325	534	1,046,106	$96,090,961

The Departments solicit comment for this collection of information related to all aspects of the estimated hour burden and costs. Specifically, the Departments seek comment related to any technical or operational difficulties associated with maintaining current and up-to-date provider network information or any out-of-network allowed amounts for covered items and services. The Departments also seek comment related to the technical and labor requirements or costs that may be required to meet the requirements proposed in this rule; specifically, any factors that could minimize the frequency of updates that health insurance issuers or TPAs would be required to make to the Allowed Amount File.

The Departments solicit comment for this collection of information related to all aspects of the estimated hour burden and costs. Specifically, the Departments seek comment related to any technical or operational difficulties associated with collecting data and maintaining any out-of-network allowed amounts for covered items and services; including, any difficulties associated with the adjudication of paid claims, incorporating covered items or services furnished by a particular out-of-network provider during the 90-day time period that begins 180 days prior to the publication date of the machine-readable file. The Departments also seek comment related to the technical and labor requirements or costs that may be required to meet the requirements proposed in this rule; specifically, any factors that could minimize the burden and costs associated with updates that health insurance issuers or TPAs would be required to make to the Allowed Amount File.

The Departments also propose that a group health plan may satisfy the proposed requirements by making available the historical amounts paid to out-of-network providers by its health insurance issuer or service provider that includes allowed amounts information on the issuer's or service provider's book of business and a plan or issuer may rely on information provided by its claims clearinghouse in aggregate. To the extent a plan or issuer is providing out-of-network historical payment information in the aggregate, the Departments further propose to apply the 10 minimum claims threshold to the aggregated claims data set, and not at the plan or issuer level.

The Departments acknowledge that as many as 95 percent of group health plans and health insurance issuers might already contract with claims clearinghouses that currently collect some or all of the information required to be disclosed under these proposed rules and might easily be able meet the requirements in these proposed rules, potentially obviating the need for the plan, issuer, or TPA to invest in IT system development. The Departments assume that these plans, issuers, and TPAs would still incur burden, albeit reduced, related to oversight and quality assurance related to any associated clearinghouse activities. The Departments seek comment on existing efficiencies, such as the use of clearinghouses that could be leveraged by plans, issuers, and TPAs related to the development and updating of the required machine-readable files and how many health insurance issuers, TPAs, or self-insured plans may already contract with clearinghouses that collect the information required and may be able to fulfill requirements in these proposed rules.

The Departments understand that plans and issuers may include "gag clauses" in their provider contracting agreements, which prevent disclosure of negotiated rates. The Departments seek comment on whether such agreements would need to be renegotiated to remove such clauses, and, if so, seek comment regarding any costs and burden associated with this action. In conjunction with these proposed rules, CMS is seeking an OMB control number and approval for the proposed information collection (OMB control number: 0938-NEW (Transparency in Coverage (CMS-10715)). CMS is proposing to require the following information collections to include the following burden. DOL and Treasury will submit their burden estimates upon approval.

2. ICRs Regarding Medical Loss Ratio (45 CFR 158.221)

HHS proposes to amend § 158.221 to allow issuers to include in the MLR numerator shared savings payments made to enrollees as a result of the enrollee choosing to obtain health care from a lower-cost provider. HHS does not anticipate that implementing this provision would require significant changes to the MLR annual reporting form and the associated burden. The burden related to this collection is currently approved under OMB Control Number 0938-1164 (Exp. 10/31/2020); Medical Loss Ratio Annual Reports, MLR Notices, and Recordkeeping Requirements.

3. Summary of Annual Burden Estimates for Proposed Requirements

TABLE 16: Estimated Three Year Average Proposed Annual Recordkeeping and Reporting Requirements

Regulation Section(s)	OMB control number	Number of Respondents	Number of Responses	Burden per Response (hours)	Total Annual Burden (hours)	Labor Cost of Reporting ($)	Mailing Cost ($)	Total Cost ($)
§§ 54.9815-2715A(b)(2)(i); 2590.715-2715A(b)(2)(i); and 147.210(b)(2) (i)	0938-NEW*	1,959	1,959	933	1,827,094	$161,494,083	$0	$161,494,083
§§ 54.9815-2715A(b)(2)(ii); 2590.715-2715A(b)(2)(ii); and 147.210(b)(2) (ii)	0938-NEW	1,306	77,400	10	19,350	$678,411	$35,604	$714,015
§§ 54.9815-2715A(c); 2590.715-2715A(c); and 147.210(c)(1) (i)	0938-NEW	1,959	16,325	637	1,247,230	$117,507,376	$0	$117,507,376
§§ 54.9815-2715A(c)(1)(i); 2590.715-2715A(c)(1)(i); and 147.210(c)(1) (ii)	0938-NEW	1,959	16,325	534	1,046,106	$96,090,961	$0	$96,090,961
Total			112,009	2,113	4,139,780	$375,770,831	$35,604	$375,806,435

* High-end three year estimated values are represented in the table and used to determine the overall estimated three-year average.

For PRA purposes the Departments are splitting the burden; where CMS will account for 50 percent of the associated costs and burdens and the Departments of Labor and Treasury will each account for 25 percent of the associated costs and burdens. The hour burden for CMS will be 2,069,890 hours with an equivalent associated cost of approximately $187,886,416 and a cost burden of $17,802. For the Departments of Labor and Treasury, each Department will account for an hour burden of 1,034,945 hours with an equivalent associated cost of approximately $93,942,708 and a cost burden of $8,901.

B. *Submission of PRA-related Comments*

The Departments have submitted a copy of these proposed rules to the OMB for its review of the rule's information collection and recordkeeping requirements. These requirements are not effective until they have been approved by OMB.

Department of Health and Human Services

To obtain copies of the supporting statement and any related forms for the proposed collections discussed earlier in this preamble, please visit CMS's Website at www.cms.hhs.gov/PaperworkReductionActof1995, or call the Reports Clearance Office at 410-786-1326.

The Departments invite public comments on these potential information collection requirements. If you wish to comment, please submit your comments electronically as specified in the ADDRESSES section of these proposed rules and identify the rule (CMS-9915-P), the ICR's CFR citation, CMS ID number, and OMB control number.

ICR-related comments are due [INSERT DATE 60-DAYS AFTER THE DATE OF PUBLICATION IN THE FEDERAL REGISTER].

C. *Regulatory Flexibility Act*

The Regulatory Flexibility Act, (5 U.S.C. 601, *et* seq.), requires agencies to prepare an initial regulatory flexibility analysis to describe the impact of proposed rules on small entities, unless the head of the agency can certify that the rule would not have a significant economic impact on a substantial number of small entities. The RFA generally defines a "small entity" as (1) a proprietary firm meeting the size standards of the Small Business Administration (SBA), (2) a not-for-profit organization that is not dominant in its field, or (3) a small government jurisdiction with a population of less than 50,000. States and individuals are not included in the definition of "small entity." HHS uses a change in revenues of more than three to five percent as its measure of significant economic impact on a substantial number of small entities.

These proposed rules propose to require that group health plans and health insurance issuers disclose to a participant, beneficiary, or enrollee (or his or her authorized representative) such individual's cost-sharing information for covered items or services from a particular provider or providers. The Departments are of the view that these issuers generally exceed the size thresholds for "small entities" established by the SBA, this, the Departments are not of the view that an initial regulatory flexibility analysis is required for such firms. ERISA covered plans are often small entities. While the Departments' are of the view that these plans would rely on the larger health insurance issuers and TPAs to comply with these proposed rules, they would still experience increased costs due to the requirements as the costs are passed onto them. However, the Departments are not of the view that the additional costs meet the significant impact requirement. These assertions are discussed later in this section of the preamble. In addition, while the requirements of this proposal do not apply to providers, providers may experience a loss in revenue as a result of the demands of price sensitive consumers and plans, and because smaller issuers may be unwilling to continue paying higher rates than larger issuers for the same items and services.

The Departments are of the view that health insurance issuers would be classified under the North American Industry Classification System code 524114 (Direct Health and Medical Insurance Carriers). According to SBA size standards, entities with average annual receipts of $41.5 million or less would be considered small entities for these North American Industry Classification System codes. Issuers could possibly be classified in 621491 (HMO Medical Centers) and, if this is the case, the SBA size standard would be $35 million or less.[118] The Departments are of the view that few, if any, insurance companies underwriting comprehensive health insurance policies (in contrast, for example, to travel insurance policies or dental discount policies) fall below these size thresholds. Based on data from MLR annual report[119] submissions for the 2017 MLR reporting year, approximately 90 out of 500 issuers of health insurance coverage nationwide had total premium revenue of $41.5 million or less. This estimate may overstate the actual number of small health insurance companies that may be affected, since over 72 percent of these small companies belong to larger holding groups, and most, if not all, of these small companies are likely to have non-health lines of business that will result in their revenues exceeding $41.5 million. The Departments are of the view that these same assumptions apply to those TPAs that would be affected by the proposed rules. The Departments do not expect any of these 90 potentially small entities to experience a change in rebates under the proposed amendments to the MLR provisions of these proposed rules in part 158. The Departments acknowledge that it may be likely that a number of small entities might enter into contracts with other entities in order to meet the requirements in the proposed rules, perhaps allowing for the development of economies of scale. Due to the lack of knowledge regarding what small entities may decide to do in order to meet these requirements and any costs they might incur related to contracts, the Departments seek comment on ways that the proposed rules will impose additional costs and burdens on small entities and how many would be likely engage in contracts to meet the requirements.

For purposes of the RFA, the Department of Labor continues to consider a small entity to be an employee benefit plan with fewer than 100 participants.[120] Further, while some large employers may have small plans, in general small employers maintain most small plans. Thus, the Departments are of the view that assessing the impact of these proposed rules on small plans is an appropriate substitute for evaluating the effect on small entities. The definition of small entity considered appropriate for this purpose differs, however, from a definition of small business that is based on size standards promulgated by the SBA (13 CFR 121.201) pursuant to the Small Business Act (15 U.S.C. 631, *et seq.*). Therefore, EBSA requests comments on the appropriateness of the size standard used in evaluating the impact of these proposed rules on small entities. Using this definition of small, about 2,160,743 of the approximately 2,327,339 plans are small entities. Using a threshold approach, if the total costs of the proposed rules were spread evenly across all 1,754 issuers, 205 TPAs, and 2,327,339 ERISA health plans, without considering size, using the three-year average costs, the per-entity costs could be $159.70 ($371,990,734/2,329,298). Instead, if those costs are spread evenly across the estimated 193.5 million[121] beneficiaries, participants, or enrollees enrolled in plans or issuers required to comply with the requirements then the average cost per covered individual would be $1.92 ($371,990,734/193.5 million). Neither the cost per entity nor the cost per covered individual is a significant impact.

In addition, section 1102(b) of the SSA (42 U.S.C. 1302) requires us to prepare a regulatory impact analysis if a rule may have a significant impact on the operations of a substantial number of small rural hospitals. This analysis must conform to the provisions of section 603 of the RFA. For purposes of section 1102(b) of the SSA, the Departments define a small rural hospital as a hospital that is located outside of a metropolitan statistical area and has fewer than 100 beds. These proposed rules would not affect small rural hospitals. Therefore, the Departments have determined that this would not have a significant impact on the operations of a substantial number of small rural hospitals.

Impact of Regulations on Small Business - Department of the Treasury

Pursuant to section 7805(f) of the Code, these proposed rules have been submitted to the Chief Counsel for Advocacy of the SBA for comment on their impact on small business.

D. *Unfunded Mandates*

Section 202 of the Unfunded Mandates Reform Act of 1995 (UMRA) requires that agencies assess anticipated costs and benefits and take certain actions before issuing a proposed rule that includes any federal mandate that may result in expenditures in any one year by a state, local, or tribal governments, in the aggregate, or by the private sector, of $100 million in 1995 dollars, updated annually for inflation. In 2019, that threshold is approximately $154 million.

State, local, or tribal governments may incur cost to enforce some of the requirements of these proposed rules. These proposed rules include instructions for disclosures that would affect private sector firms (for example, health insurance issuers offering coverage in the individual and group markets, and TPAs providing administrative services to group health plans). The Departments acknowledge that state governments could incur costs associated with enforcement of sections within these proposed rules and although the Departments have not been able to quantify all costs, the Departments expect the combined impact on state, local, or Tribal governments and the private sector to be below the threshold.

---

[118] "Table of Small Business Size Standards Matched to North American Industry Classification System Codes." U.S. Small Business Administration. Available at: https://www.sba.gov/sites/default/files/2019-08/SBA%20Table%20of%20Size%20Standards_Effective%20Aug%2019%2C%202019_Rev.pdf.

[119] "Medical Loss Ratio Data and System Resources." CCIIO. Available at https://www.cms.gov/CCIIO/Resources/Data-Resources/mlr.html.

[120] The basis for this definition is found in section 104(a)(2) of ERISA, which permits the Secretary of Labor to prescribe simplified annual reports for pension plans that cover fewer than 100 participants.

[121] EBSA estimates that in 2016 there were 135.7 million covered individuals with private sector and 44.1 million with public sector employer sponsored coverage (available at: https://www.dol.gov/sites/dolgov/files/EBSA/researchers/data/health-and-welfare/health-insurance-coverage-bulletin-2016.pdf). Kaiser Family Foundation reports 13.7 million enrollees in the individual market for the first quarter of 2019 (available at: https://www.kff.org/private-insurance/issue-brief/data-note-changes-in-enrollment-in-the-individual-health-insurance-market-through-early-2019/)

E. Federalism

Executive Order 13132 establishes certain requirements that an agency must meet when it issues a proposed rule that imposes substantial direct costs on state and local governments, preempts state law, or otherwise has federalism implications. Federal agencies promulgating regulations that have federalism implications must consult with state and local officials and describe the extent of their consultation and the nature of the concerns of state and local officials in the preamble to the regulation.

In the Departments' view, these proposed rules may have federalism implications, because it would have direct effects on the states, the relationship between national governments and states, or on the distribution of power and responsibilities among various levels of government relating to the disclosure of health insurance coverage information to consumers.

Under these proposed rules, all group health plans and health insurance issuers, including self-insured, non-federal governmental group health plans as defined in section 2791 of the PHS Act, would be required to develop an internet-based online tool or non-internet disclosure method to disclose to a participant, beneficiary, or enrollee (or an authorized representative on behalf of such individual), the consumer-specific estimated cost-sharing liability for covered items or services from a particular provider. These proposed rules also include proposals to require plans and issuers to disclose provider negotiated rates and historical data on out-of-network allowed amounts through a digital file in a machine-readable format posted publicly on an internet website. Such federal standards developed under section 2715A of the PHS Act would preempt any related state standards that require pricing information to be disclosed to the participant, beneficiary, or enrollee, or otherwise publicly disclosed to the extent the state disclosure requirements would provide less information to the consumer or the public than what is required under this rule and the statutory authority under which it is promulgated.

The Departments are of the view that these proposed rules may have federalism implications based on the required disclosure of pricing information, as the Departments are aware of at least 28 states that have passed some form of price-transparency legislation.[122] Under these state provisions, state requirements vary broadly in terms of the level of disclosure required,[123] some states list the price for each individual service, whereas some states list the aggregate costs across providers and over time to measure the price associated with an episode of illness. States also differ in terms of the dissemination of the information. For example, California mandates that uninsured patients receive estimated prices on request. In contrast, other states use websites or software applications (or apps) that allow consumers to compare prices across providers. Still, only seven states have published the pricing information of health insurance issuers on consumer-facing public websites.[124] Thus, to the extent the disclosure provision these proposed rules required additional information to be disclosed, this proposed rule would require a higher level of disclosure by plans and issuers.

In general, through section 514, ERISA supersedes state laws to the extent that they relate to any covered employee benefit plan, and preserves state laws that regulate insurance, banking, or securities. While ERISA prohibits states from regulating a plan as an insurance or investment company or bank, the preemption provisions of section 731 of ERISA and section 2724 of the PHS Act (implemented in 29 CFR 2590.731(a) and 45 CFR 146.143(a)) apply so that the HIPAA requirements (including those of PPACA) are not to be "construed to supersede any provision of states law which establishes, implements, or continues in effect any standard or requirement solely relating to health insurance issuers in connection with group health insurance coverage except to the extent that such standard or requirement prevents the application of a "requirement" of a federal standard. The conference report accompanying HIPAA indicates that this is intended to be the "narrowest" preemption of states laws (See House Conf. Rep. No. 104-736, at 205, reprinted in 1996 U.S. Code Cong. & Admin. News 2018). States may continue to apply state law requirements to health insurance issuers except to the extent that such requirements prevent the application of PPACA requirements that are the subject of this rulemaking. Accordingly, states have significant latitude to impose requirements on health insurance issuers that are more restrictive than the federal law.

In compliance with the requirement of Executive Order 13132 that agencies examine closely any policies that may have federalism implications or limit the policy making discretion of the states, the Departments have engaged in efforts to consult with and work cooperatively with affected states, including participating in conference calls with and attending conferences of the National Association of Insurance Commissioners, and consulting with state insurance officials on an individual basis. It is expected that the Departments act in a similar fashion in enforcing PPACA, including the provisions of section 2715A of the PHS Act. While developing this rule, the Departments attempted to balance the states' interests in regulating health insurance issuers with Congress' intent to provide an improved level of price transparency to consumers in every state. By doing so, it is the Departments' view that they have complied with the requirements of Executive Order 13132.

Pursuant to the requirements set forth in section 8(a) of Executive Order 13132, and by the signatures affixed to this proposed rule, the Departments certify that the Department of Treasury, Employee Benefits Security Administration and the Centers for Medicare & Medicaid Services have complied with the requirements of Executive Order 13132 for the attached proposed rule in a meaningful and timely manner.

F. Congressional Review Act

These proposed rules are subject to the Congressional Review Act provisions of the Small Business Regulatory Enforcement Fairness Act of 1996 (5 U.S.C. 801, et seq.), which specifies that before a rule can take effect, the federal agency promulgating the rule shall submit to each House of the Congress and to the Comptroller General a report containing a copy of the rule along with other specified information, and has been transmitted to the Congress and the Comptroller for review.

G. Reducing Regulation and Controlling Regulatory Costs

Executive Order 13771, titled Reducing Regulation and Controlling Regulatory Costs, was issued on January 30, 2017. Section 2(a) of Executive Order 13771 requires an agency, unless prohibited by law, to identify at least two existing regulations to be repealed when the agency publicly proposes for notice and comment, or otherwise issues, a new regulation. In furtherance of this requirement, section 2(c) of Executive Order 13771 requires that the new incremental costs associated with new regulations shall, to the extent permitted by law, be offset by the elimination of existing costs associated with at least two prior regulations.

The designation of this rule, if finalized, would be informed by public comments received; however, these proposed rules, if finalized as proposed, would be an E.O. 13771 regulatory action.[125]

IX. Statutory Authority

The Department of the Treasury regulations are proposed to be adopted pursuant to the authority contained in sections 7805 and 9833 of the Code.

---

[122] "Transparency and disclosure of health costs and provider payments: state actions." National Council of State Legislatures. March 2017. Available at:http://www.ncsl.org/reserach/health/transparency-and-disclosure-health-costs.aspx.

[123] Mehrotra, A., Chernew, M., Sinaiko, A. "Promise and Reality of Price Transparency." 14 N. Engl. J. Med. 378. April 5, 2018. Available at: https://www.nejm.org/doi/full/10.1056/NEJMhpr1715229.

[124] Evans, M. "One State's Effort to Publicize Hospital Prices Brings Mixed Results." Wall Street Journal. June 26, 2019. Available at: https://www.wsj.com/articles/one-states-effort-to-publicize-hospital-prices-brings-mixed-results-11561555562.

[125] The Departments estimate cost of approximately $877.31 million in 2020 and annual cost of approximately $127.55 million thereafter. Thus the annualized value of cost, as of 2016 and calculated over a perpetual time horizon with a 7 percent discount rate, is $128.86 million.

The Department of Labor regulations are proposed to be adopted pursuant to the authority contained in 29 U.S.C. 1135, 1185d and 1191c; and Secretary of Labor's Order 1-2011, 77 FR 1088 (Jan. 9, 2012).

The Department of Health and Human Services regulations are proposed to be adopted pursuant to the authority contained in sections 2701 through 2763, 2791, 2792 and 2794 of the PHS Act (42 U.S.C. 300gg through 300gg-63, 300gg-91, 300gg-92 and 300gg-94), as amended.

[¶ 49,821] **Proposed Amendments of Regulations (REG-112607-19)**, published in the Federal Register on December 6, 2019.

[Code Secs. 59A and 6031]

Anti-abuse tax: Base erosion: Tax credits.—Amendments of Reg. §§1.59A-2, 1.59A-3, 1.59A-7, 1.59A-9, 1.59A-10 and 1.6031(a)-1, regarding the base erosion and anti-abuse tax imposed on certain large corporate taxpayers with respect to certain payments made to foreign related parties, are proposed.

AGENCY: Internal Revenue Service (IRS), Treasury.

ACTION: Notice of proposed rulemaking.

SUMMARY: This document contains proposed regulations that provide guidance regarding the base erosion and anti-abuse tax imposed on certain large corporate taxpayers with respect to certain payments made to foreign related parties. The proposed regulations would affect corporations with substantial gross receipts that make payments to foreign related parties.

DATES: Written or electronic comments and requests for a public hearing must be received by February 4, 2019.

ADDRESSES: Submit electronic submissions via the Federal eRulemaking Portal at www.regulations.gov (indicate IRS and REG-112607-19) by following the online instructions for submitting comments. Once submitted to the Federal eRulemaking Portal, comments cannot be edited or withdrawn. The Department of the Treasury (Treasury Department) and the IRS will publish for public availability any comment received to its public docket, whether submitted electronically or in hard copy. Send hard copy submissions to: CC:PA:LPD:PR (REG-112607-19), Room 5203, Internal Revenue Service, P.O. Box 7604, Ben Franklin Station, Washington, DC 20044. Submissions may be hand-delivered Monday through Friday between the hours of 8 a.m. and 4 p.m. to CC:PA:LPD:PR (REG-112607-19), Courier's Desk, Internal Revenue Service, 1111 Constitution Avenue NW, Washington, DC 20224.

FOR FURTHER INFORMATION CONTACT: Concerning the proposed regulations, Sheila Ramaswamy, Azeka J. Abramoff, or Karen Walny at (202) 317-6938; concerning submissions of comments and requests for a public hearing, Regina Johnson at (202) 317-6901 (not toll-free numbers).

SUPPLEMENTARY INFORMATION:

Background

This document contains proposed amendments to 26 CFR part 1 under sections 59A and 6031 of the Internal Revenue Code (the "Code"). The Tax Cuts and Jobs Act, Pub. L. 115-97 (2017) (the "Act"), which was enacted on December 22, 2017, added section 59A to the Code. Section 59A imposes on each applicable taxpayer a tax equal to the base erosion minimum tax amount for the taxable year (the "base erosion and anti-abuse tax" or "BEAT").

The Act also added reporting obligations regarding this tax for 25-percent foreign-owned corporations subject to section 6038A and foreign corporations subject to section 6038C and addressed other issues for which information reporting under those sections is important to tax administration.

On December 21, 2018, the Treasury Department and the IRS published proposed regulations (REG-104259-18) under section 59A, and proposed amendments to 26 CFR part 1 under sections 383, 1502, 6038A, and 6655 in the **Federal Register** (83 FR 65956) (the "2018 proposed regulations"). On December 6, 2019, the Treasury Department and the IRS published final regulations (the "final regulations") under sections 59A, 383, 1502, 6038A, and 6655. These proposed regulations propose other regulations under sections 59A and 6031.

Explanation of Provisions

I. *Overview*

These proposed regulations provide guidance under sections 59A and 6031 regarding certain aspects of the BEAT. Part II of this Explanation of Provisions describes proposed modifications to the rules set forth in the final regulations relating to how a taxpayer determines its aggregate group for purposes of determining gross receipts and the base erosion percentage. Part III of this Explanation of Provisions describes proposed regulations providing an election to waive deductions. Part IV of this Explanation of Provisions describes proposed regulations addressing the application of the BEAT to partnerships.

II. *Determination of a Taxpayer's Aggregate Group*

For certain purposes, including the determination of gross receipts described in section 59A(e)(2) and the base erosion percentage described in section 59A(c)(4), section 59A(e)(3) and §1.59A-1(b)(1) generally aggregate a group of corporations ("aggregate group") on the basis of persons treated as a single employer under section 52(a), which treats members of the same controlled group of corporations (as defined in section 1563(a) with certain modifications) as one person. To determine gross receipts, section 59A(e)(2) requires the application of rules similar to, but not necessarily the same as, section 448(c)(3)(B), (C), and (D). The 2018 proposed regulations provided rules for determining the aggregate group for applying the gross receipts test as well as the base erosion percentage test. Generally, the 2018 proposed regulations provided that each taxpayer determines its gross receipts and base erosion percentage by reference to its own taxable year, taking into account the results of other members of its aggregate group during that taxable year. *See* 2018 proposed §1.59A-2(d)(2).

Comments to the 2018 proposed regulations recommended that the determination of gross receipts and the base erosion percentage of a taxpayer's aggregate group be made on the basis of the taxpayer's taxable year and the taxable year of each member of its aggregate group that ends with or within the applicable taxpayer's taxable year (the "with-or-within method"). In response to the comments to the 2018 proposed regulations, the final regulations generally adopt the with-or-within method. §1.59A-2(c)(3). The final regulations do not include specific rules regarding how the with-or-within method applies in certain situations. These proposed regulations provide guidance regarding certain applications of the aggregate group rules and request comments regarding these rules in light of the with-or-within method.

A. *Rules relating to the determination of gross receipts for a short taxable year*

The 2018 proposed regulations provided guidance regarding the determination of gross receipts for purposes of section 59A. In the case of a taxpayer that has a short taxable year, the 2018 proposed regulations annualized the gross receipts of the taxpayer by multiplying the gross receipts for the short taxable year by 365 and dividing the result by the number of days in the short taxable year. *See* 2018 proposed §1.59A-2(d)(7).

One comment to the 2018 proposed regulations expressed concern that determining the gross receipts of a taxpayer by annualizing a short taxable year could yield inappropriate results when combined with the rule providing that any reference to a taxpayer includes a reference to its predecessor. For example, the comment asserted that if the taxpayer has a full taxable year but a predecessor had a short taxable year, it is not clear whether the taxable year of the predecessor should be annualized first and then combined with the year of the taxpayer or whether the taxable years of the taxpayer and its predecessor should be combined first, in which case no annualization may be necessary. The final regulations do not include a rule on short taxable years. Instead, and to allow taxpayers an additional opportunity to comment, these proposed regulations provide updated guidance with respect to short taxable years (in particular, for situations when an aggregate group has a member with a short taxable year).

In the case of a taxpayer that has a short taxable year, solely for purposes of section 59A, these proposed regulations continue to annualize the gross receipts of the taxpayer by multiplying the gross receipts for the short taxable year by 365 and dividing the result by the number of days in the short taxable year. Proposed § 1.59A-2(c)(5). However, the Treasury Department and the IRS recognize that the with-or-within method in § 1.59A-2(c)(3) must be adjusted to prevent the understatement or overstatement of the gross receipts, base erosion tax benefits, and deductions of an aggregate group in the case of a taxpayer with a short taxable year. For example, the with-or-within method would completely exclude the taxable year of certain members of an aggregate group if the taxable year of those members did not end with or within the taxpayer's short taxable year.[1] In other instances, the with-or-within method combined with an annualization approach might over-count the gross receipts of other aggregate group members if the method is applied by annualizing the full taxable years of the other members of the aggregate group that end with or within the taxpayer's short taxable year. Specifically, the regulation's requirement that a taxpayer annualize gross receipts when it has a short taxable year could be read to mean that gross receipts of aggregate group members (which may have full taxable years that end with or within the taxpayer's taxable year) also be annualized on the basis of the taxpayer's short taxable year, which could result in over-counting. In light of these concerns, these proposed regulations provide that a taxpayer with a short taxable year must use a reasonable approach to determine the base erosion percentage of its aggregate group and whether the taxpayer or its aggregate group satisfies the gross receipts test and base erosion percentage in section 59A. A reasonable approach should neither over-count nor under-count the gross receipts, base erosion tax benefits, and deductions of the aggregate group of the taxpayer.

The Treasury Department and the IRS request comments on whether more specific guidance is needed, and if so, the best approach for determining the gross receipts and base erosion percentage of an aggregate group for purposes of section 59A when the applicable taxpayer or another member of an aggregate group has a short taxable year. The approach should neither over-count nor under-count the gross receipts, base erosion tax benefits, and deductions of the aggregate group. The approach should also appropriately account for short taxable years that result from a change in a taxpayer's taxable year end (in which case the preceding and following taxable years would be full taxable years) and short taxable years that result from changes in ownership, such as a joining or leaving a consolidated group (in which case the preceding or succeeding taxable year may also be a short taxable year).

B. *Members leaving and joining an aggregate group*

A member may join or leave the aggregate group of a taxpayer because of a change in ownership of the member such as a sale of the member to a third party. A comment to the 2018 proposed regulations requested clarity on whether the determination of gross receipts and the base erosion percentage of an aggregate group takes into account the gross receipts, base erosion tax benefits, and deductions of a member of the aggregate group for the period before the member joins the group or the period after the member leaves the group. In response to this comment, the proposed regulations provide guidance that clarifies the treatment of members that join or leave the aggregate group of a taxpayer.

To determine the gross receipts and the base erosion percentage of a taxpayer with respect to its aggregate group for purposes of section 59A, these proposed regulations take into account only items of members that occur during the period that they were members of the taxpayer's aggregate group. Proposed § 1.59A-2(c)(4). Items of members that occur before a member joins an aggregate group of a taxpayer or after a member leaves an aggregate group of a taxpayer are not taken into account by the taxpayer. Solely for purposes of determining which items occurred while a corporation was a member of an aggregate group under section 59A, a corporation is treated as having a deemed taxable year end when the corporation joins or leaves an aggregate group of a taxpayer. The taxpayer may determine items attributable to this deemed short taxable year by either deeming a close of the corporation's books or, in the case of items other than extraordinary items (as defined in § 1.1502-76(b)(2)(ii)(C)), making a pro-rata allocation. *See* proposed § 1.59A-2(c)(4). For an illustration of this proposed rule, see proposed § 1.59A-2(f)(2), Example 2.

C. *Consolidated groups*

A comment to the 2018 proposed regulations expressed concern that gross receipts arising from intercompany transactions (as defined in § 1.1502-13(b)(1)) might be treated as gross receipts of the selling member (S) when S deconsolidates from a consolidated group (original consolidated group) and separately joins a different aggregate group (new aggregate group). For purposes of section 59A, the comment to the 2018 proposed regulations recommended that the gross receipts resulting from intercompany transactions in which S engaged while a member of the original consolidated group should not be counted even after S becomes a member of the new aggregate group, despite S no longer being a member of the original consolidated group.

The Treasury Department and the IRS are studying whether it is appropriate to continue to eliminate gross receipts resulting from intercompany transactions when members deconsolidate and join a different aggregate group. Furthermore, the Treasury Department and the IRS are aware of more general questions regarding the proper treatment of gross receipts when members join or deconsolidate from a consolidated group. These issues are currently under study, and the proposed regulations reserve on such issues. The Treasury Department and the IRS request comments on the appropriate treatment of a deconsolidating member's gross receipts history as it relates to the original consolidated group and the acquiring consolidated group in the context of the BEAT aggregate group.

D. *Predecessors*

For purposes of determining gross receipts, the 2018 proposed regulations provided that a reference to a taxpayer includes a reference to any predecessor of the taxpayer. 2018 proposed § 1.59A-2(c)(6)(i). The Treasury Department and the IRS, however, recognize that the aggregate groups of a taxpayer and its predecessor may overlap. As a result, an interpretation of the predecessor rule that simply adds the gross receipts of the predecessor to the gross receipts of the taxpayer's aggregate group could result in double counting of the gross receipts of corporations that are members of both aggregate groups. These proposed regulations clarify that, for purposes of section 59A, the gross receipts of those corporations included in both aggregate groups are not double counted. Proposed § 1.59A-2(c)(6)(ii). The Treasury Department and the IRS request comments on appropriate methods of taking into account predecessors for purposes of determining gross receipts of an applicable taxpayer's aggregate group.

---

[1] For example, assume FC, a foreign corporation, wholly owns DC1, DC2, and DC3, each domestic corporations. DC1, DC2, and DC3 each have a calendar year taxable year. Pursuant to the with-or-within method, DC1 includes in its aggregate group for Year 1 the taxable years of DC2 and DC3 ending on December 31, Year 1. Subsequently, DC1 changes its taxable year end to November 30. Accordingly, DC1 has a short taxable year beginning January 1, Year 2 and ending November 30, Year 2. No taxable year of DC2 or DC3 ends with or within the taxable year of DC1 ending November 30, Year 2. Nonetheless, it would not be appropriate to wholly exclude the gross receipts, base erosion tax benefits, and deductions of DC2 and DC3 from the aggregate group of DC1 for the taxable year ending November 30, Year 2.

An appropriate method should avoid double-counting and address whether to take into account the taxable year of a predecessor in determining whether to annualize a short taxable year of a taxpayer.

III. *Election to Waive Allowable Deductions*

The final regulations provide that, in general, the base erosion percentage for a taxable year is computed by dividing (1) the aggregate amount of base erosion tax benefits (the "numerator") by (2) the sum of the aggregate amount of deductions allowed plus certain other base erosion tax benefits (the "denominator"). *See* § 1.59A-2(e)(3). In general, and consistent with section 59A(c)(2), the final regulations provide that a base erosion tax benefit is any deduction that is *allowed* under chapter 1 of subtitle A of the Code for the taxable year with respect to a base erosion payment. *See* § 1.59A-3(c)(1)(i). The final regulations, consistent with section 59A(d)(1), define one category of a base erosion payment as any amount paid or accrued by the taxpayer to a foreign related party of the taxpayer and with respect to which a deduction is *allowable* under chapter 1 of subtitle A of the Internal Revenue Code. § 1.59A-3(b)(1)(i).

Comments to the 2018 proposed regulations requested that the final regulations clarify that allowable deductions that a taxpayer declines to claim on its tax return are not "allowed" deductions, and therefore, the foregone deductions are not base erosion tax benefits. These proposed regulations provide that a taxpayer may forego a deduction and that those foregone deductions will not be treated as a base erosion tax benefit if the taxpayer waives the deduction for all U.S. federal income tax purposes and follows specified procedures. Proposed § 1.59A-3(c)(6). If the taxpayer waives a deduction for purposes of section 59A, these proposed regulations provide that the taxpayer cannot claim the deduction for any purpose of the Code or regulations except as otherwise provided under the proposed regulations. *See* proposed § 1.59A-3(c)(6)(ii).

The Treasury Department and the IRS are concerned that in adopting this approach, absent certain procedural rules, taxpayers that waive a deduction pursuant to the proposed regulations to reduce their amount of base erosion tax benefits could benefit by using some or all of the foregone deductions in a subsequent year, while still benefiting from the reduction of base erosion tax benefits made in the prior year. Accordingly, proposed § 1.59A-3(c)(6) provides rules to address this concern. The proposed regulations also include certain reporting rules concerning deductions that are waived pursuant to the proposed regulations, and provide guidance on the time and manner for electing to waive deductions. Proposed § 1.59A-3(c)(6)(i) and (iii).

Specifically, the proposed regulations provide that as a baseline, all deductions that could be properly claimed by a taxpayer for the taxable year, determined after giving effect to the taxpayer's permissible method of accounting and to any election, (such as the election under section 173 to capitalize circulation expenditures or the election under section 168(g)(7) to use the alternative depreciation system of depreciation), are treated as allowed deductions solely for purposes of section 59A(c)(2)(A)(i), unless a taxpayer elects to waive certain deductions. *See* proposed § 1.59A-3(c)(5) and (6). As a result, if a taxpayer does not make an election to waive a deduction that could be properly claimed by a taxpayer for the taxable year pursuant to the procedures in proposed § 1.59A-3(c)(6), and the deduction otherwise meets the definition of a base erosion tax benefit, the deduction is treated as a base erosion tax benefit for purposes of section 59A. Consequently, the deduction is taken into account in the base erosion percentage, and is taken into account as an adjustment to modified taxable income. The proposed regulations provide that if a taxpayer elects to waive certain deductions, those deductions are waived for all tax purposes (except for certain purposes as explained in part III of this Explanation of Provisions) and, thus, are not taken into account as base erosion tax benefits. Proposed § 1.59A-3(c)(6)(ii)(A)(*1*). The waiver applies only to the deduction, not to the underlying cost or expense. Thus, a waiver of any portion of a deduction associated with a particular cost or expense does not cause the corresponding portion of that cost or expense not to be a "cost" or "expense."

A taxpayer may make the election to waive deductions on its original filed Federal income tax return, by an amended return, or during the course of an examination of the taxpayer's income tax return for the relevant tax year pursuant to procedures prescribed by the Commissioner. Proposed § 1.59A-3(c)(6)(iii). Unless the Commissioner prescribes specific procedures with respect to waiving deductions during the course of an examination, the same procedures that generally apply to affirmative tax return changes during an examination will apply. The Treasury Department and the IRS request comments related to the process for submitting an election under the proposed regulations during the course of an examination. The information related to this waiver must be reported on the appropriate forms, which are expected to include Form 8991, *Tax on Base Erosion Payments of Taxpayers With Substantial Gross Receipts*, (or a successor form). Until these proposed regulations are final, a taxpayer choosing to rely on these proposed regulations may attach a statement to the Form 8991 to make this election and include the information listed in proposed § 1.59A-3(c)(6)(i) on that statement. A taxpayer makes the election on an annual basis, and the taxpayer does not need the consent of the Commissioner if the taxpayer chooses not to make the election for a subsequent taxable year. The proposed regulations provide that the election to waive a deduction pursuant to proposed § 1.59A-3(c)(6) is disregarded for determining (1) the taxpayer's overall method of accounting or the taxpayer's method of accounting for any item; (2) whether a change in the taxpayer's overall plan of accounting or the taxpayer's treatment of a material item is a change in method of accounting under section 446(e) and § 1.446-1(e); and (3) the amount allowable for depreciation or amortization for purposes of section 167(c) and section 1016(a)(2) or (3), and any other adjustment to basis under section 1016(a). Proposed § 1.59A-3(c)(6)(ii)(B)(*1*)-(*3*). The proposed regulations also provide that the election to waive deductions does not constitute a method of accounting under section 446. Proposed § 1.59A-3(c)(6)(ii)(C).

In addition, the proposed regulations provide that the waiver of deductions is treated as occurring before the allocation and apportionment of deductions under §§ 1.861-8 through -14T and 1.861-17 (such as for purposes of section 904). Proposed § 1.59A-3(c)(6)(ii)(A)(2). However, the waiver of a deduction for interest expense that is directly allocable to income produced by a particular asset should not result in the allocation and apportionment of additional interest expense to that asset. Accordingly, the proposed regulations provide that to the extent a deduction for certain interest expense is waived that would have been directly allocated and resulted in a reduction of value of any asset for purposes of allocating and apportioning other interest expense, the asset value is still reduced as if the deduction had not been waived. Proposed § 1.59A-3(c)(6)(ii)(A)(3).

The waiver of a deduction is also disregarded for purposes of applying the exclusive apportionment rule in § 1.861-17(b), in determining the geographic source where the research and experimental activities that account for more than fifty percent of the amount of the deduction for research and experimentation was performed. Proposed § 1.59A-3(c)(6)(ii)(B)(4). For example, if this exclusive apportionment rule would not apply in the absence of waiving deductions for research and experimentation performed outside the United States, then waiving those deductions will not result in the exclusive apportionment rule applying (on the basis of a smaller pool of deducted expenses, more than fifty percent of which relate to research and experimentation performed in the United States).

The waiver of a deduction is also disregarded for purposes of determining the price of a controlled transaction under section 482. Proposed § 1.59A-3(c)(6)(ii)(B)(5). Accordingly, in determining whether a deduction that a taxpayer reports on its Federal income tax return with respect to a controlled transaction clearly reflects the taxpayer's income with respect to the controlled transaction, the IRS will consider the amount waived as if it were actually deducted. In addition, if a taxpayer applies a transfer pricing method that uses costs or expenses as an input (such as the cost plus method described in § 1.482-3(d)), the costs or expenses associated with waived deductions continue to be treated as "costs" or "expenses" for purposes of the section 482 regulations because the waiver impacts the deductible amount only, not the amount of the underlying cost or expense.

Furthermore, the waiver of a deduction is disregarded for purposes of determining: (1) the amount of a taxpayer's earnings and profits, (2) any item as necessary to prevent a taxpayer from receiving the benefit of a waived deduction, and any other item that is expressly identified in published guidance. Proposed § 1.59A-3(c)(6)(ii)(B)(6)-(8).

To ensure a taxpayer is not able to reduce the amount of its base erosion tax benefits via a waiver of deductions in a prior year and then recover the waived deductions in a subsequent year by making an accounting method change, the proposed regulations provide that, by making the election to waive deductions, the taxpayer agrees that if a change in method of accounting is made with respect to an item that had been waived, the previously waived portion of the item is not taken into account in determining the amount of adjustment under section 481(a). Proposed § 1.59A-3(c)(6)(ii)(D). For an illustration of this proposed rule, see proposed § 1.59A-3(d), Example 9. More generally, the Treasury Department and the IRS are studying the treatment of changes in method of accounting and the related section 481 adjustments for purposes of the BEAT. To the extent that a negative adjustment under section 481(a) relates to an increase in an item that would be a base erosion tax benefit, it is expected that the section 481(a) adjustment would also be taken into account as a base erosion tax benefit. In addition, the Treasury Department and the IRS are considering other consequences of adjustments under section 481(a), including (a) how positive adjustments under section 481(a) are taken into account for BEAT purposes and (b) whether a waiver similar to the waiver provided in proposed § 1.59A-3(c)(6) should be permitted with respect to negative section 481(a) adjustments.

The Treasury Department and the IRS request comments regarding the election to waive deductions, including the reporting requirements and additional rules necessary to prevent a taxpayer from claiming a waived deduction in a subsequent year. The Treasury Department and the IRS also request comments on the effect of adjustments under section 481(a) on the BEAT, including in the context of waived items.

IV. *Application of the BEAT to Partnerships*

A. *Allocations by a partnership of income instead of deductions*

In general, the final regulations treat deductions allocated by the partnership to an applicable taxpayer resulting from a base erosion payment as a base erosion tax benefit. However, the Treasury Department and the IRS are cognizant that a partner in a partnership can obtain a similar economic result if the partnership allocates income items away from the partner instead of allocating a deduction to the partner through curative allocations. To the extent the partnership places a taxpayer in such an economically equivalent position by allocating less income to that partner in lieu of allocating a deduction to the partner through curative allocations, the proposed regulations provide that the partner is similarly treated as having a base erosion tax benefit to the extent of that substitute allocation. Proposed § 1.59A-7(b)(5)(v).

B. *Effectively connected income ("ECI")*

Comments to the 2018 proposed regulations recommended that contributions of depreciable (or amortizable) property by a foreign related party to a partnership (in which an applicable taxpayer is a partner) or distributions of depreciable or amortizable property by a partnership (in which a foreign related party is a partner) to an applicable taxpayer be excluded from the definition of a base erosion payment to the extent that the foreign related party would receive (or would be expected to receive) allocations of income from that partnership interest that would be taxable to the foreign related party as ECI.

The Treasury Department and the IRS are considering additional guidance to address the treatment of a contribution by a foreign person to a partnership engaged in a U.S. trade or business, as well as transfers of partnership interests by a foreign person and transfers of property by the partnership with a foreign person as a partner to a related U.S. person. The Treasury Department and the IRS request comments addressing how these issues should be addressed, including rules to ensure that the foreign partner is treating the items allocated with respect to the property and any gain from the property as ECI.

C. *Partnership anti-abuse rules*

1. Derivatives on partnership interests

Section 1.59A-9(b) of the final regulations provides that certain transactions that have a principal purpose of avoiding section 59A will be disregarded or deemed to result in a base erosion payment. These proposed regulations provide an additional anti-abuse rule relating to derivatives on partnership interests. *See* proposed § 1.59A-9(b)(5). The rule provides that a taxpayer is treated as having a direct interest in the partnership interest or asset if the taxpayer acquires a derivative on a partnership interest or asset with a principal purpose of eliminating or reducing a base erosion payment.

2. Allocations by a partnership to prevent or reduce a base erosion payment

The proposed regulations also provide an additional anti-abuse rule to prevent a partnership from allocating items of income with a principal purpose of eliminating or reducing the base erosion payments to a taxpayer not acting in a partner capacity on amounts paid to or accrued by a partnership that do not change the economic arrangement of the partners. For example, assume that a domestic corporation and a third party both pay equal amounts to a partnership with a foreign related party partner and an unrelated partner (each having equal interests in the partnership) for services. If the partnership allocates the income it receives from the domestic corporation to the unrelated partner while allocating an equivalent amount of income from the third party to the foreign related party partner with a principal purpose of eliminating the domestic corporation's base erosion payment, the domestic corporation must determine its base erosion payment as if the allocations had not been made and the partners shared the income proportionately. As a result, half of the domestic corporation's payment would be a base erosion payment.

D. *Return of a partnership with respect to base erosion payments and base erosion tax benefits*

Pursuant to section 6031 and § 1.6031(a)-1(a), a domestic partnership must file a return of partnership income for each taxable year on the form prescribed for the partnership return. Pursuant to § 1.6031(a)-1(b), with limited exceptions, a foreign partnership that has gross income that is, or is treated as, effectively connected with the conduct of a trade or business within the United States or gross income (including gains) derived from sources within the United States must file a partnership return for its taxable year in accordance with the rules for domestic partnerships (such a foreign partnership, a "reporting foreign partnership"). The partnership return must contain the information required by the prescribed form and the accompanying instructions. The IRS plans to update Form 1065, Schedule K, and Schedule K-1 to incorporate certain information that will be necessary for its partners to complete their Form 8991 or a successor form. The IRS expects that these revisions to the Form 1065, Schedule K, and Schedule K-1 will track the information required by the Form 8991.

As a result of these planned revisions, a domestic partnership and a reporting foreign partnership will be required to report the information required by Form 8991. *See* § 1.6031(a)-1(a) and (b)(1)(i). Proposed § 1.6031(a)-1(b)(7) provides that United States partners must determine the relevant information with respect to the base erosion payments and base erosion tax benefits of a foreign partnership that is not required to file a partnership return. For a partnership that is required to file a Form 1065 and Schedule K-1, the Commissioner is expected to receive sufficient information to examine the accuracy of the partners' liability under section 59A, including as a result of items allocated to the partner by the partnership. For a foreign partnership that is not required to file a Form 1065 and Schedule K-1, proposed § 1.6031(a)-1(b)(7) is intended to ensure that the Commissioner receives similar information from the partners of that foreign partnership.

Proposed Applicability Date

The rules in the section 59A proposed regulations generally apply to taxable years beginning on or after the date that final regulations are filed with the **Federal Register**. The rules in proposed §§ 1.59A-7(c)(5)(v) and (g)(2)(x) and 1.59A-9(b)(5) and apply to taxable years ending on or after December 2, 2019. As proposed, the section 59A regulations will permit taxpayers to apply the rules therein in their entirety for taxable years beginning after December 31, 2017, and before the regulations apply. See section 7805(b)(7). If a taxpayer applies the 2018 proposed regulations to a taxable year ending on or before December 6, 2019, the determination as to whether the taxpayer is applying these proposed regulations in their entirety to such taxable year is made without regard to the application of § 1.59A-2(c)(2)(ii), (c)(4), (c)(5), and (c)(6).

In addition, taxpayers may rely on the rules in the section 59A proposed regulations in their entirety for taxable years beginning after December 31, 2017, and before the final regulations are applicable.

The rules in the section 6031(a) proposed regulations generally apply to taxable years ending on or after the date that final regulations are filed with the **Federal Register**.

Special Analyses

Regulatory Planning and Review - Economic Analysis

Executive Orders 13563 and 12866 direct agencies to assess costs and benefits of available regulatory alternatives and, if regulation is necessary, to select regulatory approaches that maximize net benefits (including potential economic, environmental, public health and safety effects, distributive impacts, and equity). Executive Order 13563 emphasizes the importance of quantifying both costs and benefits, of reducing costs, of harmonizing rules, and of promoting flexibility. The Executive Order 13771 designation for any final rule resulting from the proposed regulation will be informed by comments received. The preliminary Executive Order 13771 designation for this proposed regulation is regulatory.

These proposed regulations have been designated as subject to review under Executive Order 12866 pursuant to the Memorandum of Agreement (April 11, 2018) (MOA) between the Treasury Department and the Office of Management and Budget (OMB) regarding review of tax regulations. The Office of Information and Regulatory Affairs (OIRA) has designated these proposed regulations as significant under section 1(b) of the MOA. Accordingly, these proposed regulations have been reviewed by OIRA.

A. *Background*

The Tax Cuts and Jobs Act of 2017 (the "Act") added new section 59A, which imposes a Base Erosion and Anti-Abuse Tax ("BEAT") on certain deductions paid or accrued to foreign related parties. By taxing such payments, the BEAT "aims to level the playing field between U.S. and foreign-owned multinational corporations in an administrable way." Senate Committee on Finance, Explanation of the Bill, S. Prt. 115-20, at 391 (November 22, 2017).

In plain language, the tax is levied only on corporations with substantial gross receipts (a determination referred to as the gross receipts test) and for which the relevant deductions are three percent or higher (two percent or higher in the case of certain banks or registered securities dealers) of their total deductions (with certain exceptions), a determination referred to as the base erosion percentage test. This cut-off for the base erosion percentage test is referred to in these Special Analyses as the base erosion threshold.

A taxpayer that satisfies both the gross receipts test and the base erosion percentage test is referred to as an applicable taxpayer. A taxpayer is not an applicable taxpayer, and thus does not have any BEAT liability, if its base erosion percentage is less than the base erosion threshold.

Additional features of the BEAT also enter its calculation. The BEAT operates as a minimum tax, so an applicable taxpayer is only subject to additional tax under the BEAT if the tax at the BEAT rate multiplied by the taxpayer's modified taxable income exceeds the taxpayer's regular tax liability, reduced by certain credits. Because of this latter provision, the BEAT formula has the effect of imposing the BEAT on the amount of those tax credits. In general, tax credits are subject to the BEAT except the research credit under section 41, and a portion of low income housing credits, renewable electricity production credits under section 45, and certain investment tax credits under section 46. Notably, this means that the foreign tax credit is currently subject to the BEAT. In taxable years beginning after December 31, 2025, all tax credits are subject to the BEAT.

B. *Need for the proposed regulations*

Section 59A does not explicitly state whether an amount that is permitted as a deduction under the Code or regulations but that is not claimed as a deduction on a taxpayer's tax return is potentially a base erosion tax benefit for purposes of the BEAT and the base erosion percentage test. Comments recommended that the Treasury Department and the IRS clarify the treatment of amounts that are allowable as a deduction but not claimed as a deduction on a taxpayer's tax return. These proposed regulations are needed to respond to these comments and to clarify the treatment of these amounts under section 59A. The proposed regulations are also needed to clarify certain aspects of the rules set forth in the final regulations relating to how a taxpayer determines its aggregate group for purposes of determining gross receipts and the base erosion percentage, and how the BEAT applies to partnerships.

C. *Overview of the proposed regulations*

The proposed regulations provide taxpayers an election to waive deductions that would otherwise be taken into account in determining whether the taxpayer is an applicable taxpayer subject to the BEAT. This change is analyzed in part D of these Special Analyses.

These proposed regulations also include modifications to the rules set forth in the final regulations relating to how a taxpayer determines its aggregate group for purposes of determining gross receipts and the base erosion percentage, and how the BEAT applies to partnerships. These latter modifications to the existing final rule are not expected to result in any substantial changes in taxpayer behavior.

D. *Economic Analysis*

1. Baseline

The Treasury Department and the IRS have assessed the benefits and costs of the proposed regulations compared to a no-action baseline that reflects anticipated Federal income tax-related behavior in the absence of these proposed regulations.

2. Economic Effects of the Election to Waive Deductions (Part III of the Explanation of Provisions)

a. Background and Alternatives Considered

Section 59A does not explicitly state whether an amount that is permitted as a deduction under the Code or regulations but that is not claimed as a deduction on the taxpayer's tax return is potentially a base erosion tax benefit for the purposes of the base erosion percentage test. A taxpayer may find waiving certain deductions advantageous if the waived deductions lower the taxpayer's base erosion percentage below the base erosion threshold, thus making section 59A inapplicable to the taxpayer. Comments recommended that the Treasury Department and the IRS clarify the treatment of allowable amounts that are not claimed as a deduction on the taxpayer's tax return for purposes of section 59A.

To address concerns about the treatment of these amounts permitted as deductions under law, the Treasury Department and the IRS considered two alternatives for the proposed guidance: (1) providing that all deductions that could be properly claimed by a taxpayer for the taxable year are taken into account for purposes of the base erosion percentage test (and for other purposes of the BEAT) even if a deduction is not claimed on the taxpayer's tax return (the "alternative regulatory approach"); or (2) providing that an allowable deduction that a taxpayer does not claim on its tax return is not taken into account in the base erosion percentage test or for other purposes of the BEAT, provided that certain procedural steps are followed. The proposed regulations adopt the latter approach.

Under the alternative regulatory approach, base erosion payments allowable as deductions but not claimed by a taxpayer would nonetheless be taken into account in the base erosion percentage. Thus, a taxpayer could not avoid satisfying the base erosion percentage test by not claiming certain deductions. Under the proposed regulations, base erosion payments allowable as deductions but waived by a taxpayer are not taken into account in the base erosion percentage test, assuming certain procedural steps are followed. The waived deductions are waived for all U.S. federal income tax purposes and thus, for example, the deductions are also not allowed for regular income tax purposes. If the taxpayer is not an applicable taxpayer because it waives deductions so as not to satisfy the base erosion percentage test, the taxpayer may continue to claim deductions for base erosion payments that are not waived, provided these deductions would otherwise be allowed.

b. Example

Consider a U.S.-parented multinational enterprise that satisfies the gross receipts test and that is not a bank or registered securities dealer. The U.S. corporation has gross income from domestic sources of $1000x and also has a net global intangible low-taxed income ("GILTI") inclusion of $500x.[2] The taxpayer has $870x of deductions pertinent to this example that are not base erosion tax benefits and $30x of deductions that are base erosion tax benefits. It is also assumed that the amount of foreign tax credits permitted under section 904(a) is $105x. This taxpayer's regular U.S. taxable income is $600x ($1000x + $500x - $870x - $30x), its regular U.S. tax rate is 21.0 percent, and its regular U.S. tax liability is $21x ($600x X 21% = $126x, less foreign tax credits of $105x ($126x - $105x)).

Under the alternative regulatory approach, the taxpayer is an applicable taxpayer because its base erosion percentage is 3.33 percent ($30x / $900x), which is greater than the three percent base erosion threshold. Because the taxpayer is subject to the BEAT, it must further compute its modified taxable income, which is $630x — its regular U.S. taxable income ($600x) plus its base erosion tax benefits ($30x). The taxpayer determines its base erosion minimum tax amount as the excess of the BEAT rate (10 percent) multiplied by its modified taxable income $63x ($630x X 10%) over its regular U.S. tax liability of $21x, which is equal to $42x ($63x - $21x). In this example the total U.S. tax bill is $63x ($21x of regular tax and $42x of BEAT).

Under the proposed regulations, this taxpayer would have the option to waive all or part of its deductions that are base erosion payments so that its base erosion percentage would fall below the base erosion threshold. Specifically, the taxpayer could waive $3.10x of its deductions that are base erosion payments, yielding a base erosion percentage of less than the three percent base erosion threshold (base erosion tax benefits = $26.90x ($30x - $3.10x); base erosion percentage = $26.90x/($870x + $26.90x) = 2.99%). After taking into account this waiver, the taxpayer's regular taxable income would increase to $603.10x ($1000x + $500x - $870x - $26.90x), and its regular tax liability would increase to $21.65x ($603.10x X 21% = $126.65, less foreign tax credits of $105x = $21.65x).[3] The waiver is valuable to this taxpayer because its tax bill in this simple example is lower by $41.35x ($63x - $21.65x).

This example shows the difference in tax liability caused by allowing deductions to be waived and thus, the difference between the proposed regulations and the alternative regulatory approach. The next part D.2.c of these Special Analyses discusses the behavioral incentives and economic effects that can result from this tax treatment.

c. Economic Effects of these Proposed Regulations

The proposed regulations effectively allow a taxpayer to make payments that would be base erosion payments without becoming an applicable taxpayer. This provision reduces the effective tax on base erosion payments for at least some taxpayers, relative to the alternative regulatory approach. Because of this reduction, the proposed regulations may lead to a higher amount of base erosion payments than under the alternative regulatory approach.

Any additional base erosion payments under the proposed regulations would come from taxpayers who, under the alternative regulatory approach, would not be applicable taxpayers but would be close to being applicable taxpayers; that is, they would have base erosion percentages that were close to but below the base erosion threshold.

Taxpayers that would be applicable taxpayers under the alternative regulatory approach will not increase their base erosion payments under the proposed regulations. To see this point, consider an applicable taxpayer under the alternative regulatory approach with base erosion payments of $Y. If this taxpayer were to increase its base erosion payments by $10 and reduce its non-base erosion payments by $10 (that is, it has substituted base erosion payments for non-base erosion payments), its tax bill would generally increase by $1. The fact that this taxpayer chose base erosion payments of $Y rather than $Y+10 suggests that this substitution would be worth less than $1 to the taxpayer. The substitution is not worth the increased tax. Next consider this taxpayer under the proposed regulations. If it elects to waive sufficient deductions such that it is not an applicable taxpayer, then the marginal increase in its tax bill from the hypothetized substitution is $2.10. Thus, if this increase in base erosion payments (and substitution away from non-base erosion payments) is not worthwhile to the taxpayer under the alternative regulatory approach, it will not be worthwhile under the proposed regulations.

This example suggests that to the extent that there is any increase in base erosion payments under the proposed regulations, it will not come from taxpayers that would be applicable taxpayers under the alternative regulatory approach and will instead come from those taxpayers that would not be applicable taxpayers under the alternative regulatory approach. These taxpayers would be able, under the proposed regulations, to take on activities that increase their base erosion payments but, by waiving all or part of the deduction for these activities, avoid crossing the base erosion threshold. This is the set of taxpayers that will be the source of any economic effects arising from the proposed regulations.

As a result of the ability to waive deductions in the proposed regulations, taxpayers may change business behavior in two possible ways. First, businesses may expand economic activities in the United States even if those activities result in payments to foreign related parties (i.e., base erosion payments). For example, under the alternative regulatory approach a multinational enterprise may decide not to open an office or manufacturing plant in the United States if that incremental activity also resulted in incremental base erosion payments that would cause the taxpayer to become an applicable taxpayer. Under the proposed regulations, this business can expand its activities in the U.S. and avoid becoming an applicable taxpayer, provided it waived sufficient deductions to stay below the base erosion threshold.

---

[2] For simplification of this example, the $500x GILTI income is presented as the net of the global intangible low-tax income amount of the domestic corporation under section 951A, plus the section 78 gross up amount for foreign taxes, less the GILTI deduction under section 250(a)(1)(B). The deduction under section 250(a)(1)(B) is not taken into account in determining the base erosion percentage. See section 59A(c)(4)(B)(i).

[3] Although the waiver increases the taxpayer's regular taxable income, the taxpayer's gross income (in the context of this example) is unchanged. Thus, only the tax liability needs to be compared across the regulatory approaches to determine whether the taxpayer would benefit from waiving deductions.

Second, businesses already operating in the United States may not be discouraged from structuring transactions as base erosion payments under the proposed regulations. Under the alternative regulatory approach, a business might conduct its transactions through unrelated parties rather than with a foreign related party so that its base erosion percentage would remain below the base erosion threshold. Under the proposed regulations, this business could use a foreign related party rather than an unrelated party for these transactions, without paying the BEAT, again provided it waived sufficient deductions to stay below the base erosion threshold.

In each of these cases, a business adopting these strategies would be presumed to accrue a non-tax, economic benefit from using a foreign related party rather than an unrelated party to conduct this aspect of its business. Under the proposed regulations, there is no U.S. tax-related benefit tax associated with transacting with a foreign related party and thus any decisions made by a business to make a base erosion payment would occur because of the economic advantage it provides to the business, rather than that payment being avoided, diverted or otherwise distorted because it would result in the taxpayer becoming an applicable taxpayer subject to the BEAT. This economic advantage might arise, for example, because the business has a closer relationship with the foreign related party and its transactions with the foreign related party provide enhanced managerial control. This economic benefit accruing to this business would generally be beneficial to the U.S. economy; this is particularly true in the first case described in the preceding paragraphs. While taxpayers may have compliance costs related to deciding whether to waive deductions and ensuring that procedural rules are followed, any changes in compliance costs are expected to be small because the accounting required for the relevant deductions is essentially the same under both the proposed regulations and the alternative regulatory approach.

Note that under the proposed regulations, a taxpayer would in general face a marginal tax rate that is 21 percentage points higher on its base erosion payments than on comparable deductions that are not base erosion payments. Economic analysis would conclude that the business will undertake a base erosion payment rather than a non-base erosion payment only if it provides a non-tax benefit at least this large. Businesses will choose a different mix of base erosion and non-base erosion payments under the alternative regulatory approach, but an analogous inference about the marginal value of a base erosion payment here (and thus of the difference between the proposed regulations and the alternative regulatory approach) is more complex because the marginal tax incurred by base erosion payments near the base erosion threshold depends on (i) how close the taxpayer would be to the threshold; (ii) the quantity of its base erosion payments that are below the base erosion threshold and subject to tax if the base erosion threshold is exceeded; and (iii) other factors affecting the potential BEAT liability. Because of these factors, the difference in the non-tax value to businesses of a marginal base erosion payment between the proposed regulations and alternative regulatory approach is complex and not readily inferred.

This said, as a general matter, for taxpayers who chose to waive deductions under the proposed regulations in order not to be applicable taxpayers, the Treasury Department and the IRS expect that relative to the alternative regulatory approach, the proposed regulations would tend to:

- Reduce tax costs of additional economic activity in the United States by those taxpayers in the situation where additional economic activity in the United States would tend to increase base erosion payments;

- Reduce tax-related incentives for otherwise economically inefficient business, contractual or accounting changes designed to avoid the taxpayer being an applicable taxpayer;

- Continue to fulfill the general intent and purpose of the statute by not providing tax incentives for certain large corporations to make deductible payments to foreign related parties in excess of 3 percent of the taxpayer's deductions; and

- Reduce the number of taxpayers that are applicable taxpayers and the overall amount of BEAT collected. This revenue effect is likely to be offset to some degree by the fact that some taxpayers are likely to elect to waive allowable deductions.

The Treasury Department and the IRS have not attempted to provide a quantitative estimate of the economic consequences of the proposed regulations relative to the alternative regulatory approach. Any increase in base erosion payments under the proposed regulations depends on the number of taxpayers that would be close to the base erosion threshold under the alternative regulatory approach, the quantity of base erosion payments they would have under the alternative regulatory approach, and, most importantly, the economic value provided by those base erosion payments relative to alternative economic decisions. These items are difficult to estimate with any reasonable precision in part because they involve economic activities, including potential new economic activity in the United States, that cannot be readily inferred from existing data or models available to the Treasury Department and the IRS.

In the absence of such quantitative estimates, the Treasury Department and the IRS have undertaken a qualitative analysis of the economic effects of the proposed regulations relative to the alternative regulatory approach.

The Treasury Department and the IRS solicit comments on these findings and more generally on the economic effects of these proposed regulations. The Treasury Department and the IRS particularly solicit data, other evidence, or models that could be used to enhance the rigor of the process by which the final regulations might be developed.

d. Number of Affected Taxpayers

These proposed regulations affect all corporate taxpayers that satisfy the gross receipts test, base erosion percentage test, and have base erosion payments. The Treasury Department and the IRS project that 3,500 - 4,500 taxpayers may be applicable taxpayers under the BEAT. This estimate is based on the number of filers that (1) filed the Form 1120 series of tax returns (except for the Form 1120-S), (2) filed a Form 5471 or Form 5472, and (3) reported gross receipts of at least $500 million. Because an applicable taxpayer is defined under section 59A(e)(1)(A) as a corporation other than a regulated investment company, a real estate investment trust, or an S corporation, the Treasury Department and the IRS have determined that taxpayers who filed the Form 1120 series of tax returns will be most likely to be affected by these proposed regulations. Additionally, the Treasury Department and the IRS estimated the number of filers likely to make payments to a foreign related party based on filers of the Form 1120 series of tax returns who also filed a Form 5471 or Form 5472 to determine the number of respondents. Finally, because an applicable taxpayer is defined under section 59A(e)(1)(B) as a taxpayer with average annual gross receipts of at least $500 million for the 3-taxable-year period ending with the preceding taxable year, the Treasury Department and the IRS estimated the scope of Affected Taxpayers based on the amount of gross receipts reported by taxpayers filing the Form 1120 series of tax returns.

These projections are based solely on data with respect to the taxpayer, without taking into account any members of the taxpayer's aggregate group. As many as 100,000 - 110,000 additional taxpayers may be applicable taxpayers as a result of being members of an aggregate group.[4] This estimate is based on the number of taxpayers who filed a Form 1120 and also filed a Form 5471 or a Form 5472, but without regard to the gross receipts test. Current data do not permit an estimate of the number of taxpayers that would be close to the base erosion threshold.

E. *Paperwork Reduction Act*

The collections of information in these proposed regulations with respect to section 59A are in proposed §§ 1.59A-3(c)(5), and 1.6031(a)-1(b)(7). The collection of information in proposed §§ 1.59A-3(c)(5) is an election to waive deductions allowed under the Code. The election to waive deductions is made by a taxpayer on its original or amended income tax return. A taxpayer makes the election on an annual basis by completing

---

[4] These estimates are based on current tax filings for taxable year 2017 and do not yet include the BEAT. At this time, the Treasury Department and the IRS do not have readily available data to determine whether a taxpayer that is a member of an aggregate group will meet all tests to be an applicable taxpayer for purposes of the BEAT.

Form 8991 or as provided in applicable instructions. The IRS is contemplating making additional changes to the Form 8991 to take these proposed regulations into account.

The collection of information in proposed §1.6031(a)-1(b)(7) requires a partner in a foreign partnership that: (1) is not required to file a partnership return and (2) has made a payment or accrual that is treated as a base erosion payment of a partner under §1.59A-7(b)(2), to provide the information necessary to report any base erosion payments on Form 8991. The IRS intends that this information will be collected by completing Form 8991, *Tax on Base Erosion Payments of Taxpayers With Substantial Gross Receipts*, Form 1065, and Schedule K-1. The IRS is contemplating making revisions to Form 1065, Schedule K, and Schedule K-1 to take these proposed regulations into account.

For purposes of the Paperwork Reduction Act, the reporting burden associated with the collections of information with respect to section 59A, will be reflected in the Paperwork Reduction Act Submission, associated with Form 8991 (OMB control number 1545-0123).

The current status of the Paperwork Reduction Act submissions related to BEAT is provided in the following table. The BEAT provisions are included in aggregated burden estimates for the OMB control numbers listed below which, in the case of 1545-0123, represents a total estimated burden time, including all other related forms and schedules for corporations, of 3.157 billion hours and total estimated monetized costs of $58.148 billion ($2017). The burden estimates provided in the OMB control numbers below are aggregate amounts that relate to the entire package of forms associated with the OMB control number, and will in the future include but not isolate the estimated burden of only the BEAT requirements. These numbers are therefore unrelated to the future calculations needed to assess the burden imposed by the proposed regulations. The Treasury Department and IRS urge readers to recognize that these numbers are duplicates and to guard against overcounting the burden that international tax provisions imposed prior to the Act. No burden estimates specific to the proposed regulations are currently available. The Treasury Department has not estimated the burden, including that of any new information collections, related to the requirements under the proposed regulations. Those estimates would capture both changes made by the Act and those that arise out of discretionary authority exercised in the proposed regulations. The Treasury Department and the IRS request comments on all aspects of information collection burdens related to the proposed regulations. In addition, when available, drafts of IRS forms are posted for comment at https://apps.irs.gov/app/picklist/list/draftTaxForms.htm.

Form	Type of Filer	OMB Number(s)	Status
Form 8991	Business (NEW Model)	1545-0123	Published in the FRN on 10/11/18. Public Comment period closed on 12/10/18.
			Link: https://www.federalregister.gov/documents/2018/10/09/2018-21846/proposed-collection-comment-request-for-forms-1065-1065-b-1066-1120-1120-c-1120-f-1120-h-1120-nd

Related New or Revised Tax Forms

	New	Revision of existing form	Number of respondents (2018, estimated)
Form 8991	Y		3,500 - 4,500

The number of respondents in the Related New or Revised Tax Forms table was estimated by Treasury's Office of Tax Analysis based on data from IRS Compliance Planning and Analytics using tax return data for tax years 2015 and 2016. Data for Form 8991 represent preliminary estimates of the total number of taxpayers which may be required to file the new Form 8991. Only certain large corporate taxpayers with gross receipts of at least $500 million are expected to file this form.

F. *Regulatory Flexibility Act*

It is hereby certified that these regulations will not have a significant economic impact on a substantial number of small entities within the meaning of section 601(6) of the Regulatory Flexibility Act (5 U.S.C. chapter 6). This certification is based on the fact that these regulations will primarily affect aggregate groups of corporations with average annual gross receipts of at least $500 million and that make payments to foreign related parties. Generally only large businesses both have substantial gross receipts and make payments to foreign related parties.

Notwithstanding this certification, the Treasury Department and the IRS invite comments from the public about the impact of this proposed rule on small entities.

Pursuant to section 7805(f), these regulations will be submitted to the Chief Counsel for Advocacy of the Small Business Administration for comment on their impact on small business.

G. *Unfunded Mandates Reform Act*

Section 202 of the Unfunded Mandates Reform Act of 1995 (UMRA) requires that agencies assess anticipated costs and benefits and take certain other actions before issuing a final rule that includes any Federal mandate that may result in expenditures in any one year by a state, local, or tribal government, in the aggregate, or by the private sector, of $100 million in 1995 dollars, updated annually for inflation. In 2019, that threshold is approximately $154 million. This rule does not include any Federal mandate that may result in expenditures by state, local, or tribal governments, or by the private sector in excess of that threshold.

H. *Executive Order 13132: Federalism*

Executive Order 13132 (entitled "Federalism") prohibits an agency from publishing any rule that has federalism implications if the rule either imposes substantial, direct compliance costs on state and local governments, and is not required by statute, or preempts state law, unless the agency meets the consultation and funding requirements of section 6 of the Executive Order. This proposed rule does not have federalism implications and does not impose substantial direct compliance costs on state and local governments or preempt state law within the meaning of the Executive Order.

Comments and Request for Public Hearing

Before these proposed regulations are adopted as final regulations, consideration will be given to any comments that are submitted timely to the IRS as prescribed in this preamble under the "Addresses" heading. The Treasury Department and the IRS request comments on all aspects of the proposed rules. See also parts II and III of the Explanation of Provisions (requesting specific comments related to the aggregate group rules in light of the with-or-without method and the election to waive allowable deductions, respectively) and parts II.C., II.D., and IV.B. of the Explanation of Provisions (requesting specific comments related to the appropriate treatment of a deconsolidating member's gross receipts history, appropriate methods of taking into account predecessors and successors for purposes of determining gross receipts of an applicable taxpayer's aggregate group, and the treatment of transactions involving partnerships engaged in a U.S. trade or business, respectively).

All comments will be available at www.regulations.gov or upon request. A public hearing will be scheduled if requested in writing by any person that timely submits written comments. If a public hearing is scheduled, notice of the date, time, and place for the public hearing will be published in the **Federal Register**.

Drafting Information

The principal authors of the proposed regulations are Azeka J. Abramoff, Sheila Ramaswamy and Karen Walny of the Office of Associate Chief Counsel (International). However, other personnel from the Treasury Department and the IRS participated in their development.

[¶ 49,822]   Proposed Amendments of Regulations (REG-105495-19), published in the Federal Register on December 17, 2019.

[Code Secs. 704, 861, 904, 905, 954, 960, 965, 1502, 6227 and 6689]

Deductions: Transition tax: Financial services income: Foreign tax credits: Foreign tax redeterminations.—Reg. §1.861-20 and amendments of Reg. §§1.704-1, 1.861-8, 1.861-8T, 1.861-9, 1.861-9T, 1.861-12, 1.861-12T, 1.861-14, 1.861-14T, 1.861-17, 1.904-4, 1.904-6, 1.904(b)-3, 1.904(g)-3, 1.905-3, 1.905-4, 1.905-5, 1.954-1, 1.954-2, 1.960-1, 1.960-2, 1.960-7, 1.965-5, 1.965-9, 1.1502-4, 1.1502-21, 301.6227-1 and 301.6689-1, relating to the allocation and apportionment of deductions and creditable foreign taxes, the definition of financial services income, foreign tax redeterminations, availability of foreign tax credits under the transition tax, and the application of the foreign tax credit limitation to consolidated groups, are proposed.

AGENCY: Internal Revenue Service (IRS), Treasury.

ACTION: Notice of proposed rulemaking.

SUMMARY: This document contains proposed regulations that provide guidance relating to the allocation and apportionment of deductions and creditable foreign taxes, the definition of financial services income, foreign tax redeterminations, availability of foreign tax credits under the transition tax, and the application of the foreign tax credit limitation to consolidated groups.

DATES: Written or electronic comments and requests for a public hearing must be received by [*INSERT DATE 60 DAYS AFTER PUBLICATION IN THE FEDERAL REGISTER*].

ADDRESSES: Send electronic submissions via the Federal eRulemaking Portal at www.regulations.gov (indicate IRS and REG-105495-19) by following the online instructions for submitting comments. Once submitted to the Federal eRulemaking Portal, comments cannot be edited or withdrawn. The Department of the Treasury (the "Treasury Department") and the IRS will publish for public availability any comment received to its public docket, whether submitted electronically or in hard copy. Send hard copy submissions to: CC:PA:LPD:PR (REG-105495-19), Room 5203, Internal Revenue Service, PO Box 7604, Ben Franklin Station, Washington, DC 20044. Submissions may be hand delivered Monday through Friday between the hours of 8 a.m. and 4 p.m. to CC:PA:LPD:PR (REG-105495-19), Courier's Desk, Internal Revenue Service, 1111 Constitution Avenue, NW., Washington, DC 20224.

FOR FURTHER INFORMATION CONTACT: Concerning the proposed regulations under §§1.861-8, 1.861-9(b), 1.861-12, 1.861-14, 1.861-17, and 1.954-2(h), Jeffrey P. Cowan, (202) 317-4924; concerning §§1.704-1, 1.861-9(e), 1.904-4(e), 1.904(b)-3, 1.904(g)-3, 1.1502-4, and 1.1502-21, Jeffrey L. Parry, (202) 317-4916; concerning §§1.861-20, 1.904-6, 1.960-1, and 1.960-7, Suzanne M. Walsh, (202) 317-4908; concerning §§1.904-4(c), 1.905-3, 1.905-4, 1.905-5, 1.954-1, 301.6227-1, and 301.6689-1, Larry R. Pounders, (202) 317-5465; concerning §§1.965-5 and 1.965-9, Karen J. Cate, (202) 317-4667; concerning submissions of comments and requests for a public hearing, Regina Johnson, (202) 317-6901 (not toll-free numbers).

SUPPLEMENTARY INFORMATION:

Background

On December 7, 2018, the Treasury Department and the IRS published proposed regulations (REG-105600-18) relating to foreign tax credits in the **Federal Register** (83 FR 63200) (the "2018 FTC proposed regulations"). Those regulations addressed several significant changes that the Tax Cuts and Jobs Act (Pub. L. 115-97, 131 Stat. 2054, 2208 (2017)) (the "TCJA") made with respect to the foreign tax credit rules and related rules for allocating and apportioning deductions in determining the foreign tax credit limitation. The preamble to those proposed regulations requested comments on how to modify the existing approaches for allocating and apportioning deductions, including in particular the rules under §1.861-17 for allocating and apportioning research and experimentation ("R&E") expenditures. The 2018 FTC proposed regulations are finalized in the Rules and Regulations section of this issue of the **Federal Register** (the "2019 FTC final regulations").

On June 25, 2012, the **Federal Register** published a notice of proposed rulemaking at 77 FR 37837 (the "2012 OFL proposed regulations") proposing rules for the coordination of the rules for determining high-taxed passive income with required adjustments to the foreign tax credit limitation in respect of capital gains and the allocation and recapture of overall foreign losses and overall domestic losses, as well as the coordination of the recapture of overall foreign losses on certain dispositions of property and other rules concerning overall foreign losses and overall domestic losses. The 2012 OFL proposed regulations are finalized in the 2019 FTC final regulations.

On November 7, 2007, the **Federal Register** published temporary regulations (T.D. 9362) at 72 FR 62771 and a notice of proposed rulemaking by cross-reference to the temporary regulations at 72 FR 62805 relating to sections 905(c), 986(a), and 6689. Portions of these temporary regulations are finalized in the 2019 FTC final regulations.

This document contains proposed regulations (the "proposed regulations") addressing the following issues: (1) the allocation and apportionment of deductions under sections 861 through 865, including new rules on the allocation and apportionment of R&E expenditures and certain deductions of life insurance companies; (2) the definition of financial services income under section 904(d)(2)(D); (3) the allocation and apportionment of creditable foreign taxes; (4) the interaction of the branch loss and dual consolidated loss recapture rules with sections 904(f) and (g); (5) the effect of foreign tax redeterminations of foreign corporations on the application of the high-tax exception described in section 954(b)(4) (including for purposes of determining tested income under section 951A(c)(2)(A)(i)(III)), and required notifications under section 905(c) to the IRS of foreign tax redeterminations and related penalty provisions; (6) the definition of foreign personal holding company income under section 954; (7) the application of the foreign tax credit disallowance under section 965(g); and (8) the application of the foreign tax credit limitation to consolidated groups.

Explanation of Provisions

I. *Allocation and Apportionment of Deductions and the Calculation of Taxable Income for Purposes of Section 904(a)*

A. *Stewardship expenses, litigation damages awards and settlement payments, net operating losses, and interest expense*

1. Stewardship expenses

Under §1.861-8(e)(4)(i), stewardship expenses are definitely related and allocable to dividends received or to be received from related corporations. This reflects a determination that stewardship expenses are, at least in part, intended to protect the shareholder's capital investment and thus are factually related to the income that arises from the investment. Before the enactment of the TCJA, taxpayers with foreign subsidiaries often included in their income foreign source income only when that income was distributed to the taxpayer. However, as a result of the enactment of sections 951A and 245A, a significant portion of the foreign source income of foreign subsidiaries is included in income on a current basis or not at all. The Treasury Department and the IRS are aware that some taxpayers may be interpreting the "dividends received, or to be received" phrase in §1.861-8(e)(4)(ii) to exclude the gross up amount treated as a dividend under section 78 (the "section 78 dividend"), as well as inclusions under section 951(a)(1), section 951A, and similar provisions, even though the stewardship expenses may be factually related to such gross income.

With respect to the allocation of stewardship expenses, income arising because of one's capital investment in a foreign corporation's stock ordinarily includes not only dividends, but also inclusions under sections 951 and 951A, as well as amounts included under sections 1291, 1293, and 1296 (the "passive foreign investment company provisions"). Therefore, the proposed regulations provide that stewardship expenses are allocated to dividends and inclusions received or accrued, or to be received or accrued, from related corporations.[1] Thus, stewardship expenses are also allocated to inclusions under sections 951 and 951A, section 78 dividends, and all amounts included under the passive foreign investment company provisions.

With respect to apportionment, the current regulations do not provide an explicit rule but instead provide examples of permissible methods. The Treasury Department and the IRS have determined that an explicit rule would provide certainty for taxpayers and the IRS on the appropriate methodology for apportioning stewardship expenses while ensuring that stewardship expenses are apportioned to gross income in a manner that reflects the purpose of the expenses to protect capital investments or to facilitate compliance with reporting, legal, or regulatory requirements. Therefore, the proposed regulations provide that stewardship expenses are apportioned based upon the relative values of a taxpayer's stock assets, as determined and characterized under §1.861-9T(g) (and, as relevant, §§1.861-12 and 1.861-13) for purposes of allocating and apportioning the taxpayer's interest expense. Therefore, a taxpayer will be required to use the same method to characterize and value its stock assets for purposes of allocating and apportioning its interest and stewardship expenses, and, in some cases as described in Part 1.A.2 of this Explanation of Provisions, certain damages payments. Accordingly, since the fair market value method may not be used for interest allocation and apportionment, it may also not be used for stewardship and certain damages payments. Conforming changes are also proposed with respect to §1.861-14T(e)(4), which provides rules for the treatment of stewardship expenses with respect to an affiliated group. See also §1.861-8(g)(18) (*Example 18*) for an example illustrating the application of the proposed rules for stewardship expenses.

The Treasury Department and the IRS are aware that stewardship expenses that are incurred to facilitate compliance with reporting, legal, or regulatory requirements may be more appropriately treated as definitely related to the gross income produced by the particular asset, or assets, whose ownership required the stewardship expenditure. For example, the owner of an entity in a particular jurisdiction might have unique reporting requirements not triggered by the ownership of a similar entity in a different jurisdiction. The Treasury Department and the IRS request comments regarding exceptions to the general rule for the allocation and apportionment of stewardship expenses where it is more appropriate to treat stewardship expenses as definitely related to a more limited class of gross income. Comments are also requested on whether it is more appropriate in certain cases to allocate and apportion stewardship expenses on a separate entity, rather than an affiliated group, basis.

The proposed regulations maintain the definition of stewardship expenses as a duplicative activity (as defined in §1.482-9(l)(3)(iii)) or a shareholder activity (as defined in §1.482-9(l)(3)(iv)). *See* proposed §1.861-8(e)(4)(ii)(A). In particular, shareholder activities are those that preserve the shareholder's capital investment or facilitate compliance with reporting, regulatory, or legal requirements. *See* §1.482-9(l)(3)(iv). However, the Treasury Department and the IRS are aware that it may be difficult for taxpayers to distinguish between stewardship expenses that result from oversight functions and expenses that are supportive in nature, as described in §1.861-8(b)(3), and are concerned that expenses may be misclassified as either stewardship or supportive expenses in certain cases. For example, day-to-day management activities do not give rise to stewardship expenses and are typically more supportive in nature. However, the distinction between day-to-day management and oversight may change over time as a taxpayer's investments change. Given these concerns, the Treasury Department and the IRS request comments regarding the definition of stewardship expenses and how to readily distinguish such expenses from supportive expenses that are allocated and apportioned under §1.861-8(b)(3).

The proposed regulations extend the treatment of stewardship expenses to cover expenses incurred with respect to a partnership. *See* proposed §1.861-8(e)(4)(ii)(D). Rules similar to those with respect to corporations apply to allocate and apportion stewardship expenses incurred with respect to partnerships.

Finally, the Treasury Department and the IRS are considering whether additional changes to the rules for allocating and apportioning stewardship and similar expenses are appropriate in light of the enactment of the TCJA, and in order to better reflect modern business practices that are increasingly global and mobile in nature. Comments are requested on this topic.

2. Litigation damages awards, prejudgment interest, and settlement payments

The current rule for the allocation and apportionment of legal and accounting fees and expenses in §1.861-8(e)(5) does not specifically address damages awards, prejudgment interest, or settlement payments arising from product liability and similar claims. The Treasury Department and the IRS are aware that large, unplanned, and relatively rare expenses can have a significant effect on the calculation of a taxpayer's taxable income and foreign tax credit limitation, and, in the absence of clear rules, disputes have arisen regarding the proper treatment of such expenses. Proposed §1.861-8(e)(5) provides that deductions for damages awards, prejudgment interest, and settlement payments arising from product liability and similar or related claims are allocated to the class or classes of gross income produced by the specific sales of products or services that gave rise to the claims for damage or injury. Damages, prejudgment interest, and settlement payments related to events incident to the production of goods or provision of services, such as damages for injuries caused by industrial accidents, are allocated to the class of gross income produced by the assets involved in the event and, if necessary, apportioned between groupings based on the relative value of the assets in such groupings. In the case of claims made by investors that arise from corporate negligence, fraud, or other malfeasance, the proposed regulations provide that damages, prejudgment interest, and settlement payments paid by the corporation are allocated and apportioned based on the value of all the corporation's

---

[1] Duplicative activities or shareholder activities giving rise to stewardship expenses can only be performed with respect to members of a controlled group as described in §1.482-9(l)(3)(iii)-(iv). Accordingly, relatedness in the context of stewardship expenses includes taxpayers that are members of the same controlled group as defined in §1.482-1(i)(6). A taxpayer could incur stewardship expenses with respect to a related foreign corporation that is a passive foreign investment company (in addition to a related foreign corporation that is a controlled foreign corporation).

assets. In general, the deductions are allocated and apportioned to the statutory or residual groupings to which the related income would be assigned if recognized in the taxable year in which the deductions are allowed.

3. Net operating loss deductions

Under current rules, a net operating loss deduction is allocated and apportioned in the same manner as the deductions giving rise to the net operating loss deduction. However, the rule does not specify how the statutory and residual grouping components of a net operating loss are determined. *See* § 1.861-8(e)(8). The proposed regulations provide that a net operating loss is assigned to the statutory and residual groupings by reference to the losses in each statutory or residual grouping (determined without regard to adjustments made under section 904(b)) that are not allocated to reduce income in a different grouping in the taxable year of the loss. *See* proposed § 1.861-8(e)(8)(i). Furthermore, the proposed regulations clarify that a net operating loss deduction for a taxable year is allocated and apportioned by reference to the statutory and residual grouping components of the net operating loss that is deducted in the taxable year. *See* proposed § 1.861-8(e)(8)(ii). Finally, the proposed regulations provide that except as provided in regulations, for example, in § 1.904(g)-3, a partial net operating loss deduction is treated as ratably comprising the components of the net operating loss.[2] *See* id.

In connection with the proposed regulations under section 250, comments requested clarification on the application of § 1.861-8(e)(8) with respect to net operating losses arising prior to the enactment of the TCJA when the net operating loss is deducted in a post-TCJA year for purposes of applying section 250 as the operative section. *See* 84 FR 8188 (March 6, 2019). These comments will be addressed as part of finalizing those proposed regulations.

4. Application of the exempt income/asset rule to insurance companies in connection with certain dividends and tax-exempt interest

As explained in Part II.B.2 of the Summary of Comments and Explanation of Revisions to the 2019 FTC final regulations, one comment to the 2018 FTC proposed regulations suggested that insurance companies reduce exempt income and assets to reflect prorated amounts of dividends and tax exempt interest. *See* sections 805(a)(4), 807, 812, and 832(b)(5)(B). The 2019 FTC final regulations do not address this issue, and the proposed regulations do not adopt this comment.

Under subchapter L, a nonlife insurance company includes in income its underwriting income, which consists of premiums earned on insurance contracts during the taxable year less losses incurred and expenses incurred. The proration rules reduce the company's losses incurred by the "applicable percentage" of tax exempt interest or deductible dividends received. *See* section 832(b)(5)(B). For a life insurance company, the proration rules apply in the case of tax exempt interest by reducing the closing balance of reserve items by the "policyholder's share" (currently a fixed percentage, originally intended to be the portion of tax favored investment income used to fund the company's obligations to policyholders) of tax exempt interest. *See* sections 807(b)(1)(B) and 812. Similarly, a life insurance company is allowed a dividends received deduction (DRD) for intercorporate dividends from non-affiliates only in proportion to the "company's share" of the dividends, but not for the policyholder's share. *See* section 805(a)(4)(A). Fully deductible dividends from affiliates are excluded from proration for life insurance companies if the dividends are not themselves distributions from tax exempt interest or from dividend income that would not be fully deductible if received directly by the taxpayer.

While the mechanics of the proration rules differ depending on whether a company is a life or nonlife insurance company and whether the amount relates to dividends or tax exempt interest, the purpose of those provisions is the same. That is, the policyholder's share or applicable percentage of dividends and tax exempt interest should not create a double benefit by reason of a DRD or section 103 tax exemption for interest in the first instance and a reduction to income (via increases in unpaid losses and reserves during the taxable year) in the second. Regardless of the mechanics, however, the policyholder's share and applicable percentage adjustments do not change the fact that tax exempt interest and (for a nonlife insurance company) the applicable percentage of dividends eligible for DRDs remain exempt from U.S. tax. Including those exempt amounts and the corresponding exempt assets in the apportionment formula in allocating expenses under § 1.861-8T(d)(2)(i)(B), as the comment suggests, would effectively apportion reserve deductions (which already do not include the disallowed deductions deemed to be attributable to the exempt income, except in the case of the policyholder's share of life insurance DRDs) to exempt U.S. source income, with the result that those deductions would reduce unrelated U.S. source income, in contravention of the rule in § 1.861-8T(d)(2)(i)(B). *See also Travelers Insurance Company v. United States*, 303 F.3d 1373 (2002).

The current regulations already provide the appropriate rules in this area. Section 1.861-8T(d)(2)(ii)(B) provides that the policyholder's share of dividends received by a life insurance company is treated as tax exempt income notwithstanding the partial disallowance of the DRD, and § 1.861-14T(h) provides for the direct allocation to the dividends of an amount of reserve expenses equal to the disallowed portion of the DRDs. The current regulations do not provide a special rule for either tax exempt interest of a life insurance company or DRDs and tax exempt interest of a nonlife insurance company because, when a policyholder's share or applicable percentage is accounted for as either a reserve adjustment or a reduction to losses incurred, no further modification to the generally applicable rules is required to ensure that the appropriate amount of expenses are apportioned to U.S. source income.

Nevertheless, in order to provide greater clarity, the proposed regulations provide in proposed § 1.861-8(d)(2)(ii)(B), (d)(2)(v), and (e)(16) the effect of certain deduction limitations on the treatment of income and assets generating dividends received deductions and tax exempt interest held by insurance companies. More specifically, the proposed regulations provide that in the case of insurance companies, the term exempt income includes dividends for which a deduction is provided by sections 243(a)(1) and (2) and 245, without regard to the proration rules disallowing a portion of the deduction. Similarly, the term exempt income includes tax exempt interest without regard to the proration rules. These provisions apply on a company wide basis and therefore include each separate account of the company. Two examples are provided in proposed § 1.861-8(d)(2)(v)(B) that illustrate the application of these rules.

5. Other requests for comments on expense allocation

The Treasury Department and the IRS continue to study the rules for allocating and apportioning interest deductions. In addition, the Treasury Department and the IRS expect the implementation of section 864(f) (which is effective for taxable years beginning after December 31, 2020) will have a significant impact on the effect of interest expense apportionment and will necessitate a reexamination of the existing expense allocation rules. Therefore, the Treasury Department and the IRS are studying whether further guidance with respect to allocation and apportionment of interest expense, taking into account the changes made by the TCJA and the future implementation of section 864(f), is required. Comments are requested on this topic.

The Treasury Department and the IRS are also considering whether rules providing for the capitalization and amortization of certain expenses solely for purposes of § 1.861-9 may better reflect asset values under the tax book value method. For example, solely for purposes of § 1.861-9, research and experimental expenditures and advertising expenses could be treated as if they were capitalized and amortized. Comments are requested on this topic.

---

[2] A partial net operating loss deduction occurs when the full net operating loss is not deductible in the carryover year.

As noted in Part III.B.4.iii of the Summary of Comments and Explanation of Revisions to the 2019 FTC final regulations, the Treasury Department and the IRS are studying whether additional rules for allocating and apportioning expenses to foreign branch category income or limiting the amount of the gross income reallocated as a result of certain disregarded payments are appropriate. Comments are requested on whether such special rules would more accurately reflect the business profits of a foreign branch, while maintaining administrability for taxpayers and the IRS.

B. *Certain loans made by partnerships to partners*

The 2018 FTC proposed regulations included rules addressing the source and separate category of interest income and expense related to loans to a partnership by a U.S. person (or a member of its affiliated group) that owns an interest (directly or indirectly) in the partnership. These rules were finalized in the 2019 FTC final regulations. *See* § 1.861.9(e)(8).

As discussed in Part II.C.1 of the Summary of Comments and Explanation of Revisions of the 2019 FTC final regulations, several comments to the 2018 FTC proposed regulations requested that the rules under § 1.861-9(e)(8) with respect to specified partnership loans be expanded to cover loans made by a partnership to a partner (an "upstream partnership loan"). The Treasury Department and the IRS agree with comments that rules addressing upstream partnership loans would reduce distortions that could otherwise affect the foreign tax credit limitation. Therefore, the comments are adopted in proposed § 1.861-9(e)(9)(ii), which generally provides that, to the extent the borrower in an upstream partnership loan transaction takes into account both interest expense and interest income with respect to the same loan, the interest income is assigned to the same statutory and residual groupings as those groupings from which the matching amount of interest expense is deducted, as determined under the allocation and apportionment rules in § § 1.861-9 through 1.861-13. Additionally, proposed § 1.861-9(e)(9)(i) provides that, for purposes of applying the allocation and apportionment rules, the borrower does not take into account as an asset its proportionate share of the loan, as otherwise provided under § 1.861-9(e)(2) and (3). Proposed § 1.861-9(e)(8)(iv) also applies the upstream partnership loan rules to transactions that are not loans but that give rise to deductions that are allocated and apportioned in the same manner as interest expense under § 1.861-9T(b). An anti-avoidance rule similar to the rule in § 1.861-9(e)(8)(iii) is included to cover back-to-back third-party loans that are intended to circumvent the purposes of the rules. *See* proposed § 1.861-9(e)(8)(iii). These rules are being proposed in order to provide taxpayers an additional opportunity to comment on the rule.

Additionally, the Treasury Department and the IRS are aware that some taxpayers may be converting existing partnership debt structures that were used to increase a taxpayer's foreign tax credit limitation before the issuance of § 1.861-9(e)(8) from partnership debt into partnership equity that provides for guaranteed payments for the use of capital. The taxpayer then takes the position that the guaranteed payments are neither allocated and apportioned under the rules in § 1.861-9 nor included in subpart F income by reason of § 1.954-2(h).

Guaranteed payments for the use of capital are similar to a loan from the partner to the partnership because the payment is for the use of money and is generally deductible. *See* section 707(c). Because these arrangements raise the same policy concerns as ordinary debt instruments, the proposed regulations revise § 1.861-9(b) and § 1.954-2(h)(2)(i) explicitly to provide that guaranteed payments for the use of capital described in section 707(c) are treated similarly to interest deductions for purposes of allocating and apportioning deductions under § § 1.861-8 through 1.861-14 and are treated as income equivalent to interest under section 954(c)(1)(E). No inference is intended as to whether or not § 1.861-9T(b) or § 1.954-2(h)(2) include guaranteed payments for taxable years before the proposed regulations are applicable.

C. *Treatment of assets connected with capitalized, deferred, or disallowed interest*

Section 1.861-12T(f)(1) provides that, in certain circumstances, where interest expense that is capitalized, deferred, or disallowed under a provision of the Code, the adjusted basis or fair market value of the asset to which the interest expense is connected is reduced by the principal amount of the interest that is capitalized, deferred, or disallowed. One comment with respect to the 2018 FTC proposed regulations recommended that the Treasury Department and the IRS consider narrowing the scope of the rule in § 1.861-12T(f)(1) to prevent taxpayers from taking overly expansive views of the rule in order to minimize the value of controlled foreign corporation ("CFC") stock that attracts interest expense to reduce the foreign tax credit limitation. In response to the comment, the proposed regulations clarify what it means for an asset to be connected with indebtedness, modify the existing example, and add a new example. *See* proposed § 1.861-12(f).

D. *Treatment of section 818(f) reserve expenses for consolidated groups*

Section 818(f)(1) provides that the deduction for life insurance reserves and certain other deductions ("section 818(f) expenses") are treated as items which cannot definitely be allocated to an item or class of gross income. Therefore, when a life insurance company computes its foreign tax credit limitation, its section 818(f) expenses generally reduce its U.S. source income and foreign source income ratably. However, issues arise as to how to allocate and apportion section 818(f) expenses if the life insurance company is a member of an affiliated group of corporations (including both life and nonlife members) (the group, "life-nonlife consolidated group") that join in filing a consolidated return.

The Treasury Department and the IRS are aware of at least five potential methods for allocating section 818(f) expenses in a life-nonlife consolidated group. First, the expenses might be allocated solely among items of the life insurance company that has the reserves ("separate entity method"). Second, to the extent the life insurance company has engaged in a reinsurance arrangement that constitutes an intercompany transaction (as defined in § 1.1502-13(b)(1)), the expenses might be allocated in a manner that achieves single entity treatment between the ceding member and the assuming member ("limited single entity method"). Third, the expenses might be allocated among items of all life insurance members ("life subgroup method"). Fourth, the expenses might be allocated among items of all members of the consolidated group (including both life and non-life members) ("single entity method"). Fifth, the expenses might be allocated based on a facts and circumstances analysis ("facts and circumstances method").

In response to the request for comments in the 2018 FTC proposed regulations, the Treasury Department and the IRS have received comments advocating for certain of the aforementioned allocation methods. One comment recommended an allocation method similar to the single entity method. The comment proposed that, if all members of a consolidated group were treated as a single corporation, and if that corporation would constitute a life insurance company, then section 818(f) expenses might be allocated and apportioned to all members of the consolidated group, including nonlife members of a life-nonlife consolidated group.

Two other comments disagreed with the single entity method. These comments proposed that section 818(f) expenses generally be allocated on the separate entity method. However, if the facts and circumstances demonstrate a sufficient factual relationship between the expense and the income of more than one life insurance company, these comments proposed that such expenses might be allocated based on the facts and circumstances method. The comments did not provide examples of when facts and circumstances would demonstrate a sufficient relationship to qualify for this treatment.

The Treasury Department and the IRS decline to adopt the single entity method in the proposed regulations. Section 818(f) only applies to a life insurance company; thus, section 818(f) expenses should not be allocated to nonlife members of a consolidated group. The Treasury Department and the IRS also decline to adopt the facts and circumstances method because a broad facts and circumstances approach would introduce substantial uncertainty into the tax system and would be difficult to administer.

The Treasury Department and the IRS considered adopting the life subgroup method in the proposed regulations. This method would reflect a single entity approach for life insurance companies that operate businesses and manage assets and liabilities on a group basis. Under this paradigm, section 818(f) expenses would be treated as not definitely related to an item or class of gross income of the entire life subgroup for purposes of calculating the foreign tax credit limitation, and therefore generally ratably reduce U.S. source income and foreign source income of the life subgroup.

The Treasury Department and the IRS also considered adopting the separate entity method. The separate entity method would allocate and apportion section 818(f) expenses on a separate company basis. This method is consistent with the Code because section 818(f) expenses generally are computed on a separate company basis and relate to the liabilities of a specific life insurance company. In addition, this method is consistent with the treatment of reserves when members of a consolidated group engage in an intercompany transaction. Under § 1.1502-13(e)(2)(ii)(A), direct insurance transactions between members of a consolidated group are accounted for by both members on a separate entity basis. For example, if one member provides life insurance coverage for another member with respect to its employees, the premiums, reserve increases and decreases, and death benefit payments are determined and taken into account by both members on a separate entity basis (rather than on a single entity basis under the general rules of § 1.1502-13). *See also* § 1.1502-13(e)(2)(ii)(B)(2) (providing that reserves resulting from intercompany reinsurance transactions are determined on a separate entity basis).

After considering both methods, proposed § 1.861-14(h)(1) adopts the separate entity method. As noted previously, this method generally is consistent with section 818(f) and with the separate entity treatment of reserves under § 1.1502-13(e)(2). Nevertheless, the Treasury Department and the IRS are concerned that this method may create opportunities for consolidated groups to use intercompany transactions to shift their section 818(f) expenses and achieve a more desirable foreign tax credit result. Accordingly, the Treasury Department and the IRS request comments on whether a life subgroup method more accurately reflects the relationship between section 818(f) expenses and the income producing activities of the life subgroup as a whole, and whether the life subgroup method is less susceptible to abuse because it might prevent a consolidated group from inflating its foreign tax credit limitation through intercompany transfers of assets, reinsurance transactions, or transfers of section 818(f) expenses. The Treasury Department and the IRS also request comments on whether an anti-abuse rule may be appropriate to address concerns with the separate entity method, and regarding the appropriate application of § 1.1502-13(c) to neutralize the ancillary effects of separate-entity computation of insurance reserves, such as the computation of limitations under section 904.

E. *Allocation and apportionment of R&E expenditures*

Part I.G of the Explanation of Provisions of the 2018 FTC proposed regulations discussed the interaction between the current rules for allocating and apportioning R&E expenditures and the changes made to section 904(d) by the TCJA, and requested comments on how the regulations should be revised to account for the new category in section 904(d)(1)(A) (the "section 951A category"). The comments received are addressed in this Part I.E.

1. Relevant class of gross income and application of the gross income method

Several comments to the 2018 FTC proposed regulations recommended that the regulations for allocating and apportioning R&E expenditures under § 1.861-17 be revised to preclude allocation and apportionment of R&E expenditures to the section 951A category. The comments stated that R&E expenditures are incurred by a U.S. taxpayer to develop intangible property that cannot generate income in the section 951A category, which is limited to inclusions under section 951A ("GILTI inclusions") and the related section 78 dividend in respect of deemed paid taxes. Further, to the extent a GILTI inclusion is attributable to a CFC's income derived from intangible property developed by the worldwide group, the comments stated that the intangible property must have either been developed by the CFC or a CFC affiliate (in which case the R&E expenditures were not borne by the U.S. taxpayer), or licensed or acquired by the CFC from a U.S. affiliate, which would require that the U.S. affiliate take into account an arm's length royalty, gain on transfer, or a deemed income amount under section 367(d) to which its R&E expenditures should be allocated.

The Treasury Department and the IRS agree with the comments that the rules under § 1.861-17 should be modified to reflect the fact that R&E expenditures that are deductible under section 174 generally give rise to intangible property, and that under the rules in sections 367(d) and 482, the person incurring such R&E expenditures must be compensated properly when such intangible property gives rise to income. Therefore, proposed § 1.861-17(b) provides that the rules in that section are premised on the fact that successful R&E expenditures ultimately result in the creation of intangible property (as defined in section 367(d)(4)) and, therefore, R&E expenditures ordinarily are considered deductions that are definitely related to all gross intangible income reasonably connected with the relevant Standard Industrial Classification Manual code ("SIC code") category (or categories) of the taxpayer and so are allocable to all items of gross intangible income related to the SIC code category (or categories) as a class. Gross intangible income is defined as all gross income earned by a taxpayer that is attributable, in whole or in part, to intangible property derived from R&E expenditures and does not include dividends or any amounts included under section 951, 951A, or 1293. *See* proposed § 1.861-17(b)(2). As a result, when applying § 1.861-17 to section 904 as the operative section, because a U.S. taxpayer's gross intangible income, as defined in the proposed regulations, does not include income assigned to the section 951A category, none of its R&E expenditures are allocated or apportioned to the section 951A category.

Under § 1.861-17(c) and (d), a taxpayer may elect to apportion R&E expenditures, in excess of amounts exclusively apportioned to the place the R&E is performed under § 1.861-17(b), on the basis of either sales or gross income. In contrast to the sales method, the gross income method of apportioning R&E expenditures (1) limits taxpayers to exclusively apportion only 25 percent of R&E expenditures based on the place of research activities (instead of 50 percent under the sales method), and (2) requires the apportionment to or among the statutory groupings to be at least half of what would have been apportioned under the sales method. These limits reflect concerns that the gross income method could produce inappropriate results in cases where the types of gross income recognized by the taxpayer in the statutory and residual groupings in a SIC code category are different. For example, if a taxpayer sells products incorporating its intangible property in the United States but earns royalties from licensing its intangible property used by others to make sales abroad, comparing the gross income from sales, which includes value attributable to other factors in addition to intangible property, to the gross royalty income will generally distort the extent to which the R&E expenditures produce U.S. and foreign source income from intangible property. In such cases, the gross income method is inconsistent with the general principle under § 1.861-8T(c) that the method of apportionment "reflect to a reasonably close extent the factual relationship between the deduction and the grouping of gross income." In comparison, the sales method requires that taxpayers use a single, consistent measure — gross receipts from sales and services — to attribute R&E expenditures to their various groupings and, therefore, more clearly reflects the anticipated income expected to be derived from successful R&E expenditures.

Therefore, the proposed regulations eliminate the optional gross income method and require R&E expenditures in excess of the amount exclusively apportioned under § 1.861-17(b) to be apportioned among the statutory and residual groupings within the class of gross intangible income on the basis of the relative amounts of gross receipts from sales and services in each grouping. *See* proposed § 1.861-17(d). For this purpose, gross receipts are assigned to the grouping to which the gross intangible income attributable to the sale or service is assigned. For example, where the taxpayer licenses intangible property to a CFC which, in turn, sells products or services incorporating the intangible property, the gross receipts of the CFC are assigned to a grouping based on the source and character of the related royalty included by the taxpayer. Proposed § 1.861-17(d)(1)(iii). This rule addresses concerns that the Treasury Department and the IRS have had since before the TCJA's enactment that taxpayers would assign the gross receipts from CFC sales to U.S. customers to the residual grouping for U.S. source income while arguing that the related royalty income earned by the U.S. company that owns the intangible property can be treated as foreign source income, with the mismatch resulting in an inflation of R&E expenditures apportioned to U.S. source income. The proposed regulations also clarify that the sales method applies to income from services.

Under § 1.861-17(a)(2)(ii), the relevant SIC code categories are determined by reference to the three digit classification of the SIC code. Proposed § 1.861-17(b)(3)(iv) clarifies the rules relating to goods or property that are described in the SIC code category for "wholesale trade" or "retail trade." The purpose of this rule is to match R&E expenditures with a taxpayer's core business and minimize the number of a taxpayer's SIC code categories. This rule provides that vertically integrated taxpayers that perform upstream activities (for example, extraction or manufacturing) before downstream wholesale and retail functions must aggregate their wholesale and retail R&E expenditures and sales with their R&E expenditures and sales in the most closely related three-digit SIC code category. A taxpayer cannot use a SIC code category within the wholesale or retail trade divisions unless its business is generally limited to sales-related activities. Taxpayers engaged in both wholesale and retail trade, but not related upstream activities, are not required to aggregate their wholesale and retail R&E expenditures and sales.

Comments are requested on whether a different classification method that takes into account more recent changes in the economy and business practices should be used. For example, comments are requested on whether NAICS codes would be more appropriate.

Comments to § 1.861-17 were also received in connection with the proposed regulations under section 250. *See* 84 FR 8188 (March 6, 2019). Further changes to the rules for allocating and apportioning R&E expenditures will be considered as part of addressing comments in finalizing those regulations.

2. Elimination of legally mandated R&E and increased exclusive apportionment of R&E

Under § 1.861-17(a)(4), R&E expenditures that are undertaken solely to meet legal requirements ("legally mandated R&E") imposed by a political entity and that cannot reasonably be expected to generate amounts of gross income (beyond de minimis amounts) outside a single geographic source are allocated directly to gross income within the geographic source imposing the requirement. A rule similar to the legally mandated R&E rule existed in regulations issued in 1977 that allocated and apportioned R&E expenditures ("the 1977 regulations").

Since the adoption of the legally mandated R&E rule in the 1977 regulations, the Treasury Department and the IRS have observed that taxpayers rarely rely on the legally mandated R&E rule. In particular, legal requirements for certain products may significantly overlap between multiple jurisdictions because those jurisdictions have similar legal requirements that relate to areas such as consumer safety, pollution, or pharmaceutical products. In addition, multiple jurisdictions may have similar legal requirements because of multilateral trade and investment agreements or because taxpayers choose to sell their products only in markets with similar requirements. See, for example, IRS Coordinated Issue Biotech and Pharmaceutical Industries Legally Mandated R&E Expense (June 18, 2003) (discussing the International Conference on Harmonization, subsequently the International Council for Harmonization, and its role in rationalizing and harmonizing pharmaceutical regulations in multiple jurisdictions). To reflect the changing international business environment and simplify the regulations with respect to R&E, the proposed regulations eliminate the legally mandated R&E rule.

Under § 1.861-17(b), an exclusive apportionment of R&E expenditures is made if activities representing more than 50 percent of the R&E expenditures were performed in a particular geographic location, such as the United States. Under § 1.861-17(b)(1)(ii), for taxpayers electing the gross income method, 25 percent of R&E expenditures is exclusively apportioned to the geographic location where the R&E activities accounting for more than 50 percent of the deductible expenses were incurred. Under § 1.861-17(b)(1)(i), for taxpayers electing the sales method, 50 percent of R&E expenditures are exclusively apportioned to the geographic location where the R&E activities accounting for more than 50 percent of the deductible expenses were incurred. After this initial exclusive apportionment, the remainder of the taxpayer's R&E expenditures are apportioned under either the sales or gross income methods.

The 1977 regulations also included a rule similar to a rule in the current regulations at § 1.861-17(b)(2). Under this rule, taxpayers may demonstrate to the satisfaction of the Commissioner that an even higher amount of R&E expenditures should be exclusively apportioned to a geographic location. According to the current regulations, the exclusive apportionment rules are based on the understanding that R&E may be more valuable where it is undertaken because R&E benefits products all of which may be sold in the nearest market but only some of which may be sold in foreign markets, and R&E is often used in the nearest market first before it is used in other markets. Therefore, under the increased exclusive apportionment rule, a taxpayer may establish to the satisfaction of the Commissioner that one or both of these conditions are satisfied—that is, its research is expected to have a particularly limited or long delayed application outside the geographic area where the research is performed, such that a greater amount of R&E expenditures should be initially exclusively apportioned.

Similar to the legally mandated rule, the Treasury Department and the IRS have observed that taxpayers have rarely used the current increased exclusive apportionment rule since the issuance of the 1977 regulations. Moreover, when it has been used, the facts and circumstances nature of the analysis has caused hard-to-resolve disagreements between the Commissioner and taxpayers. Changes in the international business environment have also contributed to the decreased utilization of this rule. Accordingly, the proposed regulations eliminate the increased exclusive apportionment rule.

Finally, proposed § 1.861-17(b) clarifies that the exclusive apportionment rule applies only to section 904 as the operative section. *See also* Part I.E.1 of this Explanation of Provisions (noting that comments were received in connection with proposed regulations under section 250 and that further changes will be considered as part of addressing comments in finalizing those regulations).

3. Sales made by other entities

The sales method for apportioning R&E expenditures provides that gross receipts from sales of products or provision of services within a relevant SIC code category by controlled parties of the taxpayer are taken into account in apportioning the taxpayer's R&E expenditures if the controlled party is reasonably expected to benefit from the taxpayer's research and experimentation. Under § 1.861-17(c)(3)(iv), the sales of controlled parties that enter a valid cost sharing arrangement ("CSA") with a taxpayer are excluded from the apportionment formula because the controlled party is not expected to benefit from the taxpayer's remaining R&E expenditures.

Proposed § 1.861-17 clarifies the treatment of CSAs in two respects. First, consistent with § 1.482-7, the taxpayer's R&E expenditures allocated and apportioned under § 1.861-17 do not include any amounts that are not deductible by reason of the second sentence under § 1.482-7(j)(3)(i) (relating to cost sharing transaction payments from a controlled party). Second, the proposed regulations clarify that the exclusion of the controlled party's gross receipts applies only for purposes of apportioning those R&E expenditures that are intangible development costs with respect to the CSA. If a taxpayer who enters a CSA also incurs R&E expenditures that are not intangible development costs with respect to the CSA, then those expenses would be apportioned under the generally applicable rules, including the rules concerning controlled party sales. *See* proposed § 1.861-17(d)(4)(v).

One comment suggested that § 1.861-17 be modified to provide that a taxpayer's R&E expenditures that are funded by a foreign affiliate under a contract research arrangement should be directly allocated to the taxpayer's income from such arrangements. The terms of the contract research arrangement are not clear from the comment, and it is unclear whether the described expenditures that are reimbursed by a foreign affiliate are paid or incurred by the taxpayer to develop or improve a product in connection with the taxpayer's trade or business. *See* §§ 1.174-1 and 1.174-2. If the expenditures are not paid or incurred by the taxpayer to develop or improve a product in connection with its trade or business, the taxpayer may not deduct them under section 174. As a result, § 1.861-17 would not apply to these expenditures. The expenditures would instead be allocated and apportioned under the general rules in § 1.861-8 on the basis of the factual relationship of deductions to gross income. *See* § 1.861-8(a)(2). The Treasury Department and the IRS request comments on whether contract research arrangements involving expenditures reimbursed by a foreign affiliate are generally paid or incurred by the taxpayer in connection with its trade or business such that a deduction under section 174 is allowable, and whether a special rule for such expenditures should be considered.

Another comment suggested a special rule for "licensor models" whereby CFCs pay royalties to compensate for a taxpayer's R&E expenditures. The comment suggested that in order to avoid allocation and apportionment of R&E expenditures to the section 951A category, the activities of the licensee CFC should be excluded for purposes of apportioning the licensor's R&E expenditures and should be treated similarly to cost sharing arrangements. The comment suggested in the alternative that if the CFC sales are not excluded entirely, that R&E expenditures should be netted against the royalty income to which the R&E expenditures are apportioned.

The Treasury Department and the IRS agree that R&E expenditures should be allocated and apportioned solely with respect to the gross intangible income of the taxpayer rather than the net income of a licensee, and therefore not allocated and apportioned to the section 951A category. *See* Part I.D.1 of this Explanation of Provisions. Unlike in the case of a CSA, however, a licensor earns royalties or other forms of gross intangible income from the use of its intangible property, and it would not be appropriate to exclude such royalties in allocating R&E expenditures of the licensor. The proposed regulations require the use of the sales method, which would effectively attribute R&E expenditures to the taxpayer's royalty income based on the proportion of the gross receipts of the licensees over the total gross receipts of the taxpayer and its licensees. This approach is preferable to the comment's alternative recommendation of netting R&E expenditures against the amount of royalties because taxpayers may earn different types of gross intangible income (for example, from sales of property as well as royalties) and comparing such amounts could lead to distortive results.

Finally, under § 1.861-17(c)(3)(ii) and (f)(3), sales made by controlled corporations and partnerships taken into account to apportion R&E expenditures are reduced to reflect the taxpayer's percentage ownership of such entities. This reduction is inappropriate because the taxpayer's gross intangible income is not dependent on its percentage ownership of the entity to which it transfers intangible property. The proposed regulations, therefore, eliminate the rule reducing sales of controlled corporations that are taken into account and include partnership sales to the same extent as those made by controlled corporations.

F. *Application of section 904(b) to net operating losses*

The 2018 FTC proposed regulations included a rule in § 1.904(b)-3(d) coordinating the application of section 904(b)(4) with sections 904(f) and 904(g), which apply after section 904(b)(4). This rule is finalized substantially as proposed in the 2019 FTC final regulations. However, the 2018 FTC proposed regulations did not coordinate any of the adjustments required under section 904(b) with the net operating loss provisions. Therefore, the proposed regulations include a coordination rule. Under proposed § 1.904(b)-3(d)(2), for purposes of determining the source and separate category of a net operating loss, the separate limitation loss and overall foreign loss rules of section 904(f) and the overall domestic loss rules of section 904(g) are applied without taking into account the adjustments required under section 904(b). The Treasury Department and the IRS have determined this rule is appropriate because the amount of the net operating loss eligible to be carried to another year under section 172 is not affected by the adjustments required by section 904(b).

II. *Foreign Tax Credit Limitation Under Section 904*

A. *Definition of financial services entity*

Section 904(d)(2)(D) provides that financial services income can only be received by a person "predominantly engaged in the active conduct of a banking, insurance, financing, or similar business." Under current law, the principal significance of this provision is that under section 904(d)(2)(C), passive income of such a person is not assigned to the passive category. The preamble to the 2018 FTC proposed regulations noted that the Treasury Department and the IRS were considering modifications to the gross income-based test for determining financial services entity ("FSE") status and requested comments in this regard. One comment was received requesting that any future modifications not affect the classification of income derived by a substantial (and genuinely active) financial services group. The Treasury Department and IRS agree that a substantial and genuinely active financial services group should be included in the definition of an FSE.

However, numerous places in the Code use similar concepts and, at times, the same terms, but provide different definitions (even when largely overlapping in application). The Treasury Department and IRS have determined that interpretive guidance should be simplified and made consistent where possible and appropriate. For example, section 954(h) in the subpart F rules defines "predominantly engaged in the active conduct of a banking, financing, or similar business" (which in the case of a lending or finance business, requires more than 70 percent of the gross income be derived directly from transactions with unrelated customers); section 1297(b)(2)(B) in the passive foreign investment company ("PFIC") rules defines "active conduct of an insurance business by a qualifying insurance corporation"; and section 953(e)(3) defines the term "qualifying insurance company" in order to determine the amount of passive income excluded from subpart F income as income derived in the active conduct of an insurance business under section 954(i).

In order to promote simplification and greater consistency with other Code provisions that have complementary policy objectives, proposed § 1.904-4(e)(2) modifies the definition of an FSE by adopting a definition of "predominantly engaged in the active conduct of a banking, insurance, financing, or similar business" and "income derived in the active conduct of a banking, insurance, financing, or similar business" that is generally consistent with sections 954(h), 1297(b)(2)(B), and 953(e). Conforming changes are made to the rules for affiliated groups in proposed § 1.904-4(e)(2)(ii) and partnerships in proposed § 1.904-4(e)(2)(i)(C).

Comments are requested on whether additional guidance is needed with respect to section 954(h) (including in particular section 954(h)(2)(B)(ii), which authorizes the Treasury Department to issue regulations regarding corporations not licensed as a bank in the United States) and section 952(c)(1)(B)(vi) (defining a qualified financial institution for purposes of the qualified deficit rules).

In addition, when the regulations defining an FSE were originally promulgated in 1988, section 904(d)(1)(C) assigned financial services income to its own separate category. This separate category was repealed in 2004, effective for taxable years beginning after 2006, but the rules in section 904(d)(2)(C) and (D) were retained. The proposed regulations make additional clarifying changes to reflect the repeal of the separate category for financial services income.

Finally, in 2004, a definition of financial services group was added in section 904(d)(2)(C)(ii) which was based on the definition of an affiliated group under section 1504(a) but expanded to include insurance companies and foreign corporations. While the current regulations already include foreign corporations as part of an affiliated group, proposed § 1.904-4(e)(2)(ii) conforms the definition of an affiliated group to also include insurance companies referenced in section 1504(b)(2).

B. *Allocation and apportionment of foreign income taxes*

As explained in Part III.G of the Summary of Comments and Explanation of Revisions to the 2019 FTC final regulations, the Treasury Department and the IRS have determined that additional guidance regarding the allocation and apportionment to separate categories of creditable foreign income taxes in § 1.904-6 is warranted. As a result of changes made by the TCJA, the accurate allocation and apportionment of foreign income taxes to the gross income to which they relate has taken on increased importance. See, for example, sections 245A(d), 960, 965(g), and § 1.861-8(e)(6) (allocating the deduction for foreign income taxes, including at the level of a CFC, to statutory and residual groupings). Therefore, taxpayers will benefit from increased certainty on how to match foreign income taxes with income, particularly in the case of differences in how a U.S. taxable base and foreign taxable base are computed with respect to the same transaction. Furthermore, because these rules are relevant in numerous contexts outside of section 904, the general rules in §1.904-6 (which address allocating and apportioning taxes to separate categories) have been moved to new proposed §1.861-20 and generalized to apply for purposes of allocating and apportioning foreign income taxes to statutory and residual groupings. Rules specific to the allocation and apportionment of foreign income taxes to separate categories remain in proposed §1.904-6. Conforming changes are proposed to §§1.704-1(b)(4)(viii)(*d*)(*1*) and 1.960-1(d), which currently rely on the "principles of" §1.904-6, as well as §1.965-5(b)(2) (in the case of foreign corporation taxable years beginning after December 31, 2019).

Current §1.904-6 provides that the allocation and apportionment of foreign tax expense to a section 904 separate category is made on the basis of the income as computed under foreign law on which the tax is imposed; foreign tax is allocated to the separate category to which the income included in the foreign tax base would be assigned under Federal income tax principles. *See* 1.904-6(a)(1). If the foreign tax base includes income in more than one separate category, the tax is apportioned among the separate categories on the basis of the relative amounts of foreign taxable income in each category. In making this determination, foreign law rules apply, with certain modifications, to determine the foreign law deductions that reduce the foreign law gross income to compute the foreign law amount of taxable income in each separate category. *See* §1.904-6(a)(1)(ii).

Proposed §1.861-20 adopts the principles of §1.904-6 but provides more detailed guidance on how to apply those principles, which are illustrated by several examples. Proposed §1.861-20(c) provides that foreign tax expense is allocated and apportioned among the statutory and residual groupings by first assigning the items of gross income under foreign law ("foreign gross income") on which a foreign tax is imposed to a grouping, then allocating and apportioning deductions under foreign law to that income, and finally allocating and apportioning the foreign tax among the groupings. *See* proposed §1.861-20(c).

Proposed §1.861-20(d)(1) provides a general rule for assigning foreign gross income to a statutory or residual grouping. Under this rule, a foreign gross income item is assigned to a grouping by characterizing the item under Federal income tax law. If an item of gross income or loss arises under Federal income tax law from the same transaction or realization event from which the foreign gross income item arose (a "corresponding U.S. item"), the foreign gross income item is assigned to the same statutory or residual grouping as the corresponding U.S. item. In the case of a corresponding U.S. item that is an item of loss (or zero), the foreign gross income is assigned to the same grouping to which an item of gain would be assigned had the transaction or realization event given rise to an item of gain under Federal income tax law. *See* proposed §1.861-20(d)(1).

Proposed §1.861-20(d)(2) sets forth rules for assigning a foreign gross income item to a grouping if there is no corresponding U.S. item in the U.S. taxable year in which the taxpayer paid or accrued the foreign income tax imposed on foreign taxable income that includes the foreign gross income item. Proposed §1.861-20(d)(2)(i) generally addresses the circumstance in which there is no corresponding U.S. item either because the event giving rise to the foreign gross income is a nonrecognition event under Federal income tax law or because the recognition event giving rise to the foreign gross income occurred under Federal income tax law in a different U.S. taxable year. In both cases, proposed §1.861-20(d)(2)(i) assigns the foreign gross income to the grouping to which the corresponding U.S. item would be assigned if the event giving rise to the foreign gross income resulted in the recognition of gross income or loss under Federal income tax law in the same U.S. taxable year in which the foreign income tax is paid or accrued.

Proposed §1.861-20(d)(2)(ii) provides guidance regarding the treatment of foreign gross income items that are either excluded from gross income under Federal income tax law or attributable to base differences. Under §1.861-20(d)(2)(ii)(A), with the exception of base difference items, foreign gross income that is a type of income expressly excluded from gross income under Federal income tax law is assigned to the grouping to which the gross income would be assigned if it were included in U.S. gross income. Proposed §1.861-20(d)(2)(ii)(B) provides an exclusive list of items that are excluded from U.S. gross income and that, if taxable under foreign law, are treated as base differences. The items are death benefits described in section 101, gifts and inheritances described in section 102, contributions to capital described in section 118 and the receipt of property in exchange for stock described in section 1032, the receipt of property in exchange for a partnership interest described in section 721, returns of capital described in section 301(c)(2), and distributions to partners described in section 733. The Treasury Department and the IRS have determined that foreign tax on these items, which are excluded from U.S. gross income, is particularly difficult to associate with a particular type of U.S. gross income. Accordingly, foreign tax on base difference items is assigned to the residual grouping, with the result that no credit is allowed if the tax is paid by a CFC, and the tax is assigned to the separate category described in section 904(d)(2)(H)(i) if paid (or treated as paid) by a taxpayer claiming a direct credit under section 901. Comments are requested on whether the list should be expanded to include other items that have no logical analogue to items included in U.S. gross income, or whether a different assignment of any of these types of foreign gross income would be more appropriate.

Proposed §1.861-20(d)(3) sets forth special rules that apply for purposes of assigning certain items of foreign gross income to a grouping, including rules for distributions that both Federal income tax law and foreign law recognize, certain foreign law distributions such as consent dividends, inclusions under foreign law CFC regimes, disregarded payments, inclusions from reverse hybrids, and gain on the sale of a disregarded entity.

In the case of a distribution from a non-hybrid corporation that is recognized for both Federal income tax law and foreign tax law purposes, proposed §1.861-20(d)(3)(i)(B) treats foreign gross income arising from the distribution as a dividend and as capital gain to the extent of the portions of the distribution that are, under Federal income tax law, characterized as a dividend and capital gain, respectively. The foreign gross income is assigned to the same statutory and residual groupings as the corresponding amounts of dividend and capital gain as computed for U.S. tax purposes. Foreign gross income arising from the portion of the distribution that is a return of capital under Federal income tax law is treated as a base difference under proposed §1.861-20(d)(2)(ii)(B).

If foreign law, but not Federal income tax law, recognizes a deemed distribution or consent dividend (a "foreign law distribution"), proposed §1.861-20(d)(3)(i)(C) assigns the resulting foreign gross income to a statutory or residual grouping by applying proposed §1.861-20(d)(3)(i)(B) as though Federal income tax law recognized the distribution in the U.S. taxable year in which the taxpayer paid or accrued tax with respect to the foreign law distribution. For example, if a taxpayer recognizes foreign gross income arising from a foreign law distribution, and proposed §1.861-20(d)(3)(i)(B) (as applied for purposes of section 904 as the operative section) would treat the distribution as made out of general category section 965(a) previously taxed earnings and profits if the distribution had also occurred under Federal income tax law, the foreign gross income is assigned to the general category.

If a taxpayer (including an upper-tier CFC) includes an item of foreign gross income by reason of a foreign law regime similar to the subpart F provisions under sections 951 through 959 (a "foreign law subpart F regime"), proposed §1.861-20(d)(3)(i)(D) assigns that item to the same statutory or residual grouping as the gross income (determined under the foreign law subpart F regime) of the foreign law CFC that gave rise to the foreign gross income of the taxpayer. The taxpayer's gross income included under the foreign law subpart F regime is, in other words, treated as the foreign gross income of the foreign law CFC, and the general rules of proposed §§1.861-20(d)(1) and (2) apply to characterize that foreign gross income and assign it to the statutory and residual groupings. For example, in applying proposed §1.861-20(d)(3)(i)(D) in applying section 960 as the operative section where an upper-tier CFC is the taxpayer, the upper-tier CFC's foreign law subpart F inclusion is treated as the foreign gross income of the foreign law CFC, which is treated as if it were the taxpayer. If the foreign law CFC has a corresponding U.S. item of subpart F income for which its United States shareholder elects to apply the high tax exception under section 954(b)(4), the foreign gross income and the associated foreign tax paid by the upper-tier CFC are assigned to a residual income group under §1.960-1(d). In addition, §1.904-6(f) includes a special rule assigning certain items of foreign gross income recognized by a United States shareholder of a CFC that is also a foreign law CFC to the section 951A category for purposes of applying section 904 as the operative section.

Proposed § 1.861-20(d)(3)(ii) addresses the assignment of foreign gross income arising from disregarded payments between a foreign branch (as defined in § 1.904-4(f)(3)) and its owner. If the foreign gross income item arises from a payment made by a foreign branch to its owner, proposed § 1.861-20(d)(3)(ii)(A) generally assigns the item to the statutory and residual groupings by deeming the payment to be made ratably out of the after-tax income, computed for Federal income tax purposes, of the foreign branch, and deeming the branch income to arise in the statutory and residual groupings in the same ratio as the tax book value of the assets, including stock, owned by the foreign branch. If the item of foreign gross income arises from a disregarded payment to a foreign branch from its owner, proposed § 1.861-20(d)(3)(ii)(B) generally assigns the item to the residual grouping. However, proposed § 1.861-20(d)(3)(ii)(C) assigns an item of foreign gross income attributable to gain recognized under foreign law with respect to the receipt of a disregarded payment in exchange for property under the rule in § 1.861-20(d)(2)(i). In addition, proposed § 1.904-6(b)(2) includes special rules assigning foreign gross income items arising from certain disregarded payments for purposes of applying section 904 as the operative section.

Proposed § 1.861-20(d)(3)(iii) addresses the assignment to a statutory or residual grouping of foreign gross income that a taxpayer includes by reason of its ownership of a reverse hybrid. Under this rule, the foreign gross income that a taxpayer recognizes from a reverse hybrid is assigned to the statutory and residual groupings by treating that foreign gross income as the income of the reverse hybrid and applying the general rules of proposed § 1.861-20(d). However, § 1.904-6(f) includes a special rule assigning certain items of foreign gross income recognized by a United States shareholder of a controlled foreign corporation that is a reverse hybrid to the section 951A category for purposes of applying section 904 as the operative section. The Treasury Department and the IRS request comments on whether additional rules are needed to address other fact patterns in which the U.S. and a foreign country tax different persons on the same item of income, for example, in the case of a sale-repurchase agreement.

Finally, under proposed § 1.861-20(d)(3)(iv), if a taxpayer recognizes an item of foreign gross income that is gain from the sale of a disregarded entity, and Federal income tax law characterizes the transaction as a sale of the assets of the disregarded entity, the foreign gross income is assigned to the statutory and residual groupings in the same proportion as the gain that the taxpayer would have recognized if foreign law also treated the transaction as a sale of assets.

Changes to § 1.904-6 and § 1.960-1 are proposed to clarify and, in certain cases, modify the application of proposed § 1.861-20 for purposes of computing the foreign tax credit limitation under section 904 and foreign income taxes deemed paid under section 960.

Proposed § 1.904-6(b)(1) assigns foreign gross income that is attributable to a base difference, and the associated tax, to the separate category described in section 904(d)(2)(H)(i). Proposed § 1.904-6(b)(2)(i) generally provides that if a foreign branch makes a disregarded payment to another foreign branch or to its owner that causes the taxpayer's gross income under Federal income tax law that is otherwise attributable to the foreign branch to be attributed to another foreign branch or to the foreign branch owner under § 1.904-4(f)(2)(vi)(A) or § 1.904-4(f)(2)(vi)(D), the foreign gross income that arises by reason of the disregarded payment is assigned to the same category as the reattributed U.S. gross income. Under proposed § 1.904-6(b)(2)(ii), items of foreign gross income that a taxpayer includes solely by reason of the receipt by a foreign branch of a disregarded payment from its foreign branch owner that is a United States person are generally assigned to the foreign branch category (or, in the case of a foreign branch owner that is a partnership, to the partnership's general category income that is attributable to the foreign branch). However, items of foreign gross income attributable to gain recognized under foreign law with respect to the receipt of a disregarded payment in exchange for property are characterized and assigned under the rules of § 1.861-20(d)(2)(i). Under proposed § 1.904-6(b)(3), if a taxable disposition of property acquired in a disregarded sale results in the recognition of U.S. gross income that is reattributed to or from a foreign branch under § 1.904-4(f)(2)(vi)(A) or § 1.904-4(f)(2)(vi)(D), any foreign gross income arising from that disposition of property under foreign law is assigned to the same separate category as the corresponding U.S. item of gain under § 1.861-20(d)(1) without regard to the reattribution of U.S. gross income. This rule is intended to better match income and taxes in situations where the foreign country only taxes gain that arises during the period that follows the disregarded sale.

Finally, § 1.904-6(f) addresses the circumstance in which a United States shareholder pays or accrues foreign income tax with respect to foreign gross income that it recognizes because it owns a foreign law CFC or a reverse hybrid. The foreign income tax is allocated and apportioned to a category by treating the foreign gross income of the United States shareholder as the foreign gross income of the foreign law CFC or reverse hybrid under proposed § § 1.861-20(d)(3)(i)(D) or 1.861-20(d)(3)(ii)(B). Proposed § 1.904-6(f) reassigns to the section 951A category the foreign gross income that, if the foreign law CFC or reverse hybrid recognized the foreign gross income instead of the United States shareholder, would be assigned to the general category tested income group of the foreign law CFC or reverse hybrid to which an inclusion under section 951A is attributable. The amount of the foreign gross income that is reassigned is based upon the inclusion percentage, as defined in § 1.960-2(c)(2), of the United States shareholder.

The Treasury Department and the IRS are continuing to study the allocation and apportionment of foreign income tax that is imposed on foreign gross income that is associated with the general category tested income group of a foreign law CFC or reverse hybrid under proposed § § 1.861-20(d)(3)(i)(D) and 1.861-20(d)(3)(ii)(B), respectively. Comments are requested on the proper treatment of such foreign income tax in the circumstance in which some or all of the tax is not assigned to the section 951A category under proposed § 1.904-6(f) because no inclusion is attributable to the tested income group, or the inclusion percentage of the United States shareholder is less than 100 percent. In particular, comments are requested on the interaction of proposed § 1.904-6(f) with sections 245A(g) and 909.

Proposed § 1.960-1(d)(3)(ii) makes conforming changes and in addition clarifies that, if proposed § 1.861-20 would otherwise apply to assign foreign gross income to a PTEP group that is not increased as a result of a distribution described in section 959(b), the foreign taxable income is assigned to the income group to which the income, computed under Federal income tax law, that gave rise to the PTEP would be assigned if recognized under Federal income tax law in the year in which tax was imposed.

The Treasury Department and the IRS are also studying whether additional guidance should be provided on allocating and apportioning foreign taxes described in section 903 (tax in lieu of income tax), and foreign income taxes for which the foreign taxable base is computed formulaically with respect to a unitary business. The Treasury Department and the IRS are also studying whether the rules in § 1.861-8(e)(6) for allocating and apportioning state income taxes should be revised in light of changes made by the TCJA and changes to state rules for taxing foreign income. Comments are requested on these topics.

C. Overall foreign loss recapture on property dispositions

One comment was received with respect to the 2012 OFL proposed regulations, which recommended addressing dispositions that result in additional income recognition under branch loss recapture and dual consolidated loss recapture rules. The comment pointed out that these additional income recognition amounts are determined after first determining the additional recognition amount under section 904(f)(3) and therefore recommended adding the coordination of these rules as a new Step Nine in the ordering rules of § 1.904(g)-3. The comment recommended that the additional income recognition amounts resulting from branch loss recapture and dual consolidated loss recapture should not be subject to the overall foreign loss (OFL) recapture rules.

The branch loss recapture rules under section 367(a) referenced by the comment letter were repealed by the TCJA (subject to a special savings clause that applies with respect to losses incurred before January 1, 2018) and replaced with a new set of branch loss recapture rules in section 91. One of the principal differences between the two regimes is that previously the branch loss recapture amounts were treated as foreign source income, whereas under new section 91(d) they are treated as U.S. source income. Accordingly, although the branch loss recapture amounts for losses incurred after December 31, 2017, are no longer subject to the OFL recapture rules or separate limitation loss (SLL) recapture rules, they are now potentially subject to the overall domestic loss (ODL) recapture rules, and therefore ordering rules are still needed for the application of the branch loss recapture rules, including the rules for losses incurred before January 1, 2018, that are subject to the special savings clause.

The Treasury Department and the IRS agree with the recommendation to add a new Step Nine to §1.904(g)-3 to clarify that additional income amounts recognized by reason of branch loss recapture and dual consolidated loss recapture are not taken into account for purposes of the ordering rules until after the section 904(f)(3) amounts are determined. However, the Treasury Department and the IRS do not agree that those additional income amounts should not be subject to the OFL or ODL recapture rules. The fact that a loss recapture rule may provide that the additional income amount is treated as U.S. source income does not mean it should be treated any differently than any other U.S. source income that is subject to the ODL recapture rules. The same reasoning applies to additional income amounts that are treated as foreign source income and therefore subject to the OFL recapture rules. Accordingly, Step Nine in proposed §1.904(g)-(3)(j) provides that like section 904(f)(3) recapture amounts addressed in Step Eight, the additional income recognized by reason of branch loss and dual consolidated loss recapture will be subject to the first seven steps of the ordering rules. However, Step Nine applies only to additional income amounts with respect to branch loss and dual consolidated loss recapture that are determined after taking into account an offset for a section 904(f)(3) recapture amount. For example, if a taxpayer has a dual consolidated loss recapture in a year in which there is no section 904(f)(3) recapture, then there is only one application of Steps One through Seven, which takes into account the additional income, and Steps Eight and Nine will not apply.

When Step Nine applies, the proposed regulations provide that for purposes of determining how much of the additional income with respect to branch loss and dual consolidated loss recapture will be subject to the ODL, OFL or SLL recapture rules, any increases to an ODL, OFL or SLL account balance in the current year due to the original application of Steps One through Seven (prior to the application of Steps Eight or Nine) are taken into account.

In addition, if any additional income with respect to a branch loss or dual consolidated loss recapture is foreign source income in a separate category for which there is a remaining OFL account balance after Steps One through Eight, a special rule applies for purposes of determining the OFL recapture amount under §1.904(f)-2(c) (the lesser of the maximum potential recapture or 50 percent of total foreign source income). The special rule provides that a taxpayer must first determine a hypothetical OFL recapture amount, which is the OFL recapture amount that would have been determined in the original application of Steps One through Seven (prior to the application of Steps Eight and Nine) if the additional income in Step Nine were also taken into account. From that hypothetical OFL recapture amount, the taxpayer subtracts the actual OFL recapture amount that was determined in the original application of Steps One through Seven (without taking into account the additional income in Step Nine). The remainder is then the OFL recapture amount with respect to the additional income in Step Nine. This special rule is necessary because a simple reapplication of the OFL recapture amount rules in §1.904(f)-2(c) to just the additional income in Step Nine could result in requiring an excessive amount of recapture, because the same amount of foreign source income in other separate categories may be used twice to increase the OFL recapture amount (once in the original calculation and again in the second calculation with respect to the additional income).

III. *Foreign Tax Redeterminations Under Section 905(c)*

As discussed in Part III of the Background section of the 2019 FTC final regulations, portions of the temporary regulations relating to sections 905(c), 986(a), and 6689 (TD 9362) (the "2007 temporary regulations") are being reproposed in order to provide taxpayers an additional opportunity to comment on those rules in light of the changes made by the TCJA. References in this preamble to the 2007 temporary regulations are understood to refer to the corresponding provisions of the accompanying proposed regulations, which were issued by cross-reference to the 2007 temporary regulations at 72 FR 62805.

In particular, the rules being reproposed are: (1) §1.905-3T(d)(2), which addresses foreign tax redeterminations that affect foreign taxes deemed paid under section 960, (2) §1.905-4T, which in general provides the procedural rules for how to notify the IRS of a foreign tax redetermination, and (3) §301.6689-1T, which provides rules for the penalty for failure to notify the IRS of a foreign tax redetermination. In addition, the proposed regulations contain a transition rule in proposed §§1.905-3(b)(2)(iv) and 1.905-5 to address foreign tax redeterminations of foreign corporations that relate to taxable years before the amendments made by the TCJA. *See* Part III.D of this Explanation of Provisions.

A. *Adjustments to foreign taxes paid by foreign corporations*

Section 1.905-3T(d)(2) of the 2007 temporary regulations reflects the law in effect before the TCJA, which generally required foreign tax redeterminations of foreign corporations to be taken into account by prospectively adjusting the foreign corporations' pools of post-1986 undistributed earnings and post-1986 foreign income taxes, rather than by adjusting the calculation of deemed-paid taxes and the United States shareholder's ("U.S. shareholder") U.S. tax liability in the prior year or years in which the adjusted foreign tax was included in the calculation of foreign taxes deemed paid. Section 1.905-3T(d)(3) of the 2007 temporary regulations provides exceptions to the pooling adjustment rules that required redeterminations of the U.S. shareholder's U.S. tax liability in situations where refunds or other downward adjustments to a foreign corporation's foreign tax liability would otherwise cause a substantial overstatement of deemed paid taxes. With the repeal of the pooling regime and related amendments to section 905(c) in the TJCA, the statute now requires U.S. tax redeterminations to reflect all foreign tax redeterminations, including those that result in adjustments to foreign taxes deemed paid. Accordingly, proposed §1.905-3(b)(2)(i) provides that a U.S. tax redetermination is required in all cases to account for the effect of a foreign corporation's foreign tax redetermination.

Section 1.905-3T(d)(3)(ii), illustrated by an example in §1.905-3T(d)(3)(iii), provides that the required U.S. tax redetermination is made by taking the foreign tax redetermination into account in the prior year to which the redetermined foreign tax relates, and further provides that a U.S. tax redetermination is also required for any subsequent year in which the domestic corporate shareholder received or accrued a distribution or inclusion from the foreign corporation, which under pre-TCJA law would have resulted in foreign taxes deemed paid. Under these rules, the amount of the adjusted foreign tax was deemed to "relate back" and adjust the foreign corporation's earnings and profits, as well as its creditable foreign taxes, in the adjusted year.

In any case where a U.S. tax redetermination and adjustment to deemed paid taxes is required, an adjustment to the foreign corporation's taxable income and earnings and profits in the functional currency amount of the adjusted foreign tax (whether upward to reflect a refund or downward to reflect an additional payment of foreign tax) in the relation-back year is necessary in order to coordinate the computation of the U.S. shareholder's inclusions with the amount of the section 78 dividend in the amount of the adjusted foreign taxes deemed paid. This is because under sections 954(b)(5) and 951A(c)(2)(ii), the creditable foreign tax reduces the foreign corporation's subpart F income, tested income, and earnings and profits, so that the amount included in the U.S. shareholder's income under sections 951 and 951A is an after-foreign-tax amount; the section 78 dividend prevents the effective allowance of both a deduction and a credit for an amount of foreign tax that both reduces the inclusion and is allowed as a deemed paid foreign tax credit. If the foreign corporation's deduction from income and earnings and profits in respect of foreign taxes were adjusted in a different year than the year in which its creditable foreign taxes were adjusted, the amount of foreign tax that reduces the U.S. shareholder's inclusion and the amount added to income under section 78 in respect of the deemed paid tax would not match, such that the U.S. shareholder's income would be understated or overstated by the amount of the foreign tax adjustment.

Accordingly, proposed §1.905-3(b)(2)(ii) clarifies that the required adjustments by reason of a foreign tax redetermination of a foreign corporation include not only adjustments to the amount of foreign taxes deemed paid and related section 78 dividend, but also adjustments to the foreign corporation's income and earnings and profits and the amount of the U.S. shareholder's inclusions under sections 951 and 951A in the year to which the redetermined foreign tax relates. The TCJA amendments, by eliminating deemed paid taxes under section 902 with respect to dividends and basing deemed paid taxes under section 960 with respect to subpart F and GILTI inclusions on current year income and taxes rather than multi-year pools, will require more redeterminations of U.S. tax liability to adjust deemed paid credits under section 960, but fewer adjustments to intervening years, since a foreign tax adjustment to one year will generally no longer affect the calculation of deemed paid taxes with respect to inclusions in other years. New examples at proposed §1.905-3(b)(2)(v) illustrate these rules.

Section 905(c)(1)(B) and (C) require a redetermination of U.S. tax if accrued taxes remain unpaid after two years, or if any tax paid is refunded in whole or in part. These provisions are not limited to cases in which the foreign tax redetermination reduces the amount of the foreign tax credit. Accordingly, proposed §§1.905-3(a) and 1.905-3(b)(2)(ii) also provide that the rules under section 905(c) apply in cases in which foreign tax redeterminations affect U.S. tax liability even though there may be no change to the amount of foreign tax credits originally claimed. For example, under the proposed regulations a redetermination of U.S. tax liability is required when a foreign tax redetermination affects whether or not a taxpayer is eligible for the high-tax exception under section 954(b)(4) (the "subpart F high-tax exception") in the year to which the redetermined foreign tax relates. Similarly, a foreign tax redetermination could affect the subpart F income, tested income, and earnings and profits of a CFC in the year to which the tax relates, see proposed §1.905-3(b)(2)(ii), and therefore affect the amount of a U.S. shareholder's inclusion under section 951 or section 951A with respect to the adjusted year. Corresponding amendments are proposed to the rules in §§1.904-4(c)(7) and 1.954-1(d).

B. *Foreign tax redeterminations of successor entities*

The proposed regulations at §1.905-3(b)(3) add a rule clarifying that if at the time of a foreign tax redetermination the person with legal liability for the tax (the "successor") is a different person than the person that had legal liability for the tax in the year to which the redetermined tax relates (the "original taxpayer"), the required redetermination of U.S. tax liability is made as if the foreign tax redetermination occurred in the hands of the original taxpayer. This could occur, for example, if a disregarded entity is sold to a different taxpayer, or if a CFC liquidates into another CFC that has transferee liability for the liquidated CFC's foreign tax. The proposed regulations further provide that Federal income tax principles apply to determine the tax consequences if the successor remits, or receives a refund of, a tax that in the year to which the redetermined tax relates was the legal liability of, and thus considered paid by, the original taxpayer. Thus, for example, when the original taxpayer owns the successor which remits a tax that was the legal liability of, and considered paid by, the original taxpayer (for example, if a controlled foreign corporation that was formerly a disregarded entity pays additional tax after a foreign audit), then a distribution can result from the successor to the original taxpayer. *See Herbert Enoch*, 57 T.C. 781 (1972) (finding constructive dividend when a corporation discharged its shareholder's personal liability on debt). The Treasury Department and the IRS request comments on whether additional rules are required to address situations involving predecessors or successors.

C. *Notification to the IRS of foreign tax redeterminations and related penalty provisions*

Proposed §1.905-4 contains rules for notifying the IRS of a foreign tax redetermination. Proposed §301.6689-1 contains rules regarding the penalty for failure to notify the IRS of a foreign tax redetermination. This Part III.C describes changes made to §§1.905-4 and 301.6689-1 relative to the rules that were contained in the 2007 temporary regulations.

1. Notification through amended returns

Section 1.905-4T(b)(1)(iv) of the 2007 temporary regulations provides that, if more than one foreign tax redetermination requires a redetermination of U.S. tax liability for the same taxable year of the taxpayer (the affected year) and those redeterminations occur within two consecutive taxable years, the taxpayer generally may file for the affected year one amended return, Form 1118 (Foreign Tax Credit – Corporations) or Form 1116 (Foreign Tax Credit), and one statement under §1.905-4T(c) with respect to all of the redeterminations. Proposed §1.905-4(b)(1)(iv) clarifies that, if more than one foreign tax redetermination requires a redetermination of U.S. tax liability for the same affected year and those redeterminations occur within the same taxable year or within two consecutive taxable years, the taxpayer may file for the affected year one amended return and one statement under proposed §1.905-4(c) with respect to all of the redeterminations. Proposed §1.905-4(b)(1)(iv) also provides that the due date of the amended return and statement varies depending on whether the net effect of the foreign tax redeterminations reduces or increases the U.S. tax liability in the affected taxable year.

Section 1.905-4T(b)(1)(v) of the 2007 temporary regulations provides that, if a foreign tax redetermination requires a redetermination of U.S. tax liability that otherwise would result in an additional amount of U.S. tax due, but such amount is eliminated as a result of a carryback or carryover of an unused foreign tax under section 904(c), the taxpayer may, in lieu of applying the rules of §§1.905-4T(b)(1)(i) and (b)(1)(ii), notify the IRS of such redetermination by attaching a statement to the original return for the taxpayer's taxable year in which the foreign tax redetermination occurs. Section 1.905-4T(b)(1)(v) of the 2007 temporary regulations does not apply if the foreign tax redetermination does not change the U.S. tax liability for the taxable year to which the tax relates for a reason other than the carryback or carryover of an unused foreign tax. Section 1.905-4T(b)(1)(v) of the 2007 temporary regulations also does not apply if more than one foreign tax redetermination occurring within the same taxable year or two consecutive taxable years requires a redetermination of U.S. tax liability for the same taxable year but, taking into account all such foreign tax redeterminations on a net basis, results in no additional amount of U.S. tax liability due for such taxable year.

Proposed §1.905-4(b)(1)(v) provides that, if a foreign tax redetermination (either alone or in combination with certain other foreign tax redeterminations as provided in proposed §1.905-4(b)(1)(iv)) does not result in a change to the amount of U.S. tax due for a taxable year, for reasons including but not limited to a carryover or carryback of unused foreign taxes under section 904(c), no amended return is required for such year. Instead, appropriate adjustments are made to the amounts carried over from that year (for example, unused foreign taxes). If no amended return is required for any year, the taxpayer must attach a statement containing the information described in §1.904-2(f) to the taxpayer's timely filed (with extensions) original return for the taxpayer's taxable year in which the foreign tax redetermination occurs.

2. Foreign tax redeterminations of pass-through entities

The 2007 temporary regulations did not specifically provide guidance for pass-through entities that report creditable foreign taxes to their partners, shareholders, or beneficiaries and subsequently have a foreign tax redetermination with respect to such foreign taxes. The proposed regulations provide rules whereby these entities can satisfy their obligations under section 905(c). Proposed §1.905-4(b)(2) generally provides that a pass-through entity that reports creditable foreign income tax to its partners, shareholders, or beneficiaries, is required to notify the IRS and its partners, shareholders, or beneficiaries if there is a foreign tax redetermination with respect to such foreign income tax. See proposed §1.905-4(c) for the information required to be provided with the notification.

Additionally, in 2015, Congress introduced the centralized audit partnership regime, which requires that certain adjustments be made at the level of the partnership, rather than by partners. *See* sections 6221 through 6241 (enacted in §1101 of the Bipartisan Budget Act of 2015, Public Law 114-74 ("BBA") and as amended by the Protecting Americans from Tax Hikes Act of 2015, Public Law 114-113, div Q, and by sections 201 through 207 of the Tax Technical Corrections Act of 2018, contained in Title II of Division U of the Consolidated Appropriations Act of 2018, Public Law 115-141). Under this regime, in order to make an adjustment to a partnership-related item (as defined in section 6241(2)), the partnership must file an administrative adjustment request ("AAR"). Sections 6227(d) and 6235(a) contemplate that these rules will be coordinated with the application of section 905(c).

On June 14, 2017, the Treasury Department and the IRS published in the **Federal Register** (82 FR 27334) a notice of proposed rulemaking and on November 30, 2017, the Treasury Department and the IRS published in the **Federal Register** (82 FR 56765) another notice of proposed rulemaking. Each notice of proposed rulemaking requested comments on how a partnership subject to the centralized partnership audit regime should fulfill the requirements of section 905(c). One comment was received with respect to this issue and it recommended that partnerships satisfy their obligations under section 905(c) by filing an AAR under section 6227 and by following the procedures under that section to take necessary adjustments into account. Consistent with this request and with sections 6227(d) and 6235(a), proposed § 1.905-4(b)(2)(ii) provides that if a redetermination of U.S. tax liability would require a partnership adjustment as defined in § 301.6241-1(a)(6), the partnership must file an AAR under section 6227 without regard to the time restrictions on filing an AAR in section 6227(c). *See also* § 1.6227-1(g).

The use of the AAR process, even if the period under section 6227(c) is closed, is intended to further the purpose of sections 905(c), 6227(d), 6235(a), and 6241(11). An AAR is analogous to an amended return, which is required from other taxpayers who have a foreign tax redetermination, and provides an administrable process whereby a partnership, and its partners, can satisfy their obligations under section 905(c). The Treasury Department and the IRS request comments on any further coordination that may be required between sections 905(c) and 6227 in order to carry out the purposes of the foreign tax credit and the centralized partnership audit regime.

3. Alternative notification requirements

Proposed § 1.905-4(b)(3) provides that an amended return and Form 1118 (Foreign Tax Credit—Corporations) or Form 1116 (Foreign Tax Credit), is not required to notify the IRS of a foreign tax redetermination and redetermination of U.S. tax liability if the taxpayer satisfies alternative notification requirements that may be prescribed by the IRS through forms, instructions, publications, or other guidance. For example, as provided in Notice 2016-10, 2016-1 I.R.B. 1, the Treasury Department and the IRS intend to issue regulations providing for alternative notification procedures in the case of tax refunds received by regulated investment companies making the election to pass through foreign tax credits under section 853. The Treasury Department and the IRS request comments on additional alternative approaches to complying with the notification requirements in section 905(c) that minimize burdens to both taxpayers and the IRS.

4. Foreign tax redeterminations of LB&I taxpayers

Section 1.905-4T(b)(3) of the 2007 temporary regulations provides a special rule for U.S. taxpayers under the jurisdiction of the Large and Mid-Size Business Division. The proposed regulations reflect the organization's name change to Large Business and International Division (LB&I).

Under the special rule for U.S. taxpayers under LB&I jurisdiction ("LB&I rule"), such taxpayers are required, in limited circumstances, to provide to their examiners notice of a foreign tax redetermination that requires a redetermination of U.S. tax, in lieu of filing an amended return. One of the threshold requirements of § 1.905-4T(b)(3) of the 2007 temporary regulations is that the taxpayer must provide the statement describing the foreign tax redetermination no later than 120 days after the latest of (1) the date the foreign tax redetermination occurs, (2) the opening conference of the examination for the affected taxable year, or (3) the hand-delivery or postmark date of the opening letter concerning the examination. In no case, however, can the alternative notification procedure apply if the 120-day period within which notification must be made would start after the due date of the return for the taxable year in which the foreign tax redetermination occurs.

The LB&I rule contained in the proposed regulations is generally the same as the rule in the 2007 temporary regulations, and the Explanation of Provisions of the 2007 temporary regulations contains an explanation of the rules. However, one change has been made with respect to § 1.905-4T(b)(3) of the 2007 temporary regulations. Section 1.905-4T(b)(3) provides that, if that provision applies to permit notification during an audit, in lieu of filing an amended return a taxpayer must provide to the examiner the statement described in § 1.905-4T(c) of the 2007 temporary regulations, which contains information that enables the IRS to verify and compare the original computations with respect to a claimed foreign tax credit, the revised computations resulting from the foreign tax redetermination, and the net changes resulting therefrom. In order to satisfy the requirements of § 1.905-4T(c), a taxpayer is required to recompute its U.S. tax liability during the course of an examination, rather than only at the conclusion of the audit. To minimize administrative burdens, the statement requirement at proposed § 1.905-4(b)(4)(iii) requires the taxpayer to provide to the examiner the original amount of foreign taxes paid or accrued in the year to which the foreign tax redetermination relates, the revised amount of foreign taxes paid or accrued, and documentation with respect to the revisions, including exchange rates and dates of accrual and/or payment. This information must be provided with a penalties-of-perjury declaration signed by a person authorized to sign the return of the taxpayer.

In order to clarify when the special rules for LB&I taxpayers apply, the proposed regulations reorganize certain portions of the 2007 temporary regulations into a list of conditions, all of which must be met in order for § 1.905-4(b)(4) to apply. These conditions are as follows: (1) a foreign tax redetermination occurs while the U.S. taxpayer is under the jurisdiction of LB&I (or a successor division); (2) the foreign tax redetermination results in a downward adjustment to the amount of foreign tax paid or accrued, or included in the computation of foreign taxes deemed paid; (3) the foreign tax redetermination requires a redetermination of U.S. tax liability and accordingly, but for § 1.905-4(b)(4), the taxpayer would be required to notify the IRS of such foreign tax redetermination under § 1.905-4(b)(1)(ii) by filing an amended return; (4) the return for the taxable year for which a redetermination of U.S. tax liability is required is under examination; and (5) the due date specified in § 1.905-4(b)(1)(ii) for providing notice of such foreign tax redetermination is not before the latest of the opening conference or the hand-delivery or postmark date of the opening letter concerning the examination of the return for the taxable year for which a redetermination of U.S. tax liability is required by reason of such foreign tax redetermination.

5. Penalty provisions

Section 6689 provides that a taxpayer may be subject to a penalty if it fails to notify the IRS of a foreign tax redetermination on or before the date prescribed by regulations. Section 301.6689-1T(a) (issued in TD 8210 on June 22, 1988) states that the penalty may apply if a taxpayer fails to notify the IRS of a foreign tax redetermination "on or before the date prescribed in regulations." However, the preamble of the 2007 temporary regulations, in describing section 6689, provides that, "Under section 6689, a taxpayer that fails to notify the IRS of a foreign tax redetermination in the time *and manner* prescribed by regulations for giving such notice is subject to a penalty." (Emphasis added.) Because it is implicit in section 6689 that the required notification must comply with the requirements of section 905(c), the proposed regulations conform to the preamble description in the 2007 temporary regulations. Accordingly, proposed § 301.6689-1(a) provides that the penalty may apply if a taxpayer fails to notify the IRS of a foreign tax redetermination "on or before the date and in the manner prescribed in regulations."

The penalty under section 6689 is generally computed by reference to the amount of the deficiency resulting from a foreign tax redetermination. If a partnership fails to timely file an AAR as required under proposed § 1.905-4(b)(2)(ii) such that the penalty under section 6689 is applicable there is ambiguity regarding the correct base upon which the penalty is computed because partnerships do not generally have deficiencies in chapter 1 tax. Under the centralized partnership audit regime enacted by the BBA, if an adjustment is made to a partnership-related item of a partnership that is subject to the BBA (either by the IRS or by the partnership upon the filing of an AAR), the default rule is that the partnership is liable for an imputed underpayment calculated on the adjustments, which is an approximate substitute for the amount of chapter 1 tax that would have been owed by its partners. *See* sections 6221(a) and 6225. The fact that section 6689 is silent as to the proper base for calculating a section 6689 penalty for a partnership that is subject to BBA creates a special enforcement consideration and requires clarification. Therefore, consistent with the principles of section 6233(a)(3) (which treats the imputed underpayment as an understatement or underpayment for purposes of computing a penalty) and the requirement in section 6227(d) that regulations coordinate the application of sections 905(c) and 6227, proposed § 301.6689-1 provides that in computing the amount of the penalty imposed under section 6689, the penalty is calculated on a deficiency or by reference to the amount of the imputed underpayment that results from the foreign tax redetermination.

Finally, because section 6662 may apply if a taxpayer's U.S. tax liability is understated on an original return even if section 6689 applies to a failure to notify the IRS of a subsequent foreign tax redetermination, the proposed regulations eliminate the reference in § 301.6689-1(b) to section 6653(a) (the predecessor to section 6662).

D. *Transition rule relating to the TCJA*

The TCJA repealed the pooling rules of section 902 and related provisions of section 905(c) that mandated prospective pooling adjustments to account for redeterminations of foreign taxes paid by foreign corporations that were eligible to be deemed paid by domestic corporate shareholders of the foreign corporations. Proposed §§ 1.905-3(b)(2)(iv) and 1.905-5 provide a transition rule providing that post-2017 redeterminations of pre-2018 foreign income taxes must be accounted for by adjusting the foreign corporation's taxable income and earnings and profits, post-1986 undistributed earnings, and post-1986 foreign income taxes (or pre-1987 accumulated profits and pre-1987 foreign income taxes, as applicable) in the pre-2018 year to which the redetermined foreign taxes relate. A redetermination of U.S. tax liability is required to account for the effect of the foreign tax redetermination on foreign taxes deemed paid by domestic corporate shareholders of the foreign corporation in the relation-back year and any subsequent pre-2018 year in which the domestic corporate shareholder computed a deemed-paid credit under section 902 or 960 with respect to the foreign corporation, as well as any year to which unused foreign taxes from any such year were carried. The proposed regulations generally apply the currency translation rules applicable under prior law and the notification requirements of proposed § 1.904-4 to redeterminations of U.S. tax liability required by proposed § 1.905-3(b)(2)(iv) in these circumstances.

The Treasury Department and the IRS request comments on whether an alternative adjustment to account for post-2017 foreign tax redeterminations with respect to pre-2018 taxable years of foreign corporations, such as an adjustment to the foreign corporation's taxable income and earnings and profits, post-1986 undistributed earnings, and post-1986 foreign income taxes as of the foreign corporation's last taxable year beginning before January 1, 2018, may provide for a simplified and reasonably accurate alternative.

IV. *Foreign Income Taxes Taken Into Account Under Section 954(b)(4)*

As discussed in Part III.A of this Explanation of Provisions, proposed § 1.905-3(b)(2) provides that a U.S. tax redetermination is required when a foreign tax redetermination affects whether or not a taxpayer is eligible for the subpart F high-tax exception. Proposed § 1.954-1(d)(3)(iii) therefore provides that the subpart F high-tax exception is applied by taking into account the redetermined foreign tax in the adjusted year.

The proposed regulations also include an additional clarification relating to schemes involving jurisdictions that do not impose corporate income tax on a CFC until its earnings are distributed. The Treasury Department and the IRS are aware that certain taxpayers claim that taxes are treated as paid or accrued for purposes of § 1.954-1(d)(3) even in the absence of any distribution triggering foreign tax. The IRS may challenge this position under existing law. Furthermore, the proposed regulations clarify that foreign income taxes that have not accrued because they are contingent on a future distribution are not taken into account for purposes of determining the amount of foreign income taxes paid or accrued with respect to an item of income. However, if a redetermination of U.S. tax liability is required under proposed §§ 1.905-3(a) and 1.905-3(b)(2)(ii) when tax is imposed on the foreign corporation in connection with a distribution, the redetermined foreign tax is taken into account in applying § 1.954-1(d)(3) in the adjusted year.

V. *Disallowance of Foreign Tax Credits Under Section 965(g)*

The Treasury Department and the IRS are aware that certain taxpayers may have engaged in certain transactions that are intended to avoid the disallowance of foreign tax credits under section 965(g) with respect to distributions of section 965(a) previously taxed earnings and profits or section 965(b) previously taxed earnings and profits. For example, certain U.S. shareholders of specified foreign corporations may incur foreign income taxes on distributions recognized for foreign tax purposes that are not recognized for U.S. tax purposes (for example, consent dividends). When the section 965(a) previously taxed earnings and profits or section 965(b) previously taxed earnings and profits are distributed for U.S. tax purposes, no foreign income tax is imposed by the foreign jurisdiction. The taxpayers may argue that the foreign income taxes on the foreign distributions are not associated with a distribution of section 965(a) previously taxed earnings and profits or section 965(b) previously taxed earnings and profits for U.S. tax purposes, and, accordingly, the credit need not be reduced by the section 965(g) disallowance.

Proposed § 1.965-5(b)(2) clarifies that the principles of § 1.904-6 apply in determining the extent to which foreign income taxes are attributable to distributions of section 965(a) previously taxed earnings and profits or section 965(b) previously taxed earnings and profits for purposes of § 1.965-5(b)(1). For example, under the principles of § 1.904-6, foreign withholding taxes imposed on an amount that is recognized as a dividend for foreign, but not Federal income, tax purposes are attributable to an item of income to which that amount would be assigned if recognized as a distribution for Federal income tax purposes. To the extent a distribution would be a distribution of section 965(a) previously taxed earnings and profits or section 965(b) previously taxed earnings and profits if it were recognized for U.S. tax purposes, under proposed § 1.965-5(b)(2) the tax would be associated with section 965(a) previously taxed earnings and profits or section 965(b) previously taxed earnings and profits and disallowed in part by reason of section 965(g). For foreign corporation taxable years beginning after December 31, 2019, § 1.861-20 applies in lieu of § 1.904-6.

The IRS may challenge the credits claimed for foreign income taxes imposed on distributions recognized solely for foreign tax purposes in prior years to the extent that such foreign income taxes would be considered imposed on distributions of section 965(a) previously taxed earnings and profits or section 965(b) previously taxed earnings and profits had such distributions been recognized for U.S. tax purposes.

VI. *Updates to Consolidated Foreign Tax Credit Rules*

Proposed § 1.1502-4 includes amendments to regulations under section 1502 relating to the computation of the consolidated foreign tax credit. The proposed amendments update the regulations to reflect changes in the law, such as by eliminating out-of-date references to the per-country limitation. For purposes of determining the foreign tax credit limitation, the proposed regulations also provide that the amount of foreign source income in each separate category, used as the numerator in the foreign tax credit limitation fraction, is determined by applying the rules of § 1.1502-11, as well as sections 904(f) and 904(g), on a group-wide basis, rather than applying those rules on a separate member basis and combining the results.

The proposed regulations also add new rules for purposes of determining the source and separate category of a consolidated NOL, as well as the portion of a consolidated net operating loss ("CNOL") that is apportioned to a separate return year of a member. The Treasury Department and the IRS have determined that, when characterizing a CNOL that is apportioned to a separate return year, it is generally appropriate to link the source and separate category of the CNOL with the member's assets that are expected to produce income with that same source and separate category so as to minimize the creation of loss accounts under sections 904(f) and 904(g) in the year in which the CNOL is used. The proposed regulations achieve this result formulaically through a two-step process that generally determines a CNOL's source and separate category by reference to the statutory and residual groupings described in § 1.861-8 for purposes of applying section 904 as the operative section, which are foreign source income in each separate category, and the residual grouping, which is U.S. source income.

First, the member determines a tentative apportionment, which is a proportionate share of the amount of the CNOL in each grouping based on a comparison of the value of the member's assets in that grouping to the value of the group's total assets in the grouping. Because the total of tentative apportionments of the CNOL does not necessarily equal the member's total share of the CNOL, an adjustment is provided. If the total tentative apportionments exceed the CNOL attributable to the member, the tentative apportionment in each grouping is reduced by a pro rata share of the excess, in proportion to the amount of the tentative apportionment in that grouping over the total tentative apportionments. In contrast, if the total tentative apportionments are less than the CNOL attributable to the member, the tentative apportionment in each grouping is increased by a pro rata share of that deficiency, in proportion to the remaining CNOL in that grouping (after subtracting the tentative apportionment) over the total remaining CNOL in all groupings.

VII. *Applicability Dates*

The rules in proposed §§ 1.861-8, 1.861-9, 1.861-12, 1.861-14, 1.904-4(c)(7) and (8), 1.904(b)-3, 1.954-1, and 1.954-2, generally apply to taxable years that end on or after [*INSERT DATE OF FILING IN THE FEDERAL REGISTER*].

The rules in proposed §§ 1.704-1(b)(4)(viii)(*d*)(*1*), 1.861-17, 1.861-20, 1.904-6, and 1.960-1 apply to taxable years beginning after December 31, 2019. However, taxpayers that are on the sales method for taxable years beginning after December 31, 2017, and before January 1, 2020, may rely on proposed § 1.861-17 if they apply it consistently. Therefore, a taxpayer on the sales method for its taxable year beginning in 2018 may rely on proposed § 1.861-17 but must also apply the sales method (relying on proposed § 1.861-17) for its taxable year beginning in 2019.

Proposed §§ 1.904-4(e) and 1.904(g)-3 apply to taxable years ending on or after the date the final regulations are filed with the **Federal Register**.

In general, proposed §§ 1.905-3, 1.905-4, 1.905-5, and 301.6689-1 apply to foreign tax redeterminations (as defined in § 1.905-3(a)) occurring in taxable years ending on or after [*INSERT DATE OF FILING IN THE FEDERAL REGISTER*], and to foreign tax redeterminations of foreign corporations occurring in taxable years that end with or within a taxable year of a U.S. shareholder ending on or after [*INSERT DATE OF FILING IN THE FEDERAL REGISTER*]. In the case of foreign tax redeterminations of foreign corporations, proposed § 1.905-3 is limited to foreign tax redeterminations that relate to taxable years of foreign corporations beginning after December 31, 2017, and proposed § 1.905-5 is limited to foreign tax redeterminations that relate to taxable years of foreign corporations beginning before January 1, 2018.

Proposed § 1.965-5(b)(2) applies to taxable years of foreign corporations that end on or after [*INSERT DATE OF FILING IN THE FEDERAL REGISTER*], and with respect to a United States person, to the taxable years in which or with which such taxable years of the foreign corporations end.

Proposed § 1.1502-4 applies to taxable years for which the original consolidated Federal income tax return is due (without extensions) after [*INSERT DATE OF PUBLICATION IN THE FEDERAL REGISTER*].

Special Analyses

I. *Regulatory Planning and Review*

Executive Orders 13563 and 12866 direct agencies to assess costs and benefits of available regulatory alternatives and, if regulation is necessary, to select regulatory approaches that maximize net benefits (including potential economic, environmental, public health and safety effects, distributive impacts, and equity). Executive Order 13563 emphasizes the importance of quantifying both costs and benefits, reducing costs, harmonizing rules, and promoting flexibility. The Executive Order 13771 designation for any final rule resulting from these proposed regulations will be informed by comments received.

The proposed regulations have been designated by the Office of Information and Regulatory Affairs (OIRA) as subject to review under Executive Order 12866 pursuant to the Memorandum of Agreement (MOA, April 11, 2018) between the Treasury Department and the Office of Management and Budget regarding review of tax regulations. The Office of Information and Regulatory Affairs (OIRA) has designated these proposed regulations as significant under section 1(b) of the MOA. Accordingly, these proposed regulations have been reviewed by OIRA.

A. Background and need for the proposed regulations

Before the Tax Cuts and Jobs Act (TCJA), the United States taxed its citizens, residents, and domestic corporations on their worldwide income. However, to the extent that a foreign jurisdiction and the United States taxed the same income, this framework could have resulted in double taxation. The U.S. foreign tax credit (FTC) regime alleviated potential double taxation by allowing a non-refundable credit for foreign income taxes paid or accrued that could be applied to reduce the U.S. tax on foreign source income. Although TCJA eliminated the U.S. tax on some foreign source income, the United States continues to tax other foreign source income, and to provide foreign tax credits against this U.S. tax. The changes made by TCJA to international taxation necessitate certain changes in this FTC regime.

The FTC calculation operates by defining different categories of foreign source income (a "separate category") based on the type of income.[3] Foreign taxes paid or accrued as well as deductions for expenses borne by U.S. parents and domestic affiliates that support foreign operations are also allocated to the separate categories under similar principles. The taxpayer can then use foreign tax credits allocated to each category against the U.S. tax owed on income in that category. This approach means that taxpayers who pay foreign taxes on income in one category cannot claim a credit against U.S. taxes owed on income in a different category, an important feature of the FTC regime. For example, suppose a domestic corporate taxpayer has $100 of active foreign source income in the "general category" and $100 of passive foreign source income, such as interest income, in the "passive category." It also has $50 of foreign taxes associated with the "general category" income and $0 of foreign taxes associated with the "passive category" income. The allowable FTC is determined separately for the two categories. Therefore, none of the $50 of "general category" FTCs can be used to offset U.S. tax on the "passive category" income. This taxpayer has a pre-FTC U.S. tax liability of $42 (21 percent of $200) but can claim a FTC for only $21 (21 percent of $100) of this liability, which is the U.S. tax owed with respect to active foreign source income in the general category. The $21 represents what is known as the taxpayer's foreign tax credit limitation. The taxpayer may carry the remaining $29 of foreign taxes ($50 minus $21) back to the prior taxable year and then forward for up to 10 years (until used), and is allowed a credit against U.S. tax on general category foreign source income in the carryover year, subject to certain restrictions.

The proposed regulations are needed to address changes introduced by the TCJA and to respond to outstanding issues raised in comments to the 2018 FTC proposed regulations. In particular, the comments highlighted the following areas of concern: (a) uncertainty concerning appropriate allocation of R&E expenditures across FTC categories, (b) the need to treat loans from partnerships to partners the same as loans from partners to partnerships with respect to aligning interest income to interest expense, and (c) uncertainty regarding the appropriate level of aggregation (affiliated group versus subgroup) at which expenses of insurance companies should be allocated to foreign source income. In addition, the proposed regulations are needed to expand the application of section 905(c) to cases where a foreign tax redetermination changes a taxpayer's eligibility for the high-taxed exception under subpart F and GILTI.

---

[3] Prior to the TCJA, these categories were primarily the passive income and general income categories. The TCJA added new separate categories for global intangible low-taxed income (the section 951A category) and foreign branch income.

B. Overview of the proposed regulations

These proposed regulations address the following issues: (1) the allocation and apportionment of deductions under sections 861 through 865, including new rules on the allocation and apportionment of research and experimentation (R&E) expenditures and certain deductions of life insurance companies; (2) the definition of financial services income under section 904(d)(2)(D); (3) the allocation of foreign income taxes to the foreign income to which such taxes relate; (4) the interaction of the branch loss and dual consolidated loss recapture rules with sections 904(f) and (g); (5) the effect of foreign tax redeterminations of foreign corporations on the application of the high-tax exception described in section 954(b)(4) (including for purposes of determining tested income under section 951A(c)(2)(A)(i)(III)), and required notifications under section 905(c) to the IRS of foreign tax redeterminations and related penalty provisions; (6) the definition of foreign personal holding company income under section 954; (7) the application of the foreign tax credit disallowance under section 965(g); and (8) the application of the foreign tax credit limitation to consolidated groups.

C. Economic analysis

1. Baseline

The Treasury Department and the IRS have assessed the benefits and costs of these proposed regulations relative to a no-action baseline reflecting anticipated Federal income tax-related behavior in the absence of these regulations.

2. Summary of economic effects

The proposed regulations provide certainty and clarity to taxpayers regarding the allocation of income, expenses, and foreign income taxes to the separate categories. In the absence of the enhanced specificity provided by these regulations, similarly situated taxpayers might interpret the foreign tax credit provisions of the tax code differently, potentially resulting in inefficient patterns of economic activity. For example, in the absence of the proposed regulations, one taxpayer might have chosen not to undertake research (that is, incur R&E expenses) in a particular location, based on that taxpayer's interpretation of the tax consequences of such expenditures, that another taxpayer, making a different interpretation of the tax treatment of R&E, might have chosen to pursue in that same location. If this difference in interpretations confers a competitive advantage on the less productive enterprise, U.S. economic performance may suffer. The guidance provided in these regulations helps to ensure that taxpayers face more uniform incentives when making economic decisions. In general, economic performance is enhanced when businesses face more uniform signals about tax treatment.

Because the TCJA is new, the Treasury Department and the IRS do not know with reasonable precision the tax interpretations that taxpayers might make in the absence of this guidance. To the extent that taxpayers would generally have interpreted the foreign tax credit rules as being less favorable to the taxpayer than the proposed regulations provide, the proposed regulations may result in additional international activity by these taxpayers relative to the no-action baseline. This additional activity may include both activities that are beneficial to the U.S. economy (perhaps because they represent enhanced international opportunities for businesses with U.S. owners) and activities that are not beneficial (perhaps because they are accompanied by reduced activity in the United States). In essence, the Treasury Department and the IRS recognize that additional foreign economic activity by U.S. taxpayers may be a complement or substitute to activity within the United States and that to the extent these regulations change this activity (relative to the no-action baseline or alternative regulatory approaches), a mix of results may occur.

The Treasury Department and the IRS have not undertaken quantitative estimates of the economic effects of these regulations. The Treasury Department and the IRS do not have readily available data or models to estimate with reasonable precision (i) the tax stances that taxpayers would likely take in the absence of the proposed regulations or under alternative regulatory approaches; (ii) the difference in business decisions that taxpayers might make between the proposed regulations and the no-action baseline or alternative regulatory approaches; or (iii) how this difference in those business decisions will affect measures of U.S. economic performance.

In the absence of such quantitative estimates, the Treasury Department and the IRS have undertaken a qualitative analysis of the economic effects of the proposed regulations relative to the no-action baseline and relative to alternative regulatory approaches. This analysis is presented in part I.C.3 of these Special Analyses.

3. Economic effects of specific provisions

i. Rules for allocating R&E expenditures under the sales method

a. Background

Under long-standing foreign tax credit rules, taxpayers must allocate expenditures to income categories. In the case of research and experimentation (R&E) expenditures, taxpayers can elect between a "sales method" and a "gross income method" to allocate the R&E expenses.[4]

The TCJA created some uncertainty regarding the application of the sales method because of the introduction of the section 951A category. In particular, comments raised issues regarding whether any R&E expenditures should be allocated to the section 951A category. The fact that sales by CFCs generate tested income and tested income is generally assigned to the section 951A category might imply that R&E expenditures should be allocated to the section 951A category. But the fact that royalty payments from the CFC to the U.S. taxpayer (e.g., in remuneration for IP held by the parent that is licensed to the CFC to create the products that are sold) are in the general category implies that R&E expenditures should be allocated to the general category.

The gross income method is based on a different apportionment factor (gross income) as compared to the sales method (gross receipts). However, the gross income method is subject to certain conditions that require the result to be within a certain band around the result under the sales method, because historically the Treasury Department and the IRS have considered that the gross income method could lead to anomalous results and could be more easily manipulated than the sales method.[5] The uncertainty with respect to R&E expense allocation under the sales method needed resolution, and because the gross income method is tied to the sales method, any changes to the sales method required consideration of the gross income method.

b. Options considered for the proposed regulations

The Treasury Department and the IRS considered three options with respect to the allocation of R&E expenditures to the section 951A category for purposes of calculating the FTC limitation. The first option was to confirm that R&E expenditures are allocated to the section 951A category under the sales method and to otherwise leave their treatment under the gross income method unchanged. The second option was to revise the

---

[4] If the taxpayer chooses the gross income method, 25 percent of the R&E expenditures are exclusively apportioned to the source where more than 50 percent of the taxpayer's R&E activities occur (generally the United States), and the other 75 percent is apportioned ratably. If a taxpayer chooses the sales method then 50 percent of the R&E expenditures are exclusively apportioned on the same basis, and the other 50 percent is apportioned ratably.

[5] The gross income method is more susceptible to manipulation because taxpayers can manage the type and amount of their foreign gross income by, for example, not paying a dividend and because presuming a factual relationship between the R&E expenditure and the related class of income based on the relative amounts of a taxpayer's gross income was more attenuated than a factual relationship based on sales.

sales method to provide that R&E expenditures are only allocated to the income that represents the taxpayer's return on intellectual property (thus, R&E expenditures could not be allocated to income from the taxpayer's CFC sales) and otherwise leave their treatment under the gross income method unchanged. The third option was to revise the sales method as considered in the second option and eliminate the gross income method for purposes of allocating R&E expenditures.

The proposed regulations adopt the last option. This option allows for the provision of an allocation and apportionment method for R&E expenditures that generally matches the expense reasonably with the income it generates. The matching of income and expenses generally produces a more efficient tax system contingent on the overall Code. Additionally, because this option results in no R&E expense being allocated to section 951A category income, it does not incentivize taxpayers with excess credits in the section 951A category to perform R&E through foreign subsidiaries; instead, the chosen option generally incentivizes choosing the location of R&E based on economic considerations rather than tax-related reasons, contingent on the overall Code. Finally, because the proposed regulations adopt the principle of allocating and apportioning R&E expenditures to IP-related income of the U.S. taxpayer, the gross income method is no longer relevant, because it allocates and apportions R&E expenditures to the section 951A category, and section 951A category gross income is not IP income to the U.S. taxpayer.

c. Number of affected taxpayers

The Treasury Department and the IRS have determined that the population of affected taxpayers consists of any U.S. taxpayer with R&E expenditures and foreign operations. There are around 2,500 such taxpayers in currently available tax filings from taxable years 2015 - 2017. Based on Statistics of Income data for 2014, approximately $40 billion of R&E expenses of such taxpayers were allocated to foreign source income, out of a total of $190 billion in qualified research expenses reported by such taxpayers in that year.[6]

ii. Application of section 905(c) to changes affecting the high-tax exception

a. Background

Section 905(c) provides special rules for a foreign tax redetermination (FTR), which is when the amount of foreign tax paid in an earlier year (origin year) is changed in a later year (FTR year). This redetermination may be necessary, for example, because the taxpayer gets a refund or because a foreign audit determines that the taxpayer owes additional foreign tax. Since these additional taxes (or refunds) relate to the origin year, an FTR affects a taxpayer's origin year tax position (as well as FTC carryovers from that year).

Prior to TCJA, FTRs of foreign corporations generally resulted in prospective "pooling adjustments" to foreign tax credits. Under this approach, taxpayers simply added to or reduced the amount of foreign taxes in their foreign subsidiary's FTC "pool" going forward rather than amend the deemed paid taxes claimed on their origin year return. TCJA eliminated the pooling mechanism for taxes (because the adoption of a participation exemption system along with the elimination of deferral made it unnecessary) and replaced it with a system where taxes are deemed paid each year with an inclusion or distribution of previously taxed earnings and profits ("PTEP").

The 2019 FTC final regulations make clear that an FTR of a United States taxpayer must always be accounted for in the origin year, and that the taxpayer must file an amended return reflecting any resulting change in the taxpayer's U.S. tax liability. Section 905(c) provides tools to enforce this amended return requirement. It suspends the statute of limitations with respect to the assessment of any additional U.S. tax liability that results from an FTR, and imposes a civil penalty on taxpayers who fail to notify the IRS (through an amended return) of a FTR. To reflect the repeal of the pooling mechanism, the proposed regulations generally require taxpayers to account for FTRs of foreign subsidiaries on an amended return that reflects revised foreign taxes deemed paid under section 960 and any resulting change in the taxpayer's U.S. tax liability. However, the 2019 FTC final regulations require U.S. tax redeterminations only by reason of FTRs that affect the amount of foreign tax credit taxpayers claimed in the origin year. The rules do not apply to other tax effects, such as when the FTR changes the amount of earnings and profits the taxpayer's CFC had in the origin year, or affects whether or not the CFC's income qualifies for the high-tax exception under GILTI or subpart F.

The interaction of FTRs and the high-tax exception under GILTI and subpart F increases the importance of filing an origin year amended return. In particular, FTRs can give rise to inaccurate origin year U.S. liability calculations in the absence of an amended return precisely because they can change taxpayers' eligibility for the high-tax exception. Therefore, the proposed regulations provide that the section 905(c) rules cover situations in which the FTR affects not only the amount of FTCs taxpayers claimed in the origin year, but also whether or not their CFC's income qualified for the high-tax exception.

b. Options considered for the proposed regulations

The Treasury Department and the IRS considered two options for expanding section 905(c) to cover the high-tax exception. The first option was to limit section 905(c) to changes in the amount of FTCs. The second option was to provide that section 905(c) applies in connection with the high-tax exceptions under GILTI and subpart F.

The proposed regulations adopt the second option. The first option would lead to frequent occurrences of inaccurate results with respect to the GILTI and subpart F high-tax exceptions because it is common for foreign audits to change the amount of tax paid in a prior year. Furthermore, taxpayers would have an incentive to overpay their CFC's foreign tax in the origin year, claim the high-tax exception to avoid subpart F or GILTI inclusions, wait for the 3 year statute of limitations to pass, and then claim a foreign tax refund with the foreign authorities. Without section 905(c) applying, taxpayers would have no obligation or threat of penalty for not amending the origin year return. Although there are FTC regulations that deny a credit if taxpayers make a noncompulsory payment of tax (i.e., taxpayers paid more foreign tax than is necessary under foreign law), those rules are challenging to administer. While taxpayers have the burden to prove that they were legally required to pay the tax, the IRS may need to engage foreign tax law experts to establish that the taxpayer could have successfully fought paying it.

The second option provides a more accurate tax calculation than the first option, and it is instrumental in avoiding abuse. The increased number of amended returns will increase compliance costs for taxpayers, but the Treasury Department and the IRS consider that, in light of the high-tax exception, accurate origin year tax liability calculations necessitate these increased costs; however, the Treasury Department and the IRS solicit comments on this issue.

c. Number of affected taxpayers

The Treasury Department and the IRS determined that the proposed regulations potentially affect those U.S. taxpayers that pay foreign taxes and have a redetermination of that tax. Although data reporting the number of taxpayers subject to an FTR in a given year do not exist, some taxpayers currently subject to FTRs will file amended returns. The Treasury Department and the IRS estimate that there are approximately 300 to 600 U.S. companies with foreign affiliates that file amended returns per year. However, the expansion of the section 905(c) requirement to file an amended return to instances where a FTR changes eligibility for the high-tax exception under GILTI or subpart F has the potential to significantly increase the number of taxpayers filing amended returns. The Treasury Department and the IRS have determined that a high upper bound for the number of taxpayers subject to a FTR that will be required to file amended returns (i.e., taxpayers affected by this provision) can be derived by estimating the

---

[6] Note, however, that these taxpayers might have additional R&E expenses which are not qualified R&E expenses. The tax data do not separately identify such expenses.

number of taxpayers with a potential GILTI or subpart F inclusion. Based on currently available tax filings for taxable years 2015 and 2016, there were about 15,000 C corporations with CFCs that filed at least one Form 5471 with their Form 1120 return. In addition, for the same period, there were about 30,000 individuals with CFCs that e-filed at least one Form 5471 with their Form 1040 return. In 2015 and 2016, there were about 3,000 S corporations with CFCs that filed at least one Form 5471 with their 1120S return. The identified S corporations had an estimated 150,000 shareholders, as an upper bound. Finally, the Treasury Department and the IRS estimate that there were approximately 7,000 U.S. partnerships with CFCs that e-filed at least one Form 5471 as Category 4 or 5 filers in 2015 and 2016. The identified partnerships had approximately 2 million partners, as indicated by the number of Schedules K-1 filed by the partnerships. This number includes both domestic and foreign partners, so it substantially overstates the number of partners that would actually be affected by the final regulations because it includes foreign partners.

iii. Extension of the partnership loan rule to loans from the partner to the partnership

a. Background

The 2019 FTC final regulations provide a rule that aligns interest income and expense when a U.S. partner makes a loan to the partnership. Under this matching rule, the partner's gross interest income is apportioned between U.S. and foreign sources in each separate category based on the partner's interest expense apportionment ratios. This rule minimizes the artificial increase in foreign source taxable income based solely on offsetting amounts of interest income and expense from a related party loan to a partnership. Comments in response to the 2018 FTC proposed regulations requested an equivalent rule when the partnership makes a loan to a U.S. partner.

b. Options considered for the proposed regulations:

The Treasury Department and the IRS considered two options with respect to this rule. The first option was to not provide a rule, because the abuse the Treasury Department and the IRS were concerned about was not relevant with respect to loans from the partnership to the partner. In the absence of a matching rule, the U.S. partner's U.S. source taxable income would be artificially increased but this income is not eligible to be sheltered by FTCs. The second option was to provide an identical rule for loans from the partnership to the partner as was provided in the 2019 FTC final regulations for loans from the partner to the partnership. The proposed regulations adopt the second option. This symmetry helps to ensure that similar economic transactions are treated similarly.

c. Number of affected taxpayers

The Treasury Department and the IRS consider the population of affected taxpayers to consist of any U.S. partner in a partnership which has a loan from the partnership to the partner or certain other parties related to the partner. The Treasury Department and the IRS estimate that there are approximately 450 partnerships and 5,000 partners that would be affected by this regulation.

iv. Allocation and apportionment of expenses for insurance companies

a. Background

Section 818(f) provides that for purposes of applying the expense allocation rules to life insurance companies, the deduction for policyholder dividends, reserve adjustments, death benefits, and certain other amounts are treated as items that cannot be definitely allocated to an item or class of gross income. That means, in general, that the expenses are apportioned ratably across all gross income.

Under the expense allocation rules, for most purposes, affiliated groups are treated as a single entity, although there are exceptions for certain expenses. The statute is unclear, however, about how affiliated groups are to be treated with respect to the allocation of certain expenses for insurance companies. Depending on the approach, the results could be different because the gross income categories across the affiliated group could be calculated in multiple ways. The Treasury Department and the IRS received comments and are aware that in the absence of further guidance taxpayers are likely to take opposite positions on this treatment. Some taxpayers argue that the expenses described in section 818(f) are apportioned based on the gross income of the entire affiliated group, while others argue that expenses are apportioned on a separate company or subgroup basis taking into account only the gross income of life insurance companies.

b. Options considered for the proposed regulations

The Treasury Department and the IRS are aware of at least five potential methods for allocating section 818(f) expenses in a life-nonlife consolidated group. First, the expenses might be allocated solely among items of the life insurance company that has the reserves ("separate entity method"). Second, to the extent the life insurance company has engaged in a reinsurance arrangement that constitutes an intercompany transaction (as defined in § 1.1502-13(b)(1)), the expenses might be allocated in a manner that achieves single entity treatment between the ceding member and the assuming member ("limited single entity method"). Third, the expenses might be allocated among items of all life insurance members ("life subgroup method"). Fourth, the expenses might be allocated among items of all members of the consolidated group (including both life and non-life members) ("single entity method"). Fifth, the expenses might be allocated based on a facts and circumstances analysis ("facts and circumstances method").

In response to the request for comments in the 2018 FTC proposed regulations, the Treasury Department and the IRS received comments advocating for certain of the aforementioned allocation methods. The proposed regulations adopt the separate entity method because it is consistent with section 818(f) and with the separate entity treatment of reserves under § 1.1502-13(e)(2). The Treasury Department and the IRS recognize, however, that this method may create opportunities for consolidated groups to use intercompany transactions to shift their section 818(f) expenses and achieve a more desirable foreign tax credit result. Accordingly, the Treasury Department and the IRS request comments on whether a life subgroup method more accurately reflects the relationship between section 818(f) expenses and the income producing activities of the life subgroup as a whole, and whether the life subgroup method is less susceptible to abuse because it might prevent a consolidated group from inflating its foreign tax credit limitation through intercompany transfers of assets, reinsurance transactions, or transfers of section 818(f) expenses. The Treasury Department and the IRS also request comments regarding the appropriate application of § 1.1502-13(c) to neutralize the ancillary effects of separate-entity computation of insurance reserves, such as the computation of limitations under section 904.

c. Number of affected taxpayers

The Treasury Department and the IRS have determined that the population of affected taxpayers consists of life insurance companies that are members of an affiliated group. The Treasury Department and the IRS have established that there are approximately 60 such taxpayers.

II. *Paperwork Reduction Act*

For purposes of the Paperwork Reduction Act of 1995 (44 U.S.C. 3507(d)) ("PRA"), there is a collection of information in proposed § § 1.905-4 and 1.905-5(b). When a redetermination of U.S. tax liability is required by reason of a foreign tax redetermination (FTR), the proposed regulations generally require the taxpayer to notify the IRS of the FTR and provide certain information necessary to redetermine the U.S. tax due for the year or years affected by the FTR. If there is no change in the U.S. tax liability as a result of the FTR or if the FTR is caused by certain de minimis fluctuations in foreign currency rates, the taxpayer may simply attach the notification to their next filed tax return and make any appropriate adjustments in that year. However, taxpayers are generally required to file an amended return (or an administrative adjustment request in the case of certain partnerships) for the year or years affected by the FTR along with an updated Form 1116 Foreign Tax Credit (Individual, Estate, or Trust) (covered under OMB Control Number 1545-0074 individual, or 1545-0121 estate and trust) or Form 1118 Foreign Tax Credit-Corporations (OMB Control Number 1545-0123), and a written statement providing specific information relating to the FTR. Since the burden for filing amended income tax returns and the Forms 1116 and 1118 are covered under the OMB Control Numbers listed in the prior sentence, the burden estimates for OMB Control Number 1545-1056 only cover the burden for the written statements.

For purposes of the PRA, the reporting burden associated with proposed §§1.905-4 and 1.905-5(b) will be reflected in the PRA submission associated with OMB control number 1545-1056, which is set to expire on December 31, 2020. The number of respondents to this collection was estimated at 13,000 and the total estimated burden time was estimated to be 54,000 hours and total estimated monetized costs of $2,430,540 ($2016).

For taxpayers who are required to file an amended return (along with related Form 1116 or Form 1118) in order to report an FTR, and for purposes of the PRA, the reporting burden for filing the amended return will be reflected in OMB control numbers 1545-0123 (relating to business filers, which represents a total estimated burden time, including all related forms and schedules, of 3.157 billion hours and total estimated monetized costs of $58.148 billion ($2017)), 1545-0074 (relating to individual filers, which represents a total estimated burden time, including all related forms and schedules, of 1.784 billion hours and total estimated monetized costs of $31.764 billion ($2017)), and 1545-0121 (relating to estate and trust filers, which represents a total estimated burden time, including all related forms and schedules, of 25,066,693 hours). These overall burden estimates for OMB control numbers 1545-0123, 1545-0074, and 1545-0121 include, but do not isolate, the estimated burden of the foreign tax credit-related forms as a result of the information collection in the proposed regulations. These numbers are therefore unrelated to the future calculations needed to assess the burden imposed by the proposed regulations. These burdens have also been reported for other regulations related to the taxation of cross-border income and the Treasury Department and the IRS urge readers to recognize that these numbers are duplicates and to guard against overcounting the burden that international tax provisions imposed prior to the TCJA.

As a result of the changes made in the TCJA to the foreign tax credit rules generally, and to section 905(c) specifically, the Treasury Department and the IRS anticipate that the number of respondents may increase modestly among taxpayers who file Form 1120 series returns. The possible increase in the number of respondents is due to the elimination of adjustments to pools of post-1986 earnings and profits and post-1986 foreign income taxes as an alternative to filing an amended return following the changes made in the TCJA. These changes to the burden estimate will be reflected in the PRA submission for the renewal of OMB control number 1545-1056 as well as in the OMB control numbers 1545-0074 (for individuals) and 1545-0123 (for business taxpayers).

The estimates for the number of impacted filers with respect to the collections of information described in this Part II of the Special Analyses are based on filers of income tax returns that file a Form 1065, Form 1040, or Form 1120 series because only filers of these forms are generally subject to the collection of information requirement. The IRS estimates the number of impacted filers to be the following:

	Tax Forms Impacted	
Collection of Information	Number of respondents (estimated)	Forms to which the information may be attached
§1.905-4	8,900 - 11,700	Form 1065 series, Form 1040 series, and Form 1120 series
§1.905-5(b)	8,900 11,700	Form 1065 series, Form 1040 series, and Form 1120 series

The Treasury Department and the IRS request comments on all aspects of information collection burdens related to these proposed regulations, including estimates for how much time it would take to comply with the paperwork burdens described in this Part II of the Special Analyses and ways for the IRS to minimize the paperwork burden. No burden estimates specific to the proposed regulations are currently available. The Treasury Department has not estimated the burden, including that of any new information collections, related to the requirements under the proposed regulations. Those estimates would capture both changes made by the TCJA and those that arise out of discretionary authority exercised in the proposed regulations. The Treasury Department and the IRS welcome comments on all aspects of information collection burdens related to the foreign tax credit. In addition, when available, drafts of IRS forms are posted for comment at https://apps.irs.gov/app/picklist/list/draftTaxForms.htm.

III. *Regulatory Flexibility Act*

Pursuant to the Regulatory Flexibility Act (5 U.S.C. chapter 6), it is hereby certified that the proposed regulations will not have a significant economic impact on a substantial number of small entities within the meaning of section 601(6) of the Regulatory Flexibility Act.

The proposed regulations provide guidance needed to comply with statutory changes and affect individuals and corporations claiming foreign tax credits. The domestic small business entities that are subject to the foreign tax credit rules in the Code and in the proposed regulations are generally those domestic small business entities that are at least 10 percent corporate shareholders of foreign corporations, and so are eligible to claim dividends-received deductions or compute foreign taxes deemed paid under section 960 with respect to inclusions under subpart F and section 951A from CFCs. Other aspects of these proposed regulations also affect domestic small business entities that operate in foreign jurisdictions or that have income from sources outside of the United States. Based on 2017 Statistics of Income data, the Treasury Department and the IRS computed the fraction of taxpayers owning a CFC by gross receipts size class. The smaller size classes have a relatively small fraction of taxpayers that own CFCs, which suggests that many domestic small business entities would be unaffected by these regulations.

Many of the important aspects of the proposed regulations, including all of the rules in proposed §§1.861-8(d)(2)(ii)(B), 1.904-4(c)(7), 1.904-6(f), 1.905-3(b)(2), 1.905-5, 1.954-1, 1.954-2, and 1.965-5(b)(2) apply only to U.S. persons that operate a foreign business in corporate form, and, in most cases, only if the foreign corporation is a CFC. Because it takes significant resources and investment for a business to operate outside of the United States in corporate form, and in particular to own a CFC, the owners of such businesses will infrequently be domestic small business entities, as indicated by the Table. Other provisions in the proposed regulations, including the rules in proposed §§1.861-8(d)(2)(v), 1.861-8(e)(16), 1.861-14, 1.904-4(e), 1.1502-4, and 1.1502-21, generally apply only to members of a consolidated group and insurance companies or other members of the financial services industry earning income from sources outside of the United States. It is infrequent for domestic small entities to operate as part of an affiliated group, to be taxed as an insurance company, or to constitute a financial services entity, and also earn income from sources outside of the United States. Consequently, the Treasury Department and the IRS project that the proposed regulations are unlikely to affect a substantial number of domestic small business entities, however adequate data are not available at this time to certify that a substantial number of small entities would be unaffected.

Fraction of U.S. Corporate Taxpayers reporting CFC Ownership, by Gross Receipts Size Class

Gross Receipts Size Class	Percentage with a CFC
<1 mil	0.40%
1-5 mil	0.80%
5-10 mil	2.70%

Gross Receipts Size Class	Percentage with a CFC
10-20 mil	4.50%
20-30 mil	9.30%
30-50 mil	12.00%
50-100 mil	19.70%
100-150 mil	26.80%
150-200 mil	32.50%
200-250 mil	37.40%
250-500 mil	43.70%
>=500 mil	63.50%

*Data based on 2017 Statistics of Income sample for all 1120 returns except 1120-S and return type=2 (1120-L, 1120-RIC, 1120-F, 1120-REIT, 1120-PC,1120, 1120-L Consolidated 1504c return (controlling industries 524142 and 524143),1120-PC Consolidated 1504C return (controlling industries 524156, 524159), and 1120 Section 594/1504c consolidated return (controlling industries not 524142, 524143, 524156, 524159), 1120 Non-consolidated return).

The Treasury Department and the IRS have determined that the proposed regulations will not have a significant economic impact on domestic small business entities. Based on published information from 2013, foreign tax credits as a percentage of three different tax-related measures of annual receipts (see Table for variables) by corporations are substantially less than the 3 to 5 percent threshold for significant economic impact. The amount of foreign tax credits in 2013 is an upper bound on the change in foreign tax credits resulting from the proposed regulations.

Size (by Business Receipts)	under $500,000	$500,000 under $1,000,000	$1,000,000 under $5,000,000	$5,000,000 under $10,000,000	$10,000,000 under $50,000,000	$50,000,000 under $100,000,000	$100,000,000 under $250,000,000	$250,000,000 or more
FTC/Total Receipts	0.03%	0.00%	0.00%	0.01%	0.01%	0.03%	0.09%	0.56%
FTC/(Total Receipts-Total Deductions)	0.48%	0.03%	0.04%	0.26%	0.22%	0.51%	1.20%	9.00%
FTC/Business Receipts	0.05%	0.00%	0.00%	0.01%	0.01%	0.04%	0.10%	0.64%

Source: Statistics of Income (2013) Form 1120 available at https://www.irs.gov/statistics

Although proposed § 1.905-4 contains a collection of information requirement, the small businesses that are subject to the requirements of proposed § 1.905-4 are domestic small entities with significant foreign operations. The data to assess precise counts of small entities affected by proposed § 1.905-4 are not readily available, but, as the data above suggest, a significant number of small entities are not likely to have significant foreign operations. Further, as demonstrated in the second table in this Part III, foreign tax credits do not have a significant economic impact for small business entities. Therefore, the Treasury Department and the IRS have determined that a substantial number of domestic small business entities will not be subject to proposed § 1.905-4. Moreover, as discussed in this Part III, the proposed regulations do not have a significant economic impact on small entities. Accordingly, it is hereby certified that the requirements of proposed § 1.905-4 will not have a significant economic impact on a substantial number of small entities.

Pursuant to section 7805(f), these proposed regulations will be submitted to the Chief Counsel for Advocacy of the Small Business Administration for comment on its impact on small businesses. The Treasury Department and the IRS also request comments from the public on the certifications in this Part III.

IV. *Unfunded Mandates Reform Act*

Section 202 of the Unfunded Mandates Reform Act of 1995 (UMRA) requires that agencies assess anticipated costs and benefits and take certain other actions before issuing a final rule that includes any Federal mandate that may result in expenditures in any one year by a state, local, or tribal government, in the aggregate, or by the private sector, of $100 million in 1995 dollars, updated annually for inflation. In 2019, that threshold is approximately $154 million. This proposed rule does not include any Federal mandate that may result in expenditures by state, local, or tribal governments, or by the private sector in excess of that threshold.

V. *Executive Order 13132: Federalism*

Executive Order 13132 (entitled "Federalism") prohibits an agency from publishing any rule that has federalism implications if the rule either imposes substantial, direct compliance costs on state and local governments, and is not required by statute, or preempts state law, unless the agency meets the consultation and funding requirements of section 6 of the Executive Order. This proposed rule does not have federalism implications and does not impose substantial direct compliance costs on state and local governments or preempt state law within the meaning of the Executive Order.

Comments and Request for Public Hearing

Before these proposed regulations are adopted as final regulations, consideration will be given to any comments that are submitted timely to the IRS as prescribed in this preamble under the "Addresses" heading. The Treasury Department and the IRS request comments on all aspects of the proposed rules. Additionally, the Treasury Department and the IRS have specifically requested comments in the following parts of the Explanation of Provisions: I.A.1 (various aspects of stewardship expense including definition and exceptions), I.A.5 (future implementation of section 864(f) and potential capitalization of certain expenses solely for purposes of § 1.861-9), I.D (life subgroup method), I.E.1 (different classification methods for R&E expenditures), I.E.3 (contract research arrangements), II.A (additional guidance under sections 954(h) and 952(c)(1)(B)(vi) with respect to financial services entities), II.B (the treatment of foreign tax on base differences and on income that is recognized by a different person for U.S. tax purposes, the interaction of proposed § 1.904-6(f) with sections 245A(g) and 909, and the allocation and apportionment of certain state and foreign income taxes), III.B (foreign tax redeterminations and predecessor or successor entities), III.C.1 (alternative notification requirements under section 905(c)), III.C.2 (coordination between sections 905(c) and 6227), and III.D (alternative adjustments for post-2017 foreign tax redeterminations with respect to pre-2018 taxable years of foreign corporations).

All comments will be available at www.regulations.gov or upon request. A public hearing will be scheduled if requested in writing by any person that timely submits written comments. If a public hearing is scheduled, notice of the date, time, and place for the public hearing will be published in the **Federal Register**.

Drafting Information

The principal authors of the proposed regulations are Karen J. Cate, Jeffrey P. Cowan, Jeffrey L. Parry, Larry R. Pounders, and Suzanne M. Walsh of the Office of Associate Chief Counsel (International). However, other personnel from the Treasury Department and the IRS participated in their development.

[¶ 49,823] Proposed Amendments of Regulations (REG-107431-19), published in the Federal Register on December 17, 2019.

[Code Secs. 162, 164 and 170A]

Charitable entities: Itemized deductions: State or local tax credit.—Amendments of Reg. §§ 1.162-15, 1.164-3, 1.170A-1 and 1.170A-13, updating the regulations under section 162 to reflect current law regarding the application of section 162 to a taxpayer that makes a payment or transfer to an entity described in section 170(c) for a business purpose, are proposed.

AGENCY: Internal Revenue Service (IRS), Treasury.

ACTION: Notice of proposed rulemaking and notification of public hearing.

SUMMARY: This document provides proposed amendments to the regulations under sections 162, 164, and 170 of the Internal Revenue Code (Code). First, the proposed amendments update the regulations under section 162 to reflect current law regarding the application of section 162 to a taxpayer that makes a payment or transfer to an entity described in section 170(c) for a business purpose. Second, the proposed amendments provide safe harbors under section 162 to provide certainty with respect to the treatment of payments made by business entities to an entity described in section 170(c). Third, the proposed amendments provide a safe harbor under section 164 for payments made to an entity described in section 170(c) by individuals who itemize deductions and receive or expect to receive a state or local tax credit in return. Fourth, the proposed amendments update the regulations under section 170 to reflect past guidance and case law regarding the application of the *quid pro quo* principle under section 170 to benefits received or expected to be received by a donor from a third party.

DATES: Written or electronic comments must be received by January 31, 2020. Requests to speak and outlines of topics to be discussed at the public hearing scheduled for February 20, 2020, must be received by January 31, 2020.

ADDRESSES: Submit electronic submissions via the Federal eRulemaking Portal at http://*www.regulations.gov* (indicate IRS and REG-107431-19) by following the online instructions for submitting comments. Once submitted to the Federal eRulemaking Portal, comments cannot be edited or withdrawn. The Department of the Treasury (Treasury Department) and the IRS will publish for public availability any comment received to its public docket, whether submitted electronically or in hard copy. Send hard copy submissions to: CC:PA:LPD:PR (REG-107431-19), Room 5203, Internal Revenue Service, P.O. Box 7604, Ben Franklin Station, Washington, DC 20044. Submissions may be hand-delivered Monday through Friday between the hours of 8 a.m. and 4 p.m. to CC:PA:LPD:PR (REG-107431-19), Courier's Desk, Internal Revenue Service, 1111 Constitution Avenue NW, Washington, DC 20224.

FOR FURTHER INFORMATION CONTACT: Concerning the proposed regulations, Mon L. Lam and Merrill D. Feldstein at (202) 317-4059; concerning submission of comments and requests to speak at the public hearing, Regina Johnson at (202) 317-6901 (not toll-free numbers) or fdms.database@irscounsel.treas.gov. SUPPLEMENTARY INFORMATION:

Background and Explanation of Provisions

I. Contributions in Exchange for State and Local Tax Credits

Section 170(a)(1) generally allows an itemized deduction for any "charitable contribution" paid within the taxable year. Section 170(c) defines "charitable contribution" as a "contribution or gift to or for the use of" an entity described in that section. Under section 170(c)(1), such entities include a State, a possession of the United States, or any political subdivision of the foregoing, or the District of Columbia. Section 170(c)(2) includes certain corporations, trusts, or community chests, funds, or foundations, organized and operated exclusively for religious, charitable, scientific, literary, or educational purposes, or to foster national or international amateur sports competition, or for the prevention of cruelty to children or animals. Section 1.170A-1(c)(5) of the Income Tax Regulations provides that transfers of property to an organization described in section 170(c) that bear a direct relationship to the taxpayer's trade or business and that are made with a reasonable expectation of financial return commensurate with the amount of the transfer may constitute allowable deductions as trade or business expenses rather than as charitable contributions. Section 162(a) allows a deduction for all the ordinary and necessary expenses paid or incurred during the taxable year in carrying on any trade or business. Section 162(b) provides that no deduction shall be allowed under subsection (a) for any contribution or gift that would be allowable as a deduction under section 170 were it not for the percentage limitations, the dollar limitations, or the requirements as to the time of payment set forth in that section.

Section 1.162-15(a) applies to contributions to entities described in section 170(c). Section 1.162-15(a)(1) currently provides that no deduction is allowable under section 162(a) for a contribution or gift by an individual or a corporation if any part thereof is deductible under section 170. For example, if a taxpayer makes a contribution of $5,000 and only $4,000 of this amount is deductible under section 170(a) (whether because of the percentage limitation under either section 170(b)(1) or (2), the requirement as to time of payment, or both), no deduction is allowable under section 162(a) for the remaining $1,000. However, § 1.162-15(a)(2) clarifies that the limitations provided in section 162(b) and § 1.162-15(a)(1) apply only to payments that are in fact contributions or gifts to organizations described in section 170. For example, payments by a transit company to a local hospital (which is a charitable organization within the meaning of section 170) in consideration of a binding obligation on the part of the hospital to provide hospital services and facilities for the company's employees are not contributions or gifts within the meaning of section 170 and may be deductible under section 162(a) if the requirements of section 162(a) are otherwise satisfied.

Section 164(a) allows a deduction for the payment of certain taxes, including: (1) state and local, and foreign, real property taxes; (2) state and local personal property taxes; and (3) state and local, and foreign, income, war profits, and excess profits taxes. In addition, section 164 allows a deduction for taxes not described in the preceding sentence that are paid or accrued within the taxable year in carrying on a trade or business or an activity described in section 212. Moreover, under section 164(b)(5), taxpayers may elect to deduct state and local general sales taxes in lieu of state and local income taxes.

Section 164(b)(6), as added by section 11042(a) of the Tax Cuts and Jobs Act Pub. L. 115-97, (the "TCJA") provides that in the case of an individual, deductions for foreign real property taxes are not allowable under section 164(a)(1), and the deduction for the aggregate amount of the following state and local taxes paid during the calendar year is limited to $10,000 ($5,000 in the case of a married individual filing a separate return): (1) real property taxes; (2) personal property taxes; (3) income, war profits, and excess profits taxes; and (4) general sales taxes. This limitation applies to taxable years beginning after December 31, 2017, and before January 1, 2026, and does not apply to foreign taxes described in section 164(a)(3) or to any taxes described in section 164(a)(1) and (2) that are paid or accrued in carrying on a trade or business or an activity described in section 212.

In response to the limitation in section 164(b)(6), some taxpayers have considered tax planning strategies to avoid or mitigate its effects. Some of these strategies rely on state and local tax credit programs under which states provide tax credits in return for contributions by taxpayers to entities described in section 170(c), and some state and local governments have created new programs intended to facilitate use of these strategies.

On June 11, 2018, the Treasury Department and the IRS announced their intention to propose regulations addressing the proper application of sections 164 and 170 to taxpayers who make contributions under state and local tax credit programs to entities described in section 170(c). See Notice 2018-54, 2018-24 I.R.B. 750. On August 27, 2018, proposed regulations (REG-112176-18) under sections 170 and 642(c) were published in the **Federal Register** (83 FR 43563) ("2018 proposed regulations"). The 2018 proposed regulations proposed amending § 1.170A-1(h)(3) to provide, in general, that if a taxpayer makes a payment or transfers property to or for the use of an entity described in section 170(c), and the taxpayer receives or expects to receive a state or local tax credit in return for such payment or transfer, the tax credit constitutes a return benefit to the taxpayer and reduces the taxpayer's charitable contribution deduction. The 2018 proposed regulations were premised, in part, on the *quid pro quo* principle articulated by the Supreme Court in *United States v. American Bar Endowment*, 477 U.S. 105, 116 (1986), and its progeny that "a payment of money generally cannot constitute a charitable deduction if the contributor expects a substantial benefit in return." The 2018 proposed regulations also proposed amending regulations under section 642(c), to provide a similar rule for payments made by a trust or decedent's estate.

The Treasury Department and the IRS received over 7,700 comments responding to the 2018 proposed regulations and 25 requests to speak at the public hearing, which was held on November 5, 2018. After taking into account the comments received and the concerns expressed at the public hearing, the Treasury Department and the IRS published final regulations in the **Federal Register** on June 13, 2019 (T.D. 9864, 84 FR 27513) ("the final regulations"). The final regulations retained the rules set out in the 2018 proposed regulations, with certain clarifying and technical changes. Most significantly, the final regulations retained the general rule that, if a taxpayer makes a payment or transfers property to or for the use of an entity described in section 170(c), and the taxpayer receives or expects to receive a state or local tax credit in return for such transfer, the tax credit constitutes a return benefit to the taxpayer, or *quid pro quo*, reducing the taxpayer's charitable contribution deduction. See § 1.170A-1(h)(3) of the final regulations.

In response to Notice 2018-54 and the 2018 proposed regulations, commenters raised several ancillary issues. These issues involved: (1) treatment of business entity payments to entities described in section 170(c); (2) treatment of payments by individuals with total state and local tax liabilities that were less than or equal to the section 164(b)(6) limitations; and (3) application of the *quid pro quo* principle under section 170 to benefits received or expected to be received by the donor from a party other than the donee.

Although the Treasury Department and the IRS have provided sub-regulatory safe harbors related to the first two issues (in Rev. Proc. 2019-12, 2019-04 I.R.B. 401, and Notice 2019-12, 2019-27 I.R.B. 57), the Treasury Department and the IRS believe that it is appropriate to include these safe harbors in proposed regulations and to request comments. Further, in the preamble to the final regulations, the Treasury Department and the IRS extensively addressed the third issue — whether a benefit received or expected to be received from a party other than the donee may constitute a *quid pro quo* that reduces the taxpayer's charitable contribution deduction under section 170. The preamble to the final regulations stated that the Treasury Department and the IRS would propose additional regulations setting forth a general rule for benefits received or expected to be received from third parties. Accordingly, the proposed regulations, provided herein, would amend the regulations under sections 162, 164, and 170 to provide guidance on these three issues.

II. Payments by Business Entities in Exchange for State or Local Tax Credits

After the issuance of Notice 2018-54, and continuing after the publication of the 2018 proposed regulations, the Treasury Department and the IRS received inquiries from taxpayers regarding the application of the proposed regulations to businesses that make payments to entities described in section 170(c) pursuant to state and local tax credit programs. The taxpayers sought guidance as to whether a business entity may deduct these payments under section 162 as ordinary and necessary business expenses incurred in carrying on a trade or business. In response, on September 5, 2018, the IRS released a frequently asked question ("FAQ") stating that a business taxpayer making a payment to an entity described in section 170(c) is generally permitted to deduct such payment as an ordinary and necessary business expense under section 162 if the payment is made with a business purpose. However, after the release of the FAQ, taxpayers continued to express concern about whether the business purpose requirement is met for contributions that result in a tax credit. Specifically, taxpayers asked whether payments by business entities in exchange for state and local tax credits would bear a direct relationship to the taxpayer's trade or business such that these payments would qualify as ordinary and necessary business expenses of carrying on a trade or business under section 162(a).

On December 28, 2018, the IRS issued Rev. Proc. 2019-12, providing a safe harbor under section 162 for payments made by a business entity that is a C corporation or specified passthrough entity to or for the use of an organization described in section 170(c) if the C corporation or specified passthrough entity receives or expects to receive state or local tax credits in return. The revenue procedure states that, to the extent that a C corporation receives or expects to receive a state or local tax credit in return for a payment to an organization described in section 170(c), it is reasonable to conclude that there is a direct benefit and a reasonable expectation of commensurate financial return to the C corporation's business in the form of a reduction in the state or local taxes the C corporation would otherwise be required to pay. Thus, the revenue procedure provides a safe harbor that allows a C corporation engaged in a trade or business to treat the portion of the payment that is equal to the amount of the credit received or expected to be received as meeting the requirements of an ordinary and necessary business expense under section 162.

The IRS determined that a similar analysis is appropriate in the case of a business entity other than a C corporation if (1) the business entity is regarded as separate from its owner for all Federal tax purposes under § 301.7701-3 of the Procedure and Administration Regulations ("passthrough entity"); (2) the passthrough entity operates a trade or business within the meaning of section 162; (3) the passthrough entity is subject to a state or local tax incurred in carrying on its trade or business that is imposed directly on the entity; and (4) in return for a payment to an entity described in section 170(c), the passthrough entity receives or expects to receive a state or local tax credit that the entity applies or expects to apply to offset a state or local tax other than a state or local income tax. Thus, to the extent that a specified passthrough entity makes a payment to an entity described in section 170(c) and receives or expects to receive a state or local tax credit, Rev. Proc. 2019-12 permits the passthrough entity to treat the payment as meeting the requirements of an ordinary and necessary business expense under section 162. The safe harbors for C corporations and specified passthrough entities apply only to payments of cash and cash equivalents.

In the interest of providing certainty for taxpayers, the Treasury Department and the IRS believe that it is appropriate to propose regulations to incorporate the safe harbors set out in Rev. Proc. 2019-12 and to request comments on these safe harbors. Thus, these proposed regulations propose amending § 1.162-15(a) to incorporate the Rev. Proc. 2019-12 safe harbors. These proposed regulations also propose amending § 1.170A-1(c)(5) and (h)(3)(viii) to provide cross references to § 1.162-15(a). The Treasury Department and the IRS specifically request comments on whether the safe harbors should be expanded to apply to an individual who is carrying on a trade or business or an activity described in section 212.

The proposed regulations propose additional revisions to § 1.162-15(a) to more clearly reflect the current state of the law regarding a taxpayer's payment or transfer to an entity described in section 170(c). If the taxpayer's payment or transfer bears a direct relationship to its trade or business, and the payment is made with a reasonable expectation of commensurate financial return, the payment or transfer to the section 170(c) entity may constitute an allowable deduction as a trade or business expense under section 162, rather than a charitable contribution under section 170. See § 1.170A-1(c)(5); *Marquis v. Commissioner*, 49 T.C. 695 (1968). A proposed example illustrates that this rule applies regardless of whether the taxpayer expects to receive a state or local tax credit in return.

The proposed revisions are also consistent with the decision in *American Bar Endowment*, which states that a payment to an entity described in section 170(c) may have a dual character—part charitable contribution and part business expense. 477 U.S. at 117. Under *American Bar Endowment* and § 1.170A-1(h), if a taxpayer makes a payment to an entity described under section 170(c) in an amount that exceeds the fair market value of the benefit that the taxpayer receives or expects to receive in return, and this excess amount is paid with charitable intent, the taxpayer is allowed a charitable contribution deduction under section 170 for this excess amount.

In addition, the proposed regulations propose to add a cross-reference to § 1.170A-1(h) (payments to section 170(c) entities in exchange for consideration), which provides more detailed rules for determining whether a payment, or a portion of a payment, to an entity described in section 170(c) may be deducted under section 162(a) or section 170.

III. Payments by Individuals in Exchange for State and Local Tax Credits

After publication of the 2018 proposed regulations, commenters expressed concerns that the proposed regulations would create unfair consequences for certain individuals who receive state or local tax credits in return for their payments. Specifically, commenters noted that individuals who itemize deductions for Federal income tax purposes and have total state and local tax liabilities for the taxable year of $10,000 or less ($5,000 or less in the case of a married individual filing a separate return) would be precluded from taking charitable contribution deductions to the extent that they receive state or local tax credits even though the individuals would have been able to deduct equivalent payments of state and local taxes. Thus, if these individuals chose to make a payment to a section 170(c) entity through a state or local tax credit program instead of paying tax to the state or local government, they would lose the deduction to which they would otherwise have been entitled under section 164 even after the application of the section 164(b)(6) limitation.

These state and local tax credit programs effectively offer taxpayers a choice of paying taxes to the state or local government or making a payment to a section 170(c) entity and receiving a tax credit that offsets a tax liability the taxpayer would otherwise owe to the state or local government. This situation can be analogized to situations in which an individual entitled to receive a payment from a second party directs or permits the second party to satisfy its payment obligation by making a payment to a third party. In such situations, the payment may be treated, for Federal income tax purposes, as a payment by the payor to the individual entitled to receive payment. *Cf.* Rev. Rul. 86-14, 1986-1 C.B. 304, modifying Rev. Rul. 74-75, 1974-1 C.B. 19 (payment made by an employer to a third party to discharge an obligation of an employee treated for Federal income tax purposes as made by the employer to the employee).

For these reasons, on June 11, 2019, the IRS released Notice 2019-12, announcing that the Treasury Department and the IRS intend to publish proposed regulations with a safe harbor under section 164 for individuals who make payments to section 170(c) entities in return for state or local tax credits. Under this safe harbor, an individual who itemizes deductions and who makes a payment to an entity described in section 170(c) in exchange for a state or local tax credit may treat as a payment of state or local tax for purposes of section 164 the portion of such payment for which a charitable contribution deduction is or will be disallowed under § 1.170A-1(h)(3). This treatment is allowed in the taxable year in which the payment is made, but only to the extent that the individual applies the resulting credit pursuant to applicable state or local law to offset the individual's state or local tax liability for such taxable year or the preceding taxable year. Notice 2019-12 requested comments for purposes of incorporating the safe harbor in proposed regulations.

The Treasury Department and the IRS received several comments in response to Notice 2019-12. Generally, commenters responded favorably to the safe harbor in the notice, finding that its rationale was sound and that the rule would effectively eliminate concerns that the final regulations under § 1.170A-1(h)(3) unfairly burden individuals who itemize deductions and have state and local tax liabilities that are less than the section 164(b)(6) limitation. One commenter noted that Executive Order 12866, which directs the agency issuing a regulation to identify the problem it intends to address and design the regulation in the most cost-effective manner to achieve that objective with the least amount of burden on society, further supports the safe harbor. See Executive Order 12866, section 1(b). This commenter also suggested that the IRS should track the effects of the safe harbor by requiring taxpayers to disclose state tax and local tax credits on their Form 1040, Schedule A. Alternatively, the commenter suggested that the IRS obtain this information directly from the states. Another commenter generally supported the safe harbor, but suggested that the Treasury Department and the IRS should avoid creating more safe harbor exceptions to § 1.170A-1(h)(3) of the final regulations. This commenter also expressed concerns about the application of the safe harbor when the state and local tax limitation under section 164(b)(6) expires or is modified.

Other commenters were concerned that Notice 2019-12 did not fully address the tax consequences to taxpayers who received or expected to receive state or local tax credits. Specifically, these commenters asked that the Treasury Department and the IRS provide guidance to address the treatment of state or local tax credits for Federal income tax purposes upon their sale or expiration. As noted in the preamble to the final regulations, the Treasury Department and the IRS recognize the significance and complexity of these questions. The Treasury Department and the IRS continue to study these issues and invite additional comment to inform potential future guidance on these issues.

The Treasury Department and the IRS continue to believe that the notice provides a fair, reasonable, and legally sound basis for the safe harbor for individual taxpayers, and that the safe harbor should be added to the regulations under section 164. Accordingly, these proposed regulations propose adding § 1.164-3(j) to provide a safe harbor for individuals who make a payment to or for the use of an entity described in section 170(c) in return for a state or local tax credit. These proposed regulations also propose adding § 1.170A-1(h)(3)(ix) to provide a cross reference to the safe harbor proposed under § 1.164-3(j) and to request comments.

Under these proposed regulations, an individual who itemizes deductions and who makes a payment to a section 170(c) entity in exchange for a state or local tax credit may treat as a payment of state or local tax for purposes of section 164 the portion of such payment for which a charitable contribution deduction under section 170 is or will be disallowed under § 1.170A-1(h)(3). This treatment is allowed in the taxable year in which the payment is made, but only to the extent that the resulting credit is applied pursuant to applicable state or local law to offset the individual's state or local tax liability for such taxable year or the preceding taxable year. Any unused credit permitted to be carried forward may be treated as a payment of state or local tax under section 164 in the taxable year or years for which the carryover credit is applied in accordance with state or local law. The safe harbor for individuals applies only to payments of cash and cash equivalents.

The proposed regulations are not intended to permit a taxpayer to avoid the limitations of section 164(b)(6). Therefore, the proposed regulations provide that any payment treated as a state or local tax under section 164, pursuant to the safe harbor provided in § 1.164-3(j) of the proposed regulations, is subject to the limitations on deductions in section 164(b)(6). Furthermore, the proposed regulations are not intended to permit deductions of the same payments under more than one provision. Thus, the proposed regulations provide that an individual who relies on the safe harbor in § 1.164-3(j) to deduct qualifying payments under section 164 may not also deduct the same payments under any other section of the Code.

IV. Consideration Provided by Party Other Than the Donee

Section 1.170A-1(h)(1) provides that no part of a payment that a taxpayer makes to or for the use of an organization described in section 170(c) that is in consideration for (as defined in § 1.170A-13(f)(6)) goods or services (as defined in § 1.170A-13(f)(5)) is a contribution or gift within the meaning of section 170(c) unless the taxpayer (i) intends to make a payment in an amount that exceeds the fair market value of the goods or services; and (ii) makes a payment in an amount that exceeds the fair market value of the goods or services.

Section 1.170A-1(h)(2) states that the charitable contribution deduction under section 170(a) may not exceed the amount of cash paid and the fair market value of property transferred to an organization described in section 170(c) over the fair market value of goods or services the organization provides in return. Section 1.170A-13(f)(5) defines goods or services as cash, property, services, benefits, and privileges. Section 1.170A-13(f)(6) provides that a donee provides goods or services in consideration for a taxpayer's payment if, at the time the taxpayer makes a payment to the donee, the taxpayer receives or expects to receive goods or services in exchange for that payment.

Section 1.170A-1(h)(3)(iii) defines "in consideration for" for purposes of determining whether a state or local tax credit should reduce a charitable contribution under section 170. This section provides that the term "in consideration for" shall have the meaning set forth in §1.170A-13(f)(6), except that the state or local tax credit need not be provided by the donee organization.

Some commenters on the 2018 proposed regulations interpreted the definition of "in consideration for" under §1.170A-13(f)(6) to suggest that consideration provided by a third party is disregarded in calculating the charitable contribution deduction, and that §1.170A-1(h)(3)(iii) of the proposed regulations provided an exception from this rule solely for state or local tax credits provided by third parties. Other commenters disagreed with this interpretation and suggested that the final regulations should set forth a general rule clarifying that consideration includes all benefits that a taxpayer receives or expects to receive, regardless of whether they are provided by the donee.

In the preamble to the final regulations, the Treasury Department and the IRS acknowledged that the final regulations did not address all situations in which a taxpayer makes a payment or transfers property and receives or expect to receive benefits from a party that is not the donee. Accordingly, the preamble to the final regulations indicated that the Treasury Department and the IRS intended to propose amendments to the regulations under section 170 to make clear that the *quid pro quo* principle applies regardless of whether the party providing the *quid pro quo* is the donee.

As noted in the preamble to the final regulations, in *American Bar Endowment*, 477 U.S. at 116-17, and *Hernandez v. Commissioner*, 490 U.S. 680, 691-92 (1989), the Supreme Court made clear that a payment is not a charitable contribution if the donor expects to receive a substantial benefit in return. *American Bar Endowment* and *Hernandez* did not directly address the question of benefits provided by third parties; the return benefits at issue in those cases were provided by the donees. However, the Court derived the *quid pro quo* principle in those cases from a lower court decision and a revenue ruling that directly addressed the question. See *American Bar Endowment*, 477 U.S. at 117 (citing *Singer v. United States*, 449 F.2d 413 (Ct. Cl. 1971), and Rev. Rul. 67-246, 1967-2 C.B. 104); *Hernandez*, 490 U.S. at 691 (citing *Singer*). In *Singer*, the appellate division of the Court of Claims (the predecessor to the Court of Appeals for the Federal Circuit) held that a sewing machine company was not eligible for a charitable contribution deduction for selling sewing machines to schools at a discount because the company "expected a return in the nature of future increased sales" to students. *Singer*, 449 F.2d at 423-24. In so holding, the court expressly rejected the company's argument that this expected benefit should be ignored because it would come from the students rather than from the schools. *Id*. at 422-23. The court stated, "Obviously, we cannot agree with plaintiff's distinction." *Id*.

In Rev. Rul. 67-246, Example 11, a local store agreed to award a transistor radio, worth $15, to each person who contributed $50 or more to a specific charity. The ruling concluded that if a taxpayer received a $15 radio as a result of a $100 payment to the charity, only $85 qualified as a charitable contribution deduction. It did not matter that the donor received the $15 radio from the store, a third party, rather than from the charity. This conclusion is reflected in the IRS's audit practices. See IRS Conservation Easement Audit Techniques Guide (Rev. Jan. 24, 2018, p. 16) (stating that a "quid pro quo contribution is a transfer of money or property . . . partly in exchange for goods or services in return from the charity or a third party," and "a quid pro quo may also be in the form of an indirect benefit from a third party").

Moreover, courts have ruled that a taxpayer's expectation of significant financial returns demonstrates a lack of charitable intent. For example, in *Ottawa Silica Co. v. United States*, 699 F.2d 1124 (Fed. Cir. 1983), the Federal Circuit denied a taxpayer's charitable contribution deduction for the value of land the taxpayer donated for construction of a school. The court's analysis focused on the taxpayer's expectation of benefits, and not on the source of such benefits. The court found that the taxpayer had reason to believe that construction of a school would result in the construction of new roads that would in turn increase the value of the taxpayer's retained land. The court recognized that although the taxpayer did not receive an agreement from any party that the roads would be built, the expectation of this benefit was a sufficient reason to deny the charitable contribution deduction. More recently, in *Wendell Falls Development, LLC v. Commissioner*, T.C. Memo. 2018-45, a taxpayer contributed a conservation easement that essentially restricted land for use as a park. The taxpayer expected this restriction to increase the value of the taxpayer's adjacent property. The Tax Court disallowed the taxpayer's claimed charitable contribution deduction for the easement, finding that the taxpayer contributed the easement with the expectation of receiving a substantial benefit (increased value of taxpayer's adjacent property) from the contribution, even though the expected benefit would not come from the donee. In accordance with these authorities, the source of the return benefit is immaterial in determining whether the donee at the time of the contribution expects to receive substantial benefits in return.

The *quid pro quo* principle is thus equally applicable regardless of whether the donor expects to receive the benefit from the donee or from a third party. In either case, the donor's payment is not a charitable contribution or gift to the extent that the donor expects a substantial benefit in return. Accordingly, the Treasury Department and the IRS propose amendments to §1.170A-1(h) that address a donor's payments in exchange for consideration in order for the regulation to reflect existing law. Specifically, these proposed amendments revise paragraph (h)(4) to provide definitions of "in consideration for" and "goods and services" for purposes of applying the rules in §1.170A-1(h). Under the proposed regulations, a taxpayer will be treated as receiving goods and services in consideration for a taxpayer's payment or transfer to an entity described in section 170(c) if, at the time the taxpayer makes the payment or transfer, the taxpayer receives or expects to receive goods or services in return.

The proposed regulations do not amend the language of §1.170A-13(f)(6) which discusses "in consideration for" for purposes of determining whether the taxpayer provides proper substantiation of its charitable contribution. Section 1.170A-13(f) details the requirements of a contemporaneous written acknowledgment, including a statement of whether the donee organization provides any goods or services in consideration for any cash or other property transferred to the donee organization and a description and a good faith estimate of the value of those goods or services. See §1.170A-13(f)(2)(ii) and (iii). These substantiation provisions refer only to written acknowledgments from donee organizations and do not address the application of *quid pro quo* principles to benefits received from parties other than donees. The Treasury Department and the IRS request comments on whether guidance concerning substantiation and reporting of *quid pro quo* benefits provided or expected to be provided by third parties, including state governments, would be beneficial to taxpayers in demonstrating that they have given more than they received or expected to receive and to the IRS in administering the proposed regulation. In addition, the Treasury Department and the IRS request comments regarding the manner by which donors, donees, or third parties may report or provide substantiation for the value or type of consideration received or expected to be received from third parties.

For additional clarity, the proposed regulation amends the language in §1.170A-1(h)(2)(i)(B) to clarify that the fair market value of goods and services includes the value of goods and services provided by parties other than the donee. Also, the proposed regulation adds a definition of "goods and services" that is the same as the definition in §1.170A-13(f)(5). Finally, the proposed regulation revises the cross-references defining "in consideration for" and "goods and services" in paragraphs (h)(1) and (h)(3)(iii) to be consistent with the proposed definitions provided in paragraph (h)(4).

Proposed Applicability Dates

The proposed amendments contained in §§1.162-15(a)(1) and (2) and 1.170A-1(c)(5), regarding the application of section 162 to taxpayers that make payments or transfers to entities described in section 170(c), are proposed to apply to payments or transfers on or after December 17, 2019. However, a taxpayer may rely on these proposed regulations for payments and transfers made on or after January 1, 2018 and before the date regulations finalizing these proposed regulations are published in the Federal Register.

The proposed amendment contained in §1.162-15(a)(3), regarding safe harbors for C corporations and specified passthrough entities making payments to or for the use of section 170(c) entities in exchange for state or local tax credits, is proposed to apply to payments on or after December 17, 2019. However, prior to this date, a taxpayer may continue to apply Rev. Proc. 2019-12, which applies to payments made on or after January 1, 2018.

The proposed amendments contained in §§1.164-3(j) and 1.170A-1(h)(3)(ix), regarding the safe harbor for payments by certain individuals to or for the use of section 170(c) entities, are proposed to apply to payments made on or after June 11, 2019, the date that the IRS issued Notice 2019-12, announcing it intended to publish proposed regulations with a safe harbor under section 164 for individuals who make payments to section 170(c) entities in return for state or local tax credits. However, individuals may rely on these proposed regulations for payments made after August 27, 2018, the applicability date of the final regulations, and before the date regulations finalizing these proposed regulations are published in the Federal Register.

Finally, the proposed amendments contained in §§1.170A-1(h)(1), (h)(2)(i)(B), (h)(3)(iii), and (h)(4)(i), and 1.170A-13(f)(7) clarifying "in consideration for" for purposes of applying §1.170A-1(h) are proposed to apply to payments or transfers on or after December 17, 2019.

Special Analyses

Regulatory Planning and Review – Economic Analysis

Executive Orders 13563 and 12866 direct agencies to assess costs and benefits of available regulatory alternatives and, if regulation is necessary, to select regulatory approaches that maximize net benefits (including potential economic, environmental, public health and safety effects, distributive impacts, and equity). Executive Order 13563 emphasizes the importance of quantifying both costs and benefits, of reducing costs, of harmonizing rules, and of promoting flexibility. This proposed rule is expected to be an EO 13771 regulatory action. Details on the estimated costs of this proposed rule can be found in the rule's economic analysis.

These proposed regulations have been designated as subject to review under Executive Order 12866 pursuant to the Memorandum of Agreement (April 11, 2018) between the Treasury Department and the Office of Management and Budget (OMB) regarding review of tax regulations. The Office of Information and Regulatory Affairs has designated these regulations as significant under section 1(b) of the MOA. Accordingly, the OMB has reviewed these regulations.

A. Background

Section 164 of the Code allows a deduction for certain state and local taxes paid, including state or local income and property taxes. Section 164(b)(6), added by the TCJA, generally limits an individual's deduction of these taxes to $10,000 ($5,000 in the case of a married individual filing a separate return). The limitation does not apply to foreign income taxes or to property taxes that are paid or incurred in carrying on a trade or business or an activity described in section 212. Section 162 allows a deduction for ordinary and necessary expenses paid or incurred in carrying on a trade or business. Section 170 allows a deduction for charitable contributions, specifically for payments or transfers to an entity described in section 170(c); however, the deduction must be reduced by any *quid pro quo* benefit that the taxpayer receives or expects to receive in return.

After the enactment of the TCJA, questions arose regarding the interaction of these deductions. To clarify the application of these provisions, the Treasury Department and the IRS issued guidance including: 1) Final regulations (T.D. 9864, 84 FR 27513) providing that a tax credit received or expected to be received in return for a payment or transfer to an entity described in section 170(c) (hereafter referred to as a charitable entity) is a return benefit to the taxpayer, resulting in the reduction of the charitable contribution deduction; 2) Notice 2019-12 announcing the intent to issue proposed regulations providing a safe harbor for individuals under which a charitable contribution that is disallowed because of a return benefit of a state or local tax credit may be treated as a payment of state or local tax; and 3) Rev. Proc. 2019-12 providing a safe harbor allowing as a deductible business expense certain payments by businesses to charitable organizations.

B. Need for the proposed regulations

The Treasury Department and the IRS believe that it is appropriate to propose as regulations and seek additional public comment on the safe harbors provided in Notice 2019-12 and Rev. Proc. 2019-12. In addition, comments received in response to Notice 2018-54 and the 2018 proposed regulations (guidance preceding the final regulations T.D. 9864) indicate that taxpayers will benefit from additional guidance regarding contributions to a charitable entity resulting in a return benefit from a third party.

C. Overview of the proposed regulations

First, these proposed regulations reflect the guidance in Notice 2019-12. Under the safe harbor an individual who itemizes deductions and who makes a payment to a charitable entity in exchange for a state or local tax credit may be able to claim a state and local tax deduction for the portion of the payment for which a charitable contribution deduction is or will be disallowed as a return benefit. The safe harbor for individuals applies only to payments of cash and cash equivalents. In addition, these payments are subject to the overall limitation on state and local deductions added by the TCJA. Further, any payment may be deducted under only one provision of the Code. Thus, an individual who has total state and local tax liability of $10,000 or less, and who makes a payment to a charitable entity and receives a state tax credit in return resulting in the disallowance of a charitable contribution deduction, may claim an itemized deduction for the disallowed amount, subject to other requirements of the Code.

Second, the proposed regulations incorporate into the regulations under section 162 longstanding principles from case law and existing section 170 regulations regarding a taxpayer's payment or transfer to a charitable entity. Specifically, the proposed regulations confirm that, when a taxpayer's transfer or payment bears a direct relationship to its trade or business, and that transfer or payment is made with a reasonable expectation of commensurate financial return, the transfer or payment to the charitable entity may constitute an allowable deduction under section 162, rather than under section 170. In addition, the proposed regulations incorporate the safe harbors provided by Rev. Proc. 2019-12 for certain payments by C corporations and specified passthrough entities, for cases in which the financial return is a tax credit. Thus, under the proposed regulations, a C corporation may treat the portion of the payment to a charitable entity that is equal to the amount of tax credit received or expected to be received in return as a deductible business expense under section 162. Consistent with Rev. Proc. 2019-12, the proposed regulations also provide that a specified passthrough entity may treat a payment resulting in a tax credit as a business expense if the business is regarded as separate from its owner for Federal tax purposes, if it operates a trade or business within the meaning of section 162, if it is subject to state or local tax incurred in carrying on its trade or business that is imposed directly on the passthrough entity, and if it receives or expects to receive a state or local tax credit in return for the payment.

Third, the proposed regulations clarify that a payment to a charitable entity that results in a return benefit is a *quid pro quo* for purposes of section 170, regardless of whether the donor expects to receive the benefit from the donee or from a third party. As a result, the contribution is reduced by the amount of the return benefit for purposes of determining the amount allowable as a charitable contribution deduction.

D. Economic Analysis

1. Baseline

The Treasury Department and the IRS have assessed the benefits and costs of these proposed regulations compared to a no-action baseline that reflects anticipated Federal income tax-related behavior in the absence of these proposed regulations.

2. Summary of Economic Effects

The proposed regulations reflect existing, published, Treasury Department and IRS policies. As a result, they provide some additional clarity to taxpayers by clearly articulating these existing policies as regulations. The Treasury Department does not expect any noticeable change in taxpayer behavior resulting from these regulations, but requests comments on their potential economic effects. The increased clarity, in particular the provision of safe harbors, is expected to reduce compliance burdens.

As described in the Special Analyses for the final regulations (T.D. 9864), allowing a payment that is disallowed as a charitable contribution deduction because of the receipt or expected receipt of a tax credit to be deducted as a payment of state or local tax means that payments by taxpayers with state and local tax liabilities of $10,000 or less are subject to the same tax treatment under these proposed regulations as under the TCJA (in absence of any guidance) and as under the law prior to the TCJA. (See Example 2, Table 1, T.D. 9864.) It also means that such taxpayers are not treated less favorably than taxpayers with state and local tax liabilities in excess of $10,000 or taxpayers subject to the Alternative Minimum Tax. (See Examples 1 and 3 of Table 1, T.D. 9864.)

The Treasury Department and the IRS request comments on the economic effects of the proposed regulations.

Regulatory Flexibility Act

Pursuant to the Regulatory Flexibility Act (5 U.S.C. chapter 6), it is hereby certified that this proposed rule will not have a significant economic impact on a substantial number of small entities. Although data are not readily available for the IRS and the Treasury Department to assess the number of small entities that are likely to be directly affected by the regulations, the economic impact is unlikely to be significant.

As discussed elsewhere in this preamble, the proposed rule largely updates the regulations to reflect existing law and policy. The proposed amendments would update the section 162 and section 170 regulations to reflect current law. In addition, the proposed amendments add to the regulations safe harbors under section 162 and section 164, regarding deductions when payments are made to entities described in section 170(c) and the donor receives or expects to receive a state or local tax credit in return; these safe harbors were provided previously in Internal Revenue Bulletin guidance. These regulations are expected to provide some additional certainty to taxpayers but are not expected to result in any noticeable change in taxpayer behavior. The increased certainty, and in particular the provision of safe harbors, is expected to reduce compliance burdens. Accordingly, the Treasury Department and the IRS certify that the proposed rule will not have a significant economic impact on a substantial number of small entities.

Notwithstanding this certification, the Treasury Department and the IRS invite comments about the potential impact of this proposed rule on small entities.

Pursuant to section 7805(f), the proposed regulations will be submitted to the Chief Counsel for Advocacy of the Small Business Administration for comment on its impact on small businesses.

Comments and Requests and Public Hearing

Before the regulations proposed herein are adopted as final regulations, consideration will be given to any electronic and written comments that are submitted timely to the IRS as prescribed in this preamble under the ADDRESSES heading. All comments submitted will be made available at *http://* www.regulations.gov or upon request. A public hearing has been scheduled for February, 20, 2020, beginning at 10 a.m. in the Auditorium of the Internal Revenue Building, 1111 Constitution Avenue, N.W., Washington, DC 20224. Due to building security procedures, visitors must enter at the Constitution Avenue entrance. In addition, all visitors must present photo identification to enter the building. Because of access restrictions, visitors will not be admitted beyond the immediate entrance area more than 30 minutes before the hearing starts. For information about having your name placed on the building access list to attend the hearing, see the "FOR FURTHER INFORMATION CONTACT" section of this preamble.

The rules of 26 CFR 601.601(a)(3) apply to the hearing. Persons who wish to present oral comments at the hearing must submit an outline of the topics to be discussed and the time to be devoted to each topic by January 31, 2020. Submit a signed paper or electronic copy of the outline as prescribed in this preamble under the "Addresses" heading. An agenda showing the scheduling of the speakers will be prepared after the deadline for receiving outlines has passed. Copies of the agenda will be available free of charge at the hearing.

Statement of Availability of IRS Documents

IRS Revenue Procedures, Revenue Rulings, Notices, and other guidance cited in this document are published in the Internal Revenue Bulletin (or Cumulative Bulletin) and are available from the Superintendent of Documents, U.S. Government Publishing Office, Washington, DC 20402, or by visiting the IRS website at *http://www.irs.gov.*

Drafting Information

The principal author of these proposed regulations is the Office of the Associate Chief Counsel (Income Tax and Accounting). However, other personnel from the IRS and the Treasury Department participated in their development.

[¶ 49,824]   Proposed Amendments of Regulations (REG-122180-18), published in the Federal Register on December 20, 2019.

[Code Secs. 162 and 338]

Employee remuneration: Deductions: Covered employees: Grandfather rule.—Reg. § 1.162-33, and amendments of **Reg. §§ 1.162-27 and 1.338-1**, setting forth proposed regulations under section 162(m) of the Internal Revenue Code (Code), which limits the deduction for certain employee remuneration in excess of $1,000,000 for federal income tax purposes, are proposed.

Certain Employee Remuneration in Excess of $1,000,000 under Internal Revenue Code Section 162(m)

AGENCY: Internal Revenue Service (IRS), Treasury.

ACTION: Notice of proposed rulemaking and notice of public hearing.

SUMMARY: This document sets forth proposed regulations under section 162(m) of the Internal Revenue Code (Code), which limits the deduction for certain employee remuneration in excess of $1,000,000 for federal income tax purposes. These proposed regulations implement the amendments made to section 162(m) by the Tax Cuts and Jobs Act. These proposed regulations would affect publicly held corporations. This document also provides a notice of a public hearing on these proposed regulations. **DATES:** Written or electronic comments must be received by February 18, 2020. Outlines of topics to be discussed at the public hearing scheduled for March 9, 2020, at 10 a.m. must be received by February 18, 2020.

ADDRESSES: Submit electronic submissions via the Federal eRulemaking Portal at *www.regulations.gov* (indicate IRS and REG-122180-18) by following the online instructions for submitting comments. Once submitted to the Federal eRulemaking Portal, comments cannot be edited or withdrawn. The Department of the Treasury (Treasury Department) and the IRS will publish for public availability any comment received to its public docket, whether submitted electronically or in hard copy. Send hard copy submissions to: CC:PA:LPD:PR (REG-122180-18), Room 5203, Internal Revenue Service, P.O. Box 7604, Ben Franklin Station, Washington, DC 20044. Submissions may be hand-delivered Monday through Friday between the hours of 8 a.m. and 4 p.m. to CC:PA:LPD:PR (REG-122180-18), Courier's Desk, Internal Revenue Service, 1111 Constitution Avenue NW, Washington, DC 20224.

FOR FURTHER INFORMATION CONTACT: Concerning these proposed regulations, Ilya Enkishev at (202) 317-5600; concerning submissions of comments, the hearing, and/or being placed on the building access list to attend the hearing, Regina Johnson at (202) 317-6901 (not toll-free numbers) or fdms.database@irscounsel.treas.gov.

SUPPLEMENTARY INFORMATION:

Background

This document sets forth proposed amendments to the Income Tax Regulations (26 CFR part 1) under section 162(m). Section 162(m)(1) disallows the deduction by any publicly held corporation for applicable employee remuneration paid with respect to any covered employee to the extent that such remuneration for the taxable year exceeds $1,000,000. Section 162(m) was added to the Code by section 3211(a) of the Omnibus Budget Reconciliation Act of 1993, Public Law 103-66. Proposed regulations under section 162(m) were published in the *Federal Register* on December 20, 1993 (58 FR 66310) (1993 proposed regulations). On December 2, 1994, the Treasury Department and the IRS issued amendments to the proposed regulations (59 FR 61884) (1994 proposed regulations). On December 20, 1995, the Treasury Department and the IRS issued final regulations under section 162(m) (TD 8650) (60 FR 65534) (final regulations).

Section 162(m) was amended by section 13601 of the Tax Cuts and Jobs Act (TCJA) (Pub. L. 115-97, 131 Stat. 2054, 2155 (2017)). Section 13601 of TCJA amended the definitions of covered employee, publicly held corporation, and applicable employee remuneration in section 162(m). Section 13601 also provided a transition rule applicable to certain outstanding compensatory arrangements (commonly referred to as the grandfather rule).

On August 21, 2018, the Treasury Department and the IRS released Notice 2018-68 (2018-36 I.R.B. 418), which provides guidance on certain issues under section 162(m). Specifically, the notice provides guidance on the amended rules for identifying covered employees. Furthermore, the notice provides guidance on the operation of the grandfather rule, including when a contract will be considered materially modified so that it is no longer grandfathered. Notice 2018-68 requested comments on the following issues:

- the application of the definition of publicly held corporation to foreign private issuers, including the reference to issuers that are required to file reports under section 15(d) of the Securities Exchange Act of 1934,

- the application of the definition of covered employee to an employee who was a covered employee of a predecessor of the publicly held corporation,

- the application of section 162(m) to corporations immediately after they become publicly held either, through an initial public offering or a similar business transaction, and

- the application of the Securities and Exchange Commission (SEC) executive compensation disclosure rules for determining the three most highly compensated executive officers for a taxable year that does not end on the same date as the last completed fiscal year.

In drafting these proposed regulations, the Treasury Department and the IRS have considered all comments received on the notice. See § 601.601(d)(2)(ii)(b). Commenters noted that the many examples in Notice 2018-68 were helpful in illustrating the guidance in the notice. In light of these comments, the Treasury Department and the IRS have included numerous examples in these proposed regulations to illustrate the proposed rules.

Explanation of Provisions

I. *Overview*

Section 13601 of TCJA significantly amended section 162(m). This document adds a section to the Income Tax Regulations (26 CFR part 1) to reflect these amendments. The amended section 162(m) applies to taxable years beginning after December 31, 2017, except to the extent the grandfather rule applies. Because the final regulations continue to apply to deductions related to amounts of remuneration that are grandfathered, the final regulations are retained as a separate section in the Income Tax Regulations under section 162(m).

II. *Publicly Held Corporation*

A. In General

Section 162(m)(2) defines the term "publicly held corporation." Before the amendments made by section 13601(c) of TCJA, section 162(m)(2) defined publicly held corporation as any corporation issuing any class of common equity securities required to be registered under section 12 of the Securities Exchange Act of 1934 (Exchange Act). In defining a publicly held corporation, § 1.162-27(c)(1) adds that whether a corporation is publicly held is determined based solely on whether, as of the last day of its taxable year, the corporation is subject to the reporting obligations of section 12 of the Exchange Act.

Section 13601(c) of TCJA amended the definition of publicly held corporation in section 162(m)(2) to provide that the term means any corporation which is an issuer (as defined in section 3 of the Exchange Act) the securities of which are required to be registered under section 12 of the Exchange Act, or that is required to file reports under section 15(d) of the Exchange Act. Thus, section 13601(c) of TCJA expanded the definition of publicly held corporation in two ways to include: (1) A corporation with any class of securities (rather than only a class of common equity securities) that is required to be registered under section 12 of the Exchange Act, and (2) a corporation that is required to file reports under section 15(d) of the Exchange Act.

The proposed regulations similarly define a publicly held corporation as any corporation that issues securities required to be registered under section 12 of the Exchange Act or that is required to file reports under section 15(d) of the Exchange Act. Unlike the final regulations, the proposed regulations do not focus on whether the corporation is subject to the reporting obligations of section 12 of the Exchange Act. Rather, tracking the statutory text as amended, the proposed regulations focus on whether a corporation's securities are required to be registered under section 12, or whether a corporation is required to file reports under section 15(d).

Consistent with the statutory expansion of section 162(m), Congress provided in the legislative history to TCJA that the definition of a publicly held corporation "may include certain additional corporations that are not publicly traded, such as large private C or S corporations." H. Rep. 115-466, at 490 (2017) (Conf. Rep.). See also Staff of the Joint Committee on Taxation, General Explanation of Public Law 115-97 (Blue Book), at 261 (December 20, 2018). As a result, these proposed regulations make clear that an S corporation (as defined in section 1361(a)(1)) would qualify as a publicly held corporation if it (1) issues securities required to be registered under section 12(b) of the Exchange Act, or (2) is required to file reports under section 15(d) of the Exchange Act (for example, because the S corporation has issued publicly traded debt). See Proposed § 1.162-33(c)(1)(i). Accordingly, the proposed regulations also provide that an S corporation parent of a qualified subchapter S subsidiary (as defined in section 1361(b)(3)(B)) (QSub) that issues securities required to be so registered, or is required to file such reports, likewise would qualify as a publicly held corporation. See part II.G of this Explanation of Provisions section. See also Proposed § 1.162-33(c)(1)(iv).

For ease of administration, the proposed regulations follow the approach in the final regulations and use the last day of a corporation's taxable year to determine whether it is publicly held. Accordingly, the proposed regulations provide that a corporation is publicly held if, as of the last day of its taxable year, its securities are required to be registered under section 12 of the Exchange Act or it is required to file reports under section 15(d) of the Exchange Act.

A corporation is required to register its securities under section 12 of the Exchange Act in two circumstances. First, section 12(b) of the Exchange Act requires a corporation to register its securities in order to list them for trading on a national securities exchange (15 U.S.C. 78l(b)). Second, section 12(g) of the Exchange Act requires an issuer with total assets exceeding $10 million to register a class of equity securities that is held of record by either 2,000 or more persons, or 500 or more persons who are not accredited investors (as that term is defined by the SEC) (15 U.S.C. 78l(g)).[1]

A corporation is required to file reports under section 15(d) of the Exchange Act when it offers securities for sale in a transaction subject to the registration requirements of the Securities Act of 1933 (Securities Act) and its registration statement is declared effective by the SEC. A corporation's section 15(d) filing obligation is automatically suspended when certain statutory requirements are met, and a corporation that meets other requirements established by rule may file a form with the SEC to suspend its section 15(d) filing obligation.[2] A commenter suggested that a corporation should not be considered publicly held if its obligation to file reports under section 15(d) of the Exchange Act is suspended. The proposed regulations adopt this suggestion.

In defining the term publicly held corporation under pre-amended section 162(m)(2), the final regulations included examples illustrating whether a corporation, as of the last day of its taxable year, is subject to the reporting obligations of section 12 of the Exchange Act. Similarly, these proposed regulations include examples illustrating when a corporation, as of the last day of its taxable year, is either required to file reports under section 15(d) of the Exchange Act or required to register its securities under section 12 of the Exchange Act. Even though the examples in these proposed regulations illustrate the application of the Securities Act and the Exchange Act and the rules thereunder (17 CFR part 240) for purposes of section 162(m), the examples are not intended to provide any guidance on how an issuer should apply the requirements of the Securities Act, the Exchange Act, and the rules thereunder (17 CFR part 240). Questions regarding those requirements should be directed to the SEC.

B. Subsidiaries That File Reports under Section 15(d) of the Exchange Act

Pursuant to the definition of publicly held corporation in the proposed regulations, a corporation is publicly held if, as of the last day of its taxable year, it is required to file reports under section 15(d) of the Exchange Act. A commenter suggested that if a wholly-owned subsidiary corporation of a publicly held corporation subject to section 162(m) is required to file reports under section 15(d) of the Exchange Act, then it should not be considered a publicly held corporation separately subject to section 162(m) because its parent corporation is already subject to section 162(m). According to the commenter, to consider the subsidiary a publicly held corporation would result in two sets of covered employees—one for the parent corporation and one for the subsidiary corporation. The commenter was concerned that there would be too many covered employees for the group of corporations. The proposed regulations do not adopt this suggestion because not treating the subsidiary corporation as a separate publicly held corporation is inconsistent with the text of amended section 162(m)(2), which defines a publicly held corporation as a corporation that is required to file reports under section 15(d) of the Exchange Act. This conclusion is consistent with the affiliated group rule in the final regulations (which is retained in these proposed regulations and discussed in section II.E of this preamble) providing that a publicly held subsidiary is separately subject to section 162(m) and, therefore, has its own set of covered employees. C. Foreign Private Issuers

Foreign issuers[3] may access the U.S. capital markets to raise capital or establish a trading presence for their securities. There are specific rules under the Federal securities laws that apply if a foreign issuer meets the regulatory definition of "foreign private issuer" (FPI). "Foreign private issuer" is defined in 21 CFR 240.3b-4(c). A foreign private issuer is any foreign issuer other than a foreign government, except for an issuer that has (1) more than 50% of its outstanding voting securities held of record by U.S. residents and (2) any of the following: (i) a majority of its officers and directors are citizens or residents of the United States, (ii) more than 50% of its assets are located in the United States, or (iii) its business is principally administered in the United States.

A FPI may access the U.S. capital markets or establish a trading presence in the U.S. by offering or listing its securities, often in the form of American Depositary Receipts (ADRs). An ADR is a negotiable certificate that evidences ownership of a specified number (or fraction) of the FPI's securities held by a depositary (typically, a U.S. bank). Depending on the FPI's level of participation in the U.S. capital market or trading presence, the FPI may be required to register its deposited securities (underlying the ADRs) under section 12 of the Exchange Act.

Commenters recommended that the proposed regulations provide that section 162(m) does not apply to FPIs. Before TCJA, the IRS ruled in several private letter rulings that section 162(m) does not apply to FPIs because FPIs are not required to file a summary compensation table pursuant to the reporting obligations under the Exchange Act.[4] The rationale of the rulings is that section 162(m) does not apply to FPIs because they do not have covered employees as a result of not being required to file a summary compensation table with the SEC. Commenters suggested that section 162(m) should continue to be inapplicable to FPIs because they are not required to disclose compensation of their officers on an individual basis under the Exchange Act, unless that disclosure is required by their home country. The commenters asserted that determining compensation on an individual basis (in order to determine the three most highly compensated executive officers) would require the FPIs to expend significant time and money in adopting the necessary internal legal and compliance procedures to comply with the Exchange Act requirements that are otherwise inapplicable to them.

The proposed regulations do not adopt the recommendation to exclude FPIs from the application of section 162(m). Pursuant to the definition of publicly held corporation in amended section 162(m)(2), a FPI is a publicly held corporation if it is required either to register its securities under

---

[1] In the case of an issuer that is a bank, savings and loan holding company, or bank holding company, section 12(g) of the Exchange Act requires registration if the issuer has assets exceeding $10 million and a class of equity securities held of record by 2,000 or more persons. See Exchange Act Rule 12g-1 (17 CFR 240.12g-1) regarding the requirements of section 12(g) generally, and Exchange Act Rule 12g5-1 (17 CFR 240.12g5-1) for determining record ownership of securities for purposes of Exchange Act sections 12(g) and 15(d).

[2] See Exchange Act Section 15(d) (15 U.S.C. 78o(d)), and Exchange Act Rules 15d-6 (17 CFR 240.15d-6) and 12h-3 (17 CFR 240.12h-3).

[3] The term "foreign issuer" means any issuer which is a foreign government, a national of any foreign country or a corporation or other organization incorporated or organized under the laws of any foreign country. 21 CFR 240.3b-4(b).

[4] A private letter ruling may be relied upon only by the taxpayer to whom the ruling was issued, and does not constitute generally applicable guidance. See section 11.02 of Revenue Procedure 2019-1, 2019-01 I.R.B. 157.

section 12 of the Exchange Act or to file reports under section 15(d) of the Exchange Act. The legislative history to TCJA indicates that Congress intended for section 162(m) to apply to FPIs.[5] Furthermore, the rationale of the private letter rulings, which conclude that section 162(m) does not apply to FPIs because they are not required to file a summary compensation table, is inconsistent with the definition of covered employee in amended section 162(m)(3). As discussed in section III of this preamble, under the definition of covered employee as amended by TCJA, a publicly held corporation has covered employees regardless of whether it is required to file a summary compensation table, and regardless of whether the employees appear on a summary compensation table that is filed. Accordingly, the proposed regulations do not adopt the suggestion to exclude FPIs from the application of section 162(m). The proposed regulations include examples illustrating when a FPI is a publicly held corporation. Because the calculation of compensation to determine the three highest compensated executive officers for a taxable year is made in accordance with the SEC executive compensation disclosure rules under the Exchange Act, the Treasury Department and the IRS request comments on whether a safe harbor for that determination is appropriate for FPIs that are not required to disclose compensation of their officers on an individual basis in their home countries and, if so, how that safe harbor should be designed.

D. Publicly Traded Partnerships

Partnerships may issue equity interests that are required to be registered under section 12 of the Exchange Act because they are traded on an established securities market. These partnerships are known as publicly traded partnerships (PTPs). Under section 7704(a), a PTP generally is treated as a corporation for purposes of the Code, unless its gross income meets the requirement of section 7704(c)(2). Stakeholders have asked whether a PTP that is treated as a corporation under that provision would be considered a publicly held corporation. As described in the preamble to the 1993 proposed regulations, stakeholders previously raised this issue:

> Questions have arisen as to the application of section 162(m) to certain master limited partnerships whose equity interests are required to be registered under the Exchange Act and that, beginning in 1997, may be treated as corporations for Federal income tax purposes. Whether these partnerships would be publicly held corporations within the meaning of section 162(m) and, if so, the manner in which they would satisfy the exception for performance-based compensation is currently under study and is not addressed in these proposed regulations. If necessary, guidance as to the application of section 162(m) to these entities will be provided in the future.

(58 FR 66310, 66311). The Treasury Department and the IRS have concluded that, for purposes of section 162(m), a PTP that is treated as a corporation under section 7704 (or otherwise) is a publicly held corporation if, as of the last day of its taxable year, its securities are required to be registered under section 12 of the Exchange Act or it is required to file reports under section 15(d) of the Exchange Act. A PTP that is not treated as a corporation for Federal tax purposes (for example, because it satisfies the gross income requirement under section 7704(c)(2) and is not otherwise treated as a corporation for Federal tax purposes) is not a publicly held corporation for purposes of section 162(m).

E. Affiliated Groups

In defining the term "publicly held corporation," §1.162-27(c)(1)(ii) provides that a publicly held corporation includes an affiliated group of corporations, as defined in section 1504 (determined without regard to section 1504(b)). The proposed regulations retain this rule with a modification described below. Because an affiliated group may include more than one publicly held corporation, §1.162-27(c)(1)(ii) provides that an affiliated group of corporations does not include any subsidiary that is itself a publicly held corporation. In that case, pursuant to the final regulations, the publicly held subsidiary and its subsidiaries (if any) are separately subject to section 162(m). Therefore, the parent corporation that is a publicly held corporation and the publicly held subsidiary each has its own set of covered employees. However, the final regulations do not specifically address the situation in which a parent corporation is privately held and the subsidiary is publicly held. Because the amended definition of publicly held corporation includes a corporation that is required to file reports under section 15(d) of the Exchange Act, this type of affiliated group may be more common post-TCJA. Accordingly, unlike the final regulations, which provide that a publicly held subsidiary is excluded from an affiliated group, with the result that a privately held parent is not part of an affiliated group with its publicly held subsidiary, these proposed regulations provide that an affiliated group includes a parent corporation that is privately held and its subsidiary that is publicly held. Furthermore, because an affiliated group of corporations is determined without regard to section 1504(b), an affiliated group may also include a domestic parent corporation that is publicly held and its foreign subsidiary that is not publicly held.

A covered employee of a publicly held corporation may also perform services for another member of the affiliated group. In these situations, §1.162-27(c)(1)(ii) provides that

> [i]f a covered employee is paid compensation in a taxable year by more than one member of an affiliated group, compensation paid by each member of the affiliated group is aggregated with compensation paid to the covered employee by all other members of the group. Any amount disallowed as a deduction by this section must be prorated among the payor corporations in proportion to the amount of compensation paid to the covered employee by each such corporation in the taxable year.

The proposed regulations retain this rule and include additional rules addressing the proration of the deduction disallowance in situations in which a covered employee is paid compensation in a taxable year by more than one publicly held corporation in an affiliated group. Under these rules, the amount disallowed as a deduction is determined separately with respect to each publicly held payor corporation of which the individual is a covered employee. Accordingly, in determining the deduction disallowance with respect to compensation paid to a covered employee by one publicly held payor corporation of an affiliated group, compensation paid to the covered employee by another publicly held payor corporation of the affiliated group (of which the individual is also a covered employee) is not aggregated for purposes of the deduction disallowance proration.

F. Disregarded Entities

Generally under §301.7701-2(c)(2)(i), a business entity that has a single owner and is not a corporation under §301.7701-2(b) is disregarded as an entity separate from its owner for Federal tax purposes (disregarded entity). All of the activities of a disregarded entity are therefore treated in the same manner as a sole proprietorship or as a branch or division of its owner under §301.7701-2. Section 301.7701-2(c)(2)(iv) provides that §301.7701-2(c)(2)(i) does not apply to taxes imposed under Subtitle C—Employment Taxes and Collection of Income Tax (Chapters 21, 22, 23, 23A, 24, and 25 of the Code). Because section 162(m) is in Subtitle A, the general rule in §301.7701-2(c)(2)(i) applies for purposes of section 162(m).

Nonetheless, a disregarded entity that is owned by a privately held corporation may be an issuer of securities that are required to be registered under section 12(b) of the Exchange Act or may be required to file reports under section 15(d) of the Exchange Act. The Treasury Department and the IRS have concluded that, for purposes of section 162(m), a corporation that is the owner of a disregarded entity is treated as issuing any securities issued by its disregarded entity. Accordingly, if a disregarded entity that is owned by a privately held corporation is an issuer of securities that are required to be registered under section 12(b) of the Exchange Act or is required to file reports under section 15(d) of the Exchange Act, these proposed regulations treat the privately held corporation as a publicly held corporation for purposes of section 162(m).

The Treasury Department and the IRS are aware that a corporation could form a partnership with a minority partner in an attempt to circumvent the proposed rules treating a corporation that wholly-owns a disregarded entity that issues certain securities as a publicly held corporation for

[5] The legislative history to TCJA provides that the amendment to the definition of publicly held corporation under section 162(m) "extends the applicability of section 162(m) to include . . . all foreign companies publicly traded through ADRs." House Conf. Rpt. 115-466, 489 (2017). The Blue Book similarly states that "the provision extends the applicability of section 162(m) to include all foreign companies publicly traded through ADRs." Blue Book at page 261.

purposes of section 162(m). In these circumstances, the corporation may be treated as a publicly held corporation by reason of the application of §1.701-2 or other federal income tax principles. The Treasury Department and the IRS also note that, in addition to the above-described fact pattern involving disregarded entities, §1.701-2 and other federal income tax principles may apply to any transaction in which a corporation forms a partnership in an attempt to circumvent the proposed rules.

G. Qualified Subchapter S Subsidiaries

Section 1361(b)(3)(B) defines a QSub as any domestic corporation that is not an ineligible corporation (as defined in section 1361(b)(2)) if an S corporation owns 100 percent of the stock of such corporation and the S corporation elects to treat the corporation as a QSub. Under section 1361(b)(3)(A), unless otherwise provided by regulations, a QSub is not treated as a separate corporation, and therefore all of its assets, liabilities, and items of income, deduction, and credit are treated as assets, liabilities, and such items (as the case may be) of its parent S corporation.

Like a disregarded entity, a QSub may issue securities required to be registered under section 12(b) of the Exchange Act, or be required to file reports under section 15(d) of the Exchange Act. The Treasury Department and the IRS have concluded that, for purposes of section 162(m), an S corporation that is the owner of a QSub is treated as issuing any securities that are issued by its QSub. Accordingly, if a QSub is an issuer of securities that are required to be registered under section 12(b) of the Exchange Act, or is required to file reports under section 15(d) of the Exchange Act, these proposed regulations treat the QSub's S corporation parent as a publicly held corporation for purposes of section 162(m). See Proposed §1.162-33(c)(1)(iv).

III. *Covered Employee*

A. In General

Section 162(m)(3) defines the term "covered employee." Before TCJA, section 162(m)(3) defined a covered employee as any employee of the taxpayer if (a) as of the close of the taxable year, such employee is the chief executive officer of the taxpayer or is an individual acting in such capacity, or (b) the total compensation of such employee for the taxable year is required to be reported to shareholders under the Exchange Act by reason of such employee being among the four highest compensated officers for the taxable year (other than the chief executive officer).

Section 13601(b) of TCJA amended the definition of covered employee in section 162(m)(3) to provide that a covered employee means any employee of the taxpayer if (a) the employee is the principal executive officer (PEO) or principal financial officer (PFO) of the taxpayer at any time during the taxable year, or was an individual acting in such a capacity, (b) the total compensation of the employee for the taxable year is required to be reported to shareholders under the Exchange Act by reason of such employee being among the three highest compensated officers for the taxable year (other than the PEO and PFO), or (c) the individual was a covered employee of the taxpayer (or any predecessor) for any preceding taxable year beginning after December 31, 2016. Section 13601(c) of TCJA also added flush language to provide that a covered employee includes any employee whose total compensation for the taxable year places the individual among the three highest compensated officers for the taxable year (other than any individual who is the PEO or PFO of the taxpayer at any time during the taxable year, or was an individual acting in such a capacity) even if the compensation of the officer is not required to be reported to shareholders under the Exchange Act.

The SEC executive compensation disclosure rules generally require disclosure of compensation of the three most highly compensated executive officers if they were employed at the end of the taxable year and up to two executive officers whose compensation would have been disclosed but for the fact that they were not employed at the end of the taxable year. See Item 402 of Regulation S-K, 17 CFR 229.402(a)(3). After TCJA amended the definition of covered employee, stakeholders submitted comments indicating that they would benefit from initial guidance on whether amended section 162(m)(3)(B) and the flush language to section 162(m)(3) require an employee to be employed at the end of the taxable year to qualify as a covered employee. Notice 2018-68 provided that a covered employee for any taxable year means any employee who is among the three highest compensated executive officers for the taxable year, regardless of whether the executive officer is serving at the end of the publicly held corporation's taxable year, and regardless of whether the executive officer's compensation is subject to disclosure for the last completed fiscal year under the applicable SEC rules. To reach this conclusion, consistent with Notice 2018-68, the proposed regulations rely on the flush language to section 162(m)(3), the legislative history,[6] and the SEC executive compensation disclosure rules that do not necessarily require an executive officer to be employed at the end of the fiscal year for his or her compensation to be disclosed for the year. Based on these considerations, the proposed regulations adopt the position set forth in Notice 2018-68.[7]

B. Taxable Years Not Ending on Same Date as Fiscal Years

The SEC executive compensation disclosure rules are based on a corporation's fiscal year. Usually, a corporation's fiscal and taxable years end on the same date; however, this is not always the case (for example, due to a short taxable year as a result of a corporate transaction that does not result in a short fiscal year). In these cases, the publicly held corporation will have three most highly compensated executive officers under section 162(m)(3)(B) for the short taxable year (instead of the fiscal year). In Notice 2018-68, the Treasury Department and IRS requested comments on the application of the SEC executive compensation disclosure rules to determine the three most highly compensated executive officers for a taxable year that does not end on the same date as the fiscal year for purposes of section 162(m)(3)(B). The notice provided that until additional guidance is issued, taxpayers should base their determination of the three most highly compensated executive officers for purposes of section 162(m)(3)(B) upon a reasonable good faith interpretation of the statute.

A commenter suggested that the determination of the three highest compensated executive officers should be based on the total amount of otherwise deductible remuneration. The proposed regulations do not adopt this approach. In defining covered employee, section 162(m)(3)(B) provides that the three most highly compensated executive officers are officers whose compensation is required to be (or would be required to be) reported to shareholders under the Exchange Act. Therefore, under the statutory text, the determination of the three most highly compensated executive officers is made pursuant to the rules under the Exchange Act. Accordingly, the proposed regulations provide that the amount of compensation used to identify the three most highly compensated executive officers is determined pursuant to the executive compensation disclosure rules under the Exchange Act using the taxable year as the fiscal year for purposes of making the determination. Thus, for example, if a publicly held corporation uses a calendar year fiscal year for SEC reporting purposes, but has a taxable year beginning July 1, 2019, and ending June 30, 2020, then the three most highly compensated executive officers are determined for the taxable year ending June 30, 2020, by applying the executive compensation disclosure rules under the Exchange Act as if the fiscal year ran from July 1, 2019 to June 30, 2020. The same rule applies to short taxable years. Assume in the previous example that, due to a corporate transaction, the corporation's taxable year ran from July 1, 2019, to March 31, 2020. In that situation, the three most highly compensated executive officers would be determined for the taxable year ending March 31, 2020 by applying the disclosure rules as if the fiscal year began July 1, 2019, and ended March 31, 2020. For a discussion of the proposed special applicability dates related to the determination of the three most highly compensated executive officers for a corporation whose fiscal year and taxable year do not end on the same date, see section VIII.B of this preamble.

---

[6] See House Conf. Rpt. 115-466, 489 (2017).

[7] Furthermore, in explaining the amended definition of covered employee, the Blue Book concurred with the guidance provided in Notice 2018-68. Blue Book at page 260.

C. Covered Employees Limited to Executive Officers

The SEC executive compensation disclosure rules require disclosure of compensation for certain executive officers. The term executive officer is defined in 17 CFR 240.3b-7 as follows:

The term executive officer, when used with reference to a registrant, means its president, any vice president of the registrant in charge of a principal business unit, division or function (such as sales, administration or finance), any other officer who performs a policy making function or any other person who performs similar policy making functions for the registrant. Executive officers of subsidiaries may be deemed executive officers of the registrant if they perform such policy making functions for the registrant.

Under the amended definition of covered employee, a PEO and PFO are covered employees by virtue of having those positions or acting in those capacities. The three highest compensated officers (other than the PEO or PFO) are covered employees by reason of their compensation. With respect to the three highest compensated officers for a taxable year, a commenter asked whether only an executive officer (as defined in 17 CFR 240.3b-7) may qualify as a covered employee. Because the SEC executive compensation disclosure rules that require disclosure of the three highest compensated executive officers apply only to executive officers, only an executive officer may qualify as a covered employee under section 162(m)(3)(B).

A publicly held corporation may own an interest in a partnership as discussed in section IV.B. of this preamble. Consistent with the definition of the term executive officer in 17 CFR 240.3b-7, an officer of a partnership is deemed to be an executive officer of a publicly held corporation that owns an interest in such partnership if the officer performs a policy making function for the publicly held corporation. As a deemed executive officer of the publicly held corporation, the officer of the partnership may be a covered employee under section 162(m)(3)(B) if the officer is one of the three highest compensated executive officers of the publicly held corporation.

D. Covered Employees after Separation from Service

Consistent with section 162(m)(3)(C), as amended by TCJA, Notice 2018-68 provides that a covered employee identified for taxable years beginning after December 31, 2016, will continue to be a covered employee for all subsequent taxable years. Accordingly, if an individual is a covered employee for a taxable year, the individual remains a covered employee for all subsequent taxable years, even after the individual has separated from service. For example, if a publicly held corporation makes nonqualified deferred compensation (NQDC) payments to a former PEO after separation from service, then the deduction for the payments generally would be subject to section 162(m). Notice 2018-68 based this conclusion on the statutory text in section 162(m)(3)(C) and the legislative history, which provides that

if an individual is a covered employee with respect to a corporation for a taxable year beginning after December 31, 2016, the individual remains a covered employee for all future years. Thus, an individual remains a covered employee with respect to compensation otherwise deductible for subsequent years, including for years during which the individual is no longer employed by the corporation and years after the individual has died.

(House Conf. Rpt. 115-466, 489 (2017)). The Blue Book reiterated the legislative history in explaining the amended definition of covered employee.[8]

One commenter suggested that a covered employee ceases to be a covered employee for taxable years following the taxable year in which the individual separates from service because the statutory text uses the term "employee" instead of "individual" in defining covered employee. In other words, the commenter asserted that the term "employee" in the statute should be interpreted as referring to a "current employee" instead of a "current or former employee." The commenter suggested that because this is the plain reading of the statute, the legislative history should be ignored. The proposed regulations do not adopt this suggestion. The statute gives no indication that the term "employee" is limited to a current employee, and a reference in the Code to an "employee" has frequently been interpreted in regulations as a reference to a current or a former employee.[9] Given the ambiguity in the meaning of "employee" and the legislative intent in this context to include a former employee, as evidenced by the legislative history and the Blue Book explanation of the term covered employee, the proposed regulations define employee to include a former employee.

E. Predecessor Corporation

Section 162(m)(3)(C) provides that the term "covered employee" means any employee who was a covered employee of the taxpayer for any preceding taxable year beginning after December 31, 2016. The term "covered employee" also means any employee who was a covered employee of any predecessor of the taxpayer for any preceding taxable year beginning after December 31, 2016. For clarity, these proposed regulations use the term "predecessor of a publicly held corporation" instead of "predecessor." An individual who is a covered employee for one taxable year (including a taxable year of a predecessor of a publicly held corporation) remains a covered employee for subsequent taxable years.

In certain circumstances, the term "predecessor of a publicly held corporation" includes the publicly held corporation itself if it was a publicly held corporation for a prior taxable year. Specifically, the proposed regulations provide that a predecessor of a publicly held corporation includes a publicly held corporation that, after becoming privately held, again becomes a publicly held corporation for a taxable year ending before the 36-month anniversary of the due date for the corporation's U.S. Federal income tax return (excluding any extensions) for the last taxable year for which the corporation was previously publicly held. For a discussion of the proposed special applicability date related to the definition of predecessor of a publicly held corporation as applied to a privately held corporation that was previously a publicly held corporation and again becomes a publicly held corporation, see section VIII.B of this preamble.

The proposed regulations also provide that the term "predecessor of a publicly held corporation" includes a publicly held corporation that is acquired (target corporation), or the assets of which are acquired, by another publicly held corporation (acquiror corporation) in certain transactions. Accordingly, the covered employees of the target corporation in those transactions are also covered employees of the acquiror corporation.

The proposed regulations define the term "predecessor of a publicly held corporation" by reference to the type of corporate acquisition in which a publicly held corporation is acquired. The proposed regulations describe corporate acquisitions in four categories: (1) Corporate reorganizations, (2) corporate divisions, (3) stock acquisitions, and (4) asset acquisitions. Certain transactions may fall within more than one category, but this redundancy is intended to provide certainty as to the application of these rules if a taxpayer is unsure which category covers the acquisition in question.

With respect to corporate reorganizations, the proposed regulations provide that a predecessor of a publicly held corporation includes a publicly held corporation that is acquired or that is the transferor corporation in a corporate reorganization described in section 368(a)(1). For example, if a

---

[8] The Blue Book states that, "[i]n addition, if an individual is a covered employee with respect to a corporation for a taxable year beginning after December 31, 2016, the individual remains a covered employee for all future years. Thus, an individual remains a covered employee with respect to compensation otherwise deductible for subsequent years, including for years during which the individual is no longer employed by the corporation and years after the individual has died." Blue Book at page 260.

[9] For example, under §1.105-11(c)(3)(iii), the nondiscrimination rules of section 105(h)(3) apply to former employees even though the Code uses only the term "employees."

publicly held target corporation merges into a publicly held acquiror corporation, then any covered employee of the target corporation would become a covered employee of the acquiror corporation.

With respect to corporate divisions, the proposed regulations provide that a predecessor of a publicly held corporation includes a publicly held distributing corporation that distributes or exchanges the stock of one or more controlled corporations in a transaction described in section 355(a)(1) (a 355(a)(1) transaction) if the controlled corporation is a publicly held corporation. This rule applies to the distributing corporation only with respect to covered employees of the distributing corporation who are hired by the controlled corporation (or by a corporation affiliated with the controlled corporation that received stock of the controlled corporation as a shareholder of the distributing corporation in the 355(a)(1) transaction) within the period beginning 12 months before and ending 12 months after the distribution. For example, if a publicly held distributing corporation exchanges with its shareholders the stock of a controlled corporation for stock of the distributing corporation in a 355(a)(1) transaction, and the controlled corporation is a publicly held corporation after the exchange, then any covered employee of the distributing corporation would become a covered employee of the controlled corporation if hired by the controlled corporation within the period beginning 12 months before and ending 12 months after the exchange. Furthermore, a covered employee of the distributing corporation who becomes a covered employee of the controlled corporation will remain a covered employee of the distributing corporation for all subsequent taxable years because, as discussed in section III.D of this preamble, if an individual is a covered employee for a taxable year, the individual remains a covered employee for all subsequent taxable years.

With respect to stock acquisitions, a predecessor of a publicly held corporation includes a publicly held corporation that becomes a member of an affiliated group (as defined in proposed §1.162-33(c)(1)(ii)). For example, if an affiliated group that is considered a publicly held corporation pursuant to proposed §1.162-33(c)(1)(ii) in the proposed regulations acquires a publicly held target corporation that becomes a member of the affiliated group, then the target corporation would be considered a predecessor of the affiliated group. Therefore, any covered employee of the target corporation would become a covered employee of the affiliated group.

With respect to asset acquisitions, if an acquiror corporation or one or more members of an affiliated group (acquiror group) acquires at least 80% of the operating assets (determined by fair market value on the date of acquisition) of a publicly held target corporation, then the target corporation is a predecessor of the acquiror corporation or group. For example, if an acquiror corporation acquires 80% or more of the operating assets of a publicly held target corporation, then any covered employees of the target corporation that become employees of the acquiror corporation would become covered employees of the acquiror corporation. For acquisitions of assets that occur over time, the proposed regulations provide that generally only acquisitions that occur within a 12-month period are taken into account to determine whether at least 80% of the target corporation's operating assets were acquired.

Similarly, this asset acquisition rule provides that the target is a predecessor of a publicly held corporation only with respect to a covered employee of the target corporation who is hired by the acquiror (or a corporation affiliated with the acquiror) within the period beginning 12 months before and ending 12 months after the date on which all events necessary for the acquisition have occurred.

These proposed regulations provide that the rules for determining predecessors are applied cumulatively, with the result that a predecessor of a corporation includes each predecessor of the corporation and the predecessor or predecessors of any prior predecessor or predecessors.

Also, in a similar manner to the rule for a publicly held corporation that becomes privately held, and subsequently becomes publicly held, these proposed regulations provide that a target corporation may be a predecessor corporation in certain circumstances. For example, the proposed regulations provide that if a target corporation was a publicly held corporation, subsequently becomes privately held, is then acquired by an acquiror that is not a publicly held corporation, and the acquiror becomes a publicly held corporation for a taxable year ending before the 36-month anniversary of the due date for the target corporation's U.S. Federal income tax return (excluding any extensions) for the last taxable year for which the target corporation was publicly held, then the target corporation is a predecessor of the publicly held corporation. The proposed regulations also provide a similar rule for asset acquisitions.

These proposed regulations further clarify that, in the case of an election to treat as an asset purchase either the sale, exchange, or distribution of stock pursuant to regulations under section 336(e) or the purchase of stock pursuant to regulations under section 338, the corporation is treated as the same corporation before and after the transaction for which the election is made. Similar exceptions are made to the general treatment of an election under section 336(e) and section 338 that would treat the postelection corporation as a new corporation for purposes of other rules regarding various compensation tax provisions (see §1.338-1(b)(2)(i)). These exceptions align with the other predecessor rules in these proposed regulations by treating a substantial continuation of the earlier business in the post-election corporation as continuing the pre-election corporation, so that the covered employees continue to be covered employees.

F. Disregarded Entities

Under section 162(m)(3), only employees of the taxpayer may be covered employees. When a corporation owns an entity that is disregarded as an entity separate from its owner under §301.7701-2(c)(2)(i), the corporation that is a publicly held corporation (and not its wholly-owned entity) is the taxpayer for purposes of section 162(m)(3). In that case, the covered employees of the publicly held corporation are identified pursuant to the rules discussed in sections III.A through III.E of this preamble. Accordingly, a PEO, PFO, or executive officer of a disregarded entity wholly-owned by a corporation is generally not treated as a PEO, PFO, or executive officer of the corporate owner (the publicly held corporation). However, consistent with the definition of the term executive officer in 17 CFR 240.3b-7 that treats executive officers of subsidiaries as executive officers of the registrant if the executive officers perform policy making functions for the registrant, an executive officer of a disregarded entity is treated as an executive officer of its corporate owner for the taxable year if the executive officer performs policy making functions for the corporate owner during the taxable year. These proposed regulations include examples illustrating how to determine whether employees of a disregarded entity are treated as covered employees of its publicly held corporate owner for purposes of section 162(m).

The Treasury Department and the IRS are aware that, in an attempt to circumvent the proposed rules treating a corporation that wholly-owns a disregarded entity that issues certain securities as a publicly held corporation for purposes of section 162(m), a corporation could form a partnership with a minority partner and the partnership could then employ an individual who otherwise would have been a covered employee of the corporation. In these circumstances, §1.701-2 and other federal income tax principles may apply to a transaction in which a corporation forms a partnership in an attempt to circumvent the proposed rules.

G. Qualified Subchapter S Subsidiaries

Like the case when a corporation owns a disregarded entity, when an S corporation that is a publicly held corporation owns a QSub, the S corporation, and not its QSub, is the taxpayer for purposes of section 162(m)(3). Therefore, pursuant to the rules discussed in sections III.A through III.E of this preamble, a PEO, PFO, or executive officer of such QSub generally is not treated as a PEO, PFO, or executive officer of the S corporation owner (that is, the publicly held corporation). Under these proposed regulations, an executive officer of a QSub is treated as an executive officer of its S corporation owner for the taxable year if the executive officer performs policy making functions for the S corporation owner during the taxable year. See Proposed §1.162-33(c)(2)(iv). This treatment is consistent with the definition of the term executive officer in 17 CFR 240.3b-7, which treats executive officers of subsidiaries as executive officers of the registrant if the executive officers perform policy making functions for the registrant.

IV. *Applicable Employee Remuneration*

A. In General

Section 162(m)(4) defines the term "applicable employee remuneration" with respect to any covered employee for any taxable year as the aggregate amount allowable as a deduction for such taxable year (determined without regard to section 162(m)) for remuneration for services performed by such employee (whether or not during the taxable year). Before TCJA, applicable employee remuneration did not include remuneration payable on a commission basis (as defined in section 162(m)(4)(B)) or performance-based compensation (as defined in section 162(m)(4)(C)). Section 13601(a) of TCJA amended the definition of applicable employee remuneration to eliminate these exclusions, while section 13601(d) of TCJA added a special rule for remuneration paid to beneficiaries. This special rule, set forth in section 162(m)(4)(F), provides that remuneration shall not fail to be applicable employee remuneration merely because it is includible in the income of, or paid to, a person other than the covered employee, including after the death of the covered employee.

For simplicity, when incorporating the amendments TCJA made to the definition of applicable employee remuneration, these proposed regulations use the term "compensation" instead of "applicable employee remuneration." Consistent with the amendments made by TCJA, these proposed regulations provide that compensation means the aggregate amount allowable as a deduction under chapter 1 of the Code for the taxable year (determined without regard to section 162(m)) for remuneration for services performed by a covered employee, whether or not the services were performed during the taxable year. The proposed regulations also clarify that compensation includes an amount that is includible in the income of, or paid to, a person other than the covered employee, including after the death of the covered employee.

B. Compensation Paid by a Partnership to a Covered Employee

These proposed regulations address the issue of compensation paid by a partnership (as defined for Federal tax purposes) to a covered employee of a publicly held corporation; this issue has been subject to a no-rule position for private letter rulings since 2010. Between 2006 and 2008, the IRS issued four private letter rulings addressing specific situations in which a publicly held corporation was a partner in a partnership. As part of the analysis, the private letter rulings stated that if a publicly held corporation is a partner in a partnership, then section 162(m) does not apply to the corporation's distributive share of the partnership's deduction for compensation paid by the partnership for services performed for it by a covered employee of the corporation. Therefore, the private letter rulings ruled on the facts presented that section 162(m) did not limit the otherwise deductible compensation expense of the publicly held corporation for compensation the partnership paid the covered employee. Upon further consideration, and recognizing the potential for abuse, the IRS stopped issuing private letter rulings involving section 162(m) and partnerships.[10] Stakeholders have asked the Treasury Department and the IRS to address this issue in these proposed regulations.

In relevant part, section 162(m)(1) provides that "[i]n the case of any publicly held corporation, no deduction shall be allowed under this chapter for applicable employee remuneration with respect to any covered employee." This language does not limit the application of section 162(m) to deductions for compensation paid by the publicly held corporation; it also covers the deduction for compensation paid to the corporation's covered employees by another party to the extent the corporation is allocated a share of the otherwise deductible item. For instance, if a publicly held corporate partner is allocated a distributive share of the partnership's deduction for compensation paid by the partnership, the allocated distributive share of the deduction is subject to section 162(m) even though the corporation did not directly pay the compensation to the covered employee. Thus, the publicly held corporation must take into account its distributive share of the partnership's deduction for compensation expense paid to the publicly held corporation's covered employee and aggregate that distributive share and the corporation's otherwise allowable deduction for compensation paid directly to that employee in determining the amount allowable to the corporation as a deduction for compensation under section 162(m). See § 1.702-1(a)(8)(ii) and (iii).

The Treasury Department and the IRS are aware that this issue has not been addressed in generally applicable guidance and understand taxpayers may have taken positions contrary to those set forth in these proposed regulations. Accordingly, the proposed regulations provide transition relief for current compensation arrangements, but also prohibit the formation or expansion of these types of structures for the purpose of avoiding the application of section 162(m) prior to the issuance of final regulations. Specifically, in order to ensure that compensation agreements are not formed or otherwise structured to circumvent this rule after publication of these proposed regulations and prior to the publication of the final regulations, the proposed regulations propose that the rule with respect to compensation paid by a partnership will apply to any deduction for compensation that is otherwise allowable for a taxable year ending on or after December 20, 2019 but will not apply to compensation paid pursuant to a written binding contract in effect on December 20, 2019 that is not materially modified after that date. The Treasury Department and the IRS request comments on whether similar rules should apply to trusts.

C. Compensation for Services in a Capacity other than an Executive Officer

A commenter suggested that, if a covered employee separates from service as an executive officer and subsequently performs services as a director of the publicly held corporation, then the compensation paid to the individual as a director should not be considered applicable employee remuneration for purposes of section 162(m)(4). These proposed regulations do not adopt this suggestion.

Since the enactment of section 162(m) in 1993, director fees were considered applicable employee remuneration for purposes of section 162(m)(4). In describing compensation for which the deduction is limited by section 162(m), the legislative history to the enactment of section 162(m) states:

> Unless specifically excluded, the deduction limitation applies to all remuneration for services, including cash and the cash value of all remuneration (including benefits) paid in a medium other than cash. If an individual is a covered employee for a taxable year, the deduction limitation applies to all compensation not explicitly excluded from the deduction limitation, regardless of whether the compensation is for services as a covered employee and regardless of when the compensation was earned.

House Conf. Rpt. 103-213, 585 (1993). Thus, in enacting section 162(m), Congress did not exclude compensation for services not performed as a covered employee from the deduction limitation. As stated in the preamble to the 1993 proposed regulations, "[t]he deduction limit of section 162(m) applies to any compensation that could otherwise be deducted in a taxable year, except for enumerated types of payments set forth in section 162(m)(4)" (58 FR 66310, 66310). Compensation earned by a covered employee through a non-employee position, such as director fees, was never one of the "enumerated types of payments set forth in section 162(m)(4)" and so this compensation does not fall within the exception and has always been considered applicable employee remuneration for which the deduction is limited by section 162(m).[11] The amendments to section 162(m)(4) made by TCJA did not change this aspect of the definition of applicable employee remuneration; accordingly, the proposed regulations do not adopt the commenter's suggestion.

---

[10] Initially, the IRS announced the no-rule position in 2010 in section 5.06 of Revenue Procedure 2010-3, 2010-1 I.R.B. 110, which provided that "[w]hether the deduction limit under § 162(m) applies to compensation attributable to services performed for a related partnership" was an area under study in which rulings or determination letters will not be issued until the IRS resolves the issue through publication of a revenue ruling, revenue procedure, regulations, or otherwise. Most recently, section 4.01(13) of Revenue Procedure 2019-3, 2019-01 I.R.B. 130, provides that this issue is an area in which rulings or determination letters will not ordinarily be issued.

[11] Furthermore, as explained in section II.E of this preamble, the final regulations provide that all compensation paid to a covered employee by more than one member of an affiliated group is aggregated for purposes of prorating the amount disallowed as a deduction by section 162(m). For purposes of aggregating the total compensation paid by the affiliated group, the final regulations do not exclude compensation paid for services performed by a covered employee in a capacity other than an employee (for example, as an independent contractor).

Pursuant to the amended definition of covered employee in section 162(m)(3)(C), a covered employee includes any individual who was a covered employee of the publicly held corporation (or any predecessor) for any taxable year beginning after December 31, 2016. Therefore, a covered employee remains a covered employee after separation from service. If, after separation from service as an employee, a covered employee returns to provide services to the publicly held corporation in any capacity, including as a common law employee, a director, or an independent contractor, then any deduction for compensation paid to the covered employee is subject to section 162(m).

V. *Privately Held Corporations that Become Publicly Held*

Section 162(m) applies to the deduction for compensation paid to a covered employee that is otherwise deductible for a taxable year of a publicly held corporation. These proposed regulations provide that, in the case of a corporation that is a privately held corporation that becomes a publicly held corporation, section 162(m) applies to the deduction for any compensation that is otherwise deductible for the taxable year ending on or after the date that the corporation becomes a publicly held corporation. Furthermore, the proposed regulations provide that a corporation is considered to become publicly held on the date that its registration statement becomes effective either under the Securities Act or the Exchange Act.

Commenters suggested that these proposed regulations retain the transition relief provided in the final regulations for privately held corporations that become publicly held. Commenters reasoned that corporations that become publicly held corporations need time to adjust compensation arrangements to take into account section 162(m). The proposed regulations do not adopt this suggestion.

As background, in enacting section 162(m) in 1993, Congress excepted performance-based compensation from the definition of applicable employee remuneration and, thus, the section 162(m) deduction limitation. Before TCJA, section 162(m)(4)(C) defined performance-based compensation as "any remuneration payable solely on account of the attainment of one or more performance goals, but only if—

(i) the performance goals are determined by a compensation committee of the board of directors of the taxpayer which is comprised solely of 2 or more outside directors,

(ii) the material terms under which the remuneration is to be paid, including the performance goals, are disclosed to shareholders and approved by a majority of the vote in a separate shareholder vote before the payment of such compensation, and

(iii) before any payment of such remuneration, the compensation committee referred to in clause (i) certifies that the performance goals and any other material terms were in fact satisfied.

These requirements are also set forth in §§1.162-27(e)(2) through (e)(5). In enacting section 162(m), Congress recognized that privately held corporations may have difficulty adopting compensation arrangements that satisfy the requirements for performance-based compensation. Specifically, Congress was concerned about the shareholder approval requirement. Congress also recognized that, when a corporation becomes a publicly held corporation in connection with an initial public offering (IPO), prospective shareholders who read the corporation's prospectus are aware of the compensation arrangements adopted prior to the IPO. Accordingly, Congress thought that shareholders who read the prospectus and purchase the corporation's shares are, in effect, approving the corporation's compensation arrangements. The 1993 legislative history provides as follows:

[I]n the case of a privately held company that becomes publicly held, the prospectus is subject to the rules similar to those applicable to publicly held companies. Thus, if there has been disclosure that would satisfy the rules described above, persons who buy stock in the publicly held company will be aware of existing compensation arrangements. No further shareholder approval is required of compensation arrangements existing prior to the time the company became public unless there is a material modification of such arrangements.

House Conf. Rpt. 103-213, 588 (1993). Based on the legislative history, the final regulations provided transition relief for corporations that become publicly held. Section 1.162-27(f)(1) provides that in the case of a corporation that was not a publicly held corporation and then becomes a publicly held corporation, section 162(m) "does not apply to any remuneration paid pursuant to a compensation plan or agreement that existed during the period in which the corporation was not publicly held." If a corporation becomes publicly held in connection with an IPO, then the relief provided in §1.162-27(f)(1) applies only to the extent that the prospectus accompanying the IPO disclosed information concerning the existing compensation plans or agreements and satisfied all applicable securities laws.

Section 13601(a) of TCJA amended the definition of applicable employee remuneration in section 162(m)(4) to eliminate the exception for performance-based compensation, which among other things, made shareholder approval of compensation arrangements irrelevant with respect to entitlement to the deduction. Accordingly, these proposed regulations do not retain the transition relief provided in the final regulations.

For a discussion of rules applicable to privately held corporations that previously were publicly held corporations, see section III.E. of this preamble.

VI. *Grandfather Rules*

A. In General

Section 13601(e) of TCJA generally provides that TCJA amendments to section 162(m) apply to taxable years beginning after December 31, 2017. However, it further provides that those amendments do not apply to remuneration that is provided pursuant to a written binding contract that was in effect on November 2, 2017, and that was not modified in any material respect on or after such date.

As discussed in Notice 2018-68, the text of section 13601(e) of the TJCA is almost identical to the text of pre-TCJA section 162(m)(4)(D), which provided a grandfather rule in connection with the enactment of section 162(m) in 1993. Under that grandfather rule, section 162(m) did not apply to remuneration payable under a written binding contract that was in effect on February 17, 1993, and that was not modified thereafter in any material respect before such remuneration was paid. Section 1.162-27(h) provides guidance on the definitions of written binding contract and material modification for purposes of applying the original grandfather rule, and Notice 2018-68 adopted those definitions for purposes of the grandfather rule in connection with section 13601(e) of TCJA. The proposed regulations likewise adopt those definitions. Notice 2018-68 also provided examples illustrating the use of these definitions, and many of those examples are incorporated in these proposed regulations. However, to increase clarity, the proposed regulations replace some examples from Notice 2018-68 with other examples. This replacement with new examples does not reflect a substantive change from the definitions of written binding contract and material modification provided in Notice 2018-68.

Notice 2018-68 clarified that remuneration is payable under a written binding contract that was in effect on November 2, 2017, only to the extent that the corporation is obligated under applicable law (for example, state contract law) to pay the remuneration under the contract if the employee performs services or satisfies the applicable vesting conditions. Accordingly, the TJCA amendments to section 162(m) apply to any amount of remuneration that exceeds the amount of remuneration that applicable law obligates the corporation to pay under a written binding contract that was in effect on November 2, 2017, if the employee performs services or satisfies the applicable vesting conditions.

As an alternative to the grandfather rules in Notice 2018-68, some commenters suggested that these proposed regulations adopt a safe harbor regarding the determination of whether a contract qualifies as a written binding contract so that compensation paid pursuant to the contract would be grandfathered. Under the suggested safe harbor, any arrangement in effect on or before November 2, 2017, would be treated as a written binding contract if an amount related to the compensation payable under the contract was accrued (or could have been accrued) as a cost under

Generally Accepted Accounting Principles (GAAP), regardless of whether the corporation is obligated to pay the remuneration under applicable law.

Although the Treasury Department and the IRS understand that the application of the written binding contract standard may be burdensome in certain cases and welcome the potential for simplification, the suggested safe harbor raises several issues. First, as expressed in the comment, the accrual of a cost is often based on predictions of whether the amount will be paid, which may not necessarily reflect whether the amount must be paid in all cases. This raises issues of whether costs identified correlate with the statutory standard of being paid under a legally binding contract if, in fact, the employer was not necessarily bound to pay the amounts of compensation but rather was likely to pay them. Second, the suggested safe harbor is an accounting standard based on financial statements audited by accountants. This raises issues of tax administration, including the potential for the IRS to audit for section 162(m) purposes a corporation's "audited" financial statements, and challenges IRS examiners would have in applying GAAP principles. For these reasons, the proposed regulations do not adopt this suggested safe harbor. However, the Treasury Department and the IRS welcome further comments on whether the suggested safe harbor standard would be administrable, including how it would be implemented with respect to differing positions on corporate tax returns (such as use of the standard in Notice 2018-68 and these proposed regulations) that have already been filed.

B. Compensation Subject to Discretion

Under the definition of written binding contract in Notice 2018-68 and these proposed regulations, applicable law (such as state contract law) determines the amount of compensation that a corporation is obligated to pay pursuant to a written binding contract in effect on November 2, 2017. Some commenters suggested that negative discretion be completely disregarded in determining the amount of compensation that a corporation is obligated to pay pursuant to a written binding contract. The proposed regulations do not adopt this approach, because it is contrary to the statutory text and the legislative history. See House Conf. Rpt. 115-466, 490 (2017). The Treasury Department and the IRS are aware, however, that compensation arrangements may purport to provide the corporation with a wider scope of negative discretion than applicable law permits the corporation to exercise. In that case, the negative discretion is taken into account only to the extent the corporation may exercise the negative discretion under applicable law.

One commenter asked whether an amount of compensation is grandfathered if it is paid pursuant to a written binding contract under which the corporation is obligated to recover an amount of compensation from the employee if a vesting condition is later determined not to have been satisfied. For example, a vesting condition may be based on the achievement of results reported in the financial statements. In this example, if a corporation pays a bonus based on the financial statements but the financial statements are subsequently restated and demonstrate that the vesting condition was not, in fact, satisfied, then the corporation is required to recover a portion of the bonus from the employee. If, under applicable law, the employee retains the remaining portion of the bonus then, pursuant to the grandfather rules in Notice 2018-68 and these proposed regulations, that remaining portion of the bonus is grandfathered compensation that is not subject to TCJA amendments. Similarly, if the corporation has discretion to recover compensation (in whole or in part), only the amount of compensation that the corporation is obligated to pay under applicable law that is not subject to potential recovery is grandfathered. The proposed regulations include examples illustrating these principles.

Applicable law may provide a corporation with contingent discretion to recover compensation. This issue was not addressed in Notice 2018-68. Under these proposed regulations, a corporation is not treated as currently having discretion merely because it will have discretion to recover an amount if a condition occurs subsequent to the vesting and payment of the compensation and the occurrence of the condition is objectively outside of the corporation's control. For example, pursuant to a written binding contract in effect on November 2, 2017, a corporation may be obligated under applicable law to pay $500,000 of compensation if the employee satisfies a vesting condition, but the corporation may be permitted to recover $300,000 from the employee if the employee is convicted of a felony within three calendar years from the date of payment. If the employee is not convicted of a felony within three calendar years from the date of payment, then the $500,000 is grandfathered. If, however, the employee is convicted of a felony within three years after the payment of the $500,000, then the corporation has discretion whether to recover the $300,000 from the employee. Accordingly, if the employee is convicted of a felony within three calendar years after the payment, $300,000 of the $500,000 is not grandfathered. This is true regardless of whether the corporation exercises its discretion to recover the $300,000. Because the corporation may not recover $200,000 of the $500,000 payment in any event, the $200,000 remains grandfathered regardless of whether the employee is convicted of a felony.

C. Account and Nonaccount Balance Plans

Notice 2018-68 includes examples illustrating the application of the grandfather rule to account balance plans, and those examples are incorporated into these proposed regulations. Commenters requested guidance on the application of the grandfather rule to nonaccount balance plans, and some of these commenters suggested that benefits accruing under a nonaccount balance plan after November 2, 2017, should be automatically grandfathered. The proposed regulations do not adopt this approach. Consistent with the text of section 13601(e) of TCJA providing the grandfather rule, the amount of compensation that is grandfathered under a nonaccount balance plan is the amount that the corporation is obligated to pay under applicable law on November 2, 2017. The proposed regulations include examples illustrating these rules.

Commenters also requested guidance on determining the amount of compensation that a corporation is obligated to pay under applicable law with respect to linked plan arrangements. In these arrangements, the amount payable to an employee under a NQDC plan is linked to a qualified employer plan. For example, a typical arrangement may provide that the amount of NQDC to be paid to an employee is the account balance (or an accumulated benefit) in a NQDC plan reduced by the account balance in a section 401(k) plan. These proposed regulations include an example involving this type of arrangement.

D. Earnings on Grandfathered Amounts in Account and Nonaccount Balance Plans

Notice 2018-68 includes an example illustrating the circumstances in which earnings credited to account balance plans after November 2, 2017, are grandfathered, as well as an example illustrating that those earnings are not grandfathered when the corporation retains the right under applicable law to amend the plan at any time either to stop or to reduce future credits (including earnings) to the account balance. Commenters suggested that earnings credited after November 2, 2017, on grandfathered amounts in nonaccount balance plans should also be grandfathered. The proposed regulations do not adopt the commenters' suggestion. Instead, consistent with TCJA and the guidance in Notice 2018-68, the proposed regulations provide that earnings credited after November 2, 2017, on grandfathered amounts are grandfathered only if the corporation is obligated to pay the earnings under applicable law pursuant to a written binding contract in effect on November 2, 2017.

Stakeholders asked how §1.409A-3(j)(4)(ix)(C)(3) affects the determination of whether earnings credited on a grandfathered amount after November 2, 2017, are grandfathered if the corporation retains the right under applicable law to terminate the plan at any time in compliance with section 409A. Section 1.409A-3(j)(4)(ix)(C)(3) provides that, if a service recipient terminates a NQDC plan, then the time and form of payments may be accelerated, but payment may not be made within 12 months of the date of termination of the plan. The definition of written binding contract in Notice 2018-68 and these proposed regulations provides that earnings credited after November 2, 2017, on grandfathered amounts are grandfathered only if the corporation is obligated to pay the earnings under applicable law pursuant to a written binding contract in effect on November 2, 2017. Accordingly, if, under applicable law, the corporation is obligated to continue to credit earnings for amounts under the NQDC plan during the 12 months after terminating the plan, then the earnings would be grandfathered.[12] In that case, the grandfathered amount would be the amount that the corporation is obligated to pay under applicable law as of November 2, 2017, plus the 12 months of earnings that the corporation is obligated to credit under applicable law. However, any additional amounts that become payable under the plan after November 2, 2017, and earnings on those amounts would not be grandfathered.

Applicable law and the terms of the plan determine the amount of earnings that the corporation is obligated to credit for amounts under the plan during the 12 months after plan termination. Thus, for example, with respect to a nonaccount balance plan, under applicable law, the amount of earnings that the corporation is obligated to credit might be limited to the difference between the present value of the benefit under the plan as of November 2, 2017, and any increase in present value due solely to passage of time (12 months). Furthermore, with respect to a nonaccount balance plan that provides for a formula amount (for example, the amount payable under the plan is based on the participant's final salary and years of service), the amount of earnings that the corporation is obligated to credit under applicable law might be limited to a reasonable rate of interest to reflect the time value of money during the passage of time (12 months) applied to the benefit under the plan as of November 2, 2017 (and not reflecting any additional salary increase or years of service accumulated after November 2, 2017).

E. Severance Agreements

Commenters asked about the application of the grandfather rule in Notice 2018-68 to compensation payable pursuant to a severance agreement that is a written binding contract and is in effect on November 2, 2017. Severance payable under such a contract is grandfathered only if the amount of severance is based on compensation elements the employer is obligated to pay under the contract. For example, if the amount of severance is based on final base salary, the severance is grandfathered only if the corporation is obligated to pay both the base salary and the severance under applicable law pursuant to a written binding contract in effect on November 2, 2017. For this purpose, a corporation may be obligated to pay severance under a written binding contract as of November 2, 2017, even if the employee remains employed as of November 2, 2017, but only with respect to the amount the corporation would have been required to pay if the employee had been terminated as of November 2, 2017.

Commenters also asked whether all or a portion of severance is grandfathered if a portion of the amount is based on a variable component, such as a discretionary or performance bonus. The examples in these proposed regulations illustrate that each component of the severance formula is analyzed separately to determine the amount of severance that is grandfathered. For example, the amount of severance may be equal to two times the sum of: (1) Final base salary and (2) any bonus paid within 12 months prior to separation from service. In this example, the amount of severance is based on two components, base salary and bonus. Therefore, the entire amount of severance (based on both components) is grandfathered only if, under applicable law, the corporation is obligated to pay both portions, the base salary and the bonus pursuant to a written binding contract in effect on November 2, 2017.

F. Material Modification

1. In General

These proposed regulations adopt the definition of material modification in Notice 2018-68. Under that definition, a material modification occurs when the contract is amended to increase the amount of compensation payable to the employee. Furthermore, if a written binding contract is materially modified, it is treated as a new contract entered into as of the date of the material modification. Accordingly, amounts received by an employee under the contract before a material modification are not affected, but amounts received subsequent to the material modification are treated as paid pursuant to a new contract, rather than as paid pursuant to a written binding contract in effect on November 2, 2017. The adoption of a supplemental contract or agreement that provides for increased compensation, or the payment of additional compensation, is a material modification of a written binding contract if the facts and circumstances demonstrate that the additional compensation is paid on the basis of substantially the same elements or conditions as the compensation that is otherwise paid pursuant to the written binding contract in effect on November 2, 2017. However, a material modification of a written binding contract does not include a supplemental payment that is equal to or less than a reasonable cost-of-living increase over the payment made in the preceding year under that written binding contract. In that case, only the deduction for the reasonable cost-of-living increase is subject to section 162(m) as amended by TCJA. In addition, the failure, in whole or in part, to exercise negative discretion under a contract does not result in the material modification of that contract. Finally, if amounts are paid to an employee from more than one written binding contract (or if a single written document consists of several written binding contracts), then a material modification of one written binding contract does not automatically result in a material modification of the other contracts unless the material modification affects the amounts payable under those contracts.

2. Earnings on Grandfathered Amounts that are Subsequently Deferred

Notice 2018-68 provides rules for determining whether a material modification occurs if a written binding contract in effect on November 2, 2017, is subsequently modified to defer the payment of compensation. Under those rules, which are adopted in these proposed regulations, if the contract is modified to defer the payment of compensation, any compensation paid or to be paid that is in excess of the amount that was originally payable to the employee under the contract will not be treated as resulting in a material modification if the additional amount is based on either a reasonable rate of interest or a predetermined actual investment (whether or not assets associated with the amount originally owed are actually invested therein) such that the amount payable by the employer at the later date will be based on the actual rate of return on the predetermined actual investment (including any decrease, as well as any increase, in the value of the investment). The proposed regulations provide that a predetermined actual investment means a predetermined actual investment as defined in §31.3121(v)(2)-1(d)(2)(i)(B), and also include examples illustrating these rules relating to the treatment of earnings.

However, even though the payment of earnings will not result in the contract being materially modified, this generally does not mean that the earnings are treated as grandfathered. For situations in which an employee defers an amount of grandfathered compensation after November 2, 2017, the earnings on the deferred amount are not grandfathered if, as of November 2, 2017, the corporation was not obligated under the terms of the contract to provide the deferral election and to pay the earnings on the deferred amount under applicable law. Pursuant to the definition of written binding contract in Notice 2018-68 and these proposed regulations, these earnings are not grandfathered because, as of November 2, 2017, the corporation was not obligated to pay them under applicable law.

3. Material Modification Prior to Payment of a Grandfathered Amount

Commenters asked whether a grandfathered amount of compensation is no longer considered grandfathered if the underlying compensation arrangement is materially modified after November 2, 2017, but before the payment of the grandfathered amount. Pursuant to the definition of material modification in Notice 2018-68 and these proposed regulations, if the contract is materially modified after November 2, 2017, but before the payment of a grandfathered amount of compensation, then the compensation is treated as paid pursuant to the new contract and is no longer grandfathered. For example, if, under applicable law, a corporation is obligated to pay $100,000 on December 31, 2020, under a written binding

---

[12] Section 1.409A-3(j)(4)(ix)(C) provides that if a service recipient terminates a NQDC plan (as defined in §1.409A-1(c)) for one participant, then it must terminate the NQDC plan for all participants. Given this requirement, a corporation might refrain from terminating a NQDC plan and continue to credit earnings on a grandfathered amount after November 2, 2017. If a corporation is permitted under applicable law to terminate the NQDC plan, then only the amount it would be obligated to pay under applicable law if it did terminate the NQDC plan is grandfathered.

contract in effect on November 2, 2017, then the $100,000 is grandfathered. If, on January 1, 2019, the contract is materially modified, then the $100,000 is treated as paid pursuant to a new contract and is not grandfathered.

4. Acceleration of Payment or Vesting

Under the definition of material modification in Notice 2018-68 and these proposed regulations, a modification of a written binding contract that accelerates the payment of compensation is a material modification unless the amount of compensation paid is discounted to reasonably reflect the time value of money. For example, if a corporation is obligated under applicable law to pay compensation on December 31, 2020, pursuant to a written binding contract in effect on November 2, 2017, then the compensation is grandfathered. If the corporation pays the entire amount of compensation on December 31, 2019 without a discount to reasonably reflect the time of value of money, then the entire amount of compensation is treated as paid pursuant to a new contract and is no longer grandfathered. Furthermore, any subsequent payment made pursuant to the contract is not grandfathered because the contract itself was materially modified when the prior payment was accelerated without a discount to reasonably reflect the time value of money.

Commenters asked whether accelerating the payment of compensation attributable to equity-based compensation is considered a material modification when the payment is subject to a substantial risk of forfeiture. For example, an option may be subject to a substantial risk of forfeiture if, on the date of grant, the terms of the option provide that an employee may exercise the option only after performing services for three years after the date of grant. In this example, if the terms of the option are subsequently modified to require performance of services for only two years, then the modification results in the lapse of a substantial risk of forfeiture. One might consider this a material modification because the employee may exercise the option and receive compensation attributable to the exercise earlier than provided in the terms of the option on the date of grant. However, commenters suggested that accelerating vesting of equity-based compensation should not be a material modification because the acceleration does not provide for an increase in the amount of compensation received. The commenters reasoned that the acceleration of vesting of an equity award for which the amount of compensation is always variable is unlike the acceleration of the payment of a fixed cash award in which the acceleration may always be considered an increase in compensation due to the time value of money. To support their recommendation, commenters pointed out that, with respect to incentive stock options, section 424(h)(3)(C) and § 1.424-1(e)(4)(ii) provide that acceleration of vesting of an incentive stock option is not a modification.

These proposed regulations adopt the commenters' suggestion. Specifically, these proposed regulations provide that for compensation received pursuant to the substantial vesting of restricted property, or the exercise of a stock option or stock appreciation right that do not provide for a deferral of compensation (as defined in § 1.409A-1(b)(5)(i) and (ii)), a modification of a written binding contract in effect on November 2, 2017, that results in a lapse of the substantial risk of forfeiture (as defined § 1.83-3(c)) is not considered a material modification. Likewise, with respect to other compensation arrangements, if an amount of compensation payable under a written binding contract in effect on November 2, 2017, is subject to a substantial risk of forfeiture (as defined in § 1.409A-1(d)), then a modification of the contract that results in a lapse of the substantial risk of forfeiture is not considered a material modification. Thus, for all forms of compensation, a modification to a written binding contract that accelerates vesting will not be considered a material modification.

The Treasury Department and the IRS considered alternatives to the commenters' suggestion. For example, the Treasury Department and the IRS considered an approach based on the rules under section 280G. Under those rules, an acceleration of vesting can give rise to an excess parachute payment under section 280G even if the timing of the payment is not accelerated. See § 1.280G-1, Q&A-24. In other words, the rules under section 280G are based on the principle that there is independent value attributable to the acceleration of vesting, even if the timing of the payment is unchanged. Given the limited scope of the section 162(m) grandfathering rule and its diminishing applicability over time, the Treasury Department and the IRS have determined that it is not necessary to apply that principle in this context.

G. Ordering Rule for Payments Consisting of Grandfathered and Non-Grandfathered Amounts

Some NQDC arrangements provide for a series of payments instead of a lump sum. For a NQDC arrangement that is a written binding contract entered into prior to November 2, 2017, only a portion of the amounts payable under the arrangement might be grandfathered depending on the terms of the arrangement and applicable law. To identify the grandfathered amount when payment under the arrangement is made in a series of payments, the proposed regulations provide that the grandfathered amount is allocated to the first otherwise deductible payment paid under the arrangement. If the grandfathered amount exceeds the payment, then the excess is allocated to the next otherwise deductible payment paid under the arrangement. This process is repeated until the entire grandfathered amount has been paid. For example, assume that a NQDC arrangement provides for an annual payment of $100,000 for three years, and only $120,000 is grandfathered. Pursuant to the proposed regulations, the entire $100,000 paid in the first year is grandfathered. In the second year, only $20,000 of the $100,000 payment is grandfathered; the remaining $80,000 paid in the second year is not grandfathered. In the third year, none of the $100,000 payment is grandfathered.

VII. *Coordination with Section 409A*

Section 409A addresses NQDC arrangements and sets forth certain requirements that must be met to avoid current income inclusion and certain additional income tax. NQDC arrangements must designate a time and form of payment, among other requirements, to comply with section 409A. Pursuant to § 1.409A-2(b)(7)(i), a payment may be delayed past the designated payment date to the extent that the service recipient reasonably anticipates that, if the payment were made as scheduled, the service recipient's deduction with respect to such payment would not be permitted due to the application of section 162(m).[13] Generally, a payment delayed in accordance with § 1.409A-2(b)(7)(i) must be paid no later than the service provider's first taxable year in which the deduction of such payment will not be barred by the application of section 162(m).

If any scheduled payment to a service provider in a service recipient's taxable year is delayed in accordance with § 1.409A-2(b)(7)(i), then the delay in payment is treated as a subsequent deferral election unless all scheduled payments to that service provider that could be delayed in accordance with § 1.409A-2(b)(7)(i) are also delayed.[14] A subsequent deferral election will violate section 409A if the election fails to satisfy the requirements of section 409A(a)(4)(C).[15] A similar rule under § 1.409A-1(b)(4)(ii) permits delayed payments of compensation that otherwise qualifies as a short-term deferral under § 1.409A-1(b)(4)(i) (commonly referred to as the short-term deferral exception).

Before TCJA, an individual who was a covered employee for one taxable year would not necessarily remain a covered employee for subsequent taxable years, and would not be a covered employee after separation from service. Accordingly, parties to NQDC arrangements anticipated that in these cases, pursuant to §§ 1.409A-1(b)(4)(ii) and 1.409A-2(b)(7)(i), the corporation would be able to make the payment when the individual separated from service (if not earlier), when the individual would no longer be a covered employee and the deduction for the payment would no

---

[13] In general, if a payment is delayed pursuant to § 1.409A-2(b)(7)(i), then the payment must be made either during the service provider's first taxable year in which the service recipient reasonably anticipates, or reasonably should anticipate, that the payment will not fail to be deductible because of section 162(m), if the payment is made during such year or, if later, during the period beginning on the day the service provider separates from service and ending on the later of the last day of the taxable year of the service recipient in which the separation from service occurs or the 15th day of the third month following the separation from service.

[14] See § 1.409A-2(b)(7) for additional requirements for the service recipient to delay a payment so that the delay is not treated as a subsequent deferral election, such as treating all payments to similarly situated service providers on a reasonably consistent basis.

[15] Pursuant to section 409A(a)(4)(C), a subsequent deferral election (i) must be made at least 12 months before the prior scheduled payment date, (ii) cannot be effective for at least 12 months after the date of the subsequent election, and (iii) must delay the payment at least 5 years from the original scheduled payment date.

longer be restricted due to the application of section 162(m). Because TCJA amendments to the definition of covered employee fundamentally alter the premise of §§1.409A-1(b)(4)(ii) and 1.409A-2(b)(7)(i), commenters asked whether a service recipient may delay the scheduled payment of grandfathered amounts in accordance with §§1.409A-1(b)(4)(ii) and 1.409A-2(b)(7)(i), without delaying the payment of non-grandfathered amounts, in circumstances in which the service recipient has discretion to delay the payment. Commenters stated that the service provider may not want the non-grandfathered payments delayed and that the corporation would be willing to pay those payments under the original schedule since a delay in many cases would not result in the corporation being able to deduct the payment.

The Treasury Department and the IRS have concluded that the rules should be modified to accommodate this change. Consequently, in circumstances in which the service recipient has discretion to delay the payment, a service recipient may delay the scheduled payment of grandfathered amounts in accordance with §§1.409A-1(b)(4)(ii) and 1.409A-2(b)(7)(i), without delaying the payment of non-grandfathered amounts, and the delay of the grandfathered amounts will not be treated as a subsequent deferral election. As discussed in section VI of this preamble, the amendments made to section 162(m) by TCJA do not apply to grandfathered amounts. Therefore, the deduction for amounts grandfathered under the amended section 162(m) is not subject to section 162(m) when paid to a former covered employee who separated from service. Thus, the payment of these grandfathered amounts may be delayed consistent with §§1.409A-1(b)(4)(ii) and 1.409A-2(b)(7)(i). The Treasury Department and the IRS intend to incorporate these modifications into the regulations under section 409A, and taxpayers may rely on the guidance in this paragraph of the preamble for any taxable year beginning after December 31, 2017, until the issuance of proposed regulations under section 409A incorporating these modifications and permitting taxpayers to rely on such proposed regulations under section 409A.

Even though §§1.409A-1(b)(4)(ii) and 1.409A-2(b)(7)(i) provide that the service recipient has discretion to delay a payment, and that the discretion is not required to be set forth in the written plan, the Treasury Department and the IRS understand that compensation arrangements in effect on November 2, 2017, may explicitly require the service recipient to delay a payment if the service recipient reasonably believes the deduction with respect to the payment will not be permitted under section 162(m). Commenters pointed out that with respect to a service provider who is a covered employee, non-grandfathered amounts may require the passage of a significant period of time before a payment of the entire amount would be deductible, and may possibly never become deductible if the service provider dies and the payment (or remaining amount due) is payable at death. Commenters requested that relief be provided so that compensation arrangements may be amended to no longer require the service recipient to delay a payment that the service recipient reasonably believes will not be deductible under section 162(m) without resulting in a failure to meet the requirements of section 409A. The Treasury Department and the IRS have determined that this type of relief is appropriate given the impact of TCJA amendments on application of the rules in §§1.409A-1(b)(4)(ii) and 1.409A-2(b)(7)(i). Accordingly, if a NQDC arrangement is amended to remove the provision requiring the corporation to delay a payment if the corporation reasonably anticipates at the time of the scheduled payment that the deduction would not be permitted under section 162(m), then the amendment will not result in an impermissible acceleration of payment under §1.409A-3(j), and will not be considered a material modification for purposes of the grandfather rule under the amended section 162(m). The plan amendment must be made no later than December 31, 2020. If, pursuant to the amended plan, the corporation would have been required to make a payment (or payments) prior to December 31, 2020, then the payment (or payments) must be made no later than December 31, 2020. The Treasury Department and the IRS intend to incorporate these modifications into the regulations under section 409A, and taxpayers may rely on the guidance in this paragraph of the preamble for any taxable year beginning after December 31, 2017, until the issuance of proposed regulations under section 409A incorporating these modifications and permitting taxpayers to rely on such proposed regulations under section 409A.

Amounts payable under NQDC arrangements may consist of both grandfathered amounts and non-grandfathered amounts. With respect to these arrangements, employers may apply the guidance provided in the previous two paragraphs of this preamble. Accordingly, the plan may be amended to remove the provision requiring the corporation to delay the payment of non-grandfathered amounts if it is anticipated that the corporation's deduction with respect to the payments will not be permitted under section 162(m); notwithstanding such an amendment, the corporation may continue to delay payment of the grandfathered amounts in accordance with §§1.409A-1(b)(4)(ii) and 1.409A-2(b)(7)(i).

VIII. *Proposed Applicability Dates*

A. General Applicability Date

Generally, these regulations are proposed to apply to compensation that is otherwise deductible for taxable years beginning on or after [DATE OF PUBLICATION OF THE FINAL RULE IN THE FEDERAL REGISTER]. Taxpayers may choose to rely on these proposed regulations until the applicability date of the final regulations, provided that taxpayers apply these proposed regulations consistently and in their entirety. Because these proposed regulations do not broaden the definition of "covered employee" as provided in Notice 2018-68 and do not restrict the application of the definition of "written binding contract" as provided in Notice 2018-68, except as provided by the special applicability dates described in section VIII.B of this preamble, taxpayers may no longer rely on Notice 2018-68 for taxable years ending on or after December 20, 2019, but instead may rely on these proposed regulations for those taxable years.

B. Special Applicability Dates

These regulations are proposed to include special applicability dates covering certain aspects of the following provisions of the proposed regulations:

1. Definition of covered employee.

2. Definition of predecessor of a publicly held corporation.

3. Definition of compensation.

4. Application of section 162(m) to a deduction for compensation otherwise deductible for a taxable year ending on or after a privately held corporation becomes a publicly held corporation.

5. Definitions of written binding contract and material modification.

First, the definition of covered employee is proposed to apply to taxable years ending on or after September 10, 2018, the publication date of Notice 2018-68, which provided guidance on the definition of covered employee. Notice 2018-68 also provided that the Treasury Department and the IRS anticipate that the guidance in the notice will be incorporated in future regulations that, with respect to the issues addressed in the notice, will apply to any taxable year ending on or after September 10, 2018. Because these proposed regulations adopt the definition of covered employee in Notice 2018-68, the guidance on the definition of covered employee in these proposed regulations is proposed to apply to taxable years ending on or after September 10, 2018. The Treasury Department and the IRS recognize, however, that the rules related to a corporation whose fiscal year and taxable year do not end on the same date were not discussed in Notice 2018-68. Accordingly, the proposed regulations provide that, for a corporation whose fiscal and taxable years do not end on the same date, the rule requiring the determination of the three most highly compensated executive officers to be made pursuant to the rules under the Exchange Act applies to taxable years beginning on or after December 20, 2019.

Second, the provisions defining a predecessor corporation of a publicly held corporation are proposed to apply to corporate transactions for which all events necessary for the transaction occur on or after [DATE OF PUBLICATION OF THE FINAL RULE IN THE FEDERAL REGISTER]. With respect to the rules that apply to corporations that change from publicly held to privately held status or visa-versa, the definition of the term predecessor corporation of a publicly held corporation applies to a privately held corporation that again becomes a publicly held corporation on or after December 20, 2019. Accordingly, depending on the timing of any earlier transition from a publicly held corporation to a privately held corporation, the publicly held corporation that existed before the issuance of final regulations may be treated as a predecessor of a privately held corporation that becomes a publicly held corporation after the date of issuance of final regulations. Until the applicability date of the final regulations, taxpayers may rely on the definition of predecessor of a publicly held corporation in these proposed regulations or a reasonable good faith interpretation of the term "predecessor." The Treasury Department and the IRS have determined, however, that excluding the following target corporations from the definition of the term "predecessor" in the following situations is not a reasonable good faith interpretation of the statute: (1) A publicly held target corporation the stock or assets of which are acquired by another publicly held corporation in a transaction to which section 381(a) applies, and (2) a publicly held target corporation, at least 80% of the total voting power, and at least 80% of the total value, of the stock of which is acquired by a publicly held acquiring corporation (including an affiliated group). No inference is intended regarding whether the treatment of a target corporation as other than a "predecessor" in any other situation is a reasonable good faith interpretation of the statute.

Third, as discussed in section IV.C. of this preamble, the rule that the definition of compensation in proposed §1.162-33(c)(3) includes an amount equal to the publicly held corporation's distributive share of a partnership's deduction for compensation expense attributable to the compensation paid by the partnership is proposed to apply to any deduction for compensation that is otherwise allowable for a taxable year ending on or after December 20, 2019 The Treasury Department and the IRS are aware that arrangements currently exist that reflect an understanding that the allocated deduction would not be limited by section 162(m). Accordingly, this aspect of the definition of compensation would not apply to compensation paid pursuant to a written binding contract in effect on December 20, 2019 that is not materially modified after that date.

Fourth, the guidance on the applicability of section 162(m)(1) to the deduction for any compensation otherwise deductible for a taxable year ending on or after the date when a corporation becomes a publicly held corporation is proposed to apply to corporations that become publicly held after December 20, 2019. A corporation that was not a publicly held corporation and then becomes a publicly held corporation on or before December 20, 2019 may rely on the transition relief as provided in §1.162-27(f)(1) until the earliest of the events provided in §1.162-27(f)(2).

Fifth, the definitions of written binding contract and material modification are proposed to apply to taxable years ending on or after September 10, 2018, the publication date of Notice 2018-68, which provided guidance defining these terms. Notice 2018-68 also provided that the Treasury Department and IRS anticipated that the guidance in the notice would be incorporated in future regulations that, with respect to the issues addressed in the notice, would apply to any taxable year ending on or after September 10, 2018. Because these proposed regulations adopt the definitions of the terms "written binding contract" and "material modification" that were included in Notice 2018-68, the guidance on these definitions in these proposed regulations is proposed to apply to taxable years ending on or after September 10, 2018.

Special Analyses

This regulation is not subject to review under section 6(b) of Executive Order 12866 pursuant to the Memorandum of Agreement (April 11, 2018) between the Department of the Treasury and the Office of Management and Budget regarding review of tax regulations. Pursuant to the Regulatory Flexibility Act (RFA) (5 U.S.C. chapter 6), it is hereby certified that these proposed regulations would not have a significant economic impact on a substantial number of small entities. This certification is based on the fact that section 162(m)(1) applies only to publicly held corporations (for example, corporations that list securities on a national securities exchange and are rarely small entities) and only impacts those publicly held corporations that compensate certain executive officers in excess of $1 million in a taxable year. Notwithstanding this certification that the proposed regulations would not have a significant economic impact on a substantial number of small entities, the Treasury Department and the IRS invite comments on the impacts these proposed regulations may have on small entities. Pursuant to section 7805(f) of the Code, this proposed rule has been submitted to the Chief Counsel for Advocacy of the Small Business Administration for comment on its impact on small entities.

Comments and Public Hearing

Before these proposed regulations are adopted as final regulations, consideration will be given to any comments that are submitted timely to the IRS as prescribed in this preamble under the "**ADDRESSES**" heading. Treasury and the IRS request comments on all aspects of the proposed rules. All comments will be available at *www.regulations.gov* or upon request.

A public hearing has been scheduled for March 9, 2020, beginning at 10 a.m. in the Auditorium of the Internal Revenue Building, 1111 Constitution Avenue, NW., Washington, DC. Due to building security procedures, visitors must enter at the Constitution Avenue entrance. In addition, all visitors must present photo identification to enter the building. Because of access restrictions, visitors will not be admitted beyond the immediate entrance area more than 30 minutes before the hearing starts. For more information about having your name placed on the building access list to attend the hearing, see the "**FOR FURTHER INFORMATION CONTACT**" section of this preamble.

The rules of 26 CFR 601.601(a)(3) apply to the hearing. Persons who wish to present oral comments at the hearing must submit an outline of the topics to be discussed and the time to be devoted to each topic by December 20, 2019. Submit a signed paper or electronic copy of the outline as prescribed in this preamble under the "**ADDRESSES**" heading. A period of 10 minutes will be allotted to each person for making comments. An agenda showing the scheduling of the speakers will be prepared after the deadline for receiving outlines has passed. Copies of the agenda will be available free of charge at the hearing.

Drafting Information

The principal author of these regulations is Ilya Enkishev, Office of Associate Chief Counsel (Employee Benefits, Exempt Organizations, and Employment Taxes). However, other personnel from the Treasury Department and the IRS participated in the development of these regulations.

[¶49,825] Proposed Amendments of Regulations (REG-116163-19), published in the Federal Register on December 23, 2019.

[Code Sec. 6402]

Refunds: Direct deposit refunds: Taxpayer First Act (TFA).—Amendments of Reg. §301.6402-2, concerning the procedures for identification and recovery of a misdirected direct deposit refund, are proposed.

AGENCY: Internal Revenue Service (IRS), Treasury.

ACTION: Notice of proposed rulemaking.

SUMMARY: These proposed regulations provide guidance on section 6402(n) of the Internal Revenue Code (Code), concerning the procedures for identification and recovery of a misdirected direct deposit refund. The regulations reflect changes to the law made by the Taxpayer First Act. The proposed regulations affect taxpayers who have made a claim for refund, requested the refund be issued as a direct deposit, but did not receive a refund in the account designated on the claim for refund.

DATES: Comments and requests for a public hearing must be received by February 21, 2020.

ADDRESSES: Submit electronic submissions via the Federal eRulemaking Portal at www.regulations.gov (indicate IRS and REG-116163-19) by following the online instructions for submitting comments. Once submitted to the Federal eRulemaking Portal, comments cannot be edited or withdrawn. The Department of the Treasury (Treasury Department) and the IRS will publish for public availability any comment received to its public docket, whether submitted electronically or in hard copy. Send hard copy submissions to: CC:PA:LPD:PR (REG-116163-19), Room 5203, Internal Revenue Service, P.O. Box 7604, Ben Franklin Station, Washington, DC 20044. Submissions may be hand-delivered Monday through Friday between the hours of 8 a.m. and 4 p.m. to CC:PA:LPD:PR (REG-116163-19), Courier's Desk, Internal Revenue Service, 1111 Constitution Avenue NW, Washington, DC 20224.

FOR FURTHER INFORMATION CONTACT: Concerning the proposed amendments to the regulations, Mary C. King at (202) 317-5433; concerning submissions of comments, or requests for a public hearing, Regina L. Johnson, at (202) 317-6901 (not toll-free numbers).

SUPPLEMENTARY INFORMATION:

Background

This document contains proposed amendments to 26 CFR part 301 under section 6402(n) of the Code and provides guidance on the procedures used to identify and recover tax refunds issued by electronic funds transfer (direct deposit) that were not delivered to the account designated to receive the direct deposit refund on the federal tax return or other claim for refund. These proposed regulations implement section 6402(n) of the Code, a new provision added by section 1407 of the Taxpayer First Act, Public Law 116-25, 133 Stat. 981 (2019) (TFA).

Section 6402(a) provides the Secretary of the Treasury or his delegate (Secretary) with the authority to refund the balance of an overpayment after first crediting the overpayment amount against any tax liability of the person who made the overpayment. Before any refund is issued, the balance must also be offset against certain nontax liabilities. Sections 6402(a), (c), (d), (e), and (f) require a taxpayer's overpayment to be applied to any outstanding Federal tax debt, past-due child support, Federal agency non-tax debt, State income tax obligation, or certain unemployment compensation debts owed to a state prior to crediting the overpayment to a future tax or issuing a refund. This application of a tax overpayment is called a refund offset. An offset occurs after a refund is certified by the IRS but prior to the issuance of the refund.

The procedures for making a claim for refund are set out in §301.6402-2 of the Procedure and Administration Regulations. Those regulations include procedures for the mailing of a check in payment of allowed claims for refund. See §301.6402-2(f). The procedures for sending a refund by direct deposit are set out in the Treasury Financial Manual, the Bureau of the Fiscal Service Green Book, and the regulations under 31 CFR part 210. The Treasury Financial Manual is available for downloading at the Bureau of the Fiscal Service's web site at https://tfm.fiscal.treasury.gov/home.html. The Green Book is available for downloading at the Bureau of the Fiscal Service's web site at https://www.fiscal.treasury.gov/reference-guidance/green-book/.

The IRS generally issues a refund in the manner requested on the claim for refund. This includes splitting a refund by authorizing direct deposits into multiple accounts using Form 8888, "Allocation of Refund (Including Savings Bond Purchases)." Under current procedures, if a taxpayer requests that the refund be issued as a direct deposit on a current year tax return, the IRS will generally issue the refund it determines to the account number and routing number designated on the claim. A direct deposit may be stopped or unable to be delivered for a number of reasons, including, but not limited to, an invalid routing number, rejection by a financial institution, or a processing error. If the direct deposit is stopped or returned prior to the delivery of the refund to the account designated on the claim for refund, the IRS will generally issue the refund in the form of a paper check.

Under current procedures, set out in Internal Revenue Manual (I.R.M.) sections 21.4.1, 21.4.2, and 21.4.3 and available at https://www.irs.gov/irm, a taxpayer or authorized representative may report a missing refund to the IRS by using an IRS customer service line or filing a Form 3911, "Taxpayer Statement Regarding Refund." A taxpayer or authorized representative may also report a missing refund to the IRS through the Office of the Taxpayer Advocate (commonly referred to as the Taxpayer Advocate Service (TAS)). When a missing refund is reported, the IRS will first determine if a refund was issued to the taxpayer and whether a direct deposit transaction was made. If the refund was issued as a direct deposit, the IRS will verify the accuracy of the taxpayer's account number and routing number.

If the taxpayer reports a missing refund and the IRS confirms a refund was issued, the IRS will generally conduct a refund trace to determine why the refund was not delivered to the account of the taxpayer. A refund trace is the process by which the IRS tracks stolen, lost, or misplaced refund checks or verifies a financial institution received direct deposits and may replace an authorized refund to the taxpayer if warranted. A refund trace will be initiated when a taxpayer reports a missing refund and the IRS confirms a refund was issued as a direct deposit, even if the taxpayer reports that the account information designated on the claim for refund was incorrect. A refund trace is initiated by inputting a trace code into the IRS's Integrated Data Retrieval System (IDRS), which sends a request to the Treasury Department's Bureau of the Fiscal Service (BFS) for assistance in identifying information about the account into which the refund was made.

When the BFS receives a refund trace request from the IRS for a tax refund issued as a direct deposit, the BFS asks financial institutions for assistance in verifying that the institution received the direct deposit, identifying information about the account where the refund was made, and recovery of such amounts. The correct financial institution is identified by the routing number that appears on the claim for refund. The BFS uses FS Form 150.1, which is an official request from the Treasury Department to the financial institution to recover more information regarding the direct deposit. The information requested includes whether the financial institution received the refund; whether the financial institution returned the refund, will return the refund, or if no funds are available for return; whether the refund was deposited into the account of the taxpayer on whose behalf the request is being made; and the account number and account owner's identifying information.

When the IRS determines that a refund or a portion of a refund was made by direct deposit to an account that is not the account designated on the taxpayer's claim for refund, the refund is considered to be a misdirected direct deposit refund. A misdirected direct deposit refund occurs when the IRS has caused the error, such as when the IRS mistakenly inputs an incorrect account number from the claim for refund, or when a financial institution credits the payment to an account other than the account designated in the IRS's direct deposit instruction. See 31 CFR §210.8; see also Bureau of the Fiscal Service, Green Book: A Guide to Federal Government ACH Payments, at 2-6 (2016) (where a financial institution has misdirected a payment, the financial institution may be liable to the issuing agency if there is a resulting loss by the agency). When a misdirected direct deposit refund is discovered, the IRS will issue a replacement refund to the taxpayer in the full amount of the refund that was misdirected. This replacement refund is issued regardless of whether the IRS is able to recover the misdirected direct deposit refund that the taxpayer did not receive.

Occasionally, a taxpayer or authorized representative will designate an incorrect account or routing number on the claim for refund that will cause a refund to be disbursed to an account that is not the account of the taxpayer. When the IRS determines that a refund or a portion of a refund was made by direct deposit to the account designated on the taxpayer's claim for refund, the refund is not considered to be a "misdirected direct deposit refund." Nevertheless, the IRS should generally initiate a refund trace for any reported missing refund that is issued as a direct deposit. In some instances, such as when the date of the direct deposit is less than five calendar days from when the missing refund is reported, the IRS will not initiate a refund trace immediately. Through the refund trace procedure, the IRS will coordinate with financial institutions and the BFS to request the return of a refund not deposited into the account of the taxpayer on whose behalf the request is being made. In cases when the taxpayer designates an incorrect account number on the claim for refund, the IRS will issue a replacement refund only after the IRS has recovered the original refund or a portion of the refund that was deposited in the incorrect account from the financial institution. When the financial institution returns the refund, the IRS will issue a replacement refund in the amount recovered. When the IRS has recovered only a portion of the refund that was directed to the incorrect account, only the portion recovered will be refunded to the taxpayer.

In other instances, a refund will be disbursed to the account designated to receive the refund, but the taxpayer will nevertheless not receive the refund that was disbursed. The IRS has separate procedures, reflected in I.R.M. 21.4.1, 21.4.2, and 21.4.3, to assist taxpayers whose refunds are not delivered to them despite the deposit of the refund in the account designated on the return or claim for refund. These procedures also include information on when the IRS will issue a replacement refund to victims of tax return preparer misconduct. See Form 14157-A, Tax Return Preparer Fraud or Misconduct Affidavit. However, refunds that are diverted from the correct taxpayer due to tax return preparer misconduct are not considered to be "misdirected direct deposit refunds" because they are deposited into the account listed on the claim for refund.

The TFA added section 6402(n) to the Code. Pursuant to section 6402(n)(1), the Secretary is required to establish procedures to allow taxpayers to report when a refund is not deposited into the taxpayer's account. Section 6402(n)(2) further directs the Secretary to establish procedures for coordination with financial institutions to identify the account to which a misdirected direct deposit refund has been made and to recover such refunds. Finally, under section 6402(n)(3), the Secretary is directed to establish procedures to allow a misdirected direct deposit refund to be delivered to the correct account of the taxpayer. These proposed regulations describe the procedures under section 6402(n) that will be used when a taxpayer or authorized representative notifies the IRS that the requested refund was not received. The proposed regulations adopt current IRS procedures for the reporting, identification, recovery, and delivery of misdirected direct deposit refunds.

Explanation of Provisions

I. Definitions

In §301.6402-2(g)(1) of the proposed regulations, a misdirected direct deposit refund is defined as any refund of an overpayment of tax that is disbursed as a direct deposit but is not deposited into the account designated on the claim for refund to receive the direct deposit refund. This typically occurs when the IRS mistakenly inputs an incorrect account or routing number from the claim for refund, usually as a result of a processing or computer error. A misdirected direct deposit refund can also occur if a financial institution mistakenly credits the payment to an account other than the account designated in the IRS's direct deposit instruction. These proposed regulations are intended to serve taxpayers as part of the IRS's mission to provide top quality service by increasing awareness of the IRS procedures taxpayers may use to report missing direct deposit refunds and to streamline the identification and recovery of misdirected refunds. See H.R. Rep. No. 116-39, pt. 1, at 62 (2019) (although this report is for a prior, un-enacted version of the Taxpayer First Act, H.R. 1957, 116th Cong. (2019), section 1407 of that bill and that of the bill that was passed by the same Congress as Public Law 116-25 are identical).

Not all instances where a taxpayer fails to receive a direct deposit in the account designated on the claim for refund are the result of a misdirected direct deposit refund. The requested tax refund may have instead been issued in the form of a paper check or may not have been issued at all if the IRS adjusted the requested refund amount during the processing of the tax return or offset the requested tax refund to pay certain debts. In some scenarios, the refund is disbursed as a direct deposit, but is not deposited into the account in which the taxpayer expects the refund to be deposited. This includes instances of tax return preparer misconduct and taxpayers designating an incorrect account or routing number on the claim for refund. There are no significant variances between the proposed regulations and current I.R.M. procedures with regards to refunds that are deposited into the accounts designated on the claims for refund which are ultimately not received by the taxpayer.

The proposed regulations include in the definition of a misdirected direct deposit refund only those refunds which are actually issued as a direct deposit. A misdirected direct deposit refund therefore does not include an overpayment that is credited against another outstanding tax liability of the taxpayer pursuant to section 6402(a) or that is offset pursuant to the law. A refund that is offset or applied as mandated by law is not a misdirected direct deposit refund because these actions are mandated by law.

A refund issued as a check is not a misdirected direct deposit refund merely because the taxpayer requested the refund in the form of a direct deposit. Under current procedures, there are many reasons why a requested direct deposit will be issued as a paper check, including if the financial institution rejects or returns the direct deposit or the claim for refund is filed more than a year after the close of the tax year. Additional information on reasons why a direct deposit may be rejected can be found in I.R.M. 21.4.1.5.8.1, Direct Deposit Reject Reason Codes. If a refund is issued as a check, the taxpayer may then deposit the refund into the correct account.

II. Reporting

Section 301.6402-2(g)(2) of the proposed regulations designates the method of reporting a misdirected direct deposit refund. Under current procedures, taxpayers may submit Form 3911 to the IRS to report a missing refund. The Form 3911, including any future version of the Form, should be filed in accordance with the instructions provided. Alternatively, a taxpayer may report a missing refund orally through an IRS customer service line. If the IRS is unable to verify the identity of the caller through oral statements, the taxpayer may have to submit a written request on the Form 3911 to report a missing refund. Taxpayers may also report a missing refund, after scheduling an appointment, through submission of the Form 3911 in person at a Taxpayer Assistance Center. Where a taxpayer is experiencing a hardship, the taxpayer may report a missing refund to TAS by telephone, facsimile, mail or in person.

The proposed regulations direct taxpayers to use current procedures, including by allowing missing direct deposit refunds to be reported via Form 3911, a customer service line, TAS, and at Taxpayer Assistance Centers. This continuity aids in administering the refund procedures by using processes with which the public and the IRS are familiar. Any taxpayer missing a refund or a portion of a refund made by direct deposit may use the reporting procedures set out in §301.6402-2(g)(2) of the proposed regulations. If the IRS determines a direct deposit was issued, it will initiate a refund trace for any missing refund in accordance with the procedures set out in §301.6402-2(g)(3) of the proposed regulations.

III. Coordination with Financial Institutions

Under current procedures, the IRS coordinates with the BFS as well as financial institutions to locate and recover misdirected direct deposit refunds. When a taxpayer reports a missing direct deposit refund, the IRS will review its records to determine if a refund was issued or if there are indicators on the account signifying that an offset may have occurred. If the IRS determines that a refund was issued as a direct deposit, the IRS will initiate a refund trace, which sends a refund trace inquiry to the BFS. The BFS sends an official request on FS Form 150.1 to the financial institution to search for the electronic funds transfer. FS Form 150.1 requests the financial institution to identify the account into which the refund was made, as well as the identifying information of the account holder, including name and Social Security number.

The refund trace will ask for the assistance of the financial institution in the recovery of the refund if the refund was deposited into an account in error. If the financial institution is unable or unwilling to recover the refund, the IRS will separately contact the financial institution to request assistance in recovering the refund. The financial institution may return the refund through the procedures determined by the BFS. See Bureau of the Fiscal Service, Green Book: A Guide to Federal Government ACH Payments (2016). If the refund is recovered, a credit will be added to the taxpayer's account to reflect the return of the refund.

Section 301.6402-2(g)(3) of the proposed regulations formalizes current procedures. Where a direct deposit has been misdirected, this section of the regulations proposes to require the IRS to contact banks through the BFS to obtain the information necessary to identify whether the financial institution received the refund and the owner of the deposit account to whom the deposit was disbursed. The regulations further direct the IRS to utilize either BFS procedures or directly seek the assistance of the bank holding the misdirected direct deposit refund to recover the amount.

IV. Delivery of the Refund to the Correct Account

Section 301.6402-2(g)(4) of the proposed regulations establishes that when a misdirected direct deposit refund has been identified by the IRS, the IRS will issue a replacement refund in the full amount of the refund that was misdirected. The refund will generally be issued as soon as possible to make the taxpayer whole and limit credit interest. When a financial institution has indicated that a misdirected direct deposit refund will be returned to the IRS, the IRS generally issues a replacement refund after the misdirected refund is returned. The timing of the replacement refund is calculated to ensure that a replacement refund is not issued twice as a result of a returned refund being credited back to a taxpayer's account after a replacement refund has already been issued, resulting in an erroneous refund to the taxpayer. An erroneous refund is defined as the receipt of any money from the IRS to which the recipient is not entitled.

A replacement refund will generally be issued as a paper check, which the taxpayer may deposit into the correct account. The IRS is generally unable to change the account information for a direct deposit after the information has been input. For example, where the IRS has determined the refund is a misdirected direct deposit refund because it mistakenly input the account number from a claim for refund, the IRS usually cannot correct the incorrect account number. Thus, the taxpayer will receive the refund as a paper check. The check will be sent via postal service to the address listed on the master file. If the taxpayer updates their address through the Form 3911, the check will be mailed to the updated address.

In some limited instances, such as when TAS has worked with a taxpayer to establish hardship criteria, a replacement refund may be issued as a direct deposit. In general, however, to effectively administer the issuance of a replacement refund, the taxpayer will receive the refund in the form of a check. The taxpayer may then deposit the check into the proper account.

V. Application of Procedures to Missing Refunds

Section 301.6402-2(g)(5) of the proposed regulations provides that the reporting and coordination procedures found in § 301.6402-2(g)(2) through (3)(i) of the proposed regulations for misdirected direct deposit refunds should be used for any refund issued as a direct deposit that the taxpayer believes is missing. As with a misdirected direct deposit refund, once a refund is reporting as missing the IRS will coordinate with the BFS to track the missing refund and gather available information about the account into which the refund was deposited. Section 301.6402-2(g)(5) of the proposed regulations also provides that if a missing refund or a portion of a refund is returned to the IRS resulting in an overpayment on the taxpayer's account, the IRS will issue a refund in accordance with the law. As with a misdirected direct deposit refund, such overpayment may be credited against a federal tax liability or offset against certain non-tax liabilities prior to the issuance of a refund.

Proposed Applicability Date

The applicability date for these proposed regulations applies to claims for refund filed after the date final regulations are published in the **Federal Register**.

Special Analyses

This regulation is not subject to review under section 6(b) of Executive Order 12866 pursuant to the Memorandum of Agreement (April 11, 2018) between the Department of the Treasury and the Office of Management and Budget regarding review of tax regulations.

These proposed regulations do not impose any additional information collection requirements in the form of reporting, recordkeeping requirements, or third-party disclosure requirements related to tax compliance. However, because a taxpayer or a taxpayer's representative may elect to report a missing refund using the procedures described in proposed § 301.6402-2(g)(2)(ii)(B), some taxpayers may use a form to report a missing refund. The collection of information in proposed § 301.6402-2(g)(2)(ii)(B) is through use of a Form 3911, "Taxpayer Statement Regarding Refund," and is the sole collection of information requirement established by the proposed regulations.

For the purposes of the Paperwork Reduction Act, 44 U.S.C. §§ 3501-3520, the reporting burden associated with the collection of information with respect to section 6402(n) will be reflected in Paperwork Reduction Act submissions for IRS Form 3911 (OMB Control Number 1545-1384). The estimated average time to complete Form 3911 is five minutes. However, use of a form is not required. A taxpayer may instead elect to investigate a missing refund over the telephone or in person at a Taxpayer Assistance Center and, after the IRS identifies the tax refund and informs the taxpayer that the refund was issued as a direct deposit, orally report that the already-identified refund is missing. An agency may not conduct or sponsor, and a person is not required to respond to, a collection of information unless it displays a valid control number assigned by the Office of Management and Budget.

It is hereby certified that these proposed regulations will not have a significant economic impact on a substantial number of small entities within the meaning of section 601(6) of the Regulatory Flexibility Act (5 U.S.C. chapter 6). The certification is based on the information that follows. There is no significant impact from these regulations on any small entity utilizing the procedures prescribed by these regulations to report a missing refund because there is no significant cost associated with reporting a missing refund. There is no fee charged in connection with reporting a missing refund, and the estimated time to complete a Form 3911, "Taxpayer Statement Regarding Refund," is five minutes. There are no tax consequences associated with the proposed regulations, as it merely sets forth the procedures for reporting a missing refund and describes the process the IRS uses in locating a missing refund and, in some instances, issuing a replacement refund. The process in these proposed regulations mirrors the existing process and does not change the reporting burden. Accordingly, this regulation is not expected to have a significant economic impact on a substantial number of small entities. Pursuant to section 7805(f) of the Code, this notice of proposed rulemaking will be submitted to the Chief Counsel for Advocacy of the Small Business Administration for comment on its impact on small business entities. The Treasury Department and the IRS invite comments on any impact these proposed regulations would have on small business entities.

Section 202 of the Unfunded Mandates Reform Act of 1995 requires that agencies assess anticipated costs and benefits and take certain other actions before issuing a final rule that includes any Federal mandate that may result in expenditures in any one year by a state, local, or tribal government, in the aggregate, or by the private sector, of $100 million in 1995 dollars, updated annually for inflation. In 2018, that threshold is approximately $150 million. This rule does not include any Federal mandate that may result in expenditures by state, local, or tribal governments, or by the private sector in excess of that threshold.

Executive Order 13132 (entitled Federalism) prohibits an agency from publishing any rule that has federalism implications if the rule either imposes substantial, direct compliance costs on state and local governments, and is not required by statute, or preempts state law, unless the agency meets the consultation and funding requirements of section 6 of the Executive Order. This proposed rule does not have federalism implications, and does not impose substantial direct compliance costs on state and local governments or preempt state law, within the meaning of the Executive Order.

Comments and Requests for a Public Hearing

Before these proposed amendments to the regulations are adopted as final regulations, consideration will be given to any comments that are submitted timely to the IRS as prescribed in the preamble under the "**ADDRESSES**" section. The Treasury Department and the IRS request comments on all aspects of the proposed regulations. All comments submitted will be made available at *http://www.regulations.gov* or upon request. A public hearing will be scheduled if requested in writing by any person that timely submits written comments. If a public hearing is scheduled, then notice of the date, time, and place for the public hearing will be published in the **Federal Register**.

Drafting Information

The principal author of these regulations is Mary C. King of the Office of the Associate Chief Counsel (Procedure and Administration). Other personnel from the Treasury Department and the IRS participated in the development of the regulations.

[¶ 49,826]   Proposed Amendments of Regulations (REG-100956-19), published in the Federal Register on December 30, 2019.

[Code Secs. 863, 864, 865, 937 and 1502]

Source of income: Sale of property: Nonresidents.—Reg. §1.865-3, and amendments of Reg. §§1.863-1, 1.863-2, 1.863-3, 1.863-8, 1.864-6, 1.937-2, 1.937-3 and 1.1502-13, modifying the rules for determining the source of income from sales of inventory produced within the United States and sold without the United States or vice versa, are proposed.

AGENCY: Internal Revenue Service (IRS), Treasury.

ACTION: Notice of proposed rulemaking.

SUMMARY: This document contains proposed regulations modifying the rules for determining the source of income from sales of inventory produced within the United States and sold without the United States or vice versa. These proposed regulations also contain new rules for determining the source of income from sales of personal property (including inventory) by nonresidents that are attributable to an office or other fixed place of business that the nonresident maintains in the United States. Finally, these proposed regulations modify certain rules for determining whether foreign source income is effectively connected with the conduct of a trade or business within the United States.

DATES: Comments and requests for a public hearing must be received by February 28, 2020.. ADDRESSES: Submit electronic submissions via the Federal eRulemaking Portal at www.regulations.gov (indicate IRS and REG-100956-19) by following the online instructions for submitting comments. Once submitted to the Federal eRulemaking Portal, comments cannot be edited or withdrawn. The Department of the Treasury ("Treasury Department") and the IRS will publish for public availability any comment received to its public docket, whether submitted electronically or in hard copy. Send hard copy submissions to: CC:PA:LPD:PR (REG-100956-19), Room 5203, Internal Revenue Service, P.O. Box 7604, Ben Franklin Station, Washington, DC 20044. FOR FURTHER INFORMATION CONTACT: Concerning the proposed regulations Brad McCormack, (202) 317-6911 or Anisa Afshar, (202) 317-4999; concerning submissions of comments and requests for a public hearing, Regina L. Johnson, (202) 317-6901 (not toll free numbers).

SUPPLEMENTARY INFORMATION:

Background

These regulations (the "proposed regulations") contain proposed amendments to 26 CFR part 1 revising the rules under section 863 of the Internal Revenue Code (the "Code") for determining the source of gross income from sales of certain property, and under section 864 for treating foreign source income as effectively connected with the conduct of a trade or business within the United States. Conforming revisions are made to current regulations that reference section 863. The proposed regulations also provide guidance under section 865(e)(2) and (3) regarding the source of income from the sale of personal property, including inventory property, within the meaning of section 865(i)(1) ("inventory"), by nonresidents.

The Tax Cuts and Jobs Act, Pub. L. 115-97 (2017) (the "Act"), enacted on December 22, 2017, amended section 863 of the Code, which provides special rules for determining the source of income, including income partly from within and partly from without the United States. Specifically, section 14303 of the Act amended section 863(b) to allocate or apportion income from the sale or exchange of inventory property produced (in whole or in part) by a taxpayer within and sold or exchanged without the United States or produced (in whole or in part) by the taxpayer without and sold or exchanged within the United States (collectively, "Section 863(b)(2) Sales") solely on the basis of production activities with respect to that inventory. Before the Act, section 863(b) provided that income from Section 863(b)(2) Sales would be treated as derived partly from sources within and partly from sources without the United States without providing the basis for such allocation or apportionment.

Current §1.863-3 provides rules for allocating or apportioning gross income from Section 863(b)(2) Sales. Those rules provide several methods for determining the amount of gross income from Section 863(b)(2) Sales that is attributable to production activity and the amount of gross income attributable to sales activity, with different rules then applying to source the portion of the income derived from production activity versus sales activity. *See* current §1.863-3(b). Current §1.863-3(f) provides rules for gains, profits, and income that are treated as derived partly from sources within the United States and partly from sources within a possession of the United States (generally referred to herein as a "U.S. territory").

With respect to production activity, current §1.863-3(c)(1)(ii) provides a formula for allocating or apportioning gross income where there is production activity both within and without the United States. Current §1.863-3(c)(1)(ii)(A) determines the amount of income from sources without the United States by multiplying all the income attributable to taxpayer's production activities by a fraction, the numerator of which is the average adjusted basis of production assets that are located outside the United States and the denominator of which is the average adjusted basis of all the production assets located within and without the United States. For purposes of applying this formula, the adjusted basis of production assets is determined under section 1011, which is adjusted under section 1016 for depreciation deductions allowed. Section 13201 of the Act amended section 168(k) to allow an additional first-year depreciation deduction of 100 percent of the basis of certain property placed in service after September 27, 2017, and before January 1, 2023. Therefore, certain new and used production assets placed in service and used predominantly within the United States during this period may have an adjusted basis of zero. After December 31, 2022, qualifying property placed in service before January 1, 2027 (or, in the case of certain property, January 1, 2028), is still subject to accelerated depreciation for an amount equal to the applicable percentage of the basis of the property. Section 168(k)(1) and (6). However, production assets placed in service or used predominantly without the United States, or both, do not qualify for this accelerated depreciation and must be depreciated using the straight line method under the alternative depreciation system ("ADS") of section 168(g)(2). *See* section 168(g)(1)(A).

Section 865, added to the Code as part of the Tax Reform Act of 1986, Pub. L. 99-514 (1986) (the "TRA"), provides rules for sourcing sales of personal property. The general rule of section 865(a)(1) is that income from a sale of personal property is sourced based on the residence of the seller. Section 865(b) excepts inventory from this rule and sources income from the sale of inventory generally based on either the place of sale (for purchased inventory under section 861(a)(6) or 862(a)(6)) or based on the allocation and apportionment rules of section 863 (for inventory produced by the taxpayer). The place of sale rules typically depend upon the location where title to the inventory passes from the seller to the buyer. *See* §1.861-7(c).

Section 865(c) provides special rules for sourcing gain from the sale of depreciable personal property. Under section 865(c)(1), gain from the sale of depreciable personal property that is not in excess of depreciation adjustments is allocated between sources within and without the United States by treating the same proportion of such gain as sourced within the United States as the United States depreciation adjustments (as defined in section 865(c)(3)) with respect to such property bear to the total depreciation adjustments, and by treating the remaining portion of such gain as sourced without the United States. Under section 865(c)(2), gain in excess of the depreciation adjustments is sourced as if such property were inventory.

Section 865(e)(2) provides a further overlay to these rules with respect to all sales of personal property (including inventory) by nonresidents, as that term is defined in section 865(g)(1)(B), attributable to an office or other fixed place of business in the United States. Section 865(e)(2)(A) generally provides that income from any sale of personal property attributable to such an office or other fixed place of business is sourced in the United States. An exception is provided in section 865(e)(2)(B) for a sale of inventory for use, disposition, or consumption outside the United States if a foreign office of the nonresident "materially participated" in the sale. Section 865(e)(3) provides that the "principles of section 864(c)(5) shall apply" to determine whether a nonresident has an office or other fixed place of business and whether a sale is attributable to such office or other fixed place of business. Where applicable, section 865(e)(2) applies "[n]otwithstanding any other provisions" of subchapter N, part I, including sections 863(b), 861(a)(6), and 862(a)(6).

Section 864(c) provides the general rules for determining whether income is treated as effectively connected with the conduct of a trade or business within the United States. Nonresident alien individuals, foreign corporations, and bona fide residents of a U.S. territory ("non-U.S. persons") engaged in a trade or business within the United States are generally subject to U.S. net basis taxation on income that is effectively connected with that trade or business. Section 864(c)(2) provides that income described in section 871(a)(1) or (h) or section 881(a) or (c), as well as U.S. source capital gains or losses, are determined to be effectively connected or not based on two tests—whether the income is "derived from assets" used in the non-U.S. person's trade or business or whether the activities of the trade or business were a "material factor" in the realization of the income. Section 864(c)(3) generally treats U.S. source income not described in section 864(c)(2) as effectively connected with a non-U.S. person's trade or business within the United States. Section 864(c)(4)(B) sets forth additional rules that treat certain foreign source income as effectively connected with the conduct of a U.S. trade or business if a non-U.S. person has an office or other fixed place of business within the United States to which the income is attributable, including income from certain sales of inventory as described in section 864(c)(4)(B)(iii).

Section 864(c)(5)(A) provides rules for determining whether a non-U.S. person has an office or other fixed place of business to which section 864(c)(4)(B) may apply as the result of the presence of an agent in the United States, and section 864(c)(5)(B) provides a threshold requirement for determining whether any income is attributable to such an office or other fixed place of business. Once it is determined that an office or other fixed place of business in the United States exists and income is attributable thereto, section 864(c)(5)(C) provides that the amount of income so attributable is generally the amount that is properly allocable to the office or other fixed place of business. Section 864(c)(5)(C) further provides that, with respect to certain sales of inventory described in section 864(c)(4)(B)(iii), the amount attributable to the office or fixed place of business cannot exceed the income that would otherwise have been U.S. source had the sale been made in the United States. As noted, the principles of section 864(c)(5) apply in the context of section 865(e)(2) pursuant to section 865(e)(3).

Explanation of Provisions

Consistent with the Act's changes to section 863(b)(2), these proposed regulations amend § 1.863-3 in order to properly allocate or apportion gross income from Section 863(b)(2) Sales based solely on production activity, and remove the methods for allocating or apportioning gross income between production and sales activity. In addition, because of the Act's change to section 168(k) to allow accelerated depreciation in some circumstances, these proposed regulations provide a new rule for computing the adjusted basis of production assets for purposes of applying the formula for allocating or apportioning gross income where there is production activity both within and without the United States. These proposed regulations also contain conforming amendments to other regulations that allocate or apportion income between production and sales activity. In addition, these proposed regulations make minor changes to § § 1.937-2, 1.937-3, and 1.1502-13 to update relevant cross references and examples.

These regulations also add proposed § 1.865-3 to clarify the proper scope and application of section 865(e)(2), as well as the interaction between section 865(e)(2) and section 865(c) regarding the sourcing of income from the sale of certain depreciable personal property. The proposed regulations also clarify the interaction between the section 865(e)(2) rules and the rules governing effectively connected income under section 864(c)(4)(B)(iii) and (c)(5). The proposed regulations amend § 1.864-6(c), the current rules for determining the amount of foreign source effectively connected income attributable to an office or other fixed place of business within the United States, to be consistent with the proposed sourcing rules applicable to produced inventory sales under section 865(e)(2).

I. Modification of Current § 1.863-3 and Other Regulations to Reflect the Amendments of Section 863(b) and Section 168(k)

A. Proposed changes to § 1.863-3 to reflect the amendment of section 863(b)

Before amendment by the Act, section 863(b)(2) provided that gains, profits, and income from Section 863(b)(2) Sales were sourced partly from sources within and partly from sources without the United States, but did not prescribe a particular method of allocating or apportioning between these two sources. Accordingly, current § 1.863-3 provides allocation or apportionment methods for Section 863(b)(2) Sales. Under those regulations, a taxpayer must allocate or apportion gross income from Section 863(b)(2) Sales between production activity and sales activity using one of three methods described in current § 1.863-3(b): the 50/50 method described in paragraph (b)(1), the independent factory price ("IFP") method described in paragraph (b)(2), or the books and records method described in paragraph (b)(3). Current § 1.863-3(d) provides rules for allocating and apportioning expenses to gross income from Section 863(b)(2) Sales, including a requirement to apportion expenses pro rata based on the source of gross income where the 50/50 method has been used. Current § 1.863-3(e) provides rules for electing one of these methods and the related information that a taxpayer must disclose on a tax return.

The Act amended section 863(b) to source income from Section 863(b)(2) Sales solely on the basis of the production activity with respect to the inventory sold, and as a result sales activity is no longer a relevant factor for allocating or apportioning income under that section. Therefore, these proposed regulations remove the three methods in paragraph (b) and the related election rules in paragraph (e). Proposed § 1.863-3(b) requires sourcing of Section 863(b)(2) Sales based solely on the location of production activities, consistent with section 863(b)(2), as amended. Given the elimination of the 50/50 method, the proposed regulations no longer provide for the apportionment of expenses based solely on relative gross income from U.S. and foreign sources. Instead, the proposed regulations provide that expenses are allocated and apportioned based on the generally-applicable rules in § § 1.861-8 through 1.861-17.

B. Proposed changes to § 1.863-3(e)

Proposed § 1.863-3(e) (which replaces current § 1.863-3(f)) does not provide a specific rule for sourcing gross income derived from the sale of inventory produced (in whole or in part) by the taxpayer within the United States and sold within a U.S. territory, or produced (in whole or in part) by a taxpayer in a U.S. territory and sold within the United States. Instead, proposed § 1.863-3(e) provides a cross-reference directing taxpayers to source such income under the rules provided by proposed § 1.863-3(c). Proposed § 1.863-3(e) modifies the rule for sourcing gross income derived from the purchase of personal property within a U.S. territory and its sale within the United States under section 863(b)(3). Consistent with proposed § 1.863-3(b), proposed § 1.863-3(e) removes the books and records method provided by current § 1.863-3(f)(3)(i)(B). Instead, proposed § 1.863-3(e)(3)(i) requires sourcing such income based solely upon the taxpayer's business activity.

C. *Proposed changes to §1.863-3 to reflect the amendment of section 168(k)*

Notwithstanding the changes to section 863(b) required by the Act, there remains a need for rules to allocate or apportion gross income from Section 863(b)(2) Sales between U.S. and foreign sources where, with respect to inventory, there is production activity both within and without the United States. The proposed regulations retain the existing rules in current §1.863-3(c)(1)(ii) for sourcing gross income from production activity where there is production activity both within and without the United States. The proposed regulations do not amend current §1.863-3(c)(1)(ii)(A), which determines the amount of foreign source income in such cases by multiplying the total gross income from Section 863(b)(2) Sales by a fraction, the numerator of which is the average adjusted basis of production assets located outside the United States and the denominator of which is all production assets within and without the United States. The remaining income is treated as U.S. source.

Because of the Act's change to section 168(k) to allow accelerated depreciation in some circumstances, the Treasury Department and the IRS have determined that a new rule is needed in current §1.863-3(c)(1)(ii)(B) for computing the adjusted basis of production assets for purposes of the formula for allocating or apportioning gross income where there is production activity both within and without the United States. Absent a change to the rules of current §1.863-3(c)(1)(ii)(B), the Act's modifications to the depreciation treatment of U.S. production assets will have the unintended effect of skewing the apportionment formula in favor of foreign source income because non-U.S. production assets (relative to U.S. production assets) will generally have a higher adjusted basis. Therefore, these proposed regulations modify the measurement of the basis of U.S. production assets under current §1.863-3(c)(1)(ii)(B) for purposes of the apportionment formula of proposed §1.863-3(c)(2)(i). The proposed regulations measure the basis of U.S. production assets based on ADS under section 168(g)(2) so that the basis of both U.S. and non-U.S. production assets is measured consistently on a straight line method over the same recovery period.

The Treasury Department and the IRS have determined that requiring the use of ADS for purposes of proposed §1.863-3 is consistent with other provisions of the Act that require the use of ADS. For example, sections 951A(d)(3) and 250(b)(2)(B) (by cross reference to section 951A(d)) both require the use of ADS for purposes of determining qualified business asset investment to calculate global intangible low-taxed income and foreign-derived intangible income, respectively. The use of ADS is also consistent with the interest allocation rules in §1.861-9(i)(1)(i). Nevertheless, the Treasury Department and the IRS request comments regarding the suitability of using ADS for these purposes and whether there is a more appropriate way to compare U.S. and non-U.S. production assets for purposes of proposed §1.863-3, such as the relative U.S. and non-U.S. production assets reported on the taxpayer's financial statements.

The proposed regulations do not otherwise modify the rules in current §1.863-3 for determining the location or existence of production activity, a topic the Treasury Department and the IRS may address in future guidance. The Treasury Department and the IRS request comments regarding other potential approaches to determine the location or existence of production activity or other modifications to current or proposed §1.863-3 that may be appropriate.

D. *Proposed changes to other regulations under section 863 to reflect the changes to §1.863-3*

The proposed regulations also modify current §1.863-1, current §1.863-2, and current §1.863-8 to reflect the changes to current §1.863-3. Proposed §1.863-1(b) provides special rules for allocating or apportioning gross income from the sale of natural resources, which can be a subset of inventory generally. *See* proposed §1.863-2(b). Current §1.863-1(b)(1) provides a general "export terminal" rule that allocates sales income at the export terminal, sourcing gross receipts equal to the fair market value of the natural resources at the export terminal to the location of the farm, mine, well, deposit, or uncut timber, and gross receipts in excess of that amount either to the place of sale or according to the rules in §1.863-3, depending on the circumstances.

Current §1.863-1(b)(2) provides a special rule for taxpayers performing additional production activities before the relevant product is shipped from the export terminal. The gross receipts are allocated between sources within and without the United States based on the fair market value of the product immediately before the additional production activities. Gross receipts equal to the fair market value of the natural resources immediately before the additional production activities are sourced to the location of the farm, mine, well, deposit or uncut timber, and the gross receipts in excess of that fair market value are sourced based on §1.863-3.

As it is generally no longer appropriate under section 863(b)(2) to allocate or apportion any gross income from sales of inventory, including natural resources, to sales activity, the proposed regulations modify current §1.863-1(b) to remove the export terminal rule so that, where there is no additional production activity with respect to the natural resource, all gross income from sales of natural resources inventory is based on the location of the farm, mine, oil or gas well, other natural deposit, or uncut timber from which the natural resource is derived. In other words, where there are no additional production activities, the location of the farm, mine, oil or gas well, other natural deposit, or uncut timber is considered the place of production generally.[1]

Where there are additional production activities with respect to the natural resource either within or without the jurisdiction from which the natural resource is derived, the gross income is allocated or apportioned first to the jurisdiction where the farm, mine, oil or gas well, other natural deposit, or uncut timber is located, in an amount equal to the fair market value of the product before the additional production activities. Any income in excess of that fair market value is then allocated or apportioned between sources within and without the United States under proposed §1.863-3 principles based on the location of the assets used in the additional production activities. *See* proposed §1.863-1(b)(2).

In the case of sales of natural resources by a nonresident that are attributable to an office or other fixed place of business in the United States of such nonresident, the foregoing rules are subject to the rules of section 865(e)(2) and proposed §1.865-3.

Current §1.863-8(b)(3)(ii) provides a special rule for allocating and apportioning income under section 863(d) derived from sales of property (including inventory) produced by a taxpayer if the property is produced or sold, at least in part, in space or international water. This rule requires the taxpayer to allocate gross income from such sales between production and sales activity under a 50/50 method, whereby half of the taxpayer's gross income will be considered income allocable to production activity and the remaining half of such gross income will be considered income allocable to sales activity. As it is generally no longer appropriate under section 863(b)(2) to allocate or apportion any gross income from sales of inventory produced by a taxpayer (including production in space or international water) to sales activity, the proposed regulations modify current §1.863-8(b)(3)(ii) to remove the 50/50 method and replace it with a rule that allocates gross income solely on the basis of production activity.

E. *Proposed changes to regulations under section 1502 to reflect the changes to §1.863-3*

To reflect section 863(b)(2), as amended by the Act, and the proposed regulations' amendments to §1.863-3, the proposed regulations also amend example 14 of §1.1502-13(c)(7)(ii)(N). This example illustrates the interaction between the intercompany transaction rules under current §1.1502-13 and the sourcing rules in section 863. As revised by the proposed regulations, the example continues to illustrate the same matching principles for intercompany transactions under proposed §1.1502-13 while updating the facts and analysis to reflect the changes in section 863(b)(2) and §1.863-3.

---

[1] Treasury Decision 8687, 1996-2 C.B. 47, added the export terminal rule in current §1.863-1(b) partly in response to the decision in *Phillips Petroleum Co. v. Commissioner*, 97 T.C. 30 (1991), *aff'd without published opinion*, 70 F.3d 1282 (10th Cir. 1995). These proposed regulations follow *Phillips Petroleum* in treating natural resources, once extracted, in the same way as other types of inventory and therefore subject to section 863(b)(2), as amended.

II. *Proposed Rules for Sales of Personal Property by Nonresidents*

A. *Proposed source rules under § 1.865-3 to take into account section 863(b)*

1. Interaction of Section 863(b), as Amended, with Section 865(e)(2)

In light of the changes made by the Act to section 863(b), the Treasury Department and the IRS are concerned that nonresident taxpayers may take an improper position that these changes override the application of section 865(e)(2) as it applies to sales[2] of inventory[3] produced by a nonresident taxpayer and sold through a U.S. sales office, despite the fact that section 865(e)(2) applies "[n]otwithstanding any other provisions in [sections 861 through 865]." To address this improper interpretation of section 865(e)(2), and to provide guidance for the application of section 865(e)(2) in general, the proposed regulations add proposed § 1.865-3.

Section 865, enacted in 1986 as part of the TRA, provides special sourcing rules for sales of personal property. In particular, section 865(e)(2) provides that "[n]otwithstanding any other provisions of this part," if a nonresident has an office or other fixed place of business in the United States, "income from any sale of personal property (including inventory property) attributable to such office or other fixed place of business" is U.S. source. Accordingly, to the extent that inventory income described in section 863(b)(2) is considered to be derived from a sale by a nonresident attributable to an office or other fixed place of business in the United States, section 865(e)(2) must be given effect in determining the source of the income.

For purposes of section 865(e)(2), section 865(e)(3) provides that the "principles of section 864(c)(5)" apply in determining "whether a taxpayer has an office or other fixed place of business" and "whether a sale is attributable" thereto. As described in the Background section of this preamble, section 864(c)(5)(A) provides rules for determining whether a non-U.S. person has an office or other fixed place of business to which section 864(c)(4)(B) may apply as the result of the presence of an agent in the United States, section 864(c)(5)(B) provides a threshold requirement for determining whether any income is attributable to such an office or other fixed place of business, and section 864(c)(5)(C) addresses the extent to which the income, gain, or loss is attributable to an office or other fixed place of business and includes a limitation that for sales of inventory, the income attributable to an office or other fixed place of business within the United States cannot exceed "the income which would be derived from sources within the United States if the sale or exchange were made in the United States."

Section 865(e)(2) may properly be read to treat all income from a sale of personal property by a nonresident as U.S. source so long as the sale is "attributable" to the nonresident's office or other fixed place of business in the United States. By its terms, section 865(e)(3) does not necessarily change this result because it references section 864(c)(5) only for purposes of (1) determining whether a taxpayer has an office or other fixed place of business and (2) whether a sale is attributable to such office or other fixed place of business. Section 865(e)(3) does not by its terms reference section 864(c)(5) for determining the amount of income attributable to such office or other fixed place of business. On this basis, section 865(e) may fairly be read to override section 863(b) where Section 863(b)(2) Sales of a nonresident are attributable to an office or other fixed place of business in the United States, with the result that all of the income from such sales is sourced within the United States.

On the other hand, section 865 concerns the source of income, gain, and loss, and section 865(e)(3) refers to "the principles of section 864(c)(5)," which determines "income, gain or loss" attributable to an office or other fixed place of business in the United States (as noted in subparagraphs 864(c)(5)(B) and 864(c)(5)(C), which operate together). On this basis, the Treasury Department and the IRS have determined that section 864(c)(5) may serve not only as the basis to attribute a sale to an office or other fixed place of business in the United States within the meaning of section 865(e)(2), but also as the basis, in the context of section 865(e)(2) as applicable to Section 863(b)(2) Sales, for allowing a limitation on the amount of income and gain from sales of inventory property attributable to such office or other fixed place of business and, therefore, sourced in the United States. In particular, as relevant here, section 864(c)(5)(C) limits the amount of "income, gain, or loss" from sales that meet the "material factor" threshold of section 864(c)(5)(B) to the amount of income "properly allocable" to the office or other fixed place of business in the United States[4] (which is a lesser amount of income than would be allocated based on such sale under a literal reading of section 865(e)(2) (the entire amount of income)).

The last clause of section 864(c)(5)(C) also imposes a limitation in the case of sales described in section 864(c)(4)(B)(iii) (sales outside the United States made through an office or other fixed place of business in the United States) that "the income which shall be treated as attributable to an office or other fixed place of business within the United States shall not exceed the income which would be derived from sources within the United States if the sale or exchange were made in the United States." Before the enactment of section 865(e)(2), which generally caused such sales to result in U.S. source income and hence fall outside the scope of section 864(c)(4)(B)(iii), this clause was intended to limit the application of section 864(c)(4)(B) to income from sales activities, thus excluding income from production activities. The clause did not determine how much income was attributable to sales versus production activities. Following the Act, which did not amend section 865(e)(2), the Treasury Department and the IRS continue to believe that this clause has no relevance to the determination of how much income is attributable to sales activities or to sales governed by section 865(e)(2).

By incorporating the principles of section 864(c)(5), section 865(e)(3) thus authorizes regulations that would bifurcate the income from a sale of inventory property produced by a nonresident outside the United States and sold through an office or other fixed place of business in the United States so that only the "properly allocable" amount of income from that sale is attributable to an office or other fixed place of business in the United States and treated as U.S. source. In such a case, this amount reflects the nonresident's sales activity, not its production activities, with respect to the personal property sale, which is the portion of the income that Congress intended to treat as U.S. source when it enacted section 865(e)(2) in 1986.[5] H.R. Rep. No. 99-426, at 360-61 (1985).

The 1986 legislative history of section 865(e)(2) shows that Congress intended, by enacting that provision, to repeal (in certain cases) the title passage rule that formerly controlled the source of the "sales income" from the sale of personal property, regardless of where the "sales activities" occurred. *See* H.R. Rep. No. 99-426, at 360 (1985) (providing that "[a]lthough the title passage rule operates clearly, it is manipulable"); *see also* S. Rep. No. 99-313, at 330-33 (1986). The legislative history shows that Congress rather sought to tax "income derived from sales" based on the "location of the economic activity generating the income." *See* S. Rep. No. 99-313, at 330 (1986); H.R. Rep. No. 99-426, at 360 (1985). "If the seller maintains a fixed place of business outside the seller's country of residence which materially participates in a sale, . . . the committee generally believes that the level of economic activity with respect to the sale that is associated with that place of business is high enough such that the location of that place of business should govern the source of the sales income." H.R. Rep. No. 99-426, at 360-61 (1985). These statements show, both individually and in the aggregate, that Congress enacted section 865(e)(2) with a focus upon sourcing income from sales activity based on the economic location of the activity, rather than the location of title passage. The principles of section 864(c)(5) (and in particular subparagraph (C)

---

[2] As defined in section 865(i)(2).

[3] Inventory property, as defined in section 865(i)(1).

[4] Section 864(c)(5)(C) actually states "the income; gain or loss property [sic] allocable thereto." Based on the legislative history behind The Foreign Investors Tax Act, Pub. L. 89-809 (1966), which added section 864(c) to the Code, the use of "property" in the final

bill appears to be a typographical error. The Senate Report that added this provision used the word "properly" not "property." *See* S. Rep. No. 1707 at 1275 (1966).

[5] In the case of inventory property purchased outside the United States (other than in a U.S. territory of the United States) and sold through an office or other fixed place of business in the United States, section 863(b) has no application and hence, regardless of where title passage occurs, all of the income is considered attributable to such office or other fixed place of business and sourced in the United States.

thereof) give effect to this intent through section 865(e)(3) by limiting the application of section 865(e)(2) to sales income properly allocable to the office or other fixed place of business in the United States.

Before the issuance of these proposed regulations, the Treasury Department and the IRS had never issued formal guidance on the sourcing rules of section 865(e)(2) in the case of inventory property produced outside the United States and sold within the United States. Nevertheless, in light of the statutory text of section 865(e)(2) and (3) (as well as section 864(c)(5)(C) by reference) and the legislative history of these provisions, in practice, the IRS has historically interpreted section 865(e)(2) to include a limitation that treated as U.S. source only the sales income allocable to the office or other fixed place of business in the United States reflecting the sales activity from the transaction. See, e.g., 1996 Field Service Advice (FSA) LEXIS 68 (Sept. 24, 1996); 1996 FSA LEXIS 465 (Feb. 29, 1996). This historical interpretation utilized the rules of section 863(b) before amendment by the Act (referenced in current §1.864-6(c)) to determine the amount of income allocable to the office or other fixed place of business in the United States, thereby allowing taxpayers to apply, among other rules, a 50/50 split between U.S. source income (allocable to the office or other fixed place of business in the United States and reflective of sales activity) and foreign source income (reflective of production activity) for sales subject to section 865(e)(2) (the "50/50 method"). The IRS has historically allowed the 50/50 method for establishing the amount allocable to the office or other fixed place of business in the United States (and the sales activity) under section 864(c)(5). Section 865(e)(3) incorporates into section 865(e)(2) the principles of section 864(c)(5), and so the 50/50 method approximated the effect of applying the principles of section 864(c)(5) under section 865(e)(2).

Although the Act amended section 863(b), it made no changes to section 865(e)(2), which does not explicitly reference or depend upon section 863. The 2018 Blue Book notes the absence of any change to section 865(e)(2). See 2018 Blue Book at 397 n.1798. Consistent with historical IRS practice, in its description of prior law, the 2018 Blue Book explains that although sections 863(b) and 865(e)(2) may appear to conflict, in the case of a nonresident manufacturing property without the United States for sale within the United States, the result is that "the income generally is partly U.S.-source and partly foreign-source."[6] Id. at 328 n.1519.

Further, despite the changes to section 863(b) in the Act, structurally, the bifurcated approach is maintained, and section 863(b)(2) continues to refer to inventory that is produced within the United States and sold without the United States, or produced without the United States and sold within the United States. The statutory provision preserves the distinction between sales and production economic activity. If Congress intended to eliminate the sales versus production dichotomy for all purposes, it presumably would have deleted those phrases as the new flush language (that any sale of manufactured inventory property is sourced in whole based on the location of production activities) would have made them surplusage.

In light of Congress's decision to retain the underlying structure of section 863(b)(2) and append the flush language as an overlay, the IRS's longstanding interpretation of the relationship of sections 863(b)(2) and 865(e)(2) under pre-Act law, and the fact that section 865(e)(2) was left unaltered by the Act, the Treasury Department and the IRS have determined that the relationship between section 863(b)(2) and section 865(e)(2) should not be interpreted differently before and after the Act. Thus, section 865(e)(2) should continue to apply to inventory property sales income "properly allocable" to an office or other fixed place of business in the United States (reflecting sales activity rather than production activity) just as before the Act.

As noted, the Treasury Department and the IRS understand that some nonresident taxpayers may be taking the position that, applied after the Act, the last clause of section 864(c)(5)(C) (limiting the income treated as attributable to an office or other fixed place of business in the United States to the amount that would be U.S. source if the sale were made in the United States) causes the income from the sale of inventory produced outside the United States and subject to section 865(e)(2) to be foreign source to the same extent that it would be foreign source under section 863(b), standing alone, which would cause the sourcing of both the sales and production income from the disposition to be based on the location of production activities. Such a reading cannot be correct, because it would inappropriately construe a provision (section 865(e)(2)) intended as a separate restriction on the source rule under section 863(b)(2) (and which literally can be read as entirely overriding that rule) to be determined solely by reference to the terms of such source rule itself (rather than at most in a manner giving effect to both rules). Further, such a construction would cause section 865(e)(2) to have no effect with respect to sales of inventory that are also described in section 863(b)(2), contrary to longstanding statutory construction principles. See, e.g., Watt v. Alaska, 451 U.S. 259, 267 (1981) (statutes should be read to give effect to each if it can be done so while preserving their sense and purpose).

Moreover, such a reading would, in effect, import the change in section 863(b) from the Act into section 865(e)(2), which Congress did not do. As noted, section 865(e)(2) applies "[n]otwithstanding any other provisions." Section 865(e)(3) applies the "principles" of section 864(c)(5), which reflects the sometimes imprecise fit between sections 864(c)(5) and 865(e)(2), such as the fact that section 864(c)(5) refers to "income, gain or loss," rather than a "sale," attributable to an office or other fixed place of business in the United States. The relevant principles referenced in section 865(e)(3) are those that apply for purposes of determining the income, gain, or loss attributable to an office or fixed place of business in the United States. As discussed previously in this section of the Explanation of Provisions, the last clause of section 864(c)(5)(C) is not relevant to that determination and therefore is not relevant to the application of sections 863(b) or 865(e)(2). The principles of section 864(c)(5) are those self-contained in the words of the provision itself ("properly allocable"), and not the limitation provided in the last clause of section 864(c)(5)(C) that serves a different purpose. The amendment to section 863(b)(2) did not change the traditional analysis regarding the attribution of inventory sales to an office or other fixed place of business in the United States.

In light of the foregoing, these proposed regulations clarify the application of the principles of section 864(c)(5) in the context of section 865(e)(2) and provide that sales of inventory produced outside the United States and sold through an office maintained by the nonresident in the United States must be sourced in the United States in part. 2. Overview of the Proposed Regulations under Section 865(e)(2)

Section 865(e)(2) sources the amount of income from sales described in section 865(e)(2)(A) to which the exception in section 865(e)(2)(B) does not apply (Section 865(e)(2) Sales) that is determined to be properly allocable to the nonresident's office or other fixed place of business in the United States under the principles of section 864(c)(5)(C) as referenced by section 865(e)(3). In cases where a sale of personal property is not a Section 865(e)(2) Sale, other sourcing provisions continue to apply.

Proposed §1.865-3(a) sets forth the general rule in section 865(e)(2)(A), and proposed §1.865-3(b) sets forth the exception in section 865(e)(2)(B) and cross-references the rules of §1.864-6(b)(3) to determine if a foreign office materially participated in the sale. Proposed §1.865-3(c) sets forth the rules for determining whether a nonresident has an office or other fixed place of business in the United States by incorporating the principles of §1.864-7, and whether a sale of personal property is attributable to that office or other fixed place of business in the United States by incorporating the principles of §1.864-6(b) and (c), as amended.

Proposed §1.865-3(d) then provides rules for determining the amount of income that is treated as U.S. source; the rules depend on whether the property sold is inventory (including property treated as inventory under section 865(c)(2)) or other personal property of a nonresident sold in a sale attributable to an office or other fixed place of business in the United States of the nonresident. Proposed §1.865-3(d) provides separate source rules for income from sales of inventory subject to section 865(e)(2), dependent on whether the nonresident produced the inventory (either the

---

[6] This statement appears to conflict with another statement in the 2018 Blue Book with respect to prior law to the effect that the application of section 865(e)(2) to a sale of personal property made by a nonresident attributable to its office or fixed place of business in the United States results in all income from the sale being sourced in the United States. Id. at 396-97.

default 50/50 method in paragraph (d)(2)(i) or the elective books and records method in paragraph (d)(2)(ii)), or purchased the inventory, 100 percent U.S. source income in paragraph (d)(3). Proposed § 1.865-3(d)(2)(ii) provides the books and records method that a taxpayer can elect to apply in lieu of the default 50/50 method, including the rules for making that election and the records that must be provided to the Commissioner upon request. To the extent income from either type of inventory sale is treated as U.S. source under proposed § 1.865-3(d)(2) or (3), the income will generally be effectively connected with the conduct of a U.S. trade or business under section 864(c)(3).

Proposed § 1.865-3(e) provides a cross reference to the rules in § § 1.882-4 and 1.882-5, which determine the amount of expenses that are properly allocated and apportioned to gross income effectively connected with the conduct of a trade or business in the United States.

3. The proposed rules for non-inventory property

Section 864(c)(2) applies to determine whether U.S. source gain from the sale of non-inventory property and other capital assets by a non-U.S. person is effectively connected with the conduct of a U.S. trade or business. The proposed regulations implement section 865 and provide source rules for determining whether gain is U.S. source for purposes of section 864(c)(2).

In the case of income derived from the sale of depreciable personal property, section 865(c) distinguishes between gain not in excess of depreciation adjustments and gain in excess of depreciation adjustments, and bifurcates the gain not in excess of depreciation adjustments pro rata to depreciation deductions allowable in computing taxable income from sources within the United States and without the United States. Section 865(c)(1). Gain in excess of depreciation is sourced as if such property were inventory property. Section 865(c)(2) and proposed § 1.865-3(d)(4). See section II.A.4 of this Explanation of Provisions for discussion of the sourcing of inventory property. The legislative history of section 865(c), which was enacted at the same time as section 865(e)(2), indicates that Congress intended to create a special rule for depreciable personal property to source the income derived from the sale of depreciable personal property, to the extent of prior depreciation deductions, under a recapture principle. Under this rule, gain from the sale of depreciable personal property, to the extent of prior depreciation deductions, is sourced within the United States in proportion to the extent of the depreciation deductions that were previously allocated against U.S. source income. On the other hand, the gain, to the extent of prior depreciation deductions, is sourced without the United States in proportion to the extent of the depreciation deductions that were previously allocated against foreign source income. See H.R. Rep. No. 99-426, at 364 (1985); S. Rep. No. 99-313, at 331-32 (1986); Joint Committee on Taxation, General Explanation of the Tax Reform Act of 1986 (Pub. L. 99-514), JCS-10-87, at 63 (1987). Thus, Congress intended to apply the recapture rule to source gain, not in excess of depreciation, from a sale of depreciable personal property (as opposed to sourcing that gain based on the location of the taxpayer's office).

Consistent with this legislative history, the Treasury Department and the IRS have determined that, to the extent a nonresident previously allocated depreciation deductions against foreign source income, in the event of a sale of such property through an office or other fixed place of business in the United States, the associated gain is not "properly allocable" to an office or other fixed place of business in the United States under the principles of section 864(c)(5), and therefore to such extent the sale (and gain) is not attributable to a nonresident's office or other fixed place of business in the United States under section 865(e)(2). Therefore, in the case of income subject to section 865(e)(2) from the sale of depreciable personal property, the amount of gain, not in excess of depreciation deductions, that is allocable to the nonresident's office or fixed place of business within the United States is the amount of gain that would be attributable to United States depreciation deductions under the recapture rule of section 865(c)(1). To the extent the gain exceeds prior U.S. and non-U.S. depreciation deductions, sections 865(c)(2) and 865(e)(2) apply and source that gain as if the property were inventory. Thus, the residual gain in excess of depreciation deductions is sourced under the rules of section 865(e)(2) as described in proposed § 1.865-3(d)(2) (for produced inventory, the 50/50 method and the books and records method) and (d)(3) (for purchased inventory, 100 percent U.S. source income).

4. The proposed rules for inventory

With respect to inventory purchased and sold by a nonresident in a sale attributable to an office or other fixed place of business in the United States and subject to section 865(e)(2), none of the income from the sale is attributable to production activity, and therefore, unless the exception in section 865(e)(2)(B) applies, all of the income from the sale is properly allocable to the office or other fixed place of business in the United States. Thus, the proposed regulations clarify that in these cases section 865(e)(2) causes all of the gross income derived from the disposition to be U.S. source. See § 1.865-3(d)(3).

With respect to inventory produced and sold by a nonresident in a sale attributable to an office or other fixed place of business in the United States and subject to section 865(e)(2), the Treasury Department and the IRS have determined that the disposition continues to give rise to gross income that is partly allocable to the nonresident's office or other fixed place of business in the United States (representative of the sales activity with respect to the transaction) and sourced under section 865(e)(2), with the remainder allocable to production activity and sourced under section 863(b). Therefore, these proposed regulations provide a rule specifically for Section 865(e)(2) Sales involving inventory produced by the nonresident that distinguishes generally between sales and production activities in determining the source of the income from sales of produced inventory and is consistent with the overall structure of subchapter N, part I (sections 861-865).

The Treasury Department and the IRS understand that Congress intended for the source rules to "operate clearly without the necessity for burdensome factual determinations." H.R. Rep. No. 99-426, at 360 (1985). Additionally, it is noteworthy that the "principles" of section 864(c)(5)(C), rather than the exact rules thereof, apply in the section 865(e)(2) context. Finally, the Treasury Department and the IRS are mindful of the fact that section 865(e)(2) was not modified by the Act. Before the Act, by applying the principles of current § 1.863-3(b) to determine the amount of income allocable to the office or other fixed place of business in the United States, the 50/50 method allowed for a 50 percent U.S. source result with respect to sales of produced inventory.

Based on the foregoing considerations, these proposed regulations continue to apply the 50/50 method as the general rule to treat 50 percent of a nonresident's income with respect to produced inventory sold through an office or other fixed place of business in the United States as U.S. source income attributable to the sales activity of the office maintained by the nonresident. The remaining 50 percent of the income is allocated or apportioned between U.S. and foreign sources by applying section 863(b) and the regulations thereunder (as amended by these proposed regulations) based upon the location of production activities. Thus, where inventory is produced entirely outside the United States and sold through a U.S. sales office in a transaction subject to section 865(e)(2), 50 percent of the gross income is U.S. source income allocable to the U.S. sales office or other fixed place of business, and the remaining 50 percent is foreign source income.

In prescribing the 50/50 method for dividing gross income from Section 865(e)(2) Sales between production and sales activity, the Treasury Department and the IRS appreciate that this method may not correspond precisely to the economic genesis of the gross income with respect to the sales and production activity involved. Nevertheless, the Treasury Department and the IRS have determined that this is an appropriate and administrable way to give effect to the principles of section 864(c)(5) in allocating income to the office or other fixed place of business in the United States (and focusing on sales activity) when applying section 865(e)(2). First, the 50/50 method has historically been recognized as a reasonable method for allocating income between production and sales activity. Before the Act, section 863(b) specified that income from Section 863(b)(2) Sales "be treated as derived partly from sources within and partly from sources without the United States," and imposed no standard for allocating or apportioning the income. As discussed, the 50/50 method was a commonly used and well-understood sourcing method that ensured some income was allocated or apportioned to sales activity and some to production activity under section 863(b). For example, in 1984 the Treasury Department stated that "[g]enerally, [income derived from the manufacture and sale of property] is allocated one-half on the basis of the place of manufacture and half on the basis of the place of sale." Treasury Department, Tax Reform for Fairness, Simplicity, and Economic Growth, Nov. 1984 at 364. The House, Senate, and Conference Committees each stated with respect to the TRA that "[under the 50/50 method], half of such income generally is sourced in the country of manufacture, and half of the income is sourced on the basis of the place of sale." H.R. Rep. No. 99-426, at 359 (1985); S. Rep. No. 99-313, at 329 (1986); H.R. Rep. No. 99-841, at 917 (1986) ("Conf. Rep."). Finally, the staff of the Joint Committee on Taxation has referred to the 50/50 method as the "production/marketing split" and stated that under this method "50 percent of such income generally is attributed to the place of production." Joint Committee on Taxation, Factors Affecting International Competitiveness of the United States, JCS-6-91, at 148-149 (1991). Second, the 50/50 method was the most administrable of the permissible means of applying section 865(e)(2) through the application of section 864(c)(5)(C) and current § 1.864-6(c)(2) before the Act. Therefore, these proposed regulations adopt the 50/50 method as the default method for allocating or apportioning gross income attributable to Section 865(e)(2) Sales between sources within and without the United States.

Nevertheless, the Treasury Department and the IRS are aware that some taxpayers may be able to more precisely allocate or apportion their gross income between sales and production activities based on their books of account. Taxpayers, at their election, have historically used such a "books and records" method under current § 1.863-3(b)(3) to allocate or apportion their gross income from sales of inventory between production and sales activities. Therefore, as an elective alternative to the default 50/50 method, taxpayers may continue to use a books and records method as provided in these proposed regulations. However, the proposed regulations include more detailed guidance regarding the requirements that must be met before a taxpayer will be permitted to use this method.

A taxpayer electing the books and records method must prepare and maintain records that are in existence when its return is filed regarding the allocation of gross income between sales and production activities in its books of account and indicate in a statement attached to its tax return that it elects to apply this method. As part of its records that exist when its return is filed, the taxpayer must include an explanation of how such allocation clearly reflects the taxpayer's income from production and sales activities under the principles of section 482. The Treasury Department and the IRS intend the taxpayer's explanation to allow a potential examiner to have a roadmap for understanding the method by which the taxpayer determined the allocation of gross income between the U.S. sales activities and the foreign production activities, respectively. The use of section 482 in the proposed regulations is not intended to imply that the taxpayer's explanation must satisfy the documentation requirements of section 6662(e) and § 1.6662-6(d). The taxpayer must make available its books and records for both its sales activities and its production activities and the related explanation upon request of the Commissioner. If a taxpayer fails to satisfy these requirements in full, the default 50/50 method will apply.

These proposed regulations, however, do not also provide for an elective IFP method as allowed by current § 1.863-3(b)(2). The Treasury Department and the IRS have determined that this method is applicable only in very narrow circumstances when an IFP exists and therefore has rarely been elected by taxpayers in practice. Any taxpayer that wishes to continue using an IFP could generally continue to reach a similar result by electing the books and records method and basing the allocation or apportionment in its books and records on the IFP. Nevertheless, the Treasury Department and the IRS request comments on whether the IFP or any other methods for allocating or apportioning gross income attributable to Section 865(e)(2) Sales between sources within and without the United States should be included in these regulations.

B. *Modification of current § 1.864-6(c)(2) to ensure consistency with § 1.865-3*

Section 864(c)(4)(B)(iii) generally provides that income derived from the sale of inventory (outside the United States) by a non-U.S. person through an office or other fixed place of business in the United States may be effectively connected income, notwithstanding that it would be foreign source income under the title passage rules in § 1.861-7(c). It provides an exception for inventory sold for use or consumption outside the United States, similar to the exception in section 865(e)(2)(B).

Accordingly, sections 864(c)(4)(B)(iii) and 865(e)(2), as a statutory matter, appear to overlap in their treatment of sales of inventory by non-U.S. persons through an office or other fixed place of business in the United States. This was not the case, however, in 1986 because Congress removed section 864(c)(4)(B)(iii) from the Code when section 865(e)(2) was added. The Tax Reform Act of 1986, Pub. L. 99-514 (1986) (section 1211(a) added section 865, while section 1211(b)(2) removed section 864(c)(4)(B)(iii)). Two years later, however, in the Technical and Miscellaneous Revenue Act of 1988 ("TAMRA 1988"), Congress added section 864(c)(4)(B)(iii) back to the Code, with the Senate Report to TAMRA 1988 explaining that the provision was reinstated because it "is necessary to ensure that foreign persons who have a substantial presence in the United States, who may be treated as U.S. residents for source rule purposes but as nonresidents for general purposes, are taxed on income derived from sales of inventory property." S. Rep. No. 100-445, at 239 (1988); see also Joint Committee on Taxation, Description of the Technical Correction Act of 1988, JCS-10-88, at 250 (1988); TAMRA 1988 (section 1012(d)(7) restored section 864(c)(4)(B)(iii)).

The Treasury Department and the IRS have thus determined that where both provisions potentially could apply, as in the case of foreign corporations and most nonresident alien individuals, section 865(e)(2) takes precedence over section 864(c)(4)(B)(iii) because section 865(e)(2) applies "[n]otwithstanding any other provisions of this part." Consistent with the TAMRA 1988 legislative history, the Treasury Department and the IRS have determined that section 864(c)(4)(B)(iii) applies solely to nonresident alien individuals (defined in section 7701(b)) who under section 865(g)(1) have a tax home (as defined in section 911(d)(3)) in the United States (and whose inventory sales thus would not be subject to section 865(e)(2) as those individuals would not be "nonresidents" under section 865(g)(1)(B)). Note that these nonresident alien individuals would be subject to section 864(c)(4)(B)(iii) and section 864(c)(5) only with respect to income from inventory sales that is determined to be foreign source after application of sections 861(a)(6), 862(a)(6), and 863(b) pursuant to section 865(b). Thus, for example, a nonresident alien individual engaged in a U.S. trade or business, with a tax home in the United States, who purchases inventory outside the United States and resells inventory attributable to a U.S. office (with title passing offshore) would have foreign source income under section 862(a)(6) (by reference from section 865(b)), but that foreign source income would then be subject to section 864(c)(4)(B)(iii) and section 864(c)(5) to determine the amount of the individual's foreign source effectively connected income.

Although the scope of section 864(c)(4)(B)(iii) is narrow, the Treasury Department and the IRS have determined that income from sales of inventory by these individuals should be taxable as effectively connected income to the same extent as if inventory sales by these individuals were governed by section 865(e)(2), depending on whether the inventory was either purchased abroad or produced abroad. Section 1.864-6(c)(2) is therefore modified so that it applies exclusively to this distinct class of nonresident aliens, those with a tax home in the United States who are not covered under section 865(e)(2). Further, in order for these individuals to be subject to tax to the same extent as other nonresident taxpayers under section 865(e)(2), the proposed regulations remove any current references in § 1.864-6(c)(2) to section 863(b) and § 1.863-3, thereby clarifying that the rules of section 863(b) and § 1.863-3 do not apply in the context of section 864(c)(4)(B)(iii) to treat inventory sales as exclusively giving rise to foreign source income if the inventory sold was produced exclusively outside of the United States. The proposed regulations do not modify the treatment of sales by these individuals of intangible personal property described in § 1.864-5(b)(1) or of stock or securities described in § 1.864-5(b)(2), which continue to be governed by § 1.864-6(c)(1). Current and proposed § 1.864-6(c)(2) implement the rule in section 864(c)(5)(C) that applies solely to sales of personal property described in section 864(c)(4)(B)(iii) and § 1.864-5(b)(3).

These proposed regulations also may impact the determination of qualified business income for purposes of section 199A. Section 199A(c)(3)(A)(i) provides that "qualified items of income, gain, deduction, and loss" under section 199A(c)(3) are those items that are, among other things, effectively connected with the conduct of a trade or business in the United States within the meaning of section 864(c) (subject to certain modifications). The Treasury Department and the IRS continue to study the application of section 864(c) in the context of section 199A, and request comments on this topic.

C. *U.S. income tax treaties*

The Treasury Department and the IRS are aware that under U.S. income tax treaties, the business profits of foreign treaty residents may be taxable in the United States only if the profits are attributable to a permanent establishment in the United States. With respect to taxpayers entitled to the benefits of an income tax treaty, the amount of profits attributable to a U.S. permanent establishment will not be affected by these regulations.

Proposed Applicability Date

The regulations are proposed to apply to taxable years ending on or after December 23, 2019. As proposed, the regulations will permit taxpayers to apply the rules therein in their entirety for taxable years beginning after December 31, 2017, and before these regulations apply.

In addition, taxpayers may rely on the rules in the proposed regulations for taxable years beginning after December 31, 2017, and before the final regulations are applicable, provided that the taxpayer and persons that are related (within the meaning of section 267 or 707) to the taxpayer apply the proposed regulations in their entirety. For taxable years before these regulations apply, the IRS may, where appropriate, challenge certain positions described in this preamble, including that following the amendment to section 863(b)(2) income earned by nonresidents from sales of personal property produced outside the United States and sold through an office or other fixed place of business in the United States is 100 percent foreign source.

Special Analyses

The Administrator of the Office of Information and Regulatory Affairs (OIRA), Office of Management and Budget, has determined that this proposed rule is not a significant regulatory action, as that term is defined in section 3(f) of Executive Order 12866. Therefore, OIRA has not reviewed this proposed rule pursuant to section 6(a)(3)(A) of Executive Order 12866 and the April 11, 2018, Memorandum of Agreement between the Treasury Department and the Office of Management and Budget ("OMB").

I. *Regulatory Flexibility Act*

Pursuant to the Regulatory Flexibility Act (5 U.S.C. chapter 6), it is hereby certified that these proposed regulations, if adopted, will not have a significant economic impact on a substantial number of small entities. Although data are not readily available to assess the number of small entities potentially affected, any economic impact of these regulations is unlikely to be significant. Specifically, the regulations in §§ 1.863-1 and 1.863-3 (with conforming changes in cross-referencing regulations) implement the statutory change made to section 863(b) by the Act. This change affects sales of inventory property by any taxpayer where the taxpayer produces the inventory (in whole or in part) within the United States and sells that inventory without the United States, or vice versa. The change in sourcing for those entities is attributable to the change in section 863(b) made by the Act. Proposed §§ 1.863-1 and 1.863-3 merely implement the statutory change with limited additional guidance. The Treasury Department and the IRS do not anticipate that any differences between the changes in section 863(b) made by the Act and the changes in proposed §§ 1.863-1 and 1.863-3 made by these proposed regulations will have a significant economic impact on a substantial number of small entities. Notwithstanding this certification, the Treasury Department and the IRS invite comments on the impact of this rule on small entities.

The other regulations in this publication (other than changes to ensure consistency with section 863(b)) are the proposed regulations in §§ 1.864-6 and 1.865-3. These proposed regulations solely affect non-U.S. taxpayers, which are not subject to the Regulatory Flexibility Act.

Pursuant to section 7805(f), this notice of proposed rulemaking has been submitted to the Chief Counsel for Advocacy of the Small Business Administration for comment on its impact on small businesses.

II. *Unfunded Mandates Reform Act*

Section 202 of the Unfunded Mandates Reform Act of 1995 requires that agencies assess anticipated costs and benefits and take certain other actions before issuing a final rule that includes any Federal mandate that may result in expenditures in any one year by a state, local, or tribal government, in the aggregate, or by the private sector, of $100 million in 1995 dollars, updated annually for inflation. In 2019, that threshold is approximately $154 million. These proposed regulations do not include any Federal mandate that may result in expenditures by state, local, or tribal governments, or by the private sector in excess of that threshold.

III. *Executive Order 13132: Federalism*

Executive Order 13132 (entitled "Federalism") prohibits an agency from publishing any rule that has federalism implications if the rule either imposes substantial, direct compliance costs on state and local governments, and is not required by statute, or preempts state law, unless the agency meets the consultation and funding requirements of section 6 of the Executive Order. These proposed regulations do not have federalism implications and do not impose substantial direct compliance costs on state and local governments or preempt state law within the meaning of the Executive Order.

Comments and Requests for Public Hearing

Before the proposed regulations are adopted as final regulations, consideration will be given to any comments that are submitted timely to the IRS as prescribed in this preamble under "Addresses." The Treasury Department and the IRS request comments on all aspects of the proposed rules. See also sections I.C, II.A.4, and II.B of the Explanation of Provisions (requesting specific comments related to the suitability of using ADS, other potential approaches to determine the location or existence of production activity, or other modifications to § 1.863-3 that may be appropriate; related to whether there are other suitable methods for allocating or apportioning income attributable to Section 865(e)(2) Sales between U.S. and foreign sources; and related to the impact of these proposed regulations on the determination of qualified business income for purposes of section 199A, respectively). All comments will be available at www.regulations.gov or upon request. A public hearing will be scheduled if requested in writing by any person that timely submits comments. If a public hearing is scheduled, notice of the date, time, and place for the public hearing will be published in the **Federal Register**.

Drafting Information

The principal authors of the proposed regulations are Brad McCormack and Anisa Afshar of the Office of Associate Chief Counsel (International). However, other personnel from the Treasury Department and the IRS participated in their development.

[¶ 49,827]   Partial withdrawal of notice of proposed rulemaking (REG-125710-18), published in the Federal Register on January 14, 2020.

[Code Sec. 382]

Loss limitation: Section 382 limitation: Built-in gains: Built-in losses.—Amendments of Reg. §§ 1.382-1, 1.382-2 and 1.382-7, providing guidance regarding the items of income and deduction that are included in the calculation of built-in gains and losses under section 382 of the Internal Revenue Code (Code), are proposed. Reg. §§ 1.382-2(b)(4) and 1.382-7(g), proposed on September 10, 2019, are withdrawn.

AGENCY: Internal Revenue Service (IRS), Treasury.

ACTION: Partial withdrawal of notice of proposed rulemaking; notice of proposed rulemaking.

SUMMARY: This document withdraws a portion of a notice of proposed rulemaking published in the Proposed Rules section of the **Federal Register** on September 10, 2019. That notice of proposed rulemaking contained proposed rules to provide guidance regarding the items of income and deduction that are included in the calculation of built-in gains and losses under section 382 of the Internal Revenue Code (Code). If adopted, those proposed rules would apply to any ownership change occurring after the date the Treasury decision adopting those proposed rules as a final regulation is published in the **Federal Register**. This notice of proposed rulemaking would delay the applicability of those proposed rules and provide transition relief for eligible taxpayers. The proposed regulations in this notice of proposed rulemaking would affect corporations that experience an ownership change for purposes of section 382.

DATES: Written or electronic comments must be received by March 14, 2020. Written or electronic requests for a public hearing and outlines of topics to be discussed at the public hearing must be received by March 14, 2020.

ADDRESSES: Submit electronic submissions via the Federal eRulemaking Portal at www.regulations.gov (indicate IRS and REG-125710-18) by following the online instructions for submitting comments. Once submitted to the Federal eRulemaking Portal, comments cannot be edited or withdrawn. The Department of the Treasury (Treasury Department) and the IRS will publish for public availability any comment received to its public docket, whether submitted electronically or in hard copy. Send hard copy submissions to: Internal Revenue Service, CC:PA:LPD:PR (REG-125710-18), Room 5203, Post Office Box 7604, Ben Franklin Station, Washington, DC 20044. FOR FURTHER INFORMATION CONTACT: Concerning the proposed regulations, Jonathan R. Neuville at (202) 317-5363; concerning submissions of comments or requests for a public hearing, Regina L. Johnson at (202) 317-6901 (not toll-free numbers).

SUPPLEMENTARY INFORMATION:

Background

On September 10, 2019, the Treasury Department and the IRS published in the **Federal Register** (84 FR 47455) a notice of proposed rulemaking (REG-125710-18) proposing revisions to the rules in §§ 1.382-2 and 1.382-7 (September 2019 proposed regulations). These rules would affect the determination of net built-in gains and losses and recognized built-in gains and losses under section 382(h) that, in turn, affect the limitation under section 382 on net operating losses and disallowed business interest expense under section 163(j).

Proposed §§ 1.382-2(b)(4) and 1.382-7(g)(1), as set forth in the September 2019 proposed regulations, provided that the September 2019 proposed regulations would apply to ownership changes that occur after the date the Treasury decision adopting the September 2019 proposed regulations as final regulations is published in the **Federal Register**. As noted in part II of the Background in the September 2019 proposed regulations, section V of Notice 2003-65 (2003-2 C.B. 747) provides that taxpayers may rely on either of two safe harbor approaches for applying section 382(h) to an ownership change "prior to the effective date of temporary or final regulations under section 382(h)."

Taxpayers and practitioners have expressed concern that the applicability date set forth in the September 2019 proposed regulations would impose a significant burden on taxpayers evaluating and negotiating business transactions, due to their uncertainty regarding when those transactions will close and when the September 2019 proposed regulations will be finalized. As a result, taxpayers and practitioners have requested transition relief with regard to ownership changes caused by pending transactions. In connection with this request, taxpayers and practitioners also have expressed concern that transition relief limited to transactions for which a binding agreement is in effect on or before the applicability date of final regulations would be inadequate, because pending transactions regularly are modified or delayed prior to closing.

As explained more fully in the Explanation of Provisions, this notice of proposed rulemaking modifies the applicability dates for the September 2019 proposed regulations by withdrawing the text of proposed §§ 1.382-2(b)(4) and 1.382-7(g), as set forth in the September 2019 proposed regulations, and proposing revised applicability dates.

Explanation of Provisions

I. Delay of Applicability Date and Applicability of Pre-existing Guidance

To address the concerns raised by taxpayers and practitioners, the Treasury Department and the IRS are withdrawing the text of proposed §§ 1.382-2(b)(4) and 1.382-7(g) contained in the September 2019 proposed regulations. In its place, the Treasury Department and the IRS are proposing the revised applicability date text set forth in proposed §§ 1.382-2(b)(4) and 1.382-7(g) as contained in this notice of proposed rulemaking.

The Treasury Department and the IRS do not intend there to be any gap between the date on which taxpayers can no longer rely on Notice 2003-65 and the date on which the final regulations are applicable. Other than in the case of the two exceptions described in parts II and III of this Explanation of Provisions, the applicability date of the final regulations will be 30 days after the date the Treasury decision containing such regulations is published in the **Federal Register** (delayed applicability date). As provided in this proposed regulation, Notice 2003-65 will remain applicable to ownership changes to which the final regulations do not apply.

II. Limiting Duplicative Application of Section 382

The first exception to the delayed applicability date relates to the rule in proposed § 1.382-7(d)(5), which provides that certain carryforwards of business interest expense disallowed under section 163(j) would not be treated as recognized built-in losses under section 382(h)(6)(B) if such amounts were allowable as deductions during the five-year recognition period set forth in section 382(h)(7)(A). This rule eliminates the possible duplicative application of section 382 to certain disallowed business interest expense carryforwards. Due to the noncontroversial nature of this rule, the Treasury Department and the IRS have determined that proposed § 1.382-7(d)(5) should be finalized before the remainder of the rules in the September 2019 proposed regulations, and that taxpayers should be allowed to retroactively apply this rule. To that end, the Treasury Department and IRS expect that proposed § 1.382-7(d)(5) will be finalized as part of the Treasury decision that finalizes the proposed section 163(j) regulations (see 83 FR 67490) and taxpayers will be permitted to apply the rule to prior periods. The Treasury Department and the IRS continue to actively study the remainder of the rules in the September 2019 proposed regulations.

III. Transition Relief Provisions

Under the transition relief provisions proposed in this notice of proposed rulemaking, the final regulations would not apply to certain ownership changes that occur after the delayed applicability date. As discussed in part I of this Explanation of Provisions, the delayed applicability date will be 30 days after the date these regulations are published in the **Federal Register**. In order for an ownership change after the delayed applicability date to qualify for transition relief, the ownership change must occur immediately after an owner shift or equity structure shift that occurs:

(1) Pursuant to a binding agreement in effect on or before the delayed applicability date and at all times thereafter;

(2) Pursuant to a specific transaction described in a public announcement made on or before the delayed applicability date;

(3) Pursuant to a specific transaction described in a filing with the Securities and Exchange Commission submitted on or before the delayed applicability date;

(4) By order of a court (or pursuant to a plan confirmed, or a sale approved, by order of a court) in a title 11 or similar case (as defined in section 382(l)(5)(F)), provided that the taxpayer was a debtor in a case before such court on or before the delayed applicability date; or

(5) Pursuant to a transaction described in a private letter ruling request submitted to the IRS on or before the delayed applicability date.

The relevant owner shift or equity structure shift must be a specific, identifiable transaction. For example, a stock buyback pursuant to an announced, on-going program would not qualify.

Taxpayers may continue to rely on Notice 2003-65 with respect to any ownership change qualifying for transition relief, even though the Notice will be obsoleted on the delayed applicability date. However, a taxpayer may choose to apply the final regulations to such an ownership change.

Special Analyses

These proposed regulations are not subject to review under section 6(b) of Executive Order 12866 pursuant to the Memorandum of Agreement (April 11, 2018) between the Treasury Department and the Office of Management and Budget regarding review of tax regulations.

Pursuant to the Regulatory Flexibility Act (RFA), 5 U.S.C. chapter 6, the Treasury Department and the IRS hereby certify that these proposed regulations will not have a significant economic impact on a substantial number of small entities. This proposed rule is limited to revising the proposed applicability date of proposed regulations under section 382(h) of the Internal Revenue Code that were published in the **Federal Register** (84 FR 47455) on September 10, 2019. Based on the narrow scope of corporate transactions covered by the proposed regulations' delayed applicability rules, the Treasury Department and the IRS have determined that these proposed regulations are unlikely to affect a substantial number of small entities and are unlikely to have a significant economic impact on any small entities affected.

The Treasury Department and the IRS invite comments on any impact that these regulations would have on small entities.

Pursuant to section 7805(f), this notice of proposed rulemaking has been submitted to the Chief Counsel for Advocacy of the Small Business Administration for comment on its impact on small business.

Comments and Requests for Public Hearing

The Treasury Department and the IRS appreciate the comments that taxpayers and practitioners already have provided regarding the September 2019 proposed regulations and encourage taxpayers and practitioners to provide comments on the proposed regulations contained in this notice of proposed rulemaking. In particular, the Treasury Department and the IRS request comments on whether taxpayers should be permitted to apply the final regulations to ownership changes occurring before the applicability date and what restrictions, if any, should be placed on such retroactive application.

Before these proposed regulations are adopted as final regulations, consideration will be given to any comments that are submitted timely to the Treasury Department and the IRS as prescribed in this preamble under the **"ADDRESSES"** heading. All comments will be available at http:// www.regulations.gov or upon request. A public hearing will be scheduled if requested in writing by any person that timely submits written comments. If a public hearing is scheduled, notice of the date, time, and place of the public hearing will be published in the **Federal Register**.

Statement of Availability of IRS Documents

Notice 2003-65 is published in the Internal Revenue Bulletin (or Cumulative Bulletin) and is available from the Superintendent of Documents, U.S. Government Publishing Office, Washington, DC 20402, or by visiting the IRS website at http://www.irs.gov.

Drafting Information

The principal authors of this notice of proposed rulemaking are Jonathan R. Neuville of the Office of Associate Chief Counsel (Corporate) and Kevin M. Jacobs, formerly of the Office of Associate Chief Counsel (Corporate). However, other personnel from the Treasury Department and the IRS participated in their development.

[¶ 49,828] Proposed Amendments of Regulations (REG-132741-17), published in the Federal Register on February 13, 2020.

Code Secs. 3401 and Code Sec. 3402]

Tax Cuts and Jobs Act (TCJA): Form W-4: Tax withholding: Wages.—Amendments of Reg. §§31.3401(e)-1, 31.3402(a)-1, 31.3402(b)-1, 31.3402(c)-1, 31.3402(f)(1)-1, 31.3402(f)(2)-1, 31.3402(f)(3)-1, 31.3402(f)(4)-1, 31.3402(f)(4)-2, 31.3402(f)(5)-1, 31.3402(f)(6)-1, 31.3402(g)-1, 31.3402(h)(4)-1, 31.3402(i)-1, 31.3402(i)-2, 31.3402(l)-1, 31.3402(m)-1 and 31.3402(n)-1, implementing recent changes in the Internal Revenue Code made by the Tax Cuts and Jobs Act (TCJA), and reflecting the redesigned 2020 Form W-4 and related IRS publications, are proposed.

AGENCY: Internal Revenue Service (IRS), Treasury.

ACTION: Notice of proposed rulemaking.

SUMMARY: This document sets forth proposed regulations that provide guidance for employers concerning the amount of Federal income tax to withhold from employee's wages, implementing recent changes in the Internal Revenue Code made by the Tax Cuts and Jobs Act (TCJA), and reflecting the redesigned 2020 Form W-4 and related IRS publications. These proposed regulations affect employers that pay wages subject to Federal income tax withholding and employees who receive wages subject to Federal income tax withholding.

DATES: Written (including electronic) comments and requests for a public hearing must be received by April 13, 2020.

ADDRESSES: Submit electronic submissions via the Federal eRulemaking Portal at *www.regulations.gov* (indicate IRS and REG-132741-17) by following the online instructions for submitting comments. Once submitted to the Federal eRulemaking Portal, comments cannot be edited or withdrawn. The Department of the Treasury (Treasury Department) and the Internal Revenue Service (IRS) will publish for public availability any comment received to their public docket, whether submitted electronically or in hard copy. Send hard copy submissions to: CC:PA:LPD:PR (REG-132741-17), room 5203, Internal Revenue Service, PO Box 7604, Ben Franklin Station, Washington, DC 20044.

FOR FURTHER INFORMATION CONTACT: Concerning the proposed regulations, Mikhail Zhidkov of the Office of Associate Chief Counsel (Employee Benefits, Exempt Organizations, and Employment Taxes), (202) 317-4774; concerning submission of comments or requests for a hearing, please contact Regina Johnson at (202) 317-6901 (not toll-free numbers).

SUPPLEMENTARY INFORMATION:

Background

This document sets forth proposed amendments to the Employment Tax Regulations (26 CFR part 31) under sections 3401 and 3402 of the Internal Revenue Code (Code). Generally, these proposed regulations update the regulations under sections 3401 and 3402 to conform to the changes to sections 3401 and 3402 made by the Tax Cuts and Jobs Act, Pub. L. No. 115-97, 131 Stat. 2054 (2017) (TCJA) and other legislation enacted since the regulations were last revised. In addition, these proposed regulations are designed to accommodate the redesigned 2020 Form W-4, "Employee's Withholding Certificate," and related wage withholding tables and computational procedures established by the IRS and reflected in Publication 15-T, "Federal Income Tax Withholding Methods."

General statutory and regulatory framework

Section 3402(a)(1) provides that, except as otherwise provided in section 3402, every employer making a payment of wages shall deduct and withhold from such wages a tax determined in accordance with tables or computational procedures prescribed by the Secretary of the Treasury. Section 3402(a)(1) further provides that any tables or procedures prescribed under section 3402(a)(1) shall be in such form, and provide for such amounts to be deducted and withheld, as the Secretary determines to be most appropriate to carry out the purposes of chapter 1 (imposition of individual income tax). Section 3402 sets forth certain methods of withholding but also gives the Secretary broad regulatory authority in providing for tables or computational procedures for income tax withholding.

How an employer applies the withholding tables or computational procedures generally depends on the withholding allowance certificate the employee furnishes the employer. Under section 3402(f)(5), withholding allowance certificates must be in such form and include such information as the Secretary may by regulations prescribe. Section 31.3402(f)(5)-1 of the current Employment Tax Regulations (hereinafter, "current regulations") provides that the withholding allowance certificate is the Form W-4. An employee who receives wages subject to withholding under section 3402 is required to furnish his or her employer a Form W-4 on commencement of employment or, generally, within 10 days after the employee experiences a "change of status" that reduces the "withholding allowance" to which the employee is entitled. *See* section 3402(f)(2).

An employee completes Form W-4 based on the employee's personal tax situation by applying the factors listed in section 3402(f)(1), which, for 2019 and earlier years, were incorporated into the worksheets to the Form W-4. One of those factors reflects personal exemptions. See Section 3402(f)(1)(A).[1] Also, under section 3402(f)(1)(D), an employee may take into account additional amounts under section 3402(m), which allows employees to take into account items such as itemized deductions in the manner provided under regulations prescribed by the Secretary.

Generally, for 2019 and earlier, an employee could make three entries on Form W-4 that could affect the amount of income tax withheld from the employee's wages: the employee's marital status, a number of withholding allowances based on the factors in section 3402(f)(1), and any additional amount, not otherwise required, that the employee requested to be withheld from the employee's wages. *See* sections 3402(l) (marital status), 3402(f)(1) (withholding allowance), and 3402(i) (increases in amount of withholding not otherwise required under section 3402).[2]

Once an employee completes a valid Form W-4, the employee must furnish the Form W-4 to the employer. The employer puts the Form W-4 into effect in accordance with the timing rules in section 3402(f)(3). Under § 31.3401(e)-1(b) of the current regulations, the employer is not required to ascertain whether the number of allowances an employee claims is greater than the number of withholding allowances to which the employee is entitled.[3] Once in effect, the employer generally applies the entries on an employee's Form W-4 to compute the amount of income tax to withhold from the employee's regular wages under either the percentage method of withholding or the wage bracket method of withholding. *See* section 3402(b) and (c).[4]

TCJA changes

Prior to TCJA, one withholding exemption was equal to the amount of one personal exemption provided in section 151(b), prorated to the payroll period. *See* section 3402(a)(2) (2017). TCJA enacted section 151(d)(5), which reduced the personal exemption amount to zero for the years 2018-2025. *See* TCJA section 11041(a). TCJA also increased the standard deduction under section 63, increased the child tax credit under section 24, and created a new credit under section 24 for other dependents. *See* TCJA sections 11021 and 11022.

TCJA permanently modified the wage withholding rules in section 3402(a)(2) and, replaced "withholding exemptions" with a "withholding allowance, prorated to the payroll period." *See* TCJA section 11041(c)(1). TCJA also repealed section 3401(e), which, prior to TCJA, provided, for purposes of chapter 24 (relating to collection of income tax at source on wages), that the "number of withholding exemptions claimed" meant the number of withholding exemptions claimed in a withholding exemption certificate in effect under section 3402(f) or in effect under the corresponding section of prior law, except that if no such certificate was in effect, the number of withholding exemptions claimed was considered zero. *See* TCJA section 11041(c)(2)(A).

TCJA modified section 3402(f), and defined a "withholding allowance," which is determined based on the factors listed in section 3402(f)(1). *See* TCJA section 11041(c)(2)(B). TCJA further changed the list of factors on which the withholding allowance is based and added that the withholding allowance is determined based on rules determined by the Secretary. *See* TCJA section 11041(c)(2)(B). This change to section 3402(f)(1) revised section 3402(f)(1)(C), entitling an employee to take into account the number of individuals for which the employee expects to take an income tax credit under section 24 instead of the number of individuals with respect to whom the employee reasonably expects to claim a deduction under section 151. Section 3402(f)(1)(D) also changed an employee's entitlement to take into account the standard deduction from an amount generally equal to one withholding exemption to the standard deduction allowable to such employee (one-half of the standard deduction in the case of an employee who is married and whose spouse is an employee receiving wages subject to withholding). Finally, TCJA added section 3402(f)(1)(F), which provides that the employee's withholding allowance also takes into account "whether the employee has withholding allowance certificates in effect with respect to more than one employer." *See* TCJA section 11041(c)(2)(B).

TCJA also made conforming changes to the "change of status" rules in section 3402(f)(2), changing "withholding exemptions" to "withholding allowance," struck out "exemption," and inserted "allowance" in various subsections of section 3402. This resulted in a conforming change to the statutory name of the withholding exemption certificate in section 3402(f)(5) to the withholding allowance certificate. *See* TCJA sections 11041(c)(2)(B) and (C).

TCJA amended section 3402(m) by changing the reference from "withholding allowances" to "withholding allowance." *See* TCJA sections 11041(c)(2)(D) and (E). TCJA added the section 199A deduction to the list of deductions in section 3402(m)(1) that an employee may take into account in determining the additional withholding allowance that the employee is entitled to claim on Form W-4, and struck the reference to section 62(a)(10) in section 3402(m)(1) with respect to certain payments made under divorce or separation instruments previously described in section 62(a)(10). *See* TCJA sections 11011(b)(4) and 11051(b)(2)(B). Under section 11051(c) of TCJA, there are special effective date provisions with respect to this change, which are discussed in more detail in section 7(a) of the Explanation of Provisions.

TCJA changed the rules under section 3405(a)(4) for withholding from periodic payments under section 3405(a) when no withholding allowance certificate has been furnished, changing the requirement that the default rate of withholding be determined "by treating the payee as a married individual claiming 3 withholding exemptions" to a requirement that the default rate of withholding be determined "under rules prescribed by the

---

[1] Section 151(d)(5) suspends the deduction for personal exemptions for calendar years 2018-2025.

[2] As discussed later in this preamble, an employee may also claim exemption from withholding under section 3402(n) on a valid Form W-4. Other special rules could also apply to affect the amount of tax withheld, such as for nonresident aliens or lock-in letters, discussed later in this preamble.

[3] Under § 31.3402(f)(2)-1(e) of the current regulations, an employer must disregard an "invalid" Form W-4 for purposes of computing withholding. An invalid Form W-4 is

one that includes any alteration or unauthorized addition or that the employee clearly indicates to be false.

[4] Special rules apply to "supplemental wages" under § 31.3402(g)-1 of the current regulations. In the case of supplemental wages in excess of $1,000,000, employers must disregard the entries on the employee's Form W-4 and apply a mandatory flat rate of withholding. In the case of supplemental wages of less than $1,000,000, employers may either disregard the entries on the employee's Form W-4 and withhold using the optional flat rate or may use an aggregate procedure, taking into consideration the entries on the Form W-4 furnished by the employee.

Secretary." TCJA also made conforming changes to the rules under section 3405(a) for withholding from periodic payments of pensions, annuities, and certain other deferred income, changing "exemption" to "allowance" in section 3405(a)(3) and (4).

The legislative history of TCJA states that "the Secretary of the Treasury is to develop rules to determine the amount of tax required to be withheld by employers from a taxpayer's wages." H.R. Rep. No. 115-466, at 203 (2017).

Guidance addressing TCJA and comments received

TCJA allowed the Secretary of the Treasury to administer section 3402 before January 1, 2019 without regard to the changes described above. *See* TCJA section 11041(f)(2). Nevertheless, on January 11, 2018, the Treasury Department and the IRS released Notice 1036, "Early Release Copies of the 2018 Percentage Method Tables for Income Tax Withholding," which implemented TCJA's tax rate changes, standard deduction, and suspension of the deduction under section 151. The Treasury Department and the IRS designed the 2018 withholding tables to work with the Forms W-4 that employees had already furnished their employers. On February 28, 2018, the Treasury Department and the IRS updated Form W-4, "Employee's Withholding Allowance Certificate," incorporating TCJA's changes in the 2018 Form W-4's worksheets and updated the online withholding calculator to reflect TCJA changes. Notice 2018-14, 2018-7 I.R.B. 353, published February 12, 2018, allowed continued use of the 2017 Form W-4 temporarily in 2018 and included a relief provision stating that employees who experienced changes in their tax circumstances solely attributable to TCJA were not required to furnish a new Form W-4 to their employers in 2018. Notice 2018-14 also provided that, for 2018, the rules for withholding from periodic payments under section 3405(a) when no withholding allowance certificate has been furnished would parallel the rules for prior years and would be based on treating the payee as a married individual claiming three withholding allowances.

Notice 2018-92, 2018-51 I.R.B. 1038, published December 17, 2018, addressed some of TCJA's changes to section 3402 and provided interim rules for the 2019 calendar year. Section 3 of Notice 2018-92 addressed TCJA's use of "withholding allowance" (singular) and provided that withholding allowances (plural) were to be used for the computational procedures in 2019, consistent with Form W-4 for 2019 (discussed in the next section of this preamble) and prior years. Under section 3 of Notice 2018-92, any reference to a withholding exemption in the regulations and other guidance under section 3402 was to be applied as if it were a reference to a withholding allowance. Section 11 of Notice 2018-92 solicited comments generally, but no comments on this issue were received.

Section 4 of Notice 2018-92 extended the relief provided in Notice 2018-14 for changes in tax circumstances solely attributable to TCJA. Section 5 addressed the repeal of section 3401(e), noted earlier in this preamble, and provided that an employee who fails to furnish a valid Form W-4 will be treated as single but entitled to the number of withholding allowances provided in accordance with computational procedures set forth by the IRS in Publication 15 (Circular E), "Employer's Tax Guide." For 2019, the computational procedures in Publication 15 provided that employees who fail to furnish a Form W-4 were treated as single with zero withholding allowances. One comment on this issue was received and is discussed in Section 8(a) of the Explanation of Provisions.

Section 6 of Notice 2018-92 allowed employees to include the employee's estimated deduction under section 199A in determining the additional withholding allowance under section 3402(m) that the employee is entitled to claim on Form W-4. Section 6 of Notice 2018-92 requested comments with respect to any additional items employees should be able to claim under section 3402(m), but no comments on this issue were received.

Section 7 of Notice 2018-92 allowed taxpayers to use the online withholding calculator (now called the Tax Withholding Estimator) or Publication 505, "Tax Withholding and Estimated Tax," in lieu of the Form W-4 worksheets. One comment was received on the online withholding calculator and is discussed in section 7(b) of the Explanation of Provisions.

Section 8 of Notice 2018-92 requested comments on alternative withholding methods under section 3402(h) and announced that the IRS and the Treasury Department intend to eliminate the combined income tax withholding and employee Federal Insurance Contributions Act (FICA) tax withholding tables under § 31.3402(h)(4)-1(b). No comments on this issue were received. Section 9 of Notice 2018-92 reflected a modification of the notification requirements for the withholding compliance program. Specifically, employers in receipt of a notice prescribing a maximum number of withholding allowances an employee may claim (a lock-in letter) were instructed not to send a response to the IRS when the employer no longer employs the employee (within the meaning of § 31.3402(f)(2)-1(g)(2)(iii)). One commenter thanked the Treasury Department and the IRS for the change to the notice requirements in the lock-in letter program.

Section 10 of Notice 2018-92 provided that, for 2019, the rules for withholding from periodic payments under section 3405(a) when no withholding certificate has been furnished would parallel the rules for prior years and would be based on treating the payee as a married individual claiming three withholding allowances.

2019 Form W-4 and 2019 Publication 15

In June 2018, the Treasury Department and the IRS released for public comment a draft 2019 Form W-4 and draft instructions. Unlike the relatively minor changes made to Form W-4 in recent years prior to that, the 2019 draft Form W-4 and instructions incorporated significant changes intended to improve the accuracy of income tax withholding and make the withholding system more transparent for employees. Many comments were received on the draft form and instructions. In response to comments received from stakeholders, the Treasury Department and the IRS announced on September 20, 2018, that implementation of the redesigned form would be postponed until 2020, and that the Treasury Department and the IRS would continue working closely with stakeholders as additional changes were made to the form for 2020. In addition, Notice 2018-92 announced that the 2019 Form W-4 would include minimal changes to the 2018 Form W-4 and would continue to apply section 3402 by using the existing withholding system under which employees claimed a number of withholding allowances on a valid Form W-4.

Although the 2019 Form W-4 continued the computation of withholding principally based on the number of withholding allowances the employee claimed on Form W-4, the amount of each withholding allowance for 2019, like the years before it, was set to what would have been the value of a personal or dependency exemption in section 151(b) prior to enactment of TCJA. *See* Rev. Proc. 2018-57, 2018-49 I.R.B. 827, sections 2.03 and 3.25. For calendar years 2018 through 2025, however, the exemption amount is zero.[5] *See* section 151(d)(5)(A). Moreover, the high value of each withholding allowance ($4,050 for 2017, $4,150 for 2018, and $4,200 for 2019) led to rounding errors that made it difficult for some employees to have their withholding equal their tax liability for the year. Accuracy was even more difficult to achieve for employees claiming tax credits, as these amounts first had to be converted into tax deductions and then expressed as a number of withholding allowances. In addition to limiting accuracy, the use of withholding allowances to compute withholding is not intuitive, given that wages, deductions, credits, and taxes are all expressed as dollar amounts, rather than a number of withholding allowances. Although the 2019 Form W-4 and prior Forms W-4 generally allow employees to achieve a high degree of accuracy if the employee requests an additional dollar amount to be withheld and/or uses the withholding calculator (now called the Tax Withholding Estimator) or Publication 505 in completing the Form W-4, most employees did not use these options.

---

[5] The 2019 Publication 15 (Circular E), "Employer's Tax Guide," started its income tax withholding tables for single persons at the basic standard deduction ($12,200 for 2019) for unmarried individuals minus the value of two allowances ($8,400), which is $3,800 (for an annual payroll period, and otherwise to be prorated to the payroll period). Similarly, the 2019 Publication 15 started its income tax tables for married persons at the basic standard deduction ($24,400) for married individuals filing joint returns minus the value of three allowances ($12,600), which is $11,800. Thus, the tables in Publication 15 applied section 151(d)(5)(A). The income tax withholding tables in the 2018 Publication 15 were similar.

In addition, employees with multiple withholding allowance certificates in effect, including married couples filing jointly where both spouses receive wages subject to withholding, had difficulty achieving accuracy using the Two-Earner/Multiple Jobs Worksheet. This worksheet required the employee to estimate wages at the lowest-paying job and the highest-paying job and, if applicable, reduce the withholding allowances with respect to the highest-paying job. In some cases, an employee would need to determine an additional amount to withhold from each paycheck for the highest-paying job by applying two tables in the Two-Earners/Multiple Jobs Worksheet. Despite the complexity of this approach, it did not allow employees to have their withholding equal their tax liability if there were two or more simultaneous jobs in the household, and accuracy was further reduced if new Forms W-4 were not furnished to all of the employers after the amount of wages from any employer changed. Moreover, it is unclear how many employees actually used the Two-Earners/Multiple Jobs Worksheet to compute their withholding allowances, even when it would have been advantageous for employees to do so to achieve more accurate withholding.

2020 Form W-4, Employee's Withholding Certificate

To address the limitations of the prior Form W-4, on May 31, 2019, a draft of a revised Form W-4 was released for public comment. The revised Form W-4 is intended to reduce the combined complexity of the form, instructions, and worksheets and to increase the transparency and accuracy of the withholding system. The 2020 Form W-4 uses the same underlying information as the 2019 Form W-4, but replaces complex worksheets with more straightforward questions. After extensive stakeholder feedback, the draft 2020 Form W-4 was further revised and re-released on August 8, 2019. This version was released to allow automated payroll providers sufficient time to update payroll systems, and it was announced no further substantive changes to the 2020 Form W-4 were expected. The form has been renamed from the Employee's Withholding Allowance Certificate to the Employee's Withholding Certificate. The final 2020 Form W-4 was released on December 4, 2019, and then was rereleased on December 31, 2019, to reflect a change in the medical expense deduction threshold under section 213 for 2020 made by the Further Consolidated Appropriations Act, 2020, Pub. L. 116-94, 133 Stat. 2534, 3228 (2019).

The 2020 Form W-4 does not use withholding allowances. An employee checks a filing status (single, married filing separately, head of household, married filing jointly, or qualifying widow(er)) on the Form W-4 and, as a result, will generally have the basic standard deduction corresponding to the employee's anticipated filing status on his or her income tax return taken into account in determining the amount of tax withheld from the employee's pay, in accordance with section 3402(f)(1)(E).[6] In addition, the 2020 Form W-4 streamlines the multiple jobs procedures and gives employees three options to account for a working spouse or multiple jobs held concurrently in accordance with sections 3402(f)(1)(B), (E), and (F): (1) employees may use the Tax Withholding Estimator to achieve accurate withholding; (2) employees may complete the Multiple Jobs Worksheet and enter an additional amount to withhold from the employee's pay for each pay period; or (3) employees may check the box in Step 2(c) on the 2020 Form W-4 to request withholding using higher withholding rate tables. (For married taxpayers filing jointly with two jobs held concurrently, the effect of checking the box in Step 2(c) is similar to selecting "Married, but withhold at higher Single rate" on a Form W-4 from 2019 or earlier.) The 2020 Form W-4 also allows an employee to enter dollar amounts for tax credits, other income, and deductions the employee expects to claim on his or her income tax return to reflect the permitted allowance under sections 3402(f)(1)(C) and (f)(1)(D) and the increase in the amount of withholding under section 3402(i). The Tax Withholding Estimator is expected to provide instructions on how to complete Form W-4 to take into account an employee's personal tax circumstances in a manner that helps protect the employee's privacy by limiting the entries the employee is required to make on the 2020 Form W-4. The IRS will continue to update the Tax Withholding Estimator based on user feedback and to enhance accuracy, privacy, and the employee experience.

2020 Publication 15-T, Federal Income Tax Withholding Methods

On June 7, 2019, the IRS released for public comment a draft of Publication 15-T, "Federal Income Tax Withholding Methods," which provided percentage method tables, wage bracket withholding tables, and other computational procedures for employers to use to compute withholding for employees for the 2020 calendar year, including employees who furnish a 2020 Form W-4 to be effective for 2020. After stakeholder feedback, Publication 15-T was revised and rereleased on August 13, 2019 and was rereleased on November 4, 2019. The income tax withholding tables reflecting 2020 cost-of-living adjustments were made available on November 28, 2019, for use with automated payroll systems. Publication 15-T was finalized and released on December 24, 2019.

Percentage method tables, wage bracket withholding tables, discussion on alternative withholding methods, and Tables for Withholding on Distributions of Indian Gaming Profits to Tribal Members that were formerly published in Publication 15 (Circular E), "Employer's Tax Guide," Publication 15-A, "Employer's Supplemental Tax Guide," and Publication 51, "Agricultural Employer's Tax Guide," are now published in Publication 15-T, "Federal Income Tax Withholding Methods." However, in 2020, the IRS discontinued publishing Formula Tables for Percentage Method Withholding (for Automated Payroll Systems), Wage Bracket Percentage Method Tables (for Automated Payroll Systems), and Combined Federal Income Tax, Employee Social Security Tax, and Employee Medicare Tax Withholding Tables.

In addition, the IRS has discontinued publishing Notice 1036, "Early Release Copies of the Percentage Method Tables for Income Tax Withholding," effective beginning with calendar year 2020, and instead will post information previously included in Notice 1036 in early release drafts of Publication 15 (www.irs.gov/Pub15) and Publication 15-T (www.irs.gov/Pub15T) for use by the public and payroll community. Notice 1036 was developed in 1996 before advanced release drafts of forms and publications were posted on www.irs.gov/draftforms and various product webpages. The information previously included in Notice 1036 generally will be available on www.irs.gov more quickly than Notice 1036 was made available in prior years.

2020 Form W-4P, Withholding Certificate for Pension or Annuity Payments

Section 3405(a) generally requires the payor of periodic payments from pensions, annuities, or certain other deferred income to withhold from such payments as if such payments were wages paid by an employer to an employee. Under section 3405(a)(2), an individual may elect not to have withholding apply to periodic payments from pensions, annuities, or certain other deferred income; however, such election is not available with respect to eligible rollover distributions or certain payments to be made outside of the United States or its possessions. See sections 3405(c)(1) (eligible rollover distributions) and 3405(e)(13) (certain payments to be made outside the United States or its possessions). But see proposed §31.3405(e)-1 (certain payments not considered made outside the United States).

An individual's withholding election (or election not to have withholding apply, if available), with respect to pensions, annuities, or certain other deferred income, including periodic payments under section 3405(a), generally is made using Form W-4P, Withholding Certificate for Pension or Annuity Payments. On December 13, 2019, the IRS early released a draft 2020 Form W-4P. As the early release draft indicates, the Treasury Department and the IRS do not plan to redesign the 2020 Form W-4P in the same manner as the 2020 W-4. Instead, the 2020 Form W-4P will continue to request withholding allowances and marital status, rather than filing status, with respect to periodic payments under section 3405(a). Similarly, the Step 2(c) checkbox on the 2020 Form W-4 to request withholding using a higher withholding rate table will be inapplicable for the 2020 Form W-4P. Notice 2020-3 (which the IRS released on December 18, 2019 in advance of its expected publication in the 2020-3 edition of the

---

[6] For employees who do not check the box in Step 2(c) to request withholding using higher rate tables, part of the basic standard deduction is built into the percentage method tables in Publication 15-T; the other part of the standard deduction is subtracted from the employee's wages before the tables are applied. This approach is to permit the tables to be used with Forms W-4 furnished in 2019 and prior years. Other entries on the 2020 Form W-4 can affect other additions and subtractions that determine the amount of tax withheld from the employee's pay.

Internal Revenue Bulletin) describes withholding rules under section 3405(a) for the 2020 calendar year and provides additional information regarding the 2020 Form W-4P. Publication 15-A includes further information regarding the 2020 Form W-4P and alerts taxpayers that the related withholding tables and computational procedures for the 2020 Form W-4P are included in Publication 15-T.

Explanation of Provisions

These proposed regulations incorporate the changes made by TCJA to sections 3401 and 3402 and provide flexible and administrable rules for income tax withholding from wages that work with both the 2020 Form W-4 and its related tables and computational procedures described in Publication 15-T, and Forms W-4 and related tables and computational procedures provided in 2019 and earlier years. Because the ultimate goal of income tax withholding is to achieve withholding from employee's wages that accurately reflects the provisions of chapter 1 applicable to wages and the period wages are paid, the Treasury Department and the IRS have determined that the mechanical details of income tax withholding should be provided in forms, instructions, publications, and other guidance, so that these materials can be quickly updated as needed (for legislative changes or other reasons) to give payroll processors adequate time to program their systems to withhold the proper amount of income tax from employees' pay. These proposed regulations are generally compatible with the income tax withholding system in effect for 2019, as well as the system in effect for 2020, and as discussed in the Proposed Applicability Date section of this preamble, may be relied upon by employers for withholding until final regulations are published.

The changes made by TCJA to section 3405(a) (withholding on pensions, annuities, and certain other deferred income) were addressed in Notice 2018-14 and Notice 2018-92 for the 2018 and 2019 calendar years, respectively. These proposed regulations do not address withholding under section 3405(a); instead, Notice 2020-3 describes withholding rules under section 3405(a) for the 2020 calendar year.

1. *Number of Withholding Exemptions Claimed*

In accordance with the change made by section 11041(c)(2)(A) of TCJA and as indicated in section 5 of Notice 2018-92, the proposed regulations remove §31.3401(e)-1. Because section 11041(c) of TCJA repealed section 3401(e) and generally changed the references in Chapter 24 from "withholding exemptions" to "withholding allowance," current regulations under section 3401(e) are no longer consistent with the Code. (See section 2 of this Explanation of Provisions for definitions and interchangeable terms). However, rules similar to the substantive rules currently under §31.3401(e)-1 are included in other parts of these proposed regulations. Section 5 of this Explanation of Provisions discusses the withholding allowance to which an employee is entitled, and section 6(a) of this Explanation of Provisions discusses the rules for employees who fail to furnish Forms W-4.

2. *Definitions and Interchangeable Terms*

These proposed regulations clarify that, for purposes of chapter 24 of the Code and subpart E of part 31 of the Employment Tax Regulations (relating to collection of income tax at source), any reference to withholding exemption certificates means withholding allowance certificates unless otherwise stated. Section 11041 of TCJA changed the statutory title of the withholding exemption certificate to the withholding allowance certificate. However, under section 3402(f)(4), a withholding allowance certificate in effect under section 3402(f) generally continues in effect until superseded by another such certificate that is effective under section 3402(f). Thus, the rules proposed in these regulations generally apply to both withholding exemption certificates and withholding allowance certificates.

These proposed regulations generally refer to the Form W-4 as the withholding allowance certificate, the statutory term in section 3402(f)(5). However, proposed §31.3402(f)(5)-1 provides that the Form W-4, "Employee's Withholding Certificate," previously called "Employee's Withholding Allowance Certificate," is the form prescribed for the withholding allowance certificate required to be furnished under section 3402(f)(2).

An employee is not required to furnish a new Form W-4 solely because of the 2020 Form W-4 redesign, regardless of when the employee's Form W-4 currently in effect was furnished. Similarly, an employer must generally continue to compute the amount of tax to be withheld from an employee's wages based on a valid Form W-4 furnished by the employee regardless of when the employee furnished the Form W-4 on which such computation is based.[7] The 2020 Publication 15-T provides guidance on how employers will withhold income tax, under the tables and computational procedures set forth therein, using Forms W-4 furnished and in effect on or before December 31, 2019. An employer may ask all employees first paid wages before 2020 to furnish a 2020 Form W-4, but in connection with the request the employer should explain that (1) employees are not required to furnish a new Form W-4, and (2) if the employee does not furnish a 2020 Form W-4, the amount of tax to be withheld from the employee's wages will continue to be based on the last valid Form W-4 previously furnished. 3.

Percentage Method of Withholding

Section 31.3402(b)-1 of the current regulations provides that the amount of tax to be deducted and withheld under the percentage method of withholding is determined under the applicable percentage method withholding table included in Circular E (Employer's Tax Guide) according to the instructions therein. These proposed regulations clarify that employers that use the percentage method of withholding must compute the amount of tax to be withheld based on the entry for the employee's anticipated filing status or marital status and other entries on the employee's Form W-4 using the applicable percentage method tables and computational procedures in the applicable forms, instructions, publications, and other guidance prescribed by the IRS issued for use with respect to the period in which wages are paid. In 2020, percentage method tables and computational procedures are provided in Publication 15-T.

4. *Wage Bracket Method of Withholding*

Section 31.3402(c)-1(a) of the current regulations provides that, for employers using the wage bracket withholding method, the correct amount of withholding is determined under the applicable wage bracket withholding table in the Circular E (Employer's Tax Guide) issued for use with respect to the period in which such wages are paid. These proposed regulations clarify that employers that use the wage bracket withholding method and computational procedures based on the entry for the employee's anticipated filing status or marital status and other entries on the employee's Form W-4 should use the applicable wage bracket method tables and computational procedures in forms, instructions, publications, and other guidance prescribed by the IRS issued for use with respect to the period in which wages are paid. In 2020, wage bracket method tables and computational procedures are provided in Publication 15-T. In addition, these proposed regulations update the current regulations for the change in the Form W-4 and its computational procedures and provide that employers that use wage bracket method withholding tables applicable to a daily or miscellaneous pay period must use the wage bracket withholding tables applicable to the employee's filing status or marital status.

---

[7] This rule does not apply to a Form W-4 claiming exemption from withholding, which, for a 2019 Form W-4, will expire on February 18, 2020. Under proposed §31.3402(f)(4)-1(b), if a form claiming exemption from withholding expires, and the employee does not furnish a valid Form W-4 either renewing his or her exemption or claiming a withholding allowance, the employer must treat the employee as single but having the withholding allowance provided in forms, instructions, publications, and other guidance prescribed by the IRS. Publication 15 for 2020 provides that such an employee should be treated as if the employee had checked the box for single or married filing separately in Step 1(c) and made no entries in Step 2, Step 3, or Step 4 of the 2020 Form W-4.

5. Determination and Disclosure of Filing Status

Under section 3402(l)(1), an employer must treat an employee as single unless there is in effect a withholding allowance certificate indicating that the employee is married. Although section 3402(l) speaks in terms of single and married persons and provides that an employee will be treated as single unless the employee furnishes a valid Form W-4 claiming married status, the Treasury Department and the IRS have determined that this provision does not preclude adoption of head of household status to compute withholding for certain filers because the ability to claim head of household filing status furthers the goal of accuracy in withholding and, thus, reflects the provisions of chapter 1. *See* section 3402(a)(1)(B). Under section 1(j), for calendar years 2018 through 2025,[8] there is a separate income tax rate table for taxpayers filing as head of household. Providing for a head of household filing status on the Form W-4 and providing withholding tables for head of household filing status further the goal of accuracy in withholding. An employee may select head of household filing status only if the employee reasonably expects to be eligible to claim head of household filing status under section 2(b) and §1.2-2(b) of the Income Tax Regulations on the employee's income tax return.

On the other hand, although section 1 rates applicable to unmarried individuals and married individuals filing separate returns are different at higher marginal rates, the Treasury Department and the IRS have determined that the burden of providing separate withholding tables for married individuals filing separate returns outweighs the added accuracy that would be provided by having separate filing statuses for these two categories for the Form W-4 and tables. Consequently, the proposed regulations provide for three filing statuses: single, head of household, and married filing jointly.

Section 31.3402(l)-1(a) of the current regulations provides that in computing the tax to be withheld from an employee's wages, the employer must apply the withholding table that relates to employees who are single persons unless there is in effect a withholding allowance certificate indicating that the employee is married. These proposed regulations generally incorporate the principle in §31.3402(l)-1(a) of the current regulations and provide that the employee's entry for the employee's anticipated marital status or filing status on the Form W-4 determines what table employers apply under either the percentage method of withholding or wage bracket method of withholding. Employers may generally rely on the employee's entry for filing status on the Form W-4. These proposed regulations provide, consistent with section 3402(l)(1), that an employee who fails to furnish a valid Form W-4 must be treated as single.

Under section 3402(l)(2), the employee may furnish the employer a withholding allowance certificate indicating that the employee is married only if the employee is married (determined with the application of the rules in section 3402(l)(3), discussed in more detail below). Section 31.3402(l)-1(b)(1) of the current regulations generally states that an employee's marital status determines whether the employee may select married on the Form W-4. Generally, under the current regulations, the employee's anticipated filing status on the employee's income tax return does not determine whether an employee may indicate that he or she is married on the Form W-4. These proposed regulations change this rule.

Specifically, in defining "married" under section 3402(l)(2), the Treasury Department and the IRS have determined that, in addition to the employee's marital status, the amount of tax to be withheld should also be determined by reference to the employee's anticipated filing status on the employee's income tax return because this furthers accuracy and reflects the applicable provisions of chapter 1. Under section 1(j), for calendar years 2018-2025,[9] different tax rates apply to married individuals filing joint returns than married individuals filing separate returns. Correspondingly, married individuals who anticipate filing separately should not be allowed to select married filing jointly on the Form W-4 because, otherwise, such individuals would risk being significantly underwithheld. Therefore, these proposed regulations provide that an employee may only select married filing jointly on the employee's Form W-4 if the employee (1) reasonably expects to file jointly a single return of income under Subtitle A with his or her spouse, (2) is lawfully married for federal tax purposes within the meaning of §301.7701-18(b) on the day the Form W-4 is furnished, and (3) is treated as married within the meaning of section 3402(l)(3).

Furthermore, in accordance with section 3402(l)(3)(A), these proposed regulations incorporate a rule similar to §31.3402(l)-1(c) of the current regulations and provide that an employee may not select married filing jointly filing status on the Form W-4 if the employee is legally separated from his or her spouse under a decree of divorce or separate maintenance. These proposed regulations also update §31.3402(l)-1(c)(1)(ii) of the current regulations and provide that an employee may not select married filing jointly status on the Form W-4 if the employee or the employee's spouse is, or on any preceding day within the same calendar was, a nonresident alien unless the employee has made or reasonably expects to make an election under section 6013(g)[10] in the time and manner prescribed in §1.6013-6(a)(4).

In accordance with section 3402(l)(3)(B), these proposed regulations provide that an employee may generally select married filing jointly on the Form W-4 if the employee's spouse (other than a spouse referred to in section 3402(l)(3)(A)) died during the employee's taxable year. Similarly, an employee may select married filing jointly status if the employee's spouse died during the previous two taxable years, and the employee reasonably expects as of the close of the current taxable year to be a surviving spouse as defined in section 2(a) and §1.2-2(a) of the Income Tax Regulations and claim qualifying widow(er) filing status on the employee's income tax return. This rule is similar to §31.3402(l)-1(c)(2) of the current regulations.

Under section 3402(l)(2) an employee whose marital status changes from married to single must, at such time as the Secretary may by regulations prescribe, furnish the employer with a new withholding allowance certificate. Because of the addition of head of household filing status for withholding purposes, these proposed regulations provide that an employee whose anticipated filing status changes from married filing jointly (or qualifying widow(er)) to head of household or single, must, generally, within 10 days of the change furnish his or her employer with a new Form W-4. In addition, an employee whose anticipated filing status changes from head of household to single, must generally furnish his or her employer with a new Form W-4 within 10 days of the change. However, the employee does not have to furnish a new Form W-4 within 10 days of the change of status if the amount of tax the employee expects to be withheld is greater than the amount of the employee's anticipated income tax liability. Nonetheless, in all cases, an employee whose anticipated filing status changes from married filing jointly (or qualifying widow(er)) to head of household or single (including married filing separately) or from head of household to single (including married filing separately) must furnish a new Form W-4, to take effect in the following calendar year, to his or her employer by the later of December 1 of the calendar year in which the change occurs, or within 10 days of the change.

6. Withholding Allowance

These proposed regulations provide that an employee is entitled to a "withholding allowance" as provided in section 3402(f)(1) but only if the employee furnishes a valid Form W-4 claiming the withholding allowance. This is similar to the rule in §31.3402(f)(1)-1(a) of the current regulations. In addition, these proposed regulations provide that the employer is not required to ascertain whether the withholding allowance the employee claims is greater than the allowance to which the employee is entitled.

The proposed regulations define the withholding allowance, but in accordance with section 3402(a)(1), leave the computational details to forms, instructions, publications, and other guidance prescribed by the IRS. In 2020, these computational details will be set forth in the Form W-4,

---

[8] Sections 1(b) and (i) provide separate rates for head of household filers if the rates in section 1(j) cease to apply.

[9] Sections 1(b) and (i) provide separate rates for married individuals filing joint returns if the rates in section 1(j) cease to apply.

[10] Section 6013(g) was added by section 1012 of the Tax Reform Act of 1976, P.L. 94-455, 90 Stat. 1612 (1976). Under section 6013(g)(1)(B), this election applies for purposes of chapter 24.

Publication 505, Publication 15-T, and the Tax Withholding Estimator.[11] The Treasury Department and the IRS have determined that this flexible computation of the withholding allowance is consistent with section 3402(a)(1) because it is the most appropriate way to reflect the provisions of chapter 1 applicable to wages for a given calendar year. This approach will also allow the IRS to make adjustment as appropriate to reflect any legislative changes to chapter 1 in withholding on employees' pay or based on statistical data.

Under these proposed regulations, the withholding allowance under section 3402(f)(1) is determined by reference to seven factors. First, the withholding allowance depends on whether the employee is an individual for whom a deduction is allowable under section 151. *See* section 3402(f)(1)(A). The regulations repeat the statutory language with respect to this factor. Second, if the employee is married, the withholding allowance depends on whether the employee's spouse is entitled to the section 151 deduction, or would be so entitled if the spouse were an employee receiving wages, but only if the spouse does not have in effect a Form W-4 claiming an allowance for the section 151 deduction. *See* section 3402(f)(1)(B). The first and second factors, however, have no effect on withholding for calendar years 2018 through 2025 because section 151(d)(5) suspends the deduction for personal exemptions for calendar years 2018 through 2025. Accordingly, these factors are not taken into account on the 2020 Form W-4.

Third, if the employee is married, the withholding allowance depends on whether the employee's spouse is entitled to any additional amount under section 3402(m) or would be so entitled if the employee's spouse were an employee receiving wages, but only if the spouse does not have in effect a withholding allowance certificate claiming the allowance. *See* section 3402(f)(1)(B). The 2020 Form W-4 takes this factor into account by instructing taxpayers to complete the steps corresponding to any additional amount of tax deductions or tax credits on only one Form W-4 in the household.

Fourth, the withholding allowance depends on the number of individuals for whom a credit under section 24(a) may reasonably be expected to be allowable for the calendar year. *See* section 3402(f)(1)(C). These proposed regulations clarify that this means the credit under section 24(a) that the employee reasonably expects to claim on the employee's income tax return. This includes both the child tax credit and the credit for other dependents. The proposed regulations also clarify that the employee may not take into account any credit under section 24(a) that is claimed on another Form W-4. The 2020 Form W-4 takes this factor into account in Step 3 of the form.

Fifth, the withholding allowance depends on any additional amounts the employee elects to take into account under section 3402(m), but only if the employee's spouse does not have in effect a withholding allowance certificate making this election. *See* section 3402(f)(1)(D). These proposed regulations clarify this factor and state that the withholding allowance depends on additional deductions, credits, or other items the employee takes into account under proposed §31.3402(m)-1. Specifically, proposed §31.3402(m)-1(e)(3) allows the total deductions, credits, or estimated tax payments to be claimed on only one Form W-4. This is similar to the rule in §31.3402(m)-1(f) of the current regulations. Thus, an employee or the employee's spouse may not claim an amount of a deduction, credit, or estimated tax payment in proposed §31.3402(m)-1 if that same amount is claimed on any other Form W-4 in effect for the employee or the employee's spouse.

The 2020 Form W-4 takes into account estimated tax credits for dependents allowable under proposed §31.3402(m)-1(b) in Step 3. The instructions to the 2020 Form W-4 clarify that employees may also claim other credits such as the education tax credit or the foreign tax credit in Step 3 of the 2020 Form W-4. The 2020 Form W-4 takes into account estimated tax deductions allowable under proposed §31.3402(m)-1(c) in Step 4(b), which allows employees to claim deductions such as itemized deductions, student loan interest deductions, and deductible Individual Retirement Arrangement (IRA) contributions. Employees who wish to claim these and other deductions should complete the Deductions Worksheet on page 3 of Form W-4. Finally, under proposed §31.3402(m)-1, certain employees may take into account the credit for income tax withholding under chapter 24 and may take into account estimated tax payments paid provided they take into account nonwage income and follow the instructions to the Tax Withholding Estimator.[12] As stated previously in this preamble, the IRS will continue to update the Tax Withholding Estimator. The Treasury Department and IRS also request comments on whether changes should be made to the proposed regulations so that in the future the Tax Withholding Estimator may enable employees to have all required withholding on wages while taking into account expected estimated tax payments on non-wage income to be made later in the year, and, if so, what safeguards should be added to prevent inappropriate underwithholding on wages.

Sixth, the withholding allowance depends on the standard deduction allowable to the employee (one-half of the standard deduction in the case of an employee who is married (as determined under section 7703) and whose spouse is an employee receiving wages subject to withholding). *See* section 3402(f)(1)(E). These proposed regulations define this as the basic standard deduction (as defined in section 63(c)(2)) relating to the filing status the employee reasonably expects to claim on the employee's income tax return for the calendar year for which the withholding allowance is claimed. (The additional standard deduction for the aged and blind is allowed under §31.3402(m)-1(c)(5).) The 2020 Form W-4 takes into account the basic standard deduction allowable to the employee under section 3402(f)(1)(E) by having an employee check the box for the employee's anticipated filing status in Step 1(c). The basic standard deduction for each filing status is generally applied without further adjustment if the employee completes only Step 1 (including checking the box for a particular filing status) and Step 5 (signing under penalties of perjury) on the 2020 Form W-4.[13]

Seventh, the withholding allowance depends on whether the employee has withholding allowance certificates in effect with respect to more than one employer. *See* section 3402(f)(1)(F). For this factor, these proposed regulations reference the Form W-4 and other computational instructions (such as the Tax Withholding Estimator) to determine the adjustment resulting from multiple Forms W-4 the employee, the employee's spouse, or both have or reasonably expect to have in effect with respect to one or more employers. The Treasury Department and the IRS have determined that the Form W-4 and the instructions to the form are best able to direct employees how to take this factor into account in determining their withholding allowance and completing the Form W-4 due to the variety of fact patterns and the need to adjust this rule for the future based on statistical data or changes in the law to ensure accurate withholding on wages under chapter 1.

The 2020 Form W-4 provides employees three options with respect to multiple Forms W-4. Employees may use the Tax Withholding Estimator, may enter an amount computed on the Multiple Jobs Worksheet, or may select higher withholding rate tables by checking the box in Step 2(c) of the form. If the box in Step 2(c) is checked, Publication 15-T instructs employers to prorate and apply one-half of the standard deduction and marginal rates that account for equal wages for employment held concurrently. Thus, in the case of married taxpayers filing jointly, Publication 15-T applies the parenthetical in section 3402(f)(1)(E), which allows one-half of the standard deduction to an employee who is married and whose spouse is receiving wages subject to withholding.

---

[11] The withholding allowance for nonresident alien individuals is subject to the rules in proposed §31.3402(f)(6)-1, and, for 2020, nonresident aliens will find further guidance in IRS Notice 1392, "Supplemental Form W-4 Instructions for Nonresident Aliens."

[12] An employee whose employer must withhold for that employee pursuant to a notice under proposed §31.3402(f)(2)-1(g)(2) (lock-in letter) may not take into account any credit for tax withheld on wages under section 31(a) or any estimated tax payments. Thus, an employee for whom a lock-in letter is issued may not take into account income

tax withheld to date or estimated tax payments in computing the employee's withholding allowance.

[13] An employee—other than a student from India or business apprentice from India—who identifies as a nonresident alien employee by following the instructions in Notice 1392 will not have the basic standard deduction subtracted from the employee's wages. For 2020, the Publication 15-T provides special procedures employers must use with respect to such employees.

7. Additional Withholding Allowance

These proposed regulations provide rules under which an employee determines the additional withholding allowance or additional reductions in withholding the employee is entitled to claim on a Form W-4 under section 3402(m). Under section 3402(m), in determining the additional withholding allowance or additional reductions in withholding, the employee may take into account estimated tax deductions under section 3402(m)(1), estimated tax credits under section 3402(m)(2), and such additional deductions and other items as may be specified by the Secretary in regulations under section 3402(m)(3). This additional withholding allowance and additional reductions in withholding are part of the "withholding allowance" the employee is entitled to claim as provided in section 3402(f)(1)(D).

Section 6 of Notice 2018-92 discussed section 3402(m) generally and allowed taxpayers to include the estimated deduction under section 199A in determining the additional withholding allowance or additional reductions in withholding under section 3402(m). Section 6 of Notice 2018-92 requested comments with respect to the list of items set forth in §31.3402(m)-1(b). No comments on this issue were received. The Treasury Department and the IRS again request comments with respect to section 3402(m) generally, and, specifically, with respect to the aspects of these proposed regulations described in further detail in the following sections.

a. Estimated tax deductions

These proposed regulations implement section 3402(m)(1) by continuing the rule that taxpayers may take into account estimated itemized deductions (as defined in section 63(d)) allowable under Chapter 1. These proposed regulations combine the rule in §31.3402(m)-1(b)(1) and §31.3402(m)-1(c)(3) of the current regulations and define itemized deductions in proposed §31.3402(m)-1(b)(1) by cross-referencing to section 63(d). This change updates the cross-reference to the definition of itemized deductions to conform to section 102 of the Tax Reform Act of 1986, Pub. L. No. 99-514, 100 Stat. 2085, 2101 (1987) (defining itemized deductions in section 63(d)).

These proposed regulations also implement section 3402(m)(1) by allowing employees to take into account the employee's estimated deduction under section 199A in determining the additional withholding allowance or other reductions in withholding under section 3402(m) that the employee is entitled to claim on a Form W-4. This is consistent with section 6 of Notice 2018-92.

Section 11051(b)(2)(B) of TCJA struck the reference to section 62(a)(10) (regarding certain payments made under divorce or separation instruments) in section 3402(m)(1) as a permitted estimated deduction. Under section 11051(c) of TCJA, this change generally applies to any divorce or separation instrument (as defined in section 71(b)(2) of the Code as in effect before December 22, 2017) executed after December 31, 2018, or to any divorce or separation instrument (as so defined) executed on or before December 22, 2017, and modified thereafter, if the modification expressly provides that the amendments made by section 11051 of TCJA apply to such modification. However, because these proposed regulations generally allow taxpayers to take into account deductions described in section 62 that the employee reasonably expects will be allowable on the employee's income tax return for the year such item is claimed, the Treasury Department and the IRS have determined that no special rule is necessary with respect to payments described in section 62(a)(10) for the period prior to the effective date of this change to section 3402(m)(1). Employees who, under section 11051(c) of TCJA, are eligible for the deduction described in section 62(a)(10), may generally continue to take this deduction into account in determining the employee's withholding allowance or other reductions in withholding if the employee reasonably expects this deduction to be allowable on the employee's income tax return for the year the Form W-4 is in effect.

Section 3402(m)(3) authorizes the Secretary to prescribe regulations that allow employees to take into account such additional deductions (including the additional standard deduction under section 63(c)(3) for the aged and blind) in determining the additional withholding allowance or other reductions in withholding. Under this authority, these proposed regulations allow taxpayers to take into account the estimated additional standard deduction for the aged and blind provided under section 63(c)(3) and section 63(f). These proposed regulations also allow taxpayers to take into account the estimated deduction or deductions allowed for personal exemptions under section 151. Although, under section 151(d)(5), this deduction has been suspended for the calendar years 2018 through 2025, the Treasury Department and the IRS have determined that the limited period of the suspension and the specific reference to section 151 in section 3402(f)(1)(A) necessitate including in these proposed regulations a provision for a deduction for a dependency exemption or dependency exemptions under section 151 for changes scheduled to take effect after December 31, 2025.

The Treasury Department and the IRS have also determined, consistent with §31.3402(m)-1(b) of the current regulations, that employees should be permitted to take into account estimated deductions described in section 62, with certain exceptions, in determining the employee's additional withholding allowance or other reductions in withholding under section 3402(m). The proposed regulations provide for three exceptions. First, these proposed regulations provide that employees may not take into account any estimated deduction described in section 62(a)(2) if the reimbursement or payment for the amount allowable as the deduction is excludible from wages subject to income tax withholding. For example, an employee may not take into account any expenses described in section 62(a)(2)(A) that are reimbursed under a reimbursement and expense allowance arrangement since those reimbursements are excludible from wages under §31.3401(a)-4(a). The Treasury Department and the IRS have determined that it is inappropriate to allow an employee to claim an additional withholding allowance or other reductions in withholding with respect to items that are otherwise excludible from wages.

Second, these proposed regulations provide that, in determining the employee's additional withholding allowance or other reductions in withholding, employees are not allowed to take into account estimated trade or business deductions described in section 62(a)(1), estimated deductions for the production of income that are attributable to property held for the production of rent or royalties under section 62(a)(4), or estimated deductions described in section 62(a)(5) unless these amounts result in an aggregate net loss on schedules C (Profit or Loss from Business), E (Supplemental Income and Loss), or F (Profit or Loss from Farming) of Form 1040. Third, these proposed regulations provide that employees are not allowed to take into account estimated losses from the sale or exchange of property described in section 62(a)(3) unless these amounts result in a net loss on Schedule D (Capital Gains and Losses) of Form 1040 or on the last line of Part II of Form 4797 (Sale of Business Property). These limitations on estimated deductions described in section 62(a)(1), (3), (4), and (5) are consistent with §31.3402(m)-1(b)(12) of the current regulations, which affirmatively permits taking into account the estimated deductions for these items "from" the applicable schedules. In addition, these proposed regulations continue the rule in §31.3402(m)-1(b)(7) of the current regulations and allow employees to take into account a net operating loss carryover under section 172 in determining the employee's additional withholding allowance or other reductions in withholding under section 3402(m).

b. Estimated tax credits

These proposed regulations allow an employee to take into account estimated income tax credits allowable under chapter 1 in determining the employee's additional withholding allowance or other reductions in withholding and update the cross reference in §31.3402(m)-1(b)(2) of the current regulations to conform to changes under section 471 of the Deficit Reduction Act of 1984, Pub. L. No. 98-369, 98 Stat. 494, 825 (1984). (The credit under section 24 of the Code (child tax credit) is part of the employee's withholding allowance under section 3402(f)(2)(C) and is thus not part of the employee's additional withholding allowance).

Section 31.3402(m)-1(b)(2)(i) of the current regulations does not allow an employee to take the credit for tax withheld on wages under section 31(a) into account in determining the employee's additional withholding allowance or other reductions in withholding under section 3402(m). However, section 7 of Notice 2018-92 stated that the Treasury Department and the IRS intend to update the regulations under section 3402 to explicitly allow employees to use the withholding calculator (now called the Tax Withholding Estimator) or Publication 505 to determine what entries to make on Form W-4 in lieu of completing certain worksheets included with the Form W-4. The Tax Withholding Estimator currently takes into account the amount of income tax withheld to date to estimate the amount of withholding required for the remaining payroll periods during the calendar year. Thus, the Treasury Department and the IRS have determined that employees may take into account the credit permitted under section 31(a) for income tax withheld under chapter 24 to date but only if (1) on the day the employee estimates the amount of income tax withheld, the amount has been withheld from the employee's wages (or other payments treated as wages for chapter 24 purposes, such as pension payments subject to withholding under section 3405 or certain other payments subject to backup withholding under section 3406) and (2) the employee enters this amount of tax withheld pursuant to the instructions in the Tax Withholding Estimator or Publication 505.[14]

The Treasury Department and the IRS have determined that these limitations in taking into account the credit for tax withheld are necessary to prevent employees from having a disproportionate amount of income tax withheld at the end of a calendar year. Historically, the withholding tables and procedures established under the Code are structured so that withholding from wages generally occurs evenly throughout the year. However, if an employee's employer has already withheld more Federal income tax from the employee's wages than necessary to satisfy the employee's anticipated income tax liability, employees should generally be able to take any excess amounts withheld into account.

One commenter to Notice 2018-92 suggested that the withholding calculator (now called the Tax Withholding Estimator) should include an entry accommodating an annual payroll period so a multiplier of one can be used if prior year tax information is used for the entries in the calculator. The Tax Withholding Estimator currently allows employees to enter weekly, bi-weekly, semi-monthly, and monthly payroll frequencies because those are the most common types of payroll periods used by employers. The Treasury Department and the IRS request comments on whether there is a need to provide additional payroll frequencies—other than weekly, bi-weekly, semi-monthly, and monthly—as part of the Tax Withholding Estimator. Also, the Treasury Department and the IRS note that the Tax Withholding Estimator currently asks the employee to enter the total wages the employee expects to receive this year and bases its recommendation, in part, on that annual entry. In addition, the Tax Withholding Estimator makes recommendations for the current year, and prior year information may not always be useful when employees' circumstances change.

With regard to nonresident aliens, these proposed regulations continue the rule in § 31.3402(m)-1(b)(2)(ii) of the current regulations to disregard the credit for tax withheld on nonresident aliens and foreign corporations. However, these proposed regulations update the cross-reference for the credit for tax withheld on nonresident aliens from section 32 to section 33 consistent with section 471(c) of the Deficit Reduction Act of 1984.

Finally, these proposed regulations provide that an employee may not take into account, in determining the employee's additional withholding allowance or other reductions in withholding under section 3402(m), any estimated chapter 1 tax credits the employee has claimed or expects to be refunded as a result of filing an IRS form other than the employee's individual income tax return (Form 1040). For example, an employee may not take into account an estimated credit under section 34 for certain uses of gasoline and special fuel the employee claimed or expects to claim on Form 8849, but if the employee expects to claim the section 34 credit on a Form 4136 attached to the employee's individual income tax return, the employee may take this credit into account. This rule is similar to § 31.3402(m)-1(b)(2)(iii) of the current regulations. However, under these proposed regulations, this rule applies to all chapter 1 tax credits that an employee claimed or expects to claim on an IRS form other than the employee's individual income tax return. The Treasury Department and the IRS have determined that it is inappropriate to allow an employee to take into account a chapter 1 tax credit that the taxpayer has otherwise requested to be refunded by filing an IRS form other than the employee's individual income tax return.

c. Estimated tax payments

The Treasury Department and the IRS have determined that certain estimated tax payments are "other items" referenced in section 3402(m)(3) because employees who have both wages and non-wage income, including net earnings from self-employment, should be able to take into account any estimated tax payments they already paid with respect to non-wage income if they want to have income tax withheld from their wages for the remainder of the year to apply toward tax liability with respect to non-wage income for that year. The Treasury Department and the IRS also want to ensure employees do not use estimated tax payments to inappropriately reduce required withholding on wages. Accordingly, these proposed regulations allow taxpayers to take into account, in determining the additional withholding allowance or other reductions in withholding under section 3402(m)(3), estimated tax payments paid to date if (1) the amount claimed has been paid with the payment voucher from Form 1040-ES, "Estimated Tax for Individuals" (or was otherwise designated by the taxpayer as a payment of estimated tax); (2) the employee uses the Tax Withholding Estimator and enters the amount claimed pursuant to the instructions in the Tax Withholding Estimator; and (3) in using the Tax Withholding Estimator, the employee includes all items of nonwage income the Tax Withholding Estimator prompts the employee to enter.[15] As a result, employees who desire to satisfy their tax obligations related to self-employment and other non-wage income through wage withholding rather than future estimated tax payments may use the Tax Withholding Estimator to compute the amount necessary to do so. Employees who desire to continue to pay estimated taxes in whole or in part on self-employment or other non-wage income, should not use the Tax Withholding Estimator, but should follow the instructions in Publication 505 to determine how to complete Form W-4. The Treasury Department and the IRS request comments on whether employees should be able to take into account in the Tax Withholding Estimator estimated tax payments they have not yet made but plan to make during the calendar year with regard to their non-wage income and, if so, what conditions are advisable to ensure employees do not shift required withholding on wages to estimated tax payments or inadvertently pay insufficient taxes during the calendar year so that they owe taxes when they file their tax returns and possibly face estimated tax or underpayment penalties.

d. Definitions and special rules

These proposed regulations continue the rules in § 31.3402(m)-1(c)(1) of the current regulations relating to the circumstances under which an employee may take into account, in determining the employee's additional withholding allowance or other reductions in withholding under section 3402(m), deductions, credits, and other items. Specifically, an employee may generally take into account only a particular deduction or credit (other than the credit for income tax withheld on wages) that the employee reasonably expects will be allowable for the year the estimation is made, which in no event may exceed the amount shown for that particular deduction or credit on the employee's tax return for the preceding taxable year plus a determinable additional amount. However, these proposed regulations provide that a taxpayer may not take into account any proposed adjustment relating to a disallowed tax deduction or credit that is the subject of any pending request for reconsideration, protest, request for consideration by an Appeals office, or civil action.

These proposed regulations partially incorporate the rule in the flush language of § 31.3402(m)-1(b) of the current regulations to provide that an employee must offset any deduction allowable under proposed § 31.3402(m)-1(b) with items includible in the employee's gross income for which no Federal income tax is withheld. However, unlike the rule in the flush language of § 31.3402(m)-1(b) of the current regulations, the rule in the proposed regulations is applied only with respect to deductions and not with respect to income tax credits. The Treasury Department and the IRS have determined that requiring taxpayers to apply this rule with respect to credits is mathematically cumbersome and would complicate withholding procedures for employees. In order to offset tax credits with nonwage income, employees would have to convert the credit to a deduction, and the Treasury Department and the IRS view such a procedure as undercutting the purpose of the 2020 Form W-4, which in separate steps requests dollar amounts for estimated tax credits and estimated deductions, facilitating determination of more accurate withholding. The Treasury Department and the IRS request comments with respect to this rule.

---

[14] An employee subject to a lock-in letter may not take the credit under section 31(a) into account.

[15] An employee subject to a lock-in letter may not take estimated tax payments into account.

These proposed regulations also incorporate the rules in § 31.3402(m)-1(f) of the current regulations and provide that an employee may not take into account, in determining the employee's additional withholding allowance or other reductions in withholding under section 3402(m), deductions, credits, or estimated tax payments if these deductions, credits, or estimated tax payments are claimed on another valid Form W-4 in effect with respect to another employer of the employee or an employer of the employee's spouse. These proposed regulations provide that spouses who file jointly may only claim deductions, credits, or estimated tax payments once, but these amounts may be allocated between the spouses. These proposed regulations also provide that a married employee who expects to file separately from his or her spouse and has filed separately for the preceding taxable year may take into account deductions, credits, or estimated tax payments on the basis of the employee's individual wages and allowable items. These proposed regulations further provide that an employee must follow the instructions to the Form W-4, and other forms, instructions, publications, and related guidance in determining the credits, deductions, or estimated tax payments the employee may take into account under section 3402(m). This is similar to the rule in § 31.3402(m)-1(d)(1) of the current regulations, which instructs taxpayers to compute additional allowances using the tables and instructions on Form W-4. Finally, these proposed regulations delete the examples illustrating the application of section 3402(m) and the current regulations. The Treasury Department and the IRS request comments on the need for examples that illustrate the application of these proposed regulations.

8. *Furnishing of Withholding Allowance Certificates*

As stated earlier in this preamble, these proposed regulations implement TCJA's changes to section 3402(f)(2) of the Code and conform to the redesigned 2020 Form W-4. These proposed regulations also address the circumstances under which the employee must furnish the employer a Form W-4. Under section 3402(f)(2), in no event may the employee furnish the employer a withholding allowance certificate claiming a withholding allowance in excess of the withholding allowance the employee is entitled to claim under section 3402(f)(1).

In addition, these proposed regulations restate and clarify certain longstanding special rules relating to when an employer should request each employee to furnish a new Form W-4, rules relating to inclusion of social security numbers on a Form W-4, and rules relating to invalid Forms W-4. Finally, these proposed regulations clarify longstanding rules relating to the submission of certain Forms W-4 to the IRS and rules governing when the IRS may notify the employer in writing that an employee is not entitled to claim a complete exemption from withholding or more than the maximum withholding allowance specified by the IRS in a written notice (a lock-in letter).

a. *Commencement of employment*

Under section 3402(f)(2)(A), on or before the commencement of employment with an employer, an employee must furnish the employer with a signed withholding allowance certificate relating to the withholding allowance claimed by the employee, which in no event may exceed the withholding allowance to which the employee is entitled. These proposed regulations clarify section 3402(f)(2)(A) and provide that, on or before commencement of employment, an employee must furnish the employer with a signed Form W-4 relating to the filing status the employee reasonably expects to claim on the employee's income tax return and the withholding allowance the employee is entitled to as discussed in section 6 of this Explanation of Provisions. These proposed regulations clarify that an employee may in no event furnish a Form W-4 claiming a withholding allowance in excess of the withholding allowance the employee is entitled to as determined based on the employee's reasonable expectations and the instructions provided in forms, instructions, publications, and other guidance prescribed by the IRS.

These proposed regulations also clarify that an employee who may claim exemption from withholding under section 3402(n) and proposed § 31.3402(n)-1 may furnish a Form W-4 claiming the exemption from withholding on or before commencement of employment with an employer.

As stated in section 5 of Notice 2018-92, because TCJA struck section 3401(e) but did not make any substantive changes to section 3402(l) (providing that an employee is treated as single unless the employee furnishes the employer a Form W-4 indicating the employee is married), these proposed regulations provide, with respect to wages paid on or after January 1, 2020, that an employer with an employee who failed or fails to furnish a valid Form W-4 on or before commencing employment with the employer must treat the employee as single but having the withholding allowance provided in forms, instructions, publications, and other guidance prescribed by the IRS (default rate). This rule provides flexibility to adjust the applicable default rate of withholding, if warranted based on future legislation or statistical data, to better align withholding with income tax liability.

The IRS plans to provide a default rate for employees who fail to furnish a Form W-4 and who commenced employment on or before December 31, 2019 (and were paid wages in 2019 or earlier) that differs from the default rate for employees who fail to furnish a Form W-4 and were first paid wages on or after January 1, 2020. However, for this purpose, for any employee commencing employment on or after January 1, 2020, in determining when the employee was first paid wages, the employer may choose to disregard any previous payment of wages during a prior employment relationship between the employee and the employer that had ended, such as for an employee who retired and is later rehired. In this circumstance, the employer may treat the employee who fails to furnish a Form W-4 as though the employee was first paid wages on or after January 1, 2020.

Employees hired and paid wages on or before December 31, 2019, who failed to furnish Forms W-4 have historically been treated as single and claiming zero withholding allowances. This default rate will continue to apply to these employees hired and paid wages on or before December 31, 2019, who fail to furnish a valid Form W-4. As a result employees in this situation would generally have a similar amount of income tax withheld from wages in 2020 as in 2019 (although the 2020 Publication 15-T provides percentage method and wage bracket method withholding tables that take into account 2020 cost-of-living adjustments to certain items due to inflation as required by various provisions of the Code).

On the other hand, Publication 15-T instructs employers to treat an employee who is first paid wages on or after January 1, 2020 (even if hired at the end of 2019), and who fails to furnish a Form W-4 as if the employee had checked the box for single or married filing separately in Step 1(c) and made no entries in Step 2, Step 3, or Step 4 of the 2020 Form W-4. Thus, a single filer's standard deduction with no other entries for the steps on the 2020 Form W-4 will be taken into account in determining withholding for the employee. The tables and computational instructions in Publication 15-T were adjusted accordingly. The Treasury Department and the IRS have determined that this updated default rate of withholding adequately reflects the appropriate withholding for most employees.

However, if this updated default rate were applied to wages paid in 2020 or later to those employees who were hired and paid wages on or before December 31, 2019, those employees would generally have less income tax withheld from their wages paid in 2020 or later than they did in 2019 and earlier without furnishing a new Form W-4 to their employers. Thus, these employees might be surprised by such an unexpected change in withholding when they took no action to cause the change in withholding. The Treasury Department and the IRS note that if an employee desires and is entitled to have less tax withheld from the employee's wages, the employee should furnish his or her employer a valid Form W-4 (and employees will more easily achieve accurate withholding using the 2020 Form W-4). Accordingly, while the updated default rate for employees first paid wages on or after January 1, 2020, will lead to more accurate withholding than the continued default rate for employees hired and paid wages on or before December 31, 2019, the Treasury Department and the IRS view the use of separate default rates depending on when the employee commenced employment and first received wages as appropriately balancing the desire for accurate withholding and the desire to not reduce withholding for employees with no change in circumstance or newly furnished Form W-4.

Section 11 of Notice 2018-92 solicited comments generally, and one commenter suggested that an employee who fails to furnish a Form W-4 should continue to be treated as single with zero withholding allowances because adding allowances to the employee's wages complicates the withholding system. The Treasury Department and the IRS do not agree that adding withholding allowances complicates the withholding system, especially after implementation of the redesigned 2020 Form W-4. Recognizing that the goal of the withholding system is to achieve the appropriate withholding of income tax to approximate an employee's income tax liability, the proposed regulations provide that employees who fail to furnish Form W-4 will be treated as single having the withholding allowance provided in forms, instructions, publications, or other guidance by the IRS. Withholding on these employees' wages takes into consideration statistical data concerning the tax liability of employees and is designed to avoid placing an unnecessary burden on employers. Thus, Treasury Department and the IRS will not adopt this specific comment

b. *Change of status*

Similar to the current regulations, these proposed regulations provide "change of status" rules for employees who experience changed circumstances that reduce the withholding allowance an employee is entitled to claim. In particular, these proposed regulations update the rules to reflect TCJA changes and changes in computational procedures set forth in forms, instructions and publications. *See* section 3402(f)(2)(B) and (C). As required by the Code, these proposed regulations provide that an employee is generally required to furnish a new Form W-4 to his or her employer within 10 days after the change of status if the change affects the current calendar year or by December 1 of the current calendar year to take effect in the following calendar year if the change affects the next calendar year. Due to the TCJA change in the definition of a withholding allowance and to reflect the goal of the withholding system to ensure the tax withheld approximates the employee's income tax liability while minimizing employee and employer burden, these proposed regulations provide that an employee does not have to furnish a new Form W-4 if the amount of tax the employee expects to be withheld from the employee's pay for the calendar year is greater than the amount of the employee's anticipated income tax liability.

Furthermore, because this general rule may be difficult for certain employees to apply and because the 2020 Form W-4 generally uses annual estimates of dollar amounts, the IRS and the Treasury Department have determined that requiring employees to furnish, and employers to put into effect, new Forms W-4 for small changes in circumstances would be burdensome and complex. Therefore, these proposed regulations also provide a de minimis rule with respect to changes of status under section 3402(f)(2)(B) and (C). These change of status rules apply for Forms W-4 furnished in 2019 or prior years and for Forms W-4 furnished in 2020 or later years.

Specifically, these proposed regulations provide seven circumstances under which an employee must furnish a new Form W-4 to the employer. If any of the seven circumstances apply, the employee experiences a "change of status" and must, within 10 days after the change occurs (if the change of status affects the current calendar year) or by the later of December 1 of the current calendar year or 10 days after the change occurs (if the change of status affects the next calendar year), furnish his or her employer with a new Form W-4. Notwithstanding a change in status, however, if the employee's income tax withholding for the calendar year would continue to equal or exceed the employee's anticipated income tax liability for the year, then the employee generally does not have to furnish a new Form W-4 to the employer.[16]

First, if an employee's filing status changes from married filing jointly (or qualifying widow(er)) to head of household or single (including married filing separately) or from head of household to single (including married filing separately), the proposed regulations provide that the employee experiences a change of status.

Second, if an unmarried employee commences concurrent employment with a second employer that pays wages subject to income tax withholding and selects higher withholding rate tables on the second Form W-4, the proposed regulations provide that the employee experiences a change of status with respect to the first Form W-4 if higher withholding rates were not selected on the first Form W-4. Similarly, if a married employee (1) expects to file jointly with his or her spouse, (2) no longer has only one Form W-4 on file for the employee, the employee's spouse, or both, and (3) the employee or the employee's spouse selects higher withholding rate tables on a second Form W-4, then the employee experiences a change of status with respect to the first Form W-4 if higher withholding rate tables were not selected on the first Form W-4. The higher withholding rate tables are designed to work for employees with two employers (including married employees filing jointly if both spouses are employed by employers who pay wages subject to income tax withholding). Employees with two Forms W-4 in effect who select higher withholding rate tables on one Form W-4 without selecting higher withholding rate tables on the second Form W-4 have a significant risk of having less than the amount necessary to satisfy their tax liability withheld from their wages.

Third, if an employee has multiple Forms W-4 in effect, and the employee or the employee's spouse reasonably expects an annual increase in regular wages of $10,000, the proposed regulations provide that a change of status occurs with respect to the Form W-4 on which the employee has utilized the multiple job procedures (other than selecting higher withholding rate tables) set forth in forms, instructions, publications, and other guidance. For this purpose, the proposed regulations indicate that "regular wages" means wages paid by an employer for a payroll period either at a regular periodic rate (*e.g.*, daily, hourly) or at a predetermined fixed amount. The Treasury Department and the IRS anticipate that this change of status rule will promote accuracy in withholding without imposing unnecessary burden in requiring new Forms W-4 for smaller changes in regular wages. As in prior years, in 2020, the income tax withholding tables in Publication 15-T do not adequately account for increases in regular wages for employees who utilize the multiple job procedures (other than selecting higher withholding rate tables) because these wages may be subject to a higher marginal rate of income tax on the employee's income tax return.

Fourth, if an employee claims a child tax credit on a Form W-4 and expects the number of qualifying children with respect to whom a child tax credit was claimed to decrease, the proposed regulations provide that the employee experiences a change of status with respect to the Form W-4 on which the child tax credit was claimed.

Fifth, if an employee has claimed any tax credit, including a child tax credit, and the amount of tax credits the employee reasonably expects to claim decreases by more than $500, the proposed regulations provide that the employee experiences a change of status with respect to the Form W-4 on which these tax credits are claimed.

Sixth, the proposed regulations provide that an employee experiences a change of status with respect to deductions the employee reasonably expects to claim (such as itemized deductions in excess of the basic standard deduction corresponding to the employee's claimed filing status) if the employee reasonably expects the deductions claimed on the employee's tax return to decrease by more than $2,300.

The Treasury Department and the IRS anticipate that these dollar thresholds for requiring a new Form W-4 will account for decreases in credits and deductions and will promote accuracy in the withholding system. Indeed, these threshold amounts for requiring a new Form W-4 will lead to more accuracy than the change of status rules in the current regulations that are in effect for 2019, which turn on the value of one allowance that historically has been tied to the pre-TCJA personal exemption amount, which for 2019 is $4,200.[17] Accordingly, this proposed change of status rule should help make withholding more accurate and thereby decrease the risk of underwithholding for employees.

---

[16] However, any employee whose anticipated filing status changes from married filing jointly (or qualifying widow(er)) to head of household or single (including married filing separately) or from head of household to single (including married filing separately) must furnish a new Form W-4 to take effect in the following calendar year to his or her employer by the later of December 1 of the calendar year in which the change occurs, or within 10 days of the change.

[17] Under section 3 of Notice 2018-92, an employee would experience a change of status if the employee's claimed deductions decrease by more than $4,200 or if the employee's claimed tax credits decrease by as much as $1,554 (*i.e.*, assuming the individual is taxed at the highest marginal tax rate in section 1(j) of 37%, the maximum benefit from a tax credit equivalent to $4,200 in deductions is $1,554).

Seventh, an employee experiences a change of status under the proposed regulations if he or she no longer reasonably expects to be able to claim exemption from withholding under section 3402(n) and proposed § 31.3402(n)-1. This change can occur if the employee expects to incur an income tax liability under subtitle A for either the current or the previous calendar year.

Finally, similar to the rule in § 31.3402(f)(2)-1(b)(2) of the current regulations, these proposed regulations provide that if an employee experiences a change of status that increases the employee's withholding allowance, the employee may furnish the employer with a new Form W-4 claiming the increased withholding allowance the employee is entitled to claim under proposed § 31.3402(f)(1)-1(b). Like § 31.3402(f)(2)-1(b)(3) of the current regulations, these proposed regulations also provide that if, on any day during the calendar year, the employee may claim exemption from withholding under section 3402(n) and proposed § 31.3402(n)-1, the employee may furnish the employer with a new Form W-4 claiming exemption from withholding.

c. Special rules relating to withholding allowance certificates

These proposed regulations provide that employers should request each employee to furnish a new Form W-4 for the next calendar year before December 1 of each year, in the event of a change to an employee's withholding allowance. A similar rule is in § 31.3402(f)(2)-1(c)(3) of the current regulations, which states that employers should request each employee to furnish a new Form W-4. These proposed regulations update the current "exemption status" nomenclature to "withholding allowance," which is defined in proposed § 31.3402(f)(1)-1(b).

These proposed regulations provide that an employee must include the employee's social security number on the signed Form W-4 the employee furnishes to the employer. An employee may not use a truncated social security number in completing the employee's Form W-4 because a person may not truncate his or her own taxpayer identification number on any statement or document the person furnishes to another person. *See* § 301.6109-4(b)(2)(iv). A similar rule is set forth in § 31.3402(f)(2)-1(d) of the current regulations.

These proposed regulations continue the rule that any alteration or unauthorized addition to a Form W-4 causes a Form W-4 to be invalid.[18] In addition, any oral or written statement clearly indicating that an employee's Form W-4 is false that an employee makes to the employer on or before the date on which the employee furnishes the Form W-4 causes the employee's Form W-4 to be invalid. An employer that receives an invalid Form W-4 must disregard the invalid Form W-4 for purposes of computing withholding. The employer must inform the employee that the Form W-4 is invalid and must request another Form W-4 from the employee. If the employee fails to comply with the employer's request the employer must withhold according to the employee's last valid Form W-4 in effect. If no valid Form W-4 is in effect, the employer must treat the employee as single but having the withholding allowance provided by the forms, instructions, and publications prescribed by the IRS. This treatment is consistent with default rates described in section 8(a) of this Explanation of Provisions that apply if an employee fails to furnish a valid W-4 upon commencement of employment.

These proposed regulations remove § 31.3402(f)(2)-1(f) of the current regulations, which provides that the withholding exemption certificate shall be used for purposes of withholding with respect to qualified State individual taxes, as well as Federal Tax. Section 31.3402(f)(2)-1(f) relates to a subchapter of the Code that was repealed by section 11801(a)(45) of Title XI of the Omnibus Budget Reconciliation Act of 1990, Pub. L. No. 101-508, 104 Stat. 1388-522 (repealing Subchapter E of Chapter 64).

d. Submission of certain withholding allowance certificates

These proposed regulations continue the rule in the current regulations regarding the submission of withholding exemption certificates to the IRS but update any reference to "withholding exemption certificate" to "withholding allowance certificate". Under these proposed regulations, the IRS may, by written notice or through published guidance in the IRB, request submission of a Form W-4.[19]

e. Notice of maximum withholding allowance permitted

These proposed regulations continue the rule from the current regulations regarding the notice prescribing the maximum number of withholding exemptions an employee may claim (a lock-in letter) but update any reference to "maximum number of withholding exemptions permitted" to "maximum withholding allowance." This change is consistent with TCJA's changes to section 3402(f)(1). In addition, these proposed regulations replace the term "marital status" with an employee's "filing status." These proposed regulations also replace references to "number of exemptions" with "withholding allowance" to implement TCJA's changes to section 3402(f)(1).

These proposed regulations are consistent with section 3 of Notice 2019-92, which provided that, until further guidance is issued, any reference to a withholding exemption in the regulations and guidance under section 3402 is applied as if it were a reference to a withholding allowance.[20] Proposed § 31.3402(f)(1)-1(b) prescribes the withholding allowance an employee is entitled to, and, therefore, the maximum withholding allowance the employee is entitled to is based on that definition. Correspondingly, the IRS and the Treasury Department have determined that the notices issued under § 31.3402(f)(2)-1(g)(2), including a lock-in letter or a modification notice, which the IRS may issue subsequently to a lock-in letter to modify an employee's filing status and/or permitted withholding allowance, will be updated to reflect the 2020 Form W-4 withholding procedures. These proposed regulations update the reference to the withholding allowance certificate if an employee subject to a lock-in letter requests more withholding or requests less withholding to correspond to proposed § 31.3402(f)(1)-1(b) (defining the withholding allowance to which the employee is entitled), § 31.3402(i)-1(a)(1) and (2) (providing for voluntary increases in the amount of withholding not otherwise required under section 3402), and proposed § 31.3402(l)-1(b) (providing for the filing status an employee may claim on the Form W-4). If an employer is required to apply a maximum withholding allowance prescribed by a lock-in letter or modification notice, and the employee subsequently furnishes the employer a new Form W-4, the employer must put this new Form W-4 into effect only if it requires the employer to withhold more income tax than prescribed by the lock-in letter or modification notice. If the new Form W-4 would result in less income tax being withheld from the employee's wages, the employer may not put the Form W-4 into effect.

Consistent with section 9 of Notice 2018-92, these proposed regulations eliminate the requirement that the employer send a written response to the IRS office designated in the lock-in letter that the employee is not employed by the employer. Notices issued under § 31.3402(f)(2)-1(g)(2) will continue to provide that if an employer no longer employs an employee, no action is required. These proposed regulations also include minor non-substantive changes with regard to the lock-in letter.

Finally, these proposed regulations provide for three special rules in determining the withholding allowance for employees who are subject to a lock-in letter or who request that the IRS issue a modification notice to modify a lock-in letter. First, the anticipated tax benefit from any tax credit or deduction must be offset by the anticipated tax attributable to items includible in the employee's gross income in the manner determined by the IRS. Second, the section 31(a) credit may not be taken into account. Third, estimated tax payments may not be taken into account. The Treasury

---

[18] Similar to the rule in the current regulations, proposed § 31.3402(f)(5)-1(b)(1) provides that an alteration of a Form W-4 is any deletion of the language of the jurat or other similar provision of the Form W-4 by which the employee certifies or affirms the correctness of the completed Form W-4, or any material defacing the Form W-4. Proposed § 31.3402(f)(5)-1(b)(2) provides that an unauthorized addition to a Form W-4 is any writing on the Form W-4 other than the entries requested on the Form W-4 (e.g., name, address, and filing status) or permitted by instructions or other guidance.

[19] Separate procedures apply to examination of returns, which are further discussed in § 601.105.

[20] Section 3 of Notice 2018-92 further provides, as an example, that the language in § 31.3402(f)(2)-1(g)(2)(i) providing for an IRS notification process to specify a "maximum number of withholding exemptions" an employee may claim will be applied as a reference to a maximum number of withholding allowances.

Department and the IRS have determined that these special rules are appropriate because taxpayers subject to a lock-in letter have been significantly noncompliant with wage withholding rules and requirements for payment of income tax liability. Moreover, these rules will generally be applied by the IRS in preparing any modification notice, once such notices have been revised to incorporate the 2020 Form W-4 withholding procedures, and thus concerns that apply to other employees regarding the complexity of these computations do not apply to employees subject to a lock-in letter.

9. *When a Withholding Allowance Certificate Takes Effect*

Section 31.3402(f)(3)-1 of the current regulations was last updated in 1983 by T.D. 7915, 48 F.R. 44072-01 (September 27,1983). These proposed regulations update the regulations under section 3402(f)(3) to reflect the statutory rules enacted in section 10302 of the Omnibus Reconciliation Act of 1987, Pub. L. No. 100-203, 101 Stat. 1330, 1330-429 (1987). As noted in section 2, above, these rules apply to withholding exemption certificates, and any reference to withholding allowance certificates or Forms W-4 includes a reference to a withholding exemption certificate, furnished and effective on or before December 31, 2017.

Specifically, section 3402(f)(3)(A) provides that when there is no withholding allowance certificate in effect for a particular employee, and the employee furnishes a withholding allowance certificate to the employer, the employer must put the certificate into effect as of the beginning of the first payroll period ending after the date the certificate is furnished. If the payment of wages is made without regard to a payroll period, the employer must put the withholding allowance certificate into effect as of the first payment of wages after it is furnished. These proposed regulations reiterate the statutory rule.

Under section 3402(f)(3)(B), if the employer has a valid withholding allowance certificate in effect with respect to a particular employee, and the employee furnishes a withholding allowance certificate to take effect during the calendar year, the employer must put the certificate into effect as of the beginning of the first payroll period ending (or the first payment of wages made without regard to a payroll period) on or after the 30th day after the day on which the certificate is furnished. An employer may elect to put a withholding allowance certificate into effect earlier but no earlier than on or after the day the withholding allowance certificate is furnished. An employer may not put into effect a withholding allowance certificate furnished to take effect in the next calendar year under section 3402(f)(2)(C) until the next calendar year. These proposed regulations reiterate these statutory rules.

10. *Period During Which Withholding Exemption Certificates Remain in Effect*

The proposed regulations remove § 31.3402(f)(4)-1 of the current regulations, which applies to withholding exemption certificates furnished prior to January 1, 1982. Generally, withholding exemption or allowance certificates continue in effect until replaced by a new Form W-4. The Treasury Department and the IRS have determined that the rules discussed in section 11 of this Explanation of Provisions are sufficient to account for Forms W-4 in effect under prior law.

11. *Effective Period of a Withholding Allowance Certificate*

Similar to the current regulations, the proposed regulations provide that Forms W-4 that took effect under prior law generally remain in effect until another Form W-4 is furnished. *See* section 3402(f)(4). This applies with respect to withholding exemption certificates and Forms W-4 furnished on or before December 31, 2019, including those that are in effect on December 31, 2019, that have not been superseded by a new Form W-4 furnished to be effective for 2020 or subsequent years. However, under these proposed regulations, a Form W-4 furnished by an employee subject to a lock-in letter ceases to be effective when the lock-in letter takes effect unless the Form W-4 results in more withholding than prescribed by the lock-in letter. If the employee's Form W-4 results in more withholding than prescribed by the lock-in letter, the employer should continue withholding according to the employee's Form W-4, even after the employee is released from the lock-in letter. If the employer had been withholding according to a lock-in letter, upon the employee's release from the lock-in letter, the proposed regulations provide that the employee must furnish his or her employer a new valid Form W-4 in order to ensure that withholding after release from the lock-in letter is as accurate as possible. If the employee fails to do so, the employee will be treated as single but having the withholding allowance provided in forms, instructions, publications, and other guidance prescribed by the Commissioner, in accordance with § 31.3402(f)(2)-1(a)(4). Accordingly, an employee subject to a lock-in letter and subsequently released who does not furnish a new Form W-4 would be treated as single or married filing separately in Step 1(c) of the 2020 Form W-4 with no entries in Step 2, Step 3, or Step 4 of the 2020 Form W-4, once withholding compliance notices are modified for 2020 withholding procedures.

These proposed regulations delete the cross reference in § 31.3402(f)(4)-2(b) of the current regulations to the withholding allowance under section 3402(m) because this cross-reference is designed to highlight a distinction relevant to Forms W-4 furnished before 1982. Even though this distinction is no longer relevant, these proposed regulations continue the general rule in the current regulations and provide that an employee who claims deductions, credits, or other items under section 3402(m) must furnish a new Form W-4 when he or she experiences a change of status to which the rules under proposed § 31.3402(f)(2)-1(b) (change of status that affects the current calendar year) or proposed § 31.3402(f)(2)-1(e) (change of status that affects the next calendar year) apply.

These proposed regulations continue the rule of the current regulations and provide that Forms W-4 that claim exemption from withholding under section 3402(n) generally are effective up to and including February 15 of the following year, and an employer may continue to rely on an employee's Form W-4 claiming exemption from withholding until February 16 of the following year. *See* section 3402(n) (providing in flush language that the Secretary shall by regulations provide for the coordination of the provisions of section 3402(n) and section 3402(f)). However, these proposed regulations provide that if a Form W-4 claiming exemption from withholding expires, and the employee does not furnish a valid Form W-4 either renewing his or her exemption or claiming a withholding allowance, the employer must treat the employee as single but having the withholding allowance provided in forms, instructions, publications, and other guidance prescribed by the IRS. Unlike the current regulations, these proposed regulations do not require the employer to put into effect a previously furnished valid Form W-4 when an employee's Form W-4 claiming exemption from withholding expires.

For 2020, Publication 15 instructs employers to treat employees who claimed exemption from withholding in 2019 and who do not furnish a new 2020 Form W-4 as single or married filing separately in Step 1(c) of the 2020 Form W-4 with no entries in Step 2, Step 3, or Step 4 of the 2020 Form W-4. This treatment is consistent with default rates described in section 8(a) of this Explanation of Provisions that apply if an employee fails to furnish a Form W-4 upon commencement of employment.

12. *Form and Contents of Withholding Allowance Certificates*

These proposed regulations provide that the withholding allowance certificate required to be furnished under section 3402(f)(2) is the Form W-4. The Form W-4 is called the "Employee's Withholding Certificate." Previously, for years 1972 through 2019, the Form W-4 was called the "Employee's Withholding Allowance Certificate." The name of the form was changed for the 2020 revision because the Form W-4 is no longer based on a number of withholding allowances valued at a particular dollar amount. Blank copies of paper Forms W-4 will be supplied to employers upon request to the IRS. An employer may also download and print Form W-4 from the IRS Internet site at www.irs.gov. These proposed regulations provide rules similar to § 31.3402(f)(5)-1(a) of the current regulations relating to substitute paper Forms W-4.

These proposed regulations provide that, unless provided otherwise in forms, instructions, publications, or other guidance prescribed by the IRS, only the Form W-4 revision in effect for a calendar year may be furnished by an employee in that calendar year and given legal effect by the employer as a new Form W-4 or to replace a previously furnished Form W-4. However, an employee may furnish the Form W-4 revision for the following calendar year in the current calendar year to take effect for the following calendar year. These proposed regulations provide an example illustrating this rule.

The Treasury Department and the IRS have received questions from payroll groups on the extent to which employers have to comply with revenue procedures relating to substitute forms when providing paper substitute Forms W-4 to employees. Rev. Proc. 2018-51, 2018-44 I.R.B. 721 (also published in Publication 1167, "General Rules and Specifications for Substitute Forms and Schedules") applies to any substitute paper Forms W-4. However, because the broader purpose of Rev. Proc. 2018-51 and Publication 1167 is to provide guidance on forms filed with the IRS, and the Form W-4 is generally not filed with the IRS, the Treasury Department and the IRS request comments on whether additional guidance is needed regarding substitute paper Forms W-4.

These proposed regulations also provide rules similar to § 31.3402(f)(5)-1(b) of the current regulations relating to invalid Forms W-4. However, these proposed regulations replace any reference to "withholding exemption certificate" with a reference to the "withholding allowance certificate" because of TCJA's changes to section 3402(f)(5) and clarify certain provisions. Under these proposed regulations, an unauthorized addition to a Form W-4 is any writing on the certificate other than the entries on the Form W-4 (e.g., name, address, and filing status). An unauthorized addition does not include entries on the Form W-4 permitted by the instructions or other guidance. Thus, a 2020 Form W-4 with an entry "Exempt" on Form W-4 in the space below Step 4(c) is not an unauthorized addition because this entry is permitted by the 2020 Form W-4 instructions. Similarly, an entry on the Form W-4 indicating an employee is a nonresident alien individual is not an unauthorized addition because this entry is permitted by Notice 1392, "Supplemental Form W-4 Instructions for Nonresident Aliens." The proposed regulations clarify, however, that an entry claiming exemption from withholding that is accompanied by any other entry on the Form W-4 (other than the employee's filing status) that could potentially affect the amount of income tax withheld from the employee's pay (i.e., an entry on Step 2, Step 3, or Step 4 of the 2020 Form W-4) is an unauthorized addition and, thus, a Form W-4 that includes such an entry is invalid.

In addition to all the rules under § 31.3402(f)(5)-1(c) of the current regulations related to electronic Form W-4 systems, these proposed regulations provide that an employer that maintains an electronic Form W-4 system for its employees to furnish Forms W-4 electronically must provide the employee with the same information as the current version of the official IRS Form W-4 available on irs.gov and must satisfy any requirements specified by the IRS in forms, publications, and other guidance. These proposed regulations further provide that an employer that maintains an electronic Form W-4 system for its employees must provide the employees the ability to claim exemption from withholding under section 3402(n) and must include the two certifications described in proposed § 31.3402(n)-1(a).

13. *Withholding Exemptions for Nonresident Alien Individuals*

Section 3402(f)(6) provides that a nonresident alien individual (other than an individual described in section 3401(a)(6)(A) or (B))[21] shall be entitled to only one withholding exemption. The Treasury Department and the IRS have concluded that the withholding exemption referenced in section 3402(f)(6) is the deduction allowed to the nonresident alien individual under section 151, which for 2018-2025 means zero under section 151(d)(5). These proposed regulations include this clarification.

In addition, proposed § 31.3402(f)(6)-1(a) provides that a nonresident alien individual (other than a nonresident individual treated as a resident under section 6013(g) and (h)) must follow administrative guidance such as forms, instructions, publications, or other guidance prescribed by the IRS that apply to the nonresident alien individual's withholding. For 2020, nonresident alien individuals should review and apply Notice 1392 to determine how to complete the 2020 Form W-4. Employers are instructed to apply special procedures in Publication 15-T for these individuals. The application of the procedures in the 2020 Publication 15-T depends on whether the nonresident alien individual has furnished a Form W-4 on or after January 1, 2020.

14. *Supplemental Wage Payments*

These proposed regulations provide that mandatory flat rate withholding under § 31.3402(g)-1(a)(2) is computed without regard to any entries on a Form W-4, including the expanded entries on the 2020 Form W-4. In addition, optional flat rate withholding under § 31.3402(g)-1(a)(7) applies without regard to any entries on the Form W-4 other than the entry claiming exempt status. However, employers who use the aggregate procedure for withholding on supplemental wages under § 31.3402(g)-1(a)(6) of the current regulations should take into consideration the Form W-4 (including a 2020 Form W-4) furnished by the employee.

15. *Alternative Withholding Methods*

The proposed regulations eliminate the combined income tax withholding and employee FICA tax withholding tables under § 31.3402(h)(4)-1(b) of the current regulations. The Treasury Department and the IRS announced their intention to eliminate these tables in section 8 of Notice 2018-92. No comments were received on this issue. As stated in section 8 of Notice 2018-92, although employers may withhold a combined amount of income and FICA tax, employers must still compute and report amounts of income tax and FICA tax separately on quarterly or annual employment tax returns and Forms W-2. Though use of the combined tables would generally reduce the number of computations in determining the withholding from wages for an employer, this difference in the number of computations has become less relevant with the advance in computational technology since 1970 when these tables were first provided.

Moreover, the combined tables are not consistent with these proposed regulations as applied to certain entries on the 2020 Form W-4. Specifically, income tax must be withheld with respect to an employee's entry in Step 4(a) (Other income) of the 2020 Form W-4, which applies proposed § 31.3402(i)-1(a)(2)(i). An employer must reduce wages by an employee's entry in Step 4(b) (Deductions) of the 2020 Form W-4, which applies proposed § 31.3402(m)-1(b). However, neither the entry in Step 4(a) nor the entry on Step 4(b) impacts employees' FICA tax liability under section 3101. Thus, an employer who is furnished a Form W-4 with entries on either Step 4(a) or Step 4(b) would not be able to use combined tables, which further diminishes the usefulness of this alternative withholding procedure.

Because section 8 of Notice 2018-92 announced the Treasury Department's and the IRS' intent to remove the combined income tax withholding and employee FICA tax withholding tables, this rule will be proposed with an effective date of January 1, 2020. Accordingly, the 2020 version of Publication 15-T does not include combined income tax withholding and employee FICA tax withholding tables. The Treasury Department and the IRS again request comments on alternative withholding procedures under section 3402(h) generally. However, the Treasury Department and the IRS do not consider allowing employees to base their withholding on a fixed dollar amount or percentage as consistent with section 3402(a).

---

[21] Although section 3402(f)(6) references section 3401(a)(6)(A) or (B), section 3401(a)(6) was amended so that there are no longer separately enumerated subparagraphs (A) or (B). Thus, this reference applies to section 3401(a)(6) and § 31.3401(a)(6)-1 of the current regulations.

16. *Additional Withholding*

These proposed regulations remove § 31.3402(i)-1 of the current regulations because this provision applies to agreements to withhold additional amounts of Federal income tax, not otherwise required, entered into before October 1, 1981. The Treasury Department and the IRS request comments on whether this rule should be retained.

17. *Increases in Withholding*

Section 3402(i) provides that the Secretary may by regulations provide for increases in the amount of withholding in cases in which an employee requests such changes. The current regulations express this rule as an agreement to withhold "an additional amount" from the employee's wages. See § 31.3402(i)-1(a). This rule was consistent with the format of Form W-4 for years prior to 2020 with respect to the line requesting an additional amount to be withheld from each payment of regular wages. To reflect the revised computational procedures on the 2020 Form W-4, these proposed regulations provide that, for amounts not otherwise required to be withheld from an employee's wages under section 3402, in addition to specifying an additional amount to withhold from the employee's wages, the employee may request that an additional amount be added to the employee's wages on Form W-4, so that the employer may withhold an additional amount of income tax resulting from this addition under the computational procedures prescribed by the IRS in forms, instructions, publications, and other guidance for the calendar year for which the Form W-4 is in effect. In addition, these proposed regulations provide that an employee may request an additional amount, not otherwise required, to be withheld from the employee's wages by selecting higher withholding rate tables.

These proposed regulations also clarify the circumstances under which the employer must comply with the employee's request. Employers must generally comply with the employee's request on a valid Form W-4 after the employer has withheld all amounts otherwise required to be withheld by Federal law (other than by amounts described in this section), state law, and local law (other than by state or local law that provides for voluntary withholding). The amounts withheld under section 3402(i) are considered tax required to be withheld under section 3402. Finally, these proposed regulations delete references to decreases in withholding under section 3402(i) because of statutory changes made in section 1581 of the Tax Reform Act of 1986, Pub. L. No. 99-514, 100 Stat 2085, 2766 (1987), which eliminated the option to decrease withholding by a set dollar amount from section 3402(i).

18. *Exemption from withholding*

These proposed regulations add certain clarifying rules to the rules in § 31.3402(n)-1 of the current regulations concerning claiming an exemption from withholding, and thereby propose to restore in substance rules that were formerly in the regulations. See 26 CFR 31.3402(n)-1(2005). To qualify for the exemption provided by section 3402(n) for a taxable year, an employee must certify that the employee incurred no liability for income tax imposed under subtitle A of the Code for the employee's preceding taxable year, and that the employee anticipates that he or she will incur no liability for income tax imposed under subtitle A for the current taxable year. These proposed regulations amend the current regulations to add a provision concerning when the employee is considered to incur no liability for income tax imposed under subtitle A. Specifically, § 31.3402(n)-1(c) of these proposed regulations provides that, for purposes of section 3402(n) and § 31.3402(n)-1 of the regulations, an employee is not considered to incur liability for income tax imposed under subtitle A if the amount of the tax is equal to or less than the total amount of credits against the tax that are allowable to the employee under chapter 1, other than the credits allowable under section 31 or 34. Proposed § 31.3402(n)-1(c) also provides that, for purposes of section 3402(n) and § 31.3402(n)-1, an employee who files a joint return under section 6013 is considered to incur liability for any tax shown on that return. These proposed regulations provide that an employee who is entitled to file a joint return under section 6013 shall not certify that the employee anticipates that he or she will incur no liability for income tax imposed by subtitle A for the employee's current taxable year if the statement would not be true in the event the employee files a joint return for the year, unless the employee filed a separate return for the preceding taxable year and anticipates that he or she will file a separate return for the current taxable year.

The rule concerning incurring liability for income tax imposed by Subtitle A and the rule concerning joint returns were in the regulations before 2006 (see 26 CFR 31.3402(n)-1(2005)) but were deleted by T.D. 9276, 71 FR 42049 (July 26, 2006). This deletion did not indicate a change in position by the Treasury Department and the IRS, and the position of the Treasury Department and the IRS on these issues has remained the same as reflected in Publication 505 for each year from 2007 through 2019. Restoring the rules to the regulations is intended to provide additional clarity and guidance as to the Treasury Department and the IRS position on these issues.

Proposed Applicability Date

The amendments set forth in this notice of proposed rulemaking are generally proposed to apply on the date of publication of a Treasury Decision adopting these rules as final regulations in the Federal Register. Taxpayers may rely on the rules set forth in this notice of proposed rulemaking, in their entirety, until the date a Treasury Decision adopting these regulations as final regulations is published in the Federal Register. However, proposed § 31.3402(f)(2)-1(g) relating to withholding compliance is proposed to apply as of the date the notice of proposed rulemaking is published in the Federal Register, proposed § 31.3402(f)(5)-1(a)(3) regarding the requirement to use the current version of Form W-4 is proposed to apply as of 30 days after the date the notice of proposed rulemaking is published in the Federal Register, and the proposed removal of § 31.3402(h)(4)-1(b) relating to the combined income tax withholding and employee FICA tax withholding tables is proposed to apply on and after January 1, 2020. Except with regard to the removal of § 31.3402(h)(4)-1(b), the proposed regulations provide that, under section 7805(b)(7), taxpayers may choose to apply the rules therein on or after January 1, 2020.

Paperwork Reduction Act

Any collection of information associated with this notice of proposed rulemaking has been submitted to the Office of Management and Budget for review under OMB control number 1545-0074 in accordance with the Paperwork Reduction Act of 1995 (44 U.S.C. 3507(d)). In general, the collection of information is required under § 3402 of the Internal Revenue Code (the Code). The Treasury Department and the IRS request comments on all aspects of information collection burdens related to these proposed regulations, including estimates for how much time it would take to comply with the paperwork burdens described in OMB control number 1545-0074 and ways for the IRS to minimize the paperwork burden. An agency may not conduct or sponsor and a person is not required to respond to a collection of information unless it displays a valid OMB control number.

Special Analyses

I. *Regulatory Planning and Review*

This regulation is not subject to review under section 6(b) of Executive Order 12866 pursuant to the Memorandum of Agreement (April 11, 2018) between the Department of the Treasury and the Office of Management and Budget regarding review of tax regulations.

II. *Regulatory Flexibility Act*

Under the Regulatory Flexibility Act (RFA) (5 U.S.C. chapter 6), it is hereby certified that these proposed regulations, if adopted, would not have a significant economic impact on a substantial number of small entities that are directly affected by the proposed regulations. The proposed regulations will apply to all employers that have an income tax withholding obligation and, therefore, are likely to affect a substantial number of small entities. Although the proposed regulations are likely to affect a substantial number of small entities, the economic impact of the regulations will not be significant.

These proposed regulations do not independently impact employers or employees because these regulations support both the 2019 and 2020 Form W-4 and related withholding procedures, and employees are not required to furnish a new Form W-4 solely because of the redesign of the Form W-4. Employees who have a Form W-4 on file with their employer from years prior to 2020 generally will continue to have their withholding determined based on that form. These proposed regulations incorporate the changes made by TCJA to sections 3401 and 3402 and conform the regulations to provide flexible and administrable rules for income tax withholding from wages to implement the 2020 Form W-4 and its related tables and computational procedures described in Publication 15-T, and to work with Forms W-4 provided in 2019 and earlier years. Any economic impact on small entities that have an income tax withholding obligation is generally a result of the change in underlying substantive tax rules which led to revisions in the method of computing withholding, not these proposed regulations. Because the proposed regulations preserve the option of continuing to use old Forms W-4 for existing employees who have not had significantly changed circumstances, the proposed regulations minimize impact of the statutory changes on employers, including small entities. Accordingly, Treasury and the IRS certify that this proposed rule will not have a significant economic impact on a substantial number of small entities pursuant to the Regulatory Flexibility Act (5 U.S.C. chapter 6). Notwithstanding this certification, the Treasury Department and the IRS invite comments on any impact this rule would have on small entities.

Pursuant to section 7805(f), this notice of proposed rulemaking has been submitted to the Chief Counsel for Advocacy of the Small Business Administration for comment on its impact on small business.

III. *Unfunded Mandates Reform Act*

Section 202 of the Unfunded Mandates Reform Act of 1995 (UMRA) requires that agencies assess anticipated costs and benefits and take certain other actions before issuing a final rule that includes any Federal mandate that may result in expenditures in any one year by a state, local, or tribal government, in the aggregate, or by the private sector, of $100 million in 1995 dollars, updated annually for inflation. This rule does not include any Federal mandate that may result in expenditures by state, local, or tribal governments, or by the private sector in excess of that threshold.

IV. *Executive Order 13132: Federalism*

Executive Order 13132 (entitled "Federalism") prohibits an agency from publishing any rule that has federalism implications if the rule either imposes substantial, direct compliance costs on state and local governments, and is not required by statute, or preempts state law, unless the agency meets the consultation and funding requirements of section 6 of the Executive Order. This proposed rule does not have federalism implications and does not impose substantial direct compliance costs on state and local governments or preempt state law within the meaning of the Executive Order.

Statement of Availability of IRS Documents

IRS Revenue Procedures, Revenue Rulings, and Notices cited in this preamble are published in the Internal Revenue Bulletin (or Cumulative Bulletin) and are available from the Superintendent of Documents, U.S. Government Publishing Office, Washington, DC 20402, or by visiting the IRS web site at *http://www.irs.gov*.

Comments and Requests for a Public Hearing

Before these proposed regulations are adopted as final regulations, consideration will be given to any electronic and written comments that are submitted timely to the IRS as prescribed in this preamble under the **"ADDRESSES"** heading. The Treasury Department and the IRS request comments on all aspects of the proposed rules. All comments will be available at *http://www.regulations.gov* or upon request. A public hearing will be scheduled if requested in writing by any person that timely submits written comments. If a public hearing is scheduled, notice of the date, time, and place for the public hearing will be published in the **Federal Register**. **Drafting Information**

The principal author of these proposed regulations is Mikhail Zhidkov, Office of the Associate Chief Counsel (Employee Benefits, Exempt Organizations, and Employment Taxes). Other personnel from the Treasury Department and the IRS participated in their development.

[¶ 49,829]   **Proposed Amendments of Regulations (REG-100814-19)**, published in the Federal Register on February 26, 2020.

[Code Sec. 274]

Deductions: Itemized deductions: Meals and entertainment expenses: Amusement expenses: Recreation activities.—Reg. §§1.274-11 and 1.274-12, providing guidance under section 274 of the Internal Revenue Code (Code) regarding certain statutory amendments made to section 274 by 2017 legislation, are proposed.

AGENCY: Internal Revenue Service (IRS), Treasury.

ACTION: Notice of proposed rulemaking.

SUMMARY: This document contains proposed regulations that provide guidance under section 274 of the Internal Revenue Code (Code) regarding certain statutory amendments made to section 274 by 2017 legislation. Specifically, the proposed regulations address the elimination of the deduction under section 274 for expenditures related to entertainment, amusement, or recreation activities, and provide guidance to determine whether an activity is of a type generally considered to be entertainment. The proposed regulations also address the limitation on the deduction of food and beverage expenses under section 274(k) and (n), including the applicability of the exceptions under section 274(e)(2), (3), (4), (7), (8), and (9). These proposed regulations affect taxpayers who pay or incur expenses for meals or entertainment in taxable years beginning after December 31, 2017. This document also provides notice of a public hearing on these proposed regulations.

DATES: Written or electronic comments must be received by April 11, 2020. Outlines of topics to be discussed at the public hearing scheduled for April 7, 2020, at 10 a.m. must be received by April 11, 2020. If no outlines are received by April 11, 2020, the public hearing will be cancelled.

ADDRESSES: Submit electronic submissions via the Federal Rulemaking Portal at *www.regulations.gov* (indicate IRS and REG-100814-19) by following the online instructions for submitting comments. Once submitted to the Federal Rulemaking Portal, comments cannot be edited or withdrawn. The Department of the Treasury (Treasury Department) and the Internal Revenue Service (IRS) will publish for public availability any comment received to their public docket, whether submitted electronically or in hard copy. Send hard copy submissions to: CC:PA:LPD:PR (REG-100814-19), room 5203, Internal Revenue Service, P.O. Box 7604, Ben Franklin Station, Washington, DC 20044.

FOR FURTHER INFORMATION CONTACT: Concerning the proposed regulations, call Patrick Clinton of the Office of Associate Chief Counsel (Income Tax and Accounting), (202) 317-7005; concerning the submission of comments, the hearing, or to be placed on the building access list to attend the hearing, call Regina Johnson, (202) 317-6901 (not toll-free numbers), or email fdms.database@irscounsel.treas.gov.

SUPPLEMENTARY INFORMATION:

Background

1. *Statutory Framework*

This document contains proposed regulations under section 274 of the Code that amend the Income Tax Regulations (26 CFR part 1). Section 274 was added to the Code by section 4 of the Revenue Act of 1962, Public Law 87-834 (76 Stat. 960) and has been amended numerous times over the years. In general, section 274 limits or disallows deductions for certain meal and entertainment expenditures that otherwise would be allowable under chapter 1 of the Code, primarily under section 162(a), which allows a deduction for ordinary and necessary expenses paid or incurred during the taxable year in carrying on any trade or business.

On December 22, 2017, section 274 was amended by section 13304 of Public Law 115-97 (131 Stat. 2054), commonly referred to as the Tax Cuts and Jobs Act, (TCJA) to revise the rules for deducting expenditures for meals and entertainment, effective for amounts paid or incurred after December 31, 2017.

2. *Business Meals and Entertainment*

Section 274(a)(1)(A) generally disallows a deduction for any item with respect to an activity of a type considered to constitute entertainment, amusement, or recreation (entertainment expenditures). However, prior to the amendment by the TCJA, section 274(a)(1)(A) provided exceptions to that disallowance if the taxpayer established that: (1) the item was directly related to the active conduct of the taxpayer's trade or business (directly related exception), or (2) in the case of an item directly preceding or following a substantial and bona fide business discussion (including business meetings at a convention or otherwise), the item was associated with the active conduct of the taxpayer's trade or business (business discussion exception). Section 274(e)(1) through (9) also provides exceptions to the rule in section 274(a) that disallows a deduction for entertainment expenditures. The TCJA did not change the application of the section 274(e) exceptions to entertainment expenditures.

Section 274(a)(1)(B) disallows a deduction for any item with respect to a facility used in connection with an activity referred to in section 274(a)(1)(A). Section 274(a)(2) provides that, for purposes of applying section 274(a)(1), dues or fees to any social, athletic, or sporting club or organization shall be treated as items with respect to facilities. Section 274(a)(3) disallows a deduction for amounts paid or incurred for membership in any club organized for business, pleasure, recreation, or other social purpose.

Prior to amendment by the TCJA, section 274(n)(1) generally limited the deduction of food or beverage expenses and entertainment expenditures to 50 percent of the amount that otherwise would have been allowable. Thus, under prior law, taxpayers could deduct 50 percent of meal expenses and 50 percent of entertainment expenditures that met the directly related or business discussion exception. Distinguishing between meal expenses and entertainment expenditures was unnecessary for purposes of the 50 percent limitation.

Section 13304(a)(1) of the TCJA repealed the directly related and business discussion exceptions to the general prohibition on deducting entertainment expenditures in section 274(a)(1)(A). Also, section 13304(a)(2)(D) of the TCJA amended the 50 percent limitation in section 274(n)(1) to remove the reference to entertainment expenditures. Thus, entertainment expenditures are no longer deductible unless one of the nine exceptions to section 274(a) in section 274(e) applies.

While the TCJA eliminated the deduction for entertainment expenses, Congress did not amend the provisions relating to the deductibility of business meals. Thus, taxpayers generally may continue to deduct 50 percent of the food and beverage expenses associated with operating their trade or business, including meals consumed by employees on work travel. See H.R. Rep. No. 115-466, at 407 (2017) (Conf. Rep.). However, as before the TCJA, no deduction is allowed for the expense of any food or beverages unless (a) the expense is not lavish or extravagant under the circumstances, and (b) the taxpayer (or an employee of the taxpayer) is present at the furnishing of the food or beverages. See section 274(k).

Prior to amendment by the TCJA, section 274(d) provided substantiation requirements for deductions under section 162 or 212 for any traveling expense (including meals and lodging while away from home), and for any item with respect to an activity of a type considered to constitute entertainment, amusement, or recreation or with respect to a facility used in connection with such activity. Section 13304(a)(2)(A) of the TCJA repealed the substantiation requirements for entertainment expenditures. Traveling expenses (including meals and lodging while away from home), however, remain subject to the section 274(d) substantiation requirements. Food and beverage expenses are subject to the substantiation requirements under section 162 and the requirement to maintain books and records under section 6001.

On October 15, 2018, the Treasury Department and the IRS published Notice 2018-76, 2018-42 I.R.B. 599, providing transitional guidance on the deductibility of expenses for certain business meals and requesting comments for future guidance to further clarify the treatment of business meal expenses and entertainment expenditures under section 274. Under the notice, taxpayers may deduct 50 percent of an otherwise allowable business meal expense if: (1) the expense is an ordinary and necessary expense under section 162(a) paid or incurred during the taxable year in carrying on any trade or business; (2) the expense is not lavish or extravagant under the circumstances; (3) the taxpayer, or an employee of the taxpayer, is present at the furnishing of the food or beverages; (4) the food and beverages are provided to a current or potential business customer, client, consultant, or similar business contact; and (5) in the case of food and beverages provided during or at an entertainment activity, the food and beverages are purchased separately from the entertainment, or the cost of the food and beverages is stated separately from the cost of the entertainment on one or more bills, invoices, or receipts. The notice provides that the entertainment disallowance rule may not be circumvented through inflating the amount charged for food and beverages.

The Treasury Department and the IRS received approximately 25 comments in response to Notice 2018-76. All comments were considered and are available at *www.regulations.gov* or upon request. Several of the comments addressing the notice are summarized in the Explanation of Provisions. However, comments recommending statutory revisions or addressing provisions outside the scope of these proposed regulations are not discussed in this preamble. The Treasury Department and the IRS continue to study comments on issues related to section 274 that are beyond the scope of these proposed regulations and may discuss those comments that are beyond the scope of these regulations in the final regulations or future guidance.

3. *Travel Meals*

Section 274(n)(1) generally limits the deduction of food or beverage expenses, including expenses for food or beverages consumed while away from home, to 50 percent of the amount that otherwise would have been allowable, unless one of the six exceptions to section 274(n) in section 274(e) applies. However, no deduction is allowed for the expense of any food or beverages unless (a) the expense is not lavish or extravagant under the circumstances, and (b) the taxpayer (or an employee of the taxpayer) is present at the furnishing of the food or beverages. See section 274(k). Section 274(d) provides substantiation requirements for traveling expenses, including food and beverage expenses incurred while on business travel away from home.

Section 274(m) provides additional limitations on travel expenses. Section 274(m)(1) generally limits the deduction for luxury water transportation expenses to twice the highest federal per diem rate allowable at the time of travel, and section 274(m)(2) generally disallows a deduction for expenses for travel as a form of education. Section 274(m)(3) provides that no deduction is allowed under chapter 1 of the Code (other than section 217) for travel expenses paid or incurred with respect to a spouse, dependent, or other individual accompanying the taxpayer (or an officer or employee of the taxpayer) on business travel, unless: (A) the spouse, dependent, or other individual is an employee of the taxpayer, (B) the travel of the spouse, dependent, or other individual is for a bona fide business purpose, and (C) such expenses would otherwise be deductible by the spouse, dependent, or other individual.

4. Employer-Provided Meals

Prior to amendment by the TCJA, section 274(n)(1) generally limited the deduction for food or beverage expenses to 50 percent of the amount that otherwise would have been allowable, subject to an exception in section 274(n)(2)(B) in the case of an expense for food or beverages that is excludable from the gross income of the recipient under section 132 by reason of section 132(e), relating to *de minimis* fringes. Section 132(e)(1) defines "*de minimis* fringe" as any property or service the value of which is, after taking into account the frequency with which similar fringes are provided by the employer to its employees, so small as to make accounting for it unreasonable or administratively impracticable. Section 132(e)(2) provides that the operation by an employer of any eating facility for employees is treated as a *de minimis* fringe if (1) the facility is located on or near the business premises of the employer, and (2) revenue derived from the facility normally equals or exceeds the direct operating costs of the facility. Thus, under prior law, employers generally were allowed to fully deduct an expense for food or beverages provided to their employees if the amount was excludable from the gross income of the employee as a *de minimis* fringe. However, the TCJA repealed section 274(n)(2)(B), meaning that expenses for food or beverages that are *de minimis* fringes under section 132(e) are no longer excepted from section 274(n)(1). As a result, these expenses, like other food or beverage expenses generally, are subject to the 50 percent limitation unless one of the six exceptions to section 274(n) in section 274(e) applies.

5. Section 274(e) Exceptions to Section 274(k) and (n)

Section 274(k)(2) and (n)(2)(A) provide that the limitations on the deduction of food or beverage expenses in sections 274(k)(1) and (n)(1), respectively, do not apply if the expense is described in paragraph (2), (3), (4), (7), (8), or (9) of section 274(e). Expenses described in paragraph (1), (5), and (6) of section 274(e) are not exceptions to the limitations on the deduction of food or beverage expenses in section 274(k)(1) and (n)(1). However, they are exceptions to the disallowance on deduction of entertainment expenses in section 274(a).

Section 274(e)(2) applies to expenses for goods, services, and facilities to the extent that the expenses are treated as compensation to the recipient. Section 274(e)(3) applies to expenses incurred by a taxpayer in connection with the performance of services for an employer or other person under a reimbursement or other expense allowance arrangement. Section 274(e)(4) applies to expenses for recreational, social, or similar activities for employees. Section 274(e)(7) applies to expenses for goods, services, and facilities made available to the general public. Section 274(e)(8) applies to expenses for goods or services that are sold by the taxpayer in a bona fide transaction for adequate and full consideration in money or money's worth. Section 274(e)(9) applies to expenses for goods, services, and facilities to the extent that the expenses are treated as income to a person other than an employee.

Explanation of Provisions

The proposed regulations describe and clarify the statutory requirements of section 274(a), 274(k), and 274(n), as well as the applicability of certain exceptions under section 274(e) to food or beverage expenses. To implement the TCJA's disallowance of entertainment expenditures under section 274(a), the proposed regulations add a new section at § 1.274-11 (proposed § 1.274-11) for entertainment expenditures paid or incurred after December 31, 2017. The proposed regulations also add a new section at § 1.274-12 (proposed § 1.274-12) to address food or beverage expenses under section 274(k) and 274(n) paid or incurred after December 31, 2017, including the application of the exceptions in section 274(e)(2), (3), (4), (7), (8), and (9). Specifically, proposed § 1.274-12 addresses expenses for business meals as described in Notice 2018-76, as well as expenses for other meals including travel meals and employer-provided meals.

1. Entertainment Expenditures

A. In General

Proposed § 1.274-11 restates the statutory rules under section 274(a), including the application of the entertainment deduction disallowance rule to dues or fees to any social, athletic, or sporting club or organization. The proposed regulations substantially incorporate the existing definition of entertainment in § 1.274-2(b)(1), with minor modifications to remove outdated language. The proposed regulations also confirm that the nine exceptions in section 274(e) continue to apply to entertainment expenditures under section 274(a). Finally, as described further in part I.B. of this Explanation of Provisions, the proposed regulations provide that for purposes of section 274(a), the term "entertainment" does not include food or beverages unless the food or beverages are provided at or during an entertainment activity and the costs of the food or beverages are not separately stated from the entertainment costs.

Taxpayers may continue to rely upon the existing rules in § 1.274-2, to the extent applicable and not superseded by the TCJA, for entertainment expenditures paid or incurred after December 31, 2017.

B. Separately Stated Food or Beverages not Entertainment

The proposed regulations substantially incorporate the guidance in Notice 2018-76 to distinguish between entertainment expenditures and food or beverage expenses in the context of business meals provided at or during an entertainment activity. In addition, the proposed regulations generally apply the guidance in Notice 2018-76 to all food or beverages, including travel meals and employer-provided meals, provided at or during an entertainment activity. However, in response to a comment on the notice, the proposed regulations further clarify the rules applicable to food or beverages provided at or during an entertainment activity.

Notice 2018-76 explains that in the case of food and beverages provided during or at an entertainment activity, the taxpayer may deduct 50 percent of an otherwise allowable business expense if the food and beverages are purchased separately from the entertainment, or if the cost of the food and beverages is stated separately from the cost of the entertainment on one or more bills, invoices, or receipts. The notice provides that the entertainment disallowance rule may not be circumvented through inflating the amount charged for food and beverages. Taxpayers may continue to rely on the guidance in Notice 2018-76 until these proposed regulations are finalized.

One commenter asked for clarification of the requirement in the notice that the entertainment disallowance rule may not be circumvented by inflating the amount charged for food and beverages on one or more bills, invoices, or receipts. In response, the proposed regulations provide that the amount charged for food or beverages on a bill, invoice, or receipt must reflect the venue's usual selling cost for those items if they were to be purchased separately from the entertainment, or must approximate the reasonable value of those items. Further, the proposed regulations provide that unless food or beverages provided at or during an entertainment activity are purchased separately from the entertainment, or the cost of the food or beverages is stated separately from the cost of the entertainment on one or more bills, invoices, or receipts, no allocation can be made and the entire amount is a nondeductible entertainment expenditure. Finally, in accordance with the TCJA's amendments to section 274(a)(1) specifically repealing the "directly related" and "business discussion" exceptions to the general disallowance rule for entertainment expenditures, the proposed regulations clarify that the entertainment disallowance rule applies whether or not the expenditure for the activity is related to or associated with the active conduct of the taxpayer's trade or business. The Treasury Department and the IRS request comments on these rules.

2. *Food or Beverage Expenses*

A. *Business Meal Expenses*

As noted earlier in this Explanation of Provisions, the proposed regulations substantially incorporate the guidance in Notice 2018-76 addressing business meals provided during or at an entertainment activity. The proposed regulations also incorporate other statutory requirements taxpayers must meet to deduct 50 percent of an otherwise allowable business meal expense. Specifically, the expense must not be lavish or extravagant under the circumstances and the taxpayer, or an employee of the taxpayer, must be present at the furnishing of the food or beverages.

The proposed regulations also address the general requirement in Notice 2018-76 that the food and beverages be provided to a business contact, which was described in the notice as a "current or potential business customer, client, consultant, or similar business contact." This requirement is to ensure that the meal expenses are directly connected with or pertaining to the taxpayer's trade or business, as required under section 162. One commenter on Notice 2018-76 requested a definition of "potential business contact," suggesting that the term could be interpreted broadly to include almost anyone. In response to the comment, and to conform the rule more closely to the trade or business requirement in section 162, the proposed regulations follow the definition of "business associate" as currently provided in §1.274-2(b)(2)(iii). Thus, the proposed regulations provide that the food or beverages must be provided to a "person with whom the taxpayer could reasonably expect to engage or deal in the active conduct of the taxpayer's trade or business such as the taxpayer's customer, client, supplier, employee, agent, partner, or professional adviser, whether established or prospective." In addition to clarifying this definition for purposes of determining whether a business meal expense is deductible, the proposed regulations apply this standard to the deduction of food or beverage expenses generally. In particular, the proposed regulations include employees as a type of business associate, making the standard applicable to employer-provided meals as well as to situations in which a taxpayer provides meals to both employees and non-employee business associates at the same event. The Treasury Department and the IRS request comments on this standard.

B. *Travel Meal Expenses*

Although the TCJA did not specifically amend the rules for travel expenses, the proposed regulations are intended to provide comprehensive rules for food and beverage expenses and thus apply the general rules for meal expenses from Notice 2018-76, as revised in these proposed regulations, to travel meals. In addition, the proposed regulations incorporate the substantiation requirements in section 274(d), unchanged by the TCJA, to travel meals. Finally, the proposed regulations apply the limitations in section 274(m)(3) to expenses for food or beverages paid or incurred while on travel for spouses, dependents or other individuals accompanying the taxpayer (or an officer or employee of the taxpayer) on business travel. These limitations do not apply to deductions for moving expenses under section 217. However, the TCJA amended section 217 to suspend the deduction for moving expenses for taxable years beginning after December 31, 2017, and before January 1, 2026, except with respect to certain members of the Armed Forces. Thus, the proposed regulations revise the reference to section 217 to reflect that amendment.

C. *Other Food or Beverage Expenses*

The proposed regulations apply the business meal guidance in Notice 2018-76, as revised in these proposed regulations, to food or beverage expenses generally. Under section 274(n)(1), the deduction for food or beverage expenses generally is limited to 50 percent of the amount that would otherwise be allowable. Prior to the TCJA, under section 274(n)(2)(B), expenses for food or beverages that were excludable from employee income as *de minimis* fringe benefits under section 132(e) were not subject to the 50 percent deduction limitation under section 274(n)(1) and could be fully deducted. The TCJA repealed section 274(n)(2)(B) so that expenses for food or beverages excludable from employee income under section 132(e) are subject to the section 274(n)(1) deduction limitation unless another exception under section 274(n)(2) applies.

Under section 274(k)(1), in order for food or beverage expenses to be deductible the food or beverages must not be lavish or extravagant under the circumstances and the taxpayer or an employee of the taxpayer must be present at the furnishing of the food or beverages. However, as discussed in part E of this Explanation of Provisions, section 274(e) provides six exceptions to the limitations on the deduction of food or beverages in section 274(k)(1) and 274(n)(1) and the proposed regulations explain how those exceptions apply.

In response to comments that the Treasury Department and the IRS received after enactment of the TCJA, the proposed regulations address several scenarios involving the deductibility of food or beverage expenses. For example, commenters requested guidance on the deductibility of expenses for: (i) food or beverages provided to food service workers who consume the food or beverages while working in a restaurant or catering business; (ii) snacks available to employees in a pantry, break room, or copy room; (iii) refreshments provided by a real estate agent at an open house; (iv) food or beverages provided by a seasonal camp to camp counselors; (v) food or beverages provided to employees at a company cafeteria; and (vi) food or beverages provided at company holiday parties and picnics. The Treasury Department and the IRS considered all comments received and provide examples in proposed §1.274-12(c) to address many of the factual scenarios raised by commenters.

D. *Definitions*

The proposed regulations provide that the deduction limitation rules generally apply to all food and beverages, whether characterized as meals, snacks, or other types of food or beverage items. In addition, unless one of the six exceptions under section 274(n)(2)(A) applies, the deduction limitations apply regardless of whether the food or beverages are treated as *de minimis* fringe benefits under section 132(e).

The proposed regulations define food or beverage expenses to mean the cost of food or beverages, including any delivery fees, tips, and sales tax. In the case of employer-provided meals at an eating facility, food or beverage expenses do not include expenses for the operation of the eating facility such as salaries of employees preparing and serving meals, and other overhead costs.

E. *Section 274(e) Exceptions to Section 274(k) and (n)*

Section 274(k)(2) and (n)(2)(A) provide that the limitations on deductions in section 274(k)(1) and (n)(1), respectively, do not apply to any expense described in section 274(e)(2), (3), (4), (7), (8), and (9). The proposed regulations, therefore, provide that the deduction limitations are not applicable to expenditures for business meals, travel meals, or other food or beverages that fall within one of these exceptions.

i. Expenses Treated as Compensation under Section 274(e)(2) or (e)(9)

Pursuant to section 274(e)(2), the proposed regulations provide that the limitations in section 274(k)(1) and (n)(1) do not apply to expenditures for food or beverages of an employee of the taxpayer (including food or beverages of a spouse, dependent or other individual accompanying the employee on travel described in section 274(m)(3)), to the extent the taxpayer treats the expenses as compensation to the employee on the taxpayer's income tax return as originally filed, and as wages to the employee for purposes of withholding under chapter 24 of the Code relating to collection of income tax at source on wages.

Pursuant to section 274(e)(9), the proposed regulations provide that the limitations in section 274(k)(1) and (n)(1) do not apply to expenses for food or beverages of a person who is not an employee of the taxpayer to the extent the expenses are includible in the gross income of the recipient of the food or beverages as compensation for services rendered, or as a prize or award under section 74.

The Treasury Department and the IRS are aware that some taxpayers may attempt to claim a full deduction under section 274(e)(2) or (e)(9) by including a value that is less than the amount required to be included under §1.61-21, which provides the rules for valuation of fringe benefits, or by purportedly including a value of zero, as compensation and as wages to the employee, or as includible in gross income by a person who is not an employee of the taxpayer. The proposed regulations therefore provide that expenses for food or beverages with a value that is less than the amount required to be included in gross income under §1.61-21, or for which the amount required to be included in gross income is zero, will not be considered as having been treated as compensation and as wages to the employee, or as includible in gross income by a recipient of the food or beverages who is not an employee of the taxpayer for purposes of section 274(e)(2) and (e)(9).

ii. Reimbursed Food or Beverage Expenses

Pursuant to section 274(e)(3), the proposed regulations provide that in the case of expenses for food or beverages paid or incurred by one person in connection with the performance of services for another person (whether or not the other person is an employer) under a reimbursement or other expense allowance arrangement, the limitations on deductions in section 274(k)(1) and (n)(1) apply either to the person who makes the expenditure or to the person who actually bears the expense, but not to both. Section 274(e)(3)(B) provides that if the services are performed for a person other than an employer, such as by an independent contractor, the exception in section 274(e)(3) applies only if the taxpayer, in this case, the independent contractor, accounts, to the extent provided by section 274(d), to such person. The proposed regulations therefore provide that the deduction limitations in section 274(k)(1) and (n)(1) apply to an independent contractor unless, under a reimbursement or other expense allowance arrangement, the contractor accounts to the client or customer with substantiation that satisfies the requirements of section 274(d).

iii. Recreational Expenses for Employees

Pursuant to section 274(e)(4), the proposed regulations provide that any food or beverage expense paid or incurred by a taxpayer for a recreational, social, or similar activity, primarily for the benefit of the taxpayer's employees, is not subject to the deduction limitations in section 274(k)(1) and (n)(1). However, activities that discriminate in favor of highly compensated employees, officers, shareholders or others who own a 10-percent or greater interest in the business are not considered paid or incurred primarily for the benefit of employees.

The Treasury Department and the IRS have received several questions and comments on the deductibility of food or beverage expenses for recreational, social and similar activities for employees. Many commenters requested confirmation that food or beverage expenses for company holiday parties and picnics that do not discriminate in favor of highly compensated employees are not subject to the deduction limitations in section 274(k)(1) and (n)(1) because the exception in section 274(e)(4) applies. Commenters also suggested that expenses for snacks and beverages available to all employees in a pantry, break room, or copy room are not subject to the deduction limitations in section 274(k)(1) and (n)(1) because the exception in section 274(e)(4) applies.

In response to the questions and comments received, the proposed regulations confirm the rules in the existing regulations that the exception in section 274(e)(4) applies to food or beverage expenses for company holiday parties, annual picnics, or summer outings that do not discriminate in favor of highly compensated employees. However, an example in the proposed regulations demonstrates the section 274(e)(4) exception does not apply to free food or beverages provided in a break room because the mere provision or availability of food or beverages is not a recreational, social, or similar activity, despite the fact that employees may incidentally socialize while they are in the break room.

In addition, the proposed regulations provide that the exception in section 274(e)(4) does not apply to food or beverage expenses that are excludable under section 119 as meals provided for the convenience of the employer. Because these food or beverages are, by definition, furnished for the employer's convenience, they cannot also be primarily for the benefit of the employees, even if some social activity occurs during the provision of food or beverages.

iv. Items Available to the Public

Pursuant to section 274(e)(7), the proposed regulations provide that any food or beverage expense of a taxpayer is not subject to the deduction limitations in section 274(k)(1) and (n)(1) to the extent the food or beverages are made available to the general public. In addition, the proposed regulations provide that this exception applies to the entire amount of the expense for food or beverages provided to employees if similar food or beverages are provided by the employer to, and are primarily consumed by, the general public. For this purpose, "primarily consumed" means greater than 50 percent of actual or reasonably estimated consumption, and "general public" includes, but is not limited to, customers, clients, and visitors. The proposed regulations also provide that the general public does not include employees, partners, or independent contractors of the taxpayer. Further, an exclusive list of guests also is not considered the general public. See *Churchill Downs, Inc. v. Commissioner*, 307 F.3d 423 (6th Cir. 2002).

Commenters have requested guidance as to whether the exception in section 274(e)(7) for food or beverages made available by the taxpayer to the general public applies in various situations. The Treasury Department and the IRS considered these comments and included examples in the proposed regulations to illustrate that the exception in section 274(e)(7) generally applies to the entire food or beverage expense if the food or beverages are primarily consumed by the general public.

v. Goods or Services Sold to Customers

Pursuant to section 274(e)(8), the proposed regulations provide that any expense for food or beverages that are sold to customers in a bona fide transaction for an adequate and full consideration in money or money's worth is not subject to the deduction limitations in section 274(k)(1) and (n)(1). The proposed regulations clarify that money or money's worth does not include payment through services provided.

The Treasury Department and the IRS are aware of concerns raised by commenters that it is a common business practice for employers of restaurant and food service workers to provide food or beverages at no cost or at a discount to their employees. The Joint Committee on Taxation's Bluebook on the TCJA explains that amendments made by the TCJA to limit the deduction for expenses of the employer associated with providing food or beverages to employees through an employer-operated eating facility that meets the requirements of section 132(e)(2) do not affect other exceptions to the 50-percent limitation on deductions for food or beverage expenses. For example, a restaurant or catering business may continue to deduct 100 percent of its costs for food or beverage items, purchased in connection with preparing and providing meals to its paying customers, which are also consumed at the worksite by employees who work in the employer's restaurant or catering business. Joint Committee on Taxation, *General Explanation of Public Law 115-97* (JCS-1-18), at 186 n.940 and at 188 n.956, December 2018. The proposed regulations incorporate this interpretation of the exception in section 274(e)(8).

Finally, the proposed regulations provide that for purposes of the section 274(e)(8) exception to the deduction limitations in section 274(k)(1) and (n)(1), the term "customer" includes anyone who is sold food or beverages in a bona fide transaction for an adequate and full consideration in money or money's worth. For example, employees of the taxpayer are customers when they purchase food or beverages from the taxpayer in a bona fide transaction for arm's length, fair market value prices.

Request for Comments

The Treasury Department and the IRS request comments on all aspects of these proposed regulations. Regarding entertainment expenditures under proposed §1.274-11, comments are specifically requested about the definition of entertainment, including how to distinguish entertainment from advertising and travel; the use of the objective test in defining entertainment activities; the application of the exceptions in section 274(e) to entertainment expenditures; and whether additional issues or examples should be addressed in the regulations. Regarding food or beverage expenses under proposed § 1.274-12, comments are specifically requested about the changes from Notice 2018-76 to the rules for business meals; the application of the exceptions in section 274(e) to food or beverage expenses; and whether additional issues or examples should be addressed in the regulations.

Proposed Applicability Date

Section 7805(b)(1)(A) and (B) of the Code generally provide that no temporary, proposed, or final regulation relating to the internal revenue laws may apply to any taxable period ending before the earliest of (A) the date on which the regulation is filed with the **Federal Register**, or (B) in the case of a final regulation, the date on which a proposed or temporary regulation to which the final regulation relates was filed with the **Federal Register**.

Consistent with authority provided by section 7805(b)(1)(A), these regulations are proposed to apply for taxable years that begin on or after the date of publication of a Treasury decision adopting these rules as final regulations in the **Federal Register**. Pending the issuance of the final regulations, a taxpayer may rely on these proposed regulations for entertainment expenditures and food or beverage expenses, as applicable, paid or incurred after December 31, 2017. In addition, a taxpayer may rely on the guidance in Notice 2018-76 until these proposed regulations are finalized.

Special Analyses

These proposed regulations are not subject to review under section 6(b) of Executive Order 12866 pursuant to the Memorandum of Agreement (April 11, 2018) between the Treasury Department and the Office of Management and Budget regarding review of tax regulations.

In accordance with the Regulatory Flexibility Act (5 U.S.C. chapter 6), it is hereby certified that this proposed rule will not have a significant economic impact on a substantial number of small entities. Although the rule may affect a substantial number of small entities, the economic impact of the regulations is not likely to be significant. Data are not readily available about the number of taxpayers affected, but the number is likely to be substantial for both large and small entities because the rule may affect entities that incur meal and entertainment expenses. The economic impact of these regulations is not likely to be significant, however, because these proposed regulations substantially incorporate prior guidance and otherwise clarify the application of the TCJA changes to section 274 related to meals and entertainment. The proposed regulations will assist taxpayers in understanding the changes to section 274 and make it easier for taxpayers to comply with those changes. Notwithstanding this certification, the Treasury Department and the IRS welcome comments on the impact of these regulations on small entities.

Pursuant to section 7805(f), these proposed regulations have been submitted to the Chief Counsel for Advocacy of the Small Business Administration for comment on their impact on small business.

Unfunded Mandates Reform Act

Section 202 of the Unfunded Mandates Reform Act of 1995 (UMRA) requires that agencies assess anticipated costs and benefits and take certain other actions before issuing a final rule that includes any Federal mandate that may result in expenditures in any one year by a state, local, or tribal government, in the aggregate, or by the private sector, of $100 million (updated annually for inflation). This rule does not include any Federal mandate that may result in expenditures by state, local, or tribal governments, or by the private sector in excess of that threshold.

Executive Order 13132: Federalism

Executive Order 13132 (entitled "Federalism") prohibits an agency from publishing any rule that has federalism implications if the rule either imposes substantial, direct compliance costs on state and local governments, and is not required by statute, or preempts state law, unless the agency meets the consultation and funding requirements of section 6 of the Executive order. This proposed rule does not have federalism implications and does not impose substantial direct compliance costs on state and local governments or preempt state law within the meaning of the Executive order.

Statement of Availability of IRS Documents

Notices cited in this preamble are published in the Internal Revenue Bulletin (or Cumulative Bulletin) and are available from the Superintendent of Documents, U.S. Government Publishing Office, Washington, DC 20402, or by visiting the IRS web site at *http://www.irs.gov*.

Comments

Before these proposed regulations are adopted as final regulations, consideration will be given to any electronic and written comments that are submitted timely to the IRS as prescribed in this preamble under the **"ADDRESSES"** heading. The Treasury Department and the IRS request comments on all aspects of the proposed rules. All comments will be available at *http://www.regulations.gov* or upon request.

Drafting Information

The principal author of this proposed regulation is Patrick Clinton, Office of the Associate Chief Counsel (Income Tax & Accounting). Other personnel from the Treasury Department and the IRS participated in their development.

[¶ 49,830]   **Proposed Amendments of Regulations (REG-132529-17)**, published in the Federal Register on April 2, 2020.

[Code Secs. 338, 381, 801, 806, 807, 809, 810, 816, 817A, 818, 848, 6012 and 9100]

Life insurance: Life insurance company reserves: Computation.—Reg. §§ 1.807-3, 1.807-4 and 1.816-1 and amendments of Reg. §§ 1.338-11, 1.381(c)(22)-1, 1.801-2, 1.801-5, 1.801-7, 1.801-8, 1.806-4, 1.807-1, 1.809-2, 1.809-5, 1.810-3, 1.817A-0, 1.817A-1, 1.818-2, 1.818-4, 1.848-1, 1.6012-2 and 301.9100-6T, providing guidance on the computation of life insurance reserves and the change in basis of computing certain reserves of insurance companies, are proposed.

AGENCY: Internal Revenue Service (IRS), Treasury.

ACTION: Notice of proposed rulemaking.

SUMMARY: This document contains proposed regulations that provide guidance on the computation of life insurance reserves and the change in basis of computing certain reserves of insurance companies. These proposed regulations implement recent legislative changes to the Internal Revenue Code. This document invites comments on these proposed regulations. This document affects entities taxable as insurance companies.

DATES: Written or electronic comments and requests for a public hearing must be received by June 1, 2020.

ADDRESSES: Submit electronic submissions via the Federal eRulemaking Portal at *www.regulations.gov* (indicate IRS and REG-132529-17) by following the online instructions for submitting comments. Once submitted to the Federal eRulemaking Portal, comments cannot be edited or withdrawn. The Department of the Treasury (Treasury Department) and the IRS will publish for public availability any comment received to its public docket, whether submitted electronically or in hard copy. Send hard copy submissions to: CC:PA:LPD:PR (REG-132529-17), Room 5203, Internal Revenue Service, P.O. Box 7604, Ben Franklin Station, Washington, DC 20044. FOR FURTHER INFORMATION CONTACT: Concerning the proposed regulations, Dan Phillips, (202) 317-6995; concerning submissions of comments and requests for a public hearing, Regina Johnson, (202) 317-5177 or *fdms.database@irscounsel.treas.gov* (not toll-free numbers).

SUPPLEMENTARY INFORMATION:

Background

This document contains proposed amendments to 26 CFR part 1 under sections 807 and 816 of the Internal Revenue Code (Code). Sections 807 and 816 were added to the Code by section 211(a) of the Deficit Reduction Act of 1984, Public Law 98-369, 98 Stat. 494. Section 807 was amended by sections 13513 and 13517 of the Tax Cuts and Jobs Act, Public Law 115-97, 131 Stat. 2054, 2143, 2144 (2017) (TCJA). These amendments by the TCJA apply to taxable years beginning after December 31, 2017.

This document also proposes to amend or remove the following regulations in 26 CFR: §§1.338-11, 1.381(c)(22)-1, 1.801-2, 1.801-5, 1.801-7, 1.801-8, 1.806-4, 1.807-1, 1.809-2, 1.809-5, 1.810-3, 1.817A-0, 1.817A-1, 1.818-2, 1.818-4, 1.848-1, 1.6012-2, and 301.9100-6T. These proposed changes are conforming changes to regulations that (i) relate to repealed or amended law, (ii) reference regulations that are proposed to be removed, (iii) have no future application, or (iv) relate to other regulations proposed by this document.

A. *Reserves Taken into Account in Determining Life Insurance Company Taxable Income*

Section 801(a) imposes a tax on the life insurance company taxable income of every life insurance company. Section 801(b) defines life insurance company taxable income to mean life insurance gross income, reduced by life insurance deductions. Under section 803(a)(2), life insurance gross income includes a net decrease in items described in section 807(c) as required by section 807(a). Under sections 804 and 805(a)(2), life insurance deductions include a deduction for a net increase in items as required by section 807(b).

The items described in section 807(c) are: (i) life insurance reserves (as defined in section 816(b)); (ii) unearned premiums and unpaid losses included in total reserves; (iii) amounts that are discounted at the appropriate rate of interest to satisfy obligations under insurance and annuity contracts that do not involve life, accident, or health contingencies when the computation is made; (iv) dividend accumulations and other amounts held at interest in connection with insurance and annuity contracts; (v) premiums received in advance and liabilities for premium deposit funds; and (vi) reasonable special contingency reserves under contracts of group term life insurance or group accident and health insurance that are held for retired lives, premium stabilization, or a combination of both.

B. *Life Insurance Reserves Taken into Account in Determining Premiums Earned for a Nonlife Insurance Company*

Section 831(a) generally imposes a tax on the taxable income of every insurance company other than a life insurance company (a nonlife insurance company). Section 832 defines taxable income for this purpose to be gross income (as defined in section 832(b)(1)) less allowed deductions. Section 832(b)(1) provides that gross income includes underwriting income, and section 832(b)(3) provides that underwriting income means premiums earned on insurance contracts during the taxable year less losses incurred and expenses incurred.

Under sections 832(b)(4) and 832(b)(7)(A), premiums earned on insurance contracts during the taxable year are reduced by life insurance reserves at the end of the taxable year and increased by life insurance reserves at the end of the preceding taxable year. For this purpose, life insurance reserves are defined in section 816(b) but determined under section 807(d).

C. *Method of Computing Life Insurance Reserves for Purposes of Determining Income*

1. *Prior to modification by the TCJA*

Section 807(d) sets forth rules for computing the amount of life insurance reserves for a contract for purposes of determining life insurance company taxable income and for purposes of computing premiums earned for a nonlife insurance company. Prior to amendment by the TCJA, section 807(d)(1) provided that the amount of the life insurance reserves for any contract was the greater of the net surrender value of the contract (determined under section 807(e)(1)) or the federally prescribed reserve determined under section 807(d)(2). This amount, however, could not exceed the amount that would have been taken into account with respect to the contract in determining statutory reserves (as defined in prior section 807(d)(6)).

Prior section 807(d)(2) provided that the federally prescribed reserve for a contract was computed using (i) the tax reserve method applicable to the contract, (ii) the greater of the applicable Federal interest rate or the prevailing state assumed interest rate, and (iii) the prevailing commissioners' standard tables for mortality and morbidity, adjusted as appropriate to reflect the risks (such as substandard risks) incurred under the contract that were not otherwise taken into account.

In the case of a contract to which the Commissioners' Reserve Valuation Method (CRVM) applied (generally, a life insurance contract), prior sections 807(d)(3)(A)(i) and 807(d)(3)(B)(i) provided that the tax reserve method applicable to the contract was the CRVM as prescribed by the National Association of Insurance Commissioners (NAIC) that was in effect on the date the contract was issued. Similarly, in the case of a contract to which the Commissioners' Annuity Reserve Valuation Method (CARVM) applied (generally, an annuity contract), prior sections 807(d)(3)(A)(ii) and 807(d)(3)(B)(ii) provided that the tax reserve method applicable to the contract was the CARVM as prescribed by the NAIC that was in effect on the date the contract was issued. Other parameters, such as the appropriate interest rate and mortality tables, were likewise generally determined with reference to the date the contract was issued.

Section 1.807-1 provided instructions on what mortality and morbidity tables taxpayers should have used to compute life insurance reserves for a contract for which there were no applicable commissioners' standard tables when the contract was issued. Section 1.807-1 was published as a final regulation in the **Federal Register** (54 FR 52933) on December 26, 1989 (T.D. 8278).

2. *Principle-based reserves and IRS notices*

In recent years, the NAIC has promulgated and states have adopted principle-based reserving methods to better reflect the economics of more complex life insurance and annuity products. Principle-based reserves (PBR) are intended to replace a more formulaic approach to determining policy reserves with an approach that takes into account a range of future economic conditions and more closely reflects the risks of complex insurance products. *See, e.g., Principle-Based Reserves for Life Products under the NAIC Valuation Manual*, Actuarial Standard of Practice No. 52, Actuarial Standards Board, Sept. 2017, App 1.

Federal income tax issues arose when trying to apply the requirements of prior section 807(d) to tax reserve methods that were PBR methods. It was not clear how aspects of PBR methods fit within the statutory requirements of prior section 807(d). For example, a PBR method may require reserves to be computed based on many different scenarios in which many different interest rate assumptions are made, but prior section 807(d) required the use of a single interest rate when computing the reserve for a contract.

In 2008, the IRS issued Notice 2008-18, 2008-1 C.B. 363, to alert life insurance companies that Federal tax issues might arise as a result of the then-proposed PBR methods, identify areas of concern, and invite comments on these and other issues. Several comments were received and considered.

In 2010, the IRS issued Notice 2010-29, 2010-15 I.R.B. 547, to provide interim guidance to issuers of variable annuity contracts as a result of the adoption by the NAIC of Actuarial Guideline 43 (AG 43), which describes a PBR method. The interim guidance provided, among other things, that (i) for purposes of determining whether an insurance company satisfies the 50 percent of reserves test for qualification as a life insurance company under section 816(a), the Standard Scenario Amount (SSA) determined under AG 43 is included in life insurance reserves as defined in section 816(b) and total reserves as defined in section 816(c), (ii) for purposes of applying the statutory reserve cap of section 807(d)(1), the term "statutory reserves" under prior section 807(d)(6) (current section 807(d)(4)) includes the SSA, provided the requirements of prior section 807(d)(6) are otherwise met, and (iii) for purposes of determining the amount of the reserve under prior section 807(d)(2) for contracts falling within the scope of AG 43 and issued on or after December 31, 2009, the provisions for determining the SSA are taken into account and the provisions for determining the conditional tail expectation amount (a component of AG 43) are not taken into account.

3. Modification by the TCJA

Section 13517 of the TCJA amended section 807(d)(1) to provide generally that, for purposes of determining life insurance company taxable income, the amount of the life insurance reserves for any contract (other than a contract to which section 807(d)(1)(B) applies (relating to variable contracts)), is the greater of the net surrender value of such contract or 92.81 percent of the reserve determined under section 807(d)(2). The amount of the life insurance reserve for a variable contract, as specified in amended section 807(d)(1)(B), is the sum of (i) the greater of the net surrender value of such contract or the portion of the reserve that is separately accounted for under section 817 and (ii) 92.81 percent of the excess (if any) of the reserve determined under section 807(d)(2) over the amount in clause (i).

Section 13517 of the TCJA amended prior section 807(d)(2) to provide that the amount of the reserve under section 807(d)(2) is determined using the tax reserve method applicable to such contract. Section 13517 of the TCJA also amended prior section 807(d)(3) to provide generally that the tax reserve method applicable to a contract is the method prescribed by the NAIC that applies to the contract as of the date the reserve is determined, not the date the contract was issued, as was required prior to the TCJA.

The TCJA did not change the treatment of asset adequacy reserves. Asset adequacy reserves and similar reserves that address solvency concerns of state regulators but do not meet technical actuarial requirements have long been excluded from life insurance reserves for Federal income tax purposes. *See, e.g.,* Rev. Rul. 67-435, 1967-2 C.B. 232; *Old Line Insurance Co. v. Commissioner,* 13 B.T.A. 758 (1928). The Conference Report to the TCJA states that "[a]s under present law, no deduction for asset adequacy reserves or deficiency reserves is allowed." H.R. Rep. No. 115-466, at 477 (2017) (Conference Report). *See also* Staff of the Joint Committee on Taxation, 115th Cong., General Explanation of Public Law 115-97, 235 (Comm. Print 2018) (Bluebook).

Section 13517(c)(3) of the TCJA provided a transition rule that requires any difference between (i) the amount of life insurance reserves with respect to any contract as of the close of the taxable year preceding the first taxable year beginning after December 31, 2017, computed using the method prescribed by the TCJA and (ii) the amount of such reserves computed using the method prior to the amendments by the TCJA, to be taken into account over the eight succeeding taxable years. Rev. Proc. 2019-34, 2019-35 I.R.B. 669, provides simplified procedures for an insurance company to obtain consent of the Commissioner of Internal Revenue or his delegate (Commissioner) to change its method of accounting for life insurance reserves to comply with the amendments to section 807 made by the TCJA.

D. Change in Basis of Computing Reserves

1. Prior to modification by the TCJA

a. Statutory provisions

Prior to amendment by the TCJA, section 807(f)(1) provided that if the basis for determining any item described in section 807(c) (for example, life insurance reserves) as of the close of any taxable year differed from the basis for that determination as of the close of the preceding taxable year, then so much of the difference between the amount of the items at the close of the taxable year computed on the new basis and the amount of the item at the close of the taxable year computed on the old basis, as is attributable to contracts issued before the taxable year, was taken into account ratably for each of the succeeding ten taxable years.

Prior section 807(f) was substantially similar to and replaced prior section 810(d) as enacted by the Life Insurance Company Income Tax Act of 1959, Public Law 86-69, 73 Stat. 112 (1959). By enacting prior section 810(d), Congress provided a specific treatment for adjustments resulting from a change in method of computing reserves that otherwise would have been subject to the general tax rules under section 481 for changes in method of accounting. *See, e.g., American General Life and Accident Insurance Co. v. United States,* 90-1 USTC (CCH) ¶ 50,010 (M.D. Tenn.1989)

(section 481 is a more general provision dealing with a broad variety of cases and section 810, on the other hand, is much more specific and deals with a very narrow and limited type of change in method of accounting).

If a company ceases to qualify as a life insurance company, section 807(f)(2), which was not amended by the TCJA, requires, except as provided in section 381(c)(22), that the balance of any adjustment under section 807(f) be taken into account in the taxable year preceding the taxable year in which the taxpayer no longer qualifies as a life insurance company.

b. Regulatory provisions

Regulations relating to the change in method of computing reserves were adopted under Code provisions that existed prior to their repeal by the Deficit Reduction Act of 1984. If and to the extent the Deficit Reduction Act of 1984 incorporated provisions of prior law, regulations and other guidance generally continued to serve as interpretive guides to the new provisions. H.R. Rep. No. 98-432, pt. 2, at 1401 (1984).

Section 1.801-5(c) provides that if reserves are claimed by a life insurance company then sufficient information must be filed with the return to enable the validation of the claim. Section 1.801-5(c) also requires certain information to be filed if the basis (for Federal income tax purposes) for determining the amount of the life insurance reserves as of the close of the taxable year differs from the basis for such determination as of the beginning of the taxable year. Section 1.801-5 was published as a final regulation in the **Federal Register** (25 FR 12654) on December 10, 1960 (T.D. 6513).

Section 1.806-4 describes prior section 806(b) and provides that a change in basis of computing any of the items in prior section 810(c) (the predecessor to section 807(c)) is not a change in method of accounting requiring the consent of the Secretary of the Treasury or his delegate (Secretary) under section 446(e). Section 1.806-4 was published as a final regulation in the **Federal Register** (25 FR 12654) on December 10, 1960 (T.D. 6513).

Section 1.810-3 describes how a change in basis of computing the items in prior section 810(c) should have been treated under the Code prior to its amendment by the Deficit Reduction Act of 1984. Section 1.810-3(a) provides that if the basis for determining an item in prior section 810(c) at the end of a taxable year differs from the basis for such determination at the end of the preceding taxable year, then the difference between the amount of the item computed at the end of the taxable year on the new basis and the amount of the item computed at the end of the taxable year on the old basis is generally taken into account ratably over the 10 succeeding taxable years. Example 1 of § 1.810-3(b) illustrates that if there is a change in basis of computing an item described in former section 810(c) during a taxable year, then for purposes of determining any increase or decrease in such item during the taxable year, such increase or decrease is the difference between the amount of such item computed at the beginning of the taxable year on the old basis and the amount of such item computed at the end of the taxable year on the old basis. Section 1.810-3(c) further provides that, subject to section 381(c)(22), if a company ceases to qualify as a life insurance company, the balance of any adjustment resulting from the change in method of computing reserves must be taken into account in the taxable year preceding the taxable year in which the taxpayer no longer qualifies as a life insurance company. Section 1.810-3 was published as a final regulation in the **Federal Register** (25 FR 12654) on December 10, 1960 (T.D. 6513).

Section 1.818-2(c) describes prior sections 806(b) and 810(d)(1). Section 1.818-2 was published as a final regulation in the **Federal Register** (26 FR 2781) on April 4, 1961 (T.D. 6558).

c. *IRS guidance*

The application of section 807(f) prior to its amendment by the TCJA and the application of prior section 810(d) are illustrated by Rev. Rul. 2002-6, 2002-1 C.B. 460 (inclusion of factors omitted in a previous year's determination of reserves is a change in basis under prior section 807(f) and taxpayer may correct the method on an amended return); Rev. Rul. 94-74, 1994-2 C.B. 157 (applying prior section 807(f) in several situations in which taxpayer changed the basis of computing life insurance reserves); Rev. Rul. 80-117, 1980-1 C.B. 143 (revocation of the election to recompute life insurance reserves under prior section 818(c) of a company acquired in a merger results in a recomputation of the reserves, which is a change in basis of computing the reserves subject to the 10 year spread of prior section 810(d)); Rev. Rul. 80-116, 1980-1 C.B. 141 (recomputation of life insurance reserves under prior section 818(c) of a company acquired in a merger is not a change in basis of computing reserves under prior section 810(d) because reserves must be recomputed for both beginning and end of year); Rev. Rul. 78-354, 1978-2 C.B. 190 (election of a life insurance company to recompute life insurance reserves under prior section 818(c) is terminated when company fails to qualify as a life insurance company and the required recomputation of the reserves is a change in basis of computing the reserves subject to the 10 year spread of prior section 810(d); method of nonlife insurance company taking 10 year spread into account is shown); Rev. Rul. 77-198, 1977-1 C.B. 190 (recomputation of certain reserves from a nonactuarial method to a method utilizing recognized mortality tables and assumed rates of interest is a change in basis of computing reserves under prior sections 806(b) and 810(d)); Rev. Rul. 75-308, 1975-2 C.B. 264 (change in basis of computing reserves under prior section 810(d) occurs when the addition to the reserve is made, not when the company adopts the policy to change the basis of computing reserves); Rev. Rul. 74-57, 1974-1 C.B. 163 (life insurance company that changes basis of computing reserves must take into account the entire adjustment under prior section 810(d) in the year of change if it ceases to qualify as a life insurance company in the year after the year of change); Rev. Rul. 70-568, 1970-2 C.B. 140 (recomputation of reserves under prior section 818(c) applies to contracts at beginning of year even if they are not held at end of year; prior section 810(d) does not apply to the recomputation); Rev. Rul. 70-192, 1970-1 C.B. 153 (change in assumption of when in year death benefits would be paid is a change in basis of computing reserves under prior sections 806(b) and 810 (d)); Rev. Rul. 69-444, 1969-2 C.B. 145 (an increase in life insurance reserves attributable solely to the addition of a new benefit on existing contracts is not a change in basis of computing reserves under prior sections 806(b) and 810(d)); Rev. Rul. 65-240, 1965-2 C.B. 236 (a nonlife company's change in basis of computing life insurance reserves is a change in basis of computing reserves under prior section 810(d) and is subject to the 10 year spread); Rev. Rul. 65-233, 1965-2 C.B. 228 (prior sections 806(b) and 810(d) apply in the year of a change in basis of computing reserves notwithstanding that state regulatory approval for change was not received until the following year); and Rev. Rul. 65-143, 1965-1 C.B. 261 (change in method of computing life insurance reserves from a preliminary term basis to a net level premium basis is a change in basis of computing reserves under prior sections 806(b) and 810(d); election under prior section 818(c) does not apply to life insurance contracts that are computed for statutory purposes on a net level premium basis at the end of the year of election).

d. *Nonlife insurance companies*

Section 832(b)(4) requires a nonlife insurance company to include life insurance reserves, as defined in section 816(b) and determined under section 807, in its determination of premiums earned on insurance contracts during the taxable year, which is a component of underwriting income. Section 807(f) provides rules for changing the basis for determining any item referred to in section 807(c), and life insurance reserves are referred to in section 807(c)(1). Nonlife insurance companies are required to follow the requirements in section 807(f) to change the basis of computing life insurance reserves. Rev. Rul. 65-240.

2. *Modification by the TCJA*

Section 13513 of the TCJA amended prior section 807(f) to provide that any difference between the amount of an item referred to in section 807(c) as of the close of the taxable year computed on a new basis and the amount of such item as of the close of the taxable year computed on the old basis, as is attributable to contracts issued before the taxable year, is to be taken into account under section 481 as adjustments attributable to a change in method of accounting initiated by the taxpayer and made with the consent of the Secretary.

Section 811(a), which was not amended by the TCJA, generally provides that computations made for the determination of Federal income taxes imposed by the provisions of subchapter L of chapter 1 of the Code (subchapter L) that are set forth in part I shall be made under an accrual method of accounting or, to the extent permitted under regulations, under a combination of an accrual method and any other permitted method. To the extent not inconsistent with the preceding sentence or any other provision in part I of subchapter L, these computations are to be made in a manner consistent with the manner required for the annual statement approved by the NAIC. Section 811(a) does not affect the application of section 446(e), which generally requires a taxpayer to secure the consent of the Secretary before changing the method of computing the taxpayer's taxable income. *See also* § 1.446-1(e).

After the amendment of section 807(f) by the TCJA, a life insurance company must follow the regular administrative procedures for a change in method of accounting for a change in basis of computing reserves referred to in section 807(c). *See, e.g.*, § 1.446-1(e); Rev. Proc. 2015-13, 2015-5 I.R.B. 419, Rev. Proc. 2019-43, 2019-48 I.R.B. 1107; Rev. Proc. 2002-18, 2002-1 C.B. 678. Similarly, a nonlife insurance company must follow the administrative procedures for a change in method of accounting to change its basis of computing life insurance reserves (as defined in section 816(b)).

The Conference Report explained that under the amended law "[i]ncome or loss [sic] resulting from a change in method of computing life insurance company reserves is taken into account consistent with IRS procedures, generally ratably over a four-year period, instead of over a 10-year period." Conference Report at 467. The Joint Committee on Taxation explained that a company that makes a change in method of computing life insurance company reserves is required to report and file such statements and other information as the Secretary requires under the IRS procedures for accounting method changes, including the procedures for obtaining automatic consent to change an accounting method. Bluebook at 228.

Rev. Proc. 2015-13 provides the IRS procedures for a taxpayer to obtain the advance (non-automatic) or automatic consent of the Commissioner to change a method of accounting. These procedures generally require a taxpayer to file a Form 3115, "Application for Change in Accounting Method," to change the taxpayer's method of accounting. Rev. Proc. 2019-10, 2019-02 I.R.B. 296, modified the list of automatic accounting method changes in Rev. Proc. 2018-31, 2018-22 I.R.B. 637, to add section 26.04, which provided procedures for an insurance company to obtain automatic consent of the Commissioner to change its method of accounting to comply with section 807(f) for taxable years beginning after December 31, 2017. In response to comments, section 26.04 of Rev. Proc. 2018-31 was modified and superseded by Rev. Proc. 2019-43. See section 26.04 of Rev. Proc. 2019-43 for the current procedures for an insurance company to obtain automatic consent of the Commissioner to change its method of accounting to comply with section 807(f). Rev. Proc. 2019-10 also modified Rev. Rul. 94-74 and Rev. Rul. 2002-6 to the extent their holdings are inconsistent with the general rules for changing a method of accounting under section 446(e) and § 1.446-1(e). Rev. Proc. 2002-18 provides the IRS procedures for changes in method of accounting imposed by the IRS and other procedures for resolving accounting method issues.

E. *Reporting of Reserves*

Section 13517 of the TCJA added section 807(e)(6), which provides that the Secretary shall require reporting (at such time and in such manner as the Secretary shall prescribe) with respect to the opening and closing balance of reserves and with respect to the method of computing reserves for purposes of determining income.

The Conference Report states that for this purpose the Secretary may require a life insurance company (including an affiliated group filing a consolidated return that includes a life insurance company) to report each of the line item elements of each separate account by combining them with such items from other separate accounts and the general account and report the combined amounts on a line-by-line basis. The Secretary may also provide that the reporting on a separate account by separate account basis is generally not permitted. The Conference Report further states that under existing regulatory authority, the Secretary may require e-filing or comparable filing of the returns and may require that the taxpayer provide its annual statement via a link, electronic copy, or other similar means. Conference Report at 478-79.

F. *Annual Statements and Electronically Filed Forms 1120-L and 1120-PC*

Section 6012(a)(2) generally requires that returns with respect to income taxes must be made by every corporation subject to taxation under subtitle A of the Code. Final regulations under section 6012 related to insurance companies were published in the **Federal Register** (72 FR 32794) on June 14, 2007 (T.D. 9329). Section 1.6012-2(c)(1) provides that a life insurance company must make a return on Form 1120-L, "U.S. Life Insurance Company Income Tax Return," and, except as provided in §1.6012-2(c)(4), file with its return a copy of its annual statement. Similarly, § 1.6012-2(c)(2) requires every domestic insurance company other than a life insurance company to make a return on Form 1120-PC, "U.S. Property and Casualty Insurance Company Income Tax Return," and, except as provided in §1.6012-2(c)(4), file with its return a copy of its annual statement. For these purposes, an annual statement means the annual statement, the form of which is approved by the NAIC, that is filed by an insurance company for the year with the applicable state regulators or, if the insurance company is not required to file the NAIC annual statement, a pro forma annual statement. Section 1.6012-2(c)(3) generally provides that the requirements of §1.6012-2(c)(1) and (2) concerning returns and annual statements also apply to foreign insurance companies subject to tax under section 801 or section 831.

Section 1.6012-2(c)(4) provides that if an insurance company described in §1.6012-2(c)(1), (2), or (3) files its return electronically, it should not include its annual statement with such return but that such statement (or pro forma annual statement) must be available at all times to the IRS.

Explanation of Provisions

A. *Computation of Life Insurance Reserves*

Section 1.807-1(a) of the proposed regulations provides that no asset adequacy reserve may be included in the determination of the amount of life insurance reserves under section 807(d). This proposed regulation is consistent with the law both before and after the TCJA. The substantive rules in current § 1.807-1 have no application for taxable years beginning after December 31, 2017, and therefore, are not included in § 1.807-1 of the proposed regulations.

B. *Reporting of Reserves*

Section 1.807-3 of the proposed regulations allows the IRS to require information necessary for the proper reporting of items described in section 807(c), including separate account items. This provision is consistent with section 807(e)(6), as added by the TCJA.

C. *Change in Basis of Computing Reserves*

1. Proposed Section 1.807-4

Section 1.807-4 of the proposed regulations provides guidance relating to both the change in basis of computing reserves of a life insurance company and the change in basis of computing life insurance reserves of a nonlife insurance company. Section 1.807-4(a) of the proposed regulations requires an insurance company to follow administrative procedures prescribed by the Commissioner to change the basis of computing reserves. This requirement is consistent with the Conference Report relating to section 13513 of the TCJA, which provides that a taxpayer is required to follow IRS procedures. Conference Report at 467; *see also* Bluebook at 228 (a company is required to comply with procedures for automatic method changes and to report and file statements and other information as the Secretary requires).

Section 1.807-4(b) of the proposed regulations provides that, to avoid the double counting of income or a deduction, a taxpayer that changes its basis of computing reserves is required to take into account under section 481(a) an adjustment attributable to the change in basis. The proposed regulations provide that if a taxpayer loses its insurance company status, then any remaining balance of a section 481(a) adjustment must be taken into account in the last taxable year the taxpayer was an insurance company. This proposed rule, however, would not require an insurance company to accelerate the accounting for such adjustment if it changes from a life insurance company to a nonlife insurance company or vice versa.

Section 1.807-4(c) of the proposed regulations provides that for purposes of determining any increase or decrease in items described in section 807(c) (for a life insurance company) or the amount of life insurance reserves (for a nonlife insurance company), the determination should be made for the year of change using the old basis of computing reserves and should be made in the following taxable year using the new basis of computing reserves.

Certain revenue rulings are inconsistent with section 807(f), as amended by the TCJA. Accordingly, these revenue rulings are proposed to be obsoleted for taxable years beginning on or after the date of publication of the Treasury decision adopting these rules as final regulations in the **Federal Register**. *See* Effect on Other Documents.

2. Procedure for Obtaining Automatic Consent

Section 26.04 of Rev. Proc. 2019-43 provides the current procedures for an insurance company to obtain automatic consent of the Commissioner to change its method of accounting to comply with section 807(f). In response to comments, the Treasury Department and the IRS intend to revise section 26.04 of Rev. Proc. 2019-43 as described in the following paragraphs.

First, section 26.04(2)(b)(ii) of Rev. Proc. 2019-43 provides that multiple changes during the same taxable year for the same type of contract are considered a single change in basis and the effects of such changes are netted and treated as a single section 481(a) adjustment. Section 807(f)(1), however, provides that the section 481(a) adjustment is the difference between the amount of any item referred to in section 807(c) computed on the new basis and the amount of such item computed on the old basis. Accordingly, the Treasury Department and the IRS intend to revise section 26.04 of Rev. Proc. 2019-43 to require netting of the section 481(a) adjustments at the level of each item referred to in section 807(c) so there is a single section 481(a) adjustment for each of the items referred to in section 807(c).

Second, section 26.04(1) of Rev. Proc. 2019-43 provides that the automatic change procedures apply to a nonlife insurance company. The Treasury Department and the IRS intend to revise section 26.04 of Rev. Proc. 2019-43 to clarify the manner in which nonlife insurance companies implement changes to the basis of computing life insurance reserves (as defined in section 816(b)) during a taxable year (year of change). Specifically, the clarification would provide that, if a nonlife insurance company changes the basis of computing its life insurance reserves, then for purposes of applying section 832(b)(4), (i) for the year of change, life insurance reserves at the end of the year of change with respect to contracts issued before the year of change are determined on the old basis and (ii) for the year following the year of change, life insurance reserves at the end of the preceding taxable year with respect to contracts issued before the year of change are determined on the new basis. Life insurance reserves attributable to contracts issued during the year of change and thereafter must be computed on the new basis.

D. *Definition of Life Insurance Reserves*

The TCJA modified section 807(d) to provide that, for purposes of part I of subchapter L (other than section 816), the amount of life insurance reserves for any contract (other than a variable contract) is the greater of the net surrender value of such contract or 92.81 percent of the reserve determined under the applicable tax reserve method. For any variable contract, the amount of the life insurance reserve is the sum of (i) the greater of the net surrender value of such contract or the portion of the reserve that is separately accounted for under section 817 and (ii) 92.81 percent of the excess (if any) of the reserve determined under the applicable tax reserve method over the amount in clause (i).

Section 807(d)(3) provides that the applicable tax reserve method is CRVM in the case of a contract covered by CRVM and CARVM in the case of a contract covered by CARVM. The CRVM and CARVM may be PBR methods, which may be gross premium reserves and may take into account certain expenses and other factors. Congress understood that for this purpose life insurance reserves could be determined using PBR methods. The Joint Committee on Taxation described the purpose of the TCJA's amendments to section 807(d) as "accomodat[ing] the NAIC-prescribed principle-based reserve methodology." Bluebook at 235.

Section 807(c)(1), however, provides that the reserves referred to in sections 807(a) and (b), which are the reserves taken into account in determining the gross income or deductions of a life insurance company, are "life insurance reserves (as defined in section 816(b))."

Section 816(b) generally defines life insurance reserves to be amounts that are (i) computed or estimated on the basis of recognized mortality or morbidity tables and assumed rates of interest, (ii) set aside to mature or liquidate, either by payment or reinsurance, future unaccrued claims arising from life insurance, annuity, and noncancellable accident and health insurance contracts involving, at the time with respect to which the reserves are computed, life, accident, or health contingencies, and (iii) with some exceptions, required by law. Section 816(b) (and its predecessor provisions) have been interpreted as describing a net premium reserve that does not take into account expenses or certain other factors. *See, e.g.,* Rev. Rul. 77-451, 1977-2 C.B. 224; *Maryland Casualty Co. v. United States,* 251 U.S. 342 (1920).

Thus, although Congress intended that the tax reserve method used to compute life insurance reserves under section 807(d), as amended by the TCJA, could include PBR methods, section 816(b) (by virtue of the reference in section 807(c)(1)) could be interpreted to preclude reserves determined under PBR methods from qualifying as life insurance reserves for purposes of section 807. To clarify the interaction between sections 807 and 816, § 1.816-1 of the proposed regulations provides that a reserve that meets the requirements in sections 816(b)(1) and (2) will not be disqualified as a life insurance reserve if it is determined using a method that takes into account other factors, provided that the method used to compute the reserves is a "tax reserve method" as defined in section 807(d)(3). This definition would apply to life insurance reserves taken into account by nonlife insurance companies under section 832(b)(4) and for purposes of determining an insurance company's qualification as a life insurance company under section 816.

E. *Electronic Filing of Annual Statements*

The Conference Report contemplates requiring the electronic filing of annual statements to improve reporting of insurance reserves, as necessary to carry out and enforce section 807. Conference Report at 478-79. The Treasury Department and the IRS believe that requiring an insurance company to file its annual statement electronically (if the company's Form 1120-L or Form 1120-PC is also filed electronically) is necessary to allow the IRS to better and more efficiently examine the return. Accordingly, § 1.6012-2(c) is proposed to be amended to remove the rule that prohibits an insurance company that files its Form 1120-L or Form 1120-PC electronically from filing its annual statement (or pro forma annual statement) electronically. The Treasury Department and the IRS request comments regarding potential issues that may arise in filing the annual statement (or pro forma annual statements) electronically (for example, if the size of the annual statement(s) may exceed or cause the filed return to exceed the size limits in section 2.1.2 (Submission Size) of IRS Publication 4164, *Modernized e-File (MeF) Guide for Software Developers and Transmitters, Processing Year 2020.)*

F. *Proposed Removal or Revision of Regulations with No Future Application.*

1. *In general*

This notice of proposed rulemaking proposes to remove §§ 1.801-7, 1.801-8(e), 1.806-4, 1.809-2, 1.810-3, 1.818-2(c), and 1.818-4 because these provisions provide guidance under law that has been repealed or substantially changed and will have no application after the adoption of the proposed regulations as final. Section 1.801-5(c) is proposed to be removed because its requirement that a taxpayer file certain information when it changes the basis of computing life insurance reserve is obviated by the requirement in § 1.807-4(b) of the proposed regulations that a taxpayer changing the basis of computing any item referred to in section 807(c) follow the administrative procedures prescribed by the Commissioner.

This notice of proposed rulemaking proposes to revise § 301.9100-6T to remove provisions related to elections under law that has been repealed or elections that may no longer be made.

2. *Section 1.381(c)(22)-1*

This notice of proposed rulemaking proposes to remove § 1.381(c)(22)-1(b)(6) because its requirement that an acquiring corporation take into account any net increases or net decreases in reserves of the distributor or transferor corporation under section 810(d)(1) is no longer applicable. The principle in § 1.381(c)(22)-1(b)(6), however, applies to transactions in which the distributor or transferor corporation has any remaining portion of an adjustment that was required to be taken into account over 10 years under prior section 807(f). *See* section 2.08 of Rev. Proc. 2019-10. After the amendment of section 807(f) by the TCJA, an acquiring corporation must take into account any remaining section 481(a) adjustment of the transferor or distributor corporation pursuant to the IRS's administrative procedures. *See* section 7.03 of Rev. Proc. 2015-13.

3. *Section 1.817A-1*

This notice of proposed rulemaking proposes to revise § 1.817A-1 to remove the requirement that the current market rate of interest prescribed in § 1.817A-1(a)(5) be used to determine both the life insurance reserve and the required interest (as provided in prior section 812(b)(2)(A)) during the temporary guarantee period of a non-equity indexed modified guaranteed contract (MGC).

Prior to its amendment by the TCJA, section 807(d) generally provided that life insurance reserves for a contract were determined using a rate of interest applicable when the contract was issued. Prior section 807(d)(2)(B) provided that the rate of interest to be used was the greater of the applicable Federal interest rate or the prevailing State assumed interest rate. The TCJA amended section 807(d), however, to provide that life insurance reserves for a contract are generally computed using a method applicable to the contract and in effect as of the date the reserve is determined. Section 807(d), as amended, does not prescribe a particular interest rate to be used in determining life insurance reserves. Thus, the requirement in §1.817A-1(b)(2) that the applicable interest rate to be used under section 807(d)(2)(B) to compute life insurance reserves for an MGC is a prescribed current market interest rate is now inapplicable. Additionally, the need for §1.817A-1(b)(1) to prescribe a current market interest rate to determine life insurance reserves for MGCs (as opposed to an interest rate applicable when the contract was issued) is no longer present because section 807(d), as amended, requires the use of a method in effect as of the date the reserve is determined.

Prior to its amendment by the TCJA, section 812 determined "company's share" and "policyholder's share," in part, by reference to required interest on certain reserves under section 807(c). Prior section 812(b)(2)(A) provided that the required interest was computed at the greater of the prevailing State assumed rate or the applicable Federal interest rate. The TCJA amended section 812 to provide that the "company's share" means 70% and the "policyholder's share" means 30%. Accordingly, after the TCJA's amendment of section 812, a particular interest rate is no longer needed to determine the "company's share" and the "policyholder's share."

Section 1.817A-1 also requires that the current market rate of interest prescribed in §1.817A-1(a)(5) be used to determine reserves under section 807(c)(3) for an MGC during any temporary guarantee period. Prior to amendment of section 807(c), the "appropriate rate of interest" that was otherwise required to determine reserves for MGCs under section 807(c)(3) (the highest of the applicable Federal interest rate, the prevailing State assumed interest rate, or the interest rate assumed by the company in determining the guaranteed benefit) was determined when the obligation first did not involve life, accident, or health contingencies, and was thus not necessarily a current interest rate. The TCJA, however, modified the flush language in section 807(c)(3) to provide that the "appropriate rate of interest" is the highest rate or rates permitted to be used to discount the obligations by the NAIC as of the date the reserve is determined. Because the interest rate now required to be used to determine reserves under section 807(c)(3) (in the absence of the application of §1.817A-1) is a current market interest rate, §1.817A-1 may no longer be needed to provide a current interest rate. The Treasury Department and the IRS request comments on whether the current market rate of interest prescribed by §1.817A-1 should continue to apply to reserves under section 807(c)(3) for an MGC during any temporary guarantee period.

4. Section 1.338-11

This notice of proposed rulemaking proposes to revise §1.338-11(d)(2) to reflect the change in section 807(f) made by the TCJA. Section 1.338-11(d) generally provides that when a section 338 election is made for an insurance company, new target must effectively capitalize its subsequent increase in reserves for any acquired contracts in the deemed asset sale to the extent the fair market value of certain assets acquired by new target in the deemed asset sale exceeds the adjusted grossed-up basis (AGUB) allocated to those assets (that is, to the extent of a "bargain purchase"). In the absence of this rule, new target could obtain a better tax result if it acquired understated reserves and subsequently increased them rather than acquiring adequately stated reserves.

Section 1.338-11(d) was intended to minimize incentives for sellers to defer increases in reserves. *See* T.D. 9257 (71 FR 17990). An exception to §1.338-11(d), however, is provided if new target is required by section 807(f) to spread the reserve increase over the 10 succeeding taxable years. *See* §1.338-11(d)(2)(ii). There was limited incentive for sellers to defer increases in reserves when new target was required to spread the deduction resulting from the reserve increase over 10 years, as was the case under section 807(f) prior to its amendment by the TCJA. The amendment to section 807(f) by the TCJA together with the applicable administrative procedures require a deduction resulting from a reserve increase under section 807(f) to be taken into account in one year. As a result, there is greater incentive for a seller to defer increases in reserves if new target would be allowed to take the deduction into account in one year, and the reason for providing the exception currently in §1.338-11(d)(2)(ii) no longer exists. Accordingly, this notice of proposed rulemaking proposes to remove the exception for reserve increases under section 807(f) that is currently provided in §1.338-11(d)(2)(ii).

A new §1.338-11(d)(3)(iii) is also proposed to be added so the standard used for determining when there is an additional premium under §1.338-11(d)(3) for a change in items referenced in section 807(c) is the same as that used under section 807(f). Changes in PBRs that are contemplated by the applicable method, for example, may not constitute changes in the basis of computing reserves under section 807(f) and should not result in an amount of additional premium under §1.338-11(d)(3).

G. Proposed Conforming Changes to Regulations.

This notice of proposed rulemaking proposes to revise §§1.801-2, 1.809-5, and 1.848-1 to correct references to Code provisions or regulations that have been changed, removed, or are proposed to be removed by this notice of proposed rulemaking.

Determination of Life Insurance or Annuity Contract Status for Certain Foreign-Issued Contracts

The Code contains a statutory definition of a life insurance contract under section 7702, rules applicable to certain flexible premium contracts under section 101(f), distribution on death requirements under section 72(s), and diversification requirements under section 817(h). These requirements, which reflect Congress's concern that the tax-favored treatment generally accorded life insurance and annuity contracts was available to contracts that were too investment oriented or provided for undue tax deferral, are relevant to the tax treatment of a policyholder, annuitant, or beneficiary as well as the entity that issues or reinsures a life insurance or annuity contract.

The Treasury Department and IRS received a request to promulgate regulations under section 807 that generally would provide, for purposes of subchapter L, that the determination of whether a contract issued by a non-United States insurance company and reinsured by a United States insurance company is a life insurance or annuity contract is made without regard to these statutory requirements, provided that (i) no policyholder, insured, annuitant, or beneficiary with respect to the contract is a United States person and (ii) such contract is regulated as a life insurance or annuity contract by a foreign regulator. Under the requested approach, a United States insurance company may be able to establish additional life insurance or other tax reserves for such a contract that is reinsured by a United States insurance company even if the contract does not meet these statutory requirements.

The Treasury Department and the IRS are evaluating this request, including whether to address it as part of this rulemaking. Comments are requested generally in respect of the requested change, including in respect of statutory interpretation and implications in various contexts and provisions outside of subchapter L, such as, for example, the interaction with policies underlying the Federal withholding tax provisions that could apply to reinsurance payments from a United States reinsurer to a non-United States insurer as well as the administrability of requiring a United States reinsurance company to track the residence of direct and indirect beneficial owners of any interest in the contract, policyholder, insured, annuitant, or beneficiary of a contract issued by a non-United States insurance company that it may not administer.

Proposed Applicability Dates

The rules in this notice of proposed rulemaking are proposed to apply to taxable years beginning on or after the date of publication of the Treasury decision adopting these rules as final regulations in the **Federal Register**.

A taxpayer may choose to apply §§1.807-4, 1.816-1, and 1.817A-1(b) of the final regulations to taxable years beginning after December 31, 2017, the effective date of the revision of section 807 made by the TCJA, and ending before the first taxable year that begins on or after the date of publication of the Treasury decision adopting these rules as final in the **Federal Register**. *See* section 7805(b)(7). Alternatively, a taxpayer may rely on §§ 1.807-4 and 1.816-1 of the proposed regulations for taxable years beginning after December 31, 2017, and ending before the first taxable year that begins on or after the date of publication of the Treasury decision adopting these rules as final in the **Federal Register**.

Under proposed § 1.6012-2(l), taxpayers may choose to apply § 1.6012-2(c) of the final regulations to any original Federal income tax return (including any amended return filed on or before the due date (including extensions) of such original return) timely filed on or after the date of publication of the Treasury decision adopting these rules as final in the **Federal Register**.

Effect on Other Documents

The following revenue rulings are proposed to be obsoleted for taxable years beginning on or after the date of publication of the Treasury decision adopting these rules as final regulations in the **Federal Register**: Rev. Rul. 2002-6, Rev. Rul. 94-74, Rev. Rul. 80-117, Rev. Rul. 80-116, Rev. Rul. 78-354, Rev. Rul. 77-198, Rev. Rul. 75-308, Rev. Rul. 74-57, Rev. Rul. 70-568, Rev. Rul. 70-192, Rev. Rul. 69-444, Rev. Rul. 65-240, Rev. Rul. 65-233, Rev. Rul. 65-143. Comments are requested regarding principles contained within these revenue rulings that are consistent with current section 807(f) and for which additional guidance is needed if these rulings are obsoleted.

Notice 2010-29 is proposed to be obsoleted for taxable years beginning after December 31, 2017.

Special Analyses

This regulation is not subject to review under section 6(b) of Executive Order 12866 pursuant to the Memorandum of Agreement (April 11, 2018) between the Treasury Department and the Office of Management and Budget regarding review of tax regulations.

Paperwork Reduction Act

The collection of information relating to this notice of proposed rulemaking will be submitted to the Office of Management and Budget for review under OMB Control Number 1545-0123 in accordance with the Paperwork Reduction Act of 1995 (44 U.S.C. 3507(d)).

In response to the Conference Report, § 1.6012-2 of the proposed regulations would require an insurance company to include the insurance company's annual statement (as defined in § 1.6012-2(c)(5)) with an electronically filed Federal income tax return (Form 1120-L for a life insurance company and Form 1120-PC for a nonlife insurance company). Federal income tax items of an insurance company are determined in part based upon the insurance company's annual statement. Providing the annual statement to the IRS with an electronically filed Federal income tax return is necessary to allow the IRS to better and more efficiently examine an insurance company's Federal income tax return.

In accordance with section 807(e)(6), as added by the TCJA, § 1.807-3 of the proposed regulations provides that the IRS may require reporting on Form 1120-L of the opening balance and closing balance of items described in section 807(c) (for example, life insurance reserves) and the method of computing such items for purposes of determining income. Providing this information is necessary to allow the IRS to better examine an insurance company's Federal income tax return.

For purposes of the Paperwork Reduction Act, the burden for the collection of information associated with § 1.6012-2 of the proposed regulations will be reflected in the burden on the Form 1120-L and in the burden on the Form 1120-PC (OMB Control Number 1545-0123) when the burden for each is revised to reflect the collection of information associated with § 1.6012-2 of the proposed regulations. The respondents to the collection of information are life insurance companies that file the Form 1120-L electronically and nonlife insurance companies that file the Form 1120-PC electronically.

For purposes of the Paperwork Reduction Act, the burden for the collection of information associated with § 1.807-3 of the proposed regulations will be reflected in the burden on the Form 1120-L (OMB Control Number 1545-0123) when the burden is revised to reflect the collection of information associated with § 1.807-3 of the proposed regulations. The respondents to the collection of information are life insurance companies that file a Form 1120-L.

Comments on the collection of information should be sent to the Office of Management and Budget, Attn: Desk Officer for the Department of the Treasury, Office of Information and Regulatory Affairs, Washington, DC 20503, with copies to the Internal Revenue Service, Attn: IRS Reports Clearance Officer, SE:CAR:MP:T:T:SP, Washington, DC 20224. Comments on the collection of information should be received by June 1, 2020. Comments are specifically requested concerning:

Whether the proposed collection of information is necessary for the proper performance of the functions of the IRS, including whether the information will have practical utility;

How the quality, utility, and clarity of the information to be collected may be enhanced;

How the burden of complying with the proposed collection of information may be minimized, including through the application of automated collection techniques or other forms of information technology; and

Estimates of capital or start-up costs and costs of operation, maintenance, and purchase of services to provide information.

An agency may not conduct or sponsor, and a person is not required to respond to, a collection of information unless it displays a valid control number assigned by the Office of Management and Budget.

Regulatory Flexibility Act

It is hereby certified that the proposed regulations will not have a significant economic impact on a substantial number of small entities pursuant to the Regulatory Flexibility Act (5 U.S.C. chapter 6).

Section 13517 of the TCJA added section 807(e)(6) to the Code. Under section 807(e)(6), the Secretary may require reporting (at such time and in such manner as the Secretary shall prescribe) with respect to the opening balances and the closing balances of reserves and with respect to the method of computing reserves for purposes of determining income. Section 1.807-3 of the proposed regulations would allow the IRS to require the reporting of this information on any prescribed forms, such as the Form 1120-L.

The Conference Report at 478-479 provides that, under existing authority, the Secretary may require an insurance company to provide its annual statement via a link, electronic copy, or other similar means. Section 1.6012-2(c) of the proposed regulations would require an insurance company to include the insurance company's annual statement with an electronically filed Federal income tax return (Form 1120-L for a life insurance company and Form 1120-PC for a nonlife insurance company). Under current procedures, an insurance company can only electronically file a Form 1120-L or Form 1120-PC if the insurance company is part of an affiliated group filing a consolidated return, the parent of which files a Form 1120. Although data are not readily available, the IRS and the Treasury Department expect that any reporting burden associated with § 1.6012-2(c) of the proposed regulations will fall primarily on financial and insurance firms with annual receipts greater than $41.5 million and, therefore, will not affect a substantial number of small entities. *See* 13 CFR 121.201, sector 52 (finance and insurance).

As stated in the preceding paragraph, the rule is not expected to affect a substantial number of small entities; however, even if a substantial number of small entities were affected, the economic impact of the regulation is not likely to be significant. Section 1.807-3 of the proposed regulations is limited in scope to time and manner of information reporting, and any economic impact associated with this proposed regulation is expected to be minimal. Further, the information reported to the IRS is information that the insurance company has readily available.

Notwithstanding this certification, the Treasury Department and the IRS invite comments on the impact this rule would have on small entities.

Pursuant to section 7805(f) of the Code, the notice of proposed rulemaking will be submitted to the Chief Counsel for Advocacy of the Small Business Administration for comment on its impact on small business.

Comments and Public Hearing

Before these proposed regulations are adopted as final regulations, consideration will be given to any comments that are submitted timely to the IRS as prescribed in this preamble under the **ADDRESSES** heading. The Treasury Department and the IRS request comments on all aspects of the proposed rules and the other proposed actions described herein. All comments that are submitted by the public will be available for public inspection and copying at *http://www.regulations.gov* or upon request.

A public hearing will be scheduled if requested in writing by any person that timely submits written comments. If a public hearing is scheduled, notice of the date, time, and place for the hearing will be published in the **Federal Register**.

The rules of 26 CFR 601.601(a)(3) apply to the hearing. Persons who wish to present oral comments at the hearing must submit written or electronic comments and an outline of the topics to be discussed and the time to be devoted to each topic by May 17, 2020. Such persons should submit a signed paper original and eight (8) copies or an electronic copy. A period of 10 minutes will be allotted to each person for presenting oral comments. An agenda showing the scheduling of the speakers will be prepared after the deadline for receiving outlines has passed. Copies of the agenda will be available free of charge at the hearing.

Drafting Information

The principal author of these regulations is Dan Phillips, Office of Associate Chief Counsel (Financial Institutions and Products), IRS. However, other personnel from the Treasury Department and the IRS participated in their development.

Statement of Availability of IRS Documents

The IRS notices, revenue procedures, and revenue rulings cited in this preamble are published in the Internal Revenue Bulletin (or Cumulative Bulletin) and are available from the Superintendent of Documents, U.S. Government Publishing Office, Washington, DC 20402, or by visiting the IRS website at *http://www.irs.gov*.

[¶ 49,831] Proposed Amendments of Regulations (REG-106013-19), published in the Federal Register on April 8, 2020.

[Code Secs. 245A, 881 and 951A]

Hybrid deduction: Global Intangible Low-Taxed Income (GILTI): Disqualified payment: Shareholder: Foreign corporation.—Amendments of Reg. §§ 1.245A(e)-1, 1.881-3, 1.951A-0, 1.951A-2 and 1.951A-7, adjusting hybrid deduction accounts to take into account earnings and profits of a controlled foreign corporation that are included in income by a United States shareholder, are proposed.

AGENCY: Internal Revenue Service (IRS), Treasury.

ACTION: Notice of proposed rulemaking.

SUMMARY: This document contains proposed regulations that adjust hybrid deduction accounts to take into account earnings and profits of a controlled foreign corporation that are included in income by a United States shareholder. This document also contains proposed regulations that address, for purposes of the conduit financing rules, arrangements involving equity interests that give rise to deductions (or similar benefits) under foreign law. Further, this document contains proposed regulations relating to the treatment of certain payments under the global intangible low-taxed income (GILTI) provisions. The proposed regulations affect United States shareholders of foreign corporations and persons that make payments in connection with certain hybrid arrangements.

DATES: Written or electronic comments and requests for a public hearing must be received by June 8, 2020.

ADDRESSES: Submit electronic submissions via the Federal eRulemaking Portal at www.regulations.gov (indicate IRS and REG-106013-19) by following the online instructions for submitting comments. Once submitted to the Federal eRulemaking Portal, comments cannot be edited or withdrawn. The Department of the Treasury (Treasury Department) and the IRS will publish for public availability any comment received to its public docket, whether submitted electronically or in hard copy. Send hard copy submissions to: CC:PA:LPD:PR (REG-106013-19), Room 5203, Internal Revenue Service, P.O. Box 7604, Ben Franklin Station, Washington, DC 20044. FOR FURTHER INFORMATION CONTACT: Concerning the proposed regulations under section 951A, Jorge M. Oben at (202) 317-6934; concerning all other proposed regulations, Richard F. Owens at (202) 317-6501; concerning submissions of comments or requests for a public hearing, Regina L. Johnson at (202) 317-6901 (not toll free numbers).

SUPPLEMENTARY INFORMATION:

Background

I. *Section 245A(e) - Hybrid Dividends*

Section 245A(e) was added to the Internal Revenue Code ("Code") by the Tax Cuts and Jobs Act, Pub. L. No. 115-97 (2017) (the "Act"), which was enacted on December 22, 2017. Section 245A(e) and the final regulations under section 245A(e), which are published in the Rules and Regulations section of this issue of the **Federal Register** (the "section 245A(e) final regulations"), neutralize the double non-taxation effects of a hybrid dividend or tiered hybrid dividend through either denying the section 245A(a) dividends received deduction with respect to the dividend or requiring an inclusion under section 951(a)(1)(A) with respect to the dividend, depending on whether the dividend is received by a domestic corporation or a controlled foreign corporation ("CFC"). The section 245A(e) final regulations require that certain shareholders of a CFC maintain a hybrid deduction account with respect to each share of stock of the CFC that the shareholder owns, and provide that a dividend received by the shareholder from the CFC is a hybrid dividend or tiered hybrid dividend to the extent of the sum of those accounts. A hybrid deduction account with respect to a share of stock of a CFC reflects the amount of hybrid deductions of the CFC that have been allocated to the share, reduced by the amount of hybrid deductions that gave rise to a hybrid dividend or tiered hybrid dividend.

II. *Section 1.881-3 - Conduit Financing Arrangements*

A. *In general*

Section 7701(l) of the Code authorizes the Secretary to prescribe regulations recharacterizing any multiple-party financing transaction as a transaction directly among any two or more of such parties where the Secretary determines that such recharacterization is appropriate to prevent the avoidance of any tax imposed by the Code. In prescribing such regulations, the legislative history to section 7701(l) states that "it would be within the proper scope of the provision for the Secretary to issue regulations dealing with multi-party financing transactions involving . . . equity investments." H.R. Conf. Rep. No. 103-213, at 655 (1993).

On August 11, 1995, the Treasury Department and the IRS published in the **Federal Register** final regulations (TD 8611, 60 FR 40997) that allow the IRS to disregard the participation of one or more intermediate entities in a financing arrangement where such entities are acting as conduit entities, and to recharacterize the financing arrangement as a transaction directly between the remaining parties to the financing arrangement for purposes of imposing tax under sections 871, 881, 1441 and 1442.

B. *Limited treatment of equity interests as financing transactions*

Section 1.881-3(a)(2)(i)(A) defines a financing arrangement to mean a series of transactions by which one person (the "financing entity") advances money or other property, or grants rights to use property, and another person (the "financed entity") receives money or other property, or rights to use property, if the advance and receipt are effected through one or more other persons ("intermediate entities"). Except in cases in which § 1.881-3(a)(2)(i)(B) applies (special rule to treat two or more related persons as a single intermediate entity in the absence of a financing transaction between the related persons), the regulations apply only if "financing transactions," as defined in § 1.881-3(a)(2)(ii), link the financing entity, each of the intermediate entities, and the financed entity. Section 1.881-3(a)(2)(ii)(A) and (B) limit the definition of financing transaction in the case of equity investments to stock in a corporation (or a similar interest in a partnership, trust, or other person) that is subject to certain redemption, acquisition, or payment rights or requirements ("redeemable equity").

If it is determined that an intermediate entity is participating as a conduit entity in a conduit financing arrangement, the financing arrangement may be recharacterized as a transaction directly between the remaining parties (in most cases, the financing entity and the financed entity). *See* § 1.881-3(a)(3)(ii)(A). The portion of the financed entity's payments subject to this recharacterization is determined under § 1.881-3(d)(1)(i). Under § 1.881-3(d)(1)(i), if the aggregate principal amount of the financing transactions to which the financed entity is a party exceeds the aggregate principal amount linking any of the parties to the financing arrangement, then the recharacterized portion is determined by multiplying the payment by a fraction the numerator of which is the lowest aggregate principal amount of the financing transactions linking any of the parties to the financing transaction and the denominator of which is the aggregate principal amounts linking the financed entity to the financing arrangement. Conversely, if the aggregate principal amount of the financing transactions to which the financed entity is a party is less than or equal to the aggregate principal amount of the financing transactions linking any of the parties to the financing arrangement, the entire amount of the payment is recharacterized.

C. *Hybrid instruments*

On December 22, 2008, the Treasury Department and the IRS published in the **Federal Register** (73 FR 78252) a notice of proposed rulemaking (REG-113462-08) ("2008 proposed regulations") that proposed adding § 1.881-3(a)(2)(i)(C) to the conduit financing regulations to treat an entity disregarded as an entity separate from its owner for U.S. tax purposes as a person for purposes of determining whether a conduit financing arrangement exists. The preamble to the 2008 proposed regulations provides that the Treasury Department and the IRS are also studying transactions where a financing entity advances cash or other property to an intermediate entity in exchange for a hybrid instrument (that is, an instrument treated as debt under the tax laws of the foreign country in which the intermediary is resident and equity for U.S. tax purposes), and states that they may issue separate guidance to address the treatment under § 1.881-3 of certain hybrid instruments.

The preamble to the 2008 proposed regulations presents two possible approaches to hybrid instruments and requests comments on those and other possible approaches and factors that should be considered. The first approach would treat all transactions involving hybrid instruments between a financing entity and an intermediate entity as *per se* financing transactions under § 1.881-3(a)(2)(ii)(A). The second approach would treat only certain hybrid instruments as financing transactions based on specific factors or criteria. Only one comment was received. The comment suggested that the Treasury Department and the IRS take a more targeted approach in identifying specific transactions where there is evidence of limited taxation in the intermediary jurisdiction as a direct consequence of the hybrid instrument.

On December 9, 2011, the Treasury Department and the IRS published in the **Federal Register** final regulations (TD 9562, 76 FR 76895) that adopted the 2008 proposed regulations' treatment of disregarded entities under § 1.881-3 without substantive changes. The preamble to the final regulations states that the Treasury Department and the IRS would continue to study the treatment of hybrid instruments in financing transactions.

III. *Section 951A - Global Intangible Low-Taxed Income*

Section 951A, added to the Code by the Act, requires a United States shareholder of any CFC for any taxable year to include in gross income the shareholder's global intangible low-taxed income ("GILTI inclusion amount") for such taxable year. On October 10, 2018, the Treasury Department and the IRS published in the **Federal Register** proposed regulations (REG-104390-18, 83 FR 51072) implementing section 951A. On June 21, 2019, the Treasury Department and the IRS published in the **Federal Register** final regulations ("GILTI final regulations") (TD 9866, 84 FR 29288) that adopted the proposed regulations, with revisions.

The GILTI final regulations include a rule that provides that a deduction or loss attributable to basis created by reason of a transfer of property from a CFC to a related CFC during the period after December 31, 2017, the final date for measuring earnings and profits ("E&P") for purposes of section 965, and before the date on which section 951A first applies with respect to the transferor CFC's income (for example, December 1, 2018, for a CFC with a taxable year ending November 30) (the "disqualified period," and such basis, "disqualified basis"), is allocated and apportioned solely to residual CFC gross income. *See* § 1.951A-2(c)(5)(i). Residual CFC gross income is gross income other than gross tested income, subpart F income, or income effectively connected with a trade or business in the United States. *See* § 1.951A-2(c)(5)(iii)(B). The rule also provides that any depreciation, amortization, or cost recovery allowances attributable to disqualified basis are not properly allocable to property produced or acquired for resale under section 263, 263A, or 471. *See* § 1.951A-2(c)(5)(i). The purpose of the rule is to ensure that taxpayers cannot take advantage of the disqualified period to engage in transactions that allowed taxpayers to enhance their tax attributes, including by reducing their tested income or increasing their tested loss over time, without resulting in any current tax cost. *See* 84 FR 29299.

Explanation of Provisions

I. *Rules Under Section 245A(e) to Reduce Hybrid Deduction Accounts*

A. *In general*

As discussed in part II.C.2 of the Summary of Comments and Explanation of Revisions of the section 245A(e) final regulations, the Treasury Department and the IRS have determined that hybrid deduction accounts with respect to stock of a CFC should be reduced in certain cases. In particular, the accounts should generally be reduced to the extent that earnings and profits of the CFC that have not been subject to foreign tax as a result of certain hybrid arrangements are, by reason of certain provisions (not including section 245A(e)), "included in income" in the United States (that is, taken into account in income and not offset by, for example, a deduction or credit particular to the inclusion). By adjusting the accounts in this manner, section 245A(e) neutralizes the double non-taxation effects of certain hybrid arrangements in a manner consistent with the results that would arise were the sheltered earnings and profits (that is, the earnings and profits that were not subject to foreign tax as a result of the arrangement) distributed as a dividend for which the section 245A(a) deduction is not allowed. In such a case, the dividend consisting of the sheltered earnings and profits would generally be taken into account in a United States shareholder's gross income, and the United States shareholder would generally be taxed at the U.S. corporate statutory rate and allowed neither a dividends received deduction for the dividend nor other relief particular to the dividend (such as foreign tax credits).

The proposed regulations thus provide a new rule that, as part of the end-of-the-year adjustments to a hybrid deduction account, reduces the account by three categories of amounts included in the gross income of a domestic corporation with respect to the share. *See* proposed §1.245A(e)-1(d)(4)(i)(B). The first category relates to an inclusion under section 951(a)(1)(A) ("subpart F inclusion") with respect to the share, and the second relates to a GILTI inclusion amount with respect to the share. *See* proposed §1.245A(e)-1(d)(4)(i)(B)(*1*) and (2). The third category is for inclusions under sections 951(a)(1)(B) and 956 with respect to the share, to the extent the inclusion occurs by reason of the application of section 245A(e) to the hypothetical distribution described in §1.956-1(a)(2). *See* proposed §1.245A(e)-1(d)(4)(i)(B)(3). An amount in the third category provides a dollar-for-dollar reduction of the account because, due to the lack of availability of deductions or credits particular to the amount (including foreign tax credits) to offset or reduce such amount, the entirety of such amount is assumed to be included in income in the United States. *See, for example,* §1.960-2(b)(1) (no foreign income taxes are deemed paid under section 960(a) with respect to an inclusion under section 951(a)(1)(B)).

As discussed in part I.B of this Explanation of Provisions, the entirety of an amount in the first or second category may not be included in income in the United States and, as a result, such an amount does not provide a dollar-for-dollar reduction of the account. In addition, the reduction of the account for these amounts cannot exceed the hybrid deductions allocated to the share for the taxable year multiplied by the ratio of the subpart F income or tested income, as applicable, of the CFC for the taxable year to the CFC's taxable income. *See* proposed §1.245A(e)-1(d)(4)(i)(B)(*1*)(*ii*) and (d)(4)(i)(B)(2)(*ii*); *see also* proposed §1.245A(e)-1(d)(4)(i)(B)(*1*)(*iii*) and (d)(4)(i)(B)(2)(*iii*) (in certain cases, excess amounts are allocated to other hybrid deduction accounts and reduce those accounts). This limitation is, for example, intended to prevent a subpart F inclusion for a taxable year from removing from the account hybrid deductions incurred in a prior taxable year, because such hybrid deductions generally represent an amount of prior year earnings that were not subject to foreign tax as a result of a hybrid arrangement, and the subpart F inclusion in the current year does not subject such earnings to U.S. tax (but rather, subjects certain current year earnings to U.S. tax). In addition, because hybrid deductions incurred in the current taxable year may ratably shelter from foreign tax each type of earnings of a CFC (as opposed to, for example, only sheltering from foreign tax earnings of a type that the United States views as attributable to subpart F income), the limitation is generally intended to ensure that, for example, a subpart F inclusion does not remove from the account hybrid deductions that sheltered from foreign tax current year earnings of a type that the United States views as attributable to income other than subpart F income.

B. *Adjusted subpart F and GILTI inclusions*

The proposed regulations generally reduce a hybrid deduction account with respect to a share of stock of a CFC by an "adjusted subpart F inclusion" or an "adjusted GILTI inclusion" (or both) with respect to the share. *See* proposed §1.245A(e)-1(d)(4)(i)(B)(*1*) and (2). An adjusted subpart F inclusion or an adjusted GILTI inclusion is intended to measure, in an administrable manner, the extent to which a domestic corporation's subpart F inclusion or GILTI inclusion amount is likely included in income in the United States, taking into account foreign tax credits associated with the inclusion and, in the case of a GILTI inclusion amount, the deduction under section 250(a)(1)(B).

The starting point in determining an adjusted subpart F inclusion with respect to a share of stock of a CFC is identifying a domestic corporation's pro rata share of the CFC's subpart F income, and then attributing such inclusion to particular shares of stock of the CFC. *See* proposed §1.245A(e)-1(d)(4)(ii)(A). For purposes of attributing the inclusion, the proposed regulations provide that the principles of section 951(a)(2) and §1.951-1(b) and (e) apply.

Once the amount of the subpart F inclusion attributable to the share is determined, the "associated foreign income taxes" with respect to the amount must be determined. *See* proposed §1.245A(e)-1(d)(4)(ii)(A) and (D). The term associated foreign income taxes means the amount of current year tax allocated and apportioned to the subpart F income groups of the CFC, to the extent allocated to the share. *See* proposed §1.245A(e)-1(d)(4)(ii)(D)(1) and (d)(4)(ii)(E). The computation of associated foreign income taxes does not take into account any limitations on foreign tax credits, such as under section 904, because doing so would involve considerable complexity. These rules are intended to approximate, in an administrable manner, deemed paid credits resulting from the application of section 960(a) that are eligible to be claimed with respect to the subpart F inclusion attributable to the share.

The final step is to adjust, pursuant to a two-step process, the subpart F inclusion attributable to the share, to approximate the tax effect of the associated foreign income taxes. *See* proposed §1.245A(e)-1(d)(4)(ii)(A). First, the associated foreign income taxes are added to the subpart F inclusion, to reflect that when a domestic corporation claims section 960 credits it includes in gross income under section 78 an amount equal to such credits. *See* proposed §1.245A(e)-1(d)(4)(ii)(A)(1). Second, an amount equal to the amount of income offset by the associated foreign income taxes - calculated as the associated foreign tax credits divided by the corporate tax rate - is subtracted from the sum of the amounts described in the previous sentence. *See* proposed §1.245A(e)-1(d)(4)(ii)(A)(2). The difference of the amounts is the adjusted subpart F inclusion with respect to the share.[1]

Similar rules apply for purposes of determining an adjusted GILTI inclusion with respect to a share of stock of a CFC. However, special rules account for the fact that the computation of foreign tax credits under section 960(d) takes into account a domestic corporation's inclusion percentage (as described in §1.960-2(c)(2)) and the 80 percent limit in section 960(d)(1). *See* proposed §1.245A(e)-1(d)(4)(ii)(B)(3) and (d)(4)(ii)(D)(2). In addition, a special rule accounts for the effect of a section 250 deduction that a domestic corporation may claim related to GILTI. *See* proposed §1.245A(e)-1(d)(4)(ii)(B)(2).

C. *Applicability date*

The proposed rules relating to hybrid deduction accounts are proposed to apply to taxable years ending on or after the date that final regulations are published in the **Federal Register**. For taxable years before taxable years covered by such final regulations, a taxpayer may apply the rules set forth in the final regulations, provided that it consistently applies the rules to those taxable years. *See* section 7805(b)(7). In addition, a taxpayer may rely on the proposed rules with respect to any period before the date that the proposed regulations are published as final regulations in the **Federal Register**, provided that it consistently does so.

II. *Conduit Regulations under §1.881-3 to Address Equity Interests that Give Rise to Deductions or other Benefits under Foreign Law*

A. *Overview*

Under the current conduit financing regulations, an instrument that is treated as equity for U.S. tax purposes (and is not redeemable equity described in §1.881-3(a)(2)(ii)(B)) generally will not be characterized as a financing transaction, even though the instrument gives rise to a deduction or other benefit under the tax laws of the issuer's jurisdiction. For example, an instrument that is treated as stock (that is not redeemable

---

[1] Thus, for example, in a case in which the subpart F inclusion attributable to a share is $94.75x and the associated foreign income taxes with respect to such is $5.25x, the adjusted subpart F inclusion with respect to the share would be $75x, calculated as $100x ($94.75x + $5.25x) less $25x ($5.25x ÷ 21%).

equity) for U.S. tax purposes, but as indebtedness under the laws of the issuer's jurisdiction, would not be characterized as a financing transaction under the current regulations.

The Treasury Department and the IRS have determined that these types of instruments can be used to inappropriately avoid the application of the conduit financing regulations and, therefore, the proposed regulations expand the definition of equity interests treated as a financing transaction by taking into account the tax treatment of the instrument under the tax law of the relevant foreign country, which is generally the country where the equity issuer resides. The Treasury Department and the IRS have determined that, while these types of instruments are characterized as equity for U.S. tax purposes, they still raise conduit financing concerns if they are either indebtedness under the issuer's tax law or provide benefits similar to indebtedness under the issuer's tax law. For example, a financing company may have an incentive to form a corporation in a country that allows a tax benefit, such as a notional interest deduction with respect to equity, that encourages the routing of income through the intermediary issuer in functionally the same manner as when an intermediate entity issues a debt instrument that is treated as a financing transaction under the current regulations. Similarly, a financing entity may form an intermediate corporation in a country to take advantage of the country's purported integration regime that provides a substantial refund of the issuer's corporate tax paid upon a distribution to a related shareholder, and the shareholder is not taxable on that distribution under the laws of the intermediate country. The Treasury Department and IRS have concluded that these structures raise concerns similar to those Congress intended to address when it enacted sections 267A and 245A(e) regarding arrangements that "exploit differences in the treatment of a transaction or entity under the laws of two or more tax jurisdictions . . ." *See* S. Comm. on the Budget, Reconciliation Recommendations Pursuant to H. Con. Res. 71, S. Print No. 115-20, at 389 (2017).

The Treasury Department and the IRS have determined that the conduit regulations should apply in these cases generally based on benefits that are associated with an equity interest, rather than targeting only particular transactions based on specific factors or criteria as recommended by a comment, because these arrangements are often deliberately structured and a more limited approach could be easily circumvented or difficult to administer. However, even if the equity interests of an intermediate entity are treated as a financing transaction under the proposed regulations, the intermediate entity will not be a conduit entity if, for example, its participation in the financing arrangement is not pursuant to a tax avoidance plan. *See* § 1.881-3(b).

B. *Treatment of equity interests that give rise to deductions or other benefits under foreign law*

The proposed regulations expand the types of equity interests treated as a financing transaction to include stock or a similar interest if under the tax laws of a foreign country where the issuer is a resident, the issuer is allowed a deduction or another tax benefit for an amount paid, accrued or distributed with respect to the stock or similar interest. Similarly, if the issuer maintains a taxable presence, referred to as a permanent establishment ("PE") under the laws of many foreign countries without regard to a treaty, and such country allows a deduction (including a notional deduction) for an amount paid, accrued or distributed with respect to the deemed equity or capital of the PE, the amount of the deemed equity or capital will be treated as a financing transaction. *See* proposed § 1.881-3(a)(2)(ii)(B)(*1*)(*iv*). The proposed regulations also treat stock or a similar interest as a financing transaction if a person related to the issuer, generally a shareholder or other interest holder in an entity, is entitled to a refund (including a credit) or similar tax benefit for taxes paid by the issuer to its country of residence, without regard to the person's tax liability with respect to the payment, accrual or distribution under the laws of the issuer. *See* proposed § 1.881-3(a)(2)(ii)(B)(*1*)(*v*).

An equity interest treated as a financing transaction under the proposed regulations would include, for example, stock that gives rise to a notional interest deduction under the tax laws of the foreign country in which the issuer is a tax resident or the tax laws of the country in which the issuer maintains a permanent establishment to which a financing payment is attributable. However, if an equity interest constitutes a financing transaction because the issuer is allowed a notional interest deduction and is one of the financing transactions that links a party to the financing arrangement, the proposed regulations limit the portion of the financed entity's payment that is recharacterized under § 1.881-3(d)(1)(i) to the financing transaction's principal amount as determined under § 1.881-3(d)(1)(ii), multiplied by the applicable rate used to compute the issuer's notional interest deduction in the year of the financed entity's payment. *See* proposed § 1.881-3(d)(1)(iii). This limitation is intended to recharacterize only the portion of the payment that can be traced to the notional interest deduction on the principal amount of the equity on which the notational deduction is based. Notional interest deductions may also accrue with respect to equity composed of retained earnings, not related to the financing transaction, and therefore are not taken into account under this rule.

The proposed regulations also make conforming changes to reflect the application of these rules in the context of Chapter 4 withholding (sections 1471 and 1472).

C. *Interaction with section 267A*

While the proposed conduit regulations may apply to many of the same instruments identified in the final regulations under section 267A issued in the Rules and Regulations section of this issue of the **Federal Register** (the "section 267A final regulations"), in some respects the proposed conduit regulations have a broader scope than those rules in order to prevent the use of conduit entities from inappropriately obtaining the benefits of an applicable U.S. income tax treaty. For example, the imported mismatch rules in the section 267A final regulations, in determining whether a deduction for an interest or royalty payment is disallowed by reason of the income attributable to the payment being offset by an offshore deduction, only take into account offshore deductions that produce a deduction/no inclusion ("D/NI") outcome as a result of hybridity. A D/NI outcome is not a result of hybridity if, for example, the no-inclusion occurs because the foreign tax law does not impose a corporate income tax.

The existing conduit regulations, in contrast, already apply whether or not there is a D/NI outcome with respect to an offshore financing transaction. The proposed regulations will now also cover, without regard to how the transaction is treated for U.S. tax purposes (as debt or equity), any financing transaction where the intermediate entity is allowed a deduction or other tax benefit similar to those described in the section 267A final regulations and applicable in the imported mismatch context.

D. *Applicability date*

The proposed rules relating to conduit transactions are proposed to apply to payments made on or after the date that final regulations are published in the **Federal Register**.

III. *Rules under Section 951A to Address Certain Disqualified Payments Made During the Disqualified Period*

A. *In general*

As discussed in part III of the Background of this preamble, the GILTI final regulations provide that (i) a deduction or loss attributable to disqualified basis created by reason of a transfer from a CFC to a related CFC during the disqualified period is allocated and apportioned solely to residual CFC gross income, and (ii) any depreciation, amortization, or cost recovery allowances attributable to disqualified basis are not properly allocable to property produced or acquired for resale under section 263, 263A, or 471. *See* § 1.951A-2(c)(5)(i).

The Treasury Department and the IRS understand that, in addition to the transactions circumscribed by the rules in § 1.951A-2(c)(5), taxpayers also may have entered into transactions in which, for example, a CFC that licensed property to a related CFC received pre-payments of royalties due under the license from the related CFC, which did not constitute subpart F income. Although the recipient of the prepayments ("related recipient CFC") would generally have been required to include the royalties in income upon payment during the disqualified period, when they would not have affected amounts included under section 965 with respect to the related recipient CFC and also would not have given rise to gross tested income under section 951A, the related CFC that made the pre-payment would generally only be allowed to deduct the payment over time as economic performance occurred. *See* section 461. Accordingly, the related CFC that made the pre-payment would claim deductions that reduce tested income (or increase tested loss) during taxable years to which section 951A applies, even though the corresponding income would not have been subject to tax under section 951 (including as a result of section 965) or section 951A.

The Treasury Department and the IRS have determined that the deductions attributable to pre-payments (including, but not limited to, deductions attributable to prepaid rents and royalties) should be subject to similar treatment as the final GILTI regulations' treatment of deductions or loss attributable to disqualified basis. Accordingly, proposed §1.951A-2(c)(6) treats a deduction by a CFC related to a deductible payment to a related recipient CFC during the disqualified period as allocated and apportioned solely to residual CFC gross income, as defined in §1.951A-2(c)(5)(iii)(B), and provides that any deduction related to such a payment is not properly allocable to property produced or acquired for resale under section 263, 263A, or 471, consistent with §1.951A-2(c)(5)(i) and the authority therefor described in the preamble to the final GILTI regulations. *See* 84 FR 29298-29300. This rule applies only to the extent the payments would constitute income described in section 951A(c)(2)(A)(i) and §1.951A-2(c)(1), without regard to whether section 951A applies. *See* proposed §1.951A-2(c)(6)(ii)(A).

B. *Applicability date*

The proposed rules relating to section 951A are proposed to apply to taxable years of foreign corporations ending on or after April 7, 2020, and to taxable years of United States shareholders in which or with which such taxable years end. *See* section 7805(b)(1)(B). Given the applicability date, these rules would effectively be limited to payments made during the disqualified period that give rise to deductions or loss in taxable years of foreign corporations ending on or after April 7, 2020 and would not, for example, affect payments made during the disqualified period for which the associated deduction or loss is taken into account in the year paid.

Special Analyses

I. *Regulatory Planning and Review*

Executive Orders 13771, 13563, and 12866 direct agencies to assess costs and benefits of available regulatory alternatives and, if regulation is necessary, to select regulatory approaches that maximize net benefits, including potential economic, environmental, public health and safety effects, distributive impacts, and equity. Executive Order 13563 emphasizes the importance of quantifying both costs and benefits, reducing costs, harmonizing rules, and promoting flexibility. The preliminary Executive Order 13771 designation for this proposed rulemaking is regulatory.

The proposed regulations have been designated by the Office of Management and Budget's Office of Information and Regulatory Affairs as significant under Executive Order 12866 pursuant to section 1(b) the Memorandum of Agreement (April 11, 2018) between the Treasury Department and the Office of Management and Budget regarding review of tax regulations.

A. *Background*

The Act introduced two new provisions, sections 245A(e) and 267A, that affect the treatment of hybrid arrangements and a new section, 951A, which imposes tax on United States shareholders with respect to certain earnings of their CFCs.[2] The Treasury Department and the IRS previously issued proposed regulations under sections 245A(e) and 267A and are issuing final regulations simultaneously with these current proposed regulations. The Treasury Department and IRS have also previously issued final regulations (REG-104390-18, 83 FR 51072), which provided additional rules implementing section 951A. In addition to these rules, the Treasury Department and the IRS previously provided guidance regarding conduit financing arrangements under sections 881 and 7701(l). *See* TD 8611, 60 FR 40997 and TD 9562, 76 FR 76895.

Section 245A(e) disallows the dividends received deduction (DRD) for any dividend received by a U.S. shareholder from a CFC if the dividend is a hybrid dividend. In addition, section 245A(e) treats hybrid dividends between CFCs with a common U.S. shareholder as subpart F income. The statute defines a hybrid dividend as an amount received from a CFC for which a deduction would be allowed under section 245A(a) and for which the CFC received a deduction or other tax benefit in a foreign country. This disallowance of the DRD for hybrid dividends and the treatment of hybrid dividends as subpart F income neutralizes the double non-taxation that these dividends might otherwise be produced by these dividends.[3] The section 245A(e) final regulations require that taxpayers maintain "hybrid deduction accounts" to track a CFC's (or a person related to a CFC's) hybrid deductions allowed in foreign jurisdictions across sources and years. The section 245A(e) final regulations then provide that a dividend received by a U.S. shareholder from the CFC is a hybrid dividend to the extent of the sum of those accounts.

These proposed regulations also include rules regarding conduit financing arrangements.[4] Under the current conduit financing regulations, a "financing arrangement" means a series of transactions by which one entity (the financing entity) advances money or other property to another entity (the financed entity) through one or more intermediaries. If the IRS determines that a principal purpose of such an arrangement is to avoid U.S. tax, the IRS may disregard the participation of intermediate entities. As a result, U.S.-source payments from the financed entity are, for U.S. withholding tax purposes, treated as being made directly to the financing entity.

For example, consider a foreign entity that is seeking to finance its U.S. subsidiary but is not entitled to U.S. tax treaty benefits; thus, U.S.-source payments made to this entity are not entitled to reduced withholding tax rates. Instead of lending money directly to the U.S. subsidiary, the foreign entity might loan money to an affiliate residing in a treaty jurisdiction and have the affiliate lend on to the U.S. subsidiary in order to access U.S. tax treaty benefits.

Under the current conduit financing regulations, if the IRS determines that a principal purpose of such an arrangement is to avoid U.S. tax, the IRS may disregard the participation of the affiliate. As a result, U.S.-source interest payments from the U.S. subsidiary are, for U.S. withholding tax purposes, treated as being made directly to the foreign entity.

In general, the current conduit financing regulations apply only if "financing transactions," as defined under the regulations, link the financing entity, the intermediate entities, and the financed entity. Under the current conduit financing regulations, an instrument that is equity for U.S. tax purposes generally will not be treated as a "financing transaction" unless it provides the holder significant redemption rights. This is the case even if the instrument gives rise to a deduction under the laws of the foreign jurisdiction (e.g., perpetual debt). As a result, the current conduit financing regulations would not apply, and the U.S.-source payment might be entitled to a lower rate of U.S. withholding tax.

---

[2] Hybrid arrangements are tax-avoidance tools used by certain multinational corporations (MNCs) that have operations both in the U.S. and a foreign country. These hybrid arrangements use differences in tax treatment by the U.S. and a foreign country to reduce taxes in one or both jurisdictions. Hybrid arrangements can be "hybrid entities," in which a taxpayer is treated as a flow-through or disregarded entity in one country but as a corporation in another, or "hybrid instruments," which are financial transactions that are treated as debt in one country and as equity in another.

[3] The tax treatment under which certain payments are deductible in one jurisdiction and not included in income in a second jurisdiction is referred to as a deduction/no-inclusion outcome ("D/NI outcome".)

[4] On December 22, 2008, the Treasury Department and the IRS published a notice of proposed rulemaking (REG-113462-08) ("2008 proposed regulations") that proposed adding §1.881-3(a)(2)(i)(C) to the conduit financing regulations. The preamble to the 2008 proposed regulations provides that the Treasury Department and the IRS are also studying transactions where a financing entity advances cash or other property to an intermediate entity in exchange for a hybrid instrument (that is, an instrument treated as debt under the tax laws of the foreign country in which the intermediary is resident and equity for U.S. tax purposes), and states that they may issue separate guidance to address the treatment under §1.881-3 of certain hybrid instruments.

The proposed regulations also implement items in section 951A of the Act. Section 951A provides for the taxation of global intangible low-taxed income (GILTI), effective beginning with the first taxable year of a CFC that begins after December 31. 2017. The GILTI final regulations address the treatment of a deduction or loss attributable to basis created by certain transfers of property from one CFC to a related CFC after December 31, 2017, but before the date on which section 951A first applies to the transferring CFC's income. Those regulations state that such a deduction or loss is allocated to residual CFC gross income; that is, income that is not attributable to tested income, subpart F income, or income effectively connected with a trade or business in the United States.

B. *Overview of proposed regulations*

These proposed regulations address three main issues: (i) adjustments to hybrid deduction accounts under section 245A(e) and the final regulations; (ii) conduit financing arrangements that use certain equity interests that allow the issuer a deduction or other tax benefit under foreign tax law; and (iii) certain payments between related CFCs during a disqualified period under section 951A and the GILTI final regulations.

First, the proposed regulations address adjustments to hybrid deduction accounts under section 245A(e) and the final regulations. The section 245A(e) final regulations stipulate that hybrid deduction accounts should generally be reduced to the extent that earnings and profits of the CFC that have not been subject to foreign tax as a result of certain hybrid arrangements are included in income in the United States by some provision other than section 245A(e). The proposed regulations provide new rules for reducing hybrid deduction accounts by reason of income inclusions attributable to subpart F, GILTI, and sections 951(a)(1)(B) and 956. An inclusion due to subpart F or GILTI reduces a hybrid deduction account only to the extent that the inclusion is not offset by a deduction or credit, such as a foreign tax credit, that likely will be afforded to the inclusion. Because deductions and credits are typically not available to offset income inclusions under section 951(a)(1)(B) and 956, these inclusions reduce a hybrid deduction account dollar-for-dollar.

Second, the proposed regulations address conduit financing arrangements under §1.881-3 by expanding the types of transactions classified as financing transactions. The proposed rules state that if the issuer of a financial instrument is allowed a deduction or tax benefit for an amount paid, accrued, or distributed with respect to a stock or similar interest under the tax law of the foreign jurisdiction where the issuer is a resident, then it may now be characterized as a financing transaction even though the instrument is equity for U.S. tax purposes. Accordingly, the conduit financing regulations would apply to multiple-party financing arrangements using these types of instruments, which include certain types of hybrid instruments. This change essentially aligns the conduit regulations with the policy of section 267A by discouraging the exploitation of differences in treatment of financial instruments across jurisdictions. While section 267A and the final regulations apply only if the D/NI outcome is a result of the use of a hybrid entity or instrument, the conduit financing regulations apply regardless of causation and instead look to whether there is a tax avoidance plan. Thus, this new rule will address economically similar transactions that section 267A and the section 267A final regulations do not cover.

Finally, the proposed regulations address certain payments made after December 31, 2017, but before the date of the start of the first fiscal year for the transferor CFC for which 951A applies (the "disqualified period") in which payments, such as pre-payments of royalties, create income during the disqualified period and a corresponding deduction or loss claimed in taxable years after the disqualified period. Absent the proposed regulations, those deductions or losses could have been used to reduce tested income or increase tested losses, among other benefits. However, under the proposed regulations, these deductions will no longer provide such a tax benefit, and will instead be allocated to residual CFC income, similar to deductions or losses from certain property transfers in the disqualified period under the GILTI final regulations.

C. *Need for the proposed regulations*

A failure to reduce hybrid deduction accounts by certain earnings of a CFC that are indirectly included in the income of a U.S. shareholder may result in double taxation for some taxpayers—for example, those which have subpart F or GILTI income inclusions.

Failure to address certain equity interests under the conduit financing regulations may allow some MNCs to avoid U.S. tax by shifting additional income towards conduit financing arrangements that use financial instruments treated as equity for U.S. tax purposes but as debt in a foreign jurisdiction. These arrangements are economically similar to the hybrid arrangements that are addressed by the Act and by the section 267A final regulations and to other arrangements covered by the conduit financing regulations, but they have not yet been addressed themselves.

The Treasury Department and IRS are aware that certain transactions that accelerate income, but do not give rise to a disposition of property (e.g., prepayments of royalties from a related CFC) fall outside the purview of the GILTI final regulations. In order for the Code to treat similar transactions similarly, these types of transactions need to be addressed by regulation.

D. *Economic analysis*

1. Baseline

The Treasury Department and the IRS have assessed the benefits and costs of the proposed regulations relative to a no-action baseline reflecting anticipated federal income tax-related behavior in the absence of these regulations.

2. Economic Analysis of Specific Provisions and Alternatives Considered

i. Section 245A(e) - Adjustment of hybrid deduction account

Under the final regulations, taxpayers must maintain hybrid deduction accounts to track income of a CFC that was sheltered from foreign tax due to hybrid arrangements, so that it may be included in U.S. income under section 245A(e) when paid as a dividend. The proposed regulations address how hybrid deduction accounts should be adjusted to account for earnings and profits of a CFC included in U.S. income due to certain provisions other than section 245A(e). The proposed regulations provide rules reducing a hybrid deduction account for three categories of inclusions: subpart F inclusions, GILTI inclusions, and inclusions under sections 951(a)(1)(B) and 956.

One option for addressing the treatment of earnings and profits included in U.S. income due to provisions other than section 245A(e) would be to not issue additional guidance beyond current tax rules and thus not to adjust hybrid deduction accounts to account for such inclusions. This would be the simplest approach among those considered, but under this approach, some income could be subject to double taxation in the United States. For example, if no adjustment is made, to the extent that a CFC's earnings and profits were sheltered from foreign tax as a result of certain hybrid arrangements, the section 245A DRD would be disallowed for an amount of dividends equal to the amount of the sheltered earnings and profits, even if some of the sheltered earnings and profits were included in the income of a U.S. shareholder under the subpart F rules. The U.S. shareholder would be subject to tax on both the dividends and on the subpart F inclusion. Owing to this double taxation, this approach is not proposed by the Treasury Department and the IRS.

A second option would be to reduce hybrid deduction accounts by amounts included in gross income under the three categories; that is, without regard to deductions or credits that may offset the inclusion. While this option is also relatively simple, it could lead to double non-taxation and thus would give rise to results not intended by the statute. Subpart F and GILTI inclusions may be offset by ~~and thus may not be fully taxed in the~~

United States as a result of - foreign tax credits and, in the case of GILTI, the section 250 deduction.[5] Therefore, this option for reducing hybrid deduction accounts may result in some income that was sheltered from foreign tax due to hybrid arrangements also escaping full U.S. taxation. This double non-taxation is economically inefficient because otherwise similar activities are taxed differently, incentivizing wasteful avoidance activities.

A third option, which is the option proposed by the Treasury Department and the IRS, is to reduce hybrid deduction accounts by the amount of the inclusions from the three categories, but only to the extent that the inclusions are likely not offset by foreign tax credits or, in the case of GILTI, the section 250 deduction. For subpart F and GILTI inclusions, the proposed regulations stipulate adjustments to be made to account for the foreign tax credits and the section 250 deduction available to GILTI income. These adjustments are intended to provide a precise, administrable manner for measuring the extent to which a subpart F or GILTI inclusion is included in U.S. income and not shielded by foreign tax credits or deductions. This option results in an outcome aligned with statutory intent, as it generally ensures that the section 245A DRD is disallowed (and thus a dividend is included in U.S. income without any regard for foreign tax credits) only for amounts that were sheltered from foreign tax by reason of a hybrid arrangement but that have not yet been subject to U.S. tax.

Relative to a no-action baseline, the proposed regulations provide taxpayers with new instruction regarding how to adjust hybrid deduction accounts to account for earnings and profits that are included in U.S. income by reason of certain provisions other than section 245A(e). This new instruction avoids possible double taxation. Double taxation is inconsistent with the intent and purpose of the statute and is economically inefficient because it may result in otherwise similar income streams facing different tax treatment, incentivizing taxpayers to finance operations with specific income streams and activities that may not be the most economically productive.

The Treasury Department and IRS estimate that this provision will impact an upper bound of approximately 2,000 taxpayers. This estimate is based on the top 10 percent of taxpayers (by gross receipts) that filed a domestic corporate income tax return for tax year 2017 with a Form 5471 attached, because only domestic corporations that are U.S. shareholders of CFCs are potentially affected by section 245A(e).[6]

This estimate is an upper bound on the number of large corporations affected because it is based on all transactions, even though only a portion of such transactions involve hybrid arrangements. The tax data do not report whether these reported dividends were part of a hybrid arrangement because such information was not relevant for calculating tax prior to the Act. In addition, this estimate is an upper bound because the Treasury Department and the IRS anticipate that fewer taxpayers would engage in hybrid arrangements going forward as the statute and §1.245A(e)-1 would make such arrangements less beneficial to taxpayers.

ii. Conduit financing regulations to address equity interests that give rise to deductions or other benefits under foreign law

The conduit financing regulations allow the IRS to disregard intermediate entities in a multiple-party financing arrangement for the purposes of determining withholding tax rates if the instruments used in the arrangement are considered "financing transactions." Financing transactions generally exclude instruments that are treated as equity for U.S. tax purposes unless they have significant redemption features. Thus, in the absence of further guidance, the conduit financing regulations would not apply to certain arrangements using certain hybrid instruments or other instruments that are eligible for deductions in the jurisdiction of the issuer but treated as equity under U.S. law. This would allow payments made under these arrangements to continue to be eligible for reduced withholding tax rates through a conduit structure.

One option for addressing the current disparate treatment would be to not change the conduit financing regulations, which currently treat equity as a financing transaction only if it has specific redemption features; this is the no-action baseline. This option is not proposed by the Treasury Department and the IRS, since it is inconsistent with the Treasury Department's and the IRS's ongoing efforts to address financing transactions that use hybrid instruments, as discussed in the 2008 proposed regulations.

A second option considered would be to treat as a financing transaction an instrument that is equity for U.S. tax purposes but debt for purposes of the issuer's jurisdiction of residence. This approach would prevent taxpayers from using this type of hybrid instrument to engage in treaty shopping through a conduit jurisdiction. However, this approach would not cover certain cases, such as if a jurisdiction offers a tax benefit to non-debt instruments (e.g., a notional interest deduction with respect to equity).

A third option, which is adopted in these proposed regulations, is to treat as a financing transaction any instrument that is equity for U.S. tax purposes and which entitles its issuer or its shareholder a deduction or similar tax benefit in the issuer's resident jurisdiction or in the jurisdiction where the resident has a permanent establishment. This rule is broader than the second option. It covers all instruments that give rise to deductions or similar tax benefits, such as credits, rather than only those instruments that are treated as debt. This rule also covers instruments where a financing payment is attributable to a permanent establishment of the issuer, and the tax laws of the permanent establishment's jurisdiction allow a deduction or similar treatment for the instrument. This will prevent issuers from routing transactions through their permanent establishments to avoid the anti-conduit rules. The Treasury Department and the IRS adopted this third option since it will most efficiently, and in a manner that is clear and administrable, prevent inappropriate avoidance of the conduit financing regulations. The Treasury Department and the IRS project that this third option will ensure that similar financing arrangements are treated similarly by the tax system.

Relative to a no-action baseline, the proposed regulations are likely to incentivize some taxpayers to shift away from conduit financing arrangements and hybrid arrangements. The Treasury Department and the IRS project little to no overall economic loss, or even an economic gain, from this shift because conduit arrangements are generally not economically productive arrangements and are typically pursued only for tax-related reasons. The Treasury Department and the IRS recognize, however, that as a result of these provisions, some taxpayers may face a higher effective tax rate, which may lower their economic activity.

The Treasury Department and the IRS have not undertaken more precise quantitative estimates of either of these economic effects because we do not have readily available data or models to estimate with reasonable precision: (i) the types or volume of conduit arrangements that taxpayers would likely use under the proposed regulations or under the no-action baseline; or (ii) the effects of those arrangements on businesses' overall economic performance, including possible differences in compliance costs. In the absence of such quantitative estimates, the Treasury Department and the IRS project that the proposed regulations will best enhance U.S. economic performance relative to the no-action baseline and relative to other alternative regulatory approaches and because they most comprehensively ensure that similar financing arrangements are treated similarly by the tax system.

The Treasury Department and the IRS estimate that the number of taxpayers potentially affected by the proposed conduit financing regulations will be an upper bound of approximately 7,000 taxpayers. This estimate is based on the top 10 percent of taxpayers (by gross receipts) that filed a domestic corporate income tax return with a Form 5472, "Information Return of a 25% Foreign-Owned U.S. Corporation or a Foreign Corporation Engaged in a U.S. Trade or Business," attached because primarily foreign entities that advance money or other property to a related U.S. entity through one or more foreign intermediaries are potentially affected by the conduit financing regulations.[7]

---

[5] Typically, deductions or credits are not available to offset income inclusions under sections 951(a)(1)(B) and 956, the third category addressed by the proposed regulations.

[6] Because of the complexities involved, primarily only large taxpayers engage in hybrid arrangements. The estimate that the top 10 percent of otherwise-relevant taxpay-

ers (by gross receipts) are likely to engage in hybrid arrangements is based on the judgment of the Treasury Department and IRS.

[7] Because of the complexities involved, primarily only large taxpayers engage in conduit financing arrangements. The estimate that the top 10 percent of otherwise-

This estimate is an upper bound on the number of large corporations affected because it is based on all domestic corporate arrangements involving foreign related parties, even though only a portion of such arrangements are conduit financing arrangements that use hybrid instruments. The tax data do not report whether these arrangements were part of a conduit financing arrangement because such information is not provided on tax forms. In addition, this estimate is an upper bound because the Treasury Department and the IRS anticipate that fewer taxpayers would engage in conduit financing arrangements that use hybrid instruments going forward as the proposed conduit financing regulations would make such arrangements less beneficial to taxpayers.

iii. Rules under section 951A to address certain disqualified payments made during the disqualified period

The final 951A regulations include a rule that addresses certain transactions involving asset transfers between related CFCs during the disqualified period that may have the effect of reducing GILTI inclusions due to timing differences between when a transaction occurs and when resulting deductions are claimed. The disqualified period of a CFC is the period between December 31, 2017, which is the last earnings and profits measurement date under section 965, and the beginning of the CFC's first taxable year that begins after December 31, 2017, which is the first taxable year with respect to which section 951A is effective.

The proposed regulations refine this rule to extend its applicability to other transactions for which similar timing differences can arise. For example, suppose that a CFC licensed property to a related CFC for ten years and received pre-payments of royalties during the disqualified period from the related CFC. Since these prepayments were received by the licensor CFC during the disqualified period, they would not have affected amounts included under section 965 nor given rise to GILTI tested income. However, the licensee CFC that made the payments would not have claimed the total of the corresponding deductions during the disqualified period, since the timing of deductions are generally tied to economic performance over the period of use. The licensee CFC would claim deductions over the ten years of the contract, and since these deductions would be claimed during taxable years when section 951A is in effect, these deductions would reduce GILTI tested income or increase GILTI tested loss. Thus, this type of transaction could lower overall income inclusions for the U.S. shareholder of these CFCs in a manner that does not accurately reflect the earnings of the CFCs over time.

The Treasury Department and the IRS propose that all deductions attributable to payments to a related CFC during the disqualified period should be allocated and apportioned to residual CFC gross income. These deductions will not thereby reduce tested, subpart F or effectively connected income. This rule provides similar treatment to transactions involving prepayments as the rule in the GILTI final regulations provides to asset transfers between related CFCs during the disqualified period.

Relative to a no-action baseline, the proposed regulations harmonize the treatment of similar transactions. Since this rule applies to deductions resulting from transactions that occurred during the disqualified period and not to any new transactions, the Treasury Department and the IRS do not expect changes in taxpayer behavior under the proposed regulations, relative to the no-action baseline.

The Treasury Department and the IRS estimate that the number of taxpayers potentially affected by these proposed regulations will be an upper bound of approximately 25,000 to 35,000 taxpayers. This estimate is based on filers of income tax returns with a Form 5471 attached because only filers that are U.S. shareholders of CFCs or that have at least a 10 percent ownership in a foreign corporation would be subject to section 951A. This estimate is an upper bound because it is based on all filers subject to section 951A, even though only a portion of such taxpayers may have engaged in the pre-payment transactions during the disqualified period described in the proposed regulations. Therefore, the Treasury Department and the IRS estimate that the number of taxpayers potentially affected by these proposed regulations will be substantially less than 25,000 to 35,000 taxpayers.

II. *Paperwork Reduction Act*

Pursuant to §1.6038-2(f)(14), certain U.S. shareholders of a CFC must provide information relating to the CFC and the rules of section 245A(e) on Form 5471, "Information Return of U.S. Persons With Respect to Certain Foreign Corporations," (OMB control number 1545-0123), as the form or other guidance may prescribe. The proposed regulations do not impose any additional information collection requirements relating to section 245A(e). However, the proposed regulations provide guidance regarding certain computations required under section 245A(e), and such could affect the information required to be reported on Form 5471. For purposes of the Paperwork Reduction Act of 1995 (44 U.S.C. 3507(d)) ("PRA"), the reporting burden associated with §1.6038-2(f)(14) is reflected in the PRA submission for Form 5471. See the chart at the end of this part II of this Special Analyses section for the status of the PRA submission for Form 5471. As described in the Special Analyses section the preamble to the section 245A(e) final regulations, and as set forth in the chart below, the IRS estimates the number of affected filers to be 2,000.

Pursuant to §1.6038-5, certain U.S. shareholders of a CFC must provide information relating to the CFC and the U.S. shareholder's GILTI inclusion under section 951A on new Form 8992, "U.S. Shareholder Calculation of Global Intangible Low-Taxed Income (GILTI)," (OMB control number 1545-0123), as the form or other guidance may prescribe. The proposed regulations do not impose any additional information collection requirements relating to section 951A. However, the proposed regulations provide guidance regarding computations required under section 951A for taxpayers who engaged in certain transactions during the disqualified period, and such guidance could affect the information required to be reported by these taxpayers on Form 8992. For purposes of the PRA, the reporting burden associated with the collection of information under §1.6038-5 is reflected in the PRA submission for Form 8992. See the chart at the end of this part II of this Special Analyses section for the status of the PRA submission for Form 8992. As discussed in the Special Analyses section of the preamble to the proposed regulations under section 951A (REG-104390-18, 83 FR 51072), and as set forth in the chart below, the IRS estimates the number of filers subject to §1.6038-5 to be 25,000 to 35,000. Since the proposed regulations only apply to taxpayers who engaged in certain transactions during the disqualified period, the IRS estimates that the number of filers affected by the proposed regulations and subject to the collection of information in §1.6038-5 will be significantly less than 25,000 to 35,000.

There is no existing collection of information relating to conduit financing arrangements, and the proposed regulations do not impose any new information collection requirements relating to conduit financing arrangements. Therefore, a PRA analysis is not required with respect to the proposed regulations relating to conduit financing arrangements.

As a result, the IRS estimates the number of filers affected by these proposed regulations to be the following.

Collection of information	Tax Forms Impacted	
	Number of respondents (estimated, rounded to nearest 1,000)	Forms in which information may be collected
§1.6038-2(f)(14)	2,000	Form 5471 (Schedule I)
§1.6038-5	25,000 - 35,000	Form 8992

(Footnote Continued)

relevant taxpayers (by gross receipts) are likely to engage in conduit financing arrangements is based on the judgment of the Treasury Department and IRS.

Tax Forms Impacted		
Collection of information	Number of respondents (estimated, rounded to nearest 1,000)	Forms in which information may be collected

Source: IRS data (MeF, DCS, and Compliance Data Warehouse)

The current status of the PRA submissions related to the tax forms associated with the information collections in §§ 1.6038-2(f)(14) and 1.6038-5 is provided in the accompanying table. The reporting burdens associated with the information collections in §§ 1.6038-2(f)(14) and 1.6038-5 are included in the aggregated burden estimates for OMB control number 1545-0123, which represents a total estimated burden time for all forms and schedules for corporations of 3.157 billion hours and total estimated monetized costs of $58.148 billion ($2017). The overall burden estimates provided in 1545-0123 are aggregate amounts that relate to the entire package of forms associated with the OMB control number, and are therefore not accurate for future calculations needed to assess the burden specific to certain regulations, such as the information collections under § 1.6038-2(f)(14) or § 1.6038-5. No burden estimates specific to the proposed regulations are currently available. The Treasury Department and the IRS have not identified any burden estimates, including those for new information collections, related to the requirements under the proposed regulations. The Treasury Department and the IRS estimate PRA burdens on a taxpayer-type basis rather than a provision-specific basis. Changes in those estimates will capture both changes made by the Act and those that arise out of discretionary authority exercised in the proposed regulations.

The Treasury Department and the IRS request comments on all aspects of information collection burdens related to the proposed regulations, including estimates for how much time it would take to comply with the paperwork burdens related to the forms described and ways for the IRS to minimize the paperwork burden. Proposed revisions (if any) to these forms that reflect the information collections related to the proposed regulations will be made available for public comment at https://apps.irs.gov/app/picklist/list/draftTaxForms.html and will not be finalized until after these forms have been approved by OMB under the PRA.

Form	Type of Filer	OMB Number(s)	Status
Form 5471	Business (NEW Model)	1545-0123	Published in the Federal Register on 9/30/19 (84 FR 51718). Public Comment period closed on 11/29/19. Approved by OMB through 1/31/2021.
	Link: *https://www.federalregister.gov/documents/2019/09/30/2019-21068/proposed-collection-comment-request-for-forms-1065-1066-1120-1120-c-1120-f-1120-h-1120-nd-1120-s*		
	Individual (NEW Model)	1545-0074	Published in the Federal Register on 9/30/19 (84 FR 51712). Public Comment period closed on 11/29/19. Approved by OMB through 1/31/2021.
	Link: *https://www.federalregister.gov/documents/2019/09/30/2019-21066/proposed-collection-comment-request-for-form-1040-form-1040nr-form-1040nr-ez-form-1040x-1040-sr-and-u*		
Form 8992	Business (NEW Model)	1545-0123	Published in the Federal Register on 9/30/19 (84 FR 51718). Public Comment period closed on 11/29/19. Approved by OMB through 1/31/2021.
	Link: *https://www.federalregister.gov/documents/2019/09/30/2019-21068/proposed-collection-comment-request-for-forms-1065-1066-1120-1120-c-1120-f-1120-h-1120-nd-1120-s*		

III. *Regulatory Flexibility Act*

It is hereby certified that this notice of proposed rulemaking will not have a significant economic impact on a substantial number of small entities within the meaning of section 601(6) of the Regulatory Flexibility Act (5 U.S.C. chapter 6).

These proposed regulations, if finalized, would amend certain computations required under section 245A(e) or section 951A. As discussed in the Special Analyses accompanying the preambles to the section 245A(e) final regulations and the proposed regulations under section 951A (REG-104390-18, 83 FR 51072), as well as in this part III of the Special Analyses, the Treasury Department and the IRS project that a substantial number of domestic small business entities will not be subject to sections 245A(e) and 951A, and therefore, the existing requirements in §§ 1.6038-2(f)(14) and 1.6038-5 will not have a significant economic impact on a substantial number of small entities.

The small entities that are subject to section 245A(e) and § 1.6038-2(f)(14) are controlling U.S. shareholders of a CFC that engage in a hybrid arrangement, and the small entities that are subject to section 951A and § 1.6038-5 are U.S. shareholders of a CFC. A CFC is a foreign corporation in which more than 50 percent of its stock is owned by U.S. shareholders, measured either by value or voting power. A U.S. shareholder is any U.S. person that owns 10 percent or more of a foreign corporation's stock, measured either by value or voting power, and a controlling U.S. shareholder of a CFC is a U.S. person that owns more than 50 percent of the CFC's stock.

The Treasury Department and the IRS estimate that there are only a small number of taxpayers having gross receipts below either $25 million (or $41.5 million for financial entities) who would potentially be affected by these regulations.[8] Our estimate of those entities who could potentially be affected is based on our review of those taxpayers who filed a domestic corporate income tax return in 2016 with gross receipts below either $25 million (or $41.5 million for financial institutions) who also reported dividends on a Form 5471. The Treasury Department and the IRS estimate that the number of small entities potentially affected by these regulations will be between 1 and 6 percent of all affected entities regardless of size.

The Treasury Department and the IRS cannot readily identify from these data amounts that are received pursuant to hybrid arrangements because those amounts are not separately reported on tax forms. Thus, dividends received as reported on Form 5471 are an upper bound on the amount of hybrid arrangements by these taxpayers.

The Treasury Department and the IRS estimated the upper bound of the relative cost of the statutory and regulatory hybrids provisions, as a percentage of revenue, for these taxpayers as (i) the statutory tax rate of 21 percent multiplied by dividends received as reported on Form 5471, divided by (ii) the taxpayer's gross receipts. Based on this calculation, the Treasury Department and the IRS estimate that the upper bound of the relative cost of these statutory and regulatory provisions is above 3 percent for more than half of the small entities described in the preceding paragraph. Because this estimate is an upper bound, a smaller subset of these taxpayers (including potentially zero taxpayers) is likely to have a cost above three percent of gross receipts.

Notwithstanding this certification, the Treasury Department and IRS invite comments about the impact this proposal may have on small entities.

---

[8] This estimate is limited to those taxpayers who report gross receipts above $0.

Pursuant to section 7805(f) of the Code, this notice of proposed rulemaking has been submitted to the Chief Counsel for Advocacy of the Small Business Administration for comment on its impact on small business.

Comments and Requests for Public Hearing

Before the proposed regulations are adopted as final regulations, consideration will be given to any comments that are submitted timely to the IRS as prescribed in this preamble under the "ADDRESSES" heading. The Treasury Department and the IRS request comments on all aspects of the proposed rules.

All comments will be available at *www.regulations.gov* or upon request. A public hearing will be scheduled if requested in writing by any person that timely submits written comments. If a public hearing is scheduled, then notice of the date, time, and place for the public hearing will be published in the **Federal Register**.

Drafting Information

The principal authors of these regulations are Shane M. McCarrick and Richard F. Owens of the Office of Associate Chief Counsel (International). However, other personnel from the Treasury Department and the IRS participated in their development.

[¶ 49,832]   **Proposed Amendments of Regulations (REG-117138-17)**, published in the Federal Register on April 16, 2020.

[26 CFR Part 300]

Preparer Tax Identification Number (PTIN): Tax return preparer: Tax return.—Amendments of Reg. § 300.12, relating to the imposition of certain user fees on tax return preparers, are proposed.

AGENCY: Internal Revenue Service (IRS), Treasury.

ACTION: Notice of proposed rulemaking.

SUMMARY: This document contains proposed amendments to the regulations relating to the imposition of certain user fees on tax return preparers. The proposed regulations reduce the amount of the user fee to apply for or renew a preparer tax identification number (PTIN) and affect individuals who apply for or renew a PTIN. The Independent Offices Appropriations Act of 1952 authorizes the charging of user fees.

DATES: Written or electronic comments and requests for a public hearing must be received by May 16, 2020. Requests for a public hearing must be submitted as prescribed in the "**Comments and Requests for a Public Hearing**" section.

ADDRESSES: Commenters are strongly encouraged to submit public comments electronically. Submit electronic submissions via the Federal eRulemaking Portal at www.regulations.gov (indicate IRS and REG-117138-17) by following the online instructions for submitting comments. Once submitted to the Federal eRulemaking Portal, comments cannot be edited or withdrawn. The IRS expects to have limited personnel available to process public comments that are submitted on paper through mail. Until further notice, any comments submitted on paper will be considered to the extent practicable. The Department of the Treasury (Treasury Department) and the IRS will publish for public availability any comment submitted electronically, and to the extent practicable on paper, to its public docket.

Send paper submissions to: CC:PA:LPD:PR (REG-117138-17), room 5203, Internal Revenue Service, PO Box 7604, Ben Franklin Station, Washington, D.C. 20044. FOR FURTHER INFORMATION CONTACT: Concerning the proposed regulations, Michael A. Franklin at (202) 317-6844; concerning cost methodology, Michael A. Weber at (202) 803-9738; concerning submissions of comments and/or requests for a public hearing, Regina Johnson, (202) 317-5177 (not toll-free numbers).

SUPPLEMENTARY INFORMATION:

Background and Explanation of Provisions

This document contains proposed amendments to 26 CFR part 300 regarding user fees.

Regulations require a tax return preparer who prepares all or substantially all of a tax return or claim for refund to provide a PTIN as their identifying number on any tax return or claim for refund prepared for compensation. To account for its costs of providing PTIN application and renewal services, the IRS charges a user fee to apply for or renew a PTIN. This proposal would reduce the user fee from $33 per application or renewal to $21.

A. *User Fee Authority*

The Independent Offices Appropriations Act of 1952 (IOAA), which is codified at 31 U.S.C. 9701, authorizes agencies to prescribe regulations that establish user fees for services provided by the agency. The IOAA provides that regulations implementing user fees are subject to policies prescribed by the President; these policies are set forth in the Office of Management and Budget (OMB) Circular A-25, 58 FR 38142 (July 15, 1993) (OMB Circular A-25).

Under OMB Circular A-25, Federal agencies that provide services that confer benefits on identifiable recipients are to establish user fees that recover the full cost of providing the service. An agency that seeks to impose a user fee for government-provided services must calculate the full cost of providing those services. In general, a user fee should be set at an amount that allows the agency to recover the direct and indirect costs of providing the service, unless the OMB grants an exception. OMB Circular A-25 provides that agencies are to review user fees biennially and update them as necessary.

B. *PTIN Requirement*

Section 6109(a)(4) of the Internal Revenue Code authorizes the Secretary of the Treasury or his delegate to prescribe regulations for the inclusion of a tax return preparer's identifying number on a return, statement, or other document required to be filed with the IRS. On September 30, 2010, the Treasury Department and the IRS published final regulations under section 6109 (REG-134235-08) in the **Federal Register** (TD 9501) (75 FR 60315) (PTIN regulations) to provide that, for returns or claims for refund filed after December 31, 2010, the identifying number of a tax return preparer is the individual's PTIN or such other number prescribed by the IRS in forms, instructions, or other appropriate guidance. The PTIN regulations require a tax return preparer who prepares or who assists in preparing all or substantially all of a tax return or claim for refund after December 31, 2010 to have a PTIN.

The PTIN regulations also state that the IRS will set forth in forms, instructions, or other appropriate guidance PTIN application and renewal procedures, including the requirement to pay a user fee to obtain or renew a PTIN. Pursuant to the authority granted in section 6109(c) and in accordance with § 1.6109-2(d) of the PTIN regulations, the IRS has set forth application and renewal procedures in Form W-12, *IRS Paid Preparer Tax Identification Number (PTIN) Application and Renewal,* and the Form W-12 Instructions. Individuals may also apply for or renew a PTIN and pay the user fee online at irs.gov/ptin. The annual PTIN application and renewal period generally begins in the fall of the year preceding the filing season to which the PTIN relates.

Section 1.6109-2(d) states that only individuals authorized to practice before the IRS under 31 U.S.C. 330 are eligible to obtain a PTIN. Under § 1.6109-2(h), the IRS may prescribe in forms, instructions, or other appropriate guidance exceptions to the requirements of the PTIN regulations, including the requirement that an individual must be authorized to practice before the IRS to be eligible to receive a PTIN. On December 30, 2010, the Treasury Department and the IRS released Notice 2011-6 (2011-3 IRB 315 (Jan. 17, 2011)), which stated that, until December 31, 2013, a provisional PTIN could be renewed upon proper application and payment of the applicable user fee, even if the individual holding the provisional PTIN was not authorized to practice before the IRS.

On June 3, 2011, the Treasury Department and the IRS published in the **Federal Register** (76 FR 32286) amendments to Treasury Department Circular No. 230 (31 CFR part 10), to regulate all tax return preparers under 31 U.S.C. 330. In *Loving v. IRS*, 917 F.Supp.2d 67 (D.D.C. 2013), the district court concluded that the Treasury Department and the IRS lacked statutory authority to regulate tax return preparation as practice before the IRS under 31 U.S.C. 330 and enjoined the Treasury Department and the IRS from enforcing the regulations issued under that section. The district court subsequently modified its order to clarify that the IRS's authority to require that tax return preparers obtain a PTIN is unaffected by the injunction. *Loving v. IRS*, 920 F.Supp.2d 108, 109 (D.D.C. 2013) (stating "Congress has specifically authorized the PTIN scheme by statute . . . [and that] scheme, therefore, does not fall within the scope of the injunction and may proceed as promulgated."). The United States Court of Appeals for the District of Columbia Circuit affirmed the district court's decision and order for injunction. *Loving v. IRS*, 742 F.3d 1013 (D.C. Cir. 2014).

C. *PTIN User Fee*

Final regulations (REG-139343-08) published in the **Federal Register** (TD 9503) (75 FR 60316) (initial PTIN user fee regulations) on September 30, 2010, established a $50 user fee to apply for or renew a PTIN, in addition to a portion payable directly to the contractor, which was $14.25 for new applications and $13 for renewal applications. The $50 user fee was based on an annual PTIN renewal period and an estimate that 1.2 million individuals would be applying for or renewing a PTIN each year.

The Treasury Department and the IRS determined that a $50 user fee to apply for or renew a PTIN would recover the full direct and indirect costs that the government would incur to administer the PTIN application and renewal process. As explained in the preamble to the initial PTIN user fee regulations, the projected costs included the development and maintenance of the IRS information technology system that would interface with a third-party contractor, the development and maintenance of internal applications that would have the capacity to process and administer the anticipated increase in PTIN applications, and customer service support activities, which included website development and maintenance and call center staffing to respond to questions regarding PTIN usage and renewal. The $50 user fee was also determined to recover costs for personnel, administrative, and management support needed to evaluate and address tax compliance issues of individuals applying for and renewing a PTIN, to investigate and address conduct and suitability issues, and otherwise support and enforce the programs that required an individual to apply for and renew a PTIN.

Pursuant to the guidelines in OMB Circular A-25, the IRS re-calculated its costs associated with providing PTINs in 2015. The IRS determined that the full cost of administering the PTIN program going forward was reduced from $50 to $33 per application or renewal, plus a $17 fee per application or renewal payable directly to a third-party contractor. Final regulations (REG-121496-15) published in the **Federal Register** (TD 9781) (81 FR 52766) (2016 PTIN user fee regulations) on August 10, 2016, superseded and adopted temporary regulations (TD 9742) (80 FR 66794) and established the $33 annual user fee to apply for or renew a PTIN, plus $17 per application or renewal payable directly to a third-party contractor. The reduction in the fee amount was attributable to several factors, which included the reduced number of PTIN holders (approximately 700,000) from the number originally projected (1.2 million) in 2010, which reduced associated costs; the absorption of certain development costs in the early years of the program; and the fact that certain activities that would have been conducted in relation to registered tax return preparers would not be performed. In particular, the determination of the user fee no longer included expenses for personnel who performed functions primarily related to continuing education and testing for registered tax return preparers. Additionally, expenses related to personnel who performed continuing education and testing for enrolled agents and enrolled retirement plan agents were removed from the user fee.

In 2017, the IRS again conducted a biennial review of the PTIN user fee and determined that the amount of the fee going forward should be reduced to $31 per application or renewal, plus an amount payable directly to a third-party contractor. The reduction was primarily attributable to reductions in contract support costs and salary and benefits. On June 1, 2017, before a notice of proposed rulemaking proposing to reduce the amount of the fee was issued, the IRS was enjoined from charging a PTIN user fee. In *Steele v. United States*, 260 F. Supp. 3d 52 (D.D.C. 2017), the United States District Court for the District of Columbia concluded that the Treasury Department and the IRS lacked the statutory authority to charge a PTIN user fee and enjoined the IRS from charging a PTIN user fee. The government filed an appeal and on March 1, 2019, the United States Court of Appeals for the District of Columbia Circuit reversed the district court's decision and lifted the injunction against charging the PTIN user fee. *See Montrois v. United States*, 916 F.3d 1056 (D.C. Cir. 2019) (holding that a PTIN provides tax return preparers a specific benefit by allowing them to provide an identifying number that is not a social security number on returns they prepare and stating that the permissible amount of the fee would be the same regardless of whether the specific benefit was instead the ability to prepare tax returns for compensation). The case is currently on remand in the United States District Court for the District of Columbia regarding the amount of the fee. *Id.* at 1068.

Pursuant to the guidelines in OMB Circular A-25, the IRS has re-calculated its cost of providing PTINs. The IRS has determined that the full cost of administering the PTIN program going forward has been reduced to $21 per application or renewal, plus $14.95 payable directly to a third-party contractor. The government is authorized to charge a PTIN user fee under the IOAA because, in exchange for the fee, it provides a service by issuing and maintaining PTINs, which provide tax return preparers a specific benefit by allowing them to provide an identifying number that is not a social security number on returns and to prepare returns for compensation.

D. *Calculation of User Fees Generally*

The IRS follows generally accepted accounting principles (GAAP) in calculating the full cost of administering PTIN applications and renewals. The Federal Accounting Standards Advisory Board (FASAB) is the body that establishes GAAP that apply for Federal reporting entities, such as the IRS. FASAB publishes the FASAB Handbook of Accounting Standards and Other Pronouncements, as Amended (Current Handbook), available at https://files.fasab.gov/pdffiles/2019_fasab-handbook.pdf. Current Handbook includes the *Statement of Federal Financial Accounting Standards (SFFAS) No. 4: Managerial Cost Accounting Concepts and Standards for the Federal Government. SFFAS No. 4* establishes internal costing standards to accurately measure and manage the full cost of Federal programs, and the methodology below is in accordance with *SFFAS No. 4.*

1. *Cost Center Allocation*

The IRS determines the cost of its services and the activities involved in producing them through a cost-accounting system that tracks costs to organizational units. The lowest organizational unit in the IRS's cost-accounting system is a cost center. Cost centers are usually separate offices that are distinguished by subject-matter area of responsibility or geographic region. All costs of operating a cost center are recorded in the IRS's cost-accounting system. The costs charged to a cost center are the direct costs for the cost center's activities in addition to allocated overhead. Some cost centers work on different services across the IRS and are not fully devoted to the services for which the IRS charges user fees.

2. Cost Estimation of Direct Costs

The IRS uses various cost-measurement techniques to estimate the cost attributable to the program. These techniques include using various timekeeping systems to measure the time required to accomplish activities, or using information provided by subject-matter experts on the time devoted to a program. To determine the labor and benefits cost incurred to provide the service of providing a PTIN, the IRS estimated the number of full-time employees required to conduct activities related to the costs of issuing and renewing PTINs. The number of full-time employees is based on both current employment numbers and future hiring estimates. Other direct costs associated with administering the PTIN program include contract costs and travel, training, supplies, printing, and other miscellaneous costs.

3. Overhead

When the indirect cost of a service or activity is not specifically identified from the cost-accounting system, an overhead rate is added to the identifiable direct cost to arrive at full cost. Overhead is an indirect cost of operating an organization that is not specifically identifiable with an activity. Overhead includes costs of resources that are jointly or commonly consumed by one or more organizational unit's activities but are not specifically identifiable to a single activity.

These costs can include:

- General management and administrative services of sustaining and supporting organizations.
- Facilities management and ground maintenance services (security, rent, utilities, and building maintenance).
- Procurement and contracting services.
- Financial management and accounting services.
- Information technology services.
- Services to acquire and operate property, plants, and equipment.
- Publication, reproduction, and graphics and video services.
- Research, analytical, and statistical services.
- Human resources/personnel services.
- Library and legal services.

To calculate the overhead allocable to a service, the IRS multiplies an overhead rate by the estimated direct costs. The IRS calculates the overhead rate annually based on the Statement of Net Cost included in the IRS annual financial statements. The financial statements are audited by the Government Accountability Office. The overhead rate is the ratio of the IRS's indirect costs divided by direct costs of its organizational units. Indirect costs are labor, benefits, and non-labor costs (excluding IT related to taxpayer services, enforcement, and business system modernization) from the supporting and sustaining organizational units. Direct costs are labor, benefits, and non-labor costs for the IRS's organizational units that interact directly with taxpayers.

For the PTIN user fee review, an overhead rate of 57.58 percent was used. The rate was calculated based on the FY 2019 Statement of Net Cost as follows:

Total Indirect Costs	$4,006,706,430
Total Direct Costs ÷	$6,957,940,668
Overhead Rate	57.58%

E. Calculation of PTIN User Fee

The IRS projected the direct costs associated with the PTIN program for fiscal years 2020 through 2022. Direct costs are incurred by the Return Preparer Office (RPO) and include staffing and other direct costs related to administering the PTIN program. Staffing costs relate to conducting certain suitability checks, foreign preparer processing, handling compliance and complaint activities, information technology and contract-related support, communications, budgeting and finance, and program oversight and support. The labor and benefits for the work performed related to the PTIN program is projected to be $30,816,935 in total over fiscal years 2020 through 2022. Other direct costs associated with administering the PTIN program include contract costs and travel, training, supplies, printing, and other miscellaneous costs. The total amount of these other direct costs over fiscal years 2020 through 2022 is projected to be $463,750. Total direct costs for fiscal years 2020 through 2022 are therefore projected to be $31,280,685. Adding overhead expenses to the total direct costs results in total costs of $49,292,103 as shown below:

Total Direct Costs	$ 31,280,685
Overhead (57.58%)	$ 18,011,418
Total Direct Costs and Overhead	$49,292,103

The number of users annually is estimated to be 800,000, based on numbers of PTIN holders in prior fiscal years. Dividing the total cost by the projected population of users for fiscal years 2020 through 2022 results in a cost per application of $21 as shown below:

Total Costs	$49,292,103
Number of Applications	÷ 2,400,000
Cost Per Application	$ 21

Taking into account the full amount of these costs, the amount of the PTIN user fee per application or renewal is $21. The revised amount takes into account a reduction in contract support costs, a reduction in the cost of salary and benefits, and the current fiscal year overhead rate.

A third-party contractor performs certain functions, including processing applications to obtain or renew a PTIN and operating a call center, and charges a reasonable fee, which will be set at $14.95 per application or renewal, in addition to the amount charged by the government. The third-party contractor was chosen through a competitive bidding process. The amount of the contractor portion may change in 2021 when the contract expires and will be re-computed.

Special Analyses

The OMB's Office of Information and Regulatory Analysis has determined that this regulation is significant and subject to review under section 6(b) of Executive Order 12866.

Pursuant to the Regulatory Flexibility Act (5 U.S.C. chapter 6), it is hereby certified that these proposed regulations will not have a significant economic impact on a substantial number of small entities. The proposed regulations affect all individuals who prepare or assist in preparing all or substantially all of a tax return or claim for refund for compensation. Only individuals, not businesses, can have a PTIN. Thus, the economic impact of these regulations on any small entity generally will be a result of an individual tax return preparer who is required to have a PTIN owning a small business or a small business otherwise employing an individual tax return preparer who is required to have a PTIN. The Treasury Department and the IRS estimate that approximately 800,000 individuals will apply annually for an initial or renewal PTIN. Although the final regulations will likely affect a substantial number of small entities, the economic impact on those entities is not significant. The final regulations will establish a $21 fee per application or renewal (plus $14.95 payable directly to the contractor), which is a reduction from the previously established fee of $33 (plus $17 payable directly to the contractor) per application or renewal and will not have a significant economic impact on a small entity. Accordingly, the Secretary certifies that the rule will not have a significant economic impact on a substantial number of small entities.

Pursuant to section 7805(f), this notice of proposed rulemaking has been submitted to the Chief Counsel of the Office of Advocacy of the Small Business Administration for comment on its impact on small business.

Comments and Requests for a Public Hearing

Before these proposed amendments to the regulations are adopted as final regulations, consideration will be given to comments that are submitted timely to the IRS as prescribed in the preamble under the "ADDRESSES" section. The Treasury Department and the IRS request comments on all aspects of the proposed regulations. Any electronic comments submitted, and to the extent practicable any paper comments submitted, will be made available at *www.regulations.gov* or upon request.

A public hearing will be scheduled if requested in writing by any person who timely submits electronic or written comments. Requests for a public hearing are also encouraged to be made electronically. If a public hearing is scheduled, notice of the date and time for the public hearing will be published in the **Federal Register**. Announcement 2020-4, 2020-17 IRB 1, provides that until further notice, public hearings conducted by the IRS will be held telephonically. Any telephonic hearing will be made accessible to people with disabilities.

Drafting Information

The principal author of these regulations is Michael A. Franklin, Office of the Associate Chief Counsel (Procedure and Administration). Other personnel from the Treasury Department and the IRS participated in the development of the regulations.

[¶ 49,833]   **Proposed Amendments of Regulations (REG-106864-18)**, published in the Federal Register on April 24, 2020.

[Code Secs. 170A, 509, 512 and 513]

Exempt organization: Unrelated business: Unrelated business taxable income.—Reg. §1.512(a)-6 and amendments of Reg. §§1.170A-9, 1.509(a)-3, 1.512(a)-1, 1.512(b)-1 and 1.513-1, providing guidance on how an exempt organization subject to the unrelated business income tax described in section 511 of the Internal Revenue Code (Code) determines if it has more than one unrelated trade or business, and, if so, how the exempt organization calculates unrelated business taxable income, are proposed.

AGENCY: Internal Revenue Service (IRS), Treasury.

ACTION: Notice of proposed rulemaking.

SUMMARY: This document contains proposed regulations that provide guidance on how an exempt organization subject to the unrelated business income tax described in section 511 of the Internal Revenue Code (Code) determines if it has more than one unrelated trade or business, and, if so, how the exempt organization calculates unrelated business taxable income. The proposed regulations also clarify that the definition of "unrelated trade or business" applies to individual retirement accounts. Additionally, the proposed regulations provide that inclusions of subpart F income and global intangible low-taxed income are treated in the same manner as dividends for purposes of section 512. The proposed regulations affect exempt organizations. **DATES**: Written or electronic comments and requests for a public hearing must be submitted by June 23, 2020.

ADDRESSES: Submit electronic submissions via the Federal eRulemaking Portal at *www.regulations.gov* (indicate IRS and REG-106864-18) by following the online instructions for submitting comments. Once submitted to the Federal eRulemaking Portal, comments cannot be edited or withdrawn. The Department of the Treasury (Treasury Department) and the Internal Revenue Service (IRS) will publish for public availability any comment received to its public docket, whether submitted electronically or in hard copy. Send hard copy submissions to: CC:PA:LPD:PR (REG-106864-18), Room 5203, Internal Revenue Service, P.O. Box 7604, Ben Franklin Station, Washington, DC 20044.

FOR FURTHER INFORMATION CONTACT: Concerning the proposed rules, Jonathan A. Carter at (202) 317-5800; concerning submissions of comments and requests for a public hearing, Regina Johnson at (202) 317-5177 (not toll-free numbers).

SUPPLEMENTARY INFORMATION:

Background

Under section 501(a) of the Code, organizations described in sections 401(a) and 501(c) generally are exempt from federal income taxation. However, section 511(a)(1) imposes a tax (computed as provided in section 11) on the unrelated business taxable income (UBTI) of organizations described in section 511(a)(2), which includes organizations described in sections 401(a) and 501(c) (other than a trust described in section 511(b) or an instrumentality of the United States described in section 501(c)(1)), as well as state colleges and universities. Additionally, section 511(b)(1) imposes a tax (computed as provided in section 1(e)) on the UBTI of trusts described in section 511(b)(2), which describes trusts that are exempt from federal income taxation under section 501(a) and which, if it were not for such exemption, would be subject to subchapter J of chapter 1 of the Code (relating to estates, trusts, beneficiaries, and decedents). Organizations described in section 511(a)(2) and trusts described in section 511(b)(2) are collectively called "exempt organizations" or "organizations" throughout this preamble, unless otherwise stated.[1]

Definitions of UBTI

Section 512 provides two different definitions of UBTI - one in section 512(a)(1), which applies to most exempt organizations, and one in section 512(a)(3), which applies only to social clubs described in section 501(c)(7), voluntary employees' beneficiary associations (VEBAs) described in section 501(c)(9), and supplemental unemployment compensation benefits trusts (SUBs) described in section 501(c)(17).

Section 512(a)(1) defines UBTI as the gross income derived by any exempt organization from an unrelated trade or business regularly carried on by it, less the deductions allowed by chapter 1 of the Code (chapter 1) that are directly connected with the carrying on of such trade or business,

---

[1] Section 408(e) states that an individual retirement account (IRA) is subject to the taxes imposed by section 511. Accordingly, any reference to an exempt organization in this preamble includes an IRA, without regard to whether it is a traditional IRA, Roth IRA, simplified employee pension (SEP-IRA), or savings incentive match plan for employees (SIMPLE IRA). See section 9 of this preamble for more information.

both computed with the modifications described in section 512(b). Section 513(a) generally defines "unrelated trade or business" as any trade or business the conduct of which is not substantially related (aside from the need of such exempt organization for income or funds or the use it makes of the profits derived) to the exercise or performance by such exempt organization of its charitable, educational, or other purpose or function constituting the basis for its exemption under section 501 (or, in the case of a state college or university, to the exercise or performance of any purpose or function described in section 501(c)(3)). However, in the case of a trust that is exempt from tax under section 501(a) and described in section 401(a) (qualified retirement plans) or section 501(c)(17) (SUBs), section 513(b) defines "unrelated trade or business," as any trade or business regularly carried on by such trust or by a partnership of which it is a member. Section 1.513-1(b) generally provides that, for purposes of section 513, the term "trade or business" has the same meaning as in section 162.

By contrast, section 512(a)(3)(A) defines UBTI as the gross income (excluding exempt function income), less the deductions allowed by chapter 1 that are directly connected with the production of the gross income (excluding exempt function income), both computed with the modifications described in section 512(b)(6) (net operating loss (NOL) deduction), (b)(10) (charitable contribution deduction by exempt organizations), (b)(11) (charitable contribution deduction by certain trusts), and (b)(12) (specific deduction). Accordingly, UBTI under section 512(a)(3) is not limited to the gross income derived by an exempt organization from any unrelated trade or business regularly conducted by it. Thus, any gross income that is not exempt function income (nonexempt function income) is UBTI under section 512(a)(3).

Unrelated Trades or Businesses Conducted Indirectly Through Another Entity

An exempt organization may conduct an unrelated trade or business directly or indirectly through another entity, such as a partnership (including any entity treated as a partnership for federal tax purposes). Section 512(c) provides that, if a trade or business regularly carried on by a partnership of which an exempt organization is a partner is an unrelated trade or business with respect to such exempt organization, the exempt organization includes in UBTI - subject to the exceptions, additions, and limitations of section 512(b) -its distributive share of partnership gross income (whether or not distributed) and partnership deductions directly connected with such gross income. *See* § 1.512(c)-1 (describing how UBTI is calculated in a situation in which an exempt organization's distributive share of partnership income consists of both UBTI and income that is excluded from the calculation of UBTI). In determining whether a partnership conducts a trade or business that is an unrelated trade or business with respect to an exempt organization partner, the exempt organization would use the applicable definition of "unrelated trade or business" in section 513(a) or (b). Section 512(c) applies regardless of whether an exempt organization is a general or limited partner. *See* Rev. Rul. 79-222, 1979-2 C.B. 236.

Calculation of UBTI

An exempt organization may engage in more than one unrelated trade or business. Prior to the enactment of section 512(a)(6), an exempt organization deriving gross income from the regular conduct of two or more unrelated trades or businesses calculated UBTI by determining its aggregate gross income from all such unrelated trades or businesses and reducing that amount by the aggregate deductions allowed with respect to all such unrelated trades or businesses. *See* § 1.512(a)-1(a). However, section 512(a)(6), which was added to the Code by section 13702 of Public Law 115-97, 131 Stat. 2054 (2017), commonly referred to as the Tax Cuts and Jobs Act (TCJA), enacted December 22, 2017, changed this calculation for exempt organizations with more than one unrelated trade or business so that, in the case of any exempt organization with more than one unrelated trade or business:

(A) UBTI, including for purposes of determining any NOL deduction, shall be computed separately with respect to each trade or business and without regard to section 512(b)(12) (allowing a specific deduction of $1,000),

(B) The UBTI of such exempt organization shall be the sum of the UBTI so computed with respect to each trade or business, less a specific deduction under section 512(b)(12), and

(C) For purposes of section 512(a)(6)(B), UBTI with respect to any such trade or business shall not be less than zero.

Thus, under section 512(a)(6), an exempt organization is no longer permitted to aggregate income and deductions from all unrelated trades or businesses when calculating UBTI. Section 512(a)(6) applies to taxable years beginning after December 31, 2017, but not to NOLs arising before January 1, 2018, that are carried over to taxable years beginning on or after such date. *See* section 13702(b) of the TCJA.

In August 2018, the Treasury Department and the IRS issued Notice 2018-67 (2018-36 IRB 409 (Sept. 4, 2018)), which discussed and solicited comments regarding various issues arising under section 512(a)(6) and set forth interim guidance and transition rules relating to that section. The Treasury Department and the IRS received 24 comments in response to Notice 2018-67 and considered these comments in drafting these proposed regulations. Some of these comments discussed the interaction between section 512(a)(6) and (7), which was also enacted by the TCJA and provided that an exempt organization's UBTI is increased by any amount for which a deduction is not allowable under chapter 1 by reason of section 274 and which is paid or incurred by such exempt organization for certain disallowed fringes. These comments are not discussed because section 512(a)(7) was repealed on December 20, 2019. *See* Further Consolidated Appropriations Act, 2020, Division Q, Public Law 116-94, 133 Stat. 2534 (2019) (retroactively effective to date of enactment of the TCJA). The remaining comments are discussed in the Explanation of Provisions and Comment Summary. The comments are available for public inspection upon request.

Explanation of Provisions and Summary of Comments

Section 512(a)(6) requires an exempt organization with more than one unrelated trade or business to first calculate UBTI separately with respect to each such trade or business, without regard to the specific deduction generally allowed under section 512(b)(12). The Conference Report explains that "[t]he organization's [UBTI] for the taxable year is the sum of the amounts (not less than zero) computed for each separate trade or business, less the specific deduction allowed under section 512(b)(12)." H.R. Rep. No. 115-466 (2017), at 548. Section 512(a)(6) continues to allow an NOL deduction, but "only with respect to a trade or business from which the loss arose." *Id.* Thus, the legislative history states that "a deduction from one trade or business for a taxable year may not be used to offset income from a different unrelated trade or business for the same taxable year." *Id.* at 548. Because section 512(a)(6) disallows the aggregation of income and deductions from all unrelated trades or businesses, these proposed regulations revise § 1.512(a)-1(a) to state that, in the case of an organization with more than one unrelated trade or business, UBTI is calculated separately with respect to each such trade or business as provided in new proposed § 1.512(a)-6.

Congress did not provide explicit criteria for determining whether an exempt organization has "more than one unrelated trade or business" or how to identify "separate" unrelated trades or businesses for purposes of calculating UBTI in accordance with section 512(a)(6).[2] Accordingly, these proposed regulations establish the method for determining whether an exempt organization has more than one unrelated trade or business for purposes of section 512(a)(6) and identifying separate unrelated trades or businesses for purposes of calculating UBTI under this section. These proposed regulations also clarify that, for purposes of the unrelated business income tax generally and the application of section 512(a)(6) specifically, an individual retirement plan (IRA) described in section 408(e) uses the definition of "unrelated trade or business" in section 513(b)

---

[2] The Joint Committee on Taxation's General Explanation of Pub. L. 115-97 states that "it is intended that the Secretary issue guidance concerning when an activity will be treated as a separate unrelated trade or business for purposes of [section 512(a)(6)]." Staff of the Joint Committee on Taxation, General Explanation of Pub. L. 115-97 (December 2018), at 293.

applicable to trusts. Additionally, these proposed regulations clarify that inclusions of subpart F income under section 951(a)(1)(A) and global intangible low-taxed income (GILTI) under section 951A(a) are treated in the same manner as dividends for purposes of section 512(b)(1).

1. *Separate Unrelated Trade or Business*

There is no general statutory or regulatory definition of what activities constitute a "trade or business" for purposes of the Code. Whether an activity constitutes a trade or business may vary depending on which Code section is involved. *See generally Commissioner v. Groetzinger*, 480 U.S. 23, 27 (1987). Section 1.513-1(b) of the current Treasury regulations (promulgated in 1967) states that, "for purposes of section 513, the term 'trade or business' has the same meaning it has in section 162, and generally includes any activity carried on for the production of income from the sale of goods or performance of services."

Notice 2018-67 permitted a reasonable, good-faith interpretation of sections 511 through 514, considering all the facts and circumstances, when determining whether an exempt organization has more than one unrelated trade or business for purposes of section 512(a)(6). At the same time, Notice 2018-67 stated that the Treasury Department and the IRS were considering the use of the North American Industry Classification System (NAICS) codes as a method for determining whether an exempt organization has more than one unrelated trade or business for purposes of section 512(a)(6) and for purposes of calculating UBTI under section 512(a)(6)(A). NAICS is an industry classification system for purposes of collecting, analyzing, and publishing statistical data related to the United States business economy that results from a cooperative effort between Canada, Mexico, and the United States. *See* Executive Office of the President, Office of Management and Budget, North American Industry Classification System (2017) (2017 NAICS Manual), *available at* https://www.census.gov/eos/www/naics/2017NAICS/2017_NAICS_Manual.pdf. The structure of NAICS is hierarchical, using a six-digit coding system. *Id.* at 16, 18, & 20. NAICS divides the economy into 20 sectors. *Id.* at 3. The first two digits of the code designate the sector, each of which represents a general category of economic activity, including retail trade (44-45); real estate and rental and leasing (53); health care and social assistance (62); and accommodation and food services (72). *Id.* at 16 & 20. The third digit designates the subsector; the fourth digit designates the industry group; and the fifth digit designates the NAICS industry. Any establishment is usually classified down to the NAICS five-digit industry level classification, using the classification of the industry that best matches its primary activity. When applicable, the sixth digit is used to designate the national industry, to reflect differences between the countries. A zero as the sixth digit generally indicates that the NAICS industry and the U.S. industry are the same. *Id.* at 18. Accordingly, each digit of the NAICS 6-digit codes describes an industry with increasing specificity.

In Notice 2018-67, the Treasury Department and the IRS provided that a reasonable, good-faith interpretation included using the most specific level - six-digit codes (NAICS 6-digit codes). The Treasury Department and the IRS also requested comments regarding rules to identify separate trades or businesses that achieve the intent of Congress in enacting section 512(a)(6) and that are administrable for exempt organizations and the IRS. As discussed further in section 1.a of this preamble, methods commenters suggested included devising a facts and circumstances test along with a clearly defined safe harbor, adopting principles described in various Code sections (including sections 183 and 469), using the groupings described in Form 14018, "Compliance Questionnaire Colleges and Universities," and using less than six digits of the NAICS codes.

After considering the comments, the Treasury Department and the IRS continue to view an identification method based on NAICS codes as administrable for exempt organizations and the IRS. Moreover, in response to comments regarding the burden related to the specificity of NAICS 6-digit codes, the proposed regulations provide that an exempt organization generally will identify its separate unrelated trades or businesses using the first two digits of the NAICS codes (NAICS 2-digit codes).

a. *The North American Industry Classification System (NAICS)*

Most commenters that discussed NAICS supported using the NAICS codes to identify separate unrelated trades or businesses for purposes of section 512(a)(6). Nonetheless, several commenters generally opposed this proposed method. These commenters argued that the NAICS codes were not created to define "trade or business" for UBTI purposes and therefore fail to sufficiently describe the full range of possible unrelated trades or businesses engaged in by exempt organizations. While the Treasury Department and the IRS recognize that the NAICS codes were not specifically designed for use under section 512(a)(6), the Treasury Department and the IRS continue to believe that using the NAICS codes is appropriate because NAICS "is a comprehensive [classification] system covering all economic activities." 2017 NAICS Manual, at 14. Additionally, the broad scope of activities covered by the NAICS 2-digit codes should cover all the unrelated trade or business activities conducted by exempt organizations.

The NAICS codes were developed, in coordination with Canada and Mexico, by the Office of Management and Budget (OMB) and are managed by the United States Census Bureau. The OMB reviews and updates the NAICS codes as appropriate every five years and, at times, may remove codes. *Id.* at 78. In responding to the NAICS 6-digit codes discussed in Notice 2018-67, some commenters expressed concern that the Treasury Department and the IRS do not control NAICS and that this could adversely impact organizations using the codes for tax purposes. The Treasury Department and the IRS view the proposal to use NAICS 2-digit codes as addressing this concern because the codes are revised through notice and comment rulemaking, and OMB has never revised the codes at the 2-digit level.

A few commenters noted that a recent report by the Treasury Inspector General for Tax Administration (TIGTA) determined that the NAICS codes are "unreliable for use to identify businesses that may be subject to excise tax reporting and payment." Treasury Inspector General for Tax Administration, The Affordable Care Act: An Improved Strategy is Needed to Ensure Accurate Reporting and Payment of the Medical Device Excise Tax 5 (Jul. 17, 2014). The Treasury Department and the IRS consider the situation addressed by the TIGTA report to be distinguishable from the use of the NAICS 2-digit codes to identify separate unrelated trades or businesses for purposes of section 512(a)(6). The TIGTA report addressed the IRS's efforts to determine the population of taxpayers subject to the new medical device excise tax based on the NAICS 6-digit code a taxpayer had reported on Schedule K, "Other Information," of Form 1120, "U.S. Corporation Income Tax Return" to identify the activity from which it derives the largest percentage of total receipts. TIGTA found that not every medical device manufacturer used the same NAICS 6-digit code to report the activity, such that reliance on one NAICS 6-digit code would not identify all businesses that may be subject to the tax. TIGTA also noted that the NAICS 6-digit code did not always signify a business that is engaged in taxable sales of medical devices. Here, an exempt organization will be reporting each of its separate unrelated trades or businesses using the more general NAICS 2-digit codes on Form 990-T, "Exempt Organization Business Income Tax Return," for the purpose of ensuring compliance with section 512(a)(6). As previously discussed, the NAICS 2-digit code describes a broader sector of the economy, making it more likely that taxpayers engaged in similar activities that could be described in more than one NAICS 6-digit code will nonetheless report those activities as part of the same overall sector.

i. NAICS 2-Digit Codes

As discussed in section 1 of this preamble, Notice 2018-67 permitted reliance on NAICS 6-digit codes as a method of identifying separate trades or businesses and requested comments regarding whether use of less than six digits of the NAICS codes, either alone or in combination with one or more other methods, would appropriately identify separate trades or businesses for purposes of achieving the objectives of section 512(a)(6). Nearly all the commenters making recommendations on the NAICS codes rejected the use of NAICS 6-digit codes. These commenters noted that using NAICS 6-digit codes would result in significant administrative burden because an exempt organization would have to determine which of over 1,000 NAICS 6-digit codes most accurately describes its trades or businesses. Commenters noted that many NAICS 6-digit codes may apply to more than one trade or business activity or that no NAICS 6-digit code may exist to accurately describe a trade or business activity. Additionally, these commenters argued that the use of NAICS 6-digit codes could potentially require an exempt organization to split what has traditionally been considered one unrelated trade or business activity into multiple trades or businesses.

Half of the commenters making recommendations on the NAICS codes suggested adoption of NAICS 2-digit codes, which would identify trades or businesses in 20 sectors. These commenters generally explained that use of NAICS 2-digit codes would result in broader, less subjective identification of trades or businesses that would naturally permit the aggregation of similar activities. Furthermore, one of these commenters stated that the use of fewer digits of the NAICS codes would minimize implementation costs and reduce the administrative burden on the IRS as well as exempt organizations. This commenter opined that the NAICS 2-digit codes are less likely to change over time than the NAICS codes with more digits because the specificity of the NAICS codes increases as digits are added. NAICS 3-digit codes, which one commenter recommended adopting, identify 99 subsectors. By contrast, NAICS 4-digit codes, which two commenters recommended adopting, identify 311 industry groups.

The Treasury Department and the IRS recognize that limitations exist in using NAICS as a method of identifying an exempt organization's separate unrelated trades or businesses. However, the Treasury Department and the IRS conclude that adopting the NAICS 2-digit codes will minimize those limitations and that NAICS 2-digit codes are less likely to change over time than NAICS codes with more digits. At the same time, adoption of NAICS 2-digit codes will not allow the offsetting of losses between the 20 sectors of unrelated trades or businesses. Additionally, under existing precedent, an organization must determine whether an activity is an "unrelated trade or business" within the meaning of section 513 before it determines what NAICS 2-digit code describes that "separate" unrelated trade or business. An organization cannot use losses from an activity that consistently generates losses to offset income from a profitable trade or business unless the organization can show that the loss-producing activity is conducted with the requisite profit motive. *See Portland Golf Club v. Commissioner*, 497 U.S. 154, 164 (1990) (confirming that, "[a]lthough [section 162] does not expressly require that a 'trade or business' must be carried on with an intent to profit, this Court has ruled that a taxpayer's activities fall within the scope of [section] 162 only if an intent to profit has been shown" and citing *Groetzinger*, 480 U.S. at 35); *Losantiville Country Club v. Commissioner*, 906 F.3d 468, 473-75 (6th Cir. 2018) (demonstrating profit motive without reference to profitability by applying section 183 factors).

Furthermore, the Treasury Department and the IRS conclude that use of NAICS 2-digit codes results in broader identification of trades or businesses that will minimize implementation costs and will mitigate the administrative burden on exempt organizations and the IRS that would be imposed by more detailed NAICS codes. The use of NAICS 2-digit codes should also reduce any inequity that might result from a code system that was not specifically designed to describe the business activities of exempt organizations.

For these reasons, the proposed regulations generally provide that an exempt organization will identify each of its separate unrelated trades or businesses using the first two digits of the NAICS code that most accurately describes a trade or business. The Treasury Department and the IRS request comments on whether another method, or additional methods, of identifying an exempt organization's separate unrelated trades or businesses better achieves the intent of Congress in enacting section 512(a)(6) while still being administrable for exempt organizations and the IRS.

A few commenters requested confirmation that the Treasury Department and the IRS will permit an exempt organization to rely on the NAICS code that describes all the activities of the organization. For example, NAICS describes educational services, which includes colleges, universities, and professional schools, under one NAICS 2-digit code (61).

An unrelated trade or business generally is any trade or business the conduct of which is not substantially related to the exercise or performance by such exempt organization of its charitable, educational, or other purpose or function constituting the basis for its exemption under section 501. *See* section 513(a). A NAICS code that describes all of an exempt organization's activities, even those activities that are substantially related to the exercise or performance of the exempt organization's exempt function, fails to identify the exempt organization's unrelated trades or businesses and undermines the Congressional intent in enacting section 512(a)(6). Accordingly, the proposed regulations clarify that the NAICS code chosen must identify the unrelated trade or business in which the exempt organization engages (directly or indirectly) and not the activities the conduct of which are substantially related to the exercise or performance by such exempt organization of its charitable, educational, or other purpose or function constituting the basis for its exemption under section 501 (or, in the case of an exempt organization described in section 511(a)(2)(B), to the exercise or performance of any purpose or function described in section 501(c)(3)). Thus, returning to the previous example, a college or university cannot choose NAICS code 61 for all its unrelated trade or business activities.

Similarly, one commenter requested that the Treasury Department and the IRS confirm that a qualified retirement plan can use the NAICS code describing employee benefit funds, which is included under the NAICS 2-digit code for finance and insurance (52), to describe all the plan's unrelated trades or businesses. As discussed in the Background section, qualified retirement funds are subject to the general definition of UBTI in section 512(a)(1) but the term "unrelated trade or business" is defined in a special rule for trusts under section 513(b) as "any trade or business regularly carried on by such [plan] or by a partnership of which it is a member." Accordingly, it must use the NAICS 2-digit code that most accurately describes the underlying trade or business regularly carried on by the plan or by a partnership of which it is a member. However, it appears that qualified retirement plans generally derive most, if not all, of their UBTI from investment activities, the identification of which is discussed in section 2 of this preamble, and which includes UBTI from any qualifying partnership interests (see section 2.d of this preamble) or qualifying S corporation interests (see section 4.a of this preamble). Accordingly, unless a qualified retirement plan engages directly in one or more unrelated trades or businesses or has non-qualifying partnership interests or non-qualifying S corporation interests, a qualified retirement plan will not be subject to section 512(a)(6) because it will only have one unrelated trade or business for purposes of section 512(a)(6) - its investment activities.

A social club described in section 501(c)(7) would not be able to use the NAICS 2-digit code for arts, entertainment, and recreation (71), which includes golf courses and country clubs, to identify all its unrelated trades or businesses. As explained in the Background section, social clubs are subject to the definition of UBTI in section 512(a)(3), which defines UBTI, in part, as "gross income (excluding exempt function income)" and does not refer directly to "any unrelated trade or business." However, as further explained in section 5 of this preamble, these proposed regulations apply regardless of whether an organization is subject to the definition of UBTI in section 512(a)(1) or section 512(a)(3). Accordingly, a social club must use the NAICS code that most accurately describes its unrelated trade or business activities. The social club may use the NAICS 2-digit code for arts, entertainment, and recreation (71) only to the extent such code describes its unrelated trades or businesses, such as rounds of golf played by nonmembers, the greens fees for which would result in UBTI.

At least one commenter recommended that the proposed regulations permit an exempt organization to aggregate trades or businesses that may be described by multiple NAICS codes as a single trade or business when those activities are closely related, similar in nature, and essentially conducted as a single trade or business. Although the Treasury Department and the IRS recognize that the use of more digits of the NAICS codes could result in the division of business activities traditionally conducted as one unit into more than one trade or business, the use of NAICS codes at the 2-digit level, as noted by other commenters, results in the aggregation of trades or businesses in the same economic sector. Accordingly, the Treasury Department and the IRS address this comment by adopting the use of NAICS 2-digit codes.

ii. Codes Reported Only Once

The Treasury Department and the IRS recognize that an exempt organization can have a trade or business that it operates in different, geographic areas. For example, a hospital organization may operate several hospital facilities in a geographic area (or multiple geographic areas), all of which include pharmacies that sell goods to the general public. *See* Rev. Rul. 68-375, 1968-2 C.B. 245. Pharmacies are described under the NAICS 2-digit code for retail trade (44). Although each pharmacy potentially could be considered a "separate" trade or business under section 512(a)(6), particularly if separate books and records exist for each pharmacy, the Treasury Department and the IRS recognize that devising rules to distinguish between each pharmacy trade or business would introduce additional complexity and increase the administrative burden on the hospital organization. Accordingly, the proposed regulations provide that an exempt organization will report each NAICS 2-digit code only once. Thus, even though the hospital organization in the previous example operates more than one pharmacy, the hospital organization would report all the pharmacies using the NAICS 2-digit code for retail trade (44), along with any other retail trades or businesses described by this NAICS 2-digit code, on Form 990-T as one unrelated trade or business.

iii. Erroneous Codes

The proposed regulations provide that, once an exempt organization has identified a separate unrelated trade or business using a particular NAICS 2-digit code, the organization may not change the NAICS 2-digit code describing that trade or business unless the organization can show that the NAICS 2-digit code chosen was due to an unintentional error and that another NAICS 2-digit code more accurately describes the trade or business. This limitation will apply to codes reported on the first Form 990-T filed after final regulations under section 512(a)(6) are published in the **Federal Register**. The Treasury Department and the IRS anticipate that the instructions to the Form 990-T will be revised to describe how an exempt organization provides notification of such an error. Additionally, the Treasury Department and the IRS request comments regarding whether there are other circumstances in which an exempt organization should be permitted to change NAICS 2-digit codes.

b. *New Identification Methods*

At least two commenters suggested that the proposed regulations permit the Treasury Department and the IRS the flexibility to add new methods of identifying separate unrelated trades or businesses through guidance published in the Internal Revenue Bulletin. The Treasury Department and the IRS recognize that other code systems may exist (and have not yet been identified) or may be devised in the future that better reflect the unrelated trade or business activities engaged in by exempt organizations. However, the Treasury Department and the IRS also expect that the proposed regulations provide a method of identifying separate unrelated trades or businesses that is administrable for exempt organizations and the IRS and therefore do not anticipate the need to routinely modify that method. As more experience is gained over time with the administration of section 512(a)(6), the Treasury Department and the IRS may consider additional identification methods, including the use of code systems or indices other than NAICS, and will publish guidance as needed.

c. *De Minimis Exception*

One commenter recommended that the Treasury Department and the IRS adopt a de minimis exception for exempt organizations reporting less than $100,000 of gross UBTI. Relying on statistical data published by the IRS, the commenter states that such organizations were responsible for only five percent of the total unrelated business income tax paid in 2013. This commenter argued that small exempt organizations likely lack the internal staff and the resources to implement the changes required by the enactment of section 512(a)(6) and to engage outside professionals to assist with ongoing compliance with that section.

As a result of the commenter's proposed threshold, section 512(a)(6) would not apply to more than 80 percent of the exempt organizations filing Form 990-Ts (based on the statistical data cited by the commenter). *See* Table 4. Unrelated Business Income Tax Returns: Returns with Positive Unrelated Business Taxable Income: Number of Returns, Gross Unrelated Business Income (UBI), Total Deductions, Unrelated Business Taxable Income, and Total Tax, by Type of Entity and Size of Gross UBI Tax Year 2013, *available* at https://www.irs.gov/statistics/soi-tax-stats-exempt-organizations-unrelated-business-income-ubi-tax-statistics#2. Accordingly, a supposed "de minimis" rule with a $100,000 gross UBTI threshold would effectively render section 512(a)(6) a nullity for most exempt organizations.

More importantly, as noted by the commenter, section 512(a)(6) does not provide a de minimis rule and does not provide discretionary authority for the Treasury Department and the IRS to establish one. Accordingly, even at a lower threshold, a de minimis rule would be contrary to the stated Congressional intent of not permitting exempt organizations to use losses from one unrelated trade or business to offset the gains from another unrelated trade or business. However, the Treasury Department and the IRS note that the use of NAICS 2-digit codes, along with the treatment of an exempt organization's investment activities as one unrelated trade or business (as described in section 2.a of this preamble), is expected to address many of the concerns prompting the request for a de minimis rule because smaller entities are not as likely to have more than one unrelated trade or business. The Treasury Department and the IRS therefore do not adopt this comment.

d. *Allocation of Directly Connected Deductions*

i. In General

Section 512(a)(1) permits an exempt organization with an unrelated trade or business to reduce the income from that trade or business by the deductions allowed by chapter 1 that are directly connected with the carrying on of such trade or business. To be "directly connected" with a trade or business, an item of deduction must have a proximate and primary relationship to the carrying on of the unrelated trade or business generating the gross income. *See* §1.512(a)-1(a). Expenses, depreciation, and similar items attributable solely to the conduct of an unrelated trade or business are proximately and primarily related to that trade or business and qualify to reduce income from such trade or business under section 512(a)(1) to the extent such items meet the requirements of sections 162 (trade or business expenses), 167 (depreciation), and other relevant provisions. To the extent that an exempt organization may have items of deduction that are shared between an exempt activity and an unrelated trade or business, §1.512(a)-1(c) provides special rules for allocating such expenses. For example, if facilities are used both to carry on exempt activities and to conduct unrelated trade or business activities, then expenses, depreciation, and similar items attributable to such facilities must be allocated between the two uses on a reasonable basis. *See* §1.512(a)-1(c).[3]

The allocation issues under section 512(a)(1) are also relevant under section 512(a)(6) because an exempt organization with more than one unrelated trade or business must not only allocate indirect expenses among exempt and taxable activities as described in §1.512(a)-1(c) but also among separate unrelated trades or businesses. Accordingly, Notice 2018-67 stated the Treasury Department and the IRS are considering modifying the underlying reasonable allocation method in §1.512(a)-1(c) and providing specific standards for allocating expenses relating to dual use facilities and the rules under section 512(a)(6). Notice 2018-67 requested comments regarding possible rules or defined standards for the allocation of indirect expenses between separate unrelated trades or businesses for purposes of calculating UBTI under section 512(a)(6)(A), and regarding what allocation methods should be considered "reasonable."

The three commenters addressing allocation methods generally recommended retaining the current "any reasonable method" approach. Nonetheless, one of these commenters recommended that the Treasury Department and the IRS adopt existing cost allocation rules set forth by the OMB, referred to as the Uniform Administrative Requirements, Cost Principles, and Audit Requirements for Federal Awards (2 CFR 200), and by the Financial Accounting Standards Board in the Accounting Standard Update 2016-14, both of which require allocations to be made "on a rational,

---

[3] The same method used for allocating expenses in determining taxable income must also be used when determining whether an activity is conducted with the intent to profit, and thus (as discussed further in section 5.b.iv of this preamble) whether such activity is a trade or business. *Portland Golf Club v. Commissioner*, 497 U.S. 154, 171 (1990) (stating that "in demonstrating the requisite profit motive, Portland Golf must employ the same method of allocating fixed expenses as it uses in calculating its actual loss").

reasonable, and objective basis across functional expense categories." Another commenter recommended adopting accounting methods specific to social club activities, such as a golf.

The Treasury Department and the IRS are concerned that permitting allocation methods based solely on reasonableness is difficult for the IRS to administer and may not provide certainty for taxpayers. Whether an allocation method is "reasonable" depends on all the facts and circumstances. *See Rensselaer Polytechnic Institute v. Commissioner*, 79 T.C. 967 (1982), *aff'd* 732 F.2d 1058 (2d Cir. 1984) (finding an allocation method based on actual use to be "reasonable" within the meaning of §1.512(a)-1(c)). The Treasury Department and the IRS continue to consider the allocation issue and intend to publish a separate notice of proposed rulemaking providing further guidance on this issue. Until publication of a separate notice of proposed rulemaking, these proposed regulations incorporate the existing allocation standard in §1.512(a)-1(c), which provides that an exempt organization must allocate deductions on a reasonable basis between separate unrelated trades or businesses. The proposed regulations also provide that the use of the unadjusted gross-to-gross method is not a reasonable allocation method under the general allocation rule and as incorporated for section 512(a)(6) purposes (see section 1.d.iii of this preamble). ii. State and Local Taxes and Tax Preparation Fees

At least one commenter requested guidance on the deduction of certain general expenses. This commenter recommended that tax return preparation fees be permitted as a deduction after calculation of total UBTI under section 512(a)(6)(B). The commenter argued that such expenses should not be allocated between separate unrelated trades or businesses because such expenses pertain to all the exempt organization's activities - related and unrelated.

As previously discussed, deductions are permitted under section 512(a)(1) and (3) only if two conditions are met: (1) the deduction is allowed under chapter 1; and (2) in the case of section 512(a)(1), the deduction is directly connected with the carrying on of such separate unrelated trade or business, or, in the case of section 512(a)(3), the deduction is directly connected with the production of the gross income (excluding exempt function income). Accordingly, an exempt organization may deduct only tax return preparation fees that are directly connected with a separate unrelated trade or business, in the case of an organization subject to section 512(a)(1), or that are directly connected with the production of the gross income (excluding exempt function income), in the case of an organization subject to section 512(a)(3). If such fees are directly connected with more than one separate unrelated trade or business or are also attributable to the exempt organization's related activities (or exempt function income in the case of an organization subject to section 512(a)(3)), the exempt organization must allocate such expenses as discussed in section 4.d.i of this preamble. *See* §1.512(a)-1(c). Nothing in section 512(a)(6)(B) permits either the deduction of expenses that are not otherwise deductible in calculating UBTI or the deduction of expenses after calculation of total UBTI. Thus, the Treasury Department and the IRS do not adopt this comment.

One commenter also suggested that state income taxes not directly connected with any separate unrelated trade or business resulting from the increase in UBTI under section 512(a)(7) be permitted as a deduction after calculation of total UBTI under section 512(a)(6)(B). With the repeal of section 512(a)(7), the Treasury Department and the IRS expect that exempt organizations are no longer subject to state income taxes that are not directly connected with the carrying on of a separate unrelated trade or business. If this is not the case, the Treasury Department and the IRS request examples of such state income taxes.

iii. The Unadjusted Gross-to-Gross Method is Unreasonable

The IRS has previously indicated that it will not litigate the reasonableness of the allocation method in *Rensselaer* pending revision of the Treasury regulations. 732 F.2d 1058, *action on dec.*, 1987-014 (Jun. 18, 1987). However, regarding facilities or personnel that are used both to carry on exempt activities and to conduct unrelated trade or business activities or more than one separate unrelated trade or business, the Treasury Department and the IRS have concluded that allocation of expenses, depreciation, and similar items using an unadjusted gross-to-gross method is not reasonable. In general, a gross-to-gross method of allocation uses a ratio of gross income from an unrelated trade or business activity over the total gross income from both unrelated and related activities generating the same indirect expenditures. The percentage resulting from this ratio is used to determine the percentage of the shared costs attributable to the unrelated trade or business activity (or activities).

In some circumstances, the provision of a good or service can be both related and unrelated depending on to whom the good or service is offered. For example, with respect to social clubs, the provision of goods and services to members is an exempt function whereas the provision of the same goods and services to nonmembers is a nonexempt function. Another example is a school that operates a ski facility for use in its physical education program and for recreational use by its students and the general public. Rev. Rul. 78-98, 1978-1 C.B. 167. If the social club charges nonmembers a higher price than it charges members for the same good or service or if the school charges the general public more for slope and ski lift fees than it charges its students, the gross-to-gross ratio will increase, resulting in more indirect expenses being allocated to the unrelated activity. However, no difference likely exists in the cost of providing the good or service to members versus nonmembers or in the cost of providing the ski slopes and lifts to students versus the public. Accordingly, the failure to adjust the price of the good or service offered to nonmembers or the general public for purposes of determining the allocation of indirect expenses (that is, using an unadjusted gross-to-gross method) overstates the percentage of the indirect expenses that should be allocated to the unrelated activities. *See Portland Golf*, 497 U.S. at 157 fn. 4 (indicating that a system where the taxpayer "charges nonmembers higher prices for food and drink than members are charged, even though nonmembers' meals presumably cost no more to prepare and serve" seems likely to "[overstate] the percentage of fixed costs properly attributable to nonmember sales").

When an organization charges different prices for the same good or service depending on whether the offering of the good or service is a related or unrelated activity, then such organization should adjust the per "unit" price of the good or service of the related activity to that of the unrelated activity (or activities) for the ratio created by the gross-to-gross method to appropriately account for the percentage of indirect expenses attributable to the unrelated activity. Failing to make this adjustment does not appropriately account for the portion of indirect expenses attributable to an unrelated activity and is therefore an unreasonable method for allocating expenditures under §1.512(a)-1(c). Accordingly, the proposed regulations provide that the unadjusted gross-to-gross method is not reasonable, whether under the general allocation rule or as incorporated for section 512(a)(6) purposes.

The Treasury Department and the IRS request comments regarding whether any other allocation methods should be considered unreasonable and the methods or rules that could be adopted instead of a reasonableness standard for allocations both between related and unrelated activities and between two or more separate unrelated trades or businesses.

2. *Activities in the Nature of Investments*

Several commenters expressed concern regarding the use of the NAICS codes to identify investment activities as one or more separate unrelated trades or businesses. One commenter noted that a partnership is not required to report the NAICS codes for all the trades or businesses in which it engages on the Schedule K-1 (Form 1065), "Partner's Share of Income, Deductions, Credits, etc.," provided to its partners. Another commenter expressed concern that the NAICS codes lacked specificity for purposes of sufficiently identifying an exempt organization's investment activities. Therefore, two commenters suggested that an exempt organization's investment activities be identified separately from other activities identified using the NAICS codes.

Consistent with Notice 2018-67, the proposed regulations generally permit the aggregation of the investment activities specifically listed in the proposed regulations for purposes of section 512(a)(6) to mitigate the burden on exempt organizations, particularly those with interests in multi-tier partnerships. However, under the proposed regulations, investment activities are not identified using NAICS 2-digit codes. Specifically, the proposed regulations provide that NAICS 2-digit codes are used to identify separate unrelated trades or businesses except to the extent provided in other paragraphs of the proposed regulations. Under the proposed regulations, an exempt organization's investment activities, as well as the separate unrelated trades or businesses discussed in sections 3 and 4 of this preamble, are identified as described in the proposed regulations and reported as described in the forms and instructions (see section 8 of this preamble).

a. *Investment Activities Are Treated as a Separate Unrelated Trade or Business for Purposes of Section 512(a)(6)*

As a general matter, a number of commenters suggested that the Treasury Department and the IRS should not treat an exempt organization's investment activities as an unrelated trade or business, and therefore the income and losses from these activities should not be considered for purposes of applying section 512(a)(6). The Treasury Department and the IRS have concluded that the structure and purposes of sections 511 through 514 indicate that an exempt organization's investment activities should be treated as a separate unrelated trade or business for purposes of section 512(a)(6). Section 512(a)(1) provides that UBTI means the gross income derived by an exempt organization from any unrelated trade or business regularly carried on by it. Further, section 512(a)(1) provides that an exempt organization excludes from the calculation of UBTI the amounts described in section 512(b)(1), (2), (3), and (5) - that is, dividends, interest, annuities, etc.; royalties; rents; and capital gains. If an exempt organization's investment activities were not an unrelated trade or business, exclusion of certain amounts under section 512(b), such as capital gains (and losses) under section 512(b)(5), would appear to be unnecessary. Furthermore, other income that an exempt organization may consider "investment income" - such as unrelated debt-financed income - is treated as "derived from an unrelated trade or business" under other paragraphs of section 512(b) - including section 512(b)(4). The application of section 512(a)(6) to income included in UBTI under section 512(b)(4), (13), or (17) is discussed in more detail in section 3 of this preamble.

Some commenters cited *Higgins v. Commissioner*, 312 U.S. 212 (1941), to support the position that an exempt organization's investment of its own assets is not a trade or business. However, *Higgins* is not relevant under sections 511 through 514 because it applies to individuals, not corporations or trusts. For the taxable years involved in *Higgins*, a deduction was allowed for all ordinary and necessary expenses of carrying on a trade or business, but a deduction was not allowed for personal, living, or family expenses. Congress responded to *Higgins* by enacting what is now section 212(1) to allow individuals to deduct all ordinary and necessary expenses incurred in the production or collection of income. *Estate of Rockefeller v. Commissioner*, 762 F.2d 264, 266 n.3 (2d Cir. 1985). Section 212 applies only to individuals. Corporations or trusts may deduct only "ordinary and necessary expenses paid or incurred during the taxable year in carrying on any trade or business" under section 162. Thus, no deduction for expenses directly connected with investment activities would be permitted to a corporation or trust unless its investment activities are a part of a trade or business within the meaning of section 162.

However, the Treasury Department and the IRS recognize that exempt organizations have UBTI under sections 511 through 514 from activities engaged in with an intent to make an investment rather than with the intent to actively participate in any of the unrelated trade or business activities generating the UBTI. Accordingly, Notice 2018-67 stated that, as a matter of administrative convenience, the proposed regulations would treat an exempt organization's investment activities as one trade or business for purposes of section 512(a)(6)(A) in order to permit the exempt organization to aggregate gross income and directly connected deductions from possibly multiple separate unrelated trades or businesses. After publication of Notice 2018-67, the Joint Committee on Taxation (JCT) confirmed that "it is intended that the Secretary consider whether it would be appropriate in certain cases to permit an organization that maintains an investment portfolio to treat multiple investment activities as one unrelated trade or business." Staff of the Joint Committee on Taxation, General Explanation of Pub. L. 115-97 (December 2018), at 293 (General Explanation). Consistent with Notice 2018-67 and the General Explanation, the proposed regulations provide that an exempt organization's various investment activities, as exclusively listed therein, are treated as a separate unrelated trade or business for purposes of section 512(a)(6)(A) and the proposed regulations.

b. *Exclusive List of "Investment Activities"*

Notice 2018-67 did not define the term "investment activities" but rather requested comments regarding the scope of the activities, both investment partnership interests or other investment activities, that should be included in the category of "investment activities" for purposes of section 512(a)(6). Some commenters suggested that the term "investment activities" include all passive income. Some of these commenters specifically suggested using the definition of "material participation" in section 469 as a method to identify "investment activities." However, most commenters addressing this issue suggested that the term "investment activities" should include activities that give rise to amounts included as: an item of gross income derived from an unrelated trade or business under section 512(b)(4) (debt-financed property), (13) (certain amounts received from controlled entities), and (17) (certain amounts derived from foreign corporations); gross income (or loss) from a partnership that is not directly or indirectly controlled by the exempt organization; and, with respect to controlled partnerships, an item of gross income derived from an unrelated trade or business under section 512(b)(4), (13), and (17).

In drafting these proposed regulations, the Treasury Department and the IRS considered whether to provide a general definition of the term "investment activities." However, even though other areas of the Code make a distinction between "active" and "passive" activities, those distinctions are not applicable for purposes of sections 511 through 514. Section 512(c) applies regardless of whether the exempt organization is an active or passive participant in the unrelated trade or business of the partnership or whether it is a general or limited partner. Rev. Rul. 79-222; *Service Bolt & Nut Co. v. Commissioner*, 724 F.2d 519, 523-24 (6th Cir., 1983), *aff'g*, 78 T.C. 812 (1982); *see also Leila G. Newhall Unitrust v. Commissioner*, 105 F.3d 482 (9th Cir. 1997), *aff'g*, 104 T.C. 236 (1995) (following *Service Bolt & Nut*, 724 F.2d 519). Thus, the Treasury Department and the IRS do not believe that use of the criteria for finding "material participation" under section 469 is appropriate in applying section 512(a)(6).

Rather, the proposed regulations provide an exclusive list of an exempt organization's investment activities that can be treated as one separate unrelated trade or business for purposes of section 512(a)(6). Under the proposed regulations, for most exempt organizations, such investment activities are limited to: (i) qualifying partnership interests (see section 2.d of this preamble); (ii) debt-financed properties (see section 3.a of this preamble); and (iii) qualifying S corporation interests (see section 4.a of this preamble). As discussed in section 5.b.i of this preamble, the qualifying partnership rules do not apply to social clubs described in section 501(c)(7). However, for exempt organizations subject to section 512(a)(3) (including social clubs), the proposed regulations clarify that UBTI from the investment activities of such organizations includes certain additional amounts (see section 5.a of this preamble).

The Treasury Department and the IRS will continue to consider whether the term "investment activities" can be defined more generally in a manner that is administrable and consistent with the legislative intent of section 512(a)(6). The Treasury Department and the IRS request comments regarding the specific factors that should be considered when determining whether an activity is an investment activity for purposes of section 512(a)(6).

c. *Partnership Interests*

With respect to partnership interests, the Treasury Department and the IRS stated in Notice 2018-67 that the category of "investment activities" for purposes of section 512(a)(6) should include only partnership interests in which the exempt organization does not significantly participate in any partnership trade or business. Some commenters suggested including in this category partnerships over which the exempt organization has no control, which is discussed in more detail in section 2.d of this preamble.

Other commenters suggested that this category include all limited partnerships or limited liability companies (LLCs) in which the exempt organization is a non-managing member (regardless of the exempt organization's percentage interest or other participation in the partnership). The Treasury Department and the IRS decline to adopt this comment because of the variation in state law for determining non-managing member equivalent interests and the administrative burden that reliance on state law places on the IRS. Nonetheless, as discussed in section 2.d.iii.B of this preamble, the Treasury Department and the IRS recognize that there may be rights or actions permitted by state law that are normal and routine and that do not indicate any measurable influence or control over a partnership. Accordingly, the Treasury Department and the IRS request comments on whether certain permitted rights or actions should be disregarded in determining whether a partnership interest is a qualifying partnership interest. In addition, the proposed regulations clarify that any partnership in which an exempt organization is a general partner for any federal tax purpose is not a qualifying partnership interest within the meaning of the proposed regulations, regardless of the exempt organization's percentage interest.

d. *Qualifying Partnership Interests*

Pending publication of proposed regulations, the interim rule described in Notice 2018-67 permitted an exempt organization to aggregate its UBTI from certain partnership interests with multiple trades or businesses, including trades or businesses conducted by lower-tier partnerships (qualifying partnership interest). *See* section 6.01(2) of Notice 2018-67. Additionally, the interim rule permitted the aggregation of any qualifying partnership interest (QPI) with all other QPIs, resulting in the treatment of the aggregate group of QPIs as a single trade or business for purposes of section 512(a)(6)(A). *Id.*

Although some commenters suggested retaining the interim rule as described in Notice 2018-67, the majority of commenters appeared to support retention of the interim rule but made suggestions regarding possible revisions that potentially could reduce any administrative burden associated with the rule. Consistent with these comments, the proposed regulations retain the interim rule with the modifications described in the following sections of this preamble.

i. Designation of a QPI

Like Notice 2018-67, the proposed regulations permit, but do not require, an organization to aggregate its UBTI from QPIs. *See* section 6.01(2) of Notice 2018-67. However, the proposed regulations add that, once an organization designates a partnership interest as a QPI (in accordance with forms and instructions), it cannot thereafter identify the trades or businesses conducted by the partnership that are unrelated trades or businesses with respect to the organization using NAICS 2-digit codes unless and until the partnership interest is no longer a QPI. For example, if an organization has a partnership interest that is a QPI and the organization designates that partnership interest as a QPI on its Form 990-T, the organization cannot, in the next taxable year, identify the trades or businesses of the partnership that are unrelated trades or businesses with respect to the organization using NAICS 2-digit codes. However, if in a future taxable year, the organization's partnership interest is no longer a QPI, then the organization would be required to identify the trades or business of the partnership that are unrelated trades or businesses with respect to the organization using NAICS 2-digit codes.

A partnership interest is a QPI if it meets the requirements of either the de minimis test (discussed in section 2.d.ii of this preamble) or the control test (discussed in section 2.d.iii of this preamble).

ii. The De Minimis Test

Both Notice 2018-67 and the proposed regulations provide that a partnership interest is a QPI that meets the requirements of the de minimis test if the exempt organization holds directly no more than 2 percent of the profits interest and no more than 2 percent of the capital interest. *See* section 6.02(1) of Notice 2018-67. As noted by several commenters, the 2 percent threshold for the de minimis test is consistent with the de minimis test under section 4943, which provides that a private foundation does not have excess business holdings in any corporation in which it (together with certain related private foundations described in section 4946(a)(1)(H)) owns not more than 2 percent of the voting stock and not more than 2 percent in value of all outstanding shares of all classes of stock. The Treasury Department and the IRS chose not to cross-reference the section 4943 de minimis test because that section applies only to private foundations. Nonetheless, because Congress adopted a 2 percent de minimis test under section 4943, the Treasury Department and the IRS consider a 2 percent threshold to be appropriate for purposes of the de minimis test in the proposed regulations.

However, the proposed regulations make two changes to the de minimis test provided in Notice 2018-67 to improve administrability and to provide more appropriate relief. First, as discussed in section 2.d.iv of this preamble, an exempt organization is no longer required to combine certain related interests when determining whether a partnership interest meets the requirements of the de minimis test. Second, in response to comments that the interim rule should apply to lower-tier partnerships, the proposed regulations provide that, if an exempt organization does not control a partnership in which the exempt organization holds a direct interest (directly-held partnership interest) but that directly-held partnership interest is not a QPI because the exempt organization holds more than 20 percent of the capital interest, any partnership in which the exempt organization holds an indirect interest through the directly-held partnership interest (indirectly-held partnership interest) may be a QPI if the indirectly-held partnership interest meets the requirements of the de minimis test (look-through rule). Accordingly, the proposed regulations permit (but do not require) an exempt organization to aggregate the UBTI from some indirectly-held QPIs with its directly-held QPIs. However, the look-through rule does not apply to indirectly-held QPIs that do not meet the requirements of the de minimis test but may meet the requirements of the control test.

For example, if an exempt organization directly holds 50 percent of the capital interests of a partnership that it does not control and the directly-held partnership holds 4 percent of the capital and profits interests of lower-tier partnership A and 10 percent of the capital and profits interests of lower-tier partnership B, the exempt organization can aggregate its interest in lower-tier partnership A with its other QPIs because the exempt organization indirectly holds 2 percent of the capital and profits interests of lower-tier partnership A (4 percent x 50 percent = 2 percent). However, the exempt organization may not aggregate its interest in lower-tier partnership B with its QPIs because the exempt organization indirectly holds 5 percent (10 percent x 50 percent) of the capital and profits interest of lower-tier partnership B, which does not meet the requirements of the de minimis test.

If a directly-held partnership interest is not a QPI, the general principles of section 512(c) apply and the exempt organization is required to identify the trades or businesses conducted by the directly-held partnership, and any indirectly-held partnerships, that are unrelated trades or businesses with respect to the exempt organization. The Treasury Department and the IRS expect that permitting an exempt organization to aggregate any indirectly-held partnership interests that meet the requirements of the de minimis test with all other QPIs will reduce the administrative burden on exempt organizations because there will be no need to identify each trade or business conducted by such indirectly-held partnership. However, the Treasury Department and the IRS request comments regarding the administrability of permitting the aggregation of indirectly-held partnership interests that meet the requirements of the de minimis test.

iii. The Control Test

Notice 2018-67 stated that a partnership interest is a QPI that meets the requirements of the control test if the exempt organization (i) directly holds no more than 20 percent of the capital interest; and (ii) does not have control or influence over the partnership. *See* section 6.03(1) of Notice 2018-67.

A. Percentage Interest

Numerous commenters made recommendations regarding the first prong of the control test, most of which recommend increasing the percentage threshold to 50 percent to conform with the definition of control in section 512(b)(13). Multiple commenters suggested that the percentage control requirement be eliminated entirely.

The proposed regulations retain the 20 percent threshold used in Notice 2018-67. The Treasury Department and the IRS intend the percentage threshold to be a proxy to identify partnership interests in which the exempt organization does not significantly participate in any partnership trade or business and therefore may appropriately be considered an investment activity for purposes of section 512(a)(6). The 20 percent threshold is consistent with at least one other administrative exception created for certain investment activities. *See* section 731(c)(3)(C)(i) & § 1.731-2(e). Accordingly, the proposed regulations treat a 20 percent interest in a partnership over which the exempt organization partner has no control (see section 2.d.iii.B of this preamble) as a part of the exempt organization's investment activities. However, as with the de minimis test, an exempt organization is no longer required to combine certain related interests when determining whether a partnership interest meets the 20 percent threshold under the control test (see section 2.d.iv of this preamble).

The Treasury Department and the IRS recognize that an exempt organization may have more than 20 percent of the capital interests of a partnership but the exempt organization may consider that partnership interest to be part of its investment activities raising funds for its exempt activities. However, as discussed in section 2.b of this preamble, the proposed regulations do not provide a general definition of the term "investment activities" such that a non-QPI could be aggregated with the exempt organization's other investment activities for purposes of section 512(a)(6). While the addition of the look-through rule to the de minimis test in these proposed regulations may result in the aggregation of some of the lower-tier partnership interests of a directly-held non-QPI, an exempt organization's investment intent is not sufficient to treat the overall non-QPI as part of its investment activities.

At least two commenters suggested that the capital interests in a partnership do not indicate control over a partnership. The Treasury Department and the IRS understand that a partner's percentage interest in the capital interests of a partnership does not necessarily correlate with the partner's ability to control the partnership. However, the Treasury Department and the IRS have concluded that a combination of an exempt organization's percentage capital interest in a partnership and the exempt organization's ability to control the partnership are an appropriate administrative proxy for determining whether a partnership interest is an investment activity. The use of a percentage interest, in addition to the definition of "control" discussed in section 2.d.iii.B of this preamble, provides a bright line for the evaluation of partnership interests that may be investment activities. Furthermore, because an exempt organization's percentage profits interest may change throughout the year, the proposed regulations continue to consider only an exempt organization's capital interest in a partnership for purposes of the control test.

B. Definition of "Control"

Notice 2018-67 provided that all facts and circumstances are relevant for determining whether an exempt organization has control or influence over a partnership. *See* section 6.03(3) of Notice 2018-67. Notice 2018-67 then provided three specific circumstances in which an exempt organization has control or influence. *Id.* Commenters generally appeared to support the inclusion of a facts and circumstances test. Nonetheless, numerous commenters suggested revisions to what it means for an exempt organization to have influence or control over a partnership.

First, Notice 2018-67 provided that an exempt organization has control or influence if the exempt organization may require the partnership to perform, or may prevent the partnership from performing, any act that significantly affects the operations of the partnership. Several commenters recommended that the proposed regulations clarify that the right to vote for the appointment or removal of a general partner or managing member, the ability to appoint representatives to investor committees or advisory committees, and the right to approve the selection or removal of a general partner or managing member do not evidence influence or control. These commenters explained that these rights help ensure that the general partner cannot alter a partnership without the consent of the limited partners. Similarly, other commenters requested that the proposed regulations clarify that an exempt organization will not be deemed to have influence or control over a partnership if it exercises its rights or takes actions that it is permitted to take under state law while maintaining its limited liability status in a partnership.

Second, Notice 2018-67 provided that an exempt organization has control or influence over a partnership if any of the exempt organization's officers, directors, trustees, or employees have rights to participate in the management of the partnership or conduct the partnership's business at any time, or if the exempt organization has the power to appoint or remove any of the partnership's officers, directors, trustees, or employees. One commenter stated that the presence of these rights or powers does not necessarily illustrate control. Another commenter suggested that this rule is overly restrictive and will cause many partnership interests in which an exempt organization has no influence or control to fail to meet the requirements of the control test. This commenter stated that many exempt organizations have governing board members that also work in the investment management industry and may participate in conducting the business of a partnership in which the exempt organization invests. The commenter explained that these individuals' expertise in financial management is essential for the prudent management of an exempt organization's investments. The commenter argued that a general rule based on facts and circumstances is sufficient to address situations in which an exempt organization exercises "excessive" influence or control over a partnership such that it should not be considered a QPI.

The proposed regulations retain the control rule described in Notice 2018-67 with minor modifications to address the comments described above. In particular, the proposed regulations remove the term "influence" so that the second prong of the control test provides that, if the exempt organization has 20 percent or less of the capital interests, a partnership interest is a QPI that meets the requirements of the control test if the exempt organization does not control the partnership. Consistent with Notice 2018-67, the proposed regulations provide that all the facts and circumstances are relevant for determining whether an exempt organization controls a partnership. The proposed regulations clarify that the partnership agreement is among the facts and circumstances that may be considered when making a determination of control.

The proposed regulations also list certain specific circumstances that evidence control, focusing on four discrete rights or powers. Two circumstances focus on the exempt organization's ability to perform certain actions on its own. Specifically, the proposed regulations provide that an exempt organization controls a partnership if the exempt organization, by itself, may require the partnership to perform, or may prevent the partnership from performing, any act that significantly affects the operations of the partnership or has the power to appoint or remove any of the partnership's officers or employees or a majority of directors. The remaining two circumstances focus on whether any of the exempt organization's officers, directors, trustees, or employees have rights to participate in the management of the partnership at any time or to conduct the partnership's business at any time. No exception is provided for certain professionals that may serve on the boards of both the exempt organization and partnerships in which the exempt organization is a partner.

The Treasury Department and the IRS recognize that, although these rights or powers indicate control in some situations, other facts and circumstances may tip the scale the other way. Accordingly, the Treasury Department and the IRS request comments regarding whether all these rights or powers should be weighted the same or whether there are certain circumstances in which such right or power would never indicate control.

iv. Combining Related Interests

Both the de minimis test and the control test in Notice 2018-67 required an exempt organization to own less than a certain percentage of the profits and capital interests in a partnership. *See* sections 6.02(1) (de minimis test) and 6.03(1) (control test) of Notice 2018-67. In determining the exempt organization's ownership percentage, both the de minimis test and the control test required the exempt organization to combine certain related interests (aggregation rule). *Id.* The aggregation rule in section 6.02(2)(b)(i) of Notice 2018-67 provided that, when determining an exempt organization's percentage partnership interest, the interest of a disqualified person (as defined in section 4958(f)), a supporting organization (as defined in section 509(a)(3)), or a controlled entity (as defined in section 512(b)(13)) in the same partnership would be taken into account. *See* section 6.02(2)(b)(ii) through (iv) of Notice 2018-67.

Most commenters suggested that the aggregation rule is overly burdensome and requested that it be removed. Commenters noted that many public charity boards have numerous members and argued that verifying the board members' ownership percentages, after taking into account other related interests, for every partnership interest that generates UBTI would be unreasonable, if not impossible. Additionally, these commenters stated that the exempt organization cannot usually obtain information about other partners from the partnerships in which it holds interests because of confidentiality agreements.

If the aggregation rule is retained, commenters recommended several revisions. First, two commenters suggested eliminating the aggregation rule for the de minimis test. Next, a commenter suggested only requiring aggregation of interests owned by controlled entities and persons with direct control over the exempt organization's investment decisions. Additionally, another commenter would limit aggregation with interests owned by controlled entities to those interests owned by Type I and II supporting organizations described in section 509(a)(3)(B)(i) and (ii) and exclude interests owned by Type III supporting organizations described in section 509(a)(3)(B)(iii). Finally, another commenter suggested requiring aggregation with interests owned by controlled entities but not interests owned by persons or organizations that are not controlled by the exempt organization.

The proposed regulations retain a modified aggregation rule to address situations in which an exempt organization may control a partnership through the aggregation of interests. The aggregation rule in the proposed regulations differs from the aggregation rule in Notice 2018-67 in two ways. First, the aggregation rule in the proposed regulations applies only for purposes of the control test and not for purposes of the de minimis test. Second, the proposed regulations do not require an exempt organization to take into account the interests of disqualified persons when determining the exempt organization's percentage interest in a partnership for purposes of the control test.

The proposed regulations adopt other aspects of the aggregation rule from Notice 2018-67 without change. In particular, the proposed regulations include the definitions of "supporting organization" and "controlled entity" used in Notice 2018-67, which cross-referenced sections 509(a)(3) and 512(b)(13)(D), respectively. Additionally, the proposed regulations provide that, when determining an exempt organization's percentage interest in a partnership for purposes of the control test, the interests of a supporting organization or a controlled entity in the same partnership will be taken into account. However, the Treasury Department and the IRS will continue to consider whether the aggregation of the interests of supporting organizations is appropriate in the circumstance in which the exempt organization is a supported organization that has little to no control over its supporting organizations.

v. Reliance on Schedule K-1 (Form 1065)

Notice 2018-67 provided that, in determining the exempt organization's percentage interest in a partnership, the exempt organization may rely on the Schedule K-1 (Form 1065) (or its successor) it receives from the partnership. Commenters requested various revisions to the Schedule K-1 (Form 1065) to assist in the reporting process. The Treasury Department and the IRS will consider revisions to the Schedule K-1 (Form 1065). Otherwise, the proposed regulations continue to permit reliance on Schedule K-1 (Form 1065) if the form lists the exempt organization's percentage profits interest or its percentage capital interest, or both, at the beginning and end of the year. However, the proposed regulations clarify that the exempt organization may not rely on the form to the extent that any information about the exempt organization's percentage interest is not specifically provided. For example, if the Schedule K-1 (Form 1065) an exempt organization receives from a partnership lists the exempt organization's percentage capital interest at the beginning and end of the year but lists its profits interest as "variable," the exempt organization may rely on the form only with respect to its percentage capital interest.

vi. Additional Recommended Changes

Commenters suggested additional modifications to the de minimis and control tests, including phase-in and grace periods to address changes in an exempt organization's percentage interest that are beyond the exempt organization's control. Two commenters requested that an exempt organization be permitted up to 90 days to reduce its interest in a partnership in order to satisfy the requirements of the de minimis test if the increase in interest was because of another partner's withdrawal or percentage reduction. Another commenter suggested that, if a partnership interest met the requirements of either the de minimis test or the control test in a taxable year, the partnership interest should continue to meet those requirements in the following taxable years if the exempt organization's percentage interest changed through no action of the exempt organization partner.

The proposed regulations do not adopt any of these recommended changes because the de minimis and control tests are rules of administrative convenience. Allowing greater interests due to other actions would require other safeguards and limitations that would complicate the rule and place additional administrative burdens on exempt organizations and the IRS. Nevertheless, the Treasury Department and the IRS recognize that an exempt organization may not be aware of changes in its partnership interest until it receives a Schedule K-1 (Form 1065) from the partnership at the end of the partnership's taxable year. In such a circumstance, it may be appropriate to permit a higher percentage interest in taxable years in which the increase in an exempt organization's percentage interest during a taxable year is the result of the actions of other partners. Accordingly, the Treasury Department and the IRS request comments regarding whether permitting a higher percentage interest in taxable years in which the increase occurs as the result of the actions of other partners would address these commenters' concerns.

e. *Transition Rule*

Pending publication of proposed regulations, the transition rule in Notice 2018-67 permitted an exempt organization to treat each partnership interest acquired prior to August 21, 2018, that failed to meet the requirements of either the de minimis test or the control test as one trade or business for purposes of section 512(a)(6), regardless of whether there was more than one trade or business directly or indirectly conducted by the partnership or lower-tier partnerships. *See* section 6.04 of Notice 2018-67.

Many commenters asserted that the transition rule should apply to any partnership interest held by an exempt organization regardless of the date acquired. However, in the case of a partnership that conducts more than one trade or business that is a separate unrelated trade or business with respect to the exempt organization, applying the transition rule to all partnership interests and treating each non-QPI as one trade or business would undermine the purpose of section 512(a)(6) by allowing the gains from one unrelated trade or business to offset the losses from another unrelated trade or business. Accordingly, the Treasury Department and the IRS do not accept this comment.

Other commenters suggested that the proposed regulations should clarify that, if an exempt organization acquired a partnership interest before August 21, 2018, changes in the exempt organization's percentage interest would not affect the availability of the transition rule. Accordingly, the proposed regulations clarify that a partnership interest acquired prior to August 21, 2018, will continue to meet the requirement of the transition rule even if the exempt organization's percentage interest changes on or after August 21, 2018.

The proposed regulations also include two additions to the transition rule. First, the proposed regulations permit an exempt organization to rely on the transition rule only until the first day of the organization's first taxable year beginning after the date these proposed regulations are published as final regulations (transition period). Second, the proposed regulations provide that an exempt organization may apply either the transition rule or the look-through rule, but not both, to a partnership interest that meets the requirements for both rules. During the transition period, the exempt organization must determine how a partnership interest to which it chose to apply the transition rule will be treated under the final regulations. The Treasury Department and the IRS request comments regarding whether any additional transitional relief is necessary.

3. *Inclusions of Income Derived from an Unrelated Trade or Business under Section 512(b)(4), (13), and (17)*

Section 512(b)(4), (13), and (17) require the inclusion of certain income as items of gross income derived from an unrelated trade or business if such income is unrelated debt-financed income, a specified payment from controlled entities, or certain insurance income derived from a controlled foreign corporation, respectively. In Notice 2018-67, the Treasury Department and the IRS explained that, in the absence of section 512(b)(1), (2), (3), and (5), the income described in these sections would be included in the calculation of UBTI to the extent that such amounts are "gross income derived by any organization from any unrelated trade or business . . . regularly carried on by it" under section 512(a)(1). Accordingly, the Treasury Department and the IRS stated that no distinction existed between "gross income derived by any organization from any unrelated trade or business . . . regularly carried on by it" within the meaning of section 512(a)(1) and amounts included "as an item of gross income derived from an unrelated trade or business" under section 512(b)(4), (13), and (17).

However, the Treasury Department and the IRS recognized that some interpretations of section 512(a)(6) might impose a significant burden on exempt organizations required to include certain income in UBTI under section 512(b)(4), (13), or (17), and, consequently, that aggregating income included in UBTI under these sections may be appropriate in certain circumstances. In Notice 2018-67, the Treasury Department and the IRS requested comments regarding the treatment under section 512(a)(6) of income that is not from a partnership, but that is included in UBTI under section 512(b)(4), (13), and (17).

A few commenters disagreed with the statement that there is "no distinction between 'gross income derived by any organization from any unrelated trade or business . . . regularly carried on by it' under section 512(a)(1) and amounts included in UBTI 'as an item of gross income derived from an unrelated trade or business' under section 512(b)(4), (13), and (17)." These commenters argued that amounts included as items of gross income from an unrelated trade or business under section 512(b)(4), (13), and (17) should not be subject to section 512(a)(6) because such amounts are treated as income from investment activities and not as gross income from a trade or business.

As discussed in section 2.a of this preamble, investment activities are treated as a separate unrelated trade or business for purposes of section 512(a)(6). Furthermore, section 512(b)(4), (13), and (17) each provide that income described in the provision is income derived from an unrelated trade or business. Accordingly, amounts included in UBTI under section 512(b)(4), (13), and (17) contribute to the determination of whether an organization has more than one unrelated trade or business and thus is subject to section 512(a)(6). After considering the comments received and the legislative history of each section, the Treasury Department and the IRS propose the following treatment of amounts included in UBTI under section 512(b)(4), (13), and (17) for purposes of section 512(a)(6).

a. *Unrelated Debt-Financed Income*

In the case of debt-financed property (as defined in section 514), section 512(b)(4) requires an exempt organization to include, as an item of gross income from an unrelated trade or business, any unrelated debt-financed income, determined under section 514, with respect to such debt-financed property, even if an amount received with respect to the debt-financed property would ordinarily be excluded from the calculation of UBTI under section 512(b)(1), (2), (3), or (5). Section 514(b)(1) defines the term "debt-financed property" as any property that is held to produce income and with respect to which there is acquisition indebtedness. Section 1.514(b)-1(a) clarifies that property held to produce income includes rental real estate, tangible personal property, and corporate stock. Section 1.514(a)-1(a) provides that the calculation of debt-financed taxable income is made on a property-by-property basis. Thus, as stated in Notice 2018-67, one interpretation of sections 512(b)(4) and 514 and the regulations thereunder could require each debt-financed property to be treated as a separate unrelated trade or business under section 512(a)(6).

However, the amounts excluded from the calculation of UBTI under section 512(b)(1), (2), (3), and (5) that are included in UBTI if subject to acquisition indebtedness include dividends, interest, annuities, royalties, rents, and capital gains. As acknowledged in section 2.a of this preamble, dividends, interest, annuities, royalties, rents, and capital gains generally are income from investment activities. Additionally, section 514 generally does not apply to any property to the extent that the income from such property is taken into account in computing the gross income of any unrelated trade or business (except in the case of capital gains from such property that would be excluded under section 512(b)(5)). *See* section 514(b)(1)(B). Accordingly, the Treasury Department and the IRS agree with commenters that debt-financed properties (as defined in section 514) generally are held for investment purposes. Therefore, to reduce the reporting burden on exempt organizations, the proposed regulations include all the UBTI under section 512(b)(4) from an exempt organization's debt-financed property or properties (and not just its unrelated debt-financed income arising in connection with a QPI as provided in Notice 2018-67) in the list of "investment activities" treated as a separate unrelated trade or business for purposes of section 512(a)(6).

The Treasury Department and the IRS note that rental of certain property is a trade or business that must be identified using NAICS 2-digit codes. For example, section 512(b)(3)(B) provides that rents from real and personal property are included in UBTI if more than 50 percent of the total rent received or accrued under a lease is attributable to personal property. Also, § 1.512(b)-1(c)(5) indicates that payments for the use or occupancy of rooms or other space where services are also rendered to the occupant do not constitute rent from real property. Sections 512(b)(4) and 514 do not apply where such real or personal property is purchased with debt financing because the rents from these properties will have already been included in UBTI. *See* section 514(b)(1)(B) (providing that, except in the case of income excluded under section 512(b)(5), the term "debt-financed property" does not include any property to the extent that the income from such property is taken into account in computing the gross income of any unrelated trade or business); § 1.514(b)-1(b)(2)(i). Accordingly, because rent from such real and personal property is included in UBTI, the exempt organization must identify such unrelated trade or business using the NAICS 2-digit code for real estate rental and leasing (53).

b. *Specified Payments Received from Controlled Entities*

Notwithstanding section 512(b)(1), (2), and (3), section 512(b)(13)(A) requires an exempt organization, referred to as a "controlling organization," that receives or accrues (directly or indirectly) a specified payment from another entity which it controls, referred to as a "controlled entity," to include such payment as an item of gross income derived from an unrelated trade or business to the extent such payment reduces the net unrelated income of the controlled entity (or increases any net unrelated loss of the controlled entity). *See* § 1.512(b)-1(l)(1). Section 512(b)(13)(C) defines the term "specified payment" as any interest, annuity, royalty, or rent. Accordingly, section 512(b)(13) treats certain amounts that would ordinarily be excluded from the calculation of UBTI under section 512(b)(1), (2), and (3) as income derived from an unrelated trade or business.

Commenters argued that amounts included in UBTI under section 512(b)(13) should be included with an exempt organization's other investment activities. Presumably, this argument rests on the premise that the types of payments described in section 512(b)(13)(C) — that is, any interest, annuity, royalty, or rent — might be characterized generally as "investment income." However, treating specified payments included in UBTI as income from an exempt organization's investment activities would be inconsistent with the purpose of section 512(b)(13)(A), which is to prevent a controlled entity from gaining a competitive advantage (in contravention of the purposes of section 512) through making deductible payments to a controlling organization that is exempt from tax. *See* S. Rep. No. 91-552, at 73 (1969) (explaining that certain "rental" arrangements between exempt organizations and taxable subsidiaries "enable[ ] the taxable [subsidiary] to escape nearly all of its income taxes"). Consistent with that purpose, section 512(b)(13)(A) treats a specified payment as income from an unrelated trade or business only "to the extent such payment reduces the net unrelated income of the controlled entity (or increases any net unrelated loss of the controlled entity)." Section 512(b)(13) thus views such payments as stemming from the trade or business activity of the controlled entity rather than from the "investment activity" of the controlling organization.

Further, the required degree of control of the controlling organization over the controlled entity indicates that the controlled entities are not a part of the controlling organization's otherwise appropriately characterized investment activities. In general, section 512(b)(13)(D) defines the term "control" as ownership of more than 50 percent of the stock in a corporation, of the profits interests or capital interests in a partnership, or, in any other case, of the beneficial interests in an entity. The section 318 constructive ownership rules apply when determining the ownership of stock in a corporation, and similar principles apply in determining the ownership of interests in other types of entities. As generally discussed in section 2.d.iii.B of this preamble, control over an organization suggests that such interest is not part of the exempt organization's investment activities. Accordingly, even though the controlled entity's trades or businesses might not be attributed to the controlling organization (such as in the case of a controlled corporation), the control itself indicates that the controlled entity is held as part of a trade or business other than the controlling organization's investment activities.

The plain language of section 512(b)(13) could require each specified payment to be treated as a separate unrelated trade or business under section 512(a)(6) because section 512(b)(13) requires an exempt organization to include such payment as an item of gross income derived from "an" unrelated trade or business. However, this treatment may impose a considerable administrative burden on controlling organizations that receive numerous specified payments from controlled entities, such as may be the case with a university or hospital system. Therefore, these proposed regulations permit an exempt organization to aggregate all the specified payments received from a controlled entity and to treat the payments as received from a single separate unrelated trade or business for purposes of section 512(a)(6).

In particular, the proposed regulations provide that, if an exempt organization controls another entity (within the meaning of section 512(b)(13)(D)), the specified payments from that controlled entity will be treated as gross income from a separate unrelated trade or business for purposes of section 512(a)(6). If a controlling organization receives specified payments from two different controlled entities, the payments from each controlled entity are treated as separate unrelated trades or businesses. For example, a controlling organization that receives rental payments from two controlled entities will have two separate unrelated trades or businesses, one for each controlled entity. The specified payments from a controlled entity will be treated as gross income from one unrelated trade or business regardless of whether the controlled entity engages in more than one unrelated trade or business or whether the controlling organization receives more than one type of specified payment from that controlled entity.

c. Certain Amounts Derived from Foreign Corporations

Section 512(b)(17) requires any amount included in gross income under section 951(a)(1)(A) to be included as an item of gross income derived from an unrelated trade or business to the extent the amount so included is attributable to insurance income (as defined in section 953) which, if derived directly by the exempt organization, would be treated as an unrelated trade or business. Section 953(a)(1) defines "insurance income" as any income that (A) is attributable to the issuing (or reinsuring) of an insurance or annuity contract, and (B) would (subject to certain modifications not relevant here) be taxed under subchapter L of chapter 1 if such income were the income of a domestic insurance company. Thus, section 512(b)(17) "applies a look-through rule in characterizing certain subpart F insurance income for unrelated business income tax purposes." H. R. Rep. No. 104-586 (1996), at 137.

Commenters have argued that insurance income included in UBTI under section 512(b)(17) belongs in the category of investment activities. However, like section 512(b)(13), the required degree of control of the exempt organization over the controlled foreign corporation indicates that the exempt organization's interest in a controlled foreign corporation probably is not a part of the exempt organization's otherwise appropriately characterized investment activities. In particular, section 951(a)(1)(A) applies only if a foreign corporation is a controlled foreign corporation, which section 957 defines as any foreign corporation if more than 50 percent of the total combined voting power of all classes of stock of such corporation entitled to vote or the total value of the stock of such corporation is owned, directly, indirectly, or constructively by United States shareholders. Section 951(b) defines "United States shareholder," with respect to any foreign corporation, as a United States person (within the meaning of section 7701(a)(30), which includes domestic corporations and certain trusts) who owns, directly, indirectly, or constructively, 10 percent or more of the total combined voting power of all classes of stock entitled to vote of such foreign corporation or 10 percent or more of the total value of shares of all classes of stock of such foreign corporation.

Furthermore, insurance income included in UBTI under section 512(b)(17) should not be treated as gross income from an exempt organization's investment activities because the provision of insurance generally is an unrelated trade or business. Section 501(m) provides that, in the case of an exempt organization described in section 501(c)(3) or (4) that does not provide commercial-type insurance as a substantial part of its activities, the activity of providing commercial-type insurance is treated as an unrelated trade or business (as defined in section 513). However, rather than treating insurance income from each controlled foreign corporation as income from a separate unrelated trade or business, these proposed regulations treat the provision of insurance by all controlled foreign corporations as one trade or business, regardless of whether such insurance income is received from more than one controlled foreign corporation. This approach is consistent with how NAICS would categorize the provision of insurance (52 - Finance and Insurance).

However, the proposed regulations do not permit the aggregation of an exempt organization's insurance income included in UBTI under section 512(b)(17) with any insubstantial commercial-type insurance activities conducted directly by the exempt organization because the controlled foreign corporation, not the exempt organization, is engaged in the activity giving rise to the insurance income included in UBTI under section 512(b)(17). The insurance activity is not attributed to the exempt organization and thus is distinguishable from any commercial-type insurance activity engaged in directly by the exempt organization.

4. S Corporation Interest Treated as an Interest in an Unrelated Trade or Business

An S corporation is a "small corporation" that may elect to be treated under a simplified tax regime that acts as a hybrid between the rules for corporations and the rules for pass-through entities. In general, the items of income and loss of an S corporation are taxed directly to the shareholders of that corporation. *See* section 1366(a). The types of exempt organizations that are permitted to be shareholders of an S corporation are described in section 1361(c)(2)(A)(vi) and (6). Exempt organizations permitted to be S corporation shareholders include qualified retirement plans, exempt organizations described in section 501(c)(3), and certain IRAs (including, subject to the limitation described more specifically in 1361(c)(2)(A)(vi), an IRA designated as a Roth IRA under section 408A).

For purposes of the unrelated business income tax, section 512(e) provides special rules applicable to S corporations. Section 512(e)(1)(A) provides that, if an exempt organization permitted to be an S corporation shareholder holds stock in an S corporation, such interest will be treated as an interest in an unrelated trade or business. Thus, notwithstanding any other provision in sections 511 through 514, section 512(e)(1)(B) requires an exempt organization permitted to hold S corporation stock to take the following amounts into account in computing the UBTI of such exempt organization: (i) all items of income, loss, or deduction taken into account under section 1366(a) (regarding the determination of an S corporation shareholder's tax liability); and (ii) any gain or loss on the disposition of the stock in the S corporation.

Notice 2018-67 did not address, or request comments on, the treatment of amounts taken into account in computing UBTI under section 512(e). Nonetheless, one commenter recommended that UBTI from an S corporation should be treated as income from a single trade or business regardless of the manner in which such income is earned by the S corporation. The commenter stated that having to separate all the income producing activities of an S corporation would be extremely burdensome. Accordingly, the commenter recommended that all income from an S corporation should be aggregated with the income from QPIs to ensure similar treatment of all pass-through entities. In the alternative, the commenter suggested combining all income from S corporations in which the exempt organization shareholder owns less than 50 percent of the shares with the income from QPIs.

The proposed regulations generally provide that each S corporation interest will be treated as an interest in a separate unrelated trade or business, which is consistent with the language of section 512(e)(1)(A). Accordingly, if an exempt organization has two S corporation interests (that are not qualifying S corporation interests described in section 4.a of this preamble), the exempt organization will report two trades or businesses, one for each S corporation interest. The treatment of each S corporation interest as one trade or business for purposes of section 512(a)(6) is similar to the treatment of specified payments from a controlled entity under section 512(b)(13). Furthermore, the Treasury Department and the IRS view this treatment as best serving the purposes of section 512(a)(6).

Section 512(e) provides two different rules: one for items of income, loss, or deduction taken into account under section 1366(a) and one for any gain or loss on the disposition of S corporation stock. Although these amounts could be treated as separate unrelated trades or businesses for purposes of section 512(a)(6) due to the disparate methods of inclusion in the language of section 512(e), such treatment would artificially divide each S corporation interest into two trades or businesses. The separate enumeration of the gain or loss on the disposition of S corporation stock serves to override section 512(b)(5), which would otherwise exclude such gain or loss from the calculation of UBTI, and not to indicate the existence of a separate unrelated trade or business. Accordingly, the proposed regulations provide that the UBTI from an S corporation interest is the amount described in section 512(e)(1)(B), which includes both the items of income, loss, or deduction taken into account under section 1366(a) and the gain and loss on the disposition of S corporation stock.

a. Qualifying S Corporation Interests

Notwithstanding the general rule that each S corporation interest is treated as a separate unrelated trade or business, the Treasury Department and the IRS recognize that an exempt organization may hold S corporation stock for different purposes, including investment purposes. Additionally, the look-through treatment of an S corporation is similar to the look-through treatment of a partnership. As discussed in section 2.d of this preamble, these proposed regulations permit the aggregation of QPIs to mitigate the burden on exempt organizations with interests in multi-tier partnerships. Similarly, the proposed regulations permit an exempt organization to aggregate its UBTI from an S corporation interest with its UBTI from other investment activities if the exempt organization's stock ownership (by percentage of stock ownership) in the S corporation meets the requirements provided in the de minimis test or the control test for "qualifying partnership interests." As such, if an exempt organization owns (by percentage of stock ownership) 2 percent or less of the stock in an S Corporation, or, if it owns 20 percent or less of the stock in such S corporation and meets the facts and circumstances requirements under the second prong of the control test, then such S corporation interest will be a "qualifying S corporation interest" and can be aggregated with other investment activities. When determining an exempt organization's percentage ownership of stock in an S corporation, the exempt organization must apply the same rules for combining related interests that are used to determine whether a partnership interest is a QPI. An exempt organization may rely on the Schedule K-1 (Form 1120-S) that the exempt organization receives from the S corporation when determining its percentage ownership of the stock in such S corporation.

b. Employee Stock Ownership Plans

Section 512(e)(3) provides that section 512(e) does not apply to employer securities (within the meaning of section 409(l)) held by an employee stock ownership plan (ESOP) described in section 4975(e)(7). ESOPs holding S corporation stock ("S corporation ESOPs") are subject to the limits imposed by section 409(p) on the concentration of S corporation ownership. Ownership includes shares allocated to the accounts of ESOP participants. Failing to meet the requirements of section 409(p) will result in the imposition of an excise tax on the S corporation and other adverse consequences to the ESOP and certain individuals. Although section 512(e) generally does not apply to S corporation ESOPs, the application of section 409(p) to an S corporation ESOP might give rise to UBTI. The primary means of avoiding a section 409(p) failure is for the S corporation ESOP to transfer some of its S corporation shares to a non-ESOP portion of the plan or to another qualified retirement plan of the employer. *See* § 1.409(p)-1(b)(2)(v)(A)-(B). Such a transfer may result in a significant number of S corporation shares being held by the non-ESOP portion of an S corporation ESOP or by another section 401(a) plan ("transferee plan"). The transferred shares, no longer held in an ESOP, are not described in section 512(e)(3). Accordingly, the transferee plan treats the S corporation interest resulting from the transfer of the S corporation shares as an interest in an unrelated trade or business under the general rule of section 512(e)(1) and takes the amounts described in section 512(e)(1)(B) into account in computing UBTI. The Treasury Department and IRS anticipate that a transferee plan is not likely to have more than one S corporation interest. However, whether such S corporation interest may be aggregated with the investment activities of the transferee plan will depend on whether the S corporation interest is a qualifying S corporation interest. The Treasury Department and the IRS request comments on this issue.

5. Social Clubs, Voluntary Employees' Beneficiary Associations, and Supplemental Unemployment Benefits Trusts

As noted in the Background section, section 512(a)(3) provides a special definition of UBTI for social clubs, VEBAs, and SUBs. Section 512(a)(3)(A) defines UBTI, in part, as "gross income (excluding exempt function income)." "Gross income" under section 61(a) includes "gains derived from dealings in property," "interest," "rents," "royalties," "dividends," and "annuities." *See* section 61(a)(3) through (8). Consistent with section 61(a), the gross income subject to the unrelated business income tax under section 512(a)(3) generally includes interest, annuities, dividends, royalties, rents, and capital gains because the modifications in section 512(b)(1), (2), (3), and (5) that exclude such amounts from UBTI for organizations subject to section 512(a)(1) are not available under section 512(a)(3). Accordingly, social clubs, VEBAs, and SUBs generally must include interest, dividends, royalties, rents, and capital gains in UBTI unless such amounts may be set aside for a purpose described in section 512(a)(3)(B)(i) or (ii) and therefore would be exempt function income excluded from UBTI under section 512(a)(3)(A).

Section 512(a)(3)(B) defines "exempt function income" as (1) "the gross income from dues, fees, charges, or similar amounts paid by members of the organization as consideration for providing such members or their dependents or guests goods, facilities, or services in furtherance of the purposes constituting the basis for the exemption of the organization;" and (2) "all income (other than an amount equal to the gross income derived from any unrelated trade or business regularly carried on by such organization computed as if the organization were subject to [section 512(a)(1)]) which is set aside" for one of the purposes described in section 512(a)(3)(B)(i) or (ii). Such amounts set aside include reasonable costs of administration directly connected with a purpose described in section 512(a)(3)(B)(i) or (ii).

Section 512(a)(3)(B)(i) includes in exempt function income amounts set aside for a purpose specified in section 170(c)(4), that is, exclusively for religious, charitable, scientific, literary, or educational purposes. In the case of a VEBA or SUB, section 512(a)(3)(B)(ii) includes in exempt function income amounts set aside to provide for the payment of life, sick, accident, or other benefits. Section 512(a)(3)(E) limits the amounts that may be set aside under section 512(a)(3)(B)(ii). In general, section 512(a)(3)(E)(i) provides that a set aside for any purpose described in section 512(a)(3)(B)(ii) may be taken into account as exempt function income only to the extent that such set aside does not result in an amount of assets set aside for such purpose in excess of the account limit determined under section 419A (without regard to section 419A(f)(6)) for the taxable year (not taking into account any reserve described in section 419A(c)(2)(A) for post-retirement medical benefits).

In determining what income may be set aside under 512(a)(3)(B)(i) or (ii), the income available is "all income (other than an amount equal to the gross income derived from any unrelated trade or business regularly carried on by such organization computed as if the organization were subject to [section 512(a)(1)])." This parenthetical language, by referencing "the gross income from any unrelated trade or business computed as if the organization was subject to [section 512(a)(1)]," pulls in the modifications of section 512(b) applicable to that computation. Accordingly, amounts excluded from UBTI under section 512(a) via the modifications in section 512(b) (such as interest, dividends royalties, rents, and capital gains) are available to be set aside for the purposes of section 512(a)(3)(B)(i) and (ii) and may constitute exempt function income, subject to the other applicable limitations.

For example, if a social club has interest and dividends, and does not set aside any amount of such interest or dividends for a purpose specified in section 170(c)(4), then the full amount of the interest and dividends would constitute UBTI under section 512(a)(3). However, if the social club sets aside any amount of the interest or dividends for a purpose specified in section 170(c)(4), the amount of the interest and dividends set aside would be excluded from the calculation of UBTI under section 512(a)(3)(B)(i) as exempt function income (provided that such amount set aside actually is used for a purpose specified in section 170(c)(4)). Similarly, a VEBA with interest and dividends may set aside amounts to provide for the payment of life, sick, accident, or other benefits, subject to the limitations of section 512(a)(3)(E).[4] Such amount set aside will be excluded from UBTI as exempt function income (provided that such amount actually is used to provide for the payment of benefits).

Notice 2018-67 anticipated that the rules issued regarding how an exempt organization identifies separate trades or businesses for purposes of section 512(a)(6)(A) generally would apply under both section 512(a)(1) and (3). Nonetheless, because social clubs, VEBAs, and SUBs are taxed differently than other exempt organizations under section 511, Notice 2018-67 requested comments regarding any additional considerations that should be given to how section 512(a)(6) applies within the context of section 512(a)(3), and, in particular, how the income from investment activities of these organizations should be treated for purposes of section 512(a)(6).

Commenters generally agreed that social clubs should be subject to the same rules as exempt organizations subject to section 512(a)(1) when determining whether the social club is subject to section 512(a)(6). A social club therefore would identify its unrelated trades or businesses using NAICS codes and treat the income derived from investment activities as a separate unrelated trade or business. Only one commenter addressed how section 512(a)(6) should apply to VEBAs. This commenter suggested that VEBAs would not be subject to section 512(a)(6) because the unrelated trade or business activities of the VEBA could be identified under one NAICS 6-digit code - the code for health and welfare funds (525120). However, as explained in section 1.a.i of this preamble, an exempt organization cannot use a NAICS 2-digit code describing the activities the conduct of which is substantially related to the exercise or performance by such exempt organization of the purpose or function constituting the basis for its exemption under section 501. No commenter addressed how section 512(a)(6) should apply to a SUB.

Consistent with the statement made in Notice 2018-67, the Treasury Department and the IRS have determined that a social club, VEBA, or SUB will determine whether it has more than one unrelated trade or business in the same manner as an exempt organization subject to section 512(a)(1) except as discussed in sections 5.a and b of this preamble.

a. *Investment Activities*

As discussed in section 2 of this preamble, the proposed regulations treat certain "investment activities" (that is, QPIs, qualifying S corporation interests, and debt-financed property or properties) as a separate unrelated trade or business for purposes of section 512(a)(6) and the proposed regulations. Thus, a social club, VEBA, or SUB generally will treat the investment activities specifically listed in the proposed regulations as a separate unrelated trade or business for purposes of section 512(a)(6). Nonetheless, because UBTI is defined differently for social clubs, VEBAs, and SUBs, the proposed regulations clarify that, in addition to other investment activities treated as a separate unrelated trade or business for purposes of section 512(a)(6), gross income from the investment activities of a social club, VEBA, or SUB also includes specific amounts discussed in sections 5.a.i. and ii of this preamble. The Treasury Department and the IRS request comments regarding any unintended consequences, in areas other than the unrelated business income tax, resulting from the treatment of investment activity as an unrelated trade or business for purposes of section 512(a)(6) for VEBAs and SUBs.

i. Amounts Described in Section 512(b)(1), (2), (3), and (5)

Because the modifications in section 512(b)(1), (2), (3), and (5) are not available under section 512(a)(3), social clubs, VEBAs, and SUBs generally must include interest, dividends, royalties, rents, and capital gains in UBTI under section 512(a)(3)(A) unless such amounts are set aside for a purpose described in section 512(a)(3)(B)(i) or (ii).[5] As stated in section 2.a of this preamble, interest, dividends, royalties, rents, and capital gains generally are considered income from investment activities. Accordingly, the proposed regulations provide that, for purposes of section 512(a)(6), UBTI from the investment activities of a social club, VEBA, or SUB includes any amount that would be excluded from the calculation of UBTI under section 512(b)(1), (2), (3), or (5) if the social club, VEBA, or SUB were subject to section 512(a)(1).

ii. Amounts Set Aside but Used for Another Purpose and Amounts in Excess of Account Limits

Section 512(a)(3)(B) provides that, if an amount which is attributable to income set aside for a purpose described in section 512(a)(3)(B)(i) or (ii) is used for a purpose other than one described therein, such amount shall be included in UBTI under section 512(a)(3)(A). Furthermore, with respect to a VEBA or SUB, the amount set aside may not be in excess of the set aside limit under section 512(a)(3)(E) and any amount in excess of this limit is nonexempt function income included in UBTI under section 512(a)(3)(A).

As discussed in section 5.a.i of this preamble, the amounts that may be set aside under section 512(a)(3)(B)(i) or (ii) are part of the social club, VEBA, or SUB's investment activities. Therefore, the proposed regulations also provide that UBTI from the investment activities of a social club, VEBA, or SUB includes any amount that is attributable to income set aside (and not in excess of the set aside limit described in section 512(a)(3)(E)), but not used, for a purpose described in section 512(a)(3)(B)(i) or (ii) and any amount in excess of the set aside limit described in section 512(a)(3)(E).

---

[4] *See* Treas. Reg. § 1.512(a)-5(c).

[5] As explained in the introduction to section 5 of this preamble, treating the invest-ment activities of a social club, VEBA, or SUB as an unrelated trade or business for purposes of section 512(a)(6) does not affect the amounts that may be set aside under section 512(a)(3)(B)(i) or (ii).

b. *Social Club Activities*

i. Limitation on Investment Activities

Notice 2018-67 provided that the interim and transition rules for certain partnership interests did not apply to social clubs described in section 501(c)(7), pending receipt of comments and additional consideration of the issues specific to social clubs. Section 501(c)(7) requires that "substantially all of the activities" of an organization described therein be "for pleasure, recreation, and other nonprofitable purposes." Accordingly, a social club has specific limits on the amount of nonexempt function income that may be earned without endangering its tax-exempt status. While the Code does not provide more detail, intended limits are described in legislative history. *See* S. Rep. No. 94-1318 (1976), at 4-5. Additionally, Congress did not intend social clubs to receive, within these limits, non-traditional, unrelated business income. *Id.* Accordingly, consistent with Notice 2018-67, the proposed regulations provide that the QPI rule and the transition rule do not apply to social clubs because social clubs should not be invested in partnerships that would generally be conducting nontraditional, unrelated trades or businesses that generate more than a de minimis amount of UBTI. In this regard, a partnership interest meeting the requirements of the de minimis rule in these proposed regulations is not the same as a partnership interest generating only de minimis amounts of UBTI from non-traditional, unrelated trades or businesses. Thus, the Treasury Department and the IRS do not consider the administrative convenience rationale supporting the QPI rule as relevant for social clubs.

ii. Nonmember Activities

Two commenters requested that a social club be permitted to treat all nonmember activities as one unrelated trade or business for purposes of section 512(a)(6). One of these commenters argued that a social club could not easily separate its nonmember activities into separate unrelated trades or businesses because social clubs do not generally maintain separate books and records for the various locations in which sales to nonmembers may occur, such as in dining facilities or retail stores. The other commenter added that separating a social club's nonmember activities into more than one unrelated trade or business would result in substantial administrative burden. The commenters describe the variety of activities in which social clubs engage, including food and beverage sales in club dining facilities and on club grounds (such as at pools or on golf courses and tennis courts); retail sales; greens fees; and space rental fees, whether or not they include substantial services.

As generally discussed in section 5 of this preamble, under the proposed regulations, a social club with nonmember income is subject to the same rules for identifying its unrelated trades or businesses as an organization subject to the rules of section 512(a)(1). Further, as discussed in section 1.a.i of this preamble, a social club cannot use the NAICS 2-digit code generally describing social clubs (71) to describe all its non-member income because the NAICS code used must describe its separate unrelated trade or business and not the purpose for which it is exempt. While this code may describe some of a social club's non-member income, such as greens fees, other NAICS codes are more appropriate to describe other non-member income, such as merchandise sales (45) and food and beverage services (72). Accordingly, a social club must identify its separate unrelated trades or businesses in accordance with the rule described in section 1 of this preamble like an exempt organization subject to section 512(a)(1).

iii. Nonrecurring Events

The Treasury Department and the IRS recognize that UBTI within the meaning of section 512(a)(3) includes gross income without regard to a specific determination regarding the associated activities' qualification as an unrelated trade or business (within the meaning of section 513) because UBTI under section 512(a)(3) includes "all gross income (excluding exempt function income)." For example, one commenter requested guidance on how to treat income from social club events that are not anticipated to reoccur. The commenter provides as an example the hosting of a professional golf tournament when similar tournaments are not held in the same location on an annual basis. The commenter suggested that events such that occur once, or seldom, in the life of a social club, should be classified as a single trade or business under section 512(a)(6).

As explained in section 1.a of this preamble, these proposed regulations generally require an exempt organization to identify its separate unrelated trades or businesses using the NAICS 2-digit code that most accurately describes each trade or business. Whether an infrequent or possibly nonrecurring event constitutes a separate unrelated trade or business or whether such event is part of another trade or business (including, in some cases, part of the social club's investment activities) depends on the facts and circumstances of each social club and the event at issue, including the scope of activities as part of the event. While such determination is not necessary for including such income in UBTI under section 512(a)(3), identification of separate unrelated trades or businesses is necessary for applying section 512(a)(6). The Treasury Department and the IRS request comments regarding the particular facts and circumstances that should be considered by a social club when determining whether a non-recurring event should be treated as a separate unrelated trade or business, part of a larger trade or business, or as part of a social club's investment activities for purposes of section 512(a)(6).

iv. Activities Without a Profit Motive

One commenter requested that the Treasury Department and the IRS clarify that nonmember activities conducted without intent to profit are not unrelated trades or businesses. The Treasury Department and the IRS do not address this comment in the proposed regulations because it is adequately addressed by existing precedent. *See, e.g., Portland Golf Club*, 497 U.S. at 164 (1990); Rev. Rul. 81-69, 1981-1 C.B. 351.

6. *Total UBTI and the Charitable Contribution Deduction*

Consistent with section 512(a)(6)(B), the proposed regulations provide that the total UBTI of an exempt organization with more than one unrelated trade or business is the sum of the UBTI computed with respect to each separate unrelated trade or business (as identified under the proposed regulations), less the specific deduction under section 512(b)(12). The proposed regulations also state that, for purposes of calculating an exempt organization's total UBTI, the UBTI with respect to any separate unrelated trade or business identified under the proposed regulations shall not be less than zero. *See* section 512(a)(6)(C).

Additionally, section 512(b)(10) and (11) permits exempt organizations to take the deduction under section 170 for charitable contributions whether or not the deduction is directly connected with the carrying on of an unrelated trade or business. The deduction is computed under section 170 except as otherwise provided in section 512(b)(10) and (11) and the Treasury regulations thereunder. For an exempt organization described in section 511(a), the deduction allowed by section 170 is limited to 10 percent of the exempt organization's UBTI computed without the benefit of section 512(b)(10). For a trust described in section 511(b), the deduction allowed by section 170 is limited as prescribed by section 170(b)(1)(A) and (B) determined with reference to UBTI computed without the benefit of section 512(b)(11).

At least one commenter recommended that the charitable contribution deductions permitted under section 512(b)(10) and (11) be taken against total UBTI calculated under section 512(a)(6)(B) rather than being allocated among unrelated trades or businesses. Additionally, the JCT stated that "[i]t is not intended that an exempt organization that has more than one unrelated trade or business be required to allocate its deductible charitable contributions among its various unrelated trades or businesses." General Explanation, at 293 n.1377. The Treasury Department and the IRS agree. Thus, these proposed regulations clarify in new §1.512(b)-1(g)(4) that the term "unrelated business taxable income" as used in section 512(b)(10) and (11) refers to UBTI after application of section 512(a)(6).

Under section 170(d)(1)(A), exempt organizations generally are permitted to carry over charitable contributions that exceed the organization's contribution base in a taxable year. Section 170(d)(1)(B) provides a special rule when an exempt organization has both NOL carryovers and excess contributions. In the case of an exempt organization with more than one unrelated trade or business, the function of this special rule is complicated by the requirement in section 512(a)(6)(A) to calculate NOLs separately with respect to each trade or business (see section 7 of this preamble). The Treasury Department and the IRS recognize that an ordering rule may be necessary to clarify how the special rule in section 170(d)(1)(B) operates when an exempt organization has NOL carry overs in more than one unrelated trade or business. Accordingly, the Treasury Department and the IRS request comments on this issue.

7. NOLs and UBTI

a. NOL Deduction Calculated Separately with Respect to Each Trade or Business

Section 512(b)(6), which was not changed by the TCJA, generally allows an exempt organization subject to the unrelated business income tax under section 511, including an exempt organization with more than one unrelated trade or business, to take the NOL deduction provided in section 172. Section 512(b)(6)(A) states that the NOL for any taxable year, the amount of the NOL carryback or carryover to any taxable year, and the NOL deduction for any taxable year shall be determined under section 172 without taking into account any amount of income or deduction that is excluded under section 512(b) in computing UBTI. For example, a loss attributable to an unrelated trade or business is not to be reduced by reason of the receipt of dividend income. See § 1.512(b)-1(e)(1). An NOL carryover is allowed only from a taxable year for which the taxpayer is subject to the provisions of section 511, or a corresponding provision of prior law. See section 512(b)(6)(B); § 1.512(b)-1(e)(3).

Notice 2018-67 explained that section 512(a)(6) changes how an exempt organization with more than one unrelated trade or business calculates and takes NOLs into account with respect to a trade or business. Specifically, section 512(a)(6)(A) requires such an exempt organization to calculate UBTI, "including for purposes of determining any NOL deduction," separately with respect to each trade or business for taxable years beginning after December 31, 2017. The legislative intent behind this change is to allow an NOL deduction "only with respect to a trade or business from which the loss arose." H.R. Rep. No. 115-466, at 547. Accordingly, consistent with the language of section 512(a)(6)(A) and legislative intent, the proposed regulations provide that an exempt organization with more than one unrelated trade or business determines the NOL deduction allowed by sections 172(a) and 512(b)(6) separately with respect to each of its unrelated trades or businesses. The proposed regulations clarify that, if an exempt organization has more than one unrelated trade or business, § 1.512(b)-1(e), which explains the application of section 172 within the context of the unrelated business income tax, applies separately with respect to each such unrelated trade or business. Additionally, the proposed regulations add a new paragraph to § 1.512(b)-1(e) that refers an exempt organization with more than one unrelated trade or business to new proposed § 1.512(a)-6(h) regarding the computation of the NOL deduction.

b. Coordination of NOLs

To preserve NOLs from tax years prior to the effective date of the TCJA, Congress created a special transition rule for NOLs arising in a taxable year beginning before January 1, 2018 ("pre-2018 NOLs"). Section 13702(b)(2) of the TCJA provides that section 512(a)(6)(A) does not apply to pre-2018 NOLs; rather, pre-2018 NOLs are taken against the total UBTI calculated under section 512(a)(6)(B). However, when an exempt organization has pre-2018 NOLs, which are subject to a carry-forward limitation, and NOLs arising in a taxable year beginning after December 31, 2017 ("post-2017 NOLs"), which are not, a question arises regarding the order in which such losses should be taken.

In Notice 2018-67, the Treasury Department and the IRS noted that section 512(a)(6) may have changed the order in which an organization would ordinarily take losses. For example, if section 512(a)(6) is read as a more specific ordering rule for purposes of calculating and taking the NOL deduction than the one found in section 172, post-2017 NOLs would be calculated and taken before pre-2018 NOLs because the UBTI with respect to each separate unrelated trade or business is calculated under section 512(a)(6)(A) before calculating total UBTI under section 512(a)(6)(B). Accordingly, Notice 2018-67 requested comments regarding how the NOL deduction should be taken under section 512(a)(6) by exempt organizations with more than one unrelated trade or business and, in particular, by such organizations with both pre-2018 and post-2017 NOLs. Notice 2018-67 also requested comments on the ordering of pre-2018 and post-2017 NOLs and the potential treatment of pre-2018 NOLs that may expire in a given tax year if not taken before post-2017 NOLs.

In response to Notice 2018-67, several commenters addressed possible ordering rules for organizations subject to section 512(a)(6). These commenters noted that the language should not alter the ordering rules under section 172 such that pre-2018 NOLs should be allowed prior to post-2017 NOLs, especially because pre-2018 NOLs remain subject to a carry-forward limitation.

The language of section 512(a)(6) and section 13702(b) of the TCJA do not alter the ordering rules under section 172. Accordingly, the proposed regulations provide that an exempt organization with both pre-2018 and post-2017 NOLs will deduct its pre-2018 NOLs from its total UBTI under section 512(a)(6)(B) before deducting any post-2017 NOLs with regard to a separate unrelated trade or business from the UBTI from such unrelated trade or business. The proposed regulations clarify that pre-2018 NOLs are deducted from total UBTI in the manner that results in maximum utilization of the pre-2018 NOLs in a taxable year.

c. Legislative Changes to Section 172

At the same time Congress added section 512(a)(6), it also made extensive changes to section 172. These changes included limiting the NOL deduction to 80 percent of taxable income, prohibiting the carryback of NOLs (except for certain farming losses and in the case of certain insurance companies), and allowing the indefinite carryover of NOLs. Id. However, shortly before publication of these proposed regulations, Congress enacted the Coronavirus Aid, Relief, and Economic Security Act, Public Law 116-136, 134 Stat. 281 (2020) (CARES Act). Section 2303 of the CARES Act temporarily repeals the 80 percent income limitation and permits the carryback of NOLs arising in taxable years beginning after December 31, 2017, and before January 1, 2021, to each of the five taxable years preceding the taxable year of such loss. The Treasury Department and the IRS will further consider how the changes to section 172 made by the CARES Act affect the calculation of UBTI under section 512(a)(6) and may issue additional guidance on the issue.

8. Form 990-T

One commenter suggested updating the Form 990-T to provide space for an exempt organization to disclose and describe the method chosen for identifying the separate unrelated trades or businesses being reported on Form 990-T. This commenter recommended either the addition of a "miscellaneous schedule" similar to Schedule O, "Supplemental Information to Form 990 or 990-EZ," of the Form 990, "Return of Organization Exempt from Income Tax," or the inclusion of space on the schedules to the Form 990-T to make such disclosure. This commenter also recommended that the IRS update the instructions to the Form 990-T either to include a more complete list of applicable NAICS codes or to state clearly where additional codes may be found. The Treasury Department and the IRS recognize that changes to the Form 990-T and related schedules may be necessary. In particular, the Treasury Department and the IRS recognize that additional instructions are required regarding how separate unrelated trades or businesses identified under the special rules (rather than NAICS) - such as for investment activities (see section 2 of this preamble), inclusions of income derived from certain controlled entities (see section 3 of this preamble), and non-qualifying S corporation interests (see section 4 of this preamble) - are identified on Form 990-T and related schedules. Accordingly, the IRS intends to update the Form 990-T and related schedules, and the instructions thereto, as appropriate.

9. *Individual Retirement Accounts*

As previously discussed in the Background section of this preamble, section 513(b) provides a special definition of "unrelated trade or business" for a qualified retirement plan or for a trust that is exempt from tax under section 501(c)(17) (SUB). Section 513(b) defines "unrelated trade or business," as any trade or business regularly carried on by such trust or by a partnership of which it is a member.

Notice 2018-67 stated in a footnote that, because IRAs described in section 408 are, under section 408(e), subject to the tax imposed by section 511, and IRAs are most similar to qualified retirement plans, it is reasonable to apply the definition of "unrelated trade or business" described in section 513(b) to IRAs. The footnote stated that the Treasury Department and the IRS intended to provide that the section 513(b) definition of unrelated trade or business should be used for IRAs subject to the unrelated business income tax in section 511 pursuant to section 408(e). Consistent with this statement, the proposed regulations add a new paragraph to §1.513-1 clarifying that the section 513(b) definition of "unrelated trade or business" applies to IRAs. Accordingly, §1.513-1(f) provides that an IRA will apply the definition of "unrelated trade or business" in section 513(b) when determining whether it has more than one unrelated trade or business within the meaning of section 512(a)(6). The proposed regulations make corresponding changes to §1.513(b)-1(a) to account for the new paragraph added at §1.513(b)-1(f).

10. *Inclusions of Subpart F Income and Global Intangible Low-Taxed Income*

An inclusion of subpart F income under section 951(a)(1)(A) is treated in the same manner as a dividend for purposes of section 512(b)(1). Accordingly, an inclusion of subpart F income generally is excluded from the calculation of UBTI under section 512(b)(1). Notice 2018-67 explained that Congress approved the IRS's long-standing position when Congress enacted section 512(b)(17). Furthermore, Notice 2018-67 provided that an inclusion of GILTI under section 951A(a) should be treated in the same manner as an inclusion of subpart F income under section 951(a)(1)(A) for purposes of section 512(b)(1) and therefore would be treated as a dividend that generally is excluded from UBTI. Two commenters explicitly agreed with these conclusions and one commenter requested that the Treasury Department and the IRS revise the Treasury Regulations consistent with these conclusions. Accordingly, the proposed regulations revise §1.512(b)-1(a) to clarify that an inclusion of subpart F income under section 951(a)(1)(A) is treated in the same manner as a dividend for purposes of section 512(b)(1) and that an inclusion of GILTI under section 951A(a) is treated in the same manner as an inclusion of subpart F income under section 951(a)(1)(A) for purposes of section 512(b)(1).

11. *Public Support*

A question has arisen regarding whether the enactment of section 512(a)(6) impacts the calculation of public support under sections 509(a)(1) and 170(b)(1)(A)(vi) and under section 509(a)(2). Exempt organizations described in section 501(c)(3) that are classified as publicly supported charities under these sections must calculate public support annually on Form 990, Schedule A, "Public Charity Status and Public Support." In general, public support is expressed as a percentage of support from certain public sources over total support. *See* §1.170A-9(f) (definition of section 170(b)(1)(A)(vi) organization); §1.509(a)-3 (publicly supported organizations).

Section 512(a)(6) potentially impacts two aspects of the public support test. First, section 512(a)(6) potentially impacts the calculation of total support under section 509(d), a number which is used for purposes of both section 509(a)(1) and (2). Specifically, section 509(d)(3) includes, in the calculation of total support, the organization's net income from unrelated business activities, whether or not such activities are carried on regularly as a trade or business. Although section 509(d)(3) does not specifically cross-reference section 512, the term "unrelated business activities" can be read broadly to include, but not be limited to, UBTI within the meaning of section 512. If this is the case, then an organization with more than one unrelated trade or business could be required to apply section 512(a)(6) in determining its total support, which may increase its amount of total support because the losses from one unrelated trade or business cannot offset the gains from another unrelated trade or business.

Second, section 512(a)(6) potentially impacts the not-more-than-one-third support test under section 509(a)(2)(B), which requires calculation of the excess (if any) of the amount of UBTI (as defined in section 512) over the amount of the tax imposed by section 511. Unlike section 509(d)(3), which does not cross-reference section 512, the not-more-than-one-third support test specifically cross-references section 512. Accordingly, an organization with more than one unrelated trade or business could be required to apply section 512(a)(6) when determining whether it receives more than one-third of its support from non-public sources. If this is the case, application of section 512(a)(6) in this context may result in an increase in support received from nonpublic sources, again, because of the inability to use losses from one unrelated trade or business to offset income from another unrelated trade or business.

If section 512(a)(6) applies in either context, organizations with more than one unrelated trade or business may have difficulty qualifying as publicly supported because of the potential increase in the calculated support from non-public sources as well as the potential increase in the calculated amount of total support. The Treasury Department and the IRS are not aware of any intent of Congress to change the public support test when enacting section 512(a)(6). Accordingly, the proposed regulations include revisions to §§1.170A-9(f) and 1.509(a)-3 to permit an organization with more than one unrelated trade or business to aggregate its net income and net losses from all of its unrelated business activities, including its unrelated trades or businesses within the meaning of section 512, for purposes of determining whether the organization is publicly supported. The Treasury Department and the IRS recognize that requiring different calculations for purposes of calculating public support and UBTI may impose a significant administrative burden on organizations with more than one unrelated trade or business. Accordingly, the Treasury Department and the IRS request comments regarding the application of section 512(a)(6) to the public support test.

12. *Technical Correction of Inadvertently Omitted Regulatory Language*

These proposed regulations make a technical correction to §1.512(a)-1(b). In 1967, the Treasury Department and the IRS published §1.512(a)-1 in the **Federal Register** (TD 6939, 32 FR 17660). Section 1.512(a)-1(b) explained that "[e]xpenses, depreciation and similar items attributable solely to the conduct of an unrelated business are proximately and primarily related to that business and therefore qualify for deduction to the extent that they meet the requirements of section 162, section 167, or other relevant provisions of the Internal Revenue Code." An example followed this statement providing that, "[t]hus, for example, salaries of personnel employed full-time in carrying on an unrelated business are directly connected with the conduct of the unrelated business and are deductible in computing unrelated business taxable income if they otherwise qualify for deduction under the requirements of section 162."

In 1975, the Treasury Department and the IRS revised §1.512(a)-1(b) in regulations published in the **Federal Register** (TD 7392, 40 FR 58639). The final regulations omitted from the example the following language: "[t]hus, for example, salaries of personnel employed full-time in carrying on an unrelated business are directly." However, the final regulations as published in the Cumulative Bulletin (1976-1 CB 162) contained this language. Accordingly, the Treasury Department and the IRS have concluded that this language was inadvertently omitted from the final regulations in 1975 and are making a technical correction to the regulations. Therefore, the proposed regulations include the omitted language in §1.512(a)-1(b).

Proposed Applicability Dates

These regulations are proposed to apply to taxable years beginning on or after the date these regulations are published in the **Federal Register** as final regulations. For taxable years beginning before the date these regulations are published in the **Federal Register** as final regulations, an exempt organization may rely on a reasonable, good-faith interpretation of sections 511 through 514, considering all the facts and circumstances, when identifying separate unrelated trades or businesses for purposes of section 512(a)(6)(A). In addition, for these same taxable years, an exempt organization may rely on these proposed regulations in their entirety. Alternatively, for these same taxable years, an exempt organization may rely on the methods of aggregating or identifying separate trades or businesses provided in the Notice 2018-67.

Statement of Availability of IRS Documents

For copies of recently issued Revenue Procedures, Revenue Rulings, Notices, and other guidance published in the Internal Revenue Bulletin, please visit the IRS Web site at http://www.irs.gov or the Superintendent of Documents, U.S. Government Printing Office, Washington, DC 20402.

Special Analyses

I. *Regulatory Planning and Review - Economic Analysis*

Executive Orders 12866, 13563, and 13771 direct agencies to assess costs and benefits of available regulatory alternatives and, if regulation is necessary, to select regulatory approaches that maximize net benefits (including potential economic, environmental, public health, and safety effects; distributive impacts; and equity). Executive Order 13563 emphasizes the importance of quantifying both costs and benefits, of reducing costs, of harmonizing rules, and of promoting flexibility.

The proposed regulations have been designated as significant under Executive Order 12866 pursuant to the Memorandum of Agreement (April 11, 2018) between the Treasury Department and the Office of Management and Budget (OMB) regarding review of tax regulations. The Office of Information and Regulatory Affairs (OIRA) has designated the proposed rulemaking as significant under section 1(b) of the Memorandum of Agreement. Accordingly, the proposed regulations have been reviewed by OMB. For purposes of Executive Order 13771, the proposed regulations are regulatory.

A. *Background*

Certain corporations, trusts, and other entities are exempt from Federal income taxation because of the specific functions they perform ("exempt organizations"). Examples include religious and charitable organizations. However, exempt organizations that engage in business activities that are not substantially related to their exempt purposes may have taxable income under section 511(a)(1) of the Internal Revenue Code (Code). For example, the income that a tax-exempt organization generates from the sale of advertising in its quarterly magazine is unrelated business taxable income (UBTI).

Prior to the Tax Cuts and Jobs Act (TCJA), UBTI was calculated by aggregating the net incomes from all the unrelated business activities conducted by an exempt organization. As a result, losses from one activity could be used to offset profits from another activity. New section 512(a)(6), enacted in the TCJA, provides that organizations with more than one unrelated trade or business calculate the taxable amounts separately for each trade or business so that losses only offset income from the same unrelated trade or business. The statutory language, however, does not specify standards for determining what activities would be considered the same or a different trade or business.

Previously, on September 4, 2018, the Treasury Department and the IRS published Notice 2018-67, 2018-36 I.R.B. 409 (the Notice), which discussed and solicited comments regarding various issues arising under section 512(a)(6) and set forth interim guidance and transition rules relating to that section. The Treasury Department and the IRS received 24 comments in response to the Notice. The proposed regulations consider and respond to these comments.

The proposed regulations address the need for guidance by providing rules for determining when an exempt organization has more than one unrelated trade or business and how such an exempt organization computes UBTI under new section 512(a)(6). Specifically discussed below, the proposed regulations establish guidelines for (1) identifying separate unrelated trades or businesses; and (2) in certain cases, permitting an exempt organization to treat investment activities as one unrelated trade or business for purposes of computing UBTI.

B. *Baseline*

The Treasury Department has assessed the benefits and costs of the proposed regulations relative to a no-action baseline reflecting anticipated Federal income tax-related behavior in the absence of these regulations.

C. *Affected Entities*

Prior tax law did not require reporting unrelated business income by separate activity so taxpayer counts are not available. However, the IRS estimates that less than 2 percent of exempt organizations would be affected. Potentially affected organizations are only those with more than one unrelated trade or business, a group likely to include colleges and universities, certain cultural organizations such as museums, and some tax-exempt hospitals.

Presently it is not possible to obtain accurate counts of the number of exempt organizations potentially affected by the proposed regulations, because prior law did not require disaggregation of the separate sources of UBTI and therefore the IRS does not have access to this level of detail on UBTI. Approximately 1.4 million exempt organizations filed some type of information or tax return with the IRS for fiscal year 2018.[6] Only 188,000 exempt organizations filed Form 990-T, which is used to report UBTI. While not all Form 990-T filers also file an information return with the IRS, as an upper bound estimate 14 percent of exempt organizations could be affected by the regulations. Within Form 990-T filers, only a smaller subset, primarily the largest organizations in certain categories, are expected to have more than one unrelated trade or business. Among the types of organizations expected to have more than one unrelated trade or business are colleges and universities, certain cultural organizations such as museums, and some tax-exempt hospitals.

Additional information on organizations that may be affected is provided by a 2018 Center on Nonprofits and Philanthropy (CNP) survey of 723 primarily large exempt organizations.[7] Three-hundred and thirty of these organizations reported that they had filed a Form 990-T. Of these, 70 percent had revenues over $10 million and most were educational or arts and cultural organizations. Only 46 organizations (14 percent of the surveyed organizations filing Form 990-T) reported having more than one source of UBTI and almost half of these had only two sources. Thus, the Treasury Department and the IRS project that if the CNP survey results applied to the population of Form 990-T filers, then less than 2 percent of exempt organizations would be affected by the proposed regulations and that these would tend to be large educational or arts and cultural organizations.

D. *Economic Analysis of NPRM*

The proposed regulations provide greater certainty to exempt organizations regarding how to compute UBTI and tax in response to the changes made by TCJA and adopt standards that balance the statutory intent of those changes and excessive burden that might result from some

---

[6] *See* Internal Revenue Service Research, Applied Analytics, and Statistics, Statistics of Income Division Fiscal Year Return Projections for the United States Publication 6292 (Rev. 9-2019), Projected Returns 2019-2026. Exempt organizations generally must file an annual information return with IRS. *See generally* section 6033. However, churches and small organizations are exempt from this filing requirement. *See* section 6033(a)(3).

Organizations that have more than $1,000 in gross UBTI must also file Form 990-T to calculate their UBTI and tax. *See* section 512(b)(12) (providing a $1,000 specific deduction).

[7] *See* Elizabeth Boris and Joseph Cordes, "How the TCJA's New UBIT Provisions Will Affect Nonprofits," Urban Institute Research Report, January 2019.

interpretations of such standards. They also improve economic efficiency by helping to ensure that similar exempt organizations are taxed similarly. In the absence of this guidance taxpayers might make different assumptions regarding how to calculate UBTI and tax.

This section describes the two provisions of the NPRM for which economic analysis is helpful and provides a qualitative economic analysis of each one.

i. Identifying Separate Trades or Businesses

As discussed above, section 512(a)(6) requires exempt organizations with more than one unrelated trade or business to calculate UBTI separately for each trade or business so that losses are only used to offset income from the same unrelated trade or business. The Notice stated that the Treasury Department and the IRS were considering the use of NAICS codes to identify separate unrelated trades or businesses and, in the meantime, would consider the use of NAICS 6-digit codes to be reasonable for identifying separate unrelated trades or businesses. NAICS is an industry classification system for purposes of collecting, analyzing, and publishing statistical data related to the United States business economy. Each digit of the NAICS 6-digit codes describes an industry with increasing specificity.

In the Notice, the Treasury Department and the IRS requested comments regarding methods to identify separate unrelated trades or businesses in general and the use of NAICS codes in particular. As discussed further below, several commenters pointed out potential difficulties in using NAICS 6-digit codes and suggested using NAICS 2- or 3-digit codes; that is, a higher level of aggregation of business activity. The proposed regulations allow the use of NAICS 2-digit codes, thereby addressing the concerns raised in comments received and reducing compliance burdens for exempt organizations with multiple similar types of business activity.

Several commenters stated that the NAICS codes represented a workable system for identifying a separate unrelated trade or business. Not all commenters agreed as to what level of these codes should be used to group the various activities. Most of the commenters making recommendations on the NAICS codes rejected the use of NAICS 6-digit codes. These commenters noted that using NAICS 6-digit codes would result in significant compliance burden because an exempt organization would have to determine which of over 1,000 NAICS 6-digit codes most accurately describes its trades or businesses. Commenters noted that many NAICS 6-digit codes may apply to more than one trade or business activity or that no NAICS 6-digit code may exist to accurately describe a trade or business activity. Additionally, these commenters argued that the use of NAICS 6-digit codes could potentially require an exempt organization to split what has traditionally been considered one unrelated trade or business into multiple unrelated trades or businesses. Some commenters noted they would have to incur the costs of changing their accounting systems so as to collect the information needed for separate NAICS 6-digit codes. These commenters suggested a range of code levels representing various levels of specificity from 2-digits up to 4-digits.

Reflecting comments on the Notice from potentially affected organizations, the Treasury Department and the IRS chose NAICS 2-digit codes for identifying unrelated trades or businesses. Allowing the use of NAICS 2-digit codes to identify separate unrelated trades or businesses reduces the compliance costs of affected organizations relative to the use of NAICS 6-digit codes. For example, different types of food services would be in the same NAICS 2-digit code as opposed to separate NAICS 6-digit codes. Similarly, different types of recreational activities, such as fitness centers and golf courses, would be in the same NAICS 2-digit code as opposed to separate NAICS 6-digit codes. A single facility might have elements fitting several of these categories, which could change over time when NAICS codes are revised.

The guidance provided in the proposed regulations also ensures that the tax liability is calculated similarly across taxpayers, avoiding situations where one taxpayer receives differential treatment compared to another taxpayer for fundamentally similar economic activity based on their differing reasonable, good-faith interpretation of the statute. In the absence of these proposed regulations, an exempt organization might be uncertain about whether an activity is one or more than one business activity. As a result, in the absence of the proposed regulations, similar institutions might take different positions and pay different amounts of tax, introducing economic inefficiency and inequity.

Since exempt organizations could use a reasonable and good-faith effort to interpret whether some trade and business activities would have to be reported separately, behavioral responses were likely muted. These regulations do provide greater certainty and flexibility such that compliance costs may be slightly lower for affected organizations.

The Treasury Department and the IRS solicit comments on the use of the NAICS 2-digit codes and comments that provide data, other evidence, or models that would enhance the rigor by which the final regulations might be developed.

ii. Aggregation of Investment Activities

The proposed regulation's treatment of investment activities will also provide clarity and reduce burdens for exempt organizations. By providing more explicit rules for the treatment of investment activities, the proposed regulations reduce the uncertainty about what would be acceptable under the "reasonable, good-faith interpretation" provided in the Notice. Although investment income, such as interest and dividend income, is not generally taxed as UBTI, exempt organizations may engage in certain activities that the organization considers "investments" but that generate UBTI, such as debt-financed investments or investments through partnerships. Consistent with the guidance included in the Notice, the proposed regulations allow certain of this "investment" income to be aggregated and treated as a single trade or business. The proposed regulations further expand on the notice by providing a more developed rule for partnership income and explicitly list the other types of UBTI that can be aggregated as "investment" income in response to comments requesting additional clarification. As a result, the proposed regulations reduce the compliance burdens of exempt organizations of obtaining information from partnerships and simplify the calculation of UBTI when the income is generated from "investment" activities relative to the no-action baseline.

Given these proposed regulations follow and slightly expand the guidance in the Notice, investment responses are likely to be minimal. While some exempt organizations may have perceived a need to reorganize certain investments, such as in partnerships that qualify for aggregate treatment and thereby seek offset any losses, few would have been expected to do this reorganization prior to regulations being published.

iii. Summary

The proposed regulations provide rules for determining when an exempt organization has more than one unrelated trade or business and how such an exempt organization computes UBTI. In addition, the proposed regulations provide guidelines for when an exempt organization treats its investment activities as one unrelated trade or business for purposes of computing UBTI. In the absence of guidance, affected taxpayers may face more uncertainty when calculating their tax liability, a situation generally that could lead to greater conflicts with tax administrators. The Treasury Department and the IRS project that the proposed regulations will reduce taxpayer compliance burden relative to the no-action baseline. In addition, the Treasury Department and the IRS project that these regulations will affect a small number of exempt organizations. Based on this analysis, the Treasury Department and the IRS anticipate any economic effects of the proposed regulations will be modest.

II. *Paperwork Reduction Act*

The collection of information in these proposed regulations is in §1.512(b)-6(a). This information is required to determine whether an exempt organization has more than one unrelated trade or business and therefore must report those unrelated trades or businesses on Form 990-T and related schedules. In 2018, the IRS released and invited comments on drafts of an earlier version of the Form 990-T and related schedules to give members of the public opportunity to comment on changes made to the Form 990-T, and the addition of a new schedule to report additional unrelated trades or businesses, as required by the enactment of section 512(a)(6). The IRS received no comments on the Form 990-T and related schedules during that comment period. Consequently, the IRS made Form 990-T available on January 8, 2019, and the new schedule for reporting additional unrelated trades or businesses available on January 25, 2019, for use by the public. The IRS intends that the burden of collections of information will be reflected in the burden associated with the Form 990 series under OMB approval number 1545-0047.

The paperwork burden estimate for tax-exempt organizations is reported under OMB control number 1545-0047, which represents a total estimated burden time, including all other related forms and schedules for corporations, of 52 billion hours and total estimated monetized costs of $4.17 billion ($2017). The burden estimates provided in the OMB control number are aggregate amounts that relate to the entire package of forms associated with the OMB control number and will in the future include, but not isolate, the estimated burden of these proposed regulations. These numbers are therefore unrelated to the future calculations needed to assess the burden imposed by adoption of these proposed regulations. The Treasury Department and IRS urge readers to recognize that these numbers are duplicates and to guard against overcounting the burden. No burden estimates specific to the proposed regulations are currently available. The Treasury Department has not estimated the burden, including that of any new information collections, related to the requirements under the proposed regulations. Those estimates would capture both changes made by the Act and those that arise out of discretionary authority exercised in the proposed regulations. The current status of the Paperwork Reduction Act submissions related to these proposed regulations is provided in the following table.

Form	OMB Control Number	Status
990 and related forms	1545-0047	Sixty-day notice published on 9/24/2019. Thirty-day notice published on 12/31/2019. Approved by OIRA on 2/12/2020.
	Link: *https://www.irs.gov/forms-pubs/about-form-990*	

The Treasury Department and the IRS request comments on all aspects of information collection burdens related to the proposed regulations, including estimates for how much time it would take to comply with the paperwork burdens described above for each relevant form and ways for the IRS to minimize the paperwork burden. Proposed revisions (if any) to the Form 990-T and related schedules that reflect the information collections contained in these proposed regulations will be made available for public comment at http://apps.irs.gov/app/picklist/list/draftTaxForms.html. The revised Form 990-T and related schedules will not be finalized until after these forms have been approved by OMB under the PRA. Comments on these forms can be submitted at *https://www.irs.gov/forms-pubs/comment-on-tax-forms-and-publications*.

An agency may not conduct or sponsor, and a person is not required to respond to, a collection of information unless it displays a valid control number assigned by the Office of Management and Budget.

Books or records relating to a collection of information must be retained as long as their contents may become material in the administration of any internal revenue laws. Generally, tax returns and return information are confidential, as required by 26 U.S.C. 6103.

III. *Regulatory Flexibility Act*

Pursuant to the Regulatory Flexibility Act (5 U.S.C. chapter 6) (RFA), it is hereby certified that these proposed regulations would not have a significant economic impact on a substantial number of small entities. As discussed elsewhere in this preamble, these proposed regulations apply to all exempt organizations with UBTI, but only to the extent required to determine if an exempt organization has more than one unrelated trade or business. If an exempt organization only has one unrelated trade or business, these regulations do not apply and the exempt organization determines UBTI under section 512(a)(1) or section 512(a)(3), as appropriate. If an exempt organization has more than one unrelated trade or business, these proposed regulations provide instructions for computing UBTI separately with respect to each such unrelated trade or business.

These proposed regulations are not likely to affect a substantial number of small entities. According to the IRS Data Book, 1,835,534 exempt organizations existed in 2018. Internal Revenue Service, Publication 55B, Internal Revenue Service Data Book 2018, 57 (May 2019). However, only 188,334 Form 990-Ts were filed in 2018. Internal Revenue Service, Publication 6292, Fiscal Year Return Projects for the United States: 2019-2026, Fall 2019 4 (September 2019). The IRS expects that less than 10 percent of the exempt organizations population will be affected by these proposed regulations because the exempt organizations filing Form 990-T include entities not included in the definition of "small entities," such as large hospital systems and universities. Therefore, this proposed regulation is not likely to affect a substantial number of small entities.

Even if the regulations affected a substantial number of small entities, the economic impact of this proposed rule is not likely to be significant. An organization affected by this rule, with more than one unrelated trade or business, completes Part I and Part II on page 1 of Form 990-T and completes and attaches a separate schedule for each additional unrelated trade or business. Affected taxpayers have been reporting UBTI on form 990-T for the previous two tax years. As discussed elsewhere in this preamble, these regulations would provide certainty and guidance for these organizations. In the absence of this guidance, affected taxpayers may face more uncertainty when calculating their tax liability, a situation generally that could lead to greater conflicts with tax administrators. Although affected taxpayers will have to spend time reading and understanding these regulations, the Treasury Department and the IRS project that the proposed regulations provide certainty and guidance that will reduce taxpayer compliance burden for large and small entity taxpayers.

Notwithstanding this certification, the Treasury Department and the IRS invite comments on the impact this rule may have on small entities.

Pursuant to section 7805(f), this proposed rule has been submitted to the Chief Counsel for Advocacy of the Small Business Administration for comment on its impact on small entities.

Comments and Requests for Public Hearing

Before these proposed regulations are adopted as final regulations, consideration will be given to any comments that are timely submitted to the IRS as prescribed in the preamble under the "**ADDRESSES**" section. All comments submitted will be made available at *https://www.regulations.gov* or upon request.

A public hearing on these proposed regulations will be scheduled if requested in writing by any person who timely submits written comments. If a public hearing is scheduled, notice of the date, time, and place for the public hearing will be published in the **Federal Register**.

Drafting Information

The principal author of this notice of proposed rulemaking is Stephanie N. Robbins, Office of the Chief Counsel (Employee Benefits, Exempt Organizations and Employment Taxes). However, other personnel from the Treasury Department and the IRS participated in their development.

[The next page is 93,801.]

Estate Tax Proposed Regulations—Preambles

[¶ 61,101]   Proposed Regulations, published in the *Federal Register* on December 19, 1975.

Charitable remainder trusts: Election:Extended date.—Reg. § 20.2055-2 relating to the granting of an extension to permit the reformation of charitable remainder trusts has been proposed. The proposed regulations will conform the Regulations to Section 2055(e)(3) of the Internal Revenue Code as added by Section 3, Act of October 26, 1974 (P.L. 93-483).

NOTICE OF PROPOSED RULEMAKING

Notice is hereby given that the regulations set forth in tentative form below are proposed to be prescribed by the Commissioner of Internal Revenue, with the approval of the Secretary of the Treasury or his delegate. Prior to the final adoption of such regulations, consideration will be given to any comments pertaining thereto which are submitted in writing (preferably six copies) to the Commissioner of Internal Revenue, Attention: CC:LR:T, Washington, D.C. 20224, by January 23, 1976. Pursuant to 26 CFR 601.601(b), designations of material as confidential or not to be disclosed, contained in such comments, will not be accepted. Thus, persons submitting written comments should not include therein material that they consider to be confidential or inappropriate for disclosure to the public. It will be presumed by the Internal Revenue Service that every written comment submitted to it in response to this notice of proposed rule making is intended by the person submitting it to be subject in its entirety to public inspection and copying in accordance with the procedures of 26 CFR 601.702(d)(9). Any person submitting written comments who desires an opportunity to comment orally at a public hearing on these proposed regulations should submit a request, in writing, to the Commissioner by January 23, 1976. In such case, a public hearing will be held, and notice of the time, place, and date will be published in a subsequent issue of the Federal Register, unless the person or persons who have requested a hearing withdraw their requests for a hearing before notice of the hearing has been filed with the Office of the Federal Register. The proposed regulations are to be issued under the authority contained in sections 2055(e)(3) and 7805 of the Internal Revenue Code of 1954 (68A Stat. 917; 26 U.S.C. 7805). [Signed by Donald C. Alexander, Commissioner of Internal Revenue.]

Preamble

This document contains proposed amendments to the Income Tax Regulations (26 CFR Part 1) and the Estate Tax Regulations (26 CFR Part 20) to conform such regulations to the provisions of section 2055(e)(3) as added by section 3, Act of Oct. 26, 1974 (P.L. 93-483).

Section 2055(e)(2)(A) of the Code disallows an estate tax deduction for certain transfers to charity if the transfer is not in the form either of a charitable remainder trust that complies with section 664 of the Code or a pooled income fund that complies with section 642(c)(5) of the Code.

The new amendment to section 2055 is a relief provision which, in certain limited cases, extends until December 31, 1975, the transitional period originally allowed under the Tax Reform Act of 1969 to amend or conform a trust to the provisions of section 664 of the Code.

The relief provision applies to any interest for charitable purposes which passes under a will executed before September 21, 1974, or by an inter vivos trust created after July 31, 1969, and before September 21, 1974. The will or trust must be amended to meet the requirements of section 2055(e)(2)(A) by December 31, 1975, or judicial proceedings to amend the will or trust must be begun by that date.

The proposed regulations apply the relief provision to inter vivos transfers created after July 31, 1969, which are irrevocable at the date of death. However, in general, a trust amended pursuant to these temporary regulations is treated as a charitable remainder trust from the date it would be deemed created under section 664.

The proposed regulations make provision for judicial reformation as well as nonjudicial reformation by agreement of the parties provided the agreement is binding on all parties.

The proposed regulations provide that the amending procedure under section 2055(e)(3) is available only to charitable interests which, but for the disqualifying provisions of section 2055(e)(2)(A), qualify for a deduction under section 2055. A charitable interest cannot be created by the use of this relief provision.

[¶ 61,102]   Proposed Regulation (EE-7-78), published in the *Federal Register* on July 14, 1981.

Gift taxes: Annual exclusion: Contributions to spousal individual retirement accounts.— Proposed Reg. § 25.2503-5 would conform the regulations to changes made by the Revenue Act of 1978 by providing that contributions by a working spouse to an individual retirement account for the benefit of a nonworking spouse qualify for annual gift tax exclusions to the extent that they are deductible for income tax purposes.

NOTICE OF PROPOSED RULEMAKING

AGENCY: Internal Revenue Service, Treasury.

ACTION: Notice of proposed rulemaking.

SUMMARY: This document contains proposed regulations relating to individual retirement plans and simplified employee pensions. Changes to the applicable law were made by the Employee Retirement Income Security Act of 1974, the Tax Reform Act of 1976, the Revenue Act of 1978 and the Technical Corrections Act of 1979. The regulations would provide the public with the guidance needed to comply with these Acts and would affect institutions which sponsor individual retirement plans and simplified employee pensions. The regulations also affect employers and individuals who use these plans for retirement income.

DATES: Written comments and requests for a public hearing must be delivered or mailed by September 14, 1981. The amendments have varying effective dates. The provisions relating to spousal individual retirement plans are generally effective for taxable years beginning after December 31, 1976. The provisions relating to simplified employee pensions are generally effective for taxable years beginning after December 31, 1978. The provisions defining "active participant" for individuals covered by defined benefit offset plans are effective for taxable years beginning after December 31, 1980.

ADDRESS: Send comments and requests for a public hearing to: Commissioner of Internal Revenue, Attention: CC:LR:T (EE-7-78), Washington, D.C. 20224.

FOR FURTHER INFORMATION CONTACT: William D. Gibbs of the Employee Plans and Exempt Organizations Division, Office of the Chief Counsel, Internal Revenue Service, 1111 Constitution Avenue, N.W., Washington, D.C. 20224 (Attention: CC:LR:T) (202-566-3430) (not a toll-free number).

SUPPLEMENTARY INFORMATION:

BACKGROUND

This document contains proposed amendments to the Income Tax Regulations (26 CFR Part 1), the Gift Tax Regulations (26 CFR Part 25), the Employment Tax Regulations (26 CFR Part 31), the Regulations on Pension Excise Taxes (26 CFR Part 54) and the Procedure and Administration Regulations (26 CFR Part 301) under sections 62, 219, 220, 404, 408, 409, 2503, 3121, 3306, 4973, 4974, and 6693 of the Internal Revenue Code of 1954. These amendments are proposed to conform the regulations to section 2002(d) of the Employee Retirement Income Security Act of 1974 (88 Stat. 966), section 1501 of the Tax Reform Act of 1976 (90 Stat. 1734), sections 152, 156(c) and 157 of the Revenue Act of 1978 (92 Stat. 2797, 2802, 2803), and sections 101(a)(10), 101(a)(14)(A), 101(a)(14)(B), and 101(a)(14)(E)(ii) of the Technical Corrections Act of 1979 (94 Stat. 201-205). These regulations are to be issued under the authority contained in section 7805 of the Internal Revenue Code of 1954 (68A Stat. 917; 26 U.S.C. 7805).

* * *

SPOUSAL INDIVIDUAL RETIREMENT PLANS

Internal Revenue Code section 220 allows an individual to deduct amounts contributed to an individual retirement plan maintained for the individual's benefit and an individual retirement plan maintained for the benefit of the individual's non-employed spouse. The proposed regulations set forth the type of funding arrangements which must be used and additional limitations and restrictions the individual and spouse must meet in order for the individual to obtain this deduction.

* * *

COMMENTS AND REQUESTS FOR A PUBLIC HEARING

Before adopting these proposed regulations, consideration will be given to any written comments that are submitted (preferably six copies) to the Commissioner of Internal Revenue. All comments will be available for public inspection and copying. A public hearing will be held upon written request to the Commissioner by any person who has submitted written comments. If a public hearing is held, notice of the time and place will be published in the FEDERAL REGISTER.

DRAFTING INFORMATION

The principal author of these proposed regulations is William D. Gibbs of the Employee Plans and Exempt Organizations Division of the Office of Chief Counsel, Internal Revenue Service. However, personnel from other offices of the Internal Revenue Service and Treasury Department participated in developing the regulation, both on matters of substance and style.

[¶ 61,103]   **Proposed Regulation (LR-181-76)**, published in the *Federal Register* on August 3, 1983.

Estate tax: Gross estate: Property in which decedent had interest: Shares of stock.—Proposed Reg. §20.2036-2 would conform the regulations to changes in the law made by the Tax Reform Act of 1976 (P.L. 94-455) and the Revenue Act of 1978 (P.L. 95-600) relating to the estate tax consequences of a decedent's retention of voting rights in a lifetime transfer of stock.

NOTICE OF PROPOSED RULEMAKING

AGENCY: Internal Revenue Service, Treasury.

ACTION: Notice of Proposed Rulemaking.

SUMMARY: This document contains a proposed regulation concerning the estate tax consequence of a decedent's retention of voting rights in lifetime transfers of stock. Changes to the applicable tax law were made by the Tax Reform Act of 1976 and the Revenue Act of 1978. This proposed regulation, if adopted, will provide the public with the guidance needed to comply with those Acts.

DATES: Written comments and requests for a public hearing must be delivered by October 3, 1983. This regulation is proposed to apply to stock transfers made after June 22, 1976.

ADDRESS: Send comments and requests for public hearing to: Commissioner of Internal Revenue, Attention: CC:LR:T, LR-181-76, Washington, D.C. 20224.

FOR FURTHER INFORMATION CONTACT: John R. Harman of the Legislation & Regulations Division, Office of the Chief Counsel, Internal Revenue Service, 1111 Constitution Avenue, N.W., Washington, D.C. 20224, Attention: CC:LR:T, LR-181-76, 202-566-3287, not a toll-free call.

SUPPLEMENTARY INFORMATION

BACKGROUND

This document contains a proposed estate tax regulation (26 CFR Part 20) under section 2036(b) of the Internal Revenue Code of 1954 (Code). The regulation is proposed to conform the regulations to the amendment of the Code made by section 2009(a) of the Tax Reform Act of 1976 (Pub. L. 94-455, 90 Stat. 1893) and section 702(i) of the Revenue Act of 1978 (Pub. L. 95-600, 92 Stat. 2931). The regulation, when adopted, will be issued under the authority contained in section 7805 of the Code (68A Stat. 917, 26 U.S.C. 7805).

BYRUM CASE

Prior to the Tax Reform Act of 1976, the United States Supreme Court, in *U.S. v. Byrum*, 408 U.S. 125 [72-2 USTC ¶ 12,859] (1972), held that the mere retention of the power to vote stock in a closely held corporation did not constitute the retention of enjoyment of transferred property under section 2036 of the Code. Thus, stock in which the decedent retained voting rights was not required to be included in the gross estate.

THE TAX REFORM ACT OF 1976

The Tax Reform Act of 1976 provides that, pursuant to section 2036 of the Code, the retention of voting rights in stock shall be treated as the retention of the enjoyment of transferred property if the decedent retained the voting rights for life, for any period not ascertainable without reference to the decedent's death, or for any period which does not in fact end before the decedent's death. The capacity in which the decedent can exercise voting rights is immaterial. Thus, voting power exercisable as a trustee is one type of voting right subject to the rule.

THE REVENUE ACT OF 1978

The Revenue Act of 1978 made two changes to the rule contained in the 1976 Act. First, the rule is limited to the retention of voting rights in stock of a controlled corporation. A controlled corporation is defined as a corporation in which 20 percent of the voting power is deemed owned by the decedent, applying the constructive ownership rules of section 318. Second, the 1978 Act makes it clear that the rule applies to direct and indirect transfers. Thus, if the decedent transfers cash to a trust and the trust purchases stock in a controlled corporation from the decedent (directly or indirectly), the decedent will be considered to have made a transfer of the stock. In such a transaction, if the decedent acquires the right to vote the stock, he will be treated as though he retained the right to vote the stock.

EXECUTIVE ORDER 12291 AND REGULATORY FLEXIBILITY ACT

The Commissioner of Internal Revenue has determined that this proposed rule is not a major rule as defined in Executive Order 12291. Accordingly, a Regulatory Impact Analysis is not required. The Internal Revenue Service has concluded that, although this document is a notice of proposed rulemaking that solicits public comment, the regulations proposed herein are interpretative and the notice and public procedure requirements of 5 U.S.C. 553 do not apply. Accordingly, no Regulatory Flexibility Analysis is required for this rule.

COMMENTS AND REQUESTS FOR A PUBLIC HEARING

Before adopting these proposed regulations, consideration will be given to any written comments that are submitted (preferably six copies) to the Commissioner of Internal Revenue. All comments will be available for public inspection and copying. A public hearing will be held upon written request to the Commissioner by any person who has submitted written comments. If a public hearing is held, notice of the time and place will be published in the Federal Register.

DRAFTING INFORMATION

The principal author of this proposed regulation is John R. Harman of the Legislation & Regulations Division of the Office of Chief Counsel, Internal Revenue Service. However, personnel from other offices of the Internal Revenue Service and Treasury Department participated in developing the regulation, both on matters of substance and style.

[¶ 61,104]   Proposed Regulations (LR-165-84), published in the *Federal Register* on August 20, 1985.

Income and gift tax: Below-market interest rate loans: Tax Reform Act of 1984.— Regulations detailing the federal income, estate and gift tax treatment of lenders and borrowers with respect to below-market term loans made after June 6, 1984, and below-market demand loans outstanding after such date have been proposed.

AGENCY: Internal Revenue Service, Treasury.

ACTION: Notice of proposed rulemaking.

SUMMARY: This document contains proposed regulations relating to the Federal tax treatment of both the lender and the borrower in certain below-market interest rate loan transactions. Changes to the applicable tax law were made by the Tax Reform Act of 1984. These regulations would affect taxpayers who enter into certain below-market loans and provide them with guidance needed to comply with the law.

DATES: Written comments and requests for a public hearing must be delivered or mailed by October 21, 1985. The regulations are generally proposed to be effective after June 6, 1984, for below-market term loans made after June 6, 1984, and below-market demand loans outstanding after June 6, 1984. Section 1.7872-1(c) provides special effective date rules for certain loan transactions.

ADDRESS: Send comments and requests for a public hearing to: Commissioner of Internal Revenue, Attention: CC:LR:T (LR-165-84), Washington, D.C. 20224.

FOR FURTHER INFORMATION CONTACT: Sharon L. Hall of the Legislation and Regulations Division, Office of Chief Counsel, Internal Revenue Service, 1111 Constitution Avenue, N.W., Washington, D.C. 20224, Attention: CC:LR:T, 202-566-3828 (not a toll-free call).

SUPPLEMENTARY INFORMATION:

BACKGROUND

This document contains proposed amendments to the Income Tax Regulations (26 CFR Part 1), the Estate Tax Regulations (26 CFR Part 20), the Gift Tax Regulations (26 CFR Part 25) and the Excise Tax Regulations (26 CFR Part 53) under section 7872 of the Internal Revenue Code of 1954. This document also amends the Table of OMB Control Numbers (26 CFR Part 602). These amendments are proposed to provide regulations under new section 7872, which was added to the Code by section 172 of the Tax Reform Act of 1984 (98 Stat. 699).

IN GENERAL

Prior to the enactment of section 7872, some taxpayers used interest-free loans or loans with an interest rate below the current market rate (in each case, "below-market loans") which purported to circumvent well-established rules of taxation. Thus, in family or similar situations, below-market loans have been used which purported to have the effect of avoiding taxation under the grantor trust rules and deflecting income to others. Corporations have made below-market loans to shareholders with the effect of avoiding taxation of income at the corporate level which is the economic equivalent of receiving a deduction for dividends paid to those shareholders. Employers have made below-market loans to employees with the effect of providing compensation which has not been subject to employment taxes. Interest free loans have also been used to convert non-deductible expenses into the equivalent of deductible expenses.

Section 7872 addresses these and similar practices, generally, by treating certain below-market loans described in one of the categories specified in section 7872(c) as economically equivalent to loans bearing interest at the applicable Federal rate coupled with a payment by the lender to the borrower sufficient to fund the payment of interest by the borrower. Thus, the lender is treated as making (i) a loan to the borrower in exchange for a note requiring the payment of interest at the applicable Federal rate, and (ii) a transfer of funds to the borrower in an amount generally equal to the amount of interest imputed under section 7872. In the case of term gift loans, however, the amount of money treated as transferred by the lender to the borrower, which is subject to gift tax, and the amount of the imputed interest payment by the borrower to the lender are unequal because they are computed differently under the statute.

CHARACTER AND TIMING OF TRANSFERS

The character of the imputed transfer by the lender to the borrower is determined in accordance with the substance of the transaction. For example, the transfer is treated as a gift if the transaction is in substance a gift within the meaning of the gift tax provisions of the Code, and it is treated as compensation if the purpose of the transaction is the payment of compensation. This imputed transfer is computed annually and in the case of demand loans is treated as made, generally, on December 31. In the case of term loans, however, the imputed transfer is treated as made at the time the loan is made.

The timing and amount of the imputed interest payments by the borrower to the lender depend on the character of the amount transferred by the lender to the borrower and on whether the loan is a term loan or a demand loan. The imputed interest payment in the case of gift and demand loans is computed annually and generally is treated as transferred on December 31. The imputed interest payment in the case of term loans other than gift loans is computed on the date the loan is made and is subject to the original issue discount rules of section 1272.

DEFINITION OF LOAN

Because the purpose of section 7872 is to eliminate the use of below-market loans as a vehicle for tax avoidance, the term "loan" is interpreted broadly in the regulations. Accordingly, any extension of credit or any transaction under which the owner of money permits another person to use the money for a period of time after which the money is to be transferred back to the owner or applied according to an agreement with the owner, such as a refundable deposit, is a loan for purposes of section 7872. However, only those below-market loans that are gift loans, compensation-related loans, corporation-shareholder loans, tax avoidance loans or loans to be specified as significant-effect loans (see below), are subject to the provisions of section 7872. Proposed § 1.7872-4(g) provides a special rule for a below-market loan which is made between two persons and is attributable to the relationship of a third person to either the lender or the borrower (for example, a loan by an employer to the child of an employee). In this case, the loan is restructured as two successive "indirect" loans for purposes of section 7872. In addition, the regulations provide that if a lender and a borrower use another entity as an intermediary or middleman, such as in a "back-to-back" loan transaction, for the purpose of avoiding the application of section 7872, the intermediary will be ignored and the two loans will be restructured as one loan made directly between the lender and the borrower.

Section 7872(c)(1)(B)(ii) states that loans between an independent contractor and a person for whom the independent contractor provides services are subject to section 7872. In addition, the proposed regulations define a loan to include any transaction which would be treated as a refundable deposit under current law. Accordingly, if a taxpayer makes a refundable deposit to an independent contractor in connection with the performance of services, the deposit will be subject to the imputation rules of section 7872 (unless the *de minimis* rules are applicable). The Service is aware that cash amounts are frequently deposited with independent contractors in the ordinary course of business and characterized by the parties as prepayments rather than refundable deposits. Consequently, if this characterization is appropriate, those amounts would not be subject to section 7872. The proper distinction between refundable deposits and prepayments is a factual determination, and, to assist the Service in developing guidelines for drawing this distinction, interested parties are invited to comment on this issue.

PARTNERSHIPS AND PARTNERS

The Service is aware that some taxpayers have entered into below-market loans with partnerships and that other taxpayers have achieved the economic and tax result afforded a below-market loan transaction by utilizing partnerships and the tax laws under subchapter K. The proposed regulations provide that certain below-market loans made by a partnership to a partner that are made in consideration for services performed by the partner other than in his capacity as a member of the partnership will be treated as compensation-related loans for purposes of section 7872.

The final regulations under section 7872 will further address the relationship of section 7872 to partnership transactions, such as certain purported distributions which, under the facts and circumstances, may properly be characterized as loans. The Service is considering several proposals regarding the application of section 7872 to transactions between partners and partnerships and requests interested taxpayers to submit written comments on this point.

SIGNIFICANT EFFECT LOAN

In addition to the four enumerated categories of below-market loans, section 7872(c)(1)(E) provides regulatory authority for applying section 7872 to any other below-market loan if "the interest arrangements of such loan have a significant effect on any Federal tax liability of the lender or the borrower." The Conference Report accompanying the Tax Reform Act of 1984 states, among other things, that any loan that results in the conversion of a nondeductible expense into the equivalent of a deductible expense has an effect on the tax liability of the borrower or lender. The Conference Report further provides that whether an effect is significant is determined in light of all the facts and circumstances including:

(1) Whether the items of income and deduction generated by the loan offset each other;

(2) The amount of such items;

(3) The cost to the taxpayer of complying with the provision; and

(4) Any non-tax reasons for deciding to structure the transactions as a below-market loan rather than a loan with interest at a rate equal to or greater than the applicable Federal rate and a payment by the lender to the borrower.

The Service is aware of numerous situations in which below-market loans have the potential to convert nondeductible personal expenses into the equivalent of deductible expenses. This potential is particularly apparent where interest earned on the borrowed amount may be used to compensate (or provide additional compensation to) the borrower for services or property provided to the lender. Examples of these situations include:

(1) Loans to a membership organization in lieu of part or all of a membership fee;

(2) Loans to institutions providing meals, lodging, and/or medical services (*e.g.*, continuing care facilities) in lieu of fees for such services;

(3) Loans to colleges and secondary schools in lieu of part or all of the tuition, room, and board that would otherwise be charged; and

(4) Loans to an employee or independent contractor by an employer in lieu of payment for a service provided to such employer by the employee (*e.g.*, housing, life insurance coverage, health care).

Many of these transactions have a significant potential for distortion of tax liability, especially if the amounts loaned are relatively large. The Service has decided, however, not to propose regulations treating transactions as having a significant effect until further comment is received on how the facts and circumstances test should be applied, including the proper role of the factors cited by the Conference Report. The Service intends to hold a hearing after publication of these proposed regulations, if a public hearing is requested by any person who submits written comments. The Service urges taxpayers to submit written comments and to speak on this point at that hearing. No transaction will be treated under the regulations as a significant effect loan earlier than the date that future regulations under section 7872(c)(1)(E) are published in proposed form.

EXCLUSION FROM SECTION 7872

Proposed §§1.7872-7 and 1.7872-8 provide for the exclusion of certain below-market loans from the rules of section 7872. Generally, if the amount of loans between a lender and a borrower does not exceed $10,000, section 7872 does not apply. Furthermore, in the case of gift loans of less than $100,000, directly between natural persons, the imputed interest payment by the borrower to the lender each year generally is limited to the amount of the borrower's net investment income (as defined in section 7872(d)(1)(E)) for the taxable year.

In addition, section 7872(g)(1)(C) provides regulatory authority for exempting from the application of section 7872 any class of transactions if the application of section 7872 would not have a significant effect on any Federal tax liability of the lender or the borrower. Accordingly, proposed §1.7872-5 provides that certain below-market loans which are not structured as such for tax avoidance purposes are exempted from the provisions of section 7872. If, however, such a loan is structured as one of the exempted loans for tax avoidance purposes, the Service may recharacterize the transaction according to its economic substance and apply section 7872 in accordance with its terms. Interested taxpayers are invited to comment on whether other transactions should be exempted from section 7872, and on the proper tax treatment under section 7872 of private placements of convertible debt.

Section 7872(f)(8) provides that section 7872 does not apply to any loan to which section 483 or 1274 applies. The regulations clarify that generally section 7872 does not apply to any loan to which section 483 or 1274 could apply even though the rules of those sections do not apply because of exceptions or safe harbor provisions in one of those sections. The regulations further clarify that debt instruments issued for property and payable on demand, debt instruments described in section 1273(b)(3) and debt instruments described in section 1275(b) are not subject to sections 483 and 1274 and are subject to section 7872 if those instruments are described in section 7872(c)(1)(A), (B), or (C).

Certain loans subject to section 7872 are also described in section 482 of the Code (concerning the allocation of income and deductions among related taxpayers). These regulations provide for one limited exception to section 7872 in the case of a loan which is also described in §1.482-2(a)(3), concerning indebtedness arising in the ordinary course of business out of sales, leases, or the rendition of services by or between members of a group outstanding for six months or less (the "open accounts exception"). This limited exception will expire on June 30, 1986, by which time the Service plans to have completed its review of the commercial need for an exception from section 7872 in the case of certain "open account" transactions between parties described in section 7872. The Service invites written comments on this issue.

Where an employer makes a below-market term loan to an employee in certain circumstances, the loan is treated for purposes of section 7872 as a demand loan under section 7872(f)(5). In the case where the employer disposes of his interest in the loan by sale to a third party, questions have arisen regarding the proper tax treatment of the employer, employee and third-party purchaser. The Service is considering alternative ways to resolve the issues raised in these circumstances, consistent with the following principles:

(1) The employee should remain subject to section 7872(a)(1), so long as that section would be applicable if the employer had not sold his interest in the loan; and

(2) The disposition of the loan should not present opportunities for tax avoidance that would not arise had the employer not disposed of its interest in the loan.

When promulgated, these rules may also apply to certain loans, such as employee relocation loans, which are generally exempted from the statute under § 1.7872-5. The Internal Revenue Service invites comments concerning this issue.

FOREIGN CURRENCY LOANS

The proposed regulations state that for purposes of applying the below-market loan rules to loans denominated in a foreign currency, a market rate of interest appropriate for that currency shall be used in lieu of the applicable Federal rate. However, the proposed regulations expressly leave open the question of how the imputed transfer from the borrower to the lender is to be treated for tax purposes. The Service is aware that high nominal rates of interest in currencies expected to depreciate with respect to the dollar may overstate the true cost of borrowing to a U.S. taxpayer if offsetting foreign currency gains are not taken into account. Conversely, low rates of interest in currencies expected to appreciate with respect to the dollar may understate true borrowing costs. The Service is studying this issue further, in the context of transactions governed by section 7872 as well as those governed by sections 1271 through 1275, and plans to address this issue in future regulations under these sections.

REQUEST FOR COMMENTS ON CERTAIN TRANSACTIONS

The Service is aware that numerous transactions which occur in the ordinary course of business in many industries may be characterized under section 7872(c)(1)(B) as compensation-related loans. (One example is a transaction in which a cash margin deposit is made pursuant to requirements of an exchange to a futures commission merchant or to the exchange as a condition for trading futures contracts. See § 1.7872-5 for a special temporary rule pending comments.) In order to determine whether these transactions are subject to section 7872 and whether the interest arrangements of such transaction have a significant effect on the Federal tax liability of the lender or borrower, the Service requests that taxpayers submit written comments providing a full explanation of the transactions.

The Service is also aware that other persons subject to section 7872 may enter into numerous short-term demand loans for business-related or other purposes. (One example is short-term loans resulting from the extension of credit through the use of a credit card. See § 1.7872-10(a)(b) for a special rule relating to revolving credit loans.) Because of the volume and the short-term nature of the loans in these situations, the Service is also considering whether special rules of convenience can be formulated in some circumstances to reduce the cost of compliance without creating opportunities for manipulation or tax avoidance. The Service invites comments and suggestions with respect to such possible rules of convenience, the circumstances in which they would be applicable, and any exceptions that may be necessary if such rules are adopted.

APPLICABLE FEDERAL RATE

Under the proposed regulations, the applicable Federal rate in effect at any time depends upon the Federal statutory rates established for semiannual periods and the alternate Federal rates established by the Commissioner on a monthly basis (see § 1.1274-3T). The Federal statutory rates and the alternate Federal rates are published by the Commissioner along with equivalent rates which are based on different compounding periods. The choice of the appropriate Federal statutory rate or alternate Federal rate for any loan depends upon the payment intervals or compounding periods required under the loan agreement. The regulations provide special rules to permit use of the alternate Federal rate in the case of demand loans. In addition, the proposed regulations provide special rules for certain variable interest rate loans.

UNASCERTAINABLE TERM

The proposed regulations do not address the treatment of term loans in the case where the period for which the loan is outstanding is unascertainable. For example, a loan which must be repaid when the borrower marries is a term loan outstanding for an unascertainable period of time. In order to make the calculations required by section 7872 (b), it is necessary to know the period of time that the term loan is outstanding. The Service invites comments on this issue.

OTHER ISSUES: CONSISTENCY; ESTATE AND GIFT TAX RULES; PRIVATE FOUNDATIONS

Section 7872 (g)(1)(B) provides regulatory authority for assuring that the positions of the lender and borrower are consistent as to the application or nonapplication of section 7872. Accordingly, proposed § 1.7872-11 (f) provides that the lender and the borrower each must attach a statement to their income tax returns of any taxable year in which they either have imputed income or claim a deduction for an amount imputed under section 7872.

In addition, proposed § 20.7872-1 implements section 7872 (g)(2) by prohibiting the discounting, at other than the applicable Federal rate, for estate tax purposes, of any term loan made by a decedent with donative intent after June 6, 1984. Proposed § 25.7872-1 implements section 7872(a) by providing that the amount transferred by the lender to the borrower and characterized as a gift is subject to the gift tax provisions. Finally, § 53.4941(d)-2 is amended to provide that the amount of interest on loans between a disqualified person and a private foundation is computed without regard to section 7872 for purposes of application of the excise tax imposed by that section.

EFFECTIVE DATES

In general, the provisions of section 7872 apply after June 6, 1984, to term loans made after June 6, 1984, and to demand loans outstanding after June 6, 1984. If, however, a demand loan that was outstanding after June 6, 1984, is retired before September 17, 1984, the provisions of section 7872 will not apply to the demand loan for the period ending on the date on which the loan is retired. For this purpose, the demand loan is retired by repayment, cancellation, forgiveness, modification of the interest arrangement, or some other similar action (see Internal Revenue Service News Release, IR-84-95, published August 28, 1984).

COMMENTS AND REQUESTS FOR A PUBLIC HEARING

Before adopting these proposed regulations, consideration will be given to any written comments that are submitted (preferably eight copies) to the Commissioner of Internal Revenue. All comments will be available for public inspection and copying. A public hearing will be held upon written request to the Commissioner by any person who has submitted written comments. If a public hearing is to be held, notice of the time and place will be published in the FEDERAL REGISTER.

The collection of information requirements contained in this notice of proposed rulemaking have been submitted to the Office of Management and Budget (OMB) for review under section 3504(h) of the Paperwork Reduction Act. Comments on these requirements should be sent to the Office of Information and Regulatory Affairs of OMB, Attention: Desk officer for Internal Revenue Service, New Executive Office Building, Washington, D.C. 20503. The Internal Revenue Service requests that persons submitting comments on these requirements to OMB also send copies of those comments to the Service.

SPECIAL ANALYSES

The Commissioner of Internal Revenue has determined that this proposed rule is not a major rule as defined in Executive Order 12291. Accordingly, a Regulatory Impact Analysis is not required. Although this document is a notice of proposed rulemaking that solicits public comment, the Internal Revenue Service has concluded that the proposed regulations are interpretative and that the notice and public procedure requirements of 5 U.S.C. 553 do not apply. Accordingly, these proposed regulations do not constitute regulations subject to the Regulatory Flexibility Act (5 U.S.C. chapter 6).

DRAFTING INFORMATION

The principal author of these proposed regulations is Howard A. Balikov of the Legislation and Regulations Division of the Office of Chief Counsel, Internal Revenue Service. However, personnel from other offices of the Internal Revenue Service and Treasury Department participated in developing the regulations on matters of both substance and style.

[¶ 61,105]   **Proposed Regulations (EE-148-81)**, published in the *Federal Register* on January 23, 1984.

Estate and gift tax: Annuities: Qualified plans: Employer and employee contributions.— Amendments to Reg. § 20.2039-2 and § 20.2039-4, relating to estate and gift tax treatment of employee contributions to and distributions from employee annuity plans, have been proposed. The proposed amendments would provide the public with the guidance needed to comply with changes made to the applicable law by the Economic Recovery Tax Act of 1981. Although the proposed amendments would not reflect changes made by TEFRA, they would incorporate the changes made by the 1982 Technical Corrections Act.

NOTICE OF PROPOSED RULEMAKING

AGENCY: Internal Revenue Service, Treasury.

ACTION: Notice of proposed rulemaking.

SUMMARY: This document contains proposed regulations relating to individual retirement plans, simplified employee pensions, and qualified voluntary employee contributions. Changes to the applicable law were made by the Economic Recovery Tax Act of 1981. The regulations would provide the public with the guidance needed to comply with the Act. The regulations would affect: institutions which sponsor individual retirement plans and simplified employee pensions, employers and individuals who use individual retirement plans and simplified employee pensions for retirement income, employers who maintain plans which accept qualified voluntary employee contributions and employees who make qualified voluntary employee contributions.

DATES: Written comments and requests for a public hearing must be delivered or mailed by March 23, 1984. The regulations are generally effective for taxable years beginning after December 31, 1981.

ADDRESS: Send comments and requests for a public hearing to: Commissioner of Internal Revenue, Attention: CC:LR:T (EE-148-81), Washington, D.C. 20224.

FOR FURTHER INFORMATION CONTACT: William D. Gibbs of the Employee Plans and Exempt Organizations Division, Office of the Chief Counsel, Internal Revenue Service, 1111 Constitution Avenue, N.W., Washington, D.C. 20224 (Attention: CC:LR:T) (202-566-3430) (not a toll-free number).

SUPPLEMENTARY INFORMATION:

BACKGROUND

This document contains proposed amendments to the Income Tax Regulations (26 CFR Part 20), the Gift Tax Regulations (26 CFR Part 1), the Estate Tax Regulations (26 CFR Part 25), and the Procedure and Administration Regulations (26 CFR Part 301) under sections 219, 408, 409, 415, 2039, 2517, and 6652 of the Internal Revenue Code of 1954. These amendments are proposed to conform the regulations to sections 311 (except subsection (b)) and 314(b) of the Economic Recovery Tax Act of 1981 (95 Stat. 274, 286). These regulations are to be issued under the authority contained in section 7805 of the Internal Revenue Code of 1954 (68A Stat. 917; 26 U.S.C. 7805).

INDIVIDUAL RETIREMENT PLANS

Section 219, as amended by the Economic Recovery Tax Act of 1981, allows an individual a deduction of up to the lesser of $2,000 or compensation includible in gross income for contributions to an individual retirement plan. Unlike old section 219, an individual is allowed this deduction whether or not he is an "active participant" in an employer's plan. The deduction for individual retirement plan contributions is reduced, however, by amounts which the employee contributes to an employer's plan and treats as qualified voluntary employee contributions. The remainder of the individual retirement plan rules are similar to those under prior law.

SPOUSAL INDIVIDUAL RETIREMENT ACCOUNTS

Code section 220 was deleted by the Economic Recovery Tax Act of 1981. In its place is new section 219(c), which allows an individual and his nonworking spouse to contribute up to the lesser of compensation includible in the working spouse's gross income or $2,250 to individual retirement accounts. The spouses must file a joint return to obtain this additional $250 deduction. No deduction is allowed if the spouse for whose benefit the individual retirement plan is maintained has attained age 70$\frac{1}{2}$ before the close of the taxable year.

There is no requirement, as under old law, that equal amounts be contributed to the individual retirement accounts of both spouses. However, no more than $2,000 may be contributed to the individual retirement account of either spouse.

SIMPLIFIED EMPLOYEE PENSIONS

The Economic Recovery Tax Act of 1981 increased the maximum deduction for contributions to simplified employee pensions to the lesser of 15% of compensation from the employer maintaining the simplified employee pension arrangement or the amount contributed by the employer to the simplified employee pension and included in gross income (but not in excess of $15,000). An employee may also contribute and deduct the lesser of $2,000 or compensation includible in gross income regardless of the employer's contribution to the simplified employee pension.

QUALIFIED VOLUNTARY EMPLOYEE CONTRIBUTIONS

Section 219, as amended by the Economic Recovery Tax Act of 1981, allows an individual a deduction for qualified voluntary employee contributions (QVEC's). QVEC's are voluntary contributions made by an individual as an employee under an employer's plan. The employer's plan must allow employees to make contributions which may be treated as QVEC's.

The maximum amount which can be deducted as a QVEC is the lesser of $2,000 or the compensation includible in gross income from the employer which maintains the plan which accepts the QVEC's.

Proposed § 1.219(a)-5(a) sets forth the type of plans which can accept qualified voluntary employee contributions.

Proposed § 1.219(a)-5(c) sets forth the rules a plan must follow to receive qualified voluntary employee contributions.

Additional rules for QVEC's are set forth in proposed § 1.219(a)-5(d), (e), and (f).

The reporting rules for qualified voluntary employee contributions are in proposed § 1.219(a)-5(g). This provision gives the Commissioner discretionary authority to modify the reporting requirements for these contributions. Any such modification of the reporting requirements would be subject to review by the Office of Management and Budget under the Paperwork Reduction Act of 1980.

OTHER AMENDMENTS

Conforming and technical amendments made by the Economic Recovery Tax Act of 1981 have been made to the regulations under Code sections 408, 409, 415, 2039, 2517, and 6652.

Although the Treasury Department stopped selling retirement bonds in early 1982, the regulations contain references to Code sections 405 and 409. These references apply to retirement bonds sold through early 1982 and to retirement bonds that may be sold subsequently.

These proposed regulations do not reflect amendments made to the Code by the Tax Equity and Fiscal Responsibility Act of 1982. These proposed regulations reflect changes in the applicable statutory provisions made by the Technical Corrections Act of 1982.

EXECUTIVE ORDER 12291 AND REGULATORY FLEXIBILITY ACT

The Commissioner has determined that this proposed regulation is not a major regulation for purposes of Executive Order 12291. Accordingly, a regulatory impact analysis is not required.

Although this document is a notice of proposed rulemaking which solicits public comment, the Internal Revenue Service has concluded that the regulations proposed herein are interpretative and that the notice and public procedure requirements of 5 U.S.C. 553 do not apply. Accordingly, these proposed regulations do not constitute regulations subject to the Regulatory Flexibility Act (5 U.S.C. chapter 6).

COMMENTS AND REQUESTS FOR A PUBLIC HEARING

Before adopting these proposed regulations, consideration will be given to any written comments that are submitted (preferably seven copies) to the Commissioner of Internal Revenue. All comments will be available for public inspection and copying. A public hearing will be held upon written request to the Commissioner by any person who has submitted written comments. If a public hearing is held, notice of the time and place will be published in the *Federal Register*.

The collection of information requirements contained in this notice of proposed rulemaking have been submitted to the Office of Management and Budget (OMB) for review under section 3504(h) of the Paperwork Reduction Act of 1980. Comments on these requirements should be sent to the Office of Information and Regulatory Affairs of OMB, Attention: Desk Office for Internal Revenue Service, New Executive Office Building, Washington, D.C. 20503. The Internal Revenue Service requests that persons submitting comments on these requirements to OMB also send copies of those comments to the Service.

DRAFTING INFORMATION

The principal author of these proposed regulations is William D. Gibbs of the Employee Plans and Exempt Organizations Division of the Office of Chief Counsel, Internal Revenue Service. However, personnel from other offices of the Internal Revenue Service and Treasury Department participated in developing the regulation, both on matters of substance and style.

[¶ 61,106]   **Proposed Regulations (EE-96-85)**, filed with the *Federal Register* on January 29, 1986.

Estate tax: Gross estate: Annuities: Exclusion for qualified plan and IRA benefits.— The IRS has issued temporary regulations providing guidance with respect to qualified employee benefit plans, welfare benefit funds and employees receiving benefits through such plans. The rules have also been proposed as final regulations and implement law changes enacted by the Tax Reform Act of 1984 (P.L. 98-369), including the repeal of the estate tax exclusion for qualified plan benefits under Code Sec. 2039.

NOTICE OF PROPOSED RULEMAKING

AGENCY: Internal Revenue Service, Treasury.

ACTION: Notice of proposed rulemaking by cross reference to temporary regulations.

SUMMARY: In the Rules and Regulations portion of this issue of the Federal Register, the Internal Revenue Service is issuing temporary regulations relating to effective dates and certain other issues arising under the employee benefit provisions of the Tax Reform Act of 1984. The text of those temporary regulations also serves as the comment document for this notice of proposed rulemaking.

DATES: Written comments and requests for a public hearing must be delivered or mailed by April 7, 1986. The regulations are proposed to be effective on varying dates provided in the temporary regulations.

ADDRESS: Send comments and requests for a public hearing to Commissioner of Internal Revenue, Attn: CC:LR:T (EE-96-85), 1111 Constitution Avenue, N.W., Washington, D.C. 20224.

FOR FURTHER INFORMATION CONTACT: John T. Ricotta of the Employee Plans and Exempt Organizations Division, Office of Chief Counsel, Internal Revenue Service, 1111 Constitution Ave., N.W., Washington, D.C. 20224, Attention: CC:LR:T (EE-96-85), telephone: 202-566-3544 (not a toll-free number).

SUPPLEMENTARY INFORMATION:

BACKGROUND

The temporary regulations provide guidance concerning * * * repeal of the estate tax exclusion for qualified plan benefits under section 2039 of the Code, as amended by section 525 of the Act (P.L. 98-369, 98 Stat. 873) * * *. [Portions not relevant to estate and gift taxes omitted.—CCH.] The proposed regulations are issued under the authority contained in section 7805 of the Code (26 U.S.C. § 7805). * * *

SPECIAL ANALYSES

The Commissioner of Internal Revenue has determined that this proposed rule is not a major rule as defined in Executive Order 12291 and that a Regulatory Impact Analysis is therefore not required. Although this document is a notice of proposed rulemaking which solicits public comment, the Internal Revenue Service has concluded that the regulations proposed herein are interpretative and that the notice and public procedure requirements of 5 U.S.C. 553 do not apply. Accordingly, these proposed regulations do not constitute regulations subject to the Regulatory Flexibility Act (5 U.S.C. Chapter 6).

COMMENTS AND REQUESTS FOR A PUBLIC HEARING

Before the adoption of these proposed regulations, consideration will be given to any written comments that are submitted (preferably eight copies) to the Commissioner of Internal Revenue. All comments will be available for public inspection and copying. A public hearing will be held upon written request to the Commissioner by any person who has submitted written comments. If a public hearing is held, notice of the time and place will be published in the Federal Register. The collection of information requirements contained herein have been submitted to the Office of Management and Budget (OMB) for review under section 3504(h) of the Paperwork Reduction Act. Comments on the requirements should be sent to the Office of Information and Regulatory Affairs, of OMB, Attention: Desk Officer for Internal Revenue Service, New Executive Office Building, Washington, D.C. 20503. The Internal Revenue Service requests persons submitting comments to OMB also to send copies of the comments to the Service.

[¶ 61,107]   **Proposed Regulations (LR-189-84)**, filed with the *Federal Register* on March 27, 1986.

Income and gift tax: Below-market interest rate loans.—Reg. § 1.7872-4, § 25.2512-4 and § 25.2512-8, relating to the federal income and gift tax treatment of below-market interest rate loans, have been proposed.

NOTICE OF PROPOSED RULEMAKING

AGENCY: Internal Revenue Service, Treasury.

ACTION: Notice of proposed rulemaking.

SUMMARY: This document contains proposed regulations relating to (1) the tax treatment of debt instruments issued after July 1, 1982, that contain original issue discount, (2) the imputation of and the accounting for interest with respect to sales and exchanges of property occurring after December 31, 1984, and (3) safe haven interest rates for loans or advances between commonly controlled taxpayers and safe haven leases between such taxpayers. Changes to the applicable law were made by the Tax Equity and Fiscal Responsibility Act of 1982 as amended by the Technical Corrections Act of 1982, and the Tax Reform Act of 1984 as amended by Pub. L. No. 98-612 and Pub. L. No. 99-121. The regulations would provide needed guidance to taxpayers who must comply with these provisions of the law.

DATES:

* * *

DATES FOR COMMENTS AND REQUEST FOR A PUBLIC HEARING

Written comments and request for a public hearing must be delivered or mailed by June 9, 1986.

ADDRESS: Send comments (preferably eight copies) and request for a public hearing to: Commissioner of Internal Revenue, Attention: CC:LR:T, (LR-189-84), 1111 Constitution Avenue, N.W., Washington, D.C. 20224.

FOR FURTHER INFORMATION CONTACT: Theresa E. Bearman (sections 163, 1271, 1272, 1273, 1275 and related matters), Ewan D. Purkiss (sections 446, 483, 1274 and related matters), Susan T. Baker (all matters other than those relating to sections 446, 482 and 483), or Joseph M. Rosenthal (section 482 and related matters) of the Legislation and Regulations Division, Office of Chief Counsel, Internal Revenue Service, 1111 Constitution Avenue, N.W., Washington, D.C. 20224 (Attention: CC:LR:T LR-189-84). Telephone 202-566-3829 (Bearman), 202-566-3238 (Purkiss), 202-566-3294 (Baker), 202-566-3289 (Rosenthal) (not a toll-free call).

SUPPLEMENTARY INFORMATION:

* * *

REGULATORY FLEXIBILITY ACT

Although this document is a notice of proposed rulemaking that solicits public comment, the Internal Revenue Service has concluded that the regulations proposed herein are interpretative and that the notice and public procedure requirements of 5 U.S.C. 553 do not apply. Accordingly, these proposed regulations do not constitute regulations subject to the Regulatory Flexibility Act (5 U.S.C. chapter 6).

NON-APPLICATION OF EXECUTIVE ORDER 12291

The Commissioner of Internal Revenue has determined that this proposed rule is not a major rule as defined in Executive Order 12291 and that a regulatory impact analysis therefore is not required.

COMMENTS AND REQUEST FOR A PUBLIC HEARING

Before these proposed regulations are adopted, consideration will be given to any written comments that are submitted (preferably eight copies) to the Commissioner of Internal Revenue. All comments will be available for public inspection and copying. A public hearing will be held upon written request to the Commissioner by any person who has submitted written comments. If a public hearing is held, notice of the time and place will be published in the FEDERAL REGISTER. The collection of information requirements contained herein have been submitted to the Office of Management and Budget (OMB) for review under section 3504(h) of the Paperwork Reduction Act. Comments on the requirements should be sent to the Office of Information and Regulatory Affairs of OMB, Attention: Desk Officer for Internal Revenue Service, New Executive Office Building, Washington, D.C. 20503. The Internal Revenue Service requests that persons submitting comments to OMB also send copies of the comments to the Service.

DRAFTING INFORMATION

The principal author of the proposed regulations under sections 163, 1271, 1272, 1273, and 1275 is Theresa E. Bearman of the Legislation and Regulations Division of the Office of Chief Counsel, Internal Revenue Service; the principal author of the regulations under sections 446, 483 and 1274 is Ewan D. Purkiss of the Legislation and Regulations Division of the Office of Chief Counsel, Internal Revenue Service; and the principal author of the regulations under section 482 is Joseph M. Rosenthal of the Legislation and Regulations Division of the Office of Chief Counsel, Internal Revenue Service. However, personnel from other offices of the Internal Revenue Service and the Treasury Department participated in developing the regulations on matters of both substance and style.

[¶ 61,132]   Proposed Regulations (REG-147775-06), published in the *Federal Register* on April 17, 2008.

Generation-skipping transfer tax: Returns and procedures: Allocation of exemption: Extension of time.—Regulations describing the circumstances and procedures under which an extension of time to allocate generation-skipping transfer (GST) exemption to a transfer under Code Sec. 2642, have been proposed. Currently, in accordance with Notice 2001-50, 2001-2 CB 189, requests for extension of time are governed by Reg. § 301.9100-3. The proposed regulations are intended to replace Reg. § 301.9100-3 with regard to relief under Code Sec. 2642(g)(1). Once the regulations have been adopted as final, Reg. § 301.9100-3 will be amended to provide that relief under Code Sec. 2642(g)(1) is unavailable through either Reg. §§ 301.9100-1 or 301.9100-3. Requests for extension of time under Code Sec. 2642(g)(1) apply to allocations of GST exemption under Code Sec. 2631, elections to opt out of automatic allocation under Code Secs. 2632(b)(3) and (c)(5), and elections to treat a trust as a GST trust under Code Sec. 2632(c)(5)(A)(ii). Requests for relief under Code Sec. 2642(g)(1) will be granted when it is established that the transferor or transferor's estate acted reasonably and in good faith and granting relief would not prejudice the interests of the government. In determining whether the transferor or the transferor's estate acted reasonably and in good faith, these nonexclusive factors will be considered: (1) the intent at the time of the transfer to timely allocate the GST exemption; (2) the occurrence of events beyond the control of the transferor; (3) the lack of awareness of the need to allocate the GST exemption to a transfer; (4) evidence of consistency in allocating or not allocating the GST exemption; and (5) reasonable reliance on a qualified tax professional. The following nonexclusive factors will also be considered when determining whether granting an exemption would prejudice the government: (1) whether the use of hindsight would produce an economic advantage that would have been unavailable had the election been timely made; (2) whether the delay in filing a request for relief was done with the intent to deprive the IRS of sufficient time to challenge the claimed identity of the transferor; or (3) whether the relief would cause unreasonable disruptions or difficulties in adjusting the previous GST tax consequences. Relief under Code Sec. 2642(g)(1) will not be granted when the standards of reasonableness, good faith, and lack of prejudice to the government are not met, as in the following situations: (1) granting relief would decrease a timely filed allocation of GST exemption; (2) the transferor was accurately informed in all material respects by a tax professional at the time of the transfer for which relief is requested; or (3) the IRS determines that the request is an attempt to benefit from hindsight. Relief provided under Code Sec. 2642(g)(1) will be granted through the IRS letter ruling program.

AGENCY: Internal Revenue Service (IRS), Treasury.

ACTION: Notice of proposed rulemaking and notice of public hearing.

SUMMARY: This document contains proposed regulations providing guidance under section 2642(g)(1). The proposed regulations describe the circumstances and procedures under which an extension of time will be granted under section 2642(g)(1). The proposed guidance affects individuals (or their estates) who failed to make a timely allocation of generation-skipping transfer (GST) exemption to a transfer, and individuals (or their estates) who failed to make a timely election under section 2632(b)(3) or (c)(5). This document also provides notice of a public hearing.

DATES: Written or electronic comments must be received by July 16, 2008.

Outlines of topics to be discussed at the public hearing scheduled for August 5, 2008, must be received by July 15, 2008.

ADDRESSES: Send submissions to: CC:PA:LPD:PR (REG-147775-06), Internal Revenue Service, Room 5203, PO Box 7604, Ben Franklin Station, Washington, DC 20044. Submissions may be hand delivered Monday through Friday between the hours of 8 a.m. and 4 p.m. to CC:PA:LPD:PR (REG-147775-06), 1111 Constitution Avenue NW., Washington, DC 20224; or sent electronically via the Federal eRulemaking Portal at *www.regulations.gov* (IRS-REG-147775-06). The public hearing will be held in the IRS auditorium.

FOR FURTHER INFORMATION CONTACT: Concerning the proposed regulations, Theresa M. Melchiorre, (202) 622-3090; concerning submissions of comments, the hearing, and/or to be placed on the building access list to attend the hearing, Richard Hurst at *Richard.A.Hurst @irscounsel.treas.gov* or (202) 622-7180 (not toll-free numbers).

SUPPLEMENTARY INFORMATION:

Paperwork Reduction Act

The collections of information contained in this notice of proposed rulemaking have been submitted to the Office of Management and Budget for review in accordance with the Paperwork Reduction Act of 1995 (44 U.S.C. 3507(d)). Comments on the collections of information should be sent to the **Office of Management and Budget**, Attn: Desk Officer for the Department of the Treasury, Office of Information and Regulatory Affairs, Washington, DC 20503, with copies to the **Internal Revenue Service**, Attn: IRS Reports Clearance Officer, SE:W:CAR:MP:T:T:SP, Washington, DC 20224. Comments on the collection of information should be received by June 16, 2008.

Comments are specifically requested concerning:

Whether the proposed collection of information is necessary for the proper performance of the functions of the IRS, including whether the information will have practical utility;

The accuracy of the estimated burden associated with the proposed collection of information;

How the quality, utility, and clarity of the information to be collected may be enhanced;

How the burden of complying with the proposed collection of information may be minimized, including through the application of automated collection techniques or other forms of information technology; and

Estimates of capital or start-up costs and costs of operation, maintenance, and purchase of service to provide information.

The reporting requirement in these proposed regulations is in §26.2642-7(h)(2) and (3). This information must be reported by transferors or the executors of transferors' estates requesting relief under section 2642(g)(1). This information will be used by the IRS to determine whether to grant a transferor or a transferor's estate an extension of time to: (1) allocate GST exemption, as defined in section 2631, to a transfer; (2) elect under section 2632(b)(3) (the election not to have the deemed allocation of GST exemption apply to a direct skip); (3) elect under section 2632(c)(5)(A)(i) (the election not to have the deemed allocation of GST exemption apply to an indirect skip or transfers made to a particular trust); and (4) elect under section 2632(c)(5)(A)(ii) (the election to treat any trust as a GST trust for purposes of section 2632(c)).

The following estimates are an approximation of the average time expected to be necessary for a collection of information. They are based on the information that is available to the IRS. Individual respondents may require greater or less time, depending on their particular circumstances.

Estimated total annual reporting burden: 1800 hours.

Estimated average annual burden: 2 hours.

Estimated number of respondents: 900.

Estimated annual frequency of response: When relief is requested.

An agency may not conduct or sponsor, and a person is not required to respond to, a collection of information unless it displays a valid control number assigned by the Office of Management and Budget.

Books or records relating to a collection of information must be retained as long as their contents may become material in the administration of any internal revenue law. Generally, tax returns and tax return information are confidential, as required by 26 U.S.C. 6103.

Background

The proposed regulations provide guidance on the application of section 2642(g)(1). Congress added section 2642(g)(1) to the Internal Revenue Code (Code) in section 564 of the Economic Growth and Tax Relief Reconciliation Act of 2001 (EGTRRA), (Public Law 107-16, § 564, 115 Stat. 91). This section directs the Secretary to issue regulations describing the circumstances and procedures under which an extension of time will be granted to: (1) allocate GST exemption, as defined in section 2631(a), to a transfer; (2) elect under section 2632(b)(3) (the election not to have the deemed allocation of GST exemption apply to a direct skip); (3) elect under section 2632(c)(5)(A)(i) (the election not to have the deemed allocation of GST exemption apply to an indirect skip or transfers made to a particular trust); and (4) elect under section 2632(c)(5)(A)(ii) (the election to treat any trust as a GST trust for purposes of section 2632(c)). In determining whether to grant relief, section 2642(g)(1) directs that all relevant circumstances be considered including evidence of intent contained in the trust instrument or the instrument of transfer.

The legislative history accompanying section 2642(g)(1) indicates that Congress believed that, in appropriate circumstances, an individual should be granted an extension of time to allocate GST exemption regardless of whether any period of limitations had expired. Those circumstances include situations in which the taxpayer intended to allocate GST exemption and the failure to allocate the exemption was inadvertent. H.R. Conf. Rep. No. 107-84, 202 (2001).

After the enactment of section 2642(g)(1), the IRS issued Notice 2001-50 (2001-2 CB 189), which announced that transferors may seek an extension of time to make an allocation of GST exemption. The Notice provides, generally, that relief will be granted under §301.9100-3 of the Procedure and Administration Regulations if the taxpayer satisfies the requirements of those regulations and establishes to the satisfaction of the Commissioner that the taxpayer acted reasonably and in good faith and that a grant of the requested relief will not prejudice the interests of the Government. If relief is granted under §301.9100-3 and the allocation is made, the amount of GST exemption allocated to the transfer is the Federal gift or estate tax value of the property as of the date of the transfer and the allocation is effective as of the date of the transfer. (Notice 2001-50 will be made obsolete upon the publication of the Treasury decision adopting these proposed regulations as final regulations in the **Federal Register**.)

On August 2, 2004, the IRS issued Rev. Proc. 2004-46 (2004-2 CB 142), which provides an alternate simplified method to obtain an extension of time to allocate GST exemption in certain situations. Generally, this method is available only with regard to an inter vivos transfer to a trust from which a GST may be made and only if each of the following requirements is met: (1) the transfer qualified for the gift tax annual exclusion under section 2503(b); (2) the sum of the amount of the transfer and all other gifts by the transferor to the donee in the same year did not exceed the applicable annual exclusion amount for that year; (3) no GST exemption was allocated to the transfer; (4) the taxpayer has unused GST exemption to allocate to the transfer as of the filing of the request for relief; and (5) no taxable distributions or taxable terminations have occurred as of the filing of the request for relief.

To date, the IRS has issued numerous private letter rulings under §301.9100-3 granting an extension of time to timely allocate GST exemption in situations in which transferors (or their executors) failed to allocate GST exemption to a trust on a timely filed Federal gift or estate tax return. These proposed regulations are intended to replace §301.9100-3 with regard to relief under section 2642(g)(1).

Accordingly, §301.9100-3 will be amended to provide that relief under section 2642(g)(1) cannot be obtained through the provisions of §§301.9100-1 and 301.9100-3 after the date of publication of the Treasury decision adopting these rules as final regulations in the **Federal Register**. Relief under §301.9100-2(b) (the automatic 6-month extension) will continue to be available to transferors or transferor's estates qualifying for that relief. In addition, the procedures contained in Revenue Procedure 2004-46 will remain effective for transferors within the scope of that Revenue Procedure.

Explanation of Provisions

The proposed regulations identify the standards that the IRS will apply in determining whether to grant a transferor or a transferor's estate an extension of time to: (1) allocate GST exemption, as defined in section 2631, to a transfer; (2) elect under section 2632(b)(3) (the election not to have the deemed allocation of GST exemption apply to a direct skip); (3) elect under section 2632(c)(5)(A)(i) (the election not to have the deemed allocation of GST exemption apply to an indirect skip or transfers made to a particular trust); and (4) elect under section 2632(c)(5)(A)(ii) (the election to treat any trust as a GST trust for purposes of section 2632(c)). The proposed regulations also identify situations with facts that do not satisfy the standards for granting relief and in which, as a result, an extension of time will not be granted.

If an extension of time to allocate GST exemption is granted under section 2642(g)(1), the allocation of GST exemption will be considered effective as of the date of the transfer, and the value of the property transferred for purposes of chapter 11 or chapter 12 will determine the amount of GST exemption to be allocated. If an extension of time to elect out of the automatic allocation of GST exemption under section 2632(b)(3) or (c)(5)(A)(i) is granted under section 2642(g)(1), the election will be considered effective as of the date of the transfer. If an extension of time to elect to treat any trust as a GST trust under section 2632(c)(5)(A)(ii) is granted under section 2642(g)(1), the election will be considered effective as of the date of the first (or each) transfer covered by that election.

The amount of GST exemption that may be allocated to a transfer pursuant to an extension granted under section 2642(g)(1) is limited to the amount of the transferor's unused GST exemption under section 2631(c) as of the date of the transfer. Thus, if the amount of GST exemption has increased since the date of the transfer, no portion of the increased amount may be applied by reason of the grant of relief under section 2642(g)(1) to a transfer taking place in an earlier year and prior to the effective date of that increase.

Requests for relief under section 2642(g)(1) will be granted when the taxpayer establishes to the satisfaction of the IRS that the taxpayer acted reasonably and in good faith, and that the grant of relief will not prejudice the interests of the Government. For purposes of section 2642(g)(1), the following nonexclusive list of factors will be used to determine whether a transferor or the executor of a transferor's estate acted reasonably and in good faith: (1) the intent of the transferor or the executor of the transferor's estate to timely allocate GST exemption or to timely make an election under section 2632(b)(3) or (c)(5) as evidenced in the trust instrument, instrument of transfer, or contemporaneous documents, such as Federal gift or estate tax returns or correspondence; (2) the occurrence of intervening events beyond the control of the transferor as defined in section 2652(a), or of the executor of the transferor's estate as defined in section 2203, that caused the failure to allocate GST exemption to a transfer or the failure to elect under section 2632(b)(3) or (c)(5); (3) the lack of awareness by the transferor or the executor of the transferor's estate of the need to allocate GST exemption to a transfer after exercising reasonable diligence, taking into account the experience of the transferor or the executor of the transferor's estate and the complexity of the GST issue; (4) evidence of consistency by the transferor in allocating (or not allocating) the transferor's GST exemption, although evidence of consistency may be less relevant if there is evidence of a change of circumstances or change of trust beneficiaries that would otherwise support a deviation from prior GST tax exemption allocation practices; and (5) reasonable reliance by the transferor or the executor of the transferor's estate on the advice of a qualified tax professional retained or employed by either (or both) of them, and the failure of the transferor or executor, in reliance on or consistent with that advice, to allocate GST exemption to the transfer or to make an election described in section 2632(b)(3) or (c)(5). The IRS will consider all relevant facts and circumstances in making this determination.

For purposes of section 2642(g)(1), the following nonexclusive list of factors will be used to determine whether the interests of the Government would be prejudiced: (1) the grant of requested relief would permit the use of hindsight to produce an economic advantage or other benefit that either would not have been available if the allocation or election had been timely made, or that results from the selection of one out of a number of alternatives (other than whether or not to make an allocation or election) that were available at the time the allocation or election could have been made timely; (2) if the transferor or the executor of the transferor's estate delayed the filing of the request for relief with the intent to deprive the IRS of sufficient time (by reason of the expiration or the impending expiration of the applicable statute of limitations or otherwise) to challenge the claimed identity of the transferor, the value of the transferred property that is the subject of the requested relief, or any other aspect of the transfer that is relevant for transfer tax purposes; and (3) a determination by the IRS that, in the event of a grant of relief under section 2642(g)(1), it would be unreasonably disruptive or difficult to adjust the GST tax consequences of a taxable termination or a taxable distribution that occurred between the time for making a timely allocation of GST exemption or a timely election described in section 2632(b)(3) or (c)(5) and the time at which the request for relief under section 2642(g)(1) was filed. The IRS will consider all relevant facts and circumstances in making this determination.

Relief under section 2642(g)(1) will not be granted when the standard of reasonableness, good faith and lack of prejudice to the interests of the Government is not met. This standard is not met in the following situations: (1) the transferor or the executor of the transferor's estate made an allocation of GST exemption as described in §26.2632-1(b)(4)(ii)(A)(1), or an election under section 2632(b)(3) or (c)(5), on a timely filed Federal gift or estate tax return, and the relief requested would decrease or revoke that allocation or election; (2) the transferor or the transferor's executor delayed in requesting relief in order to preclude the IRS, as a practical matter, from challenging the identity of the transferor, the value of the transferred interest on the Federal estate or gift tax return, or any other aspect of the transaction that is relevant for Federal estate or gift tax purposes; (3) the action or inaction that is the subject of the request for relief reflected or implemented the decision with regard to the allocation of GST exemption or an election described in section 2632(b)(3) or (c)(5) that was made by the transferor or executor of the transferor's estate who had been accurately informed in all material respects by a qualified tax professional retained or employed by either (or both) of them; or (4) the IRS determines that the transferor's request is an attempt to benefit from hindsight.

A request for relief under section 2642(g)(1) does not reopen, suspend or extend the period of limitations on assessment of any estate, gift, or GST tax under section 6501. Thus, the IRS may request that the transferor or the transferor's executor consent under section 6501(c)(4) to extend the period of limitations on assessment of any or all gift and GST taxes on the transfer(s) for which relief under section 2642(g)(1) has been requested. The transferor or the transferor's executor has the right to refuse to extend the period of limitations, or to limit such extension to particular issues or to a particular period of time. See section 6501(c)(4)(B).

If the grant of relief under section 2642(g)(1) results in a potential tax refund claim, no refund will be paid or credited to the taxpayer or the taxpayer's estate if, at the time of filing the request for relief, the period of limitations for filing a claim for a credit or refund of Federal gift, estate, or GST tax under section 6511 on the transfer for which relief is granted has expired.

Relief provided under section 2642(g)(1) will be granted through the IRS letter ruling program.

Proposed Effective Date

Section 26.2642-7 applies to requests for relief filed on or after the date of publication of the Treasury decision adopting these rules as final regulations in the **Federal Register**.

Availability of IRS Documents

The IRS notice and revenue procedure cited in this preamble are published in the Cumulative Bulletin and are available at www.irs.gov.

Special Analyses

It has been determined that this notice of proposed rulemaking is not a significant regulatory action as defined in Executive Order 12866. Therefore, a regulatory assessment is not required. Pursuant to the Regulatory Flexibility Act (RFA) (5 U.S.C. chapter 6), it is hereby certified that this regulation will not have a significant economic impact on a substantial number of small entities. The applicability of this rule is limited to individuals (or their estates) and trusts, which are not small entities as defined by the RFA (5 U.S.C. 601). Although it is anticipated that there may be a beneficial economic impact for some small entities, including entities that provide tax and legal services that assist individuals in the private letter ruling program, any benefit to those entities would be indirect. Further, this indirect benefit will not affect a substantial number of these small entities because only a limited number of individuals (or their estates) and trusts would submit a private letter ruling request under this rule. Therefore, only a small fraction of tax and legal services entities would generate business or benefit from this rule. Accordingly, a regulatory flexibility analysis is not required. Pursuant to section 7805(f) of the Code, this regulation has been submitted to the Chief Counsel for Advocacy of the Small Business Administration for comment on its impact on small entities.

Comments and Public Hearing

Before these proposed regulations are adopted as final regulations, consideration will be given to any written (a signed original and eight (8) copies) or electronic comments that are submitted timely to the IRS. The IRS and Treasury Department request comments on the clarity of the proposed rules and also on how they can be made easier to understand. All comments will be available for public inspection and copying.

A public hearing has been scheduled for August 5, 2008 in the IRS auditorium. Due to building security procedures, visitors must enter at the Constitution Avenue entrance. In addition, all visitors must present photo identification to enter the building. Because of access restrictions, visitors will not be admitted beyond the immediate entrance area more than 30 minutes before the hearing starts. For more information about having your name placed on the list to attend the hearing, see the "FOR FURTHER INFORMATION CONTACT" section of this preamble.

The rules of 26 CFR 601.601(a)(3) apply to the hearing. Persons who wish to present oral comments at the hearing must submit written (a signed original and eight (8) copies) or electronic comments by July 16, 2008 and an outline of the topics to be discussed and the time to be devoted to each topic by July 15, 2008. A period of 10 minutes will be allotted to each person for making comments. An agenda showing the scheduling of the speakers will be prepared after the deadline for receiving outlines has passed. Copies of the agenda will be available free of charge at the hearing.

Drafting Information

The principal author of these regulations is Theresa M. Melchiorre, Office of Chief Counsel, IRS.

[¶ 61,140]   Proposed Regulations (REG-107845-08), published in the *Federal Register* on May 7, 2009.

[*Code Secs. 642, 664, 2031, 2032, 2055, 2056A, 2512, 2522, and 7520*]

Estate, gift, and income taxes: Valuation: Limited property interests: Annuities: Interests for life: Terms of years: Reversionary interests: Actuarial tables.—Proposed amendments to Regs. §§ 1.642(c)-6, 1.664-4, 20.2031-7, 20.2055-2, 20.2056A-4, 25.2512-5, 25.2522(c)-3, 20.7520-1, 25.7520-1, and 25.7520-3, relating to the valuation tables used in valuing annuities, interests for life or term of years, and remainder and reversionary interests have been finalized. The amendments provide updated actuarial tables that reflect mortality data compiled from the 2000 census as set forth in Life Table 2000CM. The amendments made to 20.2032-1 have not yet been adopted.

[¶ 61,150]   Proposed Regulations (REG-112196-07), published in the *Federal Register* on November 18, 2011.

[*Code Sec. 2032*]

Estate tax: Gross estate: Alternate valuation.—The IRS has issued proposed regulations providing guidance regarding the alternate valuation election under Code Sec. 2032. These proposed regulations replace those issued on April 25, 2008 (NPRM REG-112196-07), which limited the use of the alternate value election to reductions due to "market conditions." Under the proposed regulations, a change in the percentage of ownership or control in an entity includible in a decedent's gross estate is irrelevant when determining the value of the decedent's interest on the alternate valuation date. Several other new rules for determining the value of interests on the alternate valuation date were added under Proposed Reg. § 20.2032-1(c)(1)(iv) and Proposed Reg. § 20.2032-1(c)(iii)(B). Proposed Reg. § 20.2032-1(c)(1)(ii) and Proposed Reg. § 20.2032-1(c)(1)(iii)(A), which provide exceptions to the general rule under Reg. § 20.2032-1(c)(1) were also added. Amended rules under Proposed Reg. § 20.2032-1(c)(2) and Proposed Reg. § 20.2032-1(c)(3) clarify when property is deemed to be disposed of for purposes of Code Sec. 2032 and the person or entity that will be treated as disposing of the property. Examples for the amended rules of Proposed Reg. § 20.2032-1(c) are provided under Proposed Reg. § 20.2032-1(c)(5). Finally, the proposed regulations revise Proposed Reg. § 20.2032-1(f) to clarify the factors that impact the fair market of the property and the effect of which will be recognized under Code Sec. 2032. Generally, the proposed regulations are applicable to the estates of decedents dying after the date that they are published as final in the Federal Register.

AGENCY: Internal Revenue Service (IRS), Treasury.

ACTION: Notice of proposed rulemaking and notice of public hearing.

SUMMARY: This document contains proposed regulations that provide guidance respecting the election to use the alternate valuation method under section 2032 of the Internal Revenue Code (Code). The proposed regulations will affect estates that file Form 706, United States Estate (and Generation-Skipping Transfer) Tax Return and elect to use the alternate valuation method. This document also provides notice of a public hearing on these proposed regulations.

DATES: Written or electronic comments must be received by February 16, 2012. Outlines of topics to be discussed at the public hearing scheduled for March 9, 2012, at 10:00 a.m. must be received by February 17, 2012.

ADDRESSES: Send submissions to: CC:PA:LPD:PR (REG-112196-07), Internal Revenue Service, Room 5203, PO Box 7604, Ben Franklin Station, Washington, DC 20044. Submissions may be hand delivered Monday through Friday between the hours of 8 a.m. and 4 p.m. to CC:PA:LPD:PR (REG-112196-07), Courier's Desk, Internal Revenue Service, 1111 Constitution Avenue NW., Washington, DC 20224; or sent electronically via the Federal eRulemaking Portal at *http:// www.regulations.gov* (IRSREG-112196-07). The public hearing will be held in the Auditorium, beginning at 10 a.m., at the Internal Revenue Building, 1111 Constitution Avenue NW, Washington, DC.

FOR FURTHER INFORMATION CONTACT: Concerning the proposed regulations, Theresa M. Melchiorre, (202) 622-3090; concerning submissions of comments, the hearing, and/or to be placed on the building access list to attend the hearing, Richard Hurst at *Richard.A.Hurst@irscounsel.treas.gov* or at (202) 622-7180 (not toll-free numbers).

SUPPLEMENTARY INFORMATION:

Background

Section 2001 imposes a tax on the transfer of the taxable estate of every decedent who is a citizen or resident of the United States. Section 2033 provides that the value of the gross estate includes the value of all property to the extent of the interest of the decedent at the time of his death. Section 2031(a) provides that the value of the decedent's gross estate includes the value at the time of the decedent's death of all property, real or personal, tangible or intangible, wherever situated. Section 2032(a) provides that the value of the gross estate may be determined, if the executor so elects, by valuing all the property includible in the gross estate as follows. Property distributed, sold, exchanged, or otherwise disposed of during the 6-month period immediately after the date of death (alternate valuation period) is valued as of the date of distribution, sale, exchange, or other disposition (transaction date). I.R.C. section 2032(a)(1). Property not distributed, sold, exchanged, or otherwise disposed of during the alternate valuation period is valued as of the date that is 6 months after the decedent's death (6-month date). I.R.C. section 2032(a)(2). Any interest or estate that is affected by the mere lapse of time is includible at its value as of the date of death (instead of any later date), with adjustment for any difference in its value as of the later date that is not due to the mere lapse of time. I.R.C. section 2032(a)(3).

Section 2031(c) was enacted by the Taxpayer Relief Act of 1997, 105 Public Law 34 section 508(a), 111 Stat. 788 (August 5, 1997). Pursuant to this section, a decedent's estate may elect to exclude from the gross estate a portion of the fair market value of property includible in the decedent's gross estate by granting a qualified conservation easement on that property after the date of the decedent's death but on or before the due date (including extensions) for filing the Form 706, United States Estate (and Generation-Skipping Transfer) Tax Return.

On April 25, 2008, a notice of proposed rulemaking (Reg-112196-07) relating to amendments to the Estate Tax Regulations (26 CFR part 20) under section 2032 of the Code was published in the **Federal Register** (73 FR 22300). Those regulations (73 FR 22300) proposed to clarify that the election to use the alternate valuation method under section 2032 is available to estates that experience a reduction in the value of the gross estate during the alternate valuation period, but only to the extent that the reduction in value is due to market conditions and not to other post-death events (events occurring during the alternate valuation period). The term "market conditions" was defined as events outside of the control of the decedent (or the decedent's executor or trustee) or other person whose property is being valued that affect the fair market value of the property includible in the decedent's gross estate. Changes in value due to mere lapse of time or to other post-death events would be ignored in determining the value of the decedent's gross estate under the alternate valuation method.

No hearing was held because no person or organization requested to speak at a hearing. However, written comments were received. Some commentators expressed concern that the proposed regulations (73 FR 22300) would create administrative problems because an estate would be required to trace property and to obtain appraisals based on hypothetical property. Some commentators stated that the current and the proposed regulations (73 FR 22300) did not adequately address the application of section 2032 to certain types of property, such as property the title to which passes at death due to contract, and to transactions carried out during the alternate valuation period between an estate and partnerships, corporations, or other entities. For example, § 20.2032-1(c)(1) does not address the consequences of the estate contributing property to a partnership during the alternate valuation period.

In addition, commentators requested guidance on the effect of a section 2032 election in calculating the portion of a trust includible in the decedent's gross estate under section 2036. This would arise in the situation where the decedent had retained the right to an annuity, unitrust, or other payment from the trust for life, for any period not ascertainable without reference to the grantor's death, or for a period that does not in fact end before the grantor's death. Further, some commentators requested guidance on the treatment of the grant, during the alternate valuation period, of a qualified conservation easement under section 2031(c).

Many commentators acknowledged that estates may enter into a transaction during the alternate valuation period that could result in the abuse of the section 2032 election. They suggested that the IRS and Treasury Department would better serve taxpayers and address any potential abuse by ensuring that the regulations address the issues described in this preamble rather than finalizing the approach taken in the proposed regulations.

In view of the comments, the Treasury Department and the IRS are withdrawing the proposed regulations (73 FR 22300) by the publication of these proposed regulations in the **Federal Register**. Nevertheless, see the background section of those proposed regulations (73 FR 22300) for a summary of the legislative history of section 2032 and the purpose for issuing these proposed regulations.

This document contains revised proposed amendments to the regulations promulgated under section 2032. These proposed regulations make irrelevant, for purposes of determining the value of property as of the transaction date or the 6-month date, whichever is applicable (alternate valuation date), the percentage of ownership or control in an entity includible in the gross estate and the extent of participation by the estate (or other holder of property includible in the gross estate) in the relevant postdeath events.

Certain provisions in the current regulations that have been in effect since 1954 are restated in the proposed regulations for purposes of clarity. The effective date of those provisions is not changed.

Explanation of Provisions

These regulations propose to amend several sections of § 20.2032-1. Generally, paragraph (c)(1)(i) identifies transactions that constitute distributions, sales, exchanges, or dispositions of property. If an estate's (or other holder's) property is subject to such a transaction during the alternate valuation period, the estate must value that property on the transaction date. The value included in the gross estate is the fair market value of that property on the date of and immediately prior to the transaction. The term "property" refers to the property includible in the decedent's gross estate under section 2033.

Sections 20.2032-1(c)(1)(ii) and (c)(1)(iii)(A) identify two exceptions to the rule in § 20.2032-1(c)(1)(i). If either exception applies, the estate may use the 6-month date and value the property held on that date. The exception in § 20.2032-1(c)(1)(ii) applies only to transactions in which an interest in a corporation, partnership, or other entity (entity) includible in the decedent's gross estate is exchanged for one or more different interests (for example, a different class of stock) in the same entity or in an acquiring or resulting entity or entities during the alternate valuation period. Such transactions may include, without limitation, reorganizations, recapitalizations, mergers, or similar transactions. This exception substitutes a fair market value test for

the corporate provisions in the current regulations. Specifically, this paragraph proposes that, if, during the alternate valuation period, the interest in an entity includible in the gross estate is exchanged for a different interest in the same entity, or in an acquiring or resulting entity or entities, and if the fair market value of the interest on the date of the exchange equals the fair market value of the property for which it was exchanged, then the transaction will not be treated as an exchange for purposes of section 2032(a)(1). As a result, the estate may use the 6-month date to value the interest in the same entity or in the acquiring or resulting entity or entities received in the exchange. For this purpose, the fair market values of the surrendered property and received interest are deemed to be equal if the difference between the fair market values of the surrendered property and the received interest does not exceed 5 percent of the fair market value of the surrendered property as of the transaction date. This section has no effect on any other provision of the Code that is applicable to the transaction. For example, the provisions of chapter 14 may apply even if the transaction does not result in a deemed exchange for section 2032 purposes as a result of satisfying the provisions of § 20.2032-1(c)(1)(ii).

Section 20.2032-1(c)(1)(iii)(A) proposes that, if, during the alternate valuation period, an estate (or other holder) receives a distribution from a business entity, bank account, or retirement trust (entity) and an interest in that entity is includible in the decedent's gross estate, the estate may use the 6-month date to value the property held in the estate if the following requirement is satisfied. The fair market value of the interest in the entity includible in the gross estate immediately before the distribution must equal the sum of the fair market value of the distributed property on the date of the distribution and the fair market value of the interest in the entity includible in the gross estate immediately after the distribution. If this requirement is not satisfied, the estate must use the fair market value as of the distribution date and immediately prior to the distribution of the entire interest in the entity includible in the gross estate. For purposes of this section, any distribution is deemed to consist first of excluded property (as defined in § 20.2032-1(d)), if any, and then of included property.

Section 20.2032-1(c)(1)(iv) proposes an aggregation rule to use in calculating the fair market value of each portion of property that is, or is deemed to be distributed, sold, exchanged, or otherwise disposed of during the alternate valuation period, and that remains in the gross estate on the 6-month date.

Section 20.2032-1(c)(1)(iii)(B) provides a special rule to use in determining the portion of a trust includible, by reason of a retained interest, in the decedent's gross estate under section 2036 as of the alternate valuation date. An example is added to § 20.2032-1(e) to illustrate this special rule and the effect of the provisions of § 20.2032-1(d) and § 20.2032-1(f)(2)(i) on this calculation.

Section 20.2032-1(c)(2) is amended to clarify when property, the title to which passes by contract or by operation of law, is deemed to be distributed, sold, exchanged, or otherwise disposed of for section 2032 purposes. Section 20.2032-1(c)(3) is amended to clarify the person or entity that will be treated as having sold, exchanged, or otherwise disposed of the property for section 2032 purposes.

Section 20.2032-1(c)(4) is added to provide that if Congress, by statute, has deemed that a post-death event has occurred on the decedent's date of death, the postdeath event will not result in a distribution, sale, exchange, or other disposition of the property for section 2032 purposes. To date, the only post-death event that satisfies this exception is the grant, during the alternate valuation period, of a conservation easement in accordance with section 2031(c). With respect to such a grant, for section 2032 purposes, the estate must determine the fair market value of the property as of the date of death and as of the alternate valuation date, taking into account the effect of the easement on each of those valuation dates.

Section 20.2032-1(c)(5) provides examples, not intended to be exclusive, illustrating the provisions of § 20.2032-1(c).

Section 20.2032-1(f) is revised to clarify the types of factors that impact the fair market value of property and the effect of which will be recognized under section 2032. This paragraph also explains and illustrates these rules.

Proposed Effective/Applicability Date

Section 20.2032-1(c)(2) except the second sentence of the introductory text, § 20.2032-1(c)(3) except § 20.2032-1(c)(3)(i)(C), the chart in *Example 1* of § 20.2032-1(e), § 20.2032-1(f)(2) except the last sentence, and the first and third sentences in § 20.2032-1(f)(2)(ii) are applicable to decedents dying after August 16, 1954. Sections 20.2032-1(a) introductory text, 20.2032-1(a)(1), 20.2032-1(a)(2), 20.2032-1(c)(1)(i), (c)(1)(ii), (c)(1)(iii), (c)(1)(iv), (c)(3)(i)(C), (c)(4), (c)(5), (f)(1), (f)(2)(i), and (f)(3), the second sentence in § 20.2032-1(c)(2) introductory text, § 20.2032-1(e) except the chart in Example 1, the last sentence in § 20.2032-1(f)(2) introductory text, and the second sentence in § 20.2032-1(f)(2)(ii) are applicable to estates of decedents dying on or after the date of publication of the Treasury decision adopting these rules as final in the **Federal Register**.

Special Analyses

It has been determined that this proposed regulation is not a significant regulatory action as defined in Executive Order 12866, as supplemented by Executive Order 13563. Therefore, a regulatory assessment is not required. It also has been determined that section 553(b) of the Administrative Procedure Act (5 U.S.C. chapter 5) does not apply to these regulations and, because these regulations do not impose on small entities a collection of information requirement, the Regulatory Flexibility Act (5 U.S.C. chapter 6) does not apply. Therefore, a Regulatory Flexibility Analysis is not required. Pursuant to section 7805(f) of the Internal Revenue Code, this regulation has been submitted to the Chief Counsel for Advocacy of the Small Business Administration for comment on its impact on small business.

Comments and Public Hearing

Before these proposed regulations are adopted as final regulations, consideration will be given to any written (a signed original and eight (8) copies) or electronic comments that are submitted timely to the IRS. The IRS and Treasury Department also request comments on the clarity of the proposed rules and how they can be made easier to understand. All comments will be available for public inspection and copying.

A public hearing has been scheduled for March 9, 2012 at 10:00 a.m. in Auditorium, Internal Revenue Building. Due to building security procedures, visitors must use the main building entrance 1111 Constitution Avenue NW, Washington, DC. In addition, all visitors must present photo identification to enter the building. Because of access restrictions, visitors will not be admitted beyond the immediate entrance area more than 30 minutes before the hearing starts. For more information about having your name placed on the list to attend the hearing, see the "FOR FURTHER INFORMATION CONTACT" section of this preamble.

The rules of 26 CFR 601.601(a)(3) apply to the hearing. Persons who wish to present oral comments at the hearing must submit written (a signed original and eight (8) copies) or electronic comments by February 16, 2012, and an outline of the topics to be discussed and the time to be devoted to each topic by February 17, 2012. A period of 10 minutes will be allotted to each person for making comments. An agenda showing the scheduling of the speakers will be prepared after the deadline for receiving outlines has passed. Copies of the agenda will be available free of charge at the hearing.

Drafting Information

The principal author of these proposed regulations is Theresa M. Melchiorre, Office of Associate Chief Counsel (Passthroughs and Special Industries).

[¶ 61,157] Proposed Regulations (REG-102837-15), published in the *Federal Register* on June 22, 2015.

[Code Secs. 2501, 2503, 2511, 2642, and 2652]

Estate, gift, generation-skipping transfer and income taxes: Taxable gifts: Transfer to ABLE accounts: Proposed regulations.—The IRS has proposed regulations that provide guidance regarding programs under the Stephen Beck, Jr., Achieving a Better Life Experience Act of 2014 (ABLE Act), which was enacted as part of the Tax Increase Prevention Act of 2014 (P.L. 113-295). The proposed regulations provide guidance on the requirements a program must satisfy in order to be a qualified ABLE program. The proposed regulations provide that any contribution by a designated beneficiary to a qualified ABLE program benefitting the designated beneficiary is not treated as a completed gift. The proposed regulations provide that any contribution by a designated beneficiary to a qualified ABLE program benefitting the designated beneficiary is not treated as a completed gift. The proposed regulations provide that contributions to an ABLE account by a person other than the designated beneficiary are treated as completed gifts to the designated beneficiary of the account, and that such gifts are neither gifts of a future interest nor a qualified transfer under Code Sec. 2503(e). Accordingly, no distribution from an ABLE account to the designated beneficiary of that account is treated as a taxable gift. Neither gift nor generation-skipping transfer (GST) tax apply to the change of a designated beneficiary of an ABLE account, as long as the new designated beneficiary is an eligible individual who is a sibling of the former designated beneficiary. The proposed regulations provide that, upon the death of the designated beneficiary, all amounts remaining in the ABLE account are includible in the designated beneficiary's gross estate for purposes of the estate tax and clarify other estate and generation-skipping tax related issues. Until the issuance of final regulations, taxpayers and qualified ABLE programs may rely on the proposed regulations.**

AGENCY: Internal Revenue Service (IRS), Treasury.

ACTION: Notice of proposed rulemaking and notice of public hearing.

SUMMARY: This document contains proposed regulations under section 529A of the Internal Revenue Code that provide guidance regarding programs under The Stephen Beck, Jr., Achieving a Better Life Experience Act of 2014. Section 529A provides rules under which States or State agencies or instrumentalities may establish and maintain a new type of tax-favored savings program through which contributions may be made to the account of an eligible disabled individual to meet qualified disability expenses. These accounts also receive favorable treatment for purposes of certain means-tested Federal programs. In addition, these proposed regulations provide corresponding amendments to regulations under sections 511 and 513, with respect to unrelated business taxable income, sections 2501, 2503, 2511, 2642 and 2652, with respect to gift and generation-skipping transfer taxes, and section 6011, with respect to reporting requirements. This document also provides notice of a public hearing on these proposed regulations.

DATES: Comments must be received by September 21, 2015. Outlines of topics to be discussed at the public hearing scheduled for October 14, 2015, at 10 am, must be received by September 21, 2015.

ADDRESSES: Send submissions to: CC:PA:LPD:PR (REG-102837-15), room 5203, Internal Revenue Service, PO Box 7604, Ben Franklin Station, Washington DC 20044. Submissions may be hand delivered Monday through Friday between the hours of 8 a.m. and 4 p.m. to CC:PA:LPD:PR (REG-102837-15), Courier's Desk, Internal Revenue Service, 1111 Constitution Avenue NW, Washington, DC, or sent electronically via the Federal eRulemaking Portal at *http://www.regulations.gov* (IRS REG-102837-15). The public hearing will be held in the Auditorium, Internal Revenue Building, 1111 Constitution Avenue, NW, Washington, DC.

FOR FURTHER INFORMATION CONTACT: Concerning the proposed regulations under section 529A, Taina Edlund or Terri Harris, (202) 317-4541, or Sean Barnett, (202) 317-5800; concerning the proposed estate and gift tax regulations, Theresa Melchiorre, (202) 317-4643; concerning the reporting provisions under section 529A, Mark Bond, (202) 317-6844; concerning submissions of comments, the hearing, and/or to be placed on the building access list to attend the hearing, call Regina Johnson, (202) 317-6901 (not toll-free numbers).

SUPPLEMENTARY INFORMATION:

Paperwork Reduction Act

The collection of information contained in this notice of proposed rulemaking has been submitted to the Office of Management and Budget for review and approval in accordance with the Paperwork Reduction Act of 1995 (44 U.S.C. 3507(d)). Comments on the collection of information should be sent to the **Office of Management and Budget**, Attn: Desk Officer for the Department of the Treasury, Office of Information and Regulatory Affairs, Washington, DC 20503, with copies to the **Internal Revenue Service**, Attn: IRS Reports Clearance Officer, SE:W:CAR:MP:T:T:SP, Washington, DC 20224. Comments on the collection of information should be received by August 18, 2015.

Comments are specifically requested concerning:

Whether the proposed collection of information is necessary for the proper performance of the functions of the Internal Revenue Service, including whether the information will have practical utility;

The accuracy of the estimated burden associated with the proposed collection of information;

How the quality, utility, and clarity of the information to be collected may be enhanced;

How the burden of complying with the proposed collection of information may be minimized, including through forms of information technology; and

Estimates of capital or start-up costs and costs of operation, maintenance, and purchase of services to provide information.

The collection of information in the proposed regulations is in §§1.529A-2, 1.529A-5, 1.529A-6 and 1.529A-7. The collection of information flows from sections 529A(d)(1), (d)(2), (d)(3), (e)(1) and (e)(2) of the Internal Revenue Code (Code). Section 529A(d)(1) requires qualified ABLE programs to provide reports to the Secretary and to designated beneficiaries with respect to contributions, distributions, the return of excess contributions, and such other matters as the Secretary may require. Section 529(d)(2) provides that the Secretary shall make available to the public reports containing aggregate information, by diagnosis and other relevant characteristics, on contributions and distributions from the qualified ABLE program. Section 529(d)(3) requires qualified ABLE programs to provide notice to the Secretary upon the establishment of an ABLE account, containing the name and State of residence of the designated beneficiary and such other information as the Secretary may require. Section 529A(e)(1) requires that a disability certification with respect to certain individuals be filed with the Secretary. Section 529A(e)(2) provides that the disability certification include a certification to the satisfaction of the Secretary that the individual has a medically determinable physical or mental impairment that occurred before the date on which the individual attained age 26 and also include a copy of a physician's diagnosis. The burden under §§1.529A-5 and 1.529A-6 is reflected in the burden under the new Form 5498-QA, "ABLE Account Contribution Information," and the new Form 1099-QA, "Distributions from ABLE Accounts," respectively.

The expected recordkeepers are programs described in section 529A, established and maintained by a State or a State agency or instrumentality and individuals with ABLE accounts.

Estimated number of recordkeepers: 10,050.

Estimated average annual burden hours per recordkeeper: 1.6 hours.

Estimated total annual recordkeeping burden: 16,080.

An agency may not conduct or sponsor, and a person is not required to respond to, a collection of information unless it displays a valid control number assigned by the Office of Management and Budget.

Books or records relating to a collection of information must be retained as long as their contents may become material in the administration of any internal revenue law. Generally, tax returns and return information are confidential, as required by 26 U.S.C. 6103.

Background

The Stephen Beck, Jr., Achieving a Better Life Experience (ABLE) Act of 2014, enacted on December 19, 2014, as part of The Tax Increase Prevention Act of 2014 (Public Law 113-295), added section 529A to the Internal Revenue Code. Congress recognized the special financial burdens borne by families raising children with disabilities and the fact that increased financial needs generally continue throughout the disabled person's lifetime. Section 101 of the ABLE Act confirms that one of the purposes of the Act is to "provide secure funding for disability-related expenses on behalf of designated beneficiaries with disabilities that will supplement, but not supplant, benefits" otherwise available to those individuals, whether through private sources, employment, public programs, or otherwise. Prior to the enactment of the ABLE Act, various types of tax-advantaged savings arrangements existed, but none adequately served the goal of promoting saving for these financial needs. Section 529A allows the creation of a qualified ABLE program by a State (or agency or instrumentality thereof) under which a separate ABLE account may be established for a disabled individual who is the designated beneficiary and owner of that account. Generally, contributions to that account are subject to both an annual and a cumulative limit, and, when made by a person other than the designated beneficiary, are treated as non-taxable gifts to the designated beneficiary. Distributions made from an ABLE account for qualified disability expenses of the designated beneficiary are not included in the designated beneficiary's gross income. The earnings portion of distributions from the ABLE account in excess of the qualified disability expenses is includible in the gross income of the designated beneficiary. An ABLE account may be used for the long-term benefit and/or short-term needs of the designated beneficiary.

Section 103 of the ABLE Act, while not a tax provision, is critical to achieving the goal of the ABLE Act of providing financial resources for the benefit of disabled individuals. Because so many of the programs that provide essential financial, occupational, and other resources and services to disabled individuals are available only to persons whose resources and income do not exceed relatively low dollar limits, section 103 generally provides that a designated beneficiary's ABLE account (specifically, its account balance, contributions to the account, and distributions from the account) is disregarded for purposes of determining the designated beneficiary's eligibility for and the amount of any assistance or benefit provided under certain means-tested Federal programs. However, in the case of the Supplemental Security Income program under title XVI of the Social Security Act, distributions for certain housing expenses are not disregarded, and the balance (including earnings) in an ABLE account is considered a resource of the designated beneficiary to the extent that balance exceeds $100,000. Section 103 also addresses the impact of an excess balance in an ABLE account on the designated beneficiary's eligibility under the Supplemental Security Income program and Medicaid.

Finally, section 104 of the ABLE Act addresses the treatment of ABLE accounts in bankruptcy proceedings.

Notice 2015-18, 2015-12 IRB 765 (March 23, 2015), provides that the section 529A guidance will confirm that the owner of the ABLE account is the designated beneficiary of the account, and that the person with signature authority over (if not the designated beneficiary of) the account may neither have nor acquire any beneficial interest in the ABLE account and must administer that account for the benefit of the designated beneficiary of that account. The Notice further provides that, in the event that state legislation creating ABLE programs enacted in accordance with section 529A prior to issuance of guidance does not fully comport with the guidance when issued, the Treasury Department and the IRS intend to provide transition relief to provide sufficient time to allow States to implement the changes necessary to avoid the disqualification of the program and of the ABLE accounts already established under the program.

The Treasury Department and the IRS reiterate that States that enact legislation creating an ABLE program in accordance with section 529A, and those individuals establishing ABLE accounts in accordance with such legislation, will not fail to receive the benefits of section 529A merely because the legislation or the account documents do not fully comport with the final regulations when they are issued. The Treasury Department and the IRS intend to provide transition relief to enable those State programs and accounts to be brought into compliance with the requirements in the final regulations, including providing sufficient time after issuance of the final regulations in order for changes to be implemented.

Explanation of Provisions

Qualification as an ABLE program

The proposed regulations provide guidance on the requirements a program must satisfy in order to be a qualified ABLE program described in section 529A. Specifically, in addition to other requirements, the program must: be established and maintained by a State or a State's agency or instrumentality; permit the establishment of an ABLE account only for a designated beneficiary who is a resident of that State, or a State contracting with that State for purposes of the ABLE program; permit the establishment of an ABLE account only for a designated beneficiary who is an eligible individual; limit a designated beneficiary to only one ABLE account, wherever located; permit contributions to an ABLE account established to meet the qualified disability expenses of the account's designated beneficiary; limit the nature and amount of contributions that can be made to an ABLE account; require a separate accounting for the ABLE account of each designated beneficiary with an ABLE account in the program; limit the designated beneficiary to no more than two opportunities in any calendar year to provide investment direction, whether directly or indirectly, for the ABLE account; and prohibit the pledging of an interest in an ABLE account as security for a loan.

Because each qualified ABLE program will have significant administrative obligations beyond what is required for the administration of qualified tuition programs under section 529 (on which section 529A was loosely modeled), and because the frequency of distributions from the ABLE accounts is likely to be far greater than those made from qualified tuition accounts, the proposed regulations expressly allow a qualified ABLE program or any of its contractors to contract with one or more Community Development Financial Institutions (CDFIs) that commonly serve disabled individuals and their families to provide one or more required services. For example, a CDFI could provide screening and verification of disabilities, certification of the qualified purpose of distributions, debit card services to facilitate distributions, and social data collection and reporting. A CDFI also may be able to obtain grants to defray the cost of administering the program. In general, if certified by the Treasury Department, a CDFI may receive a financial assistance award from the CDFI Fund that was established within the Treasury Department in 1994 to promote community development in economically distressed communities through investments in CDFIs across the country.

Established and maintained

The proposed regulations provide that a program is established by a State, or its agency or instrumentality, if the program is initiated by State statute or regulation, or by an act of a State official or agency with the authority to act on behalf of the State. A program is maintained by a State or its agency or instrumentality if: all the terms and conditions of the program are set by the State or its agency or instrumentality, and the State or its agency or instrumentality is actively involved on an ongoing basis in the administration of the program, including supervising all decisions relating to the investment of assets contributed to the program. The proposed regulations set forth factors that are relevant in determining whether a State, or its agency or instrumentality, is actively involved in the administration of the program. Included in the factors is the manner and extent to which it is permissible for the program to contract out for professional and financial services.

Establishment of an ABLE account

The proposed regulations provide that, consistent with the definition of a designated beneficiary in section 529A(e)(3), the designated beneficiary of an ABLE account is the eligible individual who establishes the account or an eligible individual who succeeded the original designated beneficiary. The proposed regulations also provide that the designated beneficiary is the owner of that account.

The Treasury Department and the IRS recognize, however, that certain eligible individuals may be unable to establish an account themselves. Therefore, the proposed regulations clarify that, if the eligible individual cannot establish the account, the eligible individual's agent under a power of attorney or, if none, his or her parent or legal guardian may establish the ABLE account for that eligible individual. For purposes of these proposed regulations, because each of these individuals would be acting on behalf of the designated beneficiary, references to actions of the designated beneficiary, such as opening or managing the ABLE account, are deemed to include the actions of any other such individual with signature authority over the ABLE account. The proposed regulations also provide that, consistent with Notice 2015-18, a person other than the designated beneficiary with signature authority over the account of the designated beneficiary may neither have, nor acquire, any beneficial interest in the account during the designated beneficiary's lifetime and must administer the account for the benefit of the designated beneficiary.

At the time an ABLE account is created for a designated beneficiary, the designated beneficiary must provide evidence that the designated beneficiary is an eligible individual as defined in section 529A(e)(1). Section 529A(e)(1) provides that an individual is an eligible individual for a taxable year if, during that year, either the individual is entitled to benefits based on blindness or disability under title II or XVI of the Social Security Act and the blindness or disability occurred before the date on which the individual attained age 26, or a disability certification meeting specified requirements is filed with the Secretary. If an individual is asserting he or she is entitled to benefits based on blindness or disability under title II or XVI of the Social Security Act and the blindness or disability occurred before the date on which the individual attained age 26, the proposed regulations provide that each qualified ABLE program may determine the evidence required to establish the individual's eligibility. For example, a qualified ABLE program could require the individual to provide a copy of a benefit verification letter from the Social Security Administration and allow the individual to certify, under penalties of perjury, that the blindness or disability occurred before the date on which the individual attained age 26.

Alternatively, the designated beneficiary must submit the disability certification when opening the ABLE account. Consistent with section 529A(e)(2), the proposed regulations provide that a disability certification is a certification by the designated beneficiary that he or she: (1) has a medically determinable physical or mental impairment, which results in marked or severe functional limitations, and which (i) can be expected to result in death or (ii) has lasted or can be expected to last for a continuous period of not less than 12 months; or (2) is blind (within the meaning of section 1614(a)(2) of the Social Security Act) and that such blindness or disability occurred before the date on which the individual attained age 26. The certification must include a copy of the individual's diagnosis relating to the individual's relevant impairment or impairments, signed by a li-

censed physician (as defined in section 1861(r) of the Social Security Act, 42 U.S.C. 1395x(r)). Consistent with other IRS filing requirements, the proposed regulations also provide that the certification must be signed under penalties of perjury.

While evidence of an individual's eligibility based on entitlement to Social Security benefits should be objectively verifiable, the sufficiency of a disability certification that an individual is an eligible individual for purposes of section 529A might not be as easy to establish. Nevertheless, the Treasury Department and the IRS wish to facilitate an eligible individual's ability to establish an ABLE account without undue delay. Therefore, the proposed regulations provide that an eligible individual must present the disability certification, accompanied by the diagnosis, to the qualified ABLE program to demonstrate eligibility to establish an ABLE account. The proposed regulations further provide that the disability certification will be deemed to be filed with the Secretary once the qualified ABLE program has received the disability certification or a disability certification has been deemed to have been received under the rules of the qualified ABLE program, which information the qualified ABLE program, as discussed further below, will file with the IRS in accordance with the filing requirements under § 1.529A-5(c)(2)(iv).

Disability determination

Consistent with section 529A(g)(4), the Treasury Department and the IRS have consulted with the Commissioner of Social Security regarding disability certifications and determinations of disability. For purposes of the disability certification, the proposed regulations provide that the phrase "marked and severe functional limitations" means the standard of disability in the Social Security Act for children claiming benefits under the Supplemental Security Income for the Aged, Blind, and Disabled (SSI) program based on disability, but without regard to the age of the individual. This phrase refers to a level of severity of an impairment that meets, medically equals, or functionally equals the listings in the Listing of Impairments (the listings) in appendix 1 of subpart P of 20 CFR part 404. (*See* 20 CFR 416.906, 416.924 and 416.926a). This listing developed and used by the Social Security Administration describes for each of the major body systems impairments that cause marked and severe functional limitations. Most body system sections are in two parts: an introduction, followed by the specific listings. The introduction contains information relevant to the use of the listings with respect to that body system, such as examples of common impairments in the body system and definitions used in the listings for that body system. The introduction may also include specific criteria for establishing a diagnosis, confirming the existence of an impairment, or establishing that an impairment satisfies the criteria of a particular listing with respect to the body system. The specific listings that follow the introduction for each body system specify the objective medical and other findings needed to satisfy the criteria of that listing. Most of the listed impairments are permanent or expected to result in death, although some listings state a specific period of time for which an impairment will meet the listing.

An impairment is medically equivalent to a listing if it is at least equal in severity and duration to the severity and duration of any listing. An impairment that does not meet or medically equal any listing may result in limitations that functionally equal the listings if it results in marked limitations in two domains of functioning or an extreme limitation in one domain of functioning, as explained in 20 CFR 416.926a. In addition, the proposed regulations provide that certain conditions, specifically those listed in the Compassionate Allowances Conditions list maintained by the Social Security Administration, are deemed to meet the requirements of an impairment sufficient for a disability certification without a physician's diagnosis, provided that the condition was present before the date on which the individual attained age 26. The proposed regulations also provide the flexibility from time to time to identify additional impairments that will be deemed to meet these requirements. The Treasury Department and the IRS request comments on what other conditions should be deemed to meet the requirements of section 529A(e)(2)(A)(i).

Change in eligible individual status

The Treasury Department and the IRS recognize that there may be circumstances in which a designated beneficiary ceases to be an eligible individual but subsequently regains that status. Consequently, the Treasury Department and the IRS believe that it is appropriate to permit continuation of the ABLE account (albeit with some changes in the applicable rules) during the period in which a designated beneficiary is not an eligible individual as long as the designated beneficiary was an eligible individual when the account was established. Therefore, if at any time a designated beneficiary no longer meets the definition of an eligible individual, his or her ABLE account remains an ABLE account to which all of the provisions of the ABLE Act continue to apply, and no (taxable) distribution of the account balance is deemed to occur. However, the proposed regulations provide that, beginning on the first day of the taxable year following the taxable year in which the designated beneficiary ceased to be an eligible individual, no contributions to the ABLE account may be accepted. If the designated beneficiary subsequently again becomes an eligible individual, then additional contributions may be accepted subject to the applicable annual and cumulative limits. In this way, the Treasury Department and the IRS intend to prevent a deemed distribution of the ABLE account (and preserve the account's qualification as an ABLE account for all purposes) if, for example, the disease that caused the impairment goes into a temporary remission, and to preserve the ABLE account with its tax-free distributions for qualified disability expenses if the impairment resumes and once again qualifies the designated beneficiary as an eligible individual. Note that expenses will not be qualified disability expenses if they are incurred at a time when a designated beneficiary is neither disabled nor blind within the meaning of §1.529A-1(b)(9)(A) or §1.529A-2(e)(1)(i).

The proposed regulations provide flexibility regarding annual recertifications. A qualified ABLE program generally must require annual recertifications that the designated beneficiary continues to satisfy the definition of an eligible individual. However, a qualified ABLE program may deem an annual recertification to have been provided in appropriate circumstances. For example, a qualified ABLE program may permit certification by an individual that he or she has a permanent disability to be considered to meet the annual requirement to present a certification to the qualified ABLE program. In other cases, a program may require all of the same evidence needed for the initial disability certification of when the account was established, may require a statement under penalties of perjury that nothing has changed that would change the original disability certification, or may incorporate some other method of ensuring that the designated beneficiary continuously qualifies as an eligible individual. Alternatively, a qualified ABLE program may identify certain impairments or categories of impairments for which recertifications will be deemed to have been made annually to the qualified ABLE program unless and until the qualified ABLE program provides otherwise (for example, if a cure is discovered for a disease that causes an impairment). An initial certification or recertification that meets the requirements of the qualified ABLE program will be deemed to have met the requirement of section 529A(e)(1)(B). The Treasury Department and the IRS request comments regarding how a qualified ABLE program will be able to demonstrate eligibility in subsequent years if it allows deemed recertifications.

Contributions to an ABLE account

The proposed regulations provide that, as a general rule, all contributions to an ABLE account must be made in cash. The proposed regulations provide that a qualified ABLE program may accept cash contributions in the form of a check, money order, credit card payment, or other similar method of payment. In addition, the proposed regulations provide that the total contributions to an ABLE account in the designated beneficiary's taxable year, other than amounts received in rollovers and program-to-program transfers, must not exceed the amount of the annual per-donee gift tax exclusion under section 2503(b) in effect for that calendar year (currently $14,000) in which the designated beneficiary's taxable year begins. Finally, a qualified ABLE program must provide adequate safeguards to ensure that total contributions to an ABLE account (including the proceeds from a preexisting ABLE account) do not exceed that State's limit for aggregate contributions under its qualified tuition program.

To implement these requirements, the proposed regulations provide that a qualified ABLE program must return contributions in excess of the annual gift tax exclusion (excess contributions) to the contributor(s), along with all net income attributable to those excess contributions. Similarly, the proposed regulations also require the return of all contributions, along with all net income attributable to those contributions, that caused an ABLE account to exceed the limit established by the State for its qualified tuition program (excess aggregate contributions). If an excess contribution or excess aggregate contribution is returned to a contributor other than the designated beneficiary, the qualified ABLE program must notify the designated beneficiary of such return at the time of the return. The proposed regulations further provide that such returns of excess contributions and excess aggregate contributions must be received by the contributor(s) on or before the due date (including extensions) of

the designated beneficiary's income tax return for the year in which the excess contributions were made or in the year the excess aggregate contributions caused amounts in the ABLE account to exceed the limit in effect under section 529A(b)(6), respectively. The proposed regulations provide rules for determining the net income attributable to a contribution made to an ABLE account, and also provide that these excess contributions and excess aggregate contributions must be returned to contributors on a last-in, first-out basis. In the case of contributions that exceed the annual gift tax exclusion, a failure to return such excess contributions within the time period discussed in this paragraph will result in the imposition on the designated beneficiary of a 6 percent excise tax under section 4973(a)(6) on the amount of excess contributions. As part of a planned revision of IRA regulations, the Treasury Department and the IRS intend to propose regulations under section 4973 to reflect that ABLE accounts are subject to section 4973.

Application of gift tax to contributions to an ABLE account

Gift tax consequences may arise from contributions to an ABLE account even though the aggregate amount of such contributions to an ABLE account from all contributors may not exceed the annual exclusion amount under section 2503(b) applicable to any single contributor. Specifically, if a contributor makes other gifts to a designated beneficiary in addition to the gift to the designated beneficiary's ABLE account, the contributor's total gifts made to the designated beneficiary in that year could give rise to a gift tax liability.

Contributions may be made by any person. The term *person* is defined in section 7701(a)(1) to include an individual, trust, estate, partnership, association, company, or corporation. Therefore, for purposes of section 529A(b)(1)(A), a person would include an individual and each of the entities described in section 7701(a)(1). Under section 2501(a)(1), the gift tax applies only to gifts by individuals, but it also applies to gifts made directly or indirectly. As a result, a gift made by a trust, estate, association, company, corporation, or partnership is treated as having been made by the owner(s) of that entity. For example, a gift from a corporation to a designated beneficiary is treated as a gift from the shareholders of the corporation to the designated beneficiary. *See Example (1)* of §25.2511-1(h). Accordingly, the proposed regulations provide that, for purposes of sections 529A(b)(1)(A) and 529A(c)(1)(C), a contribution by a corporation is treated as a gift by its shareholders and a contribution by a partnership is treated as a gift by its partners. This rule also applies to trusts, estates, associations, and companies. *See* section 2511 and §25.2511-1(c).

The legislative history of section 529A suggests that a "person" described in section 529A(b)(1)(A) includes the designated beneficiary of an ABLE account. *See* 160 CONG. REC. H7051, H8317, H8318, H8321, H8322 (2014). A person may transfer his or her property into an account, such as a bank account or a trust, for his or her benefit and retain dominion and control over the property transferred. Because an individual cannot make a transfer of property to himself or herself and a transfer of property is a fundamental requirement for a completed gift, this type of transfer from a person's own property cannot be treated as a completed gift for tax purposes. *See* §25.2511-2(b) and (c). Therefore, the proposed regulations provide that any contribution by a designated beneficiary to a qualified ABLE program benefitting the designated beneficiary is not treated as a completed gift. Because the designated beneficiary remains the owner of the account for purposes of chapter 12, if the designated beneficiary transfers the funds in the account to another person as permitted under these proposed regulations, the designated beneficiary making the transfer is the donor for purposes of chapter 12 and the transferor for generation-skipping transfer tax purposes of chapter 13.

Distributions

If distributions from an ABLE account do not exceed the designated beneficiary's qualified disability expenses, no amount is includible in the designated beneficiary's gross income. Otherwise, the earnings portion of the distributions from the ABLE account as determined in the manner provided under section 72, reduced by the product of such earnings portion and the ratio of the amount of the distributions for qualified disability expenses to total distributions, is includible in the gross income of the designated beneficiary to the extent not otherwise excluded from gross income. As required by section 529A(c)(1)(D), the proposed regulations provide that, for purposes of applying section 72 to amounts distributed from an ABLE account: (1) all distributions during a taxable year are treated as one distribution; and (2) the value of the contract, income on the contract, and investment in the contract are computed as of the close of the calendar year in which the designated beneficiary's taxable year begins.

The proposed regulations also provide that, in addition to the income tax on the portion of a distribution included in gross income, an additional tax of 10 percent of the amount includible in gross income is imposed. This additional tax does not apply, however, to distributions on or after the designated beneficiary's death or to returns of excess contributions, excess aggregate contributions, or contributions to additional purported ABLE accounts made by the due date (including extensions) of the designated beneficiary's tax return for the year in which the relevant contributions were made.

Section 529A(c)(1)(C) addresses the tax consequences of the rollover of an ABLE account to an ABLE account for the same designated beneficiary maintained under a different State's qualified ABLE program, as well as a change of designated beneficiary. The proposed regulations describe with respect to these two situations the circumstances in which amounts will not be includible in income. The first is any change of designated beneficiary if the new designated beneficiary is both (1) an eligible individual for his or her taxable year in which the change is made and (2) a sibling of the former designated beneficiary. For purposes of these proposed regulations, a sibling also includes step-siblings and half-siblings, whether by blood or by adoption. The proposed regulations provide that a qualified ABLE program must permit a change of designated beneficiary, as long as the change is made prior to the death of the former designated beneficiary and as long as the successor designated beneficiary is an eligible individual. Because the designated beneficiary will be subject to gift and/or generation-skipping transfer tax if the successor designated beneficiary is not a sibling of the designated beneficiary, the Treasury Department and the IRS request comments regarding whether the final regulations should permit States to require that a successor designated beneficiary also must be a sibling of the designated beneficiary.

The second situation in which a distribution is not included in gross income arises if a distribution to the designated beneficiary of the ABLE account is paid, not later than the 60th day after the date of the distribution, to another (or the same) ABLE account for the benefit of the designated beneficiary or for the benefit of an eligible individual who is a sibling of the designated beneficiary. However, the preceding sentence does not apply to such a distribution that occurs within 12 months of a previous rollover to another ABLE account for the same designated beneficiary.

The Treasury Department and the IRS have been asked whether a qualified tuition account under section 529 may be rolled into an ABLE account for the same designated beneficiary free of tax. Because such a distribution to the ABLE account would not constitute a qualified higher education expense under section 529, the Treasury Department and the IRS do not believe they have the authority to allow such a transfer on a tax-free basis.

In addition, the proposed regulations authorize a qualified ABLE program to allow program-to-program transfers to effectuate a change of qualified ABLE program or a change of designated beneficiary to another eligible individual. Such a direct transfer is neither a distribution taxed in accordance with section 72 nor an excess contribution. A program-to-program transfer also could be accomplished, if permitted by the qualified ABLE program, through a check delivered to the designated beneficiary but negotiable only by the qualified State program under which the new ABLE account is being established.

The Treasury Department and the IRS recognize that moving funds by use of a program-to-program transfer may be preferable to moving them by a rollover because a rollover, even if made within the permissible 60-day period, may jeopardize the designated beneficiary's eligibility for certain benefits under various means-tested programs. Moreover, a direct program-to-program transfer could facilitate the efficient transfer of all relevant information regarding the application of contribution limits and the total amount of accumulated earnings that will also apply to the new account. The Treasury Department and the IRS request comments as to whether and to what extent a qualified ABLE program should be permitted to require that funds from another State's ABLE program be accepted only through program-to-program transfers.

Qualified disability expenses

Section 529A(e)(5) defines a *qualified disability expense*. Consistent with that subsection, the proposed regulations provide that qualified disability expenses are expenses that relate to the designated beneficiary's blindness or disability and are for the benefit of that designated beneficiary in maintaining or improving his or her health, independence, or quality of life. Such expenses include, but are not limited to, expenses for education, housing, transportation, employment training and support, assistive technology and personal support services, health, prevention and wellness, financial management and administrative services, legal fees, expenses for oversight and monitoring, funeral and burial expenses, and other expenses that may be identified from time to time in future guidance published in the Internal Revenue Bulletin. As previously stated, expenses incurred at a time when a designated beneficiary is neither disabled nor blind within the meaning of the proposed regulations are not qualified disability expenses.

In order to implement the legislative purpose of assisting eligible individuals in maintaining or improving their health, independence, or quality of life, the Treasury Department and the IRS conclude that the term "qualified disability expenses" should be broadly construed to permit the inclusion of basic living expenses and should not be limited to expenses for items for which there is a medical necessity or which provide no benefits to others in addition to the benefit to the eligible individual. For example, expenses for common items such as smart phones could be considered qualified disability expenses if they are an effective and safe communication or navigation aid for a child with autism. The Treasury Department and the IRS request comments regarding what types of expenses should be considered qualified disability expenses and under what circumstances. The proposed regulations authorize the identification of additional types of qualified disability expenses in guidance published in the Internal Revenue Bulletin. *See* § 601.601(d)(2). A qualified ABLE program must establish safeguards to distinguish between distributions used for the payment of qualified disability expenses and other distributions, and to permit the identification of the amounts distributed for housing expenses as that term is defined for purposes of the Supplemental Security Income program of the Social Security Administration.

Limitation on number of ABLE accounts of a designated beneficiary

Section 529A(c)(4) generally provides that, except with respect to certain rollovers, once an ABLE account has been established for a designated beneficiary, no account subsequently established for that same designated beneficiary may qualify as an ABLE account. The proposed regulations provide that, except with respect to rollovers and program-to-program transfers, no designated beneficiary may have more than one ABLE account in existence at the same time, but provides that a prior ABLE account that has been closed does not prohibit the subsequent creation of another ABLE account for the same designated beneficiary. A qualified ABLE program must obtain a verification from the eligible individual, signed under penalties of perjury, that he or she has no other ABLE account (except in the case of a rollover or program-to-program transfer). The proposed regulations provide that, in the event that any additional ABLE account is opened for a designated beneficiary with an ABLE account already in existence, only the first such account created for that designated beneficiary qualifies as an ABLE account, and each other account is treated for all purposes as being an account of the designated beneficiary that is not an ABLE account under a qualified ABLE program. The proposed regulations also provide, however, that a return, in accordance with the rules that apply to returns of excess contributions and excess aggregate contributions under § 1.529A-2(g)(4), of the entire balance of a second or other subsequent account received by the contributor(s) on or before the due date (including extensions) for filing the designated beneficiary's income tax return for the year in which the account was opened and contributions to the second or subsequent account were made will not be treated as a gift or distribution to the designated beneficiary for purposes of section 529A.

The prohibition of multiple ABLE accounts, however, does not apply to prevent a timely rollover or program-to-program transfer of the designated beneficiary's account to an ABLE account under a different qualified ABLE program.

Residency requirements

Consistent with section 529A(b)(1)(C), the proposed regulations require that an ABLE account for a designated beneficiary may be established only under the qualified ABLE program of the State in which that designated beneficiary is a resident or with which the State of the designated beneficiary's residence has contracted for the provision of ABLE accounts. If a State does not establish and maintain a qualified ABLE program, it may contract with another State to provide an ABLE program for its residents. The statute is silent as to whether a designated beneficiary must move his or her existing ABLE account when the designated beneficiary changes his or her residence. The Treasury Department and the IRS are concerned about imposing undue administrative burdens and costs on designated beneficiaries who frequently change State residency, such as members of military families. Therefore, the proposed regulations provide that a qualified ABLE program may permit a designated beneficiary to continue to maintain his or her ABLE account that was created in that State, even after the designated beneficiary is no longer a resident of that State. However, in order to enforce the one ABLE account limitation and in accordance with section 529A(g)(1), the proposed regulations provide that, other than in the case of a rollover or a program-to-program transfer of a designated beneficiary's ABLE account, a qualified ABLE program must require the designated beneficiary to verify, under penalties of perjury, when creating an ABLE account that the account being established is the designated beneficiary's only ABLE account. For example, the eligible individual could be required to check a box providing such verification on a form used to establish the account. The Treasury Department and the IRS are concerned that without such safeguards individuals could inadvertently establish two accounts with adverse tax consequences due to the loss of ABLE account status for the second account and expect qualified ABLE programs to establish safeguards to ensure that the required limit of one ABLE account per designated beneficiary is not violated.

Investment direction

Section 529A(b)(4) states that a program shall not be treated as a qualified ABLE program unless it provides that the designated beneficiary may directly or indirectly direct the investment of any contributions to the program or any earnings thereon no more than two times in any calendar year. A program will not violate this requirement merely because it permits a designated beneficiary or a person with signature authority over a designated beneficiary's account to serve as one of the program's board members or employees, or as a board member or employee of a contractor that the program hires to perform administrative services.

Cap on contributions

Section 529A(b)(6) provides that a qualified ABLE program must provide adequate safeguards to prevent aggregate contributions on behalf of a designated beneficiary in excess of the limit established by the State under section 529(b)(6) relating to Qualified State Tuition Programs. The proposed regulations provide a safe harbor that permits a qualified ABLE program to satisfy this requirement regarding total cumulative contributions if the program prohibits any additional contributions to an account as soon as the account balance reaches the specified contribution limit under such State's program established under section 529. Once the account balance falls below the prescribed limit, contributions may resume, subject to the same limitation. The Treasury Department and the IRS believe that recommencement of contributions is appropriate based on the nature and purposes of the ABLE program.

Gift and generation-skipping transfer (GST) taxes

The proposed regulations provide that contributions to an ABLE account by a person other than the designated beneficiary are treated as completed gifts to the designated beneficiary of the account, and that such gifts are neither gifts of a future interest nor a qualified transfer under section 2503(e). Accordingly, no distribution from an ABLE account to the designated beneficiary of that account is treated as a taxable gift. Finally, neither gift nor GST taxes apply to the change of designated beneficiary of an ABLE account, as long as the new designated beneficiary is an eligible individual who is a sibling of the former designated beneficiary.

Distribution on death

The proposed regulations provide that, upon the death of the designated beneficiary, all amounts remaining in the ABLE account are includible in the designated beneficiary's gross estate for purposes of the estate tax. *See* section 2031. Further, the proposed regulations cross-reference section 2053 for purposes of determining the deductibility by the designated beneficiary's estate of amounts payable from the ABLE account to satisfy claims by creditors such as a State and also cross-reference section 2652(a)(1) for treatment of the deceased designated beneficiary as the transferor of any property remaining in the ABLE account that may pass to a beneficiary.

Pursuant to section 529A(f), a qualified ABLE program must provide that, upon the designated beneficiary's death, any State may file a claim (either with the person with signature authority over the ABLE account or the executor of the designated beneficiary's estate

as defined in section 2203) for the amount of the total medical assistance paid for the designated beneficiary under the State's Medicaid plan after the establishment of the ABLE account. The amount paid in satisfaction of such a claim is not a taxable distribution from the ABLE account. Further, the amount is to be paid only after the payment of all outstanding payments due for the qualified disability expenses of the designated beneficiary and is to be reduced by the amount of all premiums paid by or on behalf of the designated beneficiary to a Medicaid Buy-In program under that State's Medicaid plan.

Unrelated business taxable income and filing requirements

A qualified ABLE program generally is exempt from income taxation. A qualified ABLE program, however, is subject to the taxes imposed by section 511 relating to the imposition of tax on unrelated business taxable income ("UBTI"). For purposes of this tax, certain administrative and other fees do not constitute unrelated business income to the ABLE program. A qualified ABLE program is not required to file Form 990, "Return of Organization Exempt From Income Tax," but will be required to file Form 990-T, "Exempt Organization Business Income Tax Return," if a filing would be required under the rules of §§ 1.6012-2(e) and 1.6012-3(a)(5) if the ABLE program were an organization described in those sections.

Reporting requirements

The proposed regulations set forth recordkeeping and reporting requirements. A qualified ABLE program must maintain records that enable the program to account to the Secretary with respect to all contributions, distributions, returns of excess contributions or additional accounts, income earned, and account balances for any designated beneficiary's ABLE account. In addition, a qualified ABLE program must report to the Secretary the establishment of each ABLE account, including the name and residence of the designated beneficiary, and other relevant information regarding the account that is included on the new Form 5498-QA, "ABLE Account Contribution Information." It is anticipated that the qualified ABLE program will report if the eligible individual has presented an adequate disability certification, accompanied by a diagnosis, to demonstrate eligibility to establish an account. Information regarding distributions will be reported on the new Form 1099-QA, "Distributions from ABLE Accounts." The proposed regulations contain more detail on how the information must be reported.

In addition, section 529A(b)(3) requires that a qualified ABLE program provide separate accounting for each designated beneficiary. Separate accounting requires that contributions for the benefit of a designated beneficiary, as well as earnings attributable to those contributions, are allocated to that designated beneficiary's account. Whether or not a program ordinarily provides each designated beneficiary an annual account statement showing the income and transactions related to the account, the program must give this information to the designated beneficiary upon request.

Section 529A(d)(4) provides that States are required to submit electronically to the Commissioner of Social Security, on a monthly basis and in the manner specified by the Commissioner of Social Security, statements on relevant distributions and account balances from all ABLE accounts. The report of the Committee on Ways and Means (H.R. Rep. No. 113-614, pt. 1, at 15 (2014)) indicates that States should work with the Commissioner of Social Security to identify data elements for the monthly reports, including the type of qualified disability expenses.

Effective Date/Applicability Date

These regulations are proposed to be effective as of the date of publication of the Treasury decision adopting these rules as final regulations in the **Federal Register**. These rules, when adopted as final regulations, will apply to taxable years beginning after December 31, 2014. The reporting requirements of §§ 1.529A-5 through 1.529A-7 will apply to information returns required to be filed, and payee statements required to be furnished, after December 31, 2015. Until the issuance of final regulations, taxpayers and qualified ABLE programs may rely on these proposed regulations.

Special Analyses

It has been determined that this notice of proposed rulemaking is not a significant regulatory action as defined in Executive Order 12866, as supplemented by Executive Order 13563. It has also been determined that section 553(b) of the Administrative Procedure Act (5 U.S.C. chapter 5) does not apply to this regulation and, because the regulation does not impose a collection of information on small entities, the Regulatory Flexibility Act (5 U.S.C. chapter 6) does not apply. This regulation, if adopted, would primarily affect states and individuals and therefore would not have a significant economic impact on a substantial number of small entities. Therefore, a regulatory flexibility analysis is not required. Pursuant to section 7805(f) of the Internal Revenue Code, this notice of proposed rulemaking will be submitted to the Chief Counsel for Advocacy of the Small Business Administration for comment on its impact on small businesses.

Comments and Public Hearing

Before these proposed regulations are adopted as final regulations, consideration will be given to any comments that are timely submitted to the IRS as prescribed in this preamble under the "Addresses" heading. The Treasury Department and the IRS request comments on all aspects of the proposed rules. All comments will be available at *www.regulations.gov* or upon request. A public hearing will be scheduled if requested in writing by any person that timely submits written or electronic comments. If a public hearing is scheduled, notice of the date, time, and place for the hearing will be published in the **Federal Register**.

A public hearing has been scheduled for **October 14, 2015**, beginning at **10:00 am** in the Auditorium, Internal Revenue Building, 1111 Constitution Avenue, NW, Washington, DC. Due to building security procedures, visitors must enter at the Constitution Avenue entrance.

In addition, all visitors must present photo identification to enter the building. Because of access restrictions, visitors will not be admitted beyond the immediate entrance area more than 30 minutes before the hearing starts. For information about having your name placed on the building access list to attend the hearing, see the "FOR FURTHER INFORMATION CONTACT" section of this preamble.

The rules of 26 CFR 601.601(a)(3) apply to the hearing. Persons who wish to present oral comments at the hearing must submit written comments by September 21, 2015, and an outline of the topics to be discussed and the time to be devoted to each topic (signed original and eight (8) copies) by September 21, 2015. Submit a signed paper original and eight (8) copies or an electronic copy. A period of 10 minutes will be allotted to each person for making comments. An agenda showing the scheduling of the speakers will be prepared after the deadline for receiving outlines has passed. Copies of the agenda will be available free of charge at the hearing.

Drafting Information

The principal authors of these regulations are Terri Harris and Sean Barnett, Office of Associate Chief Counsel (Tax Exempt and Government Entities). However, other personnel from the Treasury Department and the IRS participated in the development of these regulations.

[¶ 61,158]   Proposed Regulations (REG-112997-10), published in the *Federal Register* on September 10, 2015.

[Code Secs. 2801, 6001, 6011, 6060, 6071, 6081, 6091, 6101, 6107, 6109, 6151, 6694, 6695, 6696 and 7701]

Tax on transfers from expatriates: Covered gifts or bequests: Proposed regulations.—Proposed regulations affecting taxpayers who received covered gifts or covered bequests from expatriates have been issued. Proposed Reg. §§ 28.2801-0-28.2801-7 implement Code Sec. 2801, as added by the Heroes Earnings Assistance and Relief Tax Act of 2008 (P.L. 111-245). In addition, administrative regulations that address filing and payment due dates, returns, extension requests, and recordkeeping requirements with respect to the tax on covered gifts or bequests from expatriates were proposed. Form 708 will be issued once the regulations are published as final regulations in the Federal Register. The due date for filing Form 708 and paying the Code Sec. 2801 tax will be provided in the final regulations. As noted in Announcement 2009-57, IRB 2009-29, 158, recipients of covered gifts or bequests will be given a reasonable period of time after the date that the final regulations are published in the Federal Register to file Form 708 and pay the tax on covered gifts or bequests received after June 17, 2008, and before the date the final regulations are published. Interest will not accrue for payment of the Code Sec. 2801 tax for any tax years until after the due date for payment, as identified in the final regulations, has passed.

AGENCY: Internal Revenue Service (IRS), Treasury.

ACTION: Notice of proposed rulemaking and notice of public hearing.

SUMMARY: This document contains proposed regulations relating to a tax on United States citizens and residents who receive gifts or bequests from certain individuals who relinquished United States citizenship or ceased to be lawful permanent residents of the United States on or after June 17, 2008. These proposed regulations affect taxpayers who receive covered gifts or covered bequests on or after the date these regulations are published as final regulations in the **Federal Register**. This document also provides notice of a public hearing on these proposed regulations.

DATES: Written or electronic comments must be received by December 8, 2015. Requests to speak and outlines of topics to be discussed at the public hearing scheduled for January 6, 2016, at 10 a.m., must be received by December 8, 2015.

ADDRESSES: Send submissions to CC:PA:LPD:PR (REG-112997-10), Room 5205, Internal Revenue Service, PO Box 7604, Ben Franklin Station, Washington, DC 20044. Submissions may be hand-delivered Monday through Friday between the hours of 8 a.m. and 4 p.m. to CC:PA:LPD:PR (REG-112997-10), Courier's Desk, Internal Revenue Service, 1111 Constitution Avenue, N.W., Washington, DC; or sent electronically via the Federal eRulemaking Portal at *http://www.regulations.gov* (IRS-REG-112997-10). The public hearing will be held in the IRS Auditorium, Internal Revenue Building, 1111 Constitution Avenue, N.W., Washington, DC.

FOR FURTHER INFORMATION CONTACT: Concerning the proposed regulations, Karlene Lesho or Leslie Finlow at (202) 317-6859; concerning the submission of comments, the public hearing, or to be placed on the building access list to attend the hearing, Oluwafunmilayo Taylor at (202) 317-6901 (not toll-free numbers) or email at Oluwafunmilayo.P.Taylor@irscounsel.treas.gov.

SUPPLEMENTARY INFORMATION:

Paperwork Reduction Act

The collections of information contained in this notice of proposed rulemaking have been submitted to the Office of Management and Budget for review in accordance with the Paperwork Reduction Act of 1995 (44 U.S.C. 3507(d)). Comments on the collection of information should be sent to the **Office of Management and Budget**, Attn:

Desk Officer for the Department of the Treasury, Office of Information and Regulatory Affairs, Washington, DC 20503, and to Clearance Officer, SE:CAR:MP:T:T:SP, Washington, DC 20224. Comments on the collection of information should be received by November 9, 2015. Comments are specifically requested concerning:

Whether the proposed collections of information are necessary for the proper performance of IRS functions, including whether the information will have practical utility;

The accuracy of the estimated burden associated with the proposed collections of information;

How the quality, utility, and clarity of the information to be collected may be enhanced;

How the burden of complying with the proposed collections of information may be minimized, including through the application of automated collection techniques or other forms of information technology; and

Estimates of capital or start-up costs of operation, maintenance, and purchase of services to provide information.

The collections of information in these proposed regulations are in §§ 28.2801-4(e), 28.2801-5(d), 28.6001-1, and 28.6011-1. The collection of information requirement in proposed regulation § 28.2801-4(e) is required in order for the IRS to verify that the U.S. person who received a covered gift or covered bequest is entitled to a reduction in the section 2801 tax for certain foreign taxes paid on the transfer and, if so, the amount of such reduction. The collection of information is mandatory to obtain a benefit. The likely respondents are individuals, domestic trusts, and foreign trusts electing to be treated as domestic trusts.

The collection of information in § 28.2801-5(d) is required to notify the IRS and the U.S. persons who are beneficiaries of a foreign trust that the trust is electing to be treated as a domestic trust for purposes of section 2801. It is also required for the IRS to verify the proper amount of section 2801 tax due and to notify the beneficiaries who are U.S. citizens or residents in the event the election terminates. This alerts the IRS and the U.S. citizens and residents who are beneficiaries that the trust will be liable for payment of the section 2801 tax while the election is in effect, but that the U.S. beneficiaries will be liable for the tax if and when the election terminates. This collection of information is necessary for the proper performance of IRS functions in the collection of the section 2801 tax. This collection of information is mandatory to obtain a benefit. The likely respondents are the trustees of foreign trusts.

The collection of information in § 28.6001-1 is required for the IRS to verify the books and records pertaining to covered gifts and covered bequests and for the proper performance of IRS functions in the collection of the section 2801 tax. It is also required to verify the receipt of covered gifts and covered bequests by U.S. persons and the value of such gifts and bequests. This collection of information is mandatory. The likely respondents are individuals and trustees of trusts.

The collection of information in § 28.6011-1 is required for the IRS to verify the receipt of a covered gift or covered bequest and other information relevant to the tax imposed under section 2801. This collection of information is necessary for the proper performance of IRS functions in the collection of the section 2801 tax. This collection of information is mandatory. The likely respondents are individuals and trustees of trusts.

Estimated total annual reporting burden: 7,000 hours.

Estimated average annual burden hours per respondent: 1 hour to prepare and attach documentation to Form 708, "U.S. Return of Gifts or Bequests from Covered Expatriates," for the reduction of tax for foreign taxes paid; 2 hours for a trustee of an electing foreign trust to make the election and notify the beneficiaries; 1 hour for the trustee of the foreign trust to prepare annual certifications; 1 hour to notify the U.S. persons who are beneficiaries of the trust that the election is terminated; and, 2 hours to prepare taxpayer records and the Form 708 to report the section 2801 tax.

Estimated number of respondents: 1,000.

Estimated annual frequency of responses: annually or less.

An agency may not conduct or sponsor, and a person is not required to respond to, a collection of information unless it displays a valid control number assigned by the Office of Management and Budget.

Books or records relating to a collection of information must be retained as long as their contents may become material in the administration of any internal revenue law. Generally, tax returns and tax return information are confidential, as required by 26 U.S.C. 6103.

Background

Section 301 of the Heroes Earnings Assistance and Relief Tax Act of 2008, Public Law 110-245 (122 Stat. 1624) (the HEART Act), added new section 877A to subtitle A of the Internal Revenue Code (Code), and new chapter 15 and new section 2801 to subtitle B, effective June 17, 2008. Prior to the addition of chapter 15, subtitle B contained chapters 11 through 14 relating to the estate tax, the gift tax, the generation-skipping transfer tax, and special valuation rules for purposes of subtitle B. New chapter 15 consists solely of section 2801.

Prior to the enactment of the HEART Act, citizens and long-term residents of the United States who expatriated to avoid U.S. taxes were subject to an alternative regime of U.S. income, estate, and gift taxes under sections 877, 2107, and 2501, respectively, for a period of 10 years following expatriation. Recognizing that citizens and residents of the United States generally are subject to estate tax on their world-wide assets at the time of death, Congress determined that it was appropriate, in the interests of tax equity, to impose a tax on U.S. citizens or residents who receive, from an expatriate, a transfer that would otherwise have escaped U.S. estate and/or gift taxes as a consequence of expatriation.

In an explanation of an earlier bill also proposing enactment of new chapter 15 and section 2801, the Report of the House Ways and Means Committee states that citizens and long-term residents of the United States have a right to physically leave the United States and relinquish their citizenship or terminate their residency. See H.R. Rep. No. 110-431 (2007). The Report states that the Committee believed that the Code should not be used to discourage individuals from relinquishing citizenship or terminating residency. At the same time, however, the Report states that the Code should not reward individuals who leave the United States. The Report concludes that an individual's decision to relinquish citizenship or terminate long-term residency should not affect the total amount of taxes imposed (that is, it should be "tax neutral"). The Report further states that, where U.S. estate or gift taxes are avoided with respect to a transfer of property to a U.S. person by reason of the expatriation of the donor, it is appropriate for the recipient to be subject to a tax similar to the donor's avoided transfer taxes.

With the enactment of sections 877A and 2801, sections 877 and 2107 apply only to individuals who relinquished United States citi-

zenship or ceased to be lawful permanent residents prior to June 17, 2008. Section 2501 generally continues to apply to any individual, resident or nonresident, including individuals who expatriate, whether or not on or after June 17, 2008. Section 2501(a)(3) and (a)(5), however, provides special rules for expatriates subject to section 877(b), which are not applicable to individuals who expatriate on or after June 17, 2008.

Section 2801 imposes a tax (section 2801 tax) on covered gifts and covered bequests received by a citizen or resident of the United States (U.S. citizen or resident) from a covered expatriate. The section 2801 tax applies with regard to any property transferred to a U.S. citizen or resident which qualifies as a covered gift or covered bequest under section 2801, regardless of whether the property transferred was acquired by the donor or decedent covered expatriate before or after expatriation.

The value of a covered gift or covered bequest is its fair market value at the time the gift or bequest is received by the U.S. citizen or resident. A U.S. citizen or resident receiving a covered gift or covered bequest (U.S. recipient) is liable for payment of the section 2801 tax imposed under this chapter. A domestic trust that receives a covered gift or covered bequest is treated as a U.S. citizen and therefore is liable for payment of the section 2801 tax. A foreign trust may elect to be treated as a domestic trust (an electing foreign trust) for this purpose; absent this election, the trust's U.S. citizen or resident beneficiaries will be taxed as distributions are made from the trust (a non-electing foreign trust).

On July 20, 2009, the Treasury Department and the IRS issued Announcement 2009-57, 2009-29 I.R.B. 158. Announcement 2009-57 put taxpayers on notice that any covered gift or covered bequest received on or after June 17, 2008, is subject to the imposition of the section 2801 tax. Announcement 2009-57 states that the IRS intends to issue guidance under section 2801 and that the due date for reporting, filing, and payment of the tax imposed under section 2801 will be included in the guidance. The announcement further provides that the guidance the IRS intends to issue will provide a reasonable period of time between the date of issuance of the guidance and the date prescribed for the filing of the return and the payment of the tax.

On October 15, 2009, the Treasury Department and the IRS released Notice 2009-85, 2009-45 I.R.B. 598. Notice 2009-85 generally provides guidance for individuals who are subject to section 877A (added to the Code together with section 2801). With respect to gifts and bequests, section 9 of Notice 2009-85 provides that gifts or bequests from a covered expatriate on or after June 17, 2008, are subject to a transfer tax under new section 2801. Section 9 of Notice 2009-85 further provides that satisfaction of the reporting and tax obligations under section 2801 for covered gifts or covered bequests received on or after June 17, 2008, is deferred pending the issuance of separate guidance by the IRS.

Explanation of Provisions

The proposed regulations amend title 26 of the Code of Federal Regulations by adding part 28 (Imposition of Tax on Gifts and Bequests from Covered Expatriates) under new section 2801 of the Code. The proposed regulations are divided into seven sections.

Section 28.2801-1 of the proposed regulations sets forth the general rules of liability for the tax imposed by section 2801(a). Section 2801 imposes a tax on United States citizens or residents who receive, directly or indirectly, covered gifts or covered bequests (including distributions from foreign trusts attributable to covered gifts and covered bequests) from a covered expatriate. For purposes of section 2801, domestic trusts and foreign trusts electing to be treated as domestic trusts are treated in the same manner as U.S. citizens.

Definitions

Section 28.2801-2 of the proposed regulations defines terms for purposes of new chapter 15. The proposed regulations define the term "citizen or resident of the United States" as an individual who is a citizen or resident of the United States under the estate and gift tax rules of chapter 11 and chapter 12, respectively, in subtitle B of the Code. Accordingly, whether an individual is a "resident" is based on domicile in the United States, notwithstanding that section 877A adopts the income tax definition of that term. The Treasury Department and the IRS believe that, because section 2801 imposes a tax subject to subtitle B, the tax definition of resident under subtitle B generally should apply for purposes of section 2801. See § § 20.0-1(b)(1) and 25.2501-1(b).

The proposed regulations generally define the term "covered gift" by reference to the definition of gift for purposes of chapter 12 of subtitle B. The proposed regulations define the term "covered bequest" as any property acquired directly or indirectly because of the death of a covered expatriate. Such property generally is property that would have been includible in the gross estate of the covered expatriate under chapter 11 of subtitle B, had the covered expatriate been a U.S. citizen or resident at the time of death.

Section 2801 defines "covered expatriate" by reference to the section 877A(g)(1) definition of that term. Section 877A(g)(1) generally provides that an individual who expatriates on or after June 17, 2008, is a covered expatriate if, on the expatriation date, (1) the individual's average annual net income tax liability is greater than $124,000 (indexed for inflation) for the previous five taxable years, (2) the individual's net worth is at least $2,000,000 (not indexed), or (3) the individual fails to certify under penalty of perjury that he or she has complied with all U.S. tax obligations for the five preceding taxable years. See section 877A(g)(1); Notice 2009-85, 2009-45 I.R.B. 598. The proposed regulations provide that, if an expatriate meets the definition of a covered expatriate, the expatriate is considered a covered expatriate for purposes of section 2801 at all times after the expatriation date, except during any period beginning after the expatriation date during which such individual is subject to United States estate or gift tax as a U.S. citizen or resident.

Additionally, the proposed regulations define for purposes of section 2801 the terms "domestic trust," "foreign trust," "electing foreign trust," "U.S. recipient," "power of appointment," and "indirect acquisition of property."

Rules and Exceptions Applicable to Covered Gifts and Covered Bequests

Section 28.2801-3 addresses the rules in section 2801(e) and includes rules and several exceptions applicable to the definitions of covered gift and covered bequest. Exceptions include taxable gifts reported on a covered expatriate's timely filed gift tax return, and property included in the covered expatriate's gross estate and reported on such expatriate's timely filed estate tax return, provided that the gift or estate tax due is timely paid. Qualified disclaimers of property made by a covered expatriate are excepted from the definitions of a covered gift and covered bequest. In addition, charitable donations that would qualify for the estate or gift tax charitable deduction are excepted from the terms "covered gift" and "covered bequest."

Section 28.2801-3(c)(4) provides that a gift or bequest to a covered expatriate's U.S. citizen spouse is excepted from the terms "covered gift" and "covered bequest" if the gift or bequest, if given by a U.S. citizen or resident, would qualify for the gift or estate tax marital deduction. In the case of a gift or bequest in trust, this means that, to the extent the gift or bequest to the trust (or to a separate share of the trust) would qualify for the estate or gift tax marital deduction, the gift or bequest is not a covered gift or covered bequest. A gift or bequest of a partial or terminable interest in property that a covered expatriate makes to his or her spouse is excepted from the definitions of a covered gift and covered bequest only to the extent that such gift or bequest is qualified terminable interest property (QTIP), as defined in section 2523(f) or section 2056(b)(7), and a valid QTIP election is made. To the extent a covered gift or covered bequest is made to a non-electing foreign trust (or to a separate share of such a trust), a distribution from the trust (or from the separate share of the trust) to the U.S. citizen spouse of the covered expatriate who funded the trust (whether in whole or in part) will not qualify for the exception. Note that gifts and bequests made by a covered expatriate to his or her noncitizen spouse are subject to an annual limit under section 2523(i). Furthermore, a bequest from a covered expatriate to his or her noncitizen surviving spouse who is a U.S. resident is not a covered bequest to the extent the bequest is made to a qualified domestic trust (QDOT) that satisfies the requirements of section 2056A and the corresponding regulations, and for which a valid QDOT election is made.

Section 28.2801-3(d) provides rules to implement section 2801(e)(4) regarding covered gifts and covered bequests made in trust, including transfers of property in trust that are subject to a general power of appointment granted by the covered expatriate. In identifying the recipient of such covered gifts and covered bequests made in trust, the proposed regulations do not adopt the gift tax rule of treating the trust beneficiary or holder of an immediate right to withdraw the property as the recipient of that property. Instead, for purposes of section 2801, the proposed regulations treat transfers in trust that constitute covered gifts and covered bequests as transfers to the trust, to be taxed under the rules in section 2801(e)(4). Specifically, the proposed regulations provide that, if a covered expatriate makes a transfer in trust and such transfer is a covered gift or covered bequest, the transfer is treated as a covered gift or covered bequest to

the trust, without regard to the beneficial interests in the trust or whether any person has a general power of appointment or a power of withdrawal over trust property. Under section 2801(e)(4), the transfer to the trust will be taxed either to the trust receiving the covered gift or covered bequest, in the case of a domestic trust or electing foreign trust, or to the U.S. beneficiaries or distributees of a non-electing foreign trust as trust distributions are made.

Section 28.2801-3(e) provides two rules addressing covered gifts and covered bequests arising from powers of appointment. First, consistent with the rules in chapters 11 and 12, the proposed regulations confirm that the exercise, release, or lapse of a covered expatriate's general power of appointment for the benefit of a U.S. citizen or resident is a covered gift or covered bequest. Second, the proposed regulations provide that a covered expatriate's grant of a general power of appointment over property not held in trust is a covered gift or covered bequest to the powerholder as soon as both the power is exercisable and the transfer of the property subject to the power is irrevocable. See also § 28.2801-4(d)(5)(ii). The preceding sentence applies only for purposes of section 2801, and should not be interpreted as having any impact on the determination of whether the grant of a general power of appointment over property not in trust is a completed gift for Federal gift tax purposes, which is a question to be resolved under chapter 12 without regard to this provision.

Liability for Section 2801 Tax

Section 28.2801-4 provides specific rules regarding who is liable for the payment of the section 2801 tax. Generally, the U.S. citizen or resident who receives the covered gift or covered bequest is liable. Similarly, the proposed regulations provide rules explaining that a domestic trust that receives a covered gift or covered bequest is treated as a U.S. citizen and thus is liable for payment of the section 2801 tax imposed under this section. An electing foreign trust also is treated as a U.S. citizen. See § § 28.2801-2(b) and 28.2801-5(d). However, a non-electing foreign trust is not liable for the section 2801 tax. Instead, a U.S. citizen or resident who receives a distribution from a non-electing foreign trust is liable for the section 2801 tax on the receipt of that distribution to the extent the distribution is attributable to covered gifts or covered bequests to that trust. Under section 2801(e)(4)(B)(ii), that U.S. citizen or resident may be entitled to a limited deduction under section 164 against income tax for the section 2801 tax paid on the distribution. The deduction is limited to the extent that the section 2801 tax is imposed on that portion of the distribution that is reported in the gross income of the U.S. citizen or resident. Section 28.2801-4(a)(3)(ii) of the proposed regulations describes how to compute that deduction.

Section 28.2801-4(a)(2)(ii) of the proposed regulations provides that, in the case of a domestic trust or an electing foreign trust, the trust's payment of the section 2801 tax for which the trust is liable does not result in a taxable distribution under section 2621 of the Code to any beneficiary of the trust for generation-skipping transfer (GST) tax purposes. This provision is consistent with the GST tax consequences of a trust's payment of tax, which differ depending upon whether the trust or the trust beneficiary is liable for the tax being paid.

Section 28.2801-4(a)(2)(iv) provides a special rule for certain non-electing foreign trusts that become domestic trusts (migrated foreign trusts). A migrated foreign trust will be treated solely for purposes of section 2801 as a domestic trust for the entire year during which the change from foreign trust to domestic trust occurred. The trust must file a timely Form 708 for the year in which the trust becomes a domestic trust and must report and pay the section 2801 tax on all covered gifts and covered bequests received by the trust during the year it becomes a domestic trust as well as on the portion of the trust's value attributable to any covered gifts and covered bequests received by the trust prior to the year in which it becomes a domestic trust determined as of December 31 of the year prior to the year it becomes a domestic trust.

Charitable Remainder Trusts

Section 28.2801-4(a)(2)(iii) of the proposed regulations provides rules for charitable remainder trusts (CRTs), as defined in section 664, contributions to which are made by covered expatriates for the benefit of one or more charitable organizations described in section 170(c) and a U.S. citizen or resident other than such a charitable organization (non-charitable U.S. citizen or resident). Section 2801(e)(3) indicates that the value of the charitable organization's remainder interest in a CRT is excluded from the definition of a covered gift or covered bequest. The value of the interest of the non-charitable U.S. citizen or resident in such contributions to the CRT is a covered gift or covered bequest, unless otherwise excluded.

Under section 664, a CRT must be a domestic trust. Accordingly, when a covered expatriate contributes a covered gift or covered bequest to a CRT, the CRT is liable for the payment of the section 2801 tax attributable to the value of the non-charitable U.S. person's interest in the trust. Section 664(d)(1)(B) and (d)(2)(B) and § 1.664-3(a)(4) of the Income Tax Regulations provide that no amount other than the annuity or unitrust amount may be paid "to or for the use of any person other than an organization described under section 170(c)." This rule has been applied in Revenue Ruling 82-128 (1982-2 CB 71) to disqualify a trust as a CRT if the trust could be required to pay estate taxes by reason of the applicable state apportionment statute. Thus, if the CRT's liability for payment of section 2801 tax attributable to the non-charitable recipient's interest in the CRT were to be deemed comparable to the CRT's liability for payment of estate tax, the CRT would not qualify as a CRT under section 664.

A CRT's liability for payment of the section 2801 tax is distinguishable from a CRT's liability for payment of estate tax because the section 2801 tax is imposed expressly on the CRT under a federal tax statute, section 2801(e)(4)(A). In addition, the section 2801 tax is imposed on the CRT as a primary obligation of the CRT, rather than an obligation imposed on the CRT for the payment of a liability belonging to or attributable to another taxpayer. Accordingly, a CRT's payment of the section 2801 tax on the portion of each transfer to the CRT that is a covered gift or covered bequest is not a distribution to or for the use of any person within the meaning of section 664(d)(1)(B) and (d)(2)(B), and the CRT's liability for such a payment will not cause the trust to be disqualified as a CRT defined in section 664. The proposed regulations confirm that the charitable remainder interest's share of each transfer to the CRT is not a covered gift or covered bequest and provide the method for computing the net covered gifts and covered bequests that are taxable to the CRT under section 2801.

Computation of Section 2801 Tax

Section 28.2801-4 of the proposed regulations also provides guidance on how to compute the section 2801 tax. Generally, the section 2801 tax is determined by reducing the total amount of covered gifts and covered bequests received during the calendar year by the section 2801(c) amount, which is the dollar amount of the per-donee exclusion in effect under section 2503(b) for that calendar year ($14,000 in 2015), and then multiplying the net amount by the highest estate or gift tax rate in effect during that calendar year. The reference to section 2503(b) in section 2801 is included solely to provide a dollar amount by which to decrease the U.S. recipient's aggregate covered gifts and covered bequests received during that calendar year to determine the amount subject to the section 2801 tax; section 2801 does not incorporate the substantive rule of section 2503(b) that applies to donors of gifts under chapter 12. The resulting tax then is reduced by any estate or gift tax paid to a foreign country with regard to those transfers. See § 28.2801-4(e).

Value of a Covered Gift or Covered Bequest

The value of a covered gift or covered bequest is the fair market value of the property on the date of its receipt by the U.S. citizen or resident. Section 28.2801-4(c) provides that the value of a covered gift is determined by applying the federal gift tax valuation principles under section 2512 and chapter 14 and the corresponding regulations. Similarly, the value of a covered bequest is determined by applying the federal estate tax valuation principles under section 2031 and chapter 14 and the corresponding regulations, but without regard to sections 2032 and 2032A.

Date of Receipt

The proposed regulations identify the date of the receipt of a covered gift or covered bequest by a U.S. citizen or resident. See § 28.2801-4(d). In general, a covered gift is received on the same date it is given for purposes of chapter 12. In general, a covered bequest is received on the date the property is distributed from the estate or covered expatriate's revocable trust. However, in the case of property that passes by operation of law or beneficiary designation upon the covered expatriate's death, the date of receipt is the date of death. The proposed regulations provide more detail with regard to the determination of the date of receipt of covered gifts and covered bequests received from a non-electing foreign trust, those received pursuant to powers of appointment, and those received indirectly.

Foreign Trusts

Section 28.2801-5 of the proposed regulations provides guidance on the treatment of foreign trusts under section 2801. If a covered gift or covered bequest is made to a foreign trust, the section 2801 tax applies to any distribution from that trust, whether of income or corpus, to a recipient that is a U.S. citizen or resident, unless the foreign trust elects to be treated as a domestic trust for purposes of section 2801. The proposed regulations define the term "distribution" broadly to include any direct, indirect, or constructive transfer from a foreign trust, including each disbursement from such a trust pursuant to the exercise, release, or lapse of a power of appointment.

Distributions from Foreign Trusts

The section 2801 tax applies only to the portion of a distribution from a non-electing foreign trust that is attributable to covered gifts and covered bequests contributed to the foreign trust. Section 28.2801-5(c) of the proposed regulations provides that the amount of the distribution attributable to covered gifts and covered bequests is determined by multiplying the total distribution by a ratio, as in effect at the time of the distribution, that is redetermined after each contribution to the trust. The proposed regulations explain how to compute that ratio and provide that each distribution from the foreign trust is considered to be made proportionally from the covered and non-covered portions of the trust, without any tracing with regard to particular assets. One effect of this rule is that the portion of a distribution from a foreign trust that is attributable to covered gifts and covered bequests contributed to the foreign trust includes the ratable portion of any appreciation and income that has accrued on the foreign trust's assets since the contribution of the covered gifts and covered bequests to the foreign trust.

Election by Foreign Trust to Be Treated as Domestic Trust

Section 2801(e)(4)(B)(iii) provides that, solely for purposes of section 2801, a foreign trust may elect to be treated as a domestic trust. Consequently, the section 2801 tax is imposed on the electing foreign trust when it receives covered gifts and covered bequests, rather than on the U.S. trust beneficiaries when distributions are made from the trust. The election may be made for a calendar year whether or not the foreign trust received a covered gift or covered bequest during that calendar year. Section 28.2801-5(d)(3) of the proposed regulations provides guidance on the time and manner of making the election. In order for an election to be valid, the trustee of the foreign trust must satisfy several requirements. The trustee must make the election on a timely filed Form 708 and, if tax is due, timely pay the section 2801 tax (as computed under § 28.2801-5(d)(3)(iii)) by the due date of the Form 708 for that year and include a computation of how the applicable ratio and tax liability were calculated. Further, the trustee must designate and authorize a U.S. agent for purposes of section 2801, and must agree to file annually a Form 708 either to certify that no covered gifts or covered bequests were received by the foreign trust during the calendar year, or to report and, if tax is due, pay the section 2801 tax on covered gifts and covered bequests received by the foreign trust during the calendar year. The trustee also must report the portion of the trust attributable to covered gifts and covered bequests and all distributions attributable to covered gifts and covered bequests made to U.S. recipients in years prior to the year of the election. Finally, the trustee must notify the permissible U.S. distributees of the trust that the trustee is making the election to be treated as a domestic trust for purposes of section 2801.

Under § 28.2801-5(d)(3)(iii), an electing foreign trust that received covered gifts or covered bequests in prior calendar years when the election to be treated as a domestic trust was not in effect also must pay the section 2801 tax liability for all prior calendar years at the time the election is made on Form 708. Such liability is based on the fair market value of the trust attributable to covered gifts and covered bequests as of the last day of the calendar year immediately preceding the year for which the election is made, using the ratio calculated and then in effect under § 28.2801-5(c). If the trustee is unable to determine the portion of the trust attributable to covered gifts and covered bequests, then the fair market value of the entire trust as of the last day of the calendar year immediately preceding the year for which the election is made is subject to the section 2801 tax.

A valid election to be treated as a domestic trust is effective as of the beginning of the calendar year for which the Form 708 is filed. The effect of a valid election is that, as of such effective date of the election and until the election is terminated, U.S. citizens and residents receiving a distribution from that foreign trust will not be subject to section 2801 tax on that distribution. Instead, the electing foreign trust, like a domestic trust, must report and pay the section 2801 tax on each covered gift and covered bequest as it is received. The election, however, will not change the section 2801 tax liability of the U.S. recipients with regard to distributions made from the trust prior to the effective date of the election. The election has no impact outside of section 2801 on the taxation or reporting of trust distributions to U.S. persons.

Dispute as to Amount of Section 2801 Tax Owed by Electing Foreign Trust

If the IRS asserts that additional section 2801 tax is due from the electing foreign trust because, for example, the trust undervalued the covered gift or covered bequest or failed to report all covered gifts and covered bequests, then the IRS will notify the trustee of the foreign trust and the U.S. agent of the additional tax due on the asserted additional value or additional covered gifts or covered bequests, including any penalties and interest, and request payment by the due date identified in the IRS letter. If the trustee of the electing foreign trust and the IRS are unable to come to an agreement and the trustee fails to timely pay the additional tax and other asserted amounts, then the election is deemed to be an "imperfect election." This means that the election terminates as of the first day of the calendar year for which the IRS asserts that the additional section 2801 tax is due. In this event, the covered gifts and covered bequests for which the return was timely filed, but only to the extent of the value on which the section 2801 tax was timely paid, are no longer considered to be covered gifts or covered bequests for purposes of determining the ratio under § 28.2801-5(c)(1), and distributions relating to such amounts will not be taxable to a U.S. citizen or resident who receives a trust distribution. However, with regard to the asserted additional value or additional covered gifts or covered bequests on which the trust did not timely pay the section 2801 tax asserted by the IRS, the foreign trust is not an electing foreign trust and thus is not the taxpayer responsible for the payment of that additional section 2801 tax. Instead, as of the effective date of the termination of the trust's election, the usual rule of section 2801(e)(4)(B) applies with regard to the taxation of distributions from foreign trusts. Specifically, the U.S. citizens or residents who receive any trust distributions on or after the effective date of the terminated election should take into consideration the additional value or additional covered gifts or covered bequests asserted by the IRS in determining the ratio under § 28.2801-5(c)(1) to be applied to such distributions. If the U.S. recipient does not take the additional value or additional covered gifts or covered bequests asserted by the IRS into consideration in computing that ratio, and the IRS challenges the computation of that ratio during its review of the U.S. recipient's Form 708 reporting the distribution, the IRS's assertion of the additional value or additional covered gifts or covered bequests then will become an issue to be resolved as part of the usual examination process for the U.S. recipient's Form 708. See § 28.2801-5(e), *Example 4.*

Termination of Status as Electing Foreign Trust

An electing foreign trust's failure to file the Form 708 on an annual basis or to timely pay its section 2801 tax terminates that foreign trust's election to be treated as a domestic trust as of the first day of the calendar year for which the certification is not timely made or for which its section 2801 tax is not timely paid. But see § 28.2801-5(d)(6) in the case of a dispute as to the amount of section 2801 tax owed by an electing foreign trust. In the event of the termination of the election, the trustee should notify the permissible U.S. distributees of the effective date of the termination and that each U.S. recipient of a distribution made from the foreign trust on or after that date is subject to the section 2801 tax to the extent the distribution is attributable to covered gifts or covered bequests. After an election is terminated, a foreign trust is not prohibited from making a new election to be treated as a domestic trust by complying with all applicable requirements.

Other Provisions

Section 28.2801-6(a) addresses how the basis rules under sections 1014, 1015(a), and 1022 impact the determination of the U.S. recipient's basis in the covered gift or covered bequest. Unlike section 1015(d), which generally allows gift tax paid on the gift to be added to the donee's basis, section 2801 does not provide a similar basis adjustment for the payment of the section 2801 tax.

Section 28.2801-6(b) clarifies the applicability of the GST tax to certain section 2801 transfers and cross-references the GST rules.

Section 28.2801-6(c) discusses the interaction of section 2801 and the information reporting provisions of sections 6039F and 6048(c). Generally, pursuant to section 6039F and Notice 97-34, 1997-1 CB 422, a U.S. person (other than an organization described in section 501(c) and exempt from tax under section 501(a)) who receives a gift or bequest (including a covered gift or covered bequest) from a foreign person (other than through a foreign trust) must report such gift or bequest on Part IV of Form 3520, "Annual Return to Report Transac-

tions with Foreign Trusts and Receipt of Certain Foreign Gifts," if the total value of such gifts and bequests exceeds a certain threshold. A U.S. citizen or resident, as defined under § 28.2801-2(b) and thus including a domestic trust as defined in § 28.2801-2(c), but not including a foreign trust that elects to be treated as a domestic trust, is included within the definition of a U.S. person for purposes of section 6039F.

Under section 6039F(c)(1)(A), if a U.S. person fails to furnish all of the information regarding the gift or bequest in accordance with the requirements of Form 3520, and any related guidance, within the time prescribed (in the case of a U.S. citizen or resident, the time for filing the Form 1040, including extensions), then, absent reasonable cause, a monthly penalty of 5 percent of the amount of the gift or bequest (not to exceed 25 percent) may be imposed until such information is furnished. In addition, the tax consequences of the receipt of such gift or bequest may be determined by the Secretary. Taxpayers should be aware that the information reported on Part IV of Form 3520, whether or not timely filed, may be considered in determining whether a U.S. citizen or resident received a covered gift or covered bequest.

Pursuant to section 6048(c) and Notice 97-34, a U.S. person must report any distributions received from a foreign trust on Part III of Form 3520. Under section 6677(a), a penalty of the greater of $10,000 or 35 percent of the gross value of the distribution may be imposed on a U.S. person who fails to timely report the distribution. A U.S. citizen or resident, as defined in § 28.2801-2(b), but not including a foreign trust that elects to be treated as a domestic trust, generally would be required to report such a distribution under section 6048(c).

Further, if adequate records are not provided to determine the treatment of such a distribution, to the extent provided in Notice 97-34, as modified by the instructions to Form 3520 and any subsequent guidance, such distribution may be treated as an accumulation distribution includible in the gross income of the distributee. Taxpayers similarly should be aware that information reported on Part III of Form 3520 may be used to determine if a U.S. citizen or resident received a trust distribution attributable to a covered gift or covered bequest.

Finally, § 28.2801-6(d) addresses the section 6662 accuracy-related penalties on underpayments of tax, the section 6651 failure to file and pay penalties, and the section 6695A penalty on substantial and gross valuation misstatements attributable to incorrect appraisals. The Treasury Department and the IRS recognize that taxpayers have had to defer their tax reporting and payment obligations with respect to covered gifts and covered bequests received after the effective date of section 2801 (as described in Notice 2009-85). Thus, there may be circumstances under which a taxpayer who received a covered gift or covered bequest in a year prior to the issuance of final regulations may have difficulty in complying with the deferred filing and payment requirements with respect to those receipts. A taxpayer who establishes that such failure in this regard is due to reasonable cause and not to willful neglect will not be subject to the section 6651 penalties for failure to file or pay. The determination of whether an exception to the other penalties applies will be made on a case-by-case basis.

Section 28.2801-7 provides guidance on the responsibility of a U.S. recipient, as defined in § 28.2801-2(e), to determine if tax under section 2801 is due. The Treasury Department and the IRS realize that, because the tax imposed by this section is imposed on the U.S. citizen or resident receiving a covered gift or covered bequest, rather than on the donor or decedent covered expatriate making the gift or bequest, U.S. taxpayers may have difficulty determining whether they are liable for any tax under section 2801. Nevertheless, the same standard of due diligence that applies to any other taxpayer to determine whether the taxpayer has a tax liability or a filing requirement also applies to U.S. citizens and residents under this section. Accordingly, it is the responsibility of each U.S. citizen or resident receiving a gift or bequest, whether directly or indirectly, from an expatriate (as defined in section 877A(g)(2)) to determine its tax obligations under section 2801. Thus, the burden is on that U.S. citizen or resident to determine whether the expatriate was a covered expatriate (as defined in section 877A(g)(1)) and, if so, whether the gift or bequest was a covered gift or covered bequest.

The Treasury Department and the IRS understand that a U.S. citizen or resident receiving a gift or bequest from an expatriate may be unable to obtain directly from the expatriate, the expatriate's attorney, the expatriate's executor, or other reliable sources the information necessary to make the above determinations. If the IRS receives a request from a U.S. citizen or resident who received a gift from an expatriate who has consented to the disclosure of certain return information to that donee, a gift from an expatriate who is deceased at the time of the request, or a bequest from an expatriate, the IRS may in certain circumstances disclose to such U.S. citizen or resident the return or return information of the donor or decedent expatriate that may assist the U.S. citizen or resident in determining whether the donor or decedent was a covered expatriate and whether the transfer was a covered gift or covered bequest. See section 6103. The types of information and requirements and procedures for requesting such information will be set forth in guidance published in the Internal Revenue Bulletin.

Although the IRS, if authorized, may disclose returns and return information upon request, the IRS will not make the determinations as to whether an expatriate from whom a gift or bequest was received was a covered expatriate or whether the gift or bequest was a covered gift or covered bequest. Furthermore, the U.S. citizen or resident receiving a gift or bequest from an expatriate may not rely on any information provided by the IRS that the U.S. citizen or resident knows or has reason to know is incorrect. These determinations are the responsibility of the U.S. citizen or resident.

The proposed regulations provide that, if a living expatriate donor does not authorize the IRS to release to a U.S. citizen or resident the donor's relevant return or return information, there is a rebuttable presumption that the expatriate donor is a covered expatriate and that each gift from that expatriate to a U.S. citizen or resident is a covered gift. A taxpayer who reasonably concludes that a gift or bequest is not subject to section 2801 and intends to rebut the presumption may choose to file a protective return to start the period for assessment of any section 2801 tax. See §§ 28.2801-7(b)(2), 28.6011-1(b).

Administrative Regulations

The proposed regulations also include administrative regulations that address filing and payment due dates, returns, extension requests, and recordkeeping requirements with respect to the section 2801 tax. See §§ 28.6001-1, 28.6011-1, 28.6060-1, 28.6071-1, 28.6081-1, 28.6091-1, 28.6101-1, 28.6107-1, 28.6109-1, 28.6151-1, 28.6694-1, 28.6694-2, 28.6694-3, 28.6694-4, 28.6695-1, 28.6696-1, 28.7701-1. Section 28.6011-1(a) provides the return requirements to report the receipt of covered gifts and covered bequests from covered expatriates using Form 708.

The Treasury Department and IRS will permit the filing of a protective Form 708, unaccompanied by any payment of tax under section 2801, in limited circumstances when a U.S. citizen or resident receives a gift or bequest from an expatriate and reasonably concludes, after exercising due diligence, that the gift or bequest is not a covered gift or covered bequest from a covered expatriate. The mere absence of information confirming that the expatriate is a covered expatriate or that the gift or bequest is a covered gift or covered bequest is not a sufficient basis for a protective return. Section

28.6011-1(b)(i) provides that filing a protective Form 708, together with the required attachments, will start the period for the assessment of any section 2801 tax.

The IRS intends to issue Form 708 once these regulations are published as final regulations in the **Federal Register**. The IRS will provide the due date for filing Form 708 and for payment of the section 2801 tax liability in the final regulations. Consistent with Announcement 2009-57, U.S. recipients will be given a reasonable period of time after the date the final regulations are published in the **Federal Register** to file the Form 708 and to pay the section 2801 tax on covered gifts and covered bequests received on or after June 17, 2008, and before the date of publication of the final regulations in the **Federal Register**. Interest will not accrue on the section 2801 tax liability for any taxable years until the due date for payment, as specified in the final regulations, has passed.

Effect on Other Documents

The following publication will be obsolete when regulations finalizing these proposed regulations are published in the **Federal Register**:

Announcement 2009-57, 2009-29 I.R.B. 158.

Special Analyses

Certain IRS regulations, including this one, are exempt from the requirements of Executive Order 12866, as supplemented and reaffirmed by Executive Order 13563. Therefore, a regulatory impact assessment is not required. It has been determined that section 553(b) of the Administrative Procedure Act (5 U.S.C. chapter 5) does not apply to these regulations. Pursuant to the Regulatory Flexibility Act (5 U.S.C. chapter 6), it is hereby certified that this regulation will not have a significant economic impact on a substantial number of small entities. This certification is based on the fact that this regulation does not affect small entities because it applies to individuals and certain trusts. Accordingly, a regulatory flexibility analysis is not required. Pursuant to section 7805(f) of the Code, these proposed regulations have been submitted to the Chief Counsel for Advocacy of the Small Business Administration for comment on their impact on small businesses.

Statement of Availability for Documents Published in the Internal Revenue Bulletin

For copies of recently issued revenue procedures, revenue rulings, notices, and other guidance published in the Internal Revenue Bulletin or Cumulative Bulletin, please visit the IRS Web site at *http://www.irs.gov*.

Drafting Information

The principal authors of these regulations are Karlene Lesho and Leslie Finlow, Office of the Associate Chief Counsel (Passthroughs and Special Industries). However, other personnel from the Treasury Department and the IRS participated in their development.

[¶ 61,166]   **Proposed Regulations, NPRM REG-106706-18**, November 23, 2018.

[Code Sec. 2010]

Estate and gift taxes: Unified credit: Difference in the basic exclusion amount: Proposed regulations.—The IRS has issued Proposed Reg. § 20.2010-1 to address the effect of the temporary increase in the basic exclusion amount used in computing estate and gift taxes. For years 2018-2025, the basic exclusion amount (BEA) is increased to $10 million, as adjusted for inflation. For years after 2025, the exclusion amount reverts to $5 million, as adjusted for inflation. The proposed regulation is intended to clarify the computation of estate tax payable in situations where the BEA was different in the year of death than when prior gifts were made. The proposed regulation would be effective on and after the date that the final regulations are published.

AGENCY: Internal Revenue Service (IRS), Treasury.

ACTION: Notice of proposed rulemaking and notification of public hearing.

SUMMARY: This document contains proposed regulations addressing the effect of recent legislative changes to the basic exclusion amount used in computing Federal gift and estate taxes. The proposed regulations will affect donors of gifts made after 2017 and the estates of decedents dying after 2017.

DATES: Written and electronic comments must be received by February 20, 2019. Outlines of topics to be discussed at the public hearing scheduled for March 13, 2019, must be received by February 20, 2019. If no outlines of topics are received by February 20, 2019, the hearing will be cancelled.

ADDRESSES: Send submissions to: CC:PA:LPD:PR (REG-106706-18), Room 5203, Internal Revenue Service, P.O. Box 7604, Ben Franklin Station, Washington, DC 20044. Submissions also may be hand delivered Monday through Friday between the hours of 8 a.m. and 5 p.m.

to: CC:PA:LPD:PR (REG-106706-18), Courier's Desk, Internal Revenue Service, 1111 Constitution Avenue, NW, Washington, DC 20224, or sent electronically via the Federal eRulemaking portal at http://www.regulations.gov (IRS REG-106706-18). The public hearing will be held in the Auditorium, Internal Revenue Service Building, 1111 Constitution Avenue, NW, Washington, DC 20224. FOR FURTHER INFORMATION CONTACT: Concerning the proposed regulations, Deborah S. Ryan, (202) 317-6859; concerning submissions of comments, the hearing, and/or to be placed on the building access list to attend the hearing, Regina L. Johnson at (202) 317-6901 (not toll-free numbers).

SUPPLEMENTARY INFORMATION:

Background

I. Overview

In computing the amount of Federal gift tax to be paid on a gift or the amount of Federal estate tax to be paid at death, the gift and estate tax provisions of the Internal Revenue Code (Code) apply a unified rate schedule to the taxpayer's cumulative taxable gifts and taxable estate on death to arrive at a net tentative tax. The net tentative tax then is reduced by a credit based on the applicable exclusion amount (AEA), which is the sum of the basic exclusion amount (BEA) within the meaning of section 2010(c)(3) of the Code and, if applicable, the deceased spousal unused exclusion (DSUE) amount within the meaning of section 2010(c)(4). In certain cases, the AEA also includes a restored exclusion amount pursuant to Notice 2017-15, 2017-6 I.R.B. 783. Prior to January 1, 2018, for estates of decedents dying and gifts made beginning in 2011, section 2010(c)(3) provided a BEA of $5 million, indexed for inflation after 2011. The credit is applied first against the gift tax, on a cumulative basis, as taxable gifts are made. To the extent that any credit remains at death, it is applied against the estate tax.

This document contains proposed regulations to amend the Estate Tax Regulations (26 CFR part 20) under section 2010(c)(3) of the Code. The proposed regulations would update § 20.2010-1 to conform to statutory changes to the determination of the BEA enacted on December 22, 2017, by sections 11002 and 11061 of the Tax Cuts and Jobs Act, Public Law 115-97, 131 Stat. 2504 (2017) (TCJA).

II. Federal Gift Tax Computation Generally

The Federal gift tax is imposed by section 2501 of the Code on an individual's transfers by gift during each calendar year. The gift tax is determined under a seven-step computation required under sections 2502 and 2505 using the rate schedule set forth in section 2001(c) as in effect for the calendar year in which the gifts are made.

First, section 2502(a)(1) requires the determination of a tentative tax (that is, a tax unreduced by a credit amount) on the sum of all taxable gifts, whether made in the current year or in one or more prior periods (Step 1).

Second, section 2502(a)(2) requires the determination of a tentative tax on the sum of the taxable gifts made in all prior periods (Step 2).

Third, section 2502(a) requires the tentative tax determined in Step 2 to be subtracted from the tentative tax determined in Step 1 to arrive at the net tentative gift tax on the gifts made in the current year (Step 3).

Fourth, section 2505(a)(1) requires the determination of a credit equal to the applicable credit amount within the meaning of section 2010(c). The applicable credit amount is the tentative tax on the AEA determined as if the donor had died on the last day of the current calendar year. The AEA is the sum of the BEA as in effect for the year in which the gift was made, any DSUE amount as of the date of the gift as computed pursuant to § 25.2505-2, and any restored exclusion amount as of the date of the gift as computed pursuant to Notice 2017-15 (Step 4).

Fifth, section 2505(a)(2) and the flush language at the end of section 2505(a) require the determination of the sum of the amounts allowable as a credit to offset the gift tax on gifts made by the donor in all preceding calendar periods. For purposes of this determination, the allowable credit for each preceding calendar period is the tentative tax, computed at the tax rates in effect for the current period, on the AEA for such prior period, but not exceeding the tentative tax on the gifts actually made during such prior period. Section 2505(c). (Step 5).

Sixth, section 2505(a) requires that the total credit allowable for prior periods determined in Step 5 be subtracted from the credit for the current period determined in Step 4. (Step 6).

Finally, section 2505(a) requires that the credit amount determined in Step 6 be subtracted from the net tentative gift tax determined in Step 3 (Step 7).

III. Federal Estate Tax Computation Generally

The Federal estate tax is imposed by section 2001(a) on the transfer of a decedent's taxable estate at death. The estate tax is determined under a five-step computation required under sections 2001 and 2010 using the same rate schedule used for gift tax purposes (thus referred to as the unified rate schedule) as in effect at the decedent's death.

First, section 2001(b)(1) requires the determination of a tentative tax (again, a tax unreduced by a credit amount) on the sum of the taxable estate and the adjusted taxable gifts, defined as all taxable gifts made after 1976 other than those included in the gross estate (Step 1).

Second, section 2001(b)(2) and (g) require the determination of a hypothetical gift tax (a gift tax reduced, but not to below zero, by the credit amounts allowable in the years of the gifts) on all post-1976 taxable gifts, whether or not included in the gross estate. The credit

amount allowable for each year during which a gift was made is the tentative tax, computed using the tax rates in effect at the decedent's death, on the AEA for that year, but not exceeding the tentative tax on the gifts made during that year. Section 2505(c). The AEA is the sum of the BEA as in effect for the year in which the gift was made, any DSUE amount as of the date of the gift as computed pursuant to § 25.2505-2, and any restored exclusion amount as of the date of the gift as computed pursuant to Notice 2017-15. This hypothetical gift tax is referred to as the gift tax payable (Step 2).

Third, section 2001(b) requires the gift tax payable determined in Step 2 to be subtracted from the tentative tax determined in Step 1 to arrive at the net tentative estate tax (Step 3).

Fourth, section 2010(a) and (c) require the determination of a credit equal to the tentative tax on the AEA as in effect on the date of the decedent's death. This credit may not exceed the net tentative estate tax. Section 2010(d). (Step 4).

Finally, section 2010(a) requires that the credit amount determined in Step 4 be subtracted from the net tentative estate tax determined in Step 3. (Step 5).

IV. TCJA Amendments

Section 11061 of the TCJA amended section 2010(c)(3) to provide that, for decedents dying and gifts made after December 31, 2017, and before January 1, 2026, the BEA is increased by $5 million to $10 million as adjusted for inflation (increased BEA). On January 1, 2026, the BEA will revert to $5 million. Thus, an individual or the individual's estate may utilize the increased BEA to shelter from gift and estate taxes an additional $5 million of transfers made during the eight-year period beginning on January 1, 2018, and ending on December 31, 2025 (increased BEA period).

In addition, section 11002 of the TCJA amended section 1(f)(3) of the Code to base the determination of annual cost-of-living adjustments, including those for gift and estate tax purposes, on the Chained Consumer Price Index for All Urban Consumers for all taxable years beginning after December 31, 2017. Section 11002 of the TCJA also made conforming changes in sections 2010(c)(3)(B)(ii), 2032A(a)(3)(B), and 2503(b)(2)(B).

Section 11061 of the TCJA also added section 2001(g)(2) to the Code, which, in addition to the necessary or appropriate regulatory authority granted in section 2010(c)(6) for purposes of section 2010(c), directs the Secretary to prescribe such regulations as may be necessary or appropriate to carry out section 2001 with respect to any difference between the BEA applicable at the time of the decedent's death and the BEA applicable with respect to any gifts made by the decedent.

V. Summary of Concerns Raised by Changes in BEA

1. In General

Given the cumulative nature of the gift and estate tax computations and the differing manner in which the credit is applied against these two taxes, commenters have raised two questions regarding a potential for inconsistent tax treatment or double taxation of transfers resulting from the temporary nature of the increased BEA. First, in cases in which a taxpayer exhausted his or her BEA and paid gift tax on a pre-2018 gift, and then either makes an additional gift or dies during the increased BEA period, will the increased BEA be absorbed by the pre-2018 gift on which gift tax was paid so as to deny the taxpayer the full benefit of the increased BEA during the increased BEA period? Second, in cases in which a taxpayer made a gift during the increased BEA period that was fully sheltered from gift tax by the increased BEA but makes a gift or dies after the increased BEA period has ended, will the gift that was exempt from gift tax when made during the increased BEA period have the effect of increasing the gift or estate tax on the later transfer (in effect, subjecting the earlier gift to tax even though it was exempt from gift tax when made)?

As discussed in the remainder of this Background section, the Treasury Department and the IRS have analyzed the statutorily required steps for determining Federal gift and estate taxes in the context of several different situations that could occur either during the increased BEA period as a result of an increase in the BEA, or thereafter as a result of a decrease in the BEA. Only in the last situation discussed below was a potential problem identified, and a change intended to correct that problem is proposed in this notice of proposed rulemaking. This preamble, however, also includes a brief explanation of the reason why no potential problem is believed to exist in any of the first three situations discussed below. For the sake of simplicity, the following discussion assumes that, as may be the more usual case, the AEA includes no DSUE or restored exclusion amount and thus, refers only to the BEA.

2. Effect of Increase in BEA on Gift Tax

The first situation considered is whether, for gift tax purposes, the increased BEA available during the increased BEA period is reduced by pre-2018 gifts on which gift tax actually was paid. This issue arises for donors, who made both pre-2018 gifts exceeding the then-applicable BEA, thus making gifts that incurred a gift tax liability, and additional gifts during the increased BEA period. The concern raised is whether the gift tax computation will apply the increased BEA to the pre-2018 gifts, thus reducing the BEA otherwise available to shelter gifts made during the increased BEA period and, in effect, allocating credit to a gift on which gift tax in fact was paid.

Step 3 of the gift tax determination requires the tentative tax on all gifts from prior periods to be subtracted from the tentative tax on the donor's cumulative gifts (including the current gift). The gifts from prior periods include the pre-2018 gifts on which gift tax was paid. In this way, the full amount of the gift tax liability on the pre-2018 gifts is removed from the current year gift tax computation, regardless of whether that liability was sheltered from gift tax by the BEA and/or was satisfied by a gift tax payment. Steps 4 through 6 of the gift tax determination then require, in effect, that the BEA for the current year be reduced by the BEA allowable in prior periods against the gifts that were made by the donor in those prior periods. The increased BEA was not available in the years when the pre-2018 gifts were made and thus, was not allowable against those gifts. Accordingly, the gift tax determination appropriately reduces the increased BEA only by the amount of BEA allowable against prior period gifts, thereby ensuring that the increased BEA is not reduced by a prior gift on which gift tax in fact was paid.

3. Effect of Increase in BEA on Estate Tax

The second situation considered is whether, for estate tax purposes, the increased BEA available during the increased BEA period is reduced by pre-2018 gifts on which gift tax actually was paid. This issue arises in the context of estates of decedents who both made pre-2018 gifts exceeding the then allowable BEA, thus making gifts that incurred a gift tax liability, and die during the increased BEA period. The concern raised is whether the estate tax computation will apply the increased BEA to the pre-2018 gifts, thus reducing the BEA otherwise available against the estate tax during the increased BEA period and, in effect, allocating credit to a gift on which gift tax in fact was paid.

Step 3 of the estate tax determination requires that the hypothetical gift tax on the decedent's post-1976 taxable gifts be subtracted from the tentative tax on the sum of the taxable estate and adjusted taxable gifts. The post-1976 taxable gifts include the pre-2018 gifts on which gift tax was paid. In this way, the full amount of the gift tax liability on the pre-2018 gifts is removed from the estate tax computation, regardless of whether that liability was sheltered from gift tax by the BEA and/or was satisfied by a gift tax payment. Step 4 of the estate tax determination then requires that a credit on the amount of the BEA for the year of the decedent's death be subtracted from the net tentative estate tax. As a result, the only time that the increased BEA enters into the computation of the estate tax is when the credit on the amount of BEA allowable in the year of the decedent's death is netted against the tentative estate tax, which in turn already has been reduced by the hypothetical gift tax on the full amount of all post-1976 taxable gifts (whether or not gift tax was paid). Thus, the increased BEA is not reduced by the portion of any prior gift on which gift tax was paid, and the full amount of the increased BEA is available to compute the credit against the estate tax.

4. Effect of Decrease in BEA on Gift Tax

The third situation considered is whether the gift tax on a gift made after the increased BEA period is inflated by a theoretical gift tax on a gift made during the increased BEA period that was sheltered from gift tax when made. If so, this would effectively reverse the benefit of the increased BEA available for gifts made during the increased BEA period. This issue arises in the case of donors who both made one or more gifts during the increased BEA period that were sheltered from gift tax by the increased BEA in effect during those years, and made a post-2025 gift. The concern raised is whether the gift tax determination on the post-2025 gift will treat the gifts made during the increased BEA period as gifts not sheltered from gift tax by the credit on the BEA, given that the post-2025 gift tax determination is based on the BEA then in effect, rather than on the increased BEA.

Just as in the first situation considered in part V(2) of this Background section, Step 3 of the gift tax determination directs that the tentative tax on gifts from prior periods be subtracted from the tentative tax on the donor's cumulative gifts (including the current gift). The gift tax from prior periods includes the gift tax attributable to the gifts made during the increased BEA period. In this way, the full amount of the gift tax liability on the increased BEA period gifts is removed from the computation, regardless of whether that liability was sheltered from gift tax by the BEA or was satisfied by a gift tax payment. All that remains is the tentative gift tax on the donor's current gift. Steps 4 through 6 of the gift tax determination then require that the credit based on the BEA for the current year be reduced by such credits allowable in prior periods. Even if the sum of the credits allowable for prior periods exceeds the credit based on the BEA in the current (post-2025) year, the tax on the current gift cannot exceed the tentative tax on that gift and thus will not be improperly inflated. The gift tax determination anticipates and avoids this situation, but no credit will be available against the tentative tax on the post-2025 gift.

5. Effect of Decrease in BEA on Estate Tax

The fourth situation considered is whether, for estate tax purposes, a gift made during the increased BEA period that was sheltered from gift tax by the increased BEA inflates a post-2025 estate tax liability. This will be the case if the estate tax computation fails to treat such gifts as sheltered from gift tax, in effect reversing the benefit of the increased BEA available for those gifts. This issue arises in the case of estates of decedents who both made gifts during the increased BEA period that were sheltered from gift tax by the increased BEA in effect during those years, and die after 2025. The concern raised is whether the estate tax computation treats the gifts made during the increased BEA period as post-1976 taxable gifts not sheltered from gift tax by the credit on the BEA, given that the post-2025 estate tax computation is based on the BEA in effect at the decedent's death rather than the BEA in effect on the date of the gifts.

In this case, the statutory requirements for the computation of the estate tax, in effect, retroactively eliminate the benefit of the increased BEA that was available for gifts made during the increased BEA period. This can be illustrated by the following examples.

Example 1. Individual A made a gift of $11 million in 2018, when the BEA was $10 million. A dies in 2026, when the BEA is $5 million, with a taxable estate of $4 million. Based on a literal application of section 2001(b), the estate tax would be approximately $3,600,000, which is equal to a 40 percent estate tax on $9 million (specifically, the $9 million being the sum of the $4 million taxable estate and $5 million of the 2018 gift sheltered from gift tax by the increased BEA). This in effect would impose estate tax on the portion of the 2018 gift that was sheltered from gift tax by the increased BEA allowable at that time.

Example 2. The facts are the same as in *Example 1*, but A dies in 2026 with no taxable estate. Based on a literal application of section 2001(b), A's estate tax is approximately $2 million, which is equal to a 40 percent tax on $5 million. Five million dollars is the amount by which, after taking into account the $1 million portion of the 2018 gift on which gift tax was paid, the 2018 gift exceeded the BEA at death. This, in effect, would impose estate tax on the portion of the 2018 gift that was sheltered from the gift tax by the excess of the 2018 BEA over the 2026 BEA.

This problem occurs as a result of the interplay between Steps 2 and 4 of the estate tax determination, and the differing amounts of BEA taken into account in those steps. Step 2 determines the credit against gift taxes payable on all post-1976 taxable gifts, whether or not included in the gross estate, using the BEA amounts allowable on the dates of the gifts but determined using date of death tax rates. Step 3 subtracts gift tax payable from the tentative tax on the sum of the taxable estate and the adjusted taxable gifts. The result is the net tentative estate tax. Step 4 determines a credit based on the BEA as in effect on the date of the decedent's death. Step 5 then reduces the net tentative estate tax by the credit determined in Step 4. If the credit amount applied at Step 5 is less than that allowable for the decedent's post-1976 taxable gifts at Step 2, the effect is to increase the estate tax by the difference between those two credit amounts. In this circumstance, the statutory requirements have the effect of imposing an estate tax on gifts made during the increased BEA period that were sheltered from gift tax by the increased BEA in effect when the gifts were made.

Explanation of Provisions

To implement the TCJA changes to the BEA under section 2010(c)(3), the proposed regulations would amend § 20.2010-1 to provide that, in the case of decedents dying or gifts made after December 31, 2017, and before January 1, 2026, the increased BEA is $10 million. The proposed regulations also would conform the rules of § 20.2010-1 to the changes made by the TCJA regarding the cost of living adjustment.

Pursuant to section 2001(g)(2), the proposed regulations also would amend § 20.2010-1 to provide a special rule in cases where the portion of the credit as of the decedent's date of death that is based on the BEA is less than the sum of the credit amounts attributable to the BEA allowable in computing gift tax payable within the meaning of section 2001(b)(2). In that case, the portion of the credit against the net tentative estate tax that is attributable to the BEA would be based upon the greater of those two credit amounts. In the view of the Treasury Department and the IRS, the most administrable solution would be to adjust the amount of the credit in Step 4 of the estate tax determination required to be applied against the net tentative estate tax. Specifically, if the total amount allowable as a credit, to the extent based solely on the BEA, in computing the gift tax payable on the decedent's post-1976 taxable gifts, whether or not included in the gross estate, exceeds the credit amount, again to the extent based solely on the BEA in effect at the date of death, the Step 4 credit would be based on the larger amount of BEA. As modified, Step 4 of the estate tax determination therefore would require the determination of a credit equal to the tentative tax on the AEA as in effect on the date of the decedent's death, where the BEA included in that AEA is the larger of (i) the BEA as in effect on the date of the decedent's death under section 2010(c)(3), or (ii) the total amount of the BEA allowable in determining Step 2 of the estate tax computation (that is, the gift tax payable).

For example, if a decedent had made cumulative post-1976 taxable gifts of $9 million, all of which were sheltered from gift tax by a BEA of $10 million applicable on the dates of the gifts, and if the decedent died after 2025 when the BEA was $5 million, the credit to be applied in computing the estate tax is that based upon the $9 million of BEA that was used to compute gift tax payable.

The proposed regulations ensure that a decedent's estate is not inappropriately taxed with respect to gifts made during the increased BEA period. Congress' grant of regulatory authority in section 2001(g)(2) to address situations in which differences exist between the BEA applicable to a decedent's gifts and the BEA applicable to the decedent's estate clearly permits the Secretary to address the situation in which a gift is made during the increased BEA period and the decedent dies after the increased BEA period ends.

Commenters have noted that this problem is similar to that involving the application of the AEA addressed in the DSUE regulations. Section 20.2010-3(b). The DSUE amount generally is what remains of a decedent's BEA that can be used to offset the gift and/or estate tax liability of the decedent's surviving spouse. At any given time, however, a surviving spouse may use only the DSUE amount from his or her last deceased spouse - thus, only until the death of any subsequent spouse. Without those regulations, if a DSUE amount was used to shelter a surviving spouse's gifts from gift tax before the death of a subsequent spouse, and if the surviving spouse also survived the subsequent spouse, those gifts would have had the effect of absorbing the DSUE amount available to the surviving spouse at death, effectively resulting in a taking back of the DSUE amount that had been allocated to the earlier gifts. The DSUE regulations resolve this problem by providing that the DSUE amount available at the surviving spouse's death is the sum of the DSUE amount from that spouse's last deceased spouse, and any DSUE amounts from other deceased spouses that were "applied to one or more taxable gifts" of the surviving spouse.

Proposed Effective Date

The amendment to § 20.2010-1 is proposed to be effective on and after the date of publication of a Treasury decision adopting these rules as final regulations in the

Federal Register

Special Analyses

These proposed regulations are not subject to review under section 6(b) of Executive Order 12866 pursuant to the Memorandum of Agreement (April 11, 2018) between the Treasury Department and the Office of Management and Budget regarding review of tax regulations.

Pursuant to the Regulatory Flexibility Act (5 U.S.C. chapter 6), it is hereby certified that these proposed regulations will not have a significant economic impact on a substantial number of small entities. These proposed regulations apply to donors of gifts made after 2017 and to the estates of decedents dying after 2017, and implement an increase in the amount that is excluded from gift and estate tax. Neither an individual nor the estate of a deceased individual is a small entity within the meaning of 5 U.S.C. 601(6). Accordingly, a regulatory flexibility analysis is not required.

Pursuant to section 7805(f) of the Internal Revenue Code, this regulation has been submitted to the Chief Counsel for Advocacy of the Small Business Administration for comment on its impact on small business.

Comments and Public Hearing

Before these proposed regulations are adopted as final regulations, consideration will be given to any written or electronic comments that are submitted timely (in the manner described under the **ADDRESSES** heading) to the IRS. The Treasury Department and the IRS request comments on all aspects of the proposed regulations. All comments will be available at http://www.regulations.gov, or upon request. A public hearing on these proposed regulations has been scheduled for March 13, 2019, beginning at 10 A.M. in the Auditorium, Internal Revenue Building, 1111 Constitution Avenue, NW, Washington, DC 20224. Due to building security procedures, visitors must enter the Constitution Avenue entrance. In addition, all visitors must present photo identification to enter the building. Because of access restrictions, visitors will not be admitted beyond the immediate entrance area more than 30 minutes before the hearing starts. For information about having your name placed on the building access list to attend the hearing, see the **FOR FURTHER INFORMATION CONTACT** section of this preamble.

The rules of 26 CFR 601.601(a)(3) apply to the hearing. Persons who wish to present oral comments at the hearing must submit comments by February 20, 2019, and submit an outline of the topics to be discussed and the time devoted to each topic by February 20, 2019.

A period of 10 minutes will be allotted to each person for making comments. Copies of the agenda will be available free of charge at the hearing.

Drafting Information

The principal author of these proposed regulations is Deborah S. Ryan, Office of the Associate Chief Counsel (Passthroughs and Special Industries). Other personnel from the Treasury Department and the IRS participated in their development.

Statement of Availability of IRS Documents

Notice 2017-15 is published in the Internal Revenue Bulletin (or Cumulative Bulletin) and is available from the Superintendent of Documents, U.S. Government Publishing Office, Washington, DC 20402, or by visiting the IRS website at http://www.irs.gov.

[The next page is 93,901.]

Excise Tax Proposed Regulations—Preambles

[¶ 62,124] **Proposed Regulations and Amendment of Regulations (PS-66-93)**, published in the Federal Register on October 19, 1994.

Excise taxes: Special fuels: Gasoline and diesel fuel: Gasohol: Compressed natural gas.—Reg. §§ 40.6302(c)-0, 40.6302(c)-1, 40.6302(c)-4, 40.9999-1, 48.4041-21, 48.4081-0—48.4081-8, 48.4221-1, 48.4221-2, 48.4221-5, 48.4222(a)-1, 48.4222(b)-1 and 48.6427-10, relating to gasohol blending and the taxes on diesel fuel and compressed natural gas, are proposed. Treasury Decision 8659 adopted the proposed regulations or proposed amendments to regulations for Reg. §§ 48.4081-0—48.4081-8, 48.4221-1, 48.4221-2, 48.4221-5, 48.4222(a)-1 and 48.4222(b)-1. Treasury Decision 8609 adopted the proposals relating to Reg. §§ 40.6302(c)-0, 40.6302(c)-1, 40.6302(c)-4 and 48.4041-21. Treasury Decision 8685 adopted the amendment to Reg. § 40.9999-1. Thus, the only proposal not yet adopted amends Reg. § 48.6427-10.

AGENCY: Internal Revenue Service (IRS), Treasury.

ACTION: Notice of proposed rulemaking and notice of public hearing.

SUMMARY: This document contains proposed regulations relating to gasohol blending and the taxes on diesel fuel and compressed natural gas. This document also proposes to remove obsolete excise tax regulations. The proposed regulations reflect and implement certain changes made by the Energy Policy Act of 1992 (the Energy Act) and the Omnibus Budget Reconciliation Act of 1993 (the 1993 Act). The proposed regulations relating to gasoline and diesel fuel affect certain blenders, enterers, industrial users, refiners, terminal operators, and throughputters. The proposed regulations relating to compressed natural gas affect persons that sell or buy compressed natural gas for use as a fuel in a motor vehicle or motorboat.

DATES: Written comments must be submitted by December 19, 1994. Outlines of comments to be presented at the public hearing scheduled for January 11, 1995, must be received by December 21, 1994.

ADDRESSES: Send submissions to: CC:DOM:CORP:T:R (PS-66-93), room 5228, Internal Revenue Service, POB 7604, Ben Franklin Station, Washington, DC 20044. In the alternative, submissions may be hand delivered between the hours of 8 a.m. and 5 p.m. to: CC:DOM.CORP:T:R (PS-66-93), Courier's Desk, Internal Revenue Service, 1111 Constitution Avenue, NW, Washington, DC. The public hearing will be held in the IRS Auditorium, Seventh Floor, 7400 Corridor, Internal Revenue Building, 1111 Constitution Avenue, NW, Washington, DC.

FOR FURTHER INFORMATION CONTACT: Concerning the proposed regulations, Frank Boland, (202) 622-3130; concerning submissions and the hearing, Carol Savage, at (202) 622-8452; (not toll-free numbers).

SUPPLEMENTARY INFORMATION:

Paperwork Reduction Act

The collections of information contained in this notice of proposed rulemaking have been submitted to the Office of Management and Budget for review in accordance with the Paperwork Reduction Act (44 U.S.C. 3504(h)). Comments on the collections of information should be sent to the Office of Management and Budget, Attn: Desk Officer for the Department of the Treasury, Office of Information and Regulatory Affairs, Washington, DC 20503, with copies to the Internal Revenue Service, Attn: IRS Reports Clearance Officer, PC:FP, Washington, DC 20224.

The collections of information in this proposed regulation are in §§ 48.4041-21 and 48.6427-10. This information is required by the IRS to verify compliance with sections 4041 and 6427 and will be used to determine whether an amount of tax, credit, or payment has been computed correctly. The likely respondents are businesses and other for-profit organizations, including small businesses and organizations.

Estimated total annual reporting burden: 10 hours.

Estimated average annual burden per respondent: 1 hour.

Estimated number of respondents: 100

Estimated annual frequency of responses: On occasion.

Explanation of provisions

Background

Effective January 1, 1994, the 1993 Act amends section 4081 to impose the diesel fuel tax in the same manner as the gasoline tax. Thus, tax is imposed on (1) the removal of gasoline and diesel fuel (collectively taxable fuel) from any refinery, (2) the removal of taxable fuel from any terminal, (3) the entry of taxable fuel into the United States for consumption, use, or warehousing, and (4) the sale of taxable fuel to an unregistered person unless there was a prior taxable removal, entry, or sale of the taxable fuel. However, tax does not apply to any entry or removal of taxable fuel transferred in bulk to a refinery or terminal if the persons involved (including the terminal operator) are registered by the IRS.

Conforming amendments to gasoline regulations

On November 30, 1993, the IRS published in the Federal Register (58 FR 63069) temporary regulations under section 4081 relating to the imposition of the diesel fuel excise tax for diesel fuel that is removed at a terminal rack, removed from a refinery, entered into the United States, or blended outside of the bulk/transfer terminal system. Those rules are similar to the rules relating to the removal, entry, or blending of gasoline under §§ 48.4081-2 and 48.4081-3.

These proposed regulations generally consolidate the rules relating to gasoline and diesel fuel into a single set of rules applicable to all taxable fuel.

Compressed natural gas

Effective October 1, 1993, section 4041(a)(3) (added to the Internal Revenue Code by section 13241(e) of the 1993 Act) imposes a tax on compressed natural gas (CNG) that is sold for use or used as a fuel in a motor vehicle or motorboat.

The proposed regulations provide rules relating to the imposition of, and liability for, the tax on CNG. These rules are similar to the regulations relating to taxes on special motor fuels imposed by section 4041.

Gasohol; tolerance rule

The gasoline tax rate is 18.4 cents per gallon (the regular rate). However, a reduction from the regular rate is allowed for gasohol (a gasoline/alcohol mixture). Before January 1, 1993, section 4081(c) treated a mixture of gasoline and alcohol as gasohol only if at least 10 percent of the mixture was alcohol. The rate reduction under pre-1993 law was 5.4 cents per gallon for gasohol containing ethanol and 6 cents per gallon for gasohol containing alcohol other than ethanol. This was equivalent to a subsidy of 54 cents or 60 cents per gallon of alcohol used to produce gasohol.

Section 48.4081-6(b)(2) provides a special rule for the application of the "at least 10 percent" requirement by allowing a tolerance for mixtures that contain less than 10 percent alcohol but at least 9.8 percent alcohol. Under the tolerance rule, a portion of the mixture equal to the number of gallons of alcohol in the mixture multiplied by 10 is considered to be gasohol. Any excess liquid in the mixture is taxed at the regular rate. Absent the tolerance rule, pre-1993 law would have taxed the entire mixture at the regular rate.

The tolerance rule accommodates operational problems associated with the blending of gasohol. For example, blenders may fail to attain the required 10-percent alcohol level because the device used to meter the amount of gasoline or alcohol added to a tank truck is imprecise or because the high-speed gasoline or alcohol pump used does not shut off at the proper moment. Blenders cannot compensate for these errors by aiming for an alcohol content in excess of 10 percent because Environmental Protection Agency (EPA) rules do not authorize the sale of gasohol containing more than 10 percent alcohol.

Effective January 1, 1993, section 1920 of the Energy Act amended section 4081(c) to allow a reduction from the regular rate for mixtures containing at least 5.7 percent alcohol but less than 7.7 percent alcohol (5.7 percent gasohol) and mixtures containing at least 7.7 percent alcohol but less than 10 percent alcohol (7.7 percent gasohol). The 5.4—and 6-cents-per-gallon rate reductions were retained for mixtures containing at least 10 percent alcohol (10 percent gasohol) and were prorated for 5.7 percent and 7.7 percent gasohol to maintain the subsidy level of 54 cents or 60 cents per gallon, respectively, for ethanol or other alcohol that is mixed with gasoline.

The proposed regulations continue the present tolerance rule for mixtures that contain less than 10 percent alcohol but at least 9.8 percent alcohol. However, a similar rule is not extended to mixtures that contain less than 7.7 or 5.7 percent alcohol because blenders can compensate for any operational problems by aiming for an alcohol content above 7.7 or 5.7 percent without violating EPA rules.

Gasohol; blender credit or payment

If a gasohol blender produces gasohol from gasoline that was taxed at the regular rate, section 6427(f) allows the gasohol blender to obtain a partial credit or payment relating to that tax. The proposed regulations provide the conditions under which a credit or payment under section 6427(f) will be allowed.

Gasohol; ETBE

The regulations under section 40 provide that alcohol used to produce ethyl tertiary butyl ether (ETBE) generally is treated as *alcohol* for purposes of the alcohol fuels credit when the ETBE is mixed with gasoline. The proposed regulations provide a similar rule with respect to alcohol used to produce ETBE for purposes of the reduced tax rates for gasohol.

For example, a gasoline/ETBE mixture would qualify as 5.7 percent gasohol if the mixture contains 12.7 percent ETBE and each gallon of ETBE is made from .45 gallon of alcohol.

Reliance on these proposed regulations

These regulations are being issued in proposed form to provide timely guidance to taxpayers and to allow interested parties appropriate opportunity to provide comments before issuance of final regulations. Although final regulations may include changes made, for example, in response to comments, taxpayers may rely on the proposed regulations until final regulations are issued. For example, alcohol used to produce ETBE is treated as *alcohol* for purposes of the gasohol tax rates.

Special Analyses

It has been determined that this notice of proposed rulemaking is not a significant regulatory action as defined in EO 12866. Therefore, a regulatory assessment is not required. It also has been determined that section 553(b) of the Administrative Procedure Act (5 U.S.C. chapter 5) and the Regulatory Flexibility Act (5 U.S.C. chapter 6) do not apply to these regulations, and, therefore, a Regulatory Flexibility Analysis is not required. Pursuant to section 7805(f) of the Internal Revenue Code, this notice of proposed rulemaking will be submitted to the Chief Counsel for Advocacy of the Small Business Administration for comment on its impact on small business.

Comments and Public Hearing

Before these proposed regulations are adopted as final regulations, consideration will be given to any written comments that are submitted timely (preferably a signed original and eight copies) to the IRS. All comments will be available for public inspection and copying.

A public hearing has been scheduled for Wednesday, January 11, 1995, at 1 p.m. in the Auditorium, Internal Revenue Building, 1111 Constitution Avenue NW, Washington, DC. Because of access restrictions, visitors will not be admitted beyond the building lobby more than 15 minutes before the hearing starts.

The rules of § 601.601(a)(3) apply to the hearing.

Persons that have submitted written comments by December 19, 1994, and want to present oral comments at the hearing must submit an outline of the topics to be discussed and the time to be devoted to each topic by December 21, 1994.

A period of 10 minutes will be allotted to each person for making comments.

An agenda showing the scheduling of the speakers will be prepared after the deadline for receiving outlines has passed. Copies of the agenda will be available free of charge at the hearing.

Drafting Information

The principal author of these regulations is Frank Boland, Office of Assistant Chief Counsel (Passthroughs and Special Industries). However, other personnel from the IRS and Treasury Department participated in their development.

[¶ 62,145]   **Notice of Proposed Rulemaking (NPRM REG-141097-02)**, published in the Federal Register on April 1, 2003.

Communications tax: Definitions: Toll service.—Reg. § 49.4252-0, relating to the definition of toll telephone service for purposes of the communications excise tax, has been proposed.

AGENCY: Internal Revenue Service (IRS), Treasury.

ACTION: Notice of proposed rulemaking.

SUMMARY: This document contains proposed regulations relating to the definition of toll telephone service for purposes of the communications excise tax. These regulations affect providers and purchasers of communications services.

DATES: Written and electronic comments and requests for a public hearing must be received by June 30, 2003.

ADDRESSES: Send submissions to: CC:ITA:RU (REG-141097-02), room 5226, Internal Revenue Service, POB 7604, Ben Franklin Station, Washington, DC 20044. Submissions may be hand delivered Monday through Friday between the hours of 8 a.m. and 5 p.m. to: CC:ITA:RU (REG-141097-02), Courier's Desk, Internal Revenue Service, 1111 Constitution Avenue, NW., Washington, DC. Alternatively, taxpayers may submit electronic comments directly to the IRS Internet site at www.irs.gov/regs.

FOR FURTHER INFORMATION CONTACT: Concerning submissions, LaNita Van Dyke, (202) 622-7180; concerning the regulations, Cynthia McGreevy (202) 622-3130 (not toll-free numbers).

SUPPLEMENTARY INFORMATION:

Background

This document contains proposed amendments to the Facilities and Services Excise Tax Regulations (26 CFR part 49) relating to the definition of toll telephone service.

Section 4251 imposes tax on amounts paid for certain communications services, including local and toll telephone service. Section 4252(b)(1) provides that toll telephone service means a telephonic quality communication for which there is a toll charge that varies in amount with the distance and elapsed transmission time of each individual communication.

Section 4252(b)(1), as enacted in 1965, describes the long distance telephone service sold to residential and most business subscribers under the 1965 Federal Communications Commission rules. At that time, the charge for a long distance telephone call increased as the duration of the call increased and generally increased as the distance between the originating telephone station and the terminating telephone station increased. By the late 1990's, most carriers had moved toward a fee structure that includes a flat per-minute rate for domestic calls.

In 1979, the Treasury Department published Rev. Rul. 79-404 (1979-2 C.B. 382), which stands for the principle that a long distance telephone call for which the charge varies with elapsed transmission time but not with distance is toll telephone service described in section 4252(b)(1).

Special Analyses

It has been determined that this notice of proposed rulemaking is not a significant regulatory action as defined in Executive Order 12866. Therefore, a regulatory assessment is not required. It also has been determined that section 553(b) of the Administrative Procedure Act (5 U.S.C. chapter 5) does not apply to these regulations and, because these regulations do not impose on small entities a collection of information requirement, the Regulatory Flexibility Act (5 U.S.C. chapter 6) does not apply. Therefore, a Regulatory Flexibility Analysis is not required. Pursuant to section 7805(f) of the Internal Revenue Code, this notice of proposed rulemaking will be submitted to the Chief Counsel for Advocacy of the Small Business Administration for comment on its impact on small business.

Comments and Requests for a Public Hearing

Before these proposed regulations are adopted as final regulations, consideration will be given to any written and electronic comments that are submitted timely to the IRS. The IRS and Treasury Department specifically request comments on the clarity of the proposed regulations and how they may be made easier to understand. All comments will be available for public inspection and copying. A public hearing may be scheduled if requested in writing by any person that timely submits written comments. If a public hearing is scheduled, notice of the date, time, and place for the hearing will be published in the Federal Register.

Drafting Information

The principal author of these regulations is Cynthia McGreevy, Office of Associate Chief Counsel (Passthroughs and Special Industries). However, other personnel from the IRS and Treasury Department participated in their development.

[¶ 62,149]   Notice of Proposed Rulemaking (REG-154000-04), published in the Federal Register on April 26, 2005.

Fuel taxes: Diesel fuel: Kerosene: Nontaxable uses: Dyed fuel: Mechanical dye injection systems.—Amendments of Reg. §§ 48.4082-1 and 48.4101-1, relating to mechanical dye injection systems for diesel fuel and kerosene, have been proposed. A public hearing on the proposals has been scheduled for July 19, 2005, beginning at 10:00 a.m., in the IRS Auditorium, Internal Revenue Building, 1111 Constitution Avenue NW, Washington, D.C. Comments on the proposals and requests to speak at the hearing must be received by June 25, 2005, and should be sent to CC:PA:LPD:PR (REG-154000-04), Room 5203, Internal Revenue Service, POB 7604, Ben Franklin Station, Washington, D.C. 20044. Alternatively, taxpayers may submit comments electronically via the IRS Internet site at www.irs.gov/regs or via the Federal eRulemaking Portal at www.regulations.gov (IRS-REG-154000-04).

AGENCY: Internal Revenue Service (IRS), Treasury.

ACTION: Notice of proposed rulemaking by cross reference to temporary regulations and notice of public hearing.

SUMMARY: In the Rules and Regulations section of this issue of the **Federal Register,** the IRS is issuing temporary regulations relating to the mechanical dye injection of diesel fuel and kerosene. The text of those regulations also serves as the text of these proposed regulations. These regulations affect certain enterers, refiners, terminal operators, and throughputters.

DATES: Written and electronic comments must be received by June 27, 2005. Requests to speak and outlines of topics to be discussed at the public hearing scheduled for July 19, 2005, must be received by June 27, 2005.

ADDRESSES: Send submissions to CC:PA:LPD:PR (REG-154000-04), room 5203, Internal Revenue Service, POB 7604, Ben Franklin Station, Washington DC 20044. Submissions may be hand-delivered Monday through Friday between the hours of 8 a.m. and 4 p.m. to: CC:PA:LPD:PR (REG-154000-04), Courier's Desk, Internal Revenue Service, 1111 Constitution Avenue, NW., Washington, DC. or submitted electronically via the IRS Internet site at: *www.irs.gov/regs* or via the Federal eRuling portal at *www.regulations.gov* (IRS and REG-154000-04). The public hearing will be held in the IRS Auditorium, Internal Revenue Building, 1111 Constitution Avenue, NW., Washington DC.

FOR FURTHER INFORMATION CONTACT: Concerning the proposed regulations, William Blodgett at (202) 622-3090; concerning submissions of comments, the hearing, and/or to be placed on the building access list to attend the hearing, Sonya Cruse at (202) 622-7180 (not toll-free numbers).

SUPPLEMENTARY INFORMATION:

Paperwork Reduction Act

The collection of information contained in this notice of proposed rulemaking has been submitted to the Office of Management and Budget for review in accordance with the Paperwork Reduction Act of 1995 (44 U.S.C. 3507(d)). Comments on the collection of information should be sent to the **Office of Management and Budget,** Attn: Desk Officer for the Department of the Treasury, Office of Information and Regulatory Affairs, Washington, DC 20503, with copies to the **Internal Revenue Service,** Attn: IRS Reports Clearance Officer, SE:W:CAR:MP:T:T:SP, Washington, DC 20224. Comments on the collection of information should be received by June 27, 2005.

Comments are specifically requested concerning:

Whether the proposed collection of information is necessary for the proper performance of the functions of the Internal Revenue Service, including whether the information will have practical utility;

The accuracy of the estimated burden associated with the proposed collection of information (see below);

How the quality, utility, and clarity of the information to be collected may be enhanced;

How the burden of complying with the proposed collection of information may be minimized, including through the application of automated collection techniques or other forms of information technology; and

Estimates of capital or start-up costs and costs of operation, maintenance, and purchase of service to provide information.

The collection of information in this proposed regulation is in §§ 48.4082-1(d)(2), 48.4082-1(d)(4), 48.4082-1(d)(6) and 48.4101-1(h)(3). This collection of information is necessary to obtain a tax benefit. The likely recordkeepers are terminal operators and enterers.

Estimated total annual reporting and/or recordkeeping burden: 1,400 hours.

Estimated average annual burden hours per recordkeeper: 7 hours.

Estimated number of respondents and/or recordkeepers: 200.

An agency may not conduct or sponsor, and a person is not required to respond to, a collection of information unless it displays a valid control number assigned by the Office of Management and Budget.

Books or records relating to a collection of information must be retained as long as their contents may become material in the administration of any internal revenue law. Generally, tax returns and tax return information are confidential, as required by 26 U.S.C. 6103.

Background

Temporary regulations in the Rules and Regulations section of this issue of the **Federal Register** amend Manufacturers and Retailers Excise Taxes Regulations (26 CFR part 48) under sections 4082 and 4101. The temporary regulations set forth requirements regarding the mechanical dye injection systems for diesel fuel and kerosene and are required by the American Jobs Creation Act of 2004. The text of those temporary regulations also serves as the text of these proposed regulations. The preamble to the temporary regulations explains the temporary regulations.

Special Analyses

It has been determined that this notice of proposed rulemaking is not a significant regulatory action as defined in Executive Order 12866. Therefore, a regulatory flexibility assessment is not required. It also has been determined that section 553(b) of the Administrative Procedure Act (5 U.S.C. chapter 5) does not apply to these regulations. It is hereby certified that the collection of information in these regulations will not have a significant economic impact on a substantial number of small entitles. This certification is based on the fact that the time required to maintain the required records and report to the IRS is minimal and will not have a significant impact on those small entitles. Therefore, a Regulatory Flexibility Analysis under the Regulatory Flexibility Act (5 U.S.C. chapter 6) is not required. Pursuant to section 7805(f) of the Internal Revenue Code, this notice of proposed rulemaking will be submitted to the Chief Counsel for Advocacy of the Small Business Administration for comment on its impact on small business.

Comments and Public Hearing

Before these proposed regulations are adopted as final regulations, consideration will be given to any written (a signed original and eight (8) copies) or electronic comments that are submitted timely to the IRS. All comments will be available for public inspection and copying.

A public hearing has been scheduled for July 19, 2005, at 10 a.m. in the IRS Auditorium, Internal Revenue Building, 1111 Constitution Ave., NW, Washington, DC. All visitors must present photo identification to enter the building. Because of access restrictions, visitors will not be admitted beyond the immediate entrance area at the Constitution Avenue entrance more than 30 minutes before the hearing starts. For information about having your name placed on the building access list to attend the hearing, see the "FOR FURTHER INFORMATION CONTACT" section of this preamble.

The rules of 26 CFR 601.601(a)(3) apply to the hearing. Persons who wish to present oral comments at the hearing must submit written comments and an outline of the topics to be discussed and the time to be devoted to each topic (signed original and eight coples (8) copies) by June 27, 2005. A period of 10 minutes will be allotted to each person for making comments. An agenda showing the scheduling of speakers will be prepared after the deadline for receiving outlines has passed. Copies of the agenda will be available free of charge at the hearing.

Drafting Information

The principal author of these regulations is William Blodgett, Office of Associate Chief Counsel (Passthroughs and Special Industries), IRS. However, other personnel from the IRS and Treasury Department participated in their development.

[¶ 62,153] Notice of Proposed Rulemaking (REG-155087-05), published in the Federal Register on July 29, 2008.

Fuel credits: Alcohol mixtures: Biodiesel mixtures: Renewable diesel mixtures: Alternative fuel mixtures: Alternative fuel.—Amendments of Reg. §§ 1.40-1, 40.0-1, 40.6302(c)-(1), 48.0-1, 48.4041-0, 48.4041-18, 48.4041-19, 48.4041-20, 48.4081-1, 48.4081-2, 48.4081-3, 48.4081-6, 48.4082-4, 48.4101-1 and 48.6427-8 are proposed. Also the following new regulations are proposed: Reg. §§ 1.40-2, 1.40A-1, 48.0-4, 48.6426-1, 48.6426-2, 48.6426-3, 48.6426-4, 48.6426-5, 48.6426-6, 48.6426-7 and 48.6427-12. The proposed regulations and proposed amendments relate to credits and payments for alcohol mixtures, biodiesel mixtures, renewable diesel mixtures, alternative fuel mixtures and alternative fuel sold for use or used as a fuel, are proposed.

AGENCY: Internal Revenue Service (IRS), Treasury.

ACTION: Notice of proposed rulemaking.

SUMMARY: This document contains proposed regulations relating to credits and payments for alcohol mixtures, biodiesel mixtures, renewable diesel mixtures, alternative fuel mixtures, and alternative fuel sold for use or used as a fuel, as well as proposed regulations relating to the definition of gasoline and diesel fuel. These regulations reflect changes made by the American Jobs Creation Act of 2004, the Energy Policy Act of 2005, the Safe, Accountable, Flexible, Efficient Transportation Equity Act: A Legacy for Users, and the Tax Technical Corrections Act of 2007. These regulations affect producers of alcohol, biodiesel, and renewable diesel; producers of alcohol, biodiesel, renewable diesel, and alternative fuel mixtures; sellers and users of alternative fuel; and certain persons liable for the tax on removals, entries, or sales of gasoline or diesel fuel.

DATES: Written or electronic comments and requests for a public hearing must be received by **May 6, 2012.**

ADDRESSES: Send submissions to CC:PA:LPD:PR (REG-155087-05), room 5203, Internal Revenue Service, PO Box 7604, Ben Franklin Station, Washington, DC 20044. Submissions may be hand delivered Monday through Friday between the hours of 8 a.m. and 4 p.m. to CC:PA:LPD:PR (REG-155087-05), Courier's Desk, Internal Revenue Service, 1111 Constitution Avenue, NW, Washington, DC, or sent electronically, via the Federal eRulemaking Portal at http://www.regulations.gov (IRS REG-155087-05).

FOR FURTHER INFORMATION CONTACT: Concerning the proposed regulations, Stephanie Bland, Taylor Cortright, or DeAnn Malone, all of whom can be reached at (202) 622-3130 (not a toll-free call); concerning the submission of comments or requests for a public hearing, Oluwafunmilayo Taylor at (202) 622-7180 (not a toll-free call).

SUPPLEMENTARY INFORMATION:

Paperwork Reduction Act

The collections of information contained in this notice of proposed rulemaking have been submitted to the Office of Management and Budget for review in accordance with the Paperwork Reduction Act of 1995 (44 U.S.C. 3507(d)). Comments on the collection of information should be sent to the **Office of Management and Budget**, Attn: Desk Officer for the Department of the Treasury, Office of Information and Regulatory Affairs, Washington, DC 20503, with copies to the Internal Revenue Service, Attn: IRS Reports Clearance Officer, SE:W:CAR:MP:T:T:SP, Washington, DC 20224. Comments on the collection of information should be received by [*INSERT DATE 60 DAYS AFTER PUBLICATION OF THIS DOCUMENT IN THE FEDERAL REGISTER*]. Comments are specifically requested concerning:

Whether the proposed collection of information is necessary for the proper performance of the functions of the Internal Revenue Service, including whether the information will have practical utility;

The accuracy of the estimated burden associated with the proposed collection of information;

How the quality, utility, and clarity of the information to be collected may be enhanced;

How the burden of complying with the proposed collection of information may be minimized, including through the application of automated collection techniques or other forms of information technology; and

Estimates of capital or start-up costs and costs of operation, maintenance, and purchase of service to provide information.

The collection of information in this proposed regulation is in § 48.6426-3(e), describing the certificate the biodiesel producer must give to the claimant of a biodiesel mixture credit or biodiesel credit; § 48.6426-3(f), describing the statement a biodiesel reseller must give to the claimant of a biodiesel mixture credit or biodiesel credit; § 48.6426-4(e), describing the certificate the renewable diesel producer must give to the claimant of a renewable diesel mixture credit or renewable diesel credit; § 48.6426-4(f), describing the statement a renewable diesel reseller must give to the claimant of a renewable diesel mixture credit or renewable diesel credit; and § 48.6426-6(c), describing the statement given to a seller of liquefied natural gas. This information is required to obtain a tax benefit. This information will be used by the IRS to substantiate claims for the tax benefits. The likely recordkeepers are business or other for-profit institutions and small businesses or organizations.

Estimated total annual reporting burden: 17,710 hours.

Estimated average annual burden hours per respondent varies from 2.5 hours to 25 hours, depending on individual circumstances, with an estimated average of 22 hours.

Estimated number of respondents: 756.

Estimated annual frequency of responses: On occasion.

An agency may not conduct or sponsor, and a person is not required to respond to, a collection of information unless it displays a valid control number assigned by the Office of Management and Budget.

Books or records relating to a collection of information must be retained as long as their contents may become material in the administration of any internal revenue law. Generally, tax returns and tax return information are confidential, as required by 26 U.S.C. 6103.

Background

The Internal Revenue Code (Code) provides incentives for certain renewable and alternative fuels. Before January 1, 2005, a reduced rate of tax applied to most alcohol-blended fuels. The American Jobs Creation Act of 2004 (Public Law 108-357) replaced the reduced rate of tax for alcohol-blended fuels with credits or payments for alcohol and alcohol mixtures that are sold for use or used as a fuel. The Act also added credits and payments for biodiesel and biodiesel mixtures sold for use or used as a fuel. Credit and payment provisions for renewable diesel, renewable diesel mixtures, alternative fuel, alternative fuel mixtures, and diesel-water fuel emulsions were added to the Code by the Energy Policy Act of 2005 (Public Law 109-58) and the Safe, Accountable, Flexible, Efficient Transportation Equity Act: A Legacy for Users (Public Law 109-59) (SAFETEA). Technical corrections to SAFETEA were made by the Tax Technical Corrections Act of 2007 (Public Law 110-172).

The incentives include a credit under section 6426 for alcohol fuel mixtures, biodiesel mixtures, renewable diesel mixtures (incorporated into section 6426 by section 40A(f)), and alternative fuel mixtures sold for use or used as a fuel and alternative fuel sold for use or used as a fuel in a motor vehicle or motorboat. The credit under section 6426 is allowed against the claimant's fuel tax liability. The incentives for these fuels also include a payment under section 6427(e) and a refundable income tax credit under section 34. The amount allowed as a payment or credit under these provisions is reduced by the claimant's excise tax liability against which a credit is allowed under section 6426. Section 40 provides a nonrefundable income tax credit for alcohol fuel mixtures, alcohol that is sold for use or used as a fuel, and for the production of alcohol by certain small ethanol producers; section 40A provides similar rules relating to biodiesel and renewable diesel. The Code includes coordination rules that limit the maximum incentive that may be claimed for any particular gallon of alcohol, biodiesel, renewable diesel, and alternative fuel. Generally, for alcohol that is ethanol, the benefit is $0.51 per gallon; for biodiesel, the incentive is $0.50 per gallon ($1.00 per gallon in the case of agri-biodiesel); for renewable diesel, the incentive is $1.00 per gallon; and, for alternative fuel, the incentive is $0.50 per gallon. In the case of small ethanol producers and small agri-biodiesel producers, however, the Code allows an additional income tax credit of $0.10 per gallon.

Notice 2005-4 (2005-1 CB 289) describes the alcohol and biodiesel credits and payments and provides general guidance for these incentives. Comments received after the publication of Notice 2005-4 requested additional guidance with regard to the biodiesel producer certificates in the case of resale, commingled biodiesel, the definition of agri-biodiesel, and the definition of a biodiesel mixture. Guidance on these issues was provided in Notice 2005-62 (2005-2 CB 443). Notice 2005-80 (2005-2 CB 953) describes the registration requirements related to diesel-water fuel emulsions. Notice 2006-92, (2006-43 IRB. 774) describes the alternative fuel credits and payments. Notice 2007-37 (2007-17 IRB 1002) provides guidance on renewable diesel. Notice 2007-97 (2007-49 IRB 1092) provides guidance on liquid hydrocarbons for purposes of the definition of alternative fuel. Comments were received in response to these notices and have been considered in the development of this notice of proposed rulemaking.

Renewable and alternative fuels; currently applicable rules.

The IRS has received numerous inquiries about the proper steps that must be taken to comply with the tax laws and to take full advantage of the tax incentives for certain renewable and alternative fuels. The following are general rules that are currently applicable and would not be changed by these proposed regulations.

Registration.

Registration by the IRS is required for each person that produces alcohol, biodiesel, renewable diesel, or blended taxable fuel or claims credits or payments with respect to alternative fuel.

Application for registration is made on Form 637, "Application for Registration (For Certain Excise Tax Activities)." A person generally may not engage in an activity for which registration is required until the IRS has approved the person's registration with respect to the activity.

Imposition of tax.

Tax is imposed on the removal of a biodiesel mixture that is diesel fuel from the terminal at the terminal rack. In the case of blended taxable fuel, tax is imposed on a blender's sale or removal of the fuel and the blender is liable for the tax. Blended taxable fuel includes diesel fuel or gasoline produced outside of the bulk transfer/terminal system by mixing an untaxed liquid, such as biodiesel or alcohol, with a taxable fuel, such as diesel fuel or gasoline, that has been previously taxed (even if only at the Leaking Underground Storage Tank Trust Fund financing rate). Thus, for example, if a person produces, outside the bulk transfer/terminal system, a biodiesel mixture that is diesel fuel, that person is liable for tax on its removal or sale of the mixture. Further, tax generally is imposed on the delivery of fuel that has not been taxed into the fuel supply tank of a motor vehicle or diesel-powered train and on the delivery of alternative fuel (liquid fuel other than gas oil, fuel oil, or taxable fuel) into the fuel supply tank of a motorboat unless the delivery of the fuel or alternative fuel is for a nontaxable purpose.

Liability for these excise taxes is reported on Form 720, "Quarterly Federal Excise Tax Return." Persons that are liable for excise taxes may also be required to make semi-monthly deposits. See Form 720 for more information on deposits.

Tax incentives for mixtures.

The excise tax credits for mixtures containing alcohol, biodiesel, renewable diesel, or alternative fuel must be claimed on Form 720, Schedule C. These credits are allowed to the extent of certain fuel tax liability. The credits are claimed by the person producing the mixture.

The mixture producer may also claim payments (or refundable income tax credits) for incentives that exceed tax liability; that is, for the amount by which the maximum incentive allowable for the mixture exceeds the credit allowed on the Form 720. Notice 2005-62 contains guidance on the computation of payment limitations. Claims for payment are made either on Form 8849, "Claim for Refund of Excise Taxes," or Schedule C, Form 720, "Quarterly Federal Excise Tax Return." (Thus, claims on Form 720 may be for both an excise tax credit and a payment.) Claims for the refundable income tax credit are made on Form 4136, "Credit for Federal Tax Paid on Fuel," which is attached to the claimant's income tax return.

Tax incentives for neat fuels.

A nonrefundable general business tax credit may be claimed for alcohol, biodiesel, and renewable diesel fuels that are not in a mixture and are used as a fuel. This is the only credit or payment allowed with respect to the use of these neat fuels as a fuel. Claims for the credit are made by the person using the renewable fuel in a trade or business or by the person that sold the fuel at retail and delivered it into a vehicle. The small ethanol producer credit and the small agri-biodiesel producer credit are also nonrefundable general business credits. Claims for nonrefundable general business credits are made on Form 6478, "Credit for Alcohol Used as Fuel," and Form 8864, "Biodiesel and Renewable Diesel Fuels Credit," attached to the claimant's income tax return.

An excise tax credit may be claimed for alternative fuel that is not in a mixture and is used as a fuel. The excise tax credit is claimed on Form 720, Schedule C. The credit is allowed to the extent of certain fuel excise tax liability. The credit is claimed by the alternative fueler (unmixed fuel). If the incentive for unmixed alternative fuel exceeds the applicable excise tax liability the excess may be claimed as a payment on Form 8849 or as a refundable income tax credit on Form 4136.

Explanation of Provisions

The proposed regulations add provisions relating to registration requirements and excise tax credits or payments for alcohol, biodiesel, renewable diesel and alternative fuel mixtures and for alternative fuel and dieselwater fuel emulsions. The regulations provide definitions and prescribe rules for claiming a credit or payment. Specifically, the regulations prescribe the conditions to allowance of a credit or payment, the content of claims for credit or payment, and the form of applicable certificates. The proposed regulations also remove obsolete regulations relating to gasohol and other alcohol fuels.

The proposed regulations generally adopt the rules of Notices 2005-4, 2005-62, 2005-80, 2006-92, 2007-37, and 2007-97. Differences between the notices and the proposed regulations are described in this preamble.

Biodiesel mixtures and liability for tax.

Notice 2005-62 provides that *biodiesel mixture* means a mixture of biodiesel and diesel fuel that contains at least 0.1 percent (by volume) of diesel fuel. That rule is unchanged by these proposed regulations.

Under existing regulations, diesel fuel does not include "excluded liquid"; biodiesel mixtures with a high concentration of biodiesel typically are classified as an excluded liquid. The definition of "excluded liquid" predates the biodiesel incentives and was intended to ensure that the diesel fuel tax was not imposed on certain liquids typically not used as fuel. The proposed regulations revise the definition of "excluded liquid" so that all biodiesel mixtures, which are generally used as a substitute for diesel fuel, will be classified as diesel fuel for tax purposes. As a result, under the proposed regulations, tax is imposed on a biodiesel mixture when it is removed from the bulk transfer/terminal system. If a biodiesel mixture is produced outside the bulk transfer/terminal system, tax is imposed on the sale or removal of the mixture by the mixture producer. The mixture producer is liable for the tax and must be registered as a blender of taxable fuel. The tax incentive for the biodiesel mixture generally must be taken as a credit against the producer's fuel tax liability and any excess over the fuel tax liability is allowable as either a payment or an income tax credit.

Also, the de minimis exception to the definition of "blended taxable fuel" is removed. Under this exception, a mixture is not blended fuel if the person creating the mixture adds less than 400 gallons of untaxed liquid to previously taxed fuel during the quarter and the operator of the vehicle using the mixture is liable for the tax on the untaxed liquid. Thus, in cases in which the untaxed liquid is alcohol, biodiesel, or alternative fuel, the exception prevents the credit for which the mixture producer is eligible from being used to offset the tax. With the removal of this exception, the same person (the producer of the mixture) will be liable for the tax and eligible for the credit that can be used to offset the tax.

Biodiesel and EPA registration requirements.

The Code defines *biodiesel* as monoalkyl esters of long chain fatty acids derived from plant or animal matter that meet (1) the registration requirements of the Environmental Protection Agency (EPA) for fuel and fuel additives and, (2) ASTM D6751. Under the proposed regulations, a product meets the EPA registration requirements if the EPA does not require the product to be registered. Thus, for example, if a biodiesel mixture is to be sold only at a marina for use in boats, the biodiesel in the mixture meets the EPA registration requirement because EPA registration requirements do not apply to fuels or fuel additives sold for use in boats.

Biodiesel certificates.

The Code provides that a claim relating to a biodiesel mixture is not allowed unless, among other conditions, the claimant obtains the prescribed certificate from the biodiesel producer. Under existing rules, as well as the proposed regulations, this certificate must be attached to the claim that is filed with the IRS. However, the proposed regulations do not require a separate certificate to accompany the claim filed by a mixture producer that is also the producer of the biodiesel in the mixture. Further, the proposed regulations require, as a condition to allowance of an excise tax credit or a payment, that the claimant obtain the certificate from a registered biodiesel producer. If the claim is for a nonrefundable general business credit, the certificate may be from the registered producer or importer.

Erroneous biodiesel certificates.

Under the Code, a claim relating to a biodiesel mixture is not allowed if the mixture does not actually contain biodiesel. Guidance was requested on whether a claim would be allowed if the claimant attached a certificate for biodiesel and the information on the certificate proved to be incorrect. The proposed regulations make clear that such a claim is not allowed even if the claim is based on a biodiesel

certificate that the claimant accepted in good faith. In such a case, however, the proposed regulations generally provide that reliance on the certificate will be treated as reasonable cause for purposes of the penalties imposed by sections 6651 (relating to failure to pay) and 6675 (relating to excessive claims).

Alternative fuel.

The Code allows a credit or payment for alternative fuel that is not in a mixture if the alternative fuel is sold for use or used as a fuel in a motor vehicle or motorboat. If the claim is based on a sale, the claimant must deliver the fuel into the fuel supply tank of the motor vehicle or motorboat or, in the case of a bulk sale, obtain the statement described in § 48.4041-5(a)(2), § 48.4041-21(b), or proposed § 48.6426-6(c).

Registration of alternative fuelers.

A person must be registered by the IRS before claiming the alternative fuel or alternative fuel mixture credit or payment. Section 34 allows a refundable income tax credit with respect to alternative fuel or an alternative fuel mixture. This credit is claimed on Form 4136 filed with the claimant's Federal income tax return. Because partnerships do not file federal income tax returns, the refundable income tax credit allowable with respect to a partnership's sale or use of alternative fuel is made by its partners. The partners may file Form 4136 with their income tax returns to claim a credit based on the information provided them on the partnership's Schedule K-1.

The proposed regulations provide that a partner in a partnership is treated as a registered alternative fueler for purposes of claims on Form 4136 if the partnership is registered for purposes of claims for an excise tax credit or payment. A partner that is treated as registered under this rule is to provide the partnership's registration number on Form 4136. These rules also apply for purposes of ultimate vendor claims by partners in partnerships that are ultimate vendors of diesel fuel or kerosene.

Small ethanol producer credit.

Section 40(a)(3) provides an income tax credit for ethanol produced by eligible small ethanol producers. The amount of ethanol that is eligible for the credit during any taxable year cannot exceed 15,000,000 gallons for any producer. A small ethanol producer generally means a person whose productive capacity for all alcohol, including alcohol for which a credit is not allowable under section 40, does not exceed 60,000,000 gallons at any time during the taxable year. Section 40(g)(5) authorizes the Secretary to prescribe regulations to prevent the credit from benefiting a person that directly or indirectly has a productive capacity for alcohol in excess of 60,000,000 gallons and to prevent any person from directly or indirectly benefiting with respect to more than 15,000,000 gallons during the taxable year. Section 40A provides similar rules with respect to the small agri-biodiesel producer credit.

The proposed regulations provide that *producer* means the person that has title to the ethanol immediately after the ethanol is created. Also, the producer must use a feedstock other than ethanol to produce the ethanol. The proposed regulations do not allow the credit for ethanol produced at the facilities of a contract manufacturer if the contract manufacturer has a direct or indirect productive capacity of more than 60,000,000 gallons of alcohol during the taxable year. Similarly, if the manufacturer does not have a productive capacity of more than 60,000,000 gallons but more than 15,000,000 gallons of ethanol is produced at the manufacturer's facilities during the taxable year, the proposed regulations allow the credit with respect to only the first 15,000,000 gallons of ethanol produced at the facilities during the taxable year. These rules apply to small agribiodiesel producers also.

Gasoline and gasoline blends.

The Code defines gasoline as including gasoline blends. The proposed regulations generally define a gasoline blend as any liquid that contains at least 0.1 percent (by volume) of finished gasoline and that is suitable for use as a fuel in a motor vehicle or motorboat. Thus, for example, E-85 (a mixture of 85 percent ethanol made from corn or other agricultural products and 15 percent gasoline) is treated as a gasoline blend. Tax is imposed on the gasoline blend when it is removed from the bulk transfer/terminal system or, if it is blended taxable fuel, when it is sold or removed by the blender. The proposed regulations also classify leaded gasoline as gasoline. Thus, for example, gasoline products that are sold as "racing gasoline" generally are treated as gasoline even though their lead content make them unsuitable for highway use.

Excise tax returns.

The privilege to file consolidated returns under section 1501 applies only to income tax returns and not to excise tax returns. The proposed regulations note this rule and also reflect the rules of §301.7701-2(c)(2)(v), which was added by TD 9356 (72 FR 45891, August 16, 2007), relating to the excise tax treatment of certain business entities that are treated as separate from their owner for income tax purposes.

Proposed effective/applicability date.

The amendments to the regulations generally are proposed to be effective on the date they are published as final regulations in the **Federal Register**.

Future regulations projects.

Future proposed regulations will address other fuel-related provisions in the American Jobs Creation Act, the Energy Policy Act, and SAFETEA. These include provisions related to kerosene used in aviation, the Leaking Underground Storage Tank Trust Fund tax, the tax on alternative fuel, and two-party exchanges.

Availability of IRS documents

IRS notices cited in this preamble are published in the Internal Revenue Bulletin or Cumulative Bulletin and are available at IRS.gov.

Special Analyses

It has been determined that this notice of proposed rulemaking is not a significant regulatory action as defined in Executive Order 12866. Therefore, a regulatory assessment is not required. It also has been determined that section 553(b) of the Administrative Procedure Act (5 U.S.C. chapter 5) does not apply to these proposed regulations. It is hereby certified that this regulation will not have a significant economic impact on a substantial number of small entities. This certification is based on IRS estimates that less than 700 small entities will be required to provide certificates each year, such certificates will be provided only on occasion, and the average annual burden per respondent will be 22 hours. The economic impact of the collection of information is limited to completing a certificate in the form prescribed by the regulations. The certificate can be completed by filling in a small number of fields with information that is readily available to the taxpayer, and completion of a certificate should generally take less than 15 minutes. Accordingly, the time and resources required to prepare and provide these certificates is minimal and will not have a significant effect on those entities providing them. Therefore, an analysis under the Regulatory Flexibility Act (5 U.S.C. chapter 6) is not required. Pursuant to section 7805(f) of the Internal Revenue Code, this notice of proposed rulemaking has been submitted to the Chief Counsel for Advocacy of the Small Business Administration for comment on its impact on small business.

Comments and Requests for a Public Hearing

Before these proposed regulations are adopted as final regulations, consideration will be given to any written (a signed original and eight (8) copies) or electronic comments that are submitted timely to the IRS. The IRS and the Treasury Department request comments on the clarity of the proposed regulations and how they may be made easier to understand. All comments will be available for public inspection and copying. A public hearing will be scheduled if requested in writing by any person that timely submits written comments. If a public hearing is scheduled, notice of the date, time, and place for the hearing will be published in the **Federal Register**.

Drafting Information

The principal authors of these regulations are Taylor Cortright and Frank Boland, Office of Associate Chief Counsel (Passthroughs and Special Industries). However, other personnel from the IRS and the Treasury Department participated in their development.

[¶ 62,166] Notice of Proposed Rulemaking (REG-103380-05), published in the Federal Register on March 31, 2016.

[Code Secs. 4051, 4052, 4061, 4071, 4072 and 4073]

Highway excise taxes.—New regulations Reg. §48.0-4, Reg. §48.4051-0, Reg. §48.4051-1, Reg. §48.4051-2 are proposed. Amendments of Reg. §41.4482(a)-1, Reg. §48.0-1, Reg. §48.0-2, Reg. §48.4041-8, Reg. §48.4061(a)-1, Reg. §48.4071-3, Reg. §48.4072-1, Reg. §48.4081-1, Reg. §48.4221-7, Reg. §48.4221-8, and Reg. §145.4052-1 are proposed. Revisions of Reg. §48.4052-1, Reg. §48.4071-1, Reg. §48.4071-2, Reg. §48.4073-1, Reg. §48.4073-2 and Reg. §145.4051-1 are proposed. Removal of Reg. §48.4071-4, Reg. §48.4073, Reg. §48.4073-3, Reg. §48.4073-4, Reg. §48.6416(c)-1 and Reg. §145.4061-1 are also proposed. The proposed regulations relate to the excise taxes imposed on the sale of highway tractors, trailers, trucks, and tires; the use of heavy vehicles on the highway; and the definition of "highway vehicle" related to these and other taxes. These proposed regulations affect manufacturers, producers, importers, dealers, retailers, and users of certain highway tractors, trailers, trucks, and tires.

Excise Tax; Tractors, Trailers, Trucks, and Tires; Definition of Highway Vehicle

AGENCY: Internal Revenue Service (IRS), Treasury.

ACTION: Notice of proposed rulemaking.

SUMMARY: This document contains proposed regulations relating to the excise taxes imposed on the sale of highway tractors, trailers, trucks, and tires; the use of heavy vehicles on the highway; and the definition of highway vehicle related to these and other taxes. These proposed regulations reflect legislative changes and court decisions regarding these topics. These proposed regulations affect manufacturers, producers, importers, dealers, retailers, and users of certain highway tractors, trailers, trucks, and tires.

DATES: Written and electronic comments and requests for a public hearing must be received by March 31, 2016.

ADDRESSES: Send submissions to: CC:PA:LPD:PR (REG-103380-05), Room 5203, Internal Revenue Service, PO Box 7604, Ben Franklin Station, Washington, DC 20044. Submissions may be hand-delivered to: CC:PA:LPD:PR Monday through Friday between the hours of 8 a.m. and 4 p.m. to: CC:PA:LPD:PR (REG-103380-05), Courier's Desk, Internal Revenue Service, 1111 Constitution Avenue, NW, Washington, DC, or sent electronically via the Federal eRulemaking Portal at *http://www.regulations.gov* (IRS REG-1103380-05).

FOR FURTHER INFORMATION CONTACT: Concerning the proposed regulations, Celia Gabrysh, at (202) 317-6855; concerning submissions of comments or a request for a hearing Regina Johnson at (202) 317-6901 (not toll-free numbers).

SUPPLEMENTARY INFORMATION:

Paperwork Reduction Act

The collection of information contained in this notice of proposed rulemaking has been submitted to the Office of Management and Budget for review in accordance with the Paperwork Reduction Act of 1995 (44 U.S.C. 3507(d)). Comments on the collection of information should be sent to the **Office of Management and Budget**, Attn: Desk Officer for the Department of the Treasury, Office of Information and Regulatory Affairs, Washington, DC 20503, with copies to the **Internal Revenue Service**, Attn: IRS Reports Clearance Officer, SE:W:CAR:MP:T:T:SP, Washington, DC 20224. Comments on the collection of information should be received by March 31, 2016. Comments are specifically requested concerning:

Whether the proposed collection of information is necessary for the proper performance of the functions of the Internal Revenue Service, including whether the information will have practical utility;

The accuracy of the estimated burden associated with the proposed collection of information;

How the quality, utility, and clarity of the information to be collected may be enhanced;

How the burden of complying with the proposed collection of information may be minimized, including through the application of automated collection techniques or other forms of information technology; and

Estimates of capital or start-up costs and costs of operation, maintenance, and purchase of services to provide information.

The collections of information in these proposed regulations are in §48.4051-1(e)(8), describing the certificate the seller of an incomplete chassis cab must have to substantiate a tax-free sale; §48.4051-1(f)(3)(ii), describing the record of gross vehicle weight (GVW) a seller of a truck, trailer, or tractor must maintain to substantiate taxable and nontaxable sales; §48.4051-1(f)(4)(ii), describing the record of gross combination weight (GCW) a seller of a tractor must maintain to substantiate taxable and nontaxable sales; §48.4052-1(c), describing the certificate a seller of a truck, trailer, or tractor for resale or long term leasing must have to substantiate a tax-free sale; § 48.4052-2(b), describing the certificate a seller of a trailer must have to avoid the four percent price markup for resale within six months; § 48.4073-1(c), describing the certificate a taxable tire manufacturer must have to make a tax-free sale to the Department of Defense or the Coast Guard; § 48.4221-7(c), describing the certificate a manufacturer must have to make a tax-free sale of a taxable tire when sold for use or in connection with the sale of another article manufactured by the purchaser and sold by the purchaser in a sale that meets the requirements of section 4221(e)(2); and § 48.4221-8(c), describing the certificate a taxable tire manufacturer must have to make a tax-free sale of taxable tires for intercity, local and school buses. This information is required to obtain a tax benefit and meet a taxpayer's recordkeeping obligations under section 6001. This information will be used by the IRS to substantiate claims for tax benefits. The likely recordkeepers are businesses.

Estimated total annual reporting and/or recordkeeping burden: 750 hours.

Estimated average annual burden hours per respondent and/or recordkeeper varies from .10 hour to .40 hours, depending on individual circumstances, with an estimated average of .25 hours.

Estimated number respondents and/or recordkeepers: 3,000.

An agency may not conduct or sponsor, and a person is not required to respond to, a collection of information unless it displays a valid control number assigned by the Office of Management and Budget.

Books or records relating to a collection of information must be retained as long as their contents may become material in the administration of any internal revenue law. Generally, tax returns and tax return information are confidential, as required by 26 U.S.C. 6103.

Background

This document contains proposed amendments to the Highway Use Tax Regulations (26 CFR part 41), the Manufacturers and Retailers Excise Tax Regulations (26 CFR part 48), and the Temporary Excise Tax Regulations Under The Highway Revenue Act of 1982 (Pub. L. 97-424) (26 CFR part 145).

Tractors, Trailers, and Trucks

Before April 1, 1983, section 4061 imposed a tax on the manufacturer's sale of certain highway-type tractors, chassis, and bodies for highway-type trailers and trucks, and related parts and accessories for these articles. The Highway Revenue Act of 1982, Pub. L. 97-424 (96 Stat. 2097) (the 1982 Act), changed this tax to a 12 percent tax under section 4051(a)(1) on the first retail sale of certain highway-type tractors and chassis and bodies for highway-type trailers and trucks. In addition, the 1982 Act replaced the tax on the manufacturer's sale of related parts and accessories with a tax on the installation of parts and accessories on a vehicle containing a taxable article within six months after the vehicle was first placed in service (unless the aggregate price of the parts and the cost of installation was less than $200). Section 4051(a)(5) provides that the sale of a truck, truck trailer, or semitrailer is to be considered as the sale of a chassis and of a body.

Under the 1982 Act, a chassis or body suitable for use with (1) a truck with a GVW of 33,000 pounds or less or (2) a trailer with a GVW of 26,000 pounds or less is generally exempt from tax. All tractors of the kind chiefly used for highway transportation in connection with trailers and semitrailers were taxable under the 1982 Act regardless of their GVW.

On April 4, 1983, temporary regulations were published in the **Federal Register** (48 FR 14361; TD 7882) to implement this new retail tax. Subsequent amendments to these regulations were published in the **Federal Register** on September 13, 1985 (50 FR 37350; TD 8050); May 12, 1988 (53 FR 16867; TD 8200); and July 1, 1998 (63 FR 35799; TD 8774). Collectively, these regulations are referred to in this preamble as "the temporary regulations."

One provision in the temporary regulations provided that tax was not imposed on tractors, chassis, and bodies when they were sold for resale or long-term lease if the buyer was registered by the IRS. Section 1434(b)(2) of the Taxpayer Relief Act of 1997, Pub. L. 105-34 (111 Stat. 788) (the 1997 Act), provided that IRS registration could not be a prerequisite for these tax-free sales. Subsequently, the temporary regulations were amended to reflect this statutory provision on March 31, 2000 (65 FR 17149; TD 8879). The 1997 Act also increased from $200 to $1,000 the aggregate dollar value of parts and accessories that may be installed on section 4051 articles without incurring a tax liability.

Section 11112 of the Safe, Accountable, Flexible, Efficient Transportation Equity Act: A Legacy for Users (SAFETEA), Pub. L. 109-59 (119 Stat. 1144), added new section 4051(a)(4), that provides an exemption for small tractors from the tax on tractors.

Tires

Before January 1, 1984, section 4071 imposed a tax on the manufacturer's sale of highway and nonhighway tires, tubes, and tread rubber. Effective that date, the 1982 Act repealed most of these taxes but retained a tax on certain heavy highway-type tires based on the weight of the tires.

Section 869 of the American Jobs Creation Act of 2004, Pub. L. 108-357 (118 Stat. 1418) (2004 Act), changed section 4071 from a tax based on the weight of a tire to a tax based on the maximum rated load capacity of a tire in excess of 3,500 pounds. A special rate of tax was provided for super single tires. A super single tire was defined as a single tire greater than 13 inches in cross-section width designed to replace two tires in a dual fitment.

Section 1364(a) of the Energy Policy Act of 2005, Pub. L. 109-58 (119 Stat. 594), amended the definition of a super single tire to exclude any tire designed for steering.

Definition of Highway Vehicle

Generally, section 4051 imposes a tax only on components of highway vehicles. Similarly, the tax imposed by section 4481 on the use of certain heavy vehicles applies only to highway vehicles. Sections 6421 and 6427 allow a credit or payment related to the tax imposed on fuel (including gasoline or diesel fuel) in many cases if the fuel is used other than as a fuel in a highway vehicle.

Existing regulations define *highway vehicle* with exceptions provided for (1) certain specially-designed mobile machinery for non-transportation functions, (2) certain vehicles specially designed for off-highway transportation, and (3) certain trailers and semitrailers specially designed to perform nontransportation functions off the public highway. Section 851 of the 2004 Act generally codified the regulatory exception for item (1) and codified, with substantial changes, the regulatory definitions of items (2) and (3).

Reason for these regulations

Many of the existing regulations relating to tractors, trailers, trucks, and tires do not reflect current law. These proposed regulations reflect changes to the Internal Revenue Code since 1982, address several court decisions, remove numerous obsolete regulations, and also afford the public the opportunity to comment on those provisions of the temporary regulations that are restated and unchanged.

Explanation of Provisions

Definition of Highway Vehicle

Proposed § 48.0-5 defines a *highway vehicle* as any self-propelled vehicle, or any truck trailer or semitrailer, designed to perform a function of transporting a load over public highways. This proposed section also provides exceptions for specified mobile machinery, off-highway vehicles, and non-transportation trailers and semitrailers for purposes of the tax on the sale of heavy vehicles (section 4051), the highway use tax (section 4481), and the credits and payments allowed for certain nontaxable uses (sections 6421 and 6427). The exception for mobile machinery restates section 4053(8) (as added by the 2004 Act) and the exceptions for off-highway vehicles and non-transportation trailers and semitrailers restate section 7701(a)(48)(A) and (B) (as added by the 2004 Act). Also, Notice 2005-4, 2005-1 C.B. 289, announced that existing regulations regarding certain vehicles specially designed for off-highway transportation would be revised so that they will not apply to calendar quarters beginning after October 22, 2004. These proposed regulations make that change.

The proposed regulations provide two examples that illustrate the definition of highway vehicle. The first example concerns the off-highway vehicle exception and characterizes an asphalt semitrailer similar to the trailers and semitrailers described in *Flow Boy, Inc. v. United States*, 83-1 U.S.T.C. ¶ 16,395, aff'd, 54 A.F.T.R.2d 84-6545, 84-1 U.S.T.C. ¶ 16,418 (10th Cir. 1984), and *Gateway Equip. Corp. v. United States*, 247 F. Supp. 2d 299 (W.D.N.Y. 2003), as a highway vehicle. Relying on the then-existing regulations, the *Flow Boy* and *Gateway* courts held that the asphalt trailers and semitrailers in question were not highway vehicles. In 2004, Congress added section 7701(a)(48) to the Code, which provides a statutory definition of the term "off-highway vehicles." Under section 7701(a)(48)(A), a vehicle is not treated as a highway vehicle if such vehicle is specially designed for the primary function of transporting a particular type of load over the public highway and because of this special design, such vehicle's capability to transport a load over the public highway is substantially limited or impaired. The enactment of section 7701(a)(48) effectively disqualified an asphalt semitrailer similar to the ones described in *Flow Boy* and *Gateway* from the off-highway exception because its special design does not substantially limit or impair its capability to transport a load over a public highway. The example in the proposed regulations illustrates the analysis of whether a vehicle is a highway vehicle under section 7701(a)(48).

The second example concerns the mobile machinery exception and reflects the decision in *Florida Power & Light Co. v. United States*, 375 F.3d 1119 (Fed. Cir. 2004), which holds that a vehicle that can perform more than one transportation function is not specially designed to serve "only" as a mobile carriage and mount. See also *Schlumberger Technology Corp. and Subsidiaries v. United States*, 55 Fed. Cl. 203 (2003).

Retail Tax on Tractors, Trailers, and Trucks

The proposed regulations reorganize and partially restate the temporary regulations that address the retail tax on tractors, trailers, and trucks. Proposed § 48.4051-1(e) revises the definitions of *tractor* and *truck* and provides a model certificate for a seller to establish the tax status of an incomplete chassis cab. If the buyer of an incomplete chassis cab certifies to the seller that the buyer will not complete the incomplete chassis cab as a taxable tractor, the seller may treat the sale of the incomplete chassis cab as the sale of a truck or small tractor. Consequently, no tax is imposed on the sale of an incomplete chassis cab when accompanied by a qualifying certificate. In the absence of this certificate, the seller must treat the sale of an incomplete chassis cab as the sale of a taxable tractor. This rule generally restates § 145.4051-1(e)(1) and is consistent with the interpretation of the existing rule in *Freightliner of Grand Rapids, Inc. v. United States*, 351 F. Supp. 2d 718, 723 (2004).

Consistent with the temporary regulations, the proposed regulations define the terms tractor and truck by reference to the primary design of a vehicle. For purposes of determining whether a vehicle is "primarily designed" as a tractor or a truck, proposed § 48.4051-1(g) also includes an example and reflects Rev. Rul. 2004-80 (2004-2 CB 164), which applied the primarily designed test to determine whether a vehicle was a tractor or a truck.

The definition of *truck trailer* in proposed § 48.4051-1(e)(4)(ii) would include any manufactured home on a frame that has axles and wheels. This definition classifies a manufactured home of the type at issue in *Horton Homes, Inc. v. United States*, 357 F.3d 1209 (11th Cir. 2004), as a truck trailer because all of its load and weight is carried on its own chassis and it is designed to be towed. A consequence of this characterization is that the vehicle that tows this manufactured home is a tractor as defined in section 4051(a)(1)(E). Thus, under the proposed regulations, *toters*, as the vehicles that tow these manufactured homes are known in the industry, would be taxable as tractors. While this result is different from the decision in *Horton Homes*, which held that toters are not taxable tractors, that decision expressly noted that "Congress did not define 'trailers or semitrailers,' [in the statute] nor has the Treasury promulgated regulations defining those terms" and thus applied a dictionary definition of the term "trailer" to determine whether toters are taxable. *Id.* at 1212 n.6. These proposed regulations fill in the regulatory gap faced by the Eleventh Circuit by providing a definition of "trailer" that will clarify the determination of whether a vehicle is a taxable tractor.

Proposed § 48.4051-1(f) provides exclusions from the tax imposed by section 4051 for certain trucks and trailers that are below a certain GVW and tractors that are below a certain GVW and a certain GCW. Proposed § 48.4051-1(f) defines GVW and GCW and also provides the related recordkeeping requirements to support these exclusions.

Proposed § 48.4051-2 modifies the temporary regulations to reflect the statutory increase in the aggregate dollar value of parts and accessories that may be installed on a taxable article without incurring a tax liability.

Proposed § 48.4052-1 supplements the existing definition of *taxable sale* to include the resale of an unused article that had been previously sold tax-free.

Chassis Characterization

The proposed regulations provide that if a chassis is a component part of a highway vehicle, the taxability of the chassis is determined independent of, and without regard to, the body that is installed on the chassis. Likewise, if a body is a component part of a highway vehicle, the taxability of the body is determined independent of, and without regard to, the chassis on which the body is installed. This proposed rule is contrary to the result in Rev. Rul. 69-205 (1969-1 CB 277), which holds that an otherwise taxable chassis is not taxable if a motorhome body is installed on the chassis. This revenue ruling predates and is inconsistent with the language in section 4051(a)(1), which lists a chassis and a body as separate taxable articles. This revenue ruling will be obsoleted after publication of the final regulations.

Taxable Tires

Effective January 1, 2005, section 4071 imposes a tax on taxable tires for each ten pounds of the maximum rated load capacity that exceeds 3,500 pounds. The proposed regulations reflect this change and remove references in existing regulations to tread rubber, inner tubes, and the determination of a tire's weight. The proposed regulations also define *rated load capacity* and *super single tire*, and address multiple load ratings and the consequences of tampering with a tire's maximum load rating. The proposed regulations also provide rules under section 4073 for making tax-free sales of tires for the exclusive use of the Department of Defense and the Coast Guard. In addition, the proposed regulations provide model certificates to support these sales, as well as sales of tires by manufacturers for use on or in connection with the sale of another article manufactured by the purchaser and sold by the purchaser in a sale that meets the requirements of section 4221(e)(2) and sales of taxable tires to be used on intercity, local, and school buses (section 4221(e)(3)).

Proposed Applicability Date

The regulations generally are proposed to apply on and after the date of publication of a Treasury decision adopting these rules as final regulations in the **Federal Register**.

Availability of IRS documents

The IRS revenue rulings and the notice cited in this preamble are published in the Internal Revenue Cumulative Bulletin and are available at *www.irs.gov*.

Special Analyses

Certain IRS regulations, including this one, are exempt from the requirements of Executive Order 12866, as supplemented and reaffirmed by Executive Order 13563. Therefore, a regulatory flexibility assessment is not required. It also has been determined that section 553(b) of the Administrative Procedure Act (5 U.S.C. chapter 5) does not apply to these regulations. It is hereby certified that the collection of information in these regulations will not have a significant economic impact on a substantial number of small entities. This certification is based on the fact that the time required to secure and maintain the required information is minimal (estimated at an average of 15 minutes) and taxpayers would ordinarily already collect and retain much of this information for other business purposes such as accounting, insurance, and marketing. Also, truck manufacturers presently provide the GVW and gross combined weight to truck dealers for purposes unrelated to federal excise tax. Therefore, a Regulatory Flexibility Analysis under the Regulatory Flexibility Act (5 U.S.C. chapter 6) is not required. Pursuant to section 7805(f) of the Internal Revenue Code, this notice of proposed rulemaking has been submitted to the Chief Counsel for Advocacy of the Small Business Administration for comment on its impact on small business.

Comments and Requests for a Public Hearing

Before these proposed regulations are adopted as final regulations, consideration will be given to any comments that are submitted timely to the IRS as prescribed in this preamble under the "Addresses" heading. The Treasury Department and the IRS request comments on all aspects of the proposed regulations. All comments will be available at *www.regulations.gov* or upon request. A public hearing may be scheduled if requested in writing by any person that timely submits written comments. If a public hearing is scheduled, notice of the date, time, and place for the hearing will be published in the **Federal Register**.

Drafting Information

The principal author of these regulations is Celia Gabrysh, Office of Associate Chief Counsel (Passthroughs and Special Industries). However, other personnel from the IRS and the Treasury Department participated in their development.

[¶ 62,167]   Notice of Proposed Rulemaking (REG-135702-15), published in the Federal Register on June 10, 2016.

[Act Sec. 9010 of the Patient Protection and Affordable Care Act (P.L. 111-148)]

Expatriate health plans.—Amendments of Reg. § 46.4377-1, Reg. § 57.2, Reg. § 57.4 and Reg. § 57.10 are proposed. The proposed regulations relate to the rules for expatriate health plans, expatriate health plan issuers, and qualified expatriates under the Expatriate Health Coverage Clarification Act of 2014 (EHCCA).

Expatriate Health Plans, Expatriate Health Plan Issuers, and Qualified Expatriates;

Excepted Benefits; Lifetime and Annual Limits; and Short-Term, Limited-Duration

Insurance

AGENCIES: Internal Revenue Service, Department of the Treasury; Employee Benefits

Security Administration, Department of Labor; Centers for Medicare & Medicaid Services,

Department of Health and Human Services.

ACTION: Proposed rule.

SUMMARY: This document contains proposed regulations on the rules for expatriate health plans, expatriate health plan issuers, and qualified expatriates under the Expatriate Health Coverage Clarification Act of 2014 (EHCCA). This document also includes proposed conforming amendments to certain regulations to implement the provisions of the EHCCA. Further, this document proposes standards for travel insurance and supplemental health insurance coverage to be considered excepted benefits and revisions to the definition of short-term, limited-duration insurance for purposes of the exclusion from the definition of individual health insurance coverage. These proposed regulations affect expatriates with health coverage under expatriate health plans and sponsors, issuers and administrators of expatriate health plans, individuals with and plan sponsors of travel insurance and supplemental health insurance coverage, and individuals with short-term, limited-duration insurance. In addition, this document proposes to amend a reference in the final regulations relating to prohibitions on lifetime and annual dollar limits and proposes to require that a notice be provided in connection with hospital indemnity and other fixed indemnity insurance in the group health insurance market for it to be considered excepted benefits.

DATES: Comments are due on or before August 10, 2016.

ADDRESSES: Comments, identified by "Expatriate Health Plans and other issues," may be submitted by one of the following methods:

Hand delivery or mail: Written comment submissions may be submitted to CC:PA:LPD:PR (REG-135702-15), Internal Revenue Service, PO Box 7604, Ben Franklin Station, Washington DC 20044. Comment submissions may be hand-delivered Monday through Friday between the hours of 8 a.m. and 4 p.m. to CC:PA:LPD:PR (REG-135702-15).

Federal eRulemaking Portal: http://www.regulations.gov. Follow the instructions for submitting comments.

Comments received will be posted without change to www.regulations.gov and available for public inspection. Any comment that is submitted will be shared with the Department of Labor (DOL) and Department of Health and Human Services (HHS). Warning: Do not include any personally identifiable information (such as name, address, or other contact information) or confidential business information that you do not want publicly disclosed. All comments may be posted on the Internet and can be retrieved by most Internet search engines. No deletions, modifications, or redactions will be made to the comments received, as they are public records. **FOR FURTHER INFORMATION CONTACT:** Concerning the proposed regulations, with respect to the treatment of expatriate health plan coverage as minimum essential coverage under section 5000A of the Internal Revenue Code, John Lovelace, at 202-317-7006; with respect to the provisions relating to the health insurance providers fee imposed by section 9010 of the Affordable Care Act, Rachel Smith, at 202-317-6855; with respect to the definition of expatriate health plans, expatriate health insurance issuers, and qualified expatriates, and the provisions relating to the market reforms (such as excepted benefits, and short-term, limited-duration coverage), R. Lisa Mojiri-Azad of the IRS Office of Chief Counsel, at 202-317-5500, Elizabeth Schumacher or Matthew Litton of the Department of Labor, at 202-693-8335, Jacob Ackerman of the Centers for Medicare & Medi-

caid Services, Department of Health and Human Services, at 301-492-4179. Concerning the submission of comments or to request a public hearing, Regina Johnson. (202) 317-6901 (not toll-free numbers).

Customer Service Information: Individuals interested in obtaining information from the Department of Labor concerning employment-based health coverage laws may call the EBSA Toll-Free Hotline, at 1-866-444-EBSA (3272) or visit the Department of Labor's website (http://www.dol.gov/ebsa). In addition, information from HHS on private health insurance for consumers can be found on the Centers for Medicare & Medicaid Services (CMS) website (www.cms.gov/cciio) and information on health reform can be found at www.HealthCare.gov.

SUPPLEMENTARY INFORMATION:

I. Background

This document contains proposed amendments to Department of the Treasury (Treasury Department) regulations at 26 CFR part 1 (Income taxes), 26 CFR part 46 (Excise taxes, Health care, Health insurance, Pensions, Reporting and recordkeeping requirements), 26 CFR part 54 (Pension and excise taxes), 26 CFR part 57 (Health insurance providers fee), and 26 CFR part 301 (relating to procedure and administration) to implement the rules for expatriate health plans, expatriate health plan issuers, and qualified expatriates under the Expatriate Health Coverage Clarification Act of 2014 (EHCCA), which was enacted as Division M of the Consolidated and Further Continuing Appropriations Act, 2015, Public Law 113-235 (128 Stat. 2130). This document also contains proposed amendments to DOL regulations at 29 CFR part 2590 and HHS regulations at 45 CFR part 147, which are substantively identical to the amendments to 26 CFR part 54.

The EHCCA generally provides that the requirements of the Affordable Care Act[1] (ACA) do not apply with respect to expatriate health plans, expatriate health insurance issuers for coverage under expatriate health plans, and employers in their capacity as plan sponsors of expatriate health plans, except that: (1) an expatriate health plan shall be treated as minimum essential coverage under section 5000A(f) of the Internal Revenue Code of 1986, as amended (the Code) and any other section of the Code that incorporates the definition of minimum essential coverage; (2) the employer shared responsibility provisions of section 4980H of the Code continue to apply; (3) the health care reporting provisions of sections 6055 and 6056 of the Code continue to apply but with certain modifications relating to the use of electronic media for required statements to enrollees; (4) the excise tax provisions of section 4980I of the Code continue to apply with respect to coverage of certain qualified expatriates who are assigned (rather than transferred) to work in the United States; and (5) the annual health insurance providers fee imposed by section 9010 of the ACA takes into account expatriate health insurance issuers for certain purposes for calendar years 2014 and 2015 only.

This document also contains proposed amendments to 26 CFR part 54, 29 CFR part 2590, and 45 CFR parts 146 and 148, which would specify conditions for travel insurance, supplemental health insurance coverage, and hospital indemnity and other fixed indemnity insurance to be considered excepted benefits. Excepted benefits are exempt from the requirements that generally apply under title XXVII of the Public Health Service Act (PHS Act), part 7 of the Employee Retirement Income Security Act of 1974, as amended (ERISA), and Chapter 100 of the Code. In addition, this document contains proposed amendments to (1) the definition of "short-term, limited-duration insurance," for purposes of the exclusion from the definition of "individual health insurance coverage" and (2) the definition of "essential health benefits," for purposes of the prohibition on annual and lifetime dollar limits in 26 CFR part 54, 29 CFR 2590, and 45 CFR parts 144 and 147.

This document clarifies an exemption set forth in 45 CFR 153.400(a)(1)(iii) related to the transitional reinsurance program. Section 1341 of the Affordable Care Act provides for the establishment of

---

[1] The Patient Protection and Affordable Care Act, Pub. L. 111-148, was enacted on March 23, 2010, and the Health Care and Education Reconciliation Act, Pub. L. 111-152, was enacted on March 30, 2010. They are collectively known as the "Affordable Care Act."

a transitional reinsurance program in each State to help pay the cost of treating high-cost enrollees in the individual market in the 2014 through 2016 benefit years. Section 1341(b)(3)(B) of the ACA and 45 CFR 153.400(a)(1) require contributing entities to make reinsurance contributions for major medical coverage that is considered to be part of a commercial book of business.

This document also contains proposed conforming amendments to 45 CFR part 158 that address the separate medical loss ratio (MLR) reporting requirements for expatriate policies that are not expatriate health plans under the EHCCA.

General Statutory Background and Enactment of ACA

The Health Insurance Portability and Accountability Act of 1996 (HIPAA), Public Law 104-191 (110 Stat. 1936), added title XXVII of the PHS Act, part 7 of ERISA, and Chapter 100 of the Code, which impose portability and nondiscrimination rules with respect to health coverage. These provisions of the PHS Act, ERISA, and the Code were later augmented by other consumer protection laws, including the Mental Health Parity Act of 1996, the Paul Wellstone and Pete Domenici Mental Health Parity and Addiction Equity Act of 2008, the Newborns' and Mothers' Health Protection Act, the Women's Health and Cancer Rights Act, the Genetic Information Nondiscrimination Act of 2008, the Children's Health Insurance Program Reauthorization Act of 2009, Michelle's Law, and the ACA.

The ACA reorganizes, amends, and adds to the provisions of part A of title XXVII of the PHS Act relating to group health plans and health insurance issuers in the group and individual markets. For this purpose, the term "group health plan" includes both insured and self-insured group health plans.[2] The ACA added section 715(a)(1) of ERISA and section 9815(a)(1) of the Code to incorporate the provisions of part A of title XXVII of the PHS Act (generally, sections 2701 through 2728 of the PHS Act) into ERISA and the Code to make them applicable to group health plans and health insurance issuers providing health insurance coverage in connection with group health plans.

Expatriate Health Plans, Expatriate Health Plan Issuers and Qualified Expatriates

Prior to the enactment of the EHCCA, employers, issuers and covered individuals had expressed concerns about the application of the ACA market reform rules to expatriate health plans and whether coverage under expatriate health plans was minimum essential coverage for purposes of section 5000A of the Code. To address these concerns on an interim basis, on March 8, 2013, the Departments of Labor, HHS, and the Treasury (collectively, the Departments[3]) issued Affordable Care Act Implementation Frequently Asked Questions (FAQs) Part XIII, Q&A-1, providing relief from the ACA market reform requirements for certain expatriate group health insurance coverage.[4] For plan years ending on or before December 31, 2015, the FAQ provides that, with respect to expatriate health plans, the Departments will consider the requirements of subtitles A and C of title I of the ACA to be satisfied if the plan and issuer comply with the pre-ACA version of title XXVII of the PHS Act. For purposes of the relief, an expatriate health plan is an insured group health plan with respect to which enrollment is limited to primary insureds who reside outside of their home country for at least six months of the plan year and any covered dependents, and its associated group health insurance coverage. The FAQ also states that coverage provided under an expatriate group health plan is a form of minimum essential coverage under section 5000A of the Code. On January 9, 2014, the Departments issued Affordable Care Act Implementation FAQs Part XVIII, Q&A-6 and Q&A-7, which extended the relief of Affordable Care Act Implementation FAQs Part XIII, Q&A-1 for insured expatriate health plans to subtitle D of title I of the ACA and also provided that the relief from the requirements of subtitles A, C, and D of title I of the ACA would apply for plan years ending on or before December 31, 2016.[5]

Subsequently, the EHCCA was enacted on December 16, 2014. Section 3(a) of the EHCCA provides that the ACA generally does not apply to expatriate health plans, employers with respect to expatriate

health plans but solely in their capacity as plan sponsors of these plans, and expatriate health insurance issuers with respect to coverage offered by such issuers under expatriate health plans. Under section 3(b) of the EHCCA, however, the ACA continues to apply to expatriate health plans with respect to the employer shared responsibility provisions of section 4980H of the Code, the reporting requirements of sections 6055 and 6056 of the Code, and the excise tax provisions of section 4980I of the Code. Section 3(b) of the EHCCA further provides that an expatriate health plan offered to primary enrollees described in sections 3(d)(3)(A) and (B) of the EHCCA shall be treated as an eligible employer sponsored plan under section 5000A(f)(2) of the Code, and that an expatriate health plan offered to primary enrollees described in section 3(d)(3)(C) of the EHCCA shall be treated as a plan in the individual market under section 5000A(f)(1)(C) of the Code. Section 3(c) of the EHCCA sets forth rules for expatriate health plans with respect to the annual health insurance providers fee imposed by section 9010 of the ACA.

Sections 4375 and 4376 of the Code impose the Patient-Centered Outcomes Research Trust Fund (PCORTF) fee only with respect to individuals residing in the United States. Final regulations regarding the PCORTF fee exempt any specified health insurance policy or applicable self-insured group health plan designed and issued specifically to cover employees who are working and residing outside the United States from the fee. The exclusion from the ACA for expatriate health plans, employers with respect to expatriate health plans but solely in their capacity as plan sponsors of these plans, and expatriate health insurance issuers with respect to coverage offered by such issuers under expatriate health plans would apply to the PCORTF fee to the extent an expatriate health plan was not already excluded from the fee.

Section 1341 of the ACA establishes a transitional reinsurance program to help stabilize premiums for non-grandfathered health insurance coverage in the individual health insurance market from 2014 through 2016. Section 1341(b)(3)(B) of the ACA and the implementing regulations at 45 CFR 153.400(a)(1) require health insurance issuers and certain self-insured group health plans ("contributing entities") to make reinsurance contributions for major medical coverage that is considered to be part of a commercial book of business. This language has been interpreted to exclude "expatriate health coverage."[6] As such, HHS regulation at 45 CFR 153.400(a)(1)(iii) provides that a contributing entity must make reinsurance contributions for lives covered by its self-insured group health plans and health insurance coverage, except to the extent that such plan or coverage is expatriate health coverage, as defined by the Secretary of HHS, or for the 2015 and 2016 benefit years only, is a self-insured group health plan with respect to which enrollment is limited to participants who reside outside of their home country for at least six months of the plan year and any covered dependents of such participants. As noted in the March 8, 2013 Affordable Care Act Implementation FAQs Part XIII, Q&A-1, the FAQ definition of "expatriate health plan" was extended to the definition of "expatriate health coverage" under 45 CFR 153.400(a)(1)(iii).

Section 3(a) of the EHCCA provides that the ACA generally does not apply to expatriate health plans, employers with respect to expatriate health plans but solely in their capacity as plan sponsors of expatriate health plans, and expatriate health insurance issuers with respect to coverage offered by such issuers under expatriate health plans. Accordingly, under the EHCCA, the transitional reinsurance program contribution obligation under section 1341 of the ACA does not apply to expatriate health plans.

Section 5000A of the Code, as added by section 1501 of the ACA, provides that, for each month, taxpayers must have minimum essential coverage, qualify for a health coverage exemption, or make an individual shared responsibility payment when filing a federal income tax return. Section 5000A(f)(1)(B) of the Code provides that minimum essential coverage includes coverage under an eligible employer-sponsored plan. Section 5000A(f)(2) of the Code and 26 CFR 1.5000A-2(c) provide that an eligible employer-sponsored plan

---

[2] The term "group health plan" is used in title XXVII of the PHS Act, part 7 of ERISA, and Chapter 100 of the Code, and is distinct from the term "health plan," as used in other provisions of title I of the ACA. The term "health plan" does not include self-insured group health plans.

[3] Note, however, that in sections under headings listing only two of the three Departments, the term "Departments" generally refers only to the two Departments listed in the heading.

[4] Frequently Asked Questions about Affordable Care Act Implementation (Part XIII), available at http://www.dol.gov/ebsa/pdf/faq-aca13.pdf and http://www.cms.gov/CCIIO/Resources/Fact-Sheets-andFAQs/ACA_implementation_faq13.html.

[5] Frequently Asked Questions about Affordable Care Act Implementation (Part XVIII), available at https://www.dol.gov/ebsa/faqs/faq-aca18.html and https://www.cms.gov/CCIIO/Resources/Fact-Sheets-and-FAQs/aca_implementation_faqs18.html.

[6] See HHS Notice of Benefit and Payment Parameters for 2014 (78 FR 15410) (March 11, 2013) and HHS Notice of Benefit and Payment Parameters for 2016 (80 FR 10750) (February 27, 2015).

means, with respect to an employee, group health insurance coverage that is a governmental plan or any other plan or coverage offered in the small or large group market within a State, or a self-insured group health plan. Under section 5000A(f)(1)(C) of the Code, minimum essential coverage includes coverage under a health plan offered in the individual market within a State.

Section 3(b)(1)(A) of the EHCCA provides that an expatriate health plan that is offered to primary enrollees who are qualified expatriates described in sections 3(d)(3)(A) and 3(d)(3)(B) of the EHCCA is treated as an eligible employer-sponsored plan within the meaning of section 5000A(f)(2) of the Code. Section 3(b)(1)(B) of the EHCCA provides that, in the case of an expatriate health plan that is offered to primary enrollees who are qualified expatriates described in section 3(d)(3)(C) of the EHCCA, the coverage is treated as a plan in the individual market within the meaning of section 5000A(f)(1)(C) of the Code, for purposes of sections 36B, 5000A and 6055 of the Code.

Under section 6055 of the Code, as added by section 1502 of the ACA, providers of minimum essential coverage must file an information return with the Internal Revenue Service (IRS) and furnish a written statement to covered individuals reporting the months that an individual had minimum essential coverage. Under section 6056 of the Code, as added by section 1514 of the ACA, an applicable large employer (as defined in section 4980H(c)(2) of the Code and 26 CFR 54.4980H-1(a)(4) and 54.4980H-2 must file an information return with the IRS and furnish a written statement to its full-time employees reporting details regarding the minimum essential coverage, if any, offered by the employer. Under both sections 6055 and 6056 of the Code, reporting entities may satisfy the requirement to furnish statements to covered individuals and employees, respectively, by electronic means only if the individual or employee affirmatively consents to receiving the statements electronically.[7]

Under section 4980H of the Code, as added by section 1513 of the ACA, an applicable large employer that does not offer minimum essential coverage to its full-time employees (and their dependents) or offers minimum essential coverage that does not meet the standards for affordability and minimum value will owe an assessable payment if a full-time employee is certified as having enrolled in a qualified health plan on an Exchange with respect to which a premium tax credit is allowed with respect to the employee.

Section 3(b)(2) of the EHCCA provides that the reporting requirements of sections 6055 and 6056 of the Code and the provisions of section 4980H of the Code relating to the employer shared responsibility provisions for applicable large employers continue to apply with respect to expatriate health plans and qualified expatriates. Section 3(b)(2) of the EHCCA provides a special rule for the use of electronic media for statements required under sections 6055 and 6056 of the Code. Specifically, the required statements may be provided to a primary insured for coverage under an expatriate health plan using electronic media unless the primary insured has explicitly refused to consent to receive the statement electronically.

Section 4980I of the Code, as added by section 9001 of the ACA, imposes an excise tax if the aggregate cost of applicable employer-sponsored coverage provided to an employee exceeds a statutory dollar limit. Section 3(b)(2) of the EHCCA provides that section 4980I of the Code continues to apply to applicable employer-sponsored coverage (as defined in section 4980I(d)(1) of the Code) of a qualified expatriate (as described in section 3(d)(3)(A)(i) of the EHCCA) who is assigned (rather than transferred) to work in the United States.

Section 9010 of the ACA imposes a fee on covered entities engaged in the business of providing health insurance for United States health risks. Section 3(c)(1) of the EHCCA excludes expatriate health plans from the health insurance providers fee imposed by section 9010 of the ACA by providing that, for calendar years after 2015, a qualified expatriate (and any spouse, dependent, or any other individual enrolled in the plan) enrolled in an expatriate health plan is not considered a United States health risk. Section 3(c)(2) of the EHCCA provides a special rule solely for purposes of determining the health insurance providers fee imposed by section 9010 of the ACA for the 2014 and 2015 fee years.

Section 162(m)(6) of the Code, as added by section 9014 of the ACA, in general, limits to $500,000 the allowable deduction for remuneration attributable to services performed by certain individuals for a covered health insurance provider. For taxable years beginning after December 31, 2012, section 162(m)(6)(C)(i) of the Code and

26 CFR 1.162-31(b)(4)(A) provide that a health insurance issuer is a covered health insurance provider if not less than 25 percent of the gross premiums that it receives from providing health insurance coverage during the taxable year are from minimum essential coverage. Section 3(a)(3) of the EHCCA provides that the provisions of the ACA (including section 162(m)(6) of the Code) do not apply to expatriate health insurance issuers with respect to coverage offered by such issuers under expatriate health plans.

Section 3(d)(2) of the EHCCA provides that an expatriate health plan means a group health plan, health insurance coverage offered in connection with a group health plan, or health insurance coverage offered to certain groups of similarly situated individuals, provided that the plan or coverage meets a number of specific requirements. Section 3(d)(2)(A) of the EHCCA provides that substantially all of the primary enrollees of an expatriate health plan must be qualified expatriates. For this purpose, primary enrollees do not include individuals who are not nationals of the United States and reside in the country of their citizenship. Section 3(d)(2)(B) of the EHCCA provides that substantially all of the benefits provided under a plan or coverage must be benefits that are not excepted benefits. Section 3(d)(2)(C) of the EHCCA provides that the plan or coverage must provide coverage for inpatient hospital services, outpatient facility services, physician services, and emergency services that are comparable to the emergency services coverage that was described in or offered under 5 U.S.C. 8903(1) for the 2009 plan year.[8] Also, coverage for these services must be provided in certain countries. For qualified expatriates described in section 3(d)(3)(A) of the EHCCA (category A) and qualified expatriates described in section 3(d)(3)(B) of the EHCCA (category B), coverage for these services must be provided in the country or countries where the individual is working, and such other country or countries as the Secretary of HHS, in consultation with the Secretary of the Treasury and the Secretary of Labor, may designate. For qualified expatriates who are members of a group of similarly situated individuals described in section 3(d)(3)(C) of the EHCCA (category C), the coverage must be provided in the country or countries that the Secretary of HHS, in consultation with the Secretary of the Treasury and the Secretary of Labor, may designate.

Section 3(d)(2)(D) of the EHCCA provides that a plan qualifies as an expatriate health plan under the EHCCA only if the plan sponsor reasonably believes that benefits under the plan satisfy a standard at least actuarially equivalent to the level provided for in section 36B(c)(2)(C)(ii) of the Code (that is, "minimum value"). Section 3(d)(2)(E) of the EHCCA provides that dependent coverage of children, if offered under the expatriate health plan, must continue to be available until the individual attains age 26 (unless the individual is the child of a child receiving dependent coverage). Section 3(d)(2)(G) of the EHCCA provides that an expatriate health plan must satisfy the provisions of title XXVII of the PHS Act, Chapter 100 of the Code, and part 7 of subtitle B of title I of ERISA, that would otherwise apply if the ACA had not been enacted. These provisions are sometimes referred to as the HIPAA portability and nondiscrimination requirements.

Section 3(d)(1) of the EHCCA provides that an expatriate health insurance issuer means a health insurance issuer that issues expatriate health plans. Section 3(d)(2)(F)(i) of the EHCCA provides that an expatriate health plan or coverage must be issued by an expatriate health plan issuer, or administered by an administrator, that together with any person in the issuer's or administrator's controlled group: (1) maintains network provider agreements that provide for direct claims payments (directly or through third-party contracts), with health care providers in eight or more countries; (2) maintains call centers (directly or through third-party contracts) in three or more countries and accepts calls in eight or more languages; (3) processes at least $ 1 million in claims in foreign currency equivalents each year; (4) makes global evacuation/repatriation coverage available; (5) maintains legal and compliance resources in three or more countries; and (6) has licenses to sell insurance in more than two countries. In addition, section 3(d)(2)(F)(ii) of the EHCCA provides that the plan or coverage must offer reimbursement for items or services under such plan or coverage in the local currency in eight or more countries.

Section 3(d)(3) of the EHCCA describes three categories of qualified expatriates. A category A qualified expatriate, under section 3(d)(3)(A) of the EHCCA, is an individual whose skills, qualifica-

---

[7] See 26 CFR 1.6055-2(a)(2)(i) and 301.6056-2(a)(2)(i).

[8] These are emergency services comparable to emergency services offered under a government-wide comprehensive health plan under the Federal Employees Health Benefits (FEHB) program prior to the enactment of the ACA.

tions, job duties, or expertise has caused the individual's employer to transfer or assign the individual to the United States for a specific and temporary purpose or assignment tied to the individual's employment and who the plan sponsor has reasonably determined requires access to health insurance and other related services and support in multiple countries, and is offered other multinational benefits on a periodic basis (such as tax equalization, compensation for cross-border moving expenses, or compensation to enable the expatriate to return to the expatriate's home country). A category B qualified expatriate, under section 3(d)(3)(B) of the EHCCA, is a primary insured who is working outside the United States for at least 180 days during a consecutive 12-month period that overlaps with the plan year. A category C qualified expatriate, under section 3(d)(3)(C) of the EHCCA, is an individual who is a member of a group of similarly situated individuals that is formed for the purpose of traveling or relocating internationally in service of one or more of the purposes listed in section 501(c)(3) or (4) of the Code, or similarly situated organizations or groups, provided the group is not formed primarily for the sale of health insurance coverage and the Secretary of HHS, in consultation with the Secretary of the Treasury and the Secretary of Labor, determines the group requires access to health insurance and other related services and support in multiple countries.

Section 3(d)(4) of the EHCCA defines the United States as the 50 States, the District of Columbia, and Puerto Rico.

Section 3(f) of the EHCCA provides that, unless otherwise specified, the requirements of the EHCCA apply to expatriate health plans issued or renewed on or after July 1, 2015.

IRS Notice 2015-43

On July 20, 2015, the Treasury Department and the IRS issued Notice 2015-43 (2015-29 IRB 73) to provide interim guidance on the implementation of the EHCCA and the application of certain provisions of the ACA to expatriate health insurance issuers, expatriate health plans, and employers in their capacity as plan sponsors of expatriate health plans. The Departments of Labor and HHS reviewed and concurred with the interim guidance of Notice 2015-43. Comments were received in response to Notice 2015-43, and these comments have been considered in drafting these proposed regulations. The relevant portions of Notice 2015-43 and the related comments are discussed in the Overview of Proposed Regulations section of this preamble.[9]

IRS Notices 2015-29 and 2016-14

On March 30, 2015, the Treasury Department and the IRS issued Notice 2015-29 (2015-15 IRB 873) to provide guidance implementing the special rule of section 3(c)(2) of the EHCCA for fee years 2014 and 2015 with respect to the health insurance providers fee imposed by section 9010 of the ACA. Notice 2015-29 defines expatriate health plan by reference to the definition of expatriate policies in the MLR final rule issued by HHS[10] (MLR final rule definition) solely for the purpose of applying the special rule for fee years 2014 and 2015. The Treasury Department and the IRS determined that the MLR final rule definition of expatriate policies was sufficiently broad to cover potential expatriate health plans described in section 3(d)(2) of the EHCCA. The MLR final rule defines expatriate policies as predominantly group health insurance policies that provide coverage to employees, substantially all of whom are: (1) working outside their country of citizenship; (2) working outside their country of citizenship and outside the employer's country of domicile; or (3) non-U.S. citizens working in their home country.

On January 29, 2016, the Treasury Department and the IRS issued Notice 2016-14 (2016-7 IRB 315) to provide guidance implementing the definition of expatriate health plan for fee year 2016 with respect to the health insurance providers fee imposed by section 9010 of the ACA. Like Notice 2015-29, Notice 2016-14 provides that the definition of expatriate health plan will be the same as provided in the MLR final rule definition, solely for the purpose of the health insurance providers fee imposed by section 9010 of the ACA for fee year 2016.[11]

The Consolidated Appropriations Act, 2016, Public Law 114-113, Division P, Title II, § 201, Moratorium on Annual Fee on Health Insurance Providers (the Consolidated Appropriations Act), sus-

pends collection of the health insurance providers fee for the 2017 calendar year. Thus, health insurance issuers are not required to pay the fee for 2017.

Excepted Benefits

Sections 2722 and 2763 of the PHS Act, section 732 of ERISA, and section 9831 of the Code provide that the respective requirements of title XXVII of the PHS Act, part 7 of ERISA, and Chapter 100 of the Code generally do not apply to the provision of certain types of benefits, known as "excepted benefits." These excepted benefits are described in section 2791(c) of the PHS Act, section 733(c) of ERISA, and section 9832(c) of the Code.

There are four statutorily enumerated categories of excepted benefits. One category, under section 2791(c)(1) of the PHS Act, section 733(c)(1) of ERISA, and section 9832(c)(1) of the Code, identifies benefits that are excepted in all circumstances, including automobile insurance, liability insurance, workers compensation, and accidental death and dismemberment coverage. Under section 2791(c)(1)(H) of the PHS Act (and the parallel provisions of ERISA and the Code), this category of excepted benefits also includes "[o]ther similar insurance coverage, specified in regulations, under which benefits for medical care are secondary or incidental to other insurance benefits."

The second category of excepted benefits is limited excepted benefits, which may include limited scope vision or dental benefits, and benefits for long-term care, nursing home care, home health care, or community-based care. Section 2791(c)(2)(C) of the PHS Act, section 733(c)(2)(C) of ERISA, and section 9832(c)(2)(C) of the Code authorize the Secretaries of HHS, Labor, and the Treasury (collectively, the Secretaries) to issue regulations establishing other, similar limited benefits as excepted benefits. The Secretaries exercised this authority previously with respect to certain health flexible spending arrangements.[12] To be an excepted benefit under this second category, the statute provides that these limited benefits must either: (1) be provided under a separate policy, certificate, or contract of insurance; or (2) otherwise not be an integral part of a group health plan, whether insured or self-insured.[13]

The third category of excepted benefits, referred to as "noncoordinated excepted benefits," includes both coverage for only a specified disease or illness (such as cancer-only policies), and hospital indemnity or other fixed indemnity insurance. These benefits are excepted under section 2722(c)(2) of the PHS Act, section 732(c)(2) of ERISA, and section 9831(c)(2) of the Code only if all of the following conditions are met: (1) the benefits are provided under a separate policy, certificate, or contract of insurance; (2) there is no coordination between the provision of such benefits and any exclusion of benefits under any group health plan maintained by the same plan sponsor; and (3) the benefits are paid with respect to any event without regard to whether benefits are provided under any group health plan maintained by the same plan sponsor. In the group market, the regulations further provide that to be hospital indemnity or other fixed indemnity insurance, the insurance must pay a fixed dollar amount per day (or per other time period) of hospitalization or illness (for example, $100/day) regardless of the amount of expenses incurred.[14]

Since the issuance of these regulations, the Departments have released FAQs to address various requests for clarification as to what types of coverage meet the conditions necessary to be hospital indemnity or other fixed indemnity insurance that are excepted benefits. Affordable Care Act Implementation FAQs Part XI, Q&A-7 clarified that group health insurance coverage in which benefits are provided in varying amounts based on the type of procedure or item, such as the type of surgery actually performed or prescription drug provided is not a hospital indemnity or other fixed indemnity insurance excepted benefit because it does not meet the condition that benefits be provided on a per day (or per other time period, such as per week) basis, regardless of the amount of expenses incurred.[15]

The fourth category, under section 2791(c)(4) of the PHS Act, section 733(c)(4) of ERISA, and section 9832(c)(4) of the Code, is supplemental excepted benefits. Benefits are supplemental excepted benefits only if they are provided under a separate policy, certificate, or contract of insurance and are Medicare supplemental health insurance (also known as Medigap), TRICARE supplemental programs, or

---

[9] See 26 CFR 601.601(d)(2)(ii)(B).

[10] 45 CFR 158.120(d)(4).

[11] See 26 CFR 601.601(d)(2)(ii)(B).

[12] 26 CFR 54.9831-1(c)(3)(v), 29 CFR 2590.732(c)(3)(v), 45 CFR 146.145(b)(3)(v).

[13] PHS Act section 2722(c)(1), ERISA section 732(c)(1), Code section 9831(c)(1).

[14] 26 CFR 54.9831-1(c)(4)(i), 29 CFR 2590.732(c)(4)(i), 45 CFR 146.145(b)(4)(i).

[15] Frequently Asked Questions about Affordable Care Act Implementation (Part XI), available at http://www.dol.gov/ebsa/faqs/faq-aca11.html and http://www.cms.gov/CCIIO/Resources/Fact-Sheets-and-FAQs/aca_implementation_faqs11.html.

"similar supplemental coverage provided to coverage under a group health plan." The phrase "similar supplemental coverage provided to coverage under a group health plan" is not defined in the statute or regulations. However, the Departments' regulations clarify that one requirement to be similar supplemental coverage is that the coverage "must be specifically designed to fill gaps in primary coverage, such as coinsurance or deductibles."[16]

In 2007 and 2008, the Departments issued guidance on the circumstances under which supplemental health insurance would be considered excepted benefits under section 2791(c)(4) of the PHS Act (and the parallel provisions of ERISA, and the Code).[17] The guidance identifies several factors the Departments will apply when evaluating whether supplemental health insurance will be considered to be "similar supplemental coverage provided to coverage under a group health plan." Specifically, the Departments' guidance provides that supplemental health insurance will be considered an excepted benefit if it is provided through a policy, certificate, or contract of insurance separate from the primary coverage under the plan and meets all of the following requirements: (1) the supplemental policy, certificate, or contract of insurance is issued by an entity that does not provide the primary coverage under the plan; (2) the supplemental policy, certificate, or contract of insurance is specifically designed to fill gaps in primary coverage, such as coinsurance or deductibles, but does not include a policy, certificate, or contract of insurance that becomes secondary or supplemental only under a coordination of benefits provision; (3) the cost of the supplemental coverage is 15 percent or less of the cost of primary coverage (determined in the same manner as the applicable premium is calculated under a COBRA continuation provision); and (4) the supplemental coverage sold in the group health insurance market does not differentiate among individuals in eligibility, benefits, or premiums based upon any health factor of the individual (or any dependents of the individual).

On February 13, 2015, the Departments issued Affordable Care Act Implementation FAQs Part XXIII, providing additional guidance on the circumstances under which health insurance coverage that supplements group health plan coverage may be considered supplemental excepted benefits.[18] The FAQ states that the Departments intend to propose regulations clarifying the circumstances under which supplemental insurance products that do not fill in cost-sharing under the primary plan are considered to be specifically designed to fill gaps in primary coverage. Specifically, the FAQ provides that health insurance coverage that supplements group health coverage by providing coverage of additional categories of benefits (as opposed to filling in cost-sharing gaps under the primary plan) would be considered to be designed to "fill in the gaps" of the primary coverage only if the benefits covered by the supplemental insurance product are not essential health benefits (EHB) in the State in which the product is being marketed. The FAQ further states that, until regulations are issued and effective, the Departments will not take enforcement action under certain conditions for failure to comply with the applicable insurance market reforms with respect to group or individual health insurance coverage that provides coverage of additional categories of benefits that are not EHBs in the applicable State. States were encouraged to exercise similar enforcement discretion.

Short-Term, Limited-Duration Insurance Coverage

Short-term limited duration insurance is a type of health insurance coverage that is designed to fill in temporary gaps in coverage when an individual is transitioning from one plan or coverage to another plan or coverage. Although short-term, limited-duration insurance is not an excepted benefit, it is similarly exempt from PHS Act requirements because it is not individual health insurance coverage. Section 2791(b)(5) of the PHS Act provides that the term "individual health insurance coverage" means health insurance coverage offered to individuals in the individual market, but does not include short-term, limited-duration insurance. The PHS Act does not define short-term, limited-duration insurance. Under existing regulations, short-

term, limited-duration insurance means "health insurance coverage provided pursuant to a contract with an issuer that has an expiration date specified in the contract (taking into account any extensions that may be elected by the policyholder without the issuer's consent) that is less than 12 months after the original effective date of the contract."[19]

Prohibition on Lifetime and Annual Limits

Section 2711 of the PHS Act, as added by the ACA, generally prohibits group health plans and health insurance issuers offering group or individual health insurance coverage from imposing lifetime and annual dollar limits on EHB, as defined in section 1302(b) of the ACA. These prohibitions apply to both grandfathered and non-grandfathered health plans, except the annual limits prohibition does not apply to grandfathered individual health insurance coverage.

Under the ACA, self-insured group health plans, large group market health plans, and grandfathered health plans are not required to offer EHB, but they generally cannot place lifetime or annual dollar limits on covered services that are considered EHB. The Departments' regulations provide that, for plan years (in the individual market, policy years) beginning on or after January 1, 2017, a plan or issuer that is not required to provide EHB may select from among any of the 51 base-benchmark plans selected by a State or applied by default pursuant to 45 CFR 156.100, or one of the three FEHBP options specified at 45 CFR 156.100(a)(3), for purposes of complying with the lifetime and annual limits prohibition in section 2711 of the PHS Act.[20]

II. Overview of the Proposed Regulations

A. Expatriate Health Plans

In General

Section 3(a) of the EHCCA provides that the ACA generally does not apply to expatriate health plans, employers with respect to expatriate health plans but solely in their capacity as plan sponsors of expatriate health plans, and expatriate health insurance issuers with respect to coverage offered by such issuers under expatriate health plans. Consistent with this provision, the proposed regulations provide that the market reform provisions enacted or amended as part of the ACA, included in sections 2701 through 2728 of the PHS Act and incorporated into section 9815 of the Code and section 715 of ERISA, do not apply to an expatriate health plan, an employer, solely in its capacity as plan sponsor of an expatriate health plan, and an expatriate health insurance issuer with respect to coverage under an expatriate health plan. Similarly, section 162(m)(6) of the Code does not apply to an expatriate health insurance issuer with respect to premiums received for coverage under an expatriate health plan. In addition, under the EHCCA, the PCORTF fee under sections 4375 and 4376 of the Code and the transitional reinsurance program fee under section 1341 of the ACA do not apply to expatriate health plans. The EHCCA excludes expatriate health plans from the health insurance providers fee imposed by section 9010 except that the EHCCA provides a special rule solely for purposes of determining the fee for the 2014 and 2015 fee years. The EHCCA also designates certain coverage by an expatriate health plan as minimum essential coverage under section 5000A(f) of the Code, and provides special rules for the application of the reporting rules under sections 6055 and 6056 of the Code to expatriate health plans.

Definition of Expatriate Health Insurance Issuer

Consistent with sections 3(d)(1) and (d)(2)(F) of the EHCCA, the proposed regulations define "expatriate health insurance issuer" as a health insurance issuer (as defined under 26 CFR 54.9801-2, 29 CFR 2590.701-2 and 45 CFR 144.103) that issues expatriate health plans and satisfies certain requirements.[21] The requirements for the issuer to be an expatriate health insurance issuer include that, in the course of its normal business operations, the issuer: (1) maintains network provider agreements that provide for direct claims payments with health care providers in eight or more countries; (2) maintains call

---

[16] 26 CFR 54.9831-1(c)(5)(i)(C), 29 CFR 2590.732(c)(5)(i)(C), and 45 CFR 146.145(b)(5)(i)(C)

[17] See EBSA Field Assistance Bulletin No. 2007-04 (available at http://www.dol.gov/ebsa/regs/fab2007-4.html); CMS Insurance Standards Bulletin 08-01 (available at http://www.cms.gov/CCIIO/Resources/Files/Downloads/hipaa_08_01_508.pdf); and IRS Notice 2008-23 (available at http://www.irs.gov/irb/2008-07_IRB/ar09.html).

[18] Frequently Asked Questions about Affordable Care Act Implementation (Part XXIII), available at http://www.dol.gov/ebsa/pdf/faq-aca23.pdf and https://www.cms.gov/CCIIO/Resources/Fact-Sheets-and-FAQs/Downloads/Supplmental-FAQ_2-13-15-final.pdf.

[19] 26 CFR 54.9801-2, 29 CFR 2590.701-2, 45 CFR 144.103

[20] 26 CFR 54.9815-2711(c), 29 CFR 2590.715-2711(c), 45 CFR 147.126(c).

[21] Section 3(d)(1) of the EHCCA provides that the term "expatriate health insurance issuer" means a health insurance issuer that issues expatriate health plans; section 3(d)(5)(A) of the EHCCA provides that the term "health insurance issuer" has the meaning given in section 2791 of the PHS Act. The definition of health insurance issuer in section 9832(b)(2) of the Code and section 733(b)(2) of ERISA and underlying regulations are substantively identical to the definition under section 2791 of the PHS Act and its underlying regulations. As discussed in the section of this preamble entitled "Definition of Expatriate Health Plan" a health insurance issuer as defined in section 2791 of the PHS Act is limited to an entity licensed to engage in the business of insurance in a State and subject to State law that regulates insurance.

centers in three or more countries, and accepts calls from customers in eight or more languages; (3) processed at least $1 million in claims in foreign currency equivalents during the preceding calendar year; (4) makes global evacuation/repatriation coverage available; (5) maintains legal and compliance resources in three or more countries; and (6) has licenses or other authority to sell insurance in more than two countries, including the United States. For purposes of meeting the $1 million threshold for claims processed in foreign currency equivalents, the proposed regulations provide that the dollar value of claims processed is determined using the Treasury Department's currency exchange rate in effect on the last day of the preceding calendar year.[22] Comments are requested regarding whether use of the calendar year as the basis for measuring the dollar amount of claims processed presents administrative challenges, and how the resulting challenges, if any, may be addressed. The proposed regulations provide that each of the applicable requirements may be satisfied by two or more entities (including one entity that is the health insurance issuer) that are members of the health insurance issuer's controlled group or through contracts between the expatriate health insurance issuer and third parties.

Definition of Expatriate Health Plan

Consistent with section 3(d)(2) of the EHCCA, the proposed regulations define "expatriate health plan" as a plan offered to qualified expatriates and that satisfies certain requirements. With respect to qualified expatriates in categories A or B, the plan must be a group health plan (whether or not insured). In contrast, with respect to qualified expatriates in category C, the plan must be health insurance coverage that is not a group health plan. In addition, consistent with section 3(d)(2)(A) of the EHCCA, the proposed regulations require that substantially all primary enrollees in the expatriate health plan must be qualified expatriates. The proposed regulations define a primary enrollee as the individual covered by the plan or policy whose eligibility for coverage is not due to that individual's status as the spouse, dependent, or other beneficiary of another covered individual. However, notwithstanding this definition, an individual is not a primary enrollee if the individual is not a national of the United States and the individual resides in his or her country of citizenship. Further, the proposed regulations provide that, for this purpose, a "national of the United States" has the meaning used in the Immigration and Nationality Act (8 U.S.C. 1101 et. seq.) and 8 CFR parts 301 to 392, including U.S. citizens. Thus, for example, an individual born in American Samoa is a national of the United States at birth for purposes of the EHCCA and the proposed regulations.

Comments in response to Notice 2015-43 requested clarification of the "substantially all" enrollment requirement, with one comment suggesting that 93 percent of the enrollees would be an appropriate threshold. In response to the request for clarification, the proposed regulations provide that a plan satisfies the "substantially all" enrollment requirement if, on the first day of the plan year, less than 5 percent of the primary enrollees (or less than 5 primary enrollees if greater) are not qualified expatriates (effectively a 95 percent threshold). Consistent with section 3(d)(2)(B) of the EHCCA, the proposed regulations further provide that substantially all of the benefits provided under an expatriate health plan must be benefits that are not excepted benefits as described in 26 CFR 54.9831-1(c), 29 CFR 2590.732(c), 45 CFR 146.145(b) and 148.220, as applicable. The Departments intend that the first day of the plan year approach, which has been used in other contexts, will be simple to administer.[23] Moreover, the 95% threshold has been used in certain other circumstances in applying a "substantially all" standard.[24] The Departments solicit comment on this regulatory approach and whether the current regulatory language is sufficient to protect against potential abuses, or whether any further anti-abuse provision is necessary.

Consistent with section 3(d)(2)(C) of the EHCCA, the proposed regulations also require that an expatriate health plan cover certain types of services. Specifically, an expatriate health plan must provide coverage for inpatient hospital services, outpatient facility services, physician services, and emergency services (comparable to emergency services coverage that was described in and offered under section 8903(1) of title 5, United States Code for plan year 2009). Coverage for such services must be available in certain countries depending on the type of qualified expatriates covered by the plan. The statute authorizes the Secretary of HHS, in consultation with the Secretary of the Treasury and Secretary of Labor, to designate other

countries where coverage for such services must be made available to the qualified expatriate.

Consistent with section 3(d)(2)(D) of the EHCCA, the proposed regulations provide that in the case of an expatriate health plan, the plan sponsor must reasonably believe that benefits provided by the plan satisfy the minimum value requirements of section 36B(c)(2)(C)(ii) of the Code.[25] For this purpose, the proposed regulations provide that the plan sponsor is permitted to rely on the reasonable representations of the issuer or administrator regarding whether benefits offered by the group health plan or issuer satisfy the minimum value requirements unless the plan sponsor knows or has reason to know that the benefits fail to satisfy the minimum value requirements. Consistent with section 3(d)(2)(D) of the EHCCA, in the case of an expatriate health plan that provides dependent coverage of children, the proposed regulations provide that such coverage must be available until the individual attains age 26, unless the individual is the child of a child receiving dependent coverage. Additionally, consistent with section 3(d)(2)(F)(ii) of the EHCCA, the plan or coverage must offer reimbursements for items or services in the local currency in eight or more countries.

Consistent with section 3(d)(2)(F) of the EHCCA, the proposed regulations also provide that the policy or coverage under an expatriate health plan must be issued by an expatriate health insurance issuer or administered by an expatriate health plan administrator. With respect to qualified expatriates in categories A or B (generally, individuals whose travel or relocation is related to their employment with an employer), the coverage must be under a group health plan (whether insured or self-insured). With respect to qualified expatriates in category C (generally, groups of similarly situated individuals travelling for certain tax-exempt purposes), the coverage must be under a policy issued by an expatriate health insurance issuer.

Finally, consistent with section 3(d)(2)(G) of the EHCCA, the proposed regulations provide that an expatriate health plan must satisfy the provisions of Chapter 100 of the Code, part 7 of subtitle B of title I of ERISA and title XXVII of the PHS Act that would otherwise apply if the ACA had not been enacted. Among other requirements, those provisions limited the ability of a group health plan or group health insurance issuer to impose preexisting condition exclusions (which are now prohibited for grandfathered and non-grandfathered group health plans and health insurance coverage offered in connection with such plans, and non-grandfathered individual health insurance coverage under the ACA), including a requirement that the period of any preexisting condition exclusion be reduced by the length of any period of creditable coverage the individual had without a 63-day break in coverage.

Prior to the enactment of the ACA, HIPAA and underlying regulations also generally required that plans and issuers provide certificates of creditable coverage when an individual ceased to be covered by a plan or policy and upon request. Following the enactment of the ACA, the regulations under these provisions have eliminated the requirement for providing certificates of creditable coverage beginning December 31, 2014, because the requirement is generally no longer relevant to plans and participants as a result of the prohibition on preexisting condition exclusions. The Departments recognize that reimposing the requirement to provide certificates of creditable coverage on expatriate health plans would only be useful in situations in which an individual transferred from one expatriate health plan to another and that reimposing the requirement on all health plans would require certificates that would be unnecessary except in limited cases, such as for an individual who ceased coverage with a health plan or policy and began coverage under an expatriate health plan that imposed a preexisting condition exclusion. Because reimposing the requirement to provide certificates of creditable coverage would be inefficient and overly broad, and relevant in only limited circumstances, the proposed regulations do not require expatriate health plans to provide certificates of creditable coverage. However, expatriate health plans imposing a preexisting condition exclusion must still comply with certain limitations on preexisting condition exclusions that would otherwise apply if the ACA had not been enacted. Therefore, the proposed regulations require expatriate health plans to ensure that individuals who enroll in the expatriate health plan are provided an opportunity to demonstrate creditable coverage to offset any preexisting condition exclusion. For example, an email from the prior issuer (or former plan administrator or plan

---

[22] The most recent Treasury Department currency exchange rate can be found at https://www.fiscal.treasury.gov/fsreports/rpt/treasRptRateExch/currentRates.htm.

[23] 26 CFR 54.9831-1(b), 29 CFR 2590.732(b), 45 CFR 146.145(b).

[24] See e.g., 26 CFR 1.460-6(d)(4)(i)(D)(1).

[25] For this purpose, generally "minimum value" takes into account the provision of "essential health benefits" as defined in section 1302(b)(1) of the Affordable Care Act.

sponsor) providing information about past coverage could be sufficient confirmation of prior creditable coverage.

Comments in response to Notice 2015-43 requested clarification of the treatment of health coverage provided by a foreign government. Specifically, comments requested that health coverage provided by a foreign government be treated as minimum essential coverage under section 5000A of the Code, and that, for purposes of the employer shared responsibility provision of section 4980H of the Code, an offer of such coverage be treated as an offer of minimum essential coverage for certain foreign employees working in the United States. These issues are generally beyond the scope of these proposed regulations. Under the existing regulations under section 5000A(f)(1)(E) of the Code, there are procedures for health benefits coverage not otherwise designated under section 5000A(f)(1) of the Code as minimum essential coverage to be recognized by the Secretary of HHS, in coordination with the Secretary of the Treasury, as minimum essential coverage. The Secretary of HHS has provided that coverage under a group health plan provided through insurance regulated by a foreign government is minimum essential coverage for expatriates who meet specified conditions.[26] Furthermore, plan sponsors of health coverage that is not recognized as minimum essential coverage through statute, regulation, or guidance may submit an application to CMS for minimum essential coverage recognition pursuant to 45 CFR 156.604.[27] For a complete list of coverage recognized by CMS as minimum essential coverage under section 5000A(f)(1)(E) of the Code, see https://www.cms.gov/CCIIO/Programs-and-Initiatives/Health-Insurance-Market-Reforms/minimum-essential-coverage.html.

Comments also requested that policies sold by non-United States health insurance issuers be treated as minimum essential coverage under section 5000A of the Code, or as expatriate health plans. Section 3(d)(5)(A) of the EHCCA specifies that the terms "health insurance issuer" and "health insurance coverage" have the meanings given those terms by section 2791 of the PHS Act. Section 2791 of the PHS Act (and parallel provisions in section 9832(b) of the Code and section 733(b) of ERISA) define those terms by reference to an entity licensed to engage in the business of insurance in a State and subject to State law that regulates insurance. Under section 2791 of the PHS Act, the term "State" means each of the several States, the District of Columbia, Puerto Rico, the Virgin Islands, Guam, American Samoa, and the Northern Mariana Islands. Consistent with those provisions, these proposed regulations limit an expatriate health insurance issuer to a health insurance issuer within the meaning of those sections (and that meets the other requirements set forth in the proposed regulations). As such, a non-United States health insurance issuer does not qualify as an expatriate health insurance issuer within the meaning of the EHCCA, and coverage issued by a non-United States issuer that is not otherwise minimum essential coverage is not minimum essential coverage pursuant to the EHCCA.

Definition of Expatriate Health Plan Administrator

The proposed regulations define "expatriate health plan administrator," with respect to self-insured coverage, as an administrator of self-insured coverage that generally satisfies the same requirements as an "expatriate health insurance issuer."

Definition of Qualified Expatriate

Consistent with section 3(d)(3) of the EHCCA, the proposed regulations define "qualified expatriate" as one of three types of individuals. The first type of qualified expatriate, a category A expatriate, is an individual who has the skills, qualifications, job duties, or expertise that has caused the individual's employer to transfer or assign the individual to the United States for a specific and temporary purpose or assignment that is tied to the individual's employment with the employer. A category A expatriate may only be an individual who: (1) the plan sponsor has reasonably determined requires access to health coverage and other related services and support in multiple countries, (2) is offered other multinational benefits on a periodic basis (such as tax equalization, compensation for cross-border moving expenses, or compensation to enable the individual to return to the individual's home country), and (3) is not a national of

the United States. The proposed regulations provide that an individual who is not expected to travel outside the United States at least one time per year during the coverage period would not reasonably "require access" to health coverage and other related services and support in multiple countries. Furthermore, under the proposed regulations, the offer of a one-time *de minimis* benefit would not meet the standard for the "periodic" offer of "other multinational benefits."

Section 3(d)(3)(B) of the EHCCA provides that a second type of qualified expatriate, a category B expatriate, is an individual who works outside the United States for a period of at least 180 days in a consecutive 12-month period that overlaps with the plan year. A comment requested that the regulations clarify that the 12-month period could either be within a single plan year, or across two consecutive plan years. Consistent with the statutory language, the proposed regulations provide that a category B expatriate is an individual who is a national of the United States and who works outside the United States for at least 180 days in a consecutive 12-month period that is within a single plan year, or across two consecutive plan years. Section 3(d)(2)(C)(ii) of the EHCCA requires an expatriate health plan provided to category B expatriates to cover certain specified services, such as inpatient and outpatient services, in the country in which the individual is "present in connection" with his employment. The Departments request comments on whether it would be helpful to provide further administrative clarification of this statutory language regarding the country or countries in which the services must be provided, and, if so, whether there are facts or circumstances that will present particular challenges in applying this rule.

Finally, consistent with section 3(d)(3)(C) of the EHCCA, the proposed regulations provide that a third type of qualified expatriate, a category C expatriate, is an individual who is a member of a group of similarly situated individuals that is formed for the purpose of traveling or relocating internationally in service of one or more of the purposes listed in section 501(c)(3) or (4) of the Code, or similarly situated organizations or groups, and meets certain other conditions.[28] A category C expatriate does not include an individual in a group that is formed primarily for the sale or purchase of health insurance coverage. To qualify as this type of qualified expatriate, the Secretary of HHS, in consultation with the Secretary of the Treasury and the Secretary of Labor, must determine that the group requires access to health coverage and other related services and support in multiple countries. The proposed regulations clarify that a category C expatriate does not include an individual whose international travel or relocation is related to employment. Thus, an individual whose travel is employment-related may be a qualified expatriate only in category A or B. The proposed regulations also provide that, in the case of a group organized to travel or relocate outside the United States, the individual must be expected to travel or reside outside the United States for at least 180 days in a consecutive 12-month period that overlaps with the policy year (or in the case of a policy year that is less than 12 months, at least half of the policy year), and in the case of a group organized to travel or relocate within the United States, the individual must be expected to travel or reside in the United States for not more than 12 months. The proposed regulations provide that a group of category C expatriates must also meet the test for having associational ties under section 2791(d)(3)(B) through (F) of the PHS Act (42 U.S.C. 300gg-91(d)(3)(B) through (F)).

For purposes of section 3(d)(3)(C)(iii) of the EHCCA, the proposed regulations provide that the Secretary of HHS, in consultation with the Secretary of the Treasury and the Secretary of Labor, has determined that, in the case of a group of similarly situated individuals that meets all of the criteria in the proposed regulations, the group requires access to health coverage and other related services and support in multiple countries.

Comments in response to Notice 2015-43 requested that category C expatriates not be limited to individuals expected to travel or reside in the United States for 12 or fewer months. While the EHCCA does not include a time limit for category C expatriates, section 3(e) of the EHCCA provides that the Departments "may promulgate regulations

---

[26] See CMS Insurance Standards Bulletin Series. CCIIO Sub-Regulatory Guidance: Process for Obtaining Recognition as Minimum Essential Coverage (Oct. 31, 2013), available at https://www.cms.gov/CCIIO/Resources/Regulations-and-Guidance/Downloads/mec-guidance-10-31-2013.pdf.

[27] See CMS Insurance Standards Bulletin Series. CCIIO Sub-Regulatory Guidance: Process for Obtaining Recognition as Minimum Essential Coverage (Oct. 31, 2013), available at https://www.cms.gov/CCIIO/Resources/Regulations-and-Guidance/

Downloads/mec-guidance-10-31-2013.pdf. See also CMS Insurance Standards Bulletin Series. CCIIO Sub-Regulatory Guidance: Minimum Essential Coverage

[28] Code section 501(c)(3) describes an organization formed for religious, charitable, scientific, public safety, literary, or educational purposes, or to foster national or international amateur sports competition, or for the prevention of cruelty to children or animals, and not for political candidate campaign or legislative purposes or propaganda. Code section 501(c)(4) describes an organization operated exclusively for the promotion of social welfare.

necessary to carry out this Act, including such rules as may be necessary to prevent inappropriate expansion of the exclusions under the Act from applicable laws and regulations." In the group market, the EHCCA and the proposed regulations define a category A expatriate with respect to a "specific and temporary purpose or assignment" tied to the individual's employment in the United States. It is the view of HHS, in consultation with the Departments of Labor and the Treasury, that similar safeguards are necessary in the individual market to prevent inappropriate expansion of the exception for category C expatriates.

Comments are requested on all aspects of the proposed definition of a category C expatriate. Comments are also requested on the time limit for category C expatriates being expected to travel or reside in the United States, and what standards, if any, may be adopted in lieu of the 12-month maximum that would ensure that the definition does not permit inappropriate expansion of the exception. For example, comments are requested on whether a "specific and temporary purpose" standard should be adopted for category C expatriates, consistent with the standard for category A expatriates, or whether category C expatriates should be expected to seek medical care outside the United States at least one time per year in order to be considered to reasonably require access to health coverage and other related services and support in multiple countries. Comments are also requested on the proposed standard with respect to category C expatriates being expected to travel or reside outside the United States for at least 180 days in a consecutive 12-month period that overlaps with the policy year, and whether there are fact patterns in which the 12-month period could either be within a single policy year, or across two consecutive policy years.

Definitions of Group Health Plan and United States

Consistent with section 3(d)(5)(A) of the EHCCA, for purposes of applying the definition of expatriate health plan, "group health plan" means a group health plan as defined under 26 CFR 54.9831-1(a)(1), 29 CFR 2590.732(a)(1) or 45 CFR 146.145(a)(1), as applicable. Consistent with section 3(d)(4) of the EHCCA, the proposed regulations define "United States" to mean the 50 States, the District of Columbia and Puerto Rico.

Section 9010 of the ACA

Section 3(c)(1) of the EHCCA provides that, for purposes of the health insurance providers fee imposed by section 9010 of the ACA, a qualified expatriate enrolled in an expatriate health plan is not a United States health risk for calendar years after 2015. Section 3(c)(2) of the EHCCA provides a special rule applicable to calendar years 2014 and 2015. The Treasury Department and the IRS issued Notices 2015-29 and 2016-14 to address the definition of expatriate health plan for purposes of the health insurance providers fee imposed by section 9010 for the 2014, 2015, and 2016 fee years. No fee is due in the 2017 fee year because the Consolidated Appropriations Act suspends collection of the health insurance providers fee imposed by section 9010 of ACA for 2017.

These proposed regulations provide that, for any fee that is due on or after the date final regulations are published in the Federal Register, a qualified expatriate enrolled in an expatriate health plan as defined in these proposed regulations is not a United States health risk. These proposed regulations also authorize the IRS to specify in guidance in the Internal Revenue Bulletin the manner of determining excluded premiums for qualified expatriates in expatriate health plans. Until the date the final regulations are published in the Federal Register, taxpayers may rely on these proposed regulations with respect to any fee that is due beginning with the 2018 fee year.

Federal Tax Provision: Section 162(m)(6) of the Code

Section 162(m)(6) of the Code, as added by section 9014 of the ACA, in general, limits to $500,000 the allowable deduction for remuneration attributable to services performed by certain individuals for a covered health insurance provider. For taxable years beginning after December 31, 2012, section 162(m)(6)(C)(i) of the Code and 26 CFR 1.162-31(b)(4)(A) provide that a health insurance issuer is a covered health insurance provider if not less than 25 percent of the gross premiums that it receives from providing health insurance coverage during the taxable year are from minimum essential coverage. Section 3(a)(3) of the EHCCA provides that the provisions of the ACA (which include section 162(m)(6) of the Code) do not apply to expatriate health insurance issuers with respect to coverage offered by such issuers under expatriate health plans. Consistent with this rule, the proposed regulations exclude from the definition of the term "premium" for purposes of section 162(m)(6) of the Code amounts received in payment for coverage under an expatriate health plan. As a result, those amounts received are included in neither the numerator nor the denominator for purposes of determining whether the 25 percent standard under section 162(m)(6)(C)(i) of the Code and 26 CFR 1.162-31(b)(4)(A) is met, and they have no impact on whether a particular issuer is a covered health insurance provider.

Federal Tax Provision: Section 4980I of the Code

Section 3(b)(2) of the EHCCA provides that section 4980I of the Code applies to employer-sponsored coverage of a qualified expatriate who is assigned, rather than transferred, to work in the United States. As amended by section 101 of Division P of the Consolidated Appropriations Act, section 4980I of the Code first applies to coverage provided in taxable years beginning after December 31, 2019. Comments in response to Notice 2015-43 requested additional guidance on what it means for an employer to assign rather than transfer an employee. These proposed regulations do not address the interaction of the EHCCA and section 4980I of the Code because the Treasury Department and the IRS anticipate that this issue will be addressed in future guidance promulgated under section 4980I of the Code.

Federal Tax Provision: Section 5000A of the Code and Minimum Essential Coverage

The proposed regulations provide that, beginning January 1, 2017, coverage under an expatriate health plan that provides coverage for a qualified expatriate qualifies as minimum essential coverage for all participants in the plan. If the expatriate health plan provides coverage to category A or category B expatriates, the coverage of any participant in the plan is treated as an eligible employer-sponsored plan under section 5000A(f)(2) of the Code. If the expatriate health plan provides coverage to category C expatriates, the coverage of any enrollee in the plan is treated as a plan in the individual market under section 5000A(f)(1)(C) of the Code.

Federal Tax Provision: Sections 6055 and 6056 of the Code

Section 3(b)(2) of the EHCCA permits the use of electronic media to provide the statements required under sections 6055 and 6056 of the Code to individuals for coverage under an expatriate health plan unless the primary insured has explicitly refused to receive the statement electronically. The proposed regulations provide that, for an expatriate health plan, the recipient is treated as having consented to receive the required statement electronically unless the recipient has explicitly refused to receive the statement in an electronic format. In addition, the proposed regulations provide that the recipient may explicitly refuse either electronically or in a paper document. For a recipient to be treated as having consented under this special rule, the furnisher must provide a notice in compliance with the general disclosure requirements under sections 6055 and 6056 that informs the recipient that the statement will be furnished electronically unless the recipient explicitly refuses to consent to receive the statement in electronic form. The notice must be provided to the recipient at least 30 days prior to the due date for furnishing of the first statement the furnisher intends to furnish electronically to the recipient. Absent receipt of this notice, a recipient will not be treated as having consented to electronic furnishing of statements. Treasury and IRS request comments on further guidance that will assist issuers and plan sponsors in providing this notice in the least burdensome manner while still ensuring that the recipient has sufficient information and opportunity to opt out of the electronic reporting if the recipient desires. For example, Treasury and the IRS specifically request comments on whether the ability to provide this notice as part of the enrollment materials for the coverage would meet these goals.

Federal Tax Provision: PCORTF Fee

The proposed regulations provide that the excise tax under sections 4375 and 4376 of the Code (the PCORTF fee) does not apply to an expatriate health plan as defined at 26 CFR 54.9831-1(f)(3). Section 4375 of the Code limits the application of the fee to policies issued to individuals residing in the United States. Existing regulations under sections 4375, 4376, and 4377 of the Code exclude coverage under a plan from the fee if the plan is designed specifically to cover primarily employees who are working and residing outside the United States. A comment requested clarification about the existing PCORTF fee exemption for plans that primarily cover employees working and residing outside the United States. Consistent with the provisions of the EHCCA, the proposed regulations expand the exclusion from the PCORTF fee to also exclude an expatriate health plan regardless of whether the plan provides coverage for qualified expatriates residing or working in or outside the United States if the plan is an expatriate health plan.

Section 1341 of the ACA: Transitional Reinsurance Program

A comment also requested that the current exclusion under the PCORTF fee regulations for individuals working and residing outside the United States be applied to the transitional reinsurance fee under section 1341 of the ACA. Existing regulations relating to section 1341 of the ACA include an exception for certain expatriate health plans,[29] including expatriate group health coverage as defined by the Secretary of HHS and, for the 2015 and 2016 benefit years, self-insured group health plans with respect to which enrollment is limited to participants who reside outside their home country for at least six months of the plan year, and any covered dependents. HHS solicits comment on whether amendments are needed to 45 CFR 153.400(a)(1)(iii) to clarify the alignment with the EHCCA and exempt all expatriate plans from the requirement to make reinsurance contributions.

Section 2718 of the PHS Act: MLR Program

Section 2718 of the PHS Act, as added by sections 1001 and 10101 of the ACA, generally requires health insurance issuers to provide rebates to consumers if issuers do not achieve specified MLRs, as well as to submit an annual MLR report to HHS. The proposed regulations provide that expatriate policies described in 45 CFR 158.120(d)(4) continue to be subject to the reporting and rebate requirements of 45 CFR Part 158, but update the description of expatriate policies in 45 CFR 158.120(d)(4) to exclude policies that are expatriate health plans under the EHCCA. Given this modification, issuers may find that the number of expatriate policies that remain subject to MLR requirements is low, and that it is administratively burdensome and there is no longer a qualitative justification for continuing separate reporting of such policies. Therefore, comments are requested on whether the treatment of expatriate policies for purposes of the MLR regulations should be amended so that expatriate policies that do not meet the definition of expatriate health plan under the EHCCA would not be required to be reported separately from other health insurance policies.

Section 833(c)(5) of the Code, as added by section 9016 of the ACA, and amended by section 102 of Division N of the Consolidated and Further Continuing Appropriations Act, 2015 (Public Law 113-235, 128 Stat. 2130), provides that section 833(a)(2) and (3) do not apply to any organization unless the organization's MLR for the taxable year was at least 85 percent. In describing the MLR computation under section 833(c)(5), the statute and implementing regulations provide that the elements in the MLR computation are to be "as reported under section 2718 of the Public Service Health Act." Accordingly, the proposed regulations under section 2718 of the PHS Act would effectively apply the EHCCA exemption to section 833(c)(5) of the Code by carving out expatriate health plans under the EHCCA from the section 833(c)(5) requirements as well.

Excepted Benefits

Supplemental Health Insurance Coverage

The proposed regulations incorporate the guidance from the Affordable Care Act Implementation FAQs Part XXIII addressing supplemental health insurance products that provide categories of benefits in addition to those in the primary coverage. Under the proposed regulations, if group or individual supplemental health insurance coverage provides benefits for items and services not covered by the primary coverage (referred to as providing "additional categories of benefits"), the coverage would be considered to be designed "to fill gaps in primary coverage," for purposes of being supplemental excepted benefits if none of the benefits provided by the supplemental policy are an EHB, as defined for purposes of section 1302(b) of the ACA, in the State in which the coverage is issued. Conversely, if any benefit provided by the supplemental policy is an EHB in the State where the coverage is issued, the insurance coverage would not be supplemental excepted benefits under the proposed regulations. This standard is proposed to apply only to the extent that the supplemental health insurance provides coverage of additional categories of benefits. Supplemental health insurance products that both fill in cost sharing in the primary coverage, such as coinsurance or deductibles, and cover additional categories of benefits that are not EHB, also would be considered supplemental excepted benefits under these proposed regulations provided all other criteria are met.

Travel Insurance

The Departments are aware that certain travel insurance products may include limited health benefits. However, these products typically are not designed as major medical coverage. Instead, the risks being insured relate primarily to: (1) the interruption or cancellation of a trip (2) the loss of baggage or personal effects; (3) damages to accommodations or rental vehicles; or (4) sickness, accident, disability, or death occurring during travel, with any health benefits usually incidental to other coverage.

Section 2791(c)(1)(H) of the PHS Act, section 733(c)(1)(H) of ERISA, and section 9832(c)(1)(H) of the Code provide that the Departments may, in regulations, designate as excepted benefits "benefits for medical care that are secondary or incidental to other insurance benefits." Pursuant to this authority, and to clarify which types of travel-related insurance products are excepted benefits under the PHS Act, ERISA, and the Code, the proposed regulations provide that certain travel-related products that provide only incidental health benefits are excepted benefits. The proposed regulations define the term "travel insurance" as insurance coverage for personal risks incident to planned travel, which may include, but is not limited to, interruption or cancellation of a trip or event, loss of baggage or personal effects, damages to accommodations or rental vehicles, and sickness, accident, disability, or death occurring during travel, provided that the health benefits are not offered on a stand-alone basis and are incidental to other coverage. For this purpose, travel insurance does not include major medical plans that provide comprehensive medical protection for travelers with trips lasting 6 months or longer, including, for example, those working overseas as an expatriate or military personnel being deployed. This definition is consistent with the definition of travel insurance under final regulations for the health insurance providers fee imposed by section 9010 of the ACA issued by the Treasury Department and the IRS,[30] which uses a modified version of the National Association of Insurance Commissioners (NAIC) definition of travel insurance.

Hospital Indemnity and Other Fixed Indemnity Insurance

These proposed regulations also include an amendment to the "noncoordinated excepted benefits" category as it relates to hospital indemnity and other fixed indemnity insurance in the group market. Since the issuance of final regulations defining excepted benefits, the Departments have become aware of some hospital indemnity and other fixed indemnity insurance policies that provide comprehensive benefits related to health care costs. In addition, although hospital indemnity and other fixed indemnity insurance under section 2791 of the PHS Act, section 733 of ERISA, and section 9832 of the Code is not intended to be major medical coverage, the Departments are aware that some group health plans that provide coverage through hospital indemnity or other fixed indemnity insurance policies that meet the conditions necessary to be an excepted benefit have made representations to participants that the coverage is minimum essential coverage under section 5000A of the Code. The Departments are concerned that some individuals may incorrectly understand these policies to be comprehensive major medical coverage that would be considered minimum essential coverage.

To avoid confusion among group health plan enrollees and potential enrollees, the proposed regulations revise the conditions necessary for hospital indemnity and other fixed indemnity insurance in the group market to be excepted benefits so that any application or enrollment materials provided to enrollees and potential enrollees at or before the time enrollees and potential enrollees are given the opportunity to enroll in the coverage must include a statement that the coverage is a supplement to, rather than a substitute for, major medical coverage and that a lack of minimum essential coverage may result in an additional tax payment. The proposed regulations include specific language that must be used by group health plans and issuers of group health insurance coverage to satisfy this notice requirement, which is consistent with the notice requirement for individual market fixed indemnity coverage under regulations issued by HHS.[31] The Departments request comments on this proposed notice requirement as well as whether any additional requirements should be added to prevent confusion among enrollees and potential enrollees regarding the limited coverage provided by hospital indemnity and other fixed indemnity insurance. The Departments anticipate that conforming changes will be made in the final regulations to ensure the notice language in the individual market is

---

[29] 45 CFR 153.400(a)(1)(iii).
[30] 26 CFR 57.2(h)(1)(i)

[31] 45 CFR 148.220(b)(4)(iv).

consistent with the notice language in the group market, and solicit comments on this approach.

Additionally, the Departments have become aware of hospital indemnity or other fixed indemnity insurance policies that provide benefits for doctors' visits at a fixed amount per visit, for prescription drugs at a fixed amount per drug, or for certain services at a fixed amount per day but in amounts that vary by the type of service. These types of policies do not meet the condition that benefits be provided on a per day (or per other time period, such as per week) basis. Accordingly, the proposed regulations clarify this standard by stating that the amount of benefits provided must be determined without regard to the type of items or services received. The proposed regulations add two examples demonstrating that group health plans and issuers of group health insurance coverage that provide coverage through hospital indemnity or fixed indemnity insurance policies that provide benefits based on the type of item or services received do not meet the conditions necessary to be an excepted benefit. The first example would incorporate into regulations guidance previously provided by the Departments in Affordable Care Act Implementation FAQs Part XI, which clarified that if a policy provides benefits in varying amounts based on the type of procedure or item received, the policy does not satisfy the condition that benefits be provided on a per day (or per other time period, such as per week) basis. The second example demonstrates that a hospital indemnity or other fixed indemnity insurance policy that provides benefits for certain services at a fixed amount per day, but in varying amounts depending on the type of service, does not meet the condition that benefits be provided on a per day (or per other time period, such as per week) basis. The Departments request comments on these examples specifically, as well as on the requirement that hospital indemnity and other fixed indemnity insurance in the group market that are excepted benefits must provide benefits on a per day (or per other time period, such as per week) basis in an amount that does not vary based on the type of items or services received. The Departments also request comments on whether the conditions for hospital indemnity or other fixed indemnity insurance to be considered excepted benefits should be more substantively aligned between the group and individual markets. For example, the requirements for hospital indemnity or other fixed indemnity insurance in the individual market could be modified to be consistent with the group market provisions of these proposed regulations by limiting payment strictly on a per-period basis and not on a per-service basis.

Specified Disease Coverage

The Departments have been asked whether a policy covering multiple specified diseases or illnesses may be considered to be excepted benefits. The statute provides that the noncoordinated excepted benefits category includes "coverage of a specified disease or illness" if the coverage meets the conditions for being offered as independent, noncoordinated benefits, and the Departments' implementing regulations identify cancer-only policies as one example of specified disease coverage.[32] The Departments are concerned that individuals who purchase a specified disease policy covering multiple diseases or illnesses (including policies that cover one overarching medical condition such as "mental illness" as opposed to a specific condition such as depression) may incorrectly believe they are purchasing comprehensive medical coverage when, in fact, these polices may not include many of the important consumer protections under the PHS Act, ERISA, and the Code. The Departments solicit comments on this issue and on whether, if such policies are permitted to be considered excepted benefits, protections are needed to ensure such policies are not mistaken for comprehensive medical coverage. For example, the Departments solicit comments on whether to limit the number of diseases or illnesses that may be covered in a specified disease policy that is considered to be excepted benefits or whether issuers should be required to disclose that such policies are not minimum essential coverage under section 5000A(f) of the Code.

Short-Term, Limited-Duration Insurance

Under existing regulations, short-term, limited-duration insurance means "health insurance coverage provided pursuant to a contract with an issuer that has an expiration date specified in the contract (taking into account any extensions that may be elected by the policyholder without the issuer's consent) that is less than 12 months after the original effective date of the contract."[33] Before enactment of the ACA, short-term, limited-duration insurance was an important means for individuals to obtain health coverage when transitioning from one job to another (and from one group health plan to another) or in a similar situation. But with the guaranteed availability of coverage and special enrollment period requirements in the individual health insurance market under the ACA, short-term, limited-duration insurance is no longer the only means to obtain transitional coverage.

The Departments recently have become aware that short-term, limited-duration insurance is being sold to address situations other than the situations that the exception was initially intended to address.[34] In some instances individuals are purchasing this coverage as their primary form of health coverage and, contrary to the intent of the 12-month coverage limitation in the current definition of short-term, limited-duration insurance, some issuers are providing renewals of the coverage that extend the duration beyond 12 months. The Departments are concerned that these policies, because they are exempt from market reforms, may have significant limitations, such as lifetime and annual dollar limits on EHBs and pre-existing condition exclusions, and therefore may not provide meaningful health coverage. Further, because these policies can be medically underwritten based on health status, healthier individuals may be targeted for this type of coverage, thus adversely impacting the risk pool for ACA-compliant coverage.

To address the issue of short-term, limited-duration insurance being sold as a type of primary coverage, the proposed regulations revise the definition of short-term, limited-duration insurance so that the coverage must be less than three months in duration, including any period for which the policyholder renews or has an option to renew with or without the issuer's consent. The proposed regulations also provide that a notice must be prominently displayed in the contract and in any application materials provided in connection with enrollment in such coverage with the following language: THIS IS NOT QUALIFYING HEALTH COVERAGE ("MINIMUM ESSENTIAL COVERAGE") THAT SATISFIES THE HEALTH COVERAGE REQUIREMENT OF THE AFFORDABLE CARE ACT. IF YOU DON'T HAVE MINIMUM ESSENTIAL COVERAGE, YOU MAY OWE AN ADDITIONAL PAYMENT WITH YOUR TAXES.

This change would align the definition more closely with the initial intent of the regulation: to refer to coverage intended to fill temporary coverage gaps when an individual transitions between primary coverage. Further, limiting the coverage to less than three months improves coordination with the exemption from the individual shared responsibility provision of section 5000A of the Code for gaps in coverage of less than three months (the short coverage gap exemption), 26 CFR 1.5000A-3. Under current law, individuals who are enrolled in short-term, limited-duration coverage instead of minimum essential coverage for three months or more are generally not eligible for the short coverage gap exemption. The proposed regulations help ensure that individuals who purchase short-term, limited-duration coverage will still be eligible for the short coverage gap exemption (assuming other requirements are met) during the temporary coverage period.

In addition to proposing to reduce the length of short-term, limited-duration insurance to less than three months, the proposed regulations add the words "with or" in front of "without the issuer's consent" to address the Departments' concern that some issuers are taking liberty with the current definition of short-term, limited-duration insurance either by automatically renewing such policies or having a simplified reapplication process with the result being that such coverage lasts much longer than 12 months and serves as an individual's primary coverage but does not contain the important protections of the ACA. As indicated above, this type of coverage should only be sold for the purpose of providing coverage on a short-term basis such as filling in coverage gaps as a result of transitioning from one group health plan to another. The addition of the words "with or" clarifies that short-term, limited-duration insurance must be less than 3 months in total taking into account any option to renew or to reapply for the same or similar coverage.

The Departments seek comment on this proposal, including information and data on the number of short-term, limited-duration insurance policies offered for sale in the market, the types of individuals who typically purchase this coverage, and the reasons for which they purchase it.

---

[32] 26 CFR 54.9831-1(c)(4), 29 CFR 2590.732(c)(4), 45 CFR 146.145(b)(4) and 148.220(b)(3).

[33] 26 CFR 54.9801-2, 29 CFR 2590.702-2, 45 CFR 144.103.

[34] See e.g., Mathews, Anna W. "Sales of Short-Term Health Policies Surge," *The Wall Street Journal* April 10, 2016, available at http://www.wsj.com/articles/sales-of-short-term-health-policies-surge-1460328539.

Definition of EHB for Purposes of the Prohibition on Lifetime and Annual Limits.

On November 18, 2015, the Departments issued final regulations implementing section 2711 of the PHS Act.[35] The final regulations provide that, for plan years beginning on or after January 1, 2017, a plan or issuer that is not required to provide EHBs must define EHB, for purposes of the prohibition on lifetime and annual dollar limits, in a manner consistent with any of the 51 EHB base-benchmark plans applicable in a State or the District of Columbia, or one of the three FEHBP base-benchmarks, as specified under 45 CFR 156.100.

The final regulations under section 2711 of the PHS Act include a reference to selecting a "base-benchmark" plan, as specified under 45 CFR 156.100, for purposes of determining which benefits cannot be subject to lifetime or annual dollar limits. The base-benchmark plan selected by a State or applied by default under 45 CFR 156.100, however, may not reflect the complete definition of EHB in the applicable State. For that reason, the Departments propose to amend the regulations at 26 CFR 54.9815-2711(c), 29 CFR 2590.715-2711(c), and 45 CFR 147.126(c) to refer to the provisions that capture the complete definition of EHB in a State. Specifically, the Departments propose to replace the phrase "in a manner consistent with one of the three Federal Employees Health Benefit Program (FEHBP) options as defined by 45 CFR 156.100(a)(3) or one of the base-benchmark plans selected by a State or applied by default pursuant to 45 CFR 156.100" in each of the regulations with the following: "in a manner that is consistent with (1) one of the EHB-benchmark plans applicable in a State under 45 CFR 156.110, and includes coverage of any additional required benefits that are considered essential health benefits consistent with 45 CFR 155.170(a)(2); or (2) one of the three Federal Employees Health Benefit Program (FEHBP) options as defined by 45 CFR 156.100(a)(3), supplemented, as necessary, to meet the standards in 45 CFR 156.110." This change reflects the possibility that base-benchmark plans, including the FEHBP plan options, could require supplementation under 45 CFR 156.110, and ensures the inclusion of State-required benefit mandates enacted on or before December 31, 2011 in accordance with 45 CFR 155.170, which when coupled with a State's EHB-benchmark plan, establish the definition of EHB in that State under regulations implementing section 1302(b) of the ACA.[36] The Departments seek comment on the requirement that, when one of the FEHBP plan options is selected as the benchmark, it would be supplemented, as needed, to ensure coverage in all ten statutory EHB categories, and the benchmark plan options that should be available for this purpose.

Proposed Applicability Date and Reliance

Except as otherwise provided herein, these proposed regulations are proposed to be applicable for plan years (or, in the individual market, policy years) beginning on or after January 1, 2017. Issuers, employers, administrators, and individuals are permitted to rely on these proposed regulations pending the applicability date of final regulations in the **Federal Register**. To the extent final regulations or other guidance is more restrictive on issuers, employers, administrators, and individuals than these proposed regulations, the final regulations or other guidance will be applied without retroactive effect and issuers, employers, administrators, and individuals will be provided sufficient time to come into compliance with the final regulations.

III. Economic Impact and Paperwork Burden

A. *Summary — Department of Labor and Department of Health and Human Services*

As stated above, the proposed regulations would provide guidance on the rules for expatriate health plans, expatriate health plan issuers, and qualified expatriates under the EHCCA. The EHCCA generally provides that the requirements of the ACA do not apply with respect to expatriate health plans, expatriate health insurance issuers for coverage under expatriate health plans, and employers in their capacity as plan sponsors of expatriate health plans.

The proposed regulations address how certain requirements relating to minimum essential coverage under section 5000A of the Code, the health care reporting provisions of sections 6055 and 6056 of the Code, and the health insurance providers fee imposed by section

9010 of the ACA continue to apply subject to certain provisions while providing that the excise tax under sections 4375 and 4376 of the Code do not apply to expatriate health plans.

The proposed regulations also propose amendments to the Departments' regulations concerning excepted benefits, which would specify the conditions for supplemental health insurance products that are designed "to fill gaps in primary coverage" by providing additional categories of benefits (as opposed to filling in gaps in cost sharing) to constitute supplemental excepted benefits, and clarify that certain travel-related insurance products that provide only incidental health benefits constitute excepted benefits. The proposed regulations also require that, to be considered hospital indemnity or other fixed indemnity insurance in the group market, any application or enrollment materials provided to participants at or before the time participants are given the opportunity to enroll in the coverage must include a statement that the coverage is a supplement to, rather than a substitute for, major medical coverage and that a lack of minimum essential coverage may result in an additional tax payment. Further, the regulations clarify that hospital indemnity and other fixed indemnity insurance must pay a fixed dollar amount per day (or per other time period, such as per week) regardless of the type of items or services received.

The regulations also propose revisions to the definition of short-term, limited-duration insurance so that the coverage has to be less than 3 months in duration (as opposed to the current definition of less than 12 months in duration), and that a notice must be prominently displayed in the contract and in any application materials provided in connection with the coverage that provides that such coverage is not minimum essential coverage.

The proposed regulations also include amendments to 45 CFR part 158 to clarify that the MLR reporting requirements do not apply to expatriate health plans under the EHCCA.

Finally, the proposed regulations propose to amend the definition of "essential health benefits" for purposes of the prohibition of annual and lifetime dollar limits for group health plans and health insurance issuers that are not required to provide essential health benefits.

The Departments are publishing these proposed regulations to implement the protections intended by the Congress in the most economically efficient manner possible. The Departments have examined the effects of this rule as required by Executive Order 13563 (76 FR 3821, January 21, 2011), Executive Order 12866 (58 FR 51735, September 1993, Regulatory Planning and Review), the Regulatory Flexibility Act (RFA) (September 19, 1980, Pub. L. 96-354), the Unfunded Mandates Reform Act of 1995 (Pub. L. 104-4), Executive Order 13132 on Federalism, and the Congressional Review Act (5 U.S.C. 804(2)).

B. *Executive Orders 12866 and 13563 — Department of Labor and Department of Health and Human Services*

Executive Order 12866 (58 FR 51735) directs agencies to assess all costs and benefits of available regulatory alternatives and, if regulation is necessary, to select regulatory approaches that maximize net benefits (including potential economic, environmental, public health and safety effects; distributive impacts; and equity). Executive Order 13563 (76 FR 3821, January 21, 2011) is supplemental to and reaffirms the principles, structures, and definitions governing regulatory review as established in Executive Order 12866.

Section 3(f) of Executive Order 12866 defines a "significant regulatory action" as an action that is likely to result in a final rule — (1) having an annual effect on the economy of $100 million or more in any one year, or adversely and materially affecting a sector of the economy, productivity, competition, jobs, the environment, public health or safety, or state, local or tribal governments or communities (also referred to as "economically significant"); (2) creating a serious inconsistency or otherwise interfering with an action taken or planned by another agency; (3) materially altering the budgetary impacts of entitlement grants, user fees, or loan programs or the rights and obligations of recipients thereof; or (4) raising novel legal or policy issues arising out of legal mandates, the President's priorities, or the principles set forth in the Executive Order.

---

[35] 80 FR 72192.

[36] In the HHS Notice of Benefit and Payment Parameters for 2016 published February 27, 2015 (80 FR 10750), HHS instructed States to select a new base-benchmark plan to take effect beginning with plan or policy years beginning in 2017. The new final EHB base-benchmark plans selected as a result of this process are publicly available at downloads.cms.gov/cciio/Final%20List%20of%20BMPs_15_10_21.pdf. Additional in-

formation about the new base-benchmark plans, including plan documents and summaries of benefits, is available at www.cms.gov/CCIIO/Resources/Data-Resources/ehb.html. The definition of EHB in each of the 50 states and the District of Columbia is based on the base-benchmark plan, and takes into account any additions to the base-benchmark plan, such as supplementation under 45 CFR 156.110, and State-required benefit mandates in accordance with 45 CFR 155.170.

A regulatory impact analysis (RIA) must be prepared for rules with economically significant effects (for example, $100 million or more in any 1 year), and a "significant" regulatory action is subject to review by the OMB. The Departments have determined that this regulatory action is not likely to have economic impacts of $100 million or more in any one year, and therefore is not significant within the meaning of Executive Order 12866. The Departments expect the impact of these proposed regulations to be limited because they do not require any additional action or impose any requirements on issuers, employers and plan sponsors.

1. *Need for Regulatory Action*

Consistent with the EHCCA, enacted as Division M of the Consolidated Clarification Continuing Appropriations Act, 2015 Public Law 113-235 (128 Stat. 2130), these proposed regulations provide that the market reform provisions enacted as part of the ACA generally do not apply to expatriate health plans, any employer solely in its capacity as a plan sponsor of an expatriate health plan, and any expatriate health insurance issuer with respect to coverage under an expatriate health plan. Further, the proposed regulations define the benefit and administrative requirements for expatriate health issuers, expatriate health plans, and qualified expatriates and provide clarification regarding the applicability of certain fee and reporting requirements under the Code.

Consistent with section 2 of the EHCCA, these proposed regulations are necessary to carry out the intent of Congress that (1) American expatriate health insurance issuers should be permitted to compete on a level playing field in the global marketplace; (2) the global competitiveness of American companies should be encouraged; and (3) in implementing the health insurance providers fee imposed by section 9010 of the ACA and other provisions of the ACA, the unique and multinational features of expatriate health plans and the United States companies that operate such plans and the competitive pressures of such plans and companies should continue to be recognized.

In response to feedback the Departments have received from stakeholders, the proposed regulations would also clarify the conditions for supplemental health insurance and travel insurance to be considered excepted benefits. These clarifications will provide health insurance issuers offering supplemental insurance coverage and travel insurance products with a clearer understanding of whether these types of coverage are subject to the market reforms under title XXVII of the PHS Act, part 7 of ERISA, and Chapter 100 of the Code. The proposed regulations also would amend the definition of short-term, limited-duration insurance and impose a new notice requirement in response to recent reports that this type of coverage is being sold for purposes other than for which the exclusion for short-term, limited duration insurance was initially intended to cover.

2. *Summary of Impacts*

These proposed regulations would implement the rules for expatriate health plans, expatriate health insurance issuers, and qualified expatriates under the EHCCA. The proposed regulations also outline the conditions for travel insurance and supplemental insurance coverage to be considered excepted benefits, and revise the definition of short-term, limited-duration insurance.

Based on the NAIC 2014 Supplemental Health Care Exhibit Report,[37] which generally uses the definition of expatriate coverage in the MLR final rule at 45 CFR 158.120(d)(4),[38] there are an estimated eight issuers (one issuer in the small group market and seven issuers in the large group market) domiciled in the United States that provide expatriate health plans for approximately 270,349 enrollees. While the Departments acknowledge that some expatriate health insurance issuers and employers in their capacity as plan sponsor of an expatriate health plan may incur costs in order to comply with certain provisions of the EHCCA and these proposed regulations, as discussed below, the Departments believe that these costs will be relatively insignificant and limited.

The vast majority of expatriate health plans described in the EHCCA would qualify as expatriate health plans under the transitional relief provided in the Departments' Affordable Care Act Implementation FAQs Part XVIII, Q&A-6 and Q&A-7. The FAQs provide that expatriate health plans with plan years ending on or before December 31, 2016 are exempt from the ACA market reforms and

provide that coverage provided under an expatriate group health plan is a form of minimum essential coverage under section 5000A of the Code. The EHCCA permanently exempts expatriate health plans with plan or policy years beginning on or after July 1, 2015 from the ACA market reform requirements and provides that coverage provided under an expatriate health plan is a form of minimum essential coverage under section 5000A of the Code.

Because the Departments believe that most, if not all, expatriate health plans described in the EHCCA would qualify as expatriate health plans under the Departments' previous guidance, and the proposed regulations codify the provisions of the EHCCA by making the temporary relief in the Departments' Affordable Care Act Implementation FAQs Part XVIII, Q&A-6 and Q&A-7 permanent for specified expatriate health plans, the Departments believe that the proposed regulations will result in only marginal, if any, impact on these plans. Furthermore, the Departments believe the proposed regulations outlining the conditions for travel insurance and supplemental insurance coverage to be considered excepted benefits are consistent with prevailing industry practice and will not result in significant cost to health insurance issuers of these products.

The Departments believe that any costs incurred by issuers of short-term, limited-duration insurance and hospital indemnity and other fixed indemnity insurance to include the required notice in application or enrollment materials will be negligible since the Departments have provided the exact text for the notice. Further, the Departments note that issuers of hospital indemnity and other fixed indemnity insurance in the individual market already provide a similar notice.

As a result, the Departments have concluded that the impacts of these proposed regulations are not economically significant. The Departments request comments on the assumptions used to evaluate the economic impact of these proposed regulations, including specific data and information on the number of expatriate health plans.

C. *Paperwork Reduction Act*

1. *Department of the Treasury.*

The collection of information in these proposed regulations are in 26 CFR 1.6055-2(a)(8) and 301.6056-2(a)(8). The collection of information in these proposed regulations relates to statements required to be furnished to a responsible individual under section 6055 of the Code and statements required to be furnished to an employee under section 6056 of the Code. The collection of information in these proposed regulations would, in accordance with the EHCCA, permit a furnisher to furnish the required statements electronically unless the recipient has explicitly refused to consent to receive the statement in an electronic format. The collection of information contained in this notice of proposed rulemaking will be taken into account and submitted to the Office of Management and Budget in accordance with the Paperwork Reduction Act of 1995 (44 U.S.C. 3507(d)) in connection with the next review of the collection of information for IRS Form 1095-B (OMB # 1545-2252) and IRS Form 1095-C (OMB # 1545-2251).

Comments on the collection of information should be sent to the Office of Management and Budget, Attn: Desk Officer for the Department of the Treasury, Office of Information and Regulatory Affairs, Washington, DC 20503, with copies to the Internal Revenue Service, Attn: IRS Reports Clearance Officer, SE:CAR:MP:T:T:SP, Washington DC 20224. Comments on the collection of information should be received by August 10, 2016. Comments are sought on whether the proposed collection of information is necessary for the proper performance of the IRS, including whether the information will have practical utility; the accuracy of the estimated burden associated with the proposed collection of information; how the quality, utility, and clarity of the information to be collected may be enhanced; how the burden of complying with the proposed collection of information may be minimized, including through the application of automated collection techniques and other forms of information technology; and estimates of capital or start-up costs and costs of operation, maintenance, and purchase of service to provide information. Comments on the collection of information should be received by August 10, 2016.

An agency may not conduct or sponsor, and a person is not required to respond to, a collection of information unless it displays a

---

[37] NAIC, 2014 Supplemental Health Care Exhibit Report, Volume 1 (2015), available at http://www.naic.org/documents/prod_serv_statistical_hcs_zb.pdf.

[38] Section 45 CFR 158.120(d)(4) defines expatriate policies as predominantly group health insurance policies that provide coverage to employees, substantially all of whom

are: (1) working outside their country of citizenship; (2) working outside their country of citizenship and outside the employer's country of domicile; or (3) non-U.S. citizens working in their home country.

valid control number assigned by the Office of Management and Budget.

Books or records relating to a collection of information must be retained as long as their contents may become material in the administration of any internal revenue law. Generally, tax returns and tax return information are confidential, as required by 26 U.S.C. 6103.

2. Department of the Treasury, Department of Labor, and Department of Health and Human Services.

The proposed regulations provide that to be considered hospital or other fixed indemnity excepted benefits in the group market for plan years beginning on or after January 1, 2017, a notice must be included in any application or enrollment materials provided to participants at or before the time participants are given the opportunity to enroll in the coverage, indicating that the coverage is a supplement to, rather than a substitute for major medical coverage and that a lack of minimum essential coverage may result in an additional tax payment. The proposed regulations also provide that to be considered short-term, limited-duration insurance for policy years beginning on or after January 1, 2017, a notice must be prominently displayed in the contract and in any application materials, stating that the coverage is not minimum essential coverage and that failure to have minimum essential coverage may result in an additional tax payment. The Departments have provided the exact text for these notice requirements and the language will not need to be customized. The burden associated with these notices is not subject to the Paperwork Reduction Act of 1995 in accordance with 5 CFR 1320.3(c)(2) because they do not contain a "collection of information" as defined in 44 U.S.C. 3502(11).

D. Regulatory Flexibility Act

The Regulatory Flexibility Act (5 U.S.C. 601 et seq.) (RFA) imposes certain requirements with respect to Federal rules that are subject to the notice and comment requirements of section 553(b) of the Administrative Procedure Act (5 U.S.C. 551 et seq.) and that are likely to have a significant economic impact on a substantial number of small entities. Unless an agency certifies that a proposed rule is not likely to have a significant economic impact on a substantial number of small entities, section 603 of RFA requires that the agency present an initial regulatory flexibility analysis at the time of the publication of the notice of proposed rulemaking describing the impact of the rule on small entities and seeking public comment on such impact. Small entities include small businesses, organizations and governmental jurisdictions.

The RFA generally defines a "small entity" as (1) a proprietary firm meeting the size standards of the Small Business Administration (SBA) (13 CFR 121.201); (2) a nonprofit organization that is not dominant in its field; or (3) a small government jurisdiction with a population of less than 50,000. (States and individuals are not included in the definition of "small entity.") The Departments use as their measure of significant economic impact on a substantial number of small entities a change in revenues of more than 3 to 5 percent.

These proposed regulations are not likely to impose additional costs on small entities. According to SBA size standards, entities with average annual receipts of $38.5 million or less would be considered small entities for these North American Industry Classification System codes. The Departments believe that, since the majority of small issuers belong to larger holding groups, many if not all are likely to have non-health lines of business that would result in their revenues exceeding $38.5 million. Therefore, the Departments certify that the proposed regulations will not have a significant impact on a substantial number of small entities. In addition, section 1102(b) of the Social Security Act requires agencies to prepare a regulatory impact analysis if a rule may have a significant economic impact on the operations of a substantial number of small rural hospitals. This analysis must conform to the provisions of section 604 of the RFA. These proposed regulations would not affect small rural hospitals. Therefore, the Departments have determined that these proposed regulations would not have a significant impact on the operations of a substantial number of small rural hospitals.

E. Special Analysis - Department of the Treasury

Certain IRS regulations, including this one, are exempt from the requirements of Executive Order 12866, as supplemented and reaffirmed by Executive Order 13563. Therefore, a regulatory impact assessment is not required. It also has been determined that section 553(b) of the Administrative Procedure Act (5 U.S.C. Chapter 5) does not apply to these regulations. For applicability of RFA, see paragraph D of this section III. Pursuant to section 7805(f) of the Code,

these regulations have been submitted to the Chief Counsel for Advocacy of the Small Business Administration for comment on their impact on small business.

F. Unfunded Mandates Reform Act

For purposes of the Unfunded Mandates Reform Act of 1995 (2 U.S.C. 1501 et seq.), as well as Executive Order 12875, these proposed rules do not include any Federal mandate that may result in expenditures by State, local, or tribal governments, or the private sector, which may impose an annual burden of $146 million adjusted for inflation since 1995.

G. Federalism — Department of Labor and Department of Health and Human Services

Executive Order 13132 outlines fundamental principles of federalism. It requires adherence to specific criteria by Federal agencies in formulating and implementing policies that have "substantial direct effects" on the States, the relationship between the national government and States, or on the distribution of power and responsibilities among the various levels of government. Federal agencies promulgating regulations that have these federalism implications must consult with State and local officials, and describe the extent of their consultation and the nature of the concerns of State and local officials in the preamble to the final regulation.

In the Departments' view, these proposed regulations do not have federalism implications, because they do not have direct effects on the States, the relationship between the national government and States, or on the distribution of power and responsibilities among various levels of government.

H. Congressional Review Act

These proposed regulations are subject to the Congressional Review Act provisions of the Small Business Regulatory Enforcement Fairness Act of 1996 (5 U.S.C. 801 et seq.), and, if finalized, will be transmitted to the Congress and to the **Comptroller General** for review in accordance with such provisions.

I. Statement of Availability of IRS Documents

IRS Revenue Procedures, Revenue Rulings notices, and other guidance cited in this document are published in the Internal Revenue Bulletin (or Cumulative Bulletin) and are available from the Superintendent of Documents, U.S. Government Printing Office, Washington, DC 20402, or by visiting the IRS website at http://www.irs.gov.

IV. Statutory Authority

The Department of the Treasury regulations are proposed to be adopted pursuant to the authority contained in sections 7805 and 9833 of the Code.

The Department of Labor regulations are proposed pursuant to the authority contained in 29 U.S.C. 1135,and 1191c; Secretary of Labor's Order 1-2011, 77 FR 1088 (Jan. 9, 2012).

The Department of Health and Human Services regulations are proposed to be adopted pursuant to the authority contained in sections 2701 through 2763, 2791, and 2792 of the PHS Act (42 U.S.C. 300gg through 300gg-63, 300gg-91, and 300gg-92), as amended.

List of Subjects

26 CFR Part 1

Income taxes.

26 CFR Part 46

Excise taxes, Health care, Health insurance, Pensions, Reporting and recordkeeping requirements.

26 CFR Part 54

Pension and excise taxes.

26 CFR Part 57

Health insurance providers fee.

26 CFR Part 301

Procedure and administration.

29 CFR Part 2590

Continuation coverage, Disclosure, Employee benefit plans, Group health plans, Health care, Health insurance, Medical child support, Reporting and recordkeeping requirements.

45 CFR Parts 144, 146 and 147

Health care, Health insurance, Reporting and recordkeeping requirements.

45 CFR Part 148

Administrative practice and procedure, Health care, Health insurance, Penalties, Reporting and recordkeeping requirements.

45 CFR Part 158

Health insurance, Medical loss ratio, Reporting and rebate requirements.

John Dalrymple

Deputy Commissioner for Services and Enforcement,

Internal Revenue Service.

Signed this 1st _day of *June*, 2016.

[¶ 62,168] Notice of Proposed Rulemaking (REG-123829-16), published in the Federal Register on December 9, 2016.
[Act Sec. 9010 of the Patient Protection and Affordable Care Act (P.L. 111-148)]

Health insurance providers: Form 8963: Electronic filing.—Amendments of Reg. §57.3 and Reg. §57.10 are proposed. The proposed regulations relate to the rules for health insurance providers fees and the electronic filing of Form 8963.

Electronic Filing of the Report of Health Insurance Provider Information

AGENCY: Internal Revenue Service (IRS), Treasury.

ACTION: Notice of proposed rulemaking.

SUMMARY: This document proposes to amend the Health Insurance Providers Fee regulations to require certain covered entities engaged in the business of providing health insurance for United States health risks to electronically file Form 8963, "Report of Health Insurance Provider Information." These proposed regulations affect those entities.

DATES: Written or electronic comments and requests for a public hearing must be received by December 9, 2016.

ADDRESSES: Send submissions to: CC:PA:LPD:PR (REG-123829-16), room 5205, Internal Revenue Service, PO Box 7604, Ben Franklin Station, Washington, DC 20044. Submissions may be hand delivered Monday through Friday between the hours of 8 a.m. and 4 p.m. to CC:PA:LPD:PR (REG-123829-16), Courier's Desk, Internal Revenue Service, 1111 Constitution Avenue, NW, Washington, DC, or sent electronically via the Federal eRulemaking Portal at http://www.regulations.gov (indicate IRS REG-123829-16). FOR FURTHER INFORMATION CONTACT: Concerning the proposed regulations, David Bergman, (202) 317-6844; concerning submissions of comments or to request a public hearing, Regina Johnson, (202) 317-6901 (not toll-free numbers).

SUPPLEMENTARY INFORMATION:

Background

This document proposes to amend the Health Insurance Providers Fee Regulations (26 CFR part 57) under section 9010 of the Patient Protection and Affordable Care Act (PPACA), Public Law 111-148 (124 Stat. 119 (2010)), as amended by section 10905 of PPACA, and as further amended by section 1406 of the Health Care and Education Reconciliation Act of 2010, Public Law 111-152 (124 Stat. 1029 (2010)) (collectively, the Affordable Care Act or ACA). All references in this preamble to section 9010 are references to the ACA.

Section 9010(a) imposes an annual fee on each covered entity engaged in the business of providing health insurance. A covered entity, defined under section 9010(c), is any entity that provides health insurance for any United States health risk during each year, subject to certain exclusions. The total aggregate amount of the fee for all covered entities is determined by statute and is called the applicable amount. *See* section 9010(e). Each covered entity's annual fee is equal to an amount that bears the same ratio to the applicable amount as the covered entity's portion of net premiums written with respect to health insurance for United States health risks that are taken into account compared to the aggregate amount of net premiums written for all covered entities that are taken into account. Section 9010(b)(2) clarifies which net premiums are taken into account for purposes of calculating the fee. A covered entity (including a controlled group) with no more than $25 million in net premiums written does not have any premiums taken into account and is not liable for a fee.

Section 9010(b)(3) requires the Secretary to calculate the amount of each covered entity's fee on a calendar year basis. To facilitate these calculations, section 9010(g)(1) requires that each covered entity must report to the Secretary the covered entity's net premiums written for health insurance for any United States health risk for the preceding calendar year by the date prescribed by the Secretary. Section 9010(g)(1) also provides the Secretary with authority to prescribe the manner in which a covered entity reports its net premiums written. The reporting requirement applies regardless of whether a covered entity will be liable for a fee. Section 9010(g)(2) imposes a penalty on a covered entity for any failure to report the required information by the date prescribed by the Secretary (determined with regard to any

extension of time for filing), unless such failure is due to reasonable cause. Section 9010(g)(3) imposes an accuracy-related penalty for understating the covered entity's net premiums written for health insurance for any United States health risk for any calendar year.

Section 57.3 of the Health Insurance Providers Fee regulations implements section 9010(g) and provides the rules for covered entities to report net premiums written for health insurance of United States health risks to the IRS. Under that section, information is reported to the IRS on Form 8963, "Report of Health Insurance Provider Information," which must be filed in accordance with the form instructions by April 15 of the year following the calendar year for which data is being reported. That section further provides that rules for the manner of reporting may be provided in guidance in the Internal Revenue Bulletin. The IRS uses the information reported on Form 8963 as part of the determination of each covered entity's annual fee under section 9010. Neither the statute nor the regulations currently specify whether Form 8963 must be submitted electronically or on paper. Covered entities currently have the option of filing the form in either manner.

Section 57.5 requires the IRS to send each covered entity notice of a preliminary fee calculation for that fee year (the calendar year in which the fee must be paid, beginning with 2014), and provides the content of that notice. Section 57.5 further provides that the timing of the notice will be provided in guidance published in the Internal Revenue Bulletin. Notice 2013-76 (2013-51 IRB 769) provides that the IRS will mail each covered entity its notice of preliminary fee calculation by June 15 of each fee year. Section 57.6 requires that a covered entity correct any errors identified after receiving the preliminary fee calculation by filing a corrected Form 8963. Notice 2013-76 provides that a corrected Form 8963 must be filed by July 15 of the fee year. The corrected Form 8963 replaces the original Form 8963 for all purposes, including the determination of whether an accuracy-related penalty applies. The covered entity remains liable for any failure to report penalty if it failed to timely submit the original Form 8963. As with the original report, the corrected Form 8963 may currently be submitted either electronically on paper.

Under §57.7(b), the IRS must send each covered entity its final fee calculation no later than August 31. The IRS validates the data on Form 8963 in performing the final calculation, and, pursuant to section 9010(b)(3); the IRS is authorized to use any other source of information to determine each covered entity's net premiums written for health insurance of United States health risks. The covered entity must pay the fee by September 30 of the fee year, as provided by section 9010(a)(2). The fee must be paid by electronic funds transfer. *See* §§57.7(d); 57.6302-1.

The Consolidated Appropriations Act of 2016 imposes a moratorium on the fee for the 2017 calendar year. P.L. 114-113, section 201. Thus, covered entities are not required to pay the fee or file Form 8963 for the 2017 fee year.

Explanation of Provisions

The IRS has now had three years of experience administering the Health Insurance Providers Fee. Based on this experience, the IRS concludes that the fee could be more efficiently administered if certain covered entities were required to file Forms 8963 and corrected Forms 8963 electronically.

The calculation of the fee is complex, and the statute requires that it be paid by the covered entity by September 30. The calculation of any one covered entity's fee depends upon the data reported on Form 8963 by all covered entities - an adjustment to one covered entity's fee affects other covered entities' fees. Covered entities need time after the end of the year to compile the information that needs to be reported. Accordingly, there is a short window of time for (1) the IRS to compile and analyze the reported information and send out preliminary letters, (2) covered entities to respond with any corrections, (3) the IRS to compile and analyze the amended reporting and issue final fee letters, and (4) covered entities to pay the fee.

Paper reporting slows this process because paper forms take time to travel through the mail. Additionally, once the paper Form 8963 (or corrected Form 8963) reaches IRS personnel, the information on the paper form must be transcribed into IRS computers to calculate the fee. Transcription of paper forms is costly and time-consuming. And, because of the nature of the fee, no entity's proposed or final assessment can be determined until all the reporting of all payers has been taken into account.

The IRS uses electronic filing in several other contexts to streamline the collection of large volumes of paper forms and to efficiently use the information provided. Electronic filing of Forms 8963 and corrected Forms 8963 would benefit the administration of the fee by significantly reducing delays and the resources needed to calculate the preliminary and final fee amounts. Electronic filing will also benefit fee payers by facilitating the process for computing the fee for all covered entities.

Accordingly, pursuant to section 9010(g)(1), which provides authority to prescribe the manner for reporting, the proposed regulations amend § 57.3(a)(2) to provide that a covered entity (including a controlled group) reporting more than $25 million in net premiums written on a Form 8963 or corrected Form 8963 must electronically file these forms after December 31, 2017. Forms 8963 reporting $25 million or less in net premiums written are not required to be electronically filed. This is because a covered entity (including a controlled group) reporting no more than $25 million in net premiums written is not liable for a fee and therefore the time constraints applicable to computation of the fee are not applicable with respect to these entities. *See* § 57.4(a)(4). The proposed regulation also provides that if a Form 8963 or corrected Form 8963 is required to be filed electronically, any subsequently filed Form 8963 filed for the same fee year must also be filed electronically, even if such subsequently filed Form 8963 reports $25 million or less in net premiums written. In addition, the proposed regulation provides that failure to electronically file will be treated as a failure to file for purposes of § 57.3(b).

Proposed Effective/Applicability Date

These amendments are proposed to apply to any covered entity reporting more than $25 million in net premiums written on any Form 8963 filed after December 31, 2017.

Special Analyses

Certain IRS regulations, including this one, are exempt from the requirements of Executive Order 12866, as supplemented and reaffirmed by Executive Order 13563. Therefore, a regulatory impact assessment is not required. It is hereby certified that the electronic filing requirement would not have a significant economic impact on a substantial number of small entities pursuant to the Regulatory Flexibility Act (5 U.S.C. chapter 6). This certification is based on the fact that the rule is expected to affect primarily larger entities because the electronic filing requirement is not met unless the filer must report more than $25 million in net premiums. Accordingly, a regulatory flexibility analysis is not required.

Pursuant to section 7805(f) of the Internal Revenue Code, this notice of proposed rulemaking has been submitted to the Chief Counsel for Advocacy of the Small Business Administration for comment on the impact on small business.

Comments and Public Hearing

Before these proposed regulations are adopted as final regulations, consideration will be given to any written or electronic comments that are submitted timely to the IRS as prescribed in this preamble under the "Addresses" heading. The Treasury Department and the IRS request comments on all aspects of the proposed rules. All comments will be available for public inspection and copying at www.regulations.gov or upon request. A public hearing will be scheduled if requested in writing by any person that timely submits written comments. If a public hearing is scheduled, notice of the date, time, and place for the public hearing will be published in the Federal Register.

Drafting Information

The principal author of the proposed regulations is David Bergman of the Office of the Associate Chief Counsel (Procedure and Administration).

[¶ 62,169] Notice of Proposed Rulemaking (REG-134438-15), published in the Federal Register on December 9, 2016.

[Act Sec. 9010 of the Patient Protection and Affordable Care Act (P.L. 111-148)]

Health insurance providers: Net premiums written: Definition.—Amendments of Reg. § 57.2 and Reg. § 57.10 are proposed. The proposed regulations relate to the definition of "net premiums written."

Health Insurance Providers Fee

AGENCY: Internal Revenue Service (IRS), Treasury.

ACTION: Notice of proposed rulemaking.

SUMMARY: This document contains proposed regulations that would modify the current definition of "net premiums written" for purposes of the fee imposed by section 9010 of the Patient Protection and Affordable Care Act, as amended. The proposed regulations will affect persons engaged in the business of providing health insurance for United States health risks.

DATES: Comments and requests for a public hearing must be received by

December 9, 2016.

ADDRESSES: Send submissions to: CC:PA:LPD:PR (REG-134438-15), room 5203, Internal Revenue Service, PO Box 7604, Ben Franklin Station, Washington, DC 20044. Submissions may be hand-delivered Monday through Friday between the hours of 8 a.m. and 4 p.m. to CC:PA:LPD:PR (REG-134438-15), Courier's Desk, Internal Revenue Service, 1111 Constitution Avenue, NW, Washington, DC 20224, or sent electronically, via the Federal eRulemaking portal at *www.regulations.gov* (IRS REG-134438-15)

FOR FURTHER INFORMATION CONTACT: Concerning the proposed regulations, Rachel S. Smith, (202) 317-6855; concerning submissions of comments and request for a hearing, Regina Johnson, (202) 317-6901 (not toll-free numbers).

SUPPLEMENTARY INFORMATION:

Background

Section 9010 of the Patient Protection and Affordable Care Act (PPACA), Public Law No. 111 148 (124 Stat. 119 (2010)), as amended by section 10905 of PPACA, and as further amended by section 1406 of the Health Care and Education Reconciliation Act of 2010, Public Law 111-152 (124 Stat. 1029 (2010)) (collectively, the Affordable Care

Act or ACA) imposes an annual fee on covered entities that provide health insurance for United States health risks. Section 9010 did not amend the Internal Revenue Code (Code) but contains cross-references to specified Code sections. In this preamble all references to section 9010 are references to section 9010 of the ACA and all references to "fee" are references to the fee imposed by section 9010.

Section 9010(a) imposes an annual fee on each covered entity engaged in the business of providing health insurance. The fee is due by the annual date specified by the Secretary, but in no event later than September 30th of each calendar year in which a fee must be paid (fee year).

Section 9010(b) requires the Secretary to determine the annual fee for each covered entity based on the ratio of the covered entity's net premiums written for health insurance for any United States health risk that are taken into account for the calendar year immediately before the fee year (data year) to the aggregate net premiums written for health insurance of United States health risks of all covered entities that are taken into account during the data year. In calculating the fee, the Secretary must determine each covered entity's net premiums written for United States health risks based on reports submitted to the Secretary by the covered entity and through the use of any other source of information available to the Secretary. Section 9010 does not define the term "net premiums written."

On November 29, 2013, the Treasury Department and the IRS published in the **Federal Register** (TD 9643; 78 FR 71476) final regulations regarding the fee (final regulations). The final regulations define *net premiums written* to mean premiums written, including reinsurance premiums written, reduced by reinsurance ceded, and reduced by ceding commissions and medical loss ratio (MLR) rebates with respect to the data year. Net premiums written do not include premiums written for indemnity reinsurance (and are not reduced by indemnity reinsurance ceded) because indemnity reinsurance is not considered health insurance for purposes of section 9010. However, net premiums written do include premiums written (and are reduced by premiums ceded) for assumption reinsurance; that is, reinsurance for which there is a novation and the reinsurer takes over the entire risk.

The preamble to the final regulations explained that, for covered entities that file the Supplemental Health Care Exhibit (SHCE) with the National Association of Insurance Commissioners (NAIC), net premiums written for health insurance generally will equal the amount reported on the SHCE as direct premiums written minus MLR rebates with respect to the data year, subject to any applicable exclusions under section 9010. The instructions to Form 8963, *Report of Health Insurance Provider Information*, provide additional information on how to determine net premiums written using the SHCE and any equivalent forms as the source of data, and can be updated to reflect changes to the SHCE.

Explanation of Provisions

The proposed regulations would amend and clarify the rules for how "net premiums written" take into account certain premium adjustments and payments.

1. *Retrospective Premium Adjustments*

Following the publication of the final regulations, the Treasury Department and the IRS received comments requesting that premium adjustments related to retrospectively rated contracts be taken into account in determining net premiums written. The NAIC's Accounting Practices and Procedures Manual Statement of Statutory Accounting Principles No. 66, *Retrospectively Rated Contracts*, defines a retrospectively rated contract as a contract which has the final policy premium calculated based on the loss experience of the insured during the term of the policy (including loss development after the term of the policy) and on the stipulated formula set forth in the policy or a formula required by law. These premium adjustments, made periodically, may involve either the payment of return premium to the insured (a "retrospectively rated contract payment") or payment of an additional premium by the insured (a "retrospectively rated contract receipt"), or both, depending on experience.

Commenters recommended that in calculating net premiums written, premiums written should be increased by retrospectively rated contract receipts and reduced by retrospectively rated contract payments. Commenters asserted that retrospectively rated contract payments are refunded to policyholders in much the same way as MLR rebates. Therefore, without an adjustment for retrospectively rated contract payments, covered entities that make these payments will bear a liability for an amount of the annual fee that correlates to premiums from which they do not actually receive an economic benefit.

In response to these comments, the proposed regulations would modify the current definition of net premiums written to account for premium adjustments related to retrospectively rated contracts, computed on an accrual basis. These amounts are received from and paid to policyholders annually based on experience. Retrospectively rated contract receipts and payments do not include changes to funds or accounts that remain under the control of the covered entity, such as changes to premium stabilization reserves.

2. *Risk Adjustment Payments and Charges*

Following the publication of the final regulations, questions also arose about the treatment of risk adjustment payments under the ACA. Section 1343 of the ACA provides a permanent risk adjustment program for certain plans in the individual and small group markets. In general, the program transfers risk adjustment funds from health insurance plans with relatively lower-risk enrollees to issuers that disproportionately attract high-risk populations, such as individuals with chronic conditions. Section 1343(a)(1) generally requires each state, or the Department of Health and Human Services (HHS) acting on behalf of the state, to assess a charge on health plans and health insurance issuers in the individual or small group markets within a state (with respect to health insurance coverage) if the actuarial risk of the enrollees of such plans or coverage for a year is less than the average actuarial risk of all enrollees in all plans or coverage in the

state for the year that are not self-insured group health plans. Section 1343(a)(2) generally requires each state, or HHS acting on behalf of the state, to make a payment to health plans and health insurance issuers in the individual or small group markets within a state (with respect to health insurance coverage) if the actuarial risk of the enrollees of such plans or coverage for a year is greater than the average actuarial risk of all enrollees in all plans and coverage in the state for the year that are not self-insured group health plans.

Although not specifically listed, net premiums written, as defined in the final regulations, include risk adjustment payments received by a covered entity under section 1343(a)(2) of the ACA and are reduced for risk adjustment charges paid by a covered entity under section 1343(a)(1) of the ACA. Nonetheless, several covered entities asked whether net premiums written included risk adjustment payments received and charges paid. Therefore, these proposed regulations add specific language to the definition of net premiums written to clarify that net premiums written include risk adjustment payments received and are reduced for risk adjustment charges paid. If a covered entity did not include risk adjustment payments received as direct premiums written on its SHCE or did not file an SHCE, these amounts are still part of net premiums written and must be reported as such on Form 8963. For this purpose, risk adjustment payments received and charges paid are computed on an accrual basis.

3. *Other Premium Adjustments*

These proposed regulations would authorize the IRS to provide rules in guidance published in the Internal Revenue Bulletin for additional amounts to be taken into account in determining net premiums written. If the Treasury Department and the IRS determine that published guidance providing additional adjustments to net premiums written is warranted, such guidance will be published in the Internal Revenue Bulletin.

Proposed Effective/Applicability Date

These regulations are proposed to apply with respect to any fee that is due on or after September 30, 2018.

Special Analyses

Certain IRS regulations, including these, are exempt from the requirements of Executive Order 12866, as supplemented and reaffirmed by Executive Order 13563. Therefore, a regulatory assessment is not required. Because these regulations do not include a collection of information, a Regulatory Flexibility Analysis under the Regulatory Flexibility Act (5 U.S.C. chapter 6) is not required. Pursuant to Code section 7805(f), this notice of proposed rulemaking will be submitted to the Chief Counsel for Advocacy of the Small Business Administration for comment on its impact on small business.

Comments and Public Hearing

Before these proposed regulations are adopted as final regulations, consideration will be given to any written (a signed original and eight (8) copies) or electronic comments that are submitted timely to the IRS. Comments are requested on all aspects of these proposed regulations. The Treasury Department and the IRS specifically request comments on the following:

1. How the adjustments to net premiums written under these proposed regulations tie to amounts reported on the SHCE.

2. Whether there should be a transition rule for premium adjustments related to retrospectively rated contracts and how any such rule should be implemented.

All comments will be available for public inspection and copying. A public hearing may be scheduled if requested in writing by any person that timely submits written comments. If a public hearing is scheduled, notice of the date, time, and place for the hearing will be published in the Federal Register.

Drafting Information

The principal author of these proposed regulations is Rachel S. Smith, IRS Office of the Associate Chief Counsel (Passthroughs and Special Industries). However, other personnel from the Treasury Department and the IRS participated in their development.